DICTIONNAIRE COMPACT

FRANÇAIS ANGLAIS

ANGLAIS FRANÇAIS

CONCISE DICTIONARY

FRENCH ENGLISH

ENGLISH FRENCH

LAROUSSE

DICTIONNAIRE COMPACT

FRANÇAIS ANGLAIS

ANGLAIS FRANÇAIS

LAROUSSE

ISBN 2-03-540040-6
Larousse/HER, Paris

Distributeur exclusif au Québec: Messageries ADP, 1751 Richardson, Montréal (Québec)

ISBN 2-03-542012-1 (hardcover edition)
ISBN 2-03-542002-2 (paperback edition)

Diffusion/Sales : Larousse Kingfisher Chambers Inc., New York

LAROUSSE

CONCISE DICTIONARY

FRENCH
ENGLISH

ENGLISH
FRENCH

LAROUSSE

Deuxième Édition / *Second Edition*

Direction de la présente édition
General Editor for this edition
Valérie Katzaros

Rédaction
Editors
Frances Illingworth
Marie Ollivier
Paloma Cabot
Peggy Loison

Informatique éditoriale
Data managment
Abdul Aziz Ndao

Direction artistique
Layout
Sophie Compagne

Première Édition / *First Edition*

Direction de l'ouvrage
General Editor
Catherine Love

Coordination éditoriale
Coordinating Editors
Wendy Lee   Patrick White   Catherine Julia

Rédaction
Editors

Florence Millar
Sabine Citron
Liliane Charrier
Valérie Dupin
Véronique Athukorala
Jean Bertrand
Françoise Fauchet
Carine Lipski
Carole Coen

Harry Campbell
Donald Watt
Karen George
Margaret Ross
Huw Davies
Sara Montgomery
Calum Short
Jane Goldie
Charlotte Boynton
Callum Brines

SOMMAIRE

CONTENTS

AU LECTEUR

La gamme COMPACT offre l'outil de travail idéal pour un large éventail de situations, allant du travail scolaire ou en auto-apprentissage au contexte quotidien du bureau.

Le COMPACT français/anglais vise à répondre rapidement et efficacement au plus grand nombre des questions posées par la lecture de l'anglais d'aujourd'hui et par la rédaction de travaux, de lettres, de rapports en anglais.

Avec plus de 100 000 mots et expressions éclairés par plus de 130 000 traductions, ce dictionnaire permet de pleinement apprécier textes littéraires et documents, de mieux comprendre la presse quotidienne ou hebdomadaire, de déchiffrer prospectus et notices, de faire une traduction rapide ou une synthèse. De nombreux sigles et noms propres, les termes les plus courants des affaires et de l'informatique, en font une référence particuliè-rement actuelle. Par le traitement clair et détaillé du vocabulaire fondamental, les exemples de constructions grammaticales, les tournures idiomatiques, les indications de sens soulignant la ou les traductions appropriées, il permet de rédiger dans la langue étrangère sans risque de contresens et sans hésitation.

Une présentation et une typographie très étudiées concourent à rendre plus aisée la consultation. Pour l'usager qui n'est plus un vrai débutant sans prétendre être un spécialiste, le COMPACT est l'ouvrage de référence pour parfaire son anglais.

N'hésitez pas à nous faire part de vos observations, questions ou critiques éventuelles ; vous contribuerez ainsi à rendre cet ouvrage encore meilleur.

L'Éditeur

TO OUR READERS

The Larousse CONCISE dictionary is the perfect companion for a wide variety of situations, from language learning at school and at home to everyday use in the office.

This French dictionary is designed to provide fast and efficient solutions to the various problems encountered when reading present-day French. It will also be an invaluable aid in preparing written work of all kinds, from schoolwork to letters and reports.

The CONCISE has over 100,000 references and 130,000 translations. It enables the user to read and enjoy a wide range of fiction and journalism, to understand trade literature, brochures and manuals, and to summarize and translate from French quickly and accurately. This entirely new dictionary also features up-to-date coverage of common abbreviations and acronyms, proper names, business terms and computing vocabulary.

Writing French accurately and confidently is no longer a problem thanks to the CONCISE 's detailed coverage of essential vocabulary, and helpful sense-markers which guide the user to the most appropriate translation.

Careful thought has gone into the presentation of the entries, both in terms of layout and typography. For the user who has moved beyond beginners' level but is not intending to pursue French at an academic level, the CONCISE is the ideal reference work.

Send us your comments or queries – you will be helping us to make this dictionary an even better book in future.

The Publisher

ABBREVIATIONS
Grammatical, register and regional labels

ABRÉVIATIONS
Étiquettes grammaticales, stylistiques et dialectales

abbreviation	*abbr/abr*	abréviation
adjective	*adj*	adjectif
adverb	*adv*	adverbe
American English	*Am*	anglais américain
slang	*arg*	argot
article	*art*	article
Australian English	*Austr*	anglais australien
auxiliary	*aux*	auxiliaire
before noun	*avant n*	avant le nom

before noun — indicates that the translation is always used attributively, i.e. directly before the noun which it modifies

avant le nom — appliqué à la traduction d'un adjectif français, indique l'emploi d'un nom anglais avec valeur d'adjectif ; souligne aussi les cas où la traduction d'un adjectif est nécessairement antéposée

Belgian French	*Belg*	belgicisme
British English	*Br*	anglais britannique
Canadian English/French	*Can*	canadianisme
compound	*comp*	nom anglais utilisé en apposition

compound — a noun used to modify another noun, e.g. **gardening** in **gardening book** or **airforce** in **airforce base**

nom anglais utilisé en apposition par exemple **gardening** dans **gardening book** ou **airforce** dans **airforce base**

comparative	*compar*	comparatif
conjunction	*conj*	conjonction
continuous	*cont*	progressif
definite	*def/déf*	défini
demonstrative	*dem/dém*	démonstratif
especially	*esp*	particulièrement
exclamation	*excl*	interjection
informal	*fam*	familier
figurative	*fig*	figuré
formal	*fml*	soutenu
inseparable	*fus*	non séparable

inseparable — shows that a phrasal verb is "fused", i.e. inseparable, e.g. **look after** where the object cannot come between the verb and the particle, e.g. **I looked after him** but not **I looked him after**

non séparable — indique qu'un verbe anglais à particule (« phrasal verb ») ne peut pas être séparé de sa particule, c'est-à-dire qu'un complément d'objet ne peut être inséré entre les deux, par exemple **I looked after him** (et non **I looked him after**)

generally, in most cases	*gen/gén*	généralement

generally, in most cases — identifies the most common translation of a word

généralement — indique la traduction la plus courante d'un mot

Swiss French	*Helv*	helvétisme
humorous	*hum*	humoristique
indefinite	*indef/indéf*	indéfini
informal	*inf*	familier
infinitive	*infin*	infinitif
exclamation	*interj*	interjection
interrogative	*interr*	interrogatif

English	Abbrev	French
invariable	*inv*	invariable

applied to a noun to indicate that the plural and singular forms are the same, e.g. **garde-boue** *m inv* : **les garde-boue**, **sheep** *pl inv* : **four sheep** ; applied to a French adjective to indicate that feminine and plural forms same as masculine, e.g. **vieux jeu** *inv* : **ils sont/elle est vieux jeu**

avec un nom, signifie que la forme du pluriel est identique à la forme du singulier, par exemple **garde-boue** *m inv* : **les garde-boue**, **sheep** *pl inv* : **four sheep** ; avec un adjectif, signifie que la forme du féminin et celle du pluriel sont identiques à la forme du masculin, par exemple **vieux jeu** *inv* : **ils sont/elle est vieux jeu**

ironic	*iro/iron*	ironique
literal	*lit/litt*	littéral

in conjunction with *fig*, shows that both a literal and figurative sense is being covered by the same translation

conjointement à l'étiquette *fig*, indique que la traduction donnée couvre à la fois le sens littéral et le sens figuré

phrase(s)	*loc*	locution(s)
adjectival phrase	*loc adj*	locution adjectivale
adverbial phrase	*loc adv*	locution adverbiale
conjunctival phrase	*loc conj*	locution conjonctive
prepositional phrase	*loc prép*	locution prépositionnelle

adjectives, adverbs, conjunctions and prepositions consisting of more than one word, e.g. **d'affilée, par dépit, en dépit de, bien que**

adjectifs, adverbes, conjonctions et prépositions composés de plusieurs mots, par exemple **d'affilée, par dépit, en dépit de, bien que**

noun	*n*	nom
feminine noun	*nf*	nom féminin
masculine noun	*nm*	nom masculin
masculine or feminine noun	*nmf*	nom masculin ou féminin

depending on gender, e.g. **dentiste** *nmf* where you would say **un dentiste** or **le dentiste** for a man and **une dentiste** or **la dentiste** for a woman

dentiste *nmf* pouvant être **un dentiste** ou **une dentiste**, selon le sexe

numeral	*num*	numéral
oneself	*o.s.*	
pejorative	*pej/péj*	péjoratif

implies disapproval, e.g. **bimbo, catty, macho**

implique une nuance dépréciative, par exemple **accoutré**

personal	*pers*	personnel
phrase(s)	*phr*	locution(s)
plural	*pl*	pluriel
possessive	*poss*	possessif
past participle	*pp*	participe passé
present participle	*ppr*	participe présent
preposition	*prep/prép*	préposition
pronoun	*pron*	pronom
past tense	*pt*	passé
	qqch	quelque chose
	qqn	quelqu'un
registered trademark	®	nom déposé

words considered to be trademarks have been designated in this dictionary by the symbol ®. However, neither the presence nor the absence of such designation should be regarded as affecting the legal status of any trademark.

les noms de marque sont désignés dans ce dictionnaire par le symbole ®. Néanmoins, ni ce symbole ni son absence éventuelle ne peuvent être considérés comme susceptibles d'avoir une incidence quelconque sur le statut légal d'une marque.

relative	*rel*	relatif
someone, somebody	*sb*	
Scottish English	*Scot*	anglais écossais
separable	*sep*	séparable

shows that a phrasal verb is separable, e.g. let in, help out where the object can come between the verb and the particle, I let her in, he helped me out — indique qu'un verbe anglais à particule (« phrasal verb ») peut être séparé de sa particule, c'est-à-dire qu'un complément d'objet peut être inséré entre les deux, par exemple I let her in, I helped him out

singular	*sg*	singulier
slang	*sl*	argot
formal	*sout*	soutenu
something	*sthg*	
subject	*subj/suj*	sujet
superlative	*superl*	superlatif
very informal	*tfam*	très familier
uncountable noun	*U*	substantif non comptable

i.e. an English noun which is never used in the plural or with "a"; used when the French word is or can be a plural, e.g. applause n (U) applaudissements mpl, battement nm beat, beating (U) — désigne en anglais les noms qui ne sont jamais utilisés au pluriel, lorsque le terme français est un pluriel ou peut être mis au pluriel, par exemple applause n (U) applaudissements mpl, battement nm beat, beating (U)

usually	*usu*	habituellement
link verb followed	*v attr*	verbe suivi d'un attribut
by a predicative adjective or noun		
verb	*vb/v*	verbe
intransitive verb	*vi*	verbe intransitif
impersonal verb	*v impers*	verbe impersonnel
(always used with the subject "it")		
very informal	*v inf*	très familier
pronominal verb	*vp*	verbe pronominal
transitive verb	*vt*	verbe transitif
vulgar, offensive	*vulg*	vulgaire, susceptible de choquer
cultural equivalent	~	équivalence culturelle
introduces a new part of speech within an entry	◇	introduit une nouvelle catégorie grammaticale dans une entrée
introduces a sub-entry, such as a plural form with its own specific meaning or a set phrase containing the headword (e.g. a phrasal verb or adverbial phrase)	◆	introduit une sous-entrée, par exemple une forme plurielle ayant un sens propre, une locution adjectivale ou adverbiale, un verbe pronominal, etc.

FIELDS LABELS

DOMAINES

administration, administrative	ADMIN	administration
aeronautics, aviation	AERON/AÉRON	aéronautique
agriculture, farming	AGR(IC)	agriculture
anatomy	ANAT	anatomie
archaeology	ARCHAEOL/ARCHÉOL	archéologie
architecture	ARCHIT	architecture
astrology	ASTROL	astrologie
astronomy	ASTRON	astronomie
automobile, cars	AUT(OM)	automobile
biology	BIOL	biologie
botany	BOT	botanique
chemistry	CHEM/CHIM	chimie
cinema, film-making	CIN(EMA)	cinéma
commerce, business	COMM	commerce
computers, computer science	COMPUT	informatique
construction,	CONSTR	construction
sewing	COUT	couture
culinary, cooking	CULIN	cuisine, art culinaire
ecology	ÉCOL	écologie
economics	ECON/ÉCON	économie
electricity	ELEC/ÉLECTR	électricité
electronics	ELECTRON/ÉLECTRON	électronique
finance, financial	FIN	finances
soccer	FTBL	football
geography, geographical	GEOGR/GÉOGR	géographie
geology, geological	GEOL/GÉOL	géologie
geometry	GEOM/GÉOM	géométrie
grammar	GRAM(M)	grammaire
history	HIST	histoire
industry	IND	industrie

FIELDS LABELS

DOMAINES

computers, computer science	INFORM	informatique
juridical, legal	JUR	juridique
linguistics	LING	linguistique
mathematics	MATH(S)	mathématiques
medicine	MED/MÉD	médecine
weather, meteorology	METEOR/MÉTÉOR	météorologie
military, armaments	MIL	domaine militaire
music	MUS	musique
mythology	MYTH	mythologie
nautical, maritime	NAUT/NAVIG	navigation
pharmacology, pharmaceutics	PHARM	pharmacologie
philosophy	PHILO	philosophie
photography	PHOT	photographie
physics	PHYS	physique
politics	POL(IT)	politique
psychology, psychiatry	PSYCH(OL)	psychologie
railways	RAIL	rail
religion	RELIG	religion
school	SCH/SCOL	domaine scolaire, éducation
sociology	SOCIOL	sociologie
stock exchange	ST EX	Bourse
technology, technical	TECH(NOL)	technique, technologie
telecommunications	TELEC/TÉLÉCOM	télécommunications
television	TV/TÉLÉ	télévision
printing, typography	TYPO	typographie
university	UNIV	université
veterinary science	VETER	médecine vétérinaire
zoology	ZOOL	zoologie

PHONETIC TRANSCRIPTION

English vowels

[ɪ] pit, big, rid
[e] pet, tend
[æ] pat, bag, mad
[ʌ] putt, cut
[ɒ] pot, log
[ʊ] put, full
[ə] mother, suppose

[iː] bean, weed
[ɑː] barn, car, laugh
[ɔː] born, lawn
[uː] loop, loose
[ɜː] burn, learn, bird

English Diphtongs

[eɪ] bay, late, great
[aɪ] buy, light, aisle
[ɔɪ] boy , foil
[əʊ] no, road, blow
[aʊ] now, shout, town
[ɪə] peer, fierce, idea
[eə] pair, bear, share
[ʊə] poor, sure, tour

Semi-vowels

you, spaniel   [j]
wet, why, twin   [w]
                              [ɥ]

Consonants

pop, people   [p]
bottle, bib   [b]
train, tip   [t]
dog, did   [d]
come, kitchen   [k]
loch   [x]
gag, great   [g]
chain, wretched   [tʃ]
jig, fridge   [dʒ]
fib, physical   [f]
vine, livid   [v]
think, fifth   [θ]

TRANSCRIPTION PHONÉTIQUE

Voyelles françaises

[i] fille, île
[e] pays, année
[ɛ] bec, aime
[a] lac, papillon
[o] drôle, aube
[ɔ] botte, automne
[u] outil, goût
[y] usage, lune
[ø] aveu, jeu
[œ] peuple, bœuf
[ə] le, je

Nasales françaises

[ɛ̃] timbre, main
[ɑ̃] champ, ennui
[ɔ̃] ongle, mon
[œ̃] parfum, brun

Semi-voyelles

yeux, lieu
ouest, oui
lui, nuit

Consonnes

prendre, grippe
bateau, rosbif
théâtre, temps
dalle, ronde
coq, quatre

garder, épilogue

physique, fort
voir, rive

TRANSCRIPCIÓN FONÉTICA

TRANSCRIPTION PHONÉTIQUE

this, with	[ð]		
seal, peace	[s]	cela, savant	
zip, his	[z]	fraise, zéro	
sheep, machine	[ʃ]	charrue, schéma	
usual, measure	[ʒ]	rouge, jabot	
how, perhaps	[h]		
metal, comb	[m]	mât, drame	
night, dinner	[n]	nager, trône	
sung, parking	[ŋ]	dancing, smoking	
	[ɲ]	agneau, peigner	
little, help	[l]	halle, lit	
right, carry	[r]	arracher, sabre	

The symbol ['] has been used to represent the French "h aspiré", e.g. hachis ['aʃi].

Le symbole ['] représente le « h aspiré » français, p. ex. hachis ['aʃi].

The symbol ['] indicates that the following syllable carries primary stress and the symbol [͵] that the following syllable carries secondary stress.

Les symboles ['] et [͵] indiquent respectivement un accent primaire et un accent secondaire sur la syllabe suivante.

The symbol [ʳ] in English phonetics indicates that the final "r" is pronounced only when followed by a word beginning with a vowel. Note that it is nearly always pronounced in American English.

Le symbole [ʳ] indique que le « r » final d'un mot anglais ne se prononce que lorsqu'il forme une liaison avec la voyelle du mot suivant ; le « r » final est presque toujours prononcé en anglais américain.

A phonetic transcription has been given where appropriate after every French headword (the main word which starts an entry). All one-word English headwords similarly have phonetics. For English compound headwords, whether hyphenated or of two or more words, phonetics are given for any element which does not appear elsewhere in the dictionary as a headword in its own right.

Une transcription phonétique – quand elle a été jugée nécessaire – suit chaque libellé (terme-vedette de l'entrée) français, ainsi que chaque libellé anglais écrit en un seul mot. Pour les mots composés anglais (avec ou sans trait d'union, et composés de deux éléments ou plus), la phonétique est présente pour ceux des éléments qui n'apparaissent pas dans le dictionnaire en tant que libellés à part entière.

A NOTE ON FRENCH VERBS

French verbs have a number (from [1] to [116]) which refers to the conjugation table given at the back of the dictionary. This number is not repeated for reflexive verbs when these are sub-entries.

VERBES FRANÇAIS

Les verbes français comportent une numérotation (de [1] à [116]) qui renvoie aux conjugaisons fournies en fin d'ouvrage. Ce chiffre n'est pas répété après les verbes pronominaux lorsqu'ils apparaissent comme sous-libellés.

A NOTE ON FRENCH COMPOUNDS

A compound is a word or expression which has a single meaning but is made up of more than one word, e.g. point of order, kiss of life, virtual reality, World Series and International Monetary Fund. It is a feature of this dictionary that English compounds appear in the A-Z list in strict alphabetical order. The compound blood pressure will therefore come after bloodless which itself follows blood group.

MOTS COMPOSÉS ANGLAIS

On désigne par composés des entités lexicales ayant un sens autonome mais qui sont composées de plus d'un mot. Nous avons pris le parti de faire figurer les composés anglais dans l'ordre alphabétique général. Le composé blood pressure est ainsi présenté après bloodless, qui suit blood group.

LISTE DES ENCADRÉS CULTURELS FRANÇAIS
LIST OF FRENCH CULTURAL BOXES

L'ACADÉMIE FRANÇAISE
ARTE
L'ASSEMBLÉE
  NATIONALE
AUDIMAT
LE FESTIVAL
  D'AVIGNON
BACCALAURÉAT
BASTILLE
BEAUBOURG
BIBLIOTHÈQUE NATIO-
  NALE DE FRANCE
BISTROT
BIZUTAGE
CAFÉ
CANAL+
LE FESTIVAL DE
  CANNES
LES CHÂTEAUX
  DE LA LOIRE
LA CINÉMATHÈQUE
  FRANÇAISE
COEFFICIENT
COHABITATION
COLLÈGE
LE COLLÈGE DE FRANCE
LA COMÉDIE-FRANÇAISE

COMITÉ D'ENTREPRISE
LE CONSEIL D'ÈTAT
LE CONSEIL DES
  MINISTRES
COQ GAULOIS
LA COUR DES COMPTES
DÉCLARATION D'IM-
  PÔTS
DEUG, DEUST
DOM-TOM
GRANDE ÉCOLE
L'ÈLYSÉE
FÊTE
FÊTE DE LA MUSIQUE
FRANCOPHONIE
IMMATRICULATION
L'INSTITUT DE FRANCE
L'INSTITUT PASTEUR
LE JOURNAL OFFICIEL
LA FÊTE DU 14 JUILLET
LOTO
LE LOUVRE
LYCÉE
MAI 68
LE MARAIS
MARIANNE
MATIGNON

LA BIBLIOTHÈQUE
  MAZARINE
MÉDECINS SANS FRON-
  TIÈRES
MINITEL
MUGUET
LE MUSÉE D'ORSAY
LE PLAN ORSEC
GRAND ET PETIT
  PALAIS
PÂQUES
PARIS
POLYTECHNIQUE
QUAI
LE QUARTIER LATIN
LA RENTRÉE
LA RÉVOLUTION FRAN-
  ÇAISE
RIVE DROITE, RIVE
  GAUCHE
TIRER LES ROIS
SÉCURITÉ SOCIALE
LE SEIZIÈME
LE SÉNAT
LA SORBONNE
VERLAN
PARC DE LA VILLETTE

LIST OF ENGLISH CULTURAL BOXES
LISTE DES ENCADRÉS CULTURELS ANGLAIS

THE ALBERT HALL
A LEVEL
APRIL FOOL'S DAY
BEST MAN
BILL OF RIGHTS
BINGO
BOOKER PRIZE
BRITISH COUNCIL
BROAD SHEET
BUILDING SOCIETY
CAUCUS
THE CHURCH OF ENGLAND
THE CITY
THE COMMONWEALTH
CONGRESS
CONSTITUTION
CONTINENTAL
  BREAKFAST
COVENT GARDEN
DEVOLUTION
DOWNING STREET

EDINBURGH FESTIVAL
EMBLEMS
ENGLISH BREAKFAST
FETE
FLEET STREET
GRAMMAR SCHOOL
GREAT BRITAIN
GUY FAWKES' NIGHT
HALLOWE'EN
HIGHLAND GAMES
HOUSE OF COMMONS
HOUSE OF LORDS
HOUSE OF
  REPRESENTATIVES
ICE CREAM VAN
L
LICENSING HOURS
PANTOMIME
PENTAGON
POLITICALLY CORRECT
POPPY DAY

PRIMARIES
PRIVY COUNCIL
PUB
PUBLIC SCHOOL
PULITZER PRIZE
SAINT PATRICK'S DAY
SENATE
SPONSORED WALK
THE STARS AND
  STRIPES
SUNDAY PAPERS
THE SUPER BOWL
SUPREME COURT
TABLOID
THANKSGIVING
THE UNION JACK
WALL STREET
THE WELSH ASSEMBLY
WESTMINSTER
WHITEHALL
YELLOW LINES

COMMENT UTILISER LE DICTIONNAIRE

I. Comment trouver le mot ou l'expression que l'on recherche

Il faut d'abord se poser plusieurs questions :
S'agit-il d'un mot isolé, d'un mot à trait d'union ou d'une abréviation ?
S'agit-il d'un nom composé ?
S'agit-il d'une expression ou d'une locution ?
S'agit-il d'un verbe pronominal ?
S'agit-il d'un verbe à particules anglais ?
S'agit-il d'une forme irrégulière ?

Mots isolés, mots à trait d'union et abréviations

En règle générale, on trouve le mot recherché à la place qui lui correspond dans l'ordre alphabétique.

Les entrées commençant par une *majuscule* apparaissent après celles qui s'écrivent de la même façon mais commencent par une minuscule.

> **réunion** [reynjɔ̃] *nf* - **1.** [séance] meeting - **2.** [jonction] union, merging.
> **Réunion** [reynjɔ̃] *nf* : **(l'île de) la ~** Réunion.

Si le mot avec majuscule et le mot avec minuscule sont liés du point de vue du sens, on trouvera la version avec majuscule sous son équivalent avec minuscule, après un losange noir (◆). Il s'agit d'un type de « sous-entrée » (voir plus bas).

> **administration** [ədˌmɪnɪ'streɪʃn] *n* administration *f*.
> ◆ **Administration** *n* **Am** : **the Administration** le gouvernement.

Les mots comportant un *trait d'union*, un *point* ou une *apostrophe* viennent après ceux qui s'écrivent de la même façon mais sans aucun de ces signes.

> **second hand** ['sekənd-] *n* [of clock] trotteuse *f*.
> **second-hand** ['sekənd-] *adj* [goods, shop] d'occasion...

Les entrées portant un *accent* se trouvent après celles qui s'écrivent de la même façon mais sans accent.

> **ou** [u] *conj* [indique une alternative, une approximation] or...
> **où** [u] *pron rel* [spatial] where...

Dans certains cas, l'entrée est suivie d'un chiffre en *exposant*. Ceci veut dire que, juste avant ou juste après, figure une autre entrée, elle aussi suivie d'un chiffre, qui

> **tear¹** [tɪəʳ] *n* larme *f* ; **in ~s** en larmes.
> **tear²** [teəʳ] (*pt* **tore**, *pp* **torn**) *vt* [rip] déchirer...

s'écrit de la même façon mais a un sens ou une prononciation totalement différents. Ce sont ce que l'on appelle des homographes. Il faut s'assurer que l'on ne se trompe pas d'entrée. Faisons donc bien attention à la catégorie grammaticale et à la prononciation. Dans l'exemple ci-dessus, les deux mots « tear » n'ont pas la même phonétique ; il faut par ailleurs se demander si l'on recherche un nom (*n*) ou un verbe transitif (*vt*).

Certains mots sont traités en sous-entrée, précédés d'un losange noir (◆). Il s'agit notamment, comme on l'a vu plus haut, de formes avec majuscule sous la forme équivalente sans majuscule, ou bien de noms placés sous un adjectif.

> **animal, e, aux** [animal, o] *adj* **- 1.** [propre à l'animal] animal *(avant n)* **- 2.** [instinctif] instinctive.
> ◆ **animal** *nm* [bête] animal ; **~ en peluche** stuffed animal...

Si l'on cherche un nom qui, au *pluriel*, a un sens différent de celui du singulier (comme **glass/glasses** en anglais), c'est sous la forme au singulier qu'on le trouvera : le mot au pluriel y figure en sous-entrée.

> **glass** [glɑːs] ◇ *n* **- 1.** [gen] verre *m* **- 2.** *(U)* [glassware] verrerie *f* ◇ *comp* [bottle, jar] en OR de verre ; [door, partition] vitré(e).
> ◆ **glasses** *npl* [spectacles] lunettes *fpl*.

Certains noms apparaissent directement au pluriel dans la liste alphabétique, soit parce qu'ils n'existent pas au singulier, soit parce que ce dernier est rare (**scissors** en anglais, **abats** en français).

Noms composés

Un nom composé est une expression dotée d'une signification globale, mais constituée de plusieurs mots (p. ex. **homme d'affaires** ou **joint venture**). Dans la partie français-anglais, on trouve ces composés dans le dictionnaire à l'entrée correspondant au premier élément. Ainsi, **homme d'affaires** sera sous **homme**. Au sein d'une entrée, les différents noms composés sont classés par ordre alphabétique, sans tenir compte de la préposition médiane ; dans l'entrée **café**, par exemple, **café au lait** vient après **café glacé** et **café en grains**.

Certains composés français dont le sens est éloigné du mot d'entrée sont mis en relief dans l'article et figurent après un losange noir (◆).

> **fuseau, x** [fyzo] *nm* **- 1.** [outil] spindle **- 2.** [pantalon] ski-pants *(pl)*.
> ◆ **fuseau horaire** *nm* time zone.

Du côté anglais, les noms composés apparaissent comme des entrées à part entière.

Il existe aussi des composés dont les deux éléments sont séparés par un trait d'union. Ils figurent dans le dictionnaire en entrée, par exemple **train-spotter** ou **time-sharing**.

> **tea break** *n* Br pause pour prendre le thé, ≈ pause-café *f*.
> **tea caddy** [-ˌkædɪ] *n* boîte *f* à thé.
> **teacake** ['tiːkeɪk] *n* Br petit pain rond avec des raisins secs.

Expressions et locutions

Par « expression » on entend un groupe de mots qui se manifestent toujours dans le même ordre et qui ont un sens global (**prendre part à qqch**, **to do sb credit**). C'est notamment le cas des expressions figurées et idiomatiques, ainsi que des proverbes (**avoir un chat dans la gorge**, **to pull sb's leg**).

Toutes les expressions sont à chercher sous le premier nom dont elles se composent (**prendre part à qqch** sous **part**, **to do sb credit** sous **credit**). S'il n'y a pas de nom dans l'expression, on cherchera sous le verbe.

Certaines expressions très figées ayant une valeur grammaticale globale (locutions) sont traitées en sous-entrée sous le premier élément signifiant, précédées du symbole ➡, de façon à mettre en relief la différence de sens et de fonction grammaticale entre la locution et l'entrée à laquelle elle se rattache.

> **part** [par] *nf* [de gâteau] portion ; [de bonheur, d'héritage] share ; [partie] part ; **réclamer sa ~** to claim one's share...
> ➡ **d'autre part** *loc adv* besides, moreover.
> ➡ **de part en part** *loc adv* right through.

Verbes pronominaux

La plupart des verbes pronominaux sont placés en sous-entrée sous la forme principale qui leur correspond après le symbole ➡.

> **cacher** [3] [kaʃe] *vt* - **1.** [gén] to hide ; **je ne vous cache pas que ...** to be honest, ... - **2.** [vue] to mask.
> ➡ **se cacher** *vp* : **se ~ (de qqn)** to hide (from sb).

Verbes à particules anglais

Les verbes à particules anglais figurent en sous-entrée sous la forme principale du verbe.

> **get** [get] (*Br pt* & *pp* **got**, *cont* -**ting**, *Am pt* **got**, *pp* **gotten**, *cont* -**ting**) *vt* [cause to do] : **to ~ sb to do sthg** faire faire qqch à qqn...
> ➡ **get along** *vi* - **1.** [manage] se débrouiller - **2.** [progress] avancer, faire des progrès - **3.** [have a good relationship] s'entendre.
> ➡ **get up** ◇ *vi* se lever ◇ *vt fus* [petition, demonstration] organiser.

Formes irrégulières

Les formes irrégulières des noms, adjectifs et verbes sont données en entrée dans le dictionnaire.

> **belle** [bɛl] *adj* & *nf* ▷ **beau**.

> **went** [went] *pt* ▷ **go**.

En outre, une liste des verbes irréguliers anglais avec leurs différentes formes figure en annexe.

II. Comment trouver la bonne traduction anglaise

Une fois que l'on aura localisé en français le mot ou l'expression recherchés, il apparaîtra peut-être qu'il existe plusieurs traductions possibles. Qu'à cela ne tienne, on trouvera dans le dictionnaire tous les éléments nécessaires pour identifier la bonne traduction.

Comment fonctionne une entrée de dictionnaire ? Examinons l'entrée **sauter**.

Les losanges blancs (◇) introduisent une catégorie grammaticale lorsqu'un même mot peut en avoir plusieurs - ici, *vi* (verbe intransitif) puis *vt* (verbe transitif). Voir la liste des abréviations p. XI.

Chaque catégorie grammaticale est alors divisée en catégories de sens, introduites par des chiffres en gras (**-1.**, **-2.**), lorsque le mot a plusieurs sens. Des indicateurs entre crochets ([bondir]) ou des indicateurs de domaine (CULIN) permettent d'identifier le sens recherché.

sauter [3] [sote] ◇ *vi* **- 1.** [bondir] to jump, to leap ; **~ à la corde** to skip ; **~ de joie** *fig* to jump for joy ; **~ au cou de qqn** *fig* to throw one's arms around sb **- 2.** [exploser] to blow up ; [fusible] to blow **- 3.** [être projeté - bouchon] to fly out ; [- serrure] to burst off ; [- bouton] to fly off **- 4.** *fam* [employé] to get the sack **- 5.** [être annulé] to be cancelled **- 6.** CULIN : **faire ~ qqch** to sauté sthg **- 7.** *loc* : **et que ça saute!** *fam* and get a move on! ◇ *vt* **- 1.** [fossé, obstacle] to jump *ou* leap over **- 2.** *fig* [page, repas] to skip.

Imaginons que l'on veuille traduire **tu as sauté un chapitre**.

La phrase à traduire comporte un verbe dont nous savons qu'il peut être soit intransitif, soit transitif ; ici, c'est le verbe *transitif* qui nous intéresse (◇ vt) puisqu'il y a un complément d'objet dans la phrase.

Examinons le sens du verbe : le contexte étant celui d'un livre, c'est dans la catégorie **-2.** que l'on trouvera la traduction souhaitée, qui est **to skip**.

Concernant le mot **chapitre**, il n'y a pas de confusion possible entre différentes catégories grammaticales. En revanche, c'est au sens **-1.** [de livre & RELIG], que se trouve la solution : **chapter**.

chapitre [ʃapitr] *nm* **- 1.** [de livre & RELIG] chapter **- 2.** [de budget] head, item **- 3.** *fig* [sujet] subject.

Il ne reste plus qu'à combiner les mots trouvés pour traduire la phrase, en mettant bien sûr le verbe **to skip** au temps et à la forme voulus : **you have skipped a chapter**.

III. Informations d'ordre culturel

Afin de mieux comprendre et de mieux parler une langue étrangère, il est nécessaire d'obtenir des informations concernant les spécificités culturelles du pays concerné. De tels renseignements ne seraient pas à leur place à l'intérieur des entrées du dictionnaire. Ainsi, le lecteur français trouvera dans la partie anglais-français des **encadrés** qui le renseigneront sur les particularités culturelles du Royaume-Uni et des États-Unis.

L'encadré EMBLEMS traite des emblèmes qui symbolisent les différentes régions du Royaume-Uni.

EMBLEMS

La Grande-Bretagne est souvent symbolisée par le personnage de Britannia, une femme en robe longue portant un bouclier au motif de l'Union Jack (drapeau du Royaume-Uni). Les emblèmes de l'Angleterre sont la rose rouge et le lion. Le pays de Galles est traditionnellement représenté par le poireau, ainsi que la jonquille ou le dragon rouge. L'emblème de l'Écosse est le chardon. Le trèfle et la harpe symbolisent l'Irlande.

HOW TO USE THE DICTIONARY

I. Finding the word or phrase you are looking for

First you can ask yourself some basic questions:
Is it a single word, a hyphenated word or an abbreviation?
Is it a compound noun?
Is it a phrase or an idiom?
Is it a reflexive verb?
Is it a phrasal verb?
Is it an irregular form?

Single words, hyphenated words and abbreviations

As a general rule you will find the word you are looking for in its alphabetical order in the dictionary, whether it is a single word, a hyphenated word or an abbreviation.

Words that are written with an *initial capital letter* appear as separate entries to another word spelt in the same way but not capitalized.

> **réunion** [reynjɔ̃] *nf* - **1.** [séance] meeting - **2.** [jonction] union, merging.
> **Réunion** [reynjɔ̃] *nf* : **(l'île de) la ~** Réunion.

If however the capitalized word is related in meaning to the non-capitalized word, it will appear as a sub-entry. Sub-entries are introduced by a black diamond and help highlight items within an entry.

> **réunionnais, e** [reynjɔnɛ, ɛz] *adj* of/from Réunion Island.
> ◆ **Réunionnais, e** *nm, f* native *ou* inhabitant of Réunion.

Words with a *hyphen*, a *full stop* or an *apostrophe* come after those spelled the same way but without any of these punctuation marks.

> **SA** (*abr de* **société anonyme**) *nf* ≃ Ltd *Br*, ≃ Inc. *Am*.
> **S.A.** (*abr de* **Son Altesse**) H.H.

Accented words come after entries that are spelt in the same way but are not accented. So you will find the entry **où** after the entry **ou**.

> **ou** [u] *conj* [indique une alternative, une approximation] or...
> **où** [u] *pron rel* [spatial] where...

Some entries are followed by a *superscript* number. These are homographs: words that are spelt in the same way but that have distinct meanings or pronunciations. You must

> **car**[1] [kar] *nm* coach *Br*, bus *Am*.
> **car**[2] [kar] *conj* for, because.

be careful to identify correctly the entry you need, either by looking at the grammatical category or the phonetic transcription.

If you are looking for a noun which in the plural has its own distinct meaning, you will find it under the singular form as a sub-entry.

> **anglais, e** [ɑ̃glɛ, ɛz] *adj* English...
> ➡ **anglaises** *nfpl* ringlets.

Some plural nouns appear as headwords when they are never or rarely used in the singular, e.g. **scissors** in English or **abats** in French

Compound nouns

A compound is a word or expression which has a single meaning but is made up of more than one word e.g. **people carrier, International Monetary Fund.**

On the English-French side of the dictionary compound nouns are to be found as separate entries in their alphabetical order in the dictionary. The compound **blood donor** will therefore come after **bloodcurdling** which itself follows **blood count.**

> **blood count** *n* numération *f* globulaire.
> **bloodcurdling** ['blʌd,kɜ:dlɪŋ] *adj* à vous glacer le sang.
> **blood donor** *n* donneur *m*, -euse *f* de sang.

On the French-English side however you should look under the first element of the compound. So, for example, you will find **homme d'affaires** at the entry **homme.** If there is more than one compound within an entry, they will appear in their alphabetical order within the entry, regardless of any preposition between the two parts of the compound. So at **café** you will find **café au lait** after **café en grains** and before **café liégeois.**

Some compounds that have distinct meanings from the main entry are treated separately as sub-entries, preceded by a black diamond.

> **fuseau, x** [fyzo] *nm* - **1.** [outil] spindle - **2.** [pantalon] ski-pants *(pl).*
> ➡ **fuseau horaire** *nm* time zone.

Phrases and idioms

Phrases and idioms, such as **avoir un chat dans la gorge** or **to pull sb's leg**, are to be found under the first noun element of the phrase. So you would look for **avoir un chat dans la gorge** at the entry **chat** and **to pull sb's leg** at **leg.**

> **chat, chatte** [ʃa, ʃat] *nm, f* cat ; **~ de gouttière** ordinary cat, alley cat *Am* ; **~ sauvage** wildcat ; **~ persan/siamois** Persian/Siamese cat ; **il n'y a pas un ~** *fam* there's not a soul ; **appeler un ~ un ~** to call a spade a spade ; **avoir d'autres ~s à fouetter** to have other fish to fry ; **avoir un ~ dans la gorge** to have a frog in one's throat.

Some very fixed phrases like **in spite of** in English or **d'autre part** in French are entered under the first noun element as sub-entries.

spite [spaɪt] ◇ n rancune f ; **to do sthg out of** OR **from ~** faire qqch par malice ◇ vt contrarier.
➡ **in spite of** prep en dépit de, malgré.

part [paːr] nf [de gâteau] portion ; [de bonheur, d'héritage] share ; [partie] part ; **réclamer sa ~** to claim one's share...
➡ **d'autre part** loc adv besides, moreover.
➡ **de part en part** loc adv right through.

French reflexive verbs

French reflexive verbs are entered under the main form as sub-entries.

cacher [3] [kaʃe] vt - **1.** [gén] to hide ; **je ne vous cache pas que ...** to be honest, ... - **2.** [vue] to mask.
➡ **se cacher** vp : **se ~ (de qqn)** to hide (from sb).

English phrasal verbs

English phrasal verbs appear as sub-entries.

amount [ə'maʊnt] n [quantity] quantité f ; **a great ~ of** beaucoup de...
➡ **amount to** vt fus - **1.** [total] s'élever à - **2.** [be equivalent to] revenir à, équivaloir à.

Irregular forms

Irregular forms of nouns, adjectives and verbs appear in the dictionary as entries with cross-references to the main form.

vieil ▷ vieux.

caught [kɔːt] pt & pp ▷ catch.

II. Finding the right translation

When you have found the word you are looking for, you will have to identify the right translation. Some entries may only have one translation, but others may be subdivided into different grammatical categories and these in turn may be subdivided into different sense categories. If a word has more than one part of speech, each grammatical category is separated and introduced by a white diamond.

skip [skɪp] (pt & pp **-ped**, cont **-ping**) ◇ n - **1.** [jump] petit saut m - **2.** Br [container] benne f ◇ vt [page, class, meal] sauter ◇ vi - **1.** [gen] sauter, sautiller - **2.** Br [over rope] sauter à la corde.

Here we can see that **skip** is a noun (n), a transitive verb (vt) and an intransitive verb (vi). See page XI for a full list of abbreviations used in the dictionary.

If you had to translate the sentence **"you've skipped a page"**, you must first decide what part of speech **skip** is in this instance. It is a verb with a direct object and therefore you must look for the translation under the transitive verb category, marked "vt". To further reassure you that this is the right category you will find the noun "page" along with other nouns that are used typically with the verb **skip** in square brackets before the translation. So the translation you need here is **sauter**.

Now look at the word **page**.

Again you must decide what part of speech the word is. Here it is a noun. You will notice that the noun category is divided again into different senses. When a word has several

> **page** [peɪdʒ] ◇ n **- 1.** [of book] page f **- 2.** [sheet of paper] feuille f ◇ vt **- 1.** [using a pager] biper **- 2.** [in airport] appeler au micro.

meanings within one part of speech, these are separated into numbered categories. To choose the right numbered sense category, you must use the information provided in the brackets to pinpoint the exact meaning of the word in its context. This may be a synonym, another word frequently used with the entry word, a label indicating the subject area (computing, business, military etc) or an indicator such as here in sense **-1.** (of book). In the sentence **"you have skipped a page"**, we may assume that it is a page in a book rather than a single sheet of paper so the correct translation is **page**. After the translation you will notice the letter "*f*" in italics. This indicates that the French noun is feminine.

You can now translate the sentence correctly, once you have conjugated the verb, as: **"tu as sauté une page"**.

To help you conjugate verbs in French, there are conjugation tables at the back of the dictionary. Each verb on the French-English side of the dictionary has a bracketed number after its phonetic transcription that refers to a conjugation model.

III. Cultural notes

In order to fully understand a foreign language it is often useful to have extra information on the culture of the country. It is not always possible to give this kind of information within a dictionary entry, but you will find boxed notes after certain entries that provide fuller explanations of certain aspects of culture. For example, on the French-English side of the dictionary there is a note describing the significance of the "grandes écoles" which have certain connotations for a native French speaker.

GRANDE ÉCOLE

The 'grandes écoles' are relatively small non-university establishments awarding highly-respected diplomas. Admission is usually only possible after two years of intensive preparatory studies and a competitive examination. Most have close links with industry. The 'grandes écoles' include l'École des hautes études commerciales, or HEC (management and business), l'École polytechnique (engineering) and l'École normale supérieure (the humanities). A diploma from a 'grande école' is comparable in prestige to an Oxbridge degree in Britain.

FRANÇAIS - ANGLAIS

FRENCH - ENGLISH

FRANÇAIS-ANGLAIS
FRENCH-ENGLISH

a¹, A [a] *nm inv* a, A ; **prouver par a + b** to prove conclusively ; **de A à Z** from beginning to end.

➤ **A - 1.** *abr de* **anticyclone - 2.** (*abr de* **ampère**) A, amp **- 3.** (*abr de* **autoroute**) M.

a² ⋄ ▷ **avoir** ⋄ (*abr de* **are**) a.

à [a] *prép* (*contraction de à + le* = **au**, *contraction de à + les* = **aux**) **- 1.** [introduisant un complément d'objet indirect] to ; **parler à qqn** to speak to sb ; **donner qqch à qqn** to give sthg to sb, to give sb sthg ; **penser à qqch** to think about sthg **- 2.** [introduisant un complément de lieu - situation] at, in ; [- direction] to ; **être à la maison/au bureau** to be at home/at the office ; **il habite à Paris/à la campagne** he lives in Paris/in the country ; **il vit au Pérou** he lives in Peru ; **aller à Paris/à la campagne/au Pérou** to go to Paris/to the country/to Peru ; **un voyage à Londres/aux Seychelles** a journey to London/to the Seychelles **- 3.** [introduisant un complément de temps] : **à onze heures** at eleven o'clock ; **au mois de février** in the month of February ; **à lundi!** see you (on) Monday! ; **à plus tard!** see you later! ; **de huit à dix heures** from eight to ten o'clock ; **se situer à une heure/à 10 kilomètres de l'aéroport** to be situated an hour/10 kilometres (away) from the airport **- 4.** [introduisant un complément de manière, de moyen] : **à haute voix** out loud, aloud ; **rire aux éclats** to roar with laughter ; **agir à son gré** to do as one pleases ; **acheter à crédit** to buy on credit ; **à pied/cheval** on foot/ horseback **- 5.** [indiquant une caractéristique] with ; **une fille aux cheveux longs** a girl with long hair ; **l'homme à l'imperméable** the man with the raincoat **- 6.** [introduisant un chiffre] : **ils sont venus à dix** ten of them came ; **un livre à**

30 **francs** a 30-franc book, a book costing 30 francs ; **la vitesse est limitée à 50 km à l'heure** the speed limit is 50 km per *ou* an hour ; **un groupe de 10 à 12 personnes** a group of 10 to 12 people, a group of between 10 and 12 people ; **deux à deux** two by two **- 7.** [marque l'appartenance] : **c'est à moi/toi/lui/elle** it's mine/yours/his/hers ; **ce vélo est à ma sœur** this bike is my sister's *ou* belongs to my sister ; **une amie à moi** a friend of mine **- 8.** [introduit le but] : **coupe à champagne** champagne goblet ; **le courrier à poster** the mail to be posted ; **appartement à vendre/louer** flat for sale/to let.

AB (*abr de* **assez bien**) *fair grade (as assessment of schoolwork).*

abaisser [4] [abese] *vt* **- 1.** [rideau, voile] to lower ; [levier, manette] to push *ou* pull down **- 2.** [diminuer] to reduce, to lower **- 3.** *sout* [avilir] to debase.

➤ **s'abaisser** *vp* **- 1.** [descendre - rideau] to fall, to come down ; [- terrain] to fall away **- 2.** [s'humilier] to demean o.s. ; **s'~ à faire qqch** to lower o.s. to do sthg.

abandon [abãdɔ̃] *nm* **- 1.** [désertion, délaissement] desertion ; **à l'~** [jardin, maison] neglected, in a state of neglect **- 2.** [renonciation] abandoning, giving up **- 3.** [cession] renunciation, giving up ; **faire ~ de qqch (au profit de qqn)** to make sthg over (to sb) **- 4.** [nonchalance, confiance] abandon.

abandonner [3] [abãdɔne] *vt* **- 1.** [quitter - femme, enfants] to abandon, to desert ; [- voiture, propriété] to abandon ; **~ son poste** to desert one's post **- 2.** [renoncer à] to give up, to abandon **- 3.** [se retirer de - course, concours] to withdraw from - **4.** [céder] : ~ **qqch à qqn** to leave sthg to sb, to leave sb sthg.

➤ **s'abandonner** *vp* - **1.** [se laisser aller] : **s'~ à qqch** to give o.s. up to sthg - **2.** [s'épancher] to pour out one's feelings.

abasourdi, e [abazurdi] *adj* stunned.

abasourdir [32] [abazurdir] *vt* to stun.

abat-jour [abaʒur] *nm inv* lampshade.

abats [aba] *nmpl* [d'animal] offal *(U)* ; [de volaille] giblets.

abattage [abataʒ] *nm* [d'arbre] felling.

abattement [abatmã] *nm* - **1.** [faiblesse physique] weakness - **2.** [désespoir] dejection - **3.** [déduction] reduction ; ~ **fiscal** tax allowance.

abattis [abati] *nmpl* giblets.

abattoir [abatwar] *nm* abattoir, slaughterhouse.

abattre [83] [abatr] *vt* - **1.** [faire tomber - mur] to knock down ; [- arbre] to cut down, to fell ; [- avion] to bring down - **2.** [tuer - gén] to kill ; [- dans un abattoir] to slaughter - **3.** [épuiser] to wear out ; [démoraliser] to demoralize.

➤ **s'abattre** *vp* : **s'~ (sur)** [toit, arbre] to crash down (on) ; [pluie] to beat down (on) ; [avion, insectes, rapaces] to swoop down (on) ; [maladie, fléau] to descend (on).

abattu, e [abaty] ◇ *pp* ➤ **abattre** ◇ *adj* - **1.** [déprimé] demoralized, dejected - **2.** [affaibli] very weak.

abbaye [abei] *nf* abbey.

abbé [abe] *nm* - **1.** [prêtre] priest - **2.** [de couvent] abbot.

abc [abese] *nm* basics *(pl)*.

abcès [apsɛ] *nm* abscess ; **crever l'~ fig** to root out the problem.

abdication [abdikasjɔ̃] *nf* abdication.

abdiquer [3] [abdike] ◇ *vt* - **1.** [renoncer à] to renounce - **2.** [suj : roi] to abdicate ◇ *vi* - **1.** [roi] to abdicate - **2.** [renoncer] to give up.

abdomen [abdɔmɛn] *nm* abdomen.

abdominal, e, aux [abdɔminal, o] *adj* abdominal.

➤ **abdominaux** *nmpl* - **1.** [muscles] abdominal *ou* stomach muscles - **2.** [exercices] : **faire des abdominaux** to do exercises for the stomach muscles.

abécédaire [abesedɛr] *nm* ABC *(book)*.

abeille [abɛj] *nf* bee.

aberrant, e [abɛrɑ̃, ɑ̃t] *adj* absurd.

aberration [abɛrasjɔ̃] *nf* aberration.

abhorrer [3] [abɔre] *vt sout* to abhor.

Abidjan [abidʒɑ̃] *n* Abidjan.

abîme [abim] *nm* abyss, gulf.

abîmer [3] [abime] *vt* [détériorer - objet] to damage ; [- partie du corps, vue] to ruin.

➤ **s'abîmer** *vp* - **1.** [gén] to be damaged ; [fruits] to go bad - **2.** *fig* [personne] : **s'~ dans** [lecture] to bury o.s. in ; [pensées] to lose o.s. in.

abject, e [abʒɛkt] *adj* despicable, contemptible.

abjurer [3] [abʒyre] *vt* RELIG to renounce.

ablatif [ablatif] *nm* ablative.

ablation [ablasjɔ̃] *nf* MÉD removal.

ablutions [ablysjɔ̃] *nfpl* : **faire ses ~** to perform one's ablutions.

abnégation [abnegasjɔ̃] *nf* selflessness.

aboie, aboies *etc* ➪ **aboyer.**

aboiement [abwamã] *nm* bark, barking *(U).*

abois [abwa] *nmpl* : **être aux ~ fig** to be in dire straits.

abolir [32] [abɔlir] *vt* to abolish.

abolition [abɔlisjɔ̃] *nf* abolition.

abominable [abɔminabl] *adj* appalling, awful.

abominablement [abɔminabləmã] *adv* - **1.** [très mal] abominably - **2.** [extrêmement] awfully.

abomination [abɔminasjɔ̃] *nf* abomination.

abondamment [abɔ̃damã] *adv* - **1.** [beaucoup] plentifully - **2.** [largement] extensively.

abondance [abɔ̃dɑ̃s] *nf* - **1.** [profusion] abundance ; **en ~** in abundance - **2.** [opulence] affluence ; **vivre dans l'~** to live in affluence.

abondant, e [abɔ̃dɑ̃, ɑ̃t] *adj* [gén] plentiful ; [végétation, chevelure] luxuriant ; [pluie] heavy.

abonder [3] [abɔ̃de] *vi* to abound, to be abundant ; ~ **en qqch** to be rich in sthg ; ~ **dans le sens de qqn** to be entirely of sb's opinion.

abonné, e [abɔne] *nm, f* - **1.** [à un journal, à une chaîne de télé] subscriber ; [à un théâtre] season-ticket holder - **2.** [à un service public] consumer.

abonnement [abɔnmã] *nm* - **1.** [à un journal, à une chaîne de télé] subscription ; [à un théâtre] season ticket - **2.** [au téléphone] rental ; [au gaz, à l'électricité] standing charge.

abonner [3] [abɔne] ➤ **s'abonner** *vp* : **s'~ à qqch** [journal, chaîne de télé] to take out a subscription to sthg ; [service public] to get connected to sthg ; [théâtre] to buy a season ticket for sthg.

abord [abɔr] *nm* : **être d'un ~ facile/difficile** to be very/not very approachable ; **au premier ~, de prime ~** at first sight ; **dès l'~** from the outset.

➤ **abords** *nmpl* [gén] surrounding area *(sg)* ; [de ville] outskirts.

d'abord *loc adv* - **1.** [en premier lieu] first - **2.** [avant tout] : **(tout) d'~** first (of all), in the first place.

abordable [abɔrdabl] *adj* [lieu] accessible ; [personne] approachable ; [de prix modéré] affordable.

abordage [abɔrdaʒ] *nm* boarding.

aborder [3] [abɔrde] <> *vi* to land <> *vt* - **1.** [personne, lieu] to approach - **2.** [question] to tackle.

aborigène [abɔriʒɛn] *adj* aboriginal.

Aborigène *nmf* (Australian) aborigine.

abouti, e [abuti] *adj* - **1.** [projet, démarche] successful - **2.** [œuvre] accomplished.

aboutir [32] [abutir] *vi* - **1.** [chemin] : **~ à/dans** to end at/in - **2.** [négociation] to be successful ; **~ à qqch** to result in sthg.

aboutissement [abutismã] *nm* outcome.

aboyer [13] [abwaje] *vi* to bark.

abracadabrant, e [abrakadabrã, ãt] *adj* preposterous.

abrasif, ive [abrazif, iv] *adj* abrasive.

abrasif *nm* abrasive.

abrégé, e [abreʒe] *adj* abridged.

abrégé *nm* résumé, summary ; **en ~** in abbreviated form.

abréger [22] [abreʒe] *vt* [visite, réunion] to cut short ; [discours] to shorten ; [mot] to abbreviate.

abreuver [5] [abrœve] *vt* [animal] to water ; **~ qqn de** *fig* to shower sb with.

s'abreuver *vp* to drink.

abreuvoir [abrœvwar] *nm* [lieu] watering place ; [installation] drinking trough.

abréviation [abrevjasjɔ̃] *nf* abbreviation.

abri [abri] *nm* shelter ; **à l'~ de** sheltered from ; *fig* safe from ; **se mettre à l'~ (de)** to shelter (from), to take shelter (from) ; **~ antiatomique** nuclear fallout shelter ; **~ de jardin** garden shed.

abricot [abriko] *nm* & *adj inv* apricot.

abricotier [abrikɔtje] *nm* apricot tree.

abriter [3] [abrite] *vt* - **1.** [protéger] : **~ qqn/qqch (de)** to shelter sb/sthg (from) - **2.** [héberger] to accommodate.

s'abriter *vp* : **s'~ (de)** to shelter (from).

abroger [17] [abrɔʒe] *vt* to repeal.

abrupt, e [abrypt] *adj* - **1.** [raide] steep - **2.** [rude] abrupt, brusque.

abruti, e [abryti] *fam* <> *adj* moronic <> *nm, f* moron.

abrutir [32] [abrytir] *vt* - **1.** [abêtir] : **~ qqn** to deaden sb's mind - **2.** [accabler] : **~ qqn de travail** to work sb silly - **3.** [étourdir] to daze.

s'abrutir *vp* - **1.** [s'épuiser] : **s'~ de travail** to work o.s. stupid - **2.** [s'abêtir] to become moronic.

abrutissant, e [abrytisã, ãt] *adj* - **1.** [bruit, travail] stupefying - **2.** [jeu, feuilleton] moronic.

abrutissement [abrytismã] *nm* - **1.** [épuisement] exhaustion - **2.** [intellectuel] mindless state.

ABS (*abr de* **Antiblockiersystem**) *nm* ABS.

absence [apsãs] *nf* - **1.** [de personne] absence ; **en l'~ de** in the absence of - **2.** [carence] lack.

absent, e [apsã, ãt] <> *adj* - **1.** [personne] : **~ (de)** [gén] away (from) ; [pour maladie] absent (from) - **2.** [regard, air] vacant, absent - **3.** [manquant] lacking <> *nm, f* absentee.

absentéisme [apsãteism] *nm* absenteeism.

absenter [3] [apsãte] **s'absenter** *vp* : **s'~ (de la pièce)** to leave (the room).

abside [apsid] *nf* apse.

absinthe [apsɛ̃t] *nf* [plante] wormwood ; [boisson] absinth.

absolu, e [apsɔly] *adj* [gén] absolute ; [décision, jugement] uncompromising.

absolu *nm* : **l'~** the Absolute ; **dans l'~** out of context.

absolument [apsɔlymã] *adv* absolutely.

absolution [apsɔlysjɔ̃] *nf* absolution.

absolutisme [apsɔlytism] *nm* absolutism.

absorbant, e [apsɔrbã, ãt] *adj* - **1.** [matière] absorbent - **2.** [occupation] absorbing.

absorber [3] [apsɔrbe] *vt* - **1.** [gén] to absorb - **2.** [manger] to take - **3.** [entreprise] to take over.

s'absorber *vp* : **s'~ dans qqch** to get *ou* become absorbed in sthg.

absorption [apsɔrpsjɔ̃] *nf* - **1.** [gén] absorption - **2.** *ÉCON* takeover.

abstenir [40] [apstənir] **s'abstenir** *vp* - **1.** [ne rien faire] : **s'~ (de qqch/de faire qqch)** to refrain (from sthg/from doing sthg) - **2.** [ne pas voter] to abstain.

abstention [apstãsjɔ̃] *nf* abstention.

abstentionnisme [apstãsjɔnism] *nm* abstaining.

abstenu, e [apstəny] *pp* ▷ **abstenir.**

abstiendrai, abstiendras *etc* ▷ **abstenir.**

abstinence [apstinãs] *nf* abstinence ; **faire ~** to abstain (from eating meat).

abstraction [apstraksjɔ̃] *nf* abstraction ; **faire ~ de** to disregard.

abstrait, e [apstrɛ, ɛt] *adj* abstract.

abstrait *nm* : **l'~** the abstract.

absurde [apsyrd] <> *adj* absurd <> *nm* : **l'~** the absurd ; **raisonnement par l'~** reductio ad absurdum.

absurdité [apsyrdite] *nf* absurdity ; **dire des ~s** to talk nonsense *(U)*.

abus [aby] *nm* abuse ; **~ de confiance** breach of trust ; **~ de pouvoir** abuse of power.

abuser [3] [abyze] ◇ *vi* - **1.** [dépasser les bornes] to go too far - **2.** [user] : **~ de** [autorité, pouvoir] to overstep the bounds of ; [femme] to take advantage of ; [temps] to take up too much of ; **~ de ses forces** to overexert o.s. ◇ *vt sout* to mislead.
◆ **s'abuser** *vp* : **s'~ sur** to delude o.s. about.

abusif, ive [abyzif, iv] *adj* - **1.** [excessif] excessive - **2.** [fautif] improper.

AC (*abr de* **appellation contrôlée**) *nf label guaranteeing quality of wine.*

acabit [akabi] *nm* : **du même ~** *péj* of the same type.

acacia [akasja] *nm* acacia.

académicien, enne [akademisjɛ̃, ɛn] *nm, f* academician ; [de l'Académie française] member of the French Academy.

académie [akademi] *nf* - **1.** *SCOL* & *UNIV* ≃ regional education authority *Br*, ≃ school district *Am* - **2.** [institut] academy ; **l'Académie française** the French Academy *(learned society of leading men and women of letters)* ; **l'Académie Goncourt** *literary society whose members choose the winner of the Prix Goncourt.*

L'ACADÉMIE FRANÇAISE

Founded in 1634 by Cardinal Richelieu, the 'Académie française' consists of forty distinguished writers known as 'les Quarante' or 'les Immortels'. Their chief task is to produce a definitive grammar and dictionary, the 9th edition of which dates from 1986, and to be the ultimate authority in matters concerning the French language.

académique [akademik] *adj* - **1.** *UNIV* academic - **2.** [conventionnel] conventional.

acajou [akaʒu] *nm* & *adj inv* mahogany.

acariâtre [akarjatr] *adj* bad-tempered, cantankerous.

acarien [akarjɛ̃] *nm* [gén] acarid ; [de poussière] dust mite.

accablant, e [akablɑ̃, ɑ̃t] *adj* - **1.** [soleil, chaleur] oppressive - **2.** [preuve, témoignage] overwhelming.

accabler [3] [akable] *vt* - **1.** [surcharger] : **~ qqn de** [travail] to overwhelm sb with ; **~ qqn d'injures** to shower sb with abuse - **2.** [accuser] to condemn.

accalmie [akalmi] *nf litt* & *fig* lull.

accaparer [3] [akapare] *vt* to monopolize ; **son travail l'accapare** his work takes up all his time.
◆ **s'accaparer** *vp* : **s'~ qqch** to seize sthg.

accéder [18] [aksede] ◆ **accéder à** *vt* - **1.** [pénétrer dans] to reach, to get to - **2.** [parvenir à] to attain - **3.** [consentir à] to comply with.

accélérateur [akseleratœr] *nm* accelerator.

accélération [akselerasjɔ̃] *nf* [de voiture, machine] acceleration ; [de projet] speeding up.

accélérer [18] [akselere] ◇ *vt* to accelerate, to speed up ◇ *vi AUTOM* to accelerate.

accent [aksɑ̃] *nm* - **1.** [gén] accent ; **~ aigu/grave/circonflexe** acute/grave/circumflex (accent) - **2.** [intonation] tone ; **~ tonique** stress ; **mettre l'~ sur** to stress, to emphasize.

accentuation [aksɑ̃tɥasjɔ̃] *nf* - **1.** [à l'écrit] accenting ; [en parlant] stress - **2.** [intensification] intensification.

accentuer [7] [aksɑ̃tɥe] *vt* - **1.** [insister sur, souligner] to emphasize, to accentuate - **2.** [intensifier] to intensify - **3.** [à l'écrit] to put the accents on ; [en parlant] to stress.
◆ **s'accentuer** *vp* to become more pronounced.

acceptable [akseptabl] *adj* satisfactory, acceptable.

acceptation [akseptasjɔ̃] *nf* acceptance.

accepter [4] [aksepte] *vt* to accept ; **~ de faire qqch** to agree to do sthg ; **~ que** *(+ subjonctif)* : **~ que qqn fasse qqch** to agree to sb doing sthg ; **je n'accepte pas qu'il me parle ainsi** I won't have him talking to me like that.

acception [aksepsjɔ̃] *nf* sense.

accès [aksɛ] *nm* - **1.** [entrée] entry ; **avoir/donner ~ à** to have/to give access to ; '**~ interdit**' 'no entry' ; '**~ réservé aux riverains**' 'residents only' - **2.** [voie d'entrée] entrance - **3.** [abord] : **être d'un ~ facile/difficile** [personne] to be approachable/unapproachable ; [livre] to be easy/difficult (to read) - **4.** [crise] bout ; **~ de colère** fit of anger.

accessible [aksesibl] *adj* - **1.** [lieu, livre] accessible ; [personne] approachable ; [prix, équipement] affordable - **2.** [sensible] : **~ à** susceptible to.

accession [aksesjɔ̃] *nf* : **~ à** [trône, présidence] accession to ; [indépendance] attainment of.

accessoire [akseswar] ◇ *nm* - **1.** [gén] accessory - **2.** [de théâtre, cinéma] prop ◇ *adj* secondary.

accessoirement [akseswarmɑ̃] *adv* if need be.

accident [aksidɑ̃] *nm* accident ; **par ~** by chance, by accident ; **~ de parcours** hiccup ;

~ **de la route/de voiture/du travail** road/car/ industrial accident ; ~ **de terrain** bump.

accidenté, e [aksidɑ̃te] <> adj - **1.** [terrain, surface] uneven - **2.** [voiture] damaged - **3.** [vie] eventful <> nm, f (gén pl) : ~ **de la route** accident victim.

accidentel, elle [aksidɑ̃tɛl] adj accidental.

accidentellement [aksidɑ̃tɛlmɑ̃] adv [rencontrer] by chance, accidentally ; [mourir] in an accident.

acclamation [aklamasjɔ̃] nf (gén pl) cheers (pl), cheering (U).

acclamer [3] [aklame] vt to cheer.

acclimatation [aklimatasjɔ̃] nf acclimatization.

acclimater [3] [aklimate] vt to acclimatize ; fig to introduce.
➡ **s'acclimater** vp : **s'~ à** to become acclimatized to.

accointances [akwɛ̃tɑ̃s] nfpl : **avoir des ~ dans/avec** péj to have contacts in/with.

accolade [akɔlad] nf - **1.** TYPO brace - **2.** [embrassade] embrace ; **donner l'~ à qqn** to embrace sb.

accoler [3] [akɔle] vt - **1.** [par accolade] to bracket together - **2.** [adjoindre] : ~ **qqch à** to add sthg to.

accommodant, e [akɔmɔdɑ̃, ɑ̃t] adj obliging.

accommodement [akɔmɔdmɑ̃] nm compromise.

accommoder [3] [akɔmɔde] vt - **1.** CULIN to prepare - **2.** [mettre en accord] : ~ **qqch à** to adapt sthg to.
➡ **s'accommoder** vp : **s'~ de** to put up with ; **s'~ à** to adapt to.

accompagnateur, trice [akɔ̃paɲatœr, tris] nm, f - **1.** MUS accompanist - **2.** [guide] guide.

accompagnement [akɔ̃paɲmɑ̃] nm - **1.** MUS accompaniment - **2.** CULIN side dish.

accompagner [3] [akɔ̃paɲe] vt - **1.** [personne] to go with, to accompany - **2.** [agrémenter] : ~ **qqch de** to accompany sthg with ; **elle accompagna sa réponse d'un sourire** she answered with a smile - **3.** MUS to accompany ; ~ **qqn au piano/à la guitare** to accompany sb on the piano/guitar.

accompli, e [akɔ̃pli] adj accomplished.

accomplir [32] [akɔ̃plir] vt to carry out.
➡ **s'accomplir** vp to come about.

accomplissement [akɔ̃plismɑ̃] nm [d'apprentissage] completion ; [de travail] fulfilment.

accord [akɔr] nm - **1.** [gén & LING] agreement ; **en ~ avec** in harmony with ; **d'un commun ~** with one accord ; ~ **à l'amiable** COMM out-of-

court settlement, mutual agreement - **2.** MUS chord - **3.** [acceptation] approval ; **donner son ~ à qqch** to approve sthg.
➡ **d'accord** <> loc adv OK, all right <> loc adj : **être d'~ (avec)** to agree (with) ; **tomber** OU **se mettre d'~** to come to an agreement, to agree.

accordéon [akɔrdeɔ̃] nm accordion ; **avoir les chaussettes en ~** to have one's socks down around one's ankles.

accorder [3] [akɔrde] vt - **1.** [donner] : ~ **qqch à qqn** to grant sb sthg - **2.** [attribuer] : ~ **qqch à qqch** to accord sthg to sthg ; ~ **de l'importance à** to attach importance to - **3.** [harmoniser] to match - **4.** GRAM : ~ **qqch avec qqch** to make sthg agree with sthg - **5.** MUS to tune.
➡ **s'accorder** vp - **1.** [gén] : **s'~ (pour faire qqch)** to agree (to do sthg) ; **s'~ à faire qqch** to be unanimous in doing sthg - **2.** [être assorti] to match - **3.** GRAM to agree.

accordeur [akɔrdœr] nm tuner.

accoster [3] [akɔste] <> vt - **1.** NAVIG to come alongside - **2.** [personne] to accost <> vi NAVIG to dock.

accotement [akɔtmɑ̃] nm [de route] shoulder ; ~ **stabilisé** hard shoulder ; ~ **non stabilisé** soft verge Br, soft shoulder Am.

accouchement [akuʃmɑ̃] nm childbirth ; ~ **sans douleur** natural childbirth.

accoucher [3] [akuʃe] vi : ~ **(de)** to give birth (to).

accouder [3] [akude] ➡ **s'accouder** vp to lean on one's elbows ; **s'~ à** to lean one's elbows on.

accoudoir [akudwar] nm armrest.

accouplement [akupləmɑ̃] nm mating, coupling.

accourir [45] [akurir] vi to run up, to rush up.

accours, accourt etc ▷ **accourir**.

accouru, e [akury] pp ▷ **accourir**.

accoutré, e [akutre] adj péj : **être bizarrement ~** to be oddly got up.

accoutrement [akutrəmɑ̃] nm péj getup.

accoutrer [3] [akutre] ➡ **s'accoutrer** vp péj : **s'~ bizarrement** to get o.s. up very strangely.

accoutumance [akutymɑ̃s] nf [adaptation] adaptation ; MÉD addiction.

accoutumé, e [akutyme] adj usual.
➡ **comme à l'accoutumée** loc adv sout as usual.

accoutumer [3] [akutyme] vt : ~ **qqn à qqn/ qqch** to get sb used to sb/sthg ; ~ **qqn à faire qqch** to get sb used to doing sthg.
➡ **s'accoutumer** vp : **s'~ à qqn/qqch** to get

used to sb/sthg ; **s'~ à faire qqch** to get used to doing sthg.

accréditation [akreditasjɔ̃] *nf* FIN accreditation.

accréditer [3] [akredite] *vt* [rumeur] to substantiate ; **~ qqn auprès de** to accredit sb to. ➤ **s'accréditer** *vp* to gain substance.

accro [akro] *fam* ◇ *adj* : **~ à** hooked on ◇ *nmf* : **c'est une ~ de la planche** she's a windsurfing freak.

accroc [akro] *nm* - **1.** [déchirure] tear ; **faire un ~ à** to tear - **2.** [incident] hitch ; **sans ~** without a hitch.

accrochage [akrɔʃaʒ] *nm* - **1.** [accident] collision - **2.** *fam* [dispute] row - **3.** [de tableaux] hanging.

accroche [akrɔʃ] *nf* COMM catch line.

accrocher [3] [akrɔʃe] *vt* - **1.** [suspendre] : **~ qqch (à)** to hang sthg up (on) - **2.** [déchirer] : **~ qqch (à)** to catch sthg (on) - **3.** [attacher] : **~ qqch (à)** to hitch sthg (to) - **4.** [heurter] to bump into - **5.** [retenir l'attention de] to attract. ➤ **s'accrocher** *vp* - **1.** [s'agripper] : **s'~ (à)** to hang on (to) ; **s'~ à qqn** *fig* to cling to sb - **2.** *fam* [se disputer] to row, to have a row - **3.** *fam* [persévérer] to stick at it.

accrocheur, euse [akrɔʃœr, øz] *adj* - **1.** [qui retient l'attention] eye-catching - **2.** [opiniâtre] tenacious.

accroire [akrwar] *vt sout* : **en faire ~ à qqn** to take sb in.

accroissement [akrwasmɑ̃] *nm* increase, growth.

accroître [94] [akrwatr] *vt* to increase. ➤ **s'accroître** *vp* to increase, to grow.

accroupir [32] [akrupir] ➤ **s'accroupir** *vp* to squat.

accru, e [akry] *pp* ▷ **accroître**.

accu [aky] *nm* : **recharger ses ~s** *fam fig* to recharge one's batteries.

accueil [akœj] *nm* - **1.** [lieu] reception - **2.** [action] welcome, reception.

accueillant, e [akœjɑ̃, ɑ̃t] *adj* welcoming, friendly.

accueillir [41] [akœjir] *vt* - **1.** [gén] to welcome - **2.** [loger] to accommodate.

acculer [3] [akyle] *vt* - **1.** [repousser] : **~ qqn contre/à** to drive sb up against/into - **2.** *fig* : **~ qqn à** [ruine, désespoir] to drive sb to ; [faute] to force sb into.

accumulateur [akymylatœr] *nm* accumulator, battery.

accumulation [akymylasjɔ̃] *nf* accumulation.

accumuler [3] [akymyle] *vt* to accumulate ; *fig* to store up. ➤ **s'accumuler** *vp* to pile up.

accusateur, trice [akyzatœr, tris] ◇ *adj* accusing ◇ *nm, f* accuser.

accusation [akyzasjɔ̃] *nf* - **1.** [reproche] accusation - **2.** JUR charge ; **mettre en ~** to indict ; **l'~** the prosecution.

accusé, e [akyze] *nm, f* accused, defendant. ➤ **accusé de réception** *nm* acknowledgement (of receipt).

accuser [3] [akyze] *vt* - **1.** [porter une accusation contre] : **~ qqn (de qqch)** to accuse sb (of sthg) - **2.** JUR : **~ qqn de qqch** to charge sb with sthg - **3.** [mettre en relief] to emphasize.

acerbe [asɛrb] *adj* acerbic.

acéré, e [asere] *adj* sharp.

acériculture [aserikyltyr] *nf* maple sugar production.

acétate [asetat] *nm* acetate.

acétone [asetɔn] *nf* acetone.

achalandé, e [aʃalɑ̃de] *adj* [en marchandises] : **bien ~** well-stocked.

acharné, e [aʃarne] *adj* [combat] fierce ; [travail] unremitting.

acharnement [aʃarnəmɑ̃] *nm* relentlessness.

acharner [3] [aʃarne] ➤ **s'acharner** *vp* - **1.** [combattre] : **s'~ contre** *ou* **après** *ou* **sur qqn** [ennemi, victime] to hound sb ; [suj : malheur] to dog sb - **2.** [s'obstiner] : **s'~ (à faire qqch)** to persist (in doing sthg).

achat [aʃa] *nm* purchase ; **faire des ~s** to go shopping ; **~ d'espace** COMM buying of (advertising) space.

acheminer [3] [aʃmine] *vt* to dispatch. ➤ **s'acheminer** *vp* : **s'~ vers** [lieu, désastre] to head for ; [solution, paix] to move towards *Br ou* toward *Am*.

acheter [28] [aʃte] *vt litt* & *fig* to buy ; **~ qqch à** *ou* **pour qqn** to buy sthg for sb, to buy sb sthg ; **~ qqch à qqn** [commerçant] to buy sthg from sb.

acheteur, euse [aʃtœr, øz] *nm, f* buyer, purchaser.

achevé, e [aʃve] *adj sout* : **d'un ridicule ~** utterly ridiculous.

achèvement [aʃɛvmɑ̃] *nm* completion.

achever [19] [aʃve] *vt* - **1.** [terminer] to complete, to finish (off) - **2.** [tuer, accabler] to finish off. ➤ **s'achever** *vp* to end, to come to an end.

achoppement [aʃɔpmɑ̃] ▷ **pierre**.

acide [asid] ◇ *adj* - **1.** [saveur] sour - **2.** [propos] sharp, acid - **3.** CHIM acid ◇ *nm* - **1.** CHIM acid ;

~ **acétique/chlorhydrique/sulfurique** acetic/hydrochloric/sulphuric acid ; ~ **aminé** amino acid - **2.** *arg drogue* acid.

acidité [asidite] *nf* - **1.** CHIM acidity - **2.** [saveur] sourness - **3.** [de propos] sharpness.

acid jazz [asiddʒaz] *nm* acid jazz.

acidulé, e [asidyle] *adj* slightly acid ; ⊳ **bonbon.**

acier [asje] *nm* steel ; ~ **inoxydable** stainless steel.

aciérie [asjeri] *nf* steelworks *(sg)*.

acné [akne] *nf* acne ; ~ **juvénile** teenage acne.

acolyte [akɔlit] *nm péj* henchman.

acompte [akɔ̃t] *nm* deposit ; **verser un** ~ to put down *ou* pay a deposit.

acoquiner [3] [akɔkine] ❧ **s'acoquiner** *vp* : **s'~ avec qqn** to gang up with sb.

à-côté [akote] *(pl* **à-côtés**) *nm* - **1.** [point accessoire] side issue - **2.** [gain d'appoint] extra.

à-coup [aku] *(pl* **à-coups**) *nm* jerk ; **par ~s** in fits and starts.

acoustique [akustik] ◇ *nf* - **1.** [science] acoustics *(U)* - **2.** [d'une salle] acoustics *(pl)* ◇ *adj* acoustic.

acquéreur [akerœr] *nm* buyer.

acquérir [39] [akerir] *vt* - **1.** [gén] to acquire - **2.** [conquérir] to win.
❧ **s'acquérir** *vp* : **s'~ qqch** to win sthg, to gain sthg.

acquiers, acquiert etc ⊳ **acquérir.**

acquiescement [akjɛsmɑ̃] *nm* approval.

acquiescer [21] [akjese] *vi* to acquiesce ; ~ **à** to agree to.

acquis, e [aki, iz] ◇ *pp* ⊳ **acquérir** ◇ *adj* - **1.** [caractère] acquired - **2.** [droit, avantage] established.
❧ **acquis** *nmpl* [connaissances] knowledge *(U)*.

acquisition [akizisjɔ̃] *nf* acquisition.

acquit [aki] *nm* receipt ; **pour** ~ COMM received ; **faire qqch par** ~ **de conscience** *fig* to do sthg to set one's mind at rest.

acquittement [akitmɑ̃] *nm* - **1.** [d'obligation] settlement - **2.** JUR acquittal.

acquitter [3] [akite] *vt* - **1.** JUR to acquit - **2.** [régler] to pay - **3.** [libérer] : ~ **qqn de** to release sb from.
❧ **s'acquitter** *vp* : **s'~ de qqch** [payer] to settle sthg ; *fig* to carry sthg out.

âcre [akr] *adj* - **1.** [saveur] bitter - **2.** [fumée] acrid.

acrimonie [akrimɔni] *nf* acrimony.

acrobate [akrɔbat] *nmf* acrobat.

acrobatie [akrɔbasi] *nf* acrobatics *(U)* ; ~**s aériennes** aerobatics *(pl)*.

acrobatique [akrɔbatik] *adj* acrobatic.

acronyme [akrɔnim] *nm* acronym.

acrylique [akrilik] *adj* & *nm* acrylic.

acte [akt] *nm* - **1.** [action] act, action ; **faire** ~ **d'autorité** to exercise one's authority ; **faire** ~ **de bonne volonté** to make a gesture of goodwill ; **faire** ~ **de candidature** to submit an application - **2.** THÉÂTRE act - **3.** JUR deed ; ~ **d'accusation** charge ; ~ **de naissance/de mariage** birth/marriage certificate ; ~ **notarié** deed executed by a notary ; ~ **de vente** bill of sale - **4.** RELIG certificate ; ~ **de baptême** baptismal certificate - **5.** loc : **faire** ~ **de présence** to put in an appearance ; **prendre** ~ **de** to note, to take note of.
❧ **actes** *nmpl* [de colloque] proceedings.

acteur, trice [aktœr, tris] *nm, f* actor *(f* actress*)*.

actif, ive [aktif, iv] *adj* [gén] active ; **la population active** the working population.
❧ **actif** *nm* - **1.** FIN assets *(pl)* - **2.** loc : **avoir qqch à son** ~ to have sthg to one's credit.

action [aksjɔ̃] *nf* - **1.** [gén] action ; **passer à l'**~ to go into action ; MIL to go into battle ; **sous l'**~ **de** under the effect of - **2.** [acte] action, act ; **bonne/mauvaise** ~ good/bad deed - **3.** JUR action, lawsuit - **4.** FIN share - **5.** RELIG : ~ **de grâces** thanksgiving.

actionnaire [aksjɔnɛr] *nmf* FIN shareholder.

actionner [3] [aksjɔne] *vt* to work, to activate.

activement [aktivmɑ̃] *adv* actively.

activer [3] [aktive] *vt* to speed up.
❧ **s'activer** *vp* to bustle about.

activisme [aktivism] *nm* activism.

activiste [aktivist] *adj* & *nmf* activist.

activité [aktivite] *nf* [gén] activity ; **en** ~ [volcan] active ; ~ **d'éveil** early learning experience ; ~ **professionnelle** job, profession.

actuaire [aktɥɛr] *nmf* actuary.

actualisation [aktɥalizasjɔ̃] *nf* [d'un texte] updating.

actualiser [3] [aktɥalize] *vt* to bring up to date.

actualité [aktɥalite] *nf* - **1.** [d'un sujet] topicality ; **être d'**~ to be topical - **2.** [événements] : **l'**~ **sportive/politique/littéraire** the current sports/political/literary scene.
❧ **actualités** *nfpl* : **les ~s** the news *(sg)*.

actuel, elle [aktɥɛl] *adj* - **1.** [contemporain, présent] current, present ; **à l'heure ~le** at the present time - **2.** [d'actualité] topical.

actuellement [aktɥɛlmã] *adv* at present, currently.

acuité [akɥite] *nf* acuteness ; ~ **visuelle** keenness of sight.

acupuncture, acuponcture [akypɔ̃ktyr] *nf* acupuncture.

adage [adaʒ] *nm* adage, saying.

adaptable [adaptabl] *adj* adaptable.

adaptateur, trice [adaptatœr, tris] *nm, f* adapter.
➤ **adaptateur** *nm* ÉLECTR adapter.

adaptation [adaptasjɔ̃] *nf* adaptation.

adapter [3] [adapte] *vt* - **1.** [gén] to adapt - **2.** [fixer] to fit ; ~ **qqch à qqch** to fit sthg to sthg.
➤ **s'adapter** *vp* : **s'~ (à)** to adapt (to).

ADD (*abr de* **analogique/digital/digital**) ADD.

additif [aditif] *nm* - **1.** [supplément] rider, additional clause - **2.** [substance] additive.

addition [adisjɔ̃] *nf* - **1.** [ajout, calcul] addition - **2.** [note] bill *Br*, check *Am*.

additionnel, elle [adisjɔnɛl] *adj* extra, additional.

additionner [3] [adisjɔne] *vt* - **1.** [mélanger] : ~ **une poudre d'eau** to add water to a powder - **2.** [chiffres] to add up.
➤ **s'additionner** *vp* to add up.

adduction [adyksjɔ̃] *nf* [des eaux, du gaz] supply.

adepte [adɛpt] *nmf* follower.

adéquat, e [adekwa, at] *adj* suitable, appropriate.

adhérence [aderãs] *nf* [de pneu] grip.

adhérent, e [aderã, ãt] ⬦ *adj* : ~ **à** which adheres *ou* sticks to ⬦ *nm, f* : ~ **(de)** member (of).

adhérer [18] [adere] *vi* - **1.** [coller] to stick, to adhere ; ~ **à** [se fixer sur] to stick *ou* adhere to ; [être d'accord avec] *fig* to support, to adhere to - **2.** [être membre] : ~ **à** to become a member of, to join.

adhésif, ive [adezif, iv] *adj* sticky, adhesive.
➤ **adhésif** *nm* adhesive.

adhésion [adezjɔ̃] *nf* - **1.** [à une idée] : ~ **(à)** support (for) - **2.** [de pneu] : **une bonne ~ à la route** good road-holding (U) - **3.** [à un parti] : ~ **(à)** membership (of).

adieu [adjø] ⬦ *interj* goodbye!, farewell! ; **dire ~ à qqch** *fig* to say goodbye to sthg ⬦ *nm (gén pl)* farewell ; **faire ses ~x à qqn** to say one's farewells to sb.

adipeux, euse [adipø, øz] *adj* [tissu] adipose ; [personne] fat.

adjacent, e [adʒasã, ãt] *adj* adjoining, adjacent.

adjectif [adʒɛktif] *nm* GRAM adjective ; ~ **attribut** predicative adjective ; ~ **épithète** attributive adjective.

adjoindre [82] [adʒwɛ̃dr] *vt* : ~ **qqch à qqch** to add sthg to sthg.
➤ **s'adjoindre** *vp* to appoint, to take on.

adjoint, e [adʒwɛ̃, ɛ̃t] ⬦ *adj* deputy (*avant n*), assistant (*avant n*) ⬦ *nm, f* deputy, assistant ; ~ **au maire** deputy mayor.

adjonction [adʒɔ̃ksjɔ̃] *nf* addition ; **sans ~ de sel/sucre/conservateurs** with no added salt/sugar/preservatives.

adjudant [adʒydã] *nm* [dans la marine] warrant officer ; [dans l'armée] company sergeant major ; ~ **chef** [dans la marine] warrant officer 1st class *Br*, chief warrant officer *Am* ; [dans l'armée] regimental sergeant major.

adjudicataire [adʒydikatɛr] *nmf* successful bidder.

adjudication [adʒydikasjɔ̃] *nf* - **1.** [vente aux enchères] sale by auction - **2.** ADMIN awarding.

adjuger [17] [adʒyʒe] *vt* : ~ **qqch (à qqn)** [aux enchères] to auction sthg (to sb) ; [décerner] to award sthg (to sb) ; **adjugé!** sold!
➤ **s'adjuger** *vp* : **s'~ qqch** to give o.s. sthg.

adjurer [3] [adʒyre] *vt sout* to implore, to beg.

adjuvant [adʒyvã] *nm* - **1.** [médicament] adjuvant - **2.** [stimulant] stimulant.

admets *etc* ▷ admettre.

admettre [84] [admɛtr] *vt* - **1.** [tolérer, accepter] to allow, to accept - **2.** [supposer] to suppose, to assume ; **admettons que** (+ *subjonctif*) supposing *ou* assuming (that) - **3.** [autoriser] to allow ; **être admis à faire qqch** to be allowed to do sthg - **4.** [accueillir, reconnaître] to admit.

administrateur, trice [administratœr, tris] *nm, f* - **1.** [gérant] administrator ; ~ **de biens** administrator of an estate ; ~ **judiciaire** receiver - **2.** [de conseil d'administration] director.

administratif, ive [administratif, iv] *adj* administrative.

administration [administrasjɔ̃] *nf* - **1.** [service public] : **l'Administration** ≃ the Civil Service - **2.** [gestion] administration.

administrer [3] [administre] *vt* - **1.** [gérer] to manage, to administer - **2.** [médicament, sacrement] to administer.

admirable [admirabl] *adj* - **1.** [personne, comportement] admirable - **2.** [paysage, spectacle] wonderful.

admirablement [admirabləmã] *adv* admirably.

admirateur, trice [admiratœr, tris] *nm, f* admirer.

admiratif, ive [admiratif, iv] *adj* admiring.

admiration [admirasjɔ̃] *nf* admiration ; **être en ~ devant qqn/qqch** to be filled with admiration for sb/sthg.

admirer [3] [admire] *vt* to admire.

admis, e [admi, iz] *pp* ⊳ **admettre**.

admissible [admisibl] ⬦ *adj* - **1.** [attitude] acceptable - **2.** *SCOL* eligible ⬦ *nmf SCOL* eligible candidate.

admission [admisjɔ̃] *nf* admission.

admonester [3] [admɔnɛste] *vt sout* to admonish.

ADN (*abr de* acide désoxyribonucléique) *nm* DNA.

ado [ado] (*abr de* adolescent) *nmf fam* teenager.

adolescence [adɔlesɑ̃s] *nf* adolescence.

adolescent, e [adɔlesɑ̃, ɑ̃t] ⬦ *adj* adolescent ⬦ *nm, f* adolescent, teenager.

adonis [adɔnis] *nm* Adonis.

adonner [3] [adɔne] ➡ **s'adonner** *vp* : **s'~ à** [sport, activité] to devote o.s. to ; [vice] to take to.

adopter [3] [adɔpte] *vt* - **1.** [gén] to adopt - **2.** [loi] to pass.

adoptif, ive [adɔptif, iv] *adj* [famille] adoptive ; [pays, enfant] adopted.

adoption [adɔpsjɔ̃] *nf* adoption ; **d'~** [pays, ville] adopted ; [famille] adoptive.

adorable [adɔrabl] *adj* adorable, delightful.

adorateur, trice [adɔratœr, tris] ⬦ *adj* adoring, worshipping *Br*, worshiping *Am* ⬦ *nm, f* - **1.** [de personne] admirer - **2.** *RELIG* worshipper *Br*, worshiper *Am*.

adoration [adɔrasjɔ̃] *nf* - **1.** [amour] adoration ; **être en ~ devant qqn** to worship sb - **2.** *RELIG* worship.

adorer [3] [adɔre] *vt* - **1.** [personne, -chose] to adore - **2.** *RELIG* to worship.

adosser [3] [adose] *vt* : **~ qqch à qqch** to place sthg against sthg.
➡ **s'adosser** *vp* : **s'~ à** *ou* **contre qqch** to lean against sthg.

adoucir [32] [adusir] *vt* - **1.** [gén] to soften - **2.** [chagrin, peine] to ease, to soothe.
➡ **s'adoucir** *vp* - **1.** [temps] to become *ou* get milder - **2.** [personne] to mellow.

adoucissant, e [adusisɑ̃, ɑ̃t] *adj* soothing.
➡ **adoucissant** *nm* softener.

adoucissement [adusismɑ̃] *nm* - **1.** [de température] : **il y a eu un ~ de la température** the weather has become milder - **2.** [de peine] soothing, easing - **3.** [de l'eau] softening.

adoucisseur [adusisœr] *nm* : **~ d'eau** water softener.

adrénaline [adrenalin] *nf* adrenalin.

adresse [adrɛs] *nf* - **1.** [gén & *INFORM*] address ; **ce restaurant est une bonne ~** this restaurant is a good place to go ; **à l'~ de** *fig* for the benefit of ; **~ électronique** e-mail address - **2.** [habileté] skill - **3.** [mot] headword.

adresser [4] [adrese] *vt* - **1.** [faire parvenir] : **~ qqch à qqn** to address sthg to sb - **2.** [envoyer] : **~ qqn à qqn** to refer sb to sb.
➡ **s'adresser** *vp* : **s'~ à** [parler à] to speak to ; [être destiné à] to be aimed at, to be intended for.

Adriatique [adriatik] *nf* : **l'~** the Adriatic.

adroit, e [adrwa, at] *adj* skilful.

adroitement [adrwatmɑ̃] *adv* skilfully.

aduler [3] [adyle] *vt* to adulate.

adulte [adylt] *nmf & adj* adult.

adultère [adyltɛr] ⬦ *nm* [acte] adultery ⬦ *adj* adulterous.

adultérin, e [adylterɛ̃, in] *adj* illegitimate.

advenir [40] [advənir] *v impers* to happen ; **qu'advient-il de ...?** what is happening to ...? ; **qu'est-il advenu de ...?** what has happened to *ou* become of ...? ; **advienne que pourra** come what may.

advenu [advəny] *pp* ⊳ **advenir**.

adverbe [advɛrb] *nm* adverb.

adversaire [advɛrsɛr] *nmf* adversary, opponent.

adverse [advɛrs] *adj* [opposé] opposing ; ⊳ **parti**.

adversité [advɛrsite] *nf* adversity.

advient ⊳ **advenir**.

advint ⊳ **advenir**.

AE (*abr de* adjoint d'enseignement) *nm* noncertified teacher.

AELE (*abr de* Association européenne de libre-échange) *nf* EFTA.

AEN (*abr de* Agence pour l'énergie nucléaire) *nf* French nuclear energy agency, ≃ AEA *Br*, ≃ AEC *Am*.

aération [aerasjɔ̃] *nf* [circulation d'air] ventilation ; [action] airing.

aéré, e [aere] *adj* - **1.** [pièce] well-ventilated ; **mal ~** stuffy - **2.** *fig* [présentation] well-spaced.

aérer [18] [aere] *vt* - **1.** [pièce, chose] to air - **2.** *fig* [présentation, mise en page] to lighten.
➡ **s'aérer** *vp* [sortir] to get some fresh air.

aérien, enne [aerjɛ̃, ɛn] *adj* - **1.** [grâce] ethereal ; [démarche] light - **2.** [câble] overhead (*avant n*) - **3.** [transports, attaque] air (*avant n*) ; **compagnie ~ne** airline (company).

aérobic [aerɔbik] *nm* aerobics *(U)*.

aérodrome [aerɔdrom] *nm* aerodrome.

aérodynamique [aerɔdinamik] ◇ *nf* aerodynamics *(U)* ◇ *adj* streamlined, aerodynamic.

aérogare [aerɔgar] *nf* - **1.** [aéroport] airport - **2.** [gare] air terminal.

aéroglisseur [aerɔglisœr] *nm* hovercraft.

aérogramme [aerɔgram] *nm* aerogramme.

aéromodélisme [aerɔmɔdelism] *nm* model aircraft making.

aéronautique [aerɔnotik] ◇ *nf* aeronautics *(U)* ◇ *adj* aeronautical.

aéronaval, e, als [aerɔnaval] *adj* air and sea *(avant n)*.

aérophagie [aerɔfaʒi] *nf* abdominal wind.

aéroport [aerɔpɔr] *nm* airport.

aéroporté, e [aerɔpɔrte] *adj* airborne.

aérosol [aerɔsɔl] *nm & adj inv* aerosol.

aérospatial, e, aux [aerɔspasjal, o] *adj* aerospace *(avant n)*.
 ➡ **aérospatiale** *nf* aerospace industry.

AF ◇ *nfpl abr de* **allocations familiales** ◇ *nf* (*abr de* **Assemblée fédérale**) (Swiss) Federal Assembly.

affabilité [afabilite] *nf* affability.

affable [afabl] *adj* - **1.** [personne] affable, agreeable - **2.** [parole] kind.

affabulation [afabylasjɔ̃] *nf* fabrication.

affaiblir [32] [afeblir] *vt litt & fig* to weaken.
 ➡ **s'affaiblir** *vp litt & fig* to weaken, to become weaker.

affaiblissement [afeblismã] *nm* weakening.

affaire [afer] *nf* - **1.** [question] matter - **2.** [situation, polémique] affair - **3.** [marché] deal ; **faire une ~** to get a bargain *ou* a good deal ; **une ~ en or** a real bargain - **4.** [entreprise] business - **5.** [procès] case - **6.** *loc* : **avoir ~ à qqn** to deal with sb ; **vous aurez ~ à moi!** you'll have me to deal with! ; **c'est l'~ d'une minute** it will only take a minute ; **faire l'~** to do nicely ; **j'en fais mon ~** leave it to me ; **tirer qqn d'~** to get sb out of trouble.
 ➡ **affaires** *nfpl* - **1.** COMM business *(U)* - **2.** [objets personnels] things, belongings - **3.** [activités] affairs ; **les ~s de l'État** affairs of state ; **les Affaires étrangères** ≃ the Foreign Office *(sg)* ; **se mêler** *ou* **s'occuper de ses ~s** to mind one's own business ; **toutes ~s cessantes** forthwith.

affairé, e [afere] *adj* busy.

affairer [4] [afere] ➡ **s'affairer** *vp* to bustle about.

affairisme [aferism] *nm* racketeering.

affaissement [afesmã] *nm* GÉOGR subsidence.

affaisser [4] [afese] ➡ **s'affaisser** *vp* - **1.** [se creuser] to subside, to sink - **2.** [tomber] to collapse.

affaler [3] [afale] ➡ **s'affaler** *vp* to collapse.

affamé, e [afame] *adj* starving.

affectation [afɛktasjɔ̃] *nf* - **1.** [attribution] : **~ de qqch à** allocation of sthg to - **2.** [nomination] appointment, posting - **3.** [manque de naturel] affectation.

affecter [4] [afɛkte] *vt* - **1.** [consacrer] : **~ qqch à** to allocate sthg to - **2.** [nommer] : **~ qqn à** to appoint sb to - **3.** [feindre] to feign - **4.** [émouvoir] to affect, to move.

affectif, ive [afɛktif, iv] *adj* emotional.

affection [afɛksjɔ̃] *nf* - **1.** [sentiment] affection ; **avoir de l'~ pour** to be fond of - **2.** [maladie] complaint.

affectionner [3] [afɛksjɔne] *vt* to be fond of.

affectivité [afɛktivite] *nf* emotions *(pl)*.

affectueusement [afɛktɥøzmã] *adv* affectionately.

affectueux, euse [afɛktɥø, øz] *adj* affectionate.

afférent, e [aferã, ãt] *adj* - **1.** JUR : **~ à qqch** pertaining *ou* relating to sthg - **2.** ANAT afferent.

affermir [32] [afermir] *vt* [gén] to strengthen ; [chairs] to tone up.
 ➡ **s'affermir** *vp* - **1.** [matière] to be strengthened ; [chairs] to be toned up - **2.** [pouvoir] to be consolidated.

affichage [afiʃaʒ] *nm* - **1.** [d'un poster, d'un avis] putting up, displaying - **2.** ÉLECTRON : **~ à cristaux liquides** LCD, liquid crystal display ; **~ numérique** digital display.

affiche [afiʃ] *nf* [gén] poster ; [officielle] notice ; **~ publicitaire** (advertising) poster ; **être à l'~** *fig* to be on.

afficher [3] [afiʃe] *vt* - **1.** [liste, poster] to put up ; [vente, réglementation] to put up a notice about - **2.** [laisser transparaître] to display, to exhibit.
 ➡ **s'afficher** *vp* : **s'~ avec qqn** to flaunt o.s. with sb.

affichette [afiʃɛt] *nf* small poster.

afficheur [afiʃœr] *nm* - **1.** [entreprise] billposter - **2.** ÉLECTRON display.

affilée [afile] ➡ **d'affilée** *loc adv* : **trois jours d'~** three days running.

affiler [3] [afile] *vt* to sharpen.

affilié, e [afilje] *adj* : **~ à** affiliated to.

affiner [3] [afine] *vt litt & fig* to refine.

➤ **s'affiner** *vp* [silhouette] to become thinner ; [devenir plus raffiné] to become more refined.

affinité [afinite] *nf* affinity ; **avoir des ~s avec** to have an affinity with.

affirmatif, ive [afirmatif, iv] *adj* **- 1.** [réponse] affirmative **- 2.** [personne] positive.

➤ **affirmatif** *adv* affirmative.

➤ **affirmative** *nf* : **dans l'affirmative** if yes, if the answer is yes ; **répondre par l'affirmative** to reply in the affirmative.

affirmation [afirmasjɔ̃] *nf* assertion.

affirmativement [afirmativmɑ̃] *adv* : **répondre ~** to answer in the affirmative.

affirmer [3] [afirme] *vt* **- 1.** [certifier] to maintain, to claim **- 2.** [exprimer] to assert.

➤ **s'affirmer** *vp* to assert o.s.

affixe [afiks] *nm* affix.

affleurer [5] [aflœre] *vi fig* to rise to the surface.

affliction [afliksjɔ̃] *nf* affliction.

affligeant, e [afliʒɑ̃, ɑ̃t] *adj* **- 1.** [désolant] saddening, distressing **- 2.** [lamentable] appalling.

affliger [17] [afliʒe] *vt sout* **- 1.** [attrister] to sadden, to distress **- 2.** [de défaut, de maladie] : **être affligé de** to be afflicted with.

➤ **s'affliger** *vp sout* : **s'~ de** to be distressed at *ou* about.

affluence [aflyɑ̃s] *nf* crowd, crowds *(pl)*.

affluent [aflyɑ̃] *nm* tributary.

affluer [3] [aflye] *vi* **- 1.** [choses] to pour in, to flood in **- 2.** [personnes] to flock **- 3.** [sang] : **~ (à)** to rush (to).

afflux [afly] *nm* **- 1.** [de liquide, dons, capitaux] flow **- 2.** [de personnes] flood.

affolant, e [afɔlɑ̃, ɑ̃t] *adj* **- 1.** [inquiétant] frightening **- 2.** [troublant] disturbing.

affolé, e [afɔle] *adj* horrified.

affolement [afɔlmɑ̃] *nm* panic.

affoler [3] [afɔle] *vt* **- 1.** [inquiéter] to terrify **- 2.** [émouvoir] to drive mad.

➤ **s'affoler** *vp* [paniquer] to panic.

affranchi, e [afrɑ̃ʃi] *adj* **- 1.** [lettre - avec timbre] stamped ; [- à la machine] franked **- 2.** [personne, esclave] liberated.

affranchir [32] [afrɑ̃ʃir] *vt* **- 1.** [lettre - avec timbre] to stamp ; [- à la machine] to frank **- 2.** *arg crime* [renseigner] to put in the picture, to fill in **- 3.** [libérer] : **~ qqn de qqch** to liberate *ou* free sb from sthg **- 4.** [esclave] to set free, to liberate.

➤ **s'affranchir** *vp* : **s'~ de qqch** [se libérer de] to free o.s. from sthg.

affranchissement [afrɑ̃ʃismɑ̃] *nm* **- 1.** [de lettre - avec timbre] stamping ; [- à la machine]

franking **- 2.** [libération] liberation, emancipation.

affres [afr] *nfpl littéraire* throes.

affréter [18] [afrete] *vt* to charter.

affreusement [afrøzmɑ̃] *adv* **- 1.** [horriblement] horribly **- 2.** [énormément] awfully.

affreux, euse [afrø, øz] *adj* **- 1.** [repoussant] horrible **- 2.** [effrayant] terrifying **- 3.** [détestable] awful, dreadful.

affriolant, e [afrijɔlɑ̃, ɑ̃t] *adj* enticing.

affront [afrɔ̃] *nm* insult, affront ; **faire un ~ à qqn** to insult sb.

affrontement [afrɔ̃tmɑ̃] *nm* confrontation.

affronter [3] [afrɔ̃te] *vt* to confront.

➤ **s'affronter** *vp* to confront each other.

affubler [3] [afyble] *vt péj* : **être affublé de** to be got up in.

➤ **s'affubler** *vp* : **s'~ de qqch** *péj* to get o.s. up in sthg.

affût [afy] *nm* : **être à l'~ (de)** to be lying in wait (for) ; *fig* to be on the lookout (for).

affûter [3] [afyte] *vt* to sharpen.

afghan, e [afgɑ̃, an] *adj* Afghan.

➤ **afghan** *nm* [langue] Afghan, Pashto.

➤ **Afghan, e** *nm, f* Afghan.

Afghanistan [afganistɑ̃] *nm* : **l'~** Afghanistan.

afin [afɛ̃] ➤ **afin de** *loc prép* in order to.

➤ **afin que** *loc conj* (+ subjonctif) so that.

AFNOR, Afnor [afnɔr] (*abr de* Association française de normalisation) *nf French industrial standards authority*, ≃ BSI *Br*, ≃ ASA *Am*.

a fortiori [afɔrsjɔri] *adv* all the more.

AFP (*abr de* Agence France-Presse) *nf French press agency*.

africain, e [afrikɛ̃, ɛn] *adj* African.

➤ **Africain, e** *nm, f* African.

afrikaner [afrikaner], **afrikaander** [afrikɑ̃der] *adj* Afrikaner.

➤ **Afrikaner, Afrikaander** *nmf* Afrikaner.

Afrique [afrik] *nf* : **l'~** Africa ; **l'~ australe** Southern Africa ; **l'~ noire** sub-Saharan Africa ; **l'~ du Nord** North Africa ; **l'~ du Sud** South Africa.

after-shave [aftœrʃev] *nm inv* & *adj inv* aftershave.

ag. *abr de* agence.

AG (*abr de* assemblée générale) *nf* GM.

agaçant, e [agasɑ̃, ɑ̃t] *adj* irritating.

agacement [agasmɑ̃] *nm* irritation.

agacer [16] [agase] *vt* to irritate.

agate [agat] *nf* agate.

âge [aʒ] *nm* age ; **à l'~ de** at the age of ; **en ~ de faire qqch** old enough to do sthg ; **en bas ~** very young ; **quel ~ as-tu?** how old are you? ; **d'un certain ~** middle-aged ; **prendre de l'~** to age ; **l'~ adulte** adulthood ; **l'~ ingrat** the awkward *ou* difficult age ; **d'un ~ avancé** elderly ; **~ de fer/de bronze** Iron/Bronze Age ; **~ mental** mental age ; **d'~ mûr** of mature years ; **~ d'or** golden age ; **~ de raison** age of reason ; **le troisième ~** [personnes] the over-sixties.

âgé, e [aʒe] *adj* old, elderly ; **être ~ de 20 ans** to be 20 years old *ou* of age ; **un enfant ~ de 3 ans** a 3-year-old child.

agence [aʒɑ̃s] *nf* agency ; **~ immobilière** estate agent's *Br*, real estate agent's *Am* ; **~ matrimoniale** marriage bureau ; **Agence nationale pour l'emploi** ≃ job centre ; **~ de publicité** advertising agency ; **~ de voyages** travel agent's, travel agency.

agencement [aʒɑ̃smɑ̃] *nm* arrangement.

agencer [16] [aʒɑ̃se] *vt* to arrange ; *fig* to put together.
➤ **s'agencer** *vp* to fit together.

agenda [aʒɛ̃da] *nm* diary.

agenouiller [3] [aʒnuje] ➤ **s'agenouiller** *vp* to kneel ; **s'~ devant** *fig* to bow down before.

agent [aʒɑ̃] *nm* agent ; **~ de change** stockbroker ; **~ commercial** sales representative ; **~ immobilier** estate agent *Br*, real estate agent *Am* ; **~ de police** police officer ; **~ de publicité** advertising agent ; **~ secret** secret agent.

agglomérat [aglɔmera] *nm* GÉOL & *fig* agglomerate.

agglomération [aglɔmerasjɔ̃] *nf* - **1.** [amas] conglomeration - **2.** [ville] conurbation ; **l'~ parisienne** the Parisian urban area.

aggloméré [aglɔmere] *nm* chipboard.

agglomérer [18] [aglɔmere] *vt* to mix together.
➤ **s'agglomérer** *vp* - **1.** [surface] to bind - **2.** [foule] to gather.

agglutiner [3] [aglytine] *vt* to stick together.
➤ **s'agglutiner** *vp* [foule] to gather, to congregate.

aggravation [agravasjɔ̃] *nf* worsening, aggravation.

aggraver [3] [agrave] *vt* to make worse.
➤ **s'aggraver** *vp* to get worse, to worsen.

agile [aʒil] *adj* agile, nimble.

agilement [aʒilmɑ̃] *adv* agilely.

agilité [aʒilite] *nf litt* & *fig* agility.

agios [aʒjo] *nmpl* FIN bank charges.

agir [32] [aʒir] *vi* - **1.** [faire, être efficace] to act - **2.** [se comporter] to behave - **3.** [influer] : **~ sur** to have an effect on.
➤ **s'agir** *v impers* : **il s'agit de ...** it's a matter of ... ; **il s'agit de faire qqch** we/you *etc* must do sthg ; **de quoi s'agit-il?** what's it about? ; **de quoi s'agit-il dans ce film/cette lettre?** what is this film/letter about?

agissements [aʒismɑ̃] *nmpl péj* schemes, intrigues.

agitateur, trice [aʒitatœr, tris] *nm, f* POLIT agitator.

agitation [aʒitasjɔ̃] *nf* agitation ; [politique, sociale] unrest.

agité, e [aʒite] *adj* - **1.** [gén] restless ; [enfant, classe] restless, fidgety ; [journée, atmosphère] hectic - **2.** [mer] rough.

agiter [3] [aʒite] *vt* - **1.** [remuer - flacon, objet] to shake ; [- drapeau, bras] to wave ; '**~ avant l'emploi**' 'shake well before use' - **2.** [énerver] to perturb.
➤ **s'agiter** *vp* [personne] to move about, to fidget ; [mer] to stir ; [population] to get restless.

agneau [aɲo] *nm* - **1.** [animal, viande] lamb ; **doux comme un ~** gentle as a lamb - **2.** [cuir] lambskin.

agonie [agɔni] *nf* [de personne] mortal agony ; *fig* death throes *(pl)* ; **être à l'~** to be at death's door.

agoniser [3] [agɔnize] *vi* [personne] to be dying ; *fig* to be on its last legs.

agoraphobie [agɔrafɔbi] *nf* agoraphobia.

agrafe [agraf] *nf* - **1.** [de bureau] staple - **2.** MÉD clip.

agrafer [3] [agrafe] *vt* - **1.** [attacher] to fasten - **2.** *fam fig* [attraper] to nab.

agrafeuse [agraføz] *nf* stapler.

agraire [agrɛr] *adj* agrarian.

agrandir [32] [agrɑ̃dir] *vt* - **1.** [élargir - gén & PHOT] to enlarge ; [- rue, écart] to widen - **2.** *fig* [développer] to expand - **3.** [faire paraître plus grand] : **~ qqch** to make sthg look bigger.
➤ **s'agrandir** *vp* - **1.** [s'étendre] to grow - **2.** *fig* [se développer] to expand.

agrandissement [agrɑ̃dismɑ̃] *nm* - **1.** [gén & PHOT] enlargement - **2.** *fig* [développement] expansion.

agréable [agreabl] *adj* pleasant, nice.

agréablement [agreabləmɑ̃] *adv* pleasantly.

agréé, e [agree] *adj* [concessionnaire, appareil] authorized.

agréer [15] [agree] *vt sout* - **1.** [accepter] : **faire**

~ qqch to have sthg accepted ; **veuillez ~ mes salutations distinguées** ou **l'expression de mes sentiments distingués** yours faithfully **- 2.** [convenir] : **~ à qqn** to suit ou please sb.

agrégat [agregal *nm* **- 1.** [aggloméré] aggregate **- 2.** *fig* & *péj* [amas] hotchpotch *Br*, hodgepodge *Am*.

agrégation [agregasjɔ̃] *nf* competitive examination for secondary school and university teachers.

agrégé, e [agreʒe] *nm, f* holder of the agrégation.

agrément [agremã] *nm* **- 1.** [caractère agréable] attractiveness ; **d'~** [jardin] ornamental ; [voyage] pleasure *(avant n)* **- 2.** [approbation] consent, approval.

agrémenter [3] [agremãte] *vt* : **~ qqch (de qqch)** to embellish sthg (with sthg).
◆ **s'agrémenter** *vp* : **s'~ de qqch** [vêtement] to be trimmed ou adorned with sthg.

agrès [agrɛ] *nmpl* SPORT gym apparatus *(U)*.

agresser [4] [agrɛse] *vt* **- 1.** [suj : personne] to attack **- 2.** *fig* [suj : bruit, pollution] to assault.

agresseur [agrɛsœr] *nm* attacker.

agressif, ive [agrɛsif, iv] *adj* aggressive.

agression [agrɛsjɔ̃] *nf* attack ; MIL & PSYCHOL aggression.

agressivement [agrɛsivmã] *adv* aggressively.

agressivité [agrɛsivite] *nf* aggressiveness.

agricole [agrikɔl] *adj* agricultural.

agriculteur, trice [agrikyltœr, tris] *nm, f* farmer.

agriculture [agrikyltyr] *nf* agriculture, farming.

agripper [3] [agripe] *vt* **- 1.** [personne] to cling ou hang on to **- 2.** [objet] to grip, to clutch.
◆ **s'agripper** *vp* : **s'~ à qqn** to cling ou hang on to sb ; **s'~ à qqch** to grip ou clutch sthg.

agroalimentaire [agroalimãter] ⬦ *adj* : industrie ~ food-processing industry ; **les produits ~s** processed foods ou foodstuffs ⬦ *nm* : **l'~** the food processing industry.

agronome [agrɔnɔm] *nmf* agronomist.

agronomie [agrɔnɔmi] *nf* agronomy.

agronomique [agrɔnɔmik] *adj* agronomic.

agrume [agrym] *nm* citrus fruit.

aguerrir [32] [agerir] *vt* to harden.
◆ **s'aguerrir** *vp* : **s'~ (contre)** to become hardened (to).

aguets [agɛ] ◆ **aux aguets** *loc adv* : être/ rester aux ~ to be ou keep on the lookout.

aguichant, e [agiʃã, ãt] *adj* enticing.

ah [a] *interj* oh!, ah! ; **ah bon?** really? ; **ah, quelle bonne surprise!** what a nice surprise!

Ah *(abr de* ampère-heure*)* ah.

ahuri, e [ayri] *adj* : être ~ (par qqch) to be taken aback (by sthg).

ahurir [32] [ayrir] *vt* [étonner] to astound.

ahurissant, e [ayrisã, ãt] *adj* astounding.

ahurissement [ayrismã] *nm* astonishment.

ai ⬥ avoir.

aide [ɛd] ⬦ *nf* **- 1.** [gén] help ; **à l'~!** help! ; **appeler (qqn) à l'~** to call (to sb) for help ; **venir en ~ à qqn** to come to sb's aid, to help sb ; **~ ménagère** home help **- 2.** [secours financier] aid ; **~ sociale** social security *Br*, welfare *Am* ⬦ *nmf* [adjoint] assistant ; **~ de camp** MIL aide-de-camp.
◆ **à l'aide de** *loc prép* with the help ou aid of.

aide-mémoire [ɛdmemwar] *nm inv* aide-mémoire ; [pour examen] revision notes *(pl)*.

aider [4] [ede] *vt* to help ; **~ qqn à faire qqch** to help sb to do sthg ; **~ à faire qqch** to help to do sthg ; **~ qqn dans qqch** to help sb with sthg ; **se faire ~ par** ou **de qqn** to be helped by sb, to get help from sb ; **~ à faire qqch** to help to do sthg.
◆ **s'aider** *vp* **- 1.** [s'assister mutuellement] to help each other **- 2.** [avoir recours] : **s'~ de** to use, to make use of.

aide-soignant, e [ɛdswaɲã, ãt] *(mpl* aides-soignants, *fpl* aides-soignantes*)* *nm, f* nursing auxiliary *Br*, nurse's aide *Am*.

aie, aies etc ⬥ avoir.

aïe [aj] *interj* **- 1.** [exprime la douleur] ow!, ouch! **- 2.** [exprime le désagrément] oh dear!, oh no!

AIEA *(abr de* **Agence internationale de l'énergie atomique***)* *nf* IAEA.

aïeul, e [ajœl] *nm, f sout* grandparent, grandfather *(f* grandmother*)*.

aïeux [ajø] *nmpl* ancestors.

aigle [ɛgl] *nm* eagle.

aiglon [ɛglɔ̃] *nm* eaglet.

aigre [ɛgr] *adj* **- 1.** [gén] sour **- 2.** [propos] harsh.

aigre-doux, aigre-douce [ɛgrədu, ɛgrədus] *adj* **- 1.** CULIN sweet-and-sour **- 2.** [propos] bittersweet.

aigrelet, ette [ɛgrəlɛ, ɛt] *adj* **- 1.** [vin] vinegary **- 2.** [voix] sharpish.

aigrement [ɛgrəmã] *adv* bitterly.

aigrette [ɛgrɛt] *nf* egret.

aigreur [ɛgrœr] *nf* **- 1.** [d'un aliment] sourness **- 2.** [d'un propos] harshness.
◆ **aigreurs d'estomac** *nfpl* heartburn *(U)*.

aigri, e [egri] *adj* embittered.

aigrir [32] [egrir] *vt* **- 1.** [aliment] to make sour **- 2.** [personne] to embitter.

◆ **s'aigrir** *vp* - **1.** [aliment] to turn sour - **2.** [personne] to become bitter.

aigu, uë [egy] *adj* - **1.** [son] high-pitched - **2.** [objet, lame] sharp ; [angle] acute - **3.** [douleur] sharp, acute - **4.** [conflit, grève] bitter - **5.** [intelligence, sens] acute, keen.

◆ **aigu** *nm* high note.

aiguillage [egɥijaʒ] *nm* [RAIL - manœuvre] shunting *Br*, switching *Am* ; [- dispositif] points *(pl) Br*, switch *Am*.

aiguille [egɥij] *nf* - **1.** [gén] needle ; ~ à tricoter knitting needle ; ~ de pin pine needle ; chercher une ~ dans une botte de foin *fig* to look for a needle in a haystack - **2.** [de pendule] hand - **3.** GÉOGR peak.

aiguiller [3] [egɥije] *vt* - **1.** RAIL to shunt *Br*, to switch *Am* - **2.** [personne, conversation] to steer, to direct.

aiguilleur [egɥijœr] *nm* - **1.** RAIL pointsman *Br*, switchman *Am* - **2.** AÉRON : ~ du ciel air traffic controller.

aiguillon [egɥijɔ̃] *nm* - **1.** [dard] sting - **2.** [stimulant] spur, incentive.

aiguiser [3] [egize] *vt litt* & *fig* to sharpen ; ~ l'appétit to whet the appetite.

aïkido, aikido [ajkido] *nm* aikido.

ail [aj] (*pl* ails OU aulx [o]) *nm* garlic *(U)* ; ~ des bois *Can* wild leek.

aile [ɛl] *nf* - **1.** [gén] wing ; battre de l'~ to be in a bad way ; donner des ~s à qqn to lend sb wings ; voler de ses propres ~s to stand on one's own two feet - **2.** [de moulin] sail.

aileron [ɛlrɔ̃] *nm* - **1.** [de requin] fin - **2.** [d'avion] aileron.

ailier [elje] *nm* winger.

aille, ailles *etc* ⊳ aller.

ailleurs [ajœr] *adv* elsewhere, somewhere *Br* OU someplace *Am* else ; elle avait l'esprit ~ *fig* her mind was on other things ; nulle part ~ nowhere *Br* OU no-place *Am* else ; partout ~ everywhere *Br* OU everyplace *Am* else.

◆ **d'ailleurs** *loc adv* moreover, besides.

◆ **par ailleurs** *loc adv* moreover, furthermore.

ailloli, aïoli [ajɔli] *nm* garlic mayonnaise.

aimable [ɛmabl] *adj* kind, nice.

aimablement [ɛmabləmɑ̃] *adv* kindly.

aimant[1], e [ɛmɑ̃, ɑ̃t] *adj* loving.

aimant[2] [ɛmɑ̃] *nm* magnet.

aimanter [3] [ɛmɑ̃te] *vt* to magnetize.

aimer [4] [eme] *vt* - **1.** [gén] to like ; ~ bien qqch/qqn to like sthg/sb, to be fond of sthg/sb ; ~ bien faire qqch to (really) like doing sthg ; ~ (à) faire qqch to like to do sthg, to

like doing sthg ; j'aime à croire que ... I like to think that ... ; elle aime qu'on l'appelle par son surnom she likes being called by her nickname ; je n'aime pas que tu rentres seule le soir I don't like you coming home alone at night ; j'aimerais (bien) que tu viennes avec moi I'd like you to come with me ; j'aimerais bien une autre tasse de café I wouldn't mind another cup of coffee ; ~ mieux qqch to prefer sthg ; ~ mieux faire qqch to prefer doing OU to do sthg - **2.** [d'amour] to love.

◆ **s'aimer** *vp* - **1.** *(emploi réfléchi)* to like o.s. - **2.** *(emploi réciproque)* to love each other ; s'~ bien to like each other.

aine [ɛn] *nf* groin.

aîné, e [ene] ◇ *adj* [plus âgé] elder, older ; [le plus âgé] eldest, oldest ◇ *nm, f* [plus âgé] older OU elder child, older OU eldest son/daughter ; [le plus âgé] oldest OU eldest child, oldest OU eldest son/daughter ; elle est mon ~e de deux ans she is two years older than me.

aînesse [enɛs] ⊳ droit.

ainsi [ɛ̃si] *adv* - **1.** [manière] in this way, like this - **2.** [valeur conclusive] thus ; ~ donc so ; et ~ de suite and so on, and so forth ; pour ~ dire so to speak ; ~ soit-il RELIG so be it, amen.

◆ **ainsi que** *loc conj* - **1.** [comme, de même que] as - **2.** [et] as well as.

aïoli = ailloli.

air [ɛr] *nm* - **1.** [gén] air ; le grand ~ the fresh air ; à l'~ libre in the open air ; en plein ~ (out) in the open air, outside ; prendre l'~ to get some (fresh) air ; en l'~ [projet] (up) in the air ; *fig* [paroles] empty ; ~ comprimé compressed air ; ~ conditionné air-conditioning ; s'envoyer en l'~ *vulg* to get laid - **2.** [apparence, mine] air, look ; il a l'~ triste he looks sad ; il a l'~ de bouder it looks as if he's sulking ; il a l'~ de faire beau it looks like being a nice day ; sans en avoir l'~ without showing it ; d'un ~ dégagé in a casual manner ; n'avoir l'~ de rien to look OU seem unremarkable, to look OU seem insignificant ; un ~ de famille a family resemblance - **3.** MUS tune.

Airbag® [ɛrbag] *nm* airbag.

aire [ɛr] *nf* - **1.** [gén] area ; ~ d'atterrissage landing strip ; ~ de jeu playground ; ~ de repos lay-by ; ~ de stationnement parking area - **2.** [nid] eyrie.

airelle [ɛrɛl] *nf* bilberry.

aisance [ɛzɑ̃s] *nf* - **1.** [facilité] ease - **2.** [richesse] : il vit dans l'~ he has an affluent lifestyle.

aise [ɛz] ◇ *nf sout* pleasure ; être à l'~ OU à son ~ [confortable] to feel comfortable ; [financièrement] to be comfortably off ; **mettez-vous à l'~** make yourself comfortable ; **mettre qqn mal à l'~** to make sb feel ill at ease *ou* uneasy ; **en prendre à son ~** to do as one likes ; **à votre ~** please yourself, as you wish <> *adj* : **être bien ~ (de faire qqch)** to be delighted (to do sthg).

◆ **aises** *nfpl* : **aimer ses ~s** to like one's (home) comforts ; **prendre ses ~s** to make o.s. comfortable.

aisé, e [eze] *adj* - **1.** [facile] easy - **2.** [riche] well-off.

aisément [ezemã] *adv* easily.

aisselle [esel] *nf* armpit.

ajonc [aʒɔ̃] *nm* gorse *(U)*.

ajournement [aʒurnəmã] *nm* adjournment, postponement.

ajourner [3] [aʒurne] *vt* - **1.** [reporter - décision etc] to postpone ; [- réunion, procès] to adjourn - **2.** [candidat] to refer.

ajout [aʒu] *nm* addition.

ajouter [3] [aʒute] *vt* to add ; **~ que** to add that ; **~ foi à qqch** *sout* to give credence to sthg.

◆ **s'ajouter** *vp* : **s'~ à qqch** to be in addition to sthg.

ajustage [aʒystaʒ] *nm* fitting.

ajusté, e [aʒyste] *adj* [coupé] fitted, tailored.

ajuster [3] [aʒyste] *vt* - **1.** [monter] : **~ qqch (à)** to fit sthg (to) - **2.** [régler] to adjust - **3.** [vêtement] to alter - **4.** [tir, coup] to aim - **5.** [arranger - coiffure, cravate] to adjust.

◆ **s'ajuster** *vp* to be adaptable.

ajusteur [aʒystœr] *nm* fitter.

alaise, alèse [alez] *nf* undersheet.

alambiqué, e [alãbike] *adj* convoluted.

alarmant, e [alarmã, ãt] *adj* alarming.

alarme [alarm] *nf* alarm ; **donner l'~** to give *ou* raise the alarm.

alarmer [3] [alarme] *vt* to alarm.

◆ **s'alarmer** *vp* to get *ou* become alarmed.

alarmiste [alarmist] <> *nmf* scaremonger <> *adj* alarmist.

albanais, e [albane, ez] *adj* Albanian.

◆ **albanais** *nm* [langue] Albanian.

◆ **Albanais, e** *nm, f* Albanian.

Albanie [albani] *nf* : **l'~** Albania.

albâtre [albatr] *nm* alabaster.

albatros [albatros] *nm* albatross.

albinos [albinos] *nmf* & *adj inv* albino.

album [albɔm] *nm* album ; **~ (de) photo** photo album.

albumine [albymin] *nf* albumin.

alcalin, e [alkalɛ̃, in] *adj* alkaline.

alchimiste [alʃimist] *nmf* alchemist.

alcool [alkɔl] *nm* alcohol ; **~ à brûler** methylated spirits *(pl)* ; **~ à 90 degrés** surgical spirit ; **~ de prune/poire** plum/pear brandy.

alcoolémie [alkɔlemi] *nf* : **taux d'~** blood alcohol level.

alcoolique [alkɔlik] *nmf* & *adj* alcoholic.

alcoolisé, e [alkɔlize] *adj* alcoholic.

alcoolisme [alkɔlism] *nm* alcoholism.

Alc(o)otest® [alkɔtest] *nm* ≃ Breathalyser® ; **passer un ~** to be breathalysed.

alcôve [alkov] *nf* recess ; **secret d'~** intimate secret.

aléa [alea] *nm* (*gén pl*) *sout* hazard.

aléatoire [aleatwar] *adj* - **1.** [avenir] uncertain - **2.** [choix] random.

alémanique [alemanik] *adj* : **Suisse ~** German-speaking (part of) Switzerland.

alentour [alãtur] *adv* around, round about.

◆ **alentours** *nmpl* surroundings ; **les ~s de la ville** the outskirts of the city ; **aux ~s de** [spatial] in the vicinity of ; [temporel] around.

alerte [alert] <> *adj* - **1.** [personne, esprit] agile, alert - **2.** [style, pas] lively <> *nf* alarm, alert ; **donner l'~** to sound *ou* give the alert ; **~ à la bombe** bomb scare ; **fausse ~** false alarm.

alerter [3] [alerte] *vt* to warn, to alert.

alèse = **alaise**.

alexandrin [aleksãdrɛ̃] *nm* alexandrine.

algèbre [alʒebr] *nf* algebra.

Alger [alʒe] *n* Algiers.

Algérie [alʒeri] *nf* : **l'~** Algeria.

algérien, enne [alʒerjɛ̃, ɛn] *adj* Algerian.

◆ **Algérien, enne** *nm, f* Algerian.

algue [alg] *nf* seaweed *(U)*.

alias [aljas] *adv* alias.

alibi [alibi] *nm* alibi.

aliénation [aljenasjɔ̃] *nf* alienation ; **~ mentale** insanity.

aliéné, e [aljene] <> *adj* - **1.** *MÉD* insane - **2.** *JUR* alienated <> *nm, f MÉD* insane person.

aliéner [18] [aljene] *vt* to alienate.

alignement [aliɲmã] *nm* alignment, lining up ; **~ sur** alignment with ; **être dans l'~ de** to be in line with.

aligner [3] [aliɲe] *vt* - **1.** [disposer en ligne] to line up, to align - **2.** [présenter] to set out - **3.** [adapter] : **~ qqch sur** to align sthg with, to bring sthg into line with.

◆ **s'aligner** *vp* to line up ; **s'~ sur** *POLIT* to align o.s. with.

aliment [alimã] *nm* [nourriture] food *(U)*.

alimentaire [alimãter] *adj* - **1.** [gén] food *(avant n)* ; **c'est juste un travail ~** I'm doing this job just for the money - **2.** *JUR* maintenance *(avant n)*.

alimentation [alimɑ̃tasjɔ̃] *nf* - **1.** [nourriture] diet ; **magasin d'~** food store - **2.** [approvisionnement] : **~ (en)** supply *ou* supplying *(U)* (of).

alimenter [3] [alimɑ̃te] *vt* - **1.** [nourrir] to feed - **2.** [approvisionner] : **~ qqch en** to supply sthg with - **3.** *fig* [entretenir] to keep going.

◆ **s'alimenter** *vp* to eat.

alinéa [alinea] *nm* - **1.** [retrait de ligne] indent - **2.** [dans un document officiel] paragraph.

aliter [3] [alite] *vt* : **être alité** to be bedridden.

◆ **s'aliter** *vp* to take to one's bed.

allaitement [aletmɑ̃] *nm* [d'enfant] breastfeeding ; [d'animal] suckling.

allaiter [4] [alete] *vt* [enfant] to breast-feed ; [animal] to suckle.

allant [alɑ̃] *nm* : **plein d'~** dynamic.

allé, e [ale] *pp* ▷ **aller**.

alléchant, e [aleʃɑ̃, ɑ̃t] *adj* mouth-watering, tempting.

allécher [18] [aleʃe] *vt* : **il a été alléché par l'odeur/la perspective** the smell/prospect made his mouth water.

allée [ale] *nf* - **1.** [dans un jardin] path ; [dans une ville] avenue - **2.** [passage] aisle - **3.** [trajet] : **~s et venues** comings and goings - **4.** *Can GOLF* fairway.

allégation [alegasjɔ̃] *nf* allegation.

allégé, e [aleʒe] *adj* [régime, produit] low-fat.

allégeance [aleʒɑ̃s] *nf* allegiance.

alléger [22] [aleʒe] *vt* - **1.** [fardeau] to lighten - **2.** [douleur] to soothe.

allégorie [alegɔri] *nf* allegory.

allègre [alɛgr] *adj* - **1.** [ton] cheerful - **2.** [démarche] jaunty.

allégresse [alegrɛs] *nf* elation.

alléguer [18] [alege] *vt* : **~ une excuse** to put forward an excuse ; **~ que** to plead (that).

Allemagne [almaɲ] *nf* : **l'~** Germany ; **l'(ex-)~ de l'Est** (former) East Germany ; **l'(ex-)~ de l'Ouest** (former) West Germany.

allemand, e [almɑ̃, ɑ̃d] *adj* German.

◆ **allemand** *nm* [langue] German.

◆ **Allemand, e** *nm, f* German ; **un Allemand de l'Est/l'Ouest** an East/a West German.

aller [31] [ale] ◇ *nm* - **1.** [trajet] outward journey - **2.** [billet] single ticket *Br*, one-way ticket *Am* ◇ *vi* - **1.** [gén] to go ; **allez!** come on! ; **allez, au revoir!** bye then! ; **vas-y!** go on! ; **allons-y!, on y va!** let's go!, off we go! - **2.** (+ *infinitif*) : **~ faire qqch** to go and do sthg ; **~ chercher les enfants à l'école** to go and fetch the children from school ;

~ travailler/se promener to go to work/for a walk - **3.** [indiquant un état] : **comment vas-tu?** how are you? ; **je vais bien** I'm very well, I'm fine ; **comment ça va? — ça va** [santé] how are you? — fine *ou* all right ; [situation] how are things? — fine *ou* all right ; **~ mieux** to be better - **4.** [convenir] : **ce type de clou ne va pas pour ce travail** this kind of nail won't do *ou* isn't suitable for this job ; **~ avec** to go with ; **~ à qqn** to suit sb ; [suj : vêtement, taille] to fit sb ; **ces couleurs ne vont pas ensemble** these colours don't go well together - **5.** *loc* : **cela va de soi, cela va sans dire** that goes without saying ; **il y a de votre vie!** your life is at stake!, your life depends on it! ; **il en va de ... comme ...** the same goes for ... as ... ; **il en va de même pour lui** the same goes for him ◇ *v aux* (+ *infinitif*) [exprime le futur proche] to be going to, will ; **je vais arriver en retard** I'm going to arrive late, I'll arrive late ; **nous allons bientôt avoir fini** we'll soon have finished.

◆ **s'en aller** *vp* - **1.** [partir] to go, to be off ; **allez-vous-en!** go away! - **2.** [disparaître] to go away.

allergie [alɛrʒi] *nf* allergy.

allergique [alɛrʒik] *adj* : **~ (à)** allergic (to).

aller-retour [alerətur] *nm* return (ticket).

alliage [aljaʒ] *nm* alloy.

alliance [aljɑ̃s] *nf* - **1.** [union - stratégique] alliance ; [- par le mariage] union, marriage ; **cousin par ~** cousin by marriage - **2.** [bague] wedding ring - **3.** [organisation] : **l'Alliance française** *organization promoting French language and culture abroad*.

allié, e [alje] ◇ *adj* : **~ (à)** allied (to) ◇ *nm, f* ally.

◆ **Alliés** *nmpl* : **les Alliés** the Allies.

allier [9] [alje] *vt* - **1.** [métaux] to alloy - **2.** [associer] to combine.

◆ **s'allier** *vp* to become allies ; **s'~ qqn** to win sb over as an ally ; **s'~ à qqn** to ally with sb.

alligator [aligatɔr] *nm* alligator.

allitération [aliterasjɔ̃] *nf* alliteration.

allô [alo] *interj* hello!

allocation [alɔkasjɔ̃] *nf* - **1.** [attribution] allocation - **2.** [aide financière] : **~ chômage** unemployment benefit *(U) Br ou* compensation *(U) Am* ; **~ logement** housing benefit *(U) Br*, rent subsidy *(U) Am* ; **~s familiales** child benefit *(U) Br*, welfare *(U) Am*.

allocution [alɔkysjɔ̃] *nf* short speech.

allongé, e [alɔ̃ʒe] *adj* - **1.** [position] : **être ~** to be lying down *ou* stretched out - **2.** [forme] elongated.

allongement [alɔ̃ʒmɑ̃] *nm* lengthening.

allonger [17] [alɔ̃ʒe] <> *vt* - **1.** [gén] to lengthen, to make longer - **2.** [jambe, bras] to stretch (out) - **3.** [personne] to lay down - **4.** *fam* [argent] to dish out - **5.** *fam* [coup] to aim <> *vi* [jours] to grow longer.

➤ **s'allonger** *vp* - **1.** [gén] to get longer - **2.** [se coucher] to lie down - **3.** [se déployer] to stretch (out).

allopathique [alɔpatik] *adj* allopathic.

allouer [6] [alwe] *vt* : ~ qqch à qqn to allocate sthg to sb.

allumage [alymaʒ] *nm* - **1.** [de feu] lighting - **2.** [d'appareil électrique] switching *ou* turning on - **3.** [de moteur] ignition.

allume-cigares [alymsigar] *nm inv* cigar lighter.

allume-gaz [alymgaz] *nm inv* gas lighter.

allumer [3] [alyme] *vt* - **1.** [lampe, radio, télévision] to turn *ou* switch on ; **allume dans la cuisine** turn the kitchen light on - **2.** [gaz] to light ; [cigarette] to light (up) - **3.** *fam* [personne] to turn on.

➤ **s'allumer** *vp* - **1.** [gén] to light up ; **s'~ de** *fig* [de joie, curiosité] to light up with - **2.** *ÉLECTR* to come *ou* go on.

allumette [alymɛt] *nf* match ; **craquer une ~** to strike a match.

allumeuse [alymøz] *nf fam péj* tease.

allure [alyr] *nf* - **1.** [vitesse] speed ; **à toute ~** at top *ou* full speed - **2.** [prestance] presence ; **avoir de l'~** to have style - **3.** [apparence générale] appearance ; **avoir une drôle d'~** to look odd ; **avoir fière ~** to cut a striking figure.

allusion [alyzjɔ̃] *nf* allusion ; **faire ~ à** to refer *ou* allude to.

almanach [almana] *nm* almanac.

aloès [alɔɛs] *nm* aloe.

aloi [alwa] *nm* : **de bon ~** [mesure] of real worth ; **de mauvais ~** [gaîté] not genuine ; [plaisanterie] in bad taste.

alors [alɔr] *adv* - **1.** [jadis] then, at that time - **2.** [à ce moment-là] then - **3.** [exprimant la conséquence] then, so ; **et ~, qu'est-ce qui s'est passé?** so what happened? ; **il va se mettre en colère — et ~?** he'll be angry — so what? - **4.** [emploi expressif] well (then) ; **~, qu'est-ce qu'on fait?** well, what are we doing? ; **ça ~!** well fancy that!

➤ **d'alors** *loc adv* at that time.

➤ **jusqu'alors** *loc adv* (up) until then.

➤ **alors que** *loc conj* - **1.** [exprimant le temps] while, when - **2.** [exprimant l'opposition] even though ; **elle est sortie ~ que c'était interdit** she went out even though it was forbidden ; **ils aiment le café ~ que nous, nous bu-** vons du thé they like coffee whereas we drink tea.

alouette [alwɛt] *nf* lark.

alourdir [32] [alurdir] *vt* - **1.** [gén] to weigh down, to make heavy - **2.** *fig* [impôts] to increase.

➤ **s'alourdir** *vp* - **1.** [taille] to get bigger - **2.** [paupières] to grow heavy.

aloyau [alwajo] *nm* sirloin.

alpage [alpaʒ] *nm* high mountain pasture.

Alpes [alp] *nfpl* : **les ~** the Alps.

alpestre [alpɛstr] *adj* alpine.

alphabet [alfabɛ] *nm* alphabet.

alphabétique [alfabetik] *adj* alphabetical.

alphabétisation [alfabetizasjɔ̃] *nf* teaching of literacy.

alphabétiser [3] [alfabetize] *vt* : ~ qqn to teach sb (how) to read and write ; **~ un pays** to eliminate illiteracy from a country.

alpin, e [alpɛ̃, in] *adj* alpine.

alpinisme [alpinism] *nm* mountaineering.

alpiniste [alpinist] *nmf* mountaineer.

Alsace [alzas] *nf* : **l'~** Alsace.

alsacien, enne [alzasjɛ̃, ɛn] *adj* Alsatian.

➤ **alsacien** *nm* [dialecte] Alsatian.

➤ **Alsacien, enne** *nm, f* Alsatian.

altération [alterasjɔ̃] *nf* - **1.** [dégradation - gén] alteration, distortion ; [- de santé] deterioration - **2.** *MUS* inflection.

altercation [altɛrkasjɔ̃] *nf* altercation.

alter ego [alterego] *nm inv* alter ego.

altérer [18] [altere] *vt* - **1.** [détériorer] to spoil - **2.** [santé] to harm, to affect ; [vérité, récit] to distort.

➤ **s'altérer** *vp* - **1.** [matière - métal] to deteriorate ; [- aliment] to go off, to spoil - **2.** [santé] to deteriorate.

alternance [alternɑ̃s] *nf* - **1.** [succession] alternation ; **en ~** alternately - **2.** *POLIT* change of government party.

alternatif, ive [alternatif, iv] *adj* - **1.** [périodique] alternating - **2.** [parallèle] alternative.

➤ **alternative** *nf* alternative.

alternativement [alternativmɑ̃] *adv* alternately.

alterner [3] [alterne] <> *vt* : **(faire) ~ qqch et qqch** to alternate sthg with sthg <> *vi* [se succéder] : **~ (avec)** to alternate (with).

altesse [altɛs] *nf* : **Son Altesse** His/Her Highness.

altier, ère [altje, ɛr] *adj* haughty.

altimètre [altimetr] *nm* altimeter.

altiport [altipɔr] *nm airport at high altitude, used especially to serve ski resorts.*

altitude [altityd] *nf* altitude, height ; **en ~** at (high) altitude ; **monter en ~** to climb to altitude ; **prendre de l'~** AÉRON to gain height *ou* altitude.

alto [alto] *nm* [MUS - voix] alto ; [- instrument] viola.

alu [aly] *fam* <> *nm* [métal] aluminium *Br*, aluminum *Am* ; [papier] aluminium *Br ou* aluminum *Am* foil, tinfoil <> *adj* : **papier ~** aluminium *Br ou* aluminum *Am* foil, tinfoil.

aluminium [alyminjɔm] *nm* aluminium *Br*, aluminum *Am*.

alunir [32] [alynir] *vi* to land on the moon.

alunissage [alynisaʒ] *nm* moon landing.

alvéole [alveɔl] *nf* - **1.** [cavité] cavity ; **~ dentaire** tooth socket - **2.** [de ruche, poumon] alveolus.

amabilité [amabilite] *nf* kindness ; **avoir l'~ de faire qqch** to be so kind as to do sthg.

amadouer [6] [amadwe] *vt* [adoucir] to tame, to pacify ; [persuader] to coax.

s'amadouer *vp* to relent.

amaigrir [32] [amegrir] *vt* to make thin *ou* thinner.

s'amaigrir *vp* to get thin *ou* thinner.

amaigrissant, e [amegrisɑ̃, ɑ̃t] *adj* slimming *(avant n) Br*, reducing *(avant n) Am*.

amaigrissement [amegrismɑ̃] *nm* loss of weight.

amalgame [amalgam] *nm* - **1.** TECHNOL amalgam - **2.** [de styles] mixture - **3.** [d'idées, de notions] : **il ne faut pas faire l'~ entre ces deux questions** the two issues must not be confused.

amalgamer [3] [amalgame] *vt* to combine.

s'amalgamer *vp* : **s'~ avec** *ou* **à** to be combined *ou* mixed with.

amande [amɑ̃d] *nf* almond ; **en ~** *fig* almond-shaped.

amandier [amɑ̃dje] *nm* almond tree.

amanite [amanit] *nf* : **~ phalloïde** death-cap (mushroom).

amant [amɑ̃] *nm* lover.

amarre [amar] *nf* rope, cable ; **larguer les ~s** [bateau] to cast off ; *fam fig* [partir] to hit the road.

amarrer [3] [amare] *vt* - **1.** NAVIG to moor - **2.** [fixer] to tie down.

amaryllis [amarilis] *nf* amaryllis.

amas [ama] *nm* pile.

amasser [3] [amase] *vt* - **1.** [objets] to pile up - **2.** [argent] to accumulate.

s'amasser *vp* - **1.** [gén] to pile up - **2.** [foule] to gather.

amateur [amatœr] *nm* - **1.** [connaisseur - d'art, de bon café] : **~ de** lover of - **2.** [non-professionnel]

amateur ; **faire qqch en ~** to do sthg as a hobby - **3.** *péj* [dilettante] amateur.

amateurisme [amatœrism] *nm* - **1.** SPORT amateurism - **2.** *péj* [dilettantisme] amateurishness.

amazone [amazon] *nf* horsewoman ; **monter en ~** to ride sidesaddle.

Amazone [amazon] *nf* : **l'~** the Amazon (River).

Amazonie [amazoni] *nf* : **l'~** the Amazon (Basin).

amazonien, enne [amazonjɛ̃, ɛn] *adj* Amazonian ; **la forêt ~ne** the Amazon rain forest.

ambages [ɑ̃baʒ] ➡ **sans ambages** *loc adv sout* without beating about the bush.

ambassade [ɑ̃basad] *nf* embassy.

ambassadeur, drice [ɑ̃basadœr, dris] *nm, f* ambassador.

ambiance [ɑ̃bjɑ̃s] *nf* atmosphere ; **il y a de l'~!** there's a good atmosphere!

ambiant, e [ɑ̃bjɑ̃, ɑ̃t] *adj* : **température ~e** room temperature.

ambidextre [ɑ̃bidɛkstr] <> *nmf* ambidextrous person <> *adj* ambidextrous.

ambigu, uë [ɑ̃bigy] *adj* ambiguous.

ambiguïté [ɑ̃biguite] *nf* ambiguity ; **sans ~** [parler, répondre] unambiguously ; [réponse, attitude] unambiguous.

ambitieux, euse [ɑ̃bisjø, øz] <> *nm, f* ambitious person <> *adj* ambitious.

ambition [ɑ̃bisjɔ̃] *nf* - **1.** *péj* [arrivisme] ambitiousness - **2.** [désir] ambition ; **avoir l'~ de faire qqch** to have an ambition to do sthg.

ambitionner [3] [ɑ̃bisjone] *vt* : **~ qqch/de faire qqch** to seek sthg/to do sthg.

ambivalent, e [ɑ̃bivalɑ̃, ɑ̃t] *adj* ambivalent.

ambre [ɑ̃br] *nm* - **1.** [couleur] amber - **2.** [matière] : **~ (gris)** ambergris.

ambré, e [ɑ̃bre] *adj* [couleur] amber.

ambulance [ɑ̃bylɑ̃s] *nf* ambulance.

ambulancier, ère [ɑ̃bylɑ̃sje, ɛr] *nm, f* ambulanceman (*f* ambulancewoman).

ambulant, e [ɑ̃bylɑ̃, ɑ̃t] *adj* travelling *(avant n)*.

âme [am] *nf* - **1.** [gén] soul ; **dans l'~** [par goût] at heart ; [accompli] through and through ; **avoir une ~ de comédien** to be a born actor ; **une bonne ~** *hum* a kind soul ; **~ sœur** soulmate ; **être l'~ de qqch** to be the heart and soul of sthg - **2.** [caractère] spirit, soul - **3.** *loc* : **en mon ~ et conscience** in all honesty ; **sans rencontrer ~ qui vive** without seeing a living soul ; **rendre l'~** to breathe one's last.

amélioration [ameljɔrasjɔ̃] nf improvement.

améliorer [3] [ameljɔre] vt to improve.

➤ **s'améliorer** vp to improve.

amen [amɛn] adv amen.

aménagement [amenaʒmã] nm - **1.** [de lieu] fitting out ; ~ **du territoire** development, planning - **2.** [de programme] planning, organizing.

aménager [17] [amenaʒe] vt - **1.** [pièce] to fit out - **2.** [programme] to plan, to organize.

amende [amãd] nf fine ; **mettre qqn à l'~** to penalize sb ; **faire ~ honorable** to admit one's mistake.

amendement [amãdmã] nm POLIT amendment.

amender [3] [amãde] vt - **1.** POLIT to amend - **2.** AGRIC to enrich.

➤ **s'amender** vp to mend one's ways.

amène [amɛn] adj sout amiable, affable.

amener [19] [amne] vt - **1.** [mener] to bring - **2.** [inciter] : ~ **qqn à faire qqch** [suj : circonstances] to lead sb to do sthg ; [suj : personne] to get sb to do sthg - **3.** [occasionner, préparer] to bring about.

➤ **s'amener** vp fam - **1.** [arriver] to turn up, to show up - **2.** [venir] to come.

aménorrhée [amenɔre] nf MÉD amenorrhoea.

amenuiser [3] [amənɥize] vt - **1.** [rendre plus petit] : **ses cheveux amenuisent son visage** her hair makes her face look thinner - **2.** [réduire] to diminish, to reduce.

➤ **s'amenuiser** vp to dwindle, to diminish.

amer, ère [amɛr] adj bitter.

amèrement [amɛrmã] adv bitterly.

américain, e [amerikɛ̃, ɛn] adj American.

➤ **américain** nm [langue] American English.

➤ **Américain, e** nm, f American.

américanisme [amerikanism] nm Americanism.

amérindien, enne [amerɛ̃djɛ̃, ɛn] adj Native American.

➤ **Amérindien, enne** nm, f Native American.

Amérique [amerik] nf : **l'~** America ; **l'~ centrale** Central America ; **l'~ du Nord** North America ; **l'~ du Sud** South America ; **l'~ latine** Latin America.

amerrir [32] [amerir] vi [hydravion] to land (on the sea) ; [cabine spatiale] to splash down.

amertume [amɛrtym] nf bitterness.

améthyste [ametist] nf amethyst.

ameublement [amœbləmã] nm [meubles] furniture ; [action de meubler] furnishing.

ameublir [32] [amœblir] vt [sol] to break up.

ameuter [3] [amœte] vt [curieux] to draw a crowd of ; [quartier, voisins] to bring out.

ami, e [ami] <> adj friendly <> nm, f - **1.** [camarade] friend ; ~ **d'enfance** childhood friend ; **petit ~** boyfriend ; **petite ~e** girlfriend - **2.** [partisan] supporter, friend.

➤ **faux ami** nm false friend.

amiable [amjabl] adj [accord] friendly, informal.

➤ **à l'amiable** loc adv & loc adj out of court.

amiante [amjãt] nm asbestos.

amibe [amib] nf amoeba.

amibien, enne [amibjɛ̃, ɛn] adj amoebic.

➤ **amibien** nm amoeba.

amical, e, aux [amikal, o] adj friendly.

➤ **amicale** nf association, club (for people with a shared interest).

amicalement [amikalmã] adv - **1.** [de façon amicale] amicably, in a friendly way - **2.** [dans une lettre] yours (ever), (with) best wishes.

amidon [amidɔ̃] nm starch.

amidonner [3] [amidɔne] vt to starch.

amincir [32] [amɛ̃sir] <> vt : ~ **qqn** to make sb look slimmer <> vi to get slimmer ou thinner.

➤ **s'amincir** vp fig [diminuer] to dwindle, to diminish.

amincissant, e [amɛ̃sisã, ãt] adj slimming.

amiral, aux [amiral, o] nm admiral.

amitié [amitje] nf - **1.** [affection] affection ; **prendre qqn en ~** to befriend sb - **2.** [rapports amicaux] friendship ; **faire ses ~s à qqn** to give sb one's good ou best wishes.

AMM (abr de Autorisation de mise sur le marché) nf official authorization for marketing a pharmaceutical product.

ammoniac, aque [amɔnjak] adj CHIM ammoniac.

➤ **ammoniac** nm ammonia.

➤ **ammoniaque** nf ammonia (water).

amnésie [amnezi] nf amnesia.

amniocentèse [amnjɔsɛ̃tɛz] nf amniocentesis.

amnistie [amnisti] nf amnesty.

amnistier [9] [amnistje] vt to amnesty.

amocher [3] [amɔʃe] vt fam to mess up.

➤ **s'amocher** vp fam to mess o.s. up.

amoindrir [32] [amwɛ̃drir] vt to diminish.

➤ **s'amoindrir** vp to dwindle, to diminish.

amollir [32] [amɔlir] vt [personne] to make soft.

➤ **s'amollir** vp [personne] to go soft.

amonceler [24] [amɔ̃sle] vt to accumulate.

s'amonceler *vp* to pile up, to accumulate.

amoncelle, amoncelles *etc* ▷ **amonceler.**

amont [amɔ̃] *nm* upstream (water) ; **en ~ de** [rivière] upriver *ou* upstream from ; *fig* prior to.

amoral, e, aux [amɔral, o] *adj* - **1.** [qui ignore la morale] amoral - **2.** [débauché] immoral.

amorce [amɔrs] *nf* - **1.** [d'explosif] priming ; [de cartouche, d'obus] cap - **2.** PÊCHE bait - **3.** *fig* [commencement] beginnings *(pl)*, germ.

amorcer [16] [amɔrse] *vt* - **1.** [explosif] to prime - **2.** PÊCHE to bait - **3.** *fig* [commencer] to begin, to initiate.
s'amorcer *vp* to begin.

amorphe [amɔrf] *adj* - **1.** [personne] lifeless - **2.** [matériau] amorphous.

amortir [32] [amɔrtir] *vt* - **1.** [atténuer - choc] to absorb ; [- bruit] to deaden, to muffle - **2.** [dette] to pay off - **3.** [achat] to write off.

amortissement [amɔrtismɑ̃] *nm* - **1.** [de choc] absorption ; [de bruit] deadening, muffling - **2.** [de dette] payment, paying off - **3.** [d'achat] writing off.

amortisseur [amɔrtisœr] *nm* AUTOM shock absorber.

amour [amur] *nm* - **1.** [gén] love ; **~ maternel/filial** maternal/filial love ; **pour l'~ de** for the love of ; **pour l'~ du ciel** for heaven's sake ; **faire l'~** to make love ; **filer le parfait ~** to live out love's dream - **2.** [jolie chose] : **un ~ de** a darling (little) - **3.** [personne] : **un ~** an angel, a dear.
amours *nfpl* [vie sentimentale] love-life ; **à tes ~s!** [toast] here's to you! ; [quand on éternue] bless you!

amouracher [3] [amurafe] **s'amouracher** *vp* : **s'~ de** to become infatuated with.

amourette [amuret] *nf* passing fancy, brief love affair.

amoureusement [amurøzmɑ̃] *adv* amorously.

amoureux, euse [amurø, øz] ◇ *adj* - **1.** [personne] in love ; **être/tomber ~ (de)** to be/fall in love (with) - **2.** [regard, geste] loving ◇ *nm, f* - **1.** [prétendant] suitor - **2.** [passionné] : **~ de** lover of ; **un ~ de la nature** a nature lover.

amour-propre [amurprɔpr] *nm* pride, self-respect.

amovible [amɔvibl] *adj* - **1.** [déplaçable] detachable, removable - **2.** [fonctionnaire] removable.

ampère [ɑ̃per] *nm* amp, ampere.

amphétamine [ɑ̃fetamin] *nf* amphetamine.

amphi [ɑ̃fi] *nm* *fam* lecture hall *ou* theatre ; **cours en ~** lecture.

amphibie [ɑ̃fibi] ◇ *nm* amphibian ◇ *adj* amphibious.

amphithéâtre [ɑ̃fiteatr] *nm* - **1.** HIST amphitheatre - **2.** [d'université] lecture hall *ou* theatre.

ample [ɑ̃pl] *adj* - **1.** [vêtement - gén] loose-fitting ; [- jupe] full - **2.** [projet] extensive ; **pour de plus ~s informations** for further details - **3.** [geste] broad, sweeping.

amplement [ɑ̃pləmɑ̃] *adv* [largement] fully, amply.

ampleur [ɑ̃plœr] *nf* - **1.** [de vêtement] fullness - **2.** [d'événement, de dégâts] extent - **3.** *loc* : **prendre toute son ~** to reach its height.

ampli [ɑ̃pli] *nm* amp.

amplificateur, trice [ɑ̃plifikatœr, tris] *adj* ÉLECTR amplifying ; **un phénomène ~ de la croissance** *fig* a phenomenon which increases growth.
amplificateur *nm* - **1.** [gén] amplifier - **2.** PHOT enlarger.

amplifier [9] [ɑ̃plifje] *vt* - **1.** [mouvement, son] to amplify ; [image] to magnify, to enlarge - **2.** [scandale] to increase ; [événement, problème] to highlight.
s'amplifier *vp* [son] to grow *ou* get louder ; *fig* [revendications, phénomène] to grow.

amplitude [ɑ̃plityd] *nf* - **1.** [de geste] fullness - **2.** [d'onde] amplitude - **3.** [de température] range.

ampoule [ɑ̃pul] *nf* - **1.** [de lampe] bulb - **2.** [sur la peau] blister - **3.** [médicament] ampoule, phial.

ampoulé, e [ɑ̃pule] *adj* *péj* pompous.

amputation [ɑ̃pytasjɔ̃] *nf* MÉD amputation.

amputer [3] [ɑ̃pyte] *vt* MÉD to amputate ; *fig* [couper] to cut (back *ou* down) ; **son article a été amputé d'un tiers** his article was cut by a third.

amulette [amylet] *nf* amulet.

amusant, e [amyzɑ̃, ɑ̃t] *adj* [drôle] funny ; [distrayant] amusing ; **c'est très ~** it's great fun.

amuse-gueule [amyzgœl] *nm inv* *fam* cocktail snack, (party) nibble.

amusement [amyzmɑ̃] *nm* amusement *(U)*.

amuser [3] [amyze] *vt* to amuse, to entertain.
s'amuser *vp* to have fun, to have a good time ; **s'~ à faire qqch** to amuse o.s. (by) doing sthg.

amygdale [amidal] *nf* tonsil.

an [ɑ̃] *nm* year ; **avoir sept ~s** to be seven

(years old) ; **l'~ dernier/prochain** last/next year ; **en l'~ 2000** in the year 2000 ; **le premier** ou **le jour de l'~** New Year's Day ; **le nouvel ~ the** New Year ; **bon ~ mal ~** taking the good years with the bad.

anabolisant [anabɔlizɑ̃] *nm* anabolic steroid.

anachronique [anakrɔnik] *adj* anachronistic.

anagramme [anagram] *nf* anagram.

ANAH (*abr de* **Agence nationale pour l'amélioration de l'habitat**) *nf national agency responsible for housing projects and restoration grants.*

anal, e, aux [anal, o] *adj* anal ; **stade ~** PSYCHOL anal phase.

analgésique [analʒezik] *nm* & *adj* analgesic.

anallergique [analɛrʒik] *adj* hypoallergenic.

analogie [analɔʒi] *nf* analogy.

analogique [analɔʒik] *adj* analogue *Br*, analog *Am*.

analogue [analɔg] <> *nm* equivalent, analogue *Br*, analog *Am* <> *adj* analogous, comparable.

analphabète [analfabɛt] *nmf* & *adj* illiterate.

analyse [analiz] *nf* - **1.** [étude] analysis ; **en dernière ~** in the final analysis - **2.** CHIM & MÉD test, analysis - **3.** [psychanalyse] analysis (*U*).

analyser [3] [analize] *vt* - **1.** [étudier, psychanalyser] to analyse *Br*, to analyze *Am* - **2.** CHIM & MÉD to test, to analyse *Br*, to analyze *Am*.

➡ **s'analyser** *vp* to be analysed ou understood ; **un tel comportement ne s'analyse pas facilement** such behaviour *Br* ou behavior *Am* is not easy to understand.

analyste [analist] *nmf* analyst.

analyste-programmeur, euse [analist-prɔgramœr, øz] (*mpl* **analystes-programmeurs**, *fpl* **analystes-programmeuses**) *nm, f* systems analyst.

analytique [analitik] *adj* analytical.

ananas [anana(s)] *nm* pineapple.

anar [anar] *nmf* & *adj fam* anarchist.

anarchie [anarʃi] *nf* - **1.** POLIT anarchy - **2.** [désordre] chaos, anarchy.

anarchique [anarʃik] *adj* anarchic.

anarchiste [anarʃist] *nmf* & *adj* anarchist.

anathème [anatɛm] *nm* anathema ; **jeter l'~ sur** *fig* & *sout* to curse.

Anatolie [anatɔli] *nf* : **l'~** Anatolia.

anatomie [anatɔmi] *nf* anatomy.

anatomique [anatɔmik] *adj* anatomical.

ancestral, e, aux [ɑ̃sɛstral, o] *adj* ancestral.

ancêtre [ɑ̃sɛtr] *nmf* [aïeul] ancestor ; *fig* [forme première] forerunner, ancestor ; *fig* [initiateur] father (*f* mother).

anchois [ɑ̃ʃwa] *nm* anchovy.

ancien, enne [ɑ̃sjɛ̃, ɛn] *adj* - **1.** [gén] old ; **l'~ franc** the old franc - **2.** (*avant n*) [précédent] former, old - **3.** [qui a de l'ancienneté] senior - **4.** [du passé] ancient ; **l'Ancien Régime** the Ancien Régime.

➡ **ancien** *nm* [mobilier] : **l'~** antiques (*pl*).

➡ **anciens** *nmpl* elders.

anciennement [ɑ̃sjɛnmɑ̃] *adv* formerly, previously.

ancienneté [ɑ̃sjɛnte] *nf* - **1.** [d'une tradition] oldness - **2.** [d'un employé] seniority.

ancre [ɑ̃kr] *nf* NAVIG anchor ; **jeter l'~** to drop anchor ; **lever l'~** to weigh anchor ; *fam* [partir] to make tracks.

ancrer [3] [ɑ̃kre] *vt* [bateau] to anchor ; *fig* [idée, habitude] to root.

Andalousie [ɑ̃daluzi] *nf* : **l'~** Andalusia.

Andes [ɑ̃d] *nfpl* : **les ~** the Andes ; **la cordillère des ~** the Andes Mountain Ranges.

Andorre [ɑ̃dɔr] *nf* : **(la principauté d')~** (the principality of) Andorra.

andouille [ɑ̃duj] *nf* - **1.** [charcuterie] *type of sausage made of chitterlings (pig's intestines eaten cold)* - **2.** *fam* [imbécile] prat, twit.

andouillette [ɑ̃dujɛt] *nf type of sausage made of chitterlings (pig's intestines) eaten hot.*

androgyne [ɑ̃drɔʒin] <> *nmf* androgynous person <> *adj* androgynous.

âne [an] *nm* - **1.** ZOOL ass, donkey - **2.** *fam* [imbécile] ass.

anéantir [32] [aneɑ̃tir] *vt* - **1.** [détruire] to annihilate ; *fig* to ruin, to wreck - **2.** [démoraliser] to crush, to overwhelm.

➡ **s'anéantir** *vp* [disparaître] to vanish.

anéantissement [aneɑ̃tismɑ̃] *nm* - **1.** [destruction] annihilation ; *fig* wrecking, ruin - **2.** [abattement] dejection.

anecdote [anɛkdɔt] *nf* anecdote.

anecdotique [anɛkdɔtik] *adj* anecdotal.

anémie [anemi] *nf* MÉD anaemia *Br*, anemia *Am* ; *fig* enfeeblement.

anémié, e [anemje] *adj* anaemic *Br*, anemic *Am*.

anémier [9] [anemje] *vt* MÉD to make anaemic *Br* ou anemic *Am* ; *fig* to weaken.

➡ **s'anémier** *vp* MÉD to become anaemic *Br* ou anemic *Am* ; *fig* to weaken.

anémique [anemik] *adj* anaemic *Br*, anemic *Am*.

anémone [anemɔn] *nf* anemone.

ânerie [anri] *nf fam* - **1.** [caractère] stupidity *(U)* - **2.** [parole, acte] : **dire/faire une** ~ to say/do something stupid.

ânesse [anɛs] *nf* she-ass, she-donkey.

anesthésie [anɛstezi] *nf* anaesthesia *Br*, anesthesia *Am* ; **sous** ~ under (the) anaesthetic *Br* ou anesthetic *Am*, under anaesthesia ; ~ **locale** local anaesthetic *Br* ou anesthetic *Am* ; ~ **générale** general anaesthetic *Br* ou anesthetic *Am*.

anesthésier [9] [anɛstezje] *vt* to anaesthetize *Br*, to anesthetize *Am*.

anesthésique [anɛstezik] *nm* & *adj* anaesthetic *Br*, anesthetic *Am*.

anesthésiste [anɛstezist] *nmf* anaesthetist *Br*, anesthetist *Am*.

aneth [anɛt] *nm* dill.

anfractuosité [ãfraktɥozite] *nf* crevice.

ange [ãʒ] *nm* angel ; ~ **gardien** guardian angel ; **être aux ~s** *fig* to be in one's seventh heaven.

angélique [ãʒelik] <> *nf* angelica <> *adj* angelic.

angélus [ãʒelys] *nm* [sonnerie] angelus (bell).

angevin, e [ãʒvɛ̃, in] *adj* - **1.** [de l'Anjou] of/from Anjou - **2.** [d'Angers] of/from Angers.
➤ **Angevin, e** *nm, f* - **1.** [de l'Anjou] person from Anjou - **2.** [d'Angers] person from Angers.

angine [ãʒin] *nf* [pharyngite] pharyngitis ; [amygdalite] tonsillitis ; ~ **de poitrine** angina (pectoris).

anglais, e [ãglɛ, ɛz] *adj* English.
➤ **anglais** *nm* [langue] English.
➤ **Anglais, e** *nm, f* Englishman (*f* Englishwoman) ; **les Anglais** the English.
➤ **anglaises** *nfpl* ringlets.
➤ **à l'anglaise** *loc adv CULIN* boiled ; **filer à l'~e** *fig* to make ou sneak off.

angle [ãgl] *nm* - **1.** [coin] corner ; ~ **mort** [zone invisible] blind spot ; **arrondir les ~s** *fig* to smooth things over - **2.** *MATHS* angle ; ~ **droit/aigu/obtus** right/acute/obtuse angle ; **voir les choses sous un certain** ~ *fig* to see things from a certain point of view.

Angleterre [ãglətɛr] *nf* : **l'**~ England.

anglican, e [ãglikã, an] *adj* & *nm, f* Anglican.

anglophone [ãglɔfɔn] <> *nmf* English-speaker <> *adj* English-speaking, anglophone.

anglo-saxon, onne [ãglosaksɔ̃, ɔn] *adj* Anglo-Saxon.
➤ **anglo-saxon** *nm* [langue] Anglo-Saxon, Old English.
➤ **Anglo-Saxon, onne** *nm, f* Anglo-Saxon.

angoisse [ãgwas] *nf* anguish.

angoissé, e [ãgwase] <> *adj* anguished <> *nmf* neurotic.

angoisser [3] [ãgwase] *vt* [effrayer] to cause anxiety to.
➤ **s'angoisser** *vp* - **1.** [être anxieux] to be overcome with anxiety - **2.** *fam* [s'inquiéter] to fret.

Angola [ãgɔla] *nm* : **l'**~ Angola.

angolais, e [ãgɔlɛ, ɛz] *adj* Angolan.
➤ **Angolais, e** *nm, f* Angolan.

angora [ãgɔra] *nm* & *adj* angora.

anguille [ãgij] *nf* eel ; **il y a** ~ **sous roche** *fig* something's up, something's going on.

anguleux, euse [ãgylø, øz] *adj* angular.

anicroche [anikrɔʃ] *nf* hitch.

animal, e, aux [animal, o] *adj* - **1.** [propre à l'animal] animal *(avant n)* - **2.** [instinctif] instinctive.
➤ **animal** *nm* - **1.** [bête] animal ; ~ **en peluche** stuffed animal ; ~ **sauvage/domestique** wild/domestic animal - **2.** *péj* [personne] lout, oaf.

animalerie [animalri] *nf* pet shop.

animateur, trice [animatœr, tris] *nm, f* - **1.** *RADIO* & *TÉLÉ* presenter - **2.** [socioculturel, sportif] activities organizer - **3.** [de manifestation] organizer.

animation [animasjɔ̃] *nf* - **1.** [de rue] activity, life ; [de conversation, visage] animation - **2.** [publicitaire] demonstration, promotion - **3.** [activités] activities *(pl)* - **4.** *CIN* animation.

animé, e [anime] *adj* [rue] lively ; [conversation, visage] animated ; [objet] animate.

animer [3] [anime] *vt* - **1.** [mettre de l'entrain dans] to animate, to liven up - **2.** [présenter] to present - **3.** [organiser des activités pour] to organize activities for.
➤ **s'animer** *vp* - **1.** [visage] to light up - **2.** [rue] to come to life, to liven up.

animisme [animism] *nm* animism.

animiste [animist] *nmf* & *adj* animist.

animosité [animozite] *nf* animosity.

anis [ani(s)] *nm BOT* anise ; *CULIN* aniseed.

anisette [anizɛt] *nf* anisette.

ankylosé, e [ãkiloze] *adj* [paralysé] stiff ; [engourdi] numb.

annales [anal] *nfpl* - **1.** [revue] review *(sg)*, journal *(sg)* - **2.** [d'examen] past papers ; **les** ~ **du bac** A-level past papers - **3.** [chronique annuelle] chronicle *(sg)*, annals ; **rester dans les** ~ *fig* to go down in history.

anneau, x [ano] *nm* - **1.** [gén] ring - **2.** [maillon] link - **3.** [de reptile] coil.
➡ **anneaux** *nmpl* SPORT rings.

année [ane] *nf* year ; **d'~ en ~** from year to year ; **souhaiter la bonne ~ à qqn** to wish sb a Happy New Year ; **~ bissextile** leap year ; **~ fiscale** financial *ou* fiscal *ou* tax year ; **~-lumière** light year ; **~ scolaire** school year.

annexe [anɛks] ◇ *nf* - **1.** [de dossier] appendix, annexe - **2.** [de bâtiment] annexe ◇ *adj* related, associated.

annexer [4] [anɛkse] *vt* - **1.** [incorporer] : **~ qqch (à qqch)** to append *ou* annex sthg (to sthg) - **2.** [pays] to annex.
➡ **s'annexer** *vp* - **1.** [s'attribuer] to grab - **2.** [s'ajouter] : **s'~ à qqch** to be associated with sthg.

annexion [anɛksjɔ̃] *nf* annexation.

annihiler [3] [aniile] *vt* [réduire à néant] to destroy, to wreck.
➡ **s'annihiler** *vp* to be destroyed, to be wrecked.

anniversaire [anivɛrse] ◇ *nm* [de mariage, mort, événement] anniversary ; [de naissance] birthday ; **bon** *ou* **joyeux ~!** happy birthday! ◇ *adj* anniversary *(avant n)*.

annonce [anɔ̃s] *nf* - **1.** [déclaration] announcement ; *fig* sign, indication - **2.** [texte] advertisement ; **~ commerciale** display ad ; **passer une ~** to place an advert *ou* advertisement ; **petite ~** classified advertisement, small ad.

annoncer [16] [anɔ̃se] *vt* - **1.** [faire savoir] to announce - **2.** [indiquer] to herald - **3.** [prédire] to predict.
➡ **s'annoncer** *vp* : **s'~ bien/mal** to look promising/unpromising ; **la crise s'annonce** there is a crisis looming.

annonceur, euse [anɔ̃sœr, øz] *nm, f* advertiser.

annonciateur, trice [anɔ̃sjatœr, tris] *adj* : **~ de qqch** heralding sthg.

Annonciation [anɔ̃sjasjɔ̃] *nf* [événement] Annunciation ; [jour] Annunciation (Day).

annoter [3] [anɔte] *vt* to annotate.

annuaire [anɥer] *nm* annual, yearbook ; **~ téléphonique** telephone directory, phone book.

annuel, elle [anɥɛl] *adj* - **1.** [tous les ans] annual, yearly - **2.** [d'une année] annual.

annuellement [anɥɛlmã] *adv* annually, yearly.

annuité [anɥite] *nf* - **1.** [paiement] annual payment, annual instalment *Br ou* installment *Am* - **2.** [année de service] year (of service).

annulaire [anyler] ◇ *nm* ring finger ◇ *adj* ring-shaped, annular.

annulation [anylasjɔ̃] *nf* - **1.** [de rendez-vous, réservation] cancellation - **2.** [de mariage] annulment.

annuler [3] [anyle] *vt* - **1.** [rendez-vous, réservation] to cancel - **2.** [mariage] to annul - **3.** [procédure] to declare invalid.
➡ **s'annuler** *vp* to cancel each other out.

anoblir [32] [anɔblir] *vt* to ennoble.

anodin, e [anɔdɛ̃, in] *adj* - **1.** [blessure] minor - **2.** [propos] harmless - **3.** [détail, personne] insignificant.

anomalie [anɔmali] *nf* anomaly.

ânon [anɔ̃] *nm* young donkey *ou* ass.

ânonner [3] [anɔne] *vt* & *vi* to recite in a drone.

anonymat [anɔnima] *nm* anonymity ; **garder l'~** to remain anonymous.

anonyme [anɔnim] ◇ *nm* [écrivain] anonymous author ◇ *adj* anonymous.

anorak [anɔrak] *nm* anorak.

anorexie [anɔreksi] *nf* anorexia.

anormal, e, aux [anɔrmal, o] ◇ *adj* - **1.** [inhabituel] abnormal, not normal - **2.** [intolérable, injuste] wrong, not right - **3.** [arriéré] (mentally) subnormal ◇ *nm, f* mental defective.

anormalement [anɔrmalmã] *adv* abnormally.

ANPE (*abr de* **Agence nationale pour l'emploi**) *nf* French national employment agency, ≃ job centre *Br* ; **s'inscrire à l'~** to register as unemployed.

anse [ãs] *nf* - **1.** [d'ustensile] handle - **2.** GÉOGR cove.

antagonisme [ãtagɔnism] *nm* antagonism.

antagoniste [ãtagɔnist] ◇ *nmf* antagonist ◇ *adj* antagonistic.

antan [ãtã] ➡ **d'antan** *loc adj littéraire* of old, of yesteryear.

antarctique [ãtarktik] *adj* Antarctic ; **le cercle polaire ~** the Antarctic Circle.
➡ **Antarctique** *nm* - **1.** [continent] : **l'~** Antarctica - **2.** [océan] : **l'~** the Antarctic (Ocean).

antécédent [ãtesedã] *nm* - **1.** *(gén pl)* [passé] history *(sg)* - **2.** GRAM antecedent.

antédiluvien, enne [ãtedilyvjɛ̃, ɛn] *adj* antediluvian, ancient.

antenne [ãtɛn] *nf* - **1.** [d'insecte] antenna, feeler ; **avoir des ~s** *fam fig* to have a sixth sense - **2.** [de télévision, de radio] aerial *Br*, antenna ; **~ parabolique** dish aerial *ou* antenna *Am*, satellite dish ; **être à l'~** to be on the air ; **hors** ~ off the air - **3.** [bâtiment] unit - **4.** [succursale] branch, office.

antépénultième [ɑ̃tepenyltjɛm] <> *nf* LING antepenultimate (syllable) <> *adj* antepenultimate.

antérieur, e [ɑ̃terjœr] *adj* - **1.** [dans le temps] earlier, previous ; ~ **à** previous *ou* prior to - **2.** [dans l'espace] front *(avant n)*.

antérieurement [ɑ̃terjœrmɑ̃] *adv* earlier, previously ; ~ **à** prior to.

anthologie [ɑ̃tɔlɔʒi] *nf* anthology.

anthracite [ɑ̃trasit] <> *nm* anthracite <> *adj inv* charcoal grey Br *ou* gray Am.

anthropologie [ɑ̃trɔpɔlɔʒi] *nf* anthropology.

anthropométrie [ɑ̃trɔpɔmetri] *nf* anthropometry.

anthropophage [ɑ̃trɔpɔfaʒ] <> *nmf* cannibal <> *adj* cannibalistic.

antiaérien, enne [ɑ̃tiaerjɛ̃, ɛn] *adj* anti-aircraft.

anti-âge [ɑ̃tiaʒ] *adj* : **crème** ~ anti-ageing cream.

antialcoolique [ɑ̃tialkɔlik] *adj* : **ligue** ~ temperance league.

antibiotique [ɑ̃tibjɔtik] *nm* & *adj* antibiotic.

antibrouillard [ɑ̃tibrujar] *nm* & *adj inv* : **(phare** *ou* **feu)** ~ fog lamp Br, foglight Am.

antibruit [ɑ̃tibrɥi] *adj inv* anti-noise ; **mur** ~ noise reduction barrier.

antibuée [ɑ̃tibɥe] ▷ **dispositif.**

antichambre [ɑ̃tiʃɑ̃br] *nf* antechamber ; **faire** ~ *fig* to wait patiently *(to see somebody)*.

anticipation [ɑ̃tisipasjɔ̃] *nf* - **1.** FIN advance ; **paiement par** ~ advance payment, payment in advance - **2.** LITTÉRATURE : **roman d'**~ science fiction novel.

anticipé, e [ɑ̃tisipe] *adj* early.

anticiper [3] [ɑ̃tisipe] <> *vt* to anticipate <> *vi* : ~ **(sur qqch)** to anticipate (sthg).

anticléricalisme [ɑ̃tiklerikalism] *nm* anticlericalism.

anticolonialisme [ɑ̃tikɔlɔnjalism] *nm* anticolonialism.

anticolonialiste [ɑ̃tikɔlɔnjalist] *nmf* & *adj* anticolonialist.

anticommunisme [ɑ̃tikɔmynism] *nm* anticommunism.

anticonformiste [ɑ̃tikɔ̃fɔrmist] *adj* & *nmf* non-conformist.

anticonstitutionnel, elle [ɑ̃tikɔ̃stitysjɔnɛl] *adj* unconstitutional.

anticorps [ɑ̃tikɔr] *nm* antibody.

anticyclone [ɑ̃tisiklɔn] *nm* anticyclone.

antidater [3] [ɑ̃tidate] *vt* to backdate.

antidémarrage [ɑ̃tidemaraʒ] *adj inv* : **système** ~ immobilizer.

antidépresseur [ɑ̃tidepresœr] *nm* & *adj m* antidepressant.

antidérapant, e [ɑ̃tiderapɑ̃, ɑ̃t] *adj* [pneu] non-skid ; [semelle, surface] non-slip.
➥ **antidérapant** *nm* [pneu] anti-skid tyre Br *ou* tire Am.

antidopage [ɑ̃tidɔpaʒ], **antidoping** [ɑ̃tidɔpiŋ] *adj inv* : **contrôle** ~ dope test, drugs test.

antidote [ɑ̃tidɔt] *nm* antidote.

anti-effraction [ɑ̃tiefraksjɔ̃] *adj inv* [dispositif] antitheft.

antigang [ɑ̃tigɑ̃g] <> *adj* ▷ **brigade** <> *nf* ≈ serious crime squad.

antigel [ɑ̃tiʒɛl] *nm inv* & *adj inv* antifreeze.

antillais, e [ɑ̃tijɛ, ɛz] *adj* West Indian.
➥ **Antillais, e** *nm, f* West Indian.

Antilles [ɑ̃tij] *nfpl* : **les** ~ the West Indies ; **aux** ~ in the West Indies.

antilope [ɑ̃tilɔp] *nf* antelope.

antimilitarisme [ɑ̃timilitarism] *nm* antimilitarism.

antimilitariste [ɑ̃timilitarist] *nmf* & *adj* antimilitarist.

antimite [ɑ̃timit] *adj inv* : **boule** ~ mothball.

antinucléaire [ɑ̃tinykleɛr] *adj* antinuclear.

Antiope [ɑ̃tjɔp] *n* information system available via the French television network, ≈ Teletext Br.

antiparasite [ɑ̃tiparazit] <> *nm* suppressor <> *adj inv* anti-interference.

antipathie [ɑ̃tipati] *nf* antipathy, hostility.

antipathique [ɑ̃tipatik] *adj* unpleasant ; **elle m'est** ~ I dislike her, I don't like her.

antipelliculaire [ɑ̃tipelikylɛr] *adj* : **shampooing** ~ anti-dandruff shampoo.

antiphrase [ɑ̃tifraz] *nf* antiphrasis.

antipode [ɑ̃tipɔd] *nm* : **être à l'**~ *ou* **aux** ~**s (de)** [lieu] to be on the other side of the world (from) ; *fig* to be diametrically opposed (to).

antipoison [ɑ̃tipwazɔ̃] ▷ **centre.**

antiquaire [ɑ̃tikɛr] *nmf* antique dealer.

antique [ɑ̃tik] *adj* - **1.** [de l'antiquité - civilisation] ancient ; [- vase, objet] antique - **2.** [vieux] antiquated, ancient.

antiquité [ɑ̃tikite] *nf* - **1.** [époque] : **l'Antiquité** antiquity - **2.** [ancienneté] great age, antiquity - **3.** [objet] antique.

antirabique [ɑ̃tirabik] *adj* : vaccin ~ rabies vaccine.

antiraciste [ɑ̃tirasist] *adj* & *nmf* antiracist.

antireflet [ɑ̃tirəflɛ] *adj inv* [surface] non-reflecting.

antirides [ɑ̃tirid] *adj inv* anti-wrinkle.

antirouille [ɑ̃tiruj] *adj inv* [traitement] rust *(avant n)* ; [revêtement, peinture] rustproof.

antisèche [ɑ̃tisɛʃ] *nf arg scol* crib *Br*, cheat sheet *Am*.

antisémite [ɑ̃tisemit] ◇ *nmf* anti-Semite ◇ *adj* anti-Semitic.

antiseptique [ɑ̃tisɛptik] *nm* & *adj* antiseptic.

antisismique [ɑ̃tisismik] *adj* earthquake-proof.

antithèse [ɑ̃titɛz] *nf* antithesis.

antitussif, ive [ɑ̃titysif, iv] *adj* cough *(avant n)*.
➤ **antitussif** *nm* cough mixture.

antiviral, aux [ɑ̃tiviral, o] *nm* antivirus.

antivol [ɑ̃tivɔl] ◇ *nm inv* anti-theft device ◇ *adj inv* anti-theft.

antre [ɑ̃tr] *nm* den, lair.

anus [anys] *nm* anus.

anxiété [ɑ̃ksjete] *nf* anxiety ; être dans l'~ to be very worried *ou* anxious.

anxieusement [ɑ̃ksjøzmɑ̃] *adv* anxiously.

anxieux, euse [ɑ̃ksjø, øz] ◇ *adj* anxious, worried ; être ~ de qqch to be worried *ou* anxious about sthg ; être ~ de faire qqch to be anxious to do sthg ◇ *nm, f* worrier.

AOC *(abr de* appellation d'origine contrôlée*)* *nf* label guaranteeing quality of French wine.

aorte [aɔrt] *nf* aorta.

août [u(t)] *nm* August ; le quinze août Assumption Day ; *voir aussi* septembre.

aoûtat [auta] *nm* harvest tick.

apaisement [apɛzmɑ̃] *nm* - **1.** [moral] comfort - **2.** [de douleur] alleviation - **3.** [de tension, de crise] calming.

apaiser [4] [apeze] *vt* - **1.** [personne] to calm down, to pacify - **2.** [conscience] to salve ; [douleur] to soothe ; [soif] to slake, to quench ; [faim] to assuage.
➤ **s'apaiser** *vp* - **1.** [personne] to calm down - **2.** [besoin] to be assuaged ; [tempête] to subside, to abate ; [douleur] to die down ; [scrupules] to be allayed.

apanage [apanaʒ] *nm sout* privilege ; être l'~ de qqn/qqch to be the prerogative of sb/sthg.

aparté [aparte] *nm* - **1.** THÉÂTRE aside - **2.** [conversation] private conversation ; prendre qqn en ~ to take sb aside.

apartheid [apartɛd] *nm* apartheid.

apathie [apati] *nf* apathy.

apathique [apatik] *adj* apathetic.

apatride [apatrid] ◇ *nmf* stateless person ◇ *adj* stateless.

apercevoir [52] [apɛrsəvwar] *vt* - **1.** [voir] to see, to catch sight of - **2.** [comprendre] to see, to perceive.
➤ **s'apercevoir** *vp* : s'~ de qqch to notice sthg ; s'~ que to notice (that).

aperçois, aperçoit *etc* ▷ apercevoir.

aperçu, e [apɛrsy] *pp* ▷ apercevoir.
➤ **aperçu** *nm* general idea ; donner un ~ de qqch to give a general idea of sthg.

apéritif, ive [aperitif, iv] *adj* which whets the appetite.
➤ **apéritif** *nm* aperitif ; prendre l'~ to have an aperitif, to have drinks *(before a meal)*.

apesanteur [apəzɑ̃tœr] *nf* weightlessness.

à-peu-près [apøprɛ] *nm inv* approximation.

aphasie [afazi] *nf* aphasia.

aphone [afɔn] *adj* voiceless.

aphorisme [afɔrism] *nm* aphorism.

aphrodisiaque [afrɔdizjak] *nm* & *adj* aphrodisiac.

aphte [aft] *nm* mouth ulcer.

API *(abr de* alphabet phonétique international*)* *nm* IPA.

apiculteur, trice [apikyltœr, tris] *nm, f* beekeeper.

apiculture [apikyltyr] *nf* beekeeping.

apitoie, apitoies *etc* ▷ apitoyer.

apitoiement [apitwamɑ̃] *nm* pity.

apitoyer [13] [apitwaje] *vt* to move to pity.
➤ **s'apitoyer** *vp* to feel pity ; s'~ sur to feel sorry for.

ap. J.-C. *(abr de* après Jésus-Christ*)* AD.

APL *(abr de* aide personnalisée au logement*)* *nf* housing benefit.

aplanir [32] [aplanir] *vt* - **1.** [aplatir] to level - **2.** *fig* [difficulté, obstacle] to smooth away, to iron out.
➤ **s'aplanir** *vp fig* [se résoudre] to be ironed out.

aplatir [32] [aplatir] *vt* [gén] to flatten ; [couture] to press flat ; [cheveux] to smooth down.
➤ **s'aplatir** *vp* - **1.** [s'écraser] to be flattened - **2.** [s'étaler] to lie flat ; s'~ devant qqn *fig* to grovel before sb.

aplomb [aplɔ̃] *nm* - **1.** [stabilité] balance - **2.** [audace] nerve, cheek ; garder/perdre son ~ to keep/lose one's nerve.

◆ **d'aplomb** *loc adv* steady ; **se tenir d'~** to be steady ; **ne pas se sentir d'~** to feel out of sorts.

apnée [apne] *nf* : **plonger en ~** to dive without breathing apparatus.

apocalypse [apɔkalips] *nf* apocalypse.

apocalyptique [apɔkaliptik] *adj* apocalyptic.

apogée [apɔʒe] *nm* ASTRON apogee ; *fig* peak.

apolitique [apɔlitik] *adj* apolitical, unpolitical.

apologie [apɔlɔʒi] *nf* justification, apology ; **faire l'~ de qqn/qqch** to praise sb/sthg.

apoplexie [apɔplɛksi] *nf* apoplexy.

apostrophe [apɔstrɔf] *nf* - **1.** [signe graphique] apostrophe - **2.** [interpellation] rude remark.

apostropher [3] [apɔstrɔfe] *vt* : **~ qqn** to speak rudely to sb.

apothéose [apɔteoz] *nf* - **1.** [consécration] great honour *Br ou* honor *Am* - **2.** [point culminant - d'un spectacle] grand finale ; [- d'une carrière] crowning glory.

apôtre [apotr] *nm* apostle, disciple ; **se faire l'~ de qqch** *fig* to be the *ou* an advocate of sthg.

Appalaches [apalaʃ] *nmpl* : **les ~** the Appalachians.

apparaissais, apparaissions *etc* ▷ apparaître.

apparaître [91] [aparɛtr] ◇ *vi* - **1.** [gén] to appear - **2.** [se dévoiler] to come to light ◇ *v impers* : **il apparaît que** it seems *ou* appears that.

apparat [apara] *nm* pomp ; **d'~** [dîner, habit] ceremonial ; **en grand ~** with great pomp and ceremony.

appareil [aparɛj] *nm* - **1.** [gén] device ; [électrique] appliance ; **porter un ~ (auditif)/(dentaire)** to wear a hearing aid/a brace - **2.** [téléphone] phone, telephone ; **qui est à l'~?** who's speaking? - **3.** [avion] aircraft - **4.** [structure] apparatus - **5.** *loc* : **dans le plus simple ~** in one's birthday suit.

◆ **appareil digestif** *nm* digestive system.

◆ **appareil photo** *nm* camera ; **~ photo numérique** digital camera.

appareillage [aparɛjaʒ] *nm* - **1.** [équipement] equipment - **2.** NAVIG getting under way.

appareiller [4] [apareje] ◇ *vt* [assortir] to match up ◇ *vi* NAVIG to get under way.

apparemment [aparamɑ̃] *adv* apparently.

apparence [aparɑ̃s] *nf* appearance ; **malgré les** *ou* **en dépit des ~s** in spite of appearances ; **sauver les ~s** to keep up appearances.

◆ **en apparence** *loc adv* seemingly, apparently.

apparent, e [aparɑ̃, ɑ̃t] *adj* - **1.** [superficiel, illusoire] apparent - **2.** [visible] visible ; **coutures ~es** top-stitched seams - **3.** [évident] obvious.

apparenté, e [aparɑ̃te] *adj* : **~ à** [personne] related to ; *fig* [ressemblant] similar to ; [affilié] affiliated to.

appariteur [aparitœr] *nm* porter *(in university)*.

apparition [aparisjɔ̃] *nf* - **1.** [gén] appearance ; **faire son ~** to make one's appearance - **2.** [vision - RELIG] vision ; [- de fantôme] apparition.

appart [apart] *(abr de* **appartement***) nm fam* flat *Br*, apartment *Am*.

appartement [apartəmɑ̃] *nm* flat *Br*, apartment *Am*.

appartenance [apartənɑ̃s] *nf* : **~ à** [famille] belonging to ; [parti] membership of.

appartenir [40] [apartənir] *vi* - **1.** [être la propriété de] : **~ à qqn** to belong to sb - **2.** [faire partie de] : **~ à qqch** to belong to sthg, to be a member of sthg ; **il ne m'appartient pas de faire ...** *fig* & *sout* it's not up to me to do ...

appartenu [apartəny] *pp inv* ▷ appartenir.

appartiendrai, appartiendrais *etc* ▷ appartenir.

apparu, e [apary] *pp* ▷ apparaître.

appât [apa] *nm* PÊCHE bait, lure.

appâter [3] [apate] *vt litt* & *fig* to lure.

appauvrir [32] [apovrir] *vt* to impoverish.

◆ **s'appauvrir** *vp* to grow poorer, to become impoverished.

appel [apɛl] *nm* - **1.** [gén] call ; **faire ~ à qqn** to appeal to sb ; **faire ~ à qqch** [nécessiter] to call for sthg ; [avoir recours à] to call on sthg ; **~ (téléphonique)** (phone) call - **2.** JUR appeal ; **faire ~** JUR to appeal ; **sans ~** final - **3.** [pour vérifier - gén] roll-call ; [- SCOL] registration ; **manquer à l'~** to be absent - **4.** COMM : **~ d'offre** invitation to tender - **5.** [signe] : **faire un ~ de phares** to flash one's headlights.

appelant [aplɑ̃] *nm* [leurre] decoy ; *Can* [sifflet] birdcall.

appelé [aple] *nm* conscript.

appeler [24] [aple] ◇ *vt* - **1.** [gén] to call ; **~ au secours** *ou* **à l'aide** to call for help - **2.** [téléphoner] to ring, to call - **3.** [exiger] to call for - **4.** [entraîner] to lead to - **5.** [nommer] : **être appelé à un poste** to be appointed to a post - **6.** [amener] : **~ qqn à faire qqch** to call on sb to do sthg ◇ *vi* [solliciter] : **en ~ à qqch** to appeal to sthg.

◆ **s'appeler** *vp* - **1.** [se nommer] to be called ;

comment cela s'appelle? what is it called? ; il s'appelle Patrick his name is Patrick, he's called Patrick - **2.** [se téléphoner] : **on s'appelle demain?** shall we talk tomorrow?

appellation [apelasjɔ̃] *nf* designation, name ; ~ **contrôlée** *guarantee that a wine conforms to certain conditions of origin, strength and quality* ; ~ **d'origine** *JUR* label of origin.

appelle, appelles *etc* ▷ appeler.

appendice [apɛ̃dis] *nm* appendix.

appendicite [apɛ̃disit] *nf* appendicitis.

appentis [apɑ̃ti] *nm* lean-to.

appesantir [32] [apəzɑ̃tir] *vt* [démarche] to slow down.

➤ **s'appesantir** *vp* - **1.** [s'alourdir] to become heavy - **2.** [insister] : **s'~ sur qqch** to dwell on sthg.

appétissant, e [apetisɑ̃, ɑ̃t] *adj* [nourriture] appetizing.

appétit [apeti] *nm* appetite ; ~ **de qqch/de faire qqch** *fig* appetite for sthg/for doing sthg ; **bon ~!** enjoy your meal! ; **couper/ ouvrir l'~ à qqn** to spoil/whet sb's appetite ; **manger de bon ~** to eat heartily.

applaudir [32] [aplodir] ◇ *vt* to applaud ◇ *vi* to clap, to applaud ; ~ **à qqch** *fig* to applaud sthg ; ~ **à tout rompre** *fig* to bring the house down.

applaudissements [aplodismɑ̃] *nmpl* applause *(U)*, clapping *(U)*.

applicable [aplikabl] *adj* : ~ **(à)** applicable (to).

application [aplikasjɔ̃] *nf* [gén & *INFORM*] application ; **mettre qqch en** ~ to apply sthg.

applique [aplik] *nf* wall lamp.

appliquer [3] [aplike] *vt* [gén] to apply ; [loi] to enforce.

➤ **s'appliquer** *vp* - **1.** [s'étaler, se poser] : **cette peinture s'applique facilement** this paint goes on easily - **2.** [concerner] : **s'~ à qqn/qqch** to apply to sb/sthg - **3.** [se concentrer] : **s'~ (à faire qqch)** to apply o.s. (to doing sthg).

appoint [apwɛ̃] *nm* - **1.** [monnaie] change ; **faire l'~** to give the right money - **2.** [aide] help, support ; **d'~** [salaire, chauffage] extra ; **lit d'~** spare bed.

appointements [apwɛ̃tmɑ̃] *nmpl* salary *(sg)*.

apport [apɔr] *nm* - **1.** [gén & *FIN*] contribution - **2.** [de chaleur] input.

apporter [3] [apɔrte] *vt* - **1.** [gén] to bring ; **ça m'a beaucoup apporté** *fig* I got a lot from it - **2.** [raison, preuve] to provide, to give - **3.** [contribuer à] to give, to bring ; [provoquer] to bring

about - **4.** [mettre - soin] to exercise ; [- attention] to give.

apposer [3] [apoze] *vt* - **1.** [affiche] to put up - **2.** [signature] to append.

apposition [apozisjɔ̃] *nf GRAM* apposition ; **en** ~ in apposition.

appréciable [apresjabl] *adj* - **1.** [notable] appreciable - **2.** [précieux] : **un grand jardin, c'est ~!** I/we really appreciate having a big garden.

appréciation [apresjasjɔ̃] *nf* - **1.** [de valeur] valuation ; [de distance, poids] estimation - **2.** [jugement] judgment - **3.** *SCOL* assessment.

apprécier [9] [apresje] *vt* - **1.** [gén] to appreciate - **2.** [évaluer] to estimate, to assess.

➤ **s'apprécier** *vp* to like one other.

appréhender [3] [apreɑ̃de] *vt* - **1.** [arrêter] to arrest - **2.** [craindre] : ~ **qqch/de faire qqch** to dread sthg/doing sthg.

appréhension [apreɑ̃sjɔ̃] *nf* apprehension.

apprenais ▷ apprendre.

apprendre [79] [aprɑ̃dr] *vt* - **1.** [étudier] to learn ; ~ **à faire qqch** to learn (how) to do sthg - **2.** [enseigner] to teach ; ~ **qqch à qqn** to teach sb sthg ; ~ **à qqn à faire qqch** to teach sb (how) to do sthg - **3.** [nouvelle] to hear of, to learn of ; ~ **que** to hear that, to learn that ; ~ **qqch à qqn** to tell sb of sthg.

apprenne ▷ apprendre.

apprenti, e [aprɑ̃ti] *nm, f* [élève] apprentice ; *fig* beginner ; ~ **sorcier** *fig* sorcerer's apprentice.

apprentissage [aprɑ̃tisaʒ] *nm* - **1.** [de métier] apprenticeship - **2.** [formation] learning ; ~ **de la vie** learning about life.

apprêter [4] [aprete] *vt* to prepare.

➤ **s'apprêter** *vp* - **1.** [être sur le point] : **s'~ à faire qqch** to get ready to do sthg - **2.** [s'habiller] : **s'~ pour qqch** to dress up for sthg.

appris, e [apri, iz] *pp* ▷ apprendre.

apprivoiser [3] [aprivwaze] *vt* to tame.

➤ **s'apprivoiser** *vp* - **1.** [animal] to become tame - **2.** [personne] to become more sociable.

approbateur, trice [aprobatœr, tris] *adj* approving.

approbation [aprobasjɔ̃] *nf* approval.

approchant, e [aprɔʃɑ̃, ɑ̃t] *adj* similar ; **quelque chose d'~** something similar.

approche [aprɔʃ] *nf* [arrivée] approach ; **à l'~ des fêtes** as the Christmas holidays draw near ; **il a pressé le pas à l'~ de la maison** he quickened his step as he approached the house.

➤ **approches** *nfpl* [abords] surrounding area *(sg)*.

approcher [3] [aprɔʃe] ⟷ *vt* - **1.** [mettre plus près] to move near, to bring near ; ~ **qqch de qqn/qqch** to move sthg near (to) sb/sthg - **2.** [aborder] to go up to, to approach ⟷ *vi* to approach, to go/come near ; **approchez!** come nearer! ; **n'approchez pas!** keep *ou* stay away! ; ~ **de** [moment, fin] to approach.

➤ **s'approcher** *vp* to come/go near, to approach ; **s'~ de qqn/qqch** to approach sb/sthg.

approfondir [32] [aprɔfɔ̃dir] *vt* - **1.** [creuser] to make deeper - **2.** [développer] to go further into.

➤ **s'approfondir** *vp* - **1.** [se creuser] to become deeper - **2.** [se compliquer] to deepen.

approprié, e [aprɔprije] *adj* : ~ **(à)** appropriate (to).

approprier [10] [aprɔprije] *vt* - **1.** [adapter] to adapt - **2.** *Belg* to clean.

➤ **s'approprier** *vp* [s'adjuger] to appropriate.

approuver [3] [apruve] *vt* - **1.** [gén] to approve of ; ~ **qqn de faire qqch** to commend sb for doing sthg - **2.** *JUR* to approve.

approvisionnement [aprɔvizjɔnmɑ̃] *nm* supplies *(pl)*, stocks *(pl)*.

approvisionner [3] [aprɔvizjɔne] *vt* - **1.** [compte en banque] to pay money into - **2.** [magasin, pays] to supply.

➤ **s'approvisionner** *vp* : **s'~ chez/à** [suj : particulier] to shop at/in ; [suj : commerçant] to get one's supplies from.

approximatif, ive [aprɔksimatif, iv] *adj* approximate, rough.

approximation [aprɔksimasjɔ̃] *nf* approximation.

approximativement [aprɔksimativmɑ̃] *adv* approximately, roughly.

appt *abr de* **appartement**.

appui [apɥi] *nm* - **1.** [soutien] support ; **à l'~ de** in support of - **2.** [de fenêtre] sill.

appuie, appuies *etc* ▷ **appuyer**.

appui-tête [apɥitɛt] *(pl* **appuis-tête)** *nm* headrest.

appuyer [14] [apɥije] ⟷ *vt* - **1.** [poser] : ~ **qqch sur/contre qqch** to lean sthg on/against sthg, to rest sthg on/against sthg - **2.** [presser] : ~ **qqch sur/contre** to press sthg on/against - **3.** *fig* [soutenir] to support ⟷ *vi* - **1.** [reposer] : ~ **sur** to lean *ou* rest on - **2.** [presser] to push ; ~ **sur** [bouton] to press - **3.** *fig* [insister] : ~ **sur** to stress - **4.** [se diriger] : ~ **sur la** *ou* **à droite** to bear right.

➤ **s'appuyer** *vp* - **1.** [se tenir] : **s'~ contre/sur** to lean against/on, to rest against/on - **2.** [se

baser] : **s'~ sur** to rely on - **3.** [compter] : **s'~ sur** to rely on, to count on - **4.** *fam* [supporter, prendre en charge] : **s'~ qqn** to put up with sb ; **s'~ qqch** to take sthg on, to take on sthg.

apr. *abr de* **après**.

âpre [apr] *adj* - **1.** [goût, discussion, combat] bitter - **2.** [ton, épreuve, critique] harsh - **3.** [concurrence] fierce.

âprement [aprəmɑ̃] *adv* bitterly, fiercely.

après [aprɛ] ⟷ *prép* - **1.** [gén] after ; ~ **avoir mangé, ils ...** after having eaten *ou* after they had eaten, they ... ; ~ **cela** after that ; ~ **quoi** after which - **2.** [indiquant l'attirance, l'attachement, l'hostilité] : **soupirer ~ qqn** to yearn for sb ; **aboyer ~ qqn** to bark at sb ; **se fâcher ~ qqn** to get angry at *ou* with sb ⟷ *adv* - **1.** [temps] afterwards ; ~, **je rentrerai à la maison** I'll go home afterwards ; **un mois ~** one month later ; **le mois d'~** the following *ou* next month - **2.** [lieu, dans un ordre, dans un rang] : **la rue d'~** the next street ; **c'est ma sœur qui vient ~** my sister's next.

➤ **après coup** *loc adv* afterwards, after the event.

➤ **après que** *loc conj* (+ *indicatif*) after ; **je le verrai ~ qu'il aura fini** I'll see him after *ou* when he's finished ; ~ **qu'ils eurent dîné, ...** after dinner *ou* after they had dined, ...

➤ **après tout** *loc adv* after all.

➤ **d'après** *loc prép* according to ; **d'~ moi** in my opinion ; **d'~ lui** according to him.

➤ **et après** *loc adv* (*employée interrogativement*) - **1.** [questionnement sur la suite] and then what? - **2.** [exprime l'indifférence] so what?

après-demain [apredmɛ̃] *adv* the day after tomorrow.

après-guerre [apregɛr] *nm* post-war years *(pl)* ; **d'~** post-war.

après-midi [apremidi] *nm inv* OU *nf inv* afternoon.

après-rasage [aprerazaʒ] *(pl* **après-rasages)** *nm & adj inv* aftershave.

après-ski [apreski] *(pl* **après-skis)** *nm* [chaussure] snow-boot.

après-soleil [apresɔlɛj] *adj inv* after-sun *(avant n)*.

après-vente [aprevɑ̃t] ▷ **service**.

âpreté [aprəte] *nf* - **1.** [de goût, discussion, combat] bitterness - **2.** [de voix, épreuve, critique] harshness - **3.** [de concurrence] ferocity.

à-propos [aprɔpo] *nm inv* [de remarque] aptness ; **faire preuve d'~** to show presence of mind.

apte [apt] *adj* : ~ **à qqch/à faire qqch** capable of sthg/of doing sthg ; ~ **(au service)** *MIL* fit (for service).

aptitude [aptityd] nf : ~ (à ou pour qqch) aptitude (for sthg) ; ~ à ou pour faire qqch ability to do ou for doing sthg.

aquagym [akwaʒim] nf aquarobics (U).

aquarelle [akwarɛl] nf watercolour.

aquarium [akwarjɔm] nm aquarium.

aquatique [akwatik] adj [plante, animal] aquatic ; [milieu, paysage] watery, marshy.

aqueduc [akdyk] nm aqueduct.

aqueux, euse [akø, øz] adj watery.

aquilin [akilɛ̃] ⊳ nez.

Aquitaine [akitɛn] nf : l'~ Aquitaine.

AR ⟨⟩ nm - 1. abr de accusé de réception - 2. (abr de aller-retour) RTN ⟨⟩ abr de arrière.

arabe [arab] ⟨⟩ adj [peuple] Arab ; [désert] Arabian ⟨⟩ nm [langue] Arabic.
➤ **Arabe** nmf Arab.

arabesque [arabɛsk] nf - 1. [ornement] arabesque - 2. [ligne sinueuse] flourish.

Arabie [arabi] nf : l'~ Arabia ; l'~ Saoudite Saudi Arabia.

arabophone [arabɔfɔn] ⟨⟩ adj Arabic-speaking ⟨⟩ nmf Arabic speaker.

arachide [araʃid] nf - 1. [plante] groundnut - 2. [graine] peanut, groundnut.

araignée [arɛɲe] nf spider ; **avoir une ~ dans le ou au plafond** fam fig to have a screw loose.
➤ **araignée de mer** nf spider crab.

araser [3] [araze] vt GÉOL to erode.

arbalète [arbalɛt] nf crossbow.

arbitrage [arbitraʒ] nm - 1. [SPORT - gén] refereeing ; [- au tennis, cricket] umpiring - 2. JUR arbitration.

arbitraire [arbitrɛr] adj arbitrary.

arbitrairement [arbitrɛrmɑ̃] adv arbitrarily.

arbitre [arbitr] nm - 1. [SPORT - gén] referee ; [- au tennis, cricket] umpire - 2. [conciliateur] arbitrator.
➤ **libre arbitre** nm free will.

arbitrer [3] [arbitre] vt - 1. [SPORT - gén] to referee ; [- au tennis, cricket] to umpire - 2. [conflit] to arbitrate.

arborer [3] [arbɔre] vt - 1. [exhiber] to display, to sport - 2. [expression] to wear.

arborescence [arbɔresɑ̃s] nf INFORM tree.

arboriculteur, trice [arbɔrikyltœr, tris] nm, f tree grower.

arboriculture [arbɔrikyltyr] nf tree growing.

arbouse [arbuz] nf arbutus berry.

arbre [arbr] nm - 1. BOT & fig tree ; ~ fruitier fruit tree ; ~ généalogique family tree ; ~ de Noël Christmas tree - 2. [axe] shaft ; ~ de transmission AUTOM drive shaft, propeller shaft.

arbrisseau, x [arbriso] nm shrub.

arbuste [arbyst] nm shrub.

arc [ark] nm - 1. [arme] bow - 2. [courbe] arc ; ~ de cercle arc of a circle - 3. ARCHIT arch.

arcade [arkad] nf - 1. ARCHIT arch ; ~s arcade (sg) - 2. ANAT : ~ sourcilière arch of the eyebrows.

arc-bouter [3] [arkbute] ➤ **s'arc-bouter** vp to brace o.s.

arceau, x [arso] nm - 1. ARCHIT arch - 2. [objet métallique] hoop.

arc-en-ciel [arkɑ̃sjɛl] (pl arcs-en-ciel) nm rainbow.

archaïque [arkaik] adj archaic.

arche [arʃ] nf ARCHIT arch.

archéologie [arkeɔlɔʒi] nf archaeology.

archéologique [arkeɔlɔʒik] adj archaeological.

archéologue [arkeɔlɔg] nmf archaeologist.

archer [arʃe] nm archer.

archet [arʃe] nm MUS bow.

archétype [arketip] nm archetype.

archevêché [arʃəveʃe] nm [charge] archbishopric ; [logement] archbishop's palace.

archevêque [arʃəvɛk] nm archbishop.

archipel [arʃipɛl] nm archipelago.

architecte [arʃitɛkt] nmf architect.

architectural, e, aux [arʃitɛktyral, o] adj architectural.

architecture [arʃitɛktyr] nf architecture ; fig structure.

archiver [3] [arʃive] vt to archive.

archives [arʃiv] nfpl [de bureau] records ; [de musée] archives.

archiviste [arʃivist] nmf archivist.

arctique [arktik] adj Arctic ; **le cercle polaire ~** the Arctic Circle.
➤ **Arctique** nm : l'~ the Arctic.

ardemment [ardamɑ̃] adv fervently, passionately.

ardent, e [ardɑ̃, ɑ̃t] adj - 1. [soleil] blazing - 2. [soif, fièvre] raging ; [passion] burning - 3. [yeux, couleur] blazing.

ardeur [ardœr] nf - 1. [vigueur] fervour, enthusiasm - 2. [chaleur] blazing heat.

ardoise [ardwaz] nf slate.

ardu, e [ardy] adj - 1. [travail] arduous ; [problème] difficult - 2. [pente] steep.

are [ar] nm 100 square metres.

aréna [arena] *nm Can* sports centre with skating rink, arena *Am*.

arène [arɛn] *nf* arena ; **l'~ politique** the political arena.

➤ **arènes** *nfpl* [romaines] amphitheatre *(sg)* ; [pour corridas] bullring *(sg)*.

arête [arɛt] *nf* - **1.** [de poisson] bone - **2.** [d'un toit, d'une montagne] ridge - **3.** [du nez] bridge.

arg. *abr de* argus.

argent [arʒã] *nm* - **1.** [métal, couleur] silver - **2.** [monnaie] money ; **~ comptant** cash ; **~ liquide** (ready) cash ; **~ de poche** pocket money ; **en avoir pour son ~** to get one's money's worth.

argenté, e [arʒãte] *adj* silvery, silver.

argenterie [arʒãtri] *nf* silverware.

argentin, e [arʒãtɛ̃, in] *adj* - **1.** [son] silvery - **2.** [d'Argentine] Argentinian.

➤ **Argentin, e** *nm, f* Argentinian.

Argentine [arʒãtin] *nf* : **l'~** Argentina.

argile [arʒil] *nf* clay.

argileux, euse [arʒilø, øz] *adj* clayey.

argot [argo] *nm* slang.

argotique [argɔtik] *adj* slang *(avant n)*, slangy.

arguer [8] [argɥe] *vi sout* [prétexter] : **~ de qqch (pour)** to put sthg forward as a reason (for).

argument [argymã] *nm* argument ; **tirer ~ de qqch** to use sthg as an argument ; **~ de vente** *COMM* selling point.

argumentation [argymãtasjɔ̃] *nf* argumentation.

argus [argys] *nm* : **coté à l'~** rated in the guide to secondhand car prices.

aride [arid] *adj litt* & *fig* arid ; [travail] thankless.

aridité [aridite] *nf* aridity.

aristocrate [aristɔkrat] *nmf* aristocrat.

aristocratie [aristɔkrasi] *nf* aristocracy.

aristocratique [aristɔkratik] *adj* aristocratic.

arithmétique [aritmetik] ⬦ *nf* arithmetic ⬦ *adj* arithmetical.

armagnac [armaɲak] *nm* armagnac.

armateur [armatœr] *nm* ship owner.

armature [armatyr] *nf* - **1.** *CONSTR* & *fig* framework - **2.** [de parapluie] frame ; [de soutien-gorge] underwiring - **3.** *MUS* key signature.

arme [arm] *nf litt* & *fig* weapon ; **~ blanche** blade ; **~ à feu** firearm ; **passer l'~ à gauche** *fam fig* to snuff it.

➤ **armes** *nfpl* - **1.** [armée] : **les ~s** the army - **2.** [blason] coat of arms *(sg)* - **3.** *loc* : **faire ses premières ~s** [apprendre] to learn the ropes ;

fourbir ses ~s to prepare for battle ; **partir avec ~s et bagages** to leave taking everything.

armée [arme] *nf* army ; **l'~ de l'air** the air force ; **l'~ de terre** the army.

➤ **Armée du salut** *nf* : **l'Armée du salut** the Salvation Army.

armement [arməmã] *nm* - **1.** [*MIL* - de personne] arming ; [- de pays] armament ; [- ensemble d'armes] arms *(pl)* ; **la course aux ~s** the arms race - **2.** [de fusil] cocking - **3.** [d'appareil photo] winding-on - **4.** [de navire] fitting-out.

Arménie [armeni] *nf* : **l'~** Armenia.

arménien, enne [armenjɛ̃, ɛn] *adj* Armenian.

➤ **arménien** *nm* [langue] Armenian.

➤ **Arménien, enne** *nm, f* Armenian.

armer [3] [arme] *vt* - **1.** [pourvoir en armes] to arm ; **être armé pour qqch/pour faire qqch** *fig* [préparé] to be equipped for sthg/to do sthg - **2.** [fusil] to cock - **3.** [appareil photo] to wind on - **4.** [navire] to fit out.

➤ **s'armer** *vp litt* & *fig* : **s'~ (de)** to arm o.s. (with).

armistice [armistis] *nm* armistice.

armoire [armwar] *nf* [gén] cupboard *Br*, closet *Am* ; [garde-robe] wardrobe ; **~ à glace** wardrobe with a mirror ; **c'est une ~ à glace!** *fam fig* he's built like a tank! ; **~ à pharmacie** medicine cabinet.

armoiries [armwari] *nfpl* coat of arms *(sg)*.

armure [armyr] *nf* armour *Br*, armor *Am*.

armurerie [armyrri] *nf* [magasin] gunsmith's (shop).

armurier [armyrje] *nm* [d'armes à feu] gunsmith ; [d'armes blanches] armourer.

ARN (*abr de* acide ribonucléique) *nm* RNA.

arnaque [arnak] *nf fam* rip-off.

arnaquer [3] [arnake] *vt fam* to do *Br*, to swindle ; **se faire ~** to be had.

aromate [arɔmat] *nm* [épice] spice ; [fine herbe] herb.

aromathérapie [arɔmaterapi] *nf* aromatherapy.

aromatique [arɔmatik] *adj* aromatic.

aromatiser [3] [arɔmatize] *vt* to flavour.

arôme [arom] *nm* - **1.** [gén] aroma ; [de fleur, parfum] fragrance - **2.** [goût] flavour.

arpège [arpɛʒ] *nm* arpeggio.

arpenter [3] [arpãte] *vt* - **1.** [marcher] to pace up and down - **2.** [terrain] to survey.

arpenteur [arpãtœr] *nm* surveyor.

arqué, e [arke] *adj* - **1.** [objet] curved - **2.** [jambe] bow *(avant n)*, bandy ; [nez] hooked ; [sourcil] arched.

arr. *abr de* **arrondissement.**

arraché [araʃe] ◆ **à l'arraché** *loc adv* : **gagner** *ou* **emporter la victoire à l'~** to snatch victory.

arrachement [araʃmɑ̃] *nm fig* wrench.

arrache-pied [araʃpje] ◆ **d'arrache-pied** *loc adv* : **travailler d'~** to work away furiously.

arracher [3] [araʃe] *vt* - **1.** [extraire - plante] to pull up *ou* out ; [- dent] to extract - **2.** [déchirer - page] to tear off *ou* out ; [- chemise, bras] to tear off - **3.** [prendre] : **~ qqch à qqn** to snatch sthg from sb ; *fig* [extorquer] to extract sthg from sb ; [susciter] to wring sthg from sb - **4.** [soustraire] : **~ qqn à** [milieu, lieu] to drag sb away from ; [lit, sommeil] to drag sb from ; [habitude, torpeur] to force sb out of ; [mort, danger] to snatch sb from.
◆ **s'arracher** *vp* - **1.** [se détacher] : **s'~ de** *ou* **à** [milieu, lieu] to drag o.s. away from ; [lit, sommeil] to drag o.s. from - **2.** [se disputer] : **s'~ qqn/qqch** to fight over sb/sthg - **3.** *fam* [partir] to split, to beat it.

arraisonner [3] [arezɔne] *vt* [navire] to stop and inspect.

arrangeant, e [arɑ̃ʒɑ̃, ɑ̃t] *adj* obliging.

arrangement [arɑ̃ʒmɑ̃] *nm* - **1.** [gén] arrangement - **2.** [accord] agreement, arrangement.

arranger [17] [arɑ̃ʒe] *vt* - **1.** [gén] to arrange - **2.** [convenir à] to suit - **3.** [régler] to settle - **4.** [améliorer] to sort out - **5.** [réparer] to fix.
◆ **s'arranger** *vp* to come to an agreement ; **s'~ pour faire qqch** to manage to do sthg ; **arrangez-vous pour être là à cinq heures** make sure you're there at five o'clock ; **cela va s'~** things will work out.

arrdt. *abr de* **arrondissement.**

arrérages [areraʒ] *nmpl* arrears.

arrestation [arɛstasjɔ̃] *nf* arrest ; **être en état d'~** to be under arrest.

arrêt [arɛ] *nm* - **1.** [d'un mouvement] stopping ; **à l'~** [véhicule] stationary ; [machine] (switched) off ; **tomber en ~ devant qqch** to stop dead in front of sthg - **2.** [interruption] interruption ; **sans ~** [sans interruption] non-stop ; [sans relâche] constantly, continually ; **être en ~ maladie** to be on sick leave ; **~ maladie** *ou* **de travail** doctor's certificate ; **~ du travail** stoppage - **3.** [station] : **~ (d'autobus)** (bus) stop ; **~ facultatif** request stop - **4.** *JUR* decision, judgment.

arrêté [arete] *nm* - **1.** *FIN* settlement - **2.** *ADMIN* order, decree ; **par ~ préfectoral** by order of the prefect.

arrêter [4] [arete] ◇ *vt* - **1.** [gén] to stop

- **2.** [cesser] : **~ de faire qqch** to stop doing sthg ; **~ de fumer** to stop smoking - **3.** [abandonner - gén] to give up ; [- école] to leave - **4.** [voleur] to arrest - **5.** [fixer] to decide on
◇ *vi* to stop.
◆ **s'arrêter** *vp* to stop ; **s'~ à qqch** : **il ne s'arrête pas à ces détails** he's not going to dwell on these details ; **s'~ de faire** to stop doing ; **s'~ chez qqn** to stay with sb.

arrhes [ar] *nfpl* deposit *(sg)*.

arrière [arjɛr] ◇ *adj inv* back, rear ; **roue ~** rear *ou* back wheel ; **marche ~** reverse gear ◇ *nm* - **1.** [partie postérieure] back ; **à l'~** at the back *Br*, in back *Am* ; **assurer ses ~s** *fig* to play safe - **2.** *SPORT* back.
◆ **en arrière** *loc adv* - **1.** [dans la direction opposée] back, backwards ; **faire un pas en ~** to take a step back *ou* backwards - **2.** [derrière, à la traîne] behind ; **rester en ~** to lag behind.
◆ **en arrière de** *loc prép* behind.

arriéré, e [arjere] *adj* - **1.** [mentalité, pays] backward - **2.** [dette] outstanding, overdue.
◆ **arriéré** *nm* arrears *(pl)*.

arrière-boutique [arjɛrbutik] *(pl* **arrière-boutiques)** *nf* back shop.

arrière-garde [arjɛrgard] *(pl* **arrière-gardes)** *nf* rearguard ; **combat d'~** *litt* & *fig* rearguard action.

arrière-goût [arjɛrgu] *(pl* **arrière-goûts)** *nm* aftertaste.

arrière-grand-mère [arjɛrgrɑ̃mɛr] *(pl* **arrière-grands-mères)** *nf* great-grandmother.

arrière-grand-père [arjɛrgrɑ̃pɛr] *(pl* **arrière-grands-pères)** *nm* great-grandfather.

arrière-pays [arjɛrpei] *nm inv* hinterland.

arrière-pensée [arjɛrpɑ̃se] *(pl* **arrière-pensées)** *nf* - **1.** [raison intéressée] ulterior motive - **2.** [réserve] : **sans ~** without reservation.

arrière-plan [arjɛrplɑ̃] *(pl* **arrière-plans)** *nm* background.

arrière-saison [arjɛrsɛzɔ̃] *(pl* **arrière-saisons)** *nf* late autumn.

arrière-train [arjɛrtrɛ̃] *(pl* **arrière-trains)** *nm* hindquarters *(pl)*.

arrimer [3] [arime] *vt* - **1.** [attacher] to secure - **2.** *NAVIG* to stow.

arrivage [arivaʒ] *nm* - **1.** [de marchandises] consignment, delivery - **2.** [de touristes] influx.

arrivant, e [arivɑ̃, ɑ̃t] *nm, f* [personne] arrival.

arrivée [arive] *nf* - **1.** [venue] arrival - **2.** *TECHNOL* inlet.

arriver [3] [arive] ◇ *vi* - **1.** [venir] to arrive ; **en ~ à faire qqch** *fig* to begin to do sthg ; **j'arrive!**

(I'm) coming! ; ~ à **Paris** to arrive in *ou* reach Paris ; **l'eau m'arrivait aux genoux** the water came up to my knees - **2.** [réussir dans la vie] to succeed, to get on - **3.** [parvenir] : ~ **à faire qqch** to manage to do sthg, to succeed in doing sthg ; **il n'arrive pas à faire ses devoirs** he can't do his homework ◇ *v impers* to happen ; **il arrive que** (+ *subjonctif*) : **il arrive qu'il soit en retard** he is sometimes late ; **il arrive à tout le monde de se décourager** we all get fed up sometimes ; **il arrive à tout le monde de se tromper** anyone can make a mistake ; **il lui arrive d'oublier quel jour on est** he sometimes forgets what day it is ; **quoi qu'il arrive** whatever happens.

arrivisme [arivism] *nm péj* ambition.

arrobas, arobas [arɔbas] *nf* [dans une adresse électronique] at.

arrogance [arɔgɑ̃s] *nf* arrogance.

arrogant, e [arɔgɑ̃, ɑ̃t] ◇ *adj* arrogant ◇ *nm, f* arrogant person.

arroger [17] [arɔʒe] ➡ **s'arroger** *vp* : **s'~ le droit de faire qqch** to take it upon o.s. to do sthg.

arrondi [arɔ̃di] *nm* [de jupe] hemline.

arrondir [32] [árɔ̃dir] *vt* - **1.** [forme] to make round - **2.** [capital] to increase - **3.** [chiffre - au-dessus] to round up ; [- en dessous] to round down.
➡ **s'arrondir** *vp* [corps, visage] to fill out.

arrondissement [arɔ̃dismɑ̃] *nm* - **1.** ADMIN arrondissement *(administrative division of a département or city)* - **2.** [de somme - au-dessus] rounding up ; [- en dessous] rounding down.

arrosage [arozaʒ] *nm* [de jardin] watering ; [de rue] spraying.

arroser [3] [aroze] *vt* - **1.** [jardin] to water, to spray - **2.** [couler à travers] to flow through - **3.** *fam* [café] : ~ **son café (avec)** to lace one's coffee (with) - **4.** *fam* [repas] to wash down - **5.** *fam* [célébrer] to celebrate - **6.** *fam* [soudoyer] : ~ **qqn** to grease sb's palm.

arrosoir [arozwar] *nm* watering can.

arsenal, aux [arsənal, o] *nm* - **1.** [de navires] naval dockyard - **2.** [d'armes] arsenal ; ~ **de pêcheur** fishing gear.

arsenic [arsənik] *nm* arsenic.

art [ar] *nm* art ; **l'~ de faire qqch** the art of doing sthg ; ~ **culinaire** art of cooking ; ~ **dramatique/graphique** dramatic/graphic art ; **le septième** ~ cinema ; **~s appliqués** applied arts ; **~s et métiers** *state-funded institution offering vocational courses by correspondence or evening classes* ; **Salon des Arts ménagers** ≃ Ideal Home Exhibition *Br* home crafts exhibition *ou* show *Am*.

art. *abr de* article.

Arte [arte] *n* Franco-German cultural television channel.

ARTE

Arte is a Franco-German cultural television channel created in 1992. It broadcasts arthouse films, documentaries and cultural discussion programmes. In Germany it is only available on cable.

artère [arter] *nf* - **1.** ANAT artery ; ~ **coronaire** coronary artery - **2.** [rue] arterial road.

artériel, elle [arterjɛl] *adj* arterial.

artériosclérose [arterjɔskleroz] *nf* arteriosclerosis.

arthrite [artrit] *nf* arthritis.

arthrose [artroz] *nf* osteoarthritis.

artichaut [artiʃo] *nm* artichoke.

article [artikl] *nm* - **1.** [gén] article ; ~ **défini/indéfini** definite/indefinite article ; ~ **de fond** feature ; **~s de bureau** office supplies - **2.** INFORM record - **3.** *loc* : **faire l'~** to make a sales pitch ; **à l'~ de la mort** at death's door.

articulation [artikylasjɔ̃] *nf* - **1.** ANAT & TECHNOL joint - **2.** [prononciation] articulation - **3.** [d'une démonstration] structure.

articulé, e [artikyle] *adj* jointed.

articuler [3] [artikyle] *vt* - **1.** [prononcer] to articulate - **2.** ANAT & TECHNOL to articulate, to joint - **3.** JUR to set out.
➡ **s'articuler** *vp* to hang together ; **s'~ sur/autour de qqch** [réflexion] to be based *ou* centred on sthg.

artifice [artifis] *nm* - **1.** [moyen astucieux] clever device *ou* trick - **2.** [tromperie] trick.

artificiel, elle [artifisjɛl] *adj* artificial.

artificiellement [artifisjɛlmɑ̃] *adv* artificially.

artillerie [artijri] *nf* MIL artillery.

artisan, e [artizɑ̃, an] *nm, f* craftsman (*f* craftswoman).
➡ **artisan** *nm* [responsable] : **être l'~ de** *fig* to be the architect of.

artisanal, e, aux [artizanal, o] *adj* craft *(avant n)* ; **fabrication ~e** cottage industry.

artisanat [artizana] *nm* [métier] craft ; [classe] craftsmen.

artiste [artist] *nmf* - **1.** [créateur] artist ; ~ **peintre** painter - **2.** [interprète] performer.

artistique [artistik] *adj* artistic.

as¹ [a] ⇨ **avoir**.

as² [as] *nm* - **1.** [carte] ace - **2.** [premier] number one - **3.** [champion] star, ace - **4.** *loc* : **être fringué comme l'~ de pique** *fam* to look like a scarecrow ; **passer à l'~** *fam* to go by the board ; **être plein aux ~** *fam* to be rolling in it.

a/s *(abr de* **aux soins de)** c/o.

AS *(abr de* **association sportive)** *nf* sports association.

ASA, Asa [aza] *(abr de* **American Standards Association)** *nf* ASA.

asc. *abr de* **ascenseur**.

ascendant, e [asãdã, ãt] *adj* rising.
➤ **ascendant** *nm* - **1.** [influence] influence, power ; **avoir de l'~ sur qqn** to have influence over sb - **2.** ASTROL ascendant.

ascenseur [asãsœr] *nm* lift *Br*, elevator *Am*.

ascension [asãsjõ] *nf* - **1.** [de montagne] ascent - **2.** [d'avion] climb - **3.** [progression] rise.
➤ **Ascension** *nf* : **l'Ascension** Ascension (Day).

ascensionnel, elle [asãsjɔnɛl] *adj* upward.

ascèse [asɛz] *nf* asceticism.

ascète [asɛt] *nmf* ascetic.

ASE *(abr de* **Agence spatiale européenne)** *nf* ESA.

aseptique [asɛptik] *adj* aseptic.

ashkénase [aʃkenaz] *adj* & *nmf* : **(Juif) ~** Ashkenazi ; **les ~s** the Ashkenazim.

asiatique [azjatik] *adj* - **1.** [de l'Asie en général] Asian - **2.** [d'Extrême-Orient] oriental.
➤ **Asiatique** *nmf* Asian.

Asie [azi] *nf* : **l'~** Asia ; **l'~ centrale** Central Asia ; **l'~ du Sud-Est** Southeast Asia.

asile [azil] *nm* - **1.** [refuge] refuge - **2.** POLIT : **demander/accorder l'~ politique** to seek/to grant political asylum - **3.** *vieilli* [psychiatrique] asylum.

asocial, e, aux [asɔsjal, o] ◇ *adj* antisocial ◇ *nm, f* social misfit.

aspect [aspɛ] *nm* - **1.** [apparence] appearance ; **d'~ agréable** nice-looking - **2.** [angle & LING] aspect - **3.** [vue] : **à l'~ de** *sout* at the sight of.

asperge [aspɛrʒ] *nf* [légume] asparagus.

asperger [17] [aspɛrʒe] *vt* : **~ qqch de qqch** to spray sthg with sthg ; **~ qqn de qqch** [arroser] to spray sb with sthg ; [éclabousser] to splash sb with sthg.
➤ **s'asperger** *vp* : **s'~ de qqch** to spray o.s. with sthg.

aspérité [asperite] *nf* [du sol] bump.

asphalte [asfalt] *nm* asphalt.

asphyxie [asfiksi] *nf* - **1.** MÉD asphyxia, suffocation - **2.** *fig* [de l'économie] paralysis.

asphyxier [9] [asfiksje] *vt* - **1.** MÉD to asphyxiate, to suffocate - **2.** *fig* [économie] to paralyse *Br*, to paralyze *Am*.
➤ **s'asphyxier** *vp* to suffocate.

aspic [aspik] *nm* [vipère] asp.

aspirant, e [aspirã, ãt] *adj* : **hotte ~e** cooker hood *Br*, cooker range *Am* ; **pompe ~e** suction pump.
➤ **aspirant** *nm* [armée] ≃ officer cadet ; [marine] ≃ midshipman.

aspirateur [aspiratœr] *nm* Hoover® *Br*, vacuum cleaner ; **passer l'~** to do the vacuuming *ou* hoovering.

aspiration [aspirasjõ] *nf* - **1.** [souffle] inhalation - **2.** TECHNOL suction - **3.** LING aspiration.
➤ **aspirations** *nfpl* aspirations.

aspirer [3] [aspire] *vt* - **1.** [air] to inhale ; [liquide] to suck up - **2.** TECHNOL to suck up, to draw up - **3.** [désirer] : **~ à qqch/à faire qqch** to aspire to sthg/to do sthg.

aspirine [aspirin] *nf* aspirin.

assagir [32] [asaʒir] *vt* to quieten down.
➤ **s'assagir** *vp* to quieten down.

assaillant, e [asajã, ãt] ◇ *adj* attacking ◇ *nm, f* assailant, attacker.

assaillir [47] [asajir] *vt* to attack, to assault ; **~ qqn de qqch** *fig* to assail *ou* bombard sb with sthg.

assainir [32] [asenir] *vt* - **1.** [logement] to clean up - **2.** [eau] to purify - **3.** ÉCON to rectify, to stabilize.

assainissement [asenismã] *nm* - **1.** [de quartier] cleaning up - **2.** [d'eau] purification - **3.** ÉCON stabilization.

assaisonnement [asɛzɔnmã] *nm* [sauce] dressing ; [condiments] seasoning.

assaisonner [3] [asɛzɔne] *vt* - **1.** [salade] to dress ; [viande, plat] to season - **2.** [propos] to season - **3.** *fam* [gronder] to tell off ; **se faire ~ par qqn** to get a (good) telling-off from sb.

assassin, e [asasɛ̃, in] *adj* provocative.
➤ **assassin** *nm* [gén] murderer ; POLIT assassin.

assassinat [asasina] *nm* [gén] murder ; POLIT assassination.

assassiner [3] [asasine] *vt* [tuer - gén] to murder ; [- POLIT] to assassinate.

assaut [aso] *nm* - **1.** [attaque] assault, attack ; **prendre d'~** [lieu] to storm ; [personne] to attack - **2.** SPORT bout - **3.** *loc* : **faire ~ de** to vie with each other in.

assécher [18] [aseʃe] *vt* to drain.
➤ **s'assécher** *vp* to become dry, to dry up.

ASSEDIC, Assedic [asedik] *(abr de* **Association pour l'emploi dans l'industrie et le commerce)** *nfpl French unemployment insurance scheme* ; **toucher les ~** to get unemployment benefit *Br ou* welfare *Am*.

assemblage [asãblaʒ] *nm* - **1.** [gén] assembly

- 2. *INFORM* : langage d'~ assembler *ou* assembly language.

assemblée [asãble] *nf* **- 1.** [réunion] meeting **- 2.** [public] gathering **- 3.** *ADMIN & POLIT* assembly ; **~ constituante** constituent assembly ; **~ consultative** advisory body ; **l'Assemblée nationale** *lower house of the French parliament.*

L'ASSEMBLÉE NATIONALE

The French parliament has two chambers : the National Assembly and the Senate. The members of the National Assembly (the 'députés') are elected in the 'élections législatives' held every five years.

assembler [asãble] *vt* **- 1.** [monter] to put together **- 2.** [réunir - objets] to gather (together) **- 3.** [associer] to connect **- 4.** [personnes - gén] to bring together, to assemble ; [- députés] to convene. ◆ **s'assembler** *vp* to gather.

assener [19] [asəne], **asséner** [18] [asene] *vt* : **~ un coup à qqn** [frapper] to strike sb, to deal sb a blow.

assentiment [asãtimã] *nm* assent ; **donner son ~ à qqch** to give one's assent to sthg.

asseoir [65] [aswar] ◇ *vt* **- 1.** [sur un siège] to put **- 2.** [fondations] to lay **- 3.** *fig* [réputation] to establish ; **~ qqch sur qqch** to base sthg on sthg ; **~ l'impôt sur le revenu** to base taxation on income ◇ *vi* : **faire ~ qqn** to seat sb, to ask sb to take a seat. ◆ **s'asseoir** *vp* to sit (down).

assermenté, e [asermãte] *adj* **- 1.** [fonctionnaire, expert] sworn **- 2.** [témoin] under oath.

assertion [asersjõ] *nf* assertion.

assesseur [asesœr] *nm* assessor.

asseyais, asseyions *etc* ▷ asseoir.

asseyez, asseyons *etc* ▷ asseoir.

assez [ase] *adv* **- 1.** [suffisamment] enough ; **~ grand pour qqch/pour faire qqch** big enough for sthg/to do sthg ; **~ de** enough ; **~ de lait/chaises** enough milk/chairs ; **il en reste juste ~** there is/are just enough left ; **en avoir ~ de qqn/qqch** to have had enough of sb/sthg, to ┌ be fed up with sb/sthg **- 2.** [plutôt] quite, rather.

assidu, e [asidy] *adj* **- 1.** [élève] diligent **- 2.** [travail] painstaking **- 3.** [empressé] : **~ (auprès de qqn)** attentive (to sb).

assiduité [asidɥite] *nf* **- 1.** [zèle] diligence **- 2.** [fréquence] : **avec ~** regularly. ◆ **assiduités** *nfpl péj & sout* attentions ; **poursuivre qqn de ses ~s** to press one's attentions on sb.

assidûment [asidymã] *adv* **- 1.** [avec zèle] assiduously, diligently **- 2.** [fréquemment] regularly.

assiégeant, e [asjeʒã, ãt] *adj* besieging. ◆ **assiégeant** *nm* besieger.

assiéger [22] [asjeʒe] *vt litt & fig* to besiege.

assiette [asjet] *nf* **- 1.** [vaisselle] plate ; **~ creuse** *ou* **à soupe** soup plate ; **~ à dessert** dessert plate ; **~ plate** dinner plate **- 2.** [de cavalier] seat **- 3.** [d'impôt] base **- 4.** *CULIN* : **~ anglaise** assorted cold meats *(pl) Br*, cold cuts *(pl) Am* ; **~ de crudités** *raw vegetables served as an hors-d'œuvre* **- 5.** *loc* : **ne pas être dans son ~** to feel off colour.

assiettée [asjete] *nf* plate, plateful.

assignation [asiɲasjõ] *nf* **- 1.** [attribution] : **~ de qqch à qqn** allocation of sthg to sb **- 2.** *JUR* summons.

assigner [3] [asiɲe] *vt* **- 1.** [fonds, tâche] : **~ qqch à qqn** to allocate *ou* assign sthg to sb **- 2.** [personne] : **~ qqn à qqch** to assign sb to sthg **- 3.** *JUR* : **~ qqn en justice** to issue a writ against sb.

assimilation [asimilasjõ] *nf* assimilation ; **~ de qqch à qqch** assimilation of sthg with sthg ; **~ de qqn à qqn** comparison of sb to sb.

assimiler [3] [asimile] *vt* **- 1.** [aliment, connaissances] to assimilate **- 2.** [confondre] : **~ qqch (à qqch)** to liken sthg (to sthg) ; **~ qqn à qqn** to compare sb to *ou* with sb. ◆ **s'assimiler** *vp* **- 1.** [se comparer] : **s'~ à qqn** to be (able to be) compared to sb **- 2.** [s'intégrer] to integrate.

assis, e [asi, iz] ◇ *pp* ▷ asseoir ◇ *adj* sitting, seated ; **place ~e** seat. ◆ **assise** *nf* **- 1.** [base] seat, seating **- 2.** *BIOL & GÉOL* stratum. ◆ **assises** *nfpl* **- 1.** *JUR* : **(cour d')~es** Crown Court *Br*, Circuit court *Am* **- 2.** [congrès] conference *(sg).*

assistance [asistãs] *nf* **- 1.** [aide] assistance ; **prêter ~ à qqn** to lend assistance to sb ; **l'Assistance publique** *French authority which manages the social services and state-owned hospitals* ; **être à l'Assistance (publique)** to be in care ; **~ technique** technical aid **- 2.** [auditoire] audience.

assistant, e [asistã, ãt] *nm, f* **- 1.** [auxiliaire] assistant ; **~e sociale** social worker **- 2.** *UNIV* assistant lecturer.

assister [3] [asiste] ◇ *vi* : **~ à qqch** to be at sthg, to attend sthg ◇ *vt* to assist.

associatif, ive [asɔsjatif, iv] *adj* **- 1.** [mémoire] associative **- 2.** [vie] community *(avant n).*

association [asɔsjasjõ] *nf* **- 1.** [gén] association ; **~ d'idées** association of ideas

- **2.** [union] society, association ; ~ **à** but non lucratif *JUR* non-profit-making *Br* ou non-profit *Am* organization ; ~ **sportive** sports club - **3.** *COMM* partnership.

associé, e [asɔsje] ◇ *adj* associated ◇ *nm, f* - **1.** [collaborateur] associate - **2.** [actionnaire] partner.

associer [9] [asɔsje] *vt* - **1.** [personnes] to bring together - **2.** [idées] to associate - **3.** [faire participer] : ~ **qqn à qqch** [inclure] to bring sb in on sthg ; [prendre pour partenaire] to make sb a partner in sthg.
➤ **s'associer** *vp* - **1.** [prendre part] : **s'~ à qqch** [participer] to join ou participate in sthg ; [partager] to share sthg - **2.** [collaborer] : **s'~ à** ou **avec qqn** to join forces with sb - **3.** [se combiner] : **s'~ à qqch** to be combined with sthg.

assoiffé, e [aswafe] *adj* thirsty ; ~ **de pouvoir** *fig* power-hungry.

assois ⊳ asseoir.

assombrir [32] [asɔ̃brir] *vt* - **1.** [plonger dans l'obscurité] to darken - **2.** *fig* [attrister] to cast a shadow over.
➤ **s'assombrir** *vp* - **1.** [devenir sombre] to grow dark - **2.** *fig* [s'attrister] to darken.

assommant, e [asɔmɑ̃, ɑ̃t] *adj pej* deadly boring.

assommer [3] [asɔme] *vt* - **1.** [frapper] to knock out - **2.** [ennuyer] to bore stiff - **3.** [de reproches] to overwhelm.

Assomption [asɔ̃psjɔ̃] *nf* : **l'~** the Assumption.

assorti, e [asɔrti] *adj* - **1.** [accordé] : **bien ~** well-matched ; **mal ~** ill-matched ; **une cravate ~e au costume** a tie which matches the suit - **2.** [varié] assorted.

assortiment [asɔrtimɑ̃] *nm* assortment, selection.

assortir [32] [asɔrtir] *vt* - **1.** [objets] : ~ **qqch à qqch** to match sthg to ou with sthg - **2.** [magasin] to stock.
➤ **s'assortir** *vp* to match ; **s'~ de qqch** to be accompanied by ou with sthg.

assoupi, e [asupi] *adj* - **1.** [endormi] dozing - **2.** *fig & littéraire* [sens, intérêt] dulled ; [passion, haine] spent ; [querelle] dormant.

assoupir [32] [asupir] *vt* - **1.** *sout* [enfant] to send to sleep - **2.** *fig & littéraire* [douleur] to soothe.
➤ **s'assoupir** *vp* - **1.** [s'endormir] to doze off - **2.** *fig & littéraire* [douleur] to die down.

assoupissement [asupismɑ̃] *nm* - **1.** [sommeil] doze - **2.** *fig & sout* : **l'~ culturel** cultural apathy.

assouplir [32] [asuplir] *vt* - **1.** [corps] to make

supple - **2.** [matière] to soften - **3.** [règlement] to relax - **4.** [caractère] to mellow.
➤ **s'assouplir** *vp* - **1.** [physiquement] to become supple - **2.** [moralement] to mellow.

assouplissement [asuplismɑ̃] *nm* - **1.** [de corps] making supple - **2.** [de matière] softening - **3.** [de règlement] easing, relaxation - **4.** [de caractère] mellowing.

assourdir [32] [asurdir] *vt* - **1.** [rendre sourd] to deafen - **2.** [abrutir] to exhaust, to wear out - **3.** [amortir] to deaden, to muffle.

assouvir [32] [asuvir] *vt* to satisfy.
➤ **s'assouvir** *vp littéraire* to be satisfied.

ASSU, Assu [asy] (*abr de* **Association du sport scolaire et universitaire**) *nf former* schools and university sports association.

assujetti, e [asyʒeti] *adj* : ~ **à l'impôt** subject to tax ou taxation.

assujettir [32] [asyʒetir] *vt* - **1.** [peuple] to subjugate - **2.** [soumettre] : ~ **qqn à qqch** to subject sb to sthg - **3.** [fixer] to secure.
➤ **s'assujettir** *vp* : **s'~ à qqch** to submit to sthg.

assumer [3] [asyme] *vt* - **1.** [fonction - exercer] to carry out ; [- prendre] to take on - **2.** [risque, responsabilité] to accept - **3.** [condition] to come to terms with - **4.** [frais] to meet.
➤ **s'assumer** *vp* to come to terms with o.s.

assurance [asyrɑ̃s] *nf* - **1.** [gén] assurance - **2.** [contrat] insurance ; **contracter** ou **prendre une ~** to take out insurance ; ~ **maladie** health insurance ; ~ **tous risques** *AUTOM* comprehensive insurance ; **~-vie** life assurance.

assuré, e [asyre] *nm, f* policy holder ; ~ **social** National Insurance contributor *Br*, Social Security contributor *Am*.

assurément [asyremɑ̃] *adv sout* certainly.

assurer [3] [asyre] *vt* - **1.** [promettre] : ~ **à qqn que** to assure sb (that) ; ~ **qqn de qqch** to assure sb of sthg - **2.** [permanence, liaison] to provide - **3.** [voiture] to insure - **4.** [paix] to ensure - **5.** [échelle] to secure, to fix.
➤ **s'assurer** *vp* - **1.** [vérifier] : **s'~ que** to make sure (that) ; **s'~ de qqch** to ensure sthg, to make sure of sthg - **2.** *COMM* : **s'~ (contre qqch)** to insure o.s. (against sthg) - **3.** [obtenir] : **s'~ qqch** to secure sthg - **4.** [se stabiliser] to steady o.s.

Assyrie [asiri] *nf* : **l'~** Assyria.

assyrien, enne [asirjɛ̃, ɛn] *adj* Assyrian.
➤ **Assyrien, enne** *nm, f* Assyrian.

astérisque [asterisk] *nm* asterisk.

asthmatique [asmatik] *nmf & adj* asthmatic.

asthme [asm] *nm MÉD* asthma.

asticot [astiko] *nm* maggot.

astigmate [astigmat] *nmf* & *adj* astigmatic.

astiquer [3] [astike] *vt* to polish.

astrakan [astrakɑ̃] *nm* astrakhan.

astral, e, aux [astral, o] *adj* astral, star *(avant n)*.

astre [astr] *nm* star.

astreignant, e [astrɛɲɑ̃, ɑ̃t] *adj* demanding.

astreindre [81] [astrɛ̃dr] *vt* : ~ **qqn à qqch** to subject sb to sthg ; ~ **qqn à faire qqch** to compel sb to do sthg.

➤ **s'astreindre** *vp* : **s'~ à qqch** to subject o.s. to sthg ; **s'~ à faire qqch** to compel o.s. to do sthg.

astreint, e [astrɛ̃, ɛt] *pp* ▷ **astreindre**.

astringent, e [astrɛ̃ʒɑ̃, ɑ̃t] *adj* astringent.

➤ **astringent** *nm* astringent.

astrologie [astrɔlɔʒi] *nf* astrology.

astrologique [astrɔlɔʒik] *adj* astrological.

astrologue [astrɔlɔg] *nm* astrologer.

astronaute [astronot] *nmf* astronaut.

astronautique [astronotik] *nf* astronautics *(U)*.

astronome [astronɔm] *nmf* astronomer.

astronomie [astronɔmi] *nf* astronomy.

astronomique [astronɔmik] *adj* astronomical.

astrophysique [astrofizik] *nf* astrophysics *(U)*.

astuce [astys] *nf* - **1.** [ruse] (clever) trick - **2.** [ingéniosité] shrewdness *(U)* - **3.** [plaisanterie] wisecrack.

astucieux, euse [astysjø, øz] *adj* - **1.** [idée] clever - **2.** [personne] shrewd.

asymétrique [asimetrik] *adj* asymmetric, asymmetrical.

atavisme [atavism] *nm* atavism.

atelier [atəlje] *nm* - **1.** [d'artisan] workshop - **2.** [de peintre] studio.

atermoiement [atɛrmwamɑ̃] *nm* - **1.** [tergiversation] procrastination - **2.** JUR postponement.

athée [ate] ⬦ *nmf* atheist ⬦ *adj* atheistic.

athénée [atene] *nm* Belg secondary school.

Athènes [atɛn] *n* Athens.

athénien, enne [atenjɛ̃, ɛn] *adj* Athenian. ➤ **Athénien, enne** *nm, f* Athenian.

athlète [atlɛt] *nmf* athlete.

athlétique [atletik] *adj* athletic.

athlétisme [atletism] *nm* athletics *(U)*.

Atlantide [atlɑ̃tid] *nf* : **l'~** Atlantis.

atlantique [atlɑ̃tik] *adj* Atlantic.

➤ **Atlantique** *nm* : **l'Atlantique** the Atlantic (Ocean).

atlas [atlas] *nm* atlas.

Atlas [atlas] *nm* : **l'~** the Atlas Mountains *(pl)*.

atmosphère [atmosfɛr] *nf* atmosphere.

atmosphérique [atmosferik] *adj* atmospheric.

atoca [atɔka] *nm* Can large cranberry.

atoll [atɔl] *nm* atoll.

atome [atom] *nm* atom ; **avoir des ~s crochus avec qqn** to be on the same wavelength as sb.

atomique [atomik] *adj* - **1.** [gén] nuclear - **2.** CHIM & PHYS atomic.

atomiseur [atomizœr] *nm* spray.

atone [atɔn] *adj* - **1.** [inexpressif] lifeless - **2.** MÉD atonic - **3.** [voyelle] unstressed.

atours [atur] *nmpl littéraire* : **paré de** *ou* **dans ses plus beaux ~** in all one's finery.

atout [atu] *nm* - **1.** [carte] trump ; ~ **cœur/ pique/trèfle/carreau** hearts/spades/clubs/ diamonds are trumps - **2.** *fig* [ressource] asset, advantage.

ATP ⬦ *nf (abr de* **Association des tennismen professionnels**) ATP ⬦ *nfpl (abr de* **arts et traditions populaires**) arts and crafts ; **musée des ~** arts and crafts museum.

âtre [ɑtr] *nm littéraire* hearth.

atroce [atrɔs] *adj* - **1.** [crime] atrocious, dreadful - **2.** [souffrance] horrific, atrocious - **3.** [temps] terrible.

atrocement [atrɔsmɑ̃] *adv* - **1.** [horriblement] horribly, terribly - **2.** [exagérément] terribly.

atrocité [atrɔsite] *nf* - **1.** [horreur] atrocity - **2.** [calomnie] insult.

atrophie [atrɔfi] *nf* atrophy.

atrophier [9] [atrɔfje] ➤ **s'atrophier** *vp* to atrophy.

attabler [3] [atable] ➤ **s'attabler** *vp* to sit down (at the table) ; **s'~ devant qqch** to sit down to sthg.

attachant, e [ataʃɑ̃, ɑ̃t] *adj* lovable.

attache [ataʃ] *nf* [lien] fastening. ➤ **attaches** *nfpl* links, connections.

attaché, e [ataʃe] *nm, f* attaché ; ~ **d'ambassade** attaché ; ~ **commercial/culturel/militaire** commercial/cultural/military attaché ; ~ **de presse** [diplomatique] press attaché ; [d'organisme, d'entreprise] press officer.

attaché-case [ataʃekɛz] *(pl* **attachés-cases**) *nm* attaché case.

attachement [ataʃmɑ̃] *nm* attachment.

attacher [3] [ataʃe] ⬦ *vt* - **1.** [lier] : ~ **qqch (à)** to fasten *ou* tie sthg (to) ; *fig* [associer] to attach sthg (to) - **2.** [paquet] to tie up - **3.** [lacet] to do up ; [ceinture de sécurité] to fasten - **4.** *fig* [émotionnellement] : ~ **qqn à** to bind sb to <> *vi CULIN* : ~ **(à)** to stick (to).

➤ **s'attacher** *vp* - **1.** [émotionnellement] : **s'~ à qqn/qqch** to become attached to sb/sthg - **2.** [se fermer] to fasten ; **s'~ avec** *OU* **par qqch** to do up *OU* fasten with sthg - **3.** [s'appliquer] : **s'~ à qqch/à faire qqch** to devote o.s. to sthg/ to doing sthg, to apply o.s. to sthg/to doing sthg.

attaquant, e [atakɑ̃, ɑ̃t] <> *adj* attacking <> *nm, f* attacker.

attaque [atak] *nf* - **1.** [gén & *MÉD*] attack ; ~ **à main armée** holdup ; *fig* : ~ **contre qqn/qqch** attack on sb/sthg - **2.** *MUS* [de note] attack - **3.** *loc* : **être d'~** to be on form ; **être/se sentir d'~ pour faire qqch** to be/feel up to doing sthg.

attaquer [3] [atake] *vt* - **1.** [gén] to attack - **2.** [*JUR* - personne] to take to court ; [- jugement] to contest - **3.** *fam* [plat] to tuck into - **4.** [tâche] to tackle.

➤ **s'attaquer** *vp* - **1.** [combattre] : **s'~ à qqn** to attack sb - **2.** *fig* : **s'~ à qqch** [tâche] to tackle sthg.

attardé, e [atarde] <> *adj* - **1.** [idées] outdated - **2.** [passants] late - **3.** [enfant] backward <> *nm, f* [enfant] backward child.

attarder [3] [atarde] ➤ **s'attarder** *vp* : **s'~ sur qqch** to dwell on sthg ; **s'~ à faire qqch** to stay on to do sthg, to stay behind to do sthg.

atteignais, atteignions *etc* ▷ **atteindre.**

atteindre [8] [atɛ̃dr] *vt* - **1.** [gén] to reach - **2.** [toucher] to hit - **3.** [affecter] to affect.

atteint, e [atɛ̃, ɛ̃t] <> *pp* ▷ **atteindre** <> *adj* - **1.** [malade] : **être ~ de** to be suffering from - **2.** *fam* [fou] touched.

➤ **atteinte** *nf* - **1.** [préjudice] : **~e à** attack on ; **porter ~e à** to undermine ; **hors d'~e** [hors de portée] out of reach ; [inattaquable] beyond reach - **2.** [effet] effect.

attelage [atlaʒ] *nm* - **1.** [chevaux] team - **2.** [harnachement] harnessing *(U)*.

atteler [24] [atle] *vt* - **1.** [animaux, véhicules] to hitch up ; [wagons] to couple - **2.** [à une tâche] : **~ qqn à** to assign sb to.

➤ **s'atteler** *vp* : **s'~ à** to get down to.

attelle [atɛl] *nf* splint.

attenant, e [atnɑ̃, ɑ̃t] *adj* : ~ **(à qqch)** adjoining (sthg).

attendre [73] [atɑ̃dr] <> *vt* - **1.** [gén] to wait for ; **le déjeuner nous attend** lunch is ready ; ~ **que** (+ *subjonctif*) : ~ **que la pluie s'arrête** to

wait for the rain to stop ; **faire ~ qqn** [personne] to keep sb waiting ; **les résultats se font ~** we're all waiting for the results - **2.** [espérer] : ~ **qqch (de qqn/qqch)** to expect sthg (from sb/sthg) - **3.** [suj : surprise, épreuve] to be in store for <> *vi* to wait ; **attends! hang on!**

➤ **s'attendre** *vp* : **s'~ à** to expect.

➤ **en attendant** *loc adv* - **1.** [pendant ce temps] meanwhile, in the meantime - **2.** [quand même] all the same.

attendrir [32] [atɑ̃drir] *vt* - **1.** [viande] to tenderize - **2.** [personne] to move.

➤ **s'attendrir** *vp* : **s'~ (sur qqn/qqch)** to be moved (by sb/sthg).

attendrissant, e [atɑ̃drisɑ̃, ɑ̃t] *adj* moving, touching.

attendrissement [atɑ̃drismɑ̃] *nm* pity.

attendrisseur [atɑ̃drisœr] *nm* meat tenderizer.

attendu, e [atɑ̃dy] *pp* ▷ **attendre.**

➤ **attendu** <> *nm JUR* reasoning *(U)* <> *prép* considering.

➤ **attendu que** *loc conj* since, considering that.

attentat [atɑ̃ta] *nm* attack ; ~ **à la bombe** bomb attack, bombing ; ~ **à la pudeur** *JUR* indecent assault.

attente [atɑ̃t] *nf* - **1.** [station] wait ; **en ~** in abeyance - **2.** [espoir] expectation ; **contre toute ~** contrary to all expectations ; **répondre aux ~s de qqn** to live up to sb's expectations.

attenter [3] [atɑ̃te] *vi* : ~ **à** [liberté, droit] to violate ; ~ **à ses jours** to attempt suicide ; ~ **à la vie de qqn** to make an attempt on sb's life.

attentif, ive [atɑ̃tif, iv] *adj* - **1.** [auditoire] : ~ **(à qqch)** attentive (to sthg) - **2.** [soin] careful, scrupulous.

attention [atɑ̃sjɔ̃] <> *nf* attention ; **à l'~ de** for the attention of ; **faire ~ à** [prudence] to be careful of ; [concentration] to pay attention to ; **porter qqch à l'~ de qqn** to bring sthg to sb's attention <> *interj* watch out!, be careful! ; '~ **chien méchant**' 'beware of the dog' ; ~ **à la marche** mind the step ; '~ **peinture fraîche**' 'wet paint'.

attentionné, e [atɑ̃sjɔne] *adj* thoughtful ; ~ **auprès de** attentive to.

attentisme [atɑ̃tism] *nm* [gén] waiting game ; *POLIT* policy of wait-and-see.

attentivement [atɑ̃tivmɑ̃] *adv* attentively, carefully.

atténuante [atenɥɑ̃t] ▷ **circonstance.**

atténuation [atenɥasjɔ̃] *nf* [de lumière] dimming ; [de propos] toning down ; [de douleur] easing ; ~ **de peine** *JUR* reduction in sentence.

atténuer [7] [atenɥe] *vt* [douleur] to ease ; [propos, ton] to tone down ; [lumière] to dim, to subdue ; [bruit] to quieten.

➤ **s'atténuer** *vp* [lumière] to dim, to fade ; [bruit] to fade ; [douleur] to ease.

atterrer [4] [atere] *vt* to stagger.

atterrir [32] [aterir] *vi* to land ; ~ **dans qqch** *fig* to land up in sthg.

atterrissage [aterisaʒ] *nm* landing ; ~ **sans visibilité** blind landing ; ~ **forcé** emergency landing.

attestation [atɛstasjɔ̃] *nf* - **1.** [certificat] certificate - **2.** [action] attestation - **3.** [preuve] proof.

attester [3] [atɛste] *vt* - **1.** [confirmer] to vouch for, to testify to - **2.** [certifier] to attest.

attifer [3] [atife] *vt* to get up.

➤ **s'attifer** *vp* to get *ou* doll o.s. up.

attique [atik] *nm ARCHIT* attic.

attirail [atiraj] *nm fam* [équipement] gear.

attirance [atirãs] *nf* attraction ; **avoir/ éprouver de l'~ pour** to be/to feel attracted to.

attirant, e [atirã, ãt] *adj* attractive.

attirer [3] [atire] *vt* - **1.** [gén] to attract - **2.** [amener vers soi] : ~ **qqn à/vers soi** to draw sb to/towards one - **3.** [provoquer] : ~ **des ennuis à qqn** to cause trouble for sb.

➤ **s'attirer** *vp* : **s'~ qqch** to bring sthg on o.s.

attiser [3] [atize] *vt* - **1.** [feu] to poke - **2.** *fig* [haine] to stir up.

attitré, e [atitre] *adj* - **1.** [habituel] usual - **2.** [titulaire - fournisseur] by appointment ; [- représentant] accredited.

attitude [atityd] *nf* - **1.** [comportement, approche] attitude - **2.** [posture] posture.

attouchement [atuʃmã] *nm* caress.

attractif, ive [atraktif, iv] *adj* - **1.** [force] magnetic - **2.** [prix] attractive.

attraction [atraksjɔ̃] *nf* - **1.** [gén] attraction - **2.** [force] : ~ **magnétique** magnetic force ; **l'~ terrestre** the earth's gravitational force.

➤ **attractions** *nfpl* - **1.** [jeux] amusements - **2.** [spectacle] attractions.

attrait [atrɛ] *nm* - **1.** [séduction] appeal - **2.** [intérêt] attraction.

➤ **attraits** *nmpl* attractions.

attrape [atrap] *nf* trick.

attrape-nigaud [atrapnigo] (*pl* **attrape-nigauds**) *nm* con.

attraper [3] [atrape] *vt* - **1.** [gén] to catch - **2.** *fam* [gronder] to tell off ; **se faire ~ (par qqn)** to get a telling-off (from sb) - **3.** [habitude, accent] to pick up - **4.** *fam* [tromper] to take in.

attrayant, e [atrɛjã, ãt] *adj* attractive.

attribuer [7] [atribɥe] *vt* - **1.** [tâche, part] : ~ **qqch à qqn** to assign *ou* allocate sthg to sb, to assign *ou* allocate sb sthg ; [privilège] to grant sthg to sb, to grant sb sthg ; [récompense] to award sthg to sb, to award sb sthg - **2.** [faute] : ~ **qqch à qqn** to attribute sthg to sb, to put sthg down to sb.

➤ **s'attribuer** *vp* - **1.** [s'approprier] to appropriate (for o.s.) - **2.** [revendiquer] to claim (for o.s.).

attribut [atriby] *nm* - **1.** [gén] attribute - **2.** *GRAM* complement.

attribution [atribysjɔ̃] *nf* - **1.** [de prix] awarding, award - **2.** [de part, tâche] allocation, assignment - **3.** [d'avantage] bestowing.

➤ **attributions** *nfpl* [fonctions] duties.

attrister [3] [atriste] *vt* to sadden.

➤ **s'attrister** *vp* to be saddened.

attroupement [atrupmã] *nm* crowd.

attrouper [3] [atrupe] ➤ **s'attrouper** *vp* to form a crowd, to gather.

au [o] ▷ à.

aubade [obad] *nf* dawn serenade.

aubaine [obɛn] *nf* piece of good fortune.

aube [ob] *nf* - **1.** [aurore] dawn, daybreak ; **à l'~** at dawn ; **à l'~ de** *fig* at the dawn of - **2.** *RELIG* alb.

aubépine [obepin] *nf* hawthorn.

auberge [obɛrʒ] *nf* [hôtel] inn ; ~ **de jeunesse** youth hostel ; **on n'est pas sorti de l'~** *fam fig* we're not out of the woods yet.

aubergine [obɛrʒin] ◇ *nf* - **1.** *BOT* aubergine *Br*, eggplant *Am* - **2.** *péj* [contractuelle] traffic warden *Br*, meter maid *Am* ◇ *adj inv* [couleur] aubergine.

aubergiste [obɛrʒist] *nmf* innkeeper.

auburn [obœrn] *adj inv* auburn.

aucun, e [okœ, yn] ◇ *adj* - **1.** [sens négatif] : **ne ... ~** no ; **il n'y a ~e voiture dans la rue** there aren't any cars in the street, there are no cars in the street ; **sans faire ~ bruit** without making a sound - **2.** [sens positif] any ; **il lit plus qu'~ autre enfant** he reads more than any other child ◇ *pron* - **1.** [sens négatif] none ; ~ **des enfants** none of the children ; ~ **d'entre nous** none of us ; ~ **(des deux)** neither (of them) - **2.** [sens positif] : **plus qu'~ de nous** more than any of us ; **d'~s** *sout* some (people).

aucunement [okynmã] *adv* not at all, in no way.

audace [odas] *nf* - **1.** [hardiesse] daring, boldness - **2.** [insolence] audacity ; **avoir l'~ de faire**

qqch to have the cheek *ou* audacity to do sthg - **3.** [innovation] daring innovation.

audacieux, euse [odasjø, øz] <> *adj* - **1.** [projet] daring, bold - **2.** [personne, geste] bold <> *nm, f* daring person.

au-dedans [odədɑ̃] *loc adv* inside.
➤ **au-dedans de** *loc prép* inside.

au-dehors [odəɔr] *loc adv* outside.
➤ **au-dehors de** *loc prép* outside.

au-delà [odəla] <> *loc adv* - **1.** [plus loin] beyond - **2.** [davantage, plus] more <> *nm* : l'~ the hereafter, the afterlife.
➤ **au-delà de** *loc prép* beyond.

au-dessous [odəsu] *loc adv* below, underneath.
➤ **au-dessous de** *loc prép* below, under.

au-dessus [odəsy] *loc adv* above.
➤ **au-dessus de** *loc prép* above, over.

au-devant [odəvɑ̃] *loc adv* ahead.
➤ **au-devant de** *loc prép* : aller ~ de to go to meet ; aller ~ du danger to court danger.

audible [odibl] *adj* audible.

audience [odjɑ̃s] *nf* - **1.** [public, entretien] audience - **2.** *JUR* hearing.

Audimat® [odimat] *nm* audience rating.

AUDIMAT
Viewing figures for French television are calculated using a device which is installed for a period of time in selected households.

audionumérique [odjɔnymerik] *adj* digital audio.

audiovisuel, elle [odjɔvizɥɛl] *adj* audiovisual.
➤ **audiovisuel** *nm* TV and radio.

audit [odit] *nm* audit ; ~ **marketing** *COMM* marketing audit.

auditeur, trice [oditœr, tris] *nm, f* listener.
➤ **auditeur** *nm* - **1.** *UNIV* : ~ **libre** *person allowed to attend lectures without being registered*, auditor *Am* - **2.** *FIN* auditor.

auditif, ive [oditif, iv] *adj* - **1.** [appareil] hearing *(avant n)* - **2.** [mémoire] auditory.

audition [odisjɔ̃] *nf* - **1.** [fait d'entendre] hearing - **2.** *JUR* examination - **3.** *THÉÂTRE* audition - **4.** *MUS* recital.

auditionner [3] [odisjɔne] *vt & vi* to audition.

auditoire [oditwar] *nm* [public] audience ; ~ **cible** *COMM* target audience.

auditorium [oditɔrjɔm] *nm* [de concert] auditorium ; [d'enregistrement] studio.

auge [oʒ] *nf* [pour animaux] trough.

augmentation [ogmɑ̃tasjɔ̃] *nf* : ~ **(de)** increase (in) ; ~ **(de salaire)** rise (in salary).

augmenter [3] [ogmɑ̃te] <> *vt* to increase ; [prix, salaire] to raise ; [personne] to give a rise to *Br*, to give a raise to *Am* <> *vi* to increase, to rise ; **le froid augmente** it's getting colder ; **la douleur augmente** the pain is getting worse.

augure [ogyr] *nm* [présage] omen ; **être de bon/mauvais** ~ to be a good/bad sign.

augurer [3] [ogyre] *vt* : ~ **bien/mal de qqch** to augur well/ill for sthg.

auguste [ogyst] *adj* august.

aujourd'hui [oʒurdɥi] *adv* today.

aulx ⊳ ail.

aumône [omon] *nf* : **faire l'~ à qqn** to give alms to sb ; **faire l'~ de qqch à qqn** *fig* to favour *Br ou* favor *Am* sb with sthg.

aumônier [omonje] *nm RELIG* chaplain.

auparavant [oparavɑ̃] *adv* - **1.** [tout d'abord] first (of all) - **2.** [avant] before, previously.

auprès [oprɛ] ➤ **auprès de** *loc prép* - **1.** [à côté de] beside, next to - **2.** [dans l'opinion de] in the eyes of - **3.** [comparé à] compared with - **4.** [en s'adressant à] to.

auquel [okɛl] ⊳ lequel.

aurai, auras *etc* ⊳ avoir.

auréole [oreɔl] *nf* - **1.** *ASTRON & RELIG* halo - **2.** [trace] ring.

auréoler [3] [oreɔle] *vt* : **être auréolé de** to be crowned with.

auriculaire [orikylɛr] *nm* little finger.

aurore [orɔr] *nf* dawn ; ~ **boréale** northern lights *(pl)*, aurora borealis ; **à l'~ de** *fig* at the dawn of.

ausculter [3] [oskylte] *vt MÉD* to sound.

auspice [ospis] *nm (gén pl)*•sign, auspice ; **sous d'heureux ~s** promisingly ; **sous les ~s de qqn** under the auspices of sb.

aussi [osi] *adv* - **1.** [pareillement, en plus] also, too ; **moi ~** me too ; **j'y vais ~** I'm going too *ou* as well ; **il parle anglais et ~ espagnol** he speaks English as well as Spanish - **2.** [dans une comparaison] : ~ ... **que** as ... as ; **il n'est pas ~ intelligent que son frère** he's not as clever as his brother ; **je n'ai jamais rien vu d'~ beau** I've never seen anything so beautiful ; ~ **léger qu'il soit**, je ne pourrai pas le porter even though it's light *ou* light though it is, I won't be able to carry it ; ~ **incroyable que cela paraisse** incredible though *ou* as it may seem - **3.** *sout* [introduisant une explication] so.
➤ **(tout) aussi bien** *loc adv* just as easily, just as well ; **j'aurais pu (tout) ~ bien refuser** I could just as easily have said no.

◆ **aussi bien ... que** loc conj as well ... as ; **tu le sais ~ bien que moi** you know as well as I do.

aussitôt [osito] adv immediately.

◆ **aussitôt que** loc conj as soon as.

austère [ostɛr] adj - **1.** [personne, vie] austere - **2.** [vêtement] severe ; [paysage] harsh.

austérité [osterite] nf - **1.** [de personne, vie] austerity - **2.** [de vêtement] severeness ; [de paysage] harshness.

austral, e [ostral] (pl **australs** OU **austraux** [ostro]) adj southern.

Australie [ostrali] nf : **l'~** Australia ; **l'~-Méridionale** South Australia ; **l'~-Occidentale** Western Australia.

australien, enne [ostraljɛ̃, ɛn] adj Australian.

◆ **Australien, -enne** nm, f Australian.

autant [otã] adv - **1.** [comparatif] : **~ que** as much as ; **ce livre coûte ~ que l'autre** this book costs as much as the other one ; **~ de** (**... que**) [quantité] as much (... as) ; [nombre] as many (... as) ; **il a dépensé ~ d'argent que moi** he spent as much money as I did ; **il y a ~ de femmes que d'hommes** there are as many women as men ; **~ il est gentil avec moi ~ il est désagréable avec elle** he is as kind to me as he is unpleasant to her - **2.** [à un tel point, en si grande quantité] so much ; [en si grand nombre] so many ; **~ de patience** so much patience ; **~ de gens** so many people ; **il ne peut pas en dire ~** he can't say the same ; **en faire ~** to do likewise - **3.** [il vaut mieux] : **~ dire la vérité** we/you etc may as well tell the truth.

◆ **autant que** loc conj : **(pour) ~ que je sache** as far as I know.

◆ **d'autant** loc adv accordingly, in proportion.

◆ **d'autant mieux** loc adv all the better ; **d'~ mieux que** all the better since.

◆ **d'autant que** loc conj : **d'~ (plus) que** all the more so since ; **d'~ moins que** all the less so since.

◆ **pour autant** loc adv for all that.

autarcie [otarsi] nf autarky.

autel [otɛl] nm altar.

auteur [otœr] nm - **1.** [d'œuvre] author - **2.** [inventeur] originator - **3.** [responsable] perpetrator.

authenticité [otãtisite] nf authenticity, genuineness.

authentifier [9] [otãtifje] vt to authenticate.

authentique [otãtik] adj authentic, genuine.

autisme [otism] nm autism.

autiste [otist] ◇ nmf autistic person ◇ adj autistic.

autistique [otistik] adj autistic.

auto [oto] nf car ; **~ tamponneuse** dodgem Br, bumper car.

autobiographie [otobjografi] nf autobiography.

autobiographique [otobjografik] adj autobiographical.

autobronzant, e [otobrõzã, ãt] adj self-tanning ; **lotion ~e** self-tanning lotion.

◆ **autobronzant** nm self-tanning product.

autobus [otobys] nm bus ; **~ à impériale** ≃ double-decker bus.

autocar [otokar] nm coach.

autochtone [otokton] nmf & adj native.

autocollant, e [otokolã, ãt] adj self-adhesive, sticky.

◆ **autocollant** nm sticker.

autocouchettes [otokuʃɛt] adj inv : **train ~** ≃ Motorail® train.

autocritique [otokritik] nf self-criticism.

autocuiseur [otokyizœr] nm pressure cooker.

autodéfense [otodefãs] nf self-defence Br, self-defense Am.

autodétermination [otodetɛrminasjõ] nf self-determination.

autodétruire [98] [otodetrɥir] ◆ **s'autodétruire** vp - **1.** [machine] to self-destruct - **2.** [personne] to destroy o.s.

autodidacte [otodidakt] ◇ nmf self-taught person ◇ adj self-taught.

autodiscipline [otodisiplin] nf self-discipline.

auto-école [otoekol] (pl **auto-écoles**) nf driving school.

autofinancement [otofinãsmã] nm self-financing.

autofocus [otofokys] nm & adj inv autofocus.

autogène [otoʒɛn] adj : **training ~** autogenic training.

autogéré, e [otoʒere] adj worker-controlled, self-managed.

autogestion [otoʒɛstjõ] nf workers' control.

autographe [otograf] ◇ nm autograph ◇ adj autograph (avant n).

autoguidé, e [otogide] adj self-guided.

automate [otomat] nm [robot] automaton.

automatique [otomatik] ◇ nm - **1.** [pistolet] automatic - **2.** TÉLÉCOM ≃ direct dialling ◇ adj automatic.

automatiquement [ɔtɔmatikmɑ̃] *adv* automatically.

automatisation [ɔtɔmatizasjɔ̃] *nf* automation.

automatisme [ɔtɔmatism] *nm* - **1.** [de machine] automatic operation - **2.** [réflexe] automatic reaction, automatism.

automédication [ɔtɔmedikasjɔ̃] *nf* self-medication.

automitrailleuse [ɔtɔmitrajøz] *nf* armoured *Br ou* armored *Am* vehicle.

automnal, e, aux [ɔtɔnal, o] *adj* autumnal, autumn *(avant n)*.

automne [ɔtɔn] *nm* autumn, fall *Am* ; **en ~** in the autumn, in the fall *Am* ; **être à l'~ de sa vie** *fig* to be in the autumn of one's life.

automobile [ɔtɔmɔbil] ⟨⟩ *nf* car, automobile *Am* ⟨⟩ *adj* [industrie, accessoires] car *(avant n)*, automobile *(avant n) Am* ; [véhicule] motor *(avant n)*.

automobiliste [ɔtɔmɔbilist] *nmf* driver, motorist *Br*.

automoteur, trice [ɔtɔmɔtœr, tris] *adj* self-propelled.
➤ **automoteur** *nm* large self-propelled river barge.
➤ **automotrice** *nf* railcar.

autonettoyant, e [ɔtɔnɛtwajɑ̃, ɑ̃t] *adj* self-cleaning.

autonome [ɔtɔnɔm] *adj* - **1.** [gén] autonomous, independent - **2.** *INFORM* off-line - **3.** [appareil] self-contained.

autonomie [ɔtɔnɔmi] *nf* - **1.** [indépendance] autonomy, independence - **2.** *AUTOM* & *AVIAT* range ; **~ de vol** *AVIAT* flight range - **3.** *POLIT* autonomy, self-government.

autonomiste [ɔtɔnɔmist] *nmf* & *adj* separatist.

autoportrait [ɔtɔpɔrtrɛ] *nm* self-portrait.

autopropulsé, e [ɔtɔprɔpylse] *adj* self-propelled.

autopsie [ɔtɔpsi] *nf* post-mortem, autopsy.

autoradio [ɔtɔradjo] *nm* car radio.

autorail [ɔtɔraj] *nm* railcar.

auto-reverse [ɔtɔrivɛrs] *adj inv* auto-reverse.

autorisation [ɔtɔrizasjɔ̃] *nf* - **1.** [permission] permission, authorization ; **avoir l'~ de faire qqch** to be allowed to do sthg ; **demander/accorder l'~ de faire qqch** to request/grant permission to do sthg - **2.** [attestation] pass, permit.

autorisé, e [ɔtɔrize] *adj* [personne] in authority ; **milieux ~s** official circles.

autoriser [3] [ɔtɔrize] *vt* to authorize, to permit ; **~ qqn à faire qqch** [permission] to give

sb permission to do sthg ; [possibilité] to permit *ou* allow sb to do sthg.

autoritaire [ɔtɔritɛr] *adj* authoritarian.

autoritarisme [ɔtɔritarism] *nm* authoritarianism.

autorité [ɔtɔrite] *nf* authority ; **faire ~** [ouvrage] to be authoritative ; [personne] to be an authority ; **faire qqch d'~** to do sthg out of hand.

autoroute [ɔtɔrut] *nf* motorway *Br*, highway *Am*, freeway *Am* ; **~ de l'information** *INFORM* information highway *ou* superhighway.

autoroutier, ère [ɔtɔrutje, ɛr] *adj* motorway *(avant n) Br*, freeway *(avant n) Am*.

auto-stop [ɔtɔstɔp] *nm* hitchhiking ; hitching ; **faire de l'~** to hitchhike, to hitch ; **prendre quelqu'un en ~** to pick up a hitchhiker.

auto-stoppeur, euse [ɔtɔstɔpœr, øz] *(mpl* **auto-stoppeurs**, *fpl* **auto-stoppeuses**) *nm, f* hitchhiker, hitcher.

autosuggestion [ɔtɔsygʒɛstjɔ̃] *nf* autosuggestion.

autour [otur] *adv* round, around.
➤ **autour de** *loc prép* - **1.** [sens spatial] round, around - **2.** [sens temporel] about, around.

autre [otr] ⟨⟩ *adj indéf* - **1.** [distinct, différent] other, different ; **je préfère une ~ marque de café** I prefer another *ou* a different brand of coffee ; **l'un et l'~ projets** both projects ; **ni l'une ni l'~ maison** neither house ; **~ chose** something else - **2.** [supplémentaire] other ; **tu veux une ~ tasse de café?** would you like another cup of coffee? - **3.** [qui est différent par une certaine supériorité] : **c'est un (tout) ~ homme que son père** he's not at all like his father, he's a different man from his father - **4.** [qui reste] other, remaining ; **les ~s passagers ont été rapatriés en autobus** the other *ou* remaining passengers were bussed home ⟨⟩ *pron indéf* : **l'~** the other (one) ; **un ~** another (one) ; **les ~s** [personnes] the others ; [objets] the others, the other ones ; **l'un à côté de l'~** side by side ; **d'une semaine à l'~** from one week to the next ; **aucun ~, nul ~, personne d'~** no one else, nobody else ; **quelqu'un d'~** somebody else, someone else ; **rien d'~** nothing else ; **l'une chante, l'~ danse** one sings and the other dances ; **l'un et l'~ sont venus** they both came, both of them came ; **l'un ou l'~ ira** one or other (of them) will go ; **ni l'un ni l'~ n'est venu** neither (of them) came.

autrefois [otrəfwa] *adv* in the past, formerly.

autrement [otrəmɑ̃] *adv* - **1.** [différemment] otherwise, differently ; **je n'ai pas pu faire**

~ **que d'y aller** I had no choice but to go ;
~ **dit** in other words - **2.** [sinon] otherwise
- **3.** sout [beaucoup plus] far more ; **je n'en suis
pas ~ étonné** it doesn't particularly surprise me.

Autriche [otriʃ] nf : **l'~** Austria.

autrichien, enne [otriʃjɛ̃, ɛn] adj Austrian.

➡ **Autrichien, enne** nm, f Austrian.

autruche [otryʃ] nf ostrich ; **avoir un estomac d'~** fig to have a cast-iron stomach ;
pratiquer la politique de l'~ fig to bury one's head in the sand.

autrui [otrɥi] pron others, other people.

auvent [ovã] nm canopy.

aux [o] ⊳ **à**.

auxiliaire [oksiljɛr] ⋄ nmf [assistant] assistant ; ~ **médical** medical auxiliary ⋄ nm
GRAM auxiliary (verb) ⋄ adj - **1.** [secondaire]
auxiliary - **2.** ADMIN assistant (avant n).

auxquels, auxquelles [okɛl] ⊳ lequel.

av. abr de **avenue.**

AV ⋄ nm (abr de **avis de virement**) notification of bank transfer ⋄ abr de **avant.**

avachi, e [avaʃi] adj - **1.** [gén] misshapen
- **2.** [personne] listless ; **il était ~ dans un fauteuil** he was slumped in an armchair.

aval, als [aval] nm backing (U), endorsement.

➡ **en aval** loc adv litt & fig downstream.

➡ **en aval de** loc prép litt & fig downstream of.

avalanche [avalãʃ] nf litt & fig avalanche.

avaler [3] [avale] vt - **1.** [gén] to swallow - **2.** fig
[supporter] to take ; **dur à ~** difficult to swallow.

avaliser [3] [avalize] vt - **1.** [traite] to endorse
- **2.** [décision, projet] to back.

avance [avãs] nf - **1.** [progression, somme d'argent]
advance - **2.** [distance, temps] lead ; **le train a
dix minutes d'~** the train is ten minutes
early ; **le train a une ~ de dix minutes sur l'horaire** the train is running ten minutes
ahead of schedule ; **prendre de l'~ (dans
qqch)** to get ahead (in sthg).

➡ **avances** nfpl : **faire des ~s à qqn** to make
advances towards sb.

➡ **à l'avance** loc adv in advance.

➡ **d'avance** loc adv in advance.

➡ **en avance** loc adv : **être en ~** to be early ;
être en ~ sur qqch to be ahead of sthg.

➡ **par avance** loc adv in advance.

avancement [avãsmã] nm - **1.** [développement]
progress - **2.** [promotion] promotion.

avancer [16] [avãse] ⋄ vt - **1.** [objet, tête] to

move forward ; [date, départ] to bring forward ; [main] to hold out - **2.** [projet, travail] to
advance - **3.** [montre, horloge] to put forward
- **4.** [argent] : ~ **qqch à qqn** to advance sb sthg
⋄ vi - **1.** [approcher] to move forward - **2.** [progresser] to advance ; ~ **dans qqch** to make
progress in sthg - **3.** [faire saillie] : ~ **(dans/sur)**
to jut out (into/over), to project (into/over)
- **4.** [montre, horloge] : **ma montre avance de dix
minutes** my watch is ten minutes fast
- **5.** [servir] : **ça n'avance à rien** that won't get
us/you anywhere.

➡ **s'avancer** vp - **1.** [s'approcher] to move forward ; **s'~ vers qqn/qqch** to move towards Br
ou toward Am sb/sthg - **2.** [prendre de l'avance] :
s'~ (dans qqch) to get ahead (in sthg)
- **3.** [s'engager] to commit o.s.

avant [avã] ⋄ prép before ⋄ adv before ;
quelques jours ~ a few days earlier ou before ; **tu connais le cinéma? ma maison se situe
un peu ~** do you know the cinema? my
house is just this side of it ; **bien ~** [spatial]
well before ; [temporel] well before ou beforehand ⋄ adj inv front ; **les roues ~** the front
wheels ⋄ nm - **1.** [partie antérieure] front
- **2.** SPORT forward.

➡ **avant de** loc prép : ~ **de faire qqch** before
doing sthg ; ~ **de partir** before leaving.

➡ **avant que** loc conj (+ subjonctif) : **je dois
parler ~ que tu partes** I must speak to you
before you leave.

➡ **avant tout** loc adv above all ; **sa carrière
passe ~ tout** his career comes first.

➡ **en avant** loc adv forward, forwards.

➡ **en avant de** loc prép in front of.

avantage [avãtaʒ] nm [gén & TENNIS] advantage ; **se montrer à son ~** to look one's best ;
~s en nature fringe benefits, perks ; **~s sociaux** welfare benefits.

avantager [17] [avãtaʒe] vt - **1.** [favoriser] to favour Br, to favor Am - **2.** [mettre en valeur] to flatter.

avantageusement [avãtaʒøzmã] adv favourably Br, favorably Am.

avantageux, euse [avãtaʒø, øz] adj - **1.** [attrayant] attractive - **2.** [profitable] profitable, lucrative - **3.** [économique - prix] reasonable
- **4.** [flatteur] flattering - **5.** sout [présomptueux] :
prendre l'air ~ to look superior.

avant-bras [avãbra] nm inv forearm.

avant-centre [avãsãtr] (pl **avants-centres**)
nm centre Br ou center Am forward.

avant-coureur [avãkurœr] ⊳ **signe.**

avant-dernier, ère [avãdɛrnje, ɛr] (mpl
avant-derniers, fpl **avant-dernières**) adj second to last, penultimate.

avant-garde [avɑ̃gard] (*pl* **avant-gardes**) *nf* - **1.** *MIL* vanguard - **2.** [idées] avant-garde ; **d'~** avant-garde.

avant-goût [avɑ̃gu] (*pl* **avant-goûts**) *nm* foretaste.

avant-hier [avɑ̃tjɛr] *adv* the day before yesterday.

avant-première [avɑ̃prəmjɛr] (*pl* **avant-premières**) *nf* preview ; **présenté en ~** [film, pièce] previewed.

avant-projet [avɑ̃prɔʒɛ] (*pl* **avant-projets**) *nm* draft.

avant-propos [avɑ̃prɔpo] *nm inv* foreword.

avant-veille [avɑ̃vɛj] (*pl* **avant-veilles**) *nf* : **l'~** two days earlier.

avare [avar] <> *nmf* miser <> *adj* miserly ; **être ~ de qqch** *fig* to be sparing with sthg.

avarice [avaris] *nf* avarice.

avarie [avari] *nf* damage (*U*).

avarié, e [avarje] *adj* rotting, bad.

avatar [avatar] *nm* [transformation] metamorphosis.
◆ **avatars** *nmpl* [mésaventures] misfortunes.

avec [avɛk] <> *prép* - **1.** [gén] with ; **~ respect** with respect, respectfully ; **c'est fait ~ du cuir** it's made from leather ; **et ~ ça?, et ~ ceci?** *fam* [dans un magasin] anything else? - **2.** [vis-à-vis de] to, towards *Br*, toward *Am* <> *adv fam* with it/him *etc* ; **tiens mon sac, je ne peux pas courir ~!** hold my bag, I can't run with it!

Ave (Maria) [ave(marja)] *nm inv* Hail Mary.

avenant, e [avnɑ̃, ɑ̃t] *adj* pleasant.
◆ **avenant** *nm* *JUR* additional clause.
◆ **à l'avenant** *loc adv* in the same vein.

avènement [avɛnmɑ̃] *nm* - **1.** [d'un roi] accession - **2.** *fig* [début] advent.

avenir [avnir] *nm* future ; **avoir de l'~** to have a future ; **d'~** [profession, concept] with a future, with prospects.
◆ **à l'avenir** *loc adv* in future.

Avent [avɑ̃] *nm* : **l'~** Advent.

aventure [avɑ̃tyr] *nf* - **1.** [gén] adventure - **2.** [liaison amoureuse] affair - **3.** *loc* : **dire la bonne ~ à qqn** to tell sb's fortune.
◆ **d'aventure** *loc adv* by (any) chance.

aventurer [3] [avɑ̃tyre] *vt* - **1.** [risquer] to risk - **2.** *sout* [remarque] to venture.
◆ **s'aventurer** *vp* to venture (out) ; **s'~ à faire qqch** *fig* to venture to do sthg.

aventureux, euse [avɑ̃tyrø, øz] *adj* - **1.** [personne, vie] adventurous - **2.** [projet] risky.

aventurier, ère [avɑ̃tyrje, ɛr] *nm, f* adventurer.

avenu [avny] *adj m* : **nul et non ~** *JUR* null and void.

avenue [avny] *nf* avenue.

avérer [18] [avere] ◆ **s'avérer** *vp* : **il s'est avéré (être) à la hauteur** he proved (to be) up to it ; **il s'est avéré (être) un musicien accompli** he proved to be an accomplished musician.

averse [avɛrs] *nf* downpour ; **~ de neige** snowflurry.

aversion [avɛrsjɔ̃] *nf* : **~ pour** aversion to, loathing for ; **prendre qqn/qqch en ~** to take an intense dislike to sb/sthg ; **avoir qqn/qqch en ~** to have an aversion to sb/sthg.

averti, e [avɛrti] *adj* - **1.** [expérimenté] experienced - **2.** [initié] : **~ (de)** informed *ou* well-informed (about).

avertir [32] [avɛrtir] *vt* - **1.** [mettre en garde] to warn - **2.** [prévenir] to inform ; **avertissez-moi dès que possible** let me know as soon as possible.

avertissement [avɛrtismɑ̃] *nm* - **1.** [gén] warning - **2.** [avis] notice, notification.

avertisseur, euse [avɛrtisœr, øz] <> *adj* warning (*avant n*) <> *nm* - **1.** [Klaxon] horn - **2.** [d'incendie] alarm.

aveu, x [avø] *nm* confession ; **de l'~ de tout le monde, c'est lui le responsable** everyone agrees that he is responsible ; **passer aux ~x** to make a confession.

aveuglant, e [avœglɑ̃, ɑ̃t] *adj* - **1.** [lumière] blinding - **2.** *fig* [vérité] blindingly obvious.

aveugle [avœgl] <> *nmf* blind person ; **les ~s** the blind <> *adj litt* & *fig* blind.

aveuglement [avœgləmɑ̃] *nm* blindness.

aveuglément [avœglemɑ̃] *adv* blindly.

aveugler [5] [avœgle] *vt* - **1.** *litt* & *fig* [priver de la vue] to blind - **2.** [fenêtre] to board up.
◆ **s'aveugler** *vp* : **s'~ sur qqn** to be blind to sb's faults.

aveuglette [avœglɛt] ◆ **à l'aveuglette** *loc adv* : **marcher à l'~** to grope one's way ; **avancer à l'~** *fig* to be in the dark.

aviateur, trice [avjatœr, tris] *nm, f* aviator.

aviation [avjasjɔ̃] *nf* - **1.** [transport aérien] aviation - **2.** *MIL* airforce.

aviculture [avikyltyr] *nf* [gén] bird-breeding ; [de volailles] poultry farming.

avide [avid] *adj* - **1.** [vorace, cupide] greedy - **2.** [désireux] : **~ (de qqch/de faire qqch)** eager (for sthg/to do sthg).

avidement [avidmɑ̃] *adv* - **1.** [avec appétit, convoitise] greedily - **2.** [avec intérêt] avidly - **3.** [avec passion] eagerly.

avidité [avidite] *nf* - **1.** [voracité, cupidité] greed - **2.** [passion] eagerness.

Avignon [aviɲɔ̃] n Avignon ; **en ~** in Avignon ; **le festival d'~** the Avignon festival.

LE FESTIVAL D'AVIGNON

Founded by Jean Vilar in 1947 and held every summer in and around Avignon, this arts festival is a showcase for new theatre and dance performances. The fringe festival, known as the 'festival off' has grown in renown over the years.

avilir [32] [avilir] vt - **1.** [personne] to degrade - **2.** [monnaie, marchandise] to devalue.

➤ **s'avilir** vp - **1.** [personne] to demean o.s. - **2.** [monnaie, marchandise] to depreciate.

aviné, e [avine] adj - **1.** [personne] inebriated - **2.** [haleine] smelling of alcohol.

avion [avjɔ̃] nm plane, aeroplane, airplane Am ; **en ~** by plane, by air ; **par ~** [courrier] airmail ; **~ de ligne** airliner ; **~ à réaction** jet (plane).

aviron [avirɔ̃] nm - **1.** [rame] oar - **2.** SPORT : **l'~** rowing.

avis [avi] nm - **1.** [opinion] opinion ; **changer d'~** to change one's mind ; **être d'~ que** to be of the opinion that ; **à mon ~** in my opinion ; **les ~ sont partagés** opinion is divided - **2.** [conseil] advice (U) - **3.** [notification] notification, notice ; **sauf ~ contraire** unless otherwise informed ; **jusqu'à nouvel ~** until further notice ; **~ de débit/crédit** debit/credit advice.

avisé, e [avize] adj [sensé] sensible ; **être bien/mal ~ de faire qqch** to be well-advised/ill-advised to do sthg.

aviser [3] [avize] ◇ vt - **1.** [informer] : **~ qqn de qqch** to inform sb of sthg - **2.** sout [apercevoir] to notice ◇ vi to reassess the situation.

➤ **s'aviser** vp - **1.** sout [s'apercevoir] : **s'~ de qqch** to notice sthg ; **s'~ que** to notice (that) - **2.** [oser] : **s'~ de faire qqch** to take it into one's head to do sthg ; **ne t'avise pas de répondre!** don't you dare answer me back!

av. J.-C. (abr de **avant Jésus-Christ**) BC.

avocat, e [avɔka, at] nm, f - **1.** JUR barrister Br, attorney-at-law Am ; **~ d'affaires** commercial lawyer ; **~ de la défense** counsel for the defence Br, defense counsel Am ; **~ général** ≈ counsel for the prosecution Br, prosecuting attorney Am - **2.** [défenseur] : **se faire l'~ de qqch** to champion sthg ; **se faire l'~ du diable** fig to play devil's advocate.

➤ **avocat** nm [fruit] avocado.

avoine [avwan] nf oats (pl).

avoir [1] [avwar] ◇ nm - **1.** [biens] assets (pl) - **2.** [document] credit note ◇ v aux to have ; **j'ai fini** I have finished ; **il a attendu pendant deux heures** he waited for two hours ◇ vt

- **1.** [posséder] to have (got) ; **il a deux enfants/les cheveux bruns** he has (got) two children/brown hair ; **la maison a un grand jardin** the house has (got) a large garden - **2.** [être âgé de] : **il a 20 ans** he is 20 (years old) ; **il a deux ans de plus que son frère** he is two years older than his brother - **3.** [obtenir] to get - **4.** [éprouver] to have ; **~ du chagrin** to feel sorrowful ; **~ de la sympathie pour qqn** to have a liking for sb ; voir aussi **faim**, **peur**, **soif** etc - **5.** loc : **se faire ~** fam to be had ou conned ; **en ~ assez (de qqch/de faire qqch)** to have had enough (of sthg/of doing sthg) ; **j'en ai pour cinq minutes** it'll take me five minutes ; **en ~ après qqn** to have (got) it in for sb.

➤ **avoir à** vi + prép [devoir] : **~ à faire qqch** to have to do sthg ; **tu n'avais pas à lui parler sur ce ton** you had no need to speak to him like that, you shouldn't have spoken to him like that ; **tu n'avais qu'à me demander** you only had to ask me ; **tu n'as qu'à y aller toi-même** just go (there) yourself, why don't you just go (there) yourself?

➤ **il y a** v impers - **1.** [présentatif] there is/are ; **il y a un problème** there's a problem ; **il y a des problèmes** there are (some) problems ; **qu'est-ce qu'il y a?** what's the matter?, what is it? ; **il n'y a qu'à en finir** we'll/you'll etc just have to have done (with it) - **2.** [temporel] : **il y a trois ans** three years ago ; **il y a longtemps de cela** that was a long time ago ; **il y a longtemps qu'il est parti** he left a long time ago.

avoisinant, e [avwazinɑ̃, ɑ̃t] adj - **1.** [lieu, maison] neighbouring Br, neighboring Am - **2.** [sens, couleur] similar.

Avoriaz [avɔrjaz] n : **le festival d'~** festival of science fiction and horror films held annually at Avoriaz in the French Alps.

avortement [avɔrtəmɑ̃] nm - **1.** MÉD abortion - **2.** fig [d'un projet] abandonment.

avorter [3] [avɔrte] vi - **1.** MÉD : **(se faire) ~** to have an abortion - **2.** [échouer] to fail.

avorton [avɔrtɔ̃] nm péj [nabot] runt.

avouer [6] [avwe] vt - **1.** [confesser] to confess (to) - **2.** [reconnaître] to admit - **3.** [déclarer] to avow.

➤ **s'avouer** vp to admit (to being) ; **s'~ vaincu** to admit defeat.

avril [avril] nm April ; voir aussi **septembre**.

AVS (abr de **assurance vieillesse et survivants**) nf Swiss pension scheme.

axe [aks] nm - **1.** GÉOM & PHYS axis - **2.** [de roue] axle - **3.** [route] : **les grands ~s** the major roads ; **~ rouge** section of the Paris road system where parking is prohibited to avoid congestion - **4.** [prolongement] : **dans l'~ de** directly in line with - **5.** [de politique, de parti] line.

axer [3] [akse] vt : ~ **qqch sur qqch** to centre Br ou center Am sthg on sthg ; ~ **qqch autour de qqch** to centre Br ou center Am sthg around sthg.

axial, e, aux [aksjal, o] adj axial.

axiome [aksjom] nm axiom.

ayant [εjɑ̃] ppr ▷ **avoir**.

ayant droit [εjɑ̃drwa] (pl **ayants droit**) nm beneficiary.

ayatollah [ajatɔla] nm ayatollah.

azalée [azale] nf azalea.

azimut [azimyt] ➡ **tous azimuts** loc adj [défense, offensive] all-out.

azote [azɔt] nm nitrogen.

aztèque [aztεk] adj Aztec.
➡ **Aztèque** nmf Aztec.

azur [azyr] nm littéraire - **1.** [couleur] azure - **2.** [ciel] skies (pl).

azyme [azim] ▷ **pain**.

B

b, B [be] nm inv b, B.
➡ **B** (abr de **bien**) good grade (as assessment on schoolwork), ≃ B.

BA (abr de **bonne action**) nf fam good deed.

baba [baba] ◇ nm - **1.** CULIN : ~ **(au rhum)** rum baba - **2.** [hippie] person practising hippie life-style and values ◇ adj inv fam : **en rester ~** to be flabbergasted.

babeurre [babœr] nm buttermilk.

babil [babil] nm [d'enfant] babble, babbling.

babiller [3] [babije] vi to babble.

babines [babin] nfpl chops ; **se lécher les ~** fig to lick one's lips.

babiole [babjɔl] nf - **1.** [objet] knick-knack - **2.** [broutille] trifling matter.

bâbord [babɔr] nm port ; **à ~** to port, on the port side.

babouin [babwɛ̃] nm baboon.

baby-foot [babifut] nm inv table football.

baby-sitter [bebisitœr] (pl **baby-sitters**) nmf baby-sitter.

baby-sitting [bebisitiŋ] (pl **baby-sittings**) nm baby-sitting ; **faire du ~** to baby-sit.

bac [bak] nm - **1.** = **baccalauréat** - **2.** [bateau] ferry - **3.** [de réfrigérateur] : ~ **à glace** ice tray ; ~ **à légumes** vegetable drawer - **4.** [d'évier] sink.

baccalauréat [bakalɔrea] nm school-leaving examinations leading to university entrance qualification.

bâche [baʃ] nf [toile] tarpaulin.

bachelier, ère [baʃəlje, εr] nm, f holder of the baccalauréat.

bachot [baʃo] vieilli = **baccalauréat**.

bachotage [baʃɔtaʒ] nm cramming.

bacille [basil] nm bacillus.

bâcler [3] [bakle] vt to botch.

bacon [bekɔn] nm bacon.

bactéricide [bakterisid] adj bactericidal.

bactérie [bakteri] nf bacterium.

badaud, e [bado, od] nm, f gawper.

badge [badʒ] nm badge.

badger [badʒe] vi [en arrivant] to clock in ou on ; [en sortant] to clock out ou off.

badigeon [badiʒɔ̃] nm whitewash.

badigeonner [3] [badiʒɔne] vt - **1.** [mur] to whitewash - **2.** [plaie] to paint - **3.** [tarte, pain] to brush.

badin, e [badɛ̃, in] adj playful.

badinage [badinaʒ] nm sout joking.

badiner [3] [badine] vi sout to joke ; **ne pas ~ avec qqch** not to treat sthg lightly.

badminton [badmintɔn] nm badminton.

BAFA, Bafa [bafa] (abr de **brevet d'aptitude aux fonctions d'animation**) nm diploma for youth leaders and workers.

baffe [baf] nf fam slap.

baffle [bafl] nm speaker.

bafouer [6] [bafwe] *vt* - **1.** [principe] to trample upon - **2.** [personne] to ridicule.

bafouille [bafuj] *nf fam* letter.

bafouiller [3] [bafuje] *vi* & *vt* to mumble.

bâfrer [3] [bafre] *fam* ⟨> *vi* to guzzle ⟨> *vt* to wolf down.

bagage [bagaʒ] *nm* - **1.** *(gén pl)* [valises, sacs] luggage *(U)*, baggage *(U)* ; **faire ses ~s** to pack ; **~s à main** hand luggage ; **plier ~** to pack one's bags (and leave) - **2.** [connaissances] (fund of) knowledge ; **~ intellectuel/ culturel** intellectual/cultural baggage.

bagagiste [bagaʒist] *nmf* [chargement des avions] baggage handler ; [à l'hôtel etc] porter ; [fabricant] travel goods manufacturer.

bagarre [bagar] *nf* brawl, fight ; **chercher la ~** *fam* to look for a fight.

bagarrer [3] [bagare] *vi* to fight.
➤ **se bagarrer** *vp* to fight.

bagarreur, euse [bagarœr, øz] ⟨> *adj* aggressive, who likes a fight ⟨> *nm, f fig* fighter.

bagatelle [bagatɛl] *nf* - **1.** [objet] trinket - **2.** [somme d'argent] : **acheter qqch pour une ~** to buy sthg for next to nothing ; **la ~ de X francs** *iron* a mere X francs - **3.** [chose futile] trifle - **4.** [sexe] : **être porté sur la ~** to be quite a one for the ladies.

bagnard [baɲar] *nm* convict.

bagne [baɲ] *nm* - **1.** [prison] labour *Br ou* labor *Am* camp - **2.** [sentence] hard labour *Br ou* labor *Am* ; **c'est le ~ ici** *fig* it's slave labour *Br ou* labor *Am* here.

bagnole [baɲɔl] *nf fam* car.

bagou(t) [bagu] *nm* patter ; **avoir du ~** to have the gift of the gab.

bague [bag] *nf* - **1.** [bijou, anneau] ring ; **~ de fiançailles** engagement ring - **2.** [de cigare] band - **3.** *TECH* : **~ de serrage** clip.

baguer [3] [bage] *vt* [oiseau, arbre] to ring.

baguette [bagɛt] *nf* - **1.** [pain] French stick - **2.** [petit bâton] stick ; **~ magique** magic wand ; **~ de tambour** drumstick ; **mener qqn à la ~** to rule sb with a rod of iron - **3.** [pour manger] chopstick - **4.** [de chef d'orchestre] baton.

Bahamas [baamas] *nfpl* : **les ~** the Bahamas ; **aux ~** in the Bahamas.

bahut [bay] *nm* - **1.** [buffet] sideboard - **2.** [coffre] chest - **3.** *arg scol* [lycée] secondary school - **4.** *fam péj* [voiture] old banger.

baie [bɛ] *nf* - **1.** [fruit] berry - **2.** *GÉOGR* bay - **3.** [fenêtre] : **~ vitrée** picture window.

baignade [bɛɲad] *nf* [action] bathing *(U)* Br, swimming *(U)* ; '**~ interdite**' 'no bathing/ swimming'.

baigner [4] [beɲe] ⟨> *vt* - **1.** [donner un bain à] to bath - **2.** [tremper, remplir] to bathe ; **baigné de soleil** bathed in sunlight ⟨> *vi* : **~ dans le luxe** to be surrounded by wealth ; **~ dans son sang** to lie in a pool of blood ; **les tomates baignaient dans l'huile** the tomatoes were swimming in oil ; **tout/ça baigne** *fam* everything's/it's great.
➤ **se baigner** *vp* - **1.** [dans la mer] to go swimming, to swim - **2.** [dans une baignoire] to have a bath.

baigneur, euse [beɲœr, øz] *nm, f* bather *Br*, swimmer.
➤ **baigneur** *nm* [poupée] baby doll.

baignoire [beɲwar] *nf* bath.

bail [baj] *(pl* **baux** [bo]) *nm* - **1.** *JUR* lease ; **renouveler un ~** to renew a lease ; **~ à loyer** residential lease ; **~ reconductible** renewable lease - **2.** *loc* : **ça fait un ~ que** *fam* it's ages since.

bâillement [bajmã] *nm* yawning *(U)*, yawn.

bâiller [3] [baje] *vi* - **1.** [personne] to yawn - **2.** [vêtement] to gape.

bailleur, eresse [bajœr, bajrɛs] *nm, f* lessor ; **~ de fonds** backer.

bâillon [bajɔ̃] *nm* gag.

bâillonner [3] [bajɔne] *vt* to gag.

bain [bɛ̃] *nm* - **1.** [gén] bath ; **faire couler un ~** to run a bath ; **prendre un ~** to have *ou* take a bath ; **~ moussant** foaming bath oil ; **~ à remous** spa bath, whirlpool bath ; **~s-douches** public baths - **2.** [dans mer, piscine] swim ; **~ de mer** sea bathing *Br ou* swimming - **3.** [de partie du corps] : **~ de bouche** mouthwash ; **~ de pieds** foot-bath - **4.** *loc* : **se mettre dans le ~** to get the hang of things ; **prendre un ~ de foule** to go on a walkabout ; **prendre un ~ de soleil** to sunbathe.

bain-marie [bɛ̃mari] *(pl* **bains-marie**) *nm* : **au ~** in a bain-marie.

baïonnette [bajɔnɛt] *nf* - **1.** [arme] bayonet - **2.** *ÉLECTR* bayonet fitting.

baise [bɛz] *nf vulg* fucking.

baisemain [bɛzmɛ̃] *nm* : **faire le ~ à qqn** to kiss sb's hand.

baiser [4] [beze] ⟨> *nm* kiss ⟨> *vt vulg* [avoir des relations sexuelles avec] to fuck ⟨> *vi vulg* to fuck.

baisse [bɛs] *nf* - **1.** [gén] : **~ (de)** drop (in), fall (in) ; **en ~** falling ; **la tendance est à la ~** there is a downward trend - **2.** *INFORM* : **~ de tension** brownout.

baisser [4] [bese] ⟨> *vt* [gén] to lower ; [radio] to turn down ; **~ le ton** to modify one's tone ; **~ les yeux** to look down ⟨> *vi* - **1.** [descendre] to go down ; **le jour baisse** it's getting dark - **2.** [santé, vue] to fail - **3.** [prix] to fall - **4.** [s'affaiblir - malade] to grow weaker ; [- talent] to decline.

◆ **se baisser** *vp* to bend down.

bajoues [baʒu] *nfpl* jowls.

bakchich [bakʃiʃ] *nm* baksheesh.

bal [bal] *nm* ball ; ~ **masqué/costumé** masked/fancy-dress ball ; ~ **populaire** *ou* **musette** *popular old-fashioned dance accompanied by accordion.*

BAL, Bal (*abr de* **boîte aux lettres (électronique)**) *nf* E-mail.

balade [balad] *nf fam* stroll ; **faire une** ~ to go for a stroll.

balader [3] [balade] ◇ *vt* - **1.** *fam* [traîner avec soi] to trail around - **2.** [emmener en promenade] to take for a walk ◇ *vi* : **envoyer** ~ **qqn** to send sb packing.

◆ **se balader** *vp fam* - **1.** [se promener - à pied] to go for a walk ; [- en voiture] to go for a drive - **2.** [traîner] to be kicking around.

baladeur, euse [baladœr, øz] *adj* wandering.

◆ **baladeur** *nm* personal stereo.

◆ **baladeuse** *nf* inspection lamp.

balafre [balafr] *nf* - **1.** [blessure] gash - **2.** [cicatrice] scar.

balafré, e [balafre] *adj* scarred.

balai [balɛ] *nm* - **1.** [de nettoyage] broom, brush ; ~ **mécanique** carpet sweeper - **2.** [d'essuie-glace] wiper blade - **3.** *fam* [an] : **il a 50 ~s** he's 50 years old.

balai-brosse [balɛbrɔs] (*pl* **balais-brosses**) *nm* (long-handled) scrubbing *Br ou* scrub *Am* brush.

balaie, balaies ⊳ **balayer**.

balance [balɑ̃s] *nf* - **1.** [instrument] scales (*pl*) ; **faire pencher la** ~ *fig* to tip the balance - **2.** *COMM* & *POLIT* balance ; ~ **des paiements/ commerciale** balance of payments/of trade ; ~ **des pouvoirs** balance of power.

◆ **Balance** *nf ASTROL* Libra ; **être Balance** to be (a) Libra.

balancement [balɑ̃smɑ̃] *nm* [mouvement - d'objet, de hanches] swaying ; [- de bras, de jambe] swinging ; [- de navire] motion.

balancer [16] [balɑ̃se] ◇ *vt* - **1.** [bouger] to swing - **2.** *fam* [lancer] to chuck - **3.** *fam* [jeter] to chuck out ◇ *vi* - **1.** *sout* [hésiter] to waver - **2.** [osciller] to swing.

◆ **se balancer** *vp* - **1.** [sur une chaise] to rock backwards and forwards - **2.** [sur une balançoire] to swing - **3.** *fam* : **se** ~ **de qqch** not to give a damn about sthg.

balancier [balɑ̃sje] *nm* - **1.** [de pendule] pendulum - **2.** [de funambule] pole.

balançoire [balɑ̃swar] *nf* [suspendue] swing ; [bascule] see-saw.

balayage [balɛjaʒ] *nm* [gén] sweeping ; *TECHNOL* scanning.

balayer [11] [balɛje] *vt* - **1.** [nettoyer] to sweep - **2.** [chasser] to sweep away - **3.** *fig* [écarter] to brush aside - **4.** [suj : radar] to scan ; [suj : projecteurs] to sweep (across).

balayette [balɛjɛt] *nf* small brush.

balayeur, euse [balɛjœr, øz] *nm, f* roadsweeper *Br*, streetsweeper *Am*.

◆ **balayeuse** *nf* [machine] roadsweeper.

balayures [balɛjyr] *nfpl* sweepings.

balbutiement [balbysimɑ̃] *nm* - **1.** [bredouillement] stammering - **2.** *fig* : ~**s** [débuts] infancy (*U*).

balbutier [9] [balbysje] ◇ *vi* - **1.** [bafouiller] to stammer - **2.** *fig* [débuter] to be in its infancy ◇ *vt* [bafouiller] to stammer (out).

balcon [balkɔ̃] *nm* - **1.** [de maison - terrasse] balcony ; [- balustrade] parapet - **2.** [de théâtre, de cinéma] circle.

balconnet [balkɔnɛ] *nm* : **soutien-gorge à** ~ half-cup bra.

baldaquin [baldakɛ̃] *nm* - **1.** *ARCHIT* canopy - **2.** ⊳ lit.

Bâle [bal] *n* Basel.

Baléares [balear] *nfpl* : **les** ~ the Balearic Islands ; **aux** ~ in the Balearic Islands.

baleine [balɛn] *nf* - **1.** [mammifère] whale - **2.** [de corset] whalebone - **3.** [de parapluie] rib.

baleinier, ère [balɛnje, ɛr] *adj* whaling (*avant n*).

◆ **baleinier** *nm* whaler.

◆ **baleinière** *nf* [bateau] whaler.

Bali [bali] *n* Bali ; **à** ~ in Bali.

balinais, e [balinɛ, ɛz] *adj* Balinese.

◆ **Balinais, e** *nm, f* Balinese (*inv*).

balisage [balizaʒ] *nm* - **1.** [action] marking out - **2.** [signaux - NAVIG] markers (*pl*), marker buoys (*pl*) ; [- AÉRON] runway lights (*pl*) ; [- AUTOM] road signs (*pl*).

balise [baliz] *nf* - **1.** *NAVIG* marker (buoy) - **2.** *AÉRON* runway light - **3.** *AUTOM* road sign - **4.** *INFORM* tag.

baliser [3] [balize] ◇ *vt* to mark out ◇ *vi fam* to be scared stiff.

balistique [balistik] ◇ *nf* ballistics (*U*) ◇ *adj* ballistic.

balivernes [balivɛrn] *nfpl* nonsense (*U*).

Balkans [balkɑ̃] *nmpl* : **les** ~ the Balkans.

ballade [balad] *nf* ballad.

ballant, e [balɑ̃, ɑ̃t] *adj* : **les bras** ~**s** arms dangling.

◆ **ballant** *nm* [mouvement] : **avoir du** ~ to sway.

ballast [balast] *nm* - **1.** [chemin de fer] ballast - **2.** *NAVIG* ballast tank.

balle [bal] *nf* - **1.** [d'arme à feu] bullet ; ~ **perdue** stray bullet - **2.** [de jeu] ball ; ~ **de ping-pong/ tennis** table-tennis/tennis ball - **3.** [de marchandises] bale - **4.** *fam* [argent] franc - **5.** *loc* : **se renvoyer la** ~ to pass the buck ; **saisir la** ~ **au bond** to jump at the chance.

ballerine [balrin] *nf* - **1.** [danseuse] ballerina - **2.** [chaussure] ballet shoe.

ballet [balɛ] *nm* [gén] ballet ; *fig* [activité intense] to-ing and fro-ing.

ballon [balɔ̃] *nm* - **1.** *JEU & SPORT* ball ; ~ **de football** football ; **le** ~ **ovale** rugby ; **le** ~ **rond** football - **2.** [montgolfière, de fête] balloon - **3.** [verre de vin] : ~ **de rouge** glass of red (wine).

ballonné, e [balɔne] *adj* : **avoir le ventre** ~, **être** ~ to be bloated.

ballot [balo] *nm* - **1.** [de marchandises] bundle - **2.** *vieilli* [imbécile] twit.

ballottage [balɔtaʒ] *nm POLIT* second ballot ; **en** ~ standing for a second ballot.

ballotter [3] [balɔte] <> *vt* to toss about ; **être ballotté entre** *fig* to be torn between <> *vi* [chose] to roll around.

ballottine [balɔtin] *nf* : ~ **de foie gras** type of galantine made with foie gras.

ball-trap [baltrap] *nm* clay pigeon shooting.

balluchon = baluchon.

balnéaire [balneɛr] *adj* : **station** ~ seaside resort.

balourd, e [balur, urd] <> *adj* clumsy <> *nm, f* clumsy idiot.

balte [balt] *adj* Baltic.
◆ **Balte** *nmf* native of the Baltic states.

Baltique [baltik] *nf* : **la** ~ the Baltic (Sea).

baluchon, balluchon [balyʃɔ̃] *nm* bundle ; **faire son** ~ *fam* to pack one's bags (and leave).

balustrade [balystrad] *nf* - **1.** [de terrasse] balustrade - **2.** [rambarde] guardrail.

bambin [bɑ̃bɛ̃] *nm* kiddie.

bambou [bɑ̃bu] *nm* - **1.** [plante] bamboo ; **pousse de** ~ bamboo shoot - **2.** [matériau] : **en** ~ bamboo (avant n).

bamboula [bɑ̃bula] *nf* : **faire la** ~ *fam* to have a wild time.

ban [bɑ̃] *nm* - **1.** [de mariage] : **publier** *OU* **afficher les** ~**s** to publish *OU* display the banns - **2.** [applaudissements] round of applause - **3.** *loc* : **être/mettre qqn au** ~ **de la société** to be outlawed/to outlaw sb (from society) ; **le** ~ **et l'arrière-**~ the whole lot of them.

banal, e, als [banal] *adj* commonplace, banal ; **pas** *OU* **peu** ~ unusual.

banaliser [3] [banalize] *vt* : **voiture banalisée** unmarked police car.
◆ **se banaliser** *vp* to become commonplace.

banalité [banalite] *nf* - **1.** [caractère banal] banality - **2.** [cliché] commonplace ; **échanger des** ~**s** to make small-talk.

banane [banan] *nf* - **1.** [fruit] banana - **2.** [sac] bum-bag - **3.** [coiffure] quiff.

bananier, ère [bananje, ɛr] *adj* banana (avant n) ; **république bananière** banana republic.
◆ **bananier** *nm* - **1.** [arbre] banana tree - **2.** [cargo] banana boat.

banc [bɑ̃] *nm* [siège] bench ; **le** ~ **des accusés** *JUR* the dock ; ~ **d'essai** test-bed ; **être au** ~ **d'essai** *fig* to be at the test stage ; ~ **des joueurs** *HOCKEY* players' bench ; ~ **de neige** *Can* snowbank ; ~ **des pénalités** *OU* **des punitions** *HOCKEY* penalty box ; ~ **de poissons** shoal of fish ; ~ **de sable** sandbank.

bancaire [bɑ̃kɛr] *adj* bank (avant n), banking (avant n).

bancal, e, als [bɑ̃kal] *adj* - **1.** [personne] lame - **2.** [meuble] wobbly - **3.** [théorie, idée] unsound.

bandage [bɑ̃daʒ] *nm* [de blessé] bandage.

bande [bɑ̃d] *nf* - **1.** [de tissu, de papier] strip ; ~ **dessinée** comic strip - **2.** [bandage] bandage ; ~ **Velpeau**® crepe bandage - **3.** [de billard] cushion ; **par la** ~ *fig* by a roundabout route - **4.** [groupe] band ; ~ **de ...!** *fam* bunch of...! ; **en** ~ in a group ; **faire** ~ **à part** to keep to o.s. - **5.** [pellicule de film] film - **6.** [d'enregistrement] tape ; ~ **audionumérique** DAT tape ; ~ **magnétique** (magnetic) tape ; ~ **originale** *CIN* original soundtrack ; ~ **vidéo** video (tape) - **7.** [voie] : ~ **d'arrêt d'urgence** hard shoulder - **8.** *RADIO* : ~ **de fréquence** waveband - **9.** *NAVIG* : **donner de la** ~ to list.

bande-annonce [bɑ̃danɔ̃s] (*pl* **bandes-annonces**) *nf* trailer.

bandeau [bɑ̃do] *nm* - **1.** [sur les yeux] blindfold - **2.** [dans les cheveux] headband.

bandelette [bɑ̃dlɛt] *nf* strip (of cloth).

bander [3] [bɑ̃de] <> *vt* - **1.** *MÉD* to bandage ; ~ **les yeux de qqn** to blindfold sb - **2.** [arc] to draw back - **3.** [muscle] to flex <> *vi* *vulg* to have a hard-on.

banderole [bɑ̃drɔl] *nf* streamer.

bande-son [bɑ̃dsɔ̃] (*pl* **bandes-son**) *nf* soundtrack.

bandit [bɑ̃di] *nm* - **1.** [voleur] bandit - **2.** [personne sans scrupules] crook.

banditisme [bɑ̃ditism] *nm* serious crime.

bandoulière [bɑ̃duljɛr] *nf* bandolier ; **en ~** across the shoulder.

bangladais, e [bɑ̃ɡladɛ, ɛz] *adj* Bangladeshi.

◆ **Bangladais, e** *nm, f* Bangladeshi.

Bangladesh [bɑ̃ɡladɛʃ] *nm* : **le ~** Bangladesh ; **au ~** in Bangladesh.

banlieue [bɑ̃ljø] *nf* suburbs *(pl)* ; **en ~** in the suburbs ; **la grande ~** the outer suburbs ; **la ~ parisienne** the Paris suburbs ; **réseau de ~** commuter *ou* suburban network.

banlieusard, e [bɑ̃ljøzar, ard] *nm, f person living in the suburbs.*

bannière [banjɛr] *nf* [étendard] banner.

bannir [32] [banir] *vt* : **~ qqn/qqch (de)** to banish sb/sthg (from).

banque [bɑ̃k] *nf* - **1.** [activité] banking - **2.** [établissement, au jeu] bank ; **Banque centrale européenne** European Central Bank ; **Banque de France** Bank of France - **3.** INFORM : **~ de données** data bank - **4.** MÉD : **~ d'organes/du sang/du sperme** organ/blood/sperm bank.

banqueroute [bɑ̃krut] *nf* bankruptcy ; **faire ~** to go bankrupt.

banquet [bɑ̃kɛ] *nm* (celebration) dinner ; [de gala] banquet.

banquette [bɑ̃kɛt] *nf* seat ; **~ arrière** back seat.

banquier, ère [bɑ̃kje, ɛr] *nm, f* banker.

banquise [bɑ̃kiz] *nf* ice field.

baobab [baɔbab] *nm* baobab.

baptême [batɛm] *nm* - **1.** RELIG baptism, christening - **2.** [première fois] : **~ de l'air** maiden flight ; **~ du feu** baptism of fire.

baptiser [3] [batize] *vt* to baptize, to christen.

baptismal, e, aux [batismal, o] *adj* baptismal ; ▷ **fonts.**

baquet [bakɛ] *nm* - **1.** [cuve] tub - **2.** [siège] bucket seat.

bar [bar] *nm* - **1.** [café, unité de pression] bar ; **~ à café** *Helv* coffee bar ; **~ à vin** wine bar - **2.** [poisson] bass.

baragouiner [3] [baraɡwine] *vt fam* - **1.** [langue] : **il baragouine le français** he speaks broken French - **2.** [bredouiller] to gabble.

baraka [baraka] *nf fam* : **avoir la ~** to be lucky.

baraque [barak] *nf* - **1.** [cabane] hut - **2.** *fam* [maison] house - **3.** [de forain] stall, stand.

baraqué, e [barake] *adj fam* well-built.

baraquement [barakmɑ̃] *nm* camp *(of huts for refugees, workers etc).*

baratin [baratɛ̃] *nm fam* smooth talk ; **faire du ~ à qqn** to sweet-talk sb.

baratiner [3] [baratine] *fam* ◇ *vt* [femme] to chat up ; [client] to give one's sales pitch to ◇ *vi* to be a smooth talker.

Barbade [barbad] *nf* : **la ~** Barbados ; **à la ~** in Barbados.

barbant, e [barbɑ̃, ɑ̃t] *adj fam* deadly dull *ou* boring.

barbare [barbar] ◇ *nm* barbarian ◇ *adj* - **1.** *péj* [non civilisé] barbarous - **2.** [cruel] barbaric.

barbarisme [barbarism] *nm* GRAM barbarism.

barbe [barb] *nf* beard ; **se laisser pousser la ~** to grow a beard ; **~ à papa** candy floss *Br*, cotton candy *Am* ; **faire qqch au nez et à la ~ de qqn** *fig* to do sthg right under sb's nose ; **quelle** *ou* **la ~!** *fam* what a drag!

barbecue [barbəkju] *nm* barbecue.

barbelé, e [barbəle] *adj* barbed ; **fil de fer ~** barbed wire.

◆ **barbelé** *nm* barbed wire *(U).*

barber [3] [barbe] *vt fam* to bore stiff.

◆ **se barber** *vp fam* to be bored stiff.

barbiche [barbiʃ] *nf* goatee (beard).

barbiturique [barbityrik] *nm* barbiturate.

barboter [3] [barbɔte] ◇ *vi* to paddle ◇ *vt fam* to nick.

barboteuse [barbɔtøz] *nf* romper-suit.

barbouillé, -e [barbuje] *adj* : **être ~, avoir l'estomac ~** to feel sick.

barbouiller [3] [barbuje] *vt* - **1.** [salir] : **~ qqch (de)** to smear sthg (with) - **2.** *péj* [peindre] to daub - **3.** *fam* [écrire sur] to scribble on.

barbu, e [barby] *adj* bearded.

◆ **barbu** *nm* bearded man.

◆ **barbue** *nf* [poisson] brill.

barda [barda] *nm* - **1.** *arg mil* kit - **2.** *fam* [attirail] gear ; **avec tout son ~** with all his/her gear.

barde [bard] ◇ *nm* [poète] bard ◇ *nf* CULIN bacon, bard.

bardé, e [barde] *adj* : **il est ~ de diplômes** he's got heaps of diplomas.

barder [3] [barde] ◇ *vt* CULIN to bard ◇ *vi fam* : **ça va ~** there'll be trouble.

barème [barɛm] *nm* [de référence] table ; [de salaires] scale.

barge [barʒ] *nf* [bateau] barge.

baril [baril] *nm* barrel ; **un ~ de pétrole** a barrel of oil.

barillet [barijɛ] *nm* - **1.** [petit baril] cask - **2.** [de revolver, de serrure] cylinder.

bariolé, e [barjɔle] *adj* multicoloured *Br*, multicolored *Am*.

barjo(t) [barʒo] *adj inv fam* nuts.

barmaid [barmɛd] *nf* barmaid.

barman [barman] (*pl* **barmans** OU **barmen** [barmɛn]) *nm* barman.

baromètre [barɔmɛtr] *nm* barometer.

baron, onne [barɔ̃, ɔn] *nm, f* baron (*f* baroness).

▸ **baron** *nm* [magnat] baron.

baroque [barɔk] ⟨> *nm* ART : **le ~** the Baroque style ⟨> *adj* - **1.** [style] baroque - **2.** [bizarre] weird.

baroud [barud] *nm* : **~ d'honneur** last stand.

barque [bark] *nf* small boat ; **savoir mener sa ~** *fig* to be well-organized.

barquette [barkɛt] *nf* - **1.** [tartelette] pastry boat - **2.** [récipient - de fruits] punnet ; [- de frites] carton ; [- de crème glacée] tub.

barrage [baraʒ] *nm* - **1.** [de rue] roadblock - **2.** CONSTR dam.

barre [bar] *nf* - **1.** [gén & JUR] bar ; **~ fixe** GYM high bar ; **~ des témoins** JUR witness box *Br* OU stand *Am* ; **c'est le coup de ~** *fig* it's a rip-off ; **avoir un coup de ~** *fig* to be shattered - **2.** NAVIG helm ; **être à la ~** NAVIG & *fig* to be at the helm - **3.** [trait] stroke - **4.** INFORM : **~ d'espacement** space bar ; **~ de menu** menu bar ; **~ d'outils** tool bar.

barreau [baro] *nm* bar ; **le ~** JUR the Bar.

barrer [3] [bare] *vt* - **1.** [rue, route] to block - **2.** [mot, phrase] to cross out - **3.** [bateau] to steer.

▸ **se barrer** *vp fam* to clear off.

barrette [barɛt] *nf* [pince à cheveux] (hair) slide *Br*, barrette *Am*.

barreur, euse [barœr, øz] *nm, f* NAVIG helmsman ; [à l'aviron] cox.

barricade [barikad] *nf* barricade ; **monter sur les ~s** *fig* to man the barricades.

barricader [3] [barikade] *vt* to barricade.

▸ **se barricader** *vp* to barricade o.s. ; **se ~ chez soi** to shut o.s. away (at home).

barrière [barjɛr] *nf* *litt* & *fig* barrier ; **~ de dégel** ban on heavy lorries on certain roads during a thaw.

barrique [barik] *nf* barrel.

barrir [32] [barir] *vi* to trumpet.

baryton [baritɔ̃] *nm* baritone.

bas, basse [ba, baz *devant nm commençant par voyelle ou h muet*, bas] *adj* - **1.** [gén] low - **2.** *péj* [vil] base, low - **3.** MUS bass.

▸ **bas** ⟨> *nm* - **1.** [partie inférieure] bottom, lower part ; **avoir/connaître des hauts et des ~** to have/go through ups and downs - **2.** [vêtement] stocking ; **~ de laine** woollen *Br* OU woolen *Am* stocking ; *fig* nest egg ⟨> *adv* low ; **à ~ ...!** down with ...! ; **parler ~** to speak in a low voice, to speak softly ; **mettre ~** [animal] to give birth.

▸ **en bas** *loc adv* at the bottom ; [dans une maison] downstairs.

▸ **en bas de** *loc prép* at the bottom of ; **attendre qqn en ~ de chez lui** to wait for sb downstairs.

▸ **bas de gamme** ⟨> *adj* downmarket ⟨> *nm* bottom of the range.

basalte [bazalt] *nm* basalt.

basané, e [bazane] *adj* tanned.

bas-bleu [bablø] (*pl* **bas-bleus**) *nm* *péj* bluestocking.

bas-côté [bakote] (*pl* **bas-côtés**) *nm* [de route] verge.

bascule [baskyl] *nf* - **1.** [balance] weighing machine - **2.** [balançoire] seesaw.

basculer [3] [baskyle] ⟨> *vi* to fall over, to overbalance ; [benne] to tip up ; **~ dans qqch** *fig* to tip over into sthg ⟨> *vt* to tip up, to tilt.

base [baz] *nf* - **1.** [partie inférieure] base ; **la ~** [d'entreprise, de syndicat] the rank and file - **2.** [principe fondamental] basis ; **à ~ de** based on ; **de ~** basic ; **une boisson à ~ d'orange** an orange-based drink ; **sur la ~ de** on the basis of - **3.** INFORM : **~ de données** database - **4.** [cosmétique] : **~ de maquillage** make-up base - **5.** *Can* : **~ de plein air** outdoor recreation area.

base-ball [bɛzbol] (*pl* **base-balls**) *nm* baseball.

baser [3] [baze] *vt* to base ; **~ qqch sur** *fig* to base sthg on.

▸ **se baser** *vp* : **sur quoi vous basez-vous pour affirmer cela?** what are you basing this statement on?

bas-fond [bafɔ̃] (*pl* **bas-fonds**) *nm* [de l'océan] shallow.

▸ **bas-fonds** *nmpl* *fig* - **1.** [de la société] dregs - **2.** [quartiers pauvres] slums.

basilic [bazilik] *nm* [plante] basil.

basilique [bazilik] *nf* basilica.

basique [bazik] *adj* basic.

basket [baskɛt] ⟨> *nm* = **basket-ball** ⟨> *nf* [chaussure] trainer *Br*, sneaker *Am* ; **lâche-moi les ~s!** *fam* *fig* get off my back!

basket-ball [baskɛtbol] *nm* basketball.

basmati [basmati] *nm* basmati (rice).

basque [bask] ⟨> *adj* Basque ; **le Pays ~** the Basque country ⟨> *nm* [langue] Basque ⟨> *nf* [vêtement] tail (*of coat*) ; **être toujours pendu aux ~s de qqn** *fam* *fig* to be always tagging along after sb.

▸ **Basque** *nmf* Basque.

bas-relief [barəljɛf] (*pl* **bas-reliefs**) *nm* bas-relief.

basse [bas] ⬦ *adj* ⬦ **bas** ⬦ *nf* MUS bass.

basse-cour [baskur] (*pl* **basses-cours**) *nf* - **1.** [volaille] poultry - **2.** [partie de ferme] farmyard.

bassement [basmɑ̃] *adv* despicably ; être ~ intéressé to be motivated by petty self-interest.

bassesse [basɛs] *nf* - **1.** [mesquinerie] baseness, meanness - **2.** [action vile] despicable act.

basset [basɛ] *nm* basset hound.

bassin [basɛ̃] *nm* - **1.** [cuvette] bowl - **2.** [pièce d'eau] (ornamental) pond - **3.** [de piscine] : petit/grand ~ children's/main pool - **4.** ANAT pelvis - **5.** GÉOL basin ; ~ houiller coalfield ; le Bassin parisien the Paris basin.

bassine [basin] *nf* bowl, basin.

bassiner [3] [basine] *vt* - **1.** [humecter] to bathe - **2.** *fam* [importuner] to bore.

bassiste [basist] *nmf* bass player.

basson [basɔ̃] *nm* [instrument] bassoon ; [personne] bassoonist.

bastide [bastid] *nf traditional farmhouse or country house in southern France ; walled town (in south-west France).*

Bastille [bastij] *nf* : **la prise de la ~** the storming of the Bastille.

BASTILLE

A state prison, the Bastille fell to the people of Paris on 14 July 1789 - today celebrated as Bastille Day. The square where the Bastille once stood is now the home of the new Paris opera house, known as 'l'Opéra-Bastille'. There are many restaurants and bars around Bastille making it a popular night spot.

---

bastingage [bastɛ̃gaʒ] *nm* (ship's) rail.

bastion [bastjɔ̃] *nm litt* & *fig* bastion.

baston [bastɔ̃] *nf tfam* punch-up.

bas-ventre [bavɑ̃tr] (*pl* **bas-ventres**) *nm* lower abdomen.

bât [ba] *nm* packsaddle ; **c'est là que le ~ blesse** *fig* that's his/her *etc* weak point.

bataille [bataj] *nf* - **1.** MIL battle - **2.** [bagarre] fight - **3.** [jeu de cartes] ≃ beggar-my-neighbour - **4.** *loc* : **en ~** [cheveux] dishevelled *Br*, disheveled *Am*.

batailler [3] [bataje] *vi* : ~ **pour qqch/pour faire qqch** to fight for sthg/to do sthg.

bataillon [batajɔ̃] *nm* MIL battalion ; *fig* horde.

bâtard, e [batar, ard] ⬦ *adj* - **1.** [enfant] illegitimate - **2.** *péj* [style, solution] hybrid ⬦ *nm, f* illegitimate child.

➤ **bâtard** *nm* - **1.** [pain] *short loaf of bread* - **2.** [chien] mongrel.

batavia [batavja] *nf* Webb lettuce.

bateau [bato] *nm* - **1.** [embarcation - gén] boat ; [- plus grand] ship ; ~ **à voile/moteur** sailing/motor boat ; ~ **de pêche** fishing boat ; **mener qqn en ~** *fig* to take sb for a ride - **2.** [de trottoir] driveway entrance (low kerb) - **3.** (en apposition inv) : **encolure ~** boat neck - **4.** (en apposition inv) [sujet, thème] well-worn ; **c'est ~!** it's the same old stuff!

bateau-mouche [batomuʃ] (*pl* **bateaux-mouches**) *nm* riverboat (on the Seine).

bateleur, euse [batlœr, øz] *nm, f* street acrobat.

bâti, e [bati] *adj* - **1.** [terrain] developed - **2.** [personne] : **bien ~** well-built.

➤ **bâti** *nm* - **1.** COUTURE tacking - **2.** CONSTR frame, framework.

batifoler [3] [batifɔle] *vi* to frolic.

bâtiment [batimɑ̃] *nm* - **1.** [édifice] building - **2.** IND : **le ~** the building trade - **3.** NAVIG ship, vessel.

bâtir [32] [batir] *vt* - **1.** CONSTR to build - **2.** *fig* [réputation, fortune] to build (up) ; [théorie, phrase] to construct - **3.** COUTURE to tack.

➤ **se bâtir** *vp* to be built.

bâtisse [batis] *nf souvent péj* house.

bâton [batɔ̃] *nm* - **1.** [gén] stick ; ~ **de réglisse** liquorice stick ; ~ **de ski** ski pole - **2.** *fam fig* 10,000 francs - **3.** *loc* : **mettre des ~s dans les roues à qqn** to put a spoke in sb's wheel ; **à ~s rompus** [conversation] rambling ; **parler à ~s rompus** to talk of this and that.

bâtonnet [batɔnɛ] *nm* rod.

bâtonnier [batɔnje] *nm* JUR ≃ President of the Bar.

batracien [batrasjɛ̃] *nm* amphibian.

battage [bataʒ] *nm* : ~ **(publicitaire** *OU* **médiatique)** (media) hype.

battant, e [batɑ̃, ɑ̃t] ⬦ *adj* : **sous une pluie ~e** in the pouring *OU* driving rain ; **le cœur ~** with beating heart ⬦ *nm, f* fighter.

➤ **battant** *nm* - **1.** [de porte] door (of double doors) ; [de fenêtre] half (of double window) - **2.** [de cloche] clapper.

batte [bat] *nf* SPORT bat.

battement [batmɑ̃] *nm* - **1.** [mouvement - d'ailes] flap, beating (U) ; [- de cœur, pouls] beat, beating (U) ; [- de cils, paupières] flutter, fluttering (U) - **2.** [bruit - de porte] banging (U) ; [- de la pluie] beating (U) - **3.** [intervalle de temps] break ; **une heure de ~** an hour free.

batterie [batri] *nf* - **1.** ÉLECTR & MIL battery ;

recharger ses ~s *fig* to recharge one's batteries - **2.** [attirail] : ~ **de cuisine** kitchen utensils *(pl)* - **3.** *MUS* drums *(pl)* - **4.** [série] : **une ~ de** a string of.

batteur [batœr] *nm* - **1.** *MUS* drummer - **2.** *CULIN* beater, whisk - **3.** [*SPORT* - de cricket] batsman ; [- de base-ball] batter.

batteuse [batøz] *nf AGRIC* thresher.

battoir [batwar] *nm* - **1.** [à tapis] carpet beater - **2.** *fig* [main] great mitt *ou* paw.

battre [83] [batr] <> *vt* - **1.** [gén] to beat ; ~ **en neige** [blancs d'œufs] to beat until stiff - **2.** [parcourir] to scour - **3.** [cartes] to shuffle <> *vi* [gén] to beat ; ~ **des cils** to blink ; ~ **des mains** to clap (one's hands).

◆ **se battre** *vp* to fight ; **se** ~ **contre qqn** to fight sb.

battu, e [baty] <> *pp* ▷ **battre** <> *adj* - **1.** [tassé] hard-packed ; **jouer sur terre** ~**e** *TENNIS* to play on clay - **2.** [fatigué] : **avoir les yeux** ~**s** to have shadows under one's eyes.

◆ **battue** *nf* - **1.** [chasse] beat - **2.** [chasse à l'homme] manhunt.

baud [bo] *nm* baud.

baudroie [bodrwa] *nf* monkfish.

baudruche [bodryʃ] *nf* - **1.** [ballon] balloon - **2.** *fig* [personne] front man.

baume [bom] *nm litt & fig* balm ; **mettre du** ~ **au cœur de qqn** to comfort sb.

baux ▷ **bail**.

bauxite [boksit] *nf* bauxite.

bavard, e [bavar, ard] <> *adj* talkative <> *nm, f* chatterbox ; *péj* gossip.

bavardage [bavardaʒ] *nm* - **1.** [papotage] chattering - **2.** *(gén pl)* [racontar] gossip *(U)*.

bavarder [3] [bavarde] *vi* to chatter ; *péj* to gossip.

bavarois, e [bavarwa, waz] *adj* Bavarian.

◆ **bavarois** *nm*, **bavaroise** *nf* [gâteau] ≃ mousse.

◆ **Bavarois, e** *nm, f* Bavarian.

bave [bav] *nf* - **1.** [salive] dribble - **2.** [d'animal] slaver - **3.** [de limace] slime.

baver [3] [bave] *vi* - **1.** [personne] to dribble - **2.** [animal] to slaver - **3.** [limace] to leave a trail - **4.** [stylo] to leak - **5.** *loc* : **en** ~ *fam* to have a hard *ou* rough time of it.

bavette [bavɛt] *nf* - **1.** [bavoir, de tablier] bib - **2.** [viande] flank - **3.** *loc* : **tailler une** ~ **(avec qqn)** *fam* to have a chinwag (with sb).

baveux, euse [bavø, øz] *adj* - **1.** [bébé] dribbling - **2.** [lettre] blurred - **3.** [omelette] runny.

Bavière [bavjɛr] *nf* : **la** ~ Bavaria.

bavoir [bavwar] *nm* bib.

bavure [bavyr] *nf* - **1.** [tache] smudge - **2.** [erreur] blunder.

bayer [3] [baje] *vi* : ~ **aux corneilles** to stand gazing into space.

bazar [bazar] *nm* - **1.** [boutique] general store - **2.** *fam* [désordre] jumble, clutter.

bazarder [3] [bazarde] *vt fam* to chuck out, to get rid of.

BCBG (*abr de* **bon chic bon genre**) *nmf & adj* *term used to describe an upper-class lifestyle reflected especially in expensive and conservative clothes* ; **il est très** ~ ≃ he's a real preppie type.

BCE (*abr de* **Banque centrale européenne**) *nf* ECB.

BCG (*abr de* **bacille Calmette-Guérin**) *nm* BCG.

bcp *abr de* **beaucoup**.

bd *abr de* **boulevard**.

BD, bédé [bede] (*abr de* **bande dessinée**) *nf* : **une** ~ a comic strip ; **la** ~ comic strips *(pl)*.

béant, e [beɑ̃, ɑ̃t] *adj* [plaie, gouffre] gaping ; [yeux] wide open.

béarnais, e [bearnɛ, ɛz] *adj* of *ou* from the Béarn.

◆ **Béarnais, e** *nm, f* native *ou* inhabitant of the Béarn.

◆ **béarnaise** *nf* : **(sauce)** ~**e** Béarnaise sauce.

béat, e [bea, at] *adj* - **1.** [content de soi] smug - **2.** [heureux] blissful.

béatement [beatmɑ̃] *adv* blissfully.

béatitude [beatityd] *nf* - **1.** *RELIG* beatitude - **2.** [bonheur] bliss.

beau, belle, beaux [bo, bɛl] *adj* (**bel** [bɛl] *devant voyelle ou h muet*) - **1.** [joli - femme] beautiful, good-looking ; [- homme] handsome, good-looking ; [- chose] beautiful - **2.** [temps] fine, good - **3.** *(toujours avant le nom)* [important] fine, excellent ; **une belle somme** a tidy sum (of money) - **4.** *iron* [mauvais] : **une belle grippe** a nasty dose of the flu ; **un** ~ **travail** a fine piece of work - **5.** *(sens intensif)* : **un** ~ **jour** one fine day - **6.** [noble] fine, noble - **7.** *loc* : **elle a** ~ **jeu de dire ça** it's easy *ou* all very well for her to say that.

◆ **beau** <> *adv* : **il fait** ~ the weather is good *ou* fine ; **j'ai** ~ **essayer ...** however hard I try ..., try as I may ... ; **j'ai** ~ **dire ...** whatever I say ... <> *nm* : **être au** ~ **fixe** to be set fair ; **avoir le moral au** ~ **fixe** *fig* to have a sunny disposition ; **faire le** ~ [chien] to sit up and beg.

◆ **belle** *nf* - **1.** [femme] lady friend - **2.** [dans un jeu] decider - **3.** *loc* : **(se) faire la belle** to escape.

bel et bien *loc adv* well and truly, actually.

de plus belle *loc adv* more than ever.

Beaubourg [bobur] *n name commonly used to refer to the Pompidou Centre.*

BEAUBOURG

Officially 'Beaubourg' refers to the area surrounding the Pompidou Centre in the Halles district of Paris but it has come to mean the Pompidou Centre itself. The unusual design of the building caused much controversy when it was built in 1977. It houses a modern art gallery, a cinema, an open-stack library and other cultural exhibits. With 8 million visitors a year it is one of the most popular monuments in Paris.

beaucoup [boku] <> *adv* - **1.** [un grand nombre] : ~ **de** a lot of, many ; **il y en a** ~ there are many *ou* a lot (of them) - **2.** [une grande quantité] : ~ **de** a lot of ; ~ **d'énergie** a lot of energy ; **il n'a pas** ~ **de temps** he hasn't a lot of *ou* much time ; **il n'en a pas** ~ he doesn't have much *ou* a lot (of it) - **3.** *(modifiant un verbe)* a lot ; **il boit** ~ he drinks a lot ; **c'est** ~ **dire** that's saying a lot - **4.** *(modifiant un adjectif comparatif)* much, a lot ; **c'est** ~ **mieux** it's much *ou* a lot better ; ~ **trop vite** much too quickly <> *pron inv* many ; **nous sommes** ~ **à penser que** ... many of us think that ...

de beaucoup *loc adv* by far.

beauf [bof] *nm* - **1.** *péj* stereotype of average French man with narrow views - **2.** *fam* [beau-frère] brother-in-law.

beau-fils [bofis] *(pl* beaux-fils) *nm* - **1.** [gendre] son-in-law - **2.** [de remariage] stepson.

beau-frère [bofrɛr] *(pl* beaux-frères) *nm* brother-in-law.

beau-père [bopɛr] *(pl* beaux-pères) *nm* - **1.** [père du conjoint] father-in-law - **2.** [de remariage] stepfather.

beauté [bote] *nf* beauty ; **de toute** ~ absolutely beautiful ; **en** ~ [magnifiquement] in great style ; *sout* [femme] ravishing.

beaux-arts [bozar] *nmpl* fine art *(sg).*

Beaux-Arts *nmpl* : **les Beaux-Arts** *French national art school.*

beaux-parents [bopar ̃ɑ] *nmpl* - **1.** [de l'homme] husband's parents, in-laws - **2.** [de la femme] wife's parents, in-laws.

bébé [bebe] <> *nm* baby ; ~ **phoque** seal pup, baby seal <> *adj inv* babyish.

bébé-éprouvette [bebeepruvɛt] *(pl* bébés-éprouvette) *nm* test-tube baby.

bébête [bebɛt] *adj* silly.

bec [bɛk] *nm* - **1.** [d'oiseau] beak - **2.** [d'instrument de musique] mouthpiece - **3.** [de casserole etc] lip ; ~ **de gaz** [réverbère] gaslamp *(in street)* ; ~ **verseur** spout - **4.** *fam* [bouche] mouth ; **ouvrir le** ~ to open one's mouth ; **clouer le** ~ **à qqn** to shut sb up.

bécane [bekan] *nf fam* - **1.** [moto, vélo] bike - **2.** [ordinateur etc] machine.

bécasse [bekas] *nf* - **1.** [oiseau] woodcock - **2.** *fam* [femme sotte] silly goose.

bécassine [bekasin] *nf* - **1.** [oiseau] snipe - **2.** *fam* [jeune fille naïve] silly little goose.

bec-de-lièvre [bɛkdəljɛvr] *(pl* becs-de-lièvre) *nm* harelip.

béchamel [beʃamɛl] *nf* : **(sauce)** ~ béchamel sauce.

bêche [bɛʃ] *nf* spade.

bêcher [4] [beʃe] *vt* to dig.

bêcheur, euse [beʃœr, øz] *nm, f fam* stuck-up person.

bécoter [3] [bekɔte] *vt fam* to snog *Br ou* smooch with.

se bécoter *vp* to snog *Br*, to smooch.

becquée [beke] *nf* : **donner la** ~ **à** to feed.

becqueter, béqueter [27] [bɛkte] *vt* to peck at.

becter [4] [bɛkte] *vi fam* to eat.

bedaine [bədɛn] *nf* potbelly.

bédé = BD.

bedeau, x [bədo] *nm* verger.

bedonnant, e [bədɔn ̃ɑ, ̃ɑt] *adj* potbellied.

bédouin, e [bedw ̃ɛ, in] *adj* Bedouin.

Bédouin, e *nm, f* Bedouin.

bée [be] *adj* : **bouche** ~ open-mouthed.

bégaiement [begɛm ̃ɑ] *nm* stammering.

bégayer [11] [begeje] <> *vi* to have a stutter *ou* stammer <> *vt* to stammer (out).

bégonia [begɔnja] *nm* begonia.

bègue [bɛg] <> *adj* : **être** ~ to have a stutter *ou* stammer <> *nmf* stutterer, stammerer.

bégueule [begœl] *fam péj* <> *adj* prudish <> *nf* prude.

béguin [beg ̃ɛ] *nm fam* : **avoir le** ~ **pour qqn** to have a crush on sb ; **avoir le** ~ **pour qqch** to be mad keen on sthg.

beige [bɛʒ] *adj* & *nm* beige.

beigne [bɛɲ] *nf fam* slap.

beignet [bɛɲɛ] *nm* fritter.

bel [bɛl] ▷ **beau.**

bêler [4] [bele] *vi* to bleat.

belette [bəlɛt] *nf* weasel.

belge [bɛlʒ] *adj* Belgian.

Belge *nmf* Belgian.

belgicisme [bɛlʒisism] *nm* [mot] Belgian word ; [tournure] Belgian expression.

Belgique [bɛlʒik] *nf* : **la ~** Belgium.

bélier [belje] *nm* - **1.** [animal] ram - **2.** [poutre] battering ram.

➤ **Bélier** *nm* ASTROL Aries ; **être Bélier** to be (an) Aries.

Belize [beliz] *nm* : **le ~** Belize ; **au ~** in Belize.

belladone [beladɔn] *nf* deadly nightshade.

bellâtre [bɛlatr] *nm péj* smoothie.

belle [bɛl] *adj & nf* ⊳ **beau.**

belle-famille [bɛlfamij] (*pl* **belles-familles**) *nf* - **1.** [de l'homme] husband's family, in-laws (*pl*) - **2.** [de la femme] wife's family, in-laws (*pl*).

belle-fille [bɛlfij] (*pl* **belles-filles**) *nf* - **1.** [épouse du fils] daughter-in-law - **2.** [de remariage] stepdaughter.

belle-mère [bɛlmɛr] (*pl* **belles-mères**) *nf* - **1.** [mère du conjoint] mother-in-law - **2.** [de remariage] stepmother.

belles-lettres [bɛlletr] *nfpl* (great) literature *(U)*.

belle-sœur [bɛlsœr] (*pl* **belles-sœurs**) *nf* sister-in-law.

belligérant, e [beliʒerã, ãt] *adj & nm, f* belligerent.

belliqueux, euse [belikø, øz] *adj* [peuple] warlike ; [humeur, tempérament] aggressive.

belote [bɔlɔt] *nf* French card game.

belvédère [bɛlvedɛr] *nm* - **1.** [construction] belvedere - **2.** [terrasse] viewpoint.

bémol [bemɔl] *adj & nm* MUS flat.

bénédictin, e [benediktɛ̃, in] ◇ *adj* Benedictine ◇ *nm, f* Benedictine ; **travail de ~** *fig* painstaking task.

➤ **Bénédictine** *nf* [liqueur] Benedictine.

bénédiction [benediksjɔ̃] *nf* blessing ; **donner sa ~** *fig* to give one's blessing to.

bénéfice [benefis] *nm* - **1.** [avantage] advantage, benefit ; **au ~ de** in aid of ; **accorder à qqn le ~ du doute** to give sb the benefit of the doubt - **2.** [profit] profit ; **~ net/brut** net/gross profit ; **intéressement aux ~s** profit-sharing ; **rapport cours-~** price-earnings ratio ; **~s commerciaux** trading profit *(sg)*.

bénéficiaire [benefisjɛr] ◇ *nmf* [gén] beneficiary ; [de chèque] payee ◇ *adj* [marge] profit *(avant n)* ; [résultat, société] profit-making.

bénéficier [9] [benefisje] *vi* : **~ de** [profiter de] to benefit from ; [jouir de] to have, to enjoy ; [obtenir] to have, to get.

bénéfique [benefik] *adj* beneficial.

Bénélux [benelyks] *nm* : **le ~** Benelux ; **les pays du ~** the Benelux countries.

benêt [bənɛ] ◇ *nm* clod ◇ *adj (seulement masculin)* silly, simple.

bénévolat [benevɔla] *nm* voluntary work.

bénévole [benevɔl] ◇ *adj* voluntary ◇ *nmf* volunteer, voluntary worker.

bénévolement [benevɔlmã] *adv* voluntarily, for nothing.

Bengale [bɛ̃gal] *nm* : **le ~** Bengal ; **au ~** in Bengal.

bénin, igne [benɛ̃, iɲ] *adj* - **1.** [maladie, accident] minor ; [tumeur] benign - **2.** *sout* [bienveillant] benign.

Bénin [benɛ̃] *nm* : **le ~** Benin ; **au ~** in Benin.

béninois, e [beninwa, waz] *adj* Beninese.

➤ **Béninois, e** *nm, f* Beninese *(inv)*.

bénir [32] [benir] *vt* - **1.** [gén] to bless - **2.** [se réjouir de] to thank God for.

bénit, e [beni, it] *adj* consecrated ; **eau ~e** holy water.

bénitier [benitje] *nm* holy water font.

benjamin, e [bɛ̃ʒamɛ̃, in] *nm, f* [de famille] youngest child ; [de groupe] youngest member.

benne [bɛn] *nf* - **1.** [de camion] tipper - **2.** [de téléphérique] car - **3.** [pour déchets] skip.

benzine [bɛ̃zin] *nf* benzine.

béotien, enne [beɔsjɛ̃, ɛn] *nm, f* philistine.

BEP, Bep (*abr de* **brevet d'études professionnelles**) *nm school-leaver's diploma (taken at age 18).*

BEPC, Bepc (*abr de* **brevet d'études du premier cycle**) *nm former school certificate (taken at age 16).*

béqueter = **becqueter.**

béquille [bekij] *nf* - **1.** [pour marcher] crutch - **2.** [d'un deux-roues] stand.

berbère [bɛrbɛr] *adj & nm* Berber.

➤ **Berbère** *nmf* Berber.

bercail [bɛrkaj] *nm* fold ; **rentrer au ~** *fig* to return to the fold.

berceau, x [bɛrso] *nm* cradle.

bercer [16] [bɛrse] *vt* - **1.** [bébé, bateau] to rock ; **son enfance a été bercée de cette musique** he was brought up on this kind of music - **2.** *fig* [tromper] : **~ qqn de** to delude sb with.

➤ **se bercer** *vp fig* : **se ~ de** to delude o.s. with ; **se ~ d'illusions** to delude o.s.

berceuse [bɛrsøz] *nf* - **1.** [chanson] lullaby - **2.** *Can* [fauteuil] rocking chair.

Bercy [bɛrsi] *n* - **1.** [ministère] *the French Ministry of Finance* - **2.** [stade] *large sports and concert hall in Paris.*

BERD, Berd [bɛrd] (*abr de* **Banque européenne pour la reconstruction et le développement**) *nf* EBRD.

béret [berɛ] *nm* beret ; **~ basque** (French) beret.

bergamote [bɛrgamɔt] *nf* bergamot orange.

berge [bɛrʒ] *nf* - **1.** [bord] bank - **2.** *fam* [an] : **il a plus de 50 ~s** he's over 50.

berger, ère [bɛrʒe, ɛr] *nm, f* shepherd (*f* shepherdess).

➤ **bergère** *nf* [canapé] wing chair.

➤ **berger allemand** *nm* alsatian *Br*, German shepherd.

bergerie [bɛrʒəri] *nf* sheepfold.

bergeronnette [bɛrʒərɔnɛt] *nf* wagtail.

Berlin [bɛrlɛ̃] *n* Berlin ; **~-Est** East Berlin ; **~-Ouest** West Berlin ; **le mur de ~** the Berlin Wall.

berline [bɛrlin] *nf* saloon (car) *Br*, sedan *Am*.

berlingot [bɛrlɛ̃go] *nm* - **1.** [de lait] carton - **2.** [bonbon] boiled sweet.

berlue [bɛrly] *nf* : **j'ai la ~!** I must be seeing things!

bermuda [bɛrmyda] *nm* bermuda shorts (*pl*).

Bermudes [bɛrmyd] *nfpl* : **les ~** Bermuda (*sg*) ; **aux ~** in Bermuda ; **le triangle des ~** the Bermuda Triangle.

bernard-l'ermite [bɛrnarlɛrmit] *nm inv* hermit crab.

berne [bɛrn] *nf* : **en ~** ≃ at half-mast.

berner [3] [bɛrne] *vt* to fool.

berrichon, onne [beriʃɔ̃, ɔn] *adj* of *ou* from the Berry.

besace [bəzas] *nf* pouch.

besicles [bezikl] *nfpl hum* specs.

besogne [bəzɔɲ] *nf* job, work (*U*) ; **aller vite en ~** *fig* to be a fast worker.

besoin [bəzwɛ̃] *nm* need ; **avoir ~ de qqch/de faire qqch** to need sthg/to do sthg ; **au ~** if necessary, if need *ou* needs be ; **être dans le ~** to be in need.

➤ **besoins** *nmpl* - **1.** [exigences] needs - **2.** *loc* : **faire ses ~s** to relieve o.s. ; **pour les ~s de la cause** for our purposes.

bestial, e, aux [bɛstjal, o] *adj* bestial, brutish.

bestiole [bɛstjɔl] *nf* (little) creature.

best-seller [bɛstselɛr] (*pl* **best-sellers**) *nm* best-seller.

bétail [betaj] *nm* cattle (*pl*).

bête [bɛt] *nf* - **1.** [animal] animal ; [insecte] insect ; **~ à bon Dieu** ladybird *Br*, ladybug *Am* ; **~ féroce** wild animal ; **~ de somme** beast of burden - **2.** *loc* : **chercher la petite ~** to nitpick ; **c'est sa ~ noire** that's his/her pet hate ⬦ *adj* - **1.** [stupide] stupid - **2.** [simple] : **c'est tout ~** there's nothing to it.

bêtement [bɛtmɑ̃] *adv* - **1.** [de façon bête] stupidly - **2.** [simplement] : **tout ~** just, quite simply.

bêtifiant, e [betifjɑ̃, ɑ̃t] *adj* idiotic.

bêtise [betiz] *nf* - **1.** [stupidité] stupidity - **2.** [action, remarque] stupid thing ; **faire/dire une ~** to do/say something stupid ; **faire des ~s** to be stupid *ou* silly.

béton [betɔ̃] *nm* - **1.** [matériau] concrete ; **~ armé** reinforced concrete - **2.** *fig* : **en ~** [argument] cast-iron.

bétonner [3] [betɔne] ⬦ *vt* to concrete ⬦ *vi* FOOTBALL to play defensively.

bétonnière [betɔnjɛr] *nf* cement mixer.

bette [bɛt], **blette** [blɛt] *nf* Swiss chard.

betterave [bɛtrav] *nf* beetroot *Br*, beet *Am* ; **~ fourragère** mangel-wurzel ; **~ sucrière** *ou* **à sucre** sugar beet.

beuglement [bøgləmɑ̃] *nm* - **1.** [de bovin] mooing (*U*), lowing (*U*) - **2.** [de radio] blaring (*U*).

beugler [5] [bøgle] *vi* - **1.** [bovin] to moo, to low - **2.** *fam* [personne] to bellow ; [radio] to blare out.

beur [bœr] *nmf* person born in France of North African immigrant parents.

beurre [bœr] *nm* - **1.** [aliment] butter ; **~ de cacahuètes** peanut butter ; **~ de cacao** cocoa butter ; **~ demi-sel** slightly-salted butter ; **~ noir** brown butter sauce - **2.** *loc* : **compter pour du ~** to count for nothing ; **faire son ~** to make one's pile ; **mettre du ~ dans les épinards** to make life a little more comfortable.

beurré, e [bœre] *adj* - **1.** [couvert de beurre] buttered - **2.** *fam* [ivre] plastered.

beurrer [5] [bœre] *vt* to butter.

beurrier, ère [bœrje, ɛr] *adj* [industrie] butter (*avant n*) ; [région] butter-producing.

beurrier [bœrje] *nm* butter dish.

beuverie [bœvri] *nf* drinking session.

bévue [bevy] *nf* blunder ; **faire** *ou* **commettre une ~** to slip up.

Beyrouth [berut] *n* Beirut ; **~-Est** East Beirut ; **~-Ouest** West Beirut.

BHV (*abr de* **Bazar de l'Hôtel de Ville**) *nm* large department store in central Paris.

biais [bjɛ] *nm* - **1.** [ligne oblique] slant ; **en** *ou* **~** [de travers] at an angle ; *fig* indirectly - **2.** COUTURE bias ; **tailler un tissu dans le ~** to cut a piece of cloth on the bias - **3.** [aspect] angle - **4.** [moyen détourné] expedient ; **par le ~ de** by means of.

biaiser [4] [bjeze] *vi fig* to dodge the issue.

bibelot [biblo] *nm* trinket, curio.

biberon [bibʀɔ̃] *nm* baby's bottle ; **nourrir au ~** to bottle-feed.

bible [bibl] *nf* bible.

bibliobus [biblijɔbys] *nm* mobile library.

bibliographie [biblijɔgʀafi] *nf* bibliography.

bibliographique [biblijɔgʀafik] *adj* bibliographical.

bibliophile [biblijɔfil] *nmf* book lover.

bibliothécaire [biblijɔtekɛʀ] *nmf* librarian.

bibliothèque [biblijɔtɛk] *nf* - **1.** [meuble] bookcase - **2.** [édifice, collection] library ; **~ municipale** public library ; **la Bibliothèque nationale de France** *the French national library.*

BIBLIOTHÈQUE NATIONALE DE FRANCE

The 'Bibliothèque nationale de France' or 'BNF' is a large copyright deposit library that includes the 'Bibliothèque nationale' or 'BN', situated in the rue de Richelieu and the 'Bibliothèque de France' or 'Bibliothèque François Mitterrand', the new and ultramodern complex in the 13th arrondissement. The 'BN' houses the library's priceless collection of manuscripts, engravings, coins medals and maps, while the bulk of the book collection is in the new complex.

biblique [biblik] *adj* biblical.

Bic® [bik] *nm* ball-point pen.

bicarbonate [bikaʀbɔnat] *nm* : **~ (de soude)** bicarbonate of soda.

bicentenaire [bisɑ̃tnɛʀ] ◇ *adj* two-hundred-year-old *(avant n)* ◇ *nm* bicentenary *Br*, bicentennial *Am*.

biceps [bisɛps] *nm* biceps.

biche [biʃ] *nf* ZOOL hind, doe.

bichonner [3] [biʃɔne] *vt* [choyer] to cosset, to pamper.

◆ se bichonner *vp* to spruce o.s. up ; [femme] to doll o.s. up.

bicolore [bikɔlɔʀ] *adj* two-coloured *Br*, two-colored *Am*.

bicoque [bikɔk] *nf péj* house.

bicorne [bikɔʀn] *nm* cocked hat.

bicyclette [bisiklɛt] *nf* bicycle ; **rouler à ~** to cycle.

bidasse [bidas] *nm fam* squaddie *Br*, grunt *Am*.

bide [bid] *nm fam* - **1.** [ventre] belly - **2.** [échec] flop.

bidet [bidɛ] *nm* - **1.** [sanitaire] bidet - **2.** *hum* [cheval] nag.

bidon [bidɔ̃] *nm* - **1.** [récipient] can - **2.** *fam* [ventre] belly - **3.** *(en apposition inv) fam* [faux] phoney *Br*, phony *Am* - **4.** *fam* [simulation] : **c'est du ~** it's (a load of) rubbish.

bidonner [3] [bidɔne] **◆ se bidonner** *vp fam* to laugh one's head off.

bidonville [bidɔ̃vil] *nm* shantytown.

bidouilleur [bidujœʀ] *nm* INFORM do-it-yourselfer.

bidule [bidyl] *nm fam* thing, thingy.

bielle [bjɛl] *nf* connecting rod.

biélorusse [bjelɔʀys] *adj* Belorussian, Byelorussian.

◆ Biélorusse *nmf* Belorussian, Byelorussian.

Biélorussie [bjelɔʀysi] *nf* : **la ~** Belorussia, Byelorussia.

bien [bjɛ̃] *(compar & superl* **mieux)** ◇ *adj inv* - **1.** [satisfaisant] good ; **il est ~ comme prof** he's a good teacher ; **il est ~, ce bureau** this is a good office - **2.** [en bonne santé] well ; **je ne me sens pas ~** I don't feel well - **3.** [joli] good-looking ; **tu ne trouves pas qu'elle est ~ comme ça?** don't you think she looks good *ou* nice like that? - **4.** [à l'aise] comfortable - **5.** [convenable] respectable ◇ *nm* - **1.** [sens moral] : **le ~** good ; **le ~ et le mal** good and evil - **2.** [intérêt] good ; **je te dis ça pour ton ~** I'm telling you this for your own good - **3.** [richesse, propriété] property, possession ; **~s de consommation** consumer goods - **4.** *loc* : **faire du ~ à qqn** to do sb good ; **dire du ~ de qqn/qqch** to speak well of sb/sthg ; **mener à ~** to bring to fruition, to complete ; **en tout ~ tout honneur** with the best of intentions ◇ *adv* - **1.** [de manière satisfaisante] well ; **on mange ~ ici** the food's good here ; **il ne s'est pas ~ conduit** he didn't behave well ; **tu as ~ fait** you did the right thing ; **tu ferais ~ d'y aller** you would be wise to go ; **c'est ~ fait!** it serves him/her *etc* right! - **2.** [sens intensif] quite, really ; **~ souvent** quite often ; **es-tu ~ sûr?** are you quite sure (about it)? ; **j'espère ~ que ...** I DO hope that ... ; **on a ~ ri** we had a good laugh ; **il y a ~ trois heures que j'attends** I've been waiting for at least three hours ; **c'est ~ aimable à vous** it's very kind *ou* good of you - **3.** [renforçant un comparatif] : **il est parti ~ plus tard** he left much later ; **on était ~ moins riches** we were a lot worse off *ou* poorer - **4.** [servant à conclure ou à introduire] : **bien, c'est fini pour aujourd'hui** well, that's it for today ; **~, je t'écoute** well, I'm listening ; **très ~, je vais avec toi** all right then, I'll go with you - **5.** [en effet] : **c'est ~ lui** it really IS him ; **c'est ~ ce que je disais** that's just what I said ◇ *interj* : **eh ~!** oh well! ; **eh ~, qu'en penses-tu?** well, what do you think?

◆ biens *nmpl* property (U).

◆ bien de, bien des *loc adj* : **~ des gens sont venus** quite a lot of people came ; **~ des fois**

many times ; **il a ~ de la chance** he's very ou really lucky ; **il a eu ~ de la peine à me convaincre** he had quite a lot of trouble convincing me.
➤ **bien entendu** *loc adv* of course.
➤ **bien que** *loc conj* (+ *subjonctif*) although, though.
➤ **bien sûr** *loc adv* of course, certainly.

bien-aimé, e [bjɛ̃neme] (*mpl* **bien-aimés**, *fpl* **bien-aimées**) *adj* & *nm, f* beloved.

bien-être [bjɛ̃nɛtr] *nm inv* - **1.** [physique] wellbeing - **2.** [matériel] wellbeing, comfort.

bienfaisance [bjɛ̃fəzɑ̃s] *nf* charity.

bienfaisant, e [bjɛ̃fəzɑ̃, ɑ̃t] *adj* beneficial.

bienfait [bjɛ̃fɛ] *nm* - **1.** [effet bénéfique] benefit - **2.** [faveur] kindness.

bienfaiteur, trice [bjɛ̃fɛtœr, tris] *nm, f* benefactor.

bien-fondé [bjɛ̃fɔ̃de] (*pl* **bien-fondés**) *nm* validity.

bienheureux, euse [bjɛ̃nørø, øz] *adj* - **1.** RELIG blessed - **2.** [heureux] happy.

biennal, e, aux [bjenal, o] *adj* biennial.
➤ **biennale** *nf* biennial festival.

bien-pensant, e [bjɛ̃pɑ̃sɑ̃, ɑ̃t] (*mpl* **bien-pensants**, *fpl* **bien-pensantes**) *adj* & *nm, f péj* conformist.

bienséance [bjɛ̃seɑ̃s] *nf* decorum.
➤ **bienséances** *nfpl* conventions.

bientôt [bjɛ̃to] *adv* soon ; **à ~!** see you soon!

bienveillance [bjɛ̃vejɑ̃s] *nf* kindness.

bienveillant, e [bjɛ̃vejɑ̃, ɑ̃t] *adj* kindly.

bienvenu, e [bjɛ̃vny] <> *adj* [qui arrive à propos] welcome <> *nm, f* : **être le ~/la ~e** to be welcome ; **soyez le ~!** welcome!
➤ **bienvenue** *nf* welcome ; **souhaiter la ~e à qqn** to welcome sb.

bière [bjɛr] *nf* - **1.** [boisson] beer ; **~ blonde** lager ; **~ brune** brown ale ; **~ pression** draught *Br* ou draft *Am* beer - **2.** [cercueil] coffin.

biffer [3] [bife] *vt sout* to cross out.

bifidus [bifidys] *nm* bifidus ; **yaourt au ~ bio** yogurt, yogurt containing bifidus.

bifteck [biftɛk] *nm* steak.

bifurcation [bifyrkasjɔ̃] *nf* [embranchement] fork ; *fig* new direction.

bifurquer [3] [bifyrke] *vi* - **1.** [route, voie ferrée] to fork - **2.** [voiture] to turn off - **3.** *fig* [personne] to branch off.

bigame [bigam] <> *adj* bigamous <> *nmf* bigamist.

bigamie [bigami] *nf* bigamy.

bigarreau, x [bigaro] *nm* cherry.

bigophone [bigɔfɔn] *nm fam vieilli* [téléphone] blower *Br*, horn *Am*.

bigorneau, x [bigɔrno] *nm* winkle.

bigot, e [bigo, ɔt] *péj* <> *adj* bigoted <> *nm, f* bigot.

bigoudi [bigudi] *nm* curler.

bigrement [bigrəmɑ̃] *adv fam vieilli* [beaucoup] a lot ; [très] very.

bijou, x [biʒu] *nm* - **1.** [joyau] jewel - **2.** *fig* [chef-d'œuvre] gem.

bijouterie [biʒutri] *nf* - **1.** [magasin] jeweller's *Br* ou jeweler's *Am* (shop) - **2.** [activité] jewellery-making *Br*, jewelry-making *Am* - **3.** [commerce] jewellery *Br* ou jewelry *Am* trade.

bijoutier, ère [biʒutje, ɛr] *nm, f* jeweller *Br*, jeweler *Am*.

Bikini® [bikini] *nm* bikini.

bilan [bilɑ̃] *nm* - **1.** FIN balance sheet ; **déposer son ~** to declare bankruptcy - **2.** [état d'une situation] state of affairs ; **faire le ~ (de)** to take stock (of) ; **~ de santé** checkup.

bilatéral, e, aux [bilateral, o] *adj* - **1.** [stationnement] on both sides (of the road) - **2.** [contrat, accord] bilateral.

bile [bil] *nf* bile ; **déverser sa ~** to vent one's spleen ; **se faire de la ~** *fam* to worry.

biliaire [biljɛr] *adj* biliary ; **calcul ~** gallstone ; **vésicule ~** gall bladder.

bilieux, euse [biljø, øz] *adj* - **1.** [teint] bilious - **2.** [tempérament] irascible.

bilingue [bilɛ̃g] <> *adj* bilingual <> *nmf* [personne] bilingual person <> *nm* [dictionnaire] bilingual dictionary.

bilinguisme [bilɛ̃gɥism] *nm* bilingualism.

billard [bijar] *nm* - **1.** [jeu] billiards (*U*) - **2.** [table de jeu] billiard table - **3.** *loc* : **passer** ou **monter sur le ~** *fam* to go under the knife.

bille [bij] *nf* - **1.** [d'enfant] marble - **2.** [de billard] ball - **3.** *fam* [tête] face - **4.** [de bois] block of wood.

billet [bijɛ] *nm* - **1.** [lettre] note ; **~ doux** love letter - **2.** [argent] : **~ (de banque)** (bank) note ; **un ~ de 100 francs** a 100-franc note - **3.** [ticket] ticket ; **~ de train/d'avion** train/plane ticket ; **~ de faveur** complimentary ticket ; **~ de loterie** lottery ticket.

billetterie [bijɛtri] *nf* - **1.** [à l'aéroport] ticket desk ; [à la gare] booking office ou hall - **2.** [bureau, service] ticket office - **3.** BANQUE cash dispenser.

billion [biljɔ̃] *nm* billion *Br*, trillion *Am*.

bimensuel, elle [bimɑ̃sɥɛl] *adj* fortnightly *Br*, twice monthly.

➡ **bimensuel** *nm* fortnightly review *Br,* semimonthly *Am.*

bimestriel, elle [bimɛstrijɛl] *adj* two-monthly.

bimoteur [bimɔtœr] ◇ *adj* twin-engined. ◇ *nm* twin-engined plane.

binaire [binɛr] *adj* binary.

biner [3] [bine] *vt* to hoe.

biniou [binju] *nm* (Breton) bagpipes *(pl).*

binocle [binɔkl] *nm* pince-nez.

➡ **binocles** *nmpl fam vieilli* specs.

bio [bjo] *adj inv* natural ; **aliments ~** whole-food, health food.

biocarburant [bjɔkarbyrɑ̃] *nm* biofuel.

biochimie [bjɔʃimi] *nf* biochemistry.

biodégradable [bjɔdegradabl] *adj* bio-degradable.

biodiversité [bjɔdivɛrsite] *nf* biodiversity.

biographie [bjɔgrafi] *nf* biography.

biographique [bjɔgrafik] *adj* biographical.

biologie [bjɔlɔʒi] *nf* biology.

biologique [bjɔlɔʒik] *adj* - **1.** *SCIENCE* biological - **2.** [naturel] organic.

biopsie [bjɔpsi] *nf* biopsy.

biorythme [bjɔritm] *nm* biorhythm.

biotechnologie [bjɔtɛknɔlɔʒi] *nf* biotechnology.

bip [bip] *nm* - **1.** [signal] tone, beep ; **parlez après le ~ (sonore)** please speak after the beep *ou* tone - **2.** [appareil] bleeper.

bipède [bipɛd] *nm* & *adj* biped.

biper [3] [bipe] *vt* to page.

bique [bik] *nf* - **1.** *fam* [chèvre] (nanny) goat - **2.** *péj* [femme] : **vieille ~** old bag.

BIRD [bœrd] (*abr de* **Banque internationale pour la reconstruction et le développement**) *nf* IBRD.

biréacteur [bireaktœr] *nm* twin-engined jet.

birman, e [birmɑ̃, an] *adj* Burmese.

➡ **birman** *nm* [langue] Burmese.

➡ **Birman, e** *nm, f* Burmese.

Birmanie [birmani] *nf* : **la ~** Burma.

bis¹, e [bi, biz] *adj* greyish-brown ; **pain ~** brown bread.

bis² [bis] ◇ *adv* - **1.** [dans adresse] : **5 ~** 5a - **2.** [à la fin d'un spectacle] encore ◇ *nm* encore.

bisannuel, elle [bizanɥɛl] *adj* biennial.

bisbille [bizbij] *nf* squabble, tiff ; **être en ~ (avec)** to be on bad terms (with).

biscornu, e [biskɔrny] *adj* - **1.** [difforme] irregularly shaped - **2.** [bizarre] weird.

biscotte [biskɔt] *nf* toasted bread sold in packets and often eaten for breakfast.

biscuit [biskɥi] *nm* - **1.** [sec] biscuit *Br,* cookie *Am* ; [salé] cracker - **2.** [gâteau] sponge.

bise [biz] *nf* - **1.** [vent] north wind - **2.** *fam* [baiser] kiss ; **grosses ~s** love and kisses.

biseau, x [bizo] *nm* bevel ; **en ~** bevelled *Br,* beleved *Am.*

bison [bizɔ̃] *nm* bison.

bisou [bizu] *nm fam* kiss.

bisque [bisk] *nf* thick soup, the ingredients of which have been pureed ; **~ de homard** lobster bisque.

bissextile [bisɛkstil] ▷ **année**.

bistouri [bisturi] *nm* lancet.

bistro(t) [bistro] *nm fam* cafe, bar.

BISTROT ▬▬▬▬

This word can refer either to a small cafe or to a cosy restaurant, especially one frequented by regulars. 'Le style bistrot' refers to a style of furnishing inspired by the chairs, tables and zinc countertops typical of the traditional 'bistrot'.

bit [bit] *nm INFORM* bit.

BIT (*abr de* **Bureau international du travail**) *nm* ILO.

bit(t)e [bit] *nf vulg* cock.

bitume [bitym] *nm* - **1.** [revêtement] asphalt - **2.** *CHIM* bitumen.

bivouac [bivwak] *nm* bivouac.

bivouaquer [3] [bivwake] *vi* to bivouac.

bizarre [bizar] *adj* strange, odd.

bizarrement [bizarmɑ̃] *adv* strangely, oddly.

bizarrerie [bizarri] *nf* strangeness.

bizutage [bizytaʒ] *nm* practical jokes played on new arrivals in a school or college.

BIZUTAGE ▬▬▬▬

In some French schools and colleges, students in fancy-dress take to the streets and play practical jokes (sometimes very cruel ones) on each other and on passers-by at the beginning of the school year. This is part of the traditional initiation ceremony known as 'bizutage'.

blabla, bla-bla [blabla] *nm inv fam* waffle.

blackbouler [3] [blakbule] *vt* - **1.** [à une élection] to blackball - **2.** *fam* [à un examen] to fail.

black-out [blakawt] *nm* blackout.

blafard, e [blafar, ard] *adj* pale.

blague [blag] *nf* - **1.** [plaisanterie] joke ; **~ à part** joking apart ; **sans ~!** no!, really? - **2.** [sac] : **~ à tabac** tobacco pouch.

blaguer [3] [blage] *fam vi* to joke.

blagueur, euse [blagœr, øz] *fam* ◇ *adj*
jokey ◇ *nm, f* joker.

blaireau, x [blɛro] *nm* - **1.** [animal] badger
- **2.** [de rasage] shaving brush.

blairer [4] [blɛre] *vt fam* : **je ne peux pas la ~** I
can't stand her.

blâme [blam] *nm* - **1.** [désapprobation] disapproval - **2.** [sanction] reprimand.

blâmer [3] [blame] *vt* - **1.** [désapprouver] to
blame - **2.** [sanctionner] to reprimand.

blanc, blanche [blɑ̃, blɑ̃ʃ] *adj* - **1.** [gén] white
- **2.** [non écrit] blank - **3.** [pâle] pale.
➤ **blanc** *nm* - **1.** [couleur] white ; **~ cassé** off-
white - **2.** [personne] white (man) - **3.** [linge de
maison] : **le ~** the (household) linen - **4.** [sur pa-
ge] blank (space) ; **en ~** [chèque] blank ; **laisser
en ~** to leave blank - **5.** [dans conversation] gap
- **6.** [de volaille] white meat - **7.** [vin] white
(wine) ; **~ de ~s** *white wine from white grapes*
- **8.** *loc* : **chauffé à ~** white-hot ; **tirer à ~** to
shoot *ou* fire blanks.
➤ **blanche** *nf* - **1.** [personne] white (woman)
- **2.** *MUS* minim.
➤ **blanc d'œuf** *nm* egg white.

blanc-bec [blɑ̃bɛk] (*pl* **blancs-becs**) *nm péj*
& *vieilli* greenhorn.

blanchâtre [blɑ̃ʃɑtr] *adj* whitish.

blanche ▷ **blanc.**

blancheur [blɑ̃ʃœr] *nf* whiteness.

blanchiment [blɑ̃ʃimɑ̃] *nm* - **1.** [décoloration]
bleaching - **2.** [coloration en blanc] whitewash-
ing ; **~ d'argent** *fig* money laundering.

blanchir [32] [blɑ̃ʃir] ◇ *vt* - **1.** [mur] to whitewash - **2.** [linge, argent] to launder - **3.** [légumes]
to blanch - **4.** [sucre] to refine ; [papier, tissu] to
bleach - **5.** *fig* [accusé] : **~ qqn de qqch** to clear
sb of sthg ◇ *vi* : **~ (de)** to go white (with).

blanchissage [blɑ̃ʃisaʒ] *nm* - **1.** [de linge]
laundering - **2.** [de sucre] refining.

blanchisserie [blɑ̃ʃisri] *nf* laundry.

blanchon [blɑ̃ʃɔ̃] *nm* Can whitecoat *(baby
seal)*.

blanquette [blɑ̃kɛt] *nf* - **1.** *CULIN* stew of veal,
lamb or chicken served in a white sauce ; **~ de
veau** veal blanquette - **2.** [vin] : **~ de Limoux**
sparkling wine from Limoux.

blasé, e [blaze] ◇ *adj* blasé ◇ *nm, f* blasé
person.

blason [blazɔ̃] *nm* coat of arms.

blasphématoire [blasfematwar] *adj* blasphemous.

blasphème [blasfɛm] *nm* blasphemy.

blasphémer [18] [blasfeme] *vt* & *vi* to blas-
pheme.

blatte [blat] *nf* cockroach.

blazer [blazɛr] *nm* blazer.

blé [ble] *nm* - **1.** [céréale] wheat, corn ; **~ en herbe** unripe corn ; **~ noir** buckwheat ; **blond
comme les ~s** with corn-coloured hair
- **2.** *fam* [argent] dough.

bled [blɛd] *nm* - **1.** [brousse] North African interior - **2.** *fam péj* [village isolé] godforsaken
place.

blême [blɛm] *adj* : **~ (de)** pale (with).

blêmir [32] [blemir] *vi* to go *ou* turn pale.

blennorragie [blenɔraʒi] *nf* gonorrhoea.

blessant, e [blɛsɑ̃, ɑ̃t] *adj* hurtful.

blessé, e [blese] *nm, f* wounded *ou* injured
person ; **un grand ~** a badly wounded *ou* injured person.

blesser [4] [blese] *vt* - **1.** [physiquement - acciden-
tellement] to injure, to hurt ; [- par arme] to
wound ; **ses chaussures lui blessent les pieds**
his shoes make his feet sore - **2.** [moralement]
to hurt.
➤ **se blesser** *vp* to injure o.s., to hurt o.s.

blessure [blesyr] *nf litt* & *fig* wound.

blet, blette [blɛ, blɛt] *adj* overripe.

blette = **bette.**

bleu, e [blø] *adj* - **1.** [couleur] blue ; **~ pâle/
pétrole/roi** pale/petrol/royal blue - **2.** [vian-
de] very rare.
➤ **bleu** *nm* - **1.** [couleur] blue - **2.** [meurtrissure]
bruise - **3.** *fam* [novice - à l'armée] raw recruit ;
[- à l'université] freshman, fresher *Br* - **4.** [froma-
ge] blue cheese - **5.** [antiseptique] : **~ de méthylène** methylene blue - **6.** [vêtement] : **~ de travail** overalls *(pl)*.

bleuet [bløɛ] *nm* cornflower ; *Can* [fruit] blueberry.

bleuetière [bløtjɛr] *nf Can* blueberry field.

bleuir [32] [bløir] *vt* & *vi* to turn blue.

bleuté, e [bløte] *adj* bluish.

blindé, e [blɛ̃de] *adj* - **1.** [véhicule] armoured
Br, armored *Am* ; [porte, coffre] armour-plated
Br, armor-plated *Am* - **2.** *fam fig* [personne]
hardened.
➤ **blindé** *nm* armoured *Br ou* armored *Am*
car.

blinder [3] [blɛ̃de] *vt* - **1.** [véhicule] to armour
Br, to armor *Am* ; [porte, coffre] to armour-
plate *Br*, to armor-plate *Am* - **2.** *fam* [endurcir]
to harden.
➤ **se blinder** *vp fam fig* to harden o.s.

blini [blini] *nm* blini.

blizzard [blizar] *nm* blizzard.

bloc [blɔk] *nm* - **1.** [gén] block ; **en ~** wholesale ; **faire ~** to unite - **2.** [assemblage] unit ;
~ d'alimentation *INFORM* power pack ; **~ opéra-**

toire operating theatre ; ~ **sanitaire** toilet block.

blocage [blɔkaʒ] *nm* - **1.** ÉCON freeze, freezing *(U)* - **2.** [de roue] locking - **3.** PSYCHOL (mental) block - **4.** CONSTR rubble.

blockhaus [blɔkos] *nm* blockhouse.

bloc-moteur [blɔkmɔtœr] *(pl* **blocs-moteurs)** *nm* engine block.

bloc-notes [blɔknɔt] *(pl* **blocs-notes)** *nm* notepad.

blocus [blɔkys] *nm* blockade.

blond, e [blɔ̃, blɔ̃d] <> *adj* fair, blond <> *nm, f* fair-haired *ou* blond man *(f* fair-haired) *ou* blonde woman.
◆ **blond** *nm* : ~ **cendré/vénitien/platine** ash/strawberry/platinum blond.
◆ **blonde** *nf* - **1.** [cigarette] Virginia cigarette - **2.** [bière] lager.

blondeur [blɔ̃dœr] *nf* blondness, fairness.

blondir [32] [blɔ̃dir] *vi* to go *ou* turn blond ; **faire ~** CULIN to fry gently without browning.

bloquer [3] [blɔke] *vt* - **1.** [porte, freins] to jam ; [roues] to lock - **2.** [route, chemin] to block ; [personne] : **être bloqué** to be stuck - **3.** [prix, salaires, crédit] to freeze - **4.** [regrouper] to combine - **5.** PSYCHOL : **être bloqué** to have a (mental) block.
◆ **se bloquer** *vp* - **1.** [se coincer] to jam - **2.** PSYCHOL : **se ~ contre** to have a (mental) block about.

blottir [32] [blɔtir] ◆ **se blottir** *vp* : **se ~ (contre)** to snuggle up (to).

blouse [bluz] *nf* - **1.** [de travail, d'écolier] smock - **2.** [chemisier] blouse.

blouser [3] [bluze] <> *vi* to be full <> *vt fam* : **~ qqn** to pull a fast one on sb.

blouson [bluzɔ̃] *nm* bomber jacket, blouson ; **~ noir** ≃ teddy boy.

blue-jean [bludʒin] *(pl* **blue-jeans** [bludʒins]) *nm* jeans *(pl).*

blues [bluz] *nm inv* blues.

bluff [blœf] *nm* bluff.

bluffer [3] [blœfe] *fam vi* & *vt* to bluff.

blush [blœʃ] *nm* blusher.

BN *nf abr de* **Bibliothèque nationale.**

BNF *nf abr de* **Bibliothèque nationale de France.**

boa [bɔa] *nm* boa.

boat people [botpipəl] *nmpl* boat people.

bob [bɔb] *nm* SPORT bob.

bobard [bɔbar] *nm fam* fib.

bobine [bɔbin] *nf* - **1.** [cylindre] reel, spool - **2.** ÉLECTR coil - **3.** *fam vieilli* [visage] face.

bobo [bɔbo] *nm (langage enfantin)* : **se faire ~** to hurt o.s. ; **j'ai ~ à la tête** my head hurts.

bobsleigh [bɔbslɛg] *nm* bobsleigh.

bocage [bɔkaʒ] *nm* - **1.** [bois] grove - **2.** GÉOGR bocage.

bocal, aux [bɔkal, o] *nm* jar.

bock [bɔk] *nm* beer mug.

body-building [bɔdibildiŋ] *nm* : **le ~** body building *(U).*

bœuf [bœf, *pl* bø] *nm* - **1.** [animal] ox - **2.** [viande] beef ; **~ bourguignon** beef stew in a red-wine sauce ; **~ en daube** beef braised in wine and stock ; **~ miroton** slices of beef reheated in stock.

bof [bɔf] *interj fam* [exprime le mépris] so what? ; [exprime la lassitude] I don't really care.

bogue [bɔg], **bug** [bʌg] *nm* INFORM bug ; **le ~ de l'an 2000** the millennium bug.

bohème [bɔɛm] <> *adj* bohemian <> *nf* : **la ~** bohemia.

Bohême [bɔɛm] *nf* : **la ~** Bohemia.

bohémien, enne [bɔemjɛ̃, ɛn] <> *adj* - **1.** [tsigane] gipsy *(avant n)* - **2.** [non-conformiste] bohemian <> *nm, f* - **1.** [tsigane] gipsy - **2.** [non-conformiste] bohemian.
◆ **Bohémien, enne** *nm, f* Bohemian.

boire [108] [bwar] <> *vt* - **1.** [s'abreuver] to drink - **2.** [absorber] to soak up, to absorb <> *vi* to drink.

bois [bwa] <> *nm* wood ; **en ~** wooden ; **~ mort** dead wood *Br,* deadwood *Am* ; **~ vert** green wood ; **chèque en ~** *fig* rubber cheque *Br,* bad check *Am* ; **petit ~** kindling ; **toucher du ~** *fam fig* to touch wood *Br,* to knock on wood *Am* <> *nmpl* - **1.** MUS woodwind *(U)* - **2.** [cornes] antlers.

boisé, e [bwaze] *adj* wooded.

boiser [3] [bwaze] *vt* to afforest.

boiserie [bwazri] *nf* panelling *(U) Br,* paneling *(U) Am.*

boisson [bwasɔ̃] *nf* - **1.** [breuvage] drink ; **~ chaude/froide** hot/cold drink ; **être pris de ~** to be intoxicated - **2.** [habitude] drink, drinking *(U).*

boîte [bwat] *nf* - **1.** [récipient] box ; **en ~** tinned *Br,* canned ; **~ de conserve** tin *Br,* can ; **~ aux lettres** [pour la réception] letterbox ; [pour l'envoi] postbox *Br,* mailbox *Am* ; **~ à musique** musical box *Br,* music box *Am* ; **~ noire** black box ; **~ postale** post office box ; **mettre qqn en ~** *fig* to pull sb's leg - **2.** AUTOM : **~ à gants** glove compartment ; **~ de vitesses** gearbox - **3.** INFORM : **~ de dialogue** dialog box ; **~ aux lettres électronique** electronic mailbox ; **~ vocale** voice mail - **4.** *fam* [entreprise] company, firm ; [lycée] school - **5.** *fam* [discothèque] : **~ (de nuit)** nightclub, club.

boiter [3] [bwate] vi - **1.** [personne] to limp - **2.** [meuble] to wobble.

boiteux, euse [bwatø, øz] ◇ adj - **1.** [personne] lame - **2.** [meuble] wobbly - **3.** fig [raisonnement] shaky ◇ nm, f lame person.

boîtier [bwatje] nm - **1.** [boîte] case - **2.** TECHNOL casing.

boitiller [3] [bwatije] vi to limp slightly.

bol [bɔl] nm - **1.** [récipient] bowl - **2.** [contenu] bowl, bowlful - **3.** loc : avoir du ~ fam to be lucky ; prendre un ~ d'air to get some fresh air.

bolet [bɔlɛ] nm boletus.

bolide [bɔlid] nm - **1.** [véhicule] racing Br ou race Am car ; comme un ~ like a rocket - **2.** ASTRON meteor.

Bolivie [bɔlivi] nf : la ~ Bolivia.

bolivien, enne [bɔlivjɛ̃, ɛn] adj Bolivian.
➥ **Bolivien, enne** nm, f Bolivian.

bombance [bɔ̃bɑ̃s] nf : faire ~ fam to have a feast.

bombardement [bɔ̃baʀdəmɑ̃] nm bombardment, bombing (U).

bombarder [3] [bɔ̃baʀde] vt - **1.** MIL to bomb - **2.** [assaillir] : ~ qqn/qqch de to bombard sb/sthg with - **3.** fam fig [nommer] : ~ qqn chef de personnel to pitchfork sb into the job of personnel manager.

bombardier [bɔ̃baʀdje] nm - **1.** [avion] bomber - **2.** [aviateur] bombardier.

bombe [bɔ̃b] nf - **1.** [projectile] bomb ; fig bombshell ; ~ atomique atomic bomb ; ~ incendiaire incendiary ou fire bomb ; ~ à retardement time bomb - **2.** [casquette] riding hat - **3.** [atomiseur] spray, aerosol - **4.** CULIN : ~ glacée (ice-cream) bombe - **5.** loc : faire la ~ to live it up.

bombé, e [bɔ̃be] adj bulging, rounded.

bomber [3] [bɔ̃be] ◇ vt - **1.** [torse] to stick out - **2.** fam [dessiner à la bombe] to spray ◇ vi - **1.** [devenir convexe] to bulge - **2.** fam [aller vite] to bomb along.

bon, bonne [bɔ̃, bɔn] (compar & superl meilleur) adj - **1.** [gén] good - **2.** [généreux] good, kind - **3.** [utilisable - billet, carte] valid - **4.** [correct] right - **5.** loc : être ~ pour qqch/pour faire qqch fam to be fit for sthg/for doing sthg ; tu es ~ pour une contravention you'll end up with ou you'll get a parking ticket ; ~ à (+ infinitif) fit to ; c'est ~ à savoir that's worth knowing.
➥ **bon** ◇ adv : à quoi ~ ...? what's the use ...? ; il fait ~ the weather's fine, it's fine ;

sentir ~ to smell good ; tenir ~ to stand firm ◇ interj - **1.** [marque de satisfaction] good! - **2.** [marque de surprise] : ah ~! really? ◇ nm - **1.** [constatant un droit] voucher ; ~ de commande order form ; ~ du Trésor FIN Treasury bill ou bond - **2.** (gén pl) [personne] : les ~s et les méchants good people and wicked people - **3.** [éléments valables] good (U).
➥ **pour de bon** loc adv seriously, really.

bonbon [bɔ̃bɔ̃] nm - **1.** [friandise] sweet Br, piece of candy Am ; ~ acidulé acid drop - **2.** Belg [gâteau] biscuit.

bonbonne [bɔ̃bɔn] nf demijohn.

bonbonnière [bɔ̃bɔnjɛʀ] nf - **1.** [boîte] sweetbox Br, candy box Am - **2.** fig [appartement] bijou flat Br ou apartment Am.

bond [bɔ̃] nm [d'animal, de personne] leap, bound ; [de balle] bounce ; faire un ~ to leap (forward) ; faire faux ~ à qqn to let sb down.

bonde [bɔ̃d] nf - **1.** [d'évier] plug - **2.** [trou] bunghole - **3.** [bouchon] bung.

bondé, e [bɔ̃de] adj packed.

bondieuserie [bɔ̃djøzʀi] nf péj - **1.** [bigoterie] religiosity - **2.** [objet] religious trinket.

bondir [32] [bɔ̃diʀ] vi - **1.** [sauter] to leap, to bound ; ~ sur qqn/qqch to pounce on sb/sthg - **2.** [s'élancer] to leap forward - **3.** fig [réagir violemment] : ~ (de) to jump (with).

bonheur [bɔnœʀ] nm - **1.** [félicité] happiness - **2.** [chance] (good) luck, good fortune ; par ~ happily, fortunately ; au petit ~ haphazardly ; porter ~ to be lucky, to bring good luck.

bonhomie [bɔnɔmi] nf good-naturedness, good nature.

bonhomme [bɔnɔm] (pl bonshommes [bɔ̃zɔm]) nm - **1.** fam péj [homme] fellow - **2.** [petit garçon] fellow - **3.** [représentation] man ; ~ de neige snowman - **4.** loc : aller son petit ~ de chemin fig to jog along.

boniche [bɔniʃ] nf péj servant, skivvy Br.

bonification [bɔnifikasjɔ̃] nf - **1.** [de terre, de vin] improvement - **2.** SPORT bonus points (pl).

bonifier [9] [bɔnifje] vt to improve.
➥ **se bonifier** vp to improve.

boniment [bɔnimɑ̃] nm - **1.** [baratin] sales talk (U) - **2.** [mensonge] (tall) story.

bonjour [bɔ̃ʒuʀ] nm hello ; [avant midi] good morning ; [après midi] good afternoon ; c'est simple comme ~ it's (as) easy as ABC.

bonne [bɔn] ◇ nf maid ◇ adj ➪ bon.

bonne-maman [bɔnmamɑ̃] (pl bonnes-mamans) nf granny, grandma.

bonnement [bɔnmɑ̃] adv : tout ~ just, simply.

bonnet [bɔnɛ] nm - **1.** [coiffure] (woolly) hat ;

~ d'âne ≃ dunce's cap ; **~ de bain** swimming cap ; **~ de nuit** *fig* [personne] misery ; **gros ~** *fig* [personne] big cheese ; **~ phrygien** Phrygian cap *(worn by the sans-culottes during the French Revolution)* **- 2.** [de soutien-gorge] cup **- 3.** *loc* : **~ blanc et blanc ~** six of one and half a dozen of the other.

bonneterie [bɔnɛtri] *nf* **- 1.** [magasin] hosier's (shop) **- 2.** [marchandise] hosiery *(U)* **- 3.** [commerce] hosiery (business *ou* trade).

bon-papa [bɔ̃papa] *(pl* **bons-papas)** *nm* grandad, grandpa.

bonsoir [bɔ̃swar] *nm* [en arrivant] hello, good evening ; [en partant] goodbye, good evening ; [en se couchant] good night.

bonté [bɔ̃te] *nf* **- 1.** [qualité] goodness, kindness ; **avoir la ~ de faire qqch** *sout* to be so good *ou* kind as to do sthg **- 2.** *(gén pl)* [acte] act of kindness.

bonus [bɔnys] *nm* [prime d'assurance] no-claims bonus.

boom [bum] *nm* boom.

boomerang [bumrãg] *nm* boomerang.

borborygme [bɔrbɔrigm] *nm* rumbling *(U).*

bord [bɔr] *nm* **- 1.** [de table, de vêtement] edge ; [de verre, de chapeau] rim ; **à ras ~s** to the brim **- 2.** [de rivière] bank ; [de lac] edge, shore ; **au ~ de la mer** at the seaside **- 3.** [de bois, jardin] edge ; [de route] edge, side **- 4.** [d'un moyen de transport] : **passer par-dessus ~** to fall overboard ; **virer de ~** *NAVIG* to tack **- 5.** *loc* : **être du même ~** *fig* to be on the same side.

➥ **à bord de** *loc prép* : **à ~ de qqch** on board sthg.

➥ **au bord de** *loc prép* at the edge of ; *fig* on the verge of.

bordeaux [bɔrdo] ◇ *nm* **- 1.** [vin] Bordeaux **- 2.** [couleur] claret ◇ *adj inv* claret.

bordée [bɔrde] *nf* broadside ; **~ d'injures** *fig* torrent of abuse ; **~ de neige** *Can* heavy snowfall.

bordel [bɔrdɛl] *nm vulg* **- 1.** [maison close] brothel **- 2.** [désordre] shambles *(sg).*

border [3] [bɔrde] *vt* **- 1.** [vêtement] : **~ qqch de** to edge sthg with **- 2.** [être en bordure de] to line **- 3.** [voile] to haul on **- 4.** [couverture, personne] to tuck in.

bordereau, x [bɔrdəro] *nm* **- 1.** [liste] schedule **- 2.** [facture] invoice **- 3.** [relevé] slip ; **~ de salaire** pay slip.

bordure [bɔrdyr] *nf* **- 1.** [bord] edge ; **en ~ de** on the edge of **- 2.** [de fleurs] border **- 3.** [de vêtement] edge, edging.

boréal, e, aux [bɔreal, o] *adj* northern.

borgne [bɔrɲ] ◇ *nmf* [personne] one-eyed person ◇ *adj* **- 1.** [personne] one-eyed **- 2.** [fe-

nêtre] with an obstructed view **- 3.** *fig* [sordide] disreputable.

borne [bɔrn] *nf* **- 1.** [marque] boundary marker ; **~ kilométrique** ≃ milestone **- 2.** [limite] limit, bounds *(pl)* ; **dépasser les ~s** to go too far ; **sans ~s** boundless **- 3.** *fam* [kilomètre] kilometre *Br*, kilometer *Am* **- 4.** *INFORM* : **~ interactive** interactive terminal.

borné, e [bɔrne] *adj* **- 1.** [horizon] limited **- 2.** [personne] narrow-minded ; [esprit] narrow.

Bornéo [bɔrneo] *n* Borneo ; **à ~** in Borneo.

borner [3] [bɔrne] *vt* [terrain] to limit ; [projet, ambition] to limit, to restrict.

➥ **se borner** *vp* : **se ~ à qqch/à faire qqch** [suj : personne] to confine o.s. to sthg/to doing sthg.

bosniaque [bɔsnjak] *adj* Bosnian.

➥ **Bosniaque** *nmf* Bosnian.

Bosnie [bɔsni] *nf* : **la ~** Bosnia.

bosquet [bɔskɛ] *nm* copse.

bosse [bɔs] *nf* **- 1.** [sur tête, sur route] bump **- 2.** [de bossu, chameau] hump **- 3.** *loc* : **avoir la ~ des maths** *fam* to have a good head for maths *Br ou* math *Am* ; **rouler sa ~** *fam* to knock around *ou* about.

bosseler [24] [bɔsle] *vt* **- 1.** [cabosser] to dent **- 2.** [travailler] to emboss.

bosser [3] [bɔse] *vi fam* to work hard.

bosseur, euse [bɔsœr, øz] *fam* ◇ *adj* hardworking ◇ *nm, f* hard worker.

bossu, e [bɔsy] ◇ *adj* hunchbacked ◇ *nm, f* hunchback.

bot [bo] ▷ **pied.**

botanique [bɔtanik] ◇ *adj* botanical ◇ *nf* : **la ~** botany.

Botswana [bɔtswana] *nm* : **le ~** Botswana ; **au ~** in Botswana.

botte [bɔt] *nf* **- 1.** [chaussure] boot ; **~ de caoutchouc** wellington (boot) *Br*, rubber boot *Am* ; **lécher les ~s de qqn** *fam* to lick sb's boots ; **en avoir plein les ~s** *fam fig* to have had a bellyful **- 2.** [de légumes] bunch **- 3.** [en escrime] thrust, lunge.

botter [3] [bɔte] *vt* **- 1.** [chausser] : **être botté de cuir** to be wearing leather boots **- 2.** *fam* [donner un coup de pied à] to boot **- 3.** *fam vieilli* [plaire à] : **ça me botte** I dig it.

bottier [bɔtje] *nm* [de bottes] bootmaker ; [de chaussures] shoemaker.

bottillon [bɔtijɔ̃] *nm* (ankle) boot.

Bottin® [bɔtɛ̃] *nm* phone book.

bottine [bɔtin] *nf* (ankle) boot.

bouc [buk] *nm* **- 1.** [animal] (billy) goat ; **~ émissaire** *fig* scapegoat **- 2.** [barbe] goatee.

boucan [bukɑ̃] *nm fam* row, racket.

bouche [buʃ] *nf* - **1.** [gén] mouth ; ~ **d'incendie** fire hydrant ; ~ **de métro** metro entrance *ou* exit - **2.** *loc* : **garder qqch pour la bonne** ~ to save sthg till last *ou* the end ; **de** ~ **à oreille** by word of mouth ; **faire la fine** ~ to be awkward, to make difficulties.

bouché, e [buʃe] *adj* - **1.** [en bouteille] bottled - **2.** *fam* [personne] dumb, thick *Br*.

bouche-à-bouche [buʃabuʃ] *nm inv* : **faire du** ~ **à qqn** to give sb mouth-to-mouth resuscitation.

bouchée [buʃe] *nf* mouthful ; ~ **à la reine** *CULIN* chicken vol-au-vent ; **pour une** ~ **de pain** *fig* for a song.

boucher[1] [3] [buʃe] *vt* - **1.** [fermer - bouteille] to cork ; [- trou] to fill (in *ou* up) - **2.** [passage, vue] to block.

➤ **se boucher** *vp* to get blocked (up) ; **se** ~ **le nez** to hold one's nose.

boucher[2]**, ère** [buʃe, ɛr] *nm, f* butcher.

boucherie [buʃri] *nf* - **1.** [magasin] butcher's (shop) ; ~ **chevaline** horse butcher's - **2.** [commerce] butchery (trade) - **3.** *fig* [carnage] slaughter.

boucherie-charcuterie [buʃriʃarkytri] (*pl* **boucheries-charcuteries**) *nf* butcher's.

bouche-trou [buʃtru] (*pl* **bouche-trous**) *nm* - **1.** [personne] : **servir de** ~ to make up (the) numbers - **2.** [objet] stopgap.

bouchon [buʃɔ̃] *nm* - **1.** [pour obturer - gén] top ; [- de réservoir] cap ; [- de bouteille] cork ; ~ **de cire** buildup of wax in the ear - **2.** [de canne à pêche] float - **3.** [embouteillage] traffic jam.

bouchonner [3] [buʃɔne] ⬦ *vt* - **1.** [cheval] to rub down - **2.** [enfant] to pamper ⬦ *vi* : **ça bouchonne sur l'autoroute** there is a traffic jam on the motorway.

boucle [bukl] *nf* - **1.** [de ceinture, soulier] buckle - **2.** [bijou] : ~ **d'oreille** earring - **3.** [de cheveux] curl - **4.** [de fleuve, d'avion & *INFORM*] loop.

bouclé, e [bukle] *adj* [cheveux] curly ; [personne] curly-haired.

boucler [3] [bukle] *vt* - **1.** [attacher] to buckle ; [ceinture de sécurité] to fasten - **2.** [fermer] to shut - **3.** *fam* [enfermer - voleur] to lock up ; [- malade] to shut away - **4.** [encercler] to seal off - **5.** [terminer] to finish.

bouclier [buklije] *nm litt* & *fig* shield.

bouddha [buda] *nm* [statuette] buddha.

➤ **Bouddha** *nm* Buddha.

bouddhisme [budism] *nm* Buddhism.

bouddhiste [budist] *nmf* & *adj* Buddhist.

bouder [3] [bude] ⬦ *vi* to sulk ⬦ *vt* [chose] to dislike ; [personne] to shun ; **elle me boude de-**puis que je lui ai fait faux-bond she has cold-shouldered me ever since I let her down.

boudeur, euse [budœr, øz] ⬦ *adj* sulky ⬦ *nm, f* sulky person.

boudin [budɛ̃] *nm* - **1.** *CULIN* blood pudding ; ~ **blanc/noir** white/black pudding - **2.** *fam péj* [personne] podge.

boudiné, e [budine] *adj* - **1.** [gros] podgy - **2.** [serré] : **être** ~ **dans ses vêtements** to be squeezed into one's clothes.

boudoir [budwar] *nm* - **1.** [salon] boudoir - **2.** [biscuit] sponge finger.

boue [bu] *nf* mud ; **traîner qqn dans la** ~**, couvrir qqn de** ~ *fig* to drag sb *ou* sb's name through the mud.

bouée [bwe] *nf* - **1.** [balise] buoy - **2.** [pour flotter] rubber ring ; ~ **de sauvetage** lifebelt.

boueux, euse [buø, øz] *adj* muddy.

➤ **boueux** *nm fam* dustman *Br*, garbage man *Am*.

bouffant, e [bufɑ̃, ɑ̃t] *adj* [manche, jupe] full ; [cheveux] bouffant.

bouffe [buf] *nf fam* grub.

bouffée [bufe] *nf* - **1.** [de fumée] puff ; [de parfum] whiff ; [d'air] breath ; ~**s de chaleur** (hot) flushes *Br*, hot flashes *Am* - **2.** [accès] surge ; ~**s délirantes** mad fits.

bouffer [3] [bufe] ⬦ *vi* [manches] to puff out ⬦ *vt fam* [manger] to eat.

bouffi, e [bufi] *adj* : ~ **(de)** swollen (with).

bouffon, onne [bufɔ̃, ɔn] *adj* farcical.

➤ **bouffon** *nm* - **1.** *HIST* jester - **2.** [pitre] clown.

bouge [buʒ] *nm péj* - **1.** [taudis] hovel - **2.** [café] dive.

bougeoir [buʒwar] *nm* candlestick.

bougeotte [buʒɔt] *nf* : **avoir la** ~ to have itchy feet.

bouger [17] [buʒe] ⬦ *vt* [déplacer] to move ⬦ *vi* - **1.** [remuer] to move ; **je ne bouge pas (de chez moi) aujourd'hui** I'm staying at home today - **2.** [vêtement] to shrink - **3.** [changer] to change - **4.** [s'agiter] : **ça bouge partout dans le monde** there is unrest all over the world.

➤ **se bouger** *vp fam* - **1.** [faire des efforts] to move *ou* shift o.s. - **2.** [se déplacer] to move (over).

bougie [buʒi] *nf* - **1.** [chandelle] candle - **2.** [de moteur] spark plug, sparking plug.

bougon, onne [bugɔ̃, ɔn] ⬦ *adj* grumpy ⬦ *nm, f* grumbler.

bougonner [3] [bugɔne] *vt* & *vi* to grumble.

bougre, esse [bugr, ɛs] *nm, f fam* [homme] bloke *Br*, guy ; [femme] (old) girl.

➤ **bougre** *nm fam* : ~ **d'andouille!** you damned idiot!, you bloody fool! *Br*.

boui-boui [bwibwi] (*pl* **bouis-bouis**) *nm fam péj* (cheap) caff.

bouillabaisse [bujabɛs] *nf* bouillabaisse (*Provençal fish soup*).

bouillant, e [bujã, ãt] *adj* - **1.** [qui bout] boiling - **2.** [très chaud] boiling hot - **3.** *fig* [ardent] fiery.

bouille [buj] *nf fam* [visage] face.

bouilleur [bujœr] *nm* : **~ de cru** small-scale distiller.

bouillie [buji] *nf* baby's cereal ; **réduire en ~** [légumes] to puree ; [personne] to reduce to a pulp.

bouillir [48] [bujir] *vi* - **1.** [aliments] to boil ; **faire ~** to boil - **2.** *fig* [personne] : **~ (de)** to seethe (with).

bouilloire [bujwar] *nf* kettle.

bouillon [bujɔ̃] *nm* - **1.** [soupe] stock - **2.** [bouillonnement] bubble ; **faire bouillir à gros ~s** to bring to a rolling boil - **3.** [bactériologique] : **~ de culture** culture medium.

bouillonner [3] [bujɔne] *vi* - **1.** [liquide] to bubble - **2.** [torrent] to foam - **3.** *fig* [personne] to seethe.

bouillotte [bujɔt] *nf* hot-water bottle.

boul. *abr de* **boulevard**.

boulanger, ère [bulãʒe, ɛr] ◇ *adj* bakery (*avant n*), baking (*avant n*) ◇ *nm, f* baker.

boulangerie [bulãʒri] *nf* - **1.** [magasin] baker's (shop) - **2.** [commerce] bakery trade.

boulangerie-pâtisserie [bulãʒripatisri] (*pl* **boulangeries-pâtisseries**) *nf* ≃ baker's (shop).

boule [bul] *nf* - **1.** [gén] ball ; [de loto] counter ; [de pétanque] bowl ; **~ de commande** INFORM trackball ; **~ de neige** snowball ; **faire ~ de neige** to snowball - **2.** *loc* : **se mettre en ~** *fam* to blow one's top ; **perdre la ~** *fam* to lose one's marbles.

◆ boules *nfpl* [jeux] *game played on bare ground with steel bowls*.

◆ boules Quiès® *nfpl* *earplugs made of wax*.

bouleau, x [bulo] *nm* silver birch.

bouledogue [buldɔg] *nm* bulldog.

boulet [bulɛ] *nm* - **1.** [munition] : **~ de canon** cannonball ; **tirer à ~s rouges sur qqn** *fig* to let fly at sb - **2.** [de forçat] ball and chain - **3.** *fig* [fardeau] millstone (round one's neck).

boulette [bulɛt] *nf* - **1.** [petite boule] pellet - **2.** [de viande] meatball.

boulevard [bulvar] *nm* - **1.** [rue] boulevard ; **les grands ~s** *Paris boulevards running from the Place de la République to la Madeleine* - **2.** THÉÂTRE light comedy (*U*).

bouleversant, e [bulvɛrsã, ãt] *adj* distressing.

bouleversement [bulvɛrsəmã] *nm* disruption.

bouleverser [3] [bulvɛrse] *vt* - **1.** [objets] to turn upside down - **2.** [modifier] to disrupt - **3.** [émouvoir] to distress.

boulier [bulje] *nm* abacus.

boulimie [bulimi] *nf* bulimia.

bouliste [bulist] *nmf* bowls player.

Boulle [bul] *n* : **l'école ~** *prestigious school training cabinetmakers*.

boulon [bulɔ̃] *nm* bolt.

boulonner [3] [bulɔne] ◇ *vt* to bolt ◇ *vi fam* to slog (away).

boulot¹, otte [bulo, ɔt] *adj* dumpy.

boulot² [bulo] *nm fam* - **1.** [travail] work - **2.** [emploi] job.

boum [bum] ◇ *interj* bang! ◇ *nm* - **1.** [bruit] bang ; **faire ~** to go bang - **2.** ÉCON & *fig* boom ◇ *nf fam vieilli* party.

bouquet [bukɛ] *nm* - **1.** [de fleurs - gén] bunch (of flowers) ; [- formel] bouquet - **2.** [crevette] prawn - **3.** [de vin] bouquet - **4.** [de feu d'artifice] crowning piece - **5.** CULIN : **~ garni** bouquet garni - **6.** TÉLÉ : **~ de programmes** multichannel package - **7.** *loc* : **ça c'est le ~!** *fam* that takes the cake *ou* biscuit *Br*!

bouquetin [buktɛ̃] *nm* ibex.

bouquin [bukɛ̃] *nm fam* book.

bouquiner [3] [bukine] *vi* & *vt fam* to read.

bouquiniste [bukinist] *nmf* secondhand bookseller.

bourbeux, euse [burbø, øz] *adj* muddy.

bourbier [burbje] *nm* [lieu] quagmire, mire ; *fig* mess.

bourbon [burbɔ̃] *nm* [whisky] bourbon.

bourde [burd] *nf* - **1.** [baliverne] rubbish (*U*) - **2.** *fam* [erreur] blunder.

bourdon [burdɔ̃] *nm* - **1.** [insecte] bumblebee - **2.** [cloche] (large) bell - **3.** [ton grave] drone - **4.** *loc* : **avoir le ~** *fam* to be (feeling) down.

bourdonnement [burdɔnmã] *nm* - **1.** [d'insecte, de voix, de moteur] buzz (*U*) - **2.** *loc* : **avoir des ~s d'oreilles** to have a ringing in one's ears.

bourdonner [3] [burdɔne] *vi* - **1.** [insecte, machine, voix] to buzz - **2.** [oreille] to ring.

bourg [bur] *nm* market town.

bourgade [burgad] *nf* village.

bourgeois, e [burʒwa, az] ◇ *adj* - **1.** [valeur] middle-class - **2.** [cuisine] plain - **3.** *péj* [personne] bourgeois ◇ *nm, f* bourgeois.

bourgeoisie [burʒwazi] *nf* ≃ middle classes (*pl*).

bourgeon [burʒɔ̃] *nm* bud.

bourgeonner [3] [burʒɔne] *vi* to bud.

bourgmestre [burgmɛstr] *nm* burgomaster.

bourgogne [burgɔɲ] *nm* Burgundy *(wine)*.

Bourgogne [burgɔɲ] *nf* : **la ~** Burgundy.

bourguignon, onne [burgiɲɔ̃, ɔn] *adj* [de Bourgogne] Burgundian.

➤ **Bourguignon, onne** *nm, f* Burgundian.

bourlinguer [3] [burlɛ̃ge] *vi fam* [voyager] to bum around the world.

bourrade [burad] *nf* thump.

bourrage [buraʒ] *nm* [de coussin] stuffing.

➤ **bourrage de crâne** *nm* - **1.** [bachotage] swotting - **2.** [propagande] brainwashing.

bourrasque [burask] *nf* gust of wind.

bourratif, ive [buratif, iv] *adj* stodgy.

bourre [bur] *nf* - **1.** [de coussin] stuffing - **2.** [de laine] flock - **3.** [de bourgeon] down - **4.** *loc* : **être à la ~** *fam* [dans travail] to be behind ; [dans activité] to be running late.

bourré, e [bure] *adj fam* - **1.** [plein] : **~ (de)** [salle] packed (with) ; *fig* chock-full (of) - **2.** [ivre] plastered.

bourreau, x [buro] *nm* - **1.** HIST executioner - **2.** [personne cruelle] torturer ; **~ de travail** workaholic.

bourrelé [burle] ⫐ **remords**.

bourrelet [burlɛ] *nm* - **1.** [de graisse] roll of fat - **2.** [de porte] draught *Br ou* draft *Am* excluder.

bourrer [3] [bure] *vt* - **1.** [remplir - coussin] to stuff ; [- pipe] to fill ; [- sac, armoire] : **~ qqch (de)** to cram sthg full (with) - **2.** *fam* [gaver] : **~ qqn (de)** to stuff sb (with) - **3.** *fam* [estomac] : **ça bourre!** it's really filling!

➤ **se bourrer** *vp fam* - **1.** [se gaver] : **se ~ (de qqch)** to stuff o.s. (with sthg) - **2.** [se soûler] : **se ~ la gueule** to get plastered.

bourricot [buriko] *nm* (small) donkey.

bourrique [burik] *nf* - **1.** [ânesse] she-ass ; **faire tourner qqn en ~** *fam fig* to drive sb up the wall - **2.** *fam* [personne] pigheaded person.

bourru, e [bury] *adj* [peu aimable] surly.

bourse [burs] *nf* - **1.** [porte-monnaie] purse ; **sans ~ délier** without spending anything - **2.** [d'études] grant.

➤ **Bourse** *nf* [marché] stock exchange, stock market ; **la Bourse de Paris** the Paris Stock Exchange ; **jouer en Bourse** to speculate on the stock exchange *ou* stock market ; **Bourse de commerce** commodity market.

boursicoter [3] [bursikɔte] *vi* to dabble (on the stock market).

boursier, ère [bursje, ɛr] ⬦ *adj* - **1.** [élève] on a grant - **2.** FIN stock-exchange, stock-market *(avant n)* ⬦ *nm, f* - **1.** [étudiant] student on a grant - **2.** FIN stockbroker.

boursouflé, e [bursufle] *adj* - **1.** [enflé] swollen - **2.** [emphatique] overblown.

boursoufler [3] [bursufle] *vt* to puff up, to swell.

➤ **se boursoufler** *vp* [peinture] to blister.

bous, bout *etc* ⫐ **bouillir**.

bousculade [buskylad] *nf* - **1.** [cohue] crush - **2.** [agitation] rush.

bousculer [3] [buskyle] *vt* - **1.** [pousser] to shove - **2.** [faire tomber] to knock over - **3.** [presser] to rush - **4.** [modifier] to overturn.

➤ **se bousculer** *vp* to jostle each other.

bouse [buz] *nf* : **~ de vache** cow dung.

bousiller [3] [buzije] *vt fam* - **1.** [abîmer] to ruin, to knacker *Br* - **2.** [bâcler] to botch.

boussole [busɔl] *nf* compass.

bout [bu] *nm* - **1.** [extrémité, fin] end ; **~ à ~** end to end ; **au ~ de** [temps] after ; [espace] at the end of ; **d'un ~ à l'autre** [de ville etc] from one end to the other ; [de livre] from beginning to end ; **~ filtre** filter tip - **2.** [morceau] bit - **3.** *loc* : **au ~ du compte** all things considered ; **à tout ~ de champ** every five minutes ; **être à ~** to be exhausted ; **il n'est pas au ~ de ses peines** his troubles are not over yet ; **à ~ de souffle** out of breath, breathless ; **être à ~ de forces** to have no strength left ; **mener qqn par le ~ du nez** to lead sb by the nose ; **à ~ portant** at point-blank range ; **pousser qqn à ~** to drive sb to distraction ; **être au ~ du rouleau** to have come to the end of the road ; **venir à ~ de** [personne] to get the better of ; [difficulté] to overcome.

➤ **bout de chou** *nm fam* poppet.

boutade [butad] *nf* [plaisanterie] jest.

boute-en-train [butɑ̃trɛ̃] *nm inv* live wire ; **il était le ~ de la soirée** he was the life and soul of the party.

bouteille [butɛj] *nf* bottle ; **mettre en ~ ou ~s** to bottle ; **prendre de la ~** *fam fig* to be getting on a bit.

boutique [butik] *nf* [gén] shop ; [de mode] boutique ; **~ hors-taxe** duty-free shop ; **fermer ~** to shut up shop ; **parler ~** to talk shop.

bouton [butɔ̃] *nm* - **1.** COUTURE button ; **~ de manchette** cuff link - **2.** [sur la peau] spot - **3.** [de porte] knob - **4.** [commutateur] switch - **5.** [bourgeon] bud.

bouton-d'or [butɔ̃dɔr] *(pl* **boutons-d'or***) nm* buttercup.

boutonner [3] [butɔne] *vt* to button (up).

➤ **se boutonner** *vp* [vêtement] to button.

boutonneux, euse [butɔnø, øz] *adj* spotty.

boutonnière [butɔnjɛr] *nf* [de vêtement] buttonhole.

bouton-pression [butɔ̃presjɔ̃] (*pl* **boutons-pression**) *nm* press-stud *Br*, snap fastener *Am*.

bouture [butyr] *nf* cutting.

bouvier [buvje] *nm* - **1.** [personne] herdsman - **2.** [chien] sheepdog.

bouvreuil [buvrœj] *nm* bullfinch.

bovidé [bɔvide] *nm* bovine.

bovin, e [bɔvɛ̃, in] *adj* bovine.
bovins *nmpl* cattle.

bowling [buliŋ] *nm* - **1.** [jeu] bowling - **2.** [lieu] bowling alley.

box [bɔks] (*pl* **boxes**) *nm* - **1.** [d'écurie] loose box - **2.** [compartiment] cubicle ; **le ~ des accusés** the dock - **3.** [parking] lock-up garage.

boxe [bɔks] *nf* boxing.

boxer¹ [3] [bɔkse] <> *vi* to box <> *vt fam* to thump.

boxer² [bɔksɛr] *nm* [chien] boxer.

boxeur [bɔksœr] *nm SPORT* boxer.

boyau [bwajo] *nm* - **1.** [chambre à air] inner tube - **2.** [corde] catgut - **3.** [galerie] narrow gallery.
boyaux *nmpl* [intestins] guts.

boycott [bɔjkɔt] *nm* boycott.

boycotter [3] [bɔjkɔte] *vt* to boycott.

boy-scout [bɔjskut] (*pl* **boy-scouts**) *nm vieilli* boy scout.

BP (*abr de* **boîte postale**) *nf* PO Box.

BPF (*abr de* **bon pour francs**) *printed on cheques before space where amount is to be inserted.*

bracelet [braslɛ] *nm* - **1.** [bijou] bracelet - **2.** [de montre] strap.

bracelet-montre [braslɛmɔ̃tr] (*pl* **bracelets-montres**) *nm* wristwatch.

braconnage [brakɔnaʒ] *nm* poaching.

braconner [3] [brakɔne] *vi* to go poaching, to poach.

braconnier [brakɔnje] *nm* poacher.

brader [3] [brade] *vt* [solder] to sell off ; [vendre à bas prix] to sell for next to nothing.

braderie [bradri] *nf* clearance sale.

braguette [bragɛt] *nf* flies (*pl*).

braille [braj] *nm* Braille.

brailler [3] [braje] <> *vi* to bawl <> *vt* to bawl (out).

braire [112] [brɛr] *vi* - **1.** [âne] to bray - **2.** *fam* [personne] to bellow.

braise [brɛz] *nf* embers (*pl*) ; **cuire sous la ~** to cook in the embers of a fire ; **de ~** *fig* fiery.

braiser [4] [breze] *vt* to braise.

bramer [3] [brame] *vi* [cerf] to bell.

brancard [brãkar] *nm* - **1.** [civière] stretcher - **2.** [de charrette] shaft ; **ruer dans les ~s** *fig* to rebel, to protest.

brancardier, ère [brãkardje, ɛr] *nm, f* stretcher-bearer.

branchage [brãʃaʒ] *nm* branches (*pl*).

branche [brãʃ] *nf* - **1.** [gén] branch - **2.** [de lunettes] arm - **3.** [de compas] leg.

branché, e [brãʃe] *adj* - **1.** *ÉLECTR* plugged in, connected - **2.** *fam* [à la mode] trendy.

branchement [brãʃmã] *nm* - **1.** [raccordement] connection, plugging in - **2.** [bifurcation] branch.

brancher [3] [brãʃe] *vt* - **1.** [raccorder & *INFORM*] to connect ; **~ qqch sur** *ÉLECTR* to plug sthg into - **2.** *fam* [orienter] to steer ; **~ qqn sur qqch** to start sb off on sthg ; **~ la conversation sur** to steer the conversation towards *Br ou* toward *Am* - **3.** *fam* [plaire] to appeal to.

branchies [brãʃi] *nfpl* [de poisson] gills.

brandade [brãdad] *nf* : **~ de morue** *creamed salt cod.*

brandir [32] [brãdir] *vt* to wave.

branlant, e [brãlã, ãt] *adj* [escalier, mur] shaky ; [meuble, dent] wobbly.

branle [brãl] *nm* : **mettre en ~** to set in motion.

branle-bas [brãlba] *nm inv* pandemonium (*U*) ; **~ de combat** action stations (*pl*).

branler [3] [brãle] <> *vt* - **1.** [hocher] : **~ la tête** to shake one's head - **2.** *tfam* [faire] : **qu'est-ce qu'il branle?** what is he playing at? <> *vi* [escalier, chaise] to be shaky ; [dent, meuble] to be wobbly.
se branler *vp vulg* to wank *Br*, to jerk off.

braquage [brakaʒ] *nm* - **1.** *AUTOM* lock - **2.** [attaque] holdup.

braquer [3] [brake] <> *vt* - **1.** [diriger] : **~ qqch sur** [arme] to aim sthg at ; [télescope] to train sthg on ; [regard] to fix sthg on - **2.** [contrarier] to antagonize - **3.** *fam* [attaquer] to hold up <> *vi* to turn (the wheel).
se braquer *vp* [personne] to take a stand.

bras [bra] *nm* - **1.** [gén] arm ; **~ dessus ~ dessous** arm in arm ; **le ~ en écharpe** with one's arm in a sling ; **~ droit** right-hand man *ou* woman ; **~ de fer** [jeu] arm wrestling ; *fig* trial of strength ; **baisser les ~** to throw in the towel ; **en ~ de chemise** in one's shirtsleeves ; **se croiser les ~** just to sit there ; **avoir le ~ long** [avoir de l'influence] to have pull - **2.** [main-d'œuvre] hand, worker - **3.** [de cours d'eau] branch ; **~ de mer** arm of the sea.

brasier [brazje] *nm* [incendie] blaze, inferno.

Brasilia [brazilja] *n* Brasilia.

67

brièveté

bras-le-corps [bralkɔr] ➤ **à bras-le-corps** *loc adv* bodily.

brassage [brasaʒ] *nm* - **1.** [de bière] brewing - **2.** *fig* [mélange] mixing.

brassard [brasar] *nm* armband.

brasse [bras] *nf* [nage] breaststroke ; ~ **coulée** breaststroke ; ~ **papillon** butterfly (stroke).

brassée [brase] *nf* armful.

brasser [3] [brase] *vt* - **1.** [bière] to brew - **2.** [mélanger] to mix - **3.** *fig* [manier] to handle.

brasserie [brasri] *nf* - **1.** [usine] brewery - **2.** [industrie] brewing (industry) - **3.** [café-restaurant] brasserie.

brasseur, euse [brasœr, øz] *nm, f* - **1.** [de bière] brewer - **2.** *fig* : ~ **d'affaires** wheeler-dealer - **3.** [nageur] breaststroke swimmer.

brassière [brasjɛr] *nf* - **1.** [de bébé] (baby's) vest *Br ou* undershirt *Am* - **2.** [gilet de sauvetage] life jacket - **3.** *Can* [soutien-gorge] bra.

bravade [bravad] *nf* bravado ; **par** ~ out of bravado.

brave [brav] ◇ *adj* - **1.** *(après n)* [courageux] brave - **2.** *(avant n)* [honnête] decent - **3.** [naïf et gentil] nice ◇ *nmf* : **mon** ~ my good man.

bravement [bravmɑ̃] *adv* - **1.** [courageusement] bravely - **2.** [résolument] determinedly.

braver [3] [brave] *vt* - **1.** [parents, règlement] to defy - **2.** [mépriser] to brave.

bravo [bravo] *interj* bravo!
➤ **bravos** *nmpl* cheers.

bravoure [bravur] *nf* bravery.

BRB (*abr de* **Brigade de répression du banditisme**) *nf French serious crime squad.*

break [brɛk] *nm* - **1.** [voiture] estate (car) *Br*, station wagon *Am* - **2.** [jazz] break - **3.** [pause] break.

brebis [brəbi] *nf* ewe ; ~ **galeuse** black sheep.

brèche [brɛʃ] *nf* - **1.** [de mur] gap - **2.** *MIL* breach - **3.** *loc* : **battre qqn en** ~ [attaquer] to knock sb down ; **battre qqch en** ~ *fig* to demolish sthg ; **être sur la** ~ to be hard at work.

bredouille [brəduj] *adj* : **être/rentrer** ~ to be/to return empty-handed.

bredouillement [brədujmɑ̃] *nm* stammering.

bredouiller [3] [brəduje] ◇ *vi* to stammer ◇ *vt* to stammer (out).

bref, brève [brɛf, brɛv] *adj* - **1.** [gén] short, brief ; **soyez** ~! make it brief! - **2.** *LING* short.
➤ **bref** *adv* in short, in a word ; **en** ~ briefly.
➤ **brève** *nf PRESSE* brief news item.

brelan [brəlɑ̃] *nm* : **un** ~ three of a kind ; **un** ~ **de valets** three jacks.

breloque [brələk] *nf* charm.

brème [brɛm] *nf* [poisson] bream.

Brésil [brezil] *nm* : **le** ~ Brazil ; **au** ~ in Brazil.

brésilien, enne [breziljɛ̃, ɛn] *adj* Brazilian.
➤ **Brésilien, enne** *nm, f* Brazilian.

Bretagne [brətaɲ] *nf* : **la** ~ Brittany.

bretelle [brətɛl] *nf* - **1.** [d'autoroute] access road, slip road *Br* - **2.** [de fusil] sling - **3.** [de pantalon] : ~**s** braces *Br*, suspenders *Am* - **4.** [de bustier] strap.

breton, onne [brətɔ̃, ɔn] *adj* Breton.
➤ **breton** *nm* [langue] Breton.
➤ **Breton, onne** *nm, f* Breton.

breuvage [brœvaʒ] *nm* [boisson] beverage.

brève ➤ **bref**.

brevet [brəvɛ] *nm* - **1.** [certificat] certificate ; ~ **de secouriste** first-aid certificate - **2.** [diplôme] diploma ; ~ **des collèges** *school certificate taken after four years of secondary education* - **3.** [d'invention] patent ; **déposer un** ~ to file a patent - **4.** *fig* [assurance] guarantee.

breveter [27] [brəvte] *vt* to patent ; **faire** ~ **qqch** to take out a patent on sthg, to patent sthg.

bréviaire [brevjɛr] *nm* breviary.

bribe [brib] *nf* [fragment] scrap, bit ; *fig* snippet ; ~**s de conversation** snatches of conversation.

bric [brik] ➤ **de bric et de broc** *loc adv* any old how.

bric-à-brac [brikabrak] *nm inv* bric-a-brac.

bricolage [brikɔlaʒ] *nm* - **1.** [travaux] do-it-yourself, DIY - **2.** [réparation provisoire] patching up.

bricole [brikɔl] *nf* - **1.** [babiole] trinket - **2.** [chose insignifiante] trivial matter.

bricoler [3] [brikɔle] ◇ *vi* to do odd jobs (around the house) ◇ *vt* - **1.** [réparer] to fix, to mend - **2.** [fabriquer] to make, to knock up *Br*.

bricoleur, euse [brikɔlœr, øz] ◇ *adj* handy (about the house) ◇ *nm, f* home handyman (*f* handywoman).

bride [brid] *nf* - **1.** [de cheval] bridle ; **à** ~ **abattue** at full tilt ; **lâcher la** ~ **à qqn** to give sb his/her head - **2.** [de chapeau] string - **3.** *COUTURE* bride, bar - **4.** *TECHNOL* flange.

bridé [bride] ➤ **œil**.

brider [3] [bride] *vt* [cheval] to bridle ; *fig* to rein (in).

bridge [bridʒ] *nm* bridge.

brie [bri] *nm* [fromage] Brie.

briefer [3] [brife] *vt* to brief.

briefing [brifiŋ] *nm* briefing.

brièvement [brijɛvmɑ̃] *adv* briefly.

brièveté [brijɛvte] *nf* brevity, briefness.

brigade [brigad] *nf* - **1.** [d'ouvriers, de soldats] brigade - **2.** [détachement] squad ; ~ **antigang** *police squad concerned with combating terrorism and organized crime* ; ~ **des mœurs/des stups** vice/drugs squad ; ~ **volante** flying squad.

brigadier [brigadje] *nm* - **1.** MIL corporal - **2.** [de police] sergeant.

brigand [brigã] *nm* - **1.** [bandit] bandit - **2.** [homme malhonnête] crook.

brigandage [brigãdaʒ] *nm* - **1.** [vol à main armée] armed robbery - **2.** [action malhonnête] robbery.

briguer [3] [brige] *vt sout* to aspire to ; ~ **un second mandat** to seek re-election.

brillamment [brijamã] *adv* [gén] brilliantly ; [réussir un examen] with flying colours.

brillant, e [brijã, ãt] *adj* - **1.** [qui brille - gén] sparkling ; [- cheveux] glossy ; [- yeux] bright - **2.** [remarquable] brilliant.

➤ **brillant** *nm* - **1.** [diamant] brilliant - **2.** [éclat] shine.

brillantine [brijãtin] *nf* brilliantine.

briller [3] [brije] *vi* to shine.

brimade [brimad] *nf* - **1.** [vexation] harassment *(U)* - **2.** [de bizutage] bullying *(U)*.

brimer [3] [brime] *vt* to victimize, to bully.

brin [brɛ̃] *nm* - **1.** [tige] twig ; ~ **d'herbe** blade of grass ; **un beau** ~ **de fille** a fine figure of a girl - **2.** [fil] strand - **3.** [petite quantité] : **un** ~ **(de)** a bit (of) ; **faire un** ~ **de toilette** to have a quick wash.

brindille [brɛ̃dij] *nf* twig.

bringue [brɛ̃g] *nf fam* binge ; **faire la** ~ to go on a binge.

bringuebaler, brinquebaler [3] [brɛ̃gbale] *vi* [voiture] to jolt along.

brio [brijo] *nm* - **1.** MUS brio - **2.** [talent] : **avec** ~ brilliantly.

brioche [brijɔʃ] *nf* - **1.** [pâtisserie] brioche - **2.** *fam* [ventre] paunch.

brioché, e [brijɔʃe] *adj* [pain] brioche-style.

brique [brik] ◇ *nf* - **1.** [pierre] brick - **2.** [emballage] carton - **3.** *fam* [argent] *10,000 francs* ◇ *adj inv* brick red.

briquer [3] [brike] *vt* to scrub.

briquet [brikɛ] *nm* (cigarette) lighter.

briqueterie [briketri] *nf* brickworks *(sg)*.

bris [bri] *nm* [destruction] breaking ; ~ **de glace** broken windows.

brisant [brizã] *nm* [écueil] reef.

➤ **brisants** *nmpl* [récif] breakers.

brise [briz] *nf* breeze.

brisé, e [brize] *adj fig* broken ; ~ **de chagrin**

overwhelmed by sorrow ; ~ **de fatigue** exhausted.

brise-glace(s) [brizglas] *nm inv* [navire] icebreaker.

brise-jet [brizʒɛ] *nm inv* nozzle *(for tap)*.

brise-lames [brizlam] *nm inv* breakwater.

brise-mottes [brizmɔt] *nm inv* harrow.

briser [3] [brize] *vt* - **1.** [gén] to break - **2.** *fig* [carrière] to ruin ; [conversation] to break off ; [espérances] to shatter.

➤ **se briser** *vp* - **1.** [gén] to break - **2.** *fig* [espoir] to be dashed ; [efforts] to be thwarted.

briseur, euse [brizœr, øz] *nm, f* : ~ **de grève** strike-breaker.

bristol [bristɔl] *nm* - **1.** [papier] Bristol board - **2.** *vieilli* [carte de visite] visiting card.

britannique [britanik] *adj* British.

➤ **Britannique** *nmf* British person, Briton ; **les Britanniques** the British.

broc [bro] *nm* jug.

brocante [brɔkãt] *nf* - **1.** [commerce] secondhand trade - **2.** [objets] secondhand goods *(pl)*.

brocanteur, euse [brɔkãtœr, øz] *nm, f* dealer in secondhand goods.

brocart [brɔkar] *nm* brocade.

broche [brɔʃ] *nf* - **1.** [bijou] brooch - **2.** CULIN spit ; **cuire à la** ~ to spit-roast - **3.** ÉLECTR & MÉD pin - **4.** [de métier à filer] spindle.

broché, e [brɔʃe] *adj* - **1.** [tissu] brocade *(avant n)*, brocaded - **2.** TYPO : **livre** ~ paperback (book).

brochet [brɔʃɛ] *nm* pike.

brochette [brɔʃɛt] *nf* - **1.** [ustensile] skewer - **2.** [plat] kebab - **3.** *fam fig* [groupe] string, row.

brochure [brɔʃyr] *nf* - **1.** [imprimé] brochure, booklet - **2.** [de livre] binding - **3.** [de tissu] brocaded pattern.

brocoli [brɔkɔli] *nm* broccoli *(U)*.

brodequin [brɔdkɛ̃] *nm* boot.

broder [3] [brɔde] *vt & vi* to embroider.

broderie [brɔdri] *nf* - **1.** [art] embroidery - **2.** [ouvrage] (piece of) embroidery.

broie, broies *etc* ▷ **broyer**.

bromure [brɔmyr] *nm* bromide.

bronche [brɔ̃ʃ] *nf* bronchus ; **j'ai des problèmes de ~s** I've got chest problems.

broncher [3] [brɔ̃ʃe] *vi* to stumble ; **sans** ~ without complaining, uncomplainingly.

bronchiolite [brɔ̃kjɔlit] *nf* bronchiolitis.

bronchite [brɔ̃ʃit] *nf* bronchitis *(U)*.

bronzage [brɔ̃zaʒ] *nm* - **1.** [de peau] tan, suntan - **2.** [de métal] bronzing.

bronzant, e [brɔ̃zã, ãt] *adj* suntan *(avant n)*.

bronze [brɔ̃z] *nm* bronze.

bronzé, e [brɔ̃ze] *adj* tanned, suntanned.
bronzer [3] [brɔ̃ze] *vi* [peau] to tan ; [personne] to get a tan.
brosse [brɔs] *nf* brush ; ~ **à cheveux** hairbrush ; ~ **à dents** toothbrush ; ~ **à habits** clothes brush ; **avoir les cheveux en** ~ to have a crew cut.
brosser [3] [brɔse] *vt* - **1.** [habits, cheveux] to brush - **2.** [paysage, portrait] to paint.
➡ **se brosser** *vp* to brush one's clothes, to brush o.s. down ; **se** ~ **les cheveux/les dents** to brush one's hair/teeth.
brou ➡ **brou de noix** *nm* - **1.** [liqueur] walnut liqueur - **2.** [teinture] walnut stain.
brouet [brue] *nm* gruel.
brouette [bruɛt] *nf* wheelbarrow.
brouhaha [bruaa] *nm* hubbub.
brouillard [brujar] *nm* [léger] mist ; [dense] fog ; ~ **givrant** freezing fog ; **être dans le** ~ *fig* to be lost.
brouille [bruj] *nf* quarrel.
brouillé, e [bruje] *adj* - **1.** [fâché] : **être** ~ **avec qqn** to be on bad terms with sb ; **être** ~ **avec qqch** *fig* to be hopeless *ou* useless at sthg - **2.** [teint] muddy - **3.** ⊏ **œuf.**
brouiller [3] [bruje] *vt* - **1.** [désunir] to set at odds, to put on bad terms - **2.** [vue] to blur - **3.** [RADIO - accidentellement] to cause interference to ; [- délibérément] to jam - **4.** [rendre confus] to muddle (up).
➡ **se brouiller** *vp* - **1.** [se fâcher] to fall out ; **se** ~ **avec qqn (pour qqch)** to fall out with sb (over sthg) - **2.** [se troubler] to become blurred - **3.** [devenir confus] to get muddled (up), to become confused - **4.** MÉTÉOR to cloud over.
brouilleur [brujœr] *nm* INFORM scrambler.
brouillon, onne [brujɔ̃, ɔn] *adj* careless, untidy.
➡ **brouillon** *nm* rough copy, draft.
broussaille [brusaj] *nf* : **les** ~**s** the undergrowth ; **en** ~ *fig* [cheveux] untidy ; [sourcils] bushy.
broussailleux, euse [brusajø, øz] *adj* - **1.** [région] scrubby - **2.** [sourcils] bushy.
brousse [brus] *nf* GÉOGR scrubland, bush.
brouter [3] [brute] *vt* to graze on ⟨⟩ *vi* - **1.** [animal] to graze - **2.** TECHNOL to judder.
broutille [brutij] *nf* trifle.
broyer [13] [brwaje] *vt* to grind, to crush.
broyeur [brwajœr] *nm* : **évier à** ~ sink with waste disposal unit.
bru [bry] *nf sout* daughter-in-law.
brucelles [brysɛl] *nfpl* - **1.** [pince] (pair of) tweezers - **2.** *Helv* [pince à épiler] (pair of) eyebrow tweezers.

brugnon [bryɲɔ̃] *nm* nectarine.
bruine [brɥin] *nf* drizzle.
bruire [105] [brɥir] *vi* [feuilles, étoffe] to rustle ; [eau] to murmur.
bruissement [brɥismã] *nm* [de feuilles, d'étoffe] rustle, rustling (U) ; [d'eau] murmur, murmuring (U).
bruit [brɥi] *nm* - **1.** [son] noise, sound ; ~ **de fond** background noise - **2.** [vacarme & TECHNOL] noise ; **faire du** ~ to make a noise ; **sans** ~ silently, noiselessly - **3.** [rumeur] rumour *Br*, rumor *Am* - **4.** [retentissement] fuss ; **faire du** ~ to cause a stir.
bruitage [brɥitaʒ] *nm* sound-effects *(pl)*.
brûlant, e [brylã, ãt] *adj* - **1.** [gén] burning (hot) ; [liquide] boiling (hot) ; [plat] piping hot - **2.** *fig* [amour, question] burning.
brûle-pourpoint [brylpurpwɛ̃] ➡ **à brûle-pourpoint** *loc adv* point-blank, straight out.
brûler [3] [bryle] ⟨⟩ *vt* - **1.** [gén] to burn ; [suj : eau bouillante] to scald ; **la fumée me brûle les yeux** the smoke is making my eyes sting - **2.** [café] to roast - **3.** [feu rouge] to drive through ; [étape] to miss out, to skip ⟨⟩ *vi* - **1.** [gén] to burn ; [maison, forêt] to be on fire - **2.** [être brûlant] to be burning (hot) ; ~ **de** *fig* to be consumed with ; ~ **de faire qqch** to be longing *ou* dying to do sthg ; ~ **de fièvre** to be running a high temperature.
➡ **se brûler** *vp* to burn o.s.
brûlis [bryli] *nm* burn-off.
brûlure [brylyr] *nf* - **1.** [lésion] burn ; ~ **au premier/troisième degré** first-degree/third-degree burn - **2.** [sensation] burning (sensation) ; **avoir des** ~**s d'estomac** to have heartburn.
brume [brym] *nf* mist.
brumeux, euse [brymø, øz] *adj* misty ; *fig* hazy.
brun, e [brœ̃, bryn] ⟨⟩ *adj* brown ; [cheveux] dark ⟨⟩ *nm, f* dark-haired man (*f* woman).
➡ **brun** *nm* [couleur] brown.
➡ **brune** *nf* - **1.** [cigarette] *cigarette made of dark tobacco* - **2.** [bière] brown ale.
brunâtre [brynatr] *adj* brownish.
brunir [32] [brynir] ⟨⟩ *vt* - **1.** [peau] to tan - **2.** [métal] to polish, to burnish ⟨⟩ *vi* [personne] to get a tan ; [peau] to tan.
Brushing® [brœʃiŋ] *nm* : **faire un** ~ **à qqn** to give sb a blow-dry, to blow-dry sb's hair.
brusque [brysk] *adj* abrupt.
brusquement [bryskəmã] *adv* abruptly.
brusquer [3] [bryske] *vt* to rush ; [élève] to push.
brusquerie [bryskəri] *nf* abruptness.

brut, e [bryt] adj - **1.** [pierre précieuse, bois] rough ; [sucre] unrefined ; [métal, soie] raw ; [champagne] extra dry ; (**pétrole**) ~ crude (oil) - **2.** fig [fait, idées] crude, raw - **3.** ÉCON gross.
➤ **brute** nf brute.

brutal, e, aux [brytal, o] adj - **1.** [violent] violent, brutal ; **être ~ avec qqn** to be brutal to sb - **2.** [soudain] sudden - **3.** [manière] blunt.

brutalement [brytalmɑ̃] adv - **1.** [violemment] brutally - **2.** [soudainement] suddenly - **3.** [sèchement] bluntly.

brutaliser [3] [brytalize] vt to mistreat.

brutalité [brytalite] nf - **1.** [violence] violence, brutality - **2.** [caractère soudain] suddenness.
➤ **brutalités** nfpl brutality (U).

Bruxelles [bry(k)sɛl] n Brussels.

bruxellois, e [brysɛlwa, az] adj of/from Brussels.
➤ **Bruxellois, e** nm, f native ou inhabitant of Brussels.

bruyamment [brɥijamɑ̃] adv noisily.

bruyant, e [brɥijɑ̃, ɑ̃t] adj noisy.

bruyère [bryjɛr] nf - **1.** [plante] heather - **2.** [lande] heathland.

BT ◇ nm (abr de **brevet de technicien**) vocational training certificate (taken at age 18) ◇ nf (abr de **basse tension**) LT.

BTA (abr de **brevet de technicien agricole**) nm agricultural training certificate (taken at age 18).

BTP (abr de **bâtiment et travaux publics**) nmpl building and public works sector.

BTS (abr de **brevet de technicien supérieur**) nm advanced vocational training certificate (taken at the end of a 2-year higher education course).

bu, e [by] pp ➩ **boire.**

BU (abr de **bibliothèque universitaire**) nf university library.

buanderie [bɥɑ̃dri] nf laundry.

buccal, e, aux [bykal, o] adj buccal ; **par voie ~e** orally.

bûche [byʃ] nf - **1.** [bois] log ; **~ de Noël** Yule log ; **prendre** ou **ramasser une ~** fam to fall flat on one's face - **2.** fam [personne] lump.

bûcher¹ [byʃe] nm - **1.** [supplice] : **le ~** the stake - **2.** [funéraire] pyre.

bûcher² [3] [byʃe] ◇ vi to swot ◇ vt to swot up.

bûcheron, onne [byʃrɔ̃, ɔn] nm, f forestry worker.

bûcheur, euse [byʃœr, øz] ◇ adj hardworking ◇ nm, f fam swot Br, grind Am.

bucolique [bykɔlik] adj pastoral.

budget [bydʒɛ] nm budget.

budgétaire [bydʒetɛr] adj budgetary ; **année ~** financial Br ou fiscal Am year.

budgétiser [3] [bydʒetize] vt to budget for.

buée [bɥe] nf [sur vitre] condensation.

buffet [byfɛ] nm - **1.** [meuble] sideboard - **2.** [repas] buffet - **3.** [café-restaurant] : **~ de gare** station buffet.

buffle [byfl] nm [animal] buffalo.

bug [bʌg] nm = **bogue.**

buis [bɥi] nm box(wood).

buisson [bɥisɔ̃] nm bush.

buissonnière [bɥisɔnjɛr] ➩ **école.**

bulbe [bylb] nm bulb.

bulgare [bylgar] adj Bulgarian.
➤ **bulgare** nm [langue] Bulgarian.
➤ **Bulgare** nmf Bulgarian.

Bulgarie [bylgari] nf : **la ~** Bulgaria.

bulldozer [byldozer] nm bulldozer.

bulle [byl] nf - **1.** [gén] bubble ; **~ de savon** soap bubble - **2.** [de bande dessinée] speech balloon - **3.** RELIG (papal) bull.

bulletin [byltɛ̃] nm - **1.** [communiqué] bulletin ; **~ (de la) météo** weather forecast ; **~ de santé** medical bulletin - **2.** [imprimé] form ; **~ de vote** ballot paper - **3.** SCOL report - **4.** [certificat] certificate ; **~ de consigne** left luggage ticket Br, luggage room ou checkroom ticket Am ; **~ de salaire** ou **de paye** pay slip.

bulletin-réponse [byltɛ̃repɔ̃s] (pl **bulletins-réponse**) nm reply form.

bungalow [bœ̃galo] nm [maison] bungalow ; [de vacances] chalet.

bunker [bunkœr] nm bunker.

buraliste [byralist] nmf - **1.** [d'un bureau de tabac] tobacconist - **2.** [préposé] clerk.

bure [byr] nf - **1.** [étoffe] coarse brown woollen cloth - **2.** [de moine] frock.

bureau [byro] nm - **1.** [gén] office ; **~ d'aide sociale** social security office ; **~ de change** bureau de change ; **~ d'études** design office ; **~ de poste** post office ; **~ de tabac** tobacconist's ; **~ de vote** polling station - **2.** [meuble] desk - **3.** [comité] committee.

bureaucrate [byrokrat] nmf bureaucrat.

bureaucratie [byrokrasi] nf bureaucracy.

bureaucratique [byrokratik] adj péj bureaucratic.

bureautique [byrotik] nf office automation.

burette [byrɛt] nf - **1.** [flacon] cruet - **2.** [de chimiste] burette - **3.** [de mécanicien] oilcan.

burin [byrɛ̃] nm - **1.** [outil] chisel - **2.** [gravure] engraving.

buriné, e [byrine] adj engraved ; [visage, traits] lined.

Burkina [byrkina] *nm* : **le ~** Burkina Faso ; **au ~** in Burkina Faso.

burkinabé [byrkinabe] *adj* from Burkina Faso.
➤ **Burkinabé** *nmf* native *ou* inhabitant of Burkina Faso.

burlesque [byrlɛsk] ◇ *adj* - **1.** [comique] funny - **2.** [ridicule] ludicrous, absurd - **3.** THÉÂTRE burlesque ◇ *nm* : **le ~** the burlesque.

burnous [byrnu] *nm* - **1.** [manteau] burnous - **2.** [de bébé] hooded cape.

burundais, e [burundɛ, ɛz] *adj* Burundian.
➤ **Burundais, e** *nm, f* Burundian.

Burundi [burundi] *nm* : **le ~** Burundi ; **au ~** in Burundi.

bus [bys] *nm* bus.

buse [byz] *nf* - **1.** [oiseau] buzzard - **2.** [tuyau] pipe, duct - **3.** *fam fig* twit **Br**, idiot.

busqué [byske] ➭ **nez**.

buste [byst] *nm* [torse] chest ; [poitrine de femme, sculpture] bust.

bustier [bystje] *nm* [corsage] strapless top ; [soutien-gorge] longline bra.

but [byt] *nm* - **1.** [point visé] target - **2.** [objectif] goal, aim, purpose ; **errer sans ~** to wander aimlessly ; **il touche au ~** he's nearly there ; **à ~ non lucratif** JUR non-profit-making **Br**, non-profit **Am** ; **aller droit au ~** to go straight to the point ; **dans le ~ de faire qqch** with the aim *ou* intention of doing sthg - **3.** SPORT goal ; **marquer un ~** to score a goal - **4.** *loc* : **de ~ en blanc** point-blank, straight out.

butane [bytan] *nm* : **(gaz) ~** butane ; [domestique] Calor gas® **Br**, butane.

buté, e [byte] *adj* stubborn.
➤ **butée** *nf* - **1.** ARCHIT abutment - **2.** TECHNOL stop.

buter [3] [byte] ◇ *vi* - **1.** [se heurter] : **~ sur/contre qqch** to stumble on/over sthg, to trip on/over sthg ; *fig* to run into/come up against sthg - **2.** SPORT to score a goal ◇ *vt* - **1.** [étayer] to support - **2.** *tfam* [tuer] to do in, to bump off.
➤ **se buter** *vp* to dig one's heels in ; **se ~ contre** *fig* to refuse to listen to.

butin [bytɛ̃] *nm* [de guerre] booty ; [de vol] loot ; [de recherche] finds *(pl)*.

butiner [3] [bytine] ◇ *vi* to collect nectar ◇ *vt* [suj : abeille] to collect nectar from ; *fig* to gather.

butoir [bytwar] *nm* - **1.** [de porte] doorstop - **2.** [de chemin de fer] buffer.

butte [byt] *nf* [colline] mound, rise ; **~ de tir** butts *(pl)* ; **être en ~ à** *fig* to be exposed to.

buvable [byvabl] *adj* [boisson] drinkable ; [ampoule] (to be) taken orally.

buvard [byvar] *nm* [papier] blotting-paper ; [sous-main] blotter.

buvette [byvɛt] *nf* - **1.** [café] refreshment room, buffet - **2.** [de station thermale] pump room.

buveur, euse [byvœr, øz] *nm, f* drinker.

buvez, buvons *etc* ➭ **boire**.

BVA (*abr de* **Brulé Ville Associés**) *n* French market research company.

BVP (*abr de* **Bureau de vérification de la publicité**) *nm* French advertising standards authority, ≃ ASA **Br**.

Byzance [bizɑ̃s] *n* - **1.** HIST Byzantium - **2.** *loc* : **c'est ~!** it's fantastic!

BZH (*abr de* **Breizh**) Brittany *(as nationality sticker on a car)*.

c¹, C [se] *nm inv* c, C.
➤ **C** - **1.** (*abr de* **celsius, centigrade**) C - **2.** (*abr de* **coulomb**) C - **3.** *abr de* **code**.

c² *abr de* **centime**.

c' ➭ **ce**.

ca *abr de* **centiare**.

CA ◇ *nm* - **1.** *abr de* **chiffre d'affaires** - **2.** *abr de* **conseil d'administration** - **3.** *abr de* **corps d'armée** ◇ *nf* (*abr de* **chambre d'agriculture**) *local government body responsible for agricultural matters.*

ça [sa] *pron dém* - **1.** [désignant un objet - éloigné] that ; [- proche] this - **2.** [sujet indéterminé] it, that ; **comment ~ va?** how are you?, how are things? ; **~ ira comme ~** that will be fine ; **~ y est** that's it ; **c'est ~** that's right - **3.** [renforcement expressif] : **où ~?** where? ; **qui ~?** who?

çà [sa] *adv* : **~ et là** here and there.

caban [kabɑ̃] *nm* reefer (jacket).

cabane [kaban] *nf* - **1.** [abri] cabin, hut ; [remise] shed ; **~ à lapins** hutch - **2.** *fam* [prison] : **en ~** in the clink.

cabanon [kabanɔ̃] *nm* - **1.** [à la campagne] cottage - **2.** [sur la plage] chalet - **3.** [cellule] padded cell - **4.** [de rangement] shed.

cabaret [kabaʀɛ] *nm* cabaret.

cabas [kaba] *nm* shopping-bag.

cabillaud [kabijo] *nm* (fresh) cod.

cabine [kabin] *nf* - **1.** [de navire, d'avion, de véhicule] cabin - **2.** [compartiment, petit local] cubicle ; ~ **d'essayage** fitting room ; ~ **téléphonique** phone box.

cabinet [kabinɛ] *nm* - **1.** [pièce] : ~ **de toilette** ≃ bathroom ; ~ **de travail** study - **2.** [toilettes] toilet - **3.** [local professionnel] office ; ~ **dentaire/ médical** dentist's/doctor's surgery *Br*, dentist's/doctor's office *Am* - **4.** [de ministre] advisers *(pl)*.
➡ **cabinets** *nmpl* toilet *(sg)*.

câble [kabl] *nm* cable ; **télévision par** ~ cable television.

câblé, e [kable] *adj* TÉLÉ equipped with cable TV.

cabosser [3] [kabɔse] *vt* to dent.

cabot [kabo] <> *adj* theatrical <> *nm* - **1.** [personne] poser - **2.** *fam* [chien] mutt.

cabotage [kabɔtaʒ] *nm* coastal navigation.

caboteur [kabɔtœʀ] *nm* [navire] coaster.

cabotin, e [kabɔtɛ̃, in] *péj* <> *adj* theatrical <> *nm, f* - **1.** *fam* [acteur] ham (actor) - **2.** [frimeur] poser.

cabri [kabʀi] *nm* kid.

cabriole [kabʀijɔl] *nf* [bond] caper ; [pirouette] somersault.

cabriolet [kabʀijɔlɛ] *nm* convertible.

CAC, Cac [kak] (*abr de* **Compagnie des agents de change**) *nf* : **l'indice ~-40** *the French stock exchange shares index.*

caca [kaka] *nm fam* pooh ; **faire** ~ to do a pooh ; ~ **d'oie** greeny-yellow.

cacahouète, cacahuète [kakawɛt] *nf* peanut.

cacao [kakao] *nm* - **1.** [poudre] cocoa (powder) - **2.** [boisson] cocoa - **3.** [graine] cocoa bean.

cachalot [kaʃalo] *nm* sperm whale.

cache [kaʃ] <> *nf* [cachette] hiding place <> *nm* - **1.** [masque] card *(for masking text etc)* - **2.** CIN & PHOT mask.

cache-cache [kaʃkaʃ] *nm inv* : **jouer à** ~ to play hide and seek.

cache-col [kaʃkɔl] *nm inv* scarf.

cachemire [kaʃmir] *nm* - **1.** [laine] cashmere - **2.** [dessin] paisley.

cache-nez [kaʃne] *nm inv* scarf.

cache-oreilles [kaʃɔʀɛj] *nm inv* earmuffs.

cache-pot [kaʃpo] *nm inv* flowerpot-holder.

cacher [3] [kaʃe] *vt* - **1.** [gén] to hide ; **je ne vous cache pas que ...** to be honest, ... - **2.** [vue] to mask.
➡ **se cacher** *vp* : **se** ~ **(de qqn)** to hide (from sb).

cache-sexe [kaʃsɛks] *nm inv* G-string.

cachet [kaʃɛ] *nm* - **1.** [comprimé] tablet, pill - **2.** [marque] postmark - **3.** [style] style, character ; **avoir du** ~ to have character - **4.** [rétribution] fee - **5.** [sceau] seal.

cacheter [27] [kaʃte] *vt* to seal.

cachette [kaʃɛt] *nf* hiding place ; **en** ~ secretly.

cachot [kaʃo] *nm* - **1.** [cellule] cell - **2.** [punition] solitary confinement.

cachotterie [kaʃɔtʀi] *nf* little secret ; **faire des ~s (à qqn)** to hide things (from sb).

cachottier, ère [kaʃɔtje, ɛʀ] <> *adj* secretive <> *nm, f* secretive person.

cachou [kaʃu] *nm* sweet taken to freshen the breath.

cacophonie [kakɔfɔni] *nf* din.

cactus [kaktys] *nm* cactus.

c.-à-d. (*abr de* **c'est-à-dire**) i.e.

cadastre [kadastʀ] *nm* [registre] ≃ land register ; [service] ≃ land registry, ≃ land office *Am*.

cadavérique [kadaveʀik] *adj* deathly.

cadavre [kadavʀ] *nm* corpse, (dead) body ; **un** ~ **ambulant** a walking skeleton.

caddie [kadi] *nm* GOLF caddie.

Caddie® [kadi] *nm* [chariot] trolley.

cadeau, x [kado] <> *nm* present, gift ; **faire** ~ **de qqch à qqn** to give sthg to sb (as a present) ; ~ **d'anniversaire** birthday present ; **il ne nous a pas fait de** ~ *fam* he didn't do us any favours <> *adj inv* : **idée** ~ gift idea ; **paquet** ~ gift-wrapped parcel.

cadenas [kadna] *nm* padlock.

cadenasser [3] [kadnase] *vt* to padlock.
➡ **se cadenasser** *vp* to padlock.

cadence [kadɑ̃s] *nf* - **1.** [rythme musical] rhythm ; **en** ~ in time - **2.** [de travail] rate.

cadencé, e [kadɑ̃se] *adj* rhythmical.

cadet, ette [kadɛ, ɛt] <> *adj* younger <> *nm, f* - **1.** [de deux enfants] younger ; [de plusieurs enfants] youngest ; **il est mon** ~ **de deux ans** he's two years younger than me ; **c'est le** ~ **de mes soucis** *fig* that's the least of my worries - **2.** SPORT junior.

cadran [kadʀɑ̃] *nm* dial ; ~ **solaire** sundial.

cadre [kadʀ] *nm* - **1.** [de tableau, de porte] frame - **2.** [contexte] context ; **dans le** ~ **de** as part of ; [limite] within the limits *ou* scope of ; **sortir du**

~ de to go beyond (the scope of) **- 3.** [décor, milieu] surroundings *(pl)* **- 4.** [responsable] : **~ moyen/supérieur** middle/senior manager ; **jeune ~ dynamique** *iron* dynamic young executive ; **être rayé des ~s** to be dismissed **- 5.** [sur formulaire] box.

cadrer [3] [kadre] ⬦ *vi* to agree, to tally ⬦ *vt* *CIN, PHOT* & *TÉLÉ* to frame.

cadreur [kadrœr, øz] *nm* cameraman.

caduc, caduque [kadyk] *adj* **- 1.** [feuille] deciduous **- 2.** [qui n'est plus valide] obsolete.

CAF ⬦ *nf* (*abr de* **Caisse d'allocations familiales**) *family allowance office* ⬦ (*abr de* **coût, assurance, fret**) cif.

cafard [kafar] *nm* **- 1.** *fam SCOL* sneak ; [à la police] grass **- 2.** [insecte] cockroach **- 3.** *fig* [mélancolie] : **avoir le ~** to feel low *ou* down.

cafarder [3] [kafarde] *vi* **- 1.** [dénoncer - *SCOL*] to sneak ; [- à la police] to grass **- 2.** [déprimer] to feel low *ou* down.

cafardeux, euse [kafardø, øz] *adj* low, down.

café [kafe] ⬦ *nm* **- 1.** [plante, boisson] coffee ; **~ crème** *coffee with frothy milk* ; **~ glacé** iced coffee ; **~ en grains** coffee beans ; **~ au lait** white coffee *(with hot milk)* ; **~ liégeois** *coffee ice cream with whipped cream poured over* ; **~ moulu** ground coffee ; **~ noir** black coffee ; **~ en poudre** *ou* **soluble** instant coffee **- 2.** [lieu] bar, café ⬦ *adj inv* coffee-coloured *Br*, coffee-colored *Am*.

> **CAFÉ**
>
> In French cafés, a small cup of strong black coffee is called 'un (petit) café', 'un express' or, colloquially, 'un petit noir'. This may be served 'serré' (extra-strong), 'léger' (weak) or 'allongé' (diluted with hot water). An 'express' with a tiny amount of milk added is called 'une noisette'. A large cup of black coffee is 'un grand café', 'un double express' or, colloquially, 'un grand noir'. Coffee with frothy, steam-heated milk is called 'un (grand/petit) crème'. The term 'café au lait' is almost never used in cafés.

caféine [kafein] *nf* caffeine ; **sans ~** caffeine-free.

cafétéria [kafeterja] *nf* cafeteria.

café-théâtre [kafeteatr] (*pl* **cafés-théâtres**) *nm* ≃ cabaret.

cafetier [kaftje] *nm* café owner.

cafetière [kaftjɛr] *nf* **- 1.** [récipient] coffee-pot **- 2.** [électrique] coffee-maker ; [italienne] percolator.

cafouiller [3] [kafuje] *vi fam* **- 1.** [s'embrouiller]

to get into a mess **- 2.** [moteur] to misfire ; *TÉLÉ* to be on the blink.

cage [kaʒ] *nf* **- 1.** [pour animaux] cage **- 2.** [dans une maison] : **~ d'escalier** stairwell **- 3.** *ANAT* : **~ thoracique** rib cage.

cageot [kaʒo] *nm* [caisse] crate.

cagibi [kaʒibi] *nm* boxroom *Br*, storage room *Am*.

cagneux, euse [kaɲø, øz] *adj* : **avoir les genoux ~** to be knock-kneed.

cagnotte [kaɲɔt] *nf* **- 1.** [caisse commune] kitty **- 2.** [économies] savings *(pl)*.

cagoule [kagul] *nf* **- 1.** [passe-montagne] balaclava **- 2.** [de moine] cowl **- 3.** [de voleur, de pénitent] hood.

cahier [kaje] *nm* **- 1.** [de notes] exercise book, notebook ; **~ de brouillon** rough book ; **~ de textes** homework book **- 2.** *COMM* : **~ des charges** specification.

cahin-caha [kaɛ̃kaa] *adv* : **aller ~** to be jogging along.

cahot [kao] *nm* bump, jolt.

cahoter [3] [kaɔte] ⬦ *vi* to jolt around ⬦ *vt* **- 1.** [secouer] to jolt **- 2.** *fig* [malmener] to knock around.

cahute [kayt] *nf* shack.

caïd [kaid] *nm* **- 1.** [chef de bande] leader **- 2.** *fam* [homme fort] big shot.

caillasse [kajas] *nf fam* loose stones *(pl)*.

caille [kaj] *nf* quail.

caillé, e [kaje] *adj* [lait] curdled ; [sang] clotted.

➡ **caillé** *nm CULIN* curds *(pl)*.

cailler [3] [kaje] *vi* **- 1.** [lait] to curdle ; [sang] to clot **- 2.** [avoir froid] to be freezing.

➡ **se cailler** *vp* **- 1.** [lait] to curdle ; [sang] to clot **- 2.** *fam* [avoir froid] : **on se caille** it's freezing.

caillot [kajo] *nm* clot.

caillou, x [kaju] *nm* **- 1.** [pierre] stone, pebble **- 2.** *fam* [pierre précieuse] rock **- 3.** *fam* [crâne] head.

caillouteux, euse [kajutø, øz] *adj* stony.

caïman [kaimɑ̃] *nm* cayman.

Caire [kɛr] *n* : **Le ~** Cairo.

caisse [kɛs] *nf* **- 1.** [boîte] crate, box ; **~ à outils** toolbox **- 2.** *TECHNOL* case **- 3.** *MUS* : **grosse ~** bass drum **- 4.** [guichet] cash desk, till ; [de supermarché] checkout, till ; **~ enregistreuse** cash register **- 5.** [recette] takings *(pl)* ; **tenir la ~** *fig* to hold the purse-strings ; **~ noire** slush fund **- 6.** [organisme] : **~ d'allocation** ≃ social security office ; **~ d'épargne** [fonds] savings fund ; [établissement] savings bank ;

~ de prévoyance contingency fund ; **~ de re-traite** pension fund.

caissette [kɛset] *nf* small box.

caissier, ère [kesje, ɛr] *nm, f* cashier.

caisson [kɛsɔ̃] *nm* - **1.** *MIL* & *TECHNOL* caisson - **2.** *ARCHIT* coffer.

cajoler [3] [kaʒɔle] *vt* to make a fuss of, to cuddle.

cajolerie [kaʒɔlri] *nf* cuddle.

cajou [kaʒu] ▷ **noix.**

cake [kɛk] *nm* fruit-cake.

cal[1] [kal] *nm* callus.

cal[2] (*abr de* **calorie**) cal.

calamar [kalamar], **calmar** [kalmar] *nm* squid.

calaminé, e [kalamine] *adj* coked up.

calamité [kalamite] *nf* disaster.

calandre [kalɑ̃dr] *nf* - **1.** [de voiture] radiator grille - **2.** [machine] calender.

calanque [kalɑ̃k] *nf* rocky inlet.

calcaire [kalkɛr] <> *adj* [eau] hard ; [sol] chalky ; [roche] limestone *(avant n)* <> *nm* limestone.

calciner [3] [kalsine] *vt* to burn to a cinder.

calcium [kalsjɔm] *nm* calcium.

calcul [kalkyl] *nm* - **1.** [opération] : **le ~** arithmetic ; **~ mental** mental arithmetic - **2.** [compte] calculation - **3.** *fig* [plan] plan ; **agir par ~** to act out of self-interest - **4.** *MÉD* : **~ (rénal)** kidney stone.

calculateur, trice [kalkylatœr, tris] *adj péj* calculating.
➡ **calculateur** *nm* computer.
➡ **calculatrice** *nf* calculator ; **calculatrice de poche** pocket calculator.

calculer [3] [kalkyle] <> *vt* - **1.** [déterminer] to calculate, to work out - **2.** [prévoir] to plan ; **mal/bien ~ qqch** to judge sthg badly/well <> *vi* - **1.** [faire des calculs] to calculate - **2.** *péj* [dépenser avec parcimonie] to count the pennies.

calculette [kalkylɛt] *nf* pocket calculator.

Calcutta [kalkyta] *n* Calcutta.

cale [kal] *nf* - **1.** [de navire] hold ; **~ sèche** dry dock - **2.** [pour immobiliser] wedge.

calé, e [kale] *adj fam* - **1.** [personne] clever, brainy ; **être ~ en** to be good at - **2.** [problème] tough.

calebasse [kalbas] *nf* gourd.

calèche [kalɛʃ] *nf* (horse-drawn) carriage.

caleçon [kalsɔ̃] *nm* - **1.** [sous-vêtement masculin] boxer shorts *(pl)*, pair of boxer shorts ; **~ long** longjohns *(pl)*, pair of longjohns - **2.** [vêtement féminin] leggings *(pl)*, pair of leggings.

Calédonie [kaledɔni] *nf* : **la ~** Caledonia.

calembour [kalɑ̃bur] *nm* pun, play on words.

calendes [kalɑ̃d] *nfpl* : **renvoyer qqch aux ~ grecques** to postpone sthg indefinitely.

calendrier [kalɑ̃drije] *nm* - **1.** [système, agenda, d'un festival] calendar - **2.** [emploi du temps] timetable - **3.** [d'un voyage] schedule.

cale-pied [kalpje] *(pl* **cale-pieds)** *nm* toe-clip.

calepin [kalpɛ̃] *nm* notebook.

caler [3] [kale] <> *vt* - **1.** [avec cale] to wedge - **2.** [stabiliser, appuyer] to prop up - **3.** *fam* [remplir] : **ça cale (l'estomac)** it's filling <> *vi* - **1.** [moteur, véhicule] to stall - **2.** *fam* [personne] to give up.

calfeutrer [3] [kalføtre] *vt* to draughtproof.
➡ **se calfeutrer** *vp* to shut o.s. up.

calibre [kalibr] *nm* - **1.** [de tuyau] diameter, bore ; [de fusil] calibre ; [de fruit, d'œuf] size ; **de gros ~** large-calibre - **2.** *fam fig* [envergure] calibre ; **du même ~** of the same calibre.

calibrer [3] [kalibre] *vt* - **1.** [machine, fusil] to calibrate - **2.** [fruit, œuf] to grade.

calice [kalis] *nm* - **1.** *RELIG* chalice - **2.** *BOT* calyx.

calicot [kaliko] *nm* - **1.** [tissu] calico - **2.** [banderole] banner.

Californie [kalifɔrni] *nf* : **la ~** California ; **la Basse ~** Lower California.

californien, enne [kalifɔrnjɛ̃, ɛn] *adj* Californian.
➡ **Californien, enne** *nm, f* Californian.

califourchon [kalifurʃɔ̃] ➡ **à califourchon** *loc adv* astride ; **être (assis) à ~ sur qqch** to sit astride sthg.

câlin, e [kalɛ̃, in] *adj* affectionate.
➡ **câlin** *nm* cuddle ; **faire un ~ à qqn** to give sb a cuddle.

câliner [3] [kaline] *vt* to cuddle.

calisson [kalisɔ̃] *nm small iced cake made with almond paste.*

calleux, euse [kalø, øz] *adj* calloused.

call-girl [kolgœrl] *(pl* **call-girls)** *nf* call girl.

calligraphie [kaligrafi] *nf* calligraphy.

callosité [kalozite] *nf* callus.

calmant, e [kalmɑ̃, ɑ̃t] *adj* soothing.
➡ **calmant** *nm* [pour la douleur] painkiller ; [pour l'anxiété] tranquillizer, sedative.

calmar ▷ **calamar.**

calme [kalm] <> *adj* quiet, calm <> *nm* - **1.** [gén] calm, calmness ; **dans le ~** quietly, calmly ; **du ~!** calm down! ; **rétablir le ~** to restore order ; **le ~ plat** [de la mer] dead calm ; **c'est le ~ plat en ce moment** *fig* things are very quiet at the moment - **2.** [absence de bruit] peace (and quiet).

calmer [3] [kalme] *vt* - **1.** [apaiser] to calm

(down) - **2.** [réduire - douleur] to soothe ; [- inquiétude] to allay.

→ **se calmer** *vp* - **1.** [s'apaiser - personne, discussion] to calm down ; [- tempête] to abate ; [- mer] to become calm - **2.** [diminuer - douleur] to ease ; [- fièvre, inquiétude, désir] to subside.

calomnie [kalɔmni] *nf* [écrits] libel ; [paroles] slander.

calomnier [9] [kalɔmnje] *vt* [par écrit] to libel ; [verbalement] to slander.

calomnieux, euse [kalɔmnjø, øz] *adj* [écrits] libellous *Br*, libelous *Am* ; [propos] slanderous.

calorie [kalɔri] *nf* calorie.

calorifère [kalɔrifɛr] ◇ *nm* stove ◇ *adj* heat-giving.

calorifique [kalɔrifik] *adj* calorific.

calorifuge [kalɔrifyʒ] ◇ *adj* insulating ◇ *nm* insulation.

calorique [kalɔrik] *adj* calorific.

calot [kalo] *nm* - **1.** [de militaire] ≈ beret - **2.** [bille] (large) marble.

calotte [kalɔt] *nf* - **1.** [bonnet] skullcap - **2.** *fam* [gifle] slap - **3.** GÉOGR : ~ **glaciaire** ice cap.

calque [kalk] *nm* - **1.** [dessin] tracing - **2.** [papier] : **(papier) ~ tracing paper - 3.** *fig* [imitation] (exact) copy ; **il est le ~ de son père** he's the spitting image of his father - **4.** [traduction] calque, loan translation.

calquer [3] [kalke] *vt* - **1.** [carte] to trace - **2.** [imiter] to copy exactly ; **~ qqch sur qqch** to model sthg on sthg - **3.** [traduire littéralement] to translate literally.

calvados [kalvados] *nm* Calvados.

calvaire [kalvɛr] *nm* - **1.** [croix] wayside cross - **2.** *fig* [épreuve] ordeal.

→ **Calvaire** *nm* : **le Calvaire** Calvary.

calviniste [kalvinist] *adj* & *nmf* Calvinist.

calvitie [kalvisi] *nf* baldness ; **~ précoce** premature baldness.

camaïeu [kamajø] *nm* monochrome ; **en ~** in monochrome, monochrome *(avant n)*.

camarade [kamarad] *nmf* - **1.** [compagnon, ami] friend ; **~ de classe** classmate ; **~ d'école** schoolfriend - **2.** POLIT comrade.

camaraderie [kamaradri] *nf* - **1.** [familiarité, entente] friendship - **2.** [solidarité] comradeship, camaraderie.

cambiste [kãbist] FIN ◇ *adj* foreign exchange *(avant n)* ◇ *nmf* foreign exchange dealer.

Cambodge [kãbɔdʒ] *nm* : **le ~** Cambodia ; **au ~** in Cambodia.

cambodgien, enne [kãbɔdʒjɛ̃, ɛn] *adj* Cambodian.

→ **Cambodgien, enne** *nm, f* Cambodian.

cambouis [kãbwi] *nm* dirty grease.

cambré, e [kãbre] *adj* arched.

cambrer [3] [kãbre] *vt* : **~ les reins** OU **la taille** to arch one's back.

→ **se cambrer** *vp* [se redresser] to arch one's back.

cambriolage [kãbrijɔlaʒ] *nm* burglary.

cambrioler [3] [kãbrijɔle] *vt* to burgle *Br*, to burglarize *Am*.

cambrioleur, euse [kãbrijɔlœr, øz] *nm, f* burglar.

cambrousse [kãbrus] *nf fam* : **en pleine ~** out in the sticks.

cambrure [kãbryr] *nf* - **1.** [de pied] instep ; **~ des reins** OU **du dos** small of the back - **2.** [de poutre] curve ; [de chaussure] arch.

came [kam] *nf* - **1.** TECHNOL cam - **2.** *tfam* [drogue] stuff.

camé, e [kame] *tfam* ◇ *adj* [drogué] stoned ◇ *nm, f* junkie.

camée [kame] *nm* cameo.

caméléon [kameleõ] *nm litt* & *fig* chameleon.

camélia [kamelja] *nm* camellia.

camelote [kamlɔt] *nf* [marchandise de mauvaise qualité] junk, rubbish *Br*.

camembert [kamãbɛr] *nm* - **1.** [fromage] Camembert - **2.** [graphique] pie chart.

caméra [kamera] *nf* - **1.** CIN & TÉLÉ camera - **2.** [d'amateur] cinecamera.

cameraman [kameraman] *(pl* **cameramen** [kameramɛn], **cameramans)** *nm* cameraman.

Cameroun [kamrun] *nm* : **le ~** Cameroon ; **au ~** in Cameroon.

camerounais, e [kamrunɛ, ɛz] *adj* Cameroonian.

→ **Camerounais, e** *nm, f* Cameroonian.

Caméscope® [kameskɔp] *nm* camcorder.

camion [kamjõ] *nm* lorry *Br*, truck *Am* ; **~ de déménagement** removal van *Br*, moving van *Am*.

camion-citerne [kamjõsitɛrn] *(pl* **camions-citernes)** *nm* tanker *Br*, tanker truck *Am*.

camionnage [kamjɔnaʒ] *nm* road haulage *Br*, trucking *Am*.

camionnette [kamjɔnɛt] *nf* van.

camionneur [kamjɔnœr] *nm* - **1.** [conducteur] lorry-driver *Br*, truck-driver *Am* - **2.** [entrepreneur] road haulier *Br*, trucker *Am*.

camisole [kamizɔl] → **camisole de force** *nf* straitjacket.

camomille [kamɔmij] *nf* - **1.** [plante] camomile - **2.** [tisane] camomile tea.

camouflage [kamuflaʒ] *nm* [déguisement] camouflage ; *fig* [dissimulation] concealment.

camoufler [3] [kamufle] *vt* [déguiser] to camouflage ; *fig* [dissimuler] to conceal, to cover up ; ~ qqch en qqch to camouflage sthg as sthg.

➤ **se camoufler** *vp* [se cacher] to hide.

camouflet [kamuflɛ] *nm littéraire* [affront] snub ; **infliger un ~ à qqn** to snub sb.

camp [kɑ̃] *nm* - **1.** [gén] camp ; **~ de concentration** concentration camp ; **~ retranché** fortified camp, fortress ; **~ de vacances** holiday camp ; **~ volant** temporary camp ; **ficher le ~** *fam* to get lost, to clear off ; **lever le ~** to break camp ; *fig* to clear off *ou* out - **2.** *SPORT* half (of the field) - **3.** [parti] side.

campagnard, e [kɑ̃paɲar, ard] <> *adj* - **1.** [de la campagne] country *(avant n)* - **2.** [rustique] rustic <> *nm, f* countryman (*f* countrywoman).

campagne [kɑ̃paɲ] *nf* - **1.** [régions rurales] country ; **à la ~** in the country ; **en rase ~** in open country ; **battre la ~** [police] to comb the countryside ; [divaguer] to wander - **2.** *MIL, POLIT & PUBLICITÉ* campaign ; **partir en ~** *POLIT* to start campaigning ; **faire ~ pour/contre** to campaign for/against ; **~ d'affichage** poster campaign ; **~ électorale** election campaign ; **~ de presse** press campaign ; **~ publicitaire** advertising campaign ; **~ de vente** sales campaign.

campanule [kɑ̃panyl] *nf* bellflower, campanula.

campé, e [kɑ̃pe] *adj* : **bien ~** [personnage] well-rounded ; [récit] well-constructed ; **être bien ~ (sur ses jambes)** to stand firmly on one's feet.

campement [kɑ̃pmɑ̃] *nm* camp, encampment.

camper [3] [kɑ̃pe] <> *vi* to camp <> *vt* - **1.** [poser solidement] to place firmly - **2.** *fig* [esquisser] to portray.

➤ **se camper** *vp* : **se ~ devant qqn/qqch** to plant o.s. in front of sb/sthg.

campeur, euse [kɑ̃pœr, øz] *nm, f* camper.

camphre [kɑ̃fr] *nm* camphor.

camphré, e [kɑ̃fre] *adj* camphorated.

camping [kɑ̃piŋ] *nm* - **1.** [activité] camping ; **faire du ~** to go camping ; **~ sauvage** camping in the wild, wilderness camping *Am* - **2.** [terrain] campsite.

camping-car [kɑ̃piŋkar] *(pl* **camping-cars)** *nm* camper, Dormobile® *Br*.

Camping-Gaz® [kɑ̃piŋgaz] *nm inv* ≈ Primus® stove.

campus [kɑ̃pys] *nm* campus.

camus [kamy] ⊏> **nez.**

Canada [kanada] *nm* : **le ~** Canada ; **au ~** in Canada.

Canadair® [kanadɛr] *nm plane equipped with water tanks to fight forest fires.*

canadianisme [kanadjanism] *nm* Canadianism.

canadien, enne [kanadjɛ̃, ɛn] *adj* Canadian.

➤ **canadienne** *nf* [veste] sheepskin jacket.

➤ **Canadien, enne** *nm, f* Canadian.

canaille [kanaj] <> *adj* - **1.** [coquin] roguish - **2.** [vulgaire] crude <> *nf* - **1.** [scélérat] scoundrel - **2.** *hum* [coquin] little devil.

canal, aux [kanal, o] *nm* - **1.** [gén] channel ; **par le ~ de qqn** *fig* [par l'entremise de] through sb ; **~ de distribution** distribution channel - **2.** [voie d'eau] canal - **3.** *ANAT* canal, duct.

➤ **Canal** *nm* : **Canal+** *French TV pay channel.*

CANAL+

Canal+ broadcasts programmes that have to be unscrambled using a special decoding unit, although for part of the day its programmes can be seen without this device.

canalisation [kanalizasjɔ̃] *nf* - **1.** [conduit] pipe - **2.** *litt & fig* [action de canaliser] channelling.

canaliser [3] [kanalize] *vt* - **1.** [cours d'eau] to canalize - **2.** *fig* [orienter] to channel.

canapé [kanape] *nm* - **1.** [siège] sofa ; **~ convertible** sofa bed - **2.** *CULIN* canapé.

canapé-lit [kanapeli] *(pl* **canapés-lits)** *nm* sofa bed.

canaque, kanak [kanak] *adj* Kanak.

➤ **Canaque** *nmf* Kanak.

canard [kanar] *nm* - **1.** [oiseau] duck - **2.** [fausse note] wrong note - **3.** *fam* [journal] rag.

canari [kanari] <> *nm* canary <> *adj inv* : **jaune ~** canary yellow.

Canaries [kanari] *nfpl* : **les ~** the Canaries ; **aux ~** in the Canaries.

Canberra [kɑ̃bera] *n* Canberra.

cancan [kɑ̃kɑ̃] *nm* - **1.** [ragot] piece of gossip ; **dire des ~s sur qqn** to spread gossip about sb - **2.** [danse] cancan.

cancaner [3] [kɑ̃kane] *vi* - **1.** [canard] to quack - **2.** [médire] to spread gossip ; **~ sur qqn** to spread gossip about sb.

cancanier, ère [kɑ̃kanje, ɛr] <> *adj* gossipy <> *nm, f* gossip.

cancer [kɑ̃ser] *nm MÉD* cancer.

➤ **Cancer** *nm* - **1.** *ASTROL* Cancer ; **être Cancer** to be (a) Cancer - **2.** *GÉOGR* : **le tropique du Cancer** the tropic of Cancer.

cancéreux, euse [kɑ̃serø, øz] <> *adj* - **1.** [personne] suffering from cancer - **2.** [tumeur] cancerous ◇ *nm, f* [personne] cancer sufferer.

cancérigène [kɑ̃seriʒɛn] *adj* carcinogenic.

cancre [kɑ̃kr] *nm fam* dunce.

cancrelat [kɑ̃krəla] *nm* cockroach.

candélabre [kɑ̃delabr] *nm* candelabra.

candeur [kɑ̃dœr] *nf* ingenuousness.

candi [kɑ̃di] *adj* : **sucre ~** (sugar) candy.

candidat, e [kɑ̃dida, at] *nm, f* : **~ (à)** candidate (for).

candidature [kɑ̃didatyr] *nf* - **1.** [à un poste] application ; **poser sa ~ pour qqch** to apply for sthg - **2.** [à une élection] candidature.

candide [kɑ̃did] *adj* ingenuous.

cane [kan] *nf* (female) duck.

caneton [kantɔ̃] *nm* (male) duckling.

canette [kanɛt] *nf* - **1.** [de fil] spool - **2.** [petite cane] (female) duckling - **3.** [de boisson - bouteille] bottle ; [- boîte] can.

canevas [kanva] *nm* - **1.** COUTURE canvas - **2.** [plan] structure.

caniche [kaniʃ] *nm* poodle.

canicule [kanikyl] *nf* heatwave.

canif [kanif] *nm* penknife.

canin, e [kanɛ̃, in] *adj* canine ; **exposition ~e** dog show.
➤ **canine** *nf* canine (tooth).

caniveau (*pl* **x**) [kanivo] *nm* gutter.

cannabis [kanabis] *nm* cannabis.

canne [kan] *nf* - **1.** [bâton] walking stick ; **~ à pêche** fishing rod - **2.** *fam* [jambe] pin.
➤ **canne à sucre** *nf* sugar cane.

canné, e [kane] *adj* cane *(avant n)*.

cannelé, e [kanle] *adj* fluted.

cannelle [kanɛl] ◇ *nf* - **1.** [aromate] cinnamon - **2.** [robinet] tap *Br*, faucet *Am* ◇ *adj inv* [couleur] cinnamon.

cannelure [kanlyr] *nf* - **1.** [de colonne] flute - **2.** BOT & GÉOL striation.

Cannes [kan] *n* Cannes ; **le festival de ~** the Cannes film festival.

cannibale [kanibal] *nmf & adj* cannibal.

cannibalisme [kanibalism] *nm* cannibalism.

canoë [kanɔe] *nm* canoe.

canoë-kayak [kanɔekajak] (*pl* **canoës-kayaks**) *nm* kayak.

canon [kanɔ̃] ◇ *nm* - **1.** [arme] gun ; HIST cannon - **2.** [tube d'arme] barrel - **3.** *fam* [verre de vin] glass (of wine) - **4.** MUS : **chanter en ~** to sing in canon - **5.** [norme & RELIG] canon ◇ *adj* ➭ **droit**.

canonique [kanɔnik] *adj* canonical ; **d'un âge ~** *fig* of a venerable age.

canoniser [3] [kanɔnize] *vt* to canonize.

canot [kanɔ] *nm* dinghy ; **~ pneumatique** inflatable dinghy ; **~ de sauvetage** lifeboat.

canotage [kanɔtaʒ] *nm* rowing, boating ; **faire du ~** to go rowing *ou* boating.

canotier [kanɔtje] *nm* - **1.** [rameur] rower - **2.** [chapeau] boater.

cantal [kɑ̃tal] *nm semi-hard cheese from the Auvergne.*

cantate [kɑ̃tat] *nf* cantata.

cantatrice [kɑ̃tatris] *nf* prima donna.

cantine [kɑ̃tin] *nf* - **1.** [réfectoire] canteen - **2.** [malle] trunk.

cantique [kɑ̃tik] *nm* hymn.

canton [kɑ̃tɔ̃] *nm* - **1.** [en France] ≈ district - **2.** [en Suisse] canton.

cantonade [kɑ̃tɔnad] ➤ **à la cantonade** *loc adv* : **parler à la ~** to speak to everyone (in general).

cantonais, e [kɑ̃tɔnɛ, ɛz] *adj* Cantonese ; **riz ~** egg fried rice.
➤ **cantonais** *nm* [langue] Cantonese.
➤ **Cantonais, e** *nm, f* native *ou* inhabitant of Canton.

cantonal, e, aux [kɑ̃tɔnal, o] *adj* - **1.** [en France] ≈ district *(avant n)* - **2.** [en Suisse] cantonal.

cantonnement [kɑ̃tɔnmɑ̃] *nm* [MIL - action] billeting ; [- lieu] billet.

cantonner [3] [kɑ̃tɔne] *vt* - **1.** MIL to quarter, to billet *Br* - **2.** [maintenir] to confine ; **~ qqn à** *ou* **dans** to confine sb to.
➤ **se cantonner** *vp* : **se ~ dans** to confine o.s. to.

cantonnier [kɑ̃tɔnje] *nm* roadman.

canular [kanylar] *nm fam* hoax.

canyon, cañon [kanjɔn, kaɲɔ̃] *nm* canyon.

canyoning [kanɔniŋ] *nm* canyoning.

CAO (*abr de* **conception assistée par ordinateur**) *nf* CAD.

caoutchouc [kautʃu] *nm* - **1.** [substance] rubber ; **en ~** rubber *(avant n)* ; **~ mousse** foam rubber - **2.** [plante] rubber plant - **3.** [élastique] elastic ou rubber band.

caoutchouteux, euse [kautʃutø, øz] adj rubbery.

cap [kap] nm - **1.** GÉOGR cape ; **le ~ de Bonne-Espérance** the Cape of Good Hope ; **le ~ Horn** Cape Horn ; **passer le ~ de qqch** fig to get through sthg ; **passer le ~ de la quarantaine** fig to turn forty - **2.** [direction] course ; **changer de ~** to change course ; **mettre le ~ sur** to head for.
◆ **Cap** nm : **Le Cap** Cape Town.

CAP (abr de **certificat d'aptitude professionnelle**) nm vocational training certificate (taken at secondary school).

capable [kapabl] adj - **1.** [apte] : **~ (de qqch/de faire qqch)** capable (of sthg/of doing sthg) - **2.** [à même] : **~ de faire qqch** likely to do sthg ; **~ de réussir** likely to succeed - **3.** JUR competent.

capacité [kapasite] nf - **1.** [de récipient] capacity - **2.** [de personne] ability - **3.** JUR [mentale] capacity - **4.** UNIV : **~ en droit** [diplôme] qualifying certificate in law gained by examination after 2 years' study.

cape [kap] nf [vêtement] cloak ; **rire sous ~** fig to laugh up one's sleeve.

CAPES, Capes [kapɛs] (abr de **certificat d'aptitude au professorat de l'enseignement du second degré**) nm secondary school teaching certificate.

capésien, enne [kapesjɛ̃, ɛn] nm, f person holding a secondary school teaching qualification.

CAPET, Capet [kapɛt] (abr de **certificat d'aptitude au professorat de l'enseignement technique**) nm specialized teaching certificate.

capharnaüm [kafarnaɔm] nm mess.

capillaire [kapilɛr] ◇ adj - **1.** [lotion] hair (avant n) - **2.** ANAT & BOT capillary ◇ nm - **1.** BOT maidenhair fern - **2.** ANAT capillary.

capillarité [kapilarite] nf PHYS capillarity.

capitaine [kapitɛn] nm captain ; **~ au long cours** NAVIG master mariner.

capitainerie [kapitɛnri] nf harbour Br ou harbor Am master's office.

capital, e, aux [kapital, o] adj - **1.** [décision, événement] major - **2.** JUR capital.
◆ **capital** nm FIN capital ; **~ d'exploitation** working capital ; **~ santé** fig reserves (pl) of health ; **~ social** authorized ou share capital.
◆ **capitale** nf [ville, lettre] capital.
◆ **capitaux** nmpl capital (U).

capitaliser [3] [kapitalize] ◇ vt FIN to capitalize ; fig to accumulate ◇ vi to save.

capitalisme [kapitalism] nm capitalism.

capitaliste [kapitalist] nmf & adj capitalist.

capiteux, euse [kapitø, øz] adj - **1.** [vin] intoxicating ; [parfum] heady - **2.** [charme] alluring.

capitonné, e [kapitɔne] adj padded ; **~ de cuir** with leather upholstery.

capituler [3] [kapityle] vi to surrender ; **~ devant qqn/qqch** to surrender to sb/sthg.

caporal, aux [kapɔral, o] nm - **1.** MIL lance corporal - **2.** [tabac] caporal.

caporal-chef [kapɔralʃɛf] (pl **caporaux-chefs** [kapɔroʃɛf]) nm corporal.

capot [kapo] ◇ adj inv [aux jeux de cartes] : **mettre qqn ~** to take all the tricks from sb ◇ nm - **1.** [de voiture] bonnet Br, hood Am - **2.** [de machine] (protective) cover.

capote [kapɔt] nf - **1.** [de voiture] hood Br, top Am - **2.** [manteau] greatcoat, overcoat - **3.** [chapeau] bonnet - **4.** fam [préservatif] : **~ (anglaise)** condom.

capoter [3] [kapɔte] vi - **1.** [se retourner] to overturn - **2.** Can [perdre la tête] to lose one's head - **3.** [échouer] to come to nothing.

câpre [kapr] nf caper.

caprice [kapris] nm whim ; **les ~s de la météo** the vagaries of the weather ; **faire des ~s** to be temperamental.

capricieux, euse [kaprisjø, øz] ◇ adj [changeant] capricious ; [coléreux] temperamental ◇ nm, f temperamental person.

capricorne [kaprikɔrn] nm ZOOL capricorn beetle.
◆ **Capricorne** nm - **1.** ASTROL Capricorn ; **être Capricorne** to be (a) Capricorn - **2.** GÉOGR : **le tropique du Capricorne** the tropic of Capricorn.

capsule [kapsyl] nf - **1.** [de bouteille] cap - **2.** ASTRON, BOT & MÉD capsule.

capter [3] [kapte] vt - **1.** [recevoir sur émetteur] to pick up - **2.** [source, rivière] to harness - **3.** fig [attention, confiance] to gain, to win.

capteur [kaptœr] nm PHYS sensor ; **~ solaire** solar panel.

captieux, euse [kapsjø, øz] adj specious.

captif, ive [kaptif, iv] ◇ adj captive ; **être ~ de qqch** fig to be a slave to sthg ◇ nm, f prisoner.

captivant, e [kaptivɑ̃, ɑ̃t] adj [livre, film] enthralling ; [personne] captivating.

captiver [3] [kaptive] vt to captivate.

captivité [kaptivite] nf captivity ; **en ~** in captivity.

capture [kaptyr] *nf* **- 1.** [action] capture **- 2.** [prise] catch.

capturer [3] [kaptyre] *vt* to catch, to capture.

capuche [kapyʃ] *nf* (detachable) hood.

capuchon [kapyʃɔ̃] *nm* **- 1.** [bonnet - d'imperméable] hood ; [- de religieux] cowl **- 2.** [bouchon] cap, top.

capucin [kapysɛ̃] *nm* RELIG Capuchin.

capucine [kapysin] *nf* [fleur] nasturtium.

capverdien, enne [kapvɛrdjɛ̃, ɛn] *adj* Cape Verdean.

Capverdien, enne *nm, f* Cape Verdean.

Cap-Vert [kapvɛr] *nm* Cape Verde.

caquelon [kaklɔ̃] *nm* fondue dish.

caquet [kakɛ] *nm* **- 1.** [de poule] cackling *(U)* **- 2.** *péj* [bavardage] chatter *(U)* ; **rabattre le ~ à** *ou* **de qqn** to shut sb up.

caqueter [27] [kakte] *vi* **- 1.** [poule] to cackle **- 2.** *péj* [personne] to chatter.

car¹ [kar] *nm* coach *Br*, bus *Am*.

car² [kar] *conj* because, for.

carabine [karabin] *nf* rifle.

carabiné, e [karabine] *adj fam* [tempête] violent ; [rhume] stinking ; [amende] heavy.

Caracas [karakas] *n* Caracas.

caraco [karako] *nm* loose blouse.

caracoler [3] [karakɔle] *vi* **- 1.** [cheval] to prance ; [cavalier] to caracole **- 2.** *fig* [sautiller] to prance about.

caractère [karaktɛr] *nm* **- 1.** [gén] character ; **avoir du ~** to have character ; **avoir mauvais ~** to be bad-tempered ; **en petits/gros ~s** in small/large print ; **~s d'imprimerie** block capitals **- 2.** [caractéristique] feature, characteristic.

caractériel, elle [karakterjɛl] ⬦ *adj* [troubles] emotional ; [personne] emotionally disturbed ⬦ *nm, f* emotionally disturbed person.

caractérisé, e [karakterize] *adj* [net] clear ; **être d'une grossièreté ~e** to be downright rude.

caractériser [3] [karakterize] *vt* to be characteristic of.

se caractériser *vp* : **se ~ par qqch** to be characterized by sthg.

caractéristique [karakteristik] ⬦ *nf* characteristic, feature ⬦ *adj* : **~ (de)** characteristic (of).

carafe [karaf] *nf* [pour vin, eau] carafe ; [pour alcool] decanter ; **rester en ~** *fam* to be left stranded.

carafon [karafɔ̃] *nm* small carafe.

caraïbe [karaib] *adj* Caribbean.

Caraïbe *nmf* Carib.

Caraïbes [karaib] *nfpl* : **les ~s** the Caribbean ; **dans les Caraïbes** in the Caribbean.

carambolage [karɑ̃bɔlaʒ] *nm* pile-up.

caramel [karamɛl] ⬦ *nm* **- 1.** CULIN caramel **- 2.** [bonbon - dur] toffee, caramel ; [- mou] fudge ⬦ *adj inv* [couleur] caramel.

caraméliser [3] [karamelize] *vt* [sucre] to caramelize ; [gâteau] to coat with caramel.

se caraméliser *vp* to caramelize.

carapace [karapas] *nf* shell ; *fig* protection, shield.

carapater [3] [karapate] **se carapater** *vp fam* to scarper, to hop it.

carat [kara] *nm* carat ; **or à 9 ~s** 9-carat gold.

caravane [karavan] *nf* **- 1.** [de camping, de désert] caravan **- 2.** [groupe de personnes] procession.

caravaning [karavaniŋ] *nm* caravanning.

carbone [karbɔn] *nm* carbon ; **(papier) ~** carbon paper.

carbonique [karbɔnik] *adj* : **gaz ~** carbon dioxide ; **neige ~** dry ice.

carboniser [3] [karbɔnize] *vt* to burn to a cinder.

carbonnade [karbɔnad] *nf* CULIN type of stew.

carburant [karbyrɑ̃] ⬦ *adj m* : **mélange ~** (fuel) mixture ⬦ *nm* fuel.

carburateur [karbyratœr] *nm* carburettor *Br*, carburetor *Am*.

carbure [karbyr] *nm* carbide.

carburer [3] [karbyre] *vi* **- 1.** [moteur] : **~ bien/mal** to be well/badly tuned **- 2.** *fam* [être en forme] to be fine.

carcajou [karkaʒu] *nm* wolverine.

carcan [karkɑ̃] *nm* HIST iron collar ; *fig* yoke.

carcasse [karkas] *nf* **- 1.** [d'animal] carcass **- 2.** [de bâtiment, navire] framework **- 3.** [de véhicule] shell.

carcéral, e, aux [karseral, o] *adj* prison *(avant n)*.

carcinome [karsinɔm] *nm* carcinoma.

cardan [kardɑ̃] *nm* universal joint.

carder [3] [karde] *vt* to card.

cardiaque [kardjak] ⬦ *adj* cardiac ; **être ~** to have a heart condition ; **crise ~** heart attack ⬦ *nmf* heart patient.

cardigan [kardigɑ̃] *nm* cardigan.

cardinal, e, aux [kardinal, o] *adj* cardinal.

cardinal *nm* **- 1.** RELIG cardinal **- 2.** [nombre] cardinal number.

cardiologue [kardjɔlɔg] *nmf* heart specialist, cardiologist.

cardio-vasculaire [kardjɔvaskylɛr] *(pl* **cardio-vasculaires)** *adj* cardiovascular.

Carême [karɛm] *nm* : **le ~** Lent.

carence [karɑ̃s] *nf* - **1.** [de personne, gouvernement] inadequacy, incompetence - **2.** [manque] : ~ **(en)** deficiency (in).

carène [karɛn] *nf* NAVIG hull.

caréner [18] [karene] *vt* - **1.** [navire] to careen - **2.** [carrosserie] to streamline.

caressant, e [karɛsɑ̃, ɑ̃t] *adj* affectionate.

caresse [karɛs] *nf* caress ; **faire une ~ à qqn** to caress sb.

caresser [4] [karese] *vt* - **1.** [personne] to caress ; [animal, objet] to stroke - **2.** *fig* [espoir] to cherish.

car-ferry [karferi] (*pl* car-ferries) *nm* car ferry.

cargaison [kargɛzɔ̃] *nf* - **1.** TRANSPORT cargo - **2.** *fam* [grande quantité] load, pile.

cargo [kargo] *nm* - **1.** [navire] freighter - **2.** [avion] cargo plane.

cari = **curry**.

caribou [karibu] *nm* caribou.

caricatural, e, aux [karikatyral, o] *adj* [récit] exaggerated.

caricature [karikatyr] *nf* - **1.** [gén] caricature - **2.** *péj* [personne] sight.

carie [kari] *nf* - **1.** MÉD caries - **2.** BOT blight.

carillon [karijɔ̃] *nm* - **1.** [cloches] bells (*pl*) - **2.** [d'horloge, de porte] chime.

carillonner [3] [karijɔne] <> *vi* to ring <> *vt* - **1.** [heure] to strike, to chime - **2.** *fig* [nouvelle] to announce.

caritatif, ive [karitatif, iv] *adj* charitable.

carlingue [karlɛ̃g] *nf* - **1.** [d'avion] cabin - **2.** [de navire] keelson.

carmélite [karmelit] *nf* Carmelite (nun).

carmin [karmɛ̃] <> *adj inv* crimson <> *nm* [couleur] crimson ; [colorant] cochineal.

carnage [karnaʒ] *nm* slaughter, carnage.

carnassier, ère [karnasje, ɛr] *adj* carnivorous.

carnassier [karnasje] *nm* carnivore.

carnaval [karnaval] *nm* carnival.

carnet [karnɛ] *nm* - **1.** [petit cahier] notebook ; ~ **d'adresses** address book ; ~ **de notes** SCOL report card - **2.** [bloc de feuilles] book ; ~ **de chèques** cheque book *Br*, checkbook *Am* ; ~ **de tickets** book of tickets.

carnivore [karnivɔr] <> *adj* carnivorous <> *nm* carnivore.

carotide [karɔtid] ANAT <> *adj* carotid <> *nf* carotid artery.

carotte [karɔt] <> *nf* carrot ; ~**s râpées** grated carrots ; ~**s Vichy** glazed carrots ; **les ~s sont cuites** *fam* they've/we've *etc* had it <> *adj inv* [couleur] carroty.

carpe [karp] <> *nf* carp ; **être muet comme une ~** *fig* not to say a word <> *nm* ANAT carpus.

carpette [karpɛt] *nf* - **1.** [petit tapis] rug - **2.** *fam péj* [personne] doormat.

carquois [karkwa] *nm* quiver.

carré, e [kare] *adj* - **1.** [gén] square ; **20 mètres ~s** 20 square metres - **2.** [franc] straightforward.

➡ **carré** *nm* - **1.** [quadrilatère] square ; **élever un nombre au ~** MATHS to square a number ; ~ **blanc** TV white square in the corner of the screen indicating that a television programme is not recommended for children ; ~ **de soie** [foulard] silk square - **2.** [sur un navire] wardroom - **3.** CARTES : **un ~ d'as** four aces - **4.** CULIN : ~ **d'agneau** rack of lamb - **5.** [petit terrain] patch, plot.

carreau (*pl* x) [karo] *nm* - **1.** [carrelage] tile - **2.** [sol] tiled floor ; **rester sur le ~** *fig* to be knocked out - **3.** [vitre] window pane - **4.** [motif carré] check ; **à ~x** [tissu] checked ; [papier] squared - **5.** CARTES diamond ; [l'atout est ~ diamonds are trumps - **6.** *loc* : **se tenir à ~** to watch one's step.

carrefour [karfur] *nm* - **1.** [de routes, de la vie] crossroads (*sg*) - **2.** [forum] forum, conference.

carrelage [karlaʒ] *nm* - **1.** [action] tiling - **2.** [surface] tiles (*pl*).

carreler [24] [karle] *vt* to tile.

carrelet [karlɛ] *nm* - **1.** [poisson] plaice - **2.** [filet de pêche] net.

carreleur [karlœr] *nm* tiler.

carrément [karemɑ̃] *adv* - **1.** [franchement] bluntly - **2.** [complètement] completely, quite - **3.** [sans hésiter] straight.

carrer [3] [kare] ➡ **se carrer** *vp* : **se ~ dans** to settle o.s. in.

carrière [karjɛr] *nf* - **1.** [profession] career ; **embrasser une ~** to take up a career ; **faire ~ qqch** to make a career (for o.s.) in sthg - **2.** [gisement] quarry.

carriériste [karjerist] *nmf péj* careerist.

carriole [karjɔl] *nf* - **1.** [petite charrette] cart - **2.** *Can* [traîneau] sleigh.

carrossable [karɔsabl] *adj* suitable for vehicles.

carrosse [karɔs] *nm* (horse-drawn) coach.

carrosserie [karɔsri] *nf* - **1.** [de voiture] bodywork, body - **2.** [industrie] coachbuilding.

carrossier [karɔsje] *nm* coachbuilder.

carrousel [karuzɛl] *nm* ÉQUITATION carousel ; ~ **d'avions** *fig* aerial display.

carrure [karyr] *nf* - **1.** [de personne] build ; *fig* stature - **2.** [de vêtement] width across the shoulders.

cartable [kartabl] *nm* schoolbag.

carte [kart] *nf* - **1.** [gén] card ; **~ d'abonnement** season ticket ; **~ bancaire** cash card *Br* ; **~ de crédit** credit card ; **~ d'étudiant** student card ; **~ graphique** INFORM graphics board ; **~ à gratter** scratch card ; **~ grise** ≃ logbook *Br*, ≃ car registration papers *Am* ; **~ d'identité** identity card ; **~ à mémoire** memory card ; **~ mère** INFORM motherboard ; **~ nominative** personal identity card ; **Carte Orange** season ticket *(for use on public transport in Paris)* ; **~ postale** postcard ; **~ à puce** smart card ; **~ de séjour** residence permit ; **~ son** INFORM soundcard ; **Carte Vermeil** card entitling senior citizens to reduced rates in cinemas, on public transport etc ; **~ de visite** visiting card *Br*, calling card *Am* ; **donner ~ blanche à qqn** *fig* to give sb a free hand - **2.** [de jeu] : **~ (à jouer)** (playing) card ; **abattre ses ~s** to lay down one's cards ; *fig* to show one's hand ; **battre les ~s** to shuffle the cards ; **brouiller les ~s** *fig* to cloud *ou* obscure the issue ; **tirer les ~s à qqn** to read sb's cards - **3.** GÉOGR map ; **~ d'état-major** ≃ Ordnance Survey map *Br*, ≃ Geological Survey map *Am* ; **~ routière** road map - **4.** [au restaurant] menu ; **à la ~** [menu] à la carte ; [horaires] flexible ; **~ des vins** wine list.

cartel [kartɛl] *nm* - **1.** ÉCON cartel - **2.** POLIT coalition.

carter [kartɛr] *nm* - **1.** [de bicyclette] chain guard - **2.** [de moteur] crankcase.

carte-réponse [kartrepɔ̃s] *(pl* **cartes-réponses)** *nf* reply card.

cartésien, enne [kartezjɛ̃, ɛn] <> *adj* - **1.** [rationnel] logical, rational - **2.** [relatif à Descartes] Cartesian <> *nm, f* Cartesian.

cartilage [kartilaʒ] *nm* cartilage.

cartilagineux, euse [kartilaʒinø, øz] *adj* - **1.** [tissu] cartilaginous - **2.** [viande] gristly.

cartographie [kartɔgrafi] *nf* cartography.

cartomancien, enne [kartɔmɑ̃sjɛ̃, ɛn] *nm, f* fortune-teller *(using cards)*.

carton [kartɔ̃] *nm* - **1.** [matière] cardboard ; **en ~** cardboard ; **~ ondulé** corrugated cardboard - **2.** [emballage] cardboard box ; **~ à dessin** portfolio - **3.** [cible] target ; **faire un ~** *fam* to target-shoot ; *fig* to take potshots - **4.** [carte] : **~ d'invitation** formal invitation.

cartonné, e [kartɔne] *adj* [livre] hardback.

carton-pâte [kartɔ̃pat] *(pl* **cartons-pâtes)** *nm* pasteboard ; **de** *ou* **en ~** cardboard.

cartouche [kartuʃ] *nf* - **1.** [gén & INFORM] cartridge - **2.** [de cigarettes] carton.

cas [ka] *nm* case ; **au ~ où** in case ; **auquel ~** in which case ; **dans** *ou* **en ce ~** in that case ; **en aucun ~** under no circumstances ; **en tout ~** in any case, anyway ; **en ~ de** in case of ; **en ~ d'urgence** in an emergency ; **en ~ de besoin** if need be ; **c'est le ~ de le dire** you've hit the nail on the head ; **le ~ échéant** if the need arises, if need be ; **~ de conscience** matter of conscience ; **~ de force majeure** emergency ; **~ social** person with social problems ; **faire grand ~ de** to set great store by.

casanier, ère [kazanje, ɛr] *adj* & *nm, f* stay-at-home.

casaque [kazak] *nf* - **1.** [veste] overblouse ; **tourner ~** *fig* to change sides - **2.** HIPPISME blouse.

cascade [kaskad] *nf* - **1.** [chute d'eau] waterfall ; *fig* stream, torrent ; **en ~** *fig* one after the other - **2.** CIN stunt.

cascadeur, euse [kaskadœr, øz] *nm, f* - **1.** [au cirque] acrobat - **2.** CIN stuntman (*f* stuntwoman).

cascher = kas(c)her.

case [kaz] *nf* - **1.** [habitation] hut - **2.** [de boîte, tiroir] compartment ; [d'échiquier] square ; [sur un formulaire] box.

casemate [kazmat] *nf* bunker.

caser [3] [kaze] *vt* - **1.** *fam* [trouver un emploi pour] to get a job for - **2.** *fam* [loger] to put up - **3.** *fam* [marier] to marry off - **4.** [placer] to put.
◆ **se caser** *vp fam* - **1.** [trouver un emploi] to get (o.s.) a job - **2.** [se marier] to get hitched - **3.** [se loger] to find a place to live.

caserne [kazɛrn] *nf* barracks.

cash [kaʃ] *nm* cash ; **payer ~** to pay (in) cash.

casher = kascher.

casier [kazje] *nm* - **1.** [compartiment] compartment ; [pour le courrier] pigeonhole - **2.** [meuble - à bouteilles] rack ; [- à courrier] set of pigeonholes - **3.** PÊCHE lobster pot.
◆ **casier judiciaire** *nm* police record ; **~ judiciaire vierge** clean (police) record.

casino [kazino] *nm* casino.

Caspienne [kaspjɛn] *n* : **la ~** the Caspian Sea.

casque [kask] *nm* - **1.** [de protection] helmet ; **~ intégral** crash helmet - **2.** [séchoir] hairdryer - **3.** [à écouteurs] headphones *(pl)*.
◆ **Casques bleus** *nmpl* : **les Casques bleus** the UN peace-keeping force.

casqué, e [kaske] *adj* wearing a helmet.

casquer [3] [kaske] *vi fam* to cough up.

casquette [kaskɛt] *nf* cap.

cassant, e [kasɑ̃, ɑ̃t] *adj* - **1.** [fragile - verre] fragile ; [- cheveux] brittle - **2.** [dur] brusque.

cassation [kasasjɔ̃] ⊳ cour.

casse [kas] <> *nf* - **1.** [action] breakage - **2.** *fam*

cassé [violence] aggro **- 3.** [de voitures] scrapyard **- 4.** TYPO : **haut/bas de ~** upper/lower case ◇ nm fam [cambriolage] break-in.

cassé, e [kase] adj **- 1.** [voûté, courbé] stooped **- 2.** [voix] trembling, breaking.

casse-cou [kasku] nmf inv [personne] daredevil.

casse-croûte [kaskrut] nm inv snack.

casse-noisettes [kasnwazɛt], **casse-noix** [kasnwa] nm inv nutcrackers (pl).

casse-pieds [kaspje] ◇ adj inv fam annoying ◇ nmf inv pain (in the neck).

casser [3] [kase] ◇ vt **- 1.** [briser] to break ; **à tout ~** fam fig [extraordinaire] fabulous, fantastic ; [tout au plus] at (the) most **- 2.** JUR to quash **- 3.** COMM : **~ les prix** to slash prices ◇ vi to break.

➤ **se casser** vp **- 1.** [se briser] to break **- 2.** [membre] : **se ~ un bras** to break one's arm **- 3.** fam [se fatiguer] to strain o.s. **- 4.** fam [s'en aller] to hop it, to push off.

casserole [kasrɔl] nf **- 1.** [ustensile] saucepan ; **à la ~** CULIN braised **- 2.** [voiture] (old) banger **- 3.** fam [instrument] : **être une vraie ~** to sound tinny **- 4.** loc : **passer à la ~** fam to be bumped off ; [sexuellement] to get laid.

casse-tête [kastɛt] nm inv **- 1.** fig [problème] headache **- 2.** [jeu] puzzle.

cassette [kasɛt] nf **- 1.** [coffret] casket **- 2.** [de musique, vidéo] cassette **- 3.** INFORM : **~ audionumérique** DAT tape.

casseur [kasœr] nm **- 1.** [cambrioleur] burglar **- 2.** [manifestant] rioting demonstrator.

cassis [kasis] nm **- 1.** [fruit] blackcurrant ; [arbuste] blackcurrant bush ; [liqueur] blackcurrant liqueur **- 2.** [sur la route] dip.

cassonade [kasɔnad] nf brown sugar.

cassoulet [kasule] nm stew of haricot beans and meat.

cassure [kasyr] nf break.

castagnettes [kastaɲɛt] nfpl castanets.

caste [kast] nf caste.

casting [kastiŋ] nm [acteurs] cast ; [sélection] casting ; **aller à un ~** to go to an audition.

castor [kastɔr] nm beaver.

castration [kastrasjɔ̃] nf castration.

castrer [3] [kastre] vt to castrate ; [chat] to neuter ; [chatte] to spay.

cataclysme [kataklism] nm cataclysm.

catacombes [katakɔ̃b] nfpl catacombs.

catadioptre [katadjɔptr], **Cataphote**® [katafɔt] nm **- 1.** [sur la route] cat's eye Br, highway reflector Am **- 2.** [de véhicule] reflector.

catalan, e [katalɑ̃, an] adj Catalan, Catalonian.

➤ **catalan** nm [langue] Catalan.

➤ **Catalan, e** nm, f Catalan, Catalonian.

Catalogne [katalɔɲ] nf : **la ~** Catalonia.

catalogue [katalɔg] nm catalogue Br, catalog Am.

cataloguer [3] [kataloge] vt **- 1.** [classer] to catalogue Br, to catalog Am **- 2.** péj [juger] to label.

catalyseur [katalizœr] nm CHIM & fig catalyst.

catalytique [katalitik] ▷ pot.

catamaran [katamarɑ̃] nm **- 1.** [voilier] catamaran **- 2.** [d'hydravion] floats (pl).

Cataphote® = catadioptre.

cataplasme [kataplasm] nm poultice.

catapulter [3] [katapylte] vt to catapult.

cataracte [katarakt] nf cataract.

catarrhe [katar] nm catarrh.

catastrophe [katastrɔf] nf disaster, catastrophe ; **atterrir en ~** to crashland ; **partir en ~** to leave in a mad rush.

catastrophé, e [katastrɔfe] adj shocked, upset.

catastrophique [katastrɔfik] adj disastrous, catastrophic.

catch [katʃ] nm wrestling.

catéchisme [kateʃism] nm catechism.

catégorie [kategɔri] nf [gén] category ; [de personnel] grade ; [de viande, fruits] quality ; **~ socioprofessionnelle** ÉCON socio-economic group.

catégorique [kategɔrik] adj categorical.

catégoriquement [kategɔrikmɑ̃] adv categorically.

caténaire [katenɛr] adj & nf catenary.

cathédrale [katedral] nf cathedral.

cathode [katɔd] nf cathode.

cathodique [katɔdik] ▷ tube.

catholicisme [katɔlisism] nm Catholicism.

catholique [katɔlik] adj Catholic ; **pas (très) ~** fig dubious, dodgy.

catimini [katimini] ➤ **en catimini** loc adv secretly.

catogan [katɔgɑ̃] nm ribbon (securing hair at the back of the neck).

cauchemar [koʃmar] nm litt & fig nightmare.

cauchemardesque [koʃmardɛsk] adj nightmarish.

caudal, e, aux [kodal, o] adj caudal, tail (avant n).

causal, e, als ou **aux** [kozal, o] adj causal.

causalité [kozalite] nf causality.

causant, e [kozɑ̃, ɑ̃t] adj : **peu ~** not very chatty.

cause [koz] *nf* - **1.** [gén] cause ; **gagner qqn à sa ~** to win sb over (to one's cause) ; **à ~ de** because of ; **pour ~ de** on account of, because of ; **et pour ~!** and for good reason! ; **faire ~ commune avec qqn** to make common cause with sb - **2.** JUR case - **3.** *loc* : **être en ~** [intérêts] to be at stake ; [honnêteté] to be in doubt *ou* in question ; **être hors de ~** to be beyond suspicion ; **remettre en ~** to challenge, to question.

causer [3] [koze] ⟷ *vt* : **~ qqch à qqn** to cause sb sthg ⟷ *vi* - **1.** [bavarder] : **~ (de)** to chat (about) - **2.** [jaser] : **~ (sur)** to gossip (about).

causerie [kozri] *nf* talk.

causette [kozɛt] *nf fam* chat ; **faire la ~ avec qqn** to have a chat with sb.

causticité [kostisite] *nf* causticness, causticity.

caustique [kostik] *adj* & *nm* caustic.

cauteleux, euse [kotlø, øz] *adj* sly.

cautériser [3] [koterize] *vt* to cauterize.

caution [kosjɔ̃] *nf* - **1.** [somme d'argent] guarantee ; **libérer qqn sous ~** JUR to free sb on bail ; **payer la ~ de qqn** to stand bail for sb - **2.** [personne] guarantor ; **se porter ~ pour qqn** to act as guarantor for sb - **3.** [soutien] support, backing.

cautionner [3] [kosjone] *vt* - **1.** [se porter garant de] to guarantee - **2.** *fig* [appuyer] to support, to back.

cavalcade [kavalkad] *nf* - **1.** [de cavaliers] cavalcade - **2.** [d'enfants] stampede.

cavale [kaval] *nf fam* : **être en ~** to be on the run.

cavaler [3] [kavale] *vi fam* [courir] to run *ou* rush around ; **~ après qqn/qqch** to chase (after) sb/sthg.

cavalerie [kavalri] *nf* - **1.** MIL cavalry - **2.** [de cirque] horses *(pl)*.

cavalier, ère [kavalje, ɛr] ⟷ *adj* - **1.** [destiné aux cavaliers] : **allée cavalière** bridle path - **2.** *sout* [impertinent] offhand ⟷ *nm, f* - **1.** [à cheval] rider - **2.** [partenaire] partner ; **faire ~ seul** *fig* to go it alone.

⟜ **cavalier** *nm* [aux échecs] knight.

cavalièrement [kavaljɛrmɑ̃] *adv* in an offhand manner.

cave [kav] ⟷ *nf* - **1.** [sous-sol] cellar - **2.** [de vins] (wine) cellar - **3.** [cabaret] cellar nightclub ⟷ *nm arg crime* outsider ⟷ *adj* [joues] hollow ; [yeux] sunken.

caveau *(pl* x) [kavo] *nm* - **1.** [petite cave] small cellar - **2.** [cabaret] nightclub - **3.** [sépulture] vault.

caverne [kavɛrn] *nf* cave.

caverneux, euse [kavɛrnø, øz] ▷ **voix**.

caviar [kavjar] *nm* caviar.

cavité [kavite] *nf* cavity.

CB (*abr de* citizen's band, canaux banalisés) *nf* CB.

cc - **1.** (*abr de* cuillère à café) tsp - **2.** *abr de* charges comprises.

CC (*abr de* corps consulaire) CC.

CCE (*abr de* Commission des communautés européennes) *nf* ECC.

CCI (*abr de* Chambre de commerce et d'industrie) *nf* CCI.

CCP (*abr de* compte chèque postal, compte courant postal) *nm* post office account, ≃ Giro *Br*.

CD *nm* - **1.** (*abr de* chemin départemental) minor road - **2.** (*abr de* compact disc) CD - **3.** (*abr de* comité directeur) steering committee - **4.** (*abr de* corps diplomatique) CD.

CDD *nm abr de* contrat à durée déterminée ; **elle est en ~** she's on a fixed term contract.

CdF *abr de* Charbonnages de France) *nmpl* French national coal board, ≃ NCB *Br*.

CDI *nm* - **1.** (*abr de* centre de documentation et d'information) *school library* - **2.** *abr de* contrat à durée indéterminée ; **elle est en ~** she's got a permanent work contract.

CD-Rom [sederɔm] (*abr de* compact disc read only memory) *nm* CD-Rom.

CDS (*abr de* Centre des démocrates sociaux) *nm French political party.*

CDU (*abr de* Classification décimale universelle) *nf* DDS.

ce [sə] ⟷ *adj dém* (**cet** [sɛt] *devant voyelle ou h muet, f* **cette** [sɛt]*, pl* **ces** [se]) [proche] this, these *(pl)* ; [éloigné] that, those *(pl)* ; **~ mois, ~ mois-ci** this month ; **cette année, cette année-là** that year ; **regarde de ~ côté-ci et pas de ~ côté-là** look on this side, not that side ⟷ *pron dém* (**c'** *devant voyelle*) **c'est** it is, it's ; **~ sont** they are, they're ; **c'est mon bureau** this is my office, it's my office ; **~ sont mes enfants** these are my children, they're my children ; **c'est à Paris** it's in Paris ; **c'était hier** it was yesterday ; **qui est-~?** who is it? ; **~ qui, ~ que** what ; **ils ont eu ~ qui leur revenait** they got what they deserved ; **..., ~ qui est étonnant** ..., which is surprising ; **elle n'achète même pas ~ dont elle a besoin** she doesn't even buy what she needs ; **vous savez bien ~ à quoi je pense** you know exactly what I'm thinking about ; **faites donc ~ pour quoi on vous paie** do what you're paid to do.

CE ⟷ *nm* - **1.** *abr de* comité d'entreprise - **2.** (*abr de* cours élémentaire) : **~1** *second year of primary school* ; **~2** *third year of pri-*

mary school ⇨ *nf* (*abr de* **Communauté européenne**) EC.

CEA (*abr de* **Commissariat à l'énergie atomique**) *nm French atomic energy commission,* ≃ AEA *Br,* ≃ AEC *Am.*

CECA, Ceca [seka] (*abr de* **Communauté européenne du charbon et de l'acier**) *nf* ECSC.

ceci [səsi] *pron dém* this ; ~ **pour vous dire que** ... this is just to say (that) ... ; ~ **n'explique pas cela** this doesn't explain that ; ~ **(étant) dit** having said that ; **à ~ près que** with the exception that, except that.

cécité [sesite] *nf* blindness.

céder [18] [sede] ⇨ *vt* - **1.** [donner] to give up ; **'cédez le passage'** 'give way' *Br,* 'yield' *Am* - **2.** [revendre] to sell ⇨ *vi* - **1.** [personne] : ~ **(à)** to give in (to), to yield (to) - **2.** [chaise, plancher] to give way.

CEDEX, Cedex [sedɛks] (*abr de* **courrier d'entreprise à distribution exceptionnelle**) *nm accelerated postal service for bulk users.*

cédille [sedij] *nf* cedilla ; **c ~** c cedilla.

cèdre [sɛdr] *nm* cedar.

CEE (*abr de* **Communauté économique européenne**) *nf* EEC.

CEI (*abr de* **Communauté d'États Indépendants**) *nf* CIS.

ceindre [81] [sɛdr] *vt* - **1.** [entourer] : ~ **qqch de qqch** to put sthg around sthg - **2.** [mettre] to put on.

ceinture [sɛtyr] *nf* - **1.** [gén] belt ; **attachez vos ~s** fasten your seat *ou* safety belts ; ~ **à enrouleur** inertia-reel seat belt ; ~ **noire** *JUDO* black belt ; ~ **de sauvetage** life belt ; ~ **de sécurité** safety *ou* seat belt ; ~ **verte** green belt ; **se serrer la ~** *fig* to tighten one's belt - **2.** *ANAT* waist - **3.** *COUTURE* waistband.

ceinturon [sɛtyrɔ̃] *nm* belt.

cela [səla] *pron dém* that ; ~ **ne vous regarde pas** it's *ou* that's none of your business ; **il y a des années de ~** that was many years ago ; **c'est ~** that's right ; ~ **dit** ... having said that ... ; **malgré ~** in spite of that, nevertheless.

célébration [selebrasjɔ̃] *nf* celebration.

célèbre [selɛbr] *adj* famous.

célébrer [18] [selebre] *vt* - **1.** [gén] to celebrate - **2.** [faire la louange de] to praise.

célébrité [selebrite] *nf* - **1.** [renommée] fame - **2.** [personne] celebrity.

céleri [sɛlri] *nm* celery ; ~ **rémoulade** *CULIN* grated celeriac in mustard dressing.

➤ **céleri rave, céleri-rave** *nm* celeriac.

célérité [selerite] *nf* speed.

céleste [selɛst] *adj* heavenly.

célibat [seliba] *nm* celibacy.

célibataire [selibatɛr] ⇨ *adj* single, unmarried ; **père** *ou* **mère ~** single parent ⇨ *nmf* single person, single man (*f* woman) ; ~ **endurci** confirmed bachelor.

celle ⇨ **celui.**

celle-ci ⇨ **celui-ci.**

celle-là ⇨ **celui-là.**

celles ⇨ **celui.**

celles-ci ⇨ **celui-ci.**

celles-là ⇨ **celui-là.**

cellier [selje] *nm* storeroom.

Cellophane® [selɔfan] *nf* Cellophane® ; **sous ~** (wrapped) in cellophane.

cellulaire [selylɛr] *adj* - **1.** *BIOL* & *TÉLÉCOM* cellular - **2.** [destiné aux prisonniers] : **régime ~** solitary confinement ; **voiture ~** prison van.

cellule [selyl] *nf* - **1.** [gén & *INFORM*] cell ; ~ **photoélectrique** photoelectric cell - **2.** [groupe] unit ; ~ **de crise** [groupe] emergency committee ; [réunion] emergency committee meeting.

cellulite [selylit] *nf* cellulite.

celluloïd [selylɔid] *nm* celluloid.

cellulose [selyloz] *nf* cellulose.

celte [sɛlt] *adj* Celtic.

➤ **Celte** *nmf* Celt.

celtique [sɛltik] ⇨ *adj* Celtic ⇨ *nm* [langue] Celtic.

celui [səlɥi] (*f* **celle** [sɛl], *mpl* **ceux** [sø], *fpl* **celles** [sɛl]) *pron dém* - **1.** [suivi d'un complément prépositionnel] the one ; **celle de devant** the one in front ; **ceux d'entre vous qui** ... those of you who ... - **2.** [suivi d'un pronom relatif] : ~ **qui** [objet] the one which *ou* that ; [personne] the one who ; **c'est celle qui te va le mieux** that's the one which *ou* that suits you best ; ~ **que vous voyez** the one (which *ou* that) you can see, the one whom you can see ; **ceux que je connais** those I know - **3.** [suivi d'un adjectif, d'un participe] the one.

celui-ci [səlɥisi] (*f* **celle-ci** [sɛlsi], *mpl* **ceux-ci** [søsi], *fpl* **celles-ci** [sɛlsi]) *pron dém* this one, these ones (*pl*).

celui-là [səlɥila] (*f* **celle-là** [sɛlla], *mpl* **ceux-là** [søla], *fpl* **celles-là** [sɛlla]) *pron dém* that one, those ones (*pl*) ; ~ ... **celui-ci** the former ... the latter.

cénacle [senakl] *nm* [coterie] circle.

cendre [sɑ̃dr] *nf* ash ; **réduire qqch en ~s** to reduce sthg to ashes.

➤ **cendres** *nfpl* [restes des morts] ashes ; **renaître de ses ~s** *fig* to rise from the ashes.

➤ **Cendres** *nfpl* : **le mercredi des Cendres** Ash Wednesday.

cendré, e [sɑ̃dre] adj [chevelure] : **blond ~** ash blond.

cendrier [sɑ̃drije] nm - **1.** [de fumeur] ashtray - **2.** [de poêle] ashpan.

cène [sɛn] nf (Holy) Communion.

➤ **Cène** nf : **la Cène** the Last Supper.

censé, e [sɑ̃se] adj : **être ~ faire qqch** to be supposed to do sthg.

censément [sɑ̃semɑ̃] adv sout supposedly.

censeur [sɑ̃sœr] nm - **1.** SCOL ≃ deputy head Br, ≃ vice-principal Am - **2.** CIN & PRESSE censor - **3.** fig [juge] critic.

censure [sɑ̃syr] nf - **1.** [presse & CIN - contrôle] censorship ; [- censeurs] censors (pl) - **2.** POLIT censure - **3.** PSYCHOL censor.

censurer [3] [sɑ̃syre] vt - **1.** CIN, PRESSE & PSYCHOL to censor - **2.** [juger] to censure.

cent [sɑ̃] ◇ adj num one hundred, a hundred ◇ nm - **1.** [nombre] a hundred ; voir aussi **six - 2.** [mesure de proportion] : **pour ~** percent ; **~ pour ~** a hundred percent - **3.** [monnaie] cent.

centaine [sɑ̃tɛn] nf - **1.** [cent unités] hundred - **2.** [un grand nombre] : **une ~ de** about a hundred ; **des ~s (de)** hundreds (of) ; **plusieurs ~s de** several hundred ; **par ~s** in hundreds.

centenaire [sɑ̃tner] ◇ adj hundred-year-old (avant n) ; **être ~** to be a hundred years old ◇ nmf centenarian ◇ nm [anniversaire] centenary Br, centennial Am.

centiare [sɑ̃tjar] nm square metre Br ou meter Am.

centième [sɑ̃tjɛm] ◇ adj num, nm ou nmf hundredth ; voir aussi **sixième** ◇ nf THÉÂTRE hundredth performance.

centigrade [sɑ̃tigrad] ➤ **degré**.

centigramme [sɑ̃tigram] nm centigram.

centilitre [sɑ̃tilitr] nm centilitre Br, centiliter Am.

centime [sɑ̃tim] nm centime.

centimètre [sɑ̃timɛtr] nm - **1.** [mesure] centimetre Br, centimeter Am ; **~ cube** cubic centimetre Br ou centimeter Am - **2.** [ruban, règle] tape measure.

central, e, aux [sɑ̃tral, o] adj central.

➤ **central** nm - **1.** TENNIS centre Br ou center Am court - **2.** [de réseau] : **~ téléphonique** telephone exchange.

➤ **centrale** nf - **1.** [usine] power plant ou station ; **~e hydroélectrique** hydroelectric power station ; **~e nucléaire** nuclear power plant ou station - **2.** [syndicale] group of affiliated trade unions - **3.** COMM : **~e d'achat** buying group.

➤ **Centrale** nf grande école training highly-qualified engineers.

centralien, enne [sɑ̃traljɛ̃, ɛn] nm, f engineering student.

centralisation [sɑ̃tralizasjɔ̃] nf centralization.

centraliser [3] [sɑ̃tralize] vt to centralize.

centre [sɑ̃tr] nm [gén] centre Br, center Am ; **~ d'accueil** reception centre Br ou center Am ; **~ aéré** outdoor centre Br ou center Am ; **~ antipoison** poison centre Br ou center Am ; **~ d'appels** call centre Br ou center Am ; **~ commercial** shopping centre Br ou mall Am ; **~ culturel** arts centre Br ou center Am ; **~ de documentation** reference library ; **~ équestre** riding school ; **~ de gravité** centre Br ou center Am of gravity ; **~ nerveux** nerve centre Br ou center Am ; **~ de rééducation** rehabilitation centre Br ou center Am.

centrer [3] [sɑ̃tre] vt to centre Br, to center Am.

centre-ville [sɑ̃trəvil] (pl **centres-villes**) nm city centre Br ou center Am, town centre Br ou center Am.

centrifuge [sɑ̃trify3] ➤ **force**.

centrifugeuse [sɑ̃trify3øz] nf - **1.** TECHNOL centrifuge - **2.** CULIN juice extractor.

centriste [sɑ̃trist] POLIT ◇ adj centre (avant n) Br, center (avant n) Am ◇ nmf centrist.

centuple [sɑ̃typl] nm : **être le ~ de qqch** to be a hundred times sthg ; **au ~** a hundredfold.

centupler [3] [sɑ̃typle] vt & vi to increase a hundredfold.

cep [sɛp] nm stock.

CEP (abr de **certificat d'études primaires**) nm school-leaving certificate formerly taken at end of primary education.

cépage [sepa3] nm (type of) vine.

cèpe [sɛp] nm cep.

cependant [səpɑ̃dɑ̃] conj however, yet.

céramique [seramik] nf - **1.** [matière, objet] ceramic - **2.** [art] ceramics (U), pottery.

cerbère [sɛrber] nm strict caretaker ou doorkeeper.

cerceau (pl x) [sɛrso] nm hoop.

cercle [sɛrkl] nm circle ; **~ d'amis** circle of friends ; **~ vicieux** vicious circle.

cerclé, e [sɛrkle] adj ringed ; **des lunettes ~es d'écaille** horn-rimmed glasses.

cercueil [sɛrkœj] nm coffin.

céréale [sereal] nf cereal.

cérébral, e, aux [serebral, o] ◇ adj - **1.** [du cerveau] cerebral - **2.** [personne, activité] intellectual ◇ nm, f intellectual.

cérémonial, als [seremɔnjal] nm ceremonial.

cérémonie [seremɔni] nf ceremony ; **sans ~**

without ceremony, informally ; **faire des ~s** to make a fuss.

cérémonieux, euse [seremɔnjø, øz] *adj* ceremonious.

CERES [sɛrɛs] (*abr de* **Centre d'études, de recherches et d'éducation socialiste**) *nm formerly the intellectual section of the French socialist party.*

cerf [sɛr] *nm* stag.

cerfeuil [sɛrfœj] *nm* chervil.

cerf-volant [sɛrvɔlɑ̃] (*pl* **cerfs-volants**) *nm* - **1.** [jouet] kite - **2.** [insecte] stag beetle.

cerise [səriz] ◇ *nf* cherry ; **~ à grappes** choke berry ; **la ~ sur le gâteau** *fig* the icing on the cake ◇ *adj inv* cherry.

cerisier [sərizje] *nm* [arbre] cherry (tree) ; [bois] cherry (wood).

CERN, Cern [sɛrn] (*abr de* **Conseil européen pour la recherche nucléaire**) *nm* CERN.

cerne [sɛrn] *nm* ring.

cerné [sɛrne] ▷ **œil**.

cerner [3] [sɛrne] *vt* - **1.** [encercler] to surround - **2.** [entourer d'un trait] to ring - **3.** *fig* [sujet] to define.

certain, e [sɛrtɛ̃, ɛn] ◇ *adj* certain ; **c'est une chose ~e** there's no doubt about it ; **être ~ de qqch** to be certain *ou* sure of sthg ; **être ~ que** to be certain *ou* sure (that) ; **je suis pourtant ~ d'avoir mis mes clés là** but I'm certain *ou* sure I left my keys there ◇ *adj indéf* (*avant n*) certain ; **il a un ~ talent** he has some talent *ou* a certain talent ; **à un ~ moment** at some point ; **~s jours** some days ; **un ~ temps** for a while ; **dans une certaine mesure** to a certain extent ; **avoir un ~ âge** to be getting on, to be past one's prime ; **c'est un monsieur d'un ~ âge** he's getting on a bit ; **un ~ M. Lebrun** a Mr Lebrun.

➤ **certains** (*fpl* **certaines**) *pron indéf pl* some.

certainement [sɛrtɛnmɑ̃] *adv* [probablement] most probably, most likely ; [bien sûr] certainly.

certes [sɛrt] *adv* of course.

certificat [sɛrtifika] *nm* - **1.** [attestation, diplôme] certificate ; **~ d'aptitude professionnelle** vocational training certificate ; **~ d'études** primary school-leaving certificate ; **~ médical** medical certificate ; **~ de scolarité** certificate of regular attendance at school or university - **2.** [référence] reference.

certifié, e [sɛrtifje] *adj* : **professeur ~** qualified teacher.

certifier [9] [sɛrtifje] *vt* - **1.** [assurer] : **~ qqch à qqn** to assure sb of sthg - **2.** [authentifier] to certify.

certitude [sɛrtityd] *nf* certainty.

cérumen [serymɛn] *nm* wax, earwax.

cerveau [sɛrvo] *nm* brain.

cervelas [sɛrvəla] *nm* saveloy.

cervelle [sɛrvɛl] *nf* - **1.** ANAT brain - **2.** [facultés mentales, aliment] brains (*pl*) - **3.** *loc* : **se brûler la ~** to blow one's brains out ; **se creuser la ~** to rack one's brains.

cervical, e, aux [sɛrvikal, o] *adj* cervical ; (**vertèbre**) **~e** cervical vertebra.

ces ▷ **ce**.

CES *nm* - **1.** (*abr de* **collège d'enseignement secondaire**) *former secondary school* - **2.** *abr de* **Contrat emploi-solidarité**.

César [sezar] *nm* : **les ~s** *French cinema awards.*

césarienne [sezarjɛn] *nf* caesarean (section).

cessante [sesɑ̃t] ▷ **affaire**.

cessation [sesasjɔ̃] *nf* suspension.

cesse [sɛs] *nf* : **n'avoir de ~ que** (+ *subjonctif*) *sout* not to rest until.

➤ **sans cesse** *loc adv* continually, constantly.

cesser [4] [sese] ◇ *vi* to stop, to cease ◇ *vt* to stop ; **~ de faire qqch** to stop doing sthg.

cessez-le-feu [seselfø] *nm inv* cease-fire.

cession [sesjɔ̃] *nf* transfer.

c'est-à-dire [setadir] *conj* - **1.** [en d'autres termes] : **~ (que)** that is (to say) - **2.** [introduit une restriction, précision, réponse] : **~ que** well ..., actually ...

cet ▷ **ce**.

cétacé [setase] *nm* cetacean.

cette ▷ **ce**.

ceux ▷ **celui**.

ceux-ci ▷ **celui-ci**.

ceux-là ▷ **celui-là**.

cévenol, e [sevnɔl] *adj* of/from the Cévennes region.

Ceylan [selɑ̃] *nm* Ceylon.

cf. (*abr de* **confer**) cf.

CFA ◇ *nf* (*abr de* **Communauté financière africaine**) : **franc ~** *currency used in former French African colonies* ◇ *nm* (*abr de* **centre de formation des apprentis**) *centre for apprenticeship training.*

CFAO (*abr de* **conception de fabrication assistée par ordinateur**) *nf* CAM.

CFC (*abr de* **chlorofluorocarbone**) *nm* CFC.

CFDT (*abr de* **Confédération française démocratique du travail**) *nf French trade union.*

CFES (*abr de* **certificat de fin d'études secondaires**) *nm* school-leaving certificate.

CFF (*abr de* **Chemins de fer fédéraux**) *nmpl* Swiss railways.

CFL (*abr de* **Chemins de fer luxembourgeois**) *nmpl* Luxembourg railways.

CFP (*abr de* **Compagnie française des pétroles**) *nf French oil company.*

CFTC (*abr de* **Confédération française des travailleurs chrétiens**) *nf French trade union.*

CGC (*abr de* **Confédération générale des cadres**) *nf French management union.*

CGT (*abr de* **Confédération générale du travail**) *nf French trade union (affiliated to the Communist party).*

ch. - 1. *abr de* **charges - 2.** *abr de* **chauffage - 3.** *abr de* **cherche.**

CH (*abr de* **Confédération helvétique**) *Switzerland (as nationality sticker on a car).*

chacal [ʃakal] *nm* jackal.

chacun, e [ʃakœ̃, yn] *pron indéf* each (one) ; [tout le monde] everyone, everybody ; **~ de nous/de vous/d'eux** each of us/you/them ; **~ pour soi** every man for himself ; **tout un ~** every one of us/them.

chagrin, e [ʃagrɛ̃, in] *adj* [personne] grieving ; [caractère, humeur] morose.
➡ **chagrin** *nm* grief ; **avoir du ~** to grieve.

chagriner [3] [ʃagrine] *vt* **- 1.** [peiner] to grieve, to distress **- 2.** [contrarier] to upset.

chahut [ʃay] *nm* uproar.

chahuter [3] [ʃayte] *vi* to cause an uproar ⬦ *vt* **- 1.** [importuner - professeur] to rag, to tease ; [- orateur] to heckle **- 2.** [bousculer] to jostle.

chahuteur, euse [ʃaytœr, øz] ⬦ *adj* disruptive, rowdy ⬦ *nm, f* **- 1.** [enfant] disruptive child **- 2.** [manifestant] heckler.

chai [ʃɛ] *nm* wine and spirits store *ou* storehouse.

chaîne [ʃɛn] *nf* **- 1.** [gén] chain ; **~ de montagnes** mountain range **- 2.** IND : **~ de fabrication/de montage** production/assembly line ; **travail à la ~** production-line work ; **produire qqch à la ~** to mass-produce sthg **- 3.** TÉLÉ channel ; **~ à péage** pay TV channel ; **~ de télévision** television channel, TV channel ; **~ thématique** specialized channel **- 4.** [appareil] stereo (system) ; **~ hi-fi** hi-fi system.
➡ **chaînes** *nfpl fig* chains, bonds.

chaînette [ʃɛnɛt] *nf* small chain.

chaînon [ʃɛnɔ̃] *nm litt* & *fig* link.

chair [ʃɛr] ⬦ *nf* flesh ; **bien en ~** plump ; **en ~ et en os** in the flesh ; **~ à saucisse** sausage meat ; **avoir la ~ de poule** to have goose pimples *ou* gooseflesh, to have goosebumps *Am* ⬦ *adj inv* flesh-coloured *Br*, flesh-colored *Am*.

chaire [ʃɛr] *nf* **- 1.** [estrade - de prédicateur] pulpit ; [- de professeur] rostrum **- 2.** UNIV chair.

chaise [ʃɛz] *nf* chair ; **~ électrique** electric

chair ; **~ haute** high chair ; **~ longue** deck-chair ; **être assis entre deux ~s** *fig* to be in an awkward situation.

chaland [ʃalɑ̃] *nm* [bateau] barge.

châle [ʃal] *nm* shawl.

chalet [ʃalɛ] *nm* **- 1.** [de montagne] chalet **- 2.** *Can* [maison de campagne] (holiday) cottage.

chaleur [ʃalœr] *nf* heat ; [agréable] warmth ; **avec ~** [accueillir] warmly ; **en ~** [animal] on heat.

chaleureusement [ʃalœrøzmɑ̃] *adv* warmly.

chaleureux, euse [ʃalœrø, øz] *adj* warm.

challenge [ʃalɑ̃ʒ] *nm* **- 1.** SPORT tournament **- 2.** *fig* [défi] challenge.

challenger [tʃalɛndʒœr] *nm* SPORT & *fig* challenger.

chaloupe [ʃalup] *nf* rowing boat *Br*, rowboat *Am*.

chalumeau [ʃalymo] *nm* **- 1.** TECHNOL blowlamp *Br*, blowtorch *Am* **- 2.** [paille] (drinking) straw.

chalutier [ʃalytje] *nm* **- 1.** [bateau] trawler **- 2.** [pêcheur] trawlerman.

chamade [ʃamad] *nf* : **battre la ~** [cœur] to pound.

chamailler [3] [ʃamaje] ➡ **se chamailler** *vp fam* to squabble.

chambardement [ʃɑ̃bardəmɑ̃] *nm fam* [bouleversement] upheaval.

chambarder [3] [ʃɑ̃barde] *vt fam* **- 1.** [pièce] to turn upside down **- 2.** [projet] to upset.

chambouler [3] [ʃɑ̃bule] *vt fam* to make a mess of, to turn upside down.

chambranle [ʃɑ̃brɑ̃l] *nm* [de porte, fenêtre] frame ; [de cheminée] mantelpiece.

chambre [ʃɑ̃br] *nf* **- 1.** [où l'on dort] : **~ (à coucher)** bedroom ; **garder la ~** to stay in one's room ; **faire ~ à part** to sleep in separate rooms ; **~ à un lit, ~ pour une personne** single room ; **~ pour deux personnes** double room ; **~ à deux lits** twin-bedded room ; **~ d'amis** spare room ; **~ d'hôte** bed and breakfast **- 2.** [local] room ; **~ forte** strongroom ; **~ froide** cold store ; **~ noire** darkroom **- 3.** JUR division ; **~ d'accusation** court of criminal appeal **- 4.** POLIT chamber, house ; **Chambre des députés** House of Commons *Br*, ≃ House of Representatives *Am* **- 5.** COMM : **~ de commerce** chamber of commerce ; **~ des métiers** guild chamber **- 6.** TECHNOL chamber ; **~ à air** [de pneu] inner tube.

chambrée [ʃɑ̃bre] *nf* room, roomful ; [de soldats] barrack room.

chambrer [3] [ʃɑ̃bre] *vt* **- 1.** [vin] to bring to

room temperature - **2.** *fam* [se moquer] : ~ **qqn** to pull sb's leg, to wind sb up *Br.*

chameau, x [ʃamo] *nm* - **1.** [mammifère] camel - **2.** *fam injurieux* [homme] pig ; [femme] cow.

chamois [ʃamwa] ⬦ *nm* chamois ; [peau] chamois (leather) ⬦ *adj inv* [couleur] fawn.

champ [ʃɑ̃] *nm* - **1.** [gén & INFORM] field ; ~ **de bataille** battlefield ; ~ **de courses** racecourse ; ~ **magnétique** magnetic field ; **fleurs des ~s** wild flowers ; ~ **visuel** field of vision *ou* view ; **laisser le ~ libre à qqn** *fig* to leave the field open *ou* clear for sb - **2.** [étendue] area ; ~ **d'action** sphere of activity.

champagne [ʃɑ̃paɲ] *nm* champagne ; ~ **rosé** pink champagne.

champagnisé [ʃɑ̃ɑɲize] ⊳ **vin.**

champenois, e [ʃɑ̃pənwa, az] *adj* : **méthode ~e** champagne-style.

champêtre [ʃɑ̃pɛtr] *adj* rural.

champignon [ʃɑ̃piɲɔ̃] *nm* - **1.** BOT & MÉD fungus ; **pousser comme des ~s** *fig* to mushroom - **2.** [comestible] mushroom ; ~ **de Paris** button mushroom ; ~ **vénéneux** toadstool - **3.** *fam* [accélérateur] accelerator ; **appuyer sur le ~** to put one's foot down *Br*, to step on the gas *Am.*

champion, onne [ʃɑ̃pjɔ̃, ɔn] ⬦ *nm, f* champion ; ~ **du monde** world champion ⬦ *adj fam* brilliant.

championnat [ʃɑ̃pjɔna] *nm* championship ; ~ **du monde** world championship.

chance [ʃɑ̃s] *nf* - **1.** [bonheur] luck (*U*) ; **avoir de la ~** to be lucky ; **ne pas avoir de ~** to be unlucky ; **bonne ~!** good luck! ; **quelle ~!** what luck!, how lucky! ; **porter ~** to bring good luck - **2.** [probabilité, possibilité] chance, opportunity ; **avoir des ~s de faire qqch** to have a chance of doing sthg ; **donner sa ~ à qqn** to give sb a chance ; **il y a peu de ~s que ...** there's not much chance that ...

chancelant, e [ʃɑ̃slɑ̃, ɑ̃t] *adj* - **1.** [titubant, bancal] unsteady - **2.** *fig* [mémoire, santé] shaky.

chanceler [24] [ʃɑ̃sle] *vi* [personne, gouvernement] to totter ; [meuble] to wobble.

chancelier [ʃɑ̃səlje] *nm* - **1.** [premier ministre] chancellor - **2.** [de consulat, d'ambassade] secretary.
➡ **Chancelier** *nm* : **le Chancelier de l'Échiquier** the Chancellor of the Exchequer.

chancellerie [ʃɑ̃sɛlri] *nf* - **1.** [ministère de la justice] chancery *Br*, Department of Justice *Am* - **2.** [en Allemagne] chancellor's office - **3.** [de consulat, d'ambassade] chancery.

chanceux, euse [ʃɑ̃sø, øz] *adj* lucky.

chancre [ʃɑ̃kr] *nm* - **1.** MÉD chancre - **2.** BOT canker.

chandail [ʃɑ̃daj] *nm* (thick) sweater.

Chandeleur [ʃɑ̃lœr] *nf* Candlemas.

chandelier [ʃɑ̃dəlje] *nm* [pour une bougie] candlestick ; [à plusieurs branches] candelabra.

chandelle [ʃɑ̃dɛl] *nf* [bougie] candle ; **dîner aux ~s** candlelit dinner ; **brûler la ~ par les deux bouts** *fig* to burn the candle at both ends ; **devoir une fière ~ à qqn** *fig* to owe sb a big favour *Br ou* favor *Am* ; **tenir la ~** to play gooseberry ; **voir trente-six ~s** *fam fig* to see stars.

change [ʃɑ̃ʒ] *nm* - **1.** [troc & FIN] exchange ; **donner le ~ à qqn** to pull the wool over sb's eyes ; **gagner au ~** to be better off ; **perdre au ~** to lose out - **2.** [couche de bébé] disposable nappy *Br*, diaper *Am.*

changeant, e [ʃɑ̃ʒɑ̃, ɑ̃t] *adj* - **1.** [temps, humeur] changeable - **2.** [reflet] shimmering.

changement [ʃɑ̃ʒmɑ̃] *nm* change ; ~ **de programme** change of plan ; ~ **de vitesse** gear lever *Br*, gearshift *Am.*

changer [17] [ʃɑ̃ʒe] ⬦ *vt* - **1.** [gén] to change ; ~ **qqch contre** to change *ou* exchange sthg for ; ~ **qqn en** to change sb into ; ~ **des francs en livres** to change francs into pounds, to exchange francs for pounds - **2.** [modifier] to change, to alter ; **ne rien ~ à qqch** not to make any changes to sthg ; **ça me/te changera** that will be a (nice) change for me/ you ⬦ *vi* - **1.** [gén] to change ; ~ **de train (à)** to change trains (at) ; ~ **d'avis** to change one's mind ; **ça changera!** that'll make a change! ; ~ **de direction** to change direction ; ~ **de place (avec qqn)** to change places (with sb) ; ~ **de vitesse** AUTOM to change gear ; ~ **de voiture** to change one's car ; **pour ~** for a change - **2.** [modifier] to change, to alter ; ~ **de comportement** to alter one's behaviour *Br ou* behavior *Am.*
➡ **se changer** *vp* - **1.** [se rhabiller] to change, to get changed - **2.** [se transformer] : **se ~ en** to change into.

changeur [ʃɑ̃ʒœr] *nm* - **1.** [personne] money-changer - **2.** [appareil] : ~ **de monnaie** change machine.

chanoine [ʃanwan] *nm* canon.

chanson [ʃɑ̃sɔ̃] *nf* song ; **c'est toujours la même ~** *fig* it's the same old story.

chansonnette [ʃɑ̃sɔnɛt] *nf* ditty.

chansonnier, ère [ʃɑ̃sɔnje, ɛr] *nm, f* cabaret singer-songwriter.

chant [ʃɑ̃] *nm* - **1.** [chanson] song, singing (*U*) ; [sacré] hymn ; ~ **du cygne** *fig* swansong ; ~ **grégorien** Gregorian chant - **2.** [art] singing.

chantage [ʃɑ̃taʒ] *nm litt* & *fig* blackmail ; **fai-**

re du ~ to use OU resort to blackmail ; **faire du ~ à qqn** to blackmail sb.

chantant, e [ʃɑ̃tɑ̃, ɑ̃t] adj - **1.** [accent, voix] lilting - **2.** [musique, air] catchy.

chanter [3] [ʃɑ̃te] <> vt - **1.** [chanson] to sing - **2.** fam [raconter] to tell - **3.** littéraire [célébrer] to sing OU to tell of ; ~ **les louanges de qqn** to sing sb's praises <> vi - **1.** [gén] to sing ; ~ **juste** to sing in tune ; ~ **faux** to sing off key - **2.** loc : faire ~ **qqn** to blackmail sb ; **si ça vous chante!** fam if you feel like it!

chanterelle [ʃɑ̃trɛl] nf [champignon] chanter-elle.

chanteur, euse [ʃɑ̃tœr, øz] nm, f singer.

chantier [ʃɑ̃tje] nm - **1.** CONSTR (building) site ; [sur la route] roadworks (pl) ; **en ~** fig in progress ; ~ **naval** shipyard, dockyard - **2.** fig [désordre] shambles (sg), mess.

Chantilly [ʃɑ̃tiji] nf : **(crème) ~** stiffly whipped cream sweetened and flavoured.

chantonner [3] [ʃɑ̃tɔne] vt & vi to hum.

chanvre [ʃɑ̃vr] nm hemp.

chaos [kao] nm chaos.

chaotique [kaɔtik] adj chaotic.

chap. (abr de chapitre) ch.

chaparder [3] [ʃaparde] vt to steal.

chapeau, x [ʃapo] nm - **1.** [coiffure] hat ; ~ **melon** bowler hat ; **tirer son ~ à qqn** to take one's hat off to sb - **2.** PRESSE introductory paragraph - **3.** loc : **chapeau!** fam nice one! ; **démarrer sur les ~x de roues** fam to take off like a bat out of hell.

chapeauter [3] [ʃapote] vt [service] to head ; [personnes] to supervise.

chapelain [ʃaplɛ̃] nm chaplain.

chapelet [ʃaplɛ] nm - **1.** RELIG rosary ; **dire son ~** to say one's rosary, to tell one's beads - **2.** [de saucisses, d'oignons] string - **3.** fig [d'injures] string, torrent.

chapelier, ère [ʃapəlje, ɛr] <> adj hat (avant n) <> nm, f [pour hommes] hatter ; [pour femmes] milliner.

chapelle [ʃapɛl] nf - **1.** [petite église] chapel ; [partie d'église] choir ; ~ **ardente** chapel of rest - **2.** [coterie] clique.

chapelure [ʃaplyr] nf (dried) breadcrumbs (pl).

chaperon [ʃaprɔ̃] nm - **1.** LITTÉRATURE : **le Petit ~ Rouge** Little Red Riding Hood - **2.** [personne] chaperone.

chapiteau [ʃapito] nm - **1.** [de colonne] capital - **2.** [de cirque] big top.

chapitre [ʃapitr] nm - **1.** [de livre & RELIG] chapter - **2.** [de budget] head, item - **3.** fig [sujet] subject.

chapitrer [3] [ʃapitre] vt sout to reprimand.

chapon [ʃapɔ̃] nm - **1.** [volaille] capon - **2.** [encas] piece of bread rubbed with garlic and oil.

chaque [ʃak] adj indéf each, every ; ~ **personne** each person, everyone ; **j'ai payé ces livres 100 francs ~** I paid 100 francs each for these books.

char [ʃar] nm - **1.** MIL : ~ **(d'assaut)** tank - **2.** [charrette] cart, waggon - **3.** [de carnaval] float - **4.** Can [voiture] car - **5.** HIST chariot.

charabia [ʃarabja] nm gibberish.

charade [ʃarad] nf charade.

charbon [ʃarbɔ̃] nm - **1.** [combustible] coal ; ~ **de bois** charcoal ; **être sur des ~s ardents** fig to be like a cat on hot bricks Br OU on a hot roof Am - **2.** [maladie] anthrax.

charbonnage [] nm coalmining ; **les ~s** collieries, coalmines.

charbonnier, ère [ʃarbɔnje, ɛr] adj coal (avant n).

➤ **charbonnier** nm - **1.** [cargo] collier - **2.** [vendeur] coal merchant ; [livreur] coalman.

charcuter [3] [ʃarkyte] vt fam péj to butcher.

charcuterie [ʃarkytri] nf - **1.** [magasin] pork butcher's - **2.** [produits] pork meat products - **3.** [commerce] pork meat trade.

charcutier, ère [ʃarkytje, ɛr] nm, f [commer-çant] pork butcher.

chardon [ʃardɔ̃] nm - **1.** [plante] thistle - **2.** [sur un mur] spikes (pl).

chardonneret [ʃardɔnrɛ] nm goldfinch.

charentais, e [ʃarɑ̃tɛ, ɛz] adj of/from Char-ente.

➤ **charentaise** nf (bedroom) slipper.

charge [ʃarʒ] nf - **1.** [fardeau] load - **2.** [fonction] office - **3.** [responsabilité] responsibility ; **être à la ~ de** [personne] to be dependent on ; **les travaux sont à la ~ du propriétaire** the owner is liable for the cost of the work ; **prendre qqch en ~** [payer] to pay (for) sthg ; [s'occuper de] to take charge of sthg ; **prendre qqn en ~** to take charge of sb - **4.** ÉLECTR, JUR & MIL charge ; **revenir à la ~** to return to the fray - **5.** loc : **j'accepte, à ~ de revanche** I accept, provided that you'll let me do the same for you some time.

➤ **charges** nfpl - **1.** [d'appartement] service charge - **2.** ÉCON expenses, costs ; ~**s sociales** ≃ employer's contributions.

chargé, e [ʃarʒe] <> adj - **1.** [véhicule, personne] : ~ **(de)** loaded (with) - **2.** [responsable] : ~ **(de)** responsible (for) - **3.** [occupé] full, busy <> nm, f : ~ **d'affaires** chargé d'affaires ; ~ **de cours** ≃ lecturer ; ~ **de mission** head of mission.

chargement [ʃarʒəmã] *nm* - **1.** [action] loading - **2.** [marchandises] load.

charger [17] [ʃarʒe] *vt* - **1.** [gén & INFORM] to load - **2.** [remplir] to fill - **3.** ÉLECTR, JUR & MIL to charge - **4.** [donner une mission à] : ~ **qqn de faire qqch** to put sb in charge of doing sthg.

se charger *vp* : **se ~ de qqn/qqch** to take care of sb/sthg, to take charge of sb/sthg ; **se ~ de faire qqch** to undertake to do sthg.

chargeur [ʃarʒœr] *nm* - **1.** ÉLECTR charger - **2.** [d'arme] magazine - **3.** [d'appareil photo] cartridge, cassette '- **4.** [personne - qui expédie une charge] shipper ; [- qui charge] docker *Br*, longshoreman *Am*, stevedore *Am*.

chariot [ʃarjo] *nm* - **1.** [charrette] handcart - **2.** [à bagages, dans un hôpital] trolley *Br*, wagon *Am* ; ~ **élévateur** forklift truck - **3.** [de machine à écrire] carriage.

charismatique [karismatik] *adj* charismatic.

charisme [karism] *nm* charisma.

charitable [ʃaritabl] *adj* charitable ; [conseil] friendly.

charité [ʃarite] *nf* - **1.** [aumône & RELIG] charity ; **faire la ~ à qqn** to give sb charity - **2.** [bonté] kindness.

charivari [ʃarivari] *nm* hullabaloo.

charlatan [ʃarlatã] *nm* péj charlatan.

charlotte [ʃarlɔt] *nf* CULIN charlotte.

charmant, e [ʃarmã, ãt] *adj* charming.

charme [ʃarm] *nm* - **1.** [séduction] charm ; **faire du ~ (à qqn)** to turn on the charm (for sb) - **2.** [enchantement] spell ; **rompre le ~** to break the spell - **3.** [arbre] ironwood, hornbeam - **4.** *loc* : **se porter comme un ~** *fam* to be as fit as a fiddle.

charmer [3] [ʃarme] *vt* to charm ; **être charmé de faire qqch** to be delighted to do sthg.

charmeur, euse [ʃarmœr, øz] ◇ *adj* charming ◇ *nm, f* charmer ; ~ **de serpents** snake charmer.

charnel, elle [ʃarnɛl] *adj* carnal.

charnier [ʃarnje] *nm* mass grave.

charnière [ʃarnjɛr] ◇ *nf* hinge ; *fig* turning point ◇ *adj* [période] transitional.

charnu, e [ʃarny] *adj* fleshy.

charognard [ʃarɔɲar] *nm* litt & fig vulture.

charogne [ʃarɔɲ] *nf* - **1.** [d'animal] carrion (*U*) - **2.** tfam [crapule - homme] bastard ; [- femme] bitch.

charpente [ʃarpãt] *nf* - **1.** [de bâtiment, de roman] framework - **2.** [ossature] frame.

charpenté, e [ʃarpãte] *adj* : **être bien ~** [personne] to be well-built ; [roman] to be well-constructed.

charpentier [ʃarpãtje] *nm* carpenter.

charretier, ère [ʃartje, ɛr] ◇ *adj* cart (avant n) ◇ *nm, f* carter ; **jurer comme un ~** to swear like a trooper.

charrette [ʃarɛt] *nf* cart.

charrier [9] [ʃarje] ◇ *vt* - **1.** to carry - **2.** fam [se moquer de] : ~ **qqn** to take sb for a ride ◇ *vi* fam [exagérer] to go too far.

charrue [ʃary] *nf* plough *Br*, plow *Am* ; **mettre la ~ avant les bœufs** fam fig to put the cart before the horse.

charte [ʃart] *nf* charter ; **l'École nationale des ~s** grande école for archivists and librarians.

charter [ʃartɛr] ◇ *nm* chartered plane ◇ *adj inv* (en apposition) charter (avant n).

chartreuse [ʃartrøz] *nf* - **1.** RELIG Carthusian monastery - **2.** [liqueur] Chartreuse.

Charybde [karibd] *n* Charybdis ; **tomber de ~ en Scylla** to go from the frying pan into the fire.

chas [ʃa] *nm* eye (of needle).

chasse [ʃas] *nf* - **1.** [action] hunting ; **aller à la ~** to go hunting ; ~ **à courre** hunting (on horseback with hounds) - **2.** [période] : **la ~ est ouverte/fermée** it's the open/close season - **3.** [domaine] : ~ **gardée** private hunting *ou* shooting preserve, *fig* preserve - **4.** [poursuite] chase ; **faire la ~ à qqch** to chase sthg ; **faire la ~ à qqn/qqch** fig to hunt (for) sb/sthg, to hunt sb/sthg down ; **prendre qqn/qqch en ~** to give chase to sb/sthg ; ~ **à l'homme** manhunt - **5.** [des cabinets] : ~ **(d'eau)** flush ; **tirer la ~** to flush the toilet.

chassé-croisé [ʃasekrwaze] (*pl* **chassés-croisés**) *nm* toing and froing.

chasse-neige [ʃasnɛʒ] *nm inv* snowplough *Br*, snowplow *Am*.

chasser [3] [ʃase] ◇ *vt* - **1.** [animal] to hunt - **2.** [faire partir - personne] to drive *ou* chase away ; [- odeur, souci] to dispel ◇ *vi* - **1.** [aller à la chasse] to go hunting, to hunt - **2.** [roues] to skid.

chasseur, euse [ʃasœr, øz] *nm, f* hunter.

chasseur *nm* - **1.** [d'hôtel] page, messenger - **2.** MIL : ~ **alpin** soldier specially trained for operations in mountainous terrain - **3.** [avion] fighter.

chasseur de têtes *nm* headhunter.

châssis [ʃasi] *nm* - **1.** [de fenêtre, de porte, de machine] frame - **2.** [de véhicule] chassis - **3.** [de tableau] stretcher.

chaste [ʃast] *adj* chaste.

chasteté [ʃastəte] *nf* chastity.

chasuble [ʃazybl] ◇ *nf* chasuble ◇ *adj* ▷ **robe**.

chat, chatte [ʃa, ʃat] *nm, f* cat ; ~ **de gouttiè-**

re ordinary cat, alley cat *Am* ; **~ sauvage** wildcat ; *Can* [raton laveur] raccoon ; **~ persan/ siamois** Persian/Siamese cat ; **il n'y a pas un ~ fam** there's not a soul ; **appeler un ~ un ~** to call a spade a spade ; **avoir d'autres ~s à fouetter** to have other fish to fry ; **avoir un ~ dans la gorge** to have a frog in one's throat.

châtaigne [ʃatɛɲ] *nf* **- 1.** [fruit] chestnut **- 2. fam** [coup] clout.

châtaignier [ʃatɛɲe] *nm* [arbre] chestnut (tree) ; [bois] chestnut.

châtain [ʃatɛ̃] *adj & nm* chestnut, chestnut-brown.

château, x [ʃato] *nm* **- 1.** [forteresse] : **~ (fort)** castle **- 2.** [résidence - seigneuriale] mansion ; [- de monarque, d'évêque] palace ; **~ de cartes** *litt & fig* house of cards ; **~ de sable** sandcastle ; **les châteaux de la Loire** the Châteaux of the Loire ; **bâtir des ~x en Espagne fig** to build castles in Spain **- 3.** [vignoble] château, vineyard **- 4.** [réservoir] : **~ d'eau** water tower.

LES CHÂTEAUX DE LA LOIRE

> These royal residences were originally built as hunting lodges in the Loire Valley during the Renaissance. The largest château is Chambord and was used by Francis I. Other notable châteaux include Chenonceaux, Azay-le-Rideau, Amboise and Blois.

chateaubriand, châteaubriant [ʃatobrijɑ̃] *nm thickest part of a fillet of beef.*

châtelain, e [ʃatlɛ̃, ɛn] *nm, f* lord (*f* lady) of the manor.

châtier [9] [ʃatje] *vt sout* **- 1.** [punir] to punish **- 2.** [polir] to refine, to hone.

chatière [ʃatjɛr] *nf* **- 1.** [pour chat] cat-flap **- 2.** [d'aération] air vent.

châtiment [ʃatimɑ̃] *nm* punishment.

chaton [ʃatɔ̃] *nm* **- 1.** [petit chat] kitten **- 2. BOT** catkin **- 3.** [de bague] setting **- 4.** [pierre] stone.

chatouiller [3] [ʃatuje] *vt* **- 1.** [faire des chatouilles à] to tickle **- 2. fig** [titiller] to titillate.

chatouilles [ʃatuj] *nfpl* tickling (U).

chatouilleux, euse [ʃatujø, øz] *adj* **- 1.** [sensible aux chatouilles] ticklish **- 2. fig** [susceptible] touchy.

chatoyant, e [ʃatwajɑ̃, ɑ̃t] *adj* [reflet, étoffe] shimmering ; [bijou] sparkling.

chatoyer [13] [ʃatwaje] *vi* [reflet, étoffe] to shimmer ; [bijou] to sparkle.

châtrer [3] [ʃatre] *vt* to castrate ; [chat] to neuter ; [chatte] to spay.

chatte ➩ **chat.**

chatterton [ʃatɛrtɔn] *nm* ÉLECTR insulating tape.

chaud, e [ʃo, ʃod] *adj* **- 1.** [gén] warm ; [de température très élevée, sensuel] hot **- 2. fig** [enthousiaste] : **être ~ pour qqch/pour faire qqch** to be keen on sthg/on doing sthg **- 3.** [animé] tense.

➩ **chaud** ⬦ *adv* : **avoir ~** to be warm *ou* hot ; **il fait ~** it's warm *ou* hot ; **manger ~** to have something hot (to eat) ; **tenir ~** to keep warm ; **j'ai eu ~** [l'échapper belle] I had a narrow *ou* lucky escape ; [avoir peur] I had a nasty shock *ou* fright ⬦ *nm* : **rester au ~** to stay in the warm ; **un ~ et froid** a chill.

chaudement [ʃodmɑ̃] *adv* warmly.

chaud-froid [ʃofrwa] (*pl* chauds-froids) *nm* poultry or game served cold in a thick white sauce glazed with jelly.

chaudière [ʃodjɛr] *nf* boiler.

chaudron [ʃodrɔ̃] *nm* cauldron.

chauffage [ʃofaʒ] *nm* **- 1.** [action] heating **- 2.** [appareil] heating (system) ; **~ central** central heating.

chauffant, e [ʃofɑ̃, ɑ̃t] *adj* heating ; **couverture ~e** electric blanket ; **plaque ~e** hotplate.

chauffard [ʃofar] *nm péj* reckless driver.

chauffe-biberon [ʃofbibrɔ̃] (*pl* chauffe-biberons) *nm* bottle-warmer.

chauffe-eau [ʃofo] *nm inv* water-heater.

chauffe-plats [ʃofpla] *nm inv* hotplate, chafing dish.

chauffer [3] [ʃofe] ⬦ *vt* [rendre chaud] to heat (up) ; **~ à blanc** to heat until white-hot ⬦ *vi* **- 1.** [devenir chaud] to heat up **- 2.** [moteur] to overheat **- 3. fam** [barder] : **ça va ~** there's going to be trouble.

➩ **se chauffer** *vp* : **se ~ à qqch** to heat one's house with sthg.

chaufferette [ʃofrɛt] *nf* **- 1.** [réchaud] hotplate, chafing dish **- 2.** [pour les pieds] footwarmer.

chaufferie [ʃofri] *nf* boiler room.

chauffeur [ʃofœr] *nm* **- 1.** AUTOM driver ; **~ du dimanche** Sunday driver ; **~ de taxi** taxi driver **- 2.** [de chaudière] stoker.

chaume [ʃom] *nm* **- 1.** [paille] thatch **- 2.** [de céréales] stubble.

chaumière [ʃomjɛr] *nf* cottage.

chaussée [ʃose] *nf* road, roadway ; '**~ déformée**' 'uneven road surface'.

chausse-pied [ʃospje] (*pl* chausse-pieds) *nm* shoehorn.

chausser [3] [ʃose] ⬦ *vt* **- 1.** [chaussures, lunettes, skis] to put on ; **~ qqn** to put sb's shoes on **- 2.** [fournir] to supply shoes to **- 3.** [suj : chaussures] to fit ⬦ *vi* : ~ **du 39** to take size 39 (shoes).

➤ **se chausser** *vp* to put one's shoes on.

chausse-trape (*pl* **chausse-trapes**), **chausse-trappe** (*pl* **chausse-trappes**) [ʃostrap] *nf* trap.

chaussette [ʃosɛt] *nf* sock.

chausseur [ʃosœr] *nm* shoemaker.

chausson [ʃosɔ̃] *nm* - **1.** [pantoufle] slipper - **2.** [de danse] ballet shoe - **3.** [de bébé] bootee - **4.** *CULIN* turnover ; ~ **aux pommes** apple turnover.

chaussure [ʃosyr] *nf* - **1.** [soulier] shoe ; ~ **basse** low-heeled shoe, flat shoe ; ~ **à crampons** [pour football, rugby] studded boot ; [pour athlétisme] spiked shoe ; ~ **de marche** [de randonnée] hiking *ou* walking boot ; [confortable] walking shoe ; ~ **montante** (ankle) boot ; ~ **à scratch** shoe with Velcro® fastenings ; ~ **de ski** ski boot ; **trouver ~ à son pied** *fam* *fig* to find Mr/Miss Right - **2.** [industrie] footwear industry.

chauve [ʃov] ⬦ *adj* [sans cheveux] bald ⬦ *nm* bald man.

chauve-souris [ʃovsuri] (*pl* **chauves-souris**) *nf* bat.

chauvin, e [ʃovɛ̃, in] ⬦ *adj* chauvinistic ⬦ *nm, f* chauvinist.

chauvinisme [ʃovinism] *nm* chauvinism.

chaux [ʃo] *nf* lime ; **blanchi à la ~** whitewashed.

chavirer [3] [ʃavire] ⬦ *vi* - **1.** [bateau] to capsize - **2.** *fig* [tourner] to spin - **3.** *fig* [échouer] to founder ⬦ *vt* - **1.** [bateau] to capsize - **2.** [meuble] to tip over.

chéchia [ʃeʃja] *nf* fez.

check-up [tʃekœp] *nm inv* check-up.

chef [ʃɛf] *nm* - **1.** [d'un groupe] head, leader ; [au travail] boss ; **en ~** in chief ; ~ **de chantier** foreman ; ~ **d'entreprise** company head ; ~ **d'État** head of state ; ~ **de fabrication** production manager ; ~ **de famille** head of the family ; ~ **de file** *POLIT* (party) leader ; ~ **de gare** stationmaster ; ~ **de marque** brand manager ; ~ **d'orchestre** conductor ; ~ **de produit** product manager ; ~ **de projet** project manager ; ~ **de rayon** departmental manager *ou* supervisor ; ~ **de service** *ADMIN* departmental manager - **2.** [cuisinier] chef - **3.** *loc* : **de son propre ~** on one's own initiative ; **opiner du ~** to nod agreement.

➤ **chef d'accusation** *nm* charge, count.

chef-d'œuvre [ʃedœvr] (*pl* **chefs-d'œuvre**) *nm* masterpiece.

chef-lieu [ʃefljø] (*pl* **chefs-lieux**) *nm* ≃ county town *Br* county seat *Am*.

cheik [ʃɛk] *nm* sheikh.

chemin [ʃəmɛ̃] *nm* - **1.** [voie] path ; ~ **vicinal** byroad, minor road - **2.** [parcours] way ; *fig* road ; **en ~** on the way ; **faire du ~** to cover a lot of ground ; *fig* to gain ground ; **rebrousser ~** to turn back ; **le ~ de croix** the way of the cross ; **prendre le ~ des écoliers** *fig* to go the long way round ; **suivre le droit ~** *fig* to stay on the straight and narrow.

➤ **chemin de fer** *nm* railway *Br*, railroad *Am*.

cheminée [ʃəmine] *nf* - **1.** [foyer] fireplace - **2.** [conduit d'usine] chimney - **3.** [encadrement] mantelpiece - **4.** [de paquebot, locomotive] funnel.

cheminement [ʃəminmɑ̃] *nm* [progression] advance ; *fig* [d'idée] development.

cheminer [3] [ʃəmine] *vi* [avancer] to make one's way ; *fig* [idée] to develop.

cheminot [ʃəmino] *nm* railwayman *Br*, railroad man *Am*.

chemise [ʃəmiz] *nf* - **1.** [d'homme] shirt ; ~ **de nuit** [de femme] nightdress - **2.** [dossier] folder.

chemiserie [ʃəmizri] *nf* [magasin] shirtmaker's ; [industrie] shirtmaking.

chemisette [ʃəmizɛt] *nf* [d'homme] short-sleeved shirt ; [de femme] short-sleeved blouse.

chemisier [ʃəmizje] *nm* - **1.** [vêtement] blouse - **2.** [marchand, fabricant] shirtmaker.

chenal, aux [ʃənal, o] *nm* [canal] channel.

chenapan [ʃənapɑ̃] *nm hum* rascal.

chêne [ʃɛn] *nm* [arbre] oak (tree) ; [bois] oak.

chenet [ʃənɛ] *nm* firedog.

chenil [ʃənil] *nm* [pour chiens] kennel.

chenille [ʃənij] *nf* - **1.** [insecte] caterpillar - **2.** [courroie] caterpillar track.

chenu, e [ʃəny] *adj littéraire* [tête, barbe] hoary.

cheptel [ʃɛptɛl] *nm* [bétail] livestock (U).

chèque [ʃɛk] *nm* cheque *Br*, check *Am* ; **faire un ~** to write a cheque *Br ou* check *Am* ; **toucher un ~** to cash a cheque *Br ou* check *Am* ; ~ **(bancaire)** (bank) cheque *Br ou* check *Am* ; ~ **barré** crossed cheque *Br ou* check *Am* ; ~ **en blanc** blank cheque *Br ou* check *Am* ; ~ **postal** post office cheque *Br ou* check *Am* ; ~ **sans provision** bad cheque *Br ou* check *Am* ; ~ **de voyage** traveller's cheque *Br*, traveler's check *Am*.

chèque-cadeau [ʃɛkkado] (*pl* **chèques-cadeaux**) *nm* gift token.

chèque-repas [ʃɛkrəpa] (*pl* **chèques-repas**), **chèque-restaurant** [ʃɛkrɛstɔrɑ̃] (*pl* **chèques-restaurant**) *nm* luncheon voucher.

chéquier [ʃekje] *nm* chequebook *Br*, checkbook *Am*.

cher, chère [ʃɛr] ◇ *adj* - **1.** [aimé] : ~ **(à qqn)** dear (to sb) ; **Cher Monsieur** [au début d'une lettre] Dear Sir ; **Chère Madame** [au début d'une lettre] Dear Madam - **2.** [produit, vie, commerçant] expensive ◇ *nm, f hum* : **mon** ~ dear.

➧ **cher** *adv* : **valoir** ~, **coûter** ~ to be expensive, to cost a lot ; **payer** ~ to pay a lot ; **je l'ai payé** ~ *litt* & *fig* it cost me a lot.

➧ **chère** *nf* : **aimer la bonne chère** *sout* to like to eat well.

chercher [3] [ʃɛrʃe] ◇ *vt* - **1.** [gén] to look for ; **vous l'aurez cherché!** you're asking for it! - **2.** [prendre] : **aller/venir** ~ **qqn** [à un rendez-vous] to (go/come and) meet sb ; [en voiture] to (go/come and) pick sb up ; **aller/venir** ~ **qqch** to (go/come and) get sthg - **3.** *fam* [atteindre] : **ça va** ~ **dans les 100 francs** it will come to about 100 francs ◇ *vi* : ~ **à faire qqch** to try to do sthg.

➧ **se chercher** *vp* to try to find o.s.

chercheur, euse [ʃɛrʃœr, øz] ◇ *adj* - **1.** [esprit] inquiring - **2.** ⊳ **tête** ◇ *nm, f* [scientifique] researcher.

chèrement [ʃɛrmɑ̃] *adv* dearly.

chéri, e [ʃeri] ◇ *adj* dear ◇ *nm, f* darling.

chérir [32] [ʃerir] *vt* [personne] to love dearly ; [chose, idée] to cherish.

cherté [ʃɛrte] *nf* high cost.

chétif, ive [ʃetif, iv] *adj* - **1.** [malingre] sickly, weak - **2.** [rabougri] stunted, puny - **3.** *littéraire* [insuffisant] meagre *Br*, meager *Am*.

cheval, aux [ʃəval, o] *nm* - **1.** [animal] horse ; **à** ~ **on** horseback ; **être à** ~ **sur qqch** [être assis] to be sitting astride sthg ; *fig* [siècles] to straddle sthg ; *fig* [tenir à] to be a stickler for sthg ; ~ **d'arçons** horse (*in gymnastics*) ; ~ **de bataille** *fig* hobby horse ; ~ **de course** racehorse ; ~ **de trait** draught *Br* ou draft *Am* horse ; **chevaux de bois** merry-go-round (*sg*) ; **monter sur ses grands chevaux** to get on one's high horse - **2.** [équitation] riding, horse-riding ; **faire du** ~ to ride - **3.** *AUTOM* : ~, ~-**vapeur** horsepower.

chevaleresque [ʃəvalrɛsk] *adj* chivalrous.

chevalerie [ʃəvalri] *nf* - **1.** [qualité] chivalry - **2.** *HIST* knighthood.

chevalet [ʃəvalɛ] *nm* [de peintre] easel.

chevalier [ʃəvalje] *nm* knight ; ~ **servant** (faithful) admirer.

chevalière [ʃəvaljɛr] *nf* [bague] signet ring.

chevalin, e [ʃəvalɛ̃, in] *adj* [de cheval] horse (*avant n*) ; *fig* horsey.

chevauchée [ʃəvoʃe] *nf* - **1.** [course] ride, horse-ride - **2.** [cavalcade] cavalcade.

chevaucher [3] [ʃəvoʃe] *vt* [être assis] to sit ou be astride.

➧ **se chevaucher** *vp* to overlap.

chevelu, e [ʃəvly] *adj* hairy.

chevelure [ʃəvlyr] *nf* [cheveux] hair.

chevet [ʃəvɛ] *nm* head (*of bed*) ; **être au** ~ **de qqn** to be at sb's bedside.

cheveu, x [ʃəvø] *nm* [chevelure] hair ; **avoir les** ~**x taillés en brosse** to have a crew cut ; **se faire couper les** ~**x** to have one's hair cut ; **s'arracher les** ~**x** to tear one's hair out ; **avoir un** ~ **sur la langue** to have a lisp ; **arriver comme un** ~ **sur la soupe** to come at an awkward moment ; **couper les** ~**x en quatre** to split hairs ; **tiré par les** ~**x** far-fetched, contrived.

cheville [ʃəvij] *nf* - **1.** *ANAT* ankle ; **il ne t'arrive pas à la** ~ *fam fig* he can't hold a candle to you - **2.** [pour fixer une vis] Rawlplug® ; ~ **ouvrière** *AUTOM* & *fig* kingpin.

chèvre [ʃɛvr] ◇ *nf* [animal] goat ; **ménager la** ~ **et le chou** to run with the hare and hunt with the hounds ◇ *nm* [fromage] goat's cheese.

chevreau, x [ʃəvro] *nm* kid.

chèvrefeuille [ʃɛvrəfœj] *nm* honeysuckle.

chevreuil [ʃəvrœj] *nm* - **1.** [animal] roe deer - **2.** *CULIN* venison.

chevron [ʃəvrɔ̃] *nm* - **1.** *CONSTR* rafter - **2.** [motif décoratif] chevron.

chevronné, e [ʃəvrɔne] *adj* [expérimenté] experienced.

chevrotant, e [ʃəvrɔtɑ̃, ɑ̃t] *adj* tremulous.

chevrotine [ʃəvrɔtin] *nf* buckshot.

chewing-gum [ʃwiŋɡɔm] (*pl* **chewing-gums**) *nm* chewing gum (*U*).

chez [ʃe] *prép* - **1.** [dans la maison de] : **il est** ~ **lui** he's at home ; **il rentre** ~ **lui** he's going home ; **être** ~ **le coiffeur/médecin** to be at the hairdresser's/doctor's ; **aller** ~ **le coiffeur/médecin** to go to the hairdresser's/doctor's ; **il va venir** ~ **nous** he is going to come to our place ou house ; **il habite** ~ **nous** he lives with us - **2.** [en ce qui concerne] : ~ **les jeunes** among young people ; ~ **les Anglais** in England - **3.** [dans les œuvres de] : ~ **Proust** in (the works of) Proust - **4.** [dans le caractère de] : **cette réaction est normale** ~ **lui** this reaction is normal for ou with him ; **ce que j'apprécie** ~ **lui, c'est sa gentillesse** what I like about him is his kindness.

chez-soi [ʃeswal] *nm inv* home, place of one's own.

chialer [3] [ʃjale] *vi fam* to blubber.

chiant, e [ʃjɑ̃, ɑ̃t] *adj tfam* - **1.** [très ennuyeux] bloody *Br* ou damned boring - **2.** [contrariant] bloody *Br* ou damned annoying ; **c'est** ~ it's a bloody *Br* ou damned pain.

chic [ʃik] ◇ *adj* (*inv en genre*) - **1.** [élégant]

smart, chic - **2.** *vieilli* [serviable] nice ◇ *nm* style ; **bon ~ bon genre** ≃ Sloaney *Br*, ≃ preppie *Am* ; **avoir le ~ pour faire qqch** to have the knack of doing sthg ◇ *interj* : **~ (alors)!** great!

chicane [ʃikan] *nf* [querelle] squabble.

chicaner [3] [ʃikane] ◇ *vt* : **~ qqn sur qqch** to quibble with sb over sthg ◇ *vi* [contester] : **~ (sur qqch)** to quibble (over *ou* about sthg).

➤ **se chicaner** *vp* to squabble, to bicker.

chiche [ʃiʃ] ◇ *adj* - **1.** [avare] mean ; **être ~ de** to be sparing with - **2.** [peu abondant] meagre *Br*, meager *Am*, scanty - **3.** *fam* [capable] : **il n'est pas ~ de le faire!** he wouldn't dare (do it)! ◇ *interj* : **chiche!** (you) want a bet?

chichement [ʃiʃmã] *adv* [pauvrement] meagrely.

chichi [ʃiʃi] *nm* : **faire des ~s** *fam* to make a fuss.

chicorée [ʃikɔre] *nf* [salade] endive ; [à café] chicory ; **~ frisée** curly endive.

chien [ʃjɛ̃] *nm* - **1.** [animal] dog ; **~ d'aveugle** guide dog ; **~ de chasse** [d'arrêt] gundog ; **~ esquimau** husky ; **~ de garde** guard dog ; **~ policier/savant** police/performing dog ; **entre ~ et loup** at dusk *ou* twilight ; **se regarder en ~s de faïence** to stare grimly at each other - **2.** [d'arme] hammer - **3.** *loc* : **avoir un mal de ~ à faire qqch** to have a lot of trouble doing sthg ; **en ~ de fusil** curled up ; **avoir du ~** to have class *ou* style.

chiendent [ʃjɛ̃dã] *nm* couch grass.

chien-loup [ʃjɛ̃lu] (*pl* **chiens-loups**) *nm* Alsatian (dog).

chienne [ʃjɛn] *nf* (female) dog, bitch.

chier [9] [ʃje] *vi vulg* to shit ; **faire ~ qqn** to get on sb's tits ; **se faire ~** to be bored shitless.

chiffe [ʃif] *nf* : **c'est une ~ molle** he's spineless, he's a weed.

chiffon [ʃifɔ̃] *nm* [linge] rag ; **parler ~s** to talk clothes.

chiffonné, e [ʃifɔne] *adj* [visage, mine] worn.

chiffonner [3] [ʃifɔne] *vt* - **1.** [vêtement] to crumple, to crease ; [papier] to crumple - **2.** *fam fig* [contrarier] to bother.

chiffonnier, ère [ʃifɔnje, ɛr] *nm, f* rag-and-bone man (*f* woman).

➤ **chiffonnier** *nm* [meuble] chiffonier.

chiffre [ʃifr] *nm* - **1.** [caractère] figure, number ; **~ arabe/romain** Arabic/Roman numeral - **2.** [montant] sum ; **~ d'affaires** COMM turnover *Br*, net revenue *Am* ; **~ rond** round number ; **~ de ventes** sales figures (*pl*) - **3.** [code secret] code.

chiffrer [3] [ʃifre] ◇ *vt* - **1.** [numéroter] to

number - **2.** [évaluer] to calculate, to assess - **3.** [coder] to encode ◇ *vi fam* to mount up.

➤ **se chiffrer** *vp* : **se ~ à** to add up to.

chignole [ʃiɲɔl] *nf* drill.

chignon [ʃiɲɔ̃] *nm* bun (*in hair*) ; **se crêper le ~** *fig* to scratch each other's eyes out.

Chili [ʃili] *nm* : **le ~** Chile ; **au ~** in Chile.

chilien, enne [ʃiljɛ̃, ɛn] *adj* Chilean.

➤ **Chilien, enne** *nm, f* Chilean.

chimère [ʃimɛr] *nf* - **1.** MYTH chimera - **2.** [illusion] illusion, dream.

chimérique [ʃimerik] *adj* - **1.** [illusoire] illusory - **2.** [rêveur] fanciful.

chimie [ʃimi] *nf* chemistry.

chimiothérapie [ʃimjɔterapi] *nf* chemotherapy.

chimique [ʃimik] *adj* chemical.

chimiquement [ʃimikmã] *adv* chemically.

chimiste [ʃimist] *nmf* chemist.

chimpanzé [ʃɛ̃pɑ̃ze] *nm* chimpanzee.

chinchilla [ʃɛ̃ʃila] *nm* chinchilla.

Chine [ʃin] *nf* : **la ~** China.

chiné, e [ʃine] *adj* mottled.

chiner [3] [ʃine] *vi* to look for bargains.

chinois, e [ʃinwa, az] *adj* Chinese.

➤ **chinois** *nm* - **1.** [langue] Chinese ; **c'est du ~** *fig* it's all Greek to me - **2.** [passoire] conical sieve.

➤ **Chinois, e** *nm, f* Chinese person ; **les Chinois** the Chinese.

chinoiserie [ʃinwazri] *nf* [objet] Chinese curio, piece of chinoiserie ; *fig* unnecessary complication.

➤ **chinoiseries** *nfpl* unnecessary complications, red tape (*sg*).

chiot [ʃjo] *nm* puppy.

chiottes [ʃjɔt] *nfpl vulg* shithouse (*sg*).

chiper [3] [ʃipe] *vt fam* [voler] to pinch, to nick *Br*.

chipie [ʃipi] *nf* vixen *péj*.

chipolata [ʃipɔlata] *nf* chipolata.

chipoter [3] [ʃipɔte] *vi* : **~ (sur)** [nourriture] to pick (at) ; [contester] to quibble (over *ou* about).

chips [ʃips] *nfpl* : **(pommes) ~** (potato) crisps *Br*, (potato) chips *Am*.

chiqué [ʃike] *nm* : **c'est du ~** it's all sham.

chiquenaude [ʃiknod] *nf* flick.

chiquer [3] [ʃike] ◇ *vt* to chew ◇ *vi* to chew tobacco.

chiromancien, enne [kirɔmãsjɛ̃, ɛn] *nm, f* palmist.

chiropraticien, enne [kirɔpratisjɛ̃, ɛn] *nm, f*, **chiropracteur** [kirɔpraktœr] *nm* chiropractor.

chirurgical, e, aux [ʃiryrʒikal, o] adj surgical.

chirurgie [ʃiryrʒi] nf surgery ; **~ esthétique** plastic surgery.

chirurgien [ʃiryrʒjɛ̃] nm surgeon.

chirurgien-dentiste [ʃiryrʒjɛ̃dãtist] (pl **chirurgiens-dentistes**) nm dental surgeon.

chiure [ʃjyr] nf : **~ (de mouche)** flyspecks (pl).

ch.-l. abr de chef-lieu.

chlinguer = schlinguer.

chlore [klɔr] nm chlorine.

chloroforme [klɔrɔfɔrm] nm chloroform.

chlorophylle [klɔrɔfil] nf chlorophyll.

chlorure [klɔryr] nm chloride.

chnoque = schnock.

choc [ʃɔk] nm - **1.** [heurt, coup] impact ; **de ~** fig shock (avant n) - **2.** [conflit] clash - **3.** [émotion] shock ; **~ opératoire** post-operative shock - **4.** (en apposition) : **images-~s** shock pictures ; **prix-~** amazing bargain.

chocolat [ʃɔkɔla] <> nm chocolate ; **~ au lait/ noir** milk/plain chocolate ; **~ à cuire/à croquer** cooking/eating chocolate ; **~ Liégeois** chocolate ice cream with Chantilly cream <> adj inv chocolate (brown).

chocolaté, e [ʃɔkɔlate] adj chocolate (flavoured).

chocolatier, ère [ʃɔkɔlatje, ɛr] <> adj chocolate (avant n) <> nm, f [fabricant] chocolate manufacturer ; [commerçant] confectioner.

➧ **chocolatière** nf [récipient] chocolate pot.

chœur [kœr] nm - **1.** [chorale] choir ; [d'opéra] fig chorus ; **chanter en ~** to sing in chorus ; **en ~** fig all together - **2.** [d'église] choir, chancel.

choir [72] [ʃwar] vt littéraire : **laisser ~ qqch** to let sthg fall ; **laisser ~ qqn** fig & littéraire to let sb down ; **se laisser ~ dans qqch** to drop ou fall into sthg.

choisi, e [ʃwazi] adj selected ; [termes, langage] carefully chosen.

choisir [32] [ʃwazir] <> vt : **~ (de faire qqch)** to choose (to do sthg) <> vi to choose.

choix [ʃwa] nm - **1.** [gén] choice ; **le livre de ton ~** any book you like ; **au ~** as you prefer ; **avoir le ~** to have the choice - **2.** [qualité] : **de premier ~** grade ou class one ; **articles de second ~** seconds.

choléra [kɔlera] nm cholera.

cholestérol [kɔlesterɔl] nm cholesterol.

chômage [ʃomaʒ] nm unemployment ; **en ~, au ~** unemployed ; **~ partiel** short time (working) ; **être mis au ~ technique** to be laid off.

chômer [3] [ʃome] <> vt to keep <> vi to be unemployed ; fig to be idle.

chômeur, euse [ʃomœr, øz] nm, f : **les ~s** the unemployed.

chope [ʃɔp] nf tankard.

choper [3] [ʃope] vt fam - **1.** [voler, arrêter] to nick Br, to pinch - **2.** [attraper] to catch.

choquant, e [ʃɔkã, ãt] adj shocking.

choquer [3] [ʃɔke] vt - **1.** [scandaliser] to shock - **2.** [traumatiser] to shake (up).

choral, e, als ou **aux** [kɔral, o] adj choral.

➧ **choral, als** nm [chant] chorale.

➧ **chorale** nf [groupe] choir.

chorégraphie [kɔregrafi] nf choreography.

choriste [kɔrist] nmf chorister.

chose [ʃoz] <> nf thing ; **c'est (bien) peu de ~** it's nothing really ; **c'est la moindre des ~s** it's the least I/we can do ; **chaque ~ en son temps** everything in good time ; **de deux ~s l'une** (it's got to be) one thing or the other ; **dire bien des ~s à qqn** to give sb one's regards ; **ne pas faire les ~s à moitié** not to do things by halves ; **parler de ~s et d'autres** to talk of this and that ; **regarder les ~s en face** to face up to things <> nm fam - **1.** [truc] thingy, whatsit - **2.** [personne] thingy, what's-his-name (f what's-her-name) <> adj inv : **se sentir (tout) ~** to feel a bit peculiar.

chou, x [ʃu] <> nm - **1.** [légume] cabbage ; **~ de Bruxelles** Brussels sprout ; **faire ~ blanc** fam fig to draw a blank - **2.** [pâtisserie] choux bun ; **~ à la crème** cream puff - **3.** [personne] : **mon ~** darling <> adj inv sweet, cute.

choucas [ʃuka] nm jackdaw.

chouchou, oute [ʃuʃu, ut] nm, f favourite ; [élève] teacher's pet.

➧ **chouchou** nm [pour les cheveux] scrunchy, scrunchie.

chouchouter [3] [ʃuʃute] vt to pet.

choucroute [ʃukrut] nf sauerkraut ; **~ garnie** sauerkraut with meat and potatoes.

chouette [ʃwɛt] <> nf [oiseau] owl <> adj fam great <> interj : **~ (alors)!** great!

chou-fleur [ʃuflœr] (pl **choux-fleurs**) nm cauliflower.

choyer [13] [ʃwaje] vt sout to pamper.

CHR (abr de centre hospitalier régional) nm regional hospital.

chrétien, enne [kretjɛ̃, ɛn] adj & nm, f Christian.

chrétienté [kretjɛ̃te] nf Christendom.

Christ [krist] nm Christ.

christianiser [3] [kristjanize] vt - **1.** [personne] to convert (to Christianity) - **2.** [pays] to christianize.

christianisme [kristjanism] *nm* Christianity.

chromatique [krɔmatik] *adj* - **1.** MUS & OPTIQUE chromatic - **2.** BIOL chromosomal.

chrome [krom] *nm* - **1.** [de voiture] chrome - **2.** CHIM chromium.

chromé, e [krome] *adj* chrome-plated ; **acier** ~ chrome steel.

chromosome [krɔmozom] *nm* chromosome.

chronique [krɔnik] <> *nf* - **1.** [annales] chronicle ; **défrayer la** ~ to be the talk of the town - **2.** PRESSE : ~ **sportive** sports section <> *adj* chronic.

chrono [krono] = **chronomètre**.

chronologie [krɔnɔlɔʒi] *nf* chronology.

chronologique [krɔnɔlɔʒik] *adj* chronological.

chronomètre [krɔnɔmɛtr] *nm* SPORT stopwatch.

chronométrer [18] [krɔnɔmetre] *vt* to time.

chronométreur [krɔnɔmetrœr] *nm* HOCKEY timekeeper.

chrysalide [krizalid] *nf* chrysalis.

chrysanthème [krizɑ̃tɛm] *nm* chrysanthemum.

CHS (*abr de* Comité d'hygiène et de sécurité) *nm* health and safety committee.

chu, e [ʃy] *pp* ⊳ **choir**.

CHU (*abr de* centre hospitalo-universitaire) *nm* teaching hospital.

chuchotement [ʃyʃɔtmɑ̃] *nm* whisper.

🠶 **chuchotements** *nmpl* whispering (U).

chuchoter [3] [ʃyʃɔte] *vt* & *vi* to whisper.

chuinter [3] [ʃɥɛ̃te] *vi* [siffler] to hiss.

chut [ʃyt] *interj* sh!, hush!

chute [ʃyt] *nf* - **1.** [gén] fall ; **faire une** ~ to (have *ou* take a) fall ; ~ **de cheveux** hair loss ; ~ **d'eau** waterfall ; ~ **libre** free fall ; ~ **de neige** snowfall ; ~ **de pierres** falling rocks ; ~ **de reins** small of the back ; **la** ~ **du mur de Berlin** the fall of the Berlin Wall - **2.** [de tissu] scrap.

chuter [3] [ʃyte] *vi* - **1.** [baisser] to fall, to drop - **2.** [tomber] to fall.

Chypre [ʃipr] *nf* Cyprus ; **à** ~ in Cyprus.

chypriote [ʃipriɔt], **cypriote** [sipriɔt] *adj* Cypriot.

🠶 **Chypriote, Cypriote** *nmf* Cypriot.

ci [si] *adv* (*après n*) : **ce livre-**~ this book ; **ces jours-**~ these days.

Ci (*abr de* curie) Ci.

CIA (*abr de* Central Intelligence Agency) *nf* CIA.

ci-après [siapre] *adv* below.

cibiste [sibist] *nmf* CB enthusiast.

cible [sibl] *nf litt* & *fig* target ; **groupe** ~ target group.

ciblé [sible] *adj* COMM targeted.

cibler [3] [sible] *vt* to target.

ciboire [sibwar] *nm* ciborium.

ciboulette [sibulɛt] *nf* chives (*pl*).

cicatrice [sikatris] *nf* scar.

cicatriser [3] [sikatrize] *vt litt* & *fig* to heal.

🠶 **se cicatriser** *vp litt* & *fig* to heal.

ci-contre [sikɔ̃tr] *adv* opposite.

CICR (*abr de* Comité international de la Croix-Rouge) *nm* IRCC.

ci-dessous [sidəsu] *adv* below.

ci-dessus [sidəsy] *adv* above.

CIDEX, Cidex [sidɛks] (*abr de* courrier individuel à distribution exceptionnelle) *nm* system grouping letter boxes in country areas.

CIDJ (*abr de* centre d'information et de documentation de la jeunesse) *nm* careers advisory service.

cidre [sidr] *nm* cider ; ~ **bouché** superior bottled cider ; ~ **doux/brut** sweet/dry cider.

CIDUNaTI [sidynati] (*abr de* Comité interprofessionnel d'information et de défense de l'union nationale des travailleurs indépendants) *nm* union of self-employed craftsmen.

Cie (*abr de* compagnie) Co.

ciel (*pl sens 1* **ciels** [sjɛl], *pl sens 2* **cieux** [sjø]) <> *nm* - **1.** [firmament] sky ; ~ **de plomb** leaden sky ; **à** ~ **ouvert** open-air ; **être au septième** ~ to be in one's seventh heaven ; **remuer** ~ **et terre (pour faire qqch)** to move heaven and earth (to do sthg) ; **tomber du** ~ *fam* to be heaven-sent *ou* a godsend - **2.** [paradis, providence] heaven ; **c'est le** ~ **qui l'envoie!** he's heaven-sent! <> *interj hum* & *sout* good heavens!

🠶 **cieux** *nmpl* heaven (*sg*).

CIEP (*abr de* Centre international d'études pédagogiques) *nm* French centre for educational research.

cierge [sjɛrʒ] *nm* RELIG (votive) candle.

cigale [sigal] *nf* cicada.

cigare [sigar] *nm* cigar.

cigarette [sigarɛt] *nf* cigarette ; ~ **blonde/brune** cigarette made from Virginia/dark tobacco.

cigarillo [sigarijo] *nm* cigarillo.

ci-gît [siʒi] *adv* here lies.

cigogne [sigɔɲ] *nf* stork.

ci-inclus, e [siɛ̃kly, yz] *adj* enclosed.

🠶 **ci-inclus** *adv* enclosed.

ci-joint, e [siʒwɛ̃, ɛ̃t] *adj* enclosed.

ci-joint adv : **veuillez trouver ~ ...** please find enclosed ...

cil [sil] nm ANAT eyelash, lash.

ciller [3] [sije] vi to blink (one's eyes) ; **sans ~ fig** without blinking.

cimaise [simɛz] nf [de salle d'exposition] gallery wall.

cime [sim] nf [d'arbre, de montagne] top ; **fig** height.

ciment [simɑ̃] nm cement.

cimenter [3] [simɑ̃te] vt to cement.

cimetière [simtjɛr] nm cemetery.

ciné [sine] nm fam cinema.

cinéaste [sineast] nmf film-maker.

ciné-club [sineklœb] (pl **ciné-clubs**) nm film club.

cinéma [sinema] nm - **1.** [salle, industrie] cinema ; **aller au ~** to go to the cinema - **2.** [art] cinema, film ; **un acteur de ~** a film star ; **~ publicitaire** COMM cinema screen advertising ; **faire du ~** to be in film ; **fig** to put on an act.

cinémathèque [sinematɛk] nf film archive ; **la Cinémathèque française** the French film institute.

LA CINÉMATHÈQUE FRANÇAISE

Founded in 1936, the 'Cinémathèque française' specializes in the conservation and restoration of films ; it also screens films for public viewing.

cinématographique [sinematɔgrafik] adj cinematographic.

cinéphile [sinefil] nmf film buff.

cinétique [sinetik] <> nf kinetics (U) <> adj kinetic.

cinglant, e [sɛ̃glɑ̃, ɑ̃t] adj litt & fig biting ; [pluie] driving.

cinglé, e [sɛ̃gle] fam <> adj nuts, nutty <> nm, f nutcase.

cingler [3] [sɛ̃gle] <> vt to lash <> vi littéraire [naviguer] to sail.

cinq [sɛ̃k] <> adj num five <> nm five ; **il était moins ~ fam** it was a near thing ; voir aussi **six**.

cinquantaine [sɛ̃kɑ̃tɛn] nf - **1.** [nombre] : **une ~ de** about fifty - **2.** [âge] : **avoir la ~** to be in one's fifties.

cinquante [sɛ̃kɑ̃t] adj num & nm fifty ; voir aussi **six**.

cinquantenaire [sɛ̃kɑ̃tnɛr] <> nmf person in his/her fifties <> nm [de personne] fiftieth birthday ; [d'événement] fiftieth anniversary ; [d'institution] golden jubilee <> adj fifty-year-old.

cinquantième [sɛ̃kɑ̃tjɛm] adj num, nm OU nmf fiftieth ; voir aussi **sixième**.

cinquième [sɛ̃kjɛm] <> adj num, nm OU nmf fifth <> nf SCOL = second year OU form Br, = seventh grade Am ; voir aussi **sixième**.

cinquièmement [sɛ̃kjɛmmɑ̃] adv fifthly, in the fifth place.

cintre [sɛ̃tr] nm - **1.** [pour vêtements] coat hanger - **2.** ARCHIT arch, curve.

cintré, e [sɛ̃tre] adj - **1.** COUTURE waisted - **2.** ARCHIT arched, vaulted.

CIO (abr de **Comité international olympique**) nm IOC.

cirage [siraʒ] nm - **1.** [action] polishing - **2.** [produit] shoe polish - **3.** loc : **être dans le ~ fam** to be in a daze.

circoncision [sirkɔ̃siʒjɔ̃] nf circumcision.

circonférence [sirkɔ̃ferɑ̃s] nf - **1.** GÉOM circumference - **2.** [pourtour] boundary.

circonflexe [sirkɔ̃flɛks] ▷ **accent.**

circonscription [sirkɔ̃skripsjɔ̃] nf district ; **~ électorale** [nationale] constituency ; [locale] ward.

circonscrire [99] [sirkɔ̃skrir] vt - **1.** GÉOM to circumscribe - **2.** [incendie, épidémie] to contain - **3.** fig [sujet] to define.

se circonscrire vp : **se ~ autour de** to be centred on OU around.

circonspect, e [sirkɔ̃spɛ, ɛkt] adj cautious.

circonspection [sirkɔ̃spɛksjɔ̃] nf caution, wariness.

circonstance [sirkɔ̃stɑ̃s] nf - **1.** [occasion] occasion - **2.** (gén pl) [contexte, conjoncture] circumstance ; **~s atténuantes** JUR mitigating circumstances ; **de ~** appropriate.

circonstancié, e [sirkɔ̃stɑ̃sje] adj detailed.

circonstanciel, elle [sirkɔ̃stɑ̃sjɛl] adj GRAM adverbial.

circuit [sirkɥi] nm - **1.** [chemin] route - **2.** [parcours touristique] tour ; **~ touristique** tourist route - **3.** SPORT & TECHNOL circuit ; **en ~ fermé** [en boucle] closed-circuit (avant n) ; fig within a limited circle ; **~ imprimé/intégré** printed/integrated circuit - **4.** ÉCON network.

circulaire [sirkylɛr] nf & adj circular.

circulation [sirkylasjɔ̃] nf - **1.** [mouvement] circulation ; **mettre en ~** to circulate ; **retirer de la ~** to withdraw from circulation ; **~ (du sang)** circulation - **2.** [trafic] traffic ; **route à grande ~** main road, trunk road Br ; **'~ alternée'** 'traffic control ahead' ; **disparaître de la ~ fig** to disappear from the scene.

circulatoire [sirkylatwar] adj circulatory.

circuler [3] [sirkyle] vi - **1.** [sang, air, argent] to circulate ; **faire ~ qqch** to circulate sthg

- **2.** [aller et venir] to move (along) ; **circulez!** move along! ; **on circule mal en ville** the traffic is bad in town - **3.** [train, bus] to run - **4.** *fig* [rumeur, nouvelle] to spread.

cire [sir] *nf* - **1.** [matière] wax ; ~ **d'abeilles** beeswax ; ~ **à cacheter** sealing wax - **2.** [encaustique] polish.

ciré, e [sire] *adj* - **1.** [parquet] polished - **2.** ⊳ **toile.**
⬥ **ciré** *nm* oilskin.

cirer [3] [sire] *vt* - **1.** to polish - **2.** *loc fam* : **(n')en avoir rien à ~ (de qqch)** not to give a dawn (about sthg) ; **j'en ai rien à ~** I don't give a damn.

cireux, euse [sirø, øz] *adj* - **1.** [pâle] waxen - **2.** [matière] waxy.
⬥ **cireuse** *nf* floor polisher.

cirque [sirk] *nm* - **1.** [gén] circus - **2.** *GÉOL* cirque - **3.** *fam fig* [désordre, chahut] chaos *(U).*

cirrhose [siroz] *nf* cirrhosis *(U).*

cisaille [sizaj] *nf* shears *(pl).*

cisaillement [sizajmɑ̃] *nm* [de métal] cutting ; [de branches] pruning.

cisailler [3] [sizaje] *vt* [métal] to cut ; [branches] to prune.

ciseau, x [sizo] *nm* chisel.
⬥ **ciseaux** *nmpl* scissors.

ciseler [25] [sizle] *vt* - **1.** [pierre, métal] to chisel - **2.** [bijou] to engrave - **3.** *fig* [parfaire] to polish (up).

ciselure [sizlyr] *nf* [bois] carving ; [objet précieux] engraving.

Cisjordanie [sizʒɔrdani] *nf* : **la ~** the West Bank.

cisjordanien, enne [sizʒɔrdanjɛ̃, ɛn] *adj* of/from the West Bank.
⬥ **Cisjordanien, enne** *nm, f* native *ou* inhabitant of the West Bank.

cistercien, enne [sistersjɛ̃, ɛn] *adj* Cistercian.
⬥ **cistercien** *nm* Cistercian.

citadelle [sitadɛl] *nf litt* & *fig* citadel.

citadin, e [sitadɛ̃, in] ⬦ *adj* city *(avant n),* urban ⬦ *nm, f* city dweller.

citation [sitasjɔ̃] *nf* - **1.** *JUR* summons *(sg)* - **2.** [extrait] quote, quotation.

cité [site] *nf* - **1.** [ville] city - **2.** [lotissement] housing estate *Br ou* project *Am* ; ~ **ouvrière** (workers') housing estate *Br ou* project *Am* ; ~ **universitaire** halls *(pl)* of residence.

cité-dortoir [sitedɔrtwar] *(pl* **cités-dortoirs)** *nf* dormitory town.

citer [3] [site] *vt* - **1.** [exemple, propos, auteur] to quote - **2.** *JUR* [convoquer] to summon - **3.** *MIL* :

être cité à l'ordre du jour to be mentioned in dispatches.

citerne [sitɛrn] *nf* - **1.** [d'eau] water tank - **2.** [cuve] tank ; ~ **à mazout** oil tank.

cité U [site] *nf fam abr de* **cité universitaire.**

citoyen, enne [sitwajɛ̃, ɛn] *nm, f* citizen.

citoyenneté [sitwajɛnte] *nf* citizenship.

citron [sitrɔ̃] ⬦ *nm* lemon ; ~ **pressé** fresh lemon juice ; ~ **vert** lime ⬦ *adj inv* lemon yellow.

citronnade [sitrɔnad] *nf* (still) lemonade.

citronnelle [sitrɔnɛl] *nf* [plante] lemon balm.

citronnier [sitrɔnje] *nm* lemon tree.

citrouille [sitruj] *nf* pumpkin.

civet [sive] *nm* stew ; ~ **de lièvre** jugged hare.

civière [sivjɛr] *nf* stretcher.

civil, e [sivil] ⬦ *adj* - **1.** [gén] civil - **2.** [non militaire] civilian ⬦ *nm, f* civilian ; **dans le ~** in civilian life ; **policier en ~** plain-clothes policeman *(f* policewoman) ; **soldat en ~** soldier in civilian clothes.

civilement [sivilmɑ̃] *adv* : **se marier ~** to get married at a registry office.

civilisation [sivilizasjɔ̃] *nf* civilization.

civilisé, e [sivilize] *adj* civilized.

civiliser [3] [sivilize] *vt* to civilize.
⬥ **se civiliser** *vp* to become civilized.

civilité [sivilite] *nf* civility.
⬥ **civilités** *nfpl sout* compliments.

civique [sivik] *adj* civic ; **instruction ~** civics *(U).*

civisme [sivism] *nm* sense of civic responsibility.

cl (*abr de* **centilitre)** cl.

clac [klak] *interj* [porte] slam! ; [taquets] click!

clafoutis [klafuti] *nm* [gâteau] *cake made from a batter poured over fruit.*

claie [klɛ] *nf* - **1.** [treillis] rack - **2.** [clôture] hurdle.

clair, e [klɛr] *adj* - **1.** [gén] clear ; **c'est ~ et net** there's no two ways about it ; **il est ~ que c'est impossible** it's clear that it's impossible, clearly it's impossible - **2.** [lumineux] bright - **3.** [pâle - couleur, teint] light ; [- tissu, cheveux] light-coloured *Br,* light-colored *Am.*
⬥ **clair** ⬦ *adv* : **voir ~ (dans qqch)** *fig* to have a clear understanding (of sthg) ⬦ *nm* : **passer le plus ~ de son temps à faire qqch** to spend most *ou* the bulk of one's time doing sthg ; **mettre** *ou* **tirer qqch au ~** to shed light upon sthg.
⬥ **clair de lune** *(pl* **clairs de lune)** *nm* moonlight *(U).*
⬥ **en clair** *loc adv TÉLÉ* unscrambled *(esp of a private TV channel).*

clairement [klɛrmɑ̃] *adv* clearly.

claire-voie [klɛrvwa] ➤ **à claire-voie** *loc adv* openwork *(avant n)*.

clairière [klɛrjɛr] *nf* clearing.

clairon [klɛrɔ̃] *nm* bugle.

claironner [3] [klɛrɔne] ◇ *vi* to play the bugle ◇ *vt fig* [crier] : ~ **qqch** to shout sthg from the rooftops.

clairsemé, e [klɛrsəme] *adj* [cheveux] thin ; [arbres] scattered ; [population] sparse.

clairvoyant, e [klɛrvwajɑ̃, ɑ̃t] *adj* perceptive.

clamer [3] [klame] *vt* to proclaim.

clameur [klamœr] *nf* clamour *Br*, clamor *Am*.

clamser [3] [klamse] *vi tfam* to kick the bucket, to snuff it *Br*.

clan [klɑ̃] *nm* clan.

clandestin, e [klɑ̃dɛstɛ̃, in] ◇ *adj* [journal, commerce] clandestine ; [activité] covert ◇ *nm, f* [étranger] illegal immigrant *ou* alien ; [voyageur] stowaway.

clandestinité [klɑ̃dɛstinite] *nf* clandestine nature ; **dans la ~** [travailler] clandestinely ; [vivre] underground.

clapet [klapɛ] *nm* - **1.** TECHNOL valve - **2.** *fam fig* [bouche] trap.

clapier [klapje] *nm* [à lapins] hutch.

clapotement [klapɔtmɑ̃], **clapotis** [klapɔti] *nm* [de vagues] lapping *(U)*.

clapoter [3] [klapɔte] *vi* [vagues] to lap.

clapotis = clapotement.

claquage [klakaʒ] *nm* MÉD strain ; **se faire un ~** to pull *ou* to strain a muscle.

claque [klak] *nf* - **1.** [gifle] slap ; **donner une ~ à qqn** to slap sb - **2.** THÉÂTRE claque - **3.** *Can* [pour chaussures] galosh, rubber *Am* - **4.** *loc* : **en avoir sa ~ (de)** *fam* to be fed up to the back teeth (with).

claqué, e [klake] *adj fam* [éreinté] whacked *Br*, bushed.

claquement [klakmɑ̃] *nm* - **1.** [de porte - qui se ferme] slam, slamming *(U)* ; [- mal fermée] banging *(U)* - **2.** [de doigts] snap, snapping *(U)*.

claquemurer [3] [klakmyre] ➤ **se claquemurer** *vp* to shut o.s up *ou* away.

claquer [3] [klake] ◇ *vt* - **1.** [fermer] to slam - **2.** : **faire ~** [langue] to click ; [doigts] to snap ; [fouet] to crack - **3.** *fam* [gifler] to slap - **4.** *fam* [dépenser] to blow - **5.** *fam* [fatiguer] to wear out ◇ *vi* - **1.** [porte, volet] to bang - **2.** *fam* [personne] to kick the bucket, to snuff it *Br* - **3.** *fam* [machine] to conk out - **4.** [ampoule] to burn out, to go.

➤ **se claquer** *vp* - **1.** [se fatiguer] to wear o.s.

out - **2.** [se déchirer] : **se ~ un muscle** to pull *ou* tear a muscle.

claquettes [klakɛt] *nfpl* [danse] tap dancing *(U)*.

clarification [klarifikasjɔ̃] *nf litt* & *fig* clarification.

clarifier [9] [klarifje] *vt litt* & *fig* to clarify. ➤ **se clarifier** *vp fig* to become clear.

clarinette [klarinɛt] *nf* [instrument] clarinet.

clarté [klarte] *nf* - **1.** [lumière] brightness - **2.** [transparence] clearness - **3.** [netteté] clarity.

classe [klas] *nf* - **1.** [gén] class ; **de grande ~** first-class, high-class ; **~ ouvrière** working class ; **~ touriste** economy class - **2.** SCOL : **aller en ~** to go to school ; **~ de neige** skiing trip *(with school)* ; **~ de rattrapage** remedial class ; **~ verte** field trip *(with school)* - **3.** [catégorie] category, type - **4.** MIL rank - **5.** *loc* : **la ou quelle ~!** *fam* first class!, fantastic! ; **faire ses ~s** MIL to do one's training.

classé, e [klase] *adj* [monument] listed.

classement [klasmɑ̃] *nm* - **1.** [rangement] filing - **2.** [classification] classification - **3.** [rang - SCOL] position ; [- SPORT] placing - **4.** [liste - SCOL] class list ; [- SPORT] final placings *(pl)* ; **~ général** overall placings *(pl)*.

classer [3] [klase] *vt* - **1.** [ranger] to file - **2.** [plantes, animaux] to classify - **3.** [cataloguer] : **~ qqn (parmi)** to label sb (as) - **4.** [attribuer un rang à] to rank.

➤ **se classer** *vp* to be classed, to rank ; **se ~ troisième** to come third.

classeur [klasœr] *nm* - **1.** [meuble] filing cabinet - **2.** [portefeuille] file, folder - **3.** [d'écolier] ring binder.

classification [klasifikasjɔ̃] *nf* classification ; **~ périodique des éléments** CHIM periodic table.

classique [klasik] ◇ *nm* - **1.** [auteur] classical author ; **les grands ~s** the great classical authors - **2.** [œuvre] classic - **3.** ART & MUS : **le ~** [musique] classical (music) ; [architecture] classical architecture ; [beaux-arts] classical art ◇ *adj* - **1.** ART & MUS classical - **2.** [sobre] classic - **3.** [habituel] classic ; **ça, c'est l'histoire ~!** it's the usual story!

clause [kloz] *nf* clause.

claustrer [3] [klostre] ➤ **se claustrer** *vp sout* to shut o.s. away *ou* up.

claustrophobie [klostrɔfɔbi] *nf* claustrophobia.

clavecin [klavsɛ̃] *nm* harpsichord.

clavicule [klavikyl] *nf* collarbone.

clavier [klavje] *nm* keyboard.

clé, clef [kle] ◇ *nf* - **1.** [gén] key ; **la ~ du mys-**

tère the key to the mystery ; **fermer qqch à ~** to lock sthg ; **~s en main** [usine] turnkey ; [logement] ready for immediate entry ; **mettre qqn/qqch sous ~** to lock sb/sthg up ; **~ de contact** AUTOM ignition key ; **mettre la ~ sous la porte** to clear out - **2.** [outil] : **~ anglaise** OU **à molette** adjustable spanner Br OU **wrench** Am, monkey wrench - **3.** MUS [signe] clef ; **~ de sol/fa** treble/bass clef ; **à la ~ de** *fig* at the end (of it all) ◇ *adj* : **industrie/rôle ~** key industry/role.

➤ **clé de voûte** *nf litt* & *fig* keystone.

clean [klin] *adj fam* [chose, lieu] neat ; [personne] clean-living.

clef = **clé.**

clématite [klematit] *nf* clematis.

clémence [klemãs] *nf* - **1.** *sout* [indulgence] clemency - **2.** *fig* [douceur] mildness.

clément, e [klemã, ãt] *adj* - **1.** [indulgent] lenient - **2.** *fig* [température] mild.

clémentine [klemãtin] *nf* clementine.

cleptomane = **kleptomane.**

clerc [klɛr] *nm* [assistant] clerk ; **~ de notaire** lawyer's clerk.

clergé [klɛrʒe] *nm* clergy.

clérical, e, aux [klerikal, o] ◇ *adj* clerical ◇ *nm, f* clericalist.

CLES, Cles [klɛs] (*abr de* **contrat local emploi-solidarité**) *nm* community work scheme for young unemployed people.

Clic-Clac® [klikklac] *nm* pull-out sofa bed.

cliché [kliʃe] *nm* - **1.** PHOT negative - **2.** [banalité] cliché.

client, e [kliã, ãt] *nm, f* - **1.** [de notaire, d'agence] client ; [de médecin] patient - **2.** [acheteur] customer - **3.** [habitué] regular (customer).

clientèle [kliãtɛl] *nf* - **1.** [ensemble des clients] customers (*pl*) ; [de profession libérale] clientele - **2.** [fait d'être client] : **accorder sa ~ à** to give one's custom to.

cligner [3] [kliɲe] ◇ *vt* : **~ les yeux** to blink ◇ *vi* : **~ de l'œil** to wink ; **~ des yeux** to blink.

clignotant, e [kliɲɔtã, ãt] *adj* [lumière] flickering.

➤ **clignotant** *nm* - **1.** AUTOM indicator ; **mettre son ~** to indicate - **2.** ÉCON & *fig* warning sign.

clignoter [3] [kliɲɔte] *vi* - **1.** [yeux] to blink - **2.** [lumière] to flicker.

climat [klima] *nm litt* & *fig* climate.

climatique [klimatik] *adj* climatic.

climatisation [klimatizasjõ] *nf* air-conditioning.

climatisé, e [klimatize] *adj* air-conditioned.

clin [klɛ̃] ➤ **clin d'œil** *nm* : **faire un ~ d'œil (à)** to wink (at) ; **en un ~ d'œil** in a flash.

clinique [klinik] ◇ *nf* clinic ◇ *adj* clinical.

clinquant, e [klɛ̃kã, ãt] *adj litt* & *fig* flashy.

➤ **clinquant** *nm* - **1.** [faux bijou] imitation jewellery (U) Br OU jewelry (U) Am - **2.** *fig* [éclat] gloss.

clip [klip] *nm* - **1.** [vidéo] pop video - **2.** [boucle d'oreilles] clip-on earring.

clique [klik] *nf péj* clique.

➤ **cliques** *nfpl* : **prendre ses ~s et ses claques** *fam* to pack one's bags (and go).

cliquer [3] [klike] *vi* INFORM to click.

cliqueter [27] [klikte] *vi* - **1.** [pièces, clés, chaînes] to jingle, to jangle - **2.** [verres] to clink.

cliquetis [klikti] *nm* - **1.** [de pièces, clés, chaînes] jingling (U), jangling (U) - **2.** [de verres] clinking (U).

clitoris [klitɔris] *nm* clitoris.

clivage [klivaʒ] *nm* - **1.** GÉOL cleavage - **2.** *fig* [division] division.

cloaque [klɔak] *nm* [lieu] cesspit.

clochard, e [klɔʃar, ard] *nm, f* tramp.

cloche [klɔʃ] ◇ *nf* - **1.** [d'église] bell - **2.** [couvercle] : **~ à fromage** glass cover for cheese - **3.** *fam* [idiot] idiot, clot Br - **4.** *(en apposition)* [jupe] flared ◇ *adj fam* : **ce qu'elle peut être ~, celle-là!** she can be a right idiot!

cloche-pied [klɔʃpje] ➤ **à cloche-pied** *loc adv* hopping ; **sauter à ~** to hop.

clocher[1] [klɔʃe] *nm* [d'église] church tower.

clocher[2] [3] [klɔʃe] *vi* : **il y a quelque chose qui cloche** there's something wrong here.

clochette [klɔʃɛt] *nf* - **1.** [petite cloche] (little) bell - **2.** [de fleur] bell.

clodo [klɔdo] *nmf fam* tramp.

cloison [klwazõ] *nf* [mur] partition.

cloisonner [3] [klwazɔne] *vt* [pièce, maison] to partition (off) ; *fig* to compartmentalize.

cloître [klwatr] *nm* cloister.

cloîtrer [3] [klwatre] *vt* - **1.** RELIG to cloister - **2.** [enfermer] to shut away (from the outside world).

➤ **se cloîtrer** *vp* - **1.** [s'enfermer] to shut o.s. away ; **se ~ dans** *fig* to retreat into - **2.** [RELIG - sœur] to enter a convent ; [- moine] to enter a monastery.

clone [klɔn] *nm* INFORM clone.

clope [klɔp] *nm* OU *nf fam* cigarette, fag Br.

clopin-clopant [klɔpɛ̃klɔpã] *adv* : **aller ~** [personne] to hobble along ; *fig* to struggle along.

clopiner [3] [klɔpine] *vi* to hobble along.

cloporte [klɔpɔrt] *nm* woodlouse.

cloque [klɔk] *nf* blister.

cloquer [3] [klɔke] *vi* to blister.

clore [113] [klɔr] *vt* to close ; [négociations] to conclude ; ~ **une session** INFORM to log out.

clos, e [klo, kloz] <> *pp* ▷ **clore** <> *adj* closed.
◆ **clos** *nm* - **1.** [terrain] enclosed field - **2.** [vignoble] vineyard.

clôture [klotyr] *nf* - **1.** [haie] hedge ; [de fil de fer] fence ; ~ **électrifiée** OU **électrique** electric fence - **2.** [fermeture] closing, closure - **3.** [fin] end, conclusion.

clôturer [3] [klotyre] *vt* - **1.** [terrain] to enclose - **2.** [négociation] to close, to conclude.

clou [klu] *nm* - **1.** [pointe] nail ; ~ **de girofle** CULIN ,clove ; **des ~s!** *fam* no chance! ; **maigre comme un** ~ as thin as a rake ; **mettre au** ~ [en gage] to pawn ; [en prison] to put in the clink - **2.** [attraction] highlight.
◆ **clous** *nmpl* pedestrian crossing *(sg)*.

clouer [3] [klue] *vt* [fixer - couvercle, planche] to nail (down) ; [- tableau, caisse] to nail (up) ; *fig* [immobiliser] : **rester cloué sur place** to be rooted to the spot ; **être cloué au lit (par)** *fam* to be laid up in bed (with).

clouté, e [klute] *adj* [vêtement] studded.

clown [klun] *nm* clown ; **faire le** ~ to clown around, to act the fool.

CLT (*abr de* **Compagnie luxembourgeoise de télévision**) *nf* Luxembourg TV company.

club [klœb] *nm* club.

cm (*abr de* **centimètre**) cm.

CM <> *nf* (*abr de* **Chambre des métiers**) chamber of commerce for trades <> *nm* (*abr de* **cours moyen**) : **~1** *fourth year of primary school* ; **~2** *fifth year of primary school.*

CNAC [knak] (*abr de* **Centre national d'art et de culture**) *nm* official name of the Pompidou Centre.

CNAM [knam] (*abr de* **Conservatoire national des arts et métiers**) *nm* science and technology school in Paris.

CNC *nm* - **1.** (*abr de* **Conseil national de la consommation**) official consumer protection organization - **2.** (*abr de* **Centre national de la cinématographie**) national cinematographic organization.

CNDP (*abr de* **Centre national de documentation pédagogique**) *nm* national organization for educational resources.

CNE (*abr de* **Caisse nationale d'épargne**) *nf* national savings bank.

CNEC [knɛk] (*abr de* **Centre national de l'enseignement par correspondance**) *nm* nation-

al education body organizing correspondence courses, ≃ Open University Br.

CNES, Cnes [knɛs] (*abr de* **Centre national d'études spatiales**) *nm* French national space research centre.

CNIL [knil] *nf abr de* **Commission nationale de l'informatique et des libertés.**

CNIT, Cnit [knit] (*abr de* **Centre national des industries et des techniques**) *nm* exhibition centre at la Défense near Paris.

CNJA (*abr de* **Centre national des jeunes agriculteurs**) *nm* young farmers' union.

CNRS (*abr de* **Centre national de la recherche scientifique**) *nm* national scientific research organization.

CNTS (*abr de* **Centre national de transfusion sanguine**) *nm* national blood transfusion centre.

CNUCED, Cnuced [knysɛd] (*abr de* **Conférence des Nations unies pour le commerce et l'industrie**) *nf* UNCTAD.

coaguler [3] [kɔagyle] <> *vt* - **1.** [sang] to clot - **2.** [lait] to curdle <> *vi* - **1.** [sang] to clot - **2.** [lait] to curdle.
◆ **se coaguler** *vp* - **1.** [sang] to clot - **2.** [lait] to curdle.

coaliser [3] [kɔalize] *vt* to group together, to unite.
◆ **se coaliser** *vp* - **1.** [s'allier] to form a coalition OU an alliance - **2.** [s'unir] to unite.

coalition [kɔalisjɔ̃] *nf* coalition.

coasser [3] [kɔase] *vi* [grenouille] to croak.

COB, Cob [kɔb] (*abr de* **Commission des opérations de Bourse**) *nf* commission for supervision of stock exchange operations, ≃ SIB Br, ≃ SEC Am.

cobalt [kɔbalt] *nm* cobalt.

cobaye [kɔbaj] *nm litt* & *fig* guinea pig.

cobra [kɔbra] *nm* cobra.

coca [kɔka] <> *nm* BOT coca <> *nf* coca extract.

Coca® [kɔka] *nm* [boisson] Coke®.

cocagne [kɔkaɲ] ▷ **mât, pays.**

cocaïne [kɔkain] *nf* cocaine.

cocaïnomane [kokainɔman] *nmf* cocaine addict.

cocarde [kɔkard] *nf* - **1.** [insigne] roundel - **2.** [distinction] rosette.

cocardier, ère [kɔkardje, ɛr] <> *adj* [chauvin] jingoistic <> *nm, f* jingoist.

cocasse [kɔkas] *adj* funny.

coccinelle [kɔksinɛl] *nf* - **1.** [insecte] ladybird Br, ladybug Am - **2.** [voiture] Beetle.

coccyx [kɔksis] *nm* coccyx.

coche [kɔʃ] *nm* : manquer le ~ *fam fig* to miss the boat.

cocher[1] [kɔʃe] *nm* coachman.

cocher[2] [3] [kɔʃe] *vt* to tick (off) *Br*, to check (off) *Am*.

cochère [kɔʃɛr] ⊳ **porte**.

cocheur [kɔʃœr] *nm Can GOLF* : ~ **d'allée** pitching wedge ; ~ **de sable** sand wedge.

cochon, onne [kɔʃɔ̃, ɔn] ◇ *adj* dirty, smutty ◇ *nm, f fam péj* pig ; **un tour de** ~ a dirty trick.
➤ **cochon** *nm* pig ; ~ **d'Inde** guinea pig ; ~ **de lait** piglet.

cochonnaille [kɔʃɔnaj] *nf fam* [charcuterie] pork.

cochonner [3] [kɔʃɔne] *vt fam* to mess up.

cochonnerie [kɔʃɔnri] *nf fam* **- 1.** [nourriture] muck *(U)* **- 2.** [chose] rubbish *(U)* **- 3.** [saleté] mess *(U)* **- 4.** [obscénité] dirty joke, smut *(U)*.

cochonnet [kɔʃɔnɛ] *nm* **- 1.** [petit cochon] piglet **- 2.** *JEU* jack.

cocker [kɔkɛr] *nm* cocker spaniel.

cockpit [kɔkpit] *nm* cockpit.

cocktail [kɔktɛl] *nm* **- 1.** [réception] cocktail party **- 2.** [boisson] cocktail **- 3.** *fig* [mélange] mixture ; ~ **Molotov** Molotov cocktail.

coco [kɔko] *nm* **- 1.** ⊳ **noix - 2.** *fam péj* [individu] bloke *Br*, guy **- 3.** *péj* [communiste] commie.

cocon [kɔkɔ̃] *nm ZOOL* & *fig* cocoon.

cocooning [kɔkuniŋ] *nm* : faire du ~ to cocoon o.s.

cocorico [kɔkɔriko] *nm* [du coq] cock-a-doodle-doo.

cocotier [kɔkɔtje] *nm* coconut tree.

cocotte [kɔkɔt] *nf* **- 1.** [marmite] casserole (dish) **- 2.** [poule] hen ; ~ **en papier** paper shape **- 3.** *péj* [courtisane] tart.

Cocotte-Minute® [kɔkɔtminyt] *nf* pressure cooker.

cocu, e [kɔky] *nm, f* & *adj fam* cuckold.

code [kɔd] *nm* **- 1.** [gén] code ; ~ **barres** bar code ; ~ **de caractères** *INFORM* character code ; ~ **civil** *ou* **Napoléon** civil code ; ~ **génétique** genetic code ; ~ **pénal** penal code ; ~ **postal** postcode *Br*, zip code *Am* ; ~ **de la route** highway code ; ~ **secret** [pour carte de crédit] PIN number **- 2.** [phares] dipped headlights *(pl)* ; **se mettre en ~s** to dip one's headlights.

codéine [kɔdein] *nf* codeine.

coder [3] [kɔde] *vt* to code.

codétenu, e [kɔdetny] *nm, f* (fellow) prisoner.

codifier [9] [kɔdifje] *vt* to codify.

coefficient [kɔefisjɑ̃] *nm* coefficient ; ~ **d'erreur** margin of error.

COEFFICIENT

In 'baccalauréat' examinations, the grade for each subject is multiplied by a 'coefficient' which is determined by the type of baccalauréat chosen. For a 'bac S', which has a scientific bias, the 'coefficient' for maths will be higher than the philosophy 'coefficient', for example.

coéquipier, ère [kɔekipje, ɛr] *nm, f* teammate.

cœur [kœr] *nm* heart ; **au** ~ **de l'hiver** in the depths of winter ; **au** ~ **de l'été** at the height of summer ; **au** ~ **du conflit** at the height of the conflict ; **de bon** ~ willingly ; **de tout son** ~ with all one's heart ; **à** ~ **ouvert** *MÉD* openheart ; **parler à** ~ **ouvert à qqn** to have a heart-to-heart with sb ; **apprendre par** ~ to learn by heart ; **avoir qqch à** ~ to have one's heart set on sthg ; **avoir bon** ~ to be kindhearted ; **avoir le** ~ **sur la main** to be bighearted ; **avoir mal au** ~ to feel sick ; **avoir un** ~ **d'artichaut** to fall in love very easily ; **en avoir le** ~ **net** to be clear in one's (own) mind ; **avoir le** ~ **serré** *ou* **gros** to have a heavy heart ; **briser** *ou* **fendre le** ~ **de qqn** to break sb's heart ; **s'en donner à** ~ **joie** [prendre beaucoup de plaisir] to have a whale of a time ; **manquer de** ~, **ne pas avoir de** ~ to be heartless ; **ne pas avoir le** ~ **de faire qqch** not to have the heart to do sthg ; **serrer qqn contre son** ~ to clasp sb to one's breast ; **soulever le** ~ **à qqn** to make sb feel sick ; **tenir à** ~ to be close to one's heart.
➤ **cœur de pierre** *nm* heart of stone.

coexistence [kɔɛgzistɑ̃s] *nf* coexistence.

coexister [3] [kɔɛgziste] *vi* to coexist.

COFACE [kɔfas] (*abr de* Compagnie française d'assurance pour le commerce extérieur) *nf* export insurance company, ≃ ECGD.

coffrage [kɔfraʒ] *nm* [pour le béton] formwork *(U)* ; [charpente] coffering.

coffre [kɔfr] *nm* **- 1.** [meuble] chest **- 2.** [de voiture] boot *Br*, trunk *Am* **- 3.** [coffre-fort] safe **- 4.** *loc* : **avoir du** ~ *fam fig* to have a lot of puff.

coffre-fort [kɔfrəfɔr] (*pl* **coffres-forts**) *nm* safe.

coffrer [3] [kɔfre] *vt* **- 1.** *fam* [emprisonner] to bang up **- 2.** *TECHNOL* to put up shuttering round.

coffret [kɔfrɛ] *nm* **- 1.** [petit coffre] casket ; ~ **à bijoux** jewellery *Br ou* jewelry *Am* box **- 2.** [de disques] boxed set.

cogestion [kɔʒɛstjɔ̃] *nf* joint management.

cogitation [kɔʒitasjɔ̃] *nf hum* cogitation.
cogiter [3] [kɔʒite] *vi hum* to cogitate.
cognac [kɔɲak] *nm* cognac, brandy.
cogner [3] [kɔɲe] <> *vt fam* to beat up <> *vi*
- **1.** [heurter] to bang - **2.** *fam* [donner des coups] to
hit - **3.** [soleil] to beat down.
➤ **se cogner** *vp* - **1.** [se heurter] to bump o.s. ;
se ~ à OU **contre qqch** to bump into sthg ; **se
~ la tête/le genou** to hit one's head/knee
- **2.** *fam* [se battre] to have a punch-up *Br*.
cohabitation [kɔabitasjɔ̃] *nf* - **1.** [de personnes]
living together, cohabitation - **2.** POLIT cohabitation.

cohabiter [3] [kɔabite] *vi* - **1.** [habiter ensemble]
to live together - **2.** POLIT to cohabit.
cohérence [kɔerɑ̃s] *nf* consistency, coher-
ence.
cohérent, e [kɔerɑ̃, ɑ̃t] *adj* - **1.** [logique] consistent, coherent - **2.** [unifié] coherent.
cohéritier, ère [kɔeritje, ɛr] *nm, f* joint heir
(*f* heiress).
cohésion [kɔezjɔ̃] *nf* cohesion.
cohorte [kɔɔrt] *nf* [groupe] troop.
cohue [kɔy] *nf* - **1.** [foule] crowd - **2.** [bousculade]
crush.
coi, coite [kwa, kwat] *adj* : **rester ~ sout** to remain silent.
coiffe [kwaf] *nf* headdress.
coiffé, e [kwafe] *adj* : **être bien/mal ~** to have
tidy/untidy hair ; **être ~ d'une casquette** to
be wearing a cap.
coiffer [3] [kwafe] *vt* - **1.** [mettre sur la tête] :
~ qqn de qqch to put sthg on sb's head
- **2.** [les cheveux] : **~ qqn** to do sb's hair - **3.** [re-
couvrir] to top, to cover - **4.** [diriger] to head.
➤ **se coiffer** *vp* - **1.** [les cheveux] to do one's
hair - **2.** [mettre sur sa tête] : **se ~ de** to wear, to
put on.
coiffeur, euse [kwafœr, øz] *nm, f* hairdresser.
➤ **coiffeuse** *nf* [meuble] dressing table.
coiffure [kwafyr] *nf* - **1.** [chapeau] hat - **2.** [che-
veux] hairstyle - **3.** [profession] hairdressing.
coin [kwɛ̃] *nm* - **1.** [angle] corner ; **au ~ du feu**
by the fireside ; **envoyer qqn au ~** to make
sb stand in the corner ; **à tous les ~s de rue**
on every street corner ; **regarder qqn du
~ de l'œil** [à la dérobée] to look at sb out of the

corner of one's eye - **2.** [parcelle, endroit] place,
spot ; **du ~ local** ; **dans le ~** in the area ;
~ de ciel bleu a patch of blue sky ; *fig* **dans un
~ de ma mémoire** in a corner of my mem-
ory ; **~ cuisine** kitchen area ; **le petit ~** *fam*
the little boys'/girls' room - **3.** [outil] wedge
- **4.** [matrice] die.
coincé, e [kwɛ̃se] *adj fam* [personne] hung up.
coincer [16] [kwɛ̃se] *vt* - **1.** [bloquer] to jam
- **2.** *fam* [prendre] to nab ; *fig* to catch out
- **3.** [acculer] to corner, to trap.
➤ **se coincer** *vp* to get stuck.
coïncidence [kɔɛ̃sidɑ̃s] *nf* coincidence.
coïncider [3] [kɔɛ̃side] *vi* to coincide.
coing [kwɛ̃] *nm* [fruit] quince.
coït [kɔit] *nm* coitus.
coke [kɔk] <> *nf* [cocaïne] coke <> *nm* [combusti-
ble] coke.
col [kɔl] *nm* - **1.** [de vêtement] collar ; **faux ~** detachable collar ; **~ roulé** polo neck *Br*,
turtleneck *Am* - **2.** [partie étroite] neck - **3.** ANAT :
~ du fémur neck of the thighbone OU
femur ; **~ de l'utérus** cervix, neck of the
womb - **4.** GÉOGR pass.
col. *abr de* **colonne**.
colchique [kɔlʃik] *nm* [plante] autumn crocus.
coléoptère [kɔleɔptɛr] *nm* beetle.
colère [kɔlɛr] *nf* - **1.** [irritation] anger ; **être/se
mettre en ~** to be/get angry ; **ravaler sa ~** to
keep one's temper - **2.** [accès d'humeur] fit of
anger OU rage ; **piquer une ~** to fly into a
rage.
coléreux, euse [kɔlerø, øz], **colérique**
[kɔlerik] *adj* [tempérament] fiery ; [personne]
quick-tempered.
colifichet [kɔlifiʃɛ] *nm* [bijou] trinket.
colimaçon [kɔlimasɔ̃] ➤ **en colimaçon** *loc
adv* spiral.
colin [kɔlɛ̃] *nm* [merlu] hake.
colin-maillard [kɔlɛ̃majar] (*pl* **colin-
maillards**) *nm* blind man's buff.
colique [kɔlik] *nf* - **1.** [gén pl] [douleur] colic (*U*)
- **2.** [diarrhée] diarrhoea.
colis [kɔli] *nm* parcel.
colistier, ère [kɔlistje, ɛr] *nm, f* fellow candidate.
coll. - **1.** *abr de* **collection** - **2.** (*abr de* **collabo-
rateurs**) : **et ~** et al.
collabo [kɔlabo] *nmf* HIST & *péj* collaborator.
collaborateur, trice [kɔlabɔratœr, tris]
nm, f - **1.** [employé] colleague - **2.** [de journal]
contributor - **3.** HIST collaborator.
collaboration [kɔlabɔrasjɔ̃] *nf* collaboration.
collaborer [3] [kɔlabɔre] *vi* - **1.** [coopérer, sous
l'Occupation] to collaborate - **2.** [participer] : **~ à**
to contribute to.

collage [kɔlaʒ] *nm* - **1.** [action] sticking, gluing - **2.** ART collage.

collant, e [kɔlɑ̃, ɑ̃t] *adj* - **1.** [substance] sticky - **2.** [vêtement] close-fitting, tight-fitting - **3.** *fam* [personne] clinging, clingy.

➡ **collant** *nm* tights *(pl)* *Br*, panty hose *(pl)* *Am*.

collatéral, e, aux [kɔlateral, o] ◇ *adj* - **1.** ANAT collateral - **2.** ARCHIT side *(avant n)* - **3.** JUR collateral ◇ *nm*, *f* collateral.

collation [kɔlasjɔ̃] *nf* [repas] snack.

colle [kɔl] *nf* - **1.** [substance] glue - **2.** [question] poser ; **poser une ~ à qqn** to set sb a (real) poser - **3.** [SCOL - interrogation] test ; [- retenue] detention ; **avoir une heure de ~** to get an hour's detention.

collecte [kɔlɛkt] *nf* collection.

collecteur, trice [kɔlɛktœr, tris] ◇ *adj* : **égout ~** main sewer ◇ *nm*, *f* : **~ de fonds** fundraiser ; **~ d'impôts** tax collector.

collectif, ive [kɔlɛktif, iv] *adj* - **1.** [responsabilité, travail] collective - **2.** [billet, voyage] group *(avant n)*.

➡ **collectif** *nm* - **1.** [équipe] team - **2.** LING collective noun - **3.** FIN : **~ budgétaire** collection of budgetary measures.

collection [kɔlɛksjɔ̃] *nf* - **1.** [d'objets, de livres, de vêtements] collection ; **faire la ~ de** to collect - **2.** COMM line.

collectionner [3] [kɔlɛksjɔne] *vt litt* & *fig* to collect.

collectionneur, euse [kɔlɛksjɔnœr, øz] *nm*, *f* collector.

collectivité [kɔlɛktivite] *nf* community ; **les ~s locales** ADMIN the local communities.

collège [kɔlɛʒ] *nm* - **1.** SCOL ≈ secondary school ; **le Collège de France** the Collège de France - **2.** [de personnes] college ; **~ électoral** electoral college.

collégial, e, aux [kɔleʒjal, o] *adj* collegial, collegiate.

➡ **collégiale** *nf* collegiate church.

collégien, enne [kɔleʒjɛ̃, ɛn] *nm*, *f* schoolboy *(f* schoolgirl).

collègue [kɔlɛg] *nmf* colleague.

coller [3] [kɔle] ◇ *vt* - **1.** [fixer - affiche] to stick (up) ; [- timbre] to stick - **2.** [appuyer] to press - **3.** INFORM to paste - **4.** *fam* [mettre] to stick, to dump - **5.** SCOL to give (a) detention to, to keep behind - **6.** [embarrasser] to catch out - **7.** *fam* [suivre] to cling to - **8.** *fam* [donner] : **~ qqch à qqn** to give sthg to sb, to give sb sthg ◇ *vi* - **1.** [adhérer] to stick - **2.** [être adapté] : **~ à qqch** [vêtement] to cling to sthg ; *fig* to fit in with sthg, to adhere to sthg - **3.** *fam* [bien se passer] to be *ou* go OK - **4.** [suivre] : **~ à** to stick close to.

➡ **se coller** *vp* - **1.** *fam* [subir] to get landed with - **2.** [se plaquer] : **se ~ contre qqn/qqch** to press o.s. against sb/sthg.

collerette [kɔlrɛt] *nf* - **1.** [de vêtement] ruff - **2.** [de tuyau] flange.

collet [kɔlɛ] *nm* - **1.** [de vêtement] collar ; **mettre la main au ~ de qqn** to grab sb by the collar *ou* the scruff of the neck ; **être ~ monté** [affecté, guindé] to be strait-laced - **2.** [piège] snare.

collier [kɔlje] *nm* - **1.** [bijou] necklace ; **~ de perles** pearl necklace - **2.** [d'animal] collar - **3.** [barbe] *fringe of beard along the jawline*.

collimateur [kɔlimatœr] *nm* : **avoir qqn dans le ~** *fam* to have sb in one's sights.

colline [kɔlin] *nf* hill.

collision [kɔlizjɔ̃] *nf* [choc] collision, crash ; **entrer en ~ avec** to collide with.

colloque [kɔlɔk] *nm* colloquium.

collusion [kɔlyzjɔ̃] *nf* collusion.

collyre [kɔlir] *nm* eye lotion.

colmater [3] [kɔlmate] *vt* - **1.** [fuite] to plug, to seal off - **2.** [brèche] to fill, to seal.

colo [kɔlo] *nf fam* children's holiday camp *Br*, summer camp *Am*.

colombage [kɔlɔ̃baʒ] *nm* half-timbering ; **à ~s** half-timbered.

colombe [kɔlɔ̃b] *nf* dove.

Colombie [kɔlɔ̃bi] *nf* : **la ~** Colombia.

colombien, enne [kɔlɔ̃bjɛ̃, ɛn] *adj* Colombian.

➡ **Colombien, enne** *nm*, *f* Colombian.

Colombo [kɔlɔ̃bo] *n* Colombo.

colon [kɔlɔ̃] *nm* settler.

côlon [kolɔ̃] *nm* colon.

colonel [kɔlɔnɛl] *nm* colonel.

colonelle [kɔlɔnɛl] *nf* colonel's wife.

colonial, e, aux [kɔlɔnjal, o] *adj* colonial.

colonialisme [kɔlɔnjalism] *nm* colonialism.

colonialiste [kɔlɔnjalist] *nmf* & *adj* colonialist.

colonie [kɔlɔni] nf - **1.** [territoire] colony - **2.** [d'expatriés] community ; **~ de vacances** holiday *Br ou* summer camp *Am.*

colonisation [kɔlɔnizasjɔ̃] nf colonization.

coloniser [3] [kɔlɔnize] vt *litt* & *fig* to colonize.

-**colonne** [kɔlɔn] nf column ; **en ~** in a line *ou* column.

➽ **colonne vertébrale** nf spine, spinal column.

colorant, e [kɔlɔrɑ̃, ɑ̃t] adj colouring *Br*, coloring *Am.*

➽ **colorant** nm colouring *Br*, coloring *Am* ; **~ alimentaire** food colouring *Br ou* coloring *Am.*

coloration [kɔlɔrasjɔ̃] nf colour *Br*, color *Am*, colouring *Br*, coloring *Am.*

coloré, e [kɔlɔre] adj - **1.** [de couleur] coloured *Br*, colored *Am* - **2.** *fig* [diversifié, imagé] colourful *Br*, colorful *Am.*

colorer [3] [kɔlɔre] vt [teindre] to colour *Br*, to color *Am* ; **~ qqch de** *fig* to colour *Br ou* color *Am* sthg with.

➽ **se colorer** vp [les cheveux] to colour *Br*, to color *Am*, to dye ; **se ~ de** *fig* to be coloured *Br ou* colored *Am* with.

coloriage [kɔlɔrjaʒ] nm - **1.** [action] colouring *Br*, coloring *Am* - **2.** [dessin] drawing.

colorier [9] [kɔlɔrje] vt to colour in *Br*, to color in *Am.*

coloris [kɔlɔri] nm shade.

colorisation [kɔlɔrizasjɔ̃] nf CIN colourization *Br*, colorization *Am.*

coloriser [3] [kɔlɔrize] vt CIN to colourize *Br*, to colorize *Am.*

colossal, e, aux [kɔlɔsal, o] adj colossal, huge.

colosse [kɔlɔs] nm - **1.** [homme] giant - **2.** [statue] colossus.

colportage [kɔlpɔrtaʒ] nm hawking.

colporter [3] [kɔlpɔrte] vt [marchandise] to hawk ; [information] to spread.

➽ **se colporter** vp [information] to spread.

colporteur, euse [kɔlpɔrtœr, øz] nm, f - **1.** [de marchandises] hawker - **2.** [de ragots] gossip.

coltiner [3] [kɔltine] ➽ **se coltiner** vp *fam* to be landed with.

colza [kɔlza] nm rape (seed).

coma [kɔma] nm coma ; **être dans le ~** to be in a coma.

comateux, euse [kɔmatø, øz] <> adj comatose <> nm, f person in a coma.

combat [kɔba] nm - **1.** [bataille] battle, fight ; **mettre/être hors de ~** to put/be out of the fight ; *fig* to put/be out of the game - **2.** *fig* [lutte] struggle - **3.** *SPORT* fight.

combatif, ive [kɔbatif, iv] adj [humeur] fighting *(avant n)* ; [troupes] willing to fight.

combativité [kɔbativite] nf fighting spirit.

combattant, e [kɔbatɑ̃, ɑ̃t] <> adj fighting *(avant n)* <> nm, f [en guerre] combatant ; [dans bagarre] fighter ; **ancien ~** veteran.

combattre [83] [kɔbatr] <> vt *litt* & *fig* to fight (against) <> vi to fight.

combattu, e [kɔbaty] pp ⊳ **combattre.**

combien [kɔbjɛ̃] <> conj how much ; **~ de** [nombre] how many ; [quantité] how much ; **~ de temps?** how long? ; **ça fait ~?** [prix] how much is that? ; [longueur, hauteur etc] how long/high etc is it? <> adv how (much) <> nm *inv* : **le ~ sommes-nous?** what date is it? ; **tous les ~?** how often?

combientième [kɔbjɛ̃tjɛm] <> nmf : **il est le ~?** where did he come? <> adj : **c'est le ~ examen qu'on passe?** that makes how many exams we've taken?

combinaison [kɔbinɛzɔ̃] nf - **1.** [d'éléments] combination - **2.** [de femme] slip - **3.** [vêtement - de mécanicien] boiler suit *Br*, overalls *(pl) Br*, overall *Am* ; [- de ski] ski suit - **4.** [de coffre] combination - **5.** [manœuvre] scheme.

combine [kɔbin] nf *fam* trick.

combiné [kɔbine] nm receiver.

combiner [3] [kɔbine] vt - **1.** [arranger] to combine - **2.** [organiser] to devise.

➽ **se combiner** vp to turn out.

comble [kɔbl] <> nm height ; **le ~ de** the height of ; **c'est un ou le ~!** that beats everything! ; **être au ~ du désespoir** to be in the depths of despair ; **être au ~ du bonheur** to be overjoyed <> adj packed.

➽ **combles** nmpl attic *(sg)*, loft *(sg)* ; **loger sous les ~s** to live in an attic.

combler [3] [kɔble] vt - **1.** [gâter] to spoil ; **~ qqn de** to shower sb with - **2.** [boucher] to fill in - **3.** [déficit] to make good ; [lacune] to fill.

combustible [kɔbystibl] <> nm fuel <> adj combustible.

combustion [kɔbystjɔ̃] nf combustion.

COMECON, Comecon [kɔmɛkɔn] *(abr de* **Council for Mutual Economic Assistance)** nm COMECON.

comédie [kɔmedi] nf - **1.** *CIN* & *THÉÂTRE* comedy ; **la Comédie-Française** the Comédie

Française ; ~ **musicale** musical ; **jouer la** ~ *fig* to put on an act - **2.** [complication] palaver.

comédien, enne [kɔmedjɛ̃, ɛn] ◇ *nm, f* [acteur] actor (*f* actress) ; *fig* & *péj* sham ◇ *adj fig* & *péj* : **être** ~ to be a sham.

COMES, Comes [kɔmɛs] (*abr de* **Commissariat à l'énergie solaire**) *nm solar energy commission.*

comestible [kɔmɛstibl] *adj* edible.
◆ **comestibles** *nmpl* food (*U*).

comète [kɔmɛt] *nf* comet ; **tirer des plans sur la** ~ *fig* to count one's chickens (before they are hatched).

comice [kɔmis] *nm* : ~ **agricole** *local farmers' meeting.*

comique [kɔmik] ◇ *nm* - **1.** THÉÂTRE comic actor - **2.** [genre] **le** ~ **comedy** ◇ *adj* - **1.** [style] comic - **2.** [drôle] comical, funny.

comité [kɔmite] *nm* committee ; **en petit** ~ *fig* with a few close friends ; ~ **d'entreprise** works council (*also organizing leisure activities).*

commandant [kɔmɑ̃dɑ̃] *nm* commander ; ~ **de bord** AÉRON captain.

commande [kɔmɑ̃d] *nf* - **1.** [de marchandises] order ; **passer une** ~ to place an order ; **sur** ~ to order ; **disponible sur** ~ available on request - **2.** TECHNOL control ; **être aux ~s (de)**, **tenir les ~s (de)** [d'avion, de machine] to be at the controls (of) ; NAVIG & *fig* to be at the helm (of) - **3.** INFORM command ; ~ **numérique** digital control.

commandement [kɔmɑ̃dmɑ̃] *nm* command ; **les dix ~s** RELIG the Ten Commandments.

commander [3] [kɔmɑ̃de] ◇ *vt* - **1.** [ordonner] to order, to command - **2.** MIL to command - **3.** [contrôler] to operate, to control - **4.** COMM to order ◇ *vi* to be in charge ; ~ **à qqn de faire qqch** to order sb to do sthg.

◆ **se commander** *vp* : **ça ne se commande pas** *fig* it is uncontrollable.

commanditaire [kɔmɑ̃ditɛr] JUR ◇ *nm* backer ◇ *adj* : **(associé)** ~ sleeping partner *Br*, silent partner *Am*.

commanditer [3] [kɔmɑ̃dite] *vt* - **1.** [entreprise] to finance - **2.** [meurtre] to put up the money for.

commando [kɔmɑ̃do] *nm* commando (unit).

comme [kɔm] ◇ *conj* - **1.** [introduisant une comparaison] like ; **il sera médecin** ~ **son père** he'll become a doctor (just) like his father ; **nous nagerons** ~ **quand nous étions en Sicile** we'll go swimming as *ou* like we did when we were in Sicily ; **il se mit à pleurer** ~ **pour m'émouvoir** he started to cry as though to move me - **2.** [exprimant la manière] as ; **fais** ~ **il te plaira** do as you wish ; ~ **tu le dis** as you say ; **il était** ~ **fou** he was like a madman ; ~ **prévu/convenu** as planned/agreed ; ~ **bon vous semble** as you think best ; ~ **ci** ~ **ça** *fam* so-so - **3.** [tel que] like, such as ; **les arbres** ~ **le marronnier** trees such as *ou* like the chestnut - **4.** [en tant que] as ; ~ **professeur, il est nul** as a teacher he's hopeless - **5.** [ainsi que] : **les filles** ~ **les garçons iront jouer au foot** both girls and boys will play football ; **l'un** ~ **l'autre sont très gentils** the one is as kind as the other, they are equally kind - **6.** [introduisant une cause] as, since ; ~ **il pleuvait nous sommes rentrés** as it was raining we went back ◇ *adv* [marquant l'intensité] how ; ~ **tu as grandi!** how you've grown! ; ~ **c'est difficile!** it's so difficult! ; **regarde** ~ **il nage bien!** (just) look what a good swimmer he is!, (just) look how well he swims!

◆ **comme si** *loc conj* as if.

◆ **comme quoi** *loc adv* to the effect that ; ~ **quoi, on ne peut pas tout prévoir** which just goes to show you can't think of everything.

◆ **quelque chose comme** *loc adv* [à peu près] something like ; **cela fait quelque chose** ~ **10 000 francs** that comes to something like 10,000 francs.

commémoration [kɔmemɔrasjɔ̃] *nf* commemoration.

commémorer [3] [kɔmemɔre] *vt* to commemorate.

commencement [kɔmɑ̃smɑ̃] *nm* beginning, start ; **au** ~ at first, in the beginning.

commencer [16] [kɔmɑ̃se] ◇ *vt* [entreprendre] to begin, to start ; [être au début de] to begin ◇ *vi* to start, to begin ; ~ **à faire qqch** to begin *ou* start to do sthg, to begin *ou* start doing sthg ; ~ **par faire qqch** to begin *ou* start by doing sthg ; ~ **mal/bien** to start badly/ well.

comment [kɔmɑ̃] ⬦ *adv* how ; **comment? what?** ; ~ **ça va?** how are you? ; ~ **cela?** how come? ⬦ *interj* : ~ **donc!** of course!, sure thing! ; **et ~!** *fam* and how!, absolutely! ⬦ *nm inv* ▷ **pourquoi.**

commentaire [kɔmɑ̃tɛr] *nm* - **1.** [explication] commentary - **2.** [observation] comment ; **sans ~!** enough said!

commentateur, trice [kɔmɑ̃tatœr, tris] *nm, f* RADIO & TÉLÉ commentator ; ~ **sportif** sports commentator.

commenter [3] [kɔmɑ̃te] *vt* to comment on.

commérage [kɔmeraʒ] *nm péj* gossip (U).

commerçant, e [kɔmɛrsɑ̃, ɑ̃t] ⬦ *adj* [rue] shopping *(avant n)* ; [quartier] commercial ; [personne] business-minded ⬦ *nm, f* shopkeeper ; **petit ~** small trader.

commerce [kɔmɛrs] *nm* - **1.** [achat et vente] commerce, trade ; **dans le ~** in the shops *Br ou* stores *Am* ; ~ **de gros/détail** wholesale/ retail trade ; ~ **électronique** electronic commerce, e-commerce ; ~ **extérieur** foreign trade - **2.** [magasin] business ; **le petit ~** small shopkeepers *(pl)* - **3.** *loc* : **être d'un ~ agréable** *sout* to be easy to get on with.

commercial, e, aux [kɔmɛrsjal, o] ⬦ *adj* [entreprise, valeur] commercial ; [politique] trade *(avant n)* ⬦ *nm, f* marketing man *(f* woman).

commercialisation [kɔmɛrsjalizasjɔ̃] *nf* marketing.

commercialiser [3] [kɔmɛrsjalize] *vt* to market.

commère [kɔmɛr] *nf péj* gossip.

commets ▷ **commettre.**

commettre [84] [kɔmɛtr] *vt* to commit.
➡ **se commettre** *vp sout* : **se ~ avec** to become involved with.

commis, e [kɔmi, iz] *pp* ▷ **commettre.**
➡ **commis** *nm* assistant ; ~ **voyageur** commercial traveller *Br ou* traveler *Am.*

commisération [kɔmizerasjɔ̃] *nf sout* commiseration.

commissaire [kɔmisɛr] *nm* commissioner ; ~ **aux comptes** auditor ; ~ **de police** (police) superintendent *Br*, (police) captain *Am.*

commissaire-priseur [kɔmisɛrprizœr] *(pl* commissaires-priseurs) *nm* auctioneer.

commissariat [kɔmisarja] *nm* : ~ **de police** police station.

commission [kɔmisjɔ̃] *nf* - **1.** [délégation] commission, committee ; ~ **d'enquête** commission of inquiry ; **la Commission nationale de l'informatique et des libertés** *watchdog committee supervising the application of data protection legislation* ; ~ **parlementaire** parliamentary committee - **2.** [message] message - **3.** [rémunération] commission.
➡ **commissions** *nfpl* shopping (U) ; **faire les ~s** to do the shopping.

commissionnaire [kɔmisjɔnɛr] *nm* [intermédiaire] agent ; [d'un message] messenger ; [d'un objet] delivery boy *ou* man.

commissure [kɔmisyr] *nf* : **la ~ des lèvres** the corner of the mouth.

commode [kɔmɔd] ⬦ *nf* chest of drawers ⬦ *adj* - **1.** [pratique - système] convenient ; [- outil] handy - **2.** [aimable] : **pas ~** awkward - **3.** [facile] easy.

commodité [kɔmɔdite] *nf* convenience.
➡ **commodités** *nfpl* [conforts] comforts.

commotion [kɔmosjɔ̃] *nf* MÉD shock ; ~ **cérébrale** concussion.

commuer [7] [kɔmɥe] *vt* : ~ **qqch en** to commute sthg to.

commun, e [kɔmœ̃, yn] *adj* - **1.** [gén] common ; [décision, effort] joint ; [salle, jardin] shared ; ~ **à** common to ; **avoir qqch en ~** to have sthg in common ; **faire qqch en ~** to do sthg together - **2.** [courant] usual, common.
➡ **commun** *nm* : **le ~** the ordinary ; **hors du ~** out of the ordinary ; **le ~ des mortels** ordinary people.
➡ **commune** *nf* town.
➡ **Commune** *nf* HIST Paris Commune.
➡ **communs** *nmpl* outhouses.

communal, e, aux [kɔmynal, o] *adj* [école] local ; [bâtiments] council *(avant n).*

communautaire [kɔmynotɛr] *adj* community *(avant n).*

communauté [kɔmynote] *nf* - **1.** [groupe] community ; **vivre en ~** to live communally - **2.** [de sentiments, d'idées] identity - **3.** POL : **la Communauté européenne** the European Community ; **la Communauté d'États indépendants** the Commonwealth of Independent States.

commune ▷ **commun.**

communément [kɔmynemɑ̃] *adv* commonly.

communiant, e [kɔmynjɑ̃, ɑ̃t] *nm, f* communicant ; **premier ~** child taking first communion.

communicatif, ive [kɔmynikatif, iv] *adj* - **1.** [rire, éternuement] infectious - **2.** [personne] communicative.

communication [kɔmynikasjɔ̃] *nf* - **1.** [gén] communication ; ~ **en entreprise** communication ; ~ **de masse** mass media - **2.** TÉLÉCOM :

~ **(téléphonique)** (phone) call ; **être en ~ avec qqn** to be talking to sb ; **obtenir la ~** to get through ; **recevoir/prendre une ~** to receive/take a (phone) call ; **~ interurbaine** long-distance (phone) call.

communier [9] [kɔmynje] vi RELIG to take communion ; **~ (dans)** fig to be united (in).

communion [kɔmynjɔ̃] nf RELIG communion ; **être en ~ avec** fig & littéraire to commune with.

communiqué [kɔmynike] nm communiqué ; **~ de presse** press release.

communiquer [3] [kɔmynike] <> vt : **~ qqch à** [information, sentiment] to pass on ou communicate sthg to ; [chaleur] to transmit sthg to ; [maladie] to pass sthg on to <> vi : **~ avec** to communicate with.
♦ **se communiquer** vp [se propager] to spread.

communisme [kɔmynism] nm communism.

communiste [kɔmynist] nmf & adj communist.

commutateur [kɔmytatœr] nm switch.

commutation [kɔmytasjɔ̃] nf - **1.** JUR : **~ de peine** commutation of sentence - **2.** TECHNOL switching.

Comores [kɔmɔr] nfpl : **les ~** the Comoro Islands, the Comoros ; **aux ~** in the Comoro Islands.

comorien, enne [kɔmɔrjɛ̃, ɛn] adj Comoran, Comorian.
♦ **Comorien, enne** nm, f Comoran, Comorian.

compact, e [kɔ̃pakt] adj - **1.** [épais, dense] dense - **2.** [petit] compact.
♦ **compact** nm [disque laser] compact disc, CD.

compagne ⊳ compagnon.

compagnie [kɔ̃paɲi] nf - **1.** [gén & COMM] company ; **fausser ~ à qqn** to slip away from sb ; **tenir ~ à qqn** to keep sb company ; **et ~** and company ; iron and the rest ; **~ aérienne** airline (company) ; **~ d'assurances** insurance company ; **~ de navigation** shipping company ; **en ~ de** in the company of - **2.** [assemblée] gathering.

compagnon [kɔ̃paɲɔ̃], **compagne** [kɔ̃paɲ] nm, f companion.
♦ **compagnon** nm HIST journeyman.

comparable [kɔ̃parabl] adj comparable.

comparaison [kɔ̃parɛzɔ̃] nf [parallèle] comparison ; **en ~ de, par ~ avec** compared with, in ou by comparison with.

comparaître [91] [kɔ̃parɛtr] vi JUR : **~ (devant)** to appear (before).

comparatif, ive [kɔ̃paratif, iv] adj comparative.
♦ **comparatif** nm GRAM comparative.

comparativement [kɔ̃parativmɑ̃] adv comparatively.

comparé, e [kɔ̃pare] adj comparative ; [mérites] relative.

comparer [3] [kɔ̃pare] vt - **1.** [confronter] : **~ (avec)** to compare (with) - **2.** [assimiler] : **~ qqch à** to compare ou liken sthg to.

comparse [kɔ̃pars] nmf péj stooge.

compartiment [kɔ̃partimɑ̃] nm compartment.

compartimenter [3] [kɔ̃partimɑ̃te] vt [meuble] to partition ; fig [administration] to compartmentalize.

comparu, e [kɔ̃pary] pp ⊳ comparaître.

comparution [kɔ̃parysjɔ̃] nf JUR appearance.

compas [kɔ̃pa] nm - **1.** [de dessin] pair of compasses, compasses (pl) - **2.** NAVIG compass.

compassé, e [kɔ̃pase] adj sout staid, stuffy.

compassion [kɔ̃pasjɔ̃] nf sout compassion.

compatible [kɔ̃patibl] adj : **~ (avec)** compatible (with).

compatir [32] [kɔ̃patir] vi : **~ (à)** to sympathize (with).

compatissant, e [kɔ̃patisɑ̃, ɑ̃t] adj sympathetic.

compatriote [kɔ̃patrijɔt] nmf compatriot, fellow countryman (f countrywoman).

compensation [kɔ̃pɑ̃sasjɔ̃] nf - **1.** [dédommagement] compensation ; **en ~** in compensation - **2.** [équilibrage] balance.

compensé, e [kɔ̃pɑ̃se] adj built-up.

compenser [3] [kɔ̃pɑ̃se] <> vt to compensate ou make up for <> vi to compensate, to make up.

compétence [kɔ̃petɑ̃s] nf - **1.** [qualification] skill, ability - **2.** JUR competence ; **cela n'entre pas dans mes ~s** that's outside my scope.

compétent, e [kɔ̃petɑ̃, ɑ̃t] adj - **1.** [capable] capable, competent - **2.** ADMIN & JUR competent ; **les autorités ~es** the relevant authorities.

compétitif, ive [kɔ̃petitif, iv] adj competitive.

compétition [kɔ̃petisjɔ̃] nf competition ; **faire de la ~** to go in for competitive sport ; **~ automobile** motor race.

compétitivité [kɔ̃petitivite] nf competitiveness.

compil [kɔ̃pil] *nf fam* compilation album.
compilation [kɔ̃pilasjɔ̃] *nf* compilation.
complainte [kɔ̃plɛ̃t] *nf* lament.
complaire [110] [kɔ̃plɛr] *vi* : ~ à qqn *sout* to please sb.
➡ **se complaire** *vp* : se ~ dans qqch/à faire qqch to revel in sthg/in doing sthg.
complaisance [kɔ̃plɛzɑ̃s] *nf* - **1.** [obligeance] kindness - **2.** [indulgence] indulgence - **3.** [autosatisfaction] : avec ~ indulgently.
complaisant, e [kɔ̃plɛzɑ̃, ɑ̃t] *adj* - **1.** [aimable] obliging, kind - **2.** [indulgent] indulgent.
complément [kɔ̃plemɑ̃] *nm* - **1.** [gén & GRAM] complement ; ~ d'information additional *ou* further information ; ~ du nom possessive phrase ; ~ d'objet direct direct object ; ~ d'objet indirect indirect object - **2.** [reste] remainder.
complémentaire [kɔ̃plemɑ̃tɛr] *adj* - **1.** [supplémentaire] supplementary - **2.** [caractères, couleurs] complementary.
complet, ète [kɔ̃plɛ, ɛt] *adj* - **1.** [gén] complete ; c'est ~! *fam* that's all I/we need ; la famille au (grand) ~ the whole family - **2.** [plein] full.
➡ **complet(-veston)** *nm* suit.
complètement [kɔ̃plɛtmɑ̃] *adv* - **1.** [vraiment] absolutely, totally - **2.** [entièrement] completely.
compléter [18] [kɔ̃plete] *vt* [gén] to complete, to complement ; [somme d'argent] to make up.
➡ **se compléter** *vp* to complement one another.
complexe [kɔ̃plɛks] <> *nm* - **1.** PSYCHOL complex ; avoir des ~s to have hang-ups, to be hung up ; sans ~ *ou* ~s well-adjusted ; ~ d'infériorité/de supériorité inferiority/ superiority complex - **2.** [ensemble] complex ; ~ hospitalier/scolaire/sportif hospital/ school/sports complex ; ~ multisalle multiplex (cinema) <> *adj* complex, complicated.
complexé, e [kɔ̃plɛkse] *adj* hung up, mixed up.
complexifier [kɔ̃plɛksifje] *vt* to make (more) complex.
complexité [kɔ̃plɛksite] *nf* complexity.
complication [kɔ̃plikasjɔ̃] *nf* intricacy, complexity.
➡ **complications** *nfpl* complications.
complice [kɔ̃plis] <> *nmf* accomplice <> *adj* [sourire, regard, air] knowing.
complicité [kɔ̃plisite] *nf* complicity.
compliment [kɔ̃plimɑ̃] *nm* compliment.

complimenter [3] [kɔ̃plimɑ̃te] *vt* to compliment.
compliqué, e [kɔ̃plike] *adj* [problème] complex, complicated ; [personne] complicated.
compliquer [3] [kɔ̃plike] *vt* to complicate.
➡ **se compliquer** *vp* to get complicated.
complot [kɔ̃plo] *nm* plot.
comploter [3] [kɔ̃plɔte] *vt* & *vi litt* & *fig* to plot.
comportement [kɔ̃pɔrtəmɑ̃] *nm* behaviour *Br*, behavior *Am*.
comportemental, e, aux [kɔ̃pɔrtəmɑ̃tal, o] *adj* behavioural *Br*, behavioral *Am*.
comporter [3] [kɔ̃pɔrte] *vt* - **1.** [contenir] to include, to contain - **2.** [être composé de] to consist of, to be made up of.
➡ **se comporter** *vp* to behave.
composant, e [kɔ̃pozɑ̃, ɑ̃t] *adj* constituent, component.
➡ **composant** *nm* component.
➡ **composante** *nf* component.
composé, e [kɔ̃poze] *adj* compound.
➡ **composé** *nm* - **1.** [mélange] combination - **2.** CHIM & LING compound.
composer [3] [kɔ̃poze] <> *vt* - **1.** [constituer] to make up, to form ; être composé de to be made up of - **2.** [créer - roman, lettre, poème] to write ; [- musique] to compose, to write - **3.** [numéro de téléphone] to dial ; [code] to key in <> *vi* to compromise.
➡ **se composer** *vp* [être constitué] : se ~ de to be composed of, to be made up of.
composite [kɔ̃pozit] <> *nm* composite <> *adj* - **1.** [disparate - mobilier] assorted, of various types ; [- foule] heterogeneous - **2.** [matériau] composite.
compositeur, trice [kɔ̃pozitœr, tris] *nm, f* - **1.** MUS composer - **2.** TYPO typesetter.
composition [kɔ̃pozisjɔ̃] *nf* - **1.** [gén] composition ; [de roman] writing, composition - **2.** TYPO typesetting - **3.** SCOL test ; ~ française French composition - **4.** [caractère] : être de bonne ~ to be good-natured.
compost [kɔ̃pɔst] *nm* compost.
composter [3] [kɔ̃pɔste] *vt* [ticket, billet] to date-stamp.
compote [kɔ̃pɔt] *nf* compote ; ~ de pommes stewed apple, apple sauce ; j'ai les jambes en ~ *fam fig* my legs feel like jelly.
compotier [kɔ̃pɔtje] *nm* fruit bowl.
compréhensible [kɔ̃preɑ̃sibl] *adj* [texte, parole] comprehensible ; *fig* [réaction] understandable.

compréhensif, ive [kɔ̃preɑ̃sif, iv] *adj* understanding.

compréhension [kɔ̃preɑ̃sjɔ̃] *nf* - **1.** [de texte] comprehension, understanding - **2.** [indulgence] understanding.

comprenais, comprenions *etc* ▷ comprendre.

comprendre [79] [kɔ̃prɑ̃dr] <> *vt* - **1.** [gén] to understand ; **je comprends!** I see! ; **se faire ~** to make o.s. understood ; **mal ~** to misunderstand - **2.** [comporter] to comprise, to consist of - **3.** [inclure] to include <> *vi* to understand.

◆ **se comprendre** *vp* to understand one another ; **ça se comprend** that's understandable.

comprenne, comprennes *etc* ▷ comprendre.

compresse [kɔ̃prɛs] *nf* compress.

compresseur [kɔ̃presœr] ▷ rouleau.

compression [kɔ̃presjɔ̃] *nf* [de gaz] compression ; *fig* cutback, reduction.

comprimé, e [kɔ̃prime] *adj* compressed.

◆ **comprimé** *nm* tablet ; **~ effervescent** effervescent tablet.

comprimer [3] [kɔ̃prime] *vt* - **1.** [gaz, vapeur] to compress - **2.** [personnes] : **être comprimés dans** to be packed into.

compris, e [kɔ̃pri, iz] <> *pp* ▷ comprendre <> *adj* - **1.** [situé] lying, contained - **2.** [inclus] : **charges (non) ~es** (not) including bills, bills (not) included ; **tout ~** all inclusive, all in ; **y ~** including.

compromets ▷ compromettre.

compromettant, e [kɔ̃prɔmetɑ̃, ɑ̃t] *adj* compromising.

compromettre [84] [kɔ̃prɔmetr] *vt* to compromise.

◆ **se compromettre** *vp* : **se ~ (avec qqn/ dans qqch)** to compromise o.s. (with sb/in sthg).

compromis, e [kɔ̃prɔmi, iz] *pp* ▷ compromettre.

◆ **compromis** *nm* compromise.

compromission [kɔ̃prɔmisjɔ̃] *nf péj* base action.

comptabiliser [3] [kɔ̃tabilize] *vt* to enter in an account.

comptabilité [kɔ̃tabilite] *nf* [comptes] accounts *(pl)* ; [service] : **la ~** accounts, the accounts department.

comptable [kɔ̃tabl] <> *nmf* accountant <> *adj* accounting *(avant n)*.

comptant [kɔ̃tɑ̃] <> *adj inv* cash, in cash <> *adv* : **payer** *ou* **régler ~** to pay cash.

◆ **au comptant** *loc adv* : **payer au ~** to pay cash.

compte [kɔ̃t] *nm* - **1.** [action] count, counting *(U)* ; [total] number ; **faire le ~ (de)** countdown ; **~ à rebours** countdown ; **~ rond** round number - **2.** *BANQUE, COMM & COMPTABILITÉ* account ; **ouvrir un ~** to open an account ; **régler un ~** to settle an account ; **~ bancaire** *ou* **en banque** bank account ; **~ courant** current account, checking account *Am* ; **~ créditeur** account in credit ; **~ débiteur** overdrawn account ; **~ de dépôt** deposit account ; **~ d'épargne** savings account ; **~ d'exploitation** operating account ; **~ postal** post office account - **3.** *loc* : **avoir son ~** to have had enough ; **être/se mettre à son ~** to be/become self-employed ; **prendre qqch en ~, tenir ~ de qqch** to take sthg into account ; **régler son ~ à qqn** *fam fig* to sort sb out ; **rendre ~ de** to account for ; **se rendre ~ de qqch** to realize sthg ; **se rendre ~ que** to realize (that) ; **s'en tirer à bon ~** to get off lightly ; **tout ~ fait** all things considered.

◆ **comptes** *nmpl* accounts ; **devoir des ~s à** to be accountable to ; **faire ses ~s** to do one's accounts ; **faire des ~s d'apothicaire** to account for every last penny ; **régler ses ~s avec qqch** to come to terms with sthg ; **régler ses ~s avec qqn** to have it out with sb.

compte-chèques (*pl* **comptes-chèques**), **compte chèques** (*pl* **comptes chèques**) [kɔ̃tʃɛk] *nm* current account, checking account *Am*.

compte-gouttes [kɔ̃tgut] *nm inv* dropper ; **au ~** *fig* sparingly.

compter [3] [kɔ̃te] <> *vt* - **1.** [dénombrer] to count - **2.** [avoir l'intention de] : **~ faire qqch** to intend to do sthg, to plan to do sthg <> *vi* - **1.** [calculer] to count - **2.** [être important] to count, to matter ; **~ pour** to count for - **3.** : **~ sur** [se fier à] to rely *ou* count on - **4.** : **~ avec** [tenir compte de] to reckon with, to take account of - **5.** : **~ parmi** [faire partie de] to be included amongst, to rank amongst.

◆ **à compter de** *loc prép* as from, starting from.

◆ **sans compter** <> *loc prép* [excepté] not including <> *loc adv* : **se dépenser sans ~** *fig* to give unsparingly of o.s.

◆ **sans compter que** *loc conj* besides which.

compte rendu (*pl* **comptes rendus**), **compte-rendu** (*pl* **comptes-rendus**) [kɔ̃trɑ̃dy] *nm* report, account.

compte-tours [kɔ̃ttur] *nm inv* rev counter, tachometer.

compteur [kɔ̃tœr] *nm* meter ; **remettre les ~s à zéro fig** to go back to square one, to start all over again.

comptine [kɔ̃tin] *nf* nursery rhyme.

comptoir [kɔ̃twar] *nm* - **1.** [de bar] bar ; [de magasin] counter - **2.** HIST trading post - **3.** Helv [foire] trade fair.

compulser [3] [kɔ̃pylse] *vt* to consult.

comte [kɔ̃t] *nm* count.

comté [kɔ̃te] *nm* - **1.** [fromage] *type of cheese similar to Gruyère* - **2.** ADMIN [au Canada] county - **3.** HIST earldom.

comtesse [kɔ̃tɛs] *nf* countess.

con, conne [kɔ̃, kɔn] *tfam* ◇ *adj* bloody **Br** ou damned stupid ◇ *nm, f* stupid bastard (*f* bitch).

Conakry [kɔnakri] *n* Conakry.

concasser [3] [kɔ̃kase] *vt* to crush ; [poivre] to grind.

concave [kɔ̃kav] *adj* concave.

concéder [18] [kɔ̃sede] *vt* : **~ qqch à** [droit, terrain] to grant sthg to ; [point, victoire] to concede sthg to ; **~ que** to admit (that), to concede (that).

concentration [kɔ̃sɑ̃trasjɔ̃] *nf* concentration.

concentré, e [kɔ̃sɑ̃tre] *adj* - **1.** [gén] concentrated - **2.** [personne] : **elle était très ~e** she was concentrating hard - **3.** ⊏▷ **lait.**
➤ **concentré** *nm* concentrate ; **~ de tomates** CULIN tomato purée.

concentrer [3] [kɔ̃sɑ̃tre] *vt* to concentrate.
➤ **se concentrer** *vp* - **1.** [se rassembler] to be concentrated - **2.** [personne] to concentrate.

concentrique [kɔ̃sɑ̃trik] *adj* concentric.

concept [kɔ̃sɛpt] *nm* concept.

concepteur, trice [kɔ̃sɛptœr, tris] *nm, f* designer.

conception [kɔ̃sɛpsjɔ̃] *nf* - **1.** [gén] conception - **2.** [d'un produit, d'une campagne] design, designing *(U).*

concernant [kɔ̃sɛrnɑ̃] *prép* regarding, concerning.

concerner [3] [kɔ̃sɛrne] *vt* to concern ; **être/ se sentir concerné par qqch** to be/feel concerned by sthg ; **en ce qui me concerne** as far as I'm concerned.

concert [kɔ̃sɛr] *nm* - **1.** MUS concert - **2.** [entente] accord ; **de ~ avec qqn** together with sb.

concertation [kɔ̃sɛrtasjɔ̃] *nf* consultation.

concerter [3] [kɔ̃sɛrte] *vt* [organiser] to devise (jointly).
➤ **se concerter** *vp* to consult (each other).

concerto [kɔ̃sɛrto] *nm* concerto.

concession [kɔ̃sesjɔ̃] *nf* - **1.** [compromis & GRAM] concession ; **faire des ~s (à qqn)** to make concessions (to sb) - **2.** [autorisation] rights *(pl)*, concession.

concessionnaire [kɔ̃sesjɔnɛr] ◇ *nmf* - **1.** [automobile] (car) dealer - **2.** [qui possède une franchise] franchise holder ◇ *adj* concessionary.

concevable [kɔ̃səvabl] *adj* conceivable.

concevoir [52] [kɔ̃səvwar] *vt* - **1.** [enfant, projet] to conceive - **2.** [comprendre] to conceive of ; **je ne peux pas ~ comment/pourquoi** I cannot conceive how/why - **3.** *sout* [éprouver] to feel.
➤ **se concevoir** *vp* to be imagined.

concierge [kɔ̃sjɛrʒ] *nmf* caretaker, concierge.

concile [kɔ̃sil] *nm* council.

conciliabule [kɔ̃siljabyl] *nm* [discussion] consultation.

conciliant, e [kɔ̃siljɑ̃, ɑ̃t] *adj* conciliating.

conciliation [kɔ̃siljasjɔ̃] *nf* - **1.** [règlement d'un conflit] reconciliation, reconciling - **2.** [accord & JUR] conciliation.

concilier [9] [kɔ̃silje] *vt* - **1.** [mettre d'accord, allier] to reconcile ; **~ qqch et** ou **avec qqch** to reconcile sthg with sthg - **2.** [gagner à sa cause] : **~ qqn à** to win sb over to.
➤ **se concilier** *vp* : **se ~ qqn** to win sb over ; **se ~ qqch** to gain sthg.

concis, e [kɔ̃si, iz] *adj* [style, discours] concise ; [personne] terse.

concision [kɔ̃sizjɔ̃] *nf* conciseness, concision.

concitoyen, enne [kɔ̃sitwajɛ̃, ɛn] *nm, f* fellow citizen.

conclu, e [kɔ̃kly] *pp* ⊏▷ **conclure.**

concluant, e [kɔ̃klyɑ̃, ɑ̃t] *adj* [convaincant] conclusive.

conclure [96] [kɔ̃klyr] ◇ *vt* to conclude ; **~ de qqch que** to conclude from sthg that ; **en ~ que** to deduce (that) ◇ *vi* : **les experts ont conclu à la folie** the experts concluded he/she was mad ; **le tribunal a conclu au suicide** the court returned a verdict of suicide.

conclusion [kɔ̃klyzjɔ̃] *nf* - **1.** [gén] conclusion ; **en arriver à la ~ que** to come to the conclusion that - **2.** [partie finale] close.

concocter [3] [kɔ̃kɔkte] *vt* to concoct.

concombre [kɔ̃kɔ̃br] *nm* cucumber.

concomitant, e [kɔ̃kɔmitɑ̃, ɑ̃t] *adj* concomitant.

concordance [kɔ̃kɔrdɑ̃s] *nf* [conformité] agreement ; **~ des temps** GRAM sequence of tenses.

concorde [kɔ̃kɔrd] *nf* concord.

Concorde® [kɔ̃kɔrd] *nm* Concorde®.

concorder [3] [kɔ̃kɔrde] *vi* - **1.** [coïncider] to agree, to coincide - **2.** [être en accord] : ~ **(avec)** to be in accordance (with) - **3.** [avoir un même but] to coincide.

concourir [45] [kɔ̃kurir] *vi* - **1.** [contribuer] : ~ **à** to work towards *Br ou* toward *Am* - **2.** [participer à un concours] to compete.

concours [kɔ̃kur] *nm* - **1.** [examen] competitive examination ; ~ **de recrutement** competitive entry examination - **2.** [compétition] competition, contest ; **hors** ~ [dans une compétition] ineligible ; *fig* exceptional ; ~ **hippique** horse show - **3.** [collaboration] help ; **avec le** ~ **de qqn** with sb's help *ou* assistance - **4.** [coïncidence] : ~ **de circonstances** combination of circumstances.

concret, ète [kɔ̃krɛ, ɛt] *adj* concrete.

concrètement [kɔ̃krɛtmɑ̃] *adv* [en réalité] in real *ou* practical terms.

concrétiser [3] [kɔ̃kretize] *vt* [projet] to give shape to ; [rêve, espoir] to give solid form to.

➤ **se concrétiser** *vp* [projet] to take shape ; [rêve, espoir] to materialize.

conçu, e [kɔ̃sy] *pp* ⊳ **concevoir**.

concubin, e [kɔ̃kybɛ̃, in] *nm, f* partner, common-law husband (*f* wife).

concubinage [kɔ̃kybinaʒ] *nm* living together, cohabitation.

concupiscent, e [kɔ̃kypisɑ̃, ɑ̃t] *adj* concupiscent.

concurremment [kɔ̃kyramɑ̃] *adv* jointly.

concurrence [kɔ̃kyrɑ̃s] *nf* - **1.** [rivalité] rivalry - **2.** ÉCON competition ; ~ **déloyale** unfair competition ; **des prix défiant toute** ~ unbeatable prices - **3.** [montant] : **jusqu'à** ~ **de** to the amount of, not exceeding.

concurrent, e [kɔ̃kyrɑ̃, ɑ̃t] ⋄ *adj* rival, competing ⋄ *nm, f* competitor.

concurrentiel, elle [kɔ̃kyrɑ̃sjɛl] *adj* competitive.

condamnable [kɔ̃danabl] *adj* reprehensible.

condamnation [kɔ̃danasjɔ̃] *nf* - **1.** JUR sentence - **2.** [dénonciation] condemnation.

condamné, e [kɔ̃dane] *nm, f* convict, prisoner.

condamner [3] [kɔ̃dane] *vt* - **1.** JUR : ~ **qqn (à)** to sentence sb (to) ; ~ **qqn à une amende** to fine sb - **2.** *fig* [obliger] : ~ **qqn à qqch** to condemn sb to sthg - **3.** [malade] : **être condamné** to be terminally ill - **4.** [interdire] to forbid - **5.** [blâmer] to condemn - **6.** [fermer] to fill in, to block up.

condensateur [kɔ̃dɑ̃satœr] *nm* condenser.

condensation [kɔ̃dɑ̃sasjɔ̃] *nf* condensation.

condensé [kɔ̃dɑ̃se] ⋄ *nm* summary ⋄ *adj* ⊳ **lait**.

condenser [3] [kɔ̃dɑ̃se] *vt* to condense.

➤ **se condenser** *vp* to condense.

condescendant, e [kɔ̃desɑ̃dɑ̃, ɑ̃t] *adj* condescending.

condescendre [73] [kɔ̃desɑ̃dr] *vi sout* : ~ **à qqch/à faire qqch** to condescend to sthg/to do sthg.

condescendu [kɔ̃desɑ̃dy] *pp inv* ⊳ **condescendre**.

condiment [kɔ̃dimɑ̃] *nm* condiment.

condisciple [kɔ̃disipl] *nm* fellow student.

condition [kɔ̃disjɔ̃] *nf* - **1.** [gén] condition ; ~ **sine qua non** essential condition ; **remplir une** ~ to fulfil a condition ; **se mettre en** ~ [physiquement] to get into shape - **2.** [place sociale] station ; **la** ~ **des ouvriers** the workers' lot.

➤ **conditions** *nfpl* - **1.** [circonstances] conditions ; ~**s de vie** living conditions ; ~**s atmosphériques** atmospheric conditions - **2.** [de paiement] terms.

➤ **à condition de** *loc prép* providing *ou* provided (that).

➤ **à condition que** *loc conj* (+ *subjonctif*) providing *ou* provided (that).

➤ **sans conditions** ⋄ *loc adj* unconditional ⋄ *loc adv* unconditionally.

conditionné, e [kɔ̃disjɔne] *adj* - **1.** [emballé] : ~ **sous vide** vacuum-packed - **2.** ⊳ **air**.

conditionnel, elle [kɔ̃disjɔnɛl] *adj* conditional.

➤ **conditionnel** *nm* GRAM conditional.

conditionnement [kɔ̃disjɔnmɑ̃] *nm* - **1.** [action d'emballer] packaging, packing - **2.** [emballage] package - **3.** PSYCHOL & TECHNOL conditioning.

conditionner [3] [kɔ̃disjɔne] *vt* - **1.** [déterminer] to govern - **2.** PSYCHOL & TECHNOL to condition - **3.** [emballer] to pack.

condoléances [kɔ̃dɔleɑ̃s] *nfpl* condolences.

conducteur, trice [kɔ̃dyktœr, tris] ⋄ *adj* conductive ⋄ *nm, f* [de véhicule] driver.

➤ **conducteur** *nm* ÉLECTR conductor.

conduire [98] [kɔ̃dɥir] ⋄ *vt* - **1.** [voiture, personne] to drive - **2.** [transmettre] to conduct - **3.** *fig* [diriger] to manage - **4.** *fig* [à la ruine, au désespoir] : ~ **qqn à qqch** to drive sb to sthg ⋄ *vi* - **1.** AUTOM to drive - **2.** [mener] : ~ **à** to lead to.

➤ **se conduire** *vp* to behave.

conduisais, conduisions *etc* ⊳ **conduire**.

conduit, e [kɔ̃dɥi, it] *pp* ⊳ **conduire**.
➤ **conduit** *nm* - **1.** [tuyau] conduit, pipe - **2.** ANAT duct, canal.
➤ **conduite** *nf* - **1.** [pilotage d'un véhicule] driving ; **~e à droite/gauche** right-hand/left-hand drive ; **~e en état d'ébriété** drunken-driving - **2.** [direction] running - **3.** [comportement] behaviour *(U) Br*, behavior *(U) Am* - **4.** [canalisation] : **~e de gaz/d'eau** gas/water main, gas/water pipe.

cône [kon] *nm* GÉOM cone.

confection [kɔ̃fɛksjɔ̃] *nf* - **1.** [réalisation] making - **2.** [industrie] clothing industry.

confectionner [3] [kɔ̃fɛksjɔne] *vt* to make.

confédéral, e, aux [kɔ̃federal, o] *adj* confederal.

confédération [kɔ̃federasjɔ̃] *nf* - **1.** [d'états] confederacy - **2.** [d'associations] confederation.

conférence [kɔ̃ferɑ̃s] *nf* - **1.** [exposé] lecture - **2.** [réunion] conference ; **~ de presse** press conference ; **~ au sommet** summit conference.

conférencier, ère [kɔ̃ferɑ̃sje, ɛr] *nm, f* lecturer.

conférer [18] [kɔ̃fere] *vt* [accorder] : **~ qqch à qqn** to confer sthg on sb.

confesse [kɔ̃fɛs] *nf* : **aller à ~** to go to confession.

confesser [4] [kɔ̃fese] *vt* - **1.** [avouer] to confess - **2.** RELIG : **~ qqn** to hear sb's confession.
➤ **se confesser** *vp* to go to confession.

confession [kɔ̃fesjɔ̃] *nf* confession.

confessionnal, aux [kɔ̃fesjɔnal, o] *nm* confessional.

confessionnel, elle [kɔ̃fesjɔnɛl] *adj* RELIG denominational.

confetti [kɔ̃feti] *nm* confetti *(U)*.

confiance [kɔ̃fjɑ̃s] *nf* confidence ; **avoir ~ en** to have confidence *ou* faith in ; **avoir ~ en soi** to be self-confident ; **en toute ~** with complete confidence ; **de ~** trustworthy ; **faire ~ à qqn/qqch** to trust sb/sthg.

confiant, e [kɔ̃fjɑ̃, ɑ̃t] *adj* - **1.** [sans méfiance] trusting - **2.** [assuré] : **~ (en qqch)** confident (of sthg).

confidence [kɔ̃fidɑ̃s] *nf* confidence ; **en ~** in confidence ; **faire des ~s à qqn** to confide in sb ; **être dans la ~** to be in the know.

confident, e [kɔ̃fidɑ̃, ɑ̃t] *nm, f* confidant (*f* confidante).

confidentiel, elle [kɔ̃fidɑ̃sjɛl] *adj* confidential.

confier [9] [kɔ̃fje] *vt* - **1.** [donner] : **~ qqn/qqch à**
qqn to entrust sb/sthg to sb - **2.** [dire] : **~ qqch à qqn** to confide sthg to sb.
➤ **se confier** *vp* : **se ~ à qqn** to confide in sb.

configuration [kɔ̃figyrasjɔ̃] *nf* TECHNOL configuration ; [conception] layout.

confiné, e [kɔ̃fine] *adj* - **1.** [air] stale ; [atmosphère] enclosed - **2.** [enfermé] shut away.

confins [kɔ̃fɛ̃] *nmpl* : **aux ~ de** on the borders of.

confirmation [kɔ̃firmasjɔ̃] *nf* confirmation.

confirmer [3] [kɔ̃firme] *vt* [certifier] to confirm ; **~ qqn dans qqch** to confirm sb in sthg ; **il n'a pas été confirmé dans ses fonctions** he was not retained in the post.
➤ **se confirmer** *vp* to be confirmed.

confiscation [kɔ̃fiskasjɔ̃] *nf* confiscation.

confiserie [kɔ̃fizri] *nf* - **1.** [magasin] sweet shop *Br*, candy store *Am*, confectioner's - **2.** [sucreries] sweets *(pl) Br*, candy *(U) Am*, confectionery *(U)*.

confiseur, euse [kɔ̃fizœr, øz] *nm, f* confectioner.

confisquer [3] [kɔ̃fiske] *vt* to confiscate.

confit, e [kɔ̃fi, it] *adj* ⊳ **fruit**.
➤ **confit** *nm* conserve.

confiture [kɔ̃fityr] *nf* jam.

conflagration [kɔ̃flagrasjɔ̃] *nf* cataclysm.

conflictuel, elle [kɔ̃fliktɥɛl] *adj* conflicting.

conflit [kɔ̃fli] *nm* - **1.** [situation tendue] clash, conflict - **2.** [entre États] conflict.

confluent [kɔ̃flyɑ̃] *nm* confluence ; **au ~ de** at the confluence of.

confondre [75] [kɔ̃fɔ̃dr] *vt* - **1.** [ne pas distinguer] to confuse - **2.** [accusé] to confound - **3.** [stupéfier] to astound.
➤ **se confondre** *vp* - **1.** [se mêler] to merge - **2.** *fig* : **se ~ en excuses** to apologize profusely ; **il s'est confondu en remerciements** he thanked me/him etc profusely.

confondu, e [kɔ̃fɔ̃dy] *pp* ⊳ **confondre**.

conformation [kɔ̃fɔrmasjɔ̃] *nf* structure.

conforme [kɔ̃fɔrm] *adj* : **~ à** in accordance with.

conformé, e [kɔ̃fɔrme] *adj* : **bien ~** well-formed ; **mal ~** ill-formed.

conformément [kɔ̃fɔrmemɑ̃] ➤ **conformément à** *loc prép* in accordance with.

conformer [3] [kɔ̃fɔrme] *vt* : **~ qqch à** to shape sthg according to.
➤ **se conformer** *vp* : **se ~ à** [s'adapter] to conform to ; [obéir] to comply with.

conformiste [kɔ̃fɔrmist] ◇ *nmf* conformist ◇ *adj* - **1.** [traditionaliste] conformist - **2.** [Anglican] Anglican.

conformité [kɔ̃fɔrmite] nf **- 1.** [ressemblance] : **~ (à)** conformity (to) **- 2.** [accord] : **être en ~ avec** to be in accordance with.

confort [kɔ̃fɔr] nm comfort ; **tout ~** with all mod cons Br, with all modern conveniences Am.

confortable [kɔ̃fɔrtabl] adj comfortable.

confortablement [kɔ̃fɔrtabləmã] adv comfortably ; **~ payé** well-paid.

conforter [3] [kɔ̃fɔrte] vt : **~ qqn (dans qqch)** to strengthen sb (in sthg).

confrère, consœur [kɔ̃frɛr, kɔ̃sœr] nm, f colleague.

confrérie [kɔ̃freri] nf brotherhood.

confrontation [kɔ̃frɔ̃tasjɔ̃] nf **- 1.** [face à face] confrontation **- 2.** [comparaison] comparison.

confronter [3] [kɔ̃frɔ̃te] vt **- 1.** [mettre face à face] to confront ; fig : **être confronté à** to be confronted ou faced with **- 2.** [comparer] to compare.

confus, e [kɔ̃fy, yz] adj **- 1.** [indistinct, embrouillé] confused **- 2.** [gêné] embarrassed ; **je suis vraiment ~** I'm really very sorry.

confusément [kɔ̃fyzemã] adj **- 1.** [pêle-mêle] in confusion **- 2.** [indistinctement] indistinctly **- 3.** [vaguement] vaguely.

confusion [kɔ̃fyzjɔ̃] nf **- 1.** [gén] confusion **- 2.** [embarras] confusion, embarrassment.

congé [kɔ̃ʒe] nm **- 1.** [arrêt de travail] leave (U) ; **~ (de) maladie** sick leave ; **~ de maternité** maternity leave **- 2.** [vacances] holiday Br, vacation Am ; **en ~** on holiday ; **~ annuel** annual leave ; **~s payés** paid holiday (U) ou holidays ou leave (U) Br, paid vacation Am ; **une journée/semaine de ~** a day/week off **- 3.** [renvoi] notice ; **donner son ~ à qqn** to give sb his/her notice ; **prendre ~ (de qqn)** sout to take one's leave (of sb).

congédier [9] [kɔ̃ʒedje] vt to dismiss.

congé-formation [kɔ̃ʒefɔrmasjɔ̃] (pl **congés-formation**) nm training leave.

congélateur [kɔ̃ʒelatœr] nm freezer.

congeler [25] [kɔ̃ʒle] vt to freeze.

congénital, e, aux [kɔ̃ʒenital, o] adj congenital.

congère [kɔ̃ʒɛr] nf snowdrift.

congestion [kɔ̃ʒɛstjɔ̃] nf congestion ; **~ pulmonaire** pulmonary congestion.

conglomérat [kɔ̃glɔmera] nm conglomerate.

Congo [kɔ̃go] nm [pays] : **le ~** the Congo ; **au ~** in the Congo ; **la République démocratique du ~** the Democratic Republic of Congo ; [fleuve] : **le ~** the Congo.

congolais, e [kɔ̃gɔlɛ, ɛz] adj Congolese.

➡ **congolais** nm CULIN coconut cake.

➡ **Congolais, e** nm, f Congolese person.

congratuler [3] [kɔ̃gratyle] vt to congratulate.

congre [kɔ̃gr] nm conger eel.

congrégation [kɔ̃gregasjɔ̃] nf congregation.

congrès [kɔ̃grɛ] nm **- 1.** [colloque] assembly **- 2.** HIST [réunion] congress.

➡ **Congrès** nm [parlement américain] : **le Congrès** Congress.

congressiste [kɔ̃gresist] nmf congress participant.

congrue [kɔ̃gry] ▷ portion.

conifère [kɔnifɛr] nm conifer.

conique [kɔnik] adj conical.

conjecture [kɔ̃ʒɛktyr] nf conjecture ; **se perdre en ~s** to lose o.s. in conjecture.

conjecturer [3] [kɔ̃ʒɛktyre] vt & vi to conjecture.

conjoint, e [kɔ̃ʒwɛ̃, ɛ̃t] ◇ adj joint ◇ nm, f spouse.

conjointement [kɔ̃ʒwɛ̃tmã] adv : **~ (avec qqn)** jointly (with sb).

conjonctif, ive [kɔ̃ʒɔ̃ktif, iv] adj **- 1.** ▷ tissu **- 2.** GRAM conjunctive.

conjonction [kɔ̃ʒɔ̃ksjɔ̃] nf conjunction ; **~ de coordination/de subordination** GRAM coordinating/subordinating conjunction.

conjonctivite [kɔ̃ʒɔ̃ktivit] nf conjunctivitis (U).

conjoncture [kɔ̃ʒɔ̃ktyr] nf ÉCON situation, circumstances (pl).

conjoncturel, elle [kɔ̃ʒɔ̃ktyrɛl] adj [situation, tendance] economic.

conjugaison [kɔ̃ʒygɛzɔ̃] nf **- 1.** [union] uniting **- 2.** GRAM conjugation.

conjugal, e, aux [kɔ̃ʒygal, o] adj conjugal.

conjuguer [3] [kɔ̃ʒyge] vt **- 1.** [unir] to combine **- 2.** GRAM to conjugate.

conjuration [kɔ̃ʒyrasjɔ̃] nf **- 1.** [conspiration] conspiracy **- 2.** [exorcisme] exorcism.

conjurer [3] [kɔ̃ʒyre] vt **- 1.** [supplier] to beg ; **je vous en conjure !** sout I beg (of) you! **- 2.** [exorciser] to exorcize **- 3.** [écarter] to avert.

➡ **se conjurer** vp to plot, to conspire.

connaissais, connaissions etc ▷ connaître.

connaissance [kɔnɛsɑ̃s] nf **- 1.** [savoir] knowledge (U) ; **à ma ~** to (the best of) my knowledge ; **en ~ de cause** with full knowledge of the facts ; **prendre ~ de qqch** to study sthg, to examine sthg **- 2.** [personne] acquaintance ; **une vieille ~** an old acquaintance ; **faire ~ (avec qqn)** to become acquainted (with sb) ; **faire la ~ de** to meet - **3.** [conscience] : **perdre/reprendre ~** to lose/regain consciousness ; **sans ~** unconscious.

connaisseur, euse [kɔnɛsœr, øz] ◇ *adj* expert *(avant n)* ◇ *nm, f* connoisseur.

connaître [91] [kɔnɛtr] *vt* - **1.** [gén] to know ; **~ qqn de nom/de vue** to know sb by name/sight - **2.** [éprouver] to experience.

➡ **se connaître** *vp* - **1.** : **s'y ~ en** [être expert] to know about ; **il s'y connaît** he knows what he's talking about/doing - **2.** [soi-même] to know o.s. - **3.** [se rencontrer] to meet (each other) ; **il se connaissent** they've met each other.

connecter [4] [kɔnɛkte] *vt* to connect.

➡ **se connecter** *vpr* to log on, to log in ; **se ~ sur Internet** to log onto the Internet.

connecteur [kɔnɛktœr] *nm* : **~ à broche** INFORM pin connector.

connerie [kɔnri] *nf tfam* stupidity *(U)* ; **faire/dire des ~s** to do/to say something bloody stupid *Br*, to do/to say something damned stupid.

connexe [kɔnɛks] *adj* related.

connexion [kɔnɛksjɔ̃] *nf* connection.

connivence [kɔnivɑ̃s] *nf* connivance ; **être de ~ (avec qqn)** to be in league (with sb).

connotation [kɔnɔtasjɔ̃] *nf* connotation.

connu, e [kɔny] ◇ *pp* ▷ **connaître** ◇ *adj* - **1.** [célèbre] well-known, famous - **2.** [su] : **~ de qqn** known to sb.

conquérant, e [kɔ̃kerɑ̃, ɑ̃t] ◇ *adj* conquering ◇ *nm, f* conqueror.

conquérir [39] [kɔ̃kerir] *vt* to conquer.

conquête [kɔ̃kɛt] *nf* conquest ; **faire la ~ de qqch** to conquer sthg ; **faire la ~ de qqn** to win sb over.

conquiers, conquiert *etc* ▷ **conquérir**.

conquis, e [kɔ̃ki, iz] *pp* ▷ **conquérir**.

consacré, e [kɔ̃sakre] *adj* - **1.** [habituel] established, accepted - **2.** RELIG consecrated.

consacrer [3] [kɔ̃sakre] *vt* - **1.** RELIG to consecrate - **2.** [employer] : **~ qqch à** to devote sthg to.

➡ **se consacrer** *vp* : **se ~ à** to dedicate o.s. to, to devote o.s. to.

consanguin, e [kɔ̃sɑ̃gɛ̃, in] *adj* : **frère ~** half-brother ; **sœur ~e** half-sister ; *voir aussi* **mariage**.

consciemment [kɔ̃sjamɑ̃] *adv* knowingly, consciously.

conscience [kɔ̃sjɑ̃s] *nf* - **1.** [connaissance & PSYCHOL] consciousness ; **avoir ~ de qqch** to be aware of sthg - **2.** [morale] conscience ; **agir selon sa ~** to follow one's conscience ; **avoir**

qqch sur la ~ to have sthg on one's conscience ; **bonne/mauvaise ~** clear/guilty conscience ; **~ professionnelle** professional integrity, conscientiousness.

consciencieusement [kɔ̃sjɑ̃sjøzmɑ̃] *adv* conscientiously.

consciencieux, euse [kɔ̃sjɑ̃sjø, øz] *adj* conscientious.

conscient, e [kɔ̃sjɑ̃, ɑ̃t] *adj* conscious ; **être ~ de qqch** [connaître] to be conscious of sthg.

conscription [kɔ̃skripsjɔ̃] *nf* conscription, draft *Am*.

conscrit [kɔ̃skri] *nm* conscript, recruit, draftee *Am*.

consécration [kɔ̃sekrasjɔ̃] *nf* - **1.** [reconnaissance] recognition ; [de droit, coutume] establishment - **2.** RELIG consecration.

consécutif, ive [kɔ̃sekytif, iv] *adj* - **1.** [successif & GRAM] consecutive - **2.** [résultant] : **~ à** resulting from.

conseil [kɔ̃sɛj] *nm* - **1.** [avis] piece of advice, advice *(U)* ; **donner un ~ OU des ~s (à qqn)** to give (sb) advice ; **suivre le ~ de qqn** to take somebody's advice - **2.** [personne] : **~ (en)** consultant (in) - **3.** [assemblée] council ; **~ d'administration** board of directors ; **~ de classe** staff meeting ; **le Conseil constitutionnel** *French government body ensuring that laws, elections and referenda are constitutional* ; **~ de discipline** disciplinary committee ; **le Conseil d'État** the (French) Council of State ; **le Conseil des ministres** ≃ the Cabinet ; **~ municipal** town council *Br*, city council *Am* ; **le Conseil supérieur de la magistrature** *French state body that appoints members of the judiciary*.

CONSEIL

LE CONSEIL D'ÉTAT
The French Council of State has 200 members. It acts both as the highest court to which the legal affairs of the state can be referred, and as a consultative body to which bills and rulings are submitted by the government prior to examination by the 'Conseil des ministres'.

LE CONSEIL DES MINISTRES
The President himself presides over the 'Conseil des ministres', which traditionally meets every Wednesday morning ; strictly speaking, when ministers assemble in the sole presence of the Prime Minister, this is known as 'le Conseil du cabinet'.

---

conseiller[1] [4] [kɔ̃seje] ◇ *vt* - **1.** [recommander] to advise ; **~ qqch à qqn** to recommend sthg to sb - **2.** [guider] to advise, to counsel ◇ *vi* [donner un conseil] : ~ **à qqn de faire qqch** to advise sb to do sthg.

conseiller², ère [kɔ̃seje, ɛr] *nm, f* **- 1.** [guide] counsellor *Br*, counselor *Am* ; ~ **matrimonial** marriage counsellor *Br* ou counselor *Am* **- 2.** [d'un conseil] councillor *Br*, councilor *Am* ; ~ **municipal** town councillor *Br*, city councilman (*f* councilwoman) *Am*.

consensuel, elle [kɔ̃sɑ̃sɥɛl] *adj* : **politique ~le** consensus politics.

consensus [kɔ̃sɛ̃sys] *nm* consensus.

consentement [kɔ̃sɑ̃tmɑ̃] *nm* consent.

consentir [37] [kɔ̃sɑ̃tir] <> *vt* **- 1.** [accorder] : ~ **qqch à qqn** to grant sb sthg **- 2.** [accepter] : ~ **que** (*+ subjonctif*) : **je consens qu'il vienne** I consent to his coming <> *vi* : ~ **à qqch** to consent to sthg.

conséquence [kɔ̃sekɑ̃s] *nf* consequence, result ; **avoir des ~s (sur qqch)** to have consequences (for sthg) ; **sans ~** [sans importance] of no importance ; **ne pas tirer à ~** to be of no consequence.

conséquent, e [kɔ̃sekɑ̃, ɑ̃t] *adj* **- 1.** [cohérent] consistent **- 2.** [important] sizeable, considerable.

➡ **par conséquent** *loc adv* therefore, consequently.

conservateur, trice [kɔ̃sɛrvatœr, tris] <> *adj* conservative <> *nm, f* **- 1.** POLIT conservative **- 2.** [administrateur] curator.

➡ **conservateur** *nm* preservative.

conservation [kɔ̃sɛrvasjɔ̃] *nf* **- 1.** [état, entretien] preservation **- 2.** [d'aliment] preserving.

conservatoire [kɔ̃sɛrvatwar] *nm* academy ; ~ **de musique** music college ; **le Conservatoire national supérieur d'art dramatique, le Conservatoire** *national drama school in Paris*.

conserve [kɔ̃sɛrv] *nf* tinned *Br* ou canned food ; **en ~** [en boîte] tinned, canned ; [en bocal] preserved, bottled.

➡ **de conserve** *loc adv* together.

conserver [3] [kɔ̃sɛrve] *vt* **- 1.** [garder, entretenir] to keep **- 2.** [entreposer - en boîte] to can ; [- en bocal] to bottle ; '~ **au frais**' 'keep in a cool place' **- 3.** [personne] : **être bien conservé** to be well-preserved.

➡ **se conserver** *vp* to keep.

considérable [kɔ̃siderabl] *adj* considerable.

considération [kɔ̃siderasjɔ̃] *nf* **- 1.** [réflexion, motivation] consideration ; **en ~ de qqch** in consideration of sthg ; **prendre qqch en ~** to take sthg into consideration **- 2.** [estime] respect.

considérer [18] [kɔ̃sidere] *vt* to consider ; **tout bien considéré** all things considered.

consigne [kɔ̃siɲ] *nf* **- 1.** [ordre] orders (*pl*)

- 2. (*gén pl*) [instruction] instructions (*pl*) **- 3.** [entrepôt de bagages] left-luggage office *Br*, checkroom *Am* ; ~ **automatique** lockers (*pl*), left-luggage lockers (*pl*) *Br* **- 4.** [somme d'argent] deposit.

consigné, e [kɔ̃siɲe] *adj* returnable.

consigner [3] [kɔ̃siɲe] *vt* **- 1.** [bagages] to leave in the left-luggage office *Br* ou checkroom *Am* ou baggage room *Am* **- 2.** *sout* [relater] to record, to set down **- 3.** MIL to confine to barracks **- 4.** *vieilli* & SCOL : ~ **qqn** to give sb detention.

consistance [kɔ̃sistɑ̃s] *nf* [solidité] consistency ; *fig* substance ; **sans ~** [fade] colourless *Br*, colorless *Am*.

consistant, e [kɔ̃sistɑ̃, ɑ̃t] *adj* **- 1.** [épais] thick **- 2.** [nourrissant] substantial **- 3.** [fondé] sound.

consister [3] [kɔ̃siste] *vi* : ~ **en** to consist of ; ~ **à faire qqch** to consist in doing sthg.

consœur ▷ confrère.

consolation [kɔ̃sɔlasjɔ̃] *nf* consolation.

console [kɔ̃sɔl] *nf* **- 1.** [table] console (table) **- 2.** INFORM : ~ **de jeux** games console ; ~ **de visualisation** VDU, visual display unit.

consoler [3] [kɔ̃sɔle] *vt* **- 1.** [réconforter] : ~ **qqn (de qqch)** to comfort sb (in sthg) **- 2.** [apaiser] to soothe.

➡ **se consoler** *vp* : **se ~ de qqch** to get over sthg.

consolider [3] [kɔ̃sɔlide] *vt litt* & *fig* to strengthen.

consommateur, trice [kɔ̃sɔmatœr, tris] *nm, f* [acheteur] consumer ; [d'un bar] customer.

consommation [kɔ̃sɔmasjɔ̃] *nf* **- 1.** [utilisation] consumption ; **faire une grande** ou **grosse ~ de** to use (up) a lot of **- 2.** [boisson] drink.

consommé, e [kɔ̃sɔme] *adj sout* consummate.

➡ **consommé** *nm* consommé.

consommer [3] [kɔ̃sɔme] <> *vt* **- 1.** [utiliser] to use (up) **- 2.** [manger] to eat ; **'à ~ avant le 5 juin 2004'** 'best before ou use by 5/6/04' **- 3.** [énergie] to consume, to use <> *vi* **- 1.** [boire] to drink **- 2.** [voiture] : **cette voiture consomme beaucoup** this car uses a lot of fuel.

consonance [kɔ̃sɔnɑ̃s] *nf* consonance ; **un nom aux ~s harmonieuses** a beautiful name.

consonne [kɔ̃sɔn] *nf* consonant.

consort [kɔ̃sɔr] ▷ prince.

➡ **consorts** *nmpl* : **et ~s** *péj* and his/their sort, and the like.

consortium [kɔ̃sɔrsjɔm] *nm* consortium.

conspirateur, trice [kɔ̃spiratœr, tris] *nm, f* conspirator.

conspiration [kɔ̃spirasjɔ̃] *nf* conspiracy.

conspirer [3] [kɔ̃spire] <> *vt* [comploter] to plot <> *vi* to conspire.

conspuer [7] [kɔ̃spɥe] *vt* to boo.

constamment [kɔ̃stamɑ̃] *adv* constantly.

constance [kɔ̃stɑ̃s] *nf* - **1.** [persévérance] perseverance ; **avoir de la ~** to be indefatigable - **2.** [permanence, fidélité] constancy.

constant, e [kɔ̃stɑ̃, ɑ̃t] *adj* constant.

constat [kɔ̃sta] *nm* - **1.** [procès-verbal] report ; **~ à l'amiable** *joint insurance statement made by drivers after an accident* ; **~ d'huissier** *affidavit made before a bailiff* - **2.** [constatation] established fact ; **faire le ~ de qqch** to note sthg ; **~ d'échec** acknowledgement of failure.

constatation [kɔ̃statasjɔ̃] *nf* - **1.** [révélation] observation - **2.** [fait retenu] finding.

constater [3] [kɔ̃state] *vt* - **1.** [se rendre compte de] to see, to note - **2.** [consigner - fait, infraction] to record ; [- décès, authenticité] to certify.

constellation [kɔ̃stelasjɔ̃] *nf* ASTRON constellation.

consternation [kɔ̃sternasjɔ̃] *nf* dismay.

consterner [3] [kɔ̃sterne] *vt* to dismay.

constipation [kɔ̃stipasjɔ̃] *nf* constipation.

constipé, e [kɔ̃stipe] *adj* - **1.** MÉD constipated - **2.** *fam fig* [manière, air] ill at ease.

constituant, e [kɔ̃stitɥɑ̃, ɑ̃t] *adj* constituent ; *voir aussi* **assemblée.**

constitué, e [kɔ̃stitɥe] *adj* - **1.** [personne] : **normalement/bien ~** of normal/sound constitution - **2.** [composé] : **~ de** consisting of, composed of - **3.** [établi par la loi] constituted.

constituer [7] [kɔ̃stitɥe] *vt* - **1.** [élaborer] to set up - **2.** [composer] to make up - **3.** [représenter] to constitute - **4.** [établir] to agree, to settle (on).

➙ **se constituer** *vp* : **se ~ de** to be made up of, to consist of ; **se ~ en** to form ; **se ~ prisonnier** to give o.s. up ; **se ~ partie civile** JUR to sue privately for damages.

constitution [kɔ̃stitɥsjɔ̃] *nf* - **1.** [création] setting up - **2.** [de pays, de corps] constitution - **3.** [composition] composition - **4.** [établissement] establishment.

constitutionnel, elle [kɔ̃stitɥsjɔnel] *adj* constitutional.

constructeur [kɔ̃stryktœr] *nm* - **1.** [fabricant] manufacturer ; [de navire] shipbuilder - **2.** [bâtisseur] builder.

constructif, ive [kɔ̃stryktif, iv] *adj* - **1.** [créateur] creative - **2.** [positif] constructive.

construction [kɔ̃stryksjɔ̃] *nf* - **1.** IND building, construction ; **~ navale** shipbuilding - **2.** [édifice] structure, building - **3.** GRAM & *fig* construction.

construire [98] [kɔ̃strɥir] *vt* - **1.** [bâtir, fabriquer] to build - **2.** [roman] to structure - **3.** [théorie, phrase] to construct.

construisais, construisions *etc* ▷ **construire.**

construit, e [kɔ̃strɥi, it] *pp* ▷ **construire.**

consul [kɔ̃syl] *nm* consul ; **~ honoraire** honorary consul.

consulat [kɔ̃syla] *nm* - **1.** [charge] consulship - **2.** [résidence] consulate.

consultatif, ive [kɔ̃syltatif, iv] *adj* consultative, advisory.

consultation [kɔ̃syltasjɔ̃] *nf* - **1.** [d'ouvrage] : **de ~ aisée** easy to use - **2.** MÉD & POLIT consultation - **3.** [d'expert] (professional) advice.

consulter [3] [kɔ̃sylte] <> *vt* - **1.** [compulser] to consult - **2.** [interroger, demander conseil à] to consult, to ask - **3.** [spécialiste] to consult, to see <> *vi* [médecin] to take *ou* hold surgery ; [avocat] to be available for consultation.

➙ **se consulter** *vp* to confer.

consumer [3] [kɔ̃syme] *vt* - **1.** *sout* [brûler] to burn, to destroy - **2.** *fig* & *littéraire* [épuiser] to consume, to eat up.

➙ **se consumer** *vp* to waste away ; **se ~ de qqch** *littéraire* to be eaten up *ou* consumed with sthg.

consumérisme [kɔ̃symerism] *nm* consumerism.

contact [kɔ̃takt] *nm* - **1.** [gén] contact ; **le ~ du marbre est froid** marble is cold to the touch ; **mettre qqn et qqn en ~, mettre qqn en ~ avec qqn** to put sb in touch with sb ; **prendre ~ avec** to make contact with ; **rester en ~ (avec)** to stay in touch (with) ; **au ~ de** on contact with ; **au ~ des jeunes** through mixing *ou* associating with young people - **2.** AUTOM ignition ; **mettre/couper le ~** to switch on/off the ignition.

contacter [3] [kɔ̃takte] *vt* to contact.

contagieux, euse [kɔ̃taʒjø, øz] <> *adj* MÉD contagious ; *fig* infectious <> *nm, f* contagious patient.

contagion [kɔ̃taʒjɔ̃] *nf* MÉD contagion ; *fig* infectiousness.

container ▷ **conteneur.**

contaminer [3] [kɔ̃tamine] *vt* [infecter] to contaminate ; *fig* to contaminate, to infect.

conte [kɔ̃t] *nm* story ; **~ de fées** fairy tale.

contemplation [kɔ̃tɑ̃plasjɔ̃] *nf* contemplation ; **rester en ~ devant** to gaze in contemplation at.

contempler [3] [kɔ̃tɑ̃ple] *vt* to contemplate.

contemporain, e [kɔ̃tɑ̃pɔrɛ̃, ɛn] ◇ adj : ~ **(de)** contemporary (with) ◇ nm, f contemporary.

contenance [kɔ̃tnɑ̃s] nf - **1.** [capacité volumique] capacity - **2.** [attitude] : **se donner une ~** to give an impression of composure ; **perdre ~** to lose one's composure.

conteneur [kɔ̃tənœr], **container** [kɔ̃tɛnɛr] nm (freight) container.

contenir [40] [kɔ̃tnir] vt to contain, to hold, to take.

➙ **se contenir** vp to contain o.s., to control o.s.

content, e [kɔ̃tɑ̃, ɑ̃t] adj - **1.** [joyeux] happy - **2.** [satisfait] : ~ **(de qqn/qqch)** happy (with sb/sthg), content (with sb/sthg) ; ~ **de faire qqch** happy to do sthg.

➙ **content** nm : **avoir son ~ de** to have one's fill of.

contentement [kɔ̃tɑ̃tmɑ̃] nm satisfaction.

contenter [3] [kɔ̃tɑ̃te] vt to satisfy.

➙ **se contenter** vp : **se ~ de qqch/de faire qqch** to content o.s. with sthg/with doing sthg ; **se ~ de peu** to be content with little.

contentieux [kɔ̃tɑ̃sjø] nm [litige] dispute ; [service] legal department.

contenu, e [kɔ̃tny] pp ▷ contenir.

➙ **contenu** nm - **1.** [de récipient] contents (pl) - **2.** [de texte, discours] content.

conter [3] [kɔ̃te] vt to tell.

contestable [kɔ̃tɛstabl] adj questionable.

contestataire [kɔ̃tɛstatɛr] ◇ nmf anti-establishment figure ◇ adj anti-establishment.

contestation [kɔ̃tɛstasjɔ̃] nf - **1.** [protestation] protest, dispute - **2.** POLIT : **la ~** anti-establishment activity.

conteste [kɔ̃tɛst] ➙ **sans conteste** loc adv unquestionably.

contester [3] [kɔ̃tɛste] ◇ vt to dispute, to contest ◇ vi to protest.

conteur, euse [kɔ̃tœr, øz] nm, f storyteller.

contexte [kɔ̃tɛkst] nm context.

contiens, contient etc ▷ contenir.

contigu, uë [kɔ̃tigy] adj : ~ **(à)** adjacent (to).

continent [kɔ̃tinɑ̃] nm continent.

continental, e, aux [kɔ̃tinɑ̃tal, o] adj continental.

contingence [kɔ̃tɛ̃ʒɑ̃s] nf (gén pl) contingency.

contingent [kɔ̃tɛ̃ʒɑ̃] nm - **1.** MIL national service conscripts (pl), draft Am - **2.** COMM quota.

contingenter [3] [kɔ̃tɛ̃ʒɑ̃te] vt to put a quota on.

continu, e [kɔ̃tiny] adj continuous.

continuation [kɔ̃tinɥasjɔ̃] nf continuation.

continuel, elle [kɔ̃tinɥɛl] adj - **1.** [continu] continuous - **2.** [répété] continual.

continuellement [kɔ̃tinɥɛlmɑ̃] adv continually.

continuer [7] [kɔ̃tinɥe] ◇ vt - **1.** [poursuivre] to carry on with, to continue (with) - **2.** [prolonger] to continue ◇ vi to continue, to go on ; ~ **à** ou **de faire qqch** to continue to do ou doing sthg.

➙ **se continuer** vp to continue, to carry on.

continuité [kɔ̃tinɥite] nf continuity.

contondant, e [kɔ̃tɔ̃dɑ̃, ɑ̃t] adj blunt.

contorsionner [3] [kɔ̃tɔrsjɔne] ➙ **se contorsionner** vp to contort (o.s.), to writhe.

contour [kɔ̃tur] nm - **1.** [limite] outline - **2.** (gén pl) [courbe] bend.

contourner [3] [kɔ̃turne] vt litt & fig to bypass, to get round.

contraceptif, ive [kɔ̃trasɛptif, iv] adj contraceptive.

➙ **contraceptif** nm contraceptive.

contraception [kɔ̃trasɛpsjɔ̃] nf contraception.

contracter [3] [kɔ̃trakte] vt - **1.** [muscle] to contract, to tense ; [visage] to contort - **2.** [maladie] to contract, to catch - **3.** [engagement] to contract ; [assurance] to take out - **4.** [moralement] to make tense ou nervous - **5.** [habitude] to pick up, to acquire.

contraction [kɔ̃traksjɔ̃] nf contraction ; [état de muscle] tenseness ; **avoir des ~s** to have contractions.

contractuel, elle [kɔ̃traktɥɛl] ◇ adj contractual ◇ nm, f traffic warden Br, traffic policeman (f policewoman) Am.

contradiction [kɔ̃tradiksjɔ̃] nf contradiction.

contradictoire [kɔ̃tradiktwar] adj contradictory ; **débat ~** open debate.

contraignais, contraignions etc ▷ contraindre.

contraignant, e [kɔ̃trɛɲɑ̃, ɑ̃t] adj restricting.

contraindre [80] [kɔ̃trɛ̃dr] vt : ~ **qqn à faire qqch** to compel ou force sb to do sthg ; **être contraint de faire qqch** to be compelled ou forced to do sthg.

➙ **se contraindre** vp - **1.** sout [se maîtriser] to contain o.s., to control o.s. - **2.** [s'obliger] : **se ~ à faire qqch** to make o.s. do sthg, to force o.s. to do sthg.

contraint, e [kɔ̃trɛ̃, ɛ̃t] ◇ pp ▷ contraindre ◇ adj forced ; ~ **et forcé** under duress.

contrainte *nf* constraint ; **sans ~e** freely.

contraire [kɔ̃trɛr] ◇ *nm* : **le ~** the opposite ; **je n'ai jamais dit le ~** I have never denied it ◇ *adj* opposite ; **~ à** [non conforme à] contrary to ; [nuisible à] harmful to, damaging to.

◆ **au contraire** *loc adv* on the contrary.

◆ **au contraire de** *loc prép* unlike.

contrairement [kɔ̃trɛrmɑ̃] ◆ **contrairement à** *loc prép* contrary to.

contrariant, e [kɔ̃trarjɑ̃, ɑ̃t] *adj* - **1.** [personne] contrary, perverse - **2.** [événement] annoying, tiresome.

contrarier [9] [kɔ̃trarje] *vt* - **1.** [contrecarrer] to thwart, to frustrate - **2.** [irriter] to annoy.

◆ **se contrarier** *vp* to contrast.

contrariété [kɔ̃trarjete] *nf* annoyance.

contraste [kɔ̃trast] *nm* contrast ; **faire ~ avec** to contrast with.

contraster [3] [kɔ̃traste] *vt* & *vi* to contrast.

contrat [kɔ̃tra] *nm* contract, agreement ; **remplir son ~** *fig* to keep *ou* fulfil one's promise ; **~ d'apprentissage** apprenticeship contract ; **~ collectif** collective agreement ; **~ à durée déterminée/indéterminée** fixed-term/permanent contract ; **Contrat emploi-solidarité** *government-sponsored contract for the unemployed involving professional training* ; **~ reconductible** renewable agreement.

contravention [kɔ̃travɑ̃sjɔ̃] *nf* [amende] fine ; **~ pour stationnement interdit** parking ticket ; **dresser une ~ à qqn** to fine sb.

contre [kɔ̃tr] ◇ *prép* - **1.** [juxtaposition, opposition] against - **2.** [proportion, comparaison] : **élu à 15 voix ~ 9** elected by 15 votes to 9 ; **parier à 10 ~ 1** to bet 10 to 1 - **3.** [échange] (in exchange) for ◇ *adv* - **1.** [juxtaposition] : **prends la rampe et appuie-toi ~** take hold of the rail and lean against it - **2.** [opposition] : **vous êtes pour ou ~?** are you for or against? ◇ *nm* ▷ **pour.**

◆ **par contre** *loc adv* on the other hand.

contre-attaque [kɔ̃tratak] (*pl* **contre-attaques**) *nf* counterattack.

contrebalancer [16] [kɔ̃trəbalɑ̃se] *vt* to counterbalance, to offset.

◆ **se contrebalancer** *vp* : **se ~ de** *fam* not to give a damn about.

contrebande [kɔ̃trəbɑ̃d] *nf* [activité] smuggling ; [marchandises] contraband ; **passer qqch en ~** to smuggle sthg.

contrebandier, ère [kɔ̃trəbɑ̃dje, ɛr] *nm, f* smuggler.

contrebas [kɔ̃trəba] ◆ **en contrebas** *loc adv* (down) below.

contrebasse [kɔ̃trəbas] *nf* - **1.** [instrument] (double) bass - **2.** [musicien] (double) bass player.

contrecarrer [3] [kɔ̃trəkare] *vt* to thwart, to frustrate.

contrecœur [kɔ̃trəkœr] ◆ **à contrecœur** *loc adv* grudgingly.

contrecoup [kɔ̃trəku] *nm* consequence.

contre-courant [kɔ̃trəkurɑ̃] ◆ **à contre-courant** *loc adv* against the current.

contredire [103] [kɔ̃trədir] *vt* to contradict.

◆ **se contredire** *vp* - **1.** (emploi réciproque) to contradict (each other) - **2.** (emploi réfléchi) to contradict o.s.

contredit, e [kɔ̃trədi, it] *pp* ▷ **contredire.**

contrée [kɔ̃tre] *nf* [pays] land ; [région] region.

contre-écrou [kɔ̃trekru] (*pl* **contre-écrous**) *nm* lock-nut.

contre-espionnage [kɔ̃trɛspjɔnaʒ] *nm* counterespionage.

contre-exemple [kɔ̃trɛgzɑ̃pl] (*pl* **contre-exemples**) *nm* example to the contrary.

contre-expertise [kɔ̃trɛkspɛrtiz] (*pl* **contre-expertises**) *nf* second (expert) opinion.

contrefaçon [kɔ̃trəfasɔ̃] *nf* [activité] counterfeiting ; [produit] forgery.

contrefaire [109] [kɔ̃trəfɛr] *vt* - **1.** [signature, monnaie] to counterfeit, to forge - **2.** [voix] to disguise.

contrefait, e [kɔ̃trəfɛ, ɛt] *adj* - **1.** [frauduleux] forged - **2.** *sout* [difforme] deformed.

contreficher [3] [kɔ̃trəfiʃe] ◆ **se contreficher** *vp* : **se ~ de** *fam* not to give a damn about.

contre-filet [kɔ̃trəfilɛ] (*pl* **contre-filets**) *nm* sirloin.

contrefort [kɔ̃trəfɔr] *nm* - **1.** [pilier] buttress - **2.** [de chaussure] back.

◆ **contreforts** *nmpl* foothills.

contre-indication [kɔ̃trɛ̃dikasjɔ̃] (*pl* **contre-indications**) *nf* contraindication.

contre-interrogatoire [kɔ̃trɛ̃terɔgatwar] (*pl* **contre-interrogatoires**) *nm* cross-examination.

contre-jour [kɔ̃trəʒur] ◆ **à contre-jour** *loc adv* against the light.

contremaître, esse [kɔ̃trəmɛtr, ɛs] *nm, f* foreman (*f* forewoman).

contremarque [kɔ̃trəmark] *nf* [pour sortir d'un spectacle] pass-out ticket.

contre-offensive [kɔ̃trɔfɑ̃siv] (*pl* **contre-offensives**) *nf* counteroffensive.

contre-OPA [kɔ̃trɔpea] *nf inv* counterbid.

contre-ordre = **contrordre.**

contrepartie [kɔ̃trəparti] *nf* - **1.** [compensation] compensation - **2.** [contraire] opposing view.
➤ **en contrepartie** *loc adv* in return.

contre-performance [kɔ̃trəpɛrfɔrmɑ̃s] (*pl* contre-performances) *nf* disappointing performance.

contrepèterie [kɔ̃trəpɛtri] *nf* spoonerism.

contre-pied [kɔ̃trəpje] *nm* : **prendre le ~ de** to do the opposite of.

contreplaqué, contre-plaqué [kɔ̃trəplake] *nm* plywood.

contrepoids [kɔ̃trəpwa] *nm litt* & *fig* counterbalance, counterweight.

contrepoint [kɔ̃trəpwɛ̃] *nm* counterpoint.

contrepoison [kɔ̃trəpwazɔ̃] *nm* antidote.

contre-pouvoir [kɔ̃trəpuvwar] (*pl* contre-pouvoirs) *nm* counterbalance.

contre-publicité [kɔ̃trəpyblisite] (*pl* contre-publicités) *nf* - **1.** [mauvaise publicité] adverse *ou* bad publicity (*U*) - **2.** [publicité offensive] negative advertising (*U*).

contrer [3] [kɔ̃tre] *vt* - **1.** [s'opposer à] to counter - **2.** CARTES to double.

contresens [kɔ̃trəsɑ̃s] *nm* - **1.** [erreur - de traduction] mistranslation ; [- d'interprétation] misinterpretation - **2.** [absurdité] nonsense (*U*).
➤ **à contresens** *loc adv litt* & *fig* the wrong way.

contresigner [3] [kɔ̃trəsiɲe] *vt* to countersign.

contretemps [kɔ̃trətɑ̃] *nm* hitch, mishap.
➤ **à contretemps** *loc adv* MUS out of time ; *fig* at the wrong moment.

contrevenant, e [kɔ̃trəvnɑ̃, ɑ̃t] *nm, f* offender.

contrevenir [40] [kɔ̃trəvnir] *vi* : **~ à** to contravene, to infringe.

contrevenu [kɔ̃trəvny] *pp inv* ➤ contrevenir.

contribuable [kɔ̃tribɥabl] *nmf* taxpayer.

contribuer [7] [kɔ̃tribɥe] *vi* : **~ à** to contribute to *ou* towards.

contribution [kɔ̃tribysjɔ̃] *nf* : **~ (à)** contribution (to) ; **mettre qqn à ~** to call on sb's services.
➤ **contributions** *nfpl* taxes ; **~s directes/indirectes** direct/indirect taxation.

contrit, e [kɔ̃tri, it] *adj* contrite.

contrôle [kɔ̃trol] *nm* - **1.** [vérification - de déclaration] check, checking (*U*) ; [- de documents, billets] inspection ; **~ d'identité** identity check ; **~ de qualité** quality control ; **~ radar** [- AUTOM] radar speed-trap ; **~ de routine** routine inspection - **2.** [maîtrise, commande] control ; **perdre le ~ de qqch** to lose control of sthg ; **~ des**

naissances birth control ; **~ des prix** price control - **3.** [salle] control room - **4.** SCOL test ; **~ continu** UNIV continuous assessment - **5.** [direction] running, supervision.

contrôler [3] [kɔ̃trole] *vt* - **1.** [vérifier - documents, billets] to inspect ; [- déclaration] to check ; [- connaissances] to test - **2.** [maîtriser, diriger] to control - **3.** TECHNOL to monitor, to control - **4.** [superviser] to supervise.
➤ **se contrôler** *vp* to control o.s.

contrôleur, euse [kɔ̃trolœr, øz] *nm, f* [de train] ticket inspector ; [d'autobus] (bus) conductor (*f* conductress) ; **~ aérien** air traffic controller.

contrordre, contre-ordre (*pl* contre-ordres) [kɔ̃trɔrdr] *nm* countermand ; **sauf ~** unless otherwise instructed.

controverse [kɔ̃trɔvɛrs] *nf* controversy.

controversé, e [kɔ̃trɔvɛrse] *adj* [personne, décision] controversial.

contumace [kɔ̃tymas] *nf* JUR : **condamné par ~** sentenced in absentia.

contusion [kɔ̃tyzjɔ̃] *nf* bruise, contusion.

conurbation [kɔnyrbasjɔ̃] *nf* conurbation.

convaincant, e [kɔ̃vɛ̃kɑ̃, ɑ̃t] *adj* convincing.

convaincre [114] [kɔ̃vɛ̃kr] *vt* - **1.** [persuader] **~ qqn (de qqch)** to convince sb (of sthg) ; **~ qqn de faire qqch** to persuade sb (to do sthg) - **2.** JUR : **~ qqn de** to find sb guilty of, to convict sb of.

convaincu, e [kɔ̃vɛ̃ky] ◇ *pp* ➤ convaincre ◇ *adj* [partisan] committed ; **d'un ton ~, d'un air ~** with conviction.

convainquais, convainquions *etc* ➤ convaincre.

convainquant [kɔ̃vɛ̃kɑ̃] *ppr* ➤ convaincre.

convalescence [kɔ̃valesɑ̃s] *nf* convalescence ; **être en ~** to be convalescing *ou* recovering.

convalescent, e [kɔ̃valesɑ̃, ɑ̃t] *adj* & *nm, f* convalescent.

convenable [kɔ̃vnabl] *adj* - **1.** [manières, comportement] polite ; [tenue, personne] decent, respectable - **2.** [approprié] suitable - **3.** [acceptable] adequate, acceptable.

convenablement [kɔ̃vnabləmɑ̃] *adv* - **1.** [s'habiller, se tenir] properly - **2.** [être payé] decently - **3.** [travailler] adequately.

convenance [kɔ̃vnɑ̃s] *nf* : **à ma/votre ~** to my/your convenience.
➤ **convenances** *nfpl* proprieties.

convenir [40] [kɔ̃vnir] *vi* - **1.** [décider] : **~ de qqch/de faire qqch** to agree on sthg/to do sthg - **2.** [plaire] : **~ à qqn** to suit sb, to be convenient for sb - **3.** [être approprié] : ~ **à** OU **pour** to be suitable for ; **il convient de ... ** it is advisable to ... - **4.** sout [admettre] : ~ **de qqch** to admit to sthg ; ~ **que** to admit (that) ; **j'en conviens** sout I admit it.

convention [kɔ̃vɑ̃sjɔ̃] nf - **1.** [règle, assemblée] convention - **2.** [accord] agreement ; ~ **collective** collective agreement.
◆ **conventions** nfpl : **les ~s** convention (sg).
◆ **de convention** loc adj conventional.

conventionné, e [kɔ̃vɑ̃sjɔnel] adj subsidized, ≃ National Health (avant n) Br.

conventionnel, elle [kɔ̃vɑ̃sjɔnel] adj conventional.

convenu, e [kɔ̃vny] ◇ pp ▷ convenir ◇ adj - **1.** [décidé] : **comme ~** as agreed - **2.** péj [stéréotypé] conventional.

convergent, e [kɔ̃vɛrʒɑ̃, ɑ̃t] adj convergent.

converger [17] [kɔ̃vɛrʒe] vi : ~ **(vers)** to converge (on).

conversation [kɔ̃vɛrsasjɔ̃] nf conversation ; **détourner la ~** to change the subject ; **être en grande ~ avec** to be deep in conversation with.

converser [3] [kɔ̃vɛrse] vi sout : ~ **(avec)** to converse (with).

conversion [kɔ̃vɛrsjɔ̃] nf - **1.** [gén] : ~ **(à/en)** conversion (to/into) - **2.** SKI kick turn.

converti, e [kɔ̃vɛrti] nm, f : **prêcher un ~** fig to preach to the converted.

convertible [kɔ̃vɛrtibl] ◇ nm [canapé-lit] sofa bed ◇ adj convertible.

convertir [32] [kɔ̃vɛrtir] vt : ~ **qqn (à)** to convert sb (to) ; ~ **qqch (en)** to convert sthg (into).
◆ **se convertir** vp : **se ~ (à)** to be converted (to).

convexe [kɔ̃vɛks] adj convex.

conviction [kɔ̃viksjɔ̃] nf conviction ; **avoir la ~ que** to be convinced (that).

conviendrai, conviendrons etc ▷ convenir.

convier [9] [kɔ̃vje] vt : ~ **qqn à** to invite sb to.

convive [kɔ̃viv] nmf guest (at a meal).

convivial, e, aux [kɔ̃vivjal, o] adj - **1.** [réunion] convivial - **2.** INFORM user-friendly.

convocation [kɔ̃vɔkasjɔ̃] nf [avis écrit] summons (sg), notification to attend.

convoi [kɔ̃vwa] nm - **1.** [de véhicules] convoy ; ~ **exceptionnel** wide load - **2.** [train] train.

convoiter [3] [kɔ̃vwate] vt to covet.

convoitise [kɔ̃vwatiz] nf covetousness.

convoler [3] [kɔ̃vɔle] ▷ noces.

convoquer [3] [kɔ̃vɔke] vt - **1.** [assemblée] to

convene - **2.** [pour un entretien] to invite - **3.** [subalterne, témoin] to summon - **4.** [à un examen] : ~ **qqn** to ask sb to attend.

convoyer [13] [kɔ̃vwaje] vt to escort.

convoyeur, euse [kɔ̃vwajœr, øz] ◇ adj escort (avant n) ◇ nm, f escort ; ~ **de fonds** security guard.

convulser [3] [kɔ̃vylse] vt to convulse.
◆ **se convulser** vp to convulse.

convulsif, ive [kɔ̃vylsif, iv] adj convulsive.

convulsion [kɔ̃vylsjɔ̃] nf convulsion.

cool [kul] adj inv fam [décontracté] laid-back, cool.

coopérant [kɔɔperɑ̃] nm - **1.** MIL person engaged in voluntary work abroad as an alternative to military service - **2.** ÉCON foreign expert working in developing country.

coopératif, ive [kɔɔperatif, iv] adj cooperative.
◆ **coopérative** nf [groupement] cooperative ; **coopérative de consommation** consumers' cooperative.

coopération [kɔɔperasjɔ̃] nf - **1.** [collaboration] cooperation ; **en ~ avec qqn** in collaboration with sb - **2.** [aide] : **la ~** ≃ overseas development.

coopérer [18] [kɔɔpere] vi : ~ **(à)** to cooperate (in).

cooptation [kɔɔptasjɔ̃] nf co-opting.

coordinateur, trice [kɔɔrdinatœr, tris] ◇ adj coordinating ◇ nm, f coordinator.

coordination [kɔɔrdinasjɔ̃] nf coordination ; voir aussi **conjonction**.

coordonnée [kɔɔrdɔne] nf - **1.** LING coordinate clause - **2.** MATHS coordinate.
◆ **coordonnées** nfpl - **1.** GÉOGR coordinates - **2.** [adresse] address and phone number, details.

coordonner [3] [kɔɔrdɔne] vt to coordinate.

copain, ine [kɔpɛ̃, in] ◇ adj friendly, matey ; **être très ~s** to be great pals ◇ nm, f [ami] friend, mate ; [petit ami] boyfriend (f girlfriend).

copeau, x [kɔpo] nm [de bois] (wood) shaving.

Copenhague [kɔpenag] n Copenhagen.

copie [kɔpi] nf - **1.** [double, reproduction] copy ; ~ **(certifiée) conforme** certified copy - **2.** [SCOL - de devoir] fair copy ; [- d'examen] paper, script.

copier [9] [kɔpje] ◇ vt [gén & INFORM] to copy ◇ vi : ~ **sur qqn** to copy from sb.

copieur, euse [kɔpjœr, øz] nm, f [étudiant] copier.
◆ **copieur** nm [photocopieur] copier, photocopier.

copieusement [kɔpjøzmɑ̃] *adv* copiously.

copieux, euse [kɔpjø, øz] *adj* copious.

copilote [kɔpilɔt] *nmf* copilot.

copine ⊳ copain.

coprocesseur [kɔprɔsesœr] *nm* : ~ **mathématique** INFORM maths *Br ou* math *Am* coprocessor.

coproducteur, trice [kɔprɔdyktœr, tris] *nm, f* [pour spectacle] coproducer.

coproduction [kɔprɔdyksjɔ̃] *nf* coproduction ; **en** ~ coproduced.

copropriétaire [kɔprɔprijeter] *nmf* coowner, joint owner.

copropriété [kɔprɔprijete] *nf* coownership, joint ownership.

copuler [3] [kɔpyle] *vi* to copulate.

copyright [kɔpirajt] *nm* copyright.

coq [kɔk] *nm* cock, cockerel ; ~ **de bruyère** grouse ; **le ~ gaulois** the French cockerel ; **~ au vin** *chicken cooked with red wine, bacon, mushrooms and shallots* ; **fier comme un ~** *fig* as proud as a peacock ; **être comme un ~ en pâte** *fig* to be in clover ; **sauter** *ou* **passer du ~ à l'âne** to jump from one subject to another.

LE COQ GAULOIS

The cockerel is the symbol of France. Its cry, 'cocorico!', is sometimes used humorously to express national pride : 'trois médailles d'or pour la France - cocorico!'.

coque [kɔk] *nf* - **1.** [de noix] shell - **2.** [de navire] hull.

coquelet [kɔklɛ] *nm* cockerel.

coquelicot [kɔkliko] *nm* poppy.

coqueluche [kɔklyʃ] *nf* whooping cough ; **être la ~ de** *fig* to be the idol *ou* darling of.

coquet, ette [kɔkɛ, ɛt] *adj* - **1.** [vêtements] smart, stylish ; [ville, jeune fille] pretty - **2.** *(avant n) hum* [important] : **la ~te somme de 100 livres** the tidy sum of £100.
➤ **coquette** *nf* flirt.

coquetier [kɔktje] *nm* eggcup.

coquetterie [kɔkɛtri] *nf* - **1.** [désir de plaire] coquettishness - **2.** [élégance] smartness, stylishness.

coquillage [kɔkijaʒ] *nm* - **1.** [mollusque] shellfish - **2.** [coquille] shell.

coquille [kɔkij] *nf* - **1.** [de mollusque, noix, œuf] shell ; ~ **de noix** [embarcation] cockleshell ; **~ Saint-Jacques** scallop ; **rentrer dans sa ~** *fig* to go back into one's shell - **2.** TYPO misprint.

coquillettes [kɔkijɛt] *nfpl* pasta shells.

coquin, e [kɔkɛ̃, in] ⋄ *adj* [sous-vêtement] sexy, naughty ; [regard, histoire] saucy ⋄ *nm, f* rascal.

cor [kɔr] *nm* - **1.** [instrument] horn ; ~ **de chasse** hunting horn - **2.** [au pied] corn.
➤ **à cor et à cri** *loc adv* : **réclamer qqch à ~ et à cri** to clamour *Br ou* clamor *Am* for sthg.

corail, aux [kɔraj, o] *nm* - **1.** [gén] coral - **2.** RAIL : **train ~** ≃ express train.
➤ **corail** *adj inv* coral (pink).

Coran [kɔrɑ̃] *nm* : **le ~** the Koran.

coranique [kɔranik] *adj* Koranic.

corbeau, x [kɔrbo] *nm* - **1.** [oiseau] crow - **2.** [délateur] writer of poison-pen letters.

corbeille [kɔrbɛj] *nf* - **1.** [panier] basket ; ~ **à papier** waste paper basket - **2.** THÉÂTRE (dress) circle - **3.** [de Bourse] stockbrokers' enclosure *(at Paris Stock Exchange)*.

corbillard [kɔrbijar] *nm* hearse.

cordage [kɔrdaʒ] *nm* - **1.** [de bateau] rigging *(U)* - **2.** [de raquette] strings *(pl)*.

corde [kɔrd] *nf* - **1.** [filin] rope ; ~ **à linge** washing *ou* clothes line ; ~ **à sauter** skipping rope - **2.** [d'instrument, arc] string ; **avoir plus d'une ~ à son arc** *fig* to have more than one string to one's bow - **3.** ANAT : **~s vocales** vocal cords - **4.** HIPPISME rails *(pl)* ; ATHLÉTISME inside (lane) - **5.** *loc* : **usé jusqu'à la ~** [vêtement] threadbare ; [histoire] well-worn, hackneyed ; **faire vibrer la ~ sensible** to strike the right chord.
➤ **cordes** *nfpl* - **1.** MUS strings - **2.** BOXE : **les ~s** the ropes - **3.** *loc* : **être dans les ~s de qqn** to be (in) sb's line ; **il tombe** *ou* **pleut des ~s** it's raining cats and dogs.

cordeau [kɔrdo] *nm* [de jardinier] line ; **tracé au ~** *fig* [route] dead straight.

cordée [kɔrde] *nf* ALPINISME roped party *(of mountaineers)*.

cordelette [kɔrdəlɛt] *nf* string.

cordial, e, aux [kɔrdjal, o] *adj* warm, cordial.
➤ **cordial, aux** *nm vieilli* tonic, pick-me-up.

cordialement [kɔrdjalmɑ̃] *adv* [saluer] warmly, cordially ; [en fin de lettre] Kind regards.

cordialité [kɔrdjalite] *nf* warmth.

cordon [kɔrdɔ̃] *nm* string, cord ; ~ **ombilical** umbilical cord ; ~ **de police** police cordon.

cordon-bleu [kɔrdɔ̃blø] *(pl* **cordons-bleus)** *nm* cordon bleu cook.

cordonnerie [kɔrdɔnri] *nf* - **1.** [magasin] shoe repairer's, cobbler's - **2.** [activité, commerce] shoe repairing.

cordonnier, ère [kɔrdɔnje, ɛr] *nm, f* shoe repairer, cobbler.

Cordoue [kɔrduĮ *n* Cordoba.

Corée [kɔre] *nf* Korea ; **la ~ du Nord/du Sud** North/South Korea.

coréen, enne [kɔreɛ̃, ɛn] *adj* Korean.
➤ **Coréen, enne** *nm, f* Korean.

coreligionnaire [kɔreliʒjɔnɛr] *nmf* fellow Jew/Christian *etc.*

coriace [kɔrjas] *adj litt* & *fig* tough.

coriandre [kɔrjɑ̃dr] *nf* coriander.

cormoran [kɔrmɔrɑ̃] *nm* cormorant.

corne [kɔrn] *nf* - **1.** [gén] horn ; [de cerf] antler ; **~ d'abondance** *fig* horn of plenty ; **~ de brume** foghorn - **2.** [callosité] hard skin *(U)*, callus.

cornée [kɔrne] *nf* cornea.

corneille [kɔrnɛj] *nf* crow.

cornélien, enne [kɔrneljɛ̃, ɛn] *adj involving the conflict between love and duty.*

cornemuse [kɔrnəmyz] *nf* bagpipes *(pl).*

corner¹ [3] [kɔrne] <> *vi* [sirène] to blare (out) <> *vt* [page] to turn down the corner of.

corner² [kɔrner] *nm* FOOTBALL corner (kick).

cornet [kɔrne] *nm* - **1.** [d'aliment] cornet, cone - **2.** [de jeu] (dice) shaker.

corniaud, corniot [kɔrnjo] *nm* - **1.** [chien] mongrel - **2.** *fam* [imbécile] twit.

corniche [kɔrniʃ] *nf* - **1.** [route] cliff road - **2.** [moulure] cornice.

cornichon [kɔrniʃɔ̃] *nm* - **1.** [condiment] gherkin - **2.** *fam* [imbécile] twit.

corniot = **corniaud**.

Cornouailles [kɔrnwaj] *nf* : **la ~** Cornwall.

corollaire [kɔrɔlɛr] *nm* corollary.

corolle [kɔrɔl] *nf* corolla.

coron [kɔrɔ̃] *nm* [village] mining village.

coronaire [kɔrɔnɛr] ⊏> **artère**.

corporation [kɔrpɔrasjɔ̃] *nf* corporate body.

corporel, elle [kɔrpɔrɛl] *adj* - **1.** [physique - besoin] bodily ; [- châtiment] corporal - **2.** JUR tangible.

corps [kɔr] *nm* - **1.** [gén] body ; **être au ~ à ~** to fight hand-to-hand ; **le ~ du délit** JUR corpus delicti ; **~ étranger** foreign body ; **~ gras** fat - **2.** [groupe] : **~ d'armée** (army) corps ; **~ diplomatique** diplomatic corps ; **le ~ électoral** the electorate ; **~ enseignant** [profession] teaching profession ; [d'école] teaching staff ; **~ expéditionnaire** task force ; **le ~ législatif** the legislative body ; **le ~ médical** the medical profession - **3.** *loc* : **à mon ~ défendant** against my will ; **faire ~ avec** to form (an integral) part of ; **se dévouer ~ et âme à** to commit o.s. body and soul to ; **se jeter** *ou* **se lancer à ~ perdu dans qqch** to throw o.s. (headlong) into sthg ; **prendre ~** to take shape ; **sombrer ~ et biens** to go down with all hands.

corpulent, e [kɔrpylɑ̃, ɑ̃t] *adj* corpulent, stout.

corpus [kɔrpys] *nm* corpus.

corpuscule [kɔrpyskyl] *nm* corpuscle.

correct, e [kɔrɛkt] *adj* - **1.** [exact] correct, right - **2.** [honnête] correct, proper - **3.** [acceptable] decent ; [travail] fair.

correctement [kɔrɛktəmɑ̃] *adv* - **1.** [sans faute] accurately - **2.** [décemment] properly.

correcteur, trice [kɔrɛktœr, tris] <> *adj* corrective <> *nm, f* - **1.** [d'examen] examiner, marker *Br*, grader *Am* - **2.** TYPO proofreader.
➤ **correcteur orthographique** *nm* spellchecker.

correctif, ive [kɔrɛktif, iv] *adj* corrective.
➤ **correctif** *nm* rider ; **apporter un ~ à qqch** to qualify sthg.

correction [kɔrɛksjɔ̃] *nf* - **1.** [d'erreur] correction - **2.** [punition] punishment ; **donner une ~ à qqn** to give sb a good hiding - **3.** [modification] correction - **4.** TYPO proofreading - **5.** [notation] marking - **6.** [qualité] correctness - **7.** [bienséance] propriety.

correctionnel, elle [kɔrɛksjɔnɛl] *adj* JUR : **tribunal ~** ≃ magistrate's court ; **peine ~le** *sentence of up to five years' imprisonment*.
➤ **correctionnelle** *nf* JUR ≃ magistrate's court ; **passer en ~le** to appear before the magistrate.

corrélation [kɔrelasjɔ̃] *nf* correlation.

correspondance [kɔrɛspɔ̃dɑ̃s] *nf* - **1.** [gén] correspondence ; **cours par ~** correspondence course - **2.** TRANSPORT connection ; **assurer la ~ avec** to connect with.

correspondant, e [kɔrɛspɔ̃dɑ̃, ɑ̃t] <> *adj* corresponding <> *nm, f* - **1.** [par lettres] penfriend, correspondent - **2.** [par téléphone] : **je vous passe votre ~** I'll put you through - **3.** PRESSE correspondent ; **de notre ~ à New York** from our New York correspondent ; **~ de guerre/de presse** war/newspaper correspondent.

correspondre [75] [kɔrɛspɔ̃dr] *vi* - **1.** [être conforme] : **~ à** to correspond to - **2.** [communiquer] to communicate - **3.** [par lettres] : **~ avec** to correspond with.
➤ **se correspondre** *vp* [s'accorder] to correspond.

correspondu, e [kɔrɛspɔ̃dy] *pp* ⊏> **correspondre**.

corrida [kɔrida] *nf* bullfight.

corridor [kɔridɔr] *nm* corridor.

corrigé [kɔriʒe] *nm* correct version.

corriger [17] [kɔriʒe] vt - **1.** TYPO to correct, to proofread - **2.** [noter] to mark - **3.** [modifier] to correct - **4.** [guérir] : ~ qqn de to cure sb of - **5.** [punir] to give a good hiding to.
◆ se corriger vp - **1.** [d'un défaut] : se ~ de to cure o.s. of - **2.** [devenir raisonnable] to mend one's ways.

corroborer [3] [kɔrɔbɔre] vt to corroborate.

corroder [3] [kɔrɔde] vt [ronger] to corrode ; fig to erode.

corrompre [78] [kɔrɔ̃pr] vt - **1.** [soudoyer] to bribe - **2.** [dépraver] to corrupt - **3.** fig [gâter] to spoil.

corrompu, e [kɔrɔ̃py] ⬥ pp ▷ **corrompre** ⬥ adj [fonctionnaire, âme] corrupt.

corrosif, ive [kɔrozif, iv] adj - **1.** [acide] corrosive - **2.** fig [ironie] biting.
◆ corrosif nm corrosive.

corrosion [kɔrozjɔ̃] nf corrosion.

corruption [kɔrypsjɔ̃] nf - **1.** [subornation] bribery ; ~ de fonctionnaire bribery of a public official - **2.** [dépravation] corruption - **3.** [décomposition] decomposition - **4.** [altération] debasing.

corsage [kɔrsaʒ] nm - **1.** [chemisier] blouse - **2.** [de robe] bodice.

corsaire [kɔrsɛr] nm - **1.** [navire, marin] corsair, privateer - **2.** [pantalon] pedal-pushers (pl).

corse [kɔrs] ⬥ adj Corsican ⬥ nm [langue] Corsican.
◆ Corse ⬥ nmf Corsican ⬥ nf : la **Corse** Corsica ; en **Corse** in Corsica.

corsé, e [kɔrse] adj [café] strong ; [vin] full-bodied ; [plat, histoire] spicy.

corser [3] [kɔrse] vt - **1.** [plat, sauce] to spice up - **2.** [histoire] to liven up - **3.** [vin] to strengthen.
◆ se corser vp [se compliquer] to get complicated ; ça se corse things are getting serious.

corset [kɔrse] nm corset ; ~ orthopédique MÉD surgical corset.

cortège [kɔrtɛʒ] nm procession ; ~ funèbre funeral procession, cortege.

cortisone [kɔrtizɔn] nf cortisone.

corvée [kɔrve] nf - **1.** MIL fatigue (duty) - **2.** [activité pénible] chore.

cosignataire [kɔsiɲatɛr] nmf JUR cosignatory.

cosinus [kɔsinys] nm cosine.

cosmétique [kɔsmetik] nm & adj cosmetic.

cosmique [kɔsmik] adj cosmic.

cosmonaute [kɔsmɔnot] nmf cosmonaut.

cosmopolite [kɔsmɔpɔlit] adj cosmopolitan.

cosmos [kɔsmos] nm - **1.** [univers] cosmos - **2.** [espace] outer space.

cosse [kɔs] nf - **1.** [de légume] pod - **2.** fam vieilli [paresse] : avoir la ~ to feel lazy.

cossu, e [kɔsy] adj - **1.** [personne] wealthy, moneyed - **2.** [maison] opulent.

Costa Rica [kɔstarika] nm : le ~ Costa Rica ; au ~ in Costa Rica.

costaricien, enne [kɔstarisjɛ̃, ɛn] adj Costa Rican.
◆ Costaricien, enne nm, f Costa Rican.

costaud (f inv OU e) [kɔsto, od] adj sturdily built.
◆ costaud nm strapping man.

costume [kɔstym] nm - **1.** [folklorique, de théâtre] costume - **2.** [vêtement d'homme] suit ; ~ trois-pièces three-piece suit.

costumé, e [kɔstyme] adj fancy-dress (avant n).

costumier, ère [kɔstymje, ɛr] nm, f THÉÂTRE wardrobe master (f mistress).

cotation [kɔtasjɔ̃] nf FIN quotation ; ~ en Bourse quoting on the stock exchange.

cote [kɔt] nf - **1.** [marque de classement] classification mark ; [marque numérale] serial number - **2.** FIN quotation - **3.** [de valeur] valuation - **4.** [de cheval] odds (pl) - **5.** [popularité] rating ; avoir la ~ (auprès de qqn) fam to be popular (with sb) - **6.** [niveau] level ; ~ d'alerte [de cours d'eau] danger level ; fig crisis point.

coté, e [kɔte] adj [estimé] popular ; être ~ to be well thought of ; être bien/mal ~ to be highly/poorly rated.

côte [kot] nf - **1.** ANAT & BOT [de bœuf] rib ; [de porc, mouton, agneau] chop ; ~ à ~ side by side - **2.** [pente] hill - **3.** [littoral] coast ; la **Côte d'Azur** the French Riviera - **4.** [tissu] : velours à ~s corduroy.

côté [kote] nm - **1.** [gén] side ; être couché sur le ~ to be lying on one's side ; être aux ~s de qqn fig to be by sb's side ; d'un ~ ..., de l'autre ~ ... on the one hand ..., on the other hand ... ; et ~ finances, ça va? fam how are things moneywise? - **2.** [endroit, direction] direction, way ; de quel ~ est-il parti? which way did he go? ; de l'autre ~ de on the other side of ; de tous ~s from all directions ; du ~ de [près de] near ; [direction] towards Br, toward Am ; [provenance] from.
◆ à côté loc adv - **1.** [lieu - gén] nearby ; [- dans la maison adjacente] next door - **2.** [cible] : tirer à ~ to shoot wide (of the target).
◆ à côté de loc prép - **1.** [proximité] beside, next to - **2.** [en comparaison avec] beside, compared to - **3.** [en dehors de] : être à ~ du sujet to be off the point.

➤ **de côté** *loc adv* - **1.** [se placer, marcher] sideways - **2.** [en réserve] aside ; **mettre/laisser qqch de ~** to put/leave sthg aside.

coteau [kɔto] *nm* - **1.** [colline] hill - **2.** [versant] slope.

Côte-d'Ivoire [kotdivwar] *nf* : **la ~** the Ivory Coast.

côtelé, e [kotle] *adj* ribbed ; **velours ~** corduroy.

côtelette [kotlɛt] *nf* [de porc, mouton, d'agneau] chop ; [de veau] cutlet.

coter [3] [kɔte] *vt* - **1.** [marquer, noter] to mark - **2.** FIN to quote - **3.** [carte, plan] to mark spot heights on.

coterie [kɔtri] *nf péj & vieilli* set, clique.

côtier, ère [kotje, ɛr] *adj* coastal.

cotisation [kɔtizasjɔ̃] *nf* [à club, parti] subscription ; [à la Sécurité sociale] contribution.

cotiser [3] [kɔtize] *vi* [à un club, un parti] to subscribe ; [à la Sécurité sociale] to contribute.

➤ **se cotiser** *vp* to club together.

coton [kɔtɔ̃] *nm* cotton ; **~ (hydrophile)** cotton wool ; **filer un mauvais ~** *fig* to be in a bad way.

cotonnade [kɔtɔnad] *nf* cotton fabric.

Coton-Tige® [kɔtɔ̃tiʒ] (*pl* **Cotons-Tiges**) *nm* cotton bud *Br*, Q-tip® *Am*.

côtoyer [13] [kotwaje] *vt* - **1.** [longer] to run alongside - **2.** fig [frôler] to verge on - **3.** fig [fréquenter] to mix with.

cotte [kɔt] *nf* HIST tunic ; **~ de mailles** coat of mail.

cou [ku] *nm* [de personne, bouteille] neck ; **se jeter au ~ de qqn**, **sauter au ~ de qqn** to throw one's arms around sb's neck ; **jusqu'au ~** *fig* up to one's eyes ; **se pendre au ~ de qqn** to hang round sb's neck.

couac [kwak] *nm* false *ou* wrong note.

couard, e [kwar, ard] *sout* ◇ *adj* cowardly ◇ *nm, f* coward.

couchage [kuʃaʒ] *nm* sleeping arrangements *(pl)* ▷ **sac.**

couchant [kuʃɑ̃] ◇ *adj* ▷ **soleil** ◇ *nm* west.

couche [kuʃ] *nf* - **1.** [de peinture, de vernis] coat, layer ; [de poussière] film, layer - **2.** [épaisseur] layer ; **~ d'ozone** ozone layer ; **en avoir** *ou* **en tenir une ~** *fam* to be (as) thick as two short planks - **3.** [de bébé] nappy *Br*, diaper *Am* - **4.** [classe sociale] stratum.

➤ **couches** *nfpl vieilli* confinement *(U)*, labour *(U) Br*, labor *(U) Am*.

➤ **fausse couche** *nf* miscarriage.

couché, e [kuʃe] *adj* : **être ~** [étendu] to be lying down ; [au lit] to be in bed.

couche-culotte [kuʃkylɔt] (*pl* **couches-culottes**) *nf* disposable nappy *Br* ou diaper *Am*.

coucher[1] [3] [kuʃe] ◇ *vt* - **1.** [enfant] to put to bed - **2.** [objet, blessé] to lay down - **3.** *sout* [inscrire] to mention ◇ *vi* - **1.** [dormir] to sleep - **2.** [passer la nuit] to spend the night ; **un nom à ~ dehors** *fam* an impossible name - **3.** *fam* [avoir des rapports sexuels] : **~ avec** to sleep with.

➤ **se coucher** *vp* - **1.** [s'allonger] to lie down - **2.** [se mettre au lit] to go to bed - **3.** [se courber] to bend over - **4.** [astre] to set.

coucher[2] [kuʃe] *nm* [d'astre] setting ; **au ~ du soleil** at sunset.

couchette [kuʃɛt] *nf* - **1.** [de train] couchette - **2.** [de navire] berth.

coucheur [kuʃœr] *nm* : **mauvais ~** *fig* awkward customer.

couci-couça [kusikusa] *adv fam* so-so.

coucou [kuku] ◇ *nm* - **1.** [oiseau] cuckoo - **2.** [pendule] cuckoo clock - **3.** *péj* [avion] crate ◇ *interj* peekaboo!

coude [kud] *nm* - **1.** [de personne, de vêtement] elbow ; **être au ~ à ~** to be shoulder to shoulder ; **jouer des ~s** to elbow people aside ; **se serrer les ~s** to stick together - **2.** [courbe] bend.

coudée [kude] *nf* : **avoir les ~s franches** to have room to move *ou* elbow room.

cou-de-pied [kudpje] (*pl* **cous-de-pied**) *nm* instep.

coudoyer [13] [kudwaje] *vt* to rub shoulders with.

coudre [86] [kudr] ◇ *vt* - **1.** [bouton] to sew on - **2.** MÉD to sew up, to stitch ◇ *vi* to sew.

coudrier [kudrije] *nm* hazel tree.

couenne [kwan] *nf* [de lard] rind.

couette [kwɛt] *nf* - **1.** [édredon] duvet - **2.** [coiffure] bunches *(pl)*.

couffin [kufɛ̃] *nm* - **1.** [berceau] Moses basket - **2.** [cabas] basket.

couille [kuj] *nf* (*gén pl*) *vulg* ball.

couiner [3] [kwine] *vi* - **1.** [animal] to squeal - **2.** [pleurnicher] to whine.

coulant, e [kulɑ̃, ɑ̃t] *adj* - **1.** [fluide] runny - **2.** [style] fluent - **3.** *fam* [indulgent] easy-going, laid-back.

coulée [kule] *nf* - **1.** [de matière liquide] : **~ de lave** lava flow ; **~ de boue** mudslide - **2.** [de métal] casting.

couler [3] [kule] ◇ *vi* - **1.** [liquide] to flow ; **faire ~ un bain** to run a bath - **2.** [beurre, fromage, nez] to run - **3.** [robinet] to drip ; [tonneau, stylo] to leak - **4.** [temps] to slip by - **5.** [navire, entreprise] to sink ◇ *vt* - **1.** [navire] to sink - **2.** [métal, bronze] to cast - **3.** *fam* [personne, entreprise] to ruin.

◆ **se couler** *vp* [se glisser] to slip ; **se la ~ douce** *fam* to have an easy life.

couleur [kulœr] ◇ *nf* - **1.** [teinte, caractère] colour *Br*, color *Am* ; **télévision en ~s** colour *Br ou* color *Am* television ; **haut en ~** [personne] high-coloured *Br*, high-colored *Am* ; [quartier, récit] colourful *Br*, colorful *Am* - **2.** [linge] coloureds *(pl) Br*, coloreds *(pl) Am* - **3.** CARTES suit - **4.** [d'opinion] leaning - **5.** *loc* : **annoncer la ~** to state one's intentions ; **en faire voir de toutes les ~s à qqn** to give sb a hard time ; **sous ~ de qqch/de faire qqch** under the guise of sthg/of doing sthg ◇ *adj inv* [télévision, pellicule] colour *(avant n) Br*, color *(avant n) Am*.

couleuvre [kulœvr] *nf* grass snake ; **avaler des ~s** *fam fig* [être impassible] to swallow insults.

coulis [kuli] *nm* CULIN puree.

coulissant, e [kulisã, ãt] *adj* sliding *(avant n)*.

coulisse [kulis] *nf* - **1.** [glissière] : **fenêtre/porte à ~** sliding window/door - **2.** COUTURE hem.

◆ **coulisses** *nfpl* THÉÂTRE wings ; **dans les ~s** *fig* behind the scenes.

coulisser [3] [kulise] *vi* to slide.

couloir [kulwar] *nm* - **1.** [corridor] corridor - **2.** GÉOGR gully - **3.** SPORT & TRANSPORT lane ; **~ aérien** air lane ; **~ d'autobus** bus lane.

coulommiers [kulɔmje] *nm soft cheese made from cow's milk.*

coulpe [kulp] *nf* : **battre sa ~** to repent one's sins openly.

coup [ku] *nm* - **1.** [choc - physique, moral] blow ; **donner un ~ de coude à qqn** to nudge sb ; **rouer qqn de ~s** to give sb a beating ; **c'est un ~ bas!** *fig* that's below the belt! ; **~ de couteau** stab *(with a knife)* ; **un ~ dur** *fig* a heavy blow ; **donner un ~ de fouet à qqn** *fig* to give sb a shot in the arm ; **~ de grâce** *litt* & *fig* coup de grâce, death-blow ; **~ de pied** kick ; **~ de poing** punch - **2.** [action nuisible] trick ; **faire un sale ~ à qqn** *fam* to play a dirty trick on sb ; **~ fourré** stab in the back - **3.** [SPORT - au tennis] stroke ; [- en boxe] blow, punch ; [- au football] kick ; **~ franc** free kick - **4.** [d'éponge, de chiffon] wipe ; **un ~ de crayon** a pencil stroke ; **donner un ~ de balai** to give the floor a sweep - **5.** [bruit] noise ; **~ de feu** shot, gunshot ; **~ de sonnette** ring ; **~ de tonnerre** thunderclap - **6.** [action spectaculaire] : **~ d'éclat** feat ; **~ d'État** coup d'état) ; **~ de théâtre** *fig* dramatic turn of events - **7.** *fam* [fois] time - **8.** *loc* : **boire un ~** to have a drink ; **donner un ~ de main à qqn** to give sb a helping hand ; **être dans le ~** [être à la mode] to be up to date ; [être au courant] to be in the know ; **faire les quatre cents ~s** to lead a wild life ; **frapper un grand ~** to strike a decisive blow ; **jeter un ~ d'œil à** to glance at ; **marquer le ~** to mark the occasion ; **en prendre un ~** to take a knock ; **tenir le ~** to hold out ; **tenter le ~** to have a go ; **valoir le ~** to be well worth it.

◆ **coup de fil** *nm* phone call.

◆ **coup de foudre** *nm* love at first sight.

◆ **coup du lapin** *nm* AUTOM whiplash *(U)*.

◆ **coup de soleil** *nm* sunburn *(U)*.

◆ **coup de téléphone** *nm* telephone *ou* phone call ; **donner** *ou* **passer un ~ de téléphone à qqn** to telephone *ou* phone sb.

◆ **coup de vent** *nm* gust of wind ; **partir en ~ de vent** to rush off.

◆ **à coup sûr** *loc adv* definitely.

◆ **du coup** *loc adv* as a result.

◆ **coup sur coup** *loc adv* one after the other.

◆ **du premier coup** *loc adv* first time, at the first attempt.

◆ **sous le coup de** *loc prép* - **1.** [sous l'action de] : **tomber sous le ~ de la loi** to be a statutory offence *Br ou* offense *Am* - **2.** [sous l'effet de] in the grip of.

◆ **tout à coup** *loc adv* suddenly.

coupable [kupabl] ◇ *adj* - **1.** [personne, pensée] guilty ; **plaider ~/non ~** JUR to plead guilty/not guilty - **2.** [action, dessein] culpable, reprehensible ; [négligence, oubli] sinful ◇ *nmf* guilty person *ou* party.

coupant, e [kupã, ãt] *adj* - **1.** [tranchant] cutting - **2.** *fig* [sec] sharp.

coupe [kup] *nf* - **1.** [verre] glass ; **~ de champagne** glass of champagne - **2.** [à fruits] dish - **3.** SPORT cup ; **Coupe du monde** World Cup - **4.** [d'arbres] felling - **5.** [de vêtement, aux cartes] cut - **6.** : **~ (de cheveux)** haircut - **7.** [plan, surface] (cross) section - **8.** [de phrase] break - **9.** [réduction] cut, cutback.

coupé, e [kupe] *adj* : **bien/mal ~** well/badly cut.

◆ **coupé** *nm* coupé.

coupe-circuit [kupsirkɥi] *(pl inv* OU **coupe-circuits)** *nm* circuit breaker.

coupe-faim [kupfɛ̃] *nm inv* appetite suppressant.

coupe-feu [kupfø] ◇ *nm inv* firebreak ◇ *adj inv* fire *(avant n)*.

coupe-gorge [kupgɔrʒ] *nm inv* dangerous place.

coupelle [kupɛl] *nf* dish.

coupe-ongles [kupɔ̃gl] *nm inv* nail clippers.

coupe-papier [kuppapje] (*pl inv* OU **coupe-papiers**) *nm* paper knife.

couper [3] [kupe] <> *vt* - **1.** [gén & INFORM] to cut - **2.** [arbre] to cut down - **3.** [pain] to slice ; [rôti] to carve - **4.** [envie, appétit] to take away - **5.** [vin] to dilute - **6.** [CARTES - avec atout] to trump ; [- paquet] to cut - **7.** [découper] to cut out - **8.** [interrompre, trancher] to cut off - **9.** [traverser] to cut across <> *vi* - **1.** [gén] to cut - **2.** [échapper] : ~ à to get out of - **3.** *loc* : ~ **court à qqch** to cut sthg short.

◆ **se couper** *vp* - **1.** [se blesser] to cut o.s. - **2.** [se croiser] to cross - **3.** [s'isoler] : **se ~ de** to cut o.s. off from.

couper-coller *nm inv* INFORM : **faire un ~** to cut and paste.

couperet [kupre] *nm* - **1.** [de boucher] cleaver - **2.** [de guillotine] blade.

couperose [kuproz] *nf* [sur le visage] blotchiness.

couperosé, e [kuproze] *adj* blotchy.

coupe-vent [kupvã] *nm inv* [vêtement] windcheater *Br*, windbreaker *Am*.

couple [kupl] *nm* [de personnes] couple ; [d'animaux] pair.

couplé, e [kuple] *adj* HIPPISME doubled.

◆ **couplé** *nm* HIPPISME double.

coupler [3] [kuple] *vt* [objets] to couple.

couplet [kuple] *nm* verse.

coupole [kupɔl] *nf* ARCHIT dome, cupola.

coupon [kupɔ̃] *nm* - **1.** [d'étoffe] remnant - **2.** FIN coupon - **3.** [billet] ticket.

coupon-réponse [kupɔ̃repɔ̃s] (*pl* **coupons-réponse**) *nm* reply coupon.

coupure [kupyr] *nf* - **1.** [gén] cut ; [billet de banque] : **petite ~** small denomination note ; **~ de courant** ÉLECTR power cut ; INFORM blackout ; **~ de presse** (press) cutting, clipping ; **~ publicitaire** commercial break - **2.** *fig* [rupture] break.

cour [kur] *nf* - **1.** [espace] courtyard ; **~ de récréation** playground - **2.** [du roi, tribunal] court ; *fig* & *hum* following ; **Cour de cassation** Court of Appeal ; **la Cour des comptes** *the French audit office* ; **Haute ~ (de justice)** High Court ; **~ martiale** court-martial - **3.** *loc* : **faire la ~ à** [femme] to court ; *fig* to charm, to woo.

courage [kuraʒ] *nm* courage ; **bon ~!** good luck! ; **prendre son ~ à deux mains** to pluck up courage ; **je n'ai pas le ~ de faire mes devoirs** I can't bring myself to do my homework.

courageusement [kuraʒøzmɑ̃] *adv* courageously.

courageux, euse [kuraʒø, øz] *adj* - **1.** [brave], brave - **2.** [qui a de l'énergie] energetic - **3.** [audacieux] bold.

couramment [kuramɑ̃] *adv* - **1.** [parler une langue] fluently - **2.** [communément] commonly.

courant, e [kurɑ̃, ɑ̃t] *adj* - **1.** [habituel] everyday *(avant n)* - **2.** [en cours] present.

◆ **courant** *nm* - **1.** [marin, atmosphérique, électrique] current ; **couper le ~** to cut off the power ; **~ d'air** draught *Br*, draft *Am* ; **~ alternatif** alternating current - **2.** [d'idées] current - **3.** [laps de temps] : **dans le ~ du mois/de l'année** in the course of the month/the year ; **~ décembre** in the course of December.

◆ **au courant** *loc adv* : **être au ~** to know (about it) ; **mettre qqn au ~ (de)** to tell sb (about) ; **tenir qqn au ~ (de)** to keep sb informed (about) ; **se mettre/se tenir au ~ (de)** to get/keep up to date (with).

courbatu, e [kurbaty] *adj* aching.

courbature [kurbatyr] *nf* ache.

courbaturé, e [kurbatyre] *adj* aching.

courbe [kurb] <> *nf* curve ; **~ de niveau** [sur une carte] contour (line) ; **~ de température** MÉD temperature curve <> *adj* curved.

courber [3] [kurbe] <> *vt* - **1.** [tige] to bend - **2.** [tête] to bow <> *vi* to bow.

◆ **se courber** *vp* - **1.** [chose] to bend - **2.** [personne] to bow, to bend down.

courbette [kurbɛt] *nf* [révérence] bow ; **faire des ~s** *fig* to bow and scrape.

coureur, euse [kurœr, øz] *nm, f* - **1.** SPORT runner ; **~ cycliste** racing cyclist - **2.** *fam* [amateur] : **~ (de jupons)** womanizer.

courge [kurʒ] *nf* - **1.** [légume] marrow *Br*, squash *Am* - **2.** *fam* [imbécile] dimwit.

courgette [kurʒɛt] *nf* courgette *Br*, zucchini *Am*.

courir [45] [kurir] <> *vi* - **1.** [aller rapidement] to run ; **~ après qqn/qqch** *fig* to chase after sb/sthg, to run after sb/sthg ; **laisse ~!** *fig* let it go! ; **faire ~ qqn** *fig* to pull sb's leg - **2.** SPORT to race - **3.** [se précipiter, rivière] to rush - **4.** [se propager] : **le bruit court que ...** rumour *Br* OU rumor *Am* has it that ... ; **faire ~ un bruit** to spread a rumour *Br* OU rumor *Am* <> *vt* - **1.** SPORT to run in - **2.** [parcourir] to roam (through) - **3.** [faire le tour de] to go round - **4.** [fréquenter - bals, musées] to do the rounds of.

couronne [kurɔn] *nf* - **1.** [ornement, autorité] crown - **2.** [de fleurs] wreath ; ~ **mortuaire** *ou* **funéraire** funeral wreath - **3.** [monnaie - de Suède, d'Islande] krona ; [- du Danemark, de Norvège] krone ; [- de la République tchèque] crown.

couronnement [kurɔnmã] *nm* - **1.** [de monarque] coronation - **2.** [d'édifice] crown - **3.** *fig* [apogée] crowning achievement.

couronner [3] [kurɔne] *vt* - **1.** [monarque] to crown - **2.** [récompenser] to give a prize to ; **être couronné de succès** *fig* to be crowned with success.

courrai, courras *etc* ▷ **courir**.

courre [kur] ▷ **chasse**.

courrier [kurje] *nm* mail, letters (*pl*) ; ~ **du cœur** agony column ; ~ **direct** COMM direct mail shot ; ~ **électronique** INFORM electronic mail, E-mail ; ~ **des lecteurs** [rubrique] letters to the editor.

courroie [kurwa] *nf* TECHNOL belt ; [attache] strap ; ~ **de transmission** driving belt ; ~ **de ventilateur** fanbelt.

courroucer [16] [kuruse] *vt littéraire* to anger.

courroux [kuru] *nm littéraire* wrath, rage.

cours [kur] ◇ ▷ **courir** ◇ *nm* - **1.** [écoulement] flow ; ~ **d'eau** waterway ; **donner** *ou* **laisser libre** ~ **à** *fig* to give free rein to - **2.** [déroulement] course ; **au** ~ **de** during, in the course of ; **en** ~ [année, dossier] current ; [affaires] in hand ; **en** ~ **de route** on the way ; **entraver le** ~ **de la justice** to hinder the course of justice ; **suivre son** ~ to take its course - **3.** FIN price ; ~ **du change** exchange rate ; **avoir** ~ [monnaie] to be legal tender - **4.** [leçon] class, lesson ; **donner des** ~ **(à qqn)** to teach (sb) ; ~ **intensifs** crash course (*sg*) ; ~ **magistral** lecture ; ~ **de rattrapage/du soir** remedial/evening class - **5.** [classe] : ~ **élémentaire** *years two and three of primary school* ; ~ **moyen** *last two years of primary school* ; ~ **préparatoire** ≃ first-year infants *Br*, ≃ nursery school *Am* - **6.** [avenue] avenue.

course [kurs] *nf* - **1.** [action] running (U) ; **au pas de** ~ at a run ; **être dans la** ~ *fig* to be in touch *ou* in the know - **2.** [compétition] race ; ~ **attelée** *ou* **sous harnais** harness race ; ~ **automobile/cycliste** car/cycle race ; ~ **à pied** (foot) race - **3.** [excursion] trip - **4.** [en taxi] journey - **5.** [mouvement] flight, course - **6.** [commission] errand ; **faire des** ~s to go shopping.

coursier, ère [kursje, ɛr] *nm, f* messenger.

coursive [kursiv] *nf* gangway.

court, e [kur, kurt] *adj* short.

➤ **court** ◇ ▷ **courir** ◇ *adv* : **être à** ~ **d'argent/d'idées/d'arguments** to be short

of money/ideas/arguments ; **prendre qqn de** ~ to catch sb unawares ; **tourner** ~ to stop suddenly ◇ *nm* : ~ **de tennis** tennis court.

court-bouillon [kurbujɔ̃] (*pl* **courts-bouillons**) *nm* court-bouillon.

court-circuit [kursirkɥi] (*pl* **courts-circuits**) *nm* short circuit.

court-circuiter [3] [kursirkɥite] *vt* ÉLECTR to short-circuit ; *fig* to bypass.

courtier, ère [kurtje, ɛr] *nm, f* broker.

courtisan, e [kurtizã, an] *nm, f* - **1.** HIST courtier - **2.** [flatteur] sycophant.

➤ **courtisane** *nf* courtesan.

courtiser [3] [kurtize] *vt* - **1.** [femme] to woo, to court - **2.** *péj* [flatter] to flatter.

court-jus [kurʒy] (*pl* **courts-jus**) *nm fam* short.

court-métrage [kurmetraʒ] (*pl* **courts-métrages**) *nm* short (film).

courtois, e [kurtwa, az] *adj* courteous.

courtoisie [kurtwazi] *nf* courtesy.

couru, e [kury] ◇ *pp* ▷ **courir** ◇ *adj* popular ; **c'est** ~ **(d'avance)** *fam fig* it's a foregone conclusion.

cousais, cousions *etc* ▷ **coudre**.

couscous [kuskus] *nm* couscous, *traditional North African dish of semolina served with a spicy stew of meat and vegetables*.

cousin, e [kuzɛ̃, in] *nm, f* cousin ; ~ **germain** first cousin.

coussin [kusɛ̃] *nm* - **1.** [de siège] cushion ; ~ **d'air** air cushion - **2.** *Can* BASE-BALL base.

coussinet [kusinɛ] *nm* - **1.** [coussin] small cushion - **2.** [de patte d'animal] pad.

cousu, e [kuzy] ◇ *pp* ▷ **coudre** ◇ *adj* : **c'est du** ~ **main** *fam fig* it's top-quality stuff ; ~ **de fil blanc** *fig* obvious.

coût [ku] *nm* cost ; **le** ~ **de la vie** the cost of living ; ~s **de distribution** COMM distribution costs.

coûtant [kutã] ▷ **prix**.

couteau, x [kuto] *nm* - **1.** [gén] knife ; ~ **à cran d'arrêt** flick knife ; ~ **de cuisine** kitchen knife ; **à couper au** ~ *fig* that you could cut with a knife ; **avoir le** ~ **sous la gorge** *fig* to have a gun to one's head ; **être à** ~x **tirés (avec qqn)** *fig* to be at daggers drawn (with sb) - **2.** [coquillage] razor shell *Br*, razor clam *Am*.

coutelas [kutla] *nm* [grand couteau] large knife.

coutellerie [kutɛlri] *nf* [industrie, produits] cutlery ; [atelier] cutlery factory ; [magasin] cutler's (shop).

coûter [3] [kute] ◇ *vi* - **1.** [valoir] to cost ; **ça coûte combien?** how much is it? ; ~ **cher** to be

expensive, to cost a lot ; *fig* to be costly ;
~ **cher à qqn** to cost sb a lot ; *fig* to cost sb
dear *ou* dearly - **2.** *fig* [être pénible] to be difficult ⬦ *vt fig* to cost.
⬥ **coûte que coûte** *loc adv* at all costs.
coûteux, euse [kutø, øz] *adj* costly, expensive.
coutume [kutym] *nf* [gén & JUR] custom ; **avoir
~ de faire qqch** to be in the habit of doing
sthg ; **la ~ veut que ...** tradition dictates that
...
coutumier, ère [kutymje, ɛr] *adj* customary ; **il est ~ du fait** he's always doing that.
couture [kutyr] *nf* - **1.** [action] sewing ; **faire de
la ~** to sew - **2.** [points] seam ; **~ apparente**
topstitching, overstitching - **3.** [activité]
dressmaking ; **haute ~** designer fashion.
couturier, ère [kutyrje, ɛr] *nm, f* couturier ;
grand ~ fashion designer, couturier.
couvée [kuve] *nf* [d'œufs] clutch ; [de poussins]
brood.
couvent [kuvã] *nm* [de sœurs] convent ; [de moi-
nes] monastery.
couver [3] [kuve] ⬦ *vt* - **1.** [œufs] to sit on
- **2.** [dorloter] to mollycoddle - **3.** [maladie] to be
sickening for ⬦ *vi* [poule] to brood ; *fig* [com-
plot] to hatch.
couvercle [kuvɛrkl] *nm* [de casserole, boîte] lid,
cover ; [de flacon, bombe, aérosol] top, cap.
couvert, e [kuvɛr, ɛrt] ⬦ *pp* ▷ **couvrir**
⬦ *adj* - **1.** [submergé] covered ; **~ de** covered
with - **2.** [habillé] dressed ; **être bien ~** to be
well wrapped up - **3.** [nuageux] overcast.
⬥ **couvert** *nm* - **1.** [abri] : **se mettre à ~** to take
shelter ; **sous le ~ de l'amitié** *fig* under a
cloak of friendship - **2.** [place à table] place
(setting) ; **mettre** *ou* **dresser le ~** to set *ou* lay
the table.
⬥ **couverts** *nmpl* cutlery *(U).*
couverture [kuvɛrtyr] *nf* - **1.** [gén] cover ;
~ sociale social security cover - **2.** [de lit]
blanket ; **~ chauffante** electric blanket ; **tirer la ~ à soi** *fam fig* to take (all) the credit
(for o.s.) - **3.** [toit] roofing *(U)* - **4.** *PRESSE* coverage.
couveuse [kuvøz] *nf* - **1.** [poule] sitting hen
- **2.** [machine] incubator.
couvre-chef [kuvrəʃɛf] *(pl* **couvre-chefs)** *nm*
hum hat.
couvre-feu [kuvrəfø] *(pl* **couvre-feux)** *nm*
curfew.
couvre-lit [kuvrəli] *(pl* **couvre-lits)** *nm* bedspread.
couvre-pied   *(pl*   **couvre-pieds)**   *nm,*
couvre-pieds *nm inv* [kuvrəpje] quilt,
eiderdown.

couvreur [kuvrœr] *nm* roofer.
couvrir [34] [kuvrir] *vt* - **1.** [gén] to cover ;
~ qqn/qqch de *litt* & *fig* to cover sb/sthg with
- **2.** [protéger] to shield - **3.** [son] to drown
(out).
⬥ **se couvrir** *vp* - **1.** [se vêtir] to wrap up - **2.** [se
recouvrir] : **se ~ de feuilles/de fleurs** to come
into leaf/blossom - **3.** [ciel] to cloud over
- **4.** [se protéger] to cover o.s.
cover-girl [kɔvœrgœrl] *(pl* **cover-girls)** *nf*
cover girl.
covoiturage [kɔvwatyraʒ] *nm* car sharing ;
pratiquer le ~ to belong to a car pool.
cow-boy [kɔbɔj] *(pl* **cow-boys)** *nm* cowboy.
coyote [kɔjɔt] *nm* coyote.
CP *nm abr de* **cours préparatoire.**
CPAM (*abr de* **caisse primaire d'assurances
maladie**) *nf national health insurance office.*
cps (*abr de* **caractères par seconde**) cps.
cpt *abr de* **comptant.**
CQFD (*abr de* **ce qu'il fallait démontrer**) QED.
crabe [krab] *nm* crab.
crac [krak] *interj* crack!
crachat [kraʃa] *nm* spit *(U).*
craché, e [kraʃe] *adj* : **c'est son père tout ~**
he's the spitting image of his father.
cracher [3] [kraʃe] ⬦ *vi* - **1.** [personne] to spit
- **2.** [crépiter] to crackle - **3.** *fam fig* [dénigrer] :
~ sur qqn to run sb down - **4.** *fam* [dédaigner] :
ne pas ~ sur qqch not to turn one's nose up
at sthg ⬦ *vt* [sang] to spit (up) ; [lave, injures] to
spit (out).
crachin [kraʃɛ̃] *nm* drizzle.
crachoir [kraʃwar] *nm* spittoon ; **tenir le ~** *fam
fig* to monopolize the conversation.
crack [krak] *nm* - **1.** [cheval] top horse - **2.** *fam*
[as] star (performer) ; **c'est un ~ en mathématiques** he's a whizz at maths *Br ou* math *Am*
- **3.** [drogue] crack.
crado [krado] *adj fam* filthy.
craie [krɛ] *nf* chalk.
craignais, craignions *etc* ▷ **craindre.**
craindre [80] [krɛ̃dr] *vt* - **1.** [redouter] to fear, to
be afraid of ; **~ de faire qqch** to be afraid of
doing sthg ; **je crains d'avoir oublié mes papiers** I'm afraid I've forgotten my papers ;
~ que (+ *subjonctif*) to be afraid (that) ; **je
crains qu'il oublie** *ou* **n'oublie** I'm afraid he
may forget - **2.** [être sensible à] to be susceptible to.
craint, e [krɛ̃, ɛ̃t] *pp* ▷ **craindre.**
crainte [krɛ̃t] *nf* fear ; **de ~ de faire qqch** for
fear of doing sthg ; **de ~ que** (+ *subjonctif*) for
fear that ; **il a fui de ~ qu'on ne le voie** he fled

for fear that he might be seen *ou* for fear of being seen.

craintif, ive [krɛtif, iv] *adj* timid.

cramer [3] [krame] *vt* & *vi fam* to burn.

➡ **se cramer** *vp fam* to burn o.s. ; **se ~ le doigt** to burn one's finger.

cramoisi, e [kramwazi] *adj* crimson.

crampe [krɑ̃p] *nf* cramp.

crampon [krɑ̃pɔ̃] *nm* - **1.** [crochet - gén] clamp ; [- pour alpinisme] crampon - **2.** *fam* [personne] (persistent) bore.

cramponner [3] [krɑ̃pɔne] ➡ **se cramponner** *vp* [s'agripper] to hang on ; **se ~ à qqn/qqch** *litt* & *fig* to cling to sb/sthg.

cran [krɑ̃] *nm* - **1.** [entaille, degré] notch, cut - **2.** *(U)* [audace] guts *(pl)* ; **avoir du ~** to have guts.

crâne [krɑn] *nm* skull ; **se mettre qqch dans le ~** *fig* to get sthg into one's head.

crâner [3] [krɑne] *vi fam* to show off.

crâneur, euse [krɑnœr, øz] *fam* ⟨⟩ *adj* boastful ⟨⟩ *nm, f* show-off.

crânien, enne [kranjɛ̃, ɛn] *adj* : **boîte ~ne** skull ; **traumatisme ~** head injury.

crapaud [krapo] *nm* toad.

crapule [krapyl] *nf* scum *(U)*.

crapuleux, euse [krapylø, øz] *adj* sordid.

craqueler [24] [krakle] *vt* to crack.
➡ **se craqueler** *vp* to crack.

craquelure [kraklyr] *nf* crack.

craquement [krakmɑ̃] *nm* crack, cracking *(U)*.

craquer [3] [krake] ⟨⟩ *vi* - **1.** [produire un bruit] to crack ; [plancher, chaussure] to creak - **2.** [se déchirer] to split - **3.** [s'effondrer - personne] to crack up ; [- régime, projet] to be falling apart - **4.** [être séduit par] : **~ pour** to fall for ⟨⟩ *vt* [allumette] to strike.

crash [kraʃ] *(pl* **crashs** OU **crashes**) *nm* crash landing.

crasse [kras] ⟨⟩ *nf* - **1.** [saleté] dirt, filth - **2.** *fam* [mauvais tour] dirty trick ⟨⟩ *adj* crass.

crasseux, euse [krasø, øz] *adj* filthy.

cratère [krater] *nm* crater.

cravache [kravaʃ] *nf* riding crop.

cravacher [3] [kravaʃe] ⟨⟩ *vt* to whip ⟨⟩ *vi fam fig* to pull out all the stops.

cravate [kravat] *nf* tie.

crawl [krol] *nm* crawl.

crayon [krɛjɔ̃] *nm* - **1.** [gén] pencil ; **~ à bille** ballpoint (pen) ; **~ de couleur** crayon ; **~ noir** pencil - **2.** TECHNOL pen ; **~ optique** light pen.

crayon-feutre [krɛjɔ̃føtr] *(pl* **crayons-feutres**) *nm* felt-tip (pen).

crayonner [3] [krɛjɔne] *vt* [dessin] to sketch.

CRDP *(abr de* **centre régional de documentation pédagogique**) *nm* local centre for educational resources.

créance [kreɑ̃s] *nf* COMM debt.

créancier, ère [kreɑ̃sje, ɛr] *nm, f* creditor.

créateur, trice [kreatœr, tris] ⟨⟩ *adj* creative ⟨⟩ *nm, f* creator.
➡ **Créateur** *nm* : **le Créateur** the Creator.

créatif, ive [kreatif, iv] *adj* creative.
➡ **créatif** *nm* ideas man, designer.

création [kreasjɔ̃] *nf* creation ; **la ~ (du monde)** RELIG the Creation.

créativité [kreativite] *nf* creativity.

créature [kreatyr] *nf* creature.

crécelle [kresɛl] *nf* rattle.

crèche [krɛʃ] *nf* - **1.** [de Noël] crib - **2.** [garderie] crèche.

crécher [18] [kreʃe] *vi fam* to crash, to kip down *Br*.

crédibiliser [3] [kredibilize] *vt* to make credible.

crédibilité [kredibilite] *nf* credibility.

crédible [kredibl] *adj* credible.

CREDIF, Crédif [kredif] *(abr de* **Centre de recherche et d'étude pour la diffusion du français**) *nm* official body promoting use of the French language.

crédit [kredi] *nm* - **1.** [gén] credit ; **faire ~ à qqn** to give sb credit ; **acheter/vendre qqch à ~** to buy/sell sthg on credit ; **~ municipal** pawnshop ; **~ relais** bridging loan - **2.** *fig* & *sout* influence.

crédit-bail [kredibaj] *(pl* **crédits-bails**) *nm* leasing.

créditer [3] [kredite] *vt* [compte] to credit ; *fig* : **~ qqn de qqch** to credit sb with sthg.

créditeur, trice [kreditœr, tris] ⟨⟩ *adj* in credit ⟨⟩ *nm, f* creditor.

credo [kredo] *nm* creed, credo.

crédule [kredyl] *adj* credulous.

crédulité [kredylite] *nf* credulity.

créer [15] [kree] *vt* - **1.** RELIG [inventer] to create - **2.** [fonder] to found, to start up - **3.** [causer] : **~ des problèmes à qqn** to create trouble for sb.

crémaillère [kremajer] *nf* - **1.** [de cheminée] trammel ; **pendre la ~** *fig* to have a housewarming (party) - **2.** TECHNOL rack.

crémation [kremasjɔ̃] *nf* cremation.

crématoire [krematwar] ⟶ **four**.

crématorium [krematɔrjɔm] *nm* crematorium *Br*, crematory *Am*.

crème [krɛm] ◇ *nf* - **1.** [gén] cream ; ~ **dépilatoire/à raser** depilatory/shaving cream ; ~ **fouettée/fraîche/glacée** whipped/fresh/ice cream ; ~ **anglaise** custard ; ~ **autobronzante** self-tanning cream ; ~ **de cassis** blackcurrant liqueur ; ~ **glacée** ice cream ; ~ **hydratante** moisturizer ; ~ **pâtissière** confectioner's custard ; ~ **renversée** custard cream *Br*, cup custard *Am* - **2.** [personne] : **la** ~ **des maris/des hommes** the best of husbands/of men ◇ *adj inv* cream.

crémerie [krɛmri] *nf* dairy.

crémeux, euse [kremø, øz] *adj* creamy.

crémier, ère [kremje, ɛr] *nm, f* dairyman (*f* dairywoman).

créneau, x [krenol *nm* - **1.** [de fortification] crenel - **2.** [pour se garer] : **faire un** ~ to reverse into a parking space - **3.** [de marché] niche - **4.** [horaire] window, gap.

crénelé, e [krɛnle] *adj* crenelated.

créole [kreɔl] *adj* & *nm* creole.

◆ **créoles** *nfpl* dangly earrings.

crêpe [krɛp] ◇ *nf* CULIN pancake ◇ *nm* [tissu] crepe.

crêper [4] [krepe] *vt* to backcomb.

crêperie [krepri] *nf* pancake restaurant.

crépi [krepi] *nm* roughcast.

crépinette [krepinɛt] *nf flat sausage*.

crépir [32] [krepir] *vt* to roughcast.

crépiter [3] [krepite] *vi* [feu, flammes] to crackle ; [pluie] to patter.

crépon [krepɔ̃] ◇ *adj* ▷ **papier** ◇ *nm* seersucker.

CREPS, Creps [krɛps] (*abr de* **centre régional d'éducation physique et sportive**) *nm regional sports centre*.

crépu, e [krepy] *adj* frizzy.

crépuscule [krepyskyl] *nm* [du jour] dusk, twilight ; *fig* twilight ; **au** ~ at dusk, at twilight.

crescendo [kreʃendo, kreʃēdo] ◇ *adv* crescendo ; **aller** ~ *fig* [bruit] to get *ou* grow louder and louder ; [dépenses, émotion] to grow apace ◇ *nm inv* MUS & *fig* crescendo.

cresson [kresɔ̃] *nm* watercress.

Crète [krɛt] *nf* : **la** ~ Crete.

crête [krɛt] *nf* - **1.** [de coq] comb - **2.** [de montagne, vague, oiseau] crest.

crétin, e [kretē, in] *fam* ◇ *adj* cretinous, idiotic ◇ *nm, f* cretin, idiot.

crétois, e [kretwa, az] *adj* Cretan.

◆ **Crétois, e** *nm, f* Cretan.

cretonne [krɔtɔn] *nf* cretonne.

creuser [3] [krøze] *vt* - **1.** [trou] to dig - **2.** [objet] to hollow out - **3.** [taille, reins] to arch - **4.** *fig* [approfondir] to go into deeply - **5.** *loc* : **ça creuse!** *fam* that gives you an appetite!

◆ **se creuser** *vp* - **1.** [devenir creux] to become hollow - **2.** *fam fig* [réfléchir] to rack one's brains - **3.** *fig* [s'élargir] to deepen, to widen.

creuset [krøzɛ] *nm* crucible ; *fig* melting pot.

creux, creuse [krø, krøz] *adj* - **1.** [vide, concave] hollow - **2.** [période - d'activité réduite] slack ; [- à tarif réduit] off-peak - **3.** [paroles] empty.

◆ **creux** *nm* - **1.** [concavité] hollow ; **le** ~ **de la main** the hollow of one's hand - **2.** [période] lull - **3.** *loc* : **être au** ~ **de la vague** *fig* to be at a low point.

crevaison [krəvɛzɔ̃] *nf* puncture.

crevant, e [krəvā, āt] *adj fam* - **1.** [fatigant] exhausting, knackering *Br* - **2.** [amusant] hilarious.

crevasse [krəvas] *nf* [de mur] crevice, crack ; [de glacier] crevasse ; [sur la main] crack.

crevé, e [krəve] *adj* - **1.** [pneu] burst, punctured - **2.** *fam* [fatigué] dead, shattered *Br*.

crève [krɛv] *nf fam* bad *ou* stinking cold ; **attraper la** ~ to catch one's death (of cold).

crève-cœur [krɛvkœr] *nm inv* heartbreak.

crever [19] [krəve] ◇ *vi* - **1.** [éclater] to burst - **2.** *tfam* [mourir] to die ; ~ **de** *fig* [jalousie, orgueil] to be bursting with ◇ *vt* - **1.** [percer] to burst - **2.** *fam* [épuiser] to wear out.

◆ **se crever** *vp fam* to wear o.s. out.

crevette [krəvɛt] *nf* : ~ **(grise)** shrimp ; ~ **(rose)** prawn.

CRF (*abr de* **Croix-Rouge française**) *nf French Red Cross*.

cri [kri] *nm* - **1.** [de personne] cry, shout ; [perçant] scream ; [d'animal] cry ; **pousser un** ~ to cry (out), to shout ; **pousser des ~s de joie** to shout for *ou* with joy ; **pousser un** ~ **de douleur** to cry out in pain ; **à grands ~s** *fig* loudly - **2.** [appel] cry ; **le dernier** ~ *fig* the latest thing ; ~ **du cœur** cri de cœur.

criailler [3] [kriaje] *vi* to scream, to squawk.

criant, e [krijā, āt] *adj* [injustice] blatant.

criard, e [krijar, ard] *adj* - **1.** [voix] strident, piercing - **2.** [couleur] loud.

crible [kribl] *nm* [instrument] sieve ; **passer qqch au** ~ *fig* to examine sthg closely.

criblé, e [krible] *adj* riddled ; **être** ~ **de dettes** to be up to one's eyes in debt.

cric [krik] *nm* jack.

cricket [krikɛt] *nm* cricket.

criée [krije] ▷ **vente**.

crier [10] [krije] ◇ *vi* - **1.** [pousser un cri] to

shout (out), to yell - **2.** [parler fort] to shout - **3.** [protester] : **~ contre** OU **après qqn** to nag sb, to go on at sb - **4.** sout [grincer] to creak <> vt to shout (out).

crime [krim] nm - **1.** [délit] crime ; **~ de lèse-majesté** fig treason (U) - **2.** [meurtre] murder ; **~ passionnel** crime of passion ; **~s contre l'humanité** crime against humanity.

Crimée [krime] nf : **la ~ the** Crimea ; **la guerre de ~** the Crimean War.

criminalité [kriminalite] nf crime.

criminel, elle [kriminɛl] <> adj criminal <> nm, f criminal ; **~ de guerre** war criminal.

crin [krɛ̃] nm [d'animal] hair ; **à tout ~** fig dyed-in-the-wool.

crinière [krinjɛr] nf mane.

crique [krik] nf creek.

criquet [krikɛ] nm locust ; [sauterelle] grasshopper.

crise [kriz] nf - **1.** MÉD attack ; **~ cardiaque** heart attack ; **~ de foie** bilious attack ; **~ de tétanie** muscle spasm - **2.** [accès] fit ; **~ de larmes** fit of tears ; **~ de nerfs** attack of nerves ; **piquer une ~** fam to have a fit, to fly off the handle - **3.** [élan] (sudden) urge - **4.** [phase critique] crisis ; **en ~** in crisis.

crispant, e [krispɑ̃, ɑ̃t] adj irritating, frustrating.

crispation [krispasjɔ̃] nf - **1.** [contraction] contraction - **2.** [agacement] irritation.

crispé, e [krispe] adj tense, on edge.

crisper [3] [krispe] vt - **1.** [contracter - visage] to tense ; [- poing] to clench - **2.** [agacer] to irritate.
◆ **se crisper** vp - **1.** [se contracter] to tense (up) - **2.** [s'irriter] to get irritated.

criss [kris] nm kris.

crisser [3] [krise] vi [pneu] to screech ; [étoffe] to rustle.

cristal, aux [kristal, o] nm crystal ; **en ~** crystal (avant n) ; **~ de roche** quartz.

cristallin, e [kristalɛ̃, in] adj - **1.** [limpide] crystal clear, crystalline - **2.** [roche] crystalline.
◆ **cristallin** nm crystalline lens.

cristalliser [3] [kristalize] vt litt & fig to crystallize.
◆ **se cristalliser** vp to crystallize.

critère [kritɛr] nm criterion.

critérium [kriterjɔm] nm qualifier.

critiquable [kritikabl] adj [décision] debatable ; [personne] open to criticism.

critique [kritik] <> adj critical <> nmf critic ; **~ d'art** art critic ; **~ littéraire** literary critic <> nf criticism ; **la ~** the critics (pl).

critiquer [3] [kritike] vt to criticize.

croasser [3] [krɔase] vi to croak, to caw.

croate [krɔat] adj Croat, Croatian.
◆ **Croate** nmf Croat, Croatian.

Croatie [krɔasi] nf : **la ~** Croatia.

croc [krɔ] nm - **1.** [de chien] fang ; **montrer les ~s** fig to bare one's teeth - **2.** [crochet] hook.

croc-en-jambe [krɔkɑ̃ʒɑ̃b] (pl crocs-en-jambe) nm : **faire un ~ à qqn** to trip sb up.

croche [krɔʃ] nf quaver Br, eighth (note) Am.

croche-pied [krɔʃpje] (pl croche-pieds) nm : **faire un ~ à qqn** to trip sb up.

crochet [krɔʃɛ] nm - **1.** [de métal] hook ; **vivre aux ~s de qqn** to live off sb - **2.** TRICOT crochet hook - **3.** TYPO square bracket - **4.** [détour] : **faire un ~** to make a detour - **5.** BOXE : **~ du gauche/du droit** left/right hook.

crocheter [28] [krɔʃte] vt to pick.

crochu, e [krɔʃy] adj [doigts] claw-like ; [nez] hooked.

croco [krɔko] nm fam crocodile (skin).

crocodile [krɔkɔdil] nm crocodile.

crocus [krɔkys] nm crocus.

croire [107] [krwar] <> vt - **1.** [chose, personne] to believe ; **à l'en ~, on n'y arrivera jamais** to hear him talk, you'd think we'd never manage it - **2.** [penser] to think ; **tu crois?** do you think so? ; **il te croyait parti** he thought you'd left ; **~ que** to think (that) <> vi : **~ à** to believe in ; **~ en** to believe in, to have faith in.
◆ **se croire** vp - **1.** [prétendre être] : **il se croit plus fort que moi** he thinks he's stronger than me ; **se ~ tout permis** to think one can get away with anything ; **s'y ~** fam to think one is it - **2.** [penser se trouver] : **on se croirait au Japon** you'd think you were in Japan.

croisade [krwazad] nf HIST & fig crusade.

croisé, e [krwaze] adj [veste] double-breasted.
◆ **croisé** nm HIST crusader.
◆ **croisée** nf - **1.** [fenêtre] casement, window - **2.** [croisement] : **à la ~e des chemins** litt & fig at a crossroads.

croisement [krwazmɑ̃] nm - **1.** [intersection] junction, intersection - **2.** BIOL cross-breeding.

croiser [3] [krwaze] <> vt - **1.** [jambes] to cross ; [bras] to fold - **2.** [passer à côté de] to pass - **3.** [chemin] to cross, to cut across - **4.** [métisser] to interbreed <> vi NAVIG to cruise.
◆ **se croiser** vp [chemins] to cross, to inter-

sect ; [personnes] to pass ; [lettres] to cross ; [regards] to meet.

croisière [krwazjɛr] *nf* cruise.

croisillon [krwazijɔ̃] *nm* : à ~s lattice *(avant n)*.

croissais, croissions *etc* ▷ **croître**.

croissance [krwasɑ̃s] *nf* growth, development ; ~ **économique** economic growth *ou* development.

croissant, e [krwasɑ̃, ɑ̃t] *adj* increasing, growing.
◆ **croissant** *nm* - **1.** [de lune] crescent - **2.** *CULIN* croissant.

croître [93] [krwatr] *vi* - **1.** [grandir] to grow - **2.** [augmenter] to increase.

croix [krwa] *nf* cross ; **en ~** in the shape of a cross ; ~ **gammée** swastika ; **mettre** *ou* **faire une ~ sur qqch** *fig* to write sthg off ; **la ~ et la bannière** *fig* the devil's own job.

Croix-Rouge [krwaruʒ] *nf* : **la ~** the Red Cross.

croquant, e [krɔkɑ̃, ɑ̃t] *adj* crisp, crunchy.
◆ **croquant** *nm vieilli* yokel.

croque-madame [krɔkmadam] *nm inv* croque-monsieur with a fried egg.

croque-mitaine [krɔkmitɛn] *(pl* **croque-mitaines)** *nm* bogeyman.

croque-monsieur [krɔkməsjø] *nm inv* toasted cheese and ham sandwich.

croque-mort [krɔkmɔr] *(pl* **croque-morts)** *nm fam* undertaker.

croquer [3] [krɔke] ◇ *vt* - **1.** [manger] to crunch - **2.** [dessiner] to sketch ; **(jolie) à ~ fig** pretty as a picture ◇ *vi* to be crunchy.

croquette [krɔkɛt] *nf* croquette.

croquis [krɔki] *nm* sketch ; **faire un ~** to make a sketch.

cross [krɔs] *nm* [exercice] cross-country (running) ; [course] cross-country race.

crosse [krɔs] *nf* - **1.** [d'évêque] crozier - **2.** [de fusil] butt - **3.** *HOCKEY* hockey stick.

crotale [krɔtal] *nm* rattlesnake.

crotte [krɔt] *nf* [de lapin etc] droppings *(pl)* ; [de chien] dirt ; **crotte!** *fam* damn!

crottin [krɔtɛ̃] *nm* [de cheval] (horse) manure.

croulant, e [krulɑ̃, ɑ̃t] ◇ *adj* crumbling ◇ *nm, f fam* (old) fogy, wrinkly.

crouler [3] [krule] *vi* to crumble ; ~ **sous** *litt* & *fig* to collapse under.

croupe [krup] *nf* rump ; **monter en ~** to ride pillion.

croupier [krupje] *nm* croupier.

croupion [krupjɔ̃] *nm ZOOL* rump ; *CULIN* parson's nose.

croupir [32] [krupir] *vi litt* & *fig* to stagnate.

CROUS, Crous [krus] *(abr de* **centre régional des œuvres universitaires et scolaires)** *nm* student representative body dealing with accommodation, catering etc.

croustade [krustad] *nf* croustade.

croustillant, e [krustijɑ̃, ɑ̃t] *adj* - **1.** [croquant - pain] crusty ; [- biscuit] crunchy - **2.** [grivois] spicy, juicy.

croustiller [3] [krustije] *vi* to be crusty.

croûte [krut] *nf* - **1.** [du pain, terrestre] crust ; **casser la ~** *fam fig* to have a bite to eat ; **gagner sa ~** *fam fig* to earn a crust - **2.** *CULIN* : **en ~** in piecrust *ou* pastry - **3.** [de fromage] rind - **4.** [de plaie] scab - **5.** *fam péj* [tableau] daub.

croûton [krutɔ̃] *nm* - **1.** [bout du pain] crust - **2.** [pain frit] crouton - **3.** *fam péj* [personne] fuddy-duddy.

croyable [krwajabl] *adj* believable ; **c'est pas ~!** it's unbelievable *ou* incredible!

croyais, croyions *etc* ▷ **croire**.

croyance [krwajɑ̃s] *nf* belief.

croyant, e [krwajɑ̃, ɑ̃t] ◇ *ppr* ▷ **croire** ◇ *adj* : **être ~** to be a believer ◇ *nm, f* believer.

CRS *(abr de* **Compagnie républicaine de sécurité)** *nm member of the French riot police* ; **on a fait appel aux ~** the riot police were called in.

cru, e [kry] ◇ *pp* ▷ **croire** ◇ *adj* - **1.** [non cuit] raw - **2.** [violent] harsh - **3.** [direct] blunt - **4.** [grivois] crude.
◆ **cru** *nm* [vin] vintage, wine ; [vignoble] vineyard ; **du ~** *fig* local ; **un grand ~** a fine wine ; **de son propre ~** *fig* of one's own devising.

crû [kry] *pp* ▷ **croître**.

cruauté [kryote] *nf* cruelty.

cruche [kryʃ] *nf* - **1.** [objet] jug - **2.** *fam péj* [personne niaise] twit.

crucial, e, aux [krysjal, o] *adj* crucial.

crucifix [krysifi] *nm* crucifix.

crucifixion [krysifiksjɔ̃] *nf* crucifixion.

cruciverbiste [krysiverbist] *nmf* crossword enthusiast.

crudité [krydite] *nf* crudeness.
◆ **crudités** *nfpl* crudités.

crue [kry] *nf* rise in the water level ; **en ~** in spate.

cruel, elle [kryɛl] *adj* cruel.

cruellement [kryɛlmɑ̃] *adv* cruelly.

crûment [krymɑ̃] *adv* - **1.** [sans ménagement] bluntly - **2.** [avec grossièreté] crudely.

crustacé [krystase] *nm* shellfish, crustacean ; ~**s** shellfish (*U*).

cryoconservation [krijɔkɔ̃sɛrvasjɔ̃] *nf* cryonics, cryopreservation *f*.

cryptage [kripta3] *nm* encryption.

crypte [kript] *nf* crypt.

crypter [kripte] *vt* to encrypt ; **chaîne cryptée** encrypted channel.

cs (*abr de* **cuillère à soupe**) tbs, tbsp.

CSA (*abr de* **Conseil supérieur de l'audiovisuel**) *nm French broadcasting supervisory body.*

CSCE (*abr de* **Conférence sur la sécurité et la coopération en Europe**) *nf* CSCE.

CSEN (*abr de* **Confédération des syndicats de l'Éducation nationale**) *nf confederation of teachers' unions.*

CSG (*abr de* **contribution sociale généralisée**) *nf income-related tax contribution.*

CSP (*abr de* **catégorie socio-professionnelle**) *nf socio-professional group.*

Cuba [kyba] *n* Cuba ; **à ~** in Cuba.

cubain, aine [kybɛ̃, ɛn] *adj* Cuban.
➤ **Cubain, aine** *nm, f* Cuban.

cube [kyb] *nm* cube ; **4 au ~ = 64** 4 cubed is 64 ; **élever au ~** MATHS to cube ; **mètre ~** cubic metre *Br ou* meter *Am*.
➤ **gros cube** *nm* big motorbike.

cubique [kybik] *adj* cubic.

cubisme [kybism] *nm* cubism.

cubitus [kybitys] *nm* ulna.

cucu(l) [kyky] *adj inv fam* silly.

cueille, cueilles *etc* ⊳ **cueillir**.

cueillette [kœjɛt] *nf* picking, harvesting.

cueilli, e [kœji] *pp* ⊳ **cueillir**.

cueillir [41] [kœjir] *vt* **- 1.** [fruits, fleurs] to pick **- 2.** *fam* [personne] to catch, to nab.

cuillère, cuiller [kɥijɛr] *nf* spoon ; **~ à café** coffee spoon ; CULIN teaspoon ; **~ à dessert** dessertspoon ; **~ à soupe** soup spoon ; CULIN tablespoon ; **petite ~** teaspoon.

cuillerée [kɥijɛre] *nf* spoonful ; **~ à café** CULIN teaspoonful ; **~ à soupe** CULIN tablespoonful.

cuir [kɥir] *nm* leather ; [non tanné] hide ; **en ~** leather (*avant n*) ; **~ chevelu** ANAT scalp.

cuirasse [kɥiras] *nf* [de chevalier] breastplate ; *fig* armour *Br*, armor *Am*.

cuirassé [kɥirase] *nm* battleship.

cuire [98] [kɥir] ◇ *vt* **- 1.** [viande, œuf] to cook ; [tarte, gâteau] to bake **- 2.** [briques, poterie] to fire ◇ *vi* **- 1.** [viande, œuf] to cook ; [tarte, gâteau] to bake ; **faire ~ qqch** to cook/bake sthg **- 2.** *fig* [personne] to roast, to be boiling ; **il vous en** **cuira!** *fig* you'll suffer (for it)!, you'll regret it!

cuisais, cuisions *etc* ⊳ **cuire**.

cuisant, e [kɥizɑ̃, ɑ̃t] *adj* [douloureux] stinging, smarting ; *fig* bitter.

cuisine [kɥizin] *nf* **- 1.** [pièce] kitchen **- 2.** [art] cooking, cookery ; **faire la ~** to do the cooking, to cook ; **~ bourgeoise** home cooking **- 3.** *fam* [combine] schemings (*pl*), schemes (*pl*) ; **~ électorale** electoral hanky-panky (*U*).

cuisiné, e [kɥizine] *adj* : **plat ~** ready-cooked meal.

cuisiner [3] [kɥizine] ◇ *vt* **- 1.** [aliment] to cook **- 2.** *fam* [personne] to grill ◇ *vi* to cook ; **bien/mal ~** to be a good/bad cook.

cuisinier, ère [kɥizinje, ɛr] *nm, f* cook.
➤ **cuisinière** *nf* cooker ; **cuisinière électrique/à gaz** electric/gas cooker.

cuissardes [kɥisard] *nfpl* [de pêcheur] waders ; [de femme] thigh boots.

cuisse [kɥis] *nf* **- 1.** ANAT thigh **- 2.** CULIN leg ; **~s de grenouille** frog's legs.

cuisson [kɥisɔ̃] *nf* cooking.

cuissot [kɥiso] *nm* haunch ; **~ de chevreuil** haunch of venison.

cuistot [kɥisto] *nm fam* cook.

cuistre [kɥistr] *littéraire* ◇ *nm* prig ◇ *adj* priggish.

cuit, e [kɥi, kɥit] ◇ *pp* ⊳ **cuire** ◇ *adj* : **bien ~** [steak] well-done ; **trop ~** overcooked, overdone ; **être ~** *fam fig* to have had it.
➤ **cuite** *nf fam* : **prendre une ~e** to get plastered *ou* smashed.

cuiter [3] [kɥite] ➤ **se cuiter** *vp fam* to get plastered *ou* smashed.

cuivre [kɥivr] *nm* **- 1.** [métal] : **~ (rouge)** copper ; **~ jaune** brass **- 2.** (*gén pl*) [objet] brass (object).
➤ **cuivres** *nmpl* : **les ~s** MUS the brass.

cuivré, e [kɥivre] *adj* [couleur, reflet] coppery ; [teint] bronzed.

cul [ky] *nm* **- 1.** *tfam* [postérieur] bum ; **avoir le ~ entre deux chaises** to be in an awkward position ; **en avoir plein le ~ de qqch** *tfam* to be sick and tired of sthg ; **être comme ~ et chemise** to be as thick as thieves **- 2.** [de bouteille] bottom ; **faire ~ sec** *fam* to down one's drink in one.

culasse [kylas] *nf* **- 1.** [d'arme à feu] breech **- 2.** AUTOM cylinder head.

culbute [kylbyt] *nf* **- 1.** [saut] somersault **- 2.** [chute] tumble, fall.

culbuter [3] [kylbyte] ◇ *vt* [objet] to knock

over ⬦ *vi* - **1.** [faire une chute] to (take a) tumble - **2.** [se renverser] to (do a) somersault.

cul-de-jatte [kydʒat] (*pl* **culs-de-jatte**) *nm* legless cripple.

cul-de-sac [kydsak] (*pl* **culs-de-sac**) *nm* dead end.

culinaire [kylinɛr] *adj* culinary.

culminant [kylminɑ̃] ⊏⊐ **point.**

culminer [3] [kylmine] *vi* [surplomber] to tower ; **~ à** [s'élever à] to reach its highest point at ; *fig* to peak at.

culot [kylo] *nm* - **1.** *fam* [toupet] cheek, nerve ; **avoir le ~ de** to have the cheek *ou* nerve to ; **avoir du ~** to have a lot of nerve - **2.** [de cartouche, ampoule] cap.

culotte [kylɔt] *nf* - **1.** [sous-vêtement féminin] knickers (*pl*), panties (*pl*), pair of knickers *ou* panties - **2.** [vêtement] : **~s courtes/longues** short/long trousers ; **porter la ~** *fam fig* to wear the trousers.

culotté, e [kylɔte] *adj* [effronté] : **elle est ~e** she's got a nerve.

culpabiliser [3] [kylpabilize] ⬦ *vt* : **~ qqn** to make sb feel guilty ⬦ *vi* to feel guilty.

culpabilité [kylpabilite] *nf* guilt.

culte [kylt] *nm* - **1.** [vénération, amour] worship - **2.** [religion] religion.

cultivateur, trice [kyltivatœr, tris] *nm, f* farmer.

cultivé, e [kyltive] *adj* [personne] educated, cultured.

cultiver [3] [kyltive] *vt* - **1.** [terre, goût, relation] to cultivate - **2.** [plante] to grow.

➥ **se cultiver** *vp* to cultivate *ou* improve one's mind.

culture [kyltyr] *nf* - **1.** AGRIC cultivation, farming ; **les ~s** cultivated land - **2.** [savoir] culture, knowledge ; **~ générale** [connaissances] general knowledge ; [éducation] general education ; **~ physique** physical training - **3.** [civilisation] culture.

culturel, elle [kyltyrɛl] *adj* cultural.

culturisme [kyltyrism] *nm* bodybuilding.

cumin [kymɛ̃] *nm* cumin.

cumul [kymyl] *nm* [de fonctions, titres] holding simultaneously ; [de salaires] drawing simultaneously.

cumuler [3] [kymyle] *vt* [fonctions, titres] to hold simultaneously ; [salaires] to draw simultaneously.

cumulus [kymylys] *nm* cumulus.

cupide [kypid] *adj* greedy.

cupidité [kypidite] *nf* greed, cupidity.

curaçao [kyraso] *nm* curaçao.

curatif, ive [kyratif, iv] *adj* curative.

cure [kyr] *nf* (course of) treatment ; **faire une ~ de fruits** to go on a fruit-based diet ; **~ d'amaigrissement** slimming course *Br*, reducing treatment *Am* ; **~ de désintoxication** [d'alcool] drying-out treatment ; [de drogue] detoxification treatment ; **~ de sommeil** sleep therapy ; **faire une ~ thermale** to take the waters.

curé [kyre] *nm* parish priest.

cure-dents [kyrdɑ̃] *nm inv* toothpick.

cure-pipes *nm inv*, **cure-pipe** *nm* (*pl inv*) [kyrpip] pipe cleaner.

curer [3] [kyre] *vt* to clean out.

➥ **se curer** *vp* : **se ~ les ongles** to clean one's nails.

curetage [kyrtaʒ] *nm* curettage.

curie [kyri] *nf* curia.

curieusement [kyrjøzmɑ̃] *adv* curiously, strangely.

curieux, euse [kyrjø, øz] ⬦ *adj* - **1.** [intéressé] curious ; **~ de qqch/de faire qqch** curious about sth/to do sth - **2.** [indiscret] inquisitive - **3.** [étrange] strange, curious ⬦ *nm, f* busybody.

curiosité [kyrjozite] *nf* curiosity.

➥ **curiosités** *nfpl* interesting sights.

curiste [kyrist] *nmf person undergoing treatment at a spa.*

curling [kœrliŋ] *nm* curling.

curriculum vitae [kyrikylɔmvite] *nm inv* curriculum vitae *Br*, résumé *Am*.

curry [kyri], **carry** [kari], **cari** [kari] *nm* - **1.** [épice] curry powder - **2.** [plat] curry.

curseur [kyrsœr] *nm* cursor.

cursus [kyrsys] *nm* degree course.

cutané, e [kytane] *adj* cutaneous, skin (*avant n*).

cuti [kyti] *nf* : **virer sa ~** *fam fig* to throw off one's shackles.

cutiréaction, cuti-réaction (*pl* **cuti-réactions**) [kytireaksjɔ̃] *nf* skin test.

cutter [kœtɛr] *nm* Stanley knife®.

cuve [kyv] *nf* - **1.** [citerne] tank - **2.** [à vin] vat.

cuvée [kyve] *nf* - **1.** [récolte] vintage - **2.** [contenu de cuve] vatful.

cuver [3] [kyve] *vt* - **1.** [faire séjourner en cuve] to put in a vat to ferment - **2.** [alcool, déception] : **~ qqch** to sleep sth off.

cuvette [kyvɛt] *nf* - **1.** [récipient] basin, bowl - **2.** [de lavabo] basin ; [de W.-C.] bowl - **3.** GÉOGR basin.

cv (*abr de* **cheval-vapeur**) [puissance] HP.

CV *nm* - **1.** (*abr de* **curriculum vitae**) CV *Br*, résumé *Am* ; **ça fera bien dans ton ~** it'll look good on your CV - **2.** (*abr de* **cheval-vapeur**) hp ; [puissance fiscale] *classification for scaling of car tax.*

CVS (*abr de* **corrigées des variations saisonnières**) *adj* seasonally adjusted.

cx *nm* [coefficient de pénétration dans l'air] drag coefficient.

cyanure [sjanyr] *nm* cyanide.

cybercafé [siberkafe] *nm* cybercafé, internet café.

cybercommerce [siberkɔmers] *nm* e-commerce.

cyberespace [siberɛspas], **cybermonde** [sibermɔd] *nm* cyberspace.

cybernaute [sibernot] *nm* (net) surfer, cybersurfer, cybernaut.

cyclable [siklabl] ▷ **piste.**

Cyclades [siklad] *nfpl* : **les ~** the Cyclades ; **dans les ~** in the Cyclades.

cyclamen [siklamen] *nm* cyclamen.

cycle [sikl] *nm* cycle ; **~ menstruel** menstrual cycle ; **premier ~** UNIV ≃ first and second year ; SCOL middle school *Br*, junior high school *Am* ; **second ~** UNIV ≃ final year *Br*, ≃ senior year *Am* ; SCOL upper school *Br*, high school *Am* ; **troisième ~** UNIV ≃ postgraduate year *ou* years.

cyclique [siklik] *adj* cyclic, cyclical.

cyclisme [siklism] *nm* cycling.

cycliste [siklist] ◇ *nmf* cyclist ◇ *adj* cycle (*avant n*).

cyclo-cross [siklokrɔs] *nm inv* cyclo-cross.

cyclomoteur [siklomɔtœr] *nm* moped.

cyclone [siklon] *nm* cyclone.

cyclothymique [siklɔtimik] *nmf* & *adj* manic-depressive.

cyclotourisme [sikloturism] *nm* cycle touring.

cygne [siɲ] *nm* swan.

cylindre [silɛ̃dr] *nm* - **1.** AUTOM & GÉOM cylinder - **2.** [rouleau] roller.

cylindrée [silɛ̃dre] *nf* engine capacity.

cylindrique [silɛ̃drik] *adj* cylindrical.

cymbale [sɛ̃bal] *nf* cymbal.

cynique [sinik] ◇ *nmf* cynic ◇ *adj* cynical.

cynisme [sinism] *nm* cynicism.

cyprès [sipre] *nm* cypress.

cypriote, Cypriote ▷ **chypriote.**

cyrillique [sirilik] *adj* Cyrillic.

cystite [sistit] *nf* cystitis (*U*).

cytise [sitiz] *nm* laburnum.

d, D [de] *nm inv* d, D.

d' ▷ **de.**

da (*abr de* **déca**) da.

d'abord [dabɔr] ▷ **abord.**

Dacca [daka] *n* Dacca.

d'accord [dakɔr] *loc adv* : **d'accord!** all right!, OK! ; **être ~ avec** to agree with.

dactylo [daktilo] *nf* [personne] typist ; [procédé] typing.

dactylographier [9] [daktilografje] *vt* to type.

dada [dada] *nm* - **1.** [cheval] gee-gee - **2.** *fam* [occupation] hobby - **3.** *fam* [idée] hobbyhorse - **4.** ART Dadaism.

dadais [dade] *nm* fool ; **un grand ~** a big *ou* great lump.

dahlia [dalja] *nm* dahlia.

Dahomey [daɔme] *nm* : **le ~** Dahomey ; **au ~** in Dahomey.

daigner [4] [deɲe] *vi* to deign.

daim [dɛ̃] *nm* - **1.** [animal] fallow deer - **2.** [peau] suede.

dais [de] *nm* canopy.

Dakar [dakar] *n* Dakar.

dal (*abr de* **décalitre**) dal.

dallage [dalaʒ] *nm* [action] paving ; [dalles] pavement.

dalle [dal] *nf* [de pierre] slab ; [de lino] tile ; **avoir la ~** *fam fig* to be famished *ou* starving ; **que ~!** *fam fig* damn all!, not a (damn) thing!

dalmatien, enne [dalmasjɛ̃, ɛn] *nm, f* dalmatian.

daltonien, enne [daltɔnjɛ̃, ɛn] ◇ *adj* colour-blind *Br*, color-blind *Am* ◇ *nm, f* colour-blind *Br ou* color-blind *Am* person.

dam¹ [dam] *nm* : **au grand ~ de** [déplaisir] to the great displeasure of.

dam² (*abr de* **décamètre**) dam.

Damas [damas] *n* Damascus.

dame [dam] *nf* - **1.** [femme] lady - **2.** CARTES & ÉCHECS queen.

➡ **dames** *nfpl* draughts *Br*, checkers *Am*.

dame-jeanne [damʒan] (*pl* dames-jeannes) *nf* demijohn.

damer [3] [dame] *vt* to pack down.

damier [damje] *nm* - **1.** [de jeu] draughtboard *Br*, checkerboard *Am* - **2.** [motif] : à ~ checked.

damnation [danasjɔ̃] *nf* damnation.

damné, e [dane] <> *adj fam* damned <> *nm, f* damned person.

damner [3] [dane] *vt* to damn.
➠ **se damner** *vp* to be damned ; **se ~ pour** *fig* to risk damnation for.

dancing [dɑ̃siŋ] *nm* dance hall.

dandiner [3] [dɑ̃dine] ➠ **se dandiner** *vp* to waddle.

dandy [dɑ̃di] *nm* dandy.

Danemark [danmark] *nm* : **le ~** Denmark ; **au ~** in Denmark.

danger [dɑ̃ʒe] *nm* danger ; **en ~** in danger ; **hors de ~** out of danger ; **courir un ~** to run a risk ; **narguer le ~** to flout danger ; **~ public** public menace.

dangereusement [dɑ̃ʒrøzmɑ̃] *adv* dangerously.

dangereux, euse [dɑ̃ʒrø, øz] *adj* dangerous.

danois, e [danwa, az] *adj* Danish.
➠ **danois** *nm* - **1.** [langue] Danish - **2.** [chien] Great Dane.
➠ **Danois, e** *nm, f* Dane.

dans [dɑ̃] *prép* - **1.** [dans le temps] in ; **je reviens ~ un mois** I'll be back in a month *ou* in a month's time - **2.** [dans l'espace] in ; **~ une boîte** in *ou* inside a box ; **c'est ~ ma chambre/mon sac** it's in my room/my bag - **3.** [avec mouvement] into ; **entrer ~ une chambre** to come into a room, to enter a room - **4.** [indiquant un état, une manière] in ; **vivre ~ la misère** to live in poverty ; **il est ~ le commerce** he's in business - **5.** [environ] : **~ les ...** about ... ; **ça coûte ~ les 200 francs** it costs about 200 francs.

dansant, e [dɑ̃sɑ̃, ɑ̃t] *adj litt* & *fig* dancing ; **soirée ~e** dance ; **thé ~** tea dance.

danse [dɑ̃s] *nf* - **1.** [art] dancing ; **~ classique/folklorique/moderne** ballet/folk/modern dancing ; **~ du ventre** belly dance - **2.** [musique] dance.

danser [3] [dɑ̃se] <> *vi* - **1.** [personne] to dance - **2.** [bateau] to bob ; [flammes] to flicker <> *vt* to dance.

danseur, euse [dɑ̃sœr, øz] *nm, f* dancer ; **en danseuse** *CYCLISME* standing on the pedals ; **~ étoile** principal dancer.

dantesque [dɑ̃tɛsk] *adj* Dantesque, Dantean.

DAO (*abr de* dessin assisté par ordinateur) *nm* CAD.

dard [dar] *nm* [d'animal] sting.

darder [3] [darde] *vt* to beat down ; **~ un regard sur** *fig* to shoot a glance at.

dare-dare [dardar] *adv fam* on the double.

Dar es-Salaam [dares.salam] *n* Dar es-Salaam.

darne [darn] *nf* [de poisson] steak.

dartre [dartr] *nf* sore.

DAT (*abr de* digital audio tape) DAT.

DATAR, Datar [datar] (*abr de* Délégation à l'aménagement du territoire et à l'action régionale) *nf* regional land development agency.

datation [datasjɔ̃] *nf* dating.

date [dat] *nf* - **1.** [jour+mois+année] date ; **~ limite de vente/de consommation** sell-by/use-by date ; **de longue ~** long-standing ; **~ de naissance** date of birth - **2.** [moment] event.

dater [3] [date] <> *vt* to date <> *vi* - **1.** [marquer] to be *ou* mark a milestone - **2.** *fam* [être démodé] to be dated.
➠ **à dater de** *loc prép* as of *ou* from.

dateur, euse [datœr, øz] *adj* date (*avant n*).
➠ **dateur** *nm* [timbre] datestamp ; [de montre] date indicator.

datif [datif] *nm GRAM* dative.

datte [dat] *nf* date.

dattier [datje] *nm* date palm.

daube [dob] *nf CULIN* ≃ stew.

dauphin [dofɛ̃] *nm* - **1.** [mammifère] dolphin - **2.** *HIST* heir apparent.

dauphine [dofin] *nf HIST* heir apparent.

daurade [dɔrad] *nf* sea bream.

davantage [davɑ̃taʒ] *adv* - **1.** [plus] more ; **~ de** more - **2.** [plus longtemps] (any) longer.

dB (*abr de* décibel) dB.

DB (*abr de* division blindée) *nf* armoured *Br ou* armored *Am* division.

DCA (*abr de* défense contre aéronefs) *nf* AA (*anti-aircraft*).

DCT (*abr de* diphtérie coqueluche tétanos) *nm* vaccine against diphtheria, tetanus and whooping cough.

DDA (*abr de* Direction départementale de l'agriculture) *nf* local offices of the Ministry of Agriculture.

DDASS, Ddass [das] (*abr de* Direction départementale d'action sanitaire et sociale) *nf* ≃ DSS *Br*, ≃ SSA *Am* ; **un enfant de la ~** a state orphan.

DDD (*abr de* digital digital digital) DDD.

DDE (*abr de* Direction départementale de

l'**Équipement**) *nf* local offices of the Ministry of the Environment.

DDT (*abr de* dichloro-dyphényl-trichloréthane) *nm* DDT.

DDTAB (*abr de* diphtérie, tétanos, typhoïde, paratyphoïde A) *nm* vaccine against diphtheria, tetanus, typhoid and paratyphoid.

de [də] (*contraction de de + le = **du** [dy], de + les = **des** [de]) ◇ *prép* - **1.** [provenance] from ; revenir ~ **Paris** to come back *ou* return from Paris ; **il est sorti ~ la maison** he left the house, he went out of the house - **2.** [avec à] : ~ ... **à** from ... to ; ~ **Paris à Tokyo** from Paris to Tokyo ; ~ **dix heures à midi** from ten o'clock to *ou* till midday ; **il y avait ~ quinze à vingt mille spectateurs** there were between fifteen and twenty thousand spectators - **3.** [appartenance] of ; **la porte du salon** the door of the sitting room, the sitting room door; **le frère ~ Pierre** Pierre's brother ; **la maison ~ mes parents** my parents' house - **4.** [indique la détermination, la qualité] : **un verre d'eau** a glass of water ; **un peignoir ~ soie** a silk dressing gown ; **un appartement ~ 60 m²** a flat 60 metres square ; **un bébé ~ trois jours** a three-day-old baby ; **une ville ~ 500 000 habitants** a town with *ou* of 500,000 inhabitants ; **le train ~ 9 h 30** the 9.30 train ◇ *article partitif* - **1.** [dans une phrase affirmative] some ; **je voudrais du vin/du lait** I'd like (some) wine/(some) milk ; **boire ~ l'eau** to drink (some) water ; **acheter des légumes** to buy some vegetables - **2.** [dans une interrogation ou une négation] any ; **ils n'ont pas d'enfants** they don't have any children, they have no children ; **avez-vous du pain?** do you have any bread?, have you got any bread? ; **voulez-vous du thé?** would you like some tea?

DE (*abr de* diplômé d'État) *adj* qualified ; **infirmière ~** qualified nurse, ≈ RGN *Br*.

dé [de] *nm* - **1.** [à jouer] dice, die - **2.** [morceau] dice, cube ; **couper en ~s** *CULIN* to dice - **3.** *COUTURE* : ~ **(à coudre)** thimble.

DEA (*abr de* diplôme d'études approfondies) *nm* postgraduate diploma.

dealer¹ [dile] *vt* to deal.

dealer² [dilœr] *nm fam* dealer.

déambuler [3] [deãbyle] *vi* to stroll (around).

débâcle [debɑkl] *nf* [débandade] rout ; *fig* collapse.

déballage [debalaʒ] *nm litt* unpacking.

déballer [3] [debale] *vt* to unpack ; *fam fig* to pour out.

débandade [debãdad] *nf* dispersal.

débaptiser [3] [debatize] *vt* to rename.

débarbouiller [3] [debarbuje] *vt* : ~ **qqn** to wash sb's face.

▸ **se débarbouiller** *vp* to wash one's face.

débarcadère [debarkadɛr] *nm* landing stage.

débardeur [debardœr] *nm* - **1.** [ouvrier] docker - **2.** [vêtement] slipover.

débarquement [debarkəmã] *nm* [de marchandises] unloading ; **le Débarquement** *HIST* the D-Day landings.

débarquer [3] [debarke] ◇ *vt* [marchandises] to unload ; [passagers & *MIL*] to land ◇ *vi* - **1.** [d'un bateau] to disembark - **2.** *MIL* to land - **3.** *fam* [arriver à l'improviste] to turn up ; *fig* to know nothing.

débarras [debara] *nm* junk room ; **bon ~!** *fig* good riddance!

débarrasser [3] [debarase] *vt* - **1.** [pièce] to clear up ; [table] to clear - **2.** [ôter] : ~ **qqn de qqch** to take sthg from sb.

▸ **se débarrasser** *vp* : **se ~ de** to get rid of.

débat [deba] *nm* debate ; **élargir le ~** to broaden *ou* widen the debate.

▸ **débats** *nmpl* debates, proceedings.

débattre [83] [debatr] ◇ *vt* to debate, to discuss ◇ *vi* : ~ **de qqch** to debate *ou* discuss sthg.

▸ **se débattre** *vp* to struggle ; **se ~ avec** *ou* **contre** *fig* to struggle with *ou* against.

débattu, e [debaty] *pp* ▷ **débattre**.

débauche [deboʃ] *nf* debauchery ; **une ~ de** *fig* a profusion of.

débauché, e [deboʃe] ◇ *adj* debauched ◇ *nm, f* debauched person.

débaucher [3] [deboʃe] *vt* - **1.** [corrompre] to debauch, to corrupt - **2.** [licencier] to make redundant.

débile [debil] ◇ *nmf* - **1.** [attardé] retarded person ; ~ **mental** mentally retarded person ; ~ **profond** profoundly retarded person - **2.** *fam* [idiot] moron ◇ *adj fam* stupid.

débilitant, e [debilitã, ãt] *adj* debilitating.

débilité [debilite] *nf* - **1.** [stupidité] stupidity - **2.** [maladie] debility, deficiency.

débiner [3] [debine] ▸ **se débiner** *vp fam* to clear off.

débit [debi] *nm* - **1.** [de marchandises] (retail) sale - **2.** [magasin] : ~ **de boissons** bar ; ~ **de tabac** tobacconist's *Br*, tobacco shop *Am* - **3.** [coupe] sawing up, cutting up - **4.** [de liquide] (rate of) flow - **5.** [élocution] delivery - **6.** *FIN* debit ; **avoir un ~ de 500 francs** to be 500 francs overdrawn.

débitant, e [debitã, ãt] *nm, f* - **1.** [de boissons]

licensed grocer - **2.** [de tabac] tobacconist *Br*, tobacco dealer *Am*.

débiter [3] [debite] *vt* - **1.** [marchandises] to sell - **2.** [arbre] to saw up ; [viande] to cut up - **3.** [suj : robinet] to have a flow of - **4.** *fam fig* [prononcer] to spout - **5.** *FIN* to debit.

débiteur, trice [debitœr, tris] ◇ *adj* - **1.** [personne] debtor *(avant n)* - **2.** *FIN* debit *(avant n)*, in the red ◇ *nm, f* debtor.

déblaiement [deblɛmɑ̃], **déblayage** [deblɛjaʒ] *nm* clearing.

déblatérer [18] [deblatere] *vi fam* [médire] : ~ **contre** to rant on about.

déblayage = **déblaiement**.

déblayer [11] [debleje] *vt* [dégager] to clear ; ~ **le terrain** *fig* to clear the ground.

débloquer [3] [debloke] ◇ *vt* - **1.** [machine] to get going again - **2.** [crédit] to release - **3.** [compte, salaires, prix] to unfreeze ◇ *vi fam* to talk rubbish.

déboguer [deboge] *vt* to debug.

déboires [debwar] *nmpl* - **1.** [déceptions] disappointments - **2.** [échecs] setbacks - **3.** [ennuis] trouble *(U)*, problems.

déboisement [debwazmɑ̃] *nm* deforestation.

déboiser [3] [debwaze] *vt* [région] to deforest ; [terrain] to clear (of trees).
➨ **se déboiser** *vp* to become deforested.

déboîter [3] [debwate] ◇ *vt* - **1.** [objet] to dislodge ; ~ **une porte** to take a door off its hinges - **2.** [membre] to dislocate ◇ *vi AUTOM* to pull out.
➨ **se déboîter** *vp* - **1.** [se démonter] to come apart ; [porte] to come off its hinges - **2.** [membre] to dislocate.

débonnaire [deboner] *adj* good-natured, easy-going.

débordant, e [debordɑ̃, ɑ̃t] *adj* - **1.** [activité] bustling - **2.** [personne] : ~ **de** [joie, vie] overflowing with ; [santé, énergie] bursting with.

débordement [debordəmɑ̃] *nm* - **1.** [de fleuve, récipient] overflowing - **2.** [de joie, tendresse] outburst.
➨ **débordements** *nmpl* excesses.

déborder [3] [deborde] ◇ *vi* [fleuve, liquide] to overflow ; *fig* to flood ; ~ **de** [vie, joie] to be bubbling with ◇ *vt* [limite] to go beyond.

débouché [debuʃe] *nm* - **1.** [issue] end - **2.** *(gén pl)* *COMM* outlet - **3.** [de carrière] prospect, opening.

déboucher [3] [debuʃe] ◇ *vt* - **1.** [bouteille] to open - **2.** [conduite, nez] to unblock ◇ *vi* : ~ **sur** [arriver] to open out into ; *fig* to lead to, to achieve.

débouler [3] [debule] ◇ *vi* [personne - arriver] to charge up ; [animal] to bolt ◇ *vt* to hurtle down.

déboulonner [3] [debulone] *vt* [statue] to dismantle.

débourser [3] [deburse] *vt* to pay out.

déboussoler [3] [debusole] *vt fam* to throw, to disorientate.

debout [dəbu] *adv* - **1.** [gén] : **être** ~ [sur ses pieds] to be standing (up) ; [réveillé] to be up ; [objet] to be standing up *ou* upright ; **mettre qqch** ~ to stand sthg up ; **se mettre** ~ to stand up ; **debout!** get up!, on your feet! - **2.** *loc* : **tenir** ~ [bâtiment] to remain standing ; [argument] to stand up ; **il ne tient pas** ~ he's asleep on his feet.

débouter [3] [debute] *vt JUR* to dismiss.

déboutonner [3] [debutone] *vt* to unbutton, to undo.
➨ **se déboutonner** *vp* [défaire ses boutons] to undo one's buttons/one's jacket *etc*.

débraillé, e [debraje] *adj* dishevelled *Br*, disheveled *Am*.

débrancher [3] [debrɑ̃ʃe] *vt* - **1.** [appareil] to unplug - **2.** [téléphone] to disconnect.

débrayage [debrɛjaʒ] *nm* - **1.** [AUTOM - pièce] clutch ; [- action] disengagement of the clutch - **2.** [arrêt de travail] stoppage.

débrayer [11] [debreje] *vi* - **1.** *AUTOM* to disengage the clutch, to declutch - **2.** [cesser le travail] to stop work.

débridé, e [debride] *adj fig & sout* [imagination, sensualité] unbridled.

débris [debri] ◇ *nm* piece, fragment ◇ *nmpl* - **1.** [restes] leftovers - **2.** *fig & littéraire* [d'armée, fortune] remains ; [d'un état] ruins.

débrouillard, e [debrujar, ard] *fam* ◇ *adj* resourceful ◇ *nm, f* resourceful person.

débrouillardise [debrujardiz] *nf fam* resourcefulness.

débrouiller [3] [debruje] *vt* - **1.** [démêler] to untangle - **2.** *fig* [résoudre] to unravel, to solve.
➨ **se débrouiller** *vp* : **se** ~ **(pour faire qqch)** to manage (to do sthg) ; **se** ~ **en anglais/math** to get by in English/maths ; **débrouille-toi!** you'll have to sort it out (by) yourself!

débroussailler [3] [debrusaje] *vt* [terrain] to clear ; *fig* to do the groundwork for.

débusquer [3] [debyske] *vt* - **1.** [gibier] to drive out - **2.** [personne] to flush out.

début [deby] *nm* beginning, start ; **au** ~ at the start *ou* beginning ; **au** ~ **de** at the beginning of ; **dès le** ~ (right) from the start.
➨ **débuts** *nmpl* debut *(sg)*.

débutant, e [debytã, ãt] *nm, f* beginner.

débuter [3] [debyte] *vi* - **1.** [commencer] : ~ **(par)** to begin (with), to start (with) - **2.** [faire ses débuts] to start out.

déca [deka] *nm fam* decaff.

deçà [dəsa] ➤ **deçà delà** *loc adv* here and there.

➤ **en deçà de** *loc prép* - **1.** [de ce côté-ci de] on this side of - **2.** [en dessous de] short of.

décacheter [27] [dekaʃte] *vt* to open.

décade [dekad] *nf* period of ten days.

décadence [dekadɑ̃s] *nf* - **1.** [déclin] decline - **2.** [débauche] decadence.

décadent, e [dekadɑ̃, ɑ̃t] *adj* decadent.

décaféiné, e [dekafeine] *adj* decaffeinated.

➤ **décaféiné** *nm* decaffeinated coffee.

décalage [dekalaʒ] *nm* gap ; *fig* gulf, discrepancy ; ~ **horaire** [entre zones] time difference ; [après un vol] jet lag.

décalcification [dekalsifikasjɔ̃] *nf* decalcification.

décalcomanie [dekalkɔmani] *nf* transfer *(adhesive)*.

décaler [3] [dekale] *vt* - **1.** [dans le temps - avancer] to bring forward ; [- retarder] to put back - **2.** [dans l'espace] to move, to shift.

➤ **se décaler** *vp* to move.

décalquer [3] [dekalke] *vt* to trace.

décamper [3] [dekɑ̃pe] *vi fam* to clear off.

décan [dekɑ̃] *nm* ASTROL one of three subdivisions of each star sign.

décanter [3] [dekɑ̃te] ◇ *vt* : **laisser** ~ [liquide] to allow to settle ; *fig* [idée] to allow to settle down *ou* become clearer ◇ *vi* [liquide] to settle ; *fig* [idées] to become clear.

➤ **se décanter** *vp* [idées] to become clear.

décapant, e [dekapɑ̃, ɑ̃t] *adj* - **1.** [nettoyant] stripping - **2.** *fig* [incisif] cutting, caustic.

➤ **décapant** *nm* (paint) stripper.

décaper [3] [dekape] *vt* to strip, to sand.

décapiter [3] [dekapite] *vt* - **1.** [personne - volontairement] to behead ; [- accidentellement] to decapitate - **2.** [arbre] to cut the top off - **3.** *fig* [organisation, parti] to remove the leader *ou* leaders of.

décapotable [dekapɔtabl] *nf* & *adj* convertible.

décapsuler [3] [dekapsyle] *vt* to take the top off, to open.

décapsuleur [3] [dekapsylœr] *nm* bottle opener.

décarcasser [3] [dekarkase] ➤ **se décarcasser** *vp fam* : **se** ~ **(à faire qqch)** to slog away (at doing sthg).

décédé, e [desede] *adj* deceased.

décéder [18] [desede] *vi* to die.

déceler [25] [desle] *vt* - **1.** [révéler] to reveal - **2.** [repérer] to detect.

décélération [deselerasjɔ̃] *nf* deceleration.

décembre [desɑ̃br] *nm* December ; *voir aussi* **septembre**.

décemment [desamɑ̃] *adv* - **1.** [convenablement] properly - **2.** [raisonnablement] reasonably.

décence [desɑ̃s] *nf* decency.

décennie [deseni] *nf* decade.

décent, e [desɑ̃, ɑ̃t] *adj* decent.

décentralisation [desɑ̃tralizasjɔ̃] *nf* decentralization.

décentraliser [3] [desɑ̃tralize] *vt* to decentralize.

décentrer [3] [desɑ̃tre] *vt* to move off-centre *Br ou* off-center *Am*.

déception [desɛpsjɔ̃] *nf* disappointment.

décerner [3] [deserne] *vt* : ~ **qqch à** to award sthg to.

décès [desɛ] *nm* death.

décevant, e [desəvɑ̃, ɑ̃t] *adj* disappointing.

décevoir [52] [desəvwar] *vt* to disappoint.

déchaîné, e [deʃene] *adj* - **1.** [vent, mer] stormy, wild - **2.** [passion] unrestrained ; [opinion publique] raging - **3.** [personne] wild.

déchaîner [4] [deʃene] *vt* [passion] to unleash ; [rires] to cause an outburst of.

➤ **se déchaîner** *vp* - **1.** [éléments naturels] to erupt - **2.** [personne] to fly into a rage.

déchanter [3] [deʃɑ̃te] *vi* to become disillusioned.

décharge [deʃarʒ] *nf* - **1.** JUR discharge - **2.** ÉLECTR discharge ; ~ **électrique** electric *Br ou* electrical *Am* shock - **3.** [reçu] receipt - **4.** [dépotoir] rubbish tip *ou* dump *Br*, garbage dump *Am* ; ~ **municipale** city/town dump.

déchargement [deʃarʒəmɑ̃] *nm* unloading.

décharger [17] [deʃarʒe] *vt* - **1.** [véhicule, marchandises] to unload - **2.** [arme - tirer] to fire, to discharge ; [- enlever la charge de] to unload - **3.** [soulager - cœur] to unburden ; [- conscience] to salve ; [- colère] to vent - **4.** [libérer] : ~ **qqn de** to release sb from.

➤ **se décharger** *vp* - **1.** ÉLECTR to go flat - **2.** [se libérer] : **se** ~ **de qqch sur** to offload sthg onto - **3.** [rivière] : **se** ~ **dans** to flow into.

décharné, e [deʃarne] *adj* [maigre] emaciated.

déchausser [3] [deʃose] *vt* : ~ **qqn** to take sb's shoes off.

➤ **se déchausser** *vp* - **1.** [personne] to take one's shoes off - **2.** [dent] to come loose.

dèche [dɛʃ] *nf fam* : **être dans la** ~ to be on one's uppers.

déchéance [deʃeãs] *nf* - **1.** [déclin] degeneration, decline - **2.** [d'un souverain] dethronement - **3.** JUR loss.

déchet [deʃɛ] *nm* [de matériau] scrap.
➡ **déchets** *nmpl* refuse *(U)*, waste *(U)* ; **~s radioactifs** radioactive waste.

déchetterie® [deʃɛtri] *nf* recycling centre *Br* ou center *Am*.

déchiffrer [3] [deʃifre] *vt* - **1.** [inscription, hiéroglyphes] to decipher ; [énigme] to unravel - **2.** MUS to sight-read.

déchiqueter [27] [deʃikte] *vt* to tear to shreds.

déchirant, e [deʃirã, ãt] *adj* heartrending.

déchirement [deʃirmã] *nm* - **1.** [division] rift, split - **2.** [souffrance morale] heartbreak, distress.

déchirer [3] [deʃire] *vt* - **1.** [papier, tissu] to tear up, to rip up - **2.** *fig* [diviser] to tear apart.
➡ **se déchirer** *vp* - **1.** [personnes] to tear each other apart - **2.** [matériau, muscle] to tear.

déchirure [deʃiryr] *nf* tear ; *fig* wrench ; **~ musculaire** MÉD torn muscle.

déchoir [71] [deʃwar] *vi sout* [s'abaisser] to demean o.s.

déchu, e [deʃy] <> *pp* ▷ **déchoir** <> *adj* - **1.** [homme, ange] fallen ; [souverain] deposed - **2.** JUR : **être ~ de** to be deprived of.

deci [dəsi] ➡ **deci-delà** *adv sout* here and there.

décibel [desibɛl] *nm* decibel.

décidé, e [deside] *adj* - **1.** [résolu] determined - **2.** [arrêté] settled.

décidément [desidemã] *adv* really.

décider [3] [deside] *vt* - **1.** [prendre une décision] : **~ (de faire qqch)** to decide (to do sthg) ; **~ que** to decide (that) - **2.** [convaincre] : **~ qqn à faire qqch** to persuade sb to do sthg - **3.** [déterminer] : **~ de qqch** to decide on sthg.
➡ **se décider** *vp* - **1.** [personne] : **se ~ (à faire qqch)** to make up one's mind (to do sthg) - **2.** [affaire] to be decided, to be settled - **3.** [choisir] : **se ~ pour** to decide on, to settle on.

décideur [desidœr] *nm* decision-maker.

décilitre [desilitr] *nm* decilitre.

décimal, e, aux [desimal, o] *adj* decimal.
➡ **décimale** *nf* decimal.

décimer [3] [desime] *vt* to decimate.

décimètre [desimɛtr] *nm* - **1.** [dixième de mètre] decimetre - **2.** [règle] ruler ; **double ~** ≃ foot rule.

décisif, ive [desizif, iv] *adj* decisive.

décision [desizjɔ̃] *nf* decision ; **prendre une ~** to take ou make a decision.

décisionnaire [desizjɔnɛr] *nmf* decision-maker.

déclamer [3] [deklame] *vt* to declaim.

déclaration [deklarasjɔ̃] *nf* - **1.** [orale] declaration, announcement ; **faire une ~** to make a statement ; **~ de guerre/d'amour** declaration of war/of love - **2.** [écrite] report, declaration ; [d'assurance] claim ; **~ de naissance/de décès** registration of birth/death ; **~ d'impôts** tax return ; **~ de revenus** statement of income.

DÉCLARATION D'IMPÔTS

People in France are required to declare their taxable earnings at the beginning of the year. Quarterly tax payments ('tiers provisionnels') are based on estimated tax for the year, the payment for the final quarter being adjusted according to the actual tax owed.

déclarer [3] [deklare] *vt* - **1.** [annoncer] to declare ; **~ que** to declare (that) - **2.** [signaler] to report ; **rien à ~** nothing to declare ; **~ une naissance** to register a birth.
➡ **se déclarer** *vp* - **1.** [se prononcer] : **se ~ pour/contre qqch** to come out in favour of/against sthg - **2.** [se manifester] to break out.

déclasser [3] [deklase] *vt* - **1.** [personne - gén] to downgrade ; [- SPORT] to relegate - **2.** [objets] to get out of order.

déclenchement [deklãʃmã] *nm* [de mécanisme] activating, setting off ; *fig* launching.

déclencher [3] [deklãʃe] *vt* [mécanisme] to activate, to set off ; *fig* to launch.
➡ **se déclencher** *vp* [mécanisme] to go off, to be activated ; *fig* to be triggered off.

déclic [deklik] *nm* - **1.** [mécanisme] trigger - **2.** [bruit] click.

déclin [deklɛ̃] *nm* - **1.** [de civilisation, population, santé] decline ; **une personnalité sur son ~** *fig* a celebrity on the wane - **2.** [fin] close.

déclinaison [deklinɛzɔ̃] *nf* GRAM declension.

décliner [3] [dekline] <> *vi* - **1.** [santé, population, popularité] to decline - **2.** [jour] to draw to a close <> *vt* - **1.** [offre, honneur] to decline ; **~ une invitation** to decline an invitation ; **~ toute responsabilité** to accept no responsibility - **2.** GRAM to decline ; *fig* [gamme de produits] to develop - **3.** [énoncer] to state.
➡ **se décliner** *vp* GRAM to decline.

déclivité [deklivite] *nf* slope, incline.

décloisonner [3] [deklwazɔne] *vt fig* to decompartmentalize.

déclouer [3] [deklue] *vt* to take the nails out of.

décocher [3] [dekɔʃe] *vt litt* & *fig* to let fly ; ~ **un regard** to shoot a glance.

décoction [dekɔksjɔ̃] *nf* decoction.

décodage [dekɔdaʒ] *nm* decoding.

décoder [3] [dekɔde] *vt* to decode.

décodeur [dekɔdœr] *nm* decoder.

décoiffer [3] [dekwafe] *vt* [cheveux] to mess up.
➤ **se décoiffer** *vp* - **1.** [cheveux] to be messed up - **2.** [enlever son chapeau] to take off one's hat.

décoincer [16] [dekwɛ̃se] *vt* - **1.** [chose] to loosen ; [mécanisme] to unjam - **2.** *fam* [personne] to loosen up.
➤ **se décoincer** *vp* - **1.** [mécanisme] to loosen - **2.** *fam fig* [personne] to loosen up.

déçois, déçoit etc ⊳ **décevoir.**

décolérer [18] [dekɔlere] *vi* : **il n'a pas décoléré** he hasn't calmed down.

décollage [dekɔlaʒ] *nm litt* & *fig* takeoff.

décollé, e [dekɔle] *adj* : **il a les oreilles ~es** his ears stick out.

décollement [dekɔlmã] *nm* : ~ **de la rétine** MÉD detachment of the retina.

décoller [3] [dekɔle] ⋄ *vt* [étiquette, timbre] to unstick ; [papier peint] to strip (off) ⋄ *vi litt* & *fig* to take off.
➤ **se décoller** *vp* [étiquette, timbre] to come unstuck ; [papier peint] to peel off.

décolleté, e [dekɔlte] *adj* [vêtement] low-cut.
➤ **décolleté** *nm* - **1.** [de personne] neck and shoulders *(pl)* - **2.** [de vêtement] neckline, neck.

décolonisation [dekɔlɔnizasjɔ̃] *nf* decolonization.

décolorant, e [dekɔlɔrã, ãt] *adj* bleaching *(avant n).*
➤ **décolorant** *nm* bleach.

décoloration [dekɔlɔrasjɔ̃] *nf* bleaching.

décolorer [3] [dekɔlɔre] *vt* [par décolorant] to bleach, to lighten ; [par usure] to fade.
➤ **se décolorer** *vp* - **1.** [se ternir] to fade - **2.** [cheveux] to bleach.

décombres [dekɔ̃br] *nmpl* debris *(U).*

décommander [3] [dekɔmãde] *vt* to cancel.
➤ **se décommander** *vp* to cancel one's appointment.

décomposé, e [dekɔ̃poze] *adj* - **1.** [pourri] decomposed - **2.** [visage] haggard ; [personne] in shock.

décomposer [3] [dekɔ̃poze] *vt* - **1.** [gén] : ~ **(en)** to break down (into) - **2.** *fig* [troubler] to distort.

➤ **se décomposer** *vp* - **1.** [se putréfier] to rot, to decompose - **2.** [se diviser] : **se ~ en** to be broken down into - **3.** *fig* [s'altérer] to be distorted.

décomposition [dekɔ̃pozisjɔ̃] *nf* - **1.** [putréfaction] decomposition - **2.** *fig* [analyse] breaking down, analysis.

décompresser [4] [dekɔ̃prese] ⋄ *vt* TECHNOL to decompress ⋄ *vi* to unwind.

décompression [dekɔ̃presjɔ̃] *nf* decompression.

décompte [dekɔ̃t] *nm* - **1.** [calcul] breakdown (of an amount) - **2.** [réduction] deduction ; **j'ai fait le ~ de ce que tu me dois** I've deducted *ou* taken off what you owe me.

décompter [3] [dekɔ̃te] *vt* to deduct.

déconcentrer [3] [dekɔ̃sãtre] *vt* - **1.** [disséminer] to decentralize - **2.** [distraire] to distract.
➤ **se déconcentrer** *vp* to be distracted.

déconcertant, e [dekɔ̃sɛrtã, ãt] *adj* disconcerting.

déconcerter [3] [dekɔ̃sɛrte] *vt* to disconcert.

déconfit, e [dekɔ̃fi, it] *adj* crestfallen.

déconfiture [dekɔ̃fityr] *nf* collapse, ruin.

décongeler [25] [dekɔ̃ʒle] *vt* to defrost.

décongestionner [3] [dekɔ̃ʒɛstjɔne] *vt* to relieve congestion in ; ~ **la circulation** to reduce traffic.

déconnecter [4] [dekɔnɛkte] *vt* to disconnect ; **être déconnecté** *fam* to be out of touch.
➤ **se déconnecter** *vp* INFORM to disconnect, to log off.

déconner [3] [dekɔne] *vi tfam* [dire] to talk rubbish ; [faire] to muck around.

déconseillé, e [dekɔ̃seje] *adj* : **c'est fortement ~** it's extremely inadvisable.

déconseiller [4] [dekɔ̃seje] *vt* : ~ **qqch à qqn** to advise sb against sthg ; ~ **à qqn de faire qqch** to advise sb against doing sthg.

déconsidérer [18] [dekɔ̃sidere] *vt* to discredit.
➤ **se déconsidérer** *vp* to be discredited.

décontaminer [3] [dekɔ̃tamine] *vt* to decontaminate.

décontenancer [16] [dekɔ̃tnãse] *vt* to put out.
➤ **se décontenancer** *vp* to be put out.

décontracté, e [dekɔ̃trakte] *adj* - **1.** [muscle] relaxed - **2.** [détendu] casual, laid-back.

décontracter [3] [dekɔ̃trakte] *vt* to relax.
➤ **se décontracter** *vp* to relax.

déconvenue [dekɔ̃vny] *nf* disappointment.

décor [dekɔr] *nm* - **1.** [cadre] scenery - **2.** [ornement] decoration **- 3.** THÉÂTRE scenery *(U)* ; CIN sets *(pl)*, décor.

décorateur, trice [dekɔratœr, tris] *nm, f* CIN & THÉÂTRE designer ; ~ **d'intérieur** interior decorator.

décoratif, ive [dekɔratif, iv] *adj* decorative.

décoration [dekɔrasjɔ̃] *nf* decoration.

décorer [3] [dekɔre] *vt* to decorate.

décortiquer [3] [dekɔrtike] *vt* [noix] to shell ; [graine] to husk ; *fig* to analyse *Br* ou analyze *Am* in minute detail.

décorum [dekɔrɔm] *nm* decorum.

découcher [3] [dekuʃe] *vi* to stay out all night.

découdre [86] [dekudr] *vt* COUTURE to unpick ; **en ~** to come to blows.

➤ **se découdre** *vp* to come unstitched.

découler [3] [dekule] *vi* : ~ **de** to follow from.

découpage [dekupaʒ] *nm* **- 1.** [action] cutting out ; [résultat] paper cutout **- 2.** CIN preparation of screenplay **- 3.** ADMIN : ~ **(électoral)** division into constituencies **- 4.** *fig* [de texte] cutting, editing.

découper [3] [dekupe] *vt* **- 1.** [couper] to cut up **- 2.** *fig* [diviser] to cut out.

➤ **se découper** *vp fig* : **se ~ sur** to stand out against.

découplé, e [dekuple] *adj* : **bien ~** well-proportioned.

découpure [dekupyr] *nf* [bord] indentations *(pl)*, jagged outline.

décourageant, e [dekuraʒɑ̃, ɑ̃t] *adj* discouraging.

découragement [dekuraʒmɑ̃] *nm* discouragement.

décourager [17] [dekuraʒe] *vt* to discourage ; ~ **qqn de qqch** to put sb off sthg ; ~ **qqn de faire qqch** to discourage sb from doing sthg.

➤ **se décourager** *vp* to lose heart.

décousu, e [dekuzy] ⬦ *pp* ⊳ **découdre** ⬦ *adj fig* [conversation] disjointed.

découvert, e [dekuvɛr, ɛrt] ⬦ *pp* ⊳ **découvrir** ⬦ *adj* [tête] bare ; [terrain] exposed.

➤ **découvert** *nm* BANQUE overdraft ; **être à ~ (de 6 000 francs)** to be (6,000 francs) overdrawn.

➤ **découverte** *nf* discovery ; **aller à la ~e de** to explore.

découvrir [34] [dekuvrir] *vt* **- 1.** [trouver, surprendre] to discover **- 2.** [ôter ce qui couvre, mettre à jour] to uncover **- 3.** [laisser voir] to reveal.

➤ **se découvrir** *vp* **- 1.** [se dévêtir] to take off one's clothes, to undress **- 2.** [ôter son chapeau]

to take off one's hat **- 3.** [ciel] to clear **- 4.** [se trouver - cousin, penchant] to discover.

décrasser [3] [dekrase] *vt* to scrub.

décrépit, e [dekrepi, it] *adj* decrepit.

décrépitude [dekrepityd] *nf* **- 1.** [de personne] decrepitude **- 2.** [d'objet] dilapidation.

decrescendo [dekreʃɛndo] ⬦ *nm inv* decrescendo ⬦ *adv* MUS decrescendo ; **aller ~** *fig* to wane.

décret [dekrɛ] *nm* decree ; ~ **ministériel** order in council.

décréter [18] [dekrete] *vt* **- 1.** ADMIN to decree **- 2.** [décider] : ~ **que** to decide that.

décrier [10] [dekrije] *vt sout* to decry.

décrire [99] [dekrir] *vt* to describe.

décrisper [3] [dekrispe] *vt* **- 1.** [personne] to put at ease **- 2.** [atmosphère] to ease.

➤ **se décrisper** *vp* to relax.

décrit, e [dekri, it] *pp* ⊳ **décrire**.

décrochement [dekrɔʃmɑ̃] *nm* **- 1.** GÉOL thrust fault **- 2.** [action] unhooking **- 3.** [partie en retrait] recess.

décrocher [3] [dekrɔʃe] ⬦ *vt* **- 1.** [enlever] to take down **- 2.** [téléphone] to pick up **- 3.** *fam* [obtenir] to land ⬦ *vi fam* [abandonner] to drop out.

➤ **se décrocher** *vp* to fall down.

décroiser [3] [dekrwaze] *vt* to unfold, to uncross.

décroissant, e [dekrwasɑ̃, ɑ̃t] *adj* [courbe] decreasing ; [influence] diminishing ; **par ordre ~** in descending order.

décroître [94] [dekrwatr] *vi* to decrease, to diminish ; [jours] to get shorter.

décrotter [3] [dekrɔte] *vt* to clean the mud off.

décru, e [dekry] *pp* ⊳ **décroître**.

➤ **décrue** *nf* drop in the water level.

décrypter [3] [dekripte] *vt* to decipher.

déçu, e [desy] ⬦ *pp* ⊳ **décevoir** ⬦ *adj* disappointed.

déculotter [3] [dekylɔte] *vt* : ~ **qqn** to take sb's trousers off.

➤ **se déculotter** *vp* to take off one's trousers.

déculpabiliser [3] [dekylpabilize] *vt* : ~ **qqn** to free sb from guilt.

➤ **se déculpabiliser** *vp* to free o.s. from guilt.

décupler [3] [dekyple] *vt* & *vi* to increase tenfold.

dédaigner [4] [dedeɲe] *vt* **- 1.** [mépriser - personne] to despise ; [- conseils, injures] to scorn **- 2.** [refuser] : ~ **de faire qqch** *sout* to disdain to do sthg ; **ne pas ~ qqch/de faire qqch** not to be above sthg/above doing sthg.

dédaigneusement [dedɛɲøzmɑ̃] *adv* disdainfully.

dédaigneux, euse [dedɛɲø, øz] *adj* disdainful.

dédain [dedɛ̃] *nm* disdain, contempt.

dédale [dedal] *nm littt* & *fig* maze.

dedans [dədɑ̃] *adv* & *nm* inside.
➤ **de dedans** *loc adv* from inside, from within.
➤ **en dedans** *loc adv* inside, within.
➤ **en dedans de** *loc prép* inside, within ; *voir aussi* **là-dedans**.

dédicace [dedikas] *nf* dedication.

dédicacer [16] [dedikase] *vt* : **~ qqch (à qqn)** to sign *ou* autograph sthg (for sb).

dédié, e [dedje] *adj* INFORM dedicated.

dédier [9] [dedje] *vt* : **~ qqch (à qqn/à qqch)** to dedicate sthg (to sb/to sthg).

dédire [103] [dedir] ➤ **se dédire** *vp sout* to go back on one's word.

dédit [dedi] *nm* JUR penalty (clause).

dédommagement [dedɔmaʒmɑ̃] *nm* compensation.

dédommager [17] [dedɔmaʒe] *vt* - **1.** [indemniser] to compensate - **2.** *fig* [remercier] to repay.

dédouanement [dedwanmɑ̃], **dédouanage** [dedwanaʒ] *nm* customs clearance.

dédouaner [3] [dedwane] *vt* [marchandises] to clear through customs.

dédoublement [dedublɔmɑ̃] *nm* halving, splitting (in two) ; **~ de la personnalité** PSYCHOL & *fig* split personality.

dédoubler [3] [deduble] *vt* to halve, to split ; [fil] to separate.
➤ **se dédoubler** *vp* - **1.** PSYCHOL & *fig* to have a split personality - **2.** *fig* & *hum* [être partout] to be in two places at once.

dédramatiser [3] [dedramatize] *vt* [événement] to play down ; [situation] to defuse.

déductible [dedyktibl] *adj* deductible.

déduction [dedyksjɔ̃] *nf* deduction.

déduire [98] [deduir] *vt* : **~ qqch (de)** [ôter] to deduct sthg (from) ; [conclure] to deduce sthg (from).

déduisais, déduisait *etc* ➞ **déduire**.

déduit, e [dedɥi, it] *pp* ➞ **déduire**.

déesse [deɛs] *nf* goddess.

DEFA, Defa [defa] (*abr de* **diplôme d'État relatif aux fonctions d'animation**) *nm* diploma for senior youth leaders.

défaillance [defajɑ̃s] *nf* - **1.** [incapacité - de ma-

chine] failure ; [- de personne, organisation] weakness - **2.** [malaise] blackout, fainting fit ; **~ cardiaque** MÉD heart failure.

défaillant, e [defajɑ̃, ɑ̃t] *adj* [faible] failing.

défaillir [47] [defajir] *vi* - **1.** [s'évanouir] to faint - **2.** [faire défaut] to fail.

défaire [109] [defɛr] *vt* - **1.** [détacher] to undo ; [valise] to unpack ; [lit] to strip - **2.** *sout* [vaincre] to defeat.
➤ **se défaire** *vp* - **1.** [ne pas tenir] to come undone - **2.** *sout* [se séparer] : **se ~ de** to get rid of.

défaisais, défaisions *etc* ➞ **défaire**.

défait, e [defɛ, ɛt] ◇ *pp* ➞ **défaire** ◇ *adj* *fig* [épuisé] haggard.
➤ **défaite** *nf* defeat.

défaitisme [defetism] *nm* defeatism.

défaitiste [defetist] *nmf* & *adj* defeatist.

défalcation [defalkasjɔ̃] *nf* deduction.

défalquer [3] [defalke] *vt* to deduct.

défasse, défasses *etc* ➞ **défaire**.

défaut [defo] *nm* - **1.** [imperfection - gén] flaw ; [- de personne] fault, shortcoming ; **~ de fabrication** manufacturing fault - **2.** [manque] lack ; **à ~ de** for lack *ou* want of ; **l'eau fait (cruellement) ~** there is a serious water shortage ; **par ~** [être jugé] in one's absence ; [calculer] to the nearest decimal point.

défaveur [defavœr] *nf* disfavour Br, disfavor Am ; **être en ~** to be out of favour Br *ou* favor Am ; **tomber en ~** to fall out of favour Br *ou* favor Am.

défavorable [defavɔrabl] *adj* unfavourable Br, unfavorable Am.

défavorisé, e [defavɔrize] *adj* disadvantaged, underprivileged.

défavoriser [3] [defavɔrize] *vt* to handicap, to penalize.

défectif, ive [defɛktiv, iv] *adj* GRAM defective.

défection [defɛksjɔ̃] *nf* - **1.** [absence] absence - **2.** [abandon] defection.

défectueux, euse [defɛktɥø, øz] *adj* faulty, defective.

défendable [defɑ̃dabl] *adj littt* & *fig* defensible.

défendais, défendions *etc* ➞ **défendre**.

défendeur, eresse [defɑ̃dœr, rɛs] *nm, f* defendant.

défendre [73] [defɑ̃dr] *vt* - **1.** [personne, opinion, client] to defend - **2.** [interdire] to forbid ; **~ qqch à qqn** to forbid sb sthg ; **~ à qqn de faire qqch** to forbid sb to do sthg ; **~ que qqn fasse qqch** to forbid sb to do sthg.
➤ **se défendre** *vp* - **1.** [se battre, se justifier] to defend o.s. - **2.** *fam* [se débrouiller] : **se ~ (en)** to

get by (in) - **3.** [nier] : **se ~ de faire qqch** to deny doing sthg - **4.** [thèse] to stand up.

défendu, e [defãdy] <> pp ⊳ **défendre** <> adj : **'il est ~ de jouer au ballon'** 'no ball games'.

défense [defãs] nf - **1.** [d'éléphant] tusk - **2.** [interdiction] prohibition, ban ; **'~ de fumer/de stationner/d'entrer'** 'no smoking/parking/ entry' ; **'~ d'afficher'** 'stick no bills' - **3.** [protection] defence Br, defense Am ; **prendre la ~ de** to stand up for ; **~ antiaérienne** MIL anti-aircraft defence Br ou defense Am ; **~ des consommateurs** consumer protection ; **la ~ nationale** MIL national defence Br ou defense Am ; **légitime ~** JUR self-defence Br, self-defense Am.

défenseur [defãsœr] nm - **1.** JUR counsel for the defence Br, defense attorney Am - **2.** [partisan] champion - **3.** HOCKEY : **~ droit** right defence Br ou defense Am ; **~ gauche** left defence Br ou defense Am.

défensif, ive [defãsif, iv] adj defensive.

◆ **défensive** nf : **être sur la défensive** to be on the defensive.

déféquer [18] [defeke] vi to defecate.

déférence [deferãs] nf deference.

déférer [18] [defere] <> vt JUR to refer <> vi sout [céder] : **~ à** to defer to.

déferlement [deferləmã] nm [de vagues] breaking ; fig surge, upsurge.

déferler [3] [deferle] vi [vagues] to break ; fig to surge.

défi [defi] nm challenge ; **mettre qqn au ~ de faire qqch** to challenge sb to do sthg ; **relever le ~** to take up the challenge.

défiance [defjãs] nf distrust, mistrust.

défiant, e [defjã, ãt] adj distrustful, mistrustful.

déficeler [24] [defisle] vt to untie.

déficience [defisjãs] nf deficiency.

déficient, e [defisjã, ãt] adj deficient.

déficit [defisit] nm - **1.** FIN deficit ; **être en ~** to be in deficit - **2.** [manque] deficiency.

déficitaire [defisiter] adj in deficit.

défier [9] [defje] vt - **1.** [braver] : **~ qqn de faire qqch** to defy sb to do sthg - **2.** vieilli [provoquer] : **~ (qqn à)** to challenge (sb to).

◆ **se défier** vp littéraire : **se ~ de qqn/qqch** to mistrust sb/sthg.

défigurer [3] [defigyre] vt - **1.** [blesser] to disfigure - **2.** [enlaidir] to deface.

défilé [defile] nm - **1.** [parade] parade ; **~ de mode** fashion parade - **2.** [couloir] defile, narrow pass.

défiler [3] [defile] vi - **1.** [dans une parade] to march past - **2.** [se succéder] to pass.

◆ **se défiler** vp fam to back out.

défini, e [defini] adj - **1.** [précis] clear, precise - **2.** GRAM definite.

définir [32] [definir] vt to define.

définitif, ive [definitif, iv] adj definitive, final.

◆ **en définitive** loc adv in the end.

définition [definisjõ] nf definition ; **par ~** by definition.

définitivement [definitivmã] adv for good, permanently.

défiscaliser [3] [defiskalize] vt to exempt from taxation.

déflagration [deflagrasjõ] nf explosion.

déflation [deflasjõ] nf deflation.

déflationniste [deflasjɔnist] adj deflationary, deflationist.

déflecteur [deflɛktœr] nm quarterlight.

déflorer [3] [deflɔre] vt [jeune fille] to deflower ; fig to taint.

défonce [defõs] nf arg drogue high.

défoncé, e [defõse] adj - **1.** [abîmé - route] with large potholes ; [- chaise] broken, broken-down - **2.** arg drogue [drogué] high, stoned.

défoncer [16] [defõse] vt [caisse, porte] to smash in ; [route] to break up ; [mur] to smash down ; [chaise] to break.

◆ **se défoncer** vp - **1.** arg drogue to trip, to get high - **2.** fam [se surpasser] to go all out, to work flat out.

déformant, e [deformã, ãt] adj distorting.

déformation [deformasjõ] nf - **1.** [d'objet, de théorie] distortion - **2.** MÉD deformity ; **~ professionnelle** mental conditioning caused by one's job.

déformer [3] [deforme] vt to distort.

◆ **se déformer** vp [changer de forme] to be distorted, to be deformed ; [se courber] to bend.

défoulement [defulmã] nm unwinding, letting off steam.

défouler [3] [defule] vt fam to unwind.

◆ **se défouler** vp fam to let off steam, to unwind.

défrayer [11] [defreje] vt [payer] : **~ qqn** to pay sb's expenses ou costs.

défricher [3] [defrife] vt [terrain] to clear ; fig [question] to do the groundwork for.

défriser [3] [defrize] vt - **1.** [cheveux] to straighten - **2.** fam fig [déplaire] to bother.

défroisser [3] [defrwase] vt to smooth out.

défunt, e [defœ̃, œ̃t] <> adj [décédé] late <> nm, f deceased.

dégagé, e [degaʒe] *adj* **- 1.** [ciel, vue] clear ; [partie du corps] bare **- 2.** [désinvolte] casual, airy **- 3.** [libre] : **~ de** free from.

dégagement [degaʒmɑ̃] *nm* **- 1.** [passage] passage **- 2.** [émanation] emission **- 3.** [évacuation] freeing, extricating.

dégager [17] [degaʒe] <> *vt* **- 1.** [odeur] to produce, to give off **- 2.** [délivrer - blessé] to free, to extricate **- 3.** [idée] to bring out **- 4.** [bénéfice] to show **- 5.** [budget] to release **- 6.** [pièce] to clear **- 7.** [libérer] : **~ qqn de** to release sb from <> *vi fam* [partir] to clear off.
 se dégager *vp* **- 1.** [se délivrer] : **se ~ de qqch** to free o.s. from sthg ; *fig* to get out of sthg **- 2.** [se désencombrer] to clear **- 3.** [émaner] to be given off **- 4.** [émerger] to emerge.

dégaine [degen] *nf fam* gawkiness *(U)*.

dégainer [4] [degene] *vt* [épée, revolver] to draw.

dégarnir [32] [degarnir] *vt* to strip, to clear.
 se dégarnir *vp* [vitrine] to be cleared ; [arbre] to lose its leaves ; **sa tête se dégarnit, il se dégarnit** he's going bald.

dégât [dega] *nm litt* & *fig* damage *(U)* ; **faire des ~s** to cause damage ; **limiter les ~s** *fig* to call a halt before things get any worse.

dégel [deʒɛl] *nm* **- 1.** [fonte des glaces] thaw **- 2.** FIN unfreezing.

dégeler [25] [deʒle] <> *vt* **- 1.** [produit surgelé] to thaw **- 2.** FIN to unfreeze **- 3.** *fig* [dérider] to warm up <> *vi* to thaw.
 se dégeler *vp fig* to thaw, to warm up.

dégénéré, e [deʒenere] *adj* & *nm, f* degenerate.

dégénérer [18] [deʒenere] *vi* to degenerate ; **~ en** to degenerate into.

dégénérescence [deʒeneresɑ̃s] *nf* degeneration, degeneracy.

dégingandé, e [deʒɛ̃gɑ̃de] *adj fam* gangling.

dégivrer [3] [deʒivre] *vt* [pare-brise] to de-ice ; [réfrigérateur] to defrost.

dégivreur [deʒivrœr] *nm* [de voiture, avion] de-icer ; [de réfrigérateur] defroster.

déglinguer [3] [deglɛ̃ge] *vt fam* to smash (to pieces).
 se déglinguer *vp fam* to fall to pieces.

déglutition [deglytisjɔ̃] *nf* swallowing.

dégonflé, e [degɔ̃fle] <> *adj* [pneu, roue] flat <> *nm, f fam* [personne] chicken, yellow-belly.

dégonfler [3] [degɔ̃fle] <> *vt* to deflate, to let down <> *vi* to go down ; **faire ~** to reduce the swelling of.
 se dégonfler *vp* **- 1.** [objet] to go down **- 2.** *fam* [personne] to chicken out.

dégorger [17] [degɔrʒe] <> *vt* **- 1.** [tuyau] to clear (out) **- 2.** [eau] to discharge **- 3.** [soie, laine] to purify <> *vi* **- 1.** [tissu] to run **- 2.** CULIN : **faire ~** to soak.

dégot(t)er [degɔte] [3] *vt fam* to dig up.
 se dégot(t)er *vp fam* to dig up for o.s.

dégouliner [3] [deguline] *vi* to trickle.

dégourdi, e [degurdi] <> *adj* clever <> *nm, f* clever person.

dégourdir [32] [degurdir] *vt* **- 1.** [membres - ankylosés] to restore the circulation to ; [- gelés] to warm up **- 2.** *fig* [déniaiser] : **~ qqn** to teach sb a thing or two.
 se dégourdir *vp* **- 1.** [membres] : **se ~ les jambes** to stretch one's legs **- 2.** *fig* [acquérir de l'aisance] to learn a thing or two.

dégoût [degu] *nm* disgust, distaste ; **le ~ de la vie** world-weariness ; **ravaler son ~** to swallow one's distaste.

dégoûtant, e [degutɑ̃, ɑ̃t] <> *adj* **- 1.** [sale] filthy, disgusting **- 2.** [révoltant, grossier] disgusting <> *nm, f* disgusting person.

dégoûté, e [degute] <> *adj* [écœuré] disgusted ; **~ de** sick of <> *nm, f* : **faire le ~** to be fussy.

dégoûter [3] [degute] *vt* to disgust ; **~ qqn de qqch/de faire qqch** to put sb off sthg/off doing sthg.

dégoutter [3] [degute] *vi* : **~ (de qqch)** to drip (with sthg).

dégradant, e [degradɑ̃, ɑ̃t] *adj* degrading.

dégradation [degradasjɔ̃] *nf* **- 1.** [de bâtiment] damage ; [du sol] erosion **- 2.** [de moral] decline **- 3.** [de personne] degradation **- 4.** [de situation] deterioration.

dégradé, e [degrade] *adj* [couleur] shading off.
 dégradé *nm* gradation ; **un ~ de bleu** a blue shading.
 en dégradé *loc adv* [cheveux] layered.

dégrader [3] [degrade] *vt* **- 1.** [officier] to degrade **- 2.** [abîmer -] to damage ; [- sol] to erode **- 3.** *fig* [avilir] to degrade, to debase.
 se dégrader *vp* **- 1.** [bâtiment, santé] to deteriorate **- 2.** *fig* [personne] to degrade o.s.

dégrafer [3] [degrafe] *vt* to undo, to unfasten.
 se dégrafer *vp* to come undone.

dégraissage [degresaʒ] *nm* **- 1.** [de vêtement] dry-cleaning **- 2.** [de personnel] trimming, cutting back.

dégraisser [4] [degrese] *vt* **- 1.** [vêtement] to dry-clean **- 2.** [personnel] to trim, to cut back.

degré [degre] *nm* **- 1.** [gén] degree ; **~s centigrades** *ou* **Celsius** degrees centigrade *ou* Celsius ; **~ de parenté** degree of kinship ;

prendre qqn/qqch au premier ~ to take sb/sthg at face value - **2.** *sout* [marche] step.

dégressif, ive [degresif, iv] *adj* : **tarif ~** decreasing price scale.

dégrèvement [degrɛvmɑ̃] *nm* tax relief.

dégriffé, e [degrife] *adj* ex-designer label *(avant n).*
◆ **dégriffé** *nm* ex-designer label garment.

dégringolade [degrɛ̃gɔlad] *nf litt* & *fig* tumble.

dégringoler [3] [degrɛ̃gɔle] *fam* <> *vt* to tumble down <> *vi* [tomber] to tumble ; *fig* to crash.

dégriser [3] [degrize] *vt sout* [désenivrer] to sober up ; **~ qqn** *fig* to bring sb to his/her senses.

dégrossir [32] [degrosir] *vt* - **1.** [matériau] to rough-hew - **2.** *fig* [affaire, question] to rough out - **3.** *fig* [personne] to polish.
◆ **se dégrossir** *vp* [personne] to become more polished.

déguenillé, e [degənije] *adj* ragged.

déguerpir [32] [degɛrpir] *vi* to clear off.

dégueulasse [degœlas] *tfam* <> *adj* - **1.** [très sale, grossier] filthy ; **blague ~** dirty joke - **2.** [très mauvais-plat] disgusting ; [-temps] lousy <> *nmf* scum *(U).*

dégueuler [5] [degœle] *vi fam* to throw up.

déguisé, e [degize] *adj* disguised ; [pour s'amuser] in fancy dress.

déguisement [degizmɑ̃] *nm* disguise ; [pour bal masqué] fancy dress.

déguiser [3] [degize] *vt* to disguise.
◆ **se déguiser** *vp* : **se ~ en** [pour tromper] to disguise o.s. as ; [pour s'amuser] to dress up as.

dégustation [degystasjɔ̃] *nf* tasting, sampling ; **~ de vin** wine tasting.

déguster [3] [degyste] <> *vt* [savourer] to taste, to sample <> *vi fam* [subir] : **il va ~!** he'll be for it!

déhancher [3] [deɑ̃ʃe] ◆ **se déhancher** *vp* [en marchant] to swing one's hips ; [en restant immobile] to put all one's weight on one leg.

dehors [dəɔr] <> *adv* outside ; **aller ~** to go outside ; **dormir ~** to sleep out of doors, to sleep out ; **jeter** *ou* **mettre qqn ~** to throw sb out <> *nm* outside <> *nmpl* : **les ~** [les apparences] appearances.
◆ **en dehors** *loc adv* outside, outwards *Br*, outward *Am.*
◆ **en dehors de** *loc prép* [excepté] apart from.

déjà [deʒa] *adv* - **1.** [dès cet instant] already - **2.** [précédemment] already, before - **3.** [au fait] : **quel est ton nom ~?** what did you say your name was? - **4.** [renforce une affirmation] : **ce n'est ~ pas si mal** that's not bad at all.

déjanter [3] [deʒɑ̃te] *vt* : **~ un pneu** to take a tyre *Br ou* tire *Am* off the rim.

déjà-vu [deʒavy] *nm inv* : **c'est du ~** it's old hat.

déjection [deʒɛksjɔ̃] *nf* [action] evacuation.
◆ **déjections** *nfpl* excrement *(U).*

déjeuner [5] [deʒœne] <> *vi* - **1.** [le matin] to have breakfast - **2.** [à midi] to have lunch <> *nm* - **1.** [repas de midi] lunch ; **~ d'affaires** business lunch - **2.** *Can* [dîner] dinner.

déjouer [6] [deʒwe] *vt* to frustrate ; **~ la surveillance de qqn** to elude sb's surveillance.

delà [dəla] <> **au-delà.**

délabré, e [delabre] *adj* ruined.

délabrement [delabrəmɑ̃] *nm* - **1.** [de bâtiment] dilapidation, ruining - **2.** [de personne] ruin.

délacer [16] [delase] *vt* to unlace, to undo.

délai [delɛ] *nm* - **1.** [temps accordé] period ; **dans un ~ de** within (a period of) ; **dans les ~s impartis** by the deadline ; **sans ~** immediately, without delay ; **~ de livraison** delivery time, lead time - **2.** [sursis] extension (of deadline).

délaissé, e [delese] *adj* abandoned.

délaisser [4] [delese] *vt* - **1.** [abandonner] to leave - **2.** [négliger] to neglect.

délassement [delasmɑ̃] *nm* relaxation.

délasser [3] [delase] *vt* to refresh.
◆ **se délasser** *vp* to relax.

délateur, trice [delatœr, tris] *nm, f* informer.

délation [delasjɔ̃] *nf* informing.

délavé, e [delave] *adj* faded.

délayage [deleja3] *nm* verbiage, waffle.

délayer [11] [deleje] *vt* - **1.** [diluer] : **~ qqch dans qqch** to mix sthg with sthg - **2.** *fig* [exposer longuement] to pad out.

Delco® [dɛlko] *nm AUTOM* distributor.

délectable [delɛktabl] *adj sout* delectable.

délectation [delɛktasjɔ̃] *nf* [plaisir] delight ; **avec ~** in delight.

délecter [4] [delɛkte] ◆ **se délecter** *vp* : **se ~ de qqch/à faire qqch** to delight in sthg/in doing sthg.

délégation [delegasjɔ̃] *nf* delegation ; **agir par ~** to be delegated to act.

délégué, e [delege] <> *adj* [personne] delegated <> *nm, f* [représentant] : **~ (à)** delegate (to) ; **~ de classe/du personnel/syndical** class/staff/trade union representative.

déléguer [18] [delege] *vt* : **~ qqn (à qqch)** to delegate sb (to sthg).

délestage [delɛsta3] *nm* - **1.** [de ballon, de navire] removal of ballast - **2.** [de circulation] (temporary) diversion.

délester [3] [delɛste] vt - **1.** [ballon, navire] to remove ballast from - **2.** [circulation routière] to set up a diversion on, to divert - **3.** fig & hum [voler] : ~ qqn de qqch to relieve sb of sthg.

délibératif, ive [deliberatif, iv] adj : avoir voix délibérative to have voting rights.

délibération [deliberasjɔ̃] nf deliberation.

délibéré, e [delibere] adj - **1.** [intentionnel] deliberate - **2.** [résolu] determined.

➤ **délibéré** nm JUR judge's deliberations (pl).

délibérément [deliberemɑ̃] adv - **1.** [en connaissance de cause] after deliberation ou due consideration - **2.** [intentionnellement] deliberately, on purpose.

délibérer [18] [delibere] vi : ~ (de ou sur) to deliberate (on ou over).

délicat, e [delika, at] adj - **1.** [gén] delicate - **2.** [aimable] thoughtful, sensitive - **3.** [exigeant] fussy, difficult ; faire le ~ to be fussy.

délicatement [delikatmɑ̃] adv delicately.

délicatesse [delikatɛs] nf - **1.** [gén] delicacy - **2.** [tact] delicacy, tact.

délice [delis] nm delight.

délicieusement [delisjøzmɑ̃] adv [agréablement] delightfully.

délicieux, euse [delisjø, øz] adj - **1.** [savoureux] delicious - **2.** [agréable] delightful.

délictueux, euse [deliktɥø, øz] adj criminal.

délié, e [delje] adj [doigts] nimble.

délier [9] [delje] vt to untie ; ~ qqn de fig & sout to release sb from.

délimitation [delimitasjɔ̃] nf - **1.** [de territoire] fixing of the boundaries - **2.** [de fonction] demarcation - **3.** fig [de sujet] definition.

délimiter [3] [delimite] vt [frontière] to fix ; fig [question, domaine] to define, to demarcate.

délinquance [delɛ̃kɑ̃s] nf delinquency ; ~ informatique cybercrime ; ~ juvénile juvenile delinquency.

délinquant, e [delɛ̃kɑ̃, ɑ̃t] ◇ adj delinquent ◇ nm, f delinquent ; petit ~ petty criminal.

déliquescent, e [delikɛsɑ̃, ɑ̃t] adj fam [personne] feeble ; vieilli [mœurs] decaying.

délirant, e [delirɑ̃, ɑ̃t] adj - **1.** MÉD delirious - **2.** [extravagant] frenzied - **3.** fam [extraordinaire] crazy.

délire [delir] nm MÉD delirium ; en ~ fig frenzied.

délirer [3] [delire] vi MÉD to be ou become delirious ; fam fig to rave.

délit [deli] nm crime, offence Br, offense Am ; en flagrant ~ red-handed, in the act ; ~ de

fuite failure to stop (after an accident) ; ~s d'initiés FIN insider trading (U).

délivrance [delivrɑ̃s] nf - **1.** [libération] freeing, release - **2.** [soulagement] relief - **3.** [accouchement] delivery.

délivrer [3] [delivre] vt - **1.** [prisonnier] to free, to release - **2.** [pays] to deliver, to free ; ~ de to free from ; fig to relieve from - **3.** [remettre] : ~ qqch (à qqn) to issue sthg (to sb) - **4.** [marchandise] to deliver.

➤ **se délivrer** vp - **1.** [se libérer] : se ~ (de) to free o.s. (from) - **2.** [passeport] to be issued.

déloger [17] [delɔʒe] vt : ~ (de) to dislodge (from).

déloyal, e, aux [delwajal, o] adj - **1.** [infidèle] disloyal - **2.** [malhonnête] unfair.

Delphes [dɛlf] n Delphi.

delta [dɛlta] nm delta.

deltaplane, delta-plane (pl deltaplanes) [dɛltaplan] nm hang glider.

déluge [delyʒ] nm - **1.** RELIG : le Déluge the Flood ; remonter au Déluge fig to go back to the year dot - **2.** [pluie] downpour, deluge ; un ~ de fig a flood of.

déluré, e [delyre] adj [malin] quick-witted ; péj [dévergondé] saucy.

démagogie [demagɔʒi] nf pandering to public opinion, demagogy.

démagogique [demagɔʒik] adj demagogic.

démagogue [demagɔg] nmf demagogue.

demain [dəmɛ̃] ◇ adv - **1.** [le jour suivant] tomorrow ; ~ matin tomorrow morning - **2.** fig [plus tard] in the future ◇ nm tomorrow ; à ~! see you tomorrow!

demande [dəmɑ̃d] nf - **1.** [souhait] request ; à la ~ générale by popular demand ; accéder à une ~ to accede to a demand - **2.** [démarche] proposal ; ~ en mariage proposal of marriage - **3.** [candidature] application ; ~ d'emploi job application ; '~s d'emploi' 'situations wanted' - **4.** [commande] order - **5.** ÉCON demand - **6.** JUR petition.

demandé, e [dəmɑ̃de] adj in demand.

demander [3] [dəmɑ̃de] ◇ vt - **1.** [réclamer, s'enquérir] to ask for ; ~ qqch à qqn to ask sb for sthg - **2.** [appeler] to call ; on vous demande à la réception/au téléphone you're wanted at reception/on the telephone ; qui demandez-vous? who do you want? - **3.** [désirer] to ask, to want ; je ne demande pas mieux I'd be only too pleased (to), I'd love to - **4.** [exiger] : tu m'en demandes trop you're asking too much of me - **5.** [nécessiter] to require - **6.** [chercher] to look for, to require ◇ vi - **1.** [réclamer] : ~ à qqn de faire qqch to ask sb to do sthg ; ne ~ qu'à ... to be ready to ... - **2.** [nécessiter] : **ce projet demande à être étudié** this project requires investigation *ou* needs investigating.

◆ **se demander** *vp* : **se ~ (si)** to wonder (if *ou* whether).

demandeur[1], **euse** [dəmɑ̃dœr, øz] *nm, f* [solliciteur] : **~ d'asile** asylum-seeker ; **~ d'emploi** job-seeker.

demandeur[2], **eresse** [dəmɑ̃dœr, drɛs] *nm, f* JUR plaintiff.

démangeaison [demɑ̃ʒɛzɔ̃] *nf* [irritation] itch, itching *(U)* ; *fam fig* urge.

démanger [17] [demɑ̃ʒe] *vi* [gratter] to itch ; **ça me démange de ...** *fig* I'm itching *ou* dying to ...

démanteler [25] [demɑ̃tle] *vt* [construction] to demolish ; *fig* to break up.

démaquillant, e [demakijɑ̃, ɑ̃t] *adj* make-up-removing *(avant n)*.

◆ **démaquillant** *nm* make-up remover.

démaquiller [3] [demakije] *vt* to remove make-up from.

◆ **se démaquiller** *vp* to remove one's make-up.

démarcation [demarkasjɔ̃] *nf* [frontière] demarcation ; *fig* separation.

démarchage [demarʃaʒ] *nm* : **~ à domicile** door-to-door selling.

démarche [demarʃ] *nf* - **1.** [manière de marcher] gait, walk - **2.** [raisonnement] approach, method - **3.** [requête] step ; **faire les ~s pour faire qqch** to take the necessary steps to do sthg.

démarcheur, euse [demarʃœr, øz] *nm, f* - **1.** [représentant] door-to-door salesman *(f* saleswoman*)* - **2.** [prospecteur] canvasser.

démarque [demark] *nf* [solde] marking down.

démarquer [3] [demarke] *vt* - **1.** [solder] to mark down - **2.** SPORT not to mark.

◆ **se démarquer** *vp* - **1.** SPORT to shake off one's marker - **2.** *fig* [se distinguer] : **se ~ (de)** to distinguish o.s. (from).

démarrage [demaraʒ] *nm* starting, start ; **~ en côte** hill start.

démarrer [3] [demare] ⬦ *vi* - **1.** [véhicule] to start (up) ; [conducteur] to drive off - **2.** SPORT to break away - **3.** *fig* [affaire, projet] to get off the ground ⬦ *vt* - **1.** [véhicule] to start (up) ; **faire ~** to start - **2.** *fam fig* [commencer] : **~ qqch** to get sthg going.

démarreur [demarœr] *nm* starter.

démasquer [3] [demaske] *vt* - **1.** [personne] to unmask - **2.** *fig* [complot, plan] to unveil.

◆ **se démasquer** *vp* to show one's true colours.

démêlant, e [demɛlɑ̃, ɑ̃t] *adj* conditioning *(avant n)*.

◆ **démêlant** *nm* conditioner.

démêlé [demɛle] *nm* quarrel ; **avoir des ~s avec la justice** to get into trouble with the law.

démêler [4] [demɛle] *vt* [cheveux, fil] to untangle ; *fig* to unravel.

◆ **se démêler** *vp* : **se ~ les cheveux** to comb out one's hair ; **se ~ de** *fig* to extricate o.s. from.

démembrer [3] [demɑ̃bre] *vt* [animal] to dismember ; *fig* [réseau] to break up.

déménagement [demenaʒmɑ̃] *nm* removal.

déménager [17] [demenaʒe] ⬦ *vt* to move ⬦ *vi* to move (house).

déménageur [demenaʒœr] *nm* removal man *Br*, mover *Am*.

démence [demɑ̃s] *nf* MÉD dementia ; [bêtise] madness.

démener [19] [demne] ◆ **se démener** *vp litt & fig* to struggle.

dément, e [demɑ̃, ɑ̃t] ⬦ *adj* MÉD demented ; *fam* [extraordinaire, extravagant] crazy ⬦ *nm, f* demented person.

démenti [demɑ̃ti] *nm* denial ; **apporter un ~ à qqch** to deny sthg (formally).

démentiel, elle [demɑ̃sjɛl] *adj* MÉD demented ; *fam* [incroyable] crazy.

démentir [37] [demɑ̃tir] *vt* - **1.** [réfuter] to deny - **2.** [contredire] to contradict.

◆ **se démentir** *vp* : **ne pas se ~ sout** to remain unchanged.

démerder [3] [demɛrde] ◆ **se démerder** *vp tfam* [se débrouiller] to (know how to) look after o.s.

démériter [3] [demerite] *vi* - **1.** [être indigne] : **~ de** to show o.s. (to be) unworthy of - **2.** [être dévalorisé] : **en quoi a-t-il démérité?** what has he done wrong? ; **~ auprès de qqn** to come down in sb's eyes *ou* estimation.

démesure [deməzyr] *nf* excess, immoderation.

démesurément [deməzyremɑ̃] *adv* excessively.

démets *etc* ▷ **démettre**.

démettre [84] [demɛtr] *vt* - **1.** MÉD to put out (of joint) - **2.** [congédier] : **~ qqn de** to dismiss sb from.

◆ **se démettre** *vp* - **1.** MÉD : **se ~ l'épaule** to put one's shoulder out (of joint) - **2.** [démissionner] : **se ~ de ses fonctions** to resign.

demeurant [dəmœrɑ̃] ◆ **au demeurant** *loc adv* all things considered.

demeure [dəmœr] *nf* - **1.** *sout* [domicile, habitation] residence - **2.** JUR : **mettre qqn en ~ (de faire qqch)** to order sb (to do sthg).
➡ **à demeure** ◇ *loc adj* permanent ◇ *loc adv* permanently.

demeuré, e [dəmœre] ◇ *adj* simple, half-witted ◇ *nm, f* half-wit.

demeurer [5] [dəmœre] *vi* - **1.** *(aux : avoir)* [habiter] to live - **2.** *(aux : être)* [rester] to remain.

demi, e [dəmi] *adj* half ; **un kilo et ~** one and a half kilos ; **il est une heure et ~e** it's half past one ; **à ~** half ; **dormir à ~** to be nearly asleep ; **ouvrir à ~** to half-open ; **faire les choses à ~** to do things by halves.
➡ **demi** *nm* - **1.** [bière] beer, ≈ half-pint *Br* - **2.** FOOTBALL midfielder ; **~ de mêlée** RUGBY scrumhalf ; **~ d'ouverture** RUGBY fly half, standoff (half).
➡ **demie** *nf* : **à la ~e** on the half-hour.

demi-bouteille [dəmibutɛj] *(pl* demi-bouteilles) *nf* half-bottle.

demi-cercle [dəmisɛrkl] *(pl* demi-cercles) *nm* semicircle ; **en ~** semicircular.

demi-douzaine [dəmiduzɛn] *(pl* demi-douzaines) *nf* half-dozen ; **une ~ (de)** half a dozen.

demi-fin, e [dəmifɛ̃, in] *(mpl* demi-fins, *fpl* demi-fines) *adj* [haricots] medium.

demi-finale [dəmifinal] *(pl* demi-finales) *nf* semifinal.

demi-frère [dəmifrɛr] *(pl* demi-frères) *nm* half-brother.

demi-gros [dəmigro] *nm* : **(commerce de) ~** cash and carry.

demi-heure [dəmijœr] *(pl* demi-heures) *nf* half an hour, half-hour.

demi-jour [dəmiʒur] *nm* half-light.

demi-journée [dəmiʒurne] *(pl* demi-journées) *nf* half a day, half-day.

démilitariser [3] [demilitarize] *vt* to demilitarize.

demi-litre [dəmilitr] *(pl* demi-litres) *nm* half a litre *Br ou* liter *Am*, half-litre *Br*, half-liter *Am*.

demi-mal [dəmimal] *(pl* demi-maux) *nm* : **ce n'est que ~** things *ou* it could have been worse.

demi-mesure [dəmiməzyr] *(pl* demi-mesures) *nf* - **1.** [quantité] half a measure - **2.** [compromis] half-measure.

demi-mot [dəmimo] ➡ **à demi-mot** *loc adv* : **comprendre à ~** to understand without things having to be spelled out.

déminage [deminaʒ] *nm* [de sol] mine clearance ; [d'eau] minesweeping.

déminer [3] [demine] *vt* to clear of mines.

demi-pension [dəmipɑ̃sjɔ̃] *(pl* demi-pensions) *nf* - **1.** [d'hôtel] half-board - **2.** [d'école] : **être en ~** to take school dinners *(pl)*.

demi-pensionnaire [dəmipɑ̃sjɔner] *(pl* demi-pensionnaires) *nmf* child who has school dinners.

demi-place [dəmiplas] *(pl* demi-places) *nf* - **1.** [pour spectacle] half-price ticket - **2.** [dans transports publics] half-fare.

démis, e [demi, iz] *pp* ➩ **démettre**.

demi-saison [dəmisεzɔ̃] *nf* : **une veste de ~** a spring/autumn jacket.

demi-sel [dəmisεl] *adj inv* slightly salted.

demi-sœur [dəmisœr] *(pl* demi-sœurs) *nf* half-sister.

demi-soupir [dəmisupir] *(pl* demi-soupirs) *nm* quaver rest *Br*, eighth note rest *Am*.

démission [demisjɔ̃] *nf* resignation ; **remettre sa ~** to hand in one's notice.

démissionnaire [demisjɔner] ◇ *nmf* person resigning ◇ *adj* resigning *(avant n)* ; [ministre] outgoing *(avant n)*.

démissionner [3] [demisjɔne] ◇ *vi* [d'un emploi] to resign ; *fig* to give up ◇ *vt hum* : **~ qqn** to give sb the boot.

demi-tarif [dəmitarif] *(pl* demi-tarifs) ◇ *adj* half-price ◇ *nm* - **1.** [tarification] half-fare - **2.** [billet] half-price ticket.

demi-teinte [dəmitɛ̃t] *(pl* demi-teintes) *nf* halftone ; **en ~, en ~s** *fig* subtle.

demi-ton [dəmitɔ̃] *(pl* demi-tons) *nm* semitone.

demi-tour [dəmitur] *(pl* demi-tours) *nm* [gén] half-turn ; MIL about-turn ; **faire ~** to turn back.

démo [demo] *nf fam* demonstration ; **faire une ~ à qqn** to give s.o. a demonstration.

démobiliser [3] [demɔbilize] *vt* MIL to demobilize ; **être démobilisé** *fig* to be demotivated.

démocrate [demɔkrat] ◇ *nmf* democrat ◇ *adj* democratic.

démocrate-chrétien, enne [demɔkratkretjɛ̃, εn] *(mpl* démocrates-chrétiens, *fpl* démocrates-chrétiennes) ◇ *adj* Christian-Democratic ◇ *nm, f* Christian Democrat.

démocratie [demɔkrasi] *nf* democracy ; **les ~s occidentales** the Western democracies.

démocratique [demɔkratik] *adj* democratic.

démocratisation [demɔkratizasjɔ̃] *nf* democratization.

démocratiser [3] [demɔkratize] *vt* to democratize.

démodé, e [demɔde] *adj* old-fashioned.
démographie [demɔgrafi] *nf* demography.
démographique [demɔgrafik] *adj* demographic.
demoiselle [dəmwazɛl] *nf* - **1.** [jeune fille] maid ; ~ **d'honneur** bridesmaid - **2.** [libellule] dragonfly.
démolir [32] [demɔlir] *vt* - **1.** [gén] to demolish - **2.** *fam* [frapper] : ~ **qqn** to smash sb's face in ; **se faire** ~ to get one's face smashed in.
démolisseur [demɔlisœr] *nm* demolition worker.
démolition [demɔlisjɔ̃] *nf* demolition ; **en** ~ in the course of being demolished.
démon [demɔ̃] *nm* - **1.** [diable, personne] devil, demon ; **le** ~ *RELIG* the Devil - **2.** *fig* : **le** ~ **de l'alcool/de la curiosité** the demon drink/curiosity ; **le** ~ **de midi** middle-aged lust.
démoniaque [demɔnjak] *adj* - **1.** [diabolique] diabolical - **2.** [possédé du démon] possessed.
démonstrateur, trice [demɔ̃stratœr, tris] *nm, f* demonstrator.
démonstratif, ive [demɔ̃stratif, iv] *adj* - **1.** [argument] convincing - **2.** [personne & *GRAM*] demonstrative.
◆ **démonstratif** *nm GRAM* demonstrative.
démonstration [demɔ̃strasjɔ̃] *nf* - **1.** [gén] demonstration - **2.** *MIL* show, demonstration.
démontable [demɔ̃tabl] *adj* collapsible.
démontage [demɔ̃taʒ] *nm* dismantling, taking to pieces ; [de moteur] stripping down.
démonté, e [demɔ̃te] *adj* [océan] raging.
démonte-pneu [demɔ̃tpnø] (*pl* **démonte-pneus**) *nm* tyre lever *Br*, tire iron *Am*.
démonter [3] [demɔ̃te] *vt* - **1.** [appareil] to dismantle, to take apart - **2.** [troubler] : ~ **qqn** to put sb out.
◆ **se démonter** *vp fam* to be put out.
démontrer [3] [demɔ̃tre] *vt* - **1.** [prouver] to prove, to demonstrate - **2.** [témoigner de] to show, to demonstrate.
démoralisant, e [demɔralizɑ̃, ɑ̃t] *adj* demoralizing.
démoraliser [3] [demɔralize] *vt* to demoralize.
◆ **se démoraliser** *vp* to lose heart.
démordre [76] [demɔrdr] *vt* : **ne pas** ~ **de** to stick to.
démordu [demɔrdy] *pp inv* ▷ **démordre**.
démotiver [3] [demɔtive] *vt* to demotivate.
démouler [3] [demule] *vt* to turn out of a mould, to remove from a mould.
démultiplication [demyltiplikasjɔ̃] *nf TECHNOL* reduction in gear ratio.

démunir [32] [demynir] *vt* to deprive.
◆ **se démunir** *vp* : **se** ~ **de** to part with.
démystifier [9] [demistifje] *vt* - **1.** [concept] to demystify - **2.** [personne] to disabuse.
dénatalité [denatalite] *nf* fall in the birthrate.
dénationaliser [3] [denasjɔnalize] *vt* to denationalize.
dénaturé, e [denatyre] *adj* - **1.** [parents] unfit - **2.** [goût] unnatural - **3.** *TECHNOL* denatured.
dénaturer [3] [denatyre] *vt* - **1.** [goût] to impair, to mar - **2.** *TECHNOL* to denature - **3.** [déformer] to distort.
dénégation [denegasjɔ̃] *nf* denial.
déneigement [denɛʒmɑ̃] *nm* snow clearance.
déneiger [23] [deneʒe] *vt* to clear snow from.
déneigeuse [deneʒøz] *nf Can* snowblower.
déni [deni] *nm* denial ; ~ **de justice** *JUR* denial of justice.
déniaiser [4] [denjeze] *vt hum & vieilli* : ~ **qqn** to teach sb a thing or two.
dénicher [3] [denife] *vt fig* - **1.** [personne] to flush out - **2.** *fam* [objet] to unearth.
denier [dənje] *nm* denier *(coin).*
◆ **deniers** *nmpl* : **les** ~**s publics** the public purse *(sg)* ; **les** ~**s de l'État** the State coffers.
dénigrer [3] [denigre] *vt* to denigrate, to run down.
dénivelé [denivle] *nm* difference in level *ou* height.
dénivellation [denivelasjɔ̃] *nf* - **1.** [différence de niveau] difference in height *ou* level - **2.** [de route] bumps *(pl)*, unevenness *(U)* - **3.** [pente] slope.
dénombrer [3] [denɔ̃bre] *vt* [compter] to count ; [énumérer] to enumerate.
dénominateur [denɔminatœr] *nm* denominator ; ~ **commun** *MATHS* & *fig* common denominator.
dénomination [denɔminasjɔ̃] *nf* name.
dénommé, e [denɔme] *adj* : **un** ~ **Robert** someone by the name of Robert.
dénoncer [16] [denɔ̃se] *vt* - **1.** [gén] to denounce ; ~ **qqn à qqn** to denounce sb to sb, to inform on sb - **2.** *fig* [trahir] to betray.
dénonciation [denɔ̃sjasjɔ̃] *nf* denunciation.
dénoter [3] [denɔte] *vt* to show, to indicate.
dénouement [denumɑ̃] *nm* - **1.** [issue] outcome - **2.** [d'un film, d'un livre] denouement.
dénouer [6] [denwe] *vt* [nœud] to untie, to undo ; *fig* to unravel.

dénoyauter [3] [denwajote] *vt* [fruit] to stone.
denrée [dɑ̃re] *nf* [produit] produce *(U)* ; **~s alimentaires** foodstuffs ; **~ rare** *fig* rare commodity.
dense [dɑ̃s] *adj* - **1.** [gén] dense - **2.** [style] condensed.
densité [dɑ̃site] *nf* density ; **~ de population** population density ; **double/haute ~** INFORM double/high density.
dent [dɑ̃] *nf* - **1.** [de personne, d'objet] tooth ; **il claquait des ~s** his teeth were chattering ; **faire ses ~s** to cut one's teeth, to teethe ; **mordre à belles ~s dans** to get one's teeth into ; **~ de lait/de sagesse** milk/wisdom tooth ; **en ~s de scie** jagged, serrated ; **avoir les ~s longues** to have high hopes ; **avoir une ~ contre qqn** to have it in for sb ; **ne rien avoir à se mettre sous la ~** to have nothing left to eat ; **ne pas desserrer les ~s** not to open one's mouth ; **grincer des ~s** to gnash one's teeth - **2.** GÉOGR peak.
dentaire [dɑ̃tɛr] *adj* dental.
dental, e, aux [dɑ̃tal, o] *adj* LING dental.
denté, e [dɑ̃te] *adj* - **1.** TECHNOL toothed ; **roue ~e** cogwheel - **2.** [feuille] dentate.
dentelé, e [dɑ̃tle] *adj* serrated, jagged.
dentelle [dɑ̃tɛl] *nf* lace *(U)*.
dentier [dɑ̃tje] *nm* - **1.** [dents] dentures *(pl)* - **2.** TECHNOL set of teeth, teeth *(pl)*.
dentifrice [dɑ̃tifris] *nm* toothpaste.
dentiste [dɑ̃tist] *nmf* dentist.
dentition [dɑ̃tisjɔ̃] *nf* teeth *(pl)*, dentition.
dénuder [3] [denyde] *vt* to leave bare ; [fil électrique] to strip.
⬥ **se dénuder** *vp* to strip (off).
dénué, e [denɥe] *adj* *sout* : **~ de** devoid of.
dénuement [denymɑ̃] *nm* destitution *(U)*.
dénutrition [denytrisjɔ̃] *nf* malnutrition.
déodorant, e [deɔdɔrɑ̃, ɑ̃t] *adj* deodorant.
⬥ **déodorant** *nm* deodorant.
déontologie [deɔ̃tɔlɔʒi] *nf* professional ethics *(pl)*.
dép. - 1. *abr de* **départ - 2.** *abr de* **département.**
dépannage [depanaʒ] *nm* repair ; **service de ~** AUT breakdown service.
dépanner [3] [depane] *vt* - **1.** [réparer] to repair, to fix - **2.** *fam* [aider] to bail out.
dépanneur, euse [depanœr, øz] *nm, f* repairman (*f* repairwoman).
⬥ **dépanneuse** *nf* [véhicule] (breakdown) recovery vehicle.
dépareillé, e [depareje] *adj* [ensemble] nonmatching ; [paire] odd.
déparer [3] [depare] *vt* to spoil.

départ [depar] *nm* - **1.** [de personne] departure, leaving ; [de véhicule] departure ; **les grands ~s** the holiday exodus *(sg)* - **2.** SPORT & *fig* start ; **faux ~** false start.
⬥ **au départ** *loc adv* to start with.
départager [17] [departaʒe] *vt* - **1.** [concurrents, opinions] to decide between - **2.** [lors d'une élection] to choose between - **3.** [séparer] to separate.
département [departəmɑ̃] *nm* - **1.** [territoire] territorial and administrative division of France - **2.** [service] department.
départemental, e, aux [departəmɑ̃tal, o] *adj* of a French *département*.
⬥ **départementale** *nf* secondary road, ≃ B road *Br*.
départir [32] [departir] ⬥ **se départir** *vp* : **ne pas se ~ de** to retain.
dépassé, e [depase] *adj* - **1.** [périmé] oldfashioned - **2.** *fam* [déconcerté] : **~ par** overwhelmed by.
dépassement [depasmɑ̃] *nm* - **1.** [en voiture] overtaking ; **~ sans visibilité** overtaking blind - **2.** FIN overspending.
dépasser [3] [depase] ⬦ *vt* - **1.** [doubler] to overtake - **2.** [être plus grand que] to be taller than - **3.** [être plus long que] to be longer than - **4.** [excéder] to exceed, to be more than - **5.** [durer plus longtemps que] : **~ une heure** to go on for more than an hour - **6.** [surpasser] to outshine - **7.** [aller au-delà de] to exceed - **8.** [franchir] to pass - **9.** *loc* : **ça me dépasse** *fam* it's beyond me ⬦ *vi* : **~ (de)** to stick out (from).
⬥ **se dépasser** *vp* to excel o.s.
dépassionner [3] [depasjɔne] *vt* to take the heat out of.
dépaysement [depeizmɑ̃] *nm* change of scene, disorientation.
dépayser [3] [depeize] *vt* - **1.** [désorienter] to disorientate *Br*, to disorient *Am* - **2.** [changer agréablement] to make a change of scene for.
dépecer [29] [depəse] *vt* - **1.** [découper] to chop up - **2.** [déchiqueter] to tear apart.
dépêche [depɛʃ] *nf* dispatch.
dépêcher [4] [depeʃe] *vt* *sout* [envoyer] to dispatch.
⬥ **se dépêcher** *vp* to hurry up ; **se ~ de faire qqch** to hurry to do sthg.
dépeignais, dépeignions *etc* ⬈ **dépeindre.**
dépeindre [81] [depɛ̃dr] *vt* to depict, to describe.
dépeint, e [depɛ̃, ɛ̃t] *pp* ⬈ **dépeindre.**
dépendance [depɑ̃dɑ̃s] *nf* - **1.** [de personne]

dependence ; **être sous la ~ de** to be dependent on - **2.** [à la drogue] dependency - **3.** [de bâtiment] outbuilding.

dépendant, e [depɑ̃dɑ̃, ɑ̃t] *adj* : **~ (de)** dependent (on).

dépendre [73] [depɑ̃dr] *vt* - **1.** [être soumis] : **~ de** to depend on ; **ça dépend** it depends - **2.** [appartenir] : **~ de** to belong to - **3.** [décrocher] to take down.

dépendu [depɑ̃dy] *pp inv* ▷ **dépendre**.

dépens [depɑ̃] *nmpl* JUR costs ; **aux ~ de qqn** at sb's expense ; **je l'ai appris à mes ~** I learned that to my cost.

dépense [depɑ̃s] *nf* - **1.** [frais] expense - **2.** FIN & *fig* expenditure *(U)* ; **les ~s publiques** public spending *(U)* - **3.** [consommation] consumption.

dépenser [3] [depɑ̃se] *vt* - **1.** [argent] to spend ; **~ sans compter** to spend lavishly - **2.** *fig* [énergie] to expend.

◆ se dépenser *vp litt* & *fig* to exert o.s.

dépensier, ère [depɑ̃sje, ɛr] *adj* extravagant.

déperdition [deperdisjɔ̃] *nf* loss ; **~ de chaleur** heat loss.

dépérir [32] [deperir] *vi* - **1.** [personne] to waste away - **2.** [santé, affaire] to decline - **3.** [plante] to wither.

dépêtrer [4] [depetre] **◆ se dépêtrer** *vp* : **se ~ de** *fam* [se dégager de] to get out of ; *fig* [se sortir de] to extricate o.s. from ; *fig* [se débarrasser de] to get rid of.

dépeuplement [depœpləmɑ̃] *nm* - **1.** [de pays] depopulation - **2.** [d'étang, de rivière, de forêt] emptying of wildlife.

dépeupler [5] [depœple] *vt* - **1.** [pays] to depopulate - **2.** [étang, rivière, forêt] to drive the wildlife from.

◆ se dépeupler *vp* - **1.** [pays] to become depopulated - **2.** [rivière, étang] to have a diminishing *ou* disappearing wildlife population.

déphasé, e [defaze] *adj* ÉLECTR out of phase ; *fam fig* out of touch.

dépiauter [3] [depjote] *vt fam* [animal] to skin ; *fig* [texte] to pull to pieces.

dépilatoire [depilatwar] *adj* : **crème ~** depilatory cream.

dépistage [depistaʒ] *nm* - **1.** [de gibier, de voleur] tracking down - **2.** [de maladie] screening ; **~ du SIDA** AIDS testing.

dépister [3] [depiste] *vt* - **1.** [gibier, voleur] to track down - **2.** [maladie] to screen for - **3.** [déjouer] to throw off the scent - **4.** *fig* [découvrir] to detect.

dépit [depi] *nm* pique, spite ; **par ~** out of pique *ou* spite.

◆ en dépit de *loc prép* in spite of.

dépité, e [depite] *adj* cross, annoyed.

déplacé, e [deplase] *adj* - **1.** [propos, attitude, présence] out of place - **2.** [personne] displaced.

déplacement [deplasmɑ̃] *nm* - **1.** [d'objet] moving ; **~ de vertèbre** MÉD slipped disc *Br ou* disk *Am* - **2.** [voyage] travelling *(U)* Br, traveling *(U)* Am ; **en ~** away on business ; **valoir le ~** *fig* to be worth going.

déplacer [16] [deplase] *vt* - **1.** [objet] to move, to shift ; *fig* [problème] to shift the emphasis of - **2.** [muter] to transfer.

◆ se déplacer *vp* - **1.** [se mouvoir - animal] to move (around) ; [- personne] to walk - **2.** [voyager] to travel - **3.** MÉD : **se ~ une vertèbre** to slip a disc *Br ou* disk *Am*.

déplaire [110] [deplɛr] *vt* - **1.** [ne pas plaire] : **cela me déplaît** I don't like it - **2.** [irriter] to displease ; **n'en déplaise à mon patron** *hum* whether my boss likes it or not.

déplaisant, e [deplɛzɑ̃, ɑ̃t] *adj sout* unpleasant.

déplaisir [deplezir] *nm sout* displeasure.

dépliant [deplijɑ̃] *nm* leaflet ; **~ touristique** tourist brochure.

déplier [10] [deplije] *vt* to unfold.

◆ se déplier *vp* to unfold.

déploiement [deplwamɑ̃] *nm* - **1.** MIL deployment - **2.** [d'ailes] spreading - **3.** [de voile] unfurling, opening - **4.** *fig* [d'efforts] display ; **un grand ~ de** a major display of.

déplorable [deplɔrabl] *adj* deplorable.

déplorer [3] [deplɔre] *vt* - **1.** [regretter] to deplore - **2.** [pleurer] to mourn.

déployer [13] [deplwaje] *vt* - **1.** [déplier - gén] to unfold ; [- plan, journal] to open ; [ailes] to spread - **2.** MIL to deploy - **3.** [mettre en œuvre] to expend - **4.** [manifester] to display.

déplu [deply] *pp* ▷ **déplaire**.

dépoitraillé, e [depwatraje] *adj fam péj* with one's shirt wide open.

dépoli, e [depɔli] *adj* [métal] tarnished ; [verre] frosted.

dépolitiser [3] [depɔlitize] *vt* to depoliticize.

déportation [depɔrtasjɔ̃] *nf* - **1.** [exil] deportation - **2.** [internement] transportation to a concentration camp.

déporté, e [depɔrte] *nm, f* - **1.** [exilé] deportee - **2.** [interné] prisoner *(in a concentration camp)*.

déporter [3] [depɔrte] *vt* - **1.** [dévier] to carry off course - **2.** [exiler] to deport - **3.** [interner] to send to a concentration camp.

déposant, e [depozɑ̃, ɑ̃t] *nm, f* - **1.** *FIN* depositor - **2.** *JUR* deponent.

déposé, e [depoze] *adj* : **marque ~e** registered trademark ; **modèle ~** patented design.

déposer [3] [depoze] ⬦ *vt* - **1.** [poser] to put down - **2.** [personne, paquet] to drop - **3.** [argent, sédiment] to deposit - **4.** *ADMIN* to register - **5.** *JUR* to file ; **~ son bilan** *FIN* to go into liquidation - **6.** [monarque] to depose - **7.** [moteur] to take out ⬦ *vi* - **1.** *JUR* to testify, to give evidence - **2.** [sédiment] to form a deposit.
⬥ **se déposer** *vp* to settle.

dépositaire [depoziter] *nmf* - **1.** *COMM* agent - **2.** [d'objet] bailee ; **~ de** *fig* person entrusted with.

déposition [depozisjɔ̃] *nf* deposition.

déposséder [18] [depɔsede] *vt* : **~ qqn de** to dispossess sb of.

dépôt [depo] *nm* - **1.** [d'objet, d'argent, de sédiment] deposit, depositing (U) ; **verser un ~ (de garantie)** to put down a deposit ; **~ d'ordures** (rubbish) dump *Br*, garbage dump *Am* - **2.** *ADMIN* registration ; **~ légal** copyright registration - **3.** [garage] depot - **4.** [entrepôt] store, warehouse - **5.** [prison] ≃ police cells *(pl)*.

dépoter [3] [depɔte] *vt* [plante] to remove from the pot.

dépotoir [depɔtwar] *nm* - **1.** [décharge] (rubbish) dump *Br*, garbage dump *Am* ; *fam fig* dump, tip - **2.** [usine] sewage works, sewage reprocessing plant.

dépouille [depuj] *nf* - **1.** [peau] hide, skin - **2.** [humaine] remains *(pl)* ; **~ mortelle** mortal remains.
⬥ **dépouilles** *nfpl* spoils.

dépouillement [depujmɑ̃] *nm* - **1.** [sobriété] austerity, sobriety - **2.** [examen] perusal ; **~ de scrutin** counting of the votes.

dépouiller [3] [depuje] *vt* - **1.** [priver] : **~ qqn (de)** to strip sb (of) - **2.** [examiner] to peruse ; **~ un scrutin** to count the votes.
⬥ **se dépouiller** *vp* : **se ~ de** to divest o.s. of.

dépourvu, e [depurvy] *adj* : **~ de** without, lacking in.
⬥ **au dépourvu** *loc adv* : **prendre qqn au ~** to catch sb unawares.

dépoussiérer [18] [depusjere] *vt* to dust (off).

dépravation [depravasjɔ̃] *nf* depravity.

dépravé, e [deprave] ⬦ *adj* depraved ⬦ *nm, f* degenerate.

dépraver [3] [deprave] *vt* to deprave.
⬥ **se dépraver** *vp* to become depraved.

dépréciation [depresjasjɔ̃] *nf* depreciation.

déprécier [9] [depresje] *vt* - **1.** [marchandise] to reduce the value of - **2.** [œuvre] to disparage.
⬥ **se déprécier** *vp* - **1.** [marchandise] to depreciate - **2.** [personne] to put o.s. down.

dépressif, ive [depresif, iv] ⬦ *adj* depressive ⬦ *nm, f* depressive (person).

dépression [depresjɔ̃] *nf* depression ; **faire de la ~** to be depressed ; **~ nerveuse** nervous breakdown.

déprimant, e [deprimɑ̃, ɑ̃t] *adj* depressing.

déprime [deprim] *nf fam* : **faire une ~** to be (feeling) down.

déprimé, e [deprime] *adj* depressed.

déprimer [3] [deprime] ⬦ *vt* to depress ⬦ *vi fam* to be (feeling) down.

déprogrammer [3] [deprɔgrame] *vt* to remove from the schedule ; *TÉLÉ* to take off the air.

dépuceler [24] [depysle] *vt fam* : **~ qqn** to take sb's virginity.

depuis [dəpɥi] ⬦ *prép* - **1.** [à partir d'une date ou d'un moment précis] since ; **je ne l'ai pas vu ~ son mariage** I haven't seen him since he got married ; **il est parti ~ hier** he's been away since yesterday ; **~ le début jusqu'à la fin** from beginning to end - **2.** [exprimant une durée] for ; **il est malade ~ une semaine** he has been ill for a week ; **~ 10 ans/longtemps** for 10 years/a long time ; **~ toujours** always - **3.** [dans l'espace] from ; **~ la route, on pouvait voir la mer** you could see the sea from the road ; **~ le premier jusqu'au dernier** from the first to the last ⬦ *adv* since (then) ; **~, nous ne l'avons pas revu** we haven't seen him since (then).
⬥ **depuis lors** *loc adv* since then.
⬥ **depuis que** *loc conj* since ; **je ne l'ai pas revu ~ qu'il s'est marié** I haven't seen him since he got married.

dépuratif, ive [depyratif, iv] *adj* cleansing, eliminating.
⬥ **dépuratif** *nm* depurative.

députation [depytasjɔ̃] *nf* - **1.** [délégation] deputation - **2.** [fonction] : **candidat à la ~** parliamentary candidate.

député [depyte] *nm* - **1.** [délégué] representative - **2.** [au parlement] member of parliament *Br*, representative *Am* ; **~ européen** Euro-MP, MEP ; **~-maire** *MP and mayor*.

députer [3] [depyte] *vt* to send as representative.

déraciner [3] [derasine] *vt litt* & *fig* to uproot.

déraillement [derajmɑ̃] *nm* derailment.

dérailler [3] [deʀaje] vi - **1.** [train] to leave the rails, to be derailed - **2.** fam fig [mécanisme] to go on the blink - **3.** fam fig [personne] to go to pieces.

dérailleur [deʀajœʀ] nm [de bicyclette] derailleur.

déraison [deʀezɔ̃] nf lack of reason.

déraisonnable [deʀezɔnabl] adj unreasonable.

déraisonner [3] [deʀezɔne] vi sout to talk nonsense.

dérangement [deʀɑ̃ʒmɑ̃] nm trouble ; **en ~** out of order.

déranger [17] [deʀɑ̃ʒe] <> vt - **1.** [personne] to disturb, to bother ; **ça vous dérange si je fume?** do you mind if I smoke? - **2.** [plan] to disrupt - **3.** [maison, pièce] to disarrange, to make untidy <> vi to be disturbing.
➠ **se déranger** vp - **1.** [se déplacer] to move - **2.** [se gêner] to put o.s. out.

dérapage [deʀapaʒ] nm [glissement] skid ; fig excess ; **~ contrôlé** controlled skid.

déraper [3] [deʀape] vi [glisser] to skid ; fig to get out of hand.

dératé, e [deʀate] nm, f fam : **courir comme un ~** to run flat out.

dératisation [deʀatizasjɔ̃] nf extermination of rats.

derechef [dəʀəʃɛf] adv sout once again.

dérèglement [deʀɛɡləmɑ̃] nm [de machine] malfunction ; [de fonction corporelle] upset.

déréglementation [deʀɛɡləmɑ̃tasjɔ̃] nf deregulation.

déréglementer [3] [deʀɛɡləmɑ̃te] vt to deregulate.

dérégler [18] [deʀeɡle] vt [mécanisme] to put out of order ; fig to upset.
➠ **se dérégler** vp [mécanisme] to go wrong ; fig to be upset ou unsettled.

dérider [3] [deʀide] vt fig : **~ qqn** to cheer sb up.
➠ **se dérider** vp to cheer up.

dérision [deʀizjɔ̃] nf derision ; **tourner qqch en ~** to hold sthg up to ridicule.

dérisoire [deʀizwaʀ] adj derisory.

dérivatif, ive [deʀivatif, iv] adj derivative.
➠ **dérivatif** nm distraction.

dérivation [deʀivasjɔ̃] nf - **1.** [de cours d'eau, circulation] diversion - **2.** LING & MATHS derivation.

dérive [deʀiv] nf - **1.** [aileron] centreboard - **2.** [mouvement] drift, drifting (U) ; **aller** ou **partir à la ~** fig to fall apart.

dérivé [deʀive] nm derivative.

dérivée [deʀive] nf MATHS derivative.

dériver [3] [deʀive] <> vt - **1.** [détourner] to di-

vert - **2.** LING to derive <> vi - **1.** [aller à la dérive] to drift - **2.** fig [découler] : **~ de** to derive from.

dériveur [deʀivœʀ] nm sailing dinghy (with centreboard).

dermato [dɛʀmato] nmf fam dermatologist.

dermatologie [dɛʀmatɔlɔʒi] nf dermatology.

dermatologue [dɛʀmatɔlɔɡ] nmf dermatologist.

dernier, ère [dɛʀnje, ɛʀ] <> adj - **1.** [gén] last ; **samedi ~** last Saturday ; **l'année dernière** last year - **2.** [ultime] last, final - **3.** [plus récent] latest <> nm, f last ; **ce ~** the latter ; **petit ~** baby of the family.
➠ **en dernier** loc adv last.

dernièrement [dɛʀnjɛʀmɑ̃] adv recently, lately.

dernier-né, dernière-née [dɛʀnjene, dɛʀnjɛʀne] (mpl **derniers-nés**, fpl **dernières-nées**) nm, f [bébé] youngest (child) ; **la dernière-née de Fiat®** fig the new Fiat®.

dérobade [deʀɔbad] nf evasion, shirking (U).

dérobé, e [deʀɔbe] adj - **1.** [volé] stolen - **2.** [caché] hidden.
➠ **à la dérobée** loc adv surreptitiously.

dérober [3] [deʀɔbe] vt sout to steal.
➠ **se dérober** vp - **1.** [se soustraire] : **se ~ à qqch** to shirk sthg - **2.** [s'effondrer] to give way.

dérogation [deʀɔɡasjɔ̃] nf [action] dispensation ; [résultat] exception.

déroger [17] [deʀɔʒe] vi : **~ à** to depart from.

dérouiller [3] [deʀuje] vt - **1.** [nettoyer] to remove the rust from - **2.** fam [frapper] : **~ qqn** to give sb a belting.
➠ **se dérouiller** vp fig to stretch (o.s.).

déroulement [deʀulmɑ̃] nm - **1.** [de bobine] unwinding - **2.** fig [d'événement] development.

dérouler [3] [deʀule] vt [fil] to unwind ; [papier, tissu] to unroll.
➠ **se dérouler** vp to take place.

déroutant, e [deʀutɑ̃, ɑ̃t] adj disconcerting, bewildering.

déroute [deʀut] nf MIL rout ; fig collapse ; **mettre en ~** to rout.

dérouter [3] [deʀute] vt - **1.** [déconcerter] to disconcert, to put out - **2.** [dévier] to divert.

derrick [deʀik] nm derrick.

derrière [dɛʀjɛʀ] <> prép & adv behind <> nm - **1.** [partie arrière] back ; **la porte de ~** the back door - **2.** [partie du corps] bottom, behind.

des [de] <> art indéf ⊳ **un** <> prép ⊳ **de**.

dès [dɛ] prép from ; **~ son arrivée** the minute he arrives/arrived, as soon as he arrives/

arrived ; ~ **l'enfance** since childhood ; ~ **1900** as far back as 1900, as early as 1900 ; ~ **maintenant** from now on ; ~ **demain** starting *ou* from tomorrow.

➤ **dès lors** *loc adv* from then on.

➤ **dès lors que** *loc conj* [puisque] since.

➤ **dès que** *loc conj* as soon as.

désabusé, e [dezabyze] *adj* disillusioned.

désaccord [dezakɔr] *nm* disagreement.

désaccordé, e [dezakɔrde] *adj* out of tune.

désaccoutumer [3] [dezakutyme] *vt* : ~ **qqn de** to get sb out of the habit of.

➤ **se désaccoutumer** *vp* : se ~ **de qqch/de faire qqch** to become unaccustomed to sthg/to doing sthg.

désaffecté, e [dezafɛkte] *adj* disused.

désaffection [dezafɛksjɔ̃] *nf* disaffection.

désagréable [dezagreabl] *adj* unpleasant.

désagréablement [dezagreabləmɑ̃] *adv* unpleasantly.

désagréger [22] [dezagreʒe] *vt* to break up.

➤ **se désagréger** *vp* to break up.

désagrément [dezagremɑ̃] *nm* annoyance.

désaltérant, e [dezalterɑ̃, ɑ̃t] *adj* thirst-quenching.

désaltérer [18] [dezaltere] <> *vt* to quench the thirst of <> *vi* to be thirst-quenching.

➤ **se désaltérer** *vp* to quench one's thirst.

désamorcer [16] [dezamɔrse] *vt* [arme] to remove the primer from ; [bombe] to defuse ; *fig* [complot] to nip in the bud.

désappointer [3] [dezapwɛte] *vt* to disappoint.

désapprendre [79] [dezaprɑ̃dr] *vt* to forget.

désapprobateur, trice [dezaprɔbatœr, tris] *adj* disapproving.

désapprobation [dezaprɔbasjɔ̃] *nf* disapproval.

désapprouver [3] [dezapruve] <> *vt* to disapprove of <> *vi* to be disapproving.

désarçonner [3] [dezarsɔne] *vt litt* & *fig* to throw.

désargenté, e [dezarʒɑ̃te] *adj* short (of money).

désarmant, e [dezarmɑ̃, ɑ̃t] *adj* disarming.

désarmement [dezarməmɑ̃] *nm* disarmament.

désarmer [3] [dezarme] <> *vt* to disarm ; [fusil] to unload <> *vi* - **1.** [pays] to disarm - **2.** *fig* [personne] to give up ; [haine] to cease.

désarroi [dezarwa] *nm* confusion.

désassorti, e [dezasɔrti] *adj* [dépareillé] non-matching.

désastre [dezastr] *nm* disaster.

désastreux, euse [dezastrø, øz] *adj* disastrous.

désavantage [dezavɑ̃taʒ] *nm* disadvantage.

désavantager [17] [dezavɑ̃taʒe] *vt* to disadvantage.

désavantageux, euse [dezavɑ̃taʒø, øz] *adj* unfavourable *Br*, unfavorable *Am*.

désaveu, x [dezavø] *nm* - **1.** [reniement] denial - **2.** [désapprobation] disapproval.

désavouer [6] [dezavwe] *vt* to disown.

➤ **se désavouer** *vp* to go back on one's word.

désaxé, e [dezakse] <> *adj* [mentalement] disordered, unhinged <> *nm, f* unhinged person.

descendance [desɑ̃dɑ̃s] *nf* - **1.** [origine] descent - **2.** [progéniture] descendants *(pl)*.

descendant, e [desɑ̃dɑ̃, ɑ̃t] *nm, f* [héritier] descendant.

descendre [73] [desɑ̃dr] <> *vt (aux : avoir)* - **1.** [escalier, pente] to go/come down ; ~ **la rue en courant** to run down the street - **2.** [rideau, tableau] to lower - **3.** [apporter] to bring/take down - **4.** *fam* [personne, avion] to shoot down <> *vi (aux : être)* - **1.** [gén] to go/come down ; [température, niveau] to fall - **2.** [passager] to get off ; ~ **d'un bus** to get off a bus ; ~ **d'une voiture** to get out of a car - **3.** [loger] : ~ **chez** to stay with ; ~ **à l'hôtel** to stay in a hotel - **4.** [être issu] : ~ **de** to be descended from - **5.** [marée] to go out.

descendu, e [desɑ̃dy] *pp* ▷ **descendre**.

descente [desɑ̃t] *nf* - **1.** [action] descent - **2.** [pente] downhill slope *ou* stretch - **3.** *fam fig* [capacité à boire] : **il a une bonne ~** he can certainly put it away - **4.** [irruption] raid - **5.** [tapis] : ~ **de lit** bedside rug.

descriptif, ive [dɛskriptif, iv] *adj* descriptive.

➤ **descriptif** *nm* [de lieu] particulars *(pl)* ; [d'appareil] specification.

description [dɛskripsjɔ̃] *nf* description.

désemparé, e [dezɑ̃pare] *adj* [personne] helpless ; [avion, navire] disabled.

désemplir [32] [dezɑ̃plir] *vi* : **ce restaurant ne désemplit pas** this restaurant is always packed.

désencombrer [3] [dezɑ̃kɔ̃bre] *vt* to clear.

désendettement [dezɑ̃dɛtmɑ̃] *nm* degearing, debt reduction.

désenfler [3] [dezɑ̃fle] *vi* to go down, to become less swollen.

désengagement [dezɑ̃gaʒmɑ̃] *nm* disengagement.

désensibiliser [3] [desãsibilize] *vt* to desensitize.

déséquilibre [dezekilibr] *nm* imbalance.

déséquilibré, e [dezekilibre] *nm, f* unbalanced person.

déséquilibrer [3] [dezekilibre] *vt* - **1.** [physiquement] : ~ **qqn** to throw sb off balance - **2.** [perturber] to unbalance.

désert, e [dezer, ert] *adj* [désertique - île] desert *(avant n)* ; [peu fréquenté] deserted.
◆ **désert** *nm* desert.

déserter [3] [dezerte] *vt* & *vi* to desert.

déserteur [dezertœr] *nm* MIL deserter ; *fig* & *péj* traitor.

désertification [dezertifikasjõ], **désertisation** [desertizasjõ] *nf* desertification ; [de région] depopulation.

désertion [dezersjõ] *nf* desertion.

désertique [dezertik] *adj* desert *(avant n)*.

désertisation = désertification.

désespérant, e [dezesperã, ãt] *adj* - **1.** [déprimant] depressing - **2.** [affligeant] hopeless.

désespéré, e [dezespere] *adj* - **1.** [regard] desperate - **2.** [situation] hopeless.

désespérément [dezesperemã] *adv* - **1.** [sans espoir] hopelessly - **2.** [avec acharnement] desperately.

désespérer [18] [dezespere] ◇ *vt* - **1.** [décourager] : ~ **qqn** to drive sb to despair - **2.** [perdre espoir] : ~ **que qqch arrive** to give up hope of sthg happening ◇ *vi* : ~ **(de)** to despair (of).
◆ **se désespérer** *vp* to despair.

désespoir [dezespwar] *nm* despair ; **en ~ de cause** as a last resort ; **faire le ~ de qqn** to be the despair of sb.

déshabillé [dezabije] *nm* negligee.

déshabiller [3] [dezabije] *vt* to undress.
◆ **se déshabiller** *vp* to undress, to get undressed.

déshabituer [7] [dezabitɥe] *vt* : ~ **qqn de faire qqch** to get sb out of the habit of doing sthg.
◆ **se déshabituer** *vp* : **se ~ de qqch** to become unaccustomed to sthg.

désherbant, e [dezerbã, ãt] *adj* weedkilling.
◆ **désherbant** *nm* weedkiller.

désherber [3] [dezerbe] *vt* & *vi* to weed.

déshérité, e [dezerite] ◇ *adj* - **1.** [privé d'héritage] disinherited - **2.** [pauvre] deprived ◇ *nm, f* [pauvre] deprived person.

déshériter [3] [dezerite] *vt* to disinherit.

déshonneur [dezonœr] *nm* disgrace.

déshonorant, e [dezonorã, ãt] *adj* dishonourable *Br*, dishonorable *Am*.

déshonorer [3] [dezonore] *vt* to disgrace, to bring disgrace on.
◆ **se déshonorer** *vp* to disgrace o.s.

déshumaniser [3] [dezymanize] *vt* to dehumanize.

déshydratation [dezidratasjõ] *nf* dehydration.

déshydrater [3] [dezidrate] *vt* to dehydrate.
◆ **se déshydrater** *vp* to become dehydrated.

desiderata [deziderata] *nmpl* requirements.

design [dizajn] ◇ *adj inv* modern ◇ *nm inv* modernism.

désignation [deziɲasjõ] *nf* - **1.** [appellation] designation, name - **2.** [nomination] appointment.

désigner [3] [deziɲe] *vt* - **1.** [choisir] to appoint - **2.** [signaler] to point out - **3.** [nommer] to designate.
◆ **se désigner** *vp* : **se ~ (volontaire) pour qqch/pour faire qqch** to volunteer for sthg/ to do sthg.

désillusion [dezilyzjõ] *nf* disillusion.

désillusionner [3] [dezilyzjone] *vt* to disillusion.

désincarné, e [dezẽkarne] *adj* - **1.** RELIG disembodied - **2.** [éthéré] unearthly.

désindustrialisation [dezẽdystrijalizasjõ] *nf* deindustrialization.

désinence [dezinãs] *nf* LING ending.

désinfectant, e [dezẽfektã, ãt] *adj* disinfectant.
◆ **désinfectant** *nm* disinfectant.

désinfecter [4] [dezẽfekte] *vt* to disinfect.

désinflation [dezẽflasjõ] *nf* disinflation.

désinformation [dezẽfɔrmasjõ] *nf* disinformation.

désintégration [dezẽtegrasjõ] *nf* [désagrégation] disintegration ; *fig* break-up.

désintégrer [18] [dezẽtegre] *vt* to break up.
◆ **se désintégrer** *vp* to disintegrate, to break up.

désintéressé, e [dezẽterese] *adj* disinterested.

désintéresser [4] [dezẽterese] ◆ **se désintéresser** *vp* : **se ~ de** to lose interest in.

désintérêt [dezẽtere] *nm* lack of interest.

désintoxication [dezẽtɔksikasjõ] *nf* detoxification.

désinvolte [dezẽvɔlt] *adj* - **1.** [à l'aise] casual - **2.** *péj* [sans-gêne] offhand.

désinvolture [dezɛ̃vɔltyr] *nf* - **1.** [légèreté] casualness - **2.** *péj* [sans-gêne] offhandedness ; **avec ~** in an offhand manner.

désir [dezir] *nm* - **1.** [souhait] desire, wish - **2.** [charnel] desire.

désirable [dezirabl] *adj* desirable.

désirer [3] [dezire] *vt* - **1.** *sout* [chose] : **~ faire qqch** to wish to do sthg ; **vous désirez?** [dans un magasin] can I help you? ; [dans un café] what can I get you? - **2.** [sexuellement] to desire - **3.** *loc* : **laisser à ~** to leave a lot to be desired.

désireux, euse [dezirø, øz] *adj sout* : **~ de faire qqch** anxious to do sthg.

désistement [dezistəmɑ̃] *nm* : **~ (de)** withdrawal (from).

désister [3] [deziste] **~ se désister** *vp* - **1.** *JUR* : **se ~ de qqch** to withdraw sthg - **2.** [se retirer] to withdraw, to stand down.

désobéir [32] [dezɔbeir] *vi* : **~ (à qqn)** to disobey (sb).

désobéissance [dezɔbeisɑ̃s] *nf* disobedience.

désobéissant, e [dezɔbeisɑ̃, ɑ̃t] *adj* disobedient.

désobligeant, e [dezɔbliʒɑ̃, ɑ̃t] *adj sout* offensive.

désodorisant, e [dezɔdɔrizɑ̃, ɑ̃t] *adj* deodorant.

~ désodorisant *nm* air freshener.

désodoriser [3] [dezɔdɔrize] *vt* to deodorize.

désœuvré, e [dezœvre] *adj* idle.

désœuvrement [dezœvrəmɑ̃] *nm* idleness.

désolant, e [dezɔlɑ̃, ɑ̃t] *adj* disappointing.

désolation [dezɔlasjɔ̃] *nf* - **1.** [destruction] desolation - **2.** *sout* [affliction] distress.

désolé, e [dezɔle] *adj* - **1.** [ravagé] desolate - **2.** [très affligé] distressed - **3.** [contrarié] very sorry.

désoler [3] [dezɔle] *vt* - **1.** [affliger] to sadden - **2.** [contrarier] to upset, to make sorry.

~ se désoler *vp* [être contrarié] to be upset.

désolidariser [3] [desɔlidarize] *vt* - **1.** [choses] : **~ qqch (de)** to disengage *ou* disconnect sthg (from) - **2.** [personnes] to estrange.

~ se désolidariser *vp* : **se ~ de** to dissociate o.s. from.

désopilant, e [dezɔpilɑ̃, ɑ̃t] *adj* hilarious.

désordonné, e [dezɔrdɔne] *adj* [maison, personne] untidy ; *fig* [vie] disorganized.

désordre [dezɔrdr] *nm* - **1.** [fouillis] untidiness ; **en ~** untidy ; **dans le ~** in random order - **2.** *fig* [confusion] disorder - **3.** [agitation] disturbances *(pl)*, disorder *(U)*.

désorganiser [3] [dezɔrganize] *vt* to disrupt.

~ se désorganiser *vp* to become disorganized.

désorienté, e [dezɔrjɑ̃te] *adj* disoriented, disorientated.

désorienter [3] [dezɔrjɑ̃te] *vt* [égarer] to disorient, to disorientate ; *fig* [déconcerter] to bewilder.

désormais [dezɔrmɛ] *adv* from now on, in future.

désosser [3] [dezɔse] *vt* to bone.

despote [dɛspɔt] *◇ nm* [chef d'État] despot ; *fig* & *péj* tyrant *◇ adj* despotic.

despotique [dɛspɔtik] *adj* despotic.

despotisme [dɛspɔtism] *nm* [gouvernement] despotism ; *fig* & *péj* tyranny.

desquels, desquelles [dekɛl] ⊳ **lequel.**

DESS (*abr de* diplôme d'études supérieures spécialisées) *nm postgraduate diploma.*

dessaisir [32] [desezir] *vt JUR* : **~ qqn d'une affaire** to withdraw a case from sb.

~ se dessaisir *vp sout* : **se ~ de qqch** to relinquish sthg.

dessaler [3] [desale] *◇ vt* [poisson] : **faire ~** to soak *◇ vi NAVIG* to capsize.

dessaouler, dessoûler [3] [desule] *◇ vt* to sober up *◇ vi* to sober up ; **ne pas ~** *fam* to be permanently plastered.

dessécher [18] [deseʃe] *vt* [peau] to dry (out) ; *fig* [cœur] to harden.

~ se dessécher *vp* [peau, terre] to dry out ; [plante] to wither ; *fig* to harden.

dessein [desɛ̃] *nm sout* intention.

~ à dessein *loc adv* intentionally, on purpose.

desserrer [4] [desere] *vt* to loosen ; [poing, dents] to unclench ; [frein] to release.

dessert [desɛr] *nm* dessert.

desserte [desɛrt] *nf* - **1.** *TRANSPORT* (transport) service - **2.** [meuble] sideboard.

desservir [38] [desɛrvir] *vt* - **1.** *TRANSPORT* to serve - **2.** [table] to clear - **3.** [désavantager] to do a disservice to.

dessin [desɛ̃] *nm* - **1.** [graphique] drawing ; **~ animé** cartoon *(film)* ; **~ humoristique** cartoon *(drawing)* ; **~ industriel** draughtsmanship *Br*, draftsmanship *Am* - **2.** *fig* [contour] outline.

dessinateur, trice [desinatœr, tris] *nm, f* artist, draughtsman (*f* draughtswoman) *Br*, draftsman (*f* draftswoman) *Am* ; **~ industriel** draughtsman *Br*, draftsman *Am*.

dessiner [3] [desine] *◇ vt* [représenter] to draw ; *fig* to outline *◇ vi* to draw.

➡ **se dessiner** *vp* [se former] to take shape ; *fig* to stand out.

dessoûler = dessaouler.

dessous [dəsu] ◇ *adv* underneath ◇ *prép* underneath, under ◇ *nm* - **1.** [partie inférieure - gén] underside ; [- d'un tissu] wrong side - **2.** *loc* : **avoir le ~** to come off worst ; **être au trente-sixième ~** to be in dire straits ; **connaître lé ~ des cartes (de)** to have inside information (on) ; **les ~ de la politique/la finance** the hidden side of politics/the financial world ◇ *nmpl* [sous-vêtements féminins] underwear (U).

➡ **en dessous** *loc adv* underneath ; [plus bas] below ; **ils habitent l'appartement d'en ~** they live in the flat below *ou* downstairs ; **agir par en ~** to act in an underhand way.

➡ **en dessous de** *loc prép* below.

dessous-de-plat [dəsudpla] *nm inv* tablemat.

dessous-de-table [dəsudtabl] *nm inv* backhander.

dessus [dəsy] ◇ *adv* on top ; **n'oubliez pas d'inscrire l'adresse ~** don't forget to write the address on it ; **faites attention à ne pas marcher ~** be careful not to walk on it ◇ *nm* - **1.** [partie supérieure] top - **2.** [étage supérieur] upstairs ; **les voisins du ~** the upstairs neighbours - **3.** *loc* : **avoir le ~** to have the upper hand ; **reprendre le ~** to get over it ; **sens ~ dessous** upside down.

➡ **en dessus** *loc adv* on top.

dessus-de-lit [dəsydli] *nm inv* bedspread.

déstabilisateur, trice [destabilizatœr, tris] *adj* destabilizing.

déstabilisation [destabilizasjɔ̃] *nf* destabilization.

déstabiliser [3] [destabilize] *vt* to destabilize.

destin [dɛstɛ̃] *nm* fate.

destinataire [dɛstinatɛr] *nmf* addressee.

destination [dɛstinasjɔ̃] *nf* - **1.** [direction] destination ; **arriver à ~** to reach one's destination ; **un avion à ~ de Paris** a plane to *ou* for Paris - **2.** [rôle] purpose.

destinée [dɛstine] *nf* destiny.

destiner [3] [dɛstine] *vt* - **1.** [consacrer] : **~ qqch à** to intend sthg for, to mean sthg for - **2.** [vouer] : **~ qqn à qqch/à faire qqch** [à un métier] to destine sb for sthg/to do sthg ; [sort] to mark sb out for sthg/to do sthg.

➡ **se destiner** *vp* : **se ~ à** to intend to go into.

destituer [7] [dɛstitɥe] *vt* to dismiss.

destitution [dɛstitysjɔ̃] *nf* dismissal.

destructeur, trice [dɛstryktœr, tris] ◇ *adj* destructive ◇ *nm, f* destroyer.

destruction [dɛstryksjɔ̃] *nf* destruction.

déstructuration [destryktyrasjɔ̃] *nf* breaking down.

déstructurer [3] [destryktyre] *vt* to break down.

désuet, ète [dezɥɛ, ɛt] *adj* [expression, coutume] obsolete ; [style, tableau] outmoded.

désuétude [dezɥetyd] *nf* : **tomber en ~** [expression, coutume] to become obsolete ; [style, tableau] to become outmoded.

désuni, e [dezyni] *adj* divided.

désunion [dezynjɔ̃] *nf* division, dissension.

désunir [32] [dezynir] *vt* [scinder] to divide, to separate ; *fig* to divide.

➡ **se désunir** *vp* [athlète] to lose one's stride.

détachable [detaʃabl] *adj* detachable, removable.

détachage [detaʃaʒ] *nm* stain removal.

détachant, e [detaʃɑ̃, ɑ̃t] *adj* stain-removing.

➡ **détachant** *nm* stain remover.

détaché, e [detaʃe] *adj* detached ; **~ à** *ou* **auprès de** seconded to.

détachement [detaʃmɑ̃] *nm* - **1.** [d'esprit] detachment - **2.** [de fonctionnaire] secondment - **3.** MIL detachment.

détacher [3] [detaʃe] *vt* - **1.** [enlever] : **~ qqch (de)** [objet] to detach sthg (from) ; *fig* to free sthg (from) ; **coupon à ~** tear-off coupon - **2.** [nettoyer] to remove stains from, to clean - **3.** [délier] to undo ; [cheveux] to untie - **4.** ADMIN : **~ qqn auprès de** to second sb to.

➡ **se détacher** *vp* - **1.** [tomber] : **se ~ (de)** to come off ; *fig* to free o.s. (from) - **2.** [se défaire] to come undone - **3.** [ressortir] : **se ~ sur** to stand out on - **4.** [se désintéresser] : **se ~ de qqn** to drift apart from sb.

détail [detaj] *nm* - **1.** [précision] detail - **2.** [description] : **faire le ~ de** to give a detailed breakdown *ou* description of - **3.** COMM : **le ~** retail.

➡ **au détail** *loc adj* & *loc adv* retail.

➡ **en détail** *loc adv* in detail.

détaillant, e [detajɑ̃, ɑ̃t] ◇ *adj* retail ◇ *nm, f* retailer.

détaillé, e [detaje] *adj* detailed.

détailler [3] [detaje] *vt* - **1.** [expliquer] to give details of - **2.** [vendre] to retail.

détaler [3] [detale] *vi* - **1.** [personne] to clear out - **2.** [animal] to bolt.

détartrant, e [detartrɑ̃, ɑ̃t] *adj* descaling.

➡ **détartrant** *nm* descaling agent.

détartrer [3] [detartre] *vt* to scale, to descale.

détaxe [detaks] *nf* : **~ (sur)** [suppression] removal of tax (from) ; [réduction] reduction in tax (on).

détecter [4] [detɛkte] *vt* to detect.

détecteur, trice [detɛktœr, tris] *adj* detecting, detector *(avant n)*.

➤ **détecteur** *nm* detector ; ~ **de fumée** smoke detector.

détection [detɛksjɔ̃] *nf* detection.

détective [detɛktiv] *nm* detective ; ~ **privé** private detective.

déteindre [81] [detɛ̃dr] ◇ *vt* to fade ◇ *vi* to fade ; ~ **sur** *fig* to rub off on ; ~ **au lavage** to run (in the wash).

déteint, e [detɛ̃, ɛt] *pp* ⊳ **déteindre.**

dételer [24] [detle] ◇ *vt* - **1.** [cheval] to unharness - **2.** [wagon] to unhitch ◇ *vi fam fig* : **sans ~** at a stretch.

détendre [73] [detɑ̃dr] *vt* - **1.** [corde] to loosen, to slacken ; *fig* to ease - **2.** [personne] to relax.

➤ **se détendre** *vp* - **1.** [se relâcher] to slacken ; *fig* [situation] to ease ; [atmosphère] to become more relaxed - **2.** [se reposer] to relax.

détendu, e [detɑ̃dy] ◇ *pp* ⊳ **détendre** ◇ *adj* - **1.** [corde] loose, slack - **2.** [personne] relaxed.

détenir [40] [detnir] *vt* - **1.** [objet] to have, to hold - **2.** [personne] to detain, to hold.

détente [detɑ̃t] *nf* - **1.** [de ressort] release - **2.** [d'une arme] trigger - **3.** [repos] relaxation - **4.** *POLIT* détente - **5.** [d'athlète] thrust - **6.** *loc* : **être dur à la ~** to be slow on the uptake.

détenteur, trice [detɑ̃tœr, tris] *nm, f* [d'objet, de secret] possessor ; [de prix, record] holder.

détention [detɑ̃sjɔ̃] *nf* - **1.** [possession] possession - **2.** [emprisonnement] detention ; ~ **préventive** remand (in custody).

détenu, e [detny] ◇ *pp* ⊳ **détenir** ◇ *adj* detained ◇ *nm, f* prisoner.

détergent, e [detɛrʒɑ̃, ɑ̃t] *adj* detergent *(avant n)*.

➤ **détergent** *nm* detergent.

détérioration [deterjɔrasjɔ̃] *nf* [de bâtiment] deterioration ; [de situation] worsening.

détériorer [3] [deterjɔre] *vt* - **1.** [abîmer] to damage - **2.** [altérer] to ruin.

➤ **se détériorer** *vp* - **1.** [bâtiment] to deteriorate ; [situation] to worsen - **2.** [s'altérer] to be spoiled.

déterminant, e [detɛrminɑ̃, ɑ̃t] *adj* decisive, determining.

➤ **déterminant** *nm* - **1.** *LING* determiner - **2.** *MATHS* determinant.

détermination [detɛrminasjɔ̃] *nf* - **1.** [défini-

tion] determining *(U)* - **2.** [fixation] determination - **3.** [résolution] decision.

déterminé, e [detɛrmine] *adj* - **1.** [quantité] given *(avant n)* - **2.** [expression] determined.

déterminer [3] [detɛrmine] *vt* - **1.** [préciser] to determine, to specify - **2.** [provoquer] to bring about ; ~ **qqn à faire qqch** to cause sb to do sthg.

➤ **se déterminer** *vp* : **se ~ à faire qqch** to decide to do sthg.

déterminisme [detɛrminism] *nm* determinism.

déterré, e [detere] *adj* : **avoir une mine de ~** to look like death warmed up.

déterrer [4] [detere] *vt* to dig up.

détersif, ive [detɛrsif, iv] *adj* detergent *(avant n)*.

➤ **détersif** *nm* detergent.

détestable [detɛstabl] *adj* dreadful.

détester [3] [detɛste] *vt* to detest.

détiendrai, détiendras *etc* ⊳ **détenir.**

détonant, e [detɔnɑ̃, ɑ̃t] *adj* explosive.

détonateur [detɔnatœr] *nm* *TECHNOL* detonator ; *fig* trigger.

détonation [detɔnasjɔ̃] *nf* detonation.

détoner [3] [detɔne] *vi* to detonate.

détonner [3] [detɔne] *vi* *MUS* to be out of tune ; [couleur] to clash ; [personne] to be out of place.

détour [detur] *nm* - **1.** [crochet] detour ; **faire un ~ (par)** to make a detour (through) - **2.** [méandre] bend ; **au ~ du chemin** at the bend in the road ; **sans ~** *fig* directly.

détourné, e [deturne] *adj* [dévié] indirect ; *fig* roundabout *(avant n)*.

détournement [deturnəmɑ̃] *nm* diversion ; ~ **d'avion** hijacking ; ~ **de fonds** embezzlement ; ~ **de mineur** corruption of a minor.

détourner [3] [deturne] *vt* - **1.** [dévier - gén] to divert ; [- avion] to hijack - **2.** [écarter] : ~ **qqn de** to distract sb from, to divert sb from - **3.** [la tête, les yeux] to turn away - **4.** [argent] to embezzle.

➤ **se détourner** *vp* to turn away ; **se ~ de** *fig* to move away from.

détracteur, trice [detraktœr, tris] *nm, f* detractor.

détraqué, e [detrake] *fam* ◇ *adj* - **1.** [déréglé] on the blink - **2.** [fou] nutty, loopy ◇ *nm, f* nutter.

détraquer [3] [detrake] *vt* *fam* [dérégler] to break ; *fig* to upset.

➤ **se détraquer** *vp* *fam* [se dérégler] to go wrong ; *fig* to become unsettled.

détrempe [detrɑ̃p] *nf* *ART* tempera.

détremper [3] [detrãpe] vt - **1.** [sol] to soften - **2.** [peinture] to thin.

détresse [detrɛs] nf distress ; **en ~** in distress.

détriment [detrimã] **➡ au détriment de** loc prép to the detriment of.

détritus [detrity(s)] nm detritus.

détroit [detrwa] nm strait ; **le ~ de Bering** the Bering Strait ; **le ~ de Gibraltar** the Strait of Gibraltar.

détromper [3] [detrɔ̃pe] vt to disabuse.
➡ se détromper vp to disabuse o.s. ; **détrompez-vous!** think again!

détrôner [3] [detrone] vt [souverain] to dethrone ; fig to oust.

détrousser [3] [detruse] vt vieilli to rob.

détruire [98] [detrчir] vt - **1.** [démolir, éliminer] to destroy - **2.** [massacrer] to wipe out - **3.** fig [anéantir] to ruin.
➡ se détruire vp to destroy o.s.

détruisais, détruise etc ⊳ **détruire**.

détruit, e [detrчi, it] pp ⊳ **détruire**.

dette [dɛt] nf debt ; **avoir des ~s** to have debts ; **la ~ publique** the national debt ; **être criblé de ~s** to be crippled by debt.

DEUG, Deug [dœg] (abr de **diplôme d'études universitaires générales**) nm university diploma taken after two years of arts courses.

DEUG, DEUST

In French universities, students take the 'DEUG' or the 'DEUST' after two years of courses. They may then take further courses leading to the 'licence' (the equivalent of a bachelor's degree).

deuil [dœj] nm [douleur, mort] bereavement ; [vêtements, période] mourning (U) ; **en ~** in mourning ; **porter le ~** to be in ou wear mourning ; **faire son ~ de qqch** fig to wave sthg goodbye.

DEUST, Deust [dœst] (abr de **diplôme d'études universitaires scientifiques et techniques**) nm university diploma taken after two years of science courses ; voir aussi **DEUG**.

deux [dø] ⋄ adj num two ; **ses ~ fils** both his sons, his two sons ; **tous les ~ jours** every other day, every two days, every second day ; **en moins de ~** fam fig in no time at all, in two ticks ⋄ nm two ; **les ~** both ; **par ~** in pairs ; voir aussi **six**.

deuxième [døzjɛm] adj num, nm ou nmf second ; voir aussi **sixième**.

deuxièmement [døzjɛmmã] adv secondly.

deux-pièces [døpjɛs] nm inv - **1.** [appartement] two-room flat Br ou apartment Am - **2.** [bikini] two-piece (swimming costume).

deux-points [døpwɛ̃] nm inv colon.

deux-roues [døru] nm inv two-wheeled vehicle.

deux-temps [døtã] nm inv MÉCANIQUE two-stroke (engine).

dévaler [3] [devale] ⋄ vt to run down ⋄ vi to hurtle down.

dévaliser [3] [devalize] vt [cambrioler - maison] to ransack ; [- personne] to rob ; fig to strip bare.

dévalorisant, e [devalɔrizã, ãt] adj demeaning.

dévalorisation [devalɔrizasjɔ̃] nf depreciation.

dévaloriser [3] [devalɔrize] vt - **1.** [monnaie] to devalue - **2.** [personne] to run ou put down.
➡ se dévaloriser vp - **1.** [monnaie] to fall in value - **2.** [personne] fig to run ou put o.s. down.

dévaluation [devalчasjɔ̃] nf devaluation.

dévaluer [7] [devalчe] ⋄ vt to devalue ⋄ vi to devalue.
➡ se dévaluer vp to devalue.

devancer [16] [dəvãse] vt - **1.** [précéder] to arrive before - **2.** [surpasser] to be in front of - **3.** [anticiper] to anticipate.

devant [dəvã] ⋄ prép - **1.** [en face de] in front of - **2.** [en avant de] ahead of, in front of ; **aller droit ~ soi** to go straight ahead ou on - **3.** [en présence de, face à] in the face of ⋄ adv - **1.** [en face] in front - **2.** [en avant] in front, ahead ⋄ nm front ; **prendre les ~s** to make the first move, to take the initiative.
➡ de devant loc adj [pattes, roues] front (avant n).

devanture [dəvãtyr] nf shop window ; **à la ~ de** on display in.

dévastateur, trice [devastatœr, tris] adj devastating.

dévastation [devastasjɔ̃] nf devastation.

dévaster [3] [devaste] vt to devastate.

déveine [devɛn] nf fam bad luck.

développement [devlɔpmã] nm - **1.** [gén] development - **2.** PHOT developing - **3.** [exposé] exposition.
➡ développements nmpl developments.

développer [3] [devlɔpe] vt to develop ; [industrie, commerce] to expand.
➡ se développer vp - **1.** [s'épanouir] to spread - **2.** ÉCON to grow, to expand.

devenir [40] [dəvnir] vi to become ; **que devenez-vous?** fig how are you doing?

devenu, e [dəvny] pp ⊳ **devenir**.

dévergondé, e [devɛʀgɔ̃de] <> adj shameless, wild <> nm, f shameless person.
dévergonder [3] [devɛʀgɔ̃de] ➡ **se dévergonder** vp to go to the bad, to get into bad ways.
déverrouiller [3] [devɛʀuje] vt - **1.** [porte] to unbolt - **2.** [arme] to release the catch of.
déverser [3] [devɛʀse] vt - **1.** [liquide] to pour out - **2.** [ordures] to tip (out) - **3.** [bombes] to unload, to drop - **4.** fig [injures] to pour out.
➡ **se déverser** vp : se ~ dans to flow into.
déversoir [devɛʀswaʀ] nm overflow.
dévêtir [44] [devetiʀ] vt sout to undress.
➡ **se dévêtir** vp sout to undress, to get undressed.
dévêtu, e [devety] pp ▷ dévêtir.
déviant, e [devjɑ̃, ɑ̃t] adj deviant.
déviation [devjasjɔ̃] nf - **1.** [gén] deviation - **2.** [d'itinéraire] diversion.
dévider [3] [devide] vt [fil] to unwind.
deviendrai, deviendras etc ▷ devenir.
devienne, devient ▷ devenir.
dévier [9] [devje] <> vi : ~ de to deviate from <> vt to divert.
devin, devineresse [dəvɛ̃, dəvinʀɛs] nm, f : je ne suis pas ~! I'm not psychic!
deviner [3] [dəvine] vt to guess.
➡ **se deviner** vp - **1.** [aller de soi] to just come naturally - **2.** [se voir] : ça se devine facilement that's easy to see.
devinette [dəvinɛt] nf riddle.
devis [dəvi] nm estimate ; faire un ~ to (give an) estimate.
dévisager [17] [deviʒaʒe] vt to stare at.
devise [dəviz] nf - **1.** [formule] motto - **2.** [monnaie] currency.
➡ **devises** nfpl [argent] currency (U).
deviser [3] [dəvize] vi - **1.** sout [parler] : ~ de ou sur to converse about - **2.** Helv [faire un devis] to estimate.
dévisser [3] [devise] <> vt to unscrew <> vi ALPINISME to fall (off).
de visu [dəvizy] adv : constater qqch ~ to see sthg with one's own eyes.
dévoiler [3] [devwale] vt to unveil ; fig to reveal.
devoir [53] [dəvwaʀ] <> nm - **1.** [obligation] duty ; faire son ~ to do one's duty - **2.** SCOL homework (U) ; faire ses ~s to do one's homework <> vt - **1.** [argent, respect] : ~ qqch (à qqn) to owe (sb) sthg - **2.** [être redevable de] : ~ qqch à qqn to owe sthg to sb ; je lui dois d'être ici it's thanks to him that I'm here - **3.** [marque l'obligation] : ~ faire qqch to have to do sthg ; je dois partir à l'heure ce soir I have

to ou must leave on time tonight ; tu devrais faire attention you should ou ought to be careful ; il n'aurait pas dû mentir he shouldn't have lied, he ought not to have lied - **4.** [marque la probabilité] : il doit faire chaud là-bas it must be hot over there ; il a dû oublier he must have forgotten - **5.** [marque le futur, l'intention] : ~ faire qqch to be (due) to do sthg, to be going to do sthg ; elle doit arriver à 6 heures she's due to arrive at 6 o'clock ; je dois voir mes parents ce week-end I'm seeing ou going to see my parents this weekend - **6.** [être destiné à] : il devait mourir trois ans plus tard he was to die three years later ; cela devait arriver it had to happen, it was bound to happen.
➡ **se devoir** vp : se ~ de faire qqch to be duty-bound to do sthg ; comme il se doit as is proper.
dévolu, e [devɔly] adj sout : ~ à allotted to.
➡ **dévolu** nm : jeter son ~ sur to set one's sights on.
dévorer [3] [devɔʀe] vt to devour ; être dévoré de fig to be eaten up by ou with.
dévot, e [devo, ɔt] <> adj devout <> nm, f devout person.
dévotion [devɔsjɔ̃] nf devotion ; avec ~ [prier] devoutly ; [soigner, aimer] devotedly ; faire ses ~s to perform one's devotions.
dévoué, e [devwe] adj devoted.
dévouement [devumɑ̃] nm devotion.
dévouer [6] [devwe] ➡ **se dévouer** vp - **1.** [se consacrer] : se ~ à to devote o.s. to - **2.** fig [se sacrifier] : se ~ pour qqch/pour faire qqch to sacrifice o.s. for sthg/to do sthg.
dévoyé, e [devwaje] adj & nm, f delinquent.
dévoyer [13] [devwaje] vt littéraire to lead astray.
➡ **se dévoyer** vp littéraire to go astray.
devrai, devras etc ▷ devoir.
dextérité [dɛksteʀite] nf dexterity, skill ; avec ~ skilfully.
dg (abr de décigramme) dg.
DG (abr de directeur général) nm GM.
DGE (abr de dotation globale d'équipement) nf state contribution to local government capital budget.
DGF (abr de dotation globale de fonctionnement) nf state contribution to local government revenue budget.
DGI (abr de Direction générale des impôts) nf central tax office.
DGSE (abr de Direction générale de la sécurité extérieure) nf French intelligence and espionage service, ≃ MI6 Br, ≃ CIA Am.
diabète [djabɛt] nm diabetes (U).

diabétique [djabetik] *nmf* & *adj* diabetic.

diable [djabl] *nm* devil ; **au ~** [loin] miles from anywhere ; **avoir le ~ au corps** to be a real handful ; **tirer le ~ par la queue** to live from hand to mouth.

diablement [djabləmã] *adv vieilli* horribly.

diablesse [djablɛs] *nf* she-devil ; [femme turbulente] shrew, vixen.

diablotin [djablɔtɛ̃] *nm* imp.

diabolique [djabɔlik] *adj* diabolical.

diabolo [djabɔlo] *nm* **- 1.** [jouet] diabolo **- 2.** [boisson] fruit cordial and lemonade ; **~ menthe** mint (cordial) and lemonade.

diacre [djakr] *nm* RELIG deacon.

diadème [djadɛm] *nm* diadem.

diagnostic [djagnɔstik] *nm* MÉD & *fig* diagnosis.

diagnostiquer [3] [djagnɔstike] *vt* MÉD & *fig* to diagnose.

diagonale [djagɔnal] *nf* diagonal ; **en ~** diagonally ; **lire en ~** *fig* to skim.

diagramme [djagram] *nm* graph.

dialecte [djalɛkt] *nm* dialect.

dialectique [djalɛktik] *nf* & *adj* dialectic.

dialogue [djalɔg] *nm* discussion ; **c'est un ~ de sourds** they're/you're *etc* never going to agree.
➤ **dialogues** *nmpl* dialogue *(sg)* Br, dialog *(sg)* Am.

dialoguer [3] [djalɔge] *vi* **- 1.** [converser] to converse **- 2.** INFORM to interact.

dialyse [djaliz] *nf* dialysis.

diamant [djamã] *nm* [pierre] diamond.

diamétralement [djametralmã] *adv* : **~ opposé** diametrically opposed.

diamètre [djamɛtr] *nm* diameter.

diantre [djãtr] *interj littéraire* & *vieilli* by Jove!

diapason [djapazɔ̃] *nm* [instrument] tuning fork ; **se mettre au ~** *fig* to get on the same wavelength.

diaphane [djafan] *adj* [peau, teint] translucent ; [tissu] diaphanous.

diaphragme [djafragm] *nm* diaphragm.

diapositive [djapozitiv] *nf* slide.

diarrhée [djare] *nf* diarrhoea.

diatribe [djatrib] *nf sout* diatribe.

dichotomie [dikɔtɔmi] *nf* dichotomy.

dico [diko] *nm fam* dictionary.

Dictaphone® [diktafɔn] *nm* Dictaphone®.

dictateur [diktatœr] *nm* dictator.

dictatorial, e, aux [diktatɔrjal, o] *adj* dictatorial.

dictature [diktatyr] *nf* dictatorship.

dictée [dikte] *nf* dictation.

dicter [3] [dikte] *vt* to dictate.

diction [diksjɔ̃] *nf* diction.

dictionnaire [diksjɔnɛr] *nm* dictionary ; **~ bilingue/encyclopédique** bilingual/encyclopedic dictionary.

dicton [diktɔ̃] *nm* saying, dictum.

didactique [didaktik] *adj* didactic.

dièse [djɛz] <> *adj* sharp ; **do/fa ~** C/F sharp <> *nm* sharp.

diesel [djezɛl] *adj inv* diesel ; **moteur ~** diesel engine.

diète [djɛt] *nf* diet ; **être à la ~** [régime] ; to be on a diet ; [jeûne] to be fasting.

diététicien, enne [djetetisjɛ̃, ɛn] *nm, f* dietician.

diététique [djetetik] <> *nf* dietetics *(U)* <> *adj* [considération, raison] dietary ; [produit, magasin] health *(avant n)*.

dieu, x [djø] *nm* god ; **comme un ~** *fig* & *hum* divinely.
➤ **Dieu** *nm* God ; **mon Dieu!** my God! ; **Dieu sait où/comment** God knows where/how ; **Dieu merci!** thank God!

diffamation [difamasjɔ̃] *nf* [écrite] libel ; [orale] slander ; **attaquer qqn en ~** to sue sb for slander/libel.

diffamatoire [difamatwar] *adj* defamatory.

différant [diferã] *pp* ➢ **différer**.

différé, e [difere] *adj* recorded.
➤ **différé** *nm* : **en ~** TÉLÉ recorded ; INFORM offline.

différemment [diferamã] *adv* differently.

différence [diferãs] *nf* difference.

différencier [9] [diferãsje] *vt* : **~ qqch de qqch** to differentiate sthg from sthg.
➤ **se différencier** *vp* : **se ~ de** to be different from.

différend [diferã] *nm* [désaccord] difference of opinion ; **avoir un ~ avec** to have a difference of opinion with.

différent, e [diferã, ãt] *adj* : **~ (de)** different (from).

différentiel, elle [diferãsjɛl] *adj* differential.

différer [18] [difere] <> *vt* [retarder] to postpone <> *vi* : **~ de** to differ from, to be different from ; **~ (selon)** to vary (according to).

difficile [difisil] <> *adj* difficult <> *nm* : **faire le/la ~** to be hard to please.

difficilement [difisilmã] *adv* with difficulty.

difficulté [difikylte] *nf* **- 1.** [complexité, peine] difficulty **- 2.** [obstacle] problem ; **en ~** in difficulty.

difforme [difɔrm] *adj* deformed.

difformité [difɔrmite] *nf* deformity.

diffraction [difraksjɔ̃] *nf* diffraction.

diffus, e [dify, yz] *adj* diffused ; *fig* vague.

diffuser [3] [difyze] *vt* - **1.** [lumière] to diffuse - **2.** [émission] to broadcast - **3.** [livres] to distribute.

diffuseur [difyzœr] *nm* - **1.** [appareil] diffuser - **2.** [de livres] distributor.

diffusion [difyzjɔ̃] *nf* - **1.** [d'émission, d'onde] broadcast - **2.** [de livres] distribution.

digérer [18] [diʒere] <> *vi* to digest <> *vt* - **1.** [repas, connaissance] to digest - **2.** *fam fig* [désagrément] to put up with.

digeste [diʒɛst] *adj* (easily) digestible.

digestible [diʒɛstibl] *adj* digestible.

digestif, ive [diʒɛstif, iv] *adj* digestive.
➡ **digestif** *nm* liqueur.

digestion [diʒɛstjɔ̃] *nf* digestion.

digital, e, aux [diʒital, o] *adj* - **1.** TECHNOL digital - **2.** ⊳ **empreinte**.
➡ **digitale** *nf* digitalis.

digne [diɲ] *adj* - **1.** [honorable] dignified - **2.** [méritant] : ~ **de** worthy of ; ~ **de foi** trustworthy.

dignement [diɲmɑ̃] *adv* with dignity.

dignitaire [diɲitɛr] *nm* dignitary ; **haut ~** mandarin.

dignité [diɲite] *nf* dignity ; **se draper dans sa ~** to stand on one's dignity.

digression [digresjɔ̃] *nf* digression.

digue [dig] *nf* dike.

diktat [diktat] *nm* diktat.

dilapider [3] [dilapide] *vt* to squander.

dilatation [dilatasjɔ̃] *nf* dilation.

dilater [3] [dilate] *vt* to dilate.
➡ **se dilater** *vp* to expand, to dilate.

dilatoire [dilatwar] *adj* delaying *(avant n)*.

dilemme [dilɛm] *nm* dilemma.

dilettante [diletɑ̃t] *nmf* dilettante ; **faire qqch en ~** to dabble in sthg.

diligence [diliʒɑ̃s] *nf* HIST & *sout* diligence.

diligent, e [diliʒɑ̃, ɑ̃t] *adj vieilli* diligent.

diluant [dilɥɑ̃] *nm* thinner.

diluer [7] [dilɥe] *vt* to dilute.

diluvien, enne [dilyvjɛ̃, ɛn] *adj* torrential.

dimanche [dimɑ̃ʃ] *nm* Sunday ; **~ des Rameaux** Palm Sunday ; *voir aussi* **samedi**.

dimension [dimɑ̃sjɔ̃] *nf* - **1.** [mesure] dimension - **2.** [taille] dimensions *(pl)*, size - **3.** *fig* [importance] magnitude ; **à la ~ de** equal to.

diminué, e [diminɥe] *adj* diminished.

diminuer [7] [diminɥe] <> *vt* [réduire] to diminish, to reduce <> *vi* [intensité] to diminish, to decrease.
➡ **se diminuer** *vp* to put o.s. down.

diminutif, ive [diminytif, iv] *adj* diminutive.
➡ **diminutif** *nm* diminutive.

diminution [diminysjɔ̃] *nf* diminution.

DIN, Din [din] *(abr de* **Deutsche Industrie Norm***)* DIN.

dinde [dɛ̃d] *nf* - **1.** [animal] turkey - **2.** *péj* [femme] stupid woman.

dindon [dɛ̃dɔ̃] *nm* turkey ; **être le ~ de la farce** *fig* to be made a fool of.

dîner [3] [dine] <> *vi* to dine <> *nm* dinner ; **~ d'affaires/aux chandelles** business/candlelit dinner.

dînette [dinɛt] *nf* doll's tea party ; **faire la ~** to have a snack ; **jouer à la ~** to have a doll's tea party.

dingue [dɛ̃g] *fam* <> *adj* - **1.** [personne] crazy - **2.** [histoire] incredible <> *nmf* loony.

dinosaure [dinozɔr] *nm* dinosaur.

diocèse [djɔsɛz] *nm* diocese.

diode [djɔd] *nf* diode.

dioptrie [djɔptri] *nf* dioptre.

dioxine [diɔksin] *nf* dioxin.

diphasé, e [difaze] *adj* two-phase.

diphtérie [difteri] *nf* diphtheria.

diphtongue [diftɔ̃g] *nf* diphthong.

diplomate [diplɔmat] <> *nmf* [ambassadeur] diplomat <> *nm* [gâteau] ≃ trifle <> *adj* diplomatic.

diplomatie [diplɔmasi] *nf* diplomacy.

diplomatique [diplɔmatik] *adj* diplomatic.

diplôme [diplom] *nm* diploma.

diplômé, e [diplome] <> *adj* : **être ~ de/en** to be a graduate of/in <> *nm, f* graduate.

dire [102] [dir] *vt* : **~ qqch (à qqn)** [parole] to say sthg (to sb) ; [vérité, mensonge, secret] to tell (sb) sthg ; **~ à qqn de faire qqch** to tell sb to do sthg ; **il m'a dit que ...** he told me (that) ... ; **cela va sans ~** that goes without saying ; **c'est vite dit** *fam* that's easy (for you/him *etc*) to say ; **c'est beaucoup ~** that's saying a lot ; **elle est vraiment difficile, et ce n'est pas peu ~** she's very difficult - and I mean difficult ; **en ~ long** *fig* to speak volumes ; **entre nous soit dit** between you and me ; **la ville proprement dite** the actual town ; **~ du bien/du mal (de)** to speak well/ill(of) ; **que dirais-tu de ...?** what would you say to ...? ; **qu'en dis-tu?** what do you think (of it)? ; **on dit que ...** they say (that) ... ; **on dirait que ...** it looks as if ... ; **on dirait de la soie** it looks like silk, you'd think it was silk ; **et ~ que je n'étais pas là!**

and to think I wasn't there! ; **ça ne me dit rien** [pas envie] I don't fancy that ; [jamais entendu] I've never heard of it.

➡ **se dire** *vp* - **1.** [penser] to think (to o.s.) - **2.** [s'employer] : **ça ne se dit pas** [par décence] you mustn't say that ; [par usage] people don't say that, nobody says that - **3.** [se traduire] : **'chat' se dit 'gato' en espagnol** the Spanish for 'cat' is 'gato'.

➡ **au dire de** *loc prép* according to.

➡ **cela dit** *loc adv* having said that.

➡ **dis donc** *loc adv fam* so ; [au fait] by the way ; [à qqn qui exagère] look here!

➡ **pour ainsi dire** *loc adv* so to speak.

➡ **à vrai dire** *loc adv* to tell the truth.

direct, e [dirɛkt] *adj* direct.

➡ **direct** *nm* - **1.** *BOXE* jab ; **un ~ du gauche** a straight left - **2.** [train] direct train - **3.** *RADIO & TÉLÉ* : **le ~** live transmission *(U)* ; **en ~** live.

directement [dirɛktəmã] *adv* directly.

directeur, trice [dirɛktœr, tris] ◇ *adj* - **1.** [dirigeant] leading ; **comité ~** steering committee - **2.** [central] guiding ◇ *nm, f* director, manager ; **~ commercial/du marketing** sales/marketing director, sales/ marketing manager ; **~ général** general manager, managing director *Br*, chief executive officer *Am* ; **~ de la communication** director of communications ; **~ du personnel** *ou* **des ressources humaines** personnel *ou* human resources manager ; **~ de thèse** *UNIV* supervisor *Br*, reader *Am* ; **~ des ventes** sales manager.

direction [dirɛksjɔ̃] *nf* - **1.** [gestion, ensemble des cadres] management ; **sous la ~ de** under the management of - **2.** [orientation] direction ; **en** *ou* **dans la ~ de** in the direction of ; **'toutes ~s'** 'all routes' - **3.** *AUTOM* steering ; **~ assistée** power steering.

directive [dirɛktiv] *nf* directive.

directorial, e, aux [dirɛktɔrjal, o] *adj* managerial.

directrice ▷ **directeur**.

dirigeable [diriʒabl] *nm* : **(ballon) ~** airship.

dirigeant, e [diriʒã, ãt] ◇ *adj* ruling ◇ *nm, f* [de pays] leader ; [d'entreprise] manager.

diriger [17] [diriʒe] *vt* - **1.** [mener - entreprise] to run, to manage ; [- orchestre] to conduct ; [- film, acteurs] to direct ; [- recherches, projet] to supervise - **2.** [conduire] to steer - **3.** [orienter] : **~ qqch sur** to aim sthg at ; **~ qqch vers** to aim sthg towards *ou* toward *Am*.

➡ **se diriger** *vp* : **se ~ vers** to go towards *Br ou* toward *Am*, to head towards *Br ou* toward *Am*.

dirigisme [diriʒism] *nm* interventionism.

disais, disions *etc* ▷ **dire**.

discal, e, aux [diskal, o] ▷ **hernie**.

discernement [disɛrnəmã] *nm* - **1.** [jugement] discernment - **2.** *sout* [distinction] distinction.

discerner [3] [disɛrne] *vt* - **1.** [distinguer] : **~ qqch de** to distinguish sthg from - **2.** [deviner] to discern.

disciple [disipl] *nmf* disciple.

disciplinaire [disiplinɛr] *adj* disciplinary ; **mesure ~** disciplinary measure.

discipline [disiplin] *nf* discipline ; **~ de fer** iron rule.

discipliné, e [disipline] *adj* disciplined.

discipliner [3] [discipline] *vt* [personne] to discipline ; [cheveux] to control.

disc-jockey [diskʒɔke] (*pl* **disc-jockeys**) *nm* disc jockey.

disco [disko] ◇ *adj inv* disco *(avant n)* ◇ *nm* disco (music).

discographie [diskɔgrafi] *nf* discography.

discontinu, e [diskɔ̃tiny] *adj* [ligne] broken ; [bruit, effort] intermittent.

discontinuer [7] [diskɔ̃tinɥe] *vi* : **sans ~** without interruption.

discordance [diskɔrdɑ̃s] *nf* discrepancy.

discordant, e [diskɔrdã, ãt] *adj* discordant.

discorde [diskɔrd] *nf* discord.

discothèque [diskɔtɛk] *nf* - **1.** [boîte de nuit] night club - **2.** [de prêt] record library.

discount [disk(a)unt] *nm* discount.

discourir [45] [diskurir] *vi* to talk at length ; **~ sur** to hold forth on.

discours [diskur] *nm* - **1.** [allocution] speech ; **faire un ~** to make a speech - **2.** *LING* : **~ direct/indirect** direct/reported speech.

discouru, e [diskury] *pp* ▷ **discourir**.

discrédit [diskredi] *nm* discredit, disrepute ; **jeter le ~ sur** to bring disgrace on.

discréditer [3] [diskredite] *vt* to discredit.

➡ **se discréditer** *vp* to discredit o.s.

discret, ète [diskrɛ, ɛt] *adj* [gén] discreet ; [réservé] reserved.

discrètement [diskrɛtmã] *adv* discreetly.

discrétion [diskresjɔ̃] *nf* - **1.** [réserve, tact, silence] discretion - **2.** [sobriété] sobriety, simplicity ; **avec ~** discreetly.

➡ **à discrétion** ◇ *loc adj* unlimited ◇ *loc adv* as much as you want.

discrétionnaire [diskresjɔnɛr] *adj* discretionary.

discrimination [diskriminasjɔ̃] *nf* discrimination ; **sans ~** indiscriminately.

discriminatoire [diskriminatwar] *adj* discriminatory.

disculper [3] [diskylpe] *vt* to exonerate.
➤ **se disculper** *vp* to exonerate o.s.

discussion [diskysjɔ̃] *nf* - **1.** [conversation, examen] discussion - **2.** [contestation, altercation] argument ; **sans ~** without argument.

discutable [diskytabl] *adj* - **1.** [contestable] questionable - **2.** [douteux] doubtful, questionable.

discutailler [3] [diskytaje] *vi fam péj* to argue over trivialities *ou* details.

discuter [3] [diskyte] ⬦ *vt* - **1.** [débattre] : **~ (de) qqch** to discuss sthg - **2.** [contester] to dispute ⬦ *vi* - **1.** [parlementer] to discuss - **2.** [converser] to talk - **3.** [contester] to argue.
➤ **se discuter** *vp* to be questionable *ou* debatable.

disert, e [dizɛr, ɛrt] *adj littéraire* articulate.

disette [dizɛt] *nf sout* [famine] famine ; *fig* [manque] shortage.

diseur, euse [dizœr, øz] *nm, f* : **~ de bonne aventure** fortune-teller.

disgrâce [disgras] *nf* disgrace.

disgracieux, euse [disgrasjø, øz] *adj* - **1.** [sans grâce] awkward, graceless - **2.** [laid] plain.

disjoindre [82] [disʒwɛ̃dr] *vt* [planches, tuiles] to take apart ; *fig* to separate, to distinguish.
➤ **se disjoindre** *vp* to come apart.

disjoint, e [disʒwɛ̃, ɛ̃t] *pp* ▷ **disjoindre**.

disjoncter [disʒɔ̃kte] *vi* - **1.** ELECTR to short-circuit - **2.** *fam* [perdre la tête] to flip, to crack up.

disjoncteur [disʒɔ̃ktœr] *nm* trip switch, circuit breaker.

dislocation [dislɔkasjɔ̃] *nf* MÉD dislocation.

disloquer [3] [dislɔke] *vt* - **1.** MÉD to dislocate - **2.** [machine, empire] to dismantle.
➤ **se disloquer** *vp* [machine] to fall apart *ou* to pieces ; *fig* [empire] to break up.

disparaissais, disparaissions *etc* ▷ **disparaître**.

disparaître [91] [disparɛtr] *vi* - **1.** [gén] to disappear, to vanish ; **disparais!** vanish! ; **faire ~** [personne] to get rid of ; [obstacle] to remove - **2.** [mourir] to die.

disparate [disparat] *adj* [éléments] disparate ; [couleurs, mobilier] badly matched.

disparité [disparite] *nf* - **1.** [écart] disparity - **2.** [différence - d'éléments] disparity ; [- de couleurs] mismatch.

disparition [disparisjɔ̃] *nf* - **1.** [gén] disappearance ; [d'espèce] extinction ; **en voie de ~** endangered - **2.** [mort] passing.

disparu, e [dispary] ⬦ *pp* ▷ **disparaître** ⬦ *nm, f* dead person, deceased.

dispatcher [3] [dispatʃe] *vt* to dispatch, to despatch.

dispendieux, euse [dispɑ̃djø, øz] *adj sout* expensive.

dispensaire [dispɑ̃sɛr] *nm* community clinic *Br*, free clinic *Am*.

dispense [dispɑ̃s] *nf* - **1.** [exemption] exemption ; **~ d'âge** special dispensation *(in the matter of age)* - **2.** [certificat] certificate of exemption.

dispenser [3] [dispɑ̃se] *vt* - **1.** [distribuer] to dispense - **2.** [exempter] : **~ qqn de qqch** [corvée] to excuse sb sthg, to let sb off sthg ; **je te dispense de tes réflexions!** *fig* spare us the comments!, keep your comments to yourself!
➤ **se dispenser** *vp* : **se ~ de qqch/de faire qqch** to get out of sthg/of doing sthg.

disperser [3] [dispɛrse] *vt* to scatter (about *ou* around) ; [collection, brume, foule] to break up ; *fig* [efforts, forces] to dissipate, to waste.
➤ **se disperser** *vp* - **1.** [feuilles, cendres] to scatter ; [brume, foule] to break up, to clear - **2.** [personne] to take on too much at once, to spread o.s. too thin.

dispersion [dispɛrsjɔ̃] *nf* scattering ; [de collection, brume, foule] breaking up ; *fig* [d'efforts, forces] waste, squandering.

disponibilité [dispɔnibilite] *nf* - **1.** [de choses] availability - **2.** [de fonctionnaire] leave of absence ; **en ~** on leave of absence - **3.** [d'esprit] alertness, receptiveness.
➤ **disponibilités** *nfpl* available funds, liquid assets.

disponible [dispɔnibl] *adj* - **1.** [place, personne] available, free - **2.** [fonctionnaire] on leave of absence.

dispos, e [dispo, oz] *adj* fresh, full of energy.

disposé, e [dispoze] *adj* : **être ~ à faire qqch** to be prepared *ou* willing to do sthg ; **être bien ~ envers qqn** to be well-disposed towards *Br ou* toward *Am* sb.

disposer [3] [dispoze] ⬦ *vt* - **1.** [arranger] to arrange - **2.** [inciter] : **~ qqn à faire qqch** to lead *ou* move sb to do sthg ⬦ *vi* : **~ de** [moyens, argent] to have available (to one), to have at one's disposal ; [chose] to have the use of ; [temps] to have free *ou* available ; **vous pouvez ~** *fig* & *sout* you may leave *ou* go.
➤ **se disposer** *vp* : **se ~ à qqch/à faire qqch** *sout* to prepare for sthg/to do sthg.

dispositif [dispozitif] *nm* [mécanisme] device, mechanism ; **~ antibuée** demister ; **~ anti-**

parasite suppressor ; ~ **de sûreté** safety device.

disposition [dispozisjɔ̃] *nf* - **1.** [arrangement] arrangement - **2.** [disponibilité] : **à la ~ de** at the disposal of, available to.

➡ **dispositions** *nfpl* - **1.** [mesures] arrangements, measures - **2.** JUR provisions - **3.** [dons] : **avoir des ~s pour** to have a gift for.

disproportion [dispʀɔpɔʀsjɔ̃] *nf* disproportion.

disproportionné, e [dispʀɔpɔʀsjɔne] *adj* out of proportion.

dispute [dispyt] *nf* argument, quarrel.

disputer [3] [dispyte] *vt* - **1.** [SPORT - course] to run ; [- match] to play - **2.** [lutter pour] to fight for.

➡ **se disputer** *vp* - **1.** [se quereller] to quarrel, to fight - **2.** SPORT to be played - **3.** [lutter pour] to fight over *ou* for.

disquaire [diskɛʀ] *nm* record dealer.

disqualification [diskalifikasjɔ̃] *nf* disqualification.

disqualifier [9] [diskalifje] *vt* to disqualify.

disque [disk] *nm* - **1.** MUS record ; [vidéo] video disc ; ~ **compact** *ou* **laser** compact disc - **2.** ANAT disc *Br*, disk *Am* - **3.** INFORM disk ; ~ **dur** hard disk - **4.** SPORT discus.

➡ **disque de stationnement** *nm* parking disc *Br* *ou* permit *Am*.

disquette [diskɛt] *nf* diskette, floppy disk ; ~ **haute/double densité** high/double density disk ; ~ **système** system diskette.

dissection [disɛksjɔ̃] *nf* dissection.

dissemblable [disɑ̃blabl] *adj* dissimilar.

dissémination [diseminasjɔ̃] *nf* - **1.** [dispersion] scattering, spreading (out) ; *fig* dissemination, spreading - **2.** [répartition] scattering.

disséminer [3] [disemine] *vt* [graines, maisons] to scatter, to spread (out) ; *fig* [idées] to disseminate, to spread.

dissension [disɑ̃sjɔ̃] *nf* dissent.

disséquer [18] [diseke] *vt litt* & *fig* to dissect.

dissertation [disɛʀtasjɔ̃] *nf* essay.

disserter [3] [disɛʀte] *vi* : ~ **sur** [à l'écrit] to write on ; [à l'oral] to speak on.

dissidence [disidɑ̃s] *nf* dissent, dissidence.

dissident, e [disidɑ̃, ɑ̃t] *adj* & *nm, f* dissident.

dissimulation [disimylasjɔ̃] *nf* - **1.** [hypocrisie] duplicity - **2.** [de la vérité] concealment.

dissimulé, e [disimyle] *adj* [hypocrite] dissembling, duplicitous.

dissimuler [3] [disimyle] *vt* to conceal.

➡ **se dissimuler** *vp* - **1.** [se cacher] to conceal

o.s., to hide - **2.** [refuser de voir] : **se ~ qqch** to close one's eyes to sthg.

dissipation [disipasjɔ̃] *nf* - **1.** [dispersion] dispersal, breaking up ; *fig* [de malentendu] clearing up ; [de craintes] dispelling - **2.** [indiscipline] indiscipline, misbehaviour *Br*, misbehavior *Am* - **3.** [dilapidation] squandering - **4.** [débauche] dissipation.

dissipé, e [disipe] *adj* - **1.** [turbulent] unruly, badly behaved - **2.** [frivole] dissipated, dissolute.

dissiper [3] [disipe] *vt* - **1.** [chasser] to break up, to clear ; *fig* to dispel - **2.** [dilapider, gâcher] to squander - **3.** [distraire] to lead astray.

➡ **se dissiper** *vp* - **1.** [brouillard, fumée] to clear - **2.** [élève] to misbehave - **3.** *fig* [malaise, fatigue] to go away ; [doute] to be dispelled.

dissocier [9] [disɔsje] *vt* - **1.** [séparer] to separate, to distinguish - **2.** CHIM to dissociate.

dissolu, e [disɔly] *adj* dissolute.

dissolution [disɔlysjɔ̃] *nf* - **1.** JUR dissolution - **2.** [mélange] dissolving - **3.** *sout* [débauche] dissipation.

dissolvais, dissolvions *etc* ⊳ **dissoudre**.

dissolvant, e [disɔlvɑ̃, ɑ̃t] *adj* solvent.

➡ **dissolvant** *nm* [solvant] solvent ; [pour vernis à ongles] nail varnish remover.

dissonance [disɔnɑ̃s] *nf* dissonance ; *fig* clash, discord.

dissoudre [87] [disudʀ] *vt* : **(faire) ~** to dissolve.

➡ **se dissoudre** *vp* - **1.** [substance] to dissolve - **2.** JUR to be dissolved.

dissous, oute [disu, ut] *pp* ⊳ **dissoudre**.

dissuader [3] [disɥade] *vt* to dissuade.

dissuasif, ive [disɥazif, iv] *adj* deterrent.

dissuasion [disɥazjɔ̃] *nf* dissuasion ; **force de ~** deterrent (effect).

dissymétrique [disimetrik] *adj* dissymmetrical.

distance [distɑ̃s] *nf* - **1.** [éloignement] distance ; **à ~** at a distance ; [télécommander] by remote control ; **à une ~ de 300 mètres** 300 metres away ; **se tenir à ~** to keep one's distance ; **garder ses ~s** to keep one's distance ; **prendre ses ~s** *fig* to stand back *ou* aloof - **2.** [intervalle] interval - **3.** [écart] gap.

distancer [16] [distɑ̃se] *vt* to outstrip.

distanciation [distɑ̃sjasjɔ̃] *nf* distance.

distancier [9] [distɑ̃sje] ➡ **se distancier** *vp* : **se ~ de** to distance o.s. from.

distant, e [distɑ̃, ɑ̃t] *adj* - **1.** [éloigné] : **une ville ~e de 10 km** a town 10 km away ; **des villes**

~es de 10 km towns 10 km apart - 2. [froid] distant.

distendre [73] [distɑ̃dr] vt [ressort, corde] to stretch ; [abdomen] to distend.
◆ **se distendre** vp to distend.

distendu, e [distɑ̃dy] pp ▷ **distendre**.

distillation [distilasjɔ̃] nf distilling, distillation.

distiller [3] [distile] vt [alcool] to distil Br, to distill Am ; [pétrole] to refine ; [miel] to secrete ; fig & littéraire to exude.

distillerie [distilri] nf [industrie] distilling ; [lieu] distillery.

distinct, e [distɛ̃, ɛkt] adj distinct.

distinctement [distɛ̃ktəmɑ̃] adv distinctly, clearly.

distinctif, ive [distɛ̃ktif, iv] adj distinctive.

distinction [distɛ̃ksjɔ̃] nf distinction.

distingué, e [distɛ̃ge] adj distinguished.

distinguer [3] [distɛ̃ge] vt - 1. [différencier] to tell apart, to distinguish - 2. [percevoir] to make out, to distinguish - 3. [rendre distinct] : ~ de to distinguish from, to set apart from.
◆ **se distinguer** vp - 1. [se différencier] : se ~ (de) to stand out (from) - 2. [s'illustrer] to distinguish o.s. - 3. [être perçu] : au loin se distinguait la côte you could make out the coast in the distance.

distraction [distraksjɔ̃] nf - 1. [inattention] inattention, absent-mindedness ; par ~ absent-mindedly - 2. [passe-temps] leisure activity.

distraire [112] [distrɛr] vt - 1. [déranger] to distract - 2. [divertir] to amuse, to entertain.
◆ **se distraire** vp to amuse o.s.

distrait, e [distrɛ, ɛt] ◇ pp ▷ **distraire** ◇ adj absent-minded.

distraitement [distrɛtmɑ̃] adv absentmindedly, absently.

distrayais, distrayons etc ▷ **distraire**.

distrayant, e [distrɛjɑ̃, ɑ̃t] adj entertaining.

distribanque [distribɑ̃k] nm cash dispenser.

distribuer [7] [distribɥe] vt to distribute ; [courrier] to deliver ; [ordres] to give out ; [cartes] to deal ; [coups, sourires] to dispense.

distributeur, trice [distribytœr, tris] nm, f distributor.
◆ **distributeur** nm - 1. AUTOM & COMM distributor - 2. [machine] : ~ (automatique) de billets BANQUE cash machine, cash dispenser ; TRANSPORT ticket machine ; ~ de boissons drinks machine.

distribution [distribysjɔ̃] nf - 1. [répartition, diffusion, disposition] distribution ; ~ du courrier postal delivery ; ~ des prix SCOL prize-giving - 2. [approvisionnement] supply - 3. CIN & THÉÂTRE cast.

district [distrikt] nm district.

dit, dite [di, dit] ◇ pp ▷ **dire** ◇ adj - 1. [appelé] known as - 2. JUR said, above - 3. [fixé] : à l'heure ~e at the appointed time.

dites, dîtes ▷ **dire**.

dithyrambique [ditirɑ̃bik] adj eulogistic.

DIU (abr de dispositif intra-utérin) nm IUD.

diurétique [djyretik] nm & adj diuretic.

diurne [djyrn] adj diurnal.

diva [diva] nf prima donna, diva.

divagation [divagasjɔ̃] nf wandering.

divaguer [3] [divage] vi to ramble.

divan [divɑ̃] nm divan (seat).

divergeant [divɛrʒɑ̃] ppr ▷ **diverger**.

divergence [divɛrʒɑ̃s] nf divergence, difference ; [d'opinions] difference.

divergent, e [divɛrʒɑ̃, ɑ̃t] adj divergent.

diverger [17] [divɛrʒe] vi to diverge ; [opinions] to differ.

divers, e [divɛr, ɛrs] adj - 1. [différent] different, various - 2. [disparate] diverse - 3. (avant n) [plusieurs] various, several - 4. PRESSE : 'divers' 'miscellaneous'.

diversement [divɛrsəmɑ̃] adv variously, in different ways.

diversification [divɛrsifikasjɔ̃] nf diversification.

diversifier [9] [divɛrsifje] vt to vary, to diversify.
◆ **se diversifier** vp to diversify.

diversion [divɛrsjɔ̃] nf diversion ; créer une ~, faire ~ to create a diversion.

diversité [divɛrsite] nf diversity.

divertir [32] [divɛrtir] vt [distraire] to entertain, to amuse.
◆ **se divertir** vp to amuse o.s., to entertain o.s.

divertissant, e [divɛrtisɑ̃, ɑ̃t] adj entertaining, amusing.

divertissement [divɛrtismɑ̃] nm - 1. [passetemps] form of relaxation - 2. MUS divertimento.

dividende [dividɑ̃d] nm dividend.

divin, e [divɛ̃, in] adj divine.

divination [divinasjɔ̃] nf divination.

divinement [divinmɑ̃] adv divinely.

divinité [divinite] nf divinity.

diviser [3] [divize] vt - 1. [gén] to divide, to split up ; ~ pour régner fig divide and rule - 2. MATHS to divide ; ~ 8 par 4 to divide 8 by 4.

se diviser *vp* - **1.** [se séparer] to divide - **2.** [diverger] to be divided.

divisible [divizibl] *adj* divisible.

division [divizjɔ̃] *nf* division ; **~ aéroportée** *MIL* airborne division.

divisionnaire [divizjɔnɛr] *adj* divisional.

divorce [divɔrs] *nm* - **1.** *JUR* divorce ; **demander le ~** to ask for a divorce, to sue for divorce - **2.** *fig* [divergence] gulf, separation.

divorcé, e [divɔrse] <> *adj* divorced <> *nm, f* divorcee, divorced person.

divorcer [16] [divɔrse] *vi* to divorce.

divulgation [divylgasjɔ̃] *nf* disclosure.

divulguer [3] [divylge] *vt* to divulge.

dix [dis] *adj num* & *nm* ten ; *voir aussi* **six.**

dix-huit [dizɥit] *adj num* & *nm* eighteen ; *voir aussi* **six.**

dix-huitième [dizɥitjɛm] *adj num, nm* OU *nmf* eighteenth ; *voir aussi* **sixième.**

dixième [dizjɛm] <> *nf SCOL* ≃ third year OU form *(at primary school)* Br, ≃ second grade Am <> *adj num, nm* OU *nmf* tenth ; *voir aussi* **sixième.**

dix-neuf [diznœf] *adj num* & *nm* nineteen ; *voir aussi* **six.**

dix-neuvième [diznœvjɛm] *adj num, nm* OU *nmf* nineteenth ; *voir aussi* **sixième.**

dix-sept [disɛt] *adj num* & *nm* seventeen ; *voir aussi* **six.**

dix-septième [disɛtjɛm] *adj num, nm* OU *nmf* seventeenth ; *voir aussi* **sixième.**

dizaine [dizɛn] *nf* - **1.** *MATHS* ten - **2.** [environ dix] : **une ~ de** about ten ; **par ~s** [en grand nombre] in their dozens.

Djakarta [dʒakarta] *n* Jakarta.

djellaba [dʒelaba] *nf* jellaba.

Djibouti [dʒibuti] *n* Djibouti.

djiboutien, enne [dʒibutjɛ̃, ɛn] *adj* of/from Djibouti.

se Djiboutien, enne *nm, f* person from Djibouti.

dm *(abr de* **décimètre***)* dm.

DM *(abr de* **deutsche Mark***)* DM.

do[1] [do] *nm inv MUS* C ; [chanté] doh.

do[2] *(abr de* **dito***)* do.

doberman [dobɛrman] *nm* Doberman (pinscher).

doc [dok] *(abr de* **documentation***) nf* literature, brochures *(pl)* ; **pouvez-vous me donner de la ~ sur cet ordinateur?** could you give me some literature about this computer?

doc. *(abr de* **document***)* doc.

docile [dosil] *adj* - **1.** [obéissant] docile - **2.** [cheveux] manageable.

docilement [dosilmã] *adv* meekly, obediently.

docilité [dosilite] *nf* obedience.

dock [dok] *nm* - **1.** [bassin] dock - **2.** [hangar] warehouse.

docker [dokɛr] *nm* docker.

docte [dokt] *adj iron* professorial.

doctement [doktəmã] *adv* [savamment] learnedly.

docteur [doktœr] *nm* - **1.** [médecin] doctor ; **~ en médecine** doctor of medicine - **2.** *UNIV* : **~ ès lettres/sciences** ≃ PhD ; **~ honoris causa** ≃ Hon. PhD.

doctoral, e, aux [doktoral, o] *adj péj* pompous, professorial.

doctorat [doktora] *nm* - **1.** [grade] doctorate ; **~ d'État** ≃ D. Litt., *higher doctorate awarded for aptitude for advanced research* ; **~ du troisième cycle** *doctorate awarded for three years' study and a work of research* - **2.** [épreuve] doctoral exam.

doctoresse [doktorɛs] *nf* woman OU lady doctor.

doctrinaire [doktrinɛr] *adj* - **1.** [dogmatique] doctrinaire - **2.** [sentencieux] sententious.

doctrine [doktrin] *nf* doctrine.

document [dokymã] *nm* document.

documentaire [dokymãtɛr] *nm* & *adj* documentary.

documentaliste [dokymãtalist] *nmf* [d'archives] archivist ; *PRESSE* & *TÉLÉ* researcher.

documentation [dokymãtasjɔ̃] *nf* - **1.** [travail] research - **2.** [documents] paperwork, papers *(pl)* - **3.** [brochures] documentation.

documenté, e [dokymãte] *adj* - **1.** [personne] well-informed - **2.** [étude] well-documented.

documenter [3] [dokymãte] *vt* to document.

se documenter *vp* to do some research.

dodeliner [3] [dodline] *vi* : **~ de la tête** to nod gently.

dodo [dodo] *nm fam* beddy-byes ; **faire ~** to sleep.

dodu, e [dody] *adj fam* [enfant, joue, bras] chubby ; [animal] plump.

dogmatique [dogmatik] *adj* dogmatic.

dogme [dogm] *nm* dogma.

dogue [dog] *nm* mastiff.

doigt [dwa] *nm* finger ; **un ~ de** (just) a drop OU finger of ; **montrer qqch du ~** to point at sthg ; **~ de pied** toe ; **être à deux ~s de faire qqch** to be within an ace of doing sthg ; **mettre le ~ dans l'engrenage** to embark on sthg, to get involved ; **se mettre le ~ dans l'œil** *fam* to be kidding o.s. ; **je m'en mords les ~s** I could kick myself (for it) ; **obéir à qqn au ~ et à l'œil** to obey sb's every whim, to be at sb's beck and call.

doigté [dwate] nm delicacy, tact.

dois ⊳ **devoir.**

doive ⊳ **devoir.**

doléances [dɔleãs] nfpl sout grievances.

dollar [dɔlar] nm dollar.

dolmen [dɔlmɛn] nm dolmen.

DOM [dɔm] (abr de **département d'outre-mer**) nm French overseas département.

domaine [dɔmɛn] nm - **1.** [propriété] estate - **2.** [secteur, champ d'activité] field, domain ; **tomber dans le ~ public** be out of copyright.

domanial, e, aux [dɔmanjal, o] adj national, state (avant n).

dôme [dom] nm - **1.** ARCHIT dome - **2.** GÉOGR rounded peak.

domestication [dɔmɛstikasjɔ̃] nf domestication.

domestique [dɔmɛstik] ◇ nmf (domestic) servant ◇ adj family (avant n) ; [travaux] household (avant n).

domestiquer [3] [dɔmɛstike] vt - **1.** [animal] to domesticate - **2.** [éléments naturels] to harness.

domicile [dɔmisil] nm - **1.** [gén] (place of) residence ; **travailler à ~** to work from ou at home ; **ils livrent à ~** they do deliveries ; **sans ~ fixe** of no fixed abode ; **élire ~** to take up residence ; **~ conjugal** JUR marital home - **2.** [d'entreprise] (registered) address.

domiciliation [dɔmisiljasjɔ̃] nf : **~ bancaire** domiciliation.

domicilié, e [dɔmisilje] adj : **~ à** (officially) resident in ou at.

dominant, e [dɔminã, ãt] adj - **1.** [qui prévaut] dominant - **2.** [qui surplombe] dominating.

⬥ dominante nf - **1.** [caractéristique] dominant feature ou characteristic - **2.** [couleur] dominant colour Br ou color Am - **3.** MUS dominant.

domination [dɔminasjɔ̃] nf - **1.** [autorité] domination, dominion - **2.** [influence] influence.

dominer [3] [dɔmine] ◇ vt - **1.** [surplomber, avoir de l'autorité sur] to dominate - **2.** [surpasser] to outclass - **3.** [maîtriser] to control, to master - **4.** fig [connaître] to master ◇ vi - **1.** [régner] to dominate, to be dominant - **2.** [prédominer] to predominate - **3.** [triompher] to be on top, to hold sway.

⬥ se dominer vp to control o.s.

dominicain, e [dɔminikɛ̃, ɛn] adj Dominican.

⬥ Dominicain, e nm, f Dominican.

dominical, e, aux [dɔminikal, o] adj Sunday (avant n).

Dominique [dɔminik] nf : **la ~** Dominica.

domino [dɔmino] nm domino.

dommage [dɔmaʒ] nm - **1.** [préjudice] harm (U) ; **~s et intérêts, ~s-intérêts** damages ; **quel ~!** what a shame! ; **c'est ~ que** (+ subjonctif) it's a pity ou shame (that) - **2.** [dégâts] damage (U).

dompter [3] [dɔ̃te] vt - **1.** [animal, fauve] to tame ; [rebelles, enfants] to subdue - **3.** fig [maîtriser] to overcome, to control.

dompteur, euse [dɔ̃tœr, øz] nm, f [de fauves] tamer.

DOM-TOM [dɔmtɔm] (abr de **départements d'outre-mer/territoires d'outre-mer**) nmpl French overseas départements and territories.

DOM-TOM

The four French overseas départements are Guadeloupe, Guyana, Martinique and Réunion. The overseas territories, New Caledonia, French Polynesia, Wallis and Futuna and French territories at the Poles, enjoy greater autonomy than the departments.

---

don [dɔ̃] nm - **1.** [cadeau] gift ; **faire ~ de** to make a gift ou present of ; **~ du sang** blood donation - **2.** [aptitude] knack.

DON [dɔn] (abr de **disque optique numérique**) nm digital optical disk.

donateur, trice [dɔnatœr, tris] nm, f donor.

donation [dɔnasjɔ̃] nf settlement.

donc [dɔ̃k] conj so ; **je disais ~ ...** so as I was saying ... ; **allons ~!** come on! ; **tais-toi ~!** will you be quiet!

donjon [dɔ̃ʒɔ̃] nm keep.

donjuanisme [dɔ̃ʒɥanism] nm womanizing.

donnant [dɔnã] **⬥ donnant donnant** loc adv fair's fair.

donne [dɔn] nf JEU deal.

donné, e [dɔne] adj given ; **c'est ~** it's a gift ; **c'est pas ~** it's not exactly cheap ; **étant ~ que** given that, considering (that).

⬥ donnée nf - **1.** INFORM & MATHS datum, piece of data ; **~es numériques** numerical data - **2.** [élément] fact, particular.

donner [3] [dɔne] ◇ vt - **1.** [gén] to give ; [se débarrasser de] to give away ; **~ qqch à qqn** to give sb sthg, to give sthg to sb ; **~ qqch à faire à qqn** to give sb sthg to do, to give sthg to sb to do ; **~ sa voiture à réparer** to leave one's car to be repaired ; **quel âge lui donnes-tu?** how old do you think he/she is? - **2.** fam [dénoncer] to shop - **3.** [occasionner] to give, to cause ; **ne rien ~** to be no use *ou* good, to be unproductive ⬦ *vi* **- 1.** [tomber] : **~ dans** to fall into ; *fig* to have a tendency towards *Br ou* toward *Am* **- 2.** [s'ouvrir] : **~ sur** to look out onto **- 3.** [produire] to yield **- 4.** [amener] : **~ à penser/entendre que** to lead sb to think/understand that.

➤ **se donner** *vp* **- 1.** [se consacrer] : **se ~ à qqch** to give *ou* devote o.s. to sthg **- 2.** [céder] : **se ~ à qqn** to give o.s. to sb.

donneur, euse [dɔnœr, øz] *nm, f* **- 1.** MÉD donor ; **~ de sang** blood donor **- 2.** CARTES dealer.

dont [dɔ̃] *pron rel* **- 1.** [complément de verbe ou d'adjectif] : **la personne ~ tu parles** the person you're speaking about, the person about whom you are speaking ; **l'accident ~ il est responsable** the accident for which he is responsible ; **c'est quelqu'un ~ on dit le plus grand bien** he's someone about whom people speak highly *(la traduction varie selon la préposition anglaise utilisée avec le verbe ou l'adjectif)* **- 2.** [complément de nom ou de pronom - relatif à l'objet] of which, whose ; [- relatif à personne] whose ; **un meuble ~ le bois est vermoulu** a piece of furniture with woodworm ; **la boîte ~ le couvercle est jaune** the box whose lid is yellow, the box with the yellow lid ; **c'est quelqu'un ~ j'apprécie l'honnêteté** he's someone whose honesty I appreciate ; **celui ~ les parents sont divorcés** the one whose parents are divorced **- 3.** [indiquant la partie d'un tout] : **plusieurs personnes ont téléphoné, ~ ton frère** several people phoned, one of which was your brother *ou* and among them was your brother ; **j'ai vu plusieurs films ~ deux étaient particulièrement intéressants** I saw several films, two of which were particularly interesting.

dopage [dɔpaʒ] *nm* doping.

dopant, e [dɔpɑ̃, ɑ̃t] *adj* stimulant.

➤ **dopant** *nm* dope *(U)*.

dope [dɔp] *nf fam* dope.

doper [3] [dɔpe] *vt* to dope.

➤ **se doper** *vp* to take stimulants.

dorade [dɔrad] = **daurade**.

doré, e [dɔre] *adj* **- 1.** [couvert de dorure] gilded, gilt ; **~ sur tranche** gilt-edged **- 2.** [couleur] golden.

dorénavant [dɔrenavɑ̃] *adv* from now on, in future.

dorer [3] [dɔre] ⬦ *vt* **- 1.** [couvrir d'or] to gild **- 2.** [peau] to tan **- 3.** CULIN to glaze ⬦ *vi* CULIN : **faire ~** to brown.

➤ **se dorer** *vp* to tan.

dorloter [3] [dɔrlɔte] *vt* to pamper, to cosset.

dormant, e [dɔrmɑ̃, ɑ̃t] *adj* [eau] still.

dormeur, euse [dɔrmœr, øz] *nm, f* sleeper.

dormir [36] [dɔrmir] *vi* **- 1.** [sommeiller] to sleep ; **~ debout** to be asleep on one's feet ; **à ~ debout** unbelievable, implausible **- 2.** [rester inactif - personne] to slack, to stand around (doing nothing) ; [- capitaux] to lie idle.

dorsal, e, aux [dɔrsal, o] *adj* dorsal.

dortoir [dɔrtwar] *nm* dormitory.

dorure [dɔryr] *nf* **- 1.** [couche d'or] gilt **- 2.** [ce qui est doré] golden *ou* gilt decoration.

doryphore [dɔrifɔr] *nm* colorado beetle.

dos [do] *nm* back ; **~ à ~** back to back ; **de ~** from behind ; **sur le ~** on one's back ; **'voir au ~'** 'see over' ; **à ~ d'âne** (riding) on a mule ; **ne rien avoir à se mettre sur le ~** to have nothing to wear ; **tourner le ~ à** [être tourné] to have one's back to ; *litt* & *fig* [se tourner] to turn one's back on ; **~ crawlé** backstroke ; **avoir bon ~** to be the one who always gets the blame ; **en avoir plein le ~** *fam* to be fed up (to the back teeth), to have had it up to here ; **se mettre qqn à ~** to put sb's back up.

DOS, Dos [dɔs] *(abr de* Disk Operating System*) nm* DOS.

dosage [dozaʒ] *nm* [de médicament] dose ; [d'ingrédient] amount.

dos-d'âne [dodɑn] *nm* bump.

dose [doz] *nf* **- 1.** [quantité de médicament] dose ; **'ne pas dépasser la ~ prescrite'** 'do not exceed the prescribed dose' **- 2.** [quantité] share ; **forcer la ~** *fam fig* to overdo it ; **une (bonne) ~ de bêtise** *fam fig* a lot of silliness ; **j'en ai eu ma ~** *fam fig* I've had enough.

doser [3] [doze] *vt* [médicament, ingrédient] to measure out ; *fig* to weigh up.

doseur [dozœr] *nm* [appareil] measure ; [de cuisine] measuring jug.

dossard [dosar] *nm* number *(on competitor's back)*.

dossier [dosje] *nm* **- 1.** [de fauteuil] back **- 2.** [documents] file, dossier ; **~ suspendu** suspension file **- 3.** [classeur] file, folder **- 4.** *fig* [question] question.

dot [dɔt] *nf* dowry.

dotation [dɔtasjɔ̃] *nf* **- 1.** JUR endowment **- 2.** ADMIN grant.

doter [3] [dɔte] *vt* [pourvoir] : **~ de** [talent] to endow with ; [machine] to equip with.

douairière [dwɛrjɛr] *nf* [veuve] dowager.

douane [dwan] *nf* **- 1.** [service, lieu] customs

(pl) ; **passer la ~** to go through customs **- 2.** [taxe] (import) duty.

douanier, ère [dwanje, ɛr] <> *adj* customs *(avant n)* <> *nm, f* customs officer.

doublage [dublaʒ] *nm* **- 1.** [renforcement] lining **- 2.** [de film] dubbing **- 3.** [d'acteur] understudying.

double [dubl] <> *adj* double <> *adv* double ; **voir ~** to see double, to have double vision <> *nm* **- 1.** [quantité] : **le ~ double - 2.** [copie] copy ; **en ~** in duplicate **- 3.** [d'une personne] double **- 4.** TENNIS doubles *(pl)*.

doublé [duble] *nm* **- 1.** [en orfèvrerie] rolled gold **- 2.** [réussite double] double.

doublement [dubləmã] <> *adv* doubly <> *nm* [de lettre] doubling.

doubler [3] [duble] <> *vt* **- 1.** [multiplier] to double **- 2.** [plier] to (fold) double **- 3.** [renforcer] : **~ (de)** to line (with) **- 4.** [dépasser] to overtake **- 5.** [film, acteur] to dub **- 6.** *fam* [trahir] to con, to double-cross **- 7.** [augmenter] to double <> *vi* **- 1.** [véhicule] to overtake **- 2.** [augmenter] to double.

➤ **se doubler** *vp* : **se ~ de** to be coupled with.

doublure [dublyr] *nf* **- 1.** [renforcement] lining **- 2.** CIN stand-in.

douce ➤ **doux**.

douceâtre [dusatr] *adj* sickly (sweet), cloying.

doucement [dusmã] *adv* **- 1.** [descendre] carefully ; [frapper] gently ; **doucement!** gently *ou* easy (does it)! **- 2.** [traiter] gently ; [parler] softly **- 3.** [médiocrement] (only) so-so.

doucereux, euse [dusrø, øz] *adj* **- 1.** [saveur] sickly (sweet), cloying **- 2.** [mielleux] smooth, suave.

doucette [dusɛt] *nf* BOT lamb's lettuce.

douceur [dusœr] *nf* **- 1.** [de saveur, parfum] sweetness **- 2.** [d'éclairage, de peau, de musique] softness **- 3.** [de climat] mildness **- 4.** [de caractère] gentleness **- 5.** [plaisir] pleasure.

➤ **douceurs** *nfpl* [friandises] sweets.

➤ **en douceur** <> *loc adv* smoothly <> *loc adj* smooth.

douche [duʃ] *nf* **- 1.** [appareil, action] shower ; **prendre une ~** to take *ou* have a shower **- 2.** *fam fig* [déception] letdown ; **~ écossaise** shock to the system.

doucher [3] [duʃe] *vt* **- 1.** [donner une douche à] : **~ qqn** to give sb a shower **- 2.** *fam fig* [décevoir] to let down.

➤ **se doucher** *vp* to take *ou* have a shower, to shower.

doudou [dudu] *nm fam* [langage enfantin] *security blanket*.

doudoune [dudun] *nf* quilted jacket.

doué, e [dwe] *adj* talented ; **être ~ pour** to have a gift for.

douer [6] [due] *vt* : **~ qqn de** to endow sb with.

douille [duj] *nf* **- 1.** [d'ampoule] socket **- 2.** [de cartouche] cartridge.

douillet, ette [dujɛ, ɛt] <> *adj* **- 1.** [confortable] snug, cosy **- 2.** [sensible] soft <> *nm, f* wimp.

douillettement [dujɛtmã] *adv* snugly.

douleur [dulœr] *nf litt & fig* pain ; **se tordre de ~** to writhe in pain ; **nous avons la ~ de vous annoncer ...** it is with great sorrow that we announce ...

douloureux, euse [dulurø, øz] *adj* **- 1.** [physiquement] painful **- 2.** [moralement] distressing **- 3.** [regard, air] sorrowful.

doute [dut] *nm* doubt ; **avoir des ~s sur** to have misgivings about ; **mettre qqch en ~** to cast doubt on sthg.

➤ **sans doute** *loc adv* no doubt ; **sans aucun ~** without (a) doubt.

douter [3] [dute] <> *vt* [ne pas croire] : **~ que** (+ *subjonctif*) to doubt (that) <> *vi* [ne pas avoir confiance] : **~ de qqn/de qqch** to doubt sb/sthg, to have doubts about sb/sthg ; **j'en doute** I doubt it.

➤ **se douter** *vp* : **se ~ de qqch** to suspect sthg ; **je m'en doutais** I thought so ; **je m'en doute** I'm not surprised.

douteux, euse [dutø, øz] *adj* **- 1.** [incertain] doubtful **- 2.** [contestable] questionable **- 3.** *péj* [mœurs] dubious ; [vêtements, personne] dubious-looking.

douves [duv] *nfpl* [de château] moat *(sg)*.

Douvres [duvr] *n* Dover.

doux, douce [du, dus] *adj* **- 1.** [éclairage, peau, musique] soft **- 2.** [saveur, parfum] sweet **- 3.** [climat, condiment] mild **- 4.** *sout* [agréable] pleasant **- 5.** [pente, regard, caractère] gentle.

➤ **doux** *loc adv* : **il fait ~** the weather is mild.

➤ **en douce** *loc adv* secretly.

douzaine [duzɛn] *nf* **- 1.** [douze] dozen **- 2.** [environ douze] : **une ~ de** about twelve.

douze [duz] *adj num & nm* twelve ; *voir aussi* **six**.

douzième [duzjɛm] *adj num, nm* OU *nmf* twelfth ; *voir aussi* **sixième**.

doyen, enne [dwajɛ̃, ɛn] *nm, f* [le plus ancien] most senior member.

DP *(abr de* **délégué du personnel**) *nm staff representative*.

DPLG *(abr de* **diplômé par le gouvernement**)

adj holder of official certificate for architects, engineers etc.

dr. (*abr de* **droite**) R, r.

Dr (*abr de* **Docteur**) Dr.

draconien, enne [drakɔnjɛ̃, ɛn] *adj* draconian.

dragage [dragaʒ] *nm* dredging.

dragée [draʒe] *nf* - **1.** [confiserie] sugared almond ; **tenir la ~ haute à qqn** to hold out against sb - **2.** [comprimé] pill.

dragon [dragɔ̃] *nm* - **1.** [monstre, personne autoritaire] dragon - **2.** [soldat] dragoon.

drague [drag] *nf* - **1.** TECHNOL dredger - **2.** *fam fig* [flirt] picking up.

draguer [3] [drage] *vt* - **1.** [nettoyer] to dredge - **2.** *fam* [personne] to chat up, to get off with.

dragueur, euse [dragœr, øz] *nm, f fam* [homme] womanizer ; **quelle dragueuse!** she's always chasing after men!

➤ **dragueur** *nm* [bateau] dredger.

drainage [drɛnaʒ] *nm* draining.

drainer [4] [drene] *vt* - **1.** [terrain, plaie] to drain - **2.** *fig* [attirer] to drain off.

dramatique [dramatik] ⟺ *nf* play ⟺ *adj* - **1.** THÉÂTRE dramatic - **2.** [grave] tragic.

dramatisation [dramatizasjɔ̃] *nf* dramatization.

dramatiser [3] [dramatize] *vt* [exagérer] to dramatize.

drame [dram] *nm* - **1.** [catastrophe] tragedy ; **faire un ~ de qqch** *fig* to make a drama of sthg - **2.** LITTÉRATURE drama.

drap [dra] *nm* - **1.** [de lit] sheet - **2.** [tissu] woollen *Br ou* woolen *Am* cloth ; **être dans de beaux ~s** *fig* to be in a real mess.

drapeau, x [drapo] *nm* flag ; **~ blanc** white flag ; **le ~ tricolore** the tricolour, the French flag ; **être sous les ~x** *fig* to be doing military service.

draper [3] [drape] *vt* to drape.

➤ **se draper** *vp* : **se ~ dans** to drape o.s. in.

draperie [drapri] *nf* - **1.** [tenture] drapery - **2.** [industrie] cloth industry.

drap-housse [draus] (*pl* **draps-housses**) *nm* fitted sheet.

drapier, ère [drapje, ɛr] ⟺ *adj* clothing (*avant n*) ⟺ *nm, f* - **1.** [fabricant] cloth manufacturer - **2.** [marchand] draper.

drastique [drastik] *adj* drastic.

drave [drav] *nf Can* drive (of floating logs).

dressage [drɛsaʒ] *nm* [d'animal] training, taming.

dresser [4] [drese] *vt* - **1.** [lever] to raise - **2.** [faire tenir] to put up - **3.** *sout* [construire] to erect - **4.** [acte, liste, carte] to draw up ; [procès-verbal]

make out - **5.** [dompter] to train - **6.** *fig* [opposer] : **~ qqn contre qqn** to set sb against sb.

➤ **se dresser** *vp* - **1.** [se lever] to stand up - **2.** [s'élever] to rise (up) ; *fig* to stand ; **se ~ contre qqch** to rise up against sthg.

dresseur, euse [drescœr, øz] *nm, f* trainer.

dressoir [dreswar] *nm* dresser.

DRH ⟺ *nf* (*abr de* **direction des ressources humaines**) personnel department ⟺ *nm* (*abr de* **directeur des ressources humaines**) personnel manager.

dribbler [3] [drible] *vi* SPORT ⟺ *vi* to dribble ⟺ *vt* : **~ qqn** to dribble past sb.

drille [drij] *nm* : **un joyeux ~** a cheery person.

driver [3] [*nm* drajvœr *vi* drajve] GOLF ⟺ *nm* driver ⟺ *vi* to drive.

drogue [drɔg] *nf* - **1.** [stupéfiant] *fig* drug ; **la ~ drugs** (*pl*) ; **~ dure** hard drug - **2.** [médicament] medicine.

drogué, e [drɔge] ⟺ *adj* drugged ⟺ *nm, f* drug addict.

droguer [3] [drɔge] *vt* [victime] to drug.

➤ **se droguer** *vp* [de stupéfiants] to take drugs.

droguerie [drɔgri] *nf* hardware shop.

droguiste [drɔgist] *nmf* : **chez le ~** at the hardware shop.

droit, e [drwa, drwat] *adj* - **1.** [du côté droit] right - **2.** [rectiligne, vertical, honnête] straight ; **~ comme un i** straight as a ramrod, bolt upright.

➤ **droit** ⟺ *adv* straight ; **tout ~** straight ahead ; **aller ~ au but** *fig* to go straight to the point ⟺ *nm* - **1.** JUR law ; **~ canon** canon law ; **~ civil** civil law ; **~ coutumier** common law ; **~ pénal** criminal law ; **de ~ commun** common-law (*avant n*) - **2.** [prérogative] right ; **avoir ~ à** to be entitled to ; **avoir le ~ de faire qqch** to be allowed to do sthg ; **être dans son ~** to be within one's rights ; **être en ~ de faire qqch** to have a right to do sthg ; **de quel ~?** by what right? ; **~ d'aînesse** birthright ; **~ d'asile** right of asylum ; **~ de grâce** power of pardon ; **~ de regard** right of access ; **~ de visite** visiting rights (*pl*), access ; **~ d'aînesse** birthright ; **~ de vote** right to vote ; **~s d'auteur** royalties ; **~s de l'homme** human rights ; **~s d'inscription** registration fees ; **à qui de ~** to the proper authority.

➤ **droite** *nf* - **1.** [gén] right, right-hand side ; **à ~e** on the right ; **à ~e de** to the right of ; **garder/serrer sa ~e** to keep to the right - **2.** POLIT : **la ~e** the right (wing) ; **de ~e** right-wing.

droitier, ère [drwatje, ɛr] ⟺ *adj* right-handed ⟺ *nm, f* right-handed person, right-hander.

droiture [drwatyr] *nf* straightforwardness.

drôle [drol] *adj* - **1.** [amusant] funny - **2.** : ~ de [bizarre] funny ; *fam* [remarquable] amazing.

drôlement [drolmã] *adv* - **1.** *fam* [très] tremendously - **2.** [bizarrement] in a strange way - **3.** [de façon amusante] in a funny way.

drôlerie [drolri] *nf* humour *Br*, humor *Am*.

dromadaire [drɔmadɛr] *nm* dromedary.

dru, e [dry] *adj* thick.
◆ **dru** *adv* : **tomber** ~ to fall heavily.

drugstore [drœgstɔr] *nm* drugstore.

druide [drɥid] *nm* druid.

ds *abr de* dans.

DST (*abr de* Direction de la surveillance du territoire) *nf* counterespionage section.

DT (*abr de* diphtérie, tétanos) *nm* vaccine against diphtheria and tetanus.

D.T.COQ. (*abr de* diphtérie, tétanos, coqueluche) *nm* vaccine against diphtheria, tetanus and whooping cough.

du ▷ de.

dû, due [dy] ◇ *pp* ▷ devoir ◇ *adj* due, owing.
◆ **dû** *nm* due ; **réclamer son** ~ to demand one's due.

dualité [dɥalite] *nf* duality.

Dubayy [dybaj] *n* Dubai.

dubitatif, ive [dybitatif, iv] *adj* doubtful.

Dublin [dyblɛ̃] *n* Dublin.

dublinois, e [dyblinwa, waz] *adj* of/from Dublin.
◆ **Dublinois, e** *nm, f* Dubliner.

duc [dyk] *nm* duke.

ducal, e, aux [dykal, o] *adj* ducal.

duché [dyʃe] *nm* duchy.

duchesse [dyʃɛs] *nf* duchess.

duel [dɥɛl] *nm* duel.

duffel-coat (*pl* duffel-coats), **duffle-coat** (*pl* duffle-coats) [dœfœlkot] *nm* duffel coat.

dûment [dymã] *adv* duly.

dumping [dœmpiŋ] *nm* COMM dumping.

dune [dyn] *nf* dune.

duo [dɥo] *nm* - **1.** MUS duet ; **en** ~ in duet - **2.** [couple] duo.

dupe [dyp] ◇ *nf* dupe ◇ *adj* gullible ; **être/ne pas être** ~ to be/not to be taken in.

duper [3] [dype] *vt sout* to dupe, to take sb in.

duplex [dyplɛks] *nm* - **1.** [appartement] split-level flat, maisonette *Br*, duplex *Am* - **2.** RADIO & TÉLÉ link-up ; **en** ~ link-up (*avant n*).

duplicata [dyplikata] *nm inv* duplicate.

duplicité [dyplisite] *nf* duplicity.

dupliquer [3] [dyplike] *vt* [document] to duplicate.

duquel [dykɛl] ▷ lequel.

dur, e [dyr] ◇ *adj* - **1.** [matière, personne, travail] hard ; [carton] stiff - **2.** [viande] tough - **3.** [climat, punition, loi] harsh ◇ *nm, f fam* : ~ (à cuire) tough nut.
◆ **dur** *adv* hard.
◆ **à la dure** *loc adv* : **coucher à la** ~e to sleep rough ; **être élevé à la** ~e to have been brought up the hard way.

durable [dyrabl] *adj* lasting.

durablement [dyrabləmã] *adv* durably.

durant [dyrã] *prép* - **1.** [pendant] for - **2.** [au cours de] during.

durcir [32] [dyrsir] ◇ *vt litt* & *fig* to harden ◇ *vi* to harden, to become hard.
◆ **se durcir** *vp litt* & *fig* to harden.

durcissement [dyrsismã] *nm* hardening.

durée [dyre] *nf* length ; **(de) longue** ~ long-lasting ; '~ **de conservation** ...' 'best before ...'.

durement [dyrmã] *adv* - **1.** [violemment] hard, vigorously - **2.** [péniblement] severely - **3.** [méchamment] harshly.

durer [3] [dyre] *vi* to last.

dureté [dyrte] *nf* - **1.** [de matériau, de l'eau] hardness - **2.** [de problème] difficulty - **3.** [d'époque, de climat, de personne] harshness - **4.** [de punition] severity.

durillon [dyrijɔ̃] *nm* [sur le pied] corn ; [sur la main] callus.

dus, dut *etc* ▷ devoir.

DUT (*abr de* diplôme universitaire de technologie) *nm* university diploma in technology.

duvet [dyvɛ] *nm* - **1.** [plumes, poils fins] down - **2.** [sac de couchage] sleeping bag.

DVD (*abr de* Digital Video ou Versatile Disc) *nm inv* DVD.

DVD-ROM [dvdrɔm] (*abr de* Digital Video ou Versatile Disc Read Only Memory) *nm* DVD-ROM.

dynamique [dinamik] ◇ *nf* - **1.** PHYS dynamics (U) - **2.** fig : ~ de groupe group dynamics (*pl*) ◇ *adj* dynamic.

dynamiser [3] [dinamize] *vt* to inspire with energy.

dynamisme [dinamism] *nm* dynamism.

dynamite [dinamit] *nf* dynamite.

dynamiter [3] [dinamite] *vt* to dynamite.

dynamo [dinamo] *nf* dynamo.

dynamomètre [dinamɔmɛtr] *nm* dynamometer.

dynastie [dinasti] *nf* dynasty.

dysenterie [disãtri] *nf* dysentery.

dyslexique [disleksik] ⬦ *nmf* dyslexic person ⬦ *adj* dyslexic.
dyspepsie [dispepsi] *nf* dyspepsia.

e, E [ə] *nm inv* e, E.
➡ **E** (*abr de* **est**) E.
EAO (*abr de* **enseignement assisté par ordinateur**) *nm* CAL.
eau, x [o] *nf* water ; **prendre l'~** to leak ; **~ douce/salée/de mer** fresh/salt/sea water ; **~ gazeuse/plate** fizzy/still water ; **~ bénite** holy water ; **~ courante** running water ; **~ distillée** distilled water ; **~ minérale** mineral water ; **~ oxygénée** hydrogen peroxide ; **~ de pluie** rainwater ; **~ de source** spring water ; **~ de toilette** toilet water ; **~x dormantes** still waters ; **les Eaux et Forêts** ≃ the Forestry Commission ; **les ~x territoriales** territorial waters ; **les ~x usées** waste water *(U)* ; **à l'~ de rose** soppy, sentimental ; **mettre** *ou* **faire venir l'~ à la bouche** to make one's mouth water ; **mettre de l'~ dans son vin** to calm down, to tone it down a bit ; **tomber à l'~** *fig* to fall through.
EAU (*abr de* **Émirats arabes unis**) *nmpl* UAE.
eau-de-vie [odvi] (*pl* **eaux-de-vie**) *nf* brandy.
eau-forte [ofɔrt] (*pl* **eaux-fortes**) *nf* etching.
ébahi, e [ebai] *adj* staggered, astounded.
ébahissement [ebaismɑ̃] *nm* amazement.
ébats [eba] *nmpl littéraire* frolics ; **~ amoureux** lovemaking *(U)*.
ébattre [83] [ebatr] ➡ **s'ébattre** *vp littéraire* to frolic.
ébauche [eboʃ] *nf* [esquisse] sketch ; *fig* outline ; **l'~ d'un sourire** the ghost of a smile.
ébaucher [3] [eboʃe] *vt* - **1.** [esquisser] to rough out - **2.** *fig* [commencer] : **~ un geste** to start to make a gesture.
ébène [ebɛn] *nf* ebony.
ébéniste [ebenist] *nm* cabinet-maker.

ébénisterie [ebenistəri] *nf* - **1.** [métier] cabinet-making - **2.** [travail] cabinet work.
éberlué, e [eberlɥe] *adj* flabbergasted.
éblouir [32] [ebluir] *vt* to dazzle.
éblouissant, e [ebluisɑ̃, ɑ̃t] *adj* dazzling.
éblouissement [ebluismɑ̃] *nm* - **1.** [aveuglement] glare, dazzle - **2.** [vertige] dizziness - **3.** [émerveillement] amazement.
ébonite [ebɔnit] *nf* vulcanite, ebonite.
éborgner [3] [ebɔrɲe] *vt* : **~ qqn** to put sb's eye out.
éboueur [ebwœr] *nm* dustman *Br*, garbage collector *Am*.
ébouillanter [3] [ebujɑ̃te] *vt* to scald.
➡ **s'ébouillanter** *vp* to scald o.s.
éboulement [ebulmɑ̃] *nm* caving in, fall.
éboulis [ebuli] *nm* mass of fallen rocks.
ébouriffer [3] [eburife] *vt* - **1.** [cheveux] to ruffle - **2.** *fam* [étonner] to amaze.
ébranler [3] [ebrɑ̃le] *vt* - **1.** [bâtiment, opinion] to shake - **2.** [gouvernement, nerfs] to weaken.
➡ **s'ébranler** *vp* [train] to move off.
ébrécher [18] [ebreʃe] *vt* [assiette, verre] to chip ; *fam fig* to break into.
ébriété [ebrijete] *nf* drunkenness.
ébrouer [3] [ebrue] ➡ **s'ébrouer** *vp* [animal] to shake o.s.
ébruiter [3] [ebrɥite] *vt* to spread.
➡ **s'ébruiter** *vp* to become known.
ébullition [ebylisjɔ̃] *nf* - **1.** [de liquide] boiling point ; **porter à ~** CULIN to bring to the boil - **2.** [effervescence] : **en ~** *fig* in a state of agitation.
écaille [ekaj] *nf* - **1.** [de poisson, reptile] scale ; [de tortue] shell - **2.** [de plâtre, peinture, vernis] flake - **3.** [matière] tortoiseshell ; **en ~** [lunettes] horn-rimmed.
écailler¹, ère [ekaje, ɛr] *nm, f* oyster seller.
écailler² [3] [ekaje] *vt* - **1.** [poisson] to scale - **2.** [huîtres] to open.
➡ **s'écailler** *vp* to flake *ou* peel off.
écarlate [ekarlat] *adj & nf* scarlet ; **devenir ~** to turn crimson *ou* scarlet.
écarquiller [3] [ekarkije] *vt* : **~ les yeux** to stare wide-eyed.
écart [ekar] *nm* - **1.** [espace] space - **2.** [temps] gap - **3.** [différence] difference - **4.** [déviation] : **faire un ~** [personne] to step aside ; [cheval] to shy ; **être à l'~** to be in the background ; *fig* : **tenir qqn à l'~ de** to keep sb out of *ou* away from - **5.** GYM : **grand ~** splits *(pl)*.
écarteler [25] [ekartəle] *vt fig* to tear apart.
écartement [ekartəmɑ̃] *nm* : **~ entre** space between.
écarter [3] [ekarte] *vt* - **1.** [bras, jambes] to open,

to spread ; **~ qqch de** to move sthg away from - **2.** [obstacle, danger] to brush aside - **3.** [foule, rideaux] to push aside ; [solution] to dismiss ; **~ qqn de** to exclude sb from.

➤ **s'écarter** *vp* - **1.** [se séparer] to part - **2.** [se détourner] : **s'~ de** to deviate from.

ecchymose [ekimoz] *nf* bruise.

ecclésiastique [eklezjastik] ◇ *nm* clergyman ◇ *adj* ecclesiastical.

écervelé, e [esɛrvəle] ◇ *adj* scatty, scatterbrained ◇ *nm, f* scatterbrain.

échafaud [eʃafo] *nm* scaffold.

échafaudage [eʃafodaʒ] *nm* - **1.** CONSTR scaffolding - **2.** [amas] pile.

échafauder [3] [eʃafode] ◇ *vt* - **1.** [empiler] to pile up - **2.** [élaborer] to construct ◇ *vi* to put up scaffolding.

échalas [eʃala] *nm* - **1.** [perche] stake, pole - **2.** *péj* [personne] beanpole.

échalote [eʃalɔt] *nf* shallot.

échancré, e [eʃɑ̃kre] *adj* - **1.** [vêtement] low-necked - **2.** [côte] indented.

échancrure [eʃɑ̃kryr] *nf* - **1.** [de robe] low neckline - **2.** [de côte] indentation.

échange [eʃɑ̃ʒ] *nm* - **1.** [de choses] exchange ; **en ~ (de)** in exchange (for) ; **~ standard** *replacement of faulty goods with the same item* ; **~ de bons procédés** exchange of favours - **2.** COMM : **les ~s** trade *(sg)* ; **libre-~** free trade.

échangeable [eʃɑ̃ʒabl] *adj* exchangeable.

échanger [17] [eʃɑ̃ʒe] *vt* - **1.** [troquer] to swap, to exchange - **2.** [marchandise] : **~ qqch (contre)** to change sthg (for) - **3.** [communiquer] to exchange.

échangeur [eʃɑ̃ʒœr] *nm* interchange.

échangisme [eʃɑ̃ʒism] *nm* [de partenaires sexuels] partner-swapping.

échantillon [eʃɑ̃tijɔ̃] *nm* [de produit, de population] sample ; *fig* example.

échantillonnage [eʃɑ̃tijɔnaʒ] *nm* [série d'échantillons] range of samples.

échappatoire [eʃapatwar] *nf* way out.

échappée [eʃape] *nf* - **1.** SPORT breakaway - **2.** [vue] vista.

échappement [eʃapmɑ̃] *nm* - **1.** AUTOM exhaust ▷ **pot** - **2.** [d'horloge] escapement.

échapper [3] [eʃape] *vi* - **1.** : **~ à** [personne, situation] to escape from ; [danger, mort] to escape ; [suj : détail, parole, sens] to escape - **2.** [glisser] : **~ de** to slip from *ou* out of ; **laisser ~** to let slip - **3.** *loc* : **l'~ belle** to have a narrow escape.

➤ **s'échapper** *vp* : **s'~ (de)** to escape (from).

écharde [eʃard] *nf* splinter.

écharpe [eʃarp] *nf* scarf ; **en ~** in a sling ; **l'~ tricolore** *mayoral sash worn by French mayors at civic functions* ; **prendre en ~** *fig* to hit on the side.

écharper [3] [eʃarpe] *vt* to rip to pieces *ou* shreds.

échasse [eʃas] *nf* [de berger, oiseau] stilt.

échassier [eʃasje] *nm* wader.

échauder [3] [eʃode] *vt* - **1.** [ébouillanter] to scald - **2.** *fam fig* [enseigner] : **~ qqn** to teach sb a lesson.

échauffement [eʃofmɑ̃] *nm* - **1.** [de moteur] overheating ; [de terre] heating up - **2.** SPORT warm-up - **3.** [surexcitation] overheating - **4.** MÉD inflammation.

échauffer [3] [eʃofe] *vt* - **1.** [chauffer] to overheat - **2.** [exciter] to excite - **3.** [énerver] to irritate.

➤ **s'échauffer** *vp* - **1.** SPORT to warm up - **2.** *fig* [s'animer] to become heated.

échauffourée [eʃofure] *nf* brawl, skirmish.

échéance [eʃeɑ̃s] *nf* - **1.** [délai] expiry ; **à courte** *ou* **brève ~** in the short term ; **à longue ~** in the long term - **2.** [date] payment date ; **arriver à ~** to fall due.

échéancier [eʃeɑ̃sje] *nm* bill-book.

échéant [eʃeɑ̃] *adj* : **le cas ~** if necessary, if need be.

échec [eʃɛk] *nm* - **1.** [insuccès] failure ; **un ~ cuisant** a bitter defeat ; **essuyer un ~** to suffer a defeat ; **être en situation d'~ scolaire** to have learning difficulties ; **tenir qqn en ~** to hold sb in check ; **voué à l'~** doomed to failure - **2.** JEU : **~ et mat** checkmate.

➤ **échecs** *nmpl* chess *(U)*.

échelle [eʃɛl] *nf* - **1.** [objet] ladder ; **~ de corde** rope ladder ; **faire la courte ~ à qqn** *lit* & *fig* to give sb a leg up - **2.** [ordre de grandeur] scale ; **à l'~ de** on the level of ; **sur une grande ~** on a large scale.

échelon [eʃlɔ̃] *nm* - **1.** [barreau] rung - **2.** *fig* [niveau] level ; **gravir les ~s (de)** to climb the rungs (of).

échelonner [3] [eʃlɔne] *vt* [espacer] to spread out.

➤ **s'échelonner** *vp* to be spread out.

écheveau, x [eʃvo] *nm* skein.

échevelé, e [eʃəvle] *adj* - **1.** [ébouriffé] dishevelled *Br*, disheveled *Am* - **2.** [frénétique] wild.

échine [eʃin] *nf* ANAT spine ; **courber l'~** *fig* to submit.

échiner [3] [eʃine] ➤ **s'échiner** *vp fam* [s'épuiser] : **s'~ (à faire qqch)** to exhaust o.s. (doing sthg).

échiquier [eʃikje] *nm* - **1.** JEU chessboard

- 2. *fig* [scène] scene ; **l'~ politique** the political scene.

écho [eko] *nm* echo ; **il se fait l'~ de la direction** he repeats what the managers say ; **rester sans ~** to get no response.

échographie [ekɔgrafi] *nf* [examen] ultrasound (scan).

échoir [70] [eʃwar] *vi* - **1.** [être dévolu] : **~ à** to fall to - **2.** [expirer] to fall due.

échoppe [eʃɔp] *nf* stall.

échouer [6] [eʃwe] *vi* - **1.** [ne pas réussir] to fail ; **~ à un examen** to fail an exam - **2.** [navire] to run aground - **3.** *fam fig* [aboutir] to end up.
➤ **s'échouer** *vp* [navire] to run aground.

échu, e [eʃy] *pp* ⊳ **échoir**.

éclabousser [3] [eklabuse] *vt* - **1.** [suj : liquide] to spatter - **2.** *fig* [compromettre] to compromise.

éclaboussure [eklabusyr] *nf* - **1.** [de liquide] splash - **2.** *fig* blot (on one's reputation).

éclair [ekler] ◇ *nm* - **1.** [de lumière] flash of lightning - **2.** *fig* [instant] : **~ de flash of ; en un ~** in a flash - **3.** [gâteau] : **~ au chocolat/café** chocolate/coffee éclair ◇ *adj inv* : **visite ~** flying visit ; **guerre ~** blitzkrieg.

éclairage [eklɛraʒ] *nm* - **1.** [lumière] lighting - **2.** *fig* [point de vue] light.

éclaircie [eklɛrsi] *nf* bright interval, sunny spell.

éclaircir [32] [eklɛrsir] *vt* - **1.** [rendre plus clair] to lighten - **2.** [rendre moins épais] to thin - **3.** *fig* [clarifier] to clarify.
➤ **s'éclaircir** *vp* - **1.** [devenir plus clair] to clear - **2.** [devenir moins épais] to thin - **3.** [se clarifier] to become clearer.

éclaircissement [eklɛrsismɑ̃] *nm* [explication] explanation.

éclairer [4] [eklere] *vt* - **1.** [de lumière] to light up - **2.** [expliquer] to clarify - **3.** *littéraire* [renseigner] : **~ qqn sur qqch** to throw light on sthg for sb.
➤ **s'éclairer** *vp* - **1.** [personne] to light one's way - **2.** [regard, visage] to light up - **3.** [situation] to become clear - **4.** [rue, ville] to light up.

éclaireur [eklɛrœr] *nm* scout ; **partir en ~** to have a scout around.

éclat [ekla] *nm* - **1.** [de verre, d'os] splinter ; [de pierre] chip ; **voler en ~s** to fly into pieces - **2.** [de lumière] brilliance - **3.** [de couleur] vividness - **4.** [beauté] radiance - **5.** [faste] splendour *Br*, splendor *Am* - **6.** [bruit] burst ; **~ de rire** burst of laughter ; **~s de voix** shouts ; **faire un ~** to cause a scandal - **7.** *loc* : **rire aux ~s** to roar *ou* shriek with laughter.

éclatant, e [eklatɑ̃, ɑ̃t] *adj* - **1.** [brillant, resplendissant] brilliant, bright ; [teint, beauté] radiant ;

~ de bursting with - **2.** [admirable] resounding - **3.** [perçant] loud.

éclater [3] [eklate] *vi* - **1.** [exploser - pneu] to burst ; [- verre] to shatter ; [- obus] to explode ; **faire ~** [ballon] to burst ; [bombe] to explode ; [pétard] to let off - **2.** [incendie, rires] to break out - **3.** [joie] to shine ; **laisser ~** to give vent to - **4.** [bijou] to sparkle, to glitter - **5.** *fig* [nouvelles, scandale] to break.
➤ **s'éclater** *vp fam* to have a great time.

éclectique [eklektik] *adj* eclectic.

éclipse [eklips] *nf* - **1.** ASTRON eclipse ; **~ de lune/soleil** eclipse of the moon/sun - **2.** *fig* [période de défaillance] eclipse - **3.** *fig* [disparition] disappearance.

éclipser [3] [eklipse] *vt* to eclipse.
➤ **s'éclipser** *vp* - **1.** ASTRON to go into eclipse - **2.** *fam* [s'esquiver] to slip away.

éclopé, e [eklɔpe] ◇ *adj* lame ◇ *nm, f* lame person.

éclore [113] [eklɔr] *vi* - **1.** [s'ouvrir - fleur] to open out, to blossom ; [- œuf] to hatch ; **faire ~** [œuf] to hatch ; *fig* [vocation] to develop - **2.** *fig* [naître] to dawn.

éclos, e [eklo, oz] *pp* ⊳ **éclore**.

éclosion [eklozjɔ̃] *nf* - **1.** [de fleur] blossoming - **2.** [d'œuf] hatching - **3.** *fig* [naissance] blossoming, birth.

écluse [eklyz] *nf* lock.

écluser [3] [eklyze] *vt* - **1.** NAVIG [- fleuve] to construct locks on ; [- bateau] to take through a lock - **2.** *fam* [boire] to knock back.

écœurant, e [ekœrɑ̃, ɑ̃t] *adj* - **1.** [gén] disgusting - **2.** [démoralisant] sickening.

écœurement [ekœrmɑ̃] *nm* - **1.** [nausée] nausea - **2.** [répugnance] disgust - **3.** [découragement] discouragement.

écœurer [5] [ekœre] *vt* - **1.** [dégoûter] to sicken, to disgust - **2.** *fig* [indigner] to sicken - **3.** [décourager] to discourage.

école [ekɔl] *nf* - **1.** [gén] school ; **aller à l'~** to go to school ; **~ communale** local primary *Br ou* grade *Am* school ; **~ maternelle** nursery school ; **~ normale** ≃ teacher training college *Br*, ≃ teachers college *Am* ; **École normale supérieure** *grande école for secondary and university teachers* ; **~ primaire/secondaire** primary/secondary school *Br*, grade/high school *Am* ; **grande ~** *specialist training establishment, entered by competitive exam and highly prestigious* ; **faire l'~ buissonnière** to play truant *Br ou* hooky *Am* ; **être à bonne ~** to be in good hands ; **faire ~** to be accepted - **2.** [éducation] schooling ; **l'~ libre** education at an école libre *(Cath-*

olic school, partly state-funded) ; **l'~ privée** private education.

GRANDE ÉCOLE

The 'grandes écoles' are relatively small non-university establishments awarding highly-respected diplomas. Admission is usually only possible after two years of intensive preparatory studies and a competitive examination. Most have close links with industry. The 'grandes écoles' include l'École des hautes études commerciales, or HEC (management and business), l'École polytechnique (engineering) and l'École normale supérieure (the humanities). A diploma from a 'grande école' is comparable in prestige to an Oxbridge degree in Britain.

écolier, ère [ekɔlje, ɛr] *nm, f* - **1.** [élève] pupil - **2.** *fig* [novice] beginner.
écolo [ekɔlɔ] *nmf fam* ecologist ; **les ~s** the Greens.
écologie [ekɔlɔʒi] *nf* ecology.
écologique [ekɔlɔʒik] *adj* ecological.
écologiste [ekɔlɔʒist] *nmf* ecologist.
écomusée [ekɔmyze] *nm* museum of the environment.
éconduire [98] [ekɔ̃dɥir] *vt* [repousser - demande] to dismiss ; [- visiteur, soupirant] to show to the door.
économat [ekɔnɔma] *nm* - **1.** [fonction] bursarship - **2.** [magasin] staff shop.
économe [ekɔnɔm] <> *nmf* bursar <> *adj* careful, thrifty ; **être ~ de** to be sparing of.
économie [ekɔnɔmi] *nf* - **1.** [science] economics *(U)* - **2.** *POLIT* economy ; **~ dirigée** state-controlled economy ; **~ de marché** market economy ; **~ mixte** mixed economy - **3.** [parcimonie] economy, thrift - **4.** *litt* & *fig* [épargne] saving ; **~s d'énergie** energy savings - **5.** *(gén pl)* [pécule] savings *(pl)* ; **faire des ~s** to save up - **6.** *(gén pl)* : **~s d'échelle** economies of scale.
économique [ekɔnɔmik] *adj* - **1.** *ÉCON* economic - **2.** [avantageux] economical.
économiquement [ekɔnɔmikmɑ̃] *adv* economically.
économiser [3] [ekɔnɔmize] *vt litt* & *fig* to save.
économiste [ekɔnɔmist] *nmf* economist.
écoper [3] [ekɔpe] <> *vt* - **1.** *NAVIG* to bale out - **2.** *fam* [sanction] : **~ (de) qqch** to get sthg <> *vi fam* [être puni] to get the blame.
écoproduit [ekɔprɔdɥi] *nm* green product.
écorce [ekɔrs] *nf* - **1.** [d'arbre] bark - **2.** [d'agrume] peel ; **~ d'orange** orange peel - **3.** *GÉOL* crust.

écorché [ekɔrʃe] *nm* - **1.** *ANAT* cut-away anatomical figure - **2.** *TECHNOL* cut-away - **3.** *loc* : **un ~ vif** a soul in torment.
écorcher [3] [ekɔrʃe] *vt* - **1.** [lapin] to skin - **2.** [bras, jambe] to scratch - **3.** *fig* [langue, nom] to mispronounce.
➤ **s'écorcher** *vp* to graze o.s.
écorchure [ekɔrʃyr] *nf* graze, scratch.
écorecharge [ekɔrəʃarʒ] *nf* ecorefill.
écorner [3] [ekɔrne] *vt* [endommager - meuble] to damage ; [- page] to dog-ear.
écossais, e [ekɔsɛ, ɛz] *adj* - **1.** [de l'Écosse] Scottish ; [whisky] Scotch - **2.** [tissu] tartan.
➤ **écossais** *nm* - **1.** [langue] Scots - **2.** [tissu] tartan.
➤ **Écossais, e** *nm, f* Scot, Scotsman (*f* Scotswoman).
Écosse [ekɔs] *nf* : **l'~** Scotland.
écosser [3] [ekɔse] *vt* to shell.
écosystème [ekɔsistɛm] *nm* ecosystem.
écot [eko] *nm* share ; **payer son ~** to pay one's share.
écotourisme [ekɔturism] *nm* ecotourism.
écoulement [ekulmɑ̃] *nm* - **1.** [gén] flow - **2.** [du temps] passing - **3.** [de marchandises] selling.
écouler [3] [ekule] *vt* to sell.
➤ **s'écouler** *vp* - **1.** [eau] to flow - **2.** [personnes] to flow out - **3.** [temps] to pass.
écourter [3] [ekurte] *vt* to shorten.
écoute [ekut] *nf* - **1.** [action d'écouter] listening ; **être à l'~ de** to be listening to - **2.** [audience] audience ; **heure de grande ~** *RADIO* peak listening time ; *TÉLÉ* peak viewing time - **3.** [surveillance] : **les ~s téléphoniques** phone tapping *(U)* ; **être sur table d'~** to have one's phone tapped.
écouter [3] [ekute] *vt* to listen to.
➤ **s'écouter** *vp fig* - **1.** [écouter soi-même] to listen to o.s. - **2.** [s'observer] to coddle o.s.
écouteur [ekutœr] *nm* [de téléphone] earpiece.
➤ **écouteurs** *nmpl* [de radio] headphones.
écoutille [ekutij] *nf* hatchway.
écrabouiller [3] [ekrabuje] *vt fam* [écraser] to crush, to squash.
écran [ekrɑ̃] *nm* - **1.** *CIN* & *INFORM* screen ; **le petit ~** television ; **~ orientable** tiltable screen ; **~ tactile** tactile screen touch - **2.** [de protection] shield ; **~ de fumée** smoke screen.
écrasant, e [ekrazɑ̃, ɑ̃t] *adj* - **1.** [lourd] crushing - **2.** *fig* [accablant] overwhelming.
écraser [3] [ekraze] <> *vt* - **1.** [comprimer - cigarette] to stub out ; [- pied] to tread on ; [- insecte, raisin] to crush - **2.** [accabler] : **~ qqn (de)** to burden sb (with) - **3.** [vaincre] to crush - **4.** [renver-

ser] to run over ◇ *vi fam* : **en ~** to sleep like a log.
➤ **s'écraser** *vp* - **1.** [avion, automobile] : **s'~ (contre)** to crash (into) - **2.** [foule] to be crushed - **3.** *fam* [se taire] to shut up.

écrémer [18] [ekreme] *vt* - **1.** [lait] to skim - **2.** *fig* [bibliothèque, collection] to cream off the best from.

écrevisse [ekrəvis] *nf* crayfish ; **rouge comme une ~** (as) red as a beetroot.

écrier [10] [ekrije] ➤ **s'écrier** *vp* to cry out.

écrin [ekrɛ̃] *nm* case.

écrire [99] [ekrir] *vt* - **1.** [phrase, livre] to write - **2.** [orthographier] to spell.
➤ **s'écrire** *vp* [s'épeler] to be spelled.

écrit, e [ekri, it] ◇ *pp* ▷ **écrire** ◇ *adj* written ; **bien/mal ~** well/badly written.
➤ **écrit** *nm* - **1.** [ouvrage] writing - **2.** [examen] written exam - **3.** [document] piece of writing.
➤ **par écrit** *loc adv* in writing.

écriteau, x [ekrito] *nm* notice.

écriture [ekrityr] *nf* - **1.** [gén] writing - **2.** *(gén pl)* COMM [comptes] books *(pl)* - **3.** BIBLE : **l'Écriture sainte** the Holy Scripture.

écrivain [ekrivɛ̃] *nm* writer, author ; **~ public** (public) letter-writer.

écrivais, écrivions *etc* ▷ **écrire**.

écrou [ekru] *nm* TECHNOL nut.

écrouer [3] [ekrue] *vt* to imprison.

écroulement [ekrulmɑ̃] *nm litt* & *fig* collapse.

écrouler [3] [ekrule] ➤ **s'écrouler** *vp litt* & *fig* to collapse.

écru, e [ekry] *adj* [naturel] unbleached.

ecstasy [ekstazi] *nm* [drogue] ecstasy.

ectoplasme [ektɔplasm] *nm* ectoplasm.

ECU [eky] *(abr de* European Currency Unit*) nm* ECU.

écu [eky] *nm* - **1.** [bouclier, armoiries] shield - **2.** [monnaie ancienne] crown - **3.** = **ECU**.

écueil [ekœj] *nm* - **1.** [rocher] reef - **2.** *fig* [obstacle] stumbling block.

écuelle [ekɥɛl] *nf* - **1.** [objet] bowl - **2.** [contenu] bowlful.

éculé, e [ekyle] *adj* - **1.** [chaussure] down-at-heel - **2.** *fig* [plaisanterie] hackneyed.

écume [ekym] *nf* - **1.** [mousse, bave] foam - **2.** *fig* [lie] dregs *(pl)*.

écumer [3] [ekyme] ◇ *vt* - **1.** [confiture] to skim - **2.** *fig* [mer, ville] to scour ◇ *vi* - **1.** [mer] to foam, to boil - **2.** [animal] to foam at the mouth - **3.** *fig* [être furieux] : **~ (de)** to boil (with).

écumoire [ekymwar] *nf* skimmer.

écureuil [ekyrœj] *nm* squirrel ; **l'Écureuil** *nickname for the Caisse d'Épargne (whose logo is a squirrel)*.

écurie [ekyri] *nf* - **1.** [pour chevaux & SPORT] stable - **2.** *fig* [local sale] pigsty.

écusson [ekysɔ̃] *nm* - **1.** [d'armoiries] coat-of-arms - **2.** MIL badge.

écuyer, ère [ekɥije, ɛr] *nm, f* [de cirque] rider.
➤ **écuyer** *nm* [de chevalier] squire.

eczéma [ɛgzema] *nm* eczema.

éd. *(abr de* édition*)* ed., edit.

edelweiss [edelvɛs] *nm* edelweiss.

éden [eden] *nm* : **un ~** a garden of Eden ; **l'Éden** the garden of Eden.

édenté, e [edɑ̃te] *adj* toothless.

EDF, Edf *(abr de* Électricité de France*) nf French national electricity company.*

édifiant, e [edifjɑ̃, ɑ̃t] *adj* edifying.

édification [edifikasjɔ̃] *nf* - **1.** [de temple, empire] building - **2.** *fig* [de fidèles] edification.

édifice [edifis] *nm* - **1.** [construction] building ; **~ public** public building - **2.** *fig* [institution] : **l'~ social** the fabric of society.

édifier [9] [edifje] *vt* - **1.** [ville, église] to build - **2.** *fig* [théorie] to construct - **3.** [personne] to edify, *iron* to enlighten.

Édimbourg [edɛ̃bur] *n* Edinburgh.

édit [edi] *nm* edict.

édit. *abr de* éditeur.

éditer [3] [edite] *vt* to publish.

éditeur, trice [editœr, tris] *nm, f* publisher.

édition [edisjɔ̃] *nf* - **1.** [profession] publishing - **2.** [de journal, de livre] edition ; **dernière ~** last edition ; **~ électronique** electronic publishing ; **~ originale** first edition.

édito [edito] *nm fam* editorial.

éditorial, aux [editɔrjal, o] *nm* leader, editorial.

éditorialiste [editɔrjalist] *nmf* leader writer, editorialist.

édredon [edrədɔ̃] *nm* eiderdown.

éducateur, trice [edykatœr, tris] ◇ *adj* educational ◇ *nm, f* teacher ; **~ spécialisé** *teacher of children with special educational needs.*

éducatif, ive [edykatif, iv] *adj* educational.

éducation [edykasjɔ̃] *nf* - **1.** [apprentissage] education ; **~ civique** civics *(U)* ; **l'Éducation nationale** ≃ the Department for Education *Br*, ≃ the Department of Education *Am* ; **~ physique** physical education ; **~ sexuelle** sex education - **2.** [parentale] upbringing - **3.** [savoir-vivre] breeding.

édulcorant [edylkɔrɑ̃] *nm* : **~ (de synthèse)** (artificial) sweetener.

édulcorer [3] [edylkɔre] vt - **1.** sout [tisane] to sweeten - **2.** fig [propos] to tone down.

éduquer [3] [edyke] vt [enfant] to bring up ; [élève] to educate.

effacé, e [efase] adj - **1.** [teinte] faded - **2.** [modeste - rôle] unobtrusive ; [- personne] self-effacing.

effacer [16] [efase] vt - **1.** [mot] to erase, to rub out ; *INFORM* to delete - **2.** [souvenir] to erase - **3.** [réussite] to eclipse.

➤ **s'effacer** vp - **1.** [s'estomper] to fade (away) - **2.** sout [s'écarter] to move aside - **3.** fig [s'incliner] to give way.

effarant, e [efarã, ãt] adj frightening.

effaré, e [efare] adj frightened, scared.

effarement [efarmã] nm fear, alarm.

effarer [3] [efare] vt to frighten, to scare.

effaroucher [3] [efaruʃe] vt - **1.** [effrayer] to scare off - **2.** [intimider] to overawe.

effectif, ive [efɛktif, iv] adj - **1.** [remède] effective - **2.** [aide] positive.

➤ **effectif** nm - **1.** *MIL* strength - **2.** [de groupe] total number.

effectivement [efɛktivmã] adv - **1.** [réellement] effectively - **2.** [confirmation] in fact.

effectuer [7] [efɛktɥe] vt [réaliser - manœuvre] to carry out ; [- trajet, paiement] to make.

➤ **s'effectuer** vp to be made.

efféminé, e [efemine] adj effeminate.

effervescence [efɛrvesãs] nf - **1.** *PHYS* effervescence - **2.** [agitation] turmoil ; **en ~** in turmoil.

effervescent, e [efɛrvesã, ãt] adj [boisson] effervescent ; fig [pays] in turmoil.

effet [efɛ] nm - **1.** [gén] effect ; **avoir pour ~ de faire qqch** to have the effect of doing sthg ; **à ~ rétroactif** *JUR* retrospective ; **rester sans ~** to be ineffective ; **sous l'~ de** under the effects of ; [alcool] under the influence of ; **faire de l'~** to have an effect ; **~ de serre** greenhouse effect - **2.** [impression recherchée] impression ; **faire son ~** to cause a stir - **3.** *COMM* [titre] bill.

➤ **en effet** loc adv in fact, indeed.

➤ **à cet effet** loc adv with this end in view.

effeuiller [5] [efœje] vt [arbre] to remove the leaves from ; [fleur] to remove the petals from.

➤ **s'effeuiller** vp [arbre] to lose its leaves ; [fleur] to lose its petals.

efficace [efikas] adj - **1.** [remède, mesure] effective - **2.** [personne, machine] efficient.

efficacité [efikasite] nf - **1.** [de remède, mesure] effectiveness - **2.** [de personne, machine] efficiency.

efficience [efisjãs] nf efficiency.

effigie [efiʒi] nf effigy.

effilé, e [efile] adj [doigt, silhouette] slim, slender ; [lame] sharp ; [voiture] streamlined.

effiler [3] [efile] vt - **1.** [tissu] to fray - **2.** [lame] to sharpen - **3.** [cheveux] to thin.

➤ **s'effiler** vp to fray.

effilocher [3] [efilɔʃe] vt to fray.

➤ **s'effilocher** vp to fray.

efflanqué, e [eflãke] adj emaciated.

effleurer [5] [eflœre] vt - **1.** [visage, bras] to brush (against) - **2.** fig [problème, thème] to touch on - **3.** fig [suj : pensée, idée] : **~ qqn** to cross sb's mind.

effluve [eflyv] nm exhalation ; fig [d'enfance, du passé] breath.

effondrement [efɔ̃drəmã] nm collapse.

effondrer [3] [efɔ̃dre] ➤ **s'effondrer** vp litt & fig to collapse.

efforcer [16] [efɔrse] ➤ **s'efforcer** vp to force o.s. ; **s'~ de faire qqch** to make an effort to do sthg.

effort [efɔr] nm - **1.** [de personne] effort ; **faire un ~** to make an effort ; **faire l'~ de faire qqch** to make the effort to do sthg ; **sans ~** [victoire] effortless - **2.** *TECHNOL* stress.

effraction [efraksjɔ̃] nf breaking in ; **entrer par ~ dans** to break into.

effrayant, e [efrejã, ãt] adj - **1.** [cauchemar] terrifying - **2.** fam [appétit, prix] tremendous, awful.

effrayer [11] [efreje] vt to frighten, to scare.

➤ **s'effrayer** vp to be frightened, to take fright.

effréné, e [efrene] adj - **1.** [course] frantic - **2.** [désir] unbridled.

effriter [3] [efrite] vt to cause to crumble.

➤ **s'effriter** vp - **1.** [mur] to crumble - **2.** fig [majorité] to be eroded.

effroi [efrwa] nm fear, dread.

effronté, e [efrɔ̃te] <> adj insolent <> nm, f insolent person.

effrontément [efrɔ̃temã] adv insolently, brazenly.

effronterie [efrɔ̃tri] nf insolence.

effroyable [efrwajabl] adj - **1.** [catastrophe, misère] appalling - **2.** [laideur] hideous.

effusion [efyzjɔ̃] nf - **1.** [de liquide] effusion ; **sans ~ de sang** without bloodshed - **2.** [de sentiments] effusiveness.

égal, e, aux [egal, o] <> adj - **1.** [équivalent] equal - **2.** [régulier] even - **3.** fam [indifférent] : **ça m'est ~, c'est ~** I don't mind <> nm, f equal ; **d'~ à ~** as an equal ; **sans ~** unequalled Br, unequaled Am.

également [egalmã] adv - **1.** [avec égalité] equally - **2.** [aussi] as well, too.

égaler [3] [egale] vt - **1.** MATHS to equal - **2.** [beauté] to match, to compare with.

égalisation [egalizasjõ] nf equalization ; SPORT equalizing Br, tying Am.

égaliser [3] [egalize] <> vt [haie, cheveux] to trim <> vi SPORT to equalize Br, to tie Am.

égalitaire [egaliter] adj egalitarian.

égalitarisme [egalitarism] nm egalitarianism.

égalité [egalite] nf - **1.** [gén] equality ; **être à** ~ to be level ou equal - **2.** [d'humeur] evenness - **3.** SPORT : être à ~ to be level.

égard [egar] nm consideration ; **à cet** ~ in this respect ; **par** ~ **pour** sout out of consideration for ; **eu** ~ **à** considering.
- **à l'égard de** loc prép with regard to, towards Br, toward Am.
- **à certains égards** loc adv in some respects.

égaré, e [egare] adj - **1.** [perdu - voyageur] lost ; [- animal] stray (avant n) - **2.** [regard, air] distraught.

égarement [egarmã] nm - **1.** [de jeunesse] wildness - **2.** [de raisonnement] aberration.

égarer [3] [egare] vt - **1.** [objet] to mislay, to lose - **2.** [personne] to mislead - **3.** fig & sout [suj : passion] to lead astray.
- **s'égarer** vp - **1.** [lettre] to get lost, to go astray ; [personne] to get lost, to lose one's way - **2.** [discussion] to wander from the point - **3.** fig & sout [personne] to stray from the point.

égayer [11] [egeje] vt - **1.** [personne] to cheer up - **2.** [pièce] to brighten up.
- **s'égayer** vp to enjoy o.s.

égérie [ezeri] nf muse.

égide [ezid] nf protection ; **sous l'** ~ **de** littéraire under the aegis of.

églantier [eglãtje] nm wild rose (bush).

églantine [eglãtin] nf wild rose.

églefin, aiglefin [egləfɛ̃] nm haddock.

église [egliz] nf church ; **aller à l'** ~ to go to church.
- **Église** nf : **l'Église** the Church ; **l'Église catholique/protestante** the Catholic/ Protestant Church.

ego [ego] nm ego.

égocentrique [egosãtrik] <> nmf selfcentred person <> adj self-centred, egocentric.

égocentrisme [egosãtrism] nm selfcentredness.

égoïsme [egoism] nm selfishness, egoism.

égoïste [egoist] <> nmf selfish person <> adj selfish, egoistic.

égorger [17] [egorze] vt - **1.** [animal, personne] to cut the throat of - **2.** fig [client] to bleed white.

égosiller [3] [egozije] → **s'égosiller** vp fam - **1.** [crier] to bawl, to shout - **2.** [chanter] to sing one's head off.

égout [egu] nm sewer.

égoutter [3] [egute] vt - **1.** [vaisselle] to leave to drain - **2.** [légumes, fromage] to drain.
- **s'égoutter** vp to drip, to drain.

égouttoir [egutwar] nm - **1.** [à légumes] colander, strainer - **2.** [à vaisselle] rack (for washing-up).

égratigner [3] [egratine] vt to scratch ; fig to have a go ou dig at.
- **s'égratigner** vp : **s'** ~ **la main** to scratch one's hand.

égratignure [egratinyr] nf scratch, graze ; fig dig.

égrener [19] [egrəne] vt - **1.** [détacher les grains de - épi, cosse] to shell ; [- grappe] to pick grapes from - **2.** [chapelet] to tell - **3.** fig [marquer] to mark.
- **s'égrener** vp - **1.** [raisins] to drop off the bunch - **2.** [personnes] to spread out.

égrillard, e [egrijar, ard] adj ribald, bawdy.

Égypte [eʒipt] nf : **l'** ~ Egypt.

égyptien, enne [eʒipsjɛ̃, ɛn] adj Egyptian.
- **égyptien** nm [langue] Egyptian.
- **Égyptien, enne** nm, f Egyptian.

égyptologie [eʒiptoloʒi] nf Egyptology.

eh [e] interj hey! ; ~ **bien** well.

éhonté, e [eõte] <> adj shameless <> nm, f shameless person.

Eiffel [efɛl] n : **la tour** ~ the Eiffel Tower.

éjaculation [eʒakylasjõ] nf ejaculation ; ~ **précoce** premature ejaculation.

éjectable [eʒɛktabl] adj : **siège** ~ ejector seat.

éjecter [4] [eʒɛkte] vt - **1.** [douille] to eject - **2.** fam [personne] to kick out.

élaboration [elaborasjõ] nf [de plan, système] working out, development.

élaboré, e [elabore] adj elaborate.

élaborer [3] [elabore] vt [plan, système] to work out, to develop.

élagage [elagaʒ] nm litt & fig pruning.

élaguer [3] [elage] vt litt & fig to prune.

élan [elã] nm - **1.** ZOOL elk - **2.** SPORT run-up ; Can GOLF swing ; **prendre son** ~ to take a run-up, to gather speed - **3.** fig [de joie] outburst.

élancé, e [elãse] adj slender.

élancement [elãsmã] nm [douleur] shooting pain.

élancer [16] [elɑ̃se] *vi MÉD* to give shooting pains.
◆ **s'élancer** *vp* - **1.** [se précipiter] to rush, to dash - **2.** *SPORT* to take a run-up - **3.** *fig* [s'envoler] to soar.

élargir [32] [elaʀʒiʀ] <> *vt* to widen ; [vêtement] to let out ; *fig* to expand <> *vi fam* [forcir] to fill out.
◆ **s'élargir** *vp* - **1.** [s'agrandir] to widen ; [vêtement] to stretch ; *fig* to expand - **2.** *fam* [grossir] to put on weight.

élargissement [elaʀʒismɑ̃] *nm* widening ; [de vêtement] letting out ; *fig* expansion.

élasticité [elastisite] *nf* - **1.** *PHYS* elasticity - **2.** [de personne, corps] flexibility.

élastique [elastik] <> *nm* - **1.** [pour attacher] elastic band - **2.** [matière] elastic <> *adj* - **1.** *PHYS* elastic - **2.** [corps] flexible - **3.** *fig* [conscience] accommodating.

élastomère [elastɔmɛʀ] *nm* elastomer.

eldorado [ɛldɔʀado] *nm* El Dorado.

électeur, trice [elɛktœʀ, tʀis] *nm, f* voter, elector.

élection [elɛksjɔ̃] *nf* - **1.** [vote] election ; ~ **partielle** by-election ; ~ **présidentielle** presidential election ; ~**s municipales** local elections - **2.** *fig* [choix] choice ; **d'~** chosen.

électoral, e, aux [elɛktɔʀal, o] *adj* electoral ; [campagne, réunion] election *(avant n)*.

électoralisme [elɛktɔʀalism] *nm* electioneering.

électorat [elɛktɔʀa] *nm* electorate.

électricien, enne [elɛktʀisjɛ̃, ɛn] *nm, f* electrician.

électricité [elɛktʀisite] *nf* electricity ; **il y a de l'~ dans l'air** *fig* the atmosphere is electric.

électrification [elɛktʀifikasjɔ̃] *nf* electrification.

électrifier [9] [elɛktʀifje] *vt* to electrify.

électrique [elɛktʀik] *adj litt* & *fig* electric.

électriser [3] [elɛktʀize] *vt litt* & *fig* to electrify.

électroaimant [elɛktʀɔɛmɑ̃] *nm* electromagnet.

électrocardiogramme [elɛktʀɔkaʀdjɔgʀam] *nm* electrocardiogram.

électrochoc [elɛktʀɔʃɔk] *nm* electroshock therapy.

électrocuter [3] [elɛktʀɔkyte] *vt* to electrocute.

électrode [elɛktʀɔd] *nf* electrode.

électroencéphalogramme [elɛktʀɔɑ̃sefalogʀam] *nm* electroencephalogram.

électrogène [elɛktʀɔʒɛn] *adj* : **groupe ~** generating unit.

électrolyse [elɛktʀɔliz] *nf* electrolysis.

électromagnétique [elɛktʀɔmaɲetik] *adj* electromagnetic.

électroménager [elɛktʀɔmenaʒe] <> *adj* : **appareil ~** household electrical appliance <> *nm* household electrical appliances *(pl)*.

électron [elɛktʀɔ̃] *nm* electron.

électronicien, enne [elɛktʀɔnisjɛ̃, ɛn] *nm, f* electronics specialist.

électronique [elɛktʀɔnik] <> *nf SCIENCE* electronics *(U)* <> *adj* electronic ; [microscope] electron *(avant n)*.

électrophone [elɛktʀɔfɔn] *nm* record player.

élégamment [elegamɑ̃] *adv* elegantly.

élégance [elegɑ̃s] *nf* - **1.** [de personne, style] elegance - **2.** [délicatesse - de solution, procédé] elegance ; [- de conduite] generosity.

élégant, e [elegɑ̃, ɑ̃t] *adj* - **1.** [personne, style] elegant - **2.** [délicat - solution, procédé] elegant ; [- conduite] generous.

élément [elemɑ̃] *nm* - **1.** [gén] element ; **les bons/mauvais ~s** the good/bad elements ; **les quatre ~s** the four elements ; **être dans son ~** to be in one's element - **2.** [de machine] component.

élémentaire [elemɑ̃tɛʀ] *adj* - **1.** [gén] elementary - **2.** [installation, besoin] basic.

éléphant [elefɑ̃] *nm* elephant.

éléphantesque [elefɑ̃tɛsk] *adj fam* gigantic.

élevage [ɛlvaʒ] *nm* breeding, rearing ; [installation] farm.

élévateur, trice [elevatœʀ, tʀis] *adj* elevator *(avant n)*.
◆ **élévateur** *nm* lift *Br*, elevator *Am*.

élévation [elevasjɔ̃] *nf* - **1.** [gén] raising ; ~ **à** *MATHS* raising to ; *fig* elevation to - **2.** [tertre] rise, mound - **3.** [de sentiments] nobility.

élevé, e [ɛlve] *adj* - **1.** [haut] high - **2.** *fig* [sentiment, âme] noble - **3.** [enfant] : **bien/mal ~** well-/badly brought up.

élève [elɛv] *nmf* - **1.** [écolier, disciple] pupil - **2.** *MIL* cadet.

élever [19] [ɛlve] *vt* - **1.** [gén] to raise - **2.** [fardeau] to lift, to raise - **3.** [statue] to put up, to erect - **4.** [à un rang supérieur] to elevate - **5.** [esprit] to improve - **6.** [enfant] to bring up - **7.** [poulets] to rear, to breed.
◆ **s'élever** *vp* - **1.** [gén] to rise - **2.** [montant] : **s'~ à** to add up to - **3.** [protester] : **s'~ contre qqn/qqch** to protest against sb/sthg.

éleveur, euse [ɛlvœʀ, øz] *nm, f* breeder.

elfe [ɛlf] *nm* elf.

élider [3] [elide] *vt* to elide.

➡ **s'élider** *vp* to be elided.
éligible [eliʒibl] *adj* eligible.
élimé, e [elime] *adj* threadbare.
élimination [eliminasjɔ̃] *nf* elimination ; **procéder par ~** to proceed by elimination.
éliminatoire [eliminatwar] ◇ *nf (gén pl)* SPORT qualifying heat *ou* round ◇ *adj* qualifying *(avant n)*.
éliminer [3] [elimine] *vt* to eliminate.
élire [106] [elir] *vt* to elect.
élisais, élisions *etc* ⊳ **élire**.
élision [elizjɔ̃] *nf* elision.
élite [elit] *nf* elite ; **d'~** choice, select.
élitiste [elitist] *nmf* & *adj* elitist.
élixir [eliksir] *nm* elixir.
elle [ɛl] *pron pers* **- 1.** [sujet - personne] she ; [- animal] it, she ; [- chose] it **- 2.** [complément - personne] her ; [- animal] it, her ; [- chose] it.
➡ **elles** *pron pers pl* **- 1.** [sujet] they **- 2.** [complément] them.
➡ **elle-même** *pron pers* [personne] herself ; [animal] itself, herself ; [chose] itself.
➡ **elles-mêmes** *pron pers pl* themselves.
ellipse [elips] *nf* **- 1.** GÉOM ellipse **- 2.** LING ellipsis.
elliptique [eliptik] *adj* elliptical.
élocution [elɔkysjɔ̃] *nf* delivery ; **défaut d'~** speech defect.
éloge [elɔʒ] *nm* **- 1.** [discours] eulogy **- 2.** [louange] praise ; **faire l'~ de qqn/qqch** [louer] to speak highly of sb/sthg ; **couvrir qqn d'~s** to shower sb with praise.
élogieux, euse [elɔʒjø, øz] *adj* laudatory.
éloigné, e [elwaɲe] *adj* distant.
éloignement [elwaɲmã] *nm* **- 1.** [mise à l'écart] removal **- 2.** [séparation] absence **- 3.** [dans l'espace, le temps] distance.
éloigner [3] [elwaɲe] *vt* **- 1.** [écarter] to move away ; **~ qqch de** to move sthg away from **- 2.** [détourner] to turn away **- 3.** [chasser] to dismiss.
➡ **s'éloigner** *vp* **- 1.** [partir] to move *ou* go away **- 2.** *fig* [du sujet] to stray from the point **- 3.** [se détacher] to distance o.s.
élongation [elɔ̃gasjɔ̃] *nf* MÉD : **~ de muscle** pulled muscle.
éloquence [elɔkɑ̃s] *nf* **- 1.** [d'orateur, d'expression] eloquence **- 2.** [de données] significance.
éloquent, e [elɔkɑ̃, ɑ̃t] *adj* **- 1.** [avocat, silence] eloquent **- 2.** [données] significant.
élu, e [ely] ◇ *pp* ⊳ **élire** ◇ *adj* POLIT elected ◇ *nm, f* **- 1.** POLIT elected representative **- 2.** RELIG chosen one ; **l'~ de son cœur** *hum ou sout* one's heart's desire.
élucider [3] [elyside] *vt* to clear up.

élucubration [elykybrasjɔ̃] *nf* raving.
éluder [3] [elyde] *vt* to evade.
Élysée [elize] *nm* : **l'~** the official residence of the French President and, by extension, the President himself.

émacié, e [emasje] *adj littéraire* emaciated.
émail, aux [emaj, emo] *nm* enamel ; **en ~** enamel, enamelled *Br*, enameled *Am*.
➡ **émaux** *nmpl* enamelwork *(U)*.
e-mail [imɛl] *(pl* **e-mails)** *nm* e-mail, E-mail.
émanation [emanasjɔ̃] *nf* emanation ; **être l'~ de** *fig* to emanate from.
émancipation [emɑ̃sipasjɔ̃] *nf* emancipation.
émanciper [3] [emɑ̃sipe] *vt* to emancipate.
➡ **s'émanciper** *vp* **- 1.** [se libérer] to become free *ou* liberated **- 2.** *fam* [se dévergonder] to become emancipated.
émaner [3] [emane] *vi* : **~ de** to emanate from.
émarger [17] [emarʒe] ◇ *vt* **- 1.** [signer] to sign **- 2.** [enlever la marge de] to trim the margins of ◇ *vi* to sign.
émasculer [3] [emaskyle] *vt* to emasculate.
emballage [ɑ̃balaʒ] *nm* packaging.
emballement [ɑ̃balmɑ̃] *nm* **- 1.** [enthousiasme] sudden craze **- 2.** [de moteur] racing *(U)*.
emballer [3] [ɑ̃bale] *vt* **- 1.** [objet] to pack (up), to wrap (up) **- 2.** [moteur] to race **- 3.** *fam* [plaire à] to thrill.
➡ **s'emballer** *vp* **- 1.** [moteur] to race **- 2.** [cheval] to bolt **- 3.** *fam* [personne - s'enthousiasmer] to get carried away ; [- s'emporter] to lose one's temper.
embarcadère [ɑ̃barkader] *nm* landing stage.
embarcation [ɑ̃barkasjɔ̃] *nf* small boat.
embardée [ɑ̃barde] *nf* swerve ; **faire une ~** to swerve.
embargo [ɑ̃bargo] *nm* embargo.
embarquement [ɑ̃barkəmɑ̃] *nm* **- 1.** [de marchandises] loading **- 2.** [de passagers] boarding ; **~ immédiat** immediate boarding.
embarquer [3] [ɑ̃barke] ◇ *vt* **- 1.** [marchandises] to load **- 2.** [passagers] to (take on) board **- 3.** *fam* [dans une voiture] to take, to give a lift to **- 4.** *fam* [arrêter] to pick up **- 5.** *fam fig* [engager] : **~ qqn dans** to involve sb in **- 6.** *fam* [emmener] to cart off ◇ *vi* : **~ (pour)** to sail (for).

s'embarquer vp - **1.** [sur un bateau] to (set) sail - **2.** fam fig [s'engager] : **s'~ dans** to get involved in.

embarras [ābaral nm - **1.** [incertitude] (state of) uncertainty ; **avoir l'~ du choix** to be spoilt for choice - **2.** [situation difficile] predicament ; **être dans l'~** to be in a predicament ; **mettre qqn dans l'~** to place sb in an awkward position ; **tirer qqn d'~** to get sb out of a tight spot - **3.** [perplexité] confusion - **4.** [gêne] embarrassment - **5.** [souci] difficulty, worry.

embarrassant, e [ābarasā, āt] adj - **1.** [encombrant] cumbersome - **2.** [délicat] embarrassing.

embarrassé, e [ābarase] adj - **1.** [encombré - pièce, bureau] cluttered ; **avoir les mains ~es** to have one's hands full - **2.** [gêné] embarrassed - **3.** [confus] confused.

embarrasser [3] [ābarase] vt - **1.** [encombrer - pièce] to clutter up ; [- personne] to hamper - **2.** [gêner] to put in an awkward position.

s'embarrasser vp - **1.** [se charger] : **s'~ de qqch** to burden o.s. with sthg ; fig to bother about sthg - **2.** [s'empêtrer] : **s'~ dans** to get tangled up in.

embauche [ābɔʃ] nf, **embauchage** [ābɔʃaʒ] nm hiring, employment.

embaucher [3] [ābɔʃe] vt - **1.** [employer] to employ, to take on - **2.** fam [occuper] : **je t'embauche!** I need your help!

embaumer [3] [ābome] <> vt - **1.** [cadavre] to embalm - **2.** [parfumer] to scent <> vi to be fragrant.

embellie [ābeli] nf [éclaircie] bright ou clear spell ; fig (temporary) improvement.

embellir [32] [ābelir] <> vt - **1.** [agrémenter] to brighten up - **2.** fig [enjoliver] to embellish <> vi [devenir plus beau] to become more attractive ; fig & hum to grow, to increase.

emberlificoter [3] [āberlifikɔte] vt fam fig to sweet-talk.

s'emberlificoter vp fam to get tangled up.

embêtant, e [ābetā, āt] adj fam annoying.

embêtement [ābetmā] nm fam trouble.

embêter [4] [ābete] vt fam [contrarier, importuner] to annoy.

s'embêter vp fam [s'ennuyer] to be bored.

emblée [āble] **d'emblée** loc adv right away.

emblème [āblɛm] nm emblem.

embobiner [3] [ābɔbine] vt - **1.** [fil] to wind - **2.** fam [personne] to fool.

emboîter [3] [ābwate] vt : **~ qqch dans qqch** to fit sthg into sthg ; **~ le pas à qqn** [suivre] to follow close on sb's heels ; fig to follow sb's lead.

s'emboîter vp to fit together.

embolie [ābɔli] nf embolism.

embonpoint [ābɔ̃pwɛ̃] nm stoutness ; **prendre de l'~** to get stout.

embouché, e [ābuʃe] adj fam : **mal ~** foulmouthed.

embouchure [ābuʃyr] nf - **1.** [d'instrument] mouthpiece - **2.** [de fleuve] mouth ; **l'~ du Rhône** the mouth of the Rhône.

embourber [3] [āburbe] **s'embourber** vp [s'enliser] to get stuck in the mud ; fig to get bogged down.

embourgeoisement [āburʒwazmā] nm [de personne] adoption of middle-class values ; [de quartier] gentrification.

embourgeoiser [3] [āburʒwaze] vt [personne] to instil Br ou instill Am middle-class values in ; [quartier] to gentrify.

s'embourgeoiser vp [personne] to adopt middle-class values ; [quartier] to become gentrified.

embout [ābu] nm [protection] tip ; [extrémité d'un tube] nozzle.

embouteillage [ābutɛjaʒ] nm - **1.** [circulation] traffic jam - **2.** [mise en bouteilles] bottling.

emboutir [32] [ābutir] vt - **1.** fam [voiture] to crash into - **2.** TECHNOL to stamp.

embranchement [ābrāʃmā] nm - **1.** [carrefour] junction - **2.** [division] branching (out) ; fig branch.

embraser [3] [ābraze] vt [incendier, éclairer] to set ablaze ; fig [d'amour] to (set on) fire, to inflame.

s'embraser vp [prendre feu, s'éclairer] to be ablaze ; fig & littéraire to be inflamed.

embrassade [ābrasad] nf embrace.

embrasse [ābras] nf tieback.

embrasser [3] [ābrase] vt - **1.** [donner un baiser à] to kiss - **2.** [étreindre] to embrace - **3.** fig [du regard] to take in.

s'embrasser vp to kiss (each other).

embrasure [ābrazyr] nf : **dans l'~ de la fenêtre** in the window.

embrayage [ābrɛjaʒ] nm - **1.** [action] engaging the clutch - **2.** [mécanisme] clutch.

embrayer [11] [ābreje] vi - **1.** AUTOM to engage the clutch - **2.** fam fig [s'engager] : **~ sur** to get onto the subject of.

embrigader [3] [ābrigade] vt to recruit.

s'embrigader vp to join.

embringuer [3] [ābrɛ̃ge] vt fam to involve.

s'embringuer vp fam : **s'~ dans** to get mixed up in.

embrocher [3] [ãbrɔʃe] *vt* to skewer.
➤ **s'embrocher** *vp fam* to stab o.s.

embrouillamini [ãbrujamini] *nm fam* muddle.

embrouille [ãbruj] *nf fam* shenanigans *(pl)*.

embrouiller [3] [ãbruje] *vt* - **1.** [mélanger] to mix (up), to muddle (up) - **2.** *fig* [compliquer] to confuse.

embruns [ãbrœ̃] *nmpl* spray (U).

embryologie [ãbrijɔlɔʒi] *nf* embryology.

embryon [ãbrijɔ̃] *nm litt* & *fig* embryo.

embryonnaire [ãbrijɔnɛr] *adj litt* & *fig* embryonic.

embûche [ãbyʃ] *nf* pitfall.

embuer [7] [ãbɥe] *vt* - **1.** [de vapeur] to steam up - **2.** [de larmes] to mist (over).

embuscade [ãbyskad] *nf* ambush.

embusquer [3] [ãbyske] *vt* - **1.** [poster] to position for an ambush - **2.** [mettre à l'abri] to post away from the front line.
➤ **s'embusquer** *vp* - **1.** [se poster] to lie in ambush - **2.** [se mettre à l'abri] to be posted away from the front line.

éméché, e [emeʃe] *adj fam* merry, tipsy.

émeraude [emrod] ◇ *nf* emerald ◇ *adj inv* (en apposition) : **vert ~** emerald (green).

émergence [emɛrʒãs] *nf* emergence.

émergent, e [emɛrʒã, ãt] *adj* : **pays ~** emerging country.

émerger [17] [emɛrʒe] *vi* - **1.** [gén] to emerge - **2.** *NAVIG* & *fig* to surface.

émeri [emri] *nm* : **papier** OU **toile ~** emery paper.

émérite [emerit] *adj* distinguished, eminent.

émerveillement [emɛrvejmã] *nm* wonder.

émerveiller [4] [emɛrveje] *vt* to fill with wonder.
➤ **s'émerveiller** *vp* : **s'~ (de)** to marvel (at).

émets ▷ émettre.

émetteur, trice [emetœr, tris] *adj* transmitting ; **poste ~** transmitter.
➤ **émetteur** *nm* [appareil] transmitter ; **~-récepteur** transmitter-receiver.

émettre [84] [emɛtr] *vt* - **1.** [produire] to emit - **2.** [diffuser] to transmit, to broadcast - **3.** [mettre en circulation] to issue - **4.** [exprimer] to express.

émeus, émeut *etc* ▷ émouvoir.

émeute [emøt] *nf* riot.

émeutier, ère [emøtje, ɛr] *nm, f* rioter.

émietter [4] [emjete] *vt* - **1.** [du pain] to crumble - **2.** [morceler] to divide up.

émigrant, e [emigrã, ãt] *adj* & *nm, f* emigrant.

émigration [emigrasjɔ̃] *nf* - **1.** [de personnes] emigration - **2.** *ZOOL* migration.

émigré, e [emigre] ◇ *adj* migrant ◇ *nm, f* emigrant.

émigrer [3] [emigre] *vi* - **1.** [personnes] to emigrate - **2.** [animaux] to migrate.

émincé, e [emɛ̃se] *adj* sliced thinly.
➤ **émincé** *nm* thin slices of meat served in a sauce.

éminemment [eminamã] *adv* eminently.

éminence [eminãs] *nf* hill.
➤ **Éminence** *nf* Eminence ; **Son Éminence** His Eminence.
➤ **éminence grise** *nf* éminence grise.

éminent, e [eminã, ãt] *adj* eminent, distinguished.

émir [emir] *nm* emir.

émirat [emira] *nm* emirate.
➤ **Émirat** *nm* : **les Émirats arabes unis** the United Arab Emirates.

émis, e [emi, iz] *pp* ▷ émettre.

émissaire [emisɛr] ◇ *nm* - **1.** [envoyé] emissary, envoy - **2.** *TECHNOL* outlet, drainage channel ◇ *adj* - **1.** *ANAT* emissary - **2.** ▷ bouc.

émission [emisjɔ̃] *nf* - **1.** [de gaz, de son etc] emission - **2.** [RADIO & TÉLÉ - transmission] transmission, broadcasting ; [- programme] programme *Br*, program *Am* - **3.** [mise en circulation] issue.

emmagasiner [3] [ãmagazine] *vt* - **1.** [stocker] to store - **2.** *fig* [accumuler] to store up.

emmailloter [3] [ãmajɔte] *vt* to wrap up.

emmanchure [ãmãʃyr] *nf* armhole.

Emmaüs [emays] *n* : **~ International** *charity organization which helps the poor and homeless.*

emmêler [4] [ãmele] *vt* - **1.** [fils] to tangle up - **2.** *fig* [idées] to muddle up, to confuse.
➤ **s'emmêler** *vp* - **1.** [fils] to get into a tangle - **2.** *fig* [personne] to get mixed up.

emménagement [ãmenaʒmã] *nm* moving in.

emménager [17] [ãmenaʒe] *vi* to move in.

emmener [19] [ãmne] *vt* to take.

emmerdant, e [ãmɛrdã, ãt] *adj tfam* bloody *Br* OU damned annoying.

emmerdement [ãmɛrdəmã] *nm tfam* hassle, bloody *Br* OU damned nuisance ; **avoir des ~s** to have problems.

emmerder [3] [ãmɛrde] *vt tfam* to piss off.
➤ **s'emmerder** *vp tfam* [s'embêter] to be bored stiff.

emmerdeur, euse [ɑ̃mɛrdœr, øz] *nm, f tfam* pain in the arse *Br ou* ass *Am.*

emmitoufler [3] [ɑ̃mitufle] *vt* to wrap up.

➡ **s'emmitoufler** *vp* to wrap o.s. up.

émoi [emwa] *nm* - **1.** *sout* [agitation] agitation, commotion ; **en ~** in turmoil - **2.** [émotion] emotion.

émollient, e [emɔljɑ̃, ɑ̃t] *adj* emollient.

➡ **émollient** *nm* emollient.

émotif, ive [emɔtif, iv] ◇ *adj* emotional ◇ *nm, f* emotional person.

émotion [emosjɔ̃] *nf* - **1.** [sentiment] emotion - **2.** [peur] fright, shock ; **donner des ~s à qqn** to give sb a fright *ou* shock.

émotionnel, elle [emosjɔnel] *adj* emotional.

émotionner [3] [emosjɔne] *vt fam* to move (to the brink of tears).

émotivité [emɔtivite] *nf* emotionalism.

émoulu, e [emuly] ⊏➤ **frais.**

émousser [3] [emuse] *vt litt* & *fig* to blunt.

➡ **s'émousser** *vp* [lame] to become blunt ; *fig* to die down, to lessen.

émoustiller [3] [emustije] *vt* - **1.** [rendre gai] to liven up - **2.** [exciter] to arouse, to excite.

émouvant, e [emuvɑ̃, ɑ̃t] *adj* moving.

émouvoir [55] [emuvwar] *vt* - **1.** [troubler] to disturb, to upset - **2.** [susciter la sympathie de] to move, to touch.

➡ **s'émouvoir** *vp* to show emotion, to be upset.

empailler [3] [ɑ̃paje] *vt* - **1.** [animal] to stuff - **2.** [chaise] to upholster (with straw).

empaler [3] [ɑ̃pale] *vt* to impale.

➡ **s'empaler** *vp* : **s'~ sur** to be impaled on *ou* upon.

empaqueter [27] [ɑ̃pakte] *vt* to pack (up), to wrap (up).

emparer [3] [ɑ̃pare] ➡ **s'emparer** *vp* : **s'~ de** [suj : personne] to seize ; [suj : sentiment] to take hold of.

empâté, e [ɑ̃pate] *adj* [visage, traits] bloated ; [bouche, langue] coated.

empâter [3] [ɑ̃pate] *vt* - **1.** [visage, traits] to fatten out - **2.** [bouche, langue] to coat, to fur up.

➡ **s'empâter** *vp* to put on weight.

empattement [ɑ̃patmɑ̃] *nm* - **1.** *AUTOM* wheelbase - **2.** *TYPO* serif.

empêchement [ɑ̃pɛʃmɑ̃] *nm* obstacle ; **j'ai un ~** something has come up.

empêcher [4] [ɑ̃peʃe] *vt* to prevent ; **~ qqn/ qqch de faire qqch** to prevent sb/sthg from doing sthg ; **~ que qqn (ne) fasse qqch** to prevent sb from doing sthg ; **(il) n'empêche que** nevertheless, all the same.

➡ **s'empêcher** *vp* : **s'~ de faire qqch** to stop o.s. doing sthg ; **je ne peux pas m'~ de pleurer** I can't help crying.

empêcheur, euse [ɑ̃peʃœr, øz] *nm, f fam* : **~ de tourner en rond** killjoy.

empeigne [ɑ̃pɛɲ] *nf* upper.

empereur [ɑ̃prœr] *nm* emperor.

empesé, e [ɑ̃pəze] *adj* - **1.** [linge] starched - **2.** *fig* [style] stiff.

empester [3] [ɑ̃pɛste] ◇ *vt* to stink out ◇ *vi* to stink.

empêtrer [4] [ɑ̃petre] *vt* : **être empêtré dans** to be tangled up in.

➡ **s'empêtrer** *vp* : **s'~ (dans)** to get tangled up (in).

emphase [ɑ̃faz] *nf péj* pomposity.

emphatique [ɑ̃fatik] *adj péj* pompous.

empiècement [ɑ̃pjɛsmɑ̃] *nm* yoke.

empiéter [18] [ɑ̃pjete] *vi* : **~ sur** to encroach on.

empiffrer [3] [ɑ̃pifre] ➡ **s'empiffrer** *vp fam* to stuff o.s.

empilement [ɑ̃pilmɑ̃], **empilage** [ɑ̃pilaʒ] *nm* [action] piling up, stacking up ; [pile] pile, stack.

empiler [3] [ɑ̃pile] *vt* - **1.** [entasser] to pile up, to stack up - **2.** *tfam* [duper] to rip off.

➡ **s'empiler** *vp* to pile up.

empire [ɑ̃pir] *nm* - **1.** *HIST* & *fig* empire ; **l'Empire** *the Empire under Napoleon I* ; **le Second Empire** the Second Empire *(under Napoleon III)* ; **pour un ~** *fig* for the world - **2.** *sout* [contrôle] influence ; **sous l'~ de** [la boisson] under the influence of ; [la colère] gripped by.

empirer [3] [ɑ̃pire] *vi* & *vt* to worsen.

empirique [ɑ̃pirik] *adj* empirical.

empirisme [ɑ̃pirism] *nm* empiricism.

emplacement [ɑ̃plasmɑ̃] *nm* [gén] site, location ; [dans un camping] place.

emplâtre [ɑ̃platr] *nm* - **1.** [pommade] plaster - **2.** *péj* [incapable] lazy lump.

emplette [ɑ̃plɛt] *nf* (gén pl) purchase ; **faire des ~s** to go shopping ; **faire l'~ de** to purchase.

emplir [32] [ɑ̃plir] *vt sout* : **~ (de)** to fill (with).

➡ **s'emplir** *vp* : **s'~ (de)** to fill (with).

emploi [ɑ̃plwa] *nm* - **1.** [utilisation] use ; **faire double ~** to be unnecessary *ou* redundant ; **~ du temps** timetable ; **mode d'~** instructions *(pl)* (for use) - **2.** [travail] job.

employé, e [ɑ̃plwaje] *nm, f* employee ; **~ de bureau** office employee *ou* worker.

employer [13] [ɑ̃plwaje] *vt* - **1.** [utiliser] to use - **2.** [salarier] to employ.

➡ **s'employer** *vp* to be used ; **s'~ à qqch** to

be working on sthg, to apply o.s. to sthg ; **s'~ à faire qqch** to apply o.s. to doing sthg.

employeur, euse [ɑ̃plwajœr, øz] *nm, f* employer.

empocher [3] [ɑ̃pɔʃe] *vt fam* to pocket.

empoignade [ɑ̃pwaɲad] *nf* row.

empoigne [ɑ̃pwaɲ] ▷ **foire.**

empoigner [3] [ɑ̃pwaɲe] *vt* - **1.** [saisir] to grasp - **2.** *fig* [émouvoir] to grip.

➣ **s'empoigner** *vp fig* to come to blows.

empoisonnant, e [ɑ̃pwazɔnɑ̃, ɑ̃t] *adj* - **1.** [ennuyeux] boring - **2.** [insupportable] irritating.

empoisonnement [ɑ̃pwazɔnmɑ̃] *nm* - **1.** [intoxication] poisoning - **2.** *fam fig* [souci] trouble *(U)*.

empoisonner [3] [ɑ̃pwazɔne] *vt* - **1.** [gén] to poison - **2.** [empuantir] to stink out - **3.** *fam* [ennuyer] to annoy, to bug.

emporté, e [ɑ̃pɔrte] *adj* short-tempered.

emportement [ɑ̃pɔrtəmɑ̃] *nm* anger.

emporte-pièce [ɑ̃pɔrtəpjɛs] *nm inv* punch.

➣ **à l'emporte-pièce** *loc adj* incisive.

emporter [3] [ɑ̃pɔrte] *vt* - **1.** [emmener] to take (away) ; **à ~** [plats] to take away, to go *Am* - **2.** [entraîner] to carry along - **3.** [arracher] to tear off, to blow off - **4.** [faire mourir] to carry off - **5.** [gagner] to win - **6.** [surpasser] : **l'~ sur** to get the better of.

➣ **s'emporter** *vp* to get angry, to lose one's temper.

empoté, e [ɑ̃pɔte] *fam* ◇ *adj* clumsy ◇ *nm, f* clumsy person.

empourprer [3] [ɑ̃purpre] ➣ **s'empourprer** *vp littéraire* to turn crimson.

empreinte [ɑ̃prɛ̃t] *nf* [trace] print ; *fig* mark, trace ; **~ génétique** genetic fingerprint ; **~s digitales** fingerprints.

empressé, e [ɑ̃prese] ◇ *adj* attentive ◇ *nm, f* attentive person.

empressement [ɑ̃prɛsmɑ̃] *nm* - **1.** [zèle] attentiveness - **2.** [enthousiasme] eagerness.

empresser [4] [ɑ̃prese] ➣ **s'empresser** *vp* : **s'~ de faire qqch** to hurry to do sthg ; **s'~ auprès de qqn** to be attentive to sb.

emprise [ɑ̃priz] *nf* - **1.** [ascendant] influence ; **sous l'~ de** [l'alcool] under the influence of ; [la colère] gripped by - **2.** *JUR* expropriation.

emprisonnement [ɑ̃prizɔnmɑ̃] *nm* imprisonment.

emprisonner [3] [ɑ̃prizɔne] *vt* - **1.** [voleur] to imprison - **2.** [partie du corps] to fit tightly round.

emprunt [ɑ̃prœ̃] *nm* - **1.** *FIN* loan ; **couvrir un ~** to guarantee a loan ; **lancer un ~** to float a

loan ; **~ d'État** government loan - **2.** *LING* & *fig* borrowing.

emprunté, e [ɑ̃prœ̃te] *adj* awkward, self-conscious.

emprunter [3] [ɑ̃prœ̃te] *vt* - **1.** [gén] to borrow ; **~ qqch à** to borrow sthg from - **2.** [route] to take.

empuantir [32] [ɑ̃pɥɑ̃tir] *vt* to stink out.

EMT (*abr de* **éducation manuelle et technique**) *nf* practical sciences *(pl)*.

ému, e [emy] ◇ *pp* ▷ **émouvoir** ◇ *adj* [personne] moved, touched ; [regard, sourire] emotional.

émulation [emylasjɔ̃] *nf* - **1.** [concurrence] rivalry - **2.** [imitation] emulation.

émule [emyl] *nmf* - **1.** [imitateur] emulator - **2.** [concurrent] rival.

émulsion [emylsjɔ̃] *nf* emulsion.

en [ɑ̃] ◇ *prép* - **1.** [temps] in ; **~ 1994** in 1994 ; **~ hiver/septembre** in winter/September - **2.** [lieu] in ; [direction] to ; **une maison ~ Suède** a house in Sweden ; **habiter ~ Sicile/ville** to live in Sicily/town ; **aller ~ Sicile/ville** to go to Sicily/town ; **aller de ville ~ ville** to go from town to town - **3.** [matière] made of ; **c'est ~ métal** it's (made of) metal ; **une théière ~ argent** a silver teapot - **4.** [état, forme, manière] : **les arbres sont ~ fleurs** the trees are in blossom ; **du sucre ~ morceaux** sugar cubes ; **du lait ~ poudre** powdered milk ; **je la préfère ~ vert** I prefer it in green ; **agir ~ traître** to behave treacherously ; **je l'ai eu ~ cadeau** I was given it as a present ; **dire qqch ~ anglais** to say sthg in English ; **~ vacances** on holiday - **5.** [moyen] by ; **~ avion/bateau/train** by plane/boat/train - **6.** [mesure] in ; **vous l'avez ~ 38?** do you have it in a 38? ; **compter ~ dollars** to calculate in dollars - **7.** [devant un participe présent] : **~ arrivant à Paris** on arriving in Paris, as he/she *etc* arrived in Paris ; **~ faisant un effort** by making an effort ; **~ mangeant** while eating ; **elle répondit ~ souriant** she replied with a smile. ◇ *pron adv* - **1.** [complément de verbe, de nom, d'adjectif] : **il s'~ est souvenu** he remembered it ; **nous ~ avons déjà parlé** we've already spoken about it ; **on ~ meurt, de ce genre de maladie** people die from this sort of illness ; **je m'~ porte garant** I'll vouch for it ; **j'~ garde un très bon souvenir** I have very happy memories of it ; **sa maison ~ est pleine** his house is full of them - **2.** [avec un indéfini, exprimant une quantité] : **j'~ connais un/plusieurs** I know one/several of them ; **j'ai du chocolat, tu ~ veux?** I've got some chocolate, do you want some? ; **tu ~ as?** have you got any?, do you have any? ; **il y ~ a plusieurs** there are several (of them) - **3**. [provenance] from there ; **j'~ viens à l'instant** I've just come from there.

ENA, Ena [ena] (*abr de* **École nationale d'administration**) *nf prestigious grande école training future government officials.*

énarque [enark] *nmf graduate of the École nationale d'administration* (*ENA*).

encablure [ɑ̃kablyr] *nf* cable length.

encadrement [ɑ̃kadrəmɑ̃] *nm* - **1**. [de tableau, porte] frame - **2**. [dans une entreprise] managerial staff ; [à l'armée] officers (*pl*) ; [à l'école] staff - **3**. [du crédit] restriction.

encadrer [3] [ɑ̃kadre] *vt* - **1**. [photo, visage] to frame - **2**. [employés] to supervise ; [soldats] to be in command of ; [élèves] to teach - **3**. [détenu] to flank - **4**. *fam* [arbre] to crash into.

encadreur [ɑ̃kadrœr] *nm* framer.

encaisse [ɑ̃kɛs] *nf* ready cash.

encaissé, e [ɑ̃kese] *adj* [vallée] deep and narrow ; [rivière] steep-banked.

encaisser [4] [ɑ̃kese] *vt* - **1**. [argent, coups, insultes] to take - **2**. [chèque] to cash - **3**. *loc* : **ne pas pouvoir ~ qqn** *fam* not to be able to stand sb.

encanailler [3] [ɑ̃kanaje] **→ s'encanailler** *vp* to slum it.

encart [ɑ̃kar] *nm* insert ; **~ publicitaire** advertising insert.

en-cas, encas [ɑ̃ka] *nm inv* snack.

encastrable [ɑ̃kastrabl] *adj* that can be fitted (in).

encastrer [3] [ɑ̃kastre] *vt* to fit.
→ s'encastrer *vp* to fit (exactly).

encaustique [ɑ̃kostik] *nf* - **1**. [cire] polish - **2**. [peinture] encaustic.

encaustiquer [3] [ɑ̃kostike] *vt* to polish.

enceinte [ɑ̃sɛ̃t] <> *adj f* pregnant ; **~ de 4 mois** 4 months pregnant <> *nf* - **1**. [muraille] wall - **2**. [espace] : **dans l'~ de** within (the confines of) - **3**. [baffle] : **~ (acoustique)** speaker.

encens [ɑ̃sɑ̃] *nm* incense.

encenser [3] [ɑ̃sɑ̃se] *vt* - **1**. [brûler de l'encens dans] to burn incense in - **2**. *fig* [louer] to flatter.

encensoir [ɑ̃sɑ̃swar] *nm* censer.

encercler [3] [ɑ̃sɛrkle] *vt* - **1**. [cerner, environner] to surround - **2**. [entourer] to circle.

enchaînement [ɑ̃ʃɛnmɑ̃] *nm* - **1**. [succession] series - **2**. [liaison] link - **3**. *MUS* progression.

enchaîner [4] [ɑ̃ʃene] <> *vt* - **1**. [attacher] to chain up - **2**. *fig* [asservir] to enslave - **3**. [coordonner] to link <> *vi* : **~ (sur)** to move on (to).
→ s'enchaîner *vp* [se suivre] to follow on from each other.

enchanté, e [ɑ̃ʃɑ̃te] *adj* - **1**. [ravi] delighted ;

~ de faire votre connaissance pleased to meet you - **2**. [ensorcelé] enchanted.

enchantement [ɑ̃ʃɑ̃tmɑ̃] *nm* - **1**. [sortilège] magic spell ; **comme par ~** as if by magic - **2**. *sout* [ravissement] delight - **3**. [merveille] wonder.

enchanter [3] [ɑ̃ʃɑ̃te] *vt* - **1**. [ensorceler, charmer] to enchant - **2**. [ravir] to delight.

enchanteur, eresse [ɑ̃ʃɑ̃tœr, trɛs] <> *adj* enchanting <> *nm, f* - **1**. [magicien] enchanter - **2**. [charmeur] charmer.

enchâsser [3] [ɑ̃ʃase] *vt* - **1**. [encastrer] to fit - **2**. [sertir] to set.

enchère [ɑ̃ʃɛr] *nf* bid ; **faire monter les ~s** to raise the bidding ; **vendre qqch aux ~s** to sell sthg at *ou* by auction.

enchérir [32] [ɑ̃ʃerir] *vi* : **~ sur** to bid higher than ; *fig & littéraire* [dépasser] to go beyond.

enchevêtrer [4] [ɑ̃ʃəvetre] *vt* [emmêler] to tangle up ; *fig* to muddle, to confuse.

enclave [ɑ̃klav] *nf* enclave.

enclencher [3] [ɑ̃klɑ̃ʃe] *vt* - **1**. [mécanisme] to engage - **2**. *fig* [projet] to set in motion.
→ s'enclencher *vp* - **1**. *TECHNOL* to engage - **2**. *fig* [commencer] to begin.

enclin, e [ɑ̃klɛ̃, in] *adj* : **~ à qqch/à faire qqch** inclined to sthg/to do sthg.

enclore [113] [ɑ̃klɔr] *vt* to fence in, to enclose.

enclos, e [ɑ̃klo, oz] *pp* ▷ **enclore**.
→ enclos *nm* enclosure.

enclume [ɑ̃klym] *nf* anvil.

encoche [ɑ̃kɔʃ] *nf* notch.

encoder [ɑ̃kɔde] *vt* to encode.

encodeur [ɑ̃kɔdœr] *nm INFORM* encoder.

encoignure [ɑ̃kwaɲyr, ɑ̃kɔɲyr] *nf* - **1**. [coin] corner - **2**. [meuble] corner cupboard.

encolure [ɑ̃kɔlyr] *nf* neck.

encombrant, e [ɑ̃kɔ̃brɑ̃, ɑ̃t] *adj* cumbersome ; *fig* [personne] undesirable.

encombre [ɑ̃kɔ̃br] **→ sans encombre** *loc adv* without a hitch.

encombré, e [ɑ̃kɔ̃bre] *adj* [lieu] busy, congested ; *fig* saturated.

encombrement [ɑ̃kɔ̃brəmɑ̃] *nm* - **1**. [d'une pièce] clutter - **2**. [d'un objet] overall dimensions (*pl*) - **3**. [embouteillage] traffic jam - **4**. *INFORM* footprint.

encombrer [3] [ɑ̃kɔ̃bre] *vt* to clutter (up).
→ s'encombrer *vp fam* : **s'~ de qqn** to be lumbered with sb *Br* ; **s'~ de qqch** to burden o.s. with sthg ; *fig* to bother about sthg.

encontre [ɑ̃kɔ̃tr] **→ à l'encontre de** *loc prép* : **aller à l'~ de** to go against, to oppose.

encorbellement [ɑ̃kɔrbɛlmɑ̃] nm corbelled structure ; **en ~** corbelled.

encorder [3] [ɑ̃kɔrde] ➧ **s'encorder** vp to rope up.

encore [ɑ̃kɔr] adv - **1.** [toujours] still ; **il dort ~** he's still asleep ; **~ un mois** one more month ; **pas ~** not yet ; **elle ne travaille pas ~** she's not working yet - **2.** [de nouveau] again ; **il m'a ~ menti** he's lied to me again ; **quoi ~?** what now? ; **l'ascenseur est en panne - ~!** the lift's out of order - not again! ; **~ de la glace?** some more ice cream? ; **~ une fois** once more, once again - **3.** [marque le renforcement] even ; **~ mieux/pire** even better/worse - **4.** [marque une restriction] : **il ne suffit pas d'être beau, ~ faut-il être intelligent** it's not enough to be good-looking, you have to be intelligent too.
➧ **et encore** loc adv : **j'ai eu le temps de prendre un sandwich, et ~!** I had time for a sandwich, but only just! ; **ça vaut 100 francs, et ~** it's worth 100 francs, if that.
➧ **mais encore** loc adv what else?
➧ **si encore** loc adv if only.
➧ **encore que** loc conj (+ subjonctif) although.

encourageant, e [ɑ̃kuraʒɑ̃, ɑ̃t] adj encouraging.

encouragement [ɑ̃kuraʒmɑ̃] nm - **1.** [parole] (word of) encouragement - **2.** [action] encouragement.

encourager [17] [ɑ̃kuraʒe] vt to encourage ; **~ qqn à faire qqch** to encourage sb to do sthg.

encourir [45] [ɑ̃kurir] vt sout to incur.

encourrai, encourras etc ▷ encourir.

encouru, e [ɑ̃kury] pp ▷ encourir.

encrasser [3] [ɑ̃krase] vt - **1.** TECHNOL to clog up - **2.** fam [salir] to make dirty ou filthy.
➧ **s'encrasser** vp - **1.** TECHNOL to clog up - **2.** fam [se salir] to get dirty ou filthy.

encre [ɑ̃kr] nf ink ; **~ de Chine** Indian Br ou India Am ink.

encrer [3] [ɑ̃kre] vt to ink.

encreur [ɑ̃krœr] ▷ tampon, rouleau.

encrier [ɑ̃krije] nm inkwell.

encroûter [3] [ɑ̃krute] ➧ **s'encroûter** vp fam to get into a rut ; **s'~ dans ses habitudes** to become set in one's ways.

enculé [ɑ̃kyle] nm vulg arsehole Br, asshole Am.

enculer [3] [ɑ̃kyle] vt vulg to bugger.

encyclique [ɑ̃siklik] nf RELIG encyclical.

encyclopédie [ɑ̃siklɔpedi] nf encyclopedia.

encyclopédique [ɑ̃siklɔpedik] adj encyclopedic.

endémique [ɑ̃demik] adj endemic.

endettement [ɑ̃dɛtmɑ̃] nm debt.

endetter [4] [ɑ̃dete] ➧ **s'endetter** vp to get into debt.

endeuiller [5] [ɑ̃dœje] vt to plunge into mourning.

endiablé, e [ɑ̃djable] adj [frénétique] frantic, frenzied.

endiguer [3] [ɑ̃dige] vt - **1.** [fleuve] to dam - **2.** fig [réprimer] to stem.

endimanché, e [ɑ̃dimɑ̃ʃe] adj in one's Sunday best.

endimancher [3] [ɑ̃dimɑ̃ʃe] ➧ **s'endimancher** vp to dress in one's Sunday best.

endive [ɑ̃div] nf chicory (U).

endoctrinement [ɑ̃dɔktrinmɑ̃] nm indoctrination.

endoctriner [3] [ɑ̃dɔktrine] vt to indoctrinate.

endommager [17] [ɑ̃dɔmaʒe] vt to damage.

endormi, e [ɑ̃dɔrmi] adj - **1.** [personne] sleeping, asleep - **2.** fig [village] sleepy ; [jambe] numb ; [passion] dormant ; fam [apathique] sluggish.

endormir [36] [ɑ̃dɔrmir] vt - **1.** [assoupir, ennuyer] to send to sleep - **2.** [anesthésier - patient] to anaesthetize Br, anesthetize Am ; [- douleur] to ease - **3.** fig [tromper] to allay - **4.** fig [affaiblir] to dull.
➧ **s'endormir** vp - **1.** [s'assoupir] to fall asleep - **2.** [s'affaiblir] to be allayed - **3.** fig [jambe] to go to sleep.

endoscopie [ɑ̃dɔskɔpi] nf endoscopy.

endosser [3] [ɑ̃dose] vt - **1.** [vêtement] to put on - **2.** FIN & JUR to endorse ; **~ un chèque** to endorse a cheque Br ou check Am - **3.** fig [responsabilité] to take on.

endroit [ɑ̃drwa] nm - **1.** [lieu, point] place ; **à quel ~?** where? - **2.** [passage] part - **3.** [côté] right side ; **à l'~** the right way round.
➧ **à l'endroit de** prép littéraire with regard to.

enduire [98] [ɑ̃dɥir] vt : **~ qqch (de)** to coat sthg (with).

enduisais, enduisions etc ▷ enduire.

enduit, e [ɑ̃dɥi, it] pp ▷ enduire.
➧ **enduit** nm coating.

endurance [ɑ̃dyrɑ̃s] nf endurance.

endurant, e [ɑ̃dyrɑ̃, ɑ̃t] adj tough, resilient.

endurci, e [ɑ̃dyrsi] adj - **1.** [aguerri] hardened - **2.** fig [insensible] hard.

endurcir [32] [ɑ̃dyrsir] vt to harden.

➤ **s'endurcir** *vp* : **s'~ à** to become hardened to.

endurer [3] [ɑ̃dyre] *vt* to endure.

énergétique [enɛrʒetik] *adj* - **1.** [ressource] energy *(avant n)* - **2.** [aliment] energy-giving.

énergie [enɛrʒi] *nf* energy ; **~ nucléaire/ solaire** nuclear/solar energy ; **~ éolienne** wind power ; **~ renouvelable** renewable energy.

énergique [enɛrʒik] *adj* [gén] energetic ; [remède] powerful ; [mesure] drastic.

énergiquement [enɛrʒikmɑ̃] *adv* energetically.

énergisant, e [enɛrʒizɑ̃, ɑ̃t] *adj* stimulating.
➤ **énergisant** *nm* tonic.

énergumène [enɛrgymɛn] *nmf* rowdy character.

énervant, e [enɛrvɑ̃, ɑ̃t] *adj* annoying, irritating.

énervé, e [enɛrve] *adj* - **1.** [irrité] annoyed, irritated - **2.** [surexcité] overexcited.

énervement [enɛrvəmɑ̃] *nm* - **1.** [irritation] irritation - **2.** [surexcitation] excitement.

énerver [3] [enɛrve] *vt* to irritate, to annoy.
➤ **s'énerver** *vp* [être irrité] to get annoyed ; [être excité] to get worked up *ou* excited.

enfance [ɑ̃fɑ̃s] *nf* - **1.** [âge] childhood ; **retomber en ~** to lapse into one's second childhood - **2.** [enfants] children *(pl)* - **3.** *fig* [débuts] infancy ; [de civilisation, de l'humanité] dawn ; **l'~ de l'art** *fig* child's play.

enfant [ɑ̃fɑ̃] *nmf* - **1.** [gén] child ; **~ illégitime** *ou* **naturel** illegitimate child ; **~ martyr** abused child ; **~ prodige** child prodigy ; **attendre un ~** to be expecting a baby - **2.** [originaire] native ; **c'est un ~ de la balle** his/her parents were in the theatre/circus *etc*.
➤ **bon enfant** *loc adj* good-natured.

enfantement [ɑ̃fɑ̃tmɑ̃] *nm littéraire* childbirth ; *fig* creation.

enfanter [3] [ɑ̃fɑ̃te] *vt littéraire* to give birth to.

enfantillage [ɑ̃fɑ̃tijaʒ] *nm* childishness *(U)*.

enfantin, e [ɑ̃fɑ̃tɛ̃, in] *adj* - **1.** [propre à l'enfance] childlike ; *péj* childish ; [jeu, chanson] children's *(avant n)* - **2.** [facile] childishly simple.

enfer [ɑ̃fɛr] *nm* - **1.** RELIG & *fig* hell ; **d'~** *fig* hellish, infernal - **2.** [de bibliothèque] restricted books department.
➤ **Enfers** *nmpl* : **les Enfers** the Underworld *(sg)*.

enfermer [3] [ɑ̃fɛrme] *vt* - **1.** [séquestrer, ranger] to shut away - **2.** *littéraire* [enclore] to enclose.

➤ **s'enfermer** *vp* to shut o.s. away *ou* up ; **s'~ dans** *fig* to retreat into.

enfilade [ɑ̃filad] *nf* row ; **en ~** in a row.

enfiler [3] [ɑ̃file] *vt* - **1.** [aiguille, sur un fil] to thread - **2.** [vêtements] to slip on.
➤ **s'enfiler** *vp fam* [ingurgiter] to put away.

enfin [ɑ̃fɛ̃] *adv* - **1.** [en dernier lieu] finally, at last ; [dans une liste] lastly - **2.** [avant une récapitulation] in a word, in short - **3.** [introduit une rectification] that is, well - **4.** [introduit une concession] anyway.

enflammé, e [ɑ̃flame] *adj* - **1.** [en flammes] burning - **2.** *fig* [déclaration, discours] passionate ; [discussion] heated.

enflammer [3] [ɑ̃flame] *vt* - **1.** [bois] to set fire to - **2.** *fig* [exalter] to inflame.
➤ **s'enflammer** *vp* - **1.** [bois] to catch fire - **2.** *fig* [s'exalter] to flare up.

enflé, e [ɑ̃fle] *adj* [style] turgid.

enfler [3] [ɑ̃fle] *vi* to swell (up).

enflure [ɑ̃flyr] *nf* [de corps] swelling.

enfoncé, e [ɑ̃fɔ̃se] *adj* deep-set.

enfoncer [16] [ɑ̃fɔ̃se] *vt* - **1.** [faire pénétrer] to drive in ; **~ qqch dans qqch** to drive sthg into sthg - **2.** [enfouir] : **~ ses mains dans ses poches** to thrust one's hands into one's pockets - **3.** [défoncer] to break down - **4.** *fam* [vaincre] to hammer, to thrash.
➤ **s'enfoncer** *vp* - **1.** : **s'~ dans** [eau, boue] to sink into ; [bois, ville] to disappear into - **2.** [céder] to give way.

enfouir [32] [ɑ̃fwir] *vt* - **1.** [cacher] to hide - **2.** [ensevelir] to bury.
➤ **s'enfouir** *vp* to bury o.s.

enfourcher [3] [ɑ̃furʃe] *vt* to get on, to mount.

enfourner [3] [ɑ̃furne] *vt* - **1.** [pain] to put in the oven - **2.** *fam* [avaler] to gobble up.

enfreignais, enfreignions *etc* ▷ **enfreindre**.

enfreindre [81] [ɑ̃frɛ̃dr] *vt* to infringe.

enfreint, e [ɑ̃frɛ̃, ɛ̃t] *pp* ▷ **enfreindre**.

enfuir [35] [ɑ̃fɥir] ➤ **s'enfuir** *vp* - **1.** [fuir] to run away - **2.** *littéraire* [passer] to slip away.

enfumer [3] [ɑ̃fyme] *vt* to fill with smoke.

enfuyais, enfuyions *etc* ▷ **enfuir**.

engagé, e [ɑ̃gaʒe] *adj* committed.

engageant, e [ɑ̃gaʒɑ̃, ɑ̃t] *adj* engaging.

engagement [ɑ̃gaʒmɑ̃] *nm* - **1.** [promesse] commitment ; **sans ~** COMM without obligation - **2.** *JUR* contract - **3.** [embauche] engagement, taking on - **4.** [MIL - de soldats] enlistment ; [- combat] engagement - **5.** FOOTBALL & RUGBY kick-off - **6.** [encouragement] encouragement.

engager [17] [ɑ̃gaʒe] ◇ *vt* - **1.** [lier] to commit - **2.** [embaucher] to take on, to engage - **3.** [faire entrer] : ~ **qqch dans** to insert sthg into - **4.** [commencer] to start - **5.** [impliquer] to involve - **6.** [encourager] : ~ **qqn à faire qqch** to urge sb to do sthg ◇ *vi* - **1.** FOOTBALL & RUGBY to kick off - **2.** [lier] : **cela n'engage à rien** there is no obligation.
➤ **s'engager** *vp* - **1.** [promettre] : **s'~ à qqch/à faire qqch** to commit o.s. to sthg/to doing sthg - **2.** MIL : **s'~ (dans)** to enlist (in) - **3.** [pénétrer] : **s'~ dans** to enter - **4.** *fig* [débuter] to begin - **5.** [militer] to be committed.

engeance [ɑ̃ʒɑ̃s] *nf littéraire* riffraff.

engelure [ɑ̃ʒlyr] *nf* chilblain.

engendrer [3] [ɑ̃ʒɑ̃dre] *vt* - **1.** *littéraire* to father - **2.** MATHS to generate - **3.** *fig* [produire] to cause, to give rise to ; [sentiment] to engender.

engin [ɑ̃ʒɛ̃] *nm* - **1.** [machine] machine - **2.** MIL missile - **3.** *fam péj* [objet] thing.

engineering [ɛnʒiniriŋ] *nm* engineering.

englober [3] [ɑ̃glɔbe] *vt* to include.

engloutir [32] [ɑ̃glutir] *vt* - **1.** [dévorer] to gobble up - **2.** [faire disparaître] to engulf - **3.** *fig* [dilapider] to squander.
➤ **s'engloutir** *vp* to be engulfed.

engluer [3] [ɑ̃glɥe] *vt* - **1.** [oiseau] to catch (using birdlime) - **2.** [piège] to smear with birdlime.
➤ **s'engluer** *vp* : **s'~ (de)** to get sticky (with) ; **s'~ (dans)** *fig* to become bogged down (in).

engorgement [ɑ̃gɔrʒəmɑ̃] *nm* - **1.** MÉD engorgement - **2.** *fig* [de marché] glutting, swamping.

engorger [17] [ɑ̃gɔrʒe] *vt* - **1.** [obstruer] to block, to obstruct - **2.** MÉD to engorge.
➤ **s'engorger** *vp* to become blocked.

engouement [ɑ̃gumɑ̃] *nm* - **1.** [enthousiasme] infatuation - **2.** MÉD strangulation (of hernia).

engouer [6] [ɑ̃gwe] ➤ **s'engouer** *vp* : **s'~ de** to become infatuated with.

engouffrer [3] [ɑ̃gufre] *vt fam* - **1.** [dévorer] to wolf down - **2.** [dilapider] to squander.
➤ **s'engouffrer** *vp* : **s'~ dans** to rush into.

engourdi, e [ɑ̃gurdi] *adj* numb ; *fig* dull.

engourdir [32] [ɑ̃gurdir] *vt* to numb ; *fig* to dull.
➤ **s'engourdir** *vp* to go numb.

engourdissement [ɑ̃gurdismɑ̃] *nm* - **1.** [raideur] numbness - **2.** [torpeur] torpor.

engrais [ɑ̃grɛ] *nm* fertilizer ; ~ **chimique** chemical fertilizer.

engraisser [4] [ɑ̃grese] ◇ *vt* - **1.** [animal] to fatten - **2.** [terre] to fertilize ◇ *vi* to put on weight.
➤ **s'engraisser** *vp fam fig* to grow fat.

engranger [17] [ɑ̃grɑ̃ʒe] *vt* - **1.** [foin] to bring in - **2.** *fig* [accumuler] to store up.

engrenage [ɑ̃grənaʒ] *nm* - **1.** TECHNOL gears *(pl)* - **2.** *fig* [circonstances] : **être pris dans l'~** to be caught up in the system.

engrosser [3] [ɑ̃grose] *vt fam* to get pregnant.

engueulade [ɑ̃gœlad] *nf fam* bawling out.

engueuler [5] [ɑ̃gœle] *vt fam* : ~ **qqn** to bawl sb out.
➤ **s'engueuler** *vp fam* to have a row, to have a slanging match *Br*.

enguirlander [3] [ɑ̃girlɑ̃de] *vt* - **1.** *fam* [gronder] to tell off - **2.** *littéraire* [décorer] to decorate.

enhardir [32] [ɑ̃ardir] *vt* to make bold.
➤ **s'enhardir** *vp* to pluck up one's courage.

ENI [eni] *(abr de École normale d'instituteurs) nf* training college for primary school teachers.

énième [enjɛm] *adj fam* : **la ~ fois** the nth time.

énigmatique [enigmatik] *adj* enigmatic.

énigme [enigm] *nf* - **1.** [mystère] enigma - **2.** [jeu] riddle.

enivrant, e [ɑ̃nivrɑ̃, ɑ̃t] *adj litt* & *fig* intoxicating.

enivrer [3] [ɑ̃nivre] *vt litt* to get drunk ; *fig* to intoxicate.
➤ **s'enivrer** *vp* : **s'~ (de)** to get drunk (on) ; *fig* to become intoxicated (with).

enjambée [ɑ̃ʒɑ̃be] *nf* stride ; **marcher à grandes ~s** to stride (along).

enjamber [3] [ɑ̃ʒɑ̃be] ◇ *vt* - **1.** [obstacle] to step over - **2.** [cours d'eau] to straddle ◇ *vi* [empiéter] : ~ **sur** to encroach on.

enjeu [ɑ̃ʒø] *nm* [mise] stake ; **quel est l'~ ici?** *fig* what's at stake here?

enjoignais, enjoignions *etc* ▷ enjoindre.

enjoindre [82] [ɑ̃ʒwɛ̃dr] *vt littéraire* : ~ **à qqn de faire qqch** to enjoin sb to do sthg.

enjoint [ɑ̃ʒwɛ̃] *pp inv* ▷ enjoindre.

enjôler [3] [ɑ̃ʒole] *vt* to coax.

enjôleur, euse [ɑ̃ʒolœr, øz] ◇ *adj* wheedling ◇ *nm, f* wheedler.

enjoliver [3] [ɑ̃ʒolive] *vt* to embellish.

enjoliveur [ɑ̃ʒolivœr] *nm* [de roue] hubcap ; [de calandre] badge.

enjoué, e [ɑ̃ʒwe] *adj* cheerful.

enlacer [16] [ɑ̃lase] *vt* - **1.** [prendre dans ses bras]

to embrace, to hug - **2.** [entourer] to wind round.
➤ **s'enlacer** *vp* - **1.** [s'entrelacer] to intertwine - **2.** [s'embrasser] to embrace, to hug.

enlaidir [32] [ãledir] ◇ *vt* to make ugly ◇ *vi* to become ugly.

enlevé, e [ãlve] *adj* : **(bien)** ~ spirited.

enlèvement [ãlɛvmã] *nm* - **1.** [action d'enlever] removal ; **l'~ des ordures (ménagères)** refuse collection - **2.** [rapt] abduction.

enlever [19] [ãlve] *vt* - **1.** [gén] to remove ; [vêtement] to take off - **2.** [prendre] : ~ **qqch à qqn** to take sthg away from sb - **3.** [obtenir] to win - **4.** [kidnapper] to abduct - **5.** *littéraire* [faire mourir] to carry off.
➤ **s'enlever** *vp* to be removable.

enliser [3] [ãlize] ➤ **s'enliser** *vp* - **1.** [s'embourber] to sink, to get stuck - **2.** *fig* [piétiner] : **s'~ dans qqch** to get bogged down in sthg.

enluminure [ãlyminyr] *nf* illumination.

ENM (*abr de* **École nationale de la magistrature**) *nf grande école training lawyers.*

enneigé, e [ãneʒe] *adj* snow-covered.

enneigement [ãnɛʒmã] *nm* snow cover ; **bulletin d'~** snow report.

ennemi, e [ɛnmi] ◇ *adj* enemy *(avant n)* ◇ *nm, f* enemy ; **passer à l'~** to defect ; **~ juré** sworn enemy ; **~ public** public enemy.

ennui [ãnɥi] *nm* - **1.** [lassitude] boredom - **2.** [contrariété] annoyance ; **l'~, c'est que ...** the annoying thing is that ... - **3.** [problème] trouble *(U)* ; **attirer des ~s à qqn** to cause trouble for sb ; **s'attirer des ~s** to cause trouble for o.s. ; **avoir des ~s** to have problems.

ennuyer [14] [ãnɥije] *vt* - **1.** [agacer, contrarier] to annoy ; **cela t'ennuierait de venir me chercher?** would you mind picking me up? - **2.** [lasser] to bore - **3.** [inquiéter] to bother.
➤ **s'ennuyer** *vp* - **1.** [se morfondre] to be bored - **2.** [déplorer l'absence] : **s'~ de qqn/qqch** to miss sb/sthg.

ennuyeux, euse [ãnɥijø, øz] *adj* - **1.** [lassant] boring - **2.** [contrariant] annoying.

énoncé [enɔ̃se] *nm* - **1.** [libellé] wording - **2.** LING utterance.

énoncer [16] [enɔ̃se] *vt* - **1.** [libeller] to word - **2.** [exposer] to expound ; [théorème] to set forth.

énonciation [enɔ̃sjasjɔ̃] *nf* - **1.** [libellé] wording - **2.** LING utterance.

enorgueillir [32] [ãnɔrgœjir] ➤ **s'enorgueillir** *vp* : **s'~ de qqch/de faire qqch** to pride o.s. on sthg/on doing sthg.

énorme [enɔrm] *adj* - **1.** *litt* & *fig* [immense] enormous - **2.** *fam fig* [incroyable] far-fetched.

énormément [enɔrmemã] *adv* enormously ; ~ **de** a great deal of.

énormité [enɔrmite] *nf* - **1.** [gigantisme] enormity - **2.** [absurdité] : **dire des ~s** to say the most awful things.

enquérir [39] [ãkerir] ➤ **s'enquérir** *vp sout* : **s'~ de qqn** to ask after sb ; **s'~ de qqch** to inquire about sthg.

enquête [ãkɛt] *nf* - **1.** [de police, recherches] investigation ; ~ **de routine** routine inquiry - **2.** [sondage] survey.

enquêter [4] [ãkete] *vi* - **1.** [police, chercheur] to investigate - **2.** [sonder] to conduct a survey.

enquêteur, euse, trice [ãkɛtœr, øz, tris] *nm, f* investigator.

enquiers, enquiert *etc* ▷ **enquérir**.

enquiquinant, e [ãkikinã, ãt] *adj fam* annoying.

enquis, e [ãki, iz] *pp* ▷ **enquérir**.

enraciner [3] [ãrasine] *vt* - **1.** [planter] to dig in - **2.** *fig* [idée, préjugé] to implant.
➤ **s'enraciner** *vp* - **1.** [plante, idée] to take root - **2.** [personne] to put down roots.

enragé, e [ãraʒe] ◇ *adj* - **1.** [chien] rabid, with rabies - **2.** *fig* [invétéré] keen ◇ *nm, f* : **c'est un ~ de football** he's mad about *ou* on football.

enrageant, e [ãraʒã, ãt] *adj* infuriating.

enrager [17] [ãraʒe] *vi* to be furious ; **faire** ~ **qqn** to infuriate sb.

enrayer [11] [ãreje] *vt* - **1.** [épidémie] to check, to stop - **2.** [mécanisme] to jam.
➤ **s'enrayer** *vp* [mécanisme] to jam.

enrégimenter [3] [ãreʒimãte] *vt* [dans l'armée] to enlist ; [dans un groupe] to enrol.

enregistrement [ãrəʒistrəmã] *nm* - **1.** [de son, d'images, d'informations] recording ; ~ **pirate** pirate recording - **2.** [inscription] registration - **3.** [à l'aéroport] check-in ; ~ **des bagages** baggage registration.

enregistrer [3] [ãrəʒistre] *vt* - **1.** [son, images, informations] to record - **2.** INFORM to store - **3.** [inscrire] to register - **4.** [à l'aéroport] to check in - **5.** *fam* [mémoriser] to make a mental note of.

enregistreur, euse [ãrəʒistrœr, øz] *adj* recording *(avant n)* ; **caisse enregistreuse** cash register.

enrhumé, e [ãryme] *adj* : **je suis** ~ I have a cold.

enrhumer [3] [ãryme] ➤ **s'enrhumer** *vp* to catch (a) cold.

enrichi, e [ãriʃi] *adj* - **1.** [personne] nouveau riche - **2.** [matériau] enriched - **3.** *fig* [orné] : ~ **de** enhanced by.

enrichir [32] [ɑ̃riʃir] vt - **1.** [financièrement] to make rich - **2.** [terre] fig to enrich.

s'enrichir vp - **1.** [financièrement] to grow rich - **2.** [sol] fig to become enriched.

enrichissant, e [ɑ̃riʃisɑ̃, ɑ̃t] adj enriching.

enrichissement [ɑ̃riʃismɑ̃] nm - **1.** [gén] enrichment - **2.** [financier] increased wealth.

enrobé, e [ɑ̃rɔbe] adj - **1.** [recouvert] : ~ de coated with - **2.** fam [grassouillet] plump.

enrober [3] [ɑ̃rɔbe] vt - **1.** [recouvrir] : ~ qqch de to coat sth with - **2.** fig [requête, nouvelle] to wrap up.

s'enrober vp to put on weight.

enrôlement [ɑ̃rolmɑ̃] nm enrolment Br, enrollment Am.

enrôler [3] [ɑ̃role] vt to enrol Br, to enroll Am ; MIL to enlist.

s'enrôler vp to enrol Br, to enroll Am ; MIL to enlist.

enroué, e [ɑ̃rwe] adj hoarse.

enrouer [6] [ɑ̃rwe] **s'enrouer** vp to become hoarse.

enroulement [ɑ̃rulmɑ̃] nm rolling up.

enrouler [3] [ɑ̃rule] vt to roll up ; ~ qqch autour de qqch to wind sthg round sthg.

s'enrouler vp - **1.** [entourer] : s'~ sur OU autour de qqch to wind around sthg - **2.** [se pelotonner] : s'~ dans qqch to wrap o.s. up in sthg.

enrouleur, euse [ɑ̃rulœr, øz] adj winding.

ENS (abr de École normale supérieure) nf grande école training secondary school and university teachers.

ensabler [3] [ɑ̃sable] vt to silt up.

s'ensabler vp to silt up.

ENSAD, Ensad [ɛnsad] (abr de École nationale supérieure des arts décoratifs) nf grande école for applied arts.

ENSAM, Ensam [ɛnsam] (abr de École nationale supérieure des arts et métiers) nf grande école for engineering.

enseignant, e [ɑ̃sɛɲɑ̃, ɑ̃t] <> adj teaching (avant n) <> nm, f teacher.

enseigne [ɑ̃sɛɲ] nf - **1.** [de commerce] sign ; ~ lumineuse neon sign - **2.** [drapeau, soldat] ensign - **3.** loc : être logé à la même ~ to be in the same boat.

à telle enseigne que loc conj so much so that.

enseignement [ɑ̃sɛɲmɑ̃] nm - **1.** [gén] teaching ; ~ primaire/secondaire primary/secondary education - **2.** [leçon] lesson.

enseigner [4] [ɑ̃sɛɲe] vt litt & fig to teach ; ~ qqch à qqn to teach sb sthg, to teach sthg to sb.

ensemble [ɑ̃sɑ̃bl] <> adv together ; aller ~ to

go together <> nm - **1.** [totalité] whole ; l'~ de all of ; idée d'~ general idea ; dans l'~ on the whole - **2.** [harmonie] unity - **3.** [vêtement] outfit - **4.** [série] collection - **5.** MATHS set - **6.** ARCHIT development ; grand ~ housing estate Br OU project Am - **7.** MUS ensemble.

ensemblier [ɑ̃sɑ̃blije] nm interior decorator ; CIN & TÉLÉ set designer.

ensemencer [16] [ɑ̃səmɑ̃se] vt - **1.** [terre] to sow - **2.** [rivière] to stock.

enserrer [4] [ɑ̃sere] vt [entourer] to encircle ; fig to imprison.

ENSET, Enset [ɛnsɛt] (abr de École nationale supérieure de l'enseignement technique) nf grande école training science and technology teachers.

ensevelir [32] [ɑ̃səvlir] vt litt & fig to bury.

s'ensevelir vp to bury o.s. (away).

ensoleillé, e [ɑ̃sɔleje] adj sunny.

ensoleillement [ɑ̃sɔlɛjmɑ̃] nm sunshine.

ensommeillé, e [ɑ̃sɔmeje] adj sleepy.

ensorceler [24] [ɑ̃sɔrsəle] vt to bewitch.

ensorcellement [ɑ̃sɔrsɛlmɑ̃] nm bewitching.

ensuite [ɑ̃sɥit] adv - **1.** [après, plus tard] after, afterwards, later - **2.** [puis] then, next, after that ; et ~? what then?, what next?

ensuivre [89] [ɑ̃sɥivr] **s'ensuivre** vp to follow ; il s'ensuit que it follows that ; et tout ce qui s'ensuit and all that that entails.

entaille [ɑ̃taj] nf cut.

entailler [3] [ɑ̃taje] vt to cut.

s'entailler vp : s'~ le doigt to cut one's finger.

entame [ɑ̃tam] nf first slice.

entamer [3] [ɑ̃tame] vt - **1.** [gâteau, fromage] to start (on) ; [bouteille, conserve] to start, to open - **2.** [capital] to dip into - **3.** [cuir, réputation] to damage - **4.** [courage] to shake.

entartrer [3] [ɑ̃tartre] vt to fur up.

s'entartrer vp to fur up.

entassement [ɑ̃tɑsmɑ̃] nm - **1.** [d'objets] pile ; [action] piling up - **2.** [de personnes] squeezing.

entasser [3] [ɑ̃tɑse] vt - **1.** [accumuler, multiplier] to pile up - **2.** [serrer] to squeeze.

s'entasser vp - **1.** [objets] to pile up - **2.** [personnes] : s'~ dans to squeeze into.

entendement [ɑ̃tɑ̃dmɑ̃] nm understanding ; dépasser l'~ (de qqn) to be beyond (sb's) comprehension.

entendeur [ɑ̃tɑ̃dœr] nm : à bon ~ salut! so be warned!

entendre [73] [ɑ̃tɑ̃dr] vt - **1.** [percevoir, écouter] to hear ; ~ dire que to hear (that) ; ~ parler de qqch to hear of OU about sthg ; à l'~ ... to hear him/her talk ... ; **qu'est-ce qu'il ne faut pas entendre!** *fam* give me a break! - **2.** *sout* [comprendre] to understand ; **laisser ~ que** to imply that ; **ne rien y ~ à qqch** not to know the first thing about sthg - **3.** *sout* [vouloir] : **~ faire qqch** to intend to do sthg - **4.** [vouloir dire] to mean.

◆ **s'entendre** *vp* - **1.** [sympathiser] : **s'~ avec qqn** to get on with sb - **2.** [s'accorder] to agree - **3.** [savoir] : **s'~ en qqch/à faire qqch** to be very good at sthg/at doing sthg ; **s'y ~** to know all about it - **4.** [être compris] to be understood ; **cela s'entend** that is understood - **5.** [s'écouter] : **on ne s'entend plus** we can't hear ourselves think.

entendu, e [ãtãdy] ◇ *pp* ▷ **entendre** ◇ *adj* - **1.** [compris] agreed, understood ; **entendu! right!, O.K.! - 2.** [complice] knowing.

entente [ãtãt] *nf* - **1.** [harmonie] understanding - **2.** [accord] agreement - **3.** [compréhension] : **à double ~** with a double meaning.

entériner [3] [ãterine] *vt* to ratify.

entérite [ãterit] *nf* enteritis (U).

enterrement [ãtɛrmã] *nm* burial.

enterrer [4] [ãtere] *vt litt & fig* to bury ; **~ sa vie de garçon** to have a stag party.

◆ **s'enterrer** *vp fig* to bury o.s. (away).

entêtant, e [ãtɛtã, ãt] *adj* heady.

en-tête [ãtɛt] (*pl* **en-têtes**) *nm* heading.

entêté, e [ãtete] ◇ *adj* stubborn ◇ *nm, f* stubborn person.

entêtement [ãtɛtmã] *nm* stubbornness.

entêter [4] [ãtete] ◆ **s'entêter** *vp* to persist ; **s'~ à faire qqch** to persist in doing sthg ; **s'~ dans qqch** to persist in sthg.

enthousiasme [ãtuzjasm] *nm* enthusiasm.

enthousiasmer [3] [ãtuzjasme] *vt* to fill with enthusiasm.

◆ **s'enthousiasmer** *vp* : **s'~ pour** to be enthusiastic about.

enthousiaste [ãtuzjast] ◇ *nmf* enthusiast ◇ *adj* enthusiastic.

enticher [3] [ãtiʃe] ◆ **s'enticher** *vp* : **s'~ de qqn/qqch** to become obsessed with sb/sthg.

entier, ère [ãtje, ɛr] *adj* whole, entire.

◆ **en entier** *loc adv* in its/their entirety.

entièrement [ãtjɛrmã] *adv* - **1.** [complètement] fully - **2.** [pleinement] wholly, entirely.

entité [ãtite] *nf* entity.

entomologie [ãtɔmɔlɔʒi] *nf* entomology.

entonner [3] [ãtɔne] *vt* [chant] to strike up.

entonnoir [ãtɔnwar] *nm* - **1.** [instrument] funnel - **2.** [cavité] crater.

entorse [ãtɔrs] *nf* MÉD sprain ; **se faire une ~ à**

la cheville/au poignet to sprain one's ankle/wrist ; **faire une ~ à** *fig* [loi, règlement] to bend.

entortiller [3] [ãtɔrtije] *vt* - **1.** [entrelacer] to twist - **2.** [envelopper] : **~ qqch autour de qqch** to wrap sthg round sthg - **3.** *fam fig* [personne] to sweet-talk.

entourage [ãturaʒ] *nm* - **1.** [milieu] entourage - **2.** [clôture] surround.

entouré, e [ãture] *adj* - **1.** [enclos] surrounded - **2.** [soutenu] popular.

entourer [3] [ãture] *vt* - **1.** [enclore, encercler] : **~ (de)** to surround (with) - **2.** *fig* [soutenir] to rally round.

◆ **s'entourer** *vp* : **s'~ de** to surround o.s. with.

entourloupette [ãturlupɛt] *nf fam* dirty trick.

entournure [ãturnyr] *nf* : **être gêné aux ~s** [financièrement] to feel the pinch ; [être mal à l'aise] to feel awkward.

entracte [ãtrakt] *nm* interval ; *fig* interlude.

entraide [ãtrɛd] *nf* mutual assistance.

entraider [4] [ãtrede] ◆ **s'entraider** *vp* to help each other.

entrailles [ãtraj] *nfpl* - **1.** [intestins] entrails - **2.** *sout* [profondeurs] depths - **3.** *fig* [siège des sentiments] soul *(sg)*.

entrain [ãtrɛ̃] *nm* drive.

entraînement [ãtrɛnmã] *nm* - **1.** [mécanisme] drive - **2.** [préparation] practice ; SPORT training ; **manquer d'~** to be out of training ; *fig* to be out of practice.

entraîner [4] [ãtrene] *vt* - **1.** TECHNOL to drive - **2.** [tirer] to pull - **3.** [susciter] to lead to - **4.** SPORT to coach - **5.** [emmener] to take along - **6.** [séduire] to influence ; **~ qqn à faire qqch** to talk sb into sthg.

◆ **s'entraîner** *vp* to practise ; SPORT to train ; **s'~ à faire qqch** to practise doing sthg.

entraîneur, euse [ãtrenœr, øz] *nm, f* trainer, coach.

◆ **entraîneuse** *nf* [dans un cabaret etc] hostess.

entrant, e [ãtrã, ãt] *adj* incoming.

entrapercevoir, entr'apercevoir [52] [ãtrapɛrsəvwar] *vt* to glimpse.

entrave [ãtrav] *nf* hobble ; *fig* obstruction.

entraver [3] [ãtrave] *vt* to hobble ; *fig* to hinder.

entre [ãtr] *prép* - **1.** [gén] between ; **~ nous** between you and me, between ourselves - **2.** [parmi] among ; **l'un d'~ nous ira** one of us will go ; **généralement ils restent ~ eux** they tend to keep themselves to themselves ; **ils se battent ~ eux** they're fighting among *ou* amongst themselves.

◆ **entre autres** *loc prép* : **~ autres (choses)**

among other things ; ~ **autres (personnes)** among others.

entrebâillement [ɑ̃trəbajmɑ̃] *nm* opening ; **dans l'~ de la porte** through the half-open door.

entrebâiller [3] [ɑ̃trəbaje] *vt* to open slightly.

entrechat [ɑ̃trəʃa] *nm* - **1.** *DANSE* entrechat - **2.** [saut] leap ; **faire des ~s** to leap about.

entrechoquer [3] [ɑ̃trəʃɔke] *vt* to bang together.

➥ **s'entrechoquer** *vp* to bang into each other.

entrecôte [ɑ̃trəkot] *nf* entrecôte.

entrecoupé, e [ɑ̃trəkupe] *adj* : ~ **de** interspersed with.

entrecouper [3] [ɑ̃trəkupe] *vt* to intersperse.

entrecroiser [3] [ɑ̃trəkrwaze] *vt* to interlace.

➥ **s'entrecroiser** *vp* to intersect.

entre-déchirer [3] [ɑ̃trədeʃire] ➥ **s'entre-déchirer** *vp* to tear each other to pieces.

entre-deux [ɑ̃trədø] *nm inv* gap, space ; **dans l'~** *fig* in the interim.

entre-deux-guerres [ɑ̃trədøgɛr] *nm inv* inter-war years.

entrée [ɑ̃tre] *nf* - **1.** [arrivée, accès] entry, entrance ; '~ **interdite**' 'no admittance' ; '~ **libre**' [dans un musée] 'admission free' ; [dans une boutique] 'browsers welcome' ; ~ **en scène** entrance - **2.** [porte] entrance ; ~ **des artistes** stage door ; ~ **de service** tradesmen's entrance - **3.** [vestibule] (entrance) hall - **4.** [billet] ticket - **5.** [plat] starter, first course - **6.** [début] onset ; ~ **en matière** introduction - **7.** [rubrique] entry - **8.** *INFORM* input, entry - **9.** *loc* : **d'~ de jeu** from the outset ; **avoir ses ~s chez qqn** to have sb's ear.

entrefaites [ɑ̃trəfɛt] *nfpl* : **sur ces ~** just at that moment.

entrefilet [ɑ̃trəfile] *nm* paragraph.

entregent [ɑ̃trəʒɑ̃] *nm* : **avoir de l'~** to know how to behave.

entrejambe, entre-jambes [ɑ̃trəʒɑ̃b] *nm* crotch.

entrelacer [16] [ɑ̃trəlase] *vt* to intertwine.

➥ **s'entrelacer** *vp* to intertwine.

entrelarder [3] [ɑ̃trəlarde] *vt* - **1.** *CULIN* to lard - **2.** *fam fig* [discours] : ~ **de** to lace with.

entremêler [4] [ɑ̃trəmele] *vt* to mix ; ~ **de** to mix with.

➥ **s'entremêler** *vp* to mingle.

entremets [ɑ̃trəmɛ] *nm* dessert.

entremettais, entremettions *etc* ➪ entremettre.

entremetteur, euse [ɑ̃trəmɛtœr, øz] *nm, f* mediator.

➥ **entremetteuse** *nf péj* go-between.

entremettre [84] [ɑ̃trəmɛtr] ➥ **s'entremettre** *vp* : **s'~ (dans)** to mediate (in).

entremis, e [ɑ̃trəmi, iz] *pp* ➪ entremettre.

entremise [ɑ̃trəmiz] *nf* intervention ; **par l'~ de** through.

entrepont [ɑ̃trəpɔ̃] *nm* steerage.

entreposer [3] [ɑ̃trəpoze] *vt* to store.

entrepôt [ɑ̃trəpo] *nm* warehouse.

entreprenais, entreprenions *etc* ➪ entreprendre.

entreprenant, e [ɑ̃trəprənɑ̃, ɑ̃t] *adj* enterprising ; [auprès des femmes] forward.

entreprendre [79] [ɑ̃trəprɑ̃dr] *vt* to undertake ; [commencer] to start ; ~ **de faire qqch** to undertake to do sthg ; ~ **qqn sur** to engage sb in conversation about.

entrepreneur, euse [ɑ̃trəprənœr, øz] *nm, f* - **1.** [de services & *CONSTR*] contractor - **2.** [patron] businessman (*f* businesswoman).

entreprenne, entreprennes *etc* ➪ entreprendre.

entrepris, e [ɑ̃trəpri, iz] *pp* ➪ entreprendre.

entreprise [ɑ̃trəpriz] *nf* - **1.** [travail, initiative] enterprise ; **libre ~** *ÉCON* free enterprise - **2.** [société] company ; ~ **nationalisée** nationalized industry.

entrer [3] [ɑ̃tre] ◇ *vi (aux : être)* - **1.** [pénétrer] to enter, to go/come in ; ~ **dans** [gén] to enter ; [pièce] to go/come into ; [bain, voiture] to get into ; *fig* [sujet] to go into ; ~ **dans un mur** to crash into a wall ; ~ **par** to go in *ou* enter by ; **entrez!** come in! ; **faire ~ qqn** to show sb in ; **faire ~ qqch** to bring sthg in - **2.** [faire partie] : ~ **dans** to go into, to be part of - **3.** [être admis, devenir membre] : ~ **à** [club, parti] to join ; ~ **dans** [les affaires, l'enseignement] to go into ; [la police, l'armée] to join ; ~ **en politique** to go into politics ; ~ **à l'université** to enter university ; ~ **à l'hôpital** to go into hospital - **4.** [être au début] : ~ **en** to start, to begin ◇ *vt (aux : avoir)* - **1.** [gén] to bring in - **2.** *INFORM* to enter, to input.

entresol [ɑ̃trəsɔl] *nm* mezzanine.

entre-temps [ɑ̃trətɑ̃] *adv* meanwhile.

entretenir [40] [ɑ̃trətnir] *vt* - **1.** [faire durer] to keep alive - **2.** [cultiver] to maintain - **3.** [soigner] to look after - **4.** [personne, famille] to support - **5.** [parler à] : ~ **qqn de qqch** to speak to sb about sthg.

➥ **s'entretenir** *vp* - **1.** [se parler] : **s'~ (de)** to talk (about) - **2.** [prendre soin de soi] to look after o.s.

entretenu, e [ɑ̃trətny] ◇ *pp* ▷ **entretenir** ◇ *adj* - **1.** [soigné] well-kept ; **bien/mal ~** well-/badly kept - **2.** [femme] kept *(avant n)*.

entretien [ɑ̃trətjɛ̃] *nm* - **1.** [de voiture, jardin] maintenance, upkeep - **2.** [conversation] discussion ; [colloque] debate ; **~ d'embauche** job interview.

entretiendrai, entretiendras *etc* ▷ entretenir.

entre-tuer [7] [ɑ̃trətɥe] ◆ **s'entre-tuer** *vp* to kill each other.

entreverrai, entreverras *etc* ▷ entrevoir.

entrevoir [62] [ɑ̃trəvwar] *vt* - **1.** [distinguer] to make out - **2.** [voir rapidement] to see briefly - **3.** *fig* [deviner] to glimpse.
◆ **s'entrevoir** *vp* - **1.** [se voir] to see each other briefly - **2.** [se profiler] to be visible.

entrevoyais, entrevoyions *etc* ▷ entrevoir.

entrevu, e [ɑ̃trəvy] *pp* ▷ entrevoir.

entrevue [ɑ̃trəvy] *nf* meeting.

entrouvert, e [ɑ̃truvɛr, ɛrt] ◇ *pp* ▷ entrouvrir ◇ *adj* half-open.

entrouvrir [34] [ɑ̃truvrir] *vt* to open partly.
◆ **s'entrouvrir** *vp* to open partly.

énumération [enymerasjɔ̃] *nf* enumeration.

énumérer [18] [enymere] *vt* to enumerate.

env. *(abr de* environ*)* approx.

envahir [32] [ɑ̃vair] *vt* - **1.** [gén & MIL] to invade - **2.** *fig* [suj : sommeil, doute] to overcome - **3.** *fig* [déranger] to intrude on.

envahissant, e [ɑ̃vaisɑ̃, ɑ̃t] *adj* - **1.** [herbes] invasive - **2.** [personne] intrusive.

envahissement [ɑ̃vaismɑ̃] *nm* invasion.

envahisseur [ɑ̃vaisœr] *nm* invader.

enveloppe [ɑ̃vlɔp] *nf* - **1.** [de lettre] envelope ; **mettre sous ~** to put in an envelope ; **~ à fenêtre** window envelope ; **~ timbrée** stamped addressed envelope - **2.** [d'emballage] covering - **3.** [membrane] membrane ; [de graine] husk - **4.** *fig & littéraire* [apparence] exterior.
◆ **enveloppe budgétaire** *nf* budget.

envelopper [3] [ɑ̃vlɔpe] *vt* - **1.** [emballer] to wrap (up) - **2.** [suj : brouillard] to envelop - **3.** [déguiser] to mask.
◆ **s'envelopper** *vp* : **s'~ dans** to wrap o.s. up in.

envenimer [3] [ɑ̃vnime] *vt* - **1.** [blessure] to infect - **2.** *fig* [querelle] to poison.
◆ **s'envenimer** *vp* - **1.** [s'infecter] to become

infected - **2.** *fig* [se détériorer] to become poisoned.

envergure [ɑ̃vɛrgyr] *nf* - **1.** [largeur] span ; [d'oiseau, d'avion] wingspan - **2.** *fig* [qualité] calibre - **3.** *fig* [importance] scope ; **prendre de l'~** to expand.

enverrai, enverras *etc* ▷ envoyer.

envers[1] [ɑ̃vɛr] *prép* towards *Br*, toward *Am* ; **~ et contre tous** in spite of all opposition.

envers[2] [ɑ̃vɛr] *nm* - **1.** [de tissu] wrong side ; [de feuillet etc] back ; [de médaille] reverse - **2.** [face cachée] other side ; **l'~ du décor** *fig* behind the scenes.
◆ **à l'envers** *loc adv* [vêtement] inside out ; [portrait, feuille] upside down ; *fig* the wrong way.

envi [ɑ̃vi] ◆ **à l'envi** *loc adv littéraire* trying to outdo each other.

enviable [ɑ̃vjabl] *adj* enviable.

envie [ɑ̃vi] *nf* - **1.** [désir] desire ; **avoir ~ de qqch/de faire qqch** to feel like sth/like doing sth, to want sth/to do sth ; **mourir d'~ de faire qqch** to be dying to do sth - **2.** [convoitise] envy ; **ce tailleur me fait ~** I'd love to buy that suit.

envier [9] [ɑ̃vje] *vt* to envy ; **n'avoir rien à ~ à qqn/à qqch** to have no reason to envy sb/sth.

envieux, euse [ɑ̃vjø, øz] ◇ *adj* envious ◇ *nm, f* envious person ; **faire des ~** to make other people envious.

environ [ɑ̃virɔ̃] *adv* [à peu près] about.

environnant, e [ɑ̃virɔnɑ̃, ɑ̃t] *adj* surrounding.

environnement [ɑ̃virɔnmɑ̃] *nm* environment.

environnemental, e, aux [ɑ̃virɔnmɑ̃tal, ol] *adj* environmental.

environnementaliste [ɑ̃virɔnmɑ̃talist] *nmf* environmentalist.

environner [3] [ɑ̃virɔne] *vt* to surround.

environs [ɑ̃virɔ̃] *nmpl* (surrounding) area *(sg)* ; **dans les ~ de** in the vicinity of ; **aux ~ de** [lieu] near ; [époque] round about, around.

envisager [17] [ɑ̃vizaʒe] *vt* to consider ; **~ de faire qqch** to be considering doing sth.

envoi [ɑ̃vwa] *nm* - **1.** [action] sending, dispatch ; **~ contre remboursement** cash on delivery - **2.** [colis] parcel.

envoie, envoies *etc* ▷ envoyer.

envol [ɑ̃vɔl] *nm* takeoff.

envolée [ɑ̃vɔle] *nf* - **1.** [d'oiseaux] *fig* flight - **2.** [augmentation] : **l'~ du dollar** the rapid rise in the value of the dollar.

envoler [3] [ɑ̃vɔle] ◆ **s'envoler** *vp* - **1.** [oiseau] to fly away - **2.** [avion] to take off - **3.** [disparaître] to disappear into thin air - **4.** [se disperser] to blow away.

envoûtement [ãvutmã] *nm* enchantment.

envoûter [3] [ãvute] *vt* to bewitch.

envoyé, e [ãvwaje] <> *adj* : **bien ~** well-aimed <> *nm, f* envoy ; **~ spécial** special correspondent.

envoyer [30] [ãvwaje] *vt* to send ; **~ qqch à qqn** [expédier] to send sb sthg, to send sthg to sb ; [jeter] to throw sb sthg, to throw sthg to sb ; **~ qqn faire qqch** to send sb to do sthg ; **~ chercher qqn/qqch** to send for sb/sthg ; **~ promener qqn** *fam fig* to send sb packing.

envoyeur, euse [ãvwajœr, øz] *nm, f* sender.

enzyme [ãzym] *nm ou nf* enzyme.

éolien, enne [eɔljɛ̃, ɛn] *adj* wind *(avant n)*.
éolienne *nf* windmill *(for generating power)*, wind turbine.

épagneul [epaɲœl] *nm* spaniel.

épais, aisse [epɛ, ɛs] *adj* - **1.** [large, dense] thick - **2.** [trapu] thickset - **3.** [grossier] crude.

épaisseur [epescœr] *nf* - **1.** [largeur, densité] thickness - **2.** *fig* [consistance] depth.

épaissir [32] [epesir] *vt* & *vi* to thicken.
s'épaissir *vp* - **1.** [liquide] to thicken - **2.** *fig* [mystère] to deepen.

épanchement [epãʃmã] *nm* - **1.** [effusion] outpouring - **2.** MÉD effusion ; **~ de synovie** water on the knee.

épancher [3] [epãʃe] *vt* to pour out.
s'épancher *vp* [se confier] to pour one's heart out.

épanoui, e [epanwi] *adj* - **1.** [fleur] in full bloom - **2.** [expression] radiant - **3.** [corps] fully formed ; **aux formes ~es** well-rounded.

épanouir [32] [epanwir] *vt* [personne] to make happy.
s'épanouir *vp* - **1.** [fleur] to open - **2.** [visage] to light up - **3.** [corps] to fill out - **4.** [personnalité] to blossom.

épanouissement [epanwismã] *nm* - **1.** [de fleur] blooming, opening - **2.** [de visage] brightening - **3.** [de corps] filling out - **4.** [de personnalité] flowering.

épargnant, e [eparɲã, ãt] <> *adj* thrifty <> *nm, f* saver ; **les petits ~s** small savers.

épargne [eparɲ] *nf* - **1.** [action, vertu] saving - **2.** [somme] savings *(pl)* ; **~ logement** savings account *(to buy property)*.

épargner [3] [eparɲe] *vt* - **1.** [gén] to spare ; **~ qqch à qqn** to spare sb sthg - **2.** [économiser] to save.
s'épargner *vp* to save *ou* spare o.s.

éparpiller [3] [eparpije] *vt* - **1.** [choses, personnes] to scatter - **2.** *fig* [forces] to dissipate.
s'éparpiller *vp* - **1.** [se disperser] to scatter - **2.** *fig* [perdre son temps] to lack focus.

épars, e [epar, ars] *adj sout* [objets] scattered ; [végétation, cheveux] sparse.

épatant, e [epatã, ãt] *adj fam* great.

épate [epat] *nf fam* : **faire de l'~** to show off.

épaté, e [epate] *adj* - **1.** [nez] flat - **2.** *fam* [étonné] amazed.

épater [3] [epate] *vt fam* [étonner] to amaze.

épaule [epol] *nf* shoulder ; **hausser les ~s** to shrug (one's shoulders) ; **~ d'agneau** CULIN shoulder of lamb.

épaulement [epolmã] *nm* - **1.** [mur] retaining wall - **2.** GÉOL escarpment.

épauler [3] [epole] <> *vi* to raise one's rifle <> *vt* to support, to back up.

épaulette [epolɛt] *nf* - **1.** MIL epaulet - **2.** [rembourrage] shoulder pad.

épave [epav] *nf* wreck.

épée [epe] *nf* sword ; **~ de Damoclès** sword of Damocles ; **coup d'~ dans l'eau** *fig* wasted effort.

épeler [24] [eple] *vt* to spell.

épépiner [3] [epepine] *vt* to seed.

éperdu, e [eperdy] *adj* [sentiment] passionate ; **~ de** [personne] overcome with.

éperdument [eperdymã] *adv* - **1.** [travailler] frantically - **2.** [aimer] passionately.

éperlan [eperlã] *nm* smelt.

éperon [eprɔ̃] *nm* [de cavalier, de montagne] spur ; [de navire] ram ; **~ rocheux** rocky outcrop.

éperonner [3] [eprɔne] *vt* to spur on.

épervier [epervje] *nm* sparrowhawk.

éphèbe [efɛb] *nm hum* Adonis.

éphémère [efemɛr] <> *adj* [bref] ephemeral, fleeting <> *nm* ZOOL mayfly.

éphéméride [efemerid] *nf* tear-off calendar.

épi [epi] *nm* - **1.** [de céréale] ear ; **~ de maïs** CULIN corn on the cob - **2.** [cheveux] tuft ; **~ rebelle** unruly tuft of hair.

épice [epis] *nf* spice.

épicé, e [epise] *adj* spicy.

épicéa [episea] *nm* spruce.

épicentre [episãtr] *nm* epicentre *Br*, epicenter *Am*.

épicer [16] [epise] *vt* - **1.** [plat] to spice - **2.** [récit] to spice up.

épicerie [episri] *nf* - **1.** [magasin] grocer's (shop) - **2.** [denrées] groceries *(pl)* ; **~ fine** delicatessen.

épicier, ère [episje, ɛr] *nm, f* grocer.

épicurien, enne [epikyrjɛ̃, ɛn] ◇ adj epicurean ◇ nm, f epicure.

épidémie [epidemi] nf epidemic.

épidémique [epidemik] adj contagious.

épiderme [epidɛrm] nm epidermis.

épidermique [epidɛrmik] adj [de l'épiderme] skin (avant n) ; **réaction ~** fig kneejerk reaction.

épier [9] [epje] vt - **1.** [espionner] to spy on - **2.** [observer] to look for.

épieu [epjø] nm - **1.** [de guerre] pike - **2.** [de chasse] spear.

épigramme [epigram] nf epigram.

épilation [epilasjɔ̃] nf hair removal ; **~ à la cire** waxing.

épilepsie [epilɛpsi] nf epilepsy.

épileptique [epilɛptik] nmf & adj epileptic.

épiler [3] [epile] vt [jambes] to remove hair from ; [sourcils] to pluck.

➡ **s'épiler** vp : **s'~ les jambes** to remove the hair from one's legs ; [à la cire] to wax one's legs ; **s'~ les sourcils** to pluck one's eyebrows.

épilogue [epilɔg] nm - **1.** [de roman] epilogue Br, epilog Am - **2.** [d'affaire] outcome.

épiloguer [3] [epilɔge] vi to hold forth.

épinards [epinar] nmpl spinach (U) ; **~s en branches** leaf spinach.

épine [epin] nf - **1.** [arbrisseau] thorn bush - **2.** [piquant - de rosier] thorn ; [- de hérisson] spine ; **tirer une ~ du pied à qqn** fig to get sb out of a tight corner.

➡ **épine dorsale** nf backbone, spine.

épineux, euse [epinø, øz] adj thorny.

épingle [epɛ̃gl] nf [instrument] pin ; **~ à cheveux** hairpin ; **~ à nourrice** OU **de sûreté** safety pin ; **monter qqch en ~** fig to blow sthg up ; **tirer son ~ du jeu** fig to extricate o.s. ; **tiré à quatre ~s** fig impeccably turned out.

épingler [3] [epɛ̃gle] vt - **1.** [fixer] to pin (up) - **2.** fam fig [arrêter] to nab, to nick Br.

épinière [epinjɛr] ⟶ **moelle**.

Épiphanie [epifani] nf Epiphany.

épique [epik] adj epic.

épiscopal, e, aux [episkɔpal, o] adj episcopal.

épiscopat [episkɔpa] nm episcopate.

épisiotomie [epizjɔtɔmi] nf episiotomy.

épisode [epizɔd] nm episode.

épisodique [epizɔdik] adj - **1.** [occasionnel] occasional - **2.** [secondaire] minor.

épistémologie [epistemɔlɔʒi] nf epistemology.

épistolaire [epistɔlɛr] adj - **1.** [échange] of letters ; **être en relations ~s avec qqn** to be in

(regular) correspondence with sb - **2.** [roman] epistolary.

épitaphe [epitaf] nf epitaph.

épithète [epitɛt] ◇ nf - **1.** GRAM attribute - **2.** [qualificatif] term ◇ adj attributive.

épître [epitr] nf epistle.

éploré, e [eplɔre] adj [personne] in tears ; [visage, air] tearful.

épluchage [eplyʃaʒ] nm - **1.** [de légumes] peeling - **2.** [de textes] dissection ; [de comptes] scrutiny.

épluche-légumes [eplyʃlegym] nm inv potato peeler.

éplucher [3] [eplyʃe] vt - **1.** [légumes] to peel - **2.** [textes] to dissect ; [comptes] to scrutinize.

épluchure [eplyʃyr] nf peelings (pl).

éponge [epɔ̃ʒ] nf sponge ; **jeter l'~** fig to throw in the towel ; **passer l'~** fig to wipe the slate clean.

éponger [17] [epɔ̃ʒe] vt - **1.** [liquide, déficit] to mop up - **2.** [visage] to mop, to wipe.

➡ **s'éponger** vp [personne] to mop o.s. ; **s'~ le front** to mop one's brow.

épopée [epɔpe] nf epic.

époque [epɔk] nf - **1.** [de l'année] time - **2.** [de l'histoire] period ; **à l'~** at the time ; **~ period** ; **la Belle Époque** ≃ the Edwardian era - **3.** GÉOL period, age.

épouiller [3] [epuje] vt to delouse.

époumoner [epumɔne] ➡ **s'époumoner** vp to shout o.s. hoarse.

épouse ⟶ **époux**.

épouser [3] [epuze] vt - **1.** [personne] to marry - **2.** [forme] to hug - **3.** fig [idée, principe] to espouse.

épousseter [27] [epuste] vt to dust.

époustouflant, e [epustuflɑ̃, ɑ̃t] adj fam amazing.

époustoufler [3] [epustufle] vt fam to flabbergast, to amaze.

épouvantable [epuvɑ̃tabl] adj dreadful.

épouvantail [epuvɑ̃taj] nm [à moineaux] scarecrow ; fig bogeyman.

épouvante [epuvɑ̃t] nf terror, horror ; **film d'~** horror film.

épouvanter [3] [epuvɑ̃te] vt to terrify.

époux, épouse [epu, epuz] nm, f spouse ; **prendre pour ~** to marry.

éprendre [79] [eprɑ̃dr] ➡ **s'éprendre** vp sout : **s'~ de** to fall in love with.

épreuve [eprœv] nf - **1.** [essai, examen] test ; **à l'~ du feu** fireproof ; **à l'~ des balles** bulletproof ; **mettre à l'~** to put to the test ; **à toute ~** unfailing ; **~ écrite/orale** written/oral test ; **~ de force** fig trial of strength - **2.** [malheur] ordeal - **3.** *SPORT* event - **4.** *TYPO* proof - **5.** *PHOT* print.

épris, e [epri, iz] <> *pp* ▷ **éprendre** <> *adj sout* : ~ **de** in love with.

éprouvant, e [epruvã, ãt] *adj* testing, trying.

éprouvé, e [epruve] *adj* - **1.** [méthode] tried and tested - **2.** [personne] sorely tried.

éprouver [3] [epruve] *vt* - **1.** [tester] to test - **2.** [ressentir] to feel - **3.** [faire souffrir] to distress ; **être éprouvé par** to be afflicted by - **4.** [difficultés, problèmes] to experience.

éprouvette [epruvet] *nf* - **1.** [tube à essai] test tube - **2.** [échantillon] sample.

EPS (*abr de* **éducation physique et sportive**) *nf* PE.

épuisant, e [epɥizã, ãt] *adj* exhausting.

épuisé, e [epɥize] *adj* - **1.** [personne, corps] exhausted - **2.** [marchandise] sold out, out of stock ; [livre] out of print.

épuisement [epɥizmãl] *nm* exhaustion ; **jusqu'à ~ des stocks** while stocks last.

épuiser [3] [epɥize] *vt* to exhaust.

épuisette [epɥizet] *nf* landing net.

épuration [epyrasjɔ̃] *nf* - **1.** [des eaux] purification - **2.** *POLIT* purge.

épure [epyr] *nf* technical drawing.

épurer [3] [epyre] *vt* - **1.** [eau, huile] to purify - **2.** *POLIT* to purge - **3.** *fig* [langage] to refine.

équarrir [32] [ekarir] *vt* - **1.** [animal] to cut up - **2.** [poutre] to square - **3.** *fig* [personne] : **mal équarri** rough, crude.

équateur [ekwatœr] *nm* equator.

Équateur [ekwatœr] *nm* : **l'~** Ecuador.

équation [ekwasjɔ̃] *nf* equation ; **~ du premier/second degré** simple/quadratic equation.

équatorial, e, aux [ekwatɔrjal, o] *adj* equatorial.

équatorien, enne [ekwatɔrjɛ̃, ɛn] *adj* Ecuadoran, Ecuadorian.

➥ Équatorien, enne *nm, f* Ecuadoran, Ecuadorian.

équerre [eker] *nf* [instrument] set square ; [en T] T-square ; **en ~** at right angles.

équestre [ekɛstr] *adj* equestrian.

équeuter [3] [ekøte] *vt* to remove the stalk *ou* stalks from.

équidistance [ekɥidistãs] *nf* equidistance ; **à ~ de ... et de ...** equidistant between ... and ...

équidistant, e [ekɥidistã, ãt] *adj* equidistant.

équilatéral, e, aux [ekɥilateral, o] *adj* equilateral.

équilibre [ekilibr] *nm* - **1.** [gén] balance ; **en ~** balanced ; **perdre l'~** to lose one's balance - **2.** [psychique] stability.

équilibré, e [ekilibre] *adj* - **1.** [personne] well-balanced - **2.** [vie] stable - **3.** *ARCHIT* : **aux proportions ~es** well-proportioned.

équilibrer [3] [ekilibre] *vt* to balance.

➥ s'équilibrer *vp* to balance each other out.

équilibriste [ekilibrist] *nmf* tightrope walker.

équipage [ekipaʒ] *nm* crew.

équipe [ekip] *nf* team ; **d'~** team (*avant n*) ; **faire ~ avec** to team up with ; **travailler en ~** to work together *ou* as a team ; **~ de secours** rescue team.

équipé, e [ekipe] *adj* : **cuisine ~e** fitted kitchen.

équipée [ekipe] *nf* - **1.** [aventure] venture - **2.** [promenade] outing.

équipement [ekipmã] *nm* - **1.** [matériel] equipment - **2.** [aménagement] facilities (*pl*) ; **plan d'~ national** national development plan ; **~s sportifs/scolaires** sports/educational facilities.

équiper [3] [ekipe] *vt* - **1.** [navire, armée] to equip - **2.** [personne, local] to equip, to fit out ; **~ qqn/qqch de** to equip sb/sthg with, to fit sb/sthg out with.

➥ s'équiper *vp* : **s'~ (de)** to equip o.s. (with).

équipier, ère [ekipje, ɛr] *nm, f* team member.

équitable [ekitabl] *adj* fair.

équitablement [ekitabləmãl] *adv* fairly.

équitation [ekitasjɔ̃] *nf* riding, horse-riding ; **faire de l'~** to go riding *ou* horse-riding, to ride.

équité [ekite] *nf* fairness.

équivalent, e [ekivalã, ãt] *adj* equivalent.

➥ équivalent *nm* equivalent.

équivaloir [60] [ekivalwar] *vi* : **~ à** to be equivalent to.

équivalu [ekivaly] *pp inv* ▷ **équivaloir**.

équivaut ▷ **équivaloir**.

équivoque [ekivɔk] <> *adj* - **1.** [ambigu] ambiguous - **2.** [mystérieux] dubious <> *nf* ambiguity ; **sans ~** unequivocal (*adj*), unequivocally (*adv*).

érable [erabl] *nm* maple.

érablière [erablijer] *nf* maple grove, sugar bush *Am*.

éradication [eradikasjɔ̃] *nf* - **1.** [suppression] eradication - **2.** [ablation] removal.

éradiquer [3] [eradike] *vt* to eradicate.

érafler [3] [eraflə] vt - **1.** [peau] to scratch - **2.** [mur, voiture] to scrape.
➤ **s'érafler** vp to scratch o.s.
éraflure [eraflyr] nf - **1.** [de peau] scratch - **2.** [de mur, voiture] scrape.
éraillé, e [eraje] adj [voix] hoarse.
ère [ɛr] nf era ; **l'an 813 de notre ~** the year 813 A.D.
érection [erɛksjɔ̃] nf erection ; **en ~** erect.
éreintant, e [erɛ̃tɑ̃, ɑ̃t] adj exhausting.
éreinter [3] [erɛ̃te] vt - **1.** [fatiguer] to exhaust - **2.** [critiquer] to pull to pieces.
érémiste [eremist] nmf fam = RMiste.
ergonomique [ɛrgɔnɔmik] adj ergonomic.
ergot [ɛrgo] nm - **1.** [de coq] spur ; **se dresser sur ses ~s** to get one's hackles up - **2.** [de mammifère] dewclaw - **3.** [de blé] ergot.
ergoter [3] [ɛrgɔte] vi to quibble.
ergothérapie [ɛrgɔterapi] nf occupational therapy.
ériger [17] [eriʒe] vt - **1.** [monument] to erect - **2.** [tribunal] to set up - **3.** fig [transformer] : **~ qqn en** to set sb up as.
➤ **s'ériger** vp : **s'~ en** to set o.s. up as.
ermite [ɛrmit] nm hermit.
éroder [3] [erɔde] vt to erode.
érogène [erɔʒɛn] adj erogenous.
érosion [erozjɔ̃] nf erosion.
érotique [erɔtik] adj erotic.
érotisme [erɔtism] nm eroticism.
errance [erɑ̃s] nf wandering.
errant, e [ɛrɑ̃, ɑ̃t] adj [chien, chat] stray (avant n).
erratum [eratɔm] (pl **errata** [erata]) nm erratum.
errements [ɛrmɑ̃] nmpl bad habits.
errer [4] [ɛre] vi to wander.
erreur [erœr] nf mistake ; **par ~** by mistake ; **sauf ~ de ma part** unless I'm mistaken ; **faire ~** to be mistaken ; **faire une ~** to make a mistake ; **~ judiciaire** miscarriage of justice.
erroné, e [erɔne] adj sout wrong.
ersatz [ɛrzats] nm inv ersatz.
éructer [3] [erykte] vi to belch.
érudit, e [erydi, it] ◇ adj erudite, learned ◇ nm, f learned person.
érudition [erydisjɔ̃] nf learning, erudition.
éruption [erypsjɔ̃] nf - **1.** MÉD rash - **2.** [de volcan] eruption.
es ⮕ **être**.
ès [ɛs] prép of (in certain titles) ; **docteur ~ lettres** ≈ PhD, doctor of philosophy.
E/S (abr de **entrée/sortie**) I/O.

ESA, Esa [ɛza] (abr de European Space Agency) nf ESA.
esbroufe [ɛzbruf] nf fam showing-off ; **faire de l'~** to show off.
escabeau, x [ɛskabo] nm - **1.** [échelle] stepladder - **2.** vieilli [tabouret] stool.
escadre [ɛskadr] nf - **1.** [navires] fleet - **2.** [avions] wing.
escadrille [ɛskadrij] nf - **1.** [navires] flotilla - **2.** [avions] flight.
escadron [ɛskadrɔ̃] nm squadron.
escalade [ɛskalad] nf - **1.** [de montagne, grille] climbing - **2.** [des prix, de violence] escalation.
escalader [3] [ɛskalade] vt to climb.
escale [ɛskal] nf - **1.** [lieu - pour navire] port of call ; [- pour avion] stopover - **2.** [arrêt - de navire] call ; [- d'avion] stopover, stop ; **~ technique** refuelling stop ; **faire ~ à** [navire] to put in at, to call at ; [avion] to stop over at.
escalier [ɛskalje] nm stairs (pl) ; **descendre/monter l'~** to go downstairs/upstairs ; **~ en colimaçon** spiral staircase ; **~ de secours** fire escape ; **~ de service** backstairs ; **~ roulant** OU **mécanique** escalator.
escalope [ɛskalɔp] nf escalope ; **~ panée** escalope in breadcrumbs.
escamotable [ɛskamɔtabl] adj - **1.** [train d'atterrissage] retractable ; [antenne] telescopic - **2.** [table] folding.
escamoter [3] [ɛskamɔte] vt - **1.** [faire disparaître] to make disappear - **2.** [voler] to lift - **3.** [rentrer] to retract - **4.** [phrase, mot] to swallow - **5.** [éluder - question] to evade ; [- objection] to get round.
escampette [ɛskɑ̃pɛt] ⮕ **poudre**.
escapade [ɛskapad] nf - **1.** [voyage] outing - **2.** [fugue] escapade.
escarbille [ɛskarbij] nf cinder.
escargot [ɛskargo] nm snail ; **comme un ~** [très lentement] at a snail's pace.
escarmouche [ɛskarmuʃ] nf skirmish.
escarpé, e [ɛskarpe] adj steep.
escarpement [ɛskarpəmɑ̃] nm - **1.** [de pente] steep slope - **2.** GÉOGR escarpment.
escarpin [ɛskarpɛ̃] nm court shoe Br, pump Am.
escarre [ɛskar] nf bedsore, pressure sore.
Escaut [ɛsko] nm : **l'~** the River Scheldt.
escient [esjɑ̃] nm : **à bon ~** advisedly ; **à mauvais ~** ill-advisedly.
esclaffer [3] [ɛsklafe] ➤ **s'esclaffer** vp to burst out laughing.
esclandre [ɛsklɑ̃dr] nm sout scene ; **faire un ~** to make a scene.
esclavage [ɛsklavaʒ] nm slavery.

esclavagisme [ɛsklavaʒism] *nm* slavery.

esclave [ɛsklav] ◇ *nmf* slave ◇ *adj* : **être ~ de** to be a slave to.

escogriffe [ɛskɔgrif] *nm fam* : **un grand ~** a beanpole.

escompte [ɛskɔ̃t] *nm* discount.

escompter [3] [ɛskɔ̃te] *vt* - **1.** [prévoir] to count on - **2.** FIN to discount.

escorte [ɛskɔrt] *nf* escort.

escorter [3] [ɛskɔrte] *vt* to escort.

escouade [ɛskwad] *nf* squad.

escrime [ɛskrim] *nf* fencing.

escrimer [3] [ɛskrime] ◆ **s'escrimer** *vp* : **s'~ à faire qqch** to work (away) at doing sthg.

escroc [ɛskro] *nm* swindler.

escroquer [3] [ɛskrɔke] *vt* to swindle ; **~ qqch à qqn** to swindle sb out of sthg.

escroquerie [ɛskrɔkri] *nf* swindle, swindling *(U)*.

eskimo, Eskimo ▷ esquimau.

ésotérique [ezɔterik] *adj* esoteric.

espace [ɛspas] *nm* space ; **~ publicitaire** advertising space ; **~ vert** green space, green area ; **~ vital** living space.

espacement [ɛspasmɑ̃] *nm* - **1.** [spatial] spacing - **2.** [temporel] spacing out.

espacer [16] [ɛspase] *vt* - **1.** [dans l'espace] to space out - **2.** [dans le temps - visites] to space out ; [- paiements] to spread out.
◆ **s'espacer** *vp* to become less frequent.

espadon [ɛspadɔ̃] *nm* - **1.** [poisson] swordfish - **2.** [épée] two-handed sword.

espadrille [ɛspadrij] *nf* espadrille.

Espagne [ɛspaɲ] *nf* : **l'~** Spain.

espagnol, e [ɛspaɲɔl] *adj* Spanish.
◆ **espagnol** *nm* [langue] Spanish.
◆ **Espagnol, e** *nm, f* Spaniard ; **les Espagnols** the Spanish.

espagnolette [ɛspaɲɔlɛt] *nf* latch *(for window or shutter)*.

espalier [ɛspalje] *nm* - **1.** [arbre] espalier - **2.** SPORT wall bars *(pl)*.

espèce [ɛspɛs] *nf* - **1.** BIOL, BOT & ZOOL species - **2.** [sorte] kind, sort ; **~ d'idiot!** you stupid fool! - **3.** [circonstance] : **en l'~** *littéraire* in the case in point.
◆ **espèces** *nfpl* cash ; **payer en ~s** to pay (in) cash.

espérance [ɛsperɑ̃s] *nf* hope ; **~ de vie** life expectancy.

espéranto [ɛsperɑ̃to] *nm* Esperanto.

espérer [18] [ɛspere] ◇ *vt* to hope for ; **~ que** to hope (that) ; **~ faire qqch** to hope to do

sthg ◇ *vi* to hope ; **~ en qqn/qqch** to trust in sb/sthg.

espiègle [ɛspjɛgl] ◇ *nmf* little rascal ◇ *adj* mischievous.

espièglerie [ɛspjɛgləri] *nf* - **1.** [malice] mischievousness - **2.** [tour, farce] prank.

espion, onne [ɛspjɔ̃, ɔn] *nm, f* spy.

espionnage [ɛspjɔnaʒ] *nm* spying ; **~ industriel** industrial espionage.

espionner [3] [ɛspjɔne] *vt* to spy on.

esplanade [ɛsplanad] *nf* esplanade.

espoir [ɛspwar] *nm* hope ; **avoir bon ~ que** to be confident that ; **nourrir l'~ de faire qqch** to live in hope of doing sthg ; **sans ~** hopeless ; **sans ~ de** without hope of.

esprit [ɛspri] *nm* - **1.** [entendement, personne, pensée] mind ; **avoir l'~ mal tourné** to have a dirty *ou* filthy mind ; **être large d'~** to be broad-minded ; **ouvrir l'~ de qqn** to open sb's eyes ; **reprendre ses ~s** to recover ; **venir à l'~ de qqn** to cross sb's mind - **2.** [attitude] spirit ; **~ de caste** class consciousness ; **~ de compétition** competitive spirit ; **~ de contradiction** argumentative nature, contrariness ; **~ critique** critical acumen ; **~ d'équipe** team spirit ; **~ maison** company spirit - **3.** [humour] wit ; **faire de l'~** to try to be funny - **4.** [fantôme] spirit, ghost.

esquif [ɛskif] *nm littéraire* skiff.

esquimau, aude, aux, eskimo [ɛskimo, od] *adj* Eskimo.
◆ **esquimau, eskimo** *nm* [langue] Eskimo.
◆ **Esquimau** *nm, f*, **Eskimo** *nmf* Eskimo *(beware : the term 'Esquimau', like its English equivalent, is often considered offensive in North America. The term 'Inuit' is preferred)*.

Esquimau®, x [ɛskimo] *nm inv* : **~ (glacé)** ice cream on a stick.

esquinter [3] [ɛskɛ̃te] *vt fam* - **1.** [abîmer] to ruin - **2.** [critiquer] to slate *Br*, to pan.
◆ **s'esquinter** *vp* : **s'~ à faire qqch** to kill o.s. doing sthg.

esquisse [ɛskis] *nf* [croquis] sketch ; *fig* [de projet] outline ; *fig* [de geste, sourire] trace.

esquisser [3] [ɛskise] *vt* to sketch ; **~ un sourire** *fig* to give a half-smile.
◆ **s'esquisser** *vp* to take shape.

esquiver [3] [ɛskive] *vt* to dodge.
◆ **s'esquiver** *vp* to slip away.

essai [ɛsɛ] *nm* - **1.** [vérification] test, testing *(U)* ; **à l'~** on trial - **2.** [tentative] attempt - **3.** [étude] **~ (sur)** essay (on) - **4.** RUGBY try.

essaie, essaies *etc* ▷ essayer.

essaim [ɛsɛ̃] *nm litt & fig* swarm.

essaimer [4] [eseme] *vi* to swarm ; *fig* to spread.

essayage [esɛjaʒ] *nm* fitting.

essayer [11] [eseje] *vt* - **1.** to try ; **~ de faire qqch** to try to do sthg ; **essaie un peu, pour voir! **go on then, why don't you try?

➤ **s'essayer** *vp* : **s'~ à qqch/à faire qqch** to try one's hand at sthg/at doing sthg.

ESSEC, Essec [esɛk] (*abr de* École supérieure des sciences économiques et commerciales) *nf grande école for management and business studies.*

essence [esɑ̃s] *nf* - **1.** [fondement, de plante] essence ; **par ~ sout** in essence - **2.** [carburant] petrol *Br*, gas *Am* ; **prendre de l'~** to get some petrol - **3.** [d'arbre] species.

essentiel, elle [esɑ̃sjɛl] *adj* - **1.** [indispensable] essential - **2.** [fondamental] basic.

➤ **essentiel** *nm* - **1.** [point] : **l'~** [le principal] the essential *ou* main thing ; [objets] the essentials *(pl)* ; **l'~ est que** (*+ subjonctif*) the essential *ou* main thing is that - **2.** [quantité] : **l'~ de** the main *ou* greater part of.

essentiellement [esɑ̃sjɛlmɑ̃] *adv* - **1.** [avant tout] above all - **2.** [par essence] essentially.

esseulé, e [esœle] *adj littéraire* forsaken.

essieu, x [esjø] *nm* axle.

essor [esɔr] *nm* flight, expansion, boom ; **en plein ~** booming ; **prendre son ~** to take flight ; *fig* to take off.

essorage [esɔraʒ] *nm* [manuel, à rouleaux] wringing (out) ; [à la machine] spin-drying.

essorer [3] [esɔre] *vt* [à la main, à rouleaux] to wring out ; [à la machine] to spin-dry ; [salade] to spin, to dry.

essoreuse [esɔrøz] *nf* [à rouleaux] mangle ; [électrique] spin-dryer ; [à salade] salad spinner.

essouffler [3] [esufle] *vt* to make breathless.

➤ **s'essouffler** *vp* to be breathless *ou* out of breath ; *fig* to run out of steam.

essuie, essuies *etc* ▷ **essuyer.**

essuie-glace [esɥiglas] (*pl* essuie-glaces) *nm* windscreen wiper *Br*, windshield wiper *Am*.

essuie-mains [esɥimɛ̃] *nm inv* hand towel.

essuie-tout [esɥitu] *nm inv* kitchen roll.

essuyer [14] [esɥije] *vt* - **1.** [sécher] to dry - **2.** [nettoyer] to wipe - **3.** *fig* [subir] to suffer.

➤ **s'essuyer** *vp* to dry o.s.

est¹ [ɛst] ◇ *nm* east ; **un vent d'~** an easterly wind ; **le vent d'~** the east wind ; **à l'~** in the east ; **à l'~ (de)** to the east (of) ◇ *adj inv* [gén] east ; [province, région] eastern.

est² [ɛ] ▷ **être.**

establishment [establiʃmɛnt] *nm* : **l'~** the Establishment.

estafette [estafɛt] *nf* dispatch-rider ; *MIL* liaison officer.

estafilade [estafilad] *nf* slash, gash.

est-allemand, e [estalmɑ̃, ɑ̃d] *adj* East German.

estaminet [estaminɛ] *nm* ≃ inn.

estampe [estɑ̃p] *nf* print.

estamper [3] [estɑ̃pe] *vt* - **1.** [monnaie] to mint - **2.** *fam* [escroquer] to fleece.

estampille [estɑ̃pij] *nf* stamp.

est-ce que [ɛskə] *adv interr* : **est-ce qu'il fait beau?** is the weather good? ; **~ vous aimez l'accordéon?** do you like the accordion? ; **où ~ tu es?** where are you?

esthète [ɛstɛt] ◇ *nmf* aesthete.

esthéticien, enne [estetisjɛ̃, ɛn] *nm, f* - **1.** [spécialiste] beautician - **2.** *PHILO* aesthetician.

esthétique [estetik] ◇ *nf* : **l'~** aesthetics (U) ◇ *adj* - **1.** [relatif à la beauté] aesthetic - **2.** [harmonieux] attractive.

estimable [estimabl] *adj* - **1.** [digne d'estime] honorable, respected - **2.** [évaluable] : **facilement/difficilement ~** easy/difficult to estimate.

estimatif, ive [estimatif, iv] *adj* estimated.

estimation [estimasjɔ̃] *nf* estimate, estimation.

estime [estim] *nf* respect, esteem ; **avoir de l'~ pour qqn** to respect sb.

estimer [3] [estime] *vt* - **1.** [expertiser] to value - **2.** [évaluer] to estimate ; **j'estime la durée du voyage à 2 heures** I reckon the journey time is 2 hours - **3.** [respecter] to respect - **4.** [penser] : **~ que** to feel (that).

➤ **s'estimer** *vp* to consider o.s.

estival, e, aux [estival, o] *adj* summer (avant n).

estivant, e [estivɑ̃, ɑ̃t] *nm, f* (summer) holiday-maker *Br ou* vacationer *Am*.

estocade [estɔkad] *nf* death blow.

estomac [estɔma] *nm* - **1.** *ANAT* stomach ; **avoir l'~ barbouillé** to feel sick ; **avoir un ~ d'autruche** *fig* to have a cast-iron digestion ; **avoir l'~ dans les talons** *fig* to be starving - **2.** [culot, cran] nerve.

estomaquer [3] [estɔmake] *vt fam* to stagger.

estomper [3] [estɔ̃pe] *vt* to blur ; *fig* [douleur] to lessen.

➤ **s'estomper** *vp* to become blurred ; *fig* [douleur] to lessen.

Estonie [ɛstɔni] nf : l'~ Estonia.
estonien, enne [ɛstɔnjɛ̃, ɛn] adj Estonian.
◆ **estonien** nm [langue] Estonian.
◆ **Estonien, enne** nm, f Estonian.
estrade [ɛstrad] nf dais.
estragon [ɛstragɔ̃] nm tarragon.
estropié, e [ɛstrɔpje] <> adj crippled
<> nm, f cripple.
estropier [9] [ɛstrɔpje] vt [personne] to cripple ; fig [nom, mot] to mispronounce.
◆ **s'estropier** vp to cripple o.s.
estuaire [ɛstyɛr] nm estuary.
estudiantin, e [ɛstydjɑ̃tɛ̃, in] adj student
(avant n).
esturgeon [ɛstyrʒɔ̃] nm sturgeon.
et [e] conj - **1.** [gén] and ; ~ **moi?** what about
me? - **2.** [dans les fractions et les nombres composés] :
vingt ~ un twenty-one ; **il y a deux ans ~ demi**
two and a half years ago ; **à deux heures**
~ demie at half past two.
ét. (abr de **étage**) fl.
ETA (abr de **Euskadi ta Askatasuna**) nf ETA.
étable [etabl] nf cowshed.
établi [etabli] nm workbench.
établir [32] [etablir] vt - **1.** [gén] to establish ;
[record] to set - **2.** [dresser] to draw up.
◆ **s'établir** vp - **1.** [s'installer] to settle - **2.** [créer
son entreprise] to set o.s. up - **3.** [s'instaurer] to become established.
établissement [etablismɑ̃] nm establishment ; ~ **hospitalier** hospital ; ~ **public** public body ; ~ **scolaire** educational establishment.
étage [etaʒ] nm - **1.** [de bâtiment] floor, storey
Br, story Am ; **à l'~** upstairs ; **un immeuble à**
quatre ~s a four-storey Br ou four-story Am
block of flats ; **au premier ~** on the first floor
Br, on the second floor Am - **2.** [de fusée] stage
- **3.** [de terrain, placard] level - **4.** [condition] : **de**
bas ~ second-rate.
étager [17] [etaʒe] vt to arrange in tiers.
◆ **s'étager** vp to be terraced.
étagère [etaʒɛr] nf - **1.** [rayon] shelf - **2.** [meuble]
shelves (pl), set of shelves.
étain [etɛ̃] nm - **1.** [métal] tin ; [alliage] pewter
- **2.** [objet] piece of pewter.
étais, était etc ▷ être.
étal [etal] (pl s ou **étaux** [eto]) nm - **1.** [éventaire]
stall - **2.** [de boucher] butcher's block.
étalage [etalaʒ] nm - **1.** [action, ensemble d'objets]
display ; **faire ~ de** fig to flaunt - **2.** [devanture]
window display.
étalagiste [etalaʒist] nmf - **1.** [décorateur]
window-dresser - **2.** [vendeur] stall-holder.

étalement [etalmɑ̃] nm - **1.** [dans l'espace]
spreading out - **2.** [dans le temps] staggering.
étaler [3] [etale] vt - **1.** [exposer] to display
- **2.** [étendre] to spread out - **3.** [dans le temps] to
stagger - **4.** [mettre une couche de] to spread
- **5.** [exhiber] to parade.
◆ **s'étaler** vp - **1.** [s'étendre] to spread - **2.** [dans
le temps] : **s'~ (sur)** to be spread (over) - **3.** fam
[s'avachir] to sprawl - **4.** fam [tomber] to come a
cropper Br, to fall flat on one's face.
étalon [etalɔ̃] nm - **1.** [cheval] stallion - **2.** [mesu-
re] standard ; **~-or** gold standard.
étalonner [3] [etalɔne] vt [graduer] to calibrate.
étamine [etamin] nf - **1.** [de fleur] stamen
- **2.** [tissu] muslin.
étanche [etɑ̃ʃ] adj watertight ; [montre]
waterproof.
étanchéité [etɑ̃ʃeite] nf watertightness.
étancher [3] [etɑ̃ʃe] vt - **1.** [sang, larmes] to
stem (the flow of) - **2.** [rendre étanche] to make
watertight - **3.** [assouvir] to quench.
étang [etɑ̃] nm pond.
étant ppr ▷ être.
étape [etap] nf - **1.** [gén] stage ; **brûler les ~s** fig
to race ahead - **2.** [halte] stop ; **faire ~ à** to
break one's journey at.
état [eta] nm - **1.** [manière d'être] state ; **être en**
~/hors d'~ de faire qqch to be in a/in no fit
state to do sthg ; **en bon/mauvais ~** in good/
poor condition ; **en ~ d'ivresse** under the
influence of alcohol ; **en ~ de marche** in
working order ; **laisser les choses en l'~** to
leave things as they stand ; **remettre en ~** to
repair ; **~ d'âme** mood ; **~ d'esprit** state of
mind ; **~ de santé** (state of) health ; **être dans**
un ~ second to be in a daze ; **~ de siège** state
of siege ; **~ stationnaire** stable condition ;
~ d'urgence state of emergency ; **être dans**
tous ses ~s fig to be in a state - **2.** [métier, statut]
status ; **de son ~** by profession ; **~ civil** ADMIN
≃ marital status - **3.** [inventaire - gén] inventory ; [- de dépenses] statement ; **faire ~ de**
qqch to give an account of sthg ; **~ des lieux**
inventory and inspection of rented property.
◆ **État** nm [nation] state ; **l'État** the State ; **État**
membre member state ; **les États du Golfe**
the Gulf States.
◆ **en tout état de cause** loc adv in any
case.
étatique [etatik] adj state (avant n).
étatiser [3] [etatize] vt to bring under state
control.
étatisme [etatism] nm state control.
état-major [etamaʒɔr] (pl **états-majors**) nm

- 1. ADMIN & MIL staff ; [de parti] leadership **- 2.** [lieu] headquarters *(pl)*.

États-Unis [etazyni] *nmpl* : **les ~ (d'Amérique)** the United States (of America) ; **aux ~** in the United States.

étau, x [eto] *nm* vice.

étayer [11] [eteje] *vt* to prop up ; *fig* to back up.

etc. (*abr de* et cætera) etc.

été [ete] ◇ *pp inv* ▷ **être** ◇ *nm* summer ; **en ~** in (the) summer ; **~ indien** Indian summer.

éteignais, éteignions *etc* ▷ **éteindre**.

éteindre [81] [etɛ̃dr] *vt* **- 1.** [incendie, bougie, cigarette] to put out ; [radio, chauffage, lampe] to turn off, to switch off **- 2.** [soif] to quench **- 3.** JUR [annuler] to extinguish.

◆ **s'éteindre** *vp* **- 1.** [feu, lampe] to go out **- 2.** [bruit, souvenir] to fade (away) **- 3.** *fig & littéraire* [personne] to pass away **- 4.** [race] to die out.

éteint, e [etɛ̃, ɛ̃t] ◇ *pp* ▷ **éteindre** ◇ *adj* **- 1.** [couleur] faded **- 2.** [voix] faint ; [regard] dull.

étendage [etɑ̃daʒ] *nm* hanging out.

étendard [etɑ̃dar] *nm* standard.

étendre [73] [etɑ̃dr] *vt* **- 1.** [déployer] to stretch ; [journal, linge] to spread (out) **- 2.** [coucher] to lay **- 3.** [appliquer] to spread **- 4.** [accroître] to extend **- 5.** *fam fig* [candidat] to fail **- 6.** [diluer] to dilute ; [sauce] to thin.

◆ **s'étendre** *vp* **- 1.** [se coucher] to lie down **- 2.** [s'étaler au loin] : **s'~ (de/jusqu'à)** to stretch (from/as far as) **- 3.** [croître] to spread **- 4.** [s'attarder] : **s'~ sur** to elaborate on.

étendu, e [etɑ̃dy] ◇ *pp* ▷ **étendre** ◇ *adj* **- 1.** [bras, main] outstretched **- 2.** [plaine, connaissances] extensive.

◆ **étendue** *nf* **- 1.** [surface] area, expanse **- 2.** [durée] length **- 3.** [importance] extent **- 4.** MUS range.

éternel, elle [etɛrnɛl] *adj* eternal ; **ce ne sera pas ~** this won't last for ever.

◆ **Éternel** *nm* : **l'Éternel** the Eternal.

éternellement [etɛrnɛlmɑ̃] *adv* eternally.

éterniser [3] [etɛrnize] *vt* [prolonger] to drag out.

◆ **s'éterniser** *vp* **- 1.** [se prolonger] to drag out **- 2.** *fam* [rester] to stay for ever.

éternité [etɛrnite] *nf* eternity ; **il y a une ~ que je ne t'ai pas vu** I haven't seen you for ages.

éternuement [etɛrnymɑ̃] *nm* sneeze.

éternuer [7] [etɛrnɥe] *vi* to sneeze.

êtes ▷ **être**.

étêter [4] [etete] *vt* to cut the head off.

éther [etɛr] *nm* ether.

éthéré, e [etere] *adj* ethereal.

Éthiopie [etjɔpi] *nf* : **l'~** Ethiopia.

éthiopien, enne [etjɔpjɛ̃, ɛn] *adj* Ethiopian.

◆ **Éthiopien, enne** *nm, f* Ethiopian.

éthique [etik] ◇ *nf* ethics (U or pl) ◇ *adj* ethical.

ethnie [ɛtni] *nf* ethnic group.

ethnique [ɛtnik] *adj* ethnic.

ethnographie [ɛtnɔgrafi] *nf* ethnography.

ethnologie [ɛtnɔlɔʒi] *nf* ethnology.

ethnologue [ɛtnɔlɔg] *nmf* ethnologist.

éthologie [etolɔʒi] *nf* ethology.

éthylique [etilik] ◇ *nmf* alcoholic ◇ *adj* alcoholic ; **alcool ~** ethyl alcohol, ethanol.

éthylisme [etilism] *nm* alcoholism.

étiez, étions *etc* ▷ **être**.

étincelant, e [etɛ̃slɑ̃, ɑ̃t] *adj* sparkling.

étinceler [24] [etɛ̃sle] *vi* to sparkle.

étincelle [etɛ̃sɛl] *nf* spark.

étioler [3] [etjɔle] ◆ **s'étioler** *vp* [plante] to wilt ; [personne] to weaken ; [mémoire] to go.

étique [etik] *adj littéraire* [plante] stunted ; [personne] skinny.

étiqueter [27] [etikte] *vt litt & fig* to label.

étiquette [etikɛt] *nf* **- 1.** [marque] *fig* label **- 2.** [protocole] etiquette.

étirer [3] [etire] *vt* to stretch.

◆ **s'étirer** *vp* to stretch.

Etna [etna] *nm* : **l'~** Mount Etna.

étoffe [etɔf] *nf* fabric, material ; **avoir l'~ de** *fig* to have the makings of.

étoffer [3] [etɔfe] *vt* to flesh out.

◆ **s'étoffer** *vp* to fill out.

étoile [etwal] *nf* star ; **l'~ du berger** the evening star ; **~ filante** shooting star ; **un trois ~s** a three-star hotel ; **à la belle ~** *fig* under the stars ; **être né sous une bonne ~** *fig* to be born under a lucky star.

◆ **étoile de mer** *nf* starfish.

étoilé, e [etwale] *adj* **- 1.** [ciel, nuit] starry ; **la bannière ~e** the Star-Spangled Banner **- 2.** [vitre, pare-brise] shattered.

étole [etɔl] *nf* stole.

étonnamment [etɔnamɑ̃] *adv* surprisingly, astonishingly.

étonnant, e [etɔnɑ̃, ɑ̃t] *adj* astonishing.

étonné, e [etɔne] *adj* surprised, astonished.

étonnement [etɔnmɑ̃] *nm* astonishment, surprise ; **au grand ~ de** to the great astonishment of.

étonner [3] [etɔne] *vt* to surprise, to astonish ; **ça m'étonnerait!** I'd be (very) surprised!

⬥ **s'étonner** *vp* : **s'~ (de)** to be surprised (by) ; **s'~ que** (+ *subjonctif*) to be surprised (that).

étouffant, e [etufɑ̃, ɑ̃t] *adj* stifling.

étouffée [etufe] ⬥ **à l'étouffée** *loc adv* steamed ; [viande] braised ; **faire cuire à l'~** to steam ; [viande] to braise.

étouffement [etufmɑ̃] *nm* - **1.** [asphyxie] suffocation - **2.** [répression] suppression.

étouffer [3] [etufe] ⬥ *vt* - **1.** [gén] to stifle - **2.** [asphyxier] to suffocate - **3.** [feu] to smother - **4.** [scandale, révolte] to suppress ⬥ *vi* to suffocate.

⬥ **s'étouffer** *vp* - **1.** [s'étrangler] to choke - **2.** *fig* [se presser, s'écraser] to stifle.

étouffoir [etufwar] *nm fam* oven.

étourderie [eturdəri] *nf* - **1.** [distraction] thoughtlessness - **2.** [bévue] careless mistake ; [acte irréfléchi] thoughtless act.

étourdi, e [eturdi] ⬥ *adj* scatterbrained ⬥ *nm, f* scatterbrain.

étourdiment [eturdimɑ̃] *adv* without thinking.

étourdir [32] [eturdir] *vt* - **1.** [assommer] to daze - **2.** [fatiguer] to wear out.

⬥ **s'étourdir** *vp* to be *ou* become dazed ; **s'~ de** to get drunk on.

étourdissant, e [eturdisɑ̃, ɑ̃t] *adj* - **1.** [fatigant] wearing - **2.** [sensationnel] stunning.

étourdissement [eturdismɑ̃] *nm* dizzy spell.

étourneau, x [eturno] *nm* starling.

étrange [etrɑ̃ʒ] *adj* strange.

étrangement [etrɑ̃ʒmɑ̃] *adv* strangely.

étranger, ère [etrɑ̃ʒe, ɛr] ⬥ *adj* - **1.** [gén] foreign - **2.** [différent, isolé] unknown, unfamiliar ; **être ~ à qqn** to be unknown to sb ; **être ~ à qqch** to have no connection with sthg ; **se sentir ~** to feel like an outsider ⬥ *nm, f* - **1.** [de nationalité différente] foreigner - **2.** [inconnu] stranger - **3.** [exclu] outsider.

⬥ **étranger** *nm* : **l'~** foreign countries (*pl*) ; **à l'~** abroad.

étrangeté [etrɑ̃ʒte] *nf* strangeness.

étranglement [etrɑ̃gləmɑ̃] *nm* - **1.** [strangulation] strangulation - **2.** [rétrécissement] constriction.

étrangler [3] [etrɑ̃gle] *vt* - **1.** [gén] to choke - **2.** [strangler] to strangle - **3.** [réprimer] to stifle - **4.** [serrer] to constrict.

⬥ **s'étrangler** *vp* - **1.** [s'étouffer] to choke - **2.** [sanglots] to catch.

étrave [etrav] *nf* stem.

être [2] [ɛtr] ⬥ *nm* being ; **les ~s vivants/ humains** living/human beings. ⬥ *v aux* - **1.** [pour les temps composés] to have/to be ; **il est parti hier** he left yesterday ; **il est déjà arrivé** he has already arrived ; **il est né en 1952** he was born in 1952 - **2.** [pour le passif] to be ; **la maison a été vendue** the house has been *ou* was sold ⬥ *v attr* - **1.** [état] to be ; **il est grand/ heureux** he's tall/happy ; **la maison est blanche** the house is white ; **il est médecin** he's a doctor ; **sois sage!** be good! - **2.** [possession] : **~ à qqn** to be sb's, to belong to sb ; **c'est à vous, cette voiture?** is this your car?, is this car yours? ; **cette maison est à lui/eux** this house is his/theirs, this is his/their house ⬥ *v impers* - **1.** [exprimant le temps] : **quelle heure est-il?** what time is it?, what's the time? ; **il est dix heures dix** it's ten past ten *Br*, it's ten after ten *Am* - **2.** [suivi d'un adjectif] : **il est ...** it is ... ; **il est inutile de** it's useless to ; **il serait bon de/que** it would be good to/if, it would be a good idea to/if ⬥ *vi* - **1.** [exister] to be ; **n'~ plus** *sout* [être décédé] to be no more - **2.** [indique une situation, un état] to be ; **il est à Paris** he's in Paris ; **nous sommes au printemps/en été** it's spring/summer - **3.** [indiquant une origine] : **il est de Paris** he's from Paris.

⬥ **être à** *v + prép* - **1.** [indiquant une obligation] : **c'est à vérifier** it needs to be checked ; **cette chemise est à laver** this shirt needs washing ; **c'est à voir** that remains to be seen - **2.** [indiquant une continuité] : **il est toujours à ne rien faire** he never does a thing ; **il est toujours à s'inquiéter** he's always worrying.

étreindre [81] [etrɛ̃dr] *vt* - **1.** [embrasser] to hug, to embrace - **2.** *fig* [tenailler] to grip, to clutch.

⬥ **s'étreindre** *vp* to embrace each other.

étreinte [etrɛ̃t] *nf* - **1.** [enlacement] embrace - **2.** [pression] stranglehold.

étrenner [4] [etrene] *vt* to use for the first time.

étrennes [etren] *nfpl* Christmas box (*sg*).

étrier [etrije] *nm* stirrup.

étriller [3] [etrije] *vt* - **1.** [cheval] to curry - **2.** [personne] to wipe the floor with ; [film] to tear to pieces.

étriper [3] [etripe] *vt* - **1.** [animal] to disembowel - **2.** *fam fig* [tuer] to murder.

⬥ **s'étriper** *vp fam* to tear each other to pieces.

étriqué, e [etrike] *adj* - **1.** [vêtement] tight ; [appartement] cramped - **2.** [esprit] narrow.

étroit, e [etrwa, at] *adj* - **1.** [gén] narrow - **2.** [intime] close - **3.** [serré] tight.

⬥ **à l'étroit** *loc adj* : **être à l'~** to be cramped.

étroitement [etrwatmɑ̃] *adv* closely.

étroitesse [etʀwatɛs] *nf* narrowness ; ~ **d'esprit** *fig* narrow-mindedness.

étude [etyd] *nf* - **1.** [gén] study ; **à l'~** under consideration ; ~ **de faisabilité** feasibility study ; ~ **médias** media research ; ~ **de marché** market research *(U)* - **2.** [de notaire - local] office ; [- charge] practice - **3.** *MUS* étude.

➤ **études** *nfpl* studies ; **faire des ~s** to study ; ~**s primaires/secondaires** primary/secondary education *(U)*.

étudiant, e [etydjɑ̃, ɑ̃t] ◇ *adj* student *(avant n)* ◇ *nm, f* student.

étudié, e [etydje] *adj* studied.

étudier [9] [etydje] *vt* to study.

étui [etɥi] *nm* case ; ~ **à cigarettes/lunettes** cigarette/glasses case.

étuve [etyv] *nf* - **1.** [local] steam room ; *fig* oven - **2.** [appareil] sterilizer.

étuvée [etyve] ➤ **à l'étuvée** *loc adv* braised ; **faire cuire à l'~** to braise.

étymologie [etimɔlɔʒi] *nf* etymology.

étymologique [etimɔlɔʒik] *adj* etymological.

eu, e [y] *pp* ▷ avoir.

E-U, E-U A (*abr de* États-Unis (d'Amérique)) *nmpl* US, USA.

eucalyptus [økaliptys] *nm* eucalyptus.

eucharistie [økaristi] *nf* Eucharist.

euh [ø] *interj* er.

eunuque [ønyk] *nm* eunuch.

euphémisme [øfemism] *nm* euphemism ; **par ~** euphemistically.

euphorie [øfɔri] *nf* euphoria.

euphorique [øfɔrik] *adj* euphoric.

euphorisant, e [øfɔrizɑ̃, ɑ̃t] *adj* exhilarating.

➤ **euphorisant** *nm* antidepressant.

eurasien, enne [øʀazjɛ̃, ɛn] *adj* Eurasian.

➤ **Eurasien, enne** *nm, f* Eurasian.

eurent ▷ avoir.

euro [øʀo] *nm* euro ; **zone ~** euro zone, euro area.

eurocentrisme [øʀosɑ̃trism] *nm* Eurocentrism.

eurocrate [øʀokrat] *nmf* Eurocrat.

eurodéputé [øʀodepyte] *nm* Euro MP.

eurodevise [øʀodəviz] *nf* Eurocurrency.

eurodollar [øʀodɔlaʀ] *nm* Eurodollar.

euromissile [øʀomisil] *nm* Euromissile.

Europe [øʀɔp] *nf* : **l'~** Europe ; **l'~ centrale** Central Europe ; **l'~ de l'Est** Eastern Europe ; **ils ont parlé de l'~ verte** they discussed agriculture in the EC.

européen, enne [øʀɔpeɛ̃, ɛn] *adj* European.

➤ **Européen, enne** *nm, f* European.

Eurovision® [øʀovizjɔ̃] *nf inv* Eurovision®.

eus, eut *etc* ▷ avoir.

eût ▷ avoir.

euthanasie [øtanazi] *nf* euthanasia.

eux [ø] *pron pers* - **1.** [sujet] they ; **ce sont ~ qui me l'ont dit** they're the ones who told me - **2.** [complément] them.

➤ **eux-mêmes** *pron pers* themselves.

eV (*abr de* électron-volt) eV.

évacuation [evakɥasjɔ̃] *nf* - **1.** [gén] evacuation - **2.** [de liquide] draining.

évacuer [7] [evakɥe] *vt* - **1.** [gén] to evacuate - **2.** [liquide] to drain.

évadé, e [evade] *nm, f* escaped prisoner.

évader [3] [evade] ➤ **s'évader** *vp* : **s'~ (de)** to escape (from).

évaluation [evalɥasjɔ̃] *nf* [action] valuation ; [résultat] estimate.

évaluer [7] [evalɥe] *vt* [distance] to estimate ; [tableau] to value ; [risque] to assess.

évanescent, e [evanesɑ̃, ɑ̃t] *adj* fleeting.

évangélique [evɑ̃ʒelik] *adj* evangelical.

évangélisation [evɑ̃ʒelizasjɔ̃] *nf* evangelizing.

évangéliser [3] [evɑ̃ʒelize] *vt* to evangelize.

évangéliste [evɑ̃ʒelist] *nm* - **1.** [auteur] Evangelist - **2.** [prédicateur] evangelist.

évangile [evɑ̃ʒil] *nm* gospel ; **l'Évangile selon Saint Jean** the Gospel according to St. John.

évanouir [32] [evanwir] ➤ **s'évanouir** *vp* - **1.** [défaillir] to faint - **2.** [disparaître] to fade.

évanouissement [evanwismɑ̃] *nm* - **1.** [syncope] fainting fit - **2.** [disparition] fading.

évaporation [evapɔrasjɔ̃] *nf* evaporation.

évaporer [3] [evapɔre] ➤ **s'évaporer** *vp* to evaporate.

évasé, e [evaze] *adj* flared.

évaser [3] [evaze] *vt* to flare.

➤ **s'évaser** *vp* to flare.

évasif, ive [evazif, iv] *adj* evasive.

évasion [evazjɔ̃] *nf* escape.

évasivement [evazivmɑ̃] *adv* evasively.

évêché [eveʃe] *nm* [territoire] diocese ; [résidence] bishop's palace.

éveil [evɛj] *nm* awakening ; **en ~** on the alert.

éveillé, e [eveje] *adj* - **1.** [qui ne dort pas] wide awake - **2.** [vif, alerte] alert.

éveiller [4] [eveje] *vt* to arouse ; [intelligence, dormeur] to awaken.

➤ **s'éveiller** vp - **1.** [dormeur] to wake, to awaken - **2.** [curiosité] to be aroused - **3.** [esprit, intelligence] to be awakened - **4.** [s'ouvrir] : **s'~ à qqch** to discover sthg.

événement [evɛnmã] nm event.

événementiel, elle [evɛnmãsjɛl] adj [histoire] factual.

éventail [evãtaj] nm - **1.** [objet] fan ; **en ~** fanshaped - **2.** [choix] range.

éventaire [evãtɛr] nm - **1.** [étalage] stall, stand - **2.** [corbeille] tray.

éventé, e [evãte] adj stale.

éventer [3] [evãte] vt - **1.** [rafraîchir] to fan - **2.** [divulguer] to give away.
➤ **s'éventer** vp - **1.** [se rafraîchir] to fan o.s. - **2.** [parfum, vin] to go stale.

éventrer [3] [evãtre] vt - **1.** [étriper] to disembowel - **2.** [fendre] to rip open.

éventualité [evãtɥalite] nf - **1.** [possibilité] possibility - **2.** [circonstance] eventuality ; **dans l'~ de** in the event of ; **parer à toute ~** to be ready for any eventuality.

éventuel, elle [evãtɥɛl] adj possible.

éventuellement [evãtɥɛlmã] adv possibly.

évêque [evɛk] nm bishop.

évertuer [7] [evɛrtɥe] ➤ **s'évertuer** vp : **s'~ à faire qqch** to strive to do sthg.

éviction [eviksjɔ̃] nf eviction.

évidemment [evidamã] adv obviously.

évidence [evidãs] nf [caractère] evidence ; [fait] obvious fact ; **à l'~** obviously ; **mettre en ~** to emphasize, to highlight ; **se rendre à l'~** to face facts.

évident, e [evidã, ãt] adj obvious ; **ce n'est pas ~** [pas facile] it's not that easy.

évider [3] [evide] vt to hollow out.

évier [evje] nm sink.

évincer [16] [evɛ̃se] vt : **~ qqn (de)** to oust sb (from).

éviter [3] [evite] vt - **1.** [esquiver] to avoid - **2.** [s'abstenir] : **~ de faire qqch** to avoid doing sthg - **3.** [épargner] : **~ qqch à qqn** to save sb sthg.
➤ **s'éviter** vp - **1.** [se bouder] to avoid each other - **2.** [s'épargner] to spare o.s.

évocateur, trice [evɔkatœr, tris] adj - **1.** [film, roman] : **~ (de)** evocative (of) - **2.** [geste, regard] meaningful.

évocation [evɔkasjɔ̃] nf evocation.

évolué, e [evɔlɥe] adj - **1.** [développé] developed - **2.** [libéral, progressiste] broad-minded.

évoluer [7] [evɔlɥe] vi - **1.** [changer] to evolve ; [personne] to change - **2.** [se mouvoir] to move about.

évolutif, ive [evɔlytif, iv] adj - **1.** [système]

evolutionary - **2.** MÉD progressive - **3.** [travail] : **un poste ~** a job with prospects.

évolution [evɔlysjɔ̃] nf - **1.** [transformation] development - **2.** BIOL evolution - **3.** MÉD progress.
➤ **évolutions** nfpl movements.

évoquer [3] [evɔke] vt - **1.** [souvenir] to evoke ; **son nom ne m'évoque rien** his name means nothing to me - **2.** [problème] to refer to - **3.** [esprits, démons] to call up.

ex [ɛks] nmf inv ex.

ex- [ɛks] préfixe ex-.

exacerbé, e [ɛgzasɛrbe] adj exacerbated.

exacerber [3] [ɛgzasɛrbe] vt to heighten.

exact, e [ɛgzakt] adj - **1.** [calcul] correct - **2.** [récit, copie] exact - **3.** [ponctuel] punctual.

exactement [ɛgzaktəmã] adv exactly.

exaction [ɛgzaksjɔ̃] nf extortion.

exactitude [ɛgzaktityd] nf - **1.** [de calcul, montre] accuracy - **2.** [ponctualité] punctuality.

ex æquo [ɛgzeko] <> adj inv & nmf inv equal <> adv equal ; **troisième ~** third equal.

exagération [ɛgzaʒerasjɔ̃] nf exaggeration.

exagéré, e [ɛgzaʒere] adj exaggerated.

exagérément [ɛgzaʒeremã] adv exaggeratedly.

exagérer [18] [ɛgzaʒere] vt & vi to exaggerate.
➤ **s'exagérer** vp to exaggerate.

exaltant, e [ɛgzaltã, ãt] adj exhilarating.

exalté, e [ɛgzalte] <> adj [sentiment] elated ; [tempérament] over-excited ; [imagination] vivid <> nm, f fanatic.

exalter [3] [ɛgzalte] vt to excite.
➤ **s'exalter** vp to get carried away.

examen [ɛgzamɛ̃] nm examination ; SCOL exam, examination ; **~ médical** medical (examination) ; **mise en ~** JUR indictment.

examinateur, trice [ɛgzaminatœr, tris] nm, f examiner.

examiner [3] [ɛgzamine] vt to examine.

exaspérant, e [ɛgzasperã, ãt] adj exasperating.

exaspération [ɛgzasperasjɔ̃] nf exasperation.

exaspérer [18] [ɛgzaspere] vt to exasperate.

exaucer [16] [ɛgzose] vt to grant ; **~ qqn** to answer sb's prayers.

ex cathedra [ɛkskatedra] loc adv with authority.

excédant, e [ɛksedã, ãt] adj exasperating.

excédent [ɛksedã] nm surplus ; **en ~** surplus (avant n) ; **~ de bagages** [dans l'avion] excess luggage *ou* baggage ; ~ **commercial** trade surplus.

excédentaire [ɛksedɑ̃tɛr] *adj* surplus *(avant n)*.

excéder [18] [ɛksede] *vt* - **1.** [gén] to exceed - **2.** [exaspérer] to exasperate.

excellemment [ɛkselamɑ̃] *adv* excellently.

excellence [ɛkselɑ̃s] *nf* excellence ; **par ~** par excellence.
→ **Excellence** *nf* : **Son Excellence** His/Her Excellency.

excellent, e [ɛkselɑ̃, ɑ̃t] *adj* excellent.

exceller [4] [ɛksele] *vi* : **~ en** *ou* **dans qqch** to excel at *ou* in sthg ; **~ à faire qqch** to excel at doing sthg.

excentré, e [ɛksɑ̃tre] *adj* : **c'est très ~** it's quite a long way out.

excentrique [ɛksɑ̃trik] <> *nmf* eccentric <> *adj* - **1.** [gén] eccentric - **2.** [quartier] outlying.

excepté, e [ɛksɛpte] *adj* : **tous sont venus, lui ~** everyone came except (for) him.
→ **excepté** *prép* apart from, except.

exception [ɛksɛpsjɔ̃] *nf* exception ; **faire ~** to be an exception ; **d'~** exceptional ; **à l'~ de** except for.

exceptionnel, elle [ɛksɛpsjɔnɛl] *adj* exceptional.

exceptionnellement [ɛksɛpsjɔnɛlmɑ̃] *adv* - **1.** [par exception] in this (one) instance - **2.** [extrêmement] exceptionally.

excès [ɛksɛ] <> *nm* excess ; **~ de vitesse** speeding ; **~ de zèle** overzealousness ; **à l'~** to excess, excessively ; **sans ~** moderately <> *nmpl* excesses.

excessif, ive [ɛksesif, iv] *adj* - **1.** [démesuré] excessive - **2.** [extrême] extreme.

excessivement [ɛksesivmɑ̃] *adv* - **1.** [démesurément] excessively - **2.** [extrêmement] extremely.

excipient [ɛksipjɑ̃] *nm* excipient.

excision [ɛksizjɔ̃] *nf* excision.

excitant, e [ɛksitɑ̃, ɑ̃t] *adj* - **1.** [stimulant, passionnant] exciting - **2.** *MÉD* stimulating.
→ **excitant** *nm* stimulant.

excitation [ɛksitasjɔ̃] *nf* - **1.** [énervement] excitement - **2.** [stimulation] encouragement - **3.** *MÉD* stimulation.

excité, e [ɛksite] <> *adj* [énervé] excited <> *nm, f* hothead.

exciter [3] [ɛksite] *vt* - **1.** [gén] to excite - **2.** [inciter] : **~ qqn (à qqch/à faire qqch)** to incite sb (to sthg/to do sthg) - **3.** *MÉD* to stimulate.
→ **s'exciter** *vp* : **s'~ (sur)** to lose one's temper (with).

exclamation [ɛksklamasjɔ̃] *nf* exclamation.

exclamer [3] [ɛksklame] → **s'exclamer** *vp* : **s'~ (devant)** to exclaim (at *ou* over).

exclu, e [ɛkskly] <> *pp* ⊳ **exclure** <> *adj* excluded <> *nm, f* outsider.

exclure [96] [ɛksklyr] *vt* to exclude ; [expulser] to expel.

exclusif, ive [ɛksklyzif, iv] *adj* exclusive ; **~ de** exclusive of.

exclusion [ɛksklyzjɔ̃] *nf* expulsion ; **à l'~ de** to the exclusion of.

exclusivement [ɛksklyzivmɑ̃] *adv* - **1.** [uniquement] exclusively - **2.** [non inclus] exclusive.

exclusivité [ɛksklyzivite] *nf* - **1.** *COMM* exclusive rights *(pl)* ; **avoir l'~ (de)** to have exclusive rights (to) - **2.** *CIN* sole screening rights *(pl)* ; **en ~** exclusively - **3.** [de sentiment] exclusiveness.

excommunier [9] [ɛkskɔmynje] *vt* to excommunicate.

excrément [ɛkskremɑ̃] *nm (gén pl)* excrement *(U)*.

excroissance [ɛkskrwasɑ̃s] *nf* excrescence.

excursion [ɛkskyrsjɔ̃] *nf* excursion ; **faire une ~** to go on a trip.

excursionniste [ɛkskyrsjɔnist] *nmf* daytripper *Br*, vacationer *Am*.

excusable [ɛkskyzabl] *adj* excusable.

excuse [ɛkskyz] *nf* excuse ; **avoir une ~** to have an excuse ; **se confondre en ~s** to apologize profusely ; **présenter ses ~s à qqn** to apologize to sb.

excuser [3] [ɛkskyze] *vt* to excuse ; **excusez-moi** [pour réparer] I'm sorry ; [pour demander] excuse me ; **se faire ~** to ask to be excused.
→ **s'excuser** *vp* [demander pardon] to apologize ; **s'~ de qqch/de faire qqch** to apologize for sthg/for doing sthg.

exécrable [ɛgzekrabl] *adj* atrocious.

exécrer [18] [ɛgzekre] *vt* to loathe.

exécutant, e [ɛgzekytɑ̃, ɑ̃t] *nm, f* - **1.** [personne] underling - **2.** *MUS* performer.

exécuter [3] [ɛgzekyte] *vt* - **1.** [réaliser] to carry out ; [tableau] to paint - **2.** *MUS* to play, to perform - **3.** [mettre à mort] to execute.
→ **s'exécuter** *vp* to comply.

exécuteur, trice [ɛgzekytœr, tris] *nm, f* : **~ testamentaire** executor.

exécutif, ive [ɛgzekytif, iv] *adj* executive.
→ **exécutif** *nm* : **l'~** the executive.

exécution [ɛgzekysjɔ̃] *nf* - **1.** [réalisation] carrying out ; [de tableau] painting ; **mettre à ~** to carry out - **2.** *MUS* performance - **3.** [mise à mort] execution.

exécutoire [ɛgzekytwar] *adj* binding.

exégèse [ɛgzeʒɛz] *nf* exegesis.

exemplaire [ɛgzãplɛr] <> *nm* copy <> *adj* exemplary.

exemple [ɛgzãpl] *nm* example ; **par ~** for example, for instance ; **ça, par ~!** [exprime la surprise] well, well!, good heavens! ; **pour l'~** as an example ; **citer qqn en ~** to quote sb as an example ; **montrer l'~** to set an example ; **prendre ~ sur qqn** to take a leaf out of sb's book ; **à l'~ de** following in the footsteps of.

exempt, e [ɛgzã, ãt] *adj* : **~ de** [dispensé de] exempt from ; [dépourvu de] free of ; **~ de taxes** tax-free *Br*, tax-exempt *Am*.

exempté, e [ɛgzãte] *adj* : **~ (de)** exempt (from).

exemption [ɛgzãpsjɔ̃] *nf* exemption.

exercer [16] [ɛgzɛrse] *vt* - **1.** [entraîner, mettre en usage] to exercise ; [autorité, influence] to exert - **2.** [métier] to carry on ; [médecine] to practise.
➤ **s'exercer** *vp* - **1.** [s'entraîner] to practise ; **s'~ à qqch/à faire qqch** to practise sthg/doing sthg - **2.** [se manifester] : **s'~ (sur** *ou* **contre)** to be exerted (on).

exercice [ɛgzɛrsis] *nm* - **1.** [gén] exercise ; **~s d'assouplissement** keep-fit exercises - **2.** [entraînement] practice - **3.** [de métier, fonction] carrying out ; **dans l'~ de ses fonctions** in the execution of one's duties ; **en ~** in office - **4.** *FIN* financial year *Br*, fiscal year *Am*.

exergue [ɛgzɛrg] *nm* inscription ; **mettre qqch en ~** to emphasize sthg.

exhalaison [ɛgzalɛzɔ̃] *nf* odour *Br*, odor *Am*.

exhaler [3] [ɛgzale] *vt littéraire* - **1.** [odeur] to give off - **2.** *fig* [colère, rage] to vent - **3.** [plainte, soupir] to utter.
➤ **s'exhaler** *vp* - **1.** [odeur] to rise - **2.** [plainte, soupir] : **s'~ de** to rise from.

exhausser [3] [ɛgzose] *vt* to raise.

exhaustif, ive [ɛgzostif, iv] *adj* exhaustive.

exhiber [3] [ɛgzibe] *vt* [présenter] to show ; [faire étalage de] to show off.
➤ **s'exhiber** *vp* to make an exhibition of o.s.

exhibitionniste [ɛgzibisjɔnist] *nmf* exhibitionist.

exhortation [ɛgzɔrtasjɔ̃] *nf* exhortation.

exhorter [3] [ɛgzɔrte] *vt* : **~ qqn à qqch/à faire qqch** to urge sb to sthg/to do sthg.

exhumer [3] [ɛgzyme] *vt* to exhume ; *fig* to unearth, to dig up.

exigeant, e [ɛgziʒã, ãt] *adj* demanding.

exigence [ɛgziʒãs] *nf* - **1.** [caractère] demanding nature - **2.** [demande] demand.

exiger [17] [ɛgziʒe] *vt* - **1.** [demander] to demand ; **~ que (+ subjonctif)** to demand that ;

~ qqch de qqn to demand sthg from sb - **2.** [nécessiter] to require.

exigible [ɛgziʒibl] *adj* payable.

exigu, ë [ɛgzigy] *adj* cramped.

exiguïté [ɛgzigɥite] *nf* lack of space.

exil [ɛgzil] *nm* exile ; **en ~** exiled.

exilé, e [ɛgzile] *nm, f* exile.

exiler [3] [ɛgzile] *vt* to exile.
➤ **s'exiler** *vp* - **1.** *POLIT* to go into exile - **2.** *fig* [partir] to go into seclusion.

existence [ɛgzistãs] *nf* existence.

existentialisme [ɛgzistãsjalism] *nm* existentialism.

existentiel, elle [ɛgzistãsjɛl] *adj* existential.

exister [3] [ɛgziste] <> *vi* to exist <> *v impers* : **il existe** [il y a] there is/are.

exode [ɛgzɔd] *nm* exodus ; **~ rural** rural depopulation.

exonération [ɛgzɔnerasjɔ̃] *nf* exemption ; **~ de qqch** exemption from sthg ; **~ d'impôts** tax exemption.

exonérer [18] [ɛgzɔnere] *vt* : **~ qqn de qqch** to exempt sb from sthg.

exorbitant, e [ɛgzɔrbitã, ãt] *adj* exorbitant.

exorbité, e [ɛgzɔrbite] ▷ **œil**.

exorciser [3] [ɛgzɔrsize] *vt* to exorcize.

exotique [ɛgzɔtik] *adj* exotic.

exotisme [ɛgzɔtism] *nm* exoticism.

expansé, e [ɛkspãse] *adj* expanded.

expansif, ive [ɛkspãsif, iv] *adj* expansive.

expansion [ɛkspãsjɔ̃] *nf* expansion ; **~ démographique** population growth.

expansionniste [ɛkspãsjɔnist] *nmf* & *adj* expansionist.

expatrié, e [ɛkspatrije] *adj* & *nm, f* expatriate.

expatrier [10] [ɛkspatrije] *vt* to expatriate.
➤ **s'expatrier** *vp* to leave one's country.

expectative [ɛkspɛktativ] *nf* : **être dans l'~** wait and see.

expectorant, e [ɛkspɛktɔrã, ãt] *adj* expectorant.
➤ **expectorant** *nm* expectorant.

expédient [ɛkspedjã] *nm* expedient ; **vivre d'~s** to live by one's wits.

expédier [9] [ɛkspedje] *vt* - **1.** [lettre, marchandise] to send, to dispatch - **2.** [personne] to get rid of ; [question] to dispose of - **3.** [travail] to dash off.

expéditeur, trice [ɛkspeditœr, tris] <> *adj* dispatching *(avant n)* <> *nm, f* sender.

expéditif, ive [ɛkspeditif, iv] *adj* quick, expeditious.

expédition [ɛkspedisjɔ̃] *nf* - **1.** [envoi] sending - **2.** [voyage, campagne militaire] expedition ; ~ **punitive** punitive raid.

expéditionnaire [ɛkspedisjɔnɛr] ⊳ **corps**.

expérience [ɛksperjɑ̃s] *nf* - **1.** [pratique] experience ; **avoir de l'~** to have experience, to be experienced - **2.** [essai] experiment ; **faire l'~ de qqch** to experience *ou* try sthg ; **tenter l'~** to try.

expérimental, e, aux [ɛksperimɑ̃tal, o] *adj* experimental.

expérimentation [ɛksperimɑ̃tasjɔ̃] *nf* experimentation.

expérimenté, e [ɛksperimɑ̃te] *adj* experienced.

expérimenter [3] [ɛksperimɑ̃te] *vt* to test.

expert, e [ɛkspɛr, ɛrt] *adj* expert ; **être ~ (en la matière)** to be an expert (on the subject).
◆ **expert** *nm* expert.

expert-comptable [ɛkspɛrkɔ̃tabl] (*pl* **experts-comptables**) *nm* chartered accountant *Br*, certified public accountant *Am*.

expertise [ɛkspɛrtiz] *nf* - **1.** [examen] expert appraisal ; [estimation] (expert) valuation - **2.** [compétence] expertise.

expertiser [3] [ɛkspɛrtize] *vt* to value ; [dégâts] to assess.

expiation [ɛkspjasjɔ̃] *nf* atonement.

expier [9] [ɛkspje] *vt* to pay for.

expiration [ɛkspirasjɔ̃] *nf* - **1.** [d'air] exhalation - **2.** [de contrat] expiry.

expirer [3] [ɛkspire] ⟨⟩ *vt* to breathe out ⟨⟩ *vi* - **1.** [personne] to pass away - **2.** [contrat] to expire.

explicable [ɛksplikabl] *adj* explicable.

explicatif, ive [ɛksplikatif, iv] *adj* explanatory.

explication [ɛksplikasjɔ̃] *nf* explanation ; **demander des ~s à qqn** to demand an explanation from sb ; ~ **de texte** (literary) criticism.

explicite [ɛksplisit] *adj* explicit.

explicitement [ɛksplisitmɑ̃] *adv* explicitly.

expliciter [3] [ɛksplisite] *vt* to make explicit.

expliquer [3] [ɛksplike] *vt* - **1.** [gén] to explain - **2.** [texte] to criticize.
◆ **s'expliquer** *vp* - **1.** [se justifier] to explain o.s. - **2.** [comprendre] to understand - **3.** [discuter] to have it out - **4.** [devenir compréhensible] to be explained, to become clear.

exploit [ɛksplwa] *nm* exploit, feat ; *iron* [maladresse] achievement.

exploitable [ɛksplwatabl] *adj* [gisement] exploitable ; [renseignement] usable ; *INFORM* machine-readable.

exploitant, e [ɛksplwatɑ̃, ɑ̃t] *nm, f* farmer.

exploitation [ɛksplwatasjɔ̃] *nf* - **1.** [mise en valeur] running ; [de mine] working - **2.** [entreprise] operation, concern ; ~ **agricole** farm - **3.** [d'une personne] exploitation.

exploiter [3] [ɛksplwate] *vt* - **1.** [gén] to exploit - **2.** [entreprise] to operate, to run.

exploiteur, euse [ɛksplwatœr, øz] *nm, f* exploiter.

explorateur, trice [ɛksplɔratœr, tris] *nm, f* explorer.

exploration [ɛksplɔrasjɔ̃] *nf* exploration.

exploratoire [ɛksplɔratwar] *adj* exploratory.

explorer [3] [ɛksplɔre] *vt* to explore.

exploser [3] [ɛksploze] *vi* to explode.

explosif, ive [ɛksplozif, iv] *adj* explosive.
◆ **explosif** *nm* explosive.

explosion [ɛksplozjɔ̃] *nf* explosion ; [de colère, joie] outburst.

expo [ɛkspo] *nf fam* exhibition.

exponentiel, elle [ɛkspɔnɑ̃sjɛl] *adj* exponential.

exportateur, trice [ɛkspɔrtatœr, tris] ⟨⟩ *adj* exporting ⟨⟩ *nm, f* exporter.

exportation [ɛkspɔrtasjɔ̃] *nf* export.

exporter [3] [ɛkspɔrte] *vt* to export.

exposant, e [ɛkspozɑ̃, ɑ̃t] *nm, f* exhibitor.
◆ **exposant** *nm* exponent.

exposé, e [ɛkspoze] *adj* - **1.** [orienté] : **bien ~** facing the sun - **2.** [vulnérable] exposed.
◆ **exposé** *nm* account ; *SCOL* talk.

exposer [3] [ɛkspoze] *vt* - **1.** [orienter, mettre en danger] to expose ; ~ **sa vie** to risk one's life - **2.** [présenter -] to display ; [- tableaux] to show, to exhibit - **3.** [expliquer] to explain, to set out.
◆ **s'exposer** *vp* : **s'~ à qqch** to expose o.s. to sthg.

exposition [ɛkspozisjɔ̃] *nf* - **1.** [présentation] exhibition - **2.** [orientation] aspect - **3.** [explication] exposition.

exposition-vente [ɛkspozisjɔ̃vɑ̃t] (*pl* **expositions-ventes**) *nf* exhibition (*where purchases can be made*).

exprès¹, esse [ɛksprɛs] *adj* [formel] formal, express.
◆ **exprès** *adj inv* [urgent] express ; **en ~** by express delivery.

exprès² [ɛksprɛ] *adv* on purpose ; **faire ~ de faire qqch** to do sthg deliberately *ou* on purpose.

express [ɛksprɛs] ◇ *nm inv* - **1.** [train] express - **2.** [café] espresso ◇ *adj inv* express.

expressément [ɛkspresemãl *adv* expressly.

expressif, ive [ɛkspresif, iv] *adj* expressive.

expression [ɛkspresjɔ̃] *nf* expression ; ~ **idiomatique** idiom, idiomatic expression ; **réduire qqch à sa plus simple** ~ *fig* to reduce sthg to its simplest form ; **selon l'**~ **consacrée** as the saying goes.

expressionnisme [ɛkspresjɔnism] *nm* expressionism.

expressivité [ɛkspresivite] *nf* expressiveness.

exprimable [ɛksprimabl] *adj* which can be expressed ; **difficilement** ~ difficult to express.

exprimer [3] [ɛksprime] *vt* [pensées, sentiments] to express ; ~ **qqch par qqch** to express sthg with sthg.
◆ **s'exprimer** *vp* to express o.s.

expropriation [ɛksproprijasjɔ̃] *nf* expropriation.

exproprier [10] [ɛksproprije] *vt* to expropriate.

expulser [3] [ɛkspylse] *vt* : ~ **(de)** to expel (from) ; [locataire] to evict (from).

expulsion [ɛkspylsjɔ̃] *nf* expulsion ; [de locataire] eviction.

expurger [17] [ɛkspyrʒe] *vt* to expurgate.

exquis, e [ɛkski, iz] *adj* - **1.** [délicieux] exquisite - **2.** [distingué, agréable] delightful.

exsangue [ɛksãg] *adj* [blême] deathly pale.

extase [ɛkstaz] *nf* ecstasy ; **tomber en** ~ **devant** to go into ecstasies over.

extasier [9] [ɛkstazje] ◆ **s'extasier** *vp* : **s'**~ **devant** to go into ecstasies over.

extatique [ɛkstatik] *adj* ecstatic.

extenseur [ɛkstãsœr] ◇ *nm* GYM chest expander ◇ *adj* ▭ **muscle**.

extensible [ɛkstãsibl] *adj* stretchable.

extensif, ive [ɛkstãsif, iv] *adj* extensive.

extension [ɛkstãsjɔ̃] *nf* - **1.** [étirement] stretching - **2.** [développement] spread - **3.** [élargissement] extension ; **par** ~ by extension ; ~ **de nom de fichier** INFORM (filename) extension.

exténuant, e [ɛkstenɥã, ãt] *adj* exhausting.

exténuer [7] [ɛkstenɥe] *vt* to exhaust.

extérieur, e [ɛksterjœr] *adj* - **1.** [au dehors] outside ; [étranger] external ; [apparent] outward - **2.** ÉCON & POLIT foreign.
◆ **extérieur** *nm* - **1.** [dehors] outside ; [de maison] exterior ; **à l'**~ **de qqch** outside sthg - **2.** ÉCON & POLIT : **l'**~ foreign countries (*pl*).

extérieurement [ɛksterjœrmãl] *adv* - **1.** [à

l'extérieur] on the outside, externally - **2.** [en apparence] outwardly.

extérioriser [3] [ɛksterjɔrize] *vt* to show.
◆ **s'extérioriser** *vp* to show one's feelings.

extermination [ɛksterminasjɔ̃] *nf* extermination.

exterminer [3] [ɛkstermine] *vt* to exterminate.

externat [ɛksternal *nm* - **1.** SCOL day school - **2.** MÉD non-resident medical studentship.

externe [ɛkstern] ◇ *nmf* - **1.** SCOL day pupil - **2.** MÉD non-resident medical student, ≃ extern Am ◇ *adj* outer, external ; ~ **à qqch** outside sthg.

extincteur [ɛkstɛ̃ktœr] *nm* (fire) extinguisher.

extinction [ɛkstɛ̃ksjɔ̃] *nf* - **1.** [action d'éteindre] putting out, extinguishing ; ~ **des feux** lights out - **2.** *fig* [disparition] extinction ; ~ **de voix** loss of one's voice.

extirper [3] [ɛkstirpe] *vt* : ~ **(de)** [épine, réponse, secret] to drag (out of) ; [plante] to uproot (from) ; [erreur, préjugé] to root out (of).
◆ **s'extirper** *vp* : **s'**~ **de qqch** to struggle out of sthg.

extorquer [3] [ɛkstɔrke] *vt* : ~ **qqch à qqn** to extort sthg from sb.

extorsion [ɛkstɔrsjɔ̃] *nf* extortion ; ~ **de fonds** extortion of money.

extra [ɛkstral ◇ *nm inv* - **1.** [employé] extra help (*U*) - **2.** [chose inhabituelle] (special) treat ◇ *adj inv* - **1.** [de qualité] top-quality - **2.** *fam* [génial] great, fantastic.

extraction [ɛkstraksjɔ̃] *nf* extraction.

extrader [3] [ɛkstrade] *vt* to extradite.

extradition [ɛkstradisjɔ̃] *nf* extradition.

extraire [112] [ɛkstrɛr] *vt* : ~ **(de)** to extract (from).
◆ **extrait** *nm* extract ; ~ **de café** coffee extract ; ~ **de naissance** birth certificate.

extralucide [ɛkstralysid] ▭ **voyant**.

extraordinaire [ɛkstraɔrdinɛr] *adj* extraordinary.

extraplat, e [ɛkstrapla, at] *adj* wafer-thin.

extrapoler [3] [ɛkstrapɔle] *vt & vi* to extrapolate.

extraterrestre [ɛkstraterɛstr] *nmf & adj* extraterrestrial.

extravagance [ɛkstravagãs] *nf* extravagance.

extravagant, e [ɛkstravagã, ãt] *adj* extravagant ; [idée, propos] wild.

extraverti, e [ɛkstraverti] *nm, f & adj* extrovert.

extrême [ɛkstrɛm] ◇ *nm* extreme ; **d'un ~ à l'autre** from one extreme to the other ◇ *adj* extreme ; [limite] furthest ; **les sports ~s** extreme sports.

extrêmement [ɛkstrɛmmɑ̃] *adv* extremely.

extrême-onction [ɛkstrɛmɔ̃ksjɔ̃] (*pl* **extrêmes-onctions**) *nf* last rites (*pl*), extreme unction.

Extrême-Orient [ɛkstrɛmɔrjɑ̃] *nm* : **l'~** the Far East.

extrémiste [ɛkstremist] *nmf* & *adj* extremist.

extrémité [ɛkstremite] *nf* - **1.** [bout] end - **2.** [situation critique] straights (*pl*) ; **à la dernière ~** *fig* at death's door.

exubérant, e [ɛgzyberɑ̃, ɑ̃t] *adj* - **1.** [personne] exuberant - **2.** [végétation] luxuriant.

exulter [3] [ɛgzylte] *vi* to exult.

exutoire [ɛgzytwar] *nm* outlet.

ex-voto [ɛksvɔto] *nm inv* votive offering.

eye-liner [ajlajnɛr] (*pl* **eye-liners**) *nm* eyeliner.

f, F [ɛf] *nm inv* f, F ; **F3** three-room flat *Br* OU apartment *Am*.

◆ **F** - **1.** *abr de* **femme** - **2.** *abr de* **féminin** - **3.** (*abr de* **Fahrenheit**) F - **4.** (*abr de* **franc**) F, Fr.

fa [fa] *nm inv* F ; [chanté] fa.

FAB [fab] (*abr de* **franco à bord**) FOB, fob.

fable [fabl] *nf* fable.

fabricant, e [fabrikɑ̃, ɑ̃t] *nm, f* manufacturer.

fabrication [fabrikasjɔ̃] *nf* manufacture, manufacturing ; **de ~ artisanale** handmade.

fabrique [fabrik] *nf* [usine] factory.

fabriquer [3] [fabrike] *vt* - **1.** [confectionner] to manufacture, to make ; **fabriqué en France** made in France - **2.** *fam* [faire] : **qu'est-ce que tu fabriques?** what are you up to? - **3.** [inventer] to fabricate.

fabulation [fabylasjɔ̃] *nf* fabrication.

fabuleusement [fabyløzmɑ̃] *adv* fabulously.

fabuleux, euse [fabylø, øz] *adj* fabulous.

fac [fak] *nf fam* college, uni *Br*.

FAC (*abr de* **franc d'avarie commune**) *adj* FGA, fga.

façade [fasad] *nf litt* & *fig* facade.

face [fas] *nf* - **1.** [visage] face ; **perdre la ~** to lose face ; **sauver la ~** to save face - **2.** [côté] side ; **faire ~ à qqch** [maison] to face sthg, to be opposite sthg ; *fig* [affronter] to face up to sthg ; **de ~** from the front ; **en ~ de qqn/qqch** opposite sb/sthg ; **d'en ~** across the street, opposite ; **~ à** facing ; **~ à qqch** [situation] faced with sthg ; **~ à ~** face to face ; **regarder qqch en ~** *fig* to face up to sthg.

face-à-face [fasafas] *nm inv* debate.

facétie [fasesi] *nf* practical joke.

facétieux, euse [fasesjø, øz] ◇ *adj* playful ◇ *nm, f* joker.

facette [fasɛt] *nf litt* & *fig* facet.

fâché, e [faʃe] *adj* - **1.** [en colère] angry ; [contrarié] annoyed - **2.** [brouillé] on bad terms.

fâcher [3] [faʃe] *vt* [mettre en colère] to anger, to make angry ; [contrarier] to annoy, to make annoyed.

◆ **se fâcher** *vp* - **1.** [se mettre en colère] : **se ~ (contre qqn)** to get angry (with sb) - **2.** [se brouiller] : **se ~ (avec qqn)** to fall out (with sb).

fâcherie [faʃri] *nf* disagreement.

fâcheux, euse [faʃø, øz] *adj* unfortunate.

facho [faʃo] *nmf* & *adj fam* fascist.

facial, e, aux [fasjal, o] *adj* facial.

faciès [fasjɛs] *nm péj* [visage] features (*pl*).

facile [fasil] *adj* - **1.** [aisé] easy ; **~ à faire/prononcer** easy to do/pronounce - **2.** [peu subtil] facile - **3.** [conciliant] easy-going ; **~ à vivre** easy to get on with.

facilement [fasilmɑ̃] *adv* easily.

facilité [fasilite] *nf* - **1.** [de tâche, problème] easiness - **2.** [capacité] ease - **3.** [dispositions] aptitude - **4.** COMM : **~s de paiement** easy (payment) terms ; **~s de crédit** credit facilities.

faciliter [3] [fasilite] *vt* to make easier.

façon [fasɔ̃] *nf* - **1.** [manière] way ; **~ de parler** figure of speech - **2.** [travail] work ; COUTURE making-up - **3.** [imitation] : **~ cuir** imitation leather.

◆ **façons** *nfpl* manner (*sg*), ways ; **faire des ~s** to make a fuss.

◆ **de façon à** *loc prép* so as to.

➤ **de façon que** (+ *subjonctif*) *loc conj* so
that.
➤ **de toute façon** *loc adv* anyway, in any
case.
➤ **sans façon** ◇ *loc adj* unpretentious
◇ *loc adv* [sincèrement] really, honestly ; [accepter] without fuss.
façonner [3] [fasɔne] *vt* - **1.** [travailler, former] to
shape - **2.** [fabriquer] to manufacture, to
make.
fac-similé [faksimile] (*pl* **fac-similés**) *nm* facsimile.
facteur, trice [faktœr, tris] *nm, f* [des postes]
postman (*f* postwoman) *Br*, mailman (*f*
mailwoman) *Am*.
➤ **facteur** *nm* - **1.** MUS [fabricant] maker ;
~ **d'orgues** organ-builder - **2.** [élément &
MATHS] factor ; ~ **rhésus** MÉD Rhesus factor ;
~ **vent** *Can* windchill factor.
factice [faktis] *adj* artificial.
faction [faksjɔ̃] *nf* - **1.** [groupe] faction - **2.** MIL :
être en *ou* **de** ~ to be on guard (duty) *ou* on
sentry duty.
factotum [faktɔtɔm] *nm* odd-job man *Br*,
odd jobber *Am*.
factuel, elle [faktɥɛl] *adj* factual.
facturation [faktyrasjɔ̃] *nf* - **1.** [action] invoicing - **2.** [bureau] invoice office.
facture [faktyr] *nf* - **1.** COMM invoice ; [de gaz,
d'électricité] bill - **2.** ART technique - **3.** MUS [fabrication] making.
facturer [3] [faktyre] *vt* COMM to invoice.
facultatif, ive [fakyltatif, iv] *adj* optional.
facultativement [fakyltativmɑ̃] *adv* optionally.
faculté [fakylte] *nf* - **1.** [don & UNIV] faculty ;
~ **de lettres/de droit/de médecine** Faculty of
Arts/Law/Medicine - **2.** [possibilité] freedom
- **3.** [pouvoir] power.
➤ **facultés** *nfpl* (mental) faculties.
fada [fada] *fam* ◇ *nm* nutcase ◇ *adj* nuts.
fadaises [fadɛz] *nfpl* drivel (*U*).
fade [fad] *adj* - **1.** [sans saveur] bland - **2.** [sans intérêt] insipid.
fagot [fago] *nm* bundle of sticks ; **de derrière
les ~s** *fig* kept for a special occasion.
fagoté, e [fagote] *adj fam* dressed.
fagoter [3] [fagote] *vt fam* to dress up.
➤ **se fagoter** *vp fam* to dress o.s. up.
Fahrenheit [farɛnajt] *n inv* Fahrenheit.
faible [fɛbl] ◇ *adj* - **1.** [gén] weak ; **être ~ en
maths** to be not very good at maths - **2.** [petit - montant, proportion] small ; [- revenu] low
- **3.** [lueur, bruit] faint ◇ *nmf* weak person ;
~ **d'esprit** feeble-minded person ◇ *nm*

weakness ; **avoir un** ~ **pour** to have a weakness for.
faiblement [fɛbləmɑ̃] *adv* - **1.** [mollement]
weakly, feebly - **2.** [imperceptiblement] faintly
- **3.** [peu] slightly.
faiblesse [fɛblɛs] *nf* - **1.** [gén] weakness ;
~ **d'esprit** feeble-mindedness - **2.** [petitesse]
smallness.
faiblir [32] [feblir] *vi* - **1.** [personne, monnaie] to
weaken - **2.** [forces] to diminish, to fail
- **3.** [tempête, vent] to die down.
faïence [fajɑ̃s] *nf* earthenware.
faignant, e = fainéant.
faille [faj] ◇ ▷ **falloir** ◇ *nf* - **1.** GÉOL fault
- **2.** [défaut] flaw.
faillible [fajibl] *adj* fallible.
faillir [46] [fajir] *vi* - **1.** [manquer] : ~ **à** [promesse]
not to keep ; [devoir] not to do - **2.** [être sur le
point de] : ~ **faire qqch** to nearly *ou* almost do
sthg.
faillite [fajit] *nf* FIN bankruptcy ; **faire** ~ to go
bankrupt ; **en** ~ bankrupt.
faim [fɛ̃] *nf* hunger ; **avoir** ~ to be hungry ;
avoir ~ **de** *fig* to hunger for ; **mourir de** ~ to be
starving ; **ne pas manger à sa** ~ not to eat
one's fill ; **rester sur sa** ~ to be still hungry ;
fig to be unsatisfied *ou* disappointed ; **avoir
une** ~ **de loup** to be starving.
fainéant, e [feneɑ̃, ɑ̃t], **feignant, e**,
faignant, e [fɛɲɑ̃, ɑ̃t] ◇ *adj* lazy, idle
◇ *nm, f* lazybones.
fainéanter [3] [feneɑ̃te] *vi* to laze about.
faire [109] [fɛr] ◇ *vt* - **1.** [fabriquer, préparer] to
make ; ~ **une maison** to build a house ; ~ **une
tarte/du café/un film** to make a tart/
coffee/a film ; ~ **qqch de qqch** [transformer] to
make sthg into sthg ; ~ **qqch de qqn** *fig* to
make sthg of sb ; **il veut en** ~ **un avocat** he
wants him to be a lawyer, he wants to
make a lawyer of him - **2.** [s'occuper à, entreprendre] to do ; **qu'est-ce qu'il fait dans la vie?**
what does he do (for a living)? ; **que fais-tu
dimanche?** what are you doing on Sunday? ; **qu'est-ce que je peux** ~ **pour vous aider?** what can I do to help you? - **3.** [étudier]
to do ; ~ **de l'anglais/des maths/du droit** to do
English/maths/law - **4.** [sport, musique] to
play ; ~ **du football/de la clarinette** to play
football/the clarinet - **5.** [effectuer] to do ; ~ **le
ménage** to do the housework ; ~ **la cuisine** to
cook, to do the cooking ; ~ **la lessive** to do
the washing - **6.** [occasionner] : ~ **de la peine à
qqn** to hurt sb ; ~ **du mal à** to harm ; ~ **du
bruit** to make a noise ; **ça m'a fait quelque
chose** it affected me ; **ça ne fait rien** it
doesn't matter - **7.** [tenir le rôle de] to be, to

play - **8.** [imiter] : ~ **le sourd/l'innocent** to act deaf/(the) innocent - **9.** [calcul, mesure] : **un et un font deux** one and one are *ou* make two ; **ça fait combien (de kilomètres) jusqu'à la mer?** how far is it to the sea? ; **la table fait 2 mètres de long** the table is 2 metres *Br ou* meters *Am* long ; **~ du 38** to take a size 38 - **10.** [coûter] to be, to cost ; **ça vous fait 50 francs en tout** that'll be 50 francs altogether - **11.** [dire] : **«tiens», fit-elle** "really", she said - **12.** : **ne ~ que** [faire sans cesse] to do nothing but ; **elle ne fait que bavarder** she does nothing but gossip, she's always gossiping ; **je ne fais que passer** I've just popped in ◇ *vi* [agir] to do, to act ; **fais vite!** hurry up! ; **que ~?** what is to be done? ; **tu ferais bien d'aller voir ce qui se passe** you ought to *ou* you'd better go and see what's happening ; **~ comme chez soi** to make o.s. at home ◇ *v attr* [avoir l'air] to look ; **~ démodé/joli** to look old-fashioned/pretty ; **ça fait jeune** it makes you look young ◇ *v substitut* to do ; **je lui ai dit de prendre une échelle mais il ne l'a pas fait** I told him to use a ladder but he didn't ; **faites! please do!** ◇ *v impers* - **1.** [climat, temps] : **il fait beau/froid** it's fine/cold ; **il fait 20 degrés** it's 20 degrees ; **il fait jour/nuit** it's light/dark ; **il fait bon se reposer** it's *ou* it feels good to have a rest - **2.** [exprime la durée, la distance] : **ça fait six mois que je ne l'ai pas vu** it's six months since I last saw him ; **ça fait six mois que je fais du portugais** I've been going to Portuguese classes for six months ; **ça fait 30 kilomètres qu'on roule sans phares** we've been driving without lights for 30 kilometres ◇ *v auxiliaire* - **1.** [à l'actif] to make ; **~ démarrer une voiture** to start a car ; **~ tomber qqch** to make sthg fall ; **l'aspirine fait baisser la fièvre** aspirin brings down the temperature ; **~ travailler qqn** to make sb work ; **~ traverser la rue à un aveugle** to help a blind man cross the road - **2.** [au passif] : **~ faire qqch (par qqn)** to have sthg done (by sb) ; **~ réparer sa voiture/nettoyer ses vitres** to have one's car repaired/one's windows cleaned.

➤ **se faire** *vp* - **1.** [avoir lieu] to take place - **2.** [être à la mode] to be in - **3.** [être convenable] : **ça ne se fait pas (de faire qqch)** it's not done (to do sthg) - **4.** [devenir] : **se ~ (+ adjectif)** to get, to become ; **il se fait tard** it's getting late ; **se ~ beau** to make o.s. beautiful - **5.** [causer] (+ nom) : **se ~ mal** to hurt o.s. ; **se ~ des amis** to make friends ; **se ~ une idée sur qqch** to get some idea about sthg - **6.** (+ infinitif) : **se ~ écraser** to get run over ; **se ~ opérer** to have an operation ; **se ~ aider (par qqn)** to get help (from sb) ; **se ~ faire un cos-**

tume to have a suit made (for o.s.) - **7.** loc : **comment se fait-il que ...?** how is it that ...?, how come ...? ; **s'en ~** to worry ; **ne vous en faites pas!** don't worry!

➤ **se faire à** *vp + prép* to get used to.

faire-part [fɛrpar] *nm inv* announcement ; **~ de naissance/mariage** birth/wedding announcement.

faire-valoir [fɛrvalwar] *nm inv* [personne] foil.

fair-play [fɛrplɛ] *adj inv* sporting ; **se montrer ~** to be sporting.

fais, fait *etc* ▷ faire.

faisable [fəzabl] *adj* feasible.

faisan, e [fəzɑ̃, an] *nm, f* pheasant.

faisandé, e [fəzɑ̃de] *adj* CULIN high.

faisceau, x [fɛso] *nm* - **1.** [rayon] beam ; **~ lumineux** beam of light - **2.** [fagot] bundle.

faiseur, euse [fəzœr, øz] *nm, f* maker ; **~ d'embarras** fusspot.

faisons ▷ faire.

fait, faite [fɛ, fɛt] ◇ *pp* ▷ faire ◇ *adj* - **1.** [fabriqué] made ; **être ~ pour** *litt* & *fig* to be made *ou* meant for ; **il n'est pas ~ pour mener cette vie** he's not cut out for this kind of life ; **ils sont ~s l'un pour l'autre** they are made for each other ; **~ sur mesure** made to measure - **2.** [physique] : **bien ~** well-built - **3.** [fromage] ripe - **4.** loc : **c'est bien ~ pour lui** (it) serves him right ; **c'en est ~ de nous** we're done for.

➤ **fait** *nm* - **1.** [acte] act ; **mettre qqn devant le ~ accompli** to present sb with a fait accompli ; **prendre qqn sur le ~** to catch sb in the act ; **~s et gestes** doings, actions - **2.** [événement] event ; **~s divers** news in brief - **3.** [réalité] fact ; **le ~ est que ...** the fact is that (that) ...

➤ **au fait** *loc adv* by the way.

➤ **en fait** *loc adv* in (actual) fact.

➤ **en fait de** *loc prép* by way of.

➤ **du fait de** *loc prép* because of.

faîte [fɛt] *nm* - **1.** [de toit] ridge - **2.** [d'arbre] top - **3.** fig [sommet] pinnacle.

faites ▷ faire.

faîtière [fɛtjɛr] *nf* skylight.

fait-tout (*pl inv*), **faitout** (*pl faitouts*) [fɛtu] *nm* stewpan.

fakir [fakir] *nm* fakir.

falaise [falɛz] *nf* cliff.

falbalas [falbala] *nmpl* furbelows.

fallacieux, euse [falasjø, øz] *adj* - **1.** [promesse] false - **2.** [argument] fallacious.

falloir [69] [falwar] *v impers* : **il me faut du temps** I need (some) time ; **il lui faudra de l'énergie** he'll need (a lot of) energy ; **il te faut un peu de repos** you need some rest ; **il**

faut que tu partes you must go *ou* leave, you'll have to go *ou* leave ; **il faut toujours qu'elle intervienne!** she always has to interfere! ; **il faut agir** we/you *etc* must act ; **il faut faire attention** we/you *etc* must be careful, we'll/you'll *etc* have to be careful ; **s'il le faut** if necessary.

➤ **s'en falloir** *v impers* : **il s'en faut de peu pour qu'il puisse acheter cette maison** he can almost afford to buy the house ; **il s'en faut de 20 cm pour que l'armoire tienne dans le coin** the cupboard is 20 cm too big to fit into the corner ; **il s'en faut de beaucoup pour qu'il ait l'examen** it'll take a lot for him to pass the exam ; **peu s'en est fallu qu'il démissionne** he very nearly resigned, he came close to resigning ; **tant s'en faut** far from it, on the contrary.

fallu [faly] *pp inv* ▷ **falloir**.

falot, e [falo, ɔt] *adj* dull.

➤ **falot** *nm* lantern.

falsification [falsifikasjɔ̃] *nf* - **1.** [de document] forgery ; [de monnaie] counterfeiting - **2.** [de produit alimentaire] adulteration.

falsifier [9] [falsifje] *vt* - **1.** [document, signature, faits] to falsify - **2.** [pensée, paroles] to misrepresent - **3.** [produit alimentaire] to adulterate.

famé, e [fame] *adj* : **mal ~** with a (bad) reputation.

famélique [famelik] *adj* half-starved.

fameusement [famøzmɑ̃] *adv fam* really.

fameux, euse [famø, øz] *adj* - **1.** [célèbre] famous - **2.** *fam* [remarquable] great ; **pas ~** not up to much, nothing great.

familial, e, aux [familjal, o] *adj* family (*avant n*).

➤ **familiale** *nf* estate car *Br*, station wagon *Am*.

familiariser [3] [familjarize] *vt* : **~ qqn avec** to familiarize sb with.

➤ **se familiariser** *vp* : **se ~ avec** to get used to.

familiarité [familjarite] *nf* familiarity.

➤ **familiarités** *nfpl* liberties.

familier, ère [familje, ɛr] *adj* familiar.

➤ **familier** *nm* regular (customer).

famille [famij] *nf* family ; [ensemble des parents] relatives, relations ; **de bonne ~** of good family ; **fonder une ~** to start a family ; **~ d'accueil** [lors d'un séjour linguistique] host family ; [pour enfant en difficulté] foster home ; **~ nombreuse** large family.

famine [famin] *nf* famine ; **crier ~** *fig* to complain of one's poverty.

fan [fan] *nmf fam* fan.

fanal, aux [fanal, o] *nm* - **1.** [de phare] beacon - **2.** [de train] headlight - **3.** [lanterne] lantern.

fanatique [fanatik] ◇ *nmf* fanatic ◇ *adj* fanatical.

fanatiser [3] [fanatize] *vt* to make fanatics out of.

fanatisme [fanatism] *nm* fanaticism.

fane [fan] *nf* - **1.** [de carotte] top - **2.** [d'arbre] fallen leaf.

faner [3] [fane] ◇ *vt* [altérer] to fade ◇ *vi* - **1.** [fleur] to wither - **2.** [beauté, couleur] to fade.

➤ **se faner** *vp* - **1.** [fleur] to wither - **2.** [beauté, couleur] to fade.

fanfare [fɑ̃far] *nf* - **1.** [orchestre] brass band - **2.** [musique] fanfare ; **en ~** noisy.

fanfaron, onne [fɑ̃farɔ̃, ɔn] ◇ *adj* boastful ◇ *nm, f* braggart.

fanfaronnade [fɑ̃farɔnad] *nf* boasting (*U*).

fanfreluche [fɑ̃frəlyʃ] *nf* trimming.

fange [fɑ̃ʒ] *nf littéraire* mire ; **traîner qqn dans la ~** to drag sb through the mire.

fanion [fanjɔ̃] *nm* pennant.

fantaisie [fɑ̃tezi] ◇ *nf* - **1.** [caprice] whim - **2.** (*U*) [goût] fancy - **3.** [imagination] imagination ; **de ~** imaginary - **4.** *MUS* fantasia ◇ *adj inv* : **chapeau ~** fancy hat ; **bijoux ~** fake jewellery *Br ou* jewelry *Am*.

fantaisiste [fɑ̃tezist] ◇ *nmf* entertainer ◇ *adj* - **1.** [fumiste] dilettante - **2.** [bizarre] fanciful.

fantasmagorique [fɑ̃tasmagɔrik] *adj* phantasmagorical, extraordinary.

fantasme [fɑ̃tasm] *nm* fantasy.

fantasmer [3] [fɑ̃tasme] *vi* to fantasize.

fantasque [fɑ̃task] *adj* - **1.** [personne] whimsical - **2.** [humeur] capricious - **3.** [chose] fantastic.

fantassin [fɑ̃tasɛ̃] *nm* infantryman.

fantastique [fɑ̃tastik] ◇ *adj* fantastic ◇ *nm* : **le ~** the fantastic.

fantoche [fɑ̃tɔʃ] ◇ *adj* puppet (*avant n*) ◇ *nm* puppet.

fantomatique [fɑ̃tɔmatik] *adj* ghostly.

fantôme [fɑ̃tom] ◇ *nm* ghost ◇ *adj* - **1.** [spectral] ghostly - **2.** [inexistant] phantom.

FAO *nf* - **1.** (*abr de* **fabrication assistée par ordinateur**) CAM - **2.** (*abr de* **Food and Agriculture Organisation**) FAO.

faon [fɑ̃] *nm* fawn.

FAP (*abr de* **franc d'avarie particulière**) *adj* FPA, fpa.

far [far] *nm* : **~ breton** *sweet flan containing plums*.

faramineux, euse [faraminø, øz] *adj fam*
- **1.** [prix] astronomical - **2.** [génial] fantastic.

farandole [farãdɔl] *nf* farandole.

farce [fars] *nf* - **1.** CULIN stuffing - **2.** [blague]
(practical) joke ; **faire une ~ à qqn** to play a
(practical) joke on sb ; **~s et attrapes** jokes
and novelties - **3.** LITTÉRATURE farce.

farceur, euse [farsœr, øz] *nm, f* (practical)
joker.

farci, e [farsi] *adj* - **1.** CULIN stuffed - **2.** *fig* [plein]
stuffed, crammed.

farcir [32] [farsir] *vt* - **1.** CULIN to stuff - **2.** [rem-
plir] : **~ qqch de** to stuff *ou* cram sthg with.
- **se farcir** *vp fam* - **1.** [faire] : **se ~ qqch** to get
stuck with sthg - **2.** [supporter] : **se ~ qqn** to
put up with sb - **3.** [manger] : **se ~ qqch** to scoff
sthg.

fard [far] *nm* make-up ; **~ à joues** blusher ;
~ à paupières eyeshadow ; **piquer un ~** *fam fig*
to blush.

fardeau, x [fardo] *nm* [poids] load ; *fig* burden.

farder [3] [farde] *vt* - **1.** [maquiller] to make up
- **2.** *fig* [masquer] to disguise.
- **se farder** *vp* to make o.s. up, to put on
one's make-up.

farfadet [farfade] *nm* sprite.

farfelu, e [farfəly] *fam* <> *adj* weird <> *nm, f*
weirdo.

farfouiller [3] [farfuje] *vi fam* to rummage.

farine [farin] *nf* flour ; **rouler qqn dans la ~** *fig*
to take sb for a ride.

farineux, euse [farinø, øz] *adj* - **1.** [aspect,
goût] floury - **2.** [aliment] farinaceous.
- **farineux** *nm* starchy food.

farniente [farnjɛnte] *nm* idleness.

farouche [faruʃ] *adj* - **1.** [animal] wild, not
tame ; [personne] shy, withdrawn - **2.** [senti-
ment] fierce.

farouchement [faruʃmã] *adv* fiercely.

fart [far(t)] *nm* (ski) wax.

farter [3] [farte] *vt* to wax.

fascicule [fasikyl] *nm* part, instalment Br,
installment Am.

fascinant, e [fasinã, ãt] *adj* - **1.** [regard] alluring, captivating - **2.** [personne, histoire] fascinating.

fascination [fasinasjõ] *nf* fascination.

fasciner [3] [fasine] *vt* to fascinate.

fascisant, e [faʃizã, ãt] *adj* fascistic.

fascisme [faʃism] *nm* fascism.

fasciste [faʃist] *nmf & adj* fascist.

fasse, fassions *etc* ⊳ **faire**.

faste [fast] <> *nm* splendour Br, splendor Am
<> *adj* [favorable] lucky.

fast-food [fastfud] (*pl* **fast-foods**) *nm* fast
food.

fastidieux, euse [fastidjø, øz] *adj* boring.

fastueux, euse [fastɥø, øz] *adj* luxurious.

fatal, e [fatal] *adj* - **1.** [mortel, funeste] fatal
- **2.** [inévitable] inevitable.

fatalement [fatalmã] *adv* inevitably.

fataliste [fatalist] <> *nmf* fatalist <> *adj* fatalistic.

fatalité [fatalite] *nf* - **1.** [destin] fate - **2.** [inéluc-
tabilité] inevitability.

fatidique [fatidik] *adj* fateful.

fatigant, e [fatigã, ãt] *adj* - **1.** [épuisant] tiring
- **2.** [ennuyeux] tiresome.

fatiguant [fatigã] *ppr* ⊳ **fatiguer**.

fatigue [fatig] *nf* tiredness ; **tomber de ~**,
être mort de ~ to be dead tired.

fatigué, e [fatige] *adj* tired ; [cœur, yeux]
strained.

fatiguer [3] [fatige] *vt* [épuiser, affecter to
tire - cœur, yeux] to strain [ennuyer] to wear out
vi - **1.** [personne] to grow tired - **2.** [moteur] to
strain.
- **se fatiguer** *vp* to get tired ; **se ~ de qqch**
to get tired of sthg ; **se ~ à faire qqch** to wear
o.s. out doing sthg.

fatras [fatra] *nm* jumble.

fatuité [fatɥite] *nf littéraire* complacency.

faubourg [fobur] *nm* suburb.

fauché, e [foʃe] *adj fam* broke, hard-up.

faucher [3] [foʃe] *vt* - **1.** [couper - herbe, blé] to
cut - **2.** *fam* [voler] : **~ qqch à qqn** to pinch sthg
from sb - **3.** [piéton] to run over - **4.** *fig* [suj :
mort, maladie] to cut down.

faucille [fosij] *nf* sickle.

faucon [fokõ] *nm* hawk.

faudra ⊳ **falloir**.

faufil [fofil] *nm* tacking *ou* basting thread.

faufiler [3] [fofile] *vt* to tack, to baste.
- **se faufiler** *vp* : **se ~ dans** to slip into ; **se
~ entre** to thread one's way between.

faune [fon] <> *nf* - **1.** [animaux] fauna - **2.** *péj*
[personnes] : **la ~ qui fréquente ce bar** the sort
of people who hang round that bar <> *nm*
MYTH faun.

faussaire [foser] *nmf* forger.

faussement [fosmã] *adv* - **1.** [à tort] wrongly
- **2.** [prétendument] falsely.

fausser [3] [fose] *vt* - **1.** [déformer] to bend
- **2.** [rendre faux] to distort.
- **se fausser** *vp* [voix] to become strained.

fausset [fose] ⊳ **voix**.

fausseté [fostel] *nf* - **1.** [hypocrisie] duplicity - **2.** [de jugement, d'idée] falsity.

faut ⊏▷ **falloir**.

faute [fot] *nf* - **1.** [erreur] mistake, error ; **faire une ~** to make a mistake *ou* an error ; **~ de calcul** miscalculation ; **~ de frappe** [à la machine à écrire] typing error ; [à l'ordinateur] keying error ; **~ de goût** error of taste ; **~ d'inattention** careless mistake ; **~ d'orthographe** spelling mistake - **2.** [méfait, infraction] offence *Br*, offense *Am* ; **prendre qqn en ~** to catch sb out ; **~ professionnelle** professional misdemeanour *Br ou* misdemeanor *Am* - **3.** TENNIS fault ; FOOTBALL foul - **4.** [responsabilité] fault ; **de ma/ta** *etc* **~** my/your *etc* fault ; **par la ~ de qqn** because of sb ; **rejeter la ~ sur qqn** to shift the blame onto sb.

➡ **faute de** *loc prép* for want *ou* lack of ; **~ de mieux** for want *ou* lack of anything better.

➡ **sans faute** ◇ *loc adv* without fail ◇ *loc adj* faultless.

fauteuil [fotœj] *nm* - **1.** [siège] armchair ; **~ à bascule** rocking chair ; **~ roulant** wheelchair - **2.** [de théâtre] seat ; **~ d'orchestre** seat in the stalls *Br ou* orchestra *Am* - **3.** [de président] chair ; [d'académicien] seat.

fauteur, trice [fotœr, tris] *nm, f* : **~ de troubles** troublemaker.

fautif, ive [fotif, iv] ◇ *adj* - **1.** [coupable] guilty - **2.** [défectueux] faulty ◇ *nm, f* guilty party.

fauve [fov] ◇ *nm* - **1.** [animal] big cat - **2.** [couleur] fawn - **3.** ART Fauve ◇ *adj* - **1.** [animal] wild - **2.** [cuir, cheveux] tawny - **3.** ART Fauvist.

fauvette [fovɛt] *nf* warbler.

faux, fausse [fo, fos] *adj* - **1.** [incorrect] wrong - **2.** [postiche, mensonger, hypocrite] false ; **~ témoignage** JUR perjury - **3.** [monnaie, papiers] forged, fake ; [bijou, marbre] imitation, fake - **4.** [injustifié] : **fausse alerte** false alarm ; **c'est un ~ problème** that's not an issue (here).

➡ **faux** ◇ *nm* [document, tableau] forgery, fake ◇ *nf* scythe ◇ *adv* : **chanter/jouer ~** MUS to sing/play out of tune ; **sonner ~** *fig* not to ring true.

faux-filet (*pl* **faux-filets**), **faux filet** (*pl* **faux filets**) [fofilɛ] *nm* sirloin.

faux-fuyant [fofɥijã] (*pl* **faux-fuyants**) *nm* excuse.

faux-monnayeur [fomɔnɛjœr] (*pl* **faux-monnayeurs**) *nm* counterfeiter.

faux-semblant [fosãblã] (*pl* **faux-semblants**) *nm* pretence *Br*, pretense *Am*.

faux-sens [fosãs] *nm inv* mistranslation.

faveur [favœr] *nf* favour *Br*, favor *Am* ; **faire une ~ à qqn** to do sb a favour *Br ou* favor *Am* ;

intercéder en ~ de qqn to intercede on sb's behalf.

➡ **à la faveur de** *loc prép* thanks to.

➡ **en faveur de** *loc prép* in favour *Br ou* favor *Am* of.

favorable [favɔrabl] *adj* : **~ (à)** favourable *Br ou* favorable *Am* (to).

favorablement [favɔrabləmã] *adv* favourably *Br*, favorably *Am*.

favori, ite [favɔri, it] *adj* & *nm, f* favourite *Br*, favorite *Am*.

➡ **favoris** *nmpl* side whiskers.

favoriser [3] [favɔrize] *vt* - **1.** [avantager] to favour *Br*, to favor *Am* - **2.** [contribuer à] to promote - **3.** [aider] to assist.

favoritisme [favɔritism] *nm* favouritism *Br*, favoritism *Am*.

fax [faks] *nm* fax.

faxer [3] [fakse] *vt* to fax.

fayot [fajo] *nm fam* [personne] creep, crawler.

FB (*abr de* **franc belge**) BF.

FBI [ɛfbiaj] (*abr de* **Federal Bureau of Investigation**) *nm* FBI.

FC (*abr de* **Football club**) *nm* FC.

FCFA (*abr de* **franc CFA**) *currency still used in former French colonies in Africa.*

FCFP (*abr de* **franc CFP**) *currency still used in former French colonies in the Pacific.*

fébrile [febril] *adj* feverish.

fébrilement [febrilmã] *adv* feverishly.

fécal, e, aux [fekal, o] ⊏▷ **matière**.

fécond, e [fekɔ̃, ɔ̃d] *adj* - **1.** [femelle, terre, esprit] fertile - **2.** [écrivain] prolific - **3.** [histoire, situation] : **~ en qqch** rich in sthg.

fécondation [fekɔ̃dasjɔ̃] *nf* fertilization ; **~ in vitro** in vitro fertilization.

féconder [3] [fekɔ̃de] *vt* - **1.** [ovule] to fertilize - **2.** [femme, femelle] to impregnate - **3.** *littéraire* [fertiliser] to make fertile.

fécondité [fekɔ̃dite] *nf* - **1.** [gén] fertility - **2.** [d'écrivain] productiveness.

fécule [fekyl] *nf* starch.

féculent, e [fekylã, ãt] *adj* starchy.

➡ **féculent** *nm* starchy food.

fédéral, e, aux [federal, o] *adj* federal.

fédéralisme [federalism] *nm* federalism.

fédératif, ive [federatif, iv] *adj* federative.

fédération [federasjɔ̃] *nf* federation.

fée [fe] *nf* fairy ; **~ du logis** model housekeeper.

feed-back [fidbak] *nm inv* feedback.

féerie [fe(e)ri] *nf* - **1.** THÉÂTRE spectacular ; CIN fantasy - **2.** [de lieu] enchantment ; [de vision] enchanting sight.

féerique [fe(e)rik] *adj* [enchanteur] enchanting.

feignais, feignions *etc* ⊳ **feindre**.

feignant, e = **fainéant**.

feindre [81] [fɛ̃dr] ◇ *vt* to feign ; ~ **de faire qqch** to pretend to do sthg ◇ *vi* to pretend.

feint, e [fɛ̃, fɛ̃t] *pp* ⊳ **feindre**.

feinte [fɛ̃t] *nf* - **1.** [ruse] ruse - **2.** FOOTBALL dummy ; BOXE feint.

fêlé, e [fele] ◇ *adj* - **1.** [assiette] cracked - **2.** *fam* [personne] cracked, loony ◇ *nm, f fam* freak, nutter.

fêler [4] [fele] *vt* to crack.
➡ **se fêler** *vp* to crack.

félicitations [felisitasjɔ̃] *nfpl* congratulations ; **avec les ~ du jury** highly commended.

féliciter [3] [felisite] *vt* to congratulate.
➡ **se féliciter** *vp* : **se ~ de** to congratulate o.s. on.

félin, e [felɛ̃, in] *adj* feline.
➡ **félin** *nm* big cat.

fêlure [felyr] *nf* crack.

femelle [fəmɛl] *nf & adj* female.

féminin, e [feminɛ̃, in] *adj* - **1.** [gén] feminine - **2.** [revue, équipe] women's *(avant n)*.
➡ **féminin** *nm* GRAM feminine.

féminiser [3] [feminize] *vt* - **1.** [efféminer] to make effeminate - **2.** BIOL to feminize.
➡ **se féminiser** *vp* - **1.** [institution] to attract more women - **2.** [homme] to become effeminate.

féminisme [feminism] *nm* feminism.

féministe [feminist] *nmf & adj* feminist.

féminité [feminite] *nf* femininity.

femme [fam] *nf* - **1.** [personne de sexe féminin] woman ; **bonne ~** *péj* woman ; **contes/ remèdes de bonne ~** old wives' tales/ remedies ; **~ d'affaires** businesswoman ; **~ de chambre** chambermaid ; **~ fatale** femme fatale ; **~ au foyer** housewife ; **~ de ménage** cleaning woman ; **~ du monde** society woman ; **~ de tête** forceful woman - **2.** [épouse] wife ; **prendre ~** *vieilli* to take a wife.

femmelette [famlɛt] *nf péj* weakling.

fémur [femyr] *nm* femur.

FEN [fɛn] *(abr de Fédération de l'éducation nationale) nf* teachers' trade union.

fenaison [fənɛzɔ̃] *nf* haymaking.

fendiller [3] [fɑ̃dije] *vt* to crack.
➡ **se fendiller** *vp* to crack.

fendre [73] [fɑ̃dr] *vt* - **1.** [bois] to split - **2.** [foule, flots] to cut through.

➡ **se fendre** *vp* - **1.** [se crevasser] to crack - **2.** *fam* [d'une somme] : **se ~ de qqch** to part with sthg.

fendu, e [fɑ̃dy] *pp* ⊳ **fendre**.

fenêtre [fənɛtr] *nf* [gén & INFORM] window ; **~ à guillotine** sash window.

fenouil [fənuj] *nm* fennel.

fente [fɑ̃t] *nf* - **1.** [fissure] crack - **2.** [interstice, de vêtement] slit.

féodal, e, aux [feɔdal, o] *adj* feudal.
➡ **féodal, aux** *nm* feudal lord.

féodalité [feɔdalite] *nf* feudalism.

fer [fɛr] *nm* iron ; **en ~, de ~** iron *(avant n)* ; **~ à cheval** horseshoe ; **~ forgé** wrought iron ; **~ de lance** spearhead ; **~ à repasser** iron ; **~ à souder** soldering iron ; **les quatre ~s en l'air** flat on one's back ; **croire qqch dur comme ~** to firmly believe sthg ; **il faut battre le ~ quand il est chaud** strike while the iron is hot ; **marquer qqn au ~ rouge** to brand sb.

ferai, feras *etc* ⊳ **faire**.

fer-blanc [fɛrblɑ̃] *(pl* **fers-blancs**) *nm* tinplate, tin ; **en ~** tin *(avant n)*.

ferblanterie [fɛrblɑ̃tri] *nf* - **1.** [commerce] tin industry - **2.** [ustensiles] tinware.

férié, e [ferje] ⊳ **jour**.

férir [ferir] *vt* : **sans coup ~** without meeting any resistance *ou* obstacle.

ferme¹ [fɛrm] *nf* farm.

ferme² [fɛrm] ◇ *adj* firm ; **être ~ sur ses jambes** to be steady on one's feet ◇ *adv* - **1.** [beaucoup] a lot - **2.** [définitivement] : **acheter/ vendre ~** to make a firm purchase/sale - **3.** *loc* : **tenir ~** to stand firm.

fermement [fɛrməmɑ̃] *adv* firmly.

ferment [fɛrmɑ̃] *nm* - **1.** [levure] ferment - **2.** *fig* [germe] seed, seeds *(pl)*.

fermentation [fɛrmɑ̃tasjɔ̃] *nf* CHIM fermentation ; *fig* ferment.

fermenter [3] [fɛrmɑ̃te] *vi* CHIM & *fig* to ferment.

fermer [3] [fɛrme] ◇ *vt* - **1.** [porte, tiroir, yeux] to close, to shut ; [rideaux] to close, to draw ; [store] to pull down ; [enveloppe] to seal - **2.** [bloquer] to close ; **~ son esprit à qqch** to close one's mind to sthg - **3.** [gaz, lumière] to turn off - **4.** [vêtement] to do up - **5.** [entreprise] to close down - **6.** [interdire] : **~ qqch à qqn** to close sthg to sb - **7.** *loc* : **la ferme!, ferme-la!** *fam* shut it! ◇ *vi* - **1.** [gén] to shut, to close - **2.** [vêtement] to do up - **3.** [entreprise] to close down.
➡ **se fermer** *vp* - **1.** [porte] to close, to shut - **2.** [plaie] to close up - **3.** [vêtement] to do up

- 4. *fig* [s'endurcir] : **se ~ (à qqch)** to close o.s. off (from sthg).

fermeté [fɛrmǝte] *nf* firmness.

fermeture [fɛrmǝtyr] *nf* **- 1.** [de porte] closing ; **~ automatique des portes** doors close automatically **- 2.** [de vêtement, sac] fastening ; **~ Éclair**® zip *Br*, zipper *Am* **- 3.** [d'établissement - temporaire] closing ; [- définitive] closure ; **~ hebdomadaire/annuelle** weekly/annual closing.

fermier, ère [fɛrmje, ɛr] <> *adj* farm *(avant n)* <> *nm, f* farmer.

fermoir [fɛrmwar] *nm* clasp.

féroce [ferɔs] *adj* [animal, appétit] ferocious ; [personne, désir] fierce.

férocement [ferɔsmã] *adv* fiercely.

férocité [ferɔsite] *nf* ferocity.

Féroé [ferɔe] *nfpl* : **les îles ~** the Faeroes ; **aux îles ~** in the Faeroes.

ferraille [fɛraj] *nf* **- 1.** [vieux fer] scrap iron *(U)* ; **bon à mettre à la ~** fit for the scrap heap **- 2.** *fam* [monnaie] loose change.

ferré, e [fɛre] *adj* **- 1.** [soulier] hobnailed **- 2.** *fam fig* [calé] : **être ~ en** to be well up on.

ferrer [4] [fɛre] *vt* **- 1.** [cheval] to shoe **- 2.** [poisson] to strike **- 3.** [soulier] to put hobnails on.

ferreux, euse [fɛrø, øz] *adj* ferrous.

ferronnerie [fɛrɔnri] *nf* **- 1.** [objet, métier] ironwork *(U)* **- 2.** [atelier] ironworks *(sg)*.

ferroviaire [fɛrɔvjer] *adj* rail *(avant n)*.

ferrugineux, euse [fɛryʒinø, øz] *adj* ferruginous.

ferrure [fɛryr] *nf* **- 1.** [de porte] fitting **- 2.** [de cheval] shoeing.

ferry-boat [fɛribot] *(pl* **ferry-boats)** *nm* ferry.

fertile [fɛrtil] *adj litt* & *fig* fertile ; **~ en** *fig* filled with, full of.

fertilisant, e [fɛrtilizã, ãt] *adj* fertilizing.

fertiliser [3] [fɛrtilize] *vt* to fertilize.

fertilité [fɛrtilite] *nf* fertility.

féru, e [fery] *adj sout* [passionné] : **être ~ de qqch** to have a passion for sthg.

férule [feryl] *nf* : **(être) sous la ~ de qqn** *sout* (to be) under sb's iron rule.

fervent, e [fɛrvã, ãt] <> *adj* [chrétien] fervent ; [amoureux, démocrate] ardent <> *nm, f* devotee.

ferveur [fɛrvœr] *nf* **- 1.** [dévotion] fervour *Br*, fervor *Am* **- 2.** [zèle] zeal.

fesse [fɛs] *nf* buttock.

fessée [fese] *nf* spanking, smack (on the bottom).

fessier, ère [fesje, ɛr] *adj* buttock *(avant n)*.
➡ **fessier** *nm* buttocks *(pl)*.

festin [fɛstɛ̃] *nm* banquet, feast.

festival, als [fɛstival] *nm* festival.

festivités [fɛstivite] *nfpl* festivities.

feston [fɛstɔ̃] *nm* **- 1.** ARCHIT festoon **- 2.** COUTURE scallop.

festoyer [13] [fɛstwaje] *vi* to feast.

fêtard, e [fɛtar, ard] *nm, f* fun-loving person.

fête [fɛt] *nf* **- 1.** [congé] holiday ; **les ~s (de fin d'année)** the Christmas holidays ; **~ légale** public holiday ; **~ nationale** national holiday **- 2.** [réunion, réception] celebration ; **~ de famille** family celebration **- 3.** [kermesse] fair ; **en ~** in festive mood ; **~ foraine** funfair ; **la ~ de l'Humanité** *annual festival organized by the Communist daily newspaper 'l'Humanité'* ; **la ~ de la Musique** *annual music festival which takes place in the streets* **- 4.** [jour de célébration - de personne] saint's day ; [- de saint] feast (day) ; **~ des mères/des pères** Mother's/Father's Day **- 5.** [soirée] party **- 6.** *loc* : **ça va être ta ~** *fam* you'll get it in the neck ; **faire ~ à qqn** to make a fuss of sb ; **faire la ~** to have a good time.

FÊTE

FÊTE

The French traditionally wish 'bonne fête' to the person who has the same name as the saint commemorated on a particular day.

FÊTE DE LA MUSIQUE

This annual music festival which began life in the 1980s is becoming increasingly popular. On 21st June in cities throughout France the streets fill with both professional and amateur musicians, playing a wide range of music from classical to jazz, from rock to rap. All of the open-air concerts are free.

Fête-Dieu [fɛtdjø] *(pl inv* OU **Fêtes-Dieu)** *nf* Corpus Christi.

fêter [4] [fete] *vt* [événement] to celebrate ; [personne] to have a party for.

fétiche [fetiʃ] *nm* **- 1.** [objet de culte] fetish **- 2.** [mascotte] mascot.

fétichisme [fetiʃism] *nm* **- 1.** [culte, perversion] fetishism **- 2.** [vénération] idolatry.

fétide [fetid] *adj* fetid.

fétu [fety] *nm* : **~ (de paille)** wisp (of straw).

feu¹, e [fø] *adj* : **~ M. X** the late Mr X ; **~ mon mari** my late husband.

feu², x [fø] *nm* **- 1.** [flamme, incendie] fire ; **au ~!** fire! ; **en ~** *litt* & *fig* on fire ; **avez-vous du ~?** have you got a light? ; **faire ~** MIL to fire ; **mettre le ~ à qqch** to set fire to sthg, to set sthg

on fire ; **prendre ~** to catch fire ; **~ de bois** wood fire ; **~ de camp** camp fire ; **~ de cheminée** chimney fire ; **~ follet** will-o'-the-wisp ; **~ de joie** bonfire ; **être pris entre deux ~x** to be caught in the crossfire ; **jouer avec le ~** to play with fire ; **mettre à ~ et à sang** to ravage **- 2.** [signal] light ; **tous ~x éteints** without any lights ; **~ rouge/vert** red/green light ; **~x de croisement** dipped headlights ; **~x de position** sidelights ; **~x de route** headlights on full beam ; **~x de stationnement** parking lights ; **donner son** OU **le ~ vert (à qqn)** to give (sb) the go-ahead **- 3.** CULIN ring Br, burner Am ; **à ~ doux/vif** on a low/high flame ; **à petit ~** gently **- 4.** CIN & THÉÂTRE light (U) **- 5.** loc : **ne pas faire long ~** not to last long.
➨ **feu d'artifice** nm firework.

feuillage [fœjaʒ] nm foliage.

feuille [fœj] nf **- 1.** [d'arbre] leaf ; **~ morte** dead leaf ; **~ de vigne** BOT vine leaf **- 2.** [page] sheet ; **~ blanche** blank sheet ; **~ de papier** sheet of paper ; **~ volante** loose leaf **- 3.** [document] form ; **~ de soins** claim form for reimbursement of medical expenses **- 4.** [journal] paper ; **~ de chou** fam péj rag.

feuillet [fœjɛ] nm page.

feuilleté, e [fœjte] adj **- 1.** CULIN : **pâte ~e** puff pastry **- 2.** GÉOL foliated.
➨ **feuilleté** nm pastry.

feuilleter [27] [fœjte] vt to flick through.

feuilleton [fœjtɔ̃] nm serial ; **~ télévisé** soap opera.

feuillu, e [fœjy] adj leafy.
➨ **feuillu** nm broad-leaved tree.

feutre [føtr] nm **- 1.** [étoffe] felt **- 2.** [chapeau] felt hat **- 3.** [crayon] felt-tip pen.

feutré, e [føtre] adj **- 1.** [garni de feutre] trimmed with felt ; [qui a l'aspect du feutre] felted **- 2.** [bruit, cri] muffled.

feutrer [3] [føtre] ◇ vt **- 1.** [garnir de feutre] to trim with felt **- 2.** [bruit, cri] to muffle ◇ vi to felt (up).
➨ **se feutrer** vp to felt (up).

feutrine [føtrin] nf lightweight felt.

fève [fɛv] nf broad bean.

février [fevrije] nm February ; voir aussi **septembre**.

FF (abr de **francs français**) FF.

FFI (abr de **Forces françaises de l'intérieur**) nfpl French Resistance forces operating within France during World War II.

FFL (abr de **Forces françaises libres**) nfpl free French Army during World War II.

FFR (abr de **Fédération française de rugby**) nf French rugby federation.

fg abr de **faubourg**.

FGEN (abr de **Fédération générale de l'éducation nationale**) nf teachers' trade union.

fi [fi] interj : **faire ~ de** to scorn.

fiabilité [fjabilite] nf reliability.

fiable [fjabl] adj reliable.

FIAC [fjak] (abr de **Foire internationale d'art contemporain**) nf international contemporary art fair held annually in Paris.

fiacre [fjakr] nm hackney carriage.

fiançailles [fjɑ̃saj] nfpl engagement (sg).

fiancé, e [fjɑ̃se] nm, f fiancé (f fiancée).

fiancer [16] [fjɑ̃se] ➨ **se fiancer** vp : **se ~ (avec)** to get engaged (to).

fiasco [fjasko] nm fiasco ; **faire ~** to be a fiasco.

fibre [fibr] nf **- 1.** ANAT, BIOL & TECHNOL fibre Br, fiber Am ; **~ optique** fibre Br OU fiber Am optics (U) ; **~ de verre** fibreglass Br OU fiberglass Am, glass fibre Br **- 2.** fig [sentiment] feeling ; **avoir la ~ maternelle** to have the maternal instinct.

fibreux, euse [fibrø, øz] adj fibrous ; [viande] stringy.

fibrome [fibrom] nm fibroma.

ficelé, e [fisle] adj fam dressed ; **être mal ~** to be scruffy.

ficeler [24] [fisle] vt [lier] to tie up.

ficelle [fisɛl] nf **- 1.** [fil] string ; **tirer les ~s** to pull the strings **- 2.** [pain] thin French stick **- 3.** (gén pl) [truc] trick.

fiche [fiʃ] nf **- 1.** [document] card ; **~ de paie** pay slip ; **~ signalétique** identification sheet ; **~ technique** technical data sheet **- 2.** ÉLECTR & TECHNOL pin.

ficher [3] [fiʃe] (pp vt sens 1 & 2 fiché, pp vt sens 3 & 4 fichu) vt **- 1.** [enfoncer] : **~ qqch dans** to stick sthg into **- 2.** [inscrire] to put on file **- 3.** fam [faire] : **qu'est-ce qu'il fiche?** what's he doing? **- 4.** fam [mettre] to put ; **~ qqn par terre** to send sb flying ; **~ qqch par terre** fig to mess OU muck sthg up ; **~ qqn dehors** OU **à la porte** to throw sb out.
➨ **se ficher** vp **- 1.** [s'enfoncer - suj : clou, pique] : **se ~ dans** to go into **- 2.** fam [se moquer] : **se ~ de** to make fun of **- 3.** fam [ne pas tenir compte] : **se ~ de** not to give a damn about **- 4.** loc : **se ~ dedans** fam to get it all wrong.

fichier [fiʃje] nm file.

fichu, e [fiʃy] adj **- 1.** fam [cassé, fini] done for **- 2.** (avant n) [désagréable] nasty **- 3.** loc : **être mal ~** fam [personne] to feel rotten ; [objet] to be badly made ; **il n'est même pas ~ de faire son lit** fam he can't even make his own bed.
➨ **fichu** nm scarf.

fictif, ive [fiktif, iv] *adj* - **1.** [imaginaire] imaginary - **2.** [faux] false - **3.** [valeur] face *(avant n)*.

fiction [fiksjɔ̃] *nf* - **1.** LITTÉRATURE fiction - **2.** [monde imaginaire] dream world.

ficus [fikys] *nm* fig-tree.

fidèle [fidɛl] ⬦ *nmf* - **1.** RELIG believer - **2.** [adepte] fan ⬦ *adj* - **1.** [loyal, exact, semblable] : ~ (**à**) faithful (to) ; ~ **à la réalité** accurate - **2.** [habitué] regular.

fidèlement [fidɛlmɑ̃] *adv* - **1.** [loyalement, exactement] faithfully - **2.** [régulièrement] regularly.

fidéliser [3] [fidelize] *vt* to attract and keep.

fidélité [fidelite] *nf* faithfulness.

Fidji [fidʒi] *n* Fiji ; **à** ~ in Fiji.

fidjien, enne [fidʒjɛ̃, ɛn] *adj* Fijian.
➡ **Fidjien, enne** *nm, f* Fijian.

fief [fjɛf] *nm* fief ; *fig* stronghold.

fieffé, e [fjefe] *adj* arrant.

fiel [fjɛl] *nm litt* & *fig* gall.

fiente [fjɑ̃t] *nf* droppings *(pl)*.

fier¹, fière [fjɛr] *adj* - **1.** [gén] proud ; ~ **de qqn/qqch** proud of sb/sthg ; ~ **de faire qqch** proud to be doing sthg - **2.** [noble] noble.

fier² [9] [fje] ➡ **se fier** *vp* : **se** ~ **à** to trust, to rely on.

fièrement [fjɛrmɑ̃] *adv* proudly.

fierté [fjɛrte] *nf* - **1.** [satisfaction, dignité] pride - **2.** [arrogance] arrogance.

fièvre [fjɛvr] *nf* - **1.** MÉD fever ; **avoir de la** ~ to have a fever ; **avoir 40 de** ~ to have a temperature of 105 (degrees) - **2.** *fig* [excitation] excitement.

fiévreusement [fjevrøzmɑ̃] *adv* feverishly.

fiévreux, euse [fjevrø, øz] *adj litt* & *fig* feverish.

fig. *abr de* **figure**.

figé, e [fiʒe] *adj* fixed.

figer [17] [fiʒe] *vt* to paralyse *Br*, to paralyze *Am* ; **être figé sur place** to be rooted to the spot.
➡ **se figer** *vp* - **1.** [s'immobiliser] to freeze - **2.** [se solidifier] to congeal.

fignoler [3] [fiɲɔle] *vt* to put the finishing touches to.

figue [fig] *nf* fig.

figuier [figje] *nm* fig-tree.

figurant, e [figyrɑ̃, ɑ̃t] *nm, f* extra.

figuratif, ive [figyratif, iv] *adj* figurative.

figuration [figyrasjɔ̃] *nf* CIN & THÉÂTRE : **faire de la** ~ to work as an extra.

figure [figyr] *nf* - **1.** [gén] figure ; **faire** ~ **de** to look like ; ~**s imposées/libres** SPORT compulsory/freestyle section ; ~ **de proue** figurehead ; *fig* leading light ; ~ **de rhétori-**que LING figure of speech ; ~ **de style** LING stylistic device - **2.** [visage] face ; **faire bonne** ~ *fig* to put on a good face.

figuré, e [figyre] *adj* [sens] figurative.
➡ **figuré** *nm* : **au** ~ in the figurative sense.

figurer [3] [figyre] ⬦ *vt* to represent ⬦ *vi* : ~ **dans/parmi** to figure in/among.

figurine [figyrin] *nf* figurine.

fil [fil] *nm* - **1.** [brin] thread ; ~ **à plomb** plumb line ; ~ **conducteur** *fig* main idea ; **c'est cousu de** ~ **blanc** it doesn't fool anybody ; **de** ~ **en aiguille** gradually ; **donner du** ~ **à retordre** *fig* to make life difficult ; **perdre le** ~ **(de qqch)** *fig* to lose the thread (of sthg) ; **ne tenir qu'à un** ~ *fig* to hang by a thread - **2.** [câble] wire ; ~ **de fer** wire ; **avoir qqn au bout du** ~ to have sb on the line - **3.** [cours] course ; **au** ~ **de** in the course of - **4.** [tissu] linen - **5.** [tranchant] edge.

filament [filamɑ̃] *nm* - **1.** ANAT & ÉLECTR filament - **2.** [végétal] fibre *Br*, fiber *Am* - **3.** [de colle, bave] thread.

filandreux, euse [filɑ̃drø, øz] *adj* [viande] stringy.

filant, e [filɑ̃, ɑ̃t] ▭ **étoile**.

filasse [filas] ⬦ *nf* tow ⬦ *adj inv* flaxen.

filature [filatyr] *nf* - **1.** [usine] mill ; [fabrication] spinning - **2.** [poursuite] tailing ; **prendre qqn en** ~ to tail sb.

file [fil] *nf* line ; **à la** ~ in a line ; **en double** ~ in two lines ; **se garer en double** ~ to double-park ; **en** ~ **indienne** in single *ou* Indian file ; **se mettre en** ~ to line up ; ~ **d'attente** queue *Br*, line *Am*.

filer [3] [file] ⬦ *vt* - **1.** [soie, coton] to spin - **2.** [personne] to tail - **3.** *fam* [donner] : ~ **qqch à qqn** to slip sthg to sb, to slip sb sthg ⬦ *vi* - **1.** [bas] to ladder *Br*, to run *Am* - **2.** [aller vite - temps, véhicule] to fly (by) - **3.** *fam* [partir] to dash off - **4.** *loc* : ~ **doux** to behave nicely.

filet [file] *nm* - **1.** [à mailles] net ; ~ **à papillons** butterfly net ; ~ **de pêche** fishing net ; ~ **de provisions** string bag ; **travailler sans** ~ *fig* to take risks ; **tendre un** ~ *fig* to set a trap - **2.** CULIN fillet *Br*, filet *Am* ; ~ **de bœuf** fillet *Br* *ou* filet *Am* of beef ; ~ **de sole** fillet *Br* *ou* filet *Am* of sole - **3.** [de liquide] drop, dash ; [de lumière] shaft - **4.** [de vis] thread.

filial, e, aux [filjal, o] *adj* filial.
➡ **filiale** *nf* ÉCON subsidiary.

filiation [filjasjɔ̃] *nf* - **1.** [lien de parenté] line - **2.** *fig* [enchaînement] logical relationship.

filière [filjɛr] *nf* - **1.** [voie] : **suivre la** ~ [professionnelle] to work one's way up ; **suivre la** ~ **hiérarchique** to go through the right channels - **2.** [réseau] network.

filiforme [filifɔrm] *adj* skinny.
filigrane [filigran] *nm* [dessin] watermark ; **en ~** *fig* between the lines.
filin [filɛ̃] *nm* rope.
fille [fij] *nf* - **1.** [enfant] daughter - **2.** [femme] girl ; **jeune ~** girl ; **~ de joie** prostitute ; **~ mère** *péj* single mother ; **vieille ~** *péj* spinster ; **courir les ~s** *fig* to chase women.
fillette [fijɛt] *nf* little girl.
filleul, e [fijœl] *nm, f* godchild.
film [film] *nm* - **1.** [gén] film ; **~ d'action** action film ; **~ catastrophe** disaster movie ; **~ culte** cult film *Br*, cult movie *Am* ; **~ d'épouvante** horror film ; **~ noir** film noir ; **~ policier** detective film - **2.** *fig* [déroulement] course.
filmer [3] [filme] *vt* to film.
filmographie [filmɔgrafi] *nf* filmography, films *(pl)*.
filon [filɔ̃] *nm* - **1.** [de mine] vein - **2.** *fam fig* [possibilité] cushy number.
filou [filu] *nm* rogue.
filouterie [filutri] *nf* fraud.
fils [fis] *nm* son ; **~ de famille** boy from a privileged background ; **~ à papa** *péj* daddy's boy ; **le ~ prodigue** the prodigal son.
filtrage [filtraʒ] *nm* filtering ; *fig* screening.
filtrant, e [filtrɑ̃, ɑ̃t] *adj* [verre] tinted.
filtre [filtr] *nm* filter ; **~ à air** *AUTOM* air filter ; **~ à café** coffee filter.
filtrer [3] [filtre] ⬦ *vt* to filter ; *fig* to screen ⬦ *vi* to filter ; *fig* to filter through.
fin, fine [fɛ̃, fin] ⬦ *adj* - **1.** [gén] fine - **2.** [partie du corps] slender ; [couche, papier] thin - **3.** [subtil] shrewd - **4.** [ouïe, vue] keen - **5.** *(avant n)* [spécialiste] expert ⬦ *adv* finely ; **~ prêt** quite ready.
➤ **fin** *nf* end ; **~ mars** at the end of March ; **mettre ~ à** to put a stop *ou* an end to ; **prendre ~** to come to an end ; **tirer** *ou* **toucher à sa ~** to draw to a close ; **~ de citation** (quote) unquote ; **~ de saison** end of season ; **arrondir ses ~s de mois** to make ends meet ; **arriver** *ou* **parvenir à ses ~s** to achieve one's ends *ou* aims ; **c'est la ~ des haricots** it's the last straw ; **mener à bonne ~** to bring to a successful conclusion ; **mettre ~ à ses jours** to put an end to one's life ; **à toutes ~s utiles** just in case.
➤ **fin de série** *nf* oddment.
➤ **à la fin** *loc adv* : **tu vas m'écouter, à la ~?** will you listen to me?
➤ **à la fin de** *loc prép* at the end of.
➤ **en fin de** *loc prép* at the end of.
➤ **sans fin** *loc adj* endless.

final, e [final] *(pl* **finals** *ou* **finaux** [fino]*) adj* final.
➤ **final(e)** *nm* *MUS* finale.
➤ **finale** *nf* - **1.** *SPORT* final - **2.** [de mot] last syllable.
finalement [finalmɑ̃] *adv* finally.
finaliser [3] [finalize] *vt* to finalize.
finaliste [finalist] *nmf & adj* finalist.
finalité [finalite] *nf sout* [fonction] purpose.
finance [finɑ̃s] *nf* finance ; **la haute ~** high finance.
➤ **finances** *nfpl* finances.
➤ **Finances** *nfpl* : **les Finances** ≈ the Treasury, the Exchequer *Br*.
financement [finɑ̃smɑ̃] *nm* financing, funding.
financer [16] [finɑ̃se] *vt* to finance, to fund.
financier, ère [finɑ̃sje, ɛr] *adj* financial.
➤ **financier** *nm* financier.
financièrement [finɑ̃sjɛrmɑ̃] *adv* financially.
finasser [3] [finase] *vi fam* to resort to tricks.
finaud, e [fino, od] *adj* wily, crafty.
fine [fin] *nf* type of brandy.
finement [finmɑ̃] *adv* - **1.** [délicatement] finely - **2.** [adroitement] cleverly - **3.** [subtilement] subtly.
finesse [fines] *nf* - **1.** [gén] fineness - **2.** [minceur] slenderness - **3.** [perspicacité] shrewdness - **4.** [subtilité] subtlety.
fini, e [fini] *adj* - **1.** *péj* [fieffé] : **un crétin ~** a complete idiot - **2.** *fam* [usé, diminué] finished - **3.** [limité] finite.
➤ **fini** *nm* [d'objet] finish.
finir [32] [finir] ⬦ *vt* - **1.** [gén] to finish, to end - **2.** [vider] to empty - **3.** *fam* [user] to wear out ⬦ *vi* - **1.** [gén] to finish, to end ; **~ par faire qqch** to do sthg eventually ; **tu vas ~ par tomber!** you're going to fall! ; **mal ~** to end badly - **2.** [arrêter] : **~ de faire qqch** to stop doing sthg ; **en ~ (avec)** to finish (with) ; **à n'en plus ~** never-ending.
finish [finiʃ] *nm* finish ; **au ~** to the finish.
finition [finisjɔ̃] *nf* - **1.** [action] finishing - **2.** [d'objet] finish.
finlandais, e [fɛ̃lɑ̃dɛ, ɛz] *adj* Finnish.
➤ **Finlandais, e** *nm, f* Finn.
Finlande [fɛ̃lɑ̃d] *nf* : **la ~** Finland.
finnois, e [finwa, az] *adj* Finnish.
➤ **finnois** *nm* [langue] Finnish.
➤ **Finnois, e** *nm, f* Finn.
FINUL, Finul [finyl] *(abr de* **Forces intérimaires des Nations unies au Liban)** *nfpl* UNIFIL.
fiole [fjɔl] *nf* flask.
fioriture [fjɔrityr] *nf* flourish.

fioul = fuel.

FIP [fip] (*abr de* **France Inter Paris**) *nf French national radio station broadcasting music and traffic information.*

firmament [firmamɑ̃] *nm* firmament.

firme [firm] *nf* firm.

fis, fit *etc* ⊳ **faire.**

FIS [fis] (*abr de* **Front islamique du salut**) *nm* : **le ~** the Islamic Salvation Front.

fisc [fisk] *nm* ≃ Inland Revenue *Br*, ≃ Internal Revenue *Am*.

fiscal, e, aux [fiskal, o] *adj* tax *(avant n)*, fiscal.

fiscaliser [3] [fiskalize] *vt* to (make) subject to tax.

fiscalité [fiskalite] *nf* tax system.

fissure [fisyr] *nf litt* & *fig* crack.

fissurer [3] [fisyre] *vt* [fendre] to crack ; *fig* to split.
⬥ **se fissurer** *vp* to crack.

fiston [fistɔ̃] *nm fam* son.

fitness [fitnɛs] *nm* keep-fit.

FIV [fiv] (*abr de* **fécondation in vitro**) *nf* IVF.

FIVETE, Fivete [fivɛt] (*abr de* **fécondation in vitro et transfert d'embryon**) *nf* GIFT ; **une ~** a test-tube baby.

fixateur, trice [fiksatœr, tris] *adj* - **1.** PHOT fixing *(avant n)* - **2.** [lotion, crème] setting *(avant n).*
⬥ **fixateur** *nm* PHOT fixer.

fixatif [fiksatif] *nm* fixative.

fixation [fiksasjɔ̃] *nf* - **1.** [action de fixer] fixing - **2.** [attache] fastening, fastener ; [de ski] binding - **3.** PSYCHOL fixation.

fixe [fiks] *adj* fixed ; [encre] permanent ; **à heure ~** at set *ou* fixed times.
⬥ **fixe** *nm* fixed salary.

fixement [fiksəmɑ̃] *adv* fixedly ; **regarder ~ qqn/qqch** to stare at sb/sthg.

fixer [3] [fikse] *vt* - **1.** [gén] to fix ; [règle] to set ; **~ son choix sur** to decide on - **2.** [monter] to hang - **3.** [regarder] to stare at - **4.** [renseigner] : **~ qqn sur qqch** to put sb in the picture about sthg ; **être fixé sur qqch** to know all about sthg.
⬥ **se fixer** *vp* to settle ; **se ~ sur** [suj : choix, personne] to settle on ; [suj : regard] to rest on.

fixité [fiksite] *nf* steadiness.

fjord [fjɔrd] *nm* fjord.

fl. (*abr de* **fleuve**) R.

FL (*abr de* **florin**) Fl, F, G.

flacon [flakɔ̃] *nm* small bottle ; **~ à parfum** perfume bottle.

flageller [4] [flaʒele] *vt* - **1.** [fouetter] to flagellate - **2.** *fig* [fustiger] to denounce.

flageoler [3] [flaʒɔle] *vi* to tremble.

flageolet [flaʒɔlɛ] *nm* - **1.** [haricot] flageolet bean - **2.** MUS flageolet.

flagornerie [flagɔrnəri] *nf* flattery.

flagrant, e [flagrɑ̃, ɑ̃t] *adj* flagrant ⊳ **délit.**

flair [flɛr] *nm* sense of smell ; **avoir du ~** *fig* to be intuitive.

flairer [4] [flɛre] *vt* to sniff, to smell ; *fig* to scent.

flamand, e [flamɑ̃, ɑ̃d] *adj* Flemish.
⬥ **flamand** *nm* [langue] Flemish.
⬥ **Flamand, e** *nm, f* Flemish person, Fleming.

flamant [flamɑ̃] *nm* flamingo ; **~ rose** pink flamingo.

flambant, e [flɑ̃bɑ̃, ɑ̃t] *adj* : **~ neuf** brand new.

flambeau, x [flɑ̃bo] *nm* torch ; *fig* flame ; **se passer le ~** *fig* to hand on the torch.

flambée [flɑ̃be] *nf* - **1.** [feu] blaze - **2.** *fig* [de colère] outburst ; [de violence] outbreak ; **il y a eu une ~ des prix** prices have sky-rocketed.

flamber [3] [flɑ̃be] ◇ *vi* - **1.** [brûler] to blaze - **2.** *fam* JEU to play for high stakes ◇ *vt* - **1.** [crêpe] to flambé - **2.** [volaille] to singe.

flamboie, flamboies *etc* ⊳ **flamboyer.**

flamboyant, e [flɑ̃bwajɑ̃, ɑ̃t] *adj* - **1.** [ciel, regard] blazing ; [couleur] flaming - **2.** ARCHIT flamboyant.

flamboyer [13] [flɑ̃bwaje] *vi* to blaze.

flamingant, e [flamɛ̃gɑ̃, ɑ̃t] *adj* - **1.** [nationaliste] Flemish-nationalist - **2.** [de langue] Flemish-speaking.
⬥ **Flamingant, e** *nm, f* - **1.** [nationaliste] Flemish nationalist - **2.** [de langue] Flemish speaker.

flamme [flam] *nf* flame ; *fig* fervour *Br*, fervor *Am*, fire.

flan [flɑ̃] *nm* baked custard.

flanc [flɑ̃] *nm* [de personne, navire, montagne] side ; [d'animal, d'armée] flank ; **à ~ de coteau** on the hillside ; **être sur le ~** *fig* to feel washed out ; **tirer au ~** *fam fig* to shirk, to skive *Br*.

flancher [3] [flɑ̃ʃe] *vi fam* to give up.

flanelle [flanɛl] *nf* flannel.

flâner [3] [flane] *vi* - **1.** [se promener] to stroll - **2.** [s'attarder] to hang about, to lounge about.

flânerie [flɑnri] *nf* stroll.

flâneur, euse [flɑnœr, øz] *nm, f* stroller.

flanquer [3] [flɑ̃ke] *vt* - **1.** *fam* [jeter] : **~ qqch par terre** to fling sthg to the ground ; **~ qqn dehors** to chuck *ou* fling sb out - **2.** *fam* [donner] : **~ une gifle à qqn** to clout sb round the ear ; **~ la frousse à qqn** to put the wind up sb

- 3. [accompagner] : **être flanqué de** to be flanked by.

se flanquer *vp fam* : **se ~ par terre** to fall flat on one's face.

flapi, e [flapi] *adj fam* dead beat.

flaque [flak] *nf* pool ; **~ (d'eau)** puddle.

flash [flaʃ] *nm* **- 1.** PHOT flash **- 2.** RADIO & TÉLÉ : **~ (d'information)** newsflash ; **~ de publicité** commercial.

flash-back [flaʃbak] (*pl inv* OU **flash-backs**) *nm* CIN flashback.

flasher [3] [flaʃe] *vi fam* : **~ sur qqn/qqch** to be turned on by sb/sthg ; **faire ~ qqn** to turn sb on.

flasque [flask] ◇ *nf* flask ◇ *adj* flabby, limp.

flatter [3] [flate] *vt* **- 1.** [louer] to flatter **- 2.** [caresser] to stroke.

se flatter *vp* to flatter o.s. ; **je me flatte de le convaincre** I flatter myself that I can convince him ; **se ~ de faire qqch** to pride o.s. on doing sthg.

flatterie [flatri] *nf* flattery.

flatteur, euse [flatœr, øz] ◇ *adj* flattering ◇ *nm, f* flatterer.

flatulence [flatylɑ̃s] *nf* flatulence, wind.

FLE, fle [flə] (*abr de* **français langue étrangère**) *nm* French as a foreign language.

fléau, x [fleo] *nm* **- 1.** *litt* & *fig* [calamité] scourge **- 2.** [instrument] flail.

flèche [flɛʃ] *nf* **- 1.** [gén] arrow **- 2.** [d'église] spire **- 3.** *fig* [critique] shaft **- 4.** *loc* : **monter en ~** to shoot up ; **partir comme une ~** to shoot off.

flécher [18] [fleʃe] *vt* to mark (with arrows).

fléchette [fleʃɛt] *nf* dart.

fléchettes *nfpl* darts *(sg)*.

fléchir [32] [fleʃir] ◇ *vt* to bend, to flex ; *fig* to sway ◇ *vi* to bend ; *fig* to weaken.

fléchissement [fleʃismɑ̃] *nm* flexing, bending ; *fig* weakening.

flegmatique [flɛgmatik] *adj* phlegmatic.

flegme [flɛgm] *nm* composure.

flemmard, e [flɛmar, ard] *fam* ◇ *adj* lazy ◇ *nm, f* lazybones *(sg)*.

flemmarder [3] [flɛmarde] *vi fam* to lounge about.

flemme [flɛm] *nf fam* laziness ; **j'ai la ~ (de sortir)** I can't be bothered (to go out).

flétan [fletɑ̃] *nm* halibut.

flétrir [32] [fletrir] *vt* [fleur, visage] to wither.

se flétrir *vp* to wither.

fleur [flœr] *nf* BOT & *fig* flower ; **en ~, en ~s** [arbre] in flower, in blossom ; **à ~s** [motif] flowered ; **la fine ~ de** *fig* the flower OU the cream of ; **~ de lys** fleur-de-lis ; **dans la ~ de l'âge** in the prime of life ; **être ~ bleue** to be a romantic, to be sentimental ; **faire une ~ à qqn** *fam* to do sb a good turn ; **avoir les nerfs à ~ de peau** to be all on edge.

fleurer [5] [flœre] *vt* : **~ bon la vanille** to have a pleasant smell of vanilla.

fleuret [flœre] *nm* foil.

fleurette [flœrɛt] *nf* : **conter ~ à qqn** *vieilli* OU *hum* to whisper sweet nothings to sb.

fleuri, e [flœri] *adj* **- 1.** [jardin, pré] in flower ; [vase] of flowers ; [tissu] flowered ; [table, appartement] decorated with flowers **- 2.** *fig* [style] flowery.

fleurir [32] [flœrir] ◇ *vi* to blossom ; *fig* to flourish ◇ *vt* [maison] to decorate with flowers ; [tombe] to lay flowers on.

fleuriste [flœrist] *nmf* florist.

fleuron [flœrɔ̃] *nm fig* jewel.

fleuve [flœv] *nm* **- 1.** [cours d'eau] river **- 2.** *(en apposition)* [interminable] lengthy, interminable ; **un discours-~** an interminable speech.

flexible [flɛksibl] *adj* flexible.

flexion [flɛksjɔ̃] *nf* **- 1.** [de genou, de poutre] bending **- 2.** LING inflexion.

flibustier [flibystje] *nm* buccaneer.

flic [flik] *nm fam* cop.

flingue [flɛ̃g] *nm fam* gun.

flinguer [3] [flɛ̃ge] *vt fam* to gun down.

se flinguer *vp fam* to blow one's brains out.

flipper[1] [flipœr] *nm* pin-ball machine.

flipper[2] [3] [flipe] *vi fam* **- 1.** [être déprimé] to feel down **- 2.** [planer] to freak out.

flirt [flœrt] *nm* **- 1.** [amourette] flirtation **- 2.** [personne] boyfriend (*f* girlfriend).

flirter [3] [flœrte] *vi* : **~ (avec qqn)** to flirt (with sb) ; **~ avec qqch** *fig* to flirt with sthg.

FLN (*abr de* **Front de libération nationale**) *nm Algerian national liberation front.*

FLNC (*abr de* **Front de libération nationale corse**) *nm Corsican national liberation front.*

FLNKS (*abr de* **Front de libération nationale kanak et socialiste**) *nm political movement in New Caledonia.*

flocon [flɔkɔ̃] *nm* flake ; **~ de neige** snowflake ; **~s d'avoine** oat flakes.

flonflon [flɔ̃flɔ̃] *nm (gén pl)* blare.

flop [flɔp] *nm* [échec] flop, failure.

flopée [flɔpe] *nf fam* : **une ~ de** heaps of, masses of.

floraison [flɔrɛzɔ̃] *nf litt* & *fig* flowering, blossoming.

floral, e, aux [flɔral, o] *adj* floral.

floralies [flɔrali] *nfpl* flower show *(sg).*

flore [flɔr] *nf* flora.

Florence [flɔrɑ̃s] *n* Florence.

Floride [flɔrid] *nf* : **la ~** Florida.

florilège [flɔrilɛʒ] *nm* anthology.

florissant, e [flɔrisɑ̃, ɑ̃t] *adj* [santé] blooming ; [économie] flourishing.

flot [flo] *nm* flood, stream ; **être à ~** [navire] to be afloat ; *fig* to be back to normal ; **couler à ~s** *fig* to flow like water.

➡ **flots** *nmpl littéraire* waves.

flottage [flɔtaʒ] *nm* floating *(of logs).*

flottaison [flɔtɛzɔ̃] *nf* floating.

flottant, e [flɔtɑ̃, ɑ̃t] *adj* - **1.** [gén] floating ; [esprit] irresolute - **2.** [robe] loose-fitting.

flotte [flɔt] *nf* - **1.** AÉRON & NAVIG fleet ; **~ aérienne** air fleet - **2.** *fam* [eau] water - **3.** *fam* [pluie] rain.

flottement [flɔtmɑ̃] *nm* - **1.** [de drapeau] fluttering - **2.** [indécision] hesitation, wavering - **3.** [de monnaie] floating.

flotter [3] [flɔte] ◇ *vi* - **1.** [sur l'eau] to float - **2.** [drapeau] to flap ; [brume, odeur] to drift - **3.** [dans un vêtement] : **tu flottes dedans** it's baggy on you ◇ *v impers fam* : **il flotte** it's raining.

flotteur [flɔtœr] *nm* [de ligne de pêche, d'hydravion] float ; [de chasse d'eau] ballcock.

flou, e [flu] *adj* - **1.** [couleur, coiffure] soft - **2.** [photo] blurred, fuzzy - **3.** [pensée] vague, woolly.

➡ **flou** *nm* [de photo] fuzziness ; [de décision] vagueness ; **le ~ artistique** CIN & PHOT soft focus ; *fig* vagueness.

flouer [3] [flue] *vt fam* to do, to swindle.

fluctuant, e [flyktɥɑ̃, ɑ̃t] *adj* fluctuating.

fluctuation [flyktɥasjɔ̃] *nf* fluctuation.

fluctuer [3] [flyktɥe] *vi* to fluctuate.

fluet, ette [flɥɛ, ɛt] *adj* [personne] thin, slender ; [voix] thin.

fluide [flɥid] ◇ *nm* - **1.** [matière] fluid - **2.** *fig* [pouvoir] (occult) power ◇ *adj* [matière] fluid ; [circulation] flowing freely.

fluidifier [9] [flɥidifje] *vt* [trafic] to improve the flow of.

fluidité [flɥidite] *nf* [gén] fluidity ; [de circulation] easy flow.

fluor [flyɔr] *nm* fluorine.

fluorescent, e [flyɔresɑ̃, ɑ̃t] *adj* fluorescent.

flûte [flyt] ◇ *nf* - **1.** MUS flute ; **~ à bec** recorder ; **~ traversière** flute - **2.** [verre] flute (glass) ; **~ à champagne** champagne flute - **3.** [pain] French stick ◇ *interj fam* bother !

flûtiste [flytist] *nmf* flautist *Br*, flutist *Am*.

fluvial, e, aux [flyvjal, o] *adj* [eaux, pêche] river *(avant n)* ; [alluvions] fluvial.

flux [fly] *nm* - **1.** [écoulement] flow ; **un ~ de** *fig* a flood of - **2.** [marée] flood tide ; **le ~ et le reflux** the ebb and flow - **3.** PHYS flux.

fluxion [flyksjɔ̃] *nf* inflammation ; **~ de poitrine** pneumonia.

FM *(abr de* **frequency modulation)** *nf* FM.

FMI *(abr de* **Fonds monétaire international)** *nm* IMF.

FN *(abr de* **Front national)** *nm* extreme right-wing French political party.

FNAC, Fnac [fnak] *(abr de* **Fédération nationale des achats des cadres)** *nf* chain of large stores selling books, records, audio and video equipment etc.

FNEF, Fnef [fnɛf] *(abr de* **Fédération nationale des étudiants de France)** *nf* students' union.

FNSEA *(abr de* **Fédération nationale des syndicats d'exploitants agricoles)** *nf* farmers' union.

FO *(abr de* **Force ouvrière)** *nf* workers' trade union.

foc [fɔk] *nm* jib.

focal, e, aux [fɔkal, o] *adj* focal.

focaliser [3] [fɔkalize] *vt* to focus.

➡ **se focaliser** *vp fig* : **se ~ sur qqch** to focus on sthg.

fœtal, e, aux [fetal, o] *adj* foetal.

fœtus [fetys] *nm* foetus.

foi [fwa] *nf* - **1.** RELIG faith - **2.** [confiance] trust ; **avoir ~ en qqn/qqch** to trust sb/sthg, to have faith in sb/sthg - **3.** *loc* : **ajouter ~ à** *sout* to lend credence to ; **faire ~** to serve as proof ; **être de bonne/mauvaise ~** to be in good/bad faith ; **ma ~ ...** well ... ; **sur la ~ de** on the strength of.

foie [fwa] *nm* ANAT & CULIN liver ; **~ de veau/de volaille** calf's/chicken liver ; **~ gras** foie gras ; **avoir les ~s** *fam fig* to be scared out of one's wits.

foin [fwɛ̃] *nm* hay ; **faire les ~s** to make hay ; **faire du ~** *fam fig* to make a din.

foire [fwar] *nf* - **1.** [fête] funfair - **2.** [exposition, salon] trade fair - **3.** *fam* [agitation] circus ; **~ d'empoigne** free-for-all ; **faire la ~** *fam fig* to have a wild time.

foirer [3] [fware] *vi fam* [projet] to fall through.

foireux, euse [fwarø, øz] *adj fam* [raté] disastrous ; [qui va rater] doomed.

fois [fwa] *nf* time ; **une ~** once ; **deux ~** twice ; **trois/quatre ~** three/four times ; **deux ~ plus long** twice as long ; **neuf ~ sur dix** nine times out of ten ; **deux ~ trois** two times three ; **cette ~** this time ; **il était une ~ ...** once upon a time there was ... ; **pour une ~ (que)** for once ; **pour la énième ~** for the umpteenth time ; **une autre ~** another time ; **une (bonne) ~** pour toutes once and for all ; **une ~ n'est pas coutume** just the once won't hurt.

➡ **à la fois** *loc adv* at the same time, at once.

➡ **des fois** *loc adv* [parfois] sometimes ; **non, mais des ~!** *fam* look here!

➡ **si des fois** *loc conj fam* if ever.

➡ **une fois que** *loc conj* once.

foison [fwazɔ̃] ➡ **à foison** *loc adv* in abundance.

foisonnement [fwazɔnmɑ̃] *nm* abundance.

foisonner [3] [fwazɔne] *vi* to abound ; **~ en** *ou* **de** to abound in.

folâtre [fɔlatr] *adj* playful.

folâtrer [3] [fɔlatre] *vi* to romp (about).

folichon, onne [fɔliʃɔ̃, ɔn] *adj* : **ça n'est pas ~** *fam* it's not much fun.

folie [fɔli] *nf litt* & *fig* madness ; **à la ~** madly ; **c'est de la ~** it's madness *ou* lunacy ; **avoir la ~ des grandeurs** to have delusions of grandeur ; **faire des ~s** *fig* to be extravagant.

folio [fɔljo] *nm* folio.

folk [fɔlk] <> *nm* folk music <> *adj inv* folk ; **la musique ~** folk music.

folklore [fɔlklɔr] *nm* [de pays] folklore ; **c'est du ~** *fig* you can't take it seriously.

folklorique [fɔlklɔrik] *adj* - **1.** [danse] folk - **2.** *fig* [situation, personne] bizarre, quaint.

folle ⊂▷ **fou**.

follement [fɔlmɑ̃] *adv* madly, wildly ; **~ amoureux** madly in love.

follet [fɔlɛ] ⊂▷ **feu**.

fomenter [3] [fɔmɑ̃te] *vt* to foment.

foncé, e [fɔ̃se] *adj* dark.

foncer [16] [fɔ̃se] <> *vt* to darken, to make darker <> *vi* - **1.** [teinte] to darken - **2.** [se ruer] : **~ sur** to rush at - **3.** *fam* [se dépêcher] to get a move on.

fonceur, euse [fɔ̃sœr, øz] <> *adj* dynamic, go-ahead <> *nm, f* dynamic person.

foncier, ère [fɔ̃sje, ɛr] *adj* - **1.** [impôt] land *(avant n)* ; **propriétaire ~** landowner - **2.** [fondamental] basic, fundamental.

foncièrement [fɔ̃sjɛrmɑ̃] *adv* basically.

fonction [fɔ̃ksjɔ̃] *nf* - **1.** [gén] function ; **faire ~ de** to act as - **2.** [profession] post ; **se démettre de ses ~s** to resign ; **entrer en ~** to take up one's post *ou* duties ; **la ~ publique** the civil service.

➡ **en fonction de** *loc prép* according to.

fonctionnaire [fɔ̃ksjɔnɛr] *nmf* [de l'État] state employee ; [dans l'administration] civil servant ; **haut ~** senior civil servant.

fonctionnariat [fɔ̃ksjɔnarja] *nm* employment by the state.

fonctionnariser [3] [fɔ̃ksjɔnarize] *vt* - **1.** [personne] to make an employee of the state - **2.** [service] to take into the public sector.

fonctionnel, elle [fɔ̃ksjɔnɛl] *adj* functional.

fonctionnement [fɔ̃ksjɔnmɑ̃] *nm* working, functioning.

fonctionner [3] [fɔ̃ksjɔne] *vi* to work, to function.

fond [fɔ̃] *nm* - **1.** [de récipient, puits, mer] bottom ; [de pièce] back ; **un ~** [petite quantité] a drop ; **sans ~** bottomless ; **au fin ~ de** in the depths of ; **de ~ en comble** from top to bottom - **2.** [substance] heart, root ; **avoir un très bon ~** to be a good person at heart ; **le ~ de ma pensée** what I really think ; **le ~ et la forme** content and form ; **aller au ~ des choses** to go to the heart *ou* root of things - **3.** [arrière-plan] background ; **~ sonore** background music.

➡ **fond d'artichaut** *nm* artichoke heart.

➡ **fond de bouteille** *nm* lees *(pl)*, dregs *(pl)*.

➡ **fond de teint** *nm* foundation.

➡ **à fond** *loc adv* - **1.** [entièrement] thoroughly ; **se donner à ~** to give one's all - **2.** [très vite] at top speed.

➡ **au fond, dans le fond** *loc adv* basically.

➡ **au fond de** *loc prép* : **au ~ de moi-même/lui-même** *etc* at heart, deep down.

fondais, fondions *etc* ⊂▷ **fondre**.

fondamental, e, aux [fɔ̃damɑ̃tal, o] *adj* fundamental.

fondamentalement [fɔ̃damɑ̃talmɑ̃] *adv* fundamentally.

fondamentaliste [fɔ̃damɑ̃talist] *nmf* & *adj* fundamentalist.

fondant, e [fɔ̃dɑ̃, ɑ̃t] *adj* [neige, glace] melting ; [aliment] which melts in the mouth.

➡ **fondant** *nm* [gâteau] fondant.

fondateur, trice [fɔ̃datœr, tris] *nm, f* founder.

fondation [fɔ̃dasjɔ̃] *nf* foundation.

➡ **fondations** *nfpl CONSTR* foundations.

fondé, e [fɔ̃de] *adj* [craintes, reproches] justified, well-founded ; **non ~** unfounded ; **être ~ à faire qqch** to have good reason to do sthg.

➡ **fondé de pouvoir** *nm* authorized representative.

fondement [fɔ̃dmɑ̃] *nm* [base, motif] foundation ; **sans ~** groundless, without foundation.

fonder [3] [fɔ̃de] *vt* - **1.** [créer] to found - **2.** [baser] : **~ qqch sur** to base sthg on ; **~ de grands espoirs sur qqn** to pin one's hopes on sb.

➤ **se fonder** *vp* : **se ~ sur** [suj : personne] to base o.s. on ; [suj : argument] to be based on.

fonderie [fɔ̃dri] *nf* [usine] foundry.

fondeur, euse [fɔ̃dœr, øz] *nm, f* SKI cross-country skier.

fondre [75] [fɔ̃dr] ◇ *vt* - **1.** [beurre, neige] to melt ; [sucre, sel] to dissolve ; [métal] to melt down - **2.** [mouler] to cast - **3.** [mêler] to blend ◇ *vi* - **1.** [beurre, neige] to melt ; [sucre, sel] to dissolve ; *fig* to melt away - **2.** [maigrir] to lose weight - **3.** [se ruer] : **~ sur** to swoop down on.

➤ **se fondre** *vp* : **se ~ dans la brume/la foule** to melt away into the fog/the crowd.

fonds [fɔ̃] ◇ *nm* - **1.** [ressources] fund ; **le Fonds monétaire international** the International Monetary Fund ; **~ de roulement** working capital - **2.** [bien immobilier] : **~ (de commerce)** business ◇ *nmpl* funds ; **~ publics/secrets** public/secret funds.

fondu, e [fɔ̃dy] *pp* ▷ **fondre**.

➤ **fondu** *nm* - **1.** [CIN - ouverture] fade-in ; [- fermeture] fade-out ; **~ enchaîné** dissolve - **2.** [de couleurs] blend.

➤ **fondue** *nf* fondue ; **~ e au fromage** OU **savoyarde** cheese fondue ; **~e bourguignonne** meat fondue.

fongicide [fɔ̃ʒisid] ◇ *nm* fungicide ◇ *adj* fungicidal.

font ▷ **faire**.

fontaine [fɔ̃tɛn] *nf* [naturelle] spring ; [publique] fountain.

fonte [fɔ̃t] *nf* - **1.** [de glace, beurre] melting ; [de métal] melting down ; **la ~ des neiges** the thaw - **2.** [alliage] cast iron ; **en ~** cast-iron.

fonts [fɔ̃] *nmpl* : **~ baptismaux** (baptismal) font *(sg)*.

foot [fut] = **football**.

football [futbol] *nm* football *Br*, soccer ; **~ américain** American football *Br*, football *Am*.

footballeur, euse [futbolœr, øz] *nm, f* footballer *Br*, soccer player.

footing [futiŋ] *nm* jogging ; **faire du ~** to go jogging.

for [fɔr] *nm* : **dans son ~ intérieur** in his/her heart of hearts.

FOR (*abr de* forint) F, Ft.

forage [fɔraʒ] *nm* drilling.

forain, e [fɔrɛ̃, ɛn] *adj* ▷ **fête**.

➤ **forain** *nm* stallholder.

forban [fɔrbɑ̃] *nm* - **1.** [corsaire] pirate - **2.** [escroc] crook.

forçat [fɔrsa] *nm* convict.

force [fɔrs] *nf* - **1.** [vigueur] strength ; **avoir de la ~** to be strong ; **en ~** [passer] by (physical) effort ; [arriver] in force ; **être une ~ de la nature** to be a human dynamo ; **être de ~ à faire qqch** to be up to doing sthg ; **c'est ce qui fait sa ~** that's where his strength lies ; **~ de caractère** strength of character ; **dans la ~ de l'âge** *fig* in the prime of life - **2.** [violence, puissance, MIL & PHYS] force ; **faire faire qqch à qqn de ~** to force sb to do sthg ; **par la ~ des choses** by force of circumstances ; **avoir ~ de loi** to have force of law ; **obtenir qqch par la ~** to obtain sthg by force ; **~ centrifuge** PHYS centrifugal force ; **~ de dissuasion** deterrent power ; **~ de frappe** strike force ; **~ d'inertie** PHYS force of inertia ; **~ de vente** COMM sales force.

➤ **forces** *nfpl* - **1.** [physique] strength *(sg)* ; **être à bout de ~s** to have no strength left ; **de toutes ses ~s** with all his/her strength ; **recouvrer ses ~s** to get one's strength back ; **reprendre des ~s** to recover one's strength - **2.** [organisation] : **les ~s armées** the armed forces ; **~s d'intervention** rapid deployment force *(sg)* ; **les ~s de l'ordre** the police *(sg)* ; **les ~s de police** the police force *(sg)*.

➤ **à force de** *loc prép* by dint of.

forcé, e [fɔrse] *adj* forced.

forcément [fɔrsemɑ̃] *adv* inevitably.

forcené, e [fɔrsəne] ◇ *adj* [haine, critique] frenzied ; [partisan] fanatical ◇ *nm, f* maniac.

forceps [fɔrsɛps] *nm* forceps *(pl)*.

forcer [16] [fɔrse] ◇ *vt* - **1.** [gén] to force ; **~ qqn à qqch/à faire qqch** to force sb into sthg/to do sthg - **2.** [admiration, respect] to compel, to command - **3.** [talent, voix] to strain ◇ *vi* : **ça ne sert à rien de ~, ça ne passe pas** there's no point in forcing it, it won't go through ; **~ sur qqch** to overdo sthg.

➤ **se forcer** *vp* [s'obliger] : **se ~ à faire qqch** to force o.s. to do sthg.

forcing [fɔrsiŋ] *nm* SPORT & *fig* pressure ; **faire du ~** to push o.s.

forcir [32] [fɔrsir] *vi* to put on weight.

forer [3] [fɔre] *vt* to drill.

forestier, ère [fɔrɛstje, ɛr] *adj* forest *(avant n)*.

➤ **forestier** *nm* forestry worker.

forêt [fɔrɛ] *nf* forest.

foreuse [fɔrøz] *nf* drill.

forfait [fɔrfɛ] *nm* - **1.** [prix fixe] fixed price ; **être au ~** [pour l'imposition] to pay an estimated amount of tax - **2.** *SPORT* : **déclarer ~** [abandonner] to withdraw ; *fig* to give up - **3.** *littéraire* [crime] heinous crime.

forfaitaire [fɔrfɛtɛr] *adj* inclusive.

forfait-vacances [fɔrfɛvakɑ̃s] (*pl* **forfaits-vacances**) *nm* package holiday.

forfanterie [fɔrfɑ̃tri] *nf* bragging.

forge [fɔrʒ] *nf* forge.

forger [17] [fɔrʒe] *vt* - **1.** [métal] to forge - **2.** *fig* [caractère] to form - **3.** [plan, excuse] to concoct.

forgeron [fɔrʒərɔ̃] *nm* blacksmith.

formaliser [3] [fɔrmalize] *vt* to formalize.

➠ **se formaliser** *vp* : **se ~ (de)** to take offence *Br ou* offense *Am* (at).

formalisme [fɔrmalism] *nm* formality.

formaliste [fɔrmalist] <> *nmf* formalist <> *adj* [milieu] conventional ; [personne] : **être ~** to be a stickler for the rules.

formalité [fɔrmalite] *nf* formality ; **les ~s d'usage** the usual formalities.

format [fɔrma] *nm* - **1.** [dimension] size ; **grand/petit ~** large/small size - **2.** *INFORM* format.

formatage [fɔrmataʒ] *nm INFORM* formatting.

formater [3] [fɔrmate] *vt INFORM* to format.

formateur, trice [fɔrmatœr, tris] <> *adj* formative <> *nm, f* trainer.

formation [fɔrmasjɔ̃] *nf* - **1.** [gén] formation - **2.** [apprentissage] training ; **~ continue** continuing education ; **~ professionnelle** vocational training.

forme [fɔrm] *nf* - **1.** [aspect] shape, form ; **en ~ de** in the shape of ; **sous ~ de** in the form of ; **sous toutes ses ~s** in all its forms ; **prendre ~** to take shape - **2.** [état] form ; **être en (pleine) ~** to be in (great) shape, to be on (top) form - **3.** *loc* : **en bonne et due ~** in due form ; **faire qqch dans les ~s** to do sthg in the correct way ; **pour la ~** for form's sake ; **sans autre ~ de procès** without further ado.

➠ **formes** *nfpl* figure *(sg)*.

formel, elle [fɔrmɛl] *adj* - **1.** [définitif, ferme] positive, definite - **2.** [poli] formal.

formellement [fɔrmɛlmɑ̃] *adv* - **1.** [refuser] positively ; [promettre] definitely - **2.** [raisonner] formally.

former [3] [fɔrme] *vt* - **1.** [gén] to form - **2.** [personnel, élèves] to train - **3.** [goût, sensibilité] to develop.

➠ **se former** *vp* - **1.** [se constituer] to form - **2.** [s'instruire] to train o.s.

Formica® [fɔrmika] *nm inv* Formica®.

formidable [fɔrmidabl] *adj* - **1.** [épatant] great, tremendous - **2.** [incroyable] incredible.

formol [fɔrmɔl] *nm* formalin.

formosan, e [fɔrmɔzɑ̃, an] *adj* Formosan.

➠ **Formosan, e** *nm, f* Formosan.

Formose [fɔrmɔz] *n* Formosa ; **à ~** in Formosa.

formulaire [fɔrmylɛr] *nm* form ; **remplir un ~** to fill in a form.

formulation [fɔrmylasjɔ̃] *nf* wording, formulation.

formule [fɔrmyl] *nf* - **1.** [expression] expression ; **~ de politesse** [orale] polite phrase ; [épistolaire] letter ending - **2.** *CHIM* & *MATHS* formula - **3.** [méthode] way, method ; **nouvelle ~** new style of show/restaurant *etc* - **4.** [slogan] : **~ publicitaire** advertising slogan.

➠ **formule 1** *nf* Formula One.

formuler [3] [fɔrmyle] *vt* to formulate, to express.

forniquer [3] [fɔrnike] *vi* to fornicate.

forsythia [fɔrsisja] *nm* forsythia.

fort, e [fɔr, fɔrt] <> *adj* - **1.** [gén] strong ; **et le plus ~, c'est que ...** and the most amazing thing about it is ... ; **c'est un peu ~!** *fam* that's a bit much! ; **c'est plus ~ que moi** I can't help it - **2.** [corpulent] heavy, big - **3.** [doué] gifted ; **être ~ en qqch** to be good at sthg - **4.** [puissant - voix] loud ; [- vent, lumière, accent] strong - **5.** [considérable] large ; **il y a de ~es chances qu'il gagne** there's a good chance he'll win <> *adv* - **1.** [frapper, battre] hard ; [sonner, parler] loud, loudly - **2.** *sout* [très] very ; **avoir ~ à faire (avec qqn)** to have a hard job (with sb) <> *nm* - **1.** [château] fort - **2.** [personne] : **un ~ en qqch** a person who is good at sthg - **3.** [spécialité] : **ce n'est pas mon ~** it's not my forte *ou* strong point.

➠ **au plus fort de** *loc prép* [hiver] in the depths of ; [tempête, dispute] at the height of.

fortement [fɔrtəmɑ̃] *adv* - **1.** [avec force] hard - **2.** [très - intéressé, ému] deeply - **3.** [beaucoup - bégayer, loucher] badly.

forteresse [fɔrtərɛs] *nf* fortress.

fortifiant, e [fɔrtifjɑ̃, ɑ̃t] *adj* fortifying.

➠ **fortifiant** *nm* tonic.

fortification [fɔrtifikasjɔ̃] *nf* fortification.

fortifier [9] [fɔrtifje] *vt* [personne, ville] to fortify ; **~ qqn dans qqch** *fig* to strengthen sb in sthg.

fortuit, e [fɔrtɥi, it] *adj* chance *(avant n)*, fortuitous.

fortune [fɔrtyn] *nf* - **1.** [richesse] fortune ; **faire ~** to make one's fortune - **2.** [hasard] luck, fortune.

fortuné, e [fɔrtyne] *adj* - **1.** [riche] wealthy - **2.** [chanceux] fortunate, lucky.

forum [fɔrɔm] *nm* forum ; **~ de discussion** *INFORM* chat room.
fosse [fos] *nf* **- 1.** [trou] pit ; **~ septique** septic tank ; **~ aux lions** lions' den ; **~ d'orchestre** orchestra pit ; **~ de sable** *Can GOLF* bunker *Br*, sand trap *Am* **- 2.** [tombe] grave ; **~ commune** common grave.
fossé [fose] *nm* ditch ; *fig* gap.
fossette [fosɛt] *nf* dimple.
fossile [fosil] ◇ *adj* fossil *(avant n)*, fossilized ◇ *nm* **- 1.** [de plante, d'animal] fossil **- 2.** *fig* & *péj* [personne] fossil, fogy.
fossoyeur, euse [foswajœr, øz] *nm, f* gravedigger.
fou, folle [fu, fɔl] ◇ *adj* (**fol** *devant voyelle ou h muet*) mad, insane ; [prodigieux] tremendous ; **être ~ de qqn/qqch** to be mad about sb/sthg ; **être ~ de joie** to be deliriously happy ; **~ à lier** raving mad ◇ *nm, f* madman (*f* madwoman) ; **~ furieux** manic ; **faire le ~** *fig* to act the fool.
foudre [fudr] *nf* lightning ; **encourir** *OU* **s'attirer les ~s de qqn** *fig* to bring down sb's wrath on o.s.
foudroyant, e [fudrwajɑ̃, ɑ̃t] *adj* **- 1.** [progrès, vitesse] lightning *(avant n)* ; [succès] stunning **- 2.** [nouvelle] devastating ; [regard] withering.
foudroyer **[13]** [fudrwaje] *vt* **- 1.** [suj : foudre] to strike ; **l'arbre a été foudroyé** the tree was struck by lightning **- 2.** *fig* [abattre] to strike down, to kill ; **~ qqn du regard** to glare at sb.
fouet [fwɛ] *nm* **- 1.** [en cuir] whip ; **de plein ~** direct ; **il prit la pluie de plein ~** the rain hit him full in the face **- 2.** *CULIN* whisk.
fouetter **[4]** [fwete] *vt* **- 1.** [gén] to whip ; [suj : pluie] to lash (against) **- 2.** [stimuler] to stimulate.
fougasse [fugas] *nf type of unleavened bread.*
fougère [fuʒɛr] *nf* fern.
fougue [fug] *nf* ardour *Br*, ardor *Am*.
fougueux, euse [fugø, øz] *adj* ardent, spirited.
fouille [fuj] *nf* **- 1.** [de personne, maison] search **- 2.** [du sol] dig, excavation.
◆ **fouilles** *nfpl fam* pockets.
fouiller **[3]** [fuje] ◇ *vt* **- 1.** [gén] to search **- 2.** *fig* [approfondir] to examine closely ◇ *vi* : **~ dans** to go through.
fouillis [fuji] *nm* jumble, muddle.
fouine [fwin] *nf* stone-marten.
fouiner **[3]** [fwine] *vi* to ferret about.
foulard [fular] *nm* scarf.
foule [ful] *nf* **- 1.** [de gens] crowd ; **en ~** in great numbers ; **attirer les ~s** *fig* to draw the crowds **- 2.** *péj* [peuple] : **la ~** the masses *(pl)* **- 3.** *fig* [multitude] : **une ~ de** masses of.
foulée [fule] *nf* [de coureur] stride ; **je suis sorti faire des courses et dans la ~ ...** I went out to do some shopping and while I was at it ...
fouler **[3]** [fule] *vt* [raisin] to press ; [sol] to walk on.
◆ **se fouler** *vp* **- 1.** *MÉD* : **se ~ le poignet/la cheville** to sprain one's wrist/ankle **- 2.** *fam fig* [se fatiguer] : **ne pas se ~** not to strain o.s.
foulure [fulyr] *nf* sprain.
four [fur] *nm* **- 1.** [de cuisson] oven ; **cuit au ~** baked ; **~ électrique/à micro-ondes** electric/microwave oven ; **~ crématoire** *HIST* oven ; **je ne peux pas être (à la fois) au ~ et au moulin** *fig* I haven't got two pairs of hands, I can't be in two places at once ; **noir comme dans un ~** *fig* black as pitch **- 2.** *THÉÂTRE* flop ; **faire un ~** to flop.
fourbe [furb] ◇ *adj* treacherous, deceitful ◇ *nmf* rogue.
fourbi [furbi] *nm fam* **- 1.** [attirail] gear **- 2.** [fouillis] mess.
fourbir **[32]** [furbir] *vt litt* & *fig* to polish.
fourbu, e [furby] *adj* tired out, exhausted.
fourche [furʃ] *nf* **- 1.** [outil] pitchfork **- 2.** [de vélo, route] fork **- 3.** *Belg SCOL* free period.
fourcher **[3]** [furʃe] *vi* **- 1.** [cheveux] to split **- 2.** *loc* : **sa langue a fourché** he made a slip of the tongue.
fourchette [furʃɛt] *nf* **- 1.** [couvert] fork **- 2.** [écart] range, bracket.
fourchu, e [furʃy] *adj* forked.
fourgon [furgɔ̃] *nm* **- 1.** [camionnette] van ; **~ cellulaire** police van *Br*, patrol wagon *Am* ; **~ mortuaire** hearse **- 2.** [ferroviaire] : **~ à bestiaux** cattle truck ; **~ postal** mail van.
fourgonnette [furgɔnɛt] *nf* small van.
fourguer **[3]** [furge] *vt fam* : **~ qqch à qqn** to palm sthg off on sb.
fourmi [furmi] *nf* [insecte] ant ; *fig* hard worker ; **avoir des ~s dans les bras/les jambes** to have pins and needles in one's arms/legs.
fourmilière [furmiljɛr] *nf* anthill.
fourmillement [furmijmɑ̃] *nm* **- 1.** [d'insectes, de personnes] swarming **- 2.** [picotement] pins and needles *(pl)*.
fourmiller **[3]** [furmije] *vi* [pulluler] to swarm ; **~ de** *fig* to be swarming with.
fournaise [furnɛz] *nf* furnace.
fourneau, x [furno] *nm* **- 1.** [cuisinière, poêle] stove **- 2.** [de fonderie] furnace **- 3.** [de pipe] bowl.
fournée [furne] *nf* batch.
fourni, e [furni] *adj* [barbe, cheveux] thick.

fournil [furnil] *nm* bakery.

fournir [32] [furnir] ◇ *vt* - **1.** [procurer] : ~ **qqch à qqn** to supply *ou* provide sb with sthg - **2.** [produire] : ~ **un effort** to make an effort - **3.** [approvisionner] : ~ **qqn (en)** to supply sb (with) ◇ *vi* : ~ **à** to provide for.

◆ **se fournir** *vp* : **se** ~ **chez/en** to get supplies from/of.

fournisseur, euse [furnisœr, øz] *nm, f* supplier ; ~ **d'accès** INFORM service provider.

fourniture [furnityr] *nf* supply, supplying (U).

◆ **fournitures** *nfpl* : ~**s de bureau** office supplies ; ~**s scolaires** school supplies.

fourrage [furaʒ] *nm* fodder.

fourrager¹, ère [furaʒe, ɛr] *adj* fodder *(avant n)*.

fourrager² [17] [furaʒe] *vi fam* : ~ **dans qqch** to rummage through sthg.

fourré [fure] *nm* thicket.

fourreau, x [furo] *nm* - **1.** [d'épée] sheath ; [de parapluie] cover - **2.** [robe] sheath dress.

fourrer [fure] *vt* - **1.** CULIN to stuff, to fill - **2.** *fam* [mettre] : ~ **qqch (dans)** to stuff sthg (into).

◆ **se fourrer** *vp* : **se** ~ **dans le pétrin** to get into a mess ; **se** ~ **une idée dans la tête** to get an idea into one's head ; **je ne savais plus où me** ~ I didn't know where to put myself.

fourre-tout [furtu] *nm inv* - **1.** [pièce] lumber-room *Br*, junk room *Am* - **2.** [sac] holdall - **3.** *fig* & *péj* [d'idées] hotch-potch.

fourreur [furœr] *nm* furrier.

fourrière [furjɛr] *nf* pound ; **mettre à la** ~ [voiture] to tow away.

fourrure [furyr] *nf* fur ; **un manteau en fausse** ~ a fake fur coat.

fourvoyer [13] [furvwaje] ◆ **se fourvoyer** *vp sout* [s'égarer] to lose one's way ; [se tromper] to go off on the wrong track.

foutaise [futɛz] *nf fam* crap (U).

foutoir [futwar] *nm fam* pigsty.

foutre [116] [futr] *vt tfam* - **1.** [mettre] to shove, to stick ; ~ **qqn dehors** *ou* **à la porte** to chuck sb out - **2.** [donner] : ~ **la trouille à qqn** to put the wind up sb ; **il lui a foutu une baffe** he thumped him one - **3.** [faire] to do ; **ne rien** ~ **de la journée** to do damn all all day ; **j'en ai rien à** ~ I don't give a toss.

◆ **se foutre** *vp tfam* - **1.** [se mettre] : **se** ~ **dans** [situation] to get o.s. into - **2.** [se moquer] : **se** ~ **de (la gueule de) qqn** to laugh at sb, to take the mickey out of sb *Br* - **3.** [ne pas s'intéresser] : **je m'en fous** I don't give a damn about it.

foutu, e [futy] *adj fam* - **1.** [maudit] bloody *Br*,

damned ; [caractère] nasty - **2.** [fait, conçu] : **bien** ~ [projet, maison] great ; **elle est bien ~e, celle-là** [femme] she's a real stunner - **3.** [perdu] : **il est** ~ he's/it's had it - **4.** [capable] : **être** ~ **de faire qqch** to be liable *ou* quite likely to do sthg.

fox-terrier [fɔkstɛrje] (*pl* **fox-terriers**) *nm* fox terrier.

foyer [fwaje] *nm* - **1.** [maison] home ; **rentrer au** ~ to go home - **2.** [famille] family ; **fonder un** ~ to set up home - **3.** [résidence] home, hostel - **4.** [point central] centre *Br*, center *Am* - **5.** [de lunettes] focus ; **verres à double** ~ bifocals.

FP (*abr de* **franchise postale**) PP.

FPA (*abr de* **formation professionnelle des adultes**) *nf* state-run adult training scheme.

FPLP (*abr de* **Front populaire de libération de la Palestine**) *nm* PFLP.

frac [frak] *nm* tails (*pl*).

fracas [fraka] *nm* roar.

fracassant, e [frakasɑ̃, ɑ̃t] *adj* [bruyant] thunderous ; *fig* staggering, sensational.

fracasser [3] [frakase] *vt* to smash, to shatter.

◆ **se fracasser** *vp* : **se** ~ **contre/sur** to crash against/into.

fraction [fraksjɔ̃] *nf* fraction.

fractionner [3] [fraksjɔne] *vt* to divide (up), to split up.

◆ **se fractionner** *vp* to split up.

fracture [fraktyr] *nf* MÉD fracture ; ~ **du crâne** fractured skull ; ~ **sociale** gap between the rich and the poor.

fracturer [3] [fraktyre] *vt* - **1.** MÉD to fracture - **2.** [coffre, serrure] to break open.

◆ **se fracturer** *vp* to break, to fracture.

fragile [fraʒil] *adj* [gén] fragile ; [peau, santé] delicate.

fragiliser [3] [fraʒilize] *vt* to weaken.

fragilité [fraʒilite] *nf* fragility.

fragment [fragmɑ̃] *nm* - **1.** [morceau] fragment - **2.** [extrait - d'œuvre] extract ; [- de conversation] snatch.

fragmentaire [fragmɑ̃tɛr] *adj* fragmentary.

fragmenter [3] [fragmɑ̃te] *vt* to fragment, to break up.

◆ **se fragmenter** *vp* to fragment, to break up.

fraîche ▷ **frais**.

fraîchement [frɛʃmɑ̃] *adv* - **1.** [récemment] recently - **2.** [froidement] coolly.

fraîcheur [frɛʃœr] *nf* - **1.** [d'air, d'accueil] coolness - **2.** [de teint, d'aliment] freshness.

fraîchir [32] [frɛʃir] *vi* to freshen.

frais, fraîche [frɛ, frɛʃ] *adj* - **1.** [air, accueil] cool ; **boisson fraîche** cold drink ; **'servir ~'**

'serve chilled' - **2.** [récent - trace] fresh ; [- en-cre] wet ; **~ émoulu (de)** fresh (from) - **3.** [teint] fresh, clear ; **~ et dispos** hale and hearty.

frais <> *nm* : **mettre qqch au ~** to put sthg in a cool place ; **prendre le ~** to take a breath of fresh air <> *nmpl* [dépenses] expenses, costs ; **aux ~ de la maison** at the company's expense ; **faire des ~** to spend a lot of money ; **rentrer dans ses ~** to cover one's expenses ; **faux ~** incidentals ; **~ d'entretien** upkeep ; **~ d'équipement** capital expenditure ; **~ fixes** fixed costs ; **~ généraux** overheads ; **~ de justice** legal costs ; **~ de représentation** entertainment allowance ; **à grands ~** at a high price ; **à peu de ~** cheaply ; **faire les ~ de qqch** to bear the brunt of sthg <> *adv* : **il fait ~** it's cool.

fraise [frɛz] *nf* - **1.** [fruit] strawberry ; **~ des bois** wild strawberry - **2.** [de dentiste] drill ; [de menuisier] bit.

fraiser [4] [freze] *vt* to countersink.

fraiseuse [frezøz] *nf* milling machine.

fraisier [frezje] *nm* - **1.** [plante] strawberry plant - **2.** [gâteau] strawberry sponge.

framboise [frãbwaz] *nf* - **1.** [fruit] raspberry - **2.** [liqueur] raspberry liqueur.

framboisier [frãbwazje] *nm* - **1.** [plante] raspberry bush - **2.** [gâteau] raspberry sponge.

franc, franche [frã, frãʃ] *adj* - **1.** [sincère] frank - **2.** [net] clear, definite.

franc *nm* franc ; **ancien/nouveau ~** old/new franc ; **~ français/belge/suisse** French/Belgian/Swiss franc.

français, e [frãsɛ, ɛz] *adj* French.

français *nm* [langue] French.

Français, e *nm, f* Frenchman (f Frenchwoman) ; **les Français** the French ; **le Français moyen** the average Frenchman.

France [frãs] *nf* : **la ~** France ; **~ 2, ~ 3** *TÉLÉ French state-owned television channels* ; **France-Inter** *RADIO radio station broadcasting mainly current affairs programmes, interviews and debates.*

franche ▷ **franc.**

franchement [frãʃmã] *adv* - **1.** [sincèrement] frankly - **2.** [nettement] clearly - **3.** [tout à fait] completely, downright.

franchir [32] [frãʃir] *vt* - **1.** [obstacle] to get over - **2.** [porte] to go through ; [seuil] to cross - **3.** [distance] to cover.

franchise [frãʃiz] *nf* - **1.** [sincérité] frankness - **2.** *COMM* franchise ; **agent en ~** franchise holder - **3.** [d'assurance] excess - **4.** [détaxe] exemption.

francilien, enne [frãsiljɛ̃, ɛn] *adj* of *ou* from the Île-de-France.

Francilien, enne *nm, f* inhabitant of the Île-de-France.

franciscain, e [frãsiskɛ̃, ɛn] *adj* & *nm, f* Franciscan.

franciser [3] [frãsize] *vt* to frenchify.

franc-jeu [frãʒø] *nm* : **jouer ~** to play fair.

franc-maçon, onne [frãmasɔ̃, ɔn] *(mpl* **francs-maçons,** *fpl* **franc-maçonnes)** *adj* masonic.

franc-maçon *nm* freemason.

franc-maçonnerie [frãmasɔnri] *(pl* **franc-maçonneries)** *nf* freemasonry *(U).*

franco [frãko] *adv* - **1.** *fam* [franchement] : **y aller ~** to go straight to the point - **2.** *COMM* : **~ à bord** free on board ; **~ de port** carriage paid.

francophile [frãkofil] *nmf* & *adj* francophile.

francophone [frãkofon] <> *adj* French-speaking <> *nmf* French speaker.

francophonie [frãkofoni] *nf* : **la ~** French-speaking nations *(pl).*

FRANCOPHONIE

This is a wide-ranging cultural and political concept involving the promotion of French-speaking communities around the world, with a view to creating a 'French Commonwealth' with a strong identity.

---

franc-parler [frãparle] *(pl* **francs-parlers)** *nm* : **avoir son ~** to speak one's mind.

franc-tireur [frãtirœr] *(pl* **francs-tireurs)** *nm* - **1.** *MIL* irregular - **2.** *fig* [indépendant] freelance ; **agir en ~** to act independently.

frange [frãʒ] *nf* fringe.

frangin, e [frãʒɛ̃, frãʒin] *nm, f fam* brother (f sister).

frangipane [frãʒipan] *nf* almond paste.

franglais [frãglɛ] *nm* Franglais.

franquette [frãkɛt] ▷ **à la bonne franquette** *loc adv* informally, without any ceremony.

frappant, e [frapã, ãt] *adj* striking.

frappe [frap] *nf* - **1.** [de monnaie] minting, striking - **2.** [à la machine] typing ; *INFORM* keying - **3.** [de boxeur] punch - **4.** *péj* [voyou] lout, yob *Br.*

frappé, e [frape] *adj* - **1.** [champagne] chilled - **2.** *fam* [personne] crazy, nutty.

frapper [3] [frape] <> *vt* - **1.** [gén] to strike - **2.** [boisson] to chill <> *vi* to knock.

frasques [frask] *nfpl* pranks, escapades.

fraternel, elle [fraternel] *adj* fraternal, brotherly.

fraterniser [3] [fratɛrnize] *vi* to fraternize.
fraternité [fratɛrnite] *nf* brotherhood.
fratricide [fratrisid] ⬧ *nmf* fratricide ⬧ *adj* fratricidal.
fraude [frod] *nf* fraud ; **passer qqch en ~** to smuggle sthg in ; **~ électorale** ballot-rigging ; **~ fiscale** tax evasion ; **~ informatique** computer crime.
frauder [3] [frode] *vt* & *vi* to cheat.
fraudeur, euse [frodœr, øz] *nm, f* cheat.
frauduleux, euse [frodylø, øz] *adj* fraudulent.
frayer [11] [freje] ⬧ *vt* : **~ la voie à qqn** to clear the way for sb ⬧ *vi* [fréquenter] : **~ avec** to associate *ou* mix with.
➡ **se frayer** *vp* : **se ~ un chemin (à travers une foule)** to force one's way through (a crowd).
frayeur [frejœr] *nf* fright, fear.
fredaines [frədɛn] *nfpl* pranks.
fredonner [3] [frədɔne] *vt* & *vi* to hum.
freezer [frizœr] *nm* freezer compartment.
frégate [fregat] *nf* - 1. [bateau] frigate - 2. [oiseau] frigate-bird.
frein [frɛ̃] *nm* - 1. AUTOM brake ; **~ à main** handbrake ; **~ moteur** engine brake - 2. *fig* [obstacle] brake, check ; **mettre un ~ à** to curb - 3. *loc* : **ronger son ~** *fig* to champ at the bit.
freinage [frɛnaʒ] *nm* braking.
freiner [4] [frene] ⬧ *vt* - 1. [mouvement, véhicule] to slow down ; [inflation, dépenses] to curb - 2. [personne] to restrain ⬧ *vi* to brake.
frelaté, e [frəlate] *adj* [vin] adulterated ; *fig* corrupt.
frêle [frɛl] *adj* - 1. [enfant, voix] frail - 2. [construction] flimsy, fragile.
frelon [frəlɔ̃] *nm* hornet.
freluquet [frəlykɛ] *nm péj* whippersnapper.
frémir [32] [fremir] *vi* - 1. [corps, personne] to tremble - 2. [eau] to simmer.
frémissement [fremismɑ̃] *nm* - 1. [de corps, personne] shiver, trembling *(U)* - 2. [d'eau] simmering.
frêne [frɛn] *nm* ash.
frénésie [frenezi] *nf* frenzy.
frénétique [frenetik] *adj* frenzied.
frénétiquement [frenetikmɑ̃] *adv* [applaudir] furiously.
fréquemment [frekamɑ̃] *adv* frequently.
fréquence [frekɑ̃s] *nf* frequency.
fréquent, e [frekɑ̃, ɑ̃t] *adj* frequent.
fréquentable [frekɑ̃tabl] *adj* respectable.
fréquentation [frekɑ̃tasjɔ̃] *nf* - 1. [d'endroit] frequenting - 2. [de personne] association.

➡ **fréquentations** *nfpl* company *(U)* ; **avoir de mauvaises ~s** to keep bad company.
fréquenté, e [frekɑ̃te] *adj* : **très ~** busy ; **c'est très bien/mal ~** the right/wrong sort of people go there.
fréquenter [3] [frekɑ̃te] *vt* - 1. [endroit] to frequent - 2. [personne] to associate with ; [petit ami] to go out with, to see.
frère [frɛr] ⬧ *nm* brother ; **faux ~** false friend ; **~ de lait** foster brother ; **grand ~** big brother ⬧ *adj* [parti, pays] sister *(avant n)*.
fresque [frɛsk] *nf* fresco.
fret [frɛ] *nm* freight.
frétiller [3] [fretije] *vi* [poisson, personne] to wriggle ; **~ de joie** *fig* to quiver with delight.
fretin [frətɛ̃] *nm* : **le menu ~** the small fry.
freudien, enne [frødjɛ̃, ɛn] *adj* Freudian.
friable [frijabl] *adj* crumbly.
friand, e [frijɑ̃, ɑ̃d] *adj* : **être ~ de** to be partial to.
➡ **friand** *nm* savoury *Br ou* savory *Am* tart-let.
friandise [frijɑ̃diz] *nf* delicacy.
fric [frik] *nm fam* cash.
fricassée [frikase] *nf* fricassee.
fric-frac [frikfrak] *nm inv fam* break-in.
friche [friʃ] *nf* fallow land ; **en ~** fallow.
fricoter [3] [frikɔte] *vt litt* & *fig* to cook up.
friction [friksjɔ̃] *nf* - 1. [massage] massage - 2. *fig* [désaccord] friction.
frictionner [3] [friksjɔne] *vt* to rub.
Frigidaire® [friʒidɛr] *nm* fridge, refrigerator.
frigide [friʒid] *adj* frigid.
frigidité [friʒidite] *nf* frigidity.
frigo [frigo] *nm fam* fridge.
frigorifié, e [frigɔrifje] *adj fam* frozen.
frigorifique [frigɔrifik] *adj* refrigerated.
frileux, euse [frilø, øz] *adj* - 1. [craignant le froid] sensitive to the cold - 2. [prudent] unadventurous.
frimas [frima] *nm littéraire* foggy winter weather.
frime [frim] *nf fam* showing off.
frimer [3] [frime] *vi fam* [bluffer] to pretend ; [se mettre en valeur] to show off.
frimeur, euse [frimœr, øz] *nmf* show-off.
frimousse [frimus] *nf fam* dear little face.
fringale [frɛ̃gal] *nf fam* : **avoir la ~** to be starving.
fringant, e [frɛ̃gɑ̃, ɑ̃t] *adj* high-spirited.
fringuer [3] [frɛ̃ge] *vt* to dress.
➡ **se fringuer** *vp fam* to get dressed.

fringues [frɛ̃g] *nfpl fam* clothes.

fripe [frip] *nf* : **les ~s** secondhand clothes.

friper [3] [fripe] *vt* to crumple.
➤ **se friper** *vp* to crumple.

fripier, ère [fripje, ɛr] *nm, f* secondhand clothes dealer.

fripon, onne [fripɔ̃, ɔn] ◇ *nm, f fam vieilli* rogue, rascal ◇ *adj* mischievous, cheeky.

fripouille [fripuj] *nf fam* scoundrel ; **petite ~** little devil.

frire [115] [frir] ◇ *vt* to fry ◇ *vi* to fry ; **faire ~ to** fry.

Frisbee® [frizbi] *nm* Frisbee®.

frise [friz] *nf* ARCHIT frieze.

frisé, e [frize] *adj* [cheveux] curly ; [personne] curly-haired.
➤ **frisée** *nf* [salade] curly endive.

friser [3] [frize] ◇ *vt* - **1.** [cheveux] to curl - **2.** *fig* [ressembler à] to border on ◇ *vi* to curl.

frisette [frizɛt] *nf* curl.

frisotter [3] [frizɔte] ◇ *vt* to crimp, to frizz ◇ *vi* to be frizzy.

frisquet [friskɛ] *adj m* : **il fait ~** it's chilly.

frisson [frisɔ̃] *nm* [gén] shiver ; [de dégoût] shudder.

frissonner [3] [frisɔne] *vi* - **1.** [trembler] to shiver ; [de dégoût] to shudder - **2.** [s'agiter - eau] to ripple ; [- feuillage] to tremble.

frit, e [fri, frit] *pp* ▷ **frire**.

frite [frit] *nf* chip *Br*, (French) fry *Am*.

friterie [fritri] *nf* ≃ chip shop *Br*.

friteuse [fritøz] *nf* deep fat fryer.

friture [frityr] *nf* - **1.** [action de frire] frying - **2.** [poisson] fried fish ; **petite ~** fried whitebait - **3.** *fam* RADIO crackle.

frivole [frivɔl] *adj* frivolous.

frivolité [frivɔlite] *nf* frivolity.

froc [frɔk] *nm* - **1.** RELIG habit - **2.** *fam* [pantalon] trousers *(pl) Br*, pants *(pl) Am*.

froid, froide [frwa, frwad] *adj litt* & *fig* cold ; **rester ~** to be unmoved.
➤ **froid** ◇ *nm* - **1.** [température] cold ; **prendre ~** to catch (a) cold ; **crever de ~** *fam* to be freezing to death ; **grand ~** intense cold ; **il fait un ~ de canard** it's freezing cold ; **n'avoir pas ~ aux yeux** *fig* to be bold *ou* adventurous - **2.** [tension] coolness ; **être en ~ (avec qqn)** to be on bad terms (with sb) ◇ *adv* : **il fait ~** it's cold ; **avoir ~** to be cold ; **manger ~** to have something cold (to eat).
➤ **à froid** *loc adv* [dire, faire] coolly, unemotionally.

froidement [frwadmɑ̃] *adv* - **1.** [accueillir]

coldly - **2.** [écouter, parler] coolly - **3.** [tuer] cold-bloodedly.

froideur [frwadœr] *nf* - **1.** [indifférence] coldness - **2.** [impassibilité] coolness.

froisser [3] [frwase] *vt* - **1.** [tissu, papier] to crumple, to crease - **2.** *fig* [offenser] to offend.
➤ **se froisser** *vp* - **1.** [tissu] to crumple, to crease - **2.** MÉD : **se ~ un muscle** to strain a muscle - **3.** [se vexer] to take offence *Br ou* offense *Am*.

frôler [3] [frole] *vt* to brush against ; *fig* to have a brush with, to come close to.

fromage [frɔmaʒ] *nm* cheese ; **~ à pâte molle/dure** soft/hard cheese ; **~ de brebis** sheep's milk ; **~ de chèvre** goat's cheese ; **~ de tête** brawn *Br*, headcheese *Am*.

fromager, ère [frɔmaʒe, ɛr] ◇ *adj* cheese *(avant n)* ◇ *nm, f* [fabricant] cheesemaker.

fromagerie [frɔmaʒri] *nf* cheese shop.

froment [frɔmɑ̃] *nm* wheat.

fronce [frɔ̃s] *nf* gather.

froncement [frɔ̃smɑ̃] *nm* : **~ de sourcils** frown.

froncer [16] [frɔ̃se] *vt* - **1.** COUTURE to gather - **2.** [plisser] : **~ les sourcils** to frown.

frondaison [frɔ̃dɛzɔ̃] *nf* - **1.** [phénomène] foliation - **2.** [feuillage] foliage.

fronde [frɔ̃d] *nf* - **1.** [arme] sling ; [jouet] catapult *Br*, slingshot *Am* - **2.** [révolte] rebellion.

frondeur, euse [frɔ̃dœr, øz] ◇ *nm, f* rebel ◇ *adj* rebellious.

front [frɔ̃] *nm* - **1.** ANAT forehead - **2.** *fig* [audace] cheek ; **avoir le ~ de faire qqch** to have the cheek to do sthg - **3.** [avant] front ; [de bâtiment] front, façade ; **~ de mer** (sea) front ; **de ~** [attaquer] head on - **4.** MÉTÉOR, MIL & POLIT front - **5.** *loc* : **faire ~ à** to face up to ; **mener plusieurs activités de ~** to do several things at the same time.

frontal, e, aux [frɔ̃tal, o] *adj* - **1.** ANAT frontal - **2.** [collision, attaque] head-on.

frontalier, ère [frɔ̃talje, ɛr] ◇ *adj* frontier *(avant n)* ; **travailleur ~** person who lives on one side of the border and works on the other ◇ *nm, f* inhabitant of border area.

frontière [frɔ̃tjɛr] ◇ *adj* border *(avant n)* ◇ *nf* frontier, border ; *fig* frontier.

frontispice [frɔ̃tispis] *nm* frontispiece.

fronton [frɔ̃tɔ̃] *nm* - **1.** ARCHIT pediment - **2.** SPORT upper part of the wall in the game of pelota.

frottement [frɔtmɑ̃] *nm* - **1.** [action] rubbing - **2.** [contact, difficulté] friction.

frotter [3] [fʀɔte] ⬦ *vt* to rub ; [parquet] to scrub ⬦ *vi* to rub, to scrape.
➡ **se frotter** *vp* - **1.** [se blottir] : **se ~ contre** *ou* **à** to rub (up) against ; **il ne faut pas s'y ~** *fig* don't cross swords with him - **2.** [se laver] to rub o.s.

frottis [fʀɔti] *nm* smear ; **~ vaginal** cervical smear.

froufrou, s [fʀufʀu] *nm* rustle, swish.
➡ **froufrous** *nmpl* [de robe] frills.

froussard, e [fʀusaʀ, aʀd] *adj* & *nm, f fam* chicken.

frousse [fʀus] *nf fam* fright ; **avoir la ~** to be scared stiff.

fructifier [9] [fʀyktifje] *vi* - **1.** [investissement] to give *ou* yield a profit ; **faire ~ son argent** to make one's money grow - **2.** [terre] to be productive - **3.** [arbre, idée] to bear fruit.

fructose [fʀyktoz] *nm* fructose.

fructueux, euse [fʀyktɥø, øz] *adj* fruitful, profitable.

frugal, e, aux [fʀygal, o] *adj* frugal.

fruit [fʀɥi] *nm litt* & *fig* fruit (U) ; **~ confit** candied fruit ; **le ~ défendu** the forbidden fruit ; **~ sec** dried fruit (U) ; **~s de mer** seafood (U).

fruité, e [fʀɥite] *adj* fruity.

fruitier, ère [fʀɥitje, ɛʀ] ⬦ *adj* [arbre] fruit *(avant n)* ⬦ *nm, f* fruiterer.
➡ **fruitier** *nm* [local] store-room for fruit.

frusques [fʀysk] *nfpl* gear (U), clobber (U).

fruste [fʀyst] *adj* uncouth.

frustrant, e [fʀystʀɑ̃, ɑ̃t] *adj* frustrating.

frustration [fʀystʀasjɔ̃] *nf* frustration.

frustré, e [fʀystʀe] ⬦ *adj* frustrated ⬦ *nm, f* frustrated person.

frustrer [3] [fʀystʀe] *vt* - **1.** [priver] : **~ qqn de** to deprive sb of - **2.** [décevoir] to frustrate.

FS *(abr de franc suisse)* SFr.

FTP *(abr de francs-tireurs et partisans) nmpl* Communist Resistance forces during World War II.

fuchsia [fyʃja] *nm* fuchsia.

fuel, fioul [fjul] *nm* - **1.** [de chauffage] fuel - **2.** [carburant] fuel oil.

fugace [fygas] *adj* fleeting.

fugitif, ive [fyʒitif, iv] ⬦ *adj* fleeting ⬦ *nm, f* fugitive.

fugue [fyg] *nf* - **1.** [de personne] flight ; **faire une ~** to run away - **2.** *MUS* fugue.

fuguer [3] [fyge] *vi* to run off *ou* away.

fugueur, euse [fygœʀ, øz] *adj* & *nm, f* runaway.

fui [fɥi] *pp inv* ⬦ **fuir**.

fuir [35] [fɥiʀ] ⬦ *vi* - **1.** [détaler] to flee - **2.** [tuyau] to leak - **3.** *fig* [s'écouler] to fly by ⬦ *vt* [éviter] to avoid, to shun.

fuis, fuit *etc* ⬦ **fuir**.

fuite [fɥit] *nf* - **1.** [de personne] escape, flight ; **en ~** on the run ; **prendre la ~** to take flight ; **mettre qqn en ~** to put sb to flight - **2.** [écoulement, d'information] leak.

fulgurant, e [fylgyʀɑ̃, ɑ̃t] *adj* - **1.** [découverte] dazzling - **2.** [vitesse] lightning *(avant n)* - **3.** [douleur] searing - **4.** *littéraire* [regard] of thunder.

fulminant, e [fylminɑ̃, ɑ̃t] *adj* [menaçant] threatening.

fulminer [3] [fylmine] *vi* - **1.** [personne] : **~ (contre)** to fulminate (against) - **2.** *CHIM* to detonate.

fumant, e [fymɑ̃, ɑ̃t] *adj* - **1.** [cheminée] smoking - **2.** [plat] steaming.

fumé, e [fyme] *adj* - **1.** *CULIN* smoked - **2.** [verres] tinted.

fumée [fyme] *nf* - **1.** [de combustion] smoke ; **partir en ~** *fig* to go up in smoke - **2.** [vapeur] steam.
➡ **fumées** *nfpl littéraire* fumes.

fumer [3] [fyme] ⬦ *vi* - **1.** [personne, cheminée] to smoke - **2.** [bouilloire, plat] to steam - **3.** *fam* [être furieux] to fume, to rage ⬦ *vt* - **1.** [cigarette, aliment] to smoke - **2.** *AGRIC* to spread manure on.

fumet [fyme] *nm* - **1.** [odeur] aroma - **2.** *CULIN* greatly reduced stock.

fumeur, euse [fymœʀ, øz] *nm, f* smoker.

fumeux, euse [fymø, øz] *adj* confused, woolly.

fumier [fymje] *nm* - **1.** *AGRIC* dung, manure - **2.** *vulg* [salaud] shit.

fumigation [fymigasjɔ̃] *nf* fumigation.

fumiste [fymist] *nmf péj* skiver *Br*, shirker.

fumisterie [fymistəʀi] *nf fam* skiving *Br*, shirking.

fumoir [fymwaʀ] *nm* - **1.** [pour aliments] smokehouse - **2.** [pièce] smoking room.

funambule [fynɑ̃byl] *nmf* tightrope walker.

funèbre [fynɛbʀ] *adj* - **1.** [de funérailles] funeral *(avant n)* - **2.** [lugubre] funereal ; [sentiments] dismal.

funérailles [fyneʀaj] *nfpl* funeral *(sg)*.

funéraire [fyneʀɛʀ] *adj* funeral *(avant n)*.

funeste [fynɛst] *adj* - **1.** [accident] fatal - **2.** [initiative, erreur] disastrous - **3.** [présage] of doom.

funiculaire [fynikylɛʀ] *nm* funicular railway.

FUNU, Funu [fyny] *(abr de Force d'urgence des Nations unies) nf* UNEF.

fur [fyʀ] ➡ **au fur et à mesure** *loc adv* as I/

you *etc* go along ; **au ~ et à mesure des besoins** as (and when) needed.

➡ **au fur et à mesure que** *loc conj* as (and when).

furax [fyraks] *adj inv fam* hopping mad.

furet [fyrɛ] *nm* - **1.** [animal] ferret - **2.** [personne] nosy parker - **3.** [jeu] hunt-the-slipper.

fureter [28] [fyrte] *vi* - **1.** [fouiller] to ferret around - **2.** [chasser] to go ferreting.

fureur [fyrœr] *nf* - **1.** [colère] fury - **2.** [passion] passion ; **faire ~** to be all the rage.

furibard, e [fyribar, ard] *adj fam* mad.

furibond, e [fyribɔ̃, ɔ̃d] *adj* furious.

furie [fyri] *nf* - **1.** [colère, agitation] fury ; **en ~** [personne] infuriated ; [éléments] raging - **2.** *fig* [femme] shrew - **3.** [passion] passion.

furieusement [fyrjøzmɑ̃] *adv* - **1.** [avec fureur] furiously - **2.** [extrêmement] tremendously.

furieux, euse [fyrjø, øz] *adj* - **1.** [personne] furious - **2.** [violent] violent - **3.** [énorme] tremendous.

furoncle [fyrɔ̃kl] *nm* boil.

furtif, ive [fyrtif, iv] *adj* furtive.

furtivement [fyrtivmɑ̃] *adv* furtively.

fus, fut *etc* ▷ être.

fusain [fyzɛ̃] *nm* - **1.** [crayon] charcoal - **2.** [dessin] charcoal drawing - **3.** [arbre] spindle tree.

fuseau, x [fyzo] *nm* - **1.** [outil] spindle - **2.** [pantalon] ski-pants *(pl)*.

➡ **fuseau horaire** *nm* time zone.

fusée [fyze] *nf* - **1.** [pièce d'artifice & AÉRON] rocket - **2.** TECHNOL spindle ; AUTOM stub axle.

fuselage [fyzlaʒ] *nm* fuselage.

fuselé, e [fyzle] *adj* [doigts] tapering ; [jambes] slender.

fuser [3] [fyze] *vi* [cri, rire] to burst forth *ou* out.

fusible [fyzibl] *nm* fuse.

fusil [fyzi] *nm* - **1.** [arme] gun ; **changer son ~ d'épaule** *fig* to change one's approach - **2.** [personne] marksman.

fusillade [fyzijad] *nf* - **1.** [combat] gunfire *(U)*, fusillade - **2.** [exécution] shooting.

fusiller [3] [fyzije] *vt* - **1.** [exécuter] to shoot ; **~ qqn du regard** *fig* to look daggers at sb - **2.** *fam* [bousiller] to muck up, to ruin.

fusil-mitrailleur [fyzimitrajœr] *(pl* **fusils-mitrailleurs)** *nm* machine gun.

fusion [fyzjɔ̃] *nf* - **1.** [gén] fusion - **2.** [fonte] smelting ; **en ~** molten - **3.** ÉCON & POLIT merger.

fusionner [3] [fyzjɔne] *vt & vi* to merge.

fustiger [17] [fystiʒe] *vt* to castigate.

fut ▷ être.

fût [fy] *nm* - **1.** [d'arbre] trunk - **2.** [tonneau] barrel, cask - **3.** [d'arme] stock - **4.** [de colonne] shaft.

futaie [fytɛ] *nf* wood.

futé, e [fyte] *fam* ◇ *adj* cunning ◇ *nm, f* sharp cookie.

futile [fytil] *adj* - **1.** [insignifiant] futile - **2.** [frivole] frivolous.

futilité [fytilite] *nf* - **1.** [d'action] futility - **2.** [vétille] triviality.

futur, e [fytyr] ◇ *adj* future *(avant n)* ; **la vie ~e** RELIG the life to come ; **~s mariés** bride-and groom-to-be ◇ *nm, f* [fiancé] intended.

➡ **futur** *nm* future ; **~ antérieur** LING future perfect.

futuriste [fytyrist] ◇ *nmf* futurist ◇ *adj* futuristic.

futurologue [fytyrɔlɔg] *nmf* futurologist.

fuyant, e [fɥijɑ̃, ɑ̃t] *adj* - **1.** [perspective, front] receding *(avant n)* - **2.** [regard] evasive.

fuyard, e [fɥijar, ard] *nm, f* runaway.

fuyez, fuyons *etc* ▷ fuir.

FV *(abr de* fréquence vocale) VF.

G

g¹, G [ʒe] *nm inv* g, G.

g² *(abr de* gauche) L, l.

➡ **G** *(abr de* giga) G.

GAB [gab] *(abr de* guichet automatique de banque) *nm* cash dispenser, ATM *Am.*

gabardine [gabardin] *nf* gabardine.

gabarit [gabari] *nm* - **1.** [appareil de mesure] gauge - **2.** [dimension] size - **3.** [valeur] calibre ; **du même ~** of the same calibre.

gabegie [gabʒi] *nf* muddle, disorder.

Gabon [gabɔ̃] *nm* : **le ~** Gabon ; **au ~** in Gabon.

gabonais, e [gabonɛ, ɛz] *adj* Gabonese.

➡ **Gabonais, e** *nm, f* Gabonese.

gâche [gaʃ] *nf* - **1.** [de serrure] striking plate - **2.** [outil] trowel.

gâcher [3] [gɑʃe] vt - **1.** [gaspiller] to waste - **2.** [gâter] to spoil - **3.** CONSTR to mix.

gâchette [gɑʃɛt] nf trigger ; **appuyer sur la ~** to pull the trigger.

gâchis [gɑʃi] nm - **1.** [gaspillage] waste (U) - **2.** [désordre] mess - **3.** CONSTR mortar.

gadelle [gadɛl] nf Can currant.

gadget [gadʒɛt] nm gadget.

gadoue [gadu] nf fam [boue] mud ; [engrais] sludge.

gaélique [gaelik] ⬦ adj Gaelic ⬦ nm Gaelic ; **~ d'Écosse** Scots Gaelic ; **~ d'Irlande** Irish Gaelic.

gaffe [gaf] nf - **1.** fam [maladresse] clanger ; **faire une ~** to drop a clanger - **2.** [outil] boat hook - **3.** loc : **faire ~** fam to take care.

gaffer [3] [gafe] ⬦ vt to hook ⬦ vi fam to put one's foot in it.

gaffeur, euse [gafœr, øz] fam ⬦ adj blundering ⬦ nm, f blunderer.

gag [gag] nm gag.

gaga [gaga] adj fam gaga, doddering.

gage [gaʒ] nm - **1.** [dépôt] pledge ; **mettre qqch en ~** to pawn sthg - **2.** [assurance, preuve] proof ; **en ~ de** as a token of - **3.** [dans jeu] forfeit.

gager [17] [gaʒe] vt : **~ que** to bet (that).

gageure [gaʒyr] nf challenge.

gagnant, e [gaɲɑ̃, ɑ̃t] ⬦ adj winning (avant n) ⬦ nm, f winner.

gagne-pain [gaɲpɛ̃] nm inv livelihood.

gagne-petit [gaɲpəti] nm inv person earning a pittance.

gagner [3] [gaɲe] vt - **1.** [salaire, argent, repos] to earn - **2.** [course, prix, affection] to win - **3.** [obtenir, économiser] to gain ; **~ du temps/de la place** to gain time/space - **4.** [vaincre] : **~ qqn de vitesse** to outpace sb - **5.** [atteindre to reach suj : feu, engourdissement] to spread to [- suj : sommeil, froid] to overcome [se concilier] to win over vi - **1.** [être vainqueur] to win - **2.** [bénéficier] to gain ; **~ à faire qqch** to be better off doing sthg ; **qu'est-ce que j'y gagne?** what do I get out of it? - **3.** [s'améliorer] : **~ en** to increase in ; **~ à être connu** to improve on acquaintance.

gagneur, euse [gaɲœr, øz] nm, f winner.

gai, e [gɛ] adj - **1.** [joyeux] cheerful, happy - **2.** [vif, plaisant] bright.

gaiement [ɡemɑ̃] adv cheerfully.

gaieté [ɡete] nf - **1.** [joie] cheerfulness ; **de ~ de cœur** enthusiastically - **2.** [vivacité] brightness.

gaillard, e [gajar, ard] ⬦ adj - **1.** [alerte] sprightly, spry - **2.** [licencieux] ribald ⬦ nm, f strapping individual.

gain [gɛ̃] nm - **1.** [profit] gain, profit - **2.** [succès] winning ; **avoir** OU **obtenir ~ de cause** to win one's case - **3.** [économie] saving.

➤ **gains** nmpl earnings.

gaine [ɡɛn] nf - **1.** [étui, enveloppe] sheath - **2.** [sous-vêtement] girdle, corset.

gaine-culotte [ɡɛnkylɔt] (pl **gaines-culottes**) nf panty girdle.

gainer [4] [ɡene] vt to sheathe.

gala [gala] nm gala, reception ; **de ~** gala (avant n).

galamment [galamɑ̃] adv politely, gallantly.

galant, e [galɑ̃, ɑ̃t] adj - **1.** [courtois] gallant - **2.** [amoureux] flirtatious.

➤ **galant** nm admirer.

galanterie [galɑ̃tri] nf - **1.** [courtoisie] gallantry, politeness - **2.** [flatterie] compliment.

galantine [galɑ̃tin] nf boned meat or poultry pressed into a loaf shape.

galaxie [galaksi] nf galaxy.

galbe [galb] nm curve.

galbé, e [galbe] adj - **1.** [objet] curved - **2.** [jambe] shapely.

gale [gal] nf MÉD scabies (U).

galère [galɛr] nf NAVIG galley ; **quelle ~!** fig what a hassle!, what a drag!

galérer [18] [galere] vi fam to have a hard time.

galerie [galri] nf - **1.** [gén] gallery ; **~ marchande** OU **commerciale** shopping arcade ; **~ de peinture** picture gallery ; **~** THÉÂTRE circle ; **amuser la ~** fig to play to the gallery - **3.** [porte-bagages] roof rack.

galet [galɛ] nm - **1.** [caillou] pebble - **2.** TECHNOL wheel, roller.

galette [galɛt] nf - **1.** CULIN pancake (made from buckwheat flour) ; **~ des Rois** cake eaten on Twelfth Night - **2.** fam [argent] dough, cash.

galeux, euse [galø, øz] ⬦ adj - **1.** MÉD scabious - **2.** ▷ **brebis** ⬦ nm, f scruffy person.

galimatias [galimatja] nm gibberish (U).

galipette [galipɛt] nf fam somersault ; **faire des ~s** to do somersaults.

Galles [gal] ▷ **pays.**

gallicisme [galisism] nm [expression] French idiom ; [dans une langue étrangère] gallicism.

gallinacé, e [galinase] adj domestic.

➤ **gallinacé** nm domestic fowl.

gallois, e [galwa, az] adj Welsh.

➤ **gallois** nm [langue] Welsh.

➤ **Gallois, e** nm, f Welshman (f Welshwoman) ; **les Gallois** the Welsh.

gallo-romain, e [galɔrɔmɛ̃, ɛn] (mp **gallo-**

romains, fpl gallo-romaines) adj Gallo-Roman.

➡ **Gallo-Romain, e** nm, f Gallo-Roman.

galoche [galɔʃ] nf clog.

galon [galɔ̃] nm - **1.** COUTURE braid (U) - **2.** MIL stripe ; **prendre du ~** fig to be promoted.

galop [galo] nm [allure] gallop ; **au ~** [cheval] at a gallop ; fig at the double.

galopade [galɔpad] nf - **1.** [de cheval] gallop - **2.** [de personne] stampede.

galopant, e [galɔpã, ãt] adj fig galloping, runaway.

galoper [3] [galɔpe] vi - **1.** [cheval] to gallop - **2.** [personne] to run about - **3.** [imagination] to run riot.

galopin [galɔpɛ̃] nm fam brat.

galvaniser [3] [galvanize] vt litt & fig to galvanize.

galvauder [3] [galvode] vt [ternir] to tarnish.

➡ **se galvauder** vp to demean o.s.

gambade [gãbad] nf leap.

gambader [3] [gãbade] vi [sautiller] to leap about ; [agneau] to gambol.

gamberger [17] [gãbɛrʒe] vi fam to think hard.

gambette [gãbɛt] nf fam leg, pin.

Gambie [gãbi] nf : **la ~** Gambia.

gambien, enne [gãbjɛ̃, ɛn] adj Gambian.

➡ **Gambien, enne** nm, f Gambian.

gamelle [gamɛl] nf - **1.** [plat] mess tin Br, kit Am - **2.** fam [chute] : **se ramasser une ~** to come a cropper.

gamin, e [gamɛ̃, in] <> adj - **1.** [espiègle] lively, mischievous - **2.** [puéril] childish <> nm, f - **1.** fam [enfant] kid - **2.** [des rues] street urchin.

gaminerie [gaminri] nf - **1.** [espièglerie] mischievousness - **2.** [enfantillage] childishness ; **faire des ~s** to be childish.

gamme [gam] nf - **1.** [série] range ; **~ de produits** product range ; **haut/bas de ~** at the top/bottom of the range - **2.** MUS scale.

Gand [gã] n Ghent.

gang [gãg] nm gang.

Gange [gãz] nm : **le ~** the (River) Ganges.

ganglion [gãglijɔ̃] nm ganglion.

gangrène [gãgrɛn] nf gangrene ; fig corruption, canker.

gangster [gãgstɛr] nm gangster ; fig crook.

gangue [gãg] nf - **1.** [de minerai] gangue - **2.** fig [carcan] straitjacket.

gant [gã] nm glove ; **~ de boxe** boxing glove ; **~ de caoutchouc** rubber glove ; **~ de crin** friction glove ; **~ de toilette** face cloth, flannel Br ; **aller comme un ~ à qqn** to fit sb like a

glove ; **prendre des ~s** to be cautious ; **prendre des ~s avec qqn** to handle sb with kid gloves.

garage [garaʒ] nm garage.

garagiste [garaʒist] nmf [propriétaire] garage owner ; [réparateur] garage mechanic.

garant, e [garã, ãt] nm, f [responsable] guarantor ; **se porter ~ de** to vouch for.

➡ **garant** nm [garantie] guarantee.

garantie [garãti] nf - **1.** [gén] guarantee - **2.** [de police d'assurance] cover.

garantir [32] [garãtir] vt - **1.** [assurer & COMM] to guarantee ; **~ à qqn que** to assure ou guarantee sb that - **2.** [protéger] : **~ qqch (de)** to protect sthg (from).

garce [gars] nf bitch.

garçon [garsɔ̃] nm - **1.** [enfant] boy ; **~ manqué** tomboy - **2.** [célibataire] : **vieux ~** confirmed bachelor - **3.** [serveur] : **~ (de café)** waiter ; **garçon! waiter!**

garçonne [garsɔn] nf : **coiffure à la ~** urchin cut.

garçonnet [garsɔnɛ] nm little boy.

garçonnière [garsɔnjɛr] nf bachelor flat Br ou apartment Am.

garde [gard] <> nf - **1.** [surveillance] protection - **2.** [veille] : **de ~** on duty ; **pharmacie de ~** duty chemist ; **~ de nuit** night duty - **3.** MIL guard ; **monter la ~** to go on guard - **4.** JUR : **avoir la ~ d'un enfant** to have custody of a child ; **~ à vue** ≃ police custody - **5.** loc : **être/se tenir sur ses ~s** to be/stay on one's guard ; **mettre qqn en ~ contre qqch** to put sb on their guard about sthg ; **prendre ~ à qqch** to watch out for sthg ; **prendre ~ à ne pas faire qqch** to take care not to do sthg ; **prendre ~ que** (+ subjonctif) to take care that ; **mise en ~** warning <> nmf keeper ; **~ du corps** bodyguard ; **~ d'enfants** childminder ; **~ forestier** forest ranger ; **le ~ des Sceaux** the Minister of Justice, ≃ Lord Chancellor Br, Attorney General Am.

➡ **Garde** nf : **la Garde républicaine** the Republican Guard.

garde-à-vous [gardavu] nm inv attention ; **se mettre au ~** to stand to attention.

garde-barrière [gardəbarjɛr] (pl **gardes-barrière** ou **gardes-barrières**) nmf level-crossing keeper.

garde-boue [gardəbu] nm inv mudguard Br, fender Am.

garde-chasse [gardəʃas] (pl **gardes-chasse** ou **gardes-chasses**) nm gamekeeper.

garde-chiourme [gardəʃjurm] (pl **gardes-**

chiourme ou **gardes-chiourmes**) *nm* warder ; *fig* slavedriver.

garde-fou [gardəfu] (*pl* **garde-fous**) *nm* railing, parapet.

garde-malade [gardəmalad] (*pl* **gardes-malades**) *nmf* nurse.

garde-manger [gardəmɑ̃ʒe] *nm inv* [pièce] pantry, larder ; [armoire] meat safe *Br*, cooler *Am*.

garde-meuble [gardəmœbl] (*pl inv* ou **garde-meubles**) *nm* warehouse.

gardénia [gardenja] *nm* gardenia.

garde-pêche [gardəpɛʃ] (*pl* **gardes-pêche**) <> *nm* [personne] water bailiff *Br*, fishwarden *Am* <> *nm inv* [bateau] fishery protection vessel.

garder [3] [garde] *vt* - **1.** [gén] to keep ; [vêtement] to keep on - **2.** [surveiller] to mind, to look after ; [défendre] to guard - **3.** [protéger] : ~ **qqn de qqch** to save sb from sthg.
➤ **se garder** *vp* - **1.** [se conserver] to keep - **2.** [se méfier] : **se ~ de qqn/qqch** to beware of sb/sthg - **3.** [s'abstenir] : **se ~ de faire qqch** to take care not to do sthg.

garderie [gardəri] *nf* crèche *Br*, day nursery *Br*, day-care center *Am*.

garde-robe [gardərɔb] (*pl* **garde-robes**) *nf* wardrobe.

gardien, enne [gardjɛ̃, ɛn] *nm, f* - **1.** [surveillant] guard, keeper ; ~ **de but** goalkeeper ; ~ **de nuit** night watchman ; ~ **de prison** prison warder ou officer - **2.** *fig* [défenseur] protector, guardian - **3.** [agent] : ~ **de la paix** policeman.

gardiennage [gardjɛnaʒ] *nm* caretaking.

gardon [gardɔ̃] *nm* roach ; **frais comme un** ~ *fig* fresh as a daisy.

gare[1] [gar] *nf* station ; ~ **maritime** harbour *Br* ou harbor *Am* station ; ~ **routière** [de marchandises] road haulage depot ; [pour passagers] bus station ; ~ **de triage** marshalling yard.

gare[2] [gar] *interj* - **1.** [attention] watch out! ; ~ **aux voleurs** watch out for pickpockets ; **sans crier** ~ *fig* without warning - **2.** [menace] : ~ **à toi!** watch out!, watch it!

garer [3] [gare] *vt* - **1.** [ranger] to park - **2.** [mettre à l'abri] to put in a safe place.
➤ **se garer** *vp* - **1.** [stationner] to park - **2.** [se ranger] to pull over - **3.** [éviter] : **se ~ de qqch** to avoid sthg.

gargariser [3] [gargarize] ➤ **se gargariser** *vp* - **1.** [se rincer] to gargle - **2.** *péj* [se délecter] : **se ~ de** to delight ou revel in.

gargarisme [gargarism] *nm* gargle.

gargote [gargɔt] *nf* cheap restaurant, greasy spoon.

gargouille [garguj] *nf* gargoyle.

gargouillement [gargujmɑ̃] *nm* gurgling (*U*).

gargouiller [3] [garguje] *vi* - **1.** [eau] to gurgle - **2.** [intestins] to rumble.

garnement [garnəmɑ̃] *nm* rascal, pest.

garni [garni] *nm vieilli* furnished accommodation (*U*) *Br* ou accommodations (*pl*) *Am*.

garnir [32] [garnir] *vt* - **1.** [équiper] to fit out, to furnish - **2.** [couvrir] : ~ **qqch (de)** to cover sthg (with) - **3.** [remplir] to fill - **4.** [orner] : ~ **qqch de** to decorate sthg with ; *COUTURE* to trim sthg with.
➤ **se garnir** *vp* to fill up.

garnison [garnizɔ̃] *nf* garrison.

garniture [garnityr] *nf* - **1.** [ornement] trimming ; [de lit] bed linen - **2.** *AUTOM* : ~ **de frein** brake lining ; ~ **(intérieure)** upholstery - **3.** [*CULIN* - pour accompagner] garnish *Br*, fixings (*pl*) *Am* ; [- pour remplir] filling ; ~ **de légumes** vegetables (*pl*).

garrigue [garig] *nf* scrub.

garrot [garo] *nm* - **1.** [de cheval] withers (*pl*) - **2.** *MÉD* tourniquet - **3.** [de torture] garrotte.

garrotter [3] [garɔte] *vt* - **1.** [attacher] to tie up - **2.** *fig* [museler] to muzzle.

gars [ga] *nm fam* - **1.** [garçon, homme] lad - **2.** [type] guy, bloke *Br*.

gascon, onne [gaskɔ̃, ɔn] *adj* Gascon.
➤ **Gascon, onne** *nm, f* Gascon.

gas-oil [gazɔjl, gazwal], **gazole** [gazɔl] *nm* diesel oil.

gaspillage [gaspijaʒ] *nm* waste.

gaspiller [3] [gaspije] *vt* to waste.

gastrique [gastrik] *adj* gastric.

gastrite [gastrit] *nf* gastritis (*U*).

gastro-entérite [gastrɔɑ̃terit] (*pl* **gastro-entérites**) *nf* gastroenteritis (*U*).

gastronome [gastrɔnɔm] *nmf* gourmet.

gastronomie [gastrɔnɔmi] *nf* gastronomy.

gastronomique [gastrɔnɔmik] *adj* gastronomic.

gâteau, x [gato] *nm* cake ; ~ **d'anniversaire** birthday cake ; ~ **de miel** honeycomb ; ~ **sec** biscuit *Br*, cookie *Am* ; **c'est du** ~ *fam* it's a piece of cake.

gâter [3] [gate] *vt* - **1.** [gén] to spoil ; [vacances, affaires] to ruin, to spoil - **2.** *iron* [combler] to be too good to ; **on est gâté!** just marvellous!
➤ **se gâter** *vp* - **1.** [aliments] to spoil, to go off - **2.** [temps] to change for the worse - **3.** [situation] to take a turn for the worse.

gâterie [gatri] *nf* treat.

gâteux, euse [gatø, øz] <> *adj* senile ; **être ~ de** *fig* to be daft about *ou* besotted with <> *nm, f* - **1.** [sénile] doddering old man (*f* woman) - **2.** [radoteur] old bore.

gâtisme [gatism] *nm* - **1.** [vieillissement] senility - **2.** [stupidité] stupidity.

GATT, Gatt [gat] (*abr de* General Agreement on Tariffs and Trade) *nm* GATT.

gauche [goʃ] <> *nf* - **1.** [côté] left, left-hand side ; **rouler sur la ~** to drive on the left ; **à ~ (de)** on the left (of) , **à ma/ta** *etc* **~** on my/ your *etc* left ; **de ~** on the left - **2.** POLIT : **la ~** the left (wing) ; **de ~** left-wing <> *nm* BOXE left <> *adj* - **1.** [côté] left - **2.** [personne] clumsy.

gauchement [goʃmã] *adv* clumsily.

gaucher, ère [goʃe, ɛr] <> *adj* left-handed <> *nm, f* left-handed person.

gauchir [32] [goʃir] <> *vi* to warp <> *vt fig* to distort.

gauchisant, e [goʃizã, ãt] *adj* leftist.

gauchisme [goʃism] *nm* leftism.

gauchiste [goʃist] <> *nmf* leftist <> *adj* left-wing.

gaufre [gofr] *nf* waffle.

gaufrer [3] [gofre] *vt* to emboss.

gaufrette [gofrɛt] *nf* wafer.

gaule [gol] *nf* - **1.** [perche] pole - **2.** [canne à pêche] fishing rod.

gauler [3] [gole] *vt* to bring *ou* shake down.

gaulliste [golist] *nmf* & *adj* Gaullist.

gaulois, e [golwa, az] *adj* - **1.** [de Gaule] Gallic - **2.** [osé] ribald.

Gaulois, e *nm, f* Gaul.

gauloiserie [golwazri] *nf* bawdy story.

gausser [3] [gose] **se gausser** *vp* : **se ~ de** *littéraire* to make fun of.

gaver [3] [gave] *vt* - **1.** [animal] to force-feed - **2.** [personne] : **~ qqn de** to feed sb full of.

se gaver *vp* : **se ~ de** to gorge o.s. on.

gay [gɛ] *adj inv* & *nm* gay.

gaz [gaz] *nm inv* gas ; **à pleins ~** *fam* AUTOM flat out ; **~ carbonique** carbon dioxide ; **~ lacrymogène** tear gas ; **~ naturel** natural gas.

Gaza [gaza] *n* Gaza ; **la bande de ~** the Gaza Strip.

gaze [gaz] *nf* gauze.

gazelle [gazɛl] *nf* gazelle.

gazer [3] [gaze] <> *vt* to gas <> *vi fam* to go at top speed ; **ça gaze!** everything's great! ; **ça gaze?** how are things?

gazette [gazɛt] *nf* newspaper, gazette.

gazeux, euse [gazø, øz] *adj* - **1.** CHIM gaseous - **2.** [boisson] fizzy.

gazoduc [gazɔdyk] *nm* gas pipeline.

gazole = gas-oil.

gazomètre [gazɔmɛtr] *nm* gasometer.

gazon [gazɔ̃] *nm* [herbe] grass ; [terrain] lawn.

gazouiller [3] [gazuje] *vi* - **1.** [oiseau] to chirp, to twitter - **2.** [bébé] to gurgle.

gazouillis [gazuji] *nm* - **1.** [d'oiseau] chirping, twittering - **2.** [de bébé] gurgling.

GB, G-B (*abr de* Grande-Bretagne) *nf* GB.

gd *abr de* grand.

GDF, Gdf (*abr de* Gaz de France) *French national gas company.*

geai [ʒɛ] *nm* jay.

géant, e [ʒeɑ̃, ɑ̃t] <> *adj* gigantic, giant <> *nm, f* giant.

geignement [ʒɛɲəmɑ̃] *nm* moaning.

geindre [81] [ʒɛ̃dr] *vi* - **1.** [gémir] to moan - **2.** *fam* [pleurnicher] to whine.

gel [ʒɛl] *nm* - **1.** MÉTÉOR frost - **2.** [d'eau] freezing - **3.** [cosmétique] gel.

gélatine [ʒelatin] *nf* gelatine.

gélatineux, euse [ʒelatinø, øz] *adj* gelatinous.

gelée [ʒəle] *nf* - **1.** MÉTÉOR frost ; **~ blanche** hoarfrost - **2.** CULIN jelly ; **en ~** in jelly ; **~ royale** royal jelly.

geler [25] [ʒəle] *vt* & *vi* - **1.** [gén] to freeze - **2.** [projet] to halt.

se geler *vp fam* to freeze.

gélule [ʒelyl] *nf* capsule.

Gémeaux [ʒemo] *nmpl* ASTROL Gemini ; **être ~** to be (a) Gemini.

gémir [32] [ʒemir] *vi* - **1.** [gén] to moan - **2.** [par déception] to groan.

gémissement [ʒemismã] *nm* - **1.** [gén] moan ; [du vent] moaning (U) - **2.** [de déception] groan.

gemme [ʒɛm] *nf* gem, precious stone.

gênant, e [ʒenã, ãt] *adj* - **1.** [encombrant] in the way - **2.** [embarrassant] awkward, embarrassing - **3.** [énervant] : **être ~** to be a nuisance.

gencive [ʒãsiv] *nf* gum.

gendarme [ʒãdarm] *nm* policeman.

gendarmerie [ʒãdarməri] *nf* - **1.** [corps] police force - **2.** [lieu] police station.

gendre [ʒãdr] *nm* son-in-law.

gène [ʒɛn] *nm* gene.

gêne [ʒɛn] *nf* - **1.** [physique] difficulty - **2.** [psychologique] embarrassment ; **être sans ~** *fam* to be a cool customer - **3.** [financière] difficulty ; **être dans la ~** to be in financial difficulties.

gêné, e [ʒene] *adj* - **1.** [physiquement] : **être ~ pour marcher** to have difficulty walking

- 2. [psychologiquement] embarrassed **- 3.** [financièrement] in financial difficulties.

généalogie [ʒenealɔʒi] *nf* genealogy.

généalogique [ʒenealɔʒik] *adj* genealogical ; **arbre ~** family tree.

gêner [4] [ʒene] *vt* **- 1.** [physiquement - gén] to be too tight for ; [- suj : chaussures] to pinch **- 2.** [moralement] to embarrass **- 3.** [incommoder] to bother **- 4.** [encombrer] to hamper.
◆ **se gêner** *vp* to put o.s out ; **ne pas se ~ pour faire qqch** to feel free to do sthg ; *hum* to make no bones about doing sthg ; **ne vous gênez pas!** *hum* don't mind me!

général, e, aux [ʒeneral, o] *adj* general ; **en ~** generally, in general ; **répétition ~e** dress rehearsal.
◆ **général** *nm* MIL general.
◆ **générale** *nf* **- 1.** THÉÀTRE dress rehearsal **- 2.** MIL alarm.

généralement [ʒeneralmã] *adv* generally.

généralisation [ʒeneralizasjɔ̃] *nf* generalization.

généraliser [3] [ʒeneralize] *vt & vi* to generalize.
◆ **se généraliser** *vp* to become general *ou* widespread.

généraliste [ʒeneralist] ⬦ *nmf* GP *Br*, family doctor ⬦ *adj* general.

généralité [ʒeneralite] *nf* **- 1.** [idée] generality **- 2.** [universalité] general nature.
◆ **généralités** *nfpl* generalities.

générateur, trice [ʒeneratœr, tris] *adj* generating.
◆ **générateur** *nm* TECHNOL generator.
◆ **génératrice** *nf* ÉLECTR generator.

génération [ʒenerasjɔ̃] *nf* generation ; **la nouvelle ~** the younger generation ; **~ spontanée** SCIENCE spontaneous generation.

générer [18] [ʒenere] *vt* to generate.

généreusement [ʒenerøzmã] *adv* generously.

généreux, euse [ʒenerø, øz] *adj* generous ; [terre] fertile.

générique [ʒenerik] ⬦ *adj* generic ; **médicament ~** MÉD generic drug ⬦ *nm* **- 1.** CIN & TÉLÉ credits *(pl)* **- 2.** MÉD generic drug.

générosité [ʒenerozite] *nf* generosity.

genèse [ʒənɛz] *nf* [création] genesis.
◆ **Genèse** *nf* BIBLE Genesis.

genêt [ʒənɛ] *nm* broom.

génétique [ʒenetik] ⬦ *adj* genetic ⬦ *nf* genetics (U).

gêneur, euse [ʒenœr, øz] *nm, f* nuisance.

Genève [ʒənɛv] *n* Geneva.

genevois, e [ʒənvwa, az] *adj* Genevan.

génial, e, aux [ʒenjal, o] *adj* **- 1.** [personne] of genius **- 2.** [idée, invention] inspired **- 3.** *fam* [formidable] : **c'est ~!** that's great!, that's terrific!

génie [ʒeni] *nm* **- 1.** [personne, aptitude] genius ; **avoir du ~** to be a genius **- 2.** MYTH spirit, genie **- 3.** TECHNOL engineering ; **le ~** MIL ≃ the Royal Engineers *Br*, ≃ the (Army) Corps of Engineers *Am* ; **~ civil** civil engineering ; **~ maritime** [corps] marine architects.

genièvre [ʒənjɛvr] *nm* juniper.

génisse [ʒenis] *nf* heifer.

génital, e, aux [ʒenital, o] *adj* genital.

géniteur, trice [ʒenitœr, tris] *nm, f* parent ; [d'animal] sire (*f* dam).

génitif [ʒenitif] *nm* genitive (case).

génocide [ʒenɔsid] *nm* genocide.

génoise [ʒenwa, az] *nf* sponge cake.

génome [ʒenom] *nm* genome *m*.

genou, x [ʒənu] *nm* knee ; **à ~x** on one's knees, kneeling ; **se mettre à ~x** to kneel (down) ; **tenir** *ou* **avoir qqn sur ses ~x** to hold sb in one's lap *ou* on one's knee ; **être à ~x devant qqn** *fig* to worship sb ; **être sur les ~x** *fam fig* to be worn out, to be on one's last legs.

genouillère [ʒənujɛr] *nf* **- 1.** [bandage] knee bandage **- 2.** SPORT kneepad.

genre [ʒɑr] *nm* **- 1.** [type] type, kind ; **en tous ~s** of all kinds ; **le ~ humain** the human race **- 2.** LITTÉRATURE genre **- 3.** [style de personne] style ; **avoir mauvais ~** to be coarse-looking **- 4.** GRAM gender.

gens [ʒɑ̃] *nmpl* people.

gentiane [ʒɑ̃sjan] *nf* gentian.

gentil, ille [ʒɑti, ij] *adj* **- 1.** [agréable] nice **- 2.** [aimable] kind, nice ; **être ~ avec qqn** to be nice *ou* kind to sb.

gentilhomme [ʒɑtijɔm] (*pl* **gentilshommes**) *nm* gentleman.

gentillesse [ʒɑtijɛs] *nf* kindness ; **avoir la ~ de faire qqch** to be so kind as to do sthg.

gentillet, ette [ʒɑtijɛ, ɛt] *adj* **- 1.** [petit et gentil] nice little **- 2.** *péj* [assez agréable] nice enough.

gentiment [ʒɑtimɑ̃] *adv* **- 1.** [sagement] nicely **- 2.** [aimablement] kindly, nicely **- 3.** *Helv* [tranquillement] calmly, quietly.

gentleman [dʒɛntləman] (*pl* **gentlemen** [dʒɛntləmɛn]) *nm* gentleman.

génuflexion [ʒenyflɛksjɔ̃] *nf* genuflexion.

géographe [ʒeɔgraf] *nmf* geographer.

géographie [ʒeɔgrafi] *nf* geography.

géographique [ʒeɔgrafik] *adj* geographical.

geôlier, ère [ʒolje, ɛr] *nm, f* gaoler.

géologie [ʒeɔlɔʒi] *nf* geology.

géologique [ʒeɔlɔʒik] *adj* geological.

géologue [ʒeɔlɔg] *nmf* geologist.

géomètre [ʒeɔmɛtr] *nmf* - **1.** [spécialiste] geometer, geometrician - **2.** [technicien] surveyor.

géométrie [ʒeɔmetri] *nf* geometry.

géométrique [ʒeɔmetrik] *adj* geometric.

géophysique [ʒeɔfizik] <> *nf* geophysics (U) <> *adj* geophysical.

géopolitique [ʒeɔpɔlitik] <> *nf* geopolitics (U) <> *adj* geopolitical.

géosphère [ʒeɔsfɛr] *nf* geosphere.

gérance [ʒerɑ̃s] *nf* management.

géranium [ʒeranjɔm] *nm* geranium.

gérant, e [ʒerɑ̃, ɑ̃t] *nm, f* manager.

gerbe [ʒɛrb] *nf* - **1.** [de blé] sheaf ; [de fleurs] spray - **2.** [d'étincelles, d'eau] shower.

gercé, e [ʒɛrse] *adj* chapped.

gerber [3] [ʒɛrbe] <> *vt* - **1.** [blé] to bind into sheaves - **2.** [sacs, caisses] to pile (up) <> *vi* - **1.** [fusée] to burst in a shower of sparks - **2.** *tfam* [vomir] to puke.

gerboise [ʒɛrbwaz] *nf* jerboa.

gercer [16] [ʒɛrse] *vt* & *vi* to crack, to chap.
➡ **se gercer** *vp* to crack, to chap.

gérer [18] [ʒere] *vt* to manage.

gériatrie [ʒerjatri] *nf* geriatrics (U).

gériatrique [ʒerjatrik] *adj* geriatric.

germain, e [ʒɛrmɛ̃, ɛn] ▷ **cousin**.

germanique [ʒɛrmanik] *adj* Germanic.

germaniste [ʒɛrmanist] *nmf* - **1.** [spécialiste] German specialist - **2.** [étudiant] German student, student of German.

germe [ʒɛrm] *nm* - **1.** BOT & MÉD germ ; [de pomme de terre] eye ; **~s de soja** beansprouts - **2.** *fig* [origine] seed, cause.

germer [3] [ʒɛrme] *vi* to germinate.

germination [ʒɛrminasjɔ̃] *nf* germination.

gérondif [ʒerɔ̃dif] *nm* [latin] gerundive ; [français] gerund.

gérontologie [ʒerɔ̃tɔlɔʒi] *nf* gerontology.

gésier [ʒezje] *nm* gizzard.

gésir [49] [ʒezir] *vi littéraire* to lie.

gestation [ʒɛstasjɔ̃] *nf* gestation ; **en ~** *fig* in gestation.

geste [ʒɛst] *nm* - **1.** [mouvement] gesture - **2.** [acte] act, deed ; **faire un ~** *fig* to make a gesture.

gesticuler [3] [ʒɛstikyle] *vi* to gesticulate.

gestion [ʒɛstjɔ̃] *nf* management ; JUR administration ; **~ d'entreprise** business adminis-

tration ; **~ de fichiers** INFORM file management.

gestionnaire [ʒɛstjɔnɛr] <> *nmf* [personne] manager <> *adj* management (avant n) <> *nm* INFORM : **~ de données** data manager.

gestuel, elle [ʒɛstɥɛl] *adj* [langage] sign (avant n).

Ghana [gana] *nm* : **le ~** Ghana.

ghanéen, enne [ganeɛ̃, ɛn] *adj* Ghanaian.
➡ **Ghanéen, enne** *nm, f* Ghanaian.

ghetto [gɛto] *nm litt* & *fig* ghetto.

ghettoïsation [gɛtoizasjɔ̃] *nf* ghettoization.

gibecière [ʒibsjɛr] *nf* game bag ; [d'écolier] satchel.

gibelotte [ʒiblɔt] *nf* rabbit cooked in white wine.

gibet [ʒibɛ] *nm* gallows (sg), gibbet.

gibier [ʒibje] *nm* game ; *fig* [personne] prey ; **du gros ~** big game ; *fig* [personne] important catch.

giboulée [ʒibule] *nf* sudden shower.

giboyeux, euse [ʒibwajø, øz] *adj* abounding in game.

Gibraltar [ʒibraltar] *nm* Gibraltar ; **à ~** in Gibraltar.

giclée [ʒikle] *nf* squirt, spurt.

gicler [3] [ʒikle] *vi* to squirt, to spurt.

gicleur [ʒiklœr] *nm* jet.

gifle [ʒifl] *nf* slap ; **donner une ~ à qqn** to slap sb.

gifler [3] [ʒifle] *vt* to slap ; *fig* [suj : vent, pluie] to whip, to lash.

GIG (abr de grand invalide de guerre) *nm* war invalid.

gigantesque [ʒigɑ̃tɛsk] *adj* gigantic.

giga-octet [ʒigaɔktɛ] *nm* INFORM gigabyte.

GIGN (abr de Groupe d'intervention de la gendarmerie nationale) *nm* special crack force of the French police, ≃ SAS Br, ≃ SWAT Am.

gigogne [ʒigɔɲ] ▷ **lit, table**.

gigolo [ʒigolo] *nm* gigolo.

gigot [ʒigo] *nm* CULIN leg.

gigoter [3] [ʒigote] *vi* to squirm, to wriggle.

gilet [ʒilɛ] *nm* - **1.** [cardigan] cardigan - **2.** [sans manches] waistcoat Br, vest Am ; **~ pare-balles** bulletproof vest ; **~ de sauvetage** life jacket.

gin [dʒin] *nm* gin.

gingembre [ʒɛ̃ʒɑ̃br] *nm* ginger.

gingivite [ʒɛ̃ʒivit] *nf* inflammation of the gums, gingivitis (U).

girafe [ʒiraf] *nf* giraffe.

giratoire [ʒiratwar] *adj* gyrating ; **sens ~** roundabout *Br*, traffic circle *Am*.

girofle [ʒirɔfl] ⊳ **clou.**

giroflée [ʒirɔfle] *nf* stock.

girolle [ʒirɔl] *nf* chanterelle.

giron [ʒirɔ̃] *nm* lap ; **le ~ familial** *fig* the bosom of one's family.

girouette [ʒirwɛt] *nf* weathercock.

gisait, gisions *etc* ⊳ **gésir.**

gisant [ʒizɑ̃] ⬠ *ppr* ⊳ **gésir** ⬠ *nm* recumbent figure *(on tomb)*.

gisement [ʒizmɑ̃] *nm* deposit.

gît ⊳ **gésir.**

gitan, e [ʒitɑ̃, an] *adj* Gipsy *(avant n)*.
⬤ **Gitan, e** *nm, f* Gipsy.

Gitane® [ʒitan] *nf* [cigarette] Gitane®.

gîte [ʒit] *nm* - **1.** [logement] : **~ (rural)** gîte, *self-catering accommodation in the country* - **2.** *littéraire* [abri] lodging ; **le ~ et le couvert** board and lodging - **3.** [du lièvre] form - **4.** [du bœuf] shin *Br*, shank *Am*.

gîter [3] [ʒite] *vi* - **1.** [lièvre] to lie - **2.** [bateau] to list.

givrant, e [ʒivrɑ̃, ɑ̃t] *adj* freezing.

givre [ʒivr] *nm* frost.

givré, e [ʒivre] *adj* - **1.** CULIN : **orange** *etc* **~e** orange *etc* sorbet *(served in the hollowed-out fruit)* - **2.** *fam* [personne] round the twist.

glabre [glabr] *adj* hairless.

glaçage [glasaʒ] *nm* - **1.** [de gâteau] icing *Br*, frosting *Am* - **2.** [de tissu] glazing.

glaçant, e [glasɑ̃, ɑ̃t] *adj* cold.

glace [glas] *nf* - **1.** [eau congelée] ice ; **rester de ~** *fig* to be unmoved ; **rompre la ~** *fig* to break the ice - **2.** [crème glacée] ice cream - **3.** [vitre -] pane ; [- de voiture] window - **4.** [miroir] mirror ; **~ sans tain** two-way mirror.
⬤ **glaces** *nfpl* ice floes.

glacé, e [glase] *adj* - **1.** [gelé] frozen - **2.** [très froid] freezing - **3.** *fig* [hostile] cold - **4.** [dessert] iced ; [viande] glazed ; [fruit] glacé.

glacer [16] [glase] *vt* - **1.** [geler, paralyser] to chill - **2.** [étoffe, papier] to glaze - **3.** [gâteau] to ice *Br*, to frost *Am*.
⬤ **se glacer** *vp* [sang] to run cold.

glaciaire [glasjɛr] *adj* glacial.

glacial, e, aux [glasjal, o] *adj litt* & *fig* icy.

glaciel, elle [glasjɛl] *adj Can* of an ice floe.
⬤ **glaciel** *nm Can* ice floe.

glacier [glasje] *nm* - **1.** GÉOGR glacier - **2.** [marchand] ice cream seller *ou* man.

glacière [glasjɛr] *nf* icebox.

glaçon [glasɔ̃] *nm* - **1.** [dans boisson] ice cube - **2.** [sur toit] icicle - **3.** *fam fig* [personne] iceberg.

glaïeul [glajœl] *nm* gladiolus.

glaire [glɛr] *nf* - **1.** MÉD phlegm - **2.** [d'œuf] white.

glaise [glɛz] *nf* clay.

glaive [glɛv] *nm* sword.

gland [glɑ̃] *nm* - **1.** [de chêne] acorn - **2.** [ornement] tassel - **3.** ANAT glans.

glande [glɑ̃d] *nf* gland ; **~ endocrine** endocrine gland.

glander [3] [glɑ̃de] *vi tfam* to bugger about.

glaner [3] [glane] *vt* to glean.

glapir [32] [glapir] *vi* to yelp, to yap.

glapissement [glapismɑ̃] *nm* yelping, yapping.

glas [gla] *nm* knell ; **sonner le ~** to toll the bell ; **sonner le ~ de** *fig* to sound the death knell for.

glaucome [glokom] *nm* glaucoma.

glauque [glok] *adj* - **1.** [couleur] bluey-green - **2.** *fam* [lugubre] gloomy - **3.** *fam* [sordide] sordid.

glissade [glisad] *nf* slip ; **faire des ~s** to slide.

glissant, e [glisɑ̃, ɑ̃t] *adj* slippery.

glissement [glismɑ̃] *nm* - **1.** [action de glisser] gliding, sliding ; **~ de terrain** landslip, landslide - **2.** *fig* [électoral] swing, shift.

glisser [3] [glise] ⬠ *vi* - **1.** [se déplacer] : **~ (sur)** to glide (over), to slide (over) - **2.** [déraper] : **~ (sur)** to slip (on) - **3.** *fig* [passer rapidement] : **~ sur** to skate over - **4.** [surface] to be slippery - **5.** [progresser] to slip ; **~ dans** to slip into, to slide into ; **~ vers** to slip towards *Br ou* toward *Am*, to slide towards *Br ou* toward *Am* ⬠ *vt* to slip ; **~ un regard à qqn** *fig* to give sb a sidelong glance.
⬤ **se glisser** *vp* to slip ; **se ~ dans** [lit] to slip *ou* slide into ; *fig* to slip *ou* creep into.

glissière [glisjɛr] *nf* runner ; **à ~** sliding ; **~ de sécurité** crash barrier.

glissoire [gliswar] *nf* slide.

global, e, aux [glɔbal, o] *adj* global.

globalement [glɔbalmɑ̃] *adv* on the whole.

globalisation [glɔbalizasjɔ̃] *nf* [d'un marché] globalization.

globalité [glɔbalite] *nf* entirety.

globe [glɔb] *nm* - **1.** [sphère, terre] globe ; **le ~ terrestre** the globe - **2.** [de verre] glass cover.

globe-trotter [glɔbtrɔtœr] (*pl* **globe-trotters**) *nmf* globe-trotter.

globule [glɔbyl] *nm* corpuscle, blood cell ; **~ blanc/rouge** white/red corpuscle.

globuleux [glɔbylø] ⊳ **œil.**

gloire [glwar] *nf* - **1.** [renommée] glory ; [de vedette] fame, stardom - **2.** [mérite] credit ; **à la ~ de** in praise of.

glorieux, euse [glɔrjø, øz] *adj* [mort, combat] glorious ; [héros, soldat] renowned.

glorifier [9] [glɔrifje] *vt* to glorify, to praise. ⬥ **se glorifier** *vp* : **se ~ de** to glory in.

gloriole [glɔrjɔl] *nf* vainglory.

glose [gloz] *nf* gloss.

gloser [3] [gloze] ⬥ *vi* : **~ sur** to gossip about ⬥ *vt* to gloss.

glossaire [glɔsɛr] *nm* glossary.

glotte [glɔt] *nf* glottis.

glouglou [gluglu] *nm* - **1.** *fam* [de liquide] gurgling - **2.** [de dindon] gobbling.

gloussement [glusmɑ̃] *nm* - **1.** [de poule] cluck, clucking *(U)* - **2.** *fam* [de personne] chortle, chuckle.

glousser [3] [gluse] *vi* - **1.** [poule] to cluck - **2.** *fam* [personne] to chortle, to chuckle.

glouton, onne [glutɔ̃, ɔn] ⬥ *adj* greedy ⬥ *nm, f* glutton.

gloutonnerie [glutɔnri] *nf* gluttony, greed.

glu [gly] *nf* - **1.** [colle] glue - **2.** *fam fig* [personne] limpet, leech.

gluant, e [glyɑ̃, ɑ̃t] *adj* sticky.

glucide [glysid] *nm* glucide.

glucose [glykoz] *nm* glucose.

gluten [glytɛn] *nm* gluten.

glycémie [glisemi] *nf* glycaemia.

glycérine [gliserin] *nf* glycerine.

glycine [glisin] *nf* wisteria.

GMT (*abr de* **Greenwich Mean Time**) GMT.

gnangnan [ɲɑ̃ɲɑ̃] *adj inv fam* spineless, wet.

GNL (*abr de* **gaz naturel liquéfié**) *nm* LNG.

gnôle [ɲol] *nf* brandy.

gnome [ɲnom] *nm* gnome.

gnon [ɲɔ̃] *nm fam* thump.

go [go] ⬥ **tout de go** *loc adv* straight.

GO (*abr de* **grandes ondes**) *nfpl* LW.

goal [gol] *nm* goalkeeper.

gobelet [gɔblɛ] *nm* beaker, tumbler.

gober [3] [gɔbe] *vt* - **1.** [avaler] to gulp down - **2.** *fam* [croire] to swallow - **3.** *fam* [aimer] : **je ne peux pas la ~** I can't stand her.

goberger [17] [gɔbɛrʒe] ⬥ **se goberger** *vp fam* - **1.** [manger] to stuff o.s. - **2.** [se prélasser] to take it easy.

godasse [gɔdas] *nf fam* shoe.

godet [gɔdɛ] *nm* - **1.** [récipient] jar, pot - **2.** *COUTURE* flare.

godiller [3] [gɔdije] *vi* - **1.** [rameur] to scull - **2.** [skieur] to wedeln.

goéland [gɔelɑ̃] *nm* gull, seagull.

goélette [gɔelɛt] *nf* schooner.

goémon [gɔemɔ̃] *nm* wrack.

gogo [gogo] ⬥ **à gogo** *loc adv fam* galore.

goguenard, e [gɔgnar, ard] *adj* mocking.

goguette [gɔgɛt] ⬥ **en goguette** *loc adv fam* a bit tight *ou* tipsy.

goinfre [gwɛ̃fr] *nmf fam* pig.

goinfrer [3] [gwɛ̃fre] ⬥ **se goinfrer** *vp* : **se ~ de** *fam* to stuff *ou* pig o.s. with.

goitre [gwatr] *nm* goitre.

golden [gɔldɛn] *nf inv* Golden Delicious.

golf [gɔlf] *nm* [sport] golf , [terrain] golf course.

golfe [gɔlf] *nm* gulf, bay ; **le ~ de Gascogne** the Bay of Biscay ; **le ~ Persique** the (Persian) Gulf.

gommage [gɔmaʒ] *nm* - **1.** [d'écriture] erasing, rubbing out - **2.** [cosmétique] face scrub.

gomme [gɔm] *nf* - **1.** [substance, bonbon] gum - **2.** [pour effacer] rubber *Br*, eraser - **3.** *loc* : **à la ~** *fam* hopeless, useless.

gommé, e [gɔme] *adj* gummed.

gommer [3] [gɔme] *vt* to rub out, to erase ; *fig* to erase.

gond [gɔ̃] *nm* hinge ; **sortir de ses ~s** *fam fig* to fly off the handle.

gondole [gɔ̃dɔl] *nf* gondola.

gondoler [3] [gɔ̃dɔle] *vi* [bois] to warp ; [carton] to curl.
⬥ **se gondoler** *vp* - **1.** [bois] to warp - **2.** *fam* [rire] to split one's sides laughing.

gonflable [gɔ̃flabl] *adj* inflatable.

gonfler [3] [gɔ̃fle] ⬥ *vt* - **1.** [ballon, pneu] to blow up, to inflate ; [rivière, poitrine, yeux] to swell ; [joues] to blow out - **2.** *fig* [grossir] to exaggerate - **3.** *loc* : **être gonflé** *fam* [être courageux] to have guts ; [exagérer] to have a cheek *ou* a nerve ⬥ *vi* to swell.
⬥ **se gonfler** *vp* - **1.** [se distendre] to swell - **2.** [être envahi] : **se ~ de** [orgueil] to swell with ; [espoir] to be filled with.

gonflette [gɔ̃flɛt] *nf fam* : **faire de la ~** to pump iron.

gonfleur [gɔ̃flœr] *nm* pump.

gong [gɔ̃g] *nm* gong.

gonzesse [gɔ̃zɛs] *nf tfam* bird, chick.

goret [gɔrɛ] *nm* - **1.** [cochon] piglet - **2.** *fam* [garçon] dirty little pig.

gorge [gɔrʒ] *nf* - **1.** [gosier, cou] throat ; **avoir la ~ serrée** to have a lump in one's throat ; **s'éclaircir la ~** to clear one's throat ; **faire des ~s chaudes de qqch** to laugh sthg to scorn ; **prendre qqn à la ~** to put sb in a difficult situation ; **rire à ~ déployée** to laugh heartily - **2.** *littéraire* [poitrine] breast, bosom - **3.** *(gén pl)* [vallée] gorge.

gorgée [gɔrʒe] *nf* mouthful ; **à petites ~s** in sips.

gorger [17] [gɔrʒe] *vt* : **~ qqn de qqch** [gaver] to stuff sb with sthg ; [combler] to heap sthg on sb ; **~ qqch de** to fill sthg with.
◆ **se gorger** *vp* : **se ~ de** to gorge o.s. on.

gorille [gɔrij] *nm* - **1.** [animal] gorilla - **2.** *fam* [personne] bodyguard.

gosier [gozje] *nm* throat, gullet.

gosse [gɔs] *nmf fam* kid.

gothique [gɔtik] *adj* - **1.** ARCHIT Gothic - **2.** TYPO : **écriture ~** Gothic script.
◆ **gothique** *nm* : **le ~** the Gothic style.

gouache [gwaʃ] *nf* gouache.

gouaille [gwaj] *nf* cheek.

goudron [gudrɔ̃] *nm* tar.

goudronner [3] [gudrɔne] *vt* to tar.

gouffre [gufr] *nm* abyss ; **le ~ de l'oubli/du désespoir** the depths of oblivion/despair ; **au bord du ~** *fig* on the edge of the abyss.

goujat [guʒa] *nm* boor.

goujaterie [guʒatri] *nf* boorishness.

goujon [guʒɔ̃] *nm* [poisson] gudgeon ; **taquiner le ~** to do a bit of fishing.

goulet [gulɛ] *nm* narrows *(pl)* ; **~ d'étranglement** bottleneck.

goulot [gulo] *nm* neck ; **boire au ~** to drink straight from the bottle.

goulu, e [guly] ◇ *adj* greedy, gluttonous ◇ *nm, f* glutton.

goulûment [gulymɑ̃] *adv* greedily.

goupille [gupij] *nf* pin.

goupiller [3] [gupije] *vt fam* to fix.
◆ **se goupiller** *vp fam* to work out.

goupillon [gupijɔ̃] *nm* - **1.** RELIG (holy water) sprinkler - **2.** [à bouteille] bottle brush.

gourd, e [gur, gurd] *adj* numb.

gourde [gurd] ◇ *nf* - **1.** [récipient] flask, water bottle - **2.** *fam* [personne] idiot, clot *Br* ◇ *adj fam* thick.

gourdin [gurdɛ̃] *nm* club.

gourer [3] [gure] ◆ **se gourer** *vp fam* to slip up.

gourgane [gurgan] *nf Can* broad bean.

gourmand, e [gurmɑ̃, ɑ̃d] ◇ *adj* greedy ; **~ de** fond of ◇ *nm, f* glutton.

gourmandise [gurmɑ̃diz] *nf* - **1.** [caractère] greed, greediness - **2.** [sucrerie] sweet thing.

gourme [gurm] *nf* - **1.** MÉD impetigo - **2.** [maladie du cheval] strangles *(U)* - **3.** *loc* : **jeter sa ~** vieilli to sow one's wild oats.

gourmet [gurmɛ] *nm* : **(fin) ~** gourmet.

gourmette [gurmɛt] *nf* chain bracelet.

gourou [guru] *nm* guru.

gousse [gus] *nf* pod ; **~ d'ail** clove of garlic.

gousset [gusɛ] *nm* [de gilet] fob pocket.

goût [gu] *nm* taste ; **au ~ du jour** fashionable ; **avoir du ~** to have taste ; **avoir le ~ de qqch** to have a taste ou liking for sthg ; **de bon ~** [élégant] tasteful, in good taste ; *hum* [bienséant] advisable ; **de mauvais ~** tasteless, in bad taste ; **il n'a ~ à rien** he doesn't feel like doing anything ; **prendre ~ à qqch** to take a liking to sthg ; **chacun ses ~s, à chacun son ~** each to his own.

goûter [3] [gute] ◇ *vt* - **1.** [déguster] to taste - **2.** [savourer] to enjoy - **3.** *littéraire* [estimer] to appreciate ◇ *vi* to have an afternoon snack ; **~ à** to taste ; **~ de** *litt* & *fig* to have a taste of ◇ *nm* afternoon snack for children, typically consisting of bread, butter, chocolate and a drink.

goutte [gut] ◇ *nf* - **1.** [de pluie, d'eau] drop ; **la ~ (d'eau) qui fait déborder le vase** fig the last straw ; **une ~ dans l'océan** a drop in the ocean ; **se ressembler comme deux ~s d'eau** to be as like as two peas in a pod - **2.** *fam* [alcool] : **la ~** the hard stuff - **3.** MÉD [maladie] gout ◇ *adv (de négation) littéraire* : **ne ... ~** not a thing, nothing ; **je n'y vois ~** I can't see a thing.
◆ **gouttes** *nfpl* MÉD drops.

goutte-à-goutte [gutagut] *nm inv* (intravenous) drip *Br*, IV *Am*.

gouttelette [gutlɛt] *nf* droplet.

gouttière [gutjɛr] *nf* - **1.** [CONSTR - horizontale] gutter ; [- verticale] drainpipe - **2.** MÉD splint.

gouvernail [guvɛrnaj] *nm* rudder.

gouvernante [guvɛrnɑ̃t] *nf* - **1.** [d'enfants] governess - **2.** [de maison] housekeeper.

gouverne [guvɛrn] *nf* AÉRON control surface ; **~ de direction** rudder ; **pour ma/ta ~** fig for my/your guidance.

gouvernement [guvɛrnəmɑ̃] *nm* government.

gouvernemental, e, aux [guvɛrnəmɑ̃tal, ol] *adj* [politique, organisation] government *(avant n)* ; [journal] pro-government.

gouverner [3] [guvɛrne] *vt* to govern.

gouverneur [guvɛrnœr] *nm* governor.

GPL (*abr de* **gaz de pétrole liquéfié**) *nm* LPG.

GQG (*abr de* **grand quartier général**) *nm* GHQ.

gr *abr de* **grade**.

GR (*abr de* **(sentier de) grande randonnée**) *nm* long-distance hiking path.

grabataire [grabatɛr] ◇ *nmf* invalid ◇ *adj* bedridden.

grabuge [grabyʒ] *nm fam* trouble.

grâce [gras] *nf* - **1.** [charme] grace ; **de bonne ~** with good grace, willingly ; **de mauvaise ~** with bad grace, reluctantly - **2.** [faveur] favour *Br*, favor *Am* ; **être dans les bonnes ~s de qqn** to be in sb's good books ; **faire ~ de qqch à qqn** to spare sb sthg - **3.** [miséricorde] mercy ; **rendre ~ à** *littéraire* to give thanks to.
➽ **de grâce** *interj* for heaven's sake!
➽ **grâce à** *loc prép* thanks to.

gracier [9] [grasje] *vt* to pardon.

gracieusement [grasjøzmã] *adv* - **1.** [avec grâce] graciously - **2.** [gratuitement] free (of charge).

gracieux, euse [grasjø, øz] *adj* - **1.** [charmant] graceful - **2.** [gratuit] free.

gracile [grasil] *adj* slender.

gradation [gradasjɔ̃] *nf* gradation.

grade [grad] *nm* [échelon] rank ; [universitaire] qualification ; **monter en ~** to be promoted ; **en prendre pour son ~** to get hauled over the coals.

gradé, e [grade] <> *adj* non-commissioned <> *nm, f* non-commissioned officer, NCO.

gradin [gradɛ̃] *nm* [de stade, de théâtre] tier ; [de terrain] terrace ; **en ~s** terraced.

graduation [graduasjɔ̃] *nf* graduation.

gradué, e [graduye] *Belg* <> *adj* [étudiant] college *(avant n)* <> *nm, f* college graduate.

graduel, elle [graduɛl] *adj* gradual ; [difficultés] increasing.

graduellement [graduɛlmã] *adv* gradually.

graduer [7] [gradue] *vt* - **1.** [récipient, règle] to graduate - **2.** *fig* [effort, travail] to increase gradually.

graffiti [grafiti] *nm inv* graffiti *(U)*.

grailler [3] [graje] *vi fam* to nosh *Br*, to chow down *Am*.

graillon [grajɔ̃] *nm péj* burnt fat.

grain [grɛ̃] *nm* - **1.** [gén] grain ; [de moutarde] seed ; [de café] bean ; **~ de raisin** grape - **2.** [point] : **~ de beauté** mole, beauty spot - **3.** [averse] squall - **4.** *fig* [petite quantité] : **un ~ de** a touch of ; **un ~ de bon sens** an ounce of common sense - **5.** *loc* : **avoir un ~** *fam* to be a bit touched ; **mettre son ~ de sel** *péj* to put one's oar in ; **veiller au ~** to be on one's guard.

graine [grɛn] *nf* - **1.** *BOT* seed ; **mauvaise ~** *fig* bad lot - **2.** *loc* : **être de la ~ de voleur** to be a thief in the making ; **en prendre de la ~** *fam* to follow my/his *etc* example ; **monter en ~** [salade] to bolt, to run to seed ; *fig* to shoot up.

grainetier, ère [grɛntje, ɛr] *nm, f* seed merchant.

graissage [grɛsaʒ] *nm* lubrication.

graisse [grɛs] *nf* - **1.** *ANAT* & *CULIN* fat - **2.** [pour lubrifier] grease.

graisser [4] [grɛse] *vt* - **1.** [machine] to grease, to lubricate - **2.** [vêtements] to get grease on.

graisseux, euse [grɛsø, øz] *adj* - **1.** [papier] greasy - **2.** [bourrelet] of fat.

grammaire [gramɛr] *nf* grammar.

grammatical, e, aux [gramatikal, o] *adj* grammatical.

grammaticalement [gramatikalmã] *adv* grammatically.

gramme [gram] *nm* gram, gramme ; **il n'a pas un ~ de jugeote** he hasn't got an ounce of common sense.

grand, e [grã, grãd] <> *adj* - **1.** [en hauteur] tall ; [en dimensions] big, large ; [en quantité, nombre] large, great ; **une ~e partie de** a large *ou* great proportion of ; **un ~ nombre de** a large *ou* great number of ; **en ~** [dimension] full-size - **2.** [âgé] grown-up ; **les ~es personnes** grown-ups ; **~ frère** big *ou* older brother ; **~e sœur** big *ou* older sister ; **il est assez ~ pour ...** he's old enough to ... - **3.** [puissant] big, leading - **4.** [important, remarquable] great ; **un ~ homme** a great man - **5.** [intense] : **un ~ blessé/brûlé** a person with serious wounds/burns ; **un ~ buveur/fumeur** a heavy drinker/smoker <> *nm, f* (gén pl) - **1.** [personnage] great man (*f* woman) ; **c'est l'un des ~s de l'électroménager** he's one of the big names in electrical appliances - **2.** [enfant] older *ou* bigger boy (*f* girl).
➽ **grand** *adv* : **voir ~** to think big.

grand-angle [grãtãgl] (*pl* **grands-angles**), **grand-angulaire** [grãtãgylɛr] (*pl* **grands-angulaires**) <> *adj* wide-angle <> *nm* wide-angle lens.

grand-chose [grãʃoz] ➽ **pas grand-chose** <> *pron indéf* not much <> *nmf inv fam* worthless person.

grand-duché [grãdyʃe] (*pl* **grands-duchés**) *nm* grand duchy.

Grande-Bretagne [grãdbrətaɲ] *nf* : **la ~** Great Britain.

grandement [grãdmã] *adv* - **1.** [beaucoup] greatly - **2.** [largement] a lot ; **avoir ~ de quoi vivre** to have plenty to live on.

grandeur [grãdœr] *nf* - **1.** [taille] size ; **~ nature** life-size, life-sized - **2.** [apogée] *fig* greatness ; **~ d'âme** *fig* magnanimity.

grand-guignolesque [grãgiɲɔlɛsk] *adj* bloodthirsty and melodramatic.

grandiloquent, e [grãdilɔkã, ãt] *adj* grandiloquent.

grandiose [grãdjoz] *adj* imposing.

grandir [32] [grãdir] <> *vt* : **~ qqn** [suj : chaussu-

res] to make sb look taller ; *fig* to increase sb's standing ⬠ *vi* [personne, plante] to grow ; [obscurité, bruit] to increase, to grow ; ~ **dans l'estime de qqn** to go up in sb's estimation.
⬠ **se grandir** *vp* to make o.s. (appear) taller ; *fig* to increase one's standing.

grandissant, e [grɑ̃disɑ̃, ɑ̃t] *adj* growing.

grand-maman [grɑ̃mamɑ̃] (*pl* **grand-mamans** OU **grands-mamans**) *nf* granny, grandma.

grand-mère [grɑ̃mɛr] (*pl* **grand-mères** OU **grands-mères**) *nf* grandmother ; *fam fig* old biddy ; ~ **maternelle/paternelle** maternal/paternal grandmother.

grand-messe [grɑ̃mɛs] (*pl* **grand-messes** OU **grands-messes**) *nf* high mass.

grand-oncle [grɑ̃tɔ̃kl] (*pl* **grands-oncles**) *nm* great-uncle.

grand-papa [grɑ̃papa] (*pl* **grands-papas**) *nm* grandpa, grandad.

grand-peine [grɑ̃pɛn] ⬠ **à grand-peine** *loc adv* with great difficulty.

grand-père [grɑ̃pɛr] (*pl* **grands-pères**) *nm* grandfather ; *fam fig* old geezer ; ~ **maternel/paternel** maternal/paternal grandfather.

grands-parents [grɑ̃parɑ̃] *nmpl* grandparents.

grand-tante [grɑ̃tɑ̃t] (*pl* **grand-tantes** OU **grands-tantes**) *nf* great-aunt.

grand-voile [grɑ̃vwal] (*pl* **grands-voiles**) *nf* mainsail.

grange [grɑ̃ʒ] *nf* barn.

granit(e) [granit] *nm* granite.

granité, e [granite] *adj* [tissu] pebble-weave.
⬠ **granité** *nm* - **1.** [tissu] pebble weave - **2.** [glace] granita.

granule [granyl] *nm* - **1.** [grain] granule - **2.** MÉD pill.

granulé, e [granyle] *adj* [surface] granular.
⬠ **granulé** *nm* tablet.

granuleux, euse [granylø, øz] *adj* granular.

grape-fruit [grɛpfrut] (*pl* **grape-fruits**) *nm* grapefruit.

graphe [graf] *nm* graph.

graphie [grafi] *nf* spelling.

graphique [grafik] ⬠ *nm* diagram ; [graphe] graph ⬠ *adj* graphic.

graphisme [grafism] *nm* - **1.** [écriture] handwriting - **2.** ART style of drawing.

graphiste [grafist] *nmf* graphic artist.

graphologie [grafɔlɔʒi] *nf* graphology.

graphologue [grafɔlɔg] *nmf* graphologist, handwriting expert.

grappe [grap] *nf* - **1.** [de fruits] bunch ; [de fleurs] stem ; ~ **de raisin** bunch of grapes - **2.** *fig* [de gens] knot.

grappiller [3] [grapije] ⬠ *vt litt* & *fig* to gather, to pick up ⬠ *vi* [financièrement] to make money.

grappin [grapɛ̃] *nm* [ancre] grapnel ; **mettre le** ~ **sur** *fig* & *péj* to get one's claws into sb.

gras, grasse [gra, gras] *adj* - **1.** [personne, animal] fat - **2.** [plat, aliment] fatty ; **matières ~ses** fats - **3.** [cheveux, mains] greasy - **4.** [sol] clayey ; [crayon] soft - **5.** *fig* [plaisanterie] crude - **6.** *fig* [rire] throaty ; [toux] phlegmy - **7.** *fig* [plante] succulent.
⬠ **gras** ⬠ *nm* - **1.** [du jambon] fat - **2.** [de jambe] soft OU fleshy part - **3.** TYPO bold (type) ⬠ *adv* : **manger** ~ to eat fatty foods ; **tousser** ~ to have a loose cough.

gras-double [gradubl] (*pl* **gras-doubles**) *nm* tripe.

grassement [grasmɑ̃] *adv* - **1.** [rire] coarsely - **2.** [payer] a lot.

grassouillet, ette [grasujɛ, ɛt] *adj fam* plump.

gratifiant, e [gratifjɑ̃, ɑ̃t] *adj* gratifying.

gratification [gratifikasjɔ̃] *nf* - **1.** [en argent] bonus - **2.** [psychologique] gratification.

gratifier [9] [gratifje] *vt* - **1.** [accorder] : ~ **qqn de qqch** to present sb with sthg, to present sthg to sb ; *fig* to reward sb with sthg - **2.** [stimuler] to gratify.

gratin [gratɛ̃] *nm* - **1.** CULIN dish sprinkled with breadcrumbs or cheese and browned ; ~ **dauphinois** sliced potatoes baked with cream and browned on top - **2.** *fam fig* [haute société] upper crust.

gratiné, e [gratine] *adj* - **1.** CULIN sprinkled with breadcrumbs or cheese and browned - **2.** *fam fig* [ardu] stiff - **3.** *fam fig* [déroutant] weird.
⬠ **gratinée** *nf* onion soup sprinkled with cheese and browned.

gratiner [3] [gratine] *vt* to sprinkle with breadcrumbs or cheese and then brown.

gratis [gratis] *adv* free.

gratitude [gratityd] *nf* : ~ **(envers)** gratitude (to OU towards).

gratte-ciel [gratsjɛl] *nm inv* skyscraper.

grattement [gratmɑ̃] *nm* scratching.

gratte-papier [gratpapje] *nm inv fam* pen-pusher.

gratter [3] [grate] ⬠ *vt* - **1.** [gén] to scratch ; [pour enlever] to scrape off - **2.** *fam* [gagner] to make - **3.** *fam* [devancer] to overtake ⬠ *vi*

- 1. [démanger] to itch, to be itchy **- 2.** *fam* [écrire] to scribble **- 3.** [frapper] : **~ à la porte** to tap at the door **- 4.** *fam* [travailler] to slave, to slog **- 5.** *fam* [jouer] : **~ de** [violon] to scrape away at ; [guitare] to strum on.

➤ **se gratter** *vp* to scratch.

grattoir [gratwar] *nm* **- 1.** [outil] scraper **- 2.** [de boîte d'allumettes] striking surface.

gratuit, e [gratyi, it] *adj* **- 1.** [entrée] free **- 2.** [hypothèse] unwarranted **- 3.** [violence] gratuitous.

gratuité [gratyite] *nf* **- 1.** [d'entrée] free nature **- 2.** [d'hypothèse] unwarranted nature.

gratuitement [gratyitmã] *adv* **- 1.** [sans payer] free, for nothing **- 2.** [sans raison] gratuitously.

gravats [grava] *nmpl* rubble *(U)*.

grave [grav] ◇ *adj* **- 1.** [attitude, faute, maladie] serious, grave ; **ce n'est pas ~** [ce n'est rien] don't worry about it **- 2.** [voix] deep **- 3.** *LING* : **accent ~** grave accent ◇ *nm (gén pl)* *MUS* low register.

graveleux, euse [gravlø, øz] *adj* **- 1.** [sol] gravelly **- 2.** [fruit] gritty **- 3.** [propos] crude.

gravement [gravmã] *adv* gravely, seriously.

graver [3] [grave] *vt* **- 1.** [gén] to engrave **- 2.** [bois] to carve **- 3.** [disque] to cut.

graveur, euse [gravœr, øz] *nm, f* engraver.

gravier [gravje] *nm* gravel *(U)*.

gravillon [gravijõ] *nm* fine gravel *(U)*.

gravir [32] [gravir] *vt* to climb.

gravité [gravite] *nf* **- 1.** [importance] seriousness, gravity ; **sans ~** not serious **- 2.** *PHYS* gravity.

graviter [3] [gravite] *vi* **- 1.** [astre] to revolve **- 2.** *fig* [évoluer] to gravitate.

gravure [gravyr] *nf* **- 1.** [technique] : **~ (sur)** engraving (on) ; **~ sur bois** woodcutting **- 2.** [reproduction] print ; [dans livre] plate.

gré [gre] *nm* **- 1.** [goût] : **à mon/son ~** for my/ his taste, for my/his liking **- 2.** [volonté] : **bon ~ mal ~** willy nilly ; **contre mon/son ~** against my/his will ; **de ~ ou de force** *fig* whether you/they *etc* like it or not ; **de mon/son plein ~** of my/his own free will ; **au ~ de qqn/qqch** at the will of sb/sthg, at the pleasure of sb/ sthg **- 3.** [gratitude] : **je vous saurais ~ de bien vouloir** ... *littéraire* I should be grateful if you would ...

grec, grecque [grɛk] *adj* Greek.

➤ **grec** *nm* [langue] Greek ; **~ ancien/moderne** ancient/modern Greek.

➤ **grecque** *nf* *CULIN* : **à la grecque** *stewed in oil (with tomatoes) and served cold.*

➤ **Grec, Grecque** *nm, f* Greek.

Grèce [grɛs] *nf* : **la ~** Greece.

gredin, e [grədɛ̃, in] *nm, f* rogue.

gréement [gremã] *nm* rigging.

green [grin] *nm* *GOLF* green.

Greenwich [grinwitʃ] *n* Greenwich ; **le méridien de ~** the Greenwich Meridian.

gréer [15] [gree] *vt* to rig.

greffe [grɛf] ◇ *nf* **- 1.** *MÉD* transplant ; [de peau] graft ; **~ du cœur** heart transplant **- 2.** *BOT* graft ◇ *nm JUR* : **~ (du tribunal)** office of the clerk of court.

greffer [4] [grefe] *vt* **- 1.** *MÉD* to transplant ; [peau] to graft ; **~ un rein/un cœur à qqn** to give sb a kidney/heart transplant **- 2.** *BOT* to graft.

➤ **se greffer** *vp* : **se ~ sur qqch** to be added to sthg.

greffier [grefje] *nm* clerk of the court.

grégaire [greger] *adj* gregarious.

grège [grɛʒ] ⊏ **soie**.

grégorien, enne [gregɔrjɛ̃, ɛn] *adj* Gregorian.

grêle [grɛl] ◇ *nf* hail ◇ *adj* **- 1.** [jambes] spindly **- 2.** [son] shrill.

grêlé, e [grele] *adj* pockmarked.

grêler [4] [grele] ◇ *v impers* to hail ; **il grêle** it's hailing ◇ *vt* to devastate by hail.

grêlon [grelõ] *nm* hailstone.

grelot [grəlo] *nm* bell.

grelotter [3] [grəlɔte] *vi* : **~ (de)** to shiver (with).

grenade [grənad] *nf* **- 1.** [fruit] pomegranate **- 2.** *MIL* grenade ; **~ lacrymogène** tear-gas grenade.

Grenade [grənad] ◇ *nf* [île] : **la ~** Grenada ; **à la ~** in Grenada ◇ *n* [ville d'Espagne] Granada.

grenadier [grənadje] *nm* **- 1.** [arbre] pomegranate tree **- 2.** *MIL* grenadier.

grenadine [grənadin] *nf* grenadine *(pomegranate syrup)*.

grenat [grəna] ◇ *nm* garnet ◇ *adj inv* dark red.

grenier [grənje] *nm* **- 1.** [de maison] attic **- 2.** [à foin] loft **- 3.** *fig* [région] breadbasket.

grenouille [grənuj] *nf* frog ; **~ de bénitier** *fig* fanatical churchgoer.

grenouillère [grənujɛr] *nf* [de bébé] all-in-one.

grenu, e [grəny] *adj* **- 1.** [cuir] grained **- 2.** [roche] granular.

grès [grɛ] *nm* **- 1.** [roche] sandstone **- 2.** [poterie] stoneware.

grésil [grezil] *nm* hail.

grésillement [grezijmɑ̃l *nm* [de friture] sizzling ; [de feu] crackling.

grésiller [3] [grezije] *vi* - **1.** [friture] to sizzle ; [feu] to crackle - **2.** [radio] to crackle.

grève [grɛv] *nf* - **1.** [arrêt du travail] strike ; **être en ~** to be on strike ; **faire ~** to strike, to go on strike ; **~ de la faim** hunger strike ; **~ générale** general strike ; **~ sauvage** wildcat strike ; **~ sur le tas** sit-down strike ; **~ tournante** rotating strike ; **~ du zèle** work-to-rule - **2.** [rivage] shore.

grever [19] [grəve] *vt* to burden ; [budget] to put a strain on.

gréviste [grevist] <> *nmf* striker <> *adj* striking.

GRH (*abr de* gestion des ressources humaines) *nf* personnel management.

gribouillage [gribujaʒ] *nm* - **1.** [écriture] scrawl - **2.** [dessin] doodle.

gribouiller [3] [gribuje] *vt* & *vi* - **1.** [écrire] to scrawl - **2.** [dessiner] to doodle.

gribouillis [gribuji] = gribouillage.

grief [grijɛf] *nm* grievance ; **faire ~ de qqch à qqn** to hold sthg against sb.

grièvement [grijɛvmɑ̃] *adv* seriously.

griffe [grif] *nf* - **1.** [d'animal] claw ; **montrer les ~s** *litt* & *fig* to show one's claws ; **tomber dans les ~s de qqn** *fig* to fall into sb's clutches - **2.** [de créateur] hallmark ; [de couturier] label - **3.** *Belg* [éraflure] scratch.

griffer [3] [grife] *vt* - **1.** [suj : chat etc] to claw - **2.** [suj : créateur] to put one's name to.

griffonner [3] [grifɔne] <> *vt* - **1.** [écrire] to scrawl - **2.** [dessiner] to make a rough sketch of <> *vi* - **1.** [écrire] to scrawl - **2.** [dessiner] to make a rough sketch.

griffure [grifyr] *nf* scratch.

grignoter [3] [griɲɔte] <> *vt* - **1.** [manger] to nibble - **2.** *fam fig* [réduire - capital] to eat away (at) - **3.** *fam fig* [gagner - avantage] to gain <> *vi* - **1.** [manger] to nibble - **2.** *fam fig* [prendre] : **~ sur** to nibble away at.

grigou [grigu] *nm fam* skinflint.

gri-gri (*pl* gris-gris), **grigri** (*pl* grigris) [grigri] *nm* talisman, charm.

gril [gril] *nm* grill ; **sur le ~** on the grill ; **être sur le ~** *fig* to be like a cat on hot bricks.

grillade [grijad] *nf* CULIN grilled meat.

grillage [grijaʒ] *nm* - **1.** [de porte, de fenêtre] wire netting - **2.** [clôture] wire fence.

grillager [17] [grijaʒe] *vt* to put wire netting on.

grille [grij] *nf* - **1.** [portail] gate - **2.** [d'orifice, de guichet] grille ; [de fenêtre] bars (*pl*) - **3.** [de mots croisés, de loto] grid - **4.** [tableau] table ; **~ des**

programmes programme *Br ou* program *Am* listings (*pl*) ; **~ des salaires** salary scale.

grille-pain [grijpɛ̃] *nm inv* toaster.

griller [3] [grije] <> *vt* - **1.** [viande] to grill *Br*, to broil *Am* ; [pain] to toast ; [café, marrons] to roast ; **~ une cigarette** *fam* to have a fag - **2.** *fig* [au soleil - personne] to burn ; [- végétation] to shrivel - **3.** [moteur] to burn out - **4.** *fam fig* [dépasser - concurrents] to outstrip ; **~ un feu rouge** to jump the lights ; **~ une étape** to rush ahead - **5.** *fig* [compromettre] to ruin ; **être grillé** to be done for <> *vi* - **1.** [viande] to grill *Br*, to broil *Am* - **2.** [ampoule] to blow - **3.** [personne] : **~ de** [envie, impatience] to be burning with ; **~ de faire qqch** to be longing to do sthg.

➤ **se griller** *vp fam* to be done for ; **se ~ auprès de qqn** to blow it with sb.

grillon [grijɔ̃] *nm* [insecte] cricket.

grimace [grimas] *nf* grimace ; **faire des ~s** to pull faces ; **faire la ~** to pull a face.

grimacer [16] [grimase] *vi* to grimace.

grimer [3] [grime] *vt* CIN & THÉÂTRE to make up.

➤ **se grimer** *vp* CIN & THÉÂTRE to make (o.s.) up.

grimoire [grimwar] *nm* [de sorcier] book of spells.

grimpant, e [grɛ̃pɑ̃, ɑ̃t] *adj* climbing (*avant n*).

grimper [3] [grɛ̃pe] <> *vt* to climb <> *vi* to climb ; **~ à un arbre/une échelle** to climb a tree/a ladder.

grimpeur, euse [grɛ̃pœr, øz] <> *adj* climbing (*avant n*) <> *nm, f* climber.

grinçant, e [grɛ̃sɑ̃, ɑ̃t] *adj* - **1.** [charnière] squeaking ; [porte, plancher] creaking - **2.** *fig* [ironie] jarring.

grincement [grɛ̃smɑ̃] *nm* [de charnière] squeaking ; [de porte, plancher] creaking ; **~s de dents** *fig* gnashing of teeth.

grincer [16] [grɛ̃se] *vi* [charnière] to squeak ; [porte, plancher] to creak.

grincheux, euse [grɛ̃ʃø, øz] <> *adj* grumpy <> *nm, f* moaner, grumbler.

gringalet [grɛ̃galɛ] *nm* weakling.

griotte [grijɔt] *nf* morello (cherry).

grippe [grip] *nf* MÉD flu (U) ; **avoir la ~** to have (the) flu ; **~ intestinale** gastric flu ; **prendre qqn/qqch en ~** *fig* to take a sudden dislike to sb/sthg.

grippé, e [gripe] *adj* [malade] : **être ~** to have flu.

gripper [3] [gripe] *vi* - **1.** [mécanisme] to jam - **2.** *fig* [processus] to stall.

➤ **se gripper** *vp* - **1.** [mécanisme] to jam - **2.** *fig* [système] to seize up.

grippe-sou [gripsu] (*pl inv* OU **grippe-sous**) *nm fam* skinflint.

gris, e [gri, griz] *adj* - **1.** [couleur] grey *Br*, gray *Am* - **2.** *fig* [morne] dismal - **3.** [saoul] tipsy.
➤ **gris** *nm* - **1.** [couleur] grey *Br*, gray *Am* - **2.** [tabac] shag.

grisaille [grizaj] *nf* - **1.** [de ciel] greyness *Br*, grayness *Am* - **2.** *fig* [de vie] dullness.

grisant, e [grizã, ãt] *adj* intoxicating.

grisâtre [grizatr] *adj* greyish *Br*, grayish *Am*.

grisé [grize] *nm* grey *Br* OU gray *Am* shading.

griser [3] [grize] *vt* to intoxicate.
➤ **se griser** *vp* : **se ~ de** [vin] to get tipsy on ; [air, succès] to get drunk on.

grisonnant, e [grizɔnã, ãt] *adj* greying *Br*, graying *Am*.

grisonner [3] [grizɔne] *vi* to turn grey *Br* OU gray *Am*.

grisou [grizu] *nm* firedamp.

grive [griv] *nf* thrush.

grivois, e [grivwa, az] *adj* ribald.

Groenland [grɔɛnlãd] *nm* : **le ~** Greenland ; **au ~** in Greenland.

grog [grɔg] *nm* (hot) toddy.

groggy [grɔgi] *adj inv* - **1.** [boxeur] groggy - **2.** *fig* [assommé] stunned.

grogne [grɔɲ] *nf* discontent, grumbling.

grognement [grɔɲmã] *nm* - **1.** [son] grunt ; [d'ours, de chien] growl - **2.** [protestation] grumble.

grogner [3] [grɔɲe] *vi* - **1.** [émettre un son] to grunt ; [ours, chien] to growl - **2.** [protester] to grumble.

grognon, onne [grɔɲõ, ɔn] *adj* grumpy.

groin [grwɛ̃] *nm* snout.

grommeler [24] [grɔmle] *vt* & *vi* to mutter.

grondement [grɔ̃dmã] *nm* [d'animal] growl ; [de tonnerre, de train] rumble ; [de torrent] roar.

gronder [3] [grɔ̃de] <> *vi* - **1.** [animal] to growl ; [tonnerre] to rumble - **2.** *littéraire* [grommeler] to mutter <> *vt* to scold.

groom [grum] *nm* page.

gros, grosse [gro, gros] <> *adj* (*gén avant n*) - **1.** [gén] large, big ; *péj* big - **2.** (*avant ou après n*) [corpulent] fat - **3.** [grossier] coarse - **4.** [fort, sonore] loud - **5.** [important, grave - ennuis] serious ; [- dépense] major - **6.** [plein] : **~ de** full of <> *nm*, *f* - **1.** [personne corpulente] fat person - **2.** [personnage important] big shot.
➤ **gros** <> *adv* [beaucoup] a lot ; **en avoir ~ sur le cœur** to be upset <> *nm* - **1.** [partie] : **le (plus) ~ (de qqch)** the main part (of sthg) ; **le (plus) ~ du travail** the bulk of the work - **2.** COMM : **le ~** wholesale.
➤ **de gros** *loc adj* COMM wholesale.

➤ **en gros** *loc adv* & *loc adj* - **1.** COMM wholesale - **2.** [en grands caractères] in large letters - **3.** [grosso modo] roughly.

groseille [grozɛj] <> *nf* currant ; **~ blanche** white currant ; **~ à maquereau** gooseberry ; **~ rouge** redcurrant <> *adj inv* red.

groseillier [grozeje] *nm* currant bush.

gros-porteur [groportœr] (*pl* **gros-porteurs**) *nm* jumbo (jet).

grosse [gros] <> *nf* - **1.** [douze douzaines] gross - **2.** JUR engrossment <> *adj* ➤ **gros**.

grossesse [grosɛs] *nf* pregnancy ; **~ extra-utérine** ectopic pregnancy ; **~ nerveuse** phantom pregnancy.

grosseur [grosœr] *nf* - **1.** [dimension, taille] size - **2.** [corpulence] fatness - **3.** MÉD lump.

grossier, ère [grosje, ɛr] *adj* - **1.** [matière] coarse - **2.** [sommaire] rough - **3.** [insolent] rude - **4.** [vulgaire] crude - **5.** [erreur] crass.

grossièrement [grosjɛrmã] *adv* - **1.** [sommairement] roughly - **2.** [vulgairement] crudely.

grossièreté [grosjɛrte] *nf* - **1.** [vulgarité] crudeness - **2.** [parole grossière] crude remark - **3.** [superficialité] superficiality.

grossir [32] [grosir] <> *vi* - **1.** [prendre du poids] to put on weight - **2.** [augmenter] to grow - **3.** [s'intensifier] to increase - **4.** [cours d'eau] to swell <> *vt* - **1.** [suj : microscope, verre] to magnify - **2.** [suj : vêtement] : **~ qqn** to make sb look fatter - **3.** [exagérer] to exaggerate.

grossissant, e [grosisã, ãt] *adj* [verre] magnifying.

grossissement [grosismã] *nm* - **1.** [de personne] increase in weight - **2.** [de loupe, de microscope] magnification - **3.** [exagération] exaggeration.

grossiste [grosist] *nmf* wholesaler.

grosso modo [grosomɔdo] *adv* roughly.

grotesque [grɔtɛsk] <> *adj* grotesque, ludicrous <> *nm* : **le ~** the grotesque.

grotte [grɔt] *nf* cave.

grouillant, e [grujã, ãt] *adj* - **1.** [foule] milling - **2.** [lieu] : **~ (de)** swarming (with).

grouiller [3] [gruje] *vi* : **~ (de)** to swarm (with).
➤ **se grouiller** *vp fam* to get a move on ; **se ~ de faire qqch** to rush to do sthg.

groupage [grupaʒ] *nm* bulking.

groupe [grup] *nm* group ; **en ~** as a group ; **~ armé** armed group ; **~ de pression** pressure group.
➤ **groupe électrogène** *nm* generator.
➤ **groupe sanguin** *nm* blood group.

groupement [grupmã] *nm* - **1.** [action] grouping - **2.** [groupe] group.

grouper [3] [grupe] *vt* to group.
➤ **se grouper** *vp* to come together.
groupie [grupi] *nmf* groupie.
groupuscule [grupyskyl] *nm* faction.
gruau [gryo] *nm* [farine] wheat flour.
grue [gry] *nf* TECHNOL & ZOOL crane ; **faire le pied de ~** *fig* to stand about.
gruger [17] [gryʒe] *vt littéraire* to dupe.
grumeau, x [grymo] *nm* lump.
grumeleux, euse [grymlø, øz] *adj* - **1.** [pâte] lumpy - **2.** [fruit] gritty - **3.** [peau] bumpy.
grunge [grʌnʒ] *adj* grunge *(modif)*.
gruyère [gryjɛr] *nm* Gruyère (cheese).
Guadeloupe [gwadlup] *nf* : **la ~** Guadeloupe ; **à la ~** in Guadeloupe.
guadeloupéen, enne [gwadlupeɛ̃, ɛn] *adj* of/from Guadeloupe.
➤ **Guadeloupéen, enne** *nm, f* native *ou* inhabitant of Guadeloupe.
Guatemala [gwatemala] *nm* : **le ~** Guatemala ; **au ~** in Guatemala.
guatémaltèque [gwatemaltɛk] *adj* Guatemalan.
➤ **Guatémaltèque** *nmf* Guatemalan.
gué [ge] *nm* ford ; **traverser à ~** to ford.
guenilles [gənij] *nfpl* rags.
guenon [gənɔ̃] *nf* female monkey.
guépard [gepar] *nm* cheetah.
guêpe [gɛp] *nf* wasp.
guêpier [gepje] *nm* wasp's nest ; *fig* hornet's nest ; **aller se fourrer dans un ~** to stir up a hornet's nest.
guère [gɛr] *adv* [peu] hardly ; **ne** *(+ verbe)* **~** [peu] hardly ; **il ne l'aime ~** he doesn't like him/her very much ; **l'appel n'a ~ eu de succès** the appeal met with very little success ; **ne** *(+ verbe)* **plus ~** : **il ne m'écrit plus ~** he hardly (ever) writes (to me) now *ou* any more ; **il n'y a ~ plus de six ans** it's barely more than six years ago ; **il n'y a ~ de** there are hardly any.
guéridon [geridɔ̃] *nm* pedestal table.
guérilla [gerija] *nf* guerrilla warfare.
guérir [32] [gerir] ⬦ *vt* to cure ; **~ qqn de** *litt* & *fig* to cure sb of ⬦ *vi* to recover, to get better.
guérison [gerizɔ̃] *nf* - **1.** [de malade] recovery - **2.** [de maladie] cure.
guérissable [gerisabl] *adj* curable.
guérisseur, euse [gerisœr, øz] *nm, f* healer.
guérite [gerit] *nf* MIL sentry box.
Guernesey [gɛrnəzɛ] *n* Guernsey ; **à ~** on Guernsey.
guerre [gɛr] *nf* - **1.** MIL & *fig* war ; **en ~** at war ;

déclarer la ~ to declare war ; **faire la ~ à un pays** to make *ou* wage war on a country ; **faire la ~ à qqch** to wage war on sthg ; **Première/Seconde Guerre mondiale** First/Second World War ; **~ civile** civil war ; **~ économique** trade war ; **~ froide** cold war ; **~ des nerfs** war of nerves ; **~ sainte** holy war - **2.** [technique] warfare *(U)* - **3.** *loc* : **à la ~ comme à la ~** you'll/we'll *etc* just have to make the best of things ; **c'est de bonne ~** that's fair enough *ou* perfectly fair ; **de ~ lasse** for the sake of peace.
guerrier, ère [gɛrje, ɛr] *adj* - **1.** [de guerre] war *(avant n)* - **2.** [peuple] warlike.
➤ **guerrier** *nm* warrior.
guerroyer [13] [gerwaje] *vi littéraire* to wage war.
guet [gɛ] *nm* : **faire le ~** to be on the look-out.
guet-apens [gɛtapɑ̃] *(pl* **guets-apens***)* *nm* ambush ; *fig* trap ; **tomber dans un ~** to fall into an ambush *ou* a trap.
guêtre [gɛtr] *nf* gaiter ; **traîner ses ~s** *fam* to lounge about.
guetter [4] [gete] *vt* - **1.** [épier] to lie in wait for - **2.** [attendre] to be on the look-out for, to watch for - **3.** [menacer] to threaten.
gueulante [gœlɑ̃t] *nf fam* uproar ; **pousser une ~** to yell (one's head off).
gueulard, e [gœlar, ard] *fam* ⬦ *adj* who shouts a lot ⬦ *nm, f* person who shouts a lot.
➤ **gueulard** *nm* TECHNOL throat.
gueule [gœl] *nf* - **1.** [d'animal, ouverture] mouth - **2.** *tfam* [bouche de l'homme] gob *Br*, yap *Am* ; **ta ~!** shut your gob!, shut it! ; **c'est une grande ~** he/she is all mouth - **3.** *fam* [visage] face - **4.** *loc* : **avoir la ~ de bois** to have a hangover ; **casser la ~ à qqn** to smash sb's face in ; **se casser la ~** *fam* [tomber] to fall flat on one's face ; **faire la ~** *fam* to pull a long face, to sulk ; **se jeter dans la ~ du loup** to enter the lion's den.
gueule-de-loup [gœldəlu] *(pl* **gueules-de-loup***)* *nf* snapdragon.
gueuler [5] [gœle] *fam* ⬦ *vt* to yell ⬦ *vi* - **1.** [crier] to yell - **2.** [protester] to kick up a stink, to scream and shout.
gueuleton [gœltɔ̃] *nm fam* blowout.
gueux, gueuse [gø, gøz] *nm, f littéraire* beggar.
gui [gi] *nm* mistletoe.
guichet [giʃɛ] *nm* counter ; [de gare, de théâtre] ticket office ; **jouer à ~s fermés** *fig* to be sold out.
guide [gid] ⬦ *nm* - **1.** [gén] guide ; **~ de mon-**

tagne mountain guide - **2.** [livre] guidebook ◇ *nf* Girl Guide *Br*, Girl Scout *Am*.
➼ **guides** *nfpl* reins.
guider [3] [gide] *vt* to guide.
guidon [gidɔ̃] *nm* handlebars *(pl)*.
guigne [giɲ] *nf fam* bad *ou* rotten luck.
guigner [3] [giɲe] *vt fam* - **1.** [regarder] to eye - **2.** [convoiter] to have one's eye on.
guignol [giɲɔl] *nm* - **1.** [marionnette] glove puppet - **2.** [théâtre] ≃ Punch and Judy show ; **faire le ~** *fig* to act *ou* play the fool.
guillemet [gijmɛ] *nm* inverted comma, quotation mark ; **entre ~s** in inverted commas *ou* quotation marks ; **ouvrir/fermer les ~s** to open/close quotation marks.
guilleret, ette [gijrɛ, ɛt] *adj* perky.
guillotine [gijɔtin] *nf* - **1.** [instrument] guillotine - **2.** [de fenêtre] sash.
guillotiner [3] [gijɔtine] *vt* to guillotine.
guimauve [gimov] *nf* - **1.** [confiserie, plante] marshmallow - **2.** *fam* [sentimentalité] mush.
guimbarde [gɛ̃bard] *nf* - **1.** *MUS* Jew's harp - **2.** *fam* [voiture] jalopy.
guindé, e [gɛ̃de] *adj* stiff.
Guinée [gine] *nf* : **la ~** Guinea ; **la ~-Bissau** Guinea-Bissau ; **la ~Équatoriale** Equatorial Guinea.
guinéen, enne [gineɛ̃, ɛn] *adj* Guinean.
➼ **Guinéen, enne** *nm, f* Guinean.
guingois [gɛ̃gwa] ➼ **de guingois** *adv sout* lopsidedly.
guinguette [gɛ̃gɛt] *nf* open-air dance floor.
guirlande [girlɑ̃d] *nf* - **1.** [de fleurs] garland - **2.** [de papier] chain ; [de Noël] tinsel (U).
guise [giz] *nf* : **à ma ~** as I please *ou* like ; **en ~ de** by way of.
guitare [gitar] *nf* guitar ; **~ électrique** electric guitar.
guitariste [gitarist] *nmf* guitarist.
Gulf Stream [gœlfstrim] *nm* : **le ~** the Gulf Stream.
gustatif, ive [gystatif, iv] *adj* : **sensibilité gustative** sense of taste.
guttural, e, aux [gytyral, o] *adj* guttural.
Guyana [gɥijana] *nf* : **la ~** Guyana.
Guyane [gɥijan] *nf* : **la ~** French Guiana.
gym [ʒim] *nf* gym (U).
gymkhana [ʒimkana] *nm* rally.
gymnase [ʒimnaz] *nm* gymnasium.
gymnaste [ʒimnast] *nmf* gymnast.
gymnastique [ʒimnastik] *nf SPORT* & *fig* gymnastics (U) ; **faire de la ~** to do keep-fit exercises ; **~ corrective** remedial gymnastics.

gynéco [ʒineko] *nmf fam* gynaecologist *Br*, gynecologist *Am*.
gynécologie [ʒinekɔlɔʒi] *nf* gynaecology *Br*, gynecology *Am*.
gynécologique [ʒinekɔlɔʒik] *adj* gynaecological *Br*, gynecological *Am*.
gynécologue [ʒinekɔlɔg] *nmf* gynaecologist *Br*, gynecologist *Am*.
gypse [ʒips] *nm* gypsum.
gyrophare [ʒirɔfar] *nm* flashing light.

h¹, H [aʃ] *nm inv* h, H ; **~ aspiré/muet** aspirate/silent h.
h² - **1.** (*abr de* **heure**) hr - **2.** (*abr de* **hecto**) h.
➼ **H** - **1.** *abr de* **homme** - **2.** (*abr de* **hydrogène**) H.
ha (*abr de* **hectare**) ha.
hab. *abr de* **habitant**.
habile [abil] *adj* skilful ; [démarche] clever.
habilement [abilmɑ̃] *adv* skilfully ; [manœuvrer] cleverly.
habileté [abilte] *nf* skill.
habiliter [3] [abilite] *vt* to authorize ; **être habilité à faire qqch** to be authorized to do sthg.
habillage [abijaʒ] *nm* - **1.** [action] dressing - **2.** [enveloppe, protection] covering.
habillé, e [abije] *adj* [tenue] dressy ; [réception] smart.
habillement [abijmɑ̃] *nm* - **1.** [action] clothing - **2.** [tenue] outfit - **3.** [profession] clothing trade.
habiller [3] [abije] *vt* - **1.** [vêtir] : **~ qqn (de)** to dress sb (in) - **2.** [suj : fournisseur] to provide with clothing ; [suj : fabricant] to make clothes for - **3.** [recouvrir] to cover.
➼ **s'habiller** *vp* - **1.** [se vêtir] to dress, to get dressed ; **s'~ de** to dress in - **2.** [se vêtir élégamment] to dress up - **3.** [se fournir en vêtements] to buy one's clothes.
habilleur, euse [abijœr, øz] *nm, f* dresser.

habit [abi] *nm* - **1.** [costume] suit ; **~ de neige** *Can* snowsuit ; **~ de soirée** evening dress - **2.** *RELIG* habit.

→ **habits** *nmpl* [vêtements] clothes.

habitable [abitabl] *adj* habitable.

habitacle [abitakl] *nm* [d'avion] cockpit ; [de voiture] passenger compartment.

habitant, e [abitɑ̃, ɑ̃t] *nm, f* - **1.** [de pays] inhabitant ; **loger chez l'~** to stay with local people - **2.** [d'immeuble] occupant - **3.** *Can* [paysan] farmer.

habitat [abita] *nm* - **1.** [conditions de logement] housing conditions *(pl)* - **2.** [mode de peuplement] settlement - **3.** [d'animal] habitat.

habitation [abitasjɔ̃] *nf* - **1.** [fait d'habiter] housing - **2.** [résidence] house, home.

habiter [3] [abite] ⋄ *vt* - **1.** [résider] to live in - **2.** [suj : passion, sentiment] to dwell within ⋄ *vi* to live ; **~ à** to live in.

habitude [abityd] *nf* - **1.** [façon de faire] habit ; **avoir l'~ de faire qqch** to be in the habit of doing sthg ; **d'~** usually ; **comme d'~** as usual ; **par ~** out of habit - **2.** [coutume] custom.

habitué, e [abitye] *nm, f* regular.

habituel, elle [abityɛl] *adj* - **1.** [coutumier] usual, customary - **2.** [caractéristique] typical.

habituellement [abityɛlmɑ̃] *adv* usually.

habituer [7] [abitye] *vt* : **~ qqn à qqch/à faire qqch** to get sb used to sthg/to doing sthg.

→ **s'habituer** *vp* : **s'~ à qqch/à faire qqch** to get used to sthg/to doing sthg.

hâbleur, euse ['ablœr, øz] *littéraire* ⋄ *adj* boastful ⋄ *nm, f* braggart.

hache ['aʃ] *nf* axe *Br*, ax *Am* ; **enterrer la ~ de guerre** *fig* to bury the hatchet.

haché, e ['aʃe] *adj* - **1.** [coupé - gén] finely chopped ; [- viande] minced *Br*, ground *Am* - **2.** [entrecoupé] jerky.

hacher [3] ['aʃe] *vt* - **1.** [couper - gén] to chop finely ; [- viande] to mince *Br*, to grind *Am* - **2.** [entrecouper] to interrupt.

hachette ['aʃɛt] *nf* hatchet.

hachis ['aʃi] *nm* : **un ~ de persil** finely chopped parsley ; **un ~ de porc** minced pork *Br*, ground pork *Am* ; **~ Parmentier** ≈ shepherd's pie, ≈ cottage pie.

hachisch = haschisch.

hachoir ['aʃwar] *nm* - **1.** [couteau] chopper - **2.** [appareil] mincer *Br*, grinder *Am* - **3.** [planche] chopping-board.

hachure ['aʃyr] *nf* hatching.

hachurer [3] ['aʃyre] *vt* to hatch.

haddock ['adɔk] *nm* smoked haddock.

hagard, e ['agar, ard] *adj* haggard.

hagiographie [aʒjɔgrafi] *nf* hagiography.

haï, e ['ai] *pp* ▷ haïr.

haie ['ɛ] *nf* - **1.** [d'arbustes] hedge - **2.** [de personnes] row ; [de soldats, d'agents de police] line ; **~ d'honneur** guard of honour *Br ou* honor *Am* - **3.** *SPORT* hurdle ; **400 mètres ~s** 400 metres *Br ou* meters *Am* hurdles.

haillons ['ajɔ̃] *nmpl* rags.

haine ['ɛn] *nf* hatred.

haineusement ['ɛnøzmɑ̃] *adv* with hatred.

haineux, euse ['ɛnø, øz] *adj* full of hatred.

haïr [33] ['air] *vt* to hate.

hais, hait *etc* ▷ haïr.

haïssable ['aisabl] *adj* hateful.

haïssais, haïssions *etc* ▷ haïr.

Haïti [aiti] *n* Haiti ; **à ~** in Haiti.

haïtien, enne [aisjɛ̃, ɛn] *adj* Haitian.

→ **Haïtien, enne** *nm, f* Haitian.

hâle ['al] *nm* tan.

hâlé, e ['ale] *adj* tanned.

haleine [alɛn] *nf* breath ; **avoir l'~ forte, avoir mauvaise ~** to have bad breath ; **courir à perdre ~** to run until one is breathless ; **hors d'~** out of breath ; **de longue ~** exacting and time-consuming ; **reprendre ~** to catch one's breath ; **tenir qqn en ~** to keep sb in suspense.

haler [3] ['ale] *vt* - **1.** [tirer] to haul in - **2.** [remorquer] to tow.

haletant, e ['altɑ̃, ɑ̃t] *adj* panting.

halètement ['alɛtmɑ̃] *nm* panting.

haleter [28] ['alte] *vi* to pant.

hall ['ol] *nm* - **1.** [vestibule, entrée] foyer, lobby - **2.** [salle publique] concourse ; **~ d'arrivée/de départ** arrival/departure hall.

halle ['al] *nf* covered market.

→ **halles** *nfpl* wholesale food market *(sg)*.

hallucinant, e [alysinɑ̃, ɑ̃t] *adj* - **1.** [incroyable] extraordinary - **2.** [grandiose] impressive.

hallucination [alysinasjɔ̃] *nf* hallucination.

halluciné, e [alysine] ⋄ *adj* crazed ⋄ *nm, f* lunatic.

hallucinogène [alysinɔʒɛn] ⋄ *nm* hallucinogen ⋄ *adj* hallucinogenic.

halo ['alo] *nm* - **1.** [cercle lumineux] halo - **2.** *fig* [rayonnement] aura.

halogène [alɔʒɛn] *nm* & *adj* halogen.

halte ['alt] ⋄ *nf* stop ; **faire ~** to stop ⋄ *interj* stop!

haltère [altɛr] *nm* dumbbell.

haltérophile [alterɔfil] ⋄ *nmf* weight-lifter ⋄ *adj* weight-lifting *(avant n)*.

haltérophilie [alterɔfili] *nf* weight-lifting.

hamac ['amak] *nm* hammock.

hamburger ['āburgœr] *nm* hamburger.

hameau, x [ˈamo] *nm* hamlet.
hameçon [amsɔ̃] *nm* fish-hook ; **mordre à l'~** *fig* to rise to the bait.
hammam [ˈamam] *nm* Turkish baths *(pl)*.
hampe [ˈɑ̃p] *nf* [de drapeau] pole.
hamster [ˈamstɛr] *nm* hamster.
hanche [ˈɑ̃ʃ] *nf* hip ; **rouler des ~s** to swing one's hips.
handball [ˈɑ̃dbal] *nm* handball.
handicap [ˈɑ̃dikap] *nm* handicap.
handicapé, e [ˈɑ̃dikape] <> *adj* handicapped ; **être ~ par qqch** *fig* to be handicapped by sthg <> *nm, f* handicapped person ; **~ mental** mentally handicapped person ; **~ moteur** spastic.
handicaper [3] [ˈɑ̃dikape] *vt* to handicap.
hangar [ˈɑ̃gar] *nm* shed ; AÉRON hangar.
hanneton [ˈantɔ̃] *nm* cockchafer.
Hanoi [ˈanɔj] *n* Hanoi.
hanter [3] [ˈɑ̃te] *vt* to haunt.
hantise [ˈɑ̃tiz] *nf* obsession ; **avoir la ~ de qqch/de faire qqch** to be obsessed by the fear of sthg/of doing sthg.
happer [3] [ˈape] *vt* - **1.** [attraper] to snap up - **2.** [accrocher] to strike.
hara-kiri [ˈarakiri] *nm* : **(se) faire ~** to commit hara-kiri.
harangue [ˈarɑ̃g] *nf* harangue.
haranguer [3] [ˈarɑ̃ge] *vt* to harangue.
haras [ˈara] *nm* stud (farm).
harassant, e [ˈarasɑ̃, ɑ̃t] *adj* exhausting.
harasser [3] [ˈarase] *vt* to exhaust.
harcèlement [ˈarsɛlmɑ̃] *nm* harassment ; **~ sexuel** sexual harassment.
harceler [25] [ˈarsəle] *vt* - **1.** [relancer] to harass - **2.** MIL to harry - **3.** [importuner] : **~ qqn (de)** to pester sb (with).
hardes [ˈard] *nfpl* old clothes.
hardi, e [ˈardi] *adj* bold, daring.
hardiesse [ˈardjɛs] *nf* boldness, daring.
hardware [ˈardwɛr] *nm* INFORM hardware.
harem [ˈarɛm] *nm* harem.
hareng [ˈarɑ̃] *nm* herring ; **~ saur** kipper.
harfang [ˈarfɑ̃] *nm* snowy owl.
hargne [ˈarɲ] *nf* spite (U), bad temper.
hargneux, euse [ˈarɲø, øz] *adj* [personne] spiteful, bad-tempered ; [remarque] spiteful, vicious.
haricot [ˈariko] *nm* bean ; **~s verts/blancs/rouges** green/haricot/kidney beans.
harmonica [armɔnika] *nm* harmonica, mouth organ.
harmonie [armɔni] *nf* - **1.** [gén] harmony ; vi-

vre en ~ **(avec qqn)** to live in harmony (with sb) - **2.** [de visage] symmetry - **3.** [fanfare] wind band.
harmonieusement [armɔnjøzmɑ̃] *adv* harmoniously.
harmonieux, euse [armɔnjø, øz] *adj* - **1.** [gén] harmonious - **2.** [voix] melodious - **3.** [traits, silhouette] regular.
harmonique [armɔnik] *adj* harmonic.
harmonisation [armɔnizasjɔ̃] *nf* - **1.** [coordination] harmonization - **2.** MUS harmonizing.
harmoniser [3] [armɔnize] *vt* MUS & *fig* to harmonize ; [salaires] to bring into line.
harmonium [armɔnjɔm] *nm* harmonium.
harnachement [ˈarnaʃmɑ̃] *nm* - **1.** [équipement de cheval] harness - **2.** [action] harnessing - **3.** *fig* [attirail] gear.
harnacher [3] [ˈarnaʃe] *vt* [cheval] to harness ; **être harnaché** *fig* to be got up.
harnais [ˈarnɛ] *nm* - **1.** [de cheval, de parachutiste] harness - **2.** TECHNOL train.
haro [ˈaro] *nm sout* : **crier ~ sur** to rail against.
harpagon [arpagɔ̃] *nm* ≈ Scrooge.
harpe [ˈarp] *nf* harp.
harpie [ˈarpi] *nf* harpy.
harpon [ˈarpɔ̃] *nm* harpoon.
harponner [3] [ˈarpɔne] *vt* - **1.** [poisson] to harpoon - **2.** *fam* [personne] to waylay.
hasard [ˈazar] *nm* chance ; **au ~** at random ; **à tout ~** on the off chance ; **par ~** by accident, by chance ; **comme par ~** *iron* as if by chance ; **si par ~** if by chance.
hasarder [3] [ˈazarde] *vt* - **1.** [tenter] to venture - **2.** [risquer] to hazard.
➤ **se hasarder** *vp* : **se ~ à faire qqch** to risk doing sthg.
hasardeux, euse [ˈazardø, øz] *adj* risky.
haschisch, haschich, hachisch [ˈaʃiʃ] *nm* hashish.
hâte [ˈat] *nf* haste ; **à la ~, en ~** hurriedly, hastily ; **avoir ~ de faire qqch** to be eager to do sthg.
hâter [3] [ˈate] *vt* - **1.** [activer] to hasten - **2.** [avancer] to bring forward.
➤ **se hâter** *vp* to hurry ; **se ~ de faire qqch** to hurry to do sthg.
hâtif, ive [ˈatif, iv] *adj* [précipité] hurried, hasty.
hauban [ˈobɑ̃] *nm* NAUT shroud.
hausse [ˈos] *nf* [augmentation] rise, increase ; **à la ~, en ~** rising.
haussement [ˈosmɑ̃] *nm* : **~ d'épaules** shrug (of the shoulders).
hausser [3] [ˈose] *vt* to raise.

haut, e [o, ot] adj - **1.** [gén] high ; ~ de 20 m 20 m high - **2.** [classe sociale, pays, région] upper - **3.** [responsable] senior.
➤ **haut** ◇ adv - **1.** [gén] high ; [placé] highly - **2.** [fort] loudly ; **dire bien ~ ce que l'on pense tout bas** to say out loud what everyone else is thinking ◇ nm - **1.** [hauteur] height ; **faire 2 m de ~** to be 2 m high ou in height - **2.** [sommet, vêtement] top - **3.** loc : **avoir ~s et des bas** to have one's ups and downs.
➤ **de haut** loc adv [avec dédain] haughtily ; **le prendre de ~** to react haughtily.
➤ **de haut en bas** loc adv from top to bottom.
➤ **du haut de** loc prép from the top of.
➤ **en haut** loc adv at the top ; [dans une maison] upstairs.
➤ **en haut de** loc prép at the top of.
➤ **là-haut** loc adv up there.

hautain, e [otɛ̃, ɛn] adj haughty.

hautbois ['obwa] nm oboe.

haut-de-forme ['odfɔrm] (pl **hauts-de-forme**) nm top hat.

haut de gamme [odgam] ◇ adj upmarket ; **une chaîne ~** a state-of-the-art hi-fi system ◇ nm top of the range.

haute-fidélité [otfidelite] (pl **hautes-fidélités**) nf high fidelity, hi-fi.

hautement ['otmɑ̃] adv highly.

hauteur ['otœr] nf height ; **à ~ d'épaule** at shoulder level ou height ; **ne pas être à la ~ de qqch** not to be up to sthg.

haut-fond ['ofɔ̃] (pl **hauts-fonds**) nm shallows (pl).

haut-fourneau ['ofurno] (pl **hauts-fourneaux**) nm blast furnace.

haut-le-cœur ['olkœr] nm inv retch ; **avoir des ~** to retch.

haut-le-corps ['olkɔr] nm inv : **avoir un ~** to start, to jump.

haut-parleur ['oparlœr] (pl **haut-parleurs**) nm loudspeaker.

havane ['avan] ◇ nm Havana cigar ◇ adj inv tobacco-coloured Br, tobacco-colored Am.

Havane ['avan] n : **La ~** Havana.

hâve ['av] adj littéraire haggard.

havre ['avr] nm [refuge] haven.

Hawaii ['awaj] n Hawaii ; **à ~** in Hawaii.

hawaiien, enne ['awajɛ̃, ɛn] adj Hawaiian.
➤ **Hawaiien, enne** nm, f Hawaiian.

Haye ['ɛ] n : **La ~** the Hague.

hayon ['ajɔ̃] nm hatchback.

HCR (abr de **Haut-commissariat des Nations unies pour les réfugiés**) nm UN-HCR.

hé ['e] interj hey!

hebdo [ɛbdo] nm fam weekly.

hebdomadaire [ɛbdɔmadɛr] nm & adj weekly.

hébergement [ebɛrʒəmɑ̃] nm accommodation Br, accommodations (pl) Am.

héberger [17] [ebɛrʒe] vt - **1.** [loger] to put up - **2.** [suj : hôtel] to take in.

hébété, e [ebete] adj dazed.

hébétement [ebetmɑ̃] nm stupor.

hébétude [ebetyd] nf littéraire stupor.

hébraïque [ebraik] adj Hebrew.

hébreu, x [ebrø] adj Hebrew.
➤ **hébreu** nm [langue] Hebrew.
➤ **Hébreu, x** nm Hebrew.

Hébrides [ebrid] nfpl : **les ~** the Hebrides ; **aux ~** in the Hebrides.

HEC (abr de (**école des**) **Hautes études commerciales**) n grande école for management and business studies.

hécatombe [ekatɔ̃b] nf litt & fig slaughter.

hectare [ɛktar] nm hectare.

hectolitre [ɛktɔlitr] nm hectolitre.

hédonisme [edɔnism] nm hedonism.

hédoniste [edɔnist] ◇ nmf hedonist ◇ adj hedonistic.

hégémonie [eʒemɔni] nf hegemony.

hégire [eʒir] nf hegira.

hein ['ɛ̃] interj fam eh?, what? ; **tu m'en veux, ~?** you're cross with me, aren't you?

hélas [elas] interj unfortunately, alas.

héler [18] ['ele] vt sout to hail.

hélice [elis] nf - **1.** [d'avion, de bateau] propeller - **2.** MATHS helix.

hélicoïdal, e, aux [elikɔidal, o] adj - **1.** [forme] spiral, helical - **2.** MATHS helical.

hélicoptère [elikɔptɛr] nm helicopter.

héliomarin, e [eljɔmarɛ̃, in] adj MÉD [cure] using sun and sea air.

héliport [elipɔr] nm heliport.

hélitreuiller [elitrœje] vt to wind to safety.

héliporté, e [elipɔrte] adj [troupes, fournitures] transported by helicopter ; [opération] helicopter (avant n).

hélium [eljɔm] nm helium.

Helsinki ['ɛlsiŋki] n Helsinki.

helvétisme [ɛlvetism] nm Swiss expression.

hem ['ɛm] interj [indique le doute] hmm.

hématologie [ematɔlɔʒi] nf haematology.

hématome [ematom] nm MÉD haematoma.

hémicycle [emisikl] *nm* POLIT : **l'~** the Assemblée Nationale.

hémiplégique [emipleʒik] *nmf* & *adj* hemiplegic.

hémisphère [emisfɛr] *nm* hemisphere ; **l'~ nord/sud** northern/southern hemisphere ; **~ cérébral** ANAT cerebral hemisphere.

hémoglobine [emɔglɔbin] *nf* haemoglobin.

hémophile [emɔfil] ◇ *nmf* haemophiliac ◇ *adj* haemophilic.

hémorragie [emɔraʒi] *nf* - **1.** MÉD haemorrhage ; **~ cérébrale** brain haemorrhage ; **~ interne** internal bleeding *(U)* - **2.** *fig* [perte, fuite] loss.

hémorroïdes [emɔrɔid] *nfpl* haemorrhoids, piles.

henné ['ene] *nm* henna.

hennir [32] ['enir] *vi* to neigh, to whinny.

hennissement ['enismã] *nm* neigh, whinny.

hep ['ɛp] *interj* hey!

hépatique [epatik] ◇ *nmf* person with liver problems ◇ *adj* liver *(avant n)*.

hépatite [epatit] *nf* MÉD hepatitis ; **~ B** hepatitis B ; **~ virale** viral hepatitis.

heptagone [ɛptagon] *nm* heptagon.

herbacé, e [ɛrbase] *adj* herbaceous.

herbage [ɛrbaʒ] *nm* pasture.

herbe [ɛrb] *nf* - **1.** BOT grass ; **mauvaise ~** weed - **2.** CULIN & MÉD herb ; **fines ~s** herbs - **3.** *fam* [marijuana] grass - **4.** *loc* : **en ~** budding ; **couper l'~ sous les pieds de qqn** to cut the ground from under sb's feet.

herbeux, euse [ɛrbø, øz] *adj* grassy.

herbicide [ɛrbisid] ◇ *nm* weedkiller, herbicide ◇ *adj* herbicidal.

herbier [ɛrbje] *nm* herbarium.

herbivore [ɛrbivɔr] ◇ *nm* herbivore ◇ *adj* herbivorous.

herboriste [ɛrbɔrist] *nmf* herbalist.

herboristerie [ɛrbɔristəri] *nf* herbalist's (shop).

herculéen, enne [ɛrkyleɛ̃, ɛn] *adj* Herculean.

hère ['ɛr] *nm* : **pauvre ~** poor wretch.

héréditaire [erediter] *adj* hereditary.

hérédité [eredite] *nf* - **1.** [génétique] heredity - **2.** [de biens, de titre] inheritance.

hérésie [erezi] *nf* heresy.

hérétique [eretik] ◇ *nmf* heretic ◇ *adj* heretical.

hérisser [3] ['erise] *vt* - **1.** [dresser] : **~ son poil** to bristle - **2.** [garnir] : **être hérissé de** [de clous] to be studded with ; *fig* [de difficultés] to be fraught with - **3.** [irriter] : **~ qqn** to get sb's back up.

hérisson ['erisɔ̃] *nm* - **1.** ZOOL hedgehog - **2.** [brosse] chimney sweep's brush.

héritage [eritaʒ] *nm* - **1.** [de biens] inheritance ; **faire un ~** to come into an inheritance ; **en ~** as an inheritance - **2.** [culturel] heritage.

hériter [3] [erite] ◇ *vi* to inherit ; **~ de qqch** to inherit sthg ◇ *vt* : **~ qqch de qqn** *litt* & *fig* to inherit sthg from sb.

héritier, ère [eritje, ɛr] *nm, f* heir (*f* heiress).

hermaphrodite [ɛrmafrɔdit] *nmf* & *adj* hermaphrodite.

hermétique [ɛrmetik] *adj* - **1.** [étanche] hermetic - **2.** [incompréhensible] inaccessible, impossible to understand - **3.** [impénétrable] impenetrable.

hermétiquement [ɛrmetikmã] *adv* hermetically.

hermétisme [ɛrmetism] *nm* [de texte] obscurity.

hermine [ɛrmin] *nf* - **1.** [animal] stoat - **2.** [fourrure] ermine.

hernie ['ɛrni] *nf* hernia ; **~ discale** slipped disc *Br* OU disk *Am*.

héroïne [erɔin] *nf* - **1.** [personne] heroine - **2.** [drogue] heroin.

héroïnomane [erɔinɔman] *nmf* heroin addict.

héroïque [erɔik] *adj* heroic.

héroïquement [erɔikmã] *adv* heroically.

héroïsme [erɔism] *nm* heroism.

héron ['erɔ̃] *nm* heron.

héros ['ero] *nm* hero.

herpès [ɛrpɛs] *nm* herpes.

herse ['ɛrs] *nf* - **1.** AGRIC harrow - **2.** [grille] portcullis.

hertz ['ɛrts] *nm inv* hertz.

hésitant, e [ezitã, ãt] *adj* hesitant.

hésitation [ezitasjɔ̃] *nf* hesitation ; **avec ~** hesitantly ; **sans ~** without hesitation, unhesitatingly.

hésiter [3] [ezite] *vi* to hesitate ; **~ entre/sur** to hesitate between/over ; **~ à faire qqch** to hesitate to do sthg.

hétéro [eterɔ] *adj* & *nmf* hetero.

hétéroclite [eterɔklit] *adj* motley.

hétérogène [eterɔʒɛn] *adj* heterogeneous.

hétérogénéité [eterɔʒeneite] *nf* heterogeneity.

hétérosexuel, elle [eterɔsɛksɥɛl] *adj & nm,*
f heterosexual.

hêtre [ˈɛtr] *nm* beech.

heure [œr] *nf* - **1.** [unité de temps] hour ; **250 km**
à l'~ 250 km per *ou* an hour ; **faire des ~s sup-**
plémentaires to work overtime - **2.** [moment
du jour] time ; **il est deux ~s** it's two o'clock ;
donner/demander l'~ à qqn to tell/ask sb the
time ; **quelle ~ est-il?** what time is it? ; **être à**
l'~ to be on time ; **mettre à l'~** [montre, pendule]
to put right ; **~ d'affluence** [dans les transports]
rush hour ; [au magasin] peak time ; **à quelle**
~? when?, (at) what time? ; **~ de battement**
break ; **~ creuse** off-peak time, slack period ;
~ d'ouverture/de fermeture opening/
closing time ; **~ de pointe** rush hour ; **~s de**
bureau office hours ; **~s de réception** office/
surgery *etc* hours - **3.** *scol* class, period
- **4.** *loc* : **à ~ fixe** at a set time ; **à l'~ actuelle** at
the present time ; **à l'~ qu'il est** at this mo-
ment in time ; **à la bonne ~!** that's wonderful! ; **à la première ~** at the crack of dawn ; **à**
toute ~ at any time ; **c'est l'~ (de faire qqch)**
it's time (to do sthg) ; **de bonne ~** early ; **de**
la première ~ right from the start ; **sur l'~** at
once.

heureusement [œrøzmɑ̃] *adv* - **1.** [par chance]
luckily, fortunately - **2.** [favorablement] successfully.

heureux, euse [œrø, øz] <> *adj* - **1.** [gén]
happy ; [favorable] fortunate ; **être ~ de faire**
qqch to be happy to do sthg - **2.** [réussi] successful, happy - **3.** *loc* : **encore ~ (que)** (+ *sub-*
jonctif) ... *fam* it's just as well (that) ... <> *nm,*
f : **faire un ~** to make somebody's day.

heurt [ˈœr] *nm* - **1.** [choc] collision, impact
- **2.** [désaccord] clash ; **sans ~s** smoothly.

heurter [3] [ˈœrte] <> *vt* - **1.** [rentrer dans - gén]
to hit ; [- suj : personne] to bump into - **2.** [offen-
ser - personne, sensibilité] to offend - **3.** [bon sens,
convenances] to go against <> *vi* : **~ contre qqch**
to bump into sthg.

~ se heurter *vp* - **1.** [gén] : **se ~ (contre)** to
collide (with) - **2.** [rencontrer] : **se ~ à qqch** to
come up against sthg.

heurtoir [ˈœrtwar] *nm* knocker.

hexagonal, e, aux [ɛgzagɔnal, o] *adj*
- **1.** *GÉOM* hexagonal - **2.** [français] French.

hexagone [ɛgzagɔn] *nm* *GÉOM* hexagon.

~ Hexagone *nm* : **l'Hexagone** (metropolitan) France.

HF (*abr de* **hautes fréquences**) HF.

hiatus [jatys] *nm inv* hiatus.

hibernation [ibɛrnasjɔ̃] *nf* hibernation.

hiberner [3] [ibɛrne] *vi* to hibernate.

hibiscus [ibiskys] *nm* hibiscus.

hibou, x [ˈibu] *nm* owl.

hic [ˈik] *nm fam* snag.

hideux, euse [ˈidø, øz] *adj* hideous.

hier [ijɛr] *adv* yesterday ; **~ matin/soir** yesterday morning/evening.

hiérarchie [ˈjerarʃi] *nf* hierarchy.

hiérarchique [ˈjerarʃik] *adj* hierarchical.

hiéroglyphe [jerɔglif] *nm* hieroglyph,
hieroglyphic.

~ hiéroglyphes *nmpl* hieroglyphics.

hilarant, e [ilarɑ̃, ɑ̃t] *adj* hilarious.

hilare [ilar] *adj* beaming.

hilarité [ilarite] *nf* hilarity ; **provoquer l'~ gé-**
nérale to give rise to general hilarity.

Himalaya [imalaja] *nm* : **l'~** the Himalayas
(pl).

himalayen, enne [imalajɛ̃, jɛn] *adj* Himalayan.

hindi [ˈindi] *nm* [langue] Hindi.

hindou, e [ɛ̃du] *adj* Hindu.

~ Hindou, e *nm, f* Hindu.

hindouisme [ɛ̃duism] *nm* Hinduism.

hippie, hippy [ˈipi] *(pl* **hippies***) nmf & adj*
hippy.

hippique [ipik] *adj* horse *(avant n)*.

hippisme [ipism] *nm* (horse) riding.

hippocampe [ipɔkɑ̃p] *nm* seahorse.

hippodrome [ipɔdrom] *nm* race-course.

hippopotame [ipɔpɔtam] *nm* hippopotamus.

hirondelle [irɔ̃dɛl] *nf* swallow.

hirsute [irsyt] *adj* [chevelure, barbe] shaggy.

hispanique [ispanik] *adj* - **1.** [gén] Hispanic
- **2.** [aux États-Unis] Spanish-American.

~ Hispanique *nmf* [aux États-Unis] Spanish
American.

hispano-américain, e [ispanɔamerikɛ̃, ɛn]
(*mpl* **hispano-américains**, *fpl* **hispano-**
américaines*) adj* Spanish-American.

~ Hispano-Américain, e *nm, f* Spanish-
American, Hispanic.

hispanophone [ispanɔfɔn] <> *nmf*
Spanish-speaker <> *adj* Spanish-
speaking.

hisser [3] [ˈise] *vt* - **1.** [voile, drapeau] to hoist
- **2.** [charge] to heave, to haul.

~ se hisser *vp* - **1.** [grimper] : **se ~ (sur)** to
heave *ou* haul o.s. up (onto) - **2.** *fig* [s'élever] :
se ~ à to pull o.s. up to.

histoire [istwar] *nf* - **1.** [science] history ;
~ ancienne/moderne/contemporaine an-
cient/modern/contemporary history ;
~ de l'art art history ; **~ de France** French
history ; **~ naturelle** natural history ; **~ sain-**

te Biblical history ; ~ **sociale/économique** social/economic history - **2.** [récit, mensonge] story ; **c'est une autre** ~ that's another story ; ~ **à dormir debout** tall story - **3.** [aventure] funny *ou* strange thing - **4.** *(gén pl)* [ennui] trouble *(U)* ; **faire des** ~**s** *fam* to make a fuss.

historien, enne [istɔrjɛ̃, ɛn] *nm, f* historian.

historique [istɔrik] *adj* - **1.** [roman, recherches] historical - **2.** [monument, événement] historic.

historiquement [istɔrikmɑ̃] *adv* historically.

hit-parade ['itparad] *(pl* **hit-parades)** *nm* : **le** ~ the charts *(pl)*.

hiver [ivɛr] *nm* winter ; **en** ~ in (the) winter.

hivernal, e, aux [ivɛrnal, o] *adj* winter *(avant n)*.

hiverner [3] [ivɛrne] *vi* to (spend the) winter.

hl *(abr de* **hectolitre)** hl.

HLM *(abr de* **habitation à loyer modéré)** *nm ou nf* low-rent, state-owned housing, ≃ council house/flat *Br*, ≃ public housing unit *Am*.

hm *(abr de* **hectomètre)** hm.

ho ['o] *interj* oh!

hobby ['ɔbi] *(pl* **hobbies)** *nm* hobby.

hochement ['ɔʃmɑ̃] *nm* : ~ **de tête** [affirmatif] nod (of the head) ; [négatif] shake of the head.

hocher [3] ['ɔʃe] *vt* : ~ **la tête** [affirmativement] to nod (one's head) ; [négativement] to shake one's head.

hochet ['ɔʃɛ] *nm* rattle.

hockey ['ɔkɛ] *nm* hockey ; ~ **sur glace** ice hockey *Br*, hockey *Am* ; ~ **sur gazon** field hockey.

holà ['ɔla] <> *interj* - **1.** [pour appeler] hey! - **2.** [pour arrêter] hold on! <> *nm* : **mettre le** ~ **à qqch** *fam* to put a stop to sthg.

holding ['ɔldiŋ] *nm ou nf* holding company.

hold-up ['ɔldœp] *nm inv* hold-up.

hollandais, e ['ɔlɑ̃dɛ, ɛz] *adj* Dutch.
➡ **hollandais** *nm* [langue] Dutch.
➡ **Hollandais, e** *nm, f* Dutchman (*f* Dutchwoman).

Hollande ['ɔlɑ̃d] *nf* : **la** ~ Holland ; **en** ~ in Holland.

holocauste [ɔlɔkost] *nm* holocaust.

hologramme [ɔlɔgram] *nm* hologram.

homard ['ɔmar] *nm* lobster ; ~ **à l'armoricaine** *ou* **l'américaine** lobster sautéed in oil with white wine, garlic and tomatoes.

home ['om] *nm* : ~ **d'enfants** holiday centre *Br ou* center *Am* for children.

homélie [ɔmeli] *nf* homily.

homéopathe [ɔmeɔpat] <> *nmf* homeopath <> *adj* homeopathic.

homéopathie [ɔmeɔpati] *nf* homeopathy.

homéopathique [ɔmeɔpatik] *adj* homeopathic.

homicide [ɔmisid] <> *nm* [meurtre] murder ; ~ **involontaire** manslaughter ; ~ **volontaire** murder <> *adj* homicidal.

hommage [ɔmaʒ] *nm* [témoignage d'estime] tribute ; **rendre** ~ **à qqn/qqch** to pay tribute to sb/sthg.
➡ **hommages** *nmpl* [salutations] respects ; **mes** ~**s** *sout* my respects.

hommasse [ɔmas] *adj péj* mannish, butch.

homme [ɔm] *nm* man ; **vêtements d'**~ menswear *(U)* ; **grand** ~ great man ; ~ **d'affaires** businessman ; ~ **d'État** statesman ; ~ **de main** hired man ; ~ **du monde** man about town ; ~ **de paille** stooge ; ~ **politique** politician ; **d'**~ **à** ~ man to man ; **comme un seul** ~ as one (man).

homme-grenouille [ɔmgrənuj] *(pl* **hommes-grenouilles)** *nm* frogman.

homme-orchestre [ɔmɔrkɛstr] *(pl* **hommes-orchestres)** *nm* one-man band.

homme-sandwich [ɔmsɑ̃dwitʃ] *(pl* **hommes-sandwiches)** *nm* sandwich man.

homogène [ɔmɔʒɛn] *adj* homogeneous.

homogénéisé, e [ɔmɔʒeneize] *adj* homogenized.

homogénéité [ɔmɔʒeneite] *nf* homogeneity.

homologue [ɔmɔlɔg] <> *nm* counterpart, opposite number <> *adj* equivalent.

homologuer [3] [ɔmɔlɔge] *vt* [ratifier] to approve ; *SPORT* to recognize, to ratify.

homonyme [ɔmɔnim] *nm* - **1.** *LING* homonym - **2.** [personne, ville] namesake.

homosexualité [ɔmɔsɛksɥalite] *nf* homosexuality.

homosexuel, elle [ɔmɔsɛksɥɛl] *adj & nm, f* homosexual.

Honduras ['ɔ̃dyras] *nm* : **le** ~ Honduras ; **au** ~ in Honduras ; **le** ~ **britannique** British Honduras.

hondurien, enne ['ɔ̃dyrjɛ̃, ɛn] *adj* Honduran.
➡ **Hondurien, enne** *nm, f* Honduran.

Hongkong, Hong Kong ['ɔ̃gkɔ̃g] *n* Hong Kong.

Hongrie ['ɔ̃gri] *nf* : **la** ~ Hungary.

hongrois, e [ˈɔ̃grwa, az] adj Hungarian.
→ **hongrois** nm [langue] Hungarian.
→ **Hongrois, e** nm, f Hungarian.

honnête [ɔnɛt] adj **- 1.** [intègre] honest **- 2.** [correct] honourable Br, honorable Am **- 3.** [convenable - travail, résultat] reasonable.

honnêtement [ɔnɛtmɑ̃] adv **- 1.** [de façon intègre, franchement] honestly **- 2.** [correctement] honourably Br, honorably Am.

honnêteté [ɔnɛtte] nf honesty.

honneur [ɔnœr] nm honour Br, honor Am ; en l'~ de in honour Br ou honor Am of ; être à l'~ to be in favour Br ou favor Am ; à qui ai-je l'~? sout to whom do I have the honour Br ou honor Am of speaking? ; faire ~ à qqn/à qqch to be a credit to sb/to sth ; faire ~ à un repas fig to do justice to a meal ; sauver l'~ to save one's honour Br ou honor Am.
→ **honneurs** nmpl honours Br, honors Am.

Honolulu [onolyly] n Honolulu.

honorable [ɔnɔrabl] adj **- 1.** [digne] honourable Br, honorable Am **- 2.** [convenable] respectable.

honorablement [ɔnɔrabləmɑ̃] adv honourably Br, honorably Am.

honoraire [ɔnɔrɛr] adj honorary.
→ **honoraires** nmpl fee (sg), fees.

honorer [3] [ɔnɔre] vt **- 1.** [vénérer, gratifier] : ~ qqn (de) to honour Br ou honor Am sb (with) **- 2.** [faire honneur à] to be a credit to **- 3.** [payer] to honour Br, to honor Am.
→ **s'honorer** vp : s'~ de qqch to pride o.s. on sth.

honorifique [ɔnɔrifik] adj honorary Br, ceremonial Am.

honte [ˈɔ̃t] nf **- 1.** [sentiment] shame ; avoir ~ de qqn/qqch to be ashamed of sb/sth ; avoir ~ de faire qqch to be ashamed of doing sth ; faire ~ à qqn to make sb (feel) ashamed **- 2.** [action scandaleuse] : c'est une ~! it's a disgrace!

honteusement [ˈɔ̃tøzmɑ̃] adv shamefully.

honteux, euse [ˈɔ̃tø, øz] adj shameful ; [personne] ashamed.

hooligan, houligan [ˈuligan] nm hooligan.

hop [ˈɔp] interj **- 1.** [pour faire sauter] hup! **- 2.** [pour stimuler] off you go!

hôpital, aux [ɔpital, o] nm hospital ; ~ militaire/psychiatrique military/psychiatric hospital ; ~ de jour outpatients unit.

hoquet [ˈɔkɛ] nm hiccup ; avoir le ~ to have (the) hiccups.

hoqueter [27] [ˈɔkte] vi to hiccup.

horaire [ɔrɛr] ◇ nm **- 1.** [de départ, d'arrivée]

timetable **- 2.** [de travail] hours (pl) (of work) ; ~ mobile ou flexible ou à la carte flexitime ◇ adj hourly.

horde [ˈɔrd] nf horde.

horions [ˈɔrjɔ̃] nmpl littéraire blows.

horizon [ɔrizɔ̃] nm **- 1.** [ligne, perspective] horizon ; à l'~ litt & fig on the horizon **- 2.** [panorama] view.

horizontal, e, aux [ɔrizɔ̃tal, o] adj horizontal.
→ **horizontale** nf MATHS horizontal ; à l'~ horizontal, in a horizontal position ; [couché] flat out.

horizontalement [ɔrizɔ̃talmɑ̃] adv horizontally.

horloge [ɔrlɔʒ] nf clock ; ~ parlante speaking clock Br, Time Am.

horloger, ère [ɔrlɔʒe, ɛr] ◇ adj clock/watch making (avant n) ◇ nm, f clock maker, watchmaker.

horlogerie [ɔrlɔʒri] nf clock/watch making.

hormis [ˈɔrmi] prép save.

hormonal, e, aux [ɔrmɔnal, o] adj hormonal.

hormone [ɔrmɔn] nf hormone.

horodateur [ɔrɔdatœr] nm [à l'usine] clock ; [au parking] ticket machine.

horoscope [ɔrɔskɔp] nm horoscope.

horreur [ɔrœr] nf horror ; avoir ~ de qqn/qqch to hate sb/sth ; avoir ~ de faire qqch to hate doing sth ; avoir qqn/qqch en ~ to hate sb/sth ; faire ~ à qqn to disgust sb ; quelle ~! how dreadful!, how awful!

horrible [ɔribl] adj **- 1.** [affreux] horrible **- 2.** fig [terrible] terrible, dreadful.

horriblement [ɔribləmɑ̃] adv horribly.

horrifiant, e [ɔrifjɑ̃, ɑ̃t] adj horrifying.

horrifier [9] [ɔrifje] vt to horrify.

horripilant, e [ɔripilɑ̃, ɑ̃t] adj exasperating.

horripiler [3] [ɔripile] vt to exasperate.

hors [ˈɔr] prép ▷ pair, service.
→ **hors de** loc prép outside ; ~ d'ici! get out of here! ; être ~ de soi to be beside o.s.

hors-bord [ˈɔrbɔr] nm inv speedboat.

hors-d'œuvre [ˈɔrdœvr] nm inv hors d'oeuvre, starter.

hors-jeu [ˈɔrʒø] nm inv & adj inv offside.

hors-la-loi [ˈɔrlalwa] nm inv outlaw.

hors-piste [ˈɔrpist] nm inv off-piste skiing.

hortensia [ɔrtɑ̃sja] nm hydrangea.

horticole [ɔrtikɔl] adj horticultural.

horticulteur, trice [ɔrtikyltœr, tris] nm, f horticulturalist.

horticulture [ɔrtikyltyr] *nf* horticulture.

hospice [ɔspis] *nm* home.

hospitalier, ère [ɔspitalje, ɛr] *adj* - **1.** [accueillant] hospitable - **2.** [relatif aux hôpitaux] hospital *(avant n)*.

hospitalisation [ɔspitalizasjɔ̃] *nf* hospitalization.

hospitaliser [3] [ɔspitalize] *vt* to hospitalize.

hospitalité [ɔspitalite] *nf* hospitality.

hostie [ɔsti] *nf* host.

hostile [ɔstil] *adj* : ~ (à) hostile (to).

hostilité [ɔstilite] *nf* hostility.
➡ **hostilités** *nfpl* hostilities.

hôte, hôtesse [ot, otɛs] *nm, f* host (*f* hostess) ; **hôtesse d'accueil** receptionist ; **hôtesse de l'air** air hostess.
➡ **hôte** *nm* [invité] guest.

hôtel [otɛl] *nm* - **1.** [d'hébergement] hotel ; **descendre à l'~** to stay at a hotel ; **~ trois étoiles** three-star hotel - **2.** [demeure] : **~ (particulier)** mansion - **3.** [établissement public] public building ; **~ de ville** town hall - **4.** [demeure] : **~ (particulier)** (private) mansion.

hôtelier, ère [otəlje, ɛr] <> *adj* hotel *(avant n)* <> *nm, f* hotelier.

hôtellerie [otɛlri] *nf* - **1.** [métier] hotel trade - **2.** [hôtel-restaurant] inn.

hot line [ɔtlain] *(pl* hot lines*) nf* hot line.

hotte [ɔt] *nf* - **1.** [panier] basket - **2.** [d'aération] hood ; **~ aspirante** extractor hood.

houblon [ublɔ̃] *nm* - **1.** *BOT* hop - **2.** [de la bière] hops *(pl)*.

houe [u] *nf* hoe.

houille [uj] *nf* coal ; **~ blanche** hydroelectric power.

houiller, ère [uje, ɛr] *adj* coal *(avant n)*.
➡ **houillère** *nf* coalmine.

houle [ul] *nf* swell.

houlette [ulɛt] *nf sout* : **sous la ~ de qqn** under the guidance of sb.

houleux, euse [ulø, øz] *adj litt & fig* turbulent.

houppe [up] *nf* - **1.** [à poudre] powder puff - **2.** [de cheveux] tuft.

houppette [upɛt] *nf* powder puff.

hourra, hurrah [ura] <> *nm* cheer <> *interj* hurrah!

house [aws], **house music** [awsmjuzik] *nf* house (music).

houspiller [3] [uspije] *vt* to tell off.

housse [us] *nf* cover ; **~ de couette** duvet cover.

houx [u] *nm* holly.

HS *(abr de* hors service*) adj* out of order ; **la télé est complètement ~** *fam* the telly's on the blink ; **je suis ~** *fam* I'm completely washed out.

HT *(abr de* hors taxe*)* <> *adj* exclusive of tax ; **300 F ~** ≃ 300 F plus VAT <> *nf (abr de* haute tension*)* HT.

HTML *(abr de* hypertext markup language*) nm INFORM* HTML.

huard [ɥar] *nm Can* loon.

hublot [yblo] *nm* - **1.** [de bateau] porthole - **2.** [de four, cuisinière] window.

huche [yʃ] *nf* : **~ à pain** bread bin *Br*, bread box *Am*.

hue [y] *interj* gee up!, giddy up!

huées [ɥe] *nfpl* boos.

huer [7] [ɥe] <> *vt* [siffler] to boo <> *vi* [chouette, hibou] to hoot.

huile [ɥil] *nf* - **1.** [gén] oil ; **~ d'arachide/d'olive** groundnut/olive oil ; **~ de coude** *fam fig* elbow grease ; **~ essentielle** essential oil ; **~ de foie de morue** cod-liver oil ; **~ de paraffine** paraffin *Br*, kerosene *Am* ; **~ solaire** suntan oil/lotion ; **jeter de l'~ sur le feu** to add fuel to the flames - **2.** [peinture] oil painting - **3.** *fam* [personnalité] bigwig.

huiler [3] [ɥile] *vt* to oil.

huileux, euse [ɥilø, øz] *adj* oily.

huilier [ɥilje] *nm* - **1.** [accessoire] oil and vinegar set - **2.** [fabricant] oil producer.

huis [ɥi] *nm littéraire* door ; **à ~ clos** *JUR* in camera.

huissier [ɥisje] *nm* - **1.** [appariteur] usher - **2.** *JUR* bailiff.

huit [ɥit] <> *adj num* eight <> *nm* eight ; **lundi en ~** a week on Monday *Br*, Monday week *Br*, a week from Monday *Am* ; *voir aussi* **six**.

huitaine [ɥitɛn] *nf* : **sous** *OU* **à ~** in a week's time, a week today.

huitième [ɥitjɛm] <> *adj num & nmf* eighth <> *nm* eighth ; **le ~ de finale** round before the quarterfinal <> *nf SCOL* ≃ second year *OU* form *(at junior school) Br*, ≃ fourth grade *Am* ; *voir aussi* **sixième**.

huître [ɥitr] *nf* oyster.

hululement = ululement.

hululer = ululer.

hum [œm] *interj* - **1.** [marque le doute] hmm! - **2.** [pour attirer l'attention] ahem!

humain, e [ymɛ̃, ɛn] *adj* - **1.** [gén] human - **2.** [sensible] humane.
➡ **humain** *nm* [être humain] human (being).

humainement [ymɛnmɑ̃] *adv* - **1.** [matériellement] humanly - **2.** [avec bonté] humanely.

humaniser [3] [ymanize] *vt* to humanize.

→ **s'humaniser** *vp* to become more human.

humaniste [ymanist] ⬦ *nmf* - **1.** [philosophe] humanist - **2.** [lettré] classicist ⬦ *adj* humanistic.

humanitaire [ymanitɛr] ⬦ *adj* humanitarian ; couloir ~ humanitarian *ou* safe corridor ⬦ *nm* : l' ~ humanitarian *ou* relief work.

humanité [ymanite] *nf* humanity.

→ **humanités** *nfpl* Belg humanities.

humanoïde [ymanɔid] *nmf* & *adj* humanoid.

humble [ãbl] *adj* humble.

humblement [œblǝmã] *adv* humbly.

humecter [4] [ymɛkte] *vt* to moisten.

→ **s'humecter** *vp* to moisten.

humer [3] ['yme] *vt* to smell.

humérus [ymerys] *nm* humerus.

humeur [ymœr] *nf* - **1.** [disposition] mood ; être de bonne/mauvaise ~ to be in a good/bad mood - **2.** [caractère] nature - **3.** *sout* [irritation] temper ; avec ~ angrily - **4.** *vieilli* & ANAT [liquide] humour Br, humor Am.

humide [ymid] *adj* [air, climat] humid ; [terre, herbe, mur] wet, damp ; [saison] rainy ; [front, yeux] moist.

humidificateur [ymidifikatœr] *nm* humidifier.

humidifier [9] [ymidifje] *vt* to humidify.

humidité [ymidite] *nf* [de climat, d'air] humidity ; [de terre, mur] dampness.

humiliant, e [ymiljã, ãt] *adj* humiliating.

humiliation [ymiljasjɔ̃] *nf* humiliation.

humilier [9] [ymilje] *vt* to humiliate.

→ **s'humilier** *vp* : s'~ devant qqn to grovel to sb.

humilité [ymilite] *nf* humility.

humoriste [ymɔrist] ⬦ *nmf* humorist ⬦ *adj* humoristic.

humoristique [ymɔristik] *adj* humorous.

humour [ymur] *nm* humour Br, humor Am ; avoir de l'~ to have a sense of humour Br *ou* humor Am ; manquer d'~ to have no sense of humour Br *ou* humor Am ; ~ noir black humour Br *ou* humor Am.

humus [ymys] *nm* humus.

huppé, e ['ype] *adj* - **1.** *fam* [société] uppercrust - **2.** [oiseau] crested.

hurlant, e ['yrlã, ãt] *adj* - **1.** [gén] howling - **2.** *fig* [couleurs] clashing.

hurlement ['yrlǝmã] *nm* howl.

hurler [3] ['yrle] *vi* - **1.** [gén] to howl - **2.** [couleurs] to clash.

hurluberlu, e [yrlybɛrly] *nm, f* fam crank.

hurrah = hourra.

hussard ['ysar] *nm* hussar.

→ **hussarde** *nf* : à la ~e brutally.

hutte ['yt] *nf* hut.

hybride [ibrid] *nm* & *adj* hybrid.

hydratant, e [idratã, ãt] *adj* moisturizing.

→ **hydratant** *nm* moisturizer.

hydratation [idratasjɔ̃] *nf* - **1.** CHIM hydration - **2.** [de peau] moisturizing.

hydrate [idrat] *nm* hydrate ; ~ de carbone carbohydrate.

hydrater [3] [idrate] *vt* - **1.** CHIM to hydrate - **2.** [peau] to moisturize.

hydraulique [idrolik] ⬦ *nf* hydraulics (U) ⬦ *adj* hydraulic.

hydravion [idravjɔ̃] *nm* seaplane, hydroplane.

hydre [idr] *nf* hydra.

hydrocarbure [idrɔkarbyr] *nm* hydrocarbon.

hydrocution [idrɔkysjɔ̃] *nf* immersion syncope.

hydroélectrique [idrɔelɛktrik] *adj* hydroelectric.

hydrogène [idrɔʒɛn] *nm* hydrogen.

hydrogéné, e [idrɔʒene] *adj* hydrogenated.

hydroglisseur [idrɔglisœr] *nm* jetfoil, hydroplane.

hydrographie [idrɔgrafi] *nf* hydrography.

hydrologie [idrɔlɔʒi] *nf* hydrology.

hydrophile [idrɔfil] *adj* - **1.** [qui absorbe] absorbent - **2.** ⊳ coton.

hyène [jɛn] *nf* hyena.

hygiène [iʒjɛn] *nf* hygiene ; ~ dentaire/intime dental/personal hygiene.

hygiénique [iʒjenik] *adj* - **1.** [sanitaire] hygienic - **2.** [bon pour la santé] healthy.

hymen [imɛn] *nm* - **1.** ANAT hymen - **2.** *littéraire* [mariage] marriage.

hymne [imn] *nm* hymn ; ~ national national anthem.

hyperbole [ipɛrbɔl] *nf* - **1.** MATHS hyperbola - **2.** LING hyperbole.

hyperglycémie [ipɛrglisemi] *nf* hyperglycaemia.

hypermarché [ipɛrmarʃe] *nm* hypermarket.

hypermétrope [ipɛrmetrɔp] ⬦ *nmf* longsighted person ⬦ *adj* longsighted.

hypersensible [ipɛrsãsibl] ⬦ *nmf* hypersensitive person ⬦ *adj* hypersensitive.

hypertension [ipɛrtãsjɔ̃] *nf* high blood

pressure, hypertension ; **faire de l'~** to have high blood pressure.

hypertexte [ipertɛkst] ◇ *adj* : **lien ~** hyperlink ◇ *nm* hypertext.

hypertrophié [ipertrɔfje] *adj* hypertrophic ; *fig* exaggerated.

hypnose [ipnoz] *nf* hypnosis.

hypnotique [ipnɔtik] *nm* & *adj* hypnotic.

hypnotiser [3] [ipnɔtize] *vt* to hypnotize ; *fig* to mesmerize.
◆ **s'hypnotiser** *vp* : **s'~ sur qqch** to be mesmerized by sthg.

hypoallergénique [ipɔalɛrʒenik] *adj* hypoallergenic.

hypocondriaque [ipɔkɔ̃drijak] *nmf* & *adj* hypochondriac.

hypocrisie [ipɔkrizi] *nf* hypocrisy.

hypocrite [ipɔkrit] ◇ *nmf* hypocrite ◇ *adj* hypocritical.

hypocritement [ipɔkritmɑ̃] *adv* hypocritically.

hypodermique [ipɔdɛrmik] *adj* hypodermic.

hypoglycémie [ipɔglisemi] *nf* hypoglycaemia.

hypokhâgne [ipɔkaɲ] *nf first year of a two-year preparatory arts course taken prior to the competitive examination for entry to the École normale supérieure.*

hypophyse [ipɔfiz] *nf* pituitary gland.

hypotension [ipɔtɑ̃sjɔ̃] *nf* low blood pressure ; **faire de l'~** to have low blood pressure.

hypoténuse [ipɔtenyz] *nf* hypotenuse.

hypothécaire [ipɔtekɛr] *adj* [prêt, contrat] mortgage *(avant n)*.

hypothèque [ipɔtɛk] *nf* mortgage ; **grevé d'~s** [maison] heavily mortgaged.

hypothéquer [18] [ipɔteke] *vt* to mortgage.

hypothèse [ipɔtɛz] *nf* hypothesis ; **dans l'~ où** assuming.

hypothétique [ipɔtetik] *adj* hypothetical.

hystérie [isteri] *nf* hysteria ; **~ collective** mass hysteria.

hystérique [isterik] ◇ *nmf* hysterical person ◇ *adj* hysterical.

Hz *(abr de* **hertz)** Hz.

i, I [i] *nm inv* i, I ; **mettre les points sur les i** to dot the i's and cross the t's.

IA *(abr de* **intelligence artificielle)** *nf* AI.

IAC *(abr de* **insémination artificielle entre conjoints)** *nf* AIH.

IAD *(abr de* **insémination artificielle par donneur extérieur)** *nf* AID.

ibérique [iberik] *adj* : **la péninsule ~** the Iberian Peninsula.

ibid. *(abr de* **ibidem)** ibid.

iceberg [ajsbɛrg] *nm* iceberg.

ici [isi] *adv* - **1.** [lieu] here ; **d'~** from around here ; **~ même** on this very spot ; **par ~** [direction] this way ; [alentour] around here ; **~-bas** here below - **2.** [temps] now ; **d'~ (à) jeudi** between now and Thursday ; **d'~ (à) une semaine** in a week's time, a week fron now ; **d'~ là** by then ; **d'~ peu** soon - **3.** [au téléphone] : **~ Jacques** Jacques speaking *ou* here.

icône [ikon] *nf* INFORM & RELIG icon.

iconique [ikɔnik] *adj* iconic.

iconoclaste [ikɔnɔklast] ◇ *nmf* iconoclast ◇ *adj* iconoclastic.

iconographie [ikɔnɔgrafi] *nf* iconography.

id. *(abr de* **idem)** id.

idéal, e [ideal] *(pl* **idéals** OU **idéaux** [ideo]) *adj* ideal.
◆ **idéal** *nm* ideal.

idéalement [idealmɑ̃] *adv* ideally.

idéalisation [idealizasjɔ̃] *nf* idealization.

idéaliser [3] [idealize] *vt* to idealize.

idéalisme [idealism] *nm* idealism.

idéaliste [idealist] ◇ *nmf* idealist ◇ *adj* idealistic.

idée [ide] *nf* idea ; **à l'~ de/que** at the idea of/that ; **avoir dans l'~ que ...** to have a feeling that ... ; **changer d'~** to change one's mind ; **ne pas avoir la moindre ~ (de)** not to have the slightest idea (about) ; **se faire des ~s** to imagine things ; **se faire des ~s sur qqn/qqch** to get ideas about sb/sthg ; **se faire une ~ de** to get an idea of ; **cela ne m'est jamais venu à l'~** it never occurred to me ; **~ fixe** obsession ; **~ de génie** brainwave ; **~s noires** black thoughts ; **~s reçues** assumptions ; **se rafraî-chir les ~s** to refresh one's memory.

idem [idɛm] *adv* idem.

identification [idɑ̃tifikasjɔ̃] *nf* : **~ (à)** identification (with).

identifier [9] [idɑ̃tifje] *vt* to identify ; **~ qqn à qqch** to identify sb with sthg.

➤ **s'identifier** *vp* : **s'~ à qqn/qqch** to identify with sb/sthg.

identique [idɑ̃tik] *adj* : **~ (à)** identical (to).

identité [idɑ̃tite] *nf* identity.

idéologie [ideɔlɔʒi] *nf* ideology.

idéologique [ideɔlɔʒik] *adj* ideological.

idiomatique [idjɔmatik] *adj* idiomatic.

idiome [idjom] *nm* idiom.

idiot, e [idjo, ɔt] <> *adj* idiotic ; *MÉD* idiot *(avant n)* <> *nm, f* idiot.

idiotie [idjɔsi] *nf* - **1.** [stupidité] idiocy - **2.** [action, parole] idiotic thing.

idoine [idwan] *adj sout* appropriate.

idolâtrer [3] [idolatre] *vt* to idolize.

idole [idɔl] *nf* idol.

IDS *(abr de* **initiative de défense stratégique)** *nf* SDI.

idylle [idil] *nf* - **1.** [amour] romance - **2.** [poème] idyll.

idyllique [idilik] *adj* [idéal] idyllic.

if [if] *nm* yew.

IFOP, Ifop [ifɔp] *(abr de* **Institut français d'opinion publique)** *nm* French market research institute.

Ifremer [ifrəmɛr] *(abr de* **Institut français de recherche pour l'exploitation de la mer)** *nm* research establishment for marine resources.

IGF *(abr de* **impôt sur les grandes fortunes)** *nm* former wealth tax.

IGH *(abr de* **immeuble de grande hauteur)** *nm* very high building.

igloo, iglou [iglu] *nm* igloo.

IGN *(abr de* **Institut géographique national)** *nm* national geographical institute, ≃ Ordnance Survey *Br.*

ignare [iɲar] <> *nmf* ignoramus <> *adj* ignorant.

ignifuge [iɲifyʒ] <> *nm* fireproofing material <> *adj* fireproof.

ignoble [iɲɔbl] *adj* - **1.** [abject] base - **2.** [hideux] vile.

ignominie [iɲɔmini] *nf* - **1.** [état] disgrace - **2.** [action] disgraceful act.

ignominieux, euse [iɲɔminjø, øz] *adj* ignominious.

ignorance [iɲɔrɑ̃s] *nf* ignorance ; **dans l'~ de** in the dark about, in ignorance of.

ignorant, e [iɲɔrɑ̃, ɑ̃t] <> *adj* ignorant ; **~ en/de qqch** ignorant of sthg <> *nm, f* ignoramus.

ignoré, e [iɲɔre] *adj* unknown.

ignorer [3] [iɲɔre] *vt* - **1.** [ne pas savoir] not to know, to be unaware of ; **~ que** not to know that - **2.** [ne pas tenir compte de] to ignore - **3.** [ne pas connaître] to have no experience of.

➤ **s'ignorer** *vp* - **1.** [se bouder] to ignore each other - **2.** [méconnaître ses possibilités] to be unaware of one's talent.

IGPN *(abr de* **Inspection générale de la police nationale)** *nf* police disciplinary body.

IGS *(abr de* **Inspection générale des services)** *nf* police disciplinary body for Paris.

il [il] *pron pers* - **1.** [sujet - personne] he ; [- animal] it, he ; [- chose] it - **2.** [sujet d'un verbe impersonnel] it ; **~ pleut** it's raining.

➤ **ils** *pron pers pl* they.

île [il] *nf* island ; **les ~s Anglo-Normandes** the Channel Islands ; **les ~s Baléares** the Balearic Islands ; **les ~s Britanniques** the British Isles ; **les ~s Canaries** the Canary Islands ; **les ~s Malouines** the Falkland Islands ; **l'~ de Man** the Isle of Man ; **l'~ Maurice** Mauritius.

illégal, e, aux [ilegal, o] *adj* illegal.

illégalité [ilegalite] *nf* - **1.** [fait d'être illégal] illegality - **2.** [action illégale] illegal act.

illégitime [ileʒitim] *adj* - **1.** [enfant] illegitimate ; [union] unlawful - **2.** [non justifié] unwarranted.

illettré, e [iletre] *adj* & *nm, f* illiterate.

illicite [ilisit] *adj* illicit.

illico [iliko] *adv fam* right away, pronto.

illimité, e [ilimite] *adj* - **1.** [sans limites] unlimited - **2.** [indéterminé] indefinite.

illisible [ilizibl] *adj* - **1.** [indéchiffrable] illegible - **2.** [incompréhensible & *INFORM*] unreadable.

illogique [ilɔʒik] *adj* illogical.

illumination [ilyminasjɔ̃] *nf* - **1.** [éclairage] lighting - **2.** [idée soudaine] inspiration.

➤ **illuminations** *nfpl* illuminations.

illuminé, e [ilymine] <> *adj* illuminated <> *nm, f péj* crank.

illuminer [3] [ilymine] *vt* to light up ; [bâtiment, rue] to illuminate.

➤ **s'illuminer** *vp* : **s'~ de joie** to light up with joy.

illusion [ilyzjɔ̃] *nf* illusion ; **se faire des ~s** to fool o.s. ; **~ d'optique** optical illusion ; **se bercer d'~s** to live in cloud cuckoo land.

illusionner [3] [ilyzjɔne] *vt* to delude.

➤ **s'illusionner** *vp* to delude o.s.

illusionniste [ilyzjɔnist] *nmf* conjurer.

illusoire [ilyzwar] adj illusory.
illustrateur, trice [ilystratœr, tris] nm, f illustrator.
illustration [ilystrasjɔ̃] nf illustration.
illustre [ilystr] adj illustrious.
illustré, e [ilystre] adj illustrated.
➡ **illustré** nm illustrated magazine.
illustrer [3] [ilystre] vt - **1.** [gén] to illustrate - **2.** [rendre célèbre] to make famous.
➡ **s'illustrer** vp to distinguish o.s.
îlot [ilo] nm - **1.** [île] small island, islet - **2.** [de maisons] block - **3.** [lieu isolé] island - **4.** fig [de résistance] pocket.
ils ⊳ il.
IMA [ima] (abr de Institut du monde arabe) nm Paris exhibition centre for Arab culture and art.
image [imaʒ] nf - **1.** [vision mentale, comparaison, ressemblance] image ; **être l'~ de qqn** to be the image of sb ; **~ de marque** [de personne] image ; [d'entreprise] corporate image - **2.** [dessin] picture ; **~ d'Épinal** sentimental picture ; fig simplistic argument/theory ; **sage comme une ~** as good as gold.
imagé, e [imaʒe] adj full of imagery.
imaginable [imaʒinabl] adj imaginable.
imaginaire [imaʒinɛr] ⟨⟩ nm : **l'~** the imaginary ⟨⟩ adj imaginary.
imaginatif, ive [imaʒinatif, iv] adj imaginative.
imagination [imaʒinasjɔ̃] nf imagination ; **avoir de l'~** to be imaginative.
➡ **imaginations** nfpl littéraire & péj [chimères] fancies.
imaginer [3] [imaʒine] vt - **1.** [supposer, croire] to imagine - **2.** [trouver] to think of.
➡ **s'imaginer** vp - **1.** [se voir] to see o.s. - **2.** [croire] to imagine.
imam [imam] nm imam.
imbattable [ɛ̃batabl] adj unbeatable.
imbécile [ɛ̃besil] ⟨⟩ nmf imbecile ⟨⟩ adj idiotic.
imbécillité [ɛ̃besilite] nf - **1.** [manque d'intelligence] imbecility - **2.** [acte, parole] stupid thing.
imberbe [ɛ̃bɛrb] adj beardless.
imbiber [3] [ɛ̃bibe] vt : **~ qqch de qqch** to soak sthg with ou in sthg.
➡ **s'imbiber** vp : **s'~ de** to soak up.
imbriqué, e [ɛ̃brike] adj overlapping.
imbriquer [3] [ɛ̃brike] ➡ **s'imbriquer** vp [se chevaucher] to overlap ; fig to intertwine.
imbroglio [ɛ̃brɔljo] nm imbroglio.
imbu, e [ɛ̃by] adj : **être ~ de** to be full of ; **être ~ de soi-même** to be full of oneself.

imbuvable [ɛ̃byvabl] adj - **1.** [eau] undrinkable - **2.** fam [personne] unbearable.
imitateur, trice [imitatœr, tris] nm, f - **1.** [comique] impersonator - **2.** péj [copieur] imitator.
imitation [imitasjɔ̃] nf imitation ; **~ imitation leather** ; **à l'~ de** in imitation of.
➡ **en imitation** loc adj imitation.
imiter [3] [imite] vt - **1.** [s'inspirer de, contrefaire] to imitate - **2.** [reproduire l'aspect de] to look (just) like.
immaculé, e [imakyle] adj immaculate ; **L'Immaculée Conception** The Immaculate Conception.
immanent, e [imanɑ̃, ɑ̃t] adj immanent ; **~ à** inherent in.
immangeable [ɛ̃mɑ̃ʒabl] adj inedible.
immanquable [ɛ̃mɑ̃kabl] adj impossible to miss ; [sort, échec] inevitable.
immanquablement [ɛ̃mɑ̃kabləmɑ̃] adv inevitably.
immatériel, elle [imaterjɛl] adj - **1.** PHILO immaterial - **2.** [beauté] unreal - **3.** [investissement] intangible.
immatriculation [imatrikylasjɔ̃] nf registration.

immatriculer [3] [imatrikyle] vt to register.
immature [imatyr] adj immature.
immaturité [imatyrite] nf immaturity.
immédiat, e [imedja, at] ⟨⟩ adj immediate ⟨⟩ nm : **dans l'~** for the time being.
immédiatement [imedjatmɑ̃] adv immediately.
immémorial, e, aux [imemɔrjal, o] adj ancient.
immense [imɑ̃s] adj immense.
immensément [imɑ̃semɑ̃] adv immensely.
immensité [imɑ̃site] nf immensity, vastness.
immerger [17] [imɛrʒe] vt to submerge.
➡ **s'immerger** vp to submerge o.s.
immérité, e [imerite] adj undeserved.
immersion [imɛrsjɔ̃] nf immersion.
immettable [ɛ̃metabl] adj unwearable.
immeuble [imœbl] ⟨⟩ nm building ⟨⟩ adj JUR real.
immigrant, e [imigrɑ̃, ɑ̃t] nm, f immigrant.
immigration [imigrasjɔ̃] nf immigration.
immigré, e [imigre] adj & nm, f immigrant.

immigrer [3] [imigre] *vi* to immigrate.

imminence [iminãs] *nf* imminence.

imminent, e [iminã, ãt] *adj* imminent.

immiscer [16] [imise] ➤ **s'immiscer** *vp* : s'~ **dans** to interfere in *ou* with.

immixtion [imiksjõ] *nf* interference.

immobile [imɔbil] *adj* - **1.** [personne, visage] motionless - **2.** [mécanisme] fixed, stationary - **3.** *fig* [figé] immovable.

immobilier, ère [imɔbilje, ɛr] *adj* : biens ~s property *(U) Br*, real estate *(U) Am* ; société immobilière property *Br ou* real estate *Am* company.
➤ **immobilier** *nm* : l'~ property *Br*, real estate *Am*.

immobilisation [imɔbilizasjõ] *nf* immobilization.
➤ **immobilisations** *nfpl* *FIN* fixed assets.

immobiliser [3] [imɔbilize] *vt* to immobilize.
➤ **s'immobiliser** *vp* to stop.

immobilisme [imɔbilism] *nm* *péj* opposition to progress.

immobilité [imɔbilite] *nf* immobility ; [de paysage, de lac] stillness.

immodéré, e [imɔdere] *adj* inordinate.

immoler [3] [imɔle] *vt* to sacrifice ; *RELIG* to immolate ; ~ **qqn/qqch à** to sacrifice sb/ sthg to.
➤ **s'immoler** *vp* to immolate o.s.

immonde [imõd] *adj* - **1.** [sale] foul - **2.** [abject] vile.

immondices [imõdis] *nfpl* waste *(U)*, refuse *(U)*.

immoral, e, aux [imɔral, o] *adj* immoral.

immoralité [imɔralite] *nf* - **1.** [dépravation] immorality - **2.** [obscénité] obscenity.

immortaliser [3] [imɔrtalize] *vt* to immortalize.
➤ **s'immortaliser** *vp* to gain immortality.

immortalité [imɔrtalite] *nf* immortality.

immortel, elle [imɔrtɛl] *adj* immortal.
➤ **immortelle** *nf* *BOT* everlasting flower.
➤ **Immortel, elle** *nm, f* *fam* member of the Académie française.

immuable [imɥabl] *adj* - **1.** [éternel - loi] immutable - **2.** [constant] unchanging.

immunisation [imynizasjõ] *nf* immunization.

immuniser [3] [imynize] *vt* - **1.** [vacciner] to immunize - **2.** *fig* [garantir] : ~ **qqn contre qqch** to make sb immune to sthg.

immunitaire [imyniter] *adj* immuno *(avant n)*.

immunité [imynite] *nf* immunity ; ~ di-

plomatique/parlementaire *fig* diplomatic/ parliamentary immunity.

immunodéficience [imynɔdefisjãs] *nf* immunodeficiency.

immunologique [imynɔlɔʒik] *adj* immunological.

impact [ɛ̃pakt] *nm* impact ; avoir de l'~ sur to have an impact on ; étude d'~ impact study.

impair, e [ɛ̃pɛr] *adj* odd.
➤ **impair** *nm* [faux-pas] gaffe.

imparable [ɛ̃parabl] *adj* - **1.** [coup] unstoppable - **2.** [argument] unanswerable.

impardonnable [ɛ̃pardɔnabl] *adj* unforgivable.

imparfait, e [ɛ̃parfɛ, ɛt] *adj* - **1.** [défectueux] imperfect - **2.** [inachevé] incomplete.
➤ **imparfait** *nm* *GRAM* imperfect (tense).

imparfaitement [ɛ̃parfɛtmã] *adv* imperfectly.

impartial, e, aux [ɛ̃parsjal, o] *adj* impartial.

impartialité [ɛ̃parsjalite] *nf* impartiality.

impartir [32] [ɛ̃partir] *vt* : ~ **qqch à qqn** *littéraire* [délai, droit] to grant sthg to sb ; [don] to bestow sthg upon sb ; [tâche] to assign sthg to sb.

impasse [ɛ̃pas] *nf* - **1.** [rue] dead end - **2.** *fig* [difficulté] impasse, deadlock ; être dans une ~ *ou* dans l'~ to be at an impasse, to be deadlocked - **3.** *SCOL & UNIV* : faire une ~ sur un sujet to give a subject a miss when revising for an exam - **4.** *JEU* : faire une ~ to finesse - **5.** *FIN* : ~ budgétaire budget deficit.

impassibilité [ɛ̃pasibilite] *nf* impassivity.

impassible [ɛ̃pasibl] *adj* impassive ; rester ~ to be *ou* remain impassive.

impatiemment [ɛ̃pasjamã] *adv* impatiently.

impatience [ɛ̃pasjãs] *nf* impatience ; bouillir d'~ to be burning with impatience.

impatient, e [ɛ̃pasjã, ãt] <> *adj* impatient ; être ~ de faire qqch to be impatient *ou* longing to do sthg <> *nmf* impatient person.

impatienter [3] [ɛ̃pasjãte] *vt* to annoy.
➤ **s'impatienter** *vp* : s'~ (de/contre) to get impatient (at/with).

impayable [ɛ̃pɛjabl] *adj fam* priceless.

impayé, e [ɛ̃peje] *adj* unpaid, outstanding.
➤ **impayé** *nm* outstanding payment.

impeccable [ɛ̃pekabl] *adj* - **1.** [parfait] impeccable, faultless - **2.** [propre] spotless, immaculate.

impénétrable [ɛ̃penetrabl] *adj* impenetrable.

impénitent, e [ɛ̃penitɑ̃, ɑ̃t] *adj* unrepentant.

impensable [ɛ̃pɑ̃sabl] *adj* unthinkable.

imper [ɛ̃pɛr] *nm fam* mac.

impératif, ive [ɛ̃peratif, iv] *adj* - **1.** [ton, air] imperious - **2.** [besoin] imperative, essential.
➡ **impératif** *nm* GRAM imperative.

impérativement [ɛ̃perativmɑ̃] *adv* : **il faut ~ faire qqch** it is imperative to do sthg.

impératrice [ɛ̃peratris] *nf* empress.

imperceptible [ɛ̃pɛrsɛptibl] *adj* imperceptible.

imperceptiblement [ɛ̃pɛrsɛptibləmɑ̃] *adv* imperceptibly.

imperfection [ɛ̃pɛrfɛksjɔ̃] *nf* imperfection.

impérial, e, aux [ɛ̃perjal, o] *adj* imperial.
➡ **impériale** *nf* top deck.

impérialisme [ɛ̃perjalism] *nm* POLIT imperialism ; *fig* dominance.

impérialiste [ɛ̃perjalist] *nmf* & *adj* imperialist.

impérieusement [ɛ̃perjøzmɑ̃] *adv* imperiously.

impérieux, euse [ɛ̃perjø, øz] *adj* - **1.** [ton, air] imperious - **2.** [nécessité] urgent.

impérissable [ɛ̃perisabl] *adj* undying.

imperméabilisation [ɛ̃pɛrmeabilizasjɔ̃] *nf* waterproofing.

imperméabiliser [3] [ɛ̃pɛrmeabilize] *vt* to waterproof.

imperméable [ɛ̃pɛrmeabl] <> *adj* waterproof ; **~ à** [étanche] impermeable to ; *fig* impervious *ou* immune to <> *nm* raincoat.

impersonnel, elle [ɛ̃pɛrsɔnɛl] *adj* impersonal.

impertinence [ɛ̃pɛrtinɑ̃s] *nf* impertinence *(U)*.

impertinent, e [ɛ̃pɛrtinɑ̃, ɑ̃t] <> *adj* impertinent <> *nm, f* impertinent person.

imperturbable [ɛ̃pɛrtyrbabl] *adj* imperturbable.

impétigo [ɛ̃petigo] *nm* impetigo.

impétueux, euse [ɛ̃petɥø, øz] *adj* - **1.** [personne, caractère] impetuous - **2.** *littéraire* [vent, torrent] raging.

impétuosité [ɛ̃petɥozite] *nf* impetuousness.

impie [ɛ̃pi] *littéraire* & *vieilli* <> *nmf* ungodly person <> *adj* impious.

impiété [ɛ̃pjete] *nf littéraire* & *vieilli* impiety.

impitoyable [ɛ̃pitwajabl] *adj* merciless, pitiless.

impitoyablement [ɛ̃pitwajabləmɑ̃] *adv* mercilessly, pitilessly.

implacable [ɛ̃plakabl] *adj* implacable.

implant [ɛ̃plɑ̃] *nm* MÉD implant.

implantation [ɛ̃plɑ̃tasjɔ̃] *nf* - **1.** [d'usine, de système] establishment - **2.** [de cheveux] implant.

implanter [3] [ɛ̃plɑ̃te] *vt* - **1.** [entreprise, système] to establish - **2.** *fig* [préjugé] to implant.
➡ **s'implanter** *vp* [entreprise] to set up ; [coutume] to become established.

implication [ɛ̃plikasjɔ̃] *nf* - **1.** [participation] : **~ (dans)** involvement (in) - **2.** *(gén pl)* [conséquence] implication.

implicite [ɛ̃plisit] *adj* implicit.

implicitement [ɛ̃plisitmɑ̃] *adv* implicitly.

impliquer [3] [ɛ̃plike] *vt* - **1.** [compromettre] : **~ qqn dans** to implicate sb in - **2.** [requérir, entraîner] to imply.
➡ **s'impliquer** *vp* : **s'~ dans** *fam* to become involved in.

implorer [3] [ɛ̃plɔre] *vt* to beseech.

imploser [3] [ɛ̃plɔze] *vi* to implode.

implosion [ɛ̃plɔzjɔ̃] *nf* implosion.

impoli, e [ɛ̃pɔli] *adj* rude, impolite.

impoliment [ɛ̃pɔlimɑ̃] *adv* rudely, impolitely.

impolitesse [ɛ̃pɔlitɛs] *nf* rudeness, impoliteness.

impondérable [ɛ̃pɔ̃derabl] *adj* imponderable.
➡ **impondérables** *nmpl* imponderables.

impopulaire [ɛ̃pɔpylɛr] *adj* unpopular.

import [ɛ̃pɔr] *nm* - **1.** COMM import - **2.** *Belg* [montant] total.

importance [ɛ̃pɔrtɑ̃s] *nf* - **1.** [gén] importance ; [de problème, montant] magnitude ; **attacher de l'~ à** to attach importance to ; **avoir de l'~** to be important ; **d'~** [non négligeable] of some importance ; **sans ~** unimportant ; [accident] minor - **2.** [de dommages] extent - **3.** [de ville] size.

important, e [ɛ̃pɔrtɑ̃, ɑ̃t] <> *adj* - **1.** [personnage, découverte, rôle] important ; [événement, changement] important, significant - **2.** [quantité, collection, somme] considerable, sizeable ; [dommages] extensive <> *nm, f* : **faire l'~** *péj* to act important.
➡ **important** *nm* : **l'~** the (most) important thing, the main thing.

importateur, trice [ɛ̃pɔrtatœr, tris] *adj* importing *(avant n)*.
➡ **importateur** *nm* importer.

importation [ɛ̃pɔrtasjɔ̃] *nf* COMM & *fig* import.

importer [3] [ɛ̃pɔrte] <> *vt* to import <> *v impers* : **~ (à)** to matter (to) ; **il importe de/que** it is important to/that ; **qu'importe!, peu importe!** it doesn't matter! ; **n'importe qui** anyone (at all) ; **n'importe quoi** anything (at all) ; **n'importe où** anywhere (at all) ; **n'importe quand** at any time (at all) ; **n'importe comment** anyhow.

import-export [ɛ̃pɔrɛkspɔr] (*pl* **imports-exports**) *nm* import-export.

importun, e [ɛ̃pɔrtœ̃, yn] <> *adj* - **1.** [indiscret] irksome, troublesome - **2.** [embarrassant] awkward <> *nmf* **vieilli** intruder.

importuner [3] [ɛ̃pɔrtyne] *vt* to irk.

imposable [ɛ̃pozabl] *adj* taxable.

imposant, e [ɛ̃pozɑ̃, ɑ̃t] *adj* imposing.

imposé, e [ɛ̃poze] <> *adj* - **1.** [contribuable] taxed - **2.** SPORT [figure] compulsory <> *nm, f* [contribuable] taxpayer.

imposer [3] [ɛ̃poze] *vt* - **1.** [gén] : ~ **qqch/qqn à qqn** to impose sthg/sb on sb - **2.** [impressionner] : **en ~ à qqn** to impress sb - **3.** [taxer] to tax.

➤ **s'imposer** *vp* - **1.** [être nécessaire] to be essential *ou* imperative - **2.** [forcer le respect] to stand out - **3.** [avoir pour règle] : **s'~ de faire qqch** to make it a rule to do sthg.

imposition [ɛ̃pozisjɔ̃] *nf* - **1.** FIN taxation - **2.** RELIG laying on.

impossibilité [ɛ̃pɔsibilite] *nf* impossibility ; **être dans l'~ de faire qqch** to find it impossible *ou* to be unable to do sthg.

impossible [ɛ̃pɔsibl] <> *adj* impossible <> *nm* : **tenter l'~** to attempt the impossible.

imposteur [ɛ̃pɔstœr] *nm* impostor.

imposture [ɛ̃pɔstyr] *nf* imposture.

impôt [ɛ̃po] *nm* tax ; **~ direct/indirect** direct/indirect tax ; **~s locaux** council tax **Br**, local tax **Am** ; **~ sur les grandes fortunes** wealth tax ; **~ sur les plus-values** capital gains tax ; **~ sur le revenu** income tax ; **être assujetti à l'~** to be subject to tax.

impotence [ɛ̃pɔtɑ̃s] *nf* infirmity.

impotent, e [ɛ̃pɔtɑ̃, ɑ̃t] <> *adj* disabled <> *nm, f* disabled person.

impraticable [ɛ̃pratikabl] *adj* - **1.** [inapplicable] impracticable - **2.** [inaccessible] impassable.

imprécation [ɛ̃prekasjɔ̃] *nf* **littéraire** imprecation.

imprécis, e [ɛ̃presi, iz] *adj* imprecise.

imprécision [ɛ̃presizjɔ̃] *nf* imprecision.

imprégner [18] [ɛ̃preɲe] *vt* [imbiber] : ~ **qqch de qqch** to soak sthg in sthg ; ~ **qqn de qqch** **fig** to fill sb with sthg.

➤ **s'imprégner** *vp* : **s'~ de qqch** [s'imbiber] to soak sthg up, **fig** to soak sthg up, to steep o.s. in sthg.

imprenable [ɛ̃prənabl] *adj* - **1.** [forteresse] impregnable - **2.** [vue] unimpeded.

imprésario, impresario [ɛ̃presarjo] *nm* impresario.

impression [ɛ̃presjɔ̃] *nf* - **1.** [gén] impression ; **avoir l'~ que** to have the impression *ou* feeling that ; **faire (une) bonne/mauvaise ~ (à)** to make a good/bad impression (on) - **2.** [de livre, tissu] printing - **3.** PHOT print.

impressionnable [ɛ̃presjɔnabl] *adj* - **1.** [émotif] impressionable - **2.** PHOT sensitive.

impressionnant, e [ɛ̃presjɔnɑ̃, ɑ̃t] *adj* - **1.** [imposant] impressive - **2.** [effrayant] frightening.

impressionner [3] [ɛ̃presjɔne] *vt* - **1.** [frapper] to impress - **2.** [choquer] to shock, to upset - **3.** [intimider] to frighten - **4.** PHOT to expose.

impressionnisme [ɛ̃presjɔnism] *nm* impressionism.

impressionniste [ɛ̃presjɔnist] *nmf & adj* impressionist.

imprévisible [ɛ̃previzibl] *adj* unforeseeable.

imprévoyance [ɛ̃prevwajɑ̃s] *nf* lack of foresight, improvidence.

imprévoyant, e [ɛ̃prevwajɑ̃, ɑ̃t] *adj* improvident.

imprévu, e [ɛ̃prevy] *adj* unforeseen.

➤ **imprévu** *nm* unforeseen situation ; **sauf ~** barring unforeseen circumstances.

imprimante [ɛ̃primɑ̃t] *nf* printer ; **~ laser/à jet d'encre/matricielle** laser/ink-jet/dot-matrix printer.

imprimé, e [ɛ̃prime] *adj* printed.

➤ **imprimé** *nm* - **1.** POSTES printed matter (U) - **2.** [formulaire] printed form - **3.** [tissu] print.

imprimer [3] [ɛ̃prime] *vt* - **1.** [texte, tissu] to print - **2.** [mouvement] to impart - **3.** [marque, empreinte] to leave.

imprimerie [ɛ̃primri] *nf* - **1.** [technique] printing - **2.** [usine] printing works (sg).

imprimeur [ɛ̃primœr] *nm* printer.

improbable [ɛ̃prɔbabl] *adj* improbable.

improductif, ive [ɛ̃prɔdyktif, iv] *adj* unproductive.

impromptu, e [ɛ̃prɔ̃pty] *adj* impromptu.

➤ **impromptu** <> *adv* impromptu <> *nm* impromptu.

imprononçable [ɛ̃prɔnɔ̃sabl] *adj* unpronounceable.

impropre [ɛ̃prɔpr] *adj* - **1.** GRAM incorrect - **2.** [inadapté] : ~ **à** unfit for.

impropriété [ɛ̃prɔprijete] *nf* [emploi erroné] incorrectness ; [expression] (language) error.

improvisation [ɛ̃prɔvizasjɔ̃] *nf* improvisation.

improviser [3] [ɛ̃prɔvize] *vt* to improvise.

s'improviser *vp* - **1.** [s'organiser] to be improvised - **2.** [devenir] : **s'~ metteur en scène** to act as director.

improviste [ɛ̃prɔvist] **~ à l'improviste** *loc adv* unexpectedly, without warning.

imprudemment [ɛ̃prydamɑ̃] *adv* rashly.

imprudence [ɛ̃prydɑ̃s] *nf* - **1.** [de personne, d'acte] rashness - **2.** [acte] rash act.

imprudent, e [ɛ̃prydɑ̃, ɑ̃t] <> *adj* rash <> *nm, f* rash person.

impubère [ɛ̃pybɛr] <> *adj* [avant la puberté] prepubescent <> *nmf* JUR ≃ minor.

impudence [ɛ̃pydɑ̃s] *nf* - **1.** [de personne, propos] impudence - **2.** [propos] impudent remark.

impudent, e [ɛ̃pydɑ̃, ɑ̃t] <> *adj* impudent <> *nm, f* impudent person.

impudeur [ɛ̃pydœr] *nf* shamelessness.

impudique [ɛ̃pydik] *adj* shameless.

impuissance [ɛ̃pɥisɑ̃s] *nf* - **1.** [incapacité] : **~ (à faire qqch)** powerlessness (to do sthg) - **2.** [sexuelle] impotence.

impuissant, e [ɛ̃pɥisɑ̃, ɑ̃t] *adj* - **1.** [incapable] : **~ (à faire qqch)** powerless (to do sthg) - **2.** [homme, fureur] impotent.

impuissant *nm* impotent man.

impulsif, ive [ɛ̃pylsif, iv] <> *adj* impulsive <> *nm, f* impulsive person.

impulsion [ɛ̃pylsjɔ̃] *nf* - **1.** [poussée, essor] impetus - **2.** [instinct] impulse, instinct - **3.** *fig* : **sous l'~ de qqn** [influence] at the prompting *ou* instigation of sb ; **sous l'~ de qqch** [effet] impelled by sthg.

impulsivement [ɛ̃pylsivmɑ̃] *adv* impulsively.

impulsivité [ɛ̃pylsivite] *nf* impulsiveness.

impunément [ɛ̃pynemɑ̃] *adv* with impunity.

impuni, e [ɛ̃pyni] *adj* unpunished.

impunité [ɛ̃pynite] *nf* impunity ; **en toute ~** with impunity.

impur, e [ɛ̃pyr] *adj* impure.

impureté [ɛ̃pyrte] *nf* impurity.

imputable [ɛ̃pytabl] *adj* - **1.** [accident, erreur] : **~ à** attributable to - **2.** FIN : **~ à** *ou* **sur** chargeable to.

imputation [ɛ̃pytasjɔ̃] *nf* - **1.** [accusation] charge - **2.** FIN charging.

imputer [3] [ɛ̃pyte] *vt* : **~ qqch à qqn/à qqch** to attribute sthg to sb/to sthg ; **~ qqch à qqch** FIN to charge sthg to sthg.

imputrescible [ɛ̃pytresibl] *adj* [bois] rotproof ; [déchets] non-degradable.

in [in] *adj inv vieilli* in, with it.

INA [ina] (*abr de* Institut national de l'audiovisuel) *nm national television archive.*

inabordable [inabɔrdabl] *adj* - **1.** [prix] prohibitive - **2.** GÉOGR inaccessible (by boat) - **3.** [personne] unapproachable.

inacceptable [inaksɛptabl] *adj* unacceptable.

inaccessible [inaksesibl] *adj* [destination, domaine, personne] inaccessible ; [objectif, poste] unattainable ; **~ à** [sentiment] impervious to.

inaccoutumé, e [inakutyme] *adj* unaccustomed.

inachevé, e [inaʃve] *adj* unfinished, uncompleted.

inactif, ive [inaktif, iv] *adj* - **1.** [sans occupation, non utilisé] idle - **2.** [sans effet] ineffective - **3.** [sans emploi] non-working.

inaction [inaksjɔ̃] *nf* inaction.

inactivité [inaktivite] *nf* - **1.** [oisiveté] inactivity - **2.** ADMIN : **en ~** out of active service.

inadapté, e [inadapte] <> *adj* - **1.** [non adapté] : **~ (à)** unsuitable (for), unsuited (to) - **2.** [asocial] maladjusted <> *nm, f* maladjusted person.

inadéquat, e [inadekwa, at] *adj* : **~ (à)** inadequate (for).

inadéquation [inadekwasjɔ̃] *nf* : **~ (à)** inadequacy (for).

inadmissible [inadmisibl] *adj* [conduite] unacceptable.

inadvertance [inadvertɑ̃s] *nf littéraire* oversight ; **par ~** inadvertently.

inaliénable [inaljenabl] *adj* inalienable.

inaltérable [inalterabl] *adj* - **1.** [matériau] stable - **2.** [sentiment] unfailing.

inamical, e, aux [inamikal, o] *adj* unfriendly.

inamovible [inamɔvibl] *adj* fixed.

inanimé, e [inanime] *adj* - **1.** [sans vie] inanimate - **2.** [inerte, évanoui] senseless.

inanité [inanite] *nf* futility.

inanition [inanisjɔ̃] *nf* : **tomber/mourir d'~** to faint with/die of hunger.

inaperçu, e [inapɛrsy] *adj* unnoticed ; **passer ~** to go *ou* pass unnoticed.

inapplicable [inaplikabl] *adj* inapplicable.

inappliqué, e [inaplike] *adj* - **1.** [étourdi] lazy, lacking in application - **2.** [inemployé] not applied *ou* practised.

inappréciable [inapresjabl] *adj* - **1.** [infime] imperceptible - **2.** [précieux] invaluable.

inapprochable [inaprɔʃabl] *adj* : **il est vraiment ~ en ce moment** you can't say anything to him at the moment.

inapproprié, e [inaprɔprije] *adj* : ~ à not appropriate for.

inapte [inapt] *adj* - **1.** [incapable] : ~ à qqch/à faire qqch incapable of sthg/of doing sthg - **2.** MIL unfit.

inaptitude [inaptityd] *nf* - **1.** [incapacité] : ~ à qqch/à faire qqch incapacity for sthg/for doing sthg - **2.** MIL unfitness.

inarticulé, e [inartikyle] *adj* inarticulate.

inassouvi, e [inasuvi] *adj* [faim] unsatisfied ; [soif] unquenched ; *fig* [sentiment] unsatisfied, unfulfilled.

inattaquable [inatakabl] *adj* - **1.** [imprenable] impregnable - **2.** [irréprochable] irreproachable, beyond reproach - **3.** [irréfutable] irrefutable.

inattendu, e [inatɑ̃dy] *adj* unexpected.

inattentif, ive [inatɑ̃tif, iv] *adj* : ~ à inattentive to.

inattention [inatɑ̃sjɔ̃] *nf* inattention ; **faute d'**~ careless mistake.

inaudible [inodibl] *adj* - **1.** [impossible à entendre] inaudible - **2.** [inécoutable] impossible to listen to.

inaugural, e, aux [inogyral, o] *adj* inaugural *(avant n)*, opening *(avant n)*.

inauguration [inogyrasjɔ̃] *nf* - **1.** [cérémonie] inauguration, opening (ceremony) - **2.** [début] dawn.

inaugurer [3] [inogyre] *vt* - **1.** [monument] to unveil ; [installation, route] to open ; [procédé, édifice] to inaugurate - **2.** [époque] to usher in.

inavouable [inavwabl] *adj* unmentionable.

inavoué, e [inavwe] *adj* unconfessed.

INC *(abr de Institut national de la consommation) nm* consumer research organization.

inca [ɛ̃ka] *adj* Inca.
→ **Inca** *nmf* Inca.

incalculable [ɛ̃kalkylabl] *adj* incalculable.

incandescence [ɛ̃kɑ̃desɑ̃s] *nf* incandescence.

incandescent, e [ɛ̃kɑ̃desɑ̃, ɑ̃t] *adj* incandescent.

incantation [ɛ̃kɑ̃tasjɔ̃] *nf* incantation.

incapable [ɛ̃kapabl] <> *nmf* - **1.** [raté] incompetent - **2.** JUR incapable person <> *adj* : ~ **de faire qqch** [inapte à] incapable of doing sthg ; [dans l'impossibilité de] unable to do sthg.

incapacité [ɛ̃kapasite] *nf* - **1.** [impossibilité] : ~ **à** *ou* **de faire qqch** inability to do sthg ; **être dans l'**~ **de** to be unable to - **2.** [invalidité] disability ; ~ **de travail** industrial disability - **3.** JUR incapacity - **4.** [incompétence] incompetence.

incarcération [ɛ̃karserasjɔ̃] *nf* incarceration.

incarcérer [18] [ɛ̃karsere] *vt* to incarcerate.

incarnation [ɛ̃karnasjɔ̃] *nf* incarnation.

incarné, e [ɛ̃karne] *adj* incarnate.

incarner [3] [ɛ̃karne] *vt* - **1.** [personnifier] to be the incarnation of - **2.** CIN & THÉÂTRE to play.
→ **s'incarner** *vp* - **1.** RELIG to be *ou* become incarnate - **2.** [se réaliser] to be incarnated - **3.** MÉD [ongle] to become ingrown.

incartade [ɛ̃kartad] *nf* misdemeanour *Br*, misdemeanor *Am*.

incassable [ɛ̃kasabl] *adj* unbreakable.

incendiaire [ɛ̃sɑ̃djɛr] <> *nmf* arsonist <> *adj* [bombe] incendiary ; *fig* inflammatory.

incendie [ɛ̃sɑ̃di] *nm* fire ; *fig* flames *(pl)* ; ~ **de forêt** forest fire.

incendier [9] [ɛ̃sɑ̃dje] *vt* - **1.** [mettre le feu à] to set alight, to set fire to - **2.** *fig* [faire rougir] to make burn - **3.** *fam* [réprimander] to tear a strip off.

incertain, e [ɛ̃sɛrtɛ̃, ɛn] *adj* - **1.** [gén] uncertain ; [temps] unsettled - **2.** [vague - lumière] dim ; [- contour] blurred.

incertitude [ɛ̃sɛrtityd] *nf* uncertainty ; **être dans l'**~ to be uncertain.

incessamment [ɛ̃sesamɑ̃] *adv* at any moment, any moment now.

incessant, e [ɛ̃sesɑ̃, ɑ̃t] *adj* incessant.

incessible [ɛ̃sesibl] *adj* inalienable.

inceste [ɛ̃sɛst] *nm* incest.

incestueux, euse [ɛ̃sɛstɥø, øz] <> *adj* - **1.** [liaison, parent] incestuous - **2.** [enfant] born of incest <> *nm, f* incestuous person.

inchangé, e [ɛ̃ʃɑ̃ʒe] *adj* unchanged.

incidemment [ɛ̃sidamɑ̃] *adv* - **1.** [accidentellement] accidentally - **2.** [entre parenthèses] in passing.

incidence [ɛ̃sidɑ̃s] *nf* - **1.** [conséquence] effect, impact *(U)* - **2.** FIN & PHYS incidence.

incident, e [ɛ̃sidɑ̃, ɑ̃t] *adj* [accessoire] incidental.
→ **incident** *nm* - **1.** [gén] incident ; [ennui] hitch ; **sans** ~ without incident *ou* a hitch ; ~ **diplomatique** diplomatic incident ; ~ **de parcours** (minor) setback - **2.** JUR point of law.

incinérateur [ɛ̃sineratœr] *nm* incinerator.

incinération [ɛ̃sinerasjɔ̃] *nf* - **1.** [de corps] cremation - **2.** [d'ordures] incineration.

incinérer [18] [ɛ̃sinere] *vt* - **1.** [corps] to cremate - **2.** [ordures] to incinerate.

incise [ɛ̃siz] *nf* LING interpolated clause.

inciser [3] [ɛ̃size] *vt* to incise, to make an incision in.

incisif, ive [ɛsizif, iv] *adj* incisive.
→ **incisive** *nf* incisor.
incision [ɛsizjɔ̃] *nf* incision.
incitation [ɛsitasjɔ̃] *nf* - **1.** [provocation] : ~ **à qqch/à faire qqch** incitement to sthg/to do sthg - **2.** [encouragement] : ~ **à qqch/à faire qqch** incentive to sthg/to do sthg.
inciter [3] [ɛsite] *vt* - **1.** [provoquer] : ~ **qqn à qqch/à faire qqch** to incite sb to sthg/to do sthg - **2.** [encourager] : ~ **qqn à faire qqch** to encourage sb to do sthg.
inclassable [ɛklasabl] *adj* unclassifiable.
inclinable [ɛklinabl] *adj* reclinable, reclining.
inclinaison [ɛklinɛzɔ̃] *nf* - **1.** [pente] incline - **2.** [de tête, chapeau] angle, tilt.
inclination [ɛklinasjɔ̃] *nf* - **1.** [salut - de tête] nod ; [- du corps entier] bow - **2.** [tendance] inclination ; **avoir une ~ à** to have an inclination *ou* a tendency to ; **avoir une ~ pour** [aimer] to have a liking for - **3.** *littéraire* [amour] (romantic) attachment.
incliner [3] [ɛkline] <> *vt* - **1.** [pencher] to tilt, to lean - **2.** [pousser] : ~ **qqn à qqch/à faire qqch** to incline sb to sthg/to do sthg <> *vi* : ~ **à qqch/à faire qqch** to be inclined to sthg/to do sthg.
→ **s'incliner** *vp* - **1.** [se pencher] to tilt, to lean - **2.** [céder] : **s'~ (devant)** to give in (to), to yield (to) - **3.** [respecter] : **s'~ devant** to bow down before.
inclure [96] [ɛklyr] *vt* [mettre dedans] : ~ **qqch dans qqch** to include sthg in sthg ; [joindre] to enclose sthg with sthg.
inclus, e [ɛkly, yz] <> *pp* ▷ **inclure** <> *adj* - **1.** [compris - taxe, frais] included ; [joint - lettre] enclosed ; **jusqu'à la page 10 ~e** up to and including page 10 - **2.** [dent] impacted - **3.** *MATHS* : **être ~ dans** to be a subset of.
inclusion [ɛklyzjɔ̃] *nf* inclusion.
inclusivement [ɛklyzivmɑ̃] *adv* inclusive.
incoercible [ɛkɔɛrsibl] *adj* *sout* uncontrollable.
incognito [ɛkɔɲito] <> *adv* incognito <> *nm* : **garder l'~** to remain incognito.
incohérence [ɛkɔerɑ̃s] *nf* [de paroles] incoherence ; [d'actes] inconsistency.
incohérent, e [ɛkɔerɑ̃, ɑ̃t] *adj* [paroles] incoherent ; [actes] inconsistent.
incollable [ɛkɔlabl] *adj* - **1.** [riz] nonstick - **2.** *fam* [imbattable] unbeatable.
incolore [ɛkɔlɔr] *adj* colourless *Br*, colorless *Am*.
incomber [3] [ɛkɔ̃be] *vi* : ~ **à qqn** to be sb's responsibility ; **il incombe à qqn de faire qqch**

(emploi impersonnel) it falls to sb *ou* it is incumbent on sb to do sthg.
incombustible [ɛkɔ̃bystibl] *adj* incombustible.
incommensurable [ɛkɔmɑ̃syrabl] *adj* - **1.** [immense] immeasurable - **2.** *MATHS* : ~ **avec** incommensurable with.
incommodant, e [ɛkɔmɔdɑ̃, ɑ̃t] *adj* unpleasant.
incommode [ɛkɔmɔd] *adj* - **1.** [heure, lieu] inconvenient - **2.** [position, chaise] uncomfortable.
incommoder [3] [ɛkɔmɔde] *vt* *sout* to trouble.
incommodité [ɛkɔmɔdite] *nf* - **1.** [d'installation] impracticality - **2.** [malaise] indisposition - **3.** [de situation] awkwardness.
incommunicable [ɛkɔmynikabl] *adj* - **1.** [indicible] inexpressible - **2.** *JUR* non-transferable.
incomparable [ɛkɔ̃parabl] *adj* - **1.** [différent] not comparable - **2.** [sans pareil] incomparable.
incomparablement [ɛkɔ̃parabləmɑ̃] *adv* incomparably.
incompatibilité [ɛkɔ̃patibilite] *nf* incompatibility ; ~ **d'humeur** (mutual) incompatibility.
incompatible [ɛkɔ̃patibl] *adj* incompatible.
incompétence [ɛkɔ̃petɑ̃s] *nf* - **1.** [incapacité] incompetence - **2.** [ignorance] : ~ **en qqch** ignorance about sthg.
incompétent, e [ɛkɔ̃petɑ̃, ɑ̃t] *adj* - **1.** [incapable] incompetent - **2.** [ignorant] : ~ **en qqch** ignorant about sthg.
incomplet, ète [ɛkɔ̃plɛ, ɛt] *adj* incomplete.
incomplètement [ɛkɔ̃plɛtmɑ̃] *adv* incompletely.
incompréhensible [ɛkɔ̃preɑ̃sibl] *adj* incomprehensible.
incompréhensif, ive [ɛkɔ̃preɑ̃sif, iv] *adj* unsympathetic.
incompréhension [ɛkɔ̃preɑ̃sjɔ̃] *nf* lack of understanding.
incompressible [ɛkɔ̃presibl] *adj* - **1.** *TECHNOL* incompressible - **2.** *fig* [dépenses] impossible to reduce - **3.** *JUR* ▷ **peine**.
incompris, e [ɛkɔ̃pri, iz] <> *adj* misunderstood, not appreciated <> *nm, f* misunderstood person.
inconcevable [ɛkɔ̃svabl] *adj* unimaginable.
inconciliable [ɛkɔ̃siljabl] *adj* irreconcilable.
inconditionnel, elle [ɛkɔ̃disjɔnɛl] <> *adj*

- 1. [total] unconditional **- 2.** [fervent] ardent ◇ *nm, f* ardent supporter *ou* admirer.

inconditionnellement [ɛ̃kɔ̃disjɔnɛlmɑ̃] *adv* unconditionally.

inconduite [ɛ̃kɔ̃dɥit] *nf littéraire* scandalous behaviour *Br ou* behavior *Am.*

inconfort [ɛ̃kɔ̃fɔr] *nm* discomfort.

inconfortable [ɛ̃kɔ̃fɔrtabl] *adj* uncomfortable.

incongru, e [ɛ̃kɔ̃gry] *adj* **- 1.** [malséant] unseemly, inappropriate **- 2.** [bizarre] incongruous.

incongruité [ɛ̃kɔ̃grɥite] *nf* **- 1.** [qualité bizarre] incongruity *(U)* **- 2.** [parole malséante] unseemly remark.

inconnu, e [ɛ̃kɔny] ◇ *adj* unknown ◇ *nm, f* stranger ; **la personne qui a eu le prix Goncourt cette année est un illustre ~ hum** no one has ever heard of the renowned winner of the prix Goncourt this year.

➤ **inconnue** *nf* **- 1.** MATHS unknown **- 2.** [variable] unknown (factor).

inconsciemment [ɛ̃kɔ̃sjamɑ̃] *adv* **- 1.** [sans en avoir conscience] unconsciously, unwittingly **- 2.** [à la légère] thoughtlessly.

inconscience [ɛ̃kɔ̃sjɑ̃s] *nf* **- 1.** [évanouissement] unconsciousness **- 2.** [légèreté] thoughtlessness.

inconscient, e [ɛ̃kɔ̃sjɑ̃, ɑ̃t] *adj* **- 1.** [évanoui, machinal] unconscious **- 2.** [irresponsable] thoughtless.

➤ **inconscient** *nm* **:** **l'~** the unconscious.

inconséquence [ɛ̃kɔ̃sekɑ̃s] *nf* inconsistency.

inconséquent, e [ɛ̃kɔ̃sekɑ̃, ɑ̃t] *adj* inconsistent.

inconsidéré, e [ɛ̃kɔ̃sidere] *adj* ill-considered, thoughtless.

inconsistant, e [ɛ̃kɔ̃sistɑ̃, ɑ̃t] *adj* **- 1.** [aliment] thin, watery **- 2.** [caractère] frivolous.

inconsolable [ɛ̃kɔ̃sɔlabl] *adj* inconsolable.

inconstance [ɛ̃kɔ̃stɑ̃s] *nf* fickleness.

inconstant, e [ɛ̃kɔ̃stɑ̃, ɑ̃t] ◇ *adj* fickle ◇ *nm, f* **vieilli** fickle heart.

incontestable [ɛ̃kɔ̃tɛstabl] *adj* unquestionable, indisputable.

incontestablement [ɛ̃kɔ̃tɛstabləmɑ̃] *adv* unquestionably, indisputably.

incontesté, e [ɛ̃kɔ̃tɛste] *adj* uncontested, unchallenged.

incontinence [ɛ̃kɔ̃tinɑ̃s] *nf* **- 1.** MÉD incontinence **- 2.** [excès] lack of restraint.

incontinent, e [ɛ̃kɔ̃tinɑ̃, ɑ̃t] *adj* **- 1.** MÉD incontinent **- 2.** [sans retenue] unrestrained.

➤ **incontinent** *adv littéraire* forthwith.

incontournable [ɛ̃kɔ̃turnabl] *adj* unavoidable.

inconvenance [ɛ̃kɔ̃vnɑ̃s] *nf* impropriety.

inconvenant, e [ɛ̃kɔ̃vnɑ̃, ɑ̃t] *adj* improper, unseemly.

inconvénient [ɛ̃kɔ̃venjɑ̃] *nm* **- 1.** [obstacle] problem ; **si vous n'y voyez pas d'~** if that is convenient (for you), if you have no objection **- 2.** [désavantage] disadvantage, drawback **- 3.** [risque] risk.

incorporation [ɛ̃kɔrpɔrasjɔ̃] *nf* **- 1.** [intégration] incorporation ; CULIN mixing, blending **- 2.** MIL enlistment.

incorporé, e [ɛ̃kɔrpɔre] *adj* [intégré] built-in.

incorporel, elle [ɛ̃kɔrpɔrɛl] *adj* **- 1.** [immatériel] incorporeal **- 2.** JUR intangible.

incorporer [3] [ɛ̃kɔrpɔre] *vt* **- 1.** [gén] to incorporate ; **~ qqch dans** to incorporate sthg into ; **~ qqch à** CULIN to mix *ou* blend sthg into **- 2.** MIL to enlist.

➤ **s'incorporer** *vp* **:** **s'~ à qqch** to become part of sthg.

incorrect, e [ɛ̃kɔrɛkt] *adj* **- 1.** [faux] incorrect **- 2.** [inconvenant] inappropriate ; [impoli] rude **- 3.** [déloyal] unfair ; **être ~ avec qqn** to treat sb unfairly.

incorrection [ɛ̃kɔrɛksjɔ̃] *nf* **- 1.** [impolitesse] impropriety **- 2.** [de langage] grammatical mistake **- 3.** [malhonnêteté] dishonesty.

incorrigible [ɛ̃kɔriʒibl] *adj* incorrigible.

incorruptible [ɛ̃kɔryptibl] *adj* incorruptible.

incrédule [ɛ̃kredyl] ◇ *nmf* **- 1.** [sceptique] sceptic *Br,* skeptic *Am* **- 2.** RELIG unbeliever ◇ *adj* **- 1.** [sceptique] incredulous, sceptical *Br,* skeptical *Am* **- 2.** RELIG unbelieving.

incrédulité [ɛ̃kredylite] *nf* **- 1.** [scepticisme] incredulity, scepticism *Br,* skepticism *Am* **- 2.** RELIG unbelief, lack of belief.

increvable [ɛ̃krəvabl] *adj* **- 1.** [ballon, pneu] puncture-proof **- 2.** *fam fig* [personne] tireless ; [machine] that will withstand rough treatment.

incriminer [3] [ɛ̃krimine] *vt* **- 1.** [personne] to incriminate **- 2.** [conduite] to condemn.

incroyable [ɛ̃krwajabl] *adj* incredible, unbelievable.

incroyablement [ɛ̃krwajabləmɑ̃] *adv* incredibly, unbelievably.

incroyant, e [ɛ̃krwajɑ̃, ɑ̃t] ◇ *adj* unbelieving ◇ *nm, f* unbeliever.

incrustation [ɛ̃krystasjɔ̃] *nf* **- 1.** [ornement] inlay **- 2.** [dépôt] deposit, fur *(U).*

incruster [3] [ɛ̃kryste] *vt* **- 1.** [insérer] **:** **~ qqch dans qqch** to inlay sthg into sthg **- 2.** [déco-

rer] : ~ **qqch de qqch** to inlay sthg with sthg
- **3.** [couvrir d'un dépôt] to fur up.
➡ **s'incruster** *vp* - **1.** [s'insérer] : **s'~ dans qqch**
to become embedded in sthg - **2.** [chaudière]
to fur up - **3.** *fam fig* [personne] to take root.

incubateur, trice [ɛ̃kybatœr, tris] *adj* incu-
bating.
➡ **incubateur** *nm* incubator.

incubation [ɛ̃kybasjɔ̃] *nf* [d'œuf, de maladie] incubation ; *fig* hatching.

inculpation [ɛ̃kylpasjɔ̃] *nf* charge ; **sous**
l'~ de on a charge of.

inculpé, e [ɛ̃kylpe] *nm, f* : **l'~** the accused.

inculper [3] [ɛ̃kylpe] *vt* to charge ; **~ qqn de**
to charge sb with.

inculquer [3] [ɛ̃kylke] *vt* : **~ qqch à qqn** to instil *Br ou* instill *Am* sthg in sb.

inculte [ɛ̃kylt] *adj* - **1.** [terre] uncultivated
- **2.** [barbe] unkempt - **3.** *péj* [personne] uneducated.

inculture [ɛ̃kyltyr] *nf* - **1.** [intellectuelle] lack of
education - **2.** [de terre] lack of cultivation.

incurable [ɛ̃kyrabl] <> *nmf* incurably ill
person <> *adj* incurable.

incurie [ɛ̃kyri] *nf* negligence.

incursion [ɛ̃kyrsjɔ̃] *nf* incursion, foray.

incurver [3] [ɛ̃kyrve] *vt* to curve.
➡ **s'incurver** *vp* to curve, to bend.

Inde [ɛ̃d] *nf* : **l'~** India.

indéboulonnable [ɛ̃debylɔnabl] *adj* : **il est**
~ hum they'll never be able to sack him.

indécence [ɛ̃desɑ̃s] *nf* - **1.** [impudeur, immoralité]
indecency - **2.** [propos] indecent remark ; [ac-
tion] indecent act.

indécent, e [ɛ̃desɑ̃, ɑ̃t] *adj* - **1.** [impudique] indecent - **2.** [immoral] scandalous.

indéchiffrable [ɛ̃deʃifrabl] *adj* - **1.** [texte, écri-
ture] indecipherable - **2.** [énigme] inexplicable - **3.** *fig* [regard] inscrutable, impenetrable.

indéchirable [ɛ̃deʃirabl] *adj* tear-proof.

indécis, e [ɛ̃desi, iz] <> *adj* - **1.** [personne - sur le
moment] undecided ; [- de nature] indecisive
- **2.** [sourire] vague - **3.** [résultat] uncertain
<> *nm, f* indecisive person.
➡ **indécis** *nmpl* [dans sondage] don't knows.

indécision [ɛ̃desizjɔ̃] *nf* indecision ; [perpé-
tuelle] indecisiveness.

indécrottable [ɛ̃dekrɔtabl] *adj fam* - **1.** [borné]
incredibly dumb - **2.** [incorrigible] hopeless.

indéfectible [ɛ̃defɛktibl] *adj* indestructible.

indéfendable [ɛ̃defɑ̃dabl] *adj* indefensible.

indéfini, e [ɛ̃defini] *adj* - **1.** [quantité, pronom]
indefinite - **2.** [sentiment] vague.
➡ **indéfini** *nm GRAM* indefinite.

indéfiniment [ɛ̃definimɑ̃] *adv* indefinitely.

indéfinissable [ɛ̃definisabl] *adj* indefinable.

indéformable [ɛ̃defɔrmabl] *adj* that retains
its shape.

indélébile [ɛ̃delebil] *adj* indelible.

indélicat, e [ɛ̃delika, at] *adj* - **1.** [mufle] indelicate - **2.** [malhonnête] dishonest.

indémaillable [ɛ̃demajabl] <> *nm* run-
resistant material <> *adj* run-resistant.

indemne [ɛ̃dɛmn] *adj* unscathed, unharmed ; **sortir ~ de qqch** to come out of
sthg unscathed *ou* unharmed.

indemnisation [ɛ̃dɛmnizasjɔ̃] *nf* compensation.

indemniser [3] [ɛ̃dɛmnize] *vt* : **~ qqn de qqch**
[perte, préjudice] to compensate sb for sthg ;
[frais] to reimburse sb for sthg.

indemnité [ɛ̃dɛmnite] *nf* - **1.** [de perte, préjudice]
compensation ; **~ de licenciement** redun-
dancy payment - **2.** [de frais] allowance ;
~ journalière daily allowance ; **~ de loge-**
ment accommodation *Br ou* housing *Am* allowance - **3.** [allocation] : **~ parlementaire** MP's
Br ou Congressman's *Am* salary.

indémodable [ɛ̃demɔdabl] *adj* : **ce style est ~**
this style doesn't date.

indéniable [ɛ̃denjabl] *adj* undeniable.

indéniablement [ɛ̃denjabləmɑ̃] *adv* un-
deniably.

indépendamment [ɛ̃depɑ̃damɑ̃] *adv* : **~ de**
[abstraction faite de] regardless *ou* irrespective
of ; [outre] apart from ; [sans rapport avec] independently of.

indépendance [ɛ̃depɑ̃dɑ̃s] *nf* independence ; **accéder à l'~** to gain independence.

indépendant, e [ɛ̃depɑ̃dɑ̃, ɑ̃t] *adj* - **1.** [gén]
independent ; [entrée] separate ; **~ de** independent of ; **~ de ma volonté** beyond my
control - **2.** [travailleur] self-employed.

indépendantiste [ɛ̃depɑ̃datist] <> *nmf* advocate of political independence <> *adj*
independence *(avant n)*.

indéracinable [ɛ̃derasinabl] *adj* [arbre] impossible to uproot ; *fig* ineradicable.

indescriptible [ɛ̃dɛskriptibl] *adj* indescribable.

indésirable [ɛ̃dezirabl] *nmf & adj* undesirable.

indestructible [ɛ̃dɛstryktibl] *adj* indestructible.

indéterminé, e [ɛ̃determine] *adj* - **1.** [indéfini]
indeterminate, indefinite - **2.** [vague] vague
- **3.** [personne] undecided.

indétrônable [ɛ̃detronabl] *adj* inoustable.

index [ɛ̃dɛks] *nm* - **1.** [doigt] index finger - **2.** [aiguille] pointer, needle - **3.** [registre] index ; **mettre à l'~** *fig* to blacklist.

indexation [ɛ̃dɛksasjɔ̃] *nf* indexing.

indexer [4] [ɛ̃dɛkse] *vt* - **1.** ÉCON : ~ **qqch sur qqch** to index sthg to sthg - **2.** [livre] to index.

indicateur, trice [ɛ̃dikatœr, tris] *adj* : poteau ~ signpost ; **panneau** ~ road sign.

➣ **indicateur** *nm* - **1.** [guide] directory, guide ; ~ **des chemins de fer** railway *Br* ou railroad *Am* timetable - **2.** TECHNOL gauge ; ~ **d'altitude** altimeter ; ~ **de vitesse** speedometer - **3.** ÉCON indicator - **4.** [de police] informer.

indicatif, ive [ɛ̃dikatif, iv] *adj* indicative.

➣ **indicatif** *nm* - **1.** RADIO & TÉLÉ signature tune - **2.** [code] : ~ **(téléphonique)** dialling code *Br*, dial code *Am* - **3.** GRAM : **l'~** the indicative.

indication [ɛ̃dikasjɔ̃] *nf* - **1.** [mention] indication - **2.** [renseignement] information *(U)* - **3.** [directive] instruction ; THÉÂTRE direction ; **sauf** ~ **contraire** unless otherwise instructed.

indice [ɛ̃dis] *nm* - **1.** [signe] sign - **2.** [dans une enquête] clue - **3.** [taux] rating ; ~ **du coût de la vie** ÉCON cost-of-living index ; ~ **des prix** ÉCON price index ; ~ **de refroidissement** *Can* windchill factor - **4.** MATHS index.

indicible [ɛ̃disibl] *adj* inexpressible.

indien, enne [ɛ̃djɛ̃, ɛn] *adj* - **1.** [d'Inde] Indian - **2.** [d'Amérique] American Indian, Native American.

➣ **Indien, enne** *nm, f* - **1.** [d'Inde] Indian - **2.** [d'Amérique] American Indian, Native American.

indifféremment [ɛ̃diferamɑ̃] *adv* indifferently.

indifférence [ɛ̃diferɑ̃s] *nf* indifference.

indifférencié, e [ɛ̃diferɑ̃sje] *adj* undifferentiated.

indifférent, e [ɛ̃diferɑ̃, ɑ̃t] ⬦ *adj* - **1.** [gén] : ~ **à** indifferent to - **2.** *sout* [égal] immaterial ⬦ *nm, f* unconcerned person.

indifférer [18] [ɛ̃difere] *vt* to be a matter of indifference to.

indigence [ɛ̃diʒɑ̃s] *nf* poverty.

indigène [ɛ̃diʒɛn] ⬦ *nmf* native ⬦ *adj* [peuple] native ; [faune, flore] indigenous.

indigent, e [ɛ̃diʒɑ̃, ɑ̃t] ⬦ *adj* [pauvre] destitute, poverty-stricken ; *fig* [intellectuellement] impoverished ⬦ *nm, f* poor person ; **les ~s** the poor, the destitute.

indigeste [ɛ̃diʒɛst] *adj* indigestible.

indigestion [ɛ̃diʒɛstjɔ̃] *nf* - **1.** [alimentaire] indigestion ; **avoir une** ~ to have indigestion

- **2.** *fig* [saturation] surfeit ; **avoir une** ~ **de** to have had one's fill of.

indignation [ɛ̃diɲasjɔ̃] *nf* indignation.

indigne [ɛ̃diɲ] *adj* : ~ **(de)** unworthy (of).

indigné, e [ɛ̃diɲe] *adj* indignant.

indigner [3] [ɛ̃diɲe] *vt* to make indignant.

➣ **s'indigner** *vp* : **s'~ de** ou **contre qqch** to get indignant about sthg ; **s'~ que** (+ *subjonctif*) to be indignant that.

indigo [ɛ̃digo] ⬦ *nm* indigo ⬦ *adj inv* indigo (blue).

indiqué, e [ɛ̃dike] *adj* - **1.** [convenable] appropriate - **2.** [recommandé] advisable ; **ce n'est pas très** ~ it's not very advisable - **3.** [fixé] appointed.

indiquer [3] [ɛ̃dike] *vt* - **1.** [désigner] to indicate, to point out ; ~ **qqn/qqch du doigt** to point at sb/sthg, to point sb/sthg out ; ~ **qqn/qqch du regard** to glance toward sb/sthg *Br*, to glance toward sb/sthg *Am* - **2.** [afficher, montrer - suj : carte, pendule, aiguille] to show, to indicate - **3.** [recommander] : ~ **qqn/qqch à qqn** to tell sb of sb/sthg, to suggest sb/sthg to sb - **4.** [dire, renseigner sur] to tell ; ~ **à qqn comment faire qqch** to tell sb how to do sthg ; **pourriez-vous m'~ l'heure?** could you tell me the time? - **5.** [fixer - heure, date, lieu] to name, to indicate - **6.** [dénoter] to indicate, to point to.

indirect, e [ɛ̃dirɛkt] *adj* [gén] indirect ; [itinéraire] roundabout.

indirectement [ɛ̃dirɛktəmɑ̃] *adv* indirectly.

indiscipline [ɛ̃disiplin] *nf* lack of discipline.

indiscipliné, e [ɛ̃disipline] *adj* - **1.** [écolier, esprit] undisciplined, unruly - **2.** *fig* [mèches de cheveux] unmanageable.

indiscret, ète [ɛ̃diskrɛ, ɛt] ⬦ *adj* indiscreet ; [curieux] inquisitive ⬦ *nm, f* indiscreet person.

indiscrètement [ɛ̃diskrɛtmɑ̃] *adv* indiscreetly ; [avec curiosité] inquisitively.

indiscrétion [ɛ̃diskresjɔ̃] *nf* indiscretion ; [curiosité] curiosity ; **sans** ~ ... without wishing to be indiscreet ...

indiscutable [ɛ̃diskytabl] *adj* unquestionable, indisputable.

indiscutablement [ɛ̃diskytabləmɑ̃] *adv* unquestionably, indisputably.

indiscuté, e [ɛ̃diskyte] *adj* undisputed, unquestioned.

indispensable [ɛ̃dispɑ̃sabl] ⬦ *adj* indispensable, essential ; ~ **à** indispensable to, essential to ; **il est** ~ **que** (+ *subjonctif*) it is essential ou vital that ; **il est** ~ **de faire qqch** it is essential ou vital to do sthg ⬦ *nm* : **l'~** the essentials *(pl)*.

indisponibilité [ɛ̃dispɔnibilite] *nf* unavailability.

indisponible [ɛ̃dispɔnibl] *adj* unavailable.

indisposé, e [ɛ̃dispoze] *adj* [malade] unwell ; **être ~e** [femme] to be indisposed.

indisposer [3] [ɛ̃dispoze] *vt* - **1.** *sout* [rendre malade] to indispose - **2.** *littéraire* [fâcher] to vex.

indisposition [ɛ̃dispozisjɔ̃] *nf* - **1.** [malaise] indisposition - **2.** [règles] period.

indissociable [ɛ̃disɔsjabl] *adj* indissociable.

indissoluble [ɛ̃disɔlybl] *adj* indissoluble.

indistinct, e [ɛ̃distɛ̃(kt), ɛ̃kt] *adj* indistinct ; [souvenir] hazy.

indistinctement [ɛ̃distɛ̃ktəmɑ̃] *adv* - **1.** [confusément] indistinctly - **2.** [indifféremment] equally well.

individu [ɛ̃dividy] *nm* individual.

individualiste [ɛ̃dividɥalist] <> *nmf* individualist <> *adj* individualistic.

individualité [ɛ̃dividɥalite] *nf* - **1.** [personne] individual - **2.** [unicité, originalité] individuality.

individuel, elle [ɛ̃dividɥɛl] *adj* individual.

individuellement [ɛ̃dividɥɛlmɑ̃] *adv* individually.

indivis, e [ɛ̃divi, iz] *adj* - **1.** [propriété] undivided - **2.** [héritier] joint ; **par ~** jointly.

indivisible [ɛ̃divizibl] *adj* indivisible.

Indochine [ɛ̃dɔʃin] *nf* : **l'~** Indochina ; **la guerre d'~** the Indochinese War.

indo-européen, enne [ɛ̃dɔœrɔpeɛ̃, ɛn] (*mpl* indo-européens, *fpl* indo-européennes) *adj* Indo-European.

indolence [ɛ̃dɔlɑ̃s] *nf* - **1.** [de personne] indolence, lethargy - **2.** [d'organisation] apathy - **3.** [de geste, regard] languidness.

indolent, e [ɛ̃dɔlɑ̃, ɑ̃t] *adj* - **1.** [personne] indolent, lethargic - **2.** [geste, regard] languid.

indolore [ɛ̃dɔlɔr] *adj* painless.

indomptable [ɛ̃dɔ̃tabl] *adj* - **1.** [animal] untamable - **2.** [personne] indomitable - **3.** [sentiment] uncontrollable.

Indonésie [ɛ̃dɔnezi] *nf* : **l'~** Indonesia.

indonésien, enne [ɛ̃dɔnezjɛ̃, ɛn] *adj* Indonesian.
➡ **indonésien** *nm* [langue] Indonesian.
➡ **Indonésien, enne** *nm, f* Indonesian.

indu, e [ɛ̃dy] *adj* - **1.** [heure] ungodly, unearthly - **2.** [dépenses, remarque] unwarranted.

indubitable [ɛ̃dybitabl] *adj* indubitable, undoubted ; **il est ~ que** it is indisputable *ou* beyond doubt that.

indubitablement [ɛ̃dybitabləmɑ̃] *adv* undoubtedly, indubitably.

induction [ɛ̃dyksjɔ̃] *nf* induction ; **par ~** by induction.

induire [98] [ɛ̃dɥir] *vt* to induce ; **~ qqn à faire qqch** to induce sb to do sthg ; **~ qqn en erreur** to mislead sb ; **en ~ que** to infer *ou* gather that.

induit, e [ɛ̃dɥi, ɥit] <> *pp* ⊳ **induire** <> *adj* - **1.** [consécutif] resulting - **2.** *ÉLECTR* induced.

indulgence [ɛ̃dylʒɑ̃s] *nf* [de juge] leniency ; [de parent] indulgence ; **avec ~** leniently/indulgently.

indulgent, e [ɛ̃dylʒɑ̃, ɑ̃t] *adj* [juge] lenient ; [parent] indulgent.

indûment [ɛ̃dymɑ̃] *adv* unduly.

industrialisation [ɛ̃dystrijalizasjɔ̃] *nf* industrialization.

industrialisé, e [ɛ̃dystrijalize] *adj* industrialized ; **pays ~** industrialized country.

industrialiser [3] [ɛ̃dystrijalize] *vt* to industrialize.
➡ **s'industrialiser** *vp* to become industrialized.

industrie [ɛ̃dystri] *nf* industry ; **~ alimentaire** food industry ; **~ automobile** car industry ; **~ chimique** chemical industry ; **~ lourde** heavy industry.

industriel, elle [ɛ̃dystrijɛl] *adj* industrial.
➡ **industriel** *nm* industrialist.

industrieux, euse [ɛ̃dystrijø, øz] *adj littéraire* industrious.

inébranlable [inebrɑ̃labl] *adj* - **1.** [roc] solid, immovable - **2.** *fig* [conviction] unshakeable.

INED, Ined [ined] (*abr de* **Institut national d'études démographiques**) *nm* national institute for demographic research.

inédit, e [inedi, it] *adj* - **1.** [texte] unpublished - **2.** [trouvaille] novel, original.
➡ **inédit** *nm* unpublished work.

ineffable [inefabl] *adj* ineffable.

ineffaçable [inefasabl] *adj* indelible.

inefficace [inefikas] *adj* - **1.** [personne, machine] inefficient - **2.** [solution, remède, mesure] ineffective.

inefficacité [inefikasite] *nf* - **1.** [de personne, machine] inefficiency - **2.** [de solution, remède, mesure] ineffectiveness.

inégal, e, aux [inegal, o] *adj* - **1.** [différent, disproportionné] unequal - **2.** [irrégulier] uneven - **3.** [changeant] changeable ; [artiste, travail] erratic.

inégalable [inegalabl] *adj* matchless.

inégalé, e [inegale] *adj* unequalled *Br*, unequaled *Am*.

inégalement [inegalmɑ̃] *adv* [gén] unequally ; [irrégulièrement] unevenly.

inégalité [inegalite] nf - **1.** [injustice, dispropor- tion] inequality ; ~s **sociales** social inequal- ities - **2.** [différence] difference, disparity - **3.** [irrégularité] unevenness - **4.** [d'humeur] changeability.

inélégant, e [inelegã, ãt] adj - **1.** [dans l'habille- ment] inelegant - **2.** fig [indélicat] discourteous.

inéligible [in(e)liʒibl] adj ineligible.

inéluctable [inelyktabl] adj inescapable.

inéluctablement [inelyktabləmã] adv in- escapably.

inénarrable [inenarabl] adj very funny.

inepte [inɛpt] adj inept.

ineptie [inɛpsi] nf - **1.** [bêtise] ineptitude - **2.** [chose idiote] nonsense (U) ; **dire des ~s** to talk nonsense.

inépuisable [inepɥizabl] adj inexhaustible.

inerte [inɛrt] adj - **1.** [corps, membre] lifeless - **2.** [personne] passive, inert - **3.** PHYS inert.

inertie [inɛrsi] nf - **1.** [manque de réaction] ap- athy, inertia - **2.** PHYS inertia.

inespéré, e [inɛspere] adj unexpected, unhoped-for.

inesthétique [inɛstetik] adj unaesthetic.

inestimable [inɛstimabl] adj : **d'une valeur ~** priceless ; fig invaluable.

inévitable [inevitabl] adj [obstacle] unavoid- able ; [conséquence] inevitable.

inévitablement [inevitabləmã] adv inevit- ably.

inexact, e [inɛgza(kt), akt] adj - **1.** [faux, incom- plet] inaccurate, inexact - **2.** [en retard] un- punctual.

inexactitude [inɛgzaktityd] nf - **1.** [erreur, im- précision] inaccuracy - **2.** [retard] unpunctual- ity.

inexcusable [inɛkskyzabl] adj unforgivable, inexcusable.

inexistant, e [inɛgzistã, ãt] adj nonexistent.

inexistence [inɛgzistãs] nf nonexistence.

inexorable [inɛgzɔrabl] adj inexorable.

inexorablement [inɛgzɔrabləmã] adv inex- orably.

inexpérience [inɛksperjãs] nf lack of ex- perience, inexperience.

inexpérimenté, e [inɛksperimãte] adj - **1.** [personne] inexperienced - **2.** [gestes] inex- pert - **3.** [produit] untested.

inexplicable [inɛksplikabl] adj inexplicable, unexplainable.

inexpliqué, e [inɛksplike] adj unexplained.

inexploré, e [inɛksplɔre] adj litt & fig unex- plored ; [mers] uncharted.

inexpressif, ive [inɛkspresif, iv] adj inex- pressive.

inexprimable [inɛksprimabl] adj inexpress- ible.

inexprimé, e [inɛksprime] adj unexpressed.

inexpugnable [inɛkspygnabl] adj impreg- nable.

inextensible [inɛkstãsibl] adj - **1.** [matériau] unstretchable - **2.** [étoffe] non-stretch.

inextinguible [inɛkstɛ̃gibl] adj [passion] inex- tinguishable ; [soif] unquenchable ; [rire] un- controllable.

in extremis [inɛkstremis] adv at the last mi- nute.

inextricable [inɛkstrikabl] adj - **1.** [fouillis] in- extricable - **2.** fig [affaire, mystère] that cannot be unravelled.

inextricablement [inɛkstrikabləmã] adv in- extricably.

infaillible [ɛ̃fajibl] adj [personne, méthode] in- fallible ; [instinct] unerring.

infaisable [ɛ̃fəzabl] adj unfeasible.

infamant, e [ɛ̃famã, ãt] adj [marché] dishon- ourable Br, dishonorable Am ; [propos] de- famatory.

infâme [ɛ̃fam] adj - **1.** [ignoble] despicable - **2.** hum ou littéraire [dégoûtant] vile.

infamie [ɛ̃fami] nf infamy.

infanterie [ɛ̃fãtri] nf infantry.

infanticide [ɛ̃fãtisid] <> nmf infanticide, child-killer <> adj infanticidal.

infantile [ɛ̃fãtil] adj - **1.** [maladie] childhood (avant n) - **2.** [médecine] for children - **3.** [com- portement] infantile.

infantiliser [3] [ɛ̃fãtilize] vt to treat like a child.

infarctus [ɛ̃farktys] nm infarction, infarct ; **~ du myocarde** coronary thrombosis, myo- cardial infarction.

infatigable [ɛ̃fatigabl] adj - **1.** [personne] tire- less - **2.** [attitude] untiring.

infatué, e [ɛ̃fatɥe] adj péj & sout : **~ de** con- ceited about ; **~ de soi-même** self- important.

infect, e [ɛ̃fɛkt] adj - **1.** [dégoûtant] vile - **2.** lit- téraire [marais] foul.

infecter [4] [ɛ̃fɛkte] vt - **1.** [eau] to contamin- ate - **2.** [plaie] to infect - **3.** [empoisonner] to poi- son.

➡ **s'infecter** vp to become infected, to turn septic.

infectieux, euse [ɛ̃fɛksjø, øz] adj infec- tious.

infection [ɛ̃fɛksjɔ̃] nf - **1.** MÉD infection - **2.** fig & péj [puanteur] stench.

inféoder [3] [ɛ̃feɔde] ➡ **s'inféoder** vp : **s'~ à** to pledge one's allegiance to.

inférer [18] [ẽfere] *vt littéraire* : ~ qqch de qqch to infer sthg from sthg.

inférieur, e [ẽferjœr] <> *adj* - **1.** [qui est en bas] lower - **2.** [dans une hiérarchie] inferior ; ~ à [qualité] inferior to ; [quantité] less than ; ~ ou égal à 8 MATHS less than or equal to 8 <> *nm, f* inferior.

infériorité [ẽferjɔrite] *nf* inferiority.

infernal, e, aux [ẽfernal, o] *adj* - **1.** [personne] fiendish - **2.** *fig* [bruit, chaleur, rythme] infernal ; [vision] diabolical.

infester [3] [ẽfeste] *vt* to infest ; **être infesté de** [rats, moustiques] to be infested with ; [touristes] to be overrun by.

infidèle [ẽfidɛl] <> *adj* - **1.** [mari, femme, ami] : ~ (à) unfaithful (to) - **2.** [traducteur, historien] inaccurate - **3.** *vieilli* & RELIG infidel <> *nmf vieilli* & RELIG infidel.

infidélité [ẽfidelite] *nf* - **1.** [trahison] infidelity ; **faire des ~s à** to be unfaithful to - **2.** [de traduction] inaccuracy - **3.** [de mémoire] unreliability.

infiltration [ẽfiltrasjɔ̃] *nf* infiltration.

infiltrer [3] [ẽfiltre] *vt* to infiltrate.

➡ **s'infiltrer** *vp* - **1.** [pluie, lumière] : **s'~ par/dans** to filter through/into - **2.** [hommes, idées] to infiltrate.

infime [ẽfim] *adj* minute, infinitesimal.

infini, e [ẽfini] *adj* - **1.** [sans bornes] infinite, boundless - **2.** MATHS, PHILO & RELIG infinite - **3.** *fig* [interminable] endless, interminable.

➡ **infini** *nm* infinity.

➡ **à l'infini** *loc adv* - **1.** MATHS to infinity - **2.** [discourir] ad infinitum, endlessly.

infiniment [ẽfinimɑ̃] *adv* extremely, immensely.

infinité [ẽfinite] *nf* infinity, infinite number.

infinitésimal, e, aux [ẽfinitezimal, o] *adj* infinitesimal.

infinitif, ive [ẽfinitif, iv] *adj* infinitive.

➡ **infinitif** *nm* infinitive.

infirme [ẽfirm] <> *adj* [handicapé] disabled ; [avec l'âge] infirm <> *nmf* disabled person ; ~ **de guerre** disabled ex-serviceman (*f* ex-servicewoman).

infirmer [3] [ẽfirme] *vt* - **1.** [démentir] to invalidate - **2.** JUR to annul.

infirmerie [ẽfirməri] *nf* infirmary.

infirmier, ère [ẽfirmje, ɛr] *nm, f* nurse ; ~ **diplômé** ≃ state-registered nurse.

infirmité [ẽfirmite] *nf* [handicap] disability ; [de vieillesse] infirmity.

inflammable [ẽflamabl] *adj* inflammable, flammable.

inflammation [ẽflamasjɔ̃] *nf* inflammation.

inflation [ẽflasjɔ̃] *nf* ÉCON inflation ; *fig* increase.

inflationniste [ẽflasjɔnist] *adj* & *nmf* inflationist.

infléchir [32] [ẽfleʃir] *vt fig* [politique] to modify.

➡ **s'infléchir** *vp* - **1.** [route] to bend - **2.** *fig* [politique] to shift.

inflexible [ẽflɛksibl] *adj* inflexible.

inflexion [ẽflɛksjɔ̃] *nf* - **1.** [de tête] nod - **2.** [de voix] inflection - **3.** [de route] bend - **4.** *fig* [de politique] shift.

infliger [17] [ẽfliʒe] *vt* : ~ qqch à qqn to inflict sthg on sb ; [amende] to impose sthg on sb.

influençable [ẽflyɑ̃sabl] *adj* easily influenced.

influence [ẽflyɑ̃s] *nf* influence ; [de médicament] effect ; **avoir de l'~ sur qqn** to have an influence on sb ; **avoir une bonne/mauvaise ~ sur** [suj : personne] to have a good/bad influence on, to be a good/bad influence on ; [suj : chose] to have a good/bad effect on ; **agir sous l'~ de qqch** to act under the influence of sthg.

influencer [16] [ẽflyɑ̃se] *vt* to influence.

influent, e [ẽflyɑ̃, ɑ̃t] *adj* influential.

influer [3] [ẽflye] *vi* : ~ **sur qqch** to influence sthg, to have an effect on sthg.

Infographie® [ẽfɔgrafi] *nf* computer graphics (*U*).

informateur, trice [ẽfɔrmatœr, tris] *nm, f* - **1.** [qui renseigne] informant - **2.** [de police] informer.

informaticien, enne [ẽfɔrmatisjẽ, ɛn] *nm, f* computer scientist.

information [ẽfɔrmasjɔ̃] *nf* - **1.** [renseignement] piece of information - **2.** [renseignements & INFORM] information (*U*) - **3.** [nouvelle] piece of news - **4.** JUR inquiry.

➡ **informations** *nfpl* MÉDIA news (*sg*).

informatique [ẽfɔrmatik] <> *nf* - **1.** [technique] computers ; ~ **de gestion** business applications (*pl*) - **2.** [science] computer science <> *adj* data-processing (*avant n*), computer (*avant n*).

informatisation [ẽfɔrmatizasjɔ̃] *nf* computerization.

informatiser [3] [ẽfɔrmatize] *vt* to computerize.

➡ **s'informatiser** *vp* to become computerized.

informe [ẽfɔrm] *adj* - **1.** [masse, vêtement, silhouette] shapeless - **2.** *fig* [projet] sketchy, rough.

informé, e [ɛ̃fɔrme] *adj* informed ; **bien/mal** ~ well/badly informed.

➤ **informé** *nm* : **jusqu'à plus ample ~** pending further information.

informel, elle [ɛ̃fɔrmɛl] *adj* informal.

informer [3] [ɛ̃fɔrme] <> *vt* to inform ; ~ **qqn sur** OU **de qqch** to inform sb about sthg <> *vi* JUR : ~ **contre qqn/sur qqch** to investigate sb/sthg.

➤ **s'informer** *vp* to inform o.s. ; **s'~ de qqch** to ask about sthg ; **s'~ sur qqch** to find out about sthg.

infortune [ɛ̃fɔrtyn] *nf* misfortune.

infortuné, e [ɛ̃fɔrtyne] *littéraire* & *vieilli* <> *adj* wretched <> *nm, f (gén pl)* unfortunate.

infos [ɛ̃fo] *(abr de* **informations***) nfpl fam* : **les ~** the news *(sg)*.

infraction [ɛ̃fraksjɔ̃] *nf* offence ; ~ **à** infringement OU breach of ; **être en ~** to be in breach of the law.

infranchissable [ɛ̃frɑ̃ʃisabl] *adj* insurmountable.

infrarouge [ɛ̃fraruʒ] *nm* & *adj* infrared.

infrastructure [ɛ̃frastryktyr] *nf* infrastructure ; ~ **hôtelière** hotel facilities *(pl)*.

infréquentable [ɛ̃frekɑ̃tabl] *adj* - **1.** [personne] : **il est ~** you shouldn't mix with him - **2.** [lieu] : **ce café est ~** it's not the kind of café you should go to.

infroissable [ɛ̃frwasabl] *adj* crease-resistant.

infructueux, euse [ɛ̃fryktɥø, øz] *adj* fruitless.

infuse [ɛ̃fyz] ⊳ **science**.

infuser [3] [ɛ̃fyze] <> *vt* - **1.** [tisane] to infuse ; [thé] to brew ; **laisser ~** to leave to infuse OU brew - **2.** *fig* & *littéraire* : ~ **qqch à qqn/qqch** to infuse sb/sthg with sthg <> *vi* [tisane] to infuse ; [thé] to brew.

infusion [ɛ̃fyzjɔ̃] *nf* infusion.

ingambe [ɛ̃gɑ̃b] *adj* spry.

ingénier [9] [ɛ̃ʒenje] ➤ **s'ingénier** *vp* : **s'~ à faire qqch** to try hard to do sthg.

ingénierie [ɛ̃ʒeniri] *nf* engineering.

ingénieur [ɛ̃ʒenjœr] *nm* engineer ; ~ **agronome/chimiste/électronicien** agricultural/chemical/electronics engineer ; ~ **des mines** mining engineer ; ~ **des ponts et chaussées** civil engineer ; ~ **du son** sound engineer ; ~ **des travaux publics** civil engineer.

ingénieux, euse [ɛ̃ʒenjø, øz] *adj* ingenious.

ingéniosité [ɛ̃ʒenjozite] *nf* ingenuity.

ingénu, e [ɛ̃ʒeny] <> *adj littéraire* [candide] artless ; *hum* & *péj* [trop candide] naïve <> *nm, f littéraire* [candide] naïve person ; THÉÂTRE ingénue ; **jouer les ~s** THÉÂTRE to play ingénue roles ; [dans la vie] to act the sweet young thing.

ingénuité [ɛ̃ʒenɥite] *nf* naïvety.

ingénument [ɛ̃ʒenymɑ̃] *adv* naïvely.

ingérable [ɛ̃ʒerabl] *adj* unmanageable.

ingérence [ɛ̃ʒerɑ̃s] *nf* : ~ **dans** interference in.

ingérer [18] [ɛ̃ʒere] *vt* to ingest.

➤ **s'ingérer** *vp* : **s'~ dans** to interfere in.

ingrat, e [ɛ̃gra, at] <> *adj* - **1.** [personne] ungrateful - **2.** [métier] thankless, unrewarding - **3.** [sol] barren - **4.** [physique] unattractive <> *nm, f* ungrateful wretch.

ingratitude [ɛ̃gratityd] *nf* ingratitude.

ingrédient [ɛ̃gredjɑ̃] *nm* ingredient.

inguérissable [ɛ̃gerisabl] *adj* incurable.

ingurgiter [3] [ɛ̃gyrʒite] *vt* - **1.** [avaler] to swallow - **2.** *fig* [connaissances] to absorb.

inhabitable [inabitabl] *adj* uninhabitable.

inhabité, e [inabite] *adj* uninhabited.

inhabituel, elle [inabitɥɛl] *adj* unusual.

inhalateur, trice [inalatœr, tris] *adj* : **appareil ~** inhaler.

➤ **inhalateur** *nm* inhaler.

inhalation [inalasjɔ̃] *nf* inhalation.

inhaler [3] [inale] *vt* to inhale, to breathe in.

inhérent, e [inerɑ̃, ɑ̃t] *adj* : ~ **à** inherent in.

inhiber [3] [inibe] *vt* to inhibit.

inhibition [inibisjɔ̃] *nf* inhibition.

inhospitalier, ère [inɔspitalje, ɛr] *adj* inhospitable.

inhumain, e [inymɛ̃, ɛn] *adj* inhuman.

inhumation [inymasjɔ̃] *nf* burial.

inhumer [3] [inyme] *vt* to bury.

inimaginable [inimaʒinabl] *adj* incredible, unimaginable.

inimitable [inimitabl] *adj* inimitable.

inimitié [inimitje] *nf* : ~ **contre** OU **à l'égard de** enmity towards *Br* OU toward *Am*.

ininflammable [inɛ̃flamabl] *adj* non-flammable.

inintelligible [inɛ̃teliʒibl] *adj* unintelligible.

inintéressant, e [inɛ̃teresɑ̃, ɑ̃t] *adj* uninteresting.

ininterrompu, e [inɛ̃terɔ̃py] *adj* [file, vacarme] uninterrupted ; [ligne, suite] unbroken ; [travail, effort] continuous.

inique [inik] *adj* iniquitous.

iniquité [inikite] *nf* iniquity.

initial, e, aux [inisjal, o] *adj* [lettre] initial.

➤ **initiale** *nf* initial.

initialement [inisjalmɑ̃l] *adv* initially.

initialiser [3] [inisjalize] *vt INFORM* to initialize.

initiateur, trice [inisjatœr, tris] ◇ *adj* innovative ◇ *nm, f* **- 1.** [maître] initiator **- 2.** [précurseur] innovator.

initiation [inisjasjɔ̃] *nf* : ~ **(à)** [discipline] introduction (to) ; [rituel] initiation (into).

initiatique [inisjatik] *adj* [rite] initiation (*avant n*).

initiative [inisjativ] *nf* initiative ; **avoir de l'~** to have initiative ; **prendre l'~ de qqch/de faire qqch** to take the initiative for sthg/in doing sthg ; **de sa propre ~** on one's own initiative.

initié, e [inisje] ◇ *adj* initiated ◇ *nm, f* initiate.

initier [9] [inisje] *vt* : ~ **qqn à** to initiate sb into.

➠ **s'initier** *vp* : **s'~ à** to familiarize o.s. with.

injecté, e [ɛ̃ʒɛkte] *adj* : **yeux ~s de sang** bloodshot eyes.

injecter [4] [ɛ̃ʒɛkte] *vt* to inject.

➠ **s'injecter** *vp* [yeux] : **s'~ (de sang)** to become bloodshot.

injection [ɛ̃ʒɛksjɔ̃] *nf* injection.

injoignable [ɛ̃ʒwaɲabl] *adj* : **j'ai essayé de lui téléphoner mais il est** ~ I tried to phone him but I couldn't get through to him *ou* reach him *ou* get hold of him.

injonction [ɛ̃ʒɔ̃ksjɔ̃] *nf* injunction.

injure [ɛ̃ʒyr] *nf* insult ; **abreuver qqn d'~s** to hurl insults at sb.

injurier [9] [ɛ̃ʒyrje] *vt* to insult.

injurieux, euse [ɛ̃ʒyrjø, øz] *adj* abusive, insulting.

injuste [ɛ̃ʒyst] *adj* unjust, unfair.

injustement [ɛ̃ʒystəmɑ̃] *adv* unjustly, unfairly.

injustice [ɛ̃ʒystis] *nf* injustice.

injustifiable [ɛ̃ʒystifjabl] *adj* unjustifiable.

injustifié, e [ɛ̃ʒystifje] *adj* unjustified.

inlassable [ɛ̃lasabl] *adj* tireless.

inlassablement [ɛ̃lasabləmɑ̃] *adv* tirelessly.

inné, e [ine] *adj* innate.

innocemment [inɔsamɑ̃] *adv* innocently.

innocence [inɔsɑ̃s] *nf* innocence.

innocent, e [inɔsɑ̃, ɑ̃t] ◇ *adj* innocent ◇ *nm, f* **- 1.** JUR innocent person **- 2.** [inoffensif, candide] innocent ; **faire l'~** *fig* to play the innocent **- 3.** *vieilli* [idiot] simpleton.

innocenter [3] [inɔsɑ̃te] *vt* **- 1.** JUR to clear **- 2.** *fig* [excuser] to justify.

innocuité [inɔkɥite] *nf* harmlessness, innocuousness.

innombrable [inɔ̃brabl] *adj* innumerable ; [foule] vast.

innovateur, trice [inɔvatœr, tris] ◇ *adj* innovatory ◇ *nm, f* innovator.

innovation [inɔvasjɔ̃] *nf* innovation.

innover [3] [inɔve] *vi* to innovate ; ~ **en matière de** to innovate in the field of.

inobservation [inɔpsɛrvasjɔ̃] *nf* inobservance.

inoccupé, e [inɔkype] *adj* **- 1.** [lieu] empty, unoccupied **- 2.** [personne, vie] idle.

inoculation [inɔkylasjɔ̃] *nf* [volontaire] inoculation ; [accidentelle] infection.

inoculer [3] [inɔkyle] *vt MÉD* : ~ **qqch à qqn** [volontairement] to inoculate sb with sthg ; [accidentellement] to infect sb with sthg.

inodore [inɔdɔr] *adj* odourless *Br*, odorless *Am*.

inoffensif, ive [inɔfɑ̃sif, iv] *adj* harmless.

inondation [inɔ̃dasjɔ̃] *nf* **- 1.** [action] flooding **- 2.** [résultat] flood.

inonder [3] [inɔ̃de] *vt* to flood ; ~ **de** *fig* to flood with.

inopérable [inɔperabl] *adj* inoperable.

inopérant, e [inɔperɑ̃, ɑ̃t] *adj* ineffective.

inopiné, e [inɔpine] *adj* unexpected.

inopinément [inɔpinemɑ̃] *adv* unexpectedly.

inopportun, e [inɔpɔrtœ̃, yn] *adj* inopportune.

inorganisé, e [inɔrganize] ◇ *adj* **- 1.** [sans organisation] disorganized **- 2.** [politiquement] independent ; [syndicalement] non-union (*avant n*) ◇ *nm, f* [politiquement] independent ; [syndicalement] non-union member.

inoubliable [inublijabl] *adj* unforgettable.

inouï, e [inwi] *adj* incredible, extraordinary.

Inox® [inɔks] *nm inv* & *adj inv* stainless steel.

inoxydable [inɔksidabl] ◇ *adj* stainless ; [casserole] stainless steel (*avant n*) ◇ *nm* stainless steel.

inqualifiable [ɛ̃kalifjabl] *adj* unspeakable.

inquiet, ète [ɛ̃kjɛ, ɛt] ◇ *adj* **- 1.** [gén] anxious **- 2.** [tourmenté] feverish ◇ *nm, f* worrier.

inquiétant, e [ɛ̃kjetɑ̃, ɑ̃t] *adj* disturbing, worrying.

inquiéter [18] [ɛ̃kjete] *vt* **- 1.** [donner du souci à] to worry **- 2.** [déranger] to disturb.

➠ **s'inquiéter** *vp* **- 1.** [s'alarmer] to be worried **- 2.** [se préoccuper] : **s'~ de** [s'enquérir de] to enquire about ; [se soucier de] to worry about.

inquiétude [ɛ̃kjetyd] *nf* anxiety, worry.

inquisiteur, trice [ɛ̃kizitœr, tris] *adj* prying.

INR (*abr de* Institut national de radiodiffusion) *nm Belgian broadcasting company.*

INRA, Inra [inra] (*abr de* Institut national de la recherche agronomique) *nm national institute for agronomic research.*

insaisissable [ɛ̃sezisabl] *adj* - **1.** [personne] elusive - **2.** *fig* [nuance] imperceptible.

insalubre [ɛ̃salybr] *adj* unhealthy.

insalubrité [ɛ̃salybrite] *nf* unhealthiness.

insanité [ɛ̃sanite] *nf* - **1.** [déraison] insanity, madness - **2.** [propos] : **dire** *ou* **proférer des ~s** to say insane things - **3.** [acte] insane act.

insatiable [ɛ̃sasjabl] *adj* insatiable.

insatisfait, e [ɛ̃satisfɛ, ɛt] <> *adj* - **1.** [personne] dissatisfied - **2.** [sentiment] unsatisfied <> *nm, f* malcontent.

inscription [ɛ̃skripsjɔ̃] *nf* - **1.** [action, écrit] inscription - **2.** [enregistrement] enrolment *Br*, enrollment *Am*, registration - **3.** *JUR* registration.

inscrire [99] [ɛ̃skrir] *vt* - **1.** [écrire] to write down ; [graver] to inscribe - **2.** [personne] : **~ qqn à qqch** to enrol *Br ou* enroll *Am* sb for sthg, to register sb for sthg ; **~ qqn sur qqch** to put sb's name down on sthg - **3.** *SPORT* [but] to score.

➤ **s'inscrire** *vp* - **1.** [personne] : **s'~ à qqch** to enrol *Br ou* enroll *Am* for sthg, to register for sthg ; **s'~ sur qqch** to put one's name down on sthg - **2.** [s'insérer] : **s'~ dans** to come within the scope of - **3.** *loc* : **s'~ en faux contre qqch** to deny sthg vigorously.

inscrit, e [ɛ̃skri, it] <> *pp* ⊳ **inscrire** <> *adj* [sur liste] registered ; **être ~ sur une liste** to have one's name on a list <> *nm, f* registered person.

inscrivais, inscrivions *etc* ⊳ **inscrire.**

INSEAD [insead] (*abr de* Institut européen d'administration) *nm European business school in Fontainebleau.*

insecte [ɛ̃sɛkt] *nm* insect.

insecticide [ɛ̃sɛktisid] *nm & adj* insecticide.

insectivore [ɛ̃sɛktivɔr] <> *adj* insectivorous <> *nm* insectivore.

insécurité [ɛ̃sekyrite] *nf* insecurity.

INSEE, Insee [inse] (*abr de* Institut national de la statistique et des études économiques) *nm national institute of statistics and information about the economy.*

insémination [ɛ̃seminasjɔ̃] *nf* insemination ; **~ artificielle** artificial insemination.

insensé, e [ɛ̃sɑ̃se] *adj* - **1.** [déraisonnable] insane - **2.** [incroyable, excentrique] extraordinary.

insensibiliser [3] [ɛ̃sɑ̃sibilize] *vt* to anaes-

thetize *Br*, to anesthetize *Am* ; **~ qqn (à)** *fig* to make sb insensitive (to).

insensibilité [ɛ̃sɑ̃sibilite] *nf* : **~ (à)** insensitivity (to).

insensible [ɛ̃sɑ̃sibl] *adj* - **1.** [gén] : **~ (à)** insensitive (to) - **2.** [imperceptible] imperceptible.

insensiblement [ɛ̃sɑ̃sibləmɑ̃] *adv* imperceptibly.

inséparable [ɛ̃separabl] *adj* : **~ (de)** inseparable (from).

➤ **inséparables** *nmpl* [perruches] lovebirds.

insérer [18] [ɛ̃sere] *vt* to insert ; **~ une annonce dans un journal** to put an advertisement in a newspaper.

➤ **s'insérer** *vp* - **1.** [s'intégrer] : **s'~ dans** to fit into - **2.** [s'attacher] to be attached.

INSERM, Inserm [inserm] (*abr de* Institut national de la santé et de la recherche médicale) *nm national institute for medical research.*

insertion [ɛ̃sɛrsjɔ̃] *nf* - **1.** [d'objet, de texte] insertion - **2.** [de personne] integration.

insidieux, euse [ɛ̃sidjø, øz] *adj* insidious.

insigne [ɛ̃siɲ] <> *nm* badge <> *adj* - **1.** *littéraire* [honneur] distinguished - **2.** *hum* [maladresse] remarkable.

insignifiant, e [ɛ̃siɲifjɑ̃, ɑ̃t] *adj* insignificant.

insinuant, e [ɛ̃sinɥɑ̃, ɑ̃t] *adj* ingratiating.

insinuation [ɛ̃sinɥasjɔ̃] *nf* insinuation, innuendo.

insinuer [7] [ɛ̃sinɥe] *vt* to insinuate, to imply.

➤ **s'insinuer** *vp* : **s'~ dans** [eau, humidité, odeur] to seep into ; *fig* [personne] to insinuate o.s. into.

insipide [ɛ̃sipid] *adj* [aliment] insipid, tasteless ; *fig* insipid.

insistance [ɛ̃sistɑ̃s] *nf* insistence ; **avec ~** insistently.

insistant, e [ɛ̃sistɑ̃, ɑ̃t] *adj* insistent.

insister [3] [ɛ̃siste] *vi* to insist ; **~ sur** to insist on ; **~ pour faire qqch** to insist on doing sthg.

insolation [ɛ̃sɔlasjɔ̃] *nf* - **1.** [malaise] sunstroke (U) - **2.** [ensoleillement] sunshine.

insolence [ɛ̃sɔlɑ̃s] *nf* insolence (U).

insolent, e [ɛ̃sɔlɑ̃, ɑ̃t] <> *adj* - **1.** [personne, acte] insolent - **2.** [joie, succès] unashamed, blatant <> *nm, f* insolent person.

insolite [ɛ̃sɔlit] *adj* unusual.

insoluble [ɛ̃sɔlybl] *adj* insoluble *Br*, insolvable *Am*.

insolvable [ɛ̃sɔlvabl] <> *adj* insolvent <> *nmf* bankrupt.

insomniaque [ɛ̃sɔmnjak] *nmf* & *adj* insomniac.

insomnie [ɛ̃sɔmni] *nf* insomnia *(U)* ; **avoir des ~s** to suffer from insomnia.

insondable [ɛ̃sɔ̃dabl] *adj* [gouffre, mystère] unfathomable ; [bêtise] abysmal.

insonore [ɛ̃sɔnɔr] *adj* soundproof.

insonorisation [ɛ̃sɔnɔrizasjɔ̃] *nf* soundproofing.

insonoriser [3] [ɛ̃sɔnɔrize] *vt* to soundproof.

insouciance [ɛ̃susjɑ̃s] *nf* **- 1.** [inconscience] : **~ (de)** lack of concern (about) **- 2.** [légèreté] carefree attitude.

insouciant, e [ɛ̃susjɑ̃, ɑ̃t] *adj* **- 1.** [sans-souci] carefree **- 2.** [inconscient] : **~ (de)** unconcerned (about).

insoumis, e [ɛ̃sumi, iz] *adj* **- 1.** [caractère] rebellious **- 2.** [peuple] unsubjugated **- 3.** [soldat] deserting.
➡ insoumis *nm* deserter.

insoumission [ɛ̃sumisjɔ̃] *nf* **- 1.** [caractère rebelle] rebelliousness **- 2.** MIL desertion.

insoupçonné, e [ɛ̃supsɔne] *adj* unsuspected.

insoutenable [ɛ̃sutnabl] *adj* **- 1.** [rythme] unsustainable **- 2.** [scène, violence] unbearable **- 3.** [théorie] untenable.

inspecter [4] [ɛ̃spɛkte] *vt* to inspect.

inspecteur, trice [ɛ̃spɛktœr, tris] *nm, f* inspector ; **~ des finances** ≃ tax inspector *Br*, ≃ Internal Revenue Service agent *Am* ; **~ de police** police inspector.

inspection [ɛ̃spɛksjɔ̃] *nf* **- 1.** [contrôle] inspection ; **faire l'~ de qqch** to inspect sthg **- 2.** [fonction] inspectorate ; **~ générale des Finances** ≃ Inland Revenue *Br*, ≃ Internal Revenue Service *Am*.

inspiration [ɛ̃spirasjɔ̃] *nf* **- 1.** [gén] inspiration ; [idée] bright idea, brainwave ; **avoir de l'~** to be inspired ; **avoir une bonne/ mauvaise ~** to have a good/bad idea **- 2.** [d'air] breathing in.

inspiré, e [ɛ̃spire] *adj* inspired ; **être bien ~ de faire qqch** be well-advised to do sthg.

inspirer [3] [ɛ̃spire] *vt* **- 1.** [gén] to inspire ; **~ qqch à qqn** to inspire sb with sthg **- 2.** [air] to breathe in, to inhale.
➡ s'inspirer *vp* [prendre modèle sur] : **s'~ de qqn/ qqch** to be inspired by sb/sthg.

instabilité [ɛ̃stabilite] *nf* **- 1.** [gén] instability **- 2.** [du temps] unsettled nature.

instable [ɛ̃stabl] ◇ *adj* **- 1.** [gén] unstable **- 2.** [vie, temps] unsettled ◇ *nmf* unstable person.

installateur, trice [ɛ̃stalatœr, tris] *nm, f* fitter.

installation [ɛ̃stalasjɔ̃] *nf* **- 1.** [de gaz, eau, électricité] installation **- 2.** [de personne - comme médecin, artisan] setting up ; [- dans appartement] settling in **- 3.** [d'appartement] fitting out **- 4.** [de rideaux, étagères] putting up ; [de meubles] putting in **- 5.** *(gén pl)* [équipement] installations *(pl)*, fittings *(pl)* ; [usine] plant *(U)* ; [de loisirs] facilities *(pl)* ; **~ électrique** wiring ; **~s sanitaires** plumbing *(U)*.

installer [3] [ɛ̃stale] *vt* **- 1.** [gaz, eau, électricité] to install *Br*, to instal *Am*, to put in **- 2.** [appartement] to fit out **- 3.** [rideaux, étagères] to put up ; [meubles] to put in **- 4.** [personne] : **~ qqn** to get sb settled, to install *Br ou* instal *Am* sb.
➡ s'installer *vp* **- 1.** [comme médecin, artisan etc] to set (o.s.) up **- 2.** [emménager] to settle in ; **s'~ chez qqn** to move in with sb **- 3.** [dans un fauteuil] to settle down **- 4.** *fig* [maladie, routine] to set in.

instamment [ɛ̃stamɑ̃] *adv* insistently.

instance [ɛ̃stɑ̃s] *nf* **- 1.** [autorité] authority **- 2.** JUR proceedings *(pl)* **- 3.** [insistance] entreaties *(pl)* ; **sur les ~s de** on the insistence of.
➡ en instance *loc adj* pending.
➡ en instance de *loc adv* on the point of ; **en ~ de divorce** waiting for a divorce.

instant [ɛ̃stɑ̃] *nm* instant ; **à l'~** [il y a peu de temps] a moment ago ; [immédiatement] this minute ; **à l'~ où** (just) as ; **à tout ~** [en permanence] at all times ; [d'un moment à l'autre] at any moment ; **pour l'~** for the moment ; **dans un ~** in a moment *ou* minute ; **dès l'~ où** from the moment (when) ; **un ~!** one moment! ; **en un ~** in a flash *ou* an instant ; **ne pas avoir un ~ de répit** not to have a moment's respite.

instantané, e [ɛ̃stɑ̃tane] *adj* **- 1.** [immédiat] instantaneous **- 2.** [soluble] instant.
➡ instantané *nm* snapshot.

instantanément [ɛ̃stɑ̃tanemɑ̃] *adv* instantaneously, at once.

instar [ɛ̃star] **➡ à l'instar de** *loc prép* following the example of.

instaurer [3] [ɛ̃stɔre] *vt* [instituer] to establish ; *fig* [peur, confiance] to instil *Br*, to instill *Am*.

instigateur, trice [ɛ̃stigatœr, tris] *nm, f* instigator.

instigation [ɛ̃stigasjɔ̃] *nf* instigation.
➡ à l'instigation de, sur l'instigation de *loc prép* at the instigation of.

instiller [3] [ɛ̃stile] *vt* **- 1.** [substance] to drip **- 2.** [sentiment] to instil *Br*, to instill *Am*.

instinct [ɛ̃stɛ̃] *nm* instinct ; **d'~** instinctively ; **~ de conservation** instinct for self-preservation ; **~ grégaire** herd instinct ; **~ maternel** maternal instinct.

instinctif, ive [ɛ̃stɛktif, iv] ◇ *adj* instinctive ◇ *nm, f* instinctive person.

instinctivement [ɛ̃stɛktivmɑ̃] *adv* instinctively.

instituer [7] [ɛ̃stitɥe] *vt* - **1.** [pratique] to institute - **2.** JUR [personne] to appoint.
◆ **s'instituer** *vp* to be set up *ou* established.

institut [ɛ̃stity] *nm* - **1.** [gén] institute ; **l'Institut (de France)** the Institut de France ; **~ médico-légal** mortuary ; **l'~ Pasteur** *important medical research centre* - **2.** [de soins] : **~ de beauté** beauty salon ; **~ dentaire** ≃ dental hospital.

INSTITUT

L'INSTITUT DE FRANCE
'L'Institut', as it is commonly known, is the learned society which includes the five 'Académies' (the 'Académie française' being one of them). Its headquarters are in the building of the same name on the banks of the Seine in Paris.
L'INSTITUT PASTEUR
This is a major research and teaching establishment specializing in microbiology and bacteriology. Its headquarters are in Paris but it has branches all over the world.

instituteur, trice [ɛ̃stitytœr, tris] *nm, f* primary school teacher *Br*, grade school teacher *Am*.

institution [ɛ̃stitysjɔ̃] *nf* - **1.** [gén] institution - **2.** [école privée] private school - **3.** JUR nomination.
◆ **institutions** *nfpl* POLIT institutions.

institutionnaliser [3] [ɛ̃stitysjɔnalize] *vt* to institutionalize.
◆ **s'institutionnaliser** *vp* to become institutionalized.

instructeur [ɛ̃stryktœr] ◇ *nm* instructor ◇ *adj* MIL : **sergent ~** drill sergeant.

instructif, ive [ɛ̃stryktif, iv] *adj* instructive, educational.

instruction [ɛ̃stryksjɔ̃] *nf* - **1.** [enseignement, savoir] education ; **avoir de l'~** to be educated ; **~ civique** civics (U) ; **~ publique** state education - **2.** [formation] training - **3.** [directive] order - **4.** JUR (pre-trial) investigation.
◆ **instructions** *nfpl* instructions.

instruire [98] [ɛ̃strɥir] *vt* - **1.** [éduquer] to teach, to instruct - **2.** *sout* [informer] to inform - **3.** JUR [affaire] to investigate ; **~ contre qqn** to investigate sb.
◆ **s'instruire** *vp* - **1.** [se former] to learn

- **2.** *sout* [s'informer] : **s'~ de qqch auprès de qqn** to find out about sthg from sb.

instruisais, instruisions *etc* ▷ **instruire.**

instruit, e [ɛ̃strɥi, it] ◇ *pp* ▷ **instruire** ◇ *adj* educated.

instrument [ɛ̃strymɑ̃] *nm* instrument ; **~ à cordes/percussion/vent** stringed/percussion/wind instrument ; **~ contondant** blunt instrument ; **~ de musique** musical instrument ; **~ de travail** tool.

instrumental, e, aux [ɛ̃strymɑ̃tal, o] *adj* instrumental.
◆ **instrumental** *nm* instrumental.

instrumentation [ɛ̃strymɑ̃tasjɔ̃] *nf* instrumentation.

instrumentiste [ɛ̃strymɑ̃tist] *nmf* instrumentalist.

insu [ɛ̃sy] ◆ **à l'insu de** *loc prép* : **à l'~ de qqn** without sb knowing ; **ils ont tout organisé à mon ~** they organized it all without my knowing.

insubmersible [ɛ̃sybmɛrsibl] *adj* unsinkable.

insubordination [ɛ̃sybɔrdinasjɔ̃] *nf* insubordination.

insubordonné, e [ɛ̃sybɔrdɔne] *adj* insubordinate.

insuccès [ɛ̃syksɛ] *nm* failure.

insuffisamment [ɛ̃syfizamɑ̃] *adv* insufficiently, inadequately.

insuffisance [ɛ̃syfizɑ̃s] *nf* - **1.** [manque] insufficiency - **2.** MÉD deficiency ; **~ cardiaque** cardiac insufficiency.
◆ **insuffisances** *nfpl* [faiblesses] shortcomings.

insuffisant, e [ɛ̃syfizɑ̃, ɑ̃t] *adj* - **1.** [en quantité] insufficient - **2.** [en qualité] inadequate, unsatisfactory.

insuffler [3] [ɛ̃syfle] *vt* - **1.** [air] to blow - **2.** *fig* [sentiment] : **~ qqch à qqn** to inspire sb with sthg.

insulaire [ɛ̃sylɛr] ◇ *nmf* islander ◇ *adj* - **1.** GÉOGR island (avant n) - **2.** *fig* [attitude] insular.

insularité [ɛ̃sylarite] *nf* insularity.

insuline [ɛ̃sylin] *nf* insulin.

insultant, e [ɛ̃syltɑ̃, ɑ̃t] *adj* insulting.

insulte [ɛ̃sylt] *nf* insult.

insulter [3] [ɛ̃sylte] *vt* to insult.
◆ **s'insulter** *vp* to insult each other.

insupportable [ɛ̃sypɔrtabl] *adj* unbearable.

insurgé, e [ɛ̃syrʒe] *adj & nm, f* insurgent, rebel.

insurger [17] [ɛ̃syrʒe] ◆ **s'insurger** *vp* to

rebel, to revolt ; **s'~ contre qqn** to rebel ou rise up against sb ; **s'~ contre qqch** to protest against sthg.

insurmontable [ɛsyrmɔ̃tabl] adj [difficulté] insurmountable ; [dégoût] uncontrollable.

insurrection [ɛsyrɛksjɔ̃] nf insurrection.

insurrectionnel, elle [ɛsyrɛksjɔnɛl] adj insurrectionary.

intact, e [ɛtakt] adj intact.

intangible [ɛtɑ̃ʒibl] adj - **1.** littéraire [impalpable] intangible - **2.** [sacré] inviolable.

intarissable [ɛtarisabl] adj inexhaustible ; il est ~ he could go on talking for ever.

intégral, e, aux [ɛtegral, o] adj - **1.** [paiement] in full ; [texte] unabridged, complete ; **bronzage** ~ all-over tan - **2.** MATHS : **calcul** ~ integral calculus.

➣ **intégrale** nf - **1.** MUS complete works *(pl)* - **2.** MATHS integral.

intégralement [ɛtegralmɑ̃] adv fully, in full.

intégralité [ɛtegralite] nf whole ; **dans son** ~ in full.

intégrant, e [ɛtegrɑ̃, ɑ̃t] ➣ **parti.**

intégration [ɛtegrasjɔ̃] nf integration.

intègre [ɛtegr] adj honest, of integrity.

intégré, e [ɛtegre] adj - **1.** [logiciel] integrated - **2.** [élément] built-in.

intégrer [18] [ɛtegre] vt [assimiler] : ~ **(à** ou **dans)** to integrate (into).

➣ **s'intégrer** vp - **1.** [s'incorporer] : **s'~ dans** ou **à** to fit into - **2.** [s'adapter] to integrate.

intégrisme [ɛtegrism] nm fundamentalism.

intégriste [ɛtegrist] nmf & adj fundamentalist.

intégrité [ɛtegrite] nf - **1.** [totalité] entirety - **2.** [honnêteté] integrity.

intellect [ɛtelɛkt] nm intellect.

intellectualisme [ɛtelɛktɥalism] nm intellectualism.

intellectuel, elle [ɛtelɛktɥɛl] adj & nm, f intellectual.

intellectuellement [ɛtelɛktɥɛlmɑ̃] adv intellectually.

intelligemment [ɛteliʒamɑ̃] adv intelligently.

intelligence [ɛteliʒɑ̃s] nf - **1.** [facultés mentales] intelligence ; ~ **artificielle** artificial intelligence - **2.** [personne] brain - **3.** [compréhension, complicité] understanding ; **agir d'~ avec qqn** to act in complicity with sb.

➣ **intelligences** nfpl secret contacts.

intelligent, e [ɛteliʒɑ̃, ɑ̃t] adj intelligent.

intelligentsia [ɛteliɡɛnsja] nf intelligentsia.

intelligible [ɛteliʒibl] adj - **1.** [voix] clear - **2.** [concept, texte] intelligible.

intello [ɛtelo] adj inv & nmf péj highbrow.

intempérance [ɛtɑ̃perɑ̃s] nf - **1.** [abus] excessiveness - **2.** [excès de plaisirs] overindulgence.

intempéries [ɛtɑ̃peri] nfpl bad weather *(U)*.

intempestif, ive [ɛtɑ̃pɛstif, iv] adj untimely.

intemporel, elle [ɛtɑ̃pɔrɛl] adj - **1.** [sans durée] timeless - **2.** littéraire [immatériel] immaterial.

intenable [ɛtənabl] adj - **1.** [chaleur, personne] unbearable - **2.** [position] untenable, indefensible.

intendance [ɛtɑ̃dɑ̃s] nf - **1.** MIL commissariat ; SCOL & UNIV bursar's office - **2.** fig [questions matérielles] housekeeping.

intendant, e [ɛtɑ̃dɑ̃, ɑ̃t] nm, f - **1.** SCOL & UNIV bursar - **2.** [de manoir] steward.

➣ **intendant** nm MIL quartermaster.

intense [ɛtɑ̃s] adj - **1.** [gén] intense - **2.** [circulation] dense.

intensément [ɛtɑ̃semɑ̃] adv intensely.

intensif, ive [ɛtɑ̃sif, iv] adj intensive.

intensification [ɛtɑ̃sifikasjɔ̃] nf intensification.

intensifier [9] [ɛtɑ̃sifje] vt to intensify.

➣ **s'intensifier** vp to intensify.

intensité [ɛtɑ̃site] nf intensity.

intenter [3] [ɛtɑ̃te] vt JUR : ~ **qqch contre** ou **à qqn** to bring sthg against sb.

intention [ɛtɑ̃sjɔ̃] nf intention ; **avoir l'~ de faire qqch** to intend to do sthg ; ~ **d'achat** COMM purchasing intention ; **agir dans une bonne** ~ to act with good intentions.

➣ **à l'intention de** loc prép for.

intentionné, e [ɛtɑ̃sjɔne] adj : **bien** ~ wellmeaning ; **mal** ~ ill-disposed.

intentionnel, elle [ɛtɑ̃sjɔnɛl] adj intentional.

intentionnellement [ɛtɑ̃sjɔnɛlmɑ̃] adv intentionally.

inter [ɛter] nm - **1.** vieilli = **interurbain** - **2.** SPORT : ~ **gauche/droit** inside left/right.

interactif, ive [ɛteraktif, iv] adj interactive.

interaction [ɛteraksjɔ̃] nf interaction.

interbancaire [ɛterbɑ̃ker] adj interbank *(avant n)*.

intercalaire [ɛterkaler] ◇ nm insert ◇ adj : **feuillet** ~ insert ; **jour** ~ extra day in a leap year.

intercaler [3] [ɛterkale] vt : ~ **qqch dans qqch** [feuillet, citation] to insert sthg in sthg ; [dans le temps] to fit sthg into sthg.

◆ **s'intercaler** *vp* : **s'~ entre** to come between.

intercéder [18] [ɛ̃tɛrsede] *vi* : **~ pour** *ou* **en faveur de qqn auprès de qqn** to intercede with sb on behalf of sb.

intercepter [4] [ɛ̃tɛrsɛpte] *vt* - **1.** [lettre, ballon] to intercept - **2.** [chaleur] to block.

intercession [ɛ̃tɛrsesjɔ̃] *nf* intercession.

interchangeable [ɛ̃tɛrʃɑ̃ʒabl] *adj* interchangeable.

interclasse [ɛ̃tɛrklas] *nm* break.

intercommunal, e, aux [ɛ̃tɛrkɔmynal, o] *adj* intermunicipal.

intercontinental, e, aux [ɛ̃tɛrkɔ̃tinɑ̃tal, o] *adj* intercontinental.

interdépartemental, e, aux [ɛ̃tɛrdepartəmɑ̃tal, o] *adj* interdepartmental.

interdépendance [ɛ̃tɛrdepɑ̃dɑ̃s] *nf* interdependence.

interdépendant, e [ɛ̃tɛrdepɑ̃dɑ̃, ɑ̃t] *adj* interdependent.

interdiction [ɛ̃tɛrdiksjɔ̃] *nf* - **1.** [défense] : '**~ de stationner**' 'strictly no parking' - **2.** [prohibition, suspension] : **~ (de)** ban (on), banning (of) ; **enfreindre/lever une ~** to break/lift a ban ; **~ de séjour** *order banning released prisoner from living in certain areas.*

interdire [103] [ɛ̃tɛrdir] *vt* - **1.** [prohiber] : **~ qqch à qqn** to forbid sb sthg ; **~ à qqn de faire qqch** to forbid sb to do sthg - **2.** [empêcher] to prevent ; **~ à qqn de faire qqch** to prevent sb from doing sthg - **3.** [d'exercer] to ban - **4.** [bloquer] to block.

◆ **s'interdire** *vp* : **s'~ qqch/de faire qqch** to refrain from sthg/from doing sthg.

interdisais, interdisions *etc* ▷ **interdire**.

interdisciplinaire [ɛ̃tɛrdisipliner] *adj* interdisciplinary.

interdise, interdises *etc* ▷ **interdire**.

interdit, e [ɛ̃tɛrdi, it] ◇ *pp* ▷ **interdire** ◇ *adj* - **1.** [défendu] forbidden ; '**film ~ aux moins de 18 ans**' ≃ '(18)' ; **il est ~ de fumer** you're not allowed to smoke - **2.** [ébahi] : **rester ~** to be stunned - **3.** [privé] : **être ~ de chéquier** to have had one's chequebook *Br ou* checkbook *Am* facilities withdrawn ; **~ de séjour** banned from entering the country.

◆ **interdit** *nm* : **jeter l'~ sur qqn** to bar sb ; **lever un ~** to lift a ban.

intéressant, e [ɛ̃teresɑ̃, ɑ̃t] ◇ *adj* - **1.** [captivant] interesting - **2.** [avantageux] advantageous, good ◇ *nm, f* : **faire l'~** *péj* to show off.

intéressé, e [ɛ̃terese] ◇ *adj* [concerné] concerned, involved ; *péj* [motivé] self-interested ◇ *nm, f* person concerned ; **le principal ~** the main person concerned.

intéressement [ɛ̃teresmɑ̃] *nm* profit-sharing (scheme).

intéresser [4] [ɛ̃terese] *vt* - **1.** [captiver] to interest ; **~ qqn à qqch** to interest sb in sthg - **2.** *COMM* [faire participer] : **~ les employés (aux bénéfices)** to give one's employees a share in the profits ; **~ qqn dans son commerce** to give sb a financial interest in one's business - **3.** [concerner] to concern.

◆ **s'intéresser** *vp* : **s'~ à qqn/qqch** to take an interest in sb/sthg, to be interested in sb/sthg.

intérêt [ɛ̃terɛ] *nm* - **1.** [gén] interest ; **~ pour** interest in ; **agir par ~** to act in one's own interest ; **avoir ~ à faire qqch** to be well advised to do sthg ; **dans l'~ général** in everyone's interest - **2.** [importance] significance - **3.** [avantage] advantage.

◆ **intérêts** *nmpl* - **1.** *FIN* interest *(sg)* ; **~s moratoires** interest on overdue payment - **2.** *COMM* : **avoir des ~s dans** to have a stake in.

interface [ɛ̃tɛrfas] *nf* *INFORM* interface ; **~ graphique** graphic interface.

interférence [ɛ̃tɛrferɑ̃s] *nf* - **1.** *PHYS & POLIT* interference - **2.** *fig* [conjonction] convergence.

interférer [18] [ɛ̃tɛrfere] *vi* - **1.** *PHYS* to interfere - **2.** *fig* [se rencontrer] to converge - **3.** *fig* [s'immiscer] : **~ dans qqch** to interfere in sthg.

intergalactique [ɛ̃tɛrgalaktik] *adj* intergalactic.

intérieur, e [ɛ̃terjœr] *adj* - **1.** [gén] inner - **2.** [de pays] domestic.

◆ **intérieur** *nm* - **1.** [gén] inside ; **de l'~** from the inside ; **à l'~ de soi-même** *fig & littéraire* inwardly ; **à l'~ (de qqch)** inside (sthg) - **2.** [de pays] interior.

intérieurement [ɛ̃terjœrmɑ̃] *adv* inwardly.

intérim [ɛ̃terim] *nm* - **1.** [période] interim period ; **assurer l'~ (de qqn)** to deputize (for sb) ; **par ~** acting - **2.** [travail temporaire] temporary *ou* casual work ; [dans un bureau] temping ; **faire de l'~**, **travailler en ~** to temp.

intérimaire [ɛ̃terimer] ◇ *adj* - **1.** [ministre, directeur] acting *(avant n)* - **2.** [employé, fonctions] temporary ◇ *nmf* - **1.** [ministre] acting minister - **2.** [employé] temp.

intérioriser [3] [ɛ̃terjɔrize] *vt* to internalize.

interjection [ɛ̃tɛrʒɛksjɔ̃] *nf* - **1.** *LING* interjection - **2.** *JUR* lodging of an appeal.

interjeter [27] [ɛ̃tɛrʒəte] *vt* *JUR* : **~ appel** to lodge an appeal.

interligne [ɛ̃tɛrliɲ] ◇ *nm* (line) spacing ;

simple/double ~ single/double spacing ⟷ *nf TYPO* lead, leading.

interlocuteur, trice [ɛ̃tɛrlɔkytœr, tris] *nm, f* - **1.** [dans conversation] speaker ; **mon** ~ the person to whom I am/was speaking - **2.** [dans négociation] negotiator.

interlope [ɛ̃tɛrlɔp] *adj* - **1.** [illégal] illegal - **2.** *fig* [louche] suspect, shady.

interloquer [3] [ɛ̃tɛrlɔke] *vt* to disconcert.

interlude [ɛ̃tɛrlyd] *nm* interlude.

intermède [ɛ̃tɛrmɛd] *nm* interlude.

intermédiaire [ɛ̃tɛrmedjɛr] ⟷ *nm* intermediary, go-between ; **sans** ~ without an intermediary ; **par l'** ~ **de qqn/qqch** through sb/sthg ⟷ *adj* intermediate.

interminable [ɛ̃tɛrminabl] *adj* neverending, interminable.

interministériel, elle [ɛ̃tɛrministerjɛl] *adj* interdepartmental.

intermittence [ɛ̃tɛrmitɑ̃s] *nf* [discontinuité] : **par** ~ intermittently, off and on.

intermittent, e [ɛ̃tɛrmitɑ̃, ɑ̃t] *adj* intermittent.

internat [ɛ̃tɛrna] *nm* - **1.** [SCOL - établissement] boarding school ; [- système] boarding - **2.** [MÉD & UNIV - concours] entrance examination ; [- période de stage] period spent as a houseman *Br ou* an intern *Am*.

international, e, aux [ɛ̃tɛrnasjɔnal, o] ⟷ *adj* international ⟷ *nm, f* SPORT international.

➡ **Internationale** *nf* - **1.** [association] International - **2.** [hymne] Internationale.

internationalisation [ɛ̃tɛrnasjɔnalizasjɔ̃] *nf* internationalization.

internaute [ɛ̃tɛrnot] *nmf* INFORM (net) surfer, cybersurfer, cybernaut.

interne [ɛ̃tɛrn] ⟷ *nmf* - **1.** [élève] boarder - **2.** MÉD & UNIV houseman *Br*, intern *Am* ⟷ *adj* - **1.** ANAT internal ; [oreille] inner - **2.** [du pays] domestic.

interné, e [ɛ̃tɛrne] *nm, f* - **1.** [prisonnier] internee - **2.** MÉD inmate *(of psychiatric hospital)*.

internement [ɛ̃tɛrnəmɑ̃] *nm* - **1.** POLIT internment - **2.** MÉD confinement *(to psychiatric hospital)*.

interner [3] [ɛ̃tɛrne] *vt* - **1.** MÉD to commit *(to psychiatric hospital)* - **2.** POLIT to intern.

Internet, internet [ɛ̃tɛrnɛt] *nm* : **(l')** ~ (the) internet, (the) Internet.

interpeller [26] [ɛ̃tɛrpəle] *vt* - **1.** [apostropher] to call *ou* shout out to - **2.** [interroger] to take in for questioning.

➡ **s'interpeller** *vp* to exchange insults.

Interphone® [ɛ̃tɛrfɔn] *nm* intercom ; [d'un immeuble] entry phone.

interplanétaire [ɛ̃tɛrplanetɛr] *adj* interplanetary.

interpoler [3] [ɛ̃tɛrpɔle] *vt* to interpolate.

interposer [3] [ɛ̃tɛrpoze] *vt* to interpose.

➡ **s'interposer** *vp* : **s'** ~ **dans qqch** to intervene in sthg ; **s'** ~ **entre qqn et qqn** to intervene *ou* come between sb and sb.

interprétariat [ɛ̃tɛrpretarja] *nm* interpreting.

interprétation [ɛ̃tɛrpretasjɔ̃] *nf* interpretation.

interprète [ɛ̃tɛrprɛt] *nmf* - **1.** [gén] interpreter - **2.** [porte-parole] spokesperson - **3.** CIN, MUS & THÉÂTRE performer.

interpréter [18] [ɛ̃tɛrprete] *vt* to interpret.

interprofessionnel, elle [ɛ̃tɛrprɔfɛsjɔnɛl] *adj* interprofessional.

interrogateur, trice [ɛ̃tɛrɔgatœr, tris] ⟷ *adj* inquiring *(avant n)* ⟷ *nm, f* SCOL & UNIV oral examiner.

interrogatif, ive [ɛ̃tɛrɔgatif, iv] *adj* - **1.** GRAM interrogative - **2.** [air, ton] inquiring *(avant n)*.

➡ **interrogatif** *nm* GRAM interrogative.

interrogation [ɛ̃tɛrɔgasjɔ̃] *nf* - **1.** [de prisonnier] interrogation ; [de témoin] questioning - **2.** [question] question ; ~ **directe/indirecte** GRAM direct/indirect question - **3.** SCOL test.

interrogatoire [ɛ̃tɛrɔgatwar] *nm* - **1.** [de police, juge] questioning - **2.** [procès-verbal] statement.

interrogeable [ɛ̃tɛrɔʒabl] *adj* : **répondeur** ~ **à distance** answerphone with remote playback facility.

interroger [17] [ɛ̃tɛrɔʒe] *vt* - **1.** [questionner] to question ; [accusé, base de données] to interrogate ; ~ **qqn (sur qqch)** to question sb (about sthg) - **2.** [faits, conscience] to examine.

➡ **s'interroger** *vp* : **s'** ~ **sur** to wonder about.

interrompre [78] [ɛ̃tɛrɔ̃pr] *vt* to interrupt.

➡ **s'interrompre** *vp* to stop.

interrompu, e [ɛ̃tɛrɔ̃py] *pp* ➡ **interrompre**.

interrupteur [ɛ̃tɛryptœr] *nm* switch ; ~ **à bascule** toggle switch.

interruption [ɛ̃tɛrypsjɔ̃] *nf* - **1.** [arrêt] break ; **sans** ~ without a break - **2.** [action] interruption.

intersection [ɛ̃tɛrsɛksjɔ̃] *nf* intersection.

intersidéral, e, aux [ɛ̃tɛrsideral, o] *adj* interstellar.

interstice [ɛ̃tɛrstis] *nm* chink, crack.

intersyndical, e, aux [ɛ̃tɛrsɛ̃dikal, o] *adj* interunion.

intertitre [ɛ̃tɛrtitr] *nm* - **1.** PRESSE subheading - **2.** CIN intertitle.

interurbain, e [ɛ̃tɛryrbɛ̃, ɛn] *adj* long-distance.
◆ **interurbain** *nm* : l'~ the long-distance telephone service.

intervalle [ɛ̃tɛrval] *nm* - **1.** [spatial] space, gap - **2.** [temporel] interval, period (of time) ; **à 6 jours d'~** after 6 days ; **dans l'~** in the meantime - **3.** MUS interval.

intervenant, e [ɛ̃tɛrvənɑ̃, ɑ̃t] *nm, f* - **1.** [orateur] speaker - **2.** JUR intervening party.

intervenir [40] [ɛ̃tɛrvənir] *vi* - **1.** [personne] to intervene ; ~ **auprès de qqn** to intervene with sb ; ~ **dans qqch** to intervene in sthg ; **faire** ~ **qqn** to bring *ou* call in sb - **2.** [événement] to take place.

intervention [ɛ̃tɛrvɑ̃sjɔ̃] *nf* - **1.** [gén] intervention - **2.** MÉD operation ; **subir une** ~ **chirurgicale** to have an operation, to have surgery - **3.** [discours] speech.

interventionniste [ɛ̃tɛrvɑ̃sjɔnist] *nmf* & *adj* interventionist.

intervenu, e [ɛ̃tɛrvəny] *pp* ▷ **intervenir**.

intervertir [32] [ɛ̃tɛrvɛrtir] *vt* to reverse, to invert.

interviendrai, interviendras *etc* ▷ **intervenir**.

intervienne, interviennes *etc* ▷ **intervenir**.

interviens, intervient *etc* ▷ **intervenir**.

interview [ɛ̃tɛrvjul] *nf* interview ; **accorder une** ~ **à qqn** to give *ou* grant an interview to sb.

interviewer[1] [ɛ̃tɛrvjuve] *vt* to interview.

interviewer[2] [ɛ̃tɛrvjuvœr] *nm* interviewer.

intestat [ɛ̃tɛstal JUR ◇ *nmf person who dies intestate* ◇ *adj* intestate.

intestin, e [ɛ̃tɛstɛ̃, in] *adj sout* internal.

intestin [ɛ̃tɛstɛ̃] *nm* intestine ; ~ **grêle** small intestine ; **gros** ~ large intestine.

intestinal, e, aux [ɛ̃tɛstinal, o] *adj* intestinal.

intime [ɛ̃tim] ◇ *nmf* close friend ◇ *adj* [gén] intimate ; [vie, journal] private.

intimement [ɛ̃timmɑ̃] *adv* - **1.** [persuadé] firmly - **2.** [lié] intimately.

intimer [3] [ɛ̃time] *vt* - **1.** [enjoindre] : ~ **qqch à qqn** to notify sb of sthg - **2.** JUR to summon.

intimidant, e [ɛ̃timidɑ̃, ɑ̃t] *adj* intimidating.

intimidation [ɛ̃timidasjɔ̃] *nf* intimidation.

intimider [3] [ɛ̃timide] *vt* to intimidate.

intimiste [ɛ̃timist] *adj* ART & LITTÉRATURE intimist.

intimité [ɛ̃timite] *nf* - **1.** [secret] depths *(pl)* - **2.** [familiarité, confort] intimacy - **3.** [vie privée] privacy ; **dans l'~** amongst friends, in private ; **dans la plus stricte** ~ in complete privacy, in private.

intitulé [ɛ̃tityle] *nm* [titre] title ; [de paragraphe] heading.

intituler [3] [ɛ̃tityle] *vt* to call, to entitle.
◆ **s'intituler** *vp* - **1.** [ouvrage] to be called *ou* entitled - **2.** [personne] to call o.s.

intolérable [ɛ̃tɔlerabl] *adj* intolerable.

intolérance [ɛ̃tɔlerɑ̃s] *nf* - **1.** [religieuse, politique] intolerance - **2.** [de l'organisme] : ~ **à qqch** inability to tolerate sthg.

intolérant, e [ɛ̃tɔlerɑ̃, ɑ̃t] *adj* intolerant.

intonation [ɛ̃tɔnasjɔ̃] *nf* intonation.

intouchable [ɛ̃tuʃabl] *nmf* & *adj* untouchable.

intoxication [ɛ̃tɔksikasjɔ̃] *nf* - **1.** [empoisonnement] poisoning ; ~ **alimentaire** food poisoning - **2.** *fig* [propagande] brainwashing.

intoxiqué, e [ɛ̃tɔksike] ◇ *adj* : ~ **(de)** addicted (to) ◇ *nm, f* addict.

intoxiquer [3] [ɛ̃tɔksike] *vt* : ~ **qqn par** [empoisonner] to poison sb with ; *fig* to indoctrinate sb with.
◆ **s'intoxiquer** *vp* to poison o.s.

intraduisible [ɛ̃tradɥizibl] *adj* - **1.** [texte] untranslatable - **2.** [sentiment] inexpressible.

intraitable [ɛ̃trɛtabl] *adj* : ~ **(sur)** inflexible (about).

intranet [ɛ̃tranɛt] *nm* intranet, Intranet.

intransigeance [ɛ̃trɑ̃ziʒɑ̃s] *nf* intransigence.

intransigeant, e [ɛ̃trɑ̃ziʒɑ̃, ɑ̃t] *adj* intransigent.

intransitif, ive [ɛ̃trɑ̃zitif, iv] *adj* intransitive.

intransportable [ɛ̃trɑ̃spɔrtabl] *adj* : **il est** ~ he/it cannot be moved.

intraveineux, euse [ɛ̃travɛnø, øz] *adj* intravenous.

intrépide [ɛ̃trepid] *adj* bold, intrepid.

intrépidité [ɛ̃trepidite] *nf* boldness.

intrigant, e [ɛ̃trigɑ̃, ɑ̃t] ◇ *adj* scheming ◇ *nm, f* schemer.

intrigue [ɛ̃trig] *nf* - **1.** [liaison amoureuse] intrigue, affair - **2.** [manœuvre] intrigue - **3.** CIN, LITTÉRATURE & THÉÂTRE plot.

intriguer [3] [ɛ̃trige] ◇ *vt* to intrigue ◇ *vi* to scheme, to intrigue.

intrinsèque [ɛ̃trɛ̃sɛk] *adj* intrinsic.

introductif, ive [ɛ̃trɔdyktif, iv] *adj* JUR introductory.

introduction [ɛ̃trɔdyksjɔ̃] *nf* - **1.** [gén] : ~ **(à)** introduction (to) - **2.** [insertion] insertion.

introduire [98] [ɛ̃trɔdu̯ir] *vt* - **1.** [gén] to introduce - **2.** [faire entrer] to show in - **3.** [insérer] to insert - **4.** INFORM to input, to enter.

➤ **s'introduire** *vp* - **1.** [pénétrer] to enter ; **s'~ dans une maison** [cambrioleur] to get into *ou* enter a house - **2.** [s'implanter] to be introduced.

introduisais, introduisions *etc* ➤ introduire.

introduit, e [ɛ̃trɔdu̯i, it] *pp* ➤ introduire.

intronisation [ɛ̃trɔnizasjɔ̃] *nf* RELIG enthronement ; *fig* establishment.

introspection [ɛ̃trɔspɛksjɔ̃] *nf* introspection.

introuvable [ɛ̃truvabl] *adj* nowhere *Br ou* no-place *Am* to be found.

introverti, e [ɛ̃trɔvɛrti] ◇ *adj* introverted ◇ *nm, f* introvert.

intrus, e [ɛ̃try, yz] ◇ *adj* intrusive ◇ *nm, f* intruder.

intrusion [ɛ̃tryzjɔ̃] *nf* - **1.** [gén & GÉOL] intrusion - **2.** [ingérence] interference.

intuitif, ive [ɛ̃tu̯itif, iv] ◇ *adj* intuitive ◇ *nm, f* intuitive person.

intuition [ɛ̃tu̯isjɔ̃] *nf* intuition ; **avoir de l'~** to be intuitive, to have intuition ; **avoir l'~ de qqch** to have an intuition about sthg.

intuitivement [ɛ̃tu̯itivmal] *adv* intuitively.

inuit [inu̯it] *adj inv* Inuit.

➤ **Inuit** *nmf* Inuit.

inusable [inyzabl] *adj* hardwearing.

inusité, e [inyzite] *adj* unusual, uncommon.

inutile [inytil] *adj* [objet, personne] useless ; [effort, démarche] pointless ; **~ d'insister** it's pointless insisting.

inutilement [inytilmal] *adv* needlessly, unnecessarily.

inutilisable [inytilizabl] *adj* unusable.

inutilisé, e [inytilize] *adj* unused.

inutilité [inytilite] *nf* [de personne, d'objet] uselessness ; [de démarche, d'effort] pointlessness.

inv. (*abr de* **invariable**) inv.

invaincu, e [ɛ̃vɛ̃ky] *adj* - **1.** SPORT unbeaten - **2.** [peuple] unconquered.

invalide [ɛ̃valid] ◇ *nmf* disabled person ; **~ de guerre** disabled soldier ; **~ du travail** industrially disabled person ◇ *adj* disabled.

invalider [3] [ɛ̃valide] *vt* to invalidate.

invalidité [ɛ̃validite] *nf* - **1.** JUR invalidity - **2.** MÉD disability.

invariable [ɛ̃varjabl] *adj* - **1.** [immuable] unchanging - **2.** GRAM invariable.

invariablement [ɛ̃varjablǝmal] *adv* invariably.

invasion [ɛ̃vazjɔ̃] *nf* invasion.

invective [ɛ̃vɛktiv] *nf* invective, abuse.

invectiver [3] [ɛ̃vɛktive] *vt* to abuse.

➤ **s'invectiver** *vp* to hurl abuse at each other.

invendable [ɛ̃vãdabl] *adj* unsaleable, unsellable.

invendu, e [ɛ̃vãdy] *adj* unsold.

➤ **invendu** (*gén pl*) *nm* remainder.

inventaire [ɛ̃vãter] *nm* - **1.** [gén] inventory ; **faire l'~ de qqch** to make an inventory of sthg - **2.** [COMM - activité] stocktaking *Br*, inventory *Am* ; [- liste] list.

inventer [3] [ɛ̃vãte] *vt* to invent.

inventeur [ɛ̃vãtœr] *nm* - **1.** [de machine] inventor - **2.** JUR [de trésor] finder.

inventif, ive [ɛ̃vãtif, iv] *adj* inventive.

invention [ɛ̃vãsjɔ̃] *nf* - **1.** [découverte, mensonge] invention - **2.** [imagination] inventiveness.

inventorier [9] [ɛ̃vãtɔrje] *vt* to make an inventory of.

invérifiable [ɛ̃verifjabl] *adj* unverifiable.

inverse [ɛ̃vɛrs] ◇ *nm* opposite, reverse ; **à l'~ de** contrary to ◇ *adj* - **1.** [sens] opposite ; [ordre] reverse ; **en sens ~ (de)** in the opposite direction (to) - **2.** [rapport] inverse.

inversement [ɛ̃vɛrsǝmal] *adv* - **1.** MATHS inversely ; **~ proportionnel à** in inverse proportion to - **2.** [au contraire] on the other hand - **3.** [vice versa] vice versa.

inverser [3] [ɛ̃vɛrse] *vt* to reverse.

inversion [ɛ̃vɛrsjɔ̃] *nf* reversal.

invertébré, e [ɛ̃vɛrtebre] *adj* invertebrate.

➤ **invertébré** *nm* invertebrate.

investigation [ɛ̃vɛstigasjɔ̃] *nf* investigation.

investir [32] [ɛ̃vɛstir] *vt* to invest ; **~ qqn d'une fonction** to invest *ou* vest sb with an office.

investissement [ɛ̃vɛstismal] *nm* investment.

investisseur, euse [ɛ̃vɛstisœr, øz] *nm, f* investor ; **~ institutionnel** institutional investor.

investiture [ɛ̃vɛstityr] *nf* investiture.

invétéré, e [ɛ̃vetere] *adj péj* inveterate.

invincible [ɛ̃vɛ̃sibl] *adj* [gén] invincible ; [difficulté] insurmountable ; [charme] irresistible.

inviolabilité [ɛ̃vjɔlabilite] *nf* - **1.** JUR inviolability - **2.** [de parlementaire] immunity - **3.** [de coffre] impregnability.

inviolable [ɛ̃vjɔlabl] *adj* - **1.** *JUR* inviolable - **2.** [parlementaire] immune - **3.** [coffre] impregnable.

invisible [ɛ̃vizibl] *adj* invisible ; **rester** ~ [personne] to stay out of sight.

invitation [ɛ̃vitasjɔ̃] *nf* : ~ (à) invitation (to) ; **à** *ou* **sur l'~ de qqn** at sb's invitation ; **sur ~** by invitation ; **décliner une ~** to turn down an invitation.

invite [ɛ̃vit] *nf* invitation.

invité, e [ɛ̃vite] <> *adj* [hôte] invited ; [professeur, conférencier] guest *(avant n)* <> *nm, f* guest.

inviter [3] [ɛ̃vite] *vt* to invite ; ~ **qqn à faire qqch** to invite sb to do sthg ; *fig* [suj : chose] to be an invitation to sb to do sthg ; **le beau temps invite à la promenade** this fine weather puts one in the mood for a walk ; **je vous invite!** it's my treat!

in vitro [invitro] > **fécondation**.

invivable [ɛ̃vivabl] *adj* unbearable.

invocation [ɛ̃vɔkasjɔ̃] *nf* invocation ; ~ **à** call for.

involontaire [ɛ̃vɔlɔ̃tɛr] *adj* - **1.** [acte] involuntary - **2.** [personne] unwilling.

involontairement [ɛ̃vɔlɔ̃tɛrmɑ̃] *adv* involuntarily, unintentionally.

invoquer [3] [ɛ̃vɔke] *vt* - **1.** [alléguer] to put forward - **2.** [citer, appeler à l'aide] to invoke ; [paix] to call for.

invraisemblable [ɛ̃vrɛsɑ̃blabl] *adj* - **1.** [incroyable] unlikely, improbable - **2.** [extravagant] incredible.

invraisemblance [ɛ̃vrɛsɑ̃blɑ̃s] *nf* improbability.

invulnérable [ɛ̃vylnerabl] *adj* invulnerable.

iode [jɔd] *nm* iodine.

iodé, e [jɔde] *adj* containing iodine.

ion [jɔ̃] *nm* ion.

IPC (*abr de* **indice des prix à la consommation**) *nm* CPI.

Ipsos [ipsos] *n* French market research institute.

IR (*abr de* **infra-rouge**) *adj* IR.

IRA [ira] (*abr de* **Irish Republican Army**) *nf* IRA.

irai, iras *etc* > **aller**.

Irak, Iraq [irak] *nm* : **l'~** Iraq.

irakien, enne, iraquien, enne [irakjɛ̃, ɛn] *adj* Iraqi.

➤ **Irakien, enne, Iraquien, enne** *nm, f* Iraqi.

Iran [irɑ̃] *nm* : **l'~** Iran.

iranien, enne [iranjɛ̃, ɛn] *adj* Iranian.

➤ **iranien** *nm* [langue] Iranian.

➤ **Iranien, enne** *nm, f* Iranian.

Iraq = **Irak**.

iraquien = **irakien**.

irascible [irasibl] *adj* irascible.

iris [iris] *nm* *ANAT* & *BOT* iris.

irisé, e [irize] *adj* iridescent.

irlandais, e [irlɑ̃dɛ, ɛz] *adj* Irish.

➤ **irlandais** *nm* [langue] Irish.

➤ **Irlandais, e** *nm, f* Irishman (*f* Irishwoman).

Irlande [irlɑ̃d] *nf* : **l'~** Ireland ; **l'~ du Nord/Sud** Northern/Southern Ireland.

ironie [irɔni] *nf* irony ; ~ **du sort** twist of fate.

ironique [irɔnik] *adj* ironic.

ironiquement [irɔnikmɑ̃] *adv* ironically.

ironiser [3] [irɔnize] *vi* to speak ironically.

IRPP (*abr de* **impôt sur le revenu des personnes physiques**) *nm* income tax.

irradiation [iradjasjɔ̃] *nf* [rayons] radiation ; [action] irradiation.

irradier [9] [iradje] <> *vi* to radiate <> *vt* to irradiate.

irraisonné, e [irɛzɔne] *adj* irrational.

irrationnel, elle [irasjɔnɛl] *adj* irrational.

irréalisable [irealizabl] *adj* unrealizable.

irréaliste [irealist] *adj* unrealistic.

irréalité [irealite] *nf* unreality.

irrecevable [irəsəvabl] *adj* inadmissible.

irréconciliable [irekɔ̃siljabl] *adj* irreconcilable.

irrécupérable [irekyperabl] *adj* - **1.** [irrécouvrable] irretrievable - **2.** [irréparable] beyond repair - **3.** *fam* [personne] beyond hope.

irrécusable [irekyzabl] *adj* unimpeachable.

irréductible [iredyktibl] <> *nmf* diehard <> *adj* - **1.** *CHIM*, *MATHS* & *MÉD* irreducible - **2.** *fig* [volonté] indomitable ; [personne] implacable ; [communiste] diehard *(avant n)*.

irréel, elle [ireɛl] *adj* unreal.

irréfléchi, e [irefleʃi] *adj* unthinking.

irréfutable [irefytabl] *adj* irrefutable.

irrégularité [iregylarite] *nf* - **1.** [gén] irregularity - **2.** [de terrain, performance] unevenness.

irrégulier, ère [iregylje, ɛr] *adj* - **1.** [gén] irregular - **2.** [terrain, surface] uneven, irregular - **3.** [employé, athlète] erratic.

irrégulièrement [iregyljɛrmɑ̃] *adv* irregularly.

irrémédiable [iremedjabl] *adj* - **1.** [irréparable] irreparable - **2.** [incurable] incurable.

irrémédiablement [iremedjabləmɑ̃] *adv* irreparably.

irremplaçable [irɑ̃plasabl] *adj* irreplaceable.

irréparable [ireparabl] <> *nm* : **commettre l'~**

to do the unforgivable <> adj - **1.** [objet] beyond repair - **2.** fig [perte, erreur] irreparable.

irrépressible [irepresibl] adj irrepressible.

irréprochable [ireprɔʃabl] adj irreproachable.

irrésistible [irezistibl] adj - **1.** [tentation, femme] irresistible - **2.** [amusant] entertaining.

irrésistiblement [irezistiblǝmā] adv irresistibly.

irrésolu, e [irezɔly] adj - **1.** [indécis] irresolute - **2.** [sans solution] unresolved.

irrespirable [irespirabl] adj - **1.** [air] unbreathable - **2.** fig [oppressant] oppressive.

irresponsable [irespɔ̃sabl] <> nmf irresponsible person <> adj irresponsible.

irrévérencieux, euse [ireverāsjø, øz] adj irreverent.

irréversible [ireversibl] adj irreversible.

irrévocable [irevɔkabl] adj irrevocable.

irrévocablement [irevɔkablǝmā] adv irrevocably.

irrigation [irigasjɔ̃] nf irrigation.

irriguer [3] [irige] vt to irrigate.

irritabilité [iritabilite] nf irritability.

irritable [iritabl] adj irritable.

irritant, e [iritā, āt] adj - **1.** [agaçant] irritating, annoying - **2.** MÉD irritant.

irritation [iritasjɔ̃] nf irritation.

irriter [3] [irite] vt - **1.** [exaspérer] to irritate, to annoy - **2.** MÉD to irritate.

➡ **s'irriter** vp to get irritated ; s'~ contre qqn/de qqch to get irritated with sb/at sthg.

irruption [irypsjɔ̃] nf - **1.** [invasion] invasion - **2.** [entrée brusque] irruption ; faire ~ dans to burst into.

ISBN (abr de International standard book number) nm ISBN.

ISF (abr de impôt de solidarité sur la fortune) nm wealth tax.

islam [islam] nm Islam.

islamique [islamik] adj Islamic.

islamisation [islamizasjɔ̃] nf Islamization.

islamiser [3] [islamize] vt to Islamize.

islandais, e [islādɛ, ɛz] adj Icelandic.

➡ **islandais** nm [langue] Icelandic.

➡ **Islandais, e** nm, f Icelander.

Islande [islād] nf : l'~ Iceland.

isocèle [izɔsɛl] adj isoceles.

isolant, e [izɔlā, āt] adj insulating.

➡ **isolant** nm insulator, insulating material.

isolateur, trice [izɔlatœr, tris] adj insulating.

➡ **isolateur** nm insulator.

isolation [izɔlasjɔ̃] nf insulation ; ~ phonique soundproofing ; ~ thermique thermal insulation.

isolationnisme [izɔlasjɔnism] nm isolationism.

isolé, e [izɔle] adj isolated.

isolement [izɔlmā] nm - **1.** [gén] isolation - **2.** CONSTR & ÉLECTR insulation.

isolément [izɔlemā] adv individually.

isoler [3] [izɔle] vt - **1.** [séparer] to isolate ; ~ qqch de qqch to isolate sthg from sthg - **2.** CONSTR & ÉLECTR to insulate ; ~ qqch du froid to insulate sthg (against the cold) ; ~ qqch du bruit to soundproof sthg.

➡ **s'isoler** vp : s'~ (de) to isolate o.s. (from).

isoloir [izɔlwar] nm polling booth.

isotherme [izɔtɛrm] <> nf isotherm <> adj isothermal.

Israël [israɛl] n Israel.

israélien, enne [israeljɛ̃, ɛn] adj Israeli.

➡ **Israélien, enne** nm, f Israeli.

israélite [israelit] adj Jewish.

➡ **Israélite** nmf Jew.

issu, e [isy] adj : être ~ de [résulter de] to emerge ou stem from ; [personne] to come from.

➡ **issue** nf - **1.** [sortie] exit ; ~e de secours emergency exit - **2.** fig [solution] way out, solution ; sans ~e hopeless - **3.** [terme] outcome ; à l'~e de at the end ou close of.

Istanbul [istaābul] n Istanbul.

isthme [ism] nm isthmus.

Italie [itali] nf : l'~ Italy.

italien, enne [italjɛ̃, ɛn] adj Italian.

➡ **italien** nm [langue] Italian.

➡ **Italien, enne** nm, f Italian.

italique [italik] <> nm - **1.** HIST & LING Italic - **2.** TYPO italics (pl) ; en ~ in italics <> adj - **1.** HIST & LING Italic - **2.** TYPO italic.

itinéraire [itinerer] nm itinerary, route.

itinérant, e [itinerā, āt] adj - **1.** [spectacle, troupe] itinerant - **2.** [ambassadeur] roving (avant n).

itou [itu] adv fam as well.

ITP (abr de ingénieur des travaux publics) nm civil engineer.

IUFM (abr de institut universitaire de formation des maîtres) nm ≃ teacher training college Br, ≃ teachers college Am.

IUP (abr de institut universitaire professionnel) nm business school.

IUT (abr de institut universitaire de technologie) nm ≃ technical college.

IVG (abr de interruption volontaire de grossesse) nf abortion.

ivoire [ivwar] nm ivory.

ivoirien, enne [ivwarjɛ̃, ɛn] *adj* of/from the Ivory Coast.
➤ **Ivoirien, enne** *nm, f* native *ou* inhabitant of the Ivory Coast.

ivre [ivr] *adj* drunk ; ~ **de colère** wild with anger ; ~ **de joie** drunk *ou* mad with joy ; ~ **mort** dead drunk.

ivresse [ivrɛs] *nf* drunkenness ; [extase] rapture.

ivrogne [ivrɔɲ] *nmf* drunkard.

ivrognerie [ivrɔɲri] *nf* drunkenness.

j, J [ʒi] *nm inv* j, J.
➤ **J - 1.** (*abr de* joule) J - **2.** *abr de* jour.

j' ⊳ **je.**

jabot [ʒabo] *nm* - **1.** [d'oiseau] crop - **2.** [de chemise] frill.

jacassement [ʒakasmã] *nm péj* chattering, jabbering.

jacasser [3] [ʒakase] *vi péj* to chatter, to jabber.

jachère [ʒaʃɛr] *nf* : **en** ~ fallow.

jacinthe [ʒasɛ̃t] *nf* hyacinth.

jacobin, e [ʒakɔbɛ̃, in] *adj* Jacobin.
➤ **Jacobin** *nm* ʜɪsт Jacobin.

Jacuzzi® [ʒakuzi] *nm* Jacuzzi®.

jade [ʒad] *nm* jade.

jadis [ʒadis] *adv* formerly, in former times.

jaguar [ʒagwar] *nm* jaguar.

jaillir [32] [ʒajir] *vi* - **1.** [liquide] to gush ; [flammes] to leap - **2.** [cri] to ring out - **3.** [personne] to spring out.

jais [ʒɛ] *nm* jet ; **noir comme le** ~, **noir de** ~ jetblack.

Jakarta = **Djakarta.**

jalon [ʒalɔ̃] *nm* marker pole ; **poser les (premiers)** ~**s de** *fig* to pave the way for.

jalonner [3] [ʒalɔne] *vt* to mark (out) ; **jalonné de** [bordé de] lined with ; *fig* punctuated with.

jalousement [ʒaluzmã] *adv* jealously.

jalouser [3] [ʒaluze] *vt* to be jealous of.

jalousie [ʒaluzi] *nf* - **1.** [envie] jealousy ; **être malade** *ou* **crever de** ~ *fig* to be green with envy - **2.** [store] blind.

jaloux, ouse [ʒalu, uz] *adj* : ~ **(de)** jealous (of).

jamaïquain, e, jamaïcain, e [ʒamaikɛ̃, ɛn] *adj* Jamaican.
➤ **Jamaïquain, e, Jamaïcain, e** *nm, f* Jamaican.

Jamaïque [ʒamaik] *nf* : **la** ~ Jamaica.

jamais [ʒamɛ] *adv* - **1.** [sens négatif] never ; **ne** ... ~, ~ **ne** never ; **je ne reviendrai** ~, ~ **je ne reviendrai** I'll never come back ; **(ne)** ... ~ **plus, plus** ~ **(ne)** never again ; **je ne viendrai** ~ **plus, plus** ~ **je ne viendrai** I'll never come here again ; **plus** ~! never again! - **2.** [sens positif] : **plus que** ~ more than ever ; **elle l'aimait plus que** ~ she loved him more than ever ; **il est plus triste que** ~ he's sadder than ever ; **si** ~ **tu le vois** if you should happen to see him, should you happen to see him.
➤ **à jamais** *loc adv* for ever.
➤ **pour jamais** *loc adv* for ever.

jambage [ʒãbaʒ] *nm* [de lettre] downstroke.

jambe [ʒãb] *nf* leg ; **courir à toutes** ~**s** to run flat out ; **il s'enfuit à toutes** ~**s** he ran away as fast as his legs would carry him ; **prendre ses** ~**s à son cou** to take to one's heels ; **tenir la** ~ **à qqn** *fam fig* to keep sb talking ; **ça me fait une belle** ~! *fam fig* that's no good to me!

jambières [ʒãbjɛr] *nfpl* [de football] shin pads ; [de cricket] pads.

jambon [ʒãbɔ̃] *nm* ham ; ~ **blanc** ham ; ~ **fumé** smoked ham ; **un** ~ **beurre** *fam* a ham sandwich.

jambonneau, x [ʒãbɔno] *nm* knuckle of ham.

jante [ʒãt] *nf* (wheel) rim.

janvier [ʒãvje] *nm* January ; *voir aussi* **septembre.**

Japon [ʒapɔ̃] *nm* : **le** ~ Japan ; **au** ~ in Japan.

japonais, e [ʒapɔnɛ, ɛz] *adj* Japanese.
➤ **japonais** *nm* [langue] Japanese.
➤ **Japonais, e** *nm, f* Japanese (person) ; **les Japonais** the Japanese.

jappement [ʒapmã] *nm* yap, yapping (*U*).

japper [3] [ʒape] *vi* to yap.

jaquette [ʒakɛt] *nf* - **1.** [vêtement] jacket - **2.** [de livre] (dust) jacket.

jardin [ʒardɛ̃] *nm* garden ; ~ **d'enfants** nursery school, kindergarten ; ~ **public** park ; ~ **zoologique** zoo.

jardinage [ʒardinaʒ] *nm* gardening.

jardiner [3] [ʒardine] *vi* to garden.

jardinet [ʒardine] *nm* small garden.

jardinier, ère [ʒardinje, ɛr] *nm, f* gardener.
➤ **jardinière** *nf* - **1.** [bac à fleurs] window box - **2.** CULIN : **jardinière de légumes** mixed vegetables (pl).

jargon [ʒargɔ̃] *nm* - **1.** [langage spécialisé] jargon - **2.** *fam* [charabia] gibberish.

jarret [ʒarɛ] *nm* - **1.** ANAT back of the knee - **2.** CULIN knuckle of veal.

jarretelle [ʒartɛl] *nf* suspender Br, garter Am.

jarretière [ʒartjɛr] *nf* garter.

jars [ʒar] *nm* gander.

jaser [3] [ʒaze] *vi* [bavarder] to gossip.

jasmin [ʒasmɛ̃] *nm* jasmine.

jatte [ʒat] *nf* bowl.

jauge [ʒoʒ] *nf* [instrument] gauge ; **~ de niveau d'huile** dipstick.

jauger [17] [ʒoʒe] *vt* to gauge.

jaunâtre [ʒonatr] *adj* yellowish.

jaune [ʒon] <> *nm* [couleur] yellow <> *adj* yellow <> *adv* : **rire ~** *fig* to force o.s. to laugh.
➤ **jaune d'œuf** *nm* (egg) yolk.

jaunir [32] [ʒonir] *vt* & *vi* to turn yellow.

jaunisse [ʒonis] *nf* MÉD jaundice ; **en faire une ~** *fam fig* [de jalousie] to be green with envy ; [de déception] to take it badly.

jaunissement [ʒonismɑ̃] *nm* yellowing.

java [ʒava] *nf* type of popular dance ; **faire la ~** *fam fig* to live it up.

Java [ʒava] *n* Java ; **à ~** in Java.

javanais, e [ʒavanɛ, ɛz] *adj* Javanese.
➤ **javanais** *nm* [langue] Javanese.
➤ **Javanais, e** *nm, f* Javanese (person) ; **les Javanais** the Javanese.

Javel [ʒavɛl] *nf* : **eau de ~** bleach.

javelliser [3] [ʒavelize] *vt* to chlorinate.

javelot [ʒavlo] *nm* javelin.

jazz [dʒaz] *nm* jazz.

J.-C. (*abr de* Jésus-Christ) J.C.

je [ʒə], **j'** (*devant voyelle et h muet*) *pron pers* I.

jean [dʒin], **jeans** [dʒins] *nm* jeans (pl), pair of jeans.

Jeep® [dʒip] *nf* Jeep®.

je-m'en-foutisme [ʒmɑ̃futism] *nm* couldn't-give-a-damn attitude.

jérémiades [ʒeremjad] *nfpl* moaning (U), whining (U).

jerrycan, jerricane [ʒerikan] *nm* jerry can.

jersey [ʒɛrzɛ] *nm* jersey ; **point de ~** stocking stitch.

Jersey [ʒɛrzɛ] *n* Jersey ; **à ~** on Jersey.

Jérusalem [ʒeryzalɛm] *n* Jerusalem.

jésuite [ʒezɥit] <> *nm* Jesuit <> *adj* Jesuit ; *péj* jesuitical.

Jésus-Christ [ʒezykri] *nm* Jesus Christ.

jet¹ [ʒɛ] *nm* - **1.** [action de jeter] throw ; **d'un seul ~** *fig* in one go - **2.** [de liquide] jet ; **~ d'eau** fountain - **3.** [esquisse] : **premier ~** rough outline *ou* draft.

jet² [dʒɛt] *nm* [avion] jet.

jetable [ʒətabl] *adj* disposable.

jetais, jetions *etc* ⊳ **jeter**.

jeté, e [ʒəte] *pp* ⊳ **jeter**.

jetée [ʒəte] *nf* jetty.

jeter [27] [ʒəte] *vt* to throw ; [se débarrasser de] to throw away ; **~ qqch à qqn** [lancer] to throw sth to sb, to throw sb sth ; [pour faire mal] to throw sth at sb ; **~ qqn dehors** to throw sb out ; **~ un coup d'œil (à)** to take a look (at).
➤ **se jeter** *vp* : **se ~ sur** to pounce on ; **se ~ dans** [suj : rivière] to flow into ; **se ~ dans les bras de qqn** to throw o.s. into sb's arms ; **se ~ à l'eau** *fig* to take the plunge.

jeton [ʒətɔ̃] *nm* - **1.** [de jeu] counter ; [de téléphone] token - **2.** *loc* : **avoir les ~s** *fam* to have the jitters.
➤ **faux-jeton** *nm* hypocrite.
➤ **jeton de présence** *nm* fees paid to non-executive directors of a company.

jette, jettes *etc* ⊳ **jeter**.

jetterai, jetteras *etc* ⊳ **jeter**.

jeu, x [ʒø] *nm* - **1.** [divertissement] play (U), playing (U) ; **par ~** for fun ; **~ de mots** play on words, pun - **2.** [régi par des règles] game ; **en ~** in (play) ; **hors ~** out (of play) ; **mettre un joueur hors ~** to put a player offside ; **~ de l'oie** ≃ snakes and ladders ; **~ de société** parlour Br *ou* parlor Am game ; **~ télévisé** game show - **3.** [d'argent] : **le ~** gambling ; **~ de hasard** game of chance - **4.** [d'échecs, de clés] set ; **~ de cartes** pack of cards - **5.** [manière de jouer - MUS] playing ; [- THÉÂTRE] acting ; [- SPORT] game - **6.** TECHNOL play ; **il y a du ~** there's a bit of play, it's rather loose - **7.** *loc* : **cacher son ~** to play one's cards close to one's chest ; **être en ~** to be at stake ; **entrer en ~** to come into play ; **entrer dans le ~ de qqn** to play sb's game.
➤ **Jeux Olympiques** *nmpl* : **les Jeux Olympiques** the Olympic Games.

jeudi [ʒødi] *nm* Thursday ; **~ saint** Maundy Thursday ; *voir aussi* **samedi**.

jeun [ʒœ̃] ➞ **à jeun** *loc adv* on an empty stomach.

jeune [ʒœn] ⟺ *adj* young ; [style, apparence] youthful ; ~ **homme/femme** young man/woman ; ~ **fille** girl ; ~**s gens** [gén] young people ; [garçons] young men ⟺ *adv* : **faire** ~ to look young ⟺ *nm* young person ; **les ~s** young people.

jeûne [ʒøn] *nm* fast.

jeûner [3] [ʒøne] *vi* to fast.

jeunesse [ʒœnɛs] *nf* - **1.** [âge] youth ; [de style, apparence] youthfulness - **2.** [jeunes gens] young people *(pl)*.

JF, jf *abr de* **jeune fille.**

JH *abr de* **jeune homme.**

jingle [dʒiŋgəl] *nm* jingle.

JO ⟺ *nm* (abr de **Journal officiel**) bulletin giving details of laws and official announcements ⟺ *nmpl* (abr de **Jeux Olympiques**) Olympic Games.

joaillerie [ʒɔajri] *nf* - **1.** [métier] jewel trade - **2.** [magasin] jeweller's *Br* ou jeweler's *Am* (shop).

joaillier, ère [ʒɔaje, ɛr] *nm, f* jeweller *Br*, jeweler *Am*.

job [dʒɔb] *nm fam* job.

jobard, e [ʒɔbar, ard] *adj fam* gullible.

jockey [ʒɔkɛ] *nm* jockey.

jogging [dʒɔgiŋ] *nm* - **1.** [activité] jogging ; **faire du** ~ to go jogging, to go for a jog - **2.** [vêtement] tracksuit, jogging suit.

joie [ʒwa] *nf* joy ; **avec** ~ with pleasure ; ~ **de vivre** joie de vivre, joy of living.

joignable [ʒwaɲabl] *adj* contactable.

joignais, joignions *etc* ➞ **joindre.**

joindre [82] [ʒwɛ̃dr] *vt* - **1.** [rapprocher] to join ; [mains] to put together ; **(ne pas) arriver à ~ les deux bouts** *fam fig* (to be unable) to make ends meet - **2.** [ajouter] : ~ **qqch (à)** to attach sthg (to) ; [adjoindre] to enclose sthg (with) - **3.** [par téléphone] to contact, to reach.
➞ **se joindre** *vp* : **se ~ à qqn** to join sb ; **se ~ à qqch** to join in sthg.

joint, e [ʒwɛ̃, ɛ̃t] *pp* ➞ **joindre.**
➞ **joint** *nm* - **1.** [d'étanchéité] seal - **2.** *fam* [drogue] joint.
➞ **joint de culasse** *nm* cylinder head gasket.

jointure [ʒwɛ̃tyr] *nf* ANAT joint.

joker [ʒɔkɛr] *nm* joker.

joli, e [ʒɔli] *adj* - **1.** [femme, chose] pretty, attractive - **2.** [somme, situation] nice - **3.** *loc* : **c'est bien ~, mais ...** that's all very well, but ... ; **c'est du ~ travail!** *iron* well done!

joliment [ʒɔlimɑ̃] *adv* - **1.** [bien] prettily, attractively ; *iron* nicely - **2.** *fam* [beaucoup] really.

jonc [ʒɔ̃] *nm* rush, bulrush.

joncher [3] [ʒɔ̃ʃe] *vt* to strew ; **être jonché de** to be strewn with.

jonction [ʒɔ̃ksjɔ̃] *nf* [de routes] junction.

jongler [3] [ʒɔ̃gle] *vi* to juggle.

jongleur, euse [ʒɔ̃glœr, øz] *nm, f* juggler.

jonquille [ʒɔ̃kij] *nf* daffodil.

Jordanie [ʒɔrdani] *nf* : **la ~** Jordan.

jordanien, enne [ʒɔrdanjɛ̃, ɛn] *adj* Jordanian.
➞ **Jordanien, enne** *nm, f* Jordanian.

jouable [ʒwabl] *adj* - **1.** SPORT playable - **2.** [situation] feasible.

joual [ʒwal] *nm* Can French-Canadian dialect.

joue [ʒu] *nf* cheek ; **tenir** ou **mettre qqn en** ~ *fig* to take aim at sb.

jouer [6] [ʒwe] ⟺ *vi* - **1.** [gén] to play ; ~ **avec qqn/qqch** to play with sb/sthg ; ~ **à qqch** [jeu, sport] to play sthg ; ~ **de** MUS to play ; **à toi de ~!** (it's) your turn! ; *fig* your move! - **2.** CIN & THÉÂTRE to act - **3.** [parier] to gamble - **4.** [s'appliquer] to apply - **5.** *loc* : ~ **des coudes** to use one's elbows ; ~ **de malchance** to be dogged by bad luck ; ~ **sur les mots** to play with words ⟺ *vt* - **1.** [carte, partie] to play - **2.** [somme d'argent] to bet, to wager ; *fig* to gamble with - **3.** [THÉÂTRE - personnage, rôle] to play ; [- pièce] to put on, to perform - **4.** [avoir à l'affiche] to show - **5.** MUS to perform, to play - **6.** *loc* : ~ **la comédie** to put on an act ; ~ **le jeu** to play the game ; ~ **un tour à qqn** to play a trick on sb.
➞ **se jouer** *vp* : **se ~ de qqch** to make light of sthg ; **se ~ de qqn** to deceive sb.

jouet [ʒwɛ] *nm* toy ; **être le ~ de** *fig* to be the victim of.

joueur, euse [ʒwœr, øz] *nm, f* - **1.** SPORT player ; ~ **de football** footballer, football player ; **être beau/mauvais** ~ to be a good/bad loser - **2.** [au casino] gambler.

jouffflu, e [ʒufly] *adj* [personne] chubby-cheeked.

joug [ʒu] *nm* yoke.

jouir [32] [ʒwir] *vi* - **1.** [profiter] : ~ **de** to enjoy - **2.** [sexuellement] to have an orgasm.

jouissance [ʒwisɑ̃s] *nf* - **1.** JUR [d'un bien] use - **2.** [sexuelle] orgasm.

joujou, x [ʒuʒu] *nm* toy.

jour [ʒur] *nm* - **1.** [unité de temps] day ; **huit ~s** a week ; **quinze ~s** a fortnight *Br*, two weeks ; **tous les ~s** every day ; **l'autre ~** the other day ; **de ~ en ~** day by day ; ~ **après** ~ day after day ; **au ~ le ~** from day to day ; **~ et nuit** night and day ; **du ~ au lendemain** overnight ; **~ pour ~ to** the day ; **le ~ de l'an** New Year's Day ; **~ chômé** public holiday ; **~ de congé** day off ; **~ férié** public holiday ; **~ de fête** holiday ; **le ~ J** D-Day ; **~ ouvrable** working day **- 2.** [lumière] daylight ; **de ~** in the daytime, by day ; **il fait ~** it's light ; **au petit ~** at the crack of dawn ; **au grand ~** in broad daylight **- 3.** [époque] day ; **le ~ où** the day (that) ; **un beau ~** one fine day ; **un de ces ~s** one of these days **- 4.** *loc* : **être à ~** to be up-to-date ; **mettre qqch à ~** to update sthg, to bring sthg up to date ; **de nos ~s** these days, nowadays ; **se faire ~** to become clear ; **sous un ~ nouveau** in a new light.

journal, aux [ʒurnal, o] *nm* **- 1.** [publication] newspaper, paper ; **le ~ officiel de la République française** *official publication in which public notices appear* **- 2.** TÉLÉ : **~ télévisé** television news **- 3.** [écrit] : **~ (intime)** diary, journal ; **~ de bord** NAVIG ship's log ; INFORM log.

LE JOURNAL OFFICIEL

This bulletin prints information about new laws and summaries of parliamentary debates, and informs the public of any important government business. New companies are obliged by law to publish an announcement in the 'journal officiel'.

journalier, ère [ʒurnalje, ɛr] *adj* daily.

journalisme [ʒurnalism] *nm* journalism.

journaliste [ʒurnalist] *nmf* journalist, reporter.

journalistique [ʒurnalistik] *adj* journalistic.

journée [ʒurne] *nf* day ; **faire la ~ continue** to work through lunch.

journellement [ʒurnɛlmɑ̃] *adv* daily.

joute [ʒut] *nf* joust ; *fig* duel.

jouxter [3] [ʒukste] *vt* to adjoin.

jovial, e, aux [ʒɔvjal, o] *adj* jovial, jolly.

jovialité [ʒɔvjalite] *nf* joviality, jolliness.

joyau, x [ʒwajo] *nm* jewel.

joyeusement [ʒwajøzmɑ̃] *adv* joyfully.

joyeux, euse [ʒwajø, øz] *adj* joyful, happy ; **~ Noël!** Merry Christmas!

JT (*abr de* journal télévisé) *nm* television news.

jubilation [ʒybilasjɔ̃] *nf* jubilation.

jubilé [ʒybile] *nm* jubilee.

jubiler [3] [ʒybile] *vi fam* to be jubilant.

jucher [3] [ʒyʃe] *vt* : **~ qqn sur qqch** to perch sb on sthg.

➤ **se jucher** *vp* : **se ~ sur qqch** to perch on sthg.

judaïque [ʒydaik] *adj* [loi] Judaic ; [tradition, religion] Jewish.

judaïsme [ʒydaism] *nm* Judaism.

judas [ʒyda] *nm* [ouverture] peephole.

Judée [ʒyde] *nf* : **la ~** Judaea, Judea.

judéo-chrétien, enne [ʒydeɔkretjɛ̃, ɛn] (*mpl* judéo-chrétiens, *fpl* judéo-chrétiennes) *adj* Judaeo-Christian.

judiciaire [ʒydisjɛr] *adj* judicial.

judicieusement [ʒydisjøzmɑ̃] *adv* judiciously.

judicieux, euse [ʒydisjø, øz] *adj* judicious.

judo [ʒydo] *nm* judo.

juge [ʒyʒ] *nm* judge ; **~ d'instruction** examining magistrate ; **~ de ligne** TENNIS line judge ; **~ de paix** justice of the peace ; **~ de touche** FOOTBALL linesman ; RUGBY touch judge.

jugé [ʒyʒe] ➤ **au jugé** *loc adv* by guesswork ; **tirer au ~** to fire blind.

jugement [ʒyʒmɑ̃] *nm* judgment ; **prononcer un ~** to pass sentence ; **~ de valeur** value judgment.

➤ **Jugement** *nm* : **le Jugement dernier** the Last Judgment.

jugeote [ʒyʒɔt] *nf fam* common sense ; **manquer de ~** to have no common sense.

juger [17] [ʒyʒe] <> *vt* to judge ; [accusé] to try ; **~ que** to judge (that), to consider (that) ; **~ qqn/qqch inutile** to consider sb/sthg useless ; **~ bon de faire qqch** to consider it appropriate to do sthg <> *vi* to judge ; **~ de qqch** to judge sthg ; **si j'en juge d'après mon expérience** judging from my experience ; **jugez de ma surprise!** imagine my surprise!

juguler [3] [ʒygyle] *vt* [maladie] to halt ; [révolte] to put down ; [inflation] to curb.

juif, ive [ʒɥif, iv] *adj* Jewish.

➤ **Juif, ive** *nm, f* Jew.

juillet [ʒɥijɛ] *nm* July ; **la fête du 14 Juillet** *national holiday to mark the anniversary of the storming of the Bastille* ; *voir aussi* **septembre**.

LA FÊTE DU 14 JUILLET

The celebrations to mark the anniversary of the storming of the Bastille begin on the 13th July with outdoor public dances ('les bals du 14 juillet') in the streets, and continue on the 14th with a military parade in the morning and a firework display in the evening.

juin [ʒɥɛ̃] *nm* June ; *voir aussi* **septembre**.

juke-box [dʒukbɔks] *nm inv* jukebox.

julienne [ʒyljɛn] *nf* : ~ **de légumes** (*clear soup with*) very thin strips of vegetable.

jumeau, elle, x [ʒymo, ɛl, o] ⟨⟩ *adj* twin (*avant n*) ⟨⟩ *nm, f* twin ; **vrais/faux ~x** identical/fraternal twins.

➠ **jumelles** *nfpl* OPTIQUE binoculars.

jumelage [ʒymlaʒ] *nm* twinning.

jumelé, e [ʒymle] *adj* [villes] twinned ; [maisons] semidetached ; **roues ~es** double wheels.

jumeler [24] [ʒymle] *vt* to twin.

jumelle ⊳ **jumeau**.

jument [ʒymɑ̃] *nf* mare.

jungle [ʒɑ̃gl] *nf* jungle.

junior [ʒynjɔr] *adj* & *nmf* SPORT junior.

junte [ʒɑ̃t] *nf* junta.

jupe [ʒyp] *nf* skirt.

jupe-culotte [ʒypkylɔt] (*pl* **jupes-culottes**) *nf* culottes (*pl*).

jupon [ʒypɔ̃] *nm* petticoat, slip.

Jura [ʒyra] *nm* : **le ~** the Jura (Mountains).

juré [ʒyre] *nm* JUR juror.

juré, e [ʒyre] *adj* : **ennemi ~** sworn enemy.

jurer [3] [ʒyre] ⟨⟩ *vt* : ~ **qqch à qqn** to swear *ou* pledge sthg to sb ; ~ **(à qqn) que ...** to swear (to sb) that ... ; ~ **de faire qqch** to swear *ou* vow to do sthg ; **je le jure** I swear ; **je vous jure!** *fam* honestly! ; **ne plus ~ que par** to swear by ⟨⟩ *vi* - **1.** [blasphémer] to swear, to curse - **2.** [ne pas aller ensemble] : ~ **(avec)** to clash (with).

➠ **se jurer** *vp* : **se ~ de faire qqch** to swear *ou* vow to do sthg.

juridiction [ʒyridiksjɔ̃] *nf* jurisdiction.

juridictionnel, elle [ʒyridiksjɔnɛl] *adj* jurisdictional.

juridique [ʒyridik] *adj* legal.

juridiquement [ʒyridikmɑ̃] *adv* legally.

jurisprudence [ʒyrisprydɑ̃s] *nf* jurisprudence ; **faire ~** to set a precedent.

juriste [ʒyrist] *nmf* lawyer.

juron [ʒyrɔ̃] *nm* swearword, oath.

jury [ʒyri] *nm* - **1.** JUR jury - **2.** [SCOL - d'examen] examining board ; [- de concours] admissions board.

jus [ʒy] *nm* - **1.** [de fruits, légumes] juice ; ~ **d'orange/de pomme** orange/apple juice - **2.** [de viande] gravy.

jusqu'au-boutiste [ʒyskobutist] *nmf* hardliner.

jusque, jusqu' [ʒysk(ə)] ➠ **jusqu'à** *loc prép* - **1.** [sens temporel] until, till ; **jusqu'à nouvel ordre** until further notice ; **jusqu'à pré-**

sent up until now, so far - **2.** [sens spatial] as far as ; **jusqu'au bout** to the end - **3.** [même] even ; **aller jusqu'à faire qqch** *fig* to go as far as to do sthg.

➠ **jusqu'à ce que** *loc conj* until, till.

➠ **jusqu'en** *loc prép* up until.

➠ **jusqu'ici** *loc adv* [lieu] up to here ; [temps] up until now, so far.

➠ **jusque-là** *loc adv* [lieu] up to there ; [temps] up until then.

justaucorps [ʒystokɔr] *nm* [maillot] leotard.

juste [ʒyst] ⟨⟩ *adj* - **1.** [équitable] fair - **2.** [exact] right, correct - **3.** [trop petit] tight ⟨⟩ *adv* - **1.** [bien] correctly, right - **2.** [exactement, seulement] just.

➠ **au juste** *loc adv* exactly.

➠ **tout juste** *loc adv* only just.

justement [ʒystəmɑ̃] *adv* - **1.** [avec raison] rightly - **2.** [précisément] exactly, precisely.

justesse [ʒystɛs] *nf* [de remarque] aptness ; [de raisonnement] soundness.

➠ **de justesse** *loc adv* only just.

justice [ʒystis] *nf* - **1.** JUR justice ; **se faire ~** [se suicider] to take one's life ; **passer en ~** to stand trial ; **rendre la ~** to dispense justice ; **rendre ~ à qqn/qqch** to do justice to sb/sthg - **2.** [équité] fairness.

justiciable [ʒystisjabl] *adj* : **être ~ de** JUR to be answerable to.

justicier, ère [ʒystisje, ɛr] *nm, f* righter of wrongs.

justifiable [ʒystifjabl] *adj* justifiable.

justificatif, ive [ʒystifikatif, iv] *adj* supporting.

➠ **justificatif** *nm* written proof (U).

justification [ʒystifikasjɔ̃] *nf* justification.

justifier [9] [ʒystifje] *vt* - **1.** [gén] to justify - **2.** TYPO : ~ **à gauche/à droite** to left-/right-justify.

➠ **se justifier** *vp* to justify o.s.

jute [ʒyt] *nm* jute.

juter [3] [ʒyte] *vi* [fruit] to be juicy.

juteux, euse [ʒytø, øz] *adj* juicy ; **une affaire juteuse** *fam* a nice little earner.

juvénile [ʒyvenil] *adj* youthful.

juxtaposé, e [ʒykstapoze] *adj* juxtaposed.

juxtaposer [3] [ʒykstapoze] *vt* to juxtapose, to place side by side.

juxtaposition [ʒykstapozisjɔ̃] *nf* juxtaposition.

k, K [ka] *nm inv* k, K.
K7 [kasɛt] (*abr de* **cassette**) *nf* cassette ; **radio-~** radiocassette.
Kaboul [kabul] *n* Kabul.
kabyle [kabil] ◇ *adj* Kabyle ◇ *nm* [langue] Kabyle.
◆ **Kabyle** *nmf* Kabyle.
Kabylie [kabili] *nf* : **la ~** Kabylia.
kaki [kaki] ◇ *nm* - **1.** [couleur] khaki - **2.** [fruit] persimmon ◇ *adj inv* khaki.
kaléidoscope [kaleidɔskɔp] *nm* kaleidoscope.
kamikaze [kamikaz] *nm* kamikaze pilot.
Kampuchéa [kãpyʃea] *nm* : **le ~** Kampuchea.
kanak = **canaque**.
kangourou [kãguru] *nm* kangaroo.
kapok [kapɔk] *nm* kapok.
karaoké [karaɔke] *nm* karaoke.
karaté [karate] *nm* karate.
karité [karite] *nm* shea.
kart [kart] *nm* go-kart.
karting [kartiŋ] *nm* go-karting.
kas(c)her [kaʃɛr], **cascher** *adj inv* kosher ; **manger ~** to eat kosher food.
Katar = **Qatar**.
Katmand(o)u [katmãdu] *n* Katmandu.
kayak [kajak] *nm* kayak.
KCS (*abr de* **couronne tchécoslovaque**) Kcs.
Kenya [kenja] *nm* : **le ~** Kenya ; **au ~** in Kenya.
kenyan, e [kenjã, an] *adj* Kenyan.
◆ **Kenyan, e** *nm, f* Kenyan.
képi [kepi] *nm* kepi.
kératine [keratin] *nf* keratin.
kermesse [kɛrmɛs] *nf* - **1.** [foire] fair - **2.** [fête de bienfaisance] fête.
kérosène [kerozɛn] *nm* kerosene.
ketchup [kɛtʃœp] *nm* ketchup.
keuf [kœf] *nm fam* cop.
keum [kœm] *nm fam* guy, bloke.
KF - **1.** *abr de* **kilofranc** - **2.** *abr de* **café**.
kg (*abr de* **kilogramme**) kg.
KGB (*abr de* **Komitet Gossoudarstvennoï Bezopasnosti**) *nm* KGB.
khâgne [kaɲ] *nf* second year of a two-year

preparatory arts course taken prior to the competitive examination for entry to the École normale supérieure.
Khartoum [kartum] *n* Khartoum.
khmer, ère [kmɛr] *adj* Khmer.
◆ **khmer** *nm* [langue] Khmer.
◆ **Khmer, ère** *nm, f* Khmer.
khôl [kol], **kohol** [kɔɔl] *nm* kohl.
kibboutz [kibuts] *nm inv* kibbutz.
kidnapper [3] [kidnape] *vt* to kidnap.
kidnappeur, euse [kidnapœr, øz] *nm, f* kidnapper.
kidnapping [kidnapiŋ] *nm* kidnap.
kif-kif [kifkif] *adj inv fam* : **c'est ~** it makes no odds *Br*, it's all the same.
kilo [kilo] *nm* kilo.
kilofranc [kilofrã] *nm one thousand francs*.
kilogramme [kilɔgram] *nm* kilogram.
kilométrage [kilɔmetraʒ] *nm* - **1.** [de voiture] ≈ mileage ; **~ illimité** ≈ unlimited mileage - **2.** [distance] distance.
kilomètre [kilɔmetr] *nm* kilometre *Br*, kilometer *Am*.
kilométrique [kilɔmetrik] *adj* kilometric.
kilo-octet [kilɔɔktɛ] *nm* **INFORM** kilobyte.
kilowatt [kilɔwat] *nm* kilowatt.
kilowatt-heure [kilɔwatœr] (*pl* **kilowatts-heures**) *nm* kilowatt-hour.
kilt [kilt] *nm* kilt.
kimono [kimɔno] *nm* kimono.
kinésithérapeute [kineziterapøt] *nmf* physiotherapist.
Kinshasa [kinʃasa] *n* Kinshasa.
kiosque [kjɔsk] *nm* - **1.** [de vente] kiosk ; **~ à journaux** newspaper kiosk - **2.** [pavillon] pavilion - **3.** [de navire] pilot house, wheelhouse.
kir [kir] *nm* *an apéritif made with white wine and blackcurrant liqueur*.
kirsch [kirʃ] *nm* cherry brandy.
kit [kit] *nm* kit ; **en ~** in kit form.
kitchenette [kitʃənɛt] *nf* kitchenette.
kitsch [kitʃ] *adj inv* kitsch.
kiwi [kiwi] *nm* - **1.** [oiseau] kiwi - **2.** [fruit] kiwi, kiwi fruit *(U)*.
Klaxon® [klaksɔ] *nm* horn.
klaxonner [3] [klaksɔne] *vi* to hoot.
kleptomane, cleptomane [klɛptɔman] *nmf* kleptomaniac.
kleptomanie [klɛptɔmani] *nf* kleptomania.
km (*abr de* **kilomètre**) km.
km/h (*abr de* **kilomètre par heure**) kph.
Ko (*abr de* **kilo-octet**) K.
K.-O. [kao] *nm* : **mettre qqn ~** to knock sb out.
koala [kɔala] *nm* koala (bear).
kohol = **khôl**.
Kosovar [kɔsɔvar] *nmf* Kosovar.

Kosovo [kɔsɔvɔ] *nm* : **le ~** Kosovo ; **au ~** in Kosovo.

kouglof, kugelhof [kuglɔf] *nm* cake made with dried fruit and almonds.

Koweït [kɔwɛt] *nm* [pays, ville] Kuwait ; **le ~** Kuwait ; **au ~** in Kuwait.

koweïtien, enne [kɔwɛtjɛ̃, ɛn] *adj* Kuwaiti.

Koweïtien, enne *nm, f* Kuwaiti.

krach [krak] *nm* crash ; **~ boursier** stock market crash.

kraft [kraft] *nm* kraft ; **papier ~** brown paper.

KRD (*abr de* **couronne danoise**) Kr, DKr.

KRN (*abr de* **couronne norvégienne**) Kr, NKr.

KRS (*abr de* **couronne suédoise**) Kr, Skr.

Kuala Lumpur [kyalalympyr] *n* Kuala Lumpur.

kugelhof = **kouglof**.

kumquat [kumkwat] *nm* kumquat.

kung-fu [kuŋfu] *nm* kung fu.

kurde [kyrd] <> *adj* Kurdish <> *nm* [langue] Kurdish.

Kurde *nmf* Kurd.

Kurdistan [kyrdistɑ̃] *nm* : **le ~** Kurdistan ; **au ~** in Kurdistan.

kWh (*abr de* **kilowatt-heure**) kW/hr.

Kyoto [kiɔtɔ] *n* Kyoto.

kyrielle [kirjɛl] *nf fam* stream ; [d'enfants] horde.

kyste [kist] *nm* cyst.

l, L [ɛl] <> *nm inv* l, L <> (*abr de* **litre**) l.

l' ⊳ **le**.

la[1] [la] *art déf* & *pron déf* ⊳ **le**.

la[2] [la] *nm inv* MUS A ; [chanté] la.

là [la] *adv* - **1.** [lieu] there ; **à 3 kilomètres de ~** 3 kilometres from there ; **passe par ~** go that way ; **c'est ~ que je travaille** that's where I work ; **je suis ~** I'm here ; **les faits sont ~** those are the facts - **2.** [temps] then ; **à quelques jours de ~** a few days later, a few days after that - **3.** [dans cela] : **la santé, tout est ~**

(good) health is everything ; **~ est le vrai problème** that's the real problem - **4.** [avec une proposition relative] : **~ où** [lieu] where ; [temps] when - **5.** *loc* : **de ~ à dire qu'elle est sympathique, il y a loin!** there's a big difference between saying that and saying that she's a nice person ; **nous en sommes ~** that's the stage we've reached ; **s'en tenir ~** to call a halt (there) ; *voir aussi* **ce, là-bas, là-dedans** *etc.*

là-bas [laba] *adv* (over) there.

label [labɛl] *nm* - **1.** [étiquette] : **~ de qualité** label guaranteeing quality - **2.** [commerce] label, brand name.

labeur [labœr] *nm sout* labour *Br*, labor *Am*.

labial, e, aux [labjal, o] *adj* labial.

labo [labo] (*abr de* **laboratoire**) *nm fam* lab.

laborantin, e [labɔrɑ̃tɛ̃, in] *nm, f* laboratory assistant.

laboratoire [labɔratwar] *nm* laboratory ; **~ d'analyses** test laboratory ; **~ de langues** language laboratory.

laborieusement [labɔrjøzmɑ̃] *adv* laboriously.

laborieux, euse [labɔrjø, øz] *adj* - **1.** [difficile] laborious - **2.** [travailleur] industrious ; **les classes laborieuses** the working class *(sg)*.

labour [labur] *nm* - **1.** [labourage] ploughing - **2.** *(gén pl)* [terres] ploughed field.

labourage [laburaʒ] *nm* ploughing.

labourer [3] [labure] *vt* - **1.** AGRIC to plough *Br*, to plow *Am* - **2.** *fig* [creuser] to make a gash in.

laboureur [laburœr] *nm* ploughman.

labrador [labradɔr] *nm* labrador.

labyrinthe [labirɛ̃t] *nm* labyrinth.

lac [lak] *nm* lake ; **les Grands Lacs** the Great Lakes ; **le ~ Léman** Lake Geneva ; **le ~ Majeur** Lake Maggiore.

lacer [16] [lase] *vt* to tie.

lacérer [18] [lasere] *vt* - **1.** [déchirer] to shred - **2.** [blesser, griffer] to slash.

lacet [lasɛ] *nm* - **1.** [cordon] lace - **2.** [de route] bend - **3.** [piège] snare.

lâche [laʃ] <> *nmf* coward <> *adj* - **1.** [nœud] loose - **2.** [personne, comportement] cowardly.

lâchement [laʃmɑ̃] *adv* like a coward/cowards.

lâcher [3] [laʃe] <> *vt* - **1.** [libérer - bras, objet] to let go of ; [- animal] to let go, to release - **2.** [émettre - son, mot] to let out, to come out with - **3.** [desserrer] to loosen - **4.** [laisser tomber] : **~ qqch** to drop sthg - **5.** *fam* [abandonner - ami] : **~ qqn** to drop sb <> *vi* to give way <> *nm* : **un ~ de** a release of.

lâcheté [laʃte] *nf* - **1.** [couardise] cowardice - **2.** [acte] cowardly act.

lâcheur, euse [lɑʃœr, øz] *nm, f fam* unreliable person.

lacis [lasi] *nm* [labyrinthe] maze.

laconique [lakɔnik] *adj* laconic.

laconiquement [lakɔnikmɑ̃] *adv* laconically.

lacrymal, e, aux [lakrimal, o] *adj* lacrimal.

lacrymogène [lakrimɔʒɛn] *adj* tear *(avant n)*.

lactation [laktasjɔ̃] *nf* lactation.

lacté, e [lakte] *adj* [régime] milk *(avant n)*.

lactique [laktik] *adj* lactic.

lacunaire [lakynɛr] *adj* [insuffisant] incomplete.

lacune [lakyn] *nf* [manque] gap.

lacustre [lakystr] *adj* [faune, plante] lake *(avant n)* ; [cité, village] on stilts.

lad [lad] *nm* stable lad.

là-dedans [ladədɑ̃] *adv* inside, in there ; **il y a quelque chose qui m'intrigue ~** there's something in that which intrigues me.

là-dessous [ladsu] *adv* underneath, under there ; *fig* behind that.

là-dessus [ladsy] *adv* on that ; **~, il partit** at that point *ou* with that, he left ; **je suis d'accord ~** I agree about that.

ladite ⊳ **ledit**.

lagon [lagɔ̃] *nm*, **lagune** [lagyn] *nf* lagoon.

Lagos [lagos] *nm* : **le ~** Lagos.

là-haut [lao] *adv* up there.

laïc, laïque [laik] ◇ *adj* lay *(avant n)* ; [juridiction] civil *(avant n)* ; [école] ·state *(avant n)* ◇ *nm, f* layman (*f* laywoman).

laïcisation [laisizasjɔ̃] *nf* secularization.

laid, e [lɛ, lɛd] *adj* - **1.** [esthétiquement] ugly - **2.** [moralement] wicked.

laideron [lɛdrɔ̃] *nm* ugly woman.

laideur [lɛdœr] *nf* - **1.** [physique] ugliness - **2.** [morale] wickedness.

laie [lɛ] *nf* ZOOL wild sow.

lainage [lɛnaʒ] *nm* [étoffe] woollen *Br ou* woolen *Am* material ; [vêtement] woolly, woollen *Br ou* woolen *Am* garment.

laine [lɛn] *nf* wool ; **~ polaire** polar fleece ; **~ de verre** glass wool ; **pure ~ vierge** pure new wool.

laineux, euse [lɛnø, øz] *adj* woolly.

lainier, ère [lɛnje, ɛr] ◇ *adj* wool *(avant n)* ◇ *nm, f* [marchand] wool merchant ; [ouvrier] wool worker.

laïque = **laïc**.

laisse [lɛs] *nf* [corde] lead, leash ; **tenir en ~** [chien] to keep on a lead *ou* leash ; **tenir qqn en ~** *fig* to keep sb on a short lead.

laissé-pour-compte, laissée-pour-compte [lesepurkɔ̃t] (*mpl* **laissés-pour-compte**, *fpl* **laissées-pour-compte**) *adj* - **1.** [article] unsold - **2.** *fig* [personne] rejected.
➡ **laissé-pour-compte** *nm* - **1.** [article] unsold item - **2.** [personne] reject.

laisser [4] [lese] ◇ *v aux (+ infinitif)* : **~ qqn faire qqch** to let sb do sthg ; **laisse-le faire** leave him alone, don't interfere ; **~ tomber qqch** *litt* & *fig* to drop sthg ; **~ tomber qqn** *fam* to drop *ou* ditch sb ; **laisse tomber!** *fam* drop it! ◇ *vt* - **1.** [gén] to leave ; **~ qqch à qqn** [léguer] to leave sthg to sb, to leave sb sthg ; **~ qqn/qqch à qqn** [confier] to leave sb/sthg with sb - **2.** [céder] : **~ qqch à qqn** to let sb have sthg - **3.** *loc* : **~ qqn tranquille** to leave sb in peace *ou* alone ; **~ à désirer** to leave something to be desired.
➡ **se laisser** *vp* : **se ~ faire** to let o.s. be persuaded ; **se ~ aller** to relax ; [dans son apparence] to let o.s. go ; **se ~ aller dans un fauteuil** to collapse into an armchair ; **se ~ aller à qqch** to indulge in sthg ; **se ~ tenter par** to be tempted by.

laisser-aller [leseale] *nm inv* carelessness.

laissez-passer [lesepase] *nm inv* pass.

lait [lɛ] *nm* - **1.** [gén] milk ; **~ de chèvre/vache** goat's/cow's milk ; **~ entier/écrémé** whole/skimmed milk ; **~ concentré** *ou* **condensé** [sucré] condensed milk ; [non sucré] evaporated milk ; **~ maternel** mother's milk ; **~ en poudre** powdered milk ; **~ de poule** egg flip - **2.** [cosmétique] : **~ démaquillant** cleansing milk *ou* lotion.

laitage [lɛtaʒ] *nm* dairy product.

laiterie [lɛtri] *nf* dairy.

laiteux, euse [lɛtø, øz] *adj* milky.

laitier, ère [lɛtje, ɛr] ◇ *adj* dairy *(avant n)* ◇ *nm, f* milkman (*f* milkwoman).
➡ **laitier** *nm* TECHNOL slag.

laiton [lɛtɔ̃] *nm* brass.

laitue [lɛty] *nf* lettuce.

laïus [lajys] *nm* long speech.

lama [lama] *nm* - **1.** ZOOL llama - **2.** RELIG lama.

lambeau, x [lɑ̃bo] *nm* - **1.** [morceau] shred ; **mettre qqch en ~x** to tear sthg to pieces *ou* shreds - **2.** *fig* [fragment] fragment.

lambiner [3] [lɑ̃bine] *vi fam* to dawdle.

lambris [lɑ̃bri] *nm* panelling *Br*, paneling *Am*.

lambswool [lɑ̃bswul] *nm* lambswool.

lame [lam] *nf* - **1.** [fer] blade ; **~ de rasoir** razor blade - **2.** [lamelle] strip - **3.** [vague] wave ; **~ de fond** groundswell.

lamé, e [lame] *adj* lamé ; ~ or/argent gold/silver lamé.
◆ **lamé** *nm* lamé ; **de** *ou* **en ~** lamé.

lamelle [lamɛl] *nf* - **1.** [de champignon] gill - **2.** [tranche] thin slice - **3.** [de verre] slide.

lamentable [lamɑ̃tabl] *adj* - **1.** [résultats, sort] appalling - **2.** [ton] plaintive.

lamentablement [lamɑ̃tabləmɑ̃] *adv* miserably.

lamentation [lamɑ̃tasjɔ̃] *nf* - **1.** [plainte] lamentation - **2.** *(gén pl)* [jérémiade] moaning *(U).*

lamenter [3] [lamɑ̃te] ◆ **se lamenter** *vp* to complain ; **se ~ sur qqch** to bemoan sthg ; **se ~ d'avoir fait qqch** to complain about having done sthg.

laminage [laminaʒ] *nm* lamination.

laminer [3] [lamine] *vt* IND to laminate ; *fig* [personne, revenus] to eat away at.

laminoir [laminwar] *nm* rolling mill.

lampadaire [lɑ̃padɛr] *nm* [d'intérieur] standard lamp *Br*, floor lamp *Am* ; [de rue] street lamp *ou* light.

lampe [lɑ̃p] *nf* lamp, light ; **~ à bronzer** sunlamp ; **~ de chevet** bedside lamp ; **~ halogène** halogen light ; **~ à incandescence** incandescent lamp ; **~ à pétrole** oil lamp ; **~ de poche** torch *Br*, flashlight *Am* ; **~ à souder** blowtorch ; **~ témoin** pilot light ; **s'en mettre plein la ~** *fam fig* to stuff o.s.

lampée [lɑ̃pe] *nf fam* swig.

lampion [lɑ̃pjɔ̃] *nm* Chinese lantern.

lampiste [lɑ̃pist] *nm* [employé, subalterne] underling, dogsbody *Br*.

lance [lɑ̃s] *nf* - **1.** [arme] spear - **2.** [de tuyau] nozzle ; **~ d'incendie** fire hose.

lancée [lɑ̃se] *nf* : **continuer sur sa ~** to keep going.

lance-flammes [lɑ̃sflam] *nm inv* flamethrower.

lancement [lɑ̃smɑ̃] *nm* - **1.** [d'entreprise, produit, navire] launching - **2.** [de javelot, projectile] throwing.

lance-pierres [lɑ̃spjɛr] *nm inv* catapult.

lancer [16] [lɑ̃se] ◇ *vt* - **1.** [pierre, javelot] to throw ; **~ qqch sur qqn** to throw sthg at sb - **2.** [fusée, produit, style] to launch - **3.** [émettre] to give off ; [cri] to let out ; [injures] to hurl ; [ultimatum] to issue - **4.** [moteur] to start up - **5.** [INFORM - programme] to start ; [- système] to boot (up) - **6.** *fig* [sur un sujet] : **~ qqn sur qqch** to get sb started on sthg ◇ *nm* - **1.** PÊCHE casting - **2.** SPORT throwing ; **~ du poids** shotput.
◆ **se lancer** *vp* - **1.** [débuter] to make a name for o.s - **2.** [s'engager] : **se ~ dans** [dépenses, explication, lecture] to embark on.

lanceur, euse [lɑ̃sœr, øz] *nm, f* SPORT thrower.
◆ **lanceur** *nm* AÉRON launcher.

lancinant, e [lɑ̃sinɑ̃, ɑ̃t] *adj* - **1.** [douleur] shooting - **2.** *fig* [obsédant] haunting - **3.** [monotone] insistent.

lanciner [3] [lɑ̃sine] ◇ *vi* to throb ◇ *vt fig* to haunt.

landau [lɑ̃do] *nm* - **1.** [d'enfant] pram - **2.** [carrosse] landau.

lande [lɑ̃d] *nf* moor.

langage [lɑ̃gaʒ] *nm* language ; **~ machine** INFORM machine language.

lange [lɑ̃ʒ] *nm* nappy *Br*, diaper *Am*.

langer [17] [lɑ̃ʒe] *vt* to change.

langoureusement [lɑ̃gurøzmɑ̃] *adv* languorously.

langoureux, euse [lɑ̃gurø, øz] *adj* languorous.

langouste [lɑ̃gust] *nf* crayfish.

langoustine [lɑ̃gustin] *nf* langoustine.

langue [lɑ̃g] *nf* - **1.** ANAT & *fig* tongue ; **tirer la ~ à qqn** to stick out one's tongue at sb ; **~ de bœuf** CULIN ox tongue ; **mauvaise ~** *fig* gossip ; **avoir la ~ bien pendue** to be a chatterbox ; **donner sa ~ au chat** to give up ; **ne pas avoir sa ~ dans sa poche** never to be at a loss for words ; **tenir sa ~** *fig* to hold one's tongue - **2.** LING language ; **de ~ française** [livre] French ; [personne] French-speaking ; **les politiciens qui parlent la ~ de bois** politicians who mouth clichés ; **~ maternelle** mother tongue ; **~ morte/vivante** dead/modern language.

langue-de-chat [lɑ̃gdəʃa] *(pl* **langues-de-chat)** *nf* light finger-biscuit.

languette [lɑ̃gɛt] *nf* tongue.

langueur [lɑ̃gœr] *nf* - **1.** [dépérissement, mélancolie] languor - **2.** [apathie] apathy.

languir [32] [lɑ̃gir] *vi* - **1.** [dépérir] : **~ (de)** to languish (with) - **2.** *sout* [attendre] to wait ; **faire ~ qqn** to keep sb waiting - **3.** *littéraire* [désirer] : **~ après** to pine for.

lanière [lanjɛr] *nf* strip.

lanoline [lanɔlin] *nf* lanolin.

lanterne [lɑ̃tɛrn] *nf* - **1.** [éclairage] lantern - **2.** [phare] light - **3.** *loc* : **éclairer la ~ de qqn** *fig* to put sb in the know ; **être la ~ rouge** *fam fig* to bring up the rear.

lanterner [3] [lɑ̃tɛrne] *vi fam* to dawdle ; **faire ~ qqn** to keep sb hanging around.

Laos [laɔs] *nm* : **le ~** Laos ; **au ~** in Laos.

laotien, enne [laosjɛ̃, ɛn] *adj* Laotian.
◆ **laotien** *nm* [langue] Laotian.

Laotien, enne *nm, f* Laotian.

lapalissade [lapalisad] *nf* statement of the obvious.

La Paz [lapaz] *n* La Paz.

laper [3] [lape] *vt* & *vi* to lap.

lapereau, x [lapro] *nm* baby rabbit.

lapidaire [lapidɛr] <> *nm* lapidary <> *adj* lapidary ; *fig* [style] terse.

lapider [3] [lapide] *vt* [tuer] to stone.

lapin, e [lapɛ̃, in] *nm, f* - **1.** CULIN & ZOOL rabbit ; ~ **de garenne** wild rabbit - **2.** *fam* [personne] : **mon ~** my darling ; **chaud ~** stud - **3.** *loc* : **poser un ~ à qqn** *fam* to stand sb up.

lapin *nm* [fourrure] rabbit fur.

lapon, onne ou **one** [lapɔ̃, ɔn] *adj* Lapp.

lapon *nm* [langue] Lapp.

Lapon, onne ou **one** *nm, f* Lapp, Laplander.

Laponie [laponi] *nf* : **la ~** Lapland.

laps [laps] *nm* : **(dans) un ~ de temps** (in) a while.

lapsus [lapsys] *nm* slip (of the tongue/pen) ; **faire un ~** to make a slip (of the tongue/pen).

laquais [lakɛ] *nm* lackey.

laque [lak] *nf* - **1.** [vernis, peinture] lacquer - **2.** [pour cheveux] hair spray, lacquer.

laqué, e [lake] *adj* lacquered.

laquelle ▷ **lequel.**

laquer [3] [lake] *vt* to lacquer.

larbin [larbɛ̃] *nm* - **1.** [domestique] servant - **2.** [personne servile] yes-man.

larcin [larsɛ̃] *nm* - **1.** [vol] larceny, theft - **2.** [butin] spoils *(pl)*.

lard [lar] *nm* - **1.** [graisse de porc] lard - **2.** [viande] bacon - **3.** *fam* [graisse d'homme] blubber.

larder [3] [larde] *vt* - **1.** CULIN to lard - **2.** *fig* [piquer] : ~ **qqn de coups/d'injures** to rain blows/insults on sb - **3.** *fig* [truffer] : ~ **qqch de** to cram sthg with.

lardon [lardɔ̃] *nm* - **1.** CULIN cube or strip of bacon - **2.** *fam* [enfant] kid.

large [larʒ] <> *adj* - **1.** [étendu, grand] wide ; ~ **de 5 mètres** 5 metres wide ; **être ~ de hanches/d'épaules** to have broad hips/shoulders - **2.** [important, considérable] large, big - **3.** [esprit, sourire] broad - **4.** [généreux - personne] generous <> *adv* amply ; **voir ~** to think big ; **ne pas en mener ~** *fig* to be afraid <> *nm* - **1.** [largeur] : **5 mètres de ~** 5 metres wide - **2.** [mer] : **le ~** the open sea ; **au ~ de la côte française** off the French coast ; **prendre le ~** [navire] to put to sea ; *fig* to be off.

largement [larʒəmɑ̃] *adv* - **1.** [diffuser, répandre]

widely ; **la porte était ~ ouverte** the door was wide open - **2.** [donner, payer] generously ; [dépasser] considerably ; [récompenser] amply ; **avoir ~ le temps** to have plenty of time - **3.** [au moins] easily.

largesse [larʒɛs] *nf* - **1.** [générosité] generosity - **2.** *(gén pl)* [don] gift.

largeur [larʒœr] *nf* - **1.** [d'avenue, de cercle] width - **2.** *fig* [d'idées, d'esprit] breadth.

largué, e [large] *adj* : **être ~** to be all at sea.

larguer [3] [large] *vt* - **1.** [voile] to unfurl - **2.** [bombe, parachutiste] to drop - **3.** *fam fig* [abandonner] to chuck ; **se faire ~** to be chucked.

larme [larm] *nf* - **1.** [pleur] tear ; **être en ~s** to be in tears ; **fondre en ~s** to burst into tears ; **pleurer à chaudes ~s** to cry bitterly ; **ravaler ses ~s** to hold back one's tears ; **rire aux ~s** to laugh until one cries ; **~s de crocodile** *fig* crocodile tears - **2.** *fam* [goutte] : **une ~ de** a drop of.

larmoyant, e [larmwajɑ̃, ɑ̃t] *adj* - **1.** [yeux, personne] tearful - **2.** *péj* [histoire] tearjerking.

larmoyer [13] [larmwaje] *vi* - **1.** [pleurer - personne] to weep ; [- yeux] to water - **2.** *péj* [se lamenter] to moan.

larron [larɔ̃] *nm vieilli* [voleur] thief.

larve [larv] *nf* - **1.** ZOOL larva - **2.** *péj* [personne] wimp.

larvé, e [larve] *adj* - **1.** MÉD larvate - **2.** [latent] latent.

laryngite [larɛ̃ʒit] *nf* laryngitis *(U)*.

larynx [larɛ̃ks] *nm* larynx.

las, lasse [lɑ, lɑs] *adj littéraire* - **1.** [fatigué] weary - **2.** [dégoûté, ennuyé] tired ; ~ **de faire qqch** tired of doing sthg ; ~ **de qqn/qqch** tired of sb/sthg.

las *interj* alas!

lascar [laskar] *nm* - **1.** [homme louche] shady character ; [homme rusé] rogue - **2.** *fam* [enfant] rascal.

lascif, ive [lasif, iv] *adj* lascivious.

laser [lazɛr] <> *nm* laser <> *adj inv* laser *(avant n)*.

lassant, e [lasɑ̃, ɑ̃t] *adj* tiresome.

lasser [3] [lase] *vt sout* [personne] to weary ; [patience] to try.

se lasser *vp* to weary ; **ne pas se ~ de qqch/de faire qqch** not to weary of sthg/of doing sthg.

lassitude [lasityd] *nf* lassitude.

lasso [laso] *nm* lasso.

lat. *(abr de* **latitude***)* lat.

latent, e [latɑ̃, ɑ̃t] *adj* latent.

latéral, e, aux [lateral, o] *adj* lateral.

latex [latɛks] *nm inv* latex.

latin, e [latɛ̃, in] *adj* Latin.

➠ **latin** *nm* [langue] Latin ; **y perdre son ~** *fig* to be at a loss.

latiniste [latinist] *nmf* [spécialiste] Latinist ; [étudiant] Latin student.

latino-américain, e [latinɔamerikɛ̃, ɛn] (*mpl* **latino-américains**, *fpl* **latino-américaines**) *adj* Latin-American, Hispanic.

latitude [latityd] *nf litt* & *fig* latitude.

latrines [latrin] *nfpl* latrines.

latte [lat] *nf* lath, slat.

lattis [lati] *nm* lathwork.

laudatif, ive [lodatif, iv] *adj* laudatory.

lauréat, e [lɔrea, at] ◇ *adj* prizewinning, winning ◇ *nm, f* prizewinner, winner.

laurier [lɔrje] *nm* BOT laurel.

➠ **lauriers** *nmpl* [gloire] laurels ; **s'endormir** OU **se reposer sur ses ~s** to rest on one's laurels.

laurier-rose [lɔrjeroz] (*pl* **lauriers-roses**) *nm* oleander.

laurier-sauce [lɔrjesos] (*pl* **lauriers-sauce**) *nm* bay (tree).

Lausanne [lozan] *n* Lausanne.

lavable [lavabl] *adj* washable.

lavabo [lavabo] *nm* **- 1.** [cuvette] basin **- 2.** (*gén pl*) [local] toilet.

lavage [lavaʒ] *nm* washing ; **~ à la main/en machine** hand/machine washing ; **~ de cerveau** *fig* brainwashing ; **subir un ~ d'estomac** MÉD to have one's stomach pumped.

lavande [lavɑ̃d] ◇ *nf* **- 1.** BOT lavender **- 2.** [eau] lavender water ◇ *adj inv* lavender (*avant n*).

lavasse [lavas] *nf fam* dishwater (U).

lave [lav] *nf* lava.

lave-glace [lavglas] (*pl* **lave-glaces**) *nm* windscreen washer *Br*, windshield washer *Am*.

lave-linge [lavlɛ̃ʒ] *nm inv* washing machine.

lavement [lavmɑ̃] *nm* enema.

laver [3] [lave] *vt* **- 1.** [nettoyer] to wash **- 2.** *fig* [disculper] : **~ qqn de qqch** to clear sb of sthg.

➠ **se laver** *vp* **- 1.** [se nettoyer] to wash o.s., to have a wash ; **se ~ les mains/les cheveux** to wash one's hands/hair **- 2.** [se disculper] : **se ~ (de)** to clear o.s. (of).

laverie [lavri] *nf* [commerce] laundry ; **~ automatique** launderette.

lavette [lavɛt] *nf* **- 1.** [brosse] washing-up brush ; [en tissu] dishcloth **- 2.** *fam* [homme] drip.

laveur, euse [lavœr, øz] *nm, f* washer ; **~ de carreaux** window cleaner (*person*).

lave-vaisselle [lavvesɛl] *nm inv* dishwasher.

lavis [lavi] *nm* [procédé] washing ; [dessin] wash (painting).

lavoir [lavwar] *nm* **- 1.** [lieu] laundry **- 2.** [bac] washtub.

laxatif, ive [laksatif, iv] *adj* laxative.

➠ **laxatif** *nm* laxative.

laxisme [laksism] *nm* laxity.

laxiste [laksist] ◇ *nmf* over-lenient person ◇ *adj* lax.

layette [lɛjɛt] *nf* layette.

le [lə], **l'** (*devant voyelle ou h muet*) (*f* **la** [la], *pl* **les** [le]) ◇ *art déf* **- 1.** [gén] the ; **~ lac** the lake ; **la fenêtre** the window ; **l'homme** the man ; **les enfants** the children **- 2.** [devant les noms abstraits] : **l'amour** love ; **la liberté** freedom ; **la vieillesse** old age **- 3.** [devant les noms géographiques] : **la France** France ; **les États-Unis** America, the United States (of America) ; **la Seine** the Seine ; **les Alpes** the Alps **- 4.** [temps] : **~ 15 janvier 1993** 15th January 1993 ; **je suis arrivé ~ 15 janvier 1993** I arrived on the 15th of January 1993 ; **~ lundi** [habituellement] on Mondays ; [jour précis] on (the) Monday **- 5.** [possession] : **se laver les mains** to wash one's hands ; **secouer la tête** to shake one's head ; **avoir les cheveux blonds** to have fair hair **- 6.** [distributif] per, a ; **10 francs ~ mètre** 10 francs per metre *Br* OU meter *Am*, 10 francs a metre *Br* OU meter *Am* ◇ *pron pers* **- 1.** [personne] him (*f* her), *pl* them ; [chose] it, *pl* them ; [animal] it, him (*f* her), *pl* them ; **je ~/la/les connais bien** I know him/her/them well ; **tu dois avoir la clé, donne-la moi** you must have the key, give it to me **- 2.** [représente une proposition] : **je ~ sais bien** I know, I'm well aware (of it) ; **je te l'avais bien dit!** I told you so!

LEA (*abr de* **langues étrangères appliquées**) *nfpl* applied modern languages.

leader [lidœr] ◇ *nm* [de parti, course] leader ◇ *adj* leading.

leadership [lidœrʃip] *nm* leadership.

lèche [lɛʃ] *nf tfam* bootlicking ; **faire de la ~ à qqn** to lick sb's boots.

léché, e [leʃe] *adj fam* [fignolé] polished.

lèchefrite [lɛʃfrit] *nf* dripping-pan.

lécher [18] [leʃe] *vt* **- 1.** [passer la langue sur, effleurer] to lick ; [suj : vague] to wash against **- 2.** *fam* [fignoler] to polish (up).

➠ **se lécher** *vp* : **se ~ les doigts** *fam* to lick one's fingers.

lèche-vitrines [lɛʃvitrin] *nm inv* window-shopping ; **faire du ~** to go window-shopping.

leçon [ləsɔ̃] *nf* - **1.** [gén] lesson ; **~s de conduite** driving lessons ; **~s particulières** private lessons *ou* classes - **2.** [conseil] advice *(U)* ; **faire la ~ à qqn** to lecture sb.

lecteur, trice [lɛktœr, tris] *nm, f* - **1.** [de livres] reader - **2.** UNIV foreign language assistant.
▸ **lecteur** *nm* - **1.** [gén] head ; **~ de cassettes/CD** cassette/CD player ; **~ laser universel** audio-video CD player - **2.** INFORM reader ; **~ de disques** disk drive.

lecture [lɛktyr] *nf* reading.

LED (*abr de* **light emitting diode**) *nf* LED.

ledit, ladite [lədi, ladit] (*mpl* **lesdits** [ledi], *fpl* **lesdites** [ledit]) *adj* the said, the aforementioned.

légal, e, aux [legal, o] *adj* legal.

légalement [legalmɑ̃] *adv* legally.

légalisation [legalizasjɔ̃] *nf* - **1.** [légitimation] legalization - **2.** [authentification] authentication.

légaliser [3] [legalize] *vt* - **1.** [rendre légal] to legalize - **2.** [certifier authentique] to authenticate.

légalisme [legalism] *nm* legalism.

légalité [legalite] *nf* - **1.** [de contrat, d'acte] legality, lawfulness - **2.** [loi] law.

légataire [legatɛr] *nmf* legatee ; **~ universel** sole legatee.

légation [legasjɔ̃] *nf* legation.

légendaire [leʒɑ̃dɛr] *adj* legendary.

légende [leʒɑ̃d] *nf* - **1.** [fable] legend - **2.** *péj* [invention] story - **3.** [de carte, de schéma] key ; [de photo] caption.

léger, ère [leʒe, ɛr] *adj* - **1.** [objet, étoffe, repas] light - **2.** [bruit, différence, odeur] slight - **3.** [alcool, tabac] low-strength - **4.** [femme] flighty - **5.** [insouciant - ton] light-hearted ; [- conduite] thoughtless.
▸ **à la légère** *loc adv* lightly, thoughtlessly.

légèrement [leʒɛrmɑ̃] *adv* - **1.** [s'habiller, poser] lightly - **2.** [agir] thoughtlessly - **3.** [blesser, remuer] slightly.

légèreté [leʒɛrte] *nf* - **1.** [d'objet, de repas, de punition] lightness - **2.** [de style] gracefulness - **3.** [de conduite] thoughtlessness - **4.** [de personne] flightiness.

légiférer [18] [leʒifere] *vi* to legislate.

légion [leʒjɔ̃] *nf* - **1.** MIL legion ; **la Légion étrangère** the Foreign Legion - **2.** [grand nombre] : **une ~ de** a host of ; **être ~** *fig* to be legion.
▸ **Légion** *nf* : **la Légion d'honneur** the Legion of Honour.

légionnaire [leʒjɔnɛr] *nm* legionary.

législateur, trice [leʒislatœr, tris] *nm, f* legislator.

législatif, ive [leʒislatif, iv] *adj* legislative.
▸ **législatif** *nm* legislature.
▸ **législatives** *nfpl* : **les législatives** the legislative elections, ≃ the general election *(sg)* Br.

législation [leʒislasjɔ̃] *nf* legislation.

législature [leʒislatyr] *nf* - **1.** [période] term of office - **2.** [corps] legislature.

légiste [leʒist] *adj* - **1.** [juriste] jurist - **2.** ⇨ **médecin**.

légitimation [leʒitimasjɔ̃] *nf* - **1.** [d'enfant] legitimization - **2.** *littéraire* [justification] justification.

légitime [leʒitim] *adj* legitimate.

légitimement [leʒitimmɑ̃] *adv* - **1.** [légalement] legitimately - **2.** [justement] fairly.

légitimer [3] [leʒitime] *vt* - **1.** [reconnaître] to recognize ; [enfant] to legitimize - **2.** [justifier] to justify.

légitimité [leʒitimite] *nf* - **1.** [de pouvoir, d'enfant] legitimacy - **2.** [de récompense] fairness.

legs [lɛg] *nm* legacy.

léguer [18] [lege] *vt* : **~ qqch à qqn** JUR to bequeath sthg to sb ; *fig* to pass sthg on to sb.

légume [legym] ◇ *nm* vegetable ◇ *nf fam* : **une grosse ~** a bigwig.

leitmotiv [lajtmɔtif, lɛtmɔtif] *nm* leitmotif.

Léman [lemɑ̃] ⇨ **lac**.

lendemain [lɑ̃dmɛ̃] *nm* - **1.** [jour] day after ; **le ~ matin** the next morning ; **au ~ de** after, in the days following - **2.** [avenir] tomorrow ; **sans ~** short-lived.

lénifiant, e [lenifjɑ̃, ɑ̃t] *adj litt* & *fig* soothing.

léniniste [leninist] *nmf* & *adj* Leninist.

lent, e [lɑ̃, lɑ̃t] *adj* slow ; **~ à faire qqch** slow to do sthg.

lente [lɑ̃t] *nf* nit.

lentement [lɑ̃tmɑ̃] *adv* slowly.

lenteur [lɑ̃tœr] *nf* slowness *(U)*.

lentille [lɑ̃tij] *nf* - **1.** BOT & CULIN lentil - **2.** [d'optique] lens ; **~s de contact** contact lenses.

léonin, e [leɔnɛ̃, in] *adj* - **1.** [du lion] leonine - **2.** [injuste] one-sided.

léopard [leɔpar] *nm* leopard.

lèpre [lɛpr] *nf* - **1.** MÉD leprosy - **2.** *fig* [mal] disease.

lépreux, euse [leprø, øz] ◇ *adj* - **1.** MÉD leprous - **2.** *fig* [mur, maison] peeling ◇ *nm, f* leper.

lequel [ləkɛl] (f **laquelle** [lakɛl], mpl **lesquels** [lekɛl], fpl **lesquelles** [lekɛl]) (contraction de à + lequel = **auquel**, de + lequel = **duquel**, à + lesquels/lesquelles = **auxquels/auxquelles**, de + lesquels/lesquelles = **desquels/desquelles**) ◇ pron rel **- 1.** [complément - personne] whom ; [- chose] which **- 2.** [sujet - personne] who ; [- chose] which ◇ pron interr : **lequel?** which (one)?

les ⊳ le.

lesbienne [lɛsbjɛn] nf lesbian.

lesdits, lesdites ⊳ ledit.

lèse-majesté [lɛzmaʒɛste] nf inv lese-majesty.

léser [18] [leze] vt **- 1.** [frustrer] to wrong **- 2.** MÉD to injure, to damage.

lésiner [3] [lezine] vi to skimp ; **ne pas ~ sur** not to skimp on.

lésion [lezjɔ̃] nf lesion.

Lesotho [lesɔtɔ] nm : **le ~** Lesotho.

lesquels, lesquelles ⊳ lequel.

lessive [lesiv] nf **- 1.** [nettoyage, linge] washing **- 2.** [produit] washing powder.

lessiver [3] [lesive] vt **- 1.** [nettoyer] to wash **- 2.** CHIM to leach **- 3.** fam [épuiser] to wipe out.

lest [lɛst] nm ballast ; **lâcher du ~** to jettison ballast ; fig to make concessions.

leste [lɛst] adj **- 1.** [agile] nimble, agile **- 2.** [licencieux] crude.

lestement [lɛstəmɑ̃] adv **- 1.** [agilement] nimbly, agilely **- 2.** [grivoisement] crudely.

lester [3] [lɛste] vt **- 1.** [garnir de lest] to ballast **- 2.** fam [charger] to fill, to cram.

letchi = litchi.

léthargie [letarʒi] nf litt & fig lethargy ; **tomber en ~** to become lethargic.

léthargique [letarʒik] adj lethargic.

letton, onne [letɔ̃, ɔn] adj Latvian.
◆ **letton** nm [langue] Latvian.
◆ **Letton, onne** nm, f Latvian.

Lettonie [letɔni] nf : **la ~** Latvia.

lettre [lɛtr] nf **- 1.** [gén] letter ; **en toutes ~s** in words, in full ; **~ d'amour** love letter ; **~ de couverture** cover note ; **~ ouverte** open letter ; **~ piégée** letter bomb ; **~ de rappel** reminder ; **~ de recommandation** (letter of) recommendation ; **passer comme une ~ à la poste** fam [entretien, examen] to go smoothly ; [personne] to get through easily **- 2.** [sens des mots] : **à la ~** to the letter.
◆ **lettres** nfpl **- 1.** [culture littéraire] letters **- 2.** UNIV arts ; **~s classiques** classics ; **~s modernes** French language and literature

- 3. [titre] : **~s de noblesse** letters patent of nobility.
◆ **lettre de change** nf bill of exchange.

leucémie [løsemi] nf leukemia.

leucocyte [løkɔsit] nm leucocyte.

leucorrhée [løkɔre] nf leucorrhoea.

leur [lœr] pron pers inv (to) them ; **je voudrais ~ parler** I'd like to speak to them ; **je ~ ai donné la lettre** I gave them the letter, I gave the letter to them.
◆ **leur** (pl **leurs**) adj poss their ; **c'est ~ tour** it's their turn ; **~s enfants** their children.
◆ **le leur** (f **la leur**, pl **les leurs**) pron poss theirs ; **il faudra qu'ils y mettent du ~** they've got to pull their weight.

leurre [lœr] nm **- 1.** [appât] lure **- 2.** fig [illusion] illusion **- 3.** fig [tromperie] deception, trap.

leurrer [5] [lœre] vt to deceive.
◆ **se leurrer** vp to deceive o.s.

levain [ləvɛ̃] nm **- 1.** CULIN : **pain au ~/sans ~** leavened/unleavened bread **- 2.** fig [germe] seeds (pl), germ.

levant [ləvɑ̃] ◇ nm east ◇ adj ⊳ soleil.

levé, e [ləve] adj [debout] up.
◆ **levée** nf **- 1.** [de scellés, difficulté] removal ; [de blocus, de siège, d'interdiction] lifting **- 2.** [de séance] close, closing **- 3.** [d'impôts, du courrier] collection **- 4.** [d'armée] raising **- 5.** [remblai] dyke **- 6.** CARTES trick.
◆ **levée de boucliers** nf (general) outcry.

lever [19] [ləve] ◇ vt **- 1.** [objet, blocus, interdiction] to lift **- 2.** [main, tête, armée] to raise **- 3.** [scellés, difficulté] to remove **- 4.** [séance] to close, to end **- 5.** [impôts, courrier] to collect **- 6.** [plan, carte] to draw (up) **- 7.** [enfant, malade] : **~ qqn** to get sb up ◇ vi **- 1.** [plante] to come up **- 2.** [pâte] to rise ◇ nm **- 1.** [d'astre] rising, rise ; **~ du jour** daybreak ; **~ du soleil** sunrise **- 2.** [de personne] : **il est toujours de mauvaise humeur au ~** he's always in a bad mood when he gets up **- 3.** THÉÂTRE : **~ de rideau** curtain, curtain-up ; fig curtain-raiser.
◆ **se lever** vp **- 1.** [personne] to get up, to rise ; [vent] to get up **- 2.** [soleil, lune] to rise ; [jour] to break **- 3.** [temps] to clear.

lève-tard [lɛvtar] nmf inv late riser.

lève-tôt [lɛvto] nmf inv early riser.

levier [ləvje] nm litt & fig lever ; **~ de vitesses** gear lever Br, gear shift Am.

lévitation [levitasjɔ̃] nf levitation.

lèvre [lɛvr] nf **- 1.** ANAT lip ; [de vulve] labium ; **être suspendu aux ~s de qqn** fig to hang on sb's every word ; **se mordre les ~s** fig to bite one's lip **- 2.** [bord] edge.

lévrier, levrette [levrije, ləvrɛt] *nm, f* greyhound.

levure [ləvyr] *nf* yeast ; ~ **chimique** baking powder.

lexical, e, aux [lɛksikal, o] *adj* lexical.

lexicographie [lɛksikɔgrafi] *nf* lexicography.

lexique [lɛksik] *nm* - **1.** [dictionnaire] glossary - **2.** [vocabulaire] vocabulary.

lézard [lezar] *nm* - **1.** [animal] lizard ; **faire le ~ fam** *fig* to bask in the sun - **2.** [peau] lizard (skin).

lézarde [lezard] *nf* crack.

lézarder [3] [lezarde] <> *vt* to crack <> *vi fam* [paresser] to bask.
 ♦ **se lézarder** *vp* to crack.

Lhassa [lasa] *n* Lhasa.

liaison [ljezɔ̃] *nf* - **1.** [jonction, enchaînement] connection - **2.** CULIN & LING liaison - **3.** [contact, relation] contact ; **avoir une ~** to have an affair ; **être/entrer en ~ avec** to be in/establish contact with ; **par ~ radio** by radio link - **4.** TRANSPORT link.

liane [ljan] *nf* creeper.

liant, e [ljɑ̃, ɑ̃t] *adj* sociable.
 ♦ **liant** *nm* - **1.** [substance] binder - **2.** [élasticité] elasticity.

liasse [ljas] *nf* bundle ; [de billets de banque] wad.

Liban [libɑ̃] *nm* : **le ~** Lebanon ; **au ~** in Lebanon.

libanais, e [libanɛ, ɛz] *adj* Lebanese.
 ♦ **Libanais, e** *nm, f* Lebanese (person) ; **les Libanais** the Lebanese.

Libé [libe] (*abr de* **Libération**) *nm* French left-of-centre newspaper.

libelle [libɛl] *nm* lampoon.

libellé [libele] *nm* wording.

libeller [4] [libele] *vt* - **1.** [chèque] to make out - **2.** [lettre] to word.

libellule [libelyl] *nf* dragonfly.

libéral, e, aux [liberal, o] <> *adj* [attitude, idée, parti] liberal <> *nm, f* POLIT liberal.

libéralement [liberalmɑ̃] *adv* liberally.

libéralisation [liberalizasjɔ̃] *nf* liberalization.

libéraliser [3] [liberalize] *vt* to liberalize.

libéralisme [liberalism] *nm* liberalism.

libéralité [liberalite] *nf* - **1.** [générosité] generosity - **2.** (*gén pl*) [don] generous gift.

libérateur, trice [liberatœr, tris] <> *adj* [rire] liberating ; **guerre libératrice** war of liberation <> *nm, f* liberator.

libération [liberasjɔ̃] *nf* - **1.** [de prisonnier] release, freeing - **2.** [de pays, de la femme] liber-

ation ; **la Libération** HIST the Liberation - **3.** [d'énergie] release.

libéré, e [libere] *nm, f* freed prisoner.

libérer [18] [libere] *vt* - **1.** [prisonnier, fonds] to release, to free - **2.** [pays, la femme] to liberate ; **~ qqn de qqch** to free sb from sthg - **3.** [passage] to clear - **4.** [énergie] to release - **5.** [instincts, passions] to give free rein to.
 ♦ **se libérer** *vp* - **1.** [se rendre disponible] to get away - **2.** [se dégager] : **se ~ de** [lien] to free o.s. from ; [engagement] to get out of.

Liberia [liberja] *nm* : **le ~** Liberia ; **au ~** in Liberia.

libérien, enne [liberjɛ̃, ɛn] *adj* Liberian.
 ♦ **Libérien, enne** *nm, f* Liberian.

libertaire [libertɛr] *nmf* & *adj* libertarian.

liberté [liberte] *nf* - **1.** [gén] freedom ; **en ~** free ; **Liberté, Égalité, Fraternité** Liberty, Equality, Fraternity ; **parler en toute ~** to speak freely ; **vivre en ~** to live in freedom ; **~ d'expression** freedom of expression ; **~ d'opinion** freedom of thought - **2.** JUR release ; **~ conditionnelle** parole ; **~ provisoire** bail ; **~ surveillée** probation - **3.** [loisir] free time.

libertin, e [libertɛ̃, in] <> *adj* [dissolu] dissolute ; [propos, livre] lewd <> *nm, f* libertine.

libertinage [libertinaʒ] *nm* [débauche] dissoluteness ; [de propos, livre] lewdness.

libidineux, euse [libidinø, øz] *adj* lecherous.

libido [libido] *nf* libido.

libraire [librɛr] *nmf* bookseller.

librairie [libreri] *nf* - **1.** [magasin] bookshop *Br*, bookstore *Am* - **2.** [commerce, activité] book trade.

librairie-papeterie [libreri-papetri] (*pl* **librairies-papeteries**) *nf* bookseller's and stationer's.

libre [libr] *adj* - **1.** [gén] free ; **~ de qqch** free from sthg ; **être ~ de faire qqch** to be free to do sthg - **2.** [école, secteur] private - **3.** [passage] clear.

libre-échange [librefɑ̃ʒ] (*pl* **libres-échanges**) *nm* free trade (*U*).

librement [librəmɑ̃] *adv* freely.

libre-penseur, euse [librəpɑ̃sœr, øz] (*mpl* **libres-penseurs**, *fpl* **libres-penseuses**) *nm, f* free-thinker.

libre-service [librəservis] (*pl* **libres-services**) *nm* - **1.** [système] : **le ~** self-service - **2.** [magasin] self-service store *ou* shop ; [restaurant] self-service restaurant.

librettiste [librɛtist] *nmf* librettist.

Libreville [librəvil] *n* Libreville.

Libye [libi] *nf* : **la ~** Libya.

libyen, enne [libjɛ̃, ɛn] *adj* Libyan.

➤ **Libyen, enne** *nm, f* Libyan.

lice [lis] *nf* : **en ~ fig** in the fray ; **entrer en ~ fig** to join the fray.

licence [lisɑ̃s] *nf* - **1.** [permis] permit ; COMM licence - **2.** UNIV (first) degree ; **~ ès lettres/en droit** ≃ Bachelor of Arts/Law degree - **3.** *littéraire* [liberté] licence ; **~ poétique** poetic licence.

licencié, e [lisɑ̃sje] ◇ *adj* - **1.** UNIV graduate *(avant n)* - **2.** [autorisé] permit-holding *(avant n)* ; COMM licensed ◇ *nm, f* - **1.** UNIV graduate - **2.** [titulaire d'un permis] permit-holder ; COMM licence-holder.

licenciement [lisɑ̃simɑ̃] *nm* dismissal ; [économique] layoff, redundancy Br.

licencier [9] [lisɑ̃sje] *vt* to dismiss ; [pour cause économique] to lay off, to make redundant Br.

licencieux, euse [lisɑ̃sjø, øz] *adj* licentious.

lichen [likɛn] *nm* lichen.

licite [lisit] *adj* lawful, legal.

licol [likɔl], **licou** [liku] *nm* halter.

licorne [likɔrn] *nf* unicorn.

licou = licol.

lie [li] *nf* [dépôt] dregs *(pl)*, sediment ; **la ~ de la société** *fig* & *littéraire* the dregs *(pl)* of society.

lié, e [lje] *adj* - **1.** [mains] bound - **2.** [amis] : **être très ~ avec** to be great friends with.

Liechtenstein [liʃtɛnʃtajn] *nm* : **le ~** Liechtenstein ; **au ~** in Liechtenstein.

liechtensteinois, e [liʃtɒuɔnʃtajnwa, az] *adj* from Liechtenstein.

➤ **Liechtensteinois, e** *nm, f* Liechtensteiner.

lie-de-vin [lidəvɛ̃] *adj inv* burgundy, wine-coloured Br, wine-colored Am.

liège [ljɛʒ] *nm* cork ; **en** *ou* **de ~** cork *(avant n)*.

liégeois, e [ljeʒwa, az] *adj* - **1.** GÉOGR of/from Liège - **2.** CULIN : **café/chocolat ~** coffee or chocolate ice cream topped with whipped cream.

lien [ljɛ̃] *nm* - **1.** [sangle] bond - **2.** [relation, affinité] bond, tie ; **avoir des ~s de parenté avec** to be related to - **3.** *fig* [enchaînement] connection, link.

lier [9] [lje] *vt* - **1.** [attacher] to tie (up) ; **~ qqn/qqch à** to tie sb/sthg to - **2.** [suj : contrat, promesse] to bind ; **~ qqn/qqch par** to bind sb/sthg by - **3.** [relier par la logique] to link, to connect ; **~ qqch à** to link sthg to, to connect sthg

with - **4.** [commencer] : **~ connaissance/conversation avec** to strike up an acquaintance/a conversation with - **5.** [suj : sentiment, intérêt] to unite - **6.** CULIN to thicken.

➤ **se lier** *vp* - **1.** [s'attacher] : **se ~ (d'amitié) avec qqn** to make friends with sb - **2.** [s'astreindre] : **se ~ par une promesse** to be bound by a promise.

lierre [ljɛr] *nm* ivy.

liesse [ljɛs] *nf* jubilation.

lieu, x [ljø] *nm* - **1.** [endroit] place ; **en ~ sûr** in a safe place ; **~ de naissance** birthplace ; **~ de perdition** den of vice ; **~ saint** holy place ; **haut ~ de qqch** *fig* centre *Br ou* center *Am* of sthg ; **en haut ~** *fig* in high places - **2.** *loc* : **avoir ~** to take place ; **avoir ~ de faire qqch** to have grounds for doing sthg ; **donner ~ à** to give rise to ; **tenir ~ de** to take the place of.

➤ **lieux** *nmpl* - **1.** [scène] scene *(sg)*, spot *(sg)* ; **sur les ~x (d'un crime/d'un accident)** at the scene (of a crime/an accident) - **2.** [domicile] premises.

➤ **lieu commun** *nm* commonplace.

➤ **au lieu de** *loc prép* : **au ~ de qqch/de faire qqch** instead of sthg/of doing sthg.

➤ **en dernier lieu** *loc adv* lastly.

➤ **en premier lieu** *loc adv* in the first place.

➤ **en second lieu** *loc adv* in the second place.

lieu-dit [ljødi] *(pl* **lieux-dits***)* *nm* locality, place.

lieue [ljø] *nf* league ; **j'étais à cent ~s de penser cela** *fig* I never thought for a moment.

lieutenant [ljøtnɑ̃] *nm* lieutenant.

lieutenant-colonel [ljøtnɑ̃kɔlɔnɛl] *(pl* **lieutenants-colonels***)* *nm* lieutenant-colonel.

lièvre [ljɛvr] *nm* hare ; **courir deux ~s à la fois** *fig* to do more than one thing at a time ; **lever un ~** *fig* to ask an awkward question.

lifter [3] [lifte] *vt* TENNIS to spin, to put a spin on.

lifting [liftiŋ] *nm* face-lift.

ligament [ligamɑ̃] *nm* ligament.

ligature [ligatyr] *nf* [MÉD - lien] ligature ; [- opération] ligation, ligature ; **~ des trompes** MÉD tubal ligation.

ligaturer [3] [ligatyre] *vt* - **1.** MÉD to ligature, to ligate - **2.** AGRIC to bind.

lige [liʒ] *adj* : **homme ~** liege man.

ligne [liɲ] *nf* - **1.** [gén] line ; **à la ~** new line *ou* paragraph ; **en ~** [personnes] in a line ; INFORM on line ; **restez en ~!** TÉLÉCOM who's speaking *ou* calling? ; **en ~ droite** as the crow flies ; **li-**

re entre les ~s *fig* to read between the lines ; dans sa **~ de mire** in one's line of sight ; **~ de départ/d'arrivée** starting/finishing line ; **~ aérienne** airline ; **~ de commande** INFORM command line ; **~ de conduite** line of conduct ; **~ de démarcation** demarcation line ; **~ directrice** guideline ; **~ de flottaison** water line ; **~s de la main** lines of the hand ; **les grandes ~s** TRANSPORT the main lines **- 2.** [forme - de voiture, meuble] lines *(pl)* **- 3.** [silhouette] : **avoir la ~** to have a good figure ; **garder la ~** to keep one's figure ; **surveiller sa ~** to watch one's waistline **- 4.** [de pêche] fishing line ; **pêcher à la ~** to go angling **- 5.** *loc* : **dans les grandes ~s** in outline ; **entrer en ~ de compte** to be taken into account.

lignée [liɲe] *nf* [famille] descendants *(pl)* ; **dans la ~ de** *fig* [d'écrivains, d'artistes] in the tradition of.

lignite [liɲit] *nm* lignite.

ligoter [3] [ligɔte] *vt* **- 1.** [attacher] to tie up ; **~ qqn à qqch** to tie sb to sthg **- 2.** *fig* [entraver] to bind.

ligue [lig] *nf* league.

liguer [3] [lige] ◆ **se liguer** *vp* to form a league ; **se ~ contre** to conspire against.

lilas [lila] *nm* & *adj inv* lilac.

limace [limas] *nf* **- 1.** ZOOL slug **- 2.** *fig* [personne] slowcoach *Br*, slowpoke *Am*.

limaille [limaj] *nf* filings *(pl)*.

limande [limɑ̃d] *nf* dab.

limbes [lɛ̃b] *nmpl* RELIG limbo *(sg)* ; **être dans les ~** *fig* to be in limbo.

lime [lim] *nf* **- 1.** [outil] file ; **~ à ongles** nail file **- 2.** BOT lime.

limer [3] [lime] *vt* [ongles] to file ; [aspérités] to file down ; [barreau] to file through.

limier [limje] *nm* **- 1.** [chien] bloodhound **- 2.** [détective] sleuth ; **fin ~** first-rate detective.

liminaire [liminɛr] *adj* introductory.

limitatif, ive [limitatif, iv] *adj* restrictive.

limitation [limitasjɔ̃] *nf* limitation ; [de naissances] control ; **~ de vitesse** speed limit.

limite [limit] ◇ *nf* **- 1.** [gén] limit ; **à la ~** [au pire] at worst ; **à la ~, j'accepterais de le voir** if pushed, I'd agree to see him **- 2.** [terme, échéance] deadline ; **~ d'âge** age limit ◇ *adj* [extrême] maximum *(avant n)* ; **cas ~** borderline case ; **date ~** deadline ; **date ~ de vente/consommation** sell-by/use-by date.
◆ **limites** *nfpl* : **sans ~s** limitless.

limité, e [limite] *adj* [peu important] limited.

limiter [3] [limite] *vt* **- 1.** [borner] to border, to bound **- 2.** [restreindre] to limit.
◆ **se limiter** *vp* **- 1.** [se restreindre] : **se ~ à**

qqch/à faire qqch to limit o.s. to sthg/to doing sthg **- 2.** [se borner] : **se ~ à** to be limited to.

limitrophe [limitrɔf] *adj* **- 1.** [frontalier] border *(avant n)* ; **être ~ de** to border on **- 2.** [voisin] adjacent.

limogeage [limɔʒaʒ] *nm* dismissal.

limoger [17] [limɔʒe] *vt* to dismiss.

limon [limɔ̃] *nm* **- 1.** GÉOL alluvium, silt **- 2.** CONSTR stringboard.

limonade [limɔnad] *nf* lemonade.

limpide [lɛ̃pid] *adj* **- 1.** [eau] limpid **- 2.** [ciel, regard] clear **- 3.** [explication, style] clear, lucid.

limpidité [lɛ̃pidite] *nf* **- 1.** [d'eau] limpidity **- 2.** [du ciel, de regard] clearness **- 3.** [d'explication, de style] clarity, lucidity.

lin [lɛ̃] *nm* **- 1.** BOT flax **- 2.** [tissu] linen.

linceul [lɛ̃sœl] *nm* shroud.

linéaire [lineɛr] *adj* **- 1.** [mesure, perspective] linear **- 2.** *fig* [récit] one-dimensional.

linge [lɛ̃ʒ] *nm* **- 1.** [lessive] washing **- 2.** [de lit, de table] linen **- 3.** [sous-vêtements] underwear ; **~ sale** dirty washing ; **laver son ~ sale en famille** not to wash one's dirty linen in public **- 4.** [morceau de tissu] cloth **- 5.** *loc* : **blanc** OU **pâle comme un ~** as white as a sheet.

lingerie [lɛ̃ʒri] *nf* **- 1.** [local] linen room **- 2.** [sous-vêtements] lingerie.

lingette [lɛ̃ʒɛt] *nf* wipe ; **~ démaquillante** eye makeup remover pad.

lingot [lɛ̃go] *nm* ingot ; **~ d'or** gold ingot.

linguiste [lɛ̃gɥist] *nmf* linguist.

linguistique [lɛ̃gɥistik] ◇ *nf* linguistics *(U)* ◇ *adj* linguistic.

linoléum [linɔleɔm] *nm* lino, linoleum.

linotte [linɔt] *nf* ZOOL linnet ; **tête de ~** *fig* featherbrain.

linteau, x [lɛ̃to] *nm* lintel.

lion, lionne [ljɔ̃, ljɔn] *nm, f* lion *(f* lioness*)*.
◆ **Lion** *nm* ASTROL Leo ; **être Lion** to be (a) Leo.

lionceau, x [ljɔ̃so] *nm* lion cub.

lipide [lipid] *nm* lipid.

lippu, e [lipy] *adj* thick-lipped.

liquéfier [9] [likefje] *vt* to liquefy.
◆ **se liquéfier** *vp* **- 1.** [matière] to liquefy **- 2.** *fig* [personne] to turn to jelly.

liqueur [likœr] *nf* liqueur.

liquidation [likidasjɔ̃] *nf* **- 1.** [de compte & BOURSE] settlement **- 2.** [de société, stock] liquidation **- 3.** *arg crime* [de témoin] liquidation, elimination **- 4.** *fam fig* [de problème] elimination.

liquide [likid] ◇ *nm* **- 1.** [substance] liquid **- 2.** [argent] cash ; **en ~** in cash ◇ *nf* LING liquid

◇ adj - **1.** [corps & LING] liquid - **2.** [en argent] cash *(avant n).*

liquider [3] [likide] vt - **1.** [compte & BOURSE] to settle - **2.** [société, stock] to liquidate - **3.** *fam* [importun] to get rid of - **4.** *arg crime* [témoin] to liquidate, to eliminate ; *fig* [problème] to eliminate, to get rid of.

liquidité [likidite] nf liquidity.
➡ **liquidités** nfpl liquid assets.

liquoreux, euse [likɔrø, øz] adj syrupy.

lire¹ [106] [lir] vt to read ; **lu et approuvé** read and approved.

lire² [lir] nf lira.

lis, lys [lis] nm lily.

lisais, lisions etc ▷ **lire¹.**

Lisbonne [lizbɔn] n Lisbon.

lise, lises etc ▷ **lire¹.**

liseré [lizre], **liséré** [lizere] nm - **1.** [ruban] binding - **2.** [bande] border, edging.

liseron [lizrɔ̃] nm bindweed.

liseuse [lizøz] nf - **1.** [couvre-livre] book cover - **2.** [signet] paper knife *(cum bookmark)* - **3.** [vêtement] bedjacket - **4.** [lampe] reading light.

lisible [lizibl] adj - **1.** [écriture] legible - **2.** [roman] readable.

lisiblement [lizibləmã] adv legibly.

lisière [lizjer] nf - **1.** [limite] edge - **2.** COUTURE selvage.

lisse [lis] ◇ nf - **1.** [rambarde] handrail - **2.** NAVIG rib ◇ adj - **1.** [surface, peau] smooth - **2.** [cheveux] straight.

lisser [3] [lise] vt - **1.** [papier, vêtements] to smooth (out) - **2.** [moustache, cheveux] to smooth (down) - **3.** [plumes] to preen.

listage [listaʒ] nm listing.

liste [list] nf list ; **~ d'attente** waiting list ; **~ électorale** electoral roll ; **~ de mariage** wedding present list ; **~ noire** blacklist ; **être sur la ~ rouge** to be ex-directory.

lister [3] [liste] vt to list.

listing [listiŋ] nm listing.

lit [li] nm - **1.** [gén] bed ; **faire son ~** to make one's bed ; **garder le ~** to stay in bed ; **se mettre au ~** to go to bed ; **~ à baldaquin** fourposter bed ; **~ de camp** camp bed ; **~ d'enfant** cot Br, crib Am ; **~ gigogne** pull-out bed ; **~ nuptial** marriage bed ; **~s jumeaux/ superposés** twin/bunk beds - **2.** JUR marriage ; **d'un premier ~** of a first marriage.

LIT *(abr de* lire italienne) L, Lit.

litanie [litani] nf litany.

litchi [litʃi], **letchi** [letʃi] nm lychee.

literie [litri] nf bedding.

lithographie [litɔgrafi] nf - **1.** [procédé] lithography - **2.** [image] lithograph.

litière [litjer] nf litter.

litige [litiʒ] nm - **1.** JUR lawsuit - **2.** [désaccord] dispute.

litigieux, euse [litiʒjø, øz] adj - **1.** JUR litigious - **2.** [douteux] disputed.

litote [litɔt] nf understatement, litotes.

litre [litr] nm - **1.** [mesure, quantité] litre Br, liter Am - **2.** [récipient] litre Br OU liter Am bottle.

litron [litrɔ̃] nm tfam litre Br OU liter Am of wine.

littéraire [literer] ◇ nmf person who is strong in arts subjects ◇ adj literary.

littéral, e, aux [literal, o] adj - **1.** [gén] literal - **2.** [écrit] written.

littéralement [literalmã] adv literally.

littérature [literatyr] nf - **1.** [gén] literature ; **~ comparée** comparative literature - **2.** [profession] writing.

littoral, e, aux [litɔral, o] adj coastal.
➡ **littoral** nm coast, coastline.

Lituanie [lituani] nf : **la ~** Lithuania.

lituanien, enne [lituanjɛ̃, ɛn] adj Lithuanian.
➡ **lituanien** nm [langue] Lithuanian.
➡ **Lituanien, enne** nm, f Lithuanian.

liturgie [lityrʒi] nf liturgy.

liturgique [lityrʒik] adj liturgical.

livide [livid] adj [blême] pallid.

livrable [livrabl] adj which can be delivered.

livraison [livrezɔ̃] nf [de marchandise] delivery ; **~ à domicile** home delivery.

livre [livr] ◇ nm - **1.** [gén] book ; **~ de bord** log, logbook ; **~ de cuisine** cookery book ; **~ électronique** e-book ; **~ d'images** picture book ; **~ de messe** missal ; **~ d'or** visitors' book ; **~ de poche** paperback ; **à ~ ouvert** *fig* at sight - **2.** [industrie] book trade ◇ nf pound ; **~ sterling** pound sterling.

livre-cassette [livrəkaset] *(pl* **livres-cassettes)** nm spoken word cassette.

livrée [livre] nf [uniforme] livery.

livrer [3] [livre] vt - **1.** COMM to deliver ; **~ qqch à qqn** [achat] to deliver sthg to sb ; *fig* [secret] to reveal OU give away sthg to sb - **2.** [coupable, complice] : **~ qqn à qqn** to hand sb over to sb - **3.** [abandonner] : **~ qqch à qqch** to give sthg over to sthg ; **~ qqn à lui-même** to leave sb to his own devices ; **~ passage à qqn** *fig* to let sb pass.
➡ **se livrer** vp - **1.** [se rendre] : **se ~ à** [police, ennemi] to give o.s. up to ; [amant] to give o.s. to - **2.** [se confier] : **se ~ à** [ami] to open up to, to

confide in **- 3.** [se consacrer] : **se ~ à** [occupation] to devote o.s. to ; [excès] to indulge in.

livresque [livrɛsk] *adj* bookish.

livret [livrɛ] *nm* **- 1.** [carnet] booklet ; **~ de caisse d'épargne** passbook, bankbook ; **~ de famille** *official family record book, given by registrar to newlyweds* ; **~ scolaire** ≃ school report **- 2.** [catalogue] catalogue *Br*, catalog *Am* **- 3.** *MUS* book, libretto.

livreur, euse [livrœr, øz] *nm, f* delivery man (*f* woman).

Ljubljana [ljublʒana] *n* Ljubljana.

LO (*abr de* **Lutte ouvrière**) *nf* left-wing political party.

lobby [lɔbi] (*pl* **lobbies**) *nm* lobby.

lobe [lɔb] *nm* **- 1.** *ANAT & BOT* lobe **- 2.** *ARCHIT* foil.

lober [3] [lɔbe] *vt* to lob.

local, e, aux [lɔkal, o] *adj* local ; [douleur] localized.
- **local** *nm* room, premises (*pl*).
- **locaux** *nmpl* premises, offices.

localement [lɔkalmɑ̃] *adv* locally.

localisation [lɔkalizasjɔ̃] *nf* **- 1.** [d'un avion, d'un bruit] location **- 2.** [d'une épidémie, d'un conflit, d'un produit multimédia] localization.

localiser [3] [lɔkalize] *vt* **- 1.** [avion, bruit] to locate **- 2.** [épidémie, conflit, produit multimédia] to localize.
- **se localiser** *vp* to be confined.

localité [lɔkalite] *nf* (small) town.

locataire [lɔkatɛr] *nmf* tenant.

locatif, ive [lɔkatif, iv] *adj* [relatif à la location] rental (*avant n*).
- **locatif** *nm GRAM* locative.

location [lɔkasjɔ̃] *nf* **- 1.** [de propriété - par propriétaire] letting *Br*, renting *Am* ; [- par locataire] renting ; [de machine] leasing ; **~ de voitures/vélos** car/bicycle hire *Br*, car/bicycle rent *Am* **- 2.** [bail] lease **- 3.** [maison, appartement] rented property **- 4.** [réservation] booking.

location-vente [lɔkasjɔ̃vɑ̃t] (*pl* **locations-ventes**) *nf* ≃ hire purchase *Br*, ≃ installment plan *Am*.

loc. cit. (*abr de* **loco citato**) loc. cit.

lock-out [lɔkaut] *nm inv* lockout.

locomoteur, trice [lɔkɔmɔtœr, tris] *adj* locomotive (*avant n*).

locomotion [lɔkɔmɔsjɔ̃] *nf* locomotion.

locomotive [lɔkɔmɔtiv] *nf* **- 1.** [machine] locomotive **- 2.** *fig* [leader] moving force.

locuteur, trice [lɔkytœr, tris] *nm, f* speaker.

locution [lɔkysjɔ̃] *nf* expression, phrase.

loden [lɔdɛn] *nm* [étoffe] loden ; [vêtement] loden overcoat.

loft [lɔft] *nm* (converted) loft.

logarithme [lɔgaritm] *nm* logarithm.

loge [lɔʒ] *nf* **- 1.** [de concierge, de francs-maçons] lodge **- 2.** [d'acteur] dressing room **- 3.** [de spectacle] box ; **être aux premières ~s** *fig* to have a ringside seat **- 4.** [d'écurie] loose box **- 5.** *ARCHIT* loggia.

logement [lɔʒmɑ̃] *nm* **- 1.** [hébergement] accommodation *Br*, accommodations (*pl*) *Am* **- 2.** [appartement] flat *Br*, apartment *Am* ; **~ de fonction** company flat *Br ou* apartment *Am*.

loger [17] [lɔʒe] *<> vi* [habiter] to live *<> vt* **- 1.** [amis, invités] to put up **- 2.** [clé] to put **- 3.** [suj : hôtel, maison] to accommodate, to take.
- **se loger** *vp* **- 1.** [trouver un logement] to find accommodation *Br ou* accommodations *Am* **- 2.** [se placer - ballon, balle] : **se ~ dans** to lodge in, to stick in ; **se ~ dans** *fig* [angoisse] to take hold of.

logeur, euse [lɔʒœr, øz] *nm, f* landlord (*f* landlady).

loggia [lɔdʒja] *nf* loggia.

logiciel [lɔʒisjɛl] *nm* software (*U*) ; **~ intégré** integrated software ; **~ de navigation** browser.

logique [lɔʒik] *<> nf* logic *<> adj* logical.

logiquement [lɔʒikmɑ̃] *adv* logically.

logis [lɔʒi] *nm* abode.

logistique [lɔʒistik] *<> nf* logistics (*pl*) *<> adj* logistic.

logo [lɔgo] *nm* logo.

logorrhée [lɔgɔre] *nf* logorrhoea.

loi [lwal] *nf* **- 1.** [gén] law ; **faire la ~** to lay down the law ; **la ~ du plus fort** might is right ; **~ de l'offre et de la demande** law of supply and demand ; **la ~ du talion** an eye for an eye ; **la ~ de 1901** *law concerning the setting up of non-profit-making organizations* **- 2.** [convention] rule.

loin [lwɛ̃] *adv* **- 1.** [dans l'espace] far ; **plus ~** further **- 2.** [dans le temps - passé] a long time ago ; [- futur] a long way off.
- **au loin** *loc adv* in the distance, far off.
- **de loin** *loc adv* **- 1.** [depuis une grande distance] from a distance ; **de très ~** from a great distance ; **de plus ~** from further away **- 2.** [assez peu] from a distance, from afar **- 3.** [de beaucoup] by far.
- **de loin en loin** *loc adv* **- 1.** [dans l'espace] here and there **- 2.** [dans le temps] every now and then, from time to time.
- **loin de** *loc prép* **- 1.** [gén] far from ; **~ de là!** *fig* far from it! **- 2.** [dans le temps] : **il n'est pas**

~ **de 9 h** it's nearly 9 o'clock, it's not far off 9 o'clock.

lointain, e [lwɛ̃tɛ̃, ɛn] *adj* - **1.** [pays, avenir, parent] distant - **2.** [ressemblance] vague.

~ **lointain** *nm* : **au** *ou* **dans le ~** in the distance.

loir [lwar] *nm* dormouse ; **dormir comme un ~** *fig* to sleep like a log.

loisible [lwazibl] *adj* : **il m'est ~ de participer** I am at liberty to take part.

loisir [lwazir] *nm* - **1.** [temps libre] leisure ; **avoir le ~ de faire qqch** *sout* to have the time to do sthg ; **à ~** [à satiété] as much as one likes ; [sans hâte] at leisure - **2.** (*gén pl*) [distractions] leisure activities (*pl*).

lombago = lumbago.

lombaire [lɔ̃bɛr] <> *nf* lumbar vertebra <> *adj* lumbar.

lombes [lɔ̃b] *nfpl* loins.

Lomé [lome] *n* Lomé.

londonien, enne [lɔ̃dɔnjɛ̃, ɛn] *adj* London (*avant n*).

~ **Londonien, enne** *nm, f* Londoner.

Londres [lɔ̃dr] *n* London.

long, longue [lɔ̃, lɔ̃g] *adj* - **1.** [gén] long - **2.** [lent] slow ; **être ~ à faire qqch** to take a long time doing sthg.

~ **long** <> *nm* - **1.** [longueur] : **4 mètres de ~** 4 metres long *ou* in length ; **de ~ en large** up and down, to and fro ; **en ~ et en large** in great detail ; (**tout**) **le ~ de** [espace] all along ; **tout le ~ du jour** the whole day long ; **tout au ~ de** [année, carrière] throughout ; **tomber de tout son ~** to go full length - **2.** [vêtement] : **le ~** long clothes (*pl*) <> *adv* - **1.** [beaucoup] : **en savoir ~ sur qqch** to know a lot about sthg - **2.** [s'habiller] : **elle est habillée trop ~** her clothes are too long.

~ **longue** *nf* - **1.** LING long vowel - **2.** MUS long note - **3.** CARTES long suit.

~ **à la longue** *loc adv* in the end.

long. (*abr de* **longitude**) long.

long-courrier [lɔ̃kurje] *adj* [navire] ocean-going ; [vol] long-haul.

longe [lɔ̃ʒ] *nf* - **1.** [courroie] halter - **2.** [viande] loin.

longer [17] [lɔ̃ʒe] *vt* - **1.** [border] to go along *ou* alongside - **2.** [marcher le long de] to walk along ; [raser] to stay close to, to hug.

longévité [lɔ̃ʒevite] *nf* longevity.

longiligne [lɔ̃ʒiliɲ] *adj* long-limbed.

longitude [lɔ̃ʒityd] *nf* longitude.

longitudinal, e, aux [lɔ̃ʒitydinal, o] *adj* longitudinal.

longtemps [lɔ̃tã] *adv* (for) a long time ;

avant ~ before long ; **il ne reviendra pas avant ~** he won't be back for some time ; **depuis ~** (for) a long time ; **il y a ~ que ...** it's been a long time since ... ; **il y a ~ qu'il est là** he's been here a long time ; **mettre ~ à faire qqch** to take a long time to do sthg ; **je n'en ai pas pour ~** I won't be long.

longue [=> **long**.

longuement [lɔ̃gmã] *adv* - **1.** [longtemps] for a long time - **2.** [en détail] at length.

longuet, ette [lɔ̃gɛ, ɛt] *adj fam* longish, a bit long.

longueur [lɔ̃gœr] *nf* length ; **faire 5 mètres de ~** to be 5 metres long ; **disposer qqch en ~** to put sthg lengthways ; **à ~ de journée/temps** the entire day/time ; **à ~ d'année** all year long ; **~ d'onde** wavelength ; **être sur la même ~ d'onde** *fig* to be on the same wavelength.

~ **longueurs** *nfpl* [de film, de livre] boring parts.

longue-vue [lɔ̃gvy] (*pl* **longues-vues**) *nf* telescope.

look [luk] *nm* look ; **avoir un ~** to have a style.

looping [lupiŋ] *nm* loop the loop.

lopin [lɔpɛ̃] *nm* : **~ (de terre)** patch *ou* plot of land.

loquace [lɔkas] *adj* loquacious.

loquacité [lɔkasite] *nf* loquacity.

loque [lɔk] *nf* - **1.** [lambeau] rag ; **en ~s** in rags - **2.** *fig* [personne] wreck.

loquet [lɔkɛ] *nm* latch.

lorgner [3] [lɔrɲe] *vt fam* - **1.** [observer] to eye - **2.** [guigner] to have one's eye on.

lorgnette [lɔrɲet] *nf* opera glasses (*pl*).

lorgnon [lɔrɲɔ̃] *nm* lorgnette.

lors [lɔr] *adv* : **depuis ~** since that time ; **~ de** at the time of.

lorsque [lɔrsk(ə)] *conj* when.

losange [lɔzãʒ] *nm* lozenge.

lot [lo] *nm* - **1.** [part] share ; [de terre] plot - **2.** [stock] batch - **3.** [prix] prize ; **le gros ~** the jackpot - **4.** *fig* [destin] fate, lot.

loterie [lɔtri] *nf* lottery ; **la Loterie nationale** the National Lottery.

loti, e [lɔti] *adj* : **être bien/mal ~** to be well/badly off.

lotion [lɔsjɔ̃] *nf* lotion ; **~ après-rasage** aftershave (lotion).

lotir [32] [lɔtir] *vt* to divide up ; **~ qqn de qqch** to allot sthg to sb.

lotissement [lɔtismã] *nm* - **1.** [terrain] plot - **2.** [division - de terrain] parcelling out.

loto [lɔto] *nm* - **1.** [jeu de société] lotto - **2.** [loterie] *popular national lottery.*

> **LOTO**
>
> Loto is a popular game of chance with large cash prizes. Printed grids ('bulletins') are available at tobacconists or special kiosks. Players mark seven numbers on the grid and pay a fee. The twice-weekly prize draw is broadcast on television. 'Loto sportif' is a version of Loto in which players bet on the football results.

lotte [lɔt] *nf* monkfish.

lotus [lɔtys] *nm* lotus.

louable [lwabl] *adj* - **1.** [méritoire] praise-worthy - **2.** [location] : **facilement/difficilement ~** easy/difficult to let *Br*, easy/difficult to rent *Am*.

louage [lwaʒ] *nm* hire *Br*, rental *Am* ; **voiture de ~** hire *Br ou* rental *Am* car.

louange [lwɑ̃ʒ] *nf* praise ; **chanter les ~s de qqn** *fig* to sing sb's praises.

loubar(d) [lubar] *nm fam* hooligan.

louche[1] [luʃ] *nf* ladle.

louche[2] [luʃ] *adj fam* [personne, histoire] suspicious.

loucher [3] [luʃe] *vi* - **1.** [être atteint de strabisme] to squint - **2.** *fam fig* [lorgner] : **~ sur** to have one's eye on.

louer [6] [lwe] *vt* - **1.** [glorifier] to praise ; **~ qqn de qqch** to praise sb for sthg - **2.** [donner en location] to rent (out) ; **à ~** for rent - **3.** [prendre en location] to rent - **4.** [réserver] to book.

◆ se louer *vp* - **1.** *sout* [se féliciter] : **se ~ de qqch/de faire qqch** to be very pleased about sthg/about doing sthg - **2.** [appartement] to be to let *Br ou* for rent *Am* - **3.** *péj* [se vanter] to sing one's own praises.

loufoque [lufɔk] *fam* <> *nmf* nutter <> *adj* nuts, crazy.

loup [lu] *nm* - **1.** [carnassier] wolf - **2.** [poisson] bass - **3.** [masque] mask - **4.** *fig* [personne] : **(vieux) ~ de mer** (old) sea dog.

loupe [lup] *nf* - **1.** [optique] magnifying glass ; **regarder qqch à la ~** *fig* to put sthg under the microscope - **2.** *BOT* burr.

louper [3] [lupe] *vt fam* [travail] to make a mess of ; [train] to miss.

loup-garou [lugaru] (*pl* **loups-garous**) *nm* werewolf.

loupiot, otte [lupjo, ɔt] *nm, f fam* kid.

lourd, e [lur, lurd] *adj* - **1.** [gén] heavy ; **~ de** *fig* full of - **2.** [tâche] difficult ; [faute] serious - **3.** [maladroit] clumsy, heavy-handed - **4.** *MÉTÉOR* close - **5.** [esprit] slow.

◆ lourd *adv* : **peser ~** to be heavy, to weigh a lot ; **il n'en fait pas ~** *fam* he doesn't do much.

lourdaud, e [lurdo, od] <> *adj* clumsy <> *nm, f* oaf.

lourdement [lurdəmɑ̃] *adv* - **1.** [pesamment] heavily - **2.** [maladroitement] heavily, clumsily ; [insister] strenuously.

lourdeur [lurdœr] *nf* - **1.** [gén] heaviness - **2.** *MÉTÉOR* closeness - **3.** [d'esprit] slowness.

loustic [lustik] *nm fam* - **1.** [enfant] kid - **2.** [farceur] joker - **3.** *péj* [type] guy.

loutre [lutr] *nf* otter.

louve [luv] *nf* she-wolf.

louveteau, x [luvto] *nm* - **1.** *ZOOL* wolf cub - **2.** [scout] cub.

louvoyer [13] [luvwaje] *vi* - **1.** *NAVIG* to tack - **2.** *fig* [tergiverser] to beat about the bush.

Louvre [luvr] *n* : **le ~** the Louvre (museum) ; **l'école du ~** art school in Paris.

> **LE LOUVRE**
>
> The Louvre houses one of the biggest museum collections in the world. It is divided into seven sections : Eastern antiquities, Greek and Roman antiquities, paintings, sculpture, objets d'art and graphic arts. The glass pyramid, added amid much controversy in 1989, provides access to the museum's underground entrances. The museum was refurbished in 1993 and extended by a wing that was previously home to the Ministry of Finance.

lover [3] [lɔve] **◆ se lover** *vp* [serpent] to coil up.

loyal, e, aux [lwajal, o] *adj* - **1.** [fidèle] loyal - **2.** [honnête] fair.

loyalement [lwajalmɑ̃] *adv* - **1.** [fidèlement] loyally - **2.** [honnêtement] fairly.

loyauté [lwajote] *nf* - **1.** [fidélité] loyalty - **2.** [honnêteté] fairness.

loyer [lwaje] *nm* rent.

LP (*abr de* **lycée professionnel**) *nm secondary school for vocational training.*

LSD (*abr de* **lysergic acid diethylamide**) *nm* LSD.

lu, e [ly] *pp* ▷ **lire**[1].

Luanda [lyɑ̃da] *n* Luanda.

lubie [lybi] *nf fam* whim.

lubricité [lybrisite] *nf* lechery.

lubrifiant, e [lybrifjɑ̃, ɑ̃t] *adj* lubricating.
◆ lubrifiant *nm* lubricant.

lubrification [lybrifikasjɔ̃] *nf* lubrication.

lubrifier [9] [lybrifje] *vt* to lubricate.

lubrique [lybrik] *adj* lewd.

lucarne [lykarn] *nf* - **1.** [fenêtre] skylight - **2.** *FOOTBALL* top corner of the net.

lucide [lysid] *adj* lucid.

lucidement [lysidmã] *adv* lucidly.

lucidité [lysidite] *nf* lucidity.

luciole [lysjɔl] *nf* firefly.

lucratif, ive [lykratif, iv] *adj* lucrative.

lucre [lykr] *nm péj* lucre.

ludique [lydik] *adj* play *(avant n)*.

ludo-éducatif [lydoedykatif] *nm* edutainment.

ludothèque [lydɔtɛk] *nf* toy library.

luette [lɥɛt] *nf* uvula.

lueur [lɥœr] *nf* - **1.** [de bougie, d'étoile] light ; **à la ~ de** by the light of - **2.** *fig* [de colère] gleam ; [de raison] spark ; **~ d'espoir** glimmer of hope.

luge [lyʒ] *nf* toboggan.

lugubre [lygybr] *adj* lugubrious.

lui¹ [lɥi] *pp inv* ⊳ luire.

lui² [lɥi] *pron pers* - **1.** [complément d'objet indirect - homme] (to) him ; [- femme] (to) her ; [- animal, chose] (to) it ; **je ~ ai parlé** I've spoken to him/to her ; **il le ~ a présenté** he introduced him to her ; **il ~ a serré la main** he shook his/her hand - **2.** [sujet, en renforcement de "il"] he ; **qui t'accompagnera? - ~** who will go with you? - he will ; **il sait de quoi je parle, ~** HE knows what I'm talking about - **3.** [objet, après préposition, comparatif - personne] him ; [- animal, chose] it ; **je n'ai vu que ~** I saw no one else but him ; **si j'étais ~ ...** if I were him ... ; **~, tout le monde le connaît** everyone knows HIM ; **sans ~** without him ; **je vais chez ~** I'm going to his place ; **elle est plus jeune que ~** she's younger than him *ou* than he is - **4.** [remplaçant 'soi' en fonction de pronom réfléchi - personne] himself ; [- animal, chose] itself ; **il est content de ~** he's pleased with himself.
➨ **lui-même** *pron pers* [personne] himself ; [animal, chose] itself.

luire [97] [lɥir] *vi* [soleil, métal] to shine ; *fig* [espoir] to glow, to glimmer.

luisais, luisions *etc* ⊳ luire.

luisant, e [lɥizã, ãt] *adj* gleaming.
➨ **luisant** *nm* sheen.

lumbago [lɔ̃bago]**, lombago** [lɔ̃bago] *nm* lumbago.

lumière [lymjɛr] *nf* - **1.** [éclairage] *fig* light ; **~ tamisée** subdued light ; **à la ~ de** by the light of ; **faire toute la ~ sur qqch** to make sthg clear ; **mettre qqch en ~** to highlight sthg - **2.** [personne] leading light ; **ce n'est pas une ~** *fam* he's/she's not very bright.

luminaire [lyminɛr] *nm* light.

luminescent, e [lyminɛsã, ãt] *adj* luminescent.

lumineux, euse [lyminø, øz] *adj* - **1.** [couleur, cadran] luminous - **2.** *fig* [visage] radiant ; [idée] brilliant - **3.** [explication] clear.

luminosité [lyminozite] *nf* - **1.** [du regard, ciel] radiance - **2.** *SCIENCE* luminosity.

lump [lœp] *nm* : **œufs de ~** lumpfish roe.

lunaire [lynɛr] *adj* - **1.** *ASTRON* lunar - **2.** *fig* [visage] moon *(avant n)* ; [paysage] lunar.

lunatique [lynatik] ⋄ *nmf* temperamental person ⋄ *adj* temperamental.

lunch [lœ̃ʃ] *nm* buffet lunch.

lundi [lœ̃di] *nm* Monday ; **~ de Pâques/Pentecôte** Easter/Whit Monday ; *voir aussi* samedi.

lune [lyn] *nf* - **1.** *ASTRON* moon ; **nouvelle ~** new moon ; **pleine ~** full moon ; **~ de miel** *fig* honeymoon ; **dans la ~** *fig* in the clouds ; **décrocher la ~** *fig* to move heaven and earth ; **promettre la ~** *fig* to promise the earth - **2.** *fam fig* [derrière] backside.

luné, e [lyne] *adj* : **être bien/mal ~** to be in a good/bad mood.

lunetier, ère [lyntje, ɛr] ⋄ *adj* spectacle-making *(avant n)* ⋄ *nm, f* optician.

lunette [lynɛt] *nf* - **1.** [ouverture] : **la ~ des W.-C.** [cuvette] the toilet bowl ; **~ arrière** rear window - **2.** *ASTRON* telescope.
➨ **lunettes** *nfpl* glasses ; **~s noires** dark glasses ; **~s de soleil** sunglasses.

lunule [lynyl] *nf* [d'ongle] half-moon.

lupanar [lypanar] *nm sout* brothel.

lupin [lypɛ̃] *nm* lupin.

lurette [lyrɛt] *nf* : **il y a belle ~ que ...** *fam* it's been ages since ...

luron, onne [lyrɔ̃, ɔn] *nm, f fam* : **un joyeux ~** a bit of a lad.

Lusaka [lyzaka] *n* Lusaka.

lusophone [lyzɔfɔn] *adj* Portuguese-speaking.

lustre [lystr] *nm* - **1.** [luminaire] chandelier - **2.** [éclat] sheen, shine ; *fig* reputation - **3.** *littéraire* [cinq ans] period of five years ; **ça fait des ~s que ...** *fig* it's been ages since ...

lustrer [3] [lystre] *vt* - **1.** [faire briller] to make shine - **2.** [user] to wear.

luth [lyt] *nm* lute.

luthérien, enne [lyterjɛ̃, ɛn] *adj & nm, f* Lutheran.

luthier [lytje] *nm* maker of stringed instruments.

lutin, e [lytɛ̃, in] *adj* mischievous.
➨ **lutin** *nm* imp.

lutrin [lytrɛ̃] *nm* lectern.

lutte [lyt] *nf* - **1.** [combat] fight, struggle ; **de haute ~** with a hard-fought struggle ; **la ~ des classes** the class struggle ; **~ d'influence** power struggle - **2.** *SPORT* wrestling.

lutter [3] [lyte] *vi* to fight, to struggle ; **~ contre** to fight (against).

lutteur, euse [lytœr, øz] *nm, f SPORT* wrestler ; *fig* fighter.

luxation [lyksasjɔ̃] *nf* dislocation.

luxe [lyks] *nm* luxury ; **de ~** luxury ; **ce n'est pas un** *OU* **du ~** *fig* it is a necessity ; **s'offrir** *OU* **se payer le ~ de** *fig* to afford the luxury of.

Luxembourg [lyksɑ̃bur] *nm* - **1.** [pays] : **le ~** Luxembourg ; **au ~** in Luxembourg - **2.** [ville] Luxembourg ; **à ~** in (the city of) Luxembourg - **3.** [jardins] : **le ~** the Luxembourg Gardens.

luxembourgeois, e [lyksɑ̃burʒwa, az] *adj* of/from Luxembourg.
➡ **Luxembourgeois, e** *nm, f* native *OU* inhabitant of Luxembourg.

luxer [3] [lykse] *vt* to dislocate.
➡ **se luxer** *vp* : **se ~ l'épaule** to dislocate one's shoulder.

luxueux, euse [lyksɥø, øz] *adj* luxurious.

luxure [lyksyr] *nf* lust.

luxuriant, e [lyksyrjɑ̃, ɑ̃t] *adj* luxuriant.

luzerne [lyzɛrn] *nf* lucerne, alfalfa.

lx (*abr de* **lux**) lx.

lycée [lise] *nm* ≃ secondary school *Br*, ≃ high school *Am* ; **~ technique/professionnel** ≃ technical/training college ; **~ pilote** experimental school.

> **LYCÉE**
>
> State secondary school in France for pupils aged 15 to 18. The school years covered go from 'seconde' through 'première' to 'terminale', the final year when pupils take the 'baccalauréat'.

lycéen, enne [liseɛ̃, ɛn] *nm, f* secondary school pupil *Br*, high school pupil *Am*.

lymphatique [lɛ̃fatik] *adj* - **1.** *MÉD* lymphatic - **2.** *fig* [apathique] sluggish.

lymphe [lɛ̃f] *nf* lymph.

lyncher [3] [lɛ̃ʃe] *vt* to lynch.

lynx [lɛ̃ks] *nm* lynx.

Lyon [ljɔ̃] *n* Lyons.

lyonnais, e [ljɔnɛ, ɛz] *adj* of/from Lyons.
➡ **Lyonnais, e** *nm, f* native *OU* inhabitant of Lyons.

lyre [lir] *nf* lyre.

lyrique [lirik] *adj* [poésie] *fig* lyrical ; [drame, chanteur, poète] lyric.

lyrisme [lirism] *nm* - **1.** [poésie] lyricism - **2.** [exaltation] enthusiasm.

lys = **lis**.

m¹, M [ɛm] ⬦ *nm inv* m, M ⬦ (*abr de* **mètre**) m.
➡ **M** - **1.** (*abr de* **maxwell**) Mx - **2.** (*abr de* **mile** (marin)) *nm* - **3.** (*abr de* **méga**) M - **4.** (*abr de* **Major**) M - **5.** (*abr de* **Monsieur**) Mr - **6.** (*abr de* **million**) M - **7.** *abr de* **masculin**.

m² (*abr de* **milli**) m.

m' ⬦ **me**.

M6 *n private television channel broadcasting a high proportion of music and aimed at a younger audience.*

ma ⬦ **mon**.

MA (*abr de* **maître auxiliaire**) *nm teacher on short-term contract.*

Maastricht [mastriʃt] *n* Maastricht ; **le traité de ~** the Maastricht treaty.

maboul, e [mabul] *fam* ⬦ *adj* crazy ⬦ *nm, f* nutter.

macabre [makabr] *adj* macabre.

macadam [makadam] *nm* [revêtement] macadam ; [route] road.

Macao [makao] *n* Macao ; **à ~** in Macao.

macaque [makak] *nm* - **1.** *ZOOL* macaque - **2.** *fam* [personne] ape.

macareux [makarø] *nm* puffin.

macaron [makarɔ̃] *nm* - **1.** [pâtisserie] macaroon - **2.** [coiffure] coil - **3.** [autocollant] sticker.

macaronis [makarɔni] *nmpl* - **1.** *CULIN* macaroni (*U*) - **2.** *tfam* [Italiens] *offensive term used with reference to Italians*, ≃ Eyeties.

macchabée [makabe] *nm tfam* stiff.

macédoine [masedwan] *nf* - **1.** *CULIN* : **~ de fruits** fruit salad ; **~ de légumes** mixed vegetables - **2.** *fig* [mélange] jumble.

macérer [18] [masere] ⬦ *vt* to steep ⬦ *vi*

- **1.** [mariner] .to steep ; **faire ~** to steep
- **2.** *fig* & *péj* [personne] to wallow.

mâche [maʃ] *nf* lamb's lettuce.

mâcher [3] [maʃe] *vt* - **1.** [mastiquer] to chew
- **2.** *TECHNOL* to chew up.

machiavélique [makjavelik] *adj* Machiavellian.

mâchicoulis [maʃikuli] *nm* machicolation.

machin [maʃɛ̃] *nm fam* [chose] thing, thingumajig.

Machin, e [maʃɛ̃, in] *nm, f fam* what's his name (*f* what's her name).

machinal, e, aux [maʃinal, o] *adj* mechanical.

machinalement [maʃinalmã] *adv* mechanically.

machination [maʃinasjɔ̃] *nf* machination.

machine [maʃin] *nf* - **1.** *TECHNOL* machine ; **~ à coudre** sewing machine ; **~ à écrire** typewriter ; **~ à laver** washing machine ; **~ à sous** fruit machine *Br*, one-armed bandit *Am* ; **~ à tricoter** knitting machine - **2.** [organisation] machinery (*U*) - **3.** *NAVIG* engine ; **faire ~ arrière** to reverse engines ; *fig* to backpedal - **4.** [locomotive] engine, locomotive.

machine-outil [maʃinuti] (*pl* **machines-outils**) *nf* machine tool.

machiner [3] [maʃine] *vt* to plot.

machiniste [maʃinist] *nm* - **1.** *CIN* & *THÉÂTRE* scene shifter - **2.** *TRANSPORT* driver.

machisme [matʃism] *nm* machismo.

macho [matʃo] *péj* <> *nm* macho man <> *adj inv* macho.

mâchoire [maʃwar] *nf* jaw ; **~ supérieure/inférieure** upper/lower jaw.

mâchonner [3] [maʃɔne] *vt* - **1.** [mâcher, mordiller] to chew - **2.** [marmonner] to mutter.

mâchouiller [3] [maʃuje] *vt fam* to chew.

maçon [masɔ̃] *nm* mason.

maçonner [3] [masɔne] *vt* [construire] to build ; [revêtir] to face ; [boucher] to brick up.

maçonnerie [masɔnri] *nf* [travaux] building ; [construction] masonry ; [franc-maçonnerie] freemasonry.

maçonnique [masɔnik] *adj* masonic.

macramé [makrame] *nm* macramé.

macrobiotique [makrɔbjɔtik] <> *nf* macrobiotics (*U*) <> *adj* macrobiotic.

macroéconomie [makrɔekɔnɔmi] *nf* macroeconomy.

maculer [3] [makyle] *vt* to stain.

Madagascar [madagaskar] *n* Madagascar ; **à ~** in Madagascar.

madame [madam] (*pl* **mesdames** [medam]) *nf*

- **1.** [titre] : **~ X** Mrs X ; **bonjour ~!** good morning! ; [dans hôtel, restaurant] good morning, madam! ; **bonjour mesdames!** good morning (ladies)! ; **Madame le Ministre n'est pas là** the Minister is out - **2.** *HIST* Madame (*title given to the wife of the brother of the King of France*).

madeleine [madlɛn] *nf small sponge cake.*

➡ **Madeleine** *nf* : **pleurer comme une Madeleine** to cry one's eyes out.

mademoiselle [madmwazɛl] (*pl* **mesdemoiselles** [medmwazɛl]) *nf* - **1.** [titre] : **~ X** Miss X ; **bonjour ~!** good morning! ; [à l'école, dans hôtel] good morning, miss! ; **bonjour mesdemoiselles!** good morning (ladies)! - **2.** *HIST* Mademoiselle (*title given to a Princess of France*).

madère [mader] *nm* Madeira (wine).

Madère [mader] *nf* Madeira ; **à ~** in Madeira.

madone [madɔn] *nf ART* & *RELIG* Madonna.

Madrid [madrid] *n* Madrid.

madrier [madrije] *nm* beam.

madrilène [madrilɛn] *adj* of/from Madrid.

➡ **Madrilène** *nmf* native *ou* inhabitant of Madrid.

maestria [maɛstrija] *nf* mastery ; **avec ~** brilliantly.

maf(f)ia [mafja] *nf* Mafia.

magasin [magazɛ̃] *nm* - **1.** [boutique] shop *Br*, store *Am* ; **en ~** in stock ; **grand ~** department store ; **faire les ~s** *fig* to go round the shops *Br ou* stores *Am* - **2.** [entrepôt] warehouse - **3.** [d'arme, d'appareil photo] magazine.

magasinage [magazinaʒ] *nm* warehousing, storing.

magasinier [magazinje] *nm* warehouseman, storeman.

magazine [magazin] *nm* magazine.

mage [maʒ] *nm* : **les Rois ~s** the Three Wise Men.

Maghreb [magrɛb] *nm* : **le ~** the Maghreb.

maghrébin, e [magrebɛ̃, in] *adj* North African.

➡ **Maghrébin, e** *nm, f* North African.

magicien, enne [maʒisjɛ̃, ɛn] *nm, f* magician.

magie [maʒi] *nf* magic ; **comme par ~** as if by magic ; **~ noire** black magic.

magique [maʒik] *adj* - **1.** [occulte] magic
- **2.** [merveilleux] magical.

magistère [maʒistɛr] *nm* authority.

magistral, e, aux [maʒistral, o] *adj* - **1.** [œuvre, habileté] masterly - **2.** [dispute, fessée] enormous - **3.** [attitude, ton] authoritative.

magistralement [maʒistralmɑ̃l] *adv* authoritatively, brilliantly.

magistrat [maʒistra] *nm* magistrate.

magistrature [maʒistratyr] *nf* magistracy, magistrature.

magma [magma] *nm* - **1.** GÉOL magma - **2.** *fig* [mélange] muddle.

magnanerie [maɲanri] *nf* - **1.** [bâtiment] silk farm - **2.** [sériciculture] silkworm breeding, sericulture.

magnanime [maɲanim] *adj* magnanimous.

magnanimité [maɲanimite] *nf* magnanimity.

magnat [maɲa] *nm* magnate, tycoon.

magner [3] [maɲe] ➡ **se magner** *vp fam* to get a move on.

magnésium [maɲezjɔm] *nm* magnesium.

magnétique [maɲetik] *adj* magnetic.

magnétiser [3] [maɲetize] *vt* - **1.** PHYS to magnetize - **2.** [hypnotiser, fasciner] to hypnotize.

magnétisme [maɲetism] *nm* - **1.** PHYS [fascination] magnetism - **2.** [hypnotisme] hypnotism.

magnéto(phone) [maɲetɔ(fɔn)] *nm* tape recorder.

magnétoscope [maɲetɔskɔp] *nm* videorecorder.

magnificence [maɲifisɑ̃s] *nf* magnificence.

magnifier [9] [maɲifje] *vt* to magnify.

magnifique [maɲifik] *adj* magnificent.

magnifiquement [maɲifikmɑ̃] *adv* magnificently.

magnitude [maɲityd] *nf* magnitude.

magnolia [maɲɔlja] *nm* magnolia.

magnum [magnɔm] *nm* magnum.

magot [mago] *nm fam* tidy sum, packet.

magouille [maguj] *nf fam* plot, scheme.

magouiller [3] [maguje] *vi fam* to plot, to scheme.

magret [magrɛ] *nm* fillet *Br*, filet *Am* ; ~ **de canard** breast of duck.

magyar, e [magjar] *adj* Magyar.

mai [mɛ] *nm* May ; **le premier ~** May Day ; **(les événements de) ~ 1968** May 1968 ; *voir aussi* **septembre**.

MAI 68

The events of May 1968 came about when student protests, coupled with widespread industrial unrest, culminated in a general strike and rioting. De Gaulle's government survived the crisis, but the issues raised made the events a turning point in French social history.

maigre [mɛgr] ◇ *adj* - **1.** [très mince] thin - **2.** [aliment] low-fat ; [viande] lean - **3.** [peu important] meagre *Br*, meager *Am* ; [végétation] sparse ◇ *adv* : **faire ~** not to eat meat ◇ *nmf* thin person ◇ *nm* lean meat.

maigrelet, ette [mɛgrəlɛ, ɛt] *adj* scrawny.

maigreur [mɛgrœr] *nf* thinness.

maigrir [32] [megrir] ◇ *vi* to lose weight ◇ *vt* : ~ **qqn** to make sb look thinner *ou* slimmer.

mailing [melin] *nm* mailing, mailshot.

maille [maj] *nf* - **1.** [de tricot] stitch ; ~ **à l'endroit/l'envers** plain/purl stitch - **2.** [de filet] mesh - **3.** *loc* : **avoir ~ à partir avec** to have a set-to with.

maillet [majɛ] *nm* mallet.

maillon [majɔ̃] *nm* link.

maillot [majo] *nm* [de sport] shirt, jersey ; ~ **de bain** swimsuit ; ~ **de corps** vest *Br*, undershirt *Am*.

main [mɛ̃] *nf* hand ; **à la ~** by hand ; **à pleines ~s** by the handful ; **de première ~** firsthand ; **de seconde ~** secondhand ; **à quatre ~s** four-handed, for four hands ; **de ~ de maître** in a masterly fashion ; **en sous ~** secretly ; **la ~ dans la ~** hand in hand ; **attaque à ~ armée** armed attack ; ~ **courante** handrail, banister ; **avoir la ~ leste** to be quick with one's hands ; **avoir/prendre qqch en ~** to have/to take sthg in hand ; **avoir qqch sous la ~** to have sthg at hand ; **demander la ~ de qqn** to ask for sb's hand (in marriage) ; **donner la ~ à qqn** to take sb's hand ; **faire ~ basse sur qqch** to help oneself to sthg ; **forcer la ~ à qqn** to force sb's hand ; **se frotter les ~s** to rub one's hands ; **haut la ~** effortlessly, hands down ; **haut les ~s!** hands up! ; **se laver les ~s de qqch** to wash one's hands of sthg ; **mettre la dernière ~ à** to put the finishing touches to ; **mettre la ~ à la pâte** to lend a helping hand ; **ne pas y aller de ~ morte** not to pull one's punches ; **passer la ~** CARTES to pass the deal ; **perdre la ~** *fig* to lose one's touch ; **remettre en ~(s) propre(s)** to hand over personally ; **en venir aux ~s** to come to blows.

main-d'œuvre [mɛ̃dœvr] *nf* labour *Br*, labor *Am*, workforce.

main-forte [mɛ̃fɔrt] *nf* : **prêter ~ à qqn** to come to sb's assistance.

mainmise [mɛ̃miz] *nf* seizure.

maint, e [mɛ̃, mɛ̃t] *adj littéraire* many a ; ~**s** many ; ~**es fois** time and time again.

maintenance [mɛ̃tnɑ̃s] *nf* maintenance.

maintenant [mɛ̃tnɑ̃] *adv* now.
➡ **maintenant que** *loc prép* now that.

maintenir [40] [mɛ̃tnir] *vt* - **1.** [soutenir] to

support ; ~ **qqn à distance** to keep sb away - **2.** [garder, conserver] to maintain - **3.** [affirmer] : ~ **que** to maintain (that).

◆ **se maintenir** vp - **1.** [durer] to last - **2.** [rester] to remain.

maintenu, e [mɛ̃tny] pp ▷ maintenir.

maintien [mɛ̃tjɛ̃] nm - **1.** [conservation] maintenance ; [de tradition] upholding ; **le ~ de l'ordre** the maintenance of law and order - **2.** [tenue] posture.

maintiendrai, maintiendras etc ▷ maintenir.

maire [mɛr] nm mayor.

mairie [meri] nf - **1.** [bâtiment] town hall Br, city hall Am - **2.** [administration] town council Br, city hall Am.

mais [mɛ] ◇ conj but ; ~ **non!** of course not! ; ~ **alors, tu l'as vu ou non?** so did you see him or not? ; **il a pleuré, ~ pleuré!** he cried, and how! ; **non ~ ça ne va pas!** that's just not on! ◇ adv but ; **vous êtes prêts? – ~ bien sûr!** are you ready? – but of course! ; ~ **certainement** but of course ; ~ **enfin** but after all ; [marquant l'impatience] really! ◇ nm : **il y a un ~** there's a hitch ou a snag ; **il n'y a pas de ~** (there are) no buts.

maïs [mais] nm maize Br, corn Am.

maison [mɛzɔ̃] nf - **1.** [habitation, lignée & ASTROL] house ; ~ **de campagne** house in the country ; ~ **individuelle** detached house ; **~s mitoyennes** semidetached houses - **2.** [foyer] home ; [famille] family ; **à la ~** [au domicile] at home ; [dans la famille] in my/your etc family - **3.** COMM company ; ~ **mère** parent company - **4.** [institut] : ~ **d'arrêt** prison ; ~ **de la culture** arts centre Br ou center Am ; ~ **de quartier** ≃ community centre Br ou center Am ; ~ **de retraite** old people's home - **5.** (en apposition) [artisanal] homemade ; [dans restaurant - vin] house (avant n).

Maison-Blanche [mɛzɔ̃blɑ̃ʃ] nf : **la ~** the White House.

maisonnée [mɛzɔne] nf household.

maisonnette [mɛzɔnɛt] nf small house.

maître, esse [mɛtr, mɛtrɛs] nm, f - **1.** [professeur] teacher ; ~ **auxiliaire** supply teacher Br, substitute teacher Am ; ~ **chanteur** blackmailer ; ~ **de conférences** UNIV ≃ senior lecturer ; ~ **d'école** schoolteacher ; ~ **nageur** swimming instructor - **2.** [modèle, artiste] fig master ; **les grands ~s** the Old Masters ; ~ **à penser** mentor ; **passer ~ dans l'art de faire qqch** to be a past master in the art of doing sthg - **3.** [dirigeant] ruler ; [d'animal] master (f mistress) ; ~ **d'hôtel** head waiter ; ~ **de maison** host ; ~ **d'œuvre** CONSTR project manager ;

fig artisan, architect ; **être ~ de soi** to be in control of oneself, to have self-control - **4.** (en apposition) [principal] main, principal.

◆ **Maître** nm form of address for lawyers.

◆ **maîtresse** nf [amie] mistress.

maître-assistant, e [mɛtrasistɑ̃, ɑ̃t] (mpl **maîtres-assistants**, fpl **maîtres-assistantes**) nm, f ≃ lecturer Br, ≃ assistant professor Am.

maître-autel [mɛtrotɛl] (pl **maîtres-autels**) nm high altar.

maîtresse ▷ maître.

maîtrisable [mɛtrizabl] adj controllable.

maîtrise [mɛtriz] nf - **1.** [sang-froid, domination] control ; ~ **de soi** self-control - **2.** [connaissance] mastery, command ; [habileté] skill - **3.** UNIV ≃ master's degree.

maîtriser [3] [mɛtrize] vt - **1.** [animal, forcené] to subdue - **2.** [émotion, réaction] to control, to master - **3.** [incendie] to bring under control - **4.** [dépenses] to curb.

◆ **se maîtriser** vp to control o.s.

majesté [maʒɛste] nf majesty.

◆ **Majesté** nf : **Sa Majesté** His/Her Majesty.

majestueux, euse [maʒɛstɥø, øz] adj majestic.

majeur, e [maʒœr] adj - **1.** [gén] major - **2.** [personne] of age.

◆ **majeur** nm middle finger.

Majeur [maʒœr] ▷ lac.

major [maʒɔr] nm - **1.** MIL ≃ adjutant - **2.** SCOL : ~ **(de promotion)** first in ou top of one's year group.

majoration [maʒɔrasjɔ̃] nf increase.

majordome [maʒɔrdɔm] nm majordomo.

majorer [3] [maʒɔre] vt to increase.

majorette [maʒɔrɛt] nf majorette.

majoritaire [maʒɔritɛr] ◇ nmf member of majority group ◇ adj majority (avant n) ; **être ~** to be in the majority.

majorité [maʒɔrite] nf majority ; **en (grande) ~** in the majority ; ~ **absolue/relative** POLIT absolute/relative majority ; ~ **civile** voting age.

Majorque [maʒɔrk] n Majorca ; **à ~** in Majorca.

majorquin, e adj Majorcan.

◆ **Majorquin, e** nm, f Majorcan.

majuscule [maʒyskyl] ◇ nf capital (letter) ; **en ~s** in capitals, in capital letters ◇ adj capital (avant n).

mal, maux [mal, mo] nm - **1.** [ce qui est contraire à la morale] evil ; **dire du ~ de qqn** to say bad things about sb - **2.** [souffrance physique] pain ; **avoir ~ au bras** to have a sore arm ; **avoir**

~ **au cœur** to feel sick ; **avoir ~ au dos** to have backache ; **avoir ~ à la gorge** to have a sore throat ; **avoir le ~ de mer** to be seasick ; **avoir ~ aux dents/à la tête** to have toothache/a headache ; **avoir des maux de tête** to get headaches ; **avoir le ~ des transports** to be travelsick ; **avoir ~ au ventre** to have (a) stomachache ; **faire ~ à qqn** to hurt sb ; **ça fait ~** it hurts ; **se faire ~** to hurt o.s. - **3.** [difficulté] difficulty ; **avoir du ~ à faire qqch** to have difficulty doing sthg ; **se donner du ~ (pour faire qqch)** to take trouble (to do sthg) - **4.** [douleur morale] pain, suffering (U) ; **avoir le ~ du pays** to be ou feel homesick ; **être en ~ de qqch** to long for sthg ; **faire du ~ (à qqn)** to hurt (sb) ; **c'est un moindre ~** it's the lesser of two evils.

➡ **mal** adv - **1.** [malade] ill ; **aller ~** not to be well ; **se sentir ~** to feel ill ; **être au plus ~** to be extremely ill - **2.** [respirer] with difficulty - **3.** [informé, se conduire] badly ; **être ~ reçu** to get a poor welcome ; **~ prendre qqch** to take sthg badly ; **~ tourner** to go wrong - **4.** loc : **de ~ en pis** from bad to worse ; **~ à propos** inappropriate ; **pas ~** not bad (adj), not badly (adv) ; **pas ~ de** quite a lot of.

malabar [malabar] nm fam big lad, well-built fellow.

malade [malad] <> nmf invalid, sick person ; **~ mental** mentally ill person <> adj - **1.** [souffrant - personne] ill, sick ; [- organe] bad ; **tomber ~** to fall ill ou sick ; **être ~ du cœur/des reins** to have heart/kidney trouble ; **être ~ d'inquiétude** fig to be sick with worry - **2.** fam [fou] crazy - **3.** fig [en mauvais état] in bad shape, in a bad way.

maladie [maladi] nf - **1.** MÉD illness ; **~ d'Alzheimer** Alzheimer's disease ; **~ de Creutzfeldt-Jakob** Creutzfeldt-Jakob disease ; **~ de Parkinson** Parkinson's disease ; **~ de la vache folle** mad cow disease ; **il en fait une ~** he's really worked up about it - **2.** [passion, manie] mania.

maladif, ive [maladif, iv] adj - **1.** [enfant] sickly - **2.** [pâleur] fig unhealthy.

maladresse [maladrɛs] nf - **1.** [inhabileté] clumsiness - **2.** [bévue] blunder.

maladroit, e [maladrwa, at] <> adj clumsy <> nm, f clumsy person.

maladroitement [maladrwatmã] adv clumsily.

mal-aimé, e [malɛme] (mpl **mal-aimés**, fpl **mal-aimées**) nm, f unloved person.

malais, e [malɛ, ɛz] adj Malay, Malaysian ; **la presqu'île Malaise** the Malay Peninsula.
➡ **malais** nm [langue] Malay.

➡ **Malais, e** nm, f Malay, Malaysian.

malaise [malɛz] nm - **1.** [indisposition] discomfort ; **avoir un ~** to feel faint - **2.** [trouble] unease (U) - **3.** [crise] discontent (U).

malaisé, e [maleze] adj difficult.

Malaisie [malɛzi] nf : **la ~** Malaya ; **en ~** in Malaya.

malappris, e [malapri, iz] <> adj uncouth, ill-mannered <> nm, f lout.

malaria [malarja] nf malaria.

malavisé, e [malavize] adj littéraire ill-advised, unwise.

malaxer [3] [malakse] vt to knead.

Malaysia [malɛzja] nf : **la ~** Malaysia ; **la ~ occidentale** Malaya.

malchance [malʃãs] nf bad luck (U) ; **jouer de ~** to be dogged by bad luck.

malchanceux, euse [malʃãsø, øz] <> adj unlucky <> nm, f unlucky person.

malcommode [malkɔmɔd] adj inconvenient ; [meuble] impractical.

Maldives [maldiv] nfpl : **les (îles) ~** the Maldives.

maldonne [maldɔn] nf misdeal ; **il y a ~** the cards have been misdealt ; fig there's been a misunderstanding.

mâle [mal] <> adj - **1.** [enfant, animal, hormone] male - **2.** [voix, assurance] manly - **3.** ÉLECTR male <> nm male.

malédiction [malediksjɔ̃] nf curse.

maléfice [malefis] nm sout evil spell.

maléfique [malefik] adj sout evil.

malencontreusement [malãkɔ̃trøzmã] adv inopportunely.

malencontreux, euse [malãkɔ̃trø, øz] adj [hasard, rencontre] unfortunate.

mal-en-point, mal en point [malãpwɛ̃] adj inv in a bad way ou sorry state.

malentendant, e [malãtãdã, ãt] <> adj hard of hearing <> nm, f person who is hard of hearing.

malentendu [malãtãdy] nm misunderstanding.

malfaçon [malfasɔ̃] nf defect.

malfaisant, e [malfəzã, ãt] adj harmful.

malfaiteur [malfɛtœr] nm criminal.

malfamé, e, mal famé, e [malfame] adj disreputable.

malformation [malfɔrmasjɔ̃] nf malformation.

malfrat [malfra] nm fam crook.

malgache [malgaʃ] adj Madagascan, Malagasy.
➡ **malgache** nm [langue] Malagasy.

➤ **Malgache** *nmf* Madagascan, Malagasy.

malgré [malgre] *prép* in spite of ; ~ **tout** [quoi qu'il arrive] in spite of everything ; [pourtant] even so, yet.

➤ **malgré que** *loc conj (+ subjonctif) fam* although, in spite of the fact that.

malhabile [malabil] *adj* clumsy.

malheur [malœr] *nm* misfortune ; **le ~** misfortune, bad luck ; **par ~** unfortunately ; **porter ~ à qqn** to bring sb bad luck ; **~ à toi!** woe betide you! ; **faire un ~** *fam fig* [faire un éclat] to do some damage ; [avoir du succès] to be a great hit.

malheureusement [malœrøzmã] *adv* unfortunately.

malheureux, euse [malœrø, øz] ⬦ *adj* - **1.** [triste] unhappy - **2.** [désastreux, regrettable] unfortunate - **3.** [malchanceux] unlucky - **4.** *(avant n)* [sans valeur] pathetic, miserable ⬦ *nm, f* - **1.** [infortuné] poor soul - **2.** [indigent] poor person.

malhonnête [malɔnɛt] ⬦ *nmf* dishonest person ⬦ *adj* - **1.** [personne, affaire] dishonest - **2.** *hum* [proposition, propos] indecent.

malhonnêteté [malɔnɛtte] *nf* - **1.** [de personne] dishonesty - **2.** [action] dishonest action.

Mali [mali] *nm* : **le ~** Mali ; **au ~** in Mali.

malice [malis] *nf* mischief ; **sans ~** without malice.

malicieux, euse [malisjø, øz] ⬦ *adj* mischievous ⬦ *nm, f* mischievous person.

malien, enne [maljɛ̃, ɛn] *adj* Malian.
➤ **Malien, enne** *nm, f* Malian.

malignité [maliɲite] *nf* - **1.** [méchanceté] malice, spite - **2.** *MÉD* malignancy.

malin, igne [malɛ̃, iɲ] ⬦ *adj* - **1.** [rusé] crafty, cunning ; **ce n'est pas ~!** *fig* that's not very clever! ; [regard, sourire] knowing - **2.** [méchant] malicious, spiteful - **3.** *MÉD* malignant ⬦ *nm, f* cunning *ou* crafty person ; **faire le ~** to show off.

malingre [malɛ̃gr] *adj* sickly.

malle [mal] *nf* [coffre] trunk ; [de voiture] boot *Br*, trunk *Am* ; **se faire la ~** *fam fig* to beat it.

malléable [maleabl] *adj* malleable.

mallette [malɛt] *nf* briefcase.

mal-logé, e [malɔʒe] *(mpl* **mal-logés,** *fpl* **mal-logées)** *nm, f* person living in poor accommodation.

malmener [19] [malmøne] *vt* - **1.** [brutaliser] to handle roughly, to ill-treat - **2.** [dominer] to have the better of.

malnutrition [malnytrisjɔ̃] *nf* malnutrition.

malodorant, e [malɔdɔrã, ãt] *adj* smelly.

malotru, e [malɔtry] *nm, f* lout.

Malouines [malwin] *nfpl* : **les (îles) ~** the Falkland Islands, the Falklands.

malpoli, e [malpɔli] ⬦ *adj* rude ⬦ *nm, f* rude person.

malpropre [malprɔpr] *adj* [sale] dirty.

malpropreté [malprɔprøte] *nf* [saleté] dirtiness.

malsain, e [malsɛ̃, ɛn] *adj* unhealthy.

malséant, e [malseã, ãt] *adj* unbecoming.

malt [malt] *nm* - **1.** [céréale] malt - **2.** [whisky] malt (whisky).

maltais, e [maltɛ, ɛz] *adj* Maltese.
➤ **maltais** *nm* [langue] Maltese.
➤ **Maltais, e** *nm, f* Maltese (person) ; **les Maltais** the Maltese.

Malte [malt] *n* Malta ; **à ~** in Malta.

maltraiter [4] [maltrete] *vt* to ill-treat ; [en paroles] to attack, to run down.

malus [malys] *nm increase in car insurance charges, due to loss of no-claims bonus.*

malveillance [malvɛjãs] *nf* spite.

malveillant, e [malvejã, ãt] *adj* spiteful.

malvenu, e [malvøny] *adj* out of place ; **être ~ de faire qqch** *sout* to be wrong to do sthg.

malversation [malversasjɔ̃] *nf* embezzlement.

malvoyant, e [malvwajã, ãt] ⬦ *adj* partially sighted ⬦ *nm, f* person who is partially sighted.

maman [mamã] *nf* mummy.

mamelle [mamɛl] *nf* teat ; [de vache] udder.

mamelon [mamlɔ̃] *nm* - **1.** [du sein] nipple - **2.** [butte] hillock.

mamie, mamy [mami] *nf* granny, grandma.

mammifère [mamifɛr] *nm* mammal.

mammographie [mamɔgrafi] *nf* mammography.

mammouth [mamut] *nm* mammoth.

mamours [mamur] *nmpl fam* billing and cooing *(U)* ; **se faire des ~** to bill and coo.

mamy = mamie.

Man [man] ➣ île.

management [manadʒmɛnt] *nm* management.

manager[1] [manadʒɛr] *nm* manager.

manager[2] [17] [manadʒe] *vt* to manage.

Managua [managwa] *n* Managua.

manche [mãʃ] ⬦ *nf* - **1.** [de vêtement] sleeve ; **sans ~s** sleeveless ; **~s courtes/longues** short/long sleeves ; **~s raglan** raglan sleeves ; **être en ~s de chemise** to be in one's shirtsleeves - **2.** [de jeu] round, game ; *TENNIS* set - **3.** *loc* : **faire la ~** *fam* to pass the hat round <> *nm* **- 1.** [d'outil] handle ; ~ **à balai** broomstick ; [d'avion] joystick **- 2.** *MUS* neck.

Manche [mɑ̃ʃ] *nf* **- 1.** [Normandie] : **la ~** the Manche (region) **- 2.** [mer] : **la ~** the English Channel **- 3.** [en Espagne] : **la ~** La Mancha.

manchette [mɑ̃ʃɛt] *nf* **- 1.** [de chemise] cuff **- 2.** [de journal] headline **- 3.** [coup] forearm blow.

manchon [mɑ̃ʃɔ̃] *nm* **- 1.** [en fourrure] muff **- 2.** *TECHNOL* casing, sleeve.

manchot, ote [mɑ̃ʃo, ɔt] <> *adj* one-armed <> *nm, f* one-armed person.
◆ **manchot** *nm* penguin.

mandarin [mɑ̃darɛ̃] *nm* **- 1.** [en Chine] mandarin **- 2.** *péj* [personnage important] mandarin **- 3.** [langue] Mandarin.

mandarine [mɑ̃darin] *nf* mandarin (orange).

mandat [mɑ̃da] *nm* **- 1.** [pouvoir, fonction] mandate **- 2.** *JUR* warrant ; ~ **d'amener** ≃ summons ; ~ **d'arrêt** ≃ arrest warrant ; ~ **de perquisition** search warrant **- 3.** [titre postal] money order ; ~ **postal** postal order *Br*, money order *Am*.

mandataire [mɑ̃datɛr] *nmf* proxy, representative.

mandat-carte [mɑ̃dakart] (*pl* **mandats-cartes**) *nm* postal order *Br*, money order *Am*.

mandater [3] [mɑ̃date] *vt* **- 1.** [personne] to appoint **- 2.** [somme] to pay by money order.

mandat-lettre [mɑ̃dalɛtr] (*pl* **mandats-lettres**) *nm* postal order *Br*, money order *Am*.

mander [3] [mɑ̃de] *vt littéraire* **- 1.** [appeler] to summon **- 2.** [faire savoir] : ~ **qqch à qqn** to inform sb of sthg.

mandibule [mɑ̃dibyl] *nf* mandible.

mandoline [mɑ̃dɔlin] *nf* mandolin.

mandrill [mɑ̃dril] *nm* mandrill.

mandrin [mɑ̃drɛ̃] *nm* [de serrage] chuck ; [de perçage] punch.

manège [manɛʒ] *nm* **- 1.** [attraction] merry-go-round, roundabout *Br*, carousel *Am* **- 2.** [de chevaux - lieu] riding school **- 3.** [manœuvre] scheme, game.

manette [manɛt] *nf* lever.

manganèse [mɑ̃ganɛz] *nm* manganese.

mangeable [mɑ̃ʒabl] *adj* edible.

mangeoire [mɑ̃ʒwar] *nf* manger.

manger [17] [mɑ̃ʒe] <> *vt* **- 1.** [nourriture] to eat **- 2.** [étoffe, fer] to eat away **- 3.** [fortune] to get through, to squander <> *vi* to eat.

mange-tout [mɑ̃ʒtu] <> *adj inv* : **haricots ~** runner beans *Br*, string beans *Am* <> *nm inv*

[haricot] runner bean *Br*, string bean *Am* ; [pois] mangetout *Br*, snow pea *Am*.

mangeur, euse [mɑ̃ʒœr, øz] *nm, f* eater ; **gros ~** big eater.

mangue [mɑ̃g] *nf* mango.

maniable [manjabl] *adj* **- 1.** [instrument] manageable **- 2.** [personne] easily influenced.

maniaque [manjak] <> *nmf* **- 1.** [méticuleux] fusspot **- 2.** [fou] maniac <> *adj* **- 1.** [méticuleux] fussy **- 2.** [fou] maniacal.

maniaquerie [manjakri] *nf* fussiness.

manichéisme [manikeism] *nm* Manicheism.

manie [mani] *nf* **- 1.** [habitude] funny habit ; **avoir la ~ de qqch/de faire qqch** to have a mania for sthg/for doing sthg **- 2.** [obsession] mania.

maniement [manimɑ̃] *nm* handling.

manier [9] [manje] *vt* [manipuler, utiliser] to handle ; *fig* [ironie, mots] to handle skilfully.

manière [manjer] *nf* **- 1.** [méthode] manner, way ; **recourir à la ~ forte** to resort to strong-arm tactics ; **de toute ~** at any rate ; **d'une ~ générale** generally speaking ; **c'est une ~ de parler** it's just my/his *etc* way of putting it **- 2.** [style propre à un artiste] style ; **à la ~ de** in the style of.
◆ **manières** *nfpl* manners ; **les bonnes ~s** good manners ; **faire des ~s** *fig* to pussyfoot around.
◆ **de manière à** *loc conj* (in order) to ; **de ~ à ce que** (+ *subjonctif*) so that.
◆ **de manière que** *loc conj* (+ *subjonctif*) in such a way that.

maniéré, e [manjere] *adj* affected.

maniérisme [manjerism] *nm* mannerism.

manif [manif] *nf fam* demo.

manifestant, e [manifɛstɑ̃, ɑ̃t] *nm, f* demonstrator.

manifestation [manifɛstasjɔ̃] *nf* **- 1.** [témoignage] expression **- 2.** [mouvement collectif] demonstration **- 3.** [apparition - de maladie] appearance.

manifeste [manifɛst] <> *nm* [déclaration] manifesto <> *adj* obvious.

manifestement [manifɛstəmɑ̃] *adv* obviously.

manifester [3] [manifɛste] <> *vt* to show, to express <> *vi* to demonstrate.
◆ **se manifester** *vp* **- 1.** [apparaître] to show *ou* manifest itself **- 2.** [se montrer] to turn up, to appear.

manigance [manigɑ̃s] *nf fam* scheme, intrigue.

manigancer [16] [manigɑ̃se] *vt fam* to plot.

Manille [manij] *n* Manila.

manioc [manjɔk] *nm* manioc.

manipulateur, trice [manipylatœr, tris] *nm, f* - **1.** [opérateur] technician - **2.** *fig* & *péj* [de personnes] manipulator.

➤ **manipulateur** *nm* TÉLÉCOM key.

manipulation [manipylasjɔ̃] *nf* - **1.** [de produits, d'explosifs] handling ; **~s génétiques** genetic engineering - **2.** *fig* & *péj* [manœuvre] manipulation *(U)*.

manipuler [3] [manipyle] *vt* - **1.** [colis, appareil] to handle - **2.** [statistiques, résultats] to falsify, to rig - **3.** *péj* [personne] to manipulate.

manivelle [manivɛl] *nf* crank.

manne [man] *nf* RELIG manna ; *fig* & *littéraire* godsend.

mannequin [mankɛ̃] *nm* - **1.** [forme humaine] model, dummy - **2.** [personne] model, mannequin.

manœuvre [manœvr] ⟨⟩ *nf* - **1.** [d'appareil, de véhicule] driving, handling ; **fausse ~** driver error ; *fig* false move - **2.** MIL manoeuvre *Br*, maneuver *Am*, exercise - **3.** [machination] ploy, scheme ⟨⟩ *nm* labourer *Br*, laborer *Am*.

manœuvrer [5] [manœvre] ⟨⟩ *vi* to manoeuvre *Br*, to maneuver *Am* ⟨⟩ *vt* - **1.** [faire fonctionner] to operate, to work ; [voiture] to manoeuvre *Br*, to maneuver *Am* - **2.** [influencer] to manipulate.

manoir [manwar] *nm* manor, country house.

manomètre [manɔmɛtr] *nm* manometer.

manquant, e [mɑ̃kɑ̃, ɑ̃t] *adj* missing.

manque [mɑ̃k] *nm* - **1.** [pénurie] lack, shortage ; **par ~ de** for want of - **2.** [de toxicomane] withdrawal symptoms *(pl)* ; **être en (état de) ~** to have *ou* experience withdrawal symptoms - **3.** [lacune] gap ; **~ à gagner** COMM loss of earnings.

➤ **à la manque** *loc adj fam* second-rate.

manqué, e [mɑ̃ke] *adj* [raté] failed ; [rendez-vous] missed.

manquement [mɑ̃kmɑ̃] *nm* : **~ (à)** breach (of).

manquer [3] [mɑ̃ke] ⟨⟩ *vi* - **1.** [faire défaut] to be lacking, to be missing ; **l'argent/le temps me manque** I don't have enough money/ time ; **tu me manques** I miss you - **2.** [être absent] : **~ (à)** to be absent (from), to be missing (from) - **3.** [échouer] to fail - **4.** [ne pas avoir assez] : **~ de qqch** to lack sthg, to be short of sthg - **5.** [faillir] : **il a manqué de se noyer** he nearly *ou* almost drowned ; **ne manquez pas de lui dire** don't forget to tell him ; **je n'y manquerai pas** I certainly will, I'll definitely do it - **6.** [ne pas respecter] : **~ à** [devoir] to fail in ; **~ à sa**

parole to break one's word ⟨⟩ *vt* - **1.** [gén] to miss - **2.** [échouer à] to bungle, to botch ⟨⟩ *v impers* : **il manque quelqu'un** somebody is missing ; **il me manque 20 francs** I'm 20 francs short ; **il ne manquait plus que ça** *fig* that's all I/you *etc* needed.

mansarde [mɑ̃sard] *nf* attic.

mansardé, e [mɑ̃sarde] *adj* attic *(avant n)*.

mansuétude [mɑ̃sɥetyd] *nf littéraire* indulgence.

mante [mɑ̃t] *nf* HIST mantle.

➤ **mante religieuse** *nf* praying mantis.

manteau, x [mɑ̃to] *nm* - **1.** [vêtement] coat ; **sous le ~** *fig* secretly, clandestinely - **2.** *fig* [de neige] mantle, blanket.

manucure [manykyr] *nmf* manicurist.

manuel, elle [manɥɛl] ⟨⟩ *adj* manual ⟨⟩ *nm, f* manual worker.

➤ **manuel** *nm* manual.

manufacture [manyfaktyr] *nf* [fabrique] factory.

manuscrit, e [manyskri, it] *adj* handwritten.

➤ **manuscrit** *nm* manuscript.

manutention [manytɑ̃sjɔ̃] *nf* handling.

manutentionnaire [manytɑ̃sjɔnɛr] *nmf* packer.

MAP *(abr de mise au point)* *nf* focusing.

mappemonde [mapmɔ̃d] *nf* - **1.** [carte] map of the world - **2.** [sphère] globe.

Maputo [mapyto] *n* Maputo.

maquereau, elle, x [makro, ɛl, o] *nm, f fam* pimp *(f* madam*)*.

➤ **maquereau** *nm* mackerel.

maquette [makɛt] *nf* - **1.** [ébauche] paste-up - **2.** [modèle réduit] model.

maquettiste [maketist] *nmf* model maker.

maquignon [makiɲɔ̃] *nm* - **1.** [marchand de chevaux] horse dealer - **2.** *péj* [homme d'affaires] crook.

maquillage [makijaʒ] *nm* - **1.** [action, produits] make-up - **2.** [falsification - gén] disguising ; [- de chiffres] doctoring ; [- de passeport] falsification.

maquiller [3] [makije] *vt* - **1.** [farder] to make up - **2.** [falsifier - gén] to disguise ; [- passeport] to falsify ; [- chiffres] to doctor.

➤ **se maquiller** *vp* to make up, to put on one's make-up.

maquilleur, euse [makijœr, øz] *nm, f* make-up artist.

maquis [maki] *nm* - **1.** [végétation] scrub, brush - **2.** HIST Maquis ; **prendre le ~** to join the Maquis - **3.** *fig* [méli-mélo] maze.

maquisard [makizar] *nm* member of the Resistance.

marabout [marabu] *nm* **- 1.** ZOOL marabou **- 2.** [guérisseur] marabout.

maraîcher, ère [mareʃe, ɛr] ⟵> *adj* market garden *(avant n)* Br, truck farming *(avant n)* Am ⟵> *nm, f* market gardener Br, truck farmer Am.

marais [marɛ] *nm* [marécage] marsh, swamp ; **~ salant** saltpan ; **le Marais** *historic district in central Paris.*

LE MARAIS

> The Marais includes the place des Vosges and the predominantly Jewish quarter around the rue des Rosiers. Typical flats in the Marais feature exposed beams and 'tomettes' (red hexagonal floor tiles).

marasme [marasm] *nm* **- 1.** [récession] stagnation **- 2.** [accablement] depression.

marathon [maratɔ̃] *nm* marathon.

marâtre [maratr] *nf vieilli* **- 1.** [mauvaise mère] bad mother **- 2.** [belle-mère] stepmother.

maraude [marod] *nf,* **maraudage** [marodaʒ] *nm* pilfering.

marbre [marbr] *nm* **- 1.** [roche, objet] marble ; **en** *ou* **de ~ marble** *(avant n)* ; **rester de ~** *fig* to remain impassive **- 2.** [dans imprimerie] stone **- 3.** Can BASE-BALL home base *ou* plate.

marbré, e [marbre] *adj* **- 1.** [gâteau] marble *(avant n)* **- 2.** [peau, teint] mottled.

marbrier [marbrije] *nm* monumental mason.

marbrure [marbryr] *nf* **- 1.** [imitation du marbre] marbling **- 2.** [sur la peau] mottling.

marc [mar] *nm* **- 1.** [eau-de-vie] *spirit distilled from grape residue* **- 2.** [de fruits] residue ; [de thé] leaves ; **~ de café** grounds *(pl)*.

marcassin [markasɛ̃] *nm* young wild boar.

marchand, e [marʃɑ̃, ɑ̃d] ⟵> *adj* [valeur] market *(avant n)* ; [prix] trade *(avant n)* ⟵> *nm, f* [commerçant] merchant ; [détaillant] shopkeeper Br, storekeeper Am ; **~ de journaux** newsagent Br, newsdealer Am ; **~ des quatre-saisons** street trader *(selling fruit and vegetables).*
➤ **marchand de sable** *nm fig* sandman.

marchandage [marʃɑ̃daʒ] *nm* bargaining.

marchander [3] [marʃɑ̃de] ⟵> *vt* **- 1.** [prix] to haggle over **- 2.** [appui] to begrudge ⟵> *vi* to bargain, to haggle.

marchandise [marʃɑ̃diz] *nf* merchandise *(U)*, goods *(pl)*.

marche [marʃ] *nf* **- 1.** [d'escalier] step **- 2.** [activité, sport] walking ; **être à deux heures de ~ (de)** to be two hours' walk *ou* a two-hour walk (from) ; **fermer la ~** to bring up the rear ; **ouvrir la ~** to lead the way ; **~ à pied** walking ; **~ à suivre** *fig* correct procedure **- 3.** [promenade] walk **- 4.** MUS march ; **~ funèbre/nuptiale** funeral/wedding march **- 5.** [déplacement - du temps, d'astre] course ; **assis dans le sens de la ~** [en train] sitting facing the engine ; **en ~ arrière** in reverse ; **faire ~ arrière** to reverse ; *fig* to backpedal, to backtrack **- 6.** [fonctionnement] running, working ; **en ~** running ; **se mettre en ~** to start (up) ; **mettre qqch en ~** to start sthg (up) ; **remettre qqch en ~** to restart sthg.

marché [marʃe] *nm* **- 1.** [gén] market ; **faire son ~** to go shopping, to do one's shopping ; **le ~ du travail** the labour Br *ou* labor Am market ; **~ cible** target market ; **~ noir** black market ; **~ aux puces** flea market **- 2.** [contrat] bargain, deal ; **(à) bon ~** cheap ; **meilleur ~** cheaper ; **par-dessus le ~** *fam fig* into the bargain.
➤ **Marché commun** *nm* : **le Marché commun** the Common Market.

marchepied [marʃəpje] *nm* [de train] step ; [escabeau] steps *(pl)* Br, stepladder ; *fig* stepping-stone.

marcher [3] [marʃe] *vi* **- 1.** [aller à pied] to walk **- 2.** [poser le pied] to step **- 3.** [avancer] : **~ sur** [ville, ennemi] to march on *ou* upon **- 4.** [fonctionner, tourner] to work ; **son affaire marche bien** his business is doing well **- 5.** *fam* [accepter] to agree **- 6.** *loc* : **faire ~ qqn** *fam* to take sb for a ride.

marcheur, euse [marʃœr, øz] *nm, f* walker.

marcottage [markɔtaʒ] *nm* layering.

mardi [mardi] *nm* Tuesday ; **~ gras** Shrove Tuesday ; *voir aussi* **samedi.**

mare [mar] *nf* pool.

marécage [marekaʒ] *nm* marsh, bog.

marécageux, euse [marekaʒø, øz] *adj* **- 1.** [terrain] marshy, boggy **- 2.** [plante] marsh *(avant n)*.

maréchal, aux [mareʃal, o] *nm* marshal.
➤ **maréchal des logis** *nm* sergeant.

maréchal-ferrant [mareʃalferɑ̃] *(pl* **maréchaux-ferrants** [mareʃoferɑ̃]) *nm* blacksmith.

maréchaussée [mareʃose] *nf vieilli* constabulary.

marée [mare] *nf* **- 1.** [de la mer] tide ; **(à) ~ haute/basse** (at) high/low tide **- 2.** *fig* [de personnes] wave, surge **- 3.** [poissons] seafood.
➤ **marée noire** *nf* oil slick.

marelle [marɛl] *nf* hopscotch.

marémoteur, trice [maremɔtœr, tris] *adj* [énergie] tidal ; [usine] tidal power *(avant n)*.

mareyeur, euse [marɛjœr, øz] *nm, f* wholesale fish merchant.

margarine [margarin] *nf* margarine.

marge [marʒ] *nf* - **1.** [espace] margin ; **vivre en ~ de la société** *fig* to live on the fringes of society - **2.** [latitude] leeway ; **~ d'erreur** margin of error ; **~ de sécurité** safety margin - **3.** *COMM* margin ; **~ bénéficiaire** profit margin ; **~ commerciale** gross margin.

margelle [marʒɛl] *nf* coping.

marginal, e, aux [marʒinal, o] <> *adj* - **1.** [gén] marginal - **2.** [groupe] dropout *(avant n)* <> *nm, f* dropout.

marginaliser [3] [marʒinalize] *vt* to marginalize.

marginalité [marʒinalite] *nf* living on the fringes of society.

margoulin [margulɛ̃] *nm fam* shark, conman.

marguerite [margərit] *nf* - **1.** *BOT* daisy - **2.** [d'imprimante] daisy wheel.

mari [mari] *nm* husband.

mariage [marjaʒ] *nm* - **1.** [union, institution] marriage ; **donner qqn en ~** to give sb away ; **~ d'amour** love match ; **~ blanc** unconsummated marriage ; **~ consanguin** marriage between blood relations ; **~ de raison** marriage of convenience - **2.** [cérémonie] wedding ; **~ civil/religieux** civil/church wedding - **3.** *fig* [de choses] blend.

Marianne [marjan] *n personification of the French Republic.*

marié, e [marje] <> *adj* married <> *nm, f* groom, bridegroom (*f* bride) ; **jeunes ~s** newlyweds.

marier [9] [marje] *vt* - **1.** [personne] to marry - **2.** *fig* [couleurs] to blend.

se marier *vp* - **1.** [personnes] to get married ; **se ~ avec qqn** to marry sb - **2.** *fig* [couleurs] to blend.

marihuana [marirwana], **marijuana** [mariʒyana] *nf* marijuana.

marin, e [marɛ̃, in] *adj* - **1.** [de la mer] sea *(avant n)* ; [faune, biologie] marine - **2.** *NAVIG* [carte, mille] nautical.

marin *nm* - **1.** [navigateur] seafarer - **2.** [matelot] sailor ; **~ pêcheur** deep-sea fisherman.

marine <> *nf* - **1.** [navigation] seamanship, navigation - **2.** [navires] navy ; **~e marchande** merchant navy *Br* ou marine *Am* ; **~e nationale** navy <> *nm* - **1.** *MIL* marine - **2.** [couleur] navy (blue) <> *adj inv* navy.

marinade [marinad] *nf* marinade.

mariner [3] [marine] <> *vt* to marinate <> *vi* - **1.** [aliment] to marinate ; **faire ~ qqch** to marinate sthg - **2.** *fam fig* [attendre] to hang around ; **faire ~ qqn** to let sb stew.

marinier [marinje] *nm* bargee *Br*, bargeman *Am*.

marinière [marinjɛr] *nf* smock.

marionnette [marjɔnɛt] *nf* puppet.

marital, e, aux [marital, o] *adj* : **autorisation ~e** husband's permission.

maritalement [maritalmɑ̃] *adv* : **vivre ~** to cohabit.

maritime [maritim] *adj* [navigation] maritime ; [ville] coastal.

marivaudage [marivodaʒ] *nm littéraire* banter.

marjolaine [marʒɔlɛn] *nf* marjoram.

mark [mark] *nm* [monnaie] mark.

marketing [marketiŋ] *nm* marketing ; **~ téléphonique** telemarketing.

marmaille [marmaj] *nf fam* brood (of kids).

marmelade [marməlad] *nf* stewed fruit ; **en ~** cooked to a pulp ; *fam fig* [nez] smashed to a pulp ; **~ d'oranges** marmalade.

marmite [marmit] *nf* [casserole] pot ; **faire bouillir la ~** *fig* to be the breadwinner.

marmiton [marmitɔ̃] *nm* kitchen boy.

marmonner [3] [marmɔne] *vt & vi* to mutter, to mumble.

marmot [marmo] *nm fam* kid.

marmotte [marmɔt] *nf* marmot.

marmotter [3] [marmɔte] *vt* to mutter, to mumble.

marner [3] [marne] *vi fam* to slog.

Maroc [marɔk] *nm* : **le ~** Morocco ; **au ~** in Morocco.

marocain, e [marɔkɛ̃, ɛn] *adj* Moroccan.

Marocain, e *nm, f* Moroccan.

maroquin [marɔkɛ̃] *nm* morocco (leather).

maroquinerie [marɔkinri] *nf* - **1.** [fabrication] fine-leather production ; [commerce] fine-leather trade - **2.** [magasin] leather-goods shop *Br* ou store *Am*.

maroquinier [marɔkinje] *nm* - **1.** [artisan]

leatherworker - **2.** [commerçant] leather-goods dealer.

marotte [marɔt] nf [dada] craze.

marquant, e [markɑ̃, ɑ̃t] adj outstanding.

marque [mark] nf - **1.** [signe, trace] mark ; fig stamp, mark - **2.** [label, fabricant] make, brand ; **de ~** designer (avant n) ; fig important ; **une grande ~** a well-known make ou brand ; **~ déposée** registered trademark ; **~ de fabrique** trademark - **3.** SPORT score ; **à vos ~s, prêts, partez!** on your marks, get set, go!, ready, steady, go! - **4.** [insigne] badge - **5.** [témoignage] sign, token ; **~ d'affection** sign ou token of affection.

marqué, e [marke] adj - **1.** [net] marked, pronounced - **2.** [personne, visage] marked.

marquer [3] [marke] ◇ vt - **1.** [gén] to mark - **2.** fam [écrire] to write down, to note down - **3.** [indiquer, manifester] to show - **4.** [SPORT - but, point] to score ; [- joueur] to mark ; **~ les points** to keep the score ◇ vi - **1.** [événement, expérience] to leave its mark - **2.** SPORT to score.

marqueterie [markɛtri] nf marquetry.

marqueur [markœr] nm - **1.** [crayon] marker (pen) - **2.** SPORT scorer.

marqueuse [markøz] nf labelling machine.

marquis, e [marki, iz] nm, f marquis (f marchioness).
➤ **marquise** nf [auvent] canopy.

Marquises [markiz] nfpl : **les ~** the Marquesas Islands.

marraine [marɛn] nf - **1.** [de filleul] godmother - **2.** [de navire] christener.

marrant, e [marɑ̃, ɑ̃t] adj fam funny.

marre [mar] adv : **en avoir ~ (de)** fam to be fed up (with).

marrer [3] [mare] ➤ **se marrer** vp fam to split one's sides.

marron, onne [marɔ̃, ɔn] adj péj [médecin] quack (avant n) ; [avocat] crooked.
➤ **marron** ◇ nm - **1.** [fruit] chestnut ; **~ glacé** candied chestnut ; **~ d'Inde** horse chestnut - **2.** [couleur] brown - **3.** fam [coup de poing] thump ◇ adj inv brown.

marronnier [marɔnje] nm chestnut tree.

mars [mars] nm March ; voir aussi **septembre**.

marseillais, e [marsɛjɛ, ɛz] adj of/from Marseilles.
➤ **Marseillais, e** nm, f native ou inhabitant of Marseilles.
➤ **Marseillaise** nf : **la Marseillaise** French national anthem.

Marseille [marsɛj] n Marseilles.

marsouin [marswɛ̃] nm porpoise.

marsupial, e, aux [marsypjal, o] adj marsupial.
➤ **marsupial** nm marsupial.

marte = martre.

marteau, x [marto] ◇ nm - **1.** [gén] hammer ; **~ piqueur**, **~ pneumatique** pneumatic drill - **2.** [heurtoir] knocker ◇ adj fam barmy.

marteau-pilon [martopilɔ̃] (pl **marteaux-pilons**) nm power hammer.

martel [martɛl] nm : **se mettre ~ en tête** to get worked up.

marteler [25] [martəle] vt - **1.** [pieu] to hammer ; [table, porte] to hammer on, to pound - **2.** [phrase] to rap out.

martial, e, aux [marsjal, o] adj martial.

martien, enne [marsjɛ̃, ɛn] adj & nm, f Martian.

martinet [martinɛ] nm - **1.** ZOOL swift - **2.** [fouet] whip.

martingale [martɛ̃gal] nf - **1.** [de vêtement] half-belt - **2.** JEU winning system.

Martini® [martini] nm Martini®.

martiniquais, e [martinikɛ, ɛz] adj of/from Martinique.
➤ **Martiniquais, e** nm, f native ou inhabitant of Martinique.

Martinique [martinik] nf : **la ~** Martinique ; **à la ~** in Martinique.

martin-pêcheur [martɛ̃pɛʃœr] (pl **martins-pêcheurs**) nm kingfisher.

martre [martr], **marte** [mart] nf marten.

martyr, e [martir] ◇ adj martyred ◇ nm, f martyr.
➤ **martyre** nm martyrdom ; **souffrir le ~e** to suffer agonies.

martyriser [3] [martirize] vt to torment.

marxisme [marksism] nm Marxism.

marxiste [marksist] nmf & adj Marxist.

mas [mas] nm country house or farm in the South of France.

mascara [maskara] nm mascara.

mascarade [maskarad] nf - **1.** [mise en scène] masquerade - **2.** [accoutrement] getup.

mascotte [maskɔt] nf mascot.

masculin, e [maskylɛ̃, in] adj [apparence & GRAM] masculine ; [métier, population, sexe] male.
➤ **masculin** nm GRAM masculine.

maso [mazo] fam ◇ nm masochist ◇ adj masochistic.

masochisme [mazɔsism] nm masochism.

masochiste [mazɔʃist] ◇ nmf masochist ◇ adj masochistic.

masque [mask] nm - **1.** [gén] mask ; **~ à gaz** gas mask ; **~ de plongée** diving mask

- 2. [crème] : **~ (de beauté)** face pack **- 3.** *fig* [façade] front, façade ; **lever le ~** *fig* to show one's true colours.

masqué, e [maske] *adj* masked.

masquer [3] [maske] *vt* **- 1.** [vérité, crime, problème] to conceal **- 2.** [maison, visage] to conceal, to hide.

massacrant, e [masakrɑ̃, ɑ̃t] *adj* : **être d'une humeur ~e** to be in a foul temper.

massacre [masakr] *nm litt & fig* massacre.

massacrer [3] [masakre] *vt* to massacre ; [voiture] to smash up.

massage [masaʒ] *nm* massage ; **faire un ~ à qqn** to give sb a massage.

masse [mas] *nf* **- 1.** [de pierre] block ; [d'eau] volume ; **tomber comme une ~** *fig* to drop like a stone **- 2.** [de gens] : **la ~** the majority ; **les ~s** the masses **- 3.** [grande quantité] : **une ~ de** masses *(pl)* OU **loads** *(pl)* of **- 4.** PHYS mass ; **~ molaire** molar weight ; **~ moléculaire** molecular weight **- 5.** ÉLECTR earth *Br*, ground *Am* **- 6.** [maillet] sledgehammer.

◆ **masse monétaire** *nf* FIN money supply.

◆ **masse salariale** *nf* payroll.

◆ **en masse** *loc adv* [venir] en masse, all together ; *fam* [acheter] in bulk.

massepain [maspɛ̃] *nm* marzipan.

masser [3] [mase] *vt* **- 1.** [assembler] to assemble **- 2.** [frotter] to massage.

◆ **se masser** *vp* **- 1.** [s'assembler] to assemble, to gather **- 2.** [se frotter] : **se ~ le bras** to massage one's arm.

masseur, euse [masœr, øz] *nm, f* [personne] masseur *(f* masseuse).

◆ **masseur** *nm* [appareil] massager.

massicot [masiko] *nm* guillotine.

massif, ive [masif, iv] *adj* **- 1.** [monument, personne, dose] massive **- 2.** [or, chêne] solid.

◆ **massif** *nm* **- 1.** [de plantes] clump **- 2.** [de montagnes] massif ; **le Massif central** the Massif Central.

massivement [masivmɑ̃] *adv* **- 1.** [construit] massively **- 2.** [répondre] en masse.

massue [masy] ◇ *adj inv* crushing ◇ *nf* club.

mastic [mastik] *nm* mastic, putty.

mastiquer [3] [mastike] *vt* **- 1.** [mâcher] to chew **- 2.** [coller] to putty.

mastoc [mastɔk] *adj inv péj* hulking.

mastodonte [mastɔdɔ̃t] *nm* **- 1.** [mammifère] mastodon **- 2.** *fam* [personne] hulk.

masturbation [mastyrbasjɔ̃] *nf* masturbation.

masturber [3] [mastyrbe] ◆ **se masturber** *vp* to masturbate.

m'as-tu-vu [matyvy] *nmf inv* show-off.

masure [mazyr] *nf* hovel.

mat, e [mat] *adj* **- 1.** [peinture, surface] matt *Br*, matte *Am* **- 2.** [peau, personne] dusky **- 3.** [bruit, son] dull **- 4.** [aux échecs] checkmated.

◆ **mat** *nm* checkmate.

mât [ma] *nm* **- 1.** NAVIG mast **- 2.** [poteau] pole, post ; **~ de cocagne** greasy pole.

match [matʃ] *(pl* matches OU matchs) *nm* match ; **(faire) ~ nul** (to) draw ; **~ aller/retour** first/second leg.

matelas [matla] *nm inv* [de lit] mattress ; **~ de crin** horsehair mattress ; **~ pneumatique** airbed.

matelassé, e [matlase] *adj* padded.

matelot [matlo] *nm* sailor.

mater [3] [mate] *vt* **- 1.** [soumettre, neutraliser] to subdue **- 2.** *fam* [regarder] to eye up.

matérialiser [3] [materjalize] ◆ **se matérialiser** *vp* [aspirations] to be realized.

matérialisme [materjalism] *nm* materialism.

matérialiste [materjalist] ◇ *nmf* materialist ◇ *adj* materialistic.

matériau, x [materjo] *nm* material.

◆ **matériaux** *nmpl* **- 1.** CONSTR material *(U)*, materials ; **~x de construction** building material OU materials **- 2.** [documents] material *(U)*.

matériel, elle [materjɛl] *adj* **- 1.** [être, substance] material, physical ; [confort, avantage, aide] material **- 2.** [considération] practical.

◆ **matériel** *nm* **- 1.** [gén] equipment *(U)* ; **~ d'exploitation** plant *(U)* ; **~ roulant** rolling stock *(U)* **- 2.** INFORM hardware *(U)*.

matériellement [materjɛlmɑ̃] *adv* materially.

maternel, elle [matɛrnɛl] *adj* maternal ; [langue] mother *(avant n)* ; **lait ~** mother's milk.

◆ **maternelle** *nf* nursery school.

materner [3] [matɛrne] *vt* to mother.

maternité [matɛrnite] *nf* **- 1.** [qualité] maternity, motherhood **- 2.** [hôpital] maternity hospital.

mathématicien, enne [matematisjɛ̃, ɛn] *nm, f* mathematician.

mathématique [matematik] *adj* mathematical.

◆ **mathématiques** *nfpl* mathematics *(U)*.

matheux, euse [matø, øz] *nm, f fam* mathematician.

maths [mat] *nfpl fam* maths *Br*, math *Am*.

matière [matjɛr] *nf* **- 1.** [substance] matter ; **~s fécales** faeces *Br*, feces *Am* ; **~s grasses** fats ;

~ **grise** grey *Br* OU gray *Am* matter - **2.** [matériau] material ; ~ **plastique** plastic ; ~**s premières** raw materials - **3.** [discipline, sujet] subject ; **en ~ de sport/littérature** as far as sport/literature is concerned - **4.** *loc* : **donner ~ à** to give cause for.

MATIF, Matif [matif] (*abr de* **Marché à terme international de France**) *nm body regulating activities on the French stock exchange.*

Matignon [matiɲɔ̃] *n* : (**l'hôtel**) ~ *building in Paris which houses the offices of the Prime Minister.*

> **MATIGNON**
>
> This term is often used to refer to the Prime Minister and his or her administrative staff : 'Matignon ne semble pas être d'accord'.

matin [matɛ̃] *nm* morning ; **le** ~ in the morning ; **ce** ~ this morning ; **à trois heures du** ~ at 3 o'clock in the morning ; **de bon** OU **de grand** ~ early in the morning ; **du** ~ **au soir** *fig* from dawn to dusk.

matinal, e, aux [matinal, o] *adj* - **1.** [gymnastique, émission] morning *(avant n)* - **2.** [personne] : **être** ~ to be an early riser.

mâtiné, e [matine] *adj* : ~ **de** [chien] crossed with ; *fig* [mélangé de] mixed with.

matinée [matine] *nf* - **1.** [matin] morning ; **faire la grasse** ~ to have a lie in - **2.** [spectacle] matinée, afternoon performance.

matines [matin] *nfpl* matins.

matois, e [matwa, az] *littéraire* ◇ *adj* wily ◇ *nm, f* wily person.

maton, onne [matɔ̃, ɔn] *nm, f fam arg crime* screw.

matou [matu] *nm* tom, tomcat.

matraquage [matrakaʒ] *nm* - **1.** [bastonnade] beating, clubbing - **2.** *fig* [intoxication] bombardment ; ~ **publicitaire** bombardment with adverts.

matraque [matrak] *nf* truncheon.

matraquer [3] [matrake] *vt* - **1.** [frapper] to beat, to club - **2.** *fig* [intoxiquer] to bombard.

matriarcal, e, aux [matrijarkal, o] *adj* matriarchal.

matriarcat [matrijarka] *nm* matriarchy.

matrice [matris] *nf* - **1.** [moule] mould - **2.** MATHS matrix - **3.** ANAT womb.

matricule [matrikyl] ◇ *nm* : (**numéro**) ~ number ◇ *nf* register.

matrimonial, e, aux [matrimɔnjal, o] *adj* matrimonial.

matrone [matrɔn] *nf péj* old bag.

maturation [matyrasjɔ̃] *nf* maturing.

mature [matyr] *adj* mature.

mâture [matyr] *nf* masts *(pl).*

maturité [matyrite] *nf* maturity ; [de fruit] ripeness.

maudire [104] [modir] *vt* to curse.

maudit, e [modi, it] ◇ *pp* ▷ **maudire** ◇ *adj* - **1.** [réprouvé] accursed - **2.** *(avant n)* [exécrable] damned ◇ *nm, f* person who is damned.

maugréer [15] [mogree] ◇ *vt* to mutter ◇ *vi* : ~ (**contre**) to grumble (about).

maure, more [mor] *adj* Moorish.
◆ **Maure, More** *nmf* Moor.

mauresque, moresque [moresk] *adj* Moorish.
◆ **Mauresque, Moresque** *nf* Moorish woman.

Maurice [moris] ▷ **île**.

mauricien, enne [morisjɛ̃, ɛn] *adj* Mauritian.
◆ **Mauricien, enne** *nm, f* Mauritian.

Mauritanie [moritani] *nf* : **la** ~ Mauritania.

mauritanien, enne [moritanjɛ̃, ɛn] *adj* Mauritanian.
◆ **Mauritanien, enne** *nm, f* Mauritanian.

mausolée [mozole] *nm* mausoleum.

maussade [mosad] *adj* - **1.** [personne, air] sullen - **2.** [temps] gloomy.

mauvais, e [move, ɛz] *adj* - **1.** [gén] bad - **2.** [moment, numéro, réponse] wrong - **3.** [mer] rough - **4.** [personne, regard] nasty.
◆ **mauvais** *adv* : **il fait** ~ the weather is bad ; **sentir** ~ to smell bad.

mauve [mov] *nm* & *adj* mauve.

mauviette [movjɛt] *nf fam* - **1.** [physiquement] weakling - **2.** [moralement] coward, wimp.

maux ▷ **mal**.

max [maks] (*abr de* **maximum**) *nm fam* : **un** ~ **de fric** loads of money ; **il en a rajouté un** ~ he went completely overboard.

max. (*abr de* **maximum**) max.

maxillaire [maksilɛr] *nm* jawbone.

maximal, e, aux [maksimal, o] *adj* maximum ; [degré] highest.

maxime [maksim] *nf* maxim.

maximum [maksimɔm] (*pl* **maxima** [maksima]) ◇ *nm* maximum ; **le** ~ **de vitesse/capacité** *etc* maximum speed/capacity *etc* ; **le** ~ **de personnes** the greatest (possible) number of people ; **au** ~ at the most ◇ *adj* maximum.

maya [maja] *adj* Mayan.
◆ **Maya** *nmf* : **les Mayas** the Maya.

mayonnaise [majɔnɛz] *nf* mayonnaise.

Mazarine [mazarin] *n* : **la bibliothèque ~** *public library in Paris.*

LA BIBLIOTHÈQUE MAZARINE

This library opened to the public in 1643, and is the oldest in France. It specializes in French history, especially local history.

mazout [mazut] *nm* fuel oil.

mazouté, e [mazute] *adj* polluted with oil.

MDM *nmpl abr de* **Médecins du monde.**

me [mə], **m'** *(devant voyelle ou h muet) pron pers* **- 1.** [complément d'objet direct] me **- 2.** [complément d'objet indirect] (to) me **- 3.** [réfléchi] myself **- 4.** [avec un présentatif] : **~ voici** here I am.

Me *(abr de* **maître)** *title for barristers,* ≃ QC *Br.*

mea culpa [meakulpa] *nm inv* : **faire son ~** *fig* to admit one's mistake.

méandre [meãdr] *nm* [de rivière] meander, bend.

◆ **méandres** *nmpl* [détours . sinueux] meanderings *(pl).*

mec [mɛk] *nm fam* guy, bloke.

mécanicien, enne [mekanisjɛ̃, ɛn] ◇ *adj* mechanized ◇ *nm, f* **- 1.** [de garage] mechanic **- 2.** [conducteur de train] train driver *Br*, engineer *Am.*

mécanique [mekanik] ◇ *nf* **- 1.** TECHNOL mechanical engineering **- 2.** MATHS & PHYS mechanics *(U)* **- 3.** [mécanisme] mechanism ◇ *adj* mechanical.

mécaniquement [mekanikmã] *adv* mechanically.

mécanisation [mekanizasjɔ̃] *nf* mechanization.

mécaniser [3] [mekanize] *vt* to mechanize.

mécanisme [mekanism] *nm* mechanism.

mécano [mekano] *nm fam* mechanic.

mécénat [mesena] *nm* patronage.

mécène [mesɛn] *nm* patron.

méchamment [meʃamã] *adv* **- 1.** [cruellement] nastily **- 2.** *fam* [beaucoup] really, terribly.

méchanceté [meʃãste] *nf* **- 1.** [attitude] nastiness **- 2.** *fam* [rosserie] nasty thing.

méchant, e [meʃã, ãt] ◇ *adj* **- 1.** [malveillant, cruel] nasty, wicked ; [animal] vicious **- 2.** [désobéissant] naughty ◇ *nm, f* **- 1.** [moralement] wicked person **- 2.** [en langage enfantin] baddy.

mèche [mɛʃ] *nf* **- 1.** [de bougie] wick **- 2.** [de cheveux] lock ; **~ rebelle** cowlick **- 3.** [de bombe] fuse **- 4.** [de perceuse] bit **- 5.** *loc* : **être de ~ avec qqn** to be hand in glove with sb ; **vendre la ~** to give the game away.

méchoui [meʃwi] *nm whole roast sheep.*

méconnaissable [mekɔnɛsabl] *adj* unrecognizable.

méconnaissance [mekɔnɛsãs] *nf* ignorance.

méconnu, e [mekɔny] *adj* unrecognized.

mécontent, e [mekɔ̃tã, ãt] ◇ *adj* unhappy ◇ *nm, f* malcontent.

mécontentement [mekɔ̃tãtmã] *nm* displeasure, annoyance.

mécontenter [3] [mekɔ̃tãte] *vt* to displease.

Mecque [mɛk] *n* : **La ~** Mecca.

mécréant, e [mekreã, ãt] *nm, f* nonbeliever.

méd. *abr de* **médecin.**

médaille [medaj] *nf* **- 1.** [pièce, décoration] medal **- 2.** [bijou] medallion **- 3.** [de chien] identification disc *Br ou* disk *Am*, tag.

médaillé, e [medaje] ◇ *adj* MIL decorated ; SPORT medal-winning *(avant n)* ◇ *nm, f* MIL holder of a medal ; SPORT medal-winner, medallist *Br*, medalist *Am.*

médaillon [medajɔ̃] *nm* **- 1.** [bijou] locket **- 2.** PRESSE : **en ~** inset **- 3.** ART & CULIN medallion.

médecin [medsɛ̃] *nm* doctor ; **~ conventionné** ≃ National Health doctor *Br* ; **~ de famille** family doctor, GP *Br* ; **~ de garde** doctor on duty, duty doctor *Br* ; **~ généraliste** general practitioner, GP *Br* ; **~ légiste** forensic scientist *Br*, medical examiner *Am* ; **votre ~ traitant** your (usual) doctor ; **Médecins du monde, Médecins sans frontières** *organizations providing medical aid to victims of war and disasters, especially in the Third World.*

MÉDECINS SANS FRONTIÈRES

MSF was created in 1971 as an international and non-political private association. It is made up of doctors and volunteer health workers and its mission is to assist war-torn populations and disaster victims.

médecine [medsin] *nf* medicine ; **~ générale** general medicine.

Medef [medɛf] *(abr de* **Mouvement des entreprises de France)** *nm* national council of French employers, ≃ CBI.

média [medja] *nm* : **les ~s** the (mass) media.

médian, e [medjã, an] *adj* median.

◆ **médiane** *nf* median.

médiateur, trice [medjatœr, tris] ◇ *adj* mediating *(avant n)* ◇ *nm, f* mediator ; [dans un conflit de travail] arbitrator.

◆ **médiateur** *nm* ADMIN ombudsman.

◆ **médiatrice** *nf* median.

médiathèque [medjatɛk] *nf* media library.

médiation [medjasjɔ̃] *nf* mediation ; [dans un conflit de travail] arbitration.

médiatique [medjatik] *adj* media *(avant n)*.

médiatisation [medjatizasjɔ̃] *nf* saturation media coverage.

médiatiser [3] [medjatize] *vt péj* to turn into a media event.

médical, e, aux [medikal, o] *adj* medical.

médicalisation [medikalizasjɔ̃] *nf* [d'établissement, de service] provision of medical equipment ; [de population] provision of medical care.

médicament [medikamɑ̃] *nm* medicine, drug.

médicamenteux, euse [medikamɑ̃tø, øz] *adj* medicinal.

médication [medikasjɔ̃] *nf* (course of) treatment.

médicinal, e, aux [medisinal, o] *adj* medicinal.

Médicis [medisis] *n* : **le prix ~** French literary prize.

médico-légal, e, aux [medikɔlegal, o] *adj* forensic.

médico-social, e, aux [medikɔsɔsjal, o] *adj* public health *(avant n)*.

médiéval, e, aux [medjeval, o] *adj* medieval.

médiocre [medjɔkr] ◇ *nmf* mediocre person ◇ *adj* mediocre.

médiocrité [medjɔkrite] *nf* mediocrity.

médire [103] [medir] *vi* to gossip ; **~ de qqn** to speak ill of sb.

médisance [medizɑ̃s] *nf* - **1.** [calomnie] slander - **2.** [ragot] piece of gossip.

médisant, e [medizɑ̃, ɑ̃t] ◇ *adj* slanderous ◇ *nm, f* slanderer, scandalmonger.

médit [medi] *pp inv* ▷ **médire**.

méditatif, ive [meditatif, iv] ◇ *adj* thoughtful, reflective ◇ *nm, f* thoughtful person.

méditation [meditasjɔ̃] *nf* meditation.

méditer [3] [medite] ◇ *vt* - **1.** [projeter] to plan ; **~ de faire qqch** to plan to do sthg - **2.** [approfondir] to meditate on ◇ *vi* : **~ (sur)** to meditate (on).

Méditerranée [mediterane] *nf* : **la ~** the Mediterranean (Sea).

méditerranéen, enne [mediteraneɛ̃, ɛn] *adj* Mediterranean.

➧ **Méditerranéen, enne** *nm, f* person from the Mediterranean.

médium [medjɔm] *nm* - **1.** [personne] medium - **2.** MUS middle register.

médius [medjys] *nm* middle finger.

méduse [medyz] *nf* jellyfish.

méduser [3] [medyze] *vt* to dumbfound.

meeting [mitiŋ] *nm* meeting ; **~ aérien** air show.

méfait [mefɛ] *nm* misdemeanour *Br*, misdemeanor *Am*, misdeed.

➧ **méfaits** *nmpl* [du temps] ravages.

méfiance [mefjɑ̃s] *nf* suspicion, distrust.

méfiant, e [mefjɑ̃, ɑ̃t] *adj* suspicious, distrustful.

méfier [9] [mefje] ➧ **se méfier** *vp* to be wary *ou* careful ; **se ~ de qqn/qqch** to distrust sb/sthg.

méga [mega] *adj fam* mega.

mégalo [megalo] *nmf* & *adj fam* megalomaniac ; **il est complètement ~** he thinks he's God.

mégalomane [megaloman] *nmf* & *adj* megalomaniac.

mégalomanie [megalomani] *nf* megalomania.

méga-octet [megaɔktɛ] *nm* megabyte.

mégaphone [megafɔn] *nm* megaphone, bullhorn *Am*.

mégapole [megapɔl] *nf* megalopolis, megacity.

mégarde [megard] ➧ **par mégarde** *loc adv* by mistake.

mégère [meʒɛr] *nf péj* shrew.

mégot [mego] *nm fam* fag-end *Br*, butt *Am*.

mégoter [3] [megɔte] *vi fam* : **~ sur qqch** to skimp on sthg.

meilleur, e [mɛjœr] ◇ *adj (compar)* better ; *(superl)* best ◇ *nm, f* best ; **c'est la ~e!** that takes the cake *ou* biscuit!

➧ **meilleur** ◇ *nm* : **le ~** the best ◇ *adv* better.

méjuger [17] [meʒyʒe] ◇ *vt* to misjudge ◇ *vi* : **~ de qqn/qqch** to underestimate sb/sthg.

➧ **se méjuger** *vp littéraire* to underestimate o.s.

mélancolie [melɑ̃kɔli] *nf* melancholy.

mélancolique [melɑ̃kɔlik] *adj* melancholy.

Mélanésie [melanezi] *nf* : **la ~** Melanesia.

mélanésien, enne [melanezjɛ̃, ɛn] *adj* Melanesian.

➧ **Mélanésien, enne** *nm, f* Melanesian.

mélange [melɑ̃ʒ] *nm* - **1.** [action] mixing ; **sans ~ fig** unadulterated - **2.** [mixture] mixture.

mélanger [17] [melɑ̃ʒe] *vt* - **1.** [mettre ensemble]

to mix - **2.** [déranger] to mix up, to muddle up.

 se mélanger *vp* - **1.** [se mêler] to mix - **2.** [se brouiller] to get mixed up.

mélangeur [melɑ̃ʒœr] *nm* - **1.** CIN mixer - **2.** : (robinet) ~ mixer tap *Br*, mixing tap *Am*.

mélasse [melas] *nf* - **1.** [liquide] treacle *Br*, molasses *(U) Am* - **2.** *fam* [mélange] mess ; **être dans la** ~ *fig* to be in a fix.

mêlée [mele] *nf* - **1.** [combat] fray - **2.** RUGBY scrum ; ~ **ouverte** ruck.

mêler [4] [mele] *vt* - **1.** [mélanger] to mix - **2.** [déranger] to muddle up, to mix up - **3.** [impliquer] : ~ **qqn à qqch** to involve sb in sthg - **4.** [joindre] : ~ **qqch à qqch** to mix *ou* combine sthg with sthg.

 se mêler *vp* - **1.** [se joindre] : **se** ~ **à** [groupe] to join - **2.** [s'ingérer] : **se** ~ **de qqch** to get mixed up in sthg ; **mêlez-vous de ce qui vous regarde!** mind your own business!

mélèze [melɛz] *nm* larch.

méli-mélo [melimelo] *(pl* **mélis-mélos)** *nm* muddle ; [d'objets] jumble.

mélo [melo] *nm fam* melodrama.

mélodie [melɔdi] *nf* melody.

mélodieux, euse [melɔdjø, øz] *adj* melodious, tuneful.

mélodique [melɔdik] *adj* melodic.

mélodramatique [melɔdramatik] *adj* melodramatic.

mélodrame [melɔdram] *nm* melodrama.

mélomane [melɔman] <> *nmf* music lover <> *adj* music-loving.

melon [məlɔ̃] *nm* - **1.** [fruit] melon - **2.** [chapeau] bowler (hat).

melting-pot [mɛltiŋpɔt] *nm* melting pot.

membrane [mɑ̃bran] *nf* membrane.

membre [mɑ̃br] <> *nm* - **1.** [du corps] limb ; **~s supérieurs/inférieurs** upper/lower limbs ; **~s antérieurs/postérieurs** front/back legs ; ~ **(viril)** male member - **2.** [personne, pays, partie] member ; ~ **fondateur** founder member <> *adj* member *(avant n)*.

mémé = **mémère.**

même [mɛm] <> *adj indéf* - **1.** [indique une identité ou une ressemblance] same ; **il a le** ~ **âge que moi** he's the same age as me - **2.** [sert à souligner] : **ce sont ses paroles ~s** those are his very words ; **elle est la bonté** ~ she's kindness itself <> *pron indéf* : **le/la** ~ the same one ; **ce sont toujours les ~s qui gagnent** it's always the same people who win ; **elle est toujours la** ~ she's always the same <> *adv* even ; **il n'est** ~ **pas diplômé** he isn't even

qualified ; **elle ne va** ~ **plus au cinéma** she doesn't even go to the cinema any more.

 de même *loc adv* similarly, likewise ; **il en va de** ~ **pour lui** the same goes for him.

 de même que *loc conj* just as.

 tout de même *loc adv* all the same.

 à même *loc prép* : **il boit à** ~ **la bouteille** he drinks (straight) from the bottle ; **s'asseoir à** ~ **le sol** to sit on the bare ground.

 à même de *loc prép* : **être à** ~ **de faire qqch** to be able to do sthg, to be in a position to do sthg.

 même si *loc conj* even if.

mémento [memɛ̃to] *nm* - **1.** [agenda] pocket diary - **2.** [ouvrage] notes *(title of school textbook)*.

mémère [memɛr], **mémé** [meme] *nf fam* - **1.** [grand-mère] granny - **2.** *péj* [vieille femme] old biddy.

mémoire [memwar] <> *nf* [gén & INFORM] memory ; **de** ~ from memory ; **avoir bonne/mauvaise** ~ to have a good/bad memory ; **avoir de la** ~ to have a good memory ; **avoir la** ~ **des chiffres/noms** to have a good memory for figures/names ; **perdre la** ~ to lose one's memory ; **se rafraîchir la** ~ to refresh one's memory ; **mettre en** ~ INFORM to store ; ~ **tampon** INFORM buffer ; ~ **virtuelle** INFORM virtual memory ; ~ **vive** INFORM random access memory ; **à la** ~ **de** in memory of ; **de** ~ **d'homme** in living memory ; **pour** ~ for the record <> *nm* - **1.** ADMIN memorandum, report - **2.** UNIV dissertation, paper.

 mémoires *nmpl* memoirs.

mémorable [memɔrabl] *adj* memorable.

mémorandum [memɔrɑ̃dɔm] *nm* - **1.** [note diplomatique] memorandum - **2.** [carnet] notebook.

mémorial, aux [memɔrjal, o] *nm* [monument] memorial.

mémorisable [memɔrizabl] *adj* INFORM storable.

mémoriser [3] [memɔrize] *vt* - **1.** [suj : personne] to memorize - **2.** INFORM to store.

menaçant, e [mənasɑ̃, ɑ̃t] *adj* threatening.

menace [mənas] *nf* : ~ **(pour)** threat (to).

menacer [16] [mənase] <> *vt* to threaten ; ~ **de faire qqch** to threaten to do sthg ; ~ **qqn de qqch** to threaten sb with sthg <> *vi* : **la pluie menace** it looks like rain.

ménage [menaʒ] *nm* - **1.** [nettoyage] housework *(U)* ; **faire le** ~ to do the housework ; **faire des ~s** to work as a cleaner - **2.** [couple] couple ; **se mettre en** ~ to set up house together ; ~ **à trois** ménage à trois - **3.** ÉCON household - **4.** *loc* : **faire bon ~ (avec)** to get on well (with).

ménagement [menaʒmɑ̃] *nm* [égards] consideration ; **sans ~** brutally.

ménager¹, ère [menaʒe, ɛr] *adj* household *(avant n)*, domestic.

◆ ménagère *nf* - **1.** [femme] housewife - **2.** [de couverts] canteen.

ménager² [17] [menaʒe] *vt* - **1.** [bien traiter] to treat gently - **2.** [économiser - réserves] to use sparingly ; [- argent, temps] to use carefully ; **~ ses forces** to conserve one's strength ; **~ sa santé** to take care of one's health - **3.** [préparer - surprise] to prepare.

◆ se ménager *vp* to take care of o.s., to look after o.s.

ménagerie [menaʒri] *nf* menagerie.

mendiant, e [mɑ̃djɑ̃, ɑ̃t] *nm, f* beggar.

mendicité [mɑ̃disite] *nf* begging.

mendier [9] [mɑ̃dje] *◇ vt* - **1.** [argent] to beg for - **2.** [éloges] to seek *◇ vi* to beg.

menées [məne] *nfpl* scheming *(U)*.

mener [19] [məne] *◇ vt* - **1.** [emmener] to take - **2.** [diriger - débat, enquête] to conduct ; [- affaires] to manage, to run ; **~ qqch à bonne fin** *ou* **à bien** to see sthg through, to bring sthg to a successful conclusion - **3.** [être en tête de] to lead *◇ vi* to lead.

meneur, euse [mənœr, øz] *nm, f* [chef] ringleader ; **~ d'hommes** born leader ; **~ de jeu** host.

menhir [menir] *nm* standing stone.

méninge [menɛ̃ʒ] *nf* meninx.

◆ méninges *nfp fam* brains.

méningite [menɛ̃ʒit] *nf* meningitis *(U)*.

ménisque [menisk] *nm* meniscus.

ménopause [menɔpoz] *nf* menopause.

menotte [mənɔt] *nf* [main] little hand.

◆ menottes *nfpl* handcuffs ; **passer les ~s à qqn** to handcuff sb.

mens ▷ mentir.

mensonge [mɑ̃sɔ̃ʒ] *nm* - **1.** [propos] lie ; **un pieux ~** a white lie - **2.** [acte] lying.

mensonger, ère [mɑ̃sɔ̃ʒe, ɛr] *adj* false.

menstruation [mɑ̃stryasjɔ̃] *nf* menstruation.

menstruel, elle [mɑ̃stryɛl] *adj* menstrual.

mensualiser [3] [mɑ̃sɥalize] *vt* to pay monthly.

mensualité [mɑ̃sɥalite] *nf* - **1.** [traite] monthly instalment **Br** *ou* installment **Am** - **2.** [salaire] (monthly) salary.

mensuel, elle [mɑ̃sɥɛl] *◇ adj* monthly *◇ nm, f* salaried employee.

◆ mensuel *nm* monthly (magazine).

mensuellement [mɑ̃sɥɛlmɑ̃] *adv* monthly, every month.

mensuration [mɑ̃syrasjɔ̃] *nf* measuring.

◆ mensurations *nfpl* measurements.

ment ▷ mentir.

mental, e, aux [mɑ̃tal, o] *adj* mental.

mentalement [mɑ̃talmɑ̃] *adv* mentally.

mentalité [mɑ̃talite] *nf* mentality.

menteur, euse [mɑ̃tœr, øz] *◇ adj* false *◇ nm, f* liar.

menthe [mɑ̃t] *nf* mint ; **~ à l'eau** peppermint cordial.

mentholé, e [mɑ̃tɔle] *adj* mentholated, menthol *(avant n)*.

menti [mɑ̃ti] *pp inv* ▷ mentir.

mention [mɑ̃sjɔ̃] *nf* - **1.** [citation] mention ; **faire ~ de qqch** to mention sthg - **2.** [note] note ; **'rayer la ~ inutile'** 'delete as appropriate' - **3.** UNIV : **avec ~** with distinction ; **avec la ~ très bien/bien/passable** ≃ with First/Second/Third Class Honours.

mentionner [3] [mɑ̃sjɔne] *vt* to mention.

mentir [37] [mɑ̃tir] *vi* : **~ (à)** to lie (to) ; **sans ~** honestly.

menton [mɑ̃tɔ̃] *nm* chin ; **~ en galoche** prominent chin ; **double ~** double chin.

menu, e [məny] *adj* [très petit] tiny ; [mince] thin.

◆ menu *◇ adv* : **hacher ~** to chop finely *◇ nm* [gén & INFORM] menu ; [repas à prix fixe] set menu ; **~ déroulant** INFORM pull-down menu ; **~ gastronomique/touristique** gourmet/tourist menu.

menuiserie [mənɥizri] *nf* - **1.** [métier] joinery, carpentry - **2.** [atelier] joinery (workshop) - **3.** [ouvrages] joinery *(U)*, carpentry *(U)*.

menuisier [mənɥizje] *nm* joiner, carpenter.

méprenais, méprenions *etc* ▷ méprendre.

méprendre [79] [meprɑ̃dr] **◆ se méprendre** *vp littéraire* : **se ~ sur** to be mistaken about ; **se ressembler à s'y ~** to be as like as two peas in a pod.

mépris, e [mepri, iz] *pp* ▷ méprendre.

◆ mépris *nm* - **1.** [dédain] : **~ (pour)** contempt (for), scorn (for) - **2.** [indifférence] : **~ de** disregard for.

◆ au mépris de *loc prép* regardless of.

méprisable [meprizabl] *adj* contemptible, despicable.

méprisant, e [meprizɑ̃, ɑ̃t] *adj* contemptuous, scornful.

méprise [mepriz] *nf* mistake, error.

mépriser [3] [meprize] *vt* to despise ; [danger, offre] to scorn.

mer [mɛr] *nf* sea ; **en ~** at sea ; **prendre la ~** to put to sea ; **haute** OU **pleine ~** open sea ; **ce n'est pas la ~ à boire** it's no big deal ; **la ~ Adriatique** the Adriatic ; **la ~ Baltique** the Baltic Sea ; **la ~ d'Irlande** the Irish Sea ; **la ~ Morte** the Dead Sea ; **la ~ Noire** the Black Sea ; **la ~ du Nord** the North Sea.

mercantile [mɛrkɑ̃til] *adj péj* mercenary.

mercenaire [mɛrsənɛr] *nm* & *adj* mercenary.

mercerie [mɛrsəri] *nf* - **1.** [articles] haberdashery *Br*, notions *(pl)* *Am* - **2.** [boutique] haberdasher's shop *Br*, notions store *Am*.

merci [mɛrsi] ◇ *interj* thank you!, thanks! ; **~ beaucoup!** thank you very much! ◇ *nm* : **~ (de** OU **pour)** thank you (for) ; **dire ~ à qqn** to thank sb, to say thank you to sb ◇ *nf* mercy ; **sans ~** merciless ; **être à la ~ de** to be at the mercy of.

mercier, ère [mɛrsje, ɛr] *nm, f* haberdasher *Br*, notions dealer *Am*.

mercredi [mɛrkrədi] *nm* Wednesday ; **~ des Cendres** Ash Wednesday ; *voir aussi* **samedi**.

mercure [mɛrkyr] *nm* mercury.

merde [mɛrd] *tfam* ◇ *nf* shit ◇ *interj* shit!

merdier [mɛrdje] *nm* *tfam* : **on est dans un ~** we're in the shit.

mère [mɛr] *nf* mother ; **~ célibataire** single OU unmarried mother ; **~ de famille** mother ; **~ indigne** unfit mother ; **~ poule** mother hen ; **~ supérieure** mother superior.

merguez [mɛrgɛz] *nf inv* North African spiced sausage.

méridien, enne [meridjɛ̃, ɛn] *adj* [ligne] meridian.

➥ **méridien** *nm* meridian.

méridional, e, aux [meridjɔnal, o] *adj* southern ; [du sud de la France] Southern (French).

➥ **Méridional, e aux** *nm, f* person from the Mediterranean ; [du sud de la France] person from the South (of France).

meringue [mərɛ̃g] *nf* meringue.

mérinos [merinos] *nm* merino.

merisier [mərizje] *nm* - **1.** [arbre] wild cherry (tree) - **2.** [bois] cherry.

méritant, e [meritɑ̃, ɑ̃t] *adj* deserving.

mérite [merit] *nm* merit ; **il a du ~ à y prendre part** it is to his credit that he is taking part.

mériter [3] [merite] *vt* - **1.** [être digne de, encourir] to deserve - **2.** [valoir] to be worth, to merit.

méritoire [meritwar] *adj* commendable.

merlan [mɛrlɑ̃] *nm* whiting.

merle [mɛrl] *nm* blackbird.

merveille [mɛrvɛj] *nf* marvel, wonder ; **à ~** marvellously *Br*, marvelously *Am*, wonder-

fully ; **la huitième ~ du monde** *hum* the eighth wonder of the world.

merveilleusement [mɛrvɛjøzmɑ̃] *adv* marvellously *Br*, marvelously *Am*, wonderfully.

merveilleux, euse [mɛrvɛjø, øz] *adj* - **1.** [remarquable, prodigieux] marvellous *Br*, marvelous *Am*, wonderful - **2.** [magique] magic, magical.

➥ **merveilleux** *nm* : **le ~** the supernatural.

mes ➥ **mon**.

mésalliance [mezaljɑ̃s] *nf* unsuitable marriage, misalliance.

mésange [mezɑ̃ʒ] *nf* ZOOL tit ; **~ bleue/charbonnière** blue/coal tit.

mésaventure [mezavɑ̃tyr] *nf* misfortune.

mesdames ➥ **madame**.

mesdemoiselles ➥ **mademoiselle**.

mésentente [mezɑ̃tɑ̃t] *nf* disagreement.

mésestimer [3] [mezɛstime] *vt* *littéraire* to underestimate.

mesquin, e [mɛskɛ̃, in] *adj* mean, petty.

mesquinerie [mɛskinri] *nf* - **1.** [étroitesse d'esprit] meanness, pettiness - **2.** [action mesquine] petty act.

mess [mɛs] *nm* mess.

message [mesaʒ] *nm* message ; **laisser un ~ à qqn** to leave a message for sb ; **~ publicitaire** commercial, spot.

messager, ère [mesaʒe, ɛr] *nm, f* messenger.

messagerie [mesaʒri] *nf* - **1.** (gén pl) [transport de marchandises] freight (U) ; **les ~s aériennes** air freight company (sg) - **2.** INFORM : **~ électronique** electronic mail ; **~ rose** computerized dating service ; **~ vocale électronique** INFORM voice messaging.

messe [mɛs] *nf* mass ; **aller à la ~** to go to mass ; **~ de minuit** midnight mass ; **faire des ~s basses** *fam* to mutter.

messie [mesi] *nm* Messiah ; *fig* saviour *Br*, savior *Am*.

messieurs ➥ **monsieur**.

mesure [məzyr] *nf* - **1.** [disposition, acte] measure, step ; **prendre des ~s** to take measures OU steps ; **~s d'austérité** austerity measures ; **~s de rétorsion** retaliatory measures - **2.** [évaluation, dimension] measurement ; **prendre les ~s de qqn/qqch** to measure sb/sthg - **3.** [étalon, récipient] measure - **4.** MUS time, tempo ; **battre la ~** to beat time - **5.** [modération] moderation - **6.** *loc* : **dans la ~ du possible** as far as possible ; **être en ~ de** to be in a position to ; **c'est sans commune ~** there's no possible comparison.

➥ **à la mesure de** *loc prép* worthy of.

➠ **à mesure que** *loc conj* as.

➠ **outre mesure** *loc adv* excessively.

➠ **sur mesure** *loc adj* custom-made ; [costume] made-to-measure.

mesuré, e [məzyre] *adj* [modéré] measured.

mesurer [3] [məzyre] *vt* - **1.** [gén] to measure ; **elle mesure 1,50 m** she's 5 feet tall ; **la table mesure 1,50 m** the table is 5 feet long - **2.** [risques, portée, ampleur] to weigh up ; ~ **ses paroles** to weigh one's words - **3.** [limiter] to limit - **4.** [proportionner] : ~ **qqch à qqch** to match sthg to sthg.

➠ **se mesurer** *vp* : **se** ~ **avec** *ou* **à qqn** to pit o.s. against sb.

métabolisme [metabɔlism] *nm* metabolism.

métairie [meteri] *nf* sharecropping farm.

métal, aux [metal, o] *nm* metal.

métallique [metalik] *adj* - **1.** [en métal] metal *(avant n)* - **2.** [éclat, son] metallic.

métallo [metalo] *nm fam* metalworker.

métallurgie [metalyrʒi] *nf* - **1.** [industrie] metallurgical industry - **2.** [technique] metallurgy.

métallurgique [metalyrʒik] *adj* metallurgical.

métallurgiste [metalyrʒist] *nm* - **1.** [ouvrier] metalworker - **2.** [industriel] metallurgist.

métamorphose [metamɔrfoz] *nf* metamorphosis.

métamorphoser [3] [metamɔrfoze] *vt* : ~ **qqn/qqch (en)** to transform sb/sthg (into).

➠ **se métamorphoser** *vp* BIOL to metamorphose ; *fig* : **se** ~ **(en)** to be transformed (into).

métaphore [metafɔr] *nf* metaphor.

métaphorique [metafɔrik] *adj* metaphorical.

métaphysique [metafizik] <> *nf* metaphysics *(U)* <> *adj* metaphysical.

métayer, ère [meteje, metɛjɛr] *nm, f* tenant farmer.

météo [meteo] *nf* - **1.** [bulletin] weather forecast - **2.** [service] ≃ Met Office *Br,* ≃ National Weather Service *Am.*

météore [meteɔr] *nm* meteor.

météorite [meteɔrit] *nm* OU *nf* meteorite.

météorologie [meteɔrɔlɔʒi] *nf* - **1.** SCIENCE meteorology - **2.** [service] ≃ Meteorological Office *Br,* ≃ National Weather Service *Am.*

météorologique [meteɔrɔlɔʒik] *adj* meteorological, weather *(avant n)*.

métèque [metɛk] *nm vulg* racist term used with reference to people from Mediterranean countries.

méthane [metan] *nm* methane.

méthode [metɔd] *nf* - **1.** [gén] method - **2.** [ouvrage - gén] manual ; [- de lecture, de langue] primer.

méthodique [metɔdik] *adj* methodical.

méthodiquement [metɔdikmɑ̃] *adv* methodically.

méthodiste [metɔdist] *nmf* & *adj* Methodist.

méthodologie [metɔdɔlɔʒi] *nf* methodology.

méthylène [metilɛn] *nm* - **1.** [alcool] methanol - **2.** CHIM methylene.

méticuleusement [metikyløzmɑ̃] *adv* meticulously.

méticuleux, euse [metikylø, øz] *adj* meticulous.

métier [metje] *nm* - **1.** [profession - manuelle] occupation, trade ; [- intellectuelle] occupation, profession ; **de son** ~ by trade ; **il est du** ~ he's in the same trade *ou* same line of work ; **avoir du** ~ to have experience - **2.** [machine] : ~ **(à tisser)** loom.

métis, isse [metis] <> *adj* - **1.** [personne] half-caste, half-breed - **2.** [tissu] cotton and linen <> *nm, f* half-caste, half-breed.

➠ **métis** *nm* [tissu] cotton-linen mix.

métissage [metisaʒ] *nm* [de personnes] interbreeding.

métisser [3] [metise] *vt* to cross, to crossbreed.

métrage [metraʒ] *nm* - **1.** [mesure] measurement, measuring - **2.** [COUTURE - coupon] length - **3.** CIN footage ; **long** ~ feature film ; **court** ~ short (film).

mètre [mɛtr] *nm* - **1.** LITTÉRATURE & MATHS metre *Br,* meter *Am* ; ~ **carré** square metre *Br ou* meter *Am* ; ~ **cube** cubic metre *Br ou* meter *Am* - **2.** [instrument] rule.

métrer [18] [metre] *vt* [terrain] to survey ; [tissu] to measure out.

métreur, euse [metrœr, øz] *nm, f* surveyor.

métrique [metrik] <> *nf* LITTÉRATURE metrics *(U)* <> *adj* - **1.** MATHS metric - **2.** LITTÉRATURE metrical.

métro [metro] *nm* underground *Br,* subway *Am.*

métronome [metrɔnɔm] *nm* metronome.

métropole [metrɔpɔl] *nf* - **1.** [ville] metropolis - **2.** [pays] home country.

métropolitain, e [metrɔpɔlitɛ̃, ɛn] *adj* metropolitan ; **la France** ~**e** metropolitan *ou* mainland France.

mets [mɛ] <> ▷ **mettre** <> *nm* CULIN dish.

mettable [mɛtabl] *adj* wearable.

mette ⊳ **mettre.**

metteur [metœr] *nm* : ~ **en ondes** RADIO producer ; ~ **en scène** THÉÂTRE producer ; CIN director.

mettre [84] [metr] *vt* - **1.** [placer] to put ; ~ **de l'eau à bouillir** to put some water on to boil - **2.** [revêtir] to put on ; **mets ta robe noire** put your black dress on ; **je ne mets plus ma robe noire** I don't wear my black dress any more - **3.** [consacrer - temps] to take ; [- argent] to spend ; ~ **longtemps à faire qqch** to take a long time to do sthg - **4.** [allumer - radio, chauffage] to put on, to switch on - **5.** [installer] to put in ; **faire** ~ **l'électricité** to have electricity put in ; **faire** ~ **de la moquette** to have a carpet put down *ou* fitted - **6.** [inscrire] to put (down) - **7.** *loc* : ~ **bas** [animal] to drop, to give birth ; **y** ~ **du sien** to do one's bit.
➤ **se mettre** *vp* - **1.** [se placer] : **où est-ce que ça se met?** where does this go? ; **se** ~ **au lit** to get into bed ; **se** ~ **à côté de qqn** to sit/stand near to sb - **2.** [devenir] : **se** ~ **en colère** to get angry - **3.** [commencer] : **se** ~ **à qqch/à faire qqch** to start sthg/doing sthg - **4.** [revêtir] to put on ; **je n'ai rien à me** ~ I haven't got a thing to wear - **5.** *fam* [se donner des coups] : **qu'est-ce qu'ils se sont mis!** they really set about each other!

meuble [mœbl] ⬦ *nm* piece of furniture ; **~s** furniture *(U)* ; **~s de bureau/jardin** office/garden furniture *(U)* ; **sauver les ~s** *fig* not to lose everything ⬦ *adj* - **1.** [terre, sol] easily worked - **2.** JUR movable.

meublé, e [mœble] *adj* furnished.
➤ **meublé** *nm* furnished room/flat *Br*, furnished apartment *Am*.

meubler [5] [mœble] ⬦ *vt* - **1.** [pièce, maison] to furnish - **2.** *fig* [occuper] : ~ **qqch (de)** to fill sthg (with) ⬦ *vi* to be decorative.
➤ **se meubler** *vp* to furnish one's home.

meuf [mœf] *nf fam* woman.

meugler [5] [mœgle] *vi* to moo.

meule [møl] *nf* - **1.** [à moudre] millstone - **2.** [à aiguiser] grindstone - **3.** [de fromage] round - **4.** AGRIC stack ; ~ **de foin** haystack.

meunier, ère [mønje, ɛr] ⬦ *adj* - **1.** [industrie] milling *(avant n)* - **2.** CULIN coated in flour and fried ⬦ *nm, f* miller *(f* miller's wife).

meurs, meurt *etc* ⊳ **mourir.**

meurtre [mœrtr] *nm* murder.

meurtrier, ère [mœrtrije, ɛr] ⬦ *adj* [épidémie, arme] deadly ; [fureur] murderous ; [combat] bloody ⬦ *nm, f* murderer.
➤ **meurtrière** *nf* ARCHIT loophole.

meurtrir [32] [mœrtrir] *vt* - **1.** [contusionner] to bruise - **2.** *fig* [blesser] to wound.

meurtrissure [mœrtrisyr] *nf* - **1.** [marque] bruise - **2.** *fig* [blessure] wound.

meute [møt] *nf* pack.

mévente [mevãt] *nf* poor sales *(pl)*.

mexicain, e [mɛksikɛ̃, ɛn] *adj* Mexican.
➤ **Mexicain, e** *nm, f* Mexican.

Mexico [mɛksiko] *n* Mexico City.

Mexique [mɛksik] *nm* : **le** ~ Mexico ; **au** ~ in Mexico.

mezzanine [mɛdzanin] *nf* mezzanine.

mezzo-soprano [mɛdzosoprano] *(pl* **mezzo-sopranos)** *nm* mezzo-soprano.

MF ⬦ *nf (abr de* **modulation de fréquence)** FM ⬦ - **1.** *(abr de* **mark finlandais)** Mk, Fmk - **2.** *abr de* **million de francs.**

Mgr *(abr de* **Monseigneur)** Mgr.

mi [mi] *nm inv* E ; [chanté] mi.

mi- [mi] ⬦ *adj inv* half ; **à la ~juin** in mid-June ⬦ *adv* half-.

miaou [mjau] *nm* miaow *Br*, meow *Am*.

miasme [mjasm] *nm (gén pl)* putrid *ou* foul smell.

miaulement [mjolmã] *nm* miaowing *Br*, meowing *Am*.

miauler [3] [mjole] *vi* to miaow *Br*, to meow *Am*.

mi-bas [miba] *nm inv* knee-sock.

mica [mika] *nm* mica.

mi-carême [mikarɛm] *nf* feast day on third Thursday in Lent.

miche [miʃ] *nf* [de pain] large round loaf.
➤ **miches** *nfpl fam* - **1.** [fesses] bum *(sg) Br*, butt *(sg) Am* - **2.** [seins] boobs.

mi-chemin [miʃmɛ̃] ➤ **à mi-chemin** *loc adv* halfway (there).

mi-clos, e [miklo, oz] *adj* half-closed.

micmac [mikmak] *nm fam* - **1.** [manigance] game, scheme - **2.** [embrouillamini] muddle, chaos.

mi-côte [mikot] ➤ **à mi-côte** *loc adv* halfway up/down the hill.

micro [mikro] ⬦ *nm* - **1.** [microphone] mike - **2.** [micro-ordinateur] micro ⬦ *nf* microcomputing.

microbe [mikrob] *nm* - **1.** MÉD microbe, germ - **2.** *péj* [avorton] (little) runt.

microbien, enne [mikrobjɛ̃, ɛn] *adj* bacterial.

microbiologie [mikrobjɔlɔʒi] *nf* microbiology.

microchirurgie [mikroʃiryrʒi] *nf* microsurgery.

microclimat [mikroklima] *nm* microclimate.

microcosme [mikrɔkɔsm] *nm* microcosm.

micro-édition [mikrɔedisjɔ̃] *nf* desktop publishing.

micro-électronique [mikrɔelεktrɔnik] ⟨> *nf* microelectronics *(U)* ⟨> *adj* microelectronic.

microfiche [mikrɔfiʃ] *nf* microfiche.

microfilm [mikrɔfilm] *nm* microfilm.

micron [mikrɔ̃] *nm* micron.

Micronésie [mikronezi] *nf* : **la ~** Micronesia ; **les États fédérés de ~** Federated States of Micronesia.

micro-ondes [mikrɔ̃d] *nfpl* microwaves ; **four à ~** microwave (oven).

micro-ordinateur [mikrɔɔrdinatœr] *(pl* **micro-ordinateurs)** *nm* micro, microcomputer.

micro-organisme [mikrɔɔrganism] *(pl* **micro-organismes)** *nm* micro-organism.

microphone [mikrɔfɔn] *nm* microphone.

microprocesseur [mikrɔprɔsesœr] *nm* microprocessor.

microprogramme [mikrɔprɔgram] *nm* IN-FORM firmware.

microscope [mikrɔskɔp] *nm* microscope ; **~ électronique** electron microscope.

microscopique [mikrɔskɔpik] *adj* microscopic.

microsillon [mikrɔsijɔ̃] *nm* LP, long-playing record.

MIDEM, Midem [midεm] *(abr de* Marché international du disque et de l'édition musicale) *nm* music industry trade fair.

midi [midi] *nm* - **1.** [période du déjeuner] lunchtime - **2.** [heure] midday, noon ; **chercher ~ à quatorze heures** to look for complications - **3.** [sud] south.
◆ **Midi** *nm* : **le Midi** the South of France.

midinette [midinεt] *nf péj* empty-headed girl.

mie [mi] *nf* - **1.** [de pain] soft part, inside - **2.** *vieilli* [bien-aimée] : **ma ~** sweetheart.

miel [mjεl] *nm* honey.

mielleux, euse [mjεlø, øz] *adj* [personne] unctuous ; [paroles, air] honeyed.

mien [mjε̃] ◆ **le mien** [*f* **la mienne** [lamjεn], *mpl* **les miens** [lemjε̃], *fpl* **les miennes** [lemjεn]) *pron poss* mine ; **les ~s** my family ; **j'y mets du ~** I put in a lot of effort.

miette [mjεt] *nf* - **1.** [de pain] crumb, breadcrumb - **2.** *(gén pl)* [débris] shreds *(pl)* ; **en ~s** in bits *ou* pieces.

mieux [mjø] ⟨> *adv* - **1.** [comparatif] : **~ (que)** better (than) ; **il travaille ~** he's working

better ; **il pourrait ~ faire** he could do better ; **il va ~** he's better ; **faire ~ de faire qqch** to do better to do sthg ; **vous feriez ~ de vous taire** you would do better to keep quiet, you would be well-advised to keep quiet ; **~ je le comprends, plus/moins j'ai envie de le lire** the better I understand it, the more/less I want to read it - **2.** [superlatif] best ; **il est le ~ payé du service** he's the best *ou* highest paid member of the department ; **le ~ qu'il peut** as best he can ⟨> *adj* better ⟨> *nm* - **1.** *(sans déterminant)* : **j'espérais ~** I was hoping for something better ; **faute de ~** for lack of anything better - **2.** *(avec déterminant)* best ; **il y a un *ou* du ~** there's been an improvement ; **faire de son ~** to do one's best.
◆ **au mieux** *loc adv* at best.
◆ **des mieux** *loc adv* : **un appareil des ~** conçus one of the best-designed devices.
◆ **pour le mieux** *loc adv* for the best.
◆ **on ne peut mieux** *loc adv* : **c'est on ne peut ~** it couldn't be better.
◆ **de mieux en mieux** *loc adv* better and better.
◆ **à qui mieux mieux** *loc adv* : **on criait à qui ~ ~** it was a case of who could shout (the) loudest.

mieux-être [mjøzetr] *nm inv* improvement.

mièvre [mjεvr] *adj* insipid.

mièvrerie [mjεvrəri] *nf* insipidness.

mignon, onne [miɲɔ̃, ɔn] ⟨> *adj* - **1.** [charmant] sweet, cute - **2.** [gentil] nice ⟨> *nm, f* darling, sweetheart.
◆ **mignon** *nm vieilli* favourite *Br*, favorite *Am*.

migraine [migrεn] *nf* headache ; MÉD migraine.

migrant, e [migrɑ̃, ɑ̃t] ⟨> *adj* migrant *(avant n)* ⟨> *nm, f* migrant.

migrateur, trice [migratœr, tris] *adj* migratory.
◆ **migrateur** *nm* migratory bird.

migration [migrasjɔ̃] *nf* migration.

mijaurée [miʒɔre] *nf* affected woman ; **faire la ~** to put on airs.

mijoter [3] [miʒɔte] ⟨> *vt* - **1.** CULIN to simmer - **2.** *fam* [tramer] to cook up ⟨> *vi* CULIN to simmer.

mi-journée [miʒurne] *nf* : **les informations de la ~** the lunchtime news.

mil¹ [mij] *nm* millet.

mil² *adj* = mille.

milan [milɑ̃] *nm* kite *(bird)*.

mildiou [mildju] *nm* mildew.

milice [milis] *nf* militia.

milicien, enne [milisjɛ̃, ɛn] *nm, f* militiaman (*f* militiawoman).

milieu, x [miljø] *nm* - **1.** [centre] middle ; **au ~ de** [au centre de] in the middle of ; [parmi] among, surrounded by ; **au beau** *ou* **en plein ~ de qqch** right in the middle of sthg - **2.** [stade intermédiaire] middle course ; **juste ~** happy medium - **3.** BIOL & SOCIOL environment ; **~ familial** family background ; **dans les ~x** autorisés in official circles - **4.** [pègre] : **le ~** the underworld - **5.** FOOTBALL : **~ de terrain** midfielder, midfield player.

militaire [militɛr] <> *nm* soldier ; **~ de carrière** professional soldier <> *adj* military.

militant, e [militɑ̃, ɑ̃t] *adj* & *nm, f* militant.

militantisme [militɑ̃tism] *nm* militancy.

militarisation [militarizasjɔ̃] *nf* militarization.

militariste [militarist] <> *nmf* militarist <> *adj* militaristic.

militer [3] [milite] *vi* to be active ; **~ pour** to militate in favour *Br ou* favor *Am* of ; **~ contre** to militate against.

milk-shake [milkʃɛk] (*pl* milk-shakes) *nm* milk shake.

mille, mil [mil] <> *nm inv* - **1.** [unité] a *ou* one thousand - **2.** [de cible] bull's-eye ; **dans le ~** on target - **3.** NAVIG : **~ marin** nautical mile - **4.** *Can* [distance] mile - **5.** *loc* : **des ~ et des cents** *fam* loads of money <> *adj inv* ; **c'est ~ fois trop** it's far too much ; **je lui ai dit ~ fois** I've told him/her a thousand times ; *voir aussi* **six.**

mille-feuille [milfœj] (*pl* mille-feuilles) *nm* ≃ vanilla slice *Br*, ≃ napoleon *Am*.

millénaire [milenɛr] <> *nm* millennium, thousand years (*pl*) <> *adj* thousand-year-old (*avant n*).

mille-pattes [milpat] *nm inv* centipede, millipede.

millésime [milezim] *nm* - **1.** [de pièce] date - **2.** [de vin] vintage, year.

millésimé, e [milezime] *adj* [vin] vintage (*avant n*).

millet [mijɛ] *nm* millet.

milliard [miljar] *nm* thousand million *Br*, billion *Am* ; **par ~s** *fig* in (their) millions.

milliardaire [miljardɛr] *nmf* multimillionaire *Br*, billionaire *Am*.

millième [miljɛm] *adj, nm* ou *nmf* thousandth ; *voir aussi* **sixième.**

millier [milje] *nm* thousand ; **un ~ de francs/personnes** about a thousand francs/people ; **des ~s de** thousands of ; **par ~s** in (their) thousands.

milligramme [miligram] *nm* milligram, milligramme.

millilitre [mililitr] *nm* millilitre *Br*, milliliter *Am*.

millimètre [milimɛtr] *nm* millimetre *Br*, millimeter *Am*.

millimétrique [milimetrik] *adj* : **papier ~** graph paper.

million [miljɔ̃] *nm* million ; **un ~ de francs** a million francs.

millionième [miljɔnjɛm] *adj, nm* ou *nmf* millionth.

millionnaire [miljɔnɛr] *nmf* millionaire.

mime [mim] <> *nm* mime <> *nmf* mime (artist).

mimer [3] [mime] *vt* - **1.** [exprimer sans parler] to mime - **2.** [imiter] to mimic.

mimétisme [mimetism] *nm* mimicry.

mimique [mimik] *nf* - **1.** [grimace] face - **2.** [geste] sign language (*U*).

mimosa [mimoza] *nm* mimosa.

min (*abr de* minute) min.

min. (*abr de* minimum) min.

MIN (*abr de* marché d'intérêt national) *nm* wholesale market for agricultural produce.

minable [minabl] *adj fam* - **1.** [misérable] seedy, shabby - **2.** [médiocre] pathetic.

minaret [minarɛ] *nm* minaret.

minauder [3] [minode] *vi* to simper.

mince [mɛ̃s] <> *adj* - **1.** [maigre - gén] thin ; [- personne, taille] slender, slim - **2.** *fig* [faible] small, meagre *Br*, meager *Am* <> *interj fam* : **~ alors!** drat!

minceur [mɛ̃sœr] *nf* - **1.** [gén] thinness ; [de personne] slenderness, slimness - **2.** *fig* [insuffisance] meagreness *Br*, meagerness *Am*.

mincir [32] [mɛ̃sir] *vi* to get thinner *ou* slimmer.

mine [min] *nf* - **1.** [expression] look ; **avoir bonne/mauvaise ~** to look well/ill ; **avoir une ~ de déterré** *fam* to look like death warmed up ; **faire grise ~** to look annoyed - **2.** [apparence] appearance ; **faire ~ de faire qqch** to make as if to do sthg ; [faire semblant] to pretend to do sthg ; **~ de rien, il est très costaud** *fam* he's very strong though he doesn't look it ; **ne pas payer de ~** to be not much to look at - **3.** [gisement] *fig* mine ; [exploitation] mining ; **~ de charbon** coalmine - **4.** [explosif] mine - **5.** [de crayon] lead.

miner [3] [mine] *vt* - **1.** MIL to mine - **2.** [ronger] to undermine, to wear away ; *fig* to wear down.

➡ **se miner** *vp* to worry o.s. sick.

minerai [minrɛ] *nm* ore.

minéral, e, aux [mineral, o] adj - **1.** CHIM inorganic - **2.** [eau, source] mineral *(avant n).*
➠ **minéral** nm mineral.

minéralisé, e [mineralize] adj mineralized.

minéralogie [mineralɔʒi] nf mineralogy.

minéralogique [mineralɔʒik] adj - **1.** AUTOM : numéro ~ registration number Br, license number Am ; **plaque** ~ numberplate Br, license plate Am - **2.** GÉOL mineralogical.

minet, ette [mine, ɛt] nm, f fam - **1.** [chat] pussy cat, pussy - **2.** [personne] trendy.

mincur, e [minœr] ⟷ adj minor ⟷ nm, f JUR minor.
➠ **mineur** nm [ouvrier] miner ; ~ **de fond** face worker.

mini abr de **minimum.**

miniature [minjatyr] ⟷ nf miniature ; **en** ~ in miniature ⟷ adj miniature.

miniaturiser [3] [minjatyrize] vt to miniaturize.

minibus [minibys] nm minibus.

minichaîne [miniʃɛn] nf portable hi-fi.

MiniDisc® [minidisk] nm MiniDisc®.

minier, ère [minje, ɛr] adj mining *(avant n).*

minijupe [miniʒyp] nf miniskirt.

minimal, e, aux [minimal, o] adj minimum.

minimalisme [minimalism] nm minimalism.

minime [minim] ⟷ nmf SPORT ≃ junior ⟷ adj minimal.

minimiser [3] [minimize] vt to minimize.

minimum [minimɔm] *(pl* **minimums** OU **minima** [minimal)* ⟷ nm - **1.** [gén & MATHS] minimum ; **au** ~ at least ; **le strict** ~ the bare minimum ; **le** ~ **vital** a living wage - **2.** JUR minimum penalty ⟷ adj minimum.

mini-ordinateur [miniɔrdinatœr] *(pl* **mini-ordinateurs)** nm minicomputer.

ministère [ministɛr] nm - **1.** [département] ministry Br, department - **2.** [cabinet] government - **3.** RELIG ministry.
➠ **ministère public** nm ≃ Crown Prosecution Service Br, ≃ District Attorney's office Am.

ministériel, elle [ministerjɛl] adj - **1.** [du ministère] departmental, ministerial Br - **2.** [pro-gouvernemental] pro-government.

ministre [ministr] nm secretary, minister Br ; ~ **délégué à** secretary for, minister of Br ; ~ **des Affaires étrangères** ≃ Foreign Secretary Br, ≃ Secretary of State Am ; ~ **des Affaires sociales** ≃ Social Services Secretary ; ~ **de l'Éducation nationale** ≃ Education Secretary ; ~ **d'État** secretary of state, cabinet minister Br ; ~ **des Finances** ≃ Chancellor of the Exchequer Br, ≃ Secretary of the Treasury Am ; ~ **de l'Intérieur** ≃ Home Secretary Br, ≃ Secretary of the Interior Am ; ~ **de la Santé** ≃ Health Secretary ; **premier** ~ prime minister.

Minitel® [minitɛl] nm teletext system run by the French national telephone company, providing an information and communication network.

MINITEL®

The domestic viewdata service run by France Télécom has become a familiar part of French life. The basic monitor and keyboard are given free of charge, and the subscriber is charged for the services used on his or her normal telephone bill. The subscriber dials a four-figure number (typically 3615) ; a code word then gives access to the particular service required. Some Minitel® services are purely informative (the weather, road conditions, news etc) ; others are interactive (enabling users to carry out bank transactions, book tickets for travel or, on the 'Minitel Rose', to look for companionship, for example). The Minitel® also serves as an electronic telephone directory (for which the call number is 11). Minitel® is being replaced more and more by the Internet.

minitéliste [minitelist] nmf Minitel® user.

minois [minwa] nm sweet (little) face.

minorer [3] [minɔre] vt to reduce.

minoritaire [minɔritɛr] ⟷ nmf member of a minority ⟷ adj minority *(avant n)* ; **être** ~ to be in the minority.

minorité [minɔrite] nf minority ; **en** ~ in the minority ; ~ **ethnique** ethnic minority.

Minorque [minɔrk] n Minorca ; **à** ~ in Minorca.

minorquin, e [minɔrkɛ̃, in] adj Minorcan.
➠ **Minorquin, e** nm, f Minorcan.

minoterie [minɔtri] nf - **1.** [moulin] flourmill - **2.** [industrie] (flour) milling industry.

minuit [minɥi] nm midnight.

minuscule [minyskyl] ⟷ nf [lettre] small letter ; **en** ~**s** in small letters ⟷ adj - **1.** [lettre] small - **2.** [très petit] tiny, minuscule.

minutage [minytaʒ] nm (precise) timing.

minute [minyt] ⟷ nf minute ; **à la** ~ at once ; **dans une** ~ in a minute ; **d'une** ~ **à l'autre** in next to no time ⟷ interj fam hang on (a minute)!

minuter [3] [minyte] vt - **1.** [chronométrer] to time (precisely) - **2.** JUR to draw up.

minuterie [minytri] nf [d'éclairage] time switch, timer.

minuteur [minytœr] *nm* timer.

minutie [minysi] *nf* [soin] meticulousness ; [précision] attention to detail ; **avec ~** [avec soin] meticulously ; [dans le détail] in minute detail.

minutieusement [minysjøzmã] *adv* [avec soin] meticulously ; [dans le détail] minutely, in minute detail.

minutieux, euse [minysjø, øz] *adj* [méticuleux] meticulous ; [détaillé] minutely detailed ; **un travail ~** a job requiring great attention to detail.

mioche [mjɔʃ] *nmf fam* kiddy.

mirabelle [mirabɛl] *nf* - **1.** [fruit] mirabelle (plum) - **2.** [alcool] plum brandy.

miracle [mirakl] *nm* miracle ; **par ~** by some *ou* a miracle, miraculously ; **croire aux ~s** to believe in miracles.

miraculé, e [mirakyle] ◇ *adj* lucky to be alive ◇ *nm, f person who is lucky to be alive.*

miraculeusement [mirakyløzmã] *adv* miraculously.

miraculeux, euse [mirakylø, øz] *adj* miraculous.

mirador [miradɔr] *nm* MIL watchtower.

mirage [miraʒ] *nm* mirage.

mire [mir] *nf* - **1.** TÉLÉ test card - **2.** [visée] : **ligne de ~** line of sight.

mirer [3] [mire] *vt* - **1.** [œuf] to candle - **2.** *littéraire* [refléter] to reflect.

➡ **se mirer** *vp littéraire* - **1.** [se regarder] to gaze at o.s. - **2.** [se refléter] to be reflected *ou* mirrored.

mirifique [mirifik] *adj* fabulous.

mirobolant, e [mirɔbɔlã, ãt] *adj* fabulous, fantastic.

miroir [mirwar] *nm* mirror ; **~ aux alouettes** *fig* lure ; **~ de poche** handbag mirror.

miroiter [3] [mirwate] *vi* to sparkle, to gleam ; **faire ~ qqch à qqn** to hold out the prospect of sthg to sb.

miroiterie [mirwatri] *nf* - **1.** [industrie] mirror manufacturing - **2.** [atelier] mirror workshop.

miroton [mirɔtõ] *nm boiled beef in an onion sauce.*

mis, mise [mi, miz] *pp* ▷ **mettre**.

misaine [mizɛn] *nf* foresail.

misanthrope [mizãtrɔp] ◇ *nmf* misanthropist, misanthrope ◇ *adj* misanthropic.

mise [miz] *nf* - **1.** [action] putting ; **~ en demeure** formal notice ; **~ à jour** updating ; **~ en liberté provisoire** JUR freeing on bail ; **~ en page** making up, composing ; **~ en plis** [coiffure] set ; **~ au point** PHOT focusing ; TECHNOL adjust-

ment ; *fig* clarification ; **~ en scène** production ; **~ en service** putting into operation - **2.** [d'argent] stake ; **sauver la ~ à qqn** *fig* to get sb out of a tight corner ; **~ de fonds** capital investment - **3.** [tenue] clothing - **4.** *loc* : **ne pas être de ~** to be unacceptable.

miser [3] [mize] ◇ *vt* to bet ◇ *vi* : **~ sur** to bet on ; *fig* to count on.

misérabilisme [mizerabilism] *nm* realism.

misérable [mizerabl] ◇ *nmf* - **1.** [pauvre] poor person - **2.** [coquin] wretch ◇ *adj* - **1.** [pauvre] poor, wretched - **2.** [déplorable] pitiful - **3.** [sans valeur] paltry, miserable.

misérablement [mizerabləmã] *adv* - **1.** [pauvrement] in poverty, wretchedly - **2.** [pitoyablement] miserably.

misère [mizer] *nf* - **1.** [indigence] poverty ; **~ noire** utter destitution - **2.** [infortune] misery - **3.** *fig* [bagatelle] trifle.

➡ **misères** *nfpl* [ennuis] woes *(pl)*, miseries *(pl)* ; **faire des ~s à qqn** *fam* to put sb through it.

miséreux, euse [mizerø, øz] ◇ *adj* poverty-stricken ◇ *nm, f* down-and-out.

miséricorde [mizerikɔrd] ◇ *nf* [clémence] mercy ◇ *interj* mercy (me)!

miséricordieux, euse [mizerikɔrdjø, øz] *adj* merciful.

misogyne [mizɔʒin] ◇ *nmf* misogynist ◇ *adj* misogynous.

misogynie [mizɔʒini] *nf* misogyny.

missel [misɛl] *nm* missal.

missile [misil] *nm* missile ; **~ balistique** ballistic missile.

mission [misjõ] *nf* mission ; **en ~** on a mission.

missionnaire [misjɔnɛr] ◇ *nmf* missionary ◇ *adj* missionary *(avant n)*.

missive [misiv] *nf* letter.

mistral [mistral] *nm strong cold wind that blows down the Rhône Valley and through Southern France.*

mitaine [mitɛn] *nf* fingerless glove.

mite [mit] *nf* (clothes) moth.

mité, e [mite] *adj* moth-eaten.

mi-temps [mitã] ◇ *nf inv* [SPORT - période] half ; [- pause] half-time ; **à la ~** at half-time ; **première/seconde ~** first/second half ◇ *nm* part-time work.

➡ **à mi-temps** *loc adj* & *loc adv* part-time.

miteux, euse [mitø, øz] *fam* ◇ *adj* seedy, dingy ◇ *nm, f* shabby person.

mitigé, e [mitiʒe] *adj* - **1.** [tempéré] lukewarm - **2.** *fam* [mélangé] mixed.

mitonner [3] [mitɔne] ◇ *vt* - **1.** [faire cuire] to

simmer - **2.** [préparer avec soin] to prepare lovingly - **3.** *fig* [affaire] to plot, to cook up ◇ *vi* *CULIN* to simmer.

➤ **se mitonner** *vp* : **se ~ qqch** to cook sthg up for o.s.

mitoyen, enne [mitwajɛ̃, ɛn] *adj* [commun] common ; [attenant] adjoining ; **mur ~** party wall.

mitrailler [3] [mitraje] *vt* - **1.** *MIL* to machinegun - **2.** *fam* [photographier] to click away at - **3.** *fig* [assaillir] : **~ qqn (de)** to bombard sb (with).

mitraillette [mitrajɛt] *nf* submachine gun.

mitrailleur [mitrajœr] *nm* machinegunner.

mitrailleuse [mitrajøz] *nf* machinegun.

mitre [mitr] *nf* - **1.** [d'évêque] mitre *Br*, miter *Am* - **2.** [de cheminée] cowl.

mi-voix [mivwa] ➤ **à mi-voix** *loc adv* in a low voice.

mixage [miksaʒ] *nm* *CIN* & *RADIO* (sound) mixing.

mixer[1], **mixeur** [miksœr] *nm* (food) mixer.

mixer[2] [3] [mikse] *vt* to mix.

mixité [miksite] *nf* coeducation.

mixte [mikst] *adj* mixed ; **mariage ~** mixed marriage.

mixture [mikstyr] *nf* - **1.** *CHIM* & *CULIN* mixture - **2.** *péj* [mélange] concoction.

MJC (*abr de* maison des jeunes et de la culture) *nf* youth and cultural centre.

ml (*abr de* millilitre) ml.

MLF (*abr de* Mouvement de libération de la femme) *nm* women's movement, ≈ NOW *Am*.

Mlle (*abr de* Mademoiselle) Miss.

mm (*abr de* millimètre) mm.

MM (*abr de* Messieurs) Messrs.

Mme (*abr de* Madame) Mrs.

mn (*abr de* minute) min.

mnémotechnique [mnemɔtɛknik] *adj* mnemonic.

MNS (*abr de* maître nageur sauveteur) *nm* lifeguard.

Mo (*abr de* méga-octet) MB.

mobile [mɔbil] ◇ *nm* - **1.** [objet] mobile - **2.** [motivation] motive ◇ *adj* - **1.** [gén] movable, mobile ; [partie, pièce] moving - **2.** [population, main-d'œuvre] mobile - **3.** [fête] movable ; [échelle] sliding.

mobilier, ère [mɔbilje, ɛr] *adj* *JUR* movable.
➤ **mobilier** *nm* furniture.

mobilisation [mɔbilizasjɔ̃] *nf* mobilization ; **~ générale** *MIL* general mobilization.

mobiliser [3] [mɔbilize] *vt* - **1.** [gén] to mobilize - **2.** [moralement] to rally.

➤ **se mobiliser** *vp* to mobilize, to rally.

mobilité [mɔbilite] *nf* mobility.

Mobylette® [mɔbilɛt] *nf* moped.

mocassin [mɔkasɛ̃] *nm* moccasin.

moche [mɔʃ] *adj fam* - **1.** [laid] ugly - **2.** [triste, méprisable] lousy, rotten.

modalité [mɔdalite] *nf* - **1.** [convention] form ; **~s de paiement** methods of payment - **2.** *JUR* clause.

mode [mɔd] ◇ *nf* - **1.** [gén] fashion ; **à la ~** fashion, fashionable ; **lancer une ~** to start a fashion ; **lancer la ~ de qqch** to start the fashion for sthg ; **passé de ~** out of fashion - **2.** [coutume] custom, style ; **à la ~ de** in the style of ◇ *nm* - **1.** [manière] mode, form ; **~ de vie** way of life - **2.** [méthode] method ; **~ d'emploi** instructions (for use) - **3.** *GRAM* mood - **4.** *MUS* mode.

modelage [mɔdlaʒ] *nm* [action] modelling.

modelé [mɔdle] *nm* - **1.** [de visage] contours (pl) - **2.** *ART* & *GÉOGR* relief.

modèle [mɔdɛl] *nm* - **1.** [gén] model ; **sur le ~ de** on the model of ; **~ déposé** patented design ; **~ réduit** scale model - **2.** *(en apposition)* [exemplaire] model *(avant n)*.

modeler [25] [mɔdle] *vt* to shape ; **~ qqch sur qqch** *fig* to model sthg on sthg.

➤ **se modeler** *vp littéraire* : **se ~ sur** *fig* to model o.s. on.

modélisme [mɔdelism] *nm* modelling *(of scale models)*.

modem [mɔdɛm] *nm* modem ; **~ d'appel** dial-in modem ; **~ fax** fax modem.

modérateur, trice [mɔderatœr, tris] *adj* moderating.
➤ **modérateur** *nm* - **1.** [personne] moderator - **2.** [mécanisme] regulator.

modération [mɔderasjɔ̃] *nf* moderation.

modéré, e [mɔdere] *adj* & *nm, f* moderate.

modérément [mɔderemɑ̃] *adv* in moderation, moderately.

modérer [18] [mɔdere] *vt* to moderate.

➤ **se modérer** *vp* to restrain o.s., to control o.s.

moderne [mɔdɛrn] ◇ *nm* : **le ~** modern things *(pl)*, (the) modern style ◇ *adj* modern ; [mathématiques] new.

modernisation [mɔdɛrnizasjɔ̃] *nf* modernization.

moderniser [3] [mɔdɛrnize] *vt* to modernize.

➤ **se moderniser** *vp* to become (more) modern.

modernisme [mɔdɛrnism] *nm* [style] modernism.

modernité [mɔdɛrnite] *nf* modernity.

modeste [mɔdɛst] *adj* modest ; [origine] humble.

modestement [mɔdɛstəmã] *adv* modestly.

modestie [mɔdɛsti] *nf* modesty ; **fausse ~** false modesty.

modicité [mɔdisite] *nf* [de prix, salaire] lowness, moderateness.

modifiable [mɔdifjabl] *adj* modifiable, alterable.

modification [mɔdifikasjɔ̃] *nf* alteration, modification.

modifier [9] [mɔdifje] *vt* to alter, to modify.
➧ **se modifier** *vp* to alter.

modique [mɔdik] *adj* modest.

modiste [mɔdist] *nf* milliner.

modulation [mɔdylasjɔ̃] *nf* modulation.

module [mɔdyl] *nm* module.

moduler [3] [mɔdyle] *vt* - **1.** [air] to warble - **2.** [structure] to adjust - **3.** *RADIO* to modulate.

modus vivendi [mɔdysviɛ̃di] *nm inv* modus vivendi.

moelle [mwal] *nf* *ANAT* marrow ; **~ osseuse** bone marrow ; **jusqu'à la ~** *fig* to the core.
➧ **moelle épinière** *nf* spinal cord.

moelleux, euse [mwalø, øz] *adj* - **1.** [canapé, tapis] soft - **2.** [fromage, vin] mellow.

moellon [mwalɔ̃] *nm* rubble stone.

mœurs [mœr(s)] *nfpl* - **1.** [morale] morals - **2.** [coutumes] customs, habits - **3.** *ZOOL* behaviour *(U)* *Br*, behavior *(U)* *Am*.

mohair [mɔɛr] *nm* mohair.

moi [mwa] ◇ *pron pers* - **1.** [objet, après préposition, comparatif] me ; **aide-~** help me ; **il me l'a dit, à ~** he told ME ; **c'est pour ~** it's for me ; **plus âgé que ~** older than me *ou* than I (am) - **2.** [sujet] I ; **non plus, je n'en sais rien** I don't know anything about it either ; **qui est là?** – (c'est) who's there? - it's me ; **je l'ai vu hier – ~ aussi** I saw him yesterday – me too ; **c'est ~ qui lui ai dit de venir** I was the one who told him to come ; **~, je n'ai rien dit!** I didn't say anything! ◇ *nm* : **le ~** the ego, the self.
➧ **moi-même** *pron pers* myself.

moignon [mwaɲɔ̃] *nm* stump.

moindre [mwɛ̃dr] ◇ *adj superl* : **le/la ~** the least ; *(avec négation)* the least *ou* slightest ; **les ~s détails** the smallest details ; **sans la ~ difficulté** without the slightest problem ; **c'est la ~ des choses** it's the least I/you *etc* could do ◇ *adj compar* less ; [prix] lower ; **à un ~ degré** to a lesser extent.

moine [mwan] *nm* monk.

moineau, x [mwano] *nm* sparrow.

moins [mwɛ̃] ◇ *adv* - **1.** [quantité] less ; **~ de** less (than) ; **~ de lait** less milk ; **~ de gens** fewer people ; **~ de dix** less than ten ; **il est un peu ~ de 10 heures** it's nearly 10 o'clock - **2.** [comparatif] : **~ (que)** less (than) ; **il est ~ vieux que ton frère** he's not as old as your brother, he's younger than your brother ; **il vient ~ souvent que Pierre** he doesn't come as often as Pierre, he comes less often than Pierre ; **bien ~ grand que** much smaller than ; **il mange, ~ il travaille** the less he eats, the less he works - **3.** [superlatif] : **le ~** (the) least ; **le ~ riche des hommes** the poorest man ; **il est le ~ fort** he's the least strong, he's the weakest ; **c'est lui qui vient le ~ souvent** he comes (the) least often ; **c'est lui qui travaille le ~** he works (the) least ; **le ~ possible** as little as possible ; **pas le ~ du monde** not in the least ◇ *prép* - **1.** [gén] minus ; **dix ~ huit font deux** ten minus eight is two, ten take away eight is two ; **il fait ~ vingt** it's twenty below, it's minus twenty - **2.** [servant à indiquer l'heure] : **il est 3 heures ~ le quart** it's quarter to 3 ; **il est ~ dix** it's ten to ◇ *nm* - **1.** [signe] minus (sign) - **2.** *loc* : **le ~ qu'on puisse dire, c'est que ...** it's an understatement to say ...
➧ **à moins de** *loc prép* : **à ~ de battre le record** unless I/you *etc* beat the record.
➧ **à moins que** *loc conj* (+ *subjonctif*) unless.
➧ **au moins** *loc adv* at least.
➧ **de moins en moins** *loc adv* less and less.
➧ **du moins** *loc adv* at least.
➧ **en moins** *loc adv* : **il a une dent en ~** he's missing *ou* minus a tooth ; **c'était le paradis, les anges en ~** it was heaven, minus the angels.
➧ **en moins de** *loc prép* in less than ; **en ~ de rien** in less than no time.
➧ **on ne peut moins** *loc adv* far from.
➧ **pour le moins** *loc adv* at (the very) least.
➧ **tout au moins** *loc adv* at (the very) least.

moins-value [mwɛ̃valy] (*pl* moins-values) *nf* capital loss.

moire [mwar] *nf* [étoffe] moiré.

moiré, e [mware] *adj* - **1.** [tissu] watered - **2.** *littéraire* [reflet] shimmering.

mois [mwa] *nm* - **1.** [laps de temps] month - **2.** [salaire] (monthly) salary ; **le treizième ~** extra month's salary - **3.** *fam* [loyer] month's rent.

moïse [mɔiz] *nm* wicker cradle.

moisi, e [mwazi] *adj* mouldy *Br*, moldy *Am*.
➧ **moisi** *nm* mould *Br*, mold *Am*.

moisir [32] [mwazir] *vi* - **1.** [pourrir] to go mouldy *Br ou* moldy *Am* - **2.** *fig* [personne] to rot.

moisissure [mwazisyr] *nf* mould *Br*, mold *Am*.

moisson [mwasɔ̃] *nf* **- 1.** [récolte] harvest ; faire la ~ *ou* les ~s to harvest, to bring in the harvest **- 2.** *fig* [d'idées, de projets] wealth.

moissonner [3] [mwasɔne] *vt* to harvest, to gather (in) ; *fig* to collect, to gather.

moissonneur, euse [mwasɔnœr, øz] *nm, f* [personne] harvester.

➤ **moissonneuse** *nf* [machine] harvester.

moissonneuse-batteuse [mwasɔnøzbatøz] (*pl* **moissonneuses-batteuses**) *nf* combine (harvester).

moite [mwat] *adj* [peau, mains] moist, sweaty ; [atmosphère] muggy.

moiteur [mwatœr] *nf* [de peau, mains] moistness ; [d'atmosphère] mugginess.

moitié [mwatje] *nf* **- 1.** [gén] half ; **à ~ vide** half-empty ; **faire qqch à ~** to half-do sthg ; **la ~ du temps** half the time ; **à la ~ de qqch** halfway through sthg ; **faire ~-~** to go halves **- 2.** [épouse, époux] : **ma/ta ~** *fam hum* my/your better half.

moka [mɔka] *nm* **- 1.** [café] mocha (coffee) **- 2.** [gâteau] coffee cake.

mol ▷ **mou.**

molaire [mɔlɛr] *nf* molar.

Moldavie [mɔldavi] *nf* : **la ~** Moldavia.

mole [mɔl] *nf* CHIM mole.

môle [mol] *nm* [quai] jetty.

moléculaire [mɔlekylɛr] *adj* molecular.

molécule [mɔlekyl] *nf* molecule.

moleskine [mɔlɛskin] *nf* imitation leather.

molester [3] [mɔlɛste] *vt* to manhandle.

molette [mɔlɛt] *nf* **- 1.** [de réglage] knurled wheel **- 2.** [outil] glasscutter.

mollasse [mɔlas] *adj fam* **- 1.** [mou] flabby **- 2.** *fig* [personne] lethargic.

mollasson, onne [mɔlasɔ̃, ɔn] *nm, f fam* (lazy) lump.

molle ▷ **mou.**

mollement [mɔlmɑ̃] *adv* **- 1.** [faiblement] weakly, feebly **- 2.** *littéraire* [paresseusement] sluggishly, lethargically.

mollesse [mɔlɛs] *nf* **- 1.** [de chose] softness **- 2.** [de personne] lethargy.

mollet [mɔlɛ] ◇ *nm* calf ◇ *adj* ▷ **œuf.**

molletière [mɔltjɛr] *adj* : **bande ~** puttee.

molleton [mɔltɔ̃] *nm* flannelette ; [pour table] felt.

mollir [32] [mɔlir] *vi* **- 1.** [physiquement, moralement] to give way **- 2.** [matière] to soften, to go soft **- 3.** [vent] to drop, to die down.

mollo [mɔlo] *adv fam* easy ; **y aller ~** to go easy, to take it easy.

mollusque [mɔlysk] *nm* **- 1.** ZOOL mollusc **- 2.** *fam fig* [personne] (lazy) lump.

molosse [mɔlɔs] *nm* **- 1.** [chien] *large ferocious dog* **- 2.** *fig* & *péj* [personne] hulking great brute *ou* fellow.

môme [mom] *fam* ◇ *nmf* [enfant] kid, youngster ◇ *nf* [jeune fille] bird *Br*, chick.

moment [mɔmɑ̃] *nm* **- 1.** [gén] moment ; **au ~ de l'accident** at the time of the accident, when the accident happened ; **au ~ de partir** just as we/you *etc* were leaving ; **au ~ où** just as ; **dans un ~** in a moment ; **d'un ~ à l'autre, à tout ~** (at) any moment, any moment now ; **ne pas avoir un ~ à soi** not to have a moment to oneself ; **à un ~ donné** at a given moment ; **par ~s** at times, now and then ; **sur le ~** at the time ; **en ce ~** at the moment ; **pour le ~** for the moment **- 2.** [durée] (short) time ; **avoir de bons ~s avec qqn** to have (some) good times with sb ; **passer un mauvais ~** to have a bad time **- 3.** [occasion] time ; **ce n'est pas le ~ (de faire qqch)** this is not the time (to do sthg) ; **c'est le ~ ou jamais** it's now or never.

➤ **du moment que** *loc prép* since, as.

momentané, e [mɔmɑ̃tane] *adj* temporary.

momentanément [mɔmɑ̃tanemɑ̃] *adv* temporarily.

momie [mɔmi] *nf* mummy.

mon [mɔ̃] (*f* **ma** [ma], *pl* **mes** [me]) *adj poss* my.

monacal, e, aux [mɔnakal, o] *adj* monastic.

Monaco [mɔnako] *n* : **(la principauté de) ~** (the principality of) Monaco.

monarchie [mɔnarʃi] *nf* monarchy ; **~ absolue/constitutionnelle** absolute/constitutional monarchy.

monarchique [mɔnarʃik] *adj* monarchical.

monarchiste [mɔnarʃist] *nmf* & *adj* monarchist.

monarque [mɔnark] *nm* monarch.

monastère [mɔnastɛr] *nm* monastery.

monastique [mɔnastik] *adj* monastic.

monceau, x [mɔ̃so] *nm* **- 1.** [tas] heap **- 2.** *fig* [de fautes, de bêtises] mass.

mondain, e [mɔ̃dɛ̃, ɛn] ◇ *adj* **- 1.** [chronique, journaliste] society (*avant n*) **- 2.** *péj* [futile] frivolous, superficial ◇ *nm, f* socialite.

mondanités [mɔ̃danite] *nfpl* **- 1.** [événements] society life (*U*) **- 2.** [paroles] small talk (*U*) ; [comportements] formalities.

monde [mɔ̃d] *nm* **- 1.** [gén] world ; **le/la plus ... au ~, le/la plus ... du ~** the most ... in the world ; **pour rien au ~** not for the world, not for all the tea in China ; **mettre un enfant au ~** to bring a child into the world ; **venir au ~**

to come into the world ; **en ce bas ~** RELIG in this world ; **l'autre ~** RELIG the other world ; **le quart ~** the Fourth World - **2.** [gens] people *(pl)* ; **beaucoup/peu de ~** a lot of/not many people ; **tout le ~** everyone, everybody - **3.** *loc* : **c'est un ~!** that's really the limit! ; **se faire un ~ de qqch** to make too much of sthg ; **se moquer du ~** to have a nerve ; **noir de ~** packed with people ; **tromper son ~** not to be what one seems.

➡ **Monde** *nm* : **le Nouveau Monde** the New World.

mondial, e, aux [mɔ̃djal, o] *adj* world *(avant n)*.

mondialement [mɔ̃djalmɑ̃] *adv* throughout *ou* all over the world.

mondialisation *nf* globalization.

monégasque [mɔnegask] *adj* of/from Monaco.

➡ **Monégasque** *nmf* native *ou* inhabitant of Monaco.

monétaire [mɔnetɛr] *adj* monetary.

monétarisme [mɔnetarism] *nm* monetarism.

mongol, e [mɔ̃gɔl] *adj* Mongolian.

➡ **mongol** *nm* [langue] Mongolian.

➡ **Mongol, e** *nm, f* Mongolian.

Mongolie [mɔ̃gɔli] *nf* : **la ~** Mongolia ; **la ~-Extérieure** Outer Mongolia ; **la ~-Intérieure** Inner Mongolia.

mongolien, enne [mɔ̃gɔljɛ̃, ɛn] ◇ *adj* Mongol *(avant n)* ◇ *nm, f* Mongol.

mongolisme [mɔ̃gɔlism] *nm* Mongolism.

mongoloïde [mɔ̃gɔlɔid] *adj* Mongol *(avant n)*.

moniteur, trice [mɔnitœr, tris] *nm, f* - **1.** [enseignant] instructor, coach ; **~ d'auto-école** driving instructor ; **~ de ski** ski instructor - **2.** [de colonie de vacances] supervisor, leader.

➡ **moniteur** *nm* [appareil & INFORM] monitor.

monnaie [mɔnɛ] *nf* - **1.** [moyen de paiement] money ; **fausse ~** forged currency, counterfeit money ; **~ d'échange** *fig* currency ; **c'est ~ courante** *fig* it's commonplace, it's common practice - **2.** [de pays] currency ; **~ unique** single currency - **3.** [pièces] change ; **avoir de la ~** to have change ; **avoir la ~** to have the change ; **rendre la ~ à qqn** to give sb his/her change ; **avoir la ~ de 100 francs** to have change of *ou* for 100 francs ; **faire (de) la ~** to get (some) change ; **menue ~** small *ou* loose change.

monnayable [mɔnɛjabl] *adj* convertible (into cash) ; *fig* valuable.

monnayer [11] [mɔnɛje] *vt* - **1.** [biens] to convert into cash - **2.** *fig* [silence] to buy.

monochrome [mɔnɔkrom] *adj* monochrome, monochromatic.

monocle [mɔnɔkl] *nm* monocle.

monocoque [mɔnɔkɔk] *nm* & *adj* [bateau] monohull.

monocorde [mɔnɔkɔrd] *adj* - **1.** MUS single-stringed - **2.** [monotone] monotonous.

monoculture [mɔnɔkyltyr] *nf* monoculture.

monogame [mɔnɔgam] *adj* monogamous.

monogamie [mɔnɔgami] *nf* monogamy.

monogramme [mɔnɔgram] *nm* monogram.

monolingue [mɔnɔlɛ̃g] *adj* monolingual.

monolithique [mɔnɔlitik] *adj* monolithic.

monologue [mɔnɔlɔg] *nm* - **1.** THÉÂTRE soliloquy - **2.** [discours individuel] monologue ; **~ intérieur** stream of consciousness.

monologuer [3] [mɔnɔlɔge] *vi* - **1.** THÉÂTRE to soliloquize - **2.** *fig* & *péj* [parler] to talk away.

monôme [mɔnom] *nm* - **1.** MATHS monomial - **2.** *arg scol* [procession] ≈ rag day procession.

mononucléose [mɔnɔnykleoz] *nf* : **~ infectieuse** glandular fever.

monoparental, e, aux [mɔnɔparɑ̃tal, o] *adj* single-parent *(avant n)*.

monophasé, e [mɔnɔfaze] *adj* ÉLECTR single-phase.

➡ **monophasé** *nm* single-phase current.

monoplace [mɔnɔplas] ◇ *nm* single-seater ◇ *adj* single-seater *(avant n)*.

monopole [mɔnɔpɔl] *nm* monopoly ; **avoir le ~ de qqch** *litt* & *fig* to have a monopoly of *ou* on sthg ; **~ d'État** state monopoly.

monopoliser [3] [mɔnɔpɔlize] *vt* to monopolize.

monorail [mɔnɔraj] ◇ *nm* monorail ◇ *adj inv* monorail *(avant n)*.

monoski [mɔnɔski] *nm* - **1.** [objet] monoski - **2.** *SPORT* monoskiing.

monospace [mɔnɔspas] *nm* people carrier *Am*, minivan.

monosyllabe [mɔnɔsilab] ◇ *nm* monosyllable ◇ *adj* monosyllabic.

monosyllabique [mɔnɔsilabik] *adj* monosyllabic.

monothéisme [mɔnɔteism] *nm* monotheism.

monotone [mɔnɔtɔn] *adj* monotonous.

monotonie [mɔnɔtɔni] *nf* monotony ; **rompre la ~** to break the monotony.

Monrovia [mɔ̃rɔvja] *n* Monrovia.

monseigneur [mɔ̃sɛɲœr] *(pl* **messeigneurs** [mesɛɲœr]*) nm* - **1.** [titre - d'évêque, de duc] His Grace ; [- de cardinal] His Eminence ; [- de prince] His (Royal) Highness **- 2.** [formule d'adresse - à évêque, à duc] Your Grace ; [- à cardinal] Your Eminence ; [- à prince] Your (Royal) Highness.

monsieur [məsjø] (*pl* **messieurs** [mesjø]) *nm* **- 1.** [titre] : ~ X Mr X ; **bonjour ~** good morning ; [dans hôtel, restaurant] good morning, sir ; **bonjour messieurs** good morning (gentlemen) ; **messieurs dames** ladies and gentlemen ; **Monsieur le Ministre n'est pas là** the Minister is out **- 2.** [homme quelconque] gentleman.

monstre [mɔ̃str] *nm* **- 1.** [gén] monster ; **~ marin** sea monster ; **~ sacré** idol **- 2.** *(en apposition) fam* [énorme] colossal.

monstrueusement [mɔ̃stryøzmɑ̃] *adv* [gros, laid] monstrously ; [intelligent] prodigiously.

monstrueux, euse [mɔ̃stryø, øz] *adj* **- 1.** [gén] monstrous **- 2.** *fig* [erreur] terrible.

monstruosité [mɔ̃stryozite] *nf* monstrosity.

mont [mɔ̃] *nm* **- 1.** *littéraire* [montagne] mountain ; **par ~s et par vaux** *fig* up hill and down dale ; **promettre ~s et merveilles** to promise the earth **- 2.** *GÉOGR* Mount ; **le ~ Blanc** Mont Blanc ; **le ~ Cervin** the Matterhorn **- 3.** *ANAT* : **~ de Vénus** mons veneris.

montage [mɔ̃taʒ] *nm* **- 1.** [assemblage] assembly ; [de bijou] setting **- 2.** *PHOT* photomontage **- 3.** *CIN* editing **- 4.** *ÉLECTR* wiring.

montagnard, e [mɔ̃taɲar, ard] <> *adj* mountain *(avant n)* <> *nm, f* mountain dweller.

montagne [mɔ̃taɲ] *nf* **- 1.** [gén] mountain ; **les ~s Rocheuses** the Rocky Mountains **- 2.** [région] : **la ~** the mountains *(pl)* ; **à la ~** in the mountains ; **en haute ~** at high altitudes ; **faire de la haute ~** to go mountain climbing **- 3.** *loc* : **se faire une ~ de qqch** to make a great song and dance about sthg.

➡ **montagnes russes** *nfpl* big dipper *(sg)*, roller coaster *(sg)*.

montagneux, euse [mɔ̃taɲø, øz] *adj* mountainous.

montant, e [mɔ̃tɑ̃, ɑ̃t] *adj* **- 1.** [mouvement] rising **- 2.** [vêtement] high-necked.

➡ **montant** *nm* **- 1.** [pièce verticale] upright **- 2.** [somme] total (amount).

mont-blanc [mɔ̃blɑ̃] (*pl* **monts-blancs**) *nm* *pureed chestnuts with whipped cream.*

mont-de-piété [mɔ̃dpjete] (*pl* **monts-de-piété**) *nm* pawnshop.

monté, e [mɔ̃te] *adj* : **être ~ en qqch** to be well off for sthg.

monte-charge [mɔ̃tʃarʒ] *nm inv* goods lift *Br*, service elevator *Am*.

montée [mɔ̃te] *nf* **- 1.** [de montagne] climb, ascent **- 2.** [de prix] rise **- 3.** [relief] slope, gradient.

Monténégro [mɔ̃tenegro] *nm* : **le ~** Montenegro.

monte-plats [mɔ̃tpla] *nm inv* dumbwaiter.

monter [3] [mɔ̃te] <> *vi (aux : être)* **- 1.** [personne] to come/go up ; [température, niveau] to rise ; [route, avion] to climb ; **~ sur qqch** to climb onto sthg **- 2.** [passager] to get on ; **~ dans un bus** to get on a bus ; **~ dans une voiture** to get into a car **- 3.** [cavalier] to ride ; **~ à cheval** to ride ; **~ à cheval sur qqch** *fig* to straddle sthg **- 4.** [marée] to go/come in <> *vt (aux : avoir)* **- 1.** [escalier, côte] to climb, to come/go up ; **~ la rue en courant** to run up the street **- 2.** [chauffage, son] to turn up **- 3.** [valise] to take/bring up **- 4.** [meuble] to assemble ; *COUTURE* to assemble, to put *ou* sew together ; [tente] to put up **- 5.** *CIN* to edit, to cut (together) **- 6.** [cheval] to mount **- 7.** [dispositif] to assemble **- 8.** *THÉÂTRE* to put on **- 9.** [société, club] to set up **- 10.** *CULIN* to beat, to whisk (up) **- 11.** *loc* : **~ qqn contre qqn** to set sb against sb.

➡ **se monter** *vp* **- 1.** [s'assembler] : **se ~ facilement** to be easy to assemble **- 2.** [atteindre] : **se ~ à** to amount to, to add up to.

monteur, euse [mɔ̃tœr, øz] *nm, f* **- 1.** *TECHNOL* fitter **- 2.** *CIN* editor.

Montevideo [mɔ̃tevideo] *n* Montevideo.

monticule [mɔ̃tikyl] *nm* mound ; *Can BASE-BALL* pitcher's mound.

montre [mɔ̃tr] *nf* watch ; **~ à quartz** quartz watch ; **~ en main** to the minute, exactly ; **contre la ~** [sport] time-trialling ; [épreuve] time trial ; **une course contre la ~** *fig* a race against time.

Montréal [mɔ̃real] *n* Montreal.

montre-bracelet [mɔ̃trəbrasle] (*pl* **montres-bracelets**) *nf* wristwatch.

montrer [3] [mɔ̃tre] *vt* **- 1.** [gén] to show ; **~ qqch à qqn** to show sb sthg, to show sthg to sb **- 2.** [désigner] to show, to point out ; **~ qqch du doigt** to point at *ou* to sthg.

➡ **se montrer** *vp* **- 1.** [se faire voir] to appear **- 2.** *fig* [se présenter] to show o.s. **- 3.** *fig* [se révéler] to prove (to be).

montreur, euse [mɔ̃trœr, øz] *nm, f* : **~ de marionnettes** puppeteer.

monture [mɔ̃tyr] *nf* **- 1.** [animal] mount **- 2.** [de lunettes] frame **- 3.** [de bijou] setting.

monument [mɔnymɑ̃] *nm* **- 1.** [gén] : **~ (à)** monument (to) ; **~ aux morts** war memorial **- 2.** *fig* & *hum* [chef-d'œuvre] masterpiece.

monumental, e, aux [mɔnymɑ̃tal, o] *adj* monumental.

moquer [3] [mɔke] ➡ **se moquer** *vp* : se ~ **de** [plaisanter sur] to make fun of, to laugh at ; [ne pas se soucier de] not to give a damn about ; **ne vous moquez pas!** don't mock!, don't laugh!

moquerie [mɔkri] *nf* mockery *(U)*, jibe.

moquette [mɔkɛt] *nf* (fitted) carpet.

moqueur, euse [mɔkœr, øz] <> *adj* mocking <> *nm, f* mocker.

moraine [mɔrɛn] *nf* moraine.

moral, e, aux [mɔral, o] *adj* moral.
➡ **moral** *nm* - **1.** [mental] : **au ~ comme au physique** mentally as well as physically - **2.** [état d'esprit] morale, spirits *(pl)* ; **avoir/ne pas avoir le ~** to be in good/bad spirits ; **remonter le ~ à qqn** to cheer sb up ; **se remonter le ~** to cheer (o.s.) up.
➡ **morale** *nf* - **1.** [science] moral philosophy, morals *(pl)* - **2.** [règle] morality - **3.** [mœurs] morals *(pl)* - **4.** [leçon] moral ; **faire la ~e à qqn** to preach at *ou* lecture sb.

moralement [mɔralmɑ̃] *adv* morally.

moralisateur, trice [mɔralizatœr, tris] <> *adj* moralizing <> *nm, f* moralizer.

moralisme [mɔralism] *nm* morality.

moraliste [mɔralist] <> *nmf* moralist <> *adj* moralistic.

moralité [mɔralite] *nf* - **1.** [gén] morality - **2.** [enseignement] morals.

moratoire [mɔratwar] *nm* moratorium.

morbide [mɔrbid] *adj* morbid.

morbidité [mɔrbidite] *nf* morbidity.

morceau, x [mɔrso] *nm* - **1.** [gén] piece ; **manger un ~ fam** to have a bite to eat ; **mettre en ~x** to pull *ou* tear to pieces ; **cracher le ~ fam fig** to spill the beans ; **emporter le ~ fam** to carry it off - **2.** [de poème, de film] passage ; **un ~ de bravoure** a purple passage.

morceler [24] [mɔrsəle] *vt* to break up, to split up.
➡ **se morceler** *vp* to break up.

morcellement [mɔrsɛlmɑ̃] *nm* breaking up, splitting up.

mordant, e [mɔrdɑ̃, ɑ̃t] *adj* biting.
➡ **mordant** *nm* [vivacité] keenness, bite.

mordicus [mɔrdikys] *adv fam* stubbornly, stoutly.

mordiller [3] [mɔrdije] *vt* to nibble.

mordoré, e [mɔrdɔre] *adj* bronze.

mordre [76] [mɔrdr] <> *vt* - **1.** [blesser] to bite - **2.** [dépasser] to go over - **3.** *fig* [entamer, ronger] to eat into *ou* away <> *vi* - **1.** [saisir avec les dents] : ~ **à** to bite - **2.** [croquer] : ~ **dans qqch** to

bite into sthg - **3.** *SPORT* : ~ **sur la ligne** to step over the line.

mordu, e [mɔrdy] <> *pp* ▷ **mordre** <> *adj* [amoureux] hooked <> *nm, f* : ~ **de foot/ski** *etc* football/ski *etc* addict.

more = maure.

moresque = mauresque.

morfondre [75] [mɔrfɔ̃dr] ➡ **se morfondre** *vp* to mope.

morgue [mɔrg] *nf* - **1.** [attitude] pride - **2.** [lieu] morgue.

moribond, e [mɔribɔ̃, ɔ̃d] <> *adj* dying <> *nm, f* dying person.

morigéner [18] [mɔriʒene] *vt littéraire* to rebuke.

morille [mɔrij] *nf* morel.

mormon, e [mɔrmɔ̃, ɔn] *adj* & *nm, f* Mormon.

morne [mɔrn] *adj* [personne, visage] gloomy ; [paysage, temps, ville] dismal, dreary.

Moroni [mɔrɔni] *n* Moroni.

morose [mɔroz] *adj* gloomy.

morosité [mɔrozite] *nf* gloominess.

morphine [mɔrfin] *nf* morphine.

morphologie [mɔrfɔlɔʒi] *nf* morphology.

morphologique [mɔrfɔlɔʒik] *adj* morphological.

morpion [mɔrpjɔ̃] *nm* - **1.** *fam MÉD* crab - **2.** *fam* [enfant] brat - **3.** [jeu] ≃ noughts and crosses *Br*, ≃ tick-tack-toe *Am*.

mors [mɔr] *nm* bit ; **prendre le ~ aux dents** to get the bit between one's teeth.

morse [mɔrs] *nm* - **1.** *ZOOL* walrus - **2.** [code] Morse (code).

morsure [mɔrsyr] *nf* bite.

mort, e [mɔr, mɔrt] <> *pp* ▷ **mourir** <> *adj* dead ; **raide ~** stone dead ; ~ **ou vif** dead or alive ; ~ **de fatigue** *fig* dead tired ; ~ **de peur** *fig* frightened to death <> *nm, f* - **1.** [cadavre] corpse, dead body - **2.** [défunt] dead person.
➡ **mort** <> *nm* - **1.** [victime] fatality - **2.** *CARTES* dummy <> *nf litt* & *fig* death ; **de ~** [silence] deathly ; **condamner qqn à ~** *JUR* to sentence sb to death ; **se donner la ~** to take one's own life, to commit suicide ; **jusqu'à ce que** ~ **s'ensuive** to death ; **en vouloir à ~ à qqn** to hate sb's guts ; ~ **naturelle/violente** natural/ violent death ; **la ~ dans l'âme** sick at heart, with a heavy heart ; **pâle comme la ~** deathly pale.

mortadelle [mɔrtadɛl] *nf* mortadella.

mortalité [mɔrtalite] *nf* mortality, death rate ; ~ **infantile** infant mortality.

mort-aux-rats [mɔrorɑ] *nf inv* rat poison.

Morte ▷ mer.

mortel, elle [mɔrtɛl] ⬦ *adj* - **1.** [humain] mortal - **2.** [accident, maladie] fatal - **3.** *fig* [ennuyeux] deadly (dull) ⬦ *nm, f* mortal.

mortellement [mɔrtɛlmɑ̃] *adv* - **1.** [à mort] fatally - **2.** [extrêmement] mortally, deeply ; **s'ennuyer ~** to be bored to death.

morte-saison [mɔrtsɛzɔ̃] (*pl* **mortes-saisons**) *nf* slack season, off-season.

mortier [mɔrtje] *nm* mortar.

mortification [mɔrtifikasjɔ̃] *nf* mortification.

mortIfier [9] [mɔrtifje] *vt* to mortify.

mort-né, e [mɔrne] (*mpl* **mort-nés,** *fpl* **mort-nées**) ⬦ *adj* [enfant] still-born ; *fig* [projet] abortive ⬦ *nm, f* still-born child.

mortuaire [mɔrtɥɛr] *adj* funeral *(avant n)*.

morue [mɔry] *nf* - **1.** *ZOOL* cod - **2.** *injurieux* [prostituée] whore.

morve [mɔrv] *nf* snot.

morveux, euse [mɔrvø, øz] ⬦ *adj* runnynosed, snotty ⬦ *nm, f* *fam* brat.

mosaïque [mɔzaik] *nf litt* & *fig* mosaic.

Moscou [mɔsku] *n* Moscow.

moscovite [mɔskɔvit] *adj* of/from Moscow.
➤ **Moscovite** *nmf* Muscovite.

mosquée [mɔske] *nf* mosque.

mot [mo] *nm* - **1.** [gén] word ; **avoir toujours le ~ pour rire** to be always able to raise a laugh ; **au bas ~** at the lowest estimate ; **à ~s couverts** in veiled terms ; **le fin ~ de l'histoire** the real story ; **~ d'esprit** witty remark ; **~ d'excuse** *SCOL* note from one's parents ; **gros ~** swearword ; **~s croisés** crossword (puzzle) *(sg)* ; **à ~,** ~ **pour ~** word for word ; **en un ~** in a word ; **avoir son ~ à dire** to have one's say ; **avoir des ~s avec qqn** to have words with sb ; **avoir le dernier ~** to have the last word ; **avoir deux ~s à dire à qqn** *fam* to give sb a piece of one's mind ; **ne pas mâcher ses ~s** not to mince one's words ; **prendre qqn au ~** to take sb at his/her word ; **en toucher un ~ à qqn** *fam* to have a word with sb - **2.** [message] note, message.

motard [mɔtar] *nm* - **1.** [motocycliste] motorcyclist - **2.** [policier] motorcycle policeman.

motel [mɔtɛl] *nm* motel.

moteur, trice [mɔtœr, tris] *adj* - **1.** [force, énergie] driving *(avant n)* ; **à quatre roues motrices** *AUTOM* with four-wheel drive - **2.** [muscles, nerfs] motor *(avant n)*.
➤ **moteur** *nm* *TECHNOL* motor, engine ; *fig* driving force ; **~ électrique** electric motor ; **~ à explosion** combustion engine ; **~ à injection** fuel-injection engine ; **~ à réaction** jet

engine ; **~ de recherche** *INFORM* search engine.
➤ **motrice** *nf* *RAIL* motor coach *Br*, motor car *Am*.

motif [mɔtif] *nm* - **1.** [raison] motive, grounds *(pl)* - **2.** [dessin, impression] motif.

motion [mɔsjɔ̃] *nf* *POLIT* motion ; **~ de censure** motion of censure.

motivant, e [mɔtivɑ̃, ɑ̃t] *adj* motivating.

motivation [mɔtivasjɔ̃] *nf* motivation.

motiver [3] [mɔtive] *vt* - **1.** [stimuler] to motivate - **2.** [justifier] to justify.

moto [mɔto] *nf* motorbike.

motocross [mɔtokrɔs] *nm* motocross.

motoculteur [mɔtokyltœr] *nm* ≃ Rotavator®.

motocyclette [mɔtosiklɛt] *nf* motorcycle, motorbike.

motocyclisme [mɔtosiklism] *nm* motorcyle racing.

motocycliste [mɔtosiklist] *nmf* motorcyclist.

motomarine [mɔtomarin] *nf* *Can* jet ski, aquaskooter *Am*.

motoneige [mɔtonɛʒ] *nf* *Can* snowmobile.

motorisé, e [mɔtorize] *adj* motorized ; **être ~** *fam* to have a car, to have wheels.

motrice ⬦ **moteur.**

motricité [mɔtrisite] *nf* motor functions *(pl)*.

motte [mɔt] *nf* : **~ (de terre)** clod, lump of earth ; **~ de beurre** slab of butter.

motus [mɔtys] *interj* not a word! ; **~ et bouche cousue!** mum's the word!

mou, molle [mu, mɔl] *adj* (**mol** *devant voyelle ou h muet*) - **1.** [gén] soft - **2.** [faible] weak - **3.** [résistance, protestation] half-hearted - **4.** *fam* [de caractère] wet, wimpy.
➤ **mou** *nm* - **1.** *fam* [personne] wimp - **2.** [de corde] : **avoir du ~** to be slack - **3.** [abats] lungs *(pl)*, lights *(pl)*.

mouchard, e [muʃar, ard] *nm, f* *fam* [personne] sneak.
➤ **mouchard** *nm* *fam* [dans camion, train] spy in the cab.

moucharder [3] [muʃarde] *vi* *fam* to sneak.

mouche [muʃ] *nf* - **1.** *ZOOL* fly ; **~ tsé-tsé** tsetse fly ; **fine ~** *fig* shrewd individual - **2.** [accessoire féminin] beauty spot - **3.** *loc* : **faire ~** to hit the bull's eye.

moucher [3] [muʃe] *vt* - **1.** [nez] to wipe ; **~ un enfant** to wipe a child's nose - **2.** [chandelle] to snuff out - **3.** *fam fig* [personne] : **~ qqn** to put sb in his/her place.
➤ **se moucher** *vp* to blow *ou* wipe one's nose.

moucheron [muʃrɔ̃] *nm* [insecte] gnat.

moucheté, e [muʃte] *adj* - **1.** [laine] flecked - **2.** [animal] spotted, speckled.

mouchoir [muʃwar] *nm* handkerchief ; **~ en papier** paper handkerchief, tissue ; **grand comme un ~ de poche** *fig* no bigger than a pocket handkerchief.

moudre [85] [mudr] *vt* to grind.

mouds ▷ **moudre**.

moue [mu] *nf* pout ; **faire la ~** to pull a face.

mouette [mwɛt] *nf* seagull.

moufle [mufl] *nf* mitten.

mouflet, ette [muflɛ, ɛt] *nm, f fam* kid, brat.

mouflon [muflɔ̃] *nm* wild sheep.

mouillage [muja3] *nm* - **1.** [coupage] watering (down) - **2.** [NAVIG - emplacement] anchorage, moorings *(pl)* ; [- manœuvre] anchoring, mooring.

mouillé, e [muje] *adj* wet.

mouiller [3] [muje] ◇ *vt* - **1.** [personne, objet] to wet ; **se mouiller ~** to get wet *ou* soaked - **2.** [vin, lait] to water down ; CULIN to add liquid to - **3.** NAVIG : **~ l'ancre** to drop anchor - **4.** LING to palatalize - **5.** *fam fig* [compromettre] to involve ◇ *vi* NAVIG to anchor.

◆ **se mouiller** *vp* - **1.** [se tremper] to get wet - **2.** *fam fig* [prendre des risques] to stick one's neck out.

mouillette [mujɛt] *nf* finger of bread, soldier.

mouise [mwiz] *nf* : **être dans la ~** *fam* to be broke.

moulage [mula3] *nm* - **1.** [action] moulding *Br*, molding *Am*, casting - **2.** [objet] cast.

moulant, e [mulɑ̃, ɑ̃t] *adj* close-fitting.

moule [mul] ◇ *nm* mould *Br*, mold *Am* ; **~ à gâteau** cake tin *Br ou* pan *Am* ; **~ à gaufre** waffle-iron ; **~ à tarte** flan dish ◇ *nf* ZOOL mussel ; **~s marinières** CULIN mussels cooked in white wine.

mouler [3] [mule] *vt* - **1.** [objet] to mould *Br*, to mold *Am* - **2.** [forme] to make a cast of - **3.** [corps] to hug.

moulin [mulɛ̃] *nm* mill ; **~ à café** coffee mill ; **~ à eau** watermill ; **~ à paroles** *fig* chatterbox ; **~ à poivre** peppermill ; **~ à scie** *Can* sawmill ; **~ à vent** windmill.

mouliner [3] [muline] *vt* [aliments] to put through a food mill.

moulinet [mulinɛ] *nm* - **1.** PÊCHE reel - **2.** [mouvement] : **faire des ~s** to whirl one's arms around.

Moulinette® [mulinɛt] *nf* food mill ; **passer qqn à la ~** *fam fig* to tear sb to pieces.

moult [mult] *adv vieilli* many.

moulu, e [muly] *adj* - **1.** [en poudre] ground - **2.** *fig* [brisé] : **être ~ (de fatigue)** to be worn out.

moulure [mulyr] *nf* moulding.

mourais, mourions *etc* ▷ **mourir**.

mourant, e [murɑ̃, ɑ̃t] ◇ *adj* - **1.** [moribond] dying - **2.** *fig* [voix] faint ◇ *nm, f* dying person.

mourir [42] [murir] *vi* - **1.** [personne] to die ; **~ de froid/soif** *fig* to be dying of cold/thirst ; **s'ennuyer à ~** to be bored to death ; **c'est à ~ de rire** it's a scream - **2.** [civilisation] to die out - **3.** [feu] to die down.

mouroir [murwar] *nm péj* old dears' home.

mouron [murɔ̃] *nm* BOT pimpernel ; **se faire du ~** *fam fig* to worry o.s. sick.

mourrai, mourras *etc* ▷ **mourir**.

mousquetaire [muskətɛr] *nm* musketeer.

moussant, e [musɑ̃, ɑ̃t] *adj* foaming.

mousse [mus] ◇ *nf* - **1.** BOT moss - **2.** [substance] foam ; **~ carbonique** foam *(for extinguishing fires)* ; **~ à raser** shaving foam - **3.** CULIN mousse ; **~ au chocolat** chocolate mousse - **4.** [matière plastique] foam rubber ◇ *nm* NAVIG cabin boy.

mousseline [muslin] ◇ *nf* muslin ◇ *adj inv* lightened with cream or milk.

mousser [3] [muse] *vi* to foam, to lather ; **se faire ~** *fam fig* to blow one's own trumpet.

mousseux, euse [musø, øz] *adj* - **1.** [shampooing] foaming, frothy - **2.** [vin, cidre] sparkling.

◆ **mousseux** *nm* sparkling wine.

mousson [musɔ̃] *nf* monsoon.

moussu, e [musy] *adj* mossy, moss-covered.

moustache [mustaʃ] *nf* moustache *Br*, mustache *Am*.

◆ **moustaches** *nfpl* [d'animal] whiskers.

moustachu, e [mustaʃy] *adj* with a moustache *Br ou* mustache *Am*.

◆ **moustachu** *nm* man with a moustache.

moustiquaire [mustikɛr] *nf* mosquito net.

moustique [mustik] *nm* mosquito.

moutard [mutar] *nm fam* kid.

moutarde [mutard] ◇ *nf* mustard ; **la ~ me monte au nez** *fig* I'm losing my temper ◇ *adj inv* mustard *(avant n)*.

mouton [mutɔ̃] *nm* - **1.** ZOOL & *fig* sheep - **2.** [viande] mutton - **3.** *fam* [poussière] piece of fluff, fluff (U) - **4.** *loc* : **revenons à nos ~s** let's get back to the subject in hand.

◆ **moutons** *nmpl* [vagues] white horses.

mouture [mutyr] *nf* - **1.** [de céréales, de café] grinding - **2.** [de thème, d'œuvre] rehash.

mouvance [muvɑ̃s] *nf* [domaine] sphere of influence.

mouvant, e [muvɑ̃, ɑ̃t] *adj* - **1.** [terrain] unstable - **2.** [situation] uncertain.

mouvement [muvmɑ̃] *nm* - **1.** [gén] movement ; **en ~** on the move ; **faux ~** clumsy *ou* awkward movement ; **~ alternatif** TECHNOL reciprocating movement - **2.** [de colère, d'indignation] burst, fit ; **~ d'humeur** fit of bad temper.

mouvementé, e [muvmɑ̃te] *adj* - **1.** [terrain] rough - **2.** [réunion, soirée] eventful.

mouvoir [54] [muvwar] *vt* to move.
➤ **se mouvoir** *vp* to move.

moyen, enne [mwajɛ̃, ɛn] *adj* - **1.** [intermédiaire] medium - **2.** [médiocre, courant] average.
➤ **moyen** *nm* means *(sg)*, way ; **par tous les ~s** by any means possible ; **y a-t-il ~ de ...?** is there any way of ...? ; **~ de communication** means of communication ; **~ d'expression** means of expression ; **~ de locomotion** *ou* **transport** means of transport ; **employer les grands ~s** to resort to extreme measures.
➤ **moyenne** *nf* average ; **en moyenne** on average ; **la moyenne** SCOL the passmark ; **la moyenne d'âge** the average age.
➤ **moyens** *nmpl* - **1.** [ressources] means ; **avoir les ~s** to be comfortably off ; **avoir les ~s de faire qqch** to have the means to do sthg ; **avec les ~s du bord** with the means at one's disposal - **2.** [capacités] powers, ability ; **faire qqch par ses propres ~s** to do sthg on one's own ; **perdre tous ses ~s** to panic.
➤ **au moyen de** *loc prép* by means of.

Moyen Âge [mwajɛnaʒ] *nm* : **le ~** the Middle Ages *(pl)*.

moyenâgeux, euse [mwajɛnaʒø, øz] *adj* medieval.

moyen-courrier [mwajɛ̃kurje] *(pl* **moyens-courriers)** ◇ *nm* medium-haul aircraft ◇ *adj* medium-haul *(avant n)*.

moyennant [mwajɛnɑ̃] *prép* for, in return for.

moyennement [mwajɛnmɑ̃] *adv* moderately, fairly.

Moyen-Orient [mwajɛnɔrjɑ̃] *nm* : **le ~** the Middle East ; **au ~** in the Middle East.

moyen-oriental, e [mwayɛnɔrjɑ̃tal] *adj* Middle Eastern.

moyeu, x [mwajø] *nm* hub.

mozambicain, e [mɔzɑ̃bikɛ̃, ɛn] *adj* Mozambican.
➤ **Mozambicain, e** *nm, f* Mozambican.

Mozambique [mɔzɑ̃bik] *nm* : **le ~** Mozambique ; **au ~** in Mozambique.

MRAP [mrap] *(abr de* **Mouvement contre le racisme, l'antisémitisme et pour la paix)** *nm pacifist anti-racist organization.*

MRG *(abr de* **Mouvement des radicaux de gauche)** *nm centre-left political party.*

ms *(abr de* **manuscrit)** ms.

MSF *(abr de* **Médecins sans frontières)** *nmpl medical association for aid to third-world countries.*

MST *nf* - **1.** *(abr de* **maladie sexuellement transmissible)** STD - **2.** *(abr de* **maîtrise de sciences et techniques)** *masters degree in science and technology.*

MT *(abr de* **moyenne tension)** MT.

mû, mue [my] *pp* ➣ **mouvoir**.

mucosité [mykozite] *nf* mucus *(U)*.

mucus [mykys] *nm* mucus *(U)*.

mue [my] *nf* - **1.** [de pelage] moulting - **2.** [de serpent] skin, slough - **3.** [de voix] breaking.

muer [7] [mɥe] *vi* - **1.** [mammifère] to moult - **2.** [serpent] to slough its skin - **3.** [voix] to break ; [jeune homme] : **il mue** his voice is breaking.
➤ **se muer** *vp littéraire* : **se ~ en** to turn into.

muesli [mysli] *nm* muesli.

muet, muette [mɥɛ, ɛt] ◇ *adj* - **1.** MÉD dumb - **2.** [silencieux] silent ; **~ d'admiration/d'étonnement** speechless with admiration/surprise - **3.** LING silent, mute ◇ *nm, f* mute, dumb person.
➤ **muet** *nm* : **le ~** CIN silent films *(pl)*.

muezzin [mɥɛdzin] *nm* muezzin.

mufle [myfl] *nm* - **1.** [d'animal] muzzle, snout - **2.** *fig* [goujat] lout.

muflerie [myfləri] *nf* loutishness.

mufti, muphti [myfti] *nm* mufti.

mugir [32] [myʒir] *vi* - **1.** [vache] to moo - **2.** [vent, sirène] to howl.

mugissement [myʒismɑ̃] *nm* - **1.** [de vache] mooing - **2.** [de vent, sirène] howling.

muguet [mygɛ] *nm* - **1.** [fleur] lily of the valley - **2.** MÉD thrush.

MUGUET

On May Day in France, bunches of lily of the valley are sold in the streets and given as presents. The flowers are supposed to bring good luck.

---

mulâtre, mulâtresse [mylatr, trɛs] *nm, f* mulatto.
➤ **mulâtre** *adj* mulatto.

mule [myl] *nf* mule.

mulet [mylɛ] *nm* - **1.** [âne] mule - **2.** [poisson] mullet.

muletier, ère [myltje, ɛr] *adj* mule *(avant n)*.

muletier *nm* muleteer.

mulot [mylo] *nm* field mouse.

multicolore [myltikɔlɔr] *adj* multicoloured.

multiculturel, elle [myltikyltyrɛl] *adj* multicultural.

multifonction [myltifɔ̃ksjɔ̃] *adj inv* multifunction.

multiforme [myltifɔrm] *adj* multiform.

multilatéral, e, aux [myltilateral, o] *adj* multilateral.

multi-media [myltimedja] *adj* INFORM multimedia.

multimillionnaire [myltimiljɔnɛr] *nmf* & *adj* multimillionaire.

multinational, e, aux [myltinasjɔnal, o] *adj* multinational.

multinationale *nf* multinational (company).

multiple [myltipl] ◇ *nm* multiple ◇ *adj* - **1.** [nombreux] multiple, numerous - **2.** [divers] many, various.

multiplication [myltiplikasjɔ̃] *nf* multiplication.

multiplicité [myltiplisite] *nf* multiplicity.

multiplier [10] [myltiplije] *vt* - **1.** [accroître] to increase - **2.** MATHS to multiply ; **X multiplié par Y égale Z** X multiplied by *ou* times Y equals Z.

se multiplier *vp* to multiply.

multipropriété [myltiprɔprijete] *nf* timeshare.

multiracial, e, aux [myltirasjal, o] *adj* multiracial.

multirisque [myltirisk] *adj* comprehensive.

multitude [myltityd] *nf* : **~ (de)** multitude (of).

municipal, e, aux [mynisipal, o] *adj* municipal.

municipales *nfpl* : **les ~es** the local government elections.

municipalité [mynisipalite] *nf* - **1.** [commune] municipality - **2.** [conseil] town council.

munir [32] [mynir] *vt* : **~ qqn/qqch de** to equip sb/sthg with.

se munir *vp* : **se ~ de** to equip o.s. with.

munitions [mynisjɔ̃] *nfpl* ammunition (U), munitions.

munster [mœ̃stɛr] *nm* strong semi-hard cheese.

muphti = mufti.

muqueuse [mykøz] *nf* mucous membrane.

mur [myr] *nm* - **1.** [gén] wall ; **~ antibruit** soundproof wall ; **~ mitoyen** party wall ; **raser les ~s** to hug the walls ; *fig* to tread warily - **2.** *fig* [obstacle] barrier, brick wall ; **~ du son** AÉRON sound barrier.

mûr, mûre [myr] *adj* ripe ; [personne] mature ; **après ~e réflexion** *fig* after careful consideration.

mûre *nf* - **1.** [de mûrier] mulberry - **2.** [de ronce] blackberry, bramble.

muraille [myraj] *nf* wall.

mural, e, aux [myral, o] *adj* wall (avant n).

mûrement [myrmɑ̃] *adv* : **après avoir ~ réfléchi** after careful consideration.

murène [myrɛn] *nf* moray eel.

murer [3] [myre] *vt* - **1.** [boucher] to wall up, to block up - **2.** [enfermer] to wall in.

se murer *vp* to shut o.s. up *ou* away ; **se ~ dans** *fig* to retreat into.

muret [myrɛ] *nm* low wall.

mûrier [myrje] *nm* - **1.** [arbre] mulberry tree - **2.** [ronce] blackberry bush, bramble bush.

mûrir [32] [myrir] *vi* - **1.** [fruits, légumes] to ripen - **2.** *fig* [idée, projet] to develop - **3.** [personne] to mature.

murmure [myrmyr] *nm* murmur.

murmurer [3] [myrmyre] *vt* & *vi* to murmur.

musaraigne [myzarɛɲ] *nf* shrew.

musarder [3] [myzarde] *vi fam* to dawdle.

musc [mysk] *nm* musk.

muscade [myskad] *nf* nutmeg.

muscadet [myskadɛ] *nm* dry white wine.

muscat [myska] *nm* - **1.** [raisin] muscat grape - **2.** [vin] sweet wine.

muscle [myskl] *nm* muscle ; **~ extenseur** extensor muscle.

musclé, e [myskle] *adj* - **1.** [personne] muscular - **2.** *fig* [mesure, décision] forceful.

muscler [3] [myskle] *vt* : **son corps** to build up one's muscles.

se muscler *vp* to build up one's muscles.

musculaire [myskylɛr] *adj* muscular.

musculation [myskylasjɔ̃] *nf* : **faire de la ~** to do muscle-building exercises.

musculature [myskylatyr] *nf* musculature.

muse [myz] *nf* muse.

museau [myzo] *nm* - **1.** [d'animal] muzzle, snout - **2.** *fam* [de personne] face.

musée [myze] *nm* museum ; [d'art] art gallery.

museler [24] [myzle] *vt litt* & *fig* to muzzle.

muselière [myzəljɛr] *nf* muzzle.

musette [myzɛt] ◇ *nf* haversack ; [d'écolier] satchel ◇ *nm* : **le ~** dance music played on the accordion.

muséum [myzeɔm] *nm* museum.

musical, e, aux [myzikal, o] *adj* - **1.** [son] musical - **2.** [émission, critique] music *(avant n)*.

music-hall [myzikol] *(pl* music-halls*)* *nm* music-hall.

musicien, enne [myzisjɛ̃, ɛn] <> *adj* musical <> *nm, f* musician.

musicographie [myzikɔgrafi] *nf* musicography.

musicologue [myzikɔlɔg] *nmf* musicologist.

musique [myzik] *nf* music ; ~ **de chambre** chamber music ; ~ **de film** film *Br* OU movie *Am* score ; **connaître la** ~ *tam fig* to know the score.

musqué, e [myske] *adj* - **1.** [parfum] musky - **2.** [animal] : **rat** ~ muskrat.

must [mœst] *nm fam* must.

musulman, e [myzylmɑ̃, an] *adj* & *nm, f* Muslim.

mutant, e [mytɑ̃, ɑ̃t] *adj* & *nm, f* mutant.

mutation [mytasjɔ̃] *nf* - **1.** BIOL mutation - **2.** *fig* [changement] transformation ; **en pleine** ~ undergoing a (complete) transformation - **3.** [de fonctionnaire] transfer.

muter [3] [myte] *vt* to transfer.

mutilation [mytilasjɔ̃] *nf* mutilation.

mutilé, e [mytile] *nm, f* disabled person.

mutiler [3] [mytile] *vt* to mutilate ; **il a été mutilé du bras droit** he lost his right arm.

mutin, e [mytɛ̃, in] *adj littéraire* impish.

  ➡ **mutin** *nm* rebel ; MIL & NAVIG mutineer.

mutiner [3] [mytine] ➡ **se mutiner** *vp* to rebel ; MIL & NAVIG to mutiny.

mutinerie [mytinri] *nf* rebellion ; MIL & NAVIG mutiny.

mutisme [mytism] *nm* silence.

mutualiste [mytɥalist] <> *nmf* mutualist <> *adj* : **société** ~ mutual insurance company.

mutualité [mytɥalite] *nf* [assurance] mutual insurance.

mutuel, elle [mytɥɛl] *adj* mutual.

  ➡ **mutuelle** *nf* mutual insurance company.

mutuellement [mytɥɛlmɑ̃] *adv* mutually.

mycose [mikoz] *nf* mycosis, fungal infection.

myocarde [mjɔkard] *nm* myocardium.

myopathie [mjɔpati] *nf* myopathy.

myope [mjɔp] <> *nmf* shortsighted person <> *adj* shortsighted, myopic.

myopie [mjɔpi] *nf* shortsightedness, myopia.

myosotis [mjozɔtis] *nm* forget-me-not.

myriade [mirjad] *nf* : **une** ~ **de** a myriad of.

myrtille [mirtij] *nf* bilberry *Br*, blueberry *Am*.

mystère [mistɛr] *nm* - **1.** [gén] mystery - **2.** *CULIN* ice cream covered in meringue and flaked almonds.

mystérieusement [misterjøzmɑ̃] *adv* mysteriously.

mystérieux, euse [misterjø, øz] *adj* mysterious.

mysticisme [mistisism] *nm* mysticism.

mystification [mistifikasjɔ̃] *nf* [tromperie] hoax, practical joke.

mystifier [9] [mistifje] *vt* [duper] to take in.

mystique [mistik] <> *nmf* mystic <> *adj* mystic, mystical.

mythe [mit] *nm* myth.

mythifier [9] [mitifje] *vt* to mythicize.

mythique [mitik] *adj* mythical.

mytho [mito] *adj fam* : **il est complètement** ~ you can't believe anything he says.

mythologie [mitɔlɔʒi] *nf* mythology.

mythologique [mitɔlɔʒik] *adj* mythological.

mythomane [mitɔman] *nmf* pathological liar.

n, N [ɛn] *nm inv* [lettre] n, N.

  ➡ **N** - **1.** (*abr de* **newton**) N - **2.** (*abr de* **nord**) N.

n' ▷ ne.

n° (*abr de* **numéro**) no.

nabot, e [nabo, ɔt] *nm, f péj* midget.

nac (*abr de* **nouvel animal de compagnie**) [nak] *nm wild animal kept as a pet.*

nacelle [nasɛl] *nf* [de montgolfière] basket.

nacre [nakr] *nf* mother-of-pearl.

nacré, e [nakre] *adj* pearly.

nage [naʒ] *nf* - **1.** [natation] swimming ; ~ **indienne** side stroke ; ~ **papillon** butterfly (stroke) ; **à la ~** CULIN *poached in wine and herbs* ; **traverser à la ~** to swim across **- 2.** *loc* : **en ~** bathed in sweat.

nageoire [naʒwar] *nf* fin.

nager [17] [naʒe] ◇ *vi* **- 1.** [se baigner] to swim **- 2.** [flotter] to float **- 3.** *fig* [dans vêtement] : **~ dans** to be lost in ; **~ dans la joie** to be incredibly happy ◇ *vt* to swim.

nageur, euse [naʒœr, øz] *nm, f* swimmer.

naguère [nagɛr] *adv littéraire* a short time ago.

naïade [najad] *nf* water nymph.

naïf, naïve [naif, iv] ◇ *adj* **- 1.** [ingénu, art] naive **- 2.** *péj* [crédule] gullible ◇ *nm, f* **- 1.** *péj* [niais] fool **- 2.** [peintre] naive painter.

nain, e [nɛ̃, nɛn] ◇ *adj* dwarf *(avant n)* ◇ *nm, f* dwarf.

Nairobi [nɛrɔbi] *n* Nairobi.

naissais, naissions *etc* ▷ **naître.**

naissance [nɛsɑ̃s] *nf* **- 1.** [de personne] birth ; **donner ~ à** to give birth to ; **de ~** [aveugle] from birth ; **le contrôle des ~s** birth control **- 2.** [endroit] source ; [du cou] nape **- 3.** *fig* [de science, nation] birth ; **donner ~ à** to give rise to ; **prendre ~ dans** to originate in.

naissant, e [nɛsɑ̃, ɑ̃t] *adj* **- 1.** [brise] rising ; [jour] dawning **- 2.** [barbe] incipient.

naître [92] [nɛtr] *vi* **- 1.** [enfant] to be born ; **elle est née en 1965** she was born in 1965 **- 2.** [espoir] to spring up ; **~ de** to arise from ; **faire ~ qqch** to give rise to sthg.

naïvement [naivmɑ̃] *adv* naively.

naïveté [naivte] *nf* **- 1.** [candeur] innocence **- 2.** *péj* [crédulité] gullibility.

naja [naʒa] *nm* cobra.

Namibie [namibi] *nf* : **la ~** Namibia.

namibien, enne [namibjɛ̃, ɛn] *adj* Namibian.

➥ **Namibien, enne** *nm, f* Namibian.

nana [nana] *nf fam* [jeune fille] girl.

nanti, e [nɑ̃ti] ◇ *adj* wealthy ◇ *nm, f* wealthy person ; **les ~s** the rich.

nantir [32] [nɑ̃tir] *vt littéraire* : **~ qqn de** to provide sb with.

➥ **se nantir** *vp littéraire* : **se ~ de** to provide o.s. with.

NAP [nap] *(abr de Neuilly Auteuil Passy)* ◇ *adj* ≃ Sloany *Br*, ≃ preppie *Am* ◇ *nf* ≃ Sloane *Br*, ≃ preppie type *Am*.

naphtaline [naftalin] *nf* mothballs *(pl)*.

nappage [napaʒ] *nm* CULIN coating.

nappe [nap] *nf* **- 1.** [de table] tablecloth, cloth **- 2.** *fig* [étendue - gén] sheet ; [- de brouillard] blanket **- 3.** [couche] layer ; **~ de mazout** *ou* **pétrole** oil slick.

napper [3] [nape] *vt* CULIN to coat.

napperon [naprɔ̃] *nm* tablemat.

naquis, naquit *etc* ▷ **naître.**

narcisse [narsis] *nm* BOT narcissus.

narcissique [narsisik] ◇ *nmf* narcissist ◇ *adj* narcissistic.

narcissisme [narsisism] *nm* narcissism.

narcodollars [narkodɔlar] *nmpl* narcodollars.

narcotique [narkɔtik] *nm* & *adj* narcotic.

narguer [3] [narge] *vt* [danger] to flout ; [personne] to scorn, to scoff at.

narine [narin] *nf* nostril.

narquois, e [narkwa, az] *adj* sardonic.

narrateur, trice [naratœr, tris] *nm, f* narrator.

narratif, ive [naratif, iv] *adj* narrative.

narration [narasjɔ̃] *nf* **- 1.** [récit] narration **- 2.** SCOL essay.

narrer [3] [nare] *vt littéraire* to narrate.

NASA, Nasa [naza] *(abr de National Aeronautics and Space Administration) nf* NASA.

nasal, e, aux [nazal, o] *adj* nasal.

nasaliser [3] [nazalize] *vt* to nasalize.

naseau, x [nazo] *nm* nostril.

nasillard, e [nazijar, ard] *adj* nasal.

nasiller [3] [nazije] *vi* **- 1.** [personne] to speak through one's nose **- 2.** [machine] to whine.

nasse [nas] *nf* keep net.

natal, e, als [natal] *adj* [d'origine] native.

natalité [natalite] *nf* birth rate.

natation [natasjɔ̃] *nf* swimming ; **faire de la ~** to swim.

natif, ive [natif, iv] ◇ *adj* **- 1.** [originaire] native *(avant n)* ; **~ de** native of **- 2.** [inné] innate ◇ *nm, f* native.

nation [nasjɔ̃] *nf* nation.

➥ **Nations unies** *nfpl* : **les Nations unies** the United Nations.

national, e, aux [nasjɔnal, o] *adj* national.

➥ **nationale** *nf* : **(route) ~e** ≃ A road *Br*, ≃ state highway *Am*.

nationalisation [nasjɔnalizasjɔ̃] *nf* nationalization.

nationaliser [3] [nasjɔnalize] *vt* to nationalize.

nationalisme [nasjɔnalism] *nm* nationalism.

nationaliste [nasjɔnalist] *nmf* & *adj* nationalist.

nationalité [nasjɔnalite] *nf* nationality , **de ~ française** of French nationality ; **double ~** dual nationality.

nativité [nativite] *nf* nativity.

natte [nat] *nf* - **1.** [tresse] plait - **2.** [tapis] mat.

natter [3] [nate] *vt* to plait.

naturalisation [natyralizasjɔ̃] *nf* - **1.** [de personne, de plante] naturalization - **2.** [taxidermie] stuffing.

naturalisé, e [natyralize] <> *adj* - **1.** [personne, plante] naturalized - **2.** [empaillé] stuffed <> *nm, f* naturalized person.

naturaliser [3] [natyralize] *vt* - **1.** [personne, plante] to naturalize ; **se faire ~** to become naturalized - **2.** [empailler] to stuff.

naturaliste [natyralist] <> *nmf* - **1.** LITTÉRATURE & ZOOL naturalist - **2.** [empailleur] taxidermist <> *adj* naturalistic.

nature [natyr] <> *nf* nature ; **par ~** by nature ; **payer en ~** to pay in kind <> *adj inv* - **1.** [simple] plain - **2.** *fam* [spontané] natural.
→ **nature morte** *nf* still life.

naturel, elle [natyrɛl] *adj* natural.
→ **naturel** *nm* - **1.** [tempérament] nature ; **être d'un ~ affable/sensible** *etc* to be affable/sensitive *etc* by nature - **2.** [aisance, spontanéité] naturalness - **3.** CULIN : **thon au ~** tuna in brine.

naturellement [natyrɛlmɑ̃] *adv* - **1.** [gén] naturally - **2.** [logiquement] rationally.

naturisme [natyrism] *nm* naturism.

naturiste [natyrist] <> *nmf* naturist <> *adj* naturist *(avant n)*, nudist *(avant n)*.

naturopathie [natyropati] *nf* naturopathy.

naufrage [nofraʒ] *nm* - **1.** [navire] shipwreck ; **faire ~** to be wrecked - **2.** *fig* [effondrement] collapse.

naufragé, e [nofraʒe] <> *adj* shipwrecked <> *nm, f* shipwrecked person.

nauséabond, e [nozeabɔ̃, ɔ̃d] *adj* nauseating.

nausée [noze] *nf* - **1.** MÉD nausea ; **avoir la ~** to feel nauseous *ou* sick ; **donner la ~ à qqn** *litt* & *fig* to make sb (feel) sick - **2.** [dégoût] disgust.

nautique [notik] *adj* nautical ; [ski, sport] water *(avant n)*.

nautisme [notism] *nm* water sports *(pl)*.

naval, e, als [naval] *adj* naval.

navarin [navarɛ̃] *nm* lamb stew.

navet [navɛ] *nm* - **1.** BOT turnip - **2.** *fam péj* [œuvre] load of rubbish.

navette [navɛt] *nf* shuttle ; **~ spatiale** AÉRON space shuttle ; **faire la ~** to shuttle.

navigable [navigabl] *adj* navigable.

navigant, e [navigɑ̃, ɑ̃t] <> *adj* navigation *(avant n)* <> *nm, f* : **les ~s** the flight crew.

navigateur, trice [navigatœr, tris] *nm, f* navigator.
→ **navigateur** *nm* INFORM browser.

navigation [navigasjɔ̃] *nf* navigation ; COMM shipping ; **~ aérienne/spatiale** air/space travel.

naviguer [3] [navige] *vi* - **1.** [voguer] to sail - **2.** [piloter] to navigate - **3.** INFORM to browse.

navire [navir] *nm* ship ; **~ de guerre** warship ; **~ marchand** merchant ship.

navrant, e [navrɑ̃, ɑ̃t] *adj* - **1.** [triste] upsetting, distressing - **2.** [regrettable, mauvais] unfortunate.

navrer [3] [navre] *vt* to upset ; **être navré de qqch/de faire qqch** to be sorry about sthg/to do sthg.

nazi, e [nazi] <> *adj* Nazi *(avant n)* <> *nm, f* Nazi.

nazisme [nazism] *nm* Nazism.

NB *(abr de Nota Bene)* NB.

NBC *(abr de nucléaire, bactériologique, chimique)* *adj* NBC.

nbreuses *abr de* **nombreuses**.

nbrx *abr de* **nombreux**.

n.c. - 1. *(abr de non communiqué)* n.a. - **2.** *(abr de non connu)* n.a.

n.d. - 1. *(abr de non daté)* n.d - **2.** *(abr de non disponible)* n.a.

N-D *(abr de Notre-Dame)* OL.

NDA *(abr de note de l'auteur)* author's note.

N'Djamena [ndʒamena] *n* N'Djamena.

NDLR *(abr de note de la rédaction)* editor's note.

NDT *(abr de note du traducteur)* translator's note.

ne [nə], **n'** *(devant voyelle ou h muet)* *adv* - **1.** [négation] ⊳ **pas²**, **plus**, **rien** *etc* - **2.** [négation implicite] : **il se porte mieux que je ~ (le) croyais** he's in better health than I thought (he would be) - **3.** [avec verbes ou expressions marquant le doute, la crainte etc] : **je crains qu'il n'oublie** I'm afraid he'll forget ; **j'ai peur qu'il n'en parle** I'm frightened he'll talk about it.

né, e [ne] *adj* born ; **~ en 1965** born in 1965 ; **~ le 17 juin** born on the 17th June ; **~ de** born to *ou* of ; **Mme X, ~e Y** Mrs X née Y ; **je ne suis pas ~ d'hier** I wasn't born yesterday.

néanmoins [neɑ̃mwɛ̃] *adv* nevertheless.

néant [neɑ̃] *nm* - **1.** [absence de valeur] worthlessness - **2.** [absence d'existence] nothingness ; **réduire à ~** to reduce to nothing.

nébuleux, euse [nebylø, øz] *adj* - **1.** [ciel] cloudy - **2.** [idée, projet] nebulous.
→ **nébuleuse** *nf* - **1.** ASTRON nebula - **2.** *fig* [groupe] nebulous group.

nécessaire [nesesɛr] ◇ adj necessary ; ~ à necessary for ; **il est ~ de faire qqch** it is necessary to do sthg ; **il est ~ que** (*+ subjonctif*) : **il est ~ qu'elle vienne** she must come ◇ nm - **1.** [biens] necessities (pl) ; **le strict ~** the bare essentials (pl) - **2.** [mesures] : **faire le ~** to do the necessary - **3.** [trousse] bag ; **~ de couture** sewing kit ; **~ de toilette** toilet bag.

nécessairement [nesesɛrmɑ̃] adv - **1.** [fatalement] necessarily, of necessity - **2.** [absolument] absolutely, positively.

nécessité [nesesite] nf - **1.** [obligation, situation] necessity ; **être dans la ~ de faire qqch** to have no choice ou alternative but to do sthg - **2.** [besoin] need.

⬥ **nécessités** nfpl necessities.

nécessiter [3] [nesesite] vt to necessitate.

nec plus ultra [nɛkplyzyltra] nm inv : **le ~ de** the last word in.

nécrologie [nekrɔlɔʒi] nf [notice] obituary ; [rubrique] deaths (pl).

nécrologique [nekrɔlɔʒik] adj obituary (avant n).

nécromancien, enne [nekrɔmɑ̃sjɛ̃, ɛn] nm, f necromancer.

nécrose [nekroz] nf necrosis.

nectar [nɛktar] nm nectar ; **~ d'abricot/de pêche** apricot/peach nectar.

nectarine [nɛktarin] nf nectarine.

néerlandais, e [neɛrlɑ̃dɛ, ɛz] adj Dutch.

⬥ **néerlandais** nm [langue] Dutch.

⬥ **Néerlandais, e** nm, f Dutchman (f Dutchwoman) ; **les Néerlandais** the Dutch.

nef [nɛf] nf - **1.** [d'église] nave - **2.** littéraire [bateau] vessel.

néfaste [nefast] adj - **1.** [jour, événement] fateful - **2.** [influence] harmful.

nèfle [nɛfl] nf medlar.

néflier [neflije] nm medlar tree.

négatif, ive [negatif, iv] adj negative.

⬥ **négatif** nm PHOT negative.

⬥ **négative** nf : **répondre par la négative** to reply in the negative.

négation [negasjɔ̃] nf - **1.** [rejet] denial - **2.** GRAM negative.

négativement [negativmɑ̃] adv negatively.

négligé, e [negliʒe] adj - **1.** [travail, tenue] untidy - **2.** [ami, jardin] neglected.

⬥ **négligé** nm - **1.** [laisser-aller] untidiness - **2.** [déshabillé] negligée.

négligeable [negliʒabl] adj negligible.

négligemment [negliʒamɑ̃] adv - **1.** [sans soin] carelessly - **2.** [avec indifférence] casually.

négligence [negliʒɑ̃s] nf - **1.** [laisser-aller] carelessness - **2.** [omission] negligence ; **par ~** out of negligence.

négligent, e [negliʒɑ̃, ɑ̃t] ◇ adj - **1.** [sans soin] careless - **2.** [indifférent] casual ◇ nm, f casual person.

négliger [17] [negliʒe] vt - **1.** [ami, jardin] to neglect ; **~ de faire qqch** to fail to do sthg - **2.** [avertissement] to ignore.

⬥ **se négliger** vp to neglect o.s.

négoce [negɔs] nm business.

négociable [negɔsjabl] adj negotiable.

négociant, e [negɔsjɑ̃, ɑ̃t] nm, f dealer.

négociateur, trice [negɔsjatœr, tris] nm, f negotiator.

négociation [negɔsjasjɔ̃] nf negotiation ; **~s de paix** peace negotiations ; **~s au sommet** summit meeting (sg).

négocier [9] [negɔsje] vt to negotiate.

nègre, négresse [nɛgr, negrɛs] nm, f negro (f negress) (beware : the terms 'nègre' and 'négresse' are considered racist).

⬥ **nègre** ◇ nm fam ghost writer ◇ adj negro (avant n) (beware : the term 'nègre' is considered racist).

négrier [negrije] nm - **1.** [esclavagiste] slave trader - **2.** fig [exploiteur] slave driver.

négro [negro] nm racist term used with reference to black people.

neige [nɛʒ] nf - **1.** [flocons] snow ; **aller à la ~** ≃ to go skiing ; **blanc comme ~** as white as snow ; fig pure as the driven snow ; **~ fabriquée** Can artificial snow - **2.** loc : **battre en ~** CULIN to beat ou whip until stiff.

⬥ **neige carbonique** nf dry ice.

neiger [23] [neʒe] v impers : **il neige** it is snowing.

neigeux, euse [neʒø, øz] adj snowy.

nénuphar [nenyfar] nm water-lily.

néo-calédonien, enne [neɔkaledɔnjɛ̃, ɛn] (mpl néo-calédoniens, fpl néo-calédoniennes) adj New Caledonian.

⬥ **Néo-Calédonien, enne** nm, f New Caledonian.

néo-colonialiste [neɔkɔlɔnjalist] (pl néo-colonialistes) nmf & adj neo-colonialist.

néologisme [neɔlɔʒism] nm neologism.

néon [neɔ̃] nm - **1.** [gaz] neon - **2.** [enseigne] neon light.

néonatal, e, als [neɔnatal] adj neonatal.

néophyte [neɔfit] ◇ nmf novice ◇ adj novice (avant n).

néo-zélandais, e [neɔzelɑ̃dɛ, ɛz] (mpl inv, fpl néo-zélandaises) adj New Zealand (avant n).

⬥ **Néo-Zélandais, e** nm, f New Zealander.

Népal [nepal] nm : **le ~** Nepal ; **au ~** in Nepal.

népalais, e [nepalɛ, ɛz] *adj* Nepalese.

➤ **népalais** *nm* [langue] Nepali, Nepalese.

➤ **Népalais, e** *nm, f* Nepalese (person) ; **les Népalais** the Nepalese.

néphrite [nefrit] *nf* nephritis.

népotisme [nepɔtism] *nm* nepotism.

nerf [nɛr] *nm* - **1.** ANAT nerve ; ~ **optique/rachidien** optic/spinal nerve - **2.** *fig* [vigueur] spirit.

➤ **nerfs** *nmpl* nerves ; **avoir les ~s solides/d'acier** to have strong nerves/nerves of steel ; **être à bout de ~s** to be at the end of one's tether ; **être sur les ~s** to be tense ; **taper sur les ~s de qqn** *fam* to get on sb's nerves.

nerveusement [nɛrvøzmɑ̃] *adv* nervously.

nerveux, euse [nɛrvø, øz] ◇ *adj* - **1.** [gén] nervous - **2.** [viande] stringy - **3.** [style] vigorous ; [voiture] nippy ◇ *nm, f* nervous person.

nervosité [nɛrvozite] *nf* nervousness.

nervure [nɛrvyr] *nf* - **1.** [de feuille, d'aile] vein - **2.** [de voûte] rib.

n'est-ce pas [nɛspɑ] *adv* : **vous me croyez, ~?** you believe me, don't you? ; **c'est délicieux, ~?** it's delicious, isn't it? ; **~ que vous vous êtes bien amusés?** you enjoyed yourselves, didn't you?

net, nette [nɛt] *adj* - **1.** [écriture, image, idée] clear - **2.** [propre, rangé] clean, neat - **3.** COMM & FIN net ; **~ d'impôt** tax-free *Br*, tax-exempt *Am* - **4.** [visible, manifeste] definite, distinct.

➤ **net** *adv* - **1.** [sur le coup] on the spot ; **s'arrêter ~** to stop dead ; **se casser ~** to break clean off - **2.** [franchement - parler] plainly.

Net [nɛt] *nm fam* : **le ~** the Net, the net ; **surfer sur le ~** to surf the Net.

nettement [nɛtmɑ̃] *adv* - **1.** [clairement] clearly - **2.** [incontestablement] definitely ; **~ mieux** definitely better ; **~ plus/moins** much more/less.

netteté [nɛtte] *nf* clearness.

nettoie, nettoies *etc* ▷ **nettoyer.**

nettoyage [netwajaʒ] *nm* [de vêtement] cleaning ; **~ à sec** dry cleaning.

nettoyant [netwajɑ̃] *nm* cleaning fluid.

nettoyer [13] [netwaje] *vt* - **1.** [gén] to clean - **2.** [grenier] to clear out - **3.** [suj : police, soldats] to clean up.

neuf¹, neuve [nœf, nœv] *adj* new ; **flambant ~** brand new.

➤ **neuf** *nm* : **vêtu de ~** wearing new clothes ; **quoi de ~?** what's new? ; **rien de ~** nothing new ; **refaire** OU **remettre à ~** to make as good as new, to refurbish.

neuf² [nœf] *adj num* & *nm* nine ; *voir aussi* **six.**

neurasthénie [nørasteni] *nf* depression.

neurasthénique [nørastenik] *nmf* & *adj* depressive.

neurochirurgie [nørɔʃiryrʒi] *nf* neurosurgery.

neuroleptique [nørɔlɛptik] ◇ *nm* neuroleptic drug ◇ *adj* neuroleptic.

neurologie [nørɔlɔʒi] *nf* neurology.

neurologique [nørɔlɔʒik] *adj* neurological.

neurologue [nørɔlɔg] *nmf* neurologist.

neuropsychiatre [nøropsikjatr] *nmf* neuropsychiatrist.

neurovégétatif, ive [nørovɛʒetatif, iv] *adj* : **système ~** nervous system.

neutralisation [nøtralizasjɔ̃] *nf* neutralization.

neutraliser [3] [nøtralize] *vt* to neutralize.

neutralité [nøtralite] *nf* neutrality.

neutre [nøtr] ◇ *nm* LING neuter ◇ *adj* - **1.** [gén] neutral - **2.** LING neuter.

neutron [nøtrɔ̃] *nm* neutron.

neuve ▷ **neuf¹.**

neuvième [nœvjɛm] ◇ *adj num, nm* OU *nmf* ninth ; *voir aussi* **sixième** ◇ *nf* SCOL ≃ first year OU form *(at junior school) Br,* ≃ third grade *Am.*

névé [neve] *nm* snowbank.

neveu, x [nəvø] *nm* nephew.

névralgie [nevralʒi] *nf* - **1.** MÉD neuralgia - **2.** [mal de tête] headache.

névralgique [nevralʒik] *adj* - **1.** [douloureux] neuralgic - **2.** *fig* [sensible] sensitive.

névrite [nevrit] *nf* neuritis.

névrose [nevroz] *nf* neurosis.

névrosé, e [nevroze] *adj* & *nm, f* neurotic.

névrotique [nevrɔtik] *adj* neurotic.

New Delhi [njudeli] *n* New Delhi.

New York [njujɔrk] *n* - **1.** [ville] New York (City) ; **à ~** in New York (City) - **2.** [état] New York State ; **dans l'État de ~** in New York State.

new-yorkais, e [njujɔrkɛ, ɛz] *(mpl inv, fpl new-yorkaises) adj* from New York.

➤ **New-Yorkais, e** *nm, f* New Yorker.

nez [ne] *nm* nose ; **saigner du ~** to have a nosebleed ; **~ aquilin** aquiline nose ; **~ busqué** hooked nose ; **~ camus** pug nose ; **~ retroussé** snub nose ; **avoir le ~ fin** to have a good sense of smell ; *fig* to have foresight ; **~ à ~** face to face ; **ça lui pend au ~** *fam* he's got it coming to him ; **faire qqch au ~ et à la barbe de qqn** to do sthg (right) under sb's nose ; **mettre le ~ dehors** to put one's nose outside ; **mettre le ~ à la fenêtre** to show one's face at the window ; **raccrocher au ~ de qqn** to hang up on sb ; **rire au ~ de qqn** to laugh in sb's face.

NF (*abr de* **Norme française**) *French industrial standard,* ≃ BS *Br.*

ni [ni] *conj* : **sans pull ~ écharpe** without a sweater or a scarf ; **je ne peux ~ ne veux venir** I neither can nor want to come.

➤ **ni ... ni** *loc corrélative* neither ... nor ; **~ lui ~ moi** neither of us ; **~ l'un ~ l'autre n'a parlé** neither of them spoke ; **je ne les aime ~ l'un ~ l'autre** I don't like either of them.

niable [njabl)] *adj* deniable.

Niagara [njagara] *nm* : **les chutes du ~** Niagara Falls.

niais, e [nje, njɛz] ◇ *adj* silly, foolish ◇ *nm, f* fool.

niaisement [njɛzmã] *adv* foolishly.

niaiserie [njɛzri] *nf* foolishness (U) ; **dire des ~s** to talk rubbish.

Niamey [njamɛ] *n* Niamey.

Nicaragua [nikaragwa] *nm* : **le ~** Nicaragua ; **au ~** in Nicaragua.

nicaraguayen, enne [nikaragwajɛ̃, ɛn] *adj* Nicaraguan.

➤ **Nicaraguayen, enne** *nm, f* Nicaraguan.

niche [niʃ] *nf* - **1.** [de chien] kennel - **2.** [de statue] niche - **3.** *fam* [farce] trick.

nicher [3] [niʃe] *vi* - **1.** [oiseaux] to nest - **2.** *fam* [personne] to live.

➤ **se nicher** *vp* to hide.

nickel [nikɛl] ◇ *nm* nickel ◇ *adj inv fam* spotless, spick and span.

niçois, e [niswa, az] *adj* of/from Nice ; **salade ~e** *salad made out of lettuce, green peppers, tuna fish, tomatoes, anchovy and hard-boiled egg.*

➤ **Niçois, e** *nm, f* native *ou* inhabitant of Nice.

Nicosie [nikɔzi] *n* Nicosia.

nicotine [nikɔtin] *nf* nicotine.

nid [ni] *nm* nest ; **~-d'abeilles** [tissu] waffle cloth ; **~ à poussière** *fig* dust trap.

➤ **nid de poule** *nm* pothole.

nièce [njɛs] *nf* niece.

nier [9] [nje] *vt* to deny.

nigaud, e [nigo, od] ◇ *adj* silly ◇ *nm, f* simpleton.

Niger [niʒɛr] *nm* - **1.** [fleuve] : **le ~** the River Niger - **2.** [État] : **le ~** Niger ; **au ~** in Niger.

Nigeria [niʒerja] *nm* : **le ~** Nigeria ; **au ~** in Nigeria.

nigérian, e [niʒerjã, an] *adj* Nigerian.

➤ **Nigérian, e** *nm, f* Nigerian.

nigérien, enne [niʒerjɛ̃, ɛn] *adj* Nigerien.

➤ **Nigérien, enne** *nm, f* Nigerien.

night-club [najtklœb] (*pl* **night-clubs**) *nm* nightclub.

Nil [nil] *nm* : **le ~** the Nile ; **le ~ Blanc** the White Nile ; **le ~ Bleu** the Blue Nile.

n'importe ⊳ **importer.**

nippes [nip] *nfpl fam* gear (U).

nippon, one [nipɔ̃, ɔn] *adj* Japanese.

➤ **Nippon, one** *nm, f* Japanese (person) ; **les Nippons** the Japanese.

nirvana [nirvana] *nm* nirvana.

nitrate [nitrat] *nm* nitrate.

nitrique [nitrik] *adj* nitric.

nitroglycérine [nitrogliserin] *nf* nitroglycerine.

niveau, x [nivo] *nm* - **1.** [gén] level ; **de même ~** *fig* of the same standard ; **~ à bulle** spirit level ; **au-dessus du ~ de la mer** above sea level ; **~ scolaire** standard of education ; **~ de vie** standard of living ; **au ~ de** at the level of ; *fig* [en ce qui concerne] as regards - **2.** LING : **~ de langue** register.

niveler [24] [nivle] *vt* to level ; *fig* to level out.

nivellement [nivɛlmã] *nm* levelling ; *fig* levelling out ; **~ par le bas** levelling down.

NN (*abr de* **nouvelle norme**) *revised standard of hotel classification.*

noble [nɔbl] ◇ *nmf* nobleman (*f* noblewoman) ◇ *adj* noble.

noblement [nɔbləmã] *adv* nobly.

noblesse [nɔblɛs] *nf* nobility.

noce [nɔs] *nf* - **1.** [mariage] wedding - **2.** [invités] wedding party - **3.** *loc* : **faire la ~** *fam* to live it up.

➤ **noces** *nfpl* wedding (*sg*) ; **convoler en justes ~s** to be married ; **elle l'a épousé en secondes ~s** he is her second husband ; **~s d'or/d'argent** golden/silver wedding (anniversary).

nocif, ive [nɔsif, iv] *adj* - **1.** [produit, gaz] noxious - **2.** *fig* [théorie, doctrine] harmful.

nocivité [nɔsivite] *nf* - **1.** [de produit, gaz] noxiousness - **2.** *fig* [de théorie, doctrine] harmfulness.

noctambule [nɔktãbyl] *nmf* night bird.

nocturne [nɔktyrn] ◇ *nm* - **1.** MUS nocturne - **2.** ZOOL night hunter ◇ *nm ou nf* - **1.** [d'un magasin] late opening ; **ouvert en ~** open late - **2.** SPORT : **match en ~** evening game ◇ *adj* - **1.** [émission, attaque] night (*avant n*) - **2.** [animal] nocturnal.

nodule [nɔdyl] *nm* nodule.

Noël [nɔɛl] *nm* Christmas ; **joyeux ~!** happy *ou* merry Christmas!

nœud [nø] *nm* - **1.** [de fil, de bois] knot ; **~ coulant**

slipknot ; **double ~** double knot **- 2.** NAVIG knot ; **filer à X ~s** NAVIG to do X knots **- 3.** *fig* & *littéraire* [attachement] bond **- 4.** [de l'action, du problème] crux **- 5.** [ornement] bow ; **~ de cravate** knot *(in one's tie)* ; **~ papillon** bow tie **- 6.** ANAT, ASTRON, ÉLECTR & RAIL node.

noie, noies *etc* ⊳ noyer.

noierai, noieras *etc* ⊳ noyer.

noir, e [nwar] *adj* **- 1.** [gén] black ; **~ de** [poussière, suie] black with **- 2.** [pièce, couloir] dark **- 3.** *fig* [pressentiment] sombre *Br*, somber *Am* **- 4.** *fig* [ivre] drunk.
  ➣ **Noir, e** *nm, f* black.
  ➣ **noir** *nm* **- 1.** [couleur] black ; **~ sur blanc** *fig* in black and white **- 2.** [obscurité] dark **- 3.** *loc* : **acheter qqch au ~** to buy sthg on the black market ; **broyer du ~** to be down in the dumps ; **travail au ~** moonlighting ; **travailler au ~** to moonlight ; **voir tout en ~** to see the dark side of everything.
  ➣ **noire** *nf* crotchet *Br*, quarter note *Am*.

noirâtre [nwaratr] *adj* blackish.

noiraud, e [nwaro, od] ⬦ *adj* swarthy ⬦ *nm, f* swarthy person.

noirceur [nwarsœr] *nf* **- 1.** *littéraire* [couleur] blackness **- 2.** *fig* [méchanceté] wickedness.

noircir [32] [nwarsir] ⬦ *vi* to darken ⬦ *vt litt* & *fig* to blacken.
  ➣ **se noircir** *vp* [devenir noir] to darken.

Noire ⊳ mer.

noise [nwaz] *nf littéraire* : **chercher ~ à qqn** to pick a quarrel with sb.

noisetier [nwaztje] *nm* hazel tree.

noisette [nwazɛt] ⬦ *nf* **- 1.** [fruit] hazelnut **- 2.** [petite quantité] : **une ~ de beurre** a knob of butter ⬦ *adj inv* hazel.

noix [nwa] *nf* **- 1.** [fruit] walnut ; **~ de cajou** cashew (nut) ; **~ de coco** coconut ; **~ de muscade** nutmeg **- 2.** [de viande] : **~ de veau** cushion of veal **- 3.** *loc* : **à la ~** *fam* dreadful.

nom [nɔ̃] *nm* **- 1.** [gén] name ; **au ~ de** in the name of ; **~ de Dieu!** *tfam* bloody hell! *Br*, God damn it! ; **~ d'un chien** *ou* **d'une pipe!** *fam* drat! ; **faux ~** false name ; **~ déposé** trade name ; **~ d'emprunt** assumed name ; **~ de famille** surname ; **~ de fichier** INFORM filename ; **~ de jeune fille** maiden name ; **traiter qqn de tous les ~s** to call sb all the names under the sun **- 2.** [prénom] (first) name **- 3.** GRAM noun ; **~ composé** compound noun ; **~ propre/commun** proper/common noun.

nomade [nɔmad] ⬦ *nmf* nomad ⬦ *adj* nomadic.

nombre [nɔ̃br] *nm* number ; **au ~ de** among ; **bon ~ de** a large number of, a good many ; **un bon ~ d'entre nous/eux** many of us/them ; **venir en ~** to come in large numbers ; **~ pair/impair** even/odd number.

nombreux, euse [nɔ̃brø, øz] *adj* **- 1.** [famille, foule] large **- 2.** [erreurs, occasions] numerous ; **peu ~** few.

nombril [nɔ̃bril] *nm* navel ; **il se prend pour le ~ du monde** he thinks the world revolves around him.

nombrilisme [nɔ̃brilism] *nm fam péj* navel-gazing.

nomenclature [nɔmɑ̃klatyr] *nf* **- 1.** [terminologie] nomenclature **- 2.** [liste] word list.

nominal, e, aux [nɔminal, o] *adj* **- 1.** [liste] of names **- 2.** [valeur, autorité] nominal **- 3.** GRAM noun *(avant n)*.

nominalement [nɔminalmɑ̃] *adv* **- 1.** [désigner] by name **- 2.** GRAM nominally.

nominatif, ive [nɔminatif, iv] *adj* [liste] of names.
  ➣ **nominatif** *nm* GRAM nominative.

nomination [nɔminasjɔ̃] *nf* nomination, appointment.

nommé, e [nɔme] ⬦ *adj* **- 1.** [désigné] named **- 2.** [choisi] appointed ⬦ *nm, f* aforementioned.

nommément [nɔmemɑ̃] *adv* [citer] by name.

nommer [3] [nɔme] *vt* **- 1.** [appeler] to name, to call **- 2.** [qualifier] to call **- 3.** [promouvoir] to appoint, to nominate **- 4.** [dénoncer, mentionner] to name.
  ➣ **se nommer** *vp* **- 1.** [s'appeler] to be called **- 2.** [se désigner] to give one's name.

non [nɔ̃] ⬦ *adv* **- 1.** [réponse négative] no **- 2.** [se rapportant à une phrase précédente] not ; **moi ~** not me ; **moi ~ plus** (and) neither am/do *etc* I ; **elle ne travaille pas aujourd'hui, moi ~ plus** she's not working today and neither am I **- 3.** [sert à demander une confirmation] : **c'est une bonne idée, ~?** it's a good idea, isn't it? **- 4.** [modifie un adjectif ou un adverbe] not ; **~ loin d'ici** not far from here ; **une difficulté ~ négligeable** a not inconsiderable problem ⬦ *nm inv* no.
  ➣ **non moins** *loc adv* no less.
  ➣ **non (pas) ... mais** *loc corrélative* not ... but ; **~ pas maigre, mais mince** not skinny but slim.
  ➣ **non plus ... mais** *loc corrélative* no longer ... but.
  ➣ **non (pas) que ... mais** *loc corrélative* not that ... but.

nonagénaire [nɔnaʒener] *nmf* & *adj* nonagenarian.

non-agression [nɔnagrɛsjɔ̃] *nf* non-aggression.

non-aligné, e [nɔnaliɲe] *adj* non-aligned ; **les pays ~s** the non-aligned countries.

nonante [nɔnɑ̃t] *adj num Belg & Helv* ninety.

non-assistance [nɔnasistɑ̃s] *nf* non-assistance ; **~ à personne en danger** failure to give assistance to a person in danger.

nonchalance [nɔ̃ʃalɑ̃s] *nf* nonchalance, casualness.

nonchalant, e [nɔ̃ʃalɑ̃, ɑ̃t] *adj* nonchalant, casual.

non-combattant, e [nɔ̃kɔ̃batɑ̃, ɑ̃t] <> *adj* noncombatant <> *nm, f* noncombatant.

non-conformiste [nɔ̃kɔ̃fɔrmist] <> *nmf* nonconformist <> *adj* unconventional.

non-conformité [nɔ̃kɔ̃fɔrmite] *nf* nonconformity.

non-dit [nɔ̃di] *nm* unvoiced feeling.

non-fumeur, euse [nɔ̃fymœr, øz] <> *nm, f* non-smoker <> *adj* non-smoking *(avant n)*.

non-ingérence [nɔ̃nɛ̃ʒerɑ̃s] *nf* noninterference.

non-inscrit, e [nɔ̃nɛ̃skri, it] *adj & nm, f POLIT* independent.

non-intervention [nɔ̃nɛ̃tɛrvɑ̃sjɔ̃] *nf* nonintervention.

non-lieu [nɔ̃ljø] *(pl* **non-lieux)** *nm JUR* dismissal through lack of evidence ; **rendre un ~** to dismiss a case for lack of evidence.

nonne [nɔn] *nf* nun.

nonobstant [nɔnɔpstɑ̃] *sout* <> *prép* notwithstanding <> *adv* nevertheless.

non-paiement [nɔ̃pɛmɑ̃] *nm* nonpayment.

non-recevoir [nɔ̃rəsəvwar] ⏵ **fin de non-recevoir** *nf JUR* objection.

non-résident, e [nɔ̃rezidɑ̃] *nm* nonresident.

non-retour [nɔ̃rətur] ⏵ **point de non-retour** *nm* point of no return.

non-sens [nɔ̃sɑ̃s] *nm inv* **- 1.** [absurdité] nonsense **- 2.** [contresens] meaningless word.

non-stop [nɔnstɔp] *adj inv* non-stop.

non-violence [nɔ̃vjɔlɑ̃s] *nf* non-violence.

non-voyant, e [nɔ̃vwajɑ̃, ɑ̃t] *nm, f* visually handicapped.

nord [nɔr] <> *nm* north ; **un vent du ~** a northerly wind ; **le vent du ~** the north wind ; **au ~** in the north ; **au ~ (de)** to the north (of) ; **le grand Nord** the frozen North ; **perdre le ~** *fam fig* to lose one's head <> *adj inv* north ; [province, région] northern.

nord-africain, e [nɔrafrikɛ̃, ɛn] *(mpl* **nord-africains,** *fpl* **nord-africaines)** *adj* North African.

⏵ **Nord-Africain, e** *nm, f* North African.

nord-américain, e [nɔramerikɛ̃, ɛn] *(mpl*

nord-américains, *fpl* **nord-américaines)** *adj* North American.

⏵ **Nord-Américain, e** *nm, f* North American.

nord-coréen, enne [nɔrkɔreɛ̃, ɛn] *(mpl* **nord-coréens,** *fpl* **nord-coréennes)** *adj* North Korean.

⏵ **Nord-Coréen, enne** *nm, f* North Korean.

nord-est [nɔrɛst] *nm & adj inv* north-east.

nordicité [nɔrdisite] *nf Can* northerliness.

nordique [nɔrdik] *adj* Nordic, Scandinavian.

⏵ **Nordique** *nmf* **- 1.** [Scandinave] Scandinavian **- 2.** *Can* North Canadian.

nord-ouest [nɔrwɛst] *nm & adj inv* north-west.

normal, e, aux [nɔrmal, o] *adj* normal.

⏵ **normale** *nf* **- 1.** [moyenne] : **la ~e** the norm **- 2.** *Can GOLF* par.

normalement [nɔrmalmɑ̃] *adv* normally, usually ; **~ il devrait déjà être arrivé** he should have arrived by now.

normalien, enne [nɔrmaljɛ̃, ɛn] *nm, f* **- 1.** [élève d'une école normale] student at teacher training college *Br ou* teachers college *Am* **- 2.** [ancien élève de l'École normale supérieure] graduate of the École normale supérieure.

normalisation [nɔrmalizasjɔ̃] *nf* **- 1.** [stabilisation] normalization **- 2.** [standardisation] standardization.

normaliser [3] [nɔrmalize] *vt* **- 1.** [situation] to normalize **- 2.** [produit] to standardize.

⏵ **se normaliser** *vp* to return to normal.

normalité [nɔrmalite] *nf* normality.

normand, e [nɔrmɑ̃, ɑ̃d] *adj* Norman.

⏵ **Normand, e** *nm, f* Norman.

Normandie [nɔrmɑ̃di] *nf* : **la ~** Normandy.

normatif, ive [nɔrmatif, iv] *adj* prescriptive.

norme [nɔrm] *nf* **- 1.** [gén] standard, norm ; **être dans la ~** to be within the norm ; **être hors ~s** to be non-standard **- 2.** [critère] criterion.

Norvège [nɔrvɛʒ] *nf* : **la ~** Norway.

norvégien, enne [nɔrveʒjɛ̃, ɛn] *adj* Norwegian.

⏵ **norvégien** *nm* [langue] Norwegian.

⏵ **Norvégien, enne** *nm, f* Norwegian.

nos ⏵ **notre.**

nostalgie [nɔstalʒi] *nf* nostalgia ; **avoir la ~ de** to feel nostalgia for.

nostalgique [nɔstalʒik] *adj* nostalgic.

nota bene [nɔtabene] *nm inv* nota bene, NB.

notable [nɔtabl] ⬦ *adj* noteworthy, notable ⬦ *nm* notable.

notablement [nɔtabləmã] *adv* notably.

notaire [nɔtɛr] *nm* ≈ solicitor *Br*, ≈ lawyer.

notamment [nɔtamã] *adv* in particular.

notarial, e, aux [nɔtarjal, o] *adj* notarial.

notarié, e [nɔtarje] *adj* ≈ drawn up by a solicitor *Br ou* lawyer.

notation [nɔtasjɔ̃] *nf* - **1.** [système] notation - **2.** [remarque] note - **3.** SCOL marking, grading *Am*.

note [nɔt] *nf* - **1.** [gén & MUS] note ; **prendre des ~s** to take notes ; **prendre qqch en ~** to make a note of sthg ; **fausse ~** MUS false note ; *fig* sour note ; **~ de bas de page** footnote ; **~ de service** memo - **2.** SCOL & UNIV mark, grade *Am* ; **avoir une bonne/mauvaise ~** to have a good/bad mark - **3.** [facture] bill ; **une ~ salée** *fam* a hefty *ou* steep bill.

noter [3] [nɔte] *vt* - **1.** [écrire] to note down - **2.** [constater] to note, to notice - **3.** SCOL & UNIV to mark, to grade *Am* - **4.** [marquer] to mark.

notice [nɔtis] *nf* instructions *(pl)* ; **~ explicative** directions for use.

notification [nɔtifikasjɔ̃] *nf* notification.

notifier [9] [nɔtifje] *vt* : **~ qqch à qqn** to notify sb of sthg.

notion [nɔsjɔ̃] *nf* - **1.** [conscience, concept] notion, concept - **2.** *(gén pl)* [rudiment] smattering *(U)*.

notoire [nɔtwar] *adj* [fait] well-known ; [criminel] notorious.

notoirement [nɔtwarmã] *adv* notoriously.

notoriété [nɔtɔrjete] *nf* - **1.** [de fait] notoriety ; **être de ~ publique** to be common *ou* public knowledge - **2.** [célébrité] fame.

notre [nɔtr] *(pl* **nos** [no]) *adj poss* our.

nôtre [nɔtr] ➤ **le nôtre** *(f* **la nôtre**, *pl* **les nôtres**) *pron poss* ours ; **les ~s** our family *(sg)* ; **serez-vous des ~s demain?** will you be joining us tomorrow? ; **il faut y mettre du ~** we'll all have to pull our weight.

Nouakchott [nuakʃɔt] *n* Nouakchott.

nouba [nuba] *nf* : **faire la ~** *fam* to paint the town red.

nouer [6] [nwe] *vt* - **1.** [corde, lacet] to tie ; [bouquet] to tie up - **2.** *fig* [gorge, estomac] to knot - **3.** *sout* [alliance, amitié] to make, to form.

➤ **se nouer** *vp* - **1.** [gorge] to tighten up - **2.** [alliance, amitié] to be formed - **3.** [intrigue] to start.

noueux, euse [nwø, øz] *adj* [bois] knotty ; [mains] gnarled.

nougat [nuga] *nm* nougat.

nouille [nuj] *nf fam péj* idiot.

➤ **nouilles** *nfpl* [pâtes] pasta *(U)*, noodles *(pl)*.

Nouméa [numea] *n* Nouméa.

nounou [nunu] *nf* nanny.

nourrice [nuris] *nf* - **1.** [garde d'enfants] nanny, child-minder ; [qui allaite] wet nurse - **2.** [réservoir] jerrycan *Br*, can *Am*.

nourrir [32] [nurir] *vt* - **1.** [gén] to feed ; **nourri-logé-blanchi** board, lodging and laundry - **2.** [sentiment, projet] to nurture - **3.** [style, esprit] to improve.

➤ **se nourrir** *vp* to eat ; **se ~ de qqch** *litt* & *fig* to live on sthg.

nourrissant, e [nurisã, ãt] *adj* nutritious, nourishing.

nourrisson [nurisɔ̃] *nm* infant.

nourriture [nurityr] *nf* food.

nous [nu] *pron pers* - **1.** [sujet] we - **2.** [objet] us. ➤ **nous-mêmes** *pron pers* ourselves.

nouveau, elle, x [nuvo, ɛl, o] (**nouvel** *devant voyelle et* h *muet*) ⬦ *adj* new ; **~x mariés** newlyweds ⬦ *nm, f* new boy *(f* new girl).

➤ **nouveau** *nm* : **il y a du ~** there's something new.

➤ **nouvelle** *nf* - **1.** [information] (piece of) news *(U)* - **2.** [court récit] short story.

➤ **nouvelles** *nfpl* news ; **les nouvelles** MÉDIA the news *(sg)* ; **il a donné de ses nouvelles** I/ we *etc* have heard from him ; **être sans nouvelles de qqn/qqch** to have no news of sb/ sthg ; **aux dernières nouvelles ...** the latest is ...

➤ **à nouveau** *loc adv* - **1.** [encore] again - **2.** [de manière différente] afresh, anew.

➤ **de nouveau** *loc adv* again.

nouveau-né, e [nuvone] *(mpl* **nouveau-nés**, *fpl* **nouveau-nées**) ⬦ *adj* newborn ⬦ *nm, f* newborn baby.

nouveauté [nuvote] *nf* - **1.** [actualité] novelty - **2.** [innovation] something new - **3.** [ouvrage] new book/film *etc*.

nouvel, nouvelle [nuvɛl] ▷ **nouveau**.

Nouvelle-Calédonie [nuvɛlkaledɔni] *nf* : **la ~** New Caledonia.

Nouvelle-Écosse [nuvɛlekɔs] *nf* : **la ~** Nova Scotia.

Nouvelle-Guinée [nuvɛlɡine] *nf* : **la ~** New Guinea.

nouvellement [nuvɛlmã] *adv* recently.

Nouvelle-Orléans [nuvɛlɔrleã] *n* : **La ~** New Orleans.

Nouvelle-Zélande [nuvɛlzelãd] *nf* : **la ~** New Zealand.

novateur, trice [nɔvatœr, tris] ⬦ *adj* innovative ⬦ *nm, f* innovator.

novembre [nɔvɑ̃br] *nm* November ; *voir aussi* **septembre**.

novice [nɔvis] ⟨⟩ *nmf* novice ⟨⟩ *adj* inexperienced.

noyade [nwajad] *nf* drowning.

noyau, x [nwajo] *nm* - **1.** [de fruit] stone, pit - **2.** ASTRON, BIOL & PHYS nucleus - **3.** *fig* [d'amis] group, circle ; [d'opposants, de résistants] cell ; **~ dur** hard core - **4.** *fig* [centre] core.

noyauter [3] [nwajote] *vt* to infiltrate.

noyé, e [nwaje] ⟨⟩ *adj* - **1.** [personne] drowned - **2.** [inondé] flooded ; **yeux ~s de larmes** eyes swimming with tears ⟨⟩ *nm, f* drowned person.

noyer [13] [nwaje] *vt* - **1.** [animal, personne] to drown ; **~ son chagrin** to drown one's sorrows - **2.** [terre, moteur] to flood - **3.** [estomper, diluer] to swamp ; [contours] to blur.
 ◆ **se noyer** *vp* - **1.** [personne] to drown - **2.** *fig* [se perdre] : **se ~ dans** to become bogged down in - **3.** [s'estomper] to be swamped.

N/Réf (*abr de* **Notre référence**) O/Ref.

NRF (*abr de* **Nouvelle Revue Française**) *nf* - **1.** [revue] *literary review* - **2.** [mouvement] *literary movement*.

nu, e [ny] *adj* - **1.** [personne] naked - **2.** [paysage, fil électrique] bare - **3.** [style, vérité] plain.
 ◆ **nu** *nm* nude ; **à ~** stripped, bare ; **mettre à ~** to strip bare.

nuage [nɥaʒ] *nm* - **1.** [gén] cloud ; **être dans les ~s** *fig* to have one's head in the clouds - **2.** [petite quantité] : **un ~ de lait** a drop of milk - **3.** [de foulard] scarf.

nuageux, euse [nɥaʒø, øz] *adj* - **1.** [temps, ciel] cloudy - **2.** *fig* [esprit] hazy.

nuance [nɥɑ̃s] *nf* - **1.** [de couleur] shade ; [de son, de sens] nuance ; **tout en ~s** extremely subtle - **2.** [touche] : **~ de** touch of, trace of.

nuancer [16] [nɥɑ̃se] *vt* - **1.** [couleurs] to shade - **2.** [pensée] to qualify.

nubile [nybil] *adj* nubile.

nucléaire [nykleɛr] ⟨⟩ *nm* nuclear energy ⟨⟩ *adj* nuclear.

nudisme [nydism] *nm* nudism, naturism.

nudiste [nydist] *nmf & adj* nudist.

nudité [nydite] *nf* - **1.** [de personne] nudity, nakedness - **2.** [de lieu, style] bareness.

nuée [nɥe] *nf* - **1.** [multitude] : **une ~ de** a horde of - **2.** *littéraire* [nuage] cloud.

nues [ny] *nfpl* : **tomber des ~** to be completely taken aback.

nui [nɥi] *pp inv* ▷ **nuire**.

nuire [97] [nɥir] *vi* : **~ à** to harm, to injure.
 ◆ **se nuire** *vp* to harm o.s.

nuisais, nuisions *etc* ▷ **nuire**.

nuisance [nɥizɑ̃s] *nf* nuisance *(U)*, harm *(U)* ; **~s sonores** noise pollution.

nuise, nuises *etc* ▷ **nuire**.

nuisette [nɥizɛt] *nf* short nightgown, baby-doll nightgown.

nuisible [nɥizibl] *adj* harmful.

nuit [nɥi] *nf* - **1.** [laps de temps] night ; **cette ~** [la nuit dernière] last night ; [la nuit prochaine] tonight ; **de ~** at night ; **bateau/vol de ~** night ferry/flight ; **passer la ~ à l'hôtel** to spend the night in a hotel ; **~ blanche** sleepless night - **2.** [obscurité] darkness, night ; **il fait ~** it's dark ; **perdu dans la ~ des temps** lost in the mists of time.

nuitamment [nɥitamɑ̃] *adv littéraire* by night.

nuitée [nɥite] *nf* overnight stay.

nul, nulle [nyl] ⟨⟩ *adj indéf (avant n) littéraire* no ⟨⟩ *adj (après n)* - **1.** [égal à zéro] nil - **2.** [sans valeur] useless, hopeless ; **c'est ~ !** *fam* it's rubbish! ; **être ~ en maths** to be hopeless *ou* useless at maths - **3.** [sans résultat] : **match ~** draw - **4.** [caduc] : **~ et non avenu** JUR null and void ⟨⟩ *nm, f péj* nonentity ⟨⟩ *pron indéf* **sout** no one, nobody.
 ◆ **nulle part** *loc adv* nowhere *Br*, no-place *Am*.

nullement [nylmɑ̃] *adv* by no means.

nullité [nylite] *nf* - **1.** [médiocrité] incompetence - **2.** *péj* [personne] nonentity - **3.** JUR invalidity, nullity.

numéraire [nymerɛr] ⟨⟩ *nm* cash ⟨⟩ *adj* [espèces] legal.

numéral, e, aux [nymeral, o] *adj* numeral.
 ◆ **numéral, aux** *nm* numeral.

numérateur [nymeratœr] *nm* numerator.

numération [nymerasjɔ̃] *nf* - **1.** MATHS numeration - **2.** MÉD : **~ globulaire** blood count.

numérique [nymerik] *adj* - **1.** [gén] numerical - **2.** INFORM digital.

numériquement [nymerikmɑ̃] *adv* numerically.

numéro [nymero] *nm* - **1.** [gén] number ; **composer** *ou* **faire un ~** to dial a number ; **faire un faux ~** to dial a wrong number ; **~ minéralogique** *ou* **d'immatriculation** registration *Br ou* license *Am* number ; **~ azur** *telephone number for which calls are charged at the local rate irrespective of the actual distance covered* ; **~ de téléphone** telephone number ; **~ vert** ≃ freefone number ; **tirer le mauvais ~** *fig* to get a raw deal - **2.** [de spectacle] act, turn ; **faire son ~** *fig* to do one's little act - **3.** *fam* [personne] : **quel ~!** what a character!

numéroter [3] [nymerote] *vt* to number.

numerus clausus [nymerysklɔzys] *nm* restricted intake of students.

numismatique [nymismatik] ⟨⟩ *nf* numismatics *(U)* ⟨⟩ *adj* numismatic.

nu-pieds [nypje] *nm inv* [sandale] sandal.

nuptial, e, aux [nypsjal, o] *adj* nuptial.

nuque [nyk] *nf* nape.

nurse [nœrs] *nf* children's nurse, nanny.

nursery [nœrsəri] *(pl* **nurseries**) *nf* - **1.** [dans un hôpital] nursery - **2.** [dans un lieu public] parent-and-baby clinic.

nutritif, ive [nytritif, iv] *adj* nutritious.

nutritionniste [nytrisjɔnist] *nmf* nutritionist, dietician.

Nylon® [nilɔ̃] *nm* nylon.

nymphe [nɛ̃f] *nf* nymph.

nymphomane [nɛ̃fɔman] *nf* & *adj* nymphomaniac.

o, O [o] *nm inv* [lettre] o, O.
➡ **O** *(abr de* **Ouest***)* W.

ô [o] *interj* oh!, O!

OACI *(abr de* **Organisation de l'aviation civile internationale***) nf* ICAO.

OAS *(abr de* **Organisation de l'armée secrète***) nf organization opposed to independence in Algeria in the 1960s.*

oasis [ɔazis] *nf* - **1.** [dans désert] oasis - **2.** *fig* [de calme] haven, oasis.

obédience [ɔbedjɑ̃s] *nf* - **1.** [appartenance] allegiance, persuasion ; **être d'~ marxiste/catholique** to be a Marxist/Catholic - **2.** [obéissance] obedience.

obéir [32] [ɔbeir] *vi* - **1.** [personne] : **~ à qqn/qqch** to obey sb/sthg - **2.** [freins] to respond.

obéissance [ɔbeisɑ̃s] *nf* obedience ; **devoir ~ à qqn** to owe sb allegiance.

obéissant, e [ɔbeisɑ̃, ɑ̃t] *adj* obedient.

obélisque [ɔbelisk] *nm* obelisk.

obèse [ɔbez] ⟨⟩ *nmf* obese person ⟨⟩ *adj* obese.

obésité [ɔbezite] *nf* obesity.

objecter [4] [ɔbʒɛkte] *vt* - **1.** [répliquer] to raise as an objection ; **~ que** to object that - **2.** [prétexter] : **~ qqch (à qqn)** to put forward sthg as an excuse (to sb).

objecteur [ɔbʒɛktœr] *nm* objector ; **~ de conscience** conscientious objector.

objectif, ive [ɔbʒɛktif, iv] *adj* objective.
➡ **objectif** *nm* - **1.** PHOT lens - **2.** [but, cible] objective, target.

objection [ɔbʒɛksjɔ̃] *nf* objection ; **faire ~ à** to object to.

objectivement [ɔbʒɛktivmɑ̃] *adv* objectively.

objectivité [ɔbʒɛktivite] *nf* objectivity.

objet [ɔbʒɛ] *nm* - **1.** [chose] object ; **~ d'art** object d'art ; **~ de valeur** valuable ; **~s trouvés** lost property office *Br*, lost and found (office) *Am* - **2.** [sujet] subject ; **être** OU **faire l'~ de** to be the subject of - **3.** [but] aim, object ; **cette réunion a pour ~ de ...** the aim of this meeting is to ... ; **sans ~** pointless.

objurgations [ɔbʒyrgasjɔ̃] *nfpl* - **1.** [remontrances] objurgations - **2.** [prières] pleas.

obligation [ɔbligasjɔ̃] *nf* - **1.** [gén] obligation ; **être dans l'~ de faire qqch** to be obliged to do sthg ; **sans ~ d'achat** COMM (with) no obligation to buy ; **avoir une ~ envers qqn** to be under an obligation to sb - **2.** FIN bond, debenture.
➡ **obligations** *nfpl* obligations, duties ; **avoir des ~s** to have obligations, to have a duty ; **~s militaires** military duties.

obligatoire [ɔbligatwar] *adj* - **1.** [imposé] compulsory, obligatory - **2.** *fam* [inéluctable] inevitable.

obligeance [ɔbliʒɑ̃s] *nf* sout obligingness ; **avoir l'~ de faire qqch** to be good OU kind enough to do sthg.

obligeant, e [ɔbliʒɑ̃, ɑ̃t] *adj* helpful, obliging.

obliger [17] [ɔbliʒe] *vt* - **1.** [forcer] : **~ qqn à qqch** to impose sthg on sb ; **~ qqn à faire qqch** to force sb to do sthg ; **être obligé de faire qqch** to be obliged to do sthg - **2.** JUR to bind - **3.** [rendre service à] to oblige.
➡ **s'obliger** *vp* : **s'~ à qqch** to impose sthg on o.s. ; **s'~ à faire qqch** to force o.s. to do sthg.

oblique [ɔblik] ⟨⟩ *adj* oblique ; **en ~** diagonally ⟨⟩ *nf* oblique line.

obliquer [3] [ɔblike] *vi* to turn off.

oblitérer [18] [ɔblitere] *vt* - **1.** [tamponner] to

cancel - **2.** MÉD to obstruct - **3.** [effacer] to obliterate.

oblong, oblongue [ɔblɔ̃, ɔ̃g] *adj* oblong.

obnubiler [3] [ɔbnybile] *vt* to obsess ; **être obnubilé par** to be obsessed with *ou* by.

obole [ɔbɔl] *nf* small contribution.

obscène [ɔpsɛn] *adj* obscene.

obscénité [ɔpsenite] *nf* obscenity.

obscur, e [ɔpskyr] *adj* - **1.** [sombre] dark - **2.** [confus] vague - **3.** [inconnu, douteux] obscure.

obscurantisme [ɔpskyrɑ̃tism] *nm* obscurantism.

obscurcir [32] [ɔpskyrsir] *vt* - **1.** [assombrir] to darken - **2.** [embrouiller] to confuse.
➤ **s'obscurcir** *vp* - **1.** [s'assombrir] to grow dark - **2.** [s'embrouiller] to become confused.

obscurément [ɔpskyremɑ̃] *adv* obscurely.

obscurité [ɔpskyrite] *nf* - **1.** [nuit] darkness - **2.** [anonymat] obscurity - **3.** [hermétisme] abstruseness.

obsédant, e [ɔpsedɑ̃, ɑ̃t] *adj* haunting.

obsédé, e [ɔpsede] <> *adj* obsessed <> *nm, f* obsessive ; **~ sexuel** sex maniac.

obséder [18] [ɔpsede] *vt* to obsess, to haunt.

obsèques [ɔpsɛk] *nfpl* funeral *(sg)*.

obséquieux, euse [ɔpsekjø, øz] *adj* obsequious.

obséquiosité [ɔpsekjozite] *nf* obsequiousness.

observance [ɔpsɛrvɑ̃s] *nf* observance.

observateur, trice [ɔpsɛrvatœr, tris] <> *adj* observant <> *nm, f* observer.

observation [ɔpsɛrvasjɔ̃] *nf* - **1.** [gén] observation ; **être en ~** MÉD to be under observation - **2.** [critique] remark - **3.** [conformité] observance.

observatoire [ɔpsɛrvatwar] *nm* - **1.** ASTRON observatory - **2.** [lieu de surveillance] observation post.

observer [3] [ɔpsɛrve] *vt* - **1.** [regarder, remarquer, respecter] to observe - **2.** [épier] to watch - **3.** [constater] : **~ que** to note that ; **faire ~ qqch à qqn** to point sthg out to sb - **4.** *sout* [attitude] to keep, to maintain.
➤ **s'observer** *vp* - **1.** [se surveiller] to be careful of one's behaviour *Br ou* behavior *Am* - **2.** [s'épier] to watch each other.

obsession [ɔpsesjɔ̃] *nf* obsession.

obsessionnel, elle [ɔpsesjɔnɛl] *adj* obsessional.

obsolète [ɔpsɔlɛt] *adj* obsolete.

obstacle [ɔpstakl] *nm* - **1.** [entrave] obstacle - **2.** *fig* [difficulté] hindrance ; **faire ~ à qqch/**qqn to hinder sthg/sb ; **rencontrer un ~** to meet an obstacle.

obstétricien, enne [ɔpstetrisjɛ̃, ɛn] *nm, f* obstetrician.

obstétrique [ɔpstetrik] *nf* obstetrics *(U)*.

obstination [ɔpstinasjɔ̃] *nf* stubbornness, obstinacy.

obstiné, e [ɔpstine] <> *adj* - **1.** [entêté] stubborn, obstinate - **2.** [acharné] dogged <> *nm, f* stubborn *ou* obstinate person.

obstinément [ɔpstinemɑ̃] *adv* - **1.** [refuser] obstinately - **2.** [travailler] doggedly.

obstiner [3] [ɔpstine] ➤ **s'obstiner** *vp* to insist ; **s'~ à faire qqch** to persist stubbornly in doing sthg ; **s'~ dans qqch** to cling stubbornly to sthg.

obstruction [ɔpstryksjɔ̃] *nf* - **1.** MÉD obstruction, blockage - **2.** POLIT & SPORT obstruction.

obstructionniste [ɔpstryksjɔnist] *nmf* & *adj* POLIT obstructionist.

obstruer [3] [ɔpstrye] *vt* to block, to obstruct.
➤ **s'obstruer** *vp* to become blocked.

obtempérer [18] [ɔptɑ̃pere] *vi* : **~ à** to comply with.

obtenir [40] [ɔptənir] *vt* to get, to obtain ; **~ qqch de qqn** to get sthg from sb ; **~ de faire qqch** to get permission to do sthg ; **~ qqch à ou pour qqn** to obtain sthg for sb.

obtention [ɔptɑ̃sjɔ̃] *nf* obtaining.

obtenu, e [ɔptəny] *pp* ➤ **obtenir.**

obtiendrai, obtiendras *etc* ➤ **obtenir.**

obtienne, obtiennes *etc* ➤ **obtenir.**

obturateur, trice [ɔptyratœr, tris] *adj* closing *(avant n).*
➤ **obturateur** *nm* - **1.** [valve] stop valve - **2.** PHOT shutter.

obturation [ɔptyrasjɔ̃] *nf* closing, sealing.

obturer [3] [ɔptyre] *vt* to close, to seal ; [dent] to fill.

obtus, e [ɔpty, yz] *adj* obtuse.

obus [ɔby] *nm* shell.

OC *(abr de* **ondes courtes)** SW.

occasion [ɔkazjɔ̃] *nf* - **1.** [possibilité, chance] opportunity, chance ; **saisir l'~ (de faire qqch)** to seize *ou* grab the chance (to do sthg) ; **rater une ~ (de faire qqch)** to miss a chance (to do sthg) ; **être l'~ de** to give rise to ; **à l'~** some time ; [de temps en temps] sometimes, on occasion ; **à la première ~** at the first opportunity - **2.** [circonstance] occasion ; **à l'~ de** on the occasion of ; **dans les grandes ~s** on important occasions - **3.** [bonne affaire] bargain.
➤ **d'occasion** *loc adv* & *loc adj* secondhand.

occasionnel, elle [ɔkazjɔnɛl] *adj* [irrégulier - visite, problème] occasional ; [- travail] casual.

occasionner [3] [ɔkazjɔne] *vt* to cause.

occident [ɔksidā] *nm* west.

➽ **Occident** *nm* : **l'Occident** the West.

occidental, e, aux [ɔksidātal, o] *adj* western.

➽ **Occidental, e, aux** *nm, f* Westerner.

occiput [ɔksipyt] *nm* back of the head.

occitan, e [ɔksitā, an] *adj* Provençal French.

➽ **occitan** *nm* [langue] Provençal French.

➽ **Occitan, e** *nm, f* speaker of Provençal French.

occlusion [ɔklyzjɔ̃] *nf* - **1.** MÉD blockage, obstruction - **2.** LING & CHIM occlusion.

occulte [ɔkylt] *adj* occult.

occulter [3] [ɔkylte] *vt* [sentiments] to conceal.

occupant, e [ɔkypā, āt] ◇ *adj* occupying ◇ *nm, f* occupant, occupier.

➽ **occupant** *nm* : **l'~** the occupying power *ou* forces *(pl)*.

occupation [ɔkypasjɔ̃] *nf* - **1.** [activité] occupation, job ; **vaquer à ses ~s** to go about one's business - **2.** MIL occupation - **3.** JUR occupancy.

➽ **Occupation** *nf* : **l'Occupation** the Occupation (of France).

occupé, e [ɔkype] *adj* - **1.** [personne] busy ; **être ~ à qqch** to be busy with sthg - **2.** [appartement, zone] occupied - **3.** [place] taken ; [toilettes] engaged ; **c'est ~** [téléphone] it's engaged *Br ou* busy *Am*.

occuper [3] [ɔkype] *vt* - **1.** [gén] to occupy - **2.** [espace] to take up - **3.** [fonction, poste] to hold - **4.** [main-d'œuvre] to employ.

➽ **s'occuper** *vp* - **1.** [s'activer] to keep o.s. busy ; **s'~ à qqch/à faire qqch** to be busy with sthg/doing sthg - **2.** : **s'~ de qqch** [se charger de] to take care of sthg, to deal with sthg ; [s'intéresser à] to take an interest in, to be interested in ; **occupez-vous de vos affaires!** mind your own business! - **3.** [prendre soin] : **s'~ de qqn** to take care of sb, to look after sb.

occurrence [ɔkyrās] *nf* - **1.** [circonstance] : **en l'~** in this case - **2.** LING occurrence.

OCDE *(abr de* **Organisation de coopération et de développement économique)** *nf* OECD.

océan [ɔseā] *nm* ocean ; **l'~ Antarctique** the Antarctic Ocean ; **l'~ Arctique** the Arctic Ocean ; **l'~ Atlantique** the Atlantic Ocean ; **l'~ Indien** the Indian Ocean ; **l'~ Pacifique** the Pacific Ocean.

Océanie [ɔseani] *nf* : **l'~** Oceania.

océanien, enne [ɔseanjē, ɛn] *adj* Oceanian.

➽ **Océanien, enne** *nm, f* Oceanian.

océanique [ɔseanik] *adj* ocean *(avant n)*.

océanographie [ɔseanɔgrafi] *nf* oceanography.

ocelot [ɔslo] *nm* ocelot.

ocre [ɔkr] *adj inv* & *nf* ochre *Br*, ocher *Am*.

octante [ɔktāt] *adj num Belg* & *Helv* eighty.

octave [ɔktav] *nf* octave.

octet [ɔktɛ] *nm* INFORM byte.

octobre [ɔktɔbr] *nm* October ; *voir aussi* **septembre**.

octogénaire [ɔktɔʒenɛr] *nmf* & *adj* octogenarian.

octogone [ɔktɔgɔn] *nm* octagon.

octroie, octroies *etc* ▷ **octroyer**.

octroyer [13] [ɔktrwaje] *vt* : **~ qqch à qqn** to grant sb sthg, to grant sthg to sb.

➽ **s'octroyer** *vp* to grant o.s., to treat o.s. to.

oculaire [ɔkylɛr] ◇ *nm* eyepiece ◇ *adj* ocular, eye *(avant n)* ; **témoin ~** eyewitness.

oculiste [ɔkylist] *nmf* ophthalmologist.

ode [ɔd] *nf* ode.

odeur [ɔdœr] *nf* smell ; **ne pas être en ~ de sainteté (auprès de)** *fig* to be out of favour *Br ou* favor *Am* (with).

odieusement [ɔdjøzmā] *adv* abominably.

odieux, euse [ɔdjø, øz] *adj* - **1.** [crime] odious, abominable - **2.** [personne, attitude] unbearable, obnoxious.

odorant, e [ɔdɔrā, āt] *adj* sweet-smelling, fragrant.

odorat [ɔdɔra] *nm* (sense of) smell.

odoriférant, e [ɔdɔriferā, āt] *adj* sweet-smelling, fragrant.

odyssée [ɔdise] *nf* odyssey.

OEA *(abr de* **Organisation des États américains)** *nf* OAS.

œdème [edɛm] *nm* oedema.

œil [œj] *(pl* **yeux** [jø]*) nm* - **1.** [gén] eye ; **yeux bridés/exorbités/globuleux** slanting/bulging/protruding eyes ; **avoir les yeux cernés** to have bags under one's eyes ; **baisser/lever les yeux** to look down/up, to lower/raise one's eyes ; **du coin de l'~** out of the corner of one's eye ; **écarquiller les yeux** to stare wide-eyed ; **à l'~ nu** to the naked eye ; **sous mes/tes etc yeux** before my/your *etc* very eyes ; **à vue d'~** visibly - **2.** [bulle de graisse] blob of grease *ou* fat - **3.** *loc* : **avoir qqch/qqn à l'~** to have one's eye on sthg/sb ; **avoir un ~ au beurre noir** to have a black eye ; **n'avoir pas froid aux yeux** not to be afraid of anything, to have plenty of nerve ; **avoir des**

yeux de lynx to have eyes like a hawk ; **ne pas avoir les yeux dans sa poche** to be very observant ; **couver qqch/qqn des yeux** to look fondly at sthg/sb, to look lovingly at sthg/sb ; **ça crève les yeux** fam it's staring you in the face, it's as plain as the nose on your face ; **ne pas en croire ses yeux** not to believe one's eyes ; **dévorer qqn/qqch des yeux** [avec insistance] to eye sb/sthg intently ; [avec convoitise] to eye sb/sthg greedily ; **faire de l'~ à qqn** fam to give sb the eye, to eye sb up ; **faire les gros yeux à qqn** to glare at sb ; **fermer les yeux sur qqch** to close one's eyes to sthg ; **mon ~!** fam like hell! ; **ouvrir l'~** to keep one's eyes open ; **se rincer l'~** fam to get an eyeful ; **cela saute aux yeux** it's obvious ; **tourner de l'~** fam to pass out.

œil-de-bœuf [œjdəbœf] (pl **œils-de-bœuf**) nm bull's eye window.

œillade [œjad] nf wink ; **lancer une ~ à qqn** to wink at sb.

œillère [œjɛr] nf eyebath.
➤ **œillères** nfpl blinkers Br, blinders Am ; **avoir des ~s** fam fig to be blinkered.

œillet [œjɛ] nm - **1.** [fleur] carnation - **2.** [de chaussure] eyelet.

œnologie [enɔlɔʒi] nf wine appreciation.

œnologue [enɔlɔg] nmf wine expert.

œsophage [ezɔfaʒ] nm oesophagus Br, esophagus Am.

œstrogène [ɛstrɔʒɛn] nm oestrogen Br, estrogen Am.

œuf [œf] nm egg ; **~ à la coque/au plat/poché** boiled/fried/poached egg ; **~ mollet/dur** soft-boiled/hard-boiled egg ; **~ de Pâques** Easter egg ; **~s brouillés** scrambled eggs ; **~s en** ou **à la neige** whipped egg whites ; **dans l'~** fig in the bud.

œuvre [œvr] ⬦ nf - **1.** [travail] work ; **être à l'~** to be working ou at work ; **se mettre à l'~** to get down to work ; **mettre qqch en ~** to make use of sthg ; [loi, accord, projet] to implement sthg - **2.** [artistique] work ; [ensemble de la production d'un artiste] works (pl) ; **~ d'art** work of art ; [organisation] charity ; **~ de bienfaisance** charity, charitable organization ⬦ nm - **1.** [d'artiste] works (pl), work - **2.** [de bâtiment] : **le gros ~** the shell.

œuvrer [5] [œvre] vi littéraire : **~ (pour)** to work (for).

OFCE (abr de **Observatoire français des conjonctures économiques**) nm economic research institute.

off [ɔf] adj inv - **1.** CIN [voix, son] off - **2.** [festival] fringe (avant n).

offensant, e [ɔfɑ̃sɑ̃, ɑ̃t] adj offensive.

offense [ɔfɑ̃s] nf - **1.** [insulte] insult - **2.** RELIG trespass.

offenser [3] [ɔfɑ̃se] vt - **1.** [personne] to offend - **2.** [bon goût] to offend against.
➤ **s'offenser** vp : **s'~ de** to take offence Br ou offense Am at, to be offended by.

offenseur [ɔfɑ̃sœr] nm offender, offending party.

offensif, ive [ɔfɑ̃sif, iv] adj offensive.
➤ **offensive** nf - **1.** MIL offensive ; **passer à l'offensive** to go on the offensive ; **prendre l'offensive** to take the offensive - **2.** fig [du froid] (sudden) onset.

offert, e [ɔfɛr, ɛrt] pp ⊳ **offrir**.

offertoire [ɔfɛrtwar] nm offertory.

office [ɔfis] nm - **1.** [bureau] office, agency ; **~ du tourisme** tourist office - **2.** [fonction] : **faire ~ de** to act as ; **remplir son ~** to do its job, to fulfil its function - **3.** RELIG service - **4.** loc : **recourir aux ~s de qqn** to turn to sb for help.
➤ **d'office** loc adv automatically, as a matter of course ; **commis d'~** officially appointed.

officialiser [3] [ɔfisjalize] vt to make official.

officiel, elle [ɔfisjɛl] adj & nm, f official.

officiellement [ɔfisjɛlmɑ̃] adv officially.

officier[1] [9] [ɔfisje] vi to officiate.

officier[2] [ɔfisje] nm officer ; **~ d'ordonnance** aide-de-camp.

officieusement [ɔfisjøzmɑ̃] adv unofficially.

officieux, euse [ɔfisjø, øz] adj unofficial.

officine [ɔfisin] nf - **1.** [pharmacie] pharmacy - **2.** péj [repaire] agency.

offrande [ɔfrɑ̃d] nf - **1.** [don] offering - **2.** RELIG offertory.

offrant [ɔfrɑ̃] nm : **au plus ~** to the highest bidder.

offre [ɔfr] nf - **1.** [proposition] offer ; [aux enchères] bid ; [pour contrat] tender ; '**~s d'emploi**' 'situations vacant', 'vacancies' ; **~ d'essai** trial offer ; **~ de lancement** introductory offer ; **~ publique d'achat** takeover bid - **2.** ÉCON supply ; **la loi de l'~ et de la demande** the law of supply and demand.

offrir [34] [ɔfrir] vt - **1.** [faire cadeau] : **~ qqch à qqn** to give sb sthg, to give sthg to sb - **2.** [proposer] : **~ qqch à qqn** to offer sb sthg ou sthg to sb ; **~ (à qqn) de faire qqch** to offer to do sthg (for sb) - **3.** [présenter] to offer, to present ; **son visage n'offrait rien d'accueillant** his/her face showed no sign of welcome.
➤ **s'offrir** vp - **1.** [croisière, livre] to treat o.s. to

- 2. [se présenter] to present itself **- 3.** [s'exposer] : **s'~ à qqch** to expose o.s. to sthg **- 4.** [se proposer] to offer one's services, to offer o.s. ; **s'~ à faire qqch** to offer to do sthg.

offset [ɔfsɛt] ◇ *adj inv* offset ◇ *nm inv* offset (lithography) ◇ *nf inv* offset press.

offshore [ɔfʃɔr] ◇ *adj inv* **- 1.** [exploitation] offshore **- 2.** *SPORT* speedboat *(avant n)* ; **bateau ~** speedboat ◇ *nm SPORT* speedboat racing.

offusquer [3] [ɔfyske] *vt* to offend.
➤ **s'offusquer** *vp* : **s'~ (de)** to take offence *Br ou* offense *Am* (at).

ogive [ɔʒiv] *nf* **- 1.** *ARCHIT* ogive ; **en ~** ribbed **- 2.** *MIL* [d'obus] head ; [de fusée] nosecone ; **~ nucléaire** nuclear warhead.

OGM *(abr de organisme génétiquement modifié) nm* GMO.

ogre, ogresse [ɔgr, ɔgrɛs] *nm, f* ogre *(f* ogress).

oh [o] ◇ *interj* oh! ; **~ la la!** dear oh dear! ◇ *nm inv* : **pousser des ~ et des ah** to ooh and ah.

ohé [ɔe] *interj* hey!

OHQ *(abr de ouvrier hautement qualifié) nm* highly skilled worker.

oie [wa] *nf* goose ; **~ blanche** *fig* innocent young girl.

oignon [ɔɲɔ̃] *nm* **- 1.** [plante] onion ; **mêle-toi de tes ~s** *fam fig* mind your own business ; **soigner qqn aux petits ~s** *fam fig* to take care of sb's every need **- 2.** [bulbe] bulb **- 3.** *MÉD* bunion.

oindre [82] [wɛ̃dr] *vt littéraire* **- 1.** [corps] to (rub with) oil **- 2.** *RELIG* to anoint.

oiseau, x [wazo] *nm* **- 1.** *ZOOL* bird ; **~ de proie** bird of prey **- 2.** *fam péj* [individu] character.

oiseau-mouche [wazomuʃ] *(pl* **oiseaux-mouches)** *nm* hummingbird.

oiseleur [waslœr] *nm* bird-catcher.

oiseux, euse [wazø, øz] *adj* pointless.

oisif, ive [wazif, iv] ◇ *adj* idle ◇ *nm, f* man of leisure *(f* woman of leisure).

oisillon [wazijɔ̃] *nm* fledgling.

oisiveté [wazivte] *nf* idleness.

oison [wazɔ̃] *nm* gosling.

OIT *(abr de Organisation internationale du travail) nf* ILO.

O.K. [ɔke] *interj fam* okay.

OL *(abr de ondes longues)* LW.

oléagineux, euse [ɔleaʒinø, øz] *adj* oléagineux.
➤ **oléagineux** *nm* oleaginous plant.

oléoduc [ɔleɔdyk] *nm* (oil) pipeline.

olfactif, ive [ɔlfaktif, iv] *adj* olfactory.

oligo-élément [ɔligoelemɑ̃] *(pl* **oligo-éléments)** *nm* trace element.

olivâtre [ɔlivatr] *adj* [verdâtre] olive-coloured *Br*, olive-colored *Am* ; [teint] sallow.

olive [ɔliv] ◇ *nf* olive ◇ *adj inv* olive, olive-green.

oliveraie [ɔlivrɛ] *nf* olive grove.

olivier [ɔlivje] *nm* [arbre] olive tree ; [bois] olive wood.

OLP *(abr de Organisation de libération de la Palestine) nf* PLO.

Olympe [ɔlɛ̃p] *nm* : **l'~** Olympus.

olympiade [ɔlɛ̃pjad] *(gén pl) nf* olympiad *(sg)*.

olympien, enne [ɔlɛ̃pjɛ̃, ɛn] *adj* Olympian.

olympique [ɔlɛ̃pik] *adj* Olympic *(avant n)*.

OM ◇ *nm (abr de Olympique de Marseille) Marseilles football team* ◇ *(abr de ondes moyennes)* MW.

Oman [ɔman] *n* Oman ; **le sultanat d'~** the Sultanate of Oman.

ombilic [ɔ̃bilik] *nm* **- 1.** [de personne] navel **- 2.** *BOT* navelwort.

ombilical, e, aux [ɔ̃bilikal, o] *adj* umbilical.

ombrage [ɔ̃braʒ] *nm* shade ; **porter ~ à qqn** *fig* to offend sb ; **prendre ~ de qqch** *fig* to take offence *Br ou* offense *Am* at sthg, to take umbrage at sthg.

ombragé, e [ɔ̃braʒe] *adj* shady.

ombrageux, euse [ɔ̃braʒø, øz] *adj* **- 1.** [personne] touchy, prickly **- 2.** [cheval] nervous, skittish.

ombre [ɔ̃br] *nf* **- 1.** [zone sombre] shade ; **faire de l'~ à qqn** to get in sb's light ; **à l'~ de** [arbre] in the shade of ; [personne] in the shadow of ; **rester dans l'~ de qqn** *fig* to live in sb's shadow ; **laisser qqch dans l'~** *fig* to deliberately ignore sthg ; **vivre dans l'~** *fig* to live in obscurity **- 2.** [forme, fantôme] shadow ; **~s chinoises** [spectacle] shadow play *ou* pantomime *(sg)* ; [jeu] Chinese shadows **- 3.** [trace] hint ; **ça ne fait pas l'~ d'un doute** there's not the shadow of a doubt **- 4.** [cosmétique] : **~ à paupières** eye shadow.

ombrelle [ɔ̃brɛl] *nf* parasol.

ombrer [3] [ɔ̃bre] *vt* **- 1.** [paupières] to put eye shadow on **- 2.** [dessin] to shade (in).

OMC *(abr de Organisation mondiale du commerce) nf* WTO.

omelette [ɔmlɛt] *nf* omelette ; **~ norvégienne** baked Alaska.

omets ▷ omettre.

omettre [84] [ɔmɛtr] *vt* to omit ; **~ de faire qqch** to omit to do sthg.

OMI (*abr de* **Organisation maritime internationale**) *nf* IMO.

omis, e [ɔmi, iz] *pp* ▷ **omettre.**

omission [ɔmisjɔ̃] *nf* omission ; **par ~** by omission.

OMM (*abr de* **Organisation météorologique mondiale**) *nf* WMO.

omnibus [ɔmnibys] ◇ *nm* stopping *ou* local train ◇ *adj inv* : **ce train est ~ pour ...** this train stops at all stations to ...

omnipotent, e [ɔmnipɔtɑ̃, ɑ̃t] *adj* omnipotent.

omniprésence [ɔmniprezɑ̃s] *nf* omnipresence.

omniprésent, e [ɔmniprezɑ̃, ɑ̃t] *adj* omnipresent.

omniscient, e [ɔmnisjɑ̃, ɑ̃t] *adj* omniscient.

omnisports [ɔmnispɔr] *adj inv* sports *(avant n)*.

omnivore [ɔmnivɔr] ◇ *nm* omnivore ◇ *adj* omnivorous.

omoplate [ɔmɔplat] *nf* [os] shoulder blade ; [épaule] shoulder.

OMS (*abr de* **Organisation mondiale de la santé**) *nf* WHO.

on [ɔ̃] *pron pers indéf* - **1.** [indéterminé] you, one ; **~ n'a pas le droit de fumer ici** you're not allowed *ou* one isn't allowed to smoke here, smoking isn't allowed here - **2.** [les gens, l'espèce humaine] they, people ; **~ vit de plus en plus vieux en Europe** people in Europe are living longer and longer - **3.** [quelqu'un] someone ; **~ vous a appelé au téléphone ce matin** there was a telephone call for you this morning - **4.** *fam* [nous] we ; **~ s'en va** we're off, we're going.

onanisme [ɔnanism] *nm* onanism.

once [ɔ̃s] *nf* : **une ~ (de)** an ounce (of).

oncle [ɔ̃kl] *nm* uncle.

onction [ɔ̃ksjɔ̃] *nf* unction.

onctueux, euse [ɔ̃ktɥø, øz] *adj* smooth.

onctuosité [ɔ̃ktɥozite] *nf* smoothness.

onde [ɔ̃d] *nf* - **1.** PHYS wave - **2.** *littéraire* [eau] : **l'~** the waters *(pl)*.

➡ **ondes** *nfpl* [radio] air *(sg)*.

ondée [ɔ̃de] *nf* shower (of rain).

on-dit [ɔ̃di] *nm inv* rumour *Br*, rumor *Am*, hearsay *(U)*.

ondoyant, e [ɔ̃dwajɑ̃, ɑ̃t] *adj* [ondulant] rippling ; [démarche] swaying.

ondoyer [13] [ɔ̃dwaje] *vi* to ripple.

ondulant, e [ɔ̃dylɑ̃, ɑ̃t] *adj* [ondoyant] undulating, wavy ; [démarche] swaying.

ondulation [ɔ̃dylasjɔ̃] *nf* - **1.** [mouvement] rippling ; [de sol, terrain] undulation - **2.** [de coiffure] wave.

ondulé, e [ɔ̃dyle] *adj* [surface] undulating ; [chevelure] wavy ; [tôle, carton] corrugated.

onduler [ɔ̃dyle] *vi* [drapeau] to ripple, to wave ; [cheveux] to be wavy ; [route] to undulate.

one-man-show [wanmanʃo] *nm inv* one-man show.

onéreux, euse [ɔnerø, øz] *adj* costly.

ONF (*abr de* **Office national des forêts**) *nm French national forestry agency*, ≃ Forestry Commission *Br*, ≃ National Forestry Service *Am*.

ONG (*abr de* **organisation non gouvernementale**) *nf* NGO.

ongle [ɔ̃gl] *nm* - **1.** [de personne] fingernail, nail ; **se faire les ~s** to do one's nails ; **se ronger les ~s** to bite one's nails - **2.** [d'animal] claw.

onglée [ɔ̃gle] *nf* : **j'ai l'~** my fingers are numb with cold.

onglet [ɔ̃gle] *nm* - **1.** [de reliure] tab - **2.** [de lame] thumbnail groove - **3.** CULIN top skirt.

onguent [ɔ̃gɑ̃] *nm* ointment.

onirique [ɔnirik] *adj* [relatif au rêve] dream *(avant n)* ; [semblable au rêve] dreamlike.

onomastique [ɔnɔmastik] ◇ *nf* onomastics *(sg)* ◇ *adj* onomastic.

onomatopée [ɔnɔmatɔpe] *nf* onomatopoeia.

ont ▷ **avoir.**

ONU, Onu [ɔny] (*abr de* **Organisation des Nations unies**) *nf* UN, UNO.

ONUDI, Onudi [ɔnydi] (*abr de* **Organisation des Nations unies pour le développement industriel**) *nf* UNIDO.

onyx [ɔniks] *nm* onyx.

onze [ɔ̃z] ◇ *adj num* eleven ◇ *nm* [chiffre & SPORT] eleven ; *voir aussi* **six.**

onzième [ɔ̃zjɛm] ◇ *adj num, nm ou nmf* eleventh ; *voir aussi* **sixième** ◇ *nf* [classe] ≃ second year *ou* form *(at primary school) Br*, ≃ first grade *Am* ; *voir aussi* **sixième.**

OP (*abr de* **ouvrier professionnel**) *nm* skilled worker.

OPA (*abr de* **offre publique d'achat**) *nf* takeover bid.

opacité [ɔpasite] *nf* opacity.

opale [ɔpal] *nf* & *adj inv* opal.

opaline [ɔpalin] *nf* opaline.

opaque [ɔpak] *adj* : **~ (à)** opaque (to).

op. cit. (*abr de* **opere citato**) op. cit.

OPE (*abr de* **offre publique d'échange**) *nf*

take-over bid where bidder offers to exchange shares.

OPEP, Opep [ɔpɛp] (*abr de* **Organisation des pays exportateurs de pétrole**) *nf* OPEC.

opéra [ɔpera] *nm* - **1.** MUS opera - **2.** [théâtre] opera house ; **l'Opéra Bastille** *opera house built on the site of the Bastille* ; **l'Opéra de Paris** the Paris Opera (House).

opérable [ɔperabl] *adj* operable.

opéra-bouffe [ɔperabuf] (*pl* **opéras-bouffes**) *nm* comic opera.

opéra-comique [ɔperakɔmik] (*pl* **opéras-comiques**) *nm* light opera.

opérateur, trice [ɔperatœr, tris] *nm, f* operator ; **~ de saisie** keyboarder.

opération [ɔperasjɔ̃] *nf* - **1.** [gén] operation - **2.** COMM deal, transaction.

opérationnel, elle [ɔperasjɔnɛl] *adj* operational.

opératoire [ɔperatwar] *adj* MÉD operating *(avant n)* ; **choc ~** post-operative shock.

opérer [18] [ɔpere] <> *vt* - **1.** MÉD to operate on - **2.** [exécuter] to carry out, to implement ; [choix, tri] to make <> *vi* [agir] to take effect ; [personne] to operate, to proceed.

➡ **s'opérer** *vp* to come about, to take place.

opérette [ɔperɛt] *nf* operetta.

ophtalmique [ɔftalmik] *adj* ophthalmic.

ophtalmologiste [ɔftalmɔlɔʒist] *nmf* ophthalmologist.

Opinel® [ɔpinɛl] *nm folding knife used especially for outdoor activities, scouting etc.*

opiner [3] [ɔpine] *vi sout* : **~ à qqch** to give one's consent to sthg.

opiniâtre [ɔpinjatr] *adj* - **1.** [caractère, personne] stubborn, obstinate - **2.** [effort] dogged ; [travail] unrelenting ; [fièvre, toux] persistent.

opiniâtreté [ɔpinjatrəte] *nf* [de caractère, personne] stubbornness, obstinacy.

opinion [ɔpinjɔ̃] *nf* opinion ; **conforter** OU **renforcer qqn dans son ~** to confirm sb's opinion ; **avoir (une) bonne/mauvaise ~ de** to have a good/bad opinion of ; **l'~ publique** public opinion.

opium [ɔpjɔm] *nm* opium.

opportun, e [ɔpɔrtœ̃, yn] *adj* opportune, timely.

opportunément [ɔpɔrtynemɑ̃] *adv* opportunely.

opportunisme [ɔpɔrtynism] *nm* opportunism.

opportuniste [ɔpɔrtynist] <> *nmf* opportunist <> *adj* opportunistic.

opportunité [ɔpɔrtynite] *nf* - **1.** [à-propos] op-

portuneness, timeliness - **2.** [occasion] opportunity.

opposant, e [ɔposɑ̃, ɑ̃t] <> *adj* opposing <> *nm, f* : **~ (à)** opponent (of).

opposé, e [ɔpoze] *adj* - **1.** [direction, côté, angle] opposite - **2.** [intérêts, opinions] conflicting ; [forces] opposing - **3.** [hostile] : **~ à** opposed to.

➡ **opposé** *nm* : **l'~** the opposite ; **à l'~ de** in the opposite direction from ; *fig* unlike, contrary to.

opposer [3] [ɔpoze] *vt* - **1.** [mettre en opposition - choses, notions] : **~ qqch (à)** to contrast sthg (with) - **2.** [mettre en présence - personnes, armées] to oppose ; **~ deux équipes** to bring two teams together ; **~ qqn à qqn** to pit OU set sb against sb - **3.** [refus, protestation, objection] to put forward ; **~ une objection à qqn** to raise an objection with sb, to put forward an objection to sb - **4.** [diviser] to divide.

➡ **s'opposer** *vp* - **1.** [contraster] to contrast - **2.** [entrer en conflit] to clash - **3.** : **s'~ à** [se dresser contre] to oppose, to be opposed to ; **s'~ à ce que qqn fasse qqch** to be opposed to sb's doing sthg.

opposition [ɔpozisjɔ̃] *nf* - **1.** [gén] opposition ; **faire ~ à** [décision, mariage] to oppose ; [chèque] to stop ; **entrer en ~ avec** to come into conflict with - **2.** JUR : **~ (à)** objection (to) - **3.** [contraste] contrast ; **par ~ à** in contrast with, as opposed to.

oppressant, e [ɔpresɑ̃, ɑ̃t] *adj* oppressive.

oppresser [4] [ɔprese] *vt* - **1.** [étouffer] to suffocate, to stifle - **2.** *fig* [tourmenter] to oppress.

oppresseur [ɔpresœr] <> *nm* oppressor <> *adj* oppressive.

oppressif, ive [ɔpresif, iv] *adj* oppressive.

oppression [ɔpresjɔ̃] *nf* - **1.** [asservissement] oppression - **2.** [malaise] tightness of the chest.

opprimé, e [ɔprime] <> *adj* oppressed <> *nm, f* oppressed person.

opprimer [3] [ɔprime] *vt* - **1.** [asservir] to oppress - **2.** [étouffer] to stifle.

opprobre [ɔprɔbr] *nm* : **jeter l'~ sur qqn** to cast opprobrium on sb.

opter [3] [ɔpte] *vi* : **~ pour** to opt for.

opticien, enne [ɔptisjɛ̃, ɛn] *nm, f* optician.

optimal, e, aux [ɔptimal, o] *adj* optimal.

optimiser [ɔptimize], **optimaliser** [3] [ɔptimalize] *vt* to optimize.

optimisme [ɔptimism] *nm* optimism.

optimiste [ɔptimist] <> *nmf* optimist <> *adj* optimistic.

optimum [ɔptimɔm] (*pl* **optimums** OU **optima** [-ma]) *nm* & *adj* optimum.

option [ɔpsjɔ̃] *nf* - **1.** [gén] option ; **prendre**

une **~ sur** FIN to take (out) an option on - **2.** [accessoire] optional extra.

optionnel, elle [ɔpsjɔnɛl] *adj* optional.

optique [ɔptik] ◇ *nf* - **1.** [science, technique] optics *(U)* - **2.** [perspective] viewpoint ; **dans l'~ de faire qqch** with a mind *ou* view to doing sthg ◇ *adj* [nerf] optic ; [verre] optical.

opulence [ɔpylɑ̃s] *nf* - **1.** [richesse] opulence ; **vivre** *ou* **nager dans l'~** to live a life of luxury - **2.** [ampleur] fullness, ampleness.

opulent, e [ɔpylɑ̃, ɑ̃t] *adj* - **1.** [riche] rich - **2.** [gros] ample.

OQ (*abr de* **ouvrier qualifié**) *nm* skilled worker.

or¹ [ɔr] *nm* - **1.** [métal, couleur] gold ; **en ~** [objet] gold *(avant n)* ; **une occasion en ~** a golden opportunity ; **une affaire en ~** [achat] an excellent bargain ; [commerce] a lucrative line of business ; **j'ai une femme en ~** I've a wonderful wife ; **~ blanc** white gold ; **~ massif** solid gold ; **~ noir** *fig* black gold ; **pour tout l'~ du monde** *fig* for all the tea in China ; **rouler sur l'~** *fig* to be rolling in it - **2.** [dorure] gilding.

or² [ɔr] *conj* [au début d'une phrase] now ; [pour introduire un contraste] well, but.

oracle [ɔrakl] *nm* oracle.

orage [ɔraʒ] *nm* - **1.** [tempête] storm ; **il y a de l'~ dans l'air** *fig* there's a storm brewing - **2.** *fig* [tumulte, revers] turmoil.

orageux, euse [ɔraʒø, øz] *adj* stormy.

oraison [ɔrɛzɔ̃] *nf* prayer ; **~ funèbre** funeral oration.

oral, e, aux [ɔral, o] *adj* oral.
◆ **oral** *nm* oral (examination) ; **~ de rattrapage** *oral examination taken after failing written exams.*

oralement [ɔralmɑ̃] *adv* orally.

orange [ɔrɑ̃ʒ] ◇ *nf* orange ; **~ pressée** freshly squeezed orange juice ◇ *nm & adj inv* [couleur] orange.

orangé, e [ɔrɑ̃ʒe] *adj* orangey.
◆ **orangé** *nm* orangey colour *Br ou* color *Am.*

orangeade [ɔrɑ̃ʒad] *nf* orange squash.

oranger [ɔrɑ̃ʒe] *nm* orange tree.

orangeraie [ɔrɑ̃ʒrɛ] *nf* orange grove.

orang-outan (*pl* **orangs-outans**), **orang-outang** (*pl* **orangs-outangs**) [ɔrɑ̃utɑ̃] *nm* orangutang.

orateur, trice [ɔratœr, tris] *nm, f* - **1.** [conférencier] speaker - **2.** [personne éloquente] orator.

orbital, e, aux [ɔrbital, o] *adj* [mouvement] orbital ; [station] orbiting.

orbite [ɔrbit] *nf* - **1.** ANAT (eye) socket - **2.** AS-

TRON & *fig* orbit ; **mettre sur ~** AÉRON to put into orbit ; *fig* to launch.

Orcades [ɔrkad] *nfpl* : **les ~** the Orkney Islands, the Orkneys.

orchestral, e, aux [ɔrkɛstral, o] *adj* orchestral.

orchestration [ɔrkɛstrasjɔ̃] *nf* orchestration.

orchestre [ɔrkɛstr] *nm* - **1.** MUS orchestra - **2.** CIN & THÉÂTRE stalls *(pl) Br,* orchestra *Am ;* **fauteuil d'~** seat in the stalls *Br,* orchestra seat *Am.*

orchestrer [3] [ɔrkɛstre] *vt litt & fig* to orchestrate.

orchidée [ɔrkide] *nf* orchid.

ordinaire [ɔrdinɛr] ◇ *adj* - **1.** [usuel, standard] ordinary, normal - **2.** *péj* [commun] ordinary, common ◇ *nm* - **1.** [moyenne] : **l'~** the ordinary - **2.** [alimentation] usual diet.
◆ **d'ordinaire** *loc adv* normally, usually.

ordinal, e, aux [ɔrdinal, o] *adj* ordinal.
◆ **ordinal, aux** *nm* ordinal (number).

ordinateur [ɔrdinatœr] *nm* computer ; **~ individuel** personal computer, PC ; **~ de poche** palmtop.

ordonnance [ɔrdɔnɑ̃s] ◇ *nf* - **1.** MÉD prescription - **2.** [de gouvernement, juge] order ◇ *nm ou nf* MIL orderly.

ordonnateur, trice [ɔrdɔnatœr, tris] *nm, f* organizer.

ordonné, e [ɔrdɔne] *adj* [maison, élève] tidy.

ordonner [3] [ɔrdɔne] *vt* - **1.** [ranger] to organize, to put in order - **2.** [enjoindre] to order, to tell ; **~ à qqn de faire qqch** to order sb to do sthg - **3.** MÉD : **~ qqch à qqn** to prescribe sb sthg - **4.** RELIG to ordain - **5.** MATHS to arrange in order.
◆ **s'ordonner** *vp* to be arranged *ou* put in order.

ordre [ɔrdr] *nm* - **1.** [gén, MIL & RELIG] order ; **par ~ alphabétique/chronologique/décroissant** in alphabetical / chronological / descending order ; **par ~ d'entrée en scène** in order of appearance ; **procéder par ~** to take one thing at a time ; **rétablir l'~** to restore order ; **rappeler qqn à l'~** to call sb to order ; **donner un ~ à qqn** to give sb an order ; **être aux ~s de qqn** to be at sb's disposal ; **intimer à qqn l'~ de faire qqch** to order sb to do sthg ; **jusqu'à nouvel ~** until further notice ; **entrer dans les ~s** RELIG to take holy orders ; **l'~ établi** the established order ; **~ de mission** MIL orders *(pl)* (*for a particular mission*) ; **l'~ public** law and order ; **troubler l'~ public** to disturb the peace - **2.** [bonne organisation] tidiness, orderliness ; **en ~** orderly, tidy ; **avoir de l'~** to

be orderly *ou* tidy ; **mettre en** ~ to put in order, to tidy (up) ; **mettre bon** ~ **à** to sort out - **3.** [catégorie] : **de premier** ~ first-rate ; **de second** ~ second-rate ; **d'**~ **privé/pratique** of a private/practical nature ; **dans un tout autre** ~ **d'idées** in a quite different connection ; **pouvez-vous me donner un** ~ **de grandeur?** can you give me some idea of the size/amount *etc* ? - **4.** [corporation] professional association ; **l'Ordre des médecins** ≃ the British Medical Association *Br*, ≃ the American Medical Association *Am* - **5.** FIN : **à l'**~ **de** payable to.
- **ordre du jour** *nm* - **1.** [de réunion] agenda ; **à l'**~ **du jour** [de réunion] on the agenda ; *fig* topical - **2.** MIL order of the day.

ordure [ɔrdyr] *nf* - **1.** *fig* [grossièreté] filth *(U)* - **2.** *péj* [personne] scum *(U)*, bastard.
- **ordures** *nfpl* [déchets] rubbish *(U) Br*, garbage *(U) Am*.

ordurier, ère [ɔrdyrje, ɛr] *adj* filthy, obscene.

orée [ɔre] *nf* edge.

oreille [ɔrɛj] *nf* - **1.** ANAT ear - **2.** [ouïe] hearing ; **avoir de l'**~ to have a good ear (for music) ; **être dur d'**~ to be hard of hearing - **3.** [de fauteuil, écrou] wing ; [de marmite, tasse] handle - **4.** *loc* : **se boucher les** ~**s** to close one's ears ; **dormir sur ses deux** ~**s** to rest easy ; **dresser** *ou* **tendre l'**~ to prick up one's ears ; **écorcher les** ~**s** to grate on the ear ; **écouter d'une** ~ **distraite, n'écouter que d'une** ~ to only half-listen ; **il ne l'entend pas de cette** ~ he's dead (set) against it ; **faire la sourde** ~ to turn a deaf ear ; **se faire tirer l'**~ to need talking round ; **prêter l'**~ **(à qqch)** to lend an ear (to sthg) ; **rebattre les** ~**s à qqn** *fam* to go on at sb.

oreiller [ɔreje] *nm* pillow.

oreillette [ɔrɛjɛt] *nf* - **1.** [du cœur] auricle - **2.** [de casquette] earflap.

oreillons [ɔrɛjɔ̃] *nmpl* mumps *(sg)*.

ores [ɔr] - **d'ores et déjà** *loc adv* from now on.

orfèvre [ɔrfɛvr] *nm* goldsmith ; [d'argent] silversmith ; **être** ~ **en la matière** *fig* to be (an) expert on the subject.

orfèvrerie [ɔrfɛvrəri] *nf* - **1.** [art] goldsmith's art ; [d'argent] silversmith's art - **2.** [commerce] goldsmith's trade ; [d'argent] silversmith's trade.

orfraie [ɔrfrɛ] *nf* sea eagle.

organdi [ɔrgɑ̃di] *nm* organdie.

organe [ɔrgan] *nm* - **1.** ANAT organ - **2.** [institution] organ, body - **3.** [mécanisme] mechanism, system ; ~**s de commande** controls - **4.** *litté-*

raire [voix] voice - **5.** *fig* [porte-parole] representative.

organigramme [ɔrganigram] *nm* - **1.** [hiérarchique] organization chart - **2.** INFORM flow chart.

organique [ɔrganik] *adj* organic.

organisateur, trice [ɔrganizatœr, tris] ◇ *adj* organizing *(avant n)* ◇ *nm, f* organizer.

organisation [ɔrganizasjɔ̃] *nf* organization ; **avoir le sens de l'**~ to be well-organized ; **Organisation mondiale du commerce** World Trade Organization.

organisé, e [ɔrganize] *adj* organized ; ~ **en qqch** organized in sthg.

organiser [ɔrganize] *vt* to organize.
- **s'organiser** *vp* - **1.** [personne] to be *ou* get organized - **2.** [prendre forme] to take shape.

organiseur [ɔrganizœr] *nm* [agenda, ordinateur] (personal) organizer.

organisme [ɔrganism] *nm* - **1.** BIOL & ZOOL organism ; ~ **génétiquement modifié** genetically modified organism - **2.** [institution] body, organization.

organiste [ɔrganist] *nmf* organist.

orgasme [ɔrgasm] *nm* orgasm.

orge [ɔrʒ] *nf* barley.

orgeat [ɔrʒa] *nm* : **sirop d'**~ barley water.

orgelet [ɔrʒəlɛ] *nm* stye.

orgie [ɔrʒi] *nf* orgy.

orgue [ɔrg] *nm* organ.
- **orgues** *nfpl* - **1.** MUS organ *(sg)* - **2.** GÉOL columns.

orgueil [ɔrgœj] *nm* pride.

orgueilleux, euse [ɔrgœjø, øz] ◇ *adj* proud ◇ *nm, f* proud person.

orient [ɔrjɑ̃] *nm* east.
- **Orient** *nm* : **l'Orient** the Orient, the East.

orientable [ɔrjɑ̃tabl] *adj* adjustable.

oriental, e, aux [ɔrjɑ̃tal, o] *adj* [région, frontière] eastern ; [d'Extrême-Orient] oriental.
- **Oriental, e aux** *nm, f* Oriental.

orientation [ɔrjɑ̃tasjɔ̃] *nf* - **1.** [direction] orientation ; **avoir le sens de l'**~ to have a good sense of direction - **2.** SCOL career ; ~ **professionnelle** careers advice, vocational guidance - **3.** [de maison] aspect - **4.** *fig* [de politique, recherche] direction, trend.

orienté, e [ɔrjɑ̃te] *adj* [tendancieux] biased.

orienter [3] [ɔrjɑ̃te] *vt* - **1.** [disposer] to position - **2.** [voyageur, élève, recherches] to guide, to direct - **3.** [navire] to steer ; [voile] to trim.
- **s'orienter** *vp* - **1.** [se repérer] to find *ou* get

one's bearings - **2.** *fig* [se diriger] : **s'~ vers** to move towards *Br ou* toward *Am*.

orifice [ɔrifis] *nm* orifice.

oriflamme [ɔriflam] *nf* banner.

origan [ɔrigɑ̃] *nm* oregano.

originaire [ɔriʒinɛr] *adj* - **1.** [natif] : **être ~ de** to originate from ; [personne] to be a native of - **2.** [premier] original.

original, e, aux [ɔriʒinal, o] ◇ *adj* - **1.** [premier, inédit] original - **2.** [singulier] eccentric ◇ *nm, f* [personne] (outlandish) character.

➡ **original, aux** *nm* [œuvre, document] original.

originalité [ɔriʒinalite] *nf* - **1.** [nouveauté] originality ; [caractéristique] original feature - **2.** [excentricité] eccentricity.

origine [ɔriʒin] *nf* - **1.** [gén] origin ; **d'~** [originel] original ; [de départ] of origin ; **pays d'~** country of origin ; **d'~ anglaise** of English origin ; **à l'~** originally - **2.** [souche] origins *(pl)* - **3.** [provenance] source.

originel, elle [ɔriʒinɛl] *adj* original.

orignal, aux [ɔriɲal, o] *nm* moose.

oripeaux [ɔripo] *nmpl* rags.

ORL ◇ *nmf* (*abr de* oto-rhino-laryngologiste) ENT specialist ◇ *nf* (*abr de* oto-rhino-laryngologie) ENT.

orme [ɔrm] *nm* elm.

ormeau, x [ɔrmo] *nm* young elm.

ornement [ɔrnəmɑ̃] *nm* - **1.** [gén & *MUS*] ornament ; **d'~** [plante, arbre] ornamental - **2.** *ARCHIT* embellishment.

ornemental, e, aux [ɔrnəmɑ̃tal, o] *adj* ornamental.

ornementation [ɔrnəmɑ̃tasjɔ̃] *nf* ornamentation.

ornementer [3] [ɔrnəmɑ̃te] *vt* to ornament.

orner [3] [ɔrne] *vt* - **1.** [décorer] : **~ (de)** to decorate (with) - **2.** [agrémenter] to adorn.

ornière [ɔrnjɛr] *nf* rut.

ornithologie [ɔrnitɔlɔʒi] *nf* ornithology.

orphelin, e [ɔrfəlɛ̃, in] ◇ *adj* orphan *(avant n)*, orphaned ; **~ de père** fatherless ; **~ de mère** motherless ◇ *nm, f* orphan.

orphelinat [ɔrfəlina] *nm* orphanage.

Orsay [ɔrsɛ] *n* : **le musée d'~** *art museum in Paris*.

LE MUSÉE D'ORSAY

This museum, a converted railway station on the banks of the Seine, houses works of art from the second half of the 19th century and the early 20th century.

ORSEC, Orsec [ɔrsɛk] (*abr de* Organisation

des secours) *adj* : **le plan ~** *disaster contingency plan*.

LE PLAN ORSEC

This plan is set in motion whenever there is a major disaster in France, such as flooding or forest fires.

ORSECRAD, Orsecrad [ɔrsɛkrad] (*abr de* Orsec en cas d'accident nucléaire) *adj* : **plan ~** *disaster contingency plan in case of nuclear accident*.

orteil [ɔrtɛj] *nm* toe ; **gros ~** big toe.

orthodontiste [ɔrtɔdɔ̃tist] *nmf* orthodontist.

orthodoxe [ɔrtɔdɔks] ◇ *adj* - **1.** *RELIG* Orthodox - **2.** [conformiste] orthodox ◇ *nmf* - **1.** *RELIG* Orthodox Christian - **2.** *POLIT* conformist.

orthodoxie [ɔrtɔdɔksi] *nf* orthodoxy.

orthogonal, e, aux [ɔrtɔgɔnal, o] *adj* orthogonal.

orthographe [ɔrtɔgraf] *nf* spelling.

orthographier [9] [ɔrtɔgrafje] *vt* to spell ; **mal ~** to misspell.

orthographique [ɔrtɔgrafik] *adj* orthographic.

orthopédique [ɔrtɔpedik] *adj* orthopaedic.

orthopédiste [ɔrtɔpedist] *nmf* orthopaedist.

orthophoniste [ɔrtɔfɔnist] *nmf* speech therapist.

ortie [ɔrti] *nf* nettle.

ortolan [ɔrtɔlɑ̃] *nm* ortolan.

orvet [ɔrvɛ] *nm* slowworm.

os [ɔs, pl o] *nm* - **1.** [gén] bone ; **~ à moelle** marrowbone ; **~ de seiche** cuttlebone - **2.** *fam fig* [difficulté] snag, hitch.

OS (*abr de* ouvrier spécialisé) *nm* semi-skilled worker.

oscillation [ɔsilasjɔ̃] *nf* oscillation ; [de navire] rocking.

oscillatoire [ɔsilatwar] *adj* swinging, oscillatory.

osciller [3] [ɔsile] *vi* - **1.** [se balancer] to swing ; [navire] to rock - **2.** [vaciller, hésiter] to waver.

osé, e [oze] *adj* daring, audacious.

oseille [ozɛj] *nf* - **1.** *BOT* sorrel - **2.** *fam* [argent] bread.

oser [3] [oze] *vt* to dare ; **~ faire qqch** to dare (to) do sthg ; **si j'ose dire** if I may say so.

osier [ozje] *nm* - **1.** *BOT* osier - **2.** [fibre] wicker.

Oslo [ɔslo] *n* Oslo.

osmose [ɔsmoz] *nf* osmosis ; **en ~ by** osmosis.

ossature [ɔsatyr] *nf* - **1.** ANAT skeleton - **2.** *fig* [structure] framework.

osselet [ɔslɛ] *nm* - **1.** ANAT ossicle - **2.** [élément de jeu] jack ; **jouer aux ~s** to play jacks.

ossements [ɔsmã] *nmpl* bones.

osseux, euse [ɔsø, øz] *adj* - **1.** ANAT & MÉD bone *(avant n)* - **2.** [maigre] bony.

ossification [ɔsifikasjɔ̃] *nf* ossification.

ossuaire [ɔsɥɛr] *nm* ossuary.

ostensible [ɔstãsibl] *adj* conspicuous.

ostensiblement [ɔstãsibləmã] *adv* conspicuously.

ostensoir [ɔstãswar] *nm* monstrance.

ostentation [ɔstãtasjɔ̃] *nf* ostentation.

ostentatoire [ɔstãtatwar] *adj* ostentatious.

ostéopathe [ɔsteɔpat] *nmf* osteopath.

ostéoporose [ɔsteɔpɔroz] *nf* MÉD osteoporosis.

ostracisme [ɔstrasism] *nm* ostracism.

otage [ɔtaʒ] *nm* hostage ; **prendre qqn en ~** to take sb hostage.

OTAN, Otan [ɔtã] *(abr de* **Organisation du traité de l'Atlantique Nord***) nf* NATO.

otarie [ɔtari] *nf* sea lion.

OTASE [ɔtaz] *(abr de* **Organisation du traité de l'Asie du sud-est***) nf* SEATO.

ôter [3] [ote] *vt* - **1.** [enlever] to take off - **2.** [soustraire] to take away - **3.** [retirer, prendre] : **~ qqch à qqn** to take sthg away from sb.
　　◆ **s'ôter** *vp fam* : **ôte-toi de là!** get out of the way!

otite [ɔtit] *nf* ear infection.

oto-rhino-laryngologie [ɔtɔrinɔlarɛ̃gɔlɔʒi] *nf* ear, nose and throat medicine, ENT.

Ottawa [ɔtawa] *n* Ottawa.

ou [u] *conj* - **1.** [indique une alternative, une approximation] or - **2.** [sinon] : **~ (bien)** or (else).
　　◆ **ou (bien) ... ou (bien)** *loc corrélative* either ... or ; **~ c'est elle, ~ c'est moi!** it's either her or me!

où [u] ◇ *pron rel* - **1.** [spatial] where ; **le village ~ j'habite** the village where I live, the village I live in ; **pose-le là ~ tu l'as trouvé** put it back where you found it ; **partout ~ vous irez** wherever you go - **2.** [temporel] that ; **le jour ~ je suis venu** the day (that) I came ◇ *adv* where ; **je vais ~ je veux** I go where I please ; **que vous alliez wherever you go** ◇ *adv interr* where? ; **~ vas-tu?** where are you going? ; **~ est la voiture?** where's the car? ; **dites-moi ~ il est allé** tell me where he's gone.
　　◆ **d'où** *loc adv* [conséquence] hence ; **d'~ on conclut que ...** from which it may be concluded that ...

OUA *(abr de* **Organisation de l'unité africaine***) nf* OAU.

Ouagadougou [wagadugu] *n* Ouagadougou.

ouailles [waj] *nfpl* flock *(sg)*.

ouais [wɛ] *interj fam* yeah!

ouananiche [wananiʃ] *nf* Can *type of freshwater salmon*.

ouaouaron [wawarɔ̃] *nm* Can bullfrog.

ouate [wat] *nf* - **1.** [pansement] cotton wool Br, cotton Am - **2.** [rembourrage] (cotton) wadding.

ouaté, e [wate] *adj* - **1.** [garni d'ouate] cotton wool Br *(avant n)*, cotton Am *(avant n)* ; [vêtement] quilted - **2.** *fig* [feutré] muffled.

oubli [ubli] *nm* - **1.** [acte d'oublier] forgetting - **2.** [négligence] omission ; [étourderie] oversight - **3.** [abnégation] : **~ de soi** self-effacement - **4.** [général] oblivion ; **tomber dans l'~** to sink into oblivion.

oublier [10] [ublije] *vt* to forget ; [laisser quelque part] to leave behind ; **~ de faire qqch** to forget to do sthg.
　　◆ **s'oublier** *vp* - **1.** [emploi passif] to be forgotten - **2.** [emploi réfléchi] to forget o.s. - **3.** *euphémisme* [chat, enfant] to have an accident.

oubliettes [ublijɛt] *nfpl* dungeon *(sg)* ; **jeter qqch aux ~** *fam fig* to shelve sthg.

oublieux, euse [ublijø, øz] *adj* forgetful.

ouest [wɛst] ◇ *nm* west ; **un vent d'~** a westerly wind ; **le vent d'~** the west wind ; **à l'~** in the west ; **à l'~ (de)** to the west (of) ◇ *adj inv* [gén] west ; [province, région] western.

ouest-allemand, e [wɛstalmã, ãd] *adj* West German.

ouf [uf] *interj* phew!

Ouganda [ugãda] *nm* : **l'~** Uganda.

ougandais, e [ugãdɛ, ɛz] *adj* Ugandan.
　　◆ **Ougandais, e** *nm, f* Ugandan.

oui [wi] ◇ *adv* yes ; **tu viens? - ~** are you coming? - yes (I am) ; **tu viens, ~ ou non?** are you coming or not?, are you coming or aren't you? ; **je crois que ~** I think so ; **faire signe que ~** to nod ; **mais ~, bien sûr que ~** yes, of course ◇ *nm inv* yes ; **pour un ~ pour un non** for no apparent reason.

ouï-dire [widir] *nm inv* : **par ~** by *ou* from hearsay.

ouïe [wi] *nf* hearing ; **avoir l'~ fine** to have excellent hearing.
　　◆ **ouïes** *nfpl* [de poisson] gills.

ouistiti [wistiti] *nm* - **1.** ZOOL marmoset - **2.** *fam* [type] bloke Br, guy.

Oulan-Bator [ulanbatɔr] *n* Ulan Bator.

ouragan [uragã] *nm* - **1.** MÉTÉOR hurricane - **2.** *fig* [tempête] storm.

ourdir [32] [urdir] *vt fig* & *littéraire* [complot] to hatch.

ourler [3] [urle] *vt* - **1.** COUTURE to hem - **2.** *littéraire* [border] to edge.

ourlet [urle] *nm* - **1.** COUTURE hem ; **faire un ~ à** to hem - **2.** [de l'oreille] helix.

ours [urs] *nm* bear ; **~ (en peluche)** teddy (bear) ; **~ polaire** polar bear.

ourse [urs] *nf* she-bear.
➠ **Ourse** *nf* : **la Grande/Petite Ourse** the Great/Little Bear.

oursin [ursɛ̃] *nm* sea urchin.

ourson [ursɔ̃] *nm* bear cub.

oust, ouste [ust] *interj fam* [dehors!] clear off! ; [vite!] get a move on!

outarde [utard] *nf* bustard.

outil [uti] *nm* tool.

outillage [utijaʒ] *nm* [équipement] tools *(pl)*, equipment.

outrage [utraʒ] *nm* - **1.** *sout* [insulte] insult ; **faire subir les derniers ~s à qqn** *fig* & *littéraire* to ravish sb - **2.** JUR : **~ aux bonnes mœurs** affront to public decency ; **~ à magistrat** contempt of court ; **~ à la pudeur** indecent behaviour *(U)* Br *ou* behavior *(U)* Am.

outrageant, e [utraʒɑ̃, ɑ̃t] *adj* insulting, offensive.

outrager [17] [utraʒe] *vt* - **1.** [offenser] to insult - **2.** [contrevenir] to offend.

outrageusement [utraʒøzmɑ̃] *adv* outrageously.

outrance [utrɑ̃s] *nf* excess ; **à ~** excessively.

outrancier, ère [utrɑ̃sje, ɛr] *adj* extravagant.

outre[1] [utr] *nf* wineskin.

outre[2] [utr] <> *prép* besides, as well as <> *adv* : **passer ~** to go on, to proceed further ; **passer ~ à qqch** to disregard sthg.
➠ **en outre** *loc adv* moreover, besides.
➠ **outre que** *loc conj* apart from the fact that.

outre-Atlantique [utratlɑ̃tik] *loc adv* across the Atlantic.

outrecuidance [utrəkɥidɑ̃s] *nf littéraire* presumptuousness.

outrecuidant, e [utrəkɥidɑ̃, ɑ̃t] *adj littéraire* presumptuous.

outre-Manche [utrəmɑ̃ʃ] *loc adv* across the Channel.

outremer [utrəmɛr] <> *nm* [pierre] lapis lazuli ; [couleur] ultramarine <> *adj inv* ultramarine.

outre-mer [utrəmɛr] *loc adv* overseas ; **d'~** overseas.

outrepasser [3] [utrəpase] *vt* to exceed.

outrer [3] [utre] *vt* [personne] to outrage.

outre-Rhin [utrərɛ̃] *loc adv* across the Rhine.

outsider [awtsajdœr] *nm* outsider.

ouvert, e [uvɛr, ɛrt] <> *pp* ▷ **ouvrir** <> *adj* - **1.** [gén] open ; **grand ~** wide open - **2.** [robinet] on, running.

ouvertement [uvɛrtəmɑ̃] *adv* openly.

ouverture [uvɛrtyr] *nf* - **1.** [gén] opening ; [d'hostilités] outbreak ; **l'~ de la chasse** the start of the hunting season ; **~ d'esprit** open-mindedness - **2.** MUS overture - **3.** PHOT aperture.
➠ **ouvertures** *nfpl* [propositions] overtures.

ouvrable [uvrabl] *adj* working ; **heures ~s** hours of business.

ouvrage [uvraʒ] *nm* - **1.** [travail] work *(U)*, task ; **se mettre à l'~** to start work - **2.** [objet produit] (piece of) work ; COUTURE work *(U)* - **3.** [livre, écrit] work ; **~ de référence** reference work.

ouvragé, e [uvraʒe] *adj* elaborate.

ouvrant, e [uvrɑ̃, ɑ̃t] *adj* : **toit ~** sunroof.

ouvré, e [uvre] *adj* : **jour ~** working day.

ouvre-boîtes [uvrəbwat] *nm inv* tin opener Br, can opener.

ouvre-bouteilles [uvrəbutɛj] *nm inv* bottle opener.

ouvreuse [uvrøz] *nf* usherette.

ouvrier, ère [uvrije, ɛr] <> *adj* [quartier, enfance] working-class ; [conflit] industrial ; [questions, statut] labour *(avant n)* Br, labor *(avant n)* Am ; **classe ouvrière** working class <> *nm, f* worker ; **~ agricole** farm worker ; **~ qualifié** skilled worker ; **~ spécialisé** semi-skilled worker.
➠ **ouvrière** *nf* ZOOL worker.

ouvrir [34] [uvrir] <> *vt* - **1.** [gén] to open ; **~ qqch à qqn** to open sthg to sb - **2.** [chemin, voie] to open up - **3.** [gaz] to turn on <> *vi* to open ; **~ par qqch** to open with sthg ; **~ sur qqch** to open onto sthg.
➠ **s'ouvrir** *vp* - **1.** [porte, fleur] to open - **2.** [route, perspectives] to open up - **3.** [personne] : **s'~ (à qqn)** to confide (in sb), to open up (to sb) - **4.** [se blesser] : **s'~ le genou** to cut one's knee open ; **s'~ les veines** to slash *ou* cut one's wrists - **5.** [se sensibiliser] : **s'~ à qqch** to start to take an interest in sthg.

ovaire [ɔvɛr] *nm* ovary.

ovale [ɔval] *adj* & *nm* oval.

ovation [ɔvasjɔ̃] *nf* ovation ; **faire une ~ à qqn** to give sb an ovation.

ovationner [3] [ɔvasjɔne] *vt* to give an ovation to.

overdose [ɔvœrdoz] *nf* overdose.

ovin, e [ɔvɛ̃, in] *adj* ovine.
➡ **ovin** *nm* sheep.

OVNI, Ovni [ɔvni] (*abr de* **objet volant non identifié**) *nm* UFO.

ovoïde [ɔvɔid] *adj* egg-shaped.

ovuler [3] [ɔvyle] *vi* to ovulate.

oxydable [ɔksidabl] *adj* liable to rust.

oxydation [ɔksidasjɔ̃] *nf* oxidation, oxidization.

oxyde [ɔksid] *nm* oxide ; **~ de carbone** carbon monoxide.

oxyder [3] [ɔkside] *vt* to oxidize.
➡ **s'oxyder** *vp* to become oxidized.

oxygène [ɔksiʒɛn] *nm* oxygen ; **ballon d'~** oxygen cylinder.

oxygéné, e [ɔksiʒene] *adj* - **1.** CHIM oxygenated ▷ **eau** - **2.** [cheveux] peroxide-blond, bleached.

oxygéner [18] [ɔksiʒene] *vt* - **1.** CHIM to oxygenate - **2.** [cheveux] to bleach, to peroxide.
➡ **s'oxygéner** *vp fam* to get some fresh air.

ozone [ozon] *nm* ozone.

P

p¹, P [pe] *nm inv* p, P.

p² - **1.** (*abr de* **pico**) p - **2.** (*abr de* **page**) p - **3.** (*abr de* **passable**) *fair grade* (*as assessment of schoolwork*), ≃ C - **4.** *abr de* **pièce**.

Pa (*abr de* **pascal**) Pa.

PA (*abr de* **petites annonces**) *nfpl* small ads.

PAC, Pac [pak] (*abr de* **politique agricole commune**) *nf* CAP.

pacage [pakaʒ] *nm* pasture.

pacemaker [pɛsmekœr] *nm* pacemaker.

pacha [paʃa] *nm* pasha ; **mener une vie de ~** *fam fig* to live a life of ease.

pachyderme [paʃidɛrm] *nm* elephant ; **les ~s** (the) pachyderms.

pacificateur, trice [pasifikatœr, tris] ◇ *adj* pacifying ◇ *nm, f* peacemaker.

pacification [pasifikasjɔ̃] *nf* pacification.

pacifier [9] [pasifje] *vt* to pacify.

pacifique [pasifik] *adj* peaceful.

Pacifique [pasifik] *nm* : **le ~** the Pacific (Ocean).

pacifiquement [pasifikmɑ̃] *adv* peacefully.

pacifiste [pasifist] *nmf & adj* pacifist.

pack [pak] *nm* pack.

package [pakadʒ] *nm* INFORM package.

packaging [pakadʒiŋ] *nm* packaging.

pacotille [pakɔtij] *nf* shoddy goods (*pl*), rubbish ; **de ~** cheap.

PACS [paks] (*abr de* **Pacte civil de solidarité**) *nm* Civil Solidarity Pact, *civil contract conferring marital rights on the contrating parties*.

pacte [pakt] *nm* pact.

pactiser [3] [paktize] *vi* : **~ avec** [faire un pacte avec] to make a pact with ; [transiger avec] to come to terms with.

pactole [paktɔl] *nm* gold mine *fig*.

paddock [padɔk] *nm* - **1.** [d'un hippodrome] paddock - **2.** *tfam* [lit] : **se mettre au ~** to hit the sack.

paddy [padi] *nm* paddy (rice).

paella [paela] *nf* paella.

paf [paf] ◇ *interj* wham! ◇ *adj inv fam* [ivre] plastered.

PAF [paf] ◇ *nf* (*abr de* **Police de l'air et des frontières**) *police authority responsible for civil aviation etc* ◇ *nm* (*abr de* **paysage audiovisuel français**) *French radio and television*.

pagaie [pagɛ] *nf* paddle.

pagaille, pagaye, pagaïe [pagaj] *nf fam* mess ; **en ~** [en désordre] in a mess ; **des fruits en ~** loads of fruit.

paganisme [paganism] *nm* paganism.

pagaye = **pagaille**.

pagayer [11] [pageje] *vi* to paddle.

pagayeur, euse [pagɛjœr, øz] *nm, f* paddler.

page [paʒ] ◇ *nf* - **1.** [feuillet] page ; **~ blanche** blank page ; **mettre en ~s** TYPO to make up (into pages) ; **~ d'accueil** INFORM home page ; **~ de garde** flyleaf - **2.** *fig* [passage] passage ; [événement] episode, page - **3.** *loc* : **être à la ~** to be up-to-date ; **tourner la ~** to turn the page ◇ *nm* page (boy).

pagination [paʒinasjɔ̃] *nf* pagination.

pagne [paɲ] *nm* loincloth.

pagode [pagɔd] *nf* pagoda.

paie¹, paies *etc* ⊳ **payer.**

paie², paye [pɛ] *nf* pay (U), wages (pl).

paiement, payement [pɛmɑ̃] *nm* payment ; **~ anticipé** advance payment.

païen, ïenne [pajɛ̃, ɛn] *adj* & *nm, f* pagan, heathen.

paierai, paieras *etc* ⊳ **payer.**

paillard, e [pajar, ard] ⇔ *adj* bawdy ⇔ *nm, f* rake (f slut).

paillasse [pajas] ⇔ *nf* - **1.** [matelas] straw mattress - **2.** [d'évier] draining board ⇔ *nm* clown.

paillasson [pajasɔ̃] *nm* - **1.** [tapis] doormat - **2.** AGRIC (roll of) matting.

paille [paj] *nf* - **1.** BOT straw ; **être sur la ~** *fam fig* to be down and out - **2.** [pour boire] straw.
⇒ **paille de fer** *nf* steel wool.

pailleté, e [pajte] *adj* sequined.

paillette [pajɛt] *nf (gén pl)* - **1.** [sur vêtements] sequin, spangle - **2.** [d'or] grain of gold dust - **3.** [de lessive, savon] flake ; **savon en ~s** soap flakes (pl).

pain [pɛ̃] *nm* - **1.** [aliment] bread ; **un ~ a** loaf ; **petit ~** (bread) roll ; **~ azyme** unleavened bread ; **~ de campagne** ≃ farmhouse loaf ; **~ au chocolat** *sweet roll with chocolate filling* ; **~ complet** wholemeal bread ; **~ d'épice** ≃ gingerbread ; **~ au lait** sweet roll, bun ; **~ de mie** sandwich loaf ; **~ perdu** ≃ French toast ; **~ de seigle** rye bread ; **~ au son** wholemeal bread ; **avoir du ~ sur la planche** *fam fig* to have a lot on one's plate ; **ôter le ~ de la bouche de qqn** *fig* to take the bread out of sb's mouth - **2.** [de savon, cire] bar - **3.** *tfam* [coup] punch.

pair, e [pɛr] *adj* even.
⇒ **pair** *nm* peer.
⇒ **paire** *nf* pair ; **une ~e de** [lunettes, ciseaux, chaussures] a pair of ; **c'est une autre ~e de manches** *fig* that's another story.
⇒ **au pair** *loc adv* for board and lodging, for one's keep ; **jeune fille au ~** au pair (girl).
⇒ **de pair** *loc adv* : **aller de ~ avec** to go hand in hand with.
⇒ **hors pair** *loc adj* unrivalled *Br*, unrivaled *Am*.

paisible [pɛzibl] *adj* peaceful.

paisiblement [pɛzibləmɑ̃] *adv* peacefully.

paître [91] [pɛtr] ⇔ *vi* to graze ⇔ *vt* to feed on.

paix [pɛ] *nf* peace ; **en ~** [en harmonie] at peace ; [tranquillement] in peace ; **avoir la ~** to have peace and quiet ; **faire la ~ avec qqn** to make peace with sb ; **ficher la ~ à qqn** *fam* to stop hassling sb ; **laisser qqn en ~** to leave sb alone *ou* in peace.

Pakistan [pakistɑ̃] *nm* : **le ~** Pakistan ; **au ~** in Pakistan.

pakistanais, e [pakistanɛ, ɛz] *adj* Pakistani.
⇒ **Pakistanais, e** *nm, f* Pakistani.

PAL, Pal [pal] *(abr de* **Phase Alternation Line)** *adj* PAL.

palabrer [3] [palabre] *vi* to have interminable discussions.

palabres [palabr] *nmpl* ou *nfpl* interminable discussions.

palace [palas] *nm* luxury hotel.

palais [palɛ] *nm* - **1.** [château] palace - **2.** [grand édifice] centre *Br*, center *Am* ; **~ des expositions** exhibition centre *Br* ou center *Am* ; **le ~ Garnier** *the (old) Paris opera house* ; **~ de justice** JUR law courts (pl) ; **le ~ du Luxembourg** *palace in Paris where the French Senate is situated* ; **~ omnisports** (multi-purpose) sports centre *Br* ou center *Am* ; **le ~ des Papes** *the Papal Palace in Avignon* ; **le Grand Palais** the Grand Palais ; **le Petit Palais** the Petit Palais - **3.** ANAT palate.

GRAND ET PETIT PALAIS

Both museums were built for the 'Exposition universelle' in 1900 on a wide tract of land between the Champs-Élysées and the Seine. The west wing of the 'Grand Palais' houses the 'Palais de la Découverte', an interactive science museum for children and adults. International art exhibitions are held in other parts of the museum. The 'Petit Palais' houses the 'Musée des Beaux-Arts' as well as other temporary art exhibitions.

palan [palɑ̃] *nm* block and tackle, hoist.

pale [pal] *nf* [de rame, d'hélice] blade.

pâle [pal] *adj* pale.

palefrenier [palfrənje] *nm* groom.

paléographie [paleografi] *nf* paleography.

paléolithique [paleolitik] ⇔ *nm* : **le ~** the Paleolithic (age) ⇔ *adj* paleolithic.

paléontologie [paleɔ̃tɔlɔʒi] *nf* paleontology.

Palerme [palɛrm] *n* Palermo.

Palestine [palɛstin] *nf* : **la ~** Palestine.

palestinien, enne [palɛstinjɛ̃, ɛn] *adj* Palestinian.
⇒ **Palestinien, enne** *nm, f* Palestinian.

palet [palɛ] *nm* HOCKEY puck.

paletot [palto] *nm* (short) overcoat.

palette [palɛt] *nf* - **1.** [de peintre] palette - **2.** CULIN shoulder - **3.** [de chariot élévateur] pallet.

palétuvier [paletyvje] *nm* mangrove.

pâleur [palœr] *nf* [de visage] pallor.

pâlichon, onne [paliʒɔ̃, ɔn] *adj fam* pale, sickly-looking.

palier [palje] *nm* - **1.** [d'escalier] landing - **2.** [étape] level - **3.** TECHNOL bearing.

pâlir [32] [palir] ⬦ *vt* to turn pale ⬦ *vi* [couleur, lumière] to fade ; [personne] to turn *ou* go pale ; **~ de** [angoisse] to turn *ou* go pale with ; [jalousie] to turn *ou* go green with.

palissade [palisad] *nf* [clôture] fence ; [de verdure] hedge.

palissandre [palisɑ̃dr] *nm* rosewood.

palliatif, ive [paljatif, iv] *adj* palliative.
⬥ **palliatif** *nm* - **1.** MÉD palliative - **2.** *fig* stopgap measure.

pallier [9] [palje] *vt* to make up for.

Palma [palma] *n* : **~ (de Majorque)** Palma (de Majorca).

palmarès [palmarɛs] *nm* - **1.** [de lauréats] list of (medal) winners, SCOL list of prizewinners - **2.** [de succès] record (of achievements).

palme [palm] *nf* - **1.** [de palmier] palm-leaf - **2.** [de nageur] flipper - **3.** [décoration, distinction] : **avec ~** MIL ≃ with bar ; **la ~ d'or** *award given to best film at the Cannes Film Festival* ; **~s académiques** *decoration awarded for services to education*.

palmé, e [palme] *adj* - **1.** BOT palmate - **2.** ZOOL web-footed ; [patte] webbed.

palmeraie [palmərɛ] *nf* palm grove.

palmier [palmje] *nm* - **1.** BOT palm tree - **2.** CULIN *sweet pastry shaped like a palm leaf*.

palmipède [palmipɛd] ⬦ *nm* web-footed bird ⬦ *adj* web-footed.

palombe [palɔ̃b] *nf* woodpigeon.

pâlot, otte [palo, ɔt] *adj* pale, sickly-looking.

palourde [palurd] *nf* clam.

palpable [palpabl] *adj* palpable, tangible.

palper [3] [palpe] *vt* - **1.** [toucher] to feel, to finger ; MÉD to palpate - **2.** *fam* [de l'argent] to get.

palpitant, e [palpitɑ̃, ɑ̃t] *adj* exciting, thrilling.

palpitation [palpitasjɔ̃] *nf* palpitation.

palpiter [3] [palpite] *vi* - **1.** [paupières] to flutter ; [cœur] to pound - **2.** [personne] : **~ de** to tremble *ou* quiver with - **3.** *littéraire* [flamme] to tremble, to quiver.

palu [paly] *nm fam* malaria.

paludisme [palydism] *nm* malaria.

pâmer [3] [pame] ⬥ **se pâmer** *vp* - **1.** *littéraire* [s'évanouir] to swoon (away) - **2.** *fig* : **se ~ de** to be overcome with.

pâmoison [pamwazɔ̃] *nf littéraire* swoon.

pampa [pɑ̃pa] *nf* pampas (*pl*).

pamphlet [pɑ̃flɛ] *nm* satirical tract.

pamplemousse [pɑ̃pləmus] *nm* grapefruit.

pan [pɑ̃] ⬦ *nm* - **1.** [de vêtement] tail - **2.** [d'affiche] piece, bit ; **~ de mur** section of wall - **3.** [d'écrou] side ⬦ *interj* bang!

panacée [panase] *nf* panacea.

panachage [panaʃaʒ] *nm* - **1.** [mélange] mix - **2.** POLIT splitting one's vote.

panache [panaʃ] *nm* - **1.** [de plumes, fumée] plume - **2.** [éclat] panache.

panaché, e [panaʃe] *adj* - **1.** [de plusieurs couleurs] multicoloured Br, multicolored Am - **2.** [mélangé] mixed.
⬥ **panaché** *nm* shandy.

panacher [3] [panaʃe] *vt* - **1.** [mélanger] to mix - **2.** POLIT : **~ une liste électorale** to split one's vote among several candidates.

panafricanisme [panafrikanism] *nm* Pan-Africanism.

panama [panama] *nm* panama (hat).

Panama [panama] *nm* - **1.** [pays] : **le ~** Panama ; **au ~** in Panama - **2.** [ville] Panama City.

panaméen, enne [panameɛ̃, ɛn], **panamien, enne** [panamjɛ̃, ɛn] *adj* Panamanian.
⬥ **Panaméen, enne**, **Panamien, enne** *nm, f* Panamanian.

panard [panar] *nm fam* foot.

panaris [panari] *nm* whitlow.

pancarte [pɑ̃kart] *nf* - **1.** [de manifestant] placard - **2.** [de signalisation] sign.

pancréas [pɑ̃kreas] *nm* pancreas.

panda [pɑ̃da] *nm* panda.

pané, e [pane] *adj* breaded, in breadcrumbs.

panégyrique [paneʒirik] *nm* panegyric.

panel [panɛl] *nm* [groupe] sample (group) ; [jury] panel.

paner [3] [pane] *vt* to coat with breadcrumbs.

panier [panje] *nm* basket ; **~ à provisions** shopping basket ; **c'est un ~ de crabes** *fig* they're always at each other's throats ; **~ à salade** CULIN salad shaker ; *fig* police van ; **mettre au ~** *fig* to throw out.

panier-repas [panjerəpa] (*pl* **paniers-repas**) *nm* packed lunch.

panini [panini] (*pl* **paninis**) *nm* panini.

panique [panik] ⬦ *nf* panic ⬦ *adj* panicky ; **être pris d'une peur ~** to be panic-stricken.

paniquer [3] [panike] *vt* & *vi* to panic.
⬥ **se paniquer** *vp fam* to panic.

panne [pan] *nf* [arrêt] breakdown ; **tomber en ~** to break down ; **~ de courant** OU **d'électricité** power failure ; **tomber en ~ d'essence** OU **en ~ sèche** to run out of petrol *Br* OU gas *Am* ; **~ de secteur** ÉLECTR mains failure.

panneau, x [pano] *nm* - **1.** [pancarte] sign ; **~ d'affichage** noticeboard *Br*, bulletin board *Am* ; [pour publicité] (advertising) hoarding *Br*, billboard *Am* ; **~ indicateur** signpost ; **~ publicitaire** (advertising) hoarding *Br*, billboard *Am* ; **~ de signalisation** road sign - **2.** [élément] panel ; **~ de commande** INFORM control panel.

panonceau, x [panɔso] *nm* - **1.** [plaque] plaque - **2.** [enseigne] sign.

panoplie [panɔpli] *nf* - **1.** [jouet] outfit - **2.** [d'armes] display - **3.** *fig* [de mesures] package.

panorama [panɔrama] *nm* [vue] view, panorama ; *fig* overview.

panoramique [panɔramik] <> *adj* panoramic <> *nm* CIN pan, panning shot.

panse [pãs] *nf* - **1.** [d'estomac] first stomach, rumen - **2.** *fam* [gros ventre] belly, paunch ; **se remplir** OU **s'en mettre plein la ~** to stuff o.s. - **3.** [partie arrondie] bulge.

pansement [pãsmã] *nm* dressing, bandage ; **~ (adhésif)** (sticking) plaster *Br*, Bandaid® *Am*.

panser [3] [pãse] *vt* - **1.** [plaie] to dress, to bandage ; [jambe] to put a dressing on, to bandage ; [avec pansement adhésif] to put a plaster *Br* OU Bandaid® *Am* on - **2.** [cheval] to groom.

pantagruélique [pãtagryelik] *adj* gargantuan.

pantalon [pãtalɔ̃] *nm* trousers *(pl)* *Br*, pants *(pl)* *Am*, pair of trousers *Br* OU pants *Am*.

pantelant, e [pãtlã, ãt] *adj* panting, gasping.

panthéisme [pãteism] *nm* pantheism.

panthéiste [pãteist] <> *nmf* pantheist <> *adj* pantheistic.

panthéon [pãteɔ̃] *nm* : **le Panthéon** the Pantheon *(where famous Frenchmen and Frenchwomen are buried)*.

panthère [pãtɛr] *nf* panther ; **~ noire** black panther.

pantin [pãtɛ̃] *nm* - **1.** [jouet] jumping jack - **2.** *péj* [personne] puppet.

pantois, e [pãtwa, az] *adj* astounded, dumbstruck ; **rester ~** to be astounded OU dumbstruck.

pantomime [pãtɔmim] *nf* - **1.** [art, pièce] mime - **2.** *fig* & *péj* [manège ridicule] : **qu'est-ce que c'est que cette ~?** what are you playing at?

pantouflard, e [pãtuflar, ard] *fam adj* & *nm, f* stay-at-home.

pantoufle [pãtufl] *nf* slipper.

panure [panyr] *nf* breadcrumbs *(pl)*, coating of breadcrumbs.

PAO *(abr de* publication assistée par ordinateur*) nf* DTP.

paon [pã] *nm* peacock ; **fier comme un ~** (as) proud as a peacock.

papa [papa] *nm* dad, daddy ; **~ gâteau** indulgent father.

papal, e, aux [papal, o] *adj* papal.

paparazzi [paparadzi] *(pl inv* OU **paparazzis)** *nm péjor* paparazzi ; **les ~s** the paparazzi.

papauté [papote] *nf* papacy.

papaye [papaj] *nf* papaya, pawpaw.

pape [pap] *nm* - **1.** RELIG pope ; **sérieux comme un ~** deadly serious - **2.** *fig* [de mouvement] leading light.

papelard [paplar] *nm fam* [papier] bit of paper.

paperasse [papras] *nf péj* - **1.** [papier sans importance] bumf *(U) Br*, papers *(pl)* - **2.** [papiers administratifs] paperwork *(U)*.

paperasserie [paprasri] *nf péj* paperwork.

papeterie [papetri] *nf* [magasin] stationer's ; [fabrique] paper mill.

papetier, ère [papetje, ɛr] *nm, f* [commerçant] stationer ; [fabricant] paper manufacturer.

papi, papy [papi] *nm* grandpa, grandad.

papier [papje] *nm* - **1.** [matière, écrit] paper ; **noircir du ~** to scribble ; **~ alu** OU **aluminium** aluminium *Br* OU aluminum *Am* foil, tinfoil ; **~ carbone** carbon paper ; **~ continu** continuous stationery ; **~ crépon** crêpe paper ; **~ d'emballage** wrapping paper ; **~ à en-tête** headed notepaper ; **~ glacé** glazed paper ; **~ hygiénique** OU **toilette** toilet paper ; **~ journal** newsprint ; [vieux journaux] newspaper ; **~ à lettres** writing paper, notepaper ; **~ mâché** papier-mâché ; **~ machine** typing paper ; **~ millimétré** graph paper ; **~ peint** wallpaper ; **~ de soie** tissue paper ; **~ thermique** thermal paper ; **~ tue-mouches** fly paper ; **~ de verre** glasspaper, sandpaper - **2.** [article de journal] article.

papiers *nmpl* : **~s (d'identité)** (identity) papers.

papier-calque [papjekalk] *(pl* **papiers-calque)** *nm* tracing paper.

papier-filtre [papjefiltr] *(pl* **papiers-filtres)** *nm* filter paper.

papier-monnaie [papjemɔnɛ] *(pl* **papiers-monnaies)** *nm* paper money.

papille [papij] *nf* : **~s gustatives** taste buds.

papillon [papijɔ̃] *nm* - **1.** ZOOL butterfly ; **~ de**

nuit moth **- 2.** [contravention] (parking) ticket **- 3.** [écrou] wing nut **- 4.** [nage] butterfly (stroke).

papillonner [3] [papijɔne] *vi* to flit about *ou* around.

papillote [papijɔt] *nf* **- 1.** [de bonbon] sweet paper *ou* wrapper *Br*, candy paper *Am* **- 2.** [de cheveux] curl paper **- 3.** *CULIN* : **en ~s** *baked in tinfoil or greaseproof paper*.

papilloter [3] [papijɔte] *vi* [lumière] to twinkle ; [yeux] to blink.

papoter [3] [papɔte] *vi fam* to chatter.

papou, e [papu] *adj* Papuan.
➤ **papou** *nm* [langue] Papuan.
➤ **Papou, e** *nm, f* Papuan.

Papouasie-Nouvelle-Guinée [papwazi-nyvɛlginel] *nf* : **la ~** Papua New Guinea.

paprika [paprika] *nm* paprika.

papy = papi.

papyrus [papirys] *nm* papyrus.

Pâque [pak] *nf* : **la ~** Passover ; *voir aussi* Pâques.

paquebot [pakbo] *nm* liner.

pâquerette [pakrɛt] *nf* daisy.

Pâques [pak] *nfpl* Easter *(sg)* ; **joyeuses ~** Happy Easter ; **île de ~** Easter Island.

> **PÂQUES**
>
> In France, Easter is symbolized not only by eggs but also by bells ; according to legend, church bells fly to Rome at Easter.

paquet [pakɛ] *nm* **- 1.** [colis] parcel **- 2.** [emballage] packet ; **~-cadeau** gift-wrapped parcel **- 3.** *loc* : **mettre le ~** *fam* to pull out all the stops, to give it all one's got.

paquetage [pakta3] *nm MIL* kit.

par [par] *prép* **- 1.** [spatial] through, by (way of) ; **passer ~ la Suède et le Danemark** to go via Sweden and Denmark ; **regarder ~ la fenêtre** to look out of the window ; **~ endroits** in places ; **~ ici/là** this/that way ; **mon cousin habite ~ ici** my cousin lives round here **- 2.** [temporel] on ; **~ un beau jour d'été** on a lovely summer's day ; **~ le passé** in the past **- 3.** [moyen, manière, cause] by ; **~ bateau/train/avion** by boat/train/plane ; **~ pitié** out of *ou* from pity ; **~ accident** by accident, by chance **- 4.** [introduit le complément d'agent] by ; **faire faire qqch ~ qqn** to have sthg done by sb **- 5.** [sens distributif] per, a ; **une heure ~ jour** one hour a *ou* per day ; **deux ~ deux** two at a time ; **marcher deux ~ deux** to walk in twos.
➤ **par-ci par-là** *loc adv* here and there.

para [para] (*abr de* **parachutiste**) *nm* para.

parabole [parabɔl] *nf* **- 1.** [récit] parable **- 2.** *MATHS* parabola.

parabolique [parabɔlik] *adj* parabolic.

paracétamol [19] [parasetamɔl] *nm* paracetamol.

parachever [19] [paraʃve] *vt* to put the finishing touches to.

parachutage [paraʃyta3] *nm* parachuting, dropping by parachute.

parachute [paraʃyt] *nm* parachute ; **~ ascensionnel** parachute *(for parascending)* ; **faire du ~ ascensionnel** to go parascending.

parachuter [3] [paraʃyte] *vt* to parachute, to drop by parachute ; **ils l'ont parachuté directeur** *fig* he was unexpectedly given the job of manager.

parachutisme [paraʃytism] *nm* parachuting.

parachutiste [paraʃytist] *nmf* parachutist ; *MIL* paratrooper.

parade [parad] *nf* **- 1.** [spectacle] parade **- 2.** [défense] parry ; *fig* riposte **- 3.** [étalage] show.

parader [3] [parade] *vi* to show off.

paradis [paradi] *nm* paradise ; **~ fiscal** tax haven ; **le Paradis terrestre** *BIBLE* the Garden of Eden ; *fig* heaven on earth.

paradisiaque [paradizjak] *adj* heavenly.

paradoxal, e, aux [paradɔksal, o] *adj* paradoxical.

paradoxalement [paradɔksalmɑ̃] *adv* paradoxically.

paradoxe [paradɔks] *nm* paradox.

parafe, paraphe [paraf] *nm* initials *(pl)*.

parafer, parapher [3] [parafe] *vt* to initial.

paraffine [parafin] *nf* paraffin *Br*, kerosene *Am* ; [solide] paraffin wax.

parages [para3] *nmpl* : **être** *ou* **se trouver dans les ~** *fig* to be in the area *ou* vicinity.

paragraphe [paragraf] *nm* paragraph.

Paraguay [paragwe] *nm* : **le ~** Paraguay ; **au ~** in Paraguay.

paraguayen, enne [paragwejɛ̃, ɛn] *adj* Paraguayan.
➤ **Paraguayen, enne** *nm, f* Paraguayan.

paraissais, paraissions *etc* ▷ paraître.

paraître [91] [parɛtr] ◇ *v attr* to look, to seem, to appear ◇ *vi* **- 1.** [se montrer] to appear **- 2.** [être publié] to come out, to be published **- 3.** [se manifester] to show (through) ; **laisser ~** to show ; **ne rien laisser ~** to let nothing show **- 4.** [briller] to be noticed ◇ *v impers* : **il paraît/paraîtrait que** it appears/would appear that ; **paraît-il** apparently, it seems.

parallèle [paralɛl] ◇ *nm* parallel ; **mettre en ~** *fig* to compare ; **établir un ~ entre** *fig* to draw a parallel between ◇ *nf* parallel (line) ◇ *adj* - **1.** [action, en maths] parallel - **2.** [marché] unofficial ; [médecine, énergie] alternative.

parallèlement [paralɛlmɑ̃] *adv* in parallel ; *fig* at the same time.

parallélépipède [paralelepipɛd] *nm* parallelepiped.

parallélisme [paralelism] *nm* parallelism ; [de roues] alignment.

parallélogramme [paralelɔgram] *nm* parallelogram.

paralysant, e [paralizɑ̃, ɑ̃t] *adj* paralysing.

paralyser [3] [paralize] *vt* to paralyse.

paralysie [paralizi] *nf* paralysis.

paralytique [paralitik] *adj* & *nmf* paralytic.

paramédical, e, aux [paramedikal, o] *adj* paramedical.

paramètre [paramɛtr] *nm* parameter.

paramilitaire [paramilitɛr] *adj* paramilitary.

parangon [parɑ̃gɔ̃] *nm littéraire* paragon.

parano [parano] *adj fam* paranoid.

paranoïa [paranɔja] *nf* paranoia.

paranoïaque [paranɔjak] ◇ *adj* paranoid ◇ *nmf* paranoiac.

paranormal, e, aux [paranɔrmal, o] *adj* paranormal.

parapente [parapɑ̃t] *nm* paragliding ; **faire du ~** to go paragliding.

parapet [parapɛ] *nm* parapet.

paraphe = parafe.

parapher = parafer.

paraphrase [parafraz] *nf* paraphrase.

paraphraser [3] [parafraze] *vt* to paraphrase.

paraplégique [parapleʒik] *nmf* & *adj* paraplegic.

parapluie [paraplɥi] *nm* umbrella ; **~ atomique** *ou* **nucléaire** nuclear umbrella.

parapsychologie [parapsikɔlɔʒi] *nf* parapsychology.

parascolaire [paraskɔlɛr] *adj* extracurricular.

parasite [parazit] ◇ *nm* parasite ◇ *adj* parasitic ; **bruits ~s** *RADIO* & *TÉLÉ* interference (U).

➤ **parasites** *nmpl* *RADIO* & *TÉLÉ* interference (U).

parasiter [3] [parazite] *vt* - **1.** [suj : ver, insecte] to live parasitically on, to parasitize - **2.** [suj : personne] to leech *ou* live off - **3.** *RADIO* & *TÉLÉ* to cause interference on.

parasol [parasɔl] *nm* parasol, sunshade.

paratonnerre [paratɔnɛr] *nm* lightning conductor *Br ou* rod *Am*.

paravent [paravɑ̃] *nm* screen.

parbleu [parblø] *interj* (but) of course!

parc [park] *nm* - **1.** [jardin] park ; [de château] grounds *(pl)* ; **~ d'attractions** amusement park ; **~ de loisirs** ≃ leisure park ; **~ national** national park ; **~ à thème** ≃ theme park - **2.** [pour l'élevage] pen ; **~ à huîtres** oyster bed - **3.** [de bébé] playpen - **4.** [de voitures] fleet ; **le ~ automobile** the number of cars on the roads.

parcelle [parsɛl] *nf* - **1.** [petite partie] fragment, particle - **2.** [terrain] parcel of land.

parce que [parsk(ə)] *loc conj* because.

parchemin [parʃəmɛ̃] *nm* parchment.

parcheminé, e [parʃəmine] *adj* wrinkled.

parcimonie [parsimɔni] *nf* parsimoniousness ; **avec ~** sparingly, parsimoniously.

parcimonieusement [parsimɔnjøzmɑ̃] *adv* parsimoniously.

parcimonieux, euse [parsimɔnjø, øz] *adj* parsimonious.

parcmètre [parkmɛtr] *nm* parking meter.

parcourir [45] [parkurir] *vt* - **1.** [région, route] to cover - **2.** [journal, dossier] to skim *ou* glance through, to scan.

parcourrai, parcourras *etc* ▷ parcourir.

parcours¹, parcourt *etc* ▷ parcourir.

parcours² [parkur] *nm* - **1.** [trajet, voyage] journey ; [itinéraire] route ; **~ du combattant** assault course ; **~ santé** *trail in the countryside where signs encourage people to do exercises for their health* - **2.** *GOLF* [terrain] course ; [trajet] round.

parcouru, e [parkury] *pp* ▷ parcourir.

par-delà [pardəla] *prép* beyond.

par-derrière [pardɛrjɛr] *adv* - **1.** [par le côté arrière] round the back - **2.** [en cachette] behind one's back.

par-dessous [pardəsu] *prép* & *adv* under, underneath.

pardessus [pardəsy] *nm inv* overcoat.

par-dessus [pardəsy] ◇ *prép* over, over the top of ; **~ tout** above all ◇ *adv* over, over the top.

par-devant [pardəvɑ̃] ◇ *prép* in front of ◇ *adv* in front.

pardi [pardi] *interj fam* of course!

pardon [pardɔ̃] ◇ *nm* forgiveness ; **demander ~** to say (one is) sorry ◇ *interj* [excuses] (I'm) sorry! ; [pour attirer l'attention] excuse me! ; **pardon?** (I beg your) pardon? *Br*, pardon me? *Am*.

pardonnable [pardɔnabl] *adj* forgiveable.

pardonner [3] [pardɔne] ◇ *vt* to forgive ; **~ qqch à qqn** to forgive sb for sthg ; **~ à qqn d'avoir fait qqch** to forgive sb for doing sthg ◇ *vi* : **ce genre d'erreur ne pardonne pas** this kind of mistake is fatal.

paré, e [pare] *adj* [prêt] ready.

pare-balles [parbal] ◇ *nm inv* [gilet] bulletproof vest ; [plaque] bullet-proof shield ◇ *adj inv* bullet-proof.

pare-brise [parbriz] *nm inv* windscreen *Br*, windshield *Am*.

pare-chocs [parʃɔk] *nm inv* bumper.

pare-feu [parfø] *nm inv* [dispositif] fireguard ; [en forêt] fire-break.

pareil, eille [parɛj] ◇ *adj* - **1.** [semblable] : **~ (à)** similar (to) - **2.** [tel] such ; **un ~ film** such a film, a film like this ; **de ~s films** such films, films like these ◇ *nm, f* : **mes ~s** my equals ; **sans ~** matchless ; **c'est du ~ au même** it comes to much the same thing ; **rendre la pareille à qqn** to pay sb back in his/her own coin, to give sb a taste of his/her own medicine.

➥ **pareil** *adv fam* the same (way).

pareillement [parɛjmã] *adv* [de même] in the same way ; [également, aussi] likewise, also.

parement [parmã] *nm* facing.

parent, e [parã, ãt] ◇ *adj* : **~ (de)** related (to) ◇ *nm, f* relative, relation ; **~ éloigné** distant relation *ou* relative.

➥ **parents** *nmpl* - **1.** [père et mère] parents, mother and father - **2.** *littéraire* [ancêtres] forefathers.

parental, e, aux [parãtal, o] *adj* parental.

parenté [parãte] *nf* - **1.** [lien, affinité] relationship - **2.** [famille] relatives *(pl)*, relations *(pl)*.

parenthèse [parãtɛz] *nf* - **1.** [digression] digression, parenthesis - **2.** *TYPO* bracket, parenthesis ; **entre ~s** in brackets ; *fig* incidentally, by the way ; **mettre entre ~s** to put in brackets, to bracket ; *fig* to put to one side ; **ouvrir/fermer la ~** to open/close brackets.

paréo [pareo] *nm* pareo.

parer [3] [pare] ◇ *vt* - **1.** *sout* [orner] to adorn - **2.** [vêtir] : **~ qqn de qqch** to dress sb up in sthg, to deck sb out in sthg ; *fig* to attribute sthg to sb - **3.** [contrer] to ward off, to parry ◇ *vi* : **~ à** [faire face à] to deal with ; [pourvoir à] to prepare for ; **~ au plus pressé** to see to what is most urgent.

➥ **se parer** *vp* to dress up, to put on all one's finery ; **se ~ de** to adorn o.s. with ; *fig* [titre] to assume.

pare-soleil [parsɔlɛj] *nm inv* sun visor.

paresse [parɛs] *nf* - **1.** [fainéantise] laziness, idleness - **2.** *MÉD* sluggishness.

paresser [4] [parɛse] *vi* to laze about *ou* around.

paresseusement [parɛsøzmã] *adv* lazily, idly.

paresseux, euse [parɛsø, øz] ◇ *adj* - **1.** [fainéant] lazy - **2.** *MÉD* sluggish ◇ *nm, f* [personne] lazy *ou* idle person.

➥ **paresseux** *nm* [animal] sloth.

parfaire [109] [parfɛr] *vt* to complete, to perfect.

parfait, e [parfɛ, ɛt] *adj* perfect.

➥ **parfait** *nm* - **1.** *CULIN* parfait - **2.** *GRAM* perfect (tense).

parfaitement [parfɛtmã] *adv* - **1.** [admirablement, très] perfectly - **2.** [marque l'assentiment] absolutely.

parfois [parfwa] *adv* sometimes.

parfum [parfœ̃] *nm* - **1.** [de fleur] scent, fragrance - **2.** [à base d'essences] perfume, scent - **3.** [de glace] flavour - **4.** *loc* : **être/mettre qqn au ~** to be/put sb in the know.

parfumé, e [parfyme] *adj* - **1.** [fleur] fragrant - **2.** [mouchoir] perfumed - **3.** [femme] : **elle est trop ~e** she's wearing too much perfume.

parfumer [3] [parfyme] *vt* - **1.** [suj : fleurs] to perfume - **2.** [mouchoir] to perfume, to scent - **3.** *CULIN* to flavour.

➥ **se parfumer** *vp* to put perfume on.

parfumerie [parfymri] *nf* perfumery.

parfumeur, euse [parfymœr, øz] *nm, f* perfumer.

pari [pari] *nm* - **1.** [entre personnes] bet ; **faire un ~** to make *ou* lay a bet ; **gagner/perdre son ~** to win/lose one's bet - **2.** [jeu] betting *(U)*.

paria [parja] *nm* pariah.

parier [9] [parje] *vt* : **~ (sur)** to bet (on) ; **je l'aurais parié!** *fig* I thought as much!

parieur [parjœr] *nm* punter.

parigot, ote [parigo, ɔt] *adj fam* Parisian.

➥ **Parigot, ote** *nm, f fam* Parisian.

Paris [pari] *n* Paris.

PARIS

The name 'Paris' followed by a number or Roman numeral refers to a Paris university : 'Paris VII' (the science faculty at Jussieu), 'Paris IV' (the Sorbonne), 'Paris X' (Nanterre university) etc.
When 'Paris' is followed by an ordinal number, this refers to an 'arrondissement' : 'Paris quinzième', 'Paris quatrième' etc.

paris-brest [paribrɛst] *nm inv choux pastry ring with cream and almonds.*

parisianisme [parizjanism] *nm* [expression] Parisian idiom ; [habitude] Parisian custom.

parisien, enne [parizjɛ̃, ɛn] *adj* [vie, société] Parisian ; [métro, banlieue, région] Paris *(avant n)*.
◆ **Parisien, enne** *nm, f* Parisian.

paritaire [paritɛr] *adj* : **commission ~** joint commission *(with both sides equally represented)*.

parité [parite] *nf* parity.

parjure [parʒyr] ◇ *nmf* [personne] perjurer ◇ *nm* [faux serment] perjury.

parjurer [3] [parʒyre] ◆ **se parjurer** *vp* to perjure o.s.

parka [parka] *nm* OU *nf* parka.

parking [parkiŋ] *nm* [parc] car park *Br*, parking lot *Am*.

parlant, e [parlã, ãt] *adj* - **1.** [qui parle] : **le cinéma ~** talking pictures ; **l'horloge ~e** *TÉLÉCOM* the speaking clock - **2.** *fig* [chiffres, données] eloquent ; [portrait] vivid.

parlement [parləmã] *nm* parliament ; **le Parlement européen** the European Parliament.

parlementaire [parləmãtɛr] ◇ *nmf* [député] member of parliament ; [négociateur] negotiator ◇ *adj* parliamentary.

parlementarisme [parləmãtarism] *nm* (system of) parliamentary government.

parlementer [3] [parləmãte] *vi* - **1.** [négocier] to negotiate, to parley - **2.** [parler longtemps] to talk at length.

parler [3] [parle] ◇ *vi* - **1.** [gén] to talk, to speak ; **les faits parlent d'eux-mêmes** the facts speak for themselves ; **~ à/avec qqn** to speak to/with sb, to talk to/with sb ; **~ de qqch à qqn** to speak OU talk to sb about sthg ; **~ de qqn/qqch** to talk about sb/sthg ; **~ de faire qqch** to talk about doing sthg ; **~ en français** to speak in French ; **~ tout seul** to talk to o.s. ; **sans ~ de** apart from, not to mention ; **à proprement ~** strictly speaking ; **~ pour ne rien dire** to talk for the sake of talking ; **tu parles!** *fam* you can say that again! ; **n'en parlons plus** we'll say no more about it - **2.** [avouer] to talk ◇ *vt* [langue] to speak ; **~ (le) français** to speak French ; **~ politique/affaires** to talk politics/business ◇ *nm* - **1.** [manière de parler] speech - **2.** [patois] dialect.
◆ **se parler** *vp* : **ils ne se parlent pas** they're not on speaking terms.

parleur [parlœr] *nm* : **beau ~** *péj* fine talker.

parloir [parlwar] *nm* parlour *Br*, parlor *Am*.

parlo(t)te [parlɔt] *nf* chat.

parme [parm] *nm* & *adj inv* violet.

parmesan [parməzã] *nm* Parmesan (cheese).

parmi [parmi] *prép* among.

parodie [parɔdi] *nf* parody.

parodier [9] [parɔdje] *vt* to parody.

paroi [parwa] *nf* - **1.** [mur] wall ; [cloison] partition ; **~ rocheuse** rock face - **2.** [de récipient] inner side.

paroisse [parwas] *nf* parish.

paroissial, e, aux [parwasjal, o] *adj* parish *(avant n)*.

paroissien, enne [parwasjɛ̃, ɛn] *nm, f* parishioner.

parole [parɔl] *nf* - **1.** [faculté de parler] : **la ~** speech - **2.** [propos, discours] : **adresser la ~ à qqn** to speak to sb ; **couper la ~ à qqn** to cut sb off ; **prendre la ~** to speak ; **donner** OU **passer la ~ à qqn** to hand over to sb - **3.** [promesse, mot] word ; **tenir ~** to keep one's word ; **donner sa ~ d'honneur** to give one's word of honour *Br* OU honor *Am* ; **croire qqn sur ~** to take sb's word for it ; **libérer qqn sur ~** to free sb on parole.
◆ **paroles** *nfpl* MUS words, lyrics.

parolier, ère [parɔlje, ɛr] *nm, f* [de chanson] lyricist ; [d'opéra] librettist.

paroxysme [parɔksism] *nm* height.

parpaing [parpɛ̃] *nm* breeze block.

parquer [3] [parke] *vt* - **1.** [animaux] to pen in OU up - **2.** [prisonniers] to shut up OU in - **3.** [voiture] to park.

parquet [parkɛ] *nm* - **1.** [plancher] parquet floor - **2.** JUR ≃ Crown Prosecution Service *Br*, ≃ District Attorney's office *Am*.

parqueter [27] [parkəte] *vt* to lay a parquet floor in.

parrain [parɛ̃] *nm* - **1.** [d'enfant] godfather - **2.** [de festival, sportif] sponsor.

parrainage [parenaʒ] *nm* sponsorship.

parrainer [4] [parene] *vt* to sponsor, to back.

parricide [parisid] ◇ *nm* [crime] parricide ◇ *adj* parricidal.

pars, part ▷ **partir**.

parsemer [19] [parsəme] *vt* : **~ (de)** to strew (with).

part [par] *nf* - **1.** [de gâteau] portion ; [de bonheur, d'héritage] share ; [partie] part ; **réclamer sa ~ to** claim one's share ; **~ de marché** ÉCON market share ; **se tailler la ~ du lion** *fig* to take the lion's share - **2.** [participation] : **prendre ~ à qqch** to take part in sthg - **3.** *loc* : **de la ~ de** from ; [appeler, remercier] on behalf of ; **c'est de**

la ~ de qui? [au téléphone] who's speaking ou calling? ; **dites-lui de ma ~ que ...** tell him from me that ... ; **ce serait bien aimable de votre ~** it would be very kind of you ; **pour ma ~** as far as I'm concerned ; **faire ~ à qqn de qqch** to inform sb of sthg ; **faire la ~ des choses** to make allowances.

➤ **à part** ◇ *loc adv* aside, separately ◇ *loc adj* exceptional ◇ *loc prép* apart from.

➤ **autre part** *loc adv* somewhere Br ou someplace Am else.

➤ **d'autre part** *loc adv* besides, moreover.

➤ **de part en part** *loc adv* right through.

➤ **de part et d'autre** *loc adv* on both sides.

➤ **d'une part ..., d'autre part** *loc corrélative* on the one hand ..., on the other hand.

➤ **quelque part** *loc adv* somewhere Br, someplace Am.

part. *abr de* particulier.

partage [partaʒ] *nm* - **1.** [action] sharing (out) - **2.** JUR distribution.

partager [17] [partaʒe] *vt* - **1.** [morceler] to divide (up) ; **être partagé** *fig* to be divided - **2.** [mettre en commun] : **~ qqch avec qqn** to share sthg with sb - **3.** [prendre part à] to share (in).

➤ **se partager** *vp* - **1.** [se diviser] to be divided - **2.** [partager son temps] to divide one's time - **3.** [se répartir] : **se ~ qqch** to share sthg between themselves/ourselves *etc.*

partance [partɑ̃s] *nf* : **en ~** outward bound ; **en ~ pour** bound for.

partant, e [partɑ̃, ɑ̃t] *adj* : **être ~ pour** to be ready for.

➤ **partant** *nm* starter.

partenaire [partənɛr] *nmf* partner ; **~s sociaux** labour Br ou labor Am and management.

partenariat [partənarja] *nm* partnership.

parterre [partɛr] *nm* - **1.** [de fleurs] (flower) bed - **2.** THÉÂTRE stalls *(pl)* Br, orchestra Am.

parti, e [parti] ◇ *pp* ▷ **partir** ◇ *adj fam* [ivre] tipsy.

➤ **parti** *nm* - **1.** POLIT party ; **~ d'opposition** opposition party - **2.** [choix, décision] course of action ; **prendre ~** to make up one's mind ; **prendre le ~ de faire qqch** to make up one's mind to do sthg ; **en prendre son ~** to be resigned ; **être de ~ pris** to be prejudiced ou biased ; **tirer ~ de** to make (good) use of - **3.** [personne à marier] match ; **un beau ~** a good match.

➤ **partie** *nf* - **1.** [élément, portion] part ; **en grande ~e** largely ; **en majeure ~e** for the most part ; **faire ~e (intégrante) de qqch** to be (an integral) part of sthg - **2.** [domaine d'activité]

field, subject - **3.** SPORT game - **4.** JUR party ; **la ~e adverse** the opposing party - **5.** *loc* : **prendre qqn à ~e** to attack sb.

➤ **parties** *nfpl fam* private parts, privates.

➤ **en partie** *loc adv* partly, in part.

partial, e, aux [parsjal, o] *adj* biased.

partialement [parsjalmɑ̃] *adv* in a biased way, with bias.

partialité [parsjalite] *nf* partiality, bias.

participant, e [partisipɑ̃, ɑ̃t] ◇ *adj* participating ◇ *nm, f* - **1.** [à réunion] participant - **2.** SPORT competitor - **3.** [à concours] entrant.

participatif, ive [partisipatif, iv] *adj* : **prêt ~** participating capital loan.

participation [partisipasjɔ̃] *nf* - **1.** [collaboration] participation - **2.** ÉCON interest ; **~ aux frais** (financial) contribution ; **~ aux bénéfices** profit-sharing ; **~ majoritaire/minoritaire** majority/minority interest.

participe [partisip] *nm* participle ; **~ passé/présent** past/present participle.

participer [3] [partisipe] *vi* : **~ à** [réunion, concours] to take part in ; [frais] to contribute to ; [bénéfices] to share in ; **~ de** *littéraire* to have some of the characteristics of.

particularisme [partikylarism] *nm* (sense of) identity.

particularité [partikylarite] *nf* distinctive feature.

particule [partikyl] *nf* - **1.** [gén & LING] particle - **2.** [nobiliaire] nobiliary particle.

particulier, ère [partikylje, ɛr] *adj* - **1.** [personnel, privé] private - **2.** [spécial] particular, special ; [propre] peculiar, characteristic ; **~ à** peculiar to, characteristic of - **3.** [remarquable] unusual, exceptional ; **cas ~** special case - **4.** [assez bizarre] peculiar.

➤ **particulier** *nm* [personne] private individual.

➤ **en particulier** *loc adv* - **1.** [seul à seul] in private - **2.** [surtout] in particular, particularly - **3.** [à part] separately.

particulièrement [partikyljɛrmɑ̃] *adv* particularly ; **tout ~** especially.

partie ▷ **parti**.

partiel, elle [parsjɛl] *adj* partial.

➤ **partiel** *nm* UNIV ≈ end-of-term exam.

partiellement [parsjɛlmɑ̃] *adv* partially, partly.

partir [43] [partir] *vi* - **1.** [personne] to go, to leave ; **~ à** to go to ; **~ pour** to leave for ; **~ de** [bureau] to leave ; [aéroport, gare] to leave from ; [hypothèse, route] to start from ; [date] to run from - **2.** [voiture] to start ; **c'est bien/mal parti** *fig* it got off on the right/wrong foot

- 3. [coup de feu] to go off ; [bouchon] to pop
- 4. [tache] to come out, to go.
➤ **à partir de** *loc prép* from.

partisan, e [partizɑ̃, an] *adj* [partial] partisan ;
être ~ de to be in favour *Br ou* favor *Am* of.
➤ **partisan** *nm* **- 1.** [adepte] supporter, advocate **- 2.** *MIL* partisan.

partitif, ive [partitif, iv] *adj* partitive.
➤ **partitif** *nm* partitive.

partition [partisjɔ̃] *nf* **- 1.** [séparation] partition
- 2. *MUS* score.

partout [partu] *adv* everywhere ; **~ ailleurs**
everywhere else ; **un peu ~** all over, everywhere.

paru, e [pary] *pp* ⊳ **paraître.**

parure [paryr] *nf* (matching) set.

parution [parysjɔ̃] *nf* publication.

parvenir [40] [parvənir] *vi* : **~ à** [atteindre] to
reach ; [obtenir] to achieve ; **~ à faire qqch** to
manage to do sthg ; **faire ~ qqch à qqn** to
send sthg to sb.

parvenu, e [parvəny] <> *pp* ⊳ **parvenir**
<> *nm, f péj* parvenu, upstart.

parviendrai, parviendras etc ⊳ **parvenir.**

parvis [parvi] *nm* square *(in front of church)*.

pas¹ [pɑ] *nm* **- 1.** [gén] step ; **allonger le ~** to
quicken one's pace ; **marquer le ~** to mark
time ; **revenir sur ses ~** to retrace one's
steps ; **~ à ~** step by step ; **au ~** cadencé in
quick time ; **à ~ de loup** *fig* stealthily ; **à
~ feutrés** *fig* with muffled footsteps **- 2.** *TECH-NOL* thread **- 3.** *loc* : **c'est à deux ~ (d'ici)** it's
very near (here), **emboîter le ~ à qqn** to fall
into step with sb ; **faire les cent ~** to pace up
and down ; **faire un faux ~** to slip ; *fig* to
make a faux pas ; **faire le premier ~** to make
the first move ; **franchir ou sauter le ~** to
take the plunge ; **(rouler) au ~** (to move) at a
snail's pace ; **sur le ~ de la porte** on the doorstep ; **tirer qqn d'un mauvais ~** to get sb out
of a tight spot.

pas² [pɑ] *adv* **- 1.** [avec ne] not ; **elle ne vient ~**
she's not *ou* she isn't coming ; **elle n'a
~ mangé** she hasn't eaten ; **je ne le connais ~**
I don't know him ; **il n'y a ~ de vin** there's no
wine, there isn't any wine ; **je préférerais ne
~ le rencontrer** I would prefer not to meet
him, I would rather not meet him **- 2.** [sans
ne] not ; **l'as-tu vu ou ~?** have you seen him
or not? ; **il est très satisfait, moi ~** he's very
pleased, but I'm not ; **sincère ou ~** (whether)
sincere or not ; **une histoire ~ drôle** a story
which isn't funny ; **~ encore** not yet ; **~ du
tout** not at all **- 3.** [avec pron indéf] : **~ un** [aucun]

none, not one ; **~ un d'eux n'est venu** none of
them *ou* not one of them came.

pascal, e [paskal] *(pl* **pascals** *ou* **pascaux** [pas-
ko]) *adj* Easter *(avant n).*
➤ **pascal** *nm* **- 1.** *INFORM* Pascal **- 2.** *PHYS* pascal.

pas-de-porte [padpɔrt] *nm inv* key money.

passable [pasabl] *adj* passable, fair.

passablement [pasabləmɑ̃] *adv* **- 1.** [assez
bien] fairly well **- 2.** [beaucoup] quite a bit.

passage [pasaʒ] *nm* **- 1.** [action - de passer] going
past ; [- de traverser] crossing ; **être de ~** to be
passing through ; **au ~** [en passant] as he/she
etc goes by ; *fig* in passing **- 2.** [endroit] passage, way ; **se frayer un ~** à travers *ou* dans to
force a way through ; '**~ interdit**' 'no entry' ;
~ clouté *ou* **pour piétons** pedestrian crossing ; **~ à niveau** level crossing *Br*, grade
crossing *Am* ; **~ protégé** *priority given to traffic on the main road* ; **~ souterrain** underpass
Br, subway *Am* **- 3.** [changement d'état] : **~ de
qqch à qqch** change *ou* transition from sthg
to sthg ; **~ à vide** dizzy spell ; *fig* bad patch
- 4. [extrait] passage.

passager, ère [pasaʒe, ɛr] <> *adj* **- 1.** [bonheur] fleeting, short-lived **- 2.** [hôte] short-
stay *(avant n)* ; **oiseau ~** bird of passage
<> *nm, f* passenger ; **~ clandestin** stowaway.

passant, e [pasɑ̃, ɑ̃t] <> *adj* busy <> *nm, f*
passer-by.
➤ **passant** *nm* [de ceinture] (belt) loop.

passation [pasasjɔ̃] *nf* **- 1.** [conclusion] signing
- 2. [transmission] hand-over ; **~ des pouvoirs**
transfer of power.

passe [pas] <> *nm* passkey <> *nf* **- 1.** [au sport]
pass **- 2.** *NAVIG* channel **- 3.** *fam* [prostitution] :
maison de ~ ≃ brothel **- 4.** *loc* : **être en ~ de
faire qqch** to be on the way to doing sthg ;
être dans une mauvaise ~ to be in a fix.

passé, e [pase] *adj* **- 1.** [qui n'est plus] past ; [précédent] : **la semaine ~e** last week ; **au cours de
la semaine ~e** in the last week ; **il est trois
heures ~es** it's gone three *Br*, it's after three
- 2. [fané] faded.
➤ **passé** <> *nm* past ; **~ composé** perfect
tense ; **~ simple** past historic <> *prép* after.

passe-droit [pasdrwa] *(pl* **passe-droits**) *nm*
privilege.

passementerie [pasmɑ̃tri] *nf* haberdashery *Br*, notions *(pl) Am*.

passe-montagne [pasmɔ̃taɲ] *(pl* **passe-
montagnes**) *nm* Balaclava (helmet).

passe-partout [paspartu] *nm inv* **- 1.** [clé]
passkey **- 2.** *(en apposition)* [tenue] all-
purpose ; [phrase] stock *(avant n)*.

passe-passe [paspas] *nm inv* : **tour de ~** [presti-digitation] conjuring trick ; *fig* [tromperie] trick.

passe-plat [paspla] (*pl* **passe-plats**) *nm* serving hatch.

passeport [paspɔr] *nm* passport.

passer [3] [pase] ◇ *vi* (aux : *être*) - **1.** [se frayer un chemin] to pass, to get past - **2.** [défiler] to go by *ou* past - **3.** [aller] to go ; **~ à** *ou* **au travers** *ou* **par** to come *ou* pass through ; **~ chez qqn** to call on sb, to drop in on sb ; **~ de qqch à qqch** [changer d'état] to go from sthg to sthg ; [changer d'activité] to change from sthg to sthg ; **~ devant** [bâtiment] to pass ; [juge] to come before ; **en passant** in passing ; **ne faire que ~** to stay only a short while - **4.** [venir - facteur] to come, to call - **5.** *SCOL* to pass, to be admitted ; **~ dans la classe supérieure** to move up, to be moved up (a class) - **6.** [être accepté] **qu'il soit toujours en retard, passe encore, mais ...** it's one thing *ou* it's all very well to be late all the time but ... - **7.** [fermer les yeux] : **~ sur qqch** to pass over sthg - **8.** [temps] to pass, to go by - **9.** [disparaître - souvenir, couleur] to fade ; [- douleur] to pass, to go away - **10.** *CIN*, *TÉLÉ* & *THÉÂTRE* to be on ; **~ à la radio/télévision** to be on the radio/ television - **11.** *CARTES* to pass - **12.** [devenir] : **~ président/directeur** to become president/ director, to be appointed president/ director - **13.** *loc* : **~ inaperçu** to pass *ou* go unnoticed ; **passons ...** let's move on ... ; **~ pour** to be regarded as ; **se faire ~ pour qqn** to pass o.s. off as sb ; **il y est passé** *fam* [mort] he kicked the bucket ; **tout son argent y passe** *fam* all his money goes on that ◇ *vt (aux : avoir)* - **1.** [franchir - frontière, rivière] to cross ; [- douane] to go through - **2.** [soirée, vacances] to spend - **3.** [sauter - ligne, tour] to miss - **4.** [défauts] : **~ qqch à qqn** to overlook sthg in sb - **5.** [faire aller - bras] to pass, to put - **6.** [peinture] to lay on, to spread - **7.** [filtrer - huile] to strain ; [- café] to filter - **8.** [film, disque] to put on - **9.** [vêtement] to slip on - **10.** [vitesses] to change ; **~ la** *ou* **en troisième** to change into third (gear) - **11.** [donner] : **~ qqch à qqn** to pass sb sthg ; *MÉD* to give sb sthg - **12.** [accord] : **~ un contrat avec qqn** to have an agreement with sb - **13.** *SCOL* & *UNIV* [examen] to sit, to take - **14.** [au téléphone] : **je vous passe Mme Ledoux** [transmettre] I'll put you through to Mme Ledoux ; [donner l'écouteur à] I'll hand you Mme Ledoux.

➤ **se passer** *vp* - **1.** [événement] to happen, to take place ; **comment ça s'est passé?** how did it go? ; **ça ne se passera pas comme ça!** I'm not putting up with that! - **2.** [s'enduire - crème] to put on - **3.** [s'abstenir] : **se ~ de qqch/de faire qqch** to do without sthg/doing sthg.

passereau [pasro] *nm* sparrow.

passerelle [pasrɛl] *nf* - **1.** [pont] footbridge - **2.** [passage mobile] gangway.

passe-temps [pastɑ̃] *nm inv* pastime.

passe-thé [paste] *nm inv* tea strainer.

passible [pasibl] *adj* : **~ de** *JUR* liable to.

passif, ive [pasif, iv] *adj* passive.

➤ **passif** *nm* - **1.** *GRAM* passive - **2.** *FIN* liabilities *(pl)*.

passion [pasjɔ̃] *nf* passion ; **avoir la ~ de qqch** to have a passion for sthg.

➤ **Passion** *nf* *MUS* & *RELIG* Passion.

passionnant, e [pasjɔnɑ̃, ɑ̃t] *adj* exciting, fascinating.

passionné, e [pasjɔne] ◇ *adj* - **1.** [personne] passionate - **2.** [récit, débat] impassioned ◇ *nm, f* passionate person ; **~ de ski/ d'échecs** *etc* skiing/chess *etc* fanatic.

passionnel, elle [pasjɔnɛl] *adj* [crime] of passion.

passionnément [pasjɔnemɑ̃] *adv* passionately.

passionner [3] [pasjɔne] *vt* [personne] to grip, to fascinate.

➤ **se passionner** *vp* : **se ~ pour** to have a passion for.

passivement [pasivmɑ̃] *adv* passively.

passivité [pasivite] *nf* passivity.

passoire [paswar] *nf* [à liquide] sieve ; [à légumes] colander.

pastel [pastɛl] ◇ *nm* pastel ◇ *adj inv* [couleur] pastel *(avant n)*.

pastèque [pastɛk] *nf* watermelon.

pasteur [pastœr] *nm* - **1.** *littéraire* [berger] shepherd - **2.** *RELIG* pastor, minister.

pasteurisation [pastœrizasjɔ̃] *nf* pasteurization.

pasteuriser [3] [pastœrize] *vt* to pasteurize.

pastiche [pastiʃ] *nm* pastiche.

pastille [pastij] *nf* [bonbon] pastille, lozenge.

pastis [pastis] *nm* aniseed-flavoured aperitif.

pastoral, e, aux [pastɔral, o] *adj* *littéraire* pastoral.

➤ **pastorale** *nf* *ART* & *LITTÉRATURE* pastoral ; *MUS* pastorale.

patagon, one [patagɔ̃, ɔn] *adj* Patagonian.

➤ **Patagon, one** *nm, f* Patagonian.

Patagonie [patagɔni] *nf* : **la ~** Patagonia.

patapouf [patapuf] *nm fam* fatty.

patate [patat] *nf* - **1.** *fam* [pomme de terre] spud - **2.** *fam* [imbécile] fathead.

➤ **patate douce** *nf* sweet potato.

patati [patati] *interj* : et ~ et patata *fam* and so on and so forth.

patatras [patatra] *interj* crash!

pataud, e [pato, od] ⟺ *adj* clumsy ⟺ *nm, f* clumsy person.

pataugeoire [patoʒwar] *nf* paddling pool.

patauger [17] [patoʒe] *vi* - **1.** [barboter] to splash about - **2.** *fam fig* [s'embrouiller] to flounder.

patch [patʃ] *nm* MÉD patch.

patchouli [patʃuli] *nm* patchouli.

patchwork [patʃwœrk] *nm* patchwork.

pâte [pat] *nf* - **1.** [à tarte] pastry ; [à pain] dough ; ~ **brisée** shortcrust pastry ; ~ **feuilletée** puff pastry ; ~ **à frire** batter ; ~ **à pain** bread dough ; ~ **à tarte** pastry - **2.** [mélange] paste ; ~ **d'amandes** almond paste ; ~ **de fruits** *jelly made from fruit paste* ; **une ~ de fruits** a fruit jelly *(sweet)* ; ~ **à modeler** modelling clay ; ~ **à papier** paper pulp - **3.** *loc* : être bonne ~ to be easy-going.

➤ **pâtes** *nfpl* pasta *(sg)*.

pâté [pate] *nm* - **1.** CULIN pâté ; ~ **de campagne** farmhouse pâté ; ~ **en croûte** *pâté baked in a pastry case* ; ~ **de foie** liver pâté ; ~ **impérial** spring roll - **2.** [tache] ink blot - **3.** [bloc] : ~ **de maisons** block (of houses).

pâtée [pate] *nf* mash, feed.

patelin [patlɛ̃] *nm fam* village, place.

patène [patɛn] *nf* paten.

patente [patɑ̃t] *nf* licence fee *(for traders and professionals)*.

patenté, e [patɑ̃te] *adj* - **1.** [commerçant] licensed - **2.** *fam* [voleur, menteur] habitual.

patère [patɛr] *nf* [portemanteau] coat hook.

paternalisme [patɛrnalism] *nm* paternalism.

paternaliste [patɛrnalist] ⟺ *nmf* paternalist ⟺ *adj* paternalistic.

paternel, elle [patɛrnɛl] *adj* [devoir, autorité] paternal ; [amour, ton] fatherly.

➤ **paternel** *nm fam* old man.

paternité [patɛrnite] *nf* paternity, fatherhood ; *fig* authorship, paternity.

pâteux, euse [patø, øz] *adj* - **1.** [aliment] doughy ; [encre] thick - **2.** [style] leaden.

pathétique [patetik] ⟺ *nm littéraire* pathos ⟺ *adj* moving, pathetic.

pathologie [patɔlɔʒi] *nf* pathology.

pathologique [patɔlɔʒik] *adj* pathological.

pathos [patos] *nm littéraire* & *péj* pathos.

patibulaire [patibylɛr] *adj péj* sinister.

patiemment [pasjamɑ̃] *adv* patiently.

patience [pasjɑ̃s] *nf* - **1.** [gén] patience ; **s'armer de** ~ to be patient, to have patience ; **perdre** ~ to lose patience - **2.** [jeu de cartes] patience *Br*, solitaire *Am*.

patient, e [pasjɑ̃, ɑ̃t] ⟺ *adj* patient ⟺ *nm, f* - **1.** [qui a de la patience] patient person - **2.** MÉD patient.

patienter [3] [pasjɑ̃te] *vi* to wait ; **'veuillez patienter'** 'please wait'.

patin [patɛ̃] *nm* - **1.** SPORT skate ; ~ **à glace/à roulettes** ice/roller skate ; **faire du** ~ **à glace/à roulettes** to go ice-/roller-skating - **2.** [de feutre] *cloth pad used under shoes to protect wooden floor*.

patinage [patinaʒ] *nm* SPORT skating ; ~ **artistique/de vitesse** figure/speed skating.

patine [patin] *nf* patina.

patiner [3] [patine] ⟺ *vi* - **1.** SPORT to skate - **2.** [véhicule] to skid ⟺ *vt* [objet] to give a patina to ; [avec vernis] to varnish.

➤ **se patiner** *vp* to take on a patina.

patineur, euse [patinœr, øz] *nm, f* skater.

patinoire [patinwar] *nf* ice *ou* skating rink.

patio [patjo, pasjo] *nm* patio.

pâtir [32] [patir] *vi* : ~ **de** to suffer the consequences of.

pâtisserie [patisri] *nf* - **1.** [gâteau] pastry - **2.** [art, métier] pastry-making - **3.** [commerce] ≃ cake shop.

pâtissier, ère [patisje, ɛr] ⟺ *adj* : **crème pâtissière** confectioner's custard ⟺ *nm, f* pastrycook.

patois [patwa] *nm* patois.

patraque [patrak] *adj fam* [personne] out of sorts.

patriarcal, e, aux [patrijarkal, o] *adj* patriarchal.

patriarcat [patrijarka] *nm* - **1.** RELIG patriarchate - **2.** SOCIOL patriarchy.

patriarche [patrijarʃ] *nm* patriarch.

patrie [patri] *nf* country, homeland ; ~ **d'adoption** country of adoption.

patrimoine [patrimwan] *nm* [familial] inheritance ; [collectif] heritage.

patriote [patrijɔt] ⟺ *nmf* patriot ⟺ *adj* patriotic.

patriotique [patrijɔtik] *adj* patriotic.

patriotisme [patrijɔtism] *nm* patriotism.

patron, onne [patrɔ̃, ɔn] *nm, f* - **1.** [d'entreprise] head - **2.** [chef] boss - **3.** RELIG patron saint.

➤ **patron** *nm* [modèle] pattern.

patronage [patrɔnaʒ] *nm* - **1.** [protection] pat-

ronage ; [de saint] protection **- 2.** [organisation] youth club.

patronal, e, aux [patrɔnal, o] *adj* [organisation, intérêts] employers' *(avant n).*

patronat [patrɔnal *nm* employers.

patronnesse [patrɔnɛs] *nf* : **(dame)** ~ *iron* patroness.

patronyme [patrɔnim] *nm* patronymic.

patronymique [patrɔnimik] *adj* patronymic.

patrouille [patruj] *nf* patrol.

patrouiller [3] [patruje] *vi* to patrol.

patte [pat] *nf* **- 1.** [d'animal] paw ; [d'oiseau] foot ; montrer ~ **blanche** *fig* to give the password ; **à quatre ~s** four-legged ; *fig* on all fours, on one's hands and knees ; **retomber sur ses ~s** *fig* to land on one's feet **- 2.** *fam* [jambe] leg ; [pied] foot ; [main] hand, paw ; **graisser la ~ à qqn** to grease sb's palm **- 3.** [favori] sideburn **- 4.** [de poche, de portefeuille] fastening.

patte-d'oie [patdwa] *(pl* **pattes-d'oie)** *nf* crow's foot.

pattemouille [patmuj] *nf* damping cloth.

pâturage [patyraʒ] *nm* [lieu] pasture land.

pâture [patyr] *nf* [nourriture] food, fodder ; *fig* intellectual nourishment ; **donner qqn/qqch en ~ à, offrir qqn/qqch en ~ à** to feed sb/sthg to.

paume [pom] *nf* **- 1.** [de main] palm **- 2.** SPORT real tennis.

paumé, e [pome] *fam* <> *adj* lost <> *nm, f* down and out.

paumer [3] [pome] *fam vt* to lose.
➠ **se paumer** *vp* to get lost.

paupérisation [poperizasjɔ̃] *nf* pauperization.

paupière [popjɛr] *nf* eyelid.

paupiette [popjɛt] *nf* thin slice of meat or fish stuffed and rolled ; **~s de veau** ≃ veal olives.

pause [poz] *nf* **- 1.** [arrêt] break ; **~-café** coffee-break **- 2.** MUS pause.

pauvre [povr] <> *nmf* poor person ; **le/la ~!** the poor thing! <> *adj* poor ; ~ **en** low in ; ~ **d'esprit** feeble-minded.

pauvrement [povrəmã] *adv* poorly.

pauvreté [povrəte] *nf* poverty.

pavage [pavaʒ] *nm* paving.

pavaner [3] [pavane] ➠ **se pavaner** *vp* to strut.

pavé, e [pave] *adj* cobbled.
➠ **pavé** *nm* **- 1.** [chaussée] : **être sur le ~** *fig* to be out on the streets ; **battre le ~** *fig* to walk the streets **- 2.** [de pierre] cobblestone, paving

stone **- 3.** *fam* [livre] tome **- 4.** [de viande] slab **- 5.** INFORM : ~ **numérique** numeric keypad.

paver [3] [pave] *vt* to pave.

pavillon [pavijɔ̃] *nm* **- 1.** [bâtiment] detached house ; ~ **de banlieue** ≃ bungalow ; ~ **de chasse** hunting lodge **- 2.** [de trompette] bell **- 3.** [d'oreille] pinna, auricle **- 4.** [drapeau] flag.

pavoiser [3] [pavwaze] <> *vt* to decorate with flags <> *vi fam* to crow.

pavot [pavo] *nm* poppy.

payable [pɛjabl] *adj* payable.

payant, e [pɛjã, ãt] *adj* **- 1.** [hôte] paying *(avant n)* **- 2.** [spectacle] with an admission charge **- 3.** *fam* [affaire] profitable.

paye = paie².

payement = paiement.

payer [11] [pɛje] <> *vt* **- 1.** [gén] to pay ; [achat] to pay for ; ~ **qqch à qqn** to buy sthg for sb, to buy sb sthg, to treat sb to sthg ; ~ **qqn de qqch** *fig* [efforts, peine] to reward sb for sthg **- 2.** [expier - crime, faute] to pay for ; **il me le paiera!** he'll pay for this! <> *vi* : ~ **(pour)** to pay (for) ; ~ **de sa poche** to pay out of one's own pocket ; ~ **de sa personne** [s'exposer au danger] to put o.s. on the line ; [se donner du mal] to put in a lot of effort ; ~ **d'audace** to risk one's all.
➠ **se payer** *vp* [s'offrir] : **se ~ qqch** to buy o.s. sthg, to treat o.s. to sthg.

payeur, euse [pɛjœr, øz] *adj* payments *(avant n).*
➠ **payeur** *nm* payer ; **mauvais ~** bad debtor.

pays [pei] *nm* **- 1.** [gén] country ; ~ **d'adoption** country of adoption ; ~ **de cocagne** *fig* land of plenty ; **les ~ de l'Est** the Eastern bloc (countries) ; ~ **natal** native land, native country ; **comme en ~ conquis** like the lord of the manor **- 2.** [région, province] region ; **être du ~** to be a local **- 3.** [village] village.
➠ **pays de Galles** *nm* : **le ~ de Galles** Wales ; **au ~ de Galles** in Wales.

paysage [peizaʒ] *nm* **- 1.** [site, vue] landscape, scenery **- 2.** [tableau] landscape **- 3.** *fig* [contexte] scene.

paysager, ère [peizaʒe, ɛr] *adj* landscaped.

paysagiste [peizaʒist] <> *nmf* **- 1.** [peintre] landscape artist **- 2.** [concepteur de parcs] landscape gardener <> *adj* landscape *(avant n).*

paysan, anne [peizã, an] <> *adj* [vie, coutume] country *(avant n)*, rural ; [organisation, revendication] farmers' *(avant n)* ; *péj* peasant *(avant n)* <> *nm, f* **- 1.** [agriculteur] (small) farmer **- 2.** *péj* [rustre] peasant.

paysannat [peizana] *nm* peasantry.

paysannerie [peizanri] *nf* peasantry, peasant class.

Pays-Bas [peibal *nmpl* : **les ~** the Netherlands ; **aux ~** in the Netherlands.

PC *nm* - **1.** (*abr de* **Parti communiste**) Communist Party - **2.** (*abr de* **personal computer**) PC - **3.** (*abr de* **prêt conventionné**) *special loan for house purchase* - **4.** (*abr de* **permis de construire**) planning permission - **5.** (*abr de* **poste de commandement**) HQ - **6.** (*abr de* **Petite Ceinture**) *bus following the inner ring road in Paris.*

pcc (*abr de* **pour copie conforme**) certified accurate.

PCF (*abr de* **Parti communiste français**) *nm* French Communist Party.

PCV (*abr de* **à percevoir**) *nm* reverse charge call.

P-DG (*abr de* **président-directeur général**) *nm* Chairman and Managing Director *Br*, Chairman and President *Am*.

p.-ê. *abr de* **peut-être.**

PEA (*abr de* **plan d'épargne en actions**) *nm* savings scheme.

péage [peaʒ] *nm* toll.

peau [po] *nf* - **1.** [gén] skin ; **~ de banane** banana skin ; **~ d'orange** orange peel ; *MÉD* ≃ cellulite ; **n'avoir que la ~ sur les os** to be just skin and bones ; **être bien/mal dans sa ~** [en général] to feel great/terrible ; [en situation] to feel at ease/ill at ease ; **risquer sa ~** to risk one's neck ; **sauver sa ~** to save one's skin - **2.** [cuir] hide, leather *(U)* ; **~ de vache** *fam fig* [homme] bastard ; [femme] bitch.

peaufiner [3] [pofine] *vt fig* [travail] to polish up.

peccadille [pekadij] *nf* peccadillo.

péché [peʃe] *nm* sin ; **les sept ~s capitaux** the seven deadly sins ; **le ~ originel** original sin ; **un ~ mignon** a weakness.

pêche [pɛʃ] *nf* - **1.** [fruit] peach ; **~ Melba** peach Melba - **2.** [activité] fishing ; [poissons] catch ; **aller à la ~** to go fishing ; **à la dandinette** jigging ; **~ sous la glace** ice fishing ; **~ à la ligne** angling ; **~ sous-marine** underwater fishing - **3.** *loc* : **avoir la ~** *fam* to feel great.

pécher [18] [peʃe] *vi* to sin ; **~ contre la bienséance** *fig* to break the rules of correct behaviour ; **~ par omission** *fig* to commit the sin of omission ; **cet exposé pèche par manque d'exemples** *fig* this report falls down because it lacks examples.

pêcher[1] [peʃe] *vt* - **1.** [poisson] to catch - **2.** *fam* [trouver] to dig up.

pêcher[2] [peʃe] *nm* peach tree.

pêcherie [peʃri] *nf* fishery, fishing ground.

pécheur, eresse [peʃœr, peʃrɛs] ◇ *adj* sinful ◇ *nm, f* sinner.

pêcheur, euse [peʃœr, øz] *nm, f* fisherman (*f* fisherwoman).

pecnot = **péquenot.**

pectine [pɛktin] *nf* pectin.

pectoral, e, aux [pɛktɔral, o] *adj* - **1.** [muscle] pectoral - **2.** [sirop] cough (*avant n*).
➡ **pectoraux** *nmpl* pectorals.

pécule [pekyl] *nm* [économies] savings (*pl*).

pécuniaire [pekynjɛr] *adj* financial.

pédagogie [pedagɔʒi] *nf* - **1.** [science] education, pedagogy - **2.** [qualité] teaching ability.

pédagogique [pedagɔʒik] *adj* educational ; [méthode] teaching (*avant n*).

pédagogue [pedagɔg] ◇ *nmf* teacher ◇ *adj* : **être ~** to be a good teacher.

pédale [pedal] *nf* - **1.** [gén] pedal ; **perdre les ~s** *fam fig* to lose one's head - **2.** *fam injr* [homosexuel] queer.

pédaler [3] [pedale] *vi* [à bicyclette] to pedal ; **~ dans la choucroute** *fam fig* to be all at sea.

pédalier [pedalje] *nm* - **1.** [de vélo] (bicycle) drive - **2.** [d'orgue] pedals (*pl*).

Pédalo® [pedalo] *nm* pedal boat.

pédant, e [pedã, ãt] ◇ *adj* pedantic ◇ *nm, f* pedant.

pédé [pede] *nm tfam péj* queer.

pédéraste [pederast] *nm* homosexual, pederast.

pédérastie [pederasti] *nf* homosexuality.

pédestre [pedɛstr] *adj* : **randonnée ~** hike, ramble ; **chemin ~** footpath.

pédiatre [pedjatr] *nmf* pediatrician.

pédiatrie [pedjatri] *nf* pediatrics *(U)*.

pédicule [pedikyl] *nm BOT* peduncle.

pédicure [pedikyr] *nmf* chiropodist.

pedigree [pedigre] *nm* pedigree.

pédophile [pedɔfil] ◇ *nm* pedophile ◇ *adj* pedophiliac.

peeling [piliŋ] *nm* face scrub.

pègre [pɛgr] *nf* underworld.

peignais, peignions *etc* ▷ **peindre.**

peigne [pɛɲ] *nm* - **1.** [démêloir, barrette] comb ; **se donner un coup de ~** to run a comb through one's hair ; **passer qqch au ~ fin** *fig* to go through sthg with a fine-tooth comb ; **sale comme un ~** *fig* filthy dirty - **2.** [de tissage] card.

peigner [4] [peɲe] *vt* - **1.** [cheveux] to comb - **2.** [fibres] to card.
➡ **se peigner** *vp* to comb one's hair.

peignoir [pɛɲwar] *nm* dressing gown *Br*, robe *Am*, bathrobe *Am* ; ~ **de bain** bathrobe.

peinard, e, pénard, e [pɛnar, ard] *adj fam* [emploi] cushy ; [personne] comfortable.

peindre [81] [pɛ̃dr] *vt* to paint ; *fig* [décrire] to depict.
◆ **se peindre** *vp* [émotion] *fig* : **se ~ sur** to be written on.

peine [pɛn] *nf* **- 1.** [châtiment] punishment, penalty ; *JUR* sentence ; **sous ~ de qqch** on pain of sthg ; **~ capitale** *OU* **de mort** capital punishment, death sentence ; **~ incompressible** sentence without remission **- 2.** [chagrin] sorrow, sadness *(U)* ; **avoir de la ~** to be sad ; **faire de la ~ à qqn** to upset sb, to distress sb **- 3.** [effort] trouble ; **se donner de la ~** to go to a lot of trouble ; **c'est ~ perdue** it's a waste of effort ; **prendre la ~ de faire qqch** to go to the trouble of doing sthg ; **ça ne vaut pas** *OU* **ce n'est pas la ~** it's not worth it **- 4.** [difficulté] difficulty ; **avoir de la ~ à faire qqch** to have difficulty *OU* trouble doing sthg ; **à grand-~** with great difficulty ; **sans ~** without difficulty, easily.
◆ **à peine** *loc adv* scarcely, hardly ; **à ~ ... que** hardly ... than ; **c'est à ~ si on se parle** we hardly speak (to each other).

peiner [4] [pene] ◇ *vt* [affliger] to distress, to sadden ◇ *vi* **- 1.** [travailler] to work hard **- 2.** [se fatiguer] to struggle, to labour *Br*, to labor *Am*.

peint, e [pɛ̃, pɛ̃t] *pp* ▷ **peindre**.

peintre [pɛ̃tr] *nm* painter ; **~ en bâtiment** painter and decorator.

peinture [pɛ̃tyr] *nf* **- 1.** [gén] painting **- 2.** [produit] paint ; **'~ fraîche'** 'wet paint'.

peinturlurer [3] [pɛ̃tyrlyre] *vt péj* to daub.
◆ **se peinturlurer** *vp péj* to plaster one's face with make-up.

péjoratif, ive [peʒɔratif, iv] *adj* pejorative.

Pékin [pekɛ̃] *n* Peking, Beijing.

pékinois, e [pekinwa, az] *adj* of/from Peking.
◆ **pékinois** *nm* **- 1.** [langue] Mandarin **- 2.** [chien] pekinese.
◆ **Pékinois, e** *nm, f* native *OU* inhabitant of Peking ; **les Pékinois** the people of Peking.

PEL, Pel [pɛl] (*abr de* **plan d'épargne logement**) *nm savings scheme offering low-interest mortgages.*

pelage [pɔlaʒ] *nm* coat, fur.

pelé, e [pɔle] *adj* **- 1.** [crâne] bald **- 2.** *fig* [colline, paysage] bare.

pêle-mêle [pɛlmɛl] *adv* pell-mell.

peler [25] [pɔle] *vt* & *vi* to peel.

pèlerin [pɛlrɛ̃] *nm* pilgrim.

pèlerinage [pɛlrinaʒ] *nm* **- 1.** [voyage] pilgrimage ; **en ~** on a pilgrimage **- 2.** [lieu] place of pilgrimage.

pèlerine [pɛlrin] *nf* cape.

pélican [pelikɑ̃] *nm* pelican.

pelisse [pɔlis] *nf* pelisse.

pelle [pɛl] *nf* **- 1.** [instrument] shovel ; **~ à tarte** pie server ; **à la ~** *fam fig* by the bucketful **- 2.** [machine] digger.

pelletée [pɛlte] *nf* shovelful.

pelleter [27] [pɛlte] *vt* to shovel.

pelleteuse [pɛltøz] *nf* mechanical digger.

pellicule [pelikyl] *nf* film.
◆ **pellicules** *nfpl* dandruff *(U)*.

pelote [pɔlɔt] *nf* **- 1.** [de laine, ficelle] ball **- 2.** *COUTURE* pin cushion.
◆ **pelote basque** *nf* pelota.

peloter [3] [plɔte] *vt fam* to paw.

peloton [plɔtɔ̃] *nm* **- 1.** [de ficelle] small ball **- 2.** [de soldats] squad ; **~ d'exécution** firing squad **- 3.** [de concurrents] pack ; **le ~ de tête** *SPORT* the leading group ; *fig* the top few.

pelotonner [3] [pɔlɔtɔne] ◆ **se pelotonner** *vp* to curl up ; **se ~ contre** to snuggle up to.

pelouse [pɔluz] *nf* **- 1.** [de jardin] lawn **- 2.** [de champ de courses] public enclosure **- 3.** *FOOTBALL* & *RUGBY* field.

peluche [pɔlyʃ] *nf* **- 1.** [jouet] soft toy, stuffed animal **- 2.** [tissu] plush **- 3.** [d'étoffe] piece of fluff.

pelucheux, euse [pɔlyʃø, øz] *adj* fluffy.

pelure [pɔlyr] *nf* **- 1.** [fruit] peel **- 2.** *fam péj* [habit] coat.

pénal, e, aux [penal, o] *adj* penal.

pénalisation [penalizasjɔ̃] *nf* penalty.

pénaliser [3] [penalize] *vt* to penalize.

pénalité [penalite] *nf* penalty.

penalty [penalti] (*pl* **penaltys** *OU* **penalties**) *nm* penalty.

pénard = peinard.

pénates [penat] *nmpl* : **regagner ses ~** *fam* to go home.

penaud, e [pɔno, od] *adj* sheepish.

penchant [pɑ̃ʃɑ̃] *nm* **- 1.** [inclination] tendency **- 2.** [sympathie] : **~ pour** liking *OU* fondness for.

pencher [3] [pɑ̃ʃe] ◇ *vi* to lean ; **~ vers** *fig* to incline towards *Br OU* toward *Am* ; **~ pour** to incline in favour *Br OU* favor *Am* of ◇ *vt* to bend.
◆ **se pencher** *vp* [s'incliner] to lean over ; [se baisser] to bend down ; **se ~ sur qqn/qqch** to

lean over sb/sthg ; **se ~ sur qqch** *fig* [problème, cas] to look into sthg.

pendable [pɑ̃dabl] *adj* : **tour ~** dirty trick ; **ce n'est pas un cas ~** it's not a hanging matter.

pendaison [pɑ̃dezɔ̃] *nf* hanging ; **~ de crémaillère** house-warming.

pendant¹, e [pɑ̃dɑ̃, ɑ̃t] *adj* - **1.** [bras] hanging, dangling - **2.** [question] pending.
◆ **pendant** *nm* - **1.** [bijou] : **~ d'oreilles** (drop) earring - **2.** [de paire] counterpart ; **se faire ~** *fig* to make a pair.

pendant² [pɑ̃dɑ̃] *prép* during.
◆ **pendant que** *loc conj* while, whilst ; **~ que j'y suis, ...** while I'm at it, ...

pendeloque [pɑ̃dlɔk] *nf* - **1.** [bijou] pendant - **2.** [de lustre] crystal.

pendentif [pɑ̃dɑ̃tif] *nm* pendant.

penderie [pɑ̃dri] *nf* wardrobe.

pendouiller [3] [pɑ̃duje] *vi fam* to dangle, to hang down.

pendre [73] [pɑ̃dr] ◇ *vi* - **1.** [être fixé en haut] : **~ (à)** to hang (from) - **2.** [descendre trop bas] to hang down ◇ *vt* - **1.** [rideaux, tableau] to hang (up), to put up - **2.** [personne] to hang.
◆ **se pendre** *vp* - **1.** [s'accrocher] : **se ~ à** to hang from - **2.** [se suicider] to hang o.s.

pendu, e [pɑ̃dy] ◇ *pp* ▷ **pendre** ◇ *adj* - **1.** [objet] hung up, hanging up ; *fig* : **il est toujours ~ au téléphone** he's never off the phone - **2.** [personne] hanged ◇ *nm, f* hanged person.

pendule [pɑ̃dyl] ◇ *nm* pendulum ◇ *nf* clock.

pendulette [pɑ̃dylɛt] *nf* small clock.

pêne [pɛn] *nm* bolt.

pénétrant, e [penetrɑ̃, ɑ̃t] *adj* penetrating ; [odeur] pervasive.

pénétration [penetrasjɔ̃] *nf* - **1.** [de projectile, d'idée] penetration - **2.** [sagacité] shrewdness.

pénétré, e [penetre] *adj* earnest ; **elle est ~e de son importance** she's full of her own importance.

pénétrer [18] [penetre] ◇ *vi* to enter ◇ *vt* - **1.** [mur, vêtement] to penetrate - **2.** *fig* [mystère, secret] to fathom out.
◆ **se pénétrer** *vp* [s'imprégner] : **se ~ d'une idée** to let an idea sink in.

pénible [penibl] *adj* - **1.** [travail] laborious - **2.** [nouvelle, maladie] painful - **3.** *fam* [personne] tiresome.

péniblement [peniblǝmɑ̃] *adv* - **1.** [avec difficulté] with difficulty, laboriously - **2.** [cruellement] painfully - **3.** [à peine] just about.

péniche [peniʃ] *nf* barge.

pénicilline [penisilin] *nf* penicillin.

péninsule [penɛ̃syl] *nf* peninsula ; **la ~ d'Arabie** the Arabian Peninsula ; **la ~ Ibérique** the Iberian peninsula.

pénis [penis] *nm* penis.

pénitence [penitɑ̃s] *nf* - **1.** [repentir] penitence - **2.** [peine, punition] penance.

pénitencier [penitɑ̃sje] *nm* prison, penitentiary *Am*.

pénitent, e [penitɑ̃, ɑ̃t] ◇ *adj* penitent ◇ *nm, f* penitent.

pénitentiaire [penitɑ̃sjɛr] *adj* prison *(avant n)*.

penne [pɛn] *nf ZOOL* quill.

pénombre [penɔ̃br] *nf* half-light.

pensable [pɑ̃sabl] *adj* : **ce n'est pas ~** it's unthinkable.

pensant, e [pɑ̃sɑ̃, ɑ̃t] *adj* thinking.

pense-bête [pɑ̃sbɛt] *(pl* **pense-bêtes***) nm* reminder.

pensée [pɑ̃se] *nf* - **1.** [idée, faculté] thought - **2.** [esprit] mind, thoughts *(pl)* ; **par la** *ou* **en ~** in one's mind *ou* thoughts - **3.** [opinion] thoughts *(pl)*, feelings *(pl)* - **4.** [doctrine] thought, thinking - **5.** *BOT* pansy.

penser [3] [pɑ̃se] ◇ *vi* to think ; **~ à qqn/qqch** [avoir à l'esprit] to think of sb/sthg, to think about sb/sthg ; [se rappeler] to remember sb/sthg ; **~ à faire qqch** [avoir à l'esprit] to think of doing sthg ; [se rappeler] to remember to do sthg ; **qu'est-ce que tu en penses?** what do you think (of it)? ; **faire ~ à qqn/qqch** to make one think of sb/sthg ; **faire ~ à qqn à faire qqch** to remind sb to do sthg ; **sans ~ à mal** without meaning any harm ; **n'y pensons plus!** let's forget it! ; **laisser** *ou* **donner à ~ (que)** to make one think (that) ; **même s'il ne dit rien, il n'en pense pas moins** even if he doesn't say anything, he's thinking it nonetheless ◇ *vt* to think ; **~ que ...** to think (that) ... ; **je pense que oui** I think so ; **je pense que non** I don't think so ; **~ faire qqch** to be planning to do sthg ; **pensez-vous!** don't be silly!

penseur [pɑ̃sœr] *nm* thinker.

pensif, ive [pɑ̃sif, iv] *adj* pensive, thoughtful.

pension [pɑ̃sjɔ̃] *nf* - **1.** [allocation] pension ; **~ alimentaire** [dans un divorce] alimony - **2.** [hébergement] board and lodgings ; **~ complète** full board ; **demi-~** half board - **3.** [hôtel] guesthouse ; **~ de famille** guesthouse, boarding house - **4.** [prix de l'hébergement] ≈ rent, keep - **5.** [internat] boarding school ;

être en ~ to be a boarder *ou* at boarding school.

pensionnaire [pãsjɔnɛr] *nmf* - **1.** [élève] boarder - **2.** [hôte payant] lodger.

pensionnat [pãsjɔna] *nm* - **1.** [internat] boarding school - **2.** [élèves] boarders *(pl)*.

pensivement [pãsivmã] *adv* pensively, thoughtfully.

pensum [pɛ̃sɔm] *nm* - **1.** [travail ennuyeux] chore - **2.** *vieilli* [punition] imposition.

pentagone [pɛ̃tagɔn] *nm* pentagon.
➡ **Pentagone** *nm* : **le Pentagone** the Pentagon.

pentathlon [pɛ̃tatlɔ̃] *nm* pentathlon.

pente [pãt] *nf* slope ; **en ~** sloping, inclined ; **être sur une mauvaise ~** *fig* to be on a downward path ; **remonter la ~** *fig* to claw one's way back again.

pentecôte [pãtkot] *nf* [juive] Pentecost ; [chrétienne] Whitsun.

pénurie [penyri] *nf* shortage.

PEP, Pep [pɛp] (*abr de* **plan d'épargne populaire**) *nm* personal pension plan.

pépé [pepe] *nm fam* - **1.** [grand-père] grandad, grandpa - **2.** [homme âgé] old man.

pépère [pepɛr] *fam* <> *nm* [grand-père] grandad, grandpa <> *adj* cushy.

pépier [9] [pepje] *vi* to chirp.

pépin [pepɛ̃] *nm* - **1.** [graine] pip - **2.** *fam* [ennui] hitch - **3.** *fam* [parapluie] umbrella, brolly *Br*.

pépinière [pepinjɛr] *nf* tree nursery ; *fig* [école, établissement] nursery.

pépiniériste [pepinjerist] *nmf* nursery man (*f* woman).

pépite [pepit] *nf* nugget.

péquenot, pecnot [pekno] *nm*, **péquenaud, e** *nm, f,* [pekno, od] *fam péj* country bumpkin.

percale [pɛrkal] *nf* percale.

perçant, e [pɛrsã, ãt] *adj* - **1.** [regard, son] piercing - **2.** [froid] bitter, biting.

percée [pɛrse] *nf* - **1.** [trouée] opening - **2.** *MIL, SPORT* & *fig* breakthrough.

percement [pɛrsəmã] *nm* opening (up) ; [d'oreilles] piercing.

perce-neige [pɛrsəneʒ] *nm inv ou nf inv* snowdrop.

perce-oreille [pɛrsɔrɛj] (*pl* **perce-oreilles**) *nm* earwig.

percepteur [pɛrsɛptœr] *nm* tax collector.

perceptible [pɛrsɛptibl] *adj* perceptible.

perception [pɛrsɛpsjɔ̃] *nf* - **1.** [d'impôts] collection - **2.** [bureau] tax office - **3.** [sensation] perception.

percer [16] [pɛrse] <> *vt* - **1.** [mur, roche] to make a hole in ; [coffre-fort] to crack - **2.** [trou] to make ; [avec perceuse] to drill - **3.** [silence, oreille] to pierce - **4.** [foule] to make one's way through - **5.** *fig* [mystère] to penetrate <> *vi* - **1.** [soleil] to break through - **2.** [abcès] to burst ; **avoir une dent qui perce** to be cutting a tooth - **3.** [réussir] to make a name for o.s., to break through.

perceuse [pɛrsøz] *nf* drill.

percevoir [52] [pɛrsəvwar] *vt* - **1.** [intention, nuance] to perceive - **2.** [retraite, indemnité] to receive - **3.** [impôts] to collect.

perchaude [pɛrʃod] *nf Can* yellow *ou* lake perch.

perche [pɛrʃ] *nf* - **1.** [poisson] perch - **2.** [de bois, métal] pole ; **tendre la ~ à qqn** *fig* to throw sb a line.

percher [3] [pɛrʃe] <> *vi* - **1.** [oiseau] to perch - **2.** *fam* [personne] to live <> *vt* to perch.
➡ **se percher** *vp* to perch.

perchiste [pɛrʃist] *nmf* - **1.** *SPORT* pole vaulter - **2.** *CIN* & *TÉLÉ* boom operator.

perchoir [pɛrʃwar] *nm* perch.

perclus, e [pɛrkly, yz] *adj* : **~ de** [rhumatismes] crippled with ; *fig* [crainte] paralysed with.

perçois, perçoit *etc* ▷ **percevoir**.

percolateur [pɛrkɔlatœr] *nm* percolator.

perçu, e [pɛrsy] *pp* ▷ **percevoir**.

percussion [pɛrkysjɔ̃] *nf* percussion.

percussionniste [pɛrkysjɔnist] *nmf* percussionist.

percutant, e [pɛrkytã, ãt] *adj* - **1.** [obus] explosive - **2.** *fig* [argument] forceful.

percuter [3] [pɛrkyte] <> *vt* to strike, to smash into <> *vi* to explode.

perdant, e [pɛrdã, ãt] <> *adj* losing <> *nm, f* loser.

perdition [pɛrdisjɔ̃] *nf* - **1.** [ruine morale] perdition - **2.** [détresse] : **en ~** in distress.

perdre [77] [pɛrdr] <> *vt* - **1.** [gén] to lose - **2.** [temps] to waste ; [occasion] to miss, to waste - **3.** [suj : bonté, propos] to be the ruin of - **4.** *loc* : **vous ne perdez rien pour attendre!** just wait until I get my hands on you! <> *vi* to lose.
➡ **se perdre** *vp* - **1.** [coutume] to die out, to become lost - **2.** [personne] to get lost, to lose one's way ; **se ~ dans les détails** *fig* to get bogged down in details.

perdreau, x [pɛrdro] *nm* young partridge.

perdrix [pɛrdri] *nf* partridge.

perdu, e [pɛrdy] <> *pp* ▷ **perdre** <> *adj* - **1.** [égaré] lost - **2.** [endroit] out-of-the-way

- **3.** [balle] stray - **4.** [emballage] non-returnable - **5.** [temps, occasion] wasted - **6.** [malade] dying - **7.** [récolte, robe] spoilt, ruined.

perdurer [3] [pɛrdyre] *vi littéraire* to endure.

père [pɛr] *nm* - **1.** [gén] father ; **mon ~** RELIG Father ; **~ de famille** father ; **de ~ en fils** from father to son - **2.** [d'animal] sire - **3.** *fam* [homme mûr] : **le ~ Martin** old Martin.
◆ **pères** *nmpl* [ancêtres] forefathers, ancestors.
◆ **père Noël** *nm* : **le ~ Noël** Father Christmas, Santa Claus.

pérégrination [peregrinasjɔ̃] *nf (gén pl)* wanderings *(pl)*.

péremption [perɑ̃psjɔ̃] *nf* time limit ; **date de ~** best-before date.

péremptoire [perɑ̃ptwar] *adj* peremptory.

pérennité [perenite] *nf* durability.

péréquation [perekwasjɔ̃] *nf* equalization.

perfectible [pɛrfɛktibl] *adj* perfectible.

perfection [pɛrfɛksjɔ̃] *nf* - **1.** [qualité] perfection ; **à la ~** to perfection - **2.** [chose parfaite] jewel, gem.

perfectionnement [pɛrfɛksjɔnmɑ̃] *nm* improvement.

perfectionner [3] [pɛrfɛksjɔne] *vt* to perfect.
◆ **se perfectionner** *vp* to improve.

perfectionnisme [pɛrfɛksjɔnism] *nm* perfectionism.

perfectionniste [pɛrfɛksjɔnist] *nmf* & *adj* perfectionist.

perfide [pɛrfid] *adj* perfidious.

perfidement [pɛrfidmɑ̃] *adv* perfidiously.

perfidie [pɛrfidi] *nf* perfidy.

perforateur, trice [pɛrfɔratœr, tris] *adj* perforating.
◆ **perforateur** *nm* punch card operator.
◆ **perforatrice** *nf* [perceuse] drill ; [de bureau] hole punch.

perforation [pɛrfɔrasjɔ̃] *nf* perforation.

perforer [3] [pɛrfɔre] *vt* to perforate.

performance [pɛrfɔrmɑ̃s] *nf* performance ; **les ~s d'une voiture** a car's performance.

performant, e [pɛrfɔrmɑ̃, ɑ̃t] *adj* - **1.** [personne] efficient - **2.** [machine] high-performance *(avant n)*.

perfusion [pɛrfyzjɔ̃] *nf* perfusion.

pergola [pɛrgɔla] *nf* pergola.

péricliter [3] [periklite] *vi* to collapse.

péridurale [peridyral] *nf* epidural.

péril [peril] *nm* peril ; **au ~ de ma vie** at the risk of my life.

périlleux, euse [perijø, øz] *adj* perilous, dangerous.

périmé, e [perime] *adj* out-of-date ; *fig* [idées] outdated.

périmètre [perimɛtr] *nm* - **1.** [contour] perimeter - **2.** [contenu] area.

périnatal, e, aux [perinatal, o] *adj* perinatal.

périnée [perine] *nm* perineum.

période [perjɔd] *nf* period.

périodique [perjɔdik] <> *nm* periodical <> *adj* periodic.

périodiquement [perjɔdikmɑ̃] *adv* periodically.

péripatéticienne [peripatetisjɛn] *nf* streetwalker.

péripétie [peripesi] *nf* event.

périphérie [periferi] *nf* - **1.** [de ville] outskirts *(pl)* - **2.** [bord] periphery ; [de cercle] circumference.

périphérique [periferik] <> *nm* - **1.** [route] ring road *Br*, beltway *Am* - **2.** INFORM peripheral device <> *adj* peripheral ; **boulevard ~** ring road *Br*, beltway *Am*.

périphrase [perifraz] *nf* periphrasis.

périple [peripl] *nm* - **1.** NAVIG voyage - **2.** [voyage] trip.

périr [32] [perir] *vi* to perish.

périscolaire [periskɔler] *adj* extracurricular.

périscope [periskɔp] *nm* periscope.

périssable [perisabl] *adj* - **1.** [denrée] perishable - **2.** *littéraire* [sentiment] transient.

péristyle [peristil] *nm* peristyle.

péritonite [peritɔnit] *nf* peritonitis.

perle [pɛrl] *nf* - **1.** [de nacre] pearl - **2.** [de bois, verre] bead - **3.** [de sang, d'eau] drop - **4.** [personne] gem - **5.** *fam* [erreur] howler.

perlé, e [pɛrle] *adj* beaded ; **grève ~e** go-slow *Br*, slowdown *Am*.

perler [3] [pɛrle] *vi* to form beads.

perlimpinpin [pɛrlɛ̃pɛ̃pɛ̃] *nm* : **poudre de ~** miracle cure.

permanence [pɛrmanɑ̃s] *nf* - **1.** [continuité] permanence ; **en ~** constantly - **2.** [service] : **être de ~ to** to be on duty - **3.** SCOL : **(salle de) ~** study room.

permanent, e [pɛrmanɑ̃, ɑ̃t] <> *adj* permanent ; [cinéma] with continuous showings ; [comité] standing *(avant n)* <> *nm, f* official.
◆ **permanente** *nf* perm.

perméable [pɛrmeabl] *adj* : **~ (à)** permeable (to) ; *fig* open (to), receptive (to).

permets ▷ **permettre**.

permettais, permettions *etc* ⊳ **per-mettre.**

permettre [84] [pɛrmɛtr] *vt* to permit, to allow ; **vous permettez?** may I? ; ~ **qqch à qqn** to allow sb sthg ; ~ **à qqn de faire qqch** to permit *ou* allow sb to do sthg.
◆ **se permettre** *vp* : **se ~ qqch** to allow o.s sthg ; [avoir les moyens de] to be able to afford sthg ; **se ~ de faire qqch** to take the liberty of doing sthg.

permis, e [pɛrmi, iz] *pp* ⊳ **permettre.**
◆ **permis** *nm* licence *Br*, license *Am*, permit ; ~ **de conduire** driving licence *Br*, driver's license *Am* ; ~ **de construire** planning permission *Br*, building permit *Am* ; ~ **de séjour** residence permit ; ~ **de travail** work permit.

permissif, ive [pɛrmisif, iv] *adj* permissive.

permission [pɛrmisjɔ̃] *nf* **- 1.** [autorisation] permission **- 2.** *MIL* leave.

permutable [pɛrmytabl] *adj* which can be changed round.

permutation [pɛrmytasjɔ̃] *nf* [de mots, figures] transposition ; *MATHS* permutation.

permuter [3] [pɛrmyte] ⟨⟩ *vt* to change round ; [mots, figures] to transpose ⟨⟩ *vi* to change, to switch.

pernicieux, euse [pɛrnisjø, øz] *adj* **- 1.** *MÉD* pernicious **- 2.** [conseil, habitude] harmful.

péroné [perɔne] *nm* fibula.

péroraison [perɔrɛzɔ̃] *nf* peroration.

pérorer [3] [perɔre] *vi péj* to hold forth.

Pérou [peru] *nm* : **le ~** Peru ; **au ~** in Peru.

perpendiculaire [pɛrpãdikylɛr] ⟨⟩ *nf* perpendicular ⟨⟩ *adj* : ~ **(à)** perpendicular (to).

perpendiculairement [pɛrpãdikylɛrmã] *adv* perpendicularly ; ~ **à** perpendicular to.

perpète, perpette [pɛrpɛt] ◆ **à perpète** *loc adv fam* [loin] miles away ; [longtemps] for ever.

perpétrer [18] [pɛrpetre] *vt* to perpetrate.

perpette = **perpète.**

perpétuel, elle [pɛrpetɥɛl] *adj* **- 1.** [fréquent, continu] perpetual **- 2.** [rente] life *(avant n)* ; [secrétaire] permanent.

perpétuellement [pɛrpetɥɛlmã] *adv* perpetually.

perpétuer [7] [pɛrpetɥe] *vt* to perpetuate.
◆ **se perpétuer** *vp* to continue ; [espèce] to perpetuate itself.

perpétuité [pɛrpetɥite] *nf* perpetuity ; **à ~** for life ; **être condamné à ~** to be sentenced to life imprisonment.

perplexe [pɛrplɛks] *adj* perplexed.

perplexité [pɛrplɛksite] *nf* perplexity.

perquisition [pɛrkizisjɔ̃] *nf* search.

perquisitionner [3] [pɛrkizisjɔne] ⟨⟩ *vi* to make a search ⟨⟩ *vt* to search, to make a search of.

perron [pɛrɔ̃] *nm* steps *(pl)* *(at entrance to building).*

perroquet [pɛrɔkɛ] *nm* [animal] parrot.

perruche [peryʃ] *nf* budgerigar.

perruque [perɥk] *nf* wig.

pers [pɛr(s)] *adj littéraire* blue-green.

persan, e [pɛrsã, an] *adj* Persian.
◆ **persan** *nm* **- 1.** [langue] Persian **- 2.** [chat] Persian (cat).
◆ **Persan, e** *nm, f* Persian.

persécuter [3] [pɛrsekyte] *vt* **- 1.** [martyriser] to persecute **- 2.** [harceler] to harass.

persécuteur, trice [pɛrsekytœr, tris] ⟨⟩ *adj* persecuting ⟨⟩ *nm, f* persecutor.

persécution [pɛrsekysjɔ̃] *nf* persecution.

persévérance [pɛrseverãs] *nf* perseverance.

persévérant, e [pɛrseverã, ãt] *adj* persevering.

persévérer [18] [pɛrsevere] *vi* : ~ **(dans)** to persevere (in).

persienne [pɛrsjɛn] *nf* shutter.

persiflage [pɛrsiflaʒ] *nm* mockery.

persifler [3] [pɛrsifle] *vt littéraire* to mock.

persifleur, euse [pɛrsiflœr, øz] ⟨⟩ *adj* mocking ⟨⟩ *nm, f* mocker.

persil [pɛrsil] *nm* parsley.

persillé, e [pɛrsije] *adj* **- 1.** [plat] with parsley **- 2.** [viande] marbled ; [fromage] veined, blue-veined.

Persique [pɛrsik] ⊳ **golfe.**

persistance [pɛrsistãs] *nf* persistence.

persistant, e [pɛrsistã, ãt] *adj* persistent ; **arbre à feuillage ~** evergreen (tree).

persister [3] [pɛrsiste] *vi* to persist ; ~ **à faire qqch** to persist in doing sthg ; ~ **dans qqch** to persist in sthg.

personnage [pɛrsɔnaʒ] *nm* **- 1.** [dignitaire] figure **- 2.** *THÉÂTRE* character ; *ART* figure **- 3.** [personnalité] image **- 4.** *péj* [individu] character, individual.

personnaliser [3] [pɛrsɔnalize] *vt* to personalize.

personnalité [pɛrsɔnalite] *nf* **- 1.** [gén] personality **- 2.** *JUR* status.

personne [pɛrsɔn] ◇ *nf* person ; ~s people ; en ~ in person, personally ; ~ âgée elderly person ; ~ morale legal entity ◇ *pron indéf* - **1.** [quelqu'un] anybody, anyone ; je me demande si ~ arrivera un jour à le convaincre I wonder if anyone will ever convince him - **2.** [aucune personne] nobody, no one ; ~ ne viendra nobody will come ; il n'y a jamais ~ there's never anybody there, nobody is ever there ; ~ d'autre nobody *ou* no one else.

personnel, elle [pɛrsɔnɛl] *adj* - **1.** [gén] personal - **2.** [égoïste] self-centred.

◆ **personnel** *nm* staff, personnel ; ~ navigant flight crew.

personnellement [pɛrsɔnɛlmɑ̃] *adv* personally.

personnification [pɛrsɔnifikasjɔ̃] *nf* personification.

personnifier [9] [pɛrsɔnifje] *vt* to personify.

perspective [pɛrspɛktiv] *nf* - **1.** ART [point de vue] perspective - **2.** [panorama] view - **3.** [éventualité] prospect.

perspicace [pɛrspikas] *adj* perspicacious.

perspicacité [pɛrspikasite] *nf* perspicacity.

persuader [3] [pɛrsɥade] *vt* : ~ qqn de qqch/de faire qqch to persuade sb of sthg/to do sthg, to convince sb of sthg/to do sthg.

◆ **se persuader** *vp* : se ~ que to persuade *ou* convince o.s. (that) ; se ~ de to persuade *ou* convince o.s. of.

persuasif, ive [pɛrsɥazif, iv] *adj* persuasive.

persuasion [pɛrsɥazjɔ̃] *nf* persuasion.

perte [pɛrt] *nf* - **1.** [gén] loss ; à ~ COMM at a loss ; ~ sèche dead loss - **2.** [gaspillage - de temps] waste ; en pure ~ for absolutely nothing - **3.** [ruine, déchéance] ruin ; courir/aller à sa ~ to be on the road to ruin.

◆ **pertes** *nfpl* [morts] losses.

◆ **à perte de vue** *loc adv* as far as the eye can see.

pertinemment [pɛrtinamɑ̃] *adv* pertinently.

pertinence [pɛrtinɑ̃s] *nf* pertinence, relevance.

pertinent, e [pɛrtinɑ̃, ɑ̃t] *adj* pertinent, relevant.

perturbateur, trice [pɛrtyrbatœr, tris] ◇ *adj* disruptive ◇ *nm, f* troublemaker.

perturbation [pɛrtyrbasjɔ̃] *nf* disruption ; ASTRON & MÉTÉOR disturbance.

perturber [3] [pɛrtyrbe] *vt* - **1.** [gén] to disrupt ; ~ l'ordre public to disturb the peace - **2.** PSYCHOL to disturb.

péruvien, enne [peryvjɛ̃, ɛn] *adj* Peruvian.

◆ **Péruvien, enne** *nm, f* Peruvian.

pervenche [pɛrvɑ̃ʃ] ◇ *nf* - **1.** BOT periwinkle - **2.** *fam* [contractuelle] traffic warden *Br*, meter maid *Am* ◇ *adj inv* (periwinkle) blue.

pervers, e [pɛrvɛr, ɛrs] ◇ *adj* - **1.** [vicieux] perverted - **2.** [effet] unwanted ◇ *nm, f* pervert.

perversion [pɛrvɛrsjɔ̃] *nf* perversion.

perversité [pɛrvɛrsite] *nf* perversity.

pervertir [32] [pɛrvɛrtir] *vt* to pervert.

◆ **se pervertir** *vp* to become perverted.

pesage [pəzaʒ] *nm* - **1.** [pesée] weighing - **2.** [de jockey] weigh-in.

pesamment [pəzamɑ̃] *adv* heavily.

pesant, e [pəzɑ̃, ɑ̃t] *adj* - **1.** [lourd] heavy - **2.** [style, architecture] ponderous.

◆ **pesant** *nm* : valoir son ~ d'or *fig* to be worth its/one's weight in gold.

pesanteur [pəzɑ̃tœr] *nf* - **1.** PHYS gravity - **2.** [lourdeur] heaviness.

pesée [pəze] *nf* - **1.** [opération] weighing - **2.** [quantité] weight - **3.** [pression] pressure, force.

pèse-lettre [pɛzlɛtr] (*pl inv* OU **pèse-lettres**) *nm* letter-scales.

pèse-personne [pɛzpɛrsɔn] (*pl inv* OU **pèse-personnes**) *nm* scales (*pl*).

peser [19] [pəze] ◇ *vt* to weigh ; tout bien pesé *fig* all things considered ◇ *vi* - **1.** [avoir un certain poids] to weigh - **2.** [être lourd] to be heavy ; ~ à qqn *fig* to weigh on sb ; ~ sur *fig* [accabler] to weigh heavy on ; *fig* [influer sur] to influence - **3.** [appuyer] : ~ sur qqch to press (down) on sthg.

◆ **se peser** *vp* to weigh o.s.

peseta [pezeta] *nf* peseta.

pessimisme [pesimism] *nm* pessimism.

pessimiste [pesimist] ◇ *nmf* pessimist ◇ *adj* pessimistic.

peste [pɛst] *nf* - **1.** MÉD plague ; craindre qqn/qqch comme la ~ *fig* to be terrified of sb/sthg ; fuir qqn/qqch comme la ~ *fig* to avoid sb/sthg like the plague - **2.** [personne] pest.

pester [3] [pɛste] *vi* : ~ (contre qqn/qqch) to curse (sb/sthg).

pesticide [pɛstisid] ◇ *nm* pesticide ◇ *adj* pesticidal.

pestiféré, e [pɛstifere] ◇ *adj* plague-stricken ◇ *nm, f* plague victim.

pestilentiel, elle [pɛstilɑ̃sjɛl] *adj* pestilential.

pet [pɛ] *nm fam* fart.

pétale [petal] *nm* petal.

pétanque [petɑ̃k] *nf* ≈ bowls (*U*).

pétant, e [petɑ̃, ɑ̃t] *adj fam* on the dot.

pétarader [3] [petarade] *vi* to backfire.

pétard [petar] *nm* - **1.** [petit explosif] banger *Br*, firecracker - **2.** *fam* [revolver] gun - **3.** *fam* [postérieur] bum *Br*, butt *Am* - **4.** *fam* [haschich] joint.

pet-de-nonne [pɛdnɔn] (*pl* **pets-de-nonne**) *nm very light fritter.*

péter [18] [pete] ◇ *vi* - **1.** *tfam* [personne] to fart - **2.** *fam* [câble, élastique] to snap ◇ *vt fam* to bust.

pète-sec [pɛtsɛk] *adj inv fam* bossy.

pétillant, e [petijɑ̃, ɑ̃t] *adj litt* & *fig* sparkling.

pétiller [3] [petije] *vi* - **1.** [vin, eau] to sparkle, to bubble - **2.** [feu] to crackle - **3.** *fig* [yeux] to sparkle ; ~ **de** [personne] to bubble with ; [yeux] to sparkle with.

petiot, e [pətjo, ɔt] ◇ *adj* teeny ◇ *nm, f* little one.

petit, e [pəti, it] ◇ *adj* - **1.** [de taille, jeune] small, little ; ~ **frère** little *ou* younger brother ; **~e sœur** little *ou* younger sister - **2.** [voyage, visite] short, little - **3.** [faible, infime - somme d'argent] small ; [- bruit] faint, slight ; **c'est une ~e nature** he/she is slightly built - **4.** [de peu d'importance, de peu de valeur] minor - **5.** [médiocre, mesquin] petty - **6.** [de rang modeste - commerçant, propriétaire, pays] small ; [- fonctionnaire] minor ; **les ~es gens** people of modest means ◇ *nm, f* - **1.** [personne de petite taille] small man (*f* woman) - **2.** [enfant] little one, child ; **bonjour, mon ~/ma ~e** good morning, my dear ; **pauvre ~!** poor little thing! ; **la classe des ~s** SCOL the infant class ◇ *nm* - **1.** [jeune animal] young (*U*) ; **faire des ~s** to have puppies/kittens *etc* - **2.** (*gén pl*) [personne modeste] little man.
➤ **petit à petit** *loc adv* little by little, gradually.

petit-beurre [p(ə)tibœr] (*pl* **petits-beurre**) *nm small biscuit.*

petit-bourgeois, petite-bourgeoise [p(ə)tiburʒwa, p(ə)titburʒwaz] (*mpl* **petits-bourgeois**, *fpl* **petites-bourgeoises**) *péj* ◇ *adj* lower middle-class ◇ *nm, f* lower middle-class person.

petit déjeuner [p(ə)tideʒøne] (*pl* **petits déjeuners**) *nm* breakfast.

petit-déjeuner [5] [p(ə)tideʒøne] *vi* to have breakfast, to breakfast.

petite-fille [p(ə)titfij] (*pl* **petites-filles**) *nf* granddaughter.

petitement [p(ə)titmɑ̃] *adv* - **1.** [être logé] in cramped conditions - **2.** [chichement - vivre] poorly - **3.** [mesquinement] pettily.

petitesse [p(ə)titɛs] *nf* - **1.** [de personne, de revenu] smallness - **2.** [d'esprit] pettiness.

petit-fils [p(ə)tifis] (*pl* **petits-fils**) *nm* grandson.

petit-four [p(ə)tifur] (*pl* **petits-fours**) *nm* petit-four.

pétition [petisjɔ̃] *nf* petition.

pétitionner [3] [petisjɔne] *vi* to petition.

petit-lait [p(ə)tilɛ] (*pl* **petits-laits**) *nm* whey.

petit-nègre [p(ə)tinɛgr] *nm inv fam* pidgin French.

petits-enfants [p(ə)tizɑ̃fɑ̃] *nmpl* grandchildren.

petit-suisse [p(ə)tisɥis] (*pl* **petits-suisses**) *nm fresh soft cheese, eaten with sugar.*

peton [pətɔ̃] *nm fam* foot.

pétrifier [9] [petrifje] *vt litt* & *fig* to petrify.
➤ **se pétrifier** *vp* to become petrified.

pétrin [petrɛ̃] *nm* - **1.** [de boulanger] kneading machine - **2.** *fam* [embarras] pickle ; **se fourrer/être dans le ~** to get into/to be in a pickle.

pétrir [32] [petrir] *vt* - **1.** [pâte, muscle] to knead - **2.** *fig* & *littéraire* [personne] to mould ; **pétri d'orgueil** filled with pride.

pétrochimie [petrɔʃimi] *nf* petrochemistry.

pétrochimique [petrɔʃimik] *adj* petrochemical.

pétrodollar [petrɔdɔlar] *nm* petrodollar.

pétrole [petrɔl] *nm* oil, petroleum ; ~ **lampant** paraffin (oil) *Br*, kerosene *Am*.

pétrolier, ère [petrɔlje, ɛr] *adj* oil (*avant n*), petroleum (*avant n*).
➤ **pétrolier** *nm* - **1.** [navire] oil tanker - **2.** [personne] oil magnate.

pétrolifère [petrɔlifɛr] *adj* oil-bearing.

pétulant, e [petylɑ̃, ɑ̃t] *adj* exuberant.

pétunia [petynja] *nm* petunia.

peu [pø] ◇ *adv* - **1.** (*avec verbe, adjectif, adverbe*) : **il a ~ dormi** he didn't sleep much, he slept little ; **c'est un livre ~ intéressant** it's not a very interesting book ; **~ souvent** not very often, rarely ; **très ~** very little - **2.** : **~ de** (+ *nom sg*) little, not much ; (+ *nom pl*) few, not many ; **il a ~ de travail** he hasn't got much work, he has little work ; **c'est (bien) ~ de chose** it's not much ; **il reste ~ de jours** there aren't many days left ; **~ d'élèves l'ont compris** few *ou* not many students understood him ; **~ de gens le connaissent** few *ou* not many know him ◇ *nm* - **1.** [petite quantité] : **le ~ de** (+ *nom sg*) the little ; (+ *nom pl*) the few ; **avec mon ~ de moyens** with the little I possess - **2.** : **un ~** a little, a bit ; **je le connais un ~** I know him slightly *ou* a little ; **un (tout)**

petit ~ a little bit ; **elle est un ~ sotte** she's a bit stupid ; **tu parles un ~ fort** you're talking a little too loudly ; **un ~ de** a little ; **un ~ de vin/patience** a little wine/patience.

→ **avant peu** *loc adv* soon, before long.

→ **depuis peu** *loc adv* recently.

→ **peu à peu** *loc adv* gradually, little by little.

→ **pour peu que** (+ *subjonctif*) *loc conj* if ever, if only.

→ **pour un peu** *loc adv* nearly, almost.

→ **si peu que** (+ *subjonctif*) *loc conj* however little.

→ **sous peu** *loc adv* soon, shortly.

peul, e [pøl] *adj* Fulani.

→ **peul** *nm* [langue] Fulani.

→ **Peul, e** *nm, f* Fulani.

peuplade [pœpladl] *nf* tribe.

peuple [pœpl] *nm* - **1.** [gén] people ; **le ~** the (common) people - **2.** *fam* [multitude] : **quel ~!** what a crowd!

peuplé, e [pœple] *adj* populated.

peuplement [pœpləmɑ̃l] *nm* - **1.** [action] populating - **2.** [population] population.

peupler [5] [pœple] *vt* - **1.** [pourvoir d'habitants - région] to populate ; [- bois, étang] to stock - **2.** [habiter, occuper] to inhabit - **3.** *fig* [remplir] to fill.

→ **se peupler** *vp* - **1.** [région] to become populated - **2.** [rue, salle] to be filled.

peuplier [pøplije] *nm* poplar.

peur [pœr] *nf* fear ; **avoir ~ de qqn/qqch** to be afraid of sb/sthg ; **avoir ~ de faire qqch** to be afraid of doing sthg ; **avoir ~ que** (+ *subjonctif*) to be afraid that ; **j'ai ~ qu'il ne vienne pas** I'm afraid he won't come ; **faire ~ à qqn** to frighten sb ; **par** *ou* **de ~ de qqch** for fear of sthg ; **par** *ou* **de ~ de faire qqch** for fear of doing sthg ; **il n'a pas ~ du ridicule** he doesn't mind making a fool of himself ; **avoir une ~ bleue de** to be scared stiff of ; **avoir plus de ~ que de mal** to be more frightened than hurt ; **laid à faire ~** horribly ugly ; **mourir de ~** to die of fright ; **prendre ~** to take fright.

peureux, euse [pœrø, øz] <> *adj* fearful, timid <> *nm, f* fearful *ou* timid person.

peut ▷ **pouvoir**.

peut-être [pøtɛtr] *adv* perhaps, maybe ; **~ qu'ils ne viendront pas, ils ne viendront ~ pas** perhaps *ou* maybe they won't come ; **~ pas** perhaps *ou* maybe not.

peux ▷ **pouvoir**.

p. ex. (*abr de* **par exemple**) e.g.

pH (*abr de* **potential of hydrogen**) *nm* pH.

phalange [falɑ̃ʒ] *nf* - **1.** ANAT phalanx - **2.** POLIT falange.

phallique [falik] *adj* phallic.

phallocrate [falɔkrat] <> *nm* male chauvinist <> *adj* male chauvinist (*avant n*) ; [milieu] male-dominated.

phallus [falys] *nm* phallus.

pharaon [faraɔ̃] *nm* pharaoh.

phare [far] <> *nm* - **1.** [tour] lighthouse - **2.** AUTOM headlight ; **~ antibrouillard** fog lamp <> *adj* landmark (*avant n*) ; **une industrie ~** a flagship *ou* pioneering industry.

pharmaceutique [farmasøtik] *adj* pharmaceutical.

pharmacie [farmasi] *nf* - **1.** [science] pharmacology - **2.** [magasin] chemist's *Br*, drugstore *Am* - **3.** [meuble] : **(armoire à) ~** medicine cupboard.

pharmacien, enne [farmasjɛ̃, ɛn] *nm, f* chemist *Br*, druggist *Am*.

pharmacologie [farmakɔlɔʒi] *nf* pharmacology.

pharyngite [farɛ̃ʒit] *nf* pharyngitis (*U*).

pharynx [farɛ̃ks] *nm* pharynx.

phase [faz] *nf* phase ; **être en ~ avec qqn** to be on the same wavelength as sb.

phénix [feniks] *nm* - **1.** MYTH phoenix - **2.** [personne] paragon.

phénoménal, e, aux [fenɔmenal, o] *adj* phenomenal.

phénomène [fenɔmɛn] *nm* - **1.** [fait] phenomenon - **2.** [être anormal] freak - **3.** *fam* [excentrique] character.

philanthropie [filɑ̃trɔpi] *nf* philanthropy.

philanthropique [filɑ̃trɔpik] *adj* philanthropic.

philatélie [filateli] *nf* philately, stamp-collecting.

philatéliste [filatelist] *nmf* philatelist, stamp-collector.

philharmonique [filarmɔnik] *adj* philharmonic.

philippin, e [filipɛ̃, in] *adj* Filipino.

→ **Philippin, e** *nm, f* Filipino.

Philippines [filipin] *nfpl* : **les ~** the Philippines ; **aux ~** in the Philippines.

philistin [filistɛ̃] *nm* philistine.

philodendron [filɔdɛ̃drɔ̃] *nm* philodendron.

philologie [filɔlɔʒi] *nf* philology.

philosophe [filɔzɔf] <> *nmf* philosopher <> *adj* philosophical.

philosopher [3] [filɔzɔfe] *vi* to philosophize.

philosophie [filɔzɔfi] *nf* philosophy.
philosophique [filɔzɔfik] *adj* philosophical.
philosophiquement [filɔzɔfikmã] *adv* philosophically.
philtre [filtr] *nm* love potion.
phlébite [flebit] *nf* phlebitis.
Phnom Penh [pnɔmpɛn] *n* Phnom Penh.
phobie [fɔbi] *nf* phobia.
phobique [fɔbik] *nmf* & *adj* phobic.
phonème [fɔnɛm] *nm* phoneme.
phonétique [fɔnetik] ◇ *nf* phonetics *(U)* ◇ *adj* phonetic.
phonétiquement [fɔnetikmã] *adv* phonetically.
phono [fɔno] *nm fam vieilli* gramophone *Br*, phonograph *Am*.
phonographe [fɔnɔgraf] *nm vieilli* gramophone *Br*, phonograph *Am*.
phoque [fɔk] *nm* seal.
phosphate [fɔsfat] *nm* phosphate.
phosphaté, e [fɔsfate] *adj* : **engrais ~** phosphate fertilizer.
phosphore [fɔsfɔr] *nm* phosphorus.
phosphorescent, e [fɔsfɔresã, ãt] *adj* phosphorescent.
photo [fɔto] ◇ *nf* - **1.** [technique] photography - **2.** [image] photo, picture ; **prendre qqn en ~** to take a photo of sb ; **~ d'identité** passport photo ; **~ noir et blanc** black and white photo ; **~ couleur** colour *Br ou* color *Am* photo ; **y'a pas ~** *fam* there's no comparison ◇ *adj inv* : **appareil ~** camera.
photocomposition [fɔtokɔ̃pozisjɔ̃] *nf* filmsetting *Br*, photocomposition *Am*.
photocopie [fɔtokɔpi] *nf* - **1.** [procédé] photocopying - **2.** [document] photocopy.
photocopier [9] [fɔtokɔpje] *vt* to photocopy.
photocopieur [fɔtokɔpjœr] *nm*, **photocopieuse** [fɔtokɔpjøz] *nf* photocopier.
photoélectrique [fɔtoelektrik] *adj* photoelectric.
photogénique [fɔtoʒenik] *adj* photogenic.
photographe [fɔtograf] *nmf* - **1.** [artiste, technicien] photographer - **2.** [commerçant] camera dealer.
photographie [fɔtografi] *nf* - **1.** [technique] photography - **2.** [cliché] photograph.
photographier [9] [fɔtografje] *vt* to photograph.
photographique [fɔtografik] *adj* photographic.

Photomaton® [fɔtɔmatɔ̃] *nm* photo booth.
photomontage [fɔtɔmɔ̃taʒ] *nm* photomontage.
photoreportage [fɔtɔrəpɔrtaʒ] *nm* PRESSE report *(consisting mainly of photographs)*.
photosensible [fɔtɔsãsibl] *adj* photosensitive.
photothèque [fɔtɔtɛk] *nf* photograph library.
phrase [fraz] *nf* - **1.** LING sentence ; **~ toute faite** stock phrase - **2.** MUS phrase.
phraséologie [frazeɔlɔʒi] *nf* phraseology ; *péj* verbiage.
phraseur, euse [frazœr, øz] *nm*, *f péj* verbose person.
phréatique [freatik] *adj* : **nappe ~** water table.
phrygien, enne [friʒjɛ̃, ɛn] *adj* Phrygian.
➧ **Phrygien, enne** *nm*, *f* Phrygian.
phtisie [ftizi] *nf vieilli* consumption.
phylloxéra, phylloxera [filɔksera] *nm* phylloxera.
physicien, enne [fizisjɛ̃, ɛn] *nm*, *f* physicist.
physiologie [fizjɔlɔʒi] *nf* physiology.
physiologique [fizjɔlɔʒik] *adj* physiological.
physiologiquement [fizjɔlɔʒikmã] *adv* physiologically.
physionomie [fizjɔnɔmi] *nf* - **1.** [faciès] face - **2.** [apparence] physiognomy.
physionomiste [fizjɔnɔmist] ◇ *nmf* person with a good memory for faces ◇ *adj* : être ~ to have a good memory for faces.
physiothérapie [fizjɔterapi] *nf natural medicine based on treatment using water, air, light etc.*
physique [fizik] ◇ *adj* physical ◇ *nf* SCIENCE physics *(U)* ◇ *nm* - **1.** [constitution] physical well-being - **2.** [apparence] physique.
physiquement [fizikmã] *adv* physically.
phytothérapie [fitɔterapi] *nf* herbal medicine.
p.i. *abr de* par intérim.
piaf [pjaf] *nm fam* sparrow.
piaffer [3] [pjafe] *vi* - **1.** [cheval] to paw the ground - **2.** [personne] to fidget.
piaillement [pjajmã] *nm* - **1.** [d'oiseau] cheeping - **2.** [d'enfant] squawking.
piailler [3] [pjaje] *vi* - **1.** [oiseaux] to cheep - **2.** [enfant] to squawk.
pianiste [pjanist] *nmf* pianist.
piano [pjano] ◇ *nm* piano ; **~ demi-queue**

baby grand (piano) ; ~ **droit** upright (piano) ; ~ **mécanique** player piano ; ~ à **queue** grand (piano) ◇ *adv* - **1.** *MUS* piano - **2.** [doucement] gently.

pianoter [3] [pjanɔte] *vi* - **1.** [jouer du piano] to plunk away (on the piano) - **2.** [sur table] to drum one's fingers.

piaule [pjol] *nf fam* [hébergement] place ; [chambre] room.

piauler [3] [pjole] *vi* - **1.** [oiseau] to cheep - **2.** [enfant] to whimper.

PIB (*abr de* **produit intérieur brut**) *nm* GDP.

pic [pik] *nm* - **1.** [outil] pick, pickaxe *Br*, pickax *Am* - **2.** [montagne] peak - **3.** [oiseau] woodpecker - **4.** : *fig* [maximum] ~ **d'audience** top (audience) ratings ; **on a observé des ~s de pollution** pollution levels reached a peak, pollution levels peaked.

➤ **à pic** *loc adv* - **1.** [verticalement] vertically ; **couler à ~** to sink like a stone - **2.** *fam fig* [à point nommé] just at the right moment.

pichenette [piʃnɛt] *nf* flick (of the finger).

pichet [piʃɛ] *nm* jug.

pickpocket [pikpɔkɛt] *nm* pickpocket.

pick-up [pikœp] *nm inv* - **1.** *vieilli* [tourne-disque] record player - **2.** [camionnette] pick-up (truck).

picoler [3] [pikɔle] *vi fam* to booze.

picorer [3] [pikɔre] *vi & vt* to peck.

picotement [pikɔtmã] *nm* prickling (U), prickle.

picoter [3] [pikɔte] *vt* - **1.** [yeux] to make sting - **2.** [pain] to peck (at).

pictogramme [piktɔgram] *nm* pictogram.

pictural, e, aux [piktyral, o] *adj* pictorial.

pic-vert = pivert.

pie [pi] ◇ *nf* - **1.** [oiseau] magpie - **2.** *fig & péj* [bavard] chatterbox ◇ *adj inv* [cheval] piebald.

pièce [pjɛs] *nf* - **1.** [élément] piece ; [de moteur] part ; **mettre en ~s** [vêtement] to tear to pieces ; [assiette, tasse] to smash to pieces ; ~ **de collection** collector's item ; ~ **détachée** spare part ; **en ~s détachées** *fig* in little bits *ou* pieces ; ~ **de musée** museum piece ; **créer/inventer qqch de toutes ~s** to create/invent sthg from start to finish - **2.** [unité] : **quinze francs ~** fifteen francs each *ou* apiece ; **acheter/vendre qqch à la ~** to buy/sell sthg singly, to buy/sell sthg separately ; **travailler à la ~** to do piece work - **3.** [document] document, paper ; ~ **à conviction** object produced as evidence, exhibit ; ~ **d'identité** identification papers (*pl*) ; ~ **justificative** written proof (*U*), supporting document - **4.** [œuvre littéraire ou musicale] piece ; ~ **(de théâtre)** play - **5.** [argent] : ~ **(de monnaie)** coin - **6.** [de maison] room - **7.** *COUTURE* patch.

➤ **pièce d'eau** *nf* large pond, ornamental lake.

➤ **pièce montée** *nf* tiered cake.

piécette [pjesɛt] *nf* small coin.

pied [pje] *nm* - **1.** [gén] foot ; **à ~** on foot ; **avoir ~** to be able to touch the bottom ; **perdre ~** *litt & fig* to be out of one's depth ; **à ~s joints** with one's feet together ; **être/marcher ~s nus** *ou* **nu-~s** to be/to go barefoot ; ~ **bot** [handicap] clubfoot - **2.** *CULIN* : ~ **de porc** pig's trotter - **3.** [base - de montagne, table] foot ; [- de verre] stem ; [- de lampe] base - **4.** [plant - de tomate] stalk ; [- de vigne] stock - **5.** *loc* : **attendre qqch/qqn de ~ ferme** to be ready for sb/sthg ; **c'est le ~** *fam* it's great ; **casser les ~s à qqn** *fam* to get on sb's nerves ; **comme un ~** [chanter, conduire] *fam* terribly ; **être au ~ du mur** to have one's back to the wall ; **être sur ~** to be (back) on one's feet, to be up and about ; **être sur un ~ d'égalité (avec)** to be on an equal footing (with) ; **faire du ~ à** to play footsie with ; **faire le ~ de grue** to wait about ; **faire des ~s et des mains** to move heaven and earth, to do one's utmost ; **faire un ~ de nez à qqn** to thumb one's nose at sb ; **ça te fera les ~s!** *fam* it'll serve you right! ; **fouler qqch aux ~s** to ride roughshod over sthg ; **se lever du bon ~/du ~ gauche** to get out of bed on the right/wrong side ; **mettre qqch sur ~** to get sthg on its feet, to get sthg off the ground ; **mettre qqn au ~ du mur** to drive sb to the wall ; **mettre les ~s dans le plat** *fam* to put one's foot in it ; **je n'ai jamais mis les ~s chez lui** I've never set foot in his house ; **au ~ de la lettre** literally, to the letter ; **de ~ en cap** from head to toe ; **ne pas savoir sur quel ~ danser** not to know which way to turn ; **ne pas se laisser marcher sur les ~s** not to let anyone tread on one's toes ; **prendre son ~** *fam* [sexuellement] to come ; *fig* to be in seventh heaven ; **retomber sur ses ~s** to land on one's feet.

➤ **en pied** *loc adj* [portrait] full-length.

pied-à-terre [pjetatɛr] *nm inv* pied-à-terre.

pied-de-biche [pjedbiʃ] (*pl* **pieds-de-biche**) *nm* - **1.** [outil] nail claw - **2.** *COUTURE* presser foot.

pied-de-poule [pjedpul] (*pl* **pieds-de-poule**) ◇ *nm* houndstooth (material) ◇ *adj inv* houndstooth (*avant n*).

piédestal, aux [pjedɛstal, o] *nm* pedestal.

piedmont = piémont.

pied-noir *(pl* **pieds-noirs)** [pjenwar] *nmf* French settler in Algeria.

piège [pjɛʒ] *nm litt* & *fig* trap ; **être pris au ~** to be trapped ; **tendre un ~** to set a trap.

piéger [22] [pjeʒe] *vt* - **1.** [animal, personne] to trap - **2.** [colis, véhicule] to boobytrap.

piémont, piedmont [pjemɔ̃] *nm* piedmont glacier/plain.

piercing [piːrsiŋ] *nm* body piercing.

pierraille [pjɛraj] *nf* loose stones *(pl).*

pierre [pjɛr] *nf* stone ; **~ d'achoppement** *fig* stumbling block ; **~ précieuse** precious stone ; **poser la première ~** CONSTR to lay the foundation stone ; *fig* to lay the foundations ; **faire d'une ~ deux coups** *fig* to kill two birds with one stone.

pierreries [pjɛrri] *nfpl* precious stones, jewels.

piété [pjete] *nf* piety.

piétiner [3] [pjetine] <> *vi* - **1.** [trépigner] to stamp (one's feet) - **2.** *fig* [ne pas avancer] to make no progress, to be at a standstill <> *vt* - **1.** [personne, parterre] to trample - **2.** *fig* [principes] to ride roughshod over.

piéton, onne [pjetɔ̃, ɔn] <> *nm, f* pedestrian <> *adj* pedestrian *(avant n).*

piétonnier, ère [pjetɔnje, ɛr] *adj* pedestrian *(avant n).*

piètre [pjɛtr] *adj* poor.

pieu, x [pjø] *nm* - **1.** [poteau] post, stake - **2.** *fam* [lit] pit *Br*, sack *Am.*

pieusement [pjøzmã] *adv* - **1.** RELIG piously - **2.** *fig* [conserver] religiously.

pieuter [3] [pjøte] ➡ **se pieuter** *vp fam* to hit the hay.

pieuvre [pjœvr] *nf* octopus ; *fig* & *péj* leech.

pieux, pieuse [pjø, pjøz] *adj* - **1.** [personne, livre] pious - **2.** [soins] devoted - **3.** [silence] reverent.

pif [pif] *nm fam* conk, hooter *Br* ; **au ~** *fig* by guesswork.

pige [piʒ] *nf* - **1.** PRESSE : **travailler à la ~** to work freelance - **2.** *fam* [an] : **avoir 30 ~s** to be 30 (years old).

pigeon [piʒɔ̃] *nm* - **1.** [oiseau] pigeon ; **~ voyageur** carrier pigeon, homing pigeon - **2.** *fam péj* [personne] sucker.

pigeonnant, e [piʒɔnã, ãt] *adj* [soutien-gorge] uplift *(avant n)* ; [poitrine] prominent.

pigeonner [3] [piʒɔne] *vt fam* to cheat.

pigeonnier [piʒɔnje] *nm* - **1.** [pour pigeons] pigeon loft, dovecote - **2.** *fig* & *vieilli* [logement] garret.

piger [17] [piʒe] *fam* <> *vt* to understand <> *vi* to catch on, to get it.

pigiste [piʒist] *nmf* freelance.

pigment [pigmã] *nm* pigment.

pigmentation [pigmãtasjɔ̃] *nf* pigmentation.

pignon [piɲɔ̃] *nm* - **1.** [de mur] gable ; **avoir ~ sur rue** *fig* to be a person of substance - **2.** [d'engrenage] gearwheel - **3.** [de pomme de pin] pine kernel.

pilaf [pilaf] ➡ **riz.**

pile [pil] <> *nf* - **1.** [de livres, journaux] pile - **2.** ÉLECTR battery - **3.** [de pièce] : **~ ou face** heads or tails <> *adv fam* on the dot ; **tomber/arriver ~** to come/to arrive at just the right time.

piler [3] [pile] <> *vt* - **1.** [amandes] to crush, to grind - **2.** *fam* [adversaire] to thrash <> *vi fam* AUTOM to jam on the brakes.

pileux, euse [pilø, øz] *adj* hairy *(avant n)* ; **système ~** hair.

pilier [pilje] *nm* - **1.** [de construction] pillar - **2.** *fig* [soutien] mainstay, pillar - **3.** *fig* & *péj* [habitué] : **c'est un ~ de bar** he's always propping up the bar - **4.** RUGBY prop (forward).

pillage [pijaʒ] *nm* looting.

pillard, e [pijar, ard] <> *nm, f* looter <> *adj* looting *(avant n).*

piller [3] [pije] *vt* - **1.** [ville, biens] to loot - **2.** *fig* [ouvrage, auteur] to plagiarize.

pilon [pilɔ̃] *nm* - **1.** [instrument] pestle ; **mettre au ~** to pulp - **2.** [de poulet] drumstick - **3.** [jambe de bois] wooden leg.

pilonner [3] [pilɔne] *vt* to pound.

pilori [pilɔri] *nm* pillory ; **mettre** OU **clouer qqn au ~** *fig* to pillory sb.

pilotage [pilɔtaʒ] *nm* piloting ; **~ automatique** automatic piloting.

pilote [pilɔt] <> *nm* - **1.** [d'avion] pilot ; [de voiture] driver ; **~ automatique** autopilot ; **~ de chasse** fighter pilot ; **~ de course** racing *Br* OU race *Am* driver ; **~ d'essai** test pilot ; **~ de ligne** airline pilot - **2.** [poisson] pilot fish <> *adj* pilot *(avant n)*, experimental.

piloter [3] [pilɔte] *vt* - **1.** [avion] to pilot ; [voiture] to drive - **2.** [personne] to show around.

pilotis [pilɔti] *nm* pile.

pilule [pilyl] *nf* pill ; **prendre la ~** to be on the pill ; **dorer la ~ à qqn** *fig* to sugar the pill for sb.

pimbêche [pɛ̃bɛʃ] *péj* <> *nf* stuck-up woman, stuck-up girl <> *adj* stuck-up.

piment [pimã] *nm* - **1.** [plante] pepper, capsicum ; **~ rouge** chilli pepper, hot red pepper - **2.** *fig* [piquant] spice ; **donner du ~ à qqch** to spice sthg up.

pimenter [3] [pimɑ̃te] *vt* - **1.** [plat] to put chillis in - **2.** *fig* [récit] to spice up.

pimpant, e [pɛ̃pɑ̃, ɑ̃t] *adj* smart.

pin [pɛ̃] *nm* pine ; **~ parasol** umbrella pine ; **~ sylvestre** Scots pine.

pin's [pinz] *nm inv* badge.

pinacle [pinakl] *nm* ARCHIT pinnacle ; **porter qqn au ~** *fig* to praise sb to the skies.

pinailler [3] [pinaje] *vi fam* to split hairs ; **~ sur** to quibble about.

pinard [pinar] *nm fam* wine, *péj* plonk *Br*, jug wine *Am*.

pince [pɛ̃s] *nf* - **1.** [grande] pliers (*pl*) - **2.** [petite] : **~ (à épiler)** tweezers (*pl*) ; **~ à linge** clothes peg *Br*, clothespin *Am* - **3.** [de crabe] pincer - **4.** *fam* [main] mitt - **5.** *fam* [jambe] : **à ~s** on foot - **6.** COUTURE dart.

pincé, e [pɛ̃se] *adj* - **1.** [air, sourire] prim - **2.** [nez] pinched.

pinceau, x [pɛ̃so] *nm* - **1.** [pour peindre] brush - **2.** *fam* [pied] foot.

pincée [pɛ̃se] *nf* pinch.

pincement [pɛ̃smɑ̃] *nm* pinching ; **~ au cœur** *fig* pang of sorrow.

pince-monseigneur [pɛ̃smɔ̃sɛɲœr] (*pl* pinces-monseigneur) *nf* jemmy *Br*, jimmy *Am*.

pince-nez [pɛ̃sne] *nm inv* pince-nez.

pincer [16] [pɛ̃se] <> *vt* - **1.** [serrer] to pinch ; MUS to pluck ; [lèvres] to purse - **2.** *fam fig* [arrêter] to nick *Br*, to catch ; **se faire ~** to get nicked *Br*, to get caught - **3.** [suj : froid] to nip <> *vi fam* - **1.** [faire froid] : **ça pince!** it's a bit nippy! - **2.** *fig* [avoir le béguin] : **en ~ pour qqn** to be crazy about sb.

➤ **se pincer** *vp* : **se ~ le doigt** to jam *ou* catch one's finger ; **se ~ le nez** to hold one's nose.

pince-sans-rire [pɛ̃ssɑ̃rir] *nmf inv* person with a deadpan face.

pincettes [pɛ̃sɛt] *nfpl* [ustensile] tongs ; **il n'est pas à prendre avec des ~** *fig* he's like a bear with a sore head.

pinçon [pɛ̃sɔ̃] *nm* pinch mark.

pinède [pinɛd], **pineraie** [pinrɛ], **pinière** [pinjɛr] *nf* pine wood.

pingouin [pɛ̃gwɛ̃] *nm* penguin.

ping-pong [piŋpɔ̃g] (*pl* ping-pongs) *nm* ping pong, table tennis.

pingre [pɛ̃gr] *péj* <> *nmf* skinflint <> *adj* stingy.

pingrerie [pɛ̃grəri] *nf péj* stinginess.

pinière = pinède.

pinson [pɛ̃sɔ̃] *nm* chaffinch ; **gai comme un ~** *fig* happy as a lark.

pintade [pɛ̃tad] *nf* guinea fowl.

pintadeau, x [pɛ̃tado] *nm* young guinea fowl.

pinte [pɛ̃t] *nf* - **1.** [mesure anglo-saxonne] pint - **2.** *vieilli* [mesure française] quart - **3.** *Helv* [débit de boissons] drinking establishment.

pin-up [pinœp] *nf inv* pinup (girl).

pioche [pjɔʃ] *nf* - **1.** [outil] pick - **2.** JEU pile.

piocher [3] [pjɔʃe] <> *vt* - **1.** [terre] to dig - **2.** JEU to take - **3.** *fig* [choisir] to pick at random <> *vi* - **1.** [creuser] to dig - **2.** JEU to pick up ; **~ dans** [tas] to delve into ; [économies] to dip into.

piolet [pjɔlɛ] *nm* ice axe *Br ou* ax *Am*.

pion, pionne [pjɔ̃, pjɔn] *nm, f fam* SCOL supervisor (*often a student who does this as a part-time job*).

➤ **pion** *nm* [aux échecs] pawn ; [aux dames] piece ; **damer le ~ à qqn** *fig* to get the better of sb ; **n'être qu'un ~** *fig* to be just a pawn in the game.

pionnier, ère [pjɔnje, ɛr] *nm, f* pioneer.

pipe [pip] *nf* pipe.

pipeau [pipo] *nm* MUS (reed) pipe ; **c'est du ~** *fam* that's nonsense.

pipeline, pipe-line [pajplajn, piplin] (*pl* pipe-lines) *nm* pipeline.

piper [3] [pipe] *vt* - **1.** [cartes] to mark ; [dés] to load - **2.** *loc* : **ne pas ~ mot** not to breathe a word.

piperade [piperad] *nf* eggs cooked with tomatoes, peppers and onions.

pipette [pipɛt] *nf* pipette.

pipi [pipi] *nm fam* wee ; **faire ~** to have a wee.

piquant, e [pikɑ̃, ɑ̃t] *adj* - **1.** [barbe, feuille] prickly - **2.** [sauce] spicy, hot - **3.** [froid] biting - **4.** *fig* [détail] spicy, juicy.

➤ **piquant** *nm* - **1.** [d'animal] spine ; [de végétal] thorn, prickle - **2.** *fig* [d'histoire] spice.

pique [pik] <> *nf* - **1.** [arme] pike - **2.** *fig* [mot blessant] barbed comment <> *nm* [aux cartes] spade.

piqué, e [pike] *adj* - **1.** [vin] sour, vinegary - **2.** [meuble] worm-eaten - **3.** [tissu] spotted, flecked - **4.** *fam* [personne] loony.

➤ **piqué** *nm* - **1.** [tissu] piqué - **2.** AÉRON dive.

pique-assiette [pikasjɛt] (*pl inv* ou **pique-assiettes**) *nmf péj* sponger.

pique-nique [piknik] (*pl* pique-niques) *nm* picnic.

pique-niquer [3] [piknike] *vi* to picnic.

piquer [3] [pike] <> *vt* - **1.** [suj : guêpe, méduse] to sting ; [suj : serpent, moustique] to bite - **2.** [avec pointe] to prick ; **~ qqch de** CULIN to stick sthg with - **3.** MÉD to give an injection to ; **se faire ~ contre** fam to have o.s. inoculated ou vaccinated against - **4.** [animal] to put down - **5.** [fleur] : **~ qqch dans** to stick sthg into - **6.** [suj : tissu, barbe] to prickle - **7.** [suj : fumée, froid] to sting - **8.** COUTURE to sting - **9.** fam [voler] to pinch - **10.** fig [curiosité] to excite, to arouse - **11.** fam [voleur, escroc] to nick Br, to catch ; **se faire ~** to get nicked Br, to get caught ⬦ vi - **1.** [ronce] to prick ; [ortie] to sting - **2.** [guêpe, méduse] to sting ; [serpent, moustique] to bite - **3.** [épice] to burn - **4.** COUTURE to machine - **5.** fam [voler] : **~ (dans)** to pinch (from) - **6.** [avion] to dive.

➤ **se piquer** vp - **1.** [avec une épingle, des ronces] to prick o.s. - **2.** [avec des orties] to sting o.s. - **3.** fam [se droguer] to shoot up - **4.** littéraire [se vexer] to become irritated - **5.** littéraire & péj [avoir la prétention] : **se ~ de qqch/de faire qqch** to pride o.s. on one's knowledge of sthg/on one's ability to do sthg.

piquet [pikɛ] nm - **1.** [pieu] peg, stake - **2.** JEU piquet.

➤ **piquet de grève** nm picket.

piqueter [27] [pikte] vt to dot, to spot.

piquette [pikɛt] nf - **1.** [vin] cheap wine ou plonk Br - **2.** fam [défaite] : **prendre une** ou **la ~** fig to get a hammering ou a thrashing.

piqûre [pikyr] nf - **1.** [de guêpe, de méduse] sting ; [de serpent, de moustique] bite - **2.** [d'ortie] sting - **3.** [injection] jab Br, shot - **4.** COUTURE stitching (U).

piranha [piraɲa], **piraya** [piraja] nm piranha.

piratage [pirataʒ] nm piracy ; INFORM hacking.

pirate [pirat] ⬦ nm - **1.** [corsaire] pirate ; **~ de l'air** hijacker, skyjacker - **2.** fig [escroc] swindler ⬦ adj pirate (avant n).

pirater [3] [pirate] vt to pirate.

piraterie [piratri] nf - **1.** [flibuste] piracy (U) - **2.** [acte] act of piracy - **3.** fig [escroquerie] swindling.

piraya = piranha.

pire [pir] ⬦ adj - **1.** [comparatif relatif] worse - **2.** [superlatif] : **le/la ~** the worst ⬦ nm : **le ~ (de)** the worst (of) ; **s'attendre au ~** to expect the worst.

Pirée [pire] nm : **Le ~** Piraeus.

pirogue [pirɔg] nf dugout canoe.

pirouette [pirwɛt] nf - **1.** [saut] pirouette - **2.** fig [faux-fuyant] prevarication, evasive answer ; **répondre par une ~** to answer evasively ; **s'en tirer par une ~** to evade the issue.

pis [pi] ⬦ adj littéraire [pire] worse ⬦ adv worse ; **de mal en ~** from bad to worse ; **de ~ en ~** worse and worse ⬦ nm udder.

pis-aller [pizale] nm inv last resort.

pisciculture [pisikyltyr] nf fish farming.

piscine [pisin] nf swimming pool ; **~ couverte/découverte** indoor/open-air swimming pool.

Pise [piz] n Pisa ; **la tour de ~** the Leaning Tower of Pisa.

pisse [pis] nf tfam pee, piss.

pisse-froid [pisfrwa] nm inv fam péj wet blanket.

pissenlit [pisɑ̃li] nm dandelion ; **manger les ~s par la racine** fig to be pushing up daisies.

pisser [3] [pise] fam ⬦ vt - **1.** [suj : personne] : **~ du sang** to pass blood - **2.** [suj : plaie] : **son genou pissait le sang** blood was gushing from his knee ⬦ vi to pee, to piss.

pissotière [pisɔtjɛr] nf fam public urinal.

pistache [pistaʃ] ⬦ nf [fruit] pistachio (nut) ⬦ adj inv [couleur] pistachio (green).

piste [pist] nf - **1.** [trace] trail ; **suivre/perdre une ~** to follow/to lose a trail ; **brouiller les ~s** fig to cover one's tracks - **2.** [zone aménagée] : **~ d'atterrissage** runway ; **~ cyclable** cycle track ; **~ de danse** dance floor ; **~ de ski** ski run - **3.** [chemin] path, track - **4.** [d'enregistrement] track.

pister [3] [piste] vt [gibier] to track ; [suspect] to tail.

pisteur [pistœr] nm ski patrol member.

pistil [pistil] nm pistil.

pistolet [pistɔlɛ] nm - **1.** [arme] pistol, gun - **2.** [à peinture] spray gun.

pistolet-mitrailleur [pistɔlɛmitrajœr] (pl **pistolets-mitrailleurs**) nm submachine gun.

piston [pistɔ̃] nm - **1.** [de moteur] piston - **2.** MUS [d'instrument] valve - **3.** fig [appui] string-pulling ; **avoir du ~** to have friends in the right places.

pistonner [3] [pistɔne] vt to pull strings for ; **se faire ~** to have strings pulled for one.

pistou [pistu] nm dish of vegetables served with sauce made from basil.

pita [pita] nf pitta (bread).

pitance [pitɑ̃s] nf péj & vieilli sustenance.

pitbull, pit-bull [pitbul] (pl **pit-bulls**) nm pitbull (terrier).

piteux, euse [pitø, øz] adj piteous.

pitié [pitje] nf pity ; **avoir ~ de qqn** to have pity on sb, to pity sb ; **sans ~** pitiless, ruthless ; **par ~** for pity's sake.

piton [pitɔ̃] nm - **1.** [clou] piton - **2.** [pic] peak.

pitoyable [pitwajabl] *adj* pitiful.

pitre [pitr] *nm* clown ; **faire le ~** to fool about.

pitrerie [pitrəri] *nf* tomfoolery.

pittoresque [pitɔrɛsk] <> *nm* : **le ~** [de description] the vividness ; [d'histoire] the amusing part <> *adj* - **1.** [région] picturesque - **2.** [détail] colourful *Br*, colorful *Am*, vivid.

pivert, pic-vert (*pl* **pic-verts**) [pivɛr] *nm* green woodpecker.

pivoine [pivwan] *nf* peony.

pivot [pivo] *nm* - **1.** [de machine, au basket] pivot - **2.** [de dent] post - **3.** [centre] *fig* mainspring.

pivotant, e [pivɔtɑ̃, ɑ̃t] *adj* [fauteuil] swivel (avant n).

pivoter [3] [pivɔte] *vi* to pivot ; [porte] to revolve ; **faire ~ qqch** to swivel sthg around, to pivot sthg.

pizza [pidza] *nf* pizza.

pizzeria [pidzerja] *nf* pizzeria.

PJ <> *nf* (*abr de* **police judiciaire**) ≃ CID *Br*, ≃ FBI *Am* <> (*abr de* **pièces jointes**) Encl.

Pl., pl. *abr de* **place**.

PL (*abr de* **poids lourd**) HGV.

placage [plakaʒ] *nm* [de bois] veneer.

placard [plakar] *nm* - **1.** [armoire] cupboard ; **mettre qqn au ~** *fam fig* to elbow sb out ; **mettre qqch au ~** *fam fig* to shelve sthg - **2.** [affiche] poster, notice - **3.** TYPO galley (proof).

placarder [3] [plakarde] *vt* [affiche] to put up, to stick up ; [mur] to placard, to stick a notice on.

place [plas] *nf* - **1.** [espace] space, room ; **prendre de la ~** to take up (a lot of) space ; **faire ~ à** [amour, haine] to give way to - **2.** [emplacement, position] position ; **changer qqch de ~** to put sthg in a different place, to move sthg ; **prendre la ~ de qqn** to take sb's place ; **ne pas tenir** ou **rester en ~** to be unable to stay still ; **à la ~ de qqn** instead of sb, in sb's place ; **à ta ~** if I were you, in your place - **3.** [siège] seat ; **céder sa ~ à qqn** to give up one's seat to sb ; **prendre ~** to take a seat ; **~ assise** seat - **4.** [rang] place - **5.** [de ville] square - **6.** [emploi] position, job ; **perdre sa ~** to lose one's job - **7.** COMM market - **8.** MIL [de garnison] garrison (town) ; **~ forte** fortified town - **9.** *loc* : **se mettre à la ~ de qqn** to put o.s. in sb's place ou shoes ; **remettre qqn à sa ~** to put sb in his/her place.

placebo [plasebo] *nm* placebo.

placement [plasmɑ̃] *nm* - **1.** [d'argent] investment - **2.** [d'employé] placing.

placenta [plasɛ̃ta] *nm* ANAT placenta.

placer [16] [plase] *vt* - **1.** [gén] to put, to place ; [invités, spectateurs] to seat ; **être bien/mal placé**

to have a good/bad seat ; **être bien/mal placé pour faire qqch** *fig* to be in a position/in no position to do sthg ; **être haut placé** *fig* to be highly placed - **2.** [mot, anecdote] to put in, to get in - **3.** [argent] to invest.

➤ **se placer** *vp* - **1.** [prendre place - debout] to stand ; [- assis] to sit (down) - **2.** *fig* [dans une situation] to put o.s. - **3.** [se classer] to come, to be.

placide [plasid] *adj* placid.

placidité [plasidite] *nf* placidity.

plafond [plafɔ̃] *nm litt* & *fig* ceiling ; **faux ~** false ceiling.

plafonner [3] [plafɔne] <> *vt* to put a ceiling in <> *vi* [prix, élève] to peak ; [avion] to reach its ceiling.

plafonnier [plafɔnje] *nm* ceiling light.

plage [plaʒ] *nf* - **1.** [de sable] beach - **2.** [ville balnéaire] resort - **3.** [d'ombre, de prix] band ; *fig* [de temps] slot - **4.** [de disque] track - **5.** [dans une voiture] : **~ arrière** back shelf.

plagiaire [plaʒjɛr] *nmf* plagiarist.

plagiat [plaʒja] *nm* plagiarism.

plagier [9] [plaʒje] *vt* to plagiarize.

plagiste [plaʒist] *nm* beach attendant.

plaid [plɛd] *nm* car rug.

plaider [4] [plede] JUR <> *vt* to plead <> *vi* to plead ; **~ contre qqn** to plead against sb ; **~ pour qqn** JUR to plead for sb ; [justifier] to plead sb's cause.

plaideur, euse [plɛdœr, øz] *nm, f* litigant.

plaidoirie [plɛdwari] *nf*, **plaidoyer** [plɛdwaje] *nm* JUR speech for the defence *Br* ou defense *Am* ; *fig* plea.

plaie [plɛ] *nf* - **1.** *litt* & *fig* wound - **2.** *fam* [personne] pest.

plaignais, plaignions *etc* ⊳ **plaindre**.

plaignant, e [plɛɲɑ̃, ɑ̃t] JUR <> *adj* litigant (avant n) <> *nm, f* plaintiff.

plaindre [80] [plɛ̃dr] *vt* to pity ; **ne pas être à ~** to be not to be pitied.

➤ **se plaindre** *vp* to complain ; **se ~ de** [souffrir de] to complain of ; [être mécontent de] to complain about.

plaine [plɛn] *nf* plain.

plain-pied [plɛ̃pje] ➤ **de plain-pied** *loc adv* - **1.** [pièce] on one floor ; **de ~ avec** *litt* & *fig* on a level with - **2.** *fig* [directement] straight.

plaint, e [plɛ̃, plɛ̃t] *pp* ⊳ **plaindre**.

plainte [plɛ̃t] *nf* - **1.** [gémissement] moan, groan ; *fig* & *litt* [du vent] moan - **2.** [doléance & JUR] complaint ; **porter ~** to lodge a complaint ; **retirer sa ~** JUR to withdraw one's action ou suit ; **~ contre X** ≃ complaint against person or persons unknown.

plaintif, ive [plɛ̃tif, iv] *adj* plaintive.

plaire [110] [plɛr] *vi* to be liked ; **il me plaît** I like him ; **ça te plairait d'aller au cinéma?** would you like to go to the cinema? ; **s'il vous/te plaît** please.
➤ **se plaire** *vp* - **1.** [s'aimer] to get on well together - **2.** [prendre plaisir] : **se ~ à faire qqch** to take pleasure in doing sthg ; **se ~ avec qqn** to enjoy being with sb ; **se ~ à Paris** to enjoy being in Paris.

plaisance [plɛzɑ̃s] ➤ **de plaisance** *loc adj* pleasure *(avant n)* ; **navigation de ~** sailing ; **port de ~** marina.

plaisancier, ère [plɛzɑ̃sje, ɛr] *nm, f* (amateur) sailor.

plaisant, e [plɛzɑ̃, ɑ̃t] *adj* pleasant.
➤ **mauvais plaisant** *nm péj* hoaxer.

plaisanter [3] [plɛzɑ̃te] ⇔ *vi* to joke ; **~ avec qqch** to joke about sthg ; **ne pas ~ avec** *ou* **sur qqch** to take sthg seriously ; **tu plaisantes?** you must be joking! ⇔ *vt sout* [personne] to tease.

plaisanterie [plɛzɑ̃tri] *nf* joke ; **c'est une ~?** *iron* you must be joking! ; **c'était une ~** *fig* it was child's play.

plaisantin [plɛzɑ̃tɛ̃] *nm* joker.

plaise ➣ **plaire**.

plaisir [plɛzir] *nm* pleasure ; **les ~s de la vie** life's pleasures ; **avoir du/prendre ~ à faire qqch** to have/to take pleasure in doing sthg ; **faire ~ à qqn** to please sb ; **avec ~** with pleasure ; **j'ai le ~ de vous annoncer que ...** I have the (great) pleasure of announcing that ... ; **pour le** *ou* **son ~** for pleasure ; **prendre un malin ~ à faire qqch** to take a malicious pleasure in doing sthg ; **se faire un ~ de faire qqch** to be only too pleased to do sthg.

plan¹, e [plɑ̃, plan] *adj* level, flat.

plan² [plɑ̃] *nm* - **1.** [dessin - de ville] map ; [- de maison] plan - **2.** [projet] plan ; **faire des ~s** to make plans ; **avoir son ~** to have something in mind - **3.** [domaine] : **sur tous les ~s** in all respects ; **sur le ~ affectif** emotionally ; **sur le ~ familial** as far as the family is concerned - **4.** [surface] : **~ d'eau** lake ; **~ de travail** work surface, worktop - **5.** GÉOM plane - **6.** CINÉMA take ; **gros ~** close-up.
➤ **plan social** *nm* redundancy scheme *ou* plan.
➤ **à l'arrière-plan** *loc adv* in the background.
➤ **au premier plan** *loc adv* - **1.** [dans l'espace] in the foreground - **2.** [dans un ordre] : **c'est au premier ~ de nos préoccupations** it's our

chief concern, it's uppermost in our minds.
➤ **de tout premier plan** *loc adj* exceptional.
➤ **en plan** *loc adv* : **laisser qqn en ~** to leave sb stranded, to abandon sb ; **il a tout laissé en ~** he dropped everything.
➤ **sur le même plan** *loc adj* on the same level.

planche [plɑ̃ʃ] *nf* - **1.** [en bois] plank ; **~ à dessin** drawing board ; **~ à neige** snowboard ; **~ à repasser** ironing board ; **~ de salut** fig mainstay ; **~ à voile** [planche] sailboard ; [sport] windsurfing ; **faire la ~** fig to float - **2.** [d'illustration] plate.
➤ **planches** *nfpl* - **1.** fig & THÉÂTRE boards ; **monter sur les ~s** to go on the stage - **2.** fam [skis] skis.

plancher¹ [plɑ̃ʃe] *nm* - **1.** [de maison, de voiture] floor ; **débarrasser le ~** fam fig to clear off - **2.** fig [limite] floor, lower limit.

plancher² [3] [plɑ̃ʃe] *vi* - **1.** arg scol to be given a test - **2.** fam fig [travailler] : **~ (sur)** to work hard (at).

planchiste [plɑ̃ʃist] *nmf* windsurfer.

plancton [plɑ̃ktɔ̃] *nm* plankton.

planer [3] [plane] *vi* - **1.** [avion, oiseau] to glide - **2.** [nuage, fumée, brouillard] to float - **3.** fig [danger] : **~ sur qqn** to hang over sb - **4.** fam fig [personne] to be out of touch with reality, to have one's head in the clouds ; **~ au-dessus de qqch** to be above sthg.

planétaire [planetɛr] *adj* - **1.** ASTRON planetary - **2.** [mondial] world *(avant n)*.

planétarium [planetarjɔm] *nm* planetarium.

planète [planɛt] *nf* planet.

planeur [planœr] *nm* glider.

planificateur, trice [planifikatœr, tris] ⇔ *adj* planning *(avant n)* ⇔ *nm, f* planner.

planification [planifikasjɔ̃] *nf* ÉCON planning.

planifier [9] [planifje] *vt* ÉCON to plan.

planisphère [planisfɛr] *nm* map of the world, planisphere.

planning [planiŋ] *nm* - **1.** [de fabrication] workflow schedule - **2.** [agenda personnel] schedule ; **~ familial** [contrôle] family planning ; [organisme] family planning clinic.

planque [plɑ̃k] *nf* fam - **1.** [cachette] hideout - **2.** fig [situation, travail] cushy number.

planquer [3] [plɑ̃ke] *vt* fam to hide.
➤ **se planquer** *vp* fam to hide.

plant [plɑ̃] *nm* - **1.** [plante] seedling - **2.** [culture] bed, patch.

plantain [plɑ̃tɛ̃] *nm* plantain.

plantaire [plɑ̃tɛr] *adj* plantar.

plantation [plɑ̃tasjɔ̃] *nf* - **1.** [exploitation - d'arbres, de coton, de café] plantation ; [- de légumes] patch - **2.** [action] planting.

plante [plɑ̃t] *nf* - **1.** BOT plant ; ~s médicinales medicinal herbs ; ~ verte *ou* d'appartement *ou* d'intérieur house *ou* pot plant - **2.** ANAT sole.

planté, e [plɑ̃te] *adj fam* - **1.** [personne] : rester ~ to be rooted to the spot - **2.** [machine] broken-down.

planter [3] [plɑ̃te] <> *vt* - **1.** [arbre, terrain] to plant ; ~ qqch de qqch to plant sthg with sthg - **2.** [clou] to hammer in, to drive in ; [pieu] to drive in ; [couteau, griffes] to stick in - **3.** [tente] to pitch - **4.** *fam fig* [laisser tomber] to dump ; **tout ~ là** to drop everything - **5.** *fig* [chapeau] to stick ; [baiser] to plant ; ~ **son regard dans celui de qqn** to look sb right in the eyes <> *vi* INFORM *fam* to crash.
◆ **se planter** *vp* - **1.** [se camper] to plant o.s. - **2.** *fam* [tomber] to go flying ; [en voiture] to have a prang - **3.** *fam* [se tromper] to be wrong.

planteur [plɑ̃tœr, øz] *nm* planter.

planton [plɑ̃tɔ̃] *nm* orderly.

plantureux, euse [plɑ̃tyrø, øz] *adj* - **1.** [repas] lavish - **2.** [femme] buxom - **3.** [terre] fertile.

plaque [plak] *nf* - **1.** [de métal, de verre, de verglas] sheet ; [de marbre] slab ; ~ **chauffante** *ou* **de cuisson** hotplate ; ~ **de chocolat** bar of chocolate - **2.** [gravée] plaque ; ~ **d'immatriculation** *ou* **minéralogique** number plate *Br*, license plate *Am* - **3.** [insigne] badge - **4.** [sur la peau] patch - **5.** [dentaire] plaque - **6.** *loc* : **être à côté de la ~** to be wide of the mark.
◆ **plaque tournante** *nf* RAIL turntable ; *fig* hub.

plaqué, e [plake] *adj* - **1.** [métal] plated ; ~ **or/argent** gold-/silver-plated - **2.** [bois] veneered.
◆ **plaqué** *nm* - **1.** [métal] : **du ~ or/argent** gold/silver plate - **2.** [bois] veneered wood.

plaquer [3] [plake] *vt* - **1.** [métal] to plate - **2.** [bois] to veneer - **3.** [aplatir] to flatten ; ~ **qqn contre qqch** to pin sb against sthg ; ~ **qqch contre qqch** to stick sthg onto sthg - **4.** RUGBY to tackle - **5.** MUS [accord] to play - **6.** *fam* [travail, personne] to chuck.
◆ **se plaquer** *vp* : **se ~ contre qqch** to flatten o.s. against sthg ; **se ~ au sol** to lie flat on the ground ; **se ~ les cheveux** to flatten (down) one's hair.

plaquette [plakɛt] *nf* - **1.** [de métal] plaque ; [de marbre] tablet - **2.** [de chocolat] bar ; [de beurre] pat - **3.** [de comprimés] packet, strip - **4.** (gén

pl) BIOL platelet - **5.** [petit livre] slim volume - **6.** AUTOM : ~ **de frein** brake pad.

plasma [plasma] *nm* plasma.

plastic [plastik] *nm* plastic explosive.

plasticage [plastikaʒ] *nm* [de coffre] blowing ; **un ~ de la banque** a bomb attack on the bank.

plastifier [9] [plastifje] *vt* to coat with plastic, to plastic-coat.

plastique [plastik] <> *adj* & *nm* plastic <> *nf* - **1.** [en sculpture] art of modelling - **2.** [beauté] form - **3.** [arts] plastic arts *(pl)*.

plastiquer [3] [plastike] *vt* to blow up *(with plastic explosives)*.

plastron [plastrɔ̃] *nm* [de chemise] shirt front.

plastronner [3] [plastrone] *vi* [parader] to swagger.

plat, e [pla, plat] *adj* - **1.** [gén] flat - **2.** [eau] still.
◆ **plat** *nm* - **1.** [partie plate] flat - **2.** [récipient] dish ; **mettre les petits ~s dans les grands** *fig* to go to town - **3.** [mets] course ; ~ **cuisiné** ready-cooked meal *ou* dish ; ~ **du jour** today's special ; ~ **préparé** ready meal ; ~ **de résistance** main course ; **en faire tout un ~** *fig* to make a song and dance about it - **4.** [plongeon] belly-flop.
◆ **à plat** *loc adv* - **1.** [horizontalement, dégonflé] flat - **2.** *fam* [épuisé] exhausted.

platane [platan] *nm* plane tree.

plateau, x [plato] *nm* - **1.** [de cuisine] tray ; ~ **de/à fromages** cheese board - **2.** [de balance] pan - **3.** GÉOGR & *fig* plateau - **4.** THÉÂTRE stage ; CIN & TÉLÉ set - **5.** [de vélo] chain wheel.

plateau-repas [platorəpa] *(pl* **plateaux-repas)** *nm* tray (of food).

plate-bande [platbɑ̃d] *(pl* **plates-bandes)** *nf* flower bed.

platée [plate] *nf* dishful, plateful.

plate-forme [platfɔrm] *(pl* **plates-formes)** *nf* - **1.** [gén] platform ; ~ **de forage** drilling platform - **2.** GÉOGR shelf.

platement [platmɑ̃] *adv* - **1.** [sans imagination] dully - **2.** [servilement] humbly.

platine [platin] <> *adj inv* platinum <> *nm* [métal] platinum <> *nf* [de tourne-disque] deck ; ~ **laser** compact disc player.

platiné, e [platine] *adj* platinum *(avant n)*.

platitude [platityd] *nf* - **1.** [médiocrité] banality - **2.** [propos sans intérêt] platitude ; **débiter des ~s** to spout platitudes.

platonique [platonik] *adj* - **1.** [amour, amitié] platonic - **2.** *littéraire* [protestation] ineffective.

plâtras [platrɑ] *nm* [gravats] rubble.

plâtre [platr] *nm* - **1.** CONSTR & MÉD plaster ; **es-**

suyer les ~s *fig* to be the first to suffer
- **2.** [sculpture] plaster cast - **3.** *péj* [fromage] :
c'est du vrai ~ it's like sawdust.

plâtrer [3] [platre] *vt* - **1.** [mur] to plaster
- **2.** *MÉD* to put in plaster.

plâtrier [platrije] ◇ *nm* plasterer ◇ *adj m* :
ouvrier ~ plasterer.

plausible [plozibl] *adj* plausible.

play-back [plebak] *nm inv* miming ; **chanter
en ~** to mime.

play-boy [plebɔj] (*pl* **play-boys**) *nm* playboy.

plèbe [plɛb] *nf* - **1.** *péj* [populace] : **la ~** the plebs
(*pl*) - **2.** *HIST* : **la ~** the plebeians (*pl*).

plébéien, enne [plebejɛ̃, ɛn] *adj* plebeian.

plébiscite [plebisit] *nm* plebiscite.

plébisciter [3] [plebisite] *vt* - **1.** *POLIT* to elect
by plebiscite - **2.** [approuver] to endorse overwhelmingly.

pléiade [plejad] *nf* pleiad.

plein, e [plɛ̃, plɛn] *adj* - **1.** [rempli, complet] full ;
c'est la ~e forme I am/they are *etc* in top
form ; **en ~e nuit** in the middle of the night ;
en ~ air in the open air ; **~ à craquer** *fig* full to
bursting - **2.** [non creux] solid - **3.** [femelle]
pregnant - **4.** *fam* [saoul] plastered.
◆ **plein** ◇ *adv fam* : **il a de l'encre ~ les doigts**
he has ink all over his fingers ; **~ de** lots of ;
en ~ dans/sur qqch right in/on sthg ◇ *nm*
- **1.** [de réservoir] full tank ; **le ~, s'il vous plaît** fill
her up please ; **faire le ~** to fill up - **2.** *loc* :
battre son ~ to be at its height.

pleinement [plɛnmã] *adv* fully, totally.

plein-temps [plɛ̃tã] (*pl* **pleins-temps**) *nm*
full-time job.

plénier, ère [plenje, ɛr] *adj* plenary.

plénipotentiaire [plenipɔtãsjer] *nm* & *adj*
plenipotentiary.

plénitude [plenityd] *nf* fullness.

pléonasme [pleɔnasm] *nm* pleonasm.

pléthorique [pletɔrik] *adj sout* [classe] over-
full.

pleurer [5] [plœre] ◇ *vi* - **1.** [larmoyer] to cry ;
~ de joie to weep for joy, to cry with joy
- **2.** *péj* [se plaindre] to whinge - **3.** [réclamer] :
~ après to cry for - **4.** [se lamenter] : **~ sur** to
lament ◇ *vt* to mourn.

pleurésie [plœrezi] *nf* pleurisy.

pleureur, euse [plœrœr, øz] ◇ *adj* whining
◇ *nm, f* whinger.
◆ **pleureuse** *nf* professional mourner.

pleurnicher [3] [plœrniʃe] *vi* to whine, to
whinge.

pleurnicheur, euse [plœrniʃœr, øz] ◇ *adj*
whining, whingeing ◇ *nm, f* whinger.

pleurs [plœr] *nmpl* : **être en ~** to be in tears.

pleut ⊳ **pleuvoir**.

pleutre [pløtr] *littéraire* ◇ *nm* coward ◇ *adj*
cowardly.

pleuvoir [68] [pløvwar] *v impers litt* & *fig* to
rain ; **il pleut** it is raining.

Plexiglas® [plɛksiglas] *nm* Plexiglas®.

plexus [plɛksys] *nm* plexus ; **~ solaire** solar
plexus.

pli [pli] *nm* - **1.** [de tissu] pleat ; [de pantalon]
crease ; **faux ~** crease - **2.** [forme] shape ;
prendre le ~ (de faire qqch) *fig* to get into the
habit (of doing sthg) - **3.** [du front] line ; [du cou]
fold - **4.** [lettre] letter ; [enveloppe] envelope ;
sous ~ séparé under separate cover - **5.** *CAR-
TES* trick - **6.** *GÉOL* fold.

pliable [plijabl] *adj* pliable.

pliant, e [plijã, ãt] *adj* folding (*avant n*).
◆ **pliant** *nm* folding chair.

plier [10] [plije] ◇ *vt* - **1.** [papier, tissu] to fold
- **2.** [vêtement, vélo] to fold (up) - **3.** [branche, bras]
to bend - **4.** *fig* [personne] : **~ qqn à sa volonté** to
bend sb to one's will ; **~ qqn à la discipline** to
impose discipline on sb ◇ *vi* - **1.** [se courber]
to bend - **2.** *fig* [céder] to bow.
◆ **se plier** *vp* - **1.** [être pliable] to fold (up) - **2.** *fig*
[se soumettre] : **se ~ à qqch** to bow to sthg.

plinthe [plɛ̃t] *nf* plinth.

plissé, e [plise] *adj* - **1.** [jupe] pleated - **2.** [peau]
wrinkled.
◆ **plissé** *nm* pleats (*pl*), pleating.

plissement [plismã] *nm* - **1.** [de front] creas-
ing ; [d'yeux] screwing up - **2.** *GÉOL* fold.

plisser [3] [plise] ◇ *vt* - **1.** *COUTURE* to pleat
- **2.** [front] to crease ; [lèvres] to pucker ; [yeux]
to screw up ◇ *vi* [étoffe] to crease.
◆ **se plisser** *vp* - **1.** [étoffe] to crease - **2.** [front]
to crease.

pliure [plijyr] *nf* - **1.** [de tissu, de papier] fold
- **2.** [d'articulation] crook.

plomb [plɔ̃] *nm* - **1.** [métal, de vitrail] lead - **2.** [de
chasse] shot ; **avoir du ~ dans l'aile** *fig* to be in a
bad way - **3.** *ÉLECTR* fuse ; **les ~s ont sauté** a
fuse has blown *ou* gone - **4.** [de pêche] sinker.

plombage [plɔ̃baʒ] *nm* - **1.** [de dent] filling
- **2.** [de ligne] weighting (with lead).

plombé, e [plɔ̃be] *adj* - **1.** [dent] filled - **2.** [li-
gne] weighted (with lead) - **3.** [teinte] leaden.

plomber [3] [plɔ̃be] *vt* - **1.** [ligne] to weight
(with lead) - **2.** [dent] to fill.
◆ **se plomber** *vp* [ciel] to become leaden.

plomberie [plɔ̃bri] *nf* plumbing.

plombier [plɔ̃bje] *nm* plumber.

plonge [plɔ̃ʒ] *nf fam* dishwashing ; **faire la ~** to wash dishes.

plongeant, e [plɔ̃ʒɑ̃, ɑ̃t] *adj* - **1.** [vue] from above - **2.** [décolleté] plunging.

plongée [plɔ̃ʒe] *nf* - **1.** [immersion] diving ; **~ sous-marine** scuba diving - **2.** CIN & PHOT high-angle shot.

plongeoir [plɔ̃ʒwar] *nm* diving board.

plongeon [plɔ̃ʒɔ̃] *nm* [dans l'eau, au football] dive ; **faire un ~** to plunge ; **faire le ~** *fig* to hit rock bottom.

plonger [17] [plɔ̃ʒe] <> *vt* - **1.** [immerger, enfoncer] to plunge ; **~ la tête sous l'eau** to put one's head under the water - **2.** *fig* [précipiter] : **~ qqn dans qqch** to throw sb into sthg ; **~ une pièce dans l'obscurité** to plunge a room into darkness <> *vi* - **1.** [dans l'eau, gardien de but] to dive - **2.** [avion, oiseau] : **~ sur** to dive (down) onto - **3.** *fig* [se lancer] to dive *ou* jump in.

➤ **se plonger** *vp* - **1.** [s'immerger] to submerge - **2.** *fig* [s'absorber] : **se ~ dans qqch** to immerse o.s. in sthg.

plongeur, euse [plɔ̃ʒœr, øz] *nm, f* - **1.** [dans l'eau] diver - **2.** [dans restaurant] dishwasher.

plot [plo] *nm* ÉLECTR contact.

plouc [pluk] *nmf* & *adj fam péj* country bumpkin.

plouf [pluf] *interj* splash!

ployer [13] [plwaje] *vt* & *vi litt* & *fig* to bend.

plu [ply] <> *pp inv* ▷ **plaire** <> *pp inv* ▷ **pleuvoir**.

pluie [plɥi] *nf* - **1.** [averse] rain *(U)* ; **sous la ~** in the rain ; **une ~ battante** driving rain ; **une ~ fine** drizzle ; **des ~s diluviennes** torrential rain ; **il fait la ~ et le beau temps** *fig* what he says goes ; **ne pas être né de la dernière ~** *fig* not to be born yesterday - **2.** *fig* [grande quantité] : **une ~ de** a shower of.

plumage [plymaʒ] *nm* plumage.

plumard [plymar] *nm fam* bed, sack *Am*.

plume [plym] <> *nf* - **1.** [d'oiseau] feather ; **y laisser/perdre des ~s** *fig* to come off badly - **2.** [pour écrire - d'oiseau] quill pen ; [- de stylo] nib ; **un homme de ~** *fig* a man of letters <> *nm fam* [plumard] bed, sack *Am*.

plumeau, x [plymo] *nm* feather duster.

plumer [3] [plyme] *vt* - **1.** [volaille] to pluck - **2.** *fam fig* & *péj* [personne] to fleece.

plumier [plymje] *nm* pencil box.

plupart [plypar] *nf* : **la ~ de** most of, the majority of ; **la ~ du temps** most of the time, mostly ; **pour la ~** mostly, for the most part.

pluralisme [plyralism] *nm* pluralism.

pluralité [plyralite] *nf* plurality.

pluridimensionnel, elle [plyridimɑ̃sjɔnɛl] *adj* multidimensional.

pluridisciplinaire [plyridisipliner] *adj* multidisciplinary.

pluriel, elle [plyrjɛl] *adj* - **1.** GRAM plural - **2.** [société] pluralist.

➤ **pluriel** *nm* plural ; **au ~** in the plural.

plus [ply(s)] <> *adv* - **1.** [quantité] more ; **je peux vous en dire ~** I can't tell you anything more ; **il a ~ de travail cette année** he has more work this year ; **il en veut ~** he wants more (of it/them) ; **beaucoup ~ de** (+ *nom sg*) a lot more, much more ; (+ *nom pl*) a lot more, many more ; **un peu ~ de** (+ *nom sg*) a little more ; (+ *nom pl*) a few more ; **il y a (un peu) ~ de 15 ans** (a little) more than 15 years ago ; **~ j'y pense, ~ je me dis que ...** the more I think about it, the more I'm sure ... - **2.** [comparaison] more ; **c'est ~ court par là** it's shorter that way ; **viens ~ souvent** come more often ; **c'est un peu ~ loin** it's a (little) bit further ; **~ jeune (que)** younger (than) ; **c'est ~ simple qu'on ne le croit** it's simpler than you think - **3.** [superlatif] : **le ~** the most ; **c'est lui qui travaille le ~** he's the hardest worker, he's the one who works (the) hardest ; **un des ses tableaux les ~ connus** one of his best-known paintings ; **le ~ souvent** the most often ; **le ~ loin** the furthest ; **le ~ souvent possible** as often as possible ; **le ~ vite possible** as quickly as possible - **4.** [négation] no more ; **~ un mot!** not another word! ; **ne ... ~** no longer, no more ; **il n'a ~ d'amis** he no longer has any friends, he has no friends any more ; **il ne vient ~ me voir** he doesn't come to see me any more, he no longer comes to see me ; **je n'y vais ~ du tout** I don't go there any more <> *nm* - **1.** [signe] plus (sign) - **2.** *fig* [atout] plus <> *prép* plus ; **trois ~ trois font six** three plus three is six, three and three are six.

➤ **au plus** *loc adv* at the most ; **tout au ~** at the very most.

➤ **de plus** *loc adv* - **1.** [en supplément, en trop] more ; **elle a cinq ans de ~ que moi** she's five years older than me - **2.** [en outre] furthermore, what's more.

➤ **de plus en plus** *loc adv* more and more.

➤ **de plus en plus de** *loc prép* more and more.

➤ **en plus** *loc adv* - **1.** [en supplément] extra - **2.** [d'ailleurs] moreover, what's more.

➤ **en plus de** *loc prép* in addition to.

➤ **ni plus ni moins** *loc adv* no more no less.

➤ **on ne peut plus** *loc adv* : **il est on ne peut ~ bête** he's as stupid as can be.

➤ **plus ou moins** *loc adv* more or less.

➤ **sans plus** *loc adv* : **elle est gentille, sans ~** she's nice, but no more than that.

plusieurs [plyzjœr] *adj indéf pl* & *pron indéf mfpl* several.

plus-que-parfait [plyskəparfɛ] *nm* GRAM pluperfect.

plus-value [plyvaly] (*pl* **plus-values**) *nf* - **1.** [d'investissement] appreciation - **2.** [excédent] surplus - **3.** [bénéfice] profit.

plutonium [plytɔnjɔm] *nm* plutonium.

plutôt [plyto] *adv* rather ; **~ que de faire qqch** instead of doing sthg, rather than doing *ou* do sthg.

pluvial, e, aux [plyvjal, o] *adj* : **eau ~e** rainwater.

pluvieux, euse [plyvjø, øz] *adj* rainy.

pluviométrie [plyvjɔmetri] *nf* rainfall measurement.

pluviosité [plyvjozite] *nf* rainfall.

p.m. (*abr de* **pour mémoire**) p.m.

PM *nf* - **1.** (*abr de* **préparation militaire**) *training before military service* - **2.** (*abr de* **police militaire**) MP.

PMA ⬦ *nf* (*abr de* **procréation médicalement assistée**) assisted reproduction ⬦ *nmpl* (*abr de* **pays les moins avancés**) LDCs.

PME (*abr de* **petite et moyenne entreprise**) *nf* SME.

PMI *nf* - **1.** (*abr de* **petite et moyenne industrie**) small industrial firm - **2.** (*abr de* **protection maternelle et infantile**) *social service concerned with child welfare.*

PMU (*abr de* **Pari mutuel urbain**) *nm system for betting on horses.*

PNB (*abr de* **produit national brut**) *nm* GNP.

pneu, x [pnø] *nm* - **1.** [de véhicule] tyre *Br*, tire *Am* ; **~ avant** front tyre *Br ou* tire *Am* ; **~ arrière** rear tyre *Br ou* tire *Am* ; **~ clouté** studded tyre *Br ou* tire *Am* ; **~-neige** winter tyre *Br ou* tire *Am* - **2.** *vieilli* [message] *letter sent by network of pneumatic tubes.*

pneumatique [pnømatik] ⬦ *nf* PHYS pneumatics (*U*) ⬦ *nm vieilli* - **1.** [de véhicule] tyre *Br*, tire *Am* - **2.** [message] *letter sent by network of pneumatic tubes* ⬦ *adj* - **1.** [fonctionnant à l'air] pneumatic - **2.** [gonflé à l'air] inflatable.

pneumonie [pnømɔni] *nf* pneumonia.

PNUD, Pnud [pnyd] (*abr de* **Programme des Nations unies pour le développement**) *nm* UNDP.

PNUE, Pnue [pny] (*abr de* **Programme des Nations unies pour l'environnement**) *nm* UNEP.

p.o. *abr de* **par ordre.**

PO (*abr de* **petites ondes**) MW.

poche [pɔʃ] *nf* - **1.** [de vêtement, de sac, d'air] pocket ; **de ~** pocket (*avant n*) ; **~ revolver** back *ou* hip pocket ; **c'est dans la ~** *fig* it's in the bag ; **faire les ~s de qqn** *fig* to go through sb's pockets ; **s'en mettre plein** *ou* **se remplir les ~s** *fig* to make a packet - **2.** [sac, sous les yeux] bag ; **faire des ~s** [vêtement] to bag.

pocher [3] [pɔʃe] *vt* - **1.** CULIN to poach - **2.** [blesser] : **~ l'œil à qqn** to give sb a black eye.

pochette [pɔʃɛt] *nf* - **1.** [enveloppe] envelope ; [d'allumettes] book ; [de photos] packet - **2.** [de disque] sleeve - **3.** [mouchoir] (pocket) handkerchief.

pochette-surprise [pɔʃɛtsyrpriz] (*pl* **pochettes-surprises**) *nf* lucky bag.

pochoir [pɔʃwar] *nm* stencil.

podium [pɔdjɔm] *nm* podium.

podologue [pɔdɔlɔg] *nmf* chiropodist, podiatrist *Am.*

poêle [pwal] ⬦ *nf* pan ; **~ à frire** frying pan ⬦ *nm* stove.

poêlée [pwale] *nf* panful.

poêlon [pwalɔ̃] *nm* casserole.

poème [pɔɛm] *nm* poem.

poésie [pɔezi] *nf* - **1.** [genre, émotion] poetry - **2.** [pièce écrite] poem.

poète [pɔɛt] ⬦ *adj* poetic ⬦ *nm* - **1.** [écrivain] poet - **2.** *fig* & *hum* [rêveur] dreamer.

poétique [pɔetik] *adj* poetic.

poétiquement [pɔetikmã] *adv* poetically.

pognon [pɔɲɔ̃] *nm* *tfam* dosh.

pogrom(e) [pɔgrɔm] *nm* pogrom.

poids [pwa] *nm* - **1.** [gén] weight ; **quel ~ fait-il?** how heavy is it/he? ; **perdre/prendre du ~** to lose/gain weight ; **vendre au ~** to sell by weight ; **avoir du ~** *fig* to carry a lot of weight ; **donner du ~ à** *fig* to lend weight to ; **~ lourd** BOXE heavyweight ; [camion] heavy goods vehicle ; **~ plume** BOXE featherweight ; **de ~** [argument] weighty ; **il ne fait pas le ~** *fig* he's not up to it - **2.** SPORT [lancer] shot.

poignant, e [pwaɲɑ̃, ɑ̃t] *adj* poignant.

poignard [pwaɲar] *nm* dagger.

poignarder [3] [pwaɲarde] *vt* to stab.

poigne [pwaɲ] *nf* grip ; *fig* authority ; **avoir de la ~** to have a strong grip ; *fig* to have authority.

poignée [pwaɲe] *nf* - **1.** [quantité, petit nombre] handful - **2.** [manche] handle.

➤ **poignée de main** *nf* handshake.

poignet [pwaɲɛ] *nm* - **1.** ANAT wrist - **2.** [de vêtement] cuff.

poil [pwal] *nm* - **1.** [du corps] hair ; **à ~** *fam* [tout nu] starkers - **2.** [d'animal] hair, coat ; **de tout ~** fig of all kinds - **3.** [de pinceau] bristle ; [de tapis] strand - **4.** fam [peu] : **il s'en est fallu d'un ~ que je réussisse** I came within a hair's breadth of succeeding - **5.** loc : **être de bon/mauvais ~** fam fig to be in a good/bad mood ; **reprendre du ~ de la bête** fig to regain strength.

poil-de-carotte [pwaldəkarɔt] adj inv fam [personne] red-headed ; [cheveux] carroty.

poiler [3] [pwale] **➡ se poiler** vp fam to kill o.s. (laughing).

poilu, e [pwaly] adj hairy.
➡ poilu nm fam French First World War soldier.

poinçon [pwɛ̃sɔ̃] nm - **1.** [outil] awl - **2.** [marque] hallmark.

poinçonner [3] [pwɛ̃sɔne] vt - **1.** [bijou] to hallmark - **2.** [billet, tôle] to punch.

poinçonneuse [pwɛ̃sɔnøz] nf punch.

poindre [82] [pwɛ̃dr] vi littéraire - **1.** [jour] to break - **2.** [plante] to come up - **3.** fig [sentiment] to break through.

poing [pwɛ̃] nm fist ; **dormir à ~s fermés** fig to sleep like a log.

point [pwɛ̃] ⬦ nm - **1.** COUTURE & TRICOT stitch ; **~s de suture** MÉD stitches - **2.** [de ponctuation] : **~ (final)** full stop Br, period Am ; **~ d'interrogation/d'exclamation** question/exclamation mark ; **~s de suspension** suspension points ; **mettre les ~s sur les i** fig to get things straight - **3.** [petite tache] dot ; **~ noir** [sur la peau] blackhead ; fig [problème] problem - **4.** [endroit] spot, point ; fig point : **~ d'appui** [support] something to lean on ; **~ chaud** POLIT key issue ; [zone dangereuse] trouble spot, hot spot ; **~ culminant** [en montagne] summit ; fig climax ; **~ d'eau** water supply point ; **~ de mire** fig focal point ; **~ névralgique** fig sensitive spot ; **~ de ralliement** rallying point ; **~ de repère** [temporel] reference point ; [spatial] landmark ; **~ de vente** point of sale, sale outlet ; **~ de vue** [panorama] viewpoint ; fig [opinion, aspect] point of view ; **avoir un ~ commun avec qqn** to have something in common with sb - **5.** [degré] point ; **au ~ que, à tel ~ que** to such an extent that ; **je ne pensais pas que cela le vexerait à ce ~** I didn't think it would make him so cross ; **être ... au ~ de faire qqch** to be so ... as to do sthg - **6.** fig [position] position ; **faire le ~** to take stock (of the situation) - **7.** [réglage] : **mettre au ~** [machine] to adjust ; [idée, projet] to finalize ; **à ~** [cuisson] just right ; **à ~ (nommé)** just in time - **8.** [question, détail] point, detail ; **~ faible** weak point - **9.** [score] point ; **marquer un ~** SPORT & fig to

score a point - **10.** [douleur] pain ; **~ de côté** stitch - **11.** [début] : **être sur le ~ de faire qqch** to be on the point of doing sthg, to be about to do sthg ; **au ~ du jour** sout at daybreak - **12.** AUTOM : **au ~ mort** in neutral - **13.** GÉOGR : **~s cardinaux** points of the compass ⬦ adv vieilli : **ne ~** not (at all) ; **ne vous en faites ~** don't worry.

pointage [pwɛ̃taʒ] nm - **1.** [au travail - d'entrée] clocking in ; [- de sortie] clocking out - **2.** [d'arme] aiming.

pointe [pwɛ̃t] nf - **1.** [extrémité] point ; [de nez] tip ; **se hausser sur la ~ des pieds** to stand on tiptoe ; **en ~** pointed ; **tailler en ~** to taper ; **se terminer en ~** to taper ; **~ d'asperge** asparagus tip - **2.** [clou] tack - **3.** [sommet] peak, summit ; **à la ~ de** fig at the peak of ; **à la ~ de la technique** at the forefront ou leading edge of technology - **4.** [accélération] : **faire ou pousser une ~ (jusqu'à)** to put on a spurt (and reach) - **5.** fig [trait d'esprit] witticism - **6.** fig [petite quantité] : **une ~** a touch of.
➡ pointes nfpl DANSE points ; **faire des ou les ~s** to dance on one's points.
➡ de pointe loc adj - **1.** [vitesse] maximum, top - **2.** [industrie, secteur] leading ; [technique] latest.

pointer [3] [pwɛ̃te] ⬦ vt - **1.** [cocher] to tick (off) - **2.** [employés - à l'entrée] to check in ; [- à la sortie] to check out - **3.** [diriger] : **~ qqch vers** to point sthg towards Br ou toward Am ; **~ qqch sur** to point sthg at ⬦ vi - **1.** [à l'usine - à l'entrée] to clock in ; [- à la sortie] to clock out - **2.** [à la pétanque] to get as close to the jack as possible - **3.** [être en pointe] to stick up - **4.** [jour] to break - **5.** fig [sentiment] to show through.
➡ se pointer vp fam to turn up.

pointillé [pwɛ̃tije] nm - **1.** [ligne] dotted line ; **en ~** [ligne] dotted ; fig [par sous-entendus] obliquely - **2.** [perforations] perforations (pl).

pointilleux, euse [pwɛ̃tijø, øz] adj : **~ (sur)** particular (about).

pointu, e [pwɛ̃ty] adj - **1.** [objet] pointed - **2.** [voix, ton] sharp - **3.** [étude, formation] specialized.

pointure [pwɛ̃tyr] nf (shoe) size.

point-virgule [pwɛ̃virgyl] (pl points-virgules) nm semi-colon.

poire [pwar] ⬦ nf - **1.** [fruit] pear ; **~ Belle-Hélène** pear ou poire Belle-Hélène ; **couper la ~ en deux** fig to compromise - **2.** MÉD : **~ à injections** syringe - **3.** fam [visage] face - **4.** fam [naïf] dope ⬦ adj fam : **être ~** to be a sucker ou a mug Br.

poireau, x [pwaro] nm leek ; **~x vinaigrette** leeks with vinaigrette dressing.

poireauter, poiroter [3] [pwarote] *vi fam* to hang around.

poirier [pwarje] *nm* pear tree ; **faire le ~** *fig* to do a headstand.

poiroter = poireauter.

pois [pwa] *nm* - **1.** BOT pea ; **~ chiche** chickpea ; **petits ~** garden peas, petits pois ; **~ de senteur** sweet pea - **2.** *fig* [motif] dot, spot ; **à ~** spotted, polka-dot.

poison [pwazɔ̃] <> *nm* [substance] poison <> *nmf fam fig* [personne] drag, pain ; [enfant] brat.

poisse [pwas] *nf fam* bad luck ; **porter la ~** to be bad luck.

poisseux, euse [pwasø, øz] *adj* sticky.

poisson [pwasɔ̃] *nm* fish ; **~ d'avril** [farce] April fool ; [en papier] *paper fish pinned to someone's back as a prank on April Fools' Day* ; **~-chat** catfish ; **~ rouge** goldfish ; **noyer le ~** *fig* to confuse the issue.

Poissons *nmpl* ASTROL Pisces *(sg)* ; **être Poissons** to be (a) Pisces.

poissonnerie [pwasɔnri] *nf* - **1.** [boutique] fish shop, fishmonger's (shop) - **2.** [métier] fish trade.

poissonneux, euse [pwasɔnø, øz] *adj* full of fish.

poissonnier, ère [pwasɔnje, ɛr] *nm, f* fishmonger.

poitevin, e [pwatvɛ̃, in] *adj* [de Poitiers] of/from Poitiers ; [du Poitou] of/from Poitou.

Poitevin, e *nm, f* [de Poitiers] person from Poitiers ; [du Poitou] person from Poitou.

poitrail [pwatraj] *nm* breast, chest.

poitrinaire [pwatrinɛr] *nmf & adj* consumptive.

poitrine [pwatrin] *nf* - **1.** [thorax] chest ; [de femme] chest, bust - **2.** [viande] breast.

poivre [pwavr] *nm* pepper ; **~ blanc** white pepper ; **~ gris, ~ noir** black pepper ; **~ et sel** *fig* pepper-and-salt.

poivrer [3] [pwavre] *vt* to put pepper on.

se poivrer *vp fam* to get plastered.

poivrier [pwavrije] *nm*, **poivrière** [pwavrijɛr] *nf* pepper pot *Br*, pepperbox *Am*.

poivron [pwavrɔ̃] *nm* pepper, capsicum ; **~ rouge/vert** red/green pepper.

poivrot, e [pwavro, ɔt] *nm, f fam* boozer.

poix [pwa] *nf* pitch.

poker [pɔkɛr] *nm* poker.

polaire [pɔlɛr] *adj* polar.

polar [pɔlar] *nm fam* thriller, whodunnit.

polariser [3] [pɔlarize] *vt* - **1.** TECHNOL to polarize - **2.** *fig* [attention] to focus.

se polariser *vp* : **se ~ sur** to be centred *ou* focussed on.

Polaroïd® [pɔlarɔid] *nm* Polaroid®.

polder [pɔldɛr] *nm* polder.

pôle [pol] *nm* pole ; **~ Nord/Sud** North/South Pole.

polémique [pɔlemik] <> *nf* controversy <> *adj* [style, ton] polemical.

polémiquer [3] [pɔlemike] *vi* to engage in controversy.

pole position [polpozisjɔ̃] *(pl* pole positions*) nf* SPORT pole position.

poli, e [pɔli] *adj* - **1.** [personne] polite - **2.** [surface] polished.

poli *nm* polish.

police [pɔlis] *nf* - **1.** [force de l'ordre] police ; **être de** *ou* **dans la ~** to be in the police ; **~ judiciaire** *plain-clothes police force responsible for criminal investigation and arrests,* ≃ CID *Br*, ≃ FBI *Am* ; **~ secours** *emergency service provided by the police* ; **~ secrète** secret police - **2.** [contrat] policy ; **~ d'assurance** insurance policy - **3.** TYPO : **~** (de caractères) font.

policé, e [pɔlise] *adj littéraire* civilized.

polichinelle [pɔliʃinɛl] *nm* - **1.** [personnage] Punch ; **secret de ~** *fig* open secret - **2.** *fam fig* [guignol] buffoon.

policier, ère [pɔlisje, ɛr] *adj* - **1.** [de la police] police *(avant n)* - **2.** [film, roman] detective *(avant n)*.

policier *nm* police officer.

policlinique [pɔliklinik] *nf* [partie d'hôpital] ≃ outpatients department.

poliment [pɔlimɑ̃] *adv* politely.

polio [pɔljo] *nf* polio.

poliomyélite [pɔljɔmjelit] *nf* poliomyelitis.

polir [32] [pɔlir] *vt* to polish.

polissage [pɔlisaʒ] *nm* polishing.

polisson, onne [pɔlisɔ̃, ɔn] <> *adj* - **1.** [chanson, propos] lewd, suggestive - **2.** [enfant] naughty <> *nm, f* [enfant] naughty child.

politesse [pɔlitɛs] *nf* - **1.** [courtoisie] politeness - **2.** [action] polite action ; **se faire des ~s** *iron* to exchange favours.

politicard, e [pɔlitikar, ard] *péj* <> *adj* politicking <> *nm, f* (political) schemer, politico.

politicien, enne [pɔlitisjɛ̃, ɛn] <> *adj péj* politicking, politically unscrupulous <> *nm, f* politician, politico.

politique [pɔlitik] <> *nf* - **1.** [de gouvernement, de personne] policy ; **~ étrangère/intérieure** foreign/domestic policy ; **pratiquer la ~ de l'autruche** *fig* to bury one's head in the sand

- 2. [affaires publiques] politics *(U)* ◇ *nm* politician ◇ *adj* **- 1.** [pouvoir, théorie] political ; homme ~ politician **- 2.** *littéraire* [choix, réponse] politic.

politiquement [pɔlitikmɑ̃] *adv* politically ; ~ **correct** politically correct, PC.

politisation [pɔlitizasjɔ̃] *nf* politicization.

politiser [3] [pɔlitize] *vt* to politicize.

politologue [pɔlitɔlɔg] *nmf* political expert *ou* analyst.

polka [pɔlka] *nf* polka.

pollen [pɔlɛn] *nm* pollen.

polluant [pɔlɥɑ̃] *nm* pollutant.

polluer [7] [pɔlɥe] *vt* to pollute.

pollution [pɔlysjɔ̃] *nf* pollution.

polo [pɔlo] *nm* **- 1.** [sport] polo **- 2.** [chemise] polo shirt.

polochon [pɔlɔʃɔ̃] *nm fam* bolster.

Pologne [pɔlɔɲ] *nf* : **la ~** Poland.

polonais, e [pɔlɔnɛ, ɛz] *adj* Polish.
➤ **polonais** *nm* [langue] Polish.
➤ **polonaise** *nf* **- 1.** [danse] polonaise **- 2.** [gâteau] *brioche with an almond filling covered in meringue*.
➤ **Polonais, e** *nm, f* Pole.

poltron, onne [pɔltrɔ̃, ɔn] ◇ *nm, f* coward ◇ *adj* cowardly.

polyamide [pɔliamid] *nm* polyamide.

polychrome [pɔlikrom] *adj* polychrome, polychromatic.

polyclinique [pɔliklinik] *nf* general hospital.

polycopie [pɔlikɔpi] *nf* duplicating.

polycopié, e [pɔlikɔpje] *adj* duplicate *(avant n)*.
➤ **polycopié** *nm* duplicated lecture notes *(pl)*.

polycopier [9] [pɔlikɔpje] *vt* to duplicate.

polyculture [pɔlikyltyr] *nf* mixed farming.

polyester [pɔliɛstɛr] *nm* polyester.

polygame [pɔligam] ◇ *nm* polygamist ◇ *adj* polygamous.

polygamie [pɔligami] *nf* polygamy.

polyglotte [pɔliglɔt] *nmf* & *adj* polyglot.

polygone [pɔligɔn] *nm* **- 1.** *MATHS* polygon **- 2.** *MIL* : ~ **de tir** rifle range.

polymère [pɔlimɛr] ◇ *nm* polymer ◇ *adj* polymeric.

polymorphe [pɔlimɔrf] *adj* polymorphous.

Polynésie [pɔlinezi] *nf* : **la ~** Polynesia ; **la ~ française** French Polynesia.

polynésien, enne [pɔlinezjɛ̃, ɛn] *adj* Polynesian.
➤ **polynésien** *nm* [langue] Polynesian.
➤ **Polynésien, enne** *nm, f* Polynesian.

polype [pɔlip] *nm* polyp.

polyphonie [pɔlifɔni] *nf* polyphony.

polysémique [pɔlisemik] *adj* polysemous, polysemic.

polystyrène [pɔlistirɛn] *nm* polystyrene.

polytechnicien, enne [pɔlitɛknisjɛ̃, ɛn] *nm, f* student or ex-student of the École Polytechnique.

Polytechnique [pɔlitɛknik] *n* : **l'École ~** prestigious engineering college.

POLYTECHNIQUE

This prestigious engineering school in Palaiseau near Paris has close connections with the Ministry of Defence. It is popularly known as 'l'X'.

polythéisme [pɔliteism] *nm* polytheism.

polythéiste [pɔliteist] ◇ *nmf* polytheist ◇ *adj* polytheistic.

polyvalent, e [pɔlivalɑ̃, ɑ̃t] *adj* **- 1.** [salle] multi-purpose **- 2.** [professeur] non-specialized **- 3.** *CHIM* & *MÉD* polyvalent **- 4.** [personne] versatile.
➤ **polyvalent** *nm* tax inspector specializing in company taxation.

pomelo [pɔmelo] *nm* grapefruit.

pommade [pɔmad] *nf* [médicament] ointment.

pommader [3] [pɔmade] *vt* to pomade.

pomme [pɔm] *nf* **- 1.** [fruit] apple ; ~ **de pin** pine *ou* fir cone **- 2.** [pomme de terre] : ~s **allumettes** very thin chips ; ~s **frites** chips *Br*, (French) fries *Am* ; ~s **vapeur** steamed potatoes **- 3.** *loc* : ~ **de discorde** bone of contention ; **tomber dans les** ~s *fam* to pass out, to faint.
➤ **pomme d'Adam** *nf* Adam's apple.

pommeau, x [pɔmo] *nm* **- 1.** [de parapluie, de canne] knob **- 2.** [de sabre] pommel.

pomme de terre [pɔmdətɛr] *nf* potato ; ~s **de terre à l'eau** boiled potatoes ; ~s **de terre au four** baked potatoes ; ~s **de terre frites** chips *Br*, (French) fries *Am* ; ~s **de terre en robe des champs** jacket potatoes ; ~s **de terre sautées** sauté potatoes.

pommelé, e [pɔmle] *adj* dappled ; **gris ~** dapple grey *Br ou* gray *Am*.

pommette [pɔmɛt] *nf* cheekbone.

pommier [pɔmje] *nm* apple tree.

pompe [pɔ̃p] *nf* **- 1.** [appareil] pump ; ~ **à essence** petrol pump *Br*, gas pump *Am* ; ~ **à incendie** fire engine *Br*, fire truck *Am* **- 2.** [magnificence] pomp, ceremony ; **en grande** ~ with great ceremony - **3.** *fam* [chaussure] shoe ; être à côté de ses ~s *fam fig* to be completely out of it.

➡ **pompes funèbres** *nfpl* undertaker's *(sg)*, funeral director's *(sg) Br*, mortician's *(sg) Am.*

Pompéi [pɔ̃peil] *n* Pompeii.

pomper [3] [pɔ̃pe] *vt* - **1.** [eau, air] to pump - **2.** [avec éponge] to soak up - **3.** *arg scol* [copier] : ~ qqch (sur qqn) to crib sthg (from sb).

pompette [pɔ̃pɛt] *adj fam* merry, tipsy.

pompeusement [pɔ̃pøzmɑ̃] *adv* pompously.

pompeux, euse [pɔ̃pø, øz] *adj* pompous.

pompier, ère [pɔ̃pje, ɛr] *adj* pretentious.

pompier [pɔ̃pje] *nm* fireman *Br*, fire fighter *Am.*

pompiste [pɔ̃pist] *nmf* petrol *Br ou* gas *Am* pump attendant.

pompon [pɔ̃pɔ̃] *nm* pompom ; **décrocher le ~** *fam fig* to take the biscuit *Br ou* cake.

pomponner [3] [pɔ̃pɔne] ➡ **se pomponner** *vp* to get dressed up.

ponce [pɔ̃s] *adj* : **pierre** ~ pumice (stone).

poncer [16] [pɔ̃se] *vt* [bois] to sand (down).

ponceuse [pɔ̃søz] *nf* sander, sanding machine.

poncif [pɔ̃sif] *nm* [banalité] commonplace, cliché.

ponction [pɔ̃ksjɔ̃] *nf* - **1.** [MÉD - lombaire] puncture ; [- pulmonaire] tapping - **2.** *fig* [prélèvement] withdrawal.

ponctionner [3] [pɔ̃ksjɔne] *vt* - **1.** [MÉD - région lombaire] to puncture ; [- poumon] to tap - **2.** *fig* [contribuable] to take money from ; [argent] to withdraw.

ponctualité [pɔ̃ktɥalite] *nf* punctuality.

ponctuation [pɔ̃ktɥasjɔ̃] *nf* punctuation.

ponctuel, elle [pɔ̃ktɥɛl] *adj* - **1.** [action] specific, selective - **2.** [personne] punctual.

ponctuellement [pɔ̃ktɥɛlmɑ̃] *adv* punctually.

ponctuer [7] [pɔ̃ktɥe] *vt* to punctuate ; ~ qqch de qqch *fig* to punctuate sthg with sthg.

pondéral, e, aux [pɔ̃deral, o] *adj* weight *(avant n).*

pondération [pɔ̃derasjɔ̃] *nf* - **1.** [de personne] level-headedness - **2.** *ÉCON* weighting.

pondéré, e [pɔ̃dere] *adj* - **1.** [personne] level-headed - **2.** *ÉCON* weighted.

Pondichéry [pɔ̃diʃeri] *n* Pondicherry.

pondre [75] [pɔ̃dr] *vt* - **1.** [œufs] to lay - **2.** *fam fig* [projet, texte] to produce.

pondu, e [pɔ̃dy] *pp* ▷ pondre.

poney [pɔnɛ] *nm* pony.

pongiste [pɔ̃ʒist] *nmf* table-tennis player.

pont [pɔ̃] *nm* - **1.** *CONSTR* bridge ; ~s et chaussées *ADMIN* ≃ highways department - **2.** [lien] link, connection ; ~ aérien airlift ; **couper les ~s avec qqn** *fig* to break with sb - **3.** [congé] day off granted by an employer to fill the gap between a national holiday and a weekend ; **faire le ~** to have a long weekend - **4.** [de navire] deck.

ponte [pɔ̃t] ⬦ *nf* [action] laying ; [œufs] clutch ⬦ *nm* - **1.** *JEU* punter - **2.** *fam* [autorité] big shot.

pontife [pɔ̃tif] *nm* pontiff.

pontifical, e, aux [pɔ̃tifikal, o] *adj* papal.

pontificat [pɔ̃tifika] *nm* pontificate.

pontifier [9] [pɔ̃tifje] *vi fam* to pontificate.

pont-levis [pɔ̃ləvi] *(pl* ponts-levis*) nm* drawbridge.

ponton [pɔ̃tɔ̃] *nm* - **1.** [plate-forme] pontoon - **2.** [chaland] lighter, barge.

pool [pul] *nm* pool.

pop [pɔp] ⬦ *nm* pop ⬦ *adj* pop *(avant n).*

pop-corn [pɔpkɔrn] *nm inv* popcorn *(U).*

pope [pɔp] *nm* priest *(in the Orthodox church).*

popeline [pɔplin] *nf* poplin.

popote [pɔpɔt] *fam* ⬦ *adj inv* homeloving ⬦ *nf* : **faire la** ~ to do the cooking ; **préparer la** ~ to prepare the meal.

populace [pɔpylas] *nf péj* mob.

populaire [pɔpylɛr] *adj* - **1.** [du peuple - volonté] popular, of the people ; [- quartier] working-class ; [- art, chanson] folk - **2.** [personne] popular.

populariser [3] [pɔpylarize] *vt* to popularize.

popularité [pɔpylarite] *nf* popularity.

population [pɔpylasjɔ̃] *nf* population ; ~ active working population.

populiste [pɔpylist] *nmf* & *adj* populist.

populo [pɔpylo] *nm fam* - **1.** [peuple] hoi polloi - **2.** [foule] crowd.

porc [pɔr] *nm* - **1.** [animal] pig, hog *Am* - **2.** *fig* & *péj* [personne] pig, swine - **3.** [viande] pork - **4.** [peau] pigskin.

porcelaine [pɔrsəlɛn] *nf* - **1.** [matière] china, porcelain - **2.** [objet] piece of china *ou* porcelain - **3.** [mollusque] cowrie shell.

porcelet [pɔrsəlɛ] *nm* piglet.

porc-épic [pɔrkepik] *(pl* porcs-épics*) nm* porcupine.

porche [pɔrʃ] *nm* porch.

porcherie [pɔrʃəri] *nf litt* & *fig* pigsty.

porcin, e [pɔrsɛ̃, in] *adj* - **1.** [élevage] pig *(avant n)* - **2.** *fig* & *péj* [yeux] piggy.
➡ **porcin** *nm* pig.

pore [pɔr] *nm* pore.

poreux, euse [pɔrø, øz] *adj* porous.

pornographie [pɔrnɔgrafi] *nf* pornography.

pornographique [pɔrnɔgrafik] *adj* pornographic.

porridge [pɔridʒ] *nm* porridge.

port [pɔr] *nm* - **1.** [lieu] port ; **arriver à bon ~** [personne] to arrive safe and sound ; [chose] to arrive in good condition ; **~ d'attache** home port ; **~ de commerce/pêche** commercial/fishing port - **2.** [fait de porter sur soi - d'objet] carrying ; [- de vêtement, décoration] wearing ; **~ d'armes** carrying of weapons - **3.** [transport] carriage ; **franco de ~** carriage paid - **4.** [allure] bearing.

portable [pɔrtabl] ⬦ *nm* TV portable ; INFORM laptop, portable ; [téléphone] mobile ⬦ *adj* - **1.** [vêtement] wearable - **2.** [ordinateur, machine à écrire] portable, laptop.

portage [pɔrtaʒ] *nm Can* NAUT portage.

portail [pɔrtaj] *nm* portal.

portant, e [pɔrtɑ̃, ɑ̃t] *adj* : **être bien/mal ~** to be in good/poor health.
➡ **portant** *nm* upright.

portatif, ive [pɔrtatif, iv] *adj* portable.

Port-au-Prince [pɔroprɛ̃s] *n* Port-au-Prince.

porte [pɔrt] *nf* - **1.** [de maison, voiture] door ; **claquer la ~** to slam the door ; **claquer/fermer la ~ au nez de qqn** to slam/shut the door in sb's face ; **écouter aux ~s** to listen at keyholes ; **être à la ~** to be locked out ; **ficher** *ou* **foutre qqn à la ~** *fam* to throw *ou* chuck sb out ; **mettre qqn à la ~** to throw sb out ; **~ cochère** carriage entrance ; **~ de communication** communicating door ; **~ d'entrée** front door ; **~ de secours** emergency exit ; **~ vitrée** glass door - **2.** AÉRON & SKI [de ville] gate ; **la ~ de Versailles** *site of a large exhibition complex in Paris where major trade fairs take place* - **3.** *fig* [de région] gateway.

porte-à-faux [pɔrtafo] *nm inv* [roche] overhang ; CONSTR cantilever ; **en ~** overhanging ; CONSTR cantilevered ; *fig* in a delicate situation.

porte-à-porte [pɔrtapɔrt] *nm inv* : **faire du ~** to sell from door to door.

porte-avions [pɔrtavjɔ̃] *nm inv* aircraft carrier.

porte-bagages [pɔrtbagaʒ] *nm inv* luggage rack ; [de voiture] roof rack.

porte-bébé [pɔrtbebe] *(pl* **porte-bébés)** *nm* baby sling, papoose.

porte-bonheur [pɔrtbɔnœr] *nm inv* lucky charm.

porte-bouteilles [pɔrtbutɛj] *nm inv* [casier] wine rack.

porte-cartes, porte-carte [pɔrtəkart] *nm inv* card holder.

porte-cigarettes [pɔrtsigaret] *nm inv* cigarette case.

porte-clefs, porte-clés [pɔrtəkle] *nm inv* keyring.

porte-couteau [pɔrtkuto] *(pl* **porte-couteaux)** *nm* knife-rest.

porte-documents [pɔrtdɔkymɑ̃] *nm inv* attaché *ou* document case.

porte-drapeau [pɔrtdrapo] *(pl* **porte-drapeaux)** *nm* standard-bearer.

portée [pɔrte] *nf* - **1.** [de missile] range ; **à ~ de** within range of ; **à ~ de main** within reach ; **à ~ de voix** within earshot ; **à ~ de vue** in sight ; **à ~ de qqn** *fig* within sb's reach ; **hors de la ~ de** out of reach of - **2.** [d'événement] impact, significance - **3.** MUS stave, staff - **4.** [de femelle] litter.

porte-fenêtre [pɔrtfənɛtr] *(pl* **portes-fenêtres)** *nf* French window *ou* door *Am*.

portefeuille [pɔrtəfœj] *nm* - **1.** [pour billets] wallet - **2.** FIN & POLIT portfolio.

porte-jarretelles [pɔrtʒartɛl] *nm inv* suspender belt *Br*, garter belt *Am*.

porte-malheur [pɔrtmalœr] *nm inv* jinx.

portemanteau, x [pɔrtmɑ̃to] *nm* [au mur] coat-rack ; [sur pied] coat stand.

portemine [pɔrtəmin] *nm* propelling pencil.

porte-monnaie [pɔrtmɔnɛ] *nm inv* purse.

porte-parapluies [pɔrtparaplɥi] *nm inv* umbrella stand.

porte-parole [pɔrtparɔl] *nm inv* spokesman (f spokeswoman) ; **~ officiel du gouvernement** official government spokesman.

porte-plume [pɔrtəplym] *nm inv* penholder.

porter [3] [pɔrte] ⬦ *vt* - **1.** [gén] to carry - **2.** [vêtement, lunettes, montre] to wear ; [barbe] to have - **3.** [nom, date, inscription] to bear - **4.** [apporter] to take - **5.** [inciter] : **~ qqn à faire qqch** to lead sb to do sthg - **6.** [inscrire] to put down, to write down ; **porté disparu** reported missing ⬦ *vi* - **1.** [s'appuyer - balcon] : **~ sur** to be supported by - **2.** [traiter] : **~ sur qqn/qqch** to be about sb/sthg **- 3.** [remarque] to strike home **- 4.** [voix, tir] to carry.

◆ **se porter** ◇ *vp* **- 1.** [se sentir] : **se ~ bien/mal** to be well/unwell **- 2.** [se diriger] : **se ~ sur** [choix, regard] to fall on ; [conversation] to turn to **- 3.** [se livrer] : **se ~ à** [violences] to carry out ; **se ~ à des extrémités** to go to extremes ◇ *v attr* : **se ~ garant de qqch** to guarantee sthg, to vouch for sthg ; **se ~ candidat à** to stand for election to *Br*, to run for *Am*.

porte-savon [pɔrtsavɔ̃] (*pl inv* OU **porte-savons**) *nm* soap dish.

porte-serviettes [pɔrtsɛrvjɛt] *nm inv* towel rail.

porteur, euse [pɔrtœr, øz] ◇ *adj* : **marché ~ COMM** growth market ; **mère porteuse** surrogate mother ; **mur ~** load-bearing wall ◇ *nm, f* **- 1.** [de message, nouvelle] bringer, bearer **- 2.** [de bagages] porter **- 3.** [détenteur - de papiers, d'actions] holder ; [- de chèque] bearer **- 4.** [de maladie] carrier.

porte-voix [pɔrtəvwa] *nm inv* megaphone, loud-hailer *Am*.

portier [pɔrtje] *nm* commissionaire.

portière [pɔrtjɛr] *nf* [de voiture, train] door.

portillon [pɔrtijɔ̃] *nm* barrier, gate.

portion [pɔrsjɔ̃] *nf* **- 1.** [de gâteau] portion, helping **- 2.** [d'héritage] portion, part ; **être réduit à la ~ congrue** *fig* to get the smallest share.

portique [pɔrtik] *nm* **- 1.** ARCHIT portico **- 2.** SPORT crossbeam *(for hanging apparatus)*.

Port-Louis [pɔrlwi] *n* Port Louis.

porto [pɔrto] *nm* port.

Porto-Novo [pɔrtonovo] *n* Porto Novo.

portoricain, e [pɔrtɔrikɛ̃, ɛn] *adj* Puerto Rican.
◆ **Portoricain, e** *nm, f* Puerto Rican.

Porto Rico [pɔrtoriko], **Puerto Rico** [pwertoriko] *n* Puerto Rico.

portrait [pɔrtrɛ] *nm* portrait ; PHOT photograph ; **être tout le ~ de qqn** *fig* to be the spitting ou very image of sb ; **faire le ~ de qqn** *fig* to describe sb.

portraitiste [pɔrtretist] *nmf* portrait painter.

portrait-robot [pɔrtrerɔbo] (*pl* **portraits-robots**) *nm* Photofit® picture, Identikit® picture.

portuaire [pɔrtɥer] *adj* port *(avant n)*, harbour *(avant n) Br*, harbor *(avant n) Am*.

portugais, e [pɔrtyge, ɛz] *adj* Portuguese.
◆ **portugais** *nm* [langue] Portuguese.
◆ **Portugais, e** *nm, f* Portuguese (person) ; **les Portugais** the Portuguese.

Portugal [pɔrtygal] *nm* : **le ~** Portugal ; **au ~** in Portugal.

POS, Pos [pɔs] (*abr de* plan d'occupation des sols) *nm* land use scheme.

pose [poz] *nf* **- 1.** [de pierre, moquette] laying ; [de papier peint, rideaux] hanging **- 2.** [position] pose ; **prendre la ~** to pose **- 3.** PHOT exposure.

posé, e [poze] *adj* sober, steady.

posément [pozemã] *adv* calmly.

poser [3] [poze] ◇ *vt* **- 1.** [mettre] to put down ; **~ qqch sur qqch** to put sthg on sthg **- 2.** [installer - rideaux, papier peint] to hang ; [- étagère] to put up ; [- moquette, carrelage] to lay **- 3.** [affirmer] to lay down, to set out **- 4.** [donner à résoudre - problème, difficulté] to pose ; **~ une question** to ask a question ; **~ sa candidature** to apply ; [- POLIT] to stand for election ◇ *vi* to pose.
◆ **se poser** *vp* **- 1.** [oiseau, avion] to land ; *fig* [choix, regard] : **se ~ sur** to fall on **- 2.** [question, problème] to arise, to come up **- 3.** [personne] : **se ~ en** to pose as.

poseur, euse [pozœr, øz] *nm, f vieilli* show-off, poser.

positif, ive [pozitif, iv] *adj* positive.

position [pozisjɔ̃] *nf* position ; **prendre ~** *fig* to take up a position, to take a stand.

positionnement [pozisjɔnmã] *nm* positioning.

positionner [3] [pozisjɔne] *vt* to position.
◆ **se positionner** *vp* to position o.s.

positivement [pozitivmã] *adv* positively.

posologie [pozɔlɔʒi] *nf* dosage.

possédant, e [posedã, ãt] ◇ *adj* property-owning *(avant n)* ◇ *nm, f* person from the property-owning classes.

possédé, e [posede] ◇ *adj* possessed ◇ *nm, f* person possessed.

posséder [18] [posede] *vt* **- 1.** [détenir - voiture, maison] to possess, to own ; [- diplôme] to have ; [- capacités, connaissances] to possess, to have **- 2.** [langue, art] to have mastered **- 3.** *fam* [personne] to have.

possesseur [posesœr] *nm* **- 1.** [de bien] possessor, owner **- 2.** [de secret, diplôme] holder.

possessif, ive [posesif, iv] *adj* possessive.
◆ **possessif** *nm* GRAM possessive.

possession [posesjɔ̃] *nf* **- 1.** [gén] possession ; **être en ma/ta** etc **~** to be in my/your etc possession ; **prendre ~ de** to take possession of ; **être en ~ de** to be in possession of ; **~ de soi** self-possession, composure **- 2.** [de langue] knowledge, command.

possibilité [posibilite] *nf* **- 1.** [gén] possibility **- 2.** [moyen] chance, opportunity.

➡ **possibilités** *nfpl* [capacités] potential *(sg)*.

possible [pɔsibl] ⬥ *adj* possible ; **c'est/ce n'est pas ~** that's possible/impossible ; **dès que** *ou* **aussitôt que ~** as soon as possible ⬥ *nm* : **faire tout son ~** to do one's utmost, to do everything possible ; **dans la mesure du ~** as far as possible.

postal, e, aux [pɔstal, o] *adj* postal.

postdater [3] [pɔstdate] *vt* to postdate.

poste [pɔst] ⬥ *nf* - **1.** [service] post *Br*, mail *Am* ; **envoyer/recevoir qqch par la ~** to send/receive sthg by post ; **~ aérienne** airmail - **2.** [bureau] post office ; **~ centrale** central post office ; **~ restante** poste restante *Br*, general delivery *Am* ⬥ *nm* - **1.** [emplacement] post ; **~ de police** police station ; **~ de secours** first-aid post ; **être fidèle au ~** *fig* to stay at one's post - **2.** [emploi] position, post - **3.** [appareil] : **~ émetteur** transmitter ; **~ de radio** radio ; **~ de télévision** television (set) - **4.** *TÉLÉCOM* extension.

poster[1] [pɔstɛr] *nm* poster.

poster[2] [3] [pɔste] *vt* - **1.** [lettre] to post *Br*, to mail *Am* - **2.** [sentinelle] to post.
➡ **se poster** *vp* to position o.s., to station o.s.

postérieur, e [pɔsterjœr] *adj* - **1.** [date] later, subsequent - **2.** [membre] hind *(avant n)*, back *(avant n)*.
➡ **postérieur** *nm hum* posterior.

postérieurement [pɔsterjœrmɑ̃] *adv* subsequently.

posteriori [pɔsterjɔri] ➡ **a posteriori** *loc adv* a posteriori.

postérité [pɔsterite] *nf* - **1.** [générations à venir] posterity - **2.** *littéraire* [descendance] descendants *(pl)*.

postface [pɔstfas] *nf* postscript.

posthume [pɔstym] *adj* posthumous.

postiche [pɔstiʃ] ⬥ *nm* hairpiece ⬥ *adj* false.

postier, ère [pɔstje, ɛr] *nm, f* post-office worker.

postillon [pɔstijɔ̃] *nm* [salive] droplet of saliva.

postillonner [3] [pɔstijɔne] *vi* to splutter.

postindustriel, elle [pɔstɛ̃dystrijɛl] *adj* post-industrial.

Post-it® [pɔstit] *nm inv* Post-it®, Post-it® note.

postmoderne [pɔstmɔdɛrn] *adj* postmodern.

postnatal, e [pɔstnatal] *(pl* **postnatals** ou **postnataux** [pɔstnato]*) adj* postnatal.

postopératoire [pɔstɔperatwar] *adj* postoperative.

post-scriptum [pɔstskriptɔm] *nm inv* postscript.

postsynchronisation [pɔstsɛ̃krɔnizasjɔ̃] *nf* dubbing.

postulant, e [pɔstylɑ̃, ɑ̃t] *nm, f* - **1.** [pour emploi] applicant - **2.** *RELIG* postulant.

postuler [3] [pɔstyle] *vt* - **1.** [emploi] to apply for - **2.** *PHILO* to postulate.

posture [pɔstyr] *nf* posture ; **être** *ou* **se trouver en mauvaise ~** *fig* to be in a difficult position.

pot [po] *nm* - **1.** [récipient] pot, jar ; [à eau, à lait] jug ; **~ de chambre** chamber pot ; **~ de fleurs** flowerpot ; **découvrir le ~ aux roses** to get to the bottom of something ; **tourner autour du ~** *fam* to beat about the bush - **2.** *AUTOM* : **~ catalytique** catalytic convertor ; **~ d'échappement** exhaust (pipe) ; [silencieux] silencer *Br*, muffler *Am* - **3.** *fam* [boisson] drink ; **boire** *ou* **prendre un ~** to have a drink ; **faire un ~** to have a drinks party - **4.** *loc fam* : **avoir du/manquer de ~** to be lucky/unlucky ; **payer plein ~** to pay full fare *ou* full whack.

potable [pɔtabl] *adj* - **1.** [liquide] drinkable ; **eau ~** drinking water - **2.** *fam* [travail] acceptable.

potache [pɔtaʃ] *nm fam* schoolkid.

potage [pɔtaʒ] *nm* soup ; **~ aux légumes** vegetable soup.

potager, ère [pɔtaʒe, ɛr] *adj* : **jardin ~** vegetable garden ; **plante potagère** vegetable.
➡ **potager** *nm* kitchen *ou* vegetable garden.

potasse [pɔtas] *nf* potash.

potasser [3] [pɔtase] *vt fam* [cours] to swot up *Br*, to bone up on *Am* ; [examen] to swot up for *Br*, to bone up for *Am*.

potassium [pɔtasjɔm] *nm* potassium.

pot-au-feu [pɔtofø] *nm inv* - **1.** [plat] *boiled beef with vegetables* - **2.** [viande] ≈ piece of stewing steak *Br ou* stewbeef *Am*.

pot-de-vin [podvɛ̃] *(pl* **pots-de-vin***) nm* bribe.

pote [pɔt] *nm fam* mate *Br*, buddy *Am*.

poteau, x [pɔto] *nm* post ; **~ de but** goalpost ; **~ indicateur** signpost ; **~ télégraphique** telegraph pole ; **coiffer qqn au ~** to pip sb at the post.

potée [pɔte] *nf pot-au-feu made with salt pork*.

potelé, e [pɔtle] *adj* plump, chubby.

potence [pɔtɑ̃s] *nf* - **1.** *CONSTR* bracket - **2.** [de pendaison] gallows *(sg)*.

potentat [pɔtɑ̃ta] *nm* potentate.

potentiel, elle [pɔtɑ̃sjɛl] *adj* potential.
➡ **potentiel** *nm* potential.

potentiellement [pɔtɑ̃sjɛlmɑ̃] *adv* potentially.

poterie [pɔtri] *nf* - **1.** [art] pottery - **2.** [objet] piece of pottery.

potiche [pɔtiʃ] *nf* - **1.** [vase] vase - **2.** *fam* [personne] figurehead.

potier, ère [pɔtje, ɛr] *nm, f* potter.

potin [pɔtɛ̃] *nm fam* [bruit] din.
➡ **potins** *nmpl fam* [ragots] gossip *(U)*.

potion [posjɔ̃] *nf* potion.

potiron [pɔtirɔ̃] *nm* pumpkin.

pot-pourri [popuri] *(pl* pots-pourris*) nm* pot-pourri.

pou, x [pu] *nm* louse.

pouah [pwa] *interj* ugh!

poubelle [pubɛl] *nf* dustbin *Br*, trashcan *Am*.

pouce [pus] *nm* - **1.** [de main] thumb ; [de pied] big toe ; **sucer son ~** to suck one's thumb ; **manger sur le ~** to grab something to eat - **2.** [mesure] inch ; **ne pas bouger/céder d'un ~** not to move/give an inch.

poudre [pudr] *nf* powder ; **~ vermifuge** worming powder ; **prendre la ~ d'escampette** to make off.

poudrerie [pudrəri] *nf Can* snowdrift.

poudreux, euse [pudrø, øz] *adj* powdery.
➡ **poudreuse** *nf* powder (snow).

poudrier [pudrije] *nm* - **1.** [boîte] powder compact - **2.** [fabricant] explosives manufacturer.

poudrière [pudrijɛr] *nf* powder magazine ; *fig* powder keg.

poudroyer [13] [pudrwaje] *vi littéraire* to rise (up) in clouds.

pouf [puf] ⟨ *nm* pouffe ⟨ *interj* thud!

pouffer [3] [pufe] *vi* : **~ (de rire)** to snigger.

pouilleux, euse [pujø, øz] ⟨ *adj* - **1.** [personne, animal] flea-ridden - **2.** [endroit] squalid ⟨ *nm, f* - **1.** [couvert de poux] person with fleas - **2.** [misérable] down-and-out.

poulailler [pulaje] *nm* - **1.** [de ferme] henhouse - **2.** *fam* THÉÂTRE gods *(sg)*.

poulain [pulɛ̃] *nm* foal ; *fig* protégé.

poulamon [pulamɔ̃] *nm Can* tomcod.

poularde [pulard] *nf* fattened chicken.

poule [pul] *nf* - **1.** ZOOL hen ; **la ~ aux œufs d'or** the goose that lays the golden egg ; **~ mouillée** wimp, wet - **2.** *fam péj* [femme] bird *Br*, broad *Am* - **3.** SPORT [compétition] round robin ; RUGBY [groupe] pool.

poulet [pulɛ] *nm* - **1.** ZOOL chicken ; **~ rôti** roast chicken ; **~ fermier** free-range chicken ; **~ de grain** corn-fed chicken - **2.** *fam* [policier] cop.

poulette [pulɛt] *nf* - **1.** ZOOL pullet - **2.** *fam péj* [fille] bird *Br*, chick *Am*.

pouliche [puliʃ] *nf* filly.

poulie [puli] *nf* pulley.

poulpe [pulp] *nm* octopus.

pouls [pu] *nm* pulse.

poumon [pumɔ̃] *nm* lung ; **à pleins ~s** deeply.

poupe [pup] *nf* stern.

poupée [pupe] *nf* - **1.** [jouet] doll - **2.** [pansement] finger bandage.

poupin, e [pupɛ̃, in] *adj* chubby.

poupon [pupɔ̃] *nm* - **1.** [bébé] little baby - **2.** [jouet] baby doll.

pouponner [3] [pupɔne] *vi* to play mother.

pouponnière [pupɔnjɛr] *nf* nursery.

pour [pur] ⟨ *prép* - **1.** [gén] for - **2.** (+ *infinitif*) : **~ faire** in order to do, (so as) to do ; **je suis venu ~ vous voir** I've come to see you ; **~ m'avoir aidé** for having helped me, for helping me - **3.** [indique un rapport] for ; **avancé ~ son âge** advanced for his/her age ; **~ moi** for my part, as far as I'm concerned ; **~ ce qui est de** as regards, with regard to ⟨ *adv* : **je suis ~** I'm (all) for it ⟨ *nm* : **le ~ et le contre** the pros and cons *(pl)*.
➡ **pour que** *loc conj* (+ *subjonctif*) so that, in order that.

pourboire [purbwar] *nm* tip.

pourceau, x [purso] *nm littéraire* swine.

pourcentage [pursɑ̃taʒ] *nm* percentage.

pourfendeur, euse [purfɑ̃dœr, øz] *nm, f littéraire* : **~ d'abus** righter of wrongs.

pourparlers [purparle] *nmpl* talks.

pourpre [purpr] ⟨ *nf* - **1.** [colorant] purple (dye) - **2.** [couleur] purple ⟨ *nm & adj* crimson.

pourquoi [purkwa] ⟨ *adv* why ; **~ pas?** why not? ; **c'est ~ ...** that's why ... ⟨ *nm inv* : **le ~ (de)** the reason (for) ; **les ~** the questions ; **le ~ et le comment** the whys and wherefores.

pourrai, pourras *etc* ▷ **pouvoir**.

pourri, e [puri] *adj* - **1.** [fruit] rotten - **2.** [personne, milieu] corrupt - **3.** [enfant] spoiled rotten, ruined.
➡ **pourri** *nm* - **1.** [de fruit] rotten part - **2.** *fam* [personne] creep.

pourrir [32] [purir] ⟨ *vt* - **1.** [matière, aliment] to rot, to spoil - **2.** [enfant] to ruin, to spoil rotten <> *vi* [matière] to rot ; [fruit, aliment] to go rot-ten *ou* bad.

pourriture [purityr] *nf* - **1.** [d'aliment] rot - **2.** *fig* [de personne, de milieu] corruption - **3.** *injurieux* [personne] bastard.

poursuis, poursuit *etc* ⊏> poursuivre.

poursuite [pursɥit] *nf* - **1.** [de personne] chase ; **se lancer à la ~ de** to set off after - **2.** [d'argent, de vérité] pursuit - **3.** [de négociations] continuation.

➤ **poursuites** *nfpl* JUR (legal) proceedings ; **engager des ~s judiciaires** to take legal action.

poursuivant, e [pursɥivã, ãt] *nm, f* pursuer.

poursuivi, e [pursɥivi] *pp* ⊏> poursuivre.

poursuivre [89] [pursɥivr] <> *vt* - **1.** [voleur] to pursue, to chase ; [gibier] to hunt - **2.** [rêve, vengeance] to pursue - **3.** [enquête, travail] to carry on with, to continue - **4.** JUR [criminel] to prosecute ; [voisin] to sue <> *vi* to go on, to carry on.

pourtant [purtã] *adv* nevertheless, even so.

pourtour [purtur] *nm* perimeter.

pourvoi [purvwa] *nm* JUR appeal ; **présenter un ~ en cassation** to take one's case to the Appeal Court.

pourvoir [64] [purvwar] <> *vt* : **~ qqn de** to provide sb with ; **~ qqch de** to equip *ou* fit sthg with <> *vi* : **~ à** to provide for.

➤ **se pourvoir** *vp* - **1.** [se munir] : **se ~ de** to provide o.s. with - **2.** JUR to appeal.

pourvoirie [purvwari] *nf* Can outfitter *(for hunting and fishing).*

pourvoyeur, euse [purvwajœr, øz] *nm, f* supplier.

pourvu, e [purvy] *pp* ⊏> pourvoir.

➤ **pourvu que** *(+ subjonctif) loc conj* - **1.** [condition] providing, provided (that) - **2.** [souhait] let's hope (that).

pousse [pus] *nf* - **1.** [croissance] growth - **2.** [bourgeon] shoot ; **~s de bambou** bamboo shoots.

poussé, e [puse] *adj* - **1.** [travail] meticulous - **2.** [moteur] souped-up.

pousse-café [puskafe] *nm inv fam* liqueur.

poussée [puse] *nf* - **1.** [pression] pressure - **2.** [coup] push - **3.** [de fièvre, inflation] rise ; **~ démographique** population increase.

pousse-pousse [puspus] *nm inv* - **1.** [voiture] rickshaw - **2.** *Helv* [poussette] pushchair.

pousser [3] [puse] <> *vt* - **1.** [personne, objet] to push ; **~ qqn à bout** *fig* to push sb to breaking point - **2.** [moteur, voiture] to drive hard - **3.** [recherches, études] to carry on, to continue

- **4.** [cri, soupir] to give - **5.** [inciter] : **~ qqn à faire qqch** to urge sb to do sthg - **6.** [au crime, au suicide] : **~ qqn à** to drive sb to <> *vi* - **1.** [exercer une pression] to push - **2.** [croître] to grow - **3.** [poursuivre son chemin] to push on - **4.** *fam* [exagérer] to overdo it.

➤ **se pousser** *vp* to move up.

poussette [puset] *nf* pushchair *Br*, stroller *Am*.

poussière [pusjer] *nf* - **1.** [gén] dust ; **mordre la ~** to bite the dust ; **réduire en ~** to reduce to dust ; **et des ~s** *fam* and a bit - **2.** *littéraire* [de mort] ashes *(pl)*.

poussiéreux, euse [pusjerø, øz] *adj* - **1.** [meuble] dusty - **2.** [teint] dull - **3.** *fig* [organisation] old-fashioned.

poussif, ive [pusif, iv] *adj fam* wheezy.

poussin [pusɛ̃] *nm* - **1.** ZOOL chick - **2.** SPORT under-11.

poussoir [puswar] *nm* push button.

poutre [putr] *nf* beam.

poutrelle [putrel] *nf* girder.

pouvoir [58] [puvwar] <> *nm* - **1.** [gén] power ; **~ d'achat** purchasing power ; **les ~s publics** the authorities - **2.** JUR proxy, power of attorney <> *vt* - **1.** [avoir la possibilité de, parvenir à] : **~ faire qqch** to be able to do sthg ; **je ne peux pas venir ce soir** I can't come tonight ; **pouvez-vous ...?** can you ...?, could you ...? ; **je n'en peux plus** [exaspéré] I'm at the end of my tether ; [fatigué] I'm exhausted ; **je/tu n'y peux rien** there's nothing I/you can do about it ; **tu aurais pu me le dire!** you might have *ou* could have told me! ; **il est on ne peut plus bête/gentil** nobody could be stupider/kinder - **2.** [avoir la permission de] : **je peux prendre la voiture?** can I borrow the car? ; **aucun élève ne peut partir** no pupil may leave - **3.** [indiquant l'éventualité] : **il peut pleuvoir** it may rain ; **vous pourriez rater votre train** you could *ou* might miss your train.

➤ **se pouvoir** *v impers* : **il se peut que je me trompe** I may be mistaken ; **cela se peut/pourrait bien** that's quite possible.

pp *(abr de* pages*)* pp.

p.p. *(abr de* par procuration*)* pp.

PQ <> *nm (abr de* papier-cul*) fam* bog paper <> - **1.** *(abr de* province de Québec*)* PQ - **2.** *(abr de* premier quartier [de lune]*)* first quarter.

Pr *(abr de* professeur*)* Prof.

PR <> *nm (abr de* Parti républicain*) French political party* <> *nf (abr de* poste restante*)* PR.

pragmatique [pragmatik] *adj* pragmatic.

pragois, e, praguois, e [pragwa, az] *adj* of/from Prague.

➤ **Pragois, e, Praguois, e** *nm, f* native *ou* inhabitant of Prague.

Prague [prag] *n* Prague.

praguois, e = pragois.

praire [prɛr] *nf* clam.

prairie [preri] *nf* meadow ; [aux États-Unis] prairie.

praline [pralin] *nf* - **1.** [amande] sugared almond - **2.** *Belg* [chocolat] chocolate.

praliné [praline] *nm* almond-flavoured sponge covered with praline.

praticable [pratikabl] ◇ *adj* - **1.** [route] passable - **2.** [plan] feasible, practicable ◇ *nm* [CIN & THÉÂTRE - plate-forme] (tray) dolly ; [- élément de décor] prop.

praticien, enne [pratisjɛ̃, ɛn] *nm, f* practitioner ; *MÉD* medical practitioner.

pratiquant, e [pratikɑ̃, ɑ̃t] ◇ *adj* practising ◇ *nm, f* practising Christian/Jew/Muslim etc.

pratique [pratik] ◇ *nf* - **1.** [expérience] practical experience - **2.** [usage] practice ; **mettre qqch en ~** to put sthg into practice ◇ *adj* practical ; [gadget, outil] handy.

pratiquement [pratikmɑ̃] *adv* - **1.** [en fait] in practice - **2.** [quasiment] practically.

pratiquer [3] [pratike] ◇ *vt* - **1.** [métier] to practise *Br*, to practice *Am* ; [sport] to do ; [jeu de ballon] to play ; [méthode] to apply ; **~ la pêche/le football** to be a keen fisherman/football player - **2.** [ouverture] to make ◇ *vi* *RELIG* to be a practising Christian/Jew/Muslim etc.

➤ **se pratiquer** *vp* - **1.** *SPORT* to be played - **2.** [politique, tradition] to be the practice ; [prix] to apply.

pré [pre] *nm* meadow.

préado [preado] *nmf fam* preadolescent.

préalable [prealabl] ◇ *adj* prior, previous ; **~ à** prior to, preceding ; **sans avis ~** without prior warning *ou* notice ◇ *nm* precondition.

➤ **au préalable** *loc adv* first, beforehand.

préalablement [prealabləmɑ̃] *adv* first, beforehand ; **~ à** prior to.

préambule [preɑ̃byl] *nm* - **1.** [introduction, propos] preamble ; **sans ~** immediately - **2.** [prélude] : **~ de** prelude to.

préau, x [preo] *nm* - **1.** [d'école] (covered) play area - **2.** [de prison] (covered) exercise yard.

préavis [preavi] *nm inv* advance notice *ou* warning.

précaire [prekɛr] *adj* [incertain] precarious.

précancéreux, euse [prekɑ̃serø, øz] *adj* precancerous.

précarité [prekarite] *nf* [instabilité] precariousness.

précaution [prekosjɔ̃] *nf* - **1.** [prévoyance] precaution ; **par ~** as a precaution ; **prendre des ~s** to take precautions - **2.** [prudence] caution.

précautionneux, euse [prekosjɔnø, øz] *adj* cautious.

précédemment [presedamɑ̃] *adv* previously, before.

précédent, e [presedɑ̃, ɑ̃t] *adj* previous.

➤ **précédent** *nm* precedent ; **sans ~** unprecedented.

précéder [18] [presede] *vt* - **1.** [dans le temps - gén] to precede ; [- suj : personne] to arrive before - **2.** [marcher devant] to go in front of - **3.** *fig* [devancer] to get ahead of.

précepte [presept] *nm* precept.

précepteur, trice [preseptœr, tris] *nm, f* (private) tutor.

préchauffer [3] [preʃofe] *vt* to preheat.

prêche [prɛʃ] *nm* sermon ; *fig* lecture.

prêcher [4] [preʃe] *vt* & *vi* to preach.

prêcheur, euse [preʃœr, øz] ◇ *adj* preaching, moralizing ◇ *nm, f* - **1.** *RELIG* preacher - **2.** *fig* [moralisateur] moralizer.

prêchi-prêcha [preʃipreʃa] *nm inv* preachifying.

précieusement [presjøzmɑ̃] *adv* preciously.

précieux, euse [presjø, øz] *adj* - **1.** [pierre, métal] precious ; [objet] valuable ; [collaborateur] invaluable, valued - **2.** *péj* [style] precious, affected.

préciosité [presjozite] *nf péj* [affectation] preciosity, affectation.

précipice [presipis] *nm* precipice.

précipitamment [presipitamɑ̃] *adv* hastily.

précipitation [presipitasjɔ̃] *nf* - **1.** [hâte] haste - **2.** *CHIM* precipitation.

➤ **précipitations** *nfpl* *MÉTÉOR* precipitation (U).

précipiter [3] [presipite] *vt* - **1.** [objet, personne] to throw, to hurl ; **~ qqn/qqch du haut de** to throw sb/sthg off, to hurl sb/sthg off - **2.** [départ] to hasten.

➤ **se précipiter** *vp* - **1.** [se jeter] to throw o.s., to hurl o.s. - **2.** [s'élancer] : **se ~ (vers qqn)** to rush *ou* hurry (towards sb) - **3.** [s'accélérer - gén] to speed up ; [- choses, événements] to move faster.

précis, e [presi, iz] *adj* - **1.** [exact] precise, accurate - **2.** [fixé] definite, precise.
➤ **précis** *nm* handbook.

précisément [presizemã] *adv* precisely, exactly.

préciser [3] [presize] *vt* - **1.** [heure, lieu] to specify - **2.** [pensée] to clarify.
➤ **se préciser** *vp* to become clear.

précision [presizjɔ̃] *nf* - **1.** [de style, d'explication] precision - **2.** [détail] detail ; **apporter** *ou* **donner des ~s** to give further information.

précité, e [presite] *adj* above-mentioned.

précoce [prekɔs] *adj* - **1.** [plante, fruit] early - **2.** [enfant] precocious.

précocité [prekɔsite] *nf* - **1.** [de plante, de saison] earliness - **2.** [d'enfant] precociousness.

préconçu, e [prekɔ̃sy] *adj* preconceived.

préconiser [3] [prekɔnize] *vt* to recommend ; **~ de faire qqch** to recommend doing sthg ; **~ que** *(+ subjonctif)* to recommend that.

précuit, e [prekɥi, it] *adj* precooked.

précurseur [prekyrsœr] ◇ *nm* precursor, forerunner ◇ *adj* precursory.

prédateur, trice [predatœr, tris] *adj* predatory.
➤ **prédateur** *nm* predator.

prédécesseur [predesesœr] *nm* predecessor.

prédécoupé, e [predekupe] *adj* pre-cut.

prédestination [predɛstinasjɔ̃] *nf* predestination.

prédestiner [3] [predɛstine] *vt* to predestine ; **être prédestiné à qqch/à faire qqch** to be predestined for sthg/to do sthg.

prédéterminer [3] [predetɛrmine] *vt* to predetermine.

prédicat [predika] *nm* predicate.

prédicateur, trice [predikatœr, tris] *nm, f* preacher.

prédication [predikasjɔ̃] *nf* preaching ; [discours] sermon.

prédiction [prediksjɔ̃] *nf* prediction.

prédilection [predilɛksjɔ̃] *nf* partiality, ; **avoir une ~ pour** to have a partiality *ou* liking for ; **de ~** favourite *(avant n)* Br, favorite *(avant n)* Am.

prédire [103] [predir] *vt* to predict.

prédisposer [3] [predispoze] *vt* : **~ qqn à qqch** to predispose sb to sthg.

prédisposition [predispozisjɔ̃] *nf* : **~ à** prédisposition to *ou* towards.

prédit, e [predi, it] *pp* ▷ **prédire**.

prédominant, e [predɔminɑ̃, ɑ̃t] *adj* predominant.

prédominer [3] [predɔmine] *vt* to predominate.

préélectoral, e, aux [preelɛktɔral, o] *adj* pre-election *(avant n)*.

préemballé, e [preɑ̃bale] *adj* prepacked.

prééminence [preeminɑ̃s] *nf* preeminence.

préemption [preɑ̃psjɔ̃] *nf* preemption.

préétabli, e [preetabli] *adj* pre-established.

préexistant, e [preɛgzistɑ̃, ɑ̃t] *adj* preexisting.

préfabriqué, e [prefabrike] *adj* - **1.** [maison] prefabricated - **2.** [accusation, sourire] false.
➤ **préfabriqué** *nm* prefabricated material.

préface [prefas] *nf* preface.

préfectoral, e, aux [prefɛktɔral, o] *adj* prefectorial.

préfecture [prefɛktyr] *nf* prefecture.

préférable [preferabl] *adj* preferable.

préféré, e [prefere] *adj* & *nm, f* favourite Br, favorite Am.

préférence [preferɑ̃s] *nf* preference ; **de ~** preferably.

préférentiel, elle [preferɑ̃sjɛl] *adj* preferential.

préférer [18] [prefere] *vt* : **~ qqn/qqch (à)** to prefer sb/sthg (to) ; **~ faire qqch** to prefer to do sthg ; **je préfère rentrer** I would rather go home, I would prefer to go home ; **je préfère ça!** I like that better!, I prefer that!

préfet [prefɛ] *nm* prefect.

préfigurer [3] [prefigyre] *vt* to prefigure.

préfixe [prefiks] *nm* prefix.

préhistoire [preistwar] *nf* prehistory.

préhistorique [preistɔrik] *adj* prehistoric.

préinscription [preɛ̃skripsjɔ̃] *nf* preregistration.

préjudice [preʒydis] *nm* harm *(U)*, detriment *(U)* ; **porter ~ à qqn** to harm sb.

préjudiciable [preʒydisjabl] *adj* : **~ (à)** harmful (to), detrimental (to).

préjugé [preʒyʒe] *nm* : **~ (contre)** prejudice (against).

prélasser [3] [prelase] ➤ **se prélasser** *vp* to lounge.

prélat [prela] *nm* prelate.

prélavage [prelavaʒ] *nm* pre-wash.

prélèvement [prelɛvmã] *nm* - **1.** MÉD removal ; [de sang] sample - **2.** FIN deduction ; **~ automatique** direct debit ; **~ mensuel**

monthly standing order ; ~s obligatoires tax and social security contributions.

prélever [19] [prelve] vt - **1.** FIN : ~ de l'argent (sur) to deduct money (from) - **2.** MÉD to remove ; ~ du sang to take a blood sample.

préliminaire [preliminɛr] adj preliminary.
◆ **préliminaires** nmpl - **1.** [de paix] preliminary talks - **2.** [de discours] preliminaries.

prélude [prelyd] nm : ~ (à) prelude (to).

préluder [3] [prelyde] vi - **1.** [marquer le début] : ~ à to be a prelude to - **2.** MUS to warm up.

prématuré, e [prematyre] ◇ adj premature ◇ nm, f premature baby.

prématurément [prematyremɑ̃] adv prematurely.

préméditation [premeditasjɔ̃] nf premeditation ; avec ~ [meurtre] premeditated ; [agir] with premeditation.

préméditer [3] [premedite] vt to premeditate ; ~ de faire qqch to plan to do sthg.

prémices [premis] nfpl sout beginnings.

premier, ère [prəmje, ɛr] ◇ adj - **1.** [gén] first ; [étage] first Br, second Am - **2.** [qualité] top - **3.** [état] original ◇ nm, f first ; être/sortir ~ to be/come first, to be/come top ; jeune ~ CIN leading man.
◆ **premier** nm [étage] first floor Br, second floor Am.
◆ **première** nf - **1.** CIN première ; THÉÂTRE première, first night - **2.** [exploit] first - **3.** [première classe] first class - **4.** SCOL ≃ lower sixth year OU form Br, ≃ eleventh grade Am - **5.** AUTOM first (gear).
◆ **premier de l'an** nm : le ~ de l'an New Year's Day.
◆ **en premier** loc adv first, firstly.

premièrement [prəmjɛrmɑ̃] adv first, firstly.

premier-né, première-née [prəmjene, prəmjɛrne] (mpl **premiers-nés**, fpl **premières-nées**) nm, f first-born (child).

prémisse [premis] nf premise.

prémolaire [premɔlɛr] nf premolar.

prémonition [premɔnisjɔ̃] nf premonition.

prémonitoire [premɔnitwar] adj premonitory.

prémunir [32] [premynir] vt : ~ qqn (contre) to protect sb (against).
◆ **se prémunir** vp to protect o.s. ; se ~ contre qqch to guard against sthg.

prenais, prenions etc ⊳ prendre.

prenant, e [prənɑ̃, ɑ̃t] ◇ vb ⊳ prendre ◇ adj - **1.** [film, histoire] absorbing - **2.** JUR : partie ~e payee.

prénatal, e [prenatal] (pl **prénatals** OU pré-

nataux [prenato]) adj antenatal ; [allocation] maternity (avant n).

prendre [79] [prɑ̃dr] ◇ vt - **1.** [gén] to take - **2.** [enlever] to take (away) ; ~ qqch à qqn to take sthg from sb - **3.** [aller chercher - objet] to get, to fetch ; [- personne] to pick up - **4.** [repas, boisson] to have ; vous prendrez quelque chose? would you like something to eat/ drink? - **5.** [voleur] to catch ; se faire ~ to get caught - **6.** [responsabilité] to take (on) ; ~ sur soi de faire qqch to take it upon o.s. to do sthg - **7.** [aborder - personne] to handle ; [- problème] to tackle ; ~ qqn par qqch to win sb over by sthg ; ~ qqn par surprise to take sb by surprise ; à tout ~ on the whole, all things considered - **8.** [réserver] to book ; [louer] to rent, to take ; [acheter] to buy - **9.** [poids] to gain, to put on - **10.** [embaucher] to take on ◇ vi - **1.** [ciment, sauce] to set - **2.** [plante, greffe] to take ; [mode] to catch on - **3.** [feu] to catch - **4.** [se diriger] : ~ à droite to turn right.
◆ **se prendre** vp - **1.** [vêtement] : se ~ à to catch on - **2.** [se considérer] : pour qui se prend-il? who does he think he is? - **3.** loc : s'en ~ à qqn [physiquement] to set about sb ; [verbalement] to take it out on sb ; je sais comment m'y ~ I know how to do it OU go about it.

preneur, euse [prənœr, øz] nm, f [locataire] lessee ; [acheteur] purchaser.

prenne, prennes etc ⊳ prendre.

prénom [prenɔ̃] nm first name.

prénommer [3] [prenɔme] vt to name, to call.
◆ **se prénommer** vp to be called.

prénuptial, e, aux [prenypsjal, o] adj premarital.

préoccupant, e [preɔkypɑ̃, ɑ̃t] adj preoccupying.

préoccupation [preɔkypasjɔ̃] nf preoccupation.

préoccupé, e [preɔkype] adj preoccupied.

préoccuper [3] [preɔkype] vt to preoccupy.
◆ **se préoccuper** vp : se ~ de qqch to be worried about sthg.

préparateur, trice [preparatœr, tris] nm, f lab OU laboratory assistant ; ~ en pharmacie chemist's assistant Br, druggist's assistant Am.

préparatifs [preparatif] nmpl preparations.

préparation [preparasjɔ̃] nf preparation.

préparatoire [preparatwar] adj preparatory.

préparer [3] [prepare] vt - **1.** [gén] to prepare ; [plat, repas] to cook, to prepare ; ~ qqn à qqch to prepare sb for sthg - **2.** [réserver] : ~ qqch à qqn to have sthg in store for sb - **3.** [congrès] to organize.

se préparer *vp* - **1.** [personne] : **se ~ à qqch/à faire qqch** to prepare for sthg/to do sthg - **2.** [tempête] to be brewing.

prépondérance [prepɔ̃derɑ̃s] *nf* : ~ **(sur)** dominance (over), supremacy (over).

prépondérant, e [prepɔ̃derɑ̃, ɑ̃t] *adj* dominating.

préposé, e [prepoze] *nm, f* (minor) official ; [de vestiaire] attendant ; [facteur] postman (*f·* postwoman) *Br*, mailman (*f* mailwoman) *Am* ; ~ à qqch person in charge of sthg.

préposer [3] [prepoze] *vt* to put in charge ; **être préposé à qqch/à faire qqch** to be (put) in charge of sthg/of doing sthg.

préposition [prepozisjɔ̃] *nf* preposition.

prépuce [prepys] *nm* foreskin.

préréglé, e [preregle] *adj* preset, preprogrammed.

préretraite [prerətrɛt] *nf* early retirement ; [allocation] early retirement pension.

prérogative [prerɔgativ] *nf* prerogative.

près [prɛ] *adv* near, close.

de près *loc adv* closely ; **regarder qqch de ~** to watch sthg closely ; **de plus/très ~** more/ very closely.

près de *loc prép* - **1.** [dans l'espace] near, close to - **2.** [dans le temps] close to ; **il est ~ de partir** he's about to leave - **3.** [presque] nearly, almost.

à peu près *loc adv* more or less, just about ; **il est à peu ~ cinq heures** it's about five o'clock.

à peu de chose(s) près *loc adv* more or less, approximately.

à ceci près que, à cela près que *loc conj* except that, apart from the fact that.

à ... près *loc adv* : **à dix centimètres ~** to within ten centimetres ; **il n'en est pas à un ou deux jours ~** a day or two more or less won't make any difference.

présage [prezaʒ] *nm* omen.

présager [17] [prezaʒe] *vt* - **1.** [annoncer] to portend - **2.** [prévoir] to predict ; **laisser ~ de qqch** to hint at sthg.

pré-salé [presale] (*pl* **prés-salés**) *nm* lamb *reared on salt marshes*.

presbyte [prɛsbit] <> *nmf* longsighted person *Br*, farsighted person *Am* <> *adj* longsighted *Br*, farsighted *Am*.

presbytère [prɛsbitɛr] *nm* presbytery.

presbytérien, enne [prɛsbiterjɛ̃, ɛn] *nm, f & adj* Presbyterian.

presbytie [prɛsbisi] *nf* longsightedness *Br*, farsightedness *Am*.

prescience [presjɑ̃s] *nf littéraire* foresight.

préscolaire [preskɔlɛr] *adj* preschool (*avant n*).

prescription [prɛskripsjɔ̃] *nf* - **1.** MÉD prescription - **2.** JUR limitation.

prescrire [99] [prɛskrir] *vt* - **1.** [mesures, conditions] to lay down, to stipulate - **2.** MÉD to prescribe.

se prescrire *vp* MÉD to be prescribed.

prescrit, e [prɛskri, it] *pp* ⊳ **prescrire**.

prescrivais, prescrivions *etc* ⊳ **prescrire**.

préséance [preseɑ̃s] *nf* precedence.

présélection [preselɛksjɔ̃] *nf* preselection ; [pour · concours] making a list of finalists, short-listing *Br*.

présélectionner [3] [preselɛksjɔne] *vt* to preselect ; [candidats] to put on a list of finalists, to short-list *Br*.

présence [prezɑ̃s] *nf* - **1.** [gén] presence ; **en ~ face to face** ; **honorer qqn de sa ~** to honour sb with one's presence ; **en ~ de** in the presence of ; **en sa** *etc* ~ in his/her *etc* presence - **2.** [compagnie] company (*U*) - **3.** [assiduité] attendance ; **feuille de ~** attendance sheet.

présence d'esprit *nf* presence of mind.

présent, e [prezɑ̃, ɑ̃t] *adj* - **1.** [gén] present ; **le ~ ouvrage** this work ; **la ~e loi** this law ; **avoir qqch ~ à l'esprit** to remember sthg - **2.** [actif] attentive, involved.

présent *nm* - **1.** [gén] present ; **faire ~ à qqn de qqch** *sout* to make sb a present of sthg ; **à ~** at present ; **à ~ que** now that ; **jusqu'à ~** up to now, so far ; **dès à ~** right away - **2.** GRAM : **le ~** the present tense.

présente *nf* : **je vous informe par la ~e que ...** I hereby inform you that ...

présentable [prezɑ̃tabl] *adj* - **1.** [d'aspect] presentable - **2.** [d'attitude] : **tu n'es pas ~** I can't take you anywhere.

présentateur, trice [prezɑ̃tatœr, tris] *nm, f* presenter.

présentation [prezɑ̃tasjɔ̃] *nf* - **1.** [de personne] : **faire les ~s** to make the introductions - **2.** [aspect extérieur] appearance ; **avoir une bonne/mauvaise ~** to be of a pleasing/ disagreeable appearance - **3.** [de papiers, de produit, de film] presentation ; **sur ~ de** on presentation of ; ~ **de la marque** brand presentation - **4.** [de magazine] layout.

présentement [prezɑ̃tmɑ̃] *adv* at the moment, at present.

présenter [3] [prezɑ̃te] <> *vt* - **1.** [gén] to

present ; [projet] to present, to submit - **2.** [invité] to introduce - **3.** [condoléances, félicitations, avantages] to offer ; [hommages] to pay ; **~ qqch à qqn** to offer sb sthg <> *vi fam* : **~ bien/mal** to make a good/bad impression.

se présenter *vp* - **1.** [se faire connaître] : **se ~ (à)** to introduce o.s. (to) - **2.** [être candidat] : **se ~ à** [élection] to stand in *Br*, to run in *Am* ; [examen] to sit *Br*, to take - **3.** [paraître] to appear - **4.** [occasion, situation] to arise, to present itself - **5.** [affaire, contrat] : **se ~ bien/mal** to look good/bad.

présentoir [prezɑ̃twar] *nm* display stand.

préservatif [prezɛrvatif] *nm* condom.

préservation [prezɛrvasjɔ̃] *nf* preservation.

préserver [3] [prezɛrve] *vt* to preserve.

se préserver *vp* : **se ~ de** to protect o.s. from.

présidence [prezidɑ̃s] *nf* - **1.** [de groupe] chairmanship - **2.** [d'État] presidency - **3.** [lieu] presidential residence *ou* palace.

président, e [prezidɑ̃, ɑ̃t] *nm, f* - **1.** [d'assemblée] chairman (*f* chairwoman) ; **~ du conseil d'administration** chairman of the board - **2.** [d'État] president ; **Monsieur/Madame le Président** Mr/Madam President ; **~ de la République** President (of the Republic) of France - **3.** JUR [de tribunal] presiding judge ; [de jury] foreman (*f* forewoman).

présidente *nf vieilli* president's wife.

président-directeur général *nm* (chairman and) managing director.

présidentiel, elle [prezidɑ̃sjɛl] *adj* presidential ; **régime ~** presidential system.

présider [3] [prezide] <> *vt* - **1.** [réunion] to chair - **2.** [banquet, dîner] to preside over <> *vi* : **~ à** to be in charge of ; *fig* to govern, to preside at.

présomptif, ive [prezɔ̃ptif, iv] *adj* : **héritier ~** heir apparent.

présomption [prezɔ̃psjɔ̃] *nf* - **1.** [hypothèse] presumption - **2.** JUR presumption - **3.** *littéraire* [prétention] presumptuousness.

présomptueux, euse [prezɔ̃ptɥø, øz] <> *adj* presumptuous <> *nm, f littéraire* presumptuous person.

presque [prɛsk] *adv* almost, nearly ; **~ rien** next to nothing, scarcely anything ; **~ jamais** hardly ever.

presqu'île [prɛskil] *nf* peninsula.

pressant, e [prɛsɑ̃, ɑ̃t] *adj* pressing.

press-book [prɛsbuk] (*pl* **press-books**) *nm* portfolio.

presse [prɛs] *nf* press ; **avoir bonne/mauvaise ~** to have a good/bad press.

pressé, e [prese] *adj* - **1.** [travail] urgent ; **aller au plus ~** to do first things first - **2.** [personne] : **être ~** to be in a hurry - **3.** [citron, orange] freshly squeezed.

presse-citron [prɛssitrɔ̃] *nm inv* lemon squeezer.

pressentiment [presɑ̃timɑ̃] *nm* premonition.

pressentir [37] [presɑ̃tir] *vt* - **1.** [événement] to have a premonition of - **2.** *sout* [personne] to sound out.

presse-papiers [prɛspapje] *nm inv* paperweight.

presse-purée [prɛspyre] *nm inv* potato masher.

presser [4] [prese] *vt* - **1.** [écraser - olives] to press ; [- citron, orange] to squeeze - **2.** [disque] to press - **3.** [dans ses bras] to squeeze - **4.** [bouton] to press, to push - **5.** *sout* [harceler] : **~ qqn de faire qqch** to press sb to do sthg ; **~ qqn de questions** to bombard sb with questions - **6.** [accélérer] to speed up ; **~ le pas** to speed up, to walk faster.

se presser *vp* - **1.** [se dépêcher] to hurry (up) ; **sans se ~** without hurrying *ou* rushing - **2.** [s'agglutiner] : **se ~ (autour de)** to crowd (around) - **3.** [se serrer] to huddle.

pressing [presiŋ] *nm* steam pressing ; [établissement] dry cleaner's.

pression [presjɔ̃] *nf* - **1.** [gén] pressure ; **exercer une ~ sur qqch** to exert pressure on sthg ; **exercer une ~ sur qqn, faire ~ sur qqn** to put pressure on sb ; **sous ~** [liquide] *fig* under pressure ; [cabine] pressurized ; **~ artérielle** blood pressure ; **~ atmosphérique** atmospheric pressure - **2.** [sur vêtement] press stud *Br*, popper *Br*, snap fastener *Am* - **3.** [bière] draught *Br ou* draft *Am* beer.

pressoir [preswar] *nm* - **1.** [machine] press - **2.** [lieu] press house.

pressurer [3] [presyre] *vt* - **1.** [objet] to press, to squeeze - **2.** *fig* [contribuable] to squeeze.

pressurisation [presyrizasjɔ̃] *nf* pressurization.

pressuriser [3] [presyrize] *vt* to pressurize.

prestance [prɛstɑ̃s] *nf* bearing ; **avoir de la ~** to have presence.

prestataire [prɛstatɛr] *nmf* - **1.** [bénéficiaire] person in receipt of benefit, claimant - **2.** [fournisseur] provider ; **~ de service** service provider.

prestation [prɛstasjɔ̃] *nf* - **1.** [allocation] benefit ; **~ en nature** payment in kind ; **~s familia-**

les ≈ family allowance **- 2.** [de comédien] performance **- 3.** [de serment] taking.

preste [prɛst] *adj littéraire* nimble.

prestement [prɛstəmɑ̃] *adv* nimbly.

prestidigitateur, trice [prɛstidiʒitatœr, tris] *nm, f* conjurer.

prestidigitation [prɛstidiʒitasjɔ̃] *nf* conjuring.

prestige [prɛstiʒ] *nm* prestige.

prestigieux, euse [prɛstiʒjø, øz] *adj* **- 1.** [magnifique] splendid **- 2.** [réputé] prestigious.

présumé, e [prezyme] *adj* presumed.

présumer [3] [prezyme] ⬦ *vt* to presume, to assume ; **~ que** to presume (that), to assume (that) ; **être présumé coupable/innocent** to be presumed guilty/innocent ⬦ *vi* : **~ de qqch** to overestimate sthg.

présupposé [presypoze] *nm* presupposition.

présupposer [3] [presypoze] *vt* to presuppose.

présure [prezyr] *nf* rennet.

prêt, e [prɛ, prɛt] *adj* ready ; **~ à qqch/à faire qqch** ready for sthg/to do sthg ; **~ à tout** ready for anything ; **~s? partez!** *SPORT* get set, go!, ready, steady, go !
➡ **prêt** *nm* [action] lending *(U)* ; [somme] loan.

prêt-à-porter [prɛtaportə] *(pl* **prêts-à-porter)** *nm* ready-to-wear clothing *(U).*

prétendant [pretɑ̃dɑ̃] *nm* **- 1.** [au trône] pretender **- 2.** [amoureux] suitor.

prétendre [73] [pretɑ̃dr] ⬦ *vt* **- 1.** [affecter] : **~ faire qqch** to claim to do sthg **- 2.** [affirmer] : **~ que** to claim (that), to maintain (that) **- 3.** *littéraire* [exiger] : **~ faire qqch** to intend to do sthg ⬦ *vi* [aspirer] : **~ à qqch** to aspire to sthg.
➡ **se prétendre** *vp* : **se ~ acteur/écrivain** to claim to be an actor/an author.

prétendu, e [pretɑ̃dy] ⬦ *pp* ➭ **prétendre** ⬦ *adj (avant n)* so-called.

prétendument [pretɑ̃dymɑ̃] *adv* supposedly.

prête-nom [prɛtnɔ̃] *(pl* **prête-noms)** *nm* front man.

prétentieux, euse [pretɑ̃sjø, øz] ⬦ *adj* pretentious ⬦ *nm, f* pretentious person.

prétention [pretɑ̃sjɔ̃] *nf* **- 1.** [suffisance] pretentiousness **- 2.** [ambition] pretension, ambition ; **avoir la ~ de faire qqch** to claim *ou* pretend to do sthg.

prêter [4] [prete] ⬦ *vt* **- 1.** [fournir] : **~ qqch (à qqn)** [objet, argent] to lend (sb) sthg ; *fig* [concours, appui] to lend (sb) sthg, to give (sb) sthg

- 2. [attribuer] : **~ qqch à qqn** to attribute sthg to sb ⬦ *vi* : **~ à** to lead to, to generate.
➡ **se prêter** *vp* : **se ~ à** [participer à] to go along with ; [convenir à] to fit, to suit.

prétérit [preterit] *nm* preterite.

prêteur, euse [pretœr, øz] ⬦ *adj* generous ⬦ *nm, f* : **~ sur gages** pawnbroker.

prétexte [pretɛkst] *nm* pretext, excuse ; **sous ~ de faire qqch/que** on the pretext of doing sthg/that, under the pretext of doing sthg/that ; **sous aucun ~** on no account.

prétexter [4] [pretɛkste] *vt* to give as an excuse.

Pretoria [pretɔrja] *n* Pretoria.

prêtre [prɛtr] *nm* priest.

prêtresse [prɛtrɛs] *nf* priestess.

preuve [prœv] *nf* **- 1.** [gén] proof **- 2.** *JUR* evidence **- 3.** [témoignage] sign, token ; **faire ~ de qqch** to show sthg ; **faire ses ~s** to prove o.s./itself.

preux [prø] ⬦ *nm* knight valiant ⬦ *adj m* valiant.

prévaloir [61] [prevalwar] *vi* [dominer] : **~ (sur)** to prevail (over).
➡ **se prévaloir** *vp* : **se ~ de** to boast about.

prévalu [prevaly] *pp inv* ➭ **prévaloir.**

prévarication [prevarikasjɔ̃] *nf sout* breach of trust.

prévaut ➭ **prévaloir.**

prévenance [prevnɑ̃s] *nf* **- 1.** [attitude] thoughtfulness, consideration **- 2.** [action] considerate *ou* thoughtful act.

prévenant, e [prevnɑ̃, ɑ̃t] *adj* considerate, attentive.

prévenir [40] [prevnir] *vt* **- 1.** [employé, élève] : **~ qqn (de)** to warn sb (about) **- 2.** [police] to inform **- 3.** [désirs] to anticipate **- 4.** [maladie] to prevent **- 5.** *littéraire* [prédisposer] : **~ qqn contre qqn** to prejudice sb against sb.

préventif, ive [prevɑ̃tif, iv] *adj* **- 1.** [mesure, médecine] preventive **- 2.** *JUR* : **être en détention préventive** to be on remand.

prévention [prevɑ̃sjɔ̃] *nf* **- 1.** [protection] : **~ (contre)** prevention (of) ; **~ routière** road safety (measures) **- 2.** *JUR* remand.

prévenu, e [prevny] ⬦ *pp* ➭ **prévenir** ⬦ *nm, f* accused, defendant.

préviendrai, préviendras *etc* ➭ **prévenir.**

prévisible [previzibl] *adj* foreseeable.

prévision [previzjɔ̃] *nf* forecast, prediction ; [de coûts] estimate ; *ÉCON* forecast ; **les ~s météorologiques** the weather forecast.

➡ **en prévision de** *loc prép* in anticipation of.

prévisionnel, elle [previzjɔnɛl] *adj* anticipatory ; **budget ~** budget estimate.

prévoir [63] [prevwar] *vt* - **1.** [s'attendre à] to expect - **2.** [prédire] to predict - **3.** [anticiper] to foresee, to anticipate - **4.** [programmer] to plan ; **n'être pas prévu** to be unforeseen ; **comme prévu** as planned, according to plan.

prévoyais, prévoyions *etc* ▷ **prévoir**.

prévoyance [prevwajɑ̃s] *nf* [de personne] foresight ; *voir aussi* **caisse**.

prévoyant, e [prevwajɑ̃, ɑ̃t] *adj* provident.

prévu, e [prevy] *pp* ▷ **prévoir**.

prie-Dieu [pridjø] *nm inv* prie-dieu.

prier [10] [prije] ◇ *vt* - **1.** RELIG to pray to - **2.** [implorer] to beg ; **(ne pas) se faire ~ (pour faire qqch)** (not) to need to be persuaded (to do sthg) ; **je vous en prie** [de grâce] please, I beg you ; [de rien] don't mention it, not at all - **3.** *sout* [demander] : **~ qqn de faire qqch** to request sb to do sthg ; **~ instamment qqn de faire qqch** to insist that sb does sthg ; **vous êtes priés de** you are requested to - **4.** *littéraire* [convier] to invite ◇ *vi* RELIG to pray.

prière [prijɛr] *nf* - **1.** [RELIG - recueillement] prayer *(U)*, praying *(U)* ; [- formule] prayer ; [- office] prayers *(pl)* - **2.** *littéraire* [demande] entreaty ; **~ de frapper avant d'entrer** please knock before entering.

prieuré [prijœre] *nm* priory.

primaire [primɛr] *adj* - **1.** [premier] : **couleur ~** primary colour *Br ou* color *Am* ; **élection ~** primary (election) ; **ère ~** Palaeozoic era ; **études ~s** primary education *(U)* - **2.** *péj* [primitif] limited.

primate [primat] *nm* - **1.** ZOOL primate - **2.** *fam* [brute] gorilla.

primauté [primote] *nf* primacy.

prime [prim] ◇ *nf* - **1.** [d'employé] bonus ; **~ d'intéressement** profit-related bonus ; **~ d'objectif** incentive bonus - **2.** [allocation - de déménagement, de transport] allowance ; [- à l'exportation] incentive - **3.** [d'assurance] premium - **4.** [cadeau] free gift ; **en ~** as a free gift ; *fig* in addition ◇ *adj* - **1.** [premier] : **de ~ abord** at first glance ; **de ~ jeunesse** in the first flush of youth - **2.** MATHS prime.

primer [3] [prime] ◇ *vi* to take precedence, to come first ◇ *vt* - **1.** [être supérieur à] to take precedence over - **2.** [récompenser] to award a prize to ; **le film a été primé au festival** the film won an award at the festival.

primerose [primroz] *nf* hollyhock.

primesautier, ère [primsotje, ɛr] *adj* impulsive.

primeur [primœr] *nf* immediacy ; **avoir la ~ de qqch** to be the first to hear sthg.

➡ **primeurs** *nfpl* early produce *(U)*.

primevère [primvɛr] *nf* primrose.

primitif, ive [primitif, iv] ◇ *adj* - **1.** [gén] primitive - **2.** [aspect] original ◇ *nm, f* primitive.

primo [primo] *adv* firstly.

primordial, e, aux [primɔrdjal, o] *adj* essential.

prince [prɛ̃s] *nm* prince ; **~ consort** prince consort.

prince-de-Galles [prɛ̃sdəgal] *nm inv* & *adj inv* Prince of Wales check.

princesse [prɛ̃sɛs] *nf* princess.

princier, ère [prɛ̃sje, ɛr] *adj* princely.

principal, e, aux [prɛ̃sipal, o] ◇ *adj* - **1.** [gén] main, principal - **2.** GRAM main ◇ *nm, f* - **1.** [important] : **le ~** the main thing - **2.** SCOL headmaster (*f* headmistress) *Br*, principal *Am*.

principalement [prɛ̃sipalmɑ̃] *adv* mainly, principally.

principauté [prɛ̃sipote] *nf* principality.

principe [prɛ̃sip] *nm* principle ; **par ~** on principle.

➡ **en principe** *loc adv* theoretically, in principle.

printanier, ère [prɛ̃tanje, ɛr] *adj* - **1.** [temps] spring-like - **2.** *fig* [humeur] bright and cheerful.

printemps [prɛ̃tɑ̃] *nm* - **1.** [saison] spring - **2.** *fig* [de la vie] springtime - **3.** *fam* [année] : **avoir 20 ~** to be 20.

priori [prijɔri] ➡ **a priori** ◇ *loc adv* in principle ◇ *nm inv* initial reaction ◇ *adj inv* a priori.

prioritaire [prijɔritɛr] *adj* - **1.** [industrie, mesure] priority *(avant n)* - **2.** AUTOM with right of way.

priorité [prijɔrite] *nf* - **1.** [importance primordiale] priority ; **en ~** first - **2.** AUTOM right of way ; **~ à droite** give way to the right.

pris, e [pri, priz] ◇ *pp* ▷ **prendre** ◇ *adj* - **1.** [place] taken ; [personne] busy ; [mains] full - **2.** [nez] blocked ; [gorge] sore - **3.** [envahi] : **~ de** seized with.

➡ **prise** *nf* - **1.** [sur barre, sur branche] grip, hold ; **lâcher ~** to let go ; *fig* to give up ; **avoir ~ sur qqch** to have hold of sthg ; **avoir ~ sur qqn** *fig* to have a hold over sb ; **être aux ~es avec** *fig* to grapple with - **2.** [action de prendre - de ville] seizure, capture ; **~e en charge** [par Sécurité sociale] (guaranteed) reimbursement ; **~e**

d'otages hostage taking ; **~e de sang** blood test ; **~e de vue** shot ; **~ e de vue** *ou* **vues** [action] filming, shooting **- 3.** [à la pêche] haul **- 4.** *ÉLECTR* : **~e (de courant)** [mâle] plug ; [femelle] socket **- 5.** [de judo] hold ; **faire une ~e à qqn** *SPORT* to get sb in a hold **- 6.** *INFORM* outlet.

priser [3] [prize] *vt* **- 1.** *sout* [apprécier] to appreciate, to value **- 2.** [aspirer] : **~ du tabac** to take snuff.

prisme [prism] *nm* prism.

prison [prizɔ̃] *nf* **- 1.** [établissement] prison **- 2.** [réclusion] imprisonment.

prisonnier, ère [prizɔnje, ɛr] ◇ *nm, f* prisoner ; **faire qqn ~** to take sb prisoner, to capture sb ◇ *adj* imprisoned ; *fig* trapped ; **être ~ de** to be the prisoner of ; *fig* to be a prisoner of *ou* a slave to.

privatif, ive [privatif, iv] *adj* **- 1.** *JUR* private **- 2.** *GRAM* privative.

privation [privasjɔ̃] *nf* deprivation.
➤ **privations** *nfpl* privations, hardships.

privatisation [privatizasjɔ̃] *nf* privatization.

privatiser [3] [privatize] *vt* to privatize.

privé, e [prive] *adj* private.
➤ **privé** *nm* **- 1.** *ÉCON* private sector **- 2.** [détective] private eye **- 3.** [intimité] : **en ~** in private ; **dans le ~** in private life.

priver [3] [prive] *vt* : **~ qqn (de)** to deprive sb (of).
➤ **se priver** *vp* **- 1.** [s'abstenir] : **se ~ de** to go *ou* do without, to deprive o.s. of ; **ne pas se ~ de faire qqch** not to hesitate to do sthg ; **ne pas se ~ de qqch** to indulge in sthg **- 2.** *(emploi absolu)* [économiser] to do *ou* go without.

privilège [privilɛʒ] *nm* privilege.
➤ **privilèges** *nmpl* : **les ~s** the privileges of the aristocracy, cities, corporations, guilds etc abolished in 1789.

privilégié, e [privileʒje] ◇ *adj* **- 1.** [personne] privileged **- 2.** [climat, site] favoured *Br*, favored *Am* ◇ *nm, f* privileged person.

privilégier [9] [privileʒje] *vt* to favour *Br*, to favor *Am*.

prix [pri] *nm* **- 1.** [coût] price ; **à** *ou* **au ~ coûtant** at cost (price) ; **~ d'achat** purchase price ; **à aucun ~** on no account ; **à ~ fixe** set-price *(avant n)* ; **au ~ fort** at a very high price ; **hors de ~** too expensive ; **à moitié ~** at half price ; **à tout ~** at all costs ; **~ d'ami** reduced price ; **~ net** net (price) ; **de revient** cost price ; **acheter** *ou* **payer qqch à ~ d'or** to pay through the nose for sthg ; **mettre la tête de qqn à ~** to put a price on sb's head ; **y mettre le ~** to pay a lot **- 2.** [importance] value **- 3.** [ré-

compense] prize ; **~ Nobel** Nobel prize ; [lauréat] Nobel prizewinner.
➤ **Grand Prix** *nm* Grand Prix.

pro [pro] *nmf* & *adj fam* pro.

probabilité [prɔbabilite] *nf* **- 1.** [chance] probability **- 2.** [vraisemblance] probability, likelihood ; **selon toute ~** in all probability.

probable [prɔbabl] *adj* probable, likely ; **il est ~ que** it is likely *ou* probable that.

probablement [prɔbabləmɑ̃] *adv* probably.

probant, e [prɔbɑ̃, ɑ̃t] *adj* convincing, conclusive.

probatoire [prɔbatwar] *adj* [période] trial *(avant n)* ; [examen] qualifying.

probité [prɔbite] *nf* integrity.

problématique [prɔblematik] ◇ *nf* problems *(pl)* ◇ *adj* problematic.

problème [prɔblɛm] *nm* problem ; **poser un ~** to cause *ou* pose a problem ; **sans ~!**, **(il n'y a) pas de ~!** *fam* no problem! ; **faux ~** imaginary problem ; **ça ne lui pose aucun ~** hum that doesn't worry him/her.

procédé [prɔsede] *nm* **- 1.** [méthode] process **- 2.** [conduite] behaviour *(U) Br*, behavior *(U) Am*.

procéder [18] [prɔsede] *vi* **- 1.** [agir] to proceed **- 2.** [exécuter] : **~ à qqch** to set about sthg ; **il sera procédé au démantèlement de l'entreprise** the company will be dismantled **- 3.** *sout* [provenir] : **~ de** to come from, to originate in.

procédure [prɔsedyr] *nf* procedure ; [démarche] proceedings *(pl)*.

procédurier, ère [prɔsedyrje, ɛr] ◇ *adj* quibbling ◇ *nm, f* quibbler.

procès [prɔsɛ] *nm* *JUR* trial ; **intenter un ~ à qqn** to sue sb ; **faire le ~ de** *fig* to make a case against.

processeur [prɔsesœr] *nm* processor.

procession [prɔsesjɔ̃] *nf* procession ; **en ~** in procession.

processus [prɔsesys] *nm* process.

procès-verbal [prɔsɛverbal] *(pl* **procès-verbaux** [prɔsɛverbo]*) nm* **- 1.** [contravention - gén] ticket ; [- pour stationnement interdit] parking ticket **- 2.** [compte-rendu] minutes *(pl)*.

prochain, e [prɔʃɛ̃, ɛn] *adj* **- 1.** [suivant] next ; **à la ~e!** *fam* see you! **- 2.** [imminent] impending.
➤ **prochain** *nm* *littéraire* [semblable] fellow man.

prochainement [prɔʃɛnmɑ̃] *adv* soon, shortly.

proche [prɔʃ] *adj* **- 1.** [dans l'espace] near ; **~ de** near, close to ; [semblable à] very similar to, closely related to ; **je me sens très ~ de ce qu'il dit** my feelings are very close *ou* similar to his - **2.** [dans le temps] imminent, near ; **dans un ~ avenir** in the immediate future - **3.** [ami, parent] close.

➤ **proches** *nmpl* : **les ~s** close friends and relatives *(sg)*.

➤ **de proche en proche** *loc adv sout* gradually.

Proche-Orient [prɔʃɔrjɑ̃] *nm* : **le ~** the Near East.

proclamation [prɔklamasjɔ̃] *nf* proclamation.

proclamer [3] [prɔklame] *vt* to proclaim, to declare.

procréation [prɔkreasjɔ̃] *nf* procreation ; **~ artificielle** artificial reproduction.

procréer [15] [prɔkree] *vt littéraire* to procreate.

procuration [prɔkyrasjɔ̃] *nf* proxy ; **par ~** by proxy.

procurer [3] [prɔkyre] *vt* : **~ qqch à qqn** [suj : personne] to obtain sthg for sb ; [suj : chose] to give *ou* bring sb sthg.

➤ **se procurer** *vp* : **se ~ qqch** to obtain sthg.

procureur [prɔkyrœr] *nm* : **~ général** chief prosecutor ; **Procureur de la République** ≃ Attorney General.

prodigalité [prɔdigalite] *nf* extravagance *(U)*.

prodige [prɔdiʒ] *nm* - **1.** [miracle] miracle - **2.** [tour de force] marvel, wonder ; **c'est un ~ d'ingéniosité** it's incredibly ingenious - **3.** [génie] prodigy.

prodigieusement [prɔdiʒjøzmɑ̃] *adv* fantastically, incredibly.

prodigieux, euse [prɔdiʒjø, øz] *adj* fantastic, incredible.

prodigue [prɔdig] *adj* [dépensier] extravagant ; **~ de** *fig* lavish with.

prodiguer [3] [prɔdige] *vt littéraire* [soins, amitié] : **~ qqch (à)** to lavish sthg (on).

producteur, trice [prɔdyktœr, tris] ◇ *nm, f* - **1.** [gén] producer - **2.** *AGRIC* producer, grower ◇ *adj* : **~ de pétrole** oil-producing *(avant n)* ; **~ d'emplois** which creates jobs.

productif, ive [prɔdyktif, iv] *adj* productive.

production [prɔdyksjɔ̃] *nf* - **1.** [gén] production ; **coût de ~** production cost ; **la ~ littéraire d'un pays** the literature of a country - **2.** [producteurs] producers *(pl)*.

productivité [prɔdyktivite] *nf* productivity.

produire [98] [prɔdɥir] *vt* - **1.** [gén] to produce - **2.** [provoquer] to cause.

➤ **se produire** *vp* - **1.** [arriver] to occur, to take place - **2.** [acteur, chanteur] to appear.

produisais, produisions *etc* ⊳ **produire.**

produit, e [prɔdɥi, it] *pp* ⊳ **produire.**

➤ **produit** *nm* - **1.** [gén] product ; **~s alimentaires** foodstuffs, foods ; **~ de beauté** cosmetic, beauty product ; **~s chimiques** chemicals ; **~ de consommation** consumer product ; **~s d'entretien** cleaning products ; **~ financier** financial product ; **~ de grande consommation** mass consumption product - **2.** [d'investissement] profit, income.

proéminent, e [prɔeminɑ̃, ɑ̃t] *adj* prominent.

prof [prɔf] *nmf fam* teacher.

profanation [prɔfanasjɔ̃] *nf* desecration.

profane [prɔfan] ◇ *nmf* - **1.** [non religieux] nonbeliever - **2.** [novice] layman ◇ *adj* - **1.** [laïc] secular - **2.** [ignorant] ignorant.

profaner [3] [prɔfane] *vt* - **1.** [église] to desecrate - **2.** *fig* [mémoire] to defile.

proférer [18] [prɔfere] *vt* to utter.

professer [4] [prɔfese] *vt* to profess.

professeur [prɔfesœr] *nm* [gén] teacher ; [dans l'enseignement supérieur] lecturer ; [titulaire] professor.

profession [prɔfesjɔ̃] *nf* - **1.** [métier] occupation ; **de ~** by trade/profession ; **sans ~** unemployed ; **~ libérale** profession - **2.** [corps de métier - libéral] profession ; [- manuel] trade.

➤ **profession de foi** *nf* - **1.** *RELIG* profession of faith - **2.** [manifeste] manifesto.

professionnel, elle [prɔfesjɔnɛl] ◇ *adj* - **1.** [gén] professional - **2.** [école] technical ; [enseignement] vocational ◇ *nm, f* professional.

professionnellement [prɔfesjɔnɛlmɑ̃] *adv* professionally.

professoral, e, aux [prɔfesɔral, o] *adj* [ton, attitude] professorial ; [corps] teaching *(avant n)*.

professorat [prɔfesɔra] *nm* teaching.

profil [prɔfil] *nm* - **1.** [de personne, d'emploi] profile ; [de bâtiment] outline ; **de ~** [visage, corps] in profile ; [objet] from the side - **2.** [coupe] section.

profiler [3] [prɔfile] *vt* to shape.

➤ **se profiler** *vp* - **1.** [bâtiment, arbre] to stand out - **2.** [solution] to emerge.

profit [prɔfi] *nm* - **1.** [avantage] benefit ; **au ~ de** in aid of ; **tirer ~ de** to profit from, to benefit from - **2.** [gain] profit.

profitable [prɔfitabl] *adj* profitable ; **être ~ à qqn** to benefit sb, to be beneficial to sb.

profiter [3] [prɔfite] vi - **1.** [tirer avantage] : ~ **de** [vacances] to benefit from ; [personne] to take advantage of ; ~ **de qqch pour faire qqch** to take advantage of sthg to do sthg ; **en** ~ to make the most of it ; **en** ~ **pour faire qqch** to take the opportunity to do sthg - **2.** [servir] : ~ **à qqn** to be beneficial to sb.

profiteroles [prɔfitrɔl] nfpl : ~ **au chocolat** chocolate profiteroles.

profiteur, euse [prɔfitœr, øz] nm, f péj profiteer.

profond, e [prɔfɔ̃, ɔ̃d] adj - **1.** [gén] deep - **2.** [pensée] deep, profound - **3.** PSYCHOL : **un débile** ~ a profoundly subnormal person.
➤ **profond** <> nm : **au plus** ~ **de** in the depths of <> adv deep.

profondément [prɔfɔ̃demɑ̃] adv - **1.** [enfoui] deep - **2.** [intensément - aimer, intéresser] deeply ; [- dormir] soundly ; **être** ~ **endormi** to be fast asleep - **3.** [extrêmement - convaincu, ému] deeply, profoundly ; [- différent] profoundly.

profondeur [prɔfɔ̃dœr] nf depth ; **en** ~ in depth ; ~ **de champ** CIN & PHOT depth of field.
➤ **profondeurs** nfpl depths.

profusion [prɔfyzjɔ̃] nf : **une** ~ **de** a profusion of ; **à** ~ in abundance, in profusion.

progéniture [prɔʒenityr] nf offspring.

progiciel [prɔʒisjɛl] nm software package.

programmable [prɔgramabl] adj programmable.

programmateur, trice [prɔgramatœr, tris] nm, f programme Br OU program Am planner.
➤ **programmateur** nm automatic control unit.

programmation [prɔgramasjɔ̃] nf - **1.** INFORM programming ; **faire de la** ~ to program ; ~ **linéaire** linear programming - **2.** RADIO & TÉLÉ programme Br OU program Am planning.

programme [prɔgram] nm - **1.** [gén] programme Br, program Am ; **le** ~ **des réjouissances** hum the treats in store ; **c'est tout un** ~ it's quite an undertaking - **2.** INFORM program ; ~ **d'application** INFORM applications program - **3.** [planning] schedule - **4.** SCOL syllabus.

programmé, e [prɔgrame] adj programmed.

programmer [3] [prɔgrame] vt - **1.** [organiser] to plan - **2.** RADIO & TÉLÉ to schedule - **3.** INFORM to program.

programmeur, euse [prɔgramœr, øz] nm, f INFORM (computer) programmer.

progrès [prɔgrɛ] nm progress (U) ; **être en** ~ to be making (good) progress ; **faire des** ~ to make progress.

progresser [4] [prɔgrese] vi - **1.** [avancer] to progress, to advance - **2.** [maladie] to spread - **3.** [élève] to make progress.

progressif, ive [prɔgresif, iv] adj progressive ; [difficulté] increasing.

progression [prɔgresjɔ̃] nf - **1.** [avancée] advance - **2.** [de maladie, du nationalisme] spread.

progressiste [prɔgresist] nmf & adj progressive.

progressivement [prɔgresivmɑ̃] adv progressively.

prohiber [3] [prɔibe] vt to ban, to prohibit.

prohibitif, ive [prɔibitif, iv] adj - **1.** [dissuasif] prohibitive - **2.** JUR prohibitory.

prohibition [prɔibisjɔ̃] nf ban, prohibition.
➤ **Prohibition** nf : **la Prohibition** HIST Prohibition.

proie [prwa] nf prey ; **être la** ~ **de qqn** fig to be the prey OU victim of sb ; **être la** ~ **de qqch** fig to be the victim of sthg ; **être en** ~ **à** [sentiment] to be prey to.

projecteur [prɔʒɛktœr] nm - **1.** [de lumière] floodlight ; THÉÂTRE spotlight - **2.** [d'images] projector.

projectile [prɔʒɛktil] nm missile.

projection [prɔʒɛksjɔ̃] nf - **1.** [gén] projection - **2.** [jet] throwing.

projectionniste [prɔʒɛksjɔnist] nmf projectionist.

projet [prɔʒɛ] nm - **1.** [perspective] plan - **2.** [étude, ébauche] draft ; ~ **de loi** bill.

projeter [27] [prɔʃte] vt - **1.** [envisager] to plan ; ~ **de faire qqch** to plan to do sthg - **2.** [missile, pierre] to throw - **3.** [film, diapositives] to show - **4.** GÉOM & PSYCHOL to project.
➤ **se projeter** vp [ombre] to be cast.

prolétaire [prɔleter] nmf & adj proletarian.

prolétariat [prɔletarja] nm proletariat.

prolétarien, enne [prɔletarjɛ̃, ɛn] adj proletarian.

prolifération [prɔliferasjɔ̃] nf proliferation.

proliférer [18] [prɔlifere] vi to proliferate.

prolifique [prɔlifik] adj prolific.

prolixe [prɔliks] adj sout wordy, verbose.

prolo [prɔlo] nmf fam prole, pleb.

prologue [prɔlɔg] nm prologue.

prolongation [prɔlɔ̃gasjɔ̃] nf [extension] extension, prolongation.
➤ **prolongations** nfpl SPORT extra time (U) ; **jouer les** ~**s** to go into extra time.

prolongement [prɔlɔ̃ʒmɑ̃] nm [de mur, quai]

extension ; **être dans le ~ de** to be a continuation of.

➡ **prolongements** *nmpl* [conséquences] repercussions.

prolonger [17] [prɔlɔ̃ʒe] *vt* - **1.** [dans le temps] : **~ qqch (de)** to prolong sthg (by) - **2.** [dans l'espace] : **~ qqch (de)** to extend sthg (by).

➡ **se prolonger** *vp* - **1.** [événement] to go on, to last - **2.** [route] to go on, to continue.

promenade [prɔmnad] *nf* - **1.** [balade] walk, stroll ; *fig* trip, excursion ; **~ en voiture** drive ; **~ à vélo** (bike) ride ; **faire une ~** to go for a walk - **2.** [lieu] promenade.

promener [19] [prɔmne] *vt* - **1.** [personne] to take out (for a walk) ; [en voiture] to take for a drive - **2.** *littéraire* [chagrin] to carry (about) - **3.** *fig* [regard, doigts] : **~ qqch sur** to run sthg over.

➡ **se promener** *vp* to go for a walk.

promeneur, euse [prɔmnœr, øz] *nm, f* walker, stroller.

promesse [prɔmɛs] *nf* - **1.** [serment] promise ; **manquer à sa ~** to break one's promise ; **tenir sa ~** to keep one's promise ; **~s en l'air** empty promises - **2.** [engagement] undertaking ; **~ d'achat/de vente** *JUR* agreement to purchase/to sell - **3.** *fig* [espérance] : **être plein de ~s** to be very promising.

promets ▷ **promettre**.

prometteur, euse [prɔmɛtœr, øz] *adj* promising.

promettre [84] [prɔmɛtr] ◇ *vt* to promise ; **~ qqch à qqn** to promise sb sthg ; **~ de faire qqch** to promise to do sthg ; **~ à qqn que** to promise sb that ◇ *vi* to be promising ; **ça promet!** *iron* that bodes well!

➡ **se promettre** *vp* : **se ~ de faire qqch** to resolve to do sthg.

promis, e [prɔmi, iz] ◇ *pp* ▷ **promettre** ◇ *adj* promised ; **~ à qqch** destined for sthg ◇ *nm, f hum* intended.

promiscuité [prɔmiskɥite] *nf* overcrowding ; **~ sexuelle** (sexual) promiscuity.

promontoire [prɔmɔ̃twar] *nm* promontory.

promoteur, trice [prɔmɔtœr, tris] *nm, f* - **1.** [novateur] instigator - **2.** [constructeur] property developer.

promotion [prɔmɔsjɔ̃] *nf* - **1.** [gén] promotion ; **~ des ventes** sales promotion ; **en ~** [produit] on special offer - **2.** *MIL* & *SCOL* year.

promotionnel, elle [prɔmɔsjɔnɛl] *adj* promotional.

promouvoir [56] [prɔmuvwar] *vt* to promote.

prompt, e [prɔ̃, prɔ̃t] *adj sout* : **~ (à faire qqch)** swift (to do sthg).

promptitude [prɔ̃tityd] *nf sout* swiftness.

promu, e [prɔmy] *pp* ▷ **promouvoir**.

promulgation [prɔmylgasjɔ̃] *nf* promulgation.

promulguer [3] [prɔmylge] *vt* to promulgate.

prôner [3] [prone] *vt sout* to advocate.

pronom [prɔnɔ̃] *nm* pronoun ; **~ personnel/possessif/relatif** personal/possessive/relative pronoun.

pronominal, e, aux [prɔnɔminal, o] *adj* pronominal.

prononcé, e [prɔnɔ̃se] *adj* marked.

➡ **prononcé** *nm* [d'arrêt] delivery ; [de sentence] passing.

prononcer [16] [prɔnɔ̃se] *vt* - **1.** *JUR* & *LING* to pronounce - **2.** [dire] to utter.

➡ **se prononcer** *vp* - **1.** [se dire] to be pronounced ; **comme ça se prononce** as it is pronounced - **2.** [trancher - assemblée] to decide, to reach a decision ; [- magistrat] to deliver a verdict ; **se ~ sur** to give one's opinion of.

prononciation [prɔnɔ̃sjasjɔ̃] *nf* - **1.** *LING* pronunciation - **2.** *JUR* pronouncement.

pronostic [prɔnɔstik] *nm* - **1.** *(gén pl)* [prévision] forecast - **2.** *MÉD* prognosis.

pronostiquer [3] [prɔnɔstike] *vt* - **1.** [annoncer] to forecast - **2.** *MÉD* to make a prognosis of.

pronostiqueur, euse [prɔnɔstikœr, øz] *nm, f* forecaster.

propagande [prɔpagɑ̃d] *nf* - **1.** [endoctrinement] propaganda - **2.** *fig* & *hum* [publicité] : **faire de la ~ pour qqch** to plug sthg.

propagation [prɔpagasjɔ̃] *nf* - **1.** [de flammes, de maladie] *fig* spread, spreading - **2.** *BIOL* & *PHYS* propagation.

propager [17] [prɔpaʒe] *vt* to spread.

➡ **se propager** *vp* to spread ; *BIOL* to be propagated ; *PHYS* to propagate.

propane [prɔpan] *nm* propane.

propension [prɔpɑ̃sjɔ̃] *nf* : **~ à qqch/à faire qqch** propensity for sthg/to do sthg.

prophète, prophétesse [prɔfɛt, prɔfetɛs] *nm, f* prophet (*f* prophetess).

➡ **Prophète** *nm* : **le Prophète** the Prophet.

prophétie [prɔfesi] *nf* prophecy.

prophétique [prɔfetik] *adj* prophetic.

prophétiser [3] [prɔfetize] *vt* to prophesy.

prophylactique [prɔfilaktik] *adj* prophylactic.

prophylaxie [prɔfilaksi] *nf* prophylaxis.

propice [prɔpis] *adj* favourable *Br*, favorable *Am* ; ~ à [changement] conducive to ; [culture, élevage] good for.

proportion [prɔpɔrsjɔ̃] *nf* proportion ; **en ~ de** in proportion to ; **toutes ~s gardées** relatively speaking.

proportionné, e [prɔpɔrsjɔne] *adj* : **bien/mal ~** well-/badly-proportioned ; **~ à** proportionate to.

proportionnel, elle [prɔpɔrsjɔnɛl] *adj* : **~ (à)** proportional (to).
➡ **proportionnelle** *nf* : **la ~le** proportional representation.

proportionnellement [prɔpɔrsjɔnɛlmɑ̃] *adv* proportionally.

propos [prɔpo] ◇ *nm* - **1.** [discours] talk - **2.** [but] intention ; **c'est à quel ~?** what is it about? ; **de ~ délibéré** deliberately, on purpose ; **hors de ~** at the wrong time ◇ *nmpl* [paroles] talk *(U)*, words ; **tenir des ~ d'une extrême banalité** to say extremely banal things.
➡ **à propos** ◇ *loc adv* - **1.** [opportunément] at (just) the right time - **2.** [au fait] by the way ◇ *loc adj* [opportun] opportune.
➡ **à propos de** *loc prép* about.

proposer [3] [prɔpoze] *vt* - **1.** [offrir] to offer, to propose ; **~ qqch à qqn** to offer sb sthg, to offer sthg to sb ; **~ à qqn de faire qqch** to offer to do sthg for sb - **2.** [suggérer] to suggest, to propose ; **~ de faire qqch** to suggest *ou* propose doing sthg - **3.** [loi, candidat] to propose.
➡ **se proposer** *vp* - **1.** [offrir ses services] to offer one's services - **2.** [décider] : **se ~ de faire qqch** to intend *ou* mean to do sthg.

proposition [prɔpozisjɔ̃] *nf* - **1.** [offre] offer, proposal ; **~ malhonnête** improper suggestion ; **faire des ~s à qqn** to proposition sb - **2.** [suggestion] suggestion, proposal - **3.** GRAM clause.
➡ **proposition de loi** *nf* bill.

propre [prɔpr] ◇ *adj* - **1.** [nettoyé] clean - **2.** [soigné] neat, tidy - **3.** [éduqué - enfant] toilet-trained ; [- animal] house-trained *Br*, housebroken *Am* - **4.** [personnel] own - **5.** [particulier] : **~ à** peculiar to - **6.** [approprié] : **~ (à)** suitable (for), appropriate (for) - **7.** [de nature] : **~ à faire qqch** capable of doing sthg - **8.** *fig* [honnête] respectable - **9.** *loc* : **nous voilà ~s!** *hum* we're in a fine mess! ◇ *nm* - **1.** [propreté] cleanness, cleanliness ; **recopier qqch au ~** to make a fair copy of sthg, to copy sthg up - **2.** [particularité] : **le ~ de** the characteristic feature of ; **avoir qqch en ~** JUR to be the sole owner of sthg.
➡ **au propre** *loc adv* LING literally.

propre-à-rien [prɔprarjɛ̃] *(pl* **propres-à-rien)** *nmf* good-for-nothing.

proprement [prɔprəmɑ̃] *adv* - **1.** [convenablement - habillé] neatly, tidily ; [- se tenir] correctly - **2.** [véritablement] completely ; **à ~ parler** strictly *ou* properly speaking ; **l'événement ~ dit** the event itself, the actual event - **3.** [exclusivement] peculiarly.

propret, ette [prɔprɛ, ɛt] *adj* neat and tidy.

propreté [prɔprəte] *nf* cleanness, cleanliness.

propriétaire [prɔprijetɛr] *nmf* - **1.** [possesseur] owner ; **~ foncier** property owner ; **~ terrien** landowner - **2.** [dans l'immobilier] landlord.

propriété [prɔprijete] *nf* - **1.** [gén] property ; **~ industrielle** JUR patent rights *(pl)* ; **~ privée** private property - **2.** [droit] ownership - **3.** [terres] property *(U)* - **4.** [convenance] suitability.

propulser [3] [prɔpylse] *vt litt* & *fig* to propel.
➡ **se propulser** *vp* to move forward, to propel o.s. forward *ou* along ; *fig* to shoot.

propulsion [prɔpylsjɔ̃] *nf* propulsion.

prorata [prɔrata] ➡ **au prorata de** *loc prép* in proportion to.

prorogation [prɔrɔgasjɔ̃] *nf* - **1.** JUR extension - **2.** POLIT adjournment.

proroger [17] [prɔrɔʒe] *vt* - **1.** JUR to extend - **2.** POLIT to adjourn.

prosaïque [prozaik] *adj* prosaic, mundane.

proscription [prɔskripsjɔ̃] *nf* [interdiction] banning, prohibition.

proscrire [99] [prɔskrir] *vt* - **1.** [interdire] to ban, to prohibit - **2.** *littéraire* [chasser] : **~ qqn (de)** to exile sb (from), to banish sb (from).

proscrit, e [prɔskri, it] ◇ *pp* ▷ **proscrire** ◇ *adj* - **1.** [interdit] banned, prohibited - **2.** *littéraire* [chassé] exiled ◇ *nm, f littéraire* exile.

proscrivais, proscrivions *etc* ▷ **proscrire**.

prose [proz] *nf* prose ; **en ~** in prose.

prosélyte [prozelit] *nmf* convert.

prosélytisme [prozelitism] *nm* proselytizing.

prospecter [4] [prɔspɛkte] *vt* - **1.** [pays, région] to prospect - **2.** COMM to canvass.

prospecteur, trice [prɔspɛktœr, tris] *nm, f* - **1.** [de ressources] prospector - **2.** COMM canvasser.

prospectif, ive [prɔspɛktif, iv] *adj* . **analyse prospective** COMM forecast.
➡ **prospective** *nf* futurology.

prospection [prɔspɛksjɔ̃] *nf* - **1.** [de ressources] prospecting - **2.** COMM canvassing.

prospectus [prɔspɛktys] *nm* (advertising) leaflet.

prospère [prɔspɛr] *adj* - **1.** [commerce] prosperous - **2.** [santé] blooming.

prospérer [18] [prɔspere] *vi* to prosper, to thrive ; [plante, insecte] to thrive.

prospérité [prɔsperite] *nf* - **1.** [richesse] prosperity - **2.** [bien-être] well-being.

prostate [prɔstat] *nf* prostate (gland).

prosterner [3] [prɔstɛrne] ➤ **se prosterner** *vp* to bow down ; **se ~ devant** to bow down before ; *fig* to kowtow to.

prostitué [prɔstitɥe] *nm* male prostitute.

prostituée [prɔstitɥe] *nf* prostitute.

prostituer [7] [prɔstitɥe] ➤ **se prostituer** *vp* to prostitute o.s.

prostitution [prɔstitysjɔ̃] *nf* prostitution.

prostration [prɔstrasjɔ̃] *nf* prostration.

prostré, e [prɔstre] *adj* prostrate.

protagoniste [prɔtagɔnist] *nmf* protagonist, hero (*f* heroine).

protecteur, trice [prɔtɛktœr, tris] <> *adj* protective <> *nm, f* - **1.** [défenseur] protector - **2.** [des arts] patron - **3.** [souteneur] pimp - **4.** Can POLIT : **le Protecteur du citoyen** the ombudsman.

protection [prɔtɛksjɔ̃] *nf* - **1.** [défense] protection ; **~ contre** protection from *ou* against ; **se mettre sous la ~ de qqn** to put o.s. under sb's protection ; **prendre qqn sous sa ~** to take sb under one's wing - **2.** [des arts] patronage.

protectionnisme [prɔtɛksjɔnism] *nm* protectionism.

protectionniste [prɔtɛksjɔnist] *nmf & adj* protectionist.

protectorat [prɔtɛktɔra] *nm* protectorate.

protégé, e [prɔteʒe] <> *adj* protected <> *nm, f* protégé.

protège-cahier [prɔteʒkaje] (*pl* **protège-cahiers**) *nm* exercise book cover.

protéger [22] [prɔteʒe] *vt* - **1.** [gén] to protect - **2.** [arts] to be a patron of.
➤ **se protéger** *vp* [se préserver] to protect o.s. ; [mettre un préservatif] to use a condom.

protéine [prɔtein] *nf* protein.

protestant, e [prɔtɛstɑ̃, ɑ̃t] *adj & nm, f* Protestant.

protestantisme [prɔtɛstɑ̃tism] *nm* Protestantism.

protestataire [prɔtɛstatɛr] <> *nmf* protest-

or <> *adj sout* [vote, écrits] protest *(avant n)* ; [cri] of protest.

protestation [prɔtɛstasjɔ̃] *nf* - **1.** [contestation] protest - **2.** *littéraire* [déclaration] protestation.

protester [3] [prɔtɛste] *vi* to protest ; **~ contre qqch** to protest against sthg, to protest sthg Am ; **~ de qqch** *littéraire* to protest sthg.

prothèse [prɔtɛz] *nf* prosthesis ; **~ dentaire** dentures *(pl)*, false teeth *(pl)*.

protide [prɔtid] *nm* protein.

protocolaire [prɔtɔkɔlɛr] *adj* [poli] conforming to etiquette.

protocole [prɔtɔkɔl] *nm* protocol.

proton [prɔtɔ̃] *nm* proton.

prototype [prɔtɔtip] *nm* prototype.

protubérance [prɔtyberɑ̃s] *nf* bulge, protuberance.

protubérant, e [prɔtyberɑ̃, ɑ̃t] *adj* bulging, protruding.

proue [pru] *nf* bows *(pl)*, prow.

prouesse [prues] *nf* feat.

prouver [3] [pruve] *vt* - **1.** [établir] to prove - **2.** [montrer] to demonstrate, to show.
➤ **se prouver** *vp* to prove to o.s.

provenance [prɔvnɑ̃s] *nf* origin ; **en ~ de** from.

provençal, e, aux [prɔvɑ̃sal, o] *adj* - **1.** [de Provence] of/from Provence - **2.** CULIN with tomatoes, garlic and onions.
➤ **provençal** *nm* [langue] Provençal.
➤ **Provençal, e, aux** *nm, f* native *ou* inhabitant of Provence.
➤ **à la provençale** *loc adv* CULIN with tomatoes, garlic and onions.

Provence [prɔvɑ̃s] *nf* : **la ~** Provence.

provenir [40] [prɔvnir] *vi* : **~ de** to come from ; *fig* to be due to, to be caused by.

provenu, e [prɔvny] *pp* ▷ **provenir**.

proverbe [prɔvɛrb] *nm* proverb.

proverbial, e, aux [prɔvɛrbjal, o] *adj* proverbial.

providence [prɔvidɑ̃s] *nf* providence ; *fig* guardian angel.
➤ **Providence** *nf* Providence.

providentiel, elle [prɔvidɑ̃sjɛl] *adj* providential.

proviendrai, proviendras *etc* ▷ **provenir**.

proviens, provient *etc* ▷ **provenir**.

province [prɔvɛ̃s] *nf* - **1.** [gén] province - **2.** [campagne] provinces *(pl)*.

provincial, e, aux [prɔvɛ̃sjal, o] *adj & nm, f* provincial.

proviseur [prɔvizœr] *nm* ≃ head Br, ≃ headteacher *Br*, ≃ headmaster (*f* headmistress) *Br*, ≃ principal *Am*.

provision [prɔvizjɔ̃] *nf* - **1.** [réserve] stock, supply ; **faire ~ de qqch** to stock up on *ou* with sthg - **2.** *FIN* retainer ▷ **chèque.**
➡ **provisions** *nfpl* provisions.

provisionnel, elle [prɔvizjɔnɛl] *adj* provisional.

provisoire [prɔvizwar] ◇ *adj* temporary ; *JUR* provisional ◇ *nm* : **ce n'est que du ~** it's only a temporary arrangement.

provisoirement [prɔvizwarmɑ̃] *adv* temporarily.

provocant, e [prɔvɔkɑ̃, ɑ̃t] *adj* provocative.

provocateur, trice [prɔvɔkatœr, tris] ◇ *adj* provocative ◇ *nm, f* agitator, troublemaker.

provocation [prɔvɔkasjɔ̃] *nf* provocation.

provoquer [3] [prɔvɔke] *vt* - **1.** [entraîner] to cause - **2.** [personne] to provoke.
➡ **se provoquer** *vp* to provoke each other.

proxénète [prɔksenɛt] *nm* pimp.

proxénétisme [prɔksenetism] *nm* pimping, procuring.

proximité [prɔksimite] *nf* - **1.** [de lieu] proximity, nearness ; **à ~ de** near - **2.** [d'événement] closeness.

prude [pryd] ◇ *nf* prude ◇ *adj* prudish.

prudemment [prydamɑ̃] *adv* cautiously.

prudence [prydɑ̃s] *nf* care, caution.

prudent, e [prydɑ̃, ɑ̃t] *adj* careful, cautious ; **sois ~!** be careful!

prud'homme [prydɔm] *nm* ≃ member of an industrial tribunal ; **Conseil de ~s** ≃ industrial tribunal.

prune [pryn] ◇ *nf* plum ; **compter pour des ~s** *fam* to count for nothing ◇ *adj inv* plum-coloured *Br*, plum-colored *Am*.

pruneau, x [pryno] *nm* - **1.** [fruit] prune - **2.** *fam* [balle] slug.

prunelle [prynɛl] *nf* *ANAT* pupil ; **j'y tiens comme à la ~ de mes yeux** it's the apple of my eye.

prunier [prynje] *nm* plum tree ; **secouer qqn comme un ~** *fam* to shake sb until his/her teeth rattle.

Prusse [prys] *nf* : **la ~** Prussia.

prussien, enne [prysjɛ̃, ɛn] *adj* Prussian.
➡ **Prussien, enne** *nm, f* Prussian.

PS¹ (*abr de* **Parti socialiste**) *nm French socialist party.*

PS², **P-S** (*abr de* **post-scriptum**) *nm* PS.

psalmodie [psalmɔdi] *nf* chanting.

psalmodier [9] [psalmɔdje] ◇ *vt* to chant ; *fig & péj* to drone ◇ *vi* to drone.

psaume [psom] *nm* psalm.

pseudonyme [psødɔnim] *nm* pseudonym.

PS-G (*abr de* **Paris St-Germain**) *nm Paris football team.*

PSIG (*abr de* **Peloton de surveillance et d'intervention de la gendarmerie**) *nm gendarmerie commando squad.*

PSU (*abr de* **Parti socialiste unifié**) *nm socialist party.*

psy [psi] *fam* ◇ *nmf* (*abr de* **psychiatre**) shrink ◇ *adj* : **elle est très ~** she's really into psychology.

psychanalyse [psikanaliz] *nf* psychoanalysis ; **faire la ~ de qqn** to psychoanalyse sb.

psychanalyser [3] [psikanalize] *vt* to psychoanalyse.

psychanalyste [psikanalist] *nmf* psychoanalyst, analyst.

psychanalytique [psikanalitik] *adj* psychoanalytic, psychoanalytical.

psyché [psife] *nf* cheval mirror.

psychédélique [psikedelik] *adj* psychedelic.

psychiatre [psikjatr] *nmf* psychiatrist.

psychiatrie [psikjatri] *nf* psychiatry.

psychiatrique [psikjatrik] *adj* psychiatric.

psychique [psifik] *adj* psychic ; [maladie] psychosomatic.

psychisme [psifism] *nm* psyche, mind.

psychodrame [psikɔdram] *nm* psychodrama ; *fig* melodrama.

psychologie [psikɔlɔʒi] *nf* psychology.

psychologique [psikɔlɔʒik] *adj* psychological.

psychologiquement [psikɔlɔʒikmɑ̃] *adv* psychologically.

psychologue [psikɔlɔg] ◇ *nmf* psychologist ◇ *adj* psychological.

psychopathe [psikɔpat] *nmf* psychopath.

psychose [psikoz] *nf* - **1.** *MÉD* psychosis - **2.** [crainte] obsessive fear.

psychosomatique [psikɔsɔmatik] *adj* psychosomatic.

psychothérapeute [psikɔterapøt] *nmf* psychotherapist.

psychothérapie [psikɔterapi] *nf* psychotherapy.

PTA (*abr de* **peseta**) Pta, P.

Pte - **1.** *abr de* **porte** - **2.** *abr de* **pointe**.

PTT (*abr de* **Postes, télécommunications et**

télédiffusion) *nfpl former French post office and telecommunications network.*

pu [py] *pp* ⤳ **pouvoir.**

puant, e [pɥɑ̃, ɑ̃t] *adj* **- 1.** [fétide] smelly, stinking **- 2.** *fam fig* [personne] bumptious, full of oneself.

puanteur [pɥɑ̃tœr] *nf* stink, stench.

pub¹ [pyb] *nf fam* ad, advert *Br* ; [métier] advertising.

pub² [pœb] *nm* pub.

pubère [pybɛr] *adj* pubescent.

puberté [pybɛrte] *nf* puberty.

pubis [pybis] *nm* [zone] pubis.

public, ique [pyblik] *adj* public.
➡ **public** *nm* **- 1.** [auditoire] audience ; **en ~** in public **- 2.** [population] public ; **grand ~** general public.

publication [pyblikasjɔ̃] *nf* publication.

publicitaire [pyblisitɛr] ⬦ *nmf* person in advertising ⬦ *adj* [campagne] advertising *(avant n)* ; [vente, film] promotional.

publicité [pyblisite] *nf* **- 1.** [domaine] advertising ; **~ comparative** comparative advertising ; **~ institutionnelle** corporate advertising ; **~ mensongère** misleading advertising, deceptive advertising ; **~ sur le lieu de vente** point-of-sale advertising, POS advertising **- 2.** [réclame] advertisement, advert **- 3.** [autour d'une affaire] publicity *(U)* **- 4.** [caractère public] public nature.

publier [10] [pyblije] *vt* **- 1.** [livre] to publish ; [communiqué] to issue, to release **- 2.** [nouvelle] to make public.

publiquement [pyblikmɑ̃] *adv* publicly.

publireportage [pyblirəpɔrtaʒ] *nm* free write-up *Br*, reading notice *Am*.

puce [pys] *nf* **- 1.** [insecte] flea **- 2.** INFORM (silicon) chip **- 3.** *fig* [terme affectueux] pet, love **- 4.** *loc* : **mettre la ~ à l'oreille de qqn** to make sb suspicious ; **secouer les ~s à qqn** *fam* to tear sb off a strip.
➡ **puces** *nfpl* : **les ~s** flea market *(sg)*.

puceau, elle, x [pyso, ɛl, o] *nm, f & adj fam* virgin.

puceron [pysrɔ̃] *nm* aphid.

pudding [pudiŋ] *nm* plum *ou* Christmas pudding.

pudeur [pydœr] *nf* **- 1.** [physique] modesty, decency **- 2.** [morale] restraint.

pudibond, e [pydibɔ̃, ɔ̃d] *adj* prudish, prim and proper.

pudibonderie [pydibɔ̃dri] *nf littéraire* prudishness, primness.

pudique [pydik] *adj* **- 1.** [physiquement] modest, decent **- 2.** [moralement] restrained.

pudiquement [pydikmɑ̃] *adv* modestly.

puer [7] [pɥe] ⬦ *vi* to stink ; **ça pue ici!** it stinks in here! ⬦ *vt* to reek of, to stink of.

puéricultrice [pɥerikyltris] *nf* nursery nurse.

puériculture [pɥerikyltyr] *nf* childcare.

puéril, e [pɥeril] *adj* childish.

puérilité [pɥerilite] *nf* childishness.

Puerto Rico = Porto Rico.

PUF, Puf [pyf] *(abr de* **Presses Universitaires de France)** *nfpl French publishing house.*

pugilat [pyʒila] *nm* fight.

pugnace [pygnas] *adj littéraire* pugnacious.

pugnacité [pygnasite] *nf littéraire* pugnacity.

puis [pɥi] *adv* then ; **et ~** [d'ailleurs] and moreover *ou* besides ; **et ~ quoi** *ou* **après?** *fam* so what?

puisard [pɥizar] *nm* cesspool.

puiser [3] [pɥize] *vt* [liquide] to draw ; **~ qqch dans qqch** *fig* to draw *ou* take sthg from sthg.

puisque [pɥiskə] *conj* **- 1.** [gén] since **- 2.** [renforce une affirmation] : **mais puisqu'il m'attend!** but he's waiting for me!

puissamment [pɥisamɑ̃] *adv* powerfully.

puissance [pɥisɑ̃s] *nf* power ; **les grandes ~s** the great powers.
➡ **en puissance** *loc adj* potential.

puissant, e [pɥisɑ̃, ɑ̃t] *adj* powerful.
➡ **puissant** *nm* : **les ~s** the powerful.

puisse, puisses *etc* ⤳ **pouvoir.**

puits [pɥi] *nm* **- 1.** [d'eau] well **- 2.** [de gisement] shaft ; **~ de mine** mine shaft ; **~ de pétrole** oil well ; **~ de sciences** *fig* fount of all knowledge.

pull [pyl], **pull-over** [pylɔvɛr] *(pl* pull-overs) *nm* jumper *Br*, sweater.

pulluler [3] [pylyle] *vi* to swarm.

pulmonaire [pylmɔnɛr] *adj* lung *(avant n)*, pulmonary.

pulpe [pylp] *nf* pulp.

pulpeux, euse [pylpø, øz] *adj* **- 1.** [fruit] pulpy ; [jus] containing pulp **- 2.** *fig* [femme] curvaceous.

pulsation [pylsasjɔ̃] *nf* beat, beating *(U)*.

pulsion [pylsjɔ̃] *nf* impulse.

pulvérisateur [pylverizatœr] *nm* spray.

pulvérisation [pylverizasjɔ̃] *nf* **- 1.** [d'insecticide] spraying **- 2.** MÉD spray ; [traitement] spraying.

pulvériser [3] [pylverize] vt - **1.** [projeter] to spray - **2.** [détruire] to pulverize ; *fig* to smash.

puma [pyma] nm puma.

punaise [pynɛz] ⬦ nf - **1.** [insecte] bug - **2.** *fig* [femme] shrew - **3.** [clou] drawing pin *Br*, thumbtack *Am* ⬦ *interj* good grief!

punch [pɔ̃ʃ] nm punch.

punching-ball [pœnʃiŋbol] (*pl* **punching-balls**) nm punchball.

puni, e [pyni] adj punished.

punir [32] [pynir] vt : ~ **qqn (de)** to punish sb (with).

punitif, ive [pynitif, iv] adj punitive.

punition [pynisjɔ̃] nf punishment.

punk [pœnk] nmf & adj inv punk.

pupille [pypij] ⬦ nf ANAT pupil ⬦ nmf [orphelin] ward ; ~ **de l'État** ≃ child in care ; ~ **de la Nation** war orphan (*in care*).

pupitre [pypitr] nm - **1.** [d'orateur] lectern ; MUS stand - **2.** TECHNOL console - **3.** [d'écolier] desk.

pur, e [pyr] adj - **1.** [gén] pure - **2.** *fig* [absolu] pure, sheer ; ~ **et simple** pure and simple - **3.** *fig* & *littéraire* [intention] honourable *Br*, honorable *Am* - **4.** [lignes] pure, clean.

purée [pyre] nf purée ; ~ **de pois** *fig* peasouper ; ~ **de pommes de terre** mashed potatoes (*pl*).

purement [pyrmɑ̃] adv purely ; ~ **et simplement** purely and simply. ↵

pureté [pyrte] nf - **1.** [gén] purity - **2.** [de sculpture, de diamant] perfection - **3.** [d'intention] honourableness.

purgatif, ive [pyrgatif, iv] adj purgative.
➡ **purgatif** nm purgative.

purgatoire [pyrgatwar] nm purgatory.

purge [pyrʒ] nf - **1.** MÉD & POLIT purge - **2.** [de radiateur] bleeding.

purger [17] [pyrʒe] vt - **1.** MÉD & POLIT to purge - **2.** [radiateur] to bleed - **3.** [peine] to serve.
➡ **se purger** vp to take a purgative.

purificateur, trice [pyrifikatœr, tris] adj purifying, cleansing.
➡ **purificateur** nm purifier.

purification [pyrifikasjɔ̃] nf purification ; ~ **ethnique** ethnic cleansing.

purifier [9] [pyrifje] vt to purify.
➡ **se purifier** vp to become pure *ou* clean ; *fig* to purify *ou* cleanse o.s.

purin [pyrɛ̃] nm slurry.

puriste [pyrist] nmf & adj purist.

puritain, e [pyritɛ̃, ɛn] ⬦ adj - **1.** [pudibond] puritanical - **2.** RELIG Puritan (*avant n*) ⬦ nm, f - **1.** [prude] puritan - **2.** RELIG Puritan.

puritanisme [pyritanism] nm puritanism ; RELIG Puritanism.

pur-sang [pyrsɑ̃] nm inv thoroughbred.

purulent, e [pyrylɑ̃, ɑ̃t] adj purulent.

pus [py] nm pus.

pusillanime [pyzilanim] adj pusillanimous.

pusillanimité [pyzilanimite] nf pusillanimity.

pustule [pystyl] nf pustule.

putain [pytɛ̃] ⬦ nf vulg - **1.** péj [prostituée] whore - **2.** péj [femme facile] tart, slag - **3.** *fig* [pour exprimer le mécontentement] : (**ce**) ~ **de ...** this/that sodding ... *Br*, this/that goddam ... *Am* ⬦ *interj* sod it! *Br*, bugger! *Br*, goddam! *Am* ; [exprime l'étonnement] (well) bugger me! *Br*, goddam it! *Am*.

pute [pyt] nf vulg péj [prostituée] whore.

putois [pytwa] nm polecat.

putréfaction [pytrefaksjɔ̃] nf putrefaction ; **en** ~ rotting, putrefying.

putréfier [9] [pytrefje] ➡ **se putréfier** vp to putrefy, to rot.

putrescent, e [pytrɛsɑ̃, ɑ̃t] adj putrescent, rotting.

putride [pytrid] adj - **1.** [corps] putrid - **2.** [odeur, miasme] fetid, foul.

putsch [putʃ] nm uprising, coup.

putschiste [putʃist] ⬦ nmf rebel ⬦ adj rebel (*avant n*).

puzzle [pœzl] nm jigsaw (puzzle).

P-V nm abr de **procès-verbal**.

PVC (abr de **polyvinyl chloride**) nm PVC.

PVD (abr de **pays en voie de développement**) nm developing country.

px (abr de **prix**) : **~ à déb.** offers.

pygmée [pigme] adj pygmy.
➡ **Pygmée** nmf Pygmy.

pyjama [piʒama] nm pyjamas (*pl*).

pylône [pilon] nm pylon.

Pyongyang [pjɔ̃ŋjɑ̃g] n Pyongyang.

pyramide [piramid] nf pyramid.

pyrénéen, enne [pireneɛ̃, ɛn] adj Pyrenean.
➡ **Pyrénéen, enne** nm, f Pyrenean.

Pyrénées [pirene] nfpl : **les** ~ the Pyrenees.

Pyrex® [pirɛks] nm Pyrex®.

pyromane [pirɔman] nmf arsonist ; MÉD pyromaniac.

pyrotechnique [pirɔtɛknik] adj firework (*avant n*), pyrotechnic.

python [pitɔ̃] nm python.

q¹, Q [ky] *nm inv* [lettre] q, Q.
q² *abr de* **quintal.**
Qatar, Katar [katar] *nm* : **le ~** Qatar.
QCM (*abr de* **questionnaire à choix multiple**) *nm* multiple choice questionnaire.
QG (*abr de* **quartier général**) *nm* HQ.
QHS (*abr de* **quartier de haute sécurité**) *nm* high-security wing.
QI (*abr de* **quotient intellectuel**) *nm* IQ.
Qom, Qum [kɔm] *n* Qom.
qqch (*abr de* **quelque chose**) sthg.
qqe *abr de* **quelque.**
qqes *abr de* **quelques.**
qqf *abr de* **quelquefois.**
qqn (*abr de* **quelqu'un**) s.o., sb.
qu' ▷ **que.**
quadragénaire [kwadraʒenɛr] ◇ *nmf* forty year old ◇ *adj* : **être ~** to be in one's forties.
quadrangulaire [kwadrãgylɛr] *adj* quadrangular.
quadrature [kwadratyr] *nf* quadrature ; **c'est la ~ du cercle** it's like trying to square the circle.
quadrichromie [kwadrikrɔmi] *nf* four-colour *Br ou* four-color *Am* printing.
quadrilatère [kwadrilatɛr] *nm* quadrilateral.
quadrillage [kadrijaʒ] *nm* - **1.** [de papier, de tissu] criss-cross pattern - **2.** [policier] combing.
quadrille [kadrij] *nm* quadrille.
quadriller [3] [kadrije] *vt* - **1.** [papier] to mark with squares - **2.** [ville - suj : rues] to criss-cross ; [- suj : police] to comb.
quadrimoteur [kwadrimɔtœr] ◇ *nm* four-engined plane ◇ *adj* four-engined.
quadriphonie [kwadrifɔni] *nf* quadraphony.
quadrupède [k(w)adrypɛd] *nm & adj* quadruped.
quadruple [k(w)adrypl] *nm & adj* quadruple.
quadruplés, ées [k(w)adryple] *nm, f pl* quadruplets, quads.
quadrupler [3] [k(w)adryple] *vt & vi* to quadruple, to increase fourfold.

quai [kɛ] *nm* - **1.** [de gare] platform - **2.** [de port] quay, wharf - **3.** [de rivière] embankment.

QUAI

"Note that the names 'Quai d'Orsay' and 'Quai des Orfèvres' are often used to refer to the government departments situated on the streets of the same name : the foreign office and the police department respectively. 'Le quai de Conti' is sometimes used to refer to the Académie française.

qualifiable [kalifjabl] *adj* [conduite, attitude] : **peu ~** indescribable.
qualificatif, ive [kalifikatif, iv] *adj* qualifying.
◆ **qualificatif** *nm* term.
qualification [kalifikasjɔ̃] *nf* - **1.** [gén] qualification - **2.** [désignation] designation.
qualifier [9] [kalifje] *vt* - **1.** [gén] to qualify ; **être qualifié pour qqch/pour faire qqch** to be qualified for sthg/to do sthg - **2.** [caractériser] : **~ qqn/qqch de qqch** to describe sb/sthg as sthg, to call sb/sthg sthg.
◆ **se qualifier** *vp* to qualify.
qualitatif, ive [kalitatif, iv] *adj* qualitative.
qualitativement [kalitativmã] *adv* qualitatively.
qualité [kalite] *nf* - **1.** [gén] quality ; **de bonne/ mauvaise ~** of good/poor quality ; **~ de vie** quality of life - **2.** [condition] position, capacity ; **en ~ de** in my/his *etc* capacity as.
quand [kã] ◇ *conj* - **1.** [lorsque, alors que] when ; **~ tu le verras, demande-lui de me téléphoner** when you see him, ask him to phone me ; **pourquoi rester ici ~ on pourrait partir en week-end?** why stay here when we could go away for the weekend? - **2.** *sout* [introduit une hypothèse] even if ◇ *adv interr* when ; **~ arriveras-tu?** when will you arrive? ; **je ne sais pas encore ~ je pars** I don't know yet when I'm leaving ; **jusqu'à ~ restez-vous?** how long are you staying for?
◆ **quand même** ◇ *loc conj sout* even though, even if ◇ *loc adv* all the same ; **je pense qu'il ne viendra pas, mais je l'inviterai ~ même** I don't think he'll come but I'll invite him all the same ; **tu pourrais faire attention ~ même!** you might at least be careful! ◇ *interj* : **~ même, à son âge!** really, at his/her age!
◆ **quand bien même** *loc conj sout* even though, even if ; **j'irai, ~ bien même je devrais y aller à pied!** I'll go, even if I have to walk!
◆ **n'importe quand** *loc adv* any time.
quant [kã] ◆ **quant à** *loc prép* as for.
quant-à-soi [kãtaswa] *nm inv* reserve ; **rester sur son ~** to remain aloof.

quantième [kɑ̃tjɛm] *nm* date.
quantifiable [kɑ̃tifjabl] *adj* quantifiable.
quantifier [9] [kɑ̃tifje] *vt* to quantify.
quantitatif, ive [kɑ̃titatif, iv] *adj* quantitative.
quantitativement [kɑ̃titativmɑ̃] *adv* quantitatively.
quantité [kɑ̃tite] *nf* - **1.** [mesure] quantity, amount - **2.** [abondance] : **(une) ~ de** a great many, a lot of ; **en ~** in large numbers ; **des exemplaires en ~** a large number of copies - **3.** LING & SCIENCE quantity.
quarantaine [karɑ̃tɛn] *nf* - **1.** [nombre] : **une ~ de** about forty - **2.** [âge] : **avoir la ~** to be in one's forties - **3.** [isolement] quarantine ; **mettre qqn en ~** *fig* to send sb to Coventry.
quarante [karɑ̃t] *adj num* & *nm* forty ; *voir aussi* **six**.
quarantième [karɑ̃tjɛm] *adj num, nm* OU *nmf* fortieth ; *voir aussi* **sixième**.
quart [kar] *nm* - **1.** [fraction] quarter ; **deux heures moins le ~** (a) quarter to two, (a) quarter of two *Am* ; **deux heures et ~** (a) quarter past two, (a) quarter after two *Am* ; **il est moins le ~** it's (a) quarter to ; **un ~ de** a quarter of ; **démarrer au ~ de tour** to start first time ; *fig* to fly off the handle ; **un ~ d'heure** a quarter of an hour ; **passer un mauvais ~ d'heure** to have a bad time of it - **2.** NAVIG watch - **3.** : **~ de finale** quarter final.
quart-arrière [kararjer] *nmf* Can SPORT quarterback.
quarté [karte] *nm system of betting involving the first four horses in a race.*
quartette [kwartet] *nm* jazz quartet.
quartier [kartje] *nm* - **1.** [de ville] area, district ; **les beaux ~s** the smart areas ; **le ~ latin** the Latin quarter ; **~ résidentiel** residential area - **2.** [de fruit] piece ; [de viande] quarter - **3.** [héraldique, de lune] quarter - **4.** (*gén pl*) MIL quarters (*pl*) ; **~ général** headquarters (*pl*) ; **avoir/donner ~ libre** to have/give permission to leave barracks ; *fig* to have/give permission to go out.

LE QUARTIER LATIN

The Latin quarter is on the left bank of the Seine and includes both the 5th and 6th arrondissements. It has been the student quarter ever since the Middle Ages when the Sorbonne was first created. As well as many prestigious schools and libraries, there are bookshops, art-house cinemas and cafés.

quartier-maître [kartjemetr] (*pl* **quartiers-maîtres**) *nm* leading seaman.

quart-monde [karmɔ̃d] (*pl* **quarts-mondes**) *nm* : **le ~** the Fourth World.
quartz [kwarts] *nm* quartz ; **montre à ~** quartz watch.
quasi [kazi] *adv* almost, nearly.
quasi- [kazi] *préfixe* near ; **~collision** near collision.
quasiment [kazimɑ̃] *adv fam* almost, nearly.
quatorze [katɔrz] *adj num* & *nm* fourteen ; *voir aussi* **six**.
quatorzième [katɔrzjɛm] *adj num, nm* OU *nmf* fourteenth ; *voir aussi* **sixième**.
quatrain [katrɛ̃] *nm* quatrain.
quatre [katr] ◇ *adj num* four ; **monter l'escalier ~ à ~** to take the stairs four at a time ; **se mettre en ~ pour qqn** to bend over backwards for sb ◇ *nm* four ; *voir aussi* **six**.
quatre-quarts [katkar] *nm inv* pound cake.
quatre-vingt = **quatre-vingts**.
quatre-vingt-dix [katrəvɛ̃dis] *adj num* & *nm* ninety ; *voir aussi* **six**.
quatre-vingt-dixième [katrəvɛ̃dizjɛm] *adj num, nm* OU *nmf* ninetieth ; *voir aussi* **sixième**.
quatre-vingtième [katrəvɛ̃tjɛm] *adj num, nm* OU *nmf* eightieth ; *voir aussi* **sixième**.
quatre-vingts, quatre-vingt [katrəvɛ̃] *adj num* & *nm* eighty ; *voir aussi* **six**.
quatrième [katrijɛm] ◇ *adj num, nm* OU *nmf* fourth ; *voir aussi* **sixième** ◇ *nf* - **1.** SCOL third year OU form *Br*, ≃ eighth grade *Am* - **2.** [en danse] fourth position.
quatuor [kwatɥɔr] *nm* quartet ; Can GOLF foursome.
que [k(ə)] ◇ *conj* - **1.** [introduit une subordonnée] that ; **je sais ~ tu mens** I know (that) you're lying ; **il a dit qu'il viendrait** he said (that) he'd come ; **il veut ~ tu viennes** he wants you to come - **2.** [introduit une hypothèse] whether ; **~ vous le vouliez ou non** whether you like it or not - **3.** [reprend une autre conjonction] : **s'il fait beau et que nous avons le temps ...** if the weather is good and we have time ... - **4.** [indique un ordre, un souhait] : **qu'il entre!** let him come in! ; **~ tout le monde sorte!** everybody out! - **5.** [après un présentatif] : **voilà/voici ~ ça recommence!** here we go again! - **6.** [comparatif - après moins, plus] than ; [- après autant, aussi, même] as ; **plus jeune ~ moi** younger than I (am) OU than me ; **elle a la même robe ~ moi** she has the same dress as I do OU as me - **7.** [seulement] : **ne ... ~** only ; **je n'ai qu'une sœur** I've only got one sister ◇ *pron rel* [chose, animal] which, that ; [personne] whom, that ; **la femme ~ j'aime** the woman (whom OU that) I love ; **le livre qu'il m'a prêté** the book (which OU that) he lent me ◇ *pron interr* what ; **~ savez-vous au juste?** what exactly do you

know? ; ~ **faire?** what can I/we/one do? ; **je me demande ~ faire** I wonder what I should do ◇ *adv excl* : **qu'elle est belle!** how beautiful she is! ; ~ **de monde!** what a lot of people!

◆ **c'est que** *loc conj* it's because ; **si je vais me coucher, c'est ~ j'ai sommeil** if I'm going to bed, it's because I'm tired.

◆ **qu'est-ce que** *pron interr* what ; **qu'est-ce ~ tu veux encore?** what else do you want?

◆ **qu'est-ce qui** *pron interr* what ; **qu'est-ce qui se passe?** what's going on?

Québec [kebɛk] *nm* - **1.** [province] : **le ~** Quebec ; **la province de** *ou* **du ~** Quebec State ; **au ~** in Quebec - **2.** [ville] Quebec ; **à ~** in (the city of) Quebec.

québécois, e [kebekwa, az] *adj* Quebec *(avant n)*.

◆ **québécois** *nm* [langue] Quebec French.

◆ **Québécois, e** *nm, f* Quebecker, Québecois.

quel [kɛl] *(f* **quelle,** *mpl* **quels,** *fpl* **quelles)** ◇ *adj interr* [personne] which ; [chose] what, which ; ~ **homme?** which man? ; ~ **est cet homme?** who is this man? ; ~ **livre voulez-vous?** what *ou* which book do you want? ; **de ~ côté es-tu?** what *ou* which side are you on? ; **je ne sais ~s sont ses projets** I don't know what his plans are ; **quelle heure est-il?** what time is it?, what's the time? ◇ *adj excl* : ~ **idiot!** what an idiot! ; **quelle honte!** the shame of it! ; ~ **beau temps!** what lovely weather! ◇ *adj indéf* : ~ **que** *(+ subjonctif)* [chose, animal] whatever ; [personne] whoever ; **il se baigne, ~ que soit le temps** he goes swimming whatever the weather ; **il refuse de voir les nouveaux arrivants, ~s qu'ils soient** he refuses to see new arrivals, whoever they may be ◇ *pron interr* which (one) ; **de vous trois, ~ est le plus jeune?** which (one) of you three is the youngest?

quelconque [kɛlkɔ̃k] *adj* - **1.** [n'importe lequel] any ; **donner un prétexte ~** to give any old excuse ; **si pour une raison ~ ...** if for any reason ... ; **une ~ observation** some remark or other - **2.** *(après n)* *péj* [banal] ordinary, mediocre.

quelque [kɛlk(ə)] ◇ *adj indéf* some ; **à ~ distance de là** some way away (from there) ; **j'ai ~s lettres à écrire** I have some *ou* a few letters to write ; **vous n'avez pas ~s livres à me montrer?** don't you have any books to show me? ; **les ~s fois où j'étais absent** the few times I wasn't there ; **les ~s 200 francs qu'il m'a prêtés** the 200 francs or so (that) he lent me ; ~ **route que je prenne** whatever route I take ; ~ **peu** somewhat, rather ◇ *adv* [environ] about ; **200 francs et ~** some *ou* about 200 francs ; **il est midi et ~** *fam* it's just after midday ; ~ **volontaire qu'il se montrât** however willing he was.

quelque chose [kɛlkəʃoz] *pron indéf* something ; ~ **de différent** something different ; ~ **d'autre** something else ; **tu veux boire ~?** do you want something *ou* anything to drink? ; **apporter un petit ~ à qqn** to give sb a little something ; **c'est ~!** [ton admiratif] it's really something! ; **cela m'a fait ~** I really felt it.

quelquefois [kɛlkəfwa] *adv* sometimes, occasionally.

quelque part [kɛlkəpar] *adv* somewhere *Br*, someplace *Am* ; **l'as-tu vu ~?** did you see him anywhere *Br* *ou* anyplace *Am*?, have you seen him anywhere *Br* *ou* anyplace *Am*?

quelques-uns, quelques-unes [kɛlkəzœ̃, yn] *pron indéf* some, a few.

quelqu'un [kɛlkœ̃] *pron indéf m* someone, somebody ; **c'est ~ d'ouvert/d'intelligent** he's/she's a frank/an intelligent person.

quémander [3] [kemɑ̃de] *vt* to beg for ; ~ **qqch à qqn** to beg sb for sthg.

qu'en-dira-t-on [kɑ̃diratɔ̃] *nm inv* *fam* tittle-tattle.

quenelle [kənɛl] *nf* very finely chopped mixture of fish or chicken cooked in stock.

quenotte [kənɔt] *nf* *fam* tooth.

querelle [kərɛl] *nf* quarrel ; **chercher ~ à qqn** to pick a quarrel with sb.

quereller [4] [kərele] ◆ **se quereller** *vp* : ~ **(avec)** to quarrel (with).

querelleur, euse [kərɛlœr, øz] ◇ *adj* quarrelsome ◇ *nm, f* quarrelsome person.

quérir [kerir] *vt littéraire* : **faire ~ qqn** to summon sb ; **aller ~ qqn** to go and fetch sb.

qu'est-ce que [kɛskə] ▷ **que.**

qu'est-ce qui [kɛski] ▷ **que.**

question [kɛstjɔ̃] *nf* question ; **y a-t-il des ~s?** (are there) any questions? ; **poser une ~ à qqn** to ask sb a question ; **il est ~ de faire qqch** it's a question *ou* matter of doing sthg ; **il n'en est pas ~** there is no question of it ; **remettre qqn/qqch en ~** to question sb/sthg, to challenge sb/sthg ; ~ **subsidiaire** tiebreaker.

questionnaire [kɛstjɔnɛr] *nm* questionnaire.

questionner [3] [kɛstjɔne] *vt* to question.

quête [kɛt] *nf* - **1.** *sout* [d'objet, de personne] quest ; **se mettre en ~ de** to go in search of - **2.** [d'aumône] : **faire la ~** to take a collection.

quêter [4] [kete] ⬦ *vi* to collect ⬦ *vt fig* to
· seek, to look for.

quetsche [kwɛtʃ] *nf* - **1.** [fruit] variety of plum
- **2.** [eau-de-vie] *type of plum brandy.*

queue [kø] *nf* - **1.** [d'animal] tail ; **faire une ~ de
poisson à qqn** *fig* & AUTOM to cut sb up ; **histoire sans ~ ni tête** *fig* cock-and-bull story
- **2.** [de fruit] stalk - **3.** [de poêle] handle - **4.** [de
liste, de classe] bottom ; [de file, peloton] rear
- **5.** [file] queue *Br*, line *Am* ; **faire la ~** to queue
Br, to stand in line *Am* ; **à la ~ leu leu** in single
file - **6.** *vulg* [sexe masculin] dick.

queue-de-cheval [kødʃəval] (*pl* **queues-de-
cheval**) *nf* ponytail.

queue-de-pie [kødpi] (*pl* **queues-de-pie**) *nf
fam* tails (*pl*).

qui [ki] ⬦ *pron rel* - **1.** *(sujet)* [personne] who ;
[chose] which, that ; **l'homme ~ parle** the man
. who's talking ; **je l'ai vu ~ passait** I saw him
pass ; **le chien ~ aboie** the barking dog, the
dog which *ou* that is barking ; **~ plus est**
(and) what's more ; **~ mieux est** even better,
better still - **2.** *(complément d'objet direct)*
who ; **tu vois ~ je veux dire** you see who I
mean ; **invite ~ tu veux** invite whoever *ou*
anyone you like - **3.** *(après une préposition)*
who, whom ; **la personne à ~ je parle** the person I'm talking to, the person to whom I'm
talking - **4.** *(indéfini)* : **~ que tu sois** whoever
you are ; **~ que ce soit** whoever it may be
⬦ *pron interr* - **1.** *(sujet)* who ; **~ es-tu?** who
are you? ; **je voudrais savoir ~ est là** I would
like to know who's there - **2.** *(complément
d'objet, après une préposition)* who, whom ;
~ demandez-vous? who do you want to
see? ; **dites-moi ~ vous demandez** tell me
who you want to see ; **à ~ vas-tu le donner?**
who are you going to give it to?, to whom
are you going to give it?
➥ **qui est-ce qui** *pron interr* who.
➥ **qui est-ce que** *pron interr* who, whom.

quiche [kiʃ] *nf* quiche.

quiconque [kikɔ̃k] ⬦ *pron indéf* anyone,
anybody ⬦ *pron rel indéf sout* anyone who,
whoever.

Quid [kwid] *n* : **le ~** *annually updated one-
volume encyclopedia of facts and figures.*

quidam [kidam] *nm fam* chap *Br*, guy *Am*.

quiétude [kjetyd] *nf* tranquillity *Br*, tranquility *Am*.

quignon [kiɲɔ̃] *nm fam* hunk.

quille [kij] *nf* - **1.** [de bateau] keel - **2.** *arg mil* : **la
~** discharge, demob *Br*.
➥ **quilles** *nfpl* - **1.** [jeu] : (jeu de) **~s** skittles (U)
- **2.** *fam* [jambes] pins.

quincaillerie [kɛ̃kajri] *nf* - **1.** [ustensiles] iron-

mongery *Br*, hardware - **2.** [magasin] ironmonger's (shop) *Br*, hardware shop - **3.** *fam
fig* [bijoux] jewellery.

quincaillier, ère [kɛ̃kaje, ɛr] *nm, f* ironmonger *Br*, hardware dealer.

quinconce [kɛ̃kɔ̃s] *nm* : **en ~** in a staggered
arrangement.

quinine [kinin] *nf* quinine.

quinquagénaire [kɛ̃kaʒenɛr] ⬦ *nmf* fifty
year old ⬦ *adj* : **être ~** to be in one's fifties.

quinquennal, e, aux [kɛ̃kenal, o] *adj* [plan]
five-year (*avant n*) ; [élection] five-yearly.

quintal, aux [kɛ̃tal, o] *nm* quintal.

quinte [kɛ̃t] *nf* MUS fifth.
➥ **quinte de toux** *nf* coughing fit.

quintessence [kɛ̃tesɑ̃s] *nf* quintessence.

quintette [kɛ̃tɛt] *nm* quintet.

quintuple [kɛ̃typl] *nm* & *adj* quintuple.

quintupler [3] [kɛ̃typle] *vt* & *vi* to quintuple, to increase fivefold.

quinzaine [kɛ̃zɛn] *nf* - **1.** [nombre] fifteen (or
so) ; **une ~ de** about fifteen - **2.** [deux semaines]
fortnight *Br*, two weeks (*pl*) ; **~ publicitaire/
commerciale** two-week advertising cam-
paign/sale.

quinze [kɛ̃z] ⬦ *adj num* fifteen ; **dans ~ jours**
in a fortnight *Br*, in two weeks ⬦ *nm*
- **1.** [chiffre] fifteen ; *voir aussi* **six** - **2.** RUGBY : **le
Quinze de France** the French fifteen.

quinzième [kɛ̃zjɛm] *adj num*, *nm ou nmf*
fifteenth ; *voir aussi* **sixième**.

quiproquo [kiprɔko] *nm* misunderstanding.

Quito [kito] *n* Quito.

quittance [kitɑ̃s] *nf* receipt.

quitte [kit] *adj* quits ; **être ~ de qqch** to be
clear of sthg ; **en être ~ pour qqch/pour faire
qqch** to get off with sthg/doing sthg ; **~ à faire qqch** even if it means doing sthg ; **~ ou
double** double or quits.

quitter [3] [kite] *vt* - **1.** [gén] to leave ; **ne quittez pas!** [au téléphone] hold the line, please!
- **2.** [fonctions] to give up - **3.** [vêtement] to take
off.
➥ **se quitter** *vp* to part.

quitus [kitys] *nm* discharge.

qui-vive [kiviv] ⬦ *interj* who goes there?
⬦ *nm inv* : **être sur le ~** to be on the alert.

quoi [kwa] ⬦ *pron rel (après prép)* : **ce à ~ je me
suis intéressé** what I was interested in ; **c'est
en ~ vous avez tort** that's where you're
wrong ; **après ~** after which ; **avoir de ~ vivre**
to have enough to live on ; **avez-vous de
~ écrire?** have you got something to write
with? ; **merci — il n'y a pas de ~** thank you

— don't mention it ⟺ *pron interr* what ; **à ~ penses-tu?** what are you thinking about? ; **je ne sais pas ~ dire** I don't know what to say ; **à ~ bon?** what's the point *ou* use? ; **~ de neuf?** what's new? ; **~ de plus?** what else? ; **décide-toi, ~!** *fam* make your mind up, will you? ; **tu viens ou ~?** *fam* are you coming or what?

➡ **quoi que** *loc conj* (+ *subjonctif*) whatever ; **~ qu'il arrive** whatever happens ; **~ qu'il dise** whatever he says ; **~ qu'il en soit** be that as it may.

quoique [kwakə] *conj* although, though.

quolibet [kɔlibɛ] *nm sout* jeer, taunt.

quorum [k(w)ɔrɔm] *nm* quorum.

quota [k(w)ɔta] *nm* quota.

quote-part [kɔtpar] (*pl* **quotes-parts**) *nf* share.

quotidien, enne [kɔtidjɛ̃, ɛn] *adj* daily.

➡ **quotidien** *nm* - **1.** [routine] daily life ; **au ~** on a day-to-day basis - **2.** [journal] daily (newspaper).

quotidiennement [kɔtidjɛnmɑ̃] *adv* daily, every day.

quotient [kɔsjɑ̃] *nm* quotient ; **~ intellectuel** intelligence quotient.

R

r¹, R [ɛr] *nm inv* [lettre] r, R.
➡ **R** (*abr de* **rand**) R.

r² *abr de* **rue**.

rab [rab] *nm fam* [portion] seconds (*pl*) ; [travail] overtime.

rabâchage [rabaʃaʒ] *nm fam* constant harping on (*U*).

rabâcher [3] [rabaʃe] ⟺ *vi fam* to harp on ⟺ *vt* to go over (and over).

rabais [rabɛ] *nm* reduction, discount ; **au ~** *péj* [artiste] third-rate ; [travailler] for a pittance.

rabaisser [4] [rabese] *vt* - **1.** [réduire] to re-

duce ; [orgueil] to humble - **2.** [personne] to belittle.

➡ **se rabaisser** *vp* - **1.** [se déprécier] to belittle o.s. - **2.** [s'humilier] : **se ~ à faire qqch** to demean o.s. by doing sthg.

rabat [raba] *nm* - **1.** [partie rabattue] flap - **2.** [de robe d'avocat] bands (*pl*).

Rabat [raba] *n* Rabat.

rabat-joie [rabaʒwa] ⟺ *nm inv* killjoy ⟺ *adj inv* : **être ~** to be a killjoy.

rabatteur, euse [rabatœr, øz] *nm, f* - **1.** [de gibier] beater - **2.** *fig & péj* [de clientèle] tout.

rabattre [83] [rabatr] *vt* - **1.** [col] to turn down - **2.** [siège] to tilt back ; [couvercle] to shut - **3.** [somme] to deduct - **4.** [gibier] to drive - **5.** *fam* [clients] to tout for - **6.** *loc* : **en ~** to climb down.

➡ **se rabattre** *vp* - **1.** [siège] to tilt back ; [couvercle] to shut - **2.** [voiture, coureur] to cut in - **3.** [se contenter] : **se ~ sur** to fall back on.

rabattu, e [rabaty] *pp* ▷ **rabattre**.

rabbin [rabɛ̃] *nm* rabbi.

rabibocher [3] [rabiboʃe] *vt* - **1.** *fam* [époux] to reconcile, to get back together - **2.** *vieilli* [voiture] to patch up.

➡ **se rabibocher** *vp fam* to make (it) up.

rabiot [rabjo] *nm fam* [portion] seconds (*pl*), more ; [travail] overtime.

râble [rabl] *nm* [de lapin] back ; *CULIN* saddle.

râblé, e [rable] *adj* stocky.

rabot [rabo] *nm* plane.

raboter [3] [rabote] *vt* to plane.

raboteux, euse [rabotø, øz] *adj* uneven, rugged.

➡ **raboteuse** *nf* planing machine.

rabougri, e [rabugri] *adj* - **1.** [plante] stunted - **2.** [personne] shrivelled, wizened.

rabrouer [3] [rabrue] *vt* to snub.

racaille [rakaj] *nf péj* riffraff.

raccommodage [rakɔmɔdaʒ] *nm* mending.

raccommoder [3] [rakɔmɔde] *vt* - **1.** [vêtement] to mend - **2.** *fam fig* [personnes] to reconcile, to get back together.

➡ **se raccommoder** *vp fam* to make (it) up.

raccompagner [3] [rakɔ̃paɲe] *vt* to see home, to take home.

raccord [rakɔr] *nm* - **1.** [liaison] join - **2.** [pièce] connector, coupling - **3.** *CIN* link.

raccordement [rakɔrdəmɑ̃] *nm* connection, linking.

raccorder [3] [rakɔrde] *vt* : **~ qqch (à)** to connect sthg (to), to join sthg (to).

➡ **se raccorder** *vp* : **se ~ par** to be connected *ou* joined by ; **se ~ à** to be connected to ; *fig* [faits] to tie in with.

raccourci [rakursi] *nm* shortcut ; **en ~** in miniature.

raccourcir [32] [rakursir] ◇ *vt* to shorten ◇ *vi* to grow shorter.

raccroc [rakro] ➡ **par raccroc** *loc adv* by a fluke.

raccrocher [3] [rakrɔʃe] ◇ *vt* to hang back up ◇ *vi* - **1.** [au téléphone] : **~ (au nez de qqn)** to hang up (on sb), to put the phone down (on sb) - **2.** *fam* [coureur] to give up.

➡ **se raccrocher** *vp* : **se ~ à** to cling to, to hang on to.

race [ras] *nf* [humaine] race ; [animale] breed ; **de ~** pedigree ; [cheval] thoroughbred.

racé, e [rase] *adj* - **1.** [animal] purebred - **2.** [voiture] of distinction.

rachat [raʃa] *nm* - **1.** [transaction] repurchase - **2.** *fig* [de péchés] atonement.

racheter [28] [raʃte] *vt* - **1.** [acheter en plus - gén] to buy another ; [- pain, lait] to buy some more - **2.** [acheter d'occasion] to buy - **3.** [acheter après avoir vendu] to buy back - **4.** *fig* [péché, faute] to atone for ; [défaut, lapsus] to make up for - **5.** [prisonnier] to ransom - **6.** [honneur] to redeem - **7.** COMM [société] to buy out.

➡ **se racheter** *vp fig* to redeem o.s.

rachitique [raʃitik] *adj* suffering from rickets.

rachitisme [raʃitism] *nm* rickets (U).

racial, e, aux [rasjal, o] *adj* racial.

racine [rasin] *nf* root ; [de nez] base ; **~ carrée/cubique** MATHS square/cube root.

racisme [rasism] *nm* racism.

raciste [rasist] *nmf & adj* racist.

racket [raket] *nm* racket.

racketter [4] [rakete] *vt* : **~ qqn** to subject sb to a protection racket.

racketteur [raketœr] *nm* racketeer.

raclée [rakle] *nf fam* hiding, thrashing.

racler [3] [rakle] *vt* to scrape ; **ce vin racle le gosier** this wine is a bit rough (on the throat).

➡ **se racler** *vp* : **se ~ la gorge** to clear one's throat.

raclette [raklet] *nf* - **1.** CULIN melted Swiss cheese served with jacket potatoes - **2.** [outil] scraper.

racloir [raklwar] *nm* scraper.

racolage [rakɔlaʒ] *nm fam péj* [par commerçant] touting ; [par prostituée] soliciting.

racoler [3] [rakɔle] *vt fam péj* [suj : commerçant] to tout for ; [suj : prostituée] to solicit.

racoleur, euse [rakɔlœr, øz] *adj fam péj* [air, sourire] come hither ; [publicité] strident.

➡ **racoleur** *nm fam péj* tout.

➡ **racoleuse** *nf fam péj* streetwalker.

racontar [rakɔ̃tar] *nm fam péj* piece of gossip.

➡ **racontars** *nmpl fam péj* tittle-tattle (U).

raconter [3] [rakɔ̃te] *vt* - **1.** [histoire] to tell, to relate ; [événement] to relate, to tell about ; **~ qqch à qqn** to tell sb sthg, to relate sthg to sb - **2.** [ragot, mensonge] to tell ; **qu'est-ce que tu racontes?** what are you on about?

racornir [32] [rakɔrnir] *vt* to harden.

➡ **se racornir** *vp* to become hard.

radar [radar] *nm* radar ; **marcher au ~** *fam* to be on automatic pilot.

rade [rad] *nf* (natural) harbour *Br ou* harbor *Am* ; **rester en ~** *fam fig* to be left stranded.

radeau, x [rado] *nm* - **1.** [embarcation] raft - **2.** [train de bois] timber raft.

radial, e, aux [radjal, o] *adj* radial.

radiateur [radjatœr] *nm* radiator.

radiation [radjasjɔ̃] *nf* - **1.** PHYS radiation - **2.** [de liste, du barreau] striking off.

radical, e, aux [radikal, o] *adj* radical.

➡ **radical** *nm* - **1.** [gén] radical - **2.** LING stem.

radicalement [radikalmɑ̃] *adv* radically.

radier [9] [radje] *vt* to strike off.

radiesthésiste [radjestezist] *nmf* diviner (by radiation).

radieux, euse [radjø, øz] *adj* radiant ; [soleil] dazzling.

radin, e [radɛ̃, in] *fam péj* ◇ *adj* stingy ◇ *nm, f* skinflint.

radiner [3] [radine] ➡ **se radiner** *vp fam* to get one's skates on, to get a move on.

radio [radjo] ◇ *nf* - **1.** [station, poste] radio ; **à la ~** on the radio ; **allumer** *ou* **mettre la ~** to switch on the radio ; **éteindre la ~** to switch off the radio ; **~ pirate** pirate radio - **2.** MÉD : **passer une ~** to have an X-ray, to be X-rayed ◇ *nm* radio operator.

radioactif, ive [radjoaktif, iv] *adj* radioactive.

radioactivité [radjoaktivite] *nf* radioactivity.

radioamateur [radjoamatœr] *nm* (radio) ham.

radiodiffuser [3] [radjodifyze] *vt* to broadcast.

radiodiffusion [radjodifyzjɔ̃] *nf* broadcasting.

radioélectrique [radjoelektrik] *adj* radio (avant n).

radiographie [radjografi] *nf* - **1.** [technique] radiography - **2.** [image] X-ray.

radiographier [9] [radjografje] *vt* to x-ray.

radiologie [radjɔlɔʒil] *nf* radiology.

radiologue [radjɔlɔg], **radiologiste** [radjɔlɔʒist] *nmf* radiologist.

radiophonique [radjɔfɔnik] *adj* radio *(avant n)*.

radioréveil *(pl* radioréveils), **radioréveil** *(pl* radios-réveils) [radjɔrevɛj] *nm* radio alarm, clock radio.

radioscopie [radjɔskɔpi] *nf* radioscopy.

radio-taxi [radjɔtaksi] *(pl* radio-taxis) *nm* radio taxi, radio-cab.

radiotéléphone [radjɔtelefɔn] *nm* cordless telephone, portable telephone.

radiotélévisé, e [radjɔtelevize] *adj* broadcast on both radio and television.

radiothérapie [radjɔterapi] *nf* radiotherapy.

radis [radi] *nm* radish ; **n'avoir plus un ~** *fig* not to have a penny *Br* OU cent *Am* (to one's name).

radium [radjɔm] *nm* radium.

radius [radjys] *nm* radius.

radotage [radɔtaʒ] *nm* rambling.

radoter [3] [radɔte] *vi* to ramble.

radouber [3] [radube] *vt* to repair.

radoucir [32] [radusir] *vt* to soften.
➤ **se radoucir** *vp* [temps] to become milder ; [personne] to calm down.

radoucissement [radusismᾶl] *nm* - **1.** [d'attitude] softening - **2.** [de température] rise ; **un ~ du temps** a spell of milder weather.

rafale [rafal] *nf* - **1.** [de vent] gust ; **en ~s** in gusts OU bursts - **2.** [de coups de feu, d'applaudissements] burst.

raffermir [32] [rafɛrmir] *vt* - **1.** [muscle] to firm up - **2.** *fig* [pouvoir] to strengthen.
➤ **se raffermir** *vp* - **1.** [muscle] to firm up - **2.** *fig* [prix, autorité] to strengthen.

raffinage [rafinaʒ] *nm* refining.

raffiné, e [rafine] *adj* refined.

raffinement [rafinmᾶl] *nm* refinement.

raffiner [3] [rafine] ◇ *vt* to refine ◇ *vi* : **~ sur** to be meticulous about.

raffinerie [rafinri] *nf* refinery.

raffoler [3] [rafɔle] *vi* : **~ de qqn/qqch** to adore sb/sthg.

raffut [rafy] *nm fam* row, racket.

rafiot, rafiau [rafjo] *nm fam péj* tub *(boat)*.

rafistoler [3] [rafistɔle] *vt fam* to patch up.

rafle [rafl] *nf* raid.

rafler [3] [rafle] *vt* to swipe.

rafraîchir [32] [rafreʃir] ◇ *vt* - **1.** [nourriture, vin] to chill, to cool ; [air] to cool - **2.** [vêtement, appartement] to smarten up ; *fig* [mémoire, idées] to refresh ; [connaissances] to brush up ◇ *vi* to cool (down).
➤ **se rafraîchir** *vp* - **1.** [se refroidir] to cool (down) - **2.** [en buvant] to have a drink.

rafraîchissant, e [rafreʃisᾶᾳ̃t] *adj* refreshing.

rafraîchissement [rafreʃismᾶl] *nm* - **1.** [de climat] cooling - **2.** [boisson] cold drink ; **prendre un ~** to have a drink - **3.** [de vêtement, d'appartement] smartening up.

raft(ing) [raft(iŋ)] *nm* whitewater rafting.

ragaillardir [32] [ragajardir] *vt fam* to buck up, to perk up.

rage [raʒ] *nf* - **1.** [fureur] rage ; **être ivre** OU **fou de ~** to be mad with rage ; **la ~ au ventre** OU **cœur** seething with rage ; **faire ~** [tempête] to rage - **2.** [manie] : **~ de faire qqch** mania for doing sthg - **3.** [maladie] rabies *(U)*.
➤ **rage de dents** *nf* (raging) toothache.

rageant, e [raʒᾶ, ᾶt] *adj fam* infuriating.

rager [17] [raʒe] *vi fam* to fume.

rageur, euse [raʒœr, øz] *adj* bad-tempered.

rageusement [raʒøzmᾶl] *adv* furiously.

raglan [raglᾶl] ◇ *nm inv* raglan coat ◇ *adj inv* raglan *(avant n)*.

ragot [rago] *nm (gén pl) fam* (malicious) rumour *Br* OU rumor *Am*, tittle-tattle *(U)*.

ragoût [ragu] *nm* stew.

ragoûtant, e [ragutᾶ, ᾶt] *adj* : **peu** OU **pas très ~** *péj* [plat] not very appetizing ; *fig* [idée] not very inviting.

rai [rɛ] *nm littéraire* [de soleil] ray.

raid [rɛd] *nm* - **1.** AÉRON, BOURSE & MIL raid ; **~ aérien** air raid - **2.** SPORT long-distance rally.

raide [rɛd] ◇ *adj* - **1.** [cheveux] straight - **2.** [tendu - corde] taut ; [- membre, cou] stiff - **3.** [pente] steep - **4.** [personne - attitude physique] stiff, starchy ; [- caractère] inflexible - **5.** *fam* [histoire] hard to swallow, far-fetched - **6.** *fam* [chanson] rude, blue - **7.** *fam* [sans le sou] broke ◇ *adv* - **1.** [abruptement] steeply - **2.** *loc* : **tomber ~ mort** to fall down dead.

raideur [rɛdœr] *nf* - **1.** [de membre] stiffness - **2.** [de personne - attitude physique] stiffness, starchiness ; [- caractère] inflexibility.

raidillon [rɛdijɔ̃] *nm* steep (section of) road.

raidir [32] [rɛdir] *vt* [muscle] to tense ; [corde] to tighten, to tauten.
➤ **se raidir** *vp* - **1.** [se contracter] to grow stiff, to stiffen - **2.** *fig* [résister] : **se ~ contre** to steel o.s. against.

raie [rɛ] *nf* - **1.** [rayure] stripe - **2.** [dans les cheveux] parting *Br*, part *Am* - **3.** [des fesses] crack - **4.** [poisson] skate.

raifort [rɛfɔr] *nm* horseradish.

rail [raj] *nm* rail ; **remettre qqn/qqch sur les ~s** to put sb/sth back on the rails, to get sb/sth back on the rails.

railler [3] [raje] *vt sout* to mock (at).
➤ **se railler** *vp* : **se ~ de** *sout* to mock (at).

raillerie [rajri] *nf sout* mockery *(U)*.

railleur, euse [rajœr, øz] *sout* ◇ *adj* mocking ◇ *nm, f* scoffer.

rainette [rɛnɛt] *nf* tree frog.

rainure [renyr] *nf* [longue] groove, channel ; [courte] slot.

raisin [rɛzɛ̃] *nm* [fruit] grapes *(pl)* ; **~ blanc/noir** white/black grapes ; **~s de Corinthe** currants ; **~s secs** raisins.

raison [rɛzɔ̃] *nf* - **1.** [gén] reason ; **perdre la ~** not to be in one's right mind ; **recouvrer la ~** to come to one's senses ; **à plus forte ~** all the more (so) ; **se faire une ~** to resign o.s. ; **~ de plus pour faire qqch** all the more reason to do sth - **2.** [justesse, équité] : **avoir ~** to be right ; **avoir ~ de faire qqch** to be right to do sth ; **avoir ~ de qqn/qqch** to get the better of sb/sth ; **donner ~ à qqn** to prove sb right.
➤ **à raison de** *loc prép* at (the rate of).
➤ **en raison de** *loc prép* owing to, because of.

raisonnable [rɛzɔnabl] *adj* reasonable.

raisonnablement [rɛzɔnabləmɑ̃] *adv* - **1.** [agir, parler] reasonably - **2.** [manger, boire] in moderation.

raisonnement [rɛzɔnmɑ̃] *nm* - **1.** [faculté] reason, power of reasoning - **2.** [argumentation] reasoning, argument.

raisonner [3] [rɛzɔne] ◇ *vt* [personne] to reason with ◇ *vi* - **1.** [penser] to reason - **2.** [discuter] : **~ avec** to reason with.
➤ **se raisonner** *vp* [personne] to be reasonable.

raisonneur, euse [rɛzɔnœr, øz] ◇ *adj* reasoning ; *péj* argumentative ◇ *nm, f* argumentative person.

rajeunir [32] [raʒœnir] ◇ *vt* - **1.** [suj : couleur, vêtement] : **~ qqn** to make sb look younger - **2.** [suj : personne] : **~ qqn de trois ans** to take three years off sb's age - **3.** [vêtement, canapé] to renovate, to do up ; [meubles] to modernize - **4.** *fig* [parti] to rejuvenate ◇ *vi* - **1.** [personne] to look younger ; [se sentir plus jeune] to feel younger *ou* rejuvenated - **2.** [faubourg] to be modernized.
➤ **se rajeunir** *vp* to lie about one's age.

rajeunissement [raʒœnismɑ̃] *nm* [de population] drop in age.

rajout [raʒu] *nm* addition.

rajouter [3] [raʒute] *vt* to add ; **en ~** *fam* to exaggerate.

rajuster [raʒyste], **réajuster** [3] [reaʒyste] *vt* to adjust ; [cravate] to straighten.
➤ **se rajuster** *vp* to straighten one's clothes.

râle [ral] *nm* moan ; [de mort] death rattle.

ralenti, e [ralɑ̃ti] *adj* slow.
➤ **ralenti** *nm* - **1.** AUTOM idling speed ; **tourner au ~** AUTOM to idle ; *fig* to tick over *Br* ; **vivre au ~** *fig* to take things easy - **2.** CIN slow motion.

ralentir [32] [ralɑ̃tir] ◇ *vt* - **1.** [allure, expansion] to slow (down) - **2.** [rythme] to slacken ◇ *vi* to slow down *ou* up.
➤ **se ralentir** *vp* to slow down *ou* up.

ralentissement [ralɑ̃tismɑ̃] *nm* - **1.** [d'allure, d'expansion] slowing (down) - **2.** [de rythme] slackening - **3.** [embouteillage] hold-up - **4.** PHYS deceleration.

râler [3] [rale] *vi* - **1.** [malade] to breathe with difficulty - **2.** *fam* [grogner] to moan.

râleur, euse [ralœr, øz] *fam* ◇ *adj* moaning *(avant n)* ◇ *nm, f* grumbler, moaner.

ralliement [ralimɑ̃] *nm* rallying.

rallier [9] [ralje] *vt* - **1.** [poste, parti] to join - **2.** [suffrages] to win - **3.** [troupes] to rally.
➤ **se rallier** *vp* to rally ; **se ~ à** [parti] to join ; [cause] to rally to ; [avis] to come round to.

rallonge [ralɔ̃ʒ] *nf* - **1.** [de table] leaf, extension - **2.** [électrique] extension (lead) - **3.** *fam* [de crédit] extension (of credit).

rallonger [17] [ralɔ̃ʒe] ◇ *vt* to lengthen ◇ *vi* to lengthen, to get longer.

rallumer [3] [ralyme] *vt* - **1.** [feu, cigarette] to relight ; *fig* [querelle] to revive - **2.** [appareil, lumière électrique] to switch (back) on again.
➤ **se rallumer** *vp* - **1.** [feu, guerre, colère] to flare up again - **2.** [lumière électrique] to come on again.

rallye [rali] *nm* rally.

RAM, Ram [ram] *(abr de Random access memory) nf* RAM.

ramadan [ramadɑ̃] *nm* Ramadan.

ramage [ramaʒ] *nm littéraire* [d'oiseau] song.
➤ **ramages** *nmpl* leafy design, foliage *(U)*.

ramassage [ramasaʒ] *nm* collection ; **~ scolaire** [action] pick-up (of school children) ; [service] school bus.

ramasse-miettes [ramasmjɛt] *nm inv* crumb-brush and tray (set).

ramasser [3] [ramase] *vt* - **1.** [récolter, réunir] to gather, to collect ; *fig* [forces] to gather - **2.** [prendre] to pick up - **3.** *fig* [pensée] to sum up - **4.** *fam* [claque, rhume] to get.

◆ **se ramasser** *vp* **- 1.** [se replier] to crouch **- 2.** *fam* [tomber, échouer] to come a cropper.

ramassis [ramasi] *nm péj* : **un ~ de** a collection of.

rambarde [rɑ̃bard] *nf* (guard) rail.

rame [ram] *nf* **- 1.** [aviron] oar **- 2.** RAIL train ; **~ de métro** underground *Br ou* subway *Am* train **- 3.** [de papier] ream **- 4.** [tuteur] stake, pole.

rameau, x [ramo] *nm* branch.
◆ **Rameaux** *nmpl* : **les Rameaux** Palm Sunday.

ramener [19] [ramne] *vt* **- 1.** [remmener] to take back **- 2.** [rapporter, restaurer] to bring back **- 3.** [remettre] to put back **- 4.** [réduire] : **~ qqch à qqch** to reduce sthg to sthg, to bring sthg down to sthg **- 5.** *loc* : **il ramène tout à lui** he sees things only in terms of how they affect him ; **la ~** *fam* to stick one's oar in.
◆ **se ramener** *vp* **- 1.** [problème] : **se ~ à** to come down to **- 2.** *fam* [arriver] to turn up.

ramequin [ramkɛ̃] *nm* ramekin.

ramer [3] [rame] *vi* **- 1.** [rameur] to row **- 2.** *fam fig* [peiner] to slog.

rameur, euse [ramœr, øz] *nm, f* rower.

rameuter [3] [ramøte] *vt* to round up.

ramier [ramje] *nm* wood pigeon.

ramification [ramifikasjɔ̃] *nf* **- 1.** [division] branch **- 2.** *(gén pl) fig* [de complot] ramification.

ramifier [9] [ramifje] ◆ **se ramifier** *vp* to branch out.

ramolli, e [ramɔli] ◇ *adj* soft ; *fig* soft (in the head) ◇ *nm, f fam fig* thicko, half-wit.

ramollir [32] [ramɔlir] *vt* **- 1.** [beurre] to soften **- 2.** *fam fig* [ardeurs] to cool.
◆ **se ramollir** *vp* **- 1.** [beurre] to go soft, to soften **- 2.** *fam fig* [courage] to weaken.

ramonage [ramɔnaʒ] *nm* chimney sweeping.

ramoner [3] [ramɔne] *vt* to sweep.

ramoneur [ramɔnœr] *nm* (chimney) sweep.

rampant, e [rɑ̃pɑ̃, ɑ̃t] *adj* **- 1.** [animal] crawling **- 2.** [plante] creeping **- 3.** *fig* [attitude] grovelling.
◆ **rampants** *nmpl arg aéron* ground staff (U).

rampe [rɑ̃p] *nf* **- 1.** [d'escalier] banister, handrail ; **lâcher la ~** *fam fig* to kick the bucket **- 2.** [d'accès] ramp ; **~ de lancement** launch pad **- 3.** THÉÂTRE : **la ~** the footlights (pl).

ramper [3] [rɑ̃pe] *vi* **- 1.** [animal, soldat, enfant] to crawl **- 2.** [plante] to creep **- 3.** *fig* [personne] : **~ devant** to grovel to **- 4.** *fig* [inquiétude] to creep.

rancard, rencard [rɑ̃kar] *nm fam* [rendez-vous] date, meeting.

rancart, rencart [rɑ̃kar] *nm* : **mettre au ~** to chuck out.

rance [rɑ̃s] ◇ *nm* : **sentir le ~** to smell rancid ◇ *adj* **- 1.** [beurre] rancid **- 2.** *fig* [idéologie] stale.

ranch [rɑ̃tʃ] *nm* ranch.

rancir [32] [rɑ̃sir] *vi* to go rancid.

rancœur [rɑ̃kœr] *nf* rancour *Br*, rancor *Am*, resentment.

rançon [rɑ̃sɔ̃] *nf* ransom ; *fig* price.

rancune [rɑ̃kyn] *nf* rancour *Br*, rancor *Am*, spite ; **garder** *ou* **tenir ~ à qqn de qqch** to hold a grudge against sb for sthg ; **sans ~!** no hard feelings!

rancunier, ère [rɑ̃kynje, ɛr] ◇ *adj* vindictive, spiteful ◇ *nm, f* vindictive *ou* spiteful person.

randonnée [rɑ̃dɔne] *nf* **- 1.** [promenade - à pied] walk ; [- à cheval, à bicyclette] ride ; [- en voiture] drive **- 2.** [activité] : **la ~** [à pied] walking ; [à cheval] riding.

randonneur, euse [rɑ̃dɔnœr, øz] *nm, f* walker, rambler.

rang [rɑ̃] *nm* **- 1.** [d'objets, de personnes] row ; **se mettre en ~ par deux** to line up in twos ; **en ~ d'oignons** *fig* in a row *ou* line **- 2.** MIL rank ; **de haut ~** high-ranking ; **se mettre sur les ~s** to be in the running ; **grossir les ~s de** to swell the ranks of **- 3.** [position sociale] station **- 4.** *Can* [peuplement rural] rural district **- 5.** *Can* [chemin] country road.

rangé, e [rɑ̃ʒe] *adj* [sérieux] well-ordered, well-behaved.

rangée [rɑ̃ʒe] *nf* row.

rangement [rɑ̃ʒmɑ̃] *nm* tidying up.

ranger [17] [rɑ̃ʒe] *vt* **- 1.** [élèves, soldats] to line up **- 2.** [chambre] to tidy **- 3.** [objets] to arrange **- 4.** [voiture] to park **- 5.** *fig* [livre, auteur] : **~ parmi** to rank among.
◆ **se ranger** *vp* **- 1.** [élèves, soldats] to line up **- 2.** [voiture] to pull in **- 3.** [piéton] to step aside **- 4.** [s'assagir] to settle down **- 5.** *fig* [se rallier] : **se ~ à** to go along with ; **se ~ à côté de** to side with.

Rangoon [rɑ̃gun] *n* Rangoon.

ranimer [3] [ranime] *vt* **- 1.** [personne] to revive, to bring round **- 2.** [feu] to rekindle **- 3.** *fig* [sentiment] to rekindle, to reawaken.
◆ **se ranimer** *vp* **- 1.** [personne] to come round, to come to **- 2.** *fig* [haine, ressentiment] to reawaken, to be renewed ; [volcan] to become active again.

rap [rap] *nm* rap (music).

rapace [rapas] ⬥ *nm* bird of prey ⬥ *adj* [cupide] rapacious, grasping.

rapacité [rapasite] *nf* rapaciousness.

rapatrié, e [rapatrije] ⬥ *nm, f* repatriated settler ⬥ *adj* repatriated.

rapatriement [rapatrimɑ̃] *nm* repatriation.

rapatrier [10] [rapatrije] *vt* to repatriate.

râpe [rap] *nf* - **1.** [de cuisine] grater ; ~ à fromage cheese grater - **2.** [de menuisier] rasp - **3.** *Helv fam* [avare] miser, skinflint.

râpé, e [rape] *adj* - **1.** *CULIN* grated - **2.** [manteau] threadbare - **3.** *fam* [raté] : **c'est ~!** we've had it!

⬥ **râpé** *nm* grated Gruyère cheese.

râper [3] [rape] *vt* - **1.** *CULIN* to grate - **2.** [bois, métal] to rasp.

rapetasser [3] [raptase] *vt fam péj* to patch up.

râpeux, euse [rapø, øz] *adj* - **1.** [tissu] rough - **2.** [vin] harsh.

raphia [rafja] *nm* raffia.

rapide [rapid] ⬥ *adj* - **1.** [gén] rapid - **2.** [train, coureur] fast - **3.** [pente] steep - **4.** [musique, intelligence] lively, quick ⬥ *nm* - **1.** [train] express (train) - **2.** [de fleuve] rapid.

rapidement [rapidmɑ̃] *adv* rapidly.

rapidité [rapidite] *nf* rapidity.

rapiécer [20] [rapjese] *vt* to patch.

rapière [rapjɛr] *nf* rapier.

rappel [rapɛl] *nm* - **1.** [de réservistes, d'ambassadeur] recall - **2.** [souvenir] reminder ; ~ à l'ordre call to order - **3.** [de paiement] back pay - **4.** [de vaccination] booster - **5.** [au spectacle] curtain call, encore - **6.** *SPORT* abseiling ; **descendre en ~** to abseil (down) - **7.** *TECHNOL* : **ressort de ~** return spring.

rappeler [24] [raple] *vt* - **1.** [gén] to call back ; ~ qqn à qqch *fig* to bring sb back to sthg - **2.** [faire penser à] : ~ qqch à qqn to remind sb of sthg ; **ça me rappelle les vacances** it reminds me of my holidays.

⬥ **se rappeler** *vp* to remember.

rappelle, rappelles *etc* ⮑ rappeler.

rappliquer [3] [raplike] *vi fam* to turn up, to show up.

rapport [rapɔr] *nm* - **1.** [corrélation] link, connection ; ~ **de causalité** causal link ; **je ne vois pas le ~** I don't see the connection - **2.** [contact] : **se mettre en ~ avec qqn** to get in touch with sb - **3.** [compte-rendu] report - **4.** [profit] return, yield - **5.** *MATHS* ratio ; **un excellent ~ qualité-prix** excellent value for money.

⬥ **rapports** *nmpl* - **1.** [relations] relations - **2.** [sexuels] : **~s (sexuels)** intercourse *(sg)* ;

avoir des ~s (sexuels) avec qqn to have sex with sb.

⬥ **par rapport à** *loc prép* in comparison to, compared with.

rapporter [3] [rapɔrte] *vt* to bring back.

⬥ **se rapporter** *vp* : **se ~ à** to refer *ou* relate to.

rapporteur, euse [rapɔrtœr, øz] ⬥ *adj* sneaky, telltale *(avant n)* ⬥ *nm, f* sneak, telltale.

⬥ **rapporteur** *nm* - **1.** [de commission] rapporteur - **2.** *GÉOM* protractor.

rapprochement [raprɔʃmɑ̃] *nm* - **1.** [d'objets, de personnes] bringing together - **2.** *fig* [entre événements] link, connection - **3.** *fig* [de pays, de parti] rapprochement, coming together.

rapprocher [3] [raprɔʃe] *vt* - **1.** [mettre plus près] : ~ qqn/qqch de qqch to bring sb/sthg nearer to sthg, to bring sb/sthg closer to sthg - **2.** *fig* [personnes] to bring together - **3.** *fig* [idée, texte] : ~ qqch (de) to compare sthg (with).

⬥ **se rapprocher** *vp* - **1.** [approcher] : **se ~ (de qqn/qqch)** to approach (sb/sthg) - **2.** [se ressembler] : **se ~ de qqch** to be similar to sthg - **3.** [se réconcilier] : **se ~ de qqn** to become closer to sb.

rapsodie = rhapsodie.

rapt [rapt] *nm* abduction.

raquette [rakɛt] *nf* - **1.** [de tennis, de squash] racket ; [de ping-pong] bat - **2.** [à neige] snowshoe.

rare [rar] *adj* - **1.** [peu commun, peu fréquent] rare ; **ses ~s amis** his few friends - **2.** [peu dense] sparse - **3.** [surprenant] unusual, surprising.

raréfaction [rarefaksjɔ̃] *nf* scarcity ; [d'air] rarefaction.

raréfier [9] [rarefje] *vt* to rarefy.

⬥ **se raréfier** *vp* to become rarefied.

rarement [rarmɑ̃] *adv* rarely.

rareté [rarte] *nf* - **1.** [de denrées, de nouvelles] scarcity - **2.** [de visites, de lettres] infrequency - **3.** [objet précieux] rarity.

rarissime [rarisim] *adj* extremely rare.

ras, e [ra, raz] *adj* - **1.** [herbe, poil] short - **2.** [mesure] full.

⬥ **ras** *adv* short ; **à ~** short ; **à ~ de** level with ; **en avoir ~ le bol** *fam* to be fed up.

⬥ **ras du cou, ras le cou** *loc adj* crew-neck, round-neck.

RAS *(abr de rien à signaler)* nothing to report.

rasade [razad] *nf* glassful.

rasage [razaʒ] *nm* shaving.

rasant, e [razã, ãt] *adj* - **1.** [lumière] low-angled - **2.** *fam* [film, discours] boring.

rascasse [raskas] *nf* scorpion fish.

rase-mottes [razmɔt] *nm inv* hedge-hopping.

raser [3] [raze] *vt* - **1.** [barbe, cheveux] to shave off - **2.** [mur, sol] to hug - **3.** [village] to raze - **4.** *fam* [personne] to bore.

➤ **se raser** *vp* - **1.** [avec rasoir] to shave - **2.** *fam* [s'ennuyer] to be bored.

raseur, euse [razœr, øz] <> *adj* boring <> *nm, f* bore.

ras-le-bol [ralbɔl] *nm inv fam* discontent ; ~! *fam* that's enough!

rasoir [razwar] <> *nm* razor ; ~ électrique electric shaver ; ~ mécanique safety razor <> *adj inv fam* boring.

rassasier [9] [rasazje] *vt* to satisfy.

➤ **se rassasier** *vp* : **se ~ de** to tire of, to have one's fill of.

rassemblement [rasãbləmã] *nm* - **1.** [d'objets] collecting, gathering - **2.** [foule] crowd, gathering - **3.** [union, parti] union - **4.** MIL parade ; **rassemblement!** fall in!

rassembler [3] [rasãble] *vt* - **1.** [personnes, documents] to collect, to gather - **2.** [courage] to summon up ; [idées] to collect.

➤ **se rassembler** *vp* - **1.** [manifestants] to assemble - **2.** [famille] to get together.

rasseoir [65] [raswar] ➤ **se rasseoir** *vp* to sit down again.

rasséréner [18] [raserene] *vt sout* to calm down.

➤ **se rasséréner** *vp sout* to recover one's serenity.

rassis, e [rasi, iz] *adj* - **1.** [pain] stale - **2.** *sout* [esprit] calm, sober.

rassurant, e [rasyrã, ãt] *adj* reassuring.

rassuré, e [rasyre] *adj* confident, at ease.

rassurer [3] [rasyre] *vt* to reassure.

➤ **se rassurer** *vp* to feel at ease *ou* reassured ; **rassurez-vous** don't worry.

rat [ra] <> *nm* rat ; **petit ~** *fig* young ballet pupil ; **être fait comme un ~** to be cornered <> *adj fam* [avare] mean, stingy.

ratage [rataʒ] *nm* bungling, messing up.

ratatiné, e [ratatine] *adj* - **1.** [fruit, personne] shrivelled - **2.** *fam fig* [vélo, bagnole] wrecked.

ratatiner [3] [ratatine] *vt* - **1.** [fruit, personne] to shrivel - **2.** *fam* [démolir] to wreck.

➤ **se ratatiner** *vp* to shrivel up, to become wrinkled.

ratatouille [ratatuj] *nf* ratatouille.

rate [rat] *nf* - **1.** [animal] female rat - **2.** [organe] spleen.

raté, e [rate] *nm, f* [personne] failure.

➤ **raté** *nm* - **1.** (*gén pl*) AUTOM misfiring (*U*) ; **faire des ~s** to misfire - **2.** *fig* [difficulté] problem.

râteau, x [rato] *nm* rake.

râtelier [ratəlje] *nm* - **1.** [à fourrage, à outils] rack ; **manger à tous les ~s** *fig* to have a finger in every pie - **2.** *fam* [dentier] false teeth (*pl*).

rater [3] [rate] <> *vt* - **1.** [train, occasion] to miss - **2.** [plat, affaire] to make a mess of ; [examen] to fail <> *vi* to go wrong.

ratification [ratifikasjɔ̃] *nf* ratification.

ratifier [9] [ratifje] *vt* to ratify.

ration [rasjɔ̃] *nf* [quantité] portion ; *fig* share ; ~ alimentaire food intake.

rationalisation [rasjonalizasjɔ̃] *nf* rationalization.

rationaliser [3] [rasjonalize] *vt* to rationalize.

rationnel, elle [rasjonɛl] *adj* rational.

rationnellement [rasjonɛlmã] *adv* rationally.

rationnement [rasjonmã] *nm* rationing ; **carte de ~** ration card.

rationner [3] [rasjone] *vt* to ration.

➤ **se rationner** *vp* to ration o.s.

ratissage [ratisaʒ] *nm* - **1.** [de jardin] raking - **2.** [de quartier] search.

ratisser [3] [ratise] *vt* - **1.** [jardin] to rake - **2.** [quartier] to search, to comb ; ~ large to cast one's net wide - **3.** *fam fig* [au jeu] to clean out - **4.** RUGBY to heel.

raton [ratɔ̃] *nm* - **1.** ZOOL young rat - **2.** *tfam* [Arabe] *racist term used with reference to North African Arabs.*

➤ **raton laveur** *nm* racoon.

raton(n)ade [ratɔnad] *nf tfam racist term used to describe an attack on North African Arab immigrants.*

RATP (*abr de* Régie autonome des transports parisiens) *nf* Paris transport authority.

rattachement [rataʃmã] *nm* uniting, joining.

rattacher [3] [rataʃe] *vt* - **1.** [attacher de nouveau] to do up, to fasten again - **2.** [relier] : ~ qqch à to join sthg to ; *fig* to link sthg with - **3.** [unir] : ~ qqn à to bind sb to.

➤ **se rattacher** *vp* : **se ~ à** to be linked to.

rattrapage [ratrapaʒ] *nm* - **1.** SCOL : **cours de ~** remedial class - **2.** [de salaires, prix] adjustment.

rattraper [3] [ratrape] *vt* - **1.** [animal, prisonnier] to recapture - **2.** [temps] : ~ le temps perdu to make up for lost time - **3.** [rejoindre] to catch up with - **4.** [bus] to catch - **5.** [erreur] to correct - **6.** [personne qui tombe] to catch.

➡ **se rattraper** *vp* - **1.** [se retenir] : **se ~ à qqn/qqch** to catch hold of sb/sthg - **2.** [compenser] to catch up - **3.** [se faire pardonner] to make amends.

rature [ratyr] *nf* alteration.

raturer [3] [ratyre] *vt* to alter.

rauque [rok] *adj* hoarse, husky.

ravagé, e [ravaʒe] *adj fam* [fou] : **être ~** to be off one's head.

ravager [17] [ravaʒe] *vt* [gén] to devastate, to ravage.

ravages [ravaʒ] *nmpl* [de troupes] ravages, devastation *(sg)* ; [d'inondation] devastation *(sg)* ; [du temps] ravages ; **faire des ~** *fig* to break hearts.

ravalement [ravalmɑ̃] *nm* cleaning, restoration.

ravaler [3] [ravale] *vt* - **1.** [façade] to clean, to restore - **2.** [personne] : **~ qqn au rang de** to lower sb to the level of - **3.** [salive] to swallow - **4.** *fig* [larmes, colère] to stifle, to hold back.

➡ **se ravaler** *vp* to debase o.s., to demean o.s.

ravaudage [ravodaʒ] *nm* mending, repairing.

ravauder [3] [ravode] *vt* to mend, to repair.

rave[1] [rav] *nf* BOT rape.

rave[2] [rɛv], **rave-party** [rɛvparti] *nf* rave (party).

ravi, e [ravi] *adj* : **~ (de)** delighted (with) ; **je suis ~ de l'avoir trouvé** I'm delighted that I found it, I'm delighted to have found it ; **je suis ~ qu'il soit venu** I'm delighted (that) he has come ; **~ de vous connaître** pleased to meet you.

ravier [ravje] *nm* small dish.

ravigotant, e [ravigɔtɑ̃, ɑ̃t] *adj fam* refreshing, stimulating.

ravigote [ravigɔt] *nf sauce of mustard, gherkins and capers.*

ravigoter [3] [ravigɔte] *vt fam* to perk up, to buck up.

ravin [ravɛ̃] *nm* ravine, gully.

raviné, e [ravine] *adj* [visage] furrowed.

raviner [3] [ravine] *vt* to gully.

raviolis [ravjɔli] *nmpl* ravioli *(U).*

ravir [32] [ravir] *vt* - **1.** [charmer] to delight ; **à ~** beautifully - **2.** *littéraire* [arracher] : **~ qqch à qqn** to rob sb of sthg.

raviser [3] [ravize] ➡ **se raviser** *vp* to change one's mind.

ravissant, e [ravisɑ̃, ɑ̃t] *adj* delightful, beautiful.

ravissement [ravismɑ̃] *nm* - **1.** [enchantement] delight - **2.** *littéraire* [rapt] rape, ravishing.

ravisseur, euse [raviscœr, øz] *nm, f* abductor.

ravitaillement [ravitajmɑ̃] *nm* [en denrées] resupplying ; [en carburant] refuelling.

ravitailler [3] [ravitaje] *vt* [en denrées] to resupply ; [en carburant] to refuel.

➡ **se ravitailler** *vp* [en denrées] to get fresh supplies ; [en carburant] to refuel.

raviver [3] [ravive] *vt* - **1.** [feu] to rekindle - **2.** [couleurs] to brighten up - **3.** *fig* [douleur] to revive - **4.** [plaie] to reopen.

ravoir [ravwar] *vt* - **1.** [jouet, livre] to get back - **2.** *fam* [linge] to get clean.

rayé, e [rɛje] *adj* - **1.** [tissu] striped - **2.** [disque, vitre] scratched - **3.** [canon] rifled.

rayer [11] [rɛje] *vt* - **1.** [disque, vitre] to scratch - **2.** [nom, mot] to cross out ; **~ qqn d'une liste** to cross sb's name off a list - **3.** [canon] to rifle.

rayon [rɛjɔ̃] *nm* - **1.** [de lumière] beam, ray ; *fig* [d'espoir] ray - **2.** *(gén pl)* [radiation] radiation *(U)* ; **~ laser** laser beam ; **~s X** X-rays - **3.** [de roue] spoke - **4.** GÉOM radius ; **dans un ~ de** *fig* within a radius of ; **~ d'action** range - **5.** [étagère] shelf - **6.** [dans un magasin] department.

rayonnage [rɛjɔnaʒ] *nm* shelving.

rayonnant, e [rɛjɔnɑ̃, ɑ̃t] *adj litt & fig* radiant.

rayonne [rɛjɔn] *nf* rayon.

rayonnement [rɛjɔnmɑ̃] *nm* - **1.** [gén] radiance ; [des arts] influence - **2.** PHYS radiation.

rayonner [3] [rɛjɔne] *vi* - **1.** [soleil] to shine ; **~ de joie** *fig* to radiate happiness - **2.** [culture] to be influential - **3.** [avenues, lignes, chaleur] to radiate - **4.** [touriste] to tour around *(from a base).*

rayure [rɛjyr] *nf* - **1.** [sur étoffe] stripe - **2.** [sur disque, sur meuble] scratch - **3.** [de fusil] groove.

raz [ra] ➡ **raz de marée** *nm* tidal wave ; POLIT & *fig* landslide.

razzia [razja] *nf fam* raid ; **faire une ~ sur** to raid, to plunder.

razzier [9] [razje] *vt* to raid, to plunder.

RBE *(abr de* revenu brut d'exploitation*) nm* gross profit.

RBL *(abr de* rouble*)* R, Rub.

R-C *abr de* rez-de-chaussée.

r.d. *(abr de* rive droite*) right (north) bank of the Seine.*

R-D *(abr de* recherche-développement*) nf* R & D.

RDA *(abr de* République démocratique allemande*) nf* GDR.

RDB (*abr de* **revenu disponible brut**) *nm* gross disposable income.

RdC *abr de* **rez-de-chaussée**.

ré [re] *nm inv MUS* D ; [chanté] re.

ré- [re] *préfixe* re-.

réabonnement [reabɔnmã] *nm* subscription renewal.

réabonner [3] [reabɔne] *vt* : ~ **qqn à** to renew sb's subscription to.

➡ **se réabonner** *vp* : **se ~ à** to renew one's subscription to.

réac [reak] *nmf & adj péj* reactionary.

réaccoutumer [3] [reakutyme] *vt* to reaccustom.

➡ **se réaccoutumer** *vp* : **se ~ à** to reaccustom o.s. to.

réacteur [reaktœr] *nm* [d'avion] jet engine ; ~ **nucléaire** nuclear reactor.

réactif, ive [reaktif, iv] *adj* reactive.

➡ **réactif** *nm* reagent.

réaction [reaksjɔ̃] *nf* : ~ **(à/contre)** reaction (to/against) ; ~ **en chaîne** chain reaction.

réactionnaire [reaksjɔner] *nmf & adj péj* reactionary.

réactiver [3] [reaktive] *vt* to reactivate.

réactualisation [reaktyalizasjɔ̃] *nf* [modernisation] updating, bringing up to date.

réactualiser [3] [reaktyalize] *vt* [moderniser] to update, to bring up to date.

réadaptation [readaptasjɔ̃] *nf* rehabilitation.

réadapter [3] [readapte] *vt* to readapt ; [accidenté] to rehabilitate.

➡ **se réadapter** *vp* : **se ~ à** to readapt to.

réaffirmer [3] [reafirme] *vt* to reaffirm.

réagir [32] [reaʒir] *vi* : ~ **(à/contre)** to react (to/against) ; ~ **sur** to affect.

réajustement [reaʒystəmã] *nm* adjustment.

réajuster = **rajuster**.

réalisable [realizabl] *adj* - **1.** [projet] feasible - **2.** *FIN* realizable.

réalisateur, trice [realizatœr, tris] *nm, f CIN & TÉLÉ* director.

réalisation [realizasjɔ̃] *nf* - **1.** [de projet] carrying out - **2.** *CIN & TÉLÉ* production.

réaliser [3] [realize] *vt* - **1.** [projet] to carry out ; [ambitions, rêves] to achieve, to realize - **2.** *CIN & TÉLÉ* to produce - **3.** [s'apercevoir de] to realize.

➡ **se réaliser** *vp* - **1.** [ambition] to be realized ; [rêve] to come true - **2.** [personne] to fulfil o.s.

réalisme [realism] *nm* realism.

réaliste [realist] ◇ *nmf* realist ◇ *adj*

- **1.** [personne, objectif] realistic - **2.** *ART & LITTÉRATURE* realist.

réalité [realite] *nf* reality ; **en ~** in reality.

reality-show, reality show [realitifo] (*pl* **reality(-) shows**) *nm* talk show focussing on real-life drama.

réaménagement [reamenaʒmã] *nm* - **1.** [de projet] restructuring - **2.** [de taux d'intérêt] readjustment.

réamorcer [16] [reamɔrse] *vt* to start up again.

réanimation [reanimasjɔ̃] *nf* resuscitation ; **en ~** in intensive care.

réanimer [3] [reanime] *vt* to resuscitate.

réapparaître [91] [reaparetr] *vi* to reappear.

réapparition [reaparisjɔ̃] *nf* reappearance.

réapprendre [79] [reaprãdr] *vt* to relearn.

réarmement [rearməmã] *nm* rearmament.

réassort [reasɔr] *nm* - **1.** [action] restocking - **2.** [result] fresh stock.

réassurance [reasyrãs] *nf* reinsurance.

rébarbatif, ive [rebarbatif, iv] *adj* - **1.** [personne, visage] forbidding - **2.** [travail] daunting.

rebâtir [32] [rəbatir] *vt* to rebuild.

rebattre [83] [rəbatr] *vt* [cartes] to reshuffle.

rebattu, e [rəbaty] ◇ *pp* ▷ **rebattre** ◇ *adj* overworked, hackneyed.

rebelle [rəbɛl] *adj* - **1.** [personne] rebellious ; [troupes] rebel (*avant n*) ; ~ **à** [discipline] unamenable to - **2.** [mèche, boucle] unruly.

rebeller [4] [rəbele] ➡ **se rebeller** *vp* : **se ~ (contre)** to rebel (against).

rébellion [rebeljɔ̃] *nf* rebellion.

rebiffer [3] [rəbife] ➡ **se rebiffer** *vp fam* : **se ~ (contre)** to rebel (against).

reblochon [rəblɔʃɔ̃] *nm* cow's-milk cheese from Haute-Savoie.

reboiser [3] [rəbwaze] *vt* to reafforest.

rebond [rəbɔ̃] *nm* bounce.

rebondi, e [rəbɔ̃di] *adj* rounded.

rebondir [32] [rəbɔ̃dir] *vi* - **1.** [objet] to bounce ; [contre mur] to rebound - **2.** *fig* [affaire] to come to life (again).

rebondissement [rəbɔ̃dismã] *nm* [d'affaire] new development.

rebord [rəbɔr] *nm* [de table] edge ; [de fenêtre] sill, ledge.

reboucher [3] [rəbuʃe] *vt* [bouteille] to put the cork back in, to recork ; [trou] to fill in.

rebours [rəbur] ➡ **à rebours** *loc adv* the wrong way ; *fig* the wrong way round, back to front.

rebouteux, euse [rəbutø, øz], **rebou-**

teur, euse [rəbutœr, øz] *nm, f fam* bonesetter.

reboutonner [3] [rəbutɔne] *vt* to rebutton.

rebrousse-poil [rəbruspwal] ⏵ **à rebrousse-poil** *loc adv* the wrong way ; **prendre qqn à ~** *fig* to rub sb up the wrong way.

rebrousser [3] [rəbruse] *vt* to brush back ; **~ chemin** *fig* to retrace one's steps.

rebuffade [rəbyfad] *nf* rebuff ; **essuyer une ~** to be rebuffed.

rébus [rebys] *nm* rebus.

rebut [rəby] *nm* scrap ; **mettre qqch au ~** to get rid of sthg, to scrap sthg.

rebutant, e [rəbytɑ̃, ɑ̃t] *adj* - **1.** [travail] disheartening - **2.** [manières] disgusting.

rebuter [3] [rəbyte] *vt* - **1.** [suj : travail] to dishearten - **2.** [suj : manières] to disgust.

récalcitrant, e [rekalsitrɑ̃, ɑ̃t] ◇ *adj* recalcitrant, stubborn ◇ *nm, f* recalcitrant.

recaler [3] [rəkale] *vt fam* to fail.

récapitulatif, ive [rekapitylatif, iv] *adj* summary *(avant n)*.
⏵ **récapitulatif** *nm* summary.

récapitulation [rekapitylasjɔ̃] *nf* recapitulation, recap.

récapituler [3] [rekapityle] *vt* to recapitulate, to recap.

recel [rəsɛl] *nm* [action] receiving *ou* handling stolen goods ; [délit] possession of stolen goods.

receler [25] [rəsəle] *vt* - **1.** [objet volé] to receive, to handle - **2.** *fig* [secret, trésor] to contain.

receleur, euse [rəsəlœr, øz] *nm, f* receiver *(of stolen goods)*.

récemment [resamɑ̃] *adv* recently.

recensement [rəsɑ̃smɑ̃] *nm* - **1.** [de population] census - **2.** [d'objets] inventory.

recenser [3] [rəsɑ̃se] *vt* - **1.** [population] to take a census of - **2.** [objets] to take an inventory of.

récent, e [resɑ̃, ɑ̃t] *adj* recent.

recentrer [3] [rəsɑ̃tre] *vt* to refocus.

récépissé [resepise] *nm* receipt.

réceptacle [reseptakl] *nm* [lieu] gathering place.

récepteur, trice [reseptœr, tris] *adj* receiving.
⏵ **récepteur** *nm* receiver.

réceptif, ive [reseptif, iv] *adj* receptive.

réception [resepsjɔ̃] *nf* - **1.** [gén] reception ; **donner une ~** to hold a reception - **2.** [de marchandises] receipt - **3.** [bureau] reception

(desk) - **4.** *SPORT* [de sauteur, skieur] landing ; [du ballon, avec la main] catch ; **bonne ~ de X** [avec le pied] X traps the ball.

réceptionnaire [resepsjɔnɛr] *nmf* - **1.** [de marchandises] receiving clerk - **2.** [à l'hôtel] head of reception.

réceptionner [3] [resepsjɔne] *vt* - **1.** [marchandises] to take delivery of - **2.** [SPORT - avec la main] to catch ; [- avec le pied] to control.

réceptionniste [resepsjɔnist] *nmf* receptionist.

récessif, ive [resesif, iv] *adj* recessive.

récession [resesjɔ̃] *nf* recession.

recette [rəsɛt] *nf* - **1.** *COMM* takings *(pl)* ; **faire ~** *fig* to be a success - **2.** *CULIN* recipe ; *fig* [méthode] recipe, formula.

recevable [rəsəvabl] *adj* - **1.** [excuse, offre] acceptable - **2.** *JUR* admissible.

receveur, euse [rəsəvœr, øz] *nm, f* - **1.** *ADMIN* : ⏵ **des impôts** tax collector ; **~ des postes** postmaster *(f* postmistress*)* - **2.** [de bus] conductor *(f* conductress*)* - **3.** [de greffe] recipient.

recevoir [52] [rəsəvwar] *vt* - **1.** [gén] to receive - **2.** [coup] to get, to receive - **3.** [invités] to entertain ; [client] to see ; **~ qqn à dîner** to have sb to dinner - **4.** *SCOL & UNIV* : **être reçu à un examen** to pass an exam.
⏵ **se recevoir** *vp SPORT* to land.

rechange [rəʃɑ̃ʒ] ⏵ **de rechange** *loc adj* spare ; *fig* alternative.

réchapper [3] [reʃape] *vi* : **~ de** to survive.

recharge [rəʃarʒ] *nf* - **1.** [cartouche] refill - **2.** [action - de batterie] recharging.

rechargeable [rəʃarʒabl] *adj* [batterie] rechargeable ; [briquet] refillable.

recharger [17] [rəʃarʒe] *vt* - **1.** [batterie] to recharge - **2.** [stylo, briquet] to refill - **3.** [arme, camion, appareil-photo] to reload.

réchaud [reʃo] *nm* (portable) stove.

réchauffé, e [reʃofe] *adj* [plat] reheated ; *fig* rehashed.

réchauffement [reʃofmɑ̃] *nm* warming (up).

réchauffer [3] [reʃofe] *vt* - **1.** [nourriture] to reheat - **2.** [personne] to warm up.
⏵ **se réchauffer** *vp* to warm up.

rêche [rɛʃ] *adj* rough.

recherche [rəʃɛrʃ] *nf* - **1.** [quête & *INFORM*] search ; **être à la ~ de** to be in search of ; **se mettre ou partir à la ~ de** to go in search of ; **faire ou effectuer des ~s** to make inquiries - **2.** *SCIENCE* research ; **faire de la ~** to do research - **3.** [raffinement] elegance.

recherché, e [rəʃɛrʃe] *adj* - **1.** [ouvrage]

sought-after - **2.** [raffiné - vocabulaire] refined ; [- mets] exquisite.

rechercher [3] [rəʃɛrʃe] *vt* - **1.** [objet, personne] to search for, to hunt for - **2.** [compagnie] to seek out.

rechigner [3] [rəʃiɲe] *vi* : ~ **à** to balk at.

rechute [rəʃyt] *nf* relapse.

rechuter [3] [rəʃyte] *vi* to relapse.

récidive [residiv] *nf* - **1.** JUR repeat offence *Br ou* offense *Am* - **2.** MÉD recurrence.

récidiver [3] [residive] *vi* - **1.** JUR to commit another offence *Br ou* offense *Am* - **2.** MÉD to recur.

récidiviste [residivist] *nmf* repeat *ou* persistent offender.

récif [resif] *nm* reef ; ~ **de corail** coral reef.

récipiendaire [resipjɑ̃dɛr] *nmf sout* - **1.** [dans assemblée] newly elected member - **2.** [de diplôme] recipient.

récipient [resipjɑ̃] *nm* container.

réciproque [resiprɔk] <> *adj* reciprocal <> *nf* : **la** ~ the reverse.

réciproquement [resiprɔkmɑ̃] *adv* mutually ; **et** ~ and vice versa.

récit [resi] *nm* story.

récital, als [resital] *nm* recital.

récitatif [resitatif] *nm* recitative.

récitation [resitasjɔ̃] *nf* recitation.

réciter [3] [resite] *vt* to recite.

réclamation [reklamasjɔ̃] *nf* complaint ; **faire/déposer une** ~ to make/lodge a complaint.

réclame [reklam] *nf* - **1.** [annonce] advert, advertisement - **2.** [publicité] : **la** ~ advertising - **3.** [promotion] : **en** ~ on special offer.

réclamer [3] [reklame] *vt* - **1.** [demander] to ask for, to request ; [avec insistance] to demand - **2.** [nécessiter] to require, to demand.

➤ **se réclamer** *vp* : **se** ~ **de** [mouvement] to identify with.

reclasser [3] [rəklase] *vt* - **1.** [dossiers] to refile - **2.** [chômeur] to find a new job for - **3.** ADMIN to regrade.

reclus, e [rəkly, yz] <> *adj sout* reclusive <> *nm, f* recluse.

réclusion [reklyzjɔ̃] *nf* imprisonment ; ~ **à perpétuité** life imprisonment.

recoiffer [3] [rəkwafe] *vt* : ~ **qqn** to do sb's hair again.

➤ **se recoiffer** *vp* to do one's hair again.

recoin [rəkwɛ̃] *nm* nook.

reçois, reçoit *etc* ▷ **recevoir**.

recoller [3] [rəkɔle] *vt* [objet brisé] to stick back together.

récolte [rekɔlt] *nf* - **1.** [AGRIC - action] harvesting (U), gathering (U) ; [- produit] harvest, crop - **2.** *fig* collection.

récolter [3] [rekɔlte] *vt* to harvest ; *fig* to collect.

recommandable [rəkɔmɑ̃dabl] *adj* commendable ; **peu** ~ undesirable.

recommandation [rəkɔmɑ̃dasjɔ̃] *nf* recommendation.

recommandé, e [rəkɔmɑ̃de] *adj* - **1.** [envoi] registered ; **envoyer qqch en** ~ to send sthg by registered post *Br ou* mail *Am* - **2.** [conseillé] advisable ; **ce n'est pas très** ~ it's not really a good idea, it's not very advisable.

recommander [3] [rəkɔmɑ̃de] *vt* to recommend ; ~ **à qqn de faire qqch** to advise sb to do sthg ; ~ **qqn à qqn** to recommend sb to sb.

➤ **se recommander** *vp* - **1.** [se réclamer] : **se** ~ **de qqn** to use sb as a referee - **2.** [invoquer la protection de] : **se** ~ **à qqn** to commend o.s. to sb - **3.** *Helv* [insister] to be persistent.

recommencement [rəkɔmɑ̃smɑ̃] *nm* new beginning.

recommencer [16] [rəkɔmɑ̃se] <> *vt* [travail] to start *ou* begin again ; [erreur] to make again ; ~ **à faire qqch** to start *ou* begin doing sthg again <> *vi* to start *ou* begin again ; **ne recommence pas!** don't do that again!

récompense [rekɔ̃pɑ̃s] *nf* reward ; **en** ~ **de** as a reward for.

récompenser [3] [rekɔ̃pɑ̃se] *vt* to reward.

recompter [3] [rəkɔ̃te] *vt* to recount.

réconciliation [rekɔ̃siljasjɔ̃] *nf* reconciliation.

réconcilier [9] [rekɔ̃silje] *vt* to reconcile.

➤ **se réconcilier** *vp* : **se** ~ **avec** to make it up with.

reconductible [rəkɔ̃dyktibl] *adj* renewable.

reconduction [rəkɔ̃dyksjɔ̃] *nf* renewal.

reconduire [98] [rəkɔ̃dɥir] *vt* - **1.** [personne] to accompany, to take - **2.** [politique, bail] to renew.

reconduit, e [rəkɔ̃dɥi, it] *pp* ▷ **reconduire**.

réconfort [rekɔ̃fɔr] *nm* comfort ; **chercher** ~ **dans** to seek comfort *ou* solace in.

réconfortant, e [rekɔ̃fɔrtɑ̃, ɑ̃t] *adj* comforting.

réconforter [3] [rekɔ̃fɔrte] *vt* to comfort.

reconnaissable [rəkɔnɛsabl] *adj* recognizable.

reconnaissance [rəkɔnɛsɑ̃s] *nf* - **1.** [gén] recognition ; ~ **de la parole/vocale** INFORM speech/voice recognition - **2.** [aveu] acknowledgment, admission ; ~ **de dette** acknowledgment of a debt, IOU - **3.** MIL reconnaissance ; **aller/partir en ~** to go out on reconnaissance - **4.** [gratitude] gratitude ; **exprimer sa ~ à qqn** to show *ou* express one's gratitude to sb.

reconnaissant, e [rəkɔnɛsɑ̃, ɑ̃t] *adj* grateful ; **je vous en suis très ~** I am very grateful to you (for it) ; **je vous serais ~ de m'aider** I would be grateful if you would help me.

reconnaître [91] [rəkɔnɛtr] *vt* - **1.** [gén] to recognize - **2.** [erreur] to admit, to acknowledge - **3.** MIL to reconnoitre.

◆ **se reconnaître** *vp* - **1.** [s'identifier] to recognize o.s. ; **se ~ dans** *ou* **en qqn** to see o.s. in sb - **2.** [s'orienter] to know where one is, to get one's bearings - **3.** [s'avouer] : **se ~ coupable** to admit one's guilt.

reconnu, e [rəkɔny] ◇ *pp* ▷ **reconnaître** ◇ *adj* well-known.

reconquérir [39] [rəkɔ̃kerir] *vt* to reconquer.

reconquête [rəkɔ̃kɛt] *nf* reconquest.

reconquis, e [rəkɔ̃ki, iz] *pp* ▷ **reconquérir.**

reconquiers, reconquiert *etc* ▷ **reconquérir.**

reconsidérer [18] [rəkɔ̃sidere] *vt* to reconsider.

reconstituant, e [rəkɔ̃stitɥɑ̃, ɑ̃t] *adj* invigorating.

◆ **reconstituant** *nm* tonic.

reconstituer [7] [rəkɔ̃stitɥe] *vt* - **1.** [puzzle] to put together - **2.** [crime, délit] to reconstruct.

reconstitution [rəkɔ̃stitysjɔ̃] *nf* - **1.** [de puzzle] putting together - **2.** [de crime, délit] reconstruction ; **~ historique** CIN & TÉLÉ dramatic reconstruction.

reconstruction [rəkɔ̃stryksjɔ̃] *nf* reconstruction, rebuilding.

reconstruire [98] [rəkɔ̃strɥir] *vt* to reconstruct, to rebuild.

reconstruit, e [rəkɔ̃strɥi, it] *pp* ▷ **reconstruire.**

reconversion [rəkɔ̃vɛrsjɔ̃] *nf* - **1.** [d'employé] redeployment - **2.** [d'usine, de société] conversion ; **opérer une ~** to restructure ; **~ économique/technique** economic/technical restructuring.

reconvertir [32] [rəkɔ̃vɛrtir] *vt* - **1.** [employé] to redeploy - **2.** [économie] to restructure.

◆ **se reconvertir** *vp* : **se ~ dans** to move into.

recopier [9] [rəkɔpje] *vt* to copy out.

record [rəkɔr] ◇ *nm* record ; **détenir/améliorer/battre un ~** to hold/improve/beat a record ◇ *adj inv* record *(avant n).*

recordman [rəkɔrdman] *(pl* **recordmen** [-mɛn]) *nm* recordholder.

recoucher [3] [rəkuʃe] *vt* to put back to bed.

◆ **se recoucher** *vp* to go back to bed.

recoudre [86] [rəkudr] *vt* to sew (up) again.

recoupement [rəkupmɑ̃] *nm* cross-check ; **par ~** by cross-checking.

recouper [3] [rəkupe] *vt* - **1.** [pain] to cut again - **2.** COUTURE to recut - **3.** *fig* [témoignages] to compare, to cross-check.

◆ **se recouper** *vp* - **1.** [lignes] to intersect - **2.** [témoignages] to match up.

recourber [3] [rəkurbe] *vt* to bend (over).

recourir [45] [rəkurir] *vi* : **~ à** [médecin, agence] to turn to ; [force, mensonge] to resort to.

recourrai, recourras *etc* ▷ **recourir.**

recours¹, recourt *etc* ▷ **recourir.**

recours² [rəkur] *nm* - **1.** [emploi] : **~ à** use of ; **avoir ~ à** [médecin, agence] to turn to ; [force, mensonge] to resort to, to have recourse to - **2.** [solution] solution, way out ; **en dernier ~** as a last resort - **3.** JUR action ; **~ en cassation** appeal ; **~ en justice** legal action ; **sans ~** without appeal ; *fig* final.

recouru [rəkury] *pp inv* ▷ **recourir.**

recouvert, e [rəkuvɛr, ɛrt] *pp* ▷ **recouvrir.**

recouvrable [rəkuvrabl] *adj* recoverable.

recouvrement [rəkuvrəmɑ̃] *nm* - **1.** [de surface] covering - **2.** [de dettes, d'impôts] collection.

recouvrer [3] [rəkuvre] *vt* - **1.** [vue, liberté] to regain - **2.** [dettes, impôts] to collect.

recouvrir [34] [rəkuvrir] *vt* - **1.** [gén] to cover ; [fauteuil] to re-cover - **2.** [personne] to cover (up).

◆ **se recouvrir** *vp* - **1.** [tuiles] to overlap - **2.** [surface] : **se ~ (de)** to be covered (with).

recracher [3] [rəkraʃe] *vt* to spit out.

récréatif, ive [rekreatif, iv] *adj* entertaining.

récréation [rekreasjɔ̃] *nf* - **1.** [détente] relaxation, recreation - **2.** SCOL break.

recréer [15] [rəkree] *vt* to recreate.

récrier [10] [rekrije] ◆ **se récrier** *vp sout* : **se ~ (à)** to exclaim (at).

récrimination [rekriminasjɔ̃] *nf* complaint.

récriminer [3] [rekrimine] *vi* to complain.

récrire [rekrir], **réécrire** [99] [reekrir] *vt* to rewrite.

recroqueviller [3] [rəkrɔkvije] ◆ **se recroqueviller** *vp* to curl up.

recru, e [rəkry] *adj* : **~ de fatigue** *littéraire* exhausted.

◆ **recrue** *nf* recruit.

recrudescence [rəkrydɛsɑ̃s] *nf* renewed outbreak.

recrutement [rəkrytmɑ̃] *nm* recruitment.

recruter [3] [rəkryte] *vt* to recruit.

rectal, e, aux [rɛktal, o] *adj* rectal.

rectangle [rɛktɑ̃gl] *nm* rectangle.

rectangulaire [rɛktɑ̃gylɛr] *adj* rectangular.

recteur [rɛktœr] *nm* SCOL *chief administrative officer of an education authority,* ≃ (Chief) Education Officer *Br.*

rectificatif, ive [rɛktifikatif, iv] *adj* correcting.
↪ **rectificatif** *nm* correction.

rectification [rɛktifikasjɔ̃] *nf* - **1.** [correction] correction - **2.** [de tir] adjustment.

rectifier [9] [rɛktifje] *vt* - **1.** [tir] to adjust - **2.** [erreur] to rectify, to correct ; [calcul] to correct.

rectiligne [rɛktiliɲ] *adj* rectilinear.

recto [rɛkto] *nm* right side ; ~ **verso** on both sides.

rectorat [rɛktɔra] *nm* SCOL *offices of the education authority,* ≃ Education Offices *Br.*

rectum [rɛktɔm] *nm* rectum.

reçu, e [rəsy] *pp* ⊳ **recevoir.**
↪ **reçu** *nm* receipt.

recueil [rəkœj] *nm* collection.

recueillement [rəkœjmɑ̃] *nm* meditation.

recueillir [41] [rəkœjir] *vt* - **1.** [fonds] to collect - **2.** [suffrages] to win - **3.** [enfant] to take in.
↪ **se recueillir** *vp* to meditate.

recuire [98] [rəkɥir] *vt* & *vi* to recook.

recul [rəkyl] *nm* - **1.** [mouvement arrière] step backwards ; MIL retreat - **2.** [d'arme à feu] recoil - **3.** [de civilisation] decline ; [d'inflation, de chômage] : ~ **(de)** downturn (in) - **4.** *fig* [retrait] : **prendre du ~** to stand back ; **avec du ~** with hindsight.

reculade [rəkylad] *nf* retreat.

reculé, e [rəkyle] *adj* distant.

reculer [3] [rəkyle] ◇ *vt* - **1.** [voiture] to back up - **2.** [date] to put back, to postpone ◇ *vi* - **1.** [aller en arrière] to move backwards ; [voiture] to reverse ; **ne ~ devant rien** *fig* to stop at nothing - **2.** [maladie, pauvreté] to be brought under control.

reculons [rəkylɔ̃] ↪ **à reculons** *adv* backwards.

récupération [rekyperasjɔ̃] *nf* [de déchets] salvage.

récupérer [18] [rekypere] ◇ *vt* - **1.** [objet] to get back - **2.** [déchets] to salvage - **3.** [idée] to pick up - **4.** [journée] to make up ◇ *vi* to recover, to recuperate.

récurer [3] [rekyre] *vt* to scour.

récurrent, e [rekyrɑ̃, ɑ̃t] *adj* recurrent.

récuser [3] [rekyze] *vt* - **1.** JUR to challenge - **2.** *sout* [refuser] to reject.
↪ **se récuser** *vp* *sout* to decline to give an opinion.

recyclage [rəsiklaʒ] *nm* - **1.** [d'employé] retraining - **2.** [de déchets] recycling.

recycler [3] [rəsikle] *vt* - **1.** [employé] to retrain - **2.** [déchets] to recycle.
↪ **se recycler** *vp* [employé] to retrain.

rédacteur, trice [redaktœr, tris] *nm, f* [de journal] subeditor ; [d'ouvrage de référence] editor ; ~ **en chef** editor-in-chief.

rédaction [redaksjɔ̃] *nf* - **1.** [de texte] editing - **2.** SCOL essay - **3.** [personnel] editorial staff.

rédactionnel, elle [redaksjɔnɛl] *adj* editorial.

reddition [redisjɔ̃] *nf* surrender.

redécouvrir [34] [rədekuvrir] *vt* to rediscover.

redéfinir [32] [rədefinir] *vt* to redefine.

redéfinition [rədefinisjɔ̃] *nf* redefinition.

redemander [3] [rədəmɑ̃de] *vt* to ask again for.

redémarrer [3] [rədemare] *vi* to start again ; *fig* to get going again.

rédempteur, trice [redɑ̃ptœr, tris] ◇ *adj* redeeming ◇ *nm, f* redeemer.

rédemption [redɑ̃psjɔ̃] *nf* redemption.

redéploiement [rədeplwamɑ̃] *nm* redeployment.

redescendre [73] [rədesɑ̃dr] ◇ *vt* (aux : avoir) - **1.** [escalier] to go/come down again - **2.** [objet - d'une étagère] to take down again ◇ *vi* (aux : être) to go/come down again.

redevable [rədəvabl] *adj* : **être ~ de 10 francs à qqn** to owe sb 10 francs ; **être ~ à qqn de qqch** [service] to be indebted to sb for sthg.

redevance [rədəvɑ̃s] *nf* [de radio, télévision] licence fee ; [téléphonique] rental (fee).

redevenir [40] [rədəvnir] *vi* to become again.

rédhibitoire [redibitwar] *adj* [défaut] crippling ; [prix] prohibitive.

rediffuser [3] [rədifyze] *vt* to broadcast again, to repeat.

rediffusion [rədifyzjɔ̃] *nf* repeat.

rédiger [17] [rediʒe] *vt* to write.

redingote [rədɛ̃gɔt] *nf* [de femme] coat ; HIST frock coat.

redire [102] [rədir] *vt* to repeat ; **avoir** OU **trouver à ~ à qqch** *fig* to find fault with sthg.

redistribuer [7] [rədistribɥe] *vt* to redistribute.

redistribution [rədistribysjɔ̃] *nf* redistribution.

redit, e [rədi, it] *pp* ⊳ **redire**.

redite [rədit] *nf* repetition.

redondance [rədɔ̃dɑ̃s] *nf* redundancy.

redonner [3] [rədɔne] *vt* to give back ; [confiance, forces] to restore.

redoublant, e [rədublɑ̃, ɑ̃t] *nm, f* pupil who is repeating a year.

redoublé, e [rəduble] *adj* : **à coups ~s** twice as hard.

redoubler [3] [rəduble] ⬦ *vt* - **1.** [syllabe] to reduplicate - **2.** [efforts] to intensify - **3.** SCOL to repeat ⬦ *vi* to intensify ; **~ d'efforts** to redouble one's efforts ; **le vent redoubla de fureur** the wind blew twice as hard.

redoutable [rədutabl] *adj* formidable.

redouter [3] [rədute] *vt* to fear.

redoux [rədu] *nm* thaw.

redressement [rədrɛsmɑ̃] *nm* - **1.** [de pays, d'économie] recovery - **2.** JUR : **~ fiscal** payment of back taxes.

redresser [4] [rədrɛse] ⬦ *vt* - **1.** [poteau, arbre] to put *ou* set upright ; **~ la tête** to raise one's head ; *fig* to hold up one's head - **2.** [situation] to set right ⬦ *vi* AUTOM to straighten up.

➤ **se redresser** *vp* - **1.** [personne] to stand *ou* sit straight - **2.** [pays] to recover.

redresseur [rədrɛsœr] *nm* : **~ de torts** righter of wrongs.

réducteur, trice [redyktœr, tris] *adj* - **1.** [de quantité] reducing - **2.** [limitatif] simplistic.

➤ **réducteur** *nm* CHIM reducing agent.

réduction [redyksjɔ̃] *nf* - **1.** [gén] reduction ; **bénéficier d'une ~** to get a reduction - **2.** MÉD setting.

réduire [98] [redɥir] ⬦ *vt* - **1.** [gén] to reduce ; **~ en** to reduce to ; **~ qqn à qqch/à faire qqch** to reduce sb to sthg/to doing sthg ; **être réduit à faire qqch** to be reduced to doing sthg - **2.** MÉD to set - **3.** *Helv* [ranger] to put away ⬦ *vi* CULIN to reduce.

➤ **se réduire** *vp* - **1.** [se restreindre] to cut down - **2.** [se ramener] : **se ~ à** to come *ou* boil down to - **3.** [se transformer] : **se ~ en** to be reduced to.

réduisais, réduisions *etc* ⊳ **réduire**.

réduit, e [redɥi, it] ⬦ *pp* ⊳ **réduire** ⬦ *adj* reduced.

➤ **réduit** *nm* - **1.** [local] small room - **2.** [renfoncement] recess.

rééchelonner [3] [reeʃlɔne] *vt* to reschedule.

réécrire = **récrire**.

rééditer [3] [reedite] *vt* - **1.** [œuvre, auteur] to re-publish - **2.** *fam* [méfaits] to give a repeat performance of.

réédition [reedisjɔ̃] *nf* new edition.

rééducation [reedykasjɔ̃] *nf* - **1.** [de membre] re-education - **2.** [de délinquant, malade] rehabilitation.

rééduquer [3] [reedyke] *vt* - **1.** [membre] to re-educate - **2.** [délinquant, malade] to rehabilitate.

réel, elle [reɛl] *adj* real.

➤ **réel** *nm* : **le ~** reality.

réélection [reelɛksjɔ̃] *nf* re-election.

réélire [106] [reelir] *vt* to re-elect.

réellement [reɛlmɑ̃] *adv* really.

réembaucher [3] [reɑ̃boʃe] *vt* to take on again.

réemploi = **remploi**.

réemployer = **remployer**.

réengager = **rengager**.

rééquilibrer [3] [reekilibre] *vt* to balance (again).

réescompte [reɛskɔ̃t] *nm* rediscount.

réessayer [reeseje], **ressayer** [rɛseje] [11] *vt* to try again.

réévaluer [7] [reevalɥe] *vt* to revalue.

réexaminer [3] [reɛgzamine] *vt* to re-examine.

réexpédier [9] [reɛkspedje] *vt* to send back.

réexporter [3] [reɛkspɔrte] *vt* to re-export.

réf. (*abr de* **référence**) ref.

refaire [109] [rəfɛr] *vt* - **1.** [faire de nouveau - travail, devoir] to do again ; [- voyage] to make again - **2.** [mur, toit] to repair - **3.** *fam* [personne] to take in.

➤ **se refaire** *vp* - **1.** [se rétablir] : **se ~ une santé** to recover (one's health) - **2.** [se réhabituer] : **~ à qqch** to get used to sthg again - **3.** *fam* [au jeu] to make up *ou* win back one's losses.

refaisais, refaisions *etc* ⊳ **refaire**.

refait, e [rəfɛ, ɛt] *pp* ⊳ **refaire**.

refasse, refasses *etc* ⊳ **refaire**.

réfection [refɛksjɔ̃] *nf* repair.

réfectoire [refɛktwar] *nm* refectory.

référé [refere] *nm* [procédure] special hearing ; [arrêt] temporary ruling ; [ordonnance] temporary injunction.

référence [referɑ̃s] *nf* reference ; **faire ~ à** to refer to.

➤ **références** *nfpl* references.

référendum [referɛ̃dɔm] *nm* referendum.

référer [18] [referel *vi* : en ~ à qqn to refer the matter to sb.
➥ **se référer** *vp* : se ~ à to refer to.
refermer [3] [rəfɛrme] *vt* to close *ou* shut again.
refiler [3] [rəfile] *vt fam* : ~ qqch à qqn [objet] to palm sthg off on sb ; [maladie] to give sthg to sb.
réfléchi, e [refleʃi] *adj* - **1.** [action] considered ; **c'est tout ~** I've made up my mind, I've decided - **2.** [personne] thoughtful - **3.** *GRAM* reflexive.
réfléchir [32] [refleʃir] ◇ *vt* - **1.** [refléter] to reflect - **2.** [penser] : ~ **que** to think *ou* reflect that ◇ *vi* to think, to reflect ; ~ à *ou* sur qqch to think about sthg.
➥ **se réfléchir** *vp* to be reflected.
réfléchissant, e [refleʃisɑ̃, ɑ̃t] *adj* reflective.
réflecteur [reflɛktœr] *nm* reflector.
reflet [rəflɛ] *nm* - **1.** [image] reflection - **2.** [de lumière] glint.
refléter [18] [rəflete] *vt* to reflect.
➥ **se refléter** *vp* - **1.** [se réfléchir] to be reflected - **2.** [transparaître] to be mirrored.
refleurir [32] [rəflœrir] *vi* - **1.** [fleurir à nouveau] to flower again - **2.** *fig* [art] to flourish again.
reflex [reflɛks] ◇ *nm* reflex camera ◇ *adj* reflex *(avant n)*.
réflexe [reflɛks] ◇ *nm* reflex ◇ *adj* reflex *(avant n)*.
réflexion [reflɛksjɔ̃] *nf* - **1.** [de lumière, d'ondes] reflection - **2.** [pensée] reflection, thought ; **à la ~** on second thoughts ; **~ faite** on reflection - **3.** [remarque] remark.
refluer [3] [rəflue] *vi* - **1.** [liquide] to flow back - **2.** [foule] to flow back ; [avec violence] to surge back.
reflux [rəfly] *nm* - **1.** [d'eau] ebb - **2.** [de personnes] backward surge.
refondre [75] [rəfɔ̃dr] *vt* - **1.** [métal] to remelt - **2.** [ouvrage] to recast.
refonte [rəfɔ̃t] *nf* - **1.** [de métal] remelting - **2.** [d'ouvrage] recasting - **3.** [d'institution, de système] overhaul, reshaping.
reforestation [rəfɔrɛstasjɔ̃] *nf* reforestation.
réformateur, trice [reformatœr, tris] ◇ *adj* reforming ◇ *nm, f* - **1.** [personne] reformer - **2.** *RELIG* Reformer.
réforme [reform] *nf* reform.
réformé, e [reforme] *adj* & *nm, f* Protestant.
➥ **réformé** *nm MIL soldier who has been invalided out.*

reformer [3] [rəforme] *vt* to re-form.
➥ **se reformer** *vp* to reform.
réformer [3] [reforme] *vt* - **1.** [améliorer] to reform, to improve - **2.** *MIL* to invalid out - **3.** [matériel] to scrap.
réformisme [reformism] *nm* reformism.
réformiste [reformist] *adj* & *nmf* reformist.
refoulé, e [rəfule] ◇ *adj* repressed, frustrated ◇ *nm, f* repressed person.
refoulement [rəfulmɑ̃] *nm* - **1.** [de personnes] repelling - **2.** *PSYCHOL* repression.
refouler [3] [rəfule] *vt* - **1.** [personnes] to repel, to repulse - **2.** *PSYCHOL* to repress.
réfractaire [refrakter] ◇ *adj* - **1.** [rebelle] insubordinate ; **~ à** resistant to ; **être ~ à la loi** to flout the law - **2.** *HIST* [prêtre] non-juring - **3.** [matière] refractory ◇ *nmf* insubordinate.
refrain [rəfrɛ̃] *nm MUS* refrain, chorus ; **c'est toujours le même ~** *fam fig* it's always the same old story.
refréner [18] [rəfrene] *vt* to check, to hold back.
➥ **se refréner** *vp* to control o.s.
réfrigérant, e [refriʒerɑ̃, ɑ̃t] *adj* - **1.** [liquide] refrigerating, refrigerant - **2.** *fam* [accueil] icy.
réfrigérateur [refriʒeratœr] *nm* refrigerator.
réfrigération [refriʒerasjɔ̃] *nf* refrigeration.
réfringent, e [refrɛ̃ʒɑ̃, ɑ̃t] *adj* refractive.
refroidir [32] [rəfrwadir] ◇ *vt* - **1.** [plat] to cool - **2.** [décourager] to discourage - **3.** *fam* [tuer] to rub out, to do in ◇ *vi* to cool.
➥ **se refroidir** *vp* - **1.** [temps] to get *ou* turn colder - **2.** [ardeur] to cool.
refroidissement [rəfrwadismɑ̃] *nm* - **1.** [de température] drop, cooling - **2.** [grippe] chill - **3.** *fig* [de sentiment] cooling off.
refuge [rəfyʒ] *nm* - **1.** [abri] refuge ; **chercher ~ auprès de qqn** to seek refuge with sb - **2.** [de montagne] hut - **3.** [sur chaussée] traffic island.
réfugié, e [refyʒje] ◇ *adj* refugee *(avant n)* ◇ *nm, f* refugee.
réfugier [9] [refyʒje] ➥ **se réfugier** *vp* to take refuge.
refus [rəfy] *nm inv* refusal ; **ce n'est pas de ~** *fam* I wouldn't say no ; **essuyer un ~** to meet with a refusal.
refuser [3] [rəfyze] *vt* - **1.** [repousser] to refuse ; **~ de faire qqch** to refuse to do sthg - **2.** [contester] : **~ qqch à qqn** to deny sb sthg

- 3. [clients, spectateurs] to turn away **- 4.** [candidat] : **être refusé** to fail.

➤ **se refuser** vp : **se ~ à faire qqch** to refuse to do sthg ; **se ~ à tout commentaire** to refuse to make any comment ; **ne rien se ~** not to stint o.s.

réfutation [refytasjɔ̃] nf refutation.
réfuter [3] [refyte] vt to refute.
regagner [3] [rəgaɲe] vt **- 1.** [reprendre] to regain, to win back **- 2.** [revenir à] to get back to.
regain [rəgɛ̃] nm **- 1.** [herbe] second crop **- 2.** [retour] : **un ~ de** a revival of, a renewal of ; **un ~ de vie** a new lease of life.
régal, als [regal] nm treat, delight.
régaler [3] [regale] vt to treat ; **c'est moi qui régale!** it's my treat!

➤ **se régaler** vp : **je me régale** [nourriture] I'm thoroughly enjoying it ; [activité] I'm having the time of my life.

regard [rəgar] nm look ; **soutenir le ~ de qqn** fig to be able to look sb straight in the eye ; **fusiller** ou **foudroyer qqn du ~** fig to glare at sb, to look daggers at sb.

➤ **au regard de** loc prép in relation to, with regard to.

➤ **en regard de** loc prép compared with.

regardant, e [rəgardɑ̃, ɑ̃t] adj **- 1.** [économe] mean **- 2.** [minutieux] : **être très/peu ~ sur qqch** to be very/not very particular about sthg.

regarder [3] [rəgarde] ◇ vt **- 1.** [observer, examiner, consulter] to look at ; [télévision, spectacle] to watch ; **~ qqn faire qqch** to watch sb doing sthg ; **~ les trains passer** to watch the trains go by **- 2.** [considérer] to consider, to regard ; **~ qqn/qqch comme** to regard sb/sthg as, to consider sb/sthg as **- 3.** [concerner] to concern ; **cela ne te regarde pas** it's none of your business ◇ vi **- 1.** [observer, examiner] to look **- 2.** [faire attention] : **sans ~ à la dépense** regardless of the expense ; **y ~ à deux fois** to think twice about it.

➤ **se regarder** vp **- 1.** [emploi réfléchi] to look at o.s. **- 2.** [emploi réciproque] to look at one another.

regarnir [32] [rəgarnir] vt to refill, to restock.
régate [regat] nf (gén pl) regatta.
régence [reʒɑ̃s] nf regency.

➤ **Régence** nf HIST : **la Régence** the Regency.

régénérer [18] [reʒenere] vt to regenerate.

➤ **se régénérer** vp to regenerate.

régent, e [reʒɑ̃, ɑ̃t] nm, f regent.
régenter [3] [reʒɑ̃te] vt : **vouloir tout ~** péj to want to be the boss.
reggae [rege] nm & adj inv reggae.

régie [reʒi] nf **- 1.** [entreprise] state-controlled company **- 2.** RADIO & TÉLÉ [pièce] control room ; CIN, THÉÂTRE & TÉLÉ [équipe] production team.
regimber [3] [rəʒɛ̃be] vi to balk.
régime [reʒim] nm **- 1.** [politique] regime ; **l'Ancien Régime** the Ancien Regime **- 2.** [administratif] system ; **~ carcéral** prison regime ; **~ de Sécurité sociale** subdivision of the French social security system applying to certain professional groups **- 3.** [alimentaire] diet ; **se mettre au/suivre un ~** to go on/to be on a diet ; **~ amincissant** slimming diet **- 4.** [de moteur] speed **- 5.** [de fleuve, des pluies] cycle **- 6.** [de bananes, dattes] bunch.
régiment [reʒimɑ̃] nm **- 1.** MIL regiment **- 2.** fam [grande quantité] : **un ~ de** masses of, loads of.
région [reʒjɔ̃] nf region ; **~ parisienne** Paris area ou region.
régional, e, aux [reʒjɔnal, o] adj regional.
régionalisation [reʒjɔnalizasjɔ̃] nf regionalization.
régionalisme [reʒjɔnalism] nm regionalism.
régionaliste [reʒjɔnalist] nmf & adj regionalist.
régir [32] [reʒir] vt to govern.
régisseur [reʒisœr] nm **- 1.** [intendant] steward **- 2.** [de théâtre] stage manager.
registre [rəʒistr] nm [gén] register ; **~ du commerce** trade register ; **~ de comptabilité** ledger ; **~s publics d'état civil** register (sg) of births, marriages and deaths.
réglable [reglabl] adj **- 1.** [adaptable] adjustable **- 2.** [payable] payable.
réglage [reglaʒ] nm adjustment, setting.
règle [rɛgl] nf **- 1.** [instrument] ruler ; **~ graduée** graduated ruler **- 2.** [principe, loi] rule ; **je suis en ~** my papers are in order ; **mets-toi en ~** get your papers in order ; **être de ~** to be the rule.

➤ **en règle générale** loc adv as a general rule.

➤ **règles** nfpl [menstruation] period (sg).

réglé, e [regle] adj **- 1.** [organisé] regular, well-ordered **- 2.** [papier] lined, ruled.
réglée [regle] adj f : **être ~** to have periods, to menstruate.
règlement [rɛgləmɑ̃] nm **- 1.** [résolution] settling ; **~ de comptes** fig settling of scores ; **~ judiciaire** liquidation **- 2.** [règle] regulation ; **observer le ~** to follow the rules ou regulations **- 3.** [paiement] settlement.

réglementaire [rɛgləmɑ̃tɛr] *adj* - **1.** [régulier] statutory - **2.** [imposé] regulation *(avant n)*.

réglementation [rɛgləmɑ̃tasjɔ̃] *nf* - **1.** [action] regulation - **2.** [ensemble de règles] regulations *(pl)*, rules *(pl)* ; ~ du travail/commerce work/commercial regulations.

réglementer [3] [rɛgləmɑ̃te] *vt* to control, to regulate.

régler [18] [regle] *vt* - **1.** [affaire, conflit] to settle, to sort out - **2.** [appareil] to adjust - **3.** [payer - note] to settle, to pay ; [- commerçant] to pay.
◆ **se régler** *vp* - **1.** [suivre] : se ~ sur qqn to model o.s. on sb - **2.** [affaire, conflit] to be sorted out, to be settled.

réglisse [reglis] *nf* liquorice.

réglo [reglo] *adj inv fam* straight.

régnant, e [rɛɲɑ̃, ɑ̃t] *adj* [monarque] reigning.

règne [rɛɲ] *nm* - **1.** [de souverain] reign ; sous le ~ de in the reign of - **2.** [pouvoir] rule - **3.** BIOL kingdom.

régner [18] [reɲe] *vi* - **1.** [souverain] to rule, to reign - **2.** [silence] to reign.

regonfler [3] [rəgɔ̃fle] *vt* - **1.** [pneu, ballon] to blow up again, to reinflate - **2.** *fam* [personne] to cheer up.

regorger [17] [rəgɔrʒe] *vi* : ~ de to be abundant in.

régresser [4] [regrese] *vi* - **1.** [sentiment, douleur] to diminish - **2.** [personne] to regress.

régressif, ive [regresif, iv] *adj* regressive, backward.

régression [regresjɔ̃] *nf* - **1.** [recul] decline - **2.** PSYCHOL regression.

regret [rəgrɛ] *nm* : ~ (de) regret (for) ; tous mes ~s I'm very sorry ; à ~ with regret ; sans ~ with no regrets ; avoir le *ou* être au ~ d'informer qqn de to be sorry *ou* to regret to inform sb of.

regrettable [rəgrɛtabl] *adj* regrettable.

regretter [4] [rəgrɛte] ◇ *vt* - **1.** [époque] to miss, to regret ; [personne] to miss - **2.** [faute] to regret ; ~ d'avoir fait qqch to regret having done sthg - **3.** [déplorer] : ~ que (+ *subjonctif*) to be sorry *ou* to regret that ◇ *vi* to be sorry.

regroupement [rəgrupmɑ̃] *nm* - **1.** [action] gathering together - **2.** [groupe] group, assembly.

regrouper [3] [rəgrupe] *vt* - **1.** [grouper à nouveau] to regroup, to reassemble - **2.** [réunir] to group together.
◆ **se regrouper** *vp* to gather, to assemble.

régulariser [3] [regylarize] *vt* - **1.** [documents] to sort out, to put in order ; [situation] to

straighten out - **2.** [circulation, fonctionnement] to regulate.

régularité [regylarite] *nf* - **1.** [gén] regularity - **2.** [de travail, résultats] consistency.

régulateur, trice [regylatœr, tris] *adj* regulating.
◆ **régulateur** *nm* regulator.

régulation [regylasjɔ̃] *nf* [contrôle] control, regulation ; ~ des naissances birth control.

réguler [3] [regyle] *vt* to regulate.

régulier, ère [regylje, ɛr] *adj* - **1.** [gén] regular - **2.** [uniforme, constant] steady, regular - **3.** [travail, résultats] consistent - **4.** [légal] legal ; être en situation régulière to have all the legally required documents - **5.** *fam* [correct] straight, above board.

régulièrement [regyljɛrmɑ̃] *adv* - **1.** [gén] regularly - **2.** [uniformément] steadily, regularly ; [étalé, façonné] evenly.

réhabilitation [reabilitasjɔ̃] *nf* rehabilitation.

réhabiliter [3] [reabilite] *vt* - **1.** [accusé] to rehabilitate, to clear ; *fig* [racheter] to restore to favour *Br ou* favor *Am* - **2.** [rénover] to restore.
◆ **se réhabiliter** *vp* to redeem o.s.

réhabituer [7] [reabitɥe] *vt* to reaccustom.
◆ **se réhabituer** *vp* : se ~ à qqch to get used to sthg again.

rehausser [3] [rəose] *vt* - **1.** [surélever] to heighten - **2.** *fig* [mettre en valeur] to enhance.

rehausseur [rəosœr] *nm* booster seat.

réimporter [3] [reɛ̃pɔrte] *vt* to reimport.

réimposer [3] [reɛ̃poze] *vt* to retax.

réimpression [reɛ̃presjɔ̃] *nf* reprinting, reprint.

réimprimer [3] [reɛ̃prime] *vt* to reprint.

rein [rɛ̃] *nm* kidney ; ~ artificiel dialysis *ou* kidney machine.
◆ **reins** *nmpl* small of the back *(sg)* ; avoir mal aux ~s to have backache ; avoir les ~s solides *fam* [être résistant] to have a strong back ; [être riche] not to be short of money.

réincarnation [reɛ̃karnasjɔ̃] *nf* reincarnation.

reine [rɛn] *nf* queen.

reine-claude [rɛnklod] *(pl* reines-claudes*)* *nf* greengage.

reinette [rɛnɛt] *nf* variety of apple similar to pippin.

réinscrire [99] [reɛ̃skrir] *vt* : ~ qqn à to re-enrol sb for.
◆ **se réinscrire** *vp* : se ~ à to re-enrol for.

réinsérer [18] [reɛ̃sere] *vt* to reinsert.
◆ **se réinsérer** *vp* to become reintegrated.

réinsertion [reɛ̃sɛrsjɔ̃] *nf* [de délinquant] rehabilitation ; [dans la vie professionnelle] reintegration.

réintégrer [18] [reɛ̃tegre] vt - **1.** [rejoindre] to return to - **2.** *JUR* to reinstate.

réintroduire [98] [reɛ̃trɔdɥir] vt to reintroduce.

réitérer [18] [reitere] vt [promesse, demande] to repeat, to reiterate ; [attaque] to repeat.

rejaillir [32] [rəʒajir] vi to splash up ; ~ sur qqn *fig* to rebound on sb.

rejet [rəʒɛ] nm - **1.** [gén] rejection - **2.** [pousse] shoot.

rejeter [27] [rəʒte] vt - **1.** [relancer] to throw back - **2.** [expulser] to bring up, to vomit - **3.** [offre, personne] to reject - **4.** [partie du corps] : ~ la tête/les bras en arrière to throw back one's head/one's arms - **5.** [imputer] : ~ la responsabilité de qqch sur qqn to lay the responsibility for sthg at sb's door.
➤ **se rejeter** vp : se ~ la faute l'un sur l'autre to blame one another for sthg ; se ~ la responsabilité (de qqch) l'un sur l'autre to hold one another responsible (for sthg).

rejeton [rəʒtɔ̃] nm offspring *(U)*.

rejette, rejettes etc ⊳ rejeter.

rejoindre [82] [rəʒwɛ̃dr] vt - **1.** [retrouver] to join - **2.** [regagner] to return to - **3.** [concorder avec] to agree with - **4.** [rattraper] to catch up with.
➤ **se rejoindre** vp - **1.** [personnes, routes] to meet - **2.** [opinions] to agree.

rejoignais, rejoignions etc ⊳ rejoindre.

rejoint, e [rəʒwɛ̃, ɛ̃t] pp ⊳ rejoindre.

réjoui, e [reʒwi] adj joyful.

réjouir [32] [reʒwir] vt to delight.
➤ **se réjouir** vp to be delighted ; se ~ de qqch to be delighted at *ou* about sthg.

réjouissance [reʒwisɑ̃s] nf rejoicing.
➤ **réjouissances** nfpl festivities.

réjouissant, e [reʒwisɑ̃, ɑ̃t] adj joyful, cheerful.

relâche [rəlɑʃ] nf - **1.** [pause] : sans ~ without respite *ou* a break - **2.** *THÉÂTRE* : demain c'est le jour de ~ we're closed tomorrow ; faire ~ to be closed.

relâché, e [rəlɑʃe] adj lax, loose.

relâchement [rəlɑʃmɑ̃] nm relaxation.

relâcher [3] [rəlɑʃe] vt - **1.** [étreinte, cordes] to loosen - **2.** [discipline, effort] to relax, to slacken - **3.** [prisonnier] to release.
➤ **se relâcher** vp - **1.** [se desserrer] to loosen - **2.** [faiblir - discipline] to become lax ; [- attention] to flag - **3.** [se laisser aller] to slacken off.

relaie, relaies etc ⊳ relayer.

relais [rəlɛ] nm - **1.** [auberge] post house ; ~ routier transport cafe - **2.** *SPORT* & *TÉLÉ* : prendre/passer le ~ to take/hand over ; **(course de)** ~ relay.

relance [rəlɑ̃s] nf - **1.** [économique] revival, boost ; [de projet] relaunch - **2.** [au jeu] stake.

relancer [16] [rəlɑ̃se] vt - **1.** [renvoyer] to throw back - **2.** [faire reprendre - économie] to boost ; [- projet] to relaunch ; [- moteur, machine] to restart.

relater [3] [rəlate] vt littéraire to relate.

relatif, ive [rəlatif, iv] adj relative ; ~ à relating to ; tout est ~ it's all relative.
➤ **relative** nf *GRAM* relative clause.

relation [rəlasjɔ̃] nf relationship ; mettre qqn en ~ avec qqn to put sb in touch with sb.
➤ **relations** nfpl - **1.** [rapport] relationship *(sg)* ; ~s sexuelles sexual relations, intercourse *(U)* - **2.** [connaissance] acquaintance ; avoir des ~s to have connections - **3.** [communication] : ~s internationales international relations ; ~s publiques public relations.

relationnel, elle [rəlasjɔnɛl] adj [problèmes] relationship *(avant n)*.

relative ⊳ relatif.

relativement [rəlativmɑ̃] adv relatively.

relativiser [3] [rəlativize] vt to relativize.

relativité [rəlativite] nf relativity.

relax, relaxe [rəlaks] adj *fam* relaxed.

relaxation [rəlaksasjɔ̃] nf relaxation.

relaxe = relax.

relaxer [3] [rəlakse] vt - **1.** [reposer] to relax - **2.** *JUR* to discharge.
➤ **se relaxer** vp to relax.

relayer [11] [rəleje] vt to relieve.
➤ **se relayer** vp to take over from one another.

relecture [rələktyr] nf second reading, rereading.

reléguer [18] [rəlege] vt to relegate.

relent [rəlɑ̃] nm - **1.** [odeur] stink, stench - **2.** *fig* [trace] whiff.

relevé, e [rəlve] adj - **1.** [style] elevated - **2.** *CULIN* spicy.
➤ **relevé** nm reading ; faire le ~ de qqch to read sthg ; ~ de compte bank statement ; ~ d'identité bancaire bank account number.

relève [rəlɛv] nf relief ; prendre la ~ to take over.

relèvement [rələvmɑ̃] nm - **1.** [redressement] rebuilding - **2.** [hausse] raising - **3.** [majoration] increase.

relever [19] [rəlve] <> vt - **1.** [redresser - personne] to help up ; [- pays, économie] to rebuild ; [- moral, niveau] to raise - **2.** [ramasser] to collect

- 3. [tête, col, store] to raise ; [manches] to push up **- 4.** [CULIN - mettre en valeur] to bring out ; [- pimenter] to season **- 5.** *fig* [récit] to liven up, to spice up **- 6.** [noter] to note down ; [compteur] to read **- 7.** [relayer] to take over from, to relieve **- 8.** [erreur] to note ◇ *vi* **- 1.** [se rétablir] : ~ de to recover from **- 2.** [être du domaine] : ~ de to come under.

➤ **se relever** *vp* **- 1.** [se mettre debout] to stand up ; [sortir du lit] to get up **- 2.** [se rétablir] : se ~ de qqch to recover from sthg, to get over sthg **- 3.** [se rehausser] to lift.

relief [rəljɛf] *nm* relief, **sans aucun** ~ completely flat ; **en** ~ in relief, raised ; **une carte en** ~ relief map ; **mettre en** ~ *fig* to enhance, to bring out.

➤ **reliefs** *nmpl* vieilli remains.

relier [9] [rəlje] *vt* **- 1.** [livre] to bind **- 2.** [attacher] : ~ qqch à qqch to link sthg to sthg **- 3.** [joindre] to connect **- 4.** *fig* [associer] to link up.

relieur, euse [rəljœr, øz] *nm, f* binder.

religieuse ▷ **religieux**.

religieusement [rəliʒjøzmɑ̃] *adv* **- 1.** [gén] religiously ; [solennellement] reverently **- 2.** [se marier] in church.

religieux, euse [rəliʒjø, øz] *adj* **- 1.** [vie, chant] religious ; [mariage] religious, church *(avant n)* **- 2.** [respectueux] reverent.

➤ **religieux** *nm* monk.

➤ **religieuse** *nf* **- 1.** RELIG nun **- 2.** CULIN : religieuse au café, religieuse au chocolat *choux pastry filled with coffee or chocolate confectioner's custard.*

religion [rəliʒjɔ̃] *nf* **- 1.** [culte] religion **- 2.** [foi] faith **- 3.** [croyance] religion, faith ; **entrer en** ~ to take one's vows.

reliquaire [rəlikɛr] *nm* reliquary.

reliquat [rəlika] *nm* balance, remainder.

relique [rəlik] *nf* relic.

relire [106] [rəlir] *vt* **- 1.** [lire] to reread **- 2.** [vérifier] to read over.

➤ **se relire** *vp* to read what one has written.

reliure [rəljyr] *nf* binding.

relogement [rələʒmɑ̃] *nm* rehousing.

reloger [17] [rələʒe] *vt* to rehouse.

relu, e [rəly] *pp* ▷ **relire**.

reluire [97] [rəlɥir] *vi* to shine, to gleam ; **faire** ~ qqch to shine *ou* polish sthg.

reluisant, e [rəlɥizɑ̃, ɑ̃t] *adj* shining, gleaming ; **peu** *ou* **pas très** ~ *fig* [avenir, situation] not all that brilliant ; [personne] shady.

remâcher [3] [rəmaʃe] *vt fig* to brood over.

remailler [3] [rəmaje] *vt* [filet] to mend ; [tricot] to darn.

remake [rimɛjk] *nm* CIN remake.

rémanent, e [remanɑ̃, ɑ̃t] *adj* residual.

remaniement [rəmanimɑ̃] *nm* restructuring ; ~ **ministériel** cabinet reshuffle.

remanier [9] [rəmanje] *vt* to restructure ; [ministère] to reshuffle.

remarier [9] [rəmarje] ➤ **se remarier** *vp* to remarry.

remarquable [rəmarkabl] *adj* remarkable.

remarquablement [rəmarkabləmɑ̃] *adv* remarkably.

remarque [rəmark] *nf* **- 1.** [observation] remark ; [critique] critical remark **- 2.** [annotation] note.

remarquer [3] [rəmarke] ◇ *vt* **- 1.** [apercevoir] to notice ; **faire** ~ qqch (à qqn) to point sthg out (to sb) ; **se faire** ~ *péj* to draw attention to o.s. **- 2.** [noter] to remark, to comment ◇ *vi* : **ce n'est pas l'idéal, remarque!** it's not ideal, mind you!

➤ **se remarquer** *vp* to be noticeable.

remballer [3] [rɑ̃bale] *vt* [marchandise] to pack up.

rembarquer [3] [rɑ̃barke] *vt* to reembark.

➤ **se rembarquer** *vp* to reembark.

rembarrer [3] [rɑ̃bare] *vt fam* to snub.

remblai [rɑ̃blɛ] *nm* embankment.

remblayer [11] [rɑ̃bleje] *vt* [hausser] to bank up ; [combler] to fill in.

rembobiner [3] [rɑ̃bɔbine] *vt* to rewind.

rembourrage [rɑ̃buraʒ] *nm* stuffing, padding.

rembourrer [3] [rɑ̃bure] *vt* to stuff, to pad.

remboursable [rɑ̃bursabl] *adj* refundable.

remboursement [rɑ̃bursəmɑ̃] *nm* refund, repayment.

rembourser [3] [rɑ̃burse] *vt* **- 1.** [dette] to pay back, to repay **- 2.** [personne] to pay back ; ~ qqn de qqch to reimburse sb for sthg.

rembrunir [32] [rɑ̃brynir] ➤ **se rembrunir** *vp* to cloud over, to become gloomy.

remède [rəmɛd] *nm litt & fig* remedy, cure.

remédier [9] [rəmedje] *vi* : ~ à qqch to put sthg right, to remedy sthg.

remembrement [rəmɑ̃brəmɑ̃] *nm* land regrouping.

remémorer [3] [rəmemɔre] ➤ **se remémorer** *vp* to recollect.

remerciement [rəmɛrsimɑ̃] *nm* thanks *(pl)* ; **une lettre de** ~ a thank-you letter ; **avec tous mes** ~**s** with all my thanks, with many thanks.

remercier [9] [rəmɛrsje] *vt* **- 1.** [dire merci à] to thank ; ~ qqn de *ou* pour qqch to thank sb for sthg ; **non, je vous remercie** no, thank you - **2.** [congédier] to dismiss.

remets [➤ **remettre**.

remettre [84] [rəmɛtr] *vt* - **1.** [replacer] to put back ; ~ **en question** to call into question ; ~ **qqn à sa place** to put sb in his place - **2.** [enfiler de nouveau] to put back on - **3.** [rétablir - lumière, son] to put back on ; ~ **qqch en marche** to restart sthg ; ~ **de l'ordre dans qqch** to tidy sthg up ; ~ **une montre à l'heure** to put a watch right ; ~ **qqch en état de marche** to put sthg back in working order - **4.** [donner] : ~ **qqch à qqn** to hand sthg over to sb ; [médaille, prix] to present sthg to sb - **5.** [ajourner] : ~ **qqch (à)** to put sthg off (until) - **6.** *fig* [reconnaître] to place - **7.** *MÉD* : ~ **qqn** to put sb back on his feet.

➤ **se remettre** *vp* - **1.** [recommencer] : **se ~ à qqch** to take up sthg again ; **se ~ à fumer** to start smoking again - **2.** [se rétablir] to get better ; **se ~ de qqch** to get over sthg - **3.** [redevenir] : **se ~ debout** to stand up again ; **le temps s'est remis au beau** the weather has cleared up - **4.** *loc* : **je m'en remets à toi** it's up to you, I'll leave it up to you.

réminiscence [reminisɑ̃s] *nf* reminiscence.

remis, e [rəmi, iz] *pp* ➤ **remettre**.

remise [rəmiz] *nf* - **1.** [action] : ~ **en jeu** throwin ; ~ **en marche** restarting ; ~ **en place** putting back in place ; ~ **en question** *ou* **cause** calling into question - **2.** [de message, colis] handing over ; [de médaille, prix] presentation - **3.** [réduction] discount ; ~ **de peine** *JUR* remission - **4.** [hangar] shed.

remiser [3] [rəmize] *vt* to put away.

rémission [remisjɔ̃] *nf* remission ; **sans ~** [punir, juger] without mercy ; [pleuvoir] unremittingly.

remmener [19] [rɑ̃mne] *vt* to take *ou* bring back.

remodeler [25] [rəmɔdle] *vt* - **1.** [forme] to remodel - **2.** [remanier] to restructure.

rémois, e [remwa, az] *adj* of/from Rheims.
➤ **Rémois, e** *nm, f* native *ou* inhabitant of Rheims.

remontant, e [rəmɔ̃tɑ̃, ɑ̃t] *adj* [tonique] invigorating.
➤ **remontant** *nm* tonic.

remontée [rəmɔ̃te] *nf* - **1.** [des eaux] rising - **2.** [de pente, rivière] ascent - **3.** *SPORT* recovery - **4.** *SKI* : ~**s mécaniques** ski-lifts - **5.** [des mineurs] bringing to the surface.

remonte-pente [rəmɔ̃tpɑ̃t] (*pl* **remonte-pentes**) *nm* ski-tow.

remonter [3] [rəmɔ̃te] <> *vt (aux : avoir)* - **1.** [escalier, pente] to go/come back up - **2.** [as-

sembler] to put together again - **3.** [manches] to turn up - **4.** [horloge, montre] to wind up - **5.** [ragaillardir] to put new life into, to cheer up
<> *vi (aux : être)* - **1.** [monter à nouveau - personne] to go/come back up ; [- baromètre] to rise again ; [- prix, température] to go up again, to rise ; [- sur vélo] to get back on ; ~ **dans une voiture** to get back into a car - **2.** [dater] : ~ **à** to date *ou* go back to.

remontoir [rəmɔ̃twar] *nm* winder.

remontrance [rəmɔ̃trɑ̃s] *nf (gén pl)* remonstrance, reprimand.

remontrer [3] [rəmɔ̃tre] *vt* to show again ; **vouloir en ~ à qqn** to try to show sb up.

remords [rəmɔr] *nm* remorse ; **être bourrelé de ~** *fam* to be conscience-stricken.

remorque [rəmɔrk] *nf* trailer ; **être en ~** to be on tow ; **être à la ~** *fig* to drag behind.

remorquer [3] [rəmɔrke] *vt* - **1.** [voiture, bateau] to tow - **2.** *fam* [personne] to drag along.

remorqueur [rəmɔrkœr] *nm* tug, tugboat.

rémoulade [remulad] *nf* remoulade (sauce).

rémouleur [remulœr] *nm* knife grinder.

remous [rəmu] <> *nm* [de bateau] wash, backwash ; [de rivière] eddy <> *nmpl fig* stir, upheaval.

rempailler [3] [rɑ̃paje] *vt* to re-cane.

rempart [rɑ̃par] *nm (gén pl)* rampart.

rempiler [3] [rɑ̃pile] <> *vt* to pile up again <> *vi fam MIL* to sign on again.

remplaçable [rɑ̃plasabl] *adj* replaceable.

remplaçant, e [rɑ̃plasɑ̃, ɑ̃t] *nm, f* [suppléant] stand-in ; *SPORT* substitute.

remplacement [rɑ̃plasmɑ̃] *nm* - **1.** [changement] replacing, replacement - **2.** [intérim] substitution ; **faire des ~s** to stand in ; [docteur] to act as a locum.

remplacer [16] [rɑ̃plase] *vt* - **1.** [gén] to replace - **2.** [prendre la place de] to stand in for ; *SPORT* to substitute.

remplir [32] [rɑ̃plir] *vt* - **1.** [gén] to fill ; ~ **de** to fill with ; ~ **qqn de joie/d'orgueil** to fill sb with happiness/pride - **2.** [questionnaire] to fill in *ou* out - **3.** [mission, fonction] to complete, to fulfil.

➤ **se remplir** *vp* to fill up.

remplissage [rɑ̃plisaʒ] *nm* - **1.** [de récipient] filling up - **2.** *fig & péj* [de texte] padding out.

remploi [rɑ̃plwa], **réemploi** [reɑ̃plwa] *nm* re-use.

remployer [rɑ̃plwaje], **réemployer** [13] [reɑ̃plwaje] *vt* to re-use.

remplumer [3] [rɑ̃plyme] ➤ **se remplu-**

mer *vp fam* - **1.** [financièrement] to get o.s. back in funds - **2.** [se rétablir] to fill out again.

remporter [3] [rɑ̃pɔrte] *vt* - **1.** [repartir avec] to take away again - **2.** [gagner] to win.

rempoter [3] [rɑ̃pɔte] *vt* to repot.

remuant, e [rəmɥɑ̃, ɑ̃t] *adj* restless, overactive.

remue-ménage [rəmymenaʒ] *nm inv* commotion, confusion.

remuer [7] [rəmɥe] ◇ *vt* - **1.** [bouger, émouvoir] to move - **2.** [café, thé] to stir ; [salade] to toss ◇ *vi* to move, to stir ; **arrête de ~ comme ça** stop being so restless.

➤ **se remuer** *vp* - **1.** [se mouvoir] to move - **2.** *fig* [réagir] to make an effort.

rémunérateur, trice [remyneratœr, tris] *adj* profitable, lucrative.

rémunération [remynerasjɔ̃] *nf* remuneration.

rémunérer [18] [remynere] *vt* - **1.** [personne] to remunerate, to pay - **2.** [activité] to pay for.

renâcler [3] [rənɑkle] *vi fam* to make a fuss ; **~ devant** *ou* **à qqch** to balk at sthg.

renaissance [rənɛsɑ̃s] *nf* rebirth.

➤ **Renaissance** *nf* : **la Renaissance** the Renaissance.

renaître [92] [rənɛtr] *vi* - **1.** [ressusciter] to come back to life, to come to life again ; **se sentir ~** to feel like a new person ; **faire ~** [passé, tradition] to revive ; **~ à la vie** to take on a new lease of life - **2.** [revenir - sentiment, printemps] to return ; [- économie] to revive, to recover.

rénal, e, aux [renal, o] *adj* renal, kidney *(avant n)*.

renard [rənar] *nm* fox.

renardeau, x [rənardo] *nm* fox cub.

rencard = rancard.

rencart = rancart.

renchérir [32] [rɑ̃ʃerir] *vi* - **1.** [augmenter] to become more expensive ; [prix] to go up - **2.** [surenchérir] : **~ sur** to add to.

renchérissement [rɑ̃ʃerismɑ̃] *nm* increase in price ; **~ des prix** price increase.

rencontre [rɑ̃kɔ̃tr] *nf* - **1.** [gén] meeting ; **faire une bonne ~** to meet somebody interesting ; **faire une mauvaise ~** to meet an unpleasant person ; **aller/venir à la ~ de qqn** to go/come to meet sb - **2.** [choc, collision] collision.

rencontrer [3] [rɑ̃kɔ̃tre] *vt* - **1.** [gén] to meet - **2.** [heurter] to strike.

➤ **se rencontrer** *vp* - **1.** [gén] to meet - **2.** [opinions] to agree.

rendement [rɑ̃dmɑ̃] *nm* [de machine, travailleur] output ; [de terre, placement] yield.

rendez-vous [rɑ̃devu] *nm inv* - **1.** [rencontre] appointment ; [amoureux] date ; **on a tous ~ au café** we're all meeting at the café ; **lors de notre dernier ~** at our last meeting ; **prendre ~ avec qqn** to make an appointment with sb ; **donner ~ à qqn** to arrange to meet sb - **2.** [lieu] meeting place.

rendormir [36] [rɑ̃dɔrmir] ➤ **se rendormir** *vp* to go back to sleep.

rendre [73] [rɑ̃dr] ◇ *vt* - **1.** [restituer] : **~ qqch à qqn** to give sthg back to sb, to return sthg to sb - **2.** [donner en retour - invitation, coup] to return - **3.** [JUR - jugement] to pronounce - **4.** [produire - effet] to produce - **5.** [vomir] to vomit, to cough up - **6.** MIL [céder] to surrender ; **~ les armes** to lay down one's arms - **7.** (+ *adj*) [faire devenir] to make ; **~ qqn fou** to drive sb mad - **8.** [exprimer] to render ◇ *vi* - **1.** [produire - champ] to yield - **2.** [vomir] to vomit, to be sick.

➤ **se rendre** *vp* - **1.** [céder, capituler] to give in ; **j'ai dû me ~ à l'évidence** I had to face facts - **2.** [aller] : **se ~ à** to go to - **3.** (+ *adj*) [se faire tel] : **se ~ utile/malade** to make o.s. useful/ill.

rêne [rɛn] *nf* rein.

renégat, e [renega, at] *nm, f sout* renegade.

renégocier [9] [renegɔsje] *vt* to renegotiate.

reneiger [23] [rəneʒe] *vi* to snow again.

renfermé, e [rɑ̃fɛrme] *adj* introverted, withdrawn.

➤ **renfermé** *nm* : **ça sent le ~** it smells stuffy in here.

renfermer [3] [rɑ̃fɛrme] *vt* [contenir] to contain.

➤ **se renfermer** *vp* to withdraw.

renfiler [3] [rɑ̃file] *vt* - **1.** [perles] to restring - **2.** [aiguille] to rethread - **3.** [vêtement] to slip on again.

renflé, e [rɑ̃fle] *adj* bulging.

renflement [rɑ̃fləmɑ̃] *nm* bulge.

renflouer [3] [rɑ̃flue] *vt* - **1.** [bateau] to refloat - **2.** *fig* [entreprise, personne] to bail out.

➤ **se renflouer** *vp fam fig* to get back on one's feet (financially).

renfoncement [rɑ̃fɔ̃smɑ̃] *nm* recess.

renfoncer [16] [rɑ̃fɔ̃se] *vt* to push (further) down.

renforcer [16] [rɑ̃fɔrse] *vt* to reinforce, to strengthen ; **cela me renforce dans mon opinion** that confirms my opinion.

renfort [rɑ̃fɔr] *nm* reinforcement ; **envoyer des ~s** to send reinforcements ; **venir en ~** to come as reinforcements ; **à grand ~ de** *fig* with the help of a lot of.

renfrogné, e [rɑ̃frɔɲe] *adj* scowling.

renfrogner [3] [rɑ̃frɔɲe] ➤ **se renfrogner** *vp* to scowl, to pull a face.

rengager [rɑ̃gaʒe], **réengager** [17] [reɑ̃gaʒe] *vt* [personnel] to take on again ⟨⟩ *vi* MIL to re-enlist, to join up again.

➤ **se rengager** *vp* MIL to re-enlist, to join up again.

rengaine [rɑ̃gɛn] *nf* - **1.** [formule répétée] (old) story - **2.** [chanson] (old) song.

rengainer [4] [rɑ̃gene] *vt* - **1.** [épée] to sheathe ; [pistolet] to put back in its holster - **2.** *fam fig* [compliment] to withold.

rengorger [17] [rɑ̃gɔrʒe] ➤ **se rengorger** *vp fig* to puff o.s. up.

reniement [rənimɑ̃] *nm* renunciation.

renier [9] [rənje] *vt* - **1.** [famille, ami] to disown - **2.** [foi, opinion] to renounce, to repudiate - **3.** [signature] to refuse to acknowledge.

renifler [3] [rənifle] ⟨⟩ *vi* to sniff ⟨⟩ *vt* to sniff ; ~ **quelque chose de louche** to smell a rat.

renne [rɛn] *nm* reindeer *(inv)*.

renom [rənɔ̃] *nm* renown, fame ; **de grand ~** of great renown, famous.

renommé, e [rənɔme] *adj* renowned, famous.

➤ **renommée** *nf* renown, fame ; **de ~e internationale** world-famous, internationally renowned.

renoncement [rənɔ̃smɑ̃] *nm* : ~ **(à)** renunciation (of).

renoncer [16] [rənɔ̃se] *vi* : ~ **à** to give up ; ~ **à comprendre qqch** to give up trying to understand sthg ; ~ **à voir qqn** to give up *ou* abandon the idea of seeing sb.

renoncule [rənɔ̃kyl] *nf* buttercup.

renouer [6] [rənwe] ⟨⟩ *vt* - **1.** [lacet, corde] to re-tie, to tie up again - **2.** [contact, conversation] to resume ⟨⟩ *vi* : ~ **avec qqn** to take up with sb again ; ~ **avec sa famille** to make it up with one's family again.

renouveau, x [rənuvo] *nm* - **1.** [transformation] revival - **2.** [regain] : **un ~ de succès** renewed success.

renouvelable [rənuvlabl] *adj* renewable ; [expérience] repeatable.

renouveler [24] [rənuvle] *vt* - **1.** [gén] to renew - **2.** [rajeunir] to revive.

➤ **se renouveler** *vp* - **1.** [être remplacé] to be renewed - **2.** [changer, innover] to have new ideas - **3.** [se répéter] to be repeated, to recur.

renouvelle, renouvelles *etc* ▷ **renouveler**.

renouvellement [rənuvɛlmɑ̃] *nm* renewal.

rénovation [renɔvasjɔ̃] *nf* renovation, restoration.

rénover [3] [renɔve] *vt* - **1.** [immeuble] to renovate, to restore - **2.** [système, méthodes] to reform.

renseignement [rɑ̃sɛɲəmɑ̃] *nm* information *(U)* ; **un ~** a piece of information ; **prendre des ~s (sur)** to make enquiries (about).

➤ **renseignements** *nmpl* - **1.** [service d'information] enquiries, information ; **appeler les ~s** TÉLÉC to call directory enquiries - **2.** [sécurité] intelligence *(U)* ; **les ~s généraux** *police department responsible for political security.*

renseigner [4] [rɑ̃sɛɲe] *vt* : ~ **qqn (sur)** to give sb information (about), to inform sb (about).

➤ **se renseigner** *vp* - **1.** [s'enquérir] to make enquiries, to ask for information - **2.** [s'informer] to find out.

rentabiliser [3] [rɑ̃tabilize] *vt* to make profitable.

rentabilité [rɑ̃tabilite] *nf* profitability ; **seuil de ~** break-even point.

rentable [rɑ̃tabl] *adj* - **1.** COMM profitable - **2.** *fam* [qui en vaut la peine] worthwhile.

rente [rɑ̃t] *nf* - **1.** [d'un capital] revenue, income ; **vivre de ses ~s** to have a private income - **2.** [pension] pension, annuity ; ~ **viagère** life annuity - **3.** [emprunt d'État] government bond.

rentier, ère [rɑ̃tje, ɛr] *nm, f* person of independent means ; **mener une vie de ~** *fig* to lead a life of leisure.

rentrée [rɑ̃tre] *nf* - **1.** [fait de rentrer] return - **2.** [reprise des activités] : **la ~ parlementaire** the reopening of parliament ; **la ~ des classes** the start of the new school year - **3.** CIN & THÉÂTRE comeback ; **faire sa ~** to make one's comeback - **4.** [recette] income ; **avoir une ~ d'argent** to come into some money.

LA RENTRÉE

The time of the year when children go back to school has considerable cultural significance in France ; coming after the long summer break or 'grandes vacances', it is the time when academic, political, social and commercial activity begin again in earnest.

rentrer [3] [rɑ̃tre] ⟨⟩ *vi (aux : être)* - **1.** [entrer de nouveau] to go/come back in ; **tout a fini par ~ dans l'ordre** everything returned to normal - **2.** [entrer] to go/come in - **3.** [revenir chez soi] to go/come back, to go/come home - **4.** [recouvrer, récupérer] : ~ **dans** to recover, to get back ; ~ **dans ses frais** to cover one's costs, to break even - **5.** [se jeter avec violence] : **~ dans** to crash into - **6.** [s'emboîter] to go in, to fit ; **~ les uns dans les autres** to fit together - **7.** [être compris] : **~ dans** to be included in - **8.** [être perçu - fonds] to come in ◇ *vt (aux : avoir)* - **1.** [mettre ou remettre à l'intérieur] to bring in ; [chemise] to tuck in - **2.** [ventre] to pull in ; [griffes] to retract, to draw in - **3.** *fig* [rage, larmes] to hold back.

renversant, e [rɑ̃vɛrsɑ̃, ɑ̃t] *adj* staggering, astounding.

renverse [rɑ̃vɛrs] *nf* : **tomber à la ~** to fall over backwards.

renversé, e [rɑ̃vɛrse] *adj* - **1.** [à l'envers] upside down - **2.** [qu'on a fait tomber] overturned - **3.** [incliné en arrière] tilted back - **4.** [stupéfait] staggered.

renversement [rɑ̃vɛrsəmɑ̃] *nm* - **1.** [inversion] turning upside down - **2.** [de situation] reversal - **3.** [de régime] overthrow - **4.** [de tête, buste] tilting back.

renverser [3] [rɑ̃vɛrse] *vt* - **1.** [mettre à l'envers] to turn upside down - **2.** [faire tomber - objet] to knock over ; [- piéton] to run over ; [- liquide] to spill - **3.** *fig* [obstacle] to overcome ; [régime] to overthrow ; [ministre] to throw out of office - **4.** [tête, buste] to tilt back - **5.** [étonner] to bowl over.

➤ **se renverser** *vp* - **1.** [incliner le corps en arrière] to lean back - **2.** [tomber] to overturn.

renvoi [rɑ̃vwa] *nm* - **1.** [licenciement] dismissal ; **notifier à qqn son ~** to give sb his/her notice - **2.** [de colis, lettre] return, sending back - **3.** [ajournement] postponement - **4.** [référence] cross-reference - **5.** JUR referral - **6.** [éructation] belch.

renvoie, renvoies *etc* ⊳ **renvoyer**.

renvoyer [30] [rɑ̃vwaje] *vt* - **1.** [faire retourner] to send back - **2.** [congédier] to dismiss - **3.** [colis, lettre] to send back, to return - **4.** [balle] to throw back - **5.** [réfléchir - lumière] to reflect ; [- son] to echo - **6.** [référer] : **~ qqn à** to refer sb to - **7.** [différer] to postpone, to put off.

réorganisation [reɔrganizasjɔ̃] *nf* reorganization.

réorganiser [3] [reɔrganize] *vt* to reorganize.

réorienter [3] [reɔrjɑ̃te] *vt* to reorient, to re-orientate.

réouverture [reuvɛrtyr] *nf* reopening.

repaire [rəpɛr] *nm* den.

repaître [91] [rəpɛtr] *vt* : **~ ses yeux (de)** to feast one's eyes (on).

➤ **se repaître** *vp* : **se ~ de** [se rassasier] to eat one's fill of ; *fig* to revel in.

répandre [74] [repɑ̃dr] *vt* - **1.** [verser, renverser] to spill ; [larmes] to shed - **2.** [diffuser, dégager] to give off - **3.** *fig* [bienfaits] to pour out ; [effroi, terreur, nouvelle] to spread.

➤ **se répandre** *vp* - **1.** [gén] to spread - **2.** [liquide] to spill - **3.** [personne] : **se ~ en injures** to let out a stream of insults ; **se ~ en remerciements** to give one's heartfelt thanks.

répandu, e [repɑ̃dy] ◇ *pp* ▷ **répandre** ◇ *adj* [opinion, maladie] widespread.

réparable [reparabl] *adj* - **1.** [objet] repairable - **2.** [erreur] that can be put right.

reparaître [91] [rəparɛtr] *vi* to reappear.

réparateur, trice [reparatœr, tris] ◇ *adj* [sommeil] refreshing ◇ *nm, f* repairer.

réparation [reparasjɔ̃] *nf* - **1.** [d'objet - action] repairing ; [- résultat] repair ; **en ~** under repair - **2.** [de faute] : **~ (de)** atonement (for) - **3.** [indemnité] reparation, compensation.

réparer [3] [repare] *vt* - **1.** [objet] to repair - **2.** [faute, oubli] to make up for ; **~ ses torts** to make amends.

reparler [3] [rəparle] *vi* : **~ de qqn/qqch** to talk about sb/sthg again ; **~ à qqn** to speak to sb again.

➤ **se reparler** *vp* to speak to each other again.

repartie [rəparti] *nf* retort ; **avoir de la ~** to be good at repartee.

repartir [43] [rəpartir] ◇ *vt littéraire* to reply ◇ *vi* - **1.** [retourner] to go back, to return - **2.** [partir de nouveau] to set off again - **3.** [recommencer] to start again.

répartir [32] [repartir] *vt* - **1.** [partager] to share out, to divide up - **2.** [dans l'espace] to spread out, to distribute - **3.** [échelonner] to spread out - **4.** [classer] to divide *ou* split up.

➤ **se répartir** *vp* to divide up.

répartition [repartisjɔ̃] *nf* - **1.** [partage] sharing out ; [de tâches] allocation - **2.** [dans l'espace] distribution.

reparu [rəpary] *pp* ▷ **reparaître**.

repas [rəpa] *nm* meal ; **prendre son ~** to eat ; **~ d'affaires** business meal, working lunch/dinner.

repassage [rəpasaʒ] *nm* ironing.

repasser [3] [rəpase] ◇ *vi (aux : être)* [passer à nouveau] to go/come back ; [film] to be on again ◇ *vt (aux : avoir)* - **1.** [frontière, montagne] to cross again, to recross - **2.** [examen] to resit - **3.** [film] to show again - **4.** *fam* [transmettre] to pass on - **5.** [linge] to iron - **6.** [leçon] to go over.

repasseuse [rəpasøz] *nf* - **1.** [ouvrière] ironer - **2.** [machine] ironing machine.

repayer [11] [rəpeje] *vt* to pay again.

repêchage [rəpɛʃaʒ] *nm* [de noyé, voiture] re-covery.

repêcher [4] [rəpeʃe] *vt* - **1.** [noyé, voiture] to fish out - **2.** *fam* [candidat] to let through.

repeindre [81] [rəpɛ̃dr] *vt* to repaint.

repeint, e [rəpɛ̃, ɛ̃t] *pp* ⊏⊐ repeindre.

repenser [3] [rəpɑ̃se] *vt* to rethink.

repentir [37] [rəpɑ̃tir] *nm* repentance.

◆ **se repentir** *vp* to repent ; **se ~ de qqch/ d'avoir fait qqch** to be sorry for sthg/for having done sthg.

repérable [rəperabl] *adj* : **difficilement ~** difficult to spot.

repérage [rəperaʒ] *nm* location.

répercussion [reperkysjɔ̃] *nf* repercussion.

répercuter [3] [reperkyte] *vt* - **1.** [lumière] to reflect ; [son] to throw back - **2.** [ordre, augmentation] to pass on.

◆ **se répercuter** *vp* - **1.** [lumière] to be reflected ; [son] to echo - **2.** [influer] : **se ~ sur** to have repercussions on.

repère [rəpɛr] *nm* [marque] mark ; [objet concret] landmark ; **point de ~** point of reference.

repérer [18] [rəpere] *vt* - **1.** [situer] to locate, to pinpoint - **2.** *fam* [remarquer] to spot ; **se faire ~** to be spotted.

◆ **se repérer** *vp fam* to find one's way around.

répertoire [repertwar] *nm* - **1.** [agenda] thumb-indexed notebook - **2.** [inventaire] catalogue *Br*, catalog *Am*, list - **3.** [de théâtre, d'artiste] repertoire - **4.** INFORM directory.

répertorier [9] [repertɔrje] *vt* to make a list of.

répéter [18] [repete] ⬦ *vt* - **1.** [gén] to repeat ; **ne pas se le faire ~ deux fois** not to have to be told twice - **2.** [leçon] to go over, to learn ; [rôle] to rehearse ⬦ *vi* to rehearse.

◆ **se répéter** *vp* - **1.** [radoter] to repeat o.s. - **2.** [se reproduire] to be repeated ; **que cela ne se répète pas!** don't let it happen again!

répétitif, ive [repetitif, iv] *adj* repetitive.

répétition [repetisjɔ̃] *nf* - **1.** [réitération] repetition - **2.** MUS & THÉÂTRE rehearsal.

repeupler [5] [rəpœple] *vt* - **1.** [région, ville] to repopulate - **2.** [forêt] to replant ; [étang] to restock.

repiquage [rəpikaʒ] *nm* - **1.** [plantation] planting out - **2.** [enregistrement] re-recording.

repiquer [3] [rəpike] ⬦ *vt* - **1.** [replanter] to plant out - **2.** [disque, cassette] to tape ⬦ *vi fam* : **~ à qqch** to take sthg up again ; **~ au plat** to have a second helping.

répit [repi] *nm* respite ; **sans ~** without respite.

replacer [16] [rəplase] *vt* - **1.** [remettre] to replace, to put back - **2.** [situer] to place, to put.

◆ **se replacer** *vp* to find new employment.

replanter [3] [rəplɑ̃te] *vt* to replant.

replat [rəpla] *nm* ledge.

replâtrer [3] [rəplatre] *vt* - **1.** [mur, fissure] to re-plaster - **2.** *fam fig* to patch up.

replet, ète [rəplɛ, ɛt] *adj* chubby.

repli [rəpli] *nm* - **1.** [de tissu] fold ; [de rivière] bend - **2.** [de troupes] withdrawal.

replier [10] [rəplije] *vt* - **1.** [plier de nouveau] to fold up again - **2.** [ramener en pliant] to fold back - **3.** [armée] to withdraw.

◆ **se replier** *vp* - **1.** [armée] to withdraw - **2.** [personne] : **se ~ sur soi-même** to withdraw into o.s. - **3.** [journal, carte] to fold.

réplique [replik] *nf* - **1.** [riposte] reply ; **sans ~** [argument] irrefutable - **2.** [d'acteur] line ; **donner la ~ à qqn** to play opposite sb - **3.** [copie] replica ; [sosie] double.

répliquer [3] [replike] ⬦ *vt* : **~ à qqn que** to reply to sb that ⬦ *vi* - **1.** [répondre] to reply ; [avec impertinence] to answer back - **2.** *fig* [riposter] to retaliate.

replonger [17] [rəplɔ̃ʒe] ⬦ *vt* to plunge back ⬦ *vi* to dive back.

◆ **se replonger** *vp* : **se ~ dans qqch** to immerse o.s. in sthg again.

répondant, e [repɔ̃dɑ̃, ɑ̃t] *nm, f* guarantor.

◆ **répondant** *nm fam* : **avoir du ~** to have money behind one.

répondeur [repɔ̃dœr] *nm* : **~ (téléphonique** OU **automatique** OU **-enregistreur)** answering machine.

répondre [75] [repɔ̃dr] ⬦ *vi* : **~ à qqn** [faire connaître sa pensée] to answer sb, to reply to sb ; [riposter] to answer sb back ; **~ à qqch** [faire une réponse] to reply to sthg, to answer sthg ; [en se défendant] to respond to sthg ; **~ au téléphone** to answer the telephone ⬦ *vt* to answer, to reply ; **~ que** to reply that, to answer that.

◆ **répondre à** *vt* - **1.** [correspondre à - besoin] to answer ; [- conditions] to meet - **2.** [ressembler à - description] to match.

◆ **répondre de** *vt* to answer for.

répondu, e [repɔ̃dy] *pp* ⊏⊐ répondre.

réponse [repɔ̃s] *nf* - **1.** [action de répondre] answer, reply ; **en ~ à votre lettre ...** in reply OU in answer OU in response to your letter ... - **2.** [solution] answer - **3.** [réaction] response.

report [rəpɔr] *nm* - **1.** [de réunion, rendez-vous] postponement - **2.** COMM [d'écritures] carrying forward - **3.** POLIT [de voix] transfer.

reportage [rəpɔrtaʒ] *nm* - **1.** [article, enquête] report - **2.** [métier] reporting.

reporter¹ [rəpɔrtɛr] *nm* reporter.

reporter² [3] [rəpɔrte] *vt* - **1.** [rapporter] to take back - **2.** [différer] : ~ **qqch à** to postpone sthg till, to put sthg off till - **3.** [somme] : ~ **(sur)** to carry forward (to) - **4.** [transférer] : ~ **sur** to transfer to.
➤ **se reporter** *vp* : **se** ~ **à** [se référer à] to refer to ; [se transporter en pensée à] to cast one's mind back to.

repos [rəpo] *nm* - **1.** [gén] rest ; **prendre un jour de** ~ to take a day off - **2.** [tranquillité] peace and quiet ; **ce n'est pas de tout** ~ it's not exactly restful - **3.** MIL : **repos!** at ease!

reposant, e [rəpozɑ̃, ɑ̃t] *adj* restful.

reposé, e [rəpoze] *adj* rested ; **à tête ~e** with a clear head.

reposer [3] [rəpoze] <> *vt* - **1.** [poser à nouveau] to put down again, to put back down - **2.** [remettre] to put back - **3.** [poser de nouveau - question] to ask again - **4.** [appuyer] to rest - **5.** [délasser] to rest, to relax <> *vi* - **1.** [pâte] to sit, to stand ; [vin] to stand - **2.** [mort] : **ici repose ...** here lies ... - **3.** [théorie] : ~ **sur** to rest on.
➤ **se reposer** *vp* - **1.** [se délasser] to rest - **2.** [faire confiance] : **se** ~ **sur qqn** to rely on sb.

repositionner [3] [rəpozisjɔne] *vt* to reposition.
➤ **se repositionner** *vp* to reposition o.s.

repoussant, e [rəpusɑ̃, ɑ̃t] *adj* repulsive.

repousser [3] [rəpuse] <> *vi* to grow again, to grow back <> *vt* - **1.** [écarter] to push away, to push back ; [l'ennemi] to repel, to drive back - **2.** [éconduire] to reject - **3.** [proposition] to reject ; to turn down - **4.** [différer] to put back, to postpone.
➤ **se repousser** *vp* [aimants] to repel one another.

repoussoir [rəpuswar] *nm* : **servir de** ~ **à qqn** to be a foil to sb.

répréhensible [repreɑ̃sibl] *adj* reprehensible.

reprenais, reprenions *etc* ➤ **reprendre**.

reprendre [79] [rəprɑ̃dr] <> *vt* - **1.** [prendre de nouveau] to take again ; **je passe te** ~ **dans une heure** I'll come by and pick you up again in an hour ; ~ **la route** to take to the road again ; ~ **haleine** to get one's breath back - **2.** [récupérer - objet prêté] to take back ; [- prisonnier, ville] to recapture - **3.** COMM [entreprise, affaire] to take over ; **ni repris ni échangé** goods may not be returned or exchanged - **4.** [se resservir] : ~ **un gâteau/de la viande** to take another cake/some more meat - **5.** [recommencer] to resume ; **'et ainsi' reprit-il ...** 'and so',

he continued ... - **6.** [retoucher] to repair ; [jupe] to alter - **7.** [corriger] to correct <> *vi* - **1.** [affaires, plante] to pick up - **2.** [recommencer] to start again.
➤ **se reprendre** *vp* - **1.** [rectifier ce qu'on a dit] to correct o.s. - **2.** [recommencer] : **se** ~ **à espérer** to find new hope ; **s'y** ~ **à plusieurs fois** to make several attempts - **3.** [se ressaisir] to pull o.s. together.

repreneur [rəprənœr] *nm person who takes over a company with the aim of revitalizing it.*

représailles [rəprezaj] *nfpl* reprisals ; **par** ~ as a reprisal, in reprisal.

représentant, e [rəprezɑ̃tɑ̃, ɑ̃t] *nm, f* representative.

représentatif, ive [rəprezɑ̃tatif, iv] *adj* representative.

représentation [rəprezɑ̃tasjɔ̃] *nf* - **1.** [gén] representation - **2.** [spectacle] performance - **3.** [métier] commercial travelling Br OU traveling Am.

représentativité [rəprezɑ̃tativite] *nf* representativeness.

représenter [3] [rəprezɑ̃te] *vt* to represent.
➤ **se représenter** *vp* - **1.** [s'imaginer] : **se** ~ **qqch** to visualize sthg - **2.** [se présenter à nouveau] : **se** ~ **à** [aux élections] to stand again at ; [à un examen] to resit, to represent.

répressif, ive [represif, iv] *adj* repressive.

répression [represjɔ̃] *nf* - **1.** [de révolte] repression - **2.** [de criminalité, d'injustices] suppression.

réprimande [reprimɑ̃d] *nf* reprimand.

réprimander [3] [reprimɑ̃de] *vt* to reprimand.

réprimer [3] [reprime] *vt* - **1.** [émotion, rire] to repress, to check - **2.** [révolte, crimes] to put down, to suppress.

repris, e [rəpri, iz] *pp* ➤ **reprendre**.
➤ **repris** *nm* : ~ **de justice** habitual criminal.

reprisage [rəprizaʒ] *nm* mending.

reprise [rəpriz] *nf* - **1.** [recommencement - des hostilités] resumption, renewal ; [- des affaires] revival, recovery ; [- de pièce] revival ; **à plusieurs ~s** on several occasions, several times - **2.** BOXE round - **3.** [accélération] acceleration - **4.** [raccommodage] mending - **5.** COMM trade-in, part exchange ; [somme payée à un locataire] *sum paid for fixtures and fittings left by outgoing tenant.*

repriser [3] [rəprize] *vt* to mend.

réprobateur, trice [reprɔbatœr, tris] *adj* reproachful.

réprobation [reprɔbasjɔ̃] *nf* disapproval.

reproche [rəprɔʃ] *nm* reproach ; **faire des ~s**

à qqn to reproach sb ; **avec ~** reproachfully ; **sans ~** blameless.

reprocher [3] [rǝprɔʃe] vt : **~ qqch à qqn** to reproach sb for sthg ; **je ne vous reproche rien** I don't reproach ou blame you for anything.

➡ **se reprocher** vp : **se ~ (qqch)** to blame o.s. (for sthg) ; **ne rien avoir à se ~** to have nothing to reproach o.s. for.

reproducteur, trice [rǝprɔdyktœr, tris] adj reproductive.

reproduction [rǝprɔdyksjɔ̃] nf reproduction ; **~ interdite** all rights (of reproduction) reserved.

reproduire [98] [rǝprɔdɥir] vt to reproduce.

➡ **se reproduire** vp - **1.** BIOL to reproduce, to breed - **2.** [se répéter] to recur.

reproduisais, reproduisions etc ⊳ **reproduire.**

reproduit, e [rǝprɔdɥi, it] pp ⊳ **reproduire.**

reprogrammer [3] [rǝprɔgrame] vt to reprogram.

reprographie [rǝprɔgrafi] nf reproduction.

réprouvé, e [repruve] ◇ adj rejected ◇ nm, f outcast.

réprouver [3] [repruve] vt [blâmer] to reprove.

reptation [rɛptasjɔ̃] nf creeping.

reptile [rɛptil] nm reptile.

repu, e [rǝpy] ◇ pp ⊳ **repaître** ◇ adj full, sated.

républicain, e [repyblikɛ̃, ɛn] adj & nm, f republican.

république [repyblik] nf republic ; **la République centrafricaine** Central African Republic ; **la République française** the French Republic ; **la République populaire de Chine** the People's Republic of China ; **la République tchèque** the Czech Republic.

répudiation [repydjasjɔ̃] nf repudiation.

répudier [9] [repydje] vt - **1.** [femme] to repudiate - **2.** [principes, engagements] to renounce.

répugnance [repyɲɑ̃s] nf - **1.** [horreur] repugnance - **2.** [réticence] reluctance ; **avoir** ou **éprouver de la ~ à faire qqch** to be reluctant to do sthg ; **avec ~** reluctantly.

répugnant, e [repyɲɑ̃, ɑ̃t] adj repugnant.

répugner [3] [repyɲe] vi : **~ à qqn** to disgust sb, to fill sb with repugnance ; **~ à faire qqch** to be reluctant to do sthg, to be loath to do sthg.

répulsion [repylsjɔ̃] nf repulsion.

réputation [repytasjɔ̃] nf reputation ; **avoir une ~ de** to have a reputation for ; **avoir la ~ d'être généreux** to have a reputation for

being generous ; **connaître qqn/qqch de ~** to know sb/sthg by reputation ; **avoir bonne/ mauvaise ~** to have a good/bad reputation.

réputé, e [repyte] adj famous, well-known ; **être ~ pour** to be famous ou well-known for.

requérir [39] [rǝkerir] vt - **1.** [nécessiter] to require, to call for - **2.** [solliciter] to solicit - **3.** JUR [réclamer au nom de la loi] to demand.

requête [rǝkɛt] nf - **1.** [prière] petition ; **à** ou **sur la ~ de** at the request of - **2.** JUR appeal - **3.** INFORM query.

requiem [rekɥijɛm] nm inv requiem.

requiers, requiert etc ⊳ **requérir.**

requin [rǝkɛ̃] nm shark.

requinquer [3] [rǝkɛ̃ke] vt fam to perk up, to buck up.

➡ **se requinquer** vp fam to perk up, to buck up.

requis, e [rǝki, iz] ◇ pp ⊳ **requérir** ◇ adj required, requisite.

réquisition [rekizisjɔ̃] nf - **1.** MIL requisition - **2.** JUR closing speech for the prosecution.

réquisitionner [3] [rekizisjɔne] vt to requisition.

réquisitoire [rekizitwar] nm JUR closing speech for the prosecution ; **~ (contre)** fig indictment (of).

RER (abr de **réseau express régional**) nm train service linking central Paris with its suburbs and airports.

rescapé, e [rɛskape] ◇ adj rescued ◇ nm, f survivor.

rescousse [rɛskus] ➡ **à la rescousse** loc adv : **venir à la ~ de qqn** to come to sb's rescue ; **appeler qqn à la ~** to call on sb for help.

réseau, x [rezo] nm network ; **~ ferroviaire/ routier** rail/road network.

réséda [rezeda] nm mignonette.

réservation [rezɛrvasjɔ̃] nf reservation.

réserve [rezɛrv] nf - **1.** [gén] reserve ; **en ~** in reserve ; **officier de ~** MIL reserve officer - **2.** [restriction] reservation ; **faire des ~s (sur)** to have reservations (about) ; **sous toute ~** ou **toutes ~s** subject to confirmation ; **sous ~ de** subject to ; **sans ~** unreservedly ; **éloges sans ~** unreserved praise - **3.** [d'animaux, de plantes] reserve ; [d'Indiens] reservation ; **~ faunique** Can wildlife reserve ; **~ naturelle** nature reserve - **4.** [local] storeroom.

réservé, e [rezɛrve] adj reserved.

réserver [3] [rezɛrve] vt - **1.** [destiner] : **~ qqch (à qqn)** [chambre, place] to reserve ou book sthg (for sb) ; fig [surprise, désagrément] to have sthg in store (for sb) - **2.** [mettre de côté, garder] : **~ qqch (pour)** to put sthg on one side (for), to keep sthg (for).

se réserver vp - **1.** [s'accorder] : **se ~ qqch** to keep sthg for o.s. ; **se ~ de faire qqch** to wait to do sthg ; **se ~ le droit de faire qqch** to reserve the right to do sthg - **2.** [se ménager] to save o.s.

réserviste [rezɛrvist] nm reservist.

réservoir [rezɛrvwar] nm - **1.** [cuve] tank - **2.** [bassin] reservoir - **3.** fig [de main-d'œuvre] reserve, pool ; [d'idées] source.

résidant, e [rezidã, ãt] adj resident.

résidence [rezidãs] nf - **1.** [habitation] residence ; **~ principale** main residence ou home ; **~ secondaire** second home ; **~ universitaire** hall of residence - **2.** [immeuble] block of luxury flats Br, luxury apartment block Am.

➤ **résidence surveillée** nf : **en ~ surveillée** under house arrest.

résident, e [rezidã, ãt] nm, f - **1.** [de pays] : **les ~s français en Écosse** French nationals resident in Scotland - **2.** [habitant d'une résidence] resident.

résidentiel, elle [rezidãsjɛl] adj residential.

résider [3] [rezide] vi - **1.** [habiter] : **~ à/dans/en** to reside in - **2.** [consister] : **~ dans** to lie in.

résidu [rezidy] nm [reste] residue ; [déchet] waste.

résiduel, elle [reziduɛl] adj residual.

résignation [reziɲasjɔ̃] nf resignation.

résigné, e [reziɲe] <> adj resigned <> nm, f resigned person.

résigner [3] [reziɲe] ➤ **se résigner** vp : **se ~ (à)** to resign o.s. (to).

résiliation [reziljasjɔ̃] nf cancellation, termination.

résilier [9] [rezilje] vt to cancel, to terminate.

résille [rezij] nf - **1.** [pour cheveux] hairnet - **2.** : **bas ~** fishnet stockings.

résine [rezin] nf resin.

résiné, e [rezine] adj flavoured with resin.

➤ **résiné** nm retsina.

résineux, euse [rezinø, øz] adj resinous.

➤ **résineux** nm conifer.

résistance [rezistãs] nf - **1.** [gén, ÉLECTR & PHYS] resistance ; **manquer de ~** to lack stamina ; **opposer une ~** to put up resistance ; **~ passive** passive resistance - **2.** [de radiateur, chaudière] element.

➤ **Résistance** nf : **la Résistance** HIST the Resistance.

résistant, e [rezistã, ãt] <> adj [personne] tough ; [tissu] hard-wearing, tough ; **être ~ au froid/aux infections** to be resistant to the cold/to infection <> nm, f [gén] resistance fighter ; [de la Résistance] member of the Resistance.

résister [3] [reziste] vi to resist ; **~ à** [attaque, désir] to resist ; [tempête, fatigue] to withstand ; [personne] to stand up to, to oppose.

résolu, e [rezɔly] <> pp ▷ **résoudre** <> adj resolute ; **être bien ~ à faire qqch** to be determined to do sthg.

résolument [rezɔlymã] adv resolutely.

résolution [rezɔlysjɔ̃] nf - **1.** [décision] resolution ; **prendre la ~ de faire qqch** to make a resolution ou to do sthg - **2.** [détermination] resolve, determination - **3.** [solution] solving.

résolvais, résolvions etc ▷ **résoudre**.

résonance [rezɔnãs] nf - **1.** ÉLECTR & PHYS resonance - **2.** fig [écho] echo.

résonner [3] [rezɔne] vi [retentir] to resound ; [renvoyer le son] to echo ; **~ de** to resound with.

résorber [3] [rezɔrbe] vt - **1.** [déficit] to absorb - **2.** MÉD to resorb.

➤ **se résorber** vp - **1.** [déficit] to be absorbed - **2.** MÉD to be resorbed.

résoudre [88] [rezudr] vt - **1.** [problème] to solve, to resolve - **2.** [décider] : **~ qqn à faire qqch** to get sb to make up his/her mind to do sthg - **3.** [décomposer] : **~ en** to break up ou resolve into.

➤ **se résoudre** vp : **se ~ à faire qqch** to make up one's mind to do sthg, to decide ou resolve to do sthg.

respect [rɛspɛ] nm respect ; **manquer de ~ à qqn** to be disrespectful to sb, to show disrespect for sb ; **sauf votre ~** with all (due) respect ; **avec tout le ~ que je vous dois** with all (due) respect, with the greatest of respect ; **tenir qqn en ~** fig to keep sb at bay.

➤ **respects** nmpl respects, regards.

respectabilité [rɛspɛktabilite] nf respectability.

respectable [rɛspɛktabl] adj respectable.

respecter [4] [rɛspɛkte] vt to respect ; **faire ~ la loi** to enforce the law.

➤ **se respecter** vp : **un professeur qui se respecte ne ferait pas cela** no self-respecting teacher would do that.

respectif, ive [rɛspɛktif, iv] adj respective.

respectivement [rɛspɛktivmã] adv respectively.

respectueusement [rɛspɛktyøzmã] adv respectfully.

respectueux, euse [rɛspɛktyø, øz] adj respectful ; **être ~ de** to have respect for.

respirable [rɛspirabl] adj : **l'air n'est plus ~** the air is no longer breathable.

respiration [rɛspirasjɔ̃] *nf* breathing *(U)* ; **retenir sa ~** to hold one's breath ; **~ artificielle** artificial respiration.

respiratoire [rɛspiratwar] *adj* respiratory.

respirer [3] [rɛspire] <> *vi* - **1.** [inspirer-expirer] to breathe - **2.** *fig* [se reposer] to get one's breath ; [être soulagé] to be able to breathe again <> *vt* - **1.** [aspirer] to breathe in - **2.** *fig* [exprimer] to exude.

resplendir [32] [rɛsplɑ̃dir] *vi* - **1.** [lune] to shine - **2.** *fig* [personne] : **~ de joie/santé** to be radiant with joy/health.

resplendissant, e [rɛsplɑ̃disɑ̃, ɑ̃t] *adj* radiant.

responsabilisation [rɛspɔ̃sabilizasjɔ̃] *nf* making sb aware of his/her responsibilities.

responsabiliser [3] [rɛspɔ̃sabilize] *vt* : **~ qqn** to make sb aware of his/her responsibilities.

responsabilité [rɛspɔ̃sabilite] *nf* - **1.** [morale] responsibility ; **décliner toute ~** to disclaim all responsibility ; **avoir la ~ de** to be responsible for, to have the responsibility of - **2.** *JUR* liability ; **~ civile** civil liability ; **~ collective/pénale** collective/criminal responsibility.

responsable [rɛspɔ̃sabl] <> *adj* - **1.** [gén] : **~ (de)** responsible (for) ; [légalement] liable (for) ; [chargé de] in charge (of), responsible (for) - **2.** [sérieux] responsible <> *nmf* - **1.** [auteur, coupable] person responsible - **2.** [dirigeant] official - **3.** [personne compétente] person in charge.

resquille [rɛskij] *nf*, **resquillage** [rɛskijaʒ] *nm* - **1.** [au théâtre etc] sneaking in without paying - **2.** [dans autobus etc] fare-dodging.

resquiller [3] [rɛskije] *vi* - **1.** [au théâtre etc] to sneak in without paying - **2.** [dans autobus etc] to dodge paying the fare.

resquilleur, euse [rɛskijœr, øz] *nm, f* - **1.** [au théâtre etc] person who sneaks in without paying - **2.** [dans autobus etc] fare-dodger.

ressac [rəsak] *nm* undertow.

ressaisir [32] [rəsezir] **se ressaisir** *vp* to pull o.s. together.

ressasser [3] [rəsase] *vt* - **1.** [répéter] to keep churning out - **2.** *fig* [mécontentement] to dwell on.

ressayer = **réessayer**.

ressemblance [rəsɑ̃blɑ̃s] *nf* [gén] resemblance, likeness ; [trait] resemblance.

ressemblant, e [rəsɑ̃blɑ̃, ɑ̃t] *adj* life-like.

ressembler [3] [rəsɑ̃ble] *vi* : **~ à** [physiquement] to resemble, to look like ; [moralement] to be like, to resemble ; **cela ne lui ressemble pas** that's not like him.

se ressembler *vp* to look alike, to resemble each other ; **qui se ressemble s'assemble** *proverbe* birds of a feather flock together *proverbe*.

ressemeler [24] [rəsəmle] *vt* to resole.

ressentiment [rəsɑ̃timɑ̃] *nm* resentment.

ressentir [37] [rəsɑ̃tir] *vt* to feel.

se ressentir *vp* : **se ~ de** [suj : travail] to show the effects of ; [suj : personne, pays] to feel the effects of.

resserre [rəsɛr] *nf* storeroom.

resserrer [4] [rəsere] *vt* - **1.** [ceinture, boulon] to tighten - **2.** *fig* [lien] to strengthen.

se resserrer *vp* - **1.** [route] to (become) narrow - **2.** [nœud, étreinte] to tighten - **3.** *fig* [relations] to grow stronger, to strengthen.

resservir [38] [rəsɛrvir] <> *vt* - **1.** [plat] to serve again ; *fig* [histoire] to trot out - **2.** [personne] to give another helping to <> *vi* to be used again.

se resservir *vp* : **se ~ de qqch** [ustensile] to use sthg again ; [plat] to take another helping of sthg.

ressort [rəsɔr] *nm* - **1.** [mécanisme] spring - **2.** *fig* [énergie] spirit - **3.** *fig* [force] force - **4.** *fig* [compétence] : **être du ~ de qqn** to be sb's area of responsibility, to come under sb's jurisdiction.

en dernier ressort *loc adv* in the last resort, as a last resort.

ressortir¹ [43] [rəsɔrtir] <> *vi* (aux : être) - **1.** [personne] to go out again - **2.** *fig* [couleur] : **~ (sur)** to stand out (against) ; **faire ~** to highlight - **3.** *fig* [résulter de] : **~ de** to emerge from <> *vt* (aux : avoir) to take *ou* get *ou* bring out again.

ressortir² [32] [rəsɔrtir] *vi* [relever] : **~ à** *JUR* to be in the province of ; *sout* [domaine] to pertain to.

ressortissant, e [rəsɔrtisɑ̃, ɑ̃t] *nm, f* national.

ressouder [3] [rəsude] *vt* to resolder ; *fig* to cement.

ressource [rəsurs] *nf* resort ; **votre seule ~ est de ...** the only course open to you is to ... ; **avoir de la ~** to be resourceful.

ressources *nfpl* - **1.** [financières] means ; **être sans ~s** to be without means - **2.** [énergétiques, de langue] resources ; **~s naturelles** natural resources - **3.** [de personne] resourcefulness *(U)*.

ressourcer [16] [rəsurse] **se ressourcer** *vp* to recharge one's batteries.

ressouvenir [40] [rəsuvnir] **se ressou-**

venir *vp littéraire* : **se ~ de qqn/qqch** to remember sb/sthg.

ressurgir [32] [rǝsyrʒir] *vi* to reappear.

ressusciter [3] [resysite] <> *vi* to rise (from the dead) ; *fig* to revive <> *vt* to bring back to life, to raise ; *fig* to revive.

restant, e [rɛstɑ̃, ɑ̃t] *adj* remaining, left.
➨ **restant** *nm* rest, remainder.

restaurant [rɛstɔrɑ̃] *nm* restaurant ; **manger au ~** to eat out ; **~ d'entreprise** staff canteen.

restaurateur, trice [rɛstɔratœr, tris] *nm, f*
- **1.** *CULIN* restaurant owner - **2.** *ART* restorer.

restauration [rɛstɔrasjɔ̃] *nf* - **1.** *CULIN* restaurant business ; **~ rapide** fast food - **2.** *ART &* *POLIT* restoration.
➨ **Restauration** *nf* : **la Restauration** the Restoration.

restaurer [3] [rɛstɔre] *vt* to restore.
➨ **se restaurer** *vp* to have something to eat.

reste [rɛst] *nm* - **1.** [de lait, temps] **le ~ (de)** the rest (of) - **2.** *MATHS* remainder ; **ne pas être en ~ (avec)** not to be outdone (by).
➨ **restes** *nmpl* - **1.** [de repas] leftovers - **2.** [de mort] remains.
➨ **au reste, du reste** *loc adv* besides.
➨ **pour le reste** *loc adv* as for the rest.

rester [3] [rɛste] <> *vi* - **1.** [dans lieu, état] to stay, to remain ; **restez calme!** stay *ou* keep calm! ; **~ sur** to retain - **2.** [se perpétuer] to endure - **3.** [subsister] to remain, to be left ; **le seul bien qui me reste** the only thing I have left - **4.** [s'arrêter] : **en ~ à qqch** to stop at sthg ; **en ~ là** to finish there - **5.** *loc* : **y ~** *fam* [mourir] to pop one's clogs <> *v impers* : **il en reste un peu** there's still a little left ; **il te reste de l'argent?** do you still have some money left? ; **il reste beaucoup à faire** there is still a lot to be done ; **il reste que ..., il n'en reste pas moins que ...** the fact remains that ... ; **reste à savoir si ...** it remains to be seen whether ...

restituer [7] [rɛstitɥe] *vt* - **1.** [objet volé] to return, to restore ; [argent] to refund, to return - **2.** [archives, texte] to reconstruct - **3.** [énergie] to release - **4.** [son] to reproduce.

restitution [rɛstitysjɔ̃] *nf* - **1.** [d'argent, objet volé] return - **2.** [d'archives, de texte] reconstruction - **3.** [d'énergie] release - **4.** [de son] reproduction.

resto [rɛsto] *nm fam* restaurant ; **les ~s du cœur** *charity food distribution centres* ; **~-U** *UNIV* university refectory, cafeteria.

Restoroute® [rɛstorut] *nm* motorway cafe *Br*, highway restaurant *Am*.

restreignais, restreignions *etc* ▷ restreindre.

restreindre [81] [rɛstrɛ̃dr] *vt* to restrict.
➨ **se restreindre** *vp* - **1.** [domaine, champ] to narrow - **2.** [personne] to cut back ; **se ~ dans qqch** to restrict sthg.

restreint, e [rɛstrɛ̃, ɛ̃t] *pp* ▷ restreindre.

restrictif, ive [rɛstriktif, iv] *adj* restrictive.

restriction [rɛstriksjɔ̃] *nf* - **1.** [condition] condition ; **sans ~** unconditionally - **2.** [limitation] restriction.
➨ **restrictions** *nfpl* [alimentaires] rationing *(U)*.

restructurer [3] [rǝstryktyre] *vt* to restructure.

résultant, e [rezyltɑ̃, ɑ̃t] *adj* resulting.
➨ **résultante** *nf* - **1.** *SCIENCE* resultant - **2.** [conséquence] consequence, outcome.

résultat [rezylta] *nm* result ; [d'action] outcome.
➨ **résultats** *nmpl* results.

résulter [3] [rezylte] <> *vi* : **~ de** to be the result of, to result from <> *v impers* : **il en résulte que ...** as a result, ...

résumé [rezyme] *nm* summary, résumé ; **en ~** [pour conclure] to sum up ; [en bref] in brief, summarized.

résumer [3] [rezyme] *vt* to summarize.
➨ **se résumer** *vp* - **1.** [suj : personne] to sum up - **2.** [se réduire] : **se ~ à qqch/à faire qqch** to come down to sthg/to doing sthg.

résurgence [rezyrʒɑ̃s] *nf* resurgence.

résurrection [rezyrɛksjɔ̃] *nf* resurrection.

rétablir [32] [retablir] *vt* - **1.** [gén] to restore ; [malade] to restore (to health) - **2.** [communications, contact] to re-establish - **3.** [dans emploi] : **~ qqn (dans)** to reinstate sb (in).
➨ **se rétablir** *vp* - **1.** [silence] to return, to be restored - **2.** [malade] to recover - **3.** *GYM* to pull o.s. up.

rétablissement [retablismɑ̃] *nm* - **1.** [d'ordre] restoration - **2.** [de communications] re-establishment - **3.** [de malade] recovery - **4.** [dans emploi] reinstatement - **5.** *GYM* pull-up.

retaper [3] [rǝtape] *vt* - **1.** [maison, canapé] to do up - **2.** [lettre] to retype - **3.** *fam* [personne] to set up.
➨ **se retaper** *vp fam* [personne] to get back on one's feet.

retard [rǝtar] *nm* - **1.** [délai] delay ; **être en ~** [sur heure] to be late ; [sur échéance] to be behind ; **avoir du ~** to be late *ou* delayed ; **se mettre en ~** to make o.s. late ; **rattraper son ~** to make up lost time ; **après bien des ~s** after much delay - **2.** [de pays, peuple, personne] backwardness.

retardataire [rətardatɛr] <> nmf - **1.** [en retard] latecomer - **2.** [enfant] backward ou retarded person <> adj - **1.** [sur heure] late - **2.** [idée, enfant] backward.

retardement [rətardəmã] nm : à ~ belatedly ; voir aussi **bombe.**

retarder [3] [rətarde] <> vt - **1.** [personne, train] to delay ; [sur échéance] to put back ; ~ **qqn dans qqch** to delay sb in sthg - **2.** [ajourner - rendez-vous] to put back ou off ; [- départ] to put back ou off, to delay - **3.** [montre] to put back <> vi - **1.** [horloge] to be slow - **2.** [ne pas être au courant] to be behind the times - **3.** [être en décalage] : ~ **sur** to be out of step ou tune with.

retendre [73] [rətãdr] vt to retighten.

retenir [40] [rətnir] vt - **1.** [physiquement - objet, personne, cri] to hold back ; [- souffle] to hold ; ~ **qqn de faire qqch** to stop ou restrain sb from doing sthg - **2.** [retarder] to keep, to detain ; ~ **qqn à dîner** to have sb stay for dinner - **3.** [montant, impôt] to keep back, to withhold - **4.** [chambre] to reserve - **5.** [leçon, cours] to remember - **6.** [projet] to accept, to adopt - **7.** [eau, chaleur] to retain - **8.** MATHS to carry - **9.** [intérêt, attention] to hold.

➤ **se retenir** vp - **1.** [s'accrocher] : **se** ~ **à** to hold onto - **2.** [se contenir] to hold on ; **se** ~ **de faire qqch** to refrain from doing sthg.

rétention [retãsjõ] nf.MÉD retention.

retentir [32] [rətãtir] vi - **1.** [son] to ring (out) - **2.** [pièce, rue] : ~ **de** to resound with - **3.** fig [fatigue, blessure] : ~ **sur** to have an effect on.

retentissant, e [rətãtisã, ãt] adj resounding.

retentissement [rətãtismã] nm - **1.** [de mesure] repercussions (pl) - **2.** [de spectacle] effect.

retenu, e [rətny] pp ▷ **retenir.**

retenue [rətny] nf - **1.** [prélèvement] deduction ; ~ **à la source** deduction at source - **2.** MATHS amount carried - **3.** SCOL detention - **4.** fig [de personne - dans relations] reticence ; [- dans comportement] restraint ; **sans** ~ without restraint.

réticence [retisãs] nf [hésitation] hesitation, reluctance ; **avec** ~ hesitantly ; **sans** ~ without hesitation.

réticent, e [retisã, ãt] adj hesitant, reluctant.

retiendrai, retiendras etc ▷ **retenir.**

retienne, retiennes etc ▷ **retenir.**

rétif, ive [retif, iv] adj restive.

rétine [retin] nf retina.

retiré, e [rətire] adj - **1.** [lieu] remote, isolated ; [vie] quiet - **2.** [personne] retired.

retirer [3] [rətire] vt - **1.** [vêtement, emballage] to take off, to remove ; [permis, jouet] to take away ; ~ **qqch à qqn** to take sthg away from sb - **2.** [plainte] to withdraw, to take back - **3.** [sortir - personne] to remove, to extricate ; [- casserole] to remove - **4.** [métal] to extract - **5.** [avantages, bénéfices] : ~ **qqch de qqch** to get ou derive sthg from sthg - **6.** [bagages, billet] to collect ; [argent] to withdraw.

➤ **se retirer** vp - **1.** [s'isoler] to withdraw, to retreat - **2.** [des affaires] : **se** ~ **(de)** to retire (from) - **3.** [refluer] to recede.

retombées [rətõbe] nfpl repercussions, fallout (sg) ; ~**s radioactives** radioactive fallout.

retomber [3] [rətõbe] vi - **1.** [gymnaste, chat] to land - **2.** [redevenir] : ~ **malade** to relapse - **3.** [pluie] to fall again - **4.** fig [colère] to die away - **5.** [cheveux] to hang down - **6.** fig [responsabilité] : ~ **sur** to fall on.

retordre [76] [rətordr] vt [linge] to wring (out) again.

rétorquer [3] [retɔrke] vt to retort ; ~ **à qqn que ...** to retort to sb that ...

retors, e [rətɔr, ɔrs] adj wily.

rétorsion [retɔrsjõ] nf retaliation ; **mesures de** ~ reprisals.

retouche [rətuʃ] nf - **1.** [de texte, vêtement] alteration - **2.** ART & PHOT touching up.

retoucher [3] [rətuʃe] vt - **1.** [texte, vêtement] to alter - **2.** ART & PHOT to touch up.

retour [rətur] nm - **1.** [gén] return ; **à mon/ton** ~ when I/you get back, on my/your return ; **au** ~ **de** [étant arrivé] on my/his etc return from ; [en cours de route] on the way back ; **être de** ~ **(de)** to be back (from) ; '~ **à l'expéditeur** ou **l'envoyeur**' 'return to sender' ; ~ **en arrière** flashback ; ~ **de chariot** carriage return ; ~ **de flamme** backfire ; ~ **de manivelle** ou **bâton** fam fig kickback ; **en** ~ in return ; **sans** ~ for ever ; **(être) sur le** ~ fig (to be) over the hill - **2.** [trajet] journey back, return journey.

retournement [rəturnəmã] nm turnaround, turnabout ; ~ **de situation** reversal.

retourner [3] [rəturne] <> vt (aux : avoir) - **1.** [carte, matelas] to turn over ; [terre] to turn (over) - **2.** [pull, poche] to turn inside out - **3.** [compliment, objet prêté] : ~ **qqch (à qqn)** to return sthg (to sb) - **4.** [lettre, colis] to send back, to return - **5.** fam fig [personne] to shake up ; **en être tout retourné** to be shaken up <> vi (aux : être) to come/go back ; ~ **à** [personne] to go back ou return to ; [objet] to be returned to ; ~ **en arrière** ou **sur ses pas** to retrace one's steps.

➤ **se retourner** vp - **1.** [basculer] to turn over

- 2. [pivoter] to turn round **- 3.** *fam fig* [s'adapter] to sort o.s. out **- 4.** [rentrer] : **s'en ~** to go back (home) **- 5.** *fig* [s'opposer] : **se ~ contre** to turn against.

retracer [16] [rətrase] *vt* **- 1.** [ligne] to redraw **- 2.** [événement] to relate.

rétracter [3] [retrakte] *vt* to retract.
➡ **se rétracter** *vp* **- 1.** [se contracter] to retract **- 2.** [se dédire] to back down.

retraduire [98] [rətradɥir] *vt* to translate again.

retrait [rətrɛ] *nm* **- 1.** [gén] withdrawal ; **~ du permis** disqualification from driving **- 2.** [de bagages] collection **- 3.** [des eaux] ebbing.
➡ **en retrait** *loc adj* & *loc adv* **- 1.** [maison] set back from the road ; **rester en ~** *fig* to hang back **- 2.** [texte] indented.

retraite [rətrɛt] *nf* **- 1.** [gén] retreat ; **battre en ~** to beat a retreat **- 2.** [cessation d'activité] retirement ; **être à la ~** to be retired ; **prendre sa ~** to retire ; **~ anticipée** early retirement **- 3.** [revenu] (retirement) pension.

retraité, e [rətrete] *adj* **- 1.** [personne] retired **- 2.** TECHNOL reprocessed *nm, f* retired person, pensioner.

retranchement [rətrɑ̃ʃmɑ̃] *nm* entrenchment ; **poursuivre** *ou* **forcer qqn dans ses derniers ~s** *fig* to drive sb into a corner.

retrancher [3] [rətrɑ̃ʃe] *vt* **- 1.** [passage] : **~ qqch (de)** to cut sthg out (from), to remove sthg (from) **- 2.** [montant] : **~ qqch (de)** to take sthg away (from), to deduct sthg (from).
➡ **se retrancher** *vp* to entrench o.s. ; **se ~ derrière/dans** *fig* to take refuge behind/in.

retransmettre [84] [rətrɑ̃smetr] *vt* to broadcast.

retransmis, e [rətrɑ̃smi, iz] *pp* ▷ retransmettre.

retransmission [rətrɑ̃smisjɔ̃] *nf* broadcast.

retravailler [3] [rətravaje] *vt* : **~ qqch** to work on sthg again *vi* to start work again.

rétrécir [32] [retresir] *vt* [tissu] to take in *vi* [tissu] to shrink.
➡ **se rétrécir** *vp* [tissu] to shrink.

rétrécissement [retresismɑ̃] *nm* **- 1.** [de vêtement] shrinkage **- 2.** MÉD stricture.

retremper [3] [rətrɑ̃pe] *vt* **- 1.** [linge] to resoak **- 2.** [acier] to requench.
➡ **se retremper** *vp* to go back into the water ; *fig* to reimmerse o.s.

rétribuer [7] [retribɥe] *vt* **- 1.** [employé] to pay **- 2.** [travail] to pay for.

rétribution [retribysjɔ̃] *nf* remuneration.

rétro [retro] *nm* **- 1.** [style] old style *ou* fash-

ion **- 2.** *fam* [rétroviseur] rear-view mirror *adj inv* old-style.

rétroactif, ive [retroaktif, iv] *adj* retrospective.

rétroactivement [retroaktivmɑ̃] *adv* retrospectively.

rétrocéder [18] [retrosede] *vt* to retrocede.

rétrocession [retrosesjɔ̃] *nf* retrocession.

rétrograde [retrograd] *adj péj* reactionary.

rétrograder [3] [retrograde] *vt* to demote *vi* **- 1.** AUTOM to change down **- 2.** [dans une hiérarchie] to move down.

rétroprojecteur [retroprojɛktœr] *nm* overhead projector.

rétrospectif, ive [retrospɛktif, iv] *adj* retrospective.
➡ **rétrospective** *nf* retrospective.

rétrospectivement [retrospɛktivmɑ̃] *adv* retrospectively.

retroussé, e [rətruse] *adj* **- 1.** [manches, pantalon] rolled up **- 2.** [nez] turned up.

retrousser [3] [rətruse] *vt* **- 1.** [manches, pantalon] to roll up **- 2.** [lèvres] to curl.

retrouvailles [rətruvaj] *nfpl* reunion (*sg*).

retrouver [3] [rətruve] *vt* **- 1.** [gén] to find ; [appétit] to recover, to regain **- 2.** [reconnaître] to recognize **- 3.** [ami] to meet, to see.
➡ **se retrouver** *vp* **- 1.** [entre amis] to meet (up) again ; **on se retrouve au café?** shall we meet up *ou* see each other at the cafe? **- 2.** [être de nouveau] to find o.s. again **- 3.** [s'orienter] to find one's way ; **ne pas s'y ~** [dans ses papiers] to be completely lost **- 4.** [erreur, style] to be found, to crop up **- 5.** [financièrement] : **s'y ~** *fam* to break even.

rétroviseur [retrovizœr] *nm* rear-view mirror.

réunification [reynifikasjɔ̃] *nf* reunification.

réunifier [9] [reynifje] *vt* to reunify.

réunion [reynjɔ̃] *nf* **- 1.** [séance] meeting **- 2.** [jonction] union, merging **- 3.** [d'amis, de famille] reunion **- 4.** [collection] collection.

Réunion [reynjɔ̃] *nf* : **(l'île de) la ~** Réunion ; **à la ~** in Réunion.

réunionnais, e [reynjɔnɛ, ɛz] *adj* of/from Réunion Island.
➡ **Réunionnais, e** *nm, f* native *ou* inhabitant of Réunion.

réunir [32] [reynir] *vt* **- 1.** [fonds] to collect **- 2.** [extrémités] to put together, to bring together **- 3.** [qualités] to combine **- 4.** [personnes to bring together - après séparation] to reunite
➡ **se réunir** *vp* **- 1.** [personnes] to meet **- 2.** [en-

treprises] to combine ; [états] to unite - **3.** [fleuves, rues] to converge.

réussi, e [reysil *adj* successful ; **c'est ~!** *fig* & *iron* congratulations!, well done!

réussir [32] [reysir] <> *vi* - **1.** [personne, affaire] to succeed, to be a success ; **~ à faire qqch** to succeed in doing sthg ; **~ un coup fumant** to pull off a master stroke - **2.** [climat] : **~ à** to agree with <> *vt* - **1.** [portrait, plat] to make a success of - **2.** [examen] to pass.

réussite [reysit] *nf* - **1.** [succès] success - **2.** [jeu de cartes] patience *Br*, solitaire *Am*.

réutiliser [3] [reytilize] *vt* to reuse.

revaloir [60] [rəvalwar] *vt* : **~ qqch à qqn** [avec reconnaissance] to repay sb for sthg ; [avec hostilité] to get even with sb for sthg.

revalorisation [rəvalɔrizasjɔ̃] *nf* [de monnaie] revaluation ; [de salaires] raising ; *fig* [d'idée] rehabilitation.

revaloriser [3] [rəvalɔrize] *vt* [monnaie] to revalue ; [salaires] to raise ; *fig* [idée, doctrine] to rehabilitate.

revanchard, e [rəvɑ̃ʃar, ard] *péj* <> *adj* of revenge <> *nm, f* advocate of revenge.

revanche [rəvɑ̃ʃ] *nf* - **1.** [vengeance] revenge ; **prendre sa ~** to take one's revenge - **2.** *SPORT* return (match).

◆ **en revanche** *loc adv* - **1.** [par contre] on the other hand - **2.** [en contrepartie] in return.

rêvasser [3] [rɛvase] *vi* to daydream.

revaudrai, revaudras *etc* ▷ revaloir.

rêve [rɛv] *nm* dream ; **de ~** *fig* dream (avant n).

rêvé, e [rɛve] *adj* ideal.

revêche [rəvɛʃ] *adj* surly.

réveil [revɛj] *nm* - **1.** [de personne] waking (up) ; *fig* awakening ; **au ~** on waking (up) - **2.** [pendule] alarm clock - **3.** [de volcan] reawakening.

réveiller [4] [reveje] *vt* - **1.** [personne] to wake up - **2.** [courage] to revive.

◆ **se réveiller** *vp* - **1.** [personne] to wake (up) - **2.** [ambitions] to reawaken.

réveillon [revejɔ̃] *nm* - **1.** [jour - de Noël] Christmas Eve ; [- de nouvel an] New Year's Eve - **2.** [repas - de Noël] Christmas Eve meal ; [- de nouvel an] New Year's Eve meal.

réveillonner [3] [revejɔne] *vi* to have a Christmas Eve/New Year's Eve meal.

révélateur, trice [revelatœr, tris] *adj* revealing.

◆ **révélateur** *nm* *PHOT* developer ; *fig* [ce qui révèle] indication.

révélation [revelasjɔ̃] *nf* - **1.** [gén] revelation - **2.** [artiste] discovery.

révéler [18] [revele] *vt* - **1.** [gén] to reveal - **2.** [artiste] to discover.

◆ **se révéler** *vp* - **1.** [apparaître] to be revealed - **2.** [s'avérer] to prove to be.

revenant [rəvnɑ̃] *nm* - **1.** [fantôme] spirit, ghost - **2.** *fam* [personne] stranger.

revendeur, euse [rəvɑ̃dœr, øz] *nm, f* retailer.

revendication [rəvɑ̃dikasjɔ̃] *nf* claim, demand.

revendiquer [3] [rəvɑ̃dike] *vt* [dû, responsabilité] to claim ; [avec force] to demand.

revendre [73] [rəvɑ̃dr] *vt* - **1.** [après utilisation] to resell - **2.** [vendre plus de] to sell more of.

revendu, e [rəvɑ̃dy] *pp* ▷ revendre.

revenir [40] [rəvnir] *vi* - **1.** [gén] to come back, to return ; **~ de** to come back from, to return from ; **~ à** to come back to, to return to ; **~ sur** [sujet] to go over again ; [décision] to go back on ; **~ à soi** to come to - **2.** [mot, sujet] to crop up - **3.** [à l'esprit] : **~ à** to come back to - **4.** [impliquer] : **cela revient au même/à dire que** ... it amounts to the same thing/to saying (that) ... - **5.** [coûter] : **~ à** to come to, to amount to ; **~ cher** to be expensive - **6.** [honneur, tâche] : **~ à** to fall to ; **c'est à lui qu'il revient de** ... it is up to him to ... - **7.** *CULIN* : **faire ~** to brown - **8.** *loc* : **sa tête ne me revient pas** I don't like the look of him/her ; **il n'en revenait pas** he couldn't get over it ; **~ de loin** to have been at death's door.

revente [rəvɑ̃t] *nf* resale.

revenu, e [rəvny] *pp* ▷ revenir.

◆ **revenu** *nm* [de pays] revenue ; [de personne] income.

rêver [4] [rɛve] <> *vi* to dream ; [rêvasser] to daydream ; **~ de/à** to dream of/about <> *vt* to dream ; **~ que** to dream (that).

réverbération [reverberasjɔ̃] *nf* reverberation.

réverbère [reverber] *nm* street lamp *ou* light.

réverbérer [18] [reverbere] *vt* to reverberate.

reverdir [32] [rəverdir] *vi* to become green again.

révérence [reverɑ̃s] *nf* - **1.** [salut] bow - **2.** *littéraire* [déférence] reverence.

révérencieux, euse [reverɑ̃sjø, øz] *adj* reverent.

révérend, e [reverɑ̃, ɑ̃d] *adj* reverend.

◆ **révérend** *nm* reverend.

révérer [18] [revere] *vt* to revere.

rêverie [rɛvri] *nf* reverie.

revers [rəver] *nm* - **1.** [de main] back ; [de pièce]

reverse ; **prendre à ~** to capture from the rear *ou* from behind ; **le ~ de la médaille** *fig* the other side of the coin **- 2.** [de veste] lapel ; [de pantalon] turn-up *Br*, cuff *Am* **- 3.** *TENNIS* backhand **- 4.** *fig* [de fortune] reversal.

reverser [3] [rəvɛrse] *vt* **- 1.** [liquide] to pour out more of **- 2.** *FIN* : **~ qqch sur** to pay sthg into ; **~ qqch dans** to invest sthg in.

réversible [reversibl] *adj* reversible.

revêtement [rəvɛtmɑ̃] *nm* surface.

revêtir [44] [rəvetir] *vt* **- 1.** [mur, surface] : **~ (de)** to cover (with) **- 2.** [aspect] to take on, to assume **- 3.** [vêtement] to put on ; [personne] to dress **- 4.** *sout* [de dignité, de pouvoir] : **~ qqn de** to invest sb with.

revêts ▷ **revêtir**.

revêtu, e [rəvety] *pp* ▷ **revêtir**.

rêveur, euse [rɛvœr, øz] ◇ *adj* dreamy ◇ *nm, f* dreamer.

reviendrai, reviendras *etc* ▷ **revenir**.

revient [rəvjɛ̃] ▷ **prix**.

revigorer [3] [rəvigɔre] *vt* to invigorate.

revirement [rəvirmɑ̃] *nm* change.

révisable [revizabl] *adj* subject to review.

réviser [3] [revize] *vt* **- 1.** [réexaminer, modifier] to revise, to review **- 2.** *SCOL* to revise **- 3.** [machine] to check.

révision [revizjɔ̃] *nf* **- 1.** [réexamen, modification] revision, review **- 2.** *SCOL* revision **- 3.** [de machine] checkup.

révisionnisme [revizjɔnism] *nm* revisionism.

révisionniste [revizjɔnist] *nmf* & *adj* revisionist.

revisser [3] [rəvise] *vt* to screw back again.

revitaliser [3] [rəvitalize] *vt* to revitalize.

revivre [90] [rəvivr] ◇ *vi* [personne] to come back to life, to revive ; *fig* [espoir] to be revived, to revive ; **faire ~** to revive ◇ *vt* to relive ; **faire ~ qqch à qqn** to bring sthg back to sb.

révocation [revɔkasjɔ̃] *nf* **- 1.** [de loi] revocation **- 2.** [de fonctionnaire] dismissal.

revoici [rəvwasi] *prép* : **me ~!** it's me again!, I'm back!

revoir [62] [rəvwar] *vt* **- 1.** [renouer avec] to see again **- 2.** [corriger, étudier] to revise *Br*, to review *Am*.

➡ **se revoir** *vp* [amis] to see each other again ; [professionnellement] to meet again.

➡ **au revoir** *interj* & *nm* goodbye.

révoltant, e [revɔltɑ̃, ɑ̃t] *adj* revolting.

révolte [revɔlt] *nf* revolt ; **inciter** *ou* **pousser qqn à la ~** to incite sb to revolt ; **être en ~ contre** to be in revolt against.

révolter [3] [revɔlte] *vt* to disgust.

➡ **se révolter** *vp* : **se ~ (contre)** to revolt (against).

révolu, e [revɔly] *adj* past ; **avoir 15 ans ~s** *ADMIN* to be over 15.

révolution [revɔlysjɔ̃] *nf* **- 1.** [gén] revolution ; **la Révolution française** the French Revolution **- 2.** *fam* [effervescence] uproar ; **en ~** in an uproar.

LA RÉVOLUTION FRANÇAISE

The French Revolution, which was precipitated by the abuses of the 'Ancien Régime' was a major turning point in French history. It was a turbulent period lasting from the storming of the Bastille in 1789 to Bonaparte's coup in 1799. The Declaration of Human Rights, the execution of Louis XVI (1792), the Terror (1793-94) and war against the other European powers were events that marked this period.

révolutionnaire [revɔlysjɔnɛr] *nmf* & *adj* revolutionary.

révolutionner [3] [revɔlysjɔne] *vt* **- 1.** [transformer] to revolutionize **- 2.** [mettre en émoi] to stir up.

revolver [revɔlvɛr] *nm* revolver.

révoquer [3] [revɔke] *vt* **- 1.** [fonctionnaire] to dismiss **- 2.** [loi] to revoke.

revue [rəvy] *nf* **- 1.** [gén] review ; **~ de presse** press review ; **passer en ~** *fig* to review **- 2.** [défilé] march-past **- 3.** [magazine] magazine **- 4.** [spectacle] revue.

révulser [3] [revylse] *vt* to disgust.

➡ **se révulser** *vp* to contort.

rewriting [rərajtiŋ] *nm* rewriting.

Reykjavik [rɛkjavik] *n* Reykjavik.

rez-de-chaussée [redʃose] *nm inv* ground floor *Br*, first floor *Am*.

rez-de-jardin [redʒardɛ̃] *nm inv* garden level.

RF *abr de* **République française**.

RFA (*abr de* **République fédérale d'Allemagne**) *nf* FRG.

RFI (*abr de* **Radio France Internationale**) *nf* *French world service radio station*.

RFO (*abr de* **Radio-télévision française d'outre-mer**) *nf* *French overseas broadcasting service*.

r.g. (*abr de* **rive gauche**) *left (south) bank of the Seine*.

RG (*abr de* **Renseignements généraux**) *nmpl* *police department responsible for political security*, ≃ *Special Branch Br*.

Rh (*abr de* **Rhésus**) Rh.

rhabiller [3] [rabije] *vt* to dress again.
 ◆ **se rhabiller** *vp* to get dressed again ; **aller se ~** *fam fig* to throw in the towel.

rhapsodie, rapsodie [rapsɔdi] *nf* rhapsody.

rhénan, e [renɑ̃, an] *adj* of/from the Rhine, Rhine *(avant n)*.

rhéostat [reɔstal] *nm* rheostat.

rhésus [rezys] *nm* rhesus (factor) ; **~ positif/négatif** rhesus positive/negative.

rhétorique [retɔrik] *nf* rhetoric.

Rhin [rɛ̃] *nm* : **le ~** the Rhine.

rhinite [rinit] *nf* rhinitis *(U)*.

rhinocéros [rinɔserɔs] *nm* rhinoceros.

rhino-pharyngite [rinɔfarɛ̃ʒit] *(pl* **rhino-pharyngites)** *nf* throat infection.

Rhodes [rɔd] *n* Rhodes ; **le colosse de ~** the Colossus of Rhodes.

rhododendron [rɔdɔdɛ̃drɔ̃] *nm* rhododendron.

Rhône [ron] *nm* : **le ~** the (River) Rhone.

rhubarbe [rybarb] *nf* rhubarb.

rhum [rɔm] *nm* rum.

rhumatisant, e [rymatizɑ̃, ɑ̃t] *adj* & *nm, f* rheumatic.

rhumatismal, e, aux [rymatismal, o] *adj* rheumatic.

rhumatisme [rymatism] *nm* rheumatism.

rhumatologue [rymatɔlɔg] *nmf* rheumatologist.

rhume [rym] *nm* cold ; **attraper un ~** to catch a cold ; **~ des foins** hay fever.

ri [ri] *pp inv* ▷ **rire**.

RI ◇ *nm* *(abr de* **régiment d'infanterie)** infantry regiment ◇ *nmpl* *(abr de* **Républicains indépendants)** *right-wing French political party*.

Riad = **Riyad**.

riant, e [rijɑ̃, ɑ̃t] *adj* smiling ; *fig* cheerful.

RIB, Rib [rib] *(abr de* **relevé d'identité bancaire)** *nm* bank account identification slip.

ribambelle [ribɑ̃bɛl] *nf* : **~ de** string of.

ricanement [rikanmɑ̃] *nm* snigger.

ricaner [3] [rikane] *vi* to snigger.

RICE, Rice [ris] *(abr de* **relevé d'identité de caisse d'épargne)** *nm savings bank account identification slip*.

richard, e [riʃar, ard] *nm, f* *fam péj* money-bags *(sg)*.

riche [riʃ] ◇ *adj* - **1.** [gén] rich ; [personne, pays] rich, wealthy ; **~ en** *ou* **de** rich in - **2.** [habit] expensive - **3.** [idée] great ◇ *nmf* rich person ; **les ~s** the rich ; **nouveau ~** nouveau riche.

richement [riʃmɑ̃] *adv* richly.

richesse [riʃɛs] *nf* - **1.** [de personne, pays] wealth *(U)* - **2.** [d'appartement] sumptuousness *(U)* - **3.** [de faune, flore] abundance ; **~ en vitamines** high vitamin content.
 ◆ **richesses** *nfpl* - **1.** [gén] wealth *(U)* - **2.** [de musée] riches.

richissime [riʃisim] *adj* super-rich.

ricin [risɛ̃] *nm* castor-oil plant ; **huile de ~** castor oil.

ricocher [3] [rikɔʃe] *vi* *litt & fig* to rebound ; [balle d'arme] to ricochet.

ricochet [rikɔʃɛ] *nm* *litt & fig* rebound ; [de balle d'arme] ricochet ; **par ~** in an indirect way.

rictus [riktys] *nm* rictus.

ride [rid] *nf* wrinkle ; [de surface d'eau] ripple.

ridé, e [ride] *adj* wrinkled.

rideau, x [rido] *nm* curtain ; **~ de fer** [frontière] Iron Curtain.

rider [3] [ride] *vt* - **1.** [peau] to wrinkle - **2.** [surface] to ruffle.
 ◆ **se rider** *vp* to become wrinkled.

ridicule [ridikyl] ◇ *adj* ridiculous ◇ *nm* : **le ~ ridicule** ; **se couvrir de ~** to make o.s. look ridiculous ; **tourner qqn/qqch en ~** to ridicule sb/sthg.

ridiculement [ridikylmɑ̃] *adv* ridiculously.

ridiculiser [3] [ridikylize] *vt* to ridicule.
 ◆ **se ridiculiser** *vp* to make o.s. look ridiculous.

ridule [ridyl] *nf* little wrinkle.

rien [rjɛ̃] ◇ *pron indéf* - **1.** [en contexte négatif] : **ne ... rien** nothing, not ... anything ; **je n'ai ~ fait** I've done nothing, I haven't done anything ; **je n'en sais ~** I don't know (anything about it), I know nothing about it ; **~ ne m'intéresse** nothing interests me ; **il n'y a plus ~ dans le réfrigérateur** there's nothing left in the fridge - **2.** [aucune chose] nothing ; **que fais-tu? — ~** what are you doing? — nothing ; **~ de nouveau** nothing new ; **~ d'autre** nothing else ; **~ du tout** nothing at all ; **~ à faire** it's no good ; **de ~!** don't mention it!, not at all! ; **pour ~** for nothing - **3.** [quelque chose] anything ; **sans ~ dire** without saying anything ◇ *nm* : **pour un ~** [se fâcher, pleurer] for nothing, at the slightest thing ; **perdre son temps à des ~s** to waste one's time with trivia ; **en un ~ de temps** in no time at all.
 ◆ **rien que** *loc adv* only, just ; **la vérité, ~ que la vérité** the truth and nothing but the truth ; **~ que l'idée des vacances la comblait** just thinking about the holiday filled her with joy.

➡ **un rien** *loc adv* a bit, a shade ; **sa robe est un ~ trop étroite** her dress is a bit too tight.

rieur, rieuse [rijœr, rijøz] *adj* cheerful.

Riga [riga] *n* Riga.

rigide [riʒid] *adj* rigid ; [muscle] tense.

rigidité [riʒidite] *nf* rigidity ; [de muscle] tenseness ; [de principes, mœurs] strictness.

rigolade [rigɔlad] *nf fam* fun (U) ; **c'est de la ~** *fig* it's a walkover.

rigolard, e [rigɔlar, ard] *adj fam* jokey, joking.

rigole [rigɔl] *nf* channel.

rigoler [3] [rigɔle] *vi fam* - **1.** [rire] to laugh - **2.** [plaisanter] : **~ (de)** to joke (about).

rigolo, ote [rigɔlo, ɔt] *fam* ◇ *adj* funny ◇ *nm, f péj* phoney *Br*, phony *Am*.

rigoriste [rigɔrist] ◇ *nmf* puritan ◇ *adj* austere, puritanical.

rigoureusement [rigurøzmɑ̃] *adv* - **1.** [punir] harshly - **2.** [vrai, ponctuel] absolutely ; **c'est ~ exact** it's the honest truth.

rigoureux, euse [rigurø, øz] *adj* - **1.** [discipline, hiver] harsh - **2.** [analyse] rigorous.

rigueur [rigœr] *nf* - **1.** [de punition] severity, harshness - **2.** [de climat] harshness - **3.** [d'analyse] rigour *Br*, rigor *Am*, exactness - **4.** *loc* : **être de ~** to be obligatory ; **tenir ~ de qqch à qqn** to hold sthg against sb.

➡ **à la rigueur** *loc adv* if necessary, if need be.

rillettes [rijet] *nfpl* potted pork, duck or goose.

rime [rim] *nf* rhyme ; **sans ~ ni raison** *fig* without rhyme or reason.

rimer [3] [rime] *vi* : **~ (avec)** to rhyme (with) ; **ça ne rime à rien** *fig* that doesn't make sense.

Rimmel® [rimɛl] *nm* mascara.

rinçage [rɛ̃saʒ] *nm* rinsing.

rince-doigts [rɛ̃sdwa] *nm inv* finger bowl.

rincer [16] [rɛ̃se] *vt* [bouteille] to rinse out ; [cheveux, linge] to rinse ; **se faire ~** *fam fig* to get a soaking.

➡ **se rincer** *vp* to rinse o.s. ; **se ~ la bouche** to rinse one's mouth.

ring [riŋ] *nm* - **1.** *BOXE* ring - **2.** *Belg* [route] bypass.

ringard, e [rɛ̃gar, ard] *fam* ◇ *adj* - **1.** [chanson] corny - **2.** [décor] naff - **3.** [acteur] second-rate - **4.** [personne] nerdy ◇ *nm, f* nerd.

ringuette [rɛ̃gɛt] *nf* ringette (women's sport similar to ice hockey).

Rio de Janeiro [rjodedʒanerɔ] *n* Rio de Janeiro.

ripaille [ripaj] *nf* : **faire ~** *fam vieilli* to have a feast.

riposte [ripɔst] *nf* - **1.** [réponse] retort, riposte - **2.** [contre-attaque] counterattack.

riposter [3] [ripɔste] ◇ *vt* : **~ que** to retort *ou* riposte that ◇ *vi* - **1.** [répondre] to riposte ; **~ à** [personne] to answer back ; [insulte] to reply to - **2.** [contre-attaquer] to counter, to retaliate.

rire [95] [rir] ◇ *nm* laugh ; **avoir un fou ~** to giggle ; **éclater de ~** to burst out laughing ◇ *vi* - **1.** [gén] to laugh ; **~ de** to laugh at - **2.** [plaisanter] : **tu veux/vous voulez ~?** you must be joking! ; **pour ~** *fam* as a joke, for a laugh.

➡ **se rire** *vp sout* : **se ~ de** to laugh at.

ris [ri] *nm* - **1.** (gén pl) *CULIN* : **~ de veau** sweetbread - **2.** *NAVIG* reef.

risée [rize] *nf* ridicule ; **être la ~ de** to be the laughing stock of.

risette [rizɛt] *nf* : **faire (une) ~ à qqn** [enfant] to give sb a nice *ou* sweet smile ; [sourire de commande] to smile politely at sb.

risible [rizibl] *adj* [ridicule] ridiculous.

risotto [rizɔto] *nm* risotto.

risque [risk] *nm* risk ; **courir un ~** to run a risk ; **prendre des ~s** to take risks ; **à tes/vos ~s et périls** at your own risk.

risqué, e [riske] *adj* - **1.** [entreprise] risky, dangerous - **2.** [plaisanterie] risqué, daring.

risquer [3] [riske] *vt* - **1.** [vie, prison] to risk ; **~ de faire qqch** to be likely to do sthg ; **je risque de perdre tout ce que j'ai** I'm running the risk of losing everything I have ; **~ que** (+ subjonctif) to take a risk that ; **cela ne risque rien** it will be all right ; **~ gros** to take a big risk ; **~ le tout pour le tout** *fig* to put everything on the line - **2.** [tenter] to venture.

➡ **se risquer** *vp* to venture ; **se ~ à faire qqch** to dare to do sthg.

risque-tout [riskətu] *nmf inv* daredevil.

rissoler [3] [risɔle] ◇ *vt* to brown ◇ *vi* to brown ; **faire ~** to brown.

ristourne [risturn] *nf* discount ; **faire une ~ à qqn** to give sb a discount.

rite [rit] *nm* - **1.** *RELIG* rite - **2.** [cérémonial] *fig* ritual.

ritournelle [riturnɛl] *nf* - **1.** *fam fig* [rabâchage] old story, old song - **2.** *MUS* ritornello.

rituel, elle [rituɛl] *adj* ritual.

➡ **rituel** *nm* ritual.

rituellement [rituɛlmɑ̃] *adv* - **1.** [selon un rite] ritually, religiously - **2.** *fig* [immuablement] unfailingly.

rivage [rivaʒ] *nm* shore.

rival, e, aux [rival, o] ◇ *adj* rival (avant n) ◇ *nm, f* rival.

rivaliser [3] [rivalize] *vi* : ~ **avec** to compete with ; ~ **de** to vie in.

rivalité [rivalite] *nf* rivalry.

rive [riv] *nf* [de rivière] bank ; **la ~ droite** [à Paris] the north bank of the Seine *(generally considered more affluent than the south bank)* ; **la ~ gauche** [à Paris] the south bank of the Seine *(generally associated with students and artists)*.

RIVE DROITE, RIVE GAUCHE

The Right (North) Bank of the Seine is traditionally associated with business and trade, and has a reputation for being more conservative than the Left Bank. The Left (South) Bank includes districts traditionally favoured by artists, students and intellectuals, and has a reputation for being bohemian and unconventional.

river [3] [rive] *vt* - **1.** [fixer] : ~ **qqch à qqch** to rivet sthg to sthg - **2.** [clou] to clinch ; **être rivé à** *fig* to be riveted *ou* glued to.

riverain, e [rivrɛ̃, ɛn] <> *adj* riverside *(avant n)* ; [de rue] roadside *(avant n)* <> *nm, f* resident.

rivet [rive] *nm* rivet.

rivière [rivjɛr] *nf* river.

➡ **rivière de diamants** *nf* diamond necklace *(with largest stone in the middle)*.

rixe [riks] *nf* fight, brawl.

Riyad, Riad [rijad] *n* Riyadh.

riz [ri] *nm* rice ; ~ **au lait** rice pudding ; ~ **pilaf** pilau rice.

riziculture [rizikyltyr] *nf* rice-growing.

rizière [rizjɛr] *nf* paddy (field).

RMC (*abr de* **Radio Monte-Carlo**) *nf* independent radio station.

RMI (*abr de* **revenu minimum d'insertion**) *nm* minimum guaranteed income *(for people with no other source of income)*.

RMiste [ɛrɛmist] *nmf* person receiving the 'RMI'.

RN (*abr de* **route nationale**) *nf* ≃ A road *Br*, ≃ State highway *Am*.

RNIS (*abr de* **réseau numérique à intégration de services**) *nm* ISDN.

ro *abr de* **recto**.

robe [rɔb] *nf* - **1.** [de femme] dress ; ~ **chasuble** pinafore dress ; ~ **de grossesse** maternity dress ; ~ **de mariée** wedding dress - **2.** [peignoir] : ~ **de chambre** dressing gown - **3.** [de magistrat] robe - **4.** [de cheval] coat - **5.** [de vin] colour *Br*, color *Am*.

robinet [rɔbinɛ] *nm* tap *Br*, faucet *Am*.

robinetterie [rɔbinɛtri] *nf* [installations] taps *(pl) Br*, faucets *(pl) Am*.

roboratif, ive [rɔbɔratif, iv] *adj sout* bracing, invigorating.

robot [rɔbo] *nm* - **1.** [gén] robot - **2.** [ménager] food processor.

robotique [rɔbɔtik] *nf* robotics *(U)*.

robotisation [rɔbɔtizasjɔ̃] *nf* automation.

robotiser [3] [rɔbɔtize] *vt* to automate.

robuste [rɔbyst] *adj* - **1.** [personne, santé] robust - **2.** [plante] hardy - **3.** [voiture] sturdy.

robustesse [rɔbystɛs] *nf* - **1.** [de personne] robustness - **2.** [de plante] hardiness - **3.** [de voiture] sturdiness.

roc [rɔk] *nm* rock.

rocade [rɔkad] *nf* bypass.

rocaille [rɔkaj] <> *nf* - **1.** [cailloux] loose stones *(pl)* - **2.** [dans un jardin] rock garden, rockery <> *adj inv* rocaille.

rocailleux, euse [rɔkajø, øz] *adj* - **1.** [terrain] rocky - **2.** *fig* [voix] harsh.

rocambolesque [rɔkɑ̃bɔlɛsk] *adj* fantastic.

roche [rɔʃ] *nf* rock.

rocher [rɔʃe] *nm* rock ; **le Rocher** the town of Monaco ; **le ~ de Gibraltar** the Rock of Gibraltar.

➡ **rocher au chocolat** *nm* nut chocolate.

rocheux, euse [rɔʃø, øz] *adj* rocky.

➡ **Rocheuses** *nfpl* : **les Rocheuses** the Rockies.

rock [rɔk] <> *nm* rock ('n' roll) <> *adj inv* rock.

rockeur, euse [rɔkœr, øz] *nm, f* - **1.** [chanteur] rock singer - **2.** [fan] rock fan.

rocking-chair [rɔkintʃɛr] *(pl* **rocking-chairs)** *nm* rocking chair.

rodage [rɔdaʒ] *nm* - **1.** [de véhicule] running-in ; **'en ~'** 'running in' - **2.** *fig* [de méthode] running-in *ou* debugging period.

rodéo [rɔdeo] *nm* rodeo ; *fig & iron* free-for-all.

roder [3] [rɔde] *vt* - **1.** [véhicule] to run in - **2.** *fam* [méthode] to run in, to debug ; [personne] to break in.

rôder [3] [rode] *vi* to prowl, to wander about.

rôdeur, euse [rodœr, øz] *nm, f* prowler.

rodomontade [rɔdɔmɔ̃tad] *nf littéraire* boasting *(U)*.

rogations [rɔgasjɔ̃] *nfpl* Rogations.

rogne [rɔɲ] *nf fam* bad temper ; **être/se mettre en ~** to be in/to get into a bad mood, to be in/to get into a temper.

rogner [3] [rɔɲe] <> *vt* - **1.** [ongles] to trim

- 2. [revenus] to eat into ◇ *vi :* **~ sur qqch** to cut down on sthg.

rognon [rɔɲɔ̃] *nm* kidney.

rognures [rɔɲyr] *nfpl* clippings, trimmings.

rogue [rɔg] *adj littéraire* arrogant.

roi [rwa] *nm* king ; **être plus royaliste que le ~** *fig* to be more Catholic than the Pope ; **tirer les ~s** to celebrate Epiphany.

➤ **Rois mages** *nmpl :* **les Rois mages** RELIG the Three Wise Men.

TIRER LES ROIS

The French traditionally celebrate Epiphany with a round, almond-flavoured pastry ('la galette des rois') containing a small porcelain figurine ('la fève', originally a dried bean). The pastry is shared out and the person who finds the 'fève' is appointed 'king' or 'queen' and given a cardboard crown to wear.

roitelet [rwatlɛ] *nm* **- 1.** [oiseau] wren **- 2.** *péj* & *vieilli* [petit roi] kinglet.

Roland-Garros [rɔlɑ̃garos] *n tennis stadium in Paris where the French Open is held.*

rôle [rol] *nm* role, part ; **jouer un ~** to play a role *ou* part ; **avoir le beau ~** *fig* to come off best.

rôle-titre [roltitr] *nm* title role.

roller [rɔl·lœr] *nm* [sport] rollerblading ; **les ~s** [patins] Rollerblades® ; **faire du ~** to go rollerblading, to rollerblade.

rollmops [rɔlmɔps] *nm* rollmop.

ROM, Rom [rɔm] (*abr de* **read only memory**) *nf* ROM.

romain, e [rɔmɛ̃, ɛn] *adj* Roman.

➤ **romain** *nm* TYPO roman.

➤ **romaine** *nf* [salade] cos (lettuce) *Br*, romaine (lettuce) *Am*.

➤ **Romain, e** *nm, f* Roman.

roman, e [rɔmɑ̃, an] *adj* **- 1.** [langue] Romance **- 2.** ARCHIT Romanesque.

➤ **roman** *nm* **- 1.** LITTÉRATURE novel ; **~ d'action** adventure novel ; **~ d'anticipation** *ou* de science fiction science fiction novel ; **~ noir** thriller **- 2.** *fig* & *iron* [exagération] story ; [aventure] saga **- 3.** ARCHIT : **le ~** the Romanesque.

romance [rɔmɑ̃s] *nf* [chanson] love song.

romancer [16] [rɔmɑ̃se] *vt* to romanticize.

romanche [rɔmɑ̃ʃ] *nm* & *adj* Romansh.

romancier, ère [rɔmɑ̃sje, ɛr] *nm, f* novelist.

romand, e [rɔmɑ̃, ɑ̃d] *adj* of/from French-speaking Switzerland.

➤ **Romand, e** *nm, f* French-speaking Swiss.

romanesque [rɔmanɛsk] *adj* **- 1.** LITTÉRATURE

novelistic **- 2.** [aventure] fabulous, storybook (*avant n*).

roman-feuilleton [rɔmɑ̃fœjtɔ̃] (*pl* **romans-feuilletons**) *nm* serial ; *fig* soap opera.

roman-fleuve [rɔmɑ̃flœv] (*pl* **romans-fleuves**) *nm* saga.

romanichel, elle [rɔmaniʃɛl] *nm, f* gipsy.

romaniste [rɔmanist] *nmf* Romanist.

roman-photo [rɔmɑ̃fɔto] (*pl* **romans-photos**) *nm* story told in photographs.

romantique [rɔmɑ̃tik] *nmf* & *adj* romantic.

romantisme [rɔmɑ̃tism] *nm* **- 1.** ART Romantic movement **- 2.** [sensibilité] romanticism.

romarin [rɔmarɛ̃] *nm* rosemary.

rombière [rɔ̃bjɛr] *nf fam péj* old biddy.

Rome [rɔm] *n* Rome.

rompre [78] [rɔ̃pr] ◇ *vt* **- 1.** *sout* [objet] to break **- 2.** [charme, marché] to break ; [fiançailles, relations] to break off **- 3.** *sout* [exercer] : **~ qqn à** to break sb into ◇ *vi* to break ; **~ avec qqn** *fig* to break up with sb ; **~ avec qqch** *fig* to break with sthg.

➤ **se rompre** *vp* to break ; **se ~ le cou/les reins** to break one's neck/back.

rompu, e [rɔ̃py] ◇ *pp* ⊏⊐ **rompre** ◇ *adj* **- 1.** [exténué] exhausted ; **~ de** exhausted by ; **~ de fatigue** exhausted **- 2.** [expérimenté] : **~ à** experienced in.

romsteck = **rumsteck**.

ronce [rɔ̃s] *nf* [arbuste] bramble.

ronchon, onne [rɔ̃ʃɔ̃, ɔn] *fam* ◇ *adj* grumpy ◇ *nm, f* grumbler.

ronchonner [3] [rɔ̃ʃɔne] *vi fam :* **~ (après)** to grumble (at).

rond, e [rɔ̃, rɔ̃d] *adj* **- 1.** [forme, chiffre] round **- 2.** [joue, ventre] chubby, plump **- 3.** *fam* [ivre] tight.

➤ **rond** ◇ *nm* **- 1.** [cercle] circle ; **en ~** in a circle *ou* ring ; **tourner en ~** *fig* to go round in circles **- 2.** [anneau] ring ; **~ de serviette** napkin ring **- 3.** *fam* [argent] : **je n'ai pas un ~** I haven't got a penny *ou* bean ◇ *adv :* **ça ne tourne pas ~** *fig* there's something up *ou* fishy.

rond-de-cuir [rɔ̃dkɥir] (*pl* **ronds-de-cuir**) *nm péj* & *vieilli* pen pusher.

ronde [rɔ̃d] *nf* **- 1.** [de surveillance] rounds (*pl*) ; [de policier] beat **- 2.** [danse] round **- 3.** MUS semibreve *Br*, whole note *Am*.

➤ **à la ronde** *loc adv :* **à des kilomètres à la ~** for miles around.

rondelet, ette [rɔ̃dlɛ, ɛt] *adj* **- 1.** [grassouillet] plump **- 2.** *fig* [somme] goodish, tidy.

rondelle [rɔ̃dɛl] *nf* **- 1.** [de saucisson] slice **- 2.** [de métal] washer **- 3.** *Can* HOCKEY puck.

rondement [rɔ̃dmɑ̃] *adv* [efficacement] effi-ciently, briskly.

rondeur [rɔ̃dœr] *nf* - **1.** [forme] roundness - **2.** [partie charnue] curve - **3.** [de caractère] open-ness.

rondin [rɔ̃dɛ̃] *nm* log.

rondouillard, e [rɔ̃dujar, ard] *adj fam* tubby.

rond-point [rɔ̃pwɛ̃] (*pl* **ronds-points**) *nm* roundabout *Br*, traffic circle *Am*.

ronflant, e [rɔ̃flɑ̃, ɑ̃t] *adj péj* grandiose.

ronflement [rɔ̃fləmɑ̃] *nm* - **1.** [de dormeur] snore - **2.** [de poêle, moteur] hum, purr.

ronfler [3] [rɔ̃fle] *vi* - **1.** [dormeur] to snore - **2.** [poêle, moteur] hum, to purr - **3.** *fam* [dor-mir] to be in a deep sleep.

ronger [17] [rɔ̃ʒe] *vt* [bois, os] to gnaw ; [métal, fa-laise] to eat away at ; *fig* to gnaw at, to eat away at.

➤ **se ronger** *vp* - **1.** [grignoter] : **se ~ les ongles** to bite one's nails - **2.** *fig* [se tourmenter] to worry, to torture o.s.

rongeur, euse [rɔ̃ʒœr, øz] *adj* gnawing, ro-dent *(avant n)*.
➤ **rongeur** *nm* rodent.

ronron [rɔ̃rɔ̃] *nm* - **1.** [de chat] purr ; [de moteur] purr, hum - **2.** *fig* & *péj* [routine] humdrum existence.

ronronnement [rɔ̃rɔnmɑ̃] *nm* [de chat] purring ; [de moteur] purring, humming.

ronronner [3] [rɔ̃rɔne] *vi* [chat] to purr ; [mo-teur] to purr, to hum.

roquefort [rɔkfɔr] *nm* Roquefort (*French blue-veined cheese*).

roquer [3] [rɔke] *vi* ÉCHECS to castle.

roquet [rɔkɛ] *nm péj* - **1.** [chien] nasty little dog - **2.** *fig* [personne] nasty little squirt.

roquette [rɔkɛt] *nf* rocket.

rosace [rɔzas] *nf* - **1.** [ornement] rose - **2.** [vitrail] rose window - **3.** [figure géométrique] rosette.

rosaire [rɔzɛr] *nm* rosary.

rosâtre [rozatr] *adj* pinkish.

rosbif [rɔsbif] *nm* - **1.** [viande] roast beef - **2.** [Anglais] *pejorative term for a British per-son*.

rose [roz] ◇ *nf* rose ; **~ trémière** hollyhock ; **frais comme une ~** fresh as a daisy ; **envoyer qqn sur les ~s** *fam fig* to send sb packing ◇ *nm* pink ◇ *adj* pink ; **~ bonbon** bright pink.
➤ **rose des vents** *nf* compass card.

rosé, e [roze] *adj* - **1.** [vin] rosé - **2.** [teinte] rosy.
➤ **rosé** *nm* rosé.
➤ **rosée** *nf* dew.

roseau, x [rozo] *nm* reed.

roseraie [rozrɛ] *nf* rose garden.

rosette [rozɛt] *nf* - **1.** [nœud] bow - **2.** [insigne] rosette.
➤ **rosette de Lyon** *nf dry pork sausage.*

rosier [rozje] *nm* rose bush.

rosir [32] [rozir] *vt* & *vi* to turn pink.

rosse [rɔs] *péj* ◇ *nf* - **1.** *vieilli* [cheval] nag - **2.** *fig* [femme] bitch, cow ; [homme] bastard ◇ *adj* nasty.

rosser [3] [rɔse] *vt* to thrash.

rosserie [rɔsri] *nf fam* nasty remark.

rossignol [rɔsiɲɔl] *nm* - **1.** [oiseau] nightin-gale - **2.** *fam fig* [article invendable] piece of rub-bish - **3.** [passe-partout] picklock.

rot [ro] *nm* burp.

rotatif, ive [rɔtatif, iv] *adj* rotary.
➤ **rotative** *nf* rotary press.

rotation [rɔtasjɔ̃] *nf* rotation.

roter [3] [rɔte] *vi fam* to burp.

rôti, e [roti] *adj* roast.
➤ **rôti** *nm* roast, joint ; **~ de veau/porc** roast veal/pork.

rotin [rɔtɛ̃] *nm* rattan.

rôtir [32] [rotir] ◇ *vt* to roast ◇ *vi* - **1.** CULIN to roast ; **faire ~** to roast - **2.** *fam fig* [avoir chaud] to be roasting.
➤ **se rôtir** *vp* : **se ~ au soleil** *fig* to bask in the sunshine.

rôtisserie [rotisri] *nf* - **1.** [restaurant] ≃ steak-house - **2.** [magasin] *shop selling roast meat.*

rôtissoire [rotiswar] *nf* spit.

rotonde [rɔtɔ̃d] *nf* - **1.** [bâtiment] rotunda - **2.** [d'autobus] back seat.

rotor [rɔtɔr] *nm* rotor.

rotule [rɔtyl] *nf* kneecap.

roturier, ère [rɔtyrje, ɛr] ◇ *adj* - **1.** [non no-ble] common - **2.** *péj* [commun] plebeian ◇ *nm, f vieilli* commoner.

rouage [rwaʒ] *nm* cog, gearwheel ; **les ~s de l'État** *fig* the wheels of State.

roublard, e [rublar, ard] *fam* ◇ *adj* cunning, crafty ◇ *nm, f* cunning *ou* crafty devil.

roublardise [rublardiz] *nf* - **1.** [caractère] cun-ning, craftiness - **2.** *vieilli* [acte] cunning *ou* crafty trick.

rouble [rubl] *nm* rouble.

roucoulement [rukulmɑ̃] *nm* cooing ; *fig* billing and cooing.

roucouler [3] [rukule] ◇ *vt* to warble ; *fig* to coo ◇ *vi* to coo ; *fig* to bill and coo.

roue [ru] *nf* - **1.** [gén] wheel ; **descendre en ~ li-bre** to freewheel downhill ; **~ arrière/avant** back/front wheel ; **~ dentée** cogwheel ; **~ de secours** spare wheel ; **un deux ~s** a two-wheeled vehicle - **2.** [de paon] : **faire la ~** to display - **3.** *GYM* cartwheel.

rouer [6] [rwe] *vt* : **~ qqn de coups** to thrash sb, to beat sb.

rouerie [ruri] *nf littéraire* - **1.** [caractère] cunning - **2.** *vieilli* [action] cunning trick.

rouet [rue] *nm* [à filer] spinning wheel.

rouge [ruʒ] <> *nm* - **1.** [couleur] red - **2.** *fam* [vin] red (wine) ; **gros ~** *fam* cheap red wine, plonk - **3.** [fard] rouge, blusher ; **~ à lèvres** lipstick - **4.** *AUTOM* : **passer au ~** to turn red ; [conducteur] to go through a red light <> *nmf POLIT & péj* Red <> *adj* - **1.** [gén] red ; **~ de** red with - **2.** [fer, tison] red-hot - **3.** *POLIT & péj* Red <> *adv* : **voir ~ fig** to see red.

rougeâtre [ruʒatr] *adj* reddish.

rougeaud, e [ruʒo, od] <> *adj* red-faced <> *nm, f* red-faced person.

rouge-gorge [ruʒgɔrʒ] (*pl* **rouges-gorges**) *nm* robin.

rougeoiement [ruʒwamɑ̃] *nm* reddening.

rougeole [ruʒɔl] *nf* measles (*sg*).

rougeoyer [13] [ruʒwaje] *vi* to turn red.

rouget [ruʒɛ] *nm* mullet.

rougeur [ruʒœr] *nf* - **1.** [teinte] redness - **2.** [de visage, de chaleur, d'effort] flush ; [de gêne] blush - **3.** [sur peau] red spot *ou* blotch.

rougir [32] [ruʒir] <> *vt* - **1.** [colorer] to turn red - **2.** [chauffer] to make red-hot <> *vi* - **1.** [devenir rouge] to turn red - **2.** [d'émotion] : **~ (de)** [de plaisir, colère] to flush (with) ; [de gêne] to blush (with) - **3.** *fig* [avoir honte] : **~ de qqch** to be ashamed of sthg.

rougissant, e [ruʒisɑ̃, ɑ̃t] *adj* [ciel] reddening ; [jeune fille] blushing.

rouille [ruj] <> *nf* - **1.** [oxyde] rust - **2.** *CULIN* spicy garlic sauce for fish soup <> *adj inv* rust.

rouiller [3] [ruje] <> *vt* to rust, to make rusty <> *vi* to rust.

  ◆ **se rouiller** *vp* to rust ; *fig* to get rusty.

roulade [rulad] *nf* - **1.** [galipette] roll - **2.** *CULIN* rolled meat.

roulant, e [rulɑ̃, ɑ̃t] *adj* - **1.** [meuble] on wheels, on castors - **2.** *RAIL* : **personnel ~** train crew.

roulé, e [rule] *adj* rolled ; **bien ~e** *fam fig* curvy, shapely.

  ◆ **roulé** *nm CULIN* ≃ swiss roll.

rouleau, x [rulo] *nm* - **1.** [gén & *TECHNOL*] roller ; **~ compresseur** steamroller ; **~ encreur** ink roller - **2.** [de papier] roll - **3.** [à pâtisserie] rolling pin - **4.** *CULIN* : **~ de printemps** spring roll.

roulé-boulé [rulebule] (*pl* **roulés-boulés**) *nm* roll.

roulement [rulmɑ̃] *nm* - **1.** [gén] rolling - **2.** [de hanches] swaying - **3.** [de personnel] rotation ; **travailler par ~** to work to a rota - **4.** [de tambour, tonnerre] roll - **5.** *TECHNOL* rolling bearing ; **~ à billes** ball bearing - **6.** *FIN* circulation.

rouler [3] [rule] <> *vt* - **1.** [déplacer] to wheel - **2.** [enrouler - tapis] to roll up ; [- cigarette] to roll - **3.** *fam* [balancer] to roll - **4.** *LING* to roll - **5.** [faire tourner sur soi] to roll - **6.** *fam fig* [duper] to swindle, to do <> *vi* - **1.** [ballon, bateau] to roll - **2.** [véhicule] to go, to run ; [suj : personne] to drive - **3.** [tonnerre] to rumble - **4.** [suj : conversation] : **~ sur** to turn on - **5.** *fam* [aller bien] : **ça roule** everything's OK *ou* going well.

  ◆ **se rouler** *vp* to roll about ; **se ~ par terre** to roll on the ground ; **se ~ en boule** to roll o.s. into a ball.

roulette [rulɛt] *nf* - **1.** [petite roue] castor ; **comme sur des ~s** *fam fig* like clockwork - **2.** [de dentiste] drill - **3.** *JEU* roulette ; **~ russe** Russian roulette.

roulis [ruli] *nm* roll.

roulotte [rulɔt] *nf* [de gitan] caravan ; [de tourisme] caravan *Br*, trailer *Am*.

roulure [rulyr] *nf fam péj* tart, whore.

roumain, e [rumɛ̃, ɛn] *adj* Romanian.

  ◆ **roumain** *nm* [langue] Romanian.

  ◆ **Roumain, e** *nm, f* Romanian.

Roumanie [rumani] *nf* : **la ~** Romania.

round [rawnd] *nm* round.

roupiller [3] [rupije] *vi fam* to snooze.

roupillon [rupijɔ̃] *nm fam* snooze.

rouquin, e [rukɛ̃, in] *fam* <> *adj* redheaded <> *nm, f* redhead.

rouspéter [18] [ruspete] *vi fam* to grumble, to moan.

rousse [▷ roux.

rousseur [rusœr] *nf* redness.

  ◆ **taches de rousseur** *nfpl* freckles.

roussi [rusi] *nm* burning ; **ça sent le ~** *fam* it's trouble's on its way.

roussir [32] [rusir] <> *vt* - **1.** [rendre roux] to turn brown ; *CULIN* to brown - **2.** [brûler légèrement] to singe <> *vi* to turn brown ; *CULIN* to brown.

routage [rutaʒ] *nm* sorting and mailing.

routard, e [rutar, ard] *nm, f fam* (hippie) traveller *Br ou* traveler *Am*.

route [rut] *nf* - **1.** [gén] road ; **~ à grande circulation** busy road ; **faire de la ~** to do a lot of mileage ; **en ~** on the way ; **en ~!** let's go! ; **mettre en ~** [démarrer] to start up ; *fig* to get under way ; **~ nationale** ≃ A road *Br*, ≃ highway *Am* ; **tenir la ~** *AUTOM* to hold the road ; *fig* to hold water - **2.** [itinéraire] route ; **montrer la ~ à qqn** to show sb the way ; **faire fausse ~** to go the wrong way ; *fig* to be on the wrong track - **3.** *fig* [voie] path.

routier, ère [rutje, ɛr] *adj* road *(avant n)*.
➡ **routier** *nm* - **1.** [chauffeur] long-distance lorry driver *Br ou* trucker *Am* - **2.** [restaurant] ≃ transport cafe *Br*, ≃ truck stop *Am*.

routine [rutin] *nf* routine.

routinier, ère [rutinje, ɛr] *adj* routine.

rouvert, e [ruvɛr, ɛrt] *pp* ➪ **rouvrir**.

rouvrir [34] [ruvrir] *vt* to reopen, to open again.
➡ **se rouvrir** *vp* to reopen, to open again.

roux, rousse [ru, rus] ◇ *adj* - **1.** [cheveux] red - **2.** [feuilles] russet, red-brown - **3.** [sucre] brown ◇ *nm, f* [personne] redhead.
➡ **roux** *nm* - **1.** [couleur] red, russet - **2.** *CULIN* roux.

royal, e, aux [rwajal, o] *adj* - **1.** [de roi] royal - **2.** [magnifique] princely.

royalement [rwajalmɑ̃] *adv* - **1.** [recevoir] royally ; [vivre] like royalty - **2.** *fig* [complètement] : **elle s'en moque ~** she couldn't care less.

royaliste [rwajalist] *nmf & adj* royalist.

royalties [rwajalti(z)] *nfpl* royalties.

royaume [rwajom] *nm* kingdom.

Royaume-Uni [rwajomyni] *nm* : **le ~** the United Kingdom.

royauté [rwajote] *nf* - **1.** [fonction] kingship - **2.** [régime] monarchy.

RP ◇ *nfpl* (*abr de* **relations publiques**) PR *(sg)* ◇ *nf* - **1.** (*abr de* **recette principale**) main post office - **2.** *abr de* **région parisienne**.

R.P. (*abr de* **révérend père**) Holy Father.

RPR (*abr de* **Rassemblement pour la République**) *nm* French political party to the right of the political spectrum.

RSVP (*abr de* **répondez s'il vous plaît**) RSVP.

RTB (*abr de* **Radio-télévision belge**) *nf* Belgian broadcasting company.

rte *abr de* **route**.

RTL (*abr de* **Radio-télévision Luxembourg**) *nf* Luxembourg broadcasting company.

RU (*abr de* **restaurant universitaire**) *nm* refectory.

ruade [ryad] *nf* kick.

Ruanda, Rwanda [ryɑ̃da] *nm* : **le ~** Rwanda ; **au ~** in Rwanda.

ruandais, e [ryɑ̃dɛ, ɛz] *adj* Rwandan.
➡ **ruandais** *nm* [langue] Rwandan.
➡ **Ruandais, e** *nm, f* Rwandan.

ruban [rybɑ̃] *nm* ribbon ; **~ adhésif** adhesive tape.

rubéole [rybeɔl] *nf* German measles *(sg)*, rubella.

rubicond, e [rybikɔ̃, ɔ̃d] *adj* rubicund.

rubis [rybi] ◇ *nm* - **1.** [pierre précieuse] ruby - **2.** [de montre] jewel - **3.** *loc* : **payer ~ sur l'ongle** to pay cash on the nail ◇ *adj inv* [couleur] ruby.

rubrique [rybrik] *nf* - **1.** [chronique] column - **2.** [dans classement] heading.

ruche [ryʃ] *nf* - **1.** [abeilles] hive - **2.** [abri] hive, beehive ; *fig* hive of activity.

rucher [ryʃe] *nm* apiary.

rude [ryd] *adj* - **1.** [surface] rough - **2.** [voix] harsh - **3.** [personne, manières] rough, uncouth - **4.** [hiver, épreuve] harsh, severe ; [tâche, adversaire] tough - **5.** [appétit] hearty.

rudement [rydmɑ̃] *adv* - **1.** [brutalement - tomber] hard ; [- répondre] harshly - **2.** *fam* [très] damn.

rudesse [rydɛs] *nf* harshness, severity.

rudimentaire [rydimɑ̃tɛr] *adj* rudimentary.

rudiments [rydimɑ̃] *nmpl* rudiments.

rudoie, rudoies *etc* ➪ **rudoyer**.

rudoyer [13] [rydwaje] *vt* to treat harshly.

rue [ry] *nf* street ; **descendre dans la ~** to take to the streets ; **jeter/mettre/être à la ~** *fig* to throw/to put/to be out on the streets ; **ne pas courir les ~s** *fig* not to grow on trees, to be thin on the ground.

ruée [rye] *nf* rush.

ruelle [ryɛl] *nf* [rue] alley, lane.

ruer [7] [rye] *vi* to kick.
➡ **se ruer** *vp* : **se ~ sur** to pounce on.

rugby [rygbi] *nm* rugby ; **~ à treize/quinze** Rugby League/Union.

rugir [32] [ryʒir] ◇ *vt* to roar, to bellow ◇ *vi* to roar ; [vent] to howl ; [personne] : **~ de** to roar with.

rugissement [ryʒismɑ̃] *nm* roar, roaring *(U)* ; [de vent] howling.

rugosité [rygozite] *nf* - **1.** [de surface] roughness - **2.** [aspérité] rough patch.

rugueux, euse [rygø, øz] *adj* rough.

ruine [rɥin] *nf* - **1.** [gén] ruin ; **tomber en ~s** to fall into ruins - **2.** [effondrement] ruin, downfall - **3.** [humaine] wreck - **4.** [acquisition] : **c'est une vraie ~** it costs me/you *etc* an arm and a leg.

ruiner [3] [rɥine] *vt* to ruin.
➡ **se ruiner** *vp* to ruin o.s., to bankrupt o.s.

ruineux, euse [rɥinø, øz] *adj* ruinous.

ruisseau, x [rɥiso] *nm* - **1.** [cours d'eau] stream ; **des ~x de larmes** floods of tears - **2.** *fig & péj* [caniveau] gutter.

ruisseler [24] [rɥisle] *vi* : ~ **(de)** to stream (with).

ruissellement [rɥisɛlmɑ̃] *nm* streaming.

rumba [rumba] *nf* rumba.

rumeur [rymœr] *nf* - **1.** [bruit] murmur - **2.** [nouvelle] rumour *Br*, rumor *Am*.

ruminant [ryminɑ̃] *nm* ruminant.

ruminer [3] [rymine] *vt* to ruminate ; *fig* to mull over.

rumsteck, romsteck [rɔmstɛk] *nm* rump steak.

rupestre [rypɛstr] *adj* - **1.** ART cave *(avant n)*, rock *(avant n)* - **2.** BOT rock *(avant n)*.

rupin, e [rypɛ̃, in] *fam* ⬦ *adj* plush ⬦ *nm, f* moneybags *(sg)*.

rupture [ryptyr] *nf* - **1.** [cassure] breaking - **2.** *fig* [changement] abrupt change ; **en ~ de ban avec** *fig* at odds with - **3.** [manque] : **être en ~ de stock** to be out of stock - **4.** [de négociations, fiançailles] breaking off ; [de contrat] breach - **5.** [amoureuse] breakup, split.

rural, e, aux [ryral, o] ⬦ *adj* country *(avant n)*, rural ⬦ *nm, f* country-dweller.

ruse [ryz] *nf* - **1.** [habileté] cunning, craftiness - **2.** [subterfuge] ruse.

rusé, e [ryze] ⬦ *adj* cunning, crafty ⬦ *nm, f* cunning *ou* crafty person.

ruser [3] [ryze] *vi* to use trickery.

rush [rœʃ] *(pl* rushs *ou* rushes) *nm* rush.

russe [rys] ⬦ *adj* Russian ⬦ *nm* [langue] Russian.
⬦ **Russe** *nmf* Russian.

Russie [rysi] *nf* : **la ~** Russia.

rustine [rystin] *nf* small rubber patch for repairing bicycle tyres.

rustique [rystik] ⬦ *nm* [style] rustic style ⬦ *adj* rustic.

rustre [rystr] *péj* ⬦ *nmf* lout ⬦ *adj* loutish.

rut [ryt] *nm* : **être en ~** [mâle] to be rutting ; [femelle] to be on heat.

rutabaga [rytabaga] *nm* swede, rutabaga *Am*.

rutilant, e [rytilɑ̃, ɑ̃t] *adj* [brillant] gleaming.

rutiler [3] [rytile] *vi* to gleam.

R-V *abr de* **rendez-vous.**

Rwanda = **Ruanda.**

rythme [ritm] *nm* - **1.** MUS rhythm ; **en ~** in rhythm - **2.** [de travail, production] pace, rate ; **au ~ de** at the rate of ; **~ cardiaque** heart rate.

rythmer [3] [ritme] *vt* to give rhythm to.

rythmique [ritmik] ⬦ *nf* rhythmics *(U)* ⬦ *adj* rhythmical.

S

s¹, S [ɛs] *nm inv* - **1.** [lettre] s, S - **2.** [forme] zigzag.
⬦ **S** *(abr de* **Sud)** S.

s² *(abr de* **seconde)** s.

s' ⊳ **se, si.**

s/ *abr de* **sur.**

sa ⊳ **son².**

SA *(abr de* **société anonyme)** *nf* ≃ Ltd *Br*, ≃ Inc. *Am*.

S.A. *(abr de* **Son Altesse)** H.H.

sabayon [sabajɔ̃] *nm* zabaglione.

sabbat [saba] *nm* - **1.** RELIG Sabbath - **2.** [de sorciers] sabbath.

sabbatique [sabatik] *adj* - **1.** RELIG Sabbath *(avant n)* - **2.** [congé] sabbatical.

sable [sabl] ⬦ *nm* sand ; **de ~** [plage] sandy ; [tempête] sand *(avant n)* ; **~s mouvants** quicksand *(sg)*, quicksands ⬦ *adj inv* [couleur] sandy.

sablé, e [sable] *adj* - **1.** [route] sandy - **2.** CULIN : **gâteau ~** ≃ shortbread *(U)*.
⬦ **sablé** *nm* ≃ shortbread *(U)*.

sabler [3] [sable] *vt* - **1.** [route] to sand - **2.** [façade] to sandblast - **3.** [boire] : **~ le champagne** to crack a bottle of champagne.

sableux, euse [sablø, øz] *adj* sandy.
⬦ **sableuse** *nf* sandblaster.

sablier [sablije] *nm* hourglass.

sablière [sablijɛr] *nf* - **1.** [carrière] sand quarry - **2.** [poutre] stringer.

sablonneux, euse [sablɔnø, øz] *adj* sandy.

saborder [3] [sabɔrde] *vt* [navire] to scuttle ; *fig* [entreprise] to wind up ; *fig* [projet] to scupper.
⬦ **se saborder** *vp* - **1.** [navire] to be scuttled - **2.** *fig* [entreprise] to wind up.

sabot [sabo] *nm* - **1.** [chaussure] clog - **2.** [de cheval] hoof - **3.** AUTOM : **~ de Denver** wheel clamp, Denver boot ; **~ de frein** brake shoe.

sabotage [sabotaʒ] *nm* - **1.** [volontaire] sabotage - **2.** [bâclage] bungling.

saboter [3] [sabote] *vt* - **1.** [volontairement] to sabotage - **2.** [bâcler] to bungle.

saboteur, euse [sabɔtœr, øz] *nm, f* MIL & POLIT saboteur.

sabre [sabr] *nm* sabre *Br*, saber *Am*.

sabrer [3] [sabre] *vt* - **1.** vieilli [avec sabre] to cut down - **2.** *fam* [biffer] to slash - **3.** *fam* [critiquer] to slam - **4.** *fam* [candidat] to fail.

sac [sak] *nm* - **1.** [gén] bag ; [pour grains] sack ; [contenu] bag, bagful, sack, sackful ; **~ de couchage** sleeping bag ; **~ à dos** rucksack ; **~ à main** handbag ; **~ de voyage** travelling *Br* OU traveling *Am* bag ; **vider son ~** *fig* to get it off one's chest - **2.** *fam* [10 francs] 10 francs - **3.** *littéraire* [pillage] sack ; **mettre à ~** [ville] to sack ; [maison] to ransack.

saccade [sakad] *nf* jerk.

saccadé, e [sakade] *adj* jerky.

saccage [sakaʒ] *nm* havoc.

saccager [17] [sakaʒe] *vt* - **1.** [piller] to sack - **2.** [dévaster] to destroy.

saccharine [sakarin] *nf* saccharin.

SACEM, Sacem [sasɛm] (*abr de* **Société des auteurs, compositeurs et éditeurs de musique**) *nf society that safeguards the rights of French writers and musicians.*

sacerdoce [sasɛrdɔs] *nm* priesthood ; *fig* vocation.

sacerdotal, e, aux [sasɛrdɔtal, o] *adj* priestly.

sachant *ppr* ⮕ **savoir.**

sache, saches *etc* ⮕ **savoir.**

sachet [saʃɛ] *nm* [de bonbons] bag ; [de shampooing] sachet ; **~ de thé** teabag.

sacoche [sakɔʃ] *nf* - **1.** [de médecin, d'écolier] bag - **2.** [de cycliste] pannier.

sac-poubelle [sakpubɛl] (*pl* **sacs-poubelle**) *nm* [petit] dustbin liner ; [grand] rubbish bag *Br*, garbage bag *Am*.

sacquer, saquer [3] [sake] *vt fam* - **1.** [renvoyer] to sack *Br*, to fire - **2.** [élève] to fail - **3.** *loc* : **je ne peux pas le ~** I can't stand OU stomach him.

sacraliser [3] [sakralize] *vt* to hold as sacred.

sacre [sakr] *nm* [de roi] coronation ; [d'évêque] consecration.

sacré, e [sakre] *adj* - **1.** [gén] sacred - **2.** RELIG [ordres, écritures] holy - **3.** (*avant n*) *fam* [maudit] bloody *Br* (*avant n*), goddam *Am* (*avant n*) - **4.** (*avant n*) [considérable] : **un ~ ...** a hell of a ...

sacrement [sakrəmɑ̃] *nm* sacrament ; **les derniers ~s** the last rites.

sacrément [sakremɑ̃] *adv fam vieilli* dashed.

sacrer [3] [sakre] *vt* - **1.** [roi] to crown ; [évêque] to consecrate - **2.** *fig* [déclarer] to hail.

sacrifice [sakrifis] *nm* sacrifice ; **faire un ~/des ~s** *fig* to make a sacrifice/sacrifices.

sacrifié, e [sakrifje] *adj* - **1.** [personne] sacrificed - **2.** [prix] giveaway (*avant n*).

sacrifier [9] [sakrifje] ⬦ *vt* [gén] to sacrifice ; **~ qqch pour qqn/qqch** to sacrifice sthg for sb/sthg ; **~ qqch pour faire qqch** to sacrifice sthg to do sthg ; **~ qqn/qqch à** to sacrifice sb/sthg to ⬦ *vi littéraire* [se conformer] : **~ à** to conform to.
⬦ **se sacrifier** *vp* : **se ~ à/pour** to sacrifice o.s. to/for.

sacrilège [sakrilɛʒ] ⬦ *nm* sacrilege ⬦ *nmf* sacrilegious person ⬦ *adj* sacrilegious.

sacristain [sakristɛ̃] *nm* sacristan.

sacristie [sakristi] *nf* sacristy.

sacro-saint, e [sakrosɛ̃, ɛ̃t] *adj hum* sacrosanct.

sadique [sadik] ⬦ *nmf* sadist ⬦ *adj* sadistic.

sadisme [sadism] *nm* sadism.

sadomasochiste [sadomazoʃist] ⬦ *nmf* sadomasochist ⬦ *adj* sadomasochistic.

safari [safari] *nm* safari ; **~-photo** photographic safari.

SAFER, Safer [safɛr] (*abr de* **Société d'aménagement foncier et d'établissement régional**) *nf agency entitled to buy land and earmark it for agricultural use.*

safran [safrɑ̃] ⬦ *nm* - **1.** [épice] saffron - **2.** NAVIG rudder blade ⬦ *adj inv* [couleur] saffron.

saga [saga] *nf* saga.

sagace [sagas] *adj* sagacious.

sagacité [sagasite] *nf* sagacity.

sagaie [sagɛ] *nf* assegai.

sage [saʒ] ⬦ *adj* - **1.** [personne, conseil] wise, sensible - **2.** [enfant, chien] good - **3.** [goûts] modest ; [propos, vêtement] sober ⬦ *nm* wise man, sage.

sage-femme [saʒfam] (*pl* **sages-femmes**) *nf* midwife.

sagement [saʒmɑ̃] *adv* - **1.** [avec bon sens] wisely, sensibly - **2.** [docilement] like a good girl/boy.

sagesse [saʒɛs] *nf* - **1.** [bon sens] wisdom, good sense - **2.** [docilité] good behaviour *Br* OU behavior *Am*.

Sagittaire [saʒitɛr] *nm* ASTROL Sagittarius ; **être ~** to be (a) Sagittarius.

sagouin, e [sagwɛ̃, in] *nm, f fam* slob.
⬦ **sagouin** *nm* ZOOL squirrel monkey.

Sahara [saara] *nm* : **le ~** the Sahara ; **au ~** in the Sahara ; **le ~ occidental** the Western Sahara.

saharien, enne [saarjɛ̃, ɛn] *adj* Saharan.
➤ **saharienne** *nf* safari jacket.
➤ **Saharien, enne** *nm, f* Saharan.

saignant, e [sɛɲɑ̃, ɑ̃t] *adj* - **1.** [blessure] bleeding - **2.** [viande] rare, underdone - **3.** *fam fig* [critique] hurtful.

saignée [seɲe] *nf* - **1.** *vieilli* & MÉD bloodletting, bleeding - **2.** [pli du bras] crook of the arm - **3.** [sillon - dans un sol] ditch ; [- dans un mur] groove.

saignement [sɛɲmɑ̃] *nm* bleeding.

saigner [4] [seɲe] <> *vt* - **1.** [malade, animal] to bleed - **2.** [financièrement] : ~ **qqn (à blanc)** to bleed sb (white) <> *vi* to bleed ; **je saigne du nez** my nose is bleeding, I've got a nosebleed.
➤ **se saigner** *vp* : **se ~ pour qqn** *fig* to bleed o.s. white for sb.

saillant, e [sajɑ̃, ɑ̃t] *adj* - **1.** [proéminent] projecting, protruding ; [muscles] bulging ; [pommettes] prominent - **2.** *fig* [événement] salient, outstanding.

sailli, e [saji] *pp* ⊳ **saillir**[1], **saillir**[2].

saillie [saji] *nf* - **1.** [avancée] projection ; **en ~** projecting - **2.** ZOOL covering.

saillir[1] [50] [sajir] *vi* [balcon] to project, to protrude ; [muscles] to bulge.

saillir[2] [32] [sajir] *vt* ZOOL to cover.

sain, e [sɛ̃, sɛn] *adj* - **1.** [gén] healthy ; **~ et sauf** safe and sound - **2.** [lecture] wholesome - **3.** [fruit] fit to eat ; [mur, gestion] sound.

saindoux [sɛ̃du] *nm* lard.

sainement [sɛnmɑ̃] *adv* - **1.** [vivre] healthily - **2.** [raisonner] soundly.

saint, e [sɛ̃, sɛ̃t] <> *adj* - **1.** [sacré] holy ; **le Saint-Esprit** the Holy Spirit ; **la Saint-Sylvestre** New Year's Eve ; **la Sainte Vierge** the Blessed Virgin - **2.** [pieux] saintly - **3.** [extrême] : **avoir une ~e horreur de qqch** to detest sthg <> *nm, f* saint ; **le ~ des ~s** *fig* the holy of holies.

saint-bernard [sɛbɛrnar] *nm inv* - **1.** [chien] St Bernard - **2.** *fig* [personne] good Samaritan.

saintement [sɛ̃tmɑ̃] *adv* : **vivre ~** to lead a saintly life.

saint-émilion [sɛ̃temiljɔ̃] *nm inv* red wine *from the Bordeaux region.*

sainte-nitouche [sɛ̃tnituʃ] *(pl* **saintes-nitouches)** *nf péj* : **c'est une ~** butter wouldn't melt in her mouth.

sainteté [sɛ̃te] *nf* holiness.
➤ **Sainteté** *nf* : **Sa Sainteté** His Holiness.

saint-glinglin [sɛ̃glɛ̃glɛ̃] ➤ **à la saint-glinglin** *loc adv fam* till Doomsday.

saint-honoré [sɛ̃tɔnɔre] *nm inv choux pastry ring filled with confectioner's custard.*

Saint-Marin [sɛ̃marɛ̃] *n* San Marino ; **à ~** in San Marino.

saint-marinais, e [sɛ̃marinɛ, ɛz] *adj* of/ from San Marino.
➤ **Saint-Marinais, e** *nm, f* native *ou* inhabitant of San Marino.

Saint-Père [sɛ̃pɛr] *nm* Holy Father.

Saint-Pétersbourg [sɛ̃petɛrsbur] *n* Saint Petersburg.

saint-pierre [sɛ̃pjɛr] *nm inv* [poisson] John Dory.

Saint-Pierre [sɛ̃pjɛr] *n* : **la basilique ~** Saint Peter's Basilica.

Saint-Siège [sɛ̃sjɛʒ] *nm* : **le ~** the Holy See.

sais, sait *etc* ⊳ **savoir.**

saisie [sezi] *nf* - **1.** FISC & JUR distraint, seizure - **2.** INFORM input ; **erreur de ~** input error ; **~ de données** data capture.

saisir [32] [sezir] *vt* - **1.** [empoigner] to take hold of ; [avec force] to seize ; **~ qqn à la gorge** to seize *ou* grab sb by the throat - **2.** FIN & JUR to seize, to distrain - **3.** INFORM to capture - **4.** [comprendre] to grasp - **5.** [suj : sensation, émotion] to grip, to seize - **6.** [surprendre] : **être saisi par** to be struck by - **7.** CULIN to seal.
➤ **se saisir** *vp* : **se ~ de qqn/qqch** to seize sb/ sthg, to grab sb/sthg.

saisissant, e [sezisɑ̃, ɑ̃t] *adj* - **1.** [spectacle] gripping ; [ressemblance] striking - **2.** [froid] biting.

saisissement [sezismɑ̃] *nm* [émotion] emotion.

saison [sɛzɔ̃] *nf* season ; **la belle ~** the summer months *(pl)* ; **c'est la bonne/mauvaise ~ pour** it's the right/wrong time of year for ; **la ~ des amours** the mating season ; **en/ hors ~** in/out of season ; **la haute/basse/ morte ~** the high/low/off season.

saisonnalité [sɛzɔnalite] *nf* seasonal nature.

saisonnier, ère [sɛzɔnje, ɛr] <> *adj* seasonal <> *nm, f* seasonal worker.

saké [sake] *nm* sake.

salace [salas] *adj* salacious.

salade [salad] *nf* - **1.** [plante] lettuce - **2.** [plat] (green) salad ; **~ de fruits** fruit salad ; **~ niçoise** *salad containing anchovies and tuna* - **3.** *fam fig* [méli-mélo] mess - **4.** *fam fig* [baratin] story ; **raconter des ~s** to tell stories ; **vendre sa ~** to lay it on thick.

saladier [saladje] *nm* salad bowl.

salaire [salɛr] *nm* - **1.** [rémunération] salary, wage ; **~ brut/net/de base** gross/net/basic salary, gross/net/basic wage - **2.** *fig* [récompense] reward.

salaison [salɛzɔ̃] *nf* - **1.** [procédé] salting - **2.** [aliment] salted food.

salamalecs [salamalɛk] *nmpl fam péj* bowing and scraping (U).

salamandre [salamɑ̃dr] *nf* [animal] salamander.

salami [salami] *nm* salami.

salant [salɑ̃] ⊳ marais.

salarial, e, aux [salarjal, o] *adj* wage (avant n).

salariat [salarja] *nm* - **1.** [système] paid employment - **2.** [salariés] wage-earners (pl).

salarié, e [salarje] ◇ *adj* - **1.** [personne] wage-earning - **2.** [travail] paid ◇ *nm, f* salaried employee.

salaud [salo] *vulg* ◇ *nm* bastard ◇ *adj m* shitty.

sale [sal] *adj* - **1.** [linge, mains] dirty ; [couleur] dirty, dingy - **2.** *(avant n)* [type, gueule, coup] nasty ; [tour, histoire] dirty ; [bête, temps] filthy.

salé, e [sale] *adj* - **1.** [eau, saveur] salty ; [beurre] salted ; [viande, poisson] salt *(avant n)*, salted - **2.** *fig* [histoire] spicy - **3.** *fam fig* [addition, facture] steep.
◆ **salé** *nm* - **1.** [aliment salé] savoury *Br ou* savory *Am* food - **2.** [porc] salt pork.

salement [salmɑ̃] *adv* - **1.** [malproprement] dirtily, disgustingly - **2.** *fam* [très] bloody *Br*, damn.

saler [3] [sale] *vt* - **1.** [gén] to salt - **2.** *fam fig* [note] to bump up.

saleté [salte] *nf* - **1.** [malpropreté] dirtiness, filthiness - **2.** [crasse] dirt (U), filth (U) ; **faire des ~s** to make a mess - **3.** *fam* [pacotille] junk (U), rubbish (U) - **4.** *fam* [maladie] bug - **5.** [obscénité] dirty thing, obscenity ; **il m'a dit des ~s** he used obscenities to me - **6.** [action] disgusting thing ; **faire une ~ à qqn** to play a dirty trick on sb - **7.** *fam péj* [personne] nasty piece of work.

salière [saljer] *nf* saltcellar ; **~-poivrière** cruet.

salin, e [salɛ̃, in] *adj* saline ; [eau] salt *(avant n)*.

salir [32] [salir] *vt* - **1.** [linge, mains] to (make) dirty, to soil - **2.** *fig* [réputation, personne] to sully.
◆ **se salir** *vp* to get dirty.

salissant, e [salisɑ̃, ɑ̃t] *adj* - **1.** [tissu] easily soiled - **2.** [travail] dirty, messy.

salissure [salisyr] *nf* stain.

salivaire [saliver] *adj* salivary.

salive [saliv] *nf* saliva ; **dépenser beaucoup de** ~ *fig* to talk nineteen to the dozen ; **perdre sa** ~ *fig* to waste one's breath.

saliver [3] [salive] *vi* to salivate.

salle [sal] *nf* - **1.** [pièce] room ; **en** ~ [dans un café] inside ; ~ **d'attente** waiting room ; ~ **de bains** bathroom ; ~ **de cinéma** cinema ; ~ **de classe** classroom ; ~ **d'eau, ~ de douches** shower room ; ~ **d'embarquement** gate lounge ; ~ **des machines** engine room ; ~ **à manger** dining room ; ~ **non-fumeur** ≃ no smoking area ; ~ **d'opération** operating theatre *Br ou* room *Am* ; ~ **de séjour** living room ; ~ **de spectacle** theatre *Br*, theater *Am* ; ~ **des ventes** saleroom *Br*, salesroom *Am* - **2.** [de spectacle] auditorium - **3.** [public] audience, house ; **jouer à ~ pleine** to play to a full house ; **faire ~ comble** to have a full house.

salmigondis [salmigɔ̃di] *nm* hotchpotch *Br*, hodgepodge *Am*.

salmis [salmi] *nm* half-roasted game or poultry finished in wine sauce.

salmonellose [salmɔneloz] *nf* salmonella poisoning.

salon [salɔ̃] *nm* - **1.** [de maison] lounge *Br*, living room - **2.** [commerce] : ~ **de coiffure** hairdressing salon, hairdresser's ; ~ **de thé** tearoom - **3.** [foire-exposition] show.

salopard [salɔpar] *nm tfam* bastard.

salope [salɔp] *nf vulg* bitch.

saloper [3] [salɔpe] *vt fam* to mess up, to make a mess of.

saloperie [salɔpri] *nf fam* - **1.** [pacotille] rubbish (U) - **2.** [maladie] bug - **3.** [saleté] junk (U), rubbish (U) ; **faire des ~s** to make a mess - **4.** [action] dirty trick ; **faire des ~s à qqn** to play dirty tricks on sb - **5.** [propos] dirty comment.

salopette [salɔpɛt] *nf* [d'ouvrier] overalls (pl) ; [à bretelles] dungarees (pl) *Br*, overalls *Am*.

salpêtre [salpɛtr] *nm* saltpetre *Br*, saltpeter *Am*.

salsa [salsa] *nf* salsa.

salsifis [salsifi] *nm* salsify.

SALT [salt] *(abr de Strategic Arms Limitation Talks)* SALT.

saltimbanque [saltɛ̃bɑ̃k] *nmf* acrobat.

salubre [salybr] *adj* healthy.

salubrité [salybrite] *nf* healthiness ; **la ~ publique** public health.

saluer [7] [salɥe] *vt* - **1.** [accueillir] to greet - **2.** [dire au revoir à] to take one's leave of - **3.** *MIL & fig* to salute.
◆ **se saluer** *vp* to say hello/goodbye (to one another).

salut [saly] <> nm - **1.** [de la main] wave ; [de la tête] nod ; [propos] greeting - **2.** MIL salute - **3.** [d'acteur] bow - **4.** [sauvegarde] safety - **5.** RELIG salvation <> interj fam [bonjour] hi! ; [au revoir] bye!, see you!

salutaire [salyter] adj - **1.** [conseil, expérience] salutary - **2.** [remède, repos] beneficial.

salutation [salytasjɔ̃] nf littéraire salutation, greeting.

➡ **salutations** nfpl : veuillez agréer, Monsieur, mes ~s distinguées OU mes sincères ~s sout yours faithfully, yours sincerely.

salutiste [salytist] nmf & adj Salvationist.

Salvador [salvadɔr] nm : le ~ El Salvador ; au ~ in El Salvador.

salvadorien, enne [salvadɔrjɛ̃, ɛn] adj Salvadorian.

➡ **Salvadorien, enne** nm, f Salvadorian.

salve [salv] nf salvo.

Salzbourg [salzbur] n Salzburg.

samaritain, e [samaritɛ̃, ɛn] adj Samaritan.

➡ **samaritain** nm Helv first-aid worker.

samba [sãba] nf samba.

samedi [samdi] nm Saturday ; nous sommes partis ~ we left on Saturday ; ~ 13 septembre Saturday 13th September ; ~ dernier/prochain last/next Saturday ; ~ matin/midi/après-midi/soir Saturday morning/lunchtime/afternoon/evening ; de/du ~ Saturday (avant n) ; le ~ d'avant the Saturday before ; le ~ on Saturdays ; ~ en huit a week on Saturday, Saturday week ; ~ en quinze two weeks on Saturday ; un ~ sur deux every other Saturday ; nous sommes OU c'est ~ it's Saturday (today) ; tous les ~s every Saturday.

Samoa [samɔa] n Samoa ; à ~ in Samoa.

samoan, e [samɔ̃a, an] adj Samoan.

➡ **Samoan, e** nm, f Samoan.

samouraï, samuraï [samuraj] nm samurai.

samovar [samɔvar] nm samovar.

SAMU, Samu [samy] (abr de Service d'aide médicale d'urgence) nm French ambulance and emergency service, ≈ Ambulance Brigade Br, ≈ Paramedics Am.

samuraï = samouraï.

sanatorium [sanatɔrjɔm] nm sanatorium.

sanctifier [9] [sãktifje] vt - **1.** [rendre saint] to sanctify - **2.** [révérer] to hallow.

sanction [sãksjɔ̃] nf sanction ; fig [conséquence] penalty, price ; prendre des ~s contre to impose sanctions on.

sanctionner [3] [sãksjɔne] vt to sanction.

sanctuaire [sãktɥer] nm - **1.** [d'église] sanctuary - **2.** [lieu saint] shrine.

sandale [sãdal] nf sandal.

sandalette [sãdalɛt] nf sandal.

Sandow® [sãdo] nm - **1.** [attache] elastic cable (for securing luggage etc) - **2.** AÉRON catapult.

sandwich [sãdwitʃ] (pl sandwiches OU sandwichs) nm sandwich ; être pris en ~ entre fam to be sandwiched between.

sang [sã] nm blood ; en ~ bleeding ; pur-~ thoroughbred ; dans le ~ fig in the blood ; le faire du mauvais ~ OU un ~ d'encre fig to get really worried OU upset ; suer ~ et eau fig to sweat blood.

sang-froid [sãfrwa] nm inv calm ; de ~ in cold blood ; perdre/garder son ~ to lose/to keep one's head.

sanglant, e [sãglã, ãt] adj bloody ; fig cruel.

sangle [sãgl] nf strap ; [de selle] girth.

➡ **sangles** nfpl webbing (U).

sangler [3] [sãgle] vt [attacher] to strap ; [cheval] to girth.

sanglier [sãglije] nm boar.

sanglot [sãglo] nm sob ; éclater en ~s to burst into sobs.

sangloter [3] [sãglɔte] vi to sob.

sangria [sãgrija] nf sangria.

sangsue [sãsy] nf leech ; fig [personne] bloodsucker.

sanguin, e [sãgɛ̃, in] adj - **1.** ANAT blood (avant n) - **2.** [rouge - visage] ruddy ; [- orange] blood (avant n) - **3.** [emporté] quick-tempered.

➡ **sanguine** nf - **1.** [dessin] red chalk drawing - **2.** [fruit] blood orange.

sanguinaire [sãginer] adj - **1.** [tyran] bloodthirsty - **2.** [lutte] bloody.

sanguinolent, e [sãginɔlã, ãt] adj stained with blood.

Sanisette® [sanizɛt] nf automatic public toilet, superloo Br.

sanitaire [saniter] <> nm bathroom fittings and plumbing <> adj - **1.** [service, mesure] health (avant n) - **2.** [installation, appareil] bathroom (avant n).

➡ **sanitaires** nmpl toilets and showers.

sans [sã] <> prép without ; ~ argent without any money ; ~ faire un effort without making an effort <> adv : passe-moi mon manteau, je ne veux pas sortir ~ pass me my coat, I don't want to go out without it.

➡ **sans que** loc conj : ~ que vous le sachiez without your knowing.

sans-abri [sãzabri] nmf inv homeless person.

San Salvador [sɑ̃salvadɔr] *n* San Salvador.

sanscrit [sɑ̃skri] *nm* Sanskrit.

sans-emploi [sɑ̃zɑ̃plwa] *nmf inv* unemployed person.

sans-gêne [sɑ̃ʒɛn] ⟨⟩ *nm inv* [qualité] rudeness, lack of consideration ⟨⟩ *nmf inv* [personne] rude *ou* inconsiderate person ⟨⟩ *adj inv* rude, inconsiderate.

sans-le-sou [sɑ̃lsu] *nmf inv fam* person who is broke *ou* hard up.

sans-logis [sɑ̃lɔʒi] *nmf inv* homeless person.

sansonnet [sɑ̃sɔnɛ] *nm* starling.

sans-papiers [sɑ̃papje] *nmf immigrant without proper identity or working papers.*

sans-plomb [sɑ̃plɔ̃] *nm inv* unleaded (petrol *Br ou* gas *Am*), lead-free petrol *Br ou* gas *Am*.

santal [sɑ̃tal] *nm* sandalwood.

santé [sɑ̃te] *nf* health ; **recouvrer la ~** to get one's health back ; **~ de fer** strong *ou* iron constitution ; **à ta/votre ~!** cheers!, good health! ; **boire à la ~ de qqn** to drink sb's health, to toast sb.

santiag [sɑ̃tjag] *nf* cowboy boot.

Santiago [sɑ̃tjago] *n* Santiago.

santon [sɑ̃tɔ̃] *nm* figure placed in Christmas crib.

Santorin [sɑ̃tɔrɛ̃] *n* Santorini.

São Paulo [saopolo] *n* - **1.** [ville] São Paulo - **2.** [État] : **l'État de ~** São Paulo (State).

saoudien, enne [saudjɛ̃, ɛn] *adj* Saudi (Arabian).
➤ **Saoudien, enne** *nm, f* Saudi (Arabian).

saoul = **soûl**.

saouler = **soûler**.

saper [3] [sape] *vt* to undermine.
➤ **se saper** *vp fam* to dress o.s. up.

sapeur [sapœr] *nm* sapper.

sapeur-pompier [sapœrpɔ̃pje] (*pl* **sapeurs-pompiers**) *nm* fireman, fire fighter.

saphir [safir] *nm* sapphire.

sapin [sapɛ̃] *nm* - **1.** [arbre] fir, firtree ; **~ de Noël** Christmas tree - **2.** [bois] fir, deal *Br*.

sapinière [sapinjɛr] *nf* fir forest.

sapristi [sapristi] *interj fam* goodness me!, my goodness!

saquer = **sacquer**.

S.A.R. (*abr de* **son altesse royale**) H.R.H.

sarabande [sarabɑ̃d] *nf* - **1.** [danse] saraband - **2.** *fam* [vacarme] din, racket.

Sarajevo [sarajɛvo] *n* Sarajevo.

sarbacane [sarbakan] *nf* [arme] blowpipe *Br*, blowgun *Am* ; [jouet] peashooter.

sarcasme [sarkasm] *nm* sarcasm.

sarcastique [sarkastik] *adj* sarcastic.

sarcler [3] [sarkle] *vt* to weed.

sarcloir [sarklwar] *nm* hoe.

sarcophage [sarkɔfaʒ] *nm* sarcophagus.

Sardaigne [sardɛɲ] *nf* : **la ~** Sardinia.

sarde [sard] *adj* Sardinian.
➤ **Sarde** *nmf* Sardinian.

sardine [sardin] *nf* sardine ; **~s à l'huile** sardines in oil ; **être serrés comme des ~s** *fam fig* to be packed like sardines.

sardinerie [sardinri] *nf* sardine cannery.

sardonique [sardɔnik] *adj* sardonic.

SARL, Sarl (*abr de* **société à responsabilité limitée**) *nf* limited liability company ; **Leduc, ~** ≃ Leduc Ltd.

sarment [sarmɑ̃] *nm* - **1.** [de vigne] shoot - **2.** [tige] stem.

sarrasin, e [sarazɛ̃, in] *adj* Saracen.
➤ **sarrasin** *nm* buckwheat.
➤ **Sarrasin, e** *nm, f* Saracen.

sarrau [saro] *nm* smock.

sarriette [sarjɛt] *nf* savory.

sas [sas] *nm* - **1.** AÉRON & NAVIG airlock - **2.** [d'écluse] lock - **3.** [tamis] sieve.

S.A.S. (*abr de* **son altesse sérénissime**) H.S.H.

satané, e [satane] *adj* (*avant n*) *fam* damned.

satanique [satanik] *adj* satanic.

satellisation [satelizasjɔ̃] *nf* - **1.** [de fusée] putting into orbit - **2.** [de pays] becoming a satellite.

satelliser [3] [satelize] *vt* - **1.** [fusée] to put into orbit - **2.** [pays] to make a satellite.

satellite [satelit] ⟨⟩ *nm* satellite ; **par ~** by satellite ; **~-relais** telecommunications satellite ⟨⟩ *adj* satellite (*avant n*).

satiété [sasjete] *nf* : **à ~** [boire, manger] one's fill ; [répéter] ad nauseam.

satin [satɛ̃] *nm* satin.

satiné, e [satine] *adj* satin (*avant n*) ; [peau] satiny-smooth.
➤ **satiné** *nm* satin-like quality.

satinette [satinɛt] *nf* - **1.** [coton et soie] satinet - **2.** [coton seul] sateen.

satire [satir] *nf* satire.

satirique [satirik] *adj* satirical.

satisfaction [satisfaksjɔ̃] *nf* satisfaction.

satisfaire [109] [satisfɛr] *vt* to satisfy ; **~ à** [condition, revendication] to meet, to satisfy ; [engagement] to fulfil.

➡ **se satisfaire** *vp* : **se ~ de** to be satisfied with.

satisfaisait, satisfaisions *etc* ▷ **satisfaire**.

satisfaisant, e [satisfəzɑ̃, ɑ̃t] *adj* - **1.** [travail] satisfactory - **2.** [expérience] satisfying.

satisfait, e [satisfɛ, ɛt] ◇ *pp* ▷ **satisfaire** ◇ *adj* satisfied ; **être ~ de** to be satisfied with ; **'~ ou remboursé'** 'satisfaction guaranteed or your money back'.

satisfasse, satisfasses *etc* ▷ **satisfaire**.

saturation [satyʀasjɔ̃] *nf* saturation.

saturé, e [satyʀe] *adj* : **~ (de)** saturated (with).

saturer [3] [satyʀe] *vt* : **~ qqch (de)** to saturate sthg (with).

saturne [satyʀn] *nm vieilli* lead.

➡ **Saturne** *nf* ASTRON Saturn.

satyre [satiʀ] *nm* satyr ; *fig* sex maniac.

sauce [sos] *nf* - **1.** CULIN sauce ; **en ~** in a sauce ; **~ hollandaise** hollandaise sauce ; **~ tartare** tartare sauce ; **~ tomate/blanche/piquante** tomato/white/spicy sauce - **2.** *fig* [accompagnement] presentation ; **mettre qqn à toutes les ~s** to use sb as a dogsbody.

saucer [16] [sose] *vt* - **1.** [assiette] to wipe - **2.** *fam* [personne] : **se faire ~** to get soaked.

saucière [sosjɛʀ] *nf* sauceboat.

saucisse [sosis] *nf* - **1.** CULIN sausage ; **~ de Francfort** frankfurter ; **~ sèche** dried sausage - **2.** *fam vieilli* & AÉRON barrage balloon.

saucisson [sosisɔ̃] *nm* slicing sausage.

saucissonner [3] [sosisɔne] ◇ *vi fam* to have a picnic ◇ *vt* - **1.** [colis] to truss up - **2.** [baguette] slice up.

sauf¹, sauve [sof, sov] *adj* [personne] safe, unharmed ; *fig* [honneur] saved, intact.

sauf² [sof] *prép* - **1.** [à l'exclusion de] except, apart from - **2.** [sous réserve de] barring ; **~ que** except (that).

sauf-conduit [sofkɔ̃dɥi] (*pl* **sauf-conduits**) *nm* safe-conduct.

sauge [soʒ] *nf* - **1.** CULIN sage - **2.** [plante ornementale] salvia.

saugrenu, e [sogʀəny] *adj* ridiculous, nonsensical.

saule [sol] *nm* willow ; **~ pleureur** weeping willow.

saumâtre [somatʀ] *adj* - **1.** [eau] brackish - **2.** *fig* [plaisanterie] distasteful.

saumon [somɔ̃] ◇ *nm* salmon ◇ *adj inv* salmon pink.

saumoné, e [somɔne] *adj* salmon (*avant n*).

saumure [somyʀ] *nf* brine.

sauna [sona] *nm* sauna.

saupoudrer [3] [sopudʀe] *vt* : **~ qqch de** to sprinkle sthg with.

saupoudreuse [sopudʀøz] *nf* dredger.

saur [sɔʀ] ▷ **hareng**.

saurai, sauras *etc* ▷ **savoir**.

saurien [soʀjɛ̃] *nm* saurian.

saut [so] *nm* - **1.** [bond] leap, jump - **2.** SPORT : **~ en hauteur** high jump ; **~ en longueur** long jump, broad jump *Am* ; **~ à l'élastique** bungee-jumping ; **faire du ~ à l'élastique** to go bungee-jumping - **3.** [visite] : **faire un ~ chez qqn** *fig* to pop in and see sb - **4.** INFORM : **~ de page** page break.

saute [sot] *nf* sudden change ; **avoir des ~s d'humeur** to have mood swings, to be temperamental.

sauté, e [sote] *adj* sautéed.

➡ **sauté** *nm* : **~ de veau** sautéed veal.

saute-mouton [sotmutɔ̃] *nm inv* : **jouer à ~** to play leapfrog.

sauter [3] [sote] ◇ *vi* - **1.** [bondir] to jump, to leap ; **~ à la corde** to skip ; **~ d'un sujet à l'autre** *fig* to jump from one subject to another ; **~ de joie** *fig* to jump for joy ; **~ au cou de qqn** *fig* to throw one's arms around sb - **2.** [exploser] to blow up ; [fusible] to blow - **3.** [être projeté - bouchon] to fly out ; [- serrure] to burst off ; [- bouton] to fly off ; [- chaîne de vélo] to come off - **4.** *fam* [employé] to get the sack - **5.** [être annulé] to be cancelled - **6.** CULIN : **faire ~ qqch** to sauté sthg - **7.** *loc* : **et que ça saute!** *fam* and get a move on! ◇ *vt* - **1.** [fossé, obstacle] to jump *ou* leap over - **2.** *fig* [page, repas] to skip - **3.** *vulg* [personne] : **~ qqn** to have it off with sb.

sauterelle [sotʀɛl] *nf* - **1.** ZOOL grasshopper - **2.** *fam fig* [personne] beanpole.

sauterie [sotʀi] *nf vieilli* do, party.

sauternes [sotɛʀn] *nm sweet dessert wine*.

sauteur, euse [sotœʀ, øz] ◇ *adj* [insecte] jumping (*avant n*) ◇ *nm, f* [athlète] jumper.

➡ **sauteur** *nm* [cheval] jumper.

➡ **sauteuse** *nf* CULIN frying pan.

sautiller [3] [sotije] *vi* to hop.

sautoir [sotwaʀ] *nm* - **1.** [bijou] chain ; **~ de perles** string of pearls ; **porter qqch en ~** to wear sthg on a chain round one's neck - **2.** SPORT jumping area.

sauvage [sovaʒ] ◇ *adj* - **1.** [plante, animal] wild - **2.** [farouche - animal familier] shy, timid ; [- personne] unsociable - **3.** [conduite, haine] savage ◇ *nmf* - **1.** [solitaire] recluse - **2.** *péj* [brute, indigène] savage.

sauvagement [sovaʒmɑ̃] *adv* savagely.

sauvageon, onne [sovaʒɔ̃, ɔn] *nm, f* little savage.

sauvagerie [sovaʒri] *nf* - **1.** [férocité] brutality, savagery - **2.** [insociabilité] unsociableness.

sauvagine [sovaʒin] *nf littéraire* wildfowl.

sauve ⊳ **sauf¹**.

sauvegarde [sovgard] *nf* - **1.** [protection] safeguard - **2.** *INFORM* saving ; [copie] backup.

sauvegarder [3] [sovgarde] *vt* - **1.** [protéger] to safeguard - **2.** *INFORM* to save ; [copier] to back up.

sauve-qui-peut [sovkipø] ◇ *nm inv* [débandade] stampede ◇ *interj* every man for himself!

sauver [3] [sove] *vt* - **1.** [gén] to save ; **~ qqn/ qqch de** to save sb/sthg from, to rescue sb/ sthg from ; **~ qqn de** *MÉD* to cure sb of - **2.** [navire, biens] to salvage.

➡ **se sauver** *vp* : **se ~ (de)** to run away (from) ; [prisonnier] to escape (from).

sauvetage [sovtaʒ] *nm* - **1.** [de personne] rescue - **2.** [de navire, biens] salvage.

sauveteur [sovtœr] *nm* rescuer.

sauvette [sovɛt] ➡ **à la sauvette** *loc adv* hurriedly, at great speed.

sauveur [sovœr] *nm* saviour *Br*, savior *Am*.

SAV [sav] (*abr de* **service après-vente**) *nm* after-sales service.

savamment [savamɑ̃] *adv* - **1.** [avec érudition] learnedly - **2.** [avec habileté] skilfully, cleverly.

savane [savan] *nf* savanna.

savant, e [savɑ̃, ɑ̃t] *adj* - **1.** [érudit] scholarly - **2.** [habile] skilful, clever - **3.** [animal] performing *(avant n)*.

➡ **savant** *nm* scientist.

savarin [savarɛ̃] *nm* ring-shaped cake containing rum.

savate [savat] *nf* - **1.** [pantoufle] worn-out slipper ; [soulier] worn-out shoe - **2.** *SPORT* kick boxing - **3.** *fam fig* [personne] clumsy oaf.

saveur [savœr] *nf* flavour *Br*, flavor *Am* ; *fig* savour *Br*, savor *Am*.

savoir [59] [savwar] ◇ *vt* - **1.** [gén] to know ; **faire ~ qqch à qqn** to tell sb sthg, to inform sb of sthg ; **si j'avais su ...** had I but known ..., if I had only known ... ; **sans le ~** unconsciously, without being aware of it ; **en ~ long sur qqn/qqch** to know a lot about sb/ sthg ; **tu (ne) peux pas ~** *fam* you have no idea ; **pas que je sache** not as far as I know ; **(ne pas) ~ de quoi il retourne** (not) to know what it's all about - **2.** [être capable de] to know how to ; **sais-tu conduire?** can you drive? ◇ *nm* learning.

➡ **à savoir** *loc conj* namely, that is.

savoir-faire [savwarfɛr] *nm inv* know-how, expertise.

savoir-vivre [savwarvivr] *nm inv* good manners *(pl)*.

savon [savɔ̃] *nm* - **1.** [matière] soap ; [pain] cake *ou* bar of soap - **2.** *fam* [réprimande] telling-off ; **passer un ~ à qqn** to give sb a telling-off.

savonner [3] [savɔne] *vt* - **1.** [linge] to soap - **2.** *fam* [enfant] to tell off.

➡ **se savonner** *vp* to soap o.s.

savonnette [savɔnɛt] *nf* guest soap.

savonneux, euse [savɔnø, øz] *adj* soapy.

savourer [3] [savure] *vt* to savour *Br*, to savor *Am*.

savoureux, euse [savurø, øz] *adj* - **1.** [mets] tasty - **2.** *fig* [anecdote] juicy.

savoyard, e [savwajar, ard] *adj* of/from Savoy.

➡ **Savoyard, e** *nm, f* native *ou* inhabitant of Savoy.

saxophone [saksɔfɔn] *nm* saxophone.

saxophoniste [saksɔfɔnist] *nmf* saxophonist, saxophone player.

saynète [sɛnɛt] *nf* playlet.

SBB (*abr de* **Schweizerische Bundesbahn**) *Swiss federal railways*.

sbire [sbir] *nm péj* henchman.

sc. (*abr de* **scène**) sc.

s/c (*abr de* **sous couvert de**) c/o.

scabreux, euse [skabrø, øz] *adj* - **1.** [propos] shocking, indecent - **2.** [entreprise] risky.

scalp [skalp] *nm* - **1.** [action] scalping - **2.** [trophée] scalp.

scalpel [skalpɛl] *nm* scalpel.

scalper [3] [skalpe] *vt* to scalp.

scampi [skɑ̃pi] *nmpl* scampi *(U)*.

scandale [skɑ̃dal] *nm* - **1.** [fait choquant] scandal - **2.** [indignation] uproar - **3.** [tapage] scene ; **faire du** *ou* **un ~** to make a scene.

scandaleusement [skɑ̃daløzmɑ̃] *adj* scandalously, outrageously.

scandaleux, euse [skɑ̃dalø, øz] *adj* scandalous, outrageous.

scandaliser [3] [skɑ̃dalize] *vt* to shock, to scandalize.

➡ **se scandaliser** *vp* to be shocked, to be scandalized.

scander [3] [skɑ̃de] *vt* - **1.** [vers] to scan - **2.** [slogan] to chant.

scandinave [skɑ̃dinav] *adj* Scandinavian.

➡ **Scandinave** *nmf* Scandinavian.

Scandinavie [skãdinavi] *nf* : **la ~** Scandinavia.

scanner[1] [4] [skane] *vt* to scan.

scanner[2] [skanɛr] *nm* scanner.

scaphandre [skafãdr] *nm* - **1.** [de plongeur] diving suit ; **~ autonome** aqualung - **2.** [d'astronaute] spacesuit.

scaphandrier [skafãdrije] *nm* deep-sea diver.

scarabée [skarabe] *nm* beetle, scarab.

scarlatine [skarlatin] *nf* scarlet fever.

scarole [skarɔl] *nf* endive.

scatologique [skatɔlɔʒik] *adj* scatological.

sceau, x [so] *nm* seal ; *fig* stamp, hallmark ; **sous le ~ du secret** *fig* under the seal of secrecy.

scélérat, e [selera, at] *littéraire* ◇ *adj* wicked ◇ *nm, f* villain ; *péj* rogue, rascal.

sceller [4] [sele] *vt* - **1.** [gén] to seal - **2.** CONSTR [fixer] to embed.

scellés [sele] *nmpl* seals ; **sous ~** sealed.

scénario [senarjo] *nm* - **1.** CIN, LITTÉRATURE & THÉÂTRE [canevas] scenario - **2.** CIN & TÉLÉ [découpage, synopsis] screenplay, script - **3.** *fig* [rituel] pattern.

scénariste [senarist] *nmf* scriptwriter.

scène [sɛn] *nf* - **1.** [gén] scene ; **~ de ménage** domestic row *ou* scene - **2.** [estrade] stage ; **entrée en ~** THÉÂTRE entrance ; *fig* appearance ; **mettre en ~** THÉÂTRE to stage ; CIN to direct.

scénique [senik] *adj* theatrical.

scepticisme [sɛptisism] *nm* scepticism *Br*, skepticism *Am*.

sceptique [sɛptik] ◇ *nmf* sceptic *Br*, skeptic *Am* ◇ *adj* - **1.** [incrédule] sceptical *Br*, skeptical *Am* - **2.** PHILO sceptic *Br*, skeptic *Am*.

sceptre [sɛptr] *nm* sceptre *Br*, scepter *Am*.

SCH (*abr de* **schilling**) S, Sch.

schah, shah [ʃa] *nm* shah.

schéma [ʃema] *nm* - **1.** [diagramme] diagram - **2.** [résumé] outline.

schématique [ʃematik] *adj* - **1.** [dessin] diagrammatic - **2.** [interprétation, exposé] simplified.

schématiquement [ʃematikmã] *adv* - **1.** [par dessin] diagrammatically - **2.** [en résumé] briefly.

schématisation [ʃematizasjɔ̃] *nf* - **1.** [présentation graphique] diagrammatic representation - **2.** *péj* [généralisation] oversimplification.

schématiser [3] [ʃematize] *vt* - **1.** [présenter en schéma] to represent diagrammatically - **2.** *péj* [généraliser] to oversimplify.

schisme [ʃism] *nm* - **1.** RELIG schism - **2.** [d'opinion] split.

schiste [ʃist] *nm* shale.

schizo [skizo] *adj fam* schizophrenic.

schizoïde [skizɔid] *adj* schizoid.

schizophrène [skizɔfrɛn] *nmf* & *adj* schizophrenic.

schizophrénie [skizɔfreni] *nf* schizophrenia.

schizophrénique [skizɔfrenik] *adj* schizophrenic.

schlinguer, chlinguer [3] [ʃlɛ̃ge] *vi tfam* to stink.

schnock, chnoque [ʃnɔk] *nm fam* : **du ~!** dummy!, dimwit!

schuss [ʃus] ◇ *nm* schuss ◇ *adv* : **descendre (tout) ~** to schuss down.

sciatique [sjatik] ◇ *nf* sciatica ◇ *adj* sciatic.

scie [si] *nf* - **1.** [outil] saw ; **~ à métaux** hacksaw ; **~ sauteuse** jigsaw - **2.** [rengaine] catchphrase - **3.** *fam* [personne] bore.

sciemment [sjamã] *adv* knowingly.

science [sjãs] *nf* - **1.** [connaissances scientifiques] science ; **~s humaines** *ou* **sociales** UNIV social sciences ; **~s naturelles** SCOL biology (*sg*) - **2.** [érudition] knowledge ; **avoir la ~ infuse** *fig* to know a lot - **3.** [art] art.

science-fiction [sjãsfiksjɔ̃] *nf* science fiction.

sciences-po [sjãspo] *nfpl* UNIV political science (*sg*).

➤ **Sciences-Po** *n* grande école for political science.

scientifique [sjãtifik] ◇ *nmf* scientist ◇ *adj* scientific.

scientifiquement [sjãtifikmã] *adv* scientifically.

scientisme [sjãtism] *nm* Christian Science.

scier [9] [sje] *vt* - **1.** [branche] to saw - **2.** *fam* [personne] to stagger.

scierie [siri] *nf* sawmill.

scinder [3] [sɛ̃de] *vt* : **~ (en)** to split (into), to divide (into).

➤ **se scinder** *vp* : **se ~ (en)** to split (into), to divide (into).

scintillant, e [sɛ̃tijã, ãt] *adj* sparkling.

scintillement [sɛ̃tijmã] *nm* sparkle.

scintiller [3] [sɛ̃tije] *vi* to sparkle.

scission [sisjɔ̃] *nf* split.

sciure [sjyr] *nf* sawdust.

sclérose [skleroz] *nf* sclerosis ; *fig* ossification ; **~ en plaques** multiple sclerosis.

sclérosé, e [sklerozel] ◇ adj sclerotic ; fig ossified ◇ nm, f person suffering from sclerosis ; fig person set in his/her ways.

scléroser [3] [skleroze] ➤ **se scléroser** vp to become sclerotic ; fig to become ossified.

scolaire [skɔlɛr] adj school (avant n) ; péj bookish.

scolarisable [skɔlarizabl] adj of school age.

scolarisation [skɔlarizasjɔ̃] nf schooling.

scolariser [3] [skɔlarize] vt to provide with schooling.

scolarité [skɔlarite] nf schooling ; **prolonger la ~** to raise the school-leaving age ; **frais de ~** SCOL school fees ; UNIV tuition fees.

scolastique [skɔlastik] ◇ nf scholasticism ◇ adj scholastic.

scoliose [skɔljoz] nf curvature of the spine.

scoop [skup] nm scoop.

scooter [skutœr] nm scooter ; **~ des mers** jet ski ; **~ des neiges** snowmobile.

scorbut [skɔrbyt] nm scurvy.

score [skɔr] nm - **1.** SPORT score - **2.** POLIT result.

scorie [skɔri] nf - **1.** (gén pl) GÉOL scoria - **2.** IND slag (U) ; fig dregs (pl).

scorpion [skɔrpjɔ̃] nm scorpion.

➤ **Scorpion** nm ASTROL Scorpio ; **être Scorpion** to be (a) Scorpio.

scotch [skɔtʃ] nm [alcool] whisky, Scotch.

Scotch® [skɔtʃ] nm [adhésif] ≃ Sellotape® Br, ≃ Scotch tape® Am.

scotcher [3] [skɔtʃe] vt to sellotape Br, to scotch-tape Am.

scout, e [skut] adj scout (avant n).

➤ **scout** nm scout.

scoutisme [skutism] nm scouting.

Scrabble® [skrabl] nm Scrabble®.

scratcher (se) [skratʃe] vpr fam to crash ; **se ~ contre un arbre** to crash into a tree.

scribe [skrib] nm HIST scribe.

scribouillard, e [skribujar, ard] nm, f péj pen pusher.

script [skript] nm - **1.** TYPO printing, print - **2.** CIN & TÉLÉ script.

scripte [skript] nmf CIN & TÉLÉ continuity person.

scriptural, e, aux [skriptyral, o] adj : **monnaie ~e** substitute money.

scrotum [skrɔtɔm] nm scrotum.

scrupule [skrypyl] nm scruple ; **avec ~** scrupulously ; **sans ~s** [être] unscrupulous ; [agir] unscrupulously.

scrupuleusement [skrypyløzmɑ̃] adv scrupulously.

scrupuleux, euse [skrypylø, øz] adj scrupulous.

scrutateur, trice [skrytatœr, tris] adj searching.

➤ **scrutateur** nm POLIT ≃ scrutineer Br, ≃ teller Am.

scruter [3] [skryte] vt to scrutinize.

scrutin [skrytɛ̃] nm - **1.** [vote] ballot ; **dépouiller un ~** to count the votes - **2.** [système] voting system ; **~ majoritaire** first-past-the-post system ; **~ proportionnel** proportional representation system.

sculpter [3] [skylte] vt to sculpt.

sculpteur [skyltœr] nm sculptor.

sculptural, e, aux [skyltyral, o] adj sculptural ; fig statuesque.

sculpture [skyltyr] nf sculpture.

sdb abr de **salle de bains**.

SDF (abr de **sans domicile fixe**) nmf : **les ~** the homeless.

SDN (abr de **Société des Nations**) nf League of Nations.

se [sə], **s'** (devant voyelle ou h muet) pron pers - **1.** (réfléchi) [personne] oneself, himself (f herself), (pl) themselves ; [chose, animal] itself, (pl) themselves ; **elle ~ regarde dans le miroir** she looks at herself in the mirror - **2.** (réciproque) each other, one another ; **elles ~ sont parlé** they spoke to each other ou to one another ; **ils ~ sont rencontrés hier** they met yesterday - **3.** (passif) : **ce produit ~ vend bien/partout** this product is selling well/is sold everywhere - **4.** [remplace l'adjectif possessif] : **~ laver les mains** to wash one's hands ; **~ couper le doigt** to cut one's finger.

S.E. (abr de **son excellence**) H.E.

séance [seɑ̃s] nf - **1.** [réunion] meeting, sitting, session ; **lever la ~** fig to adjourn the meeting ou session ; **~ extraordinaire** special session, extraordinary meeting - **2.** [période] session ; [de pose] sitting - **3.** CIN & THÉÂTRE performance - **4.** fam [scène] performance - **5.** loc : **~ tenante** right away, forthwith.

séant, e [seɑ̃, ɑ̃t] adj fitting, seemly.

➤ **séant** nm : **se dresser** ou **se mettre sur son ~** littéraire to sit up.

seau, x [so] nm - **1.** [récipient] bucket ; **~ à glace** ice bucket - **2.** [contenu] bucketful.

sébile [sebil] nf (begging) bowl.

sébum [sebɔm] nm sebum.

sec, sèche [sɛk, sɛʃ] adj - **1.** [gén] dry - **2.** [fruits] dried - **3.** [alcool] neat - **4.** [personne - maigre] lean ; [- austère] austere - **5.** fig [cœur] hard ; [voix, ton] sharp - **6.** [sans autre prestation] : **vol ~** flight only - **7.** *fam* : **être ~ sur un sujet** to have nothing to say on a subject.

◆ **sec** ◇ *adv* - **1.** [beaucoup] : **boire ~** to drink heavily - **2.** [frapper] hard - **3.** [démarrer] sharply - **4.** *loc* : **aussi ~** *fam* right away ; **être à ~** [puits] to be dry *ou* dried up ; *fam* [personne] to be broke ◇ *nm* : **tenir au ~** to keep in a dry place.

sécable [sekabl] *adj* divisible.

SECAM, Secam [sekam] (*abr de* **procédé séquentiel à mémoire**) *nm & adj* French TV broadcasting system.

sécateur [sekatœr] *nm* secateurs (*pl*).

sécession [sesesjɔ̃] *nf* secession ; **faire ~ (de)** to secede (from).

séchage [seʃaʒ] *nm* drying.

sèche [sɛʃ] *nf fam* cigarette, fag *Br*.

sèche-cheveux [sɛʃʃəvø] *nm inv* hairdryer.

sèche-linge [sɛʃlɛ̃ʒ] *nm inv* tumble-dryer.

sécher [18] [seʃe] ◇ *vt* - **1.** [linge] to dry - **2.** *arg scol* [cours] to skip, to skive off *Br* ◇ *vi* - **1.** [linge] to dry - **2.** [peau] to dry out ; [rivière] to dry up - **3.** *arg scol* [ne pas savoir répondre] to dry up.

sécheresse [seʃrɛs] *nf* - **1.** [de terre, climat, style] dryness - **2.** [absence de pluie] drought - **3.** [de réponse] curtness.

séchoir [seʃwar] *nm* - **1.** [local] drying shed - **2.** [tringle] airer, clotheshorse - **3.** [électrique] dryer ; **~ à cheveux** hairdryer.

second, e [səgɔ̃, ɔ̃d] ◇ *adj num* second ; **dans un état ~** dazed ◇ *nm, f* second ; *voir aussi* **sixième.**

◆ **second** *nm* [assistant] assistant.

◆ **seconde** *nf* - **1.** [unité de temps & *MUS*] second ; **une ~e!** just a second! - **2.** *SCOL* ≃ fifth year *ou* form *Br*, ≃ tenth grade *Am* - **3.** *TRANSPORT* second class.

secondaire [səgɔ̃dɛr] ◇ *nm* : **le ~** *GÉOL* the Mesozoic ; *SCOL* secondary education ; *ÉCON* the secondary sector ◇ *adj* - **1.** [gén & *SCOL*] secondary ; **effets ~s** *MÉD* side effects - **2.** *GÉOL* Mesozoic.

seconder [3] [səgɔ̃de] *vt* to assist.

secouer [6] [səkwe] *vt* - **1.** [gén] to shake - **2.** *fam* [réprimander] to shake up.

◆ **se secouer** *vp fam* to snap out of it.

secourable [səkurabl] *adj* helpful ; **main ~** helping hand.

secourir [45] [səkurir] *vt* [blessé, miséreux] to help ; [personne en danger] to rescue.

secourisme [səkurism] *nm* first aid.

secouriste [səkurist] *nmf* first-aid worker.

secourrai, secourras *etc* ▷ **secourir.**

secours¹, secourt *etc* ▷ **secourir.**

secours² [səkur] *nm* - **1.** [aide] help ; **appeler au ~** to call for help ; **les ~** emergency services ; **au ~!** help! ; **porter ~ à qqn** to help sb ; **voler au ~ de qqn** *fig* to rush to sb's aid - **2.** [dons] aid, relief - **3.** [renfort] relief, reinforcements (*pl*) - **4.** [soins] aid ; **les premiers ~** first aid (*U*).

◆ **de secours** *loc adj* - **1.** [trousse, poste] first-aid (*avant n*) - **2.** [éclairage, issue] emergency (*avant n*) - **3.** [roue] spare.

secouru, e [səkury] *pp* ▷ **secourir.**

secousse [səkus] *nf* - **1.** [mouvement] jerk, jolt - **2.** *fig* [bouleversement] upheaval ; [psychologique] shock - **3.** [tremblement de terre] tremor.

secret, ète [səkrɛ, ɛt] *adj* - **1.** [gén] secret - **2.** [personne] reticent.

◆ **secret** *nm* - **1.** [gén] secret ; **être/mettre qqn dans le ~ de** to be/let sb in on the secret of ; **... dont il a le ~** ... which he alone knows ; **~ d'alcôve** pillow talk (*U*) ; **~ d'État** official secret, state secret ; **~ professionnel** confidentiality - **2.** [discrétion] secrecy ; **dans le plus grand ~** in the utmost secrecy.

◆ **au secret** *loc adv JUR* in solitary confinement.

secrétaire [səkreter] ◇ *nmf* [personne] secretary ; **~ de direction** executive secretary ; **~ d'État** minister of state ; **~ général** *COMM* company secretary ; **~ de rédaction** subeditor ◇ *nm* [meuble] writing desk, secretaire.

secrétariat [səkretarja] *nm* - **1.** [bureau] secretary's office ; [d'organisation internationale] secretariat - **2.** [personnel] secretarial staff ; **assurer le ~ de qqn** to act as sb's secretary - **3.** [métier] secretarial work.

secrètement [səkrɛtmɑ̃] *adv* secretly.

sécréter [18] [sekrete] *vt* to secrete ; *fig* to exude.

sécrétion [sekresjɔ̃] *nf* secretion.

sectaire [sɛkter] *nmf & adj* sectarian.

sectarisme [sɛktarism] *nm* sectarianism.

secte [sɛkt] *nf* sect.

secteur [sɛktœr] *nm* - **1.** [zone] area ; **se trouver dans le ~** *fam* to be somewhere *Br ou* someplace *Am* around - **2.** *ADMIN* district - **3.** *ÉCON, GÉOM* & *MIL* sector ; **~ privé/public** private/public sector ; **~ primaire/secondaire/tertiaire** primary/secondary/tertiary sector - **4.** *ÉLECTR* mains ; **sur ~** off *ou* from the mains.

section [sɛksjɔ̃] *nf* - **1.** [gén] section ; [de parti] branch - **2.** [action] cutting - **3.** *MIL* platoon.

sectionnement [sɛksjɔnmɑ̃] *nm* - **1.** *fig* [division] division into sections - **2.** [coupure] severing.

sectionner [3] [sɛksjɔne] vt - **1.** fig [diviser] to divide into sections - **2.** [trancher] to sever.

➤ **se sectionner** vp to split, to be severed.

sectoriel, elle [sɛktɔrjɛl] adj sector (avant n), sector-based.

sectorisation [sɛktɔrizasjɔ̃] nf division into sectors.

sectoriser [3] [sɛktɔrize] vt to divide into sectors.

Sécu [seky] fam abr de **Sécurité sociale.**

séculaire [sekylɛr] adj [ancien] age-old.

séculariser [3] [sekylarize] vt to secularize.

séculier, ère [sekylje, ɛr] adj secular.

secundo [sɔgɔ̃do] adv in the second place, secondly.

sécurisant, e [sekyrizɑ̃, ɑ̃t] adj [milieu] secure ; [attitude] reassuring.

sécuriser [3] [sekyrize] vt : ~ qqn to make sb feel secure.

sécurité [sekyrite] nf - **1.** [d'esprit] security - **2.** [absence de danger] safety ; **la ~ routière** road safety ; **en toute ~** safe and sound - **3.** [dispositif] safety catch - **4.** [organisme] : **la Sécurité sociale** ≈ the DSS Br, ≈ the Social Security Am.

SÉCURITÉ SOCIALE ▬▬▬▬▬

The 'Sécu', as it is popularly known, created in 1945-46, provides public health benefits, pensions, maternity leave etc. These benefits are paid for by obligatory insurance contributions ('cotisations') made by employers ('cotisations patronales') and employees ('cotisations salariales'). Many French people have complementary health insurance provided by a 'mutuelle', which guarantees payment of all or part of the expenses not covered by the 'Sécurité sociale'.

sédatif, ive [sedatif, iv] adj sedative.

➤ **sédatif** nm sedative.

sédentaire [sedɑ̃tɛr] <> nmf sedentary person ; [casanier] stay-at-home <> adj [personne, métier] sedentary ; [casanier] stay-at-home.

sédentarisation [sedɑ̃tarizasjɔ̃] nf settlement (process).

sédentariser [3] [sedɑ̃tarize] ➤ **se sédentariser** vp [tribu] to settle, to become settled.

sédentarité [sedɑ̃tarite] nf settled state.

sédiment [sedimɑ̃] nm sediment.

sédimentaire [sedimɑ̃tɛr] adj sedimentary.

sédimentation [sedimɑ̃tasjɔ̃] nf sedimentation.

séditieux, euse [sedisjø, øz] littéraire <> adj seditious <> nm, f rebel.

sédition [sedisjɔ̃] nf sedition.

séducteur, trice [sedyktœr, tris] <> adj seductive <> nm, f seducer (f seductress).

séduction [sedyksjɔ̃] nf - **1.** [action] seduction - **2.** [attrait] seductive power.

séduire [98] [seduir] vt - **1.** [plaire à] to attract, to appeal to - **2.** [abuser de] to seduce.

séduisais, séduisions etc ▷ **séduire.**

séduisant, e [seduizɑ̃, ɑ̃t] adj attractive.

séduit, e [sedui, it] pp ▷ **séduire.**

séfarade [sefarad] <> nmf Sephardi <> adj Sephardic.

segment [sɛgmɑ̃] nm - **1.** GÉOM segment - **2.** TECHNOL : ~ **de frein** brake shoe ; ~ **de piston** piston ring - **3.** COMM : ~ **de marché** market segment.

segmentation [sɛgmɑ̃tasjɔ̃] nf segmentation.

segmenter [3] [sɛgmɑ̃te] vt to segment.

ségrégation [segregasjɔ̃] nf segregation.

ségrégationniste [segregasjɔnist] nmf & adj segregationist.

seiche [sɛʃ] nf cuttlefish.

seigle [sɛgl] nm rye.

seigneur [sɛɲœr] nm lord ; **faire le grand ~** fig to throw money about ; **vivre en grand ~** fig to live like a lord.

➤ **Seigneur** nm : **le Seigneur** the Lord.

seigneurial, e, aux [sɛɲœrjal, o] adj lordly ; HIST seigneurial.

sein [sɛ̃] nm breast ; fig bosom ; **donner le ~ (à un bébé)** to breast-feed (a baby).

➤ **au sein de** loc prép within.

Seine [sɛn] nf : **la ~** the (River) Seine.

séisme [seism] nm earthquake.

SEITA, Seita [sejta] (abr de **Société nationale d'exploitation industrielle des tabacs et allumettes**) nf French tobacco and match manufacturer.

seize [sɛz] adj num & nm sixteen ; voir aussi **six.**

seizième [sɛzjɛm] adj num, nm OU nmf sixteenth ; **le ~** wealthy district of Paris ; voir aussi **sixième.**

LE SEIZIÈME ▬▬▬▬▬

This term often refers to an upper-class social background, lifestyle, way of dressing etc.

séjour [seʒur] nm - **1.** [durée] stay ; **interdit de ~**

≈ banned ; ~ **linguistique** stay abroad (to develop language skills) - **2.** [pièce] living room.

séjourner [3] [seʒurne] vi to stay.

sel [sɛl] nm salt ; fig piquancy ; **gros ~** coarse salt.

➤ **sels** nmpl smelling salts ; **~s de bain** bath salts.

sélect, e [selɛkt] adj fam select.

sélecteur [selɛktœr] nm - **1.** [dispositif] selector ; **~ de température** thermostat - **2.** [de moto] gear-change lever.

sélectif, ive [selɛktif, iv] adj selective.

sélection [selɛksjɔ̃] nf selection.

sélectionné, e [selɛksjɔne] adj selected.

sélectionner [3] [selɛksjɔne] vt to select, to pick.

sélectionneur, euse [selɛksjɔnœr, øz] nm, f selector.

sélectivement [selɛktivmɑ̃] adv selectively.

self [sɛlf] nm fam self-service (cafeteria).

self-control [sɛlfkɔ̃trɔl] nm inv self-control.

self-made-man [sɛlfmɛdman] (pl **self-made-men** [sɛlfmɛdmɛn]) nm self-made man.

self-service [sɛlfsɛrvis] (pl **self-services**) nm self-service cafeteria.

selle [sɛl] nf - **1.** [gén] saddle ; **se mettre en ~** to mount - **2.** [toilettes] : **aller à la ~** to open one's bowels.

seller [4] [sele] vt to saddle.

sellerie [sɛlri] nf - **1.** [commerce] saddlery - **2.** [lieu] tack room.

sellette [sɛlɛt] nf hot seat ; **mettre qqn/être sur la ~** fig to put sb/be in the hot seat.

sellier [selje] nm saddler.

selon [səlɔ̃] prép - **1.** [conformément à] in accordance with - **2.** [d'après] according to ; **c'est ~** fam fig that (all) depends.

➤ **selon que** loc conj depending on whether.

S.Em (abr de son éminence) H.E.

semailles [səmaj] nfpl - **1.** [action] sowing (U) - **2.** [période] sowing season (sg).

semaine [səmɛn] nf - **1.** [période] week ; **à la ~** [être payé] by the week ; **en ~** during the week ; **la ~ sainte** Holy Week ; **faire qqch à la petite ~** fig to do sthg on a short-term basis - **2.** [salaire] weekly wage.

semainier, ère [səmenje, ɛr] nm, f person on duty for the week.

➤ **semainier** nm - **1.** [bijou] seven-band bracelet - **2.** [meuble] small chest of drawers - **3.** [calendrier] desk diary.

sémantique [semɑ̃tik] ⬥ nf semantics (U) ⬥ adj semantic.

sémaphore [semafɔr] nm - **1.** NAVIG semaphore - **2.** RAIL semaphore, semaphore signals (pl).

semblable [sɑ̃blabl] ⬥ nm [prochain] fellow man ; **il n'a pas son ~** there's nobody like him ⬥ adj - **1.** [analogue] similar ; **~ à** like, similar to - **2.** (avant n) [tel] such.

semblant [sɑ̃blɑ̃] nm : **un ~ de** a semblance of ; **faire ~ (de faire qqch)** to pretend (to do sthg).

sembler [3] [sɑ̃ble] ⬥ vi to seem ⬥ v impers : **il (me/te) semble que** it seems (to me/you) that.

semelle [səmɛl] nf - **1.** [de chaussure - dessous] sole ; [- à l'intérieur] insole ; **~s compensées** platform soles - **2.** [de ski] underside - **3.** CONSTR foundation ; [de poutre] flange - **4.** loc : **battre la ~** to stamp one's feet to keep warm ; **ne pas quitter qqn d'une ~** to stick to sb like glue.

semence [səmɑ̃s] nf - **1.** [graine] seed - **2.** [sperme] semen (U).

semer [19] [səme] vt - **1.** [planter] fig to sow - **2.** [répandre] to scatter ; **~ qqch de** to scatter sthg with, to strew sthg with - **3.** fam [se débarrasser de] to shake off - **4.** fam [perdre] to lose.

semestre [səmɛstr] nm half year, six-month period ; SCOL semester.

semestriel, elle [səmɛstrijɛl] adj - **1.** [qui a lieu tous les six mois] half-yearly, six-monthly - **2.** [qui dure six mois] six months', six-month.

semeur, euse [səmœr, øz] nm, f sower ; fig disseminator.

semi-automatique [səmiotɔmatik] adj semiautomatic.

semi-fini, e [səmifini] adj semi-finished.

semi-liberté [səmiliberte] (pl **semi-libertés**) nf temporary release from prison.

sémillant, e [semijɑ̃, ɑ̃t] adj vivacious.

séminaire [seminɛr] nm - **1.** RELIG seminary - **2.** UNIV [colloque] seminar.

séminal, e, aux [seminal, o] adj seminal.

séminariste [seminarist] nm seminarist.

sémiologie [semjɔlɔʒi] nf semiology.

semi-public, ique [səmipyblik] adj semi-public.

semi-remorque [səmirəmɔrk] (pl **semi-remorques**) nm articulated lorry Br, semi-trailer Am.

semis [səmi] nm - **1.** [méthode] sowing broadcast - **2.** [terrain] seedbed - **3.** [plant] seedling.

sémite [semit] adj Semitic.

➤ **Sémite** *nmf* Semite.

sémitique [semitik] *adj* Semitic.

semoir [səmwar] *nm* - **1.** [machine] drill - **2.** [sac] seedbag.

semonce [səmɔ̃s] *nf* - **1.** [réprimande] reprimand - **2.** MIL : coup de ~ warning shot.

semoule [səmul] *nf* semolina.

sempiternel, elle [sɑ̃pitɛrnɛl] *adj* eternal.

sénat [sena] *nm* senate ; **le Sénat** *upper house of the French parliament.*

LE SÉNAT

The Senate is the upper house of the French parliament. Its members are elected for a nine-year mandate by the Deputies of the Assemblée nationale and certain other government officials. The President of the Senate may deputize for the President of the Republic. The powers of the Senate are almost as extensive as those of the Assemblée nationale, although the latter is empowered to override the decisions of the Senate in cases where the two houses disagree.

sénateur [senatœr] *nm* senator.

Sénégal [senegal] *nm* : **le ~** Senegal ; **au ~** in Senegal.

sénégalais, e [senegalɛ, ɛz] *adj* Senegalese.

➤ **Sénégalais, e** *nm, f* Senegalese person.

sénile [senil] *adj* senile.

sénilité [senilite] *nf* senility.

senior [senjɔr] SPORT ⬦ *nmf* senior ⬦ *adj* senior.

sens¹, sent *etc* ▷ **sentir.**

sens² [sɑ̃s] ⬦ *nm* - **1.** [fonction, instinct, raison] sense ; **avoir un sixième ~** to have sixth sense ; **avoir le ~ de l'humour** to have a sense of humour *Br ou* humor *Am* ; **avoir le ~ de l'orientation** to have a (good) sense of direction ; **bon ~** good sense ; **tomber sous le ~** *fig* to be perfectly obvious - **2.** [opinion, avis] : **abonder dans le ~ de qqn** to agree completely with sb ; **à mon ~** to my way of thinking, to my mind - **3.** [direction] direction ; **dans le ~ de la longueur** lengthways ; **dans le ~ de la marche** in the direction of travel ; **dans le ~ des aiguilles d'une montre** clockwise ; **dans le ~ contraire des aiguilles d'une montre** anticlockwise *Br*, counterclockwise *Am* ; **en ~ inverse** in the opposite direction ; **~ dessus dessous** upside down ; **~ giratoire** roundabout *Br*, traffic circle *Am* ; **~ interdit** *ou* **unique** one-way street - **4.** [signification] meaning ; **cela n'a pas de ~!** it's nonsensical! ; **dans** *ou* **en un ~** in one sense ; **à double**

~ with a double meaning ; **au ~ strict du terme** strictly speaking ; **vide de ~** meaningless ; **en ce ~ que** in the sense that ; **~ propre/figuré** literal/figurative sense ⬦ *nmpl* senses.

sensation [sɑ̃sasjɔ̃] *nf* - **1.** [perception] sensation, feeling ; **à ~** sensational ; **faire ~** to cause a sensation - **2.** [impression] feeling.

sensationnel, elle [sɑ̃sasjɔnɛl] *adj* sensational.

sensé, e [sɑ̃se] *adj* sensible.

sensément [sɑ̃semɑ̃] *adv* sensibly.

sensibilisation [sɑ̃sibilizasjɔ̃] *nf* - **1.** MÉD & PHOT sensitization - **2.** *fig* [du public] consciousness raising.

sensibiliser [3] [sɑ̃sibilize] *vt* - **1.** MÉD & PHOT to sensitize - **2.** *fig* [public] : **~ (à)** to make aware (of).

sensibilité [sɑ̃sibilite] *nf* : **~ (à)** sensitivity (to).

sensible [sɑ̃sibl] *adj* - **1.** [gén] : **~ (à)** sensitive (to) ; **~ à la vue** visible ; **~ à l'ouïe** audible - **2.** [notable] considerable, appreciable.

sensiblement [sɑ̃sibləmɑ̃] *adv* - **1.** [à peu près] more or less - **2.** [notablement] appreciably, considerably.

sensiblerie [sɑ̃sibləri] *nf péj* [morale] sentimentality ; [physique] squeamishness.

sensoriel, elle [sɑ̃sɔrjɛl] *adj* sensory.

sensualité [sɑ̃sɥalite] *nf* [lascivité] sensuousness ; [charnelle] sensuality.

sensuel, elle [sɑ̃sɥɛl] *adj* - **1.** [charnel] sensual - **2.** [lascif] sensuous.

sentence [sɑ̃tɑ̃s] *nf* - **1.** [jugement] sentence - **2.** [maxime] adage.

sentencieux, euse [sɑ̃tɑ̃sjø, øz] *adj péj* sententious.

senteur [sɑ̃tœr] *nf littéraire* perfume.

senti, e [sɑ̃ti] ⬦ *pp* ▷ **sentir** ⬦ *adj* : **bien ~** [mots] well-chosen.

sentier [sɑ̃tje] *nm* path ; **sortir des ~s battus** *fig* to go off the beaten track.

sentiment [sɑ̃timɑ̃] *nm* feeling ; **j'ai le ~ de l'avoir déjà vu** I have the feeling that I've seen him before ; **plein de bons ~s** full of good intentions ; **veuillez agréer, Monsieur, l'expression de mes ~s distingués/cordiaux/les meilleurs** yours faithfully/sincerely/truly.

sentimental, e, aux [sɑ̃timɑ̃tal, o] ⬦ *adj* - **1.** [amoureux] love *(avant n)* - **2.** [sensible, romanesque] sentimental ⬦ *nm, f* sentimentalist.

sentimentalisme [sɑ̃timɑ̃talism] *nm* sentimentalism.

sentinelle [sɑ̃tinɛl] *nf* sentry.

sentir [37] [sɑ̃tir] ⬦ *vt* - **1.** [percevoir - par l'odorat] to smell ; [- par le goût] to taste ; [- par le toucher] to feel - **2.** [exhaler - odeur] to smell of - **3.** [colère, tendresse] to feel - **4.** [affectation, plagiat] to smack of - **5.** [danger] to sense, to be aware of ; ~ **que** to feel (that) - **6.** [beauté] to feel, to appreciate - **7.** *loc* : **je ne peux pas le** ~ *fam* I can't stand him ; **le/la ~ passer** *fam* to really feel it ⬦ *vi* : ~ **bon/mauvais** to smell good/bad.

➡ **se sentir** ⬦ *v attr* : **se ~ bien/fatigué** to feel well/tired ; **se ~ la force de faire qqch** to feel strong enough to do sthg ⬦ *vp* [être perceptible] : **ça se sent!** you can really tell!

seoir [67] [swar] ⬦ *vi sout* [aller bien] : ~ **à qqn** to become sb ⬦ *v impers* : **comme il sied** as is fitting.

Séoul [seul] *n* Seoul.

séparable [separabl] *adj* separable.

séparation [separasjɔ̃] *nf* separation.

séparatisme [separatism] *nm* separatism.

séparatiste [separatist] *nmf* separatist.

séparé, e [separe] *adj* - **1.** [intérêts] separate - **2.** [couple] separated.

séparément [separemã] *adv* separately.

séparer [3] [separe] *vt* - **1.** [gén] : ~ **(de)** to separate (from) - **2.** [suj : divergence] to divide - **3.** [maison] : ~ **(en)** to divide (into).

➡ **se séparer** *vp* - **1.** [se défaire] : **se ~ de** to part with - **2.** [conjoints] to separate, to split up ; **se ~ de** to separate from, to split up with - **3.** [participants] to disperse - **4.** [route] : **se ~ (en)** to split (into), to divide (into).

sépia [sepja] ⬦ *nf* - **1.** [matière] sepia - **2.** [dessin] sepia (drawing) ⬦ *adj inv* sepia.

sept [sɛt] *adj num* & *nm* seven ; *voir aussi* **six**.

septante [sɛptɑ̃t] *adj num inv* Belg & Helv seventy.

septembre [sɛptɑ̃br] *nm* September ; **de ~** September *(avant n)* ; **en ~, au mois de ~** in September ; **début ~, au début du mois de ~** at the beginning of September ; **fin ~, à la fin du mois de ~** at the end of September ; **d'ici ~** by September ; **(à la) mi-~** (in) mid-September ; **le premier/deux/dix ~** the first/second/tenth of September.

septennat [sɛptena] *nm* seven-year term (of office).

septentrional, e, aux [sɛptɑ̃trijɔnal, o] *adj* northern.

septicémie [sɛptisemi] *nf* septicaemia *Br*, septicemia *Am*, blood poisoning.

septième [sɛtjɛm] ⬦ *adj num, nm* OU *nmf* seventh ; *voir aussi* **sixième** ⬦ *nf* SCOL ≃ third

year OU form *(at junior school)* Br, ≃ fifth grade Am.

septièmement [sɛtjɛmmã] *adv* seventhly, in (the) seventh place.

septique [sɛptik] *adj* [infecté] septic.

septuagénaire [sɛptɥaʒenɛr] ⬦ *nmf* 70-year-old ⬦ *adj* : **être ~** to be in one's seventies.

sépulcral, e, aux [sepylkral, o] *adj* sepulchral.

sépulcre [sepylkr] *nm* sepulchre Br, sepulcher Am.

sépulture [sepyltyr] *nf* - **1.** [lieu] burial place - **2.** [inhumation] burial.

séquelle [sekɛl] *nf (gén pl)* aftermath ; MÉD aftereffect.

séquence [sekɑ̃s] *nf* sequence ; CARTES run, sequence.

séquentiel, elle [sekɑ̃sjɛl] *adj* sequential.

séquestration [sekɛstrasjɔ̃] *nf* - **1.** [de personne] confinement - **2.** [de biens] impoundment.

séquestre [sekɛstr] *nm* JUR pound ; **mettre** OU **placer sous ~** to impound.

séquestrer [3] [sekɛstre] *vt* - **1.** [personne] to confine - **2.** [biens] to impound.

serai, seras *etc* ⬒ **être**.

sérail [seraj] *nm* seraglio.

serbe [sɛrb] *adj* Serbian.

➡ **Serbe** *nmf* Serb.

Serbie [sɛrbi] *nf* : **la ~** Serbia.

serbo-croate [sɛrbɔkrɔat] *(pl* serbo-croates*)* ⬦ *nm* [langue] Serbo-Croat ⬦ *adj* Serbo-Croat, Serbo-Croatian.

➡ **Serbo-Croate** *nmf* Serbo-Croat speaker.

serein, e [sərɛ̃, ɛn] *adj* - **1.** [calme] serene - **2.** [impartial] calm, dispassionate.

sereinement [sərɛnmã] *adv* serenely, calmly.

sérénade [serenad] *nf* - **1.** MUS serenade - **2.** *fam* [tapage] hullabaloo.

sérénité [serenite] *nf* serenity.

serf, serve [sɛrf, sɛrv] *nm, f* serf.

serge [sɛrʒ] *nf* serge.

sergent [sɛrʒɑ̃] *nm* sergeant.

sergent-chef [sɛrʒɑ̃ʃɛf] *(pl* sergents-chefs*)* *nm* staff sergeant.

sériciculture [serisikyltyr] *nf* silkworm farming.

série [seri] *nf* - **1.** [gén] series *(sg)* ; ~ B CIN & TÉLÉ B movie - **2.** SPORT rank ; [au tennis] seeding - **3.** COMM & IND : **produire qqch en ~** to mass-produce sthg ; **de ~** standard ; **hors ~**

custom-made ; *fig* outstanding, extraordinary.

➤ **série noire** *nf* - **1.** [roman] : **un roman de ~ noire** a detective novel ; **c'est un vrai personnage de ~ noire** he's like something out of a detective novel - **2.** [catastrophes] chapter of accidents.

sérier [9] [serje] *vt* to classify.

sérieusement [serjøzmɑ̃] *adv* seriously.

sérieux, euse [serjø, øz] *adj* - **1.** [grave] serious - **2.** [digne de confiance] reliable ; [client, offre] genuine - **3.** [consciencieux] responsible ; **ce n'est pas ~** it's irresponsible - **4.** [considérable] considerable.

➤ **sérieux** *nm* - **1.** [application] sense of responsibility - **2.** [gravité] seriousness ; **garder son ~** to keep a straight face ; **prendre qqn/qqch au ~** to take sb/sthg seriously ; **se prendre au ~** to take o.s. (too) seriously.

sérigraphie [serigrafi] *nf* silk-screen printing.

serin, e [sərɛ̃, in] *nm, f* - **1.** [oiseau] canary - **2.** *fam* [niais] idiot, twit *Br*.

seriner [3] [sərine] *vt fam* [rabâcher] : **~ qqch à qqn** to drum sthg into sb.

seringue [sərɛ̃g] *nf* syringe.

serment [sermɑ̃] *nm* - **1.** [affirmation solennelle] oath ; **prêter ~** to take an oath ; **sous ~** on *ou* under oath ; **~ d'Hippocrate** Hippocratic oath - **2.** [promesse] vow, pledge.

sermon [sermɔ̃] *nm litt* & *fig* sermon.

sermonner [3] [sermɔne] *vt* to lecture.

SERNAM, Sernam [sernam] (*abr de* Service national de messageries) *nm* rail delivery service, ≃ Red Star® *Br*.

séronégatif, ive [serɔnegatif, iv] *adj* HIV-negative.

séropositif, ive [serɔpozitif, iv] *adj* HIV-positive.

séropositivité [serɔpozitivite] *nf* HIV infection.

serpe [serp] *nf* billhook.

serpent [serpɑ̃] *nm* ZOOL snake ; **~ à sonnette** *ou* **sonnettes** rattlesnake.

➤ **serpent monétaire** *nm* (currency) snake.

serpenter [3] [serpɑ̃te] *vi* to wind.

serpentin [serpɑ̃tɛ̃] *nm* - **1.** [de papier] streamer - **2.** [tuyau] coil.

serpillière [serpijer] *nf* floor cloth.

serpolet [serpɔle] *nm* wild thyme.

serre [ser] *nf* [bâtiment] greenhouse, glasshouse.

➤ **serres** *nfpl* ZOOL talons, claws.

serré, e [sere] *adj* - **1.** [écriture] cramped ; [tissu] closely-woven ; [rangs] serried - **2.** [style] dense, concise - **3.** [vêtement, chaussure] tight - **4.** [discussion] closely argued ; [match] close-fought - **5.** [poing, dents] clenched ; **la gorge ~e** with a lump in one's throat ; **j'en avais le cœur ~** *fig* it was heartbreaking - **6.** [café] strong.

➤ **serré** *adv* : **jouer ~** to be cautious.

serrement [sermɑ̃] *nm* - **1.** [de main] handshake - **2.** [de cœur] anguish - **3.** [de gorge] tightening.

serrer [4] [sere] ◇ *vt* - **1.** [saisir] to grip, to hold tight ; **~ la main à qqn** to shake sb's hand ; **~ qqn dans ses bras** to hug sb - **2.** *fig* [rapprocher] to bring together ; **~ les rangs** to close ranks - **3.** [poing, dents] to clench ; [lèvres] to purse ; *fig* [cœur] to wring - **4.** [suj : vêtement, chaussure] to be too tight for - **5.** [vis, ceinture] to tighten - **6.** [trottoir, bordure] to hug ◇ *vi* AUTOM : **~ à droite/gauche** to keep right/left.

➤ **se serrer** *vp* - **1.** [se blottir] : **se ~ contre** to huddle up to *ou* against ; **se ~ autour de** to crowd *ou* press around - **2.** [se rapprocher] to squeeze up - **3.** [poing] to tighten.

serre-tête [sertet] *nm inv* headband.

serrure [seryr] *nf* lock.

serrurerie [seryrri] *nf* - **1.** [métier] locksmith's trade - **2.** [ouvrage] metalwork.

serrurier [seryrje] *nm* locksmith.

sers, sert *etc* ⊳ servir.

sertir [32] [sertir] *vt* - **1.** [pierre précieuse] to set - **2.** TECHNOL [assujettir] to crimp.

sérum [serɔm] *nm* serum.

servage [servaʒ] *nm* serfdom ; *fig* bondage.

servante [servɑ̃t] *nf* - **1.** [domestique] maidservant - **2.** TECHNOL tool rest.

serve ⊳ serf.

serveur, euse [servœr, øz] *nm, f* - **1.** [de restaurant] waiter (*f* waitress) ; [de bar] barman (*f* barmaid) - **2.** CARTES dealer - **3.** TENNIS server.

➤ **serveur** *nm* INFORM server.

servi, e [servi] *pp* ⊳ servir.

serviable [servjabl] *adj* helpful, obliging.

service [servis] *nm* - **1.** [gén] service ; **être en ~** to be in use, to be set up ; **mettre en ~** to set up ; **hors ~** out of order - **2.** [travail] duty ; **pendant le ~** while on duty ; **être de ~** to be on duty - **3.** [département] department ; **~ de réanimation** intensive care (unit) ; **~ de renseignements** intelligence service ; **~ d'ordre** police and stewards (*at a demonstration*) - **4.** MIL : **~ (militaire)** military *ou* national service - **5.** [aide, assistance] favour *Br*, favor *Am* ; **rendre un ~ à qqn** to do sb a favour *Br ou* favor *Am* ; **rendre ~** to be helpful ; **~ après-vente** after-sales service - **6.** [à table] : **premier/deuxième ~** first/second sitting - **7.** [pourboire] service (charge) ; **~ compris/non compris** service included/not included - **8.** [assortiment - de porcelaine] service, set ; [- de linge] set.

serviette [sɛrvjɛt] *nf* - **1.** [de table] serviette, napkin - **2.** [de toilette] towel ; **~ de bain** bath towel - **3.** [porte-documents] briefcase.

➡ **serviette hygiénique** *nf* sanitary towel *Br ou* napkin *Am*.

serviette-éponge [sɛrvjɛtepɔ̃ʒ] (*pl* **serviettes-éponges**) *nf* terry towel.

servile [sɛrvil] *adj* - **1.** [gén] servile - **2.** [traduction, imitation] slavish.

servir [38] [sɛrvir] ⬦ *vt* - **1.** [gén] to serve ; **~ qqch à qqn** to serve sb sthg, to help sb to sthg ; **qu'est-ce que je vous sers?** what can I get you? - **2.** [avantager] to serve (well), to help ⬦ *vi* - **1.** [avoir un usage] to be useful *ou* of use ; **ça peut toujours/encore ~** it may/may still come in useful - **2.** [être utile] : **~ à qqch/à faire qqch** to be used for sthg/for doing sthg ; **ça ne sert à rien** it's pointless - **3.** [tenir lieu] : **~ de** [personne] to act as ; [chose] to serve as - **4.** [domestique] to be in service - **5.** *MIL & SPORT* to serve - **6.** *CARTES* to deal.

➡ **se servir** *vp* - **1.** [prendre] : **se ~ (de)** to help o.s. (to) ; **servez-vous!** help yourself! - **2.** [utiliser] : **se ~ de qqn/qqch** to use sb/sthg.

serviteur [sɛrvitœr] *nm* servant.

servitude [sɛrvityd] *nf* - **1.** [esclavage] servitude - **2.** (*gén pl*) [contrainte] constraint - **3.** *JUR* easement.

ses ⊳ **son²**.

sésame [sezam] *nm* - **1.** *BOT* sesame - **2.** *fig* [formule magique] : **~ ouvre-toi** open sesame.

session [sesjɔ̃] *nf* - **1.** [d'assemblée] session, sitting - **2.** *UNIV* exam session - **3.** *INFORM* : **ouvrir une ~** to log in *ou* on ; **fermer** *ou* **clore une ~** to log out *ou* off.

set [sɛt] *nm* - **1.** *TENNIS* set - **2.** [napperon] : **~ (de table)** set of table *ou* place mats.

setter [setɛr] *nm* setter.

seuil [sœj] *nm litt & fig* threshold ; **~ de rentabilité** *COMM* breakeven point.

seul, e [sœl] ⬦ *adj* - **1.** [isolé] alone ; **~ à ~** alone (together), privately - **2.** [sans compagnie] alone, by o.s. ; **parler tout ~** to talk to o.s. - **3.** [sans aide] on one's own, by o.s. - **4.** [unique] : **le ~ ...** the only ... ; **un ~ ...** a single ... ; **pas un ~ ...** not one ..., not a single ... - **5.** [esseulé] lonely ⬦ *nm, f* : **le ~** the only one ; **un ~** a single one, only one.

seulement [sœlmɑ̃] *adv* - **1.** [gén] only ; [exclusivement] only, solely - **2.** [même] even.

➡ **non seulement ... mais (encore)** *loc corrélative* not only ... but (also).

sève [sɛv] *nf* - **1.** *BOT* sap - **2.** *fig* [vigueur] vigour *Br*, vigor *Am*.

sévère [sevɛr] *adj* severe.

sévèrement [sevɛrmɑ̃] *adv* severely.

sévérité [severite] *nf* severity.

sévices [sevis] *nmpl sout* ill treatment (*U*).

Séville [sevij] *n* Seville.

sévir [32] [sevir] *vi* - **1.** [gouvernement] to act ruthlessly *ou* severely - **2.** [épidémie, guerre] to rage - **3.** [punir] to give out a punishment.

sevrage [səvraʒ] *nm* - **1.** [d'enfant] weaning - **2.** [de toxicomane] withdrawal.

sevrer [19] [səvre] *vt* to wean ; **~ qqn de** *fig* to deprive sb of.

sexagénaire [sɛksaʒenɛr] ⬦ *nmf* sixty-year-old ⬦ *adj* : **être ~** to be in one's sixties.

sex-appeal [sɛksapil] *nm* sex appeal.

S.Exc (*abr de* **son excellence**) H.E.

sexe [sɛks] *nm* - **1.** [gén] sex ; **le ~ fort/faible** *fam fig* the stronger/weaker sex - **2.** [organe] genitals (*pl*).

sexisme [sɛksism] *nm* sexism.

sexiste [sɛksist] *nmf & adj* sexist.

sexologie [sɛksɔlɔʒi] *nf* sexology.

sexologue [sɛksɔlɔg] *nmf* sexologist.

sex-shop [sɛksʃɔp] (*pl* **sex-shops**) *nm* sex shop.

sextant [sɛkstɑ̃] *nm* sextant.

sextuple [sɛkstypl] ⬦ *nm* : **le ~ de 3** 6 times 3 ⬦ *adj* sixfold.

sexualité [sɛksɥalite] *nf* sexuality.

sexuel, elle [sɛksɥɛl] *adj* sexual.

sexuellement [sɛksɥɛlmɑ̃] *adv* sexually.

sexy [sɛksi] *adj inv fam* sexy.

seyais, seyait *etc* ⊳ **seoir**.

seyant, e [sɛjɑ̃, ɑ̃t] *adj* becoming.

Seychelles [seʃɛl] *nfpl* : **les ~** the Seychelles ; **aux ~** in the Seychelles.

SFIO (*abr de* **Section française de l'internationale ouvrière**) *nf former name of the French socialist party*.

SG *abr de* **secrétaire général**.

SGEN (*abr de* **Syndicat général de l'éducation nationale**) *nm teachers' trade union*.

shah = **schah**.

shaker [ʃekɛr] *nm* cocktail shaker.

shampoing = **shampooing**.

shampooiner = shampouiner.

shampooineur = shampouineur.

shampooing [ʃɑ̃pwɛ̃] *nm* shampoo.

shampouiner, shampooiner [3] [ʃɑ̃pwine] *vt* to shampoo.

shampouineur, euse, shampooineur, euse [ʃɑ̃pwinœr, øz] *nm, f* shampooer.

Shanghai [ʃɑ̃gaj] *n* Shanghai.

shérif [ʃerif] *nm* sheriff.

sherry [ʃeri] *nm* sherry.

shetland [ʃetlɑ̃d] *nm* **- 1.** [laine] Shetland wool **- 2.** [cheval] Shetland pony.

Shetland [ʃetlɑ̃d] *nfpl* : **les ~** the Shetlands.

shooter [3] [ʃute] *vi* to shoot ; **~ dans qqch** *fam* to kick sthg.
➤ **se shooter** *vp fam arg drogue* to shoot up.

shopping [ʃɔpiŋ] *nm* shopping ; **faire du ~** to go (out) shopping.

short [ʃɔrt] *nm* shorts *(pl)*, pair of shorts.

show [ʃo] *nm* show.

show-business [ʃobiznɛs] *nm inv* show business.

si¹ [si] *nm inv* **MUS** B ; [chanté] ti.

si² [si] ◇ *adv* **- 1.** [tellement] so ; **elle est ~ belle** she is so beautiful ; **il roulait ~ vite qu'il a eu un accident** he was driving so fast (that) he had an accident ; **ce n'est pas ~ facile que ça** it's not as easy as that ; **~ vieux qu'il soit** however old he may be, old as he is **- 2.** [oui] yes ; **tu n'aimes pas le café? — ~** don't you like coffee? — yes, I do ◇ *conj* **- 1.** [gén] if ; **~ tu veux, on y va** we'll go if you want ; **~ tu faisais cela, je te détesterais** I would hate you if you did that ; **~ seulement** if only **- 2.** [dans une question indirecte] if, whether ; **dites-moi ~ vous venez** tell me if *ou* whether you're coming ◇ *nm inv* : **il y a toujours des ~ et des mais** there are always ifs and buts.
➤ **si bien que** *loc conj* so that, with the result that.
➤ **si tant est que** *loc conj (+ subjonctif)* providing, provided (that).

SI *nm* **- 1.** (*abr de* **syndicat d'initiative**) tourist office **- 2.** (*abr de* **système international**) SI.

siamois, e [sjamwa, az] *adj* Siamese ; **frères ~, sœurs ~es** **MÉD** Siamese twins ; *fig* inseparable companions.
➤ **Siamois, e** *nm, f vieilli* Siamese person.

Sibérie [siberi] *nf* : **la ~** Siberia.

sibérien, enne [siberjɛ̃, ɛn] *adj* Siberian.
➤ **Sibérien, enne** *nm, f* Siberian.

sibyllin, e [sibilɛ̃, in] *adj* enigmatic.

sic [sik] *adv* sic.

SICAV, Sicav [sikav] (*abr de* **société d'investissement à capital variable**) *nf* **- 1.** [société] unit trust, mutual fund **- 2.** [action] share in a unit trust.

Sicile [sisil] *nf* : **la ~** Sicily.

sicilien, enne [sisiljɛ̃, ɛn] *adj* Sicilian.
➤ **Sicilien, enne** *nm, f* Sicilian.

Sicob [sikɔb] (*abr de* **Salon des industries, du commerce et de l'organisation du bureau**) *nm* : **le ~** annual information technology fair in Paris.

SIDA, Sida [sida] (*abr de* **syndrome immunodéficitaire acquis**) *nm* AIDS.

side-car [sidkar] (*pl* **side-cars**) *nm* sidecar.

sidéen, enne [sideɛ̃, ɛn] *nm, f* person with AIDS.

sidéral, e, aux [sideral, o] *adj* sidereal.

sidérant, e [siderɑ̃, ɑ̃t] *adj fam* staggering.

sidérer [18] [sidere] *vt fam* to stagger.

sidérurgie [sideryrʒi] *nf* **- 1.** [industrie] iron and steel industry **- 2.** [technique] iron and steel metallurgy.

sidérurgique [sideryrʒik] *adj* steel *(avant n)*.

sidérurgiste [sideryrʒist] *nmf* steelworker.

sidologue [sidɔlɔg] *nmf* AIDS specialist.

siècle [sjɛkl] *nm* **- 1.** [cent ans] century ; **l'affaire du ~** the bargain of the century **- 2.** [époque, âge] age ; **le ~ des lumières** the (Age of) Enlightenment ; **le ~ de l'atome** the atomic age **- 3.** *(gén pl) fam* [longue durée] ages *(pl)* ; **ça fait des ~s que ...** it's ages since ...

sied, siéra *etc* ▷ seoir.

siège [sjɛʒ] *nm* **- 1.** [meuble & **POLIT**] seat ; **~ avant/arrière** front/back seat ; **~ éjectable** ejector seat **- 2.** **MIL** siege ; **lever le ~** to lift the siege **- 3.** [d'organisme] headquarters, head office ; **~ social** registered office **- 4.** **MÉD** : **se présenter par le ~** to be in the breech position **- 5.** **JUR** bench.

siéger [22] [sjeʒe] *vi* **- 1.** [juge, assemblée] to sit **- 2.** *littéraire* [mal] to have its seat ; [maladie] to be located.

sien [sjɛ̃] ➤ **le sien** (*f* **la sienne** [lasjɛn], *mpl* **les siens** [lesjɛ̃], *fpl* **les siennes** [lesjɛn]) *pron poss* [d'homme] his ; [de femme] hers ; [de chose, d'animal] its ; **les ~s** his/her family ; **faire des siennes** to be up to one's usual tricks.

sierra [sjera] *nf* sierra.

sieste [sjɛst] *nf* siesta.

sifflant, e [siflɑ̃, ɑ̃t] *adj* [son] whistling ; [voix] hissing ; **LING** sibilant.

sifflement [sifləmɑ̃] *nm* [son] whistling ; [de serpent] hissing.

siffler [3] [sifle] ◇ *vi* to whistle ; [serpent] to

hiss <> *vt* - **1.** [air de musique] to whistle - **2.** [femme] to whistle at - **3.** [chien] to whistle (for) - **4.** [acteur] to boo, to hiss - **5.** *fam* [verre] to knock back.

sifflet [siflɛ] *nm* whistle.
➤ **sifflets** *nmpl* hissing (U), boos.

sifflotement [siflɔtmɑ̃] *nm* whistling.

siffloter [3] [siflɔte] *vi* & *vt* to whistle.

sigle [sigl] *nm* acronym, (set of) initials.

signal, aux [siɲal, o] *nm* - **1.** [geste, son] signal ; ~ **d'alarme** alarm (signal) ; ~ **de détresse** distress signal ; **donner le ~ (de)** to give the signal (for) - **2.** [panneau] sign.

signalement [siɲalmɑ̃] *nm* description.

signaler [3] [siɲale] <> *vt* - **1.** [fait] to point out ; **rien à ~** nothing to report - **2.** [à la police] to denounce <> *vi* [à train, navire] : ~ **à** to signal to.
➤ **se signaler** *vp* : **se ~ par** to become known for, to distinguish o.s. by.

signalétique [siɲaletik] *adj* identifying.

signalisation [siɲalizasjɔ̃] *nf* - **1.** [action] signposting - **2.** [panneaux] signs (pl) ; [au sol] (road) markings (pl) ; *NAVIG* signals (pl).

signataire [siɲatɛr] *nmf* signatory.

signature [siɲatyr] *nf* - **1.** [nom, marque] signature - **2.** [acte] signing.

signe [siɲ] *nm* - **1.** [gén] sign ; **être ~ de** to be a sign of ; **en ~ de** as a sign of ; **être né sous le ~ de** *ASTROL* to be born under the sign of ; **être placé sous le ~ de** *fig* [conférence, transaction] to be marked by ; ~ **avant-coureur** advance indication ; ~ **de ralliement** rallying symbol ; ~ **de reconnaissance** means of recognition ; **~s extérieurs de richesse** outward signs of wealth ; **c'est bon/mauvais ~** it's a good/bad sign ; **donner ~ de vie** to get in touch - **2.** [trait] mark ; ~ **distinctif** characteristic ; ~ **particulier** distinguishing mark.

signer [3] [siɲe] *vt* to sign.
➤ **se signer** *vp* to cross o.s.

signet [siɲɛ] *nm* bookmark *(attached to spine of book)*.

significatif, ive [siɲifikatif, iv] *adj* significant.

signification [siɲifikasjɔ̃] *nf* - **1.** [sens] meaning - **2.** *JUR* service (of documents).

signifier [9] [siɲifje] *vt* - **1.** [vouloir dire] to mean - **2.** [faire connaître] to make known - **3.** *JUR* to serve notice of.

silence [silɑ̃s] *nm* - **1.** [gén] silence ; **garder le ~ (sur)** to remain silent (about) ; ~ **de glace** stony silence ; ~ **de mort** deathly hush ; **passer qqch sous ~** *fig* to avoid mentioning sthg - **2.** *MUS* rest.

silencieusement [silɑ̃sjøzmɑ̃] *adv* in silence, silently.

silencieux, euse [silɑ̃sjø, øz] *adj* - **1.** [lieu, appareil] quiet - **2.** [personne - taciturne] quiet ; [- muet] silent.
➤ **silencieux** *nm* silencer.

silex [silɛks] *nm* flint.

silhouette [silwɛt] *nf* - **1.** [de personne] silhouette ; [de femme] figure ; [d'objet] outline - **2.** *ART* silhouette.

silice [silis] *nf* silica.

siliceux, euse [silisø, øz] *adj* silicious, siliceous.

silicium [silisjɔm] *nm* silicon.

silicone [silikɔn] *nf* silicone.

sillage [sijaʒ] *nm* wake.

sillon [sijɔ̃] *nm* - **1.** [tranchée, ride] furrow - **2.** [de disque] groove.

sillonner [3] [sijɔne] *vt* - **1.** [champ] to furrow - **2.** [ciel] to crisscross.

silo [silo] *nm* silo.

simagrées [simagre] *nfpl* *péj* : **faire des ~** to make a fuss.

simiesque [simjɛsk] *adj* simian.

similaire [similɛr] *adj* similar.

similarité [similarite] *nf* similarity.

simili [simili] <> *nm* - **1.** *fam* [imitation] imitation ; **en ~** imitation *(avant n)* - **2.** [de photogravure] halftone plate *ou* block <> *nf fam* halftone illustration.

similicuir [similikɥir] *nm* imitation leather.

similitude [similityd] *nf* similarity.

simple [sɛ̃pl] <> *adj* - **1.** [gén] simple ; ~ **d'esprit** simple-minded - **2.** [ordinaire] ordinary - **3.** [billet] : **un aller ~** a single ticket <> *nm TENNIS* singles *(sg)*.
➤ **simples** *nmpl* medicinal plants *ou* herbs.

simplement [sɛ̃pləmɑ̃] *adv* simply ; **tout ~** quite simply, just.

simplet, ette [sɛ̃plɛ, ɛt] *adj* - **1.** [personne] simple - **2.** *péj* [raisonnement] simplistic.

simplicité [sɛ̃plisite] *nf* simplicity ; **d'une ~ enfantine** childishly simple.

simplificateur, trice [sɛ̃plifikatœr, tris] *adj* simplifying.

simplification [sɛ̃plifikasjɔ̃] *nf* simplification.

simplifier [9] [sɛ̃plifje] *vt* to simplify.

simplisme [sɛ̃plism] *nm* *péj* oversimplification.

simpliste [sɛ̃plist] *adj* *péj* simplistic.

simulacre [simylakr] *nm* - **1.** [semblant] : **un ~ de** a pretence of, a sham - **2.** [action simulée] enactment.

simulateur, trice [simylatœr, tris] *nm, f* pretender ; [de maladie] malingerer.

➠ **simulateur** *nm* TECHNOL simulator.

simulation [simylasjɔ̃] *nf* - **1.** [gén] simulation - **2.** [comédie] shamming, feigning ; [de maladie] malingering.

simuler [3] [simyle] *vt* - **1.** [gén] to simulate - **2.** [feindre] to feign, to sham.

simultané, e [simyltane] *adj* simultaneous.

simultanéité [simyltaneite] *nf* simultaneousness.

simultanément [simyltanemɑ̃] *adv* simultaneously.

Sinaï [sinaj] *n* : le ~ Sinai ; le mont ~ Mount Sinai.

sincère [sɛ̃sɛr] *adj* sincere.

sincèrement [sɛ̃sɛrmɑ̃] *adv* - **1.** [franchement] honestly, sincerely ; ~ **vôtre** yours sincerely - **2.** [vraiment] really, truly.

sincérité [sɛ̃serite] *nf* sincerity ; **en toute** ~ in all sincerity.

sinécure [sinekyr] *nf* sinecure ; **ce n'est pas une** ~ *fam fig* it's not exactly a cushy job.

sine qua non [sinekwanɔn] *adj* : **condition** ~ prerequisite.

Singapour [sɛ̃gapur] *n* Singapore ; **à** ~ in Singapore.

singe [sɛ̃ʒ] *nm* ZOOL monkey ; [de grande taille] ape.

singer [17] [sɛ̃ʒe] *vt* - **1.** [personne] to mimic, to ape - **2.** [sentiment] to feign.

singerie [sɛ̃ʒri] *nf* - **1.** [grimace] face - **2.** [manières] fuss (U).

singulariser [3] [sɛ̃gylarize] *vt* to draw OU call attention to.

➠ **se singulariser** *vp* to draw OU call attention to o.s.

singularité [sɛ̃gylarite] *nf* - **1.** *littéraire* [bizarrerie] strangeness - **2.** [particularité] peculiarity.

singulier, ère [sɛ̃gylje, ɛr] *adj* - **1.** *sout* [bizarre] strange ; [spécial] uncommon - **2.** GRAM singular - **3.** [d'homme à homme] : **combat** ~ single combat.

➠ **singulier** *nm* GRAM singular.

singulièrement [sɛ̃gyljɛrmɑ̃] *adv* - **1.** *littéraire* [bizarrement] strangely - **2.** [beaucoup, très] particularly.

sinistre [sinistr] ⬦ *nm* - **1.** [catastrophe] disaster - **2.** JUR damage (U) ⬦ *adj* - **1.** [personne, regard] sinister ; [maison, ambiance] gloomy - **2.** (avant n) *péj* [crétin, imbécile] dreadful, terrible.

sinistré, e [sinistre] ⬦ *adj* [région] disaster (avant n), disaster-stricken ; [famille] disaster-stricken ⬦ *nm, f* disaster victim.

sinistrose [sinistroz] *nf* pessimism.

sinologue [sinɔlɔg] *nmf* Sinologist, Chinawatcher.

sinon [sinɔ̃] *conj* - **1.** [autrement] or else, otherwise - **2.** [sauf] except, apart from - **3.** [si ce n'est] if not.

sinueux, euse [sinɥø, øz] *adj* winding ; *fig* tortuous.

sinuosité [sinɥozite] *nf* bend, twist.

sinus [sinys] *nm* - **1.** ANAT sinus - **2.** MATHS sine.

sinusite [sinyzit] *nf* sinusitis (U).

sionisme [sjɔnism] *nm* Zionism.

sioniste [sjɔnist] *nmf & adj* Zionist.

siphon [sifɔ̃] *nm* - **1.** [tube] siphon - **2.** [bouteille] soda siphon.

siphonné, e [sifɔne] *adj fam* [fou] batty, crackers.

siphonner [3] [sifɔne] *vt* to siphon.

sire [sir] *nm* - **1.** HIST lord - **2.** *loc* : **un triste** ~ a sad character.

➠ **Sire** *nm* Sire.

sirène [sirɛn] *nf* siren.

sirocco [sirɔko] *nm* sirocco.

sirop [siro] *nm* syrup ; ~ **d'érable** maple syrup ; ~ **de grenadine** (syrup of) grenadine ; ~ **de menthe** mint cordial ; ~ **d'orgeat** barley water ; ~ **contre la toux** cough mixture *ou* syrup.

siroter [3] [sirote] *vt fam* to sip.

SIRPA, Sirpa [sirpa] (*abr de* **Service d'information et de renseignement du public de l'armée**) *nm French army public information service.*

sirupeux, euse [sirypø, øz] *adj* syrupy.

sis, e [si, siz] *adj* JUR located.

sismique [sismik] *adj* seismic.

sismographe [sismɔgraf] *nm* seismograph.

sismologie [sismɔlɔʒi] *nf* seismology.

site [sit] *nm* - **1.** [emplacement] site ; ~ **archéologique/historique** archaeological/historic site ; ~ **naturel** unspoiled site - **2.** [paysage] beauty spot - **3.** INFORM : ~ **Web** web site, Web site.

sitôt [sito] *adv* : ~ **après** immediately after ; **pas de** ~ not for some time, not for a while ; ~ **arrivé, ...** as soon as I/he *etc* arrived, ... ; ~ **dit, ~ fait** no sooner said than done.

➠ **sitôt que** *loc conj* as soon as.

situation [sitɥasjɔ̃] *nf* - **1.** [position, emplacement] position, location - **2.** [contexte, circonstance] situation ; ~ **de famille** marital status ; **être en** ~ **de faire qqch** to be in a position to do sthg - **3.** [emploi] job, position - **4.** FIN financial statement.

situer [7] [sitɥe] vt - **1.** [maison] to site, to situate ; **bien/mal situé** well/badly situated - **2.** [sur carte] to locate - **3.** fam [personne] to size up.

➤ **se situer** vp [scène] to be set ; [dans classement] to be.

SIVOM, Sivom [sivɔm] (abr de **Syndicat intercommunal à vocation multiple**) nm group of local authorities pooling public services.

six [sis en fin de phrase, si devant consonne ou h aspiré, siz devant voyelle ou h muet] <> adj num six ; **il a ~ ans** he is six (years old) ; **il est ~ heures** it's six (o'clock) ; **le ~ janvier** (on) the sixth of January ; **daté du ~ septembre** dated the sixth of September ; **Charles Six** Charles the Sixth ; **page ~** page six <> nm inv - **1.** [gén] six ; **~ de pique** six of spades - **2.** [adresse] (number) six - **3.** SPORT : **le ~** number six <> pron six ; **ils étaient ~** there were six of them ; **ils sont venus à ~** six (of them) came ; **couper/partager en ~** to cut/divide into six ; **~ par ~** six at a time ; **~ d'entre eux/nous/vous** six of them/us/you ; **cinq sur ~** five out of six.

sixième [sizjɛm] <> adj num sixth <> nmf sixth ; **arriver/se classer ~** to come (in)/to be placed sixth <> nf SCOL ≃ first year ou form Br, ≃ sixth grade Am ; **être en ~** to be in the first year ou form Br, to be in sixth grade Am ; **entrer en ~** to go to secondary school <> nm - **1.** [part] : **le/un ~ de** one/a sixth of ; **cinq ~s** five sixths - **2.** [arrondissement] sixth arrondissement - **3.** [étage] sixth floor Br, seventh floor Am.

sixièmement [sizjɛmmɑ̃] adv sixthly, in (the) sixth place.

six-quatre-deux [siskatdø] ➤ **à la six-quatre-deux** loc adv fam in a slapdash way.

Skaï® [skaj] nm inv leatherette.

skateboard [skɛtbɔrd] nm skateboard.

sketch [skɛtʃ] (pl **sketches**) nm sketch (in a revue etc).

ski [ski] nm - **1.** [objet] ski - **2.** [sport] skiing ; **faire du ~** to ski ; **~ acrobatique/alpin/de fond** freestyle/alpine/cross-country skiing ; **~ nautique** water-skiing.

skier [10] [skje] vi to ski.

skieur, euse [skjœr, øz] nm, f skier.

skipper [skipœr] nm - **1.** [capitaine] skipper - **2.** [barreur] helmsman.

slalom [slalɔm] nm - **1.** SKI slalom ; **~ géant/spécial** giant/special slalom - **2.** [zigzags] : **faire du ~** to zigzag.

slalomer [3] [slalɔme] vi - **1.** SKI to slalom - **2.** [zigzaguer] to zigzag.

slave [slav] adj Slavonic.
➤ **Slave** nmf Slav.

slip [slip] nm briefs (pl) ; **~ de bain** [d'homme] swimming trunks (pl) ; [de femme] bikini bottoms (pl).

s.l.n.d. (abr de **sans lieu ni date**) date and origin unknown.

sloche [slɔʃ] nf Can slush.

slogan [slɔgɑ̃] nm slogan.

slovaque [slɔvak] <> adj Slovak <> nm [langue] Slovak.
➤ **Slovaque** nmf Slovak.

Slovaquie [slɔvaki] nf : **la ~** Slovakia.

slovène [slɔvɛn] <> adj Slovenian <> nm [langue] Slovenian.
➤ **Slovène** nmf Slovenian.

Slovénie [slɔveni] nf : **la ~** Slovenia.

slow [slo] nm slow dance.

SM, S-M (abr de **sado-masochisme**) nm S & M.

SM (abr de **sa majesté**) HM.

SMAG, Smag [smag] (abr de **salaire minimum agricole garanti**) nm guaranteed minimum wage for agricultural workers.

smala(h) [smala] nf - **1.** [de chef arabe] retinue - **2.** fam [famille] brood.

smasher [3] [sma(t)ʃe] vi TENNIS to smash (the ball).

SME (abr de **Système monétaire européen**) nm EMS.

SMIC, Smic [smik] (abr de **salaire minimum interprofessionnel de croissance**) nm index-linked guaranteed minimum wage.

smicard, e [smikar, ard] <> adj minimum-wage-earning <> nm, f minimum-wage earner.

smiley [smaili] nm smiley.

smocks [smɔk] nmpl smocking (U).

smoking [smɔkiŋ] nm dinner jacket, tuxedo Am.

SMUR, Smur [smyr] (abr de **Service médical d'urgence et de réanimation**) nm French ambulance and emergency unit.

SNC (abr de **service non compris**) service not included.

SNCB (abr de **Société nationale des chemins de fer belges**) nf Belgian railways board, ≃ BR Br.

SNCF (abr de **Société nationale des chemins de fer français**) nf French railways board, ≃ BR Br.

SNES, Snes [snɛs] (abr de **Syndicat national de l'enseignement secondaire**) nm secondary school teachers' union.

Sne-sup [snɛsyp] (*abr de* **Syndicat national de l'enseignement supérieur**) *nm university teachers' union*.

SNI (*abr de* **Syndicat national des instituteurs**) *nm primary school teachers' union*.

SNJ (*abr de* **Syndicat national des journalistes**) *nm national union of journalists*.

snob [snɔb] <> *nmf* snob <> *adj* snobbish.

snober [3] [snɔbe] *vt* to snub, to cold-shoulder.

snobinard, e [snɔbinar, ard] *fam péj* <> *adj* rather snobbish <> *nm, f* a bit of a snob.

snobisme [snɔbism] *nm* snobbery, snobbishness.

SNSM (*abr de* **Société nationale de sauvetage en mer**) *nf national sea-rescue association*.

soap opera [sopɔpera] (*pl* **soap operas**), **soap** [sop] (*pl* **soaps**) *nm* soap (opera).

sobre [sɔbr] *adj* **- 1.** [personne] temperate **- 2.** [style] sober ; [décor, repas] simple.

sobrement [sɔbrəmã] *adv* **- 1.** [boire] in moderation **- 2.** [se vêtir] soberly.

sobriété [sɔbrijete] *nf* sobriety.

sobriquet [sɔbrikɛ] *nm* nickname.

soc [sɔk] *nm* ploughshare Br, plowshare Am.

sociabilité [sɔsjabilite] *nf* sociability.

sociable [sɔsjabl] *adj* sociable.

social, e, aux [sɔsjal, o] *adj* **- 1.** [rapports, classe, service] social **- 2.** COMM : **capital ~** share capital ; **raison ~e** company name.
<> **social** *nm* : **le ~** social affairs (*pl*).

social-démocrate, sociale-démocrate [sɔsjaldemɔkrat] (*mpl* **sociaux-démocrates** [sɔsjodemɔkrat], *fpl* **sociales-démocrates**) <> *nmf* social democrat <> *adj* social democratic.

socialement [sɔsjalmã] *adv* socially.

socialisation [sɔsjalizasjɔ̃] *nf* **- 1.** [développement social] socialization **- 2.** POLIT nationalization.

socialiser [3] [sɔsjalize] *vt* **- 1.** [enfant] to socialize **- 2.** POLIT to nationalize.

socialisme [sɔsjalism] *nm* socialism.

socialiste [sɔsjalist] *nmf* & *adj* socialist.

sociétaire [sɔsjetɛr] *nmf* member.

société [sɔsjete] *nf* **- 1.** [communauté, classe sociale, groupe] society ; **en ~** in society ; **la haute ~** high society ; **~ secrète** secret society **- 2.** SPORT club **- 3.** [présence] company, society **- 4.** COMM company, firm ; **~ de bourse** securities house, brokerage firm ; **~ mère** parent company ; **~ en participation** joint-venture

company ; **~ de personnes** partnership, joint-stock company Am.

socioculturel, elle [sɔsjɔkyltyrɛl] *adj* social and cultural.

socio-économique [sɔsjɔekɔnɔmik] *adj* socioeconomic.

sociologie [sɔsjɔlɔʒi] *nf* sociology.

sociologique [sɔsjɔlɔʒik] *adj* sociological.

sociologue [sɔsjɔlɔg] *nmf* sociologist.

socioprofessionnel, elle [sɔsjɔprɔfesjɔnɛl] *adj* socioprofessional.

socle [sɔkl] *nm* **- 1.** [de statue] plinth, pedestal **- 2.** [de lampe] base **- 3.** GÉOGR : **~ continental** continental shelf.

socquette [sɔkɛt] *nf* ankle *ou* short sock.

soda [sɔda] *nm* fizzy drink.

sodium [sɔdjɔm] *nm* sodium.

sodomie [sɔdɔmi] *nf* buggery, sodomy.

sodomiser [3] [sɔdɔmize] *vt* to sodomize.

sœur [sœr] *nf* **- 1.** [gén] sister ; **grande/petite ~** big/little sister ; **~ de lait** foster sister **- 2.** RELIG nun, sister.

sofa [sɔfa] *nm* sofa.

Sofia [sɔfja] *n* Sofia.

SOFRES, Sofres [sɔfrɛs] (*abr de* **Société française d'enquête par sondages**) *nf French opinion poll company*.

software [sɔftwɛr] *nm* software.

soi [swa] *pron pers* oneself ; **chacun pour ~** every man for himself ; **en ~** in itself, per se ; **cela va de ~** that goes without saying ; **il va de ~ que** it goes without saying that.
<> **chez soi** *loc adv* at home ; **se sentir chez ~** to feel at home.
<> **soi-même** *pron pers* oneself.

soi-disant [swadizã] <> *adj inv* (*avant n*) so-called <> *adv fam* supposedly.

soie [swa] *nf* **- 1.** [textile] silk ; **en ~** silk ; **~ grège** raw silk ; **~ sauvage** wild silk **- 2.** [poil] bristle.

soierie [swari] *nf* **- 1.** (*gén pl*) [textile] silk **- 2.** [industrie] silk trade.

soif [swaf] *nf* thirst ; **~ (de)** *fig* thirst (for), craving (for) ; **avoir ~** to be thirsty ; **étancher sa ~** to quench one's thirst ; **jusqu'à plus ~** to excess ; *fig* until one has had one's fill.

soigné, e [swaɲe] *adj* **- 1.** [travail] meticulous **- 2.** [personne] well-groomed ; [jardin, mains] well-cared-for **- 3.** *fam fig* [cuite, raclée] awful, massive.

soigner [3] [swaɲe] *vt* **- 1.** [suj : médecin] to treat ; [suj : infirmière, parent] to nurse **- 2.** [invités, jardin, mains] to look after **- 3.** [travail, présentation] to take care over.

➤ **se soigner** *vp* to take care of o.s., to look after o.s.

soigneur [swaɲœr] *nm SPORT* trainer ; *BOXE* second.

soigneusement [swaɲøzmã] *adv* carefully.

soigneux, euse [swaɲø, øz] *adj* - **1.** [personne] tidy, neat - **2.** [travail] careful ; ~ **de** careful with.

soin [swɛ̃] *nm* - **1.** [attention] care ; **avoir** *OU* **prendre ~ de** to take care of, to look after ; **avoir** *OU* **prendre ~ de faire qqch** to be sure to do sthg ; **aux bons ~s de** in the care of, in the hands of ; **avec ~** carefully ; **sans ~** [procéder] carelessly ; [travail] careless ; **être aux petits ~s pour qqn** *fig* to wait on sb hand and foot - **2.** [souci] concern.

➤ **soins** *nmpl* care *(U)* ; **les premiers ~s** first aid *(sg)*.

soir [swar] *nm* evening ; **demain ~** tomorrow evening *OU* night ; **le ~** in the evening ; **à ce ~!** see you tonight!

soirée [sware] *nf* - **1.** [soir] evening ; **en ~** *CIN* & *THÉÂTRE* evening *(avant n)* - **2.** [réception] party ; **de ~** evening *(avant n)* ; **charmante ~!** *iron* wonderful evening!

sois ▷ être.

soit¹ [swat] *adv* so be it.

soit² [swa] ◇ *vb* ▷ être ◇ *conj* - **1.** [c'est-à-dire] in other words, that is to say - **2.** *MATHS* [étant donné] : ~ **une droite AB** given a straight line AB.

➤ **soit ... soit** *loc corrélative* either ... or.

➤ **soit que ... soit que** *loc corrélative (+ subjonctif)* whether ... or (whether).

soixantaine [swasɑ̃tɛn] *nf* - **1.** [nombre] : **une ~ (de)** about sixty, sixty-odd - **2.** [âge] : **avoir la ~** to be in one's sixties.

soixante [swasɑ̃t] ◇ *adj num* sixty ; **les années ~** the Sixties ◇ *nm* sixty ; *voir aussi* **six.**

soixante-dix [swasɑ̃tdis] ◇ *adj num* seventy ; **les années ~** the Seventies ◇ *nm* seventy ; *voir aussi* **six.**

soixante-dixième [swasɑ̃tdizjɛm] *adj num, nm OU nmf* seventieth ; *voir aussi* **sixième.**

soixante-huitard, e [swasɑ̃tɥitar, ard] ◇ *adj* of May 1968 ◇ *nm, f person who participated in the events of May 1968.*

soixantième [swasɑ̃tjɛm] *adj num, nm OU nmf* sixtieth ; *voir aussi* **sixième.**

soja [sɔʒa] *nm* soya.

sol [sɔl] *nm* - **1.** [terre] ground - **2.** [de maison] floor - **3.** [territoire] soil - **4.** *MUS* G ; [chanté] so.

solaire [sɔlɛr] *adj* - **1.** [énergie, four] solar - **2.** [crème] sun *(avant n).*

solarium [sɔlarjɔm] *nm* solarium.

soldat [sɔlda] *nm* - **1.** *MIL* soldier ; [grade] private ; **le ~ inconnu** the Unknown Soldier - **2.** [jouet] (toy) soldier ; ~ **de plomb** tin soldier, toy soldier.

solde [sɔld] ◇ *nm* - **1.** [de compte, facture] balance ; ~ **créditeur/débiteur** credit/debit balance - **2.** [rabais] : **en ~** [acheter] in a sale ◇ *nf MIL* pay ; **à la ~ de qqn** *fig* in the pay of sb.

➤ **soldes** *nmpl* sales.

solder [3] [sɔlde] *vt* - **1.** [compte] to close - **2.** [marchandises] to sell off.

➤ **se solder** *vp* : **se ~ par** *FIN* to show ; *fig* [aboutir] to end in.

soldeur, euse [sɔldœr, øz] *nm, f buyer and seller of discount goods.*

sole [sɔl] *nf* sole ; ~ **meunière** *sole coated with flour and fried in butter.*

solécisme [sɔlesism] *nm* solecism.

soleil [sɔlɛj] *nm* - **1.** [astre, motif] sun ; ~ **couchant/levant** setting/rising sun ; **sous un ~ de plomb** *fig* in the blazing sun - **2.** [lumière, chaleur] sun, sunlight ; **au ~** in the sun ; **en plein ~** right in the sun ; **il fait (du) ~** it's sunny ; **prendre le ~** to sunbathe - **3.** [tournesol] sunflower.

solennel, elle [sɔlanɛl] *adj* - **1.** [cérémonieux] ceremonial - **2.** [grave] solemn - **3.** *péj* [pompeux] pompous.

solennellement [sɔlanɛlmã] *adv* - **1.** [avec importance] ceremonially - **2.** [avec sérieux] solemnly.

solennité [sɔlanite] *nf* - **1.** [gravité] solemnity - **2.** [raideur] stiffness, formality - **3.** [fête] special occasion.

Solex® [sɔlɛks] *nm* ≃ moped.

solfège [sɔlfɛʒ] *nm* : **apprendre le ~** to learn the rudiments of music.

solfier [9] [sɔlfje] *vt* to sol-fa.

solidaire [sɔlidɛr] *adj* - **1.** [lié] : **être ~ de qqn** to be behind sb, to show solidarity with sb - **2.** [relié] interdependent, integral.

solidariser [3] [sɔlidarize] ➤ **se solidariser** *vp* : **se ~ (avec)** to show solidarity (with).

solidarité [sɔlidarite] *nf* [entraide] solidarity ; **par ~** [se mettre en grève] in sympathy.

solide [sɔlid] ◇ *adj* - **1.** [état, corps] solid - **2.** [construction] solid, sturdy - **3.** [personne] sturdy, robust ; ~ **sur ses jambes** steady on one's feet - **4.** [argument] solid, sound - **5.** [relation] stable, strong ◇ *nm* solid ; **il nous faut du ~** *fig* we need something solid *OU* concrete.

solidement [sɔlidmã] *adv* - **1.** [gén] firmly - **2.** [attaché] firmly, securely.

solidifier [9] [sɔlidifje] *vt* - **1.** [ciment, eau] to solidify - **2.** [structure] to reinforce.
➡ **se solidifier** *vp* to solidify.

solidité [sɔlidite] *nf* - **1.** [de matière, construction] solidity - **2.** [de mariage] stability, strength - **3.** [de raisonnement, d'argument] soundness.

soliloque [sɔlilɔk] *nm sout* soliloquy.

soliste [sɔlist] *nmf* soloist.

solitaire [sɔliter] ◇ *adj* - **1.** [de caractère] solitary - **2.** [esseulé, retiré] lonely ◇ *nmf* [personne] loner, recluse ◇ *nm* [jeu, diamant] solitaire.

solitude [sɔlityd] *nf* - **1.** [isolement] loneliness - **2.** [retraite] solitude.

solive [sɔliv] *nf* joist.

sollicitation [sɔlisitasjɔ̃] *nf* (*gén pl*) entreaty.

solliciter [3] [sɔlisite] *vt* - **1.** [demander - entretien, audience] to request ; [- attention, intérêt] to seek ; ~ **qqch de qqn** to ask sb for sthg, to seek sthg from sb - **2.** [s'intéresser à] : **être sollicité** to be in demand - **3.** [faire appel à] : ~ **qqn pour faire qqch** to appeal to sb to do sthg.

sollicitude [sɔlisityd] *nf* solicitude, concern.

solo [sɔlo] ◇ *nm* solo ; **en ~** solo ◇ *adj* solo (*avant n*).

solstice [sɔlstis] *nm* : ~ **d'été/d'hiver** summer/winter solstice.

solubilité [sɔlybilite] *nf* solubility.

soluble [sɔlybl] *adj* - **1.** [matière] soluble ; [café] instant - **2.** *fig* [problème] solvable.

soluté [sɔlyte] *nm* solution.

solution [sɔlysjɔ̃] *nf* - **1.** [résolution] solution, answer ; **chercher/trouver la ~** to seek/to find the solution, to seek/to find the answer ; ~ **de facilité** easy answer, easy way out - **2.** [liquide] solution.
➡ **solution de continuité** *nf* break ; **sans ~ de continuité** without a break.

solutionner [3] [sɔlysjɔne] *vt* to solve.

solvabilité [sɔlvabilite] *nf* solvency.

solvable [sɔlvabl] *adj* solvent, creditworthy.

solvant [sɔlvɑ̃] *nm* solvent.

somali = somalien.

Somalie [sɔmali] *nf* : **la ~** Somalia.

somalien, enne [sɔmaljɛ̃, ɛn], **somali, e** [sɔmali] *adj* Somali.
➡ **Somalien, enne, Somali, e** *nm, f* Somali.

sombre [sɔ̃br] *adj* - **1.** [couleur, costume, pièce] dark - **2.** *fig* [pensées, avenir] dark, gloomy - **3.** *fig* [complot] murky - **4.** (*avant n*) *fam* [profond] : **c'est un ~ crétin** he's a prize idiot.

sombrer [3] [sɔ̃bre] *vi* to sink ; ~ **dans** *fig* to sink into.

sommaire [sɔmer] ◇ *adj* - **1.** [explication] brief - **2.** [exécution] summary - **3.** [installation] basic ◇ *nm* summary.

sommairement [sɔmɛrmɑ̃] *adv* - **1.** [expliquer] briefly - **2.** [délibérer] summarily - **3.** [peu - vêtu] scantily ; [- meublé] basically.

sommation [sɔmasjɔ̃] *nf* - **1.** [assignation] summons (*sg*) - **2.** [ordre - de payer] demand ; [- de se rendre] warning.

somme [sɔm] ◇ *nf* - **1.** [addition] total, sum ; **faire la ~ de plusieurs choses** to add up several things - **2.** [d'argent] sum, amount - **3.** [ouvrage] overview ◇ *nm* nap.
➡ **en somme** *loc adv* in short.
➡ **somme toute** *loc adv* when all's said and done.

sommeil [sɔmɛj] *nm* sleep ; **avoir ~** to be sleepy ; **tomber de ~** to be asleep on one's feet ; **dormir d'un ~ de plomb** *fig* to be in a deep sleep.

sommeiller [4] [sɔmeje] *vi* - **1.** [personne] to doze - **2.** *fig* [qualité] to be dormant.

sommelier, ère [sɔməlje, ɛr] *nm, f* wine waiter (*f* wine waitress).

sommer [3] [sɔme] *vt* : ~ **qqn de faire qqch** *sout* to order sb to do sthg.

sommes ➡ être.

sommet [sɔme] *nm* - **1.** [de montagne] summit, top - **2.** *fig* [de hiérarchie] top ; [de perfection] height ; **conférence au ~** summit (meeting *ou* conference) - **3.** GÉOM apex.

sommier [sɔmje] *nm* base, bed base.

sommité [sɔmite] *nf* - **1.** [personne] leading light - **2.** BOT head.

somnambule [sɔmnɑ̃byl] ◇ *nmf* sleepwalker ◇ *adj* : **être ~** to be a sleepwalker.

somnifère [sɔmnifer] *nm* sleeping pill.

somnolence [sɔmnɔlɑ̃s] *nf* sleepiness, drowsiness.

somnolent, e [sɔmnɔlɑ̃, ɑ̃t] *adj* [personne] sleepy, drowsy ; *fig* [vie] dull ; *fig* [économie] sluggish.

somnoler [3] [sɔmnɔle] *vi* to doze.

somptueusement [sɔ̃ptɥøzmɑ̃] *adv* sumptuously, lavishly.

somptueux, euse [sɔ̃ptɥø, øz] *adj* sumptuous, lavish.

somptuosité [sɔ̃ptɥozite] *nf* lavishness (U).

son¹ [sɔ̃] *nm* - **1.** [bruit] sound ; **au ~ de** to the sound of ; ~ **et lumière** son et lumière - **2.** [céréale] bran.

son² [sɔ̃] (*f* **sa** [sa], *pl* **ses** [se]) *adj poss* - **1.** [possesseur défini - homme] his ; [- femme] her ; [- chose, animal] its ; **il aime ~ père** he loves his father ; **elle aime ses parents** she loves her parents ; **la ville a perdu ~ charme** the town has lost its charm - **2.** [possesseur indéfini] one's ; [après «chacun», «tout le monde» etc] his/her, their.

sonar [sɔnar] *nm* sonar.

sonate [sɔnat] *nf* sonata.

sondage [sɔ̃daʒ] *nm* - **1.** [enquête] poll, survey ; **~ d'opinion** opinion poll - **2.** TECHNOL drilling - **3.** MÉD probing.

sonde [sɔ̃d] *nf* - **1.** MÉTÉOR sonde ; [spatiale] probe - **2.** MÉD probe - **3.** NAVIG sounding line - **4.** TECHNOL drill.

sondé, e [sɔ̃de] *nm, f* poll respondent.

sonder [3] [sɔ̃de] *vt* - **1.** MÉD & NAVIG to sound - **2.** [terrain] to drill - **3.** *fig* [opinion, personne] to sound out.

sondeur, euse [sɔ̃dœr, øz] *nm, f* pollster. ◆ **sondeur** *nm* TECHNOL sounder.

songe [sɔ̃ʒ] *nm littéraire* dream ; **en ~** in a dream.

songer [17] [sɔ̃ʒe] ◇ *vt* : **~ que** to consider that ◇ *vi* : **~ à** to think about.

songeur, euse [sɔ̃ʒœr, øz] *adj* pensive, thoughtful.

sonnant, e [sɔnɑ̃, ɑ̃t] *adj* : **à six heures ~es** at six o'clock sharp.

sonné, e [sɔne] *adj* - **1.** [passé] : **il est trois heures ~es** it's gone three o'clock ; **il a quarante ans bien ~s** *fam fig* he's the wrong side of forty - **2.** *fig* [étourdi] groggy - **3.** *fam fig* [fou] cracked.

sonner [3] [sɔne] ◇ *vt* - **1.** [cloche] to ring - **2.** [retraite, alarme] to sound - **3.** [domestique] to ring for - **4.** *fam fig* [siffler] : **je ne t'ai pas sonné!** who asked you! ◇ *vi* - **1.** [gén] to ring ; **~ chez qqn** to ring sb's bell ; **~ faux** to be out of tune ; *fig* to ring false - **2.** [jouer] : **~ de** to sound.

sonnerie [sɔnri] *nf* - **1.** [bruit] ringing - **2.** [mécanisme] striking mechanism - **3.** [signal] call.

sonnet [sɔnɛ] *nm* sonnet.

sonnette [sɔnɛt] *nf* bell.

sono [sɔno] *nf fam* [de salle] P.A. (system) ; [de discothèque] sound system.

sonore [sɔnɔr] *adj* - **1.** CIN & PHYS sound (*avant n*) - **2.** [voix, rire] ringing, resonant - **3.** [salle] resonant.

sonorisation [sɔnɔrizasjɔ̃] *nf* - **1.** [action - de film] addition of the soundtrack ; [- de salle] wiring for sound - **2.** [matériel - de salle] public address system, P.A. (system) ; [- de discothèque] sound system.

sonoriser [3] [sɔnɔrize] *vt* - **1.** [film] to add the soundtrack to - **2.** [salle] to wire for sound.

sonorité [sɔnɔrite] *nf* - **1.** [de piano, voix] tone - **2.** [de salle] acoustics (*pl*).

sont ▷ être.

sophisme [sɔfism] *nm* sophism.

sophistication [sɔfistikasjɔ̃] *nf* sophistication.

sophistiqué, e [sɔfistike] *adj* sophisticated.

soporifique [sɔpɔrifik] ◇ *adj* soporific ◇ *nm* sleeping drug, soporific.

soprano [sɔprano] (*pl* **sopranos** OU **soprani** [sɔprani]) *nm* OU *nmf* soprano.

sorbet [sɔrbɛ] *nm* sorbet.

sorbetière [sɔrbətjɛr] *nf* ice-cream maker.

sorbier [sɔrbje] *nm* sorb, service tree.

Sorbonne [sɔrbɔn] *nf* : **la ~** the Sorbonne (*highly respected Paris university*).

LA SORBONNE

The Sorbonne is the oldest university in Paris. It includes the arts and law faculties. It is also known as 'Paris IV'. The term 'la Sorbonne nouvelle' refers to the arts faculty at Censier, also known as 'Paris III'.

---

sorcellerie [sɔrsɛlri] *nf* witchcraft, sorcery.

sorcier, ère [sɔrsje, ɛr] ◇ *nm, f* sorcerer (*f* witch) ◇ *adj* : **ce n'est pas ~** *fig* there's no magic involved.

sordide [sɔrdid] *adj* squalid ; *fig* sordid.

Sorlingues [sɔrlɛ̃g] *nfpl* : **les (îles) ~** the Scilly Isles.

sornettes [sɔrnɛt] *nfpl* nonsense (*U*).

sors ▷ sortir.

sort [sɔr] *nm* - **1.** [maléfice] spell ; **jeter un ~ (à qqn)** to cast a spell (on sb) - **2.** [destinée] fate ; **faire un ~ à qqch** *fam fig* to polish sthg off - **3.** [condition] lot - **4.** [hasard] : **le ~** fate ; **tirer au ~** to draw lots.

sortable [sɔrtabl] *adj* presentable ; **tu n'es pas ~!** I can't take you anywhere!

sortant, e [sɔrtɑ̃, ɑ̃t] *adj* - **1.** [numéro] winning - **2.** [président, directeur] outgoing (*avant n*).

sorte [sɔrt] ◇ *nf* sort, kind ; **une ~ de** a sort of, a kind of ; **toutes ~s de** all kinds of, all sorts of ; **de la ~** in that way, in that manner ; **de telle ~ que** so that, in such a way that ; **en quelque ~** in a way, as it were ; **faire en ~ que** to see to it that ◇ *vb* ▷ sortir.

sortie [sɔrti] *nf* - **1.** [issue] exit, way out ; [d'eau, d'air] outlet ; **~ d'autoroute** motorway junction OU exit ; **~ de secours** emergency exit - **2.** [départ] : **c'est la ~ de l'école** it's hometime ; **à la ~ du travail** when work finishes, after work **- 3.** [de produit] launch, launching ; [de disque] release ; [de livre] publication **- 4.** *(gén pl)* [dépense] outgoings *(pl)*, expenditure *(U)* **- 5.** [excursion] outing ; [au cinéma, au restaurant] evening *ou* night out ; **faire une ~** to go out **- 6.** MIL sortie **- 7.** [écoulement - de liquide, gaz] escape **- 8.** INFORM : **~ imprimante** printout ; **~ papier** hard copy.

sortie-de-bain [sɔrtidbɛ̃] *(pl* **sorties-de-bain***) nf* bathrobe.

sortilège [sɔrtilɛʒ] *nm* spell.

sortir [43] [sɔrtir] ◇ *vi (aux : être)* **- 1.** [de la maison, du bureau etc] to leave, to go/come out ; **~ de** to go/come out of, to leave **- 2.** [pour se distraire] to go out **- 3.** *fig* [quitter] : **~ de** [réserve, préjugés] to shed **- 4.** *fig* [de maladie] : **~ de** to get over, to recover from ; [coma] to come out of **- 5.** [film, livre, produit] to come out ; [disque] to be released **- 6.** [au jeu - carte, numéro] to come up **- 7.** [s'écarter de] : **~ de** [sujet] to get away from ; [légalité, compétence] to be outside **- 8.** *loc* : **~ de l'ordinaire** to be out of the ordinary ; **ça m'est complètement sorti de la tête** it went clean out of my mind ; **d'où il sort, celui-là?** where did HE spring from? ◇ *vt (aux : avoir)* **- 1.** [gén] : **~ qqch (de)** to take sthg out (of) **- 2.** [de situation difficile] to get out, to extract **- 3.** [produit] to launch ; [disque] to bring out, to release ; [livre] to bring out, to publish **- 4.** *fam* [bêtise] to come up with.

◆ **se sortir** *vp fig* [de pétrin] to get out ; **s'en ~** [en réchapper] to come out of it ; [y arriver] to get through it.

SOS *nm* SOS ; **lancer un ~** to send out an SOS.

sosie [sɔzi] *nm* double.

sot, sotte [so, sɔt] ◇ *adj* silly, foolish ◇ *nm, f* fool.

sottement [sɔtmɑ̃] *adv* stupidly, foolishly.

sottise [sɔtiz] *nf* stupidity *(U)*, foolishness *(U)* ; **dire/faire une ~** to say/do something stupid.

sottisier [sɔtizje] *nm collection of howlers.*

sou [su] *nm* : **être sans le ~** to be penniless ; **je n'ai pas le premier ~ pour acheter une voiture** I really can't afford a car.

◆ **sous** *nmpl fam* money *(U)* ; **être près de ses ~s** to be tightfisted ; **parler gros ~s** to talk big money.

souahéli = swahili.

soubassement [subasmɑ̃] *nm* base.

soubresaut [subrəso] *nm* **- 1.** [de voiture] jolt **- 2.** [de personne] start.

soubrette [subrɛt] *nf* maid.

souche [suʃ] *nf* **- 1.** [d'arbre] stump ; **dormir comme une ~** *fig* to sleep like a log **- 2.** [de carnet] counterfoil, stub **- 3.** [de famille] founder ; **de vieille ~** of old stock **- 4.** LING root.

souci [susi] *nm* **- 1.** [tracas] worry ; **se faire du ~** to worry **- 2.** [préoccupation] concern ; **c'est le dernier** *ou* **le cadet de mes ~s** that's the least of my worries **- 3.** [fleur] marigold.

soucier [9] [susje] ◆ **se soucier** *vp* : **se ~ de** to care about.

soucieux, euse [susjø, øz] *adj* **- 1.** [préoccupé] worried, concerned **- 2.** [concerné] : **être ~ de qqch/de faire qqch** to be concerned about sthg/about doing sthg.

soucoupe [sukup] *nf* **- 1.** [assiette] saucer **- 2.** [vaisseau] : **~ volante** flying saucer.

soudain, e [sudɛ̃, ɛn] *adj* sudden.
◆ **soudain** *adv* suddenly, all of a sudden.

soudainement [sudɛnmɑ̃] *adv* suddenly.

Soudan [sudɑ̃] *nm* : **le ~** the Sudan ; **au ~** in the Sudan.

soudanais, e [sudanɛ, ɛz] *adj* Sudanese.
◆ **Soudanais, e** *nm, f* Sudanese person.

soude [sud] *nf* soda ; **~ caustique** caustic soda.

souder [3] [sude] *vt* **- 1.** TECHNOL to weld, to solder **- 2.** MÉD to knit **- 3.** *fig* [unir] to bind together.

soudeur, euse [sudœr, øz] *nm, f* [personne] welder, solderer.
◆ **soudeuse** *nf* [machine] welding machine.

soudoyer [13] [sudwaje] *vt* to bribe.

soudure [sudyr] *nf* **- 1.** TECHNOL welding ; [résultat] weld ; **faire la ~** *fig* to bridge the gap **- 2.** MÉD knitting.

souffert, e [sufɛr, ɛrt] *pp* ▷ **souffrir**.

souffle [sufl] *nm* **- 1.** [respiration] breathing ; [expiration] puff, breath ; **un ~ d'air** *fig* a breath of air, a puff of wind **- 2.** *fig* [inspiration] inspiration **- 3.** [d'explosion] blast **- 4.** MÉD : **~ au cœur** heart murmur **- 5.** *loc* : **avoir le ~ coupé** to have one's breath taken away ; **couper le ~ à qqn** to take sb's breath away ; **retenir son ~** to hold one's breath.

soufflé, e [sufle] *adj* **- 1.** CULIN soufflé *(avant n)* **- 2.** *fam fig* [étonné] flabbergasted.
◆ **soufflé** *nm* soufflé ; **~ au fromage** cheese soufflé.

souffler [3] [sufle] ◇ *vt* **- 1.** [bougie] to blow out **- 2.** [verre] to blow **- 3.** [vitre] to blow out, to shatter **- 4.** [chuchoter] : **~ qqch à qqn** to whisper sthg to sb **- 5.** *fam* [prendre] : **~ qqch à qqn** to pinch sthg from sb ◇ *vi* **- 1.** [gén] to blow **- 2.** [respirer] to puff, to pant.

soufflerie [suflɔri] nf - **1.** [d'orgue] bellows (sg) - **2.** AÉRON wind tunnel.

soufflet [suflɛ] nm - **1.** [instrument] bellows (sg) - **2.** [de train] connecting corridor, concertina vestibule - **3.** COUTURE gusset - **4.** littéraire [claque] slap.

souffleur, euse [suflœr, øz] nm, f THÉÂTRE prompt.

➡ **souffleur** nm [de verre] blower.

➡ **souffleuse** nf : **souffleuse (à neige)** snowblower.

souffrance [sufrɑ̃s] nf suffering.

souffrant, e [sufrɑ̃, ɑ̃t] adj poorly.

souffre-douleur [sufrɔdulœr] nm inv whipping boy.

souffreteux, euse [sufrɔtø, øz] adj sickly.

souffrir [34] [sufrir] ◇ vi to suffer ; ~ **de** to suffer from ; ~ **du dos/cœur** to have back/heart problems ◇ vt - **1.** [ressentir] to suffer - **2.** littéraire [supporter] to stand, to bear.

soufi [sufi] adj inv Sufic.

➡ **Soufi** nm Sufi.

soufisme [sufism] nm Sufism.

soufre [sufr] nm sulphur Br, sulfur Am ; **sentir le ~** fig to smack of heresy.

souhait [swɛ] nm wish ; **tous nos ~s de** our best wishes for ; **à ~** to perfection ; **à tes/vos ~s!** bless you!

souhaitable [swetabl] adj desirable ; **il est ~ que** (+ subjonctif) it is desirable that ...

souhaiter [4] [swete] vt : ~ **qqch** to wish for sthg ; ~ **faire qqch** to hope to do sthg ; ~ **qqch à qqn** to wish sb sthg ; ~ **à qqn de faire qqch** to hope that sb does sthg ; **souhaiter que ...** (+ subjonctif) to hope that ...

souiller [3] [suje] vt littéraire [salir] to soil ; fig & sout to sully.

souillon [sujɔ̃] nf péj slut.

souillure [sujyr] nf littéraire - **1.** (gén pl) [déchet] waste (U) - **2.** fig [morale] stain.

souk [suk] nm souk ; fam fig chaos.

soul [sul] nf inv & adj inv MUS soul.

soûl, e, saoul, e [su, sul] adj drunk ; **être ~ de** fig to be drunk on.

➡ **soûl** nm : **tout mon/son ~** fig to my/his/her heart's content.

soulagement [sulaʒmɑ̃] nm relief.

soulager [17] [sulaʒe] vt - **1.** [gén] to relieve - **2.** [véhicule] to lighten.

➡ **se soulager** vp - **1.** [se libérer] to find relief - **2.** [satisfaire un besoin naturel] to relieve o.s.

soûler, saouler [3] [sule] vt - **1.** fam [enivrer] : ~ **qqn** to get sb drunk ; fig to intoxicate sb - **2.** fig & péj [de plaintes] : ~ **qqn** to bore sb silly.

➡ **se soûler** vp fam to get drunk.

soûlerie [sulri] nf drinking spree.

soulèvement [sulevmɑ̃] nm uprising.

soulever [19] [sulve] vt - **1.** [fardeau, poids] to lift ; [rideau] to raise - **2.** fig [question] to raise, to bring up - **3.** fig [enthousiasme] to generate, to arouse ; [tollé] to stir up ; ~ **qqn contre** to stir sb up against - **4.** [foule] to stir.

➡ **se soulever** vp - **1.** [s'élever] to raise o.s., to lift o.s. - **2.** [se révolter] to rise up.

soulier [sulje] nm shoe ; **être dans ses petits ~s** fig to feel awkward.

souligner [3] [suliɲe] vt - **1.** [par un trait] to underline - **2.** fig [insister sur] to underline, to emphasize - **3.** [mettre en valeur] to emphasize.

soumets ▷ soumettre.

soumettre [84] [sumɛtr] vt - **1.** [astreindre] : ~ **qqn à** to subject sb to - **2.** [ennemi, peuple] to subjugate - **3.** [projet, problème] : ~ **qqch (à)** to submit sthg (to).

➡ **se soumettre** vp : **se ~ (à)** to submit (to).

soumis, e [sumi, iz] ◇ pp ▷ soumettre ◇ adj submissive.

soumission [sumisjɔ̃] nf submission.

soupape [supap] nf valve ; ~ **de sûreté** safety valve.

soupçon [supsɔ̃] nm - **1.** [suspicion, intuition] suspicion ; **être au-dessus/à l'abri de tout ~** to be above/free from all suspicion - **2.** fig [quantité] : **un ~ de** a hint of.

soupçonner [3] [supsɔne] vt [suspecter] to suspect ; ~ **qqn de qqch/de faire qqch** to suspect sb of sthg/of doing sthg ; ~ **que** (+ subjonctif) to suspect that.

soupçonneux, euse [supsɔnø, øz] adj suspicious.

soupe [sup] nf - **1.** CULIN soup ; ~ **à l'oignon** onion soup ; ~ **populaire** soup kitchen ; **être ~ au lait** fig to have a quick temper ; **cracher dans la ~** fig to bite the hand that feeds - **2.** fam fig [neige] slush.

soupente [supɑ̃t] nf cupboard under the stairs.

souper [3] [supe] ◇ nm supper ◇ vi to have supper ; **en avoir soupé de qqch/de faire qqch** fam fig to be sick and tired of sthg/of doing sthg.

soupeser [19] [supɔze] vt - **1.** [poids] to feel the weight of - **2.** fig [évaluer] to weigh up.

soupière [supjɛr] nf tureen.

soupir [supir] nm - **1.** [souffle] sigh ; **pousser un ~** to let out ou give a sigh ; **rendre le dernier**

~ to breathe one's last - **2.** MUS crotchet rest Br, quarter-note rest Am.

soupirail, aux [supiraj, o] nm barred basement window (for ventilation purposes).

soupirant [supirã] nm suitor.

soupirer [3] [supire] ⬦ vt to sigh ⬦ vi - **1.** [souffler] to sigh - **2.** fig & littéraire [rechercher] : ~ après qqch to sigh for sthg, to yearn after sthg.

souple [supl] adj - **1.** [gymnaste] supple - **2.** [pas] lithe - **3.** [paquet, col] soft - **4.** [tissu, cheveux] flowing - **5.** [tuyau, horaire, caractère] flexible.

souplesse [suplɛs] nf - **1.** [de gymnaste] suppleness - **2.** [flexibilité - de tuyau] pliability, flexibility ; [- de matière] suppleness - **3.** [de personne] flexibility.

sourate = surate.

source [surs] nf - **1.** [gén] source ; tenir de bonne ~ ou de ~ sûre to have sthg on good authority ou from a reliable source ; puiser à la ~ fig to go to the source ; ça coule de ~ fig it's obvious - **2.** [d'eau] spring ; prendre sa ~ à to rise in.

sourcier, ère [sursje, ɛr] nm, f water diviner.

sourcil [sursi] nm eyebrow ; froncer les ~s to frown.

sourcilière [sursiljɛr] ⬦ arcade.

sourciller [3] [sursije] vi : sans ~ without batting an eyelid.

sourcilleux, euse [sursijø, øz] adj fussy, finicky.

sourd¹, e [sur, surd] ⬦ adj - **1.** [personne] deaf ; être/rester ~ à qqch fig to be/to remain deaf to sthg - **2.** [bruit, voix] muffled - **3.** [douleur] dull - **4.** [lutte, hostilité] silent ⬦ nm, f deaf person.

sourd², sourdait etc ⬦ sourdre.

sourdement [surdəmã] adv - **1.** [avec un bruit sourd] dully - **2.** fig [secrètement] silently.

sourdine [surdin] nf mute ; en ~ [sans bruit] softly ; [secrètement] in secret ; mettre une ~ à qqch to tone sthg down.

sourd-muet, sourde-muette [surmɥɛ, surdmɥɛt] (mpl sourds-muets, fpl sourdes-muettes) ⬦ adj deaf-mute, deaf and dumb ⬦ nm, f deaf-mute, deaf and dumb person.

sourdre [73] [surdr] vi to well up.

souriant, e [surjã, ãt] adj smiling, cheerful.

souriceau [suriso] nm baby mouse.

souricière [surisjɛr] nf mousetrap ; fig trap.

sourire [95] [surir] ⬦ vi to smile ; ~ à qqn to smile at sb ; fig [campagne] to appeal to sb ;

[destin, chance] to smile on sb ; ~ de qqn/qqch [être amusé par] to smile at sb/sthg ⬦ nm smile ; garder le ~ to keep smiling.

souris [suri] nf - **1.** INFORM & ZOOL mouse - **2.** [viande] knuckle - **3.** fam fig [fille] bird Br, chick Am.

sournois, e [surnwa, az] ⬦ adj - **1.** [personne] underhand - **2.** fig [maladie, phénomène] unpredictable ⬦ nm, f underhanded person.

sournoisement [surnwazmã] adv in an underhand way.

sous [su] prép - **1.** [gén] under ; nager ~ l'eau to swim underwater ; ~ la pluie in the rain ; ~ cet aspect ou angle from that point of view - **2.** [dans un délai de] within ; ~ huit jours within a week.

sous-alimentation [suzalimãtasjɔ̃] nf malnutrition, undernourishment.

sous-alimenté, e [suzalimãte] adj malnourished, underfed.

sous-bois [subwa] nm inv undergrowth.

sous-chef [suʃɛf] (pl sous-chefs) nm second-in-command.

souscripteur, trice [suskriptœr, tris] nm, f subscriber.

souscription [suskripsjɔ̃] nf subscription.

souscrire [99] [suskrir] ⬦ vt to sign ⬦ vi : ~ à to subscribe to.

sous-cutané, e [sukytane] adj MÉD subcutaneous.

sous-développé, e [sudevlope] adj ÉCON underdeveloped ; fig & péj backward.

sous-directeur, trice [sudirɛktœr, tris] (mpl sous-directeurs, fpl sous-directrices) nm, f assistant manager (f assistant manageress).

sous-employé, e [suzãplwaje] adj underemployed.

sous-ensemble [suzãsãbl] (pl sous-ensembles) nm subset.

sous-entendre [73] [suzãtãdr] vt to imply.

sous-entendu [suzãtãdy] (pl sous-entendus) nm insinuation.

sous-équipé, e [suzekipe] adj under-equipped.

sous-estimer [3] [suzɛstime] vt to underestimate, to underrate.
➤ se sous-estimer vp to underrate o.s.

sous-évaluer [7] [suzevalɥe] vt to underestimate.

sous-exploiter [3] [suzɛksplwate] vt to underexploit.

sous-exposer [3] [suzɛkspoze] vt to underexpose.

sous-fifre [sufifr] (*pl* **sous-fifres**) *nm fam* underling.

sous-jacent, e [suʒasɑ̃, ɑ̃t] *adj* underlying.

sous-lieutenant [suljøtnɑ̃] (*pl* **sous-lieutenants**) *nm* MIL sub-lieutenant.

sous-location [sulɔkasjɔ̃] (*pl* **sous-locations**) *nf* subletting.

sous-louer [6] [sulwe] *vt* to sublet.

sous-main [sumɛ̃] *nm inv* desk blotter.

sous-marin, e [sumarɛ̃, in] *adj* underwater *(avant n)*.
➡ **sous-marin** (*pl* **sous-marins**) *nm* submarine.

sous-œuvre [suzœvr] ➡ **en sous-œuvre** *loc adv* : **reprise en ~** underpinning.

sous-officier [suzɔfisje] (*pl* **sous-officiers**) *nm* non-commissioned officer.

sous-ordre [suzɔrdr] (*pl* **sous-ordres**) *nm* - **1.** [personne] subordinate - **2.** [espèce] suborder.

sous-payer [11] [supeje] *vt* to underpay.

sous-peuplé, e [supœple] *adj* underpopulated.

sous-préfecture [suprefɛktyr] (*pl* **sous-préfectures**) *nf* sub-prefecture.

sous-préfet [suprefɛ] (*pl* **sous-préfets**) *nm* sub-prefect.

sous-produit [suprɔdɥi] (*pl* **sous-produits**) *nm* - **1.** [objet] by-product - **2.** *fig* [imitation] pale imitation.

sous-secrétaire [susəkretɛr] (*pl* **sous-secrétaires**) *nm* : **~ d'État** Under-Secretary of State.

soussigné, e [susiɲe] ⬦ *adj* : **je ~** I the undersigned ; **nous ~s** we the undersigned ⬦ *nm, f* undersigned.

sous-sol [susɔl] (*pl* **sous-sols**) *nm* - **1.** [de bâtiment] basement - **2.** [naturel] subsoil.

sous-tasse [sutas] (*pl* **sous-tasses**) *nf* saucer.

sous-tendre [73] [sutɑ̃dr] *vt* to underpin.

sous-titre [sutitr] (*pl* **sous-titres**) *nm* subtitle.

sous-titrer [3] [sutitre] *vt* to subtitle.

soustraction [sustraksjɔ̃] *nf* MATHS subtraction.

soustraire [112] [sustrɛr] *vt* - **1.** [retrancher] : **~ qqch de** to subtract sthg from - **2.** *sout* [voler] : **~ qqch de qqch** to remove sthg from sthg ; **~ qqch à qqn** to take sthg away from sb - **3.** [faire échapper] : **~ qqn à qqch** to shield sb from sthg.
➡ **se soustraire** *vp* : **se ~ à** to escape from.

sous-traitance [sutrɛtɑ̃s] (*pl* **sous-traitances**) *nf* subcontracting ; **donner qqch en ~** to subcontract sthg.

sous-traitant, e [sutrɛtɑ̃, ɑ̃t] *adj* subcontracting.
➡ **sous-traitant** (*pl* **sous-traitants**) *nm* subcontractor.

sous-traiter [4] [sutrɛte] *vt* to subcontract.

soustrayais, soustrayions *etc* ▷ **soustraire**.

sous-verre [suvɛr] *nm inv* picture or document framed between a sheet of glass and a rigid backing.

sous-vêtement [suvɛtmɑ̃] (*pl* **sous-vêtements**) *nm* undergarment ; **~s** underwear *(U)*, underclothes.

soutane [sutan] *nf* cassock.

soute [sut] *nf* hold.

soutenable [sutnabl] *adj* - **1.** [défendable] tenable - **2.** [supportable] bearable.

soutenance [sutnɑ̃s] *nf* viva.

souteneur [sutnœr] *nm* procurer.

soutenir [40] [sutnir] *vt* - **1.** [immeuble, personne] to support, to hold up - **2.** [effort, intérêt] to sustain - **3.** [encourager] to support ; POLIT to back, to support - **4.** [affirmer] : **~ que** to maintain (that) - **5.** [résister à] to withstand ; [regard, comparaison] to bear.
➡ **se soutenir** *vp* - **1.** [se maintenir] to hold o.s. up, to support o.s. - **2.** [s'aider] to support each other, to back each other (up).

soutenu, e [sutny] *adj* - **1.** [style, langage] elevated - **2.** [attention, rythme] sustained - **3.** [couleur] vivid.

souterrain, e [sutɛrɛ̃, ɛn] *adj* underground.
➡ **souterrain** *nm* underground passage.

soutien [sutjɛ̃] *nm* support ; **apporter son ~ à** to give one's support to ; **~ de famille** breadwinner.

soutien-gorge [sutjɛ̃gɔrʒ] (*pl* **soutiens-gorge**) *nm* bra.

soutirer [3] [sutire] *vt* - **1.** [liquide] to decant - **2.** *fig* [tirer] : **~ qqch à qqn** to extract sthg from sb.

souvenance [suvnɑ̃s] *nf littéraire* recollection.

souvenir [40] [suvnir] *nm* - **1.** [réminiscence, mémoire] memory ; **en ~ de** in memory of ; **rappeler qqn au bon ~ de qqn** to remember sb to sb ; **avec mes meilleurs ~s** with kind regards - **2.** [objet] souvenir.
➡ **se souvenir** *vp* [ne pas oublier] : **se ~ de qqch/de qqn** to remember sthg/sb ; **se ~ que** to remember (that).

souvent [suvɑ̃] adv often ; **le plus ~** more often than not.

souvenu, e [suvny] pp ▷ **souvenir**.

souverain, e [suvrɛ̃, ɛn] ⬦ adj - **1.** [remède, état] sovereign - **2.** [indifférence] supreme ⬦ nm, f [monarque] sovereign, monarch.

souverainement [suvrɛnmɑ̃] adv - **1.** [extrêmement] intensely - **2.** [avec autorité] regally - **3.** [absolument - bon] supremely ; [- parfait] absolutely.

souveraineté [suvrɛnte] nf sovereignty.

souviendrai, souviendras etc ▷ **souvenir**.

souvienne, souviennes etc ▷ **souvenir**.

souviens, souvient etc ▷ **souvenir**.

soviet [sɔvjɛt] nm soviet ; **Soviet suprême** Supreme Soviet.

soviétique [sɔvjetik] adj Soviet.
➡ **Soviétique** nmf Soviet (citizen).

soviétologue [sɔvjetɔlɔg] nmf Kremlinologist.

soyeux, euse [swajø, øz] adj silky.

soyez ▷ **être**.

SPA (abr de **Société protectrice des animaux**) nf French society for the protection of animals, ≈ RSPCA Br, ≈ SPCA Am.

spacieux, euse [spasjø, øz] adj spacious.

spaghettis [spagɛti] nmpl spaghetti (U).

sparadrap [sparadra] nm sticking plaster.

spartiate [sparsjat] adj [austère] Spartan ; **à la ~** fig in a Spartan fashion.
➡ **spartiates** nfpl [sandales] Roman sandals.

spasme [spasm] nm spasm.

spasmodique [spasmɔdik] adj spasmodic.

spasmophilie [spasmɔfili] nf spasmophilia.

spatial, e, aux [spasjal, o] adj space (avant n).

spatio-temporel, elle [spasjɔtɑ̃pɔrɛl] adj spatio-temporal.

spatule [spatyl] nf - **1.** [ustensile] spatula - **2.** [de ski] tip.

speaker, speakerine [spikœr, spikrin] nm, f announcer.

spécial, e, aux [spesjal, o] adj - **1.** [particulier] special ; **~ à** special to - **2.** fam [bizarre] peculiar.

spécialement [spesjalmɑ̃] adv - **1.** [exprès] specially - **2.** [particulièrement] particularly, especially ; **pas ~** fam not particularly, not specially.

spécialisation [spesjalizasjɔ̃] nf specialization.

spécialiser [3] [spesjalize] vt to specialize.
➡ **se spécialiser** vp : **se ~ (dans)** to specialize (in).

spécialiste [spesjalist] nmf specialist.

spécialité [spesjalite] nf speciality.

spécieux, euse [spesjø, øz] adj littéraire specious.

spécification [spesifikasjɔ̃] nf specification.

spécificité [spesifisite] nf specificity.

spécifier [9] [spesifje] vt to specify.

spécifique [spesifik] adj specific.

spécifiquement [spesifikmɑ̃] adv specifically.

spécimen [spesimɛn] nm - **1.** [représentant] specimen - **2.** [exemplaire] sample.

spectacle [spɛktakl] nm - **1.** [représentation] show - **2.** [domaine] show business, entertainment - **3.** [tableau] spectacle, sight ; **se donner en ~** fig to make a spectacle ou an exhibition of o.s.

spectaculaire [spɛktakylɛr] adj spectacular.

spectateur, trice [spɛktatœr, tris] nm, f - **1.** [témoin] witness - **2.** [de spectacle] spectator.

spectre [spɛktr] nm - **1.** [fantôme] spectre Br, specter Am ; **le ~ de** fig the spectre Br ou specter Am of - **2.** PHYS spectrum.

spéculateur, trice [spekylatœr, tris] nm, f speculator.

spéculatif, ive [spekylatif, iv] adj speculative.

spéculation [spekylasjɔ̃] nf speculation.

spéculer [3] [spekyle] vi : **~ sur** FIN to speculate in ; fig [miser] to count on.

speech [spitʃ] (pl **speeches**) nm speech.

speed [spid] adj hyper ; **il est très ~** he's really hyper.

speeder [spide] vi fam to hurry.

spéléologie [speleɔlɔʒi] nf [exploration] potholing ; [science] speleology.

spéléologue [speleɔlɔg] nmf [explorateur] potholer ; [scientifique] speleologist.

spencer [spɛnsɛr] nm short fitted jacket or coat.

spermatozoïde [spɛrmatɔzɔid] nm sperm, spermatozoon.

sperme [spɛrm] nm sperm, semen.

sphère [sfɛr] nf sphere ; **les hautes ~s de** the higher reaches of ; **~ d'influence** sphere of influence.

sphérique [sferik] adj spherical.

sphincter [sfɛ̃ktɛr] *nm* sphincter.

sphinx [sfɛ̃ks] *nm inv* - **1.** MYTH & *fig* sphinx - **2.** ZOOL hawk moth.

spirale [spiral] *nf* spiral ; **en ~** spiral.

spiritisme [spiritism] *nm* spiritualism.

spiritualité [spiritɥalite] *nf* spirituality.

spirituel, elle [spiritɥɛl] *adj* - **1.** [de l'âme, moral] spiritual - **2.** [vivant, drôle] witty.

spirituellement [spiritɥɛlmɑ̃] *adv* - **1.** [moralement] spiritually - **2.** [avec humour] wittily.

spiritueux [spiritɥø] *nm* spirit.

spleen [splin] *nm littéraire* spleen.

splendeur [splɑ̃dœr] *nf* - **1.** [beauté, prospérité] splendour *Br*, splendor *Am* - **2.** [merveille] : c'est une ~! it's magnificent!

splendide [splɑ̃did] *adj* magnificent, splendid.

spolier [9] [spɔlje] *vt* to despoil.

spongieux, euse [spɔ̃ʒjø, øz] *adj* spongy.

sponsor [spɔ̃sɔr] *nm* sponsor.

sponsoring [spɔ̃sɔriŋ] *nm* sponsoring.

sponsorisation [spɔ̃sɔrizasjɔ̃] *nf* sponsoring, sponsorship.

sponsoriser [3] [spɔ̃sɔrize] *vt* to sponsor.

spontané, e [spɔ̃tane] *adj* spontaneous.

spontanéité [spɔ̃taneite] *nf* spontaneity.

spontanément [spɔ̃tanemɑ̃] *adv* spontaneously.

sporadique [spɔradik] *adj* sporadic.

sporadiquement [spɔradikmɑ̃] *adv* sporadically.

sport [spɔr] ⬦ *nm* sport ; **de ~** sports *(avant n)* ; **~ d'équipe/de combat** team/combat sport ; **~s d'hiver** winter sports ; **aller aux ~s d'hiver** to go on a skiing holiday ⬦ *adj inv* - **1.** [vêtement] sports *(avant n)* - **2.** [fair play] sporting.

sportif, ive [spɔrtif, iv] ⬦ *adj* - **1.** [association, résultats] sports *(avant n)* - **2.** [personne, physique] sporty, athletic - **3.** [fair play] sportsmanlike, sporting ⬦ *nm, f* sportsman *(f* sportswoman).

spot [spɔt] *nm* - **1.** [lampe] spot, spotlight - **2.** [publicité] : **~ (publicitaire)** commercial, advert.

SPOT, Spot [spɔt] *(abr de* satellite pour l'observation de la terre) *nm* earth observation satellite.

sprint [sprint] *nm* [SPORT - accélération] spurt ; [- course] sprint ; **piquer un ~** *fam* to put on a spurt.

sprinter¹ [3] [sprinte] *vi* to sprint.

sprinter² [sprintœr] *nm* sprinter.

squale [skwal] *nm* dogfish.

square [skwar] *nm* small public garden.

squash [skwaʃ] *nm* squash.

squat [skwat] *nm* squat.

squatter¹ [skwatœr] *nm* squatter.

squatter² [3] [skwate] ⬦ *vt* to squat in ⬦ *vi* to squat.

squelette [skəlɛt] *nm* skeleton.

squelettique [skəletik] *adj* - **1.** [corps] emaciated - **2.** [exposé] sketchy, skeletal.

Sri Lanka [ʃrilɑ̃ka] *nm* : **le ~** Sri Lanka ; **au ~** in Sri Lanka.

sri lankais, e [ʃrilɑ̃kɛ, ɛz] *adj* Sri Lankan.
➡ **Sri Lankais, e** *nm, f* Sri Lankan.

SS ⬦ *nf* - **1.** *(abr de* Sécurité sociale) ≃ DSS *Br*, ≃ SSA *Am* - **2.** *(abr de* SchutzStaffel) SS ; **un ~** a member of the SS ⬦ *(abr de* steamship) SS.

S.S. *(abr de* Sa Sainteté) H.H.

SSR *(abr de* Société suisse romande) *nf* French-language Swiss broadcasting company.

St *(abr de* saint) St.

stabilisateur, trice [stabilizatœr, tris] *adj* stabilizing.

stabilisation [stabilizasjɔ̃] *nf* stabilization.

stabiliser [3] [stabilize] *vt* - **1.** [gén] to stabilize ; [meuble] to steady - **2.** [terrain] to make firm.
➡ **se stabiliser** *vp* - **1.** [véhicule, prix, situation] to stabilize - **2.** [personne] to settle down.

stabilité [stabilite] *nf* stability.

stable [stabl] *adj* - **1.** [gén] stable - **2.** [meuble] steady, stable.

stade [stad] *nm* - **1.** [terrain] stadium - **2.** [étape & MÉD] stage ; **en être au ~ de/où** to reach the stage of/at which.

Stade de France *nm* Stade de France, *stadium built for the 1998 World Cup in the north of Paris.*

staff [staf] *nm* staff.

stage [staʒ] *nm* SCOL work placement ; [sur le temps de travail] in-service training ; **faire un ~** [cours] to go on a training course ; [expérience professionnelle] to go on a work placement.

stagiaire [staʒjɛr] ⬦ *nmf* trainee ⬦ *adj* trainee *(avant n)*.

stagnant, e [stagnɑ̃, ɑ̃t] *adj* stagnant.

stagnation [stagnasjɔ̃] *nf* stagnation.

stagner [3] [stagne] *vi* to stagnate.

stakhanoviste [stakanɔvist] *nmf* & *adj* Stakhanovite, hard worker.

stalactite [stalaktit] *nf* stalactite.

stalagmite [stalagmit] *nf* stalagmite.

stalle [stal] *nf* stall.

stand [stãd] *nm* - **1.** [d'exposition] stand - **2.** [de fête] stall ; ~ **de tir** shooting range, firing range.

standard [stãdar] <> *adj inv* standard <> *nm* - **1.** [norme] standard - **2.** [téléphonique] switchboard.

standardisation [stãdardizasjõ] *nf* standardization.

standardiser [3] [stãdardize] *vt* to standardize.

standardiste [stãdardist] *nmf* switchboard operator.

standing [stãdiŋ] *nm* standing ; **immeuble de grand** ~ prestigious block of flats ; **quartier de grand** ~ select district.

staphylocoque [stafilɔkɔk] *nm* staphylococcus.

star [star] *nf* CIN star.

starlette [starlet] *nf* starlet.

starter [starter] *nm* AUTOM choke ; **mettre le** ~ to pull the choke out.

starting-block [startiŋblɔk] (*pl* **starting-blocks**) *nm* starting-block.

start up [startɔp] *nf* start up.

station [stasjõ] *nf* - **1.** [arrêt - de bus] stop ; [- de métro] station ; **à quelle** ~ **dois-je descendre?** which stop do I get off at? ; ~ **de taxis** taxi stand - **2.** [installations] station ; ~ **d'épuration** sewage treatment plant ; ~ **spatiale** space station - **3.** [ville] resort ; ~ **balnéaire** seaside resort ; ~ **de ski/de sports d'hiver** ski/winter sports resort ; ~ **thermale** spa (town) - **4.** [position] position ; ~ **debout** standing position - **5.** INFORM : ~ **de travail** work station.

stationnaire [stasjɔner] *adj* stationary.

stationnement [stasjɔnmã] *nm* parking ; '~ **interdit**' 'no parking' ; ~ **en épi** angle *ou* angled parking.

stationner [3] [stasjɔne] *vi* to park.

station-service [stasjõservis] (*pl* **stations-service**) *nf* service station, petrol station *Br*, gas station *Am*.

statique [statik] *adj* static.

statisticien, enne [statistisjẽ, ɛn] *nm, f* statistician.

statistique [statistik] <> *adj* statistical <> *nf* - **1.** [science] statistics (*U*) - **2.** [donnée] statistic.

statistiquement [statistikmã] *adv* statistically.

statuaire [statчer] *nf & adj* statuary.

statue [staty] *nf* statue.

statuer [7] [statчe] *vi* : ~ **sur** to give a decision on.

statuette [statчet] *nf* statuette.

statu quo [statykwo] *nm inv* status quo.

stature [statyr] *nf* stature.

statut [staty] *nm* status.
statuts *nmpl* statutes.

statutaire [statyter] *adj* statutory.

Ste (*abr de* sainte) St.

Sté (*abr de* société) Co.

steak [stɛk] *nm* steak ; ~ **frites** steak and chips ; ~ **haché** mince ; ~ **tartare** steak tartare.

stèle [stɛl] *nf* stele.

stellaire [steler] *adj* stellar.

stencil [stensil] *nm* stencil.

sténo [steno] <> *nmf* stenographer <> *nf* shorthand.

sténodactylo [stenɔdaktilo] *nmf* shorthand typist.

sténodactylographie [stenɔdaktilɔgrafi] *nf* shorthand typing.

sténographe [stenɔgraf] *nmf* stenographer.

sténographie [stenɔgrafi] *nf* shorthand ; **en** ~ in shorthand.

sténographier [9] [stenɔgrafje] *vt* to take down in shorthand.

sténographique [stenɔgrafik] *adj* shorthand (*avant n*).

sténotypiste [stenɔtipist] *nmf* stenotypist.

stentor [stãtɔr] ▷ **voix**.

steppe [stɛp] *nf* steppe.

stéréo [stereo] <> *adj inv* stereo <> *nf* stereo ; **en** ~ in stereo.

stéréotype [stereɔtip] *nm* stereotype.

stéréotypé, e [stereɔtipe] *adj* stereotyped.

stérile [steril] *adj* - **1.** [personne] sterile, infertile ; [terre] barren - **2.** *fig* [inutile - discussion] sterile ; [- efforts] futile - **3.** MÉD sterile.

stérilet [sterilɛ] *nm* IUD, intra-uterine device.

stérilisateur [sterilizatœr] *nm* sterilizer.

stérilisation [sterilizasjõ] *nf* sterilization.

stériliser [3] [sterilize] *vt* to sterilize.

stérilité [sterilite] *nf litt & fig* sterility ; [d'efforts] futility.

sterling [sterliŋ] *adj inv & nm inv* sterling.

sternum [sternɔm] *nm* breastbone, sternum.

stéthoscope [stetɔskɔp] *nm* stethoscope.

steward [stiwart] *nm* steward.

stick [stik] *nm* [tube] stick ; **de la colle en ~** a stick of glue ; **un déodorant en ~** a stick deodorant.

stigmate [stigmat] *nm (gén pl)* mark, scar.
→ **stigmates** *nmpl* RELIG stigmata.

stigmatiser [3] [stigmatize] *vt littéraire* [dénoncer] to denounce.

stimulant, e [stimylɑ̃, ɑ̃t] *adj* stimulating.
→ **stimulant** *nm* - **1.** [remontant] stimulant - **2.** [motivation] incentive, stimulus.

stimulateur [stimylatœr] *nm* : **~ cardiaque** pacemaker.

stimulation [stimylasjɔ̃] *nf* stimulation.

stimuler [3] [stimyle] *vt* to stimulate.

stipuler [3] [stipyle] *vt* : **~ que** to stipulate (that).

stock [stɔk] *nm* stock ; **en ~** in stock ; **tout un ~ de** *fig* & *iron* a whole stock of, plenty of.

stockage [stɔkaʒ] *nm* - **1.** [de marchandises] stocking - **2.** INFORM storage.

stocker [3] [stɔke] *vt* - **1.** [marchandises] to stock - **2.** INFORM to store.

Stockholm [stɔkɔlm] *n* Stockholm.

stoïcisme [stɔisism] *nm* - **1.** PHILO Stoicism - **2.** *fig* [courage] stoicism.

stoïque [stɔik] *nmf* Stoic *adj* stoical.

stoïquement [stɔikmɑ̃] *adv* stoically.

stomacal, e, aux [stɔmakal, o] *adj* stomach *(avant n)*.

stomatologie [stɔmatɔlɔʒi] *nf* stomatology.

stomatologiste [stɔmatɔlɔʒist], **stomatologue** [stɔmatɔlɔg] *nmf* stomatologist.

stop [stɔp] *interj* stop! ; **dis-moi ~!** say when! *nm* - **1.** [feu] brake-light - **2.** [panneau] stop sign - **3.** [auto-stop] hitch-hiking, hitching ; **faire du ~** to hitch, to hitch-hike ; **on y est allé en ~** we hitch-hiked *ou* hitched there.

stopper [3] [stɔpe] *vt* - **1.** [arrêter] to stop, to halt - **2.** COUTURE to repair by invisible mending *vi* to stop.

store [stɔr] *nm* - **1.** [de fenêtre] blind - **2.** [de magasin] awning.

strabisme [strabism] *nm* squint ; **être atteint de ~** to (have a) squint.

strangulation [strɑ̃gylasjɔ̃] *nf* strangulation.

strapontin [strapɔ̃tɛ̃] *nm* - **1.** [siège] pulldown seat - **2.** *fig* [position] minor role.

strass [stras] *nm* paste.

stratagème [strataʒɛm] *nm* stratagem.

strate [strat] *nf* stratum.

stratège [strateʒ] *nm* strategist.

stratégie [strateʒi] *nf* strategy.

stratégique [strateʒik] *adj* strategic.

stratifié, e [stratifje] *adj* - **1.** GÉOL stratified - **2.** TECHNOL laminated.

stratosphère [stratɔsfɛr] *nf* stratosphere.

stress [strɛs] *nm* stress.

stressant, e [strɛsɑ̃, ɑ̃t] *adj* stressful.

stressé, e [strɛse] *adj* stressed.

stresser [4] [strɛse] *vt* : **~ qqn** to cause sb stress, to put sb under stress *vi* to be stressed.

Stretch® [strɛtʃ] *nm inv* stretch material.

stretching [strɛtʃiŋ] *nm* SPORT stretching, stretching exercises *(pl)*.

strict, e [strikt] *adj* - **1.** [personne, règlement] strict - **2.** [sobre] plain - **3.** [absolu - minimum] bare, absolute ; [- vérité] absolute ; **dans la plus ~e intimité** strictly in private ; **au sens ~ du terme** in the strict sense of the word.

strictement [striktəmɑ̃] *adv* - **1.** [rigoureusement] strictly - **2.** [sobrement] plainly, soberly.

strident, e [stridɑ̃, ɑ̃t] *adj* strident, shrill.

stridulation [stridylasjɔ̃] *nf* chirping.

strie [stri] *(gén pl)* *nf* - **1.** [sillon] groove ; [en relief] ridge - **2.** [rayure] streak.

strié, e [strije] *adj* - **1.** [rayé] striped - **2.** GÉOL striated.

strier [10] [strije] *vt* to streak.

string [striŋ] *nm* G-string.

strip-tease [striptiz] *(pl* **strip-teases)** *nm* striptease.

strip-teaseuse [striptizøz] *(pl* **strip-teaseuses)** *nf* stripper.

striure [strijyr] *nf* - **1.** [sillons] grooves *(pl)* ; [en relief] ridges *(pl)* - **2.** [rayures] streaks *(pl)*.

strophe [strɔf] *nf* verse.

structural, e, aux [stryktyral, o] *adj* structural.

structuralisme [stryktyralism] *nm* structuralism.

structure [stryktyr] *nf* structure ; **~ ou ~s d'accueil** reception facilities.

structurel, elle [stryktyrɛl] *adj* structural.

structurer [3] [stryktyre] *vt* to structure.
→ **se structurer** *vp* to be/become structured.

strychnine [striknin] *nf* strychnine.

stuc [styk] *nm* stucco.

studieusement [stydjøzmɑ̃] *adv* studiously.

studieux, euse [stydjø, øz] *adj* - **1.** [personne] studious - **2.** [vacances] study *(avant n)*.

studio [stydjo] *nm* - **1.** CIN, PHOT & TÉLÉ studio

- 2. [appartement] studio flat *Br*, studio apartment *Am*.

stupéfaction [stypefaksjɔ̃] *nf* astonishment, stupefaction.

stupéfait, e [stypefɛ, ɛt] *adj* astounded, stupefied.

stupéfiant, e [stypefjɑ̃, ɑ̃t] *adj* astounding, stunning.

➤ **stupéfiant** *nm* narcotic, drug.

stupéfier [9] [stypefje] *vt* to astonish, to stupefy.

stupeur [stypœr] *nf* **- 1.** [stupéfaction] astonishment **- 2.** *MÉD* stupor.

stupide [stypid] *adj* **- 1.** *péj* [abruti] stupid **- 2.** [insensé - mort] senseless ; [- accident] stupid **- 3.** *littéraire* [interdit] stunned.

stupidement [stypidmɑ̃] *adv* stupidly.

stupidité [stypidite] *nf* stupidity ; **faire/dire des ~s** to do/say something stupid.

style [stil] *nm* **- 1.** [gén] style ; **de ~ period** *(avant n)* ; **~ Empire/Louis XIII** Empire/Louis XIII Style ; **~ de vie** lifestyle **- 2.** *GRAM* : **~ direct/indirect** direct/indirect speech.

styliser [3] [stilize] *vt* to stylize.

stylisme [stilism] *nm* *COUTURE* design, designing.

styliste [stilist] *nmf* *COUTURE* designer.

stylistique [stilistik] ⬦ *adj* stylistic ⬦ *nf* stylistics *(U)*.

stylo [stilo] *nm* pen ; **~ bille** ballpoint (pen) ; **~ plume** fountain pen.

stylo-feutre [stiloføtr] *(pl* stylos-feutres*)* *nm* felt-tip pen.

su, e [sy] *pp* ⬑ savoir.

➤ **au su et au vu de** *loc prép* under the eyes of.

suave [sɥav] *adj* [voix] smooth ; [parfum] sweet.

suavité [sɥavite] *nf* pleasantness.

subalpin, e [sybalpɛ̃, in] *adj* subalpine.

subalterne [sybaltɛrn] ⬦ *nmf* subordinate, junior ⬦ *adj* [rôle] subordinate ; [employé] junior.

subaquatique [sybakwatik] *adj* underwater.

subconscient, e [sybkɔ̃sjɑ̃, ɑ̃t] *adj* subconscious.

➤ **subconscient** *nm* subconscious.

subdiviser [3] [sybdivize] *vt* to subdivide.

➤ **se subdiviser** *vp* to be subdivided.

subdivision [sybdivizjɔ̃] *nf* subdivision.

subir [32] [sybir] *vt* **- 1.** [conséquences, colère] to suffer ; [personne] to put up with **- 2.** [opération, épreuve, examen] to undergo **- 3.** [dommages, per-

tes] to sustain, to suffer ; **~ une hausse** to be increased.

subit, e [sybi, it] *adj* sudden.

subitement [sybitmɑ̃] *adv* suddenly.

subjectif, ive [sybʒɛktif, iv] *adj* **- 1.** [personnel, partial] subjective **- 2.** *MÉD* : **troubles ~s** symptoms.

subjectivité [sybʒɛktivite] *nf* subjectivity.

subjonctif [sybʒɔ̃ktif] *nm* subjunctive.

subjuguer [3] [sybʒyge] *vt* to captivate.

sublimation [syblimasjɔ̃] *nf* sublimation.

sublime [syblim] *adj* sublime.

sublimer [3] [syblime] *vt* to sublimate.

submerger [17] [sybmɛrʒe] *vt* **- 1.** [inonder] to flood **- 2.** [envahir] to overcome, to overwhelm **- 3.** [déborder] to overwhelm ; **être submergé de travail** to be swamped with work.

submersible [sybmɛrsibl] *nm* & *adj* submersible.

subodorer [3] [sybɔdɔre] *vt* *fam* to smell, to scent.

subordination [sybɔrdinasjɔ̃] *nf* subordination.

subordonné, e [sybɔrdɔne] ⬦ *adj* *GRAM* subordinate, dependent ⬦ *nm, f* subordinate.

➤ **subordonnée** *nf* *GRAM* subordinate clause.

subordonner [3] [sybɔrdɔne] *vt* **- 1.** [chose] : **~ qqch à qqch** to make sthg dependent on sthg **- 2.** [personne] : **~ qqn à qqn** to subordinate sb to sb.

subornation [sybɔrnasjɔ̃] *nf* bribing, subornation.

suborner [3] [sybɔrne] *vt* **- 1.** *littéraire* [séduire] to lead astray **- 2.** *JUR* to bribe, to suborn.

subreptice [sybrɛptis] *adj* surreptitious.

subrepticement [sybrɛptismɑ̃] *adv* surreptitiously.

subroger [17] [sybrɔʒe] *vt* *JUR* to substitute.

subséquent, e [sypsekɑ̃, ɑ̃t] *adj* *sout* subsequent.

subside [sypsid] *nm* *(gén pl)* grant, subsidy.

subsidiaire [sypsidjɛr] *adj* subsidiary.

subsistance [sybzistɑ̃s] *nf* subsistence ; **pourvoir à la ~ de sa famille** to support one's family.

subsister [3] [sybziste] *vi* **- 1.** [chose] to remain **- 2.** [personne] to live, to subsist.

subsonique [sypsɔnik] *adj* subsonic.

substance [sypstɑ̃s] *nf* **- 1.** [matière] substance **- 2.** [essence] gist ; **en ~** in substance.

substantiel, elle [sypstɑ̃sjɛl] *adj* substantial.

substantif [sypstãtif] *nm* noun.

substituer [7] [sypstituɥe] *vt* : **~ qqch à qqch** to substitute sthg for sthg.

➡ **se substituer** *vp* : **se ~ à** [personne] to stand in for, to substitute for ; [chose] to take the place of.

substitut [sypstity] *nm* **- 1.** [remplacement] substitute **- 2.** JUR deputy public prosecutor.

substitution [sypstitysjɔ̃] *nf* substitution.

substrat [sypstra] *nm* **- 1.** [de récit, réflexion] basis **- 2.** GÉOL & LING substratum **- 3.** CHIM substrate.

subterfuge [sypterfyʒ] *nm* subterfuge.

subtil, e [syptil] *adj* subtle.

subtilement [syptilmã] *adv* subtly.

subtiliser [3] [syptilize] *vt* to steal.

subtilité [syptilite] *nf* subtlety.

subtropical, e, aux [syptropikal, o] *adj* subtropical.

suburbain, e [sybyrbɛ̃, ɛn] *adj* suburban.

subvenir [40] [sybvənir] *vi* : **~ à** to meet, to cover ; **~ aux besoins de qqn** to meet sb's needs.

subvention [sybvãsjɔ̃] *nf* grant, subsidy.

subventionner [3] [sybvãsjɔne] *vt* to give a grant to, to subsidize.

subvenu, e [sybvəny] *pp* ▷ **subvenir**.

subversif, ive [sybversif, iv] *adj* subversive.

subversion [sybversjɔ̃] *nf* subversion.

subviendrai, subviendras *etc* ▷ **subvenir**.

subviens, subvient *etc* ▷ **subvenir**.

suc [syk] *nm* **- 1.** [d'arbre] sap ; [de fruit, viande] juice ; **~ gastrique** gastric juices *(pl)* **- 2.** *littéraire* [quintessence] essence.

succédané [syksedane] *nm* substitute.

succéder [18] [syksede] *vt* : **~ à** [suivre] to follow ; [remplacer] to succeed, to take over from.

➡ **se succéder** *vp* to follow one another.

succès [syksɛ] *nm* **- 1.** [gén] success ; **avoir du ~** to be very successful ; **avoir un ~ fou** (auprès de) to be very successful (with) ; **à ~** hit *(avant n)* ; **sans ~** [essai] unsuccessful ; [essayer] unsuccessfully ; **avec ~** [essai] successful ; [essayer] successfully ; **se tailler un franc ~** *fig* to be a great *ou* huge success **- 2.** [chanson, pièce] hit **- 3.** [conquête] conquest.

successeur [syksesœr] *nm* **- 1.** [gén] successor **- 2.** JUR successor, heir.

successif, ive [syksesif, iv] *adj* successive.

succession [syksesjɔ̃] *nf* **- 1.** [gén] succession ; **une ~ de** a succession of ; **prendre la ~ de qqn** to take over from sb, to succeed sb

- 2. JUR succession, inheritance ; **droits de ~** death duties.

successivement [syksesivmã] *adv* successively.

succinct, e [syksɛ̃, ɛ̃t] *adj* **- 1.** [résumé] succinct **- 2.** [repas] frugal.

succinctement [syksɛ̃tmã] *adv* **- 1.** [résumer] succinctly **- 2.** [manger] frugally.

succion [syksjɔ̃, sysjɔ̃] *nf* suction, sucking.

succomber [3] [sykɔ̃be] *vi* : **~ (à)** to succumb (to).

succulent, e [sykylã, ãt] *adj* delicious.

succursale [sykyrsal] *nf* branch.

sucer [16] [syse] *vt* to suck.

sucette [sysɛt] *nf* [friandise] lolly *Br*, lollipop ; **~ au caramel** caramel lollipop.

suçon [sysɔ̃] *nm* lovebite, hickey *Am*.

sucre [sykr] *nm* sugar ; **~ cristallisé** granulated sugar ; **~ glace** icing sugar *Br*, confectioner's sugar *Am* ; **~ en morceaux** lump sugar ; **~ d'orge** barley sugar ; **~ en poudre**, **~ semoule** caster sugar ; **casser du ~ sur le dos de qqn** *fam fig* to talk about sb behind his/her back.

sucré, e [sykre] *adj* [goût] sweet.

sucrer [3] [sykre] *vt* **- 1.** [café, thé] to sweeten, to sugar **- 2.** *fam* [permission] to withdraw ; [passage, réplique] to cut ; **~ qqch à qqn** to take sthg away from sb.

➡ **se sucrer** *vp fam* **- 1.** [se servir en sucre] to take some sugar **- 2.** [s'octroyer une part] to line one's pockets.

sucrerie [sykrəri] *nf* **- 1.** [usine] sugar refinery **- 2.** [friandise] sweet *Br*, candy *Am*.

sucrette [sykret] *nf* sweetener.

sucrier [sykrije] *nm* sugar bowl.

sucrier, ère [sykrije, ɛr] *adj* sugar *(avant n)*.

sud [syd] ◇ *nm* south ; **un vent du ~** a southerly wind ; **le vent du ~** the south wind ; **au ~** in the south ; **au ~ (de)** to the south (of) ◇ *adj inv* [gén] south ; [province, région] southern.

sud-africain, e [sydafrikɛ̃, ɛn] *(mpl* sud-africains, *fpl* sud-africaines) *adj* South African.

➡ **Sud-Africain, e** *nm, f* South African.

sud-américain, e [sydamerikɛ̃, ɛn] *(mpl* sud-américains, *fpl* sud-américaines) *adj* South American.

➡ **Sud-Américain, e** *nm, f* South American.

sudation [sydasjɔ̃] *nf* sweating.

sud-coréen, enne [sydkɔreɛ̃, ɛn] *(mpl* sud-coréens, *fpl* sud-coréennes) *adj* South Korean.

Sud-Coréen, enne nm, f South Korean.

sud-est [sydɛst] nm & adj inv southeast.

sud-ouest [sydwɛst] nm & adj inv south-west.

Suède [sɥɛd] nf : **la ~** Sweden.

suédois, e [sɥedwa, az] adj Swedish.

suédois nm [langue] Swedish.

Suédois, e nm, f Swede.

suée [sɥe] nf fam sweat.

suer [7] [sɥe] ◇ vi [personne] to sweat ; **faire ~ qqn** fam fig to give sb a hard time ; **se faire ~** fam fig to be bored to tears ◇ vt to exude.

sueur [sɥœr] nf sweat ; **être en ~** to be sweating ; **avoir des ~s froides** fig to be in a cold sweat.

Suez [sɥɛz] n : **le canal de ~** the Suez Canal.

suffi [syfi] pp inv ▷ suffire.

suffire [100] [syfir] ◇ vi - **1.** [être assez] : **~ pour qqch/pour faire qqch** to be enough for sthg/to do sthg, to be sufficient for sthg/to do sthg ; **ça suffit!** that's enough! - **2.** [satisfaire] : **~ à** to be enough for ◇ v impers : **il suffit de ...** all that is necessary is ..., all that you have to do is ... ; **il suffit d'un moment d'inattention pour que ...** it only takes a moment of carelessness for ... ; **il lui suffit de donner sa démission** all he has to do is resign ; **il suffit que** (+ subjonctif) : **il suffit que vous lui écriviez** all (that) you need do is write to him.

se suffire vp : **se ~ à soi-même** to be self-sufficient.

suffisais ▷ suffire.

suffisamment [syfizamɑ̃] adv sufficiently.

suffisance [syfizɑ̃s] nf [vanité] self-importance.

suffisant, e [syfizɑ̃, ɑ̃t] adj - **1.** [satisfaisant] sufficient - **2.** [vaniteux] self-important.

suffise ▷ suffire.

suffixe [syfiks] nm suffix.

suffocant, e [syfɔkɑ̃, ɑ̃t] adj - **1.** [chaleur, fumée] suffocating - **2.** fig [nouvelle, révélation] astonishing, incredible.

suffocation [syfɔkasjɔ̃] nf suffocation.

suffoquer [3] [syfɔke] ◇ vt - **1.** [suj : chaleur, fumée] to suffocate - **2.** fig [suj : colère] to choke ; [suj : nouvelle, révélation] to astonish, to stun ◇ vi to choke ; **~ de** fig to choke with.

suffrage [syfraʒ] nm vote ; **rallier tous les ~s** to win all the votes ; **recueillir des ~s** to win votes ; **~ indirect/restreint/universel** indirect/restricted/universal suffrage.

suffragette [syfraʒɛt] nf suffragette.

suggérer [18] [sygʒere] vt - **1.** [proposer] to suggest ; **~ qqch à qqn** to suggest sthg to sb ;

~ à qqn de faire qqch to suggest that sb (should) do sthg - **2.** [faire penser à] to evoke.

suggestif, ive [sygʒɛstif, iv] adj - **1.** [musique] evocative - **2.** [pose, photo] suggestive.

suggestion [sygʒɛstjɔ̃] nf suggestion.

suicidaire [sɥisider] adj suicidal.

suicide [sɥisid] ◇ nm suicide ◇ adj suicide (avant n).

suicider [3] [sɥiside] **se suicider** vp to commit suicide, to kill o.s.

suie [sɥi] nf soot.

suif [sɥif] nm tallow.

suintant, e [sɥɛ̃tɑ̃, ɑ̃t] adj [mur] sweating ; [plaie] weeping.

suintement [sɥɛ̃tmɑ̃] nm - **1.** [de mur] sweating ; [de plaie] weeping - **2.** [d'eau] seeping, oozing.

suinter [3] [sɥɛ̃te] vi - **1.** [eau, sang] to ooze, to seep - **2.** [surface, mur] to sweat ; [plaie] to weep.

suis[1] ▷ être.

suis[2], suit etc ▷ suivre.

suisse [sɥis] ◇ adj Swiss ◇ nm RELIG verger.

Suisse ◇ nf [pays] : **la ~** Switzerland ; **la ~ allemande/italienne/romande** German-/Italian-/French- speaking Switzerland ◇ nmf [personne] Swiss (person) ; **les Suisses** the Swiss.

en suisse loc adv fam alone, on one's own.

Suissesse [sɥisɛs] nf Swiss woman.

suite [sɥit] nf - **1.** [de liste, feuilleton] continuation - **2.** [série - de maisons, de succès] series ; [- d'événements] sequence - **3.** [succession] : **prendre la ~ de** [personne] to succeed, to take over from ; [affaire] to take over ; **à la ~** one after the other ; **à la ~ de** fig following - **4.** [escorte] retinue - **5.** MUS suite - **6.** [appartement] suite.

suites nfpl consequences.

de suite loc adv - **1.** [l'un après l'autre] in succession - **2.** [immédiatement] immediately.

par la suite loc adv afterwards.

par suite de loc prép owing to, because of.

suivais, suivions etc ▷ suivre.

suivant, e [sɥivɑ̃, ɑ̃t] ◇ adj next, following ◇ nm, f next ou following one ; **au ~!** next!

suivant prép according to ; **~ que** according to whether.

suiveur [sɥivœr] nm follower.

suivi, e [sɥivi] ◇ pp ▷ suivre ◇ adj - **1.** [visites] regular ; [travail] sustained ; [qualité] consistent - **2.** [raisonnement] coherent.

suivi nm follow-up.

suivre [89] [sɥivr] ◇ vt - **1.** [gén] to follow ; **'faire ~'** 'please forward' ; **à ~** to be con-

tinued - **2.** [suj : médecin] to treat <> *vi* - **1.** *SCOL*
to keep up - **2.** [venir après] to follow.
➡ **se suivre** *vp* to follow one another.

sujet, ette [syʒɛ, ɛt] <> *adj* : **être ~ à qqch** to
be subject *ou* prone to sthg ; **être ~ à faire
qqch** to be apt *ou* liable to do sthg ; **être ~ à
caution** *fig* to be unconfirmed <> *nm, f* [de
souverain] subject.
➡ **sujet** *nm* - **1.** [gén] subject ; **c'est à quel ~?**
what is it about? ; **~ de conversation** topic of
conversation ; **au ~ de** about, concerning
- **2.** [motif] : **~ de** cause for, reason for.

sulfate [sylfat] *nm* sulphate *Br*, sulfate *Am*.

sulfure [sylfyr] *nm* sulphide *Br*, sulfide *Am*.

sulfureux, euse [sylfyrø, øz] *adj* sulphur-
ous *Br*, sulfurous *Am*.

sulfurique [sylfyrik] *adj* sulphuric *Br*, sulfuric *Am*.

sulfurisé, e [sylfyrize] *adj* : **papier ~** greaseproof paper.

sultan, e [syltã, an] *nm, f* sultan (*f* sultana).

sultanat [syltana] *nm* sultanate.

Sumatra [symatra] *n* Sumatra ; **à ~** in Sumatra.

summum [sɔmɔm] *nm* summit, height.

super [sypɛr] *fam* <> *adj inv* super, great
<> *nm* four star (petrol) *Br*, premium *Am*.

superbe [sypɛrb] <> *adj* superb ; [enfant, fem-
me] beautiful <> *nf littéraire* pride, arrogance.

superbement [sypɛrbəmã] *adv* superbly.

supercarburant [sypɛrkarbyrã] *nm* high-
octane petrol *Br ou* gasoline *Am*.

supercherie [sypɛrʃəri] *nf* deception, trickery.

superfétatoire [sypɛrfetatwar] *adj littéraire*
superfluous.

superficie [sypɛrfisi] *nf* - **1.** [surface] area
- **2.** *fig* [aspect superficiel] surface.

superficiel, elle [sypɛrfisjɛl] *adj* superficial.

superficiellement [sypɛrfisjɛlmã] *adv*
superficially.

superflu, e [sypɛrfly] *adj* superfluous.
➡ **superflu** *nm* superfluity.

superforme [sypɛrfɔrm] *nf fam* top form,
top shape.

super-huit [sypɛrɥit] *nm inv* super-eight.

supérieur, e [syperjœr] <> *adj* - **1.** [étage]
upper - **2.** [intelligence, qualité] superior ; **~ à**
superior to ; [température] higher than, above
- **3.** [dominant - équipe] superior ; [- cadre] senior
- **4.** [*SCOL* - classe] upper, senior ; [- enseignement]
higher - **5.** *péj* [air] superior <> *nm, f* superior.

supériorité [syperjɔrite] *nf* superiority.

superlatif [sypɛrlatif] *nm* superlative.

supermarché [sypɛrmarʃe] *nm* supermarket.

superposable [sypɛrpozabl] *adj* stacking
(*avant n*).

superposer [3] [sypɛrpoze] *vt* to stack.
➡ **se superposer** *vp* to be stacked ; *GÉOL* to
be superposed.

superposition [sypɛrpozisjɔ̃] *nf* - **1.** [action
- d'objets] stacking - **2.** [état] superposition
- **3.** *fig* [d'influences] combination.

superproduction [sypɛrprɔdyksjɔ̃] *nf* spectacular.

superpuissance [sypɛrpɥisãs] *nf* superpower.

supersonique [sypɛrsɔnik] *adj* supersonic.

superstar [sypɛrstar] *nf fam* superstar.

superstitieux, euse [sypɛrstisjø, øz] <> *adj*
superstitious <> *nm, f* superstitious person.

superstition [sypɛrstisjɔ̃] *nf* - **1.** [croyance]
superstition - **2.** [obsession] obsessive attachment.

superviser [3] [sypɛrvize] *vt* to supervise.

supervision [sypɛrvizjɔ̃] *nf* supervision.

supplanter [3] [syplãte] *vt* to supplant.

suppléance [sypleãs] *nf* supply post *Br*, substitute post *Am*.

suppléant, e [sypleã, ãt] <> *adj* acting
(*avant n*), temporary <> *nm, f* substitute,
deputy.

suppléer [15] [syplee] <> *vt* - **1.** *littéraire* [caren-
ce] to compensate for - **2.** [personne] to stand
in for <> *vi* : **~ à** to compensate for, to make
up for.

supplément [syplemã] *nm* - **1.** [surplus] : **un
~ de détails** additional details, extra details
- **2.** *PRESSE* supplement - **3.** [de billet] extra
charge ; **en ~** extra.

supplémentaire [syplemãtɛr] *adj* extra,
additional.

supplication [syplikasjɔ̃] *nf* plea.

supplice [syplis] *nm* torture ; *fig* [souffrance]
torture, agony ; **être un ~** to be agony ; **être
au ~** to be in agony *ou* torment ; **mettre qqn
au ~** to torture sb ; **~ de Tantale** torture.

supplicié, e [syplisje] *nm, f* victim of torture.

supplier [10] [syplije] *vt* : **~ qqn de faire qqch**
to beg *ou* implore sb to do sthg ; **je t'en** *ou*
vous en supplie I beg *ou* implore you.

supplique [syplik] *nf* petition.

support [sypɔr] *nm* - **1.** [socle] support, base

-.2. *fig* [de communication] medium ; ~**s audiovi-suels** audiovisual aids ; ~ **pédagogique** teaching aid ; ~ **publicitaire** advertising medium.

supportable [sypɔrtabl] *adj* - **1.** [douleur] bearable - **2.** [conduite] tolerable, acceptable.

supporter¹ [3] [sypɔrte] *vt* - **1.** [soutenir, encourager] to support - **2.** [endurer] to bear, to stand ; ~ **que** (+ *subjonctif*) : **il ne supporte pas qu'on le contredise** he cannot bear being contradicted - **3.** [résister à] to withstand.

➤ **se supporter** *vp* [se tolérer] to bear *ou* stand each other.

supporter² [sypɔrter] *nm* supporter.

supposé, e [sypoze] *adj* [montant] estimated ; [criminel] alleged.

supposer [3] [sypoze] *vt* - **1.** [imaginer] to suppose, to assure ; **en supposant que** (+ *subjonctif*), **à** ~ **que** (+ *subjonctif*) supposing (that) - **2.** [impliquer] to imply, to presuppose.

supposition [sypozisjɔ̃] *nf* supposition, assumption.

suppositoire [sypozitwar] *nm* suppository.

suppôt [sypo] *nm littéraire* henchman ; ~ **du diable** *ou* **de satan** fiend.

suppression [sypresjɔ̃] *nf* - **1.** [de permis de conduire] withdrawal ; [de document] suppression - **2.** [de mot, passage] deletion - **3.** [de loi, poste] abolition.

supprimer [3] [syprime] *vt* - **1.** [document] to suppress ; [obstacle, difficulté] to remove - **2.** [mot, passage] to delete - **3.** [loi, poste] to abolish - **4.** [témoin] to do away with, to eliminate - **5.** [permis de conduire, revenus] : ~ **qqch à qqn** to take sthg away from sb - **6.** [douleur] to take away, to suppress.

suppurer [3] [sypyre] *vi* to suppurate.

supputation [sypytasjɔ̃] *nf* calculation, computation.

supputer [3] [sypyte] *vt littéraire* to calculate, to compute.

supranational, e, aux [sypranasjɔnal, o] *adj* supranational.

suprématie [sypremasi] *nf* supremacy.

suprême [syprɛm] <> *adj* - **1.** [gén] supreme - **2.** *sout* [dernier - moment, pensée] last <> *nm fillets in a cream sauce.*

suprêmement [syprɛmmɑ̃] *adv* supremely.

sur [syr] *prép* - **1.** [position - dessus] on ; [- au-dessus de] above, over ; ~ **la table** on the table - **2.** [direction] towards *Br*, toward *Am* ; ~ **la droite/gauche** on the right/left, to the right/left - **3.** [distance] : **travaux** ~ **10 kilomètres** roadworks for 10 kilometres *Br ou* kilo-meters *Am* - **4.** [d'après] by ; **juger qqn** ~ **sa mine** to judge sb by his/her appearance - **5.** [grâce à] on ; **il vit** ~ **les revenus de ses parents** he lives on *ou* off his parents' income - **6.** [au sujet de] on, about - **7.** [proportion] out of ; [mesure] by ; **9** ~ **10** 9 out of 10 ; **un mètre** ~ **deux** one metre *Br ou* meter *Am* by two ; **un jour** ~ **deux** every other day ; **une fois** ~ **deux** every other time.

➤ **sur ce** *loc adv* whereupon.

sûr, e [syr] *adj* - **1.** [sans danger] safe - **2.** [digne de confiance - personne] reliable, trustworthy ; [- goût] reliable, sound ; [- investissement] sound - **3.** [certain] sure, certain ; ~ **de** sure of ; ~ **et certain** absolutely certain ; ~ **de soi** self-confident.

surabondance [syrabɔ̃dɑ̃s] *nf* over-abundance.

surabondant, e [syrabɔ̃dɑ̃, ɑ̃t] *adj* over-abundant.

surabonder [3] [syrabɔ̃de] *vi littéraire* to overabound.

suractivité [syraktivite] *nf* hyperactivity.

suraigu, ë [syregy] *adj* high-pitched, shrill.

surajouter [3] [syraʒute] *vt* to add (on top).

➤ **se surajouter** *vp* to be added (on top).

suralimenter [3] [syralimɑ̃te] *vt* - **1.** [personne] to overfeed - **2.** [moteur] to supercharge.

suranné, e [syrane] *adj littéraire* old-fashioned, outdated.

surate [syrat], **sourate** [surat] *nf* sura.

surcharge [syrʃarʒ] *nf* - **1.** [de poids] excess load ; [de bagages] excess weight - **2.** *fig* [surcroît] : **une** ~ **de travail** extra work - **3.** [surabondance] surfeit - **4.** [de document] alteration - **5.** [de timbre] surcharge.

surcharger [17] [syrʃarʒe] *vt* - **1.** [véhicule, personne] : ~ **(de)** to overload (with) - **2.** [texte] to alter extensively - **3.** [timbre] to surcharge.

surchauffe [syrʃof] *nf* overheating.

surchauffer [3] [syrʃofe] *vt* to overheat.

surclasser [3] [syrklase] *vt* to outclass.

surconsommation [syrkɔ̃sɔmasjɔ̃] *nf* over-consumption.

surcroît [syrkrwa] *nm* : **un** ~ **de travail/ d'inquiétude** additional work/anxiety ; **de** *ou* **par** ~ moreover, what is more.

surdimensionné, e [syrdimɑ̃sjɔne] *adj* oversize(d).

surdi-mutité [syrdimytite] *nf* deaf-muteness.

surdité [syrdite] *nf* deafness.

surdose [syrdoz] *nf* overdose.

surdoué, e [syrdwe] *adj* exceptionally *ou* highly gifted.

sureau, x [syro] *nm* elder.

sureffectif [syrefɛktif] *nm* overmanning, overstaffing.

surélever [19] [syrɛlve] *vt* to raise, to heighten.

sûrement [syrmã] *adv* - **1.** [certainement] certainly ; **~ pas!** *fam* no way!, definitely not! - **2.** [sans doute] certainly, surely - **3.** [sans risque] surely, safely.

surenchère [syrɑ̃ʃer] *nf* higher bid ; *fig* overstatement, exaggeration ; **faire de la ~** *fig* to try to go one better.

surenchérir [32] [syrɑ̃ʃerir] *vi* to bid higher , *fig* to try to go one better.

surendetté, e [syrɑ̃dete] *adj* overindebted.

surendettement [syrɑ̃dɛtmɑ̃] *nm* overindebtedness.

surestimer [3] [syrɛstime] *vt* - **1.** [exagérer] to overestimate - **2.** [surévaluer] to overvalue.
  ➤ **se surestimer** *vp* to overestimate o.s.

sûreté [syrte] *nf* - **1.** [sécurité] safety ; **en ~** safe ; **de ~** safety *(avant n)* - **2.** [fiabilité] reliability - **3.** *JUR* surety.
  ➤ **Sûreté** *nf* : **la Sûreté (nationale)** ≃ C.I.D. *Br*, ≃ F.B.I. *Am*.

surexcitation [syrɛksitasjɔ̃] *nf* overexcitement.

surexciter [3] [syrɛksite] *vt* to overexcite.

surexposer [3] [syrɛkspoze] *vt* to overexpose.

surf [sœrf] *nm* surfing ; **~ des neiges** snowboarding.

surface [syrfas] *nf* - **1.** [extérieur, apparence] surface ; **faire ~** *litt & fig* to surface ; **en ~** superficially - **2.** [superficie] surface area.
  ➤ **grande surface** *nf* hypermarket.
  ➤ **moyenne surface** *nf* high-street store.

surfait, e [syrfɛ, ɛt] *adj* overrated.

surfer [3] [sœrf] *vi* - **1.** *SPORT* to go surfing - **2.** *INFORM* to surf.

surfeur, euse [sœrfœr, øz] *nm, f* surfer.

surfiler [3] [syrfile] *vt* to oversew.

surfin, e [syrfɛ̃, in] *adj* superfine, extra fine.

surgelé, e [syrʒəle] *adj* frozen.
  ➤ **surgelé** *nm* frozen food.

surgeler [25] [syrʒəle] *vt* to freeze.

surgir [32] [syrʒir] *vi* to appear suddenly ; *fig* [difficulté] to arise, to come up.

surhomme [syrɔm] *nm* superman.

surhumain, e [syrymɛ̃, ɛn] *adj* superhuman.

surimposer [3] [syrɛ̃poze] *vt* to overtax *(financially)*.

surimpression [syrɛ̃presjɔ̃] *nf* double exposure.

Surinam(e) [syrinam] *nm* : **le ~** Surinam ; **au ~** in Surinam.

surinfection [syrɛ̃fɛksjɔ̃] *nf* secondary infection.

surjet [syrʒɛ] *nm* overcasting stitch.

sur-le-champ [syrləʃɑ̃] *loc adv* immediately, straightaway.

surlendemain [syrlɑ̃dmɛ̃] *nm* : **le ~** two days later ; **le ~ de mon départ** two days after I left.

surligner [3] [syrline] *vt* to highlight.

surligneur [syrlinœr] *nm* highlighter (pen).

surmenage [syrmənaʒ] *nm* overwork.

surmener [19] [syrməne] *vt* to overwork.
  ➤ **se surmener** *vp* to overwork.

surmontable [syrmɔ̃tabl] *adj* surmountable.

surmonter [3] [syrmɔ̃te] *vt* - **1.** [obstacle, peur] to overcome, to surmount - **2.** [suj : statue, croix] to surmount, to top.

surnager [17] [syrnaʒe] *vi* - **1.** [flotter] to float (on the surface) - **2.** *fig* [subsister] to remain, to survive.

surnaturel, elle [syrnatyrɛl] *adj* supernatural.
  ➤ **surnaturel** *nm* : **le ~** the supernatural.

surnom [syrnɔ̃] *nm* nickname.

surnombre [syrnɔ̃br] ➤ **en surnombre** *loc adv* too many.

surnommer [3] [syrnɔme] *vt* to nickname.

surpasser [3] [syrpase] *vt* to surpass, to outdo.
  ➤ **se surpasser** *vp* to surpass *ou* excel o.s.

surpayer [11] [syrpeje] *vt* [personne] to overpay ; [article] to pay too much for.

surpeuplé, e [syrpœple] *adj* overpopulated.

surpeuplement [syrpœpləmɑ̃] *nm* overpopulation.

surplace [syrplas] *nm* : **faire du ~** [voiture] to be stuck in traffic).

surplis [syrpli] *nm* surplice.

surplomb [syrplɔ̃] ➤ **en surplomb** *loc adj* overhanging.

surplomber [3] [syrplɔ̃be] <> *vt* to overhang <> *vi* to be out of plumb.

surplus [syrply] *nm* - **1.** [excédent] surplus - **2.** [magasin] army surplus store.
  ➤ **au surplus** *loc adv* besides, what is more.

surpopulation [syrpɔpylasjɔ̃] *nf* overpopulation.

surprenant, e [syrprənɑ̃, ɑ̃t] *adj* surprising, amazing.

surprendrai, surprendras *etc* ⊳ surprendre.

surprendre [79] [syrprɑ̃dr] *vt* - **1.** [voleur] to catch (in the act) - **2.** [secret] to overhear - **3.** [prendre à l'improviste] to surprise, to catch unawares - **4.** [étonner] to surprise, to amaze.
➡ **se surprendre** *vp* : **se ~ à faire qqch** to catch o.s. doing sthg.

surpris, e [syrpri, iz] *pp* ⊳ surprendre.

surprise [syrpriz] ◇ *nf* surprise ; **par ~** by surprise ; **faire une ~ à qqn** to give sb a surprise ◇ *adj* [inattendu] surprise *(avant n)* ; **grève ~** lightning strike.

surproduction [syrprɔdyksjɔ̃] *nf* overproduction.

surréalisme [syrrealism] *nm* surrealism.

surréel, elle [syrreɛl] *adj littéraire* surreal.

sursaut [syrso] *nm* - **1.** [de personne] jump, start ; **en ~** with a start - **2.** [d'énergie] burst, surge.

sursauter [3] [syrsote] *vi* to start, to give a start.

surseoir [66] [syrswar] *vi* : **~ à qqch** to postpone *ou* defer sthg.

sursis [syrsi] *nm* JUR & *fig* reprieve ; **six mois avec ~** six months' suspended sentence ; **en ~** in remission.

sursitaire [syrsiter] *nmf* MIL *person whose call-up has been deferred.*

surtaxe [syrtaks] *nf* surcharge.

surtension [syrtɑ̃sjɔ̃] *nf* INFORM power surge.

surtout [syrtu] *adv* - **1.** [avant tout] above all - **2.** [spécialement] especially, particularly ; **~ pas** certainly not.
➡ **surtout que** *loc conj fam* especially as.

survécu [syrveky] *pp* ⊳ survivre.

surveillance [syrvɛjɑ̃s] *nf* supervision ; [de la police, de militaire] surveillance ; **être sous ~** to be under surveillance ; **Direction de la ~ du territoire** counterespionage section.

surveillant, e [syrvɛjɑ̃, ɑ̃t] *nm, f* supervisor ; [de prison] guard, warder *Br.*

surveiller [4] [syrveje] *vt* - **1.** [enfant] to watch, to keep an eye on ; [suspect] to keep a watch on - **2.** [travaux] to supervise ; [examen] to invigilate - **3.** [ligne, langage] to watch.
➡ **se surveiller** *vp* to watch o.s.

survenir [40] [syrvənir] *vi* - **1.** [personne] to arrive unexpectedly - **2.** [incident] to occur.

survenu, e [syrvəny] *pp* ⊳ survenir.

survêtement [syrvɛtmɑ̃] *nm* tracksuit.

survie [syrvi] *nf* [de personne] survival.

surviendrai, surviendras *etc* ⊳ survenir.

survient ⊳ survenir.

survivant, e [syrvivɑ̃, ɑ̃t] ◇ *nm, f* survivor ◇ *adj* surviving.

survivre [90] [syrvivr] *vi* to survive ; **~ à** [personne] to outlive, to survive ; [accident, malheur] to survive.

survol [syrvɔl] *nm* - **1.** [de territoire] flying over - **2.** [de texte] skimming through.

survoler [3] [syrvɔle] *vt* - **1.** [territoire] to fly over - **2.** [texte] to skim (through).

sus [sy(s)] *interj* : **~ à l'ennemi!** at the enemy!
➡ **en sus** *loc adv* moreover, in addition ; **en ~ de** over and above, in addition to.

susceptibilité [syseptibilite] *nf* touchiness, sensitivity.

susceptible [syseptibl] *adj* - **1.** [ombrageux] touchy, sensitive - **2.** [en mesure de] : **~ de faire qqch** liable *ou* likely to do sthg ; **~ d'amélioration, ~ d'être amélioré** open to improvement.

susciter [3] [sysite] *vt* - **1.** [admiration, curiosité] to arouse - **2.** [ennuis, problèmes] to create ; **~ qqch à qqn** *sout* to make *ou* cause sthg for sb.

susdit, e [sysdi, it] ◇ *adj* above-mentioned ◇ *nm, f* above-mentioned (person).

susnommé, e [sysnɔme] ◇ *adj* above-named ◇ *nm, f* above-named (person).

suspect, e [syspɛ, ɛkt] ◇ *adj* - **1.** [personne] suspicious ; **~ de qqch** suspected of sthg - **2.** [douteux] suspect ◇ *nm, f* suspect.

suspecter [4] [syspɛkte] *vt* to suspect, to have one's suspicions about ; **~ qqn de qqch/de faire qqch** to suspect sb of sthg/of doing sthg.

suspendre [73] [syspɑ̃dr] *vt* - **1.** [lustre, tableau] to hang (up) ; **~ au plafond/au mur** to hang from the ceiling/on the wall - **2.** [pourparlers] to suspend ; [séance] to adjourn ; [journal] to suspend publication of - **3.** [fonctionnaire, constitution] to suspend - **4.** [jugement] to postpone, to defer.
➡ **se suspendre** *vp* : **se ~ à** to hang from.

suspendu, e [syspɑ̃dy] ◇ *pp* ⊳ suspendre ◇ *adj* - **1.** [fonctionnaire] suspended - **2.** [séance] adjourned - **3.** [lustre, tableau] : **~ au plafond/au mur** hanging from the ceiling/on the wall - **4.** [véhicule] : **bien/mal ~** with good/bad suspension.

suspens [syspɑ̃] ➡ **en suspens** *loc adv* in abeyance.

suspense [syspɑ̃s, syspɛns] *nm* suspense.

suspension [syspɑ̃sjɔ̃] *nf* - **1.** [gén] suspension ; **en ~** in suspension, suspended - **2.** [de combat] halt ; [d'audience] adjournment - **3.** [lustre] light fitting.

suspicieux, euse [syspisjø, øz] *adj* suspicious.

suspicion [syspisjɔ̃] *nf* suspicion.

sustentation [systɑ̃tasjɔ̃] *nf* AÉRON lift.

sustenter [3] [systɑ̃te] ◆ **se sustenter** *vp* hum & sout to take sustenance.

susurrer [3] [sysyre] *vt* & *vi* to murmur.

suture [sytyr] *nf* suture.

suzeraineté [syzrɛnte] *nf* suzerainty.

svastika, swastika [zvastika], *nm* swastika.

svelte [zvɛlt] *adj* slender.

sveltesse [zvɛltɛs] *nf* slenderness.

SVP *abr de* **s'il vous plaît**.

swahili, e [swaili], **souahéli, e** [swaeli] *adj* Swahili.
◆ **swahili, souahéli** *nm* [langue] Swahili.

swastika = svastika.

Swaziland [swazilɑ̃d] *nm* : **le ~** Swaziland.

sweat-shirt [switʃœrt] (*pl* **sweat-shirts**) *nm* sweatshirt.

Sydney [sidnɛ] *n* Sydney.

syllabe [silab] *nf* syllable.

sylphide [silfid] *nf* sylph.

sylvestre [silvɛstr] *adj littéraire* forest *(avant n)* ⊳ **pin**.

sylviculture [silvikyltyr] *nf* forestry.

symbiose [sɛ̃bjoz] *nf* symbiosis.

symbole [sɛ̃bɔl] *nm* symbol.

symbolique [sɛ̃bɔlik] ◇ *adj* - **1.** [figure] symbolic - **2.** [geste, contribution] token *(avant n)* - **3.** [rémunération] nominal ◇ *nf* - **1.** [système] system of symbols - **2.** [interprétation] interpretation.

symboliquement [sɛ̃bɔlikmɑ̃] *adv* symbolically.

symboliser [3] [sɛ̃bɔlize] *vt* to symbolize.

symbolisme [sɛ̃bɔlism] *nm* symbolism.

symétrie [simetri] *nf* symmetry.

symétrique [simetrik] *adj* symmetrical.

symétriquement [simetrikmɑ̃] *adv* symmetrically.

sympa [sɛ̃pa] *adj fam* [personne] likeable, nice ; [soirée, maison] pleasant, nice ; [ambiance] friendly.

sympathie [sɛ̃pati] *nf* - **1.** [pour personne, projet] liking ; **avoir de la ~ pour qqn** to have a liking for sb, to be fond of sb ; **accueillir un projet avec ~** to look sympathetically *ou* favourably on a project - **2.** [condoléances] sympathy.

sympathique [sɛ̃patik] *adj* - **1.** [personne] likeable, nice ; [soirée, maison] pleasant, nice ; [ambiance] friendly - **2.** ANAT & MÉD sympathetic.

sympathisant, e [sɛ̃patizɑ̃, ɑ̃t] ◇ *adj* sympathizing ◇ *nm, f* sympathizer.

sympathiser [3] [sɛ̃patize] *vi* to get on well ; **~ avec qqn** to get on well with sb.

symphonie [sɛ̃fɔni] *nf* symphony.

symphonique [sɛ̃fɔnik] *adj* [musique] symphonic ; [concert, orchestre] symphony *(avant n)*.

symposium [sɛ̃pozjɔm] *nm* symposium.

symptomatique [sɛ̃ptɔmatik] *adj* symptomatic.

symptôme [sɛ̃ptom] *nm* symptom.

synagogue [sinagɔg] *nf* synagogue.

synchrone [sɛ̃krɔn] *adj* synchronous.

synchronique [sɛ̃krɔnik] *adj* synchronic.

synchronisation [sɛ̃krɔnizasjɔ̃] *nf* synchronization.

synchroniser [3] [sɛ̃krɔnize] *vt* to synchronize.

syncope [sɛ̃kɔp] *nf* - **1.** [évanouissement] blackout ; **tomber en ~** to faint - **2.** MUS syncopation.

syncopé, e [sɛ̃kɔpe] *adj* syncopated.

syndic [sɛ̃dik] *nm* [de copropriété] representative.

syndical, e, aux [sɛ̃dikal, o] *adj* - **1.** [délégué, revendication] (trade) union *(avant n)* - **2.** [patronal] : **chambre ~e** employers' association.

syndicalisme [sɛ̃dikalism] *nm* - **1.** [mouvement] trade unionism - **2.** [activité] (trade) union activity.

syndicaliste [sɛ̃dikalist] ◇ *nmf* trade unionist ◇ *adj* (trade) union *(avant n)*.

syndicat [sɛ̃dika] *nm* [d'employés, d'agriculteurs] (trade) union ; [d'employeurs, de propriétaires] association.
◆ **syndicat d'initiative** *nm* tourist office.

syndiqué, e [sɛ̃dike] ◇ *adj* unionized ◇ *nm, f* (trade) union member, trade unionist.

syndiquer [3] [sɛ̃dike] *vt* to unionize.
◆ **se syndiquer** *vp* - **1.** [personne] to join a (trade) union - **2.** [groupe] to form a (trade) union.

syndrome [sɛ̃drom] *nm* syndrome.

synergie [sinɛrʒi] *nf* synergy, synergism.

synode [sinɔd] *nm* synod ; **le saint-~** the holy synod.

synonyme [sinɔnim] ◇ *nm* synonym ◇ *adj* synonymous.

synoptique [sinɔptik] *adj* synoptic.

synovie [sinɔvi] ⊳ **épanchement**.

syntagme [sɛ̃tagm] *nm* phrase.

syntaxe [sɛ̃taks] *nf* syntax.

synthé [sɛ̃te] *nm fam* synth.

synthèse [sɛ̃tɛz] *nf* - **1.** [opération & *CHIM*] synthesis - **2.** [exposé] overview.

synthétique [sɛ̃tetik] *adj* - **1.** [vue] overall - **2.** [produit] synthetic - **3.** [personne] : **avoir l'esprit ~** to have a gift for summing things up.

synthétiser [3] [sɛ̃tetize] *vt* to synthesize.

synthétiseur [sɛ̃tetizœr] *nm* synthesizer.

syphilis [sifilis] *nf* syphilis.

Syrie [siri] *nf* : **la ~** Syria.

syrien, enne [sirjɛ̃, ɛn] *adj* Syrian.
- **Syrien, enne** *nm, f* Syrian.

systématique [sistematik] *adj* systematic.

systématiquement [sistematikmɑ̃] *adv* systematically.

systématiser [3] [sistematize] *vt* to systematize.
- **se systématiser** *vp* to be/become systematic.

système [sistɛm] *nm* system ; **~ bureautique** *INFORM* office automation system ; **~ expert** *INFORM* expert system ; **~ d'exploitation** *INFORM* operating system ; **le ~ D** resourcefulness ; **~ nerveux** nervous system ; **~ solaire** solar system.

t, T [te] *nm inv* t, T.

t' ▷ **te.**

ta ▷ **ton²**.

TAA (*abr de* train autos accompagnées) *nm* car-sleeper train, ≃ Motorail® *Br*.

tabac [taba] *nm* - **1.** [plante, produit] tobacco ; **~ blond** mild *ou* Virginia tobacco ; **~ brun** dark tobacco ; **~ gris** shag ; **à priser** snuff - **2.** [magasin] tobacconist's - **3.** *loc* : **faire un ~** to be a huge hit ; **passer à ~** *fam* to beat up, to do over.

tabagie [tabaʒi] *nf* - **1.** [pièce] smoke-filled room - **2.** *Can* [bureau de tabac] tobacconist's.

tabagisme [tabaʒism] *nm* - **1.** [intoxication] nicotine addiction - **2.** [habitude] smoking.

tabasser [3] [tabase] *vt fam* to beat up, to do over.

tabatière [tabatjɛr] *nf* snuffbox.

tabernacle [tabɛrnakl] *nm* tabernacle.

table [tabl] *nf* - **1.** [meuble] table ; **à ~!** lunch/dinner *etc* is ready! ; **être à ~** to be at table, to be having a meal ; **se mettre à ~** to sit down to eat ; *fig* to come clean ; **dresser** *ou* **mettre la ~** to lay the table ; **quitter la ~** to leave the table ; **~ de chevet** *ou* **de nuit** bedside table ; **~ basse** coffee table ; **~ gigogne** nest of tables ; **~ de jeu** *ou* **à jouer** gaming table ; **~ d'opération** operating table ; **~ roulante** trolley ; **~ de travail** desk - **2.** [nourriture] : **les plaisirs de la ~** good food.
- **table des matières** *nf* contents (*pl*), table of contents.
- **table de multiplication** *nf* (multiplication) table.
- **table ronde** *nf* [conférence] round table.

tableau, x [tablo] *nm* - **1.** [peinture] painting, picture, *fig* [description] picture ; **~ de maître** old master ; **noircir le ~** *fig* to paint a gloomy picture - **2.** *THÉÂTRE* scene - **3.** [panneau] board ; **~ d'affichage** notice board *Br*, bulletin board *Am* ; **~ de bord** *AÉRON* instrument panel ; *AUTOM* dashboard ; **~ noir** blackboard - **4.** [liste] register ; **~ de chasse** bag ; **~ d'honneur** honours board - **5.** [de données] table.

tablée [table] *nf* table.

tabler [3] [table] *vi* : **~ sur** to count *ou* bank on.

tablette [tablɛt] *nf* - **1.** [planchette] shelf - **2.** [de chewing-gum] stick ; [de chocolat] bar.

tableur [tablœr] *nm INFORM* spreadsheet.

tablier [tablije] *nm* - **1.** [de cuisinière] apron ; [d'écolier] smock - **2.** [de magasin] shutter ; [de cheminée] flue-shutter - **3.** [de pont] roadway, deck.

tabloïd(e) [tabloid] *nm* tabloid.

tabou, e [tabu] *adj* taboo.
- **tabou** *nm* taboo.

taboulé [tabule] *nm* Lebanese dish of bulgur wheat, onions, tomatoes and herbs.

tabouret [taburɛ] *nm* stool ; **~ de bar/de cuisine/de piano** bar/kitchen/piano stool.

tabulateur [tabylatœr] *nm* tabulator, tab.

tac [tak] *nm* : **du ~ au ~** tit for tat.

TAC (*abr de* train auto-couchettes) *nm* car-sleeper train, ≃ Motorail® *Br*.

tache [taʃ] *nf* - **1.** [de pelage] marking ; [de peau] mark ; **~ de rousseur** *ou* **de son** freckle - **2.** [de couleur, lumière] spot, patch - **3.** [sur nappe, vêtement] stain ; **faire ~ d'huile** *fig* to gain ground **- 4.** *littéraire* [morale] blemish.

tâche [taʃ] *nf* task ; **travailler à la ~** to do piecework ; **faciliter la ~ de qqn** to make sb's task easier ; **se tuer à la ~** *fig* to work o.s. to death.

tacher [3] [taʃe] *vt* **- 1.** [nappe, vêtement] to stain, to mark **- 2.** *fig* [réputation] to tarnish.

➧ **se tacher** *vp* **- 1.** [enfant] to get one's clothes dirty **- 2.** [nappe] to stain, to mark.

tâcher [3] [taʃe] ⟨⟩ *vt* : **tâche que ça soit parfait** try to make sure it's perfect ⟨⟩ *vi* : **~ de faire qqch** to try to do sthg.

tâcheron [3] [taʃrɔ̃] *nm péj* drudge.

tacheter [27] [taʃte] *vt* to spot, to speckle.

tachycardie [takikardi] *nf* tachycardia.

tacite [tasit] *adj* tacit.

tacitement [tasitmɑ̃] *adv* tacitly.

taciturne [tasityrn] *adj* taciturn.

tacot [tako] *nm fam* jalopy, heap.

tact [takt] *nm* [délicatesse] tact ; **avoir du ~** to be tactful ; **manquer de ~** to be tactless.

tacticien, enne [taktisjɛ̃, ɛn] *nm, f* tactician.

tactile [taktil] *adj* tactile.

tactique [taktik] ⟨⟩ *adj* tactical ⟨⟩ *nf* tactics *(pl)*.

tænia = ténia.

taf [taf] *nm fam* work.

taffe [taf] *nf fam* drag, puff.

taffetas [tafta] *nm* **- 1.** [tissu] taffeta **- 2.** [sparadrap] plaster.

tag [tag] *nm identifying name written with a spray can on walls, the sides of trains etc.*

tagine = tajine.

tagliatelles [taljatɛl] *nfpl* tagliatelle *(U).*

tagueur, euse [tagœr, øz] *nm, f person who sprays their 'tag' on walls, the sides of trains etc.*

Tahiti [taiti] *n* Tahiti ; **à ~** in Tahiti.

tahitien, enne [taisjɛ̃, ɛn] *adj* Tahitian.

➧ **tahitien** *nm* [langue] Tahitian.

➧ **Tahitien, enne** *nm, f* Tahitian.

taïaut, tayaut [tajo] *interj* tally-ho.

Taibei, T'ai-pei [tajpɛ] *n* Taipei.

taie [tɛ] *nf* **- 1.** [enveloppe] : **~ (d'oreiller)** pillowcase, pillow slip **- 2.** [sur œil] leucoma, opaque spot.

taïga [tajga] *nf* taiga.

taillader [3] [tajade] *vt* to gash.

taille [taj] *nf* **- 1.** [action - de pierre, diamant] cutting ; [- d'arbre, de haie] pruning **- 2.** [stature] height ; **être de ~ à faire qqch** *fig* to be capable of doing sthg **- 3.** [mesure, dimensions] size ; **vous faites quelle ~?** what size are you?, what size do you take? ; **ce n'est pas à ma ~** it doesn't fit me ; **de ~** sizeable, considerable **- 4.** [milieu du corps] waist ; **avoir une ~ de guêpe** *fig* to be wasp-waisted.

taille-crayon [tajkrɛjɔ̃] *(pl* **taille-crayons)** *nm* pencil sharpener.

tailler [3] [taje] *vt* **- 1.** [couper - chair, pierre, diamant] to cut ; [- arbre, haie] to prune ; [- crayon] to sharpen ; [- bois] to carve **- 2.** [vêtement] to cut out.

➧ **se tailler** *vp* **- 1.** [obtenir] to achieve **- 2.** *fam* [se sauver] to beat it, to clear off.

tailleur [tajœr] *nm* **- 1.** [couturier] tailor **- 2.** [vêtement] (lady's) suit **- 3.** [de diamants, pierre] cutter **- 4.** *loc* : **s'asseoir en ~** to sit cross-legged.

tailleur-pantalon [tajœrpɑ̃talɔ̃] *(pl* **tailleurs-pantalons)** *nm* trouser suit *Br,* pantsuit *Am.*

taillis [taji] *nm* coppice, copse.

tain [tɛ̃] *nm* silvering ; **miroir sans ~** two-way mirror.

taire [111] [tɛr] *vt* to conceal.

➧ **se taire** *vp* **- 1.** [rester silencieux] to be silent *ou* quiet **- 2.** [cesser de s'exprimer] to fall silent ; **faire se ~ qqn** to make sb be quiet ; **tais-toi!** shut up! **- 3.** [orchestre] to fall silent ; [cris] to cease.

taisais, taisions *etc* ▷ taire.

taise, taises *etc* ▷ taire.

Taiwan [tajwan] *n* Taiwan ; **à ~** in Taiwan.

taiwanais, e [tajwanɛ, ɛz] *adj* Taiwanese.

➧ **Taiwanais, e** *nm, f* Taiwanese.

tajine, tagine [taʒin] *nm North African stew of mutton steamed with a variety of vegetables.*

talc [talk] *nm* talcum powder.

talent [talɑ̃] *nm* talent ; **avoir du ~** to be talented, to have talent ; **les jeunes ~s** young talent *(U).*

talentueux, euse [talɑ̃tɥø, øz] *adj* talented.

talion [taljɔ̃] *nm* : **la loi du ~** an eye for an eye (and a tooth for a tooth).

talisman [talismɑ̃] *nm* talisman.

talkie-walkie [tɔkiwɔki] *(pl* **talkies-walkies)** *nm* walkie-talkie.

taloche [talɔʃ] *nf fam* [gifle] slap.

talon [talɔ̃] *nm* **- 1.** [gén] heel ; **~s aiguilles/ hauts** stiletto/high heels ; **~s plats** low *ou* flat heels ; **~ d'Achille** Achilles' heel ; **être/ marcher sur les ~s de qqn** *fig* to be/to follow hard on sb's heels ; **tourner les ~s** *fig* to turn on one's heel - **2.** [de chèque] counterfoil, stub - **3.** CARTES stock.

talonner [3] [talɔne] vt - **1.** [suj : poursuivant] to be hard on the heels of - **2.** [suj : créancier] to harry, to hound.

talonnette [talɔnɛt] nf - **1.** [de chaussure] heel cushion, heel-pad - **2.** [de pantalon] binding *(to reinforce trouser bottoms)*.

talquer [3] [talke] vt to put talcum powder on.

talus [taly] nm embankment.

tamarin [tamarɛ̃] nm [fruit] tamarind.

tamarinier [tamarinje] nm tamarind tree.

tamaris [tamaris], **tamarix** [tamariks] nm tamarisk.

tambouille [tābuj] nf fam - **1.** [plat] grub - **2.** [cuisine] cooking.

tambour [tābur] nm - **1.** [instrument, cylindre] drum ; sans ~ ni trompette *fig* without any fuss ; ~ battant *fig* briskly - **2.** [musicien] drummer - **3.** [porte à tourniquet] revolving door - **4.** [à broder] embroidery hoop.

tambourin [tāburɛ̃] nm - **1.** [à grelots] tambourine - **2.** [tambour] tambourin.

tambouriner [3] [tāburine] <> vt to drum <> vi : ~ **sur** OU **à** to drum on ; ~ **contre** to drum against.

tamis [tami] nm - **1.** [crible] sieve - **2.** [de raquette] strings *(pl)*.

Tamise [tamiz] nf : **la ~** the Thames.

tamisé, e [tamize] adj [éclairage] subdued.

tamiser [3] [tamize] vt - **1.** [farine] to sieve - **2.** [lumière] to filter.

tampon [tāpɔ̃] nm - **1.** [bouchon] stopper, plug - **2.** [éponge] pad ; ~ **à récurer** scourer - **3.** [de coton, d'ouate] pad ; ~ **hygiénique** OU **périodique** tampon - **4.** [cachet] stamp ; ~ **encreur** inking pad - **5.** litt & fig [amortisseur] buffer.

tamponner [3] [tāpɔne] vt - **1.** [document] to stamp - **2.** [plaie] to dab.
➡ **se tamponner** vp to crash into each other.

tamponneuse [tāpɔnøz] ▷ **auto**.

tam-tam [tamtam] *(pl* **tam-tams)** nm tom-tom.

tancer [16] [tāse] vt *littéraire* to rebuke.

tanche [tāʃ] nf tench.

tandem [tādɛm] nm - **1.** [vélo] tandem - **2.** [duo] pair ; **en ~** together, in tandem.

tandis [tādi] ➡ **tandis que** loc conj - **1.** [pendant que] while - **2.** [alors que] while, whereas.

tangage [tāgaʒ] nm pitching, pitch.

tangent, e [tāʒā, āt] adj : ~ **à** MATHS tangent

to, tangential to ; **c'était ~** *fig* it was close, it was touch and go.
➡ **tangente** nf tangent.

tangible [tāʒibl] adj tangible.

tango [tāgo] nm tango.

tanguer [3] [tāge] vi to pitch.

tanière [tanjɛr] nf den, lair.

tanin, tannin [tanɛ̃] nm tannin.

tank [tāk] nm tank.

tannage [tanaʒ] nm tanning.

tannant, e [tanā, āt] adj fam [assommant] irritating, maddening.

tanner [3] [tane] vt - **1.** [peau] to tan - **2.** fam [personne] to pester, to annoy.

tannerie [tanri] nf - **1.** [usine] tannery - **2.** [opération] tanning.

tanneur [tanœr] nm - **1.** [ouvrier] tanner - **2.** [commerçant] leather merchant.

tannin = tanin.

tant [tā] adv - **1.** [quantité] : ~ **de** so much ; ~ **de travail** so much work - **2.** [nombre] : ~ **de** so many ; ~ **de livres/d'élèves** so many books/pupils - **3.** [tellement] such a lot, so much ; **il l'aime ~** he loves her so much - **4.** [quantité indéfinie] so much ; **ça coûte ~** it costs so much ; **à ~ pour cent** at so many per cent - **5.** [un jour indéfini] : **votre lettre du ~** your letter of such-and-such a date - **6.** [comparatif] : ~ **que** as much as - **7.** [valeur temporelle] : ~ **que** [aussi longtemps que] as long as ; [pendant que] while.
➡ **en tant que** loc conj as ; **en ~ que tel** as such.
➡ **tant bien que mal** loc adv after a fashion, somehow or other.
➡ **tant mieux** loc adv so much the better ; ~ **mieux pour lui** good for him.
➡ **tant pis** loc adv too bad ; ~ **pis pour lui** too bad for him.
➡ **(un) tant soit peu** loc adv the slightest bit.

Tantale [tātal] ▷ **supplice**.

tante [tāt] nf - **1.** [parente] aunt - **2.** tfam péj [homosexuel] poof Br, fairy.

tantinet [tātinɛ] nm : **un ~ exagéré/trop long** a bit exaggerated/too long.

tantôt [tāto] adv - **1.** [parfois] sometimes - **2.** vieilli [après-midi] this afternoon.

Tanzanie [tāzani] nf : **la ~** Tanzania.

tanzanien, enne [tāzanjɛ̃, ɛn] adj Tanzanian.
➡ **Tanzanien, enne** nm, f Tanzanian.

TAO *(abr de* **traduction assistée par ordinateur)** nf CAT.

taoïsme [taɔism] nm Taoism.

taon [tã] *nm* horsefly.

tapage [tapaʒ] *nm* - **1.** [bruit] row ; ~ **nocturne** ≈ disturbance of the peace - **2.** *fig* [battage] fuss *(U).*

tapageur, euse [tapaʒœr, øz] *adj* - **1.** [hôte, enfant] rowdy - **2.** [style] flashy - **3.** [liaison, publicité] blatant.

tapant, e [tapã, ãt] *adj* : **à six heures** ~ *ou* ~**es** at six sharp *ou* on the dot.

tape [tap] *nf* slap.

tape-à-l'œil [tapalœj] <> *adj inv* flashy <> *nm inv* show.

tapenade [tapɔnad] *nf pounded anchovies with capers, olives and tuna fish.*

taper [3] [tape] <> *vt* - **1.** [personne, cuisse] to slap ; ~ **(un coup) à la porte** to knock at the door - **2.** [à la machine] to type - **3.** *fam* [demander de l'argent à] : ~ **qqn de** to touch sb for <> *vi* - **1.** [frapper] to hit ; ~ **du poing sur** to bang one's fist on ; ~ **dans ses mains** to clap - **2.** [à la machine] to type - **3.** *fam* [soleil] to beat down - **4.** *fig* [critiquer] : ~ **sur qqn** to knock sb - **5.** *fam* [puiser] : ~ **dans** to dip into.
◆ **se taper** *vp fam* - **1.** [chocolat, vin] to put away - **2.** [corvée] to be landed with.

tapette [tapɛt] *nf* - **1.** [à tapis] carpet beater - **2.** [à mouches] flyswatter - **3.** *tfam péj* [homosexuel] poof *Br*, fairy.

tapinois [tapinwa] ◆ **en tapinois** *loc adv* furtively.

tapioca [tapjɔka] *nm* tapioca.

tapir¹ [tapir] *nm* ZOOL tapir.

tapir² [32] [tapir] ◆ **se tapir** *vp* - **1.** [se blottir] to crouch ; *fig* [sentiment] to be hidden ; **une maison tapie au creux de la vallée** *fig* a house hidden away in the valley - **2.** [se cacher] to retreat.

tapis [tapi] *nm* - **1.** [gén] carpet ; [de gymnase] mat ; ~ **roulant** [pour bagages] conveyor belt ; [pour personnes] travolator ; ~ **de sol** groundsheet ; **dérouler le ~ rouge** *fig* to roll out the red carpet ; **mettre un sujet sur le ~** *fig* to bring up a subject - **2.** INFORM : ~ **de souris** mouse mat.

tapis-brosse [tapibrɔs] (*pl* **tapis-brosses**) *nm* doormat.

tapisser [3] [tapise] *vt* : ~ **(de)** to cover (with).

tapisserie [tapisri] *nf* [de laine] tapestry ; [papier peint] wallpaper ; **faire ~** *fig* to be a wallflower.

tapissier, ère [tapisje, ɛr] *nm, f* - **1.** [artisan] tapestry maker - **2.** [décorateur] (interior) decorator - **3.** [commerçant] upholsterer.

tapotement [tapɔtmã] *nm* tapping.

tapoter [3] [tapɔte] <> *vt* to tap ; [joue] to pat <> *vi* : ~ **sur** to tap on.

tapuscrit [tapyskri] *nm* typescript.

taquet [takɛ] *nm* - **1.** [butée] stop, catch - **2.** [loquet] latch.

taquin, e [takɛ̃, in] <> *adj* teasing <> *nm, f* tease.

taquiner [3] [takine] *vt* - **1.** [suj : personne] to tease - **2.** [suj : douleur] to worry.

taquinerie [takinri] *nf* teasing.

tarabiscoté, e [tarabiskɔte] *adj* elaborate.

tarabuster [3] [tarabyste] *vt* - **1.** [suj : personne] to badger - **2.** [suj : idée] to niggle at.

tarama [tarama] *nm* taramasalata.

tarauder [3] [tarode] *vt* to tap ; *fig* to torment.

tard [tar] *adv* late ; **plus ~** later ; **au plus ~** at the latest ; **sur le ~** [en fin de journée] late in the day ; [dans la vie] late in life.

tarder [3] [tarde] <> *vi* : ~ **à faire qqch** [attendre pour] to delay *ou* put off doing sthg ; [être lent à] to take a long time to do sthg ; **ne pas ~ à faire qqch** not to take long to do sthg ; **le feu ne va pas ~ à s'éteindre** it won't be long before the fire goes out ; **elle ne devrait plus ~ maintenant** she should be here any time now <> *v impers* : **il me tarde de te revoir/qu'il vienne** I am longing to see you again/for him to come.

tardif, ive [tardif, iv] *adj* - **1.** [heure] late - **2.** [excuse] belated.

tardivement [tardivmã] *adv* [arriver] late ; [s'excuser] belatedly.

tare [tar] *nf* - **1.** [défaut] defect - **2.** [de balance] tare - **3.** *fam péj* [personne] cretin.

taré, e [tare] <> *adj* - **1.** [héréditairement] tainted ; *fig* flawed - **2.** *fam péj* [idiot] cracked <> *nm, f* - **1.** [héréditaire] degenerate - **2.** *fam péj* [idiot] cretin.

tarentule [tarãtyl] *nf* tarantula.

targette [tarʒɛt] *nf* bolt.

targuer [3] [targe] ◆ **se targuer** *vp sout* : **se ~ de qqch/de faire qqch** to boast about sthg/about doing sthg.

tarif [tarif] *nm* - **1.** [prix - de restaurant, café] price ; [- de service] rate, price ; [douanier] tariff ; ~**s postaux** postage rates ; **demi-~** half rate *ou* price ; **plein ~** full rate *ou* price ; ~ **dégressif** decreasing rate ; ~ **préférentiel** preferential rate ; ~ **réduit** reduced price ; [au cinéma, théâtre] concession - **2.** [tableau] price list.

tarifaire [tarifɛr] *adj* tariff *(avant n).*

tarifer [3] [tarife] *vt* to fix the price *ou* rate for.

tarification [tarifikasjɔ̃] *nf* fixing of the price *ou* rate.

tarir [32] [tarir] ◇ *vt* to dry up ◇ *vi* to dry up ; **elle ne tarit pas d'éloges sur son professeur** she never stops praising her teacher.
◆ **se tarir** *vp* to dry up.

tarot [taro] *nm* tarot.
◆ **tarots** *nmpl* tarot cards.

tartare [tartar] *adj* Tartar ; **sauce ~** tartare sauce ; **steak ~** steak tartare.
◆ **Tartare** *nmf* Tartar.

tarte [tart] ◇ *nf* - **1.** [gâteau] tart ; **~ aux pommes** apple tart ; **~ tatin** ≃ upside-down apple cake - **2.** *fam fig* [gifle] slap - **3.** *loc* : **c'est pas de la ~!** *fam* it's no joke *ou* picnic! ; **~ à la crème** *CIN* custard pie ; [sujet, propos] hackneyed ◇ *adj* (*avec ou sans accord*) *fam* [idiot] stupid.

tartelette [tartəlɛt] *nf* tartlet.

tartine [tartin] *nf* - **1.** [de pain] piece of bread and butter ; **~ de confiture** piece of bread and jam ; **~ grillée** piece of toast - **2.** *fam fig* [laïus] : **en mettre une ~** *ou* **des ~s** to write reams.

tartiner [3] [tartine] *vt* - **1.** [pain] to spread ; **chocolat/fromage à ~** chocolate/cheese spread - **2.** *fam fig* [pages] to cover.

tartre [tartr] *nm* - **1.** [de dents, vin] tartar - **2.** [de chaudière] fur, scale.

tartuf(f)e [tartyf] *nm* hypocrite.

tas [ta] *nm* heap ; **un ~ de** a lot of ; **apprendre sur le ~** *fig* to learn on the job.

tasse [tas] *nf* cup ; **~ à café/à thé** coffee/tea cup ; **~ de café/de thé** cup of coffee/tea ; **boire la ~** *fig* to get a mouthful of water.

tasseau, x [taso] *nm* bracket.

tassement [tasmã] *nm* - **1.** [de neige] compression ; [de fondations] settling - **2.** *fig* [diminution] decline.

tasser [3] [tase] *vt* - **1.** [neige] to compress, to pack down - **2.** [vêtements, personnes] : **~ qqn/qqch dans** to stuff sb/sth into.
◆ **se tasser** *vp* - **1.** [fondations] to settle - **2.** *fig* [vieillard] to shrink - **3.** [personnes] to squeeze up - **4.** *fam fig* [situation] to settle down.

taste-vin [tastəvɛ̃], **tâte-vin** [tatvɛ̃] *nm inv* tasting cup.

tata [tata] *nf* auntie.

tâter [3] [tate] ◇ *vt* to feel ; *fig* to sound out ◇ *vi* : **~ de** to have a taste of.
◆ **se tâter** *vp fam fig* [hésiter] to be in two minds.

tâte-vin = **taste-vin**.

tatillon, onne [tatijɔ̃, ɔn] ◇ *adj* finicky ◇ *nm, f* finicky person.

tâtonnement [tatɔnmã] *nm* - **1.** [action] groping - **2.** (*gén pl*) [tentative] trial and error (*U*).

tâtonner [3] [tatɔne] *vi* to grope around.

tâtons [tatɔ̃] ◆ **à tâtons** *loc adv* : **marcher/procéder à ~** to feel one's way.

tatou [tatu] *nm* armadillo.

tatouage [tatwaʒ] *nm* - **1.** [action] tattooing - **2.** [dessin] tattoo.

tatouer [6] [tatwe] *vt* to tattoo.

taudis [todi] *nm* slum.

taulard = **tôlard**.

taule = **tôle**.

taulier = **tôlier**.

taupe [top] *nf litt & fig* mole ; **être myope comme une ~** *fig* to be as blind as a bat.

taupinière [topinjɛr] *nf* molehill.

taureau, x [tɔro] *nm* [animal] bull ; **prendre le ~ par les cornes** to take the bull by the horns.
◆ **Taureau** *nm ASTROL* Taurus ; **être Taureau** to be (a) Taurus.

tauromachie [tɔrɔmaʃi] *nf* bullfighting.

taux [to] *nm* rate ; [de cholestérol, d'alcool] level ; **~ de change** exchange rate ; **~ d'escompte** rate of discount ; **~ d'intérêt** interest rate ; **~ de natalité** birth rate.

taverne [tavɛrn] *nf* tavern.

taxation [taksasjɔ̃] *nf* taxation.

taxe [taks] *nf* tax ; **hors ~** *COMM* exclusive of tax, before tax ; [boutique, achat] duty-free ; **toutes ~s comprises** inclusive of tax ; **~ sur la valeur ajoutée** value added tax.

taxer [3] [takse] *vt* - **1.** [imposer] to tax - **2.** [fixer] : **~ le prix de qqch à** to fix the price of sthg at - **3.** *fam* [traiter] : **~ qqn de qqch** to call sb sthg - **4.** [accuser] : **~ qqn de qqch** to accuse sb of sthg - **5.** *fam* [prendre] : **~ qqch à qqn** to cadge sthg off *ou* from sb.

taxi [taksi] *nm* - **1.** [voiture] taxi - **2.** [chauffeur] taxi driver.

taxidermiste [taksidɛrmist] *nmf* taxidermist.

taximètre [taksimɛtr] *nm* meter.

taxinomie [taksinɔmi] *nf* taxonomy.

Taxiphone® [taksifɔn] *nm* pay phone.

tayaut = **taïaut**.

TB, tb (*abr de* **très bien**) VG.

TBE, tbe (*abr de* **très bon état**) vgc.

TCA (*abr de* **taxe sur le chiffre d'affaires**) *nf* tax on turnover.

TCF (*abr de* **Touring Club de France**) *nm* French motorists' club, ≃ AA *Br*, ≃ AAA *Am*.

Tchad [tʃad] *nm* : **le ~** Chad ; **au ~** in Chad.

tchadien, enne [tʃadjɛ̃, ɛn] *adj* of/from Chad.

➤ **tchadien** *nm* [langue] Chadic.

➤ **Tchadien, enne** *nm, f* person from Chad.

tchador [tʃadɔr] *nm* chador.

tchatche [tʃatʃ] *nf fam* : **avoir la ~** to have the gift of the gab.

tchatcher [tʃatʃe] *vi fam* to chat (away).

tchécoslovaque [tʃekɔslɔvak] *adj* Czechoslovakian.

➤ **Tchécoslovaque** *nmf* Czechoslovak.

Tchécoslovaquie [tʃekɔslɔvaki] *nf* : **la ~** Czechoslovakia.

tchèque [tʃɛk] <> *adj* Czech <> *nm* [langue] Czech.

➤ **Tchèque** *nmf* Czech.

tchétchène [tʃetʃɛn] *adj* Chechen.

➤ **Tchétchène** *nmf* Chechen.

Tchétchénie [tʃetʃeni] *nf* : **la ~** Chechnya.

TCS (*abr de* **Touring Club de Suisse**) *nm Swiss motorists' club*, ≈ AA *Br*, ≈ AAA *Am*.

TD (*abr de* **travaux dirigés**) *nmpl* supervised practical work.

TdF (*abr de* **Télévision de France**) *nf French broadcasting authority.*

te [tə], **t'** *pron pers* - **1.** [complément d'objet direct] you - **2.** [complément d'objet indirect] (to) you - **3.** [réfléchi] yourself - **4.** [avec un présentatif] : **~ voici!** here you are!

té [te] *nm* T-square.

technicien, enne [tɛknisjɛ̃, ɛn] *nm, f* - **1.** [professionnel] technician - **2.** [spécialiste] : **~ (de)** expert (in).

technicité [tɛknisite] *nf* - **1.** [de produit] technical nature - **2.** [avance technologique] technological sophistication - **3.** [savoir-faire] skill.

technico-commercial, e [tɛknikokɔmɛrsjal] (*mpl* **technico-commerciaux**, *fpl* **technico-commerciales**) <> *adj* sales engineer (*avant n*) <> *nm, f* sales engineer.

Technicolor® [tɛknikɔlɔr] *nm* Technicolor®.

technique [tɛknik] <> *adj* technical <> *nf* technique.

techniquement [tɛknikmã] *adv* technically.

techno [tɛkno] *adj* & *nf* techno.

technocrate [tɛknɔkrat] *nmf* technocrat.

technologie [tɛknɔlɔʒi] *nf* technology ; **de haute ~** high-tech.

technologique [tɛknɔlɔʒik] *adj* technological.

technologue [tɛknɔlɔg], **technologiste** [tɛknɔlɔʒist] *nmf* technologist.

teck, tek [tɛk] *nm* teak.

teckel [tɛkɛl] *nm* dachshund.

tectonique [tɛktɔnik] <> *adj* tectonic <> *nf* tectonics (*U*) ; **la ~ des plaques** plate tectonics.

TEE (*abr de* **Trans-Europ-Express**) *nm* TEE.

teen-ager [tinedʒœr] (*pl* **teen-agers**) *nmf* teenager.

tee-shirt (*pl* **tee-shirts**), **T-shirt** (*pl* **T-shirts**) [tiʃœrt] *nm* T-shirt.

Téflon® [teflɔ̃] *nm* Teflon®.

TEG (*abr de* **taux effectif garanti**) *nm* APR.

Téhéran [teerã] *n* Tehran.

teignais, teignions *etc* ▷ teindre.

teigne [tɛɲ] *nf* - **1.** [mite] moth - **2.** *MÉD* ringworm - **3.** *fam fig* & *péj* [femme] cow ; [homme] bastard.

teigneux, euse [tɛɲø, øz] *fam fig* & *péj* <> *adj* : **être teigneuse** [femme] to be a cow ; **être ~** [homme] to be a bastard <> *nm, f* [femme] cow ; [homme] bastard.

teindre [81] [tɛ̃dr] *vt* to dye.

➤ **se teindre** *vp* : **se ~ les cheveux** to dye one's hair.

teint, e [tɛ̃, tɛ̃t] <> *pp* ▷ teindre <> *adj* dyed.

➤ **teint** *nm* - **1.** [carnation] complexion - **2.** [couleur] : **tissu bon** *ou* **grand ~** colourfast *Br ou* colorfast *Am* material ; **bon ~** *fig* staunch, dyed-in-the-wool.

➤ **teinte** *nf* colour *Br*, color *Am* ; **une ~e de** *fig* a hint of.

teinté, e [tɛ̃te] *adj* tinted ; **~ de** *fig* tinged with.

teinter [3] [tɛ̃te] *vt* to stain.

➤ **se teinter** *vp* : **se ~ de** to become tinged with.

teinture [tɛ̃tyr] *nf* - **1.** [action] dyeing - **2.** [produit] dye.

➤ **teinture d'iode** *nf* tincture of iodine.

teinturerie [tɛ̃tyrri] *nf* - **1.** [pressing] dry cleaner's - **2.** [métier] dyeing.

teinturier, ère [tɛ̃tyrje, ɛr] *nm, f* - **1.** [de pressing] dry cleaner - **2.** [technicien] dyer.

tek = teck.

tel [tɛl] (*f* **telle**, *mpl* **tels**, *fpl* **telles**) <> *adj* - **1.** [valeur indéterminée] such-and-such a ; **~ et ~** such-and-such a - **2.** [semblable] such ; **un ~ homme** such a man ; **une telle générosité** such generosity ; **de telles gens** such people ; **je n'ai rien dit de ~** I never said anything of the sort - **3.** [valeur emphatique ou intensive] such ; un ~ génie such a genius ; un ~ bonheur such happiness - **4.** [introduit un exemple ou une énumération] : ~ **(que)** such as, like - **5.** [introduit une comparaison] like ; **il est ~ que je l'avais toujours rêvé** he's just like I always dreamt he would be ; ~ **quel** as it is/ was etc ⋄ pron indéf : ~ **veut marcher, tandis que ~ autre veut courir** one will want to walk, while another will want to run ; **une telle m'a dit qu'il était parti** someone or other told me he'd left.

➠ **à tel point que** loc conj to such an extent that.

➠ **de telle manière que** loc conj in such a way that.

➠ **de telle sorte que** loc conj with the result that, so that.

tél. (abr de téléphone) tel.

télé [tele] nf fam TV, telly Br.

téléachat [teleaʃa] nm teleshopping.

téléacteur, trice [teleaktœr, tris] nm, f telesalesperson.

télébenne [telebɛn], **télécabine** [telekabin] nf cable car.

Télécarte® [telekart] nf phonecard.

télécharger [17] [teleʃarʒe] vt to download.

télécommande [telekɔmɑ̃d] nf remote control.

télécommander [3] [telekɔmɑ̃de] vt to operate by remote control ; fig to mastermind.

télécommunication [telekɔmynikasjɔ̃] nf telecommunications (pl).

téléconférence [telekɔ̃ferɑ̃s] nf teleconference.

télécopie [telekɔpi] nf fax.

télécopieur [telekɔpjœr] nm fax (machine).

télédiffuser [3] [teledifyze] vt to televise.

télédiffusion [teledifyzjɔ̃] nf televising.

télédistribution [teledistribysjɔ̃] nf cable television.

télé-enseignement [teleɑ̃sɛɲmɑ̃] (pl **télé-enseignements**) nm distance learning.

téléfilm [telefilm] nm film made for television.

télégramme [telegram] nm telegram.

télégraphe [telegraf] nm telegraph.

télégraphie [telegrafi] nf telegraphy.

télégraphier [9] [telegrafje] vt to telegraph.

télégraphique [telegrafik] adj [fil, poteau] telegraph (avant n) ; **en style ~** in telegraphic style, in telegraphese.

télégraphiste [telegrafist] nmf - **1.** [technicien]

telegraphist - **2.** [employé] telegraph boy (f telegraph girl).

téléguidage [telegidaʒ] nm remote control.

téléguider [3] [telegide] vt to operate by remote control ; fig to mastermind.

téléinformatique [teleɛ̃fɔrmatik] nf INFORM data communication.

télématique [telematik] ⋄ nf telematics (U) ⋄ adj telematic.

téléobjectif [teleɔbʒɛktif] nm telephoto lens (sg).

télépathie [telepati] nf telepathy.

télépathique [telepatik] adj telepathic.

téléphérique [teleferik] nm cableway.

téléphone [telefɔn] nm telephone ; ~ **à carte** cardphone ; ~ **cellulaire** cellular telephone ; ~ **sans fil** cordless telephone ; ~ **rouge** hotline ; ~ **de voiture** carphone.

téléphoner [3] [telefɔne] ⋄ vt to telephone, to phone ⋄ vi to telephone, to phone ; ~ **à qqn** to telephone sb, to phone sb (up).

téléphonique [telefɔnik] adj telephone (avant n), phone (avant n).

téléphoniste [telefɔnist] nmf (telephone) operator, telephonist Br.

téléprospection [teleprɔspɛksjɔ̃] nf telemarketing.

télescopage [teleskɔpaʒ] nm - **1.** [de véhicules] concertinaing - **2.** fig [d'idées] cross-fertilization.

télescope [teleskɔp] nm telescope.

télescoper [3] [teleskɔpe] vt [véhicule] to crash into.

➠ **se télescoper** vp - **1.** [véhicules] to concertina - **2.** fig [idées] to influence each other.

télescopique [teleskɔpik] adj - **1.** [antenne] telescopic - **2.** [planète] visible only by telescope.

téléscripteur [teleskriptœr] nm teleprinter Br, teletypewriter Am.

télésiège [telesjɛʒ] nm chairlift.

téléski [teleski] nm ski tow.

téléspectateur, trice [telespɛktatœr, tris] nm, f (television) viewer.

télésurveillance [telesyrvejɑ̃s] nf remote surveillance.

Télétex® [teletɛks] nm teletex.

télétravail, aux [teletravaj, o] nm teleworking.

télétravailleur, euse [teletravajœr, øz] nm, f teleworker.

Télétype® [teletip] nm Teletype®.

téléviser [3] [televize] vt to televise.

téléviseur [televizœr] *nm* television (set).

télévision [televizjɔ̃] *nf* television ; **à la ~** on television ; **~ câblée** cable television ; **~ numérique** digital television.

télévisuel, elle [televizɥεl] *adj* television *(avant n)*.

télex [telεks] *nm inv* telex.

télexer [4] [telεkse] *vt* to telex.

tellement [tεlmɑ̃] *adv* - **1.** [si, à ce point] so ; (+ *comparatif*) so much ; **~ plus jeune que** so much younger than ; **pas ~** not especially, not particularly ; **ce n'est plus ~ frais/populaire** it's no longer all that fresh/popular - **2.** [autant] : **~ de** [personnes, objets] so many ; [gentillesse, travail] so much - **3.** [tant] so much ; **elle a ~ changé** she's changed so much ; **je ne comprends rien ~ il parle vite** he talks so quickly that I can't understand a word.

téloche [telɔʃ] *nf fam* telly.

téméraire [temerεr] ◇ *adj* - **1.** [audacieux] bold - **2.** [imprudent] rash ◇ *nmf* hothead.

témérité [temerite] *nf* - **1.** [audace] boldness - **2.** [imprudence] rashness.

témoignage [temwaɲaʒ] *nm* - **1.** JUR testimony, evidence *(U)* ; **faux ~** perjury - **2.** [gage] token, expression ; **en ~ de** as a token of - **3.** [récit] account.

témoigner [3] [temwaɲe] ◇ *vt* - **1.** [manifester] to show, to display - **2.** JUR : **~ que** to testify that ◇ *vi* - **1.** JUR to testify ; **~ contre** to testify against ; **~ en faveur de qqn** to testify in sb's favour *Br ou* favor *Am* - **2.** : **~ de** [être le signe de] to show ; [certifier] to testify (as) to.

témoin [temwɛ̃] ◇ *nm* - **1.** [gén] witness ; **être ~ de qqch** to be a witness to sthg, to witness sthg ; **prendre qqn à ~ (de)** to call on sb as a witness (of) ; **~ à charge** JUR witness for the prosecution ; **~ oculaire** eyewitness - **2.** INFORM indicator - **3.** *littéraire* [marque] : **~ de** evidence *(U)* of - **4.** SPORT baton ◇ *adj* [appartement] show *(avant n)*.

tempe [tɑ̃p] *nf* temple.

tempérament [tɑ̃peramɑ̃] *nm* temperament ; **avoir du ~** to be hot-blooded.

tempérance [tɑ̃perɑ̃s] *nf* temperance, moderation.

tempérant, e [tɑ̃perɑ̃, ɑ̃t] *adj* temperate.

température [tɑ̃peratyr] *nf* temperature ; **avoir de la ~** to have a temperature ; **prendre sa ~** to take one's temperature.

tempéré, e [tɑ̃pere] *adj* - **1.** [climat] temperate - **2.** [personne] even-tempered.

tempérer [18] [tɑ̃pere] *vt* - **1.** [adoucir] to temper ; *fig* [enthousiasme, ardeur] to moderate

- **2.** *fig & littéraire* [douleur, peine] to attenuate, to soothe.

tempête [tɑ̃pεt] *nf* storm ; **une ~ de** *fig* a storm of ; **~ de sable** sandstorm.

tempêter [4] [tɑ̃pεte] *vi* to rage.

tempétueux, euse [tɑ̃petɥø, øz] *adj littéraire* stormy ; *fig* tempestuous.

temple [tɑ̃pl] *nm* - **1.** HIST temple - **2.** [protestant] church.

tempo [tεmpo] *nm* tempo.

temporaire [tɑ̃pɔrεr] *adj* temporary.

temporairement [tɑ̃pɔrεrmɑ̃] *adv* temporarily.

temporel, elle [tɑ̃pɔrεl] *adj* - **1.** [défini dans le temps] time *(avant n)* - **2.** [terrestre] temporal.

temporisateur, trice [tɑ̃pɔrizatœr, tris] ◇ *adj* - **1.** [stratégie] delaying *(avant n)* - **2.** [personne] who stalls *ou* delays ◇ *nm, f* person who stalls *ou* delays.

temporiser [3] [tɑ̃pɔrize] *vi* to play for time, to stall.

temps [tɑ̃] *nm* - **1.** [gén] time ; **à plein ~** fulltime ; **à mi-~** half-time ; **à ~ partiel** parttime ; **en un ~ record** in record time ; **au** *ou* **du ~ où** (in the days) when ; **de mon ~** in my day ; **ça prend un certain ~** it takes some time ; **ces ~-ci, ces derniers ~** these days ; **pendant ce ~** meanwhile ; **les premiers ~** at the beginning ; **en ~ utile** in due course ; **en ~ de guerre/paix** in wartime/peacetime ; **il est grand ~ de partir** it is high time that we left ; **il était ~!** *iron* and about time too! ; **avoir le ~ de faire qqch** to have time to do sthg ; **gagner du ~** to save time ; **passer le ~** to pass the time ; **~ libre** free time ; **~ mort** SPORT stoppage time, injury time ; *fig* break, pause ; **à ~** in time ; **de ~ à autre** now and then *ou* again ; **de ~ en ~** from time to time ; **en même ~** at the same time ; **tout le ~** all the time, the whole time ; **tuer le ~** to kill time ; **avoir tout son ~** to have all the time in the world ; **ne pas laisser à qqn le ~ de se retourner** not to give sb the time to catch his/her breath ; **rattraper le ~ perdu** to catch up on *ou* make up for lost time ; **par les ~ qui courent** in this day and age - **2.** MUS beat - **3.** GRAM tense - **4.** MÉTÉOR weather ; **gros ~** rough weather *ou* conditions ; **un ~ de chien** foul weather.

tenable [tənabl] *adj* bearable.

tenace [tənas] *adj* - **1.** [gén] stubborn - **2.** *fig* [odeur, rhume] lingering - **3.** [colle] strong.

ténacité [tenasite] *nf* - **1.** [d'odeur] lingering nature - **2.** [de préjugé, personne] stubbornness.

tenailler [3] [tənaje] *vt* to torment.

tenailles [tənaj] *nfpl* pincers.

tenancier, ère [tənãsje, ɛr] *nm, f* manager (*f* manageress).

tenant, e [tənã,ãt] *nm, f* : **~ du titre** title holder.

◆ **tenant** *nm* - **1.** (*gén pl*) [d'une opinion] supporter - **2.** *loc* : **d'un seul ~** in one piece, intact ; **les ~s et les aboutissants** [d'une affaire] the ins and outs, the full details.

tendance [tãdãs] *nf* - **1.** [disposition] tendency ; **avoir ~ à qqch/à faire qqch** to have a tendency to sthg/to do sthg, to be inclined to sthg/to do sthg - **2.** [économique, de mode] trend.

tendancieusement [tãdãsjøzmã] *adv* tendentiously.

tendancieux, euse [tãdãsjø, øz] *adj* tendentious.

tendeur [tãdœr] *nm* - **1.** [sangle] elastic strap (*for fastening luggage etc*) - **2.** [appareil] wire-strainer - **3.** [de bicyclette] chain adjuster - **4.** [de tente] runner.

tendinite [tãdinit] *nf* tendinitis.

tendon [tãdɔ̃] *nm* tendon ; **~ d'Achille** Achilles' tendon.

tendre[1] [tãdr] ◇ *adj* - **1.** [gén] tender - **2.** [matériau] soft - **3.** [couleur] delicate ◇ *nmf* tender-hearted person.

tendre[2] [73] [tãdr] ◇ *vt* - **1.** [corde] to tighten - **2.** [muscle] to tense - **3.** [objet, main] : **~ qqch à qqn** to hold out sthg to sb - **4.** [bâche] to hang - **5.** [piège] to set (up) ◇ *vi* : **~ à/vers** [évoluer vers] to tend to/towards ; [viser à] to aim at.

◆ **se tendre** *vp* to tighten ; *fig* [relations] to become strained.

tendrement [tãdrəmã] *adv* tenderly.

tendresse [tãdrɛs] *nf* - **1.** [affection] tenderness - **2.** [indulgence] sympathy.

◆ **tendresses** *nfpl* : **se faire des ~s** to be loving with each other.

tendron [tãdrɔ̃] *nm part of veal rib*.

tendu, e [tãdy] ◇ *pp* ▷ **tendre**[2] ◇ *adj* - **1.** [fil, corde] taut - **2.** [pièce] : **~ de** [velours] hung with ; [papier peint] covered with - **3.** [personne] tense - **4.** [atmosphère, rapports] strained - **5.** [main] outstretched.

ténèbres [tenɛbr] *nfpl* darkness (*sg*), shadows ; *fig* depths.

ténébreux, euse [tenebrø, øz] *adj* - **1.** *littéraire* [forêt] dark, shadowy - **2.** *fig* [dessein, affaire] mysterious - **3.** [personne] serious, solemn.

teneur [tənœr] *nf* content ; [de traité] terms (*pl*) ; **~ en alcool/cuivre** alcohol/copper content.

ténia, tænia [tenja] *nm* tapeworm.

tenir [40] [tənir] ◇ *vt* - **1.** [objet, personne, solution] to hold - **2.** [garder, conserver, respecter] to keep - **3.** [gérer - boutique] to keep, to run - **4.** [apprendre] : **~ qqch de qqn** to have sthg from sb - **5.** [considérer] : **~ qqn pour** to regard sb as ◇ *vi* - **1.** [être solide] to stay up, to hold together - **2.** [durer] to last - **3.** [pouvoir être contenu] to fit - **4.** [être attaché] : **~ à** [personne] to care about ; [privilèges] to value - **5.** [vouloir absolument] : **~ à faire qqch** to insist on doing sthg - **6.** [ressembler] : **~ de** to take after - **7.** [relever de] : **~ de** to have something of - **8.** [dépendre de] : **il ne tient qu'à toi de ...** it's entirely up to you to ... - **9.** *loc* : **~ bon** to stand firm ; **qu'à cela ne tienne** it *ou* that doesn't matter ; **tiens!** [en donnant] here! ; [surprise] well, well! ; [pour attirer attention] look!

◆ **se tenir** *vp* - **1.** [réunion] to be held - **2.** [personnes] to hold one another ; **se ~ par la main** to hold hands - **3.** [être présent] to be - **4.** [être cohérent] to make sense - **5.** [se conduire] to behave (o.s.) - **6.** [se retenir] : **se ~ (à)** to hold on (to) - **7.** [se borner] : **s'en ~ à** to stick to.

tennis [tenis] ◇ *nm* - **1.** [sport] tennis - **2.** [terrain] tennis court ◇ *nmpl* tennis shoes.

tennisman [tenisman] (*pl* **tennismen** [tenismen]) *nm* tennis player.

ténor [tenɔr] ◇ *adj* [instrument de musique] tenor (*avant n*) ◇ *nm* - **1.** [chanteur] tenor - **2.** *fig* [vedette] : **un ~ de la politique** a political star performer.

tensioactif, ive [tãsjɔaktif, iv] *adj* surface-active.

tension [tãsjɔ̃] *nf* - **1.** [contraction, désaccord] tension - **2.** *MÉD* pressure ; **avoir de la ~** to have high blood pressure ; **~ artérielle** blood pressure - **3.** *ÉLECTR* voltage ; **haute/basse ~** high/low voltage.

tentaculaire [tãtakylɛr] *adj fig* sprawling.

tentacule [tãtakyl] *nm* tentacle.

tentant, e [tãtã, ãt] *adj* tempting.

tentateur, trice [tãtatœr, tris] ◇ *adj* tempting ◇ *nm, f* tempter (*f* temptress).

tentation [tãtasjɔ̃] *nf* temptation.

tentative [tãtativ] *nf* attempt ; **~ d'homicide** attempted murder ; **~ de suicide** suicide attempt.

tente [tãt] *nf* tent.

◆ **tente à oxygène** *nf* oxygen tent.

tenter [3] [tãte] *vt* - **1.** [entreprendre] : **~ qqch/de faire qqch** to attempt sthg/to do sthg - **2.** [plaire] to tempt ; **être tenté par qqch/de faire qqch** to be tempted by sthg/to do sthg.

tenture [tãtyr] *nf* hanging.

tenu, e [təny] ◇ *pp* ▷ **tenir** ◇ *adj* - **1.** [obligé] : **être ~ à qqch** to be bound by sthg ; **être**

~ **de faire qqch** to be required *ou* obliged to do sthg **- 2.** [en ordre] : **bien/mal** ~ [maison] well/badly kept.

ténu, e [teny] *adj* **- 1.** [fil] fine ; *fig* [distinction] tenuous **- 2.** [voix] thin.

tenue [təny] *nf* **- 1.** [entretien] running ; ~ **de la comptabilité** bookkeeping **- 2.** [manières] good manners *(pl)* **- 3.** [maintien du corps] posture **- 4.** [costume] dress ; ~ **réglementaire** regulation uniform ; ~ **de soirée** evening dress ; **être en petite** ~ to be scantily dressed.

tenue de route *nf* roadholding.

tequila [tekila] *nf* tequila.

ter [tɛr] ◇ *adv* MUS three times ◇ *adj* : **12** ~ **12B.**

térébenthine [terebɑ̃tin] *nf* turpentine.

Tergal® [tɛrgal] *nm* ≃ Terylene®.

tergiversation [tɛrʒiversasjɔ̃] *nf* shilly-shallying *(U).*

tergiverser [3] [tɛrʒiverse] *vi* to shillyshally.

terme [tɛrm] *nm* **- 1.** [fin] end ; **mettre un** ~ **à** to put an end *ou* a stop to **- 2.** [de grossesse] term ; **mener une grossesse à** ~ to go full term ; **avant** ~ prematurely **- 3.** [échéance] time limit ; [de loyer] rent day ; **à** ~ FIN forward *(avant n)* ; **à court/moyen/long** ~ [calculer] in the short/medium/long term ; [projet] short-/medium-/long-term **- 4.** [mot, élément] term.

termes *nmpl* **- 1.** [expressions] words ; **en d'autres** ~**s** in other words **- 2.** [de contrat] terms **- 3.** [relations] : **être en bons/mauvais** ~**s avec qqn** to be on good/bad terms with sb.

terminaison [tɛrminɛzɔ̃] *nf* GRAM ending.

terminaison nerveuse *nf* nerve ending.

terminal, e, aux [tɛrminal, o] *adj* **- 1.** [au bout] final **- 2.** MÉD [phase] terminal.

terminal, aux *nm* terminal.

terminale *nf* SCOL ≃ upper sixth year *ou* form *Br*, ≃ twelfth grade *Am*.

terminer [3] [tɛrmine] *vt* to end, to finish ; [travail, repas] to finish ; ~ **qqch par** to finish sthg with.

se terminer *vp* to end, to finish ; **se** ~ **par** to end *ou* finish with ; **se** ~ **en** to end in.

terminologie [tɛrminɔlɔʒi] *nf* terminology.

terminus [tɛrminys] *nm* terminus.

termite [tɛrmit] *nm* termite.

termitière [tɛrmitjɛr] *nf* termite nest.

ternaire [tɛrnɛr] *adj* CHIM & MATHS ternary ; LITTÉRATURE & MUS triple.

terne [tɛrn] *adj* dull.

ternir [32] [tɛrnir] *vt* to dirty ; [métal, réputation] to tarnish.

se ternir *vp* to get dirty ; [métal, réputation] to tarnish.

terrain [tɛrɛ̃] *nm* **- 1.** [sol] soil ; **tout** ~ all-terrain ; **vélo tout** ~ mountain bike **- 2.** [surface] piece of land ; ~ **vague** waste ground *(U) ou* land *(U)* **- 3.** [emplacement - de football, rugby] pitch ; [- de golf] course ; ~ **d'aviation** airfield ; ~ **de camping** campsite **- 4.** MIL terrain **- 5.** *fig* [domaine] ground ; **en** ~ **glissant** *fig* on shaky ground **- 6.** *loc* : **céder du** ~ **à qqn** to give ground to sb ; **déblayer le** ~ *fig* to clear the ground ; **gagner du** ~ to gain ground ; **gagner du** ~ **sur qqn** to gain on sb ; **sur le** ~ in the field.

terrasse [tɛras] *nf* terrace.

terrassement [tɛrasmɑ̃] *nm* [action] excavation.

terrasser [3] [tɛrase] *vt* [suj : personne] to bring down ; [suj : émotion] to overwhelm ; [suj : maladie] to conquer.

terrassier [tɛrasje] *nm* labourer *Br*, laborer *Am*.

terre [tɛr] *nf* **- 1.** [monde] world **- 2.** [sol] ground ; **par** ~ on the ground ; **sous** ~ underground ; ~ **à** ~ *fig* down-to-earth **- 3.** [matière] earth, soil ; ~ **cuite** terracotta ; ~ **glaise** clay **- 4.** [propriété] land *(U)* **- 5.** [territoire, continent] land ; **sur la** ~ **ferme** on dry land ; ~ **natale** native land **- 6.** ÉLECTR earth *Br*, ground *Am*.

Terre *nf* : **la Terre** Earth ; **la Terre promise** the Promised Land ; **la Terre Sainte** the Holy Land.

terreau [tɛro] *nm* compost.

terre-neuve [tɛrnœv] *nm inv* Newfoundland (dog).

Terre-Neuve [tɛrnœv] *nf* Newfoundland ; **à** ~ in Newfoundland.

terre-plein [tɛrplɛ̃] *(pl* terre-pleins*) nm* platform.

terrer [4] [tɛre] **se terrer** *vp* to go to earth.

terrestre [tɛrɛstr] *adj* **- 1.** [croûte, atmosphère] of the earth **- 2.** [animal, transport] land *(avant n)* **- 3.** [plaisir, paradis] earthly **- 4.** [considérations] worldly.

terreur [tɛrœr] *nf* terror.

terreux, euse [tɛrø, øz] *adj* **- 1.** [substance, goût] earthy **- 2.** [mains, teint] muddy.

terri = terril.

terrible [tɛribl] *adj* **- 1.** [gén] terrible **- 2.** [appétit, soif] terrific, enormous ; **avoir un travail** ~ to have a terrific *ou* an enormous amount of work **- 3.** *fam* [excellent] brilliant.

terriblement [tɛribləmɑ̃] *adv* terribly.

terrien, enne [tɛrjɛ̃, ɛn] ◇ *adj* - **1.** [foncier] : propriétaire ~ landowner - **2.** [vertu] rural ◇ *nm, f* [habitant de la Terre] earthling.

terrier [tɛrje] *nm* - **1.** [tanière] burrow - **2.** [chien] terrier.

terrifier [9] [tɛrifje] *vt* to terrify.

terril [tɛril], **terri** [tɛri] *nm* slag heap.

terrine [tɛrin] *nf* terrine.

territoire [tɛritwar] *nm* - **1.** [pays, zone] territory - **2.** ADMIN area.

➡ **territoire d'outre-mer** *nm* (French) overseas territory.

territorial, e, aux [tɛritɔrjal, o] *adj* territorial.

terroir [tɛrwar] *nm* - **1.** [sol] soil - **2.** [région rurale] country ; **du** ~ rural.

terroriser [3] [tɛrɔrize] *vt* to terrorize.

terrorisme [tɛrɔrism] *nm* terrorism.

terroriste [tɛrɔrist] ◇ *nmf* terrorist ◇ *adj* terrorist *(avant n)*.

tertiaire [tɛrsjɛr] ◇ *nm* tertiary sector ◇ *adj* tertiary.

tertio [tɛrsjo] *adv* third, thirdly.

tes ▷ ton².

tesson [tɛsɔ̃] *nm* piece of broken glass.

test [tɛst] *nm* test ; ~ **de grossesse** pregnancy test.

testament [tɛstamɑ̃] *nm* will ; *fig* legacy.

➡ **Testament** *nm* : **Ancien/Nouveau Testament** Old/New Testament.

testamentaire [tɛstamɑ̃tɛr] *adj* of a will.

tester [3] [tɛste] ◇ *vt* to test ◇ *vi* to make a will.

testicule [tɛstikyl] *nm* testicle.

tétaniser [3] [tetanize] *vt* to cause to go into spasm ; *fig* to paralyse *Br*, to paralyze *Am*.

tétanos [tetanos] *nm* tetanus.

têtard [tɛtar] *nm* tadpole.

tête [tɛt] *nf* - **1.** [gén] head ; **de la** ~ **aux pieds** from head to foot *ou* toe ; **la** ~ **en bas** head down ; **la** ~ **la première** head first ; **calculer qqch de** ~ to calculate sthg in one's head ; **50 francs par** ~ ~ 50 francs a head *ou* each ; ~ **chercheuse** homing head ; ~ **d'écriture** INFORM write head ; ~ **de lecture** INFORM read head ; ~ **de liste** POLIT main candidate ; ~ **de mort** death's head ; **piquer une** ~ *fam* to have *ou* go for a dip ; **se casser la** ~ **pour faire qqch** *fam fig* to kill o.s. doing sthg ; **se laver la** ~ to wash one's hair ; **se payer la** ~ **de qqn** *fam* to make fun of sb, to take the mickey out of sb ; **avoir la grosse** ~ *fam* to be big-headed ; **être** ~ **en l'air** to have one's head in the clouds ; **avoir la** ~ **sur les épaules** to have a good head on one's shoulders ; **faire la** ~ to sulk ; **garder la** ~ **froide** to keep a cool head ; **perdre la** ~ to lose one's head ; **tenir** ~ **à qqn** to stand up to sb - **2.** [visage] face - **3.** [devant - de cortège, peloton] head, front ; **de** ~ [voiture] front *(avant n)* ; *fig* [personne] high-powered ; **en** ~ [- SPORT] in the lead.

tête-à-queue [tɛtakø] *nm inv* spin.

tête-à-tête [tɛtatɛt] *nm inv* tête-à-tête ; **en** ~ alone.

tête-bêche [tɛtbɛʃ] *loc adv* head to tail.

tête-de-nègre [tɛtdənɛgr] *adj inv* dark brown.

tétée [tete] *nf* feed.

tétine [tetin] *nf* - **1.** [de biberon, mamelle] nipple, teat - **2.** [sucette] dummy *Br*, pacifier *Am*.

téton [tetɔ̃] *nm* - **1.** *fam* [sein] breast - **2.** TECHNOL nipple.

Tétrabrick® [tetrabrik] *nm* carton.

tétralogie [tetralɔʒi] *nf* tetralogy.

tétraplégique [tetrapleʒik] *adj* quadriplegic.

têtu, e [tety] *adj* stubborn.

teuf-teuf [tœftœf] *nm inv* old banger.

teuton, onne [tøtɔ̃, ɔn] *péj* ◇ *adj* Teutonic ◇ *nm, f* Teuton.

tex mex [tɛksmɛks] ◇ *adj* Tex Mex ◇ *nm* Tex Mex food.

texte [tɛkst] *nm* - **1.** [écrit] wording ; **dans le** ~ in the original ; ~ **intégral** unabridged text ; ~ **de loi** legal text - **2.** [imprimé] text - **3.** [extrait] passage.

textile [tɛkstil] ◇ *adj* textile *(avant n)* ◇ *nm* - **1.** [matière] textile - **2.** [industrie] : **le** ~ **textiles** *(pl)*, the textile industry.

texto [tɛksto] *adv fam* word for word.

textuel, elle [tɛkstɥɛl] *adj* - **1.** [analyse] textual ; [citation] exact ; **il a dit ça,** ~ those were his very *ou* exact words - **2.** [traduction] literal.

textuellement [tɛkstɥɛlmɑ̃] *adv* verbatim.

texture [tɛkstyr] *nf* texture.

TF1 (*abr de* Télévision Française 1) *nf* French independent television company.

TG (*abr de* Trésorerie générale) *nf* local finance office.

TGI *abr de* tribunal de grande instance.

TGV (*abr de* train à grande vitesse) *nm* French high-speed train.

thaï [taj] *nm* & *adj inv* Thai.

➡ **Thaï** *nm, f* Thai.

thaïlandais, e [tajlɑ̃dɛ, ɛz] *adj* Thai.

➡ **Thaïlandais, e** *nm, f* Thai.

Thaïlande [tajlɑ̃d] *nf* : **la** ~ Thailand.

thalasso(thérapie) [talasɔ(terapi)] nf seawater therapy.

thaumaturge [tomatyrʒ] nm *littéraire* miracle worker.

thé [te] nm tea ; ~ **au citron/lait** tea with lemon/milk ; ~ **nature** tea without milk, black tea.

théâtral, e, aux [teatral, o] adj - **1.** [saison] theatre (avant n) - **2.** [ton] theatrical.

théâtralement [teatralmã] adv theatrically.

théâtre [teatr] nm - **1.** [bâtiment, représentation] theatre - **2.** [troupe] theatre company - **3.** [art] : **faire du** ~ to be on the stage ; **adapté pour le** ~ adapted for the stage - **4.** [œuvre] plays (pl) - **5.** [lieu] scene ; ~ **d'opérations** MIL theatre of operations.

théière [tejɛr] nf teapot.

théine [tein] nf caffeine.

thématique [tematik] ◇ adj thematic ◇ nf themes (pl).

thème [tɛm] nm - **1.** [sujet & MUS] theme - **2.** SCOL prose.

➡ **thème astral** nm birth chart.

théocratie [teɔkrasi] nf theocracy.

théologie [teɔlɔʒi] nf theology.

théologien, enne [teɔlɔʒjɛ̃, ɛn] nm, f theologian.

théologique [teɔlɔʒik] adj theological.

théorème [teɔrɛm] nm theorem.

théoricien, enne [teɔrisjɛ̃, ɛn] nm, f theoretician.

théorie [teɔri] nf theory ; **en** ~ in theory.

théorique [teɔrik] adj theoretical.

théoriquement [teɔrikmã] adv theoretically.

théoriser [3] [teɔrize] ◇ vt to theorize about ◇ vi : ~ **(sur)** to theorize (about).

thérapeute [terapøt] nmf therapist.

thérapeutique [terapøtik] ◇ adj therapeutic ◇ nf therapy.

thérapie [terapi] nf therapy.

thermal, e, aux [tɛrmal, o] adj thermal.

thermalisme [tɛrmalism] nm ≃ hydrotherapy.

thermes [tɛrm] nmpl thermal baths.

thermique [tɛrmik] adj thermal.

thermodynamique [tɛrmɔdinamik] ◇ adj thermodynamic ◇ nf thermodynamics (U).

thermomètre [tɛrmɔmɛtr] nm [instrument] thermometer.

thermonucléaire [tɛrmɔnykleɛr] adj thermonuclear.

Thermos® [tɛrmos] nm OU nf Thermos® (flask).

thermostat [tɛrmɔsta] nm thermostat.

thésard, e [tezar, ard] nm, f fam PhD student.

thésauriser [3] [tezɔrize] ◇ vt to hoard ◇ vi to hoard money.

thésaurus, thesaurus [tezɔrys] nm inv thesaurus.

thèse [tɛz] nf - **1.** [opinion] argument ; **pièce/ roman à** ~ drama/novel of ideas - **2.** PHILO & UNIV thesis ; ~ **de doctorat** doctorate - **3.** [théorie] theory.

thon [tɔ̃] nm tuna.

thoracique [tɔrasik] adj thoracic ▷ **cage.**

thorax [tɔraks] nm thorax.

thriller [srilœr, trilœr] nm thriller.

thrombose [trɔ̃boz] nf thrombosis.

thune, tune [tyn] nf fam cash (U), dough (U).

thym [tɛ̃] nm thyme.

thyroïde [tirɔid] nf thyroid (gland).

TI abr de tribunal d'instance.

Tibet [tibɛ] nm : **le** ~ Tibet ; **au** ~ in Tibet.

tibétain, e [tibetɛ̃, ɛn] adj Tibetan.

➡ **Tibétain, e** nm, f Tibetan.

tibia [tibja] nm tibia.

tic [tik] nm tic.

ticket [tikɛ] nm ticket ; ~ **de caisse** (till) receipt ; ~ **modérateur** proportion of medical expenses payable by the patient ; ~ **de rationnement** ration coupon ; ~-**repas** ≈ luncheon voucher ; **avoir un** ~ **avec qqn** fam fig to have made a hit with sb.

tic-tac [tiktak] ◇ interj tick-tock! ◇ nm inv tick-tock.

tiédasse [tjedas] adj péj tepid.

tiède [tjed] ◇ adj - **1.** [boisson, eau] tepid, lukewarm - **2.** [vent] mild - **3.** fig [accueil] lukewarm ◇ adv : **à boire** ~ serve lukewarm.

tièdement [tjedmã] adv half-heartedly.

tiédeur [tjedœr] nf - **1.** [chaleur modérée] tepidness - **2.** fig [de climat] mildness - **3.** fig [indifférence] half-heartedness.

tiédir [32] [tjedir] ◇ vt to warm ◇ vi to become warm ; **faire** ~ **qqch** to warm sthg.

tien [tjɛ̃] ➡ **le tien** (f **la tienne** [latjɛn], mpl **les tiens** [letjɛ̃], fpl **les tiennes** [letjɛn]) pron poss yours ; **les** ~**s** your family ; **mets-y du** ~! make an effort! ; **à la tienne!** cheers! ; **tu en encore fais des tiennes!** you've been up to your tricks again!

tiendrai, tiendras etc ▷ tenir.

tienne ◇ vb ▷ tenir ◇ pron poss ▷ **tien.**

tiens, tient etc ▷ tenir.

tierce [tjɛrs] ◇ nf - **1.** MUS third - **2.** CARTES & ESCRIME tierce - **3.** TYPO final proof ◇ adj ▷ tiers.

tiercé [tjɛrse] nm system of betting involving the first three horses in a race.

tiers, tierce [tjɛr, tjɛrs] adj : **une tierce personne** a third party.
➡ **tiers** nm - **1.** [étranger] outsider, stranger - **2.** [tierce personne] third party ; **assurance au ~** third-party insurance - **3.** [de fraction] : **le ~ de** one-third of ; **~ provisionnel** thrice-yearly income tax payment based on estimated tax due for the previous year.

tiers-monde [tjɛrmɔ̃d] nm : **le ~** the Third World.

tiers-mondisation [tjɛrmɔ̃dizasjɔ̃] nf : **la ~ de ce pays** this country's economic degeneration to Third World levels.

tiers-mondiste [tjɛrmɔ̃dist] ◇ adj favouring the Third World ◇ nmf champion of the Third World.

tiers-payant [tjɛrpɛjɑ̃] nm system by which a proportion of the fee for medical treatment is paid directly to the hospital, doctor or pharmacist by the patient's insurer.

tifs [tif] nmpl fam hair (U).

TIG (abr de **travail d'intérêt général**) nm community service.

tige [tiʒ] nf - **1.** [de plante] stem, stalk - **2.** [de bois, métal] rod.

tignasse [tiɲas] nf fam mop (of hair).

tigre [tigr] nm tiger ; **jaloux comme un ~** fig fiercely jealous.

tigré, e [tigre] adj - **1.** [rayé] striped ; [chat] tabby (avant n) - **2.** [tacheté] spotted ; [cheval] piebald.

tigresse [tigrɛs] nf tigress.

tilleul [tijœl] nm lime (tree).

tilt [tilt] nm : **faire ~** fam fig to ring a bell.

timbale [tɛ̃bal] nf - **1.** [gobelet] (metal) cup ; **décrocher la ~** fig to hit the jackpot - **2.** CULIN timbale - **3.** MUS kettledrum.

timbrage [tɛ̃braʒ] nm postmarking.

timbre [tɛ̃br] nm - **1.** [gén] stamp - **2.** [de voix] timbre - **3.** [de bicyclette] bell.

timbré, e [tɛ̃bre] ◇ adj - **1.** [papier, enveloppe] stamped - **2.** [voix] resonant - **3.** fam [fou] barmy, doolally ◇ nm, f fam loony.

timbrer [3] [tɛ̃bre] vt to stamp.

timide [timid] ◇ adj - **1.** [personne] shy

- 2. [protestation, essai] timid - **3.** [soleil] uncertain ◇ nmf shy person.

timidement [timidmɑ̃] adv shyly ; [protester] timidly.

timidité [timidite] nf - **1.** [de personne] shyness - **2.** [de protestation] timidness.

timing [tajmiŋ] nm - **1.** [emploi du temps] schedule - **2.** [organisation] timing.

timonier [timɔnje] nm helmsman.

timoré, e [timɔre] adj fearful, timorous.

tintamarre [tɛ̃tamar] nm fam racket.

tintement [tɛ̃tmɑ̃] nm [de cloche, d'horloge] chiming ; [de pièces] jingling.

tinter [3] [tɛ̃te] vi - **1.** [cloche, horloge] to chime - **2.** [pièces] to jingle.

tintin [tɛ̃tɛ̃] interj fam no way!, not a chance!

tintouin [tɛ̃twɛ̃] nm fam - **1.** [vacarme] racket - **2.** [souci] worry.

TIP (abr de **titre interbancaire de paiement**) nm payment slip for bills, ≃ bank giro payment slip Br.

tique [tik] nf tick.

tiquer [3] [tike] vi fam : **~ (sur)** to wince (at).

tir [tir] nm - **1.** [SPORT - activité] shooting ; [- lieu] : **(centre de) ~** shooting range ; **~ à l'arc** archery ; **~ au but** penalty shoot-out ; **~ au pigeon** clay pigeon shooting - **2.** [trajectoire] shot - **3.** [salve] fire (U) - **4.** [manière, action de tirer] firing.

TIR (abr de **transports internationaux routiers**) international road transport agreement allowing lorries to avoid customs until they reach their destination.

tirade [tirad] nf - **1.** THÉÂTRE soliloquy - **2.** [laïus] tirade.

tirage [tiraʒ] nm - **1.** [de journal] circulation ; [de livre] print run ; **à grand ~** mass circulation ; **~ limité** limited edition - **2.** [du loto] draw ; **~ au sort** drawing lots - **3.** [de cheminée] draught Br, draft Am - **4.** [de vin] drawing off - **5.** loc : **il y a du tirage** fam fig there is some friction.

tiraillement [tirajmɑ̃] nm (gén pl) - **1.** [crampe] cramp - **2.** fig [conflit] conflict.

tirailler [3] [tiraje] ◇ vt - **1.** [tirer sur] to tug (at) - **2.** fig [écarteler] : **être tiraillé par/entre qqch** to be torn by/between sthg ◇ vi to fire wildly.

tirailleur [tirajœr] nm skirmisher.

Tirana [tirana] n Tirane.

tire [tir] nf - **1.** fam [voiture] wheels (pl) - **2.** loc : **vol à la ~** fam pickpocketing ; **voleur à la ~** fam pickpocket.

tiré, e [tire] *adj* [fatigué] : **avoir les traits ~s** *ou* **le visage ~** to look drawn.

tire-au-flanc [tiroflɑ̃] *nm inv fam* shirker, skiver *Br*.

tire-botte [tirbɔt] (*pl* **tire-bottes**) *nm* bootjack.

tire-bouchon [tirbuʃɔ̃] (*pl* **tire-bouchons**) *nm* corkscrew.
➤ **en tire-bouchon** *loc adv* corkscrew (*avant n*).

tire-bouchonner [3] [tirbuʃɔne] ◇ *vt* to twiddle ◇ *vi* to get *ou* become twisted.

tire-d'aile [tirdɛl] ➤ **à tire d'aile** *loc adv* as quickly as possible.

tire-fesses [tirfɛs] *nm inv fam* ski-tow.

tire-lait [tirlɛ] *nm inv* breast pump.

tire-larigot [tirlarigo] ➤ **à tire-larigot** *loc adv fam* to one's heart's content.

tirelire [tirlir] *nf* moneybox.

tirer [3] [tire] ◇ *vt* **- 1.** [gén] to pull ; [rideaux] to draw ; [tiroir] to pull open **- 2.** [tracer - trait] to draw ; [- plan] to draw up **- 3.** [revue, livre] to print **- 4.** [avec arme] to fire **- 5.** [faire sortir - vin] to draw off ; **~ qqn de** *litt* & *fig* to help *ou* get sb out of ; **~ un revolver/un mouchoir de sa poche** to pull a gun/a handkerchief out of one's pocket ; **~ la langue** to stick out one's tongue **- 6.** [aux cartes, au loto] to draw **- 7.** [plaisir, profit] to derive **- 8.** [déduire - conclusion] to draw ; [- leçon] to learn **- 9.** *loc* : **~ qqch au clair** to shed light on sthg ◇ *vi* **- 1.** [tendre] : **~ sur** to pull on *ou* at **- 2.** [aspirer] : **~ sur** [pipe] to draw *ou* pull on **- 3.** [couleur] : **bleu tirant sur le vert** greenish blue **- 4.** [cheminée] to draw **- 5.** [avec arme] to fire, to shoot **- 6.** *SPORT* to shoot.
➤ **se tirer** *vp* **- 1.** *fam* [s'en aller] to push off **- 2.** [se sortir] : **se ~ de** to get o.s. out of ; **s'en ~** *fam* to escape.

tiret [tirɛ] *nm* dash.

tirette [tirɛt] *nf* **- 1.** [planchette] leaf **- 2.** *Belg* [fermeture] zip *Br*, zipper *Am* **- 3.** [commande] lever.

tireur, euse [tirœr, øz] *nm, f* [avec arme] gunman ; **~ d'élite** marksman (*f* markswoman).
➤ **tireur** *nm* [de chèque] drawer.
➤ **tireuse** *nf* : **tireuse de cartes** fortune teller.

tiroir [tirwar] *nm* drawer.

tiroir-caisse [tirwarkɛs] (*pl* **tiroirs-caisses**) *nm* till.

tisane [tizan] *nf* herb tea.

tison [tizɔ̃] *nm* ember.

tisonnier [tizɔnje] *nm* poker.

tissage [tisaʒ] *nm* weaving.

tisser [3] [tise] *vt litt* & *fig* to weave ; [suj : araignée] to spin.

tisserand, e [tisrɑ̃, ɑ̃d] *nm, f* weaver.

tissu [tisy] *nm* **- 1.** [étoffe] cloth, material **- 2.** *BIOL* tissue ; **~ adipeux** adipose tissue ; **~ conjonctif** connective tissue.

tissu-éponge [tisyepɔ̃ʒ] (*pl* **tissus-éponges**) *nm* towelling (*U*) *Br*, toweling (*U*) *Am*.

titan [titɑ̃] *nm* Titan ; **de ~** *fig* titanic.

titiller [3] [titije] *vt* to titillate.

titrage [titraʒ] *nm* **- 1.** [d'œuvre, de film] titling **- 2.** [de liquide] titration.

titre [titr] *nm* **- 1.** [gén] title **- 2.** [de presse] headline ; **gros ~** headline **- 3.** [universitaire] diploma, qualification **- 4.** *JUR* title ; **~ de propriété** title deed **- 5.** *FIN* security **- 6.** [de monnaie] fineness **- 7.** *loc* : **à ~ gracieux** *ou* **gratuit** free of charge ; **à ~ indicatif** for information ; **à aucun ~** on any account, in any way ; **à juste ~** with just cause, justifiably so.
➤ **titre de transport** *nm* ticket.
➤ **à titre de** *loc prép* : **à ~ d'exemple** by way of example ; **à ~ d'information** for information.
➤ **au même titre que** *loc prép* in the same way that.
➤ **en titre** *loc adj* **- 1.** [titulaire] titular **- 2.** [attitré] official.

titrer [3] [titre] *vt* **- 1.** [œuvre] to title **- 2.** [liquide] to titrate.

tituber [3] [titybe] *vi* to totter.

titulaire [titylɛr] ◇ *adj* [employé] permanent ; *UNIV* with tenure ◇ *nmf* [de passeport, permis] holder ; [de poste, chaire] occupant.

titulariser [3] [titylarize] *vt* to give tenure to.

TNP (*abr de* **traité de non-prolifération**) *nm* NPT.

TNT (*abr de* **trinitrotoluène**) *nm* TNT.

toast [tost] *nm* **- 1.** [pain grillé] toast (*U*) **- 2.** [discours] toast ; **porter un ~ à** to drink a toast to.

toasteur [tostœr] *nm* toaster.

toboggan [tɔbɔgɑ̃] *nm* **- 1.** [traîneau] toboggan **- 2.** [de terrain de jeu] slide ; [de piscine] chute **- 3.** *AUTOM* flyover *Br*, overpass *Am*.

toc [tɔk] ◇ *interj* : **et ~!** so there! ◇ *nm fam* : **c'est du ~** it's fake ; **en ~** fake (*avant n*) ◇ *adj inv* rubbishy.

tocsin [tɔksɛ̃] *nm* alarm bell.

Togo [tɔgo] *nm* : **le ~** Togo ; **au ~** in Togo.

togolais, e [tɔgɔlɛ, ɛz] *adj* Togolese.
➤ **Togolais, e** *nm, f* Togolese person ; **les Togolais** the Togolese.

tohu-bohu [tɔybɔy] *nm* commotion.

toi [twa] *pron pers* you.
➤ **toi-même** *pron pers* yourself.

toile [twal] *nf* - **1.** [étoffe] cloth ; [de lin] linen ; ~ **cirée** oilcloth - **2.** [tableau] canvas, picture - **3.** NAVIG [voilure] sails *(pl)*.
➤ **toile d'araignée** *nf* spider's web.
➤ **toile de fond** *nf* backdrop.
➤ **Toile** *nf* : **la Toile** INFORM the Web, the web.

toilettage [twaletaʒ] *nm* grooming.

toilette [twalet] *nf* - **1.** [de personne, d'animal] washing ; **faire sa** ~ to (have a) wash - **2.** [parure, vêtements] outfit, clothes *(pl)* - **3.** [de monument, voiture] cleaning - **4.** [de texte] tidying up.
➤ **toilettes** *nfpl* toilet *(sg)*, toilets.

toise [twaz] *nf* height gauge.

toiser [3] [twaze] *vt* to eye (up and down).
➤ **se toiser** *vp* to eye each other up and down.

toison [twazɔ̃] *nf* - **1.** [pelage] fleece - **2.** [chevelure] mop (of hair).

toit [twa] *nm* roof ; ~ **ouvrant** sunroof.

toiture [twatyr] *nf* roof, roofing.

Tokyo [tɔkjo] *n* Tokyo.

tôlard, e, taulard, e [tolar, ard] *nm, f* *tfam* jailbird, con.

tôle [tol] *nf* - **1.** [de métal] sheet metal ; ~ **ondulée** corrugated iron - **2.** *tfam* [prison] nick *Br*, clink.

tolérable [tɔlerabl] *adj* - **1.** [comportement] excusable - **2.** [douleur] bearable, tolerable.

tolérance [tɔlerɑ̃s] *nf* - **1.** [gén] tolerance - **2.** [liberté] concession.

tolérant, e [tɔlerɑ̃, ɑ̃t] *adj* - **1.** [large d'esprit] tolerant - **2.** [indulgent] liberal.

tolérer [18] [tɔlere] *vt* to tolerate.
➤ **se tolérer** *vp* to put up with *ou* tolerate each other.

tôlier, ère, taulier, ère [tolje, ɛr] *nm, f* *tfam* [propriétaire] hotel owner.

tollé [tɔle] *nm* protest ; **soulever un** ~ **général** *fig* to cause a general outcry.

tomate [tɔmat] *nf* tomato ; ~**s à la provençale** baked or fried tomatoes with herbs, breadcrumbs and garlic.

tombal, e, aux [tɔ̃bal, o] *adj* : **pierre** ~**e** gravestone.

tombant, e [tɔ̃bɑ̃, ɑ̃t] *adj* [moustaches] drooping ; [épaules] sloping.

tombe [tɔ̃b] *nf* - **1.** [fosse] grave, tomb - **2.** [pierre] gravestone, tombstone.

tombeau, x [tɔ̃bo] *nm* tomb ; **rouler à** ~ **ouvert** *fig* to drive at breakneck speed.

tombée [tɔ̃be] *nf* fall ; **à la** ~ **du jour** *ou* **de la nuit** at nightfall.

tomber [3] [tɔ̃be] ⟨⟩ *vi (aux : être)* - **1.** [gén] to fall ; **faire** ~ **qqn** to knock sb over *ou* down ; ~ **raide mort** to drop down dead ; **je suis tombé de haut** *fig* you could have knocked me down with a feather ; ~ **bien** [robe] to hang well ; *fig* [visite, personne] to come at a good time - **2.** [cheveux] to fall out - **3.** [nouvelle] to break - **4.** [diminuer - prix] to drop, to fall ; [- fièvre, vent] to drop ; [- jour] to come to an end ; [- colère] to die down - **5.** [devenir brusquement] : ~ **malade** to fall ill ; ~ **amoureux** to fall in love ; **être bien/mal tombé** to be lucky/unlucky - **6.** [trouver] : ~ **sur** to come across - **7.** [attaquer] : ~ **sur** to set about - **8.** [se placer] : ~ **sous** [loi, juridiction] to come *ou* fall under ; ~ **sous la main** to come to hand - **9.** [date, événement] to fall on ⟨⟩ *vt (aux : avoir) fam* [séduire] to lay.

tombeur [tɔ̃bœr] *nm fam fig* womanizer, Casanova.

tombola [tɔ̃bɔla] *nf* raffle.

tome [tɔm] *nm* volume.

tomme [tɔm] *nf* : ~ **(de Savoie)** *semi-hard cow's milk cheese from Savoy*.

tommette [tɔmet] *nf* terracotta floor tile.

ton¹ [tɔ̃] *nm* - **1.** [de voix] tone ; **hausser/baisser le** ~ to raise/lower one's voice - **2.** MUS key ; **donner le** ~ to give the chord ; *fig* to set the tone.

ton² [tɔ̃] *(f* **ta** [ta]*, pl* **tes** [te]*) adj poss* your.

tonalité [tɔnalite] *nf* - **1.** MUS tonality - **2.** *fig* [impression] tone - **3.** [au téléphone] dialling tone.

tondeuse [tɔ̃døz] *nf* [à cheveux] clippers *(pl)* ; ~ **(à gazon)** mower, lawnmower.

tondre [75] [tɔ̃dr] *vt* [gazon] to mow ; [mouton] to shear ; [caniche, cheveux] to clip ; **se laisser** *ou* **se faire** ~ **par qqn** *fig* to be fleeced by sb.

tondu, e [tɔ̃dy] *adj* [caniche, cheveux] clipped ; [pelouse] mown.

tonicité [tɔnisite] *nf* [des muscles] tone.

tonifiant, e [tɔnifjɑ̃, ɑ̃t] *adj* [climat] invigorating, bracing ; [lecture] stimulating.

tonifier [9] [tɔnifje] *vt* [peau] to tone ; [esprit] to stimulate.

tonique [tɔnik] ⟨⟩ *adj* - **1.** [boisson] tonic *(avant n)* ; [froid] bracing ; [lotion] toning - **2.** LING & MUS tonic ⟨⟩ *nm* MÉD tonic ⟨⟩ *nf* MUS tonic, keynote.

tonitruant, e [tɔnitryɑ̃, ɑ̃t] *adj* booming.

tonnage [tɔnaʒ] *nm* tonnage.

tonnant, e [tɔnɑ̃, ɑ̃t] *adj* thundering, thunderous.

tonne [tɔn] *nf* - **1.** [1000 kg] tonne - **2.** [grande quantité] : **des** ~**s de tons** *ou* loads of - **3.** [tonneau] tun.

tonneau, x [tɔno] *nm* - **1.** [baril] barrel, cask - **2.** [de voiture] roll - **3.** NAVIG ton.

tonnelet [tɔnlɛ] *nm* keg, small cask.

tonnelle [tɔnɛl] *nf* bower, arbour.

tonner [3] [tɔne] *vi* to thunder.

tonnerre [tɔnɛr] *nm* thunder ; **coup de ~** thunderclap ; *fig* bombshell ; **du ~** *fam fig* terrific, great.

tonsure [tɔ̃syr] *nf* tonsure.

tonte [tɔ̃t] *nf* [de mouton] shearing ; [de gazon] mowing ; [de caniche, cheveux] clipping.

tonton [tɔ̃tɔ̃] *nm* uncle.

tonus [tɔnys] *nm* - **1.** [dynamisme] energy - **2.** [de muscle] tone.

top [tɔp] <> *nm* [signal] beep <> *adj* : **être au ~ niveau** to be at the top (level).

➤ **top secret** *adj inv* top secret.

topaze [tɔpaz] *nf* topaz.

toper [3] [tɔpe] *vi* : **tope-là!** right, you're on!

topinambour [tɔpinãbur] *nm* Jerusalem artichoke.

topique [tɔpik] <> *adj* pertinent <> *nm* topical *ou* local remedy.

topo [tɔpo] *nm fam* spiel ; **c'est toujours le même ~** *fig* it's always the same old story.

topographie [tɔpɔgrafi] *nf* topography.

topographique [tɔpɔgrafik] *adj* topographical.

toponymie [tɔpɔnimi] *nf* toponymy.

toquade [tɔkad] *nf* : **~ (pour)** [personne] crush (on) ; [style, mode] craze (for).

toque [tɔk] *nf* [de juge, de jockey] cap ; [de cuisinier] hat.

toqué, e [tɔke] *fam* <> *adj* : **~ (de)** crazy (about), nuts (about) <> *nm, f* nutter, nutcase.

torche [tɔrʃ] *nf* torch ; **~ électrique** (electric) torch *Br*, flashlight *Am*.

torcher [3] [tɔrʃe] *vt fam* - **1.** [assiette, fesses] to wipe - **2.** [travail] to dash off - **3.** [bouteille] to polish off.

➤ **se torcher** *vp tfam* to wipe one's bottom.

torchis [tɔrʃi] *nm* daub *(building material)*.

torchon [tɔrʃɔ̃] *nm* - **1.** [serviette] cloth - **2.** *fam* [travail] mess - **3.** *fam* [journal] rag.

tordant, e [tɔrdã, ãt] *adj fam* hilarious.

tord-boyaux [tɔrbwajo] *nm inv fam* gutrot.

tordre [76] [tɔrdr] *vt* - **1.** [gén] to twist - **2.** [linge] to wring (out).

➤ **se tordre** *vp* : **se ~ la cheville** to twist one's ankle ; **se ~ de douleur** *fig* to be racked with pain ; **se ~ de rire** *fam fig* to double up with laughter.

tordu, e [tɔrdy] <> *pp* ▷ **tordre** <> *adj fam* [bizarre, fou] crazy ; [esprit] warped <> *nm, f fam* nutcase.

toréador [tɔreadɔr], **torero** [tɔrero] *nm* bullfighter.

tornade [tɔrnad] *nf* tornado.

torpeur [tɔrpœr] *nf* torpor.

torpille [tɔrpij] *nf* - **1.** MIL torpedo - **2.** [poisson] torpedo, electric ray.

torpiller [3] [tɔrpije] *vt* to torpedo.

torpilleur [tɔrpijœr] *nm* torpedo boat.

torréfaction [tɔrefaksjɔ̃] *nf* roasting.

torréfier [9] [tɔrefje] *vt* to roast.

torrent [tɔrã] *nm* torrent ; **pleuvoir à ~s** *fig* to pour down ; **un ~ de** *fig* [injures] a stream of ; [lumière, larmes] a flood of.

torrentiel, elle [tɔrãsjɛl] *adj* torrential.

torride [tɔrid] *adj* torrid.

tors, e [tɔr, tɔrs] *adj* twisted.

torse [tɔrs] *nm* chest ; **bomber le ~** to puff *ou* throw out one's chest ; *fig* to puff up (with pride).

torsade [tɔrsad] *nf* - **1.** [de cheveux] twist, coil - **2.** [de pull] cable.

torsader [3] [tɔrsade] *vt* to twist.

torsion [tɔrsjɔ̃] *nf* twisting ; PHYS torsion.

tort [tɔr] *nm* - **1.** [erreur] fault ; **avoir ~** to be wrong ; **avoir ~ de faire qqch** to be wrong to do sthg ; **parler à ~ et à travers** to talk nonsense ; **être dans son** *ou* **en ~** to be in the wrong ; **reconnaître ses ~s** to acknowledge one's faults ; **à ~** wrongly ; **à ~ ou à raison** rightly or wrongly - **2.** [préjudice] wrong ; **causer** *ou* **faire du ~ à qqn** to wrong sb.

torticolis [tɔrtikɔli] *nm* stiff neck.

tortillement [tɔrtijmã] *nm* wriggling, writhing.

tortiller [3] [tɔrtije] <> *vt* [enrouler] to twist ; [moustache] to twirl <> *vi* : **~ des hanches** to swing one's hips ; **il n'y a pas à ~** *fig* there's no getting out of it.

➤ **se tortiller** *vp* to writhe, to wriggle.

tortionnaire [tɔrsjɔnɛr] <> *nmf* torturer <> *adj* given to torture.

tortue [tɔrty] *nf* tortoise ; *fig* slowcoach *Br*, slowpoke *Am*.

tortueux, euse [tɔrtɥø, øz] *adj* winding, twisting ; *fig* tortuous.

torture [tɔrtyr] *nf* torture ; **sous la ~** under torture.

torturer [3] [tɔrtyre] *vt* to torture.

➤ **se torturer** *vp* to torment o.s. ; **se ~ pour** to agonize over.

torve [tɔrv] *adj* : œil *ou* regard ~ threatening look.

tôt [to] *adv* - **1.** [de bonne heure] early - **2.** [vite] soon, early ; **ce n'est pas trop ~!** *fam* and about time too! ; **~ ou tard** sooner or later.
➤ **au plus tôt** *loc adv* at the earliest.

total, e, aux [tɔtal, o] *adj* total.
➤ **total** *nm* total ; **au ~** in total ; *fig* on the whole, all in all.

totalement [tɔtalmã] *adv* totally.

totaliser [3] [tɔtalize] *vt* - **1.** [additionner] to add up, to total - **2.** [réunir] to have a total of.

totalitaire [tɔtaliter] *adj* totalitarian.

totalitarisme [tɔtalitarism] *nm* totalitarianism.

totalité [tɔtalite] *nf* whole ; **la ~ de** [inscrits] all (of) ; [classe] the whole of, the entire ; **en ~** entirely.

totem [tɔtɛm] *nm* totem.

touareg, ègue [twarɛg] *adj* Tuareg.
➤ **touareg** *nm* [langue] Tuareg.
➤ **Touareg, ègue** *nm, f* Tuareg.

toubib [tubib] *nmf fam* doc.

toucan [tukã] *nm* toucan.

touchant, e [tuʃã, ãt] *adj* touching.

touche [tuʃ] *nf* - **1.** [de clavier] key ; **~ alphanumérique** alphanumeric key ; **~ de fonction** function key - **2.** [de peinture] stroke - **3.** *fig* [note] : **une ~ de** a touch of - **4.** *fam* [allure] appearance, look - **5.** PÊCHE bite ; **faire une ~** to make a hit - **6.** [FOOTBALL - ligne] touch line ; [- remise en jeu] throw-in ; [RUGBY - ligne] touch (line) ; [- remise en jeu] line-out ; **être mis/rester sur la ~** *fig* to be left/to stay on the sidelines - **7.** ESCRIME hit.

touche-à-tout [tuʃatu] *nmf inv* [adulte] dabbler ; [enfant] : **c'est un petit ~** he's into everything.

toucher [3] [tuʃe] ◇ *nm* : **le ~** the (sense of) touch ; **au ~** to the touch ◇ *vt* - **1.** [palper, émouvoir] to touch - **2.** [rivage, correspondant] to reach ; [cible] to hit - **3.** [salaire] to get, to be paid ; [chèque] to cash ; [gros lot] to win - **4.** [concerner] to affect, to touch on ◇ *vi* : **~ à** to touch ; [problème] to touch on ; [inconscience, folie] to border *ou* verge on ; [maison] to adjoin ; **~ à sa fin** to draw to a close.
➤ **se toucher** *vp* [maisons] to be adjacent (to each other), to adjoin (each other).

touffe [tuf] *nf* tuft.

touffu, e [tufy] *adj* [forêt] dense ; [barbe] bushy.

touiller [3] [tuje] *vt fam* [mélanger] to stir ; [salade] to toss.

toujours [tuʒur] *adv* - **1.** [continuité, répétition] always ; **ils s'aimeront ~** they will always love one another, they will love one another forever ; **~ plus** more and more ; **~ moins** less and less - **2.** [encore] still - **3.** [de toute façon] anyway, anyhow.
➤ **de toujours** *loc adj* : **ce sont des amis de ~** they are lifelong friends.
➤ **pour toujours** *loc adv* forever, for good.
➤ **toujours est-il que** *loc conj* the fact remains that.

toundra [tundra] *nf* tundra.

toupet [tupɛ] *nm* - **1.** [de cheveux] quiff *Br*, tuft of hair - **2.** *fam fig* [aplomb] cheek ; **avoir du ~, ne pas manquer de ~** *fam* to have a cheek.

toupie [tupi] *nf* (spinning) top.

tour [tur] ◇ *nm* - **1.** [périmètre] circumference ; **faire le ~ de** to go round ; **faire un ~** to go for a walk/drive *etc* ; **faire le ~ du propriétaire** to go on a tour of inspection ; **~ d'horizon** survey ; **~ de piste** SPORT lap ; **~ de taille** waist measurement - **2.** [rotation] turn ; **fermer à double ~** to double-lock ; **à ~ de bras** *fig* non-stop ; **en un ~ de main** *fig* in the twinkling of an eye - **3.** [plaisanterie] trick ; **jouer un bon/mauvais ~ à qqn** to play a joke/dirty trick on sb ; **~ de force** amazing feat - **4.** [succession] turn ; **c'est à mon ~** it's my turn ; **j'ai fait la cuisine/la vaisselle** *etc* **plus souvent qu'à mon ~** I've done more than my fair share of cooking/washing-up *etc* ; **~ de scrutin** ballot, round of voting ; **à ~ de rôle** in turn ; **~ à ~** alternately, in turn - **5.** [d'événements] turn - **6.** [de potier] wheel ◇ *nf* - **1.** [monument, de château] tower ; [immeuble] tower-block *Br*, high-rise *Am* - **2.** ÉCHECS rook, castle.
➤ **tour de contrôle** *nf* control tower.

tourbe [turb] *nf* peat.

tourbière [turbjɛr] *nf* peat bog.

tourbillon [turbijɔ̃] *nm* - **1.** [de vent] whirlwind ; **un ~ de** a whirl of - **2.** [de poussière, fumée] swirl - **3.** [d'eau] whirlpool - **4.** *fig* [agitation] hurly-burly.

tourbillonnant, e [turbijɔnã, ãt] *adj* swirling, whirling.

tourbillonner [3] [turbijɔne] *vi* to whirl, to swirl ; *fig* to whirl (round).

tourelle [turɛl] *nf* turret.

tourisme [turism] *nm* tourism.

tourista [turista] *nf* traveller's *Br ou* traveler's *Am* tummy.

touriste [turist] ◇ *nmf* tourist ; **en ~** as a tourist ◇ *adj* tourist *(avant n)*.

touristique [turistik] *adj* tourist *(avant n)*.

tourment [turmã] *nm sout* torment.

tourmente [turmɑ̃t] *nf* - **1.** *littéraire* [tempête] storm, tempest - **2.** *fig* turmoil.

tourmenter [3] [turmɑ̃te] *vt* to torment.
◆ **se tourmenter** *vp* to worry o.s., to fret.

tournage [turnaʒ] *nm* CIN shooting.

tournailler [3] [turnaje] *vi fam* to prowl about ; **~ autour de qqn/qqch** to hover around sb/sthg.

tournant, e [turnɑ̃, ɑ̃t] *adj* [porte] revolving ; [fauteuil] swivel *(avant n)* ; [pont] swing *(avant n)*.
◆ **tournant** *nm* bend ; *fig* turning point ; **je l'attends au ~** *fam fig* I'll get even with him/ her.

tourné, e [turne] *adj* - **1.** [lait] sour, off - **2.** *loc* : **bien ~** [lettre] well-worded ; [personne] shapely ; **mal ~** [lettre] badly-worded ; [personne] unattractive ; [esprit] warped.

tournebroche [turnəbrɔʃ] *nm* spit.

tourne-disque [turnədisk] *(pl* **tournedisques)** *nm* record player.

tournedos [turnədo] *nm* steak taken from the thickest part of the fillet.

tournée [turne] *nf* - **1.** [voyage] tour - **2.** *fam* [consommations] round - **3.** *fam* [correction] thrashing, hiding.

tourner [3] [turne] ◇ *vt* - **1.** [gén] to turn - **2.** [pas, pensées] to turn, to direct - **3.** [obstacle, loi] to get round - **4.** CIN to shoot - **5.** *fig* [formuler] : **bien ~ qqch** to put sthg well ◇ *vi* - **1.** [gén] to turn ; [moteur] to turn over ; [planète] to revolve ; **~ autour de qqn** *fig* to hang around sb ; **~ autour du pot** OU **du sujet** *fig* to beat about the bush ; **'tournez s'il vous plaît'** 'please turn over' - **2.** *fam* [entreprise] to tick over - **3.** [lait] to go off.
◆ **se tourner** *vp* to turn (right) round ; **se ~ vers** to turn towards *Br* OU toward *Am*.

tournesol [turnəsɔl] *nm* - **1.** [plante] sunflower - **2.** [colorant] litmus.

tourneur, euse [turnœr, øz] *nm, f* turner, lathe operator.

tournevis [turnəvis] *nm* screwdriver.

tournicoter [3] [turnikɔte] *vi fam* to wander up and down.

tourniquet [turnikɛ] *nm* - **1.** [entrée] turnstile - **2.** MÉD tourniquet.

tournis [turni] *nm fam* : **avoir le ~** to feel dizzy OU giddy ; **donner le ~ à qqn** to make sb dizzy OU giddy.

tournoi [turnwa] *nm* tournament.

tournoiement [turnwamɑ̃] *nm* wheeling, whirling.

tournoyer [13] [turnwaje] *vi* to wheel, to whirl.

tournure [turnyr] *nf* - **1.** [apparence] turn ; **prendre ~** to take shape - **2.** [formulation] form ; **~ de phrase** turn of phrase.

tour-opérateur [turɔperatœr] *(pl* **tour-opérateurs)** *nm* tour operator.

tourte [turt] *nf* pie.

tourteau, x [turto] *nm* - **1.** [crabe] crab - **2.** [pour bétail] oil cake.

tourtereau [turtəro] *nm* young turtledove.
◆ **tourtereaux** *nmpl fam fig* [amoureux] lovebirds.

tourterelle [turtərɛl] *nf* turtledove.

tourtière [turtjɛr] *nf* pie-dish.

tous ▷ tout.

Toussaint [tusɛ̃] *nf* : **la ~** All Saints' Day.

tousser [3] [tuse] *vi* to cough.

toussotement [tusɔtmɑ̃] *nm* coughing.

toussoter [3] [tusɔte] *vi* to cough.

tout [tu] *(f* **toute** [tut], *mpl* **tous** [tus], *fpl* **toutes** [tut]) ◇ *adj qualificatif* - **1.** *(avec substantif singulier déterminé)* all ; **~ le vin** all the wine ; **~ un gâteau** a whole cake ; **toute la journée/ la nuit** all day/night, the whole day/night ; **toute sa famille** all his family, his whole family - **2.** *(avec pronom démonstratif)* : **~ ceci/ cela** all this/that ; **~ ce que je sais** all I know ◇ *adj indéf* - **1.** [exprime la totalité] all ; **tous les gâteaux** all the cakes ; **toutes les femmes** all the women ; **tous les deux** both of us/them *etc* ; **tous les trois** all three of us/them *etc* - **2.** [chaque] every ; **tous les jours** every day ; **tous les deux ans** every two years ; **tous les combien?** how often? - **3.** [n'importe quel] any ; **à toute heure** at any time ◇ *pron indéf* everything, all ; **je t'ai ~ dit** I've told you everything ; **ils voulaient tous la voir** they all wanted to see her ; **ce sera ~?** will that be all ; **c'est ~** that's all.
◆ **tout** ◇ *adv* - **1.** [entièrement, tout à fait] very, quite ; **~ jeune/près** very young/near ; **ils étaient ~ seuls** they were all alone ; **~ en haut** right at the top ; **~ à côté de moi** right next to me - **2.** [avec un gérondif] : **~ en marchant** while walking ◇ *nm* : **un ~** a whole ; **le ~ est de ...** the main thing is to ... ; **risquer le ~ pour le ~** to risk everything.
◆ **du tout au tout** *loc adv* completely, entirely.
◆ **pas du tout** *loc adv* not at all.
◆ **tout à fait** *loc adv* - **1.** [complètement] quite, entirely - **2.** [exactement] exactly.
◆ **tout à l'heure** *loc adv* - **1.** [futur] in a little while, shortly ; **à ~ à l'heure!** see you later! - **2.** [passé] a little while ago.
◆ **tout de suite** *loc adv* immediately, at once.

tout-à-l'égout [tutalegu] *nm inv* mains drainage.

toutefois [tutfwa] *adv* however.

toutou [tutu] *nm fam* doggie.

tout-petit [tup(ə)ti] (*pl* **tout-petits**) *nm* toddler, tot.

tout-puissant, toute-puissante [tupɥisã, tutpɥisãt] (*mpl* **tout-puissants**, *fpl* **toutes-puissantes**) *adj* omnipotent, all-powerful.
◆ **Tout-Puissant** *nm* : **le Tout-Puissant** the Almighty.

tout-venant [tuvnã] *nm inv* : **le ~** ordinary people *(pl)*.

toux [tu] *nf* cough.

toxicité [tɔksisite] *nf* toxicity.

toxicologie [tɔksikɔlɔʒi] *nf* toxicology.

toxicomane [tɔksikɔman] *nmf* drug addict.

toxicomanie [tɔksikɔmani] *nf* drug addiction.

toxine [tɔksin] *nf* toxin.

toxique [tɔksik] *adj* toxic.

TP ◇ *nmpl* (*abr de* **travaux publics**) civil engineering ◇ *nm* (*abr de* **Trésor public**) *public revenue office*.

TPG (*abr de* **trésorier payeur général**) *nm* paymaster.

tps *abr de* **temps**.

trac [trak] *nm* nerves *(pl)* ; THÉÂTRE stage fright ; **avoir le ~** to get nervous ; THÉÂTRE to get stage fright.

tracas [traka] *nm* worry.

tracasser [3] [trakase] *vt* to worry, to bother.
◆ **se tracasser** *vp* to worry.

tracasserie [trakasri] *nf* annoyance.

tracassier, ère [trakasje, ɛr] *adj* irksome.

trace [tras] *nf* - **1.** [d'animal] track - **2.** [de brûlure, fatigue] mark - **3.** (*gén pl*) [vestige] trace - **4.** [très petite quantité] : **une ~ de** a trace of - **5.** SKI trail ; **~ directe** direct descent.

tracé [trase] *nm* [lignes] plan, drawing ; [de parcours] line.

tracer [16] [trase] ◇ *vt* - **1.** [dessiner, dépeindre] to draw - **2.** [route, piste] to mark out ; **~ la voie/le chemin à qqn** *fig* to show sb the way ◇ *vi fam* to belt along.

traceur [trasœr] *nm* INFORM plotter.

trachée-artère [traʃeartɛr] (*pl* **trachées-artères**) *nf* windpipe, trachea.

trachéite [trakeit] *nf* throat infection.

tract [trakt] *nm* leaflet.

tractations [traktasjɔ̃] *nfpl* negotiations, dealings.

tracter [3] [trakte] *vt* to tow.

tracteur [traktœr] *nm* tractor.

traction [traksjɔ̃] *nf* - **1.** [action de tirer] towing, pulling ; **~ avant/arrière** front-/rear-wheel drive - **2.** TECHNOL tensile stress - **3.** [SPORT - au sol] press-up Br, push-up Am ; [- à la barre] pull-up.

tradition [tradisjɔ̃] *nf* tradition ; **renouer avec la ~** to revive a tradition.

traditionaliste [tradisjɔnalist] *nmf* & *adj* traditionalist.

traditionnel, elle [tradisjɔnɛl] *adj* - **1.** [de tradition] traditional - **2.** [habituel] usual.

traditionnellement [tradisjɔnɛlmã] *adv* traditionally.

traducteur, trice [tradyktœr, tris] *nm, f* translator.
◆ **traducteur** *nm* INFORM translator.

traduction [tradyksjɔ̃] *nf* - **1.** [gén] translation - **2.** *littéraire* [expression] rendering.

traduire [98] [tradɥir] *vt* - **1.** [texte] to translate ; **~ qqch en français/anglais** to translate sthg into French/English - **2.** [révéler - crise] to reveal, to betray ; [- sentiments, pensée] to render, to express - **3.** JUR : **~ qqn en justice** to bring sb before the courts.

traduisible [tradɥizibl] *adj* translatable.

trafic [trafik] *nm* - **1.** [de marchandises] traffic, trafficking - **2.** [circulation] traffic.
◆ **trafic d'influence** *nm* corruption, taking bribes.

trafiquant, e [trafikã, ãt] *nm, f* trafficker, dealer.

trafiquer [3] [trafike] ◇ *vt* - **1.** [falsifier] to tamper with - **2.** *fam* [manigancer] : **qu'est-ce que tu trafiques?** what are you up to? ◇ *vi* to be involved in trafficking ; **~ de qqch** to traffic in sthg.

tragédie [traʒedi] *nf* tragedy.

tragédien, enne [traʒedjɛ̃, ɛn] *nm, f* tragedian (*f* tragedienne), tragic actor (*f* actress).

tragi-comédie [traʒikɔmedi] (*pl* **tragi-comédies**) *nf* tragicomedy.

tragi-comique [traʒikɔmik] *adj* tragicomic, tragicomical.

tragique [traʒik] ◇ *adj* tragic ◇ *nm* - **1.** [auteur] tragedian - **2.** [caractère] : **le ~** tragedy ; **prendre qqch au ~** to act as if sthg were a tragedy ; **tourner au ~** to take a tragic turn.

tragiquement [traʒikmã] *adv* tragically.

trahir [32] [trair] *vt* - **1.** [gén] to betray - **2.** [suj : moteur] to let down ; [suj : forces] to fail - **3.** [pensée] to misrepresent.
◆ **se trahir** *vp* to give o.s. away.

trahison [traizɔ̃] *nf* - **1.** [gén] betrayal - **2.** JUR treason.

train [trɛ̃] *nm* - **1.** TRANSPORT train ; ~ **corail** express ; ~ **(à) grande vitesse** high-speed train - **2.** AÉRON : ~ **d'atterrissage** landing gear - **3.** [allure] pace - **4.** [série] **un** ~ **de** a series of - **5.** *fam* [postérieur] backside, butt *Am* - **6.** *loc* : **être en** ~ *fig* to be on form.

➥ **train de vie** *nm* lifestyle.

➥ **en train de** *loc prép* : **être en** ~ **de** lire/travailler to be reading/working.

traînailler [trɛnaje], **traînasser** [3] [trɛnase] *vi fam* - **1.** [vagabonder] to loaf about - **2.** [être lent] to dawdle.

traînant, e [trɛnɑ̃, ɑ̃t] *adj* - **1.** [robe] trailing - **2.** [voix] drawling ; [démarche] dragging.

traînard, e [trɛnar, ard] *nm, f fam* straggler ; *fig* slowcoach *Br*, slowpoke *Am*.

traînasser = traînailler.

traîne [trɛn] *nf* - **1.** [de robe] train - **2.** PÊCHE dragnet - **3.** *Can* : ~ **sauvage** toboggan - **4.** *loc* : être à la ~ to lag behind.

traîneau, x [trɛno] *nm* sleigh, sledge.

traînée [trɛne] *nf* - **1.** [trace] trail ; **se répandre comme une** ~ **de poudre** *fig* to spread like wildfire - **2.** *tfam péj* [prostituée] tart, whore.

traîner [4] [trɛne] <> *vt* - **1.** [tirer, emmener] to drag - **2.** [trimbaler] to lug around, to cart around - **3.** [maladie] to be unable to shake off <> *vi* - **1.** [personne] to dawdle - **2.** [maladie, affaire] to drag on ; ~ **en longueur** to drag - **3.** [robe] to trail - **4.** [vêtements, livres] to lie around *ou* about.

➥ **se traîner** *vp* - **1.** [personne] to drag o.s. along - **2.** [jour, semaine] to drag.

training [trɛniŋ] *nm* - **1.** [entraînement] training - **2.** [survêtement] tracksuit top.

train-train [trɛ̃trɛ̃] *nm fam* routine, daily grind.

traire [112] [trɛr] *vt* - **1.** [vache] to milk - **2.** [lait] to draw.

trait [trɛ] *nm* - **1.** [ligne] line, stroke ; ~ **d'union** hyphen ; **tirer un** ~ **sur qqch** *fig* to put sthg behind one - **2.** (*gén pl*) [de visage] feature ; **ressembler à qqn** ~ **pour** ~ to be the spitting image of sb, to be exactly like sb - **3.** [caractéristique] trait, feature ; ~ **de caractère** character trait - **4.** [acte] act ; ~ **de génie** brainwave - **5.** *loc* : **avoir** ~ **à** to be to do with, to concern.

➥ **d'un trait** *loc adv* [boire, lire] in one go.

traitant, e [trɛtɑ̃, ɑ̃t] *adj* [shampooing, crème] medicated ▷ **médecin**.

traite [trɛt] *nf* - **1.** [de vache] milking - **2.** COMM bill, draft - **3.** [d'esclaves] : **la** ~ **des noirs** the

slave trade ; **la** ~ **des blanches** the white slave trade.

➥ **d'une seule traite** *loc adv* without stopping, in one go.

traité [trete] *nm* - **1.** [ouvrage] treatise - **2.** POLIT treaty ; ~ **de non-prolifération** non-proliferation treaty.

traitement [trɛtmɑ̃] *nm* - **1.** [gén & MÉD] treatment ; **mauvais** ~ ill-treatment ; ~ **de faveur** special treatment - **2.** [rémunération] wage - **3.** IND & INFORM processing ; ~ **anti-rouille** rustproofing ; ~ **de texte** word processing ; ~ **de la parole** speech processing - **4.** [de problème] handling.

traiter [4] [trete] <> *vt* - **1.** [gén & MÉD] to treat ; **se faire** ~ MÉD to be treated ; **bien/mal** ~ **qqn** to treat sb well/badly - **2.** [qualifier] : ~ **qqn d'imbécile/de lâche** *etc* to call sb an imbecile/a coward *etc* - **3.** [question, thème] to deal with - **4.** IND & INFORM to process <> *vi* - **1.** [négocier] to negotiate - **2.** [livre] : ~ **de** to deal with.

traiteur [trɛtœr] *nm* caterer.

traître, esse [trɛtr, ɛs] <> *adj* treacherous <> *nm, f* traitor.

traîtreusement [trɛtrøzmɑ̃] *adv* treacherously.

traîtrise [trɛtriz] *nf* - **1.** [déloyauté] treachery - **2.** [acte] act of treachery.

trajectoire [traʒɛktwar] *nf* trajectory, path ; *fig* path.

trajet [traʒɛ] *nm* - **1.** [distance] distance - **2.** [itinéraire] route - **3.** [voyage] journey.

trame [tram] *nf* weft ; *fig* framework.

tramer [3] [trame] *vt sout* to plot.

➥ **se tramer** <> *vp* to be plotted <> *v impers* : **il se trame quelque chose** there's something afoot.

tramontane [tramɔ̃tan] *nf strong cold wind that blows through Languedoc-Roussillon in southwest France.*

trampoline [trɑ̃pɔlin] *nm* trampoline.

tram(way) [tram(wɛ)] *nm* tram *Br*, streetcar *Am*.

tranchant, e [trɑ̃ʃɑ̃, ɑ̃t] *adj* - **1.** [instrument] sharp - **2.** [personne] assertive - **3.** [ton] curt.

➥ **tranchant** *nm* edge ; **à double** ~ *fig* two-edged.

tranche [trɑ̃ʃ] *nf* - **1.** [de gâteau, jambon] slice ; ~ **d'âge** *fig* age bracket ; ~ **de vie** *fig* slice of life - **2.** [de livre, pièce] edge - **3.** [période] part, section ; ~ **horaire** time-slot - **4.** [de revenus] portion ; [de paiement] instalment *Br*, installment *Am* ; [fiscale] bracket.

tranchée [trɑ̃ʃe] *nf* MIL trench.

trancher [3] [trãʃe] ◇ *vt* [couper] to cut ; [pain, jambon] to slice ; **~ la question** *fig* to settle the question ◇ *vi* **- 1.** *fig* [décider] to decide **- 2.** [contraster] : **~ avec** *ou* **sur** to contrast with.

tranchoir [trãʃwar] *nm* **- 1.** [couteau] chopper **- 2.** [planche] chopping board.

tranquille [trãkil] *adj* **- 1.** [endroit, vie] quiet ; **laisser qqn/qqch ~** to leave sb/sthg alone ; **se tenir/rester ~** to keep/remain quiet **- 2.** [rassuré] at ease, easy ; **soyez ~** don't worry.

tranquillement [trãkilmã] *adv* **- 1.** [sans s'agiter] quietly **- 2.** [sans s'inquiéter] calmly.

tranquillisant, e [trãkilizã, ãt] *adj* **- 1.** [nouvelle] reassuring **- 2.** [médicament] tranquillizing.
➜ **tranquillisant** *nm* tranquillizer *Br*, tranquilizer *Am*.

tranquilliser [3] [trãkilize] *vt* to reassure.
➜ **se tranquilliser** *vp* to set one's mind at rest.

tranquillité [trãkilite] *nf* **- 1.** [calme] peacefulness, quietness **- 2.** [sérénité] peace, tranquillity *Br*, tranquility *Am* ; **~ d'esprit** peace of mind.

transaction [trãzaksjɔ̃] *nf* transaction.

transactionnel, elle [trãzaksjɔnɛl] *adj* **- 1.** *PSYCHOL* transactional **- 2.** *JUR* compromise *(avant n)*.

transalpin, e [trãzalpɛ̃, in] *adj* transalpine.

transat [trãzat] ◇ *nm* deckchair ◇ *nf* transatlantic race.

transatlantique [trãzatlãtik] ◇ *adj* transatlantic ◇ *nm* transatlantic liner ◇ *nf* transatlantic race.

transbahuter [3] [trãsbayte] *vt fam* to hump *ou* lug along.

transbordement [trãsbɔrdəmã] *nm* transfer.

transcendant, e [trãsãdã, ãt] *adj fam* [extraordinaire] special, great.

transcender [3] [trãsãde] *vt* to transcend.
➜ **se transcender** *vp* to surpass o.s.

transcoder [3] [trãskɔde] *vt* to transcribe.

transcription [trãskripsjɔ̃] *nf* [de document & *MUS*] transcription ; [dans un autre alphabet] transliteration ; **~ phonétique** phonetic transcription.

transcrire [99] [trãskrir] *vt* [document & *MUS*] to transcribe ; [dans un autre alphabet] to transliterate.

transcrit, e [trãskri, it] *pp* ▷ **transcrire**.

transe [trãs] *nf* : **être en ~** *fig* to be beside o.s.
➜ **transes** *nfpl sout* agony (*U*).

transférer [18] [trãsfere] *vt* to transfer.

transfert [trãsfɛr] *nm* transfer.

transfigurer [3] [trãsfigyre] *vt* to transfigure.

transformable [trãsfɔrmabl] *adj* convertible.

transformateur, trice [trãsfɔrmatœr, tris] *adj* **- 1.** *IND* processing *(avant n)* **- 2.** *fig* [pouvoir, action] for change.
➜ **transformateur** *nm* transformer.

transformation [trãsfɔrmasjɔ̃] *nf* **- 1.** [de pays, personne] transformation **- 2.** *IND* processing **- 3.** *RUGBY* conversion.

transformer [3] [trãsfɔrme] *vt* **- 1.** [gén] to transform ; [magasin] to convert ; **~ qqch en** to turn sthg into **- 2.** *IND & RUGBY* to convert.
➜ **se transformer** *vp* : **se ~ en monstre/papillon** to turn into a monster/butterfly.

transfuge [trãsfyʒ] *nmf* renegade.

transfuser [3] [trãsfyze] *vt* [sang] to transfuse.

transfusion [trãsfyzjɔ̃] *nf* : **~ (sanguine)** (blood) transfusion.

transgénique [trãsʒenik] *adj* transgenic.

transgresser [4] [trãsgrese] *vt* [loi] to infringe ; [ordre] to disobey.

transgression [trãsgresjɔ̃] *nf* infringement, transgression.

transhumance [trãzymãs] *nf* transhumance.

transi, e [trãzi] *adj* : **être ~ de** to be paralysed *Br ou* paralyzed *Am*, to be transfixed with ; **être ~ de froid** to be chilled to the bone.

transiger [17] [trãziʒe] *vi* : **~ (sur)** to compromise (on).

transistor [3] [trãzistɔr] *nm* transistor.

transit [trãzit] *nm* transit ; **en ~** in transit.

transitaire [trãzitɛr] *nm* forwarding agent.

transiter [3] [trãzite] ◇ *vt* to forward ◇ *vi* to pass in transit ; **~ par** to pass through.

transitif, ive [trãzitif, iv] *adj* transitive.

transition [trãzisjɔ̃] *nf* transition ; **sans ~** with no transition, abruptly.

transitivité [trãzitivite] *nf* transitivity.

transitoire [trãzitwar] *adj* [passager] transitory.

translucide [trãslysid] *adj* translucent.

transmettre [84] [trãsmetr] *vt* **- 1.** [message, salutations] : **~ qqch (à)** to pass sthg on (to) **- 2.** [tradition, propriété] : **~ qqch (à)** to hand sthg down (to) **- 3.** [fonction, pouvoir] : **~ qqch (à)** to hand sthg over (to) **- 4.** [maladie] : **~ qqch (à)** to transmit sthg (to), to pass sthg on (to) **- 5.** [concert, émission] to broadcast.

se transmettre *vp* **- 1.** [maladie] to be passed on, to be transmitted **- 2.** [nouvelle] to be passed on **- 3.** [courant, onde] to be transmitted **- 4.** [tradition] to be handed down.

transmis, e [trɑ̃smi, iz] *pp* ▷ **transmettre.**

transmissible [trɑ̃smisibl] *adj* **- 1.** [patrimoine] transferable **- 2.** [maladie] transmissible.

transmission [trɑ̃smisjɔ̃] *nf* **- 1.** [de biens] transfer **- 2.** [de maladie] transmission **- 3.** [de message] passing on **- 4.** [de tradition] handing down.

transocéanique [trɑ̃zɔseanik] *adj* transoceanic.

transparaître [91] [trɑ̃sparetr] *vi* to show.

transparence [trɑ̃sparɑ̃s] *nf* transparency ; **par ~** against the light.

transparent, e [trɑ̃sparɑ̃, ɑ̃t] *adj* transparent.

transparent *nm* transparency.

transpercer [16] [trɑ̃spɛrse] *vt* to pierce ; *fig* [suj : froid, pluie] to go right through.

transpiration [trɑ̃spirasjɔ̃] *nf* [sueur] perspiration.

transpirer [3] [trɑ̃spire] *vi* **- 1.** [suer] to perspire **- 2.** *fig* [se divulguer] to leak out.

transplant [trɑ̃splɑ̃] *nm* MÉD transplant.

transplantation [trɑ̃splɑ̃tasjɔ̃] *nf* **- 1.** [d'arbre, de population] transplanting **- 2.** MÉD transplant.

transplanter [3] [trɑ̃splɑ̃te] *vt* to transplant.

transport [trɑ̃spɔr] *nm* transport (U) ; **~ aérien** air transport ; **~ ferroviaire** rail transport ; **~ maritime** sea transport ; **~s en commun** public transport (sg).

transportable [trɑ̃spɔrtabl] *adj* [marchandise] transportable ; [blessé] fit to be moved.

transporter [3] [trɑ̃spɔrte] *vt* **- 1.** [marchandises, personnes] to transport **- 2.** *fig* [enthousiasmer] to delight ; **être transporté de joie/bonheur** to be beside o.s. with joy/happiness.

transporteur [trɑ̃spɔrtœr] *nm* **- 1.** [personne] carrier ; **~ routier** road haulier *Br ou* hauler *Am* **- 2.** [machine] conveyor.

transposer [3] [trɑ̃spoze] *vt* **- 1.** [déplacer] to transpose **- 2.** [adapter] : **~ qqch (à)** to adapt sthg (for).

transposition [trɑ̃spozisjɔ̃] *nf* **- 1.** [déplacement] transposition **- 2.** [adaptation] : **~ (à)** adaptation (for).

transsexuel, elle [trɑ̃ssɛksɥɛl] *adj & nm, f* transsexual.

transvaser [3] [trɑ̃svaze] *vt* to decant.

transversal, e, aux [trɑ̃sversal, o] *adj*
- 1. [coupe] cross (avant n) **- 2.** [chemin] running at right angles, cross (avant n) *Am* **- 3.** [vallée] transverse.

transversalité [trɑ̃sversalite] *nf* transversality.

trapèze [trapɛz] *nm* **- 1.** GÉOM trapezium **- 2.** GYM trapeze **- 3.** ANAT trapezius.

trapéziste [trapezist] *nmf* trapeze artist.

trappage [trapaʒ] *nm Can* trapping.

trappe [trap] *nf* **- 1.** [ouverture] trapdoor **- 2.** [piège] trap.

trappeur [trapœr] *nm* trapper.

trapu, e [trapy] *adj* **- 1.** [personne] stocky, solidly built **- 2.** [édifice] squat.

traquenard [traknar] *nm* trap ; *fig* trap, pitfall.

traquer [3] [trake] *vt* [animal] to track ; [personne, faute] to track *ou* hunt down.

traumatisant, e [tromatizɑ̃, ɑ̃t] *adj* traumatizing.

traumatiser [3] [tromatize] *vt* to traumatize.

traumatisme [tromatism] *nm* traumatism.

traumatologie [tromatɔlɔʒi] *nf* ≃ casualty department.

travail [travaj] *nm* **- 1.** [gén] work (U) ; **se mettre au ~** to get down to work ; **demander du ~** [projet] to require some work ; **abattre du ~** *fig* to get through a lot of work ; **mâcher le ~ à qqn** *fig* to spoon-feed sb **- 2.** [tâche, emploi] job ; **~ intérimaire** temporary work ; **~ au noir** moonlighting ; **~ précaire** casual labour *Br ou* labor *Am* **- 3.** [du métal, du bois] working **- 4.** [de la mémoire] workings (pl) **- 5.** [phénomène - du bois] warping ; [- du temps, fermentation] action **- 6.** MÉD : **être en ~** to be in labour *Br ou* labor *Am* ; **entrer en ~** to go into labour *Br ou* labor *Am*.

travaux *nmpl* **- 1.** [d'aménagement] work (U) ; [routiers] roadworks ; **travaux publics** civil engineering (sg) **- 2.** SCOL : **travaux dirigés** class work ; **travaux manuels** arts and crafts ; **travaux pratiques** practical work (U).

travaux d'approche *nmpl* preliminary work (U).

travaillé, e [travaje] *adj* **- 1.** [matériau] wrought, worked **- 2.** [style] laboured *Br*, labored *Am* **- 3.** [tourmenté] : **être ~ par** to be tormented by.

travailler [3] [travaje] ◇ *vi* **- 1.** [gén] to work ; **~ chez/dans** to work at/in ; **~ à qqch** to work on sthg ; **~ à temps partiel** to work part-time **- 2.** [métal, bois] to warp ◇ *vt* **- 1.** [étudier] to work at *ou* on ; [piano] to practise **- 2.** [essayer de convaincre] to work on

- 3. [suj : idée, remords] to torment **- 4.** [matière] to work, to fashion.

travailleur, euse [travajœr, øz] <> *adj* hard-working <> *nm, f* worker ; **~ à domicile** homeworker ; **~ émigré** migrant worker ; **~ indépendant** self-employed person.

travailliste [travajist] <> *nmf* member of the Labour Party <> *adj* Labour *(avant n)*.

travée [trave] *nf* **- 1.** [de bâtiment] bay **- 2.** [de sièges] row.

traveller [travlœr] *nm inv* traveller's cheque *Br*, traveler's check *Am*.

travelling [travliŋ] *nm* [mouvement] travelling *Br ou* traveling *Am* shot.

travelo [travlo] *nm tfam* drag queen.

travers [traver] *nm* failing, fault.

◆ **à travers** *loc adv* & *loc prép* through.

◆ **au travers** *loc adv* through ; **passer au ~** *fig* to escape.

◆ **au travers de** *loc prép* through.

◆ **de travers** *loc adv* **- 1.** [irrégulièrement - écrire] unevenly ; **marcher de ~** to stagger **- 2.** [nez, escalier] crooked **- 3.** [obliquement] sideways ; **regarder qqn de ~** *fig* to look askance at sb **- 4.** [mal] wrong ; **aller de ~** to go wrong ; **comprendre qqch de ~** to misunderstand sthg ; **prendre qqch de ~** to take sthg the wrong way.

◆ **en travers** *loc adv* crosswise.

◆ **en travers de** *loc prép* across.

traverse [travers] *nf* **- 1.** [de chemin de fer] sleeper, tie *Am* **- 2.** [chemin] short cut.

traversée [traverse] *nf* crossing.

traverser [3] [traverse] *vt* **- 1.** [rue, mer, montagne] to cross ; [ville] to go through **- 2.** [peau, mur] to go through, to pierce **- 3.** [crise, période] to go through.

traversin [traversɛ̃] *nm* bolster.

travestir [32] [travestir] *vt* **- 1.** [déguiser] to dress up **- 2.** *fig* [vérité, idée] to distort.

◆ **se travestir** *vp* **- 1.** [pour bal] to wear fancy dress **- 2.** [en femme] to put on drag.

travestissement [travestismã] *nm* **- 1.** [pour bal] wearing fancy dress **- 2.** [en femme] putting on drag **- 3.** *fig* [de vérité] distortion.

trayeuse [trejøz] *nf* milking machine.

trébucher [3] [trebyʃe] *vi* : **~ (sur/contre)** to stumble (over/against).

trèfle [trefl] *nm* **- 1.** [plante] clover ; **~ à quatre feuilles** four-leaved clover **- 2.** [carte] club ; [famille] clubs *(pl)*.

tréfonds [trefɔ̃] *nm littéraire* depths *(pl)*.

treillage [trejaʒ] *nm* [clôture] trellis (fencing).

treille [trej] *nf* **- 1.** [vigne] climbing vine **- 2.** [tonnelle] trellised vines *(pl)*, vine arbour.

treillis [treji] *nm* **- 1.** [clôture] trellis (fencing) **- 2.** [toile] canvas **- 3.** MIL combat uniform.

treize [trez] *adj num* & *nm* thirteen ; *voir aussi* **six**.

treizième [trezjɛm] *adj num, nm ou nmf* thirteenth ; **~ mois** *bonus corresponding to an extra month's salary which is paid annually* ; *voir aussi* **sixième**.

trekking [trekiŋ] *nm* trek.

tréma [trema] *nm* diaeresis *Br*, dieresis *Am*.

tremblant, e [trãblã, ãt] *adj* **- 1.** [personne - de froid] shivering ; [- d'émotion] trembling, shaking ; **être tout ~** to be trembling *ou* shaking **- 2.** [voix] quavering **- 3.** [lumière] flickering.

tremble [trãbl] *nm* aspen.

tremblement [trãbləmã] *nm* **- 1.** [de corps] trembling **- 2.** [de voix] quavering **- 3.** [de feuilles] fluttering.

◆ **tremblement de terre** *nm* earthquake.

trembler [3] [trãble] *vi* **- 1.** [personne - de froid] to shiver ; [- d'émotion] to tremble, to shake **- 2.** *fig* & *sout* [avoir peur] to fear ; **~ que** *(+ subjonctif)* to fear (that) ; **~ de faire qqch** to be scared to do sthg **- 3.** [voix] to quaver **- 4.** [lumière] to flicker **- 5.** [terre] to shake.

tremblotant, e [trãblɔtã, ãt] *adj* **- 1.** [personne] trembling **- 2.** [voix] quavering **- 3.** [lumière] flickering.

trembloter [3] [trãblɔte] *vi* **- 1.** [personne] to tremble **- 2.** [voix] to quaver **- 3.** [lumière] to flicker.

trémière [tremjer] ▷ **rose**.

trémolo [tremɔlo] *nm* tremolo ; **avoir des ~s dans la voix** *hum* to have a quaver in one's voice.

trémousser [3] [tremuse] ◆ **se trémousser** *vp* to jig up and down.

trempe [trãp] *nf* **- 1.** [envergure] calibre ; **de sa ~** of his/her calibre **- 2.** *fam* [coups] thrashing.

tremper [3] [trãpe] <> *vt* **- 1.** [mouiller] to soak ; **faire ~** to soak **- 2.** [plonger] : **~ qqch dans** to dip sthg into **- 3.** [métal] to harden, to quench <> *vi* **- 1.** [linge] to soak **- 2.** [se compromettre] : **~ dans** to be involved in.

◆ **se tremper** *vp* **- 1.** [se mouiller] to get soaking wet **- 2.** [se plonger] to have a quick dip.

trempette [trãpet] *nf* : **faire ~** [se baigner] to go for a dip ; [avec biscuit] to dunk.

tremplin [trãplɛ̃] *nm litt* & *fig* springboard ; SKI ski jump.

trench-coat [trɛnʃkot] *(pl* **trench-coats***) nm* trench coat.

trentaine [trãten] *nf* **- 1.** [nombre] : **une ~ de**

about thirty - **2.** [âge] : **avoir la ~** to be in one's thirties.

trente [trãt] ◇ *adj num* thirty ; **~-trois tours** LP, long-playing record ◇ *nm* thirty ; **être/ se mettre sur son ~ et un** *fig* to be in/to put on one's Sunday best ; *voir aussi* **six.**

trentième [trãtjem] *adj num, nm* OU *nmf* thirtieth ; *voir aussi* **sixième.**

trépaner [3] [trepane] *vt* MÉD to trepan.

trépas [trepa] *nm littéraire* demise.

trépasser [3] [trepase] *vi littéraire* to pass away.

trépidant, e [trepidã, ãt] *adj* [vie] hectic.

trépidation [trepidasjɔ̃] *nf* [vibration] vibration.

trépied [trepje] *nm* - **1.** [support] tripod - **2.** [meuble] three-legged stool/table.

trépignement [trepiɲmã] *nm* stamping.

trépigner [3] [trepiɲe] *vi* to stamp one's feet.

très [trɛ] *adv* very ; **~ malade** very ill ; **~ bien** very well ; **être ~ aimé** to be much *ou* greatly liked ; **avoir ~ peur/faim** to be very frightened/hungry ; **j'ai ~ envie de** ... I'd very much like to ...

trésor [trezɔr] *nm* treasure ; **mon ~** *fig* my precious.
➡ **Trésor** *nm* : **le Trésor public** the public revenue department.
➡ **trésors** *nmpl* riches, treasures ; **des ~s de** *fig* a wealth *(sg)* of.

trésorerie [trezɔrri] *nf* - **1.** [service] accounts department - **2.** [gestion] accounts *(pl)* - **3.** [fonds] finances *(pl)*, funds *(pl)*.

trésorier, ère [trezɔrje, ɛr] *nm, f* treasurer.

tressaillement [tresajmã] *nm* [de joie] thrill ; [de douleur] wince.

tressaillir [47] [tresajir] *vi* - **1.** [de joie] to thrill ; [de douleur] to wince - **2.** [sursauter] to start, to jump.

tressauter [3] [tresote] *vi* [sursauter] to jump, to start ; [dans véhicule] to be tossed about ; **faire ~** to toss *ou* jolt about.

tresse [trɛs] *nf* - **1.** [de cheveux] plait - **2.** [de rubans] braid.

tresser [4] [trese] *vt* - **1.** [cheveux] to plait - **2.** [osier] to braid - **3.** [panier, guirlande] to weave.

tréteau, x [treto] *nm* trestle.

treuil [trœj] *nm* winch, windlass.

trêve [trɛv] *nf* - **1.** [cessez-le-feu] truce - **2.** *fig* [répit] rest, respite ; **~ de plaisanteries/de sottises** that's enough joking/nonsense.

➡ **sans trêve** *loc adv* relentlessly, unceasingly.

tri [tri] *nm* [de lettres] sorting ; [de candidats] selection ; **faire le ~ dans qqch** *fig* to sort sthg out.

triage [trijaʒ] *nm* [de lettres] sorting ; [de candidats] selection.

triangle [trijãgl] *nm* triangle ; **~ isocèle** isosceles triangle ; **~ rectangle** right-angled triangle.

triangulaire [trijãgylɛr] *adj* triangular.

triathlon [trijatlɔ̃] *nm* triathlon.

tribal, e, aux [tribal, o] *adj* tribal.

tribord [tribɔr] *nm* starboard ; **à ~** on the starboard side, to starboard.

tribu [triby] *nf* tribe.

tribulations [tribylasjɔ̃] *nfpl* tribulations, trials.

tribun [tribɛ̃] *nm* - **1.** HIST tribune - **2.** [orateur] popular orator.

tribunal, aux [tribynal, o] *nm* - **1.** JUR court ; **~ correctionnel** ≃ Magistrates' Court *Br*, ≃ County Court *Am* ; **~ pour enfants** juvenile court ; **~ d'exception** special court ; **~ de grande instance** ≃ Crown Court *Br*, ≃ Circuit Court *Am* ; **~ d'instance** ≃ Magistrates' Court *Br*, ≃ County Court *Am* ; **~ de police** police court - **2.** *fig* & *littéraire* [jugement] judgment.

tribune [tribyn] *nf* - **1.** [d'orateur] platform - **2.** (*gén pl*) [de stade] stand - **3.** *fig* [lieu d'expression] forum ; **~ libre** PRESSE opinion column.

tribut [triby] *nm littéraire* tribute.

tributaire [tribytɛr] *adj* : **être ~ de** to depend *ou* be dependent on.

tricentenaire [trisãtner] ◇ *adj* three-hundred-year-old ◇ *nm* tricentennial.

triceps [trisɛps] *nm* triceps.

triche [triʃ] *nf fam* cheating.

tricher [3] [triʃe] *vi* - **1.** [au jeu, à un examen] to cheat - **2.** [mentir] : **~ sur** to lie about.

tricherie [triʃri] *nf* cheating.

tricheur, euse [triʃœr, øz] *nm, f* cheat.

tricolore [trikɔlɔr] *adj* - **1.** [à trois couleurs] three-coloured *Br*, three-colored *Am* - **2.** [français] French.

tricot [triko] *nm* - **1.** [vêtement] jumper *Br*, sweater ; **~ de corps** vest *Br*, undershirt *Am* - **2.** [ouvrage] knitting ; **faire du ~** to knit - **3.** [étoffe] knitted fabric, jersey.

tricoter [3] [trikɔte] *vi* & *vt* to knit.

tricycle [trisikl] *nm* tricycle.

trident [tridã] *nm* - **1.** MYTH trident - **2.** [fourche] pitchfork.

tridimensionnel, elle [tridimãsjɔnɛl] *adj* three-dimensional.

triennal, e, aux [trienal, o] *adj* - **1.** [mandat] three-year - **2.** [élection] three-yearly.

trier [10] [trije] *vt* - **1.** [classer] to sort out - **2.** [sélectionner] to select ; ~ **sur le volet** to handpick.

trifouiller [3] [trifuje] *vi fam* to rummage around.

trigonométrie [trigɔnɔmetri] *nf* trigonometry.

trilingue [trilɛ̃g] <> *nmf* person who is trilingual <> *adj* trilingual.

trille [trij] *nm* trill.

trilogie [trilɔʒi] *nf* trilogy.

trim. - **1.** (*abr de* **trimestre**) quarter - **2.** (*abr de* **trimestriel**) quarterly.

trimaran [trimarã] *nm* trimaran.

trimbaler [3] [trɛ̃bale] *vt fam* [personne] to trail around ; [chose] to cart around. <>
  se trimbaler *vp fam* to trail around.

trimer [3] [trime] *vi fam* to slave away.

trimestre [trimɛstr] *nm* - **1.** [période] term - **2.** [loyer] quarter's rent ; [rente] quarter's income.

trimestriel, elle [trimɛstrijɛl] *adj* [loyer, magazine] quarterly ; SCOL end-of-term *(avant n)*.

trimoteur [trimɔtœr] <> *nm* three-engined plane <> *adj* three-engined.

tringle [trɛ̃gl] *nf* rod ; ~ **à rideaux** curtain rod.

trinité [trinite] *nf littéraire* trinity. <>
  Trinité *nf* : **la Trinité** the Trinity.

trinquer [3] [trɛ̃ke] *vi* - **1.** [boire] to toast, to clink glasses ; ~ **à** to drink to - **2.** *fam* [personne] to get the worst of it ; [voiture] to be damaged.

trio [trijo] *nm* trio.

triomphal, e, aux [trijɔ̃fal, o] *adj* [succès] triumphal ; [accueil] triumphant.

triomphalement [trijɔ̃falmã] *adv* - **1.** [en triomphe] in triumph - **2.** [fièrement] triumphantly.

triomphalisme [trijɔ̃falism] *nm* triumphalism.

triomphant, e [trijɔ̃fã, ãt] *adj* [équipe] winning ; [air] triumphant.

triomphateur, trice [trijɔ̃fatœr, tris] <> *adj* triumphant <> *nm, f* victor.

triomphe [trijɔ̃f] *nm* triumph.

triompher [3] [trijɔ̃fe] *vi* - **1.** [gén] to triumph ; ~ **de** to triumph over ; **faire ~ qqch** to ensure the success of sthg - **2.** [crier victoire] to rejoice.

trip [trip] *nm arg drogue* trip.

triparti, e [triparti], **tripartite** [tripartit] *adj* tripartite.

tripatouiller [3] [tripatuje] *vt fam* - **1.** [fruits] to paw - **2.** [texte, compte] to fiddle with.

tripes [trip] *nfpl* - **1.** [d'animal, de personne] guts ; **prendre qqn aux ~** *fam fig* to get sb in the guts - **2.** CULIN tripe *(sg)*.

triperie [tripri] *nf* - **1.** [commerce] tripe trade - **2.** [boutique] tripe shop - **3.** [aliments] tripe.

tripier, ère [tripje, ɛr] *nm, f* tripe butcher.

triple [tripl] <> *adj* triple <> *nm* : **le ~ (de)** three times as much (as).

triplé, ées [triple] *nm* - **1.** [au turf] bet on three horses winning in three different races - **2.** SPORT [trois victoires] hat-trick of victories. <>
  triplés *nm, f pl* triplets.

triplement [triplemã] <> *adv* trebly <> *nm* threefold increase, tripling.

tripler [3] [triple] *vt & vi* to triple.

triporteur [tripɔrtœr] *nm* tricycle *(used for deliveries)*.

tripot [tripo] *nm péj* gambling-den.

tripotage [tripɔtaʒ] *nm (gén pl) fam* [manigances] fiddling *(U)*.

tripoter [3] [tripɔte] <> *vt* - **1.** *fam* [stylo, montre] to play with - **2.** *vulg* [femme] to feel up <> *vi fam* : ~ **dans** [fouiller dans] to rummage about in ; [trafiquer] to dabble in.

tripous, tripoux [tripu] *nmpl stuffed tripe.*

triptyque [triptik] *nm* triptych.

trique [trik] *nf* cudgel.

triste [trist] *adj* - **1.** [personne, nouvelle] sad ; **être ~ de qqch/de faire qqch** to be sad about sthg/about doing sthg - **2.** [paysage, temps] gloomy ; [couleur] dull - **3.** *(avant n)* [lamentable] sorry.

tristement [tristəmã] *adv* - **1.** [d'un air triste] sadly - **2.** [lugubrement] gloomily - **3.** [de façon regrettable] sadly, regrettably ; ~ **célèbre** notorious.

tristesse [tristɛs] *nf* - **1.** [de personne, nouvelle] sadness - **2.** [de paysage, temps] gloominess.

tristounet, ette [tristunɛ, ɛt] *adj fam* - **1.** [personne] sad - **2.** *péj* [humeur] gloomy.

trithérapie [triterapi] *nf* combination therapy.

triton [tritɔ̃] *nm* triton.

triturer [3] [trityre] *vt* - **1.** [sel] to grind - **2.** *fam* [mouchoir] to knead. <>
  se triturer *vp fam* : **se ~ l'esprit** *ou* **les méninges** to rack one's brains.

trivial, e, aux [trivjal, o] *adj* - **1.** [banal] trivial - **2.** *péj* [vulgaire] crude, coarse.

trivialité [trivjalite] *nf* - **1.** [banalité] triviality - **2.** *péj* [vulgarité] vulgar *ou* coarse expression.

tr/mn, tr/min (*abr de* **tour par minute**) r/min, rpm.

troc [trɔk] *nm* - **1.** [échange] exchange - **2.** [système économique] barter.

troène [trɔɛn] *nm* privet.

troglodyte [trɔglɔdit] *nm* cave dweller, troglodyte.

trogne [trɔɲ] *nf fam* [visage] mug.

trognon [trɔɲɔ̃] <> *nm* [de fruit] core <> *adj inv fam* [mignon] sweet, cute.

troïka [trɔika] *nf* troika.

trois [trwa] <> *nm* three <> *adj num* three ; *voir aussi* **six** ; **les ~-huit** shift work ; **~ fois rien** *fig* nothing at all ; **les ~ jours** *MIL* induction course preceding military service (*now lasting one day*).

trois étoiles [trwazetwal] <> *adj* three-star (*avant n*) <> *nm* three-star hotel/restaurant.

troisième [trwazjɛm] <> *adj num* & *nmf* third <> *nm* third ; [étage] third floor *Br*, fourth floor *Am* <> *nf* - **1.** *SCOL* ≃ fourth year *ou* form *Br*, ≃ ninth grade *Am* - **2.** [vitesse] third (gear) ; *voir aussi* **sixième**.

troisièmement [trwazjɛmmɑ̃] *adv* thirdly.

trois-mâts [trwama] *nm inv* three-master.

trois-quarts [trwakar] *nm inv RUGBY* three-quarter.

trolley(bus) [trɔlɛ(bys)] *nm* trolleybus.

trombe [trɔ̃b] *nf* water spout ; **passer en ~** *fig* to zoom past, to speed past ; **des ~s d'eau** torrential rain (*U*).

trombone [trɔ̃bɔn] *nm* - **1.** [agrafe] paper clip - **2.** [instrument] trombone ; **~ à coulisse** slide trombone - **3.** [joueur] trombone player, trombonist.

trompe [trɔ̃p] *nf* - **1.** [instrument] trumpet - **2.** [d'éléphant] trunk - **3.** [d'insecte] proboscis - **4.** *ANAT* tube.

trompe-l'œil [trɔ̃plœj] *nm inv* - **1.** [peinture] trompe-l'oeil ; **en ~** done in trompe-l'oeil - **2.** [apparence] deception.

tromper [3] [trɔ̃pe] *vt* - **1.** [personne] to deceive ; [époux] to be unfaithful to, to deceive - **2.** [vigilance] to elude - **3.** *littéraire* [espoirs] to fall short of - **4.** [faim] to stave off.

  se tromper *vp* to make a mistake, to be mistaken ; **se ~ de jour/maison** to get the wrong day/house.

tromperie [trɔ̃pri] *nf* deception.

trompette [trɔ̃pɛt] *nf* trumpet.

trompettiste [trɔ̃petist] *nmf* trumpeter.

trompeur, euse [trɔ̃pœr, øz] <> *adj* - **1.** [personne] deceitful - **2.** [calme, apparence] deceptive <> *nm, f* deceitful person.

trompeusement [trɔ̃pøzmɑ̃] *adv* - **1.** [hypocritement] deceitfully - **2.** [apparemment] deceptively.

tronc [trɔ̃] *nm* - **1.** [d'arbre, de personne] trunk - **2.** [d'église] collection box - **3.** [de veine, nerf] stem.

  tronc commun *nm* [de programmes] common element *ou* feature ; *SCOL* core syllabus.

tronche [trɔ̃ʃ] *nf fam péj* [visage] mug.

tronçon [trɔ̃sɔ̃] *nm* - **1.** [morceau] piece, length - **2.** [de route, de chemin de fer] section.

tronçonner [3] [trɔ̃sɔne] *vt* to cut into pieces.

tronçonneuse [trɔ̃sɔnøz] *nf* chain saw.

trône [tron] *nm* throne.

trôner [3] [trone] *vi* - **1.** [personne] to sit enthroned ; [objet] to have pride of place - **2.** *hum* [faire l'important] to lord it.

tronquer [3] [trɔ̃ke] *vt* to truncate.

trop [tro] *adv* - **1.** (*devant adj, adv*) too ; **~ vieux/loin** too old/far ; **nous étions ~ nombreux** there were too many of us ; **avoir ~ chaud/froid/peur** to be too hot/cold/frightened - **2.** (*avec verbe*) too much ; **il mange ~** he eats too much ; **nous étions ~** there were too many of us ; **je n'aime pas ~ le chocolat** I don't like chocolate very much ; **on ne se voit plus ~** we don't really see each other any more ; **sans ~ savoir pourquoi** without really knowing why - **3.** (*avec complément*) : **~ de** [quantité] too much ; [nombre] too many.

  en trop, de trop *loc adv* too much/many ; **10 francs de ~** *ou* **en ~** 10 francs too much ; **une personne de ~** *ou* **en ~** one person too many ; **être de ~** [personne] to be in the way, to be unwelcome.

trophée [trofe] *nm* trophy.

tropical, e, aux [trɔpikal, o] *adj* tropical.

tropique [trɔpik] *nm* tropic ; **~ du Cancer/du Capricorne** Tropic of Cancer/Capricorn.

  tropiques *nmpl* tropics.

trop-perçu [trɔpersy] (*pl* **trop-perçus**) *nm* excess payment.

trop-plein [trɔplɛ̃] (*pl* **trop-pleins**) *nm* - **1.** [excès] excess ; *fig* excess, surplus - **2.** [déversoir] overflow.

troquer [3] [trɔke] *vt* : **~ qqch (contre)** to barter sthg (for) ; *fig* to swap sthg (for).

troquet [trɔke] *nm fam* (small) café.

trot [trɔ] *nm* trot ; **au ~** at a trot ; **au ~!** *fam fig* at the double!

trotter [3] [trɔte] *vi* - **1.** [cheval] to trot - **2.** [personne] to run around.

trotteur, euse [trɔtœr, øz] *nm, f* trotter.
➡ **trotteuse** *nf* second hand.

trottiner [3] [trɔtine] *vi* to trot.

trottinette [trɔtinɛt] *nf* child's scooter.

trottoir [trɔtwar] *nm* pavement *Br*, sidewalk *Am* ; **faire le ~** *fam fig* to walk the streets.

trou [tru] *nm* - **1.** [gén] hole ; **~ d'aération** air vent ; **~ d'air** air pocket ; **~ de serrure** keyhole - **2.** [manque, espace vide] gap ; **~ de mémoire** memory lapse - **3.** *fam* [prison] nick *Br*, clink.

troublant, e [trublɑ̃, ɑ̃t] *adj* disturbing.

trouble [trubl] ◇ *adj* - **1.** [eau] cloudy - **2.** [image, vue] blurred - **3.** [affaire] shady ◇ *nm* - **1.** [désordre] trouble, discord - **2.** [gêne] confusion ; [émoi] agitation - **3.** *(gén pl)* [dérèglement] disorder ; **~s moteurs** motor disorders ; **~s respiratoires** respiratory disorders.
➡ **troubles** *nmpl* [sociaux] unrest *(U)*.

trouble-fête [trubləfɛt] *nmf inv* spoilsport.

troubler [3] [truble] *vt* - **1.** [eau] to cloud, to make cloudy - **2.** [image, vue] to blur - **3.** [sommeil, événement] to disrupt, to disturb - **4.** [esprit, raison] to cloud - **5.** [inquiéter, émouvoir] to disturb - **6.** [rendre perplexe] to trouble.
➡ **se troubler** *vp* - **1.** [eau] to become cloudy - **2.** [personne] to become flustered.

trouée [true] *nf* gap ; *MIL* breach.

trouer [3] [true] *vt* - **1.** [chaussette] to make a hole in - **2.** *fig* [silence] to disturb.

troufion [trufjɔ̃] *nm fam* soldier.

trouillard, e [trujar, ard] *fam* ◇ *adj* yellow, chicken ◇ *nm, f* chicken.

trouille [truj] *nf fam* fear, terror.

troupe [trup] *nf* - **1.** *MIL* troop - **2.** [d'amis] group, band ; [de singes] troop - **3.** *THÉÂTRE* theatre group.

troupeau, x [trupo] *nm* [de vaches, d'éléphants] herd ; [de moutons, d'oies] flock ; *péj* [de personnes] herd.

trousse [trus] *nf* case, bag ; **~ de secours** first-aid kit ; **~ de toilette** toilet bag.
➡ **trousses** *nfpl* : **avoir qqn à ses ~s** *fig* to have sb hot on one's heels ; **être aux ~s de qqn** *fig* to be hot on the heels of sb.

trousseau, x [truso] *nm* - **1.** [de mariée] trousseau - **2.** [de clefs] bunch.

trousser [3] [truse] *vt* - **1.** [manches] to roll up ; [jupe] to hitch up - **2.** *CULIN* to truss.

trouvaille [truvaj] *nf* - **1.** [découverte] find, discovery - **2.** [invention] new idea.

trouver [3] [truve] ◇ *vt* to find ; **~ que** to feel (that) ; **~ qqch à qqn** to think sb has sthg ; **~ bon/mauvais que ...** to think (that) it is right/wrong that ... ; **~ qqch à faire/à dire** *etc* to find sthg to do/say *etc* ; **~ à s'occuper** to find something to do ◇ *v impers* : **il se trouve que ...** the fact is that ...
➡ **se trouver** *vp* - **1.** [dans un endroit] to be - **2.** [dans un état] to find o.s. - **3.** [se sentir] to feel ; **se ~ mal** [s'évanouir] to faint.

truand [tryɑ̃] *nm* crook.

truander [3] [tryɑ̃de] *vt fam* to rip off.

trublion [tryblijɔ̃] *nm* troublemaker.

truc [tryk] *nm* - **1.** [combine] trick - **2.** *fam* [chose] thing, thingamajig ; **ce n'est pas son ~** it's not his thing.

trucage = **truquage**.

truchement [tryʃmɑ̃] *nm* : **par le ~ de qqn** through sb.

trucider [3] [tryside] *vt fam hum* to bump off.

truculence [trykylɑ̃s] *nf* vividness, colourfulness *Br*, colorfulness *Am*.

truculent, e [trykylɑ̃, ɑ̃t] *adj* colourful *Br*, colorful *Am*.

truelle [tryɛl] *nf* trowel.

truffe [tryf] *nf* - **1.** [champignon] truffle ; **~ en chocolat** chocolate truffle - **2.** [museau] muzzle.

truffer [3] [tryfe] *vt* - **1.** [volaille] to garnish with truffles - **2.** *fig* [discours] : **~ de** to stuff with.

truie [trɥi] *nf* sow.

truite [trɥit] *nf* trout.

truquage, trucage [tryka3] *nm* - **1.** [d'élections] rigging - **2.** *CIN* (special) effect.

truquer [3] [tryke] *vt* - **1.** [élections] to rig - **2.** *CIN* to use special effects in.

trust [trœst] *nm* - **1.** [groupement] trust - **2.** [entreprise] corporation.

ts *abr de* **tous**.

tsar [tsar], **tzar** [dzar] *nm* tsar.

tsé-tsé [tsetse] ▷ **mouche**.

tsigane = **tzigane**.

TSVP *(abr de* **tournez s'il vous plaît)** PTO.

tt *abr de* **tout**.

TT, TTA *(abr de* **transit temporaire [autorisé])** *registration for vehicles bought in France for tax-free export by non-residents.*

tt conf. *abr de* **tout confort**.

ttes *abr de* **toutes**.

TTX *(abr de* **traitement de texte)** WP.

tu¹, e [ty] *pp* ⊳ **taire.**

tu² [ty] *pron pers* you ; **dire ~ à qqn** to use the "tu" form to sb.

TU (*abr de* **temps universel**) *nm* UT, GMT.

tuant, e [tɥɑ̃, ɑ̃t] *adj* - **1.** [épuisant] exhausting - **2.** [énervant] tiresome.

tuba [tyba] *nm* - **1.** MUS tuba - **2.** [de plongée] snorkel.

tube [tyb] *nm* - **1.** [gén] tube ; **~ cathodique** cathode ray tube ; **à pleins ~s** *fig* [chanter, crier] at the top of one's voice ; [mettre la musique] at full blast - **2.** *fam* [chanson] hit.

➡ **tube digestif** *nm* digestive tract.

tubercule [tybɛrkyl] *nm* - **1.** BOT tuber - **2.** ANAT tubercle.

tuberculeux, euse [tybɛrkylø, øz] <> *adj* tubercular <> *nm, f* tuberculosis sufferer.

tuberculose [tybɛrkyloz] *nf* tuberculosis.

tubulaire [tybylɛr] *adj* tubular.

tue-mouches [tymuʃ] ⊳ **papier.**

tuer [7] [tɥe] *vt* to kill.

➡ **se tuer** *vp* - **1.** [se suicider] to kill o.s. - **2.** [par accident] to die - **3.** *fig* [s'épuiser] : **se ~ à faire qqch** to wear o.s. out doing sthg.

tuerie [tyri] *nf* slaughter.

tue-tête [tytɛt] ➡ **à tue-tête** *loc adv* at the top of one's voice.

tueur, euse [tɥœr, øz] *nm, f* - **1.** [meurtrier] killer ; **~ à gages** hit man ; **~ en série** serial killer - **2.** [dans abattoir] slaughterer.

tuile [tɥil] *nf* - **1.** [de toit] tile - **2.** *fam* [désagrément] blow.

tulipe [tylip] *nf* tulip.

tulle [tyl] *nm* tulle.

tuméfié, e [tymefje] *adj* swollen.

tumeur [tymœr] *nf* tumour *Br*, tumor *Am*.

tumoral, e, aux [tymɔral, o] *adj* tumorous.

tumulte [tymylt] *nm* - **1.** [désordre] hubbub - **2.** *littéraire* [trouble] tumult.

tumultueux, euse [tymyltɥø, øz] *adj* stormy.

tune = **thune.**

tuner [tynɛr] *nm* tuner.

tungstène [tœ̃kstɛn] *nm* tungsten.

tunique [tynik] *nf* tunic.

Tunis [tynis] *n* Tunis.

Tunisie [tynizi] *nf* : **la ~** Tunisia.

tunisien, enne [tynizjɛ̃, ɛn] *adj* Tunisian.

➡ **Tunisien, enne** *nm, f* Tunisian.

tunnel [tynɛl] *nm* tunnel.

TUP [typ] (*abr de* **titre universel de paiement**) *nm payment slip formerly used to settle bills.*

tuque [tyk] *nf Can* wool hat, tuque *Can*.

turban [tyrbɑ̃] *nm* turban.

turbin [tyrbɛ̃] *nm fam* : **aller au ~** to go to work.

turbine [tyrbin] *nf* turbine.

turbo [tyrbo] *nm* OU *nf* turbo.

turboréacteur [tyrbɔreaktœr] *nm* turbojet.

turbot [tyrbo] *nm* turbot.

turbotrain [tyrbɔtrɛ̃] *nm* turbotrain.

turbulence [tyrbylɑ̃s] *nf* - **1.** [de personne] boisterousness - **2.** MÉTÉOR turbulence.

turbulent, e [tyrbylɑ̃, ɑ̃t] *adj* boisterous.

turc, turque [tyrk] *adj* Turkish.

➡ **turc** *nm* [langue] Turkish.

➡ **Turc, Turque** *nm, f* Turk.

turf [tœrf] *nm* [activité] : **le ~** racing.

turfiste [tœrfist] *nmf* racegoer.

turkmène [tyrkmɛn] <> *adj* Turkmen <> *nm* [langue] Turkmen.

➡ **Turkmène** *nmf* Turkoman.

turlupiner [3] [tyrlypine] *vt fam* to nag.

turnover [tœrnɔvœr] *nm* turnover.

turpitude [tyrpityd] *nf* [littéraire] turpitude.

turque ⊳ **turc.**

Turquie [tyrki] *nf* : **la ~** Turkey.

turquoise [tyrkwaz] *nf & adj inv* turquoise.

tutelle [tytɛl] *nf* - **1.** JUR guardianship - **2.** [dépendance] supervision ; **sous la ~ des Nations unies** under United Nations supervision - **3.** [protection] protection.

tuteur, trice [tytœr, tris] *nm, f* guardian.

➡ **tuteur** *nm* [pour plante] stake.

tutoiement [tytwamɑ̃] *nm* use of "tu".

tutoyer [13] [tytwaje] *vt* : **~ qqn** to use the "tu" form to sb.

tutu [tyty] *nm* tutu.

tuyau, x [tɥijo] *nm* - **1.** [conduit] pipe ; **~ d'arrosage** hosepipe - **2.** *fam* [renseignement] tip.

tuyauter [3] [tɥijote] *vt fam* to give a tip to.

tuyauterie [tɥijotri] *nf* piping (U), pipes (pl).

TV (*abr de* **télévision**) *nf* TV.

TVA (*abr de* **taxe à la valeur ajoutée**) *nf* ≃ VAT.

TVHD (*abr de* **télévision haute définition**) *nf* HDTV.

tweed [twid] *nm* tweed.

twin-set [twinsɛt] (*pl* **twin-sets**) *nm* twin set *Br*, sweater set *Am*.

tympan [tɛ̃pɑ̃] *nm* - **1.** ANAT eardrum - **2.** ARCHIT tympanum.

type [tip] <> *nm* - **1.** [exemple caractéristique] perfect example ; **il est le ~ parfait du professeur** he's the classic example of a teacher - **2.** [genre] type ; **avoir le ~ nordique/médi-**

terranéen to have Nordic/Mediterranean features **- 3.** *fam* [individu] guy, bloke ⬦ *adj inv* [caractéristique] typical.

typé, e [tipe] *adj* : **il est bien** *ou* **très ~** he has all the characteristic features.

typhoïde [tifɔid] ⬦ *nf* typhoid ⬦ *adj* : **fièvre ~** typhoid fever.

typhon [tifɔ̃] *nm* typhoon.

typhus [tifys] *nm* typhus.

typique [tipik] *adj* typical.

typiquement [tipikmɑ̃] *adv* typically.

typographe [tipɔgraf] *nmf* typographer.

typographie [tipɔgrafi] *nf* typography.

typographique [tipɔgrafik] *adj* typographical.

typologie [tipɔlɔʒi] *nf* typology.

tyran [tirɑ̃] *nm* tyrant.

tyrannie [tirani] *nf* tyranny.

tyrannique [tiranik] *adj* tyrannical.

tyranniser [3] [tiranize] *vt* to tyrannize.

tyrolien, enne [tirɔljɛ̃, ɛn] *adj* Tyrolean.
➡ **tyrolienne** *nf* [air] Tyrolienne.
➡ **Tyrolien, enne** *nm, f* Tyrolean.

tzar = tsar.

tzigane [dzigan], **tsigane** [tsigan] ⬦ *nmf* gipsy ⬦ *adj* gipsy *(avant n)*.

u, U [y] *nm inv* u, U.

ubiquité [ybikɥite] *nf* ubiquity ; **je n'ai pas le don d'~** I can't be everywhere (at once).

UDF (*abr de* **Union pour la démocratie française**) *nf* French political party to the right of the political spectrum.

UE (*abr de* **Union européenne**) *nf* EU.

UEFA (*abr de* **Union of European Football Associations**) *nf* UEFA.

UEO (*abr de* **Union de l'Europe occidentale**) *nf* WEU.

UER *nf* **- 1.** (*abr de* **unité d'enseignement et de recherche**) *former name for a university department* **- 2.** (*abr de* **Union européenne de radiodiffusion**) EBU.

UFC (*abr de* **Union fédérale des consommateurs**) *nf* French consumers' association.

UFR (*abr de* **unité de formation et de recherche**) *nf* university department.

UHF (*abr de* **ultra-haute fréquence**) *nf* UHF.

UHT (*abr de* **ultra-haute température**) *nf* UHT.

Ukraine [ykrɛn] *nf* : **l'~** the Ukraine.

ukrainien, enne [ykrɛnjɛ̃, ɛn] *adj* Ukrainian.
➡ **ukrainien** *nm* [langue] Ukrainian.
➡ **Ukrainien, enne** *nm, f* Ukrainian.

ulcère [ylsɛr] *nm* ulcer.

ulcérer [18] [ylsere] *vt* **- 1.** MÉD to ulcerate **- 2.** *sout* [mettre en colère] to enrage.
➡ **s'ulcérer** *vp* to ulcerate, to fester.

ulcéreux, euse [ylserø, øz] *adj* [plaie] ulcerous ; [organe] ulcerated.

ULM (*abr de* **ultra léger motorisé**) *nm* microlight.

Ulster [ylstɛr] *nm* : **l'~** Ulster.

ultérieur, e [ylterjœr] *adj* later, subsequent.

ultérieurement [ylterjœrmɑ̃] *adv* later, subsequently.

ultimatum [yltimatɔm] *nm* ultimatum.

ultime [yltim] *adj* ultimate, final.

ultramoderne [yltramɔdɛrn] *adj* ultramodern.

ultrasensible [yltrasɑ̃sibl] *adj* [personne] ultra-sensitive ; [pellicule] high-speed.

ultrason [yltrasɔ̃] *nm* ultrasound *(U)*.

ultraviolet, ette [yltravjɔlɛ, ɛt] *adj* ultraviolet.
➡ **ultraviolet** *nm* ultraviolet.

ululement, hululement [ylylmɑ̃] *nm* hoot, hooting *(U)*.

ululer, hululer [3] [ylyle] *vi* to hoot.

un [œ̃] (*f* **une** [yn]) ⬦ *art indéf* a, an *(devant voyelle)* ; **~ homme** a man ; **~ livre** a book ; **une femme** a woman ; **une pomme** an apple ⬦ *pron indéf* one ; **l'~ de mes amis** one of my friends ; **les ~s les autres** one another ; **l'~ ..., l'autre** one ..., the other ; **les ~s ..., les autres** some ..., others ; **l'~ et l'autre** both (of them) ; **l'~ ou l'autre** either (of them) ; **ni l'~ ni l'autre** neither one nor the other, neither (of them) ⬦ *adj num* one ; **une personne à la fois** one person at a time ⬦ *nm* one ; *voir aussi* **six**.

une nf : **faire la/être à la une** PRESSE to make the/to be on the front page ; **ne faire ni une ni deux** not to think twice.

unanime [ynanim] adj unanimous.

unanimement [ynanimmɑ̃] adv unanimously.

unanimité [ynanimite] nf unanimity ; **faire l'~** to be unanimously approved ; **à l'~** unanimously.

underground [œndœrgraɔnd] <> nm inv underground <> adj inv underground (avant n).

UNEF, Unef [ynɛf] (abr de **Union nationale des étudiants de France**) nf students' union, ≈ NUS Br.

UNESCO, Unesco [ynɛsko] (abr de **United Nations Educational, Scientific and Cultural Organization**) nf UNESCO.

uni, e [yni] adj - 1. [joint, réuni] united - 2. [famille, couple] close - 3. [surface, mer] smooth ; [route] even - 4. [étoffe, robe] plain, self-coloured Br, self-colored Am.

UNICEF, Unicef [ynisɛf] (abr de **United Nations International Children's Emergency Fund**) nm UNICEF.

unicité [ynisite] nf littéraire uniqueness.

unième [ynjɛm] adj num : **cinquante et ~** fifty-first.

unificateur, trice [ynifikatœr, tris] adj unifying.

unification [ynifikasjɔ̃] nf unification.

unifier [9] [ynifje] vt - 1. [régions, parti] to unify - 2. [programmes] to standardize.
◆ **s'unifier** vp to unite, to unify.

uniforme [ynifɔrm] <> adj uniform ; [régulier] regular <> nm uniform.

uniformément [ynifɔrmemɑ̃] adv uniformly.

uniformisation [ynifɔrmizasjɔ̃] nf standardization.

uniformiser [3] [ynifɔrmize] vt - 1. [couleur] to make uniform - 2. [programmes, lois] to standardize.

uniformité [ynifɔrmite] nf - 1. [gén] uniformity ; [de mouvement] regularity - 2. [monotonie] monotony.

unijambiste [yniʒɑ̃bist] <> adj one-legged <> nmf one-legged person.

unilatéral, e, aux [ynilateral, o] adj unilateral ; **stationnement ~** parking on only one side of the street.

unilatéralement [ynilateralmɑ̃] adv unilaterally.

union [ynjɔ̃] nf - 1. [de couleurs] blending - 2. [mariage] union ; **~ conjugale** marriage ; **~ libre** cohabitation - 3. [de pays] union ; [de syndicats] confederation ; **~ douanière** customs union - 4. [entente] unity.
◆ **Union européenne** nf European Union.
◆ **Union soviétique** nf : **l'(ex-)Union soviétique** the (former) Soviet Union.

unique [ynik] adj - 1. [seul - enfant, veston] only ; [- préoccupation] sole - 2. [principe, prix] single - 3. [exceptionnel] unique ; **tu es vraiment ~!** iron you're priceless!

uniquement [ynikmɑ̃] adv - 1. [exclusivement] only, solely - 2. [seulement] only, just.

unir [32] [ynir] vt - 1. [assembler - mots, qualités] to put together, to combine ; [- pays] to unite ; **~ qqch à** [pays] to unite sthg with ; [mot, qualité] to combine sthg with - 2. [réunir - partis, familles] to unite - 3. [marier] to unite, to join in marriage.
◆ **s'unir** vp - 1. [s'associer] to unite, to join together - 2. [se joindre - rivières] to merge ; [- couleurs] to go together - 3. [se marier] to be joined in marriage.

unisexe [yniseks] adj unisex.

unisson [ynisɔ̃] nm unison ; **à l'~** in unison.

unitaire [yniter] adj - 1. [à l'unité] : **prix ~** unit price - 2. [manifestation, politique] joint (avant n).

unité [ynite] nf - 1. [cohésion] unity - 2. COMM, MATHS & MIL unit ; **à l'~** COMM unit (avant n).
◆ **unité centrale** nf INFORM central processing unit.
◆ **unité de valeur** nf university course unit, ≈ credit.

univers [yniver] nm universe ; fig world.

universaliser [3] [yniversalize] vt to universalize, to make universal.
◆ **s'universaliser** vp to become universal.

universalité [yniversalite] nf universality.

universel, elle [yniversel] adj universal.

universellement [yniverselmɑ̃] adv universally.

universitaire [yniversiter] <> adj university (avant n) <> nmf academic.

université [yniversite] nf university.

univoque [ynivɔk] adj - 1. [mot, tournure] unambiguous - 2. [relation] one-to-one Br, one-on-one Am.

uppercut [ypɛrkyt] nm uppercut.

uranium [yranjɔm] nm uranium.

urbain, e [yrbɛ̃, ɛn] adj - 1. [de la ville] urban - 2. littéraire [affable] urbane.

urbanisation [yrbanizasjɔ̃] nf urbanization.

urbaniser [3] [yrbanize] *vt* to urbanize.
➤ **s'urbaniser** *vp* to become urbanized *ou* built up.

urbanisme [yrbanism] *nm* town planning.

urbanité [yrbanite] *nf* urbanity.

urée [yre] *nf* urea.

urémie [yremi] *nf* uraemia.

urgence [yrʒɑ̃s] *nf* - **1.** [de mission] urgency - **2.** MÉD emergency ; **les ~s** the casualty department *(sg)*.
➤ **d'urgence** *loc adv* immediately.

urgent, e [yrʒɑ̃, ɑ̃t] *adj* urgent.

urinaire [yrinɛr] *adj* urinary.

urine [yrin] *nf* urine.

uriner [3] [yrine] *vi* to urinate.

urinoir [yrinwar] *nm* urinal.

urne [yrn] *nf* - **1.** [vase] urn - **2.** [de vote] ballot box ; **aller aux ~s** to go to the polls.

urologie [yrɔlɔʒi] *nf* urology.

URSS *(abr de* **Union des républiques socialistes soviétiques)** *nf* : **l'(ex-)~** the (former) USSR.

URSSAF, Urssaf [yrsaf] *(abr de* **Union pour le recouvrement des Cotisations de la sécurité sociale et des allocations familiales)** *nf administrative body responsible for collecting social security funds.*

urticaire [yrtikɛr] *nf* urticaria, hives *(pl)*.

Uruguay [yrygwɛ] *nm* : **l'~** Uruguay.

uruguayen, enne [yrygwejɛ̃, ɛn] *adj* Uruguayan.
➤ **Uruguayen, enne** *nm, f* Uruguayan.

us [ys] *nmpl* : **les ~ et coutumes** the ways and customs.

USA *(abr de* **United States of America)** *nmpl* USA.

usage [yzaʒ] *nm* - **1.** [gén] use ; **faire ~ de qqch** to use sthg ; **en ~** in use ; **à l'~** [à l'emploi] with use ; [vêtement] with wear ; **à l'~ de qqn** for (the use of) sb ; **à ~ externe/interne** for external/internal use ; **hors d'~** out of action - **2.** [coutume] custom ; **d'~** customary - **3.** LING usage.

usagé, e [yzaʒe] *adj* worn, old.

usager [yzaʒe] *nm* user ; **les ~s de la route** road-users.

usé, e [yze] *adj* - **1.** [détérioré] worn ; **eaux ~es** waste water *(sg)* - **2.** [personne] worn-out - **3.** [plaisanterie] hackneyed, well-worn.

user [3] [yze] ◇ *vt* - **1.** [consommer] to use - **2.** [vêtement] to wear out - **3.** [forces] to use up ; [santé] to ruin ; [personne] to wear out ◇ *vi* - **1.** [se servir] : **~ de** [charme] to use ; [droit, privilège] to exercise - **2.** [traiter] : **en ~ bien avec qqn** *littéraire* to treat sb well.
➤ **s'user** *vp* - **1.** [chaussure] to wear out - **2.** [personne] to wear o.s. out - **3.** [amour] to burn itself out.

usinage [yzinaʒ] *nm* - **1.** [façonnage] machining - **2.** [fabrication] manufacturing.

usine [yzin] *nf* factory.

usiner [3] [yzine] *vt* - **1.** [façonner] to machine - **2.** [fabriquer] to manufacture.

usité, e [yzite] *adj* in common use ; **très/peu ~** commonly/rarely used.

ustensile [ystɑ̃sil] *nm* implement, tool ; **~s de cuisine** kitchen utensils.

usuel, elle [yzɥɛl] *adj* common, usual.

usuellement [yzɥɛlmɑ̃] *adv* usually, ordinarily.

usufruit [yzyfrɥi] *nm* usufruct.

usuraire [yzyrɛr] *adj* usurious.

usure [yzyr] *nf* - **1.** [de vêtement, meuble] wear ; [de forces] wearing down ; **avoir qqn à l'~** *fam* to wear sb down ; **obtenir qqch à l'~** to get sthg through sheer persistence - **2.** [intérêt] usury.

usurier, ère [yzyrje, ɛr] *nm, f* usurer.

usurpateur, trice [yzyrpatœr, tris] ◇ *adj* usurping *(avant n)* ◇ *nm, f* usurper.

usurpation [3] [yzyrpasjɔ̃] *nf* usurpation.

usurper [3] [yzyrpe] *vt* to usurp.

ut [yt] *nm inv* C.

UTA *(abr de* **Union des transporteurs aériens)** *nf French airline company.*

utérin, ine [yterɛ̃, in] *adj* uterine.

utérus [yterys] *nm* uterus, womb.

utile [ytil] *adj* useful ; **être ~ à qqn** to be useful *ou* of help to sb, to help sb.

utilement [ytilmɑ̃] *adv* usefully, profitably.

utilisable [ytilizabl] *adj* usable.

utilisateur, trice [ytilizatœr, tris] *nm, f* user ; **~ étranger** INFORM unauthorized user.

utilisation [ytilizasjɔ̃] *nf* use.

utiliser [3] [ytilize] *vt* to use.

utilitaire [ytilitɛr] ◇ *adj* - **1.** [pratique] utilitarian ; [véhicule] commercial - **2.** *péj* [préoccupations] material ; [caractère] materialistic ◇ *nm* INFORM utility (program).

utilité [ytilite] *nf* - **1.** [usage] usefulness - **2.** JUR : **entreprise d'~ publique** public utility ; **organisme d'~ publique** registered charity - **3.** *loc* : **jouer les ~s** THÉÂTRE to play bit parts ; *fig* to play second fiddle.

utopie [ytɔpi] *nf* - **1.** [idéal] utopia - **2.** [projet irréalisable] unrealistic idea.

utopique [ytɔpik] *adj* utopian.

utopiste [ytɔpist] *nmf* utopian.

UV ⇔ *nf* (*abr de* **unité de valeur**) *university course unit*, ≃ credit ⇔ (*abr de* **ultraviolet**) UV.

v, V [ve] *nm inv* v, V ; **pull en v** V-neck sweater.

v.[1] - **1.** (*abr de* **vers**) LITTÉRATURE v. - **2.** (*abr de* **verset**) v. - **3.** (*abr de* **vers**) [environ] approx.

v.[2], **V.** *abr de* **voir.**

va [va] ⇔ ▷ **aller** ⇔ *interj* : courage, **~!** come on, cheer up! ; **~ donc!** come on! ; **~ pour 50 francs/demain** OK, let's say 50 francs/tomorrow.

VA (*abr de* **voltampère**) VA.

vacance [vakɑ̃s] *nf* vacancy ; **~ du pouvoir** power vacuum.
  ➡ **vacances** *nfpl* holiday *Br (sg)*, vacation *Am (sg)* ; **bonnes ~s!** have a good holiday! ; **être/partir en ~s** to be/go on holiday ; **les grandes ~s** the summer holidays.

vacancier, ère [vakɑ̃sje, ɛr] *nm, f* holiday-maker *Br*, vacationer *Am*.

vacant, e [vakɑ̃, ɑ̃t] *adj* [poste] vacant ; [logement] vacant, unoccupied.

vacarme [vakarm] *nm* racket, din.

vacataire [vakatɛr] ⇔ *adj* [employé] temporary ⇔ *nmf* temporary worker.

vacation [vakasjɔ̃] *nf* [d'expert] session.

vaccin [vaksɛ̃] *nm* vaccine.

vaccination [vaksinasjɔ̃] *nf* vaccination.

vacciner [3] [vaksine] *vt* : **~ qqn (contre)** MÉD to vaccinate sb (against) ; *fam fig* to make sb immune (to).

vache [vaʃ] ⇔ *nf* - **1.** ZOOL cow - **2.** [cuir] cowhide - **3.** *fam péj* [femme] cow ; [homme] pig - **4.** *loc* : **la ~!** hell! ⇔ *adj fam* rotten.

vachement [vaʃmɑ̃] *adv fam* bloody *Br*, dead *Br*, real *Am*.

vacherie [vaʃri] *nf fam* nastiness ; **faire/dire une ~** to do/say something nasty.

vacherin [vaʃrɛ̃] *nm* [dessert] meringue filled with ice-cream and fruit.

vachette [vaʃɛt] *nf* - **1.** [jeune vache] calf - **2.** [cuir] calfskin.

vacillant, e [vasijɑ̃, ɑ̃t] *adj* - **1.** [jambes, fondations] unsteady ; [lumière] flickering - **2.** [mémoire, santé] failing ; [caractère] wavering, indecisive.

vaciller [3] [vasije] *vi* - **1.** [jambes, fondations] to shake ; [lumière] to flicker ; **~ sur ses jambes** to be unsteady on one's legs - **2.** [mémoire, santé] to fail.

vacuité [vakɥite] *nf sout* [de propos] emptiness, vacuousness.

vade-mecum [vademekɔm] *nm inv* vade mecum.

vadrouille [vadruj] *nf fam* : **être/partir en ~** to be/to go off gallivanting.

va-et-vient [vaevjɛ̃] *nm inv* - **1.** [de personnes] comings and goings (*pl*), toing and froing - **2.** [de balancier] to-and-fro movement - **3.** : **(porte) ~** swing door - **4.** ÉLECTR two-way switch.

vagabond, e [vagabɔ̃, ɔ̃d] ⇔ *adj* - **1.** [chien] stray ; [vie] vagabond (*avant n*) - **2.** [humeur] restless ⇔ *nm, f* [rôdeur] vagrant, tramp ; *littéraire* [voyageur] wanderer.

vagabondage [vagabɔ̃daʒ] *nm* [délit] vagrancy ; [errance] wandering, roaming.

vagabonder [3] [vagabɔ̃de] *vi* - **1.** [personne] to wander, to roam - **2.** [esprit, imagination] to wander.

vagin [vaʒɛ̃] *nm* vagina.

vaginal, e, aux [vaʒinal, o] *adj* vaginal.

vaginite [vaʒinit] *nf* vaginitis.

vagir [32] [vaʒir] *vi* to cry, to wail.

vagissement [vaʒismɑ̃] *nm* cry, wail.

vague [vag] ⇔ *adj* - **1.** [idée, promesse] vague - **2.** [vêtement] loose-fitting - **3.** (*avant n*) [quelconque] : **il a un ~ travail dans un bureau** he has some job or other in an office - **4.** (*avant n*) [cousin] distant ⇔ *nf* wave ; **une ~ de** [touristes, immigrants] a wave of ; [d'enthousiasme] a surge of ; **une ~ de froid** a cold spell ; **la nouvelle ~** the new wave ; **~ de chaleur** heatwave ⇔ *nm* : **rester dans le ~** *fig* to remain vague ; **avoir du ~ à l'âme** *fig* to be wistful.

vaguelette [vaglɛt] *nf* ripple, wave.

vaguement [vagmɑ̃] *adv* vaguely.

vahiné [vaine] *nf* Tahitian woman.

vaillamment [vajamɑ̃] *adv* bravely, valiantly.

vaillance [vajɑ̃s] *nf littéraire* bravery, courage ; MIL valour *Br*, valor *Am*.

vaillant, e [vajɑ̃, ɑ̃t] *adj* - **1.** [enfant, vieillard] hale and hearty - **2.** *littéraire* [héros] valiant.

vain, e [vɛ̃, vɛn] *adj* - **1.** [inutile] vain, useless ; **en ~** in vain, to no avail - **2.** *littéraire* [vaniteux] vain.

vaincre [114] [vɛ̃kr] *vt* - **1.** [ennemi] to defeat - **2.** [obstacle, peur] to overcome.

vaincu, e [vɛ̃ky] ◇ *pp* ⊳ **vaincre** ◇ *adj* defeated ; **s'avouer ~** to admit defeat ◇ *nm, f* defeated person.

vainement [vɛnmɑ̃] *adv* vainly.

vainqueur [vɛ̃kœr] ◇ *nm* - **1.** [de combat] conqueror, victor - **2.** SPORT winner ◇ *adj m* victorious, conquering.

vairon [vɛrɔ̃] ◇ *adj m* - **1.** [yeux] of different colours - **2.** [cheval] wall-eyed ◇ *nm* minnow.

vais ⊳ aller.

vaisseau, x [vɛso] *nm* - **1.** NAVIG vessel, ship ; **~ spatial** AÉRON spaceship - **2.** ANAT vessel - **3.** ARCHIT nave.

vaisselier [vɛsəlje] *nm* dresser.

vaisselle [vɛsɛl] *nf* crockery ; **faire** OU **laver la ~** to do the dishes, to wash up.

val [val] (*pl* **vals** OU **vaux** [vo]) *nm* valley.

valable [valablǝ] *adj* - **1.** [passeport] valid - **2.** [raison, excuse] valid, legitimate - **3.** [œuvre] good, worthwhile.

valériane [valerjan] *nf* valerian.

valet [valɛ] *nm* - **1.** [serviteur] servant ; **~ de chambre** manservant, valet ; **~ de pied** footman - **2.** *fig* & *péj* [homme servile] lackey - **3.** CARTES jack, knave.

valeur [valœr] *nf* - **1.** [gén & MUS] value ; **avoir de la ~** to be valuable ; **prendre de la ~** to increase in value ; **perdre de sa ~** to lose its value ; **mettre en ~** [talents] to bring out ; [terre] to exploit ; **~ absolue** absolute value ; **~ ajoutée** ÉCON added value ; **de (grande) ~** [chose] (very) valuable ; [personne] of (great) worth OU merit - **2.** (*gén pl*) BOURSE stocks and shares (*pl*), securities (*pl*) - **3.** [mérite] worth, merit - **4.** *fig* [importance] value, importance - **5.** [équivalent] : **la ~ de** the equivalent of.
➤ **valeurs** *nfpl* [critères de référence] values.

valeureusement [valœrøzmɑ̃] *adv* valorously.

valeureux, euse [valœrø, øz] *adj* valorous.

validation [validasjɔ̃] *nf* validation, authentication.

valide [valid] *adj* - **1.** [personne] spry - **2.** [contrat] valid.

valider [3] [valide] *vt* to validate, to authenticate.

validité [validite] *nf* validity.

valise [valiz] *nf* case, suitcase ; **faire sa ~/ses ~s** to pack one's case/cases ; *fam fig* [partir] to pack one's bags ; **~ diplomatique** diplomatic bag.

vallée [vale] *nf* valley.

vallon [valɔ̃] *nm* small valley.

vallonné, e [valone] *adj* undulating.

valoir [60] [valwar] ◇ *vi* - **1.** [gén] to be worth ; **ça vaut combien?** how much is it? ; **que vaut ce film?** is this film any good? ; **ne rien ~** not to be any good, to be worthless ; **ça vaut mieux** *fam* that's best ; **ça ne vaut pas la peine** it's not worth it ; **faire ~** [vues] to assert ; [talent] to show - **2.** [règle] : **~ pour** to apply to, to hold good for ◇ *vt* [médaille, gloire] to bring, to earn ◇ *v impers* : **il vaudrait mieux que nous partions** it would be better if we left, we'd better leave.
➤ **se valoir** *vp* to be equally good/bad.

valorisant, e [valɔrizɑ̃, ɑ̃t] *adj* good for one's image.

valorisation [valɔrizasjɔ̃] *nf* [d'immeuble, de région] development ; **~ de soi** good self-image.

valoriser [3] [valɔrize] *vt* [immeuble, région] to develop ; [individu, société] to improve the image of.

valse [vals] *nf* waltz ; *fam fig* [de personnel] reshuffle.

valser [3] [valse] *vi* to waltz ; **envoyer ~ qqch** *fam fig* to send sthg flying ; **envoyer ~ qqn** *fam fig* [employé] to give sb the elbow.

valseur, euse [valsœr, øz, danseur] *nm, f* waltzer.

valu [valy] *pp inv* ⊳ **valoir**.

valve [valv] *nf* valve.

vamp [vɑ̃p] *nf* vamp.

vamper [3] [vɑ̃pe] *vt fam* to vamp.

vampire [vɑ̃pir] *nm* - **1.** [fantôme] vampire - **2.** *fig* [personne avide] vulture - **3.** ZOOL vampire bat.

vampiriser [3] [vɑ̃pirize] *vt fig* to control.

van [vɑ̃] *nm* [fourgon] horsebox *Br*, horsecar *Am*.

vandale [vɑ̃dal] *nmf* vandal.

vandalisme [vɑ̃dalism] *nm* vandalism.

vanille [vanij] *nf* vanilla.

vanillé, e [vanije] *adj* vanilla *(avant n)*.

vanité [vanite] *nf* vanity.

vaniteux, euse [vanitø, øz] <> *adj* vain, conceited <> *nm, f* vain *ou* conceited person.

vanity-case [vanitikez] *(pl* **vanity-cases)** *nm* vanity case.

vanne [van] *nf* - **1.** [d'écluse] lockgate - **2.** *fam* [remarque] gibe.

vanné, e [vane] *adj fam* [personne] dead beat.

vanner [3] [vane] *vt* - **1.** [grain] to winnow - **2.** *fam* [fatiguer] to wear out - **3.** *fam* [se moquer de] to make gibes at, to have a go at.

vannerie [vanri] *nf* basketwork, wickerwork.

vannier [vanje] *nm* basket maker.

vantail, aux [vɑ̃taj, o] *nm* [de porte] leaf ; [d'armoire] door.

vantard, e [vɑ̃tar, ard] <> *adj* bragging, boastful <> *nm, f* boaster.

vantardise [vɑ̃tardiz] *nf* boasting *(U)*, bragging *(U)*.

vanter [3] [vɑ̃te] *vt* to vaunt.
➤ **se vanter** *vp* to boast, to brag ; **se ~ de qqch** to boast *ou* brag about sthg ; **se ~ de faire qqch** to boast *ou* brag about doing sthg.

Vanuatu [vanwaty] *nm* Vanuatu.

va-nu-pieds [vanypje] *nmf inv fam* beggar.

vapes [vap] *nfpl fam* : **être dans les ~** to have one's head in the clouds ; **tomber dans les ~** to pass out.

vapeur [vapœr] <> *nf* - **1.** [d'eau] steam ; **à la ~** steamed ; **bateau à ~** steamboat, steamer ; **locomotive à ~** steam engine ; **renverser la ~** NAVIG to reverse engines ; *fig* to backpedal - **2.** [émanation] vapour *Br*, vapor *Am* <> *nm* steamer.
➤ **vapeurs** *nfpl* - **1.** [émanations] fumes - **2.** *loc vieilli* : **avoir ses ~s** to have the vapours *Br ou* vapors *Am*.

vapocuiseur [vapɔkɥizœr] *nm* pressure cooker.

vaporeux, euse [vapɔrø, øz] *adj* - **1.** *littéraire* [ciel, lumière] hazy - **2.** [tissu] filmy.

vaporisateur [vapɔrizatœr] *nm* - **1.** [atomiseur] spray, atomizer - **2.** IND vaporizer.

vaporisation [vapɔrizasjɔ̃] *nf* - **1.** [de parfum, déodorant] spraying - **2.** PHYS vaporization.

vaporiser [3] [vapɔrize] *vt* - **1.** [parfum, déodorant] to spray - **2.** PHYS to vaporize.
➤ **se vaporiser** *vp* to vaporize.

vaquer [3] [vake] *vi* : **~ à** to see to, to attend to.

varappe [varap] *nf* rock climbing.

varappeur, euse [varapœr, øz] *nm, f* (rock) climber.

varech [varɛk] *nm* kelp.

vareuse [varøz] *nf* - **1.** [veste] loose-fitting jacket - **2.** [de marin] pea jacket - **3.** [d'uniforme] tunic.

variable [varjabl] <> *adj* - **1.** [temps] changeable - **2.** [distance, résultats] varied, varying - **3.** [température] variable <> *nf* variable.

variante [varjɑ̃t] *nf* variant.

variateur [varjatœr] *nm* ÉLECTR dimmer switch.

variation [varjasjɔ̃] *nf* variation.

varice [varis] *nf* varicose vein.

varicelle [varisɛl] *nf* chickenpox.

varié, e [varje] *adj* - **1.** [divers] various - **2.** [non monotone] varied, varying.

varier [9] [varje] *vt* & *vi* to vary.

variété [varjete] *nf* variety.
➤ **variétés** *nfpl* variety show *(sg)*.

variole [varjɔl] *nf* smallpox.

variqueux, euse [varikø, øz] *adj* varicose.

Varsovie [varsɔvi] *n* Warsaw ; **le pacte de ~** the Warsaw Pact.

vas ⤳ aller.

vasculaire [vaskylɛr] *adj* vascular.

vase [vaz] <> *nm* vase ; **en ~ clos** *fig* in a vacuum <> *nf* mud, silt.

vasectomie [vazɛktɔmi] *nf* vasectomy.

vaseline [vazlin] *nf* Vaseline®, petroleum jelly.

vaseux, euse [vazø, øz] *adj* - **1.** [fond] muddy, silty - **2.** *fam* [personne] under the weather - **3.** *fam* [raisonnement, article] woolly.

vasistas [vazistas] *nm* fanlight.

vasque [vask] *nf* - **1.** [de fontaine] basin - **2.** [coupe] bowl.

vassal, e, aux [vasal, o] *nm, f* vassal.

vaste [vast] *adj* vast, immense.

Vatican [vatikɑ̃] *nm* : **le ~** the Vatican ; **l'État de la cité du ~** Vatican City ; **au ~** in Vatican City.

va-tout [vatu] *nm inv* : **jouer son ~** *fig* to stake one's all.

vaudeville [vodvil] *nm* vaudeville.

vaudevillesque [vodvilɛsk] *adj* ludicrous.

vaudou [vodu] *nm* voodoo.

vaudrait ⤳ valoir.

vau-l'eau [volo] ➤ **à vau-l'eau** *loc adv littéraire* with the flow ; **aller à ~** *fig* to go down the drain.

vaurien, enne [vɔrjɛ̃, ɛn] *nm, f* good-for-nothing.

vaut ⊳ **valoir**.

vautour [votur] *nm* vulture.

vautrer [3] [votre] ➤ **se vautrer** *vp* [dans la boue, dans la débauche] to wallow ; [sur l'herbe, dans un fauteuil] to sprawl.

va-vite [vavit] ➤ **à la va-vite** *loc adv fam* in a rush.

vd *abr de* vend.

VDQS (*abr de* vin délimité de qualité supérieure) *nm* label indicating quality of wine.

vds *abr de* vends.

veau, x [vo] *nm* - **1.** [animal] calf ; **le Veau d'or** the golden calf - **2.** [viande] veal - **3.** [peau] calfskin - **4.** *péj* [personne] lump.

vecteur [vɛktœr] *nm* - **1.** GÉOM vector - **2.** [intermédiaire] vehicle ; MÉD carrier.

vécu, e [veky] ⊳ *pp* ⊳ **vivre** ⊳ *adj* real.

vedettariat [vədɛtarja] *nm* stardom.

vedette [vədɛt] *nf* - **1.** NAVIG patrol boat - **2.** [star] star ; **mettre en ~** *fig* to turn the spotlight on.

végétal, e, aux [veʒetal, o] *adj* [huile] vegetable (*avant n*) ; [cellule, fibre] plant (*avant n*).

végétalien, enne [veʒetaljɛ̃, ɛn] *adj* & *nm, f* vegan.

végétarien, enne [veʒetarjɛ̃, ɛn] *adj* & *nm, f* vegetarian.

végétarisme [veʒetarism] *nm* vegetarianism.

végétatif, tive [veʒetatif, iv] *adj* vegetative ; *fig* & *péj* vegetable-like.

végétation [veʒetasjɔ̃] *nf* vegetation. ➤ **végétations** *nfpl* adenoids.

végéter [18] [veʒete] *vi* to vegetate.

véhémence [veemɑ̃s] *nf* vehemence.

véhément, e [veemɑ̃, ɑ̃t] *adj* vehement.

véhicule [veikyl] *nm* vehicle ; **~ banalisé** unmarked vehicle.

véhiculer [3] [veikyle] *vt* to transport ; *fig* to convey.

veille [vɛj] *nf* - **1.** [jour précédent] day before, eve ; **la ~ au soir** the previous evening, the evening before ; **la ~ de mon anniversaire** the day before my birthday ; **la ~ de Noël** Christmas Eve ; **à la ~ de** *fig* on the eve of - **2.** [éveil] wakefulness ; [privation de sommeil] sleeplessness - **3.** [garde] : **être de ~** to be on night duty.

veillée [veje] *nf* - **1.** [soirée] evening - **2.** [de mort] watch.

veiller [4] [veje] ⊳ *vi* - **1.** [rester éveillé] to stay up - **2.** [rester vigilant] : **~ à qqch** to look after sthg ; **~ à faire qqch** to see that sthg is done ; **~ sur** to watch over ⊳ *vt* to sit up with.

veilleur [vejœr] *nm* : **~ de nuit** night watchman.

veilleuse [vejøz] *nf* - **1.** [lampe] nightlight - **2.** AUTOM sidelight - **3.** [de chauffe-eau] pilot light.

veinard, e [vɛnar, ard] *fam* ⊳ *adj* lucky ⊳ *nm, f* lucky devil.

veine [vɛn] *nf* - **1.** [gén] vein ; **en ~ de** in the mood for ; **s'ouvrir les ~s** to slash one's wrists ; **se saigner aux quatre ~s** *fig* to bleed o.s. white - **2.** [de marbre] vein ; [de bois] grain - **3.** [filon] seam, vein - **4.** *fam* [chance] luck ; **avoir de la ~** to be lucky ; **avoir une ~ de cocu** *fig* to have the luck of the devil.

veiné, e [vene] *adj* [marbre] veined ; [bois] grained.

veineux, euse [venø, øz] *adj* - **1.** ANAT venous - **2.** [marbre] veined ; [bois] grainy.

veinule [venyl] *nf* venule.

Velcro® [vɛlkro] *nm* Velcro®.

vêler [4] [vele] *vi* to calve.

vélin [velɛ̃] *nm* vellum.

véliplanchiste [veliplɑ̃ʃist] *nmf* windsurfer.

velléitaire [veleitɛr] ⊳ *nmf* indecisive person ⊳ *adj* indecisive.

velléité [veleite] *nf* whim.

vélo [velo] *nm fam* bike ; **faire du ~** to go cycling.

véloce [velɔs] *adj* swift.

vélocité [velɔsite] *nf* swiftness, speed.

vélodrome [velɔdrom] *nm* velodrome.

vélomoteur [velɔmɔtœr] *nm* light motorcycle.

velours [vəlur] *nm* velvet.

velouté, e [vəlute] *adj* velvety. ➤ **velouté** *nm* - **1.** [de peau] velvetiness - **2.** [potage] cream soup ; **~ d'asperges** cream of asparagus soup.

velu, e [vəly] *adj* hairy.

venaison [vənɛzɔ̃] *nf* venison.

vénal, e, aux [venal, o] *adj* venal.

vénalité [venalite] *nf* venality.

venant [vənɑ̃] ➤ **à tout venant** *loc adv* to all comers.

vendange [vɑ̃dɑ̃ʒ] *nf* - **1.** [récolte] grape harvest, wine harvest - **2.** [raisins] grape crop - **3.** [période] : **les ~s** (grape) harvest time *(sg)*.

vendanger [17] [vɑ̃dɑ̃ʒe] ◇ *vt* to harvest grapes from ◇ *vi* to harvest the grapes.

vendangeur, euse [vɑ̃dɑ̃ʒœr, øz] *nm, f* grape-picker.

vendetta [vɑ̃detal *nf* vendetta.

vendeur, euse [vɑ̃dœr, øz] *nm, f* salesman (*f* saleswoman).

vendre [73] [vɑ̃dr] *vt* to sell ; **'à ~'** 'for sale'.
♦ **se vendre** *vp* - **1.** [maison, produit] to be sold - **2.** *péj* [se laisser corrompre] to sell o.s. - **3.** [se trahir] to give o.s. away.

vendredi [vɑ̃drədi] *nm* Friday ; **Vendredi Saint** Good Friday ; *voir aussi* **samedi**.

vends ▷ **vendre**.

vendu, e [vɑ̃dy] ◇ *pp* ▷ **vendre** ◇ *adj* - **1.** [cédé] sold - **2.** [corrompu] corrupt ◇ *nm, f* traitor.

venelle [vənɛl] *nf* alley.

vénéneux, euse [venenø, øz] *adj* poisonous.

vénérable [venerabl] *adj* venerable.

vénération [venerasjɔ̃] *nf* veneration, reverence.

vénérer [18] [venere] *vt* to venerate, to revere.

vénerie [vɛnri] *nf* hunting.

vénérien, enne [venerjɛ̃, ɛn] *adj* venereal.

Venezuela [venezɥela] *nm* : **le ~** Venezuela ; **au ~** in Venezuela.

vénézuélien, enne [venezɥeljɛ̃, ɛn] *adj* Venezuelan.
♦ **Vénézuélien, enne** *nm, f* Venezuelan.

vengeance [vɑ̃ʒɑ̃s] *nf* vengeance.

venger [17] [vɑ̃ʒe] *vt* to avenge.
♦ **se venger** *vp* to get one's revenge ; **se ~ de qqn** to take revenge on sb ; **se ~ de qqch** to take revenge for sthg ; **se ~ sur** to take it out on.

vengeur, vengeresse [vɑ̃ʒœr, vɑ̃ʒrɛs] ◇ *adj* vengeful ◇ *nm, f* avenger.

véniel, elle [venjɛl] *adj* venial.

venimeux, euse [vənimø, øz] *adj* venomous.

venin [vənɛ̃] *nm* venom.

venir [40] [vənir] *vi* to come ; [plante, arbre] to come on ; **~ de** [personne, mot] to come from ; [échec] to be due to ; **~ à** [maturité] to reach ; [question, sujet] to come to ; **il lui vient à l'épaule** he comes up to his/her shoulder ; **~ de faire qqch** to have just done sthg ; **je viens de la voir** I've just seen her ; **s'il venait à mourir ...**

if he was to die ... ; **où veux-tu en ~ ?** what are you getting at?
♦ **s'en venir** *vp littéraire* to come (along).

Venise [vəniz] *n* Venice.

vénitien, enne [venisjɛ̃, ɛn] *adj* Venetian.
♦ **Vénitien, enne** *nm, f* Venetian.

vent [vɑ̃] *nm* wind ; **il fait** *ou* **il y a du ~** headwind ; **~ contraire** headwind ; **dans le ~** trendy ; **avoir ~ de** *fig* to get wind of ; **bon ~ !** *fig* good riddance! ; **contre ~s et marées** *fig* come hell or high water.

vente [vɑ̃t] *nf* - **1.** [cession, transaction] sale ; **en ~** on sale , **en ~ libre** available over the counter ; **~ de charité** (charity) bazaar ; **~ par correspondance** mail order ; **~ à la criée** sale by auction ; **~ en demi-gros** cash-and-carry ; **~ au détail** retail sales ; **~ directe** direct selling ; **~ aux enchères** auction ; **~ en gros** wholesale sales - **2.** [service] sales (department) - **3.** [technique] selling.

venteux, euse [vɑ̃tø, øz] *adj* windy.

ventilateur [vɑ̃tilatœr] *nm* fan.

ventilation [vɑ̃tilasjɔ̃] *nf* - **1.** [de pièce] ventilation - **2.** FIN breakdown.

ventiler [3] [vɑ̃tile] *vt* - **1.** [pièce] to ventilate - **2.** FIN to break down.

ventouse [vɑ̃tuz] *nf* - **1.** [de caoutchouc] suction pad ; [d'animal] sucker - **2.** MÉD cupping glass - **3.** TECHNOL air vent.

ventral, e, aux [vɑ̃tral, o] *adj* ventral.

ventre [vɑ̃tr] *nm* [de personne] stomach ; **avoir/prendre du ~** to have/be getting (a bit of) a paunch ; **avoir le ~ ballonné** to have a bloated stomach ; **à plat ~** flat on one's stomach ; **à terre** *fig* flat out ; **avoir quelque chose dans le ~** *fig* to have guts.

ventricule [vɑ̃trikyl] *nm* ventricle.

ventriloque [vɑ̃trilɔk] *nmf* ventriloquist.

ventripotent, e [vɑ̃tripɔtɑ̃, ɑ̃t] *adj fam* potbellied.

ventru, e [vɑ̃try] *adj* - **1.** *fam* [personne] potbellied - **2.** [cruche] round ; [commode] bow-fronted.

venu, e [vəny] ◇ *pp* ▷ **venir** ◇ *adj* : **bien ~** welcome ; **mal ~** unwelcome ; **il serait mal ~ de faire cela** it would be improper to do that ◇ *nm, f* : **nouveau ~** newcomer.
♦ **venue** *nf* coming, arrival.

vêpres [vɛpr] *nfpl* vespers.

ver [vɛr] *nm* worm ; **~ luisant** glow-worm ; **~ à soie** silkworm ; **~ solitaire** tapeworm ; **~ de terre** earthworm ; **nu comme un ~** *fig* stark naked ; **tirer les ~s du nez à qqn** *fig* to worm information out of sb.

véracité [verasite] *nf* truthfulness.

véranda [verɑ̃da] *nf* veranda.

verbal, e, aux [vɛrbal, o] *adj* - **1.** [promesse, violence] verbal - **2.** *GRAM* verb *(avant n)*.

verbalement [vɛrbalmɑ̃] *adv* verbally.

verbaliser [3] [vɛrbalize] <> *vt* to verbalize <> *vi* to make out a report.

verbe [vɛrb] *nm* - **1.** *GRAM* verb ; ~ **impersonnel** impersonal verb - **2.** *littéraire* [langage] words *(pl)*, language.

verbeux, euse [vɛrbø, øz] *adj* wordy, verbose.

verbiage [vɛrbjaʒ] *nm* verbiage.

verdâtre [vɛrdɑtr] *adj* greenish.

verdeur [vɛrdœr] *nf* - **1.** [de personne] vigour *Br*, vigor *Am*, vitality - **2.** [de langage] crudeness - **3.** [de fruit] tartness ; [de vin] acidity - **4.** [de bois] greenness.

verdict [vɛrdikt] *nm* verdict.

verdir [32] [vɛrdir] *vt* & *vi* to turn green.

verdoyant, e [vɛrdwajɑ̃, ɑ̃t] *adj* green.

verdoyer [13] [vɛrdwaje] *vi* to turn green.

verdure [vɛrdyr] *nf* - **1.** [végétation] greenery - **2.** [couleur] greenness - **3.** [légumes verts] green vegetables *(pl)*, greens *(pl)*.

véreux, euse [verø, øz] *adj* worm-eaten, maggoty ; *fig* shady.

verge [vɛrʒ] *nf* - **1.** *ANAT* penis - **2.** *littéraire* [baguette] rod, stick.

verger [vɛrʒe] *nm* orchard.

vergeture [vɛrʒətyr] *nf* stretchmark.

verglacé, e [vɛrglase] *adj* icy.

verglas [vɛrgla] *nm* (black) ice.

vergogne [vɛrgɔɲ] ~ **sans vergogne** *loc adv* shamelessly.

vergue [vɛrg] *nf* yard.

véridique [veridik] *adj* truthful.

vérifiable [verifjabl] *adj* verifiable.

vérificateur, trice [verifikatœr, tris] <> *adj* : **comptable** ~ auditor <> *nm, f* inspector.

vérification [verifikasjɔ̃] *nf* - **1.** [contrôle] check, checking - **2.** [confirmation] proof, confirmation.

vérifier [9] [verifje] *vt* - **1.** [contrôler] to check - **2.** [confirmer] to prove, to confirm. ~ **se vérifier** *vp* to prove accurate.

vérin [verɛ̃] *nm* jack.

véritable [veritabl] *adj* real ; [ami] true ; **du cuir/de l'or** ~ real leather/gold.

véritablement [veritabləmɑ̃] *adv* really.

vérité [verite] *nf* - **1.** [chose vraie, réalité, principe]

truth '*(U)* ; **dire ses quatre ~s à qqn** *fam* to tell sb a few home truths - **2.** [sincérité] sincerity - **3.** [ressemblance - de reproduction] accuracy ; [- de personnage, portrait] trueness to life. ~ **en vérité** *loc adv* actually, really.

verlan [vɛrlɑ̃] *nm* back slang.

vermeil, eille [vɛrmɛj] *adj* scarlet. ~ *nm* silver-gilt.

vermicelle [vɛrmisɛl] *nm* vermicelli *(U)*.

vermifuge [vɛrmifyʒ] *nm* [pour chat, chien] worm tablet.

vermillon [vɛrmijɔ̃] *nm* & *adj inv* vermilion.

vermine [vɛrmin] *nf* - **1.** [parasites] vermin - **2.** *fig* [canaille] rat.

vermisseau, x [vɛrmiso] *nm* - **1.** [ver] small worm - **2.** *fig* [être chétif] runt.

vermoulu, e [vɛrmuly] *adj* riddled with woodworm ; *fig* moth-eaten.

vermouth [vɛrmut] *nm* vermouth.

vernaculaire [vɛrnakylɛr] *adj* vernacular.

verni, e [vɛrni] *adj* - **1.** [bois] varnished - **2.** [souliers] : **chaussures ~es** patent-leather shoes - **3.** *fam* [chanceux] lucky.

vernir [32] [vɛrnir] *vt* to varnish.

vernis [vɛrni] *nm* varnish ; *fig* veneer ; ~ **à ongles** nail polish *ou* varnish.

vernissage [vɛrnisaʒ] *nm* - **1.** [de meuble] varnishing - **2.** [d'exposition] private viewing.

vérole [verɔl] *nf MÉD* : **petite** ~ smallpox.

verrat [vera] *nm* boar.

verre [vɛr] *nm* - **1.** [matière, récipient] glass ; [quantité] glassful, glass ; ~ **dépoli** frosted glass ; ~ **ballon** brandy glass ; ~ **à dents** tooth mug *ou* glass ; ~ **à moutarde** mustard jar ; ~ **à pied** long-stemmed glass ; ~ **à vin** wine glass - **2.** [optique] lens ; **porter des ~s** to wear glasses ; ~**s antireflet** anti-glare coated lenses ; ~**s de contact** contact lenses ; ~ **grossissant** magnifying glass ; ~**s progressifs** progressive lenses, progressives - **3.** [boisson] drink ; **boire un** ~ to have a drink.

verrerie [vɛrri] *nf* - **1.** [fabrication] glass-making - **2.** [usine] glassworks *(sg)* - **3.** [objets] glassware.

verrier [vɛrje] *nm* glass-maker.

verrière [vɛrjɛr] *nf* - **1.** [pièce] conservatory - **2.** [toit] glass roof.

verroterie [vɛrɔtri] *nf* coloured *Br* ou colored *Am* glass beads *(pl)*.

verrou [vɛru] *nm* bolt ; **mettre qqn/être sous les ~s** to put sb/to be behind bars.

verrouillage [vɛrujaʒ] *nm* AUTOM : **~ central** central locking.

verrouiller [3] [vɛruje] *vt* - **1.** [porte] to bolt - **2.** [personne] to lock up.

➤ **se verrouiller** *vp* to lock o.s. in.

verrue [vɛry] *nf* wart ; **~ plantaire** verruca.

vers[1] [vɛr] ◇ *nm* line ◇ *nmpl* : **en ~** in verse ; **faire des ~** to write poetry.

vers[2] [vɛr] *prép* - **1.** [dans la direction de] towards *Br*, toward *Am* - **2.** [aux environs de - temporel] around, about ; [- spatial] near ; **~ la fin du mois** towards *Br* ou toward *Am* the end of the month.

Versailles [vɛrsaj] *n* Versailles ; **le château de ~** (the Palace of) Versailles.

versant [vɛrsɑ̃] *nm* side.

versatile [vɛrsatil] *adj* changeable, fickle.

verse [vɛrs] ➤ **à verse** *loc adv* : **pleuvoir à ~** to pour down.

versé, e [vɛrse] *adj* : **être ~ dans** to be versed ou well-versed in.

Verseau [vɛrso] *nm* ASTROL Aquarius ; **être ~** to be (an) Aquarius.

versement [vɛrsəmɑ̃] *nm* payment.

verser [3] [vɛrse] ◇ *vt* - **1.** [eau] to pour ; [larmes, sang] to shed - **2.** [argent] to pay ◇ *vi* to overturn, to tip over ; **~ dans** *fig* to lapse into.

verset [vɛrse] *nm* verse.

verseur, euse [vɛrsœr, øz] *adj* pouring *(avant n).*

➤ **verseur** *nm* pourer.

➤ **verseuse** *nf* pot, jug *(for coffee maker).*

versification [vɛrsifikasjɔ̃] *nf* versification.

version [vɛrsjɔ̃] *nf* - **1.** [gén] version ; **~ française/originale** French/original version - **2.** [traduction] translation *(into mother tongue).*

verso [vɛrso] *nm* back.

versus [vɛrsys] *prép* versus.

vert, e [vɛr, vɛrt] *adj* - **1.** [couleur, fruit, légume, bois] green - **2.** *fig* [vieillard] spry, sprightly - **3.** [réprimande] sharp - **4.** [à la campagne] : **le tou-**

risme ~ country holidays *(pl)* - **5.** *fam* [histoire] smutty ; **(en entendre) des ~es et des pas mûres** (to hear) all sorts of awful things.

➤ **vert** *nm* - **1.** [couleur] green ; **~ bouteille/d'eau/pomme/tendre** bottle/sea/apple/soft green - **2.** [verdure] : **se mettre au ~** to take a break in the country.

➤ **Verts** *nmpl* : **les Verts** POLIT the Greens.

vert-de-gris [vɛrdəgri] ◇ *nm* verdigris ◇ *adj* grey-green *Br*, gray-green *Am*.

vertébral, e, aux [vɛrtebral, o] *adj* vertebral.

vertèbre [vɛrtɛbr] *nf* vertebra.

vertébré, e [vɛrtebre] *adj* vertebrate.

➤ **vertébré** *nm* vertebrate.

vertement [vɛrtəmɑ̃] *adv* sharply.

vertical, e, aux [vɛrtikal, o] *adj* vertical.

➤ **verticale** *nf* vertical ; **à la ~e** [descente] vertical ; [descendre] vertically.

verticalement [vɛrtikalmɑ̃] *adv* vertically.

vertige [vɛrtiʒ] *nm* - **1.** [peur du vide] vertigo ; **donner le ~ à qqn** to make sb dizzy - **2.** [étourdissement] dizziness ; *fig* intoxication ; **avoir des ~s** to suffer from ou have dizzy spells.

vertigineux, euse [vɛrtiʒinø, øz] *adj* - **1.** *fig* [vue, vitesse] breathtaking - **2.** [hauteur] dizzy.

vertu [vɛrty] *nf* - **1.** [morale, chasteté] virtue ; **de petite ~** of easy virtue - **2.** [pouvoir] properties *(pl)*, power.

➤ **en vertu de** *loc prép* in accordance with.

vertueusement [vɛrtɥøzmɑ̃] *adv* virtuously.

vertueux, euse [vɛrtɥø, øz] *adj* virtuous.

verve [vɛrv] *nf* eloquence ; **être en ~** to be particularly eloquent.

verveine [vɛrvɛn] *nf* - **1.** [plante] verbena - **2.** [infusion] verbena tea.

vésicule [vezikyl] *nf* vesicle ; **~ biliaire** gall bladder.

Vespa® [vɛspa] *nf* scooter.

vespasienne [vɛspazjɛn] *nf* public urinal.

vespéral, e, aux [vɛsperal, o] *adj littéraire* evening *(avant n).*

vessie [vesi] *nf* bladder.

veste [vɛst] *nf* - **1.** [vêtement] jacket ; **~ croisée/droite** double-/single-breasted jacket ; **retourner sa ~** *fam fig* to change one's colours - **2.** *fam* [échec] : **ramasser** ou **prendre une ~** to come a cropper.

vestiaire [vɛstjɛr] *nm* - **1.** [au théâtre] cloakroom - **2.** *(gén pl)* SPORT changing-room, locker-room.

vestibule [vɛstibyl] *nm* [pièce] hall, vestibule.

vestige [vɛstiʒ] *nm (gén pl)* [de ville] remains *(pl)* ; *fig* [de civilisation, grandeur] vestiges *(pl)*, relic.

vestimentaire [vɛstimɑ̃tɛr] *adj* [industrie] clothing *(avant n)* ; [dépense] on clothes ; **détail ~** accessory.

veston [vɛstɔ̃] *nm* jacket.

vêtement [vɛtmɑ̃] *nm* garment, article of clothing ; **~s** clothing *(U)*, clothes.

vétéran [veterɑ̃] *nm* veteran.

vétérinaire [veterinɛr] <> *adj* veterinary *(avant n)* <> *nmf* vet, veterinary surgeon.

vétille [vetij] *nf* triviality.

vêtir [44] [vetir] *vt* to dress.

▸ **se vêtir** *vp* to dress, to get dressed.

vétiver [vetivɛr] *nm* vetiver.

veto [veto] *nm inv* veto ; **mettre son ~ à qqch** to veto sthg.

véto [veto] *nmf fam* vet.

vêtu, e [vety] <> *pp* ▷ **vêtir** <> *adj* : **~ (de)** dressed (in) ; **à demi-~** half-dressed.

vétuste [vetyst] *adj* dilapidated.

vétusté [vetyste] *nf* dilapidation.

veuf, veuve [vœf, vœv] <> *adj* widowed <> *nm, f* widower *(f* widow).

veuille *etc* ▷ **vouloir**.

veule [vøl] *adj* spineless.

veulerie [vølri] *nf* spinelessness.

veut ▷ **vouloir**.

veuvage [vœvaʒ] *nm* [de femme] widowhood ; [d'homme] widowerhood.

veuve ▷ **veuf**.

veux ▷ **vouloir**.

vexant, e [vɛksɑ̃, ɑ̃t] *adj* - **1.** [contrariant] annoying, vexing - **2.** [blessant] hurtful.

vexation [vɛksasjɔ̃] *nf* [humiliation] insult.

vexatoire [vɛksatwar] *adj* offensive.

vexer [4] [vɛkse] *vt* to offend.

▸ **se vexer** *vp* to take offence *Br ou* offense *Am*.

VF *(abr de* version française) *nf indicates that a film has been dubbed into French.*

VHF *(abr de* very high frequency) *nf* VHF.

via [vja] *prép* via.

viabiliser [3] [vjabilize] *vt* to service.

viabilité [vjabilite] *nf* - **1.** [de route] passable state - **2.** [d'entreprise, organisme] viability.

viable [vjabl] *adj* viable.

viaduc [vjadyk] *nm* viaduct.

viager, ère [vjaʒe, ɛr] *adj* life *(avant n)*.

▸ **viager** *nm* life annuity ; **mettre qqch en ~** to sell sthg in return for a life annuity.

viande [vjɑ̃d] *nf* meat ; **~ blanche** white meat ; **~ froide** cold meat ; **~ rouge** red meat.

viatique [vjatik] *nm* - **1.** RELIG : **recevoir le ~** to receive the last rites *(pl)* - **2.** *littéraire* [soutien] lifeline.

vibrant, e [vibrɑ̃, ɑ̃t] *adj* - **1.** [corde] vibrating - **2.** *fig* [discours] stirring.

vibraphone [vibrafɔn] *nm* vibraphone.

vibration [vibrasjɔ̃] *nf* vibration.

vibratoire [vibratwar] *adj* vibratory.

vibrer [3] [vibre] *vi* - **1.** [trembler] to vibrate - **2.** *fig* [être ému] : **~ (de)** to be stirred (with).

vibromasseur [vibromasœr] *nm* vibrator.

vicaire [vikɛr] *nm* curate.

vice [vis] *nm* - **1.** [de personne] vice - **2.** [d'objet] fault, defect ; **~ caché** hidden flaw ; **~ de forme** JUR flaw.

vice-consul [viskɔ̃syl] *(pl* vice-consuls) *nm* vice-consul.

vice-présidence [visprezidɑ̃s] *(pl* vice-présidences) *nf* POLIT vice-presidency ; [de société] vice-chairmanship.

vice-président, e [visprezidɑ̃, ɑ̃t] *(mpl* vice-présidents, *fpl* vice-présidentes) *nm, f* POLIT vice-president ; [de société] vice-chairman *(f* vice-chairwoman).

vice versa [vis(e)vɛrsa] *loc adv* vice versa.

vichy [viʃi] *nm* - **1.** [étoffe] gingham - **2.** [eau] vichy (water).

vicié, e [visje] *adj* [air] polluted, tainted.

vicier [9] [visje] *vt* - **1.** [air] to pollute, to taint - **2.** JUR to invalidate.

vicieux, euse [visjø, øz] *adj* - **1.** [personne, conduite] perverted, depraved - **2.** [animal] restive - **3.** [attaque] underhand - **4.** *sout* [prononciation, locution] incorrect.

vicinal, e, aux [visinal, o] ▷ **chemin**.

vicissitudes [visisityd] *nfpl* vicissitudes.

vicomte, vicomtesse [vikɔ̃t, vikɔ̃tɛs] *nm, f* viscount *(f* viscountess).

victime [viktim] *nf* victim ; [blessé] casualty.

victoire [viktwar] *nf* MIL victory ; POLIT & SPORT win, victory ; **chanter ou crier ~** to boast of one's success.

victorieux, euse [viktɔrjø, øz] *adj* - **1.** MIL victorious ; POLIT & SPORT winning *(avant n)*, victorious - **2.** [air] triumphant.

victuailles [viktɥaj] *nfpl* provisions.

vidange [vidɑ̃ʒ] *nf* - **1.** [action] emptying,

draining - **2.** AUTOM oil change - **3.** [mécanisme] waste outlet.

◆ **vidanges** *nfpl* sewage *(U)*.

vidanger **[17]** [vidɑ̃ʒe] *vt* to empty, to drain.

vide [vid] ◇ *nm* - **1.** [espace] void ; *fig* [néant, manque] emptiness - **2.** [absence d'air] vacuum ; **conditionné sous ~** vacuum-packed - **3.** [ouverture] gap, space - **4.** *loc* : **faire le ~** [se détendre] to have some time on one's own ; **parler dans le ~** [sans objet] to talk aimlessly ; [sans auditeur] to talk to a brick wall *ou* to o.s. ; **regarder dans le ~** to stare into space ◇ *adj* empty ; **~ de** *fig* devoid of.

◆ **à vide** *loc adj* & *loc adv* empty.

vidéo [video] ◇ *nf* video ◇ *adj inv* video *(avant n)*.

vidéocassette [videɔkasɛt] *nf* video cassette.

vidéoconférence [videokɔ̃ferɑ̃s] = **visioconférence.**

vidéodisque [videɔdisk] *nm* videodisc.

vide-ordures [vidɔrdyr] *nm inv* rubbish chute.

vidéosurveillance [videɔsyrvɛjɑ̃s] *nf* video surveillance.

vidéothèque [videɔtɛk] *nf* video library.

vidéotransmission [videɔtrɑ̃smisjɔ̃] *nf* video transmission.

vide-poches [vidpɔʃ] *nm inv* - **1.** [chez soi] tidy - **2.** [de voiture] glove compartment.

vide-pomme [vidpɔm] (*pl inv* OU **vide-pommes**) *nm* apple corer.

vider **[3]** [vide] *vt* - **1.** [rendre vide] to empty - **2.** [évacuer] : **~ les lieux** to vacate the premises - **3.** [poulet] to clean - **4.** *fam* [personne - épuiser] to drain ; [- expulser] to chuck out.

◆ **se vider** *vp* - **1.** [eaux] : **se ~ dans** to empty into, to drain into - **2.** [baignoire, salle] to empty.

videur [vidœr] *nm* bouncer.

vie [vi] *nf* - **1.** [gén] life ; **attenter à la ~ de qqn** to make an attempt on sb's life ; **coûter la ~ à qqn** to cost sb his/her life ; **sauver la ~ à qqn** to save sb's life ; **être en ~** to be alive ; **être entre la ~ et la mort** to be at death's door ; **sa ~ durant** for one's entire life ; **à ~** for life ; **une ~ de chien** *fam* a dog's life ; **mener la ~ dure à qqn** to make sb's life hell ; **prendre la ~ du bon côté** to look on the bright side of life ; **voir la ~ en rose** to see life through rose-coloured *Br ou* rose-colored *Am* spectacles ; **enterrer sa ~ de garçon** to have a stag party *ou* night - **2.** [subsistance] cost of living ; **gagner sa ~** to earn one's living.

vieil ▻ **vieux.**

vieillard [vjɛjar] *nm* old man.

vieille ▻ **vieux.**

vieillerie [vjɛjri] *nf* [objet] old thing.

vieillesse [vjɛjɛs] *nf* - **1.** [fin de la vie] old age - **2.** [vieillards] : **la ~** old people *(pl)*.

vieilli, e [vjeji] *adj* [mode, attitude] dated.

vieillir **[32]** [vjejir] ◇ *vi* - **1.** [personne] to grow old, to age ; **~ bien/mal** to age well/badly - **2.** CULIN to mature, to age - **3.** [tradition, idée] to become dated *ou* outdated ◇ *vt* - **1.** [suj : coiffure, vêtement] : **~ qqn** to make sb look older - **2.** [suj : personne] : **ils m'ont vieilli de cinq ans** they said I was five years older than I actually am.

◆ **se vieillir** *vp* [d'apparence] to make o.s. look older ; [dans les propos] to say one is older than one really is.

vieillissement [vjejismɑ̃] *nm* - **1.** [de personne] ageing - **2.** [de mot, d'idée] obsolescence - **3.** [de vin, fromage] maturing, ageing.

vieillot, otte [vjejo, ɔt] *adj* old-fashioned.

vielle [vjɛl] *nf* hurdy-gurdy.

Vienne [vjɛn] *n* - **1.** [en France] Vienne - **2.** [en Autriche] Vienna.

viennois, e [vjenwa, az] *adj* Viennese ; **pain ~** Vienna loaf.

◆ **Viennois, e** *nm, f* Viennese.

vierge [vjɛrʒ] ◇ *nf* virgin ; **la (Sainte) Vierge** the Virgin (Mary) ◇ *adj* - **1.** [personne] virgin - **2.** [terre] virgin ; [page] blank ; [casier judiciaire] clean ; **~ de** unsullied by.

◆ **Vierge** *nf* ASTROL Virgo ; **être Vierge** to be (a) Virgo.

Viêt Nam [vjɛtnam] *nm* : **le ~** Vietnam ; **au ~** in Vietnam ; **le Nord ~** North Vietnam ; **le Sud ~** South Vietnam.

vietnamien, enne [vjɛtnamjɛ̃, ɛn] *adj* Vietnamese.

◆ **vietnamien** *nm* [langue] Vietnamese.

◆ **Vietnamien, enne** *nm, f* Vietnamese person.

vieux, vieille [vjø, vjɛj] ◇ *adj (vieil devant voyelle ou h muet)* old ; **se faire ~** to get old ; **~ jeu** old-fashioned ◇ *nm, f* - **1.** [personne âgée] old man (*f* woman) ; **les ~** the old ; **un petit ~** a little old man - **2.** *fam* [ami] : **mon ~** old chap *ou* boy *Br*, old buddy *Am* ; **ma vieille** old girl - **3.** *tfam* [parent] old man (*f* woman) ; **ses ~** his folks ◇ *nm* [meubles] antique furniture.

vif, vive [vif, viv] *adj* - **1.** [preste - enfant] lively ; [- imagination] vivid - **2.** [couleur, œil] bright ; **rouge/jaune ~** bright red/yellow - **3.** [reproche] sharp ; [discussion] bitter - **4.** *sout* [vivant] alive - **5.** [douleur, déception] acute ; [intérêt] keen ; [amour, haine] intense, deep.

◆ **vif** *nm* - **1.** JUR living person - **2.** PÊCHE live bait - **3.** *loc* : **entrer dans le ~ du sujet** to get to the heart of the matter ; **piquer au ~** to touch a raw nerve ; **prendre qqn sur le ~** to catch sb red-handed ; **une photo prise sur le ~** an action photograph.

◆ **à vif** *loc adj* [plaie] open ; **j'ai les nerfs à ~** *fig* my nerves are frayed.

vif-argent [vifarʒɑ̃] *nm inv* quicksilver ; *fig* [personne] live wire.

vigie [viʒi] *nf* - **1.** [NAVIG - personne] look-out ; [- poste] crow's nest - **2.** RAIL observation box.

vigilance [viʒilɑ̃s] *nf* vigilance.

vigilant, e [viʒilɑ̃, ɑ̃t] *adj* vigilant, watchful.

vigile [viʒil] *nm* watchman.

vigne [viɲ] *nf* - **1.** [plante] vine, grapevine - **2.** [plantation] vineyard.

◆ **vigne vierge** *nf* Virginia creeper.

vigneron, onne [viɲərɔ̃, ɔn] *nm, f* wine grower.

vignette [viɲɛt] *nf* - **1.** [timbre] label ; [de médicament] price sticker *(for reimbursement by the social security services)* ; AUTOM tax disc *Br*, license sticker *Am* - **2.** [motif] vignette.

vignoble [viɲɔbl] *nm* - **1.** [plantation] vineyard - **2.** [vignes] vineyards *(pl)*.

vigoureusement [vigurøzmɑ̃] *adv* vigorously.

vigoureux, euse [vigurø, øz] *adj* [corps, personne] vigorous ; [bras, sentiment] strong.

vigueur [vigœr] *nf* vigour *Br*, vigor *Am*.

◆ **en vigueur** *loc adj* in force.

vil, e [vil] *adj* vile, base.

vilain, e [vilɛ̃, ɛn] *adj* - **1.** [gén] nasty - **2.** [laid] ugly.

◆ **vilain** *nm* - **1.** HIST villein - **2.** *fam* [grabuge] : **il y aura du ~** there's going to be trouble.

vilebrequin [vilbrəkɛ̃] *nm* - **1.** [outil] brace and bit - **2.** AUTOM crankshaft.

vilenie [vileni] *nf* - **1.** [caractère] vileness, baseness - **2.** [action] vile deed ; [parole] vile comment.

vilipender [3] [vilipɑ̃de] *vt littéraire* to vilify.

villa [vila] *nf* villa.

village [vilaʒ] *nm* village ; **~ de vacances** holiday village *Br*, vacation village *Am*.

villageois, e [vilaʒwa, az] ◇ *adj* rustic ◇ *nm, f* villager.

ville [vil] *nf* [petite, moyenne] town ; [importante] city ; **aller en ~** to go into town ; **habiter en ~** to live in town ; **~ champignon** town which

has mushroomed ; **~ dortoir/nouvelle** dormitory/new town ; **~ d'eau** spa (town).

villégiature [vileʒjatyr] *nf* holiday.

Villette [vilɛt] *n* : **la ~** *a cultural complex in north Paris (including a science museum, theatre and park).*

Vilnious [vilnjus] *n* Vilnius.

vin [vɛ̃] *nm* wine ; **~ blanc/rosé/rouge** white/rosé/red wine ; **~ champagnisé** champagne-style wine ; **~ résiné** retsina ; **~ de table** table wine.

◆ **vin d'honneur** *nm* reception.

vinaigre [vinɛgr] *nm* vinegar ; **~ de framboise/de vin** raspberry/wine vinegar ; **~ balsamique** balsamic vinegar ; **tourner au ~** *fig* to turn sour.

vinaigrer [4] [vinegre] *vt* to put vinegar on.

vinaigrette [vinegret] *nf* oil and vinegar dressing.

vinasse [vinas] *nf péj* plonk.

vindicatif, ive [vɛ̃dikatif, iv] *adj* vindictive.

vindicte [vɛ̃dikt] *nf* : **~ publique** JUR justice.

vingt [vɛ̃] *adj num* & *nm* twenty ; *voir aussi* **six.**

vingtaine [vɛ̃tɛn] *nf* : **une ~ de** about twenty.

vingtième [vɛ̃tjɛm] *adj num, nm* OU *nmf* twentieth ; *voir aussi* **sixième.**

vinicole [vinikɔl] *adj* wine-growing, wine-producing.

vinification [vinifikasjɔ̃] *nf* wine-making.

viol [vjɔl] *nm* - **1.** [de femme] rape ; **au ~!** rape! - **2.** [de sépulture] desecration ; [de sanctuaire] violation.

violacé, e [vjɔlase] *adj* purplish.

violation [vjɔlasjɔ̃] *nf* violation, breach ; **~ de domicile** unauthorized entry.

viole [vjɔl] *nf* viol.

violemment [vjɔlamɑ̃] *adv* - **1.** [frapper] violently - **2.** [rétorquer] sharply.

violence [vjɔlɑ̃s] *nf* violence ; **se faire ~** to force o.s.

violent, e [vjɔlɑ̃, ɑ̃t] *adj* - **1.** [personne, tempête] violent - **2.** *fig* [douleur, angoisse, chagrin] acute ; [haine, passion] violent - **3.** *fam* [excessif] annoying.

violenter [3] [vjɔlɑ̃te] *vt* to assault sexually.

violer [3] [vjɔle] *vt* - **1.** [femme] to rape - **2.** [loi, traité] to break - **3.** [sépulture] to desecrate ; [sanctuaire] to violate.

violet, ette [vjɔlɛ, ɛt] *adj* purple ; [pâle] violet.

➡ **violet** *nm* purple ; [pâle] violet.

violette [vjɔlɛt] *nf* violet.

violeur [vjɔlœr] *nm* rapist.

violon [vjɔlɔ̃] *nm* - **1.** [instrument] violin ; **accorder ses ~s** *fig* to come to an agreement - **2.** [musicien] violin (player) - **3.** *fam* [prison] nick *Br*, clink.

➡ **violon d'Ingres** *nm* hobby.

violoncelle [vjɔlɔ̃sɛl] *nm* - **1.** [instrument] cello - **2.** [musicien] cello (player).

violoncelliste [vjɔlɔ̃selist] *nmf* cellist.

violoneux [vjɔlɔnø] *nm* fiddler.

violoniste [vjɔlɔnist] *nmf* violinist.

VIP (*abr de* **very important person**) *nm* VIP.

vipère [vipɛr] *nf* viper.

virage [viraʒ] *nm* - **1.** [sur route] bend ; **négocier un ~** to negotiate a bend ; **prendre un ~** to take a bend ; **~ sans visibilité** blind corner ; **~ en épingle à cheveux** hairpin bend - **2.** [changement] turn - **3.** *CHIM* colour *Br* OU color *Am* change - **4.** *MÉD* positive reaction.

viral, e, aux [viral, o] *adj* viral.

virée [vire] *nf fam* : **faire une ~** [en voiture] to go for a spin ; [dans bars] ≃ to go on a pub crawl.

virement [virmɑ̃] *nm* - **1.** *FIN* transfer ; **~ bancaire/postal** bank/giro transfer ; **~ automatique** automatic transfer - **2.** *NAVIG* : **~ (de bord)** tacking.

virer [3] [vire] ◇ *vi* - **1.** [tourner] : **~ à droite/à gauche** to turn right/left - **2.** [étoffe] to change colour *Br* OU color *Am* ; **~ au blanc/jaune** to go white/yellow - **3.** *PHOT* to tone - **4.** *MÉD* to react positively ◇ *vt* - **1.** *FIN* to transfer - **2.** *fam* [renvoyer] to kick out.

virevolte [virvɔlt] *nf* - **1.** [mouvement] twirl - **2.** *fig* [volte-face] about-turn, U-turn.

virevolter [3] [virvɔlte] *vi* - **1.** [tourner] to twirl OU spin round - **2.** *fig* [changer de sujet] to flit from one subject to another.

virginal, e, aux [virʒinal, o] *adj* virginal.

virginité [virʒinite] *nf* - **1.** [de personne] virginity - **2.** [de sentiment] purity.

virgule [virgyl] *nf* [entre mots] comma ; [entre chiffres] (decimal) point.

viril, e [viril] *adj* virile.

virilité [virilite] *nf* virility.

virologie [virɔlɔʒi] *nf* virology.

virtualité [virtɥalite] *nf* potentiality, possibility.

virtuel, elle [virtɥɛl] *adj* potential ; **animal ~** cyberpet.

virtuellement [virtɥɛlmɑ̃] *adv* - **1.** [potentiellement] potentially - **2.** [pratiquement] virtually.

virtuose [virtɥoz] *nmf* virtuoso.

virtuosité [virtɥozite] *nf* virtuosity.

virulence [virylɑ̃s] *nf* virulence.

virulent, e [virylɑ̃, ɑ̃t] *adj* virulent.

virus [virys] *nm* INFORM & MÉD virus ; *fig* bug.

vis [vis] *nf* screw ; **serrer la ~ à qqn** *fig* to put the screws on sb.

visa [viza] *nm* visa ; **~ de censure** censor's certificate.

visage [vizaʒ] *nm* face ; **à ~ découvert** *fig* openly.

visagiste [vizaʒist] *nmf* beautician.

vis-à-vis [vizavi] *nm* - **1.** [personne] person sitting opposite - **2.** [tête-à-tête] encounter - **3.** [immeuble] : **avoir un ~** to have a building opposite.

➡ **vis-à-vis de** *loc prép* - **1.** [en face de] opposite - **2.** [en comparaison de] beside, compared with - **3.** [à l'égard de] towards *Br*, toward *Am*.

viscéral, e, aux [viseral, o] *adj* - **1.** ANAT visceral - **2.** *fam* [réaction] gut *(avant n)* ; [haine, peur] deep-seated.

viscère [visɛr] *nm* (*gén pl*) innards *(pl)*.

viscose [viskoz] *nf* viscose.

viscosité [viskozite] *nf* - **1.** [de liquide] viscosity - **2.** [de surface] stickiness.

visé, e [vize] *adj* - **1.** [concerné] concerned - **2.** [vérifié] stamped.

visée [vize] *nf* - **1.** [avec arme] aiming - **2.** (*gén pl*) *fig* [intention, dessein] aim.

viser [3] [vize] ◇ *vt* - **1.** [cible] to aim at - **2.** *fig* [poste] to aspire to, to aim for ; [personne] to be directed OU aimed at - **3.** *fam* [fille, voiture] to get a load of - **4.** [document] to check, to stamp ◇ *vi* to aim, to take aim ; **~ à** to aim at ; **~ à faire qqch** to aim to do sthg, to be intended to do sthg ; **~ haut** *fig* to aim high ; **ne pas ~ juste** not to aim accurately, to aim wide.

viseur [vizœr] *nm* - **1.** [d'arme] sights *(pl)* - **2.** PHOT viewfinder.

visibilité [vizibilite] *nf* visibility.

visible [vizibl] *adj* - **1.** [gén] visible - **2.** [personne] : **il n'est pas ~** he's not seeing visitors.

visiblement [vizibləmɑ̃] *adv* visibly.

visière [vizjɛr] *nf* - **1.** [de casque] visor - **2.** [de casquette] peak - **3.** [de protection] eyeshade.

visioconférence [vizjokɔ̃ferɑ̃s], **vidéoconférence** [videokɔ̃ferɑ̃s] *nf* videoconference.

vision [vizjɔ̃] *nf* - **1.** [faculté] eyesight, vision - **2.** [représentation] view, vision - **3.** [mirage] vision.

visionnaire [vizjɔnɛr] *nmf* & *adj* visionary.

visionner [3] [vizjɔne] *vt* to view.

visionneuse [vizjɔnøz] *nf* viewer.

visite [vizit] *nf* - **1.** [chez un ami, officielle] visit ; **avoir de la ~** *ou* **une ~** to have visitors ; **rendre ~ à qqn** to pay sb a visit - **2.** [MÉD - à l'extérieur] call, visit ; [- à l'hôpital] rounds *(pl)* ; **passer une ~ médicale** to have a medical - **3.** [de monument] tour - **4.** [d'expert] inspection.

visiter [3] [vizite] *vt* - **1.** [en touriste] to tour - **2.** [malade, prisonnier] to visit.

visiteur, euse [vizitœr, øz] *nm, f* visitor.

vison [vizɔ̃] *nm* mink.

visqueux, euse [viskø, øz] *adj* - **1.** [liquide] viscous - **2.** [surface] sticky - **3.** *péj* [personne, manières] slimy, smarmy.

visser [3] [vise] *vt* - **1.** [planches] to screw together - **2.** [couvercle] to screw down - **3.** [bouchon] to screw in ; [écrou] to screw on - **4.** *fam fig* [enfant] to keep a tight rein on.

visualisation [vizɥalizasjɔ̃] *nf* INFORM display mode.

visualiser [3] [vizɥalize] *vt* - **1.** [gén] to visualize - **2.** INFORM to display ; TECHNOL to make visible.

visuel, elle [vizɥɛl] *adj* visual.
➠ **visuel** *nm* INFORM visual display unit ; **~ graphique** graphical display unit.

visuellement [vizɥɛlmɑ̃] *adv* visually.

vital, e, aux [vital, o] *adj* vital.

vitalité [vitalite] *nf* vitality.

vitamine [vitamin] *nf* vitamin.

vitaminé, e [vitamine] *adj* with added vitamins, vitamin-enriched.

vite [vit] *adv* - **1.** [rapidement] quickly, fast ; **fais ~!** hurry up! ; **avoir ~ fait de faire qqch** to have been quick to do sthg - **2.** [tôt] soon.

vitesse [vites] *nf* - **1.** [gén] speed ; **prendre de la ~** to pick up *ou* gather speed ; **prendre**

qqn de ~ *fig* to outstrip sb ; **à toute ~** at top speed ; **~ de croisière** cruising speed - **2.** AUTOM gear ; **changer de ~** to change gear ; **en quatrième ~** *fam fig* at the double.

viticole [vitikɔl] *adj* wine-growing.

viticulteur, trice [vitikyltœr, tris] *nm, f* wine-grower.

viticulture [vitikyltyr] *nf* wine-growing.

vitrage [vitraʒ] *nm* - **1.** [vitres] windows *(pl)* - **2.** [toit] glass roof.

vitrail, aux [vitraj, o] *nm* stained-glass window.

vitre [vitr] *nf* - **1.** [de fenêtre] pane of glass, windowpane - **2.** [de voiture, train] window.

vitré, e [vitre] *adj* glass *(avant n)*.

vitrer [3] [vitre] *vt* to glaze.

vitreux, euse [vitrø, øz] *adj* - **1.** [roche] vitreous - **2.** [œil, regard] glassy, glazed.

vitrier [vitrije] *nm* glazier.

vitrification [vitrifikasjɔ̃] *nf* - **1.** [de parquet] sealing and varnishing - **2.** [d'émail] vitrification.

vitrifier [9] [vitrifje] *vt* - **1.** [parquet] to seal and varnish - **2.** [émail] to vitrify.

vitrine [vitrin] *nf* - **1.** [de boutique] (shop) window ; *fig* showcase ; **lécher les ~s** to go window-shopping - **2.** [meuble] display cabinet.

vitriol [vitrijɔl] *nm* vitriol.

vitupération [vityperasjɔ̃] *nf* vituperation.

vitupérer [18] [vitypere] *vt* to rail against.

vivable [vivabl] *adj* [appartement] livable-in ; [situation] bearable, tolerable ; [personne] : **il n'est pas ~** he's impossible to live with.

vivace [vivas] *adj* - **1.** [plante] perennial ; [arbre] hardy - **2.** *fig* [haine, ressentiment] deep-rooted, entrenched ; [souvenir] enduring.

vivacité [vivasite] *nf* - **1.** [promptitude - de personne] liveliness, vivacity ; **~ d'esprit** quick-wittedness - **2.** [de coloris, teint] intensity, brightness - **3.** [de propos] sharpness.

vivant, e [vivɑ̃, ɑ̃t] *adj* - **1.** [en vie] alive, living - **2.** [enfant, quartier] lively - **3.** [souvenir] still fresh - **4.** *fig* [preuve] living.
➠ **vivant** *nm* - **1.** [vie] : **du ~ de qqn** in sb's lifetime - **2.** [personne] : **les ~s** the living ; **un bon ~** *fig* a person who enjoys (the good things in) life.

vivarium [vivarjɔm] *nm* vivarium.

vivats [viva] *nmpl* cheers, cheering *(sg)*.

vive[1] [viv] *nf* [poisson] weever.

vive[2] [viv] *interj* three cheers for ; **~ le roi!** long live the King!

vivement [vivmɑ̃] ◇ *adv* - **1.** [agir] quickly - **2.** [répondre] sharply - **3.** [affecter] deeply ◇ *interj* : ~ **les vacances!** roll on the holidays! ; ~ **que l'été arrive** I'll be glad when summer comes, summer can't come quick enough.

vivier [vivje] *nm* - **1.** [de poissons] fish pond ; [dans un restaurant] fish tank - **2.** *fig* [concentration] breeding-ground.

vivifiant, e [vivifjɑ̃, ɑ̃t] *adj* invigorating, bracing.

vivifier [9] [vivifje] *vt* to invigorate.

vivipare [vivipar] *adj* viviparous.

vivisection [vivisɛksjɔ̃] *nf* vivisection.

vivoter [3] [vivɔte] *vi* - **1.** [personne] to live from hand to mouth - **2.** [affaire, commerce] to struggle to survive.

vivre [90] [vivr] ◇ *vi* to live ; [être en vie] to be alive ; ~ **de** to live on ; **faire** ~ **sa famille** to support one's family ; **être difficile/facile à** ~ to be hard/easy to get on with ; **avoir vécu** to have seen life ◇ *vt* - **1.** [passer] to spend - **2.** [éprouver] to experience ◇ *nm* : **le** ~ **et le couvert** board and lodging.

➤ **vivres** *nmpl* provisions ; **couper les** ~**s à qqn** *fig* to cut off sb's livelihood.

vivrier, ère [vivrije, ɛr] *adj* : **culture vivrière** food crops *(pl)*.

vizir [vizir] *nm* vizier.

VL (*abr de* **véhicule lourd**) *nm* HGV.

vlan [vlɑ̃] *interj* wham!, bang!

vo *abr de* **verso**.

VO (*abr de* **version originale**) *nf indicates that a film has not been dubbed.*

vocable [vɔkabl] *nm* term.

vocabulaire [vɔkabylɛr] *nm* - **1.** [gén] vocabulary - **2.** [livre] lexicon, glossary.

vocal, e, aux [vɔkal, o] *adj* : **ensemble** ~ choir ; ▷ **corde**.

vocalise [vɔkaliz] *nf* : **faire des** ~**s** to do singing exercises.

vocaliser [3] [vɔkalize] *vi* to do singing exercises.

vocatif [vɔkatif] *nm* vocative (case).

vocation [vɔkasjɔ̃] *nf* - **1.** [gén] vocation - **2.** [d'organisation] mission.

vocifération [vɔsiferasjɔ̃] *nf* shout, scream.

vociférer [18] [vɔsifere] *vt* to shout, to scream.

vodka [vɔdka] *nf* vodka.

vœu, x [vø] *nm* - **1.** *RELIG* [résolution] vow ; **faire le** ~ **de faire qqch** to vow to do sthg ; **faire** ~ **de** silence to take a vow of silence - **2.** [souhait, requête] wish.

➤ **vœux** *nmpl* greetings ; **meilleurs** ~**x** best wishes ; **tous nos** ~**x de bonheur** our best wishes for your future happiness.

vogue [vɔg] *nf* vogue, fashion ; **en** ~ fashionable, in vogue.

voguer [3] [vɔge] *vi littéraire* to sail.

voici [vwasi] *prép* - **1.** [pour désigner, introduire] here is/are ; **le** ~ here he/it is ; **les** ~ here they are ; **vous cherchiez des allumettes?** — **en** ~ were you looking for matches? — **there are some here** ; **l'homme que** ~ this man (here) ; ~ **ce qui s'est passé** this is what happened - **2.** [il y a] : ~ **trois mois** three months ago ; ~ **quelques années que je ne l'ai pas vu** I haven't seen him for some years (now), it's been some years since I last saw him.

voie [vwa] *nf* - **1.** [route] road ; **route à deux** ~**s** two-lane road ; ~ **navigable** waterway ; **la** ~ **publique** the public highway ; ~ **sans issue** no through road ; ~ **privée** private road - **2.** [rails] track, line ; [quai] platform ; ~ **ferrée** railway line *Br*, railroad line *Am* ; ~ **de garage** siding ; *fig* dead-end job - **3.** [mode de transport] route ; **par la** ~ **maritime/aérienne** by sea/air - **4.** *ANAT* passage, tract ; **par** ~ **buccale** *ou* **orale** orally, by mouth ; **par** ~ **rectale** by rectum ; ~ **respiratoire** respiratory tract - **5.** *fig* [chemin] : **être en bonne** ~ to be going well ; **être sur la bonne/mauvaise** ~ to be on the right/wrong track ; **mettre qqn sur la** ~ to put sb on the right track ; **ouvrir la** ~ to pave the way ; **la** ~ **royale** *fig* the high road (to success) ; **trouver sa** ~ to find one's feet - **6.** [filière, moyen] means *(pl)* ; **suivre la** ~ **hiérarchique** to go through the official channels *(pl)*.

➤ **voie de fait** *nf* assault.

➤ **Voie lactée** *nf* : **la Voie lactée** the Milky Way.

➤ **en voie de** *loc prép* on the way *ou* road to ; **en** ~ **de développement** developing.

voilà [vwala] *prép* - **1.** [pour désigner] there is/ are ; **le** ~ there he/it is ; **les** ~ there they are ; **me** ~ that's me, there I am ; **le** ~ **qui arrive** (look) he's here ; **vous cherchiez de l'encre?** — **en** ~ you were looking for ink? — there is some (over) there ; **la maison que** ~ that house (there) ; **nous** ~ **arrivés** we've arrived - **2.** [reprend ce dont on a parlé] that is ; [introduit ce dont on va parler] this is ; ~ **ce que j'en pense** this is/that is what I think ; ~ **tout** that's all ; **et** ~**!** there we are! - **3.** [il y a] : ~ **dix jours** ten days ago ; ~ **dix ans que je le connais** I've known him for ten years (now).

voilage [vwalaʒ] *nm* - **1.** [rideau] net curtain - **2.** [garniture] veil.

voile [vwal] <> *nf* - **1.** [de bateau] sail ; **mettre les ~s** *fam fig* to do a bunk, to scarper - **2.** [activité] sailing <> *nm* - **1.** [textile] voile - **2.** [coiffure] veil ; **lever le ~ sur** *fig* to lift the veil on - **3.** [de brume] mist - **4.** PHOT fogging (U) - **5.** MÉD shadow.

voilé, e [vwale] *adj* - **1.** [visage, allusion] veiled - **2.** [ciel, regard] dull - **3.** [roue] buckled - **4.** PHOT fogged - **5.** [son, voix] muffled.

voiler [3] [vwale] *vt* - **1.** [visage] to veil - **2.** [vérité, sentiment] to hide - **3.** [suj : brouillard, nuages] to cover - **4.** [roue] to buckle.

⇒ **se voiler** *vp* - **1.** [femme] to wear a veil - **2.** [ciel] to cloud over ; [yeux] to mist over - **3.** [roue] to buckle.

voilette [vwalɛt] *nf* veil.

voilier [vwalje] *nm* [bateau] sailing boat, sailboat *Am*.

voilure [vwalyr] *nf* - **1.** [de bateau] sails *(pl)* - **2.** [d'avion] wings *(pl)* - **3.** [de parachute] canopy.

voir [62] [vwar] <> *vt* - **1.** [gén] to see ; **je l'ai vu tomber** I saw him fall ; **faire ~ qqch à qqn** to show sb sthg ; **avoir assez vu qqn** *fam* to be fed up with sb ; **ne rien avoir à ~ avec** *fig* to have nothing to do with ; **je te vois bien papa!** I can just see you as a father! ; **essaie un peu, pour ~!** go on, just try it! ; **voyons, ...** [en réfléchissant] let's see, ... ; **ni vu ni connu** *fam* without anyone being any the wiser - **2.** [dossier, affaire] to look at *ou* into, to go over <> *vi* to see.

⇒ **se voir** *vp* - **1.** [se regarder] to see o.s., to watch o.s. - **2.** [se rencontrer] to see one another *ou* each other - **3.** [se remarquer] to be obvious, to show ; **ça se voit!** you can tell!

voire [vwar] *adv* even.

voirie [vwari] *nf* - **1.** ADMIN ≃ Department of Transport - **2.** [décharge] rubbish dump *Br*, garbage dump *Am*.

voisin, e [vwazɛ̃, in] <> *adj* - **1.** [pays, ville] neighbouring *Br*, neighboring *Am* ; [maison] next-door - **2.** [idée] similar <> *nm, f* neighbour *Br*, neighbor *Am* ; **~ de palier** next-door neighbour *Br ou* neighbor *Am (in a flat)*.

voisinage [vwazinaʒ] *nm* - **1.** [quartier] neighbourhood *Br*, neighborhood *Am* - **2.** [environs] vicinity - **3.** [relations] : **rapports de bon ~** (good) neighbourliness *Br ou* neighborliness *Am*.

voisiner [3] [vwazine] *vi* : **~ avec** to be next to.

voiture [vwatyr] *nf* - **1.** [automobile] car ; **~ de fonction** company car ; **~ de location** hire

car ; **~ d'occasion/de sport** second-hand/ sports car - **2.** [de train] carriage.

⇒ **voiture d'enfant** *nf* pram *Br*, baby carriage *Am*.

voix [vwa] *nf* - **1.** [gén] voice ; **~ caverneuse** hollow voice ; **~ de fausset** falsetto voice ; **~ de stentor** stentorian voice ; **~ de ténor** tenor voice ; **~ off** voice-over ; **à mi-~** in an undertone ; **à ~ basse** in a low voice, quietly ; **à ~ haute** [parler] in a loud voice ; [lire] aloud ; **de vive ~** in person ; **avoir ~ au chapitre** *fig* to have a say in the matter - **2.** [suffrage] vote ; **recueillir des ~** to win *ou* get votes.

Vojvodine [vojvodin] *nf* : **la ~** Vojvodina.

vol [vɔl] *nm* - **1.** [d'oiseau, avion] flight ; **attraper qqch au ~** to catch sthg in mid-air ; **~ à voile** gliding ; **à ~ d'oiseau** as the crow flies ; **en plein ~** in flight - **2.** [groupe d'oiseaux] flight, flock - **3.** [délit] theft ; **~ avec effraction** breaking and entering ; **~ à l'étalage** shoplifting.

vol. (*abr de* volume) vol.

volage [vɔlaʒ] *adj littéraire* fickle.

volaille [vɔlaj] *nf* : **la ~** poultry, (domestic) fowl.

volant, e [vɔlɑ̃, ɑ̃t] *adj* - **1.** [qui vole] flying ; **personnel ~** aircrew - **2.** [mobile] : **feuille ~e** loose sheet.

⇒ **volant** *nm* - **1.** [de voiture] steering wheel - **2.** [de robe] flounce - **3.** [de badminton] shuttlecock.

volatil, e [vɔlatil] *adj* volatile.

⇒ **volatile** *nm* (domestic) fowl.

volatiliser [3] [vɔlatilize] ⇒ **se volatiliser** *vp* to volatilize ; *fig* to vanish into thin air.

vol-au-vent [vɔlovɑ̃] *nm inv* vol-au-vent.

volcan [vɔlkɑ̃] *nm* volcano ; *fig* spitfire ; **être assis sur un ~** *fig* to be sitting on the edge of a volcano.

volcanique [vɔlkanik] *adj* volcanic ; *fig* [tempérament] fiery.

volcanologue = vulcanologue.

volée [vɔle] *nf* - **1.** [d'oiseau] flight - **2.** [de flèches] volley ; **une ~ de coups** a hail of blows - **3.** FOOTBALL & TENNIS volley - **4.** *fam* [gifle] thrashing, hiding.

voler [3] [vɔle] <> *vi* to fly <> *vt* [personne] to rob ; [chose] to steal ; **~ qqch à qqn** to steal sthg from sb.

volet [vɔlɛ] *nm* - **1.** [de maison] shutter - **2.** [de dépliant] leaf ; [d'émission] part - **3.** INFORM drive door.

voleter [27] [vɔlte] *vi* - **1.** [papillon] to flit *ou* flutter about - **2.** [robe] to flutter.

voleur, euse [vɔlœr, øz] <> *adj* thieving <> *nm, f* thief ; **au ~!** stop thief!

volière [vɔljɛr] *nf* aviary.

volley-ball [vɔlɛbol] (*pl* **volley-balls**) *nm* volleyball.

volleyeur, euse [vɔlɛjœr, øz] *nm, f* volleyball player.

volontaire [vɔlɔ̃tɛr] ◇ *nmf* volunteer ◇ *adj* - **1.** [omission] deliberate ; [activité] voluntary - **2.** [enfant] strong-willed.

volontairement [vɔlɔ̃tɛrmɑ̃] *adv* deliberately ; [offrir] voluntarily.

volontariat [vɔlɔ̃tarja] *nm* voluntary service *(in armed forces)*.

volontariste [vɔlɔ̃tarist] *nmf* & *adj* voluntarist.

volonté [vɔlɔ̃te] *nf* - **1.** [vouloir] will ; à ~ unlimited, as much as you like ; **les dernières ~s** last wishes ; **faire les quatre ~s de qqn** *fam fig* to obey sb's every whim - **2.** [disposition] : **bonne ~** willingness, good will ; **mauvaise ~** unwillingness - **3.** [détermination] willpower.

volontiers [vɔlɔ̃tje] *adv* - **1.** [avec plaisir] with pleasure, gladly, willingly - **2.** [affable, bavard] naturally.

volt [vɔlt] *nm* volt.

voltage [vɔltaʒ] *nm* voltage.

volte [vɔlt] *nf* - **1.** [de cheval] volt, volte - **2.** *littéraire* [pirouette] pirouette.

volte-face [vɔltəfas] *nf inv* about-turn *Br*, about-face *Am* ; *fig* U-turn, about-turn *Br*, about-face *Am*.

voltige [vɔltiʒ] *nf* - **1.** [au trapèze] trapeze work ; **haute ~** flying trapeze act ; *fam fig* mental gymnastics *(U)* - **2.** [à cheval] circus riding - **3.** [en avion] aerobatics *(U)*.

voltiger [17] [vɔltiʒe] *vi* - **1.** [acrobate] to perform on a flying trapeze - **2.** [insecte, oiseau] to flit *ou* flutter about - **3.** [feuilles] to flutter about.

voltigeur [vɔltiʒœr] *nm* - **1.** [acrobate] trapeze artist - **2.** *MIL* light infantryman - **3.** *Can BASE-BALL* : **~ gauche/droit** left/right fielder ; **~ du centre** centre fielder.

volubile [vɔlybil] *adj* voluble.

volubilis [vɔlybilis] *nm* morning glory.

volubilité [vɔlybilite] *nf* volubility.

volume [vɔlym] *nm* volume.

volumineux, euse [vɔyminø, øz] *adj* voluminous, bulky.

volupté [vɔlypte] *nf* [sensuelle] sensual *ou* voluptuous pleasure ; [morale, esthétique] delight.

voluptueusement [vɔlyptɥøzmɑ̃] *adv* voluptuously.

voluptueux, euse [vɔlyptɥø, øz] *adj* voluptuous.

volute [vɔlyt] *nf* - **1.** [de fumée] wreath - **2.** *ARCHIT* volute, helix.

vomi [vɔmi] *nm fam* vomit.

vomir [32] [vɔmir] *vt* - **1.** [aliments] to bring up - **2.** [fumées] to belch, to spew (out) ; [injures] to spit out.

vomissement [vɔmismɑ̃] *nm* - **1.** [action] vomiting - **2.** [vomissure] vomit.

vomitif, ive [vɔmitif, iv] *adj* emetic ; *fam fig* revolting, sickening.
➡ **vomitif** *nm* emetic.

vont ➡ aller.

vorace [vɔras] *adj* voracious.

voracement [vɔrasmɑ̃] *adv* voraciously.

voracité [vɔrasite] *nf* voracity.

vos ➡ votre.

votant, e [vɔtɑ̃, ɑ̃t] *nm, f* voter.

vote [vɔt] *nm* vote ; **~ à main levée** (ballot by) show of hands ; **~ secret, ~ à bulletins secrets** secret ballot.

voter [3] [vɔte] ◇ *vi* to vote ◇ *vt POLIT* to vote for ; [crédits] to vote ; [loi] to pass.

votre [vɔtr] (*pl* **vos** [vo]) *adj poss* your.

vôtre [votr] ➡ **le vôtre** (*f* **la vôtre**, *pl* **les vôtres**) *pron poss* yours ; **les ~s** your family ; **vous et les ~s** people like you ; **je suis des ~s** I'm on your side ; **vous devriez y mettre du ~** you ought to pull your weight ; **à la ~!** your good health!

vouer [6] [vwe] *vt* - **1.** [promettre, jurer] : **~ qqch à qqn** to swear *ou* vow sthg to sb - **2.** [consacrer] to devote - **3.** [condamner] : **être voué à** to be doomed to.
➡ **se vouer** *vp* : **se ~ à** to dedicate *ou* devote o.s. to.

vouloir [57] [vulwar] ◇ *vt* - **1.** [gén] to want ; **voulez-vous boire quelque chose?** would you like something to drink? ; **veux-tu te taire!** will you be quiet! ; **je voudrais savoir** I would like to know ; **~ que** (+ subjonctif) : **je veux qu'il parte** I want him to leave ; **~ qqch de qqn/qqch** to want sthg from sb/sthg ; **combien voulez-vous de votre maison?** how much do you want for your house? ; **ne pas ~ de qqn/qqch** not to want sb/sthg ; **je veux bien** I don't mind ; **si tu veux** if you like, if you want ; **comme tu veux!** as you like! ; **veuillez vous asseoir** please take a seat ; **sans le ~** without meaning *ou* wishing to, unintentionally - **2.** [suj : coutume] to demand - **3.** [s'attendre à] to expect ; **que voulez-vous que j'y fasse?** what do you want me to do about it? - **4.** *loc* : **~ dire** to mean ; **si on veut** more or

less, if you like ; **en ~** to be a real go-getter ; **en ~ à qqn** to have a grudge against sb ; **tu l'auras voulu!** on your own head (be it)!
◇ *nm* : **le bon ~ de qqn** sb's good will.

➡ **se vouloir** *vp* : **elle se veut différente** she thinks she's different ; **s'en ~ de faire qqch** to be cross with o.s. for doing sthg.

voulu, e [vuly] ◇ *pp* ▷ **vouloir** ◇ *adj* - **1.** [requis] requisite - **2.** [délibéré] intentional.

vous [vu] *pron pers* - **1.** [sujet, objet direct] you ; **dire ~ à qqn** to use the "vous" form to sb - **2.** [objet indirect] (to) you - **3.** [après préposition, comparatif] you - **4.** [réfléchi] yourself, *(pl)* yourselves.

➡ **vous-même** *pron pers* yourself.
➡ **vous-mêmes** *pron pers* yourselves.

voûte [vut] *nf* - **1.** ARCHIT vault ; *fig* arch ; **la ~ céleste** the sky - **2.** ANAT : **~ du palais** roof of the mouth ; **~ plantaire** arch (of the foot).

voûter [3] [vute] *vt* to arch over, to vault.
➡ **se voûter** *vp* to be *ou* become stooped.

vouvoiement [vuvwamã] *nm* use of the "vous" form.

vouvoyer [13] [vuvwaje] *vt* : **~ qqn** to use the 'vous' form to sb.

voyage [vwajaʒ] *nm* journey, trip ; **les ~s** travel *(sg)*, travelling *(U)* Br, traveling *(U)* Am ; **bon ~!** bon voyage!, have a good *ou* safe journey! ; **partir en ~** to go away, to go on a trip ; **~ d'affaires** business trip ; **~ organisé** package tour ; **~ de noces** honeymoon.

voyager [17] [vwajaʒe] *vi* to travel.

voyageur, euse [vwajaʒœr, øz] *nm, f* traveller Br, traveler Am ; **~ de commerce** commercial traveller Br *ou* traveler Am.

voyagiste [vwajaʒist] *nm* tour operator.

voyance [vwajãs] *nf* clairvoyance.

voyant, e [vwajã, ãt] ◇ *adj* loud, gaudy ◇ *nm, f* [devin] seer ; **~e extralucide** clairvoyant.
➡ **voyant** *nm* [lampe] light ; AUTOM indicator (light) ; **~ d'essence/d'huile** petrol/oil warning light.

voyelle [vwajɛl] *nf* vowel.

voyeur, euse [vwajœr, øz] *nm, f* voyeur, Peeping Tom.

voyeurisme [vwajœrism] *nm* voyeurism.

voyou [vwaju] *nm* - **1.** [garnement] urchin - **2.** [loubard] lout.

VPC *(abr de* **vente par correspondance)** *nf* mail order sales.

vrac [vrak] ➡ **en vrac** *loc adv* - **1.** [sans emballage] loose - **2.** [en désordre] higgledy-piggledy - **3.** [au poids] in bulk.

vrai, e [vrɛ] *adj* - **1.** [histoire] true ; **c'est** *ou* **il est ~ que ...** it's true that ... ; **c'est pas ~!** *fam* never!, I don't believe it! - **2.** [or, perle, nom] real - **3.** [personne] natural - **4.** [ami, raison] real, true.
➡ **vrai** *nm* : **le ~** truth ; **être dans le ~** to be right ; **à ~ dire, à dire ~** to tell the truth.

vraiment [vrɛmã] *adv* really.

vraisemblable [vrɛsãblabl] *adj* likely, probable ; [excuse] plausible.

vraisemblablement [vrɛsãblabləmã] *adv* probably, in all probability.

vraisemblance [vrɛsãblãs] *nf* likelihood, probability ; [d'excuse] plausibility ; **contre toute ~** implausibly ; **selon toute ~** in all probability.

V/Réf *(abr de* **Votre référence)** your ref.

vrille [vrij] *nf* - **1.** BOT tendril - **2.** [outil] gimlet - **3.** [spirale] spiral.

vriller [3] [vrije] ◇ *vi* - **1.** [avion] to spin - **2.** [parachute] to twist ◇ *vt* to bore into.

vrombir [32] [vrɔbir] *vi* to hum.

vrombissement [vrɔbismã] *nm* humming *(U)*.

VRP *(abr de* **voyageur, représentant, placier)** *nm* rep.

VTT *(abr de* **vélo tout terrain)** *nm* mountain bike.

vu, e [vy] ◇ *pp* ▷ **voir** ◇ *adj* - **1.** [perçu] : **être bien/mal ~** to be acceptable/unacceptable - **2.** [compris] clear.
➡ **vu** *prép* given, in view of.
➡ **vue** *nf* - **1.** [sens, vision] sight, eyesight - **2.** [regard] gaze ; **à première ~e** at first sight ; **à ~e** on sight ; **de ~e** by sight ; **en ~e** [vedette] in the public eye ; **à ~e de nez** at a rough guess ; **à ~e d'œil** visibly ; **en mettre plein la ~e à qqn** *fam fig* to dazzle sb ; **perdre qqn de ~e** to lose touch with sb - **3.** [panorama, idée] view ; **~e d'ensemble** *fig* overview ; **avoir qqn/qqch en ~e** to have sb/sthg in mind - **4.** CIN ▷ **prise.**
➡ **vues** *nfpl* plans ; **avoir des ~es sur** to have designs on, to have one's eye on.
➡ **en vue de** *loc prép* with a view to.
➡ **vu que** *loc conj* given that, seeing that.

vulcaniser [3] [vylkanize] *vt* to vulcanize.

vulcanologue [vylkanɔlɔg], **volcanologue** [vɔlkanɔlɔg] *nmf* vulcanologist, volcanologist.

vulgaire [vylgɛr] *adj* - **1.** [grossier] vulgar, coarse - **2.** *(avant n)* *péj* [quelconque] common - **3.** [courant] common, popular.

vulgairement [vylgɛrmã] *adv* - **1.** [grossière-**

ment] vulgarly, coarsely **- 2.** [couramment] commonly, popularly.

vulgarisation [vylgarizasjɔ̃] *nf* popularization.

vulgariser [3] [vylgarize] *vt* to popularize.

vulgarité [vylgarite] *nf* vulgarity, coarseness.

vulnérabilité [vylnerabilite] *nf* vulnerability.

vulnérable [vylnerabl] *adj* vulnerable.

vulve [vylv] *nf* vulva.

VVF (*abr de* village vacances famille) *nm state-subsidized holiday village.*

vx *abr de* vieux.

w, W [dublǝve] *nm inv* w, W.

wagon [vagɔ̃] *nm* carriage ; **~ fumeurs** smoking carriage ; **~ de marchandises** goods wagon *ou* truck ; **~ non-fumeurs** non-smoking carriage ; **~de première/seconde classe** first-class/second-class carriage.

wagon-citerne [vagɔ̃sitɛrn] (*pl* **wagons-citernes**) *nm* tank wagon.

wagon-lit [vagɔ̃li] (*pl* **wagons-lits**) *nm* sleeping car, sleeper.

wagonnet [vagɔne] *nm* small truck.

wagon-restaurant [vagɔ̃rɛstɔrɑ̃] (*pl* **wagons-restaurants**) *nm* restaurant *ou* dining car.

Walkman® [wɔkman] *nm* personal stereo, Walkman®.

wallon, onne [walɔ̃, ɔn] *adj* Walloon.
◆ **wallon** *nm* [langue] Walloon.
◆ **Wallon, onne** *nm, f* Walloon.

Wallonie [walɔni] *nf* : **la ~** Southern Belgium (*where French and Walloon are spoken*).

wapiti [wapiti] *nm* wapiti.

Washington [waʃiŋtɔn] *n* **- 1.** [ville] Washington DC **- 2.** [État] Washington State.

water-polo [watɛrpolo] *nm* water polo.

waterproof [watɛrpruːf] *adj inv* waterproof.

watt [wat] *nm* watt.

Wb (*abr de* weber) Wb.

W.-C. [vese] (*abr de* water closet) *nmpl* WC (*sg*), toilets.

Web [wɛb] *nm* : **le ~** the Web, the web.

webmestre [wɛbmɛstr], **webmaster** [wɛbmastœr] *nm* webmaster.

week-end [wikɛnd] (*pl* **week-ends**) *nm* weekend ; **bon ~!** have a good *ou* nice weekend! ; **partir en ~** to go away for the weekend.

Wellington [wɛliŋtɔn] *n* Wellington.

western [wɛstɛrn] *nm* western.

Wh (*abr de* wattheure) Wh.

whisky [wiski] (*pl* **whiskies**) *nm* whisky ; **~ sec** straight *ou* neat whisky.

whist [wist] *nm* whist.

white-spirit [wajtspirit] (*pl* **white-spirits**) *nm* white spirit.

wok [wɔk] *nm* wok.

WWW (*abr de* World Wide Web) *nf* WWW.

WYSIWYG [wiziwig] (*abr de* what you see is what you get) WYSIWYG.

x, X [iks] *nm inv* x, X ; **l'X** *prestigious engineering college in Paris.*

xénophobe [gzenofɔb] ◇ *nmf* xenophobe ◇ *adj* xenophobic.

xénophobie [gzenofɔbi] *nf* xenophobia.

xérès [gzerɛs, xerɛs] *nm* sherry.

xylophone [ksilɔfɔn] *nm* xylophone.

youpi [jupi] *interj* yippee!
youyou [juju] *nm* dinghy.
Yo-yo® [jɔjɔ] *nm inv* yo-yo.
yucca [juka] *nm* yucca.

y¹, Y [igrɛk] *nm inv* y, Y.
y² [i] ◇ *adv* [lieu] there ; **j'y vais demain** I'm going there tomorrow ; **mets-y du sel** put some salt in it ; **va voir sur la table si les clefs y sont** go and see if the keys are on the table ; **on ne peut pas couper cet arbre, des oiseaux y ont fait leur nid** you can't cut down that tree, some birds have built their nest there *ou* in it ; **ils ont ramené des vases anciens et y ont fait pousser des fleurs exotiques** they brought back some antique vases and grew exotic flowers in them ◇ *pron (la traduction varie selon la préposition utilisée avec le verbe)* : **pensez-y** think about it ; **n'y comptez pas** don't count on it ; **j'y suis!** I've got it! ; *voir aussi* **aller, avoir** *etc.*

yacht [jɔt] *nm* yacht.
yacht-club [jɔtklœb] *(pl* **yacht-clubs)** *nm* yacht club.
Yaoundé [jaunde] *n* Yaoundé.
yaourt [jaurt], **yogourt, yoghourt** [jɔgurt] *nm* yoghurt ; **~ aux fruits/nature** fruit/plain yoghurt.
yaourtière [jaurtjɛr] *nf* yoghurt maker.
Yémen [jemɛn] *nm* : **le ~** Yemen ; **au ~ in** Yemen.
yéménite [jemenit] *adj* Yemeni.
→ Yéménite *nmf* Yemeni.
yen [jɛn] *nm* yen.
yeux ▷ **œil.**
yé-yé [jeje] *vieilli* ◇ *nmf inv* pop fan ◇ *adj inv* pop *(avant n).*
yiddish [jidiʃ] *nm inv* & *adj inv* Yiddish.
yoga [jɔga] *nm* yoga.
yoghourt = **yaourt.**
yogi [jɔgi] *nm* yogi.
yogourt = **yaourt.**
yougoslave [jugɔslav] *adj* Yugoslav, Yugoslavian.
→ Yougoslave *nmf* Yugoslav, Yugoslavian.
Yougoslavie [jugɔslavi] *nf* : **la ~** Yugoslavia ; **l'ex-~** the former Yugoslavia.

z, Z [zɛd] *nm inv* z, Z.
ZAC, Zac [zak] *(abr de* **zone d'aménagement concerté)** *nf* area earmarked for local government planning project.
ZAD, Zad [zad] *(abr de* **zone d'aménagement différé)** *nf* area earmarked for future development.
Zagreb [zagrɛb] *n* Zagreb.
Zaïre [zair] *nm* : **le ~** Zaïre ; **au ~ in** Zaïre.
zaïrois, e [zairwa, az] *adj* Zairian.
→ Zaïrois, e *nm, f* Zairian.
zakouski [zakuski] *nmpl* zakuski, zakouski.
Zambie [zãbi] *nf* : **la ~** Zambia.
zambien, enne [zãbjɛ̃, ɛn] *adj* Zambian.
→ Zambien, enne *nm, f* Zambian.
zapper [3] [zape] *vi* to zap, to channel-hop.
zappeur, euse [zapœr, øz] *nm, f* channel hopper, zapper.
zapping [zapiŋ] *nm* zapping, channel-hopping.
zèbre [zɛbr] *nm* zebra ; **un drôle de ~** *fam fig* an oddball.
zébrer [18] [zebre] *vt* to streak, to stripe.
zébrure [zebryr] *nf* **- 1.** [de pelage] stripe **- 2.** [marque] weal.
zébu [zeby] *nm* zebu.
ZEC [zɛk] *(abr de* **zone d'exploitation contrôlée)** *nf Can* controlled harvesting zone.
zélateur, trice [zelatœr, tris] *nm, f* zealot.
zèle [zɛl] *nm* zeal ; **faire du ~** *péj* to be over-zealous.
zélé, e [zele] *adj* zealous.
zen [zɛn] ◇ *nm* Zen ◇ *adj inv* Zen ; **rester ~** to keep cool.

zénith [zenit] *nm* zenith ; **être au ~ de** *fig* to be at the height *ou* peak of.

ZEP, Zep [zɛp] (*abr de* **zone d'éducation prioritaire**) *nf* designated area with special educational needs.

zéro [zero] <> *nm* - **1.** [chiffre] zero, nought ; [énoncé dans un numéro de téléphone] O *Br*, zero *Am* - **2.** [nombre] nought, nothing ; **deux buts à ~** two goals to nil - **3.** [de graduation] freezing point, zero ; **à ~** at zero ; **au-dessus/au-dessous de ~** above/below (zero) ; **avoir le moral à ~** *fig* to be *ou* feel down ; **repartir à** *ou* **de ~** to start again from scratch - **4.** *fam* [personne] dead loss <> *adj* : **~ faute** no mistakes.

zeste [zɛst] *nm* peel, zest ; **~ de citron** lemon peel *ou* zest.

zézaiement [zezɛmɑ̃] *nm* lisp.

zézayer [11] [zezeje] *vi* to lisp.

ZI *abr de* **zone industrielle**.

zibeline [ziblin] *nf* sable.

zieuter, zyeuter [3] [zjøte] *vt fam* to get an eyeful of.

ZIF, Zif [zif] (*abr de* **zone d'intervention foncière**) *nf* area earmarked for local government planning project.

zigoto [zigoto] *nm fam* : **un drôle de ~** an oddball.

zigouiller [3] [ziguje] *vt fam* to bump off.

zigzag [zigzag] *nm* zigzag ; **en ~** winding.

zigzaguer [3] [zigzage] *vi* to zigzag (along).

Zimbabwe [zimbabwe] *nm* : **le ~** Zimbabwe ; **au ~** in Zimbabwe.

zimbabwéen, enne [zimbabweɛ̃, ɛn] *adj* Zimbabwean.

➥ **Zimbabwéen, enne** *nm, f* Zimbabwean.

zinc [zɛ̃g] *nm* - **1.** [matière] zinc - **2.** *fam* [comptoir] bar - **3.** *fam* [avion] crate.

zinzin [zɛ̃zɛ̃] *adj fam* cracked.

Zip® [zip] *nm* zip *Br*, zipper *Am*.

zipper [3] [zipe] *vt* to zip up.

zizanie [zizani] *nf* : **semer la ~** *fig* to sow discord.

zizi [zizi] *nm fam* willy *Br*, peter *Am*.

zodiacal, e, aux [zodjakal, o] *adj* [signe] of the zodiac ; [position] in the zodiac.

zodiaque [zodjak] *nm* zodiac.

zombi [zɔ̃bi] *nm fam* zombie.

zona [zona] *nm* shingles (*U*).

zone [zon] *nf* - **1.** [région] zone, area ; **~ d'action** area of operations ; **~ bleue** restricted parking zone ; **~ érogène** erogenous zone ; **~ franche** free zone ; **~ industrielle** industrial estate *Br ou* park *Am* ; **~ piétonne** *ou* **piétonnière** pedestrian precinct *Br ou* zone *Am* - **2.** *fam* [faubourg] : **la ~** the slum belt.

zoner [3] [zone] *vi* to hang about, to hang around.

zoo [zo(o)] *nm* zoo.

zoologie [zɔɔlɔʒi] *nf* zoology.

zoologiste [zɔɔlɔʒist] *nmf* zoologist.

zoom [zum] *nm* - **1.** [objectif] zoom (lens) - **2.** [gros plan] zoom.

zoophile [zɔɔfil] <> *nmf* person who practises bestiality <> *adj* of *ou* relating to bestiality.

zoulou, e [zulu] *adj* Zulu.

➥ **Zoulou, e** *nm, f* : **les Zoulous** the Zulus.

zozo [zozo] *nm fam* mug.

zozoter [3] [zozote] *vi* to lisp.

ZUP, Zup [zyp] (*abr de* **zone à urbaniser en priorité**) *nf* area earmarked for urgent urban development.

Zurich [zyrik] *n* Zörich.

zut [zyt] *interj fam* damn!

zyeuter = **zieuter**.

zygomatique [zigomatik] *adj* zygomatic.

Vivre au Royaume-Uni et aux États-Unis

SOMMAIRE

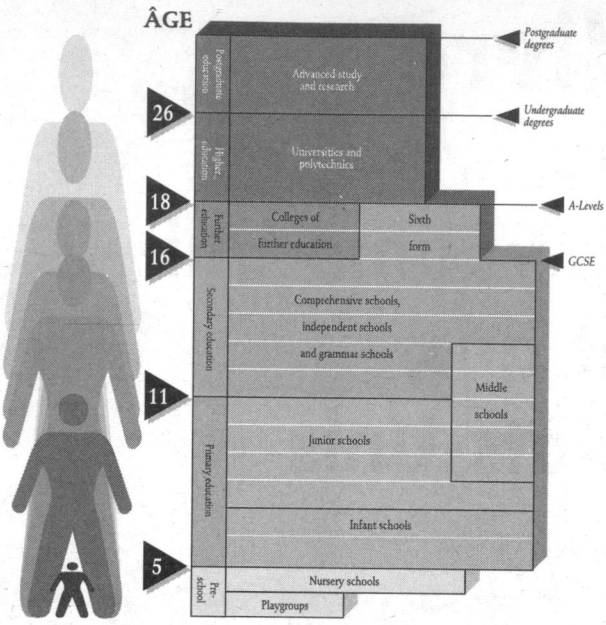

Au Royaume-Uni, l'enseignement est obligatoire pour les enfants âgés de 5 à 16 ans. Le système éducatif est très décentralisé et pris en charge en grande partie par l'administration régionale. Il s'organise de la façon suivante :

Enseignement préscolaire (jusqu'à 5 ans) Cette première étape n'est pas obligatoire, mais il est possible d'inscrire les enfants, à partir de 2 ans, dans une *nursery school* publique ou privée. Beaucoup d'enfants vont aussi dans des *playgroups* (garderies) animés par les parents eux-mêmes.

Enseignement primaire (5-11 ans) Il est dispensé dans les *primary schools,* qui se divisent normalement en *infant schools* (5-7 ans) et *junior schools* (7-11 ans), souvent dans les mêmes locaux. Dans certaines régions, il existe des *middle schools* pour les enfants de 8 à 13 ans, qui vont ensuite dans une *upper secondary school*. Certaines écoles primaires privées reçoivent le nom de *prep schools* ou *preparatory schools*.

Enseignement secondaire (11-16/18 ans) Il se fait dans des établissements publics ou privés de plusieurs types :

▶ **comprehensive schools** Il s'agit d'écoles financées par l'État et généralement mixtes. La majorité des jeunes Britanniques sont inscrits dans ces *comprehensive schools*.

▶ **independent schools** Ces établissements privés, financés par des droits de scolarité, sont communément appelés *private schools* ou *public schools*. Ils accueillent une petite proportion du nombre total d'élèves (environ 6 %) ; on trouve parmi eux des écoles prestigieuses telles qu' Eton ou Harrow.

▶ **grammar schools** Ce sont des écoles secondaires recevant une aide de l'État mais pouvant être privées, réputées dispenser un enseignement de qualité. L'admission se fait sur concours ou sur dossier. Moins de 5% des élèves fréquentent ce type d'école.

Programmes
Pendant les cinq premières années du secondaire, la plupart des élèves suivent un programme national *(national curriculum)* prescrit par le gouvernement. Vers l'âge de 16 ans, la majorité des élèves passent l'examen du *General Certificate of Secondary Education (GCSE)*, à l'issue duquel, qu'ils l'aient réussi ou pas, la moitié d'entre eux environ arrêtent leurs études.

▶ **A-levels** Ceux qui souhaitent entrer dans l'enseignement supérieur doivent faire encore deux ans d'études et préparer l'examen du *GCE Advanced Level* (ou *A-levels*) en Angleterre, au pays de Galles et en Irlande du Nord, le plus souvent dans trois matières de leur choix. En Écosse, où le système éducatif est différent, on passe un examen appelé *Highers*.

Further education (16-18 ans)
Ce terme désigne les années d'études postérieures à la fin de l'enseignement obligatoire. Ceux qui préparent les *A-levels* peuvent rester dans le même établissement, dans une classe appelée *sixth form,* ou bien s'inscrire dans un autre établissement. Ces études sont très souvent à caractère professionnel ; elles se font dans des *colleges of further education,* des écoles des beaux-arts, des établissements agricoles, etc.

Oxbridge

Les universités d'Oxford et de Cambridge (connues sous le nom collectif d'*Oxbridge*), fondées toutes deux au XIIe siècle, se distinguent en cela des autres universités britanniques, issues de l'expansion de l'enseignement supérieur dans les années 1960 –ce sont ce que l'on appelle les *redbrick universities*– ou de la promotion au statut d'université au début des années 1990, des ex-*polytechnics,* spécialisées dans les filières techniques. Bien qu'aujourd'hui la moitié environ des étudiants d'Oxford et de Cambridge viennent de lycées publics, les diplômés de ces deux établissements sont toujours considérés comme des privilégiés, en raison de leur surreprésentation dans certains milieux professionnels influents tels que la finance, la politique, les médias et les professions juridiques.

Enseignement supérieur (18-26 ans)
Les universités délivrent des *undergraduate degrees* (licence ou maîtrise) en lettres, sciences, sciences humaines, droit et médecine. Pour entrer à l'université, il faut avoir obtenu à l'examen des *A-levels* de bonne notes dans un nombre minimal de matières. Le nombre total de places dans les universités étant limité, la concurrence est féroce. Il existe un système de bourses accordées par les autorités régionales jusqu'au niveau licence, mais elles sont parfois insuffisantes et doivent être complétées par une contribution des parents ou un emprunt étudiant à taux réduit. Les *undergraduate degrees* durent en moyenne trois ans. Les étudiants ayant réussi leurs examens finals reçoivent leur diplôme lors de la cérémonie de *graduation*. Ceux qui souhaitent faire un troisième cycle deviennent des *postgraduates* et entreprennent un cursus de recherche conduisant à l'obtention d'un *higher degree* ou d'un *doctorate* (doctorat).

Cours pour adultes
Ils sont dispensés par les *colleges of further education* et les départements de formation continue des universités. Les adultes peuvent également s'inscrire aux cours par correspondance de l'*Open University,* fondée en 1969, et obtenir un diplôme d'*undergraduate* ou de *postgraduate,* même sans qualification préalable.

L e terme «Royaume-Uni» est en fait l'abréviation de «Royaume-Uni de Grande-Bretagne et d'Irlande du Nord» *(United Kingdom of Great Britain and Northern Ireland)*. La Grande-Bretagne se compose

Région	Superficie (kilomètres carrés)	Population
■ Angleterre	130 400	46 161 000
■ Pays de Galles	20 800	2 798 000
■ Écosse	78 800	4 957 000
■ Irlande du Nord	14 000	1 583 000

de l'Angleterre, du pays de Galles et de l'Écosse. Quant à l'expression «îles Britanniques», elle désigne le groupe d'îles composé de la Grande-Bretagne, de l'Irlande et de dépendances telles que les îles Anglo-Normandes et l'île de Man. Les quatre régions qui forment le Royaume-Uni ont un gouvernement commun, bien qu'il existe un Parlement écossais et une Assemblée galloise qui gèrent les affaires intérieures dans ces deux régions. Chacune de ces nations a une identité culturelle à part. Le pays de Galles possède sa propre langue, le gallois, d'origine celte, même si l'anglais reste la langue dominante. L'Écosse jouit d'une plus grande autonomie que le pays de Galles, avec un système éducatif et un système judiciaire indépendants. Le gaélique, langue écossaise elle aussi d'origine celte, est moins répandu que le gallois. L'Irlande est coupée en deux politiquement, et la population d'Irlande du Nord est majoritairement protestante, alors que celle de la république d'Irlande, ou *Éire* en gaélique, est majoritairement catholique.

Géographie
Le Royaume-Uni est environ deux fois plus petit que la France. Il y a à peu près 1 000 km entre la côte sud de l'Angleterre et l'extrémité nord de l'Écosse (hors îles), et moins de 500 km d'est en ouest au point le plus large. En Angleterre, l'intérieur des terres est plat et de faible altitude, alors que le relief est nettement plus élevé en Écosse et au pays de Galles. L'Irlande du Nord et l'Écosse ne sont éloignées l'une de l'autre, en leur point le plus proche, que d'une vingtaine de kilomètres. Les paysages d'Irlande du Nord se caractérisent par des montagnes peu élevées et des champs vallonnés. Quatre-vingt-dix pour cent de la population britannique sont concentrés dans les agglomérations urbaines comprises entre Londres et Manchester.

Administration régionale
Le Royaume-Uni se divise en unités administratives appelées *counties* (ou *regions* en Écosse), elles-mêmes divisées en *districts* :

❏ L'Angleterre et le pays de Galles possèdent 6 *metropolitan counties* qui couvrent les principales agglomérations urbaines (Greater Manchester, Merseyside, South Yorkshire, Tyne and Wear, West Midlands et West Yorkshire) et sont eux-mêmes découpés en 36 *metropolitan districts*. Il existe également 39 *non-metropolitan counties* (zones rurales) divisés en 296 *non-metropolitan districts*.

❏ Greater London (Londres et banlieue) est composé de 32 *boroughs* plus la *Corporation of the City of London,* qui correspond au quartier d'affaires de Londres.

❏ L'Écosse a un système de *unitary authorities,* au nombre de 29, plus 3 *island councils* (Orcades, Shetland et îles de l'Ouest).

❏ L'Irlande du Nord possède 26 *district councils,* sans autre subdivision administrative.

La plupart des *counties, regions, districts* et *boroughs* disposent d'un conseil de représentants élu au niveau local, renouvelé tous les quatre ans.

La plupart des Britanniques citent, parmi leurs activités favorites, les soirées passées chez soi avec des amis, les sorties au restaurant, au cinéma ou au pub. Le théâtre et les boîtes de nuit sont également très appréciés. Depuis quelques années, l'aérobic et la gymnastique connaissent un énorme succès. Pour bien des gens, la sortie traditionnelle du dimanche, en voiture et en famille, reste la conclusion idéale du week-end.

Jours fériés

Ils sont parfois appelés *bank holidays,* car les banques sont fermées ces jours-là.

▶ **Noël** est la période de vacances la plus importante. Les cadeaux sont échangés le jour de Noël, autour de l'arbre ; le dîner typique se compose d'une dinde farcie, de pommes de terre au four et de légumes. Le 26 décembre, ou *Boxing Day,* est une journée que l'on passe à regarder la télévision ou à rendre visite aux parents et amis.

▶ le **Nouvel An** est célébré de façon systématique. À minuit, il est de rigueur de chanter *Auld Lang Syne*.

▶ les **pantomimes**, ou *pantos,* sont des spectacles comiques inspirés de contes traditionnels (*Cendrillon, Jack et le haricot magique,* etc.) qui attirent petits et grands durant la période des fêtes. Il est fréquent que des vedettes du petit écran s'y produisent.

Jours fériés	
1er janvier	New Year's Day
2 janvier	New Year Bank Holiday (Écosse)
17 mars	St Patrick's Day (Irlande du Nord)
mars/avril	Good Friday (Vendredi saint ; sauf Écosse)
1er lundi de mai	May Day
dernier lundi de mai	Spring Bank Holiday (sauf Écosse)
12 juillet	Battle of the Boyne (Irlande du Nord)
1er lundi d'août	Summer Bank Holiday (Écosse)
dernier lundi d'août	Summer Bank Holiday (sauf Écosse)
25 décembre	Christmas Day
26 décembre	Boxing Day

▶ **Pâques** est, avec Noël, la seule fête religieuse célébrée au Royaume-Uni mais est avant tout synonyme de jour férié. Le dimanche de Pâques, les enfants reçoivent des œufs en chocolat.

Pubs

Le pub *(public house)* est une composante essentielle de la vie sociale. Les pubs traditionnels sont souvent divisés en *public bar* (où les places assises sont rares) et *lounge bar,* plus confortables. En général, on commande les consommations au comptoir et on règle tout de suite. On ne donne pas de pourboire aux serveurs. De nombreux établissements proposent des divertissements tels que fléchettes, billard, karaoké ou musique en direct.

Off-licences

Ce terme désigne les magasins de vins et spiritueux, dont la plupart sont ouverts de 10 h à 22 h, du lundi au samedi.

Restaurants

On trouve au Royaume-Uni de nombreux restaurants et cafés où la cuisine, qu'elle soit britannique ou étrangère, est de qualité. Quant aux plats à emporter, la préférence de bien des gens va toujours au traditionnel *fish and chips* (poisson et frites). Les repas proposés dans les pubs sont généralement d'un bon rapport qualité-prix. L'addition comporte parfois une majoration d'environ 10 % pour le service ; dans le cas contraire, on laisse un pourboire compris entre 10 et 15 %.

La télévision est de loin le loisir le plus populaire au Royaume-Uni, et la plupart des foyers possèdent au moins un téléviseur couleur. La télévision et la radio britanniques sont renommées pour leur neutralité politique.

Chaînes de télévision
Il existe cinq chaînes de télévision à diffusion nationale.

▶ la **BBC** *(British Broadcasting Corporation)* émet sur deux canaux nationaux, *BBC1* et *BBC2*. *BBC1* produit des émissions grand public de qualité, avec des dramatiques, du sport, de l'actualité, des films et des émissions comiques. *BBC2* est orientée vers une production plus culturelle et plus thématique ; elle diffuse par exemple des émissions éducatives, dont celles de l'*Open University*.

▶ **ITV** *(Independent Television,* également appelée *Channel 3)* chapeaute 15 chaînes régionales privées. La programmation d'*ITV* est plus ou moins semblable à celle de *BBC1*.

▶ **Channel 4** est une chaîne privée nationale (sauf au pays de Galles) dont la vocation est de produire des émissions à contenu spécialisé, pour des groupes plus restreints. Son équivalent au pays de Galles est la chaîne *S4C Welsh Fourth Channel* qui émet en gallois.

▶ **Channel 5** est une chaîne privée dont l'image est plus jeune et plus dynamique que celle de ses rivales.

Satellite et câble
La télévision par satellite est dominée par *British Sky Broadcasting (BskyB),* qui retransmet des manifestations sportives, des films, des émissions d'actualité, de téléachat et des jeux. D'autres sociétés proposent une programmation du même type, sur des chaînes gratuites ou à péage, ainsi que des services plus pointus tels que films à la carte, télévision interactive et accès à Internet. La télévision hertzienne continue d'attirer la grande majorité des spectateurs, mais les sociétés de satellite et de câble cherchent à augmenter leur part de marché en introduisant progressivement la diffusion numérique.

Télétexte
Ce système d'information électronique sur écran de télévision permet, par l'intermédiaire de la télécommande, de visualiser des bulletins d'information ainsi que des nouvelles sportives, des informations sur l'état des routes, la météo et les programmes télévisés. Le système de la *BBC* s'appelle *Ceefax*® et celui d'*ITV Teletext*®.

Radio
Il existe cinq stations de radio à diffusion nationale qui dépendent de la *BBC,* parallèlement à des services propres à l'Écosse, au pays de Galles et à l'Irlande du Nord. Il existe aussi deux stations nationales privées : *Classic FM* et *Virgin Radio 1215 AM*. La *BBC* possède 39 antennes régionales en Angleterre et dans les îles Anglo-Normandes, et on compte plus de 100 stations régionales privées.

Stations nationales du réseau BBC

■ **Radio 1** (1053/1089 kHz OM; 97.6–99.8 MHz FM) Musique pop et rock ; actualité et état des routes. Tous les jours de 5 h à 2 h.

■ **Radio 2** (88–90.2 MHz FM) Variétés, divertissements, émissions humoristiques et art. Bulletins d'information. 24 heures sur 24.

■ **Radio 3** (1215 kHz OM; 90.2–92.4 MHz FM) Musique classique, dramatiques, reportages, cricket. De 7 h à 2 h 30.

■ **Radio 4** (198 kHz GO; 92.4–94.6 MHz FM) Principale station non musicale. Actualité, reportages, dramatiques et divertissements. De 6 h à 0 h 30.

■ **Radio 5 Live** (693/909 kHz OM) Actualité et sport 24 heures sur 24.

Presse Quelque 56 % des Britanniques achètent un quotidien. Outre les quotidiens et journaux du dimanche nationaux, certaines villes ont un journal du soir, et il existe de nombreux quotidiens régionaux tels que *The Scotsman* (Édimbourg), le *South Wales Echo* (Cardiff) ou *The Belfast Telegraph*. Aux divers quotidiens viennent s'ajouter des centaines de publications hebdomadaires ou bimensuelles. Il est courant de se faire livrer un quotidien tôt le matin par son vendeur de journaux habituel.

Presse nationale et tirages

Quotidiens – presse populaire				Jounaux du dimanche – presse populaire			
The Sun (1964)	D	3 952 000	T	News of the World (1843)	D	4 550 000	T
Daily Mirror (1903)	G	2 432 000	T	The Sunday Mirror (1963)	D	2 440 000	T
Daily Mail (1896)	D	1 802 000	T	The People (1881)	D	1 996 000	T
Daily Express (1900)	D	1 245 000	T	The Mail on Sunday (1982)	D	1 963 000	T
Daily Record (1895)	C/G	742 000	T	The Sunday Express (1918)	D	1 343 000	GF
Daily Star (1978)	D	656 000	T	Sunday Sport (1988)	D	301 000	T

Quotidiens – presse de qualité				Jounaux du dimanche – presse de qualité			
Daily Telegraph (1855)	D	1 024 000	GF	The Sunday Times (1822)	D	1 134 000	GF
The Times (1785)	D	629 000	GF	Sunday Telegraph (1961)	D	651 000	GF
The Guardian (1821)	G	365 000	GF	The Observer (1791)	G	427 000	GF
The Independent (1986)	C/G	275 000	GF	The Independent on Sunday			
Financial Times (1888)	C	168 000	GF	(1990)	C/G	297 000	GF

entre parenthèses = date de fondation •Tendance politique : D = droite G = gauche
C = centre •T = tabloïd GF = grand format

▶ la presse britannique se divise en deux catégories : tabloïds et journaux grand format. Les journaux dits «de qualité» *(quality)* sont publiés en grand format *(broadsheet)*, bien que certains d'entre eux, *The Times* par exemple, comportent des cahiers au format tabloïd, en général consacrés à des sujets autres que l'actualité. Ces quotidiens traitent de l'actualité nationale et internationale, des nouvelles financières, des arts, de la culture et du sport. Les journaux populaires portent le nom de *tabloids* en raison de leur format plus réduit. Les articles de fond y sont remplacés par des faits divers abondamment illustrés, où la vie privée des personnalités côtoie les crimes les plus sordides. Les tabloïds ont des ventes beaucoup plus importantes que la presse grand format.

▶ la **politique** est un sujet qui n'apparaît pas du tout dans les colonnes des journaux les plus populaires, mais on peut dire que la majorité des journaux britanniques sont de droite. La relation entre les tendances politiques des lecteurs et celles de leur journal favori n'est pourtant pas systématique.

▶ les **journaux du dimanche** sont d'un format plus imposant que les quotidiens, car ils comportent souvent deux ou trois cahiers différents ainsi qu'un magazine sur papier glacé couleur appelé *colour supplement*.

Magazines Il en existe un large éventail, du très sérieux magazine d'actualité *The Economist* à l'album de bandes dessinées *Viz*. Les magazines les plus vendus sont les programmes télé, *Reader's Digest, Computer Shopper, What Car* et *National Geographic*. Les revues féminines bon marché telles que *Woman's Own, Best* ou *Prima* se vendent aussi à des millions d'exemplaires.

Dans les industries de transformation, la semaine de travail officielle est de 38 à 40 heures, et dans les bureaux, de 35 à 38 heures. Pour désigner la semaine de 35 heures on parle souvent de *9 to 5*. Toutefois, dans certains secteurs tels que les hôpitaux, l'industrie hôtelière ou la restauration, la moyenne hebdomadaire peut atteindre 50 à 60 heures.

▶ **horaires flexibles** Ce système est utilisé notamment dans les bureaux. Les employés sont tenus d'être présents pendant certaines plages fixes *(core time)*, par exemple de 9 h à 11 h 30 et de 13 h 30 à 16 h. Pour compléter leur emploi du temps, ils peuvent commencer plus tôt leur journée, travailler pendant l'heure du déjeuner ou finir plus tard.

▶ **heures supplémentaires** Le tarif normal est en général majoré de 25 % pour les jours de semaine et les samedis, et de 50 % pour les dimanches.

Congés La plupart des Britanniques ont 4 à 6 semaines de congés payés par an. Aux congés annuels viennent s'ajouter les jours fériés.

Salaires Les salariés reçoivent un salaire mensuel et se voient remettre un bulletin de salaire *(wage slip)* portant le détail de la somme brute et des prélèvements, par exemple, impôt sur le revenu, sécurité sociale et parfois caisse de retraite de l'entreprise. Les travailleurs manuels et les travailleurs temporaires reçoivent souvent une paie hebdomadaire en liquide, qui leur est généralement remise le vendredi, dans un *pay packet* qui comprend le détail de la rémunération et des prélèvements.

Impôt sur le revenu Le fisc britannique *(Inland Revenue)* recouvre l'impôt sur l'ensemble des revenus annuels du contribuable. L'année fiscale va du 6 avril au 5 avril de l'année suivante. La plupart des contribuables n'ont pas à remplir de déclaration, l'impôt étant prélevé à la source par l'employeur selon le système du *Pay-As-You-Earn (PAYE)*. Les travailleurs indépendants, en revanche, paient l'impôt rétroactivement sur la base des informations fournies dans leur déclaration de revenus et étayées par des relevés de comptes.

National Insurance Le système public de prestations sociales est financé en partie par les cotisations dites *National Insurance (NI) contributions,* qui donnent droit à une retraite, et généralement aux allocations chômage et autres prestations. Les cotisations sont obligatoires pour la plupart des personnes résidant au Royaume-Uni et sont le plus souvent prélevées à la source.

Chômage Pour percevoir les allocations, il faut avoir payé les cotisations de sécurité sociale en entier pendant un certain temps. Les personnes n'ayant pas droit aux allocations chômage peuvent demander à percevoir d'autres prestations telles que l'*Income Support*. Les *Jobcentres* affichent quelques offres d'emploi, conseillent les demandeurs dans leurs recherches, les aident à remplir les formulaires de demande de prestations et à se préparer pour les entretiens d'embauche.

Les États-Unis d'Amérique couvrent 9 364 000 km² (avec l'Alaska et Hawaii), ce qui en fait le quatrième plus grand pays du monde. Avec 252 177 000 habitants, sa population est la troisième du monde après celles de la Chine et de l'Inde. L'Alaska et les îles Hawaii dépendent des États-Unis, tout comme certaines îles ou groupes d'îles du Pacifique et de la mer des Antilles, telles que Porto Rico, Guam, les îles Vierges et les Samoa.

Les 10 agglomérations les plus importantes		
Ville	**Population**	**État**
■ Los Angeles	8 863 000	Californie
■ New York	8 547 000	New York
■ Chicago	6 070 000	Illinois
■ Philadelphia	4 857 000	Pennsylvanie
■ Detroit	4 382 000	Michigan
■ Washington DC	3 923 000	
■ Houston	3 302 000	Texas
■ Atlanta	2 834 000	Géorgie
■ Riverside-San Bernadino	2 589 000	Californie
■ Dallas	2 553 000	Texas

Régions On en distingue quatre:

❏ *le Nord-Est* – Delaware, Nouvelle-Angleterre (Connecticut, New Hampshire, Maine, Massachusetts, Rhode Island et Vermont), New Jersey, New York, Pennsylvanie, Maryland et Washington DC.

❏ *le Midwest* – Dakota du Nord, Dakota du Sud, Illinois, Indiana, Iowa, Kansas, Michigan, Minnesota, Missouri, Nebraska, Ohio et Wisconsin.

❏ *le Sud* – Alabama, Arkansas, Caroline du Nord, Caroline du Sud, Floride, Géorgie, Kentucky, Louisiane, Mississippi, Oklahoma, Tennessee, Texas, Virginie et Virginie-Occidentale.

❏ *l'Ouest* – Alaska, Arizona, Californie, Colorado, Hawaii, Idaho, Montana, Nevada, Nouveau-Mexique, Oregon, Utah, Washington et Wyoming.

Gouvernement fédéral et gouvernement de l'État

Les États-Unis sont une république fédérale composée de 50 États plus le *District of Columbia,* zone située à l'intérieur de l'État du Maryland mais devenue le territoire de la capitale, Washington DC.

❏ *Le gouvernement fédéral* se compose du président d'un Parlement bicaméral, le Congrès (*Congress* comprenant la *House of Representatives* et le *Senate*) et de la Cour suprême *(Supreme Court)*. Il est responsable des questions de défense, des affaires étrangères, de l'émission de monnaie et de la réglementation du commerce entre les États.

❏ *Les gouvernements des États* sont semblables au gouvernement fédéral. Ils ont à leur tête un gouverneur *(Governor)* et un Congrès *(State Congress)* bicaméral. Ils sont compétents en matière de fiscalité, de santé, d'éducation et de législation civile et criminelle.

❏ *Les États* sont découpés administrativement en *counties,* eux-mêmes divisés en *municipalities* (p. ex. villes, *boroughs*). La plupart des villes sont gérées par un maire élu et un conseil municipal *(city council)*.

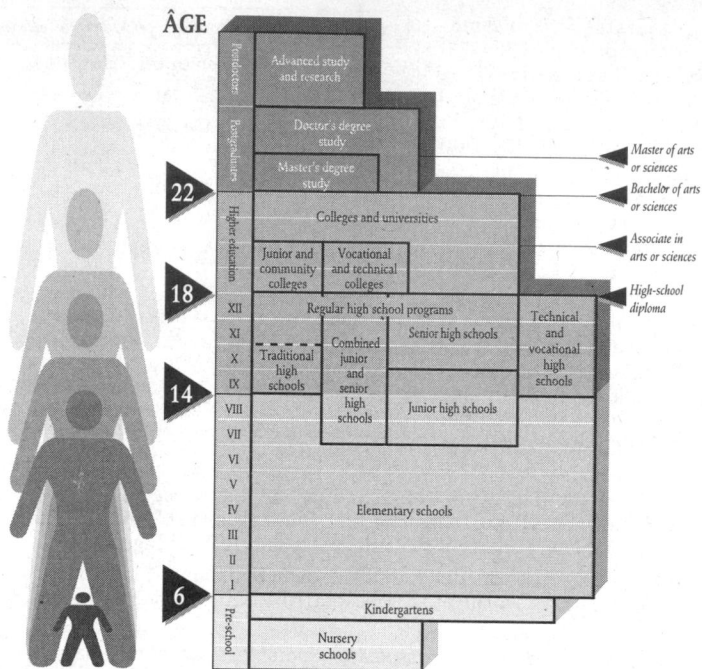

L e gouvernement fédéral américain n'exerce qu'un contrôle très réduit sur le système éducatif, dont la structure diffère selon les régions. En règle générale, la plupart des établissements primaires, secondaires et de niveau universitaire sont mixtes et publics, mais 25 % environ des écoles et 45 % environ des *colleges* sont aux mains de groupes privés ou d'institutions religieuses. Dans la plupart des États, l'enseignement est gratuit pendant douze ans à partir du *kindergarten* (c'est-à-dire à partir de l'âge de 4 ou 5 ans). L'enseignement est le plus souvent obligatoire, de l'âge de 5 ou 6 ans jusqu'à 16 ou 18 ans. Les grandes lignes du système éducatif américain sont les suivantes :

Enseignement préscolaire (jusqu'à 5 ans) Environ 35 % des
enfants de 3 et 4 ans vont à la *nursery school,* et pratiquement tous ceux de 4 et 5 ans vont au *kindergarten.*

Enseignement primaire (6-13 ans) et secondaire (jusqu'à 18 ans)
Le nombre d'années passées dans chacun de ces cycles varie d'un État à l'autre. Les cas de figure les plus courants sont les suivants :

- ❑ six ans d'*elementary school,* puis trois ans de *junior high school* et trois ans de *senior high school.*
- ❑ huit ans d'*elementary school* puis quatre ans de *high school.*
- ❑ quatre ou cinq ans d'*elementary school* puis quatre ans de *middle school* et quatre ans de *high school.*

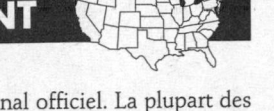

Programmes Il n'y a pas de programme national officiel. La plupart des élèves de *high school* suivent un tronc commun auquel ils peuvent, dans les années supérieures, ajouter des options *(electives)* dans des matières classiques ou plus techniques, selon l'orientation choisie.

Examens Les deux dernières années de *high school* sont sanctionnées par des examens, mais ceux-ci n'ont pas autant d'importance que dans certains autres pays, car les élèves sont soumis à un contrôle continu durant toute leur scolarité, portant sur le travail de l'année, les débats et les devoirs sur table ; une moyenne appelée *Grades Point Average (GPA)* est ainsi obtenue. Ceux qui désirent faire des études universitaires peuvent passer des examens nationaux tels que l'*American College Test (ACT)* ou le *Scholastic Aptitude Test (SAT),* organisés par des institutions privées comme le *College Entrance Examination Board* et l'*Educational Testing Service.* Les résultats de ces examens plus le *GPA* servent à sélectionner les étudiants pour l'entrée dans les *colleges,* les *graduate schools* et les écoles professionnelles.

Écoles privées Environ 12 % des enfants américains vont dans une école primaire ou secondaire privée et payante. Les années sont structurées de la même façon que dans le système public, mais les programmes sont établis de telle sorte que le plus grand nombre possible d'étudiants soient admis dans les universités et les *colleges* les plus prestigieux, comme ceux de l'*Ivy League* ou des *Seven Sisters*.

Terminologie

	High School		College
	âge	année	âge
■ freshman	14–15	9e	18
■ sophomore	15–16	10e	19
■ junior	16–17	11e	20
■ senior	17–18	12e	21

Graduation La douzième année d'études se termine par une cérémonie de remise des diplômes (*graduation* ou *commencement*), pour laquelle les étudiants portent une toque et une toge.

Enseignement supérieur (18-26 ans) Plus de la moitié des diplômés des *high schools* entrent dans l'enseignement supérieur. Il existe trois niveaux d'études : *undergraduate* (licence), *graduate* (maîtrise) et *postgraduate* (troisième cycle). De nombreux établissements publics et privés proposent ces formations : *colleges* publics, *community* ou *junior colleges* (deux années d'études), *undergraduate colleges* (quatre années), instituts techniques, ainsi que les prestigieuses universités et *graduate schools*.

Établissements les plus prestigieux

Universités	Colleges
Ivy League	*Seven Sisters*
Brown	Barnard
Columbia	Bryn Mawr
Cornell	Mount
Holyoke	
Dartmouth	Radcliffe
Harvard	Smith
Univ. of Pennsylvania	Vassar
Princeton	Wellesley
Yale	

Cours pour adultes Ce terme désigne aussi bien les cours d'alphabétisation que les études universitaires ou professionnelles. Des millions d'adultes suivent des cours, à temps partiel ou à temps plein, dans des universités ou des *colleges* (où 40 % des étudiants ont plus de 25 ans), des écoles techniques, professionnelles, etc.

Les États-Unis détiennent le record du nombre de téléviseurs par habitant. Pratiquement chaque foyer possède au moins un poste, et 70 % en possèdent au moins deux. La famille moyenne regarde la télévision sept heures par jour. Le prime time, de 19 h à 23 h, attire quelque 85 millions de téléspectateurs.

Chaînes de télévision
Il existe quatre réseaux nationaux commerciaux :

❏ *American Broadcasting Company (ABC)*
❏ *Columbia Broadcasting Service (CBS)*
❏ *National Broadcasting Company (NBC)*
❏ *Fox TV*

Ces réseaux récoltent environ 70 % des chiffres d'audience en prime time. Le nombre total de chaînes commerciales est de 1 300, et il existe aussi 400 chaînes non commerciales, dont certaines à caractère éducatif. La plus grande partie des chaînes commerciales dépendent d'un réseau national et diffusent ses émissions. Ce n'est pas le cas des quelque 400 chaînes indépendantes, souvent thématiques. La plupart des chaînes américaines émettent 24 heures sur 24.

Programmation des réseaux
Il s'agit avant tout de jeux, de talk-shows, de sitcoms, de téléfilms et de classiques du cinéma. Les seules retransmissions en direct sont les bulletins d'information locaux et les grands événements sportifs tels que la finale du Super Bowl (football américain).

Publicité et chiffres d'audience
Le système des réseaux se fonde avant tout sur la publicité (jusqu'à 15 minutes par heure). Le facteur déterminant de leur fonctionnement est l'audience, mesurée chaque jour. En effet, toute chute des chiffres d'audience effraie les annonceurs et entraîne une chute des revenus de la publicité.

Câble et satellite
Environ 60 % des foyers américains sont câblés. Dans chaque grande ville, il existe en moyenne 35 chaînes câblées en plus des réseaux nationaux et de *PBS*. Contrairement aux réseaux, la télévision par câble n'est pas soumise à la réglementation fédérale, ce qui fait que le contenu des émissions est parfois dérangeant, notamment sur les chaînes «à accès public». Les chaînes câblées sont généralement thématiques (sport, films, religion, actualité – p. ex. *CNN* –, téléachat, musique – p. ex. *MTV*). Le territoire américain est couvert par une vingtaine de satellites, chacun pouvant transmettre jusqu'à 24 chaînes (le plus souvent câblées). Les hôtels, bars et boîtes de nuit sont souvent équipés d'une antenne parabolique pour la retransmission d'événements sportifs en direct.

Public Broadcasting Service
PBS est un réseau non commercial financé par le gouvernement fédéral et des sociétés privées. Les émissions de *PBS* sont de meilleure qualité que celles des chaînes commerciales, notamment les dramatiques et les émissions pour enfants.

Radio
Il existe aux États-Unis plus de 10 000 stations de radio. Dans les grandes villes, on compte parfois jusqu'à 100 stations différentes. Beaucoup de stations dépendent de réseaux nationaux tels qu'*ABC, NBC* ou *CBS*. Ce système existe également au niveau régional, avec plus de 100 réseaux, souvent très spécialisés, qui émettent par exemple en langue étrangère. Les

réseaux non commerciaux *National Public Radio* (*NPR*, consacré à l'actualité) et `American Public Radio* (*APR*, consacré aux divertissements) diffusent des émissions «sérieuses». Comme *PBS*, ces deux réseaux sont financés par des subventions et des participations privées.

Presse Il se publie aux États-Unis environ 1 700 quotidiens et 850 journaux du dimanche, dont le tirage cumulé dépasse 68 millions d'exemplaires ; s'y ajoutent quelque 7 500 hebdomadaires et bimensuels. Les minorités ethniques ont également leurs propres journaux. La plupart des Américains achètent les

> ### Sigles radio
>
> Les stations de radio sont désignées par un sigle de quatre lettres, p. ex. **KLMN** ou **SBNS**. Les noms de stations de l'est du Mississippi et des Rocheuses commencent par un W, et celles de l'ouest par un K. Le sigle est généralement suivi de **AM** ou **FM** selon le cas, p. ex. **WBNS FM**.

journaux pour les bandes dessinées *(funnies)*, le sport, la mode, les faits divers et les nouvelles locales.

▶ **y a-t-il une presse nationale ?** La plus grande partie de la presse américaine est de type régional, à l'exception du *Christian Science Monitor, USA Today* et du *Wall Street Journal,* de certains quotidiens régionaux tels que le *New York Times,* le *Washington Post* ou le *Los Angeles Times,* qui ont des éditions nationales. *USA Today* est le principal quotidien grand public, avec ses photos en couleurs et sa couverture exhaustive des événements sportifs ; il est vendu chaque jour à plus de 5 millions d'exemplaires. Le *Wall Street Journal* publie quatre éditions régionales ; principal journal financier, il a le plus gros tirage de toute la presse américaine. Parmi les journaux régionaux de qualité, on peut citer également le *Boston Globe,* le *Chicago Tribune* ou le *San Francisco Herald.*

> ### Où acheter son journal
>
> Un tiers des Américains se font livrer leur journal à domicile. Les journaux sont également vendus dans les kiosques et dans les distributeurs, les galeries marchandes, les gares ferroviaires et routières. C'est un système basé sur la confiance, l'acheteur étant censé n'emporter qu'un exemplaire après avoir inséré le montant requis.

▶ **tabloïds et journaux grand format** Les lecteurs ont le choix entre grand format «sérieux» et tabloïds très illustrés. La plupart des villes américaines ont leur tabloïd : Boston a son *Herald,* Chicago son *Sun Times,* New York son *Daily News.* Les deux hebdomadaires les plus pittoresques sont le *National Enquirer* et le *National Examiner* ; ils ont une prédilection pour la vie privée des célébrités, les régimes alimentaires fantaisistes, etc.

▶ **les journaux du dimanche** coûtent jusqu'à trois fois plus cher que les éditions de la semaine. La plupart des quotidiens ont une édition dominicale avec de nombreux suppléments.

Magazines Les newsmagazines hebdomadaires tels que *Newsweek, Time* ou *US News and World Report,* qui traitent en profondeur l'actualité nationale et internationale, se vendent très bien.

Newsletters Ces bulletins, disponibles sur abonnement, s'adressent à un lectorat ciblé. Les sujets traités vont des informations boursières aux bonnes affaires, en passant par les potins du monde de l'industrie, l'astrologie, les voyages, etc. Ce sont probablement les publications les plus lues.

La plupart des employés travaillent 40 à 45 heures par semaine et jusqu'à 53 heures dans les industries de transformation. Habituellement, les horaires vont de 8 h à 17 h, avec une heure de pause-déjeuner.

▶ **horaires flexibles** Ce système est moins fréquent qu'au Royaume-Uni.

▶ **heures supplémentaires** Le tarif horaire est majoré de 50 % lorsqu'il y a dépassement des 40 heures hebdomadaires normales. Pour beaucoup d'employés de bureau, il n'existe aucune législation en la matière.

Congés La norme est une ou deux semaines de congés payés par an. Le total annuel augmente avec l'ancienneté.

Impôt sur le revenu Il en existe en fait deux : l'impôt fédéral et l'impôt au niveau de chaque État. Ils sont recouvrés par l'*Internal Revenue Service (IRS)*. La fraude fiscale est considérée comme un délit grave. L'employeur déduit l'impôt directement sur le salaire de l'employé ; c'est le *withholding*. La somme retenue est ensuite déduite du total réellement dû, calculé à la remise de la déclaration d'impôts. Les contribuables bénéficient également de certains dégrèvements *(tax breaks)*. Le montant de l'impôt varie selon les États, certains n'en prélevant pas du tout. Il est en général plus bas que l'impôt fédéral.

Sécurité sociale La *Social Security* couvre la retraite, le veuvage, l'invalidité et les soins médicaux Une carte de Sécurité sociale avec un numéro d'immatriculation à neuf chiffres est délivrée à chaque citoyen américain et à chaque résident étranger. Pour avoir droit aux prestations, il faut avoir eu un emploi pendant une certaine durée. Les contributions sont payées par l'employeur et l'employé à raison d'un certain pourcentage du salaire brut ; elles sont le plus souvent déduites à la source par l'employeur. Les travailleurs indépendants paient leurs cotisations une fois par an, en même temps que leurs impôts sur le revenu.

Chômage Une caisse d'assurance administrée par le gouvernement fédéral et les États verse aux demandeurs d'emploi des allocations hebdomadaires pendant une période limitée, en général 26 semaines. Le montant des allocations dépend des revenus obtenus précédemment.

Permis de séjour

Tous les étrangers ne résidant pas aux États-Unis et désirant entrer dans le pays doivent demander un visa. Il en existe deux catégories : *immigrant visa* (de résidence permanente) et *non-immigrant visa* (de résidence temporaire). Les détenteurs d'un *immigrant visa* se voient délivrer une *Alien Registration Receipt Card,* communément appelée *Green Card.* On peut obtenir celle-ci par mariage, parce que l'on est parent proche d'un citoyen américain, ou par son travail. Son détenteur a le droit de vivre et de travailler de façon permanente aux États-Unis et il peut demander la citoyenneté américaine au bout de cinq ans. Les résidents permanents n'ont pas le droit de vote, n'ont pas accès au haut fonctionnariat, ni à certaines professions.

Jours fériés Outre ceux de la fédération tout entière, de nombreux États ont leurs propres jours fériés.

▶ **Noël et le Nouvel An** Il est fréquent d'organiser des soirées pour Noël, et durant toute la période des fêtes beaucoup d'Américains reçoivent parents et amis.

▶ **Pâques**, pour les enfants, est associé à l'*Easter bunny* (petit lapin de Pâques), qui dépose chez eux, le matin de Pâques, des paniers plein de friandises et d'œufs en chocolat.

▶ **Thanksgiving** commémore la première récolte des colons de Plymouth, en 1621, après un hiver d'épreuves et de famine. C'est l'occasion, pour les familles américaines, de se retrouver pour le traditionnel dîner composé de dinde farcie accompagnée de patates douces, de sauce aux airelles et de courges, suivi d'une tarte au potiron et aux pommes.

Jours fériés nationaux	
1er janvier	New Year's Day
3e lundi de janvier	Martin Luther King Day
3e lundi de février	Presidents' Day (anniversaires de Lincoln, 12 février, et de Washington, 22 février)
Dernier lundi de mai	Memorial Day (victimes de la guerre)
4 juillet	Independence Day
1er lundi de septembre	Labour Day
2e lundi d'octobre	Columbus Day
11 novembre	Veterans' Day
4e jeudi de novembre	Thanksgiving
25 décembre	Christmas Day

Clubs et associations Ils sont nombreux et constituent, avec les activités à caractère confessionnel, l'essentiel de la vie sociale et de la vie de l'entreprise. On trouve parmi eux l'*American Legion* (anciens combattants), les *country clubs* (complexes sportifs et de loisirs), les francs-maçons, les *Shriners* (hauts responsables francs-maçons), les *Jaycees* (de «JC», *Junior Chamber of Commerce,* ou chambre de commerce des jeunes).

Bars Il en existe de nombreux types, selon le style et la clientèle. Les Américains aiment, en règle générale, la musique à fort volume et le karaoké. Les endroits où se produisent des groupes font parfois payer un droit d'entrée. Il est d'usage de laisser un pourboire d'environ 15 à 20 % du montant de l'addition.

Restaurants On trouve de multiples restaurants, du prestigieux établissement gastronomique à l'humble relais routier en passant par toutes sortes de restaurants ethniques et exotiques. La famille moyenne y laisse 40 % de son budget annuel. Les portions sont très généreuses. En règle générale, le service n'est pas compris dans l'addition et il est d'usage de laisser un pourboire d'environ 15 à 20 % du montant hors taxes.

Sport Les Américains sont de grands amateurs de sport, qu'ils en pratiquent un eux-mêmes ou qu'ils soient simples spectateurs. Les activités les plus répandues sont la natation, le cyclisme, le ski, la pêche, le jogging, la randonnée et l'aérobic. Les sports qui attirent le plus de spectateurs sont le base-ball, sport national, le football américain et le basket-ball.

CONVERTISSEUR

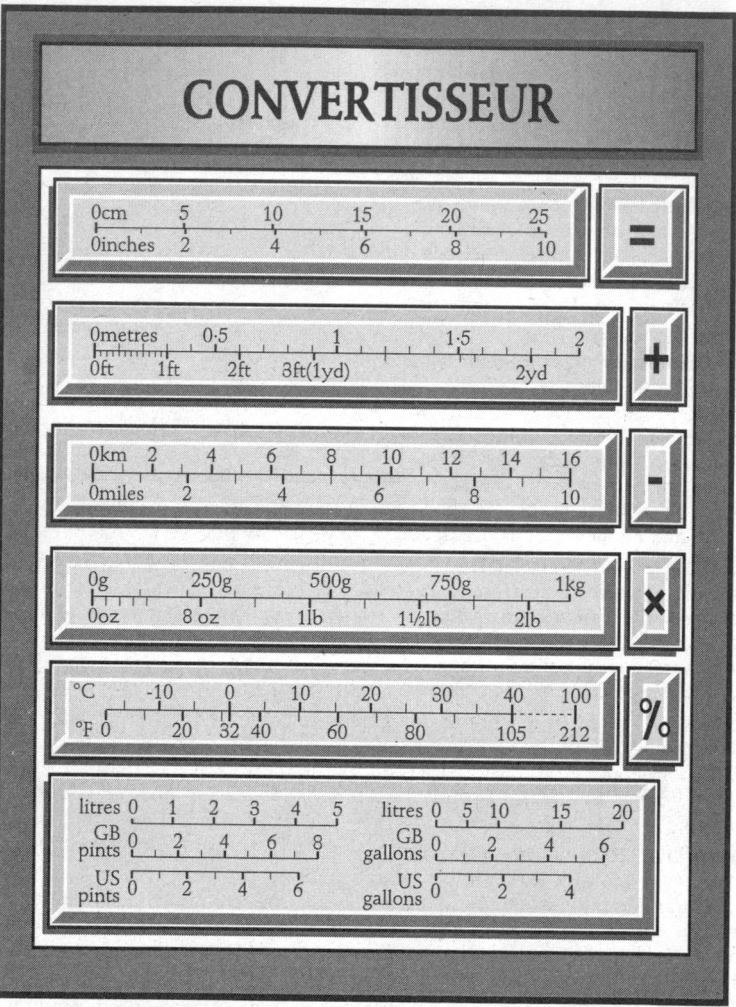

Living in France, Belgium, Switzerland, and Quebec

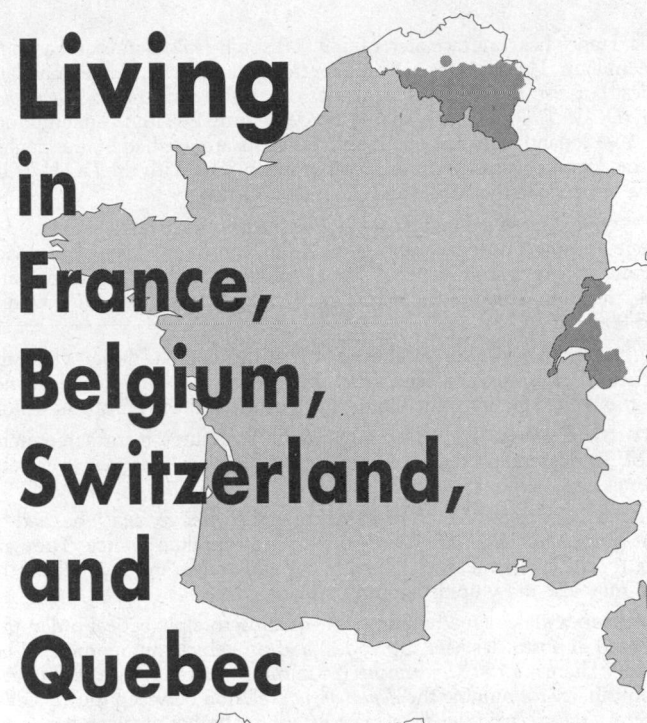

CONTENTS

FRANCE France has a surface area of 549 000 square kilometres and a population of 59 million. This includes not only metropolitan France, i.e. the mainland plus Corsica, but also the overseas territories called the *départements et territoires d'outre-mer (DOM-TOM)*. France shares borders with Belgium, Luxembourg, Germany, Switzerland, Italy and Spain and its coasts are washed by the English Channel, the Atlantic Ocean and the Mediterranean Sea. With the *DOM-TOM* it also has a presence in the Pacific and the Indian Oceans.

Administration is centralized in the capital, Paris. Although a law was passed in 1983 to increase power at local and regional level, there remains a clear divide between Paris and the rest of France. With 11 million people living in Paris and its suburbs, the capital dwarfs the next-largest cities, Marseilles (801 000) and Lyons (415 000).

In 1958 the current Constitution established the Fifth Republic, under which the independence of the executive, legislature and judiciary is guaranteed. France belongs to the United Nations, the Council of Europe and the European Union.

Division of Power French administrative structures form a hierarchy made up of (in descending order of size) *régions, départements, communes* and *arrondissements.*

▶ ***Régions*** are administered by a regional council *(conseil régional),* headed by a president *(président).* There are 22 regions in metropolitan France. They are responsible for the economic, social, health, cultural and scientific affairs of the region, and may also draw up development plans.

▶ ***Départements*** are assigned a number according to alphabetical order; this number is used in postcodes (*Am*: zip codes) and on vehicle numberplates (*Am*: license plates). There are 100 *départements* (96 in metropolitan France and 4 overseas). Responsibility for running the *département* is shared between the President of the General Council *(président du conseil général),* the body managing the *département*'s affairs, and the Prefect *(préfet),* who is appointed by the Cabinet to be the Government's representative within the *département.* The town where administrative power is centred is known as the *chef-lieu.* The mandate of the *conseil général* ranges from the upkeep of museums and monuments, managing schools, keeping up the artistic life of the *département* and providing social security, to maintaining the road network.

▶ ***Communes*** form the basic administrative unit. There are 36 000 in all, and they vary greatly in size. Each is administered by a mayor, his or her staff and town councillors elected by local residents for a period of six years. They are responsible for the upkeep of the museums and monuments of the *commune,* issue building permits and oversee nursery and primary schools. Paris, Lyons and Marseilles, which are *communes* in their own right, are subdivided into *arrondissements.*

The Executive

▶ **The President of the Republic (*président de la République*)** is the French head of state and is elected by the people for a period of seven years. He appoints the Prime Minister *(Premier ministre)* and chairs cabinet meetings every Wednesday in the Élysée Palace. He is head of the armed forces and has the power to call a referendum and dissolve the National Assembly *(see below).*

▶ **The French Government** (*Am*: Cabinet) is made up of the Prime Minister, with his or her ministers and Secretaries of State. The Prime Minister may give certain members of the Government the title of *ministre d'État,* which means that they take precedence over the other ministers, even though they are not in charge of any specific department.

▶ **The Prime Minister** is appointed by the President of the Republic and is always a member of the majority party in the National Assembly. As well as having overall responsibility for government affairs, he is in charge of defence and has the power to propose new laws.

French Institutions and their Locations	
■ residence of the President of the Republic	palais de l'Élysée
■ residence of the Prime Minister	hôtel Matignon
■ Ministry of the Interior	place Beauvau
■ Ministry of Foreign Affairs	quai d'Orsay
■ Justice Ministry	place Vendôme
■ National Assembly	palais Bourbon
■ Senate	palais du Luxembourg

The Legislature The French Parliament is made up of a lower house, the National Assembly *(Assemblée nationale),* and an upper house, the Senate *(Sénat).*

▶ **The National Assembly** has 577 members, known as *députés,* who are elected by universal suffrage for a period of five years. They sit every Wednesday during the parliamentary session, which runs from October to June.

▶ **The Senate** has 319 members, known as *sénateurs,* who are elected by an electoral college of *députés* and members of the *conseil général* of each *département.* They are elected for a period of nine years; every three years, however, one-third of the *sénateurs* come up for re-election. The President of the Senate *(président du Sénat)* stands in for the President of the Republic if he is unable to fulfil his duties.

▶ **The role of Parliament** is to pass laws and vote on the national budget. Members debate the performance of the Government and, like the Prime Minister, may propose new laws.

▶ **The Constitutional Council (Conseil constitutionnel)** consists of nine members who serve for a period of nine years. It is responsible for ensuring that the Constitution is respected.

Main Political Parties	
■ *Parti communiste* (Communist party)	PC
■ *Parti socialiste* (left of centre)	PS
■ *Génération écologie* (green party)	
■ *Les Verts* (green party)	
■ *Union pour la démocratie française* (right of centre)	UDF
■ *Rassemblement pour la République* (right of centre)	RPR
■ *Front national* (far right)	FN

Elections To be eligible to vote in France, and thus receive a voter's card *(carte d'électeur),* you must be a French national, be over 18 years of age, and not have a criminal record.

▶ **The first-past-the-post system** usually involves two rounds of voting. If a candidate does not achieve an absolute majority in the first round, i.e. more than 50% of the votes, then a second round is held. In this second round, the candidate who gains the most votes wins. This form of ballot is used in presidential and general elections.

▶ **Proportional representation** means that seats are allocated in proportion to the number of votes obtained. This form of ballot is used in particular in regional and European elections.

▶ **Local elections** use different systems depending on the size of the commune: first-past-the-post in small *communes*, and proportional representation in larger ones.

The Judiciary The Justice Minister *(ministre de la Justice)* also has the title Guardian of the Seals *(garde des Sceaux)*. The French Constitution guarantees the independence of a public and free legal system in which every defendant has the right to a lawyer, irrespective of his or her means. Any case can go to appeal and be retried in the Appeal Court *(Cour d'appel)*.

▶ **Civil courts** hear disputes between private individuals. Cases are dealt with by a *tribunal d'instance* or, if they are more complicated, by a *tribunal de grande instance*. There are also special courts such as the *tribunaux de commerce* which deal with industrial disputes, *tribunaux des baux ruraux* which rule on agricultural disputes, *tribunaux des affaires de la Sécurité sociale* for social security matters, and *conseils de prud'hommes*, which are local industrial tribunals.

▶ **Criminal courts** differ according to the offence being tried. The legal system distinguishes between *crimes* (crimes such as treason, murder, manslaughter and robbery with violence) and *délits* (offences such as fraud, resisting arrest and forgery). *Délits* are ruled on by *tribunaux de police* or *tribunaux correctionnels*, which can impose fines and prison sentences. *Crimes* are dealt with by *Cours d'assises*, which sit in the main town of each *département*. They can acquit defendants or impose punishments ranging from fines to life imprisonment.

▶ **The High Court (Haute cour de justice)** sits in cases where the President or members of the Government *(Am:* Cabinet) are impeached.

▶ ***Tribunaux administratifs*** are bodies to which individuals may appeal if they feel aggrieved by a decision of the French civil service, or if they believe the law has been violated. There are 30 of these courts. Appeals against rulings made here may be taken to the *Conseil d'État*.

▶ **A criminal record *(casier judiciaire)*** disqualifies you from working in the civil service, banking or insurance, and from voting.

BELGIUM Belgium has a surface area of 30 518 square kilometres and a population of approximately 10 million. Its capital, Brussels, houses the headquarters of the European Parliament. The Belgian Constitution states that the country is made up of three linguistic and cultural communities (French, Flemish and German) and three regions (Flanders in the north, Wallonia in the south, and the area around Brussels). Belgium has a complex institutional structure in which the Government devolves a lot of power to federal bodies. It is a constitutional and parliamentary monarchy.

The Executive The executive consists of the King and the Government *(Am:* Cabinet), headed by a Prime Minister appointed by the monarch. The Government must have majority support in both chambers of the Belgian Parliament. To ensure equality, there are equal numbers of French-speaking and Dutch-speaking ministers.

The Legislature The Belgian Parliament consists of an upper and a lower chamber, the Senate *(Sénat)* and the House of Representatives *(Chambre des* *représentants),* which together with the King have the power to pass laws.

The Judiciary The Belgian legal system is quite similar to that of France. Magistrates are appointed by the King.

SWITZERLAND The Swiss Confederation has a surface area of 41 293 square kilometres and a population of 7 million. It can be divided into a German-speaking part including the capital Bern; a French-speaking part; and the canton of Ticino, where Italian is spoken. Romansch is the official language in the canton of Graubünden (Grisons). Switzerland is a parliamentary republic divided into 23 self-governing districts known as *cantons,* three of which are themselves divided into *demi-cantons.*

The Executive Executive power is exercised by the Federal Council *(Conseil fédéral),* made up of seven members elected by the representatives of the two chambers of the Swiss Parliament. From within its ranks a President is elected for a period of one year to represent Switzerland at home and abroad.

The Legislature The Swiss Parliament, the Federal Assembly *(Assemblée fédérale),* consists of two chambers: the *Conseil des États* and the *Conseil national.*

Referenda In Switzerland referenda are widely used to amend laws and even the Constitution itself.

QUEBEC Quebec is the largest of the ten Canadian provinces, occupying 1 540 680 square kilometres. The population is just under 7 million but only 2.5% of the land is inhabited. The official language is French. Although the capital, Quebec City, is the administrative centre, the business and cultural heart of the province beats in Montreal. In 1995 the pro-independence movement lost a referendum on independence from Canada by a tiny margin.

National Administration The head of state is the British Queen, represented by the Governor-General, a Canadian appointed by the monarch on the advice of the Canadian Prime Minister. Parliament consists of the Queen, the Senate *(Sénat)* and the House of Commons *(Chambre des communes).*

▶ **The Senate** has 104 members, 24 from Quebec. Senators are appointed by the Prime Minister and the Cabinet. The Senate can introduce, amend or reject a law as long as it does not relate to the budget.

▶ **The House of Commons** has 282 members, 75 from Quebec. They are elected by universal suffrage in a one-round first-past-the-post system *(see p4).*

▶ **The Prime Minister** chooses his or her ministers and has the power to dismiss them. Usually an MP, he is the leader of the party with the most seats and, together with his Cabinet, is responsible for drawing up laws. His Government *(Am:* administration) is responsible to the House of Commons and must resign if a vote of no confidence is passed or if his party loses its majority.

Provincial Administration Quebec is ruled by a Legislative Assembly and has its own Constitution. All bills receive sanction by the Lieutenant Governor, who represents the Queen, before becoming law. The Assembly devolves power to city, town, village and district authorities. Executive power lies with the *Conseil exécutif,* or Council of Ministers, presided over by the Prime Minister of Quebec.

The Legal System The Canadian legal system is independent. Almost all the courts are administered by the individual provinces, but judges are appointed by the national Government.

FRANCE France has a centralized education system, controlled by the *ministère de l'Éducation nationale* (Ministry for National Education), which has the highest budget of all the ministries. A department of the Ministry called the *secrétariat d'État aux Universités* is responsible for higher education. Five different levels of education can be identified: *école maternelle* (nursery school), *école primaire* or *élémentaire* (primary school), *collège* (between the ages of 11 and 15), *lycée* (between 15 and 18), and *le supérieur* (higher education).

Centralization The curriculum is drawn up by the Government and is handed down to schools in an official publication called *le Bulletin officiel de l'Éducation nationale*. The country is divided into 28 educational areas known as *académies*, each presided over by a *recteur*. The dates of school terms are set by the Ministry. Christmas holidays (*Am*: vacations) and the two months of summer holidays are the same throughout the country. There are also breaks in February, in spring and around 1 November (*la Toussaint* or All Saints' Day). The exact dates of these holidays depend on which part of France you live in: for these purposes the country is split into three zones, and the order in which each zone takes its holidays changes every year.

School Year	
■ term one	September to December
■ term two	January to March
■ term three	April to June

Public and Private Education Education in France is public, non-denominational and free from *maternelle* to *lycée*. Attendance is obligatory between the ages of 6 and 16. Nursery and primary schools are run by a head teacher known as a *maître-directeur*, and are managed by the local town councils. The head teacher of a *collège* is known as a *principal* and his or her school is the responsibility of the *département*. In *lycées* the head teacher is called a *proviseur* and these schools receive their funding from the region. All teachers and administrative staff are civil servants paid by the State.

Running in parallel to the state system there are private schools, which are said to be *sous contrat* ('under contract'). This means that the teachers are paid by the State and teach the national curriculum. Some private schools are denominational and are owned by religious orders. A small number of private schools are *hors contrat*. These establishments own their premises, recruit and pay staff themselves and are not obliged to teach the national curriculum.

▶ **The *carte scolaire*** is a list of state schools divided by region. Students are assigned a school depending on where they live.

▶ **Grants** are awarded to students for all types of school if their parents have low incomes.

The Recruitment of Teachers Teachers are recruited after graduating from university (three years' study) and studying for two years at a teacher training college called an *IUFM* (*institut universitaire de formation des maîtres*). All prospective teachers follow a core curriculum and then sit an exam depending on their intended career. The different types of teacher are:

❑ *professeurs d'écoles* (at nursery and primary school level)

❑ *professeurs de collège* and *professeurs de lycée* (at secondary school level), who have to pass the *CAPES* teaching diploma or hold an *agrégation*, the highest qualification of all, and specialize in one subject

❑ *maîtres auxiliaires* (supply (*Am*: substitute) teachers), who are not government employees and have less strict training requirements.

From Nursery to *Lycée*

▶ **Nursery school (2–6)** is optional, but almost all children attend.

▶ **Primary school (6–11)** is structured in five levels: *le cours préparatoire* (*CP*), *cours élémentaires 1* and *2* (*CE1* and *CE2*), and *cours moyens 1* and *2* (*CM1* and *CM2*). Here pupils acquire reading, writing and arithmetic skills.

▶ **Collège (11–15)** involves four years' study culminating in the first national exam taken by students, the *brevet national des collèges*. After the exam, students choose which subject area they want to specialize in and hence which type of *lycée* they attend.

▶ **Lycée (15–18)** leads after three years' study to the school-leaving certificate (*Am*: high-school diploma), the *baccalauréat* (or *bac*, as it is commonly known), whatever type of *lycée* students opt for. A *lycée professionnel* prepares students for specific vocational

Grades at Baccalauréat	
■ *mention passable*	10–12 out of 20
■ *mention assez bien*	12–14 out of 20
■ *mention bien*	14–16 out of 20
■ *mention très bien*	more than 16 out of 20

bac courses, a *lycée général* offers general and vocational courses, and a *lycée technologique* specializes in technical subjects. There are two parts to the exam: the first, which consists of written and oral French tests, is taken at the end of the second year of *lycée*; and in the second part, taken at the end of the final year (called *la terminale*), students take oral and written exams in their other subjects. Successful completion of the *bac* qualifies students to enter university. There are 12 types of *bac*: three general (literature, *série L;* science, *série S;* and economics and social studies, *série ES*) and nine technical. *Lycées professionnels* offer other courses leading to vocational diplomas called the *CAP (certificat d'aptitude professionnelle)* and the *BEP (brevet d'études professionnelles),* which are completed earlier than the *bac*.

Higher Education

▶ **BTS (brevets de technicien supérieur)** are vocational diplomas awarded after two years' study at a *lycée* or a private school.

▶ **Universities and IUTs (instituts universitaires de technologie)** are open to all holders of a general or technical *baccalauréat*. Students pay no course fees (*Am*: tuition), and degrees are nationally recognized. After two years students take an exam, and if they pass they receive the *DEUG (diplôme d'études universitaires générales)* and may go on to take a *licence* (one year's study) or a *maîtrise* (two years' study). Those students who are interested in going on to do research, and possibly a doctorate, may then take one of two courses, the *DEA (diplôme d'études approfondies)* or the *DESS (diplôme d'études supérieures spécialisées).* The final qualification from an *IUT* is known as the *DUT (diplôme universitaire de technologie).* Establishments called *IUPs (instituts universitaires professionnels)* have been set up in an attempt to forge closer links between higher education and local businesses. The most illustrious French university remains the Sorbonne in Paris.

▶ **Classes préparatoires** are two years of study available in some lycées after the *bac* which prepare students to take entrance exams for the *grandes* *écoles* (see below). The first year of the literature course is known as the *lettres supérieures*, or more colloquially the *hypokhâgne*, and the second as the *première supérieure* or *khâgne*. There are also science classes and mathematics courses, *mathématiques supérieures* and *mathématiques spéciales*.

▶ **The *grandes écoles*** are prestigious establishments whose students are selected by competitive examination after the *classes préparatoires*. Graduates

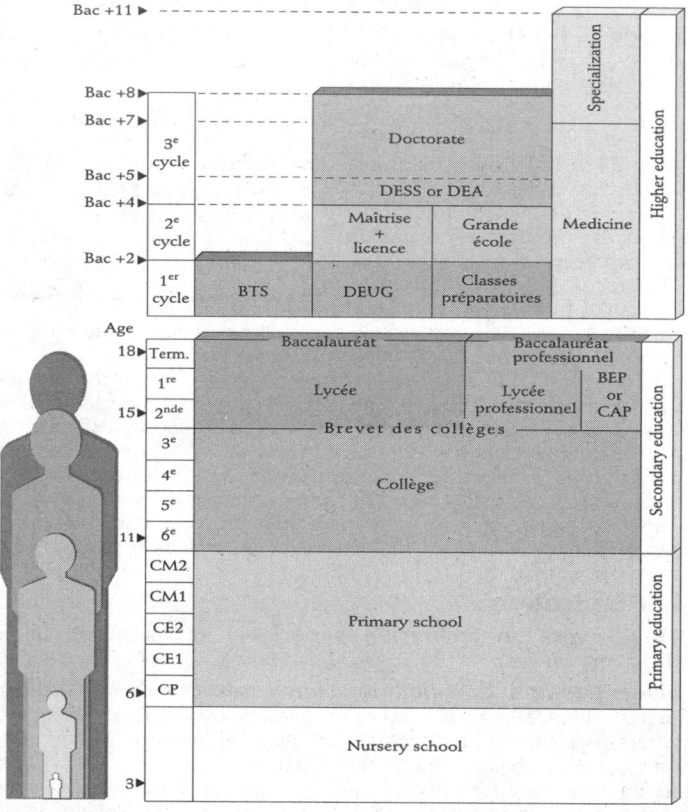

become senior civil servants, politicians, directors of large companies, engineers and academics. The most famous schools are the *Polytechnique*, the *Centrale*, the *Mines* and the *Arts et Métiers*, which all specialize in engineering; the *ENA (École nationale d'administration)*, which trains senior civil servants; and the *ENS (École normale supérieure)*, which trains high-ranking teachers and researchers. They are public and free, and students are in some cases paid a salary.

▶ **The *CNED (Centre national d'enseignement à distance)*** administers distance-learning, running correspondence courses at all levels.

BELGIUM Each linguistic community organizes and funds its own education system.

Full-time and Part-time Learning School attendance is obligatory between the ages of 6 and 18. During the last two years of this period students can study part-time while they complete an apprenticeship. Those students who want to go on to higher education, however, must study full-time in an *athénée*, the Belgian equivalent of a *lycée*, from the ages of 16 to 18 and take the university entrance exam, the *DAES (diplôme d'aptitude à accéder à l'enseignement supérieur)*.

Higher Education There are three universities in the French-speaking part of Belgium, plus one with courses in a limited number of subjects. In addition to the universities, there are seven other types of establishment running specialized vocational courses, e.g. in agriculture, nursing etc.

SWITZERLAND Each Swiss *canton* is responsible for its own education system.

Compulsory Schooling This lasts for nine years. The length of time spent in primary schools varies from four to six years depending on the *canton*. Students then go on to enter the *degré secondaire I*. German classes are compulsory from primary school.

Further Education Depending on their ability, students may choose either to follow a vocational course or to enter the *degré secondaire II*. The latter option is more popular in the French-speaking part of the country. Vocational courses all involve work placements in addition to studies at college. The *degré secondaire II* is followed either at secondary schools called *gymnases*, which prepare students to take the *maturité*, the Swiss equivalent of the *baccalauréat*, or at *écoles de degré diplôme (EDD)* where students follow a two- or three-year vocational course.

Higher Education As well as the universities, *écoles supérieures* offer courses in technical subjects, tourism or art, and *hautes écoles* run courses with a high research component.

QUEBEC In Canada each province is responsible for its own education system. As 80% of the population of Quebec is French-speaking, most classes are in French.

Compulsory Schooling At primary level school is compulsory for six years, and at secondary level for five years.

Pre-university Education After these 11 years, students may leave school or enter a *collège d'enseignement général et professionnel (cégep)* where they take either a two-year general course leading to university entrance, or a three-year vocational course leading to the job market.

Universities In Quebec universities enjoy a high degree of independence and award their own degrees. There are four French-speaking universities and three English-speaking ones. Successful students receive a qualification called a *baccalauréat* after three years. They may then study for a further two years, leading to a specialized master's degree *(maîtrise)*, and continue for three years more to gain a doctorate.

FRANCE France is the fourth largest economic power in the world and belongs to the G7 (the group of the seven most industrialized countries). Its annual gross national product (GNP) is approximately $18 000 per person.

The System in Action
The working population of France represents 43% of all inhabitants.

▶ **The primary sector** consists mostly of agriculture, and employs only 6% of the working population. Cereals are grown mostly in the Paris Basin and Picardy, and the biggest wine-producing areas are the region around Bordeaux, the Rhône valley and Burgundy.

▶ **The secondary sector**, which includes industry and construction, employs about 30% of the labour force. Nuclear power now accounts for 74% of electricity production. Most successful are the telecommunications, railway rolling stock and aerospace industries.

▶ **The tertiary sector** is continually expanding and covers banks, commerce, transport, administration and service industries.

▶ **International trade** is mainly with the European Union, Japan and the USA. France is the fourth largest exporter in the world; its main exports are machinery, cars, foodstuffs, clothing and luxury goods. Its main imports are oil, gas, machinery, cars, motorcycles, hi-fi equipment and optical instruments.

The World of Work
Employment law in France is determined by the Constitution, the *code du travail* and international agreements and treaties.

▶ **Working hours** are fixed by law at 39 hours per week, with a daily maximum of 10 hours. Employees may work an extra 130 hours per year, paid at a higher rate. Paid annual holiday is 30 working days.

▶ **Salaries** are paid monthly. Many companies offer an annual bonus, known as the *treizième mois* as it is equal to an extra month's salary, and a holiday (*Am*: vacation) bonus. There is a minimum wage, the *SMIC (salaire minimum interprofessionnel de croissance)*, which is adjusted annually on 1 July.

▶ **Workers who are made redundant** (*Am*: laid off) are entitled to claim benefit (*Am*: unemployment) for six months; this is provided jointly by the employer, the Government and the *ASSEDIC (Association pour l'emploi dans l'industrie et le commerce* – an association

Public Holidays	
■ 1 January	
■ Easter Monday	
■ 1 May	Labour Day
■ 8 May	Armistice Day 1945
■ Ascension Day	
■ Whit Monday	
■ 14 July	Bastille Day
■ 15 August	the Assumption
■ 1 November	All Saints' Day
■ 11 November	Armistice Day 1918
■ 25 December	Christmas

providing insurance against unemployment). People no longer able to claim unemployment benefit from the *ASSEDIC* are entitled to the *RMI (revenu minimum d'insertion)*, an allowance from the State providing claimants with a guaranteed minimum income.

▶ **Strikes** are legal in France for all employees, including civil servants. However, 'lockouts' (temporary closure of a company by an employer to impose certain working conditions or salary levels) are illegal.

Banking Banks in France are as a rule open from 9 a.m. to 5 p.m., with a break from noon to 2 p.m. They close during long weekends.

Currency The French unit of currency is the franc (F). One franc equals 100 centimes (c). There are coins to the value of 5c, 10c, 20c, 50c, 1F, 2F, 5F, 10F and 20F, and notes to the value of 20F, 50F, 100F, 200F and 500F.

BELGIUM Although a small country with a small population, Belgium is rich. Its annual GNP is $15 000 per person.

Agriculture In Belgium agriculture consists mainly of pig- and cattle-breeding. Belgian farmers are making a net loss.

Industry The once dominant coal industry in Belgium is in decline. A total of 63% of the country's energy comes from nuclear power. The automobile industry is flourishing, as many multinationals have set up in the country.

Banking Banks are as a rule open between 9 a.m. and 3 or 3.30 p.m., Monday to Friday, although some branches also open on Saturday mornings. Paying by cheque is still the most common means of payment.

Currency The unit of currency is the Belgian franc (FB). One Belgian franc equals 100 centimes (c).

SWITZERLAND With an annual GNP of $36 000 per person, this tiny country is one of the richest in the world. Its wealth comes from industry and, in particular, the many banks established there.

Agriculture Four times more land is used for cattle-breeding than for crops, with dairy farming predominating, but Swiss farmers still make a net loss.

Industry This consists mainly of chemicals, precision instruments and watchmaking. Switzerland exports mostly to Germany, France and Italy.

Banking Zürich, in the German-speaking part of Switzerland, is considered one of the biggest financial centres in the world. Switzerland owes its wealth to its stable currency, its highly developed banking infrastructure and the discretion for which its banks are famous.

Currency The unit of currency is the Swiss franc (FS). One Swiss franc equals 100 centimes (c).

QUEBEC Quebec is twentieth in the list of world economies, and eleventh in terms of standard of living. Although it has 63.5% of its population in employment, this is still lower than the national average.

Agriculture Just 4% of the working population is employed in agriculture, but farming is very productive and technologically advanced. Quebec meets 65% of its food requirements and also exports a lot, in particular cereals.

Industry Industry accounts for 19.3% of the working population. The most dynamic sectors are electrical and electronic goods, timber, papermaking, metal processing and plastics.

Banking The province's financial centre and stock market are based in Montreal. Banks are open from 10 a.m. to 3 p.m., Monday to Wednesday; from 10 a.m. to 6 p.m., Thursdays and Fridays; and are closed at weekends.

Currency The unit of currency is the Canadian dollar ($). One Canadian dollar equals 100 cents (c).

FRANCE The French enjoy freedom of the press. Most of the news which appears in the French media is gathered by the news agency *Agence France-Presse (AF-P)*.

The Press Newspapers are sold in kiosks, newsagents' (both *tabacs* and *maisons de la presse*) and some bookshops. It is also possible to subscribe.

▶ **The national press** is distributed throughout the country. Some newspapers like *Le Monde* appear in the evening, and others like *Le Figaro* or *Libération* in the morning. *Le Monde* also publishes monthly supplements on specific subject areas such as education, music and diplomacy.

▶ **The regional press** devotes many of its pages to local news, as well as covering national and international events.

▶ **Magazines** covering current affairs, such as the weeklies *Le Point*, *L'Express* and *Le Nouvel Observateur*, are particularly favoured by the French. Other well-known magazines such as *Paris Match* specialize in stories about celebrities. On Saturdays *Le Figaro* publishes three colour supplements (a current affairs magazine, a women's magazine and a TV magazine). Women's magazines, such as *Elle* and *Marie-Claire*, also have large circulations. There is a growing number of specialist magazines on a wide range of subjects such as cars (e.g. *L'Action automoto*), sport (e.g. *France-Football*, *Tennis Magazine*), food (e.g. *Gault-Millau Magazine*) and interior decoration (e.g. *Art et Décoration*, *Maisons Côté Sud*).

▶ **Press consortiums** now own many French newspapers. Some of the biggest groups are *Hachette–Filipacchi*, *Hersant*, *Prisma Presse* and *Bayard Presse*.

Radio and Television French radio and television are financed by a licence fee, advertising revenue and a sponsorship system. Although radio and TV are state monopolies, there are many independent channels existing alongside the publicly owned ones.

▶ **State-owned radio stations** are part of *Radio France*. The national station with the most listeners is *France-Inter*, which broadcasts a mix of light entertainment and news. Other stations include *France Info*, a round-the-clock news station; *France-Culture*, which specializes in documentaries and arts programmes; and

Frequencies (Long Wave) of Main Radio Stations	
■ *France-Inter*	162 kHz
■ *Europe 1*	183 kHz
■ *RTL*	216 kHz
■ *RMC*	234 kHz

FIP, which broadcasts uninterrupted music and short news bulletins from its 47 regional studios. *Radio France Internationale (RFI)*, which broadcasts worldwide in French and foreign languages, and *RFO*, which serves the *DOM-TOM*, are both state-owned but independent from *Radio France*.

▶ *Radios périphériques* are independent stations broadcasting programmes in French from outside the country, e.g. from Germany or Luxembourg. The most popular are *Europe 1*, *RTL* and *Radio Monte-Carlo (RMC)*.

▶ **Independent radio stations** include *Europe 2* and *NRJ*, which are targeted at teenagers, and stations catering for specific communities such as *Radio Beur* (for North Africans living in France).

▶ **Public television** is run by two channels in France: *France 2* and *France 3*.

France 2 broadcasts mostly news and drama, while *France 3* specializes in arts programmes relayed from regional studios.

▶ **Arte and La Cinquième** share a television frequency. *Arte* is a Franco-German arts channel. Its programmes start at 7 p.m, and when *Arte* is off the air, an educational channel called *La Cinquième* broadcasts instead.

▶ **Independent channels** are headed in popularity by *TF1*, which broadcasts news, sport, films and light entertainment. Other channels include *M6*, which shows American series, soap operas and music videos, and *Canal +*. In order to receive *Canal +*, viewers must pay a subscription, in return for which they are given a decoder which unscrambles the signal.

French Television Channels
■ *TF1*
■ *France 2*
■ *France 3*
■ *M6*
■ *Canal +*
■ *La Cinquième/Arte*

▶ **The *Conseil supérieur de l'audiovisuel* (CSA)** is an independent body whose function is to guarantee the independence of the public sector, to encourage competition and to ensure programme quality.

BELGIUM There are about 20 French-language daily newspapers in Belgium, including *Le Soir*, *La Lanterne* and *La Gazette de Liège*, plus a large number of weeklies and magazines.

The public French-language broadcasting body is *Radio Télévision belge francophone (RTBF)*, which gets 80% of its funding from the State but also receives advertising revenue. It has two channels. Belgians may subscribe to the Belgian version of *Canal +*, *Canal + Belgique*, and there are also cable television networks.

SWITZERLAND The multilingual nature of Switzerland is reflected in its media. Of the 103 daily newspapers available in the country, 80 are in German, 18 in French and 5 in Italian. The most widely read papers in Geneva are *La Suisse*, *La Tribune de Genève* and *Le Journal de Genève*, while in Lausanne *Le Matin* is the most popular.

The Swiss national broadcasting company has three German channels, three French and one Italian.

QUEBEC

The Press Of the 559 magazines and newspapers available in Quebec, 72.6% are in French, 13.4% are in English and 10.3% are bilingual. The most popular French-language daily papers in Montreal are *La Presse*, *Le Devoir* and *Le Journal de Montréal*, and in Quebec City *Le Soleil* and *Le Journal de Québec*.

Radio There are 116 radio stations in Quebec, 104 of which broadcast in French. Most of them are privately owned.

Television Of the 35 channels in Quebec, 17 are private companies and 18 are state-owned. *Radio Québec*, the main French-language network, has three channels, *les Téléviseurs Associés (TVA)* has ten, and Radio Canada nine. Montreal and much of Quebec City have a cable network, via which viewers have access to a number of foreign programmes, as well as round-the-clock information services (on, for example, traffic conditions and the weather).

FRANCE The French spend about 10.5% of their income on entertainment.

Sport Just 10% of French people play sport on a regular basis, although this percentage is higher among teenagers, who enjoy football (*Am*: soccer), tennis and judo.

▶ **Motor racing** is watched by a large number of French people, both on television and live at circuits like Le Mans.

▶ **Cycling** too is popular. The best-known cycle race, perhaps in the world, is the Tour de France, which takes place every year in July.

▶ **Football** (*Am*: soccer) enjoys a high standing in France, where almost every town and village have their own team. The national league has two divisions. The best-supported French teams are *Paris-Saint-Germain,* also known as *PSG,* Nantes, Monaco and *Olympique de Marseille,* usually referred to as *OM.*

▶ **Horse racing** and betting on horse races are very popular in France. The most famous race courses are at Saint-Cloud, Maisons-Laffitte, Longchamp and Chantilly.

▶ **Rugby**'s heartland is the southwest, where Toulouse, Agen and Lourdes all have successful teams. The highlight of the international season is the Five Nations Championship, which France contests with England, Scotland, Wales and Ireland.

▶ **Skiing** is enjoyed by 9.5% of French people, who make use of the excellent opportunities for winter sports offered in the Alps and the Pyrenees.

▶ **Tennis** is a well-established sport in France, with over 10 000 clubs. The French Open, *les Internationaux de France*, is held every year in June at the Roland Garros stadium in Paris and is one of the major world tournaments.

▶ **Yachting** has been made popular by famous French sailors such as Éric Tabarly, Olivier de Kersauson and Florence Arthaud. There is now a lot of interest in transatlantic and single-handed round-the-world races.

▶ **Regional sports** like *pétanque*, which originated in the South of France, and pelota (*pelote basque*) from the Basque Country are minority sports, but have become a part of French culture. *Pétanque* is played with metal bowls and a small wooden ball called a *cochonnet* (the jack); the object is to throw the bowls as close to the jack as possible. The most common version of pelota is played with a ball called a *pelote* which is thrown against a wall.

Arts

▶ **Music** is particularly enjoyed by French teenagers, 50% of whom play a musical instrument, the piano and guitar being the most popular. Paris is home to large concert halls such as Pleyel and Gaveau, and music hall theatres such as Olympia. Jazz festivals are usually held in the South of France in places like Antibes and Juan-les-Pins. Most French cities have an opera house; indeed, Paris has two, the Palais Garnier and the Bastille. During the *fête de la Musique*, which takes place every year on 21 June, both amateur and professional musicians take to the streets to give free concerts.

▶ **The largest ballet school in France** is also housed in the Palais Garnier. Students of this school are commonly referred to as *les petits rats de l'Opéra*. Ballets from the repertory are performed every year.

▶ **Theatre** companies like the independent *Comédie-Française* (the national theatre company), *Théâtre de l'Europe* (also known as *l'Odéon*), *Chaillot* and *TEP (Théâtre de l'Est parisien)* are based in Paris. Strasbourg, however, is also home to a national theatre company, the *TNS (Théâtre national de Strasbourg)*. Members of the *Comédie-Française* are often former students of the Paris music school, the *Conservatoire de Paris*. Two of the highlights of the theatrical year are the *Festival d'Avignon* in July and the *Festival d'automne* held in Paris. There is an annual awards ceremony, *les Molières*, at which the best plays and actors of the year are rewarded.

▶ **Cinema** is highly regarded in France. The most famous film festival takes place every year in Cannes, where the *palme d'or* (golden palm) is given to the best film. The *festival d'Avoriaz*, held in a ski resort in the Alps, is dedicated to science fiction; the *festival de Cognac* to detective films; and the *festival de Deauville* to American films. The French equivalent of the American Oscars ceremony is called *les Césars*.

▶ **Architecture** was a particular concern of the late President Mitterrand. A major programme was initiated 20 years ago to erect modern public buildings in Paris and the rest of France. The most notable results include the futuristic office block *l'Arche de la Défense*, the opera house *l'Opéra de la Bastille*, the pyramid outside the *Louvre* and the *Institut du monde arabe*.

▶ **Museums** number 1400, 34 of which are national. As well as permanent collections, they also house temporary exhibitions. Some museums, like the Grand Palais, are devoted entirely to special exhibitions.

▶ **The price of books** in France is regulated by the Government in an attempt to encourage people to buy them. The most prestigious annual literary prize is the *prix Goncourt*, judged by a jury of ten authors. The *Académie française* is the body responsible for setting models for use of the French language and for producing the definitive reference work, *le Dictionnaire de l'Académie française*.

Tourism

▶ **Annual holidays** (*Am*: vacations) are taken by two-thirds of French people, usually in summer, although there is a growing trend towards taking a skiing holiday.

Most Popular Tourist Attractions
■ Pompidou Centre
■ Eiffel Tower
■ Louvre
■ Cité des sciences de la Villette
■ Versailles

▶ **The theme parks** *Euro Disneyland* and *Parc Astérix* outside Paris have had huge amounts of money poured into them, but investment has not paid off as well as had been hoped. *Futuroscope* near Poitiers draws large numbers to its more educationally orientated attractions.

▶ **Hotels** in France are assessed by the Ministry of Tourism (*ministère du Tourisme*) and awarded a number of stars from 1 to 4, depending on the level of comfort they afford. The best hotels are classified as four-star *luxe*. Times are hard for small, traditional, family-run hotels which are facing stiff competition from inexpensive alternatives like *chambres d'hôtes* (bed and breakfast accommodation in someone's house) and *gîtes ruraux* (converted farmhouses or outbuildings which can be rented).

▶ **Restaurants** must display their menu and prices always include a service charge. Different systems (stars, forks, chefs' hats) are used to categorize restaurants by different specialist guides, the most illustrious and authoritative of which is the *Guide Michelin*.

BELGIUM Cycling is the biggest sport in Belgium. The use of bicycles is encouraged by the large number of cycle lanes and paths. Hiking on the 4500 kilometres of waymarked (*Am*: marked) paths throughout the country, and skiing in winter in the Ardennes are also popular. Many of the cartoons (*bandes dessinées*) enjoyed around the world are of Belgian origin, e.g. Tintin, Lucky Luke and Gaston Lagaffe. Tourist attractions in Belgium include carnivals, and the many traditional celebrations, often with a historical or religious theme, that take place between March and September. Belgium is renowned throughout the world for its chocolates but it also exports beer, notably that brewed by Trappist monks and *gueuze* (a strong beer that has been brewed twice), Spa mineral water and fruit cordials. The archetypal Belgian dish is *moules-frites* (mussels and chips, *Am*: fries).

SWITZERLAND The most popular sports in Switzerland are mountaineering and winter sports. The big ski resorts are in the German-speaking part of the country. Lakeland regions have, however, done much to develop water sports and have succeeded in attracting a large number of tourists. In the arts, one of the highlights of the year is the jazz festival in Montreux which draws top musicians from all over the world. The most famous Swiss foods are cheeses such as *Emmental* and *Vacherin*, and chocolate.

QUEBEC

Sport Most sports clubs in Quebec belong to the *Regroupement Loisir Québec*. Winter sports predominate, and include Alpine skiing (there are 1170 runs in the province); cross-country skiing in the national parks or at special centres; and snowmobiling, which is particularly popular and accessible as there are 30 000 kilometres of marked tracks. In summer, water sports like canoeing, whitewater rafting, sailing and jet-skiing are widely practised on the many lakes and rivers. Cycling is gaining in popularity year by year, helped by a network of 1600 kilometres of cycle lanes and paths.

Parks and Nature Reserves There are 19 nature reserves (three of which are managed by the Canadian Government) where hunting is banned, and 18 wildlife reserves where fishing is permitted and hunting is regulated. Camping is allowed and there are chalets which can be rented.

Arts Many music and drama festivals are held in the province, such as the classical music festival in Lanaudière and the famous *Festival du Théâtre des Amériques*. 'Barn theater' (plays put on in villages) is also popular. Montreal has an internationally renowned symphony orchestra, and mention should also be made of the many singer-songwriters who sing in French. Quebec has a lively film industry but suffers from small audiences and is in constant need of government aid. Film dubbing is a growth sector.

Tourism Hotels in Quebec are classified according to a star system by a national body called Canada Select. Staying in a *gîte du passant* (bed and breakfast accommodation at somebody's house) is also popular.

Cuisine The Québecois use different words from the French to talk about mealtimes: *déjeuner* for breakfast, *dîner* for lunch and *souper* for dinner. Maple syrup is probably the most typical food product and is widely used.

ENGLISH - FRENCH

ANGLAIS - FRANÇAIS

a¹ (pl as OR a's), **A** (pl As OR A's) [eɪ] n [letter] a m inv, A m inv ; **to get from A to B** aller d'un point à un autre ; **from A to Z** de A à Z, depuis A jusqu'à Z.
◆ **A** n - **1.** MUS la m inv - **2.** SCH [mark] A m inv.

a² [stressed eɪ, unstressed ə] (before vowel or silent 'h' **an** [stressed æn, unstressed ən]) indef art - **1.** [gen] un (une) ; **a boy** un garçon ; **a table** une table ; **an orange** une orange - **2.** [referring to occupation] : **to be a doctor/lawyer/plumber** être médecin/avocat/plombier - **3.** [instead of the number one] un (une) ; **a hundred/thousand pounds** cent/mille livres - **4.** [to express prices, ratios etc] : **20p a kilo** 20p le kilo ; **£10 a person** 10 livres par personne ; **twice a week/month** deux fois par semaine/mois ; **50 km an hour** 50 km à l'heure - **5.** [preceding person's name] un certain (une certaine) ; **a Mr Jones** un certain M. Jones.

a. abbr of **acre.**

A-1 adj inf excellent(e).

A4 n Br format m A4.

AA ◇ adj abbr of **antiaircraft** ◇ n - **1.** (abbr of Automobile Association) automobile club britannique, ≃ ACF m, ≃ TCF m - **2.** (abbr of Associate in Arts) diplôme universitaire américain de lettres - **3.** (abbr of Alcoholics Anonymous) Alcooliques Anonymes mpl.

AAA n - **1.** (abbr of Amateur Athletics Association) fédération britannique d'athlétisme - **2.** (abbr of American Automobile Association) automobile club américain, ≃ ACF m, ≃ TCF m.

AAUP (abbr of American Association of University Professors) n syndicat universitaire américain des professeurs d'université.

AB ◇ n Am abbr of **Bachelor of Arts** ◇ abbr of **Alberta.**

aback [ə'bæk] adv : **to be taken ~** être décontenancé(e).

abacus ['æbəkəs] (pl -**cuses** [-kəsi:z] OR -**ci** [-saɪ]) n boulier m, abaque m.

abandon [ə'bændən] ◇ vt abandonner ◇ n : **with ~** avec abandon.

abandoned [ə'bændənd] adj abandonné(e).

abashed [ə'bæʃt] adj confus(e).

abate [ə'beɪt] vi [storm, fear] se calmer ; [noise] faiblir.

abattoir ['æbətwɑːʳ] n abattoir m.

abbess ['æbes] n abbesse f.

abbey ['æbɪ] n abbaye f.

abbot ['æbət] n abbé m.

abbreviate [ə'briːvɪeɪt] vt abréger.

abbreviation [ə,briːvɪ'eɪʃn] n abréviation f.

ABC n - **1.** [alphabet] alphabet m - **2.** fig [basics] B.A.-Ba m, abc m - **3.** (abbr of American Broadcasting Company) chaîne de télévision américaine.

abdicate ['æbdɪkeɪt] vt & vi abdiquer.

abdication [,æbdɪ'keɪʃn] n abdication f.

abdomen ['æbdəmən] n abdomen m.

abdominal [æb'dɒmɪnl] adj abdominal(e).

abduct [əb'dʌkt] vt enlever.

abduction [æb'dʌkʃn] n enlèvement m.

aberration [,æbə'reɪʃn] n aberration f.

abet [ə'bet] (pt & pp -**ted** ; cont -**ting**) vt ▷ **aid.**

abeyance [ə'beɪəns] n : **in ~** en attente.

abhor [əb'hɔːʳ] (pt & pp -**red** ; cont -**ring**) vt exécrer, abhorrer.

abhorrent [əb'hɒrənt] *adj* répugnant(e).

abide [ə'baɪd] *vt* supporter, souffrir.

➤ **abide by** *vt fus* respecter, se soumettre à.

abiding [ə'baɪdɪŋ] *adj* [lasting - feeling, interest] constant(e) ; [- memory] éternel(elle), impérissable.

ability [ə'bɪlətɪ] (*pl* -ies) *n* - **1.** [capacity, capability] aptitude *f* ; **to do sthg to the best of one's ~** faire qqch de son mieux - **2.** [skill] talent *m*.

abject ['æbdʒekt] *adj* - **1.** [poverty] noir(e) - **2.** [person] pitoyable ; [apology] servile.

ablaze [ə'bleɪz] *adj* - **1.** [on fire] en feu - **2.** fig [bright] : **to be ~ with** être resplendissant(e) de.

able ['eɪbl] *adj* - **1.** [capable] : **to be ~ to do sthg** pouvoir faire qqch - **2.** [accomplished] compétent(e).

able-bodied [-,bɒdɪd] *adj* en bonne santé, valide.

ablutions [ə'bluːʃnz] *npl fml* ablutions *fpl*.

ably ['eɪblɪ] *adv* avec compétence, habilement.

ABM (*abbr of* **anti-ballistic missile**) *n* ABM *m*.

abnormal [æb'nɔːml] *adj* anormal(e).

abnormality [,æbnɔː'mælətɪ] (*pl* -ies) *n* - **1.** [gen] anomalie *f* - **2.** MED malformation *f*.

abnormally [æb'nɔːməlɪ] *adv* anormalement.

aboard [ə'bɔːd] <> *adv* à bord <> *prep* [ship, plane] à bord ; [bus, train] dans.

abode [ə'bəʊd] *n fml* : **of no fixed ~** sans domicile fixe.

abolish [ə'bɒlɪʃ] *vt* abolir.

abolition [,æbə'lɪʃn] *n* abolition *f*.

A-bomb (*abbr of* **atom bomb**) *n* bombe *f* atomique.

abominable [ə'bɒmɪnəbl] *adj* abominable.

abominable snowman *n* : **the ~** l'abominable homme *m* des neiges.

abominably [ə'bɒmɪnəblɪ] *adv* abominablement.

aborigine [,æbə'rɪdʒənɪ] *n* aborigène *mf* d'Australie.

abort [ə'bɔːt] <> *vt* - **1.** [pregnancy] interrompre - **2.** fig [plan, project] abandonner, faire avorter - **3.** COMPUT abandonner <> *vi* COMPUT abandonner.

abortion [ə'bɔːʃn] *n* avortement *m*, interruption *f* (volontaire) de grossesse ; **to have an ~** se faire avorter.

abortive [ə'bɔːtɪv] *adj* manqué(e).

abound [ə'baʊnd] *vi* - **1.** [be plentiful] abonder - **2.** [be full] : **to ~ with** OR **in** abonder en.

about [ə'baʊt] <> *adv* - **1.** [approximately] environ, à peu près ; **~ fifty/a hundred/a thousand** environ cinquante/cent/mille ; **at ~ five o'clock** vers cinq heures ; **I'm just ~ ready** je suis presque prêt - **2.** [referring to place] : **to run ~** courir çà et là ; **to leave things lying ~** laisser traîner des affaires ; **to walk ~** aller et venir, se promener - **3.** [on the point of] : **to be ~ to do sthg** être sur le point de faire qqch <> *prep* - **1.** [relating to, concerning] au sujet de ; **a film ~ Paris** un film sur Paris ; **what is it ~?** de quoi s'agit-il? ; **to talk ~ sthg** parler de qqch - **2.** [referring to place] : **his belongings were scattered ~ the room** ses affaires étaient éparpillées dans toute la pièce ; **to wander ~ the streets** errer de par les rues.

about-turn Br, **about-face** Am *n* MIL demitour *m* ; fig volte-face *f inv*.

above [ə'bʌv] <> *adv* - **1.** [on top, higher up] audessus - **2.** [in text] ci-dessus, plus haut - **3.** [more, over] plus ; **children aged 5 and ~** les enfants âgés de 5 ans et plus OR de plus de 5 ans <> *prep* - **2.** [on top of, higher up than] audessus de - **2.** [more than] plus de - **3.** [too good for] : **to be ~ doing sthg** ne pas s'abaisser à faire qqch.

➤ **above all** *adv* avant tout.

aboveboard [ə,bʌv'bɔːd] *adj* honnête.

abracadabra [,æbrəkə'dæbrə] *excl* abracadabra!

abrasion [ə'breɪʒn] *n fml* [on skin] écorchure *f*, égratignure *f*.

abrasive [ə'breɪsɪv] <> *adj* [substance] abrasif(ive) ; fig caustique, acerbe <> *n* abrasif *m*.

abreast [ə'brest] *adv* de front, côte à côte.

➤ **abreast of** *prep* : **to keep ~ of** se tenir au courant de.

abridged [ə'brɪdʒd] *adj* abrégé(e).

abroad [ə'brɔːd] *adv* à l'étranger.

abrupt [ə'brʌpt] *adj* - **1.** [sudden] soudain(e), brusque - **2.** [brusque] abrupt(e).

abruptly [ə'brʌptlɪ] *adv* - **1.** [suddenly] brusquement - **2.** [brusquely] abruptement.

ABS (*abbr of* **Antiblockiersystem**) *n* ABS *m*.

abscess ['æbsɪs] *n* abcès *m*.

abscond [əb'skɒnd] *vi* s'enfuir.

abseil ['æbseɪl] *vi* descendre en rappel.

absence ['æbsəns] *n* absence *f* ; **in the ~ of** [thing] faute de.

absent ['æbsənt] *adj* : **~ (from)** absent(e) (de) ; **to be ~ without leave** MIL être en absence irrégulière.

absentee [,æbsən'tiː] *n* absent *m*, -e *f*.

absenteeism [,æbsən'tiːɪzm] n absentéisme m.

absent-minded ['maɪndɪd] adj distrait(e).

absent-mindedly [-'maɪndɪdlɪ] adv distraitement.

absinth(e) ['æbsɪnθ] n absinthe f.

absolute ['æbsəluːt] adj - 1. [complete - fool, disgrace] complet(ète) - 2. [totalitarian - ruler, power] absolu(e).

absolutely ['æbsə'luːtlɪ] adv absolument.

absolute majority n majorité f absolue.

absolution [,æbsə'luːʃn] n absolution f.

absolve [əb'zɒlv] vt : to ~ sb (from) absoudre qqn (de).

absorb [əb'zɔːb] vt absorber ; [information] retenir, assimiler ; to be ~ed in sthg être absorbé(e) dans qqch.

absorbent [əb'zɔːbənt] adj absorbant(e).

absorbing [əb'zɔːbɪŋ] adj captivant(e).

absorption [əb'zɔːpʃn] n absorption f.

abstain [əb'steɪn] vi : to ~ (from) s'abstenir (de).

abstemious [æb'stiːmjəs] adj fml frugal(e), sobre.

abstention [əb'stenʃn] n abstention f.

abstinence ['æbstɪnəns] n abstinence f.

abstract [adj & n 'æbstrækt , vb æb'strækt] ⇔ adj abstrait(e) ⇔ n [summary] résumé m, abrégé m ⇔ vt [summarize] résumer.

abstraction [æb'strækʃn] n - 1. [distractedness] distraction f - 2. [abstract idea] abstraction f.

abstruse [æb'struːs] adj abstrus(e).

absurd [əb'sɜːd] adj absurde.

absurdity [əb'sɜːdətɪ] (pl -ies) n absurdité f.

absurdly [əb'sɜːdlɪ] adv absurdement.

ABTA ['æbtə] (abbr of Association of British Travel Agents) n association des agences de voyage britanniques.

Abu Dhabi [,æbuː'dɑːbɪ] n Abou Dhabi.

abundance [ə'bʌndəns] n abondance f; in ~ en abondance.

abundant [ə'bʌndənt] adj abondant(e).

abundantly [ə'bʌndəntlɪ] adv - 1. [clear, obvious] parfaitement, tout à fait - 2. [exist, grow] en abondance.

abuse [n ə'bjuːs, vb ə'bjuːz] ⇔ n (U) - 1. [offensive remarks] insultes fpl, injures fpl - 2. [maltreatment] mauvais traitement m ; child ~ mauvais traitements infligés aux enfants ; physical ~ sévices mpl corporels ; sexual ~ abus mpl sexuels - 3. [of power, drugs etc] abus m ⇔ vt - 1. [insult] insulter, injurier - 2. [maltreat] maltraiter - 3. [power, drugs etc] abuser de.

abusive [ə'bjuːsɪv] adj grossier(ère), injurieux(euse).

abut [ə'bʌt] (pt & pp -ted ; cont -ting) vi [adjoin] : to ~ on to être contigu(ë) à.

abysmal [ə'bɪzml] adj épouvantable, abominable.

abysmally [ə'bɪzməlɪ] adv abominablement.

abyss [ə'bɪs] n abîme m, gouffre m.

Abyssinia [,æbɪ'sɪnjə] n Abyssinie f; in ~ en Abyssinie.

Abyssinian [,æbɪ'sɪnɪən] ⇔ adj abyssinien(enne) ⇔ n Abyssinien m, -enne f.

a/c (abbr of account (current)) cc.

AC n - 1. (abbr of athletics club) club britannique d'athlétisme - 2. (abbr of alternating current) courant m alternatif.

acacia [ə'keɪʃə] n acacia m.

academic [,ækə'demɪk] ⇔ adj - 1. [of college, university] universitaire - 2. [person] intellectuel(elle) - 3. [question, discussion] théorique ⇔ n universitaire mf.

academic year n année f scolaire OR universitaire.

academy [ə'kædəmɪ] (pl -ies) n - 1. [school, college] école f; ~ of music conservatoire m - 2. [institution, society] académie f.

ACAS ['eɪkæs] (abbr of Advisory Conciliation and Arbitration Service) n organisme britannique de conciliation des conflits du travail.

accede [æk'siːd] vi - 1. [agree] : to ~ to agréer, donner suite à - 2. [monarch] : to ~ to the throne monter sur le trône.

accelerate [ək'seləreɪt] vi - 1. [car, driver] accélérer - 2. [inflation, growth] s'accélérer.

acceleration [ək,selə'reɪʃn] n accélération f.

accelerator [ək'seləreɪtə'] n accélérateur m.

accelerator board, accelerator card n COMPUT carte f accélérateur OR accélératrice.

accent ['æksent] n accent m.

accentuate [æk'sentjueɪt] vt accentuer.

accept [ək'sept] vt - 1. [gen] accepter ; [for job, as member of club] recevoir, admettre - 2. [agree] : to ~ that ... admettre que ...

acceptable [ək'septəbl] adj acceptable.

acceptably [ək'septəblɪ] adv convenablement.

acceptance [ək'septəns] n - 1. [gen] acceptation f - 2. [for job, as member of club] admission f.

accepted [ək'septɪd] adj [ideas, fact] reconnu(e).

access ['ækses] ⇔ n - 1. [entry, way in] accès m ;

to gain ~ to avoir accès à - **2.** [opportunity to use, see] : **to have ~ to** sthg avoir qqch à sa disposition, disposer de qqch ◇ *vt* COMPUT avoir accès à.

accessibility [ək,sesə'bɪlətɪ] *n* - **1.** [of place] accessibilité *f* - **2.** [availability] accès *m*.

accessible [ək'sesəbl] *adj* - **1.** [reachable - place] accessible - **2.** [available] disponible.

accession [æk'seʃn] *n* [of monarch] accession *f*.

accessory [ək'sesərɪ] (*pl* -**ies**) *n* - **1.** [of car, vacuum cleaner] accessoire *m* - **2.** JUR complice *mf*.

➡ **accessories** *npl* accessoires *mpl*.

access road *n* Br [to motorway] bretelle *f* de raccordement OR d'accès.

access time *n* COMPUT temps *m* d'accès.

accident ['æksɪdənt] *n* accident *m* ; **~ and emergency department** Br (service *m* des) urgences *fpl* ; **by ~** par hasard, par accident.

accidental [,æksɪ'dentl] *adj* accidentel(elle).

accidentally [,æksɪ'dentəlɪ] *adv* - **1.** [drop, break] par mégarde - **2.** [meet] par hasard.

accident-prone *adj* prédisposé(e) aux accidents.

acclaim [ə'kleɪm] ◇ *n* (*U*) éloges *mpl* ◇ *vt* louer.

acclamation [,æklə'meɪʃn] (*U*) *n* acclamation *f*.

acclimatize, -ise [ə'klaɪmətaɪz], **acclimate** Am ['ækləmeɪt] *vi* : **to ~ (to)** s'acclimater (à).

accolade ['ækəleɪd] *n* accolade *f* ; **the ultimate ~** la consécration suprême.

accommodate [ə'kɒmədeɪt] *vt* - **1.** [provide room for] loger - **2.** [oblige - person, wishes] satisfaire.

accommodating [ə'kɒmədeɪtɪŋ] *adj* obligeant(e).

accommodation Br [ə,kɒmə'deɪʃn] *n*, **accommodations** Am [ə,kɒmə'deɪʃnz] *npl* logement *m* ; **office ~** bureaux *mpl*.

accompaniment [ə'kʌmpənɪmənt] *n* MUS accompagnement *m*.

accompanist [ə'kʌmpənɪst] *n* MUS accompagnateur *m*, -trice *f*.

accompany [ə'kʌmpənɪ] (*pt* & *pp* -**ied**) *vt* - **1.** [gen] accompagner - **2.** MUS : **to ~ sb (on)** accompagner qqn (à).

accomplice [ə'kʌmplɪs] *n* complice *mf*.

accomplish [ə'kʌmplɪʃ] *vt* accomplir.

accomplished [ə'kʌmplɪʃt] *adj* accompli(e).

accomplishment [ə'kʌmplɪʃmənt] *n* - **1.** [action] accomplissement *m* - **2.** [achievement] réussite *f*.

➡ **accomplishments** *npl* talents *mpl*.

accord [ə'kɔːd] *n* : **to do** sthg **of one's own ~** faire qqch de son propre chef OR de soi-même ; **to be in ~ with** être d'accord avec ; **with one ~** d'un commun accord.

accordance [ə'kɔːdəns] *n* : **in ~ with** conformément à.

according [ə'kɔːdɪŋ] ➡ **according to** *prep* - **1.** [as stated or shown by] d'après ; **to go ~ to plan** se passer comme prévu - **2.** [with regard to] suivant, en fonction de.

accordingly [ə'kɔːdɪŋlɪ] *adv* - **1.** [appropriately] en conséquence - **2.** [consequently] par conséquent.

accordion [ə'kɔːdjən] *n* accordéon *m*.

accordionist [ə'kɔːdjənɪst] *n* accordéoniste *mf*.

accost [ə'kɒst] *vt* accoster.

account [ə'kaʊnt] *n* - **1.** [with bank, shop, company] compte *m* - **2.** [report] compte-rendu *m* - **3.** phr : **to call sb to ~** demander des comptes à qqn ; **to give a good ~ of o.s.** faire bonne impression ; **to take ~ of** sthg, **to take** sthg **into ~** prendre qqch en compte ; **to be of no ~** n'avoir aucune importance ; **on no ~** sous aucun prétexte, en aucun cas.

➡ **accounts** *npl* [of business] comptabilité *f*, comptes *mpl* ; **to do the ~s** faire les comptes.

➡ **by all accounts** *adv* d'après ce que l'on dit, au dire de tous.

➡ **on account of** *prep* à cause de.

➡ **account for** *vt fus* - **1.** [explain] justifier, expliquer ; **has everyone been ~ed for?** personne n'a été oublié? - **2.** [represent] représenter.

accountability [ə,kaʊntə'bɪlətɪ] (*U*) *n* responsabilité *f*.

accountable [ə'kaʊntəbl] *adj* - **1.** [responsible] : **~ (for)** responsable (de) - **2.** [answerable] : **to be ~ to** rendre compte à, rendre des comptes à.

accountancy [ə'kaʊntənsɪ] *n* comptabilité *f*.

accountant [ə'kaʊntənt] *n* comptable *mf*.

accounting [ə'kaʊntɪŋ] *n* comptabilité *f*.

accoutrements Br [ə'kuːtrəmənts], **accouterments** Am [ə'kuːtərmənts] *npl* fml attirail *m*.

accredited [ə'kredɪtɪd] *adj* attitré(e).

accrue [ə'kruː] *vi* [money] fructifier ; [interest] courir.

accumulate [ə'kjuːmjʊleɪt] ◇ *vt* accumuler, amasser ◇ *vi* s'accumuler.

accumulation [ə,kjuːmjʊ'leɪʃn] *n* - **1.** (*U*) [act of accumulating] accumulation *f* - **2.** [things accumulated] amas *m*.

accuracy ['ækjʊrəsɪ] n - **1.** [of description, report] exactitude f - **2.** [of weapon, typist, figures] précision f.

accurate ['ækjʊrət] adj - **1.** [description, report] exact(e) - **2.** [weapon, typist, figures] précis(e).

accurately ['ækjʊrətlɪ] adv - **1.** [truthfully - describe, report] fidèlement - **2.** [precisely - aim] avec précision ; [- type] sans faute.

accusation [,ækjuː'zeɪʃn] n accusation f.

accuse [ə'kjuːz] vt : to ~ sb of sthg/of doing sthg accuser qqn de qqch/de faire qqch.

accused [ə'kjuːzd] (pl inv) n JUR : the ~ l'accusé m, -e f.

accusing [ə'kjuːzɪŋ] adj accusateur(trice).

accusingly [ə'kjuːzɪŋlɪ] adv d'une manière accusatrice.

accustomed [ə'kʌstəmd] adj : to be ~ to sthg/ to doing sthg avoir l'habitude de qqch/de faire qqch.

ace [eɪs] ◇ n as m ; to be within an ~ of fig être à deux doigts de ◇ adj [top-class] de haut niveau.

acerbic [ə'sɜːbɪk] adj acerbe.

acetate ['æsɪteɪt] n acétate m.

acetic acid [ə'siːtɪk-] n acide m acétique.

acetone ['æsɪtəʊn] n acétone f.

acetylene [ə'setɪliːn] n acétylène m.

ACGB (abbr of Arts Council of Great Britain) n organisme public britannique d'aide à la création artistique.

ache [eɪk] ◇ n douleur f ◇ vi - **1.** [back, limb] faire mal ; my head ~s j'ai mal à la tête - **2.** fig [want] : to be aching for sthg/to do sthg mourir d'envie de qqch/de faire qqch.

achieve [ə'tʃiːv] vt [success, victory] obtenir, remporter ; [goal] atteindre ; [ambition] réaliser ; [fame] parvenir à.

achievement [ə'tʃiːvmənt] n - **1.** [success] réussite f - **2.** [of goal, objective] réalisation f.

Achilles' heel [ə'kɪliːz-] n talon m d'Achille.

Achilles' tendon n tendon m d'Achille.

acid ['æsɪd] ◇ adj lit & fig acide ◇ n acide m.

acid house n MUS house f (music).

acidic [ə'sɪdɪk] adj acide.

acidity [ə'sɪdətɪ] n acidité f.

acid jazz n MUS acid jazz m.

acid rain (U) n pluies fpl acides.

acid test n fig épreuve f décisive.

acknowledge [ək'nɒlɪdʒ] vt - **1.** [fact, situation, person] reconnaître - **2.** [letter] : to ~ (receipt of) accuser réception de - **3.** [greet] saluer.

acknowledg(e)ment [ək'nɒlɪdʒmənt] n

- **1.** [gen] reconnaissance f - **2.** [letter] accusé m de réception.

➡ **acknowledg(e)ments** npl [in book] remerciements mpl.

ACLU (abbr of American Civil Liberties Union) n ligue américaine des droits du citoyen.

acme ['ækmɪ] n apogée m.

acne ['æknɪ] n acné f.

acorn ['eɪkɔːn] n gland m.

acoustic [ə'kuːstɪk] adj acoustique.

➡ **acoustics** npl [of room] acoustique f.

acoustic guitar n guitare f sèche.

ACPO (abbr of Association of Chief Police Officers) n syndicat d'officiers supérieurs de la police britannique.

acquaint [ə'kweɪnt] vt : to ~ sb with sthg mettre qqn au courant de qqch ; to be ~ed with sb connaître qqn.

acquaintance [ə'kweɪntəns] n - **1.** [person] connaissance f - **2.** [with person] : to make sb's ~ faire la connaissance de qqn.

acquiesce [,ækwɪ'es] vi : to ~ (to OR in sthg) donner son accord (à qqch).

acquiescence [,ækwɪ'esns] n consentement m.

acquire [ə'kwaɪəʳ] vt acquérir.

acquired taste [ə'kwaɪəd-] n : it's an ~ on finit par aimer ça.

acquisition [,ækwɪ'zɪʃn] n acquisition f.

acquisitive [ə'kwɪzɪtɪv] adj avide de possessions.

acquit [ə'kwɪt] (pt & pp -ted ; cont -ting) vt - **1.** JUR acquitter - **2.** [perform] : to ~ o.s. well/ badly bien/mal se comporter.

acquittal [ə'kwɪtl] n acquittement m.

acre ['eɪkəʳ] n = demi-hectare m (= 4046,9 m²).

acreage ['eɪkərɪdʒ] n superficie f, aire f.

acrid ['ækrɪd] adj [taste, smell] âcre ; fig acerbe.

acrimonious [,ækrɪ'məʊnjəs] adj acrimonieux(euse).

acrobat ['ækrəbæt] n acrobate mf.

acrobatic [,ækrə'bætɪk] adj acrobatique.

➡ **acrobatics** npl acrobatie f.

acronym ['ækrənɪm] n acronyme m.

across [ə'krɒs] ◇ adv - **1.** [from one side to the other] en travers ; to run ~ traverser en courant - **2.** [in measurements] : the river is 2 km ~ la rivière mesure 2 km de large - **3.** [in crossword] : 21 ~ 21 horizontalement - **4.** phr : to get sthg ~ (to sb) faire comprendre qqch (à qqn) ◇ prep - **1.** [from one side to the other] d'un côté à l'autre de, en travers de ; to walk ~ the road traverser la route ; to run ~ the road traverser la route en courant ; there's a bridge ~ the river il y a un pont sur la riviè-

re - **2.** [on the other side of] de l'autre côté de ; **the house ~ the road** la maison d'en face.
← **across from** *prep* en face de.
across-the-board *adj* général(e).
acrylic [ə'krılık] <> *adj* acrylique <> *n* acrylique *m*.
act [ækt] <> *n* - **1.** [action, deed] acte *m* ; **to catch sb in the ~** prendre qqn sur le fait ; **to catch sb in the ~ of doing sthg** surprendre qqn en train de faire qqch - **2.** JUR loi *f* - **3.** [of play, opera] acte *m* ; [in cabaret etc] numéro *m* ; fig [pretence] : **to put on an ~** jouer la comédie - **4.** phr : **to get in on the ~** s'y mettre ; **to get one's ~ together** se reprendre en main <> *vi* - **1.** [gen] agir - **2.** [behave] se comporter ; **to ~ as if** se conduire comme si, se comporter comme si ; **to ~ like** se conduire comme, se comporter comme - **3.** [in play, film] jouer ; fig [pretend] jouer la comédie - **4.** [function] : **to ~ as** [person] être ; [object] servir de ; **to ~ for sb, to ~ on behalf of sb** représenter qqn <> *vt* [part] jouer ; **to ~ the fool** faire l'imbécile ; **~ your age!** ce n'est plus de ton âge!
← **act out** *vt sep* - **1.** [feelings, thoughts] exprimer - **2.** [event] mimer.
← **act up** *vi* faire des siennes.
ACT (abbr of **American College Test**) *n* examen américain de fin d'études secondaires.
acting ['æktıŋ] <> *adj* par intérim, provisoire <> *n* [in play, film] interprétation *f*.
action ['ækʃn] *n* - **1.** [gen] action *f* ; **to take ~** agir, prendre des mesures ; **to put sthg into ~** mettre qqch à exécution ; **in ~** [person] en action ; [machine] en marche ; **out of ~** [person] hors de combat ; [machine] hors service, hors d'usage ; **to be killed in ~** mourir au combat - **2.** JUR procès *m*, action *f* ; **to bring an ~ against sb** intenter un procès à OR contre qqn, intenter une action contre qqn.
action group *n* groupe *m* de pression.
action movie *n* film *m* d'action.
action replay *n* répétition *f* immédiate (au ralenti).
activate ['æktıveıt] *vt* mettre en marche.
active ['æktıv] *adj* - **1.** [gen] actif(ive) ; [encouragement] vif (vive) - **2.** [volcano] en activité.
actively ['æktıvlı] *adv* activement.
active service *n* : **to be killed on ~** mourir au champ d'honneur.
activist ['æktıvıst] *n* activiste *mf*.
activity [æk'tıvətı] (*pl* **-ies**) *n* activité *f*.
act of God *n* catastrophe *f* naturelle.
actor ['æktər] *n* acteur *m*.
actress ['æktrıs] *n* actrice *f*.
actual ['æktʃʊəl] *adj* réel(elle) ; **the ~ ceremo-**

ny **starts at ten a.m.** la cérémonie proprement dite commence à dix heures.
actuality [ˌæktʃʊ'ælətı] *n* : **in ~** en fait.
actually ['æktʃʊəlı] *adv* - **1.** [really, in truth] vraiment - **2.** [by the way] au fait.
actuary ['æktjʊərı] (*pl* **-ies**) *n* actuaire *mf*.
actuate ['æktjʊeıt] *vt* mettre en marche.
acuity [ə'kjuːətı] *n* acuité *f*.
acumen ['ækjʊmen] *n* flair *m* ; **business ~** le sens des affaires.
acupuncture ['ækjʊpʌŋktʃər] *n* acupuncture *f*, acuponcture *f*.
acute [ə'kjuːt] *adj* - **1.** [severe - pain, illness] aigu(ë) ; [- danger] sérieux(euse), grave - **2.** [perceptive - person, mind] perspicace - **3.** [keen - eyesight] perçant(e) ; [- hearing] fin(e) ; [- sense of smell] développé(e) - **4.** MATH : **~ angle** angle *m* aigu - **5.** LING : **e ~** e accent aigu.
acute accent *n* accent *m* aigu.
acutely [ə'kjuːtlı] *adv* [extremely] extrêmement.
ad [æd] (abbr of **advertisement**) *n* inf [in newspaper] annonce *f* ; [on TV] pub *f*.
AD (abbr of **Anno Domini**) ap. J.-C.
adage ['ædıdʒ] *n* adage *m*.
adamant ['ædəmənt] *adj* : **to be ~** être inflexible.
Adam's apple ['ædəmz-] *n* pomme *f* d'Adam.
adapt [ə'dæpt] <> *vt* adapter <> *vi* : **to ~ (to)** s'adapter (à)
adaptability [ə,dæptə'bılətı] *n* souplesse *f*.
adaptable [ə'dæptəbl] *adj* [person] souple.
adaptation [ˌædæp'teıʃn] *n* [of book, play] adaptation *f*.
adapter, adaptor [ə'dæptər] *n* [ELEC - for several devices] prise *f* multiple ; [- for foreign plug] adaptateur *m*.
ADC *n* - **1.** abbr of **aide-de-camp - 2.** (abbr of **Aid to Dependent Children**) aux États-Unis, aide pour enfants assistés - **3.** (abbr of **analogue-digital converter**) CAN *m*.
add [æd] *vt* - **1.** [gen] : **to ~ sthg (to)** ajouter qqch (à) - **2.** [numbers] additionner.
← **add in** *vt sep* ajouter.
← **add on** *vt sep* : **to ~ sthg on (to)** ajouter qqch (à) ; [charge, tax] rajouter qqch (à).
← **add to** *vt fus* ajouter à, augmenter.
← **add up** <> *vt sep* additionner <> *vi* inf [make sense] : **it doesn't ~ up** c'est pas logique.
← **add up to** *vt fus* se monter à, s'élever à.
addendum [ə'dendəm] (*pl* **-da** [-də]) *n* addenda *m inv*.
adder ['ædər] *n* vipère *f*.

addict ['ædɪkt] *n* lit & fig drogué *m*, -e *f* ; drug ~ drogué.

addicted [ə'dɪktɪd] *adj* : ~ **(to)** drogué(e)(à) ; fig passionné(e)(de).

addiction [ə'dɪkʃn] *n* : ~ **(to)** dépendance *f* (à) ; fig penchant *m* (pour).

addictive [ə'dɪktɪv] *adj* qui rend dépendant(e).

Addis Ababa ['ædɪs'æbəbə] *n* Addis-Ababa, Addis-Abeba.

addition [ə'dɪʃn] *n* addition *f* ; in ~ **(to)** en plus (de).

additional [ə'dɪʃənl] *adj* supplémentaire.

additive ['ædɪtɪv] *n* additif *m*.

addled ['ædld] *adj* - **1.** [egg] pourri(e) - **2.** [brain] embrouillé(e).

add-on COMPUT <> *adj* supplémentaire <> *n* dispositif *m* supplémentaire.

address [ə'dres] <> *n* - **1.** [place] adresse *f* - **2.** [speech] discours *m* <> *vt* - **1.** [gen] adresser - **2.** [meeting, conference] prendre la parole à - **3.** [problem, issue] aborder, examiner ; to ~ o.s. to s'attaquer à.

address book *n* carnet *m* d'adresses.

addressee [,ædre'si:] *n* destinataire *mf*.

Aden ['eɪdn] *n* Aden.

adenoids ['ædɪnɔɪdz] *npl* végétations *fpl*.

adept ['ædept] *adj* : ~ **(at)** doué(e)(pour).

adequacy ['ædɪkwəsɪ] *n* - **1.** [of amount] quantité *f* nécessaire - **2.** [of person] compétence *f*.

adequate ['ædɪkwət] *adj* adéquat(e).

adequately ['ædɪkwətlɪ] *adv* - **1.** [sufficiently] suffisamment - **2.** [well enough] de façon satisfaisante OR adéquate.

adhere [əd'hɪəʳ] *vi* - **1.** [stick] : to ~ **(to)** adhérer (à) - **2.** [observe] : to ~ to obéir à - **3.** [keep] : to ~ to adhérer à.

adherence [əd'hɪərəns] *n* : ~ to adhésion *f* à.

adhesive [əd'hi:sɪv] <> *adj* adhésif(ive) <> *n* adhésif *m*.

adhesive tape *n* ruban *m* adhésif.

ad hoc [,æd'hɒk] *adj* ad hoc.

ad infinitum [,ædɪnfɪ'naɪtəm] *adv* à l'infini.

adjacent [ə'dʒeɪsənt] *adj* : ~ **(to)** adjacent(e)(à), contigu(ë)(à).

adjective ['ædʒɪktɪv] *n* adjectif *m*.

adjoin [ə'dʒɔɪn] *vt* être contigu(ë) à, toucher.

adjoining [ə'dʒɔɪnɪŋ] <> *adj* voisin(e) <> *prep* attenant à.

adjourn [ə'dʒɜːn] <> *vt* ajourner <> *vi* suspendre la séance.

adjournment [ə'dʒɜːnmənt] *n* ajournement *m*.

Adjt (*abbr of* adjutant) adjt.

adjudge [ə'dʒʌdʒ] *vt* déclarer.

adjudicate [ə'dʒuːdɪkeɪt] <> *vt* juger, décider <> *vi* : to ~ **(on** OR **upon)** se prononcer (sur).

adjudication [ə,dʒuːdɪ'keɪʃn] *n* jugement *m*.

adjunct ['ædʒʌŋkt] *n* complément *m*.

adjust [ə'dʒʌst] <> *vt* ajuster, régler <> *vi* : to ~ **(to)** s'adapter (à).

adjustable [ə'dʒʌstəbl] *adj* réglable.

adjustable spanner *n* clé *f* universelle.

adjusted [ə'dʒʌstɪd] *adj* : to be well ~ être (bien) équilibré(e).

adjustment [ə'dʒʌstmənt] *n* - **1.** [modification] ajustement *m* ; TECH réglage *m* ; to make an ~ to apporter une modification à - **2.** [change in attitude] : ~ **(to)** adaptation *f* (à).

adjutant ['ædʒʊtənt] *n* adjudant *m*.

ad lib [,æd'lɪb] (*pt* & *pp* ad-libbed ; *cont* ad-libbing) <> *adj* improvisé(e) <> *adv* à volonté <> *n* improvisation *f*.

➟ **ad-lib** *vi* improviser.

adman ['ædmæn] (*pl* -men [-men]) *n* publicitaire *m*.

admin ['ædmɪn] (*abbr of* administration) *n* Br inf administration *f*.

administer [əd'mɪnɪstəʳ] *vt* - **1.** [company, business] administrer, gérer - **2.** [justice, punishment] dispenser - **3.** [drug, medication] administrer.

administration [əd,mɪnɪ'streɪʃn] *n* administration *f*.

➟ **Administration** *n* Am : the Administration le gouvernement.

administrative [əd'mɪnɪstrətɪv] *adj* administratif(ive).

administrator [əd'mɪnɪstreɪtəʳ] *n* administrateur *m*, -trice *f*.

admirable ['ædmərəbl] *adj* admirable.

admirably ['ædmərəblɪ] *adv* admirablement.

admiral ['ædmərəl] *n* amiral *m*.

Admiralty ['ædmərəltɪ] *n* Br : the ~ le ministère de la Marine.

admiration [,ædmə'reɪʃn] *n* admiration *f*.

admire [əd'maɪəʳ] *vt* admirer.

admirer [əd'maɪərəʳ] *n* admirateur *m*, -trice *f*.

admiring [əd'maɪərɪŋ] *adj* admiratif(ive).

admiringly [əd'maɪərɪŋlɪ] *adv* avec admiration.

admissible [əd'mɪsəbl] *adj* JUR recevable.

admission [əd'mɪʃn] *n* - **1.** [permission to enter]

admission f - **2.** [to museum etc] entrée f
- **3.** [confession] confession f, aveu m ; **by his/
her** etc **own ~** de son propre aveu.

admit [əd'mɪt] (pt & pp -**ted** ; cont -**ting**) <> vt
- **1.** [confess] reconnaître ; **to ~ (that)** ... reconnaître que ... ; **to ~ doing sthg** reconnaître
avoir fait qqch ; **to ~ defeat** fig s'avouer
vaincu(e) - **2.** [allow to enter, join] admettre ; **~s
two** [on ticket] valable pour deux personnes ;
to be admitted to hospital Br OR **to the hospital**
Am être admis(e) à l'hôpital <> vi : **to ~ to**
admettre, reconnaître.

admittance [əd'mɪtəns] n admission f ; **to
gain ~ to** parvenir à, entrer dans ; **'no ~'**
'entrée interdite'.

admittedly [əd'mɪtɪdlɪ] adv de l'aveu général.

admixture [æd'mɪkstʃəʳ] n mélange m.

admonish [əd'mɒnɪʃ] vt réprimander.

ad nauseam [,æd'nɔːzɪæm] adv [talk] à n'en
plus finir.

ado [ə'duː] n : **without further** OR **more ~** sans
plus de cérémonie.

adolescence [,ædə'lesns] n adolescence f.

adolescent [,ædə'lesnt] <> adj adolescent(e) ; pej puéril(e) <> n adolescent m, -e
f.

adopt [ə'dɒpt] vt adopter.

adoption [ə'dɒpʃn] n adoption f.

adoptive [ə'dɒptɪv] adj adoptif(ive).

adorable [ə'dɔːrəbl] adj adorable.

adoration [,ædə'reɪʃn] n adoration f.

adore [ə'dɔːʳ] vt adorer.

adoring [ə'dɔːrɪŋ] adj [person] adorateur(trice) ; [look] d'adoration.

adorn [ə'dɔːn] vt orner.

adornment [ə'dɔːnmənt] n décoration f.

ADP (abbr of **automatic data processing**) n
traitement automatique de données.

adrenalin [ə'drenəlɪn] n adrénaline f.

Adriatic [,eɪdrɪ'ætɪk] n : **the ~ (Sea)** l'Adriatique f, la mer Adriatique.

adrift [ə'drɪft] <> adj à la dérive <> adv : **to
go ~** fig aller à la dérive.

adroit [ə'drɔɪt] adj adroit(e).

ADT (abbr of **Atlantic Daylight Time**) n heure
d'été de la côte est des États-Unis.

adulation [,ædjuː'leɪʃn] n adulation f.

adult ['ædʌlt] <> adj - **1.** [gen] adulte - **2.** [films,
literature] pour adultes <> n adulte mf.

adult education n enseignement m pour
adultes.

adulterate [ə'dʌltəreɪt] vt frelater.

adulteration [ə,dʌltə'reɪʃn] n frelatage m.

adulterer [ə'dʌltərəʳ] n personne f adultère.

adultery [ə'dʌltərɪ] n adultère m.

adulthood ['ædʌlthʊd] n âge m adulte.

advance [əd'vɑːns] <> n - **1.** [gen] avance f
- **2.** [progress] progrès m <> comp à l'avance
<> vt - **1.** [gen] avancer - **2.** [improve] faire progresser OR avancer <> vi - **1.** [gen] avancer
- **2.** [improve] progresser.

➤ **advances** npl : **to make ~s to sb** [sexual] faire des avances à qqn ; [business] faire des
propositions à qqn.

➤ **in advance** adv à l'avance.

➤ **in advance of** prep - **1.** [in front of] en avance sur - **2.** [prior to] en avance de, avant.

advanced [əd'vɑːnst] adj avancé(e) ; **~ in
years** euphemism d'un âge avancé.

advancement [əd'vɑːnsmənt] n - **1.** [promotion] avancement m - **2.** [progress] progrès m.

advantage [əd'vɑːntɪdʒ] n : **~ (over)** avantage m (sur) ; **to be to one's ~** être à son avantage ; **to take ~ of sthg** profiter de qqch ; **to
take ~ of sb** exploiter qqn.

advantageous [,ædvən'teɪdʒəs] adj avantageux(euse).

advent ['ædvənt] n avènement m.

➤ **Advent** n RELIG Avent m.

Advent calendar n calendrier m de
l'Avent.

adventure [əd'ventʃəʳ] n aventure f.

adventure holiday n circuit m aventure.

adventure playground n terrain m
d'aventures.

adventurer [əd'ventʃərəʳ] n aventurier m,
-ère f.

adventurous [əd'ventʃərəs] adj aventureux(euse).

adverb ['ædvɜːb] n adverbe m.

adversary ['ædvəsərɪ] (pl -**ies**) n adversaire
mf.

adverse ['ædvɜːs] adj défavorable.

adversely ['ædvɜːslɪ] adv de façon défavorable.

adversity [əd'vɜːsətɪ] n adversité f.

advert ['ædvɜːt] Br = **advertisement**.

advertise ['ædvətaɪz] <> vt COMM faire de la
publicité pour ; [event] annoncer <> vi faire
de la publicité ; **to ~ for sb/sthg** chercher
qqn/qqch par voie d'annonce.

advertisement [əd'vɜːtɪsmənt] n [in newspaper] annonce f ; COMM & fig publicité f.

advertiser ['ædvətaɪzəʳ] n annonceur m.

advertising ['ædvətaɪzɪŋ] n (U) publicité f.

advertising agency n agence f de publicité.

advertising campaign *n* campagne *f* de publicité.

advice [əd'vaɪs] *n (U)* conseils *mpl* ; **a piece of** ~ un conseil ; **to give sb** ~ donner des conseils à qqn ; **to take sb's** ~ suivre les conseils de qqn.

advice note *n* avis *m*.

advisability [əd͵vaɪzə'bɪlətɪ] *n* bien-fondé *m*.

advisable [əd'vaɪzəbl] *adj* conseillé(e), recommandé(e).

advise [əd'vaɪz] ◇ *vt* - **1.** [give advice to] : **to** ~ **sb to do sthg** conseiller à qqn de faire qqch ; **to** ~ **sb against sthg** déconseiller qqch à qqn ; **to** ~ **sb against doing sthg** déconseiller à qqn de faire qqch - **2.** [professionally] : **to** ~ **sb on sthg** conseiller qqn sur qqch - **3.** [inform] : **to** ~ **sb (of sthg)** aviser qqn (de qqch) ◇ *vi* - **1.** [give advice] : **to** ~ **against sthg/against doing sthg** déconseiller qqch/de faire qqch - **2.** [professionally] : **to** ~ **on sthg** conseiller sur qqch.

advisedly [əd'vaɪzɪdlɪ] *adv* en connaissance de cause, délibérément.

adviser Br, **advisor** Am [əd'vaɪzə^r] *n* conseiller *m*, -ère *f*.

advisory [əd'vaɪzərɪ] *adj* consultatif(ive) ; **in an** ~ **capacity** OR **role** à titre consultatif.

advocacy ['ædvəkəsɪ] *n* plaidoyer *m*.

advocate [*n* 'ædvəkət, *vb* 'ædvəkeɪt] ◇ *n* - **1.** JUR avocat *m*, -e *f* - **2.** [supporter] partisan *m* ◇ *vt* préconiser, recommander.

advt. *abbr of* advertisement.

AEA (*abbr of* **Atomic Energy Authority**) *n* commission britannique à l'énergie nucléaire, ≃ CEA *f*.

AEC (*abbr of* **Atomic Energy Commission**) *n* commission américaine à l'énergie nucléaire, ≃ CEA *f*.

AEEU (*abbr of* **Amalgamated Engineering and Electrical Union**) *n* syndicat britannique d'ingénieurs et d'électriciens.

Aegean [iː'dʒiːən] *n* : **the** ~ **(Sea)** la mer Égée.

aegis ['iːdʒɪs] *n* : **under the** ~ **of** sous l'égide de.

Aeolian Islands *npl* : **the** ~ les îles *fpl* Éoliennes.

aeon Br, **eon** Am ['iːən] *n* fig éternité *f*.

aerial ['eərɪəl] ◇ *adj* aérien(enne) ◇ *n* Br antenne *f*.

aerobatics [͵eərəʊ'bætɪks] *n (U)* acrobatie *f* aérienne.

aerobics [eə'rəʊbɪks] *n (U)* aérobic *m*.

aerodrome ['eərədrəʊm] *n* aérodrome *m*.

aerodynamic [͵eərəʊdaɪ'næmɪk] *adj* aérodynamique.
➤ **aerodynamics** ◇ *n (U)* aérodynamique *f* ◇ *npl* [aerodynamic qualities] aérodynamisme *m*.

aerogramme ['eərəgræml] *n* aérogramme *m*.

aeronautics [͵eərə'nɔːtɪks] *n (U)* aéronautique *f*.

aeroplane ['eərəpleɪn] *n* Br avion *m*.

aerosol ['eərəsɒl] *n* aérosol *m*.

aerospace ['eərəʊspeɪs] *n* : **the** ~ **industry** l'industrie *f* aérospatiale.

aesthete, esthete Am ['iːsθiːt] *n* esthète *mf*.

aesthetic, esthetic Am [iːs'θetɪk] *adj* esthétique.

aesthetically, esthetically Am [iːs'θetɪklɪ] *adv* esthétiquement.

aesthetics, esthetics Am [iːs'θetɪks] *n (U)* esthétique *f*.

afar [ə'fɑː^r] *adv* : **from** ~ de loin.

AFB (*abbr of* **Air Force Base**) *n* aux États-Unis, base de l'armée de l'air.

AFDC (*abbr of* **Aid to Families with Dependent Children**) *n* aux États-Unis, aide pour les familles d'enfants assistés.

affable ['æfəbl] *adj* affable.

affair [ə'feə^r] *n* - **1.** [gen] affaire *f* - **2.** [extramarital relationship] liaison *f*.
➤ **affairs** *npl* affaires *fpl*.

affect [ə'fekt] *vt* - **1.** [influence] avoir un effet OR des conséquences sur - **2.** [emotionally] affecter, émouvoir - **3.** [put on] affecter.

affectation [͵æfek'teɪʃn] *n* affectation *f*.

affected [ə'fektɪd] *adj* affecté(e).

affection [ə'fekʃn] *n* affection *f*.

affectionate [ə'fekʃnət] *adj* affectueux(euse).

affectionately [ə'fekʃnətlɪ] *adv* affectueusement.

affidavit [͵æfɪ'deɪvɪt] *n* déclaration écrite sous serment.

affiliate [*n* & *comp* ə'fɪlɪeɪt, *vb* ə'fɪlɪət] ◇ *n* affilié *m*, -e *f* ◇ *vt* : **to be** ~**d to** OR **with** être affilié(e) à.

affiliation [ə͵fɪlɪ'eɪʃn] *n* affiliation *f*.

affinity [ə'fɪnətɪ] (*pl* -ies) *n* affinité *f* ; **to have an** ~ **with sb** avoir des affinités avec qqn.

affirm [ə'fɜːml] *vt* - **1.** [declare] affirmer - **2.** [confirm] confirmer.

affirmation [͵æfə'meɪʃn] *n* - **1.** [declaration] affirmation *f* - **2.** [confirmation] confirmation *f*.

affirmative [ə'fɜːmətɪv] ◇ adj affirmatif(ive) ◇ n : in the ~ par l'affirmative.

affix [ə'fɪks] vt [stamp] coller.

afflict [ə'flɪkt] vt affliger ; **to be ~ed with** souffrir de.

affliction [ə'flɪkʃn] n affliction f.

affluence ['æfluəns] n prospérité f.

affluent ['æfluənt] adj riche.

affluent society n société f d'abondance.

afford [ə'fɔːd] vt - **1.** [buy, pay for] : **to be able to ~ sthg** avoir les moyens d'acheter qqch - **2.** [spare] : **to be able to ~ the time (to do sthg)** avoir le temps (de faire qqch) - **3.** [harmful, embarrassing thing] : **to be able to ~ sthg** pouvoir se permettre qqch - **4.** [provide, give] procurer.

affordable [ə'fɔːdəbl] adj que l'on peut se permettre.

afforestation [æ,fɒrɪ'steɪʃn] n boisement m.

affray [ə'freɪ] n Br bagarre f.

affront [ə'frʌnt] ◇ n affront m, insulte f ◇ vt insulter, faire un affront à.

Afghan ['æfgæn], **Afghani** [æf'gænɪ] ◇ adj afghan(e) ◇ n Afghan m, -e f.

Afghan hound n lévrier m afghan.

Afghani = Afghan.

Afghanistan [æf'gænɪstæn] n Afghanistan m ; **in ~** en Afghanistan.

afield [ə'fiːld] adv : **far ~** loin.

AFL-CIO (abbr of American Federation of Labor and Congress of Industrial Organizations) n confédération syndicale américaine.

afloat [ə'fləʊt] adj lit & fig à flot.

afoot [ə'fʊt] adj en préparation.

aforementioned [ə'fɔː,menʃənd], **aforesaid** [ə'fɔːsed] adj susmentionné(e).

afraid [ə'freɪd] adj - **1.** [frightened] : **to be ~ (of)** avoir peur (de) ; **to be ~ of doing** OR **to do sthg** avoir peur de faire qqch - **2.** [reluctant, apprehensive] : **to be ~ of** craindre - **3.** [in apologies] : **to be ~ (that)** ... regretter que ... ; **I'm ~ so/not** j'ai bien peur que oui/non.

afresh [ə'freʃ] adv de nouveau.

Africa ['æfrɪkə] n Afrique f ; **in ~** en Afrique.

African ['æfrɪkən] ◇ adj africain(e) ◇ n Africain m, -e f.

African American n Noir américain m, Noire américaine f.

Afrikaans [,æfrɪ'kɑːns] n afrikaans m.

Afrikaner [,æfrɪ'kɑːnəʳ] n Afrikaner mf.

aft [ɑːft] adv sur OR à l'arrière.

AFT (abbr of American Federation of Teachers) n syndicat américain d'enseignants.

after ['ɑːftəʳ] ◇ prep - **1.** [gen] après ; **~ you!** après vous! ; **to shout ~ sb** crier après OR contre qqn ; **to be ~ sb/sthg** inf [in search of] chercher qqn/qqch ; **to name sb ~ sb** Br donner à qqn le nom de qqn - **2.** Am [telling the time] : **it's twenty ~ three** il est trois heures vingt ◇ adv après ◇ conj après que.

➤ **afters** npl Br inf dessert m.

➤ **after all** adv après tout.

afterbirth ['ɑːftəbɜːθ] n placenta m.

aftercare ['ɑːftəkeəʳ] n postcure f.

aftereffects ['ɑːftərɪ,fekts] npl suites fpl, répercussions fpl.

afterlife ['ɑːftəlaɪf] (pl -lives [-laɪvz]) n vie f future.

aftermath ['ɑːftəmæθ] n conséquences fpl, suites fpl.

afternoon [,ɑːftə'nuːn] n après-midi m inv ; **in the ~** l'après-midi ; **good ~** bonjour.

➤ **afternoons** adv l'après-midi.

aftershave ['ɑːftəʃeɪv] n après-rasage m.

aftershock ['ɑːftəʃɒk] n réplique f.

aftertaste ['ɑːftəteɪst] n lit & fig arrière-goût m.

afterthought ['ɑːftəθɔːt] n pensée f OR réflexion f après coup.

afterward(s) ['ɑːftəwəd(z)] adv après.

again [ə'gen] adv encore une fois, de nouveau ; **to do ~** refaire ; **to say ~** répéter ; **to start ~** recommencer ; **~ and ~** à plusieurs reprises ; **all over ~** une fois de plus ; **time and ~** maintes et maintes fois ; **half as much ~** à moitié autant ; **(twice) as much ~** deux fois autant ; **come ~?** inf comment?, pardon? ; **then** OR **there ~** d'autre part.

against [ə'genst] prep & adv contre ; **(as) ~** contre.

age [eɪdʒ] (cont ageing OR aging) ◇ n - **1.** [gen] âge m ; **she's 20 years of ~** elle a 20 ans ; **what ~ are you?** quel âge avez-vous? ; **to be of ~** Am avoir l'âge légal pour consommer de l'alcool dans un lieu public ; **to be under ~** être mineur(e) ; **to come of ~** atteindre sa majorité - **2.** [old age] vieillesse f - **3.** [in history] époque f ◇ vt & vi vieillir.

➤ **ages** npl : **~s ago** il y a une éternité ; **I haven't seen him for ~s** je ne l'ai pas vu depuis une éternité.

aged [adj sense 1 eɪdʒd, adj sense 2 & npl 'eɪdʒɪd] ◇ adj - **1.** [of stated age] : **~ 15** âgé(e) de 15 ans - **2.** [very old] âgé(e), vieux (vieille) ◇ npl : **the ~** les personnes fpl âgées.

age group n tranche f d'âge.

ageing ['eɪdʒɪŋ] ◇ adj vieillissant(e) ◇ n vieillissement m.

ageless ['eɪdʒlɪs] *adj* sans âge.

agency ['eɪdʒənsɪ] (*pl* -ies) *n* - 1. [business] agence *f*; **employment ~** agence OR bureau *m* de placement ; **travel ~** agence de voyages - 2. [organization] organisme *m*.

agenda [ə'dʒendə] (*pl* -s) *n* ordre *m* du jour.

agent ['eɪdʒənt] *n* agent *m*.

age-old *adj* antique.

aggravate ['ægrəveɪt] *vt* - 1. [make worse] aggraver - 2. [annoy] agacer.

aggravating ['ægrəveɪtɪŋ] *adj* [annoying] agaçant(e).

aggravation [,ægrə'veɪʃn] *n* - 1. (U) [trouble] agacements *mpl* - 2. [annoying thing] agacement *m*.

aggregate ['ægrɪgət] <> *adj* total(e) <> *n* - 1. [total] total *m* - 2. [material] agrégat *m*.

aggression [ə'greʃn] *n* agression *f*.

aggressive [ə'gresɪv] *adj* agressif(ive).

aggressively [ə'gresɪvlɪ] *adv* d'une manière agressive.

aggressor [ə'gresəʳ] *n* agresseur *m*.

aggrieved [ə'gri:vd] *adj* blessé(e), froissé(e).

aggro ['ægrəʊ] *n* Br inf enquiquinement *m*.

aghast [ə'gɑ:st] *adj* : **~ (at sthg)** atterré(e)(par qqch).

agile [Br 'ædʒaɪl, Am 'ædʒəl] *adj* agile.

agility [ə'dʒɪlətɪ] *n* agilité *f*.

aging = ageing.

agitate ['ædʒɪteɪt] <> *vt* - 1. [disturb] inquiéter - 2. [shake] agiter <> *vi* : **to ~ for/against** faire campagne pour/contre.

agitated ['ædʒɪteɪtɪd] *adj* agité(e)

agitation [,ædʒɪ'teɪʃn] *n* - 1. [anxiety] agitation *f* - 2. POL campagne *f*.

agitator ['ædʒɪteɪtəʳ] *n* agitateur *m*, -trice *f*.

AGM (*abbr of* annual general meeting) *n* Br AGA *f*.

agnostic [æg'nɒstɪk] <> *adj* agnostique <> *n* agnostique *mf*.

ago [ə'gəʊ] *adv* : **a long time ~** il y a longtemps ; **three days ~** il y a trois jours.

agog [ə'gɒg] *adj* : **to be ~ (with)** être en ébullition (à propos de).

agonize, -ise ['ægənaɪz] *vi* : **to ~ over** OR **about sthg** se tourmenter au sujet de qqch.

agonized ['ægənaɪzd] *adj* atroce.

agonizing ['ægənaɪzɪŋ] *adj* déchirant(e).

agonizingly ['ægənaɪzɪŋlɪ] *adv* [difficult etc] extrêmement.

agony ['ægənɪ] (*pl* -ies) *n* - 1. [physical pain] douleur *f* atroce ; **to be in ~** souffrir le martyre

- 2. [mental pain] angoisse *f*; **to be in ~** être angoissé(e), être torturé(e) par l'angoisse.

agony aunt *n* Br inf personne qui tient la rubrique du courrier du cœur.

agony column *n* Br inf courrier *m* du cœur.

agoraphobia [,ægərə'fəʊbjə] *n* agoraphobie *f*.

agree [ə'gri:] <> *vi* - 1. [concur] : **to ~ (with/about)** être d'accord (avec/au sujet de) ; **~ on** [price, terms] convenir de - 2. [consent] : **to ~ (to sthg)** donner son consentement (à qqch) - 3. [be consistent] concorder - 4. [food] : **to ~ with** réussir à - 5. GRAMM : **to ~ (with)** s'accorder (avec) <> *vt* - 1. [price, conditions] accepter, convenir de - 2. [concur, concede] : **to ~ (that)** ... admettre que ... - 3. [arrange] : **to ~ to do sthg** se mettre d'accord pour faire qqch.

agreeable [ə'grɪəbl] *adj* - 1. [pleasant] agréable - 2. [willing] : **to be ~ to** consentir à.

agreeably [ə'grɪəblɪ] *adv* agréablement.

agreed [ə'gri:d] *adj* : **to be ~ (on sthg)** être d'accord (à propos de qqch).

agreement [ə'gri:mənt] *n* - 1. [gen] accord *m*; **to be in ~ (with)** être d'accord (avec) ; **to reach an ~** parvenir à un accord - 2. [consistency] concordance *f*.

agricultural [,ægrɪ'kʌltʃərəl] *adj* agricole.

agriculture ['ægrɪkʌltʃəʳ] *n* agriculture *f*.

aground [ə'graʊnd] *adv* : **to run ~** s'échouer.

ah [ɑ:] *excl* ah!

aha [ɑ:'hɑ:] *excl* ah, ah!

ahead [ə'hed] *adv* - 1. [in front] devant, en avant ; **to go/be sent on ~** partir/être envoyé (envoyé) e en avant ; **right ~, straight ~** droit devant - 2. [in better position] en avance ; **Scotland are ~ by two goals to one** l'Écosse mène par deux à un ; **to get ~** [be successful] réussir - 3. [in time] à l'avance ; **the months ~** les mois à venir.

 ahead of *prep* - 1. [in front of] devant - 2. [in time] avant ; **~ of schedule** [work] en avance sur le planning ; **~ of time** en avance.

ahoy [ə'hɔɪ] *excl* NAUT ohé! ; **ship ~!** ohé, du bateau!

AI *n* - 1. (*abbr of* Amnesty International) AI *m* - 2. (*abbr of* artificial intelligence) IA *f* - 3. *abbr of* artificial insemination.

AIB (*abbr of* Accident Investigation Bureau) *n* commission d'enquête sur les accidents en Grande-Bretagne.

aid [eɪd] <> *n* aide *f*; **with the ~ of** [person] avec l'aide de ; [thing] à l'aide de ; **to go to the ~ of sb** OR **to sb's ~** aller à l'aide de qqn ; **in ~ of** au profit de <> *vt* - 1. [help] aider - 2. JUR : **~ and abet** être complice de.

AID n - **1.** (abbr of **artificial insemination by donor**) IAD f - **2.** (abbr of **Agency for International Development**) AID f.

aide [eɪd] n POL aide mf.

aide-de-camp [eɪddə'kɑ̃ː] (pl **aides-de-camp** [,eɪdz-]) n aide m de camp.

AIDS, Aids [eɪdz] (abbr of **acquired immune deficiency syndrome**) ◇ n SIDA m, sida m ◇ comp : ~ **specialist** sidologue mf ; ~ **patient** sidéen m, -enne f.

AIH (abbr of **artificial insemination by husband**) n IAC f.

ail [eɪl] vi souffrir.

ailing ['eɪlɪŋ] adj - **1.** [ill] souffrant(e) - **2.** fig [economy, industry] dans une mauvaise passe.

ailment ['eɪlmənt] n maladie f.

aim [eɪm] ◇ n - **1.** [objective] but m, objectif m - **2.** [in firing gun, arrow] : **to take** ~ **at** viser ◇ vt - **1.** [gun, camera] : **to** ~ **sthg at** braquer qqch sur - **2.** fig : **to be** ~**ed at** [plan, campaign etc] être destiné(e) à, viser ; [criticism] être dirigé(e) contre ◇ vi : **to** ~ **(at)** viser ; **to** ~ **at** OR **for** fig viser ; **to** ~ **to do sthg** viser à faire qqch.

aimless ['eɪmlɪs] adj [person] désœuvré(e) ; [life] sans but.

aimlessly ['eɪmlɪslɪ] adv sans but.

ain't [eɪnt] inf = am not, are not, is not, have not, has not.

air [eəʳ] ◇ n - **1.** [gen] air m ; **to throw sthg into the** ~ jeter qqch en l'air ; **by** ~ [travel] par avion ; **to be (up) in the** ~ fig [plans] être vague ; **to clear the** ~ fig dissiper les malentendus - **2.** RADIO & TV : **on the** ~ à l'antenne ◇ comp [transport] aérien(enne) ◇ vt - **1.** [gen] aérer - **2.** [make publicly known] faire connaître OR communiquer - **3.** [broadcast] diffuser ◇ vi sécher.

➤ **airs** npl : ~**s and graces** manières fpl ; **to give o.s.** ~**s, to put on** ~**s** prendre de grands airs.

airbag ['eəbæg] n AUT Airbag® m.

airbase ['eəbeɪs] n base f aérienne.

airbed ['eəbed] n Br matelas m pneumatique.

airborne ['eəbɔːn] adj - **1.** [troops etc] aéroporté(e) ; [seeds] emporté(e) par le vent - **2.** [plane] qui a décollé.

airbrake ['eəbreɪk] n frein m à air comprimé.

airbus ['eəbʌs] n airbus m.

air-conditioned [-kən'dɪʃnd] adj climatisé(e), à air conditionné.

air-conditioning [-kən'dɪʃnɪŋ] n climatisation f.

aircraft ['eəkrɑːft] (pl inv) n avion m.

aircraft carrier n porte-avions m inv.

air cushion n coussin m pneumatique OR gonflable.

airfield ['eəfiːld] n terrain m d'aviation.

airforce ['eəfɔːs] ◇ n armée f de l'air ◇ comp aérien(enne).

air freight n fret m aérien.

airgun ['eəgʌn] n carabine f OR fusil m à air comprimé.

airhostess ['eə,həʊstɪs] n hôtesse f de l'air.

airily ['eərəlɪ] adv à la légère.

airing ['eərɪŋ] n : **to give sthg an** ~ aérer qqch ; fig [opinions] exposer qqch.

airing cupboard n Br placard m séchoir.

airlane ['eəleɪn] n couloir m aérien.

airless ['eəlɪs] adj [room] qui sent le renfermé.

airletter ['eəletəʳ] n lettre f par avion.

airlift ['eəlɪft] ◇ n pont m aérien ◇ vt transporter par pont aérien.

airline ['eəlaɪn] n compagnie f aérienne.

airliner ['eəlaɪnəʳ] n [short-distance] (avion m) moyen-courrier m ; [long-distance] (avion) long-courrier m.

airlock ['eəlɒk] n - **1.** [in tube, pipe] poche f d'air - **2.** [airtight chamber] sas m.

airmail ['eəmeɪl] n poste f aérienne ; **by** ~ par avion.

airman ['eəmən] (pl -men [-mən]) n [aviator] aviateur m.

air mattress n matelas m pneumatique.

airplane ['eəpleɪn] n Am avion m.

airplay ['eəpleɪ] n RADIO : **to get a lot of** ~ passer beaucoup à la radio.

air pocket n trou m d'air.

airport ['eəpɔːt] ◇ n aéroport m ◇ comp de l'aéroport.

air raid n raid m aérien, attaque f aérienne.

air-raid shelter n abri m antiaérien.

air rifle n carabine f à air comprimé.

airship ['eəʃɪp] n (ballon m) dirigeable m.

airsick ['eəsɪk] adj : **to be** ~ avoir le mal de l'air.

airspace ['eəspeɪs] n espace m aérien.

airspeed ['eəspiːd] n vitesse f vraie (d'un avion).

air steward n steward m.

air stewardess n hôtesse f de l'air.

airstrip ['eəstrɪp] n piste f (d'atterrissage).

air terminal n aérogare f.

airtight ['eətaɪt] adj hermétique.

airtime ['eətaɪm] n RADIO temps m d'antenne.

air-to-air adj [missile, rocket] air-air (inv).

air-traffic control n contrôle m du trafic (aérien).

air-traffic controller n aiguilleur m (du ciel).

air travel n déplacement m OR voyage m par avion.

airwaves ['eəweɪvz] npl ondes fpl (hertziennes).

airy ['eərɪ] (compar -ier ; superl -iest) adj - **1.** [room] aéré(e) - **2.** [notions, promises] chimérique, vain(e) - **3.** [nonchalant] nonchalant(e).

aisle [aɪl] n allée f ; [in plane] couloir m.

ajar [ə'dʒɑːr] adj entrouvert(e).

AK abbr of Alaska.

aka (abbr of also known as) alias.

akin [ə'kɪn] adj : to be ~ to être semblable à.

AL abbr of Alabama.

Alabama [,ælə'bæmə] n Alabama m ; in ~ dans l'Alabama.

alabaster [,ælə'bɑːstər] n albâtre m.

alacrity [ə'lækrətɪ] n empressement m.

alarm [ə'lɑːm] <> n - **1.** [fear] alarme f, inquiétude f - **2.** [device] alarme f ; fire ~ sirène f d'incendie ; to raise OR sound the ~ donner OR sonner l'alarme <> vt alarmer, alerter.

alarm clock n réveil m, réveille-matin m inv.

alarming [ə'lɑːmɪŋ] adj alarmant(e), inquiétant(e).

alarmingly [ə'lɑːmɪŋlɪ] adv d'une manière alarmante OR inquiétante.

alarmist [ə'lɑːmɪst] adj alarmiste.

alas [ə'læs] excl hélas!

Alaska [ə'læskə] n Alaska m ; in ~ en Alaska.

Albania [æl'beɪnjə] n Albanie f ; in ~ en Albanie.

Albanian [æl'beɪnjən] <> adj albanais(e) <> n - **1.** [person] Albanais m, -e f - **2.** [language] albanais m.

albatross ['ælbətrɒs] (pl inv OR -es [-iːz]) n albatros m.

albeit [ɔːl'biːɪt] conj bien que (+ subjunctive).

Alberta [æl'bɜːtə] n Alberta f.

Albert Hall ['ælbət-] n : the ~ salle de concert à Londres.

albino [æl'biːnəʊ] (pl -s) <> n albinos mf <> comp albinos (inv).

album ['ælbəm] n album m.

albumen ['ælbjʊmɪn] n [of egg] albumen m.

alchemy ['ælkəmɪ] n alchimie f.

alcohol ['ælkəhɒl] n alcool m.

alcoholic [,ælkə'hɒlɪk] <> adj [person] alcoolique ; [drink] alcoolisé(e) <> n alcoolique mf.

alcoholism ['ælkəhɒlɪzm] n alcoolisme m.

alcopop ['ælkəʊpɒp] n boisson gazeuse faiblement alcoolisée.

alcove ['ælkəʊv] n alcôve f.

alderman ['ɔːldəmən] (pl -men [-mən]) n conseiller m municipal.

ale [eɪl] n bière f.

alert [ə'lɜːt] <> adj - **1.** [vigilant] vigilant(e) - **2.** [perceptive] vif (vive), éveillé(e) - **3.** [aware] : to be ~ to être conscient(e) de <> n [warning] alerte f ; on the ~ [watchful] sur le qui-vive ; MIL en état d'alerte <> vt alerter ; to ~ sb to sthg avertir qqn de qqch.

Aleutian Islands [ə'luːʃən-] npl : the ~ les îles fpl Aléoutiennes.

A level (abbr of Advanced level) n ≃ baccalauréat m.

Alexandria [,ælɪg'zɑːndrɪə] n Alexandrie f.

alfalfa [æl'fælfə] n luzerne f.

alfresco [æl'freskəʊ] adj & adv en plein air.

algae ['ældʒiː] npl algues fpl.

algebra ['ældʒɪbrə] n algèbre f.

Algeria [æl'dʒɪərɪə] n Algérie f ; in ~ en Algérie.

Algerian [æl'dʒɪərɪən] <> adj algérien(enne) <> n Algérien m, -enne f.

Algiers [æl'dʒɪəz] n Alger.

algorithm ['ælgərɪðm] n algorithme m.

alias ['eɪlɪəs] (pl -es [-iːz]) <> adv alias <> n faux nom m, nom d'emprunt.

alibi ['ælɪbaɪ] n alibi m.

alien ['eɪlɪən] <> adj - **1.** [gen] étranger(ère) - **2.** [from outer space] extraterrestre <> n

- 1. [from outer space] extraterrestre *mf* **- 2.** JUR [foreigner] étranger *m*, -ère *f*.

alienate ['eɪljəneɪt] *vt* aliéner.

alienation [,eɪljə'neɪʃn] *n* PSYCH aliénation *f*.

alight [ə'laɪt] <> *adj* allumé(e), en feu <> *vi* **- 1.** [bird etc] se poser **- 2.** [from bus, train] : **to ~ from** descendre de.

align [ə'laɪn] *vt* **- 1.** [line up] aligner **- 2.** [ally] : **to ~ o.s. with sb** s'aligner sur qqn.

alignment [ə'laɪnmənt] *n* alignement *m*.

alike [ə'laɪk] <> *adj* semblable <> *adv* de la même façon ; **to look ~** se ressembler.

alimentary canal [,ælɪmentərɪ-] *n* tube *m* digestif.

alimony ['ælɪmənɪ] *n* pension *f* alimentaire.

A-line *adj* trapèze *(inv)*.

alive [ə'laɪv] *adj* **- 1.** [living] vivant(e), en vie **- 2.** [practice, tradition] vivace ; **to keep ~** préserver **- 3.** [lively] plein(e) de vitalité ; **to come ~** [story, description] prendre vie ; [person, place] s'animer **- 4.** [aware] : **to be ~ to sthg** être conscient(e) de qqch **- 5.** [full of] : **to be ~ with sthg** grouiller de, pulluler de.

alkali ['ælkəlaɪ] *(pl* **-s** OR **-es)** *n* alcali *m*.

alkaline ['ælkəlaɪn] *adj* alcalin(e).

all [ɔːl] <> *adj* **- 1.** *(with sg noun)* tout (toute) ; **~ day/night/evening** toute la journée/la nuit/la soirée ; **~ the drink** toute la boisson ; **~ the time** tout le temps **- 2.** *(with pl noun)* tous (toutes) ; **~ the boxes** toutes les boîtes ; **~ men** tous les hommes ; **~ three died** ils sont morts tous les trois, tous les trois sont morts <> *pron* **- 1.** *(sg)* [the whole amount] tout *m* ; **she drank it ~, she drank ~ of it** elle a tout bu **- 2.** *(pl)* [everybody, everything] tous (toutes) ; **~ of them came, they ~ came** ils sont tous venus **- 3.** *(with superl)* :... **of ~** ... de tous (toutes) ; **I like this one best of ~** je préfère celui-ci entre tous ; **hers was the best/worst essay of ~** sa dissertation était la meilleure/la pire de toutes **- 4.** : **above ~** [> **above** ; **after ~** [> **after** ; **at ~** [> **at** <> *adv* **- 1.** [entirely] complètement ; **I'd forgotten ~ about that** j'avais complètement oublié cela ; **~ alone** tout seul (toute seule) ; **that's ~ very well, but ...** tout cela est bien beau, mais ... **- 2.** [in sport, competitions] : **the score is five ~** le score est cinq partout **- 3.** *(with compar)* : **to run ~ the faster** courir d'autant plus vite ; **~ the better** d'autant mieux.

~ all but *adv* presque, pratiquement.

~ all in all *adv* dans l'ensemble.

~ all that *adv* si ... que ça ; **it's not ~ that interesting** ce n'est pas si intéressant que ça.

~ in all *adv* en tout.

Allah ['ælə] *n* Allah *m*.

all-around Am = **all-round**.

allay [ə'leɪ] *vt* [fears, anger] apaiser, calmer ; [doubts] dissiper.

all clear *n* signal *m* de fin d'alerte ; fig feu *m* vert.

allegation [,ælɪ'geɪʃn] *n* allégation *f* ; **to make ~s (about)** faire des allégations (sur).

allege [ə'ledʒ] *vt* prétendre, alléguer ; **to ~ (that) ...** prétendre que ..., alléguer que ... ; **she is ~d to have done it** on prétend qu'elle l'a fait.

alleged [ə'ledʒd] *adj* prétendu(e).

allegedly [ə'ledʒɪdlɪ] *adv* prétendument.

allegiance [ə'liːdʒəns] *n* allégeance *f*.

allegorical [,ælɪ'gɒrɪkl] *adj* allégorique.

allegory ['ælɪgərɪ] *(pl* **-ies)** *n* allégorie *f*.

alleluia [,ælɪ'luːjə] *excl* alléluia!

allergic [ə'lɜːdʒɪk] *adj* : **~ (to)** allergique (à) ; **to be ~ to hard work** hum être allergique au travail.

allergy ['ælədʒɪ] *(pl* **-ies)** *n* allergie *f* ; **to have an ~ to sthg** être allergique à qqch.

alleviate [ə'liːvɪeɪt] *vt* apaiser, soulager.

alley(way) ['ælɪ(weɪ)] *n* [street] ruelle *f* ; [in garden] allée *f*.

alliance [ə'laɪəns] *n* alliance *f*.

allied ['ælaɪd] *adj* **- 1.** MIL allié(e) **- 2.** [related] connexe.

alligator ['ælɪgeɪtər] *(pl inv* OR **-s)** *n* alligator *m*.

all-important *adj* capital(e), crucial(e).

all-in *adj* Br [price] global(e).

~ all in <> *adv* [inclusive] tout compris <> *adj* inf [tired] crevé(e).

all-in wrestling *n* lutte *f* libre.

alliteration [ə,lɪtə'reɪʃn] *n* allitération *f*.

all-night *adj* [party etc] qui dure toute la nuit ; [bar etc] ouvert(e) toute la nuit.

allocate ['æləkeɪt] *vt* [money, resources] : **to ~ sthg (to sb)** attribuer qqch (à qqn).

allocation [,ælə'keɪʃn] *n* **- 1.** [gen] attribution *f* **- 2.** [share of money] somme *f* allouée.

allot [ə'lɒt] *(pt* & *pp* **-ted ;** *cont* **-ting)** *vt* [job] assigner ; [money, resources] attribuer ; [time] allouer.

allotment [ə'lɒtmənt] *n* **- 1.** Br [garden] jardin *m* ouvrier *(loué par la commune)* **- 2.** [sharing out] attribution *f* **- 3.** [share] part *f*.

all-out *adj* [effort] maximum *(inv)* ; [war] total(e).

allow [ə'laʊ] *vt* **- 1.** [permit - activity, behaviour] autoriser, permettre ; **to ~ sb to do sthg** permettre à qqn de faire qqch, autoriser qqn à faire qqch ; **~ me** permettez-moi **- 2.** [set

aside - money, time] prévoir - **3.** [officially accept]
accepter - **4.** [concede] : **to ~ that** ... admettre
que ...
◆ **allow for** *vt fus* tenir compte de.

allowable [ə'lauəbl] *adj* admissible.

allowance [ə'lauəns] *n* - **1.** [money received] indemnité *f;* **maternity ~** allocation *f* de maternité - **2.** Am [pocket money] argent *m* de poche - **3.** FIN : **tax ~** ≈ abattement *m* fiscal
- **4.** [excuse] : **to make ~s for sb** faire preuve
d'indulgence envers qqn ; **to make ~s for
sthg** prendre qqch en considération.

alloy ['ælɔɪ] *n* alliage *m*.

all-powerful *adj* tout-puissant (toute-
puissante).

all right ◇ *adv* bien ; [in answer - yes] d'accord ; **~, let's go!** bon, on y va? ◇ *adj*
- **1.** [healthy] en bonne santé ; [unharmed] sain
et sauf (saine et sauve) - **2.** inf [acceptable, satis-
factory] : **it was ~** c'était pas mal ; **that's ~** [never
mind] ce n'est pas grave - **3.** [allowable] : **is it ~ if
...?** ça ne vous dérange pas si ...?

all-round Br, **all-around** Am *adj* - **1.** [multi-
skilled] doué(e) dans tous les domaines
- **2.** [comprehensive] complet(ète).

all-rounder [-'raundə^r] *n* - **1.** [versatile person] :
to be an ~ être bon (bonne) en tout - **2.** SPORT
sportif complet *m*, sportive complète *f*.

all-time *adj* [record] sans précédent.

allude [ə'lu:d] *vi* : **to ~ to** faire allusion à.

allure [ə'ljuə^r] *n* charme *m*.

alluring [ə'ljuərɪŋ] *adj* séduisant(e).

allusion [ə'lu:ʒn] *n* allusion *f*.

ally [*n* 'ælaɪ, *vb* ə'laɪ] (*pl* **-ies** ; *pt* & *pp* **-ied**) ◇ *n*
allié *m*, -e *f* ◇ *vt* : **to ~ o.s. with** s'allier à.

almanac ['ɔ:lmənæk] *n* almanach *m*.

almighty [ɔ:l'maɪtɪ] *adj* inf [noise] terrible.
◆ **Almighty** *n* : **the Almighty** le Tout-
Puissant.

almond ['ɑ:mənd] *n* [nut] amande *f;* **~ (tree)**
amandier *m*.

almond paste *n* pâte *f* d'amande.

almost ['ɔ:lməust] *adv* presque ; **I ~ missed
the bus** j'ai failli rater le bus.

alms [ɑ:mz] *npl* dated aumône *f*.

aloft [ə'lɒft] *adv* - **1.** [in the air] en l'air - **2.** NAUT
dans la mâture.

alone [ə'ləun] ◇ *adj* seul(e) ; **all ~** tout seul
(toute seule) ◇ *adv* seul ; **to leave sthg ~** ne
pas toucher à qqch ; **leave me ~!** laisse-moi
tranquille! ; **to go it ~** faire cavalier seul.

along [ə'lɒŋ] ◇ *adv* : **to walk ~** se promener ; **to move ~** avancer ; **can I come ~ (with
you)?** est-ce que je peux venir (avec vous)?

◇ *prep* le long de ; **to run/walk ~ the street**
courir/marcher le long de la rue.
◆ **all along** *adv* depuis le début.
◆ **along with** *prep* ainsi que.

alongside [ə‚lɒŋ'saɪd] ◇ *prep* le long de, à
côté de ; [person] à côté de ◇ *adv* bord à
bord.

aloof [ə'lu:f] ◇ *adj* distant(e) ◇ *adv* : **to remain ~ (from)** garder ses distances (vis-
à-vis de).

aloud [ə'laud] *adv* à voix haute, tout haut.

alpaca [æl'pækə] *n* alpaga *m*.

alphabet ['ælfəbet] *n* alphabet *m*.

alphabetical [‚ælfə'betɪkl] *adj* alphabétique ; **in ~ order** par ordre alphabétique.

alphabetically [‚ælfə'betɪklɪ] *adv* par ordre
alphabétique.

alphabetize, -ise ['ælfəbətaɪz] *vt* classer
par ordre alphabétique.

alphanumeric [‚ælfənju:'merɪk] *adj* alphanumérique.

alphanumeric key *n* COMPUT touche *f* alphanumérique.

alpine ['ælpaɪn] *adj* alpin(e).

Alps [ælps] *npl* : **the ~** les Alpes *fpl*.

already [ɔ:l'redɪ] *adv* déjà.

alright [‚ɔ:l'raɪt] = **all right**.

Alsace [æl'sæs] *n* Alsace *f;* **in ~** en Alsace.

Alsatian [æl'seɪʃn] ◇ *adj* alsacien(enne)
◇ *n* - **1.** [person] Alsacien *m*, -enne *f* - **2.** [dog]
berger *m* allemand.

also ['ɔ:lsəu] *adv* aussi.

also-ran *n* [person] perdant *m*, -e *f*.

Alta. *abbr of* **Alberta**.

altar ['ɔ:ltə^r] *n* autel *m*.

alter ['ɔ:ltə^r] ◇ *vt* changer, modifier ; **to
have a dress/suit ~ed** faire retoucher une
robe/un costume ◇ *vi* changer.

alteration [‚ɔ:ltə'reɪʃn] *n* modification *f*,
changement *m; **to make an ~ OR ~s to sthg**
changer OR modifier qqch

altercation [‚ɔ:ltə'keɪʃn] *n* altercation *f*.

alter ego ['ɔ:ltə-] (*pl* **-s**) *n* alter ego *m*.

alternate [*adj* Br ɔ:l'tɜ:nət, Am 'ɔ:ltərnət, *vb*
'ɔ:ltərneɪt] ◇ *adj* alterné(e), alternatif(ive) ;
~ days tous les deux jours, un jour sur
deux ◇ *vt* faire alterner ◇ *vi* : **to ~ (with)**
alterner (avec) ; **to ~ between sthg and sthg**
passer de qqch à qqch.

alternately [ɔ:l'tɜ:nətlɪ] *adv* alternativement.

alternating current ['ɔ:ltəneɪtɪŋ-] *n* courant *m* alternatif.

alternation [‚ɔ:ltə'neɪʃn] *n* alternance *f*.

alternative [ɔːl'tɜːnətɪv] <> adj - **1.** [different] autre - **2.** [non-traditional - society] parallèle ; [- art, energy] alternatif(ive) <> n - **1.** [between two solutions] alternative f - **2.** [other possibility] : ~ **(to)** solution f de remplacement (à) ; **to have no** ~ ne pas avoir le choix ; **to have no** ~ **but to do sthg** ne pas avoir d'autre choix que de faire qqch.

alternatively [ɔːl'tɜːnətɪvlɪ] adv ou bien.

alternative medicine n médecine f parallèle OR douce.

alternator ['ɔːltəneɪtəʳ] n ELEC alternateur m.

although [ɔːl'ðəʊ] conj bien que (+ subjunctive).

altitude ['æltɪtjuːd] n altitude f.

alto ['æltəʊ] (pl -s) <> n - **1.** [male voice] hautecontre f - **2.** [female voice] contralto m <> comp alto.

altogether [ˌɔːltə'geðəʳ] adv - **1.** [completely] entièrement, tout à fait - **2.** [considering all things] tout compte fait - **3.** [in all] en tout.

altruism ['æltruɪzm] n altruisme m.

altruistic [ˌæltrʊ'ɪstɪk] adj altruiste.

aluminium Br [ˌæljʊ'mɪnɪəm], **aluminum** Am [ə'luːmɪnəm] <> n aluminium m <> comp en aluminium ; ~ **foil** papier m aluminium.

alumnus [ə'lʌmnəs] (pl -ni [-naɪ]) n ancien étudiant m, ancienne étudiante f (d'une université).

always ['ɔːlweɪz] adv toujours.

Alzheimer's disease ['ælts,haɪməz -] n maladie f d'Alzheimer.

am [æm] ⊏> be.

a.m. (abbr of ante meridiem) : at **3** ~ à 3h (du matin).

AM (abbr of amplitude modulation) n AM f.

AMA (abbr of American Medical Association) n ordre américain des médecins.

amalgam [ə'mælgəm] n amalgame m.

amalgamate [ə'mælgəmeɪt] vt & vi [unite] fusionner.

amalgamation [əˌmælgə'meɪʃn] n [of companies] fusion f.

amass [ə'mæs] vt amasser.

amateur ['æmətəʳ] <> adj amateur (inv) ; pej d'amateur <> n amateur m.

amateurish [ˌæmətə'rɪʃ] adj d'amateur.

amaze [ə'meɪz] vt étonner, stupéfier.

amazed [ə'meɪzd] adj stupéfait(e).

amazement [ə'meɪzmənt] n stupéfaction f.

amazing [ə'meɪzɪŋ] adj - **1.** [surprising] étonnant(e), ahurissant(e) - **2.** [wonderful] excellent(e).

amazingly [ə'meɪzɪŋlɪ] adv étonnamment.

Amazon ['æməzn] n - **1.** [river] : **the** ~ l'Amazone f - **2.** [region] : **the** ~ **(Basin)** l'Amazonie f ; **in the** ~ en Amazonie ; **the** ~ **rainforest** la forêt amazonienne.

Amazonian [ˌæmə'zəʊnjən] adj amazonien(enne).

ambassador [æm'bæsədəʳ] n ambassadeur m, -drice f.

amber ['æmbəʳ] <> adj - **1.** [amber-coloured] ambré(e) - **2.** Br [traffic light] orange (inv) <> n - **1.** [substance] ambre m - **2.** [colour - of traffic light] orange m <> comp [made of amber] d'ambre.

ambiance ['æmbɪəns] = **ambience**.

ambidextrous [ˌæmbɪ'dekstrəs] adj ambidextre.

ambience ['æmbɪəns] n ambiance f.

ambiguity [ˌæmbɪ'gjuːətɪ] (pl -ies) n ambiguïté f.

ambiguous [æm'bɪgjʊəs] adj ambigu(ë).

ambiguously [æm'bɪgjʊəslɪ] adv de façon ambiguë.

ambition [æm'bɪʃn] n ambition f.

ambitious [æm'bɪʃəs] adj ambitieux(euse).

ambivalence [æm'bɪvələns] n ambivalence f.

ambivalent [æm'bɪvələnt] adj ambivalent(e).

amble ['æmbl] vi déambuler.

ambulance ['æmbjʊləns] <> n ambulance f <> comp : ~ **man** ambulancier m ; ~ **woman** ambulancière f.

ambush ['æmbʊʃ] <> n embuscade f <> vt tendre une embuscade à.

ameba [ə'miːbə] Am n = **amoeba**.

ameliorate [ə'miːljəreɪt] fml <> vt améliorer <> vi s'améliorer.

amen [ˌɑː'men] excl amen!

amenable [ə'miːnəbl] adj : ~ **(to)** ouvert(e)(à).

amend [ə'mend] vt modifier ; [law] amender.
◆ **amends** npl : **to make ~s (for)** se racheter (pour).

amendment [ə'mendmənt] n modification f ; [to law] amendement m.

amenities [ə'miːnətɪz] npl aménagements mpl, équipements mpl.

America [ə'merɪkə] n Amérique f ; **in** ~ en Amérique.
◆ **Americas** npl : **the ~s** les Amériques.

American [ə'merɪkn] <> adj américain(e) <> n Américain m, -e f.

American Indian n Indien m, -enne f d'Amérique, Amérindien m, -enne f.

Americanism [ə'merɪkənɪzm] n américanisme m.

americanize, -ise [ə'merɪkənaɪz] vt américaniser.

amethyst ['æmɪθɪst] n améthyste f.

Amex ['æmeks] n (abbr of **American Stock Exchange**) deuxième place boursière des États-Unis.

amiable ['eɪmjəbl] adj aimable.

amiably ['eɪmjəblɪ] adv aimablement.

amicable ['æmɪkəbl] adj amical(e).

amicably ['æmɪkəblɪ] adv amicalement.

amid(st) [ə'mɪd(st)] prep au milieu de, parmi.

amino acid [ə'miːnəʊ-] n acide m aminé.

amiss [ə'mɪs] ◇ adj : **is there anything ~?** y a-t-il quelque chose qui ne va pas? ◇ adv : **to take sthg ~** prendre qqch de travers.

Amman [ə'mɑːn] n Amman.

ammo ['æməʊ] n (U) inf munitions fpl.

ammonia [ə'məʊnjə] n [liquid] ammoniaque f.

ammunition [,æmjʊ'nɪʃn] (U) n - **1.** MIL munitions fpl - **2.** fig [argument] argument m.

ammunition dump n dépôt m de munitions.

amnesia [æm'niːzjə] n amnésie f.

amnesty ['æmnəstɪ] (pl -ies) n amnistie f.

Amnesty International n Amnesty International f.

amniocentesis [,æmnɪəʊsen'tiːsɪs] n amniocentèse f.

amoeba, ameba Am [ə'miːbə] amibe f.

amok [ə'mɒk] adv : **to run ~** être pris(e) d'une crise de folie furieuse.

among(st) [ə'mʌŋ(st)] prep parmi, entre ; **~ other things** entre autres (choses).

amoral [,eɪ'mɒrəl] adj amoral(e).

amorous ['æmərəs] adj amoureux(euse).

amorphous [ə'mɔːfəs] adj informe.

amortize [æn'mɔːtaɪz] vt FIN amortir.

amount [ə'maʊnt] n - **1.** [quantity] quantité f ; **a great ~ of** beaucoup de - **2.** [sum of money] somme f, montant m.

➡ **amount to** vt fus - **1.** [total] s'élever à - **2.** [be equivalent to] revenir à, équivaloir à.

amp [æmp] n - **1.** abbr of **ampere** - **2.** inf (abbr of **amplifier**) ampli m.

amperage ['æmpərɪdʒ] n intensité f de courant.

ampere ['æmpeəʳ] n ampère m.

ampersand ['æmpəsænd] n esperluette f.

amphetamine [æm'fetəmiːn] n amphétamine f.

amphibian [æm'fɪbɪən] n batracien m.

amphibious [æm'fɪbɪəs] adj amphibie.

amphitheatre Br, **amphitheater** Am ['æmfɪ,θɪətəʳ] n amphithéâtre m.

ample ['æmpl] adj - **1.** [enough] suffisamment de, assez de - **2.** [large] ample.

amplification [,æmplɪfɪ'keɪʃn] n - **1.** [of sound] amplification f - **2.** [of idea, statement] développement m.

amplifier ['æmplɪfaɪəʳ] n amplificateur m.

amplify ['æmplɪfaɪ] (pt & pp -ied) ◇ vt - **1.** [sound] amplifier - **2.** [idea, statement] développer ◇ vi : **to ~ on sthg** développer qqch.

amply ['æmplɪ] adv - **1.** [sufficiently] amplement - **2.** [considerably] largement.

ampoule Br, **ampule** Am ['æmpuːl] n ampoule f.

amputate ['æmpjʊteɪt] vt & vi amputer.

amputation [,æmpjʊ'teɪʃn] n amputation f.

Amsterdam [,æmstə'dæm] n Amsterdam.

amt abbr of **amount**.

Amtrak ['æmtræk] n société nationale de chemins de fer aux États-Unis.

amuck [ə'mʌk] = **amok**.

amulet ['æmjʊlɪt] n amulette f.

amuse [ə'mjuːz] vt - **1.** [make laugh] amuser, faire rire - **2.** [entertain] divertir, distraire ; **to ~ o.s. (by doing sthg)** s'occuper (à faire qqch).

amused [ə'mjuːzd] adj - **1.** [laughing] amusé(e) ; **to be ~ at OR by sthg** trouver qqch amusant - **2.** [entertained] : **to keep o.s. ~** s'occuper.

amusement [ə'mjuːzmənt] n - **1.** [laughter] amusement m - **2.** [diversion, game] distraction f.

amusement arcade n galerie f de jeux.

amusement park n parc m d'attractions.

amusing [ə'mjuːzɪŋ] adj amusant(e).

an [stressed æn, unstressed ən] ▷ **a**.

ANA n - **1.** (abbr of **American Newspaper Association**) syndicat américain de la presse écrite - **2.** (abbr of **American Nurses Association**) syndicat américain d'infirmiers.

anabolic steroid [,ænə'bɒlɪk-] n (stéroïde m) anabolisant m.

anachronism [ə'nækrənɪzm] n anachronisme m.

anachronistic [ə,nækrə'nɪstɪk] adj anachronique.

anaemia Br, **anemia** Am [ə'niːmjə] n anémie f.

anaemic Br, **anemic** Am [ə'niːmɪk] adj anémique ; fig & pej fade, plat(e).

anaesthesia Br, **anesthesia** Am [ˌænɪs'θiːzjə] n anesthésie f.

anaesthetic Br, **anesthetic** Am [ˌænɪs'θetɪk] n anesthésique m ; **under ~** sous anesthésie ; **local/general ~** anesthésie f locale/générale.

anaesthetist Br, **anesthetist** Am [æ'niːsθətɪst] n anesthésiste mf.

anaesthetize, -ise Br, **anesthetize** Am [æ'niːsθətaɪz] vt anesthésier.

anagram ['ænəgræm] n anagramme f.

anal ['eɪnl] adj anal(e).

analgesic [ˌænæl'dʒiːsɪk] ◇ adj analgésique ◇ n analgésique m.

analog Am = analogue.

analogous [ə'næləgəs] adj : **~ (to)** analogue (à).

analogue Br, **analog** Am ['ænəlɒg] ◇ adj [watch, clock] analogique ◇ n analogue m.

analogy [ə'nælədʒɪ] (pl **-ies**) n analogie f ; **to draw an ~ with/between** faire une comparaison avec/entre ; **by ~** par analogie.

analyse Br, **-yze** Am ['ænəlaɪz] vt analyser.

analysis [ə'næləsɪs] (pl **-ses** [-siːz]) n analyse f ; **in the final** OR **last ~** en dernière analyse.

analyst ['ænəlɪst] n analyste mf.

analytic(al) [ˌænə'lɪtɪk(l)] adj analytique.

analyze Am = analyse.

anarchic [æ'nɑːkɪk] adj anarchique.

anarchist ['ænəkɪst] n anarchiste mf.

anarchy ['ænəkɪ] n anarchie f.

anathema [ə'næθəmə] n anathème m.

anatomical [ˌænə'tɒmɪkl] adj anatomique.

anatomy [ə'nætəmɪ] (pl **-ies**) n anatomie f.

ANC (abbr of **African National Congress**) n ANC m.

ancestor ['ænsestə^r] n lit & fig ancêtre m.

ancestral home [æn'sestrəl-] n demeure f ancestrale.

ancestry ['ænsestrɪ] (pl **-ies**) n - **1.** [past] ascendance f - **2.** (U) [ancestors] ancêtres mpl.

anchor ['æŋkə^r] ◇ n ancre f ; **to drop/weigh ~** jeter/lever l'ancre ◇ vt - **1.** [secure] ancrer - **2.** TV présenter ◇ vi NAUT jeter l'ancre.

anchorage ['æŋkərɪdʒ] n - **1.** NAUT mouillage m - **2.** [means of securing] ancrage m.

anchorman ['æŋkəmæn] (pl **-men** [-men]) n TV présentateur m.

anchorwoman ['æŋkə,wʊmən] (pl **-women** [-,wɪmɪn]) n TV présentatrice f.

anchovy ['æntʃəvɪ] (pl inv OR **-ies**) n anchois m.

ancient ['eɪnʃənt] adj - **1.** [monument etc] historique ; [custom] ancien(enne) - **2.** hum [car etc] antique ; [person] vieux (vieille).

ancillary [æn'sɪlərɪ] adj auxiliaire.

and [stressed ænd, unstressed ənd, ən] conj - **1.** [as well as, plus] et - **2.** [in numbers] : **one hundred ~ eighty** cent quatre-vingts ; **six ~ a half** six et demi - **3.** [to] : **come ~ see!** venez voir! ; **try ~ come** essayez de venir ; **wait ~ see** vous verrez bien.

➡ **and so on, and so forth** adv et ainsi de suite.

Andes ['ændiːz] npl : **the ~** les Andes fpl.

Andorra [æn'dɔːrə] n Andorre f ; **in ~** en Andorre.

androgynous [æn'drɒdʒɪnəs] adj androgyne.

android ['ændrɔɪd] n androïde m.

anecdote ['ænɪkdəʊt] n anecdote f.

anemia Am = anaemia.

anemic Am = anaemic.

anemone [ə'nemənɪ] n anémone f.

anesthetic etc Am = anaesthetic etc.

anew [ə'njuː] adv : **to start ~** recommencer (à zéro).

angel ['eɪndʒəl] n ange m.

Angeleno [ˌændʒə'liːnəʊ] n habitant de Los Angeles.

angelic [æn'dʒelɪk] adj angélique.

anger ['æŋgə^r] ◇ n colère f ◇ vt fâcher, irriter.

angina [æn'dʒaɪnə] n angine f de poitrine.

angle ['æŋgl] ◇ n - **1.** [gen] angle m ; **at an ~** de travers, en biais - **2.** [point of view] point m de vue, angle m ◇ vi pêcher (à la ligne) ; **to ~ for** fig [invitation, compliments] chercher à obtenir, quêter.

angler ['æŋglə^r] n pêcheur m (à la ligne).

Anglican ['æŋglɪkən] ◇ adj anglican(e) ◇ n anglican m, -e f.

anglicism ['æŋglɪsɪzml] n anglicisme m.

angling ['æŋglɪŋ] n pêche f à la ligne.

Anglo- ['æŋgləʊ] prefix anglo-.

Anglo-Saxon ◇ adj anglo-saxon(onne) ◇ n - **1.** [person] Anglo-saxon m, -onne f - **2.** [language] anglo-saxon m.

Angola [æŋ'gəʊlə] n Angola m ; **in ~** en Angola.

Angolan [æŋ'gəʊlən] ◇ adj angolais(e) ◇ n Angolais m, -e f.

angora [æŋ'gɔːrə] n angora m.

angrily ['æŋgrəlɪ] adv avec colère.

angry [ˈæŋgrɪ] (*compar* **-ier** ; *superl* **-iest**) *adj* [person] en colère, fâché(e) ; [words, quarrel] violent(e) ; **to be ~ with** OR **at sb** être en colère OR fâché contre qqn ; **to get ~** se mettre en colère, se fâcher.

angst [æŋst] *n* anxiété *f*.

anguish [ˈæŋgwɪʃ] *n* angoisse *f*.

anguished [ˈæŋgwɪʃt] *adj* angoissé(e).

angular [ˈæŋgjʊləʳ] *adj* anguleux(euse).

animal [ˈænɪml] ◇ *n* animal *m* ; pej brute *f* ◇ *adj* animal(e).

animate [ˈænɪmət] *adj* animé(e), vivant(e).

animated [ˈænɪmeɪtɪd] *adj* animé(e).

animated cartoon *n* dessin *m* animé.

animation [ˌænɪˈmeɪʃn] *n* animation *f*.

animatronics [ˌænɪməˈtrɒnɪks] *n* (U) CIN animatronique *f*.

animosity [ˌænɪˈmɒsətɪ] (*pl* **-ies**) *n* animosité *f*.

aniseed [ˈænɪsiːd] *n* anis *m*.

ankle [ˈæŋkl] ◇ *n* cheville *f* ◇ *comp* : **~ socks** socquettes *fpl* ; **~ boots** bottines *fpl*.

annals [ˈænlz] *npl* annales *fpl*.

annex(e) [ˈæneks] ◇ *n* [building] annexe *f* ◇ *vt* annexer.

annexation [ˌænekˈseɪʃn] *n* annexion *f*.

annihilate [əˈnaɪəleɪt] *vt* anéantir, annihiler.

annihilation [əˌnaɪəˈleɪʃn] *n* anéantissement *m*.

anniversary [ˌænɪˈvɜːsərɪ] (*pl* **-ies**) *n* anniversaire *m*.

annotate [ˈænəteɪt] *vt* annoter.

announce [əˈnaʊns] *vt* annoncer.

announcement [əˈnaʊnsmənt] *n* **- 1.** [statement] déclaration *f* ; [in newspaper] avis *m* **- 2.** (U) [act of stating] annonce *f*.

announcer [əˈnaʊnsəʳ] *n* RADIO & TV speaker *m*, speakerine *f*.

annoy [əˈnɔɪ] *vt* agacer, contrarier.

annoyance [əˈnɔɪəns] *n* contrariété *f*.

annoyed [əˈnɔɪd] *adj* mécontent(e), agacé(e) ; **to get ~** se fâcher ; **to be ~ at sthg** être contrarié(e) par qqch ; **to be ~ with sb** être fâché(e) contre qqn.

annoying [əˈnɔɪɪŋ] *adj* agaçant(e), énervant(e).

annual [ˈænjʊəl] ◇ *adj* annuel(elle) ◇ *n* **- 1.** [plant] plante *f* annuelle **- 2.** [book - gen] publication *f* annuelle ; [- for children] album *m*.

annual general meeting *n* assemblée *f* générale annuelle.

annually [ˈænjʊəlɪ] *adv* annuellement.

annuity [əˈnjuːɪtɪ] (*pl* **-ies**) *n* rente *f*.

annul [əˈnʌl] (*pt* & *pp* **-led** ; *cont* **-ling**) *vt* annuler ; [law] abroger.

annulment [əˈnʌlmənt] *n* annulation *f* ; [of law] abrogation *f*.

annum [ˈænəm] *n* : **per ~** par an.

Annunciation [əˌnʌnsɪˈeɪʃn] *n* : **the ~** l'Annonciation *f*.

anode [ˈænəʊd] *n* anode *f*.

anoint [əˈnɔɪnt] *vt* oindre.

anomalous [əˈnɒmələs] *adj* anormal(e).

anomaly [əˈnɒmətlɪ] (*pl* **-ies**) *n* anomalie *f*.

anon. [əˈnɒn] (*abbr of* **anonymous**) anon.

anonymity [ˌænəˈnɪmətɪ] *n* anonymat *m*.

anonymous [əˈnɒnɪməs] *adj* anonyme.

anonymously [əˈnɒnɪməslɪ] *adv* anonymement.

anorak [ˈænəræk] *n* anorak *m*.

anorexia (nervosa) [ˌænəˈreksɪə(nɜːˈvəʊsə)] *n* anorexie *f* mentale.

anorexic [ˌænəˈreksɪk] ◇ *adj* anorexique ◇ *n* anorexique *mf*.

another [əˈnʌðəʳ] ◇ *adj* **- 1.** [additional] : **~ apple** encore une pomme, une pomme de plus, une autre pomme ; **in ~ few minutes** dans quelques minutes ; **(would you like) ~ drink?** (voulez-vous) encore un verre? **- 2.** [different] : **~ job** un autre travail ◇ *pron* **- 1.** [additional one] un autre (une autre), encore un (encore une) ; **one after ~** l'un après l'autre (l'une après l'autre) **- 2.** [different one] un autre (une autre) ; **one ~** l'un l'autre (l'une l'autre).

ANSI (*abbr of* **American National Standards Institute**) *n* association américaine de normalisation.

answer [ˈɑːnsəʳ] ◇ *n* **- 1.** [gen] réponse *f* ; **in ~ to** en réponse à **- 2.** [to problem] solution *f* ◇ *vt* répondre à ; **to ~ the door** aller ouvrir la porte ; **to ~ the phone** répondre au téléphone ◇ *vi* [reply] répondre.

➤ **answer back** ◇ *vt sep* répondre à ◇ *vi* répondre.

➤ **answer for** *vt fus* être responsable de, répondre de.

answerable [ˈɑːnsərəbl] *adj* : **~ to sb/for sthg** responsable devant qqn/de qqch.

answering machine [ˈɑːnsərɪŋ-] *n* répondeur *m*.

ant [ænt] *n* fourmi *f*.

antacid [ˌæntˈæsɪd] *n* (médicament *m*) alcalin *m*.

antagonism [æn'tægənizm] *n* antagonisme *m*, hostilité *f*.

antagonist [æn'tægənist] *n* antagoniste *mf*, adversaire *mf*.

antagonistic [æn,tægə'nistik] *adj* [hostile] hostile.

antagonize, -ise [æn'tægənaiz] *vt* éveiller l'hostilité de.

Antarctic [æn'tɑːktik] <> *n* : the ~ l'Antarctique *m* ; in the ~ dans l'Antarctique <> *adj* antarctique.

Antarctica [æn'tɑːktikə] *n* Antarctique *m*, le continent *m* antarctique.

Antarctic Circle *n* : the ~ le cercle polaire antarctique.

Antarctic Ocean *n* : the ~ l'océan *m* Antarctique, l'océan Austral.

ante ['ænti] *n* inf fig : to up OR raise the ~ faire monter les enchères.

anteater ['ænt,iːtəʳ] *n* tamanoir *m*, fourmilier *m*.

antecedent [,ænti'siːdənt] *n* antécédent *m*.

antediluvian [,æntidi'luːvjən] *adj* antédiluvien(enne).

antelope ['æntiləup] (*pl inv* OR **-s**) *n* antilope *f*.

antenatal [,ænti'neitl] *adj* prénatal(e).

antenatal clinic *n* service *m* de consultation prénatale.

antenna [æn'tenə] (*pl sense 1* **-nae** [-niː], *pl sense 2* **-s**) *n* **- 1.** [of insect] antenne *f* **- 2.** Am [for TV, radio] antenne *f*.

anteroom ['æntirum] *n* antichambre *f*.

anthem ['ænθəm] *n* hymne *m*.

anthill ['ænthil] *n* fourmilière *f*.

anthology [æn'θɒlədʒi] (*pl* **-ies**) *n* anthologie *f*.

anthrax ['ænθræks] *n* charbon *m*.

anthropologist [,ænθrə'pɒlədʒist] *n* anthropologue *mf*.

anthropology [,ænθrə'pɒlədʒi] *n* anthropologie *f*.

anti- ['ænti] *prefix* anti-.

antiaircraft [,ænti'eəkrɑːft] *adj* antiaérien(enne).

antiapartheid [,æntiə'pɑːtheit] *adj* antiapartheid *(inv)*.

antiballistic missile [,æntibə'listik-] *n* missile *m* antibalistique.

antibiotic [,æntibai'ɒtik] *n* antibiotique *m*.

antibody ['ænti,bɒdi] (*pl* **-ies**) *n* anticorps *m*.

anticipate [æn'tisipeit] *vt* **- 1.** [expect] s'attendre à, prévoir **- 2.** [request, movement] antici-

per ; [competitor] prendre de l'avance sur **- 3.** [look forward to] savourer à l'avance.

anticipation [æn,tisi'peiʃn] *n* [expectation] attente *f* ; [eagerness] impatience *f* ; in ~ avec impatience ; in ~ of en prévision de ; thanking you in ~ en vous remerciant d'avance.

anticlimax [,ænti'klaimæks] *n* déception *f*.

anticlockwise [,ænti'klɒkwaiz] *adj* & *adv* Br dans le sens inverse des aiguilles d'une montre.

antics ['æntiks] *npl* **- 1.** [of children, animals] gambades *fpl* **- 2.** pej [of politicians etc] bouffonneries *fpl*.

anticyclone [,ænti'saikləun] *n* anticyclone *m*.

antidepressant [,æntidi'presnt] *n* antidépresseur *m*.

antidote ['æntidəut] *n* lit & fig : ~ (to) antidote *m* (contre).

antifreeze ['æntifriːz] *n* antigel *m*.

Antigua [æn'tiːgə] *n* Antigua.

antihero ['ænti,hiərəu] (*pl* **-es**) *n* antihéros *m*.

antihistamine [,ænti'histəmin] *n* antihistaminique *m*.

antinuclear [,ænti'njuːkliəʳ] *adj* antinucléaire.

antipathy [æn'tipəθi] *n* : ~ (to OR towards) antipathie *f* (pour).

antipersonnel ['ænti,pɜːsə'nel] *adj* MIL antipersonnel *(inv)*.

antiperspirant [,ænti'pɜːspərənt] *n* déodorant *m* antiperspirant.

Antipodes [æn'tipədiːz] *npl* : the ~ l'Australie *f* et la Nouvelle-Zélande.

antiquarian [,ænti'kweəriən] <> *adj* : ~ bookshop librairie *f* spécialisée dans les éditions anciennes <> *n* amateur *m* d'antiquités.

antiquated ['æntikweitid] *adj* dépassé(e).

antique [æn'tiːk] <> *adj* ancien(enne) <> *n* [object] objet *m* ancien ; [piece of furniture] meuble *m* ancien.

antique dealer *n* antiquaire *mf*.

antique shop *n* magasin *m* d'antiquités.

antiquity [æn'tikwəti] (*pl* **-ies**) *n* antiquité *f*.

anti-Semitic [-si'mitik] *adj* antisémite.

anti-Semitism [-semitizəm] *n* antisémitisme *m*.

antiseptic [,ænti'septik] <> *adj* antiseptique <> *n* désinfectant *m*.

antisocial [,ænti'səuʃl] *adj* **- 1.** [against society] antisocial(e) **- 2.** [unsociable] peu sociable, sauvage.

antistatic [,ænti'stætik] *adj* antistatique.

antitank [ˌæntɪ'tæŋk] *adj* antichar *(inv)*.

antithesis [æn'tɪθɪsɪs] *(pl* **-ses** [-siːz]*) n* opposé *m*, antithèse *f*.

antlers [ˌæntləz] *npl* bois *mpl (de cervidés)*.

antonym ['æntənɪm] *n* antonyme *m*.

Antwerp ['æntwɜːp] *n* Anvers.

anus ['eɪnəs] *n* anus *m*.

anvil ['ænvɪl] *n* enclume *f*.

anxiety [æŋ'zaɪətɪ] *(pl* **-ies**) *n* - **1.** [worry] anxiété *f* - **2.** [cause of worry] souci *m* - **3.** [keenness] désir *m* farouche.

anxious ['æŋkʃəs] *adj* - **1.** [worried] anxieux(euse), très inquiet(ète) ; **to be ~ about** se faire du souci au sujet de - **2.** [keen] : **to be ~ to do sthg** tenir à faire qqch ; **to be ~ that** tenir à ce que *(+ subjunctive)*.

anxiously ['æŋkʃəslɪ] *adv* avec anxiété.

any ['enɪ] ⬦ *adj* - **1.** *(with negative)* de, d' ; **I haven't got ~ money/tickets** je n'ai pas d'argent/de billets ; **he never does ~ work** il ne travaille jamais - **2.** [some - with sg noun] du, de l', de la ; [- with pl noun] des ; **have you got ~ money/milk/cousins?** est-ce que vous avez de l'argent/du lait/des cousins? - **3.** [no matter which] n'importe quel (n'importe quelle) ; **~ box will do** n'importe quelle boîte fera l'affaire ; *see also* **case** ; *see also* **day** ; *see also* **moment** ; *see also* **rate** ⬦ *pron* - **1.** *(with negative)* en ; **I didn't buy ~ (of them)** je n'en ai pas acheté ; **I didn't know ~ of the guests** je ne connaissais aucun des invités - **2.** [some] en ; **do you have ~?** est-ce que vous en avez? ; **can ~ of you change a tyre?** est-ce que l'un d'entre vous sait changer un pneu? ; **if ~** si tant est qu'il y en ait ; **few, if ~, are likely to be successful** il y en a très peu, si tant est qu'il y en ait, qui ont une chance de réussir - **3.** [no matter which one or ones] n'importe lequel (n'importe laquelle) ; **take ~ you like** prenez n'importe lequel/laquelle, prenez celui/celle que vous voulez ⬦ *adv* - **1.** *(with negative)* : **I can't see it ~ more** je ne le vois plus ; **I can't stand it ~ longer** je ne peux plus le supporter - **2.** [some, a little] un peu ; **do you want ~ more potatoes?** voulez-vous encore des pommes de terre? ; **are you finding the course ~ easier now?** est-ce que tu trouves le cours un peu plus facile maintenant? ; **is that ~ better/different?** est-ce que c'est mieux/différent comme ça?

anybody ['enɪˌbɒdɪ] = **anyone**.

anyhow ['enɪhaʊ] *adv* - **1.** [in spite of that] quand même, néanmoins - **2.** [carelessly] n'importe comment - **3.** [in any case] de toute façon.

anyone ['enɪwʌn] *pron* - **1.** *(in negative sentences)* : **I didn't see ~** je n'ai vu personne - **2.** *(in questions)* quelqu'un - **3.** [any person] n'importe qui.

anyplace ['enɪpleɪs] Am = **anywhere**.

anything ['enɪθɪŋ] *pron* - **1.** *(in negative sentences)* : **I didn't see ~** je n'ai rien vu - **2.** *(in questions)* quelque chose ; **~ else?** [in shop] et avec ceci? - **3.** [any object, event] n'importe quoi ; **if ~ happens ...** s'il arrive quoi que ce soit ...

➡ **anything but** *adv* pas du tout.

anyway ['enɪweɪ] *adv* [in any case] de toute façon.

anywhere ['enɪweəʳ], **anyplace** Am ['enɪpleɪs] *adv* - **1.** *(in negative sentences)* : **I haven't seen him ~** je ne l'ai vu nulle part - **2.** *(in questions)* quelque part - **3.** [any place] n'importe où - **4.** [any amount, number] : **~ between 5,000 and 10,000** quelque chose entre 5000 et 10000.

Anzac ['ænzæk] *(abbr of* **Australia-New Zealand Army Corps***) n* soldat australien ou néo-zélandais.

AOB, a.o.b. *(abbr of* **any other business***)* divers.

Apache [ə'pætʃɪ] *n* Apache *mf*.

apart [ə'pɑːt] *adv* - **1.** [separated] séparé(e), éloigné(e) ; **to keep ~** séparer ; **we're living ~** nous sommes séparés - **2.** [to one side] à l'écart - **3.** [in several parts] : **to take sthg ~** démonter qqch ; **to fall ~** tomber en morceaux - **4.** [aside] : **joking ~** sans plaisanter, plaisanterie à part.

➡ **apart from** *prep* - **1.** [except for] à part, sauf - **2.** [as well as] en plus de, outre.

apartheid [ə'pɑːtheɪt] *n* apartheid *m*.

apartment [ə'pɑːtmənt] *n* appartement *m*.

apartment building *n* Am immeuble *m* *(d'habitation)*.

apathetic [ˌæpə'θetɪk] *adj* apathique.

apathy ['æpəθɪ] *n* apathie *f*.

APB *(abbr of* **all points bulletin***) n* message radiodiffusé par la police concernant une personne recherchée.

ape [eɪp] ⬦ *n* singe *m* ⬦ *vt* singer.

Apennines ['æpɪnaɪnz] *npl* : **the ~** l'Apennin *m*, les Apennins *mpl*.

aperitif [əpera'tiːf] *n* apéritif *m*.

aperture ['æpəˌtjʊəʳ] *n* - **1.** [hole, opening] orifice *m*, ouverture *f* - **2.** PHOT ouverture *f*.

apex ['eɪpeks] *(pl* **-es** [-iːz] OR **apices** ['eɪpɪsiːz]*) n* sommet *m*.

APEX ['eɪpeks] *(abbr of* **advance purchase excursion***) n* Br : **~ ticket** billet *m* APEX.

aphid ['eɪfɪd] n puceron m

aphorism ['æfərɪzm] n aphorisme m.

aphrodisiac [,æfrə'dɪzɪæk] n aphrodisiaque m.

apices ['eɪpɪsi:z] pl ⊳ **apex**.

apiece [ə'pi:s] adv [for each person] chacun(e), par personne ; [for each thing] chacun(e), pièce (inv).

aplomb [ə'plɒm] n aplomb m, assurance f.

APO (abbr of Army Post Office) n service postal de l'armée.

apocalypse [ə'pɒkəlɪps] n apocalypse f.

apocalyptic [ə,pɒkə'lɪptɪk] adj apocalyptique.

apogee ['æpədʒi:] n apogée m.

apolitical [,eɪpə'lɪtɪkəl] adj apolitique.

apologetic [ə,pɒlə'dʒetɪk] adj [letter etc] d'excuse ; **to be ~ about** sthg s'excuser de qqch.

apologetically [ə,pɒlə'dʒetɪklɪ] adv en s'excusant, pour s'excuser.

apologize, -ise [ə'pɒlədʒaɪz] vi s'excuser ; **to ~ to** sb **(for** sthg) faire des excuses à qqn (pour qqch).

apology [ə'pɒlədʒɪ] (pl -ies) n excuses fpl.

apoplectic [,æpə'plektɪk] adj - **1.** MED apoplectique - **2.** inf [very angry] hors de soi.

apoplexy ['æpəpleksɪ] n apoplexie f.

apostle [ə'pɒsl] n RELIG apôtre m.

apostrophe [ə'pɒstrəfɪ] n apostrophe f.

appal Br (pt & pp -led ; cont -ling), **appall** Am [ə'pɔ:l] vt horrifier.

Appalachian [,æpə'leɪtʃjən] n : **the ~s, the ~ Mountains** les (monts mpl) Appalaches mpl.

appall Am = **appal**.

appalled [ə'pɔ:ld] adj horrifié(e).

appalling [ə'pɔ:lɪŋ] adj épouvantable.

appallingly [ə'pɔ:lɪŋlɪ] adv épouvantablement.

apparatus [,æpə'reɪtəs] (pl inv OR -es [-i:z]) n - **1.** [device] appareil m, dispositif m - **2.** (U) [in gym] agrès mpl - **3.** [system, organization] appareil m.

apparel [ə'pærəl] n Am habillement m.

apparent [ə'pærənt] adj - **1.** [evident] évident(e) ; **for no ~ reason** sans raison particulière - **2.** [seeming] apparent(e).

apparently [ə'pærəntlɪ] adv - **1.** [it seems] à ce qu'il paraît - **2.** [seemingly] apparemment, en apparence.

apparition [,æpə'rɪʃn] n apparition f.

appeal [ə'pi:l] ◇ vi - **1.** [request] : **to ~ (to** sb **for** sthg) lancer un appel (à qqn pour obtenir qqch) - **2.** [make a plea] : **to ~ to** faire appel à - **3.** JUR : **to ~ (against)** faire appel (de) - **4.** [attract, interest] : **to ~ to** sb plaire à qqn ; **it ~s to me** ça me plaît ◇ n - **1.** [request] appel m - **2.** JUR appel m - **3.** [charm, interest] intérêt m, attrait m.

appealing [ə'pi:lɪŋ] adj - **1.** [attractive] attirant(e), sympathique - **2.** [pleading] suppliant(e).

appear [ə'pɪə'] vi - **1.** [gen] apparaître ; [book] sortir, paraître - **2.** [seem] sembler, paraître ; **to ~ to be/do** sembler être/faire ; **it would ~ (that)** ... il semblerait que ... - **3.** [in play, film etc] jouer - **4.** JUR comparaître.

appearance [ə'pɪərəns] n - **1.** [gen] apparition f ; **to make an ~** se montrer ; **to put in an ~** faire acte de présence - **2.** [look] apparence f, aspect m ; **by** OR **to all ~s** selon toute apparence ; **to keep up ~s** sauver les apparences.

appease [ə'pi:z] vt apaiser.

appeasement [ə'pi:zmənt] n apaisement m.

append [ə'pend] vt ajouter ; [signature] apposer.

appendage [ə'pendɪdʒ] n appendice m.

appendices [ə'pendɪsi:z] pl ⊳ **appendix**.

appendicitis [ə,pendɪ'saɪtɪs] n (U) appendicite f.

appendix [ə'pendɪks] (pl -dixes [-dɪksi:z] OR -dices [-dɪsi:z]) n appendice m ; **to have one's ~ out** OR **removed** se faire opérer de l'appendicite.

appertain [,æpə'teɪn] vi fml : **to ~ to** se rapporter à.

appetite ['æpɪtaɪt] n - **1.** [for food] : **~ (for)** appétit m (pour) - **2.** fig [enthusiasm] : **~ (for)** goût m (de OR pour).

appetizer, -iser ['æpɪtaɪzə'] n [food] amusegueule m inv ; [drink] apéritif m.

appetizing, -ising ['æpɪtaɪzɪŋ] adj [food] appétissant(e).

applaud [ə'plɔ:d] ◇ vt - **1.** [clap] applaudir - **2.** [approve] approuver, applaudir à ◇ vi applaudir.

applause [ə'plɔ:z] n (U) applaudissements mpl.

apple ['æpl] n pomme f ; **she's the ~ of her father's eye** inf son père tient à elle comme à la prunelle de ses yeux.

apple pie n tourte f aux pommes.

apple tree n pommier m.

appliance [ə'plaɪəns] n [device] appareil m ; **domestic ~** appareil ménager.

applicable [ə'plɪkəbl] *adj :* ~ **(to)** applicable (à).

applicant ['æplɪkənt] *n :* ~ **(for)** [job] candidat *m*, -e *f* (à) ; [state benefit] demandeur *m*, -euse *f* (de).

application [ˌæplɪ'keɪʃn] *n* - **1.** [gen] application *f* - **2.** [for job etc] : ~ **(for)** demande *f* (de).

application form *n* [for post] dossier *m* de candidature, UNIV dossier *m* d'inscription.

applications program [ˌæplɪ'keɪʃns -] *n* COMPUT programme *m* d'application.

applicator ['æplɪkeɪtəʳ] *n* [for lotion, glue etc] applicateur *m*.

applied [ə'plaɪd] *adj* [science] appliqué(e).

appliqué [ə'pliːkeɪ] *n* application *f*.

apply [ə'plaɪ] (*pt & pp* -**ied**) <> *vt* appliquer ; **to** ~ **o.s. (to sthg)** s'appliquer (à qqch) ; **to** ~ **one's mind (to sthg)** s'appliquer (à qqch) ; **to** ~ **the brakes** freiner <> *vi* - **1.** [for work, grant] : **to** ~ **(for)** faire une demande (de) ; **to** ~ **for a job** faire une demande d'emploi ; **to** ~ **to sb (for sthg)** s'adresser à qqn (pour obtenir qqch) - **2.** [be relevant] : **to** ~ **(to)** s'appliquer (à), concerner.

appoint [ə'pɔɪnt] *vt* - **1.** [to job, position] : **to** ~ **sb (as sthg)** nommer qqn (qqch) ; **to** ~ **sb to sthg** nommer qqn à qqch - **2.** [time, place] fixer.

appointment [ə'pɔɪntmənt] *n* - **1.** [to job, position] nomination *f*, désignation *f* ; 'by ~ **to Her Majesty the Queen**' 'fournisseur de sa Majesté la Reine' - **2.** [job, position] poste *m*, emploi *m* - **3.** [arrangement to meet] rendezvous *m* ; **to make an** ~ prendre un rendezvous ; **by** ~ sur rendez-vous.

apportion [ə'pɔːʃn] *vt* répartir.

apposite ['æpəzɪt] *adj* pertinent(e), approprié(e).

appraisal [ə'preɪzl] *n* évaluation *f*.

appraise [ə'preɪz] *vt* évaluer.

appreciable [ə'priːʃəbl] *adj* [difference] sensible ; [amount] appréciable.

appreciably [ə'priːʃəblɪ] *adv* sensiblement.

appreciate [ə'priːʃɪeɪt] <> *vt* - **1.** [value, like] apprécier, aimer - **2.** [recognize, understand] comprendre, se rendre compte de - **3.** [be grateful for] être reconnaissant(e) de <> *vi* FIN prendre de la valeur.

appreciation [əˌpriːʃɪ'eɪʃn] *n* - **1.** [liking] contentement *m* - **2.** [understanding] compréhension *f* - **3.** [gratitude] reconnaissance *f* - **4.** FIN augmentation *f* de valeur - **5.** [of novel, play etc] critique *f*.

appreciative [ə'priːʃjətɪv] *adj* [person] reconnaissant(e) ; [remark] élogieux(euse).

apprehend [ˌæprɪ'hend] *vt* fml [arrest] appréhender, arrêter.

apprehension [ˌæprɪ'henʃn] *n* [anxiety] appréhension *f*, crainte *f*.

apprehensive [ˌæprɪ'hensɪv] *adj* inquiet(ète) ; **to be** ~ **about sthg** appréhender OR craindre qqch.

apprehensively [ˌæprɪ'hensɪvlɪ] *adv* avec appréhension.

apprentice [ə'prentɪs] <> *n* apprenti *m*, -e *f* <> *vt* : **to be** ~**d to sb** être apprenti(e) chez qqn.

apprenticeship [ə'prentɪsʃɪp] *n* apprentissage *m*.

appro. ['æprəʊ] (*abbr of* **approval**) *n* inf : **on** ~ à condition, à l'essai.

approach [ə'prəʊtʃ] <> *n* - **1.** [gen] approche *f* - **2.** [method] démarche *f*, approche *f* - **3.** [to person] : **to make an** ~ **to sb** faire une proposition à qqn <> *vt* - **1.** [come near to - place, person, thing] s'approcher de - **2.** [ask] : **to** ~ **sb about sthg** aborder qqch avec qqn ; COMM entrer en contact avec qqn au sujet de qqch - **3.** [tackle - problem] aborder <> *vi* s'approcher.

approachable [ə'prəʊtʃəbl] *adj* accessible.

approaching [ə'prəʊtʃɪŋ] *adj* qui approche.

approbation [ˌæprə'beɪʃn] *n* approbation *f*.

appropriate [*adj* ə'prəʊprɪət, *vb* ə'prəʊprɪeɪt] <> *adj* [clothing] convenable ; [action] approprié(e) ; [moment] opportun(e) <> *vt* - **1.** JUR s'approprier - **2.** [allocate] affecter.

appropriately [ə'prəʊprɪətlɪ] *adv* [dress] convenablement ; [behave] de manière appropriée.

appropriation [əˌprəʊprɪ'eɪʃn] *n* - **1.** [taking] appropriation *f* - **2.** [allocation] affectation *f*.

approval [ə'pruːvl] *n* approbation *f* ; **on** ~ COMM à condition, à l'essai.

approve [ə'pruːv] <> *vi* : **to** ~ **(of sthg)** approuver (qqch) ; **I don't** ~ **of him** il me déplaît <> *vt* [ratify] approuver, ratifier.

approved [ə'pruːvd] *adj* approuvé(e), agréé(e).

approving [ə'pruːvɪŋ] *adj* approbateur(trice).

approx. [ə'prɒks] (*abbr of* **approximately**) approx., env.

approximate [*adj* ə'prɒksɪmət, *vb* ə'prɒksɪmeɪt] <> *adj* approximatif(ive) <> *vi* : **to** ~ **to** se rapprocher de.

approximately [ə'prɒksɪmətlɪ] *adv* à peu près, environ.

approximation [əˌprɒksɪ'meɪʃn] *n* : ~ **(to)** approximation *f* (de).

Apr. (abbr of **April**) avr.

APR n - **1.** (abbr of **annualized percentage rate**) TEG m - **2.** (abbr of **annual purchase rate**) taux m annuel.

après-ski [ˌæpreɪˈskiː] n (U) activités fpl après-ski.

apricot [ˈeɪprɪkɒt] ◇ n abricot m ◇ comp à l'abricot.

April [ˈeɪprəl] n avril m ; see also **September.**

April Fools' Day n le 1er avril.

APRIL FOOLS' DAY

En Grande-Bretagne, le 1er avril est l'occasion de canulars en tous genres ; par contre, la tradition du poisson en papier n'existe pas.

apron [ˈeɪprən] n - **1.** [clothing] tablier m ; **to be tied to sb's ~ strings** inf être toujours dans les jupes de qqn - **2.** AERON aire f de stationnement.

apropos [ˈæprəpəʊ] ◇ adj pertinent(e), à propos ◇ prep : **~ (of)** à propos (de).

apt [æpt] adj - **1.** [pertinent] pertinent(e), approprié(e) - **2.** [likely] : **to be ~ to do sthg** avoir tendance à faire qqch.

Apt. (abbr of **apartment**) appt.

APT (abbr of **advanced passenger train**) n ≃ TGV m.

aptitude [ˈæptɪtjuːd] n aptitude f, disposition f ; **to have an ~ for** avoir des dispositions pour.

aptitude test n test m d'aptitude.

aptly [ˈæptlɪ] adv avec justesse, à propos.

aqualung [ˈækwəlʌŋ] n scaphandre m autonome.

aquamarine [ˌækwəməˈriːn] n [colour] bleu vert m inv.

aquaplane [ˈækwəpleɪn] vi Br AUT faire de l'aquaplaning.

aquarium [əˈkweərɪəm] (pl **-riums** OR **-ria** [-rɪə]) n aquarium m.

Aquarius [əˈkweərɪəs] n Verseau m ; **to be (an) ~** être Verseau.

aquarobics [ˌækwəˈrəʊbɪks] n aquagym f.

aquatic [əˈkwætɪk] adj - **1.** [animal, plant] aquatique - **2.** [sport] nautique.

aqueduct [ˈækwɪdʌkt] n aqueduc m.

AR abbr of **Arkansas.**

ARA (abbr of **Associate of the Royal Academy**) n membre associé de la RA.

Arab [ˈærəb] ◇ adj arabe ◇ n - **1.** [person] Arabe mf - **2.** [horse] pur-sang m arabe.

Arabia [əˈreɪbjə] n Arabie f.

Arabian [əˈreɪbjən] adj d'Arabie, arabe.

Arabian desert n : **the ~** le désert d'Arabie.

Arabian Peninsula n : **the ~** la péninsule d'Arabie.

Arabian Sea n : **the ~** la mer d'Arabie, la mer d'Oman.

Arabic [ˈærəbɪk] ◇ adj arabe ◇ n arabe m.

Arabic numeral n chiffre m arabe.

arable [ˈærəbl] adj arable.

ARAM (abbr of **Associate of the Royal Academy of Music**) n membre associé de l'académie britannique de musique.

arbiter [ˈɑːbɪtər] n fml arbitre m.

arbitrary [ˈɑːbɪtrərɪ] adj arbitraire.

arbitrate [ˈɑːbɪtreɪt] vi arbitrer.

arbitration [ˌɑːbɪˈtreɪʃn] n arbitrage m ; **to go to ~** recourir à l'arbitrage.

arc [ɑːk] n arc m.

ARC (abbr of **AIDS-related complex**) n ARC m.

arcade [ɑːˈkeɪd] n - **1.** [for shopping] galerie f marchande - **2.** [covered passage] arcades fpl.

arch [ɑːtʃ] ◇ adj malicieux(euse), espiègle ◇ n - **1.** ARCHIT arc m, voûte f - **2.** [of foot] voûte f plantaire, cambrure f ◇ vt cambrer, arquer ◇ vi former une voûte.

arch- [ɑːtʃ] prefix grand(e), principal(e).

archaeological [ˌɑːkɪəˈlɒdʒɪkl] adj archéologique.

archaeologist [ˌɑːkɪˈɒlədʒɪst] n archéologue mf.

archaeology [ˌɑːkɪˈɒlədʒɪ] n archéologie f.

archaic [ɑːˈkeɪɪk] adj archaïque.

archangel [ˈɑːkˌeɪndʒəl] n archange m.

archbishop [ˌɑːtʃˈbɪʃəp] n archevêque m.

archduchess [ˌɑːtʃˈdʌtʃɪs] n archiduchesse f.

archduke [ˌɑːtʃˈdjuːk] n archiduc m.

arched [ɑːtʃt] adj - **1.** ARCHIT cintré(e), courbé(e) - **2.** [curved] arqué(e), cambré(e).

archenemy [ˌɑːtʃˈenɪmɪ] (pl **-ies**) n ennemi m numéro un.

archeology etc [ˌɑːkɪˈɒlədʒɪ] = **archaeology** etc.

archer [ˈɑːtʃər] n archer m.

archery [ˈɑːtʃərɪ] n tir m à l'arc.

archetypal [ˌɑːkɪˈtaɪpl] adj typique.

archetype [ˈɑːkɪtaɪp] n archétype m.

archipelago [ˌɑːkɪˈpelɪɡəʊ] (pl **-es** OR **-s**) n archipel m.

architect [ˈɑːkɪtekt] n lit & fig architecte m.

architectural [ˌɑːkɪˈtektʃərəl] adj architectural(e).

architecture [ˈɑːkɪtektʃəʳ] n [gen & COMPUT] architecture f.

archive file [ˈɑːkaɪv-] n COMPUT fichier m archives.

archives [ˈɑːkaɪvz] npl archives fpl.

archivist [ˈɑːkɪvɪst] n archiviste mf.

archway [ˈɑːtʃweɪ] n passage m voûté.

ARCM (abbr of Associate of the Royal College of Music) n membre associé du conservatoire de musique britannique.

Arctic [ˈɑːktɪk] <> adj - **1.** GEOGR arctique - **2.** inf [very cold] glacial(e) <> n : the ~ l'Arctique m ; in the ~ dans l'Arctique.

Arctic Circle n : the ~ le cercle arctique.

Arctic Ocean n : the ~ l'océan m Arctique.

ardent [ˈɑːdənt] adj fervent(e), passionné(e).

ardour Br, **ardor** Am [ˈɑːdəʳ] n ardeur f, ferveur f.

arduous [ˈɑːdjʊəs] adj ardu(e).

are [weak form əʳ, strong form ɑːʳ] ⊏> be.

area [ˈeərɪə] n - **1.** [region] région f ; landing ~ aire f d'atterrissage ; parking ~ aire f de stationnement ; in the ~ dans la région ; in the ~ of [approximately] environ, à peu près - **2.** [surface size] aire f, superficie f - **3.** [of knowledge, interest etc] domaine m.

area code n indicatif m de zone.

arena [əˈriːnə] n lit & fig arène f.

aren't [ɑːnt] = are not.

Argentina [ˌɑːdʒənˈtiːnə] n Argentine f ; in ~ en Argentine.

Argentine [ˈɑːdʒəntaɪn], **Argentinian** [ˌɑːdʒənˈtɪnɪən] <> adj argentin(e) <> n Argentin m, -e f.

arguable [ˈɑːgjʊəbl] adj discutable, contestable.

arguably [ˈɑːgjʊəblɪ] adv : she's ~ the best on peut soutenir qu'elle est la meilleure.

argue [ˈɑːgjuː] <> vi - **1.** [quarrel] : to ~ (with sb about sthg) se disputer (avec qqn à propos de qqch) - **2.** [reason] : to ~ (for/against) argumenter (pour/contre) <> vt débattre de, discuter de ; to ~ that soutenir OR maintenir que.

argument [ˈɑːgjʊmənt] n - **1.** [quarrel] dispute f ; to have an ~ (with sb) se disputer (avec qqn) - **2.** [reason] argument m - **3.** (U) [reasoning] discussion f, débat m.

argumentative [ˌɑːgjʊˈmentətɪv] adj querelleur(euse), batailleur(euse).

aria [ˈɑːrɪə] n aria f.

arid [ˈærɪd] adj lit & fig aride.

Aries [ˈeəriːz] n Bélier m ; to be (an) ~ être Bélier.

arise [əˈraɪz] (pt arose ; pp arisen [əˈrɪzn]) vi [appear] surgir, survenir ; to ~ from résulter de, provenir de ; if the need ~s si le besoin se fait sentir.

aristocracy [ˌærɪˈstɒkrəsɪ] (pl -ies) n aristocratie f.

aristocrat [Br ˈærɪstəkræt, Am əˈrɪstəkræt] n aristocrate mf.

aristocratic [Br ˌærɪstəˈkrætɪk, Am əˌrɪstəˈkrætɪk] adj aristocratique.

arithmetic [əˈrɪθmətɪk] n arithmétique f.

Arizona [ˌærɪˈzəʊnə] n Arizona m ; in ~ dans l'Arizona.

ark [ɑːk] n arche f.

Arkansas [ˈɑːkənsɔː] n Arkansas m ; in ~ dans l'Arkansas.

arm [ɑːm] <> n - **1.** [of person, chair] bras m ; ~ in ~ bras dessus bras dessous ; to chance one's ~ fig tenter le coup ; to keep sb at ~'s length fig tenir qqn à distance ; to twist sb's ~ fig forcer la main à qqn - **2.** [of garment] manche f - **3.** [of organization] section f, aile f <> vt armer.

➡ **arms** npl armes fpl ; to take up ~s prendre les armes ; to be up in ~s about sthg s'élever contre qqch.

armada [ɑːˈmɑːdə] n armada f.

armadillo [ˌɑːməˈdɪləʊ] (pl -s) n tatou m.

Armageddon [ˌɑːməˈgedn] n Armageddon m.

armaments [ˈɑːməmənts] npl [weapons] matériel m de guerre, armements mpl.

armchair [ˈɑːmtʃeəʳ] n fauteuil m.

armed [ɑːmd] adj lit & fig : ~ (with) armé(e)(de).

armed forces npl forces fpl armées.

Armenia [ɑːˈmiːnjə] n Arménie f ; in ~ en Arménie.

Armenian [ɑːˈmiːnjən] <> adj arménien(enne) <> n - **1.** [person] Arménien m, -enne f - **2.** [language] arménien m.

armhole [ˈɑːmhəʊl] n emmanchure f.

armistice [ˈɑːmɪstɪs] n armistice m.

armour Br, **armor** Am [ˈɑːməʳ] n - **1.** [for person] armure f - **2.** [for military vehicle] blindage m.

armoured Br, **armored** Am [ˈɑːməd] adj MIL blindé(e).

armoured car [ˌɑːməd-] n voiture f blindée.

armour-plated [-ˈpleɪtɪd] adj blindé(e).

armoury Br, **armory** Am [ˈɑːmərɪ] (pl -ies) n arsenal m.

armpit [ˈɑːmpɪt] n aisselle f.

armrest [ˈɑːmrest] n accoudoir m.

arms control [ˈɑːmz-] n contrôle m des armements.

army [ˈɑːmɪ] (pl -ies) n lit & fig armée f.

A road n Br route f nationale.

aroma [əˈrəʊmə] n arôme m.

aromatherapy [əˌrəʊməˈθerəpɪ] n aromathérapie f.

aromatic [ˌærəˈmætɪk] adj aromatique.

arose [əˈrəʊz] pt ▷ arise.

around [əˈraʊnd] ⬦ adv - **1.** [about, round] : to walk ~ se promener ; to lie ~ [clothes etc] traîner - **2.** [on all sides] (tout) autour - **3.** [near] dans les parages - **4.** [in circular movement] : to turn ~ se retourner - **5.** phr : he has been ~ inf il n'est pas né d'hier, il a de l'expérience ⬦ prep - **1.** [gen] autour de ; to walk ~ a garden/town faire le tour d'un jardin/ d'une ville ; all ~ the country dans tout le pays - **2.** [near] : ~ here par ici - **3.** [approximately] environ, à peu près.

arousal [əˈraʊzl] n éveil m.

arouse [əˈraʊz] vt - **1.** [excite - feeling] éveiller, susciter ; [- person] exciter - **2.** [wake] réveiller.

arrange [əˈreɪndʒ] vt - **1.** [flowers, books, furniture] arranger, disposer - **2.** [event, meeting etc] organiser, fixer ; to ~ to do sthg convenir de faire qqch ; she ~d for him to come to Edinburgh elle a fait le nécessaire pour qu'il vienne à Édimbourg - **3.** MUS arranger.

arranged marriage [əˈreɪndʒd-] n mariage m arrangé.

arrangement [əˈreɪndʒmənt] n - **1.** [agreement] accord m, arrangement m ; to come to an ~ s'entendre, s'arranger - **2.** [of furniture, books] arrangement m ; **flower** ~ composition f florale - **3.** MUS arrangement m.

arrangements npl dispositions fpl, préparatifs mpl ; to make ~s prendre des mesures OR dispositions.

array [əˈreɪ] ⬦ n - **1.** [of objects] étalage m - **2.** COMPUT tableau m ⬦ vt [ornaments etc] disposer.

arrears [əˈrɪəz] npl [money owed] arriéré m ; to be in ~ [late] être en retard ; [owing money] avoir des arriérés.

arrest [əˈrest] ⬦ n [by police] arrestation f ; under ~ en état d'arrestation ⬦ vt - **1.** [gen] arrêter - **2.** fml [sb's attention] attirer, retenir.

arresting [əˈrestɪŋ] adj [striking] frappant(e), saisissant(e).

arrival [əˈraɪvl] n - **1.** [gen] arrivée f ; late ~ [of train etc] retard m - **2.** [person - at airport, hotel] arrivant m, -e f ; new ~ [person] nouveau venu

m, nouvelle venue f ; [baby] nouveau-né m, nouveau-née f.

arrive [əˈraɪv] vi arriver ; [baby] être né(e) ; to ~ at [conclusion, decision] arriver à.

arrogance [ˈærəgəns] n arrogance f.

arrogant [ˈærəgənt] adj arrogant(e).

arrogantly [ˈærəgəntlɪ] adv avec arrogance.

arrow [ˈærəʊ] n flèche f.

arrowroot [ˈærəʊruːt] n arrow-root m.

arse Br [ɑːs], **ass** Am [æs] n v inf cul m.

arsenic [ˈɑːsnɪk] n arsenic m.

arsenal [ˈɑːsənl] n arsenal m.

arson [ˈɑːsn] n incendie m criminel OR volontaire.

arsonist [ˈɑːsənɪst] n incendiaire mf.

art [ɑːt] ⬦ n art m ⬦ comp [exhibition] d'art ; [college] des beaux-arts ; ~ **student** étudiant m, -e f d'une école des beaux-arts.

◆ arts ⬦ npl - **1.** SCH & UNIV lettres fpl - **2.** [fine arts] : the ~s les arts mpl ⬦ comp SCH & UNIV de lettres ; ~s student étudiant m, -e f en lettres.

art deco [-ˈdekəʊ] n art m déco.

artefact [ˈɑːtɪfækt] = artifact.

arterial [ɑːˈtɪərɪəl] adj - **1.** [blood] artériel(elle) - **2.** [road] à grande circulation.

arteriosclerosis [ɑːˌtɪərɪəʊsklɪəˈrəʊsɪs] n artériosclérose f.

artery [ˈɑːtərɪ] (pl -ies) n artère f.

artful [ˈɑːtfʊl] adj rusé(e), malin(igne).

art gallery n [public] musée m d'art ; [for selling paintings] galerie f d'art.

art house n cinéma m d'art et d'essai.

art-house adj [cinema, film] d'art et d'essai.

arthritic [ɑːˈθrɪtɪk] adj arthritique.

arthritis [ɑːˈθraɪtɪs] n arthrite f.

artic [ɑːˈtɪk] (abbr of articulated lorry) n Br inf semi-remorque m.

artichoke [ˈɑːtɪtʃəʊk] n artichaut m.

article [ˈɑːtɪkl] n article m ; ~ of clothing vêtement m.

articled clerk [ˈɑːtɪkld-] n Br avocat m stagiaire.

articles of association [ˈɑːtɪklz-] npl statuts mpl d'une société.

articulate [adj ɑːˈtɪkjʊlət, vb ɑːˈtɪkjʊleɪt] ⬦ adj [person] qui sait s'exprimer ; [speech] net (nette), distinct(e) ⬦ vt [thought, wish] formuler.

articulated lorry [ɑːˈtɪkjʊleɪtɪd-] n Br semi-remorque m.

articulation [ɑːˌtɪkjʊˈleɪʃn] n articulation f.

artifact [ˈɑːtɪfækt] n objet m fabriqué.

artifice ['ɑ:tɪfɪs] n - **1.** [trick] artifice m, ruse f - **2.** [trickery] ingéniosité f, habileté f.

artificial [,ɑ:tɪ'fɪʃl] adj - **1.** [not natural] artificiel(elle) - **2.** [insincere] affecté(e).

artificial insemination n insémination f artificielle.

artificial intelligence n intelligence f artificielle.

artificially [,ɑ:tɪ'fɪʃəlɪ] adv artificiellement.

artificial respiration n respiration f artificielle.

artillery [ɑ:'tɪlərɪ] n artillerie f.

artisan [,ɑ:tɪ'zæn] n artisan m.

artist ['ɑ:tɪst] n artiste mf.

artiste [ɑ:'ti:st] n artiste mf.

artistic [ɑ:'tɪstɪk] adj [person] artiste ; [style etc] artistique.

artistically [ɑ:'tɪstɪklɪ] adv avec art, de façon artistique.

artistry ['ɑ:tɪstrɪ] n art m, talent m artistique.

artless ['ɑ:tlɪs] adj naturel(elle), ingénu(e).

art nouveau [,ɑ:nu:'vəʊ] n art m nouveau.

ARV (abbr of American Revised Version) n traduction américaine de la Bible.

as [unstressed əz, stressed æz] ◇ conj - **1.** [referring to time] comme, alors que ; **she rang (just) ~ I was leaving** elle m'a téléphoné au moment même où OR juste comme je partais ; **~ time goes by** à mesure que le temps passe, avec le temps - **2.** [referring to manner, way] comme ; **do ~ I say** fais ce que je (te) dis ; **~ it is** déjà ; **she's working too hard ~ it is** elle travaille déjà assez dur comme ça ; **~ it turns out** finalement, en fin de compte ; **~ things stand** les choses étant ce qu'elles sont - **3.** [introducing a statement] comme ; **~ you see,...** comme tu le vois,... ; **~ you know,...** comme tu le sais,... - **4.** [because] comme ◇ prep - **1.** [referring to function, characteristic] en, comme, en tant que ; **I'm speaking ~ your friend** je te parle en ami ; **he made a name ~ an actor** il s'est fait un nom comme acteur ; **she works ~ a nurse** elle est infirmière - **2.** [referring to attitude, reaction] : **it came ~ a shock** cela nous a fait un choc ; **she treats it ~ a game** elle prend ça à la rigolade ◇ adv (in comparisons) : **~ rich ~** aussi riche que ; **~ red ~ a tomato** rouge comme une tomate ; **he's ~ tall ~ I am** il est aussi grand que moi ; **twice ~ big ~** deux fois plus gros que ; **~ much/many ~** autant que ; **~ much wine/ many chocolates ~** autant de vin/de chocolats que.

◆ **as it were** adv pour ainsi dire.

◆ **as for** prep quant à.

◆ **as from, as of** prep dès, à partir de.

◆ **as if, as though** conj comme si ; **it looks ~ if** OR **~ though it will rain** on dirait qu'il va pleuvoir.

◆ **as to** prep - **1.** [concerning] en ce qui concerne, au sujet de - **2.** = **as for.**

AS ◇ n (abbr of Associate in/of Science) diplômé en sciences ◇ abbr of American Samoa.

ASA (abbr of American Standards Association) n association américaine de normalisation, ≈ AFNOR f.

a.s.a.p. (abbr of as soon as possible) d'urgence, dans les meilleurs délais.

asbestos [æs'bestəs] n asbeste m, amiante m.

asbestosis [,æsbes'təʊsɪs] n asbestose f.

ascend [ə'send] vt & vi monter ; **to ~ the throne** monter sur le trône.

ascendancy [ə'sendənsɪ] n ascendant m.

ascendant [ə'sendənt] n : **to be in the ~** avoir le dessus.

ascendency [ə'sendənsɪ] = **ascendancy.**

ascending [ə'sendɪŋ] adj croissant(e) ; **in ~ order** en ordre croissant.

ascension [ə'senʃn] n ascension f.

◆ **Ascension** n RELIG l'Ascension f.

Ascension Island n île f de l'Ascension.

ascent [ə'sent] n lit & fig ascension f.

ascertain [,æsə'teɪn] vt établir.

ascetic [ə'setɪk] ◇ adj ascétique ◇ n ascète mf.

ASCII ['æskɪ] (abbr of American Standard Code for Information) n ASCII m.

ascorbic acid [ə'skɔ:bɪk-] n acide m ascorbique.

ascribe [ə'skraɪb] vt : **to ~ sthg to** attribuer qqch à ; [blame] imputer qqch à.

ASCU (abbr of Association of State Colleges and Universities) n association des établissements universitaires d'État aux États-Unis.

ASE (abbr of American Stock Exchange) n la Bourse américaine.

aseptic [,eɪ'septɪk] adj aseptique.

asexual [,eɪ'sekʃʊəl] adj asexué(e).

ash [æʃ] n - **1.** [from cigarette, fire] cendre f - **2.** [tree] frêne m.

◆ **ashes** npl cendres fpl.

ASH [æʃ] (abbr of Action on Smoking and Health) n ligue antitabac britannique.

ashamed [ə'ʃeɪmd] adj honteux(euse), confus(e) ; **to be ~ of** avoir honte de ; **to be ~ to do sthg** avoir honte de faire qqch.

ashcan ['æʃkæn] n Am poubelle f.

ashen-faced ['æʃn‚feɪst] adj blême.

ashore [ə'ʃɔːʳ] adv à terre.

ashtray ['æʃtreɪ] n cendrier m.

Ash Wednesday n le mercredi des Cendres.

Asia [Br 'eɪʃə, Am 'eɪʒə] n Asie f ; **in ~** en Asie.

Asia Minor n Asie f Mineure.

Asian [Br 'eɪʃn, Am 'eɪʒn] ◇ adj asiatique ◇ n [person] Asiatique mf.

Asiatic [‚eɪʒɪ'ætɪk] adj asiatique.

aside [ə'saɪd] ◇ adv - 1. [to one side] de côté ; **to move ~** s'écarter ; **to take sb ~** prendre qqn à part ; **to brush** OR **sweep sthg ~** balayer OR repousser qqch - 2. [apart] à part ; **~ from** à l'exception de ◇ n - 1. [in play] aparté m - 2. [remark] réflexion f, commentaire m.

ask [ɑːsk] ◇ vt - 1. [gen] demander ; **to ~ sb sthg** demander qqch à qqn ; **he ~ed me my name** il m'a demandé mon nom ; **to ~ sb for sthg** demander qqch à qqn ; **to ~ sb to do sthg** demander à qqn de faire qqch ; **if you ~ me ...** si tu veux mon avis ... - 2. [put - question] poser - 3. [invite] inviter ◇ vi demander.

‣ **ask after** vt fus demander des nouvelles de.

‣ **ask for** vt fus - 1. [person] demander à voir - 2. [thing] demander

askance [ə'skæns] adv : **to look ~ at sb** regarder qqn d'un air désapprobateur.

askew [ə'skjuː] adj [not straight] de travers.

asking price ['ɑːskɪŋ-] n prix m demandé.

asleep [ə'sliːp] adj endormi(e) ; **to fall ~** s'endormir ; **to be fast** OR **sound ~** dormir profondément OR à poings fermés.

ASLEF ['æzlef] (abbr of **Associated Society of Locomotive Engineers and Firemen**) n syndicat des cheminots en Grande-Bretagne.

AS level (abbr of **Advanced Supplementary level**) n [in UK] examen facultatif complétant les A levels.

ASM (abbr of **air-to-surface missile**) n ASM m.

asparagus [ə'spærəgəs] n (U) asperges fpl.

aspartame ['æspərteɪm] n aspartame m.

ASPCA (abbr of **American Society for the Prevention of Cruelty to Animals**) n société américaine protectrice des animaux.

aspect ['æspekt] n - 1. [gen] aspect m - 2. [of building] orientation f.

aspen ['æspən] n tremble m.

aspersions [ə'spɜːʃnz] npl : **to cast ~ on** jeter le discrédit sur.

asphalt ['æsfælt] n asphalte m.

asphyxiate [əs'fɪksɪeɪt] vt asphyxier.

aspic ['æspɪk] n aspic m.

aspirate ['æspərət] adj LING aspiré(e).

aspiration [‚æspə'reɪʃn] n aspiration f.

aspire [ə'spaɪəʳ] vi : **to ~ to sthg/to do sthg** aspirer à qqch/à faire qqch.

aspirin ['æsprɪn] n aspirine f.

aspiring [ə'spaɪərɪŋ] adj : **she was an ~ writer** elle avait pour ambition de devenir écrivain.

ass [æs] n - 1. [donkey] âne m - 2. Br inf [idiot] imbécile mf, idiot m, -e f - 3. Am v inf = **arse**.

assail [ə'seɪl] vt assaillir.

assailant [ə'seɪlənt] n assaillant m, -e f.

assassin [ə'sæsɪn] n assassin m.

assassinate [ə'sæsɪneɪt] vt assassiner.

assassination [ə‚sæsɪ'neɪʃn] n assassinat m.

assault [ə'sɔːlt] ◇ n - 1. MIL : **~ (on)** assaut m (de), attaque f (de) - 2. [physical attack] : **~ (on sb)** agression f (contre qqn) ; **~ and battery** JUR coups mpl et blessures ◇ vt [attack - physically] agresser ; [- sexually] violenter.

assault course n parcours m du combattant.

assemble [ə'sembl] ◇ vt - 1. [gather] réunir - 2. [fit together] assembler, monter ◇ vi se réunir, s'assembler.

assembly [ə'semblɪ] (pl -ies) n - 1. [gen] assemblée f - 2. [fitting together] assemblage m.

assembly language n COMPUT langage m d'assemblage.

assembly line n chaîne f de montage.

assent [ə'sent] ◇ n consentement m, assentiment m ◇ vi : **to ~ (to)** donner son consentement OR assentiment (à).

assert [ə'sɜːt] vt - 1. [fact, belief] affirmer, soutenir - 2. [authority] imposer ; **to ~ o.s.** s'imposer.

assertion [ə'sɜːʃn] n [claim] assertion f, affirmation f.

assertive [ə'sɜːtɪv] adj assuré(e).

assess [ə'ses] vt évaluer, estimer.

assessment [ə'sesmənt] n - 1. [opinion] opinion f - 2. [calculation] évaluation f, estimation f.

assessor [ə'sesəʳ] n [of tax] contrôleur m (des impôts).

asset ['æset] n avantage m, atout m ; **she will be an ~ to the company** sa compétence sera un atout pour la société.

‣ **assets** npl COMM actif m.

asset-stripping [-‚strɪpɪŋ] n rachat d'une société pour en récupérer l'actif.

assiduous [ə'sɪdjʊəs] adj assidu(e).

assiduously [əˈsɪdjʊəslɪ] *adv* assidûment.

assign [əˈsaɪn] *vt* - **1.** [allot] : **to ~ sthg (to)** assigner qqch (à) - **2.** [give task to] : **to ~ sb (to sthg/to do sthg)** nommer qqn (à qqch/pour faire qqch).

assignation [ˌæsɪgˈneɪʃn] *n* rendez-vous *m* (amoureux).

assignment [əˈsaɪnmənt] *n* - **1.** [task] mission *f* ; SCH devoir *m* - **2.** [act of assigning] attribution *f*.

assimilate [əˈsɪmɪleɪt] *vt* assimiler.

assimilation [əˌsɪmɪˈleɪʃn] *n* assimilation *f*.

assist [əˈsɪst] *vt* : **to ~ sb (with sthg/in doing sthg)** aider qqn (dans qqch/à faire qqch) ; [professionally] assister qqn (dans qqch/pour faire qqch).

assistance [əˈsɪstəns] *n* aide *f* ; **to be of ~ (to)** être utile (à).

assistant [əˈsɪstənt] <> *n* assistant *m*, -e *f* ; (shop) ~ vendeur *m*, -euse *f* <> *comp* : ~ **editor** rédacteur en chef adjoint *m*, rédactrice en chef adjointe *f* ; ~ **manager** sous-directeur *m*, -trice *f*.

associate [*adj* & *n* əˈsəʊʃɪət, *vb* əˈsəʊʃɪeɪt] <> *adj* associé(e) <> *n* associé *m*, -e *f* <> *vt* : **to ~ sb/sthg (with)** associer qqn/qqch (à) ; **to be ~d with** être associé(e) à <> *vi* : **to ~ with sb** fréquenter qqn.

association [əˌsəʊsɪˈeɪʃn] *n* association *f* ; **in ~ with** avec la collaboration de.

assonance [ˈæsənəns] *n* assonance *f*.

assorted [əˈsɔːtɪd] *adj* varié(e).

assortment [əˈsɔːtmənt] *n* mélange *m*.

Asst. *abbr of* **assistant.**

assuage [əˈsweɪdʒ] *vt* [thirst, hunger] assouvir ; [grief] soulager.

assume [əˈsjuːm] *vt* - **1.** [suppose] supposer, présumer - **2.** [power, responsibility] assumer - **3.** [appearance, attitude] adopter.

assumed name [əˈsjuːmd-] *n* nom *m* d'emprunt.

assuming [əˈsjuːmɪŋ] *conj* en supposant que.

assumption [əˈsʌmpʃn] *n* - **1.** [supposition] supposition *f* - **2.** [of power] prise *f*.

Assumption *n* RELIG : **the Assumption** l'Assomption *f*.

assurance [əˈʃʊərəns] *n* - **1.** [gen] assurance *f* - **2.** [promise] garantie *f*, promesse *f*.

assure [əˈʃʊər] *vt* : **to ~ sb (of)** assurer qqn (de).

assured [əˈʃʊəd] *adj* assuré(e).

AST (*abbr of* **Atlantic Standard Time**) *n* heure d'hiver de la côte est des États-Unis.

asterisk [ˈæstərɪsk] *n* astérisque *m*.

astern [əˈstɜːn] *adv* NAUT en poupe.

asteroid [ˈæstərɔɪd] *n* astéroïde *m*.

asthma [ˈæsmə] *n* asthme *m*.

asthmatic [æsˈmætɪk] <> *adj* asthmatique <> *n* asthmatique *mf*.

astigmatism [æˈstɪgmətɪzm] *n* astigmatisme *m*.

astonish [əˈstɒnɪʃ] *vt* étonner.

astonishing [əˈstɒnɪʃɪŋ] *adj* étonnant(e).

astonishment [əˈstɒnɪʃmənt] *n* étonnement *m*.

astound [əˈstaʊnd] *vt* stupéfier.

astounding [əˈstaʊndɪŋ] *adj* stupéfiant(e).

astrakhan *n* astrakan *m*.

astray [əˈstreɪ] *adv* : **to go ~** [become lost] s'égarer ; **to lead sb ~** détourner qqn du droit chemin.

astride [əˈstraɪd] <> *adv* à cheval, à califourchon <> *prep* à cheval OR califourchon sur.

astringent [əˈstrɪndʒənt] <> *adj* astringent(e) <> *n* astringent *m*.

astrologer [əˈstrɒlədʒər] *n* astrologue *mf*.

astrological [ˌæstrəˈlɒdʒɪkl] *adj* astrologique.

astrologist [əˈstrɒlədʒɪst] = **astrologer.**

astrology [əˈstrɒlədʒɪ] *n* astrologie *f*.

astronaut [ˈæstrənɔːt] *n* astronaute *mf*.

astronomer [əˈstrɒnəmər] *n* astronome *mf*.

astronomical [ˌæstrəˈnɒmɪkl] *adj* astronomique.

astronomy [əˈstrɒnəmɪ] *n* astronomie *f*.

astrophysics [ˌæstrəʊˈfɪzɪks] *n* astrophysique *f*.

astute [əˈstjuːt] *adj* malin(igne).

asunder [əˈsʌndər] *adv* literary : **to tear ~** déchirer en deux.

ASV (*abbr of* **American Standard Version**) *n* traduction américaine de la Bible.

asylum [əˈsaɪləm] *n* asile *m*.

asymmetrical [ˌeɪsɪˈmetrɪkl] *adj* asymétrique.

at [*unstressed* ət, *stressed* æt] *prep* - **1.** [indicating place, position] à ; **they arrived ~ the airport** ils sont arrivés à l'aéroport ; ~ **my father's** chez mon père ; ~ **home** à la maison, chez soi ; ~ **school** à l'école ; ~ **work** au travail - **2.** [indicating direction] vers ; **to look ~ sb** regarder qqn ; **to smile ~ sb** sourire à qqn ; **to shoot ~ sb** tirer sur qqn - **3.** [indicating a particular time] à ; ~ **midnight/noon/eleven o'clock** à minuit/midi/onze heures ; ~ **night** la nuit ; ~ **Christmas/Easter** à Noël/Pâques - **4.** [indicating age, speed, rate] à ; ~ **52 (years of age)** à 52 ans ; ~ **100 mph** à 160 km/h **- 5.** [indicating price] : ~ **£50 a pair** 50 livres la paire **- 6.** [indicating particular state, condition] en ; ~ **peace/war** en paix/guerre ; **to be ~ lunch/dinner** être en train de déjeuner/dîner **- 7.** [indicating tentativeness, noncompletion] : **to snatch ~ sthg** essayer de saisir qqch ; **to nibble ~ sthg** grignoter qqch **- 8.** *(after adjectives)* : **amused/appalled/puzzled ~ sthg** diverti(e)/effaré(e)/intrigué(e) par qqch ; **delighted ~ sthg** ravi(e) de qqch ; **to be bad/good ~ sthg** être mauvais(e)/bon (bonne) en qqch.

➠ **at all** *adv* **- 1.** *(with negative)* : **not ~ all** [when thanked] je vous en prie ; [when answering a question] pas du tout ; **she's not ~ all happy** elle n'est pas du tout contente **- 2.** [in the slightest] : **anything ~ all** will do n'importe quoi fera l'affaire ; **do you know her ~ all?** est-ce que vous la connaissez?

ATC (*abbr of* **Air Training Corps**) *n unité de formation de l'armée de l'air britannique.*

ate [Br et, Am eɪt] *pt* ▷ **eat.**

atheism ['eɪθɪɪzm] *n* athéisme *m*.

atheist ['eɪθɪɪst] *n* athée *mf*.

Athenian [ə'θiːnjən] ◇ *adj* athénien(enne) ◇ *n* Athénien *m*, -enne *f*.

Athens ['æθɪnz] *n* Athènes.

athlete ['æθliːt] *n* athlète *mf*.

athlete's foot *n (U)* mycose *f*.

athletic [æθ'letɪk] *adj* athlétique.

➠ **athletics** *npl* athlétisme *m*.

Atlantic [ət'læntɪk] ◇ *adj* atlantique ◇ *n* : **the ~ (Ocean)** l'océan *m* Atlantique, l'Atlantique *m*.

Atlantis [ət'læntɪs] *n* Atlantide *f*.

atlas ['ætləs] *n* atlas *m*.

Atlas ['ætləs] *n* : **the ~ Mountains** l'Atlas *m*.

atm. (*abbr of* **atmosphere**) atm.

ATM (*abbr of* **automatic teller machine**) *n* DAB *m*.

atmosphere ['ætmə,sfɪər] *n* atmosphère *f*.

atmospheric [,ætməs'ferɪk] *adj* **- 1.** [pressure, pollution etc] atmosphérique **- 2.** [film, music etc] d'ambiance.

atoll ['ætɒl] *n* atoll *m*.

atom ['ætəm] *n* **- 1.** TECH atome *m* **- 2.** fig [tiny amount] grain *m*, parcelle *f*.

atom bomb *n* bombe *f* atomique.

atomic [ə'tɒmɪk] *adj* atomique.

atomic bomb = atom bomb.

atomic energy *n* énergie *f* atomique.

atomic number *n* nombre *m* OR numéro *m* atomique.

atomizer, -iser ['ætəmaɪzər] *n* atomiseur *m*, vaporisateur *m*.

atone [ə'təun] *vi* : **to ~ for** racheter.

atonement [ə'təunmənt] *n* : ~ **(for)** réparation *f* (de).

A to Z *n* plan *m* de ville.

ATP (*abbr of* **Association of Tennis Professionals**) *n* ATP *f*.

atrocious [ə'trəuʃəs] *adj* [very bad] atroce, affreux(euse).

atrocity [ə'trɒsətɪ] (*pl* **-ies**) *n* [terrible act] atrocité *f*.

attach [ə'tætʃ] *vt* **- 1.** [gen] : **to ~ sthg (to)** attacher qqch (à) **- 2.** [letter etc] joindre.

attaché [ə'tæʃeɪ] *n* attaché *m*, -e *f*.

attaché case *n* attaché-case *m*.

attached [ə'tætʃt] *adj* **- 1.** [fastened on] attaché(e) **- 2.** [letter etc] joint(e) **- 3.** [for work, job] : ~ **to** rattaché(e) à **- 4.** [fond] : ~ **to** attaché(e) à.

attachment [ə'tætʃmənt] *n* **- 1.** [device] accessoire *m* **- 2.** [fondness] : ~ **(to)** attachement *m* (à).

attack [ə'tæk] ◇ *n* **- 1.** [physical, verbal] : ~ **(on)** attaque *f* (contre) **- 2.** [of illness] crise *f* ◇ *vt* **- 1.** [gen] attaquer **- 2.** [job, problem] s'attaquer à ◇ *vi* attaquer.

attacker [ə'tækər] *n* **- 1.** [assailant] agresseur *m* **- 2.** SPORT attaquant *m*, -e *f*.

attain [ə'teɪn] *vt* atteindre, parvenir à.

attainment [ə'teɪnmənt] *n* **- 1.** [of success, aims etc] réalisation *f* **- 2.** [skill] talent *m*.

attempt [ə'tempt] ◇ *n* : ~ **(at)** tentative *f* (de) ; ~ **on sb's life** tentative d'assassinat ◇ *vt* tenter, essayer ; **to ~ to do sthg** essayer OR tenter de faire qqch.

attend [ə'tend] ◇ *vt* **- 1.** [meeting, party] assister à **- 2.** [school, church] aller à ◇ *vi* **- 1.** [be present] être présent(e) **- 2.** [pay attention] : **to ~ (to)** prêter attention à.

➠ **attend to** *vt fus* **- 1.** [deal with] s'occuper de, régler **- 2.** [look after - customer] s'occuper de ; [- patient] soigner.

attendance [ə'tendəns] *n* **- 1.** [number present] assistance *f*, public *m* **- 2.** [presence] présence *f*.

attendant [ə'tendənt] ◇ *adj* [problems] qui en découle ◇ *n* [at museum, car park] gardien *m*, -enne *f*; [at petrol station] pompiste *mf*; **swimming-pool ~** maître *m* nageur.

attention [ə'tenʃn] ◇ *n (U)* **- 1.** [gen] attention *f*; **to bring sthg to sb's ~**, **to draw sb's ~ to sthg** attirer l'attention de qqn sur qqch ; **to attract** OR **catch sb's ~** attirer l'attention de qqn ; **to pay ~ to** prêter attention à ; **for the**

~ of COMM à l'attention de - **2.** [care] soins *mpl*, attentions *fpl* - **3.** MIL : **to stand to** ~ se mettre au garde-à-vous <> *excl* MIL garde-à-vous!

attentive [ə'tentɪv] *adj* attentif(ive).

attentively [ə'tentɪvlɪ] *adv* attentivement.

attenuate [ə'tenjʋeɪt] <> *vt* atténuer <> *vi* s'atténuer.

attest [ə'test] <> *vt* attester, certifier <> *vi* : **to** ~ **to** témoigner de.

attic ['ætɪk] *n* grenier *m*.

attire [ə'taɪə'] *n (U)* fml tenue *f*.

attitude ['ætɪtjuːd] *n* - **1.** [gen] : ~ **(to** OR **towards)** attitude *f* (envers) - **2.** [posture] pose *f*

attn. (*abbr of* **for the attention of**) à l'attention de.

attorney [ə'tɜːnɪ] *n* Am avocat *m*, -e *f*.

attorney general (*pl* **attorneys general**) *n* ministre *m* de la Justice.

attract [ə'trækt] *vt* attirer ; **to be ~ed to** être attiré(e) par.

attraction [ə'trækʃn] *n* - **1.** [gen] attraction *f* ; ~ **to sb** attirance *f* envers qqn - **2.** [of thing] attrait *m*.

attractive [ə'træktɪv] *adj* [person] attirant(e), séduisant(e) ; [thing, idea] attrayant(e), séduisant(e) ; [investment] intéressant(e).

attractively [ə'træktɪvlɪ] *adv* [decorated, arranged] de manière attrayante ; [smile, dressed] de manière séduisante.

attributable [ə'trɪbjʋtəbl] *adj* : ~ **to** dû (due) à, attribuable à.

attribute [*vb* ə'trɪbjuːt, *n* 'ætrɪbjuːt] <> *vt* : **to** ~ **sthg to** attribuer qqch à <> *n* attribut *m*.

attribution [ˌætrɪ'bjuːʃn] *n* : ~ **(to)** attribution *f* (à).

attrition [ə'trɪʃn] *n* usure *f* ; **war of** ~ guerre *f* d'usure.

attuned [ə'tjuːnd] *adj* : ~ **to** accoutumé(e) à ; [ears] habitué(e) à.

Atty. Gen. *abbr of* **Attorney General.**

ATV *n* - **1.** (*abbr of* **Associated Television**) société britannique de télévision - **2.** (*abbr of* **all terrain vehicle**) véhicule tout-terrain.

atypical [ˌeɪ'tɪpɪkl] *adj* atypique.

atypically [ˌeɪ'tɪpɪklɪ] *adv* pas typiquement.

aubergine ['əʋbəʒiːn] *n* Br aubergine *f*.

auburn ['ɔːbən] *adj* auburn (inv).

auction ['ɔːkʃn] <> *n* vente *f* aux enchères ; **at** OR **by** ~ aux enchères ; **to put sthg up for** ~ mettre qqch (dans une vente) aux enchères <> *vt* vendre aux enchères.

➤ **auction off** *vt sep* vendre aux enchères.

auctioneer [ˌɔːkʃə'nɪə'] *n* commissaire-priseur *m*.

audacious [ɔː'deɪʃəs] *adj* audacieux(euse).

audacity [ɔː'dæsətɪ] *n* audace *f*.

audible ['ɔːdəbl] *adj* audible.

audience ['ɔːdjəns] *n* - **1.** [of play, film] public *m*, spectateurs *mpl* ; [of TV programme] téléspectateurs *mpl* - **2.** [formal meeting] audience *f*.

audio ['ɔːdɪəʋ] *adj* audio (inv).

audio frequency *n* audiofréquence *f*.

audiotyping ['ɔːdɪəʋˌtaɪpɪŋ] *n* audiotypie *f*.

audiotypist ['ɔːdɪəʋˌtaɪpɪst] *n* audiotypiste *mf*.

audiovisual [ˌɔːdɪəʋvɪzjʋəl] *adj* audiovisuel(elle).

audit ['ɔːdɪt] <> *n* audit *m*, vérification *f* des comptes <> *vt* vérifier, apurer.

audition [ɔː'dɪʃn] <> *n* THEATRE audition *f* ; CINEMA bout *m* d'essai <> *vi* : **to** ~ **for** passer une audition pour.

auditor ['ɔːdɪtə'] *n* auditeur *m*, -trice *f*.

auditorium [ˌɔːdɪ'tɔːrɪəm] (*pl* **-riums** OR **-ria** [-rɪə]) *n* salle *f*.

au fait [ˌəʋ'feɪ] *adj* : **to be** ~ **with sthg** être au fait de qqch, connaître qqch.

Aug. *abbr of* **August.**

augment [ɔːg'ment] *vt* augmenter, accroître.

augur ['ɔːgə'] *vi* : **to** ~ **well/badly** être de bon/ mauvais augure.

august [ɔː'gʌst] *adj* auguste, noble.

August ['ɔːgəst] *n* août *m* ; see also **September.**

Auld Lang Syne [ˌɔːldlæŋ'saɪn] *n* chant traditionnel britannique correspondant à « ce n'est qu'un au revoir, mes frères ».

aunt [ɑːnt] *n* tante *f*.

auntie, aunty ['ɑːntɪ] (*pl* **-ies**) *n* inf tata *f*, tantine *f*.

au pair [ˌəʋ'peə'] *n* jeune fille *f* au pair.

aura ['ɔːrə] *n* atmosphère *f*.

aural ['ɔːrəl] *adj* auditif(ive).

aurally ['ɔːrəlɪ] *adv* : ~ **handicapped** mal entendant(e).

auspices ['ɔːspɪsɪz] *npl* : **under the** ~ **of** sous les auspices de.

auspicious [ɔː'spɪʃəs] *adj* prometteur(euse).

Aussie ['ɒzɪ] *inf* <> *adj* australien(enne) <> *n* Australien *m*, -enne *f*.

austere [ɒ'stɪə'] *adj* austère.

austerity [ɒ'sterətɪ] *n* austérité *f*.

austerity measures *npl* restrictions *fpl*.

Australasia [ˌɒstrə'leɪʒə] *n* Australasie *f*.

Australia [ɒ'streɪljə] *n* Australie *f*; **in ~** en Australie.

Australian [ɒ'streɪljən] ⬦ *adj* australien(enne) ⬦ *n* Australien *m*, -enne *f*.

Austria ['ɒstrɪə] *n* Autriche *f*; **in ~** en Autriche.

Austrian ['ɒstrɪən] ⬦ *adj* autrichien(enne) ⬦ *n* Autrichien *m*, -enne *f*.

AUT (*abbr of* **Association of University Teachers**) *n* syndicat britannique d'enseignants universitaires.

authentic [ɔː'θentɪk] *adj* authentique.

authenticate [ɔː'θentɪkeɪt] *vt* établir l'authenticité de.

authentication [ɔːˌθentɪ'keɪʃn] *n* authentification *f*.

authenticity [ˌɔːθen'tɪsətɪ] *n* authenticité *f*.

author ['ɔːθəʳ] *n* auteur *m*.

authoritarian [ɔːˌθɒrɪ'teərɪən] *adj* autoritaire.

authoritative [ɔː'θɒrɪtətɪv] *adj* **- 1.** [person, voice] autoritaire **- 2.** [study] qui fait autorité.

authority [ɔː'θɒrətɪ] (*pl* **-ies**) *n* **- 1.** [organization, power] autorité *f*; **to be in ~** être le/la responsable **- 2.** [permission] autorisation *f* **- 3.** [expert]: **~ (on sthg)** expert *m*, -e *f* (en qqch) **- 4.** *phr*: **to have it on good ~** le tenir de bonne source OR de source sûre.

➤ **authorities** *npl*: **the authorities** les autorités *fpl*.

authorize, -ise ['ɔːθəraɪz] *vt*: **to ~ sb (to do sthg)** autoriser qqn (à faire qqch).

Authorized Version *n*: **the ~** la Bible de 1611.

authorship ['ɔːθəʃɪp] *n* paternité *f*.

autistic [ɔː'tɪstɪk] *adj* [child] autiste ; [behaviour] autistique.

auto ['ɔːtəʊ] (*pl* **-s**) *n* Am auto *f*, voiture *f*.

autobiographical ['ɔːtəˌbaɪə'græfɪkl] *adj* autobiographique.

autobiography [ˌɔːtəbaɪ'ɒgrəfɪ] (*pl* **-ies**) *n* autobiographie *f*.

autocrat ['ɔːtəkræt] *n* autocrate *m*.

autocratic [ˌɔːtə'krætɪk] *adj* autocratique.

autocross ['ɔːtəʊkrɒs] *n* Br auto-cross *m*.

Autocue® ['ɔːtəʊkjuː] *n* Br téléprompteur *m*.

autograph ['ɔːtəgrɑːf] ⬦ *n* autographe *m* ⬦ *vt* signer.

Automat® ['ɔːtəmæt] *n* Am restaurant où les plats sont vendus dans des distributeurs automatiques.

automata [ɔː'tɒmətə] *pl* ⟼ **automaton**.

automate ['ɔːtəmeɪt] *vt* automatiser.

automatic [ˌɔːtə'mætɪk] ⬦ *adj* **- 1.** [gen] automatique **- 2.** [gesture] machinal(e) ⬦ *n* **- 1.** [car] voiture *f* à transmission automatique **- 2.** [gun] automatique *m* **- 3.** [washing machine] lave-linge *m* automatique.

automatically [ˌɔːtə'mætɪklɪ] *adv* **- 1.** [gen] automatiquement **- 2.** [move, reply] machinalement.

automatic pilot *n* lit & fig pilote *m* automatique.

automation [ˌɔːtə'meɪʃn] *n* automatisation *f*, automation *f*.

automaton [ɔː'tɒmətən] (*pl* **-tons** OR **-ta** [-tə]) *n* lit & fig automate *m*.

automobile ['ɔːtəməbiːl] *n* Am automobile *f*.

automotive [ˌɔːtə'məʊtɪv] *adj* automobile.

autonomous [ɔː'tɒnəməs] *adj* autonome.

autonomy [ɔː'tɒnəmɪ] *n* autonomie *f*.

autopilot [ˌɔːtəʊ'paɪlət] = **automatic pilot**.

autopsy ['ɔːtɒpsɪ] (*pl* **-ies**) *n* autopsie *f*.

autumn ['ɔːtəm] ⬦ *n* automne *m*; **in ~** en automne ⬦ *comp* d'automne.

autumnal [ɔː'tʌmnəl] *adj* automnal(e).

auxiliary [ɔːg'zɪljərɪ] (*pl* **-ies**) ⬦ *adj* auxiliaire ⬦ *n* auxiliaire *mf*.

Av. (*abbr of* **avenue**) av.

AV ⬦ *n abbr of* **Authorized Version** ⬦ *abbr of* **audiovisual.**

avail [ə'veɪl] ⬦ *n*: **to no ~** en vain, sans résultat ⬦ *vt*: **to ~ o.s. of** profiter de.

availability [əˌveɪlə'bɪlətɪ] *n* disponibilité *f*.

available [ə'veɪləbl] *adj* disponible.

avalanche ['ævəlɑːnʃ] *n* lit & fig avalanche *f*.

avant-garde [ˌævɒŋ'gɑːd] *adj* d'avant-garde.

avarice ['ævərɪs] *n* avarice *f*.

avaricious [ˌævə'rɪʃəs] *adj* avare.

avdp. (*abbr of* **avoirdupois**) système avoirdupois.

Ave. (*abbr of* **avenue**) av.

avenge [ə'vendʒ] *vt* venger.

avenue ['ævənjuː] *n* avenue *f*.

average ['ævərɪdʒ] ⬦ *adj* moyen(enne) ⬦ *n* moyenne *f*; **on ~** en moyenne ⬦ *vt*: **the cars were averaging 90 mph** les voitures roulaient en moyenne à 150 km/h.

➤ **average out** ⬦ *vt sep* établir la moyenne de ⬦ *vi*: **to ~ out at** donner la moyenne de.

averse [ə'vɜːs] *adj*: **I'm not ~ to the occasional drink** hum je ne dis pas non à un verre de temps en temps.

aversion [ə'vɜːʃn] *n*: **~ (to)** aversion *f* (pour).

avert [ə'vɜːt] *vt* **- 1.** [avoid] écarter ; [accident] empêcher **- 2.** [eyes, glance] détourner.

aviary ['eɪvjərɪ] (pl -ies) n volière f.

aviation [ˌeɪvɪ'eɪʃn] n aviation f.

aviator ['eɪvɪeɪtəʳ] n dated aviateur m, -trice f.

avid ['ævɪd] adj : ~ (for) avide (de).

avocado [ˌævə'kɑːdəʊl (pl -s OR -es) n : ~ (pear) avocat m.

avoid [ə'vɔɪd] vt éviter ; to ~ doing sthg éviter de faire qqch.

avoidable [ə'vɔɪdəbl] adj qui peut être évité(e).

avoidance [ə'vɔɪdəns] n ⊳ tax avoidance.

avowed [ə'vaʊd] adj - 1. [supporter, opponent] déclaré(e) - 2. [aim, belief] avoué(e).

AVP (abbr of assistant vice-president) n vice-président adjoint.

AWACS ['eɪwæks] (abbr of airborne warning and control system) n AWACS m.

await [ə'weɪt] vt attendre.

awake [ə'weɪk] (pt awoke OR awaked ; pp awoken) ⋄ adj - 1. [not sleeping] réveillé(e) ; are you ~? tu dors? ; to be wide ~ être complètement réveillé(e) - 2. fig [aware] : ~ to conscient(e) de ⋄ vt - 1. [wake up] réveiller - 2. fig [feeling] éveiller ⋄ vi - 1. [wake up] se réveiller - 2. fig [feeling] s'éveiller.

awakening [ə'weɪknɪŋ] n - 1. [from sleep] réveil m ; a rude ~ un réveil brutal - 2. fig [of feeling] éveil m.

award [ə'wɔːd] ⋄ n - 1. [prize] prix m - 2. [compensation] dommages-intérêts mpl ⋄ vt : to ~ sb sthg, to ~ sthg to sb [prize] décerner qqch à qqn ; [compensation, free kick] accorder qqch à qqn.

aware [ə'weəʳ] adj : to be ~ of sthg se rendre compte de qqch, être conscient(e) de qqch ; to be ~ that se rendre compte que, être conscient que ; politically ~ politisé(e).

awareness [ə'weənɪs] n (U) conscience f.

awash [ə'wɒʃ] adj lit & fig : ~ (with) inondé(e) (de).

away [ə'weɪ] ⋄ adv - 1. [in opposite direction] : to move OR walk ~ (from) s'éloigner (de) ; to look ~ détourner le regard ; to turn ~ se détourner - 2. [in distance] : we live 4 miles ~ (from here) nous habitons à 6 kilomètres (d'ici) ; to keep sb ~ empêcher qqn de s'approcher - 3. [in time] : the elections are a month ~ les élections se dérouleront dans un mois - 4. [absent] absent(e) ; she's ~ on holiday elle est partie en vacances - 5. [in safe place] : to put sthg ~ ranger qqch - 6. [so as to be gone or used up] : to fade ~ disparaître ; to give sthg ~ donner qqch, faire don de qqch ; to take sthg ~ emporter qqch - 7. [continuously] : to be

working ~ travailler sans arrêt ⋄ adj SPORT [team, fans] de l'équipe des visiteurs ; ~ game match m à l'extérieur.

awe [ɔː] n respect m mêlé de crainte ; to be in ~ of sb être impressionné(e) par qqn.

awesome ['ɔːsəm] adj impressionnant(e).

awestruck ['ɔːstrʌk] adj impressionné(e).

awful ['ɔːfʊl] adj - 1. [terrible] affreux(euse) - 2. inf [very great] : an ~ lot (of) énormément (de).

awfully ['ɔːflɪ] adv inf [bad, difficult] affreusement ; [nice, good] extrêmement.

awhile [ə'waɪl] adv un moment.

awkward ['ɔːkwəd] adj - 1. [clumsy] gauche, maladroit(e) - 2. [embarrassed] mal à l'aise, gêné(e) - 3. [difficult - person, problem, task] difficile - 4. [inconvenient] incommode - 5. [embarrassing] embarrassant(e), gênant(e).

awkwardly ['ɔːkwədlɪ] adv - 1. [move etc] gauchement, maladroitement - 2. [with embarrassment] avec gêne OR embarras.

awkwardness ['ɔːkwədnɪs] n - 1. [of person, movement] gaucherie f, maladresse f - 2. [embarrassment] gêne f, embarras m.

awl [ɔːl] n poinçon m, alène f.

awning ['ɔːnɪŋ] n - 1. [of tent] auvent m - 2. [of shop] banne f

awoke [ə'wəʊk] pt ⊳ awake.

awoken [ə'wəʊkn] pp ⊳ awake.

AWOL ['eɪwɒl] (abbr of absent without leave) : to be/go ~ MIL être/partir en absence irrégulière.

awry [ə'raɪ] ⋄ adj de travers ⋄ adv : to go ~ aller de travers, mal tourner.

axe Br, **ax** Am [æks] ⋄ n hache f ; to have an ~ to grind prêcher pour sa paroisse ⋄ vt [project] abandonner ; [jobs] supprimer.

axes ['æksiːz] pl ⊳ axis.

axiom ['æksɪəm] n axiome m.

axis ['æksɪs] (pl axes ['æksiːz]) n axe m.

axle ['æksl] n essieu m.

ayatollah [ˌaɪə'tɒlə] n ayatollah m.

aye [aɪ] ⋄ adv oui ⋄ n oui m, [in voting] voix f pour.

AYH (abbr of American Youth Hostels) n association américaine des auberges de jeunesse.

AZ abbr of Arizona.

azalea [ə'zeɪljə] n azalée f.

Azerbaijan [ˌæzəbaɪ'dʒɑːn] n Azerbaïdjan m.

Azerbaijani [ˌæzəbaɪ'dʒɑːnɪ] ⋄ adj azerbaïdjanais(e) ⋄ n Azerbaïdjanais m, -e f.

Azeri [ə'zerɪ] ⋄ adj azeri(e) ⋄ n Azeri mf.

Azores [ə'zɔːz] npl : **the ~** les Açores fpl ; **in the ~** aux Açores.

AZT (abbr of **azidothymidine**) n AZT f.

Aztec ['æztek] ◇ adj aztèque ◇ n Aztèque mf.

azure ['æʒəʳ] adj azuré(e), bleu(e) d'azur.

B

b (pl **b's** OR **bs**), **B** (pl **B's** OR **Bs**) [biː] n [letter] b m inv, B m inv.
◆ **B** n - **1.** MUS si m - **2.** SCH [mark] B m inv.

b. abbr of **born**.

BA n - **1.** abbr of **Bachelor of Arts** - **2.** (abbr of **British Academy**) organisme public d'aide à la recherche dans le domaine des lettres - **3.** (abbr of **British Airways**) compagnie aérienne britannique.

BAA (abbr of **British Airports' Authority**) n organisme autonome responsable des aéroports en Grande-Bretagne.

babble ['bæbl] ◇ n [of voices] murmure m, rumeur f ◇ vi [person] babiller.

babe [beɪb] n - **1.** literary [baby] bébé m - **2.** Am inf [term of affection] chéri m, -e f.

baboon [bə'buːn] n babouin m.

baby ['beɪbɪ] (pl **-ies**) n - **1.** [child] bébé m - **2.** inf [darling] chéri m, -e f.

baby boomer [-,buːməʳ] n Am personne née pendant le baby-boom d'après-guerre.

baby buggy n - **1.** Br [foldable pushchair] poussette f - **2.** Am = **baby carriage**.

baby carriage n Am landau m.

babyish ['beɪbɪɪʃ] adj puéril(e), enfantin(e).

baby-minder n Br nourrice f.

baby-sit vi faire du baby-sitting.

baby-sitter [-,sɪtəʳ] n baby-sitter mf.

bachelor ['bætʃələʳ] n célibataire m.

Bachelor of Arts n [degree] ≃ licence f en OR ès lettres ; [person] ≃ licencié m, -e f en OR ès lettres.

Bachelor of Science n [degree] ≃ licence f

en OR ès sciences ; [person] ≃ licencié m, -e f en OR ès science.

bachelor's degree n ≃ licence f.

back [bæk] ◇ adv - **1.** [backwards] en arrière ; **to step/move ~** reculer ; **to push ~** repousser ; **to tie one's hair ~** attacher ses cheveux en arrière - **2.** [to former position or state] : **I'll be ~ at five** je rentrerai OR serai de retour à dix-sept heures ; **I'd like my money ~** [in shop] je voudrais me faire rembourser ; **to go ~** retourner ; **to come ~** revenir, rentrer ; **to drive ~** rentrer en voiture ; **to go ~ to sleep** se rendormir ; **to go ~ and forth** [person] faire des allées et venues ; **to be ~ (in fashion)** revenir à la mode - **3.** [in time] : **to think ~ (to)** se souvenir (de) - **4.** [in return] : **to phone** OR **call ~** rappeler ; **to write ~** répondre ; **to pay sb ~** rembourser qqn ◇ n - **1.** [of person, animal] dos m ; **to break the ~ of a job** faire le plus gros d'un travail ; **behind sb's ~** fig derrière le dos de qqn ; **to stab sb in the ~** fig poignarder qqn dans le dos ; **to put sb's ~ up** casser les pieds de qqn ; **to turn one's ~ on sb/sthg** ignorer qqn/qqch - **2.** [of door, book, hand] dos m ; [of head] derrière m ; [of envelope, cheque] revers m ; [of page] verso m ; [of chair] dossier m ; **to know somewhere like the ~ of one's hand** connaître un endroit comme sa poche - **3.** [of room, fridge] fond m ; [of car] arrière m ; **it's the ~ of beyond** Br c'est un trou perdu - **4.** SPORT arrière m ◇ adj (in compounds) - **1.** [at the back] de derrière ; [seat, wheel] arrière (inv) ; [page] dernier(ère) - **2.** [overdue] : **~ rent** arriéré m de loyer ◇ vt - **1.** [reverse] reculer - **2.** [support] appuyer, soutenir - **3.** [bet on] parier sur, miser sur ◇ vi reculer.
◆ **back to back** adv - **1.** [stand] dos à dos - **2.** [happen] l'un après l'autre.
◆ **back to front** adv à l'envers.
◆ **back away** vi reculer.
◆ **back down** vi céder.
◆ **back off** vi reculer.
◆ **back onto** vt Br : **the house ~s onto the park** l'arrière de la maison donne sur le parc.
◆ **back out** vi [of promise etc] se dédire.
◆ **back up** ◇ vt sep - **1.** [support - claim] appuyer, soutenir ; [- person] épauler, soutenir - **2.** [reverse] reculer - **3.** COMPUT sauvegarder, faire une copie de sauvegarde de ◇ vi [reverse] reculer.

backache ['bækeɪk] n : **to have ~** avoir mal aux reins OR au dos.

backbencher [,bæk'bentʃəʳ] n Br POL député qui n'a aucune position officielle au gouvernement ni dans aucun parti.

backbenches [ˌbæk'bentʃɪz] *npl* Br POL bancs *mpl* des députés sans portefeuille.

backbiting ['bækbaɪtɪŋ] *n* médisance *f*.

backbone ['bækbəʊn] *n* épine *f* dorsale, colonne *f* vertébrale ; fig [main support] pivot *m*.

backbreaking ['bæk,breɪkɪŋ] *adj* éreintant(e).

back burner *n :* to put sthg on the ~ mettre qqch en veilleuse.

backchat Br ['bæktʃæt], **backtalk** Am ['bæktɔːk] *n* inf insolence *f*.

backcloth ['bækklɒθ] Br = backdrop.

backcomb ['bækkəʊm] *vt* Br crêper.

back copy *n* vieux numéro *m* (d'un journal).

backdate [ˌbæk'deɪt] *vt* antidater.

back door *n* porte *f* de derrière ; to get a job through OR by the ~ fig obtenir un emploi par relations.

backdrop ['bækdrɒp] *n* lit & fig toile *f* de fond.

backer ['bækə'] *n* commanditaire *m*, bailleur *m* de fonds.

backfire [ˌbæk'faɪə'] *vi* - **1.** AUT pétarader - **2.** [plan] : to ~ (on sb) se retourner (contre qqn).

backgammon ['bæk,gæmən] *n* backgammon *m*, ≃ jacquet *m*.

background ['bækgraʊnd] ⬦ *n* - **1.** [in picture, view] arrière-plan *m* ; in the ~ dans le fond, à l'arrière-plan ; fig au second plan - **2.** [of event, situation] contexte *m* - **3.** [upbringing] milieu *m* ⬦ *comp* [music, noise] de fond ; ~ reading/information lectures/informations générales *(pour un certain sujet)*.

backhand ['bækhænd] *n* revers *m*.

backhanded ['bækhændɪd] *adj* fig ambigu(ë), équivoque.

backhander ['bækhændə'] *n* Br inf pot-de-vin *m*.

backing ['bækɪŋ] *n* - **1.** [support] soutien *m* - **2.** [lining] doublage *m* - **3.** MUS accompagnement *m*.

back issue = back number.

backlash ['bæklæʃ] *n* contrecoup *m*, choc *m* en retour.

backless ['bæklɪs] *adj* [dress etc] décolleté(e) dans le dos.

backlog ['bæklɒg] *n :* ~ (of work) arriéré *m* de travail, travail *m* en retard.

back number *n* vieux numéro *m*.

backpack ['bækpæk] *n* sac *m* à dos.

backpacker ['bækpækə'] *n* randonneur *m*, -euse *f (avec sac à dos)*.

backpacking ['bækpækɪŋ] *n :* to go ~ faire de la randonnée *(avec sac à dos)*.

back passage *n* euphemism rectum *m*.

back pay *n* rappel *m* de salaire.

backpedal [ˌbæk'pedl] (Br *pt* & *pp* -led ; cont -ling, Am *pt* & *pp* -ed ; cont -ing) *vi* fig : to ~ (on) faire marche OR machine arrière (sur).

back seat *n* [in car] siège *m* OR banquette *f* arrière ; to take a ~ fig jouer un rôle secondaire.

back-seat driver *n* personne qui n'arrête pas de donner des conseils au conducteur.

backside [ˌbæk'saɪd] *n* inf postérieur *m*, derrière *m*.

backslash ['bækslæʃ] *n* COMPUT barre *f* oblique inversée.

backslide [ˌbæk'slaɪd] (*pt* & *pp* -slid) *vi* rechuter, récidiver.

backspace ['bækspeɪs] ⬦ *n* [key] touche *f* de retour en arrière ⬦ *vi* [in typing] reculer d'un espace.

backstage [ˌbæk'steɪdʒ] *adv* dans les coulisses.

back street *n* petite rue *f*.

back-street abortion *n* avortement *m* clandestin.

backstroke ['bækstrəʊk] *n* dos *m* crawlé.

backtalk Am = backchat.

backtrack ['bæktræk] = backpedal.

backup ['bækʌp] ⬦ *adj* - **1.** [plan, team] de secours, de remplacement - **2.** COMPUT de sauvegarde ⬦ *n* - **1.** [gen] aide *f*, soutien *m* - **2.** COMPUT (copie *f* de) sauvegarde *f*.

backward ['bækwəd] ⬦ *adj* - **1.** [movement, look] en arrière - **2.** [country] arriéré(e) ; [person] arriéré, attardé(e) ⬦ *adv* Am = backwards.

backward-looking [-ˌlʊkɪŋ] *adj* pej rétrograde.

backwards ['bækwədz], **backward** Am ['bækwəd] *adv* [move, go] en arrière, à reculons ; [read list] à rebours, à l'envers ; ~ and forwards [movement] de va-et-vient, d'avant en arrière et d'arrière en avant ; to walk ~ and forwards aller et venir.

backwash ['bækwɒʃ] *n* remous *m*.

backwater ['bæk,wɔːtə'] *n* fig désert *m*.

backwoods ['bækwʊdz] *npl* fig : to live in the ~ of France habiter la France profonde.

backyard [ˌbæk'jɑːd] *n* - **1.** Br [yard] arrière-cour *f* - **2.** Am [garden] jardin *m* de derrière.

bacon ['beɪkən] *n* bacon *m*.

bacteria [bæk'tɪərɪə] *npl* bactéries *fpl*.

bacteriology [bæk,tɪərɪ'ɒlədʒɪ] n bactériologie f.

bad [bæd] (compar **worse** ; superl **worst**) ◇ adj - **1.** [not good] mauvais(e) ; **to be ~ at** sthg être mauvais en qqch ; **to go from ~ to worse** aller de mal en pis, empirer ; **too ~!** dommage! ; **not ~** pas mal - **2.** [unhealthy] malade ; **smoking is ~ for you** fumer est mauvais pour la santé ; **I'm feeling ~** je ne suis pas dans mon assiette - **3.** [serious] : **a ~ cold** un gros rhume - **4.** [rotten] pourri(e), gâté(e) ; **to go ~** se gâter, s'avarier - **5.** [guilty] : **to feel ~ about** sthg se sentir coupable de qqch - **6.** [naughty] méchant(e) ◇ adv Am = **badly**.

bad blood n ressentiment m, rancune f.

bad cheque n chèque m sans provision.

bad debt n créance f irrécouvrable.

bade [bæd] pt ▷ **bid.**

bad feeling n (U) rancœur f.

badge [bædʒ] n - **1.** [metal, plastic] badge m - **2.** [sewn-on] écusson m.

badger ['bædʒə'] ◇ n blaireau m ◇ vt : **to ~ sb (to do** sthg) harceler qqn (pour qu'il fasse qqch).

badly ['bædlɪ] (compar **worse** ; superl **worst**) adv - **1.** [not well] mal ; **to think ~ of sb** penser du mal de qqn - **2.** [seriously - wounded] grièvement ; [- affected] gravement, sérieusement ; **to be ~ in need of** sthg avoir vraiment OR absolument besoin de qqch.

badly-off adj - **1.** [poor] pauvre, dans le besoin - **2.** [lacking] : **to be ~ for** sthg manquer de qqch.

bad-mannered [-'mænəd] adj [child] mal élevé(e) ; [shop assistant] impoli(e).

badminton ['bædmɪntən] n badminton m.

bad-mouth vt inf casser du sucre sur le dos de.

badness ['bædnɪs] n [of behaviour] méchanceté f.

bad-tempered [-'tempəd] adj - **1.** [by nature] qui a mauvais caractère - **2.** [in a bad mood] de mauvaise humeur.

baffle ['bæfl] vt déconcerter, confondre.

baffling ['bæflɪŋ] adj déconcertant(e).

bag [bæg] (pt & pp **-ged** ; cont **-ging**) ◇ n - **1.** [gen] sac m ; **she's a ~ of bones** elle n'a que la peau sur les os ; **it's in the ~** inf c'est dans la poche, l'affaire est dans le sac ; **to pack one's ~s** fig plier bagage - **2.** [handbag] sac m à main ◇ vt - **1.** [put into bags] mettre en sac, ensacher - **2.** Br inf [reserve] garder.

➡ **bags** npl - **1.** [under eyes] poches fpl - **2.** inf [lots] : **~s of** plein OR beaucoup de.

bagel ['beɪgəl] n petit pain en couronne.

baggage ['bægɪdʒ] n (U) bagages mpl.

baggage car n Am fourgon m (d'un train).

baggage reclaim n retrait m des bagages.

baggage room n Am consigne f.

baggy ['bægɪ] (compar **-ier** ; superl **-iest**) adj ample.

Baghdad [bæg'dæd] n Bagdad.

bag lady n inf clocharde f.

bagpipes ['bægpaɪps] npl cornemuse f.

bagsnatcher ['bægsnætʃə'] n voleur m, -euse f à la tire.

bah [bɑː] excl bah!

Bahamas [bə'hɑːməz] npl : **the ~** les Bahamas fpl ; **in the ~** aux Bahamas.

Bahrain, Bahrein [bɑː'reɪn] n Bahreïn m, Bahrayn m ; **in ~** au Bahreïn.

Bahraini, Bahreini [bɑː'reɪnɪ] ◇ adj bahreïni(e) ◇ n Bahreïni m, -e f.

Bahrein [bɑː'reɪn] = **Bahrain.**

bail [beɪl] n (U) caution f ; **on ~** sous caution.

➡ **bail out** ◇ vt sep - **1.** [pay bail for] se porter garant(e) de - **2.** fig [rescue] tirer d'affaire ◇ vi [from plane] sauter (en parachute).

bailiff ['beɪlɪf] n huissier m.

bait [beɪt] ◇ n appât m ; **to rise to** OR **take the ~** fig mordre à l'hameçon ◇ vt - **1.** [put bait on] appâter - **2.** [tease] tourmenter.

baize [beɪz] n feutrine f.

bake [beɪk] ◇ vt - **1.** CULIN faire cuire au four - **2.** [clay, bricks] cuire ◇ vi [food] cuire au four.

baked beans [beɪkt-] npl haricots mpl blancs à la tomate.

baked potato [beɪkt-] n pomme f de terre en robe des champs OR de chambre.

Bakelite® ['beɪkəlaɪt] n Bakélite® f.

baker ['beɪkə'] n boulanger m, -ère f ; **~'s (shop)** boulangerie f.

bakery ['beɪkərɪ] (pl **-ies**) n boulangerie f.

baking ['beɪkɪŋ] ◇ adj inf : **it's a ~ hot day!** on cuit aujourd'hui! ◇ n cuisson f.

baking powder n levure f (chimique).

baking tin n [for cakes] moule m à gâteau ; [for meat] plat m à rôtir.

balaclava (helmet) [,bælə'klɑːvə-] n Br passe-montagne m.

balance ['bæləns] ◇ n - **1.** [equilibrium] équilibre m ; **to keep/lose one's ~** garder/perdre l'équilibre ; **off ~** déséquilibré(e) - **2.** fig [counterweight] contrepoids m ; [of evidence] poids m, force f - **3.** [scales] balance f ; **to be** OR **hang in the ~** fig être en balance - **4.** FIN solde m ◇ vt - **1.** [keep in balance] maintenir en équilibre - **2.** [compare] : **to ~** sthg **against** sthg mettre qqch et qqch en balance - **3.** [in accounting] : **to ~ a budget** équilibrer un budget ; **to ~ the books** clôturer les comptes, dresser le bilan ⬦ *vi* - **1.** [maintain equilibrium] se tenir en équilibre - **2.** [budget, accounts] s'équilibrer.

➡ **on balance** *adv* tout bien considéré.

balanced ['bælənst] *adj* [fair] juste, impartial(e).

balanced diet [ˌbælənst-] *n* alimentation *f* équilibrée.

balance of payments *n* balance *f* des paiements.

balance of power *n* équilibre *m* OR balance *f* des forces.

balance of trade *n* balance *f* commerciale.

balance sheet *n* bilan *m*.

balancing act *n* fig acrobaties *fpl*.

balcony ['bælkənɪ] (*pl* **-ies**) *n* balcon *m*.

bald [bɔːld] *adj* - **1.** [head, man] chauve - **2.** [tyre] lisse - **3.** fig [blunt] direct(e).

bald eagle *n* aigle *m* à tête blanche (*cet oiseau est le symbole des États-Unis et figure sur le sceau officiel*).

balding ['bɔːldɪŋ] *adj* qui devient chauve.

baldness ['bɔːldnɪs] *n* calvitie *f*.

bale [beɪl] *n* balle *f*.

➡ **bale out** Br ⬦ *vt sep* [boat] écoper, vider ⬦ *vi* [from plane] sauter en parachute.

Balearic Islands [ˌbælɪˈærɪk-], **Balearics** [ˌbælɪˈærɪks] *npl* : **the ~** les Baléares *fpl* ; **in the ~** aux Baléares.

baleful ['beɪlfʊl] *adj* sinistre.

Bali ['bɑːlɪ] *n* Bali *m* ; **in ~** à Bali.

balk [bɔːk] *vi* : **to ~ (at)** hésiter OR reculer (devant).

Balkan ['bɔːlkən] *adj* balkanique.

Balkans ['bɔːlkənz], **Balkan States** ['bɔːlkən-] *npl* : **the ~** les Balkans *mpl*, les États *mpl* balkaniques ; **in the ~** dans les Balkans.

ball [bɔːl] *n* - **1.** [round shape] boule *f* ; [in game] balle *f* ; [football] ballon *m* ; **to be on the ~** fig connaître son affaire, s'y connaître ; **to play ~ with sb** fig coopérer avec qqn ; **to start the ~ rolling** fig lancer la discussion - **2.** [of foot] plante *f* - **3.** [dance] bal *m* ; **to have a ~** fig bien s'amuser.

➡ **balls** vulg ⬦ *npl* [testicles] couilles *fpl* ⬦ *n* (U) [nonsense] conneries *fpl*.

ballad ['bæləd] *n* ballade *f*.

ball-and-socket joint *n* TECH rotule *f*.

ballast ['bæləst] *n* lest *m*.

ball bearing *n* roulement *m* à billes.

ball boy *n* ramasseur *m* de balles.

ballcock ['bɔːlkɒk] *n* (robinet *m* à) flotteur *m*.

ballerina [ˌbæləˈriːnə] *n* ballerine *f*.

ballet ['bæleɪ] *n* - **1.** (U) [art of dance] danse *f* - **2.** [work] ballet *m*.

ballet dancer *n* danseur *m*, -euse *f* de ballet.

ball game *n* - **1.** Am [baseball match] match *m* de base-ball - **2.** inf [situation] : **it's a whole new ~** c'est une autre paire de manches.

ball girl *n* ramasseuse *f* de balles.

ballistic missile [bəˈlɪstɪk-] *n* missile *m* balistique.

ballistics [bəˈlɪstɪks] *n* (U) balistique *f*.

ballocks ['bɒ gt'ləks] = **bollocks**.

balloon [bəˈluːn] ⬦ *n* - **1.** [gen] ballon *m* - **2.** [in cartoon] bulle *f* ⬦ *vi* [swell] gonfler.

ballooning [bəˈluːnɪŋ] *n* : **to go ~** faire une ascension en ballon.

ballot ['bælət] ⬦ *n* - **1.** [voting paper] bulletin *m* de vote - **2.** [voting process] scrutin *m* ⬦ *vt* appeler à voter ⬦ *vi* : **to ~ for sthg** voter pour qqch.

ballot box *n* - **1.** [container] urne *f* - **2.** [voting process] scrutin *m*.

ballot paper *n* bulletin *m* de vote.

ball park *n* Am terrain *m* de base-ball.

ball-park figure *n* inf chiffre *m* approximatif.

ballpoint (pen) ['bɔːlpɔɪnt-] *n* stylo *m* à bille.

ballroom ['bɔːlrʊm] *n* salle *f* de bal.

ballroom dancing *n* (U) danse *f* de salon.

balls-up Br, **ball-up** Am *n* v inf : **to make a ~ of sthg** saloper qqch.

balm [bɑːm] *n* baume *m*.

balmy ['bɑːmɪ] (*compar* **-ier** ; *superl* **-iest**) *adj* doux (douce).

baloney [bəˈləʊnɪ] *n* (U) inf foutaises *fpl*, bêtises *fpl*.

BALPA ['bælpə] (*abbr of* **British Airline Pilots' Association**) *n* syndicat britannique des pilotes de ligne.

balsa(wood) ['bɒlsə(wʊd)] *n* balsa *m*.

balsam ['bɔːlsəm] *n* baume *m*.

balsamic vinegar [bɔːlˈsæmɪk] *n* vinaigre *m* balsamique.

balti ['bɔːltɪ] *n* [pan] récipient métallique utilisé dans la cuisine indienne ; [food] plat épicé préparé dans un 'balti'.

Baltic ['bɔːltɪk] ⬦ *adj* [port, coast] de la Baltique ⬦ *n* : **the ~ (Sea)** la Baltique.

Baltic Republic *n* : **the ~s** les républiques *fpl* baltes.

Baltic State n : **the ~s** les pays mpl baltes.
balustrade [ˌbæləs'treɪd] n balustrade f.
bamboo [bæm'buː] n bambou m.
bamboozle [bæm'buːzl] vt inf embobiner.
ban [bæn] (pt & pp **-ned** ; cont **-ning**) <> n interdiction f ; **there is a ~ on smoking** il est interdit de fumer <> vt interdire ; **to ~ sb from doing sthg** interdire à qqn de faire qqch.
banal [bə'nɑːl] adj pej banal(e), ordinaire.
banana [bə'nɑːnə] n banane f.
banana republic n république f bananière.
banana split n banana split m.
band [bænd] n - **1.** [MUS - rock] groupe m ; [- military] fanfare f ; [- jazz] orchestre m - **2.** [group, strip] bande f - **3.** [stripe] rayure f - **4.** [range] tranche f.
band together vi se grouper, s'unir.
bandage ['bændɪdʒ] <> n bandage m, bande f <> vt mettre un pansement OR un bandage sur.
Band-Aid® n pansement m adhésif.
bandan(n)a [bæn'dænə] n bandana m.
b and b, B and B n abbr of bed and breakfast.
bandeau ['bændəʊ] (pl **-x** [-z]) n bandeau m.
bandit ['bændɪt] n bandit m.
bandmaster ['bænd,mɑːstər] n chef m d'orchestre.
band saw n scie f à ruban.
bandsman ['bændzmən] (pl **-men** [-mən]) n musicien m (d'orchestre).
bandstand ['bændstænd] n kiosque m à musique.
bandwagon ['bændwægən] n : **to jump on the ~** suivre le mouvement.
bandy ['bændɪ] (compar **-ier** ; superl **-iest** ; pt & pp **-ied**) adj qui a les jambes arquées.
bandy about, bandy around vt sep répandre, faire circuler.
bandy-legged [-ˌlegd] adj = bandy.
bane [beɪn] n : **he's the ~ of my life** c'est le fléau de ma vie.
bang [bæŋ] <> adv - **1.** [exactly] : **~ in the middle** en plein milieu ; **to be ~ on time** être pile à l'heure - **2.** inf [away] : **~ goes my holiday!** mes vacances sont tombées à l'eau! OR dans le lac <> n - **1.** [blow] coup m violent - **2.** [of gun etc] détonation f ; [of door] claquement m ; **to go with a ~** inf fig être du tonnerre <> vt frapper violemment ; [door] claquer ; **to ~ one's head/knee** se cogner la tête/le genou <> vi - **1.** [knock] : **to ~ on** frapper à - **2.** [make a loud noise - gun etc] détoner ; [- door]

claquer - **3.** [crash] : **to ~ into** se cogner contre <> excl boum!
bangs npl Am frange f.
bang down vt sep poser violemment.
banger ['bæŋər] n Br - **1.** inf [sausage] saucisse f - **2.** inf [old car] vieille guimbarde f, vieux tacot m - **3.** [firework] pétard m.
Bangkok [ˌbæŋ'kɒk] n Bangkok.
Bangladesh [ˌbæŋglə'deʃ] n Bangladesh m ; **in ~** au Bangladesh.
Bangladeshi [ˌbæŋglə'deʃɪ] <> adj bangladais(e), bangladeshi <> n Bangladais m, -e f, Bangladeshi mf.
bangle ['bæŋgl] n bracelet m.
banish ['bænɪʃ] vt bannir.
banister ['bænɪstər] n, **banisters** ['bænɪstəz] npl rampe f.
banjo ['bændʒəʊ] (pl **-s** OR **-es**) n banjo m.
bank [bæŋk] <> n - **1.** FIN & fig banque f - **2.** [of river, lake] rive f, bord m - **3.** [of earth] talus m - **4.** [of clouds] masse f ; [of fog] nappe f <> vt FIN mettre OR déposer à la banque <> vi - **1.** FIN : **to ~ with** avoir un compte à - **2.** [plane] tourner.
bank on vt fus compter sur.
bank account n compte m en banque.
bank balance n solde m bancaire.
bankbook ['bæŋkbʊk] n livret m de banque.
bank card = banker's card.
bank charges npl frais mpl bancaires.
bank draft n traite f bancaire.
banker ['bæŋkər] n banquier m.
banker's card n Br carte f d'identité bancaire.
banker's order n Br prélèvement m automatique.
bank holiday n Br jour m férié.
banking ['bæŋkɪŋ] n : **to go into ~** travailler dans la banque.
banking house n banque f, établissement m bancaire.
bank loan n emprunt m (bancaire).
bank manager n directeur m, -trice f de banque.
bank note n billet m de banque.
bank rate n taux m d'escompte.
bankrupt ['bæŋkrʌpt] <> adj failli(e) ; **to go ~** faire faillite <> n failli m, -e f <> vt mettre en faillite.
bankruptcy ['bæŋkrəptsɪ] (pl **-ies**) n - **1.** [gen] faillite f - **2.** fig [lack] : **moral ~** manque m de crédibilité.
bank statement n relevé m de compte.
banner ['bænər] n banderole f.

bannister(s) ['bænɪstə(z)] = **banister(s)**.

banns [bænz] *npl* : **to publish the ~** publier les bans.

banquet ['bæŋkwɪt] *n* banquet *m*.

bantam ['bæntəm] *n* poule *f* naine.

bantamweight ['bæntəmweɪt] *n* poids *m* coq.

banter ['bæntəʳ] <> *n (U)* plaisanterie *f*, badinage *m* <> *vi* plaisanter, badiner.

BAOR (*abbr of* **British Army of the Rhine**) *n* forces britanniques en Allemagne.

bap [bæp] *n* Br petit pain *m*.

baptism ['bæptɪzm] *n* baptême *m* ; **~ of fire** baptême du feu.

Baptist ['bæptɪst] *n* baptiste *mf*.

baptize, -ise [*Br* bæp'taɪz, *Am* 'bæptaɪz] *vt* baptiser.

bar [bɑːʳ] (*pt* & *pp* **-red** ; *cont* **-ring**) <> *n* - **1.** [piece - of gold] lingot *m* ; [- of chocolate] tablette *f* ; **a ~ of soap** une savonnette - **2.** [length of wood, metal] barre *f* ; **to be behind ~s** être derrière les barreaux OR sous les verrous - **3.** *fig* [obstacle] obstacle *m* - **4.** [pub] bar *m* - **5.** [counter of pub] comptoir *m*, zinc *m* - **6.** MUS mesure *f* <> *vt* - **1.** [door, road] barrer ; [window] mettre des barreaux à ; **to ~ sb's way** barrer la route OR le passage à qqn - **2.** [ban] interdire, défendre ; **to ~ sb (from)** interdire à qqn (de) <> *prep* sauf, excepté ; **~ none** sans exception.
  ➤ **Bar** *n* JUR : **the Bar** Br le barreau ; Am les avocats *mpl*.

Barbados [bɑː'beɪdɒs] *n* Barbade *f* ; **in ~** à la Barbade.

barbarian [bɑː'beərɪən] *n* barbare *mf*.

barbaric [bɑː'bærɪk] *adj* barbare.

barbarous ['bɑːbərəs] *adj* barbare.

barbecue ['bɑːbɪkjuː] <> *n* barbecue *m* <> *vt* griller sur un barbecue.

barbed ['bɑːbd] *adj* barbelé(e) ; **fig** [comment] acerbe, acide.

barbed wire [bɑːbd-] *n (U)* fil *m* de fer barbelé.

barber ['bɑːbəʳ] *n* coiffeur *m* (pour hommes) ; **~'s (shop)** salon *m* de coiffure (pour hommes) ; **to go to the ~'s** aller chez le coiffeur.

barbiturate [bɑː'bɪtjʊrət] *n* barbiturique *m*.

Barcelona [ˌbɑːsɪ'leʊnə] *n* Barcelone.

bar chart, bar graph Am *n* diagramme *m* en bâtons.

bar code *n* code *m* à barres, code-barres *m*.

bare [beəʳ] <> *adj* - **1.** [feet, arms etc] nu(e) ; [trees, hills etc] dénudé(e) - **2.** [absolute, minimum] : **the ~ facts** les simples faits ; **the ~ minimum** le strict minimum ; **the ~ essentials** le strict nécessaire - **3.** [empty] vide - **4.** [mere] : **it cost us a ~ £10** cela nous a coûté simplement 10 livres <> *vt* découvrir ; **to ~ one's teeth** montrer les dents.

bareback ['beəbæk] <> *adj* qui monte à cru OR à nu <> *adv* à cru, à nu.

barefaced ['beəfeɪst] *adj* éhonté(e).

barefoot(ed) [ˌbeə'fʊt(ɪd)] <> *adj* aux pieds nus <> *adv* nu-pieds, pieds nus.

bareheaded [ˌbeə'hedɪd] <> *adj* nu-tête *(inv)* <> *adv* nu-tête.

barelegged [ˌbeə'legd] <> *adj* aux jambes nues <> *adv* les jambes nues.

barely ['beəlɪ] *adv* [scarcely] à peine, tout juste.

bargain ['bɑːgɪn] <> *n* - **1.** [agreement] marché *m* ; **into the ~** en plus, par-dessus le marché - **2.** [good buy] affaire *f*, occasion *f* <> *vi* négocier ; **to ~ with sb for sthg** négocier qqch avec qqn.
  ➤ **bargain for, bargain on** *vt fus* compter sur, prévoir.

bargaining ['bɑːgɪnɪŋ] *n (U)* [haggling] marchandage *m*, [negotiating] négociations *fpl*.

bargaining power *n* influence *f* sur les négociations.

barge [bɑːdʒ] <> *n* péniche *f* <> *vi* inf : **to ~ past sb** bousculer qqn ; **to ~ into sb** rentrer dans qqn.
  ➤ **barge in** *vi* inf : **to ~ in (on)** interrompre.

barge pole *n* : **I wouldn't touch it with a ~** inf je ne m'y frotterais pas.

bar graph Am = **bar chart**.

baritone ['bærɪtəʊn] *n* baryton *m*.

barium meal *n* Br baryte *f*.

bark [bɑːk] <> *n* - **1.** [of dog] aboiement *m* ; **his ~ is worse than his bite** inf il n'est pas si terrible qu'il en a l'air - **2.** [on tree] écorce *f* <> *vt* [subj : person] aboyer <> *vi* [dog] : **to ~ (at)** aboyer (après).

barking ['bɑːkɪŋ] *n (U)* aboiement *m*.

barley ['bɑːlɪ] *n* orge *f*.

barley sugar *n* Br sucre *m* d'orge.

barley water *n* Br orgeat *m*.

barmaid ['bɑːmeɪd] *n* barmaid *f*, serveuse *f* de bar.

barman ['bɑːmən] (*pl* **-men** [-mən]) *n* barman *m*, serveur *m* de bar.

barmy ['bɑːmɪ] (*compar* **-ier** ; *superl* **-iest**) *adj* Br inf toqué(e), timbré(e).

barn [bɑːn] *n* grange *f*.

barnacle ['bɑːnəkl] *n* anatife *m*, bernache *f*.

barn dance *n* - **1.** [occasion] soirée *f* de danse

campagnarde **- 2. Br** [type of dance] danse *f* campagnarde.

barn owl *n* chouette *f*.

barometer [bə'rɒmɪtəʳ] *n* lit & fig baromètre *m*.

baron ['bærən] *n* baron *m ;* **press/oil ~ fig** baron *m* de la presse/du pétrole, magnat *m* de la presse/du pétrole.

baroness ['bærənɪs] *n* baronne *f*.

baronet ['bærənɪt] *n* baronnet *m*.

baroque [bə'rɒk] *adj* baroque.

barrack ['bærək] *vt* **Br** huer, conspuer.
➤ **barracks** *npl* caserne *f*.

barracking ['bærəkɪŋ] *n* **Br** chahut *m*, huée *f*.

barracuda [,bærə'kuːdə] *n* barracuda *m*.

barrage ['bærɑːʒ] *n* **- 1.** [of firing] barrage *m* **- 2.** [of questions etc] avalanche *f*, déluge *m* **- 3. Br** [dam] barrage *m*

barred [bɑːd] *adj* [window] à barreaux.

barrel ['bærəl] *n* **- 1.** [for beer, wine] tonneau *m*, fût *n ~ 2.* [for oil] baril *m* **- 3.** [of gun] canon *m*.

barre! organ *n* orgue *m* de Barbarie.

barren ['bærən] *adj* stérile.

barrette [bə'ret] *n* **Am** barrette *f*.

barricade [,bærɪ'keɪd] ◇ *n* barricade *f* ◇ *vt* barricader ; **to ~ o.s. in** se barricader.

barrier ['bærɪəʳ] *n* lit & fig barrière *f*.

barrier cream *n* **Br** crème *f* protectrice.

barring ['bɑːrɪŋ] *prep* sauf.

barrister ['bærɪstəʳ] *n* **Br** avocat *m*, -e *f*.

barroom ['bɑːruːm] *n* **Am** bar *m*.

barrow ['bærəʊ] *n* brouette *f*.

bar stool *n* tabouret *m* de bar.

Bart. *abbr* of **baronet.**

bartender ['bɑːtendəʳ] *n* **Am** barman *m*.

barter ['bɑːtəʳ] ◇ *n* troc *m* ◇ *vt :* **to ~ sthg (for)** troquer **OR** échanger qqch (contre) ◇ *vi* faire du troc.

base [beɪs] ◇ *n* base *f* ◇ *vt* baser ; **to ~ sthg on OR upon** baser **OR** fonder qqch sur ◇ *adj* indigne, ignoble.

baseball ['beɪsbɔːl] *n* base-ball *m*.

baseball cap *n* casquette *f* de base-ball.

base camp *n* camp *m* de base.

Basel ['bɑːzl] *n* Bâle.

baseless ['beɪslɪs] *adj* sans fondement.

baseline ['beɪslaɪn] *n* ligne *f* de fond.

basement ['beɪsmənt] *n* sous-sol *m*.

base metal *n* dated métal *m* vil.

base rate *n* taux *m* de base.

bases ['beɪsiːz] *pl* ⊳ **basis.**

bash [bæʃ] *inf* ◇ *n* **- 1.** [painful blow] coup *m* **- 2.** [attempt] : **to have a ~** tenter le coup

- 3. [party] fête *f*, boum *f* ◇ *vt* **- 1.** [hit - gen] frapper, cogner ; [- car] percuter **- 2.** [criticize] critiquer, attaquer.

bashful ['bæʃfʊl] *adj* timide.

basic ['beɪsɪk] *adj* fondamental(e) ; [vocabulary, salary] de base.
➤ **basics** *npl* **- 1.** [rudiments] éléments *mpl*, bases *fpl* **- 2.** [essential foodstuffs] aliments *mpl* de première nécessité.

BASIC ['beɪsɪk] (*abbr of* **Beginner's All-purpose Symbolic Instruction Code**) *n* basic *m*.

basically ['beɪsɪklɪ] *adv* **- 1.** [essentially] au fond, fondamentalement **- 2.** [really] en fait.

basic rate *n* **Br** taux *m* de base.

basic wage *n* salaire *m* de base.

basil ['bæzl] *n* basilic *m*.

basin ['beɪsn] *n* **- 1. Br** [bowl - for cooking] terrine *f ;* [- for washing] cuvette *f* **- 2.** [in bathroom] lavabo *m* **- 3. GEOGR** bassin *m*.

basis ['beɪsɪs] (*pl* **-ses** [-siːz]) *n* base *f* ; **on the ~ of** sur la base de ; **on a regular ~** de façon régulière ; **to be paid on a weekly/monthly ~** toucher un salaire hebdomadaire/ mensuel.

bask [bɑːsk] *vi :* **to ~ in the sun** se chauffer au soleil ; **to ~ in sb's approval** fig jouir de la faveur de qqn.

basket ['bɑːskɪt] *n* corbeille *f ;* [with handle] panier *m*.

basketball ['bɑːskɪtbɔːl] ◇ *n* basket-ball *m*, basket *m* ◇ *comp* de basket.

basketwork ['bɑːskɪtwɜːk] *n* vannerie *f*.

basking shark ['bɑːskɪŋ-] *n* requin *m* pèlerin.

Basle [bɑːl] = Basel.

basmati (rice) [,bæz'mætɪ (-)] *n* (riz *m*)basmati *m*.

Basque [bɑːsk] ◇ *adj* basque ◇ *n* **- 1.** [person] Basque *mf* **- 2.** [language] basque *m*.

bass¹ [beɪs] ◇ *adj* bas (basse) ◇ *n* **- 1.** [singer] basse *f* **- 2.** [double bass] contrebasse *f* **- 3.** = bass guitar.

bass² [bæs] (*pl inv* OR **-es** [-iːz]) *n* [fish] perche *f*.

bass clef [beɪs-] *n* clef *f* de fa.

bass drum [beɪs-] *n* grosse caisse *f*.

basset (hound) ['bæsɪt-] *n* basset *m*.

bass guitar [beɪs-] *n* basse *f*.

bassoon [bə'suːn] *n* basson *m*.

bastard ['bɑːstəd] *n* **- 1.** [illegitimate child] bâtard *m*, -e *f*, enfant naturel *m*, enfant naturelle *f* **- 2.** v inf [unpleasant person] salaud *m*, saligaud *m*.

baste [beɪst] *vt* arroser.

bastion ['bæstɪən] n bastion m.

BASW (abbr of British Association of Social Workers) n syndicat britannique des travailleurs sociaux.

bat [bæt] (pt & pp -ted ; cont -ting) ◇ n - **1.** [animal] chauve-souris f - **2.** [for cricket, baseball] batte f ; [for table-tennis] raquette f - **3. phr** : to do sthg off one's own ~ faire qqch de son propre chef ◇ vt [ball] frapper (avec la batte) ◇ vi manier la batte.

batch [bætʃ] n - **1.** [of papers] tas m, liasse f ; [of letters, applicants] série f - **2.** [of products] lot m.

batch file n COMPUT fichier m de commandes.

batch processing n COMPUT traitement m par lots.

bated ['beɪtɪd] adj : with ~ breath en retenant son souffle.

bath [bɑːθ] ◇ n - **1.** [bathtub] baignoire f - **2.** [act of washing] bain m ; to have OR take a bath prendre un bain ◇ vt baigner, donner un bain à.

➤ **baths** npl Br piscine f.

bath chair n fauteuil m roulant.

bath cube n sels mpl de bain (en forme de cube).

bathe [beɪð] ◇ vt - **1.** [wound] laver - **2.** [subj : light, sunshine] : to be ~d in OR with être baigné(e) de ◇ vi - **1.** [swim] se baigner - **2.** Am [take a bath] prendre un bain.

bather ['beɪðər] n baigneur m, -euse f.

bathing ['beɪðɪŋ] n (U) baignade f.

bathing cap n bonnet m de bain.

bathing costume, bathing suit n maillot m de bain.

bathing trunks npl slip m OR caleçon m de bain.

bath mat n tapis m de bain.

bath oil n huile f de bain.

bathrobe ['bɑːθrəʊb] n [made of towelling] sortie f de bain ; [dressing gown] peignoir m.

bathroom ['bɑːθrʊm] n - **1.** Br [room with bath] salle f de bains - **2.** Am [toilet] toilettes fpl.

bath salts npl sels mpl de bain.

bath towel n serviette f de bain.

bathtub ['bɑːθtʌb] n baignoire f.

batik [bə'tiːk] n batik m.

baton ['bætən] n - **1.** [of conductor] baguette f - **2.** [in relay race] témoin m - **3.** Br [of policeman] bâton m, matraque f.

baton charge n Br [by police] charge f à la matraque.

batsman ['bætsmən] (pl -men [-mən]) n batteur m.

battalion [bə'tæljən] n bataillon m.

batten ['bætn] n planche f, latte f.

➤ **batten down** vt fus : to ~ down the hatches fermer les écoutilles.

batter ['bætər] ◇ n (U) pâte f ◇ vt battre.

➤ **batter down** vt sep [door] abattre.

battered ['bætəd] adj - **1.** [child, woman] battu(e) - **2.** [car, hat] cabossé(e).

battering ['bætərɪŋ] n : to take a ~ fig être ébranlé(e).

battering ram n bélier m.

battery ['bætərɪ] (pl -ies) n batterie f ; [of calculator, toy] pile f.

battery charger n chargeur m.

battery hen n poulet m de batterie.

battle ['bætl] ◇ n - **1.** [in war] bataille f - **2.** [struggle] : ~ (for/against/with) lutte f (pour/contre/avec), combat m (pour/contre/avec) ; ~ of wits joute f d'esprit ; that's half the ~ le plus dur est fait ; to be fighting a losing ~ mener un combat perdu d'avance ◇ vi : to ~ (for/against/with) se battre (pour/contre/avec), lutter (pour/contre/avec).

battledress ['bætldres] n Br tenue f de combat.

battlefield ['bætlfiːld], **battleground** ['bætlgraʊnd] n - **1.** MIL champ m de bataille - **2.** fig [controversial subject] polémique f.

battlements ['bætlmənts] npl remparts mpl.

battleship ['bætlʃɪp] n cuirassé m.

bauble ['bɔːbl] n babiole f, colifichet m.

baud [bɔːd] n COMPUT baud m.

baud rate n COMPUT vitesse f de transmission.

baulk [bɔːk] = balk.

Bavaria [bə'veərɪə] n Bavière f ; in ~ en Bavière.

Bavarian [bə'veərɪən] ◇ adj bavarois(e) ◇ n Bavarois m, -e f.

bawdy ['bɔːdɪ] (compar -ier ; superl -iest) adj grivois(e), salé(e).

bawl [bɔːl] vt & vi brailler.

bay [beɪ] n - **1.** GEOGR baie f - **2.** [for loading] aire f (de chargement) - **3.** [for parking] place f (de stationnement) - **4.** [horse] cheval m bai - **5. phr** : to keep sb/sthg at ~ tenir qqn/qqch à distance, tenir qqn/qqch en échec ◇ vi hurler.

bay leaf n feuille f de laurier.

bayonet ['beɪənɪt] n baïonnette f.

bay tree n laurier m.

bay window n fenêtre f en saillie.

bazaar [bə'zɑːʳ] *n* - **1.** [market] bazar *m* - **2.** Br [charity sale] vente *f* de charité.

bazooka [bə'zuːkə] *n* bazooka *m*.

BB (*abbr of* **Boys' Brigade**) *n mouvement chrétien de la jeunesse en Grande-Bretagne.*

B & B *n abbr of* **bed and breakfast.**

BBC (*abbr of* **British Broadcasting Corporation**) *n office national britannique de radiodiffusion.*

BC - **1.** (*abbr of* **before Christ**) av. J.-C. - **2.** *abbr of* **British Columbia.**

BCG (*abbr of* **Bacillus Calmette-Guérin**) *n* BCG *m*.

BD (*abbr of* **Bachelor of Divinity**) *n* [degree] ≈ licence *f* de théologie ; [person] ≈ licencié(e) en théologie.

BDS (*abbr of* **Bachelor of Dental Science**) *n* [degree] ≈ licence *f* de chirurgie dentaire ; [person] ≈ licencié *m*, -e *f* en chirurgie dentaire.

be [biː] (*pt* was OR were ; *pp* been) ⟨> *aux vb* - **1.** (*in combination with ppr : to form cont tense*) : **what is he doing?** qu'est-ce qu'il fait? ; **it's snowing** il neige ; **they've been promising reform for years** ça fait des années qu'ils nous promettent des réformes - **2.** (*in combination with pp : to form passive*) être ; **to ~ loved** être aimé(e) ; **there was no one to ~ seen** il n'y avait personne - **3.** (*in question tags*) : **she's pretty, isn't she?** elle est jolie, n'est-ce pas? ; **the meal was delicious, wasn't it?** le repas était délicieux, non? OR vous n'avez pas trouvé? - **4.** (*followed by 'to' + infin*) : **the firm is to ~ sold** on va vendre la société ; **I'm to ~ promoted** je vais avoir de l'avancement ; **you're not to tell anyone** ne le dis à personne ⟨> *copulative vb* - **1.** (*with adj, n*) être ; **to ~ a doctor/lawyer/plumber** être médecin/avocat/plombier ; **she's intelligent/attractive** elle est intelligente/jolie ; **I'm hot/cold** j'ai chaud/froid ; **~ quiet!** tais-toi! ; **1 and 1 are 2** 1 et 1 font 2 - **2.** (*referring to health*) aller, se porter ; **to ~ seriously ill** être gravement malade ; **she's better now** elle va mieux maintenant ; **how are you?** comment allez-vous? - **3.** (*referring to age*) : **how old are you?** quel âge avez-vous? ; **I'm 20 (years old)** j'ai 20 ans - **4.** (*cost*) coûter, faire ; **how much was it?** combien cela a-t-il coûté?, combien ça faisait? ; **that will ~ £10, please** cela fait 10 livres, s'il vous plaît ⟨> *vi* - **1.** [exist] être, exister ; **~ that as it may** quoi qu'il en soit - **2.** (*referring to place*) être ; **Toulouse is in France** Toulouse se trouve OR est en France ; **he will ~ here tomorrow** il sera là demain - **3.** (*referring to movement*) aller, être ; **I've been to the cinema** j'ai été OR je suis allé au cinéma ⟨> *v impers* - **1.** [referring to time,

dates, distance] être ; **it's two o'clock** il est deux heures ; **it's 3 km to the next town** la ville voisine est à 3 km - **2.** [referring to the weather] faire ; **it's hot/cold** il fait chaud/froid ; **it's windy** il y a du vent - **3.** [for emphasis] : **it's me/Paul/the milkman** c'est moi/Paul/le laitier.

B/E *abbr of* **bill of exchange.**

beach [biːtʃ] ⟨> *n* plage *f* ⟨> *vt* échouer.

beach ball *n* ballon *m* de plage.

beach buggy *n* buggy *m*.

beachcomber ['biːtʃ,kəʊməʳ] *n* ramasseur d'objets trouvés sur la plage.

beachhead ['biːtʃhed] *n* MIL tête *f* de pont.

beachwear ['biːtʃweəʳ] *n* (U) tenue *f* de plage.

beacon ['biːkən] *n* - **1.** [warning fire] feu *m*, fanal *m* - **2.** [lighthouse] phare *m* - **3.** [radio beacon] radiophare *m*.

bead [biːd] *n* - **1.** [of wood, glass] perle *f* - **2.** [of sweat] goutte *f*.

beaded ['biːdɪd] *adj* orné(e) de perles.

beading ['biːdɪŋ] *n* (U) baguette *f* de recouvrement.

beady ['biːdɪ] (*compar* -**ier** ; *superl* -**iest**) *adj* : **~ eyes** petits yeux perçants.

beagle ['biːgl] *n* beagle *m*.

beak [biːk] *n* bec *m*.

beaker ['biːkəʳ] *n* gobelet *m*.

be-all *n* : **the ~ and end-all** la seule chose qui compte.

beam [biːm] ⟨> *n* - **1.** [of wood, concrete] poutre *f* - **2.** [of light] rayon *m* ⟨> *vt* [signal, news] transmettre ⟨> *vi* - **1.** [smile] faire un sourire radieux - **2.** [shine] rayonner.

beaming ['biːmɪŋ] *adj* - **1.** [smiling] radieux(euse) - **2.** [shining] rayonnant(e).

bean [biːn] *n* [gen] haricot *m* ; [of coffee] grain *m* ; **to be full of ~s** *inf* péter le feu ; **to spill the ~s** *inf* manger le morceau.

beanbag ['biːnbæg] *n* [chair] sacco *m*.

beanshoot ['biːnʃuːt], **beansprout** ['biːnsprɑʊt] *n* germe *m* OR pousse *f* de soja.

bear [beəʳ] (*pt* bore ; *pp* borne) ⟨> *n* - **1.** [animal] ours *m* - **2.** ST EX baissier *m* ⟨> *vt* - **1.** [carry] porter - **2.** [support, tolerate] supporter ; **I can't ~ Christmas** je n'aime pas Noël ; **to ~ responsibility (for)** assumer OR prendre la responsabilité (de) - **3.** [child] donner naissance à - **4.** [feeling] : **to ~ sb a grudge** garder rancune à qqn - **5.** FIN [interest] rapporter ⟨> *vi* : **to ~ left/right** se diriger vers la gauche/la droite ; **to bring pressure/influence to ~ on sb** exercer une pression/une influence sur qqn.

➡ **bear down** *vi* : **to ~ down on sb/sthg** s'approcher de qqn/qqch de façon menaçante.

🔹 **bear out** *vt sep* confirmer, corroborer.

🔹 **bear up** *vi* tenir le coup.

🔹 **bear with** *vt fus* être patient(e) avec.

bearable ['beǝrǝbl] *adj* [tolerable] supportable.

beard [bɪǝd] *n* barbe *f*.

bearded ['bɪǝdɪd] *adj* barbu(e).

bearer ['beǝrǝ'] *n* - **1.** [gen] porteur *m*, -euse *f* - **2.** [of passport] titulaire *mf*.

bear hug *n* inf : **to give sb a ~** serrer qqn très fort.

bearing ['beǝrɪŋ] *n* - **1.** [connection] : **~ (on)** rapport *m* (avec) - **2.** [deportment] allure *f*, maintien *m* - **3.** TECH [for shaft] palier *m* ; **rolling ~** roulement *m* - **4.** [on compass] orientation *f* ; **to get one's ~s** s'orienter, se repérer.

bear market *n* ST EX marché *m* à la baisse.

bearskin ['beǝskɪn] *n* - **1.** [fur] peau *f* d'ours - **2.** [hat] bonnet *m* à poil.

beast [biːst] *n* - **1.** [animal] bête *f* - **2.** inf pej [person] brute *f*.

beastly ['biːstlɪ] (*compar* **-ier** ; *superl* **-iest**) *adj* dated [person] malveillant(e), cruel(elle) ; [headache, weather] épouvantable.

beat [biːt] (*pt* **beat** ; *pp* **beaten**) ◇ *n* - **1.** [of heart, drum, wings] battement *m* - **2.** MUS [rhythm] mesure *f*, temps *m* - **3.** [of policeman] ronde *f* ◇ *adj* inf crevé(e) ◇ *vt* - **1.** [gen] battre ; **it ~s me** inf ça me dépasse - **2.** [reach ahead of] : **they ~ us to it** ils nous ont devancés, ils sont arrivés avant nous - **3.** [be better than] être bien mieux que, valoir mieux que - **4.** phr : **~ it!** inf décampe!, fiche le camp! ◇ *vi* battre.

🔹 **beat down** ◇ *vi* - **1.** [sun] taper, cogner - **2.** [rain] s'abattre ◇ *vt sep* [seller] faire baisser son prix à.

🔹 **beat off** *vt sep* [resist] repousser.

🔹 **beat up** *vt sep* inf tabasser, passer à tabac.

beaten ['biːtn] *adj* battu(e).

beater ['biːtǝ'] *n* - **1.** [for eggs] batteur *m*, fouet *m* - **2.** [for carpet] tapette *f* - **3.** [of wife, child] bourreau *m*.

beating ['biːtɪŋ] *n* - **1.** [blows] raclée *f*, rossée *f* - **2.** [defeat] défaite *f* ; **that will take some ~!** inf on ne pourra sans doute jamais faire mieux.

beating up (*pl* **beatings up**) *n* inf passage *m* à tabac.

beatnik ['biːtnɪk] *n* beatnik *mf*.

beat-up *adj* inf déglingué(e).

beautician [bjuː'tɪʃn] *n* esthéticien *m*, -enne *f*.

beautiful ['bjuːtɪfʊl] *adj* - **1.** [gen] beau (belle) - **2.** inf [very good] joli(e).

beautifully ['bjuːtǝflɪ] *adv* - **1.** [attractively - dressed] élégamment ; [- decorated] avec goût - **2.** inf [very well] parfaitement, à la perfection.

beauty ['bjuːtɪ] (*pl* **-ies**) ◇ *n* - **1.** [gen] beauté *f* - **2.** inf [very good thing] merveille *f* ◇ *comp* [products etc] de beauté.

beauty contest *n* concours *m* de beauté.

beauty parlour *n* institut *m* de beauté.

beauty queen *n* reine *f* de beauté.

beauty salon = **beauty parlour**.

beauty spot *n* - **1.** [picturesque place] site *m* pittoresque - **2.** [on skin] grain *m* de beauté.

beaver ['biːvǝ'] *n* castor *m*.

🔹 **beaver away** *vi* travailler d'arrache-pied.

becalmed [bɪ'kɑːmd] *adj* [ship] encalminé(e).

became [bɪ'keɪm] *pt* ⊳ **become**.

because [bɪ'kɒz] *conj* parce que.

🔹 **because of** *prep* à cause de.

béchamel sauce [,beɪʃǝ'mel-] *n* sauce *f* béchamel, béchamel *f*.

beck [bek] *n* : **to be at sb's ~ and call** être aux ordres OR à la disposition de qqn.

beckon ['bekǝn] ◇ *vt* - **1.** [signal to] faire signe à - **2.** fig [draw, attract] séduire ◇ *vi* [signal] : **to ~ to sb** faire signe à qqn.

become [bɪ'kʌm] (*pt* **became** ; *pp* **become**) *vi* devenir ; **to ~ quieter** se calmer ; **to ~ irritated** s'énerver ; **what has ~ of them?** que sont-ils devenus?

becoming [bɪ'kʌmɪŋ] *adj* - **1.** [attractive] seyant(e), qui va bien - **2.** [appropriate] convenable.

BECTU ['bektuː] (*abbr of* **Broadcasting, Entertainment, Cinematograph and Theatre Union**) *n* syndicat britannique des techniciens des médias audiovisuels.

bed [bed] (*pt* & *pp* **-ded** ; *cont* **-ding**) *n* - **1.** [to sleep on] lit *m* ; **to go to ~** se coucher ; **to go to ~ with sb** euphemism coucher avec qqn ; **to make the ~** faire le lit - **2.** [flowerbed] parterre *m* ; **it's not a ~ of roses** fig ce n'est pas tout rose - **3.** [of sea, river] lit *m*, fond *m*.

🔹 **bed down** *vi* coucher, se coucher.

BEd [,biː'ed] (*abbr of* **Bachelor of Education**) *n* [degree] ≃ licence *f* de sciences de l'éducation ; [person] ≃ licencié *m*, -e *f* en sciences de l'éducation.

bed and breakfast *n* ≃ chambre *f* d'hôte.

bed-bath *n* toilette *f* d'un malade.

bedbug ['bedbʌg] *n* punaise *f*.

bedclothes [ˈbedkləʊðz] *npl* draps *mpl* et couvertures *fpl*.

bedcover [ˈbedˌkʌvəʳ] *n* couvre-lit *m*, dessus-de-lit *m inv*.

bedding [ˈbedɪŋ] *n (U)* = **bedclothes**.

bedding plant *n* plant *m* à repiquer.

bedeck [bɪˈdek] *vt* : to ~ sthg with parer OR orner qqch de.

bedevil [bɪˈdevl] (Br *pt* & *pp* -led ; *cont* -ling, Am *pt* & *pp* -ed ; *cont* -ing) *vt* : to be bedevilled with être surchargé(e) de.

bedfellow [ˈbedˌfeləʊ] *n* fig partenaire *mf*.

bedlam [ˈbedləm] *n* pagaille *f*.

bed linen *n (U)* draps *mpl* et taies *fpl*.

Bedouin, Beduin [ˈbeduɪn] <> *adj* bédouin(e) <> *n* Bédouin *m*, -e *f*.

bedpan [ˈbedpæn] *n* bassin *m*.

bedraggled [bɪˈdrægld] *adj* [person] débraillé(e) ; [hair] embroussaillé(e).

bedridden [ˈbedˌrɪdn] *adj* grabataire.

bedrock [ˈbedrɒk] *n (U)* - **1.** GEOL soubassement *m* - **2.** fig [basis] base *f*, fondement *m*.

bedroom [ˈbedrʊm] *n* chambre *f* (à coucher).

Beds [bedz] (*abbr of* **Bedfordshire**) *comté anglais*.

bedside [ˈbedsaɪd] *n* chevet *m*.

bedside manner *n* [of doctor] comportement *m* envers les malades.

bed-sit(ter) *n* Br chambre *f* meublée.

bedsore [ˈbedsɔːʳ] *n* escarre *f*.

bedspread [ˈbedspred] *n* couvre-lit *m*, dessus-de-lit *m inv*.

bedtime [ˈbedtaɪm] *n* heure *f* du coucher.

Beduin [ˈbeduɪn] = **Bedouin**.

bed-wetting [ˌwetɪŋ] *n* énurésie *f*, incontinence *f* nocturne.

bee [biː] *n* abeille *f* ; to have a ~ in one's bonnet (about) avoir une idée fixe (à propos de).

Beeb [biːb] *n* Br inf : the ~ la BBC.

beech [biːtʃ] *n* hêtre *m*.

beef [biːf] *n* bœuf *m*.

➤ **beef up** *vt sep* inf [strengthen] renforcer ; [story] corser.

beefburger [ˈbiːfˌbɜːgəʳ] *n* hamburger *m*.

Beefeater [ˈbiːfˌiːtəʳ] *n* hallebardier *m* (de la Tour de Londres).

beefsteak [ˈbiːfˌsteɪk] *n* bifteck *m*.

beehive [ˈbiːhaɪv] *n* - **1.** [for bees] ruche *f* - **2.** [hairstyle] coiffure *f* en forme de dôme.

beekeeper [ˈbiːˌkiːpəʳ] *n* apiculteur *m*, -trice *f*.

beeline [ˈbiːlaɪn] *n* : to make a ~ for inf aller tout droit OR directement vers.

been [biːn] *pp* ▷ be.

beep [biːp] inf <> *n* bip *m* ; [on anwering machine] bip sonore <> *vi* faire bip.

beer [bɪəʳ] *n* bière *f*.

beer garden *n* terrasse *f*, jardin attenant à un pub.

beeswax [ˈbiːzwæks] *n* cire *f* d'abeille.

beet [biːt] *n* betterave *f*.

beetle [ˈbiːtl] *n* scarabée *m*.

beetroot [ˈbiːtruːt] *n* betterave *f*.

befall [bɪˈfɔːl] (*pt* befell [-ˈfell], *pp* befallen [-ˈfɔːlən]) literary <> *vt* advenir à <> *vi* arriver, survenir.

befit [bɪˈfɪt] (*pt* & *pp* -ted ; *cont* -ting) *vt* seoir à.

before [bɪˈfɔːʳ] <> *adv* auparavant, avant ; **I've never been there ~** je n'y suis jamais allé(e) ; **I've seen it ~** je l'ai déjà vu ; **the year ~** l'année d'avant OR précédente <> *prep* - **1.** [in time] avant - **2.** [in space] devant <> *conj* avant de (+ *infin*), avant que (+ *subjunctive*) ; **~ leaving** avant de partir ; **~ you leave** avant que vous ne partiez.

beforehand [bɪˈfɔːhænd] *adv* à l'avance.

befriend [bɪˈfrend] *vt* prendre en amitié.

befuddled [bɪˈfʌdld] *adj* [confused] embrouillé(e).

beg [beg] (*pt* & *pp* -ged ; *cont* -ging) <> *vt* - **1.** [money, food] mendier - **2.** [favour] solliciter, quémander ; [forgiveness] demander ; **to ~ sb to do sthg** prier OR supplier qqn de faire qqch ; **to ~ sb for sthg** implorer qqch de qqn <> *vi* - **1.** [for money, food] : **to ~ (for sthg)** mendier (qqch) - **2.** [plead] supplier ; **to ~ for** [forgiveness etc] demander.

began [bɪˈgæn] *pt* ▷ begin.

beggar [ˈbegəʳ] *n* mendiant *m*, -e *f*.

begin [bɪˈgɪn] (*pt* began ; *pp* begun ; *cont* -ning) <> *vt* commencer ; **to ~ doing** OR **to do sthg** commencer OR se mettre à faire qqch <> *vi* commencer ; **to ~ with** pour commencer, premièrement.

beginner [bɪˈgɪnəʳ] *n* débutant *m*, -e *f*.

beginning [bɪˈgɪnɪŋ] *n* début *m*, commencement *m*.

begonia [bɪˈgəʊnjə] *n* bégonia *m*.

begrudge [bɪˈgrʌdʒ] *vt* - **1.** [envy] : **to ~ sb sthg** envier qqch à qqn - **2.** [do unwillingly] : **to ~ doing sthg** rechigner à faire qqch.

beguile [bɪˈgaɪl] *vt* [charm] séduire.

beguiling [bɪˈgaɪlɪŋ] *adj* [charming] séduisant(e).

begun [bɪ'gʌn] *pp* ⊳ begin.

behalf [bɪ'hɑːf] *n* : on ~ of Br, in ~ of Am de la part de, au nom de.

behave [bɪ'heɪv] ⟨⟩ *vt* : to ~ o.s. bien se conduire OR se comporter ⟨⟩ *vi* - **1.** [in a particular way] se conduire, se comporter - **2.** [acceptably] bien se tenir.

behaviour Br, **behavior** Am [bɪ'heɪvjəʳ] *n* conduite *f*, comportement *m*.

behaviourism Br, **behaviorism** Am [bɪ'heɪvjərɪzml] *n* béhaviorisme *m*.

behead [bɪ'hed] *vt* décapiter.

beheld [bɪ'held] *pt* & *pp* ⊳ behold.

behind [bɪ'haɪnd] ⟨⟩ *prep* - **1.** [gen] derrière - **2.** [in time] en retard sur ; **they arrived two hours ~ us** ils sont arrivés deux heures après nous ⟨⟩ *adv* - **1.** [gen] derrière - **2.** [in time] en retard ; **to leave sthg ~** oublier qqch ; **to stay ~** rester ; **to be ~ with sthg** être en retard dans qqch ⟨⟩ *n* inf derrière *m*, postérieur *m*.

behold [bɪ'həʊld] (*pt* & *pp* **beheld**) *vt* literary voir, regarder.

beige [beɪʒ] ⟨⟩ *adj* beige ⟨⟩ *n* beige *m* ; **in ~** en beige.

Beijing [ˌbeɪ'dʒɪŋ] *n* Beijing.

being ['biːɪŋ] *n* - **1.** [creature] être *m* - **2.** [existence] : **in ~** existant(e) ; **to come into ~** voir le jour, prendre naissance.

Beirut [ˌbeɪ'ruːt] *n* Beyrouth ; **East ~** Beyrouth-Est ; **West ~** Beyrouth-Ouest.

belated [bɪ'leɪtɪd] *adj* tardif(ive).

belatedly [bɪ'leɪtɪdlɪ] *adv* tardivement.

belch [beltʃ] ⟨⟩ *n* renvoi *m*, rot *m* ⟨⟩ *vt* [smoke, fire] vomir, cracher ⟨⟩ *vi* - **1.** [person] éructer, roter - **2.** [smoke, fire] cracher, vomir.

beleaguered [bɪ'liːɡəd] *adj* assiégé(e) ; fig harcelé(e), tracassé(e).

belfry ['belfrɪ] (*pl* -ies) *n* beffroi *m*, clocher *m*.

Belgian ['beldʒən] ⟨⟩ *adj* belge ⟨⟩ *n* Belge *mf*.

Belgium ['beldʒəm] *n* Belgique *f* ; **in ~** en Belgique.

Belgrade [ˌbel'ɡreɪd] *n* Belgrade.

belie [bɪ'laɪ] (*cont* **belying**) *vt* - **1.** [disprove] démentir - **2.** [give false idea of] donner une fausse idée de.

belief [bɪ'liːf] *n* - **1.** [faith, certainty] : **~ (in)** croyance *f* (en) ; **beyond ~** incroyable - **2.** [principle, opinion] opinion *f*, conviction *f* ; **in the ~ that** persuadé(e) OR convaincu(e) que.

believable [bɪ'liːvəbl] *adj* croyable.

believe [bɪ'liːv] ⟨⟩ *vt* croire ; **~ it or not** tu ne me croiras peut-être pas ⟨⟩ *vi* croire ; **to**

~ in sb croire en qqn ; **to ~ in sthg** croire à qqch.

believer [bɪ'liːvəʳ] *n* - **1.** RELIG croyant *m*, -e *f* - **2.** [in idea, action] : **~ in** partisan *m*, -e *f* de.

Belisha beacon [bɪ'liːʃə-] *n* Br globe lumineux indiquant un passage clouté.

belittle [bɪ'lɪtl] *vt* dénigrer, rabaisser.

Belize [be'liːz] *n* Belize *m* ; **in ~** au Belize.

bell [bel] *n* [of church] cloche *f* ; [handbell] clochette *f* ; [on door] sonnette *f* ; [on bike] timbre *m* ; **the name rings a ~** ce nom me dit quelque chose.

bell-bottoms *npl* pantalon *m* à pattes d'éléphant.

bellhop ['belhɒp] *n* Am groom *m*, chasseur *m*.

belligerence [bɪ'lɪdʒərəns] *n* belligérance *f*.

belligerent [bɪ'lɪdʒərənt] *adj* - **1.** [at war] belligérant(e) - **2.** [aggressive] belliqueux(euse).

bellow ['beləʊ] ⟨⟩ *vt* [order] hurler, brailler ⟨⟩ *vi* - **1.** [person] brailler, beugler - **2.** [bull] beugler.

bellows ['beləʊz] *npl* soufflet *m*.

bell push *n* Br bouton *m* de sonnette.

bell-ringer *n* carillonneur *m*, -euse *f*.

belly ['belɪ] (*pl* -ies) *n* [of person] ventre *m* ; [of animal] panse *f*.

bellyache ['belɪeɪk] ⟨⟩ *n* mal *m* de ventre ⟨⟩ *vi* inf râler, rouspéter.

belly button *n* inf nombril *m*.

belly dancer *n* danseuse *f* orientale.

belong [bɪ'lɒŋ] *vi* - **1.** [be property] : **to ~ to sb** appartenir OR être à qqn - **2.** [be member] : **to ~ to sthg** être membre de qqch - **3.** [be in right place] être à sa place ; **that chair ~s here** ce fauteuil va là.

belongings [bɪ'lɒŋɪŋz] *npl* affaires *fpl*.

Belorussia [ˌbeləʊ'rʌʃə] *n* Biélorussie *f* ; **in ~** en Biélorussie.

beloved [bɪ'lʌvd] ⟨⟩ *adj* bien-aimé(e) ⟨⟩ *n* bien-aimé *m*, -e *f*.

below [bɪ'ləʊ] ⟨⟩ *adv* - **1.** [lower] en dessous, en bas - **2.** [in text] ci-dessous - **3.** NAUT en bas ⟨⟩ *prep* sous, au-dessous de ; **to be ~ sb in rank** occuper un rang inférieur à qqn.

belt [belt] ⟨⟩ *n* - **1.** [for clothing] ceinture *f* ; **that was below the ~** inf c'était un coup bas ; **to tighten one's ~** fig se serrer la ceinture ; **under one's ~** fig à son actif - **2.** TECH courroie *f* - **3.** [of land, sea] région *f* ⟨⟩ *vt* inf flanquer une raclée à ⟨⟩ *vi* Br inf [car] rouler à toute blinde OR à pleins gaz ; [person] foncer.

⬥ **belt out** *vt sep* inf [song] beugler.

⬥ **belt up** *vi* Br inf la fermer, la boucler.

beltway ['belt,weɪ] *n* **Am** route *f* périphérique.

bemused [bɪ'mju:zd] *adj* perplexe.

bench [bentʃ] *n* - **1.** [gen & POL] banc *m* - **2.** [in lab, workshop] établi *m*.

bend [bend] (*pt* & *pp* **bent**) ⬦ *n* - **1.** [in road] courbe *f*, virage *m* - **2.** [in pipe, river] coude *m* - **3.** phr : **round the ~** inf dingue, fou (folle) ⬦ *vt* - **1.** [arm, leg] plier - **2.** [wire, fork etc] tordre, courber ⬦ *vi* [person] se baisser, se courber ; [tree, rod] plier ; **to ~ over backwards for sb** se mettre en quatre pour qqn.

➤ **bends** *npl :* **the ~s** la maladie des caissons.

bendy ['bendɪ] (*compar* -**ier** ; *superl* -**iest**) *adj* **Br** flexible.

beneath [bɪ'ni:θ] ⬦ *adv* dessous, en bas ⬦ *prep* - **1.** [under] sous - **2.** [unworthy of] indigne de.

benediction [,benɪ'dɪkʃn] *n* bénédiction *f*.

benefactor ['benɪfæktəʳ] *n* bienfaiteur *m*.

benefactress ['benɪfæktrɪs] *n* bienfaitrice *f*.

beneficial [,benɪ'fɪʃl] *adj :* **~ (to sb)** salutaire (à qqn) ; **~ (to sthg)** utile (à qqch).

beneficiary [,benɪ'fɪʃərɪ] (*pl* -**ies**) *n* bénéficiaire *mf*.

benefit ['benɪfɪt] ⬦ *n* - **1.** [advantage] avantage *m ;* **for the ~ of** dans l'intérêt de ; **to be to sb's ~, to be of ~ to sb** être dans l'intérêt de qqn - **2.** ADMIN [allowance of money] allocation *f*, prestation *f* ⬦ comp : **~ performance** représentation *f* de bienfaisance ⬦ *vt* profiter à, être avantageux pour ⬦ *vi :* **to ~ from** tirer avantage de, profiter de.

Benelux ['benɪlʌks] *n* Bénélux *m ;* **the ~ countries** les pays du Bénélux.

benevolent [bɪ'nevələnt] *adj* bienveillant(e).

BEng [,bi:'endʒ] (*abbr of* **Bachelor of Engineering**) *n* [degree] ≃ licence *f* de mécanique ; [person] ≃ licencié(e) en mécanique.

Bengal [,beŋ'gɔːl] *n* Bengale *m ;* **in ~** au Bengale ; **the Bay of ~** le golfe du Bengale.

benign [bɪ'naɪn] *adj* - **1.** [person] gentil(ille), bienveillant(e) - **2.** MED bénin(igne)

Benin [be'ni:n] *n* Bénin *m ;* **in ~** au Bénin.

bent [bent] ⬦ *pt* & *pp* ⬅ **bend** ⬦ *adj* - **1.** [wire, bar] tordu(e) - **2.** [person, body] courbé(e), voûté(e) - **3.** **Br** inf [dishonest] véreux(euse) - **4.** [determined] : **to be ~ on doing sthg** vouloir absolument faire qqch, être décidé(e) à faire qqch ⬦ *n :* **~ (for)** penchant *m* (pour).

bequeath [bɪ'kwi:ð] *vt* lit & fig léguer.

bequest [bɪ'kwest] *n* legs *m*.

berate [bɪ'reɪt] *vt* réprimander.

Berber ['bɜːbəʳ] ⬦ *adj* berbère ⬦ *n* - **1.** [person] Berbère *mf* - **2.** [language] berbère *m*.

bereaved [bɪ'riːvd] (*pl inv*) ⬦ *adj* endeuillé(e), affligé(e) ⬦ *n :* **the ~** la famille du défunt.

bereavement [bɪ'riːvmənt] *n* deuil *m*.

bereft [bɪ'reft] *adj* literary : **~ of** privé(e) de.

beret ['bereɪ] *n* béret *m*.

Bering Sea ['berɪŋ-] *n :* **the ~** la mer de Béring.

Bering Strait ['berɪŋ-] *n :* **the ~** le détroit de Béring.

berk [bɜːk] *n* **Br** inf idiot *m*, -e *f*, andouille *f*.

Berks [bɑːks] (*abbr of* **Berkshire**) comté anglais.

Berlin [bɜː'lɪn] *n* Berlin ; **East ~** Berlin-Est ; **West ~** Berlin-Ouest ; **the ~ Wall** le mur de Berlin.

Berliner [bɜː'lɪnə] *n* Berlinois *m*, -e *f*.

berm [bɜːm] *n* **Am** bas-côté *m*.

Bermuda [bə'mju:də] *n* Bermudes *fpl ;* **in ~** aux Bermudes.

Bermuda shorts *npl* bermuda *m*.

Bern [bɜːn] *n* Berne.

berry ['berɪ] (*pl* -**ies**) *n* baie *f*.

berserk [bə'zɜːk] *adj :* **to go ~** devenir fou furieux (folle furieuse).

berth [bɜːθ] ⬦ *n* - **1.** [in harbour] poste *m* d'amarrage, mouillage *m* - **2.** [in ship, train] couchette *f* - **3.** phr : **to give sb a wide ~** éviter qqn ⬦ *vt* [ship] amener à quai ⬦ *vi* [ship] accoster, se ranger à quai.

beseech [bɪ'siːtʃ] (*pt* & *pp* **besought** OR **beseeched**) *vt* literary : **to ~ sb (to do sthg)** implorer OR supplier qqn (de faire qqch).

beset [bɪ'set] (*pt* & *pp* **beset** ; *cont* -**ting**) ⬦ *adj :* **~ with** OR **by** [doubts etc] assailli(e) de ; **the plan is ~ with risks** le plan comporte une multitude de risques ⬦ *vt* assaillir.

beside [bɪ'saɪd] *prep* - **1.** [next to] à côté de, auprès de - **2.** [compared with] comparé(e) à, à côté de - **3.** phr : **to be ~ o.s. with anger** être hors de soi ; **to be ~ o.s. with joy** être fou (folle) de joie.

besides [bɪ'saɪdz] ⬦ *adv* en outre, en plus ⬦ *prep* en plus de.

besiege [bɪ'siːdʒ] *vt* - **1.** [town, fortress] assiéger - **2.** fig [trouble, annoy] assaillir, harceler ; **to be ~d with** être assailli(e) OR harcelé(e) de.

besotted [bɪ'sɒtɪd] *adj :* **~ (with sb)** entiché(e) (de qqn).

besought [bɪ'sɔːt] *pt* & *pp* ⬅ **beseech**.

bespectacled [bɪ'spektəkld] *adj* qui porte des lunettes, à lunettes.

bespoke [bɪ'spəʊk] *adj* Br [clothes] fait(e) sur mesure ; [tailor] à façon.

best [best] ◇ *adj* le meilleur (la meilleure) ◇ *adv* le mieux ◇ *n* le mieux ; **to do one's ~** faire de son mieux ; **all the ~!** meilleurs souhaits! ; **to be for the ~** être pour le mieux ; **to make the ~ of sthg** s'accommoder de qqch, prendre son parti de qqch ; **he wants the ~ of both worlds** il veut le beurre et l'argent du beurre.
➡ **at best** *adv* au mieux.

bestial ['bestjəl] *adj* bestial(e).

best man *n* garçon *m* d'honneur.

BEST MAN

Dans les pays anglo-saxons, le garçon d'honneur présente l'alliance au marié et prononce un discours lors de la réception de mariage.

bestow [bɪ'stəʊ] *vt fml* : **to ~ sthg on sb** conférer qqch à qqn.

best-seller *n* [book] best-seller *m*.

best-selling *adj* à succès.

bet [bet] (*pt & pp* bet OR -ted ; *cont* -ting) ◇ *n* pari *m* ; **it's a safe ~ that ...** *fig* il est certain que ... ; **to hedge one's ~s** se couvrir ◇ *vt* parier ◇ *vi* parier ; **I wouldn't ~ on it** *fig* je n'en suis pas si sûr(e) ; **you ~!** *inf* un peu!, et comment!

beta-blocker ['bi:tə,blɒkəʳ] *n* bêtabloquant *m*.

Bethlehem ['beθlɪhem] *n* Bethléem.

betray [bɪ'treɪ] *vt* trahir.

betrayal [bɪ'treɪəl] *n* - **1.** [of person] trahison *f* - **2.** : **~ of trust** abus *m* de confiance - **3.** [of secret] révélation *f*.

betrothed [bɪ'trəʊðd] *adj dated* : **~ (to)** fiancé(e) (à).

better ['betəʳ] ◇ *adj (compar of good)* meilleur(e) ; **to get ~** s'améliorer ; [after illness] se remettre, se rétablir ◇ *adv. (compar of well)* mieux ; **I'd ~ leave** il faut que je parte, je dois partir ; **you'd ~ let your mother know** tu ferais mieux de le dire à ta mère ◇ *n* meilleur *m*, -e *f* ; **to get the ~ of sb** avoir raison de qqn ◇ *vt* améliorer ; **to ~ o.s.** s'élever.

better half *n inf* moitié *f*.

better off *adj* - **1.** [financially] plus à son aise - **2.** [in better situation] mieux.
➡ **better-off** *npl* : **the better-off** les gens riches OR aisés.

betting ['betɪŋ] *n (U)* paris *mpl*.

betting shop *n Br* ≃ bureau *m* de P.M.U.

between [bɪ'twi:n] ◇ *prep* entre ; **he sat (in) ~ Paul and Anne** il s'est assis entre Paul et Anne ◇ *adv* : **(in) ~** [in space] au milieu ; [in time] dans l'intervalle.

bevelled Br, **beveled** Am ['bevld] *adj* biseauté(e).

beverage ['bevərɪdʒ] *n fml* boisson *f*.

bevy ['bevɪ] (*pl* -ies) *n* bande *f*, troupe *f*.

beware [bɪ'weəʳ] *vi* : **to ~ (of)** prendre garde (à), se méfier (de) ; **~ of ...** attention à ...

bewildered [bɪ'wɪldəd] *adj* déconcerté(e), perplexe.

bewildering [bɪ'wɪldərɪŋ] *adj* déconcertant(e), déroutant(e).

bewitched [bɪ'wɪtʃt] *adj* ensorcelé(e), enchanté(e).

bewitching [bɪ'wɪtʃɪŋ] *adj* charmeur(euse), ensorcelant(e).

beyond [bɪ'jɒnd] ◇ *prep* - **1.** [in space] au-delà de - **2.** [in time] après, plus tard que - **3.** [exceeding] au-dessus de ; **it's ~ my control** je n'y peux rien ; **it's ~ my responsibility** cela n'entre pas dans le cadre de mes responsabilités ◇ *adv* au-delà.

b/f *abbr of* brought forward.

bhp *abbr of* brake horsepower.

bi- [baɪ] *prefix* bi-.

biannual [baɪ'ænjʊəl] *adj* semestriel(elle).

bias ['baɪəs] *n* - **1.** [prejudice] préjugé *m*, parti pris - **2.** [tendency] tendance *f*.

biased ['baɪəst] *adj* partial(e) ; **to be ~ towards sb/sthg** favoriser qqn/qqch ; **to be ~ against sb/sthg** défavoriser qqn/qqch.

bib [bɪb] *n* [for baby] bavoir *m*, bavette *f*.

Bible ['baɪbl] *n* : **the ~** la Bible.
➡ **bible** *n* bible *f*.

biblical ['bɪblɪkl] *adj* biblique.

bibliography [,bɪblɪ'ɒgrəfɪ] (*pl* -ies) *n* bibliographie *f*.

bicarbonate of soda [baɪ'kɑ:bənət-] *n* bicarbonate *m* de soude.

bicentenary Br [,baɪsen'ti:nərɪ] (*pl* -ies), **bicentennial** Am [,baɪsen'tenjəl] *n* bicentenaire *m*.

biceps ['baɪseps] (*pl inv*) *n* biceps *m*.

bicker ['bɪkəʳ] *vi* se chamailler.

bickering ['bɪkərɪŋ] *n (U)* chamailleries *fpl*.

bicycle ['baɪsɪkl] ◇ *n* bicyclette *f*, vélo *m* ◇ *vi* aller à bicyclette OR vélo.

bicycle path *n* piste *f* cyclable.

bicycle pump *n* pompe *f* à vélo.

bid [bɪd] (*pt & pp vt sense 1 & vi* bid ; *cont* bidding ; *pt vt senses 2 & 3* bid OR bade ; *pp vt* senses 2 & 3 **bid** OR **bidden** ; *cont* **bidding**) ◇ *n* - **1.** [attempt] tentative *f* - **2.** [at auction] enchère *f* - **3.** COMM offre *f* ◇ *vt* - **1.** [at auction] faire une enchère de - **2.** literary [request] : **to ~ sb do sthg** prier qqn de faire qqch - **3.** fml [say] : **to ~ sb good morning** souhaiter le bonjour à qqn ◇ *vi* - **1.** [at auction] : **to ~ (for)** faire une enchère (pour) - **2.** [attempt] : **to ~ for sthg** briguer qqch.

bidder ['bɪdəʳ] *n* enchérisseur *m*, -euse *f*.

bidding ['bɪdɪŋ] *n (U)* enchères *fpl*.

bide [baɪd] *vt :* **to ~ one's time** attendre son heure OR le bon moment.

bidet ['biːdeɪ] *n* bidet *m*.

biennial [baɪ'enɪəl] ◇ *adj* biennal(e) ◇ *n* plante *f* bisannuelle.

bier [bɪəʳ] *n* bière *f*.

bifidus ['bɪfɪdəs] *n* bifidus *m*.

bifocals [ˌbaɪ'fəʊklz] *npl* lunettes *fpl* bifocales.

BIFU ['bɪfuː] (*abbr of* The Banking, Insurance and Finance Union) *n syndicat britannique des employés du secteur financier.*

big [bɪg] (*compar* **-ger** ; *superl* **-gest**) *adj* - **1.** [gen] grand(e) - **2.** [in amount, bulk - box, problem, book] gros (grosse) - **3.** phr : **to do things in a ~ way** faire les choses en grand.

bigamist ['bɪgəmɪst] *n* bigame *mf*.

bigamy ['bɪgəmɪ] *n* bigamie *f*.

Big Apple *n :* **the ~** *surnom de New York.*

Big Ben [-'ben] *n* Big Ben.

big business *n (U)* les grandes entreprises *fpl*.

big cat *n* fauve *m*.

big deal inf ◇ *n :* **it's no ~** ce n'est pas dramatique ; **what's the ~?** où est le problème? ◇ *excl* tu parles!, et alors?

Big Dipper [-'dɪpəʳ] *n* - **1.** Br [rollercoaster] montagnes *fpl* russes - **2.** Am ASTRON : **the ~** la Grande Ourse.

big end *n* tête *f* de bielle.

big fish *n* inf fig huile *f*, gros bonnet *m*.

big game *n* gros gibier *m*.

big hand *n* - **1.** [on clock] grande aiguille *f* - **2.** inf [applause] : **let's give him a ~** applaudissons-le bien fort.

bighead ['bɪghed] *n* inf crâneur *m*, -euse *f*.

bigheaded [ˌbɪg'hedɪd] *adj* inf crâneur(euse).

big-hearted [-'hɑːtɪd] *adj* qui a du cœur.

big money *n* inf : **to make ~** se faire du pognon.

big mouth *n* inf grande gueule *f ;* **she's got a ~** elle ne sait pas tenir sa langue.

big name *n* inf personne *f* connue, célébrité *f*.

bigot ['bɪgət] *n* sectaire *mf*.

bigoted ['bɪgətɪd] *adj* sectaire.

bigotry ['bɪgətrɪ] *n* sectarisme *m*.

big shot *n* inf huile *f*, grosse légume *f*.

big time *n* inf : **to make the ~** réussir, arriver en haut de l'échelle.

big toe *n* gros orteil *m*.

big top *n* chapiteau *m*.

big wheel *n* - **1.** Br [at fairground] grande roue *f* - **2.** inf [big shot] huile *f*, grosse légume *f*.

bigwig ['bɪgwɪg] *n* inf huile *f*, gros bonnet *m*.

bike [baɪk] *n* inf - **1.** [bicycle] vélo *m*, bécane *f* - **2.** [motorcycle] bécane *f*, moto *f*.

bikeway ['baɪkweɪ] *n* Am piste *f* cyclable.

bikini [bɪ'kiːnɪ] *n* Bikini® *m*.

bilateral [ˌbaɪ'lætərəl] *adj* bilatéral(e).

bilberry ['bɪlbərɪ] (*pl* **-ies**) *n* myrtille *f*.

bile [baɪl] *n* - **1.** [fluid] bile *f* - **2.** [anger] mauvaise humeur *f*.

bilingual [baɪ'lɪŋgwəl] *adj* bilingue.

bilious ['bɪljəs] *adj* - **1.** [sickening] écœurant(e) - **2.** [nauseous] qui a envie de vomir.

bill [bɪl] ◇ *n* - **1.** [statement of cost] : **~ (for)** note *f* OR facture *f* (de) ; [in restaurant] addition *f* (de) - **2.** [in parliament] projet *m* de loi - **3.** [of show, concert] programme *m* - **4.** Am [banknote] billet *m* de banque - **5.** [poster] : '**post** OR **stick no ~s**' 'défense d'afficher' - **6.** [beak] bec *m* - **7.** phr : **to be given a clean ~ of health** être déclaré(e) en parfait état de santé ◇ *vt* [invoice] : **to ~ sb (for)** envoyer une facture à qqn (pour).

billboard ['bɪlbɔːd] *n* panneau *m* d'affichage.

billet ['bɪlɪt] ◇ *n* logement *m* (chez l'habitant) ◇ *vt* loger, cantonner.

billfold ['bɪlfəʊld] *n* Am portefeuille *m*.

billiards ['bɪljədz] *n* billard *m*.

billion ['bɪljən] *num* - **1.** Am [thousand million] milliard *m* - **2.** Br [million million] billion *m*.

billionaire [ˌbɪljə'neəʳ] *n* milliardaire *mf*.

bill of exchange *n* effet *m* OR lettre *f* de change.

bill of lading *n* connaissement *m*.

Bill of Rights *n :* **the ~** *les dix premiers amendements à la Constitution américaine.*

BILL OF RIGHTS

Ces amendements garantissent, entre autres droits, la liberté d'expression, de religion et de réunion.

bill of sale *n* acte *m* de vente.

billow ['bɪləʊ] ◇ *n* nuage *m*, volute *f* ◇ *vi* [smoke, steam] tournoyer ; [skirt, sail] se gonfler.

billycan ['bɪlɪkæn] *n* gamelle *f*.

billy goat ['bɪlɪ-] *n* bouc *m*.

bimbo ['bɪmbəʊ] (*pl* -s OR -es) *n* inf pej : she's a bit of a ~ c'est le genre 'pin-up'.

bimonthly [,baɪ'mʌnθlɪ] ◇ *adj* - **1.** [every two months] bimestriel(elle) - **2.** [twice a month] bimensuel(elle) ◇ *adv* - **1.** [every two months] tous les deux mois - **2.** [twice a month] deux fois par mois.

bin [bɪn] ◇ *n* - **1.** Br [for rubbish] poubelle *f* - **2.** [for grain, coal] coffre *m* - **3.** [for bread] huche *f*, boîte *f* ◇ *vt* inf balancer.

binary ['baɪnərɪ] *adj* binaire.

bind [baɪnd] (*pt* & *pp* bound) ◇ *vt* - **1.** [tie up] attacher, lier - **2.** [unite - people] lier - **3.** [bandage] panser - **4.** [book] relier - **5.** [constrain] contraindre, forcer ◇ *n* inf - **1.** Br [nuisance] corvée *f* - **2.** [difficult situation] : to be in a bit of a ~ être dans le pétrin.

◆ **bind over** *vt sep* : to be bound over être sommé(e) d'observer une bonne conduite.

binder ['baɪndə'] *n* - **1.** [machine] lieuse *f* - **2.** [person] relieur *m*, -euse *f* - **3.** [cover] classeur *m*.

binding ['baɪndɪŋ] ◇ *adj* qui lie OR engage ; [agreement] irrévocable ◇ *n* - **1.** [on book] reliure *f* - **2.** [on dress, tablecloth] liséré *m*.

binge [bɪndʒ] inf ◇ *n* : to go on a ~ prendre une cuite ◇ *vi* : to ~ on sthg se gaver OR se bourrer de qqch.

bingo ['bɪŋgəʊ] *n* bingo *m*, ≃ loto *m*.

BINGO

Ce jeu d'argent, très populaire en Grande-Bretagne, consiste à cocher des chiffres sur une carte jusqu'à ce qu'elle soit remplie ; il est souvent pratiqué dans d'anciens cinémas ou des salles municipales.

---

bin-liner *n* Br sac-poubelle *m*.

binoculars [bɪ'nɒkjʊləz] *npl* jumelles *fpl*.

biochemistry [,baɪəʊ'kemɪstrɪ] *n* biochimie *f*.

biodegradable [,baɪəʊdɪ'greɪdəbl] *adj* biodégradable.

biodiversity [,baɪəʊdaɪ'vɜːsətɪ] *n* biodiversité *f*.

biographer [baɪ'ɒgrəfə'] *n* biographe *mf*.

biographic(al) [,baɪə'græfɪk(l)] *adj* biographique.

biography [baɪ'ɒgrəfɪ] (*pl* -ies) *n* biographie *f*.

biological [,baɪə'lɒdʒɪkl] *adj* biologique ; [washing powder] aux enzymes.

biological weapon *n* arme *f* biologique.

biologist [baɪ'ɒlədʒɪst] *n* biologiste *mf*.

biology [baɪ'ɒlədʒɪ] *n* biologie *f*.

bionic [baɪ'ɒnɪk] *adj* bionique.

bionics [baɪ'ɒnɪks] *n* bionique *f*.

biopic ['baɪəʊpɪk] *n* inf film *m* biographique.

biopsy ['baɪɒpsɪ] (*pl* -ies) *n* biopsie *f*.

biotechnology [,baɪəʊtek'nɒlədʒɪ] *n* biotechnologie *f*.

bipartite [,baɪ'pɑːtaɪt] *adj* bipartite.

biplane ['baɪpleɪn] *n* biplan *m*.

birch [bɜːtʃ] *n* - **1.** [tree] bouleau *m* - **2.** [stick] : the ~ la verge, le fouet.

bird [bɜːd] *n* - **1.** [creature] oiseau *m* ; to kill two ~s with one stone faire d'une pierre deux coups - **2.** inf [woman] gonzesse *f*.

birdcage ['bɜːdkeɪdʒ] *n* cage *f* à oiseaux.

birdie ['bɜːdɪ] *n* - **1.** [bird] petit oiseau *m* - **2.** GOLF birdie *m*.

bird of paradise *n* oiseau *m* de paradis, paradisier *m*.

bird of prey *n* oiseau *m* de proie.

birdseed ['bɜːdsiːd] *n* graine *f* pour oiseaux.

bird's-eye view *n* vue *f* aérienne.

bird-watcher [-,wɒtʃə'] *n* observateur *m*, -trice *f* d'oiseaux.

Biro® ['baɪərəʊ] *n* stylo *m* à bille.

birth [bɜːθ] *n* lit & fig naissance *f* ; to give ~ (to) donner naissance (à).

birth certificate *n* acte *m* OR extrait *m* de naissance.

birth control *n* (U) régulation *f* OR contrôle *m* des naissances.

birthday ['bɜːθdeɪ] ◇ *n* anniversaire *m* ◇ *comp* [party, present etc] d'anniversaire.

birthmark ['bɜːθmɑːk] *n* tache *f* de vin.

birthplace ['bɜːθpleɪs] *n* lieu *m* de naissance.

birthrate ['bɜːθreɪt] *n* (taux *m* de) natalité *f*.

birthright ['bɜːθraɪt] *n* droit *m* de naissance OR du sang.

Biscay ['bɪskeɪ] *n* : the Bay of ~ le golfe de Gascogne.

biscuit ['bɪskɪt] *n* Br gâteau *m* sec, biscuit *m* ; Am scone *m*.

bisect [baɪ'sekt] *vt* couper OR diviser en deux.

bisexual [,baɪ'sekʃʊəl] ◇ *adj* bisexuel(elle) ◇ *n* bisexuel *m*, -elle *f*.

bishop ['bɪʃəp] *n* - **1.** RELIG évêque *m* - **2.** [in chess] fou *m*.

bison [ˈbaɪsn] (*pl inv* OR **-s**) *n* bison *m*.

bistro [ˈbiːstrəʊ] (*pl* **-s**) *n* bistro *m*.

bit [bɪt] ◇ *pt* ▷ **bite** ◇ *n* - **1.** [small piece - of paper, cheese etc] morceau *m*, bout *m* ; [- of book, film] passage *m* ; **I just want a ~** je n'en veux qu'un petit peu ; **~s and pieces** Br petites affaires *fpl* OR choses *fpl* ; **to fall to ~s** tomber en morceaux ; **to take sthg to ~s** démonter qqch - **2.** [amount] : **a ~ of** un peu de ; **a ~ of shopping** quelques courses ; **it's a ~ of a nuisance** c'est un peu embêtant ; **a ~ of trouble** un petit problème ; **quite a ~ of** pas mal de, beaucoup de - **3.** [short time] : **for a ~** pendant quelque temps - **4.** [of drill] mèche *f* - **5.** [of bridle] mors *m* - **6.** COMPUT bit *m* - **7.** phr : **to do one's ~** Br faire sa part ; **every ~ as ... as** tout aussi ... que ; **it's all a ~ much** [overwhelming] c'en est trop ; **it's a ~ much** c'est un peu fort ; **not a ~** [not at all] pas du tout.

➥ **a bit** *adv* un peu ; **I'm a ~ tired** je suis un peu fatigué(e).

➥ **bit by bit** *adv* petit à petit, peu à peu.

bitch [bɪtʃ] ◇ *n* - **1.** [female dog] chienne *f* - **2.** vinf pej [woman] salope *f*, garce *f* ◇ *vi* inf rouspéter, râler ; **to ~ about sb** casser du sucre sur le dos de qqn.

bitchy [bɪtʃɪ] (*compar* **-ier** ; *superl* **-iest**) *adj* inf vache, rosse.

bite [baɪt] (*pt* **bit** ; *pp* **bitten**) ◇ *n* - **1.** [act of biting] morsure *f*, coup *m* de dent - **2.** inf [food] : **to have a ~ (to eat)** manger un morceau - **3.** [wound] piqûre *f* - **4.** Br [sharp flavour] piquant *m* ◇ *vt* - **1.** [subj : person, animal] mordre - **2.** [subj : insect, snake] piquer, mordre ◇ *vi* - **1.** [animal, person] : **to ~ (into)** mordre (dans) ; **to ~ off sthg** arracher qqch d'un coup de dents ; **to ~ off more than one can chew** fig avoir les yeux plus gros que le ventre - **2.** [insect, snake] mordre, piquer - **3.** [grip] adhérer, mordre - **4.** fig [take effect] se faire sentir.

biting [ˈbaɪtɪŋ] *adj* - **1.** [very cold] cinglant(e), piquant(e) - **2.** [humour, comment] mordant(e), caustique.

bit part *n* petit rôle *m*, utilités *fpl*.

bitten [ˈbɪtn] *pp* ▷ **bite**.

bitter [ˈbɪtər] ◇ *adj* - **1.** [gen] amer(ère) ; **to the ~ end** jusqu'au bout - **2.** [icy] glacial(e) - **3.** [argument] violent(e) ◇ *n* Br *bière relativement amère, à forte teneur en houblon.*

bitter lemon *n* Schweppes® *m* au citron.

bitterly [ˈbɪtəlɪ] *adv* - **1.** [of weather] : **it's ~ cold** il fait un froid de canard - **2.** [disappointed] cruellement ; [cry, complain] amèrement ; [criticize] âprement, violemment.

bitterness [ˈbɪtənɪs] *n* - **1.** [gen] amertume *f* - **2.** [of wind, weather] âpreté *f*.

bittersweet [ˈbɪtəswiːt] *adj* [taste] aigredoux(-douce) ; [memory] doux-amer(-amère).

bitty [ˈbɪtɪ] (*compar* **-ier** ; *superl* **-iest**) *adj* Br inf décousu(e).

bitumen [ˈbɪtjumɪn] *n* bitume *m*.

bivouac [ˈbɪvʊæk] (*pt* & *pp* **-ked** ; *cont* **-king**) ◇ *n* bivouac *m* ◇ *vi* bivouaquer.

biweekly [ˌbaɪˈwiːklɪ] ◇ *adj* - **1.** [every two weeks] bimensuel(elle) - **2.** [twice a week] bi-hebdomadaire ◇ *adv* - **1.** [every two weeks] tous les quinze jours - **2.** [twice a week] deux fois par semaine.

bizarre [bɪˈzɑːr] *adj* bizarre.

bk - **1.** *abbr of* **bank** - **2.** *abbr of* **book**.

bl *abbr of* **bill of lading**.

BL *n* - **1.** (*abbr of* **Bachelor of Law(s)**) [degree] ≃ licence *f* de droit, ≃ [person] licencié *m*, -e *f* en OR ès droit - **2.** (*abbr of* **Bachelor of Letters**) [degree] ≃ licence *f* de lettres, ≃ [person] licencié *m*, -e *f* en OR ès lettres - **3.** (*abbr of* **Bachelor of Literature**) [degree] ≃ licence *f* de littérature, ≃ [person] licencié *m*, -e *f* en OR ès littérature.

blab [blæb] (*pt* & *pp* **-bed** ; *cont* **-bing**) *vi* inf lâcher le morceau.

black [blæk] ◇ *adj* noir(e) ; **~ and blue** [person, body] couvert(e) de bleus ; **~ and white** [films, photos] noir et blanc ◇ *n* - **1.** [colour] noir *m* - **2.** [person] noir *m*, -e *f* - **3.** phr : **in ~ and white** [in writing] noir sur blanc, par écrit ; **in the ~** [financially solvent] solvable, sans dettes ◇ *vt* Br [boycott] boycotter.

➥ **black out** ◇ *vt sep* - **1.** [city etc] faire le black-out dans - **2.** [TV programme] faire le black-out sur ◇ *vi* [faint] s'évanouir.

blackball [ˈblækbɔːl] *vt* blackbouler.

black belt *n* ceinture *f* noire.

blackberry [ˈblækbərɪ] (*pl* **-ies**) *n* mûre *f*.

blackbird [ˈblækbɜːd] *n* merle *m*.

blackboard [ˈblækbɔːd] *n* tableau *m* (noir).

black box *n* [flight recorder] boîte *f* noire.

black comedy *n* comédie *f* d'humour noir.

blackcurrant [ˌblækˈkʌrənt] *n* cassis *m*.

black economy *n* économie *f* parallèle.

blacken [ˈblækn] ◇ *vt* - **1.** [make dark] noircir - **2.** fig [reputation] ternir ◇ *vi* s'assombrir.

black eye *n* œil *m* poché OR au beurre noir.

blackhead [ˈblækhed] *n* point *m* noir.

black hole *n* trou *m* noir.

black ice *n* verglas *m*.

blackjack ['blækdʒæk] n - **1.** [card game] vingt-et-un m - **2.** Am [weapon] matraque f.

blackleg ['blækleg] n pej jaune m.

blacklist ['blæklɪst] ◇ n liste f noire ◇ vt mettre sur la liste noire.

black magic n magie f noire.

blackmail ['blækmeɪl] ◇ n lit & fig chantage m ◇ vt - **1.** [for money] faire chanter - **2.** fig [emotionally] faire du chantage à.

blackmailer ['blækmeɪlə^r] n maître-chanteur m.

Black Maria n inf panier m à salade.

black mark n fig mauvais point m.

black market n marché m noir.

blackout ['blækaʊt] n - **1.** MIL & PRESS black-out m - **2.** [power cut] panne f d'électricité - **3.** [fainting fit] évanouissement m.

Black Power n mouvement séparatiste noir né dans les années 60 aux États-Unis.

black pudding n Br boudin m.

Black Sea n : the ~ la mer Noire.

black sheep n brebis f galeuse.

blacksmith ['blæksmɪθ] n forgeron m ; [for horses] maréchal-ferrant m.

black spot n AUT point m noir.

black-tie adj [dinner] habillé, en smoking.

bladder ['blædə^r] n vessie f.

blade [bleɪd] n - **1.** [of knife, saw] lame f - **2.** [of propeller] pale f - **3.** [of grass] brin m.

Blairism ['bleərɪzm] n politique du Premier ministre britannique socialiste Tony Blair.

blame [bleɪm] ◇ n responsabilité f, faute f ; to take the ~ for sthg endosser la responsabilité de qqch ◇ vt blâmer, condamner ; to ~ sthg on rejeter la responsabilité de qqch sur, imputer qqch à ; to ~ sb/sthg for sthg reprocher qqch à qqn/qqch ; to be to ~ for sthg être responsable de qqch.

blameless ['bleɪmlɪs] adj [person] innocent(e) ; [life] irréprochable.

blanch [blɑːntʃ] ◇ vt blanchir ◇ vi blêmir, pâlir.

blancmange [blə'mɒndʒ] n blanc-manger m.

bland [blænd] adj - **1.** [person] terne - **2.** [food] fade, insipide - **3.** [music, style] insipide.

blank [blæŋk] ◇ adj - **1.** [sheet of paper] blanc (blanche) ; [wall] nu(e) - **2.** fig [look] vide, sans expression ◇ n - **1.** [empty space] blanc m - **2.** [cartridge] cartouche f à blanc - **3.** phr : to draw a ~ faire chou blanc.

blank cheque n chèque m en blanc ; fig carte f blanche.

blanket ['blæŋkɪt] ◇ adj global(e), géné-

ral(e) ◇ n - **1.** [for bed] couverture f - **2.** [of snow] couche f, manteau m ; [of fog] nappe f ◇ vt recouvrir.

blanket bath n Br toilette f d'un malade.

blankly ['blæŋklɪ] adv [stare] avec les yeux vides.

blank verse n (U) vers mpl blancs OR non rimés.

blare [bleə^r] vi hurler ; [radio] beugler.

➤ **blare out** vi hurler, beugler.

blasé [Br 'blɑːzeɪ, Am ˌblɑː'zeɪ] adj blasé(e).

blasphemous ['blæsfəməs] adj [words] blasphématoire ; [person] blasphémateur(trice).

blasphemy ['blæsfəmɪ] (pl -ies) n blasphème m.

blast [blɑːst] ◇ n - **1.** [explosion] explosion f - **2.** [of air, from bomb] souffle m ◇ vt [hole, tunnel] creuser à la dynamite ◇ excl Br inf zut!, mince!

➤ **(at) full blast** adv [play music etc] à pleins gaz OR tubes ; [work] d'arrache-pied.

➤ **blast off** vi SPACE être mis à feu, décoller.

blasted ['blɑːstɪd] adj inf fichu(e), maudit(e).

blast furnace n haut fourneau m.

blast-off n SPACE mise f à feu, lancement m.

blatant ['bleɪtənt] adj criant(e), flagrant(e).

blatantly ['bleɪtəntlɪ] adv d'une manière flagrante.

blaze [bleɪz] ◇ n - **1.** [fire] incendie m - **2.** fig [of colour, light] éclat m, flamboiement m ; in a ~ of publicity à grand renfort de publicité ◇ vi - **1.** [fire] flamber - **2.** fig [with colour] flamboyer.

blazer ['bleɪzə^r] n blazer m.

blazing ['bleɪzɪŋ] adj - **1.** [sun, heat] ardent(e) ; ~ hot torride, brûlant(e) - **2.** [row] violent(e).

bleach [bliːtʃ] ◇ n eau f de Javel ◇ vt [hair] décolorer ; [clothes] blanchir.

bleached [bliːtʃt] adj décoloré(e).

bleachers ['bliːtʃəz] npl Am SPORT gradins mpl.

bleak [bliːk] adj - **1.** [future] sombre - **2.** [place, weather, face] lugubre, triste.

bleary ['blɪərɪ] (compar -ier ; superl -iest) adj [eyes] trouble, voilé(e).

bleary-eyed [ˌblɪərɪ'aɪd] adj aux yeux troubles.

bleat [bliːt] ◇ n bêlement m ◇ vi bêler ; fig [person] se plaindre, geindre.

bleed [bliːd] (pt & pp bled [bled]) ◇ vi saigner ◇ vt [radiator etc] purger.

bleep [bliːp] ◇ n bip m, bip-bip m ◇ vt appeler avec un bip, biper ◇ vi faire bip-bip.

bleeper ['bliːpə^r] n bip m, biper m.

blemish [ˈblemɪʃ] ◇ *n* lit & fig défaut *m* ◇ *vt* [reputation] souiller, tacher.

blend [blend] ◇ *n* mélange *m* ◇ *vt :* to ~ sthg (with) mélanger qqch (avec OR à) ◇ *vi :* to ~ (with) se mêler (à OR avec).

◆ **blend in** *vi* se fondre.

◆ **blend into** *vt fus* se fondre dans.

blender [ˈblendər] *n* mixer *m*.

bless [bles] (*pt* & *pp* **-ed** OR **blest**) *vt* bénir ; to be ~ed with [talent etc] être doué(e) de ; [children] avoir la chance OR le bonheur d'avoir ; ~ you! [after sneezing] à vos souhaits! ; [thank you] merci mille fois!

blessed [ˈblesɪd] *adj* - **1.** RELIG saint(e), béni(e) - **2.** [relief, silence] merveilleux(euse) - **3.** inf [blasted] fichu(e), maudit(e).

blessing [ˈblesɪŋ] *n* lit & fig bénédiction *f* ; a ~ in disguise une bonne chose en fin de compte ; to count one's ~s s'estimer heureux(euse) de ce que l'on a ; a mixed ~ quelque chose qui a du bon et du mauvais.

blest [blest] *pt* & *pp* ▷ **bless**.

blew [bluː] *pt* ▷ **blow**.

blight [blaɪt] ◇ *n* - **1.** [plant disease] rouille *f*, charbon *m* - **2.** fig [scourge] fléau *m*, calamité *f* ◇ *vt* gâcher, briser.

blimey [ˈblaɪmɪ] *excl* Br inf zut alors!, mince alors!

blind [blaɪnd] ◇ *adj* - **1.** lit & fig aveugle ; to be ~ to sthg ne pas voir qqch - **2.** Br inf [for emphasis] : it doesn't make a ~ bit of difference to me cela m'est complètement égal ◇ *adv :* ~ drunk complètement rond(e), bourré(e) ◇ *n* [for window] store *m* ◇ *npl :* the ~ les aveugles *mpl* ◇ *vt* aveugler ; to ~ sb to sthg fig cacher qqch à qqn.

blind alley *n* lit & fig impasse *f*.

blind corner *n* virage *m* sans visibilité.

blind date *n* rendez-vous avec quelqu'un qu'on ne connaît pas.

blinders [ˈblaɪndəz] *npl* Am œillères *fpl*.

blindfold [ˈblaɪndfəʊld] ◇ *adv* les yeux bandés ◇ *n* bandeau *m* ◇ *vt* bander les yeux à.

blinding [ˈblaɪndɪŋ] *adj* - **1.** [light] aveuglant(e) - **2.** [obvious] évident(e), manifeste.

blindly [ˈblaɪndlɪ] *adv* [unseeingly] à l'aveuglette, [without thinking] aveuglément.

blindness [ˈblaɪndnɪs] *n* cécité *f* ; ~ (to sthg) fig aveuglement *m* (devant qqch).

blind spot *n* - **1.** AUT angle *m* mort - **2.** fig [inability to understand] blocage *m*.

blinis [ˈblɪniːz] *npl* blinis *mpl*.

blink [blɪŋk] ◇ *n* - **1.** [of eyes] clignement *m* - **2.** [of light] clignotement *m* - **3.** phr : on the ~ [machine] détraqué(e) ◇ *vt* - **1.** [eyes] cligner - **2.** Am AUT : to ~ one's lights faire un appel de phares ◇ *vi* - **1.** [person] cligner des yeux - **2.** [light] clignoter.

blinkered [ˈblɪŋkəd] *adj :* to be ~ lit & fig avoir des œillères.

blinkers [ˈblɪŋkəz] *npl* Br œillères *fpl*.

blinking [ˈblɪŋkɪŋ] *adj* Br inf sacré(e), fichu(e).

blip [blɪp] *n* - **1.** [sound] bip *m* - **2.** [on radar] spot *m* - **3.** fig [temporary problem] problème *m* passager.

bliss [blɪs] *n* bonheur *m* suprême, félicité *f*.

blissful [ˈblɪsfʊl] *adj* [day, silence] merveilleux(euse), divin(e) ; [ignorance] total(e).

blissfully [ˈblɪsfʊlɪ] *adv* [smile] d'un air heureux ; [happy, unaware] parfaitement.

blister [ˈblɪstər] ◇ *n* [on skin] ampoule *f*, cloque *f* ◇ *vi* - **1.** [skin] se couvrir d'ampoules - **2.** [paint] cloquer, se boursoufler.

blistering [ˈblɪstərɪŋ] *adj* [sun] brûlant(e), ardent(e) ; [attack] caustique, cinglant(e).

blister pack *n* blister *m*.

blithe [blaɪð] *adj* - **1.** [unworried] insouciant(e) - **2.** dated [cheerful] joyeux(euse), gai(e).

blithely [ˈblaɪðlɪ] *adv* gaiement, joyeusement.

blitz [blɪts] *n* - **1.** MIL bombardement *m* aérien - **2.** Br fig : to have a ~ on sthg s'attaquer à qqch.

blizzard [ˈblɪzəd] *n* tempête *f* de neige.

BLM (*abbr of* **Bureau of Land Management**) *n* service de l'aménagement du territoire aux États-Unis.

bloated [ˈbləʊtɪd] *adj* - **1.** [face] bouffi(e), boursouflé(e) - **2.** [with food] ballonné(e).

blob [blɒb] *n* - **1.** [drop] goutte *f* - **2.** [indistinct shape] forme *f* ; a ~ of colour une tache de couleur.

bloc [blɒk] *n* bloc *m*.

block [blɒk] ◇ *n* - **1.** [building] : office ~ immeuble *m* de bureaux ; ~ of flats Br immeuble *m* - **2.** Am [of buildings] pâté *m* de maisons ; it's five ~s from here c'est cinq rues plus loin - **3.** [of stone, ice] bloc *m* - **4.** [obstruction] blocage *m* - **5.** : ~ and tackle palan *m*, moufle *f* ◇ *vt* - **1.** [road, pipe, view] boucher - **2.** [prevent] bloquer, empêcher.

◆ **block off** *vt sep* [road] barrer ; [pipe, entrance] boucher.

◆ **block out** *vt sep* - **1.** [from mind] chasser - **2.** [light] empêcher d'entrer.

◆ **block up** ◇ *vt sep* boucher ◇ *vi* se boucher.

blockade [blɒ'keɪd] ◇ n blocus m ◇ vt faire le blocus de.

blockage ['blɒkɪdʒ] n obstruction f.

block booking n location f en bloc.

blockbuster ['blɒkbʌstəʳ] n inf [book] best-seller m ; [film] film m à succès, superproduction f.

block capitals npl majuscules fpl d'imprimerie.

blockhead ['blɒkhed] n inf crétin m, -e f, imbécile mf.

block letters npl majuscules fpl d'imprimerie.

block release n Br stage de formation de plusieurs semaines.

block vote n Br vote m groupé.

bloke [bləʊk] n Br inf type m.

blond [blɒnd] adj blond(e).

blonde [blɒnd] ◇ adj blond(e) ◇ n [woman] blonde f.

blood [blʌd] n sang m ; **in cold ~** de sang-froid ; **it made my ~ boil** cela m'a mis(e) dans une colère noire ; **it made my ~ run cold** cela m'a glacé le sang ; **it's in his ~** fig il a cela dans le sang ; **new** OR **fresh ~** fig sang frais.

blood bank n banque f de sang.

bloodbath ['blʌdbɑːθ, pl -bɑːðz] n bain m de sang, massacre m.

blood brother n frère m de sang.

blood cell n globule m.

blood count n numération f globulaire.

bloodcurdling ['blʌdˌkɜːdlɪŋ] adj à vous glacer le sang.

blood donor n donneur m, -euse f de sang.

blood group n groupe m sanguin.

bloodhound ['blʌdhaʊnd] n limier m.

bloodless ['blʌdlɪs] adj - 1. [face, lips] exsangue, pâle - 2. [coup, victory] sans effusion de sang.

bloodletting ['blʌdˌletɪŋ] n [killing] tuerie f.

blood money n prix m du sang.

blood orange n orange f sanguine.

blood poisoning n septicémie f.

blood pressure n tension f artérielle ; **to have high ~** faire de l'hypertension.

blood relation, blood relative n parent m, -e f par le sang.

bloodshed ['blʌdʃed] n carnage m.

bloodshot ['blʌdʃɒt] adj [eyes] injecté(e) de sang.

blood sports npl la chasse.

bloodstained ['blʌdsteɪnd] adj taché(e) de sang, ensanglanté(e).

bloodstream ['blʌdstriːm] n sang m.

blood test n prise f de sang, examen m du sang.

bloodthirsty ['blʌdˌθɜːstɪ] adj sanguinaire.

blood transfusion n transfusion f sanguine.

blood type n groupe m sanguin.

blood vessel n vaisseau m sanguin.

bloody ['blʌdɪ] (compar -ier ; superl -iest) ◇ adj - 1. [gen] sanglant(e) - 2. Br v inf foutu(e) ; **you ~ idiot!** espèce de con! ◇ adv Br v inf vachement.

bloody-minded [-'maɪndɪd] adj Br inf contrariant(e).

bloom [bluːm] ◇ n fleur f ◇ vi fleurir.

blooming ['bluːmɪŋ] ◇ adj - 1. Br inf [to show annoyance] sacré(e), fichu(e) - 2. [person] éclatant(e), resplendissant(e) ◇ adv Br inf sacrément.

blossom ['blɒsəm] ◇ n [of tree] fleurs fpl ; **in ~** en fleur(s) ◇ vi - 1. [tree] fleurir - 2. fig [person] s'épanouir.

blot [blɒt] (pt & pp -ted ; cont -ting) ◇ n lit & fig tache f ◇ vt - 1. [paper] faire des pâtés sur - 2. [ink] sécher.
  ● **blot out** vt sep voiler, cacher ; [memories] effacer.

blotchy ['blɒtʃɪ] (compar -ier ; superl -iest) adj couvert(e) de marbrures OR taches.

blotting paper ['blɒtɪŋ-] n (U) (papier m) buvard m.

blouse [blaʊz] n chemisier m.

blouson ['bluːzˌgɒtˈnl] n Br blouson m.

blow [bləʊ] (pt blew ; pp blown) ◇ vi - 1. [gen] souffler - 2. [in wind] : **to ~ off** s'envoler ; **the door blew open** la porte s'ouvrit à la volée ; **the door blew shut** la porte a claqué - 3. [fuse] sauter ◇ vt - 1. [subj : wind] faire voler, chasser - 2. [clear] : **to ~ one's nose** se moucher - 3. [trumpet] jouer de, souffler dans ; **to ~ a whistle** donner un coup de sifflet, siffler - 4. [bubbles] faire - 5. inf [money] claquer ◇ n [hit] coup m ; **to come to ~s** en venir aux mains ; **to soften the ~** fig adoucir le coup ; **to strike a ~ for** fig servir la cause de.
  ● **blow out** ◇ vt sep souffler ◇ vi - 1. [candle] s'éteindre - 2. [tyre] éclater.
  ● **blow over** vi se calmer.
  ● **blow up** ◇ vt sep - 1. [inflate] gonfler - 2. [with bomb] faire sauter - 3. [photograph] agrandir ◇ vi exploser.

blow-by-blow adj fig détaillé(e).

blow-dry <> *n* Brushing® *m* <> *vt* faire un Brushing® à.

blowfly ['bləʊflaɪ] (*pl* **-flies**) *n* mouche *f* bleue, mouche de la viande.

blowgun ['bləʊgʌn] Am = **blowpipe**.

blowlamp Br ['bləʊlæmp], **blowtorch** ['bləʊtɔ:tʃ] *n* chalumeau *m*, lampe *f* à souder.

blown [bləʊn] *pp* ⊳ **blow**.

blowout ['bləʊaʊt] *n* - **1**. [of tyre] éclatement *m* - **2**. inf [big meal] grande bouffe *f*, gueuleton *m*.

blowpipe Br ['bləʊpaɪp], **blowgun** Am ['bləʊgʌn] *n* sarbacane *f*.

blowtorch = **blowlamp**.

blowzy ['blaʊzɪ] *adj* Br négligé(e).

BLS (*abbr of* **Bureau of Labor Statistics**) *n* institut de statistiques du travail aux États-Unis.

blubber ['blʌbər] <> *n* graisse *f* de baleine <> *vi* pej chialer, pleurer comme un veau.

bludgeon ['blʌdʒən] *vt* matraquer.

blue [blu:] <> *adj* - **1**. [colour] bleu(e) - **2**. inf [sad] triste, cafardeux(euse) - **3**. [pornographic] porno (*inv*) <> *n* bleu *m* ; **in ~** en bleu ; **out of the ~** [happen] subitement ; [arrive] à l'improviste.

➤ **blues** *npl* : **the ~s** MUS le blues ; inf [sad feeling] le blues, le cafard.

blue baby *n* enfant *m* bleu.

bluebell ['blu:bel] *n* jacinthe *f* des bois.

blueberry ['blu:bərɪ] *n* myrtille *f*.

bluebird ['blu:bɜ:d] *n* oiseau *m* bleu.

blue-black *adj* bleu noir (*inv*).

blue-blooded [-'blʌdɪd] *adj* de sang noble, qui a du sang bleu.

bluebottle ['blu:,bɒtl] *n* mouche *f* bleue, mouche de la viande.

blue cheese *n* (fromage *m*) bleu *m*.

blue chip *n* ST EX valeur *f* sûre, titre *m* de premier ordre.

➤ **blue-chip** *comp* de premier ordre.

blue-collar *adj* manuel(elle).

blue-eyed boy [-aɪd-] *n* inf chouchou *m*.

blue jeans *npl* Am blue-jean *m*, jean *m*.

blue moon *n* : **once in a ~** tous les trente-six du mois.

blueprint ['blu:prɪnt] *n* photocalque *m* ; fig plan *m*, projet *m*.

bluestocking ['blu:,stɒkɪŋ] *n* pej bas-bleu *m*.

blue tit *n* Br mésange *f* bleue.

bluff [blʌf] <> *adj* franc (franche) <> *n* - **1**. [deception] bluff *m* ; **to call sb's ~** prendre qqn au mot - **2**. [cliff] falaise *f* à pic <> *vt* bluf-

fer, donner le change à <> *vi* faire du bluff, bluffer.

blunder ['blʌndər] <> *n* gaffe *f*, bévue *f* <> *vi* - **1**. [make mistake] faire une gaffe, commettre une bévue - **2**. [move clumsily] avancer d'un pas maladroit.

blundering ['blʌndərɪŋ] *adj* maladroit(e).

blunt [blʌnt] <> *adj* - **1**. [knife] émoussé(e) ; [pencil] épointé(e) ; [object, instrument] contondant(e) - **2**. [person, manner] direct(e), carré(e) <> *vt* lit & fig émousser.

bluntly ['blʌntlɪ] *adv* carrément, brutalement.

bluntness ['blʌntnɪs] *n* brusquerie *f*.

blur [blɜ:r] (*pt* & *pp* **-red** ; *cont* **-ring**) <> *n* forme *f* confuse, tache *f* floue <> *vt* - **1**. [vision] troubler, brouiller - **2**. [distinction] rendre moins net (nette).

blurb [blɜ:b] *n* texte *m* publicitaire.

blurred [blɜ:d] *adj* - **1**. [photograph] flou(e) - **2**. [vision] trouble - **3**. [distinction] peu net (nette), vague.

blurt [blɜ:t] ➤ **blurt out** *vt sep* laisser échapper.

blush [blʌʃ] <> *n* rougeur *f* <> *vi* rougir.

blusher ['blʌʃər] *n* fard *m* à joues, blush *m*.

bluster ['blʌstər] <> *n* (U) propos *mpl* coléreux <> *vi* tempêter.

blustery ['blʌstərɪ] *adj* venteux(euse).

Blvd (*abbr of* **Boulevard**) bd, boul.

BM *n* - **1**. (*abbr of* **Bachelor of Medicine**) [degree] ≃ licence *f* de médecine, ≃ [person] licencié en médecine, -e *f* en médecine - **2**. (*abbr of* **British Museum**) grand musée et bibliothèque célèbre, situés à Londres.

BMA (*abbr of* **British Medical Association**) *n* ordre britannique des médecins.

BMJ (*abbr of* **British Medical Journal**) *n* organe de la BMA.

B-movie *n* film *m* de série B.

BMus ['bi:'mʌz] (*abbr of* **Bachelor of Music**) *n* [degree] ≃ licence *f* de musique, ≃ [person] licencié en musique, -e *f* en musique.

BMX (*abbr of* **bicycle motorcross**) *n* bicross *m*.

BO *abbr of* **body odour**.

boa constrictor ['bəʊəkən'strɪktər] *n* boa *m* constricteur.

boar [bɔ:r] *n* - **1**. [male pig] verrat *m* - **2**. [wild pig] sanglier *m*.

board [bɔ:d] <> *n* - **1**. [plank] planche *f* - **2**. [for notices] panneau *m* d'affichage - **3**. [for games - gen] tableau *m* ; [- for chess] échiquier *m* - **4**. [blackboard] tableau *m* (noir) - **5**. [of company] : **~ (of directors)** conseil *m* d'administration - **6**. [committee] comité *m*, conseil *m* - **7**. Br [at hotel, guesthouse] pension f; ~ **and lodging** pension ; **full** ~ pension complète ; **half** ~ demi-pension f - **8.** : **on** ~ [on ship, plane, bus, train] à bord - **9. phr** : **to take sthg on** ~ [knowledge] assimiler qqch ; [advice] accepter qqch ; **above** ~ régulier(ère), dans les règles ; **across the** ~ [agreement etc] général(e) ; [apply] de façon générale ; **to go by the** ~ aller à vau-l'eau, être abandonné(e) ; **to sweep the** ~ tout rafler OR gagner ⬦ **vt** [ship, aeroplane] monter à bord de ; [train, bus] monter dans.

boarder ['bɔːdə'] n - **1.** [lodger] pensionnaire mf - **2.** [at school] interne mf, pensionnaire mf.

board game n jeu m de société.

boarding card ['bɔːdɪŋ-] n carte f d'embarquement.

boardinghouse ['bɔːdɪŋhaʊs, pl -haʊzɪz] n pension f de famille.

boarding school ['bɔːdɪŋ-] n pensionnat m, internat m.

board meeting n réunion f du conseil d'administration.

Board of Trade n Br : **the** ~ ≃ le ministère m du Commerce.

boardroom ['bɔːdrʊm] n salle f du conseil (d'administration).

boardwalk ['bɔːdwɔːk] n Am trottoir m en planches.

boast [bəʊst] ⬦ n vantardise f, fanfaronnade f ⬦ **vt** [special feature] s'enorgueillir de ⬦ **vi** : **to** ~ **(about)** se vanter (de).

boastful ['bəʊstfʊl] adj vantard(e), fanfaron(onne).

boat [bəʊt] n [large] bateau m ; [small] canot m, embarcation f ; **by** ~ en bateau ; **to rock the** ~ semer le trouble ; **to be in the same** ~ être logé(e) à la même enseigne.

boater ['bəʊtə'] n [hat] canotier m.

boating ['bəʊtɪŋ] n canotage m.

boatswain ['bəʊsn] n maître m d'équipage.

boat train n train qui assure la correspondance avec le bateau.

bob [bɒb] (pt & pp **-bed** ; cont **-bing**) ⬦ n - **1.** [hairstyle] coupe f au carré - **2.** Br inf dated [shilling] shilling m - **3.** = **bobsleigh** ⬦ **vi** [boat, ship] tanguer.

bobbin ['bɒbɪn] n bobine f.

bobble [bɒbl] n pompon m.

bobby ['bɒbɪ] (pl **-ies**) n Br inf agent m de police.

bobby pin n Am pince f à cheveux.

bobby socks, bobby sox npl Am socquettes fpl (de fille).

bobsleigh ['bɒbsleɪ] n bobsleigh m.

bode [bəʊd] vi literary : **to** ~ **ill/well (for)** être de mauvais/bon augure (pour).

bodice ['bɒdɪs] n corsage m.

bodily ['bɒdɪlɪ] ⬦ adj [needs] matériel(elle) ; [pain] physique ⬦ adv [lift, move] à bras-le-corps.

body ['bɒdɪ] (pl **-ies**) n - **1.** [of person] corps m ; **to keep** ~ **and soul together** subsister - **2.** [corpse] corps m, cadavre m ; **over my dead** ~! il faudra d'abord me passer sur le corps! - **3.** [organization] organisme m, organisation f - **4.** [of car] carrosserie f ; [of plane] fuselage m - **5.** (U) [of wine] corps m - **6.** (U) [of hair] volume m - **7.** [garment] body m.

body building n culturisme m.

bodyguard ['bɒdɪgɑːd] n garde m du corps.

body odour n odeur f corporelle.

body piercing n piercing m.

body search n fouille f corporelle.

body shop n - **1.** [garage] atelier m - **2.** Am inf [gym] club m de gym.

body stocking n justaucorps m.

bodywork ['bɒdɪwɜːk] n carrosserie f.

boffin ['bɒfɪn] n Br inf savant m.

bog [bɒg] n - **1.** [marsh] marécage m - **2.** Br v inf [toilet] chiottes fpl.

bogey ['bəʊgɪ] n GOLF bogey m.

bogged down [bɒgd-] adj - **1.** fig [in work] : ~ **(in)** submergé(e) (de) - **2.** [car etc] : ~ **(in)** enlisé(e) (dans).

boggle ['bɒgl] vi : **the mind** ~**s!** ce n'est pas croyable!, on croit rêver!

boggy ['bɒgɪ] adj marécageux(euse).

bogie ['bəʊgɪ] n RAIL bogie m.

Bogotá [ˌbɒgə'tɑː] n Bogotá.

bogus ['bəʊgəs] adj faux (fausse), bidon (inv).

Bohemia [bəʊ'hiːmjə] n Bohême f ; **in** ~ en Bohême.

bohemian [bəʊ'hiːmjən] ⬦ adj [person] bohème ; [lifestyle] de bohème ⬦ n bohème mf.
➤ **Bohemian** ⬦ adj bohémien(enne) ⬦ n Bohémien m, -enne f.

boil [bɔɪl] ⬦ n - **1.** MED furoncle m - **2.** [boiling point] : **to bring sthg to the** ~ porter qqch à ébullition ; **to come to the** ~ venir à ébullition ⬦ **vt** - **1.** [water, food] faire bouillir - **2.** [kettle] mettre sur le feu ⬦ **vi** [water] bouillir.
➤ **boil away** vi [evaporate] s'évaporer.
➤ **boil down to** vt fus fig revenir à, se résumer à.
➤ **boil over** vi - **1.** [liquid] déborder - **2.** fig [feelings] exploser.

boiled ['bɔɪld] adj bouilli(e) ; ~ **egg** œuf m à la coque ; ~ **sweet** Br bonbon m (à sucer).

boiler [ˈbɔɪləʳ] n chaudière f.

boiler suit n Br bleu m de travail.

boiling [ˈbɔɪlɪŋ] adj **- 1.** [liquid] bouillant(e) **- 2.** inf [weather] très chaud(e), torride ; [person] : **I'm ~ (hot)!** je crève de chaleur! **- 3.** [angry] : **~ with rage** en rage, écumant(e) de rage.

boiling point n point m d'ébullition.

boisterous [ˈbɔɪstərəs] adj turbulent(e), remuant(e).

bold [bəʊld] adj **- 1.** [confident] hardi(e), audacieux(euse) **- 2.** [lines, design] hardi(e) ; [colour] vif (vive), éclatant(e) **- 3.** TYPO : **~ type** OR **print** caractères mpl gras.

boldly [ˈbəʊldlɪ] adv hardiment, avec audace.

Bolivia [bəˈlɪvɪə] n Bolivie f ; **in ~** en Bolivie.

Bolivian [bəˈlɪvɪən] <> adj bolivien(enne) <> n Bolivien m, -enne f.

bollard [ˈbɒlɑːd] n [on road] borne f.

bollocks [ˈbɒləks] Br vinf <> npl couilles fpl <> excl quelles conneries!

Bolshevik [ˈbɒlʃɪvɪk] <> adj bolchevique <> n bolchevique mf.

bolster [ˈbəʊlstəʳ] <> n [pillow] traversin m <> vt renforcer, affirmer.

bolster up vt sep soutenir, appuyer.

bolt [bəʊlt] <> n **- 1.** [on door, window] verrou m **- 2.** [type of screw] boulon m <> adv : **~ upright** droit(e) comme un piquet <> vt **- 1.** [fasten together] boulonner **- 2.** [close - door, window] verrouiller, fermer au verrou **- 3.** [food] engouffrer, engloutir <> vi [run] détaler.

bomb [bɒm] <> n bombe f <> vt bombarder.

bombard [bɒmˈbɑːd] vt MIL & fig : **to ~ (with)** bombarder (de).

bombardment [bɒmˈbɑːdmənt] n bombardement m.

bombastic [bɒmˈbæstɪk] adj pompeux(euse).

bomb disposal squad n équipe f de déminage.

bomber [ˈbɒməʳ] n **- 1.** [plane] bombardier m **- 2.** [person] plastiqueur m.

bomber jacket n blouson m d'aviateur.

bombing [ˈbɒmɪŋ] n bombardement m.

bombproof [ˈbɒmpruːf] adj à l'épreuve des bombes.

bombshell [ˈbɒmʃel] n fig bombe f.

bombsite [ˈbɒmsaɪt] n lieu m bombardé.

bona fide [ˌbəʊnəˈfaɪdɪ] adj véritable, authentique ; [offer] sérieux(euse).

bonanza [bəˈnænzə] n aubaine f, filon m.

bond [bɒnd] <> n **- 1.** [between people] lien m **- 2.** [promise] engagement m **- 3.** FIN bon m, titre m <> vt **- 1.** [glue] : **to ~ sthg to sthg** coller qqch sur qqch **- 2.** fig [people] unir <> vi **- 1.** [stick together] : **to ~ (together)** être collé(e) (ensemble) **- 2.** fig [people] établir des liens.

bondage [ˈbɒndɪdʒ] n servitude f, esclavage m.

bonded warehouse [ˈbɒgtˈndɪd-] n entrepôt m de douane.

bone [bəʊn] <> n os m ; [of fish] arête f ; **~ of contention** pomme f de discorde ; **to feel** OR **know sthg in one's ~s** avoir le pressentiment de qqch ; **to make no ~s about sthg** ne pas cacher qqch <> vt [meat] désosser ; [fish] enlever les arêtes de.

bone china n porcelaine f tendre.

bone-dry adj tout à fait sec (sèche).

bone-idle adj paresseux(euse) comme une couleuvre OR un lézard.

boneless [ˈbəʊnlɪs] adj [meat] sans os ; [fish] sans arêtes.

bone marrow n moelle f osseuse.

bonfire [ˈbɒnˌfaɪəʳ] n [for fun] feu m de joie ; [to burn rubbish] feu.

bonfire night n Br le 5 novembre (commémoration de la tentative de Guy Fawkes de faire sauter le Parlement en 1605).

bongo [ˈbɒŋgəʊ] (pl -s OR -es) n : **~ (drum)** bongo m.

Bonn [bɒn] n Bonn.

bonnet [ˈbɒnɪt] n **- 1.** Br [of car] capot m **- 2.** [hat] bonnet m.

bonny [ˈbɒnɪ] (compar -ier ; superl -iest) adj Scot beau (belle), joli(e).

bonus [ˈbəʊnəs] (pl -es [-iːz]) n **- 1.** [extra money] prime f, gratification f **- 2.** fig [added advantage] plus m.

bonus issue n Br FIN émission f d'actions gratuites.

bony [ˈbəʊnɪ] (compar -ier ; superl -iest) adj **- 1.** [person, hand, face] maigre, osseux(euse) **- 2.** [meat] plein(e) d'os ; [fish] plein(e) d'arêtes.

boo [buː] (pl -s) <> excl hou! <> n huée f <> vt & vi huer.

boob [buːb] n inf [mistake] gaffe f, bourde f.

boobs npl Br v inf nichons mpl.

boob tube n **- 1.** Br [garment] bustier m **- 2.** Am inf télé f.

booby prize [ˈbuːbɪ-] n prix m de consolation.

booby trap [ˈbuːbɪ-] n **- 1.** [bomb] objet m piégé **- 2.** [practical joke] farce f.

booby-trap *vt* piéger.

boogie ['buːgɪ] *inf* <> *n* : **to have a ~** danser <> *vi* danser.

book [bʊk] <> *n* - **1.** [for reading] livre *m* ; **to do sthg by the ~** faire qqch selon les règles ; **to throw the ~ at sb** passer un savon à qqn - **2.** [of stamps, tickets, cheques] carnet *m* ; [of matches] pochette *f* <> *vt* - **1.** [reserve - gen] réserver ; [- performer] engager ; **to be fully ~ed** être complet(ète) - **2.** *inf* [subj : police] coller un PV à - **3.** Br FTBL prendre le nom de <> *vi* réserver.

books *npl* COMM livres *mpl* de comptes ; **to do the ~s** tenir les livres ; **to be in sb's bad ~s** être mal vu(e) de qqn ; **to be in sb's good ~s** être dans les petits papiers de qqn.

book in <> *vt sep* réserver une chambre à <> *vi* [at hotel] prendre une chambre.

book up *vt sep* réserver, retenir.

bookable ['bʊkəbl] *adj* Br [seats, tickets] qu'on peut réserver OR louer.

bookbinding ['bʊk,baɪndɪŋ] *n* reliure *f*.

bookcase ['bʊkkeɪs] *n* bibliothèque *f*.

book club *n* club *m* de livres.

bookends ['bʊkendz] *npl* serre-livres *m inv*, presse-livres *m inv*.

Booker Prize ['bʊkə-] *n* : **the ~** prix littéraire britannique.

BOOKER PRIZE

Le « Booker Prize » est le prix littéraire britannique le plus connu ; créé en 1969, il est accordé chaque année au meilleur roman d'expression anglaise découvert par un éditeur britannique.

bookie ['bʊkɪ] *n inf* bookmaker *m*, book *m*.

booking ['bʊkɪŋ] *n* - **1.** [reservation] réservation *f* - **2.** Br FTBL : **to get a ~** recevoir un carton jaune.

booking clerk *n* préposé *m*, -e *f* à la location OR la vente des billets.

booking office *n* bureau *m* de réservation OR location.

bookish ['bʊkɪʃ] *adj* [person] studieux(euse), qui aime la lecture.

bookkeeper ['bʊk,kiːpər] *n* comptable *mf*.

bookkeeping ['bʊk,kiːpɪŋ] *n* comptabilité *f*.

booklet ['bʊklɪt] *n* brochure *f*.

bookmaker ['bʊk,meɪkər] *n* bookmaker *m*.

bookmark ['bʊkmɑːk] *n* signet *m*.

bookseller ['bʊk,selər] *n* libraire *mf*.

bookshelf ['bʊkʃelf] (*pl* **-shelves** [-ʃelvz]) *n* rayon *m* OR étagère *f* à livres.

bookshop Br ['bʊkʃɒp], **bookstore** Am ['bʊkstɔːr] *n* librairie *f*.

bookstall ['bʊkstɔːl] *n* Br kiosque *m* (à journaux).

bookstore ['bʊkstɔːr] = **bookshop**.

book token *n* chèque-livre *m*.

bookworm ['bʊkwɜːm] *n* rat *m* de bibliothèque.

boom [buːm] <> *n* - **1.** [loud noise] grondement *m* - **2.** [in business, trade] boom *m* - **3.** NAUT bôme *f* - **4.** [for TV camera, microphone] girafe *f*, perche *f* <> *vi* - **1.** [make noise] gronder - **2.** [business, trade] être en plein essor OR en hausse.

boomerang ['buːməræŋ] *n* boomerang *m*.

boon [buːn] *n* avantage *m*, bénédiction *f*.

boor [bʊər] *n* butor *m*, rustre *m*.

boorish ['bʊərɪʃ] *adj* rustre, grossier(ère).

boost [buːst] <> *n* [to production, sales] augmentation *f* ; [to economy] croissance *f* ; **to give a ~ to** stimuler <> *vt* - **1.** [production, sales] accroître, stimuler - **2.** [popularity] accroître, renforcer ; **to ~ sb's spirits** OR **morale** remonter le moral à qqn.

booster ['buːstər] *n* MED rappel *m*.

booster seat *n* AUT (siège *m*) rehausseur *m*.

boot [buːt] <> *n* - **1.** [for walking, sport] chaussure *f* - **2.** [fashion item] botte *f* - **3.** Br [of car] coffre *m* <> *vt* inf flanquer des coups de pied à.

to boot *adv* par-dessus le marché, en plus.

boot out *vt sep* inf flanquer à la porte.

booth [buːð] *n* - **1.** [at fair] baraque *f* foraine - **2.** [telephone booth] cabine *f* - **3.** [voting booth] isoloir *m*.

bootleg ['buːtleg] *adj* inf [recording] pirate ; [whisky etc] de contrebande.

bootlegger ['buːt,legər] *n* inf contrebandier *m* d'alcool.

booty ['buːtɪ] *n* butin *m*.

booze [buːz] *inf* <> *n* (U) alcool *m*, boisson *f* alcoolisée <> *vi* picoler, lever le coude.

boozer ['buːzər] *n* inf - **1.** [person] picoleur *m*, -euse *f* - **2.** Br [pub] pub *m*.

bop [bɒp] (*pt & pp* **-ped** ; *cont* **-ping**) *inf* <> *n* - **1.** [hit] coup *m* - **2.** [disco, dance] boum *f* <> *vt* [hit] taper, donner un coup à <> *vi* [dance] danser.

border ['bɔːdər] <> *n* - **1.** [between countries] frontière *f* - **2.** [edge] bord *m* - **3.** [in garden] bordure *f* <> *vt* - **1.** [country] toucher à, être limitrophe de - **2.** [edge] border.

border on *vt fus* friser, être voisin(e) de.

borderline ['bɔːdəlaɪn] <> *adj* : **~ case** cas *m*

limite ⬦ *n* fig limite *f*, ligne *f* de démarcation.

bore [bɔːʳ] ⬦ *pt* ⊳ **bear** ⬦ *n* - **1.** [person] raseur *m*, -euse *f* ; [situation, event] corvée *f* - **2.** [of gun] calibre *m* ⬦ *vt* - **1.** [not interest] ennuyer, raser ; **to ~ sb stiff** OR **to tears** OR **to death** ennuyer qqn à mourir - **2.** [drill] forer, percer.

bored [bɔːd] *adj* [person] qui s'ennuie ; [look] d'ennui ; **to be ~ with** en avoir assez de ; **I'm ~ with this book** ce livre m'ennuie.

boredom [ˈbɔːdəm] *n* (U) ennui *m*.

boring [ˈbɔːrɪŋ] *adj* ennuyeux(euse), assommant(e).

born [bɔːn] *adj* né(e) ; **to be ~** naître ; **I was ~ in 1965** je suis né(e) en 1965 ; **when were you ~?** quelle est ta date de naissance? ; **~ and bred** né(e) et élevé(e).

born-again Christian *adj* [Christian] évangéliste *mf*.

borne [bɔːn] *pp* ⊳ **bear**.

Borneo [ˈbɔːnɪəʊ] *n* Bornéo *m* ; **in ~** à Bornéo.

borough [ˈbʌrə] *n* municipalité *f*.

borrow [ˈbɒrəʊ] *vt* emprunter ; **to ~ sthg (from sb)** emprunter qqch (à qqn).

borrower [ˈbɒrəʊəʳ] *n* emprunteur *m*, -euse *f*.

borrowing [ˈbɒrəʊɪŋ] *n* (U) emprunt *m*.

borstal [ˈbɔːstl] *n* Br maison *f* de redressement.

Bosnia [ˈbɒznɪə] *n* Bosnie *f* ; **in ~** en Bosnie.

Bosnia-Herzegovina [-ˌhɜːtsəɡəˈviːnə] *n* Bosnie-Herzégovine *f*.

Bosnian [ˈbɒznɪən] ⬦ *adj* bosniaque ⬦ *n* Bosniaque *mf*.

bosom [ˈbʊzəm] *n* poitrine *f*, seins *mpl* ; fig sein *m* ; **~ friend** ami *m* intime.

Bosporus [ˈbɒspərəs], **Bosphorus** [ˈbɒsfərəs] *n* : **the ~** le Bosphore.

boss [bɒs] ⬦ *n* patron *m*, -onne *f*, chef *m* ; **to be one's own ~** travailler à son compte ⬦ *vt* pej donner des ordres à, régenter.
⬦ **boss about, boss around** *vt sep* pej donner des ordres à, régenter.

bossy [ˈbɒsɪ] (*compar* **-ier** ; *superl* **-iest**) *adj* autoritaire.

bosun [ˈbəʊsn] = **boatswain**.

botanic(al) [bəˈtænɪk(l)] *adj* botanique.

botanical garden *n* jardin *m* botanique.

botanist [ˈbɒtənɪst] *n* botaniste *mf*.

botany [ˈbɒtənɪ] *n* botanique *f*.

botch [bɒtʃ] ⬦ **botch up** *vt sep* inf bousiller, saboter.

both [bəʊθ] ⬦ *adj* les deux ⬦ *pron* : **~ (of them)** (tous) les deux ((toutes) les deux) ;

~ of us are coming on vient tous les deux ⬦ *adv* : **she is ~ intelligent and amusing** elle est à la fois intelligente et drôle.

bother [ˈbɒðəʳ] ⬦ *vt* - **1.** [worry] ennuyer, inquiéter ; **to ~ o.s. (about)** se tracasser (au sujet de) ; **I can't be ~ed to do it** je n'ai vraiment pas envie de le faire - **2.** [pester, annoy] embêter ; **I'm sorry to ~ you** excusez-moi de vous déranger ⬦ *vi* : **to ~ about sthg** s'inquiéter de qqch ; **don't ~ (to do it)** ce n'est pas la peine (de le faire) ; **don't ~ getting up** ne vous donnez pas la peine de vous lever ⬦ *n* (U) embêtement *m* ; **I hope I'm not putting you to any ~** j'espère que je ne vous cause pas trop de dérangement ; **it's no ~ at all** cela ne me dérange OR m'ennuie pas du tout.

bothered [ˈbɒðəd] *adj* inquiet(ète).

Botswana [bɒˈtswɑːnə] *n* Botswana *m* ; **in ~** au Botswana.

bottle [ˈbɒtl] ⬦ *n* - **1.** [gen] bouteille *f* ; [for medicine, perfume] flacon *m* ; [for baby] biberon *m* - **2.** (U) Br inf [courage] cran *m*, culot *m* ⬦ *vt* [wine etc] mettre en bouteilles ; [fruit] mettre en bocal.
⬦ **bottle out** *vi* Br inf se dégonfler.
⬦ **bottle up** *vt sep* [feelings] refouler, contenir.

bottle bank *n* container *m* pour verre usagé.

bottled [ˈbɒtld] *adj* en bouteille.

bottle-feed *vt* nourrir au biberon.

bottleneck [ˈbɒtlnek] *n* - **1.** [in traffic] bouchon *m*, embouteillage *m* - **2.** [in production] goulet *m* d'étranglement.

bottle-opener *n* ouvre-bouteilles *m inv*, décapsuleur *m*.

bottle party *n* soirée *f* (*où chacun apporte quelque chose à boire*).

bottom [ˈbɒtəm] ⬦ *adj* - **1.** [lowest] du bas - **2.** [in class] dernier(ère) ⬦ *n* - **1.** [of bottle, lake, garden] fond *m* ; [of page, ladder, street] bas *m* ; [of hill] pied *m* - **2.** [of scale] bas *m* ; [of class] dernier *m*, -ère *f* - **3.** [buttocks] derrière *m* - **4.** [cause] : **what's at the ~ of it?** qu'est-ce qui en est la cause? ; **to get to the ~ of sthg** aller au fond de qqch, découvrir la cause de qqch.
⬦ **bottom out** *vi* atteindre son niveau le plus bas.

bottomless [ˈbɒtəmlɪs] *adj* - **1.** [very deep] sans fond - **2.** [endless] inépuisable.

bottom line *n* fig : **the ~** l'essentiel *m*.

botulism [ˈbɒtjʊlɪzm] *n* botulisme *m*

bough [baʊ] *n* branche *f*.

bought [bɔːt] pt & pp ⊳ **buy**.
boulder ['bəʊldəʳ] n rocher m.
boulevard ['buːləvɑːd] n boulevard m.
bounce [baʊns] ◇ vi **- 1.** [ball] rebondir ; [person] sauter **- 2.** [light] être réfléchi(e) ; [sound] être renvoyé(e) **- 3.** inf [chèque] être sans provision ◇ vt [ball] faire rebondir ◇ n rebond m.
➤ **bounce back** vi fig se remettre vite.
bouncer ['baʊnsəʳ] n inf videur m.
bouncy ['baʊnsɪ] (compar -ier ; superl -iest) adj **- 1.** [lively] dynamique **- 2.** [ball] qui rebondit , [bed] élastique, souple.
bound [baʊnd] ◇ pt & pp ⊳ **bind** ◇ adj **- 1.** [certain] : **he's ~ to win** il va sûrement gagner ; **she's ~ to see it** elle ne peut pas manquer de le voir **- 2.** [obliged] : **to be ~ to do sthg** être obligé(e) OR tenu(e) de faire qqch ; **I'm ~ to say/admit** je dois dire/reconnaître **- 3.** [for place] : **to be ~ for** [subj : person] être en route pour ; [subj : plane, train] être à destination de ◇ n [leap] bond m, saut m ◇ vt : **to be ~ed by** [subj : field] être limité(e) OR délimité(e) par ; [subj : country] être limitrophe de ◇ vi [leap] bondir, sauter.
➤ **bounds** npl limites fpl ; **out of ~s** interdit, défendu.
boundary ['baʊndərɪ] (pl -ies) n [gen] frontière f ; [of property] limite f, borne f.
boundless ['baʊndlɪs] adj illimité(e), sans bornes.
bountiful ['baʊntɪfʊl] adj literary [ample] abondant(e).
bounty ['baʊntɪ] n literary [generosity] générosité f, libéralité f.
bouquet [buˈkeɪ] n bouquet m.
bourbon ['bɜːbən] n bourbon m.
bourgeois ['bɔːʒwɑː] adj pej bourgeois(e).
bout [baʊt] n **- 1.** [of illness] accès m ; **a ~ of flu** une grippe **- 2.** [session] période f ; **a ~ of drinking** une beuverie **- 3.** [boxing match] combat m.
boutique [buːˈtiːk] n boutique f.
bow¹ [baʊ] ◇ n **- 1.** [in greeting] révérence f **- 2.** [of ship] proue f, avant m ◇ vt [head] baisser, incliner ◇ vi **- 1.** [make a bow] saluer **- 2.** [defer] : **to ~ to** s'incliner devant.
➤ **bow down** vi s'incliner.
➤ **bow out** vi tirer sa révérence.
bow² [bəʊ] n **- 1.** [weapon] arc m **- 2.** MUS archet m **- 3.** [knot] nœud m.
bowels ['baʊəlz] npl intestins mpl ; fig entrailles fpl.
bowl [bəʊl] ◇ n **- 1.** [container - gen] jatte f, saladier m ; [- small] bol m ; [- for washing up] cuvet-

te f ; **sugar ~** sucrier m **- 2.** [of toilet, sink] cuvette f ; [of pipe] fourneau m ◇ vt CRICKET lancer ◇ vi CRICKET lancer la balle.
➤ **bowls** n (U) boules fpl (sur herbe).
➤ **bowl over** vt sep lit & fig renverser.
bow-legged [ˌbəʊˈlegɪd] adj aux jambes arquées.
bowler ['bəʊləʳ] n **- 1.** CRICKET lanceur m **- 2.** : **~ (hat)** chapeau m melon.
bowling ['bəʊlɪŋ] n (U) bowling m.
bowling alley n [building] bowling m ; [alley] piste f de bowling.
bowling green n terrain m de boules (sur herbe).
bow tie [bəʊ-] n nœud m papillon.
bow window [bəʊ-] n fenêtre f en saillie.
box [bɒks] ◇ n **- 1.** [gen] boîte f **- 2.** THEATRE loge f **- 3.** Br inf [television] : **the ~** la télé ◇ vi boxer, faire de la boxe.
➤ **box in** vt sep **- 1.** [trap] coincer **- 2.** [enclose - pipes etc] encastrer.
boxed [bɒkst] adj en boîte, en coffret.
boxer ['bɒksəʳ] n **- 1.** [fighter] boxeur m **- 2.** [dog] boxer m.
boxer shorts npl boxer-short m.
boxing ['bɒksɪŋ] n boxe f.
Boxing Day n jour des étrennes en Grande-Bretagne (le 26 décembre).
boxing glove n gant m de boxe.
boxing ring n ring m.
box junction n Br carrefour m à l'accès réglementé.
box number n numéro m d'annonce, référence f.
box office n bureau m de location.
boxroom ['bɒksrʊm] n Br débarras m.
boy [bɔɪ] ◇ n **- 1.** [male child] garçon m **- 2.** inf [male friend] : **I'm going out with the ~s tonight** je sors avec mes potes ce soir ◇ excl inf : **(oh) ~!** ben, mon vieux!, ben, dis-donc!
boycott ['bɔɪkɒt] ◇ n boycott m, boycottage m ◇ vt boycotter.
boyfriend ['bɔɪfrend] n copain m, petit ami m.
boyish ['bɔɪɪʃ] adj **- 1.** [appearance - of man] gamin(e) ; [- of woman] de garçon **- 2.** [behaviour] garçonnier(ère).
boy scout n scout m, éclaireur m.
Bp (abbr of Bishop) Mgr.
Br (abbr of brother) RELIG F.
BR (abbr of British Rail) n ≃ SNCF f.
bra [brɑː] n soutien-gorge m.
brace [breɪs] ◇ n **- 1.** [on teeth] appareil m

(dentaire) - **2.** [on leg] appareil *m* orthopédique - **3.** [pair] paire *f*, couple *m* ⬦ *vt* - **1.** [steady] soutenir, consolider ; **to ~ o.s.** s'accrocher, se cramponner - **2.** fig [prepare] : **to ~ o.s. (for sthg)** se préparer (à qqch).

➥ **braces** *npl* Br bretelles *fpl*.

bracelet ['breɪslɪt] *n* bracelet *m*.

bracing ['breɪsɪŋ] *adj* vivifiant(e).

bracken ['brækn] *n* fougère *f*.

bracket ['brækɪt] ⬦ *n* - **1.** [support] support *m* - **2.** [parenthesis - round] parenthèse *f* ; [- square] crochet *m ;* **in ~s** entre parenthèses/crochets - **3.** [group] : **age/income ~** tranche *f* d'âge/de revenus ⬦ *vt* - **1.** [enclose in brackets] mettre entre parenthèses/crochets - **2.** [group] : **to ~ sb/sthg (together) with** mettre qqn/qqch dans le même groupe que.

brackish ['brækɪʃ] *adj* saumâtre.

brag [bræg] (*pt* & *pp* **-ged** ; *cont* **-ging**) *vi* se vanter.

braid [breɪd] ⬦ *n* - **1.** [on uniform] galon *m* - **2.** [of hair] tresse *f*, natte *f* ⬦ *vt* [hair] tresser, natter.

braille [breɪl] *n* braille *m*.

brain [breɪn] *n* cerveau *m ;* **he's got money on the ~** il ne pense qu'à l'argent.

➥ **brains** *npl* [intelligence] intelligence *f ;* **to pick sb's ~s** faire appel aux lumières de qqn ; **to rack** Br OR **cudgel** Am **one's ~s** se creuser la tête OR la cervelle.

brainchild ['breɪntʃaɪld] *n* inf idée *f* personnelle, invention *f* personnelle.

brain death *n* mort *f* cérébrale, coma *m* dépassé.

brain drain *n* fuite *f* OR exode *m* des cerveaux.

brainless ['breɪnlɪs] *adj* stupide.

brainstorm ['breɪnstɔːm] *n* - **1.** Br [mental aberration] moment *m* d'aberration - **2.** Am [brilliant idea] idée *f* géniale OR de génie.

brainstorming ['breɪnˌstɔːmɪŋ] *n* brainstorming *m*.

brainteaser ['breɪnˌtiːzəʳ] *n* colle *f*.

brainwash ['breɪnwɒʃ] *vt* faire un lavage de cerveau à.

brainwave ['breɪnweɪv] *n* idée *f* géniale OR de génie.

brainy ['breɪnɪ] (*compar* **-ier** ; *superl* **-iest**) *adj* inf intelligent(e).

braise [breɪz] *vt* braiser.

brake [breɪk] ⬦ *n* lit & fig frein *m* ⬦ *vi* freiner.

brake horsepower *n* puissance *f* de freinage.

brake light *n* stop *m*, feu *m* arrière.

brake lining *n* garniture *f* de frein.

brake pedal *n* (pédale *f* de) frein *m*.

brake shoe *n* sabot *m* OR patin *m* de frein.

bramble ['bræmbl] *n* [bush] ronce *f* ; [fruit] mûre *f*.

bran [bræn] *n* son *m*.

branch [brɑːntʃ] ⬦ *n* - **1.** [of tree, subject] branche *f* - **2.** [of railway] bifurcation *f*, embranchement *m* - **3.** [of company] filiale *f*, succursale *f ;* [of bank] agence *f* ⬦ *vi* bifurquer.

➥ **branch off** *vi* bifurquer.

➥ **branch out** *vi* [person, company] étendre ses activités, se diversifier.

branch line *n* RAIL ligne *f* secondaire.

brand [brænd] ⬦ *n* - **1.** COMM marque *f* - **2.** fig [type, style] type *m*, genre *m* ⬦ *vt* - **1.** [cattle] marquer au fer rouge - **2.** fig [classify] : **to ~ sb (as) sthg** étiqueter qqn comme qqch, coller à qqn l'étiquette de qqch.

brandish ['brændɪʃ] *vt* brandir.

brand leader *n* marque *f* dominante.

brand name *n* marque *f*.

brand-new *adj* flambant neuf (flambant neuve), tout neuf (toute neuve).

brandy ['brændɪ] (*pl* **-ies**) *n* cognac *m*.

brash [bræʃ] *adj* effronté(e).

Brasilia [brə'zɪljə] *n* Brasilia.

brass [brɑːs] *n* - **1.** [metal] laiton *m*, cuivre *m* jaune - **2.** MUS : **the ~** les cuivres *mpl*.

brass band *n* fanfare *f*.

brasserie ['bræsərɪ] *n* brasserie *f*.

brassiere [Br 'bræsɪəʳ, Am brə'zɪr] *n* soutien-gorge *m*.

brass knuckles *npl* Am coup-de-poing *m* américain.

brass tacks *npl* inf : **to get down to ~** en venir aux choses sérieuses.

brat [bræt] *n* inf pej sale gosse *m*.

bravado [brə'vɑːdəʊ] *n* bravade *f*.

brave [breɪv] ⬦ *adj* courageux(euse), brave ⬦ *n* guerrier *m* indien, brave *m* ⬦ *vt* braver, affronter.

bravely ['breɪvlɪ] *adv* courageusement, vaillamment.

bravery ['breɪvərɪ] *n* courage *m*, bravoure *f*.

bravo [ˌbrɑː'vəʊ] *excl* bravo!

brawl [brɔːl] *n* bagarre *f*, rixe *f*.

brawn [brɔːn] *n* (U) - **1.** [muscle] muscle *m* - **2.** Br [meat] fromage *m* de tête.

brawny ['brɔ:nɪ] (*compar* -**ier** ; *superl* -**iest**) *adj* musclé(e).

bray [breɪ] *vi* [donkey] braire.

brazen ['breɪznl *adj* [person] effronté(e), impudent(e) ; [lie] éhonté(e).

➤ **brazen out** *vt sep :* **to ~ it out** crâner.

brazier ['breɪzjəʳ] *n* brasero *m*.

Brazil [brə'zɪl] *n* Brésil *m* ; **in ~** au Brésil.

Brazilian [brə'zɪljən] ◇ *adj* brésilien(enne) ◇ *n* Brésilien *m*, -enne *f*.

brazil nut *n* noix *f* du Brésil.

breach [bri:tʃ] ◇ *n* - **1**. [of law, agreement] infraction *f*, violation *f*; [of promise] rupture *f*; **to be in ~ of sthg** enfreindre OR violer qqch ; **~ of confidence** abus *m* de confiance ; **~ of contract** rupture *f* de contrat - **2**. [opening, gap] trou *m*, brèche *f*; **to step into the ~** remplacer quelqu'un au pied levé - **3**. [in friendship, marriage] brouille *f* ◇ *vt* - **1**. [agreement, contract] rompre - **2**. [make hole in] faire une brèche dans.

breach of the peace *n* atteinte *f* à l'ordre public.

bread [bred] *n* pain *m* ; **~ and butter** tartine *f* beurrée, pain beurré ; *fig* gagne-pain *m*.

bread bin Br, **bread box** Am *n* boîte *f* à pain.

breadboard ['bredbɔ:d] *n* planche *f* à pain.

bread box Am = **bread bin**.

breadcrumbs ['bredkrʌmz] *npl* chapelure *f*.

breaded ['bredɪd] *adj* pané(e).

breadline ['bredlaɪn] *n :* **to be on the ~** être sans ressources OR sans le sou.

breadth [bretθ] *n* - **1**. [width] largeur *f* - **2**. *fig* [scope] ampleur *f*, étendue *f*.

breadwinner ['bred,wɪnəʳ] *n* soutien *m* de famille.

break [breɪk] (*pt* broke ; *pp* broken) ◇ *n* - **1**. [gap] : **~ (in)** trouée *f* (dans) - **2**. [fracture] fracture *f* - **3**. [change] : **a ~ with tradition** une rupture d'avec les traditions - **4**. [pause - open] pause *f*; [- at school] récréation *f*; **to take a ~** [short] faire une pause ; [longer] prendre des jours de congé ; **without a ~** sans interruption ; **to have a ~ from doing sthg** arrêter de faire qqch - **5**. inf [luck] : **(lucky)** ~ chance *f*, veine *f* - **6**. literary [of day] : **at ~ of day** au point du jour, à l'aube - **7**. COMPUT [key] break *m* ◇ *vt* - **1**. [gen] casser, briser ; **to ~ one's arm/leg** se casser le bras/la jambe ; **the river broke its banks** la rivière est sortie de son lit ; **to ~ a habit** se défaire d'une (mauvaise) habitude ; **to ~ sb's hold** se dégager de l'étreinte de qqn ; **to ~ a record** battre un record ; **to ~ a strike** briser une grève - **2**. [inter-

rupt - journey] interrompre ; [- contact, silence] rompre - **3**. [not keep - law, rule] enfreindre, violer ; [- promise] manquer à - **4**. [tell] : **to ~ the news (of sthg to sb)** annoncer la nouvelle (de qqch à qqn) - **5**. TENNIS : **to ~ sb's serve** prendre le service de qqn ◇ *vi* - **1**. [gen] se casser, se briser ; **to ~ loose** OR **free** se dégager, s'échapper - **2**. [pause] s'arrêter, faire une pause - **3**. [day] poindre, se lever - **4**. [weather] se gâter - **5**. [wave] se briser - **6**. [voice - with emotion] se briser ; [- at puberty] muer - **7**. [news] se répandre, éclater - **8**. phr : **to ~ even** rentrer dans ses frais.

➤ **break away** *vi* - **1**. [escape] s'échapper - **2**. [end relationship] : **to ~ away (from sb)** abandonner (qqn), quitter (qqn).

➤ **break down** ◇ *vt sep* - **1**. [destroy - barrier] démolir ; [- door] enfoncer - **2**. [analyse] analyser - **3**. [substance] décomposer ◇ *vi* - **1**. [car, machine] tomber en panne ; [resistance] céder ; [negotiations] échouer - **2**. [emotionally] fondre en larmes, éclater en sanglots - **3**. [decompose] se décomposer.

➤ **break in** ◇ *vi* - **1**. [burglar] entrer par effraction - **2**. [interrupt] : **to ~ in (on sb/sthg)** interrompre (qqn/qqch) ◇ *vt sep* - **1**. [horse] dresser ; [person] rompre, accoutumer - **2**. [shoes] faire.

➤ **break into** *vt fus* - **1**. [subj : burglar] entrer par effraction dans - **2**. [begin] : **to ~ into song/applause** se mettre à chanter/applaudir - **3**. [become involved in] : **to ~ into a market** pénétrer un marché ; **to ~ into the music business** percer dans la chanson.

➤ **break off** ◇ *vt sep* - **1**. [detach] détacher - **2**. [talks, relationship] rompre ; [holiday] interrompre ◇ *vi* - **1**. [become detached] se casser, se détacher - **2**. [stop talking] s'interrompre, se taire - **3**. [stop working] faire une pause, s'arrêter de travailler.

➤ **break out** *vi* - **1**. [begin - fire] se déclarer ; [- fighting] éclater - **2**. [skin, person] : **to ~ out in spots** se couvrir de boutons - **3**. [escape] : **to ~ out (of)** s'échapper (de), s'évader (de).

➤ **break through** ◇ *vt fus* [subj : sun] percer ; **she broke through the crowd** elle se fraya un chemin à travers la foule ◇ *vi* [sun] percer.

➤ **break up** ◇ *vt sep* - **1**. [into smaller pieces] mettre en morceaux - **2**. [end - marriage, relationship] détruire ; [- fight, party] mettre fin à ◇ *vi* - **1**. [into smaller pieces - gen] se casser en morceaux ; [- ship] se briser - **2**. [end - marriage, relationship] se briser ; [- talks, party] prendre fin ; [- school] finir, fermer ; **to ~ up (with sb)** rompre (avec qqn) - **3**. [crowd] se disperser.

➤ **break with** *vt fus* rompre avec.

breakable ['breɪkəbl] *adj* cassable, fragile.

breakage ['breɪkɪdʒ] *n* bris *m*.

breakaway ['breɪkəweɪ] *adj* [faction etc] dissident(e).

break dancing *n* smurf *m*.

breakdown ['breɪkdaʊn] *n* - **1.** [of vehicle, machine] panne *f;* [of negotiations] échec *m;* [in communications] rupture *f;* **nervous ~** dépression *f* nerveuse - **2.** [analysis] détail *m*.

breaker ['breɪkəʳ] *n* [wave] brisant *m*.

breakeven [ˌbreɪk'iːvn] *n* seuil *m* de rentabilité.

breakfast ['brekfəst] ◇ *n* petit déjeuner *m* ◇ *vi* : **to ~ (on)** déjeuner (de).

breakfast cereal *n* céréales *fpl*.

breakfast television *n* **Br** télévision *f* du matin.

break-in *n* cambriolage *m*.

breaking ['breɪkɪŋ] *n :* **~ and entering JUR** entrée *f* par effraction.

breaking point *n* limite *f*.

breakneck ['breɪknek] *adj :* **at ~ speed** à fond de train.

breakthrough ['breɪkθruː] *n* percée *f*.

breakup ['breɪkʌp] *n* [of marriage, relationship] rupture *f*.

breakup value *n* **COMM** valeur *f* liquidative.

bream [briːm] (*pl inv* OR **-s**) *n* brème *f*.

breast [brest] *n* - **1.** [of woman] sein *m;* [of man] poitrine *f* - **2.** [meat of bird] blanc *m* - **3.** **phr : to make a clean ~ of it** tout avouer.

breast-feed *vt* & *vi* allaiter.

breast pocket *n* poche *f* de poitrine.

breaststroke ['breststrəʊk] *n* brasse *f*.

breath [breθ] *n* souffle *m*, haleine *f;* **to take a deep ~** inspirer profondément ; **to go out for a ~ of (fresh) air** sortir prendre l'air ; **she/ it was a ~ of fresh air** elle représentait/ c'était une véritable bouffée d'oxygène ; **out of ~** hors d'haleine, à bout de souffle ; **to get one's ~ back** reprendre haleine OR son souffle ; **to hold one's ~** lit & fig retenir son souffle ; **it took my ~ away** cela m'a coupé le souffle.

breathable ['briːðəbl] *adj* respirable.

breathalyse Br, -yze Am ['breθəlaɪz] *vt* ≃ faire subir l'Alcootest® à.

Breathalyser® Br, -yzer® Am *n* Alcootest® *m*.

breathe [briːð] ◇ *vi* respirer ; **I can ~ more easily now** fig je respire maintenant ◇ *vt* - **1.** [inhale] respirer - **2.** [exhale - smell] souffler des relents de.

◆ **breathe in** ◇ *vi* inspirer ◇ *vt sep* aspirer.

◆ **breathe out** *vi* expirer.

breather ['briːðəʳ] *n* inf moment *m* de repos OR répit.

breathing ['briːðɪŋ] *n* respiration *f*, souffle *m*.

breathing space *n* fig répit *m*.

breathless ['breθlɪs] *adj* - **1.** [out of breath] hors d'haleine, essoufflé(e) - **2.** [with excitement] fébrile, fiévreux(euse).

breathtaking ['breθˌteɪkɪŋ] *adj* à vous couper le souffle.

breath test *n* Alcootest® *m*.

breed [briːd] (*pt* & *pp* bred [bred]) ◇ *n* lit & fig race *f*, espèce *f* ◇ *vt* - **1.** [animals, plants] élever - **2.** fig [suspicion, contempt] faire naître, engendrer ◇ *vi* se reproduire.

breeder ['briːdəʳ] *n* éleveur *m*, -euse *f*.

breeder reactor *n* surgénérateur *m*.

breeding ['briːdɪŋ] *n* (U) - **1.** [of animals, plants] élevage *m* - **2.** [manners] bonnes manières *fpl*, savoir-vivre *m*.

breeding-ground *n* fig terrain *m* propice.

breeze [briːz] ◇ *n* brise *f* ◇ *vi :* **to ~ in/out** [quickly] entrer/sortir en coup de vent ; [casually] entrer/sortir d'un air désinvolte.

breezeblock ['briːzblɒk] *n* **Br** parpaing *m*.

breezy ['briːzɪ] (*compar* **-ier** *; superl* **-iest**) *adj* - **1.** [windy] venteux(euse) - **2.** [cheerful] jovial(e), enjoué(e).

Breton ['bretn] ◇ *adj* breton(onne) ◇ *n* - **1.** [person] Breton *m*, -onne *f* - **2.** [language] breton *m*.

brevity ['brevɪtɪ] *n* brièveté *f*.

brew [bruː] ◇ *vt* [beer] brasser ; [tea] faire infuser ; [coffee] préparer, faire ◇ *vi* - **1.** [tea] infuser ; [coffee] se faire - **2.** fig [trouble, storm] se préparer, couver.

brewer ['bruːəʳ] *n* brasseur *m*.

brewery ['bruəri] (*pl* **-ies**) *n* brasserie *f*.

briar ['braɪəʳ] *n* églantier *m*.

bribe [braɪb] ◇ *n* pot-de-vin *m* ◇ *vt :* **to ~ sb (to do sthg)** soudoyer qqn (pour qu'il fasse qqch).

bribery ['braɪbərɪ] *n* corruption *f*.

bric-a-brac ['brɪkəbræk] *n* bric-à-brac *m*.

brick [brɪk] *n* brique *f*.

◆ **brick up** *vt sep* murer.

bricklayer ['brɪkˌleɪəʳ] *n* maçon *m*.

brickwork ['brɪkwɜːk] *n* briquetage *m*.

bridal ['braɪdl] *adj* [dress] de mariée ; [suite etc] nuptial(e).

bride [braɪd] n mariée f.

bridegroom ['braɪdgrʊm] n marié m.

bridesmaid ['braɪdzmeɪd] n demoiselle f d'honneur.

bridge [brɪdʒ] ⬦ n - **1.** [gen] pont m ; **I'll cross that ~ when I come to it** chaque chose en son temps - **2.** [on ship] passerelle f - **3.** [of nose] arête f - **4.** [card game, for teeth] bridge m ⬦ vt fig [gap] réduire.

bridging loan ['brɪdʒɪŋ-] n Br crédit-relais m.

bridle ['braɪdl] ⬦ n bride f ⬦ vt mettre la bride à, brider ⬦ vi : **to ~ (at sthg)** se rebiffer (contre qqch).

bridle path n piste f cavalière.

brief [briːf] ⬦ adj - **1.** [short] bref (brève), court(e) ; **in ~** en bref, en deux mots - **2.** [revealing] très court(e) ⬦ n - **1.** JUR affaire f, dossier m - **2.** Br [instructions] instructions fpl ⬦ vt : **to ~ sb (on)** [bring up to date] mettre qqn au courant (de) ; [instruct] briefer qqn (sur).

⬥ **briefs** npl slip m.

briefcase ['briːfkeɪs] n serviette f.

briefing ['briːfɪŋ] n instructions fpl, briefing m.

briefly ['briːflɪ] adv - **1.** [for a short time] un instant - **2.** [concisely] brièvement.

Brig. abbr of **brigadier**.

brigade [brɪ'geɪd] n brigade f ; **fire ~** pompiers mpl.

brigadier [ˌbrɪgə'dɪəʳ] n général m de brigade.

bright [braɪt] adj - **1.** [room] clair(e) ; [light, colour] vif (vive) ; [sunlight] éclatant(e) ; [eyes, future] brillant(e) - **2.** [intelligent] intelligent(e).

⬥ **brights** npl Am inf feux mpl de route, phares mpl.

⬥ **bright and early** adv de bon matin.

brighten ['braɪtn] vi - **1.** [become lighter] s'éclaircir - **2.** [face, mood] s'éclairer.

⬥ **brighten up** ⬦ vt sep égayer ⬦ vi - **1.** [person] s'égayer, s'animer - **2.** [weather] se dégager, s'éclaircir.

brightly ['braɪtlɪ] adv - **1.** [shine] avec éclat - **2.** [coloured] vivement - **3.** [cheerfully] gaiement.

brightness ['braɪtnɪs] n [of light, colour] éclat m ; [of TV] intensité f.

brilliance ['brɪljəns] n - **1.** [cleverness] intelligence f - **2.** [of colour, light] éclat m.

brilliant ['brɪljənt] adj - **1.** [gen] brillant(e) - **2.** [colour] éclatant(e) - **3.** inf [wonderful] super (inv), génial(e).

brilliantly ['brɪljəntlɪ] adv - **1.** [cleverly] bril-

lamment - **2.** [coloured] vivement - **3.** [shine] avec éclat.

Brillo pad® ['brɪləʊ-] n ≃ tampon m Jex®.

brim [brɪm] (pt & pp **-med** ; cont **-ming**) ⬦ n bord m ⬦ vi : **to ~ with** lit & fig être plein(e) de.

⬥ **brim over** vi : **to ~ over (with)** lit & fig déborder (de).

brine [braɪn] n saumure f.

bring [brɪŋ] (pt & pp **brought**) vt - **1.** [person] amener ; [object] apporter - **2.** [cause - happiness, shame] entraîner, causer ; **to ~ sthg to an end** mettre fin à qqch - **3.** JUR : **to ~ charges against sb** porter plainte contre qqn ; **to be brought to trial** comparaître en justice - **4.** phr : **I couldn't ~ myself to do it** je ne pouvais me résoudre à le faire.

⬥ **bring about** vt sep causer, provoquer.

⬥ **bring along** vt sep [person] amener ; [object] apporter.

⬥ **bring around** vt sep [make conscious] ranimer.

⬥ **bring back** vt sep - **1.** [object] rapporter ; [person] ramener - **2.** [memories] rappeler - **3.** [reinstate] rétablir.

⬥ **bring down** vt sep - **1.** [plane] abattre ; [government] renverser - **2.** [prices] faire baisser.

⬥ **bring forward** vt sep - **1.** [gen] avancer - **2.** [in bookkeeping] reporter.

⬥ **bring in** vt sep - **1.** [law] introduire - **2.** [money - subj : person] gagner ; [- subj : deal] rapporter - **3.** JUR [verdict] rendre.

⬥ **bring off** vt sep [plan] réaliser, réussir ; [deal] conclure, mener à bien.

⬥ **bring on** vt sep [cause] provoquer, causer ; **you've brought it on yourself** tu l'as cherché.

⬥ **bring out** vt sep - **1.** [product] lancer ; [book] publier, faire paraître - **2.** [cause to appear] faire ressortir.

⬥ **bring round, bring to** = **bring around**.

⬥ **bring up** vt sep - **1.** [raise - children] élever - **2.** [mention] mentionner - **3.** [vomit] rendre, vomir.

brink [brɪŋk] n : **on the ~ of** au bord de, à la veille de.

brisk [brɪsk] adj - **1.** [quick] vif (vive), rapide - **2.** [busy] : **business is ~** les affaires marchent bien - **3.** [manner, tone] déterminé(e) - **4.** [wind] frais (fraîche).

brisket ['brɪskɪt] n poitrine f de bœuf.

briskly ['brɪsklɪ] adv - **1.** [quickly] d'un bon pas - **2.** [efficiently, confidently] avec détermination.

bristle ['brɪsl] ⬦ n poil m ⬦ vi lit & fig se hérisser.

⬥ **bristle with** vt fus grouiller de.

bristly ['brɪslɪ] (compar -ier ; superl -iest) adj aux poils raides.

Brit [brɪt] (abbr of Briton) n inf Britannique mf.

Britain ['brɪtn] n Grande-Bretagne f ; in ~ en Grande-Bretagne.

British ['brɪtɪʃ] <> adj britannique <> npl : the ~ les Britanniques mpl.

British Columbia [kə'lʌmbɪə] n Colombie-Britannique f ; in ~ en Colombie-Britannique.

British Council n : the ~ organisme culturel public.

BRITISH COUNCIL

> Le British Council est chargé de promouvoir la langue et la culture anglaises, et de renforcer les liens culturels avec les autres pays.

Britisher ['brɪtɪʃəʳ] n Am Anglais m, -e f, Britannique mf.

British Isles npl : the ~ les îles fpl Britanniques.

British Rail n société des chemins de fer britanniques, ≈ SNCF f.

British Summer Time n heure f d'été (en Grande-Bretagne).

British Telecom [-'telɪkɒm] n société britannique de télécommunications.

Briton ['brɪtn] n Britannique mf.

Britpop ['brɪtpɒp] n tendance musicale des années 1990 en Grande-Bretagne.

Brittany ['brɪtənɪ] n Bretagne f ; in ~ en Bretagne.

brittle ['brɪtl] adj fragile.

Bro [brəʊ] = Br.

broach [brəʊtʃ] vt [subject] aborder.

broad [brɔːd] adj - 1. [wide - gen] large ; [- range, interests] divers(e), varié(e) - 2. [description] général(e) - 3. [hint] transparent(e) ; [accent] prononcé(e).

➡ **in broad daylight** adv en plein jour.

B road n Br route f départementale.

broad bean n fève f, gourgane f Can.

broadcast ['brɔːdkɑːst] (pt & pp broadcast) <> n RADIO & TV émission f <> vt RADIO radiodiffuser, diffuser ; TV téléviser.

broadcaster ['brɔːdkɑːstəʳ] n personnalité f de la télévision/de la radio.

broadcasting ['brɔːdkɑːstɪŋ] n (U) RADIO radiodiffusion f ; TV télévision f.

broaden ['brɔːdn] <> vt élargir <> vi s'élargir.

➡ **broaden out** <> vt sep élargir <> vi s'élargir, s'étendre.

broadly ['brɔːdlɪ] adv - 1. [generally] généralement ; ~ speaking généralement parlant - 2. [smile] jusqu'aux oreilles.

broadly-based [-'beɪst] adj varié(e), divers(e).

broadminded [ˌbrɔːd'maɪndɪd] adj large d'esprit.

broadsheet ['brɔːdʃiːt] n journal m de qualité.

BROADSHEET

> Les principaux journaux nationaux de qualité en Grande-Bretagne sont les suivants :
> The Guardian (tendance centre-gauche)
> The Independent
> The Daily Telegraph (tendance conservatrice)
> The Times (tendance centre-droite).
> The Financial Times

brocade [brə'keɪd] n brocart m.

broccoli ['brɒkəlɪ] n brocoli m.

brochure ['brəʊʃəʳ] n brochure f, prospectus m.

brogues [brəʊgz] npl chaussures lourdes souvent ornées de petits trous.

broil [brɔɪl] vt Am griller, faire cuire au gril.

broiler ['brɔɪləʳ] n - 1. [young chicken] poulet m (à rôtir) - 2. Am [pan] gril m.

broke [brəʊk] <> pt ⊳ break <> adj inf fauché(e) ; to go ~ [company] faire faillite ; to go for ~ risquer le tout pour le tout.

broken ['brəʊkn] <> pp ⊳ break <> adj - 1. [gen] cassé(e) ; to have a ~ leg avoir la jambe cassée - 2. [interrupted - journey, sleep] interrompu(e) ; [- line] brisé(e) - 3. [promise] non respecté(e) - 4. [marriage] brisé(e), détruit(e) ; [home] désuni(e) - 5. [hesitant] : to speak in ~ English parler un anglais hésitant.

broken-down adj - 1. [not working] en panne - 2. [dilapidated] délabré(e).

broker ['brəʊkəʳ] n courtier m ; (insurance) ~ assureur m, courtier m d'assurances.

brokerage ['brəʊkərɪdʒ] n courtage m.

brolly ['brɒlɪ] (pl -ies) n Br inf pépin m.

bronchitis [brɒŋ'kaɪtɪs] n (U) bronchite f.

bronze [brɒnz] <> adj [colour] (couleur) bronze (inv) <> n - 1. [gen] bronze m - 2. = bronze medal <> comp en bronze.

bronzed [br gt'nzd] adj bronzé(e).

bronze medal n médaille f de bronze.

brooch [brəʊtʃ] n broche f.

brood [bruːd] <> n - 1. [of animals] couvée f - 2. fig [of children] nichée f, marmaille f <> vi :

to ~ (over OR about sthg) ressasser (qqch), remâcher (qqch).

broody ['bru:dɪ] (compar -ier ; superl -iest) adj - **1.** [sad] triste, cafardeux(euse) - **2.** [hen] couveuse.

brook [brʊk] ◇ n ruisseau m ◇ vt fml tolérer, souffrir.

broom [bru:m] n balai m.

broomstick ['bru:mstɪk] n manche m à balai.

Bros, bros (abbr of brothers) Frères.

broth [brɒθ] n bouillon m.

brothel ['brɒθl] n bordel m.

brother ['brʌðəʳ] ◇ n frère m ◇ excl Am inf ben, dis-donc!

brotherhood ['brʌðəhʊdl] n - **1.** [companionship] fraternité f - **2.** [organization] confrérie f, société f.

brother-in-law (pl brothers-in-law) n beau-frère m.

brotherly ['brʌðəlɪ] adj fraternel(elle).

brought [brɔːt] pt & pp ⊏▷ bring.

brow [braʊ] n - **1.** [forehead] front m - **2.** [eyebrow] sourcil m ; to knit one's ~s froncer les sourcils - **3.** [of hill] sommet m.

browbeat ['braʊbiːt] (pt browbeat ; pp -en) vt rudoyer, brutaliser.

browbeaten ['braʊbiːtn] adj opprimé(e), tyrannisé(e).

brown [braʊn] ◇ adj - **1.** [colour] brun(e), marron (inv) ; ~ bread pain m bis - **2.** [tanned] bronzé(e), hâlé(e) ◇ n [colour] marron m, brun m ; in ~ en marron ◇ vt [food] faire dorer.

Brownie (Guide) ['braʊnɪ-] n ≃ jeannette f

Brownie point ['braʊnɪ-] n bon point m.

brown paper n papier m d'emballage, papier kraft.

brown rice n riz m complet.

brown sugar n sucre m roux.

browse [braʊz] ◇ vi - **1.** [look] : I'm just browsing [in shop] je ne fais que regarder ; to ~ through [magazines etc] feuilleter - **2.** [animal] brouter - **3.** COMPUT naviguer ◇ vt [file, document] parcourir ; to ~ a site COMPUT naviguer sur un site.

browser ['braʊzəʳ] n navigateur m, browser m.

bruise [bru:z] ◇ n bleu m ◇ vt - **1.** [skin, arm] se faire un bleu à ; [fruit] taler - **2.** fig [pride] meurtrir, blesser ◇ vi [person] se faire un bleu ; [fruit] se taler.

bruised [bru:zd] adj - **1.** [skin, arm] qui a des bleus ; [fruit] talé(e) - **2.** fig [pride] meurtri(e), blessé(e).

Brum [brʌm] n Br inf surnom donné à la ville de Birmingham.

Brummie, Brummy ['brʌmɪ] n Br inf habitant de Birmingham.

brunch [brʌntʃ] n brunch m.

Brunei ['bru:naɪ] n Brunei m ; in ~ au Brunei.

brunette [bru:'net] n brunette f.

brunt [brʌnt] n : to bear OR take the ~ of subir le plus gros de.

brush [brʌʃ] ◇ n - **1.** [gen] brosse f ; [of painter] pinceau m - **2.** [encounter] : to have a ~ with the police avoir des ennuis avec la police ◇ vt - **1.** [clean with brush] brosser - **2.** [move with hand] : he ~ed away some crumbs il a enlevé quelques miettes (avec sa main) - **3.** [touch lightly] effleurer.

➤ **brush aside** vt sep fig écarter, repousser.

➤ **brush off** vt sep [dismiss] envoyer promener.

➤ **brush up** ◇ vt sep [revise] réviser ◇ vi : to ~ up on sthg réviser qqch.

brushed [brʌʃt] adj [metal] poli(e) ; [cotton, nylon] peigné(e).

brush-off n inf : to give sb the ~ envoyer promener qqn.

brush-up n inf : to have a wash and ~ se donner un coup de peigne.

brushwood ['brʌʃwʊd] n (U) brindilles fpl.

brushwork ['brʌʃwɜːk] n [of painter] touche f.

brusque [bru:sk] adj brusque.

Brussels ['brʌslz] n Bruxelles.

brussels sprout n chou m de Bruxelles.

brutal ['bru:tl] adj brutal(e).

brutality [bru:'tælətɪ] (pl -ies) n brutalité f.

brutalize, -ise ['bru:təlaɪz] vt brutaliser.

brute [bru:t] ◇ adj [force] brutal(e) ◇ n brute f.

bs abbr of bill of sale.

BS (abbr of Bachelor of Science) n (titulaire d'une) licence de sciences.

BSA (abbr of Boy Scouts of America) n association américaine de scouts.

BSc (abbr of Bachelor of Science) n (titulaire d'une) licence de sciences.

BSE (abbr of bovine spongiform encephalopathy) n EBS f.

BSI (abbr of British Standards Institution) n association britannique de normalisation, ≃ AFNOR f.

B-side n face f B.

BST - 1. (abbr of British Summer Time) heure d'été britannique - **2.** (abbr of British Standard Time) heure officielle britannique.

Bt. *abbr of* baronet.

BT (*abbr of* **British Telecom**) *n* société britannique de télécommunications.

btu (*abbr of* **British thermal unit**) *n* unité de chaleur (1055 joules).

bubble ['bʌbl] ◇ *n* bulle *f* ◇ *vi* - **1.** [liquid] faire des bulles, bouillonner - **2.** fig [person] : **to ~ with** déborder de.

bubble bath *n* bain *m* moussant.

bubble gum *n* bubble-gum *m*.

bubblejet printer ['bʌbldʒet-] *n* imprimante *f* à jet d'encre.

bubbly ['bʌblɪ] (*compar* **-ier** ; *superl* **-iest**) ◇ *adj* - **1.** [water] pétillant(e) - **2.** fig [lively] plein(e) de vie ◇ *n* inf champagne *m*.

Bucharest [ˌbjuːkəˈrest] *n* Bucarest.

buck [bʌk] ◇ *n* - **1.** [male animal] mâle *m* - **2.** inf [dollar] dollar *m* ; **to make a fast ~** gagner facilement du fric - **3.** inf [responsibility] : **the ~ stops here** maintenant, j'en prends la responsabilité ; **to pass the ~** refiler la responsabilité ◇ *vt* - **1.** [subj : horse] désarçonner d'une ruade - **2.** inf [trend] : **to ~ the trend** aller à contre-courant ◇ *vi* [horse] ruer.

◆ **buck up** inf ◇ *vt sep* - **1.** [improve] : **~ your ideas up!** reprenez-vous! - **2.** [cheer up] : **to ~ sb up** remonter le moral à qqn ◇ *vi* - **1.** [hurry up] se remuer, se dépêcher - **2.** [cheer up] ne pas se laisser abattre.

bucket ['bʌkɪt] *n* - **1.** [gen] seau *m* - **2.** inf fig [lots] : **~s of rain** des trombes d'eau ; **he has ~s of charm** il a énormément de charme ; **she has ~s of money** elle est pleine aux as.

Buckingham Palace ['bʌkɪŋəm-] *n* le palais de Buckingham (*résidence officielle du souverain britannique*).

buckle ['bʌkl] ◇ *n* boucle *f* ◇ *vt* - **1.** [fasten] boucler - **2.** [bend] voiler ◇ *vi* [wheel] se voiler ; [knees, legs] se plier.

◆ **buckle down** *vi* : **to ~ down (to)** s'atteler (à).

Bucks [bʌks] (*abbr of* **Buckinghamshire**) comté anglais.

buckshot ['bʌkʃɒt] *n* chevrotine *f*.

buckskin ['bʌkskɪn] *n* (*U*) peau *f* de daim.

buckteeth [ˌbʌk'tiːθ] *npl* dents *fpl* en avant.

buckwheat ['bʌkwiːt] *n* blé *m* noir.

bud [bʌd] (*pt* & *pp* **-ded** ; *cont* **-ding**) ◇ *n* bourgeon *m* ; **to nip sthg in the ~** fig écraser OR étouffer qqch dans l'œuf ◇ *vi* bourgeonner.

Budapest [ˌbjuːdəˈpest] *n* Budapest.

Buddha ['budə] *n* Bouddha *m*.

Buddhism ['budɪzm] *n* bouddhisme *m*.

Buddhist ['budɪst] ◇ *adj* bouddhiste ◇ *n* bouddhiste *mf*.

budding ['bʌdɪŋ] *adj* [writer, artist] en herbe.

buddy ['bʌdɪ] (*pl* **-ies**) *n* inf pote *m*.

budge [bʌdʒ] ◇ *vt* faire bouger ◇ *vi* bouger.

budgerigar ['bʌdʒərɪgɑːʳ] *n* perruche *f*.

budget ['bʌdʒɪt] ◇ *adj* [holiday, price] pour petits budgets ◇ *n* budget *m ;* **the Budget** Br le budget ◇ *vt* budgétiser ◇ *vi* préparer un budget.

◆ **budget for** *vt fus* prévoir.

budget account *n* Br compte-crédit *m*.

budgetary ['bʌdʒɪtrɪ] *adj* budgétaire.

budgie ['bʌdʒɪ] *n* inf perruche *f*.

Buenos Aires [ˌbwenəsˈaɪrɪz] *n* Buenos Aires.

buff [bʌf] ◇ *adj* [brown] chamois (*inv*) ◇ *n* inf [expert] mordu *m*, -e *f*.

buffalo ['bʌfələu] (*pl inv* OR **-es** OR **-s**) *n* buffle *m*.

buffer ['bʌfəʳ] *n* - **1.** [gen] tampon *m* - **2.** COMPUT mémoire *f* tampon.

buffer state *n* État *m* tampon.

buffet[1] [Br 'bufeɪ, Am bəˈfeɪ] *n* [food, cafeteria] buffet *m*.

buffet[2] ['bʌfɪt] *vt* [physically] frapper.

buffet car ['bufeɪ-] *n* wagon-restaurant *m*.

buffoon [bəˈfuːn] *n* bouffon *m*.

bug [bʌg] (*pt* & *pp* **-ged** ; *cont* **-ging**) ◇ *n* - **1.** [insect] punaise *f* - **2.** inf [germ] microbe *m* - **3.** inf [listening device] micro *m* - **4.** COMPUT bogue *m*, bug *m* - **5.** [enthusiasm] : **the travel ~** le virus des voyages ◇ *vt* - **1.** inf [telephone] mettre sur table d'écoute ; [room] cacher des micros dans - **2.** inf [annoy] embêter.

bugbear ['bʌgbeəʳ] *n* cauchemar *m*.

bugger ['bʌgəʳ] Br v inf ◇ *n* - **1.** [person] con *m*, conne *f* - **2.** [job] : **this job's a real ~!** ce travail est vraiment chiant! ◇ *excl* merde! ◇ *vt* : **~ it!** merde alors!

◆ **bugger off** *vi* : **~ off!** fous le camp!

buggy ['bʌgɪ] (*pl* **-ies**) *n* - **1.** [carriage] boghei *m* - **2.** [pushchair] poussette *f ;* Am [pram] landau *m*.

bugle ['bjuːgl] *n* clairon *m*.

build [bɪld] (*pt* & *pp* **built**) ◇ *vt* lit & fig construire, bâtir ◇ *n* carrure *f*.

◆ **build into** *vt sep* - **1.** CONSTR encastrer - **2.** [include in] inclure dans.

◆ **build on, build upon** ◇ *vt fus* [success] tirer avantage de ◇ *vt sep* [base on] baser sur.

◆ **build up** ◇ *vt sep* [business] développer ; [reputation] bâtir ; **to ~ up one's strength** re-

prendre des forces ◇ *vi* [clouds] s'amonceler ; [traffic] augmenter.
builder ['bɪldəʳ] *n* entrepreneur *m*.
building ['bɪldɪŋ] *n* bâtiment *m*.
building and loan association *n* Am *société d'épargne et de financement immobilier.*
building block *n* - **1.** [toy] cube *m* - **2.** fig [ele-
ment] élément *m*, composante *f*.
building contractor *n* entrepreneur *m*.
building site *n* chantier *m*.
building society *n* Br ≃ société *f* d'épargne et de financement immobilier.

> **BUILDING SOCIETY**
>
> Les « building societies » fonctionnent
> comme des banques, mais n'ont pas de sys-
> tème de compensation. Établissements
> consentant des prêts immobiliers aux parti-
> culiers, elles jouent un rôle important dans
> la vie en Grande-Bretagne.

buildup ['bɪldʌp] *n* [increase] accroissement
m.
built [bɪlt] ◇ *pt* & *pp* ⊳ **build** ◇ *adj* [person]
bâti(e).
built-in *adj* - **1.** CONSTR encastré(e) - **2.** [inher-
ent] inné(e).
built-up *adj* : ~ **area** agglomération *f*.
bulb [bʌlb] *n* - **1.** ELEC ampoule *f* - **2.** BOT oignon
m - **3.** [of thermometer] cuvette *f*.
bulbous ['bʌlbəs] *adj* bulbeux(euse).
Bulgaria [bʌl'geərɪə] *n* Bulgarie *f*; **in ~** en
Bulgarie.
Bulgarian [bʌl'geərɪən] ◇ *adj* bulgare ◇ *n*
- **1.** [person] Bulgare *mf* - **2.** [language] bulgare
m.
bulge [bʌldʒ] ◇ *n* - **1.** [lump] bosse *f* - **2.** [in sales
etc] croissance *f* soudaine ◇ *vi* : **to ~ (with)**
être gonflé (de).
bulging ['bʌldʒɪŋ] *adj* [pocket, bag] bourré(e),
plein(e) à craquer ; [muscles] gonflé(e).
bulimia (nervosa) [bjʊ'lɪmɪə-] *n* boulimie
f.
bulk [bʌlk] ◇ *n* - **1.** [mass] volume *m* - **2.** [of per-
son] corpulence *f* - **3.** COMM : **in ~** en gros
- **4.** [majority] : **the ~ of** le plus gros de ◇ *adj*
en gros.
bulk buying *n* (U) achat *m* en gros.
bulkhead ['bʌlkhed] *n* cloison *f*.
bulky ['bʌlkɪ] (*compar* -**ier** ; *superl* -**iest**) *adj*
volumineux(euse).
bull [bʊl] *n* - **1.** [male cow] taureau *m* ; [male elephant, seal] mâle *m* - **2.** ST EX haussier *m* - **3.** (U)
esp Am v inf [nonsense] conneries *fpl*.

bulldog ['bʊldɒg] *n* bouledogue *m*.
bulldog clip *n* pince *f* à dessin.
bulldoze ['bʊldəʊz] *vt* - **1.** CONSTR passer au
bulldozer - **2.** fig [force] : **to ~ one's way** forcer
son chemin ; **to ~ sb into doing sthg** contraindre OR forcer qqn à faire qqch.
bulldozer ['bʊldəʊzəʳ] *n* bulldozer *m*.
bullet ['bʊlɪt] *n* [for gun] balle *f*.
bulletin ['bʊlətɪn] *n* bulletin *m*.
bulletin board *n* esp Am tableau *m* d'affichage.
bullet-proof *adj* pare-balles (*inv*).
bullfight ['bʊlfaɪt] *n* corrida *f*.
bullfighter ['bʊl,faɪtəʳ] *n* toréador *m*.
bullfighting ['bʊl,faɪtɪŋ] *n* (U) courses *fpl* de
taureaux ; [art] tauromachie *f*.
bullfinch ['bʊlfɪntʃ] *n* bouvreuil *m*.
bullion ['bʊljən] *n* (U) : **gold ~** or *m* en barres.
bullish ['bʊlɪʃ] *adj* ST EX à la hausse.
bull market *n* ST EX marché *m* à la hausse.
bullock ['bʊlək] *n* bœuf *m*.
bullring ['bʊlrɪŋ] *n* arène *f*.
bullrush ['bʊlrʌʃ] = **bulrush**.
bull's-eye *n* centre *m*.
bullshit ['bʊlʃɪt] (*pt* & *pp* -**ted** ; *cont* -**ting**)
vulg ◇ *n* (U) conneries *fpl* ◇ *vi* dire des
conneries.
bull terrier *n* bull-terrier *m*.
bully ['bʊlɪ] (*pl* -**ies**, *pt* & *pp* -**ied**) ◇ *n* tyran *m*
◇ *vt* tyranniser, brutaliser ; **to ~ sb into
doing sthg** forcer OR obliger qqn à faire qqch.
bullying ['bʊlɪŋ] *n* (U) brimades *fpl*.
bulrush ['bʊlrʌʃ] *n* jonc *m*.
bum [bʌm] (*pt* & *pp* -**med** ; *cont* -**ming**) *n*
- **1.** inf [bottom] derrière *m* - **2.** inf pej [tramp]
clochard *m* - **3.** inf [idler] bon à rien *m*.
◆ **bum around** *vi* inf - **1.** [waste time] perdre
son temps - **2.** [travel aimlessly] se balader.
bumblebee ['bʌmblbiː] *n* bourdon *m*.
bumbling ['bʌmblɪŋ] *adj* inf empoté(e).
bumf [bʌmf] (U) Br *n* inf paperasses *fpl*.
bump [bʌmp] ◇ *n* - **1.** [lump] bosse *f* - **2.** [knock,
blow] choc *m* - **3.** [noise] bruit *m* sourd ◇ *vt*
[head etc] cogner ; [car] heurter ◇ *vi* [car] : **to
~ along** cahoter.
◆ **bump into** *vt fus* [meet by chance] rencontrer par hasard.
◆ **bump off** *vt sep* inf liquider.
◆ **bump up** *vt sep* inf faire grimper.
bumper ['bʌmpəʳ] ◇ *adj* [harvest, edition] ex-
ceptionnel(elle) ◇ *n* - **1.** AUT pare-chocs *m*
inv - **2.** Am RAIL tampon *m*.
bumper-to-bumper *adj* pare-chocs contre pare-chocs.

bumph [bʌmf] = bumf.

bumptious [ˈbʌmpʃəs] *adj* suffisant(e).

bumpy [ˈbʌmpɪ] (*compar* -ier ; *superl* -iest) *adj* - **1.** [surface] défoncé(e) - **2.** [ride] cahoteux(euse) ; [sea crossing] agité(e).

bun [bʌn] *n* - **1.** [cake] petit pain *m* aux raisins ; [bread roll] petit pain au lait - **2.** [hairstyle] chignon *m*.

bunch [bʌntʃ] ◇ *n* [of people] groupe *m* ; [of flowers] bouquet *m* ; [of grapes] grappe *f* ; [of bananas] régime *m* ; [of keys] trousseau *m* ◇ *vt* grouper ◇ *vi* se grouper.
➭ **bunches** *npl* [hairstyle] couettes *fpl*.

bundle [ˈbʌndl] ◇ *n* [of clothes] paquet *m* ; [of notes, newspapers] liasse *f* ; [of wood] fagot *m* ◇ *vt* [put roughly - person] entasser ; [- clothes] fourrer, entasser.
➭ **bundle off** *vt sep* [person] envoyer en hâte.
➭ **bundle up** *vt sep* [clothes] mettre en tas ; [newspapers] mettre en liasse ; [wood] mettre en fagot.

bundled software *n* (U) COMPUT logiciel *m* inclus à l'achat d'un ordinateur.

bung [bʌŋ] ◇ *n* bonde *f* ◇ *vt* Br inf envoyer.

bungalow [ˈbʌŋɡələʊ] *n* bungalow *m*.

bunged up [bʌŋd-] *adj* bouché(e).

bungee-jumping [ˈbʌndʒɪ-] *n* saut *m* à l'élastique.

bungle [ˈbʌŋɡl] *vt* gâcher, bâcler.

bunion [ˈbʌnjən] *n* oignon *m*.

bunk [bʌŋk] *n* - **1.** [bed] couchette *f* - **2.** (U) inf [nonsense] foutaises *fpl* - **3.** phr : **to do a ~** inf mettre les voiles.

bunk bed *n* lit *m* superposé.

bunker [ˈbʌŋkə^r] *n* - **1.** GOLF & MIL bunker *m* - **2.** [for coal] coffre *m*.

bunkhouse [ˈbʌŋkhaʊs, *pl* -haʊzɪz] *n* dortoir *m*.

bunny [ˈbʌnɪ] (*pl* -ies) *n* : ~ **(rabbit)** lapin *m*.

bunny hill *n* Am SKI piste *f* pour débutants.

Bunsen burner *n* bec *m* Bunsen.

bunting [ˈbʌntɪŋ] *n* (U) guirlandes *fpl* (de drapeaux).

buoy [Br bɔɪ, Am ˈbuːɪ] *n* bouée *f*.
➭ **buoy up** *vt sep* [encourage] soutenir.

buoyancy [ˈbɔɪənsɪ] *n* - **1.** [ability to float] flottabilité *f* - **2.** fig [optimism] entrain *m*.

buoyant [ˈbɔɪənt] *adj* - **1.** [able to float] qui flotte - **2.** fig [person] enjoué(e) ; [economy] florissant(e) ; [market] ferme.

burden [ˈbɜːdn] ◇ *n* lit & fig : ~ **(on)** charge *f* (pour), fardeau *m* (pour) ◇ *vt* : **to ~ sb with** [responsibilities, worries] accabler qqn de.

bureau [ˈbjʊərəʊ] (*pl* -x [-z]) *n* - **1.** Br [desk] bureau *m* ; Am [chest of drawers] commode *f* - **2.** [office] bureau *m* - **3.** Am POL service *m* (gouvernemental).

bureaucracy [bjʊəˈrɒkrəsɪ] (*pl* -ies) *n* bureaucratie *f*.

bureaucrat [ˈbjʊərəkræt] *n* bureaucrate *mf*.

bureaucratic [ˌbjʊərəˈkrætɪk] *adj* bureaucratique.

bureaux [ˈbjʊərəʊz] *pl* ➭ **bureau**.

burger [ˈbɜːɡə^r] *n* hamburger *m*.

burglar [ˈbɜːɡlə^r] *n* cambrioleur *m*, -euse *f*.

burglar alarm *n* système *m* d'alarme.

burglarize Am = burgle.

burglary [ˈbɜːɡlərɪ] (*pl* -ies) *n* cambriolage *m*.

burgle [ˈbɜːɡl], **burglarize** Am [ˈbɜːɡləraɪz] *vt* cambrioler.

Burgundy [ˈbɜːɡəndɪ] *n* Bourgogne *f* ; **in ~** en Bourgogne.

burial [ˈberɪəl] *n* enterrement *m*.

burial ground *n* cimetière *m*.

burk [bɜːk] *n* Br inf idiot *m*, -e *f*.

Burkina Faso [bɜːˌkiːnəˈfæsəʊ] *n* Burkina *m* ; **in ~** au Burkina.

burly [ˈbɜːlɪ] (*compar* -ier ; *superl* -iest) *adj* bien charpenté(e).

Burma [ˈbɜːmə] *n* Birmanie *f*.

Burmese [ˌbɜːˈmiːz] ◇ *adj* birman(e) ◇ *n* - **1.** [person] Birman *m*, -e *f* - **2.** [language] birman *m*.

burn [bɜːn] (*pt* & *pp* burnt OR -ed) ◇ *vt* brûler ; **to ~ o.s.** se brûler ; **I've ~ed my hand** je me suis brûlé la main ◇ *vi* brûler ; **my skin ~s easily** j'attrape facilement des coups de soleil ; **to ~ with** fig brûler de ◇ *n* brûlure *f*.
➭ **burn down** ◇ *vt sep* [building, town] incendier ◇ *vi* - **1.** [building] brûler complètement - **2.** [fire] baisser d'intensité.
➭ **burn out** ◇ *vt sep* [exhaust] : **to ~ o.s. out** s'user ◇ *vi* [fire] s'éteindre.
➭ **burn up** ◇ *vt sep* [fuel] brûler ◇ *vi* [satellite] se désintégrer (sous l'effet de la chaleur).

burner [ˈbɜːnə^r] *n* brûleur *m*.

burning [ˈbɜːnɪŋ] *adj* - **1.** [on fire] en flammes - **2.** [very hot] brûlant(e) ; [cheeks, face] en feu - **3.** [passion, desire] ardent(e) ; [interest] passionné(e) ; ~ **question** question *f* brûlante.

burnish [ˈbɜːnɪʃ] *vt* astiquer, polir.

Burns' Night [bɜːnz-] *n* fête célébrée en l'honneur du poète écossais Robert Burns, le 25 janvier.

burnt [bɜːnt] *pt* & *pp* ➭ **burn**.

burnt-out *adj* - **1.** [building, car etc] détruit(e) (par le feu) - **2.** fig [person] usé(e).

burp [bɜːp] *inf* ⬦ *n* rot *m* ⬦ *vi* roter.

burrow [ˈbʌrəʊ] ⬦ *n* terrier *m* ⬦ *vi* - **1.** [dig] creuser un terrier - **2.** fig [search] fouiller.

bursar [ˈbɜːsəʳ] *n* intendant *m*, -e *f*.

bursary [ˈbɜːsərɪ] (*pl* -ies) *n* Br [scholarship, grant] bourse *f*.

burst [bɜːst] (*pt* & *pp* burst) ⬦ *vi* - **1.** [gen] éclater - **2.** [door, lid] : **to ~ open** ouvrir violemment ⬦ *vt* faire éclater ⬦ *n* [of gunfire] rafale *f* ; [of enthusiasm] élan *m* ; **a ~ of applause** un tonnerre d'applaudissements.

➤ **burst into** *vt fus* - **1.** [room] faire irruption dans - **2.** [begin suddenly] : **to ~ into tears** fondre en larmes ; **to ~ into song** se mettre tout d'un coup à chanter ; **to ~ into flames** prendre feu.

➤ **burst out** *vt fus* [say suddenly] s'exclamer ; **to ~ out laughing** éclater de rire ; **to ~ out crying** fondre en larmes.

bursting [ˈbɜːstɪŋ] *adj* - **1.** [full] plein(e), bourré(e) - **2.** [with emotion] : **~ with** débordé(e) de - **3.** [eager] : **to be ~ to do sthg** mourir d'envie de faire qqch.

Burundi [bʊˈrʊndɪ] *n* Burundi *m* ; **in ~** au Burundi.

bury [ˈberɪ] (*pt* & *pp* -ied) *vt* - **1.** [in ground] enterrer ; **to ~ o.s. in sthg** fig se plonger dans qqch - **2.** [hide] cacher, enfouir.

bus [bʌs] *n* autobus *m*, bus *m* ; [long-distance] car *m* ; **by ~** en autobus/car.

bus conductor *n* receveur *m*, -euse *f* d'autobus.

bus driver *n* conducteur *m*, -trice *f* d'autobus.

bush [bʊʃ] *n* - **1.** [plant] buisson *m* - **2.** [open country] : **the ~** la brousse - **3.** phr : **she doesn't beat about the ~** elle n'y va pas par quatre chemins.

bushel [ˈbʊʃl] *n* boisseau *m*.

bushy [ˈbʊʃɪ] (*compar* -ier ; *superl* -iest) *adj* touffu(e).

business [ˈbɪznɪs] ⬦ *n* - **1.** (U) [commerce] affaires *fpl* ; **we do a lot of ~ with them** nous travaillons beaucoup avec eux ; **she's in the publishing ~** elle est dans l'édition ; **on ~** pour affaires ; **to mean ~** inf ne pas plaisanter ; **to go out of ~** fermer, faire faillite - **2.** [company, duty] affaire *f* ; **he had no ~ to tell you that** ce n'était pas à lui de vous le dire ; **mind your own ~!** inf occupe-toi de tes oignons ! - **3.** [affair, matter] histoire *f*, affaire *f* ⬦ *comp* [meeting] d'affaires ; **~ hours** heures *fpl* ouvrables.

business address *n* adresse *f* de travail.

business card *n* carte *f* de visite.

business class *n* classe *f* affaires.

businesslike [ˈbɪznɪslaɪk] *adj* efficace.

businessman [ˈbɪznɪsmæn] (*pl* -men [-men]) *n* homme *m* d'affaires.

business school *n* école *f* de commerce.

business trip *n* voyage *m* d'affaires.

businesswoman [ˈbɪznɪsˌwʊmən] (*pl* -women [-ˌwɪmɪn]) *n* femme *f* d'affaires.

busker [ˈbʌskəʳ] *n* Br chanteur *m*, -euse *f* des rues.

bus lane *n* voie *f* des bus.

bus shelter *n* Abribus® *m*.

bus station *n* gare *f* routière.

bus stop *n* arrêt *m* de bus.

bust [bʌst] (*pt* & *pp* bust OR -ed) ⬦ *adj* inf - **1.** [broken] foutu(e) - **2.** [bankrupt] : **to go ~** faire faillite ⬦ *n* - **1.** [bosom] poitrine *f* - **2.** [statue] buste *m* - **3.** police sl [raid] descente *f* ⬦ *vt* - **1.** inf [break] péter - **2.** police sl [arrest] arrêter ; [raid] faire une descente à.

bustle [ˈbʌsl] ⬦ *n* (U) [activity] remue-ménage *m* ⬦ *vi* s'affairer.

bustling [ˈbʌslɪŋ] *adj* [place] qui bourdonne d'activité.

bust-up *n* inf - **1.** [quarrel] engueulade *f* - **2.** [of marriage, relationship] rupture *f*.

busy [ˈbɪzɪ] (*compar* -ier ; *superl* -iest) ⬦ *adj* - **1.** [gen] occupé(e) ; **to be ~ doing sthg** être occupé à faire qqch - **2.** [life, week] chargé(e) ; [town, office] animé(e) - **3.** esp Am TELEC [engaged] occupé(e) ⬦ *vt* : **to ~ o.s. (doing sthg)** s'occuper (à faire qqch).

busybody [ˈbɪzɪˌbɒdɪ] (*pl* -ies) *n* pej mouche *f* du coche.

busy signal *n* Am TELEC tonalité *f* « occupé ».

but [bʌt] ⬦ *conj* mais ; **I'm sorry, ~ I don't agree** je suis désolé, mais je ne suis pas d'accord ; **~ now let's talk about you** mais parlons plutôt de toi ⬦ *prep* sauf, excepté ; **everyone was at the party ~ Jane** tout le monde était à la soirée sauf Jane ; **he has no one ~ himself to blame** il ne peut s'en prendre qu'à lui-même ⬦ *adv* fml seulement, ne ... que ; **had I ~ known!** si j'avais su ! ; **we can ~ try** on peut toujours essayer ; **she has ~ recently joined the firm** elle n'est entrée dans la société que depuis peu.

➤ **but for** *prep* sans ; **~ for her** sans elle.

➤ **but then** *adv* mais ; **... ~ then I've known him for years** ... mais il faut dire OR il est vrai que je le connais depuis des années.

butane [ˈbjuːteɪn] *n* butane *m*.

butch [bʊtʃ] *adj* inf [woman] hommasse.

butcher [ˈbʊtʃəʳ] ⬦ *n* boucher *m* ; **~'s (shop)**

boucherie *f* ⬦ *vt* - **1.** [animal] abattre - **2.** fig [massacre] massacrer.

butchery [ˈbʊtʃərɪ] *n* lit & fig boucherie *f*.

butler [ˈbʌtləʳ] *n* maître *m* d'hôtel *(chez un particulier)*.

butt [bʌt] ⬦ *n* - **1.** [of cigarette, cigar] mégot *m* - **2.** [of rifle] crosse *f* - **3.** [for water] tonneau *m* - **4.** [of joke, criticism] cible *f* ⬦ *vt* donner un coup de tête à.

➤ **butt in** *vi* [interrupt] : **to ~ in on sb** interrompre qqn ; **to ~ in on sthg** s'immiscer *or* s'imposer dans qqch.

butter [ˈbʌtəʳ] ⬦ *n* beurre *m ;* **~ wouldn't melt in her mouth** inf on lui donnerait le bon Dieu sans confession ⬦ *vt* beurrer.

➤ **butter up** *vt sep* inf passer de la pommade à.

butter bean *n* haricot *m* beurre.

buttercup [ˈbʌtəkʌp] *n* bouton *m* d'or.

butter dish *n* beurrier *m*.

buttered [ˈbʌtəd] *adj* [bread] beurré(e).

butterfingers [ˈbʌtə͵fɪŋgəz] *(pl inv)* *n* inf maladroit *m*, -e *f*.

butterfly [ˈbʌtəflaɪ] *(pl* -ies) *n* SWIMMING & ZOOL papillon *m ;* **to have butterflies in one's stomach** avoir le trac.

buttermilk [ˈbʌtəmɪlk] *n* babeurre *m*.

butterscotch [ˈbʌtəskɒtʃ] *n* caramel *m* dur.

buttocks [ˈbʌtəks] *npl* fesses *fpl*.

button [ˈbʌtn] ⬦ *n* - **1.** [gen] bouton *m* - **2.** Am [badge] badge *m* ⬦ *vt* = **button up**.

➤ **button up** *vt sep* boutonner.

buttonhole [ˈbʌtnhəʊl] ⬦ *n* - **1.** [hole] boutonnière *f* - **2.** Br [flower] fleur *f* à la boutonnière ⬦ *vt* inf coincer.

button mushroom *n* champignon *m* de Paris.

buttress [ˈbʌtrɪs] ⬦ *n* contrefort *m* ⬦ *vt* [wall] soutenir, étayer.

buxom [ˈbʌksəm] *adj* bien en chair.

buy [baɪ] *(pt & pp* bought) ⬦ *vt* acheter ; **to ~ sthg from sb** acheter qqch à qqn ⬦ *n :* **a good ~** une bonne affaire.

➤ **buy in** *vt sep* Br stocker.

➤ **buy into** *vt fus* acquérir des parts dans.

➤ **buy off** *vt sep :* **to ~ sb off** acheter le silence de qqn.

➤ **buy out** *vt sep* - **1.** COMM racheter la part de - **2.** [from army] : **to ~ o.s. out** se racheter.

➤ **buy up** *vt sep* acheter en masse.

buyer [ˈbaɪəʳ] *n* acheteur *m*, -euse *f*.

buyer's market *n* marché *m* acheteur.

buyout [ˈbaɪaʊt] *n* rachat *m*.

buzz [bʌz] ⬦ *n* - **1.** [of insect] bourdonnement *m* - **2.** inf [telephone call] : **to give sb a ~** passer

un coup de fil à qqn ⬦ *vi :* **to ~ (with)** bourdonner (de) ⬦ *vt* [on intercom] appeler.

➤ **buzz off** *vi* Br inf : **~ off!** file!, fous le camp!

buzzard [ˈbʌzəd] *n* - **1.** Br [hawk] buse *f* - **2.** Am [vulture] urubu *m*.

buzzer [ˈbʌzəʳ] *n* sonnerie *f*.

buzzing [ˈbʌzɪŋ] *n* [of insect] bourdonnement *m ;* [of machine] ronronnement *m*.

buzzword [ˈbʌzwɜːd] *n* inf mot *m* à la mode.

by [baɪ] ⬦ *prep* - **1.** [indicating cause, agent] par ; **caused/written/killed ~** causé/écrit/tué par - **2.** [indicating means, method, manner] : **to dine ~ candlelight** dîner aux chandelles ; **to pay ~ cheque** payer par chèque ; **to travel ~ bus/ train/plane/ship** voyager en bus/par le train/en avion/en bateau ; **he's a lawyer ~ profession** il est avocat de son métier ; **~ doing sthg** en faisant qqch ; **~ nature** de nature, de tempérament - **3.** [to explain a word or expression] par ; **what do you mean ~ "all right"?** qu'est-ce que tu veux dire par « très bien »? - **4.** [beside, close to] près de ; **~ the sea** au bord de la mer ; **I sat ~ her bed** j'étais assis à son chevet - **5.** [past] : **to pass ~ sb/sthg** passer devant qqn/qqch ; **to drive ~ sb/sthg** passer en voiture devant qqn/qqch - **6.** [via, through] par ; **come in ~ the back door** entrez par la porte de derrière - **7.** [at or before a particular time] avant, pas plus tard que ; **I'll be there ~ eight** j'y serai avant huit heures ; **~ 1914 it was all over** en 1914 c'était fini ; **~ now** déjà - **8.** [during] : **~ day** le *or* de jour ; **~ night** la *or* de nuit - **9.** [according to] selon, suivant ; **~ law** conformément à la loi - **10.** [in arithmetic] par ; **divide/multiply 20 ~ 2** divisez/multipliez 20 par 2 - **11.** [in measurements] : **2 metres ~ 4** 2 mètres sur 4 - **12.** [in quantities, amounts] à ; **~ the yard** au mètre ; **~ the thousands** par milliers ; **paid ~ the day/ week/month** payé à la journée/à la semaine/au mois ; **to cut prices ~ 50%** réduire les prix de 50 % - **13.** [indicating gradual change] : **week ~ week** de semaine en semaine ; **day ~ day** jour après jour, de jour en jour ; **one ~ one** un à un, un par un - **14.** phr : **(all) ~ oneself** (tout) seul ((toute) seule) ; **I'm all ~ myself today** je suis tout seul aujourd'hui ⬦ *adv* ▷ **go, pass** etc.

bye(-bye) [baɪ(baɪ)] *excl* inf au revoir!, salut!

bye-election = **by-election**.

byelaw [ˈbaɪlɔː] = **bylaw**.

by-election *n* élection *f* partielle.

Byelorussia [bɪ͵eləʊˈrʌʃə] = **Belorussia**.

bygone [ˈbaɪgɒn] *adj* d'autrefois.

➤ **bygones** *npl :* **to let ~s be ~s** oublier le passé.

bylaw ['baɪlɔː] *n* arrêté *m*.

by-line *n* PRESS signature *f*.

bypass ['baɪpɑːs] ◇ *n* - **1.** [road] route *f* de contournement - **2.** MED : ~ **(operation)** pontage *m* ◇ *vt* [town, difficulty] contourner ; [subject] éviter.

by-product *n* - **1.** [product] dérivé *m* - **2.** fig [consequence] conséquence *f*.

bystander ['baɪˌstændə'] *n* spectateur *m*, -trice *f*.

byte [baɪt] *n* COMPUT octet *m*.

byword ['baɪwɜːd] *n* [symbol] : **to be a ~ for** être synonyme de.

C

c¹ (*pl* **c's** OR **cs**), **C** (*pl* **C's** OR **Cs**) [siː] *n* [letter] c *m* inv, C *m* inv.

➡ **C** *n* - **1.** MUS do *m* - **2.** SCH [mark] C *m* inv - **3.** (*abbr of* **Celsius, centigrade**) C.

c² [siː] - **1.** (*abbr of* **century**) s. - **2.** (*abbr of* **cent(s)**) ct.

c., ca. *abbr of* circa.

c/a - **1.** *abbr of* **credit account** - **2.** *abbr of* **current account**.

CA ◇ *n* - **1.** *abbr of* **chartered accountant** - **2.** (*abbr of* **Consumers' Association**) *union de défense des consommateurs* ◇ - **1.** *abbr of* **Central America** - **2.** *abbr of* **California**.

CAA *n* - **1.** (*abbr of* **Civil Aviation Authority**) *direction britannique de l'aviation civile* - **2.** (*abbr of* **Civil Aeronautics Authority**) *direction américaine de l'aviation civile*.

cab [kæb] *n* - **1.** [taxi] taxi *m* - **2.** [of lorry] cabine *f*.

CAB (*abbr of* **Citizens' Advice Bureau**) *n service britannique d'information et d'aide au consommateur*.

cabaret ['kæbəreɪ] *n* cabaret *m*.

cabbage ['kæbɪdʒ] *n* [vegetable] chou *m*.

cabbie, cabby ['kæbɪ] *n* inf chauffeur *m* de taxi.

caber ['keɪbə'] *n* Scot : **tossing the ~** *lancement*

d'un tronc d'arbre (épreuve des 'Highland Games').

cabin ['kæbɪn] *n* - **1.** [on ship, plane] cabine *f* - **2.** [house] cabane *f*.

cabin class *n* seconde classe *f*.

cabin cruiser *n* bateau *m* de croisière.

cabinet ['kæbɪnɪt] *n* - **1.** [cupboard] meuble *m* - **2.** POL cabinet *m*.

cabinet-maker *n* ébéniste *m*.

cabinet minister *n* ministre *m*.

cable ['keɪbl] ◇ *n* câble *m* ◇ *vt* [news] câbler ; [person] câbler à.

cable car *n* téléphérique *m*.

cablegram ['keɪblgræm] *n* câblogramme *m*.

cable railway *n* funiculaire *m*.

cable television, cable TV *n* télévision *f* par câble.

caboodle [kə'buːdl] *n* inf : **the whole ~** et tout le tremblement.

cache [kæʃ] ◇ *n* - **1.** [store] cache *f* - **2.** COMPUT mémoire-cache *f*, antémémoire *f* ◇ *vt* COMPUT stocker dans la mémoire-cache.

cachet ['kæʃeɪ] *n* cachet *m*.

cackle ['kækl] ◇ *n* - **1.** [of hen] caquet *m* - **2.** [of person] jacassement *m* ◇ *vi* - **1.** [hen] caqueter - **2.** [person] jacasser.

cacophony [kæ'kɒfənɪ] *n* cacophonie *f*.

cactus ['kæktəs] (*pl* **-tuses** [-təsiːz] OR **-ti** [-taɪ]) *n* cactus *m*.

CAD (*abbr of* **computer-aided design**) *n* CAO *f*.

caddie ['kædɪ] ◇ *n* caddie *m* ◇ *vi* : **to ~ for sb** servir de caddie à qqn.

caddy ['kædɪ] (*pl* **-ies**) *n* boîte *f* à thé.

cadence ['keɪdəns] *n* [of voice] intonation *f*.

cadet [kə'det] *n* élève *m* officier.

cadge [kædʒ] Br inf ◇ *vt* : **to ~ sthg off** OR **from sb** taper qqn de qqch ◇ *vi* : **to ~ off** OR **from sb** taper qqn.

Cadiz [kə'dɪz] *n* Cadix.

Caesar ['siːzə'] *n* César *m*.

caesarean (section) [sɪ'zeərɪən-] Br, **cesarean (section)** Am *n* césarienne *f*.

CAF (*abbr of* **cost and freight**) C et F.

cafe, café ['kæfeɪ] *n* café *m*.

cafeteria [ˌkæfɪ'tɪərɪə] *n* cafétéria *f*.

cafetière [kæfə'tjeə'] *n* cafetière *f* à piston.

caffeine ['kæfiːn] *n* caféine *f*.

cage [keɪdʒ] *n* [for animal] cage *f*.

caged [keɪdʒd] *adj* en cage.

cagey ['keɪdʒɪ] (*compar* **-ier** ; *superl* **-iest**) *adj* inf discret(ète).

cagoule [kə'guːl] *n* Br K-way® *m* inv.

cahoots [kə'huːts] n inf : **to be in ~ (with)** être de mèche (avec).

CAI (abbr of **computer-aided instruction**) n EAO m.

cairn [keən] n [pile of rocks] cairn m.

Cairo ['kaɪərəʊ] n Le Caire.

cajole [kə'dʒəʊl] vt : **to ~ sb (into doing sthg)** enjôler qqn (pour qu'il fasse qqch).

cake [keɪk] n - **1.** CULIN gâteau m ; [of fish, potato] croquette f ; **it's a piece of ~** inf fig c'est du gâteau ; **to sell like hot ~s** se vendre comme des petits pains ; **you can't have your ~ and eat it** on ne peut pas avoir le beurre et l'argent du beurre - **2.** [of soap] pain m.

caked [keɪkt] adj : **~ with mud** recouvert(e) de boue séchée.

cake tin Br, **cake pan** Am n moule m à gâteau.

cal [kæl] (abbr of **calorie**) n cal.

calamine lotion [,kæləmaɪn-] n (U) lotion f à la calamine.

calamitous [kə'læmɪtəs] adj catastrophique.

calamity [kə'læmətɪ] (pl **-ies**) n calamité f.

calcium ['kælsɪəm] n calcium m.

calculate ['kælkjʊleɪt] vt - **1.** [result, number] calculer ; [consequences] évaluer - **2.** [plan] : **to be ~d to do sthg** être calculé(e) pour faire qqch.

calculate on vi : **to ~ on sthg** compter sur qqch ; **to ~ on doing sthg** compter faire qqch.

calculated ['kælkjʊleɪtɪd] adj calculé(e).

calculating ['kælkjʊleɪtɪŋ] adj pej calculateur(trice).

calculation [,kælkjʊ'leɪʃn] n calcul m.

calculator ['kælkjʊleɪtəʳ] n calculatrice f.

calculus ['kælkjʊləs] n calcul m.

calendar ['kælɪndəʳ] n calendrier m.

calendar month n mois m (de calendrier).

calendar year n année f civile.

calf [kɑːf] (pl **calves** [kɑːvz]) n - **1.** [of cow, leather] veau m ; [of elephant] éléphanteau m ; [of seal] bébé m phoque ; [ANAT mollet m.

caliber ['kælɪbəʳ] Am = **calibre**.

calibrate ['kælɪbreɪt] vt [scale] étalonner ; [gun] calibrer.

calibre, caliber Am ['kælɪbəʳ] n calibre m.

calico ['kælɪkəʊ] n calicot m.

California [,kælɪ'fɔːnjə] n Californie f ; **in ~** en Californie.

Californian [,kælɪ'fɔːnjən] <> adj californien(enne) <> n Californien m, -enne f.

calipers Am = **callipers**.

call [kɔːl] <> n - **1.** [cry] appel m, cri m - **2.** TELEC appel m (téléphonique) ; **I'll give you a ~** je t'appellerai - **3.** [summons, invitation] appel m ; **to be on ~** [doctor etc] être de garde - **4.** [visit] visite f ; **to pay a ~ on sb** rendre visite à qqn - **5.** [demand] : **~ (for)** demande f (de) <> vt - **1.** [name, summon, phone] appeler ; **what's this thing ~ed?** comment ça s'appelle ce truc? ; **she's ~ed Joan** elle s'appelle Joan ; **let's ~ it £10** disons 10 livres - **2.** [label] : **he ~ed me a liar** il m'a traité de menteur - **3.** [shout] appeler, crier - **4.** [announce - meeting] convoquer ; [- strike] lancer ; [- flight] appeler ; [- election] annoncer <> vi - **1.** [shout - person] crier ; [- animal, bird] pousser un cri/des cris - **2.** TELEC appeler ; **who's ~ing?** qui est à l'appareil? - **3.** [visit] passer.

call back <> vt sep rappeler <> vi - **1.** TELEC rappeler - **2.** [visit again] repasser.

call by vi inf passer.

call for vt fus - **1.** [collect - person] passer prendre ; [- package, goods] passer chercher - **2.** [demand] demander.

call in <> vt sep - **1.** [expert, police etc] faire venir - **2.** COMM [goods] rappeler ; FIN [loan] exiger le remboursement de <> vi passer.

call off vt sep - **1.** [cancel] annuler ; **to ~ off a strike** rapporter un ordre de grève - **2.** [dog] rappeler.

call on vt fus - **1.** [visit] passer voir - **2.** [ask] : **to ~ on sb to do sthg** demander à qqn de faire qqch.

call out <> vt sep - **1.** [police, doctor] appeler - **2.** [order to strike] : **they ~ed the workers out** ils ont donné la consigne de grève aux ouvriers - **3.** [cry out] crier <> vi [cry out] crier.

call round vi passer.

call up vt sep - **1.** MIL & TELEC appeler - **2.** COMPUT rappeler.

call box n Br cabine f (téléphonique).

caller ['kɔːləʳ] n - **1.** [visitor] visiteur m, -euse f - **2.** TELEC demandeur m.

call girl n call-girl f.

calligraphy [kə'lɪgrəfɪ] n calligraphie f.

call-in n Am RADIO & TV programme m à ligne ouverte.

calling ['kɔːlɪŋ] n - **1.** [profession] métier m - **2.** [vocation] vocation f.

calling card n Am carte f de visite.

callipers Br, **calipers** Am ['kælɪpəz] npl - **1.** MATH compas m - **2.** MED appareil m orthopédique.

callous ['kæləs] adj dur(e).

callously ['kæləslɪ] adv durement.

callousness ['kæləsnɪs] n dureté f.

call-up *n* Br ordre *m* de mobilisation.

callus ['kæləs] (*pl* **-es** [-i:zl]) *n* cal *m*, durillon *m*.

calm [kɑːm] ◇ *adj* calme ◇ *n* calme *m* ◇ *vt* calmer.

◆ **calm down** ◇ *vt sep* calmer ◇ *vi* se calmer.

calmly ['kɑːmlı] *adv* calmement.

calmness ['kɑːmnıs] *n* calme *m*.

Calor gas® ['kælə°-] *n* Br butane *m*.

calorie ['kælərı] *n* calorie *f*.

calorific [ˌkælə'rıfık] *adj* calorifique.

calve [kɑːv] *vi* vêler.

calves [kɑːvz] *pl* ⊏> **calf.**

cam [kæm] *n* came *f*.

CAM (*abbr of* **computer-aided manufacturing**) *n* FAO *f*.

camaraderie [ˌkæmə'rɑːdərı] *n* camaraderie *f*.

camber ['kæmbə°] *n* [of road] bombement *m*.

Cambodia [kæm'bəʊdjə] *n* Cambodge *m*; **in ~** au Cambodge.

Cambodian [kæm'bəʊdjən] ◇ *adj* cambodgien(enne) ◇ *n* Cambodgien *m*, -enne *f*.

Cambs (*abbr of* **Cambridgeshire**) *comté anglais*.

camcorder ['kæmˌkɔːdə°] *n* Caméscope® *m*.

came [keım] *pt* ⊏> **come.**

camel ['kæml] ◇ *adj* ocre (*inv*) ◇ *n* chameau *m*.

camellia [kə'miːljə] *n* camélia *m*.

cameo ['kæmıəʊ] (*pl* **-s**) *n* **- 1.** [jewellery] camée *m* **- 2.** CINEMA & THEATRE courte apparition *f* (d'une grande vedette).

camera ['kæmərə] *n* PHOT appareil-photo *m*; CINEMA & TV caméra *f*; **video ~** caméra vidéo.

◆ **in camera** *adv* à huis clos.

cameraman ['kæmərəmæn] (*pl* **-men** [-men]) *n* cameraman *m*.

Cameroon [ˌkæmə'ruːn] *n* Cameroun *m*; **in ~** au Cameroun.

Cameroonian [ˌkæmə'ruːnıən] ◇ *adj* camerounais(e) ◇ *n* Camerounais *m*, -e *f*.

camisole ['kæmısəʊl] *n* camisole *f*.

camomile ['kæməmaıl] ◇ *n* camomille *f* ◇ *comp* : **~ tea** infusion *f* de camomille.

camouflage ['kæməflɑːʒ] ◇ *n* camouflage *m* ◇ *vt* camoufler.

camp [kæmp] ◇ *n* camp *m* ◇ *vi* camper.

◆ **camp out** *vi* camper.

campaign [kæm'peın] ◇ *n* campagne *f* ◇ *vi* : **to ~ (for/against)** mener une campagne (pour/contre).

campaigner [kæm'peınə°] *n* militant *m*, -e *f*.

camp bed *n* lit *m* de camp.

camper ['kæmpə°] *n* **- 1.** [person] campeur *m*, -euse *f* **- 2.** [vehicle] : **~ (van)** camping-car *m*.

campground ['kæmpgraʊnd] *n* Am terrain *m* de camping.

camphor ['kæmfə°] *n* camphre *m*.

camping ['kæmpıŋ] *n* camping *m*; **to go ~** faire du camping.

camping site, campsite ['kæmpsaıt] *n* (terrain *m* de) camping *m*.

campus ['kæmpəs] (*pl* **-es** [-i:zl]) *n* campus *m*.

camshaft ['kæmʃɑːft] *n* arbre *m* à cames.

can[1] [kæn] (*pt & pp* **-ned**; *cont* **-ning**) ◇ *n* [of drink, food] boîte *f*; [of oil] bidon *m*; [of paint] pot *m* ◇ *vt* mettre en boîte.

can[2] [weak form kən, strong form kæn] (*pt & conditional* **could**; *negative* **cannot** OR **can't**) *modal vb* **- 1.** [be able to] pouvoir; **~ you come to lunch?** tu peux venir déjeuner?; **she couldn't come** elle n'a pas pu venir; **I ~'t** OR **cannot afford it** je ne peux pas me le payer; **~ you see/hear/smell something?** tu vois/entends/sens quelque chose? **- 2.** [know how to] savoir; **I ~ play the piano** je sais jouer du piano; **~ you drive/cook?** tu sais conduire/cuisiner?; **I ~ speak French** je parle le français **- 3.** [indicating permission, in polite requests] pouvoir; **you ~ use my car if you like** tu peux prendre ma voiture si tu veux; **we ~'t wear jeans to work** on ne peut pas aller au travail en jeans; **~ I speak to John, please?** est-ce que je pourrais parler à John, s'il vous plaît? **- 4.** [indicating disbelief, puzzlement] pouvoir; **what ~ she have done with it?** qu'est-ce qu'elle a bien pu en faire?; **we ~'t just leave him here** on ne peut tout de même pas le laisser ici; **you ~'t be serious!** tu ne parles pas sérieusement! **- 5.** [indicating possibility] : **I could see you tomorrow** je pourrais vous voir demain; **the train could have been cancelled** peut-être que le train a été annulé **- 6.** [indicating usual state or behaviour] : **she ~ be a bit difficult sometimes** elle peut parfois être (un peu) difficile; **Edinburgh ~ be very chilly** il peut faire très froid à Édimbourg, il arrive qu'il fasse très froid à Édimbourg.

Canada ['kænədə] *n* Canada *m*; **in ~** au Canada.

Canadian [kə'neıdjən] ◇ *adj* canadien(enne) ◇ *n* Canadien *m*, -enne *f*.

canal [kə'næl] *n* canal *m*.

Canaries [kə'neərız] *npl* : **the ~** les Canaries *fpl*.

canary [kə'neərı] (*pl* **-ies**) *n* canari *m*.

Canary Islands *npl :* the ~ les îles *fpl* Canaries ; **in the** ~ aux Canaries.

cancan ['kænkæn] *n* cancan *m*.

cancel ['kænsl] (Br *pt* & *pp* **-led** ; *cont* **-ling**, Am *pt* & *pp* **-ed** ; *cont* **-ing**) *vt* **- 1.** [gen] annuler ; [appointment, delivery] décommander **- 2.** [stamp] oblitérer ; [cheque] faire opposition à.

➤ **cancel out** *vt sep* annuler ; **to** ~ **each other out** s'annuler.

cancellation [ˌkænsə'leɪʃn] *n* annulation *f*.

cancer ['kænsər] ◇ *n* cancer *m* ◇ *comp :* ~ **patient** cancéreux *m*, -euse *f* ; ~ **research** lutte *f* contre le cancer ; ~ **ward** service *m* de cancérologie.

➤ **Cancer** *n* Cancer *m* ; **to be (a) Cancer** être Cancer.

cancerous ['kænsərəs] *adj* cancéreux(euse).

candelabra [ˌkændɪ'lɑːbrə] *n* candélabre *m*.

C and F, C & F (*abbr of* **cost and freight**) C et F.

candid ['kændɪd] *adj* franc (franche).

candidacy ['kændɪdəsɪ] *n* candidature *f*.

candidate ['kændɪdət] *n :* ~ **(for)** candidat *m*, -e *f* (pour).

candidature ['kændɪdətʃər] *n* candidature *f*.

candidly ['kændɪdlɪ] *adv* franchement.

candidness ['kændɪdnɪs] = **candour**.

candied ['kændɪd] *adj* confit(e).

candle ['kændl] *n* bougie *f*, chandelle *f* ; **to burn the** ~ **at both ends** *inf* brûler la chandelle par les deux bouts.

candlelight ['kændllaɪt] *n* lueur *f* d'une bougie OR d'une chandelle.

candlelit ['kændllɪt] *adj* aux chandelles.

candlestick ['kændlstɪk] *n* bougeoir *m*.

candour Br, **candor** Am ['kændər] *n* franchise *f*.

candy ['kændɪ] (*pl* **-ies**) *n* **- 1.** (U) [confectionery] confiserie *f* **- 2.** [sweet] bonbon *m*.

candyfloss ['kændɪflɒs] *n* Br barbe *f* à papa.

cane [keɪn] ◇ *n* **- 1.** (U) [for furniture] rotin *m* **- 2.** [walking stick] canne *f* **- 3.** [for punishment] : **the** ~ la verge **- 4.** [for supporting plant] tuteur *m* ◇ *comp* en rotin ◇ *vt* fouetter.

cane sugar *n* sucre *m* de canne.

canine ['keɪnaɪn] ◇ *adj* canin(e) ◇ *n :* ~ **(tooth)** canine *f*.

canister ['kænɪstər] *n* [for film, tea] boîte *f* ; [for gas, smoke] bombe *f*.

cannabis ['kænəbɪs] *n* cannabis *m*.

canned [kænd] *adj* **- 1.** [food, drink] en boîte **- 2.** *inf fig* [music] enregistré(e) ; [laughter] préenregistré(e).

cannelloni [ˌkænɪ'ləʊnɪ] *n* cannelloni *m*.

cannery ['kænərɪ] (*pl* **-ies**) *n* conserverie *f*.

cannibal ['kænɪbl] *n* cannibale *mf*.

cannibalize, -ise ['kænɪbəlaɪz] *vt* cannibaliser.

cannon ['kænən] (*pl inv* OR **-s**) *n* canon *m*.

➤ **cannon into** *vt fus* Br percuter.

cannonball ['kænənbɔːl] *n* boulet *m* de canon.

cannot ['kænɒt] *fml* ⊏⊐ **can²**.

canny ['kænɪ] (*compar* **-ier** ; *superl* **-iest**) *adj* [shrewd] adroit(e).

canoe [kə'nuː] (*pt* & *pp* **-d** ; *cont* **canoeing**) ◇ *n* canoë *m*, kayak *m* ◇ *vi* faire du canoë.

canoeing [kə'nuːɪŋ] *n* (U) canoë-kayak *m*.

canon ['kænən] *n* canon *m*.

canonize, -ise ['kænənaɪz] *vt* canoniser.

canoodle [kə'nuːdl] *vi* Br *inf* se faire des mamours.

can opener *n* ouvre-boîtes *m inv*.

canopy ['kænəpɪ] (*pl* **-ies**) *n* **- 1.** [over bed] ciel *m* de lit, baldaquin *m* ; [over seat] dais *m* **- 2.** [of trees, branches] voûte *f*.

cant [kænt] *n* (U) paroles *fpl* hypocrites.

can't [kɑːnt] = **cannot**.

Cantab. (*abbr of* **cantabrigiensis**) *de l'université de Cambridge.*

Cantabrian Mountains [kæn'teɪbrɪən-] *npl :* the ~ les monts *mpl* Cantabriques.

cantaloup Br, **cantaloupe** Am ['kæntəluːp] *n* cantaloup *m*.

cantankerous [kæn'tæŋkərəs] *adj* hargneux(euse).

canteen [kæn'tiːn] *n* **- 1.** [restaurant] cantine *f* **- 2.** [box of cutlery] ménagère *f*.

canter ['kæntər] ◇ *n* petit galop *m* ◇ *vi* aller au petit galop.

Canterbury ['kæntəbrɪ] *n* Cantorbéry.

cantilever ['kæntɪliːvər] *n* cantilever *m*.

Canton [kæn'tɒn] *n* Canton.

Cantonese [ˌkæntə'niːz] ◇ *adj* cantonais(e) ◇ *n* [language] cantonais *m*.

canvas ['kænvəs] *n* toile *f* ; **under** ~ [in a tent] sous la tente.

canvass ['kænvəs] ◇ *vt* **- 1.** POL [person] solliciter la voix de **- 2.** [opinion] sonder ◇ *vi* POL solliciter des voix.

canvasser ['kænvəsər] *n* **- 1.** POL agent *m* électoral **- 2.** [for opinion poll] sondeur *m*, -euse *f*.

canvassing ['kænvəsɪŋ] *n* **- 1.** POL démarchage *m* électoral **- 2.** [for opinion poll] sondage *m*.

canyon ['kænjən] *n* canyon *m*, cañon *m*.

canyoning ['kænjənɪŋ] *n* canyoning *m*.

cap [kæp] (*pt* & *pp* **-ped** ; *cont* **-ping**) ◇ *n*

- 1. [hat - gen] casquette *f; swimming ~* bonnet *m* de bain ; **to go ~ in hand to sb** se présenter humblement devant qqn - **2.** [of pen] capuchon *m;* [of bottle] capsule *f;* [of lipstick] bouchon *m* - **3.** Br [contraceptive device] diaphragme *m* ◇ *vt* - **1.** [top] : **to be capped with** être coiffé(e) de - **2.** [outdo] : **to ~ it all** pour couronner le tout.

CAP (*abbr of* **Common Agricultural Policy**) *n* PAC *f.*

capability [ˌkeɪpə'bɪlətɪ] (*pl* -ies) *n* capacité *f.*

capable ['keɪpəbl] *adj* : **~ (of)** capable (de).

capably ['keɪpəblɪ] *adv* avec compétence.

capacious [kə'peɪʃəs] *adj* fml vaste.

capacitor [kə'pæsɪtəʳ] *n* condensateur *m.*

capacity [kə'pæsɪtɪ] (*pl* -ies) ◇ *n* - **1.** (U) [limit] capacité *f*, contenance *f;* **full to ~** plein, comble ; **to work at full ~** [factory] travailler à plein rendement ; **seating ~** nombre *m* de places (assises) - **2.** [ability] : **~ (for)** aptitude *f* (à) - **3.** [role] qualité *f;* **in my ~ as ...** en ma qualité de ... ; **in an advisory ~** en tant que conseiller ◇ *comp* : **~ audience** salle *f* comble.

cape [keɪp] *n* - **1.** GEOGR cap *m* - **2.** [cloak] cape *f.*

Cape Canaveral [-kə'nævərəl] *n* le cap Canaveral.

Cape Cod *n* le cap Cod.

Cape Horn *n* le cap Horn.

Cape of Good Hope *n :* **the ~** le cap de Bonne-Espérance.

caper ['keɪpəʳ] ◇ *n* - **1.** CULIN câpre *f* - **2.** inf [dishonest activity] coup *m*, combine *f* ◇ *vi* gambader.

Cape Town *n* Le Cap.

Cape Verde [-vɜːd] *n :* **the ~ Islands** les îles *fpl* du Cap-Vert ; **in ~** au Cap-Vert.

capillary [kə'pɪlərɪ] (*pl* -ies) *n* capillaire *m.*

capita ⊳ **per capita.**

capital ['kæpɪtl] ◇ *adj* - **1.** [letter] majuscule - **2.** [offence] capital(e) ◇ *n* - **1.** [of country] : **~ (city)** capitale *f* - **2.** TYPO : **~ (letter)** majuscule *f;* **in ~s** en lettres majuscules - **3.** (U) [money] capital *m;* **to make ~ (out) of** fig tirer profit de.

capital allowance *n* amortissement *m* fiscal pour investissement.

capital assets *npl* actif *m* immobilisé, immobilisations *fpl.*

capital expenditure *n* (U) dépenses *fpl* d'investissement.

capital gains tax *n* impôt *m* sur les plus-values.

capital goods *npl* biens *mpl* d'équipement.

capital-intensive *adj* à fort coefficient de capitaux.

capitalism ['kæpɪtəlɪzm] *n* capitalisme *m.*

capitalist ['kæpɪtəlɪst] ◇ *adj* capitaliste ◇ *n* capitaliste *mf.*

capitalize, -ise ['kæpɪtəlaɪz] *vi :* **to ~ on** tirer parti de.

capital punishment *n* peine *f* capitale OR de mort.

capital stock *n* capital *m* social.

capital transfer tax *n* droits *mpl* de mutation.

Capitol ['kæpɪtl] *n :* **the ~** le Capitole.

Capitol Hill ['kæpɪtl-] *n* siège du Congrès à Washington.

capitulate [kə'pɪtjʊleɪt] *vi* capituler.

capitulation [kə,pɪtjʊ'leɪʃn] *n* capitulation *f.*

cappuccino [ˌkæpʊ'tʃiːnəʊ] (*pl* -s) *n* cappuccino *m.*

capricious [kə'prɪʃəs] *adj* capricieux(euse).

Capricorn ['kæprɪkɔːn] *n* Capricorne *m;* **to be (a) ~** être Capricorne.

caps [kæps] (*abbr of* **capital letters**) *npl* cap.

capsicum ['kæpsɪkəm] *n* poivron *m.*

capsize [kæp'saɪz] ◇ *vt* faire chavirer ◇ *vi* chavirer.

capsule ['kæpsjuːl] *n* - **1.** [gen] capsule *f* - **2.** MED gélule *f.*

Capt. (*abbr of* **captain**) cap.

captain ['kæptɪn] ◇ *n* capitaine *m* ◇ *vt* - **1.** [ship] commander - **2.** [sports team] être le capitaine de.

caption ['kæpʃn] *n* légende *f.*

captivate ['kæptɪveɪt] *vt* captiver.

captivating ['kæptɪveɪtɪŋ] *adj* captivant(e).

captive ['kæptɪv] ◇ *adj* captif(ive) ◇ *n* captif *m*, -ive *f.*

captivity [kæp'tɪvətɪ] *n* (U) : **in ~** en captivité *f.*

captor ['kæptəʳ] *n* ravisseur *m*, -euse *f.*

capture ['kæptʃəʳ] ◇ *vt* - **1.** [person, animal] capturer ; [city] prendre ; [market] conquérir - **2.** [attention, imagination] captiver - **3.** [subj : painting, photo] rendre - **4.** COMPUT saisir ◇ *n* [of person, animal] capture *f;* [of city] prise *f.*

car [kɑːʳ] ◇ *n* - **1.** AUT voiture *f* - **2.** RAIL wagon *m*, voiture *f* ◇ *comp* [door, accident] de voiture ; [industry] automobile.

Caracas [kə'rækəs] *n* Caracas.

carafe [kə'ræf] *n* carafe *f.*

caramel [ˈkærəmel] n caramel m.

caramelize, -ise [ˈkærəməlaɪz] vi se caraméliser.

carat [ˈkærət] n Br carat m ; 24-~ gold or à 24 carats.

caravan [ˈkærəvæn] ◇ n [gen] caravane f ; [towed by horse] roulotte f ◇ comp [holiday] en caravane.

caravanning [ˈkærəvænɪŋ] n Br caravaning m.

caravan site n Br camping m pour caravanes.

caraway seed [ˈkærəweɪ-] n graine f de carvi.

carbohydrate [ˌkɑːbəʊˈhaɪdreɪt] n CHEM hydrate m de carbone.

◆ **carbohydrates** npl [in food] glucides mpl.

carbon [ˈkɑːbən] n - **1.** [element] carbone m - **2.** = carbon copy - **3.** = carbon paper.

carbonated [ˈkɑːbəneɪtɪd] adj [mineral water] gazeux(euse).

carbon copy n - **1.** [document] carbone m - **2.** fig [exact copy] réplique f.

carbon dating [-ˈdeɪtɪŋ] n datation f au carbone 14.

carbon dioxide [-daɪˈɒksaɪd] n gaz m carbonique.

carbon fibre n fibre f de carbone.

carbon monoxide n oxyde m de carbone.

carbon paper n (U) (papier m) carbone m.

car-boot sale n Br brocante en plein air où les coffres des voitures servent d'étal.

carburettor Br, **carburetor** Am [ˌkɑːbəˈretəʳ] n carburateur m.

carcass [ˈkɑːkəs] n [of animal] carcasse f.

carcinogenic [ˌkɑːsɪnəˈdʒenɪk] adj carcinogène.

card [kɑːd] n - **1.** [gen] carte f ; to play one's ~s right fig bien jouer son jeu ; to put OR lay one's ~s on the table fig jouer cartes sur table - **2.** (U) [cardboard] carton m.

◆ **cards** npl : to play ~s jouer aux cartes.

◆ **on the cards** Br, **in the cards** Am adv inf : it's on the ~s that ... il y a de grandes chances pour que ...

cardamom [ˈkɑːdəməm] n cardamome f.

cardboard [ˈkɑːdbɔːd] ◇ n (U) carton m ◇ comp en carton.

cardboard box n boîte f en carton.

card-carrying adj : ~ member membre m.

card catalog n Am fichier m.

cardiac [ˈkɑːdɪæk] adj cardiaque.

cardiac arrest n arrêt m du cœur.

cardigan [ˈkɑːdɪgən] n cardigan m.

cardinal [ˈkɑːdɪnl] ◇ adj cardinal(e) ◇ n RELIG cardinal m.

cardinal number, cardinal numeral n nombre m cardinal.

card index n Br fichier m.

cardiograph [ˈkɑːdɪəgrɑːf] n cardiographe m.

cardiology [ˌkɑːdɪˈɒlədʒɪ] n cardiologie f.

cardiovascular [ˌkɑːdɪəʊˈvæskjʊləʳ] adj cardiovasculaire.

cardphone [ˈkɑːdfəʊn] n Br téléphone m à carte.

cardsharp [ˈkɑːdˌʃɑːp] n tricheur professionnel m, tricheuse professionnelle f.

card table n table f de jeu.

card vote n Br vote m par carte (chaque carte comptant pour le nombre de voix d'adhérents représentés).

care [keəʳ] ◇ n - **1.** (U) [protection, attention] soin m, attention f ; to be in ~ Br être à l'Assistance publique ; to take ~ of [look after] s'occuper de ; to take ~ (to do sthg) prendre soin (de faire qqch) ; take ~! faites bien attention à vous! - **2.** [cause of worry] souci m ◇ vi - **1.** [be concerned] se sentir concerné(e) ; to ~ about se soucier de - **2.** [mind] : I don't ~ ça m'est égal ; who ~s? qu'est-ce que ça peut faire? ; I couldn't ~ less inf je m'en moque pas mal.

◆ **care of** prep chez.

◆ **care for** vt fus dated [like] aimer.

CARE [keəʳ] (abbr of Cooperative for American Relief Everywhere) n organisation humanitaire américaine.

career [kəˈrɪəʳ] ◇ n carrière f ◇ comp de carrière ◇ vi aller à toute vitesse.

careerist [kəˈrɪərɪst] n pej carriériste mf.

careers [kəˈrɪəz] comp [office, teacher] d'orientation.

careers adviser n conseiller m, -ère f d'orientation.

career woman n femme f qui privilégie sa carrière.

carefree [ˈkeəfriː] adj insouciant(e).

careful [ˈkeəfʊl] adj - **1.** [cautious] prudent(e) ; to be ~ to do sthg prendre soin de faire qqch, faire attention à faire qqch ; be ~! fais attention! ; to be ~ with one's money regarder à la dépense - **2.** [work] soigné(e) ; [worker] consciencieux(euse).

carefully [ˈkeəflɪ] adv - **1.** [cautiously] prudemment - **2.** [thoroughly] soigneusement.

careless [ˈkeəlɪs] adj - **1.** [work] peu soigné(e) ; [driver] négligent(e) - **2.** [unconcerned] insouciant(e).

carelessly ['keəlɪslɪ] *adv* - **1.** [inattentively] sans faire attention - **2.** [unconcernedly] avec insouciance.

carelessness ['keəlɪsnɪs] *n* - **1.** [inattention] manque *m* d'attention - **2.** [lack of concern] insouciance *f*.

carer ['keərəʳ] *n personne qui s'occupe d'un parent malade ou handicapé.*

caress [kə'res] *◇ n* caresse *f ◇ vt* caresser.

caretaker ['keə,teɪkəʳ] *n* Br gardien *m*, -enne *f*.

caretaker government *n* gouvernement *m* intérimaire.

car ferry *n* ferry *m*.

cargo ['kɑːgəʊ] *(pl -es* OR *-s) ◇ n* cargaison *f ◇ comp :* ~ **ship** cargo *m*.

car hire *n* Br location *f* de voitures.

Carib ['kærɪb] *n* Caraïbe *mf*.

Caribbean [Br kærɪ'biːən, Am kə'rɪbɪən] *◇ adj* caraïbe *◇ n :* **the** ~ **(Sea)** la mer des Caraïbes OR des Antilles ; **in the** ~ dans les Caraïbes.

caribou ['kærɪbuː] *(pl inv* OR *-s) n* caribou *m*.

caricature ['kærɪkə,tjʊəʳ] *◇ n* - **1.** [cartoon] caricature *f* - **2.** [travesty] parodie *f ◇ vt* caricaturer.

caries ['keəriːz] *n* carie *f*.

caring ['keərɪŋ] *adj* bienveillant(e).

caring professions *npl :* **the** ~ les professions *fpl* de santé.

carnage ['kɑːnɪdʒ] *n* carnage *m*.

carnal ['kɑːnl] *adj* literary charnel(elle).

carnation [kɑː'neɪʃn] *n* œillet *m*.

carnival ['kɑːnɪvl] *n* carnaval *m*.

carnivore ['kɑːnɪvɔːʳ] *n* carnivore *mf*.

carnivorous [kɑː'nɪvərəs] *adj* carnivore.

carol ['kærəl] *n :* **(Christmas)** ~ chant *m* de Noël.

carouse [kə'raʊz] *vi* faire la fête.

carousel [,kærə'sel] *n* - **1.** [at fair] manège *m* - **2.** [at airport] carrousel *m*.

carp [kɑːp] *(pl inv* OR *-s) ◇ n* carpe *f ◇ vi :* **to** ~ **(about sthg)** critiquer (qqch).

car park *n* Br parking *m*.

Carpathians [kɑː'peɪθɪənz] *npl :* **the** ~ les Carpates *fpl ;* **in the** ~ dans les Carpates.

carpenter ['kɑːpəntəʳ] *n* [on building site, in shipyard] charpentier *m ;* [furniture-maker] menuisier *m*.

carpentry ['kɑːpəntrɪ] *n* [on building site, in ship-

yard] charpenterie *f ;* [furniture-making] menuiserie *f*.

carpet ['kɑːpɪt] *◇ n* lit & fig tapis *m ;* **(fitted)** ~ moquette *f ;* **to sweep sthg under the** ~ fig tirer le rideau sur qqch *◇ vt* [floor] recouvrir d'un tapis ; [with fitted carpet] recouvrir de moquette, moquetter ; ~**ed with snow** fig recouvert d'un tapis de neige.

carpet slipper *n* pantoufle *f*.

carpet sweeper [-,swiːpəʳ] *n* balai *m* mécanique.

car phone *n* téléphone *m* pour automobile.

car pool *n* Br [fleet of cars] parc *m* de voitures.

carport ['kɑː,pɔːt] *n* appentis *m* (pour voitures).

car rental *n* Am location *f* de voitures.

carriage ['kærɪdʒ] *n* - **1.** [of train, horsedrawn] voiture *f* - **2.** *(U)* [transport of goods] transport *m ;* ~ **paid** OR **free** Br franco de port ; ~ **forward** Br en port dû - **3.** [on typewriter] chariot *m* - **4.** *(U)* literary [bearing] port *m*.

carriage clock *n* pendule *f* de voyage *(décorative).*

carriage return *n* retour *m* chariot.

carriageway ['kærɪdʒweɪ] *n* Br chaussée *f*.

carrier ['kærɪəʳ] *n* - **1.** COMM transporteur *m* - **2.** [of disease] porteur *m*, -euse *f* - **3.** MIL : (aircraft) ~ porte-avions *m inv* - **4.** [on bicycle] porte-bagages *m inv* - **5.** = **carrier bag**.

carrier bag *n* sac *m* (en plastique).

carrier pigeon *n* pigeon *m* voyageur.

carrion ['kærɪən] *n (U)* charogne *f*.

carrot ['kærət] *n* carotte *f*.

carry ['kærɪ] *(pt & pp -ied) ◇ vt* - **1.** [subj : person, wind, water] porter ; [subj : vehicle] transporter - **2.** [disease] transmettre - **3.** [responsibility] impliquer ; [consequences] entraîner ; **this offence carries a fine of £50** ce délit entraîne une amende de 50 livres - **4.** [motion, proposal] voter - **5.** [baby] attendre - **6.** MATH retenir *◇ vi* [sound] porter.

◆ **carry away** *vt fus :* **to get carried away** s'enthousiasmer.

◆ **carry forward** *vt sep* FIN reporter.

◆ **carry off** *vt sep* - **1.** [plan] mener à bien - **2.** [prize] remporter.

◆ **carry on** *◇ vt fus* continuer ; **to** ~ **on doing sthg** continuer à OR de faire qqch *◇ vi* - **1.** [continue] continuer ; **to** ~ **on with sthg** continuer qqch - **2.** inf [make a fuss] faire des histoires - **3.** inf [have a love affair] : **to** ~ **on with sb** avoir une liaison avec qqn.

◆ **carry out** *vt fus* [task] remplir ; [plan, order]

exécuter ; [experiment] effectuer ; [investigation] mener.

➤ **carry through** *vt sep* [accomplish] réaliser.

carryall ['kærɪɔːl] *n* Am fourre-tout *m inv*.

carrycot ['kærɪkɒt] *n* couffin *m*.

carry-on *n* Br inf : **what a ~!** quelle histoire!

carry-out *n* plat *m* à emporter.

carsick ['kɑːˌsɪk] *adj* : **to be ~** être malade en voiture.

cart [kɑːt] <> *n* charrette *f* <> *vt* inf traîner.

carte blanche *n* carte *f* blanche.

cartel [kɑːˈtel] *n* cartel *m*.

cartilage ['kɑːtɪlɪdʒ] *n* cartilage *m*.

carton ['kɑːtn] *n* - **1.** [box] boîte *f* en carton - **2.** [of cream, yoghurt] pot *m*; [of milk] carton *m*.

cartoon [kɑːˈtuːn] *n* - **1.** [satirical drawing] dessin *m* humoristique - **2.** [comic strip] bande *f* dessinée - **3.** [film] dessin *m* animé.

cartoonist [kɑːˈtuːnɪst] *n* - **1.** [of satirical drawings] dessinateur *m*, -trice *f* humoristique - **2.** [of comic strips] dessinateur *m*, -trice *f* de bandes dessinées.

cartridge ['kɑːtrɪdʒ] *n* - **1.** [for gun, pen] cartouche *f* - **2.** [for camera] chargeur *m* - **3.** [for record player] tête *f* de lecture

cartridge paper *n* papier-cartouche *m*.

cartwheel ['kɑːtwiːl] *n* [movement] roue *f*.

carve [kɑːv] <> *vt* - **1.** [wood, stone] sculpter ; [design, name] graver - **2.** [slice - meat] découper <> *vi* découper.

➤ **carve out** *vt sep* fig se tailler.

➤ **carve up** *vt sep* fig diviser.

carving ['kɑːvɪŋ] *n* [of wood] sculpture *f*; [of stone] ciselure *f*.

carving knife *n* couteau *m* à découper.

car wash *n* [process] lavage *m* de voitures ; [place] station *f* de lavage de voitures.

Casablanca [ˌkæsəˈblæŋkə] *n* Casablanca.

cascade [kæˈskeɪd] <> *n* [waterfall] cascade *f* <> *vi* [water] tomber en cascade.

case [keɪs] *n* - **1.** [gen] cas *m*; **to be the ~** être le cas ; **in ~ of** en cas de ; **in that ~** dans ce cas ; **in which ~** auquel cas ; **as** OR **whatever the ~ may be** selon le cas ; **a ~ in point** un bon exemple - **2.** [argument] : **~ (for/against)** arguments *mpl* (pour/contre) - **3.** JUR affaire *f*, procès *m* - **4.** [container - gen] caisse *f*; [- for glasses etc] étui *m* - **5.** Br [suitcase] valise *f*.

➤ **in any case** *adv* quoi qu'il en soit, de toute façon.

➤ **in case** <> *conj* au cas où <> *adv* : **(just) in ~** à tout hasard.

case-hardened [-ˈhɑːdnd] *adj* [person] endurci(e).

case history *n* MED antécédents *mpl*.

case study *n* étude *f* de cas.

cash [kæʃ] <> *n (U)* - **1.** [notes and coins] liquide *m*; **to pay (in) ~** payer comptant OR en espèces - **2.** inf [money] sous *mpl*, fric *m* - **3.** [payment] : **~ in advance** paiement *m* à l'avance ; **~ on delivery** paiement à la livraison <> *vt* encaisser.

➤ **cash in** *vi* inf : **to ~ in on** tirer profit de.

cash and carry *n* libre-service *m* de gros, cash-and-carry *m*.

cashbook ['kæʃbʊk] *n* livre *m* de caisse.

cash box *n* caisse *f*.

cash card *n* carte *f* de retrait.

cash crop *n* culture *f* de rapport.

cash desk *n* Br caisse *f*.

cash discount *n* remise *f* OR rabais *m* au comptant.

cash dispenser [-dɪˌspensəʳ] *n* distributeur *m* automatique de billets.

cashew (nut) ['kæʃuː-] *n* noix *f* de cajou.

cash flow *n* marge *f* d'auto-financement, cash-flow *m*.

cashier [kæˈʃɪəʳ] *n* caissier *m*, -ère *f*.

cashless ['kæʃlɪs] *adj* : **~ pay system** système *m* de paiement électronique ; **~ society** société *f* de l'argent virtuel.

cash machine *n* distributeur *m* de billets.

cashmere [kæʃˈmɪəʳ] <> *n* cachemire *m* <> *comp* en OR de cachemire.

cash payment *n* paiement *m* comptant, versement *m* en espèces.

cash point, cashpoint *n* - **1.** [cash dispenser] distributeur *m* (automatique de billets), DAB *m* - **2.** [shop counter] caisse *f*.

cash price *n* prix *m* comptant.

cash register *n* caisse *f* enregistreuse.

cash sale *n* vente *f* au comptant.

casing ['keɪsɪŋ] *n* revêtement *m*; TECH boîtier *m*.

casino [kəˈsiːnəʊ] *(pl* -s) *n* casino *m*.

cask [kɑːsk] *n* tonneau *m*.

casket ['kɑːskɪt] *n* - **1.** [for jewels] coffret *m* - **2.** Am [coffin] cercueil *m*.

Caspian Sea ['kæspɪən-] *n* : **the ~** la (mer) Caspienne.

casserole ['kæsərəʊl] *n* - **1.** [stew] ragoût *m* - **2.** [pan] cocotte *f*.

cassette [kæˈset] *n* [of magnetic tape] cassette *f*; PHOT recharge *f*.

cassette deck *n* platine *f* à cassettes.

cassette player *n* lecteur *m* de cassettes.

cassette recorder *n* magnétophone *m* à cassettes.

cassock ['kæsək] *n* soutane *f*.

cast [kɑːst] (*pt* & *pp* cast) ⇔ *n* [CINEMA & THEATRE - actors] acteurs *mpl* ; [- list of actors] distribution *f* ⇔ *vt* - **1.** [throw] jeter ; **to ~ doubt on** sthg jeter le doute sur qqch ; **to ~ a spell (on)** jeter un sort (à) - **2.** CINEMA & THEATRE donner un rôle à - **3.** [vote] : **to ~ one's vote** voter - **4.** [metal] couler ; [statue] mouler.

➤ **cast about, cast around** *vi* : **to ~ about for** sthg chercher qqch.

➤ **cast aside** *vt sep* fig écarter, rejeter.

➤ **cast off** ⇔ *vt sep* [old practices] se défaire de ⇔ *vi* NAUT larguer les amarres.

castanets [,kæstə'nets] *npl* castagnettes *fpl*.

castaway ['kɑːstəweɪ] *n* naufragé *m*, -e *f*.

caste [kɑːst] *n* caste *f*.

caster ['kɑːstə^r] *n* [wheel] roulette *f*.

caster sugar *n* Br sucre *m* en poudre.

castigate ['kæstɪgeɪt] *vt* fml châtier, punir.

casting ['kɑːstɪŋ] *n* [for film, play] distribution *f*.

casting vote *n* voix *f* prépondérante.

cast iron *n* fonte *f*.

➤ **cast-iron** *adj* - **1.** [made of cast iron] en OR de fonte - **2.** [will] de fer ; [alibi] en béton.

castle ['kɑːsl] *n* - **1.** [building] château *m* - **2.** CHESS tour *f*.

castoffs ['kɑːst gt·fs] *npl* vieilles frusques *fpl*.

castor ['kɑːstə^r] = **caster**.

castor oil *n* huile *f* de ricin.

castor sugar = **caster sugar**.

castrate [kæ'streɪt] *vt* châtrer.

castration [kæ'streɪʃn] *n* castration *f*.

casual ['kæʒʊəl] *adj* - **1.** [relaxed, indifferent] désinvolte - **2.** [offhand] sans-gêne - **3.** [chance] fortuit(e) - **4.** [clothes] décontracté(e), sport *(inv)* - **5.** [work, worker] temporaire.

casually ['kæʒʊəlɪ] *adv* [in a relaxed manner] avec désinvolture ; **~ dressed** habillé simplement.

casualty ['kæʒjʊəltɪ] (*pl* -ies) *n* - **1.** [dead person] mort *m*, -e *f*, victime *f* ; [injured person] blessé *m*, -e *f* ; [of road accident] accidenté *m*, -e *f* - **2.** = **casualty department**.

casualty department *n* service *m* des urgences.

cat [kæt] *n* - **1.** [domestic] chat *m* ; **to be like a ~ on hot bricks** Br OR **on a hot tin roof** Am être sur des charbons ardents ; **to let the ~ out of the bag** vendre la mèche ; **to put the ~ among the pigeons** Br jeter un pavé dans la mare ; **to rain ~s and dogs** pleuvoir des cordes ; **the ~'s whiskers** Br le nombril du monde - **2.** [wild] fauve *m*.

cataclysmic [,kætə'klɪzmɪk] *adj* catastrophique.

catacombs ['kætəkuːmz] *npl* catacombes *fpl*.

Catalan ['kætə,læn] ⇔ *adj* catalan(e) ⇔ *n* - **1.** [person] Catalan *m*, -e *f* - **2.** [language] catalan *m*.

catalogue Br, **catalog** Am ['kætəlɒg] ⇔ *n* [gen] catalogue *m* ; [in library] fichier *m* ⇔ *vt* cataloguer.

Catalonia [,kætə'ləʊnɪə] *n* Catalogne *f* ; **in ~** en Catalogne.

Catalonian [,kætə'ləʊnɪən] ⇔ *adj* catalan(e) ⇔ *n* [person] Catalan *m*, -e *f*.

catalyst ['kætəlɪst] *n* lit & fig catalyseur *m*.

catalytic convertor [,kætə'lɪtɪkkən'vɜːtə^r] *n* pot *m* catalytique.

catamaran [,kætəmə'ræn] *n* catamaran *m*.

catapult ['kætəpʌlt] Br ⇔ *n* - **1.** [hand-held] lance-pierres *m inv* - **2.** HISTORY [machine] catapulte *f* ⇔ *vt* lit & fig catapulter.

cataract ['kætərækt] *n* cataracte *f*.

catarrh [kə'tɑː^r] *n* catarrhe *m*.

catastrophe [kə'tæstrəfɪ] *n* catastrophe *f*.

catastrophic [,kætə'strɒfɪk] *adj* catastrophique.

cat burglar *n* Br monte-en-l'air *m inv*.

catcall ['kætkɔːl] *n* sifflet *m*.

catch [kætʃ] (*pt* & *pp* caught) ⇔ *vt* - **1.** [gen] attraper ; **to ~ sight** OR **a glimpse of** apercevoir ; **to ~ sb's attention** attirer l'attention de qqn ; **to ~ sb's imagination** séduire qqn ; **to ~ the post** Br arriver à temps pour la levée - **2.** [discover, surprise] prendre, surprendre ; **to ~ sb doing sthg** surprendre qqn à faire qqch - **3.** [hear clearly] saisir, comprendre - **4.** [trap] : **I caught my finger in the door** je me suis pris le doigt dans la porte - **5.** [strike] frapper ⇔ *vi* - **1.** [become hooked, get stuck] se prendre - **2.** [fire] prendre, partir ⇔ *n* - **1.** [of ball, thing caught] prise *f* - **2.** [fastener - of box] fermoir *m* ; [- of window] loqueteau *m* ; [- of door] loquet *m* - **3.** [snag] hic *m*, entourloupette *f*.

➤ **catch at** *vt fus* attraper, essayer d'attraper.

➤ **catch on** *vi* - **1.** [become popular] prendre - **2.** inf [understand] : **to ~ on (to sthg)** piger (qqch).

➤ **catch out** *vt sep* [trick] prendre en défaut, coincer.

➤ **catch up** ⇔ *vt sep* rattraper ⇔ *vi* : **to ~ up on sthg** rattraper qqch.

➤ **catch up with** *vt fus* rattraper.

catch-22 [-twentɪ'tuː] *n* : it's a ~ situation on ne peut pas s'en sortir.

catch-all *adj* fourre-tout *(inv)*.

catching ['kætʃɪŋ] *adj* contagieux(euse).

catchment area ['kætʃmənt-] *n* Br [of school] secteur *m* de recrutement scolaire ; [of hospital] circonscription *f* hospitalière.

catchphrase ['kætʃfreɪz] *n* rengaine *f*.

catchword ['kætʃwɜːd] *n* slogan *m*.

catchy ['kætʃɪ] *(compar* -ier ; *superl* -iest) *adj* facile à retenir, entraînant(e).

catechism ['kætəkɪzm] *n* catéchisme *m*.

categorical [,kætɪ'gɒrɪkl] *adj* catégorique.

categorically [,kætɪ'gɒrɪklɪ] *adv* catégoriquement.

categorize, -ise ['kætəgəraɪz] *vt* [classify] : **to ~ sb (as sthg)** cataloguer qqn (en tant que OR comme).

category ['kætəgərɪ] *(pl* -ies) *n* catégorie *f*.

cater ['keɪtəʳ] *vi* [provide food] s'occuper de la nourriture, prévoir les repas.

◆ **cater for** *vt fus* Br - **1.** [tastes, needs] pourvoir à, satisfaire ; [customers] s'adresser à - **2.** [anticipate] prévoir.

◆ **cater to** *vt fus* satisfaire.

caterer ['keɪtərəʳ] *n* traiteur *m*.

catering ['keɪtərɪŋ] *n* [trade] restauration *f*.

caterpillar ['kætəpɪləʳ] *n* chenille *f*.

caterpillar tracks *npl* chenille *f*.

cat flap *n* Br chatière *f*.

catharsis [kə'θɑːsɪs] *(pl* -ses [-siːz]) *n* catharsis *f*.

cathedral [kə'θiːdrəl] *n* cathédrale *f*.

catheter ['kæθɪtəʳ] *n* cathéter *m*.

cathode ray tube *n* tube *m* cathodique.

Catholic ['kæθlɪk] ◇ *adj* catholique ◇ *n* catholique *mf*.

◆ **catholic** *adj* [tastes] éclectique.

Catholicism [kə'θɒlɪsɪzm] *n* catholicisme *m*.

catkin ['kætkɪn] *n* chaton *m*.

Catseyes® ['kætsaɪz] *npl* Br catadioptres *mpl*.

catsuit ['kætsuːt] *n* Br combinaison-pantalon *f*.

catsup ['kætsəp] *n* Am ketchup *m*.

cattle ['kætl] *npl* bétail *m*.

cattle grid *n* Br grille incluse dans le sol empêchant le bétail mais ivs les véhicules de passer.

catty ['kætɪ] *(compar* -ier ; *superl* -iest) *adj* inf pej [spiteful] rosse, vache.

catwalk ['kætwɔːk] *n* passerelle *f*.

Caucasian [kɔː'keɪzjən] ◇ *adj* caucasien(enne) ◇ *n* - **1.** GEOGR Caucasien *m*, -enne *f* - **2.** [white person] Blanc *m*, Blanche *f*.

Caucasus ['kɔːkəsəs] *n* : **the ~** le Caucase.

caucus ['kɔːkəs] *n* - **1.** Am POL comité *m* électoral *(d'un parti)* - **2.** Br POL comité *m* *(d'un parti)*.

CAUCUS

Les « Caucuses » aux États-Unis sont d'immenses rassemblements politiques, au cours desquels les deux partis nationaux américains choisissent leurs candidats et définissent leurs objectifs.

---

caught [kɔːt] *pt & pp* ▷ catch.

cauliflower ['kɒlɪ,flaʊəʳ] *n* chou-fleur *m*.

causal ['kɔːzl] *adj* causal(e).

cause [kɔːz] ◇ *n* cause *f* ; **I have no ~ for complaint** je n'ai pas à me plaindre, je n'ai pas lieu de me plaindre ; **to have ~ to do sthg** avoir lieu OR des raisons de faire qqch ; **to ~ a sensation** faire sensation ◇ *vt* causer ; **to ~ sb to do sthg** faire faire qqch à qqn ; **to ~ sthg to be done** faire faire qqch.

causeway ['kɔːzweɪ] *n* chaussée *f*.

caustic ['kɔːstɪk] *adj* caustique.

caustic soda *n* soude *f* caustique.

cauterize, -ise ['kɔːtəraɪz] *vt* MED cautériser.

caution ['kɔːʃn] ◇ *n* - **1.** (U) [care] précaution *f*, prudence *f* - **2.** [warning] avertissement *m* - **3.** Br JUR réprimande *f* ◇ *vt* - **1.** [warn] : **to ~ sb against doing sthg** déconseiller à qqn de faire qqch - **2.** [subj : policeman] *informer un suspect que tout ce qu'il dira peut être retenu contre lui* ; **to ~ sb for sthg** réprimander qqn pour qqch.

cautionary ['kɔːʃənərɪ] *adj* [tale] édifiant(e).

cautious ['kɔːʃəs] *adj* prudent(e).

cautiously ['kɔːʃəslɪ] *adv* avec prudence, prudemment.

cautiousness ['kɔːʃəsnɪs] *n* prudence *f*, circonspection *f*.

cavalier [,kævə'lɪəʳ] *adj* [offhand] cavalier(ère).

cavalry ['kævlrɪ] *n* cavalerie *f*.

cave [keɪv] *n* caverne *f*, grotte *f*.

◆ **cave in** *vi* - **1.** [roof, ceiling] s'affaisser - **2.** [yield] : **to ~ in (to sthg)** capituler OR céder (devant qqch).

caveman ['keɪvmæn] *(pl* -men [-men]) *n* homme *m* des cavernes.

cavern ['kævən] *n* caverne *f*.

cavernous ['kævənəs] *adj* [room, building] immense.

caviar(e) ['kævɪɑːʳ] n caviar m.

caving ['keɪvɪŋ] n Br spéléologie f; **to go ~** faire de la spéléologie.

cavity ['kævətɪ] (pl **-ies**) n cavité f.

cavity wall insulation n Br isolation f des murs creux.

cavort [kə'vɔːt] vi gambader.

cayenne (pepper) [keɪ'en-] n poivre m de cayenne.

CB n **- 1.** (abbr of citizens' band) CB f **- 2.** (abbr of Companion of (the Order of) the Bath) distinction honorifique britannique.

CBC (abbr of Canadian Broadcasting Corporation) n office national canadien de radiodiffusion.

CBE (abbr of Companion of (the Order of) the British Empire) n distinction honorifique britannique.

CBI n abbr of Confederation of British Industry.

CBS (abbr of Columbia Broadcasting System) n chaîne de télévision américaine.

cc ⬦ n (abbr of cubic centimetre) cm³ ⬦ (abbr of carbon copy) pcc.

CC n abbr of county council.

CCTV n abbr of closed circuit television.

CD ⬦ n (abbr of compact disc) CD m ⬦ **- 1.** abbr of civil defence **- 2.** (abbr of Corps Diplomatique) CD.

CDI (abbr of compact disc interactive) n CDI m.

CD player n lecteur m de CD.

Cdr. abbr of commander.

CD-ROM [ˌsiːdiːˈrɒm] (abbr of compact disc read only memory) n CD-ROM m, CD-Rom m.

CDT (abbr of Central Daylight Time) n heure d'été du centre des États-Unis.

CDV (abbr of compact disc video) n CD vidéo m.

CDW abbr of collision damage waiver.

CE abbr of Church of England.

cease [siːs] fml ⬦ vt cesser ; **to ~ doing** OR **to do sthg** cesser de faire qqch ⬦ vi cesser.

cease-fire n cessez-le-feu m inv.

ceaseless ['siːslɪs] adj fml incessant(e), continuel(elle).

ceaselessly ['siːslɪslɪ] adv fml sans arrêt OR cesse, continuellement.

cedar (tree) ['siːdəʳ-] n cèdre m.

cede [siːd] vt céder.

cedilla [sɪ'dɪlə] n cédille f.

CEEB (abbr of College Entry Examination Board) n commission d'admission dans l'enseignement supérieur aux États-Unis.

Ceefax® ['siːfæks] n Br télétexte m de la BBC.

ceilidh ['keɪlɪ] n manifestations informelles avec chants, contes et danses en Écosse et en Irlande.

ceiling ['siːlɪŋ] n lit & fig plafond m.

celebrate ['selɪbreɪt] ⬦ vt **- 1.** [gen] célébrer, fêter **- 2.** RELIG célébrer ⬦ vi faire la fête.

celebrated ['selɪbreɪtɪd] adj célèbre.

celebration [ˌselɪˈbreɪʃn] n **- 1.** (U) [activity, feeling] fête f, festivités fpl **- 2.** [event] festivités fpl.

celebrity [sɪ'lebrətɪ] (pl **-ies**) n célébrité f.

celeriac [sɪ'lerɪæk] n céleri-rave m.

celery ['selərɪ] n céleri m (en branches).

celestial [sɪ'lestjəl] adj céleste.

celibacy ['selɪbəsɪ] n célibat m.

celibate ['selɪbət] adj célibataire.

cell [sel] n [gen & COMPUT] cellule f.

cellar ['seləʳ] n cave f.

cellist ['tʃelɪst] n violoncelliste mf.

cello ['tʃeləʊ] (pl **-s**) n violoncelle m.

Cellophane® ['seləfeɪn] n Cellophane® f.

cellphone ['selfəʊn], **cellular phone** ['seljʊləʳ-] n téléphone m cellulaire.

cellulite ['seljʊlaɪt] n cellulite f.

Celluloid® ['seljʊlɔɪd] n celluloïd® m.

cellulose ['seljʊləʊs] n cellulose f.

Celsius ['selsɪəs] adj Celsius (inv).

Celt [kelt] n Celte m.

Celtic ['keltɪk] ⬦ adj celte ⬦ n [language] celte m.

cement [sɪ'ment] ⬦ n ciment m ⬦ vt lit & fig cimenter.

cement mixer n bétonnière f.

cemetery ['semɪtrɪ] (pl **-ies**) n cimetière m.

cenotaph ['senətɑːf] n cénotaphe m.

censor ['sensəʳ] ⬦ n censeur m ⬦ vt censurer.

censorship ['sensəʃɪp] n censure f.

censure ['senʃəʳ] ⬦ n blâme m, critique f ⬦ vt blâmer, critiquer.

census ['sensəs] (pl **-es** [-iːzl]) n recensement m.

cent [sent] n cent m.

centenary Br [sen'tiːnərɪ] (pl **-ies**), **centennial** Am [sen'tenjəl] n centenaire m.

center Am = centre.

centigrade ['sentɪɡreɪd] adj centigrade.

centigram(me) ['sentɪɡræm] n centigramme m.

centilitre Br, **centiliter** Am ['sentɪˌliːtəʳ] n centilitre m.

centimetre Br, **centimeter** Am ['sentɪˌmiːtəʳ] n centimètre m.

centipede ['sentɪpiːd] n mille-pattes m inv.

central ['sentrəl] adj central(e) ; **~ to** essentiel(elle) à ; **Central Europe** Europe f centrale.

Central African <> adj centrafricain(e) <> n Centrafricain m, -e f.

Central African Republic n : **the ~** la République centrafricaine ; **in the ~** en République centrafricaine.

Central America n Amérique f centrale ; **in ~** en Amérique centrale.

Central American <> adj centraméricain(e) <> n Centraméricain m, -e f.

Central Asia n Asie f centrale ; **in ~** en Asie centrale.

central government n l'État m (par opposition aux pouvoirs régionaux).

central heating n chauffage m central.

centralization [ˌsentrəlaɪˈzeɪʃn] n centralisation f.

centralize, -ise ['sentrəlaɪz] vt centraliser.

centralized ['sentrəlaɪzd] adj centralisé(e).

central locking [-ˈlɒkɪŋ] n AUT verrouillage m centralisé.

centrally ['sentrəlɪ] adv centralement.

centrally heated adj équipé(e) du chauffage central.

central nervous system n système m nerveux central.

central processing unit n COMPUT unité f centrale (de traitement).

central reservation n Br AUT terre-plein m central.

centre Br, **center** Am ['sentəʳ] <> n centre m ; **~ of attention** centre d'attraction, point m de mire ; **~ of gravity** centre de gravité <> adj - 1. [middle] central(e) ; **a ~ parting** une raie au milieu - 2. POL du centre, centriste <> vt centrer.

⏵ **centre around, centre on** vt fus se concentrer sur.

centre back n FTBL arrière m central.

centre-fold n [poster] photo f de pin-up.

centre forward n FTBL avant-centre m inv.

centre half n FTBL arrière m central.

centrepiece Br, **centerpiece** Am ['sentəpiːs] n - 1. [decoration] milieu m de table - 2. fig [principal element] élément m principal.

centre-spread n double page f centrale.

centrifugal force [sentrɪˈfjuːɡl-] n force f centrifuge.

century ['sentʃʊrɪ] (pl -ies) n siècle m.

CEO (abbr of chief executive officer) n Am président-directeur général m.

ceramic [sɪˈræmɪk] adj en céramique.

⏵ **ceramics** npl [objects] objets mpl en céramique.

cereal ['sɪərɪəl] n céréale f.

cerebral ['serɪbrəl] adj cérébral(e).

cerebral palsy n paralysie f cérébrale.

ceremonial [ˌserɪˈməʊnjəl] <> adj [dress] de cérémonie ; [duties] honorifique <> n cérémonial m.

ceremonious [ˌserɪˈməʊnjəs] adj solennel(elle).

ceremony ['serɪmənɪ] (pl -ies) n - 1. [event] cérémonie f - 2. (U) [pomp, formality] cérémonies fpl ; **without ~** sans cérémonie ; **to stand on ~** faire des cérémonies.

cert [sɜːt] n Br inf : **it's a (dead) ~** c'est tout ce qu'il y a de sûr, c'est couru.

cert. abbr of certificate.

certain ['sɜːtn] adj - 1. [gen] certain(e) ; **he is ~ to be late** il est certain qu'il sera en retard, il sera certainement en retard ; **to be ~ of sthg/of doing sthg** être assuré de qqch/de faire qqch, être sûr de qqch/de faire qqch ; **to make ~** vérifier ; **to make ~ of** s'assurer de ; **I know for ~ that ...** je suis sûr OR certain que ... ; **to a ~ extent** jusqu'à un certain point, dans une certaine mesure - 2. [named person] : **a ~ ...** un certain (une certaine) ...

certainly ['sɜːtnlɪ] adv certainement.

certainty ['sɜːtntɪ] (pl -ies) n certitude f.

CertEd [sɜːt'ed] (abbr of Certificate in Education) n diplôme universitaire en sciences de l'éducation.

certifiable [ˌsɜːtɪˈfaɪəbl] adj [mad] bon (bonne) à enfermer.

certificate [səˈtɪfɪkət] n certificat m.

certification [ˌsɜːtɪfɪˈkeɪʃn] n certification f.

certified ['sɜːtɪfaɪd] adj [teacher] diplômé(e) ; [document] certifié(e).

certified mail n Am envoi m recommandé.

certified public accountant n Am expert-comptable m.

certify ['sɜːtɪfaɪ] (pt & pp -ied) vt - 1. [declare true] : **to ~ (that)** certifier OR attester que - 2. [give certificate to] diplômer - 3. [declare insane] déclarer mentalement aliéné(e) ; **you should be certified!** on devrait t'enfermer!

cervical [sə'vaɪkl] adj [cancer] du col de l'utérus.

cervical smear n frottis m vaginal.

cervix ['sɜːvɪks] (pl -ices [-ɪsiːz]) n col m de l'utérus.

cesarean (section) [sɪ'zeərɪən-] = caesarean (section).

cessation [se'seɪʃn] n cessation f.

cesspit ['sespɪt], **cesspool** ['sespuːl] n fosse f d'aisance.

CET (abbr of Central European Time) n heure d'Europe centrale.

cf. (abbr of confer) cf.

c/f abbr of carried forward.

CFC (abbr of chlorofluorocarbon) n CFC m.

cg (abbr of centigram) cg.

CG n abbr of coastguard.

C & G (abbr of City and Guilds) n diplôme britannique d'enseignement technique.

CGA (abbr of colour graphics adapter) n adapteur m graphique couleur CGA.

CGT n abbr of capital gains tax.

ch (abbr of central heating) ch. cent.

ch. (abbr of chapter) chap.

CH (abbr of Companion of Honour) n distinction honorifique britannique.

Chad [tʃæd] n Tchad m ; **in ~** au Tchad.

chafe [tʃeɪf] <> vt [rub] irriter <> vi - **1.** [skin] être irrité(e) - **2.** [person] : **to ~ at** s'irriter OR s'énerver de.

chaff [tʃɑːf] (U) n balle f.

chaffinch ['tʃæfɪntʃ] n pinson m.

chain [tʃeɪn] <> n chaîne f ; **~ of events** suite f OR série f d'événements ; **~ of office** chaîne f OR insigne de la fonction de maire) <> vt [person, animal] enchaîner ; [object] attacher avec une chaîne.

chain letter n chaîne f.

chain reaction n réaction f en chaîne.

chain saw n tronçonneuse f.

chain-smoke vi fumer cigarette sur cigarette.

chain-smoker n grand fumeur m, grande fumeuse f.

chain store n grand magasin m (à succursales multiples).

chair [tʃeər] <> n - **1.** [gen] chaise f ; [armchair] fauteuil m - **2.** [university post] chaire f - **3.** [of meeting] présidence f ; **to take the ~** présider <> vt [meeting] présider ; [discussion] diriger.

chair lift n télésiège m.

chairman ['tʃeəmən] (pl -men [-mən]) n président m.

chairmanship ['tʃeəmənʃɪp] n présidence f.

chairperson ['tʃeə,pɜːsn] (pl -s) n président m, -e f.

chairwoman ['tʃeə,wʊmən] (pl -women [-,wɪmɪn]) n présidente f.

chaise longue [ʃeɪz'lɒŋ] (pl chaises longues [ʃeɪz'lɒŋ]) n méridienne f.

chalet ['ʃæleɪ] n chalet m.

chalice ['tʃælɪs] n calice m.

chalk [tʃɔːk] n craie f.
- **by a long chalk** adv de loin.
- **not by a long chalk** adv loin s'en faut, loin de là.
- **chalk up** vt sep [victory, success] remporter.

chalkboard ['tʃɔːkbɔːd] n Am tableau m (noir).

challenge ['tʃælɪndʒ] <> n défi m <> vt - **1.** [to fight, competition] : **she ~d me to a race/a game of chess** elle m'a défié à la course/aux échecs ; **to ~ sb to do sthg** défier qqn de faire qqch - **2.** [question] mettre en question OR en doute.

challenger ['tʃælɪndʒər] n challenger m.

challenging ['tʃælɪndʒɪŋ] adj - **1.** [task, job] stimulant(e) - **2.** [look, tone of voice] provocateur(trice).

chamber ['tʃeɪmbər] n [gen] chambre f.
- **chambers** npl [of barrister, judge] cabinet m.

chambermaid ['tʃeɪmbəmeɪd] n femme f de chambre.

chamber music n musique f de chambre.

chamber of commerce n chambre f de commerce.

chamber orchestra n orchestre m de chambre.

chameleon [kə'miːljən] n caméléon m.

chamois¹ ['ʃæmwɑː] (pl inv) n [animal] chamois m.

chamois² ['ʃæmɪ] n : **~ (leather)** peau f de chamois.

champ [tʃæmp] <> n inf champion m, -onne f <> vi [horse] ronger, mâchonner.

champagne [,ʃæm'peɪn] n champagne m.

champion ['tʃæmpjən] n champion m, -onne f.

championship ['tʃæmpjənʃɪp] n championnat m.

chance [tʃɑːns] <> n - **1.** (U) [luck] hasard m ; **by ~** par hasard ; **if by any ~** si par hasard - **2.** [likelihood] chance f ; **she didn't stand a ~ (of doing sthg)** elle n'avait aucune chance (de faire qqch) ; **on the off ~** à tout hasard - **3.** [opportunity] occasion f - **4.** [risk] risque m ; **to take a ~** risquer le coup ; **to take a ~ on do-**

ing sthg se risquer à faire qqch ◇ *adj* fortuit(e), accidentel(elle) ◇ *vt* - **1.** [risk] risquer ; **to ~ it** tenter sa chance - **2.** literary [happen] : **to ~ to do sthg** faire qqch par hasard.

chancellor [ˈtʃɑːnsələᵣ] *n* - **1.** [chief minister] chancelier *m* - **2.** UNIV président *m*, -e *f* honoraire.

Chancellor of the Exchequer *n* Br Chancelier *m* de l'Échiquier, ≃ ministre *m* des Finances.

chancy [ˈtʃɑːnsɪ] (*compar* -ier ; *superl* -iest) *adj* inf [risky] risqué(e).

chandelier [ˌʃændəˈlɪəᵣ] *n* lustre *m*.

change [tʃeɪndʒ] ◇ *n* - **1.** [gen] : **~ (in sb/in sthg)** changement *m* (en qqn/de qqch) ; **~ of clothes** vêtements *mpl* de rechange ; **to make a ~** changer (un peu) ; **for a ~** pour changer (un peu) - **2.** [money] monnaie *f* ◇ *vt* - **1.** [gen] changer ; **to ~ sthg into sthg** changer OR transformer qqch en qqch ; **to ~ one's mind** changer d'avis - **2.** [jobs, trains, sides] changer de ; **to ~ hands** COMM changer de main - **3.** [money - into smaller units] faire la monnaie de ; [- into different currency] changer ◇ *vi* - **1.** [gen] changer - **2.** [change clothes] se changer ; **to ~ into another pair of trousers** changer de pantalon - **3.** [be transformed] : **to ~ into** se changer en.

➡ **change over** *vi* [convert] : **to ~ over from/to** passer de/à

changeable [ˈtʃeɪndʒəbl] *adj* [mood] changeable ; [weather] variable.

changed [tʃeɪndʒd] *adj* changé(e).

change machine *n* distributeur *m* de monnaie.

change of life *n* : **the ~** le retour *m* d'âge.

changeover [ˈtʃeɪndʒˌəʊvəᵣ] *n* : **~ (to)** passage *m* (à), changement *m* (pour).

change purse *n* Am porte-monnaie *m* inv.

changing [ˈtʃeɪndʒɪŋ] *adj* changeant(e).

changing room *n* SPORT vestiaire *m* ; [in shop] cabine *f* d'essayage.

channel [ˈtʃænl] (Br *pt* & *pp* -led ; *cont* -ling, Am *pt* & *pp* -ed ; *cont* -ing) ◇ *n* - **1.** TV chaîne *f* ; RADIO station *f* - **2.** [for irrigation] canal *m* ; [duct] conduit *m* - **3.** [on river, sea] chenal *m* ◇ *vt* lit & fig canaliser.

➡ **Channel** *n* : **the (English) Channel** la Manche.

➡ **channels** *npl* : **to go through the proper ~s** suivre OR passer la filière.

Channel Islands *npl* : **the ~** les îles *fpl* Anglo-Normandes ; **in the ~** dans les îles Anglo-Normandes.

Channel tunnel *n* : **the ~** le tunnel sous la Manche.

chant [tʃɑːnt] ◇ *n* chant *m* ◇ *vt* - **1.** RELIG chanter - **2.** [words, slogan] scander ◇ *vi* - **1.** RELIG chanter - **2.** [repeat words] scander des mots/des slogans.

chaos [ˈkeɪɒs] *n* chaos *m*.

chaotic [keɪˈɒtɪk] *adj* chaotique.

chap [tʃæp] *n* Br inf [man] type *m*.

chapat(t)i [tʃəˈpætɪ] *n* galette *f* de pain indienne.

chapel [ˈtʃæpl] *n* chapelle *f*.

chaperon(e) [ˈʃæpərəʊn] ◇ *n* chaperon *m* ◇ *vt* chaperonner.

chaplain [ˈtʃæplɪn] *n* aumônier *m*.

chapped [tʃæpt] *adj* [skin, lips] gercé(e).

chapter [ˈtʃæptəᵣ] *n* chapitre *m*.

char [tʃɑːᵣ] (*pt* & *pp* -red ; *cont* -ring) ◇ *n* Br [cleaner] femme *f* de ménage ◇ *vt* [burn] calciner ◇ *vi* [work as cleaner] faire des ménages.

character [ˈkærəktəᵣ] *n* - **1.** [gen] caractère *m* ; **her behaviour is out of ~** ce comportement ne lui ressemble pas - **2.** [in film, book, play] personnage *m* - **3.** inf [eccentric] phénomène *m*, original *m*.

character code *n* COMPUT code *m* de caractère.

characteristic [ˌkærəktəˈrɪstɪk] ◇ *adj* caractéristique ◇ *n* caractéristique *f*.

characteristically [ˌkærəktəˈrɪstɪklɪ] *adv* de façon caractéristique.

characterization [ˌkærəktəraɪˈzeɪʃn] *n* caractérisation *f*.

characterize, -ise [ˈkærəktəraɪz] *vt* caractériser.

charade [ʃəˈrɑːd] *n* farce *f*.

➡ **charades** *n* (U) charades *fpl*.

charcoal [ˈtʃɑːkəʊl] *n* [for drawing] charbon *m* ; [for burning] charbon de bois.

chard [tʃɑːd] *n* bette *f*, blette *f*.

charge [tʃɑːdʒ] ◇ *n* - **1.** [cost] prix *m* ; **free of ~** gratuit ; **admission ~** prix d'entrée ; **delivery ~** frais *mpl* de port - **2.** JUR accusation *f*, inculpation *f* - **3.** [responsibility] : **to take ~ of** se charger de ; **to be in ~ of, to have ~ of** être responsable de ; **in ~** responsable - **4.** ELEC & MIL charge *f* ◇ *vt* - **1.** [customer, sum] faire payer ; **they ~ £5 for admission** le prix d'entrée est 5 livres ; **how much do you ~?** vous prenez combien ? ; **to ~ sthg to sb** mettre qqch sur le compte de qqn - **2.** [suspect, criminal] : **to ~ sb (with)** accuser qqn (de) - **3.** ELEC & MIL charger ◇ *vi* - **1.** [ask in payment] :

they don't ~ for delivery ils livrent gratuitement - **2.** [rush] se précipiter, foncer.

chargeable ['tʃɑ:dʒəbl] adj - **1.** [costs] : ~ **to** à la charge de - **2.** [offence] qui entraîne une inculpation.

charge account n compte m crédit.

charge card n carte f de compte crédit (auprès d'un magasin).

charged [tʃɑ:dʒd] adj [emotional] chargé(e).

charge hand n Br chef m d'équipe.

charge nurse n Br infirmier m, -ère f en chef.

charger ['tʃɑ:dʒəʳ] n - **1.** [for batteries] chargeur m - **2.** literary [soldier's horse] cheval m de bataille.

charge sheet n Br procès-verbal m.

chariot ['tʃærɪət] n char m.

charisma [kə'rɪzmə] n charisme m.

charismatic [ˌkærɪz'mætɪk] adj charismatique.

charitable ['tʃærətəbl] adj - **1.** [person, remark] charitable - **2.** [organization] de charité.

charity ['tʃærətɪ] (pl -ies) n charité f.

charlatan ['ʃɑ:lətən] n charlatan m.

charm [tʃɑ:m] ⬦ n charme m ⬦ vt charmer.

charm bracelet n bracelet m à breloques.

charmer ['tʃɑ:məʳ] n charmeur m, -euse f.

charming ['tʃɑ:mɪŋ] adj charmant(e).

charmingly ['tʃɑ:mɪŋlɪ] adv [attractive etc] de façon charmante ; [smile, dressed] avec charme.

charred [tʃɑ:d] adj calciné(e).

chart [tʃɑ:t] ⬦ n - **1.** [diagram] graphique m, diagramme m - **2.** [map] carte f ; **weather ~** carte f météorologique ⬦ vt - **1.** [plot, map] porter sur une carte - **2.** fig [record] retracer.
➤ **charts** npl : **the ~s** le hit-parade.

charter ['tʃɑ:təʳ] ⬦ n [document] charte f ⬦ vt [plane, boat] affréter.

chartered accountant [ˌtʃɑ:təd-] n Br expert-comptable m.

charter flight n vol m charter.

chart-topping adj Br qui est en tête du hit-parade.

chary ['tʃeərɪ] (compar -ier ; superl -iest) adj : **to be ~ of doing sthg** hésiter à faire qqch.

chase [tʃeɪs] ⬦ n [pursuit] poursuite f, chasse f ; **to give ~** poursuivre ⬦ vt - **1.** [pursue] poursuivre - **2.** [drive away] chasser - **3.** fig [money, jobs] faire la chasse à ⬦ vi : **to ~ after sb/sthg** courir après qqn/qqch.
➤ **chase up** vt sep Br [person, information] rechercher, faire la chasse à.

chaser ['tʃeɪsəʳ] n [drink] verre d'alcool qu'on prend après une bière.

chasm ['kæzm] n lit & fig abîme m.

chassis ['ʃæsɪ] (pl inv) n châssis m.

chaste [tʃeɪst] adj chaste.

chasten ['tʃeɪsn] vt châtier.

chastise [tʃæ'staɪz] vt fml [scold] punir, châtier.

chastity ['tʃæstətɪ] n chasteté f.

chat [tʃæt] (pt & pp -ted ; cont -ting) ⬦ n causerie f, bavardage m ; **to have a ~** causer, bavarder ⬦ vi causer, bavarder.
➤ **chat up** vt sep Br inf baratiner.

chatline ['tʃætlaɪn] n [gen] réseau m téléphonique (payant) ; [for sexual encounters] téléphone m rose.

chat room n COMPUT forum m de discussion.

chat show n Br talk-show m.

chatter ['tʃætəʳ] ⬦ n - **1.** [of person] bavardage m - **2.** [of animal, bird] caquetage m ⬦ vi - **1.** [person] bavarder - **2.** [animal, bird] jacasser, caqueter - **3.** [teeth] : **his teeth were ~ing** il claquait des dents.

chatterbox ['tʃætəbɒks] n inf moulin m à paroles. .

chatty ['tʃætɪ] (compar -ier ; superl -iest) adj [person] bavard(e) ; [letter] plein(e) de bavardages.

chauffeur ['ʃəʊfəʳ] ⬦ n chauffeur m ⬦ vt conduire.

chauvinist ['ʃəʊvɪnɪst] n - **1.** [sexist] macho m - **2.** [nationalist] chauvin m, -e f.

chauvinistic ['ʃəʊvɪ'nɪstɪk] adj - **1.** [sexist] macho, machiste - **2.** [nationalistic] chauvin(e).

cheap [tʃi:p] ⬦ adj - **1.** [inexpensive] pas cher (chère), bon marché (inv) - **2.** [at a reduced price - fare, rate] réduit(e) ; [- ticket] à prix réduit - **3.** [low-quality] de mauvaise qualité - **4.** [joke, comment] facile ⬦ adv (à) bon marché ⬦ n : **on the ~** pour pas cher.

cheapen ['tʃi:pn] vt [degrade] rabaisser.

cheaply ['tʃi:plɪ] adv à bon marché, pour pas cher.

cheapness ['tʃi:pnɪs] n - **1.** [low cost] bas prix m - **2.** [low quality] mauvaise qualité f - **3.** [joke, comment] facilité f.

cheapskate ['tʃi:pskeɪt] n inf grigou m.

cheat [tʃi:t] ⬦ n tricheur m, -euse f ⬦ vt tromper ; **to ~ sb out of sthg** escroquer qqch à qqn ; **to feel ~ed** se sentir lésé OR frustré ⬦ vi - **1.** [in game, exam] tricher - **2.** inf [be unfaithful] : **to ~ on sb** tromper qqn.

cheating ['tʃi:tɪŋ] n tricherie f.

Chechnya ['tʃetʃnɪə] n Tchétchénie f.

check [tʃek] <> n - **1.** [inspection, test] : ~ **(on)** contrôle m (de) - **2.** [restraint] : ~ **(on)** frein m (à), restriction f(sur) ; **to put a ~ on sthg** freiner qqch ; **to keep** OR **hold sthg in ~** [emotions] maîtriser qqch - **3.** Am [bill] note f - **4.** [pattern] carreaux mpl - **5.** Am = **cheque** <> vt - **1.** [test, verify] vérifier ; [passport, ticket] contrôler - **2.** [restrain, stop] enrayer, arrêter <> vi : **to ~ (for sthg)** vérifier (qqch) ; **to ~ on sthg** vérifier OR contrôler qqch.

check in <> vt sep [luggage, coat] enregistrer <> vi - **1.** [at hotel] signer le registre - **2.** [at airport] se présenter à l'enregistrement.

check off vt sep pointer, cocher.

check out <> vt sep - **1.** [luggage, coat] retirer - **2.** [investigate] vérifier <> vi [from hotel] régler sa note.

check up vi : **to ~ up on sb** prendre des renseignements sur qqn ; **to ~ up (on sthg)** vérifier (qqch).

checkbook Am = **chequebook**.

checked [tʃekt] adj à carreaux.

checkered Am = **chequered**.

checkers ['tʃekəz] n (U) Am jeu m de dames.

check guarantee card n Am carte f bancaire.

check-in n enregistrement m.

checking account ['tʃekɪŋ-] n Am compte m courant.

checklist ['tʃeklɪst] n liste f de contrôle.

checkmate ['tʃekmeɪt] n échec et mat m.

checkout ['tʃekaʊt] n [in supermarket] caisse f.

checkpoint ['tʃekpɔɪnt] n [place] (poste m de) contrôle m.

checkup ['tʃekʌp] n MED bilan m de santé, check-up m.

Cheddar (cheese) ['tʃedə^r-] n (fromage m de) cheddar m.

cheek [tʃiːk] <> n - **1.** [of face] joue f - **2.** inf [impudence] culot m <> vt inf être insolent(e) avec.

cheekbone ['tʃiːkbəʊn] n pommette f.

cheekily ['tʃiːkɪlɪ] adv avec insolence.

cheekiness ['tʃiːkɪnɪs] n insolence f.

cheeky ['tʃiːkɪ] (compar -ier ; superl -iest) adj insolent(e), effronté(e).

cheer [tʃɪə^r] <> n [shout] acclamation f <> vt - **1.** [shout for] acclamer - **2.** [gladden] réjouir <> vi applaudir.

cheers excl - **1.** [said before drinking] santé! - **2.** inf [goodbye] salut!, ciao!, tchao! - **3.** inf [thank you] merci.

cheer on vt sep encourager.

cheer up <> vt sep remonter le moral à <> vi s'égayer.

cheerful ['tʃɪəfʊl] adj joyeux(euse), gai(e).

cheerfully ['tʃɪəfʊlɪ] adv - **1.** [joyfully] joyeusement, gaiement - **2.** [willingly] de bon gré OR cœur.

cheerfulness ['tʃɪəfʊlnɪs] n gaieté f.

cheering ['tʃɪərɪŋ] <> adj [news, story] réconfortant(e) <> n (U) acclamations fpl.

cheerio [,tʃɪərɪ'əʊ] excl inf au revoir!, salut!

cheerleader ['tʃɪə,liːdə^r] n meneur m, -euse f.

cheerless ['tʃɪəlɪs] adj morne, triste.

cheery ['tʃɪərɪ] (compar -ier ; superl -iest) adj joyeux(euse).

cheese [tʃiːz] n fromage m.

cheeseboard ['tʃiːzbɔːd] n plateau m à fromage.

cheeseburger ['tʃiːz,bɜːgə^r] n cheeseburger m, hamburger m au fromage.

cheesecake ['tʃiːzkeɪk] n CULIN gâteau m au fromage blanc, cheesecake m.

cheesy ['tʃiːzɪ] (compar -ier ; superl -iest) adj [tasting of cheese] au goût de fromage.

cheetah ['tʃiːtə] n guépard m.

chef [ʃef] n chef m.

chemical ['kemɪkl] <> adj chimique <> n produit m chimique.

chemically ['kemɪklɪ] adv chimiquement.

chemical weapons npl armes fpl chimiques.

chemist ['kemɪst] n - **1.** Br [pharmacist] pharmacien m, -enne f ; **~'s (shop)** pharmacie f - **2.** [scientist] chimiste mf.

chemistry ['kemɪstrɪ] n chimie f.

chemotherapy [,kiːməʊ'θerəpɪ] n chimiothérapie f.

cheque Br, **check** Am [tʃek] n chèque m ; **to pay by ~** payer par chèque.

cheque account n compte m chèques.

chequebook Br, **checkbook** Am ['tʃekbʊk] n chéquier m, carnet m de chèques.

cheque card n Br carte f bancaire.

chequered Br ['tʃekəd], **checkered** Am ['tʃekərd] adj - **1.** [patterned] à carreaux - **2.** fig [career, life] mouvementé(e).

Chequers ['tʃekəz] n résidence secondaire officielle du Premier ministre britannique.

cherish ['tʃerɪʃ] vt chérir ; [hope] nourrir, caresser.

cherished ['tʃerɪʃt] adj cher (chère).

cherry ['tʃerɪ] (pl -ies) n [fruit] cerise f ; ~ **(tree)** cerisier m.

cherub ['tʃerəb] (pl -s OR -im [-ɪm]) n chérubin m.

chervil ['tʃɜːvɪl] n cerfeuil m.

Ches. (abbr of Cheshire) comté anglais.

chess [tʃes] n échecs mpl.

chessboard ['tʃesbɔːd] n échiquier m.

chessman ['tʃesmæn] (pl -men [-men]) n pièce f.

chest [tʃest] n - 1. ANAT poitrine f ; to get sthg off one's ~ inf déballer ce qu'on a sur le cœur - 2. [box] coffre m.

chesterfield ['tʃestəfiːld] n canapé m.

chestnut ['tʃesnʌt] <> adj [colour] châtain (inv) <> n [nut] châtaigne f ; ~ (tree) châtaignier m.

chest of drawers (pl chests of drawers) n commode f.

chesty ['tʃestɪ] (compar -ier ; superl -iest) adj [cough] de poitrine.

chevron ['ʃevrən] n chevron m.

chew [tʃuː] <> n [sweet] bonbon m (à mâcher) <> vt mâcher.

➤ **chew over** vt sep fig [think over] ruminer, remâcher.

➤ **chew up** vt sep mâchouiller.

chewing gum ['tʃuːɪŋ-] n chewing-gum m.

chewy [tʃuːɪ] (compar -ier ; superl -iest) adj [food] difficile à mâcher.

chic [ʃiːk] <> adj chic (inv) <> n chic m.

chicanery [ʃɪ'keɪnərɪ] n (U) chicane f.

chick [tʃɪk] n [baby bird] oisillon m.

chicken ['tʃɪkɪn] <> adj inf [cowardly] froussard(e) <> n - 1. [bird, food] poulet m ; it's a ~ and egg situation c'est l'histoire de la poule et de l'œuf - 2. inf [coward] froussard m, -e f.

➤ **chicken out** vi inf se dégonfler.

chickenfeed ['tʃɪkɪnfiːd] n (U) fig bagatelle f.

chickenpox ['tʃɪkɪnpɒks] n (U) varicelle f.

chicken wire n grillage m.

chickpea ['tʃɪkpiː] n pois m chiche.

chicory ['tʃɪkərɪ] n [vegetable] endive f.

chide [tʃaɪd] (pt chided OR chid [tʃɪd], pp chid OR chidden ['tʃɪdn]) vt literary : to ~ sb (for sthg) réprimander qqn (à propos de qqch).

chief [tʃiːf] <> adj - 1. [main - aim, problem] principal(e) - 2. [head] en chef <> n chef m.

chief constable n Br commissaire m de police divisionnaire.

chief executive n directeur général m, directrice générale f.

➤ **Chief Executive** n Am : the Chief Executive le président des États-Unis.

chief justice n président m de la Cour Suprême (des États-Unis).

chiefly ['tʃiːflɪ] adv - 1. [mainly] principalement - 2. [above all] surtout.

chief of staff n chef m d'état-major.

chief superintendent n Br commissaire m de police principal.

chieftain ['tʃiːftən] n chef m.

chiffon ['ʃɪfɒn] n mousseline f.

chihuahua [tʃɪ'wɑːwə] n chihuahua m.

chilblain ['tʃɪlbleɪn] n engelure f.

child [tʃaɪld] (pl children ['tʃɪldrən]) n enfant mf.

childbearing ['tʃaɪld,beərɪŋ] n maternité f.

child benefit n (U) Br ≃ allocations fpl familiales.

childbirth ['tʃaɪldbɜːθ] n (U) accouchement m.

childhood ['tʃaɪldhʊd] n enfance f.

childish ['tʃaɪldɪʃ] adj pej puéril(e), enfantin(e).

childishly ['tʃaɪldɪʃlɪ] adv pej de façon puérile.

childless ['tʃaɪldlɪs] adj sans enfants.

childlike ['tʃaɪldlaɪk] adj enfantin(e), d'enfant.

childminder ['tʃaɪld,maɪndər] n Br gardienne f d'enfants, nourrice f.

child prodigy n enfant mf prodige.

childproof ['tʃaɪldpruːf] adj [container] qui ne peut pas être ouvert par les enfants ; ~ lock verrouillage m de sécurité pour enfants.

children ['tʃɪldrən] pl ⊏— child.

children's home n maison f d'enfants.

Chile ['tʃɪlɪ] n Chili m ; in ~ au Chili.

Chilean ['tʃɪlɪən] <> adj chilien(enne) <> n Chilien m, -enne f.

chili ['tʃɪlɪ] = chilli.

chill [tʃɪl] <> adj frais (fraîche) <> n - 1. [illness] coup m de froid - 2. [in temperature] : there's a ~ in the air le fond de l'air est frais - 3. [feeling of fear] frisson m <> vt - 1. [drink, food] mettre au frais - 2. [person] faire frissonner <> vi [drink, food] rafraîchir.

chilli ['tʃɪlɪ] (pl -es) n [vegetable] piment m.

chilling ['tʃɪlɪŋ] adj - 1. [very cold] glacial(e) - 2. [frightening] qui glace le sang.

chilli powder n poudre f de piment.

chilly ['tʃɪlɪ] (compar -ier ; superl -iest) adj froid(e) ; to feel ~ avoir froid ; it's ~ il fait froid.

chime [tʃaɪm] <> n [of bell, clock] carillon m

◇ vt [time] sonner ◇ vi [bell, clock] carillonner.

chimney ['tʃɪmnɪ] n cheminée f.

chimneypot ['tʃɪmnɪpɒt] n mitre f de cheminée.

chimneysweep ['tʃɪmnɪswiːp] n ramoneur m.

chimp(anzee) [tʃɪmp(ən'ziː)] n chimpanzé m.

chin [tʃɪn] n menton m.

china ['tʃaɪnə] ◇ n porcelaine f ◇ comp en porcelaine.

China ['tʃaɪnə] n Chine f ; in ~ en Chine ; the People's Republic of ~ la République populaire de Chine.

china clay n kaolin m.

China Sea n : the ~ la mer de Chine.

Chinatown ['tʃaɪnətaʊn] n quartier m chinois.

chinchilla [tʃɪn'tʃɪlə] n chinchilla m.

Chinese [ˌtʃaɪ'niːz] ◇ adj chinois(e) ◇ n [language] chinois m ◇ npl : the ~ les Chinois mpl.

Chinese cabbage n chou m chinois.

Chinese lantern n lanterne f vénitienne.

Chinese leaves npl Br = **Chinese cabbage**.

chink [tʃɪŋk] ◇ n - **1.** [narrow opening] fente f - **2.** [sound] tintement m ◇ vi tinter.

chinos ['tʃiːnəʊz] npl pantalon de grosse toile beige porté à l'origine par les militaires de l'armée de l'air américaine.

chintz [tʃɪnts] ◇ n chintz m ◇ comp de chintz.

chinwag ['tʃɪnwæg] n inf : to have a ~ tailler une bavette.

chip [tʃɪp] (pt & pp -**ped** ; cont -**ping**) ◇ n - **1.** Br [fried potato] frite f ; Am [potato crisp] chip m - **2.** [of glass, metal] éclat m ; [of wood] copeau m - **3.** [flaw] ébréchure f - **4.** [microchip] puce f - **5.** [for gambling] jeton m - **6.** phr : **when the ~s are down** en cas de coup dur ; **to have a ~ on one's shoulder** en avoir gros sur le cœur ◇ vt [cup, glass] ébrécher.

◆ **chip in** inf ◇ vt fus [contribute] contribuer ◇ vi - **1.** [contribute] contribuer - **2.** [interrupt] mettre son grain de sel.

◆ **chip off** vt sep enlever petit morceau par petit morceau.

chip-based [-beɪst] adj COMPUT à puce.

chipboard ['tʃɪpbɔːd] n aggloméré m.

chipmunk ['tʃɪpmʌŋk] n tamia m.

chipolata [ˌtʃɪpə'lɑːtə] n chipolata f.

chipped [tʃɪpt] adj [flawed] ébréché(e).

chippings ['tʃɪpɪŋz] npl [on road] gravillons

mpl ; [of wood] copeaux mpl ; '**loose** ~' 'attention gravillons'.

chip shop n Br friterie f.

chiropodist [kɪ'rɒpədɪst] n pédicure mf.

chiropody [kɪ'rɒpədɪ] n podologie f.

chirp [tʃɜːp] vi [bird] pépier ; [cricket] chanter.

chirpy ['tʃɜːpɪ] (compar -**ier** ; superl -**iest**) adj gai(e).

chisel ['tʃɪzl] (Br pt & pp -**led** ; cont -**ling**, Am pt & pp -**ed** ; cont -**ing**) ◇ n [for wood] ciseau m ; [for metal, rock] burin m ◇ vt ciseler.

chit [tʃɪt] n [note] note f, reçu m.

chitchat ['tʃɪttʃæt] n (U) inf bavardage m.

chivalrous ['ʃɪvlrəs] adj chevaleresque.

chivalry ['ʃɪvlrɪ] n (U) - **1.** literary [of knights] chevalerie f - **2.** [good manners] galanterie f.

chives [tʃaɪvz] npl ciboulette f.

chivy, chivvy ['tʃɪvɪ] (pt & pp -**ied**) vt inf harceler ; **to ~ sb along** faire se dépêcher qqn.

chloride ['klɔːraɪd] n chlorure m.

chlorinated ['klɔːrɪneɪtɪd] adj chloré(e).

chlorine ['klɔːriːn] n chlore m.

chlorofluorocarbon ['klɔːrəʊˌflɔːrəʊ'kɑːbən] n chlorofluorocarbone m.

chloroform ['klɒrəfɔːm] n chloroforme m.

chlorophyll ['klɒrəfɪl] n chlorophylle f.

choc-ice ['tʃɒkaɪs] n Br Esquimau® m.

chock [tʃɒk] n cale f.

chock-a-block, **chock-full** adj inf : ~ (**with**) plein(e) à craquer (de).

chocolate ['tʃɒkələt] ◇ n chocolat m ◇ comp au chocolat.

choice [tʃɔɪs] ◇ n choix m ; **we had no ~ but to accept** nous ne pouvions pas faire autrement que d'accepter ; **by** OR **from** ~ par choix ◇ adj de choix.

choir ['kwaɪə'] n chœur m.

choirboy ['kwaɪəbɔɪ] n jeune choriste m.

choke [tʃəʊk] ◇ n AUT starter m ◇ vt - **1.** [strangle] étrangler, étouffer - **2.** [block] obstruer, boucher ◇ vi s'étrangler.

◆ **choke back** vt fus [anger] étouffer ; [tears] refouler.

cholera ['kɒlərə] n choléra m.

cholesterol [kə'lestərɒl] n cholestérol m.

choose [tʃuːz] (pt **chose**, pp **chosen**) ◇ vt - **1.** [select] choisir ; **there's little** OR **not much to ~ between them** ils se valent - **2.** [decide] : **to ~ to do sthg** décider OR choisir de faire qqch ◇ vi [select] : **to ~ (from)** choisir (parmi OR entre).

choos(e)y ['tʃuːzɪ] (compar -ier ; superl -iest) adj difficile.

chop [tʃɒp] (pt & pp -ped ; cont -ping) ◇ n - **1.** CULIN côtelette f - **2.** [blow] coup m (de hache etc) ; **he's for the ~** fig il va sûrement se faire saquer ◇ vt - **1.** [wood] couper ; [vegetables] hacher - **2.** inf fig [funding, budget] réduire - **3.** phr : **to ~ and change** changer sans cesse d'avis.
➤ **chops** npl inf babines fpl.
➤ **chop down** vt sep [tree] abattre.
➤ **chop up** vt sep couper en morceaux.

chopper ['tʃɒpə'] n - **1.** [axe] couperet m - **2.** inf [helicopter] hélico m.

chopping board ['tʃ ɡt·pɪŋ-] n hachoir m.

choppy ['tʃɒpɪ] (compar -ier ; superl -iest) adj [sea] agité(e).

chopsticks ['tʃɒpstɪks] npl baguettes fpl.

choral ['kɔːrəl] adj choral(e).

chord [kɔːd] n MUS accord m ; **to strike a ~ with sb** toucher qqn.

chore [tʃɔːʳ] n corvée f ; **household ~s** travaux mpl ménagers.

choreographer [ˌkɒrɪ'ɒɡrəfəʳ] n chorégraphe mf.

choreography [ˌkɒrɪ'ɒɡrəfɪ] n chorégraphie f.

chortle ['tʃɔːtl] vi glousser.

chorus ['kɔːrəs] ◇ n - **1.** [part of song] refrain m - **2.** [singers] chœur m - **3.** fig [of praise, complaints] concert m ◇ vt répondre en chœur.

chose [tʃəʊz] pt ⊳ choose.

chosen ['tʃəʊzn] pp ⊳ choose.

choux pastry [ʃuː-] n pâte f à choux.

chow [tʃaʊ] n [dog] chow-chow m.

chowder ['tʃaʊdəʳ] n [of fish] soupe f de poisson ; [of seafood] soupe aux fruits de mer.

Christ [kraɪst] ◇ n Christ m ◇ excl Seigneur!, bon Dieu!

christen ['krɪsn] vt - **1.** [baby] baptiser - **2.** [name] nommer.

christening ['krɪsnɪŋ] ◇ n baptême m ◇ comp de baptême.

Christian ['krɪstʃən] ◇ adj - **1.** RELIG chrétien(enne) - **2.** [kind] charitable ◇ n chrétien m, -enne f.

Christianity [ˌkrɪstɪ'ænətɪ] n christianisme m.

Christian name n prénom m.

Christmas ['krɪsməs] ◇ n Noël m ; **happy** OR **merry ~!** joyeux Noël! ◇ comp de Noël.

Christmas cake n Br gâteau m de Noël.

Christmas card n carte f de Noël.

Christmas cracker n Br diablotin m.

Christmas Day n jour m de Noël.

Christmas Eve n veille f de Noël.

Christmas Island n l'île f Christmas ; **on ~** à l'île Christmas.

Christmas pudding n Br pudding m (de Noël).

Christmas stocking n ≃ soulier m de Noël.

Christmastime ['krɪsməstaɪm] n : **at ~** à Noël.

Christmas tree n arbre m de Noël.

chrome [krəʊm], **chromium** ['krəʊmɪəm] ◇ n chrome m ◇ comp chromé(e).

chromosome ['krəʊməsəʊm] n chromosome m.

chronic ['krɒnɪk] adj [illness, unemployment] chronique ; [liar, alcoholic] invétéré(e).

chronically ['krɒnɪklɪ] adv de façon chronique.

chronicle ['krɒnɪkl] ◇ n chronique f ◇ vt faire la chronique de.

chronological [ˌkrɒnə'lɒdʒɪkl] adj chronologique.

chronologically [ˌkrɒnə'lɒdʒɪklɪ] adv chronologiquement.

chronology [krə'nɒlədʒɪ] n chronologie f.

chrysalis ['krɪsəlɪs] (pl -lises [-lɪsiːz]) n chrysalide f.

chrysanthemum [krɪ'sænθəməm] (pl -s) n chrysanthème m.

chubbiness ['tʃʌbɪnɪs] n rondeur f

chubby ['tʃʌbɪ] (compar -bier ; superl -biest) adj [cheeks, face] joufflu(e) ; [person, hands] potelé(e).

chuck [tʃʌk] vt inf - **1.** [throw] lancer, envoyer - **2.** [job, boyfriend] laisser tomber.
➤ **chuck away, chuck out** vt sep inf jeter, balancer.

chuckle ['tʃʌkl] ◇ n petit rire m ◇ vi glousser.

chuffed [tʃʌft] adj Br inf : **~ (with sthg/to do sthg)** ravi(e) (de qqch/de faire qqch).

chug [tʃʌɡ] (pt & pp -ged ; cont -ging) vi [train] faire teuf-teuf.

chum [tʃʌm] n inf copain m, copine f.

chummy ['tʃʌmɪ] (compar -mier ; superl -miest) adj inf : **to be ~ with sb** être copain (copine) avec qqn.

chump [tʃʌmp] n inf imbécile mf.

chunk [tʃʌŋk] n gros morceau m.

chunky ['tʃʌŋkɪ] (compar -ier ; superl -iest) adj

[person, furniture] trapu(e) ; [sweater, jewellery] gros (grosse).

church [tʃɜːtʃ] n - **1.** [building] église f; **to go to ~** aller à l'église ; [Catholics] aller à la messe - **2.** [organization] Église f.

churchgoer [ˈtʃɜːtʃˌgəʊəʳ] n pratiquant m, -e f.

churchman [ˈtʃɜːtʃmən] (pl **-men** [-mən]) n membre m du clergé, ecclésiastique m.

Church of England n : **the ~** l'Église d'Angleterre.

THE CHURCH OF ENGLAND

L'Église d'Angleterre (de confession anglicane) est l'Église officielle de la Grande-Bretagne ; son chef laïc est le souverain, son chef spirituel l'archevêque de Cantorbéry.

Church of Scotland n : **the ~** l'Église f d'Écosse.

churchyard [ˈtʃɜːtʃjɑːd] n cimetière m.

churlish [ˈtʃɜːlɪʃ] adj grossier(ère).

churn [tʃɜːn] ⬦ n - **1.** [for making butter] baratte f - **2.** [for milk] bidon m ⬦ vt [stir up] battre ⬦ vi : **my stomach was ~ing** j'avais l'estomac tout retourné.

➡ **churn out** vt sep inf produire en série.

➡ **churn up** vt sep battre.

chute [ʃuːt] n glissière f; **rubbish ~** vide-ordures m inv.

chutney [ˈtʃʌtnɪ] n chutney m.

CI abbr of **Channel Islands.**

CIA (abbr of **Central Intelligence Agency**) n CIA f.

CIB (abbr of **Criminal Investigation Branch**) n la police judiciaire américaine.

cicada [sɪˈkɑːdə] n cigale f.

CID (abbr of **Criminal Investigation Department**) n la police judiciaire britannique.

cider [ˈsaɪdəʳ] n cidre m.

CIF (abbr of **cost, insurance and freight**) CAF, caf.

cigar [sɪˈgɑːʳ] n cigare m.

cigarette [ˌsɪgəˈret] n cigarette f.

cigarette butt n mégot m.

cigarette end Br = **cigarette butt.**

cigarette holder n fume-cigarette m inv.

cigarette lighter n briquet m.

cigarette paper n papier m à cigarettes.

C-in-C n abbr of **commander-in-chief.**

cinch [sɪntʃ] n inf : **it's a ~** c'est un jeu d'enfants.

cinder [ˈsɪndəʳ] n cendre f.

cinderblock [ˈsɪndəblɒgtˌk] n Am parpaing m.

Cinderella [ˌsɪndəˈrelə] n Cendrillon f.

cine-camera [ˈsɪnɪ-] n caméra f.

cine-film [ˈsɪnɪ-] n film m.

cinema [ˈsɪnəmə] n cinéma m.

cinematic [ˌsɪnɪˈmætɪk] adj cinématographique.

cinnamon [ˈsɪnəmən] n cannelle f.

cipher [ˈsaɪfəʳ] n [secret writing] code m.

circa [ˈsɜːkə] prep environ.

circle [ˈsɜːkl] ⬦ n - **1.** [gen] cercle m; **to come full ~** revenir à son point de départ ; **to go round in ~s** fig tourner en rond - **2.** [in theatre, cinema] balcon m ⬦ vt - **1.** [draw a circle round] entourer (d'un cercle) - **2.** [move round] faire le tour de ⬦ vi [plane] tourner en rond.

circuit [ˈsɜːkɪt] n - **1.** [gen & ELEC] circuit m - **2.** [lap] tour m ; [movement round] révolution f.

circuit board n plaquette f (de circuits imprimés).

circuit breaker n disjoncteur m.

circuitous [səˈkjuːɪtəs] adj indirect(e).

circular [ˈsɜːkjʊləʳ] ⬦ adj - **1.** [gen] circulaire - **2.** [argument] qui tourne en rond ⬦ n [letter] circulaire f; [advertisement] prospectus m.

circulate [ˈsɜːkjʊleɪt] ⬦ vi - **1.** [gen] circuler - **2.** [socialize] se mêler aux invités ⬦ vt [rumour] propager ; [document] faire circuler.

circulation [ˌsɜːkjʊˈleɪʃn] n - **1.** [gen] circulation f - **2.** PRESS tirage m.

circumcise [ˈsɜːkəmsaɪz] vt circoncire.

circumcision [ˌsɜːkəmˈsɪʒn] n circoncision f.

circumference [səˈkʌmfərəns] n circonférence f.

circumflex [ˈsɜːkəmfleks] n : **~ (accent)** accent m circonflexe.

circumnavigate [ˌsɜːkəmˈnævɪgeɪt] vt : **to ~ the world** faire le tour du monde en bateau.

circumscribe [ˈsɜːkəmskraɪb] vt fml [restrict] limiter.

circumspect [ˈsɜːkəmspekt] adj circonspect(e).

circumstances [ˈsɜːkəmstənsɪz] npl circonstances fpl ; **under OR in no ~** en aucun cas ; **under OR in the ~** en de telles circonstances.

circumstantial [ˌsɜːkəmˈstænʃl] adj fml : **~ evidence** preuve f indirecte.

circumvent [ˌsɜːkəmˈvent] vt fml [law, rule] tourner.

circus [ˈsɜːkəs] n cirque m.

cirrhosis [sɪˈrəʊsɪs] n cirrhose f.

CIS (abbr of **Commonwealth of Independent States**) n CEI f.

cissy ['sɪsɪ] (*pl* **-ies**) *n* Br inf femmelette *f*.

cistern ['sɪstən] *n* **- 1.** Br [inside roof] réservoir *m* d'eau **- 2.** [in toilet] réservoir *m* de chasse d'eau.

citation [saɪ'teɪʃn] *n* citation *f*.

cite [saɪt] *vt* citer.

citizen ['sɪtɪzn] *n* **- 1.** [of country] citoyen *m*, -enne *f* **- 2.** [of town] habitant *m*, -e *f*.

Citizens' Advice Bureau *n service britannique d'information et d'aide au consommateur.*

Citizens' Band *n* fréquence radio réservée au public, citizen band *f*.

citizenship ['sɪtɪznʃɪp] *n* citoyenneté *f*.

citric acid ['sɪtrɪk-] *n* acide *m* citrique.

citrus fruit ['sɪtrəs-] *n* agrume *m*.

city ['sɪtɪ] (*pl* **-ies**) *n* ville *f*, cité *f*.
➤ **City** *n* Br : **the City** la City (*quartier financier de Londres*).

THE CITY

La City, quartier financier de la capitale, est une circonscription administrative autonome de Londres ayant sa propre police. Le terme « the City » est souvent employé pour désigner le monde britannique de la finance.

city centre *n* centre-ville *m*.

city hall *n* Am ≃ mairie *f*, ≃ hôtel *m* de ville.

city technology college *n* Br *établissement d'enseignement technique du secondaire subventionné par les entreprises.*

civic ['sɪvɪk] *adj* [leader, event] municipal(e) ; [duty, pride] civique.

civic centre *n* Br centre *m* administratif municipal.

civics ['sɪvɪks] *n* (*U*) instruction *f* civique.

civil ['sɪvl] *adj* **- 1.** [public] civil(e) **- 2.** [polite] courtois(e), poli(e).

civil defence *n* protection *f* civile.

civil disobedience *n* résistance *f* passive à la loi.

civil engineer *n* ingénieur *m* des travaux publics.

civil engineering *n* génie *m* civil.

civilian [sɪ'vɪljən] *◇ n* civil *m*, -e *f ◇ comp* civil(e).

civility [sɪ'vɪlətɪ] *n* politesse *f*.

civilization [ˌsɪvəlaɪ'zeɪʃn] *n* civilisation *f*.

civilize, -ise ['sɪvɪlaɪz] *vt* civiliser.

civilized ['sɪvɪlaɪzd] *adj* civilisé(e).

civil law *n* droit *m* civil.

civil liberties *npl* libertés *fpl* civiques.

civil list *n* Br liste *f* civile (*allouée à la famille royale par le Parlement britannique*).

civil rights *npl* droits *mpl* civils.

civil servant *n* fonctionnaire *mf*.

civil service *n* fonction *f* publique.

civil war *n* guerre *f* civile.

CJD *n abbr of* Creutzfeldt-Jakob disease.

cl (*abbr of* centilitre) cl.

clad [klæd] *adj* literary [dressed] : **~ in** vêtu(e) de.

cladding ['klædɪŋ] *n* Br revêtement *m*.

claim [kleɪm] *◇ n* **- 1.** [for pay etc] revendication *f* ; [for expenses, insurance] demande *f* **- 2.** [right] droit *m* ; **to lay ~ to sthg** revendiquer qqch **- 3.** [assertion] affirmation *f ◇ vt* **- 1.** [ask for] réclamer **- 2.** [responsibility, credit] revendiquer **- 3.** [maintain] prétendre *◇ vi* : **to ~ for sthg** faire une demande d'indemnité pour qqch ; **to ~ (on one's insurance)** faire une déclaration de sinistre.

claimant ['kleɪmənt] *n* [to throne] prétendant *m*, -e *f* ; [of state benefit] demandeur *m*, -eresse *f*, requérant *m*, -e *f*.

claim form *n* [for expenses] note *f* de frais ; [for insurance] formulaire *m* de déclaration de sinistre.

clairvoyant [kleə'vɔɪənt] *◇ adj* [person] qui a des dons de double vue *◇ n* voyant *m*, -e *f*.

clam [klæm] (*pt & pp* **-med** ; *cont* **-ming**) *n* palourde *f*.
➤ **clam up** *vi* inf la boucler.

clamber ['klæmbə'] *vi* grimper.

clammy ['klæmɪ] (*compar* **-mier** ; *superl* **-miest**) *adj* [skin] moite ; [weather] lourd et humide.

clamor ['klæmə'] Am = clamour.

clamorous ['klæmərəs] *adj* bruyant(e).

clamour Br, **clamor** Am ['klæmə'] *◇ n* (*U*) **- 1.** [noise] cris *mpl* **- 2.** [demand] revendication *f* bruyante *◇ vi* : **to ~ for sthg** demander qqch à cor et à cri.

clamp [klæmp] *◇ n* [gen] pince *f*, agrafe *f* ; [for carpentry] serre-joint *m* ; MED clamp *m ◇ vt* **- 1.** [gen] serrer **- 2.** AUT poser un sabot de Denver à.
➤ **clamp down** *vi* : **to ~ down (on)** sévir (contre).

clampdown ['klæmpdaʊn] *n* : **~ (on)** répression *f* (contre).

clan [klæn] *n* clan *m*.

clandestine [klæn'destɪn] *adj* clandestin(e).

clang [klæŋ] *◇ n* bruit *m* métallique *◇ vi* émettre un bruit métallique.

clanger ['klæŋə'] *n* Br inf gaffe *f*.

clank [klæŋk] ⇔ n cliquetis m ⇔ vi cliqueter.

clap [klæp] (pt & pp **-ped** ; cont **-ping**) ⇔ n - **1.** [of hands] applaudissement m, battement m (de main) - **2.** [of thunder] coup m ⇔ vt - **1.** [hands] : **to ~ one's hands** applaudir, taper des mains - **2.** inf [place] mettre ; **to ~ eyes on sb** apercevoir qqn ⇔ vi applaudir, taper des mains.

clapboard ['klæpbɔːd] n Am bardeau m.

clapped-out [klæpt-] adj Br inf déglingué(e).

clapperboard ['klæpəbɔːd] n claquette f.

clapping ['klæpɪŋ] n (U) applaudissements mpl.

claptrap ['klæptræp] n (U) inf sottises fpl.

claret ['klærət] n - **1.** [wine] bordeaux m rouge - **2.** [colour] bordeaux m inv.

clarification [,klærɪfɪ'keɪʃn] n [explanation] éclaircissement m, clarification f.

clarify ['klærɪfaɪ] (pt & pp **-ied**) vt [explain] éclaircir, clarifier.

clarinet [,klærə'net] n clarinette f.

clarity ['klærətɪ] n clarté f.

clash [klæʃ] ⇔ n - **1.** [of interests, personalities] conflit m - **2.** [fight, disagreement] heurt m, affrontement m - **3.** [noise] fracas m ⇔ vi - **1.** [fight, disagree] se heurter - **2.** [differ, conflict] entrer en conflit - **3.** [coincide] : **to ~ (with sthg)** tomber en même temps (que qqch) - **4.** [colours] jurer - **5.** [cymbals etc] résonner.

clasp [klɑːsp] ⇔ n [on necklace etc] fermoir m ; [on belt] boucle f ⇔ vt [hold tight] serrer ; **to ~ hands** se serrer la main.

class [klɑːs] ⇔ n - **1.** [gen] classe f - **2.** [lesson] cours m, classe f - **3.** [category] catégorie f ; **to be in a ~ of one's own** être d'une tout autre classe ⇔ comp de classe ⇔ vt classer.

class-conscious adj pej snob (inv).

classic ['klæsɪk] ⇔ adj classique ⇔ n classique m.

➤ **classics** npl humanités fpl.

classical ['klæsɪkl] adj classique.

classical music n musique f classique.

classification [,klæsɪfɪ'keɪʃn] n classification f.

classified ['klæsɪfaɪd] adj [information, document] classé secret (classée secrète).

classified ad n petite annonce f.

classify ['klæsɪfaɪ] (pt & pp **-ied**) vt classifier, classer.

classless ['klɑːslɪs] adj sans distinctions sociales.

classmate ['klɑːsmeɪt] n camarade mf de classe.

classroom ['klɑːsrʊm] n (salle f de) classe f.

classy ['klɑːsɪ] (compar **-ier** ; superl **-iest**) adj inf chic (inv).

clatter ['klætər] ⇔ n cliquetis m ; [louder] fracas m ⇔ vi [metal object] cliqueter.

clause [klɔːz] n - **1.** [in document] clause f - **2.** GRAMM proposition f.

claustrophobia [,klɔːstrə'fəʊbjə] n claustrophobie f.

claustrophobic [,klɔːstrə'fəʊbɪk] adj - **1.** [atmosphere] qui rend claustrophobe - **2.** [person] claustrophobe.

claw [klɔː] ⇔ n - **1.** [of cat, bird] griffe f - **2.** [of crab, lobster] pince f ⇔ vt griffer ⇔ vi [person] : **to ~ at** s'agripper à.

➤ **claw back** vt sep Br [money] récupérer.

clay [kleɪ] n argile f.

clay pigeon shooting n ball-trap m.

clean [kliːn] ⇔ adj - **1.** [not dirty] propre - **2.** [sheet of paper, driving licence] vierge ; [reputation] sans tache ; **to come ~ about sthg** inf confesser qqch - **3.** [joke] de bon goût - **4.** [smooth] net (nette) ⇔ adv : **I ~ forgot** j'ai complètement oublié ⇔ vt nettoyer ; **to ~ one's teeth** se brosser OR laver les dents ⇔ vi faire le ménage ⇔ n : **to give sthg a ~** nettoyer qqch.

➤ **clean out** vt sep - **1.** [room, drawer] nettoyer à fond - **2.** inf fig [person] nettoyer.

➤ **clean up** ⇔ vt sep [clear up] nettoyer ⇔ vi inf [make a profit] ramasser de l'argent.

cleaner ['kliːnər] n - **1.** [person] personne f qui fait le ménage ; **window ~** laveur m, -euse f de vitres - **2.** [substance] produit m d'entretien - **3.** [machine] appareil m de nettoyage - **4.** [shop] : **~'s** pressing m.

cleaning ['kliːnɪŋ] n nettoyage m.

cleaning lady n femme f de ménage.

cleanliness ['klenlɪnɪs] n propreté f.

cleanly ['kliːnlɪ] adv [cut] nettement.

cleanness ['kliːnnɪs] n propreté f.

cleanse [klenz] vt - **1.** [skin, wound] nettoyer - **2.** fig [make pure] purifier ; **to ~ sb/sthg of** délivrer qqn/qqch de.

cleanser ['klenzər] n [detergent] détergent m ; [for skin] démaquillant m.

clean-shaven [-'ʃeɪvn] adj rasé(e) de près.

cleanup ['kliːnʌp] n nettoyage m.

clear [klɪər] ⇔ adj - **1.** [gen] clair(e) ; [glass, plastic] transparent(e) ; [difference] net (nette) ; **to make sthg ~ (to sb)** expliquer qqch clairement (à qqn) ; **to make it ~ that** préciser que ; **to make o.s. ~** bien se faire comprendre - **2.** [voice, sound] qui s'entend nettement - **3.** [road, space] libre, dégagé(e) ; **we have two ~ days to get there** on a deux jours entiers pour y aller **- 4.** [not guilty] : **to have a ~ conscience** avoir la conscience tranquille ◇ adv : **to stand ~** s'écarter ; **to stay ~ of sb/sthg, to steer ~ of sb/sthg** éviter qqn/qqch ◇ n : **in the ~** [out of danger] hors de danger ; [free from suspicion] au-dessus de tout soupçon ◇ vt **- 1.** [road, path] dégager ; [table] débarrasser ; **to ~ one's throat** s'éclaircir la voix **- 2.** [obstacle, fallen tree] enlever **- 3.** [jump] sauter, franchir **- 4.** [debt] s'acquitter de **- 5.** [authorize] donner le feu vert à **- 6.** JUR innocenter **- 7.** [cheque] compenser ◇ vi [fog, smoke] se dissiper , [weather, sky] s'éclaircir.

➡ **clear away** vt sep [plates] débarrasser ; [books] enlever.

➡ **clear off** vi Br inf dégager.

➡ **clear out** ◇ vt sep [cupboard] vider ; [room] ranger ◇ vi inf [leave] dégager.

➡ **clear up** ◇ vt sep **- 1.** [tidy] ranger **- 2.** [mystery, misunderstanding] éclaircir ◇ vi **- 1.** [weather] s'éclaircir **- 2.** [tidy up] tout ranger.

clearance ['klɪərəns] n **- 1.** [of rubbish] enlèvement m ; [of land] déblaiement m **- 2.** [permission] autorisation f **- 3.** [free space] dégagement m.

clearance sale n soldes mpl.

clear-cut adj net (nette).

clear-headed [-'hedɪd] adj lucide.

clearing ['klɪərɪŋ] n [in wood] clairière f.

clearing bank n Br banque f de clearing.

clearing house n **- 1.** [organization] bureau m central **- 2.** [bank] chambre f de compensation.

clearing up n rangement m.

clearly ['klɪəlɪ] adv **- 1.** [distinctly, lucidly] clairement **- 2.** [obviously] manifestement.

clearout ['klɪəraʊt] n esp Br inf (grand) nettoyage m.

clear-sighted adj qui voit juste.

clearway ['klɪəweɪ] n Br route où le stationnement n'est autorisé qu'en cas d'urgence.

cleavage ['kliːvɪdʒ] n **- 1.** [between breasts] décolleté m **- 2.** [division] division f.

cleaver ['kliːvər] n couperet m.

clef [klef] n clef f.

cleft [kleft] n fente f.

cleft palate n fente f de la voûte du palais.

clematis ['klemətɪs] n clématite f.

clemency ['klemənsɪ] n clémence f.

clementine ['kleməntaɪn] n clémentine f.

clench [klentʃ] vt serrer.

clergy ['klɜːdʒɪ] npl : **the ~** le clergé.

clergyman ['klɜːdʒɪmən] (pl -men [-mən]) n membre m du clergé.

cleric ['klerɪk] n membre m du clergé.

clerical ['klerɪkl] adj **- 1.** ADMIN de bureau **- 2.** RELIG clérical(e).

clerk [Br klɑːk, Am klɜːrk] n **- 1.** [in office] employé m, -e f de bureau **- 2.** JUR clerc m **- 3.** Am [shop assistant] vendeur m, -euse f.

clever ['klevər] adj **- 1.** [intelligent - person] intelligent(e) ; [- idea] ingénieux(euse) **- 2.** [skilful] habile, adroit(e).

cleverly ['klevəlɪ] adv **- 1.** [intelligently] intelligemment **- 2.** [skilfully] habilement.

cleverness ['klevənɪs] n **- 1.** [intelligence] intelligence f **- 2.** [skill] habileté f

cliché ['kliːʃeɪ] n cliché m.

click [klɪk] ◇ n [of lock] déclic m ; [of tongue, heels] claquement m ◇ vt faire claquer ◇ vi **- 1.** [heels] claquer ; [camera] faire un déclic **- 2.** inf fig [become clear] : **it ~ed** cela a fait tilt **- 3.** COMPUT cliquer.

client ['klaɪənt] n client m, -e f.

clientele [,kliːən'tel] n clientèle f.

cliff [klɪf] n falaise f.

cliffhanger ['klɪf,hæŋər] n inf épisode m à suspense.

climactic [klaɪ'mæktɪk] adj [point] culminant(e).

climate ['klaɪmɪt] n climat m.

climatic [klaɪ'mætɪk] adj climatique.

climax ['klaɪmæks] n [culmination] apogée m.

climb [klaɪm] ◇ n ascension f, montée f ◇ vt [tree, rope] monter à ; [stairs] monter ; [wall, hill] escalader ◇ vi **- 1.** [person] monter, grimper ; **they ~ed over the fence** ils se passèrent par-dessus la barrière **- 2.** [plant] grimper ; [road] monter ; [plane] prendre de l'altitude **- 3.** [increase] augmenter.

➡ **climb down** vi fig reconnaître qu'on a tort.

climb-down n reculade f.

climber ['klaɪmər] n **- 1.** [person] alpiniste mf, grimpeur m, -euse f **- 2.** [plant] plante f grimpante.

climbing ['klaɪmɪŋ] n [rock climbing] escalade f ; [mountain climbing] alpinisme m.

climbing frame n Br cage f à poules.

climes [klaɪmz] npl : **in sunnier ~** sous des cieux plus cléments.

clinch [klɪntʃ] vt [deal] conclure.

cling [klɪŋ] (pt & pp clung) vi **- 1.** [hold tightly] : **to ~ (to)** s'accrocher (à), se cramponner (à) **- 2.** [clothes] : **to ~ (to)** coller (à).

clingfilm ['klɪŋfɪlm] n Br film m alimentaire transparent.

clinging ['klɪŋɪŋ] adj lit & fig collant(e).

clinic ['klɪnɪk] *n* [building] centre *m* médical, clinique *f*.

clinical ['klɪnɪkl] *adj* - **1.** MED clinique - **2.** fig [attitude] froid(e).

clinically ['klɪnɪklɪ] *adv* MED cliniquement.

clink [klɪŋk] ◇ *n* cliquetis *m* ◇ *vi* tinter.

clip [klɪp] (*pt* & *pp* -**ped** ; *cont* -**ping**) ◇ *n* - **1.** [for paper] trombone *m* ; [for hair] pince *f* ; [of earring] clip *m* ; TECH collier *m* - **2.** [excerpt] extrait *m* ◇ *vt* - **1.** [fasten] attacher - **2.** [nails] couper ; [hedge] tailler ; [newspaper cutting] découper - **3.** inf [hit] : **to ~ sb round the ear** flanquer une gifle à qqn.

clipboard ['klɪpbɔːd] *n* écritoire *f* à pince, clipboard *m*.

clip-on *adj* [badge etc] à pince ; **~ earrings** clips *mpl*.

clipped [klɪpt] *adj* [voice] saccadé(e).

clippers ['klɪpəz] *npl* [for hair] tondeuse *f* ; [for nails] pince *f* à ongles ; [for hedge] cisaille *f* à haie ; [for pruning] sécateur *m*.

clipping ['klɪpɪŋ] *n* [from newspaper] coupure *f*.

clique [kliːk] *n* clique *f*.

cloak [kləʊk] ◇ *n* - **1.** [garment] cape *f* - **2.** fig [for secret] couverture *f* ◇ *vt* : **to be ~ed in** être entouré(e) de.

cloak-and-dagger *adj* : **a ~ story** un roman d'espionnage.

cloakroom ['kləʊkrʊm] *n* - **1.** [for clothes] vestiaire *m* - **2.** Br [toilets] toilettes *fpl*.

clobber ['klɒbəʳ] inf ◇ *n* (U) Br - **1.** [belongings] affaires *fpl* - **2.** [clothes] vêtements *mpl* ◇ *vt* [hit] frapper, tabasser.

clock [klɒk] *n* - **1.** [large] horloge *f* ; [small] pendule *f* ; **round the ~** [work, be open] 24 heures sur 24 ; **to put the ~ back** retarder l'horloge ; fig revenir en arrière ; **to put the ~ forward** avancer l'horloge - **2.** AUT [mileometer] compteur *m*.

◆ **clock in, clock on** *vi* Br [at work] pointer *(à l'arrivée)*.

◆ **clock off, clock out** *vi* Br [at work] pointer *(à la sortie)*.

◆ **clock up** *vt fus* [miles] faire, avaler.

clockwise ['klɒkwaɪz] *adj* & *adv* dans le sens des aiguilles d'une montre.

clockwork ['klɒkwɜːk] ◇ *n* : **to go like ~** fig aller OR marcher comme sur des roulettes ◇ *comp* [toy] mécanique.

clod [klɒd] *n* [of earth] motte *f*.

clog [klɒg] (*pt* & *pp* -**ged** ; *cont* -**ging**) *vt* boucher.

◆ **clogs** *npl* sabots *mpl*.

◆ **clog up** ◇ *vt sep* boucher ◇ *vi* se boucher.

clogged [klɒgd] *adj* bouché(e).

cloister ['klɔɪstəʳ] *n* [passage] cloître *m*.

cloistered ['klɔɪstəd] *adj* cloîtré(e).

clone [kləʊn] ◇ *n* [gen & COMPUT] clone *m* ◇ *vt* cloner.

close¹ [kləʊs] ◇ *adj* - **1.** [near] : **~ (to)** proche (de), près (de) ; **a ~ friend** un ami intime (une amie intime) ; **~ to tears** au bord des larmes ; **~ up, ~ to** de près ; **~ by, ~ at hand** tout près ; **that was a ~ shave** OR **thing** OR **call** on l'a échappé belle - **2.** [link, resemblance] fort(e) ; [cooperation, connection] étroit(e) - **3.** [questioning] serré(e) ; [examination] minutieux(euse) ; **to keep a ~ watch on sb/sthg** surveiller qqn/qqch de près ; **to pay ~ attention** faire très attention ; **to have a ~ look at sb/sthg** regarder qqn/qqch de près - **4.** [weather] lourd(e) ; [air in room] renfermé(e) - **5.** [result, contest, race] serré(e) ◇ *adv* : **~ (to)** près (de) ; **~ up, ~ together** se rapprocher ◇ *n* [street] cul-de-sac *m*.

◆ **close on, close to** *prep* [almost] près de.

close² [kləʊz] ◇ *vt* - **1.** [gen] fermer ; **to ~ one's eyes** fermer les yeux - **2.** [end] clore ◇ *vi* - **1.** [shop, bank] fermer ; [door, lid] (se) fermer - **2.** [end] se terminer, finir ◇ *n* fin *f* ; **to bring sthg to a ~** mettre fin à qqch.

◆ **close down** *vt sep* & *vi* fermer.

◆ **close in** *vi* [night, fog] descendre ; [person] : **~ in (on)** approcher OR se rapprocher (de).

◆ **close off** *vt fus* [road] barrer.

close-cropped [,kləʊs-] *adj* ras(e).

closed [kləʊzd] *adj* fermé(e).

closed circuit television *n* télévision *f* en circuit fermé.

closedown ['kləʊzdaʊn] *n* - **1.** Br RADIO & TV fin *f* (des émissions) - **2.** [of factory] fermeture *f*.

closed shop *n* atelier qui n'embauche que du personnel syndiqué.

close-fitting [,kləʊs-] *adj* près du corps.

close-knit [,kləʊs-] *adj* (très) uni(e).

closely ['kləʊslɪ] *adv* [listen, examine, watch] de près ; [resemble] beaucoup ; **to be ~ related to** OR **with** être proche parent de ; **to work ~ with sb** travailler en étroite collaboration avec qqn.

closeness ['kləʊsnɪs] *n* - **1.** [nearness] proximité *f* - **2.** [intimacy] intimité *f*.

closeout ['kləʊzaʊt] *n* Am liquidation *f*.

close quarters [,kləʊs-] *npl* : **at ~** de près.

close season [,kləʊs-] *n* Br fermeture *f* de la chasse OR de la pêche.

closet ['klɒzɪt] ◇ *n* Am [cupboard] placard *m* ◇ *adj* inf non avoué(e) ◇ *vt* : **to be ~ed with sb** être enfermé(e) avec qqn.

close-up ['kləʊs-] n gros plan m.

closing ['kləʊzɪŋ] adj [stages, remarks] final(e) ; [speech] de clôture.

closing price n prix m de clôture.

closing time ['kləʊzɪŋ-] n heure f de fermeture.

closure ['kləʊʒəʳ] n fermeture f.

clot [klɒt] (pt & pp -ted ; cont -ting) ◇ n - **1.** [of blood, milk] caillot m - **2.** Br inf [fool] empoté m, -e f ◇ vi [blood] coaguler.

cloth [klɒθ] n - **1.** (U) [fabric] tissu m - **2.** [duster] chiffon m ; [for drying] torchon m.

clothe [kləʊð] vt fml [dress] habiller ; **~d in** habillé(e) de.

clothes [kləʊðz] npl vêtements mpl, habits mpl ; **to put one's ~ on** s'habiller ; **to take one's ~ off** se déshabiller.

clothes basket n panier m à linge.

clothes brush n brosse f à habits.

clotheshorse ['kləʊðhɔːs] n séchoir m à linge.

clothesline ['kləʊðzlaɪn] n corde f à linge.

clothes peg Br, **clothespin** Am ['kləʊðzpɪn] n pince f à linge.

clothing ['kləʊðɪŋ] n (U) vêtements mpl, habits mpl.

clotted cream ['klɒtɪd-] n Br crème épaisse, spécialité de la Cornouailles.

cloud [klaʊd] ◇ n nuage m ; **to be under a ~** être mal vu ◇ vt - **1.** [mirror] embuer - **2.** fig [memory, happiness] gâcher ; **to ~ the issue** brouiller les cartes.

◆ **cloud over** vi - **1.** [sky] se couvrir - **2.** [face] s'assombrir.

cloudburst ['klaʊdbɜːst] n trombe f d'eau.

cloudless ['klaʊdlɪs] adj sans nuages.

cloudy ['klaʊdɪ] (compar -ier ; superl -iest) adj - **1.** [sky, day] nuageux(euse) - **2.** [liquid] trouble.

clout [klaʊt] inf ◇ n - **1.** [blow] coup m - **2.** (U) [influence] poids m, influence f ◇ vt donner un coup à.

clove [kləʊv] n : **a ~ of garlic** une gousse d'ail.

◆ **cloves** npl [spice] clous mpl de girofle.

clover ['kləʊvəʳ] n trèfle m.

cloverleaf ['kləʊvəliːf] (pl -leaves [-liːvz]) n [plant] feuille f de trèfle.

clown [klaʊn] ◇ n - **1.** [performer] clown m - **2.** [fool] pitre m ◇ vi faire le pitre.

cloying ['klɔɪɪŋ] adj - **1.** [smell] écœurant(e) - **2.** [sentimentality] à l'eau de rose.

club [klʌb] (pt & pp -bed ; cont -bing) ◇ n - **1.** [organization, place] club m - **2.** [weapon] mas-

sue f - **3.** : (golf) ~ club m - **4.** [playing card] trèfle m ◇ comp [member, fees] du club ◇ vt matraquer.

◆ **clubs** npl CARDS trèfle m ; **the six of ~s** le six de trèfle.

◆ **club together** vi se cotiser.

club car n Am RAIL wagon-restaurant m.

club class n classe f club.

clubhouse ['klʌbhaʊs, pl -haʊzɪz] n club m, pavillon m.

cluck [klʌk] vi glousser.

clue [kluː] n - **1.** [in crime] indice m ; **I haven't (got) a ~ (about)** je n'ai aucune idée (sur) - **2.** [answer] : **the ~ to** sthg la solution de qqch - **3.** [in crossword] définition f.

clued-up [kluːd-] adj Br inf calé(e).

clueless ['kluːlɪs] adj Br inf qui n'a aucune idée.

clump [klʌmp] ◇ n - **1.** [of trees, bushes] massif m, bouquet m - **2.** [sound] bruit m sourd ◇ vi : **to ~ about** marcher d'un pas lourd.

clumsily ['klʌmzɪlɪ] adv - **1.** [ungracefully] gauchement, maladroitement - **2.** [tactlessly] sans tact.

clumsy ['klʌmzɪ] (compar -ier ; superl -iest) adj - **1.** [ungraceful] gauche, maladroit(e) - **2.** [tool, object] peu pratique - **3.** [tactless] sans tact.

clung [klʌŋ] pt & pp ▷ cling.

cluster ['klʌstəʳ] ◇ n [group] groupe m ◇ vi [people] se rassembler ; [buildings etc] être regroupé(e).

clutch [klʌtʃ] ◇ n AUT embrayage m ◇ vt agripper ◇ vi : **to ~ at** s'agripper à.

◆ **clutches** npl : **in the ~es of** dans les griffes de.

clutch bag n pochette f.

clutter ['klʌtəʳ] ◇ n désordre m ; **in a ~** en désordre ◇ vt mettre en désordre.

cm (abbr of centimetre) n cm.

CNAA (abbr of Council for National Academic Awards) n organisme non universitaire délivrant des diplômes en Grande-Bretagne.

CND (abbr of Campaign for Nuclear Disarmament) n mouvement pour le désarmement nucléaire.

c/o (abbr of care of) a/s.

co- [kəʊ] prefix co-.

Co. - **1.** (abbr of Company) Cie - **2.** abbr of County.

CO ◇ n - **1.** abbr of commanding officer - **2.** (abbr of Commonwealth Office) secrétariat d'État au Commonwealth - **3.** abbr of conscientious objector ◇ abbr of Colorado

coach [kəʊtʃ] ◇ n - **1.** [bus] car m, autocar m - **2.** RAIL voiture f - **3.** [horsedrawn] carrosse m

- **4.** SPORT entraîneur *m* - **5.** [tutor] répétiteur *m*, -trice *f* ⬦ *vt* - **1.** SPORT entraîner - **2.** [tutor] donner des leçons (particulières) à.

coaching [ˈkəʊtʃɪŋ] *n (U)* - **1.** SPORT entraînement *m* - **2.** [tutoring] leçons *fpl* particulières.

coach trip *n* Br excursion *f* en autocar.

coagulate [kəʊˈægjʊleɪt] *vi* coaguler.

coal [kəʊl] *n* charbon *m*.

coalesce [ˌkəʊəˈles] *vi* s'unir.

coalface [ˈkəʊlfeɪs] *n* front *m* de taille.

coalfield [ˈkəʊlfiːld] *n* bassin *m* houiller.

coal gas *n* gaz *m*.

coalition [ˌkəʊəˈlɪʃn] *n* coalition *f*.

coalman [ˈkəʊlmæn] *(pl* -men [-men]) *n* Br charbonnier *m*.

coalmine [ˈkəʊlmaɪn] *n* mine *f* de charbon.

coalminer [ˈkəʊlˌmaɪnəʳ] *n* mineur *m*.

coalmining [ˈkəʊlˌmaɪnɪŋ] *n* charbonnage *m*.

coarse [kɔːs] *adj* - **1.** [rough - cloth] grossier(ère) ; [- hair] épais(aisse) ; [- skin] granuleux(euse) - **2.** [vulgar] grossier(ère).

coarse fishing *n* Br pêche *f* en eau douce *(à l'exclusion du saumon)*.

coarsen [ˈkɔːsn] ⬦ *vt* rendre grossier(ère) ⬦ *vi* devenir grossier(ère).

coast [kəʊst] ⬦ *n* côte *f* ⬦ *vi* [in car, on bike] avancer en roue libre.

coastal [ˈkəʊstl] *adj* côtier(ère).

coaster [ˈkəʊstəʳ] *n* [small mat] dessous *m* de verre.

coastguard [ˈkəʊstgɑːd] *n* - **1.** [person] garde-côte *m* - **2.** [organization] : **the ~** la gendarmerie maritime.

coastline [ˈkəʊstlaɪn] *n* côte *f*.

coat [kəʊt] ⬦ *n* - **1.** [garment] manteau *m* - **2.** [of animal] pelage *m* - **3.** [layer] couche *f* ⬦ *vt* : **to ~ sthg (with)** recouvrir qqch (de) ; [with paint etc] enduire qqch (de).

coat hanger *n* cintre *m*.

coating [ˈkəʊtɪŋ] *n* couche *f* ; CULIN glaçage *m*.

coat of arms *(pl* coats of arms) *n* blason *m*.

coauthor [kəʊˈɔːθəʳ] *n* co-auteur *m*.

coax [kəʊks] *vt* : **to ~ sb (to do** OR **into doing sthg)** persuader qqn (de faire qqch) à force de cajoleries.

coaxial cable [ˌkəʊˈæksɪəl-] *n* COMPUT câble *m* co-axial.

cob [kɒb] *n* ⬥ **corn**.

cobalt [ˈkəʊbɔːlt] *n* cobalt *m*.

cobble [ˈkɒbl] ⬥ **cobble together** *vt sep* [agreement, book] bricoler ; [speech] improviser.

cobbled [ˈkɒbld] *adj* pavé(e).

cobbler [ˈkɒbləʳ] *n* cordonnier *m*.

cobbles [ˈkɒblz], **cobblestones** [ˈkɒblstəʊnz] *npl* pavés *mpl*.

Cobol [ˈkəʊbɒl] (*abbr of* Common Business Oriented Language) *n* COBOL *m*.

cobra [ˈkəʊbrə] *n* cobra *m*.

cobweb [ˈkɒbweb] *n* toile *f* d'araignée.

Coca-Cola® [ˌkəʊkəˈkəʊlə] *n* Coca-Cola® *m inv*.

cocaine [kəʊˈkeɪn] *n* cocaïne *f*.

cock [kɒk] ⬦ *n* - **1.** [male chicken] coq *m* - **2.** [male bird] mâle *m* ⬦ *vt* - **1.** [gun] armer - **2.** [head] incliner.

⬥ **cock up** *vt sep* Br vinf faire merder.

cock-a-hoop *adj* inf ravi(e).

cockatoo [ˌkɒkəˈtuː] *(pl* -s) *n* cacatoès *m*.

cockerel [ˈkɒkrəl] *n* jeune coq *m*.

cocker spaniel *n* cocker *m*.

cockeyed [ˈkɒkaɪd] *adj* inf - **1.** [lopsided] de travers - **2.** [foolish] complètement fou (folle).

cockfight [ˈkɒkfaɪt] *n* combat *m* de coqs.

cockle [ˈkɒkl] *n* [shellfish] coque *f*.

Cockney [ˈkɒknɪ] *(pl* Cockneys) ⬦ *n* - **1.** [person] Cockney *mf (personne issue des quartiers populaires de l'est de Londres)* - **2.** [dialect, accent] cockney *m* ⬦ *comp* cockney *(inv)*.

cockpit [ˈkɒkpɪt] *n* [in plane] cockpit *m*.

cockroach [ˈkɒkrəʊtʃ] *n* cafard *m*.

cocksure [ˌkɒkˈʃɔːʳ] *adj* trop sûr(e) de soi.

cocktail [ˈkɒkteɪl] *n* cocktail *m*.

cocktail dress *n* robe *f* de soirée.

cocktail shaker [-ˌʃeɪkəʳ] *n* shaker *m*.

cocktail stick *n* bâtonnet *m* à apéritif.

cock-up *n* vinf : **to make a ~** se planter.

cocky [ˈkɒkɪ] *(compar* -ier ; *superl* -iest) *adj* inf suffisant(e).

cocoa [ˈkəʊkəʊ] *n* cacao *m*.

coconut [ˈkəʊkənʌt] *n* noix *f* de coco.

cocoon [kəˈkuːn] ⬦ *n* lit & fig cocon *m* ⬦ *vt* fig [person] couver.

cod [kɒd] *(pl* inv) *n* morue *f*.

COD - **1.** *abbr of* cash on delivery - **2.** *abbr of* collect on delivery.

code [kəʊd] ⬦ *n* code *m* ⬦ *vt* coder.

coded [ˈkəʊdɪd] *adj* codé(e).

codeine [ˈkəʊdiːn] *n* codéine *f*.

code name *n* nom *m* de code.

code of practice *n* déontologie *f*.

cod-liver oil *n* huile *f* de foie de morue.

codswallop [ˈkɒdzˌwɒləp] *n (U)* Br inf bêtises *fpl*.

co-ed [kəʊˈed] ⬦ *adj abbr of* coeducational ⬦ *n* - **1.** (*abbr of* coeducational student) *étu-*

diante d'une université mixte américaine
- 2. (*abbr of* **coeducational school**) *école mixte britannique.*

coeducational [ˌkəʊedjuːˈkeɪʃənl] *adj* mixte.

coefficient [ˌkəʊɪˈfɪʃnt] *n* coefficient *m*.

coerce [kəʊˈɜːs] *vt :* **to ~ sb (into doing sthg)** contraindre qqn (à faire qqch).

coercion [kəʊˈɜːʃn] *n* coercition *f*.

coexist [ˌkəʊɪgˈzɪst] *vi* coexister.

coexistence [ˌkəʊɪgˈzɪstəns] *n* coexistence *f*.

C. of C. (*abbr of* **chamber of commerce**) *n* CC *f*.

C of E *abbr of* **Church of England.**

coffee [ˈkɒfɪ] *n* café *m*.

coffee bar *n* Br café *m*.

coffee beans *npl* grains *mpl* de café.

coffee break *n* pause-café *f*.

coffee cup *n* tasse *f* à café.

coffee mill *n* moulin *m* à café.

coffee morning *n* Br *réunion matinale pour prendre le café.*

coffeepot [ˈkɒfɪpɒt] *n* cafetière *f*.

coffee shop *n* **- 1.** Br [shop] café *m* **- 2.** Am [restaurant] ≈ café-restaurant *m*.

coffee table *n* table *f* basse.

coffee-table book *n* beau livre *m*.

coffers [ˈkɒgtˈfəz] *npl* coffres *mpl*.

coffin [ˈkɒfɪn] *n* cercueil *m*.

cog [kɒg] *n* [tooth on wheel] dent *f* ; [wheel] roue *f* dentée ; **a ~ in the machine** fig un simple rouage.

cogent [ˈkəʊdʒənt] *adj* convaincant(e).

cogitate [ˈkɒdʒɪteɪt] *vi* fml réfléchir.

cognac [ˈkɒnjæk] *n* cognac *m*.

cognitive [ˈkɒgnɪtɪv] *adj* cognitif(ive).

cogwheel [ˈkɒgwiːl] *n* roue *f* dentée.

cohabit [ˌkəʊˈhæbɪt] *vi* fml cohabiter.

coherent [kəʊˈhɪərənt] *adj* cohérent(e).

coherently [kəʊˈhɪərəntlɪ] *adv* de façon cohérente.

cohesion [kəʊˈhiːʒn] *n* cohésion *f*.

cohesive [kəʊˈhiːsɪv] *adj* cohésif(ive).

cohort [ˈkəʊhɔːt] *n* cohorte *f*.

COHSE [ˈkəʊzɪ] (*abbr of* **Confederation of Health Service Employees**) *n ancien syndicat britannique des employés des services de santé.*

COI (*abbr of* **Central Office of Information**) *n service public britannique d'information en Grande-Bretagne.*

coil [kɔɪl] <> *n* **- 1.** [of rope etc] rouleau *m* ; [one loop] boucle *f* **- 2.** ELEC bobine *f* **- 3.** Br [contracep-

tive device] stérilet *m* <> *vt* enrouler <> *vi* s'enrouler.

➤ **coil up** *vt sep* enrouler.

coiled [kɔɪld] *adj* enroulé(e).

coin [kɔɪn] <> *n* pièce *f* (de monnaie) <> *vt* [word] inventer ; **to ~ a phrase** pour employer un lieu commun.

coinage [ˈkɔɪnɪdʒ] *n* **- 1.** (U) [currency] monnaie *f* **- 2.** [new word] néologisme *m*.

coin-box *n* Br cabine *f* (publique) à pièces.

coincide [ˌkəʊɪnˈsaɪd] *vi* coïncider.

coincidence [kəʊˈɪnsɪdəns] *n* coïncidence *f*.

coincidental [kəʊˌɪnsɪˈdentl] *adj* de coïncidence.

coincidentally [kəʊˌɪnsɪˈdentəlɪ] *adv* par hasard.

coin-operated [-ˈɒpəˌreɪtɪd] *adj* automatique.

coitus [ˈkəʊɪtəs] *n* coït *m*.

coke [kəʊk] *n* **- 1.** [fuel] coke *m* **- 2.** drugs sl coco *f*, coke *f*.

Coke® [kəʊk] *n* Coca® *m*.

Col. (*abbr of* **colonel**) Col.

cola [ˈkəʊlə] *n* cola *m*.

COLA [ˈkəʊlə] (*abbr of* **cost-of-living adjustment**) *n actualisation des salaires, indemnités etc en fonction du coût de la vie.*

colander [ˈkʌləndəˈ] *n* passoire *f*.

cold [kəʊld] <> *adj* froid(e) ; **it's ~** il fait froid ; **to be ~** avoir froid ; **to get ~** [person] avoir froid ; [hot food] refroidir ; **une boisson fraîche~** [person] avoir froid <> *n* **- 1.** [illness] rhume *m* ; **to catch (a) ~** attraper un rhume, s'enrhumer **- 2.** [low temperature] froid *m*.

cold-blooded [-ˈblʌdɪd] *adj* **- 1.** [animal] à sang-froid **- 2.** fig [killer] sans pitié ; [murder] de sang-froid.

cold cream *n* cold-cream *m*.

cold cuts *npl* esp Am assiette *f* anglaise.

cold feet *npl :* **to have** OR **get ~** inf avoir la trouille.

cold-hearted [-ˈhɑːtɪd] *adj* insensible.

coldly [ˈkəʊldlɪ] *adv* froidement.

coldness [ˈkəʊldnɪs] *n* froideur *f*.

cold shoulder *n :* **to give sb the ~** inf être froid(e) avec qqn.

cold sore *n* bouton *m* de fièvre.

cold storage *n :* **to put sthg into ~** [food] mettre qqch en chambre froide.

cold sweat *n* sueur *f* froide.

cold war *n :* **the ~** la guerre froide.

coleslaw [ˈkəʊlslɔː] *n* chou *m* cru mayonnaise.

colic [ˈkɒlɪk] *n* colique *f*.

collaborate [kə'læbəreɪt] *vi* collaborer.

collaboration [kə,læbə'reɪʃn] *n* collaboration *f*.

collaborative [kə'læbərətɪv] *adj* fait(e) en collaboration OR en commun.

collaborator [kə'læbəreɪtəʳ] *n* collaborateur *m*, -trice *f*.

collage ['kɒlɑːʒ] *n* collage *m*.

collagen ['kɒlədʒən] *n* collagène *m*.

collapse [kə'læps] ◇ *n* [gen] écroulement *m*, effondrement *m*; [of marriage] échec *m* ◇ *vi* - **1.** [building, person] s'effondrer, s'écrouler; [marriage] échouer - **2.** [fold up] être pliant(e).

collapsible [kə'læpsəbl] *adj* pliant(e).

collar ['kɒləʳ] ◇ *n* - **1.** [on clothes] col *m* - **2.** [for dog] collier *m* - **3.** TECH collier *m*, bague *f* ◇ *vt inf* [detain] coincer.

collarbone ['kɒləbəʊn] *n* clavicule *f*.

collate [kə'leɪt] *vt* collationner.

collateral [kɒ'lætərəl] *n* (U) nantissement *m*.

collation [kə'leɪʃn] *n* collation *f*.

colleague ['kɒliːg] *n* collègue *mf*.

collect [kə'lekt] ◇ *vt* - **1.** [gather together - gen] rassembler, recueillir; [- wood etc] ramasser; **to ~ o.s.** se reprendre - **2.** [as a hobby] collectionner - **3.** [go to get] aller chercher, passer prendre - **4.** [money] recueillir; [taxes] percevoir; **~ on delivery** Am paiement à la livraison ◇ *vi* - **1.** [crowd, people] se rassembler - **2.** [dust, leaves, dirt] s'amasser, s'accumuler - **3.** [for charity, gift] faire la quête ◇ *adv* Am TELEC : **to call (sb) ~** téléphoner (à qqn) en PCV.

➤ **collect up** *vt sep* ramasser.

collectable [kə'lektəbl] ◇ *adj* prisé(e) (par les collectionneurs) ◇ *n* objet *m* prisé par les collectionneurs.

collected [kə'lektɪd] *adj* - **1.** [calm] posé(e), maître de soi - **2.** LITERATURE : **~ works** œuvres *fpl* complètes.

collecting [kə'lektɪŋ] *n* (U) [hobby] fait *m* de collectionner.

collection [kə'lekʃn] *n* - **1.** [of objects] collection *f* - **2.** LITERATURE recueil *m* - **3.** [of rubbish] ramassage *m*; [of taxes] perception *f* - **4.** [of money] quête *f* - **5.** [of mail] levée *f*.

collective [kə'lektɪv] ◇ *adj* collectif(ive) ◇ *n* coopérative *f*.

collective bargaining *n* (U) négociations *de convention collective*.

collectively [kə'lektɪvlɪ] *adv* collectivement.

collective ownership *n* propriété *f* collective.

collector [kə'lektəʳ] *n* - **1.** [as a hobby] collec-

tionneur *m*, -euse *f* - **2.** [of debts, rent] encaisseur *m*; **~ of taxes** percepteur *m*.

collector's item *n* pièce *f* de collection.

college ['kɒlɪdʒ] *n* - **1.** [gen] ≃ école *f* d'enseignement (technique) supérieur - **2.** [of university] *maison communautaire d'étudiants sur un campus universitaire*.

college of education *n* ≃ institut *m* de formation de maîtres.

collide [kə'laɪd] *vi* : **to ~ (with)** entrer en collision (avec).

collie ['kɒlɪ] *n* colley *m*.

colliery ['kɒljərɪ] (*pl* -ies) *n* mine *f*.

collision [kə'lɪʒn] *n* - **1.** [crash] : **~ (with/between)** collision *f* (avec/entre) ; **to be on a ~ course (with)** fig aller au-devant de l'affrontement (avec) - **2.** fig [conflict] conflit *m*.

collision damage waiver *n* rachat *m* de franchise.

colloquial [kə'ləʊkwɪəl] *adj* familier(ère).

collude [kə'luːd] *vi* : **to ~ with sb** comploter avec qqn.

collusion [kə'luːʒn] *n* : **in ~ with** de connivence avec.

cologne [kə'ləʊn] *n* eau *f* de cologne.

Colombia [kə'lɒmbɪə] *n* Colombie *f*; **in ~** en Colombie.

Colombian [kə'lɒmbɪən] ◇ *adj* colombien(enne) ◇ *n* Colombien *m*, -enne *f*.

Colombo [kə'lʌmbəʊ] *n* Colombo.

colon ['kəʊlən] *n* - **1.** ANAT côlon *m* - **2.** [punctuation mark] deux-points *m inv*.

colonel ['kɜːnl] *n* colonel *m*.

colonial [kə'ləʊnjəl] *adj* colonial(e).

colonialism [kə'ləʊnjəlɪzm] *n* colonialisme *m*.

colonist ['kɒlənɪst] *n* colon *m*.

colonize, -ise ['kɒlənaɪz] *vt* coloniser.

colonnade [,kɒlə'neɪd] *n* colonnade *f*.

colony ['kɒlənɪ] (*pl* -ies) *n* colonie *f*.

color *etc* Am = **colour** *etc*.

Colorado [,kɒlə'rɑːdəʊ] *n* Colorado *m*; **in ~** dans le Colorado.

colorado beetle *n* doryphore *m*.

colossal [kə'lɒsl] *adj* colossal(e).

colostomy [kə'lɒstəmɪ] (*pl* -ies) *n* colostomie *f*.

colour Br, **color** Am ['kʌləʳ] ◇ *n* couleur *f*; **in ~** en couleur ◇ *adj* en couleur ◇ *vt* - **1.** [food, liquid etc] colorer; [with pen, crayon] colorier - **2.** [dye] teindre - **3.** fig [judgment] fausser ◇ *vi* rougir.

➤ **colours** *npl* [flag, of team] couleurs *fpl*.

➤ **colour in** *vt sep* colorier.

colour bar *n* discrimination *f* raciale.

colour-blind *adj* daltonien(enne).

colour-coded *adj* codé(e) par couleur.

coloured Br, **colored** Am ['kʌləd] *adj* de couleur ; **brightly ~** de couleur vive.

colourfast Br, **colorfast** Am ['kʌləfɑːst] *adj* grand teint *(inv)*.

colourful Br, **colorful** Am ['kʌləfʊl] *adj* - **1.** [gen] coloré(e) - **2.** [person, area] haut(e) en couleur.

colouring Br, **coloring** Am ['kʌlərɪŋ] *n* - **1.** [dye] colorant *m* - **2.** *(U)* [complexion] teint *m*.

colourless Br, **colorless** Am ['kʌlələs] *adj* - **1.** [not coloured] sans couleur, incolore - **2.** *fig* [uninteresting] terne.

colour scheme *n* combinaison *f* de couleurs.

colour supplement *n* Br supplément *m* illustré.

colt [kəʊlt] *n* [young horse] poulain *m*.

column ['kɒləm] *n* - **1.** [gen] colonne *f* - **2.** PRESS [article] rubrique *f*.

columnist ['kɒləmnɪst] *n* chroniqueur *m*.

coma ['kəʊmə] *n* coma *m*.

comatose ['kəʊmətəʊs] *adj* comateux(euse).

comb [kəʊm] ⬦ *n* [for hair] peigne *m* ⬦ *vt* - **1.** [hair] peigner - **2.** [search] ratisser.

combat ['kɒmbæt] ⬦ *n* combat *m* ⬦ *vt* combattre.

combative ['kɒmbətɪv] *adj* combatif(ive).

combination [,kɒmbɪ'neɪʃn] *n* combinaison *f*.

combination lock *n* serrure *f* à combinaison.

combination therapy *n* trithérapie *f*.

combine [*vb* kəm'baɪn, *n* 'kɒmbaɪn] ⬦ *vt* [gen] rassembler ; [pieces] combiner ; **to ~ sthg with sthg** [two substances] mélanger qqch avec OR à qqch ; *fig* allier qqch à qqch ⬦ *vi* COMM & POL : **to ~ (with)** fusionner (avec) ⬦ *n* - **1.** [group] cartel *m* - **2.** = **combine harvester.**

combine   harvester [-'hɑːvɪstəʳ] *n* moissonneuse-batteuse *f*.

combustible [kəm'bʌstəbl] *adj* combustible.

combustion [kəm'bʌstʃn] *n* combustion *f*.

come [kʌm] (*pt* came ; *pp* come) *vi* - **1.** [move] venir ; [arrive] arriver, venir ; **the news came as a shock** la nouvelle m'a/lui a *etc* fait un choc ; **coming!** j'arrive! ; **the time has ~** le moment est venu ; **he doesn't know whether he's coming or going** *fig* il ne sait plus où il en est - **2.** [reach] : **to ~ up to** arriver à, monter jusqu'à ; **the water came up to my knees** l'eau m'arrivait aux genoux ; **to ~ down to** des-

cendre OR tomber jusqu'à - **3.** [happen] arriver, se produire ; **~ what may** quoi qu'il arrive ; **how did you ~ to fail your exam?** comment as-tu fait pour échouer à ton examen? - **4.** [become] : **to ~ true** se réaliser ; **to ~ undone** se défaire ; **to ~ unstuck** se décoller - **5.** [begin gradually] : **to ~ to do sthg** en arriver à OR en venir à faire qqch - **6.** [be placed in order] venir, être placé(e) ; **P ~s before Q** P vient avant Q, P précède Q ; **who came first?** qui a été placé premier? ; **she came second in the exam** elle était deuxième à l'examen - **7.** *v inf* [sexually] jouir - **8.** *phr* : **~ to think of it** maintenant que j'y pense, réflexion faite.

⬝➤ **to come** *adv* à venir ; **in (the) days/years to ~** dans les jours/années à venir.

⬝➤ **come about** *vi* [happen] arriver, se produire.

⬝➤ **come across** ⬦ *vt fus* tomber sur, trouver par hasard ⬦ *vi* [speaker, message] faire de l'effet ; **you don't ~ across very well** tu présentes mal ; **to ~ across as being sincere** donner l'impression d'être sincère.

⬝➤ **come along** *vi* - **1.** [arrive by chance] arriver - **2.** [improve - work] avancer ; [- student] faire des progrès ; **the project is coming along nicely** le projet avance bien - **3.** *phr* : **~ along!** [expressing encouragement] allez! ; [hurry up] allez, dépêche-toi!

⬝➤ **come apart** *vi* - **1.** [fall to pieces] tomber en morceaux - **2.** [come off] se détacher.

⬝➤ **come at** *vt fus* [attack] attaquer.

⬝➤ **come back** *vi* - **1.** [in talk, writing] : **to ~ back to sthg** revenir à qqch - **2.** [memory] : **to ~ back (to sb)** revenir (à qqn) - **3.** [become fashionable again] redevenir à la mode.

⬝➤ **come by** *vt fus* - **1.** [get, obtain] trouver, dénicher - **2.** Am [visit, drop in on] : **they came by the house** ils sont passés à la maison.

⬝➤ **come down** *vi* - **1.** [decrease] baisser - **2.** [descend] descendre.

⬝➤ **come down to** *vt fus* se résumer à, se réduire à.

⬝➤ **come down with** *vt fus* [cold, flu] attraper.

⬝➤ **come forward** *vi* se présenter.

⬝➤ **come from** *vt fus* venir de.

⬝➤ **come in** *vi* - **1.** [enter] entrer - **2.** [arrive, be received] arriver - **3.** [be involved] jouer un rôle ; **I don't see where I ~ in** je ne vois pas quel rôle je vais jouer.

⬝➤ **come in for** *vt fus* [criticism] être l'objet de.

⬝➤ **come into** *vt fus* - **1.** [inherit] hériter de - **2.** [begin to be] : **to ~ into being** prendre naissance, voir le jour ; **to ~ into sight** apparaître.

⬝➤ **come of** *vt fus* [result from] résulter de.

come off *vi* - **1.** [button, label] se détacher ; [stain] s'enlever - **2.** [joke, attempt] réussir - **3.** [person] : **to ~ off well/badly** bien/mal s'en tirer - **4. phr : ~ off it!** inf et puis quoi encore!, non mais sans blague!

come on *vi* - **1.** [start] commencer, apparaître - **2.** [start working - light, heating] s'allumer - **3.** [progress, improve] avancer, faire des progrès - **4. phr : ~ on!** [expressing encouragement] allez! ; [hurry up] allez, dépêche-toi! ; [expressing disbelief] allons donc!

come out *vi* - **1.** [become known] être découvert(e) - **2.** [appear - product, book, film] sortir, paraître ; [- sun, moon, stars] paraître - **3.** [in exam, race etc] finir, se classer - **4.** [go on strike] faire grève - **5.** [declare publicly] : **to ~ out for/ against sthg** se déclarer pour/contre qqch - **6.** [photograph] réussir.

come out in *vt fus* : **to ~ out in spots** avoir une éruption.

come over *vt fus* [subj : sensation, emotion] envahir ; **I don't know what's ~ over her** je ne sais pas ce qui lui a pris.

come round *vi* - **1.** [change opinion] changer d'avis - **2.** [regain consciousness] reprendre connaissance, revenir à soi - **3.** [happen] venir, revenir.

come through <> *vt fus* survivre à <> *vi* - **1.** [arrive] arriver - **2.** [survive] s'en tirer.

come to <> *vt fus* - **1.** [reach] : **to ~ to an end** se terminer, prendre fin ; **to ~ to power** arriver au pouvoir ; **to ~ to a decision** arriver à *OR* prendre une décision - **2.** [amount to] s'élever à <> *vi* [regain consciousness] revenir à soi, reprendre connaissance.

come under *vt fus* - **1.** [be governed by] être soumis(e) à - **2.** [heading] se trouver sous - **3.** [suffer] : **to ~ under attack (from)** être en butte aux attaques (de).

come up *vi* - **1.** [be mentioned] survenir - **2.** [be imminent] approcher - **3.** [happen unexpectedly] se présenter - **4.** [sun] se lever.

come up against *vt fus* se heurter à.

come upon *vt fus* [find] tomber sur.

come up to *vt fus* - **1.** [approach - in space] s'approcher de ; [- in time] : **we're coming up to Christmas** Noël approche - **2.** [equal] répondre à.

come up with *vt fus* [answer, idea] proposer.

comeback ['kʌmbæk] *n* come-back *m ;* **to make a ~** [fashion] revenir à la mode ; [actor etc] revenir à la scène.

Comecon ['kɒmɪkɒn] (*abbr of* Council for Mutual Economic Aid) *n* Comecon *m.*

comedian [kə'miːdjən] *n* [comic] comique *m ;* THEATRE comédien *m.*

comedienne [kə,miːdɪ'en] *n* [comic] actrice *f* comique ; THEATRE comédienne *f.*

comedown ['kʌmdaʊn] *n* inf : **it was a ~ for her** elle est tombée bien bas pour faire ça.

comedy ['kɒmədɪ] (*pl* **-ies**) *n* comédie *f.*

comely ['kʌmlɪ] *adj* literary attrayant(e).

come-on *n* : **to give sb the ~** inf essayer d'aguicher qqn.

comet ['kɒmɪt] *n* comète *f.*

come-uppance [,kʌm'ʌpəns] *n* : **to get one's ~** inf recevoir ce qu'on mérite.

comfort ['kʌmfət] <> *n* - **1.** *(U)* [ease] confort *m ;* **that was too close for ~** c'était moins cinq - **2.** [luxury] commodité *f* - **3.** [solace] réconfort *m,* consolation *f* <> *vt* réconforter, consoler.

comfortable ['kʌmftəbl] *adj* - **1.** [gen] confortable - **2.** fig [person - at ease, financially] à l'aise - **3.** [after operation, accident] : **he's ~** son état est stationnaire.

comfortably ['kʌmftəblɪ] *adv* - **1.** [sit, sleep] confortablement - **2.** [without financial difficulty] à l'aise ; **~ off** à l'aise - **3.** [win] aisément.

comforter ['kʌmfətəʳ] *n* - **1.** [person] soutien *m* moral - **2.** Am [quilt] édredon *m.*

comforting ['kʌmfətɪŋ] *adj* [thought, words] réconfortant(e).

comfort station *n* Am toilettes *fpl* publiques.

comfy ['kʌmfɪ] (*compar* **-ier** ; *superl* **-iest**) *adj* inf confortable.

comic ['kɒmɪk] <> *adj* comique, amusant(e) <> *n* - **1.** [comedian] comique *m,* actrice *f* comique - **2.** [magazine] bande *f* dessinée.

comics *npl* Am [in newspaper] bandes *fpl* dessinées.

comical ['kɒmɪkl] *adj* comique, drôle.

comic strip *n* bande *f* dessinée.

coming ['kʌmɪŋ] <> *adj* [future] à venir, futur(e) <> *n* : **~s and goings** allées et venues *fpl.*

comma ['kɒmə] *n* virgule *f.*

command [kə'mɑːnd] <> *n* - **1.** [order] ordre *m* - **2.** *(U)* [control] commandement *m ;* **in ~ of** MIL à la tête de ; fig en possession de - **3.** [of language, subject] maîtrise *f ;* **to have at one's ~** [language] maîtriser ; [resources] avoir à sa disposition - **4.** COMPUT commande *f* <> *vt* - **1.** [order] : **to ~ sb to do sthg** ordonner *OR* commander à qqn de faire qqch - **2.** MIL [control] commander - **3.** [deserve - respect] inspirer ; [- attention, high price] mériter.

commandant [,kɒmən'dænt] *n* commandant *m.*

commandeer [,kɒmən'dɪəʳ] *vt* réquisitionner.

commander [kə'mɑːndəʳ] n - **1.** [in army] commandant m - **2.** [in navy] capitaine m de frégate.

commander-in-chief (pl commanders-in-chief) n commandant m en chef.

commanding [kə'mɑːndɪŋ] adj - **1.** [lead, position] dominant(e) - **2.** [voice, manner] impérieux(euse).

commanding officer n commandant m.

commandment [kə'mɑːndmənt] n RELIG commandement m.

command module n module m de commande.

commando [kə'mɑːndəʊ] (pl -s OR -es) n commando m.

command performance n représentation de gala organisée à la demande d'un chef d'État.

commemorate [kə'meməreɪt] vt commémorer.

commemoration [kə,memə'reɪʃn] n commémoration f.

commemorative [kə'memərətɪv] adj commémoratif(ive).

commence [kə'mens] fml <> vt commencer, entamer ; **to ~ doing sthg** commencer à faire qqch <> vi commencer.

commencement [kə'mensmənt] n fml commencement m, début m.

commend [kə'mend] vt - **1.** [praise] : **to ~ sb (on** OR **for)** féliciter qqn (de) - **2.** [recommend] : **to ~ sthg (to sb)** recommander qqch (à qqn).

commendable [kə'mendəbl] adj louable.

commendation [ˌkɒmen'deɪʃn] n : **to get a ~ for sthg** être récompensé(e) pour qqch.

commensurate [kə'menʃərət] adj fml : **~ with** correspondant(e) à.

comment ['kɒment] <> n commentaire m, remarque f ; **no ~!** sans commentaire! <> vt : **to ~ that** remarquer que <> vi : **to ~ (on)** faire des commentaires OR remarques (sur).

commentary ['kɒməntrɪ] (pl -ies) n commentaire m.

commentate ['kɒmənteɪt] vi RADIO & TV : **to ~ (on)** faire un reportage (sur).

commentator ['kɒmənteɪtəʳ] n commentateur m, -trice f.

commerce ['kɒmɜːs] n (U) commerce m, affaires fpl.

commercial [kə'mɜːʃl] <> adj commercial(e) <> n publicité f, spot m publicitaire.

commercial bank n banque f commerciale OR de commerce.

commercial break n publicités fpl.

commercial college n école f de secrétariat.

commercialism [kə'mɜːʃəlɪzm] n mercantilisme m.

commercialize, -ise [kə'mɜːʃəlaɪz] vt commercialiser.

commercialized [kə'mɜːʃəlaɪzd] adj commercial(e).

commercially [kə'mɜːʃəlɪ] adv commercialement.

commercial television n Br chaînes fpl (de télévision) privées OR commerciales.

commercial traveller n Br dated voyageur m OR représentant m de commerce.

commercial vehicle n Br véhicule m utilitaire.

commie ['kɒmɪ] inf pej <> adj coco <> n coco mf.

commiserate [kə'mɪzəreɪt] vi : **to ~ with sb** témoigner de la compassion pour qqn.

commiseration [kə,mɪzə'reɪʃn] n compassion f.

commission [kə'mɪʃn] <> n - **1.** [money, investigative body] commission f - **2.** [order for work] commande f <> vt [work] commander ; **to ~ sb to do sthg** charger qqn de faire qqch.

commissionaire [kə,mɪʃə'neəʳ] n Br chasseur m.

commissioned officer [kə'mɪʃənd-] n officier m.

commissioner [kə'mɪʃnəʳ] n - **1.** [in police] commissaire m - **2.** [commission member] membre m d'une commission

commit [kə'mɪt] (pt & pp -ted ; cont -ting) vt - **1.** [crime, sin etc] commettre ; **to ~ suicide** se suicider - **2.** [promise - money, resources] allouer ; **to ~ o.s. (to sthg/to doing sthg)** s'engager (à qqch/à faire qqch) - **3.** [consign] : **to ~ sb to prison** faire incarcérer qqn ; **to ~ sthg to memory** apprendre qqch par cœur.

commitment [kə'mɪtmənt] n - **1.** (U) [dedication] engagement m - **2.** [responsibility] obligation f.

committed [kə'mɪtɪd] adj [writer, politician] engagé(e) ; [Christian] convaincu(e) ; **he's ~ to his work** il fait preuve d'engagement dans son travail.

committee [kə'mɪtɪ] n commission f, comité m.

commode [kə'məʊd] n [with chamber pot] chaise f percée.

commodity [kə'mɒdətɪ] (pl -ies) n marchandise f.

commodity exchange n bourse f des matières premières.

common ['kɒmən] ⟨⟩ adj - **1.** [frequent] courant(e) - **2.** [shared] : ~ **(to)** commun(e) (à) - **3.** [ordinary] banal(e) ; **the ~ man** Monsieur m tout-le-monde - **4.** Br pej [vulgar] vulgaire ⟨⟩ n [land] terrain m communal.
➤ **in common** adv en commun.

commoner ['kɒmənəʳ] n roturier m, -ère f.

common good n : **for the ~** dans l'intérêt général.

common ground n fig terrain m d'entente.

common knowledge n : **it is ~ that ...** il est de notoriété publique que ...

common land n (U) terrain m communal.

common law n droit m coutumier.
➤ **common-law** adj : **common-law wife** concubine f.

commonly ['kɒmənlɪ] adv [generally] d'une manière générale, généralement.

Common Market n : **the ~** le Marché commun.

commonplace ['kɒmənpleɪs] adj banal(e), ordinaire.

common room n [staffroom] salle f des professeurs ; [for students] salle commune.

Commons ['kɒmənz] npl Br : **the ~** les Communes fpl, la Chambre des Communes.

common sense n (U) bon sens m.

Commonwealth ['kɒmənwelθ] n : **the ~** le Commonwealth.

Commonwealth of Independent States n : **the ~** la Communauté des États Indépendants.

commotion [kə'məʊʃn] n remue-ménage m.

communal ['kɒmjʊnl] adj [kitchen, garden] commun(e) ; [life etc] communautaire, collectif(ive).

commune [n 'kɒmju:n vb kə'mju:n] ⟨⟩ n communauté f ⟨⟩ vi : **to ~ with** communier avec.

communicate [kə'mju:nɪkeɪt] vt & vi communiquer.

communicating [kə'mju:nɪkeɪtɪŋ] adj [rooms]

communicant(e) ; ~ **door** porte f de communication.

communication [kə,mju:nɪ'keɪʃn] n contact m ; TÉLEC communication f.
➤ **communications** npl moyens mpl de communication.

communication cord n Br sonnette f d'alarme.

communications satellite n satellite m de communication.

communicative [kə'mju:nɪkətɪv] adj [talkative] communicatif(ive).

communicator [kə'mju:nɪkeɪtəʳ] n : **to be a good ~** avoir le don de la communication ; **to be a bad ~** avoir des difficultés de communication.

communion [kə'mju:njən] n communion f.
➤ **Communion** n (U) RELIG communion f.

communiqué [kə'mju:nɪkeɪ] n communiqué m.

Communism ['kɒmjʊnɪzm] n communisme m.

Communist ['kɒmjʊnɪst] ⟨⟩ adj communiste ⟨⟩ n communiste mf.

community [kə'mju:nətɪ] (pl -ies) n communauté f.

community centre n foyer m municipal.

community charge n Br ≃ impôts mpl locaux.

community home n Br centre m d'éducation surveillée.

community policing n ≃ îlotage m.

community service n (U) travail m d'intérêt général.

community spirit n esprit m de communauté.

commutable [kə'mju:təbl] adj JUR commuable.

commutation ticket [,kɒmju:'teɪʃn] n Am carte f de transport.

commute [kə'mju:t] ⟨⟩ vt JUR commuer ⟨⟩ vi [to work] faire la navette pour se rendre à son travail.

commuter [kə'mju:təʳ] n personne qui fait tous les jours la navette de banlieue en ville pour se rendre à son travail.

commy ['kɒmɪ] (pl -ies) = commie.

Comoro Islands npl : **the ~** les îles fpl Comores ; **in the ~** aux îles Comores.

compact [adj & vb kəm'pækt, n 'kɒmpækt] ⟨⟩ adj compact(e) ⟨⟩ n - **1.** [for face powder] poudrier m - **2.** Am AUT : ~ **(car)** petite voiture f ⟨⟩ vt tasser, rendre compact.

compact disc n compact m (disc m), disque m compact.

compact disc player n lecteur m de disques compacts.

companion [kəmˈpænjən] n [person] camarade mf; **travelling** ~ compagnon m, compagne f de voyage.

companionable [kəmˈpænjənəbl] adj sociable.

companionship [kəmˈpænjənʃɪp] n compagnie f.

company [ˈkʌmpənɪ] (pl **-ies**) n **- 1.** [COMM - gen] société f; [- insurance, airline, shipping company] compagnie f **- 2.** [companionship] compagnie f; **to keep sb** ~ tenir compagnie à qqn ; **to part** ~ **(with)** se séparer (de) **- 3.** [of actors] troupe f.

company car n voiture f de fonction.

company director n directeur m, -trice f.

company secretary n secrétaire général m, secrétaire générale f.

comparable [ˈkɒmprəbl] adj : ~ **(to** OR **with)** comparable (à).

comparative [kəmˈpærətɪv] adj **- 1.** [relative] relatif(ive) **- 2.** [study, in grammar] comparatif(ive).

comparatively [kəmˈpærətɪvlɪ] adv [relatively] relativement.

compare [kəmˈpeəʳ] <> vt : **to** ~ **sb/sthg (with), to** ~ **sb/sthg (to)** comparer qqn/qqch (avec), comparer qqn/qqch (à) ; **-d with** OR **to** par rapport à <> vi : **to** ~ **(with)** être comparable (à) ; **to** ~ **favourably/unfavourably with** supporter/ne pas supporter la comparaison avec.

comparison [kəmˈpærɪsn] n comparaison f; **in** ~ **with** OR **to** en comparaison de, par rapport à.

compartment [kəmˈpɑːtmənt] n compartiment m.

compartmentalize, -ise [ˌkɒmpɑːtˈmentəlaɪz] vt compartimenter.

compass [ˈkʌmpəs] n [magnetic] boussole f. ➡ **compasses** npl : **(a pair of) ~es** un compas.

compassion [kəmˈpæʃn] n compassion f.

compassionate [kəmˈpæʃənət] adj compatissant(e).

compatibility [kəmˌpætəˈbɪlətɪ] n [gen & COMPUT] : ~ **(with)** compatibilité f (avec).

compatible [kəmˈpætəbl] adj [gen & COMPUT] : ~ **(with)** compatible (avec).

compatriot [kəmˈpætrɪət] n compatriote mf.

compel [kəmˈpel] (pt & pp **-led** ; cont **-ling**) vt **- 1.** [force] : **to** ~ **sb (to do sthg)** contraindre OR obliger qqn (à faire qqch) **- 2.** [cause - sympathy, attention etc] susciter.

compelling [kəmˈpelɪŋ] adj [forceful] irrésistible.

compendium [kəmˈpendɪəm] (pl **-diums** OR **-dia** [-dɪə]) n [book] abrégé m.

compensate [ˈkɒmpenseɪt] <> vt : **to** ~ **sb for sthg** [financially] dédommager OR indemniser qqn de qqch <> vi : **to** ~ **for sthg** compenser qqch.

compensation [ˌkɒmpenˈseɪʃn] n **- 1.** [money] : ~ **(for)** dédommagement m (pour) **- 2.** [way of compensating] : ~ **(for)** compensation f (pour).

compere [ˈkɒmpeəʳ] Br <> n animateur m, -trice f <> vt présenter, animer.

compete [kəmˈpiːt] vi **- 1.** [vie - people] : **to** ~ **with sb for sthg** disputer qqch à qqn ; **to** ~ **for sthg** se disputer qqch **- 2.** COMM : **to** ~ **(with)** être en concurrence (avec) ; **to** ~ **for sthg** se faire concurrence pour qqch **- 3.** [take part] être en compétition.

competence [ˈkɒmpɪtəns] n (U) [proficiency] compétence f, capacité f.

competent [ˈkɒmpɪtənt] adj compétent(e).

competently [ˈkɒmpɪtəntlɪ] adv avec compétence.

competing [kəmˈpiːtɪŋ] adj [theories etc] opposé(e).

competition [ˌkɒmpɪˈtɪʃn] n **- 1.** (U) [rivalry] rivalité f, concurrence f **- 2.** (U) COMM concurrence f **- 3.** [race, contest] concours m, compétition f.

competitive [kəmˈpetətɪv] adj **- 1.** [person] qui a l'esprit de compétition ; [match, sport] de compétition ; ~ **examination** concours m **- 2.** [COMM - goods] compétitif(ive) ; [- manufacturer] concurrentiel(elle).

competitively [kəmˈpetətɪvlɪ] adv **- 1.** [play] dans un esprit de compétition **- 2.** COMM : ~ **priced** à un prix compétitif.

competitor [kəmˈpetɪtəʳ] n concurrent m, -e f.

compilation [ˌkɒmpɪˈleɪʃn] n compilation f.

compile [kəmˈpaɪl] vt rédiger.

complacency [kəmˈpleɪsnsɪ] n autosatisfaction f.

complacent [kəmˈpleɪsnt] adj content(e) de soi.

complacently [kəmˈpleɪsntlɪ] adv d'une manière hautaine ; [say] d'un ton hautain.

complain [kəmˈpleɪn] vi **- 1.** [moan] : **to** ~ **(about)** se plaindre (de) **- 2.** MED : **to** ~ **of** se plaindre de.

complaining [kəmˈpleɪnɪŋ] adj [customer] mécontent(e).

complaint [kəmˈpleɪnt] n **- 1.** [gen] plainte f;

[in shop] réclamation f - **2.** MED affection f, maladie f.

complement [n 'kɒmplɪmənt, vb 'kɒmplɪˌment] <> n - **1.** [accompaniment] accompagnement m - **2.** [number] effectif m ; full ~ effectif complet - **3.** GRAMM complément m <> vt aller bien avec.

complementary [ˌkɒmplɪ'mentərɪ] adj complémentaire.

complete [kəm'pliːt] <> adj - **1.** [gen] complet(ète) ; ~ with doté(e) de, muni(e) de - **2.** [finished] achevé(e) <> vt - **1.** [make whole] compléter - **2.** [finish] achever, terminer - **3.** [questionnaire, form] remplir.

completely [kəm'pliːtlɪ] adv complètement.

completion [kəm'pliːʃn] n achèvement m.

complex ['kɒmpleks] <> adj complexe <> n [mental, of buildings] complexe m.

complexion [kəm'plekʃn] n teint m ; of all ~s fig de tous bords.

complexity [kəm'pleksətɪ] (pl -ies) n complexité f.

compliance [kəm'plaɪəns] n : ~ (with) conformité f (à).

compliant [kəm'plaɪənt] adj docile.

complicate ['kɒmplɪkeɪt] vt compliquer.

complicated ['kɒmplɪkeɪtɪd] adj compliqué(e).

complication [ˌkɒmplɪ'keɪʃn] n complication f.

complicity [kəm'plɪsətɪ] n : ~ (in) complicité f (dans).

compliment [n 'kɒmplɪmənt, vb 'kɒmplɪˌment] <> n compliment m <> vt : to ~ sb (on) féliciter qqn (de).

➡ **compliments** npl fml compliments mpl.

complimentary [ˌkɒmplɪ'mentərɪ] adj - **1.** [admiring] flatteur(euse) - **2.** [free] gratuit(e).

complimentary ticket n billet m de faveur.

compliments slip n papillon m (joint à un envoi etc).

comply [kəm'plaɪ] (pt & pp -ied) vi : to ~ with se conformer à.

component [kəm'pəʊnənt] n composant m.

compose [kəm'pəʊz] vt - **1.** [gen] composer ; to be ~d of se composer de, être composé de - **2.** [calm] : to ~ o.s. se calmer.

composed [kəm'pəʊzd] adj [calm] calme.

composer [kəm'pəʊzə'] n compositeur m, -trice f.

composite ['kɒmpəzɪt] <> adj composite <> n composite m.

composition [ˌkɒmpə'zɪʃn] n composition f.

compost [Br 'kɒmpɒst, Am 'kɒmpəʊst] n compost m.

composure [kəm'pəʊʒə'] n sang-froid m, calme m.

compound [adj & n 'kɒmpaʊnd, vb kəm'paʊnd] <> adj composé(e) <> n - **1.** CHEM & LING composé m - **2.** [enclosed area] enceinte f <> vt - **1.** [mixture, substance] : to be ~ed of se composer de, être composé(e) de - **2.** [difficulties] aggraver.

compound fracture n fracture f multiple.

compound interest n intérêt m composé.

comprehend [ˌkɒmprɪ'hend] vt [understand] comprendre.

comprehension [ˌkɒmprɪ'henʃn] n compréhension f.

comprehensive [ˌkɒmprɪ'hensɪv] <> adj - **1.** [account, report] exhaustif(ive), détaillé(e) - **2.** [insurance] tous-risques (inv) <> n = **comprehensive school.**

comprehensively [ˌkɒmprɪ'hensɪvlɪ] adv [study, cover] exhaustivement.

comprehensive school n établissement secondaire britannique d'enseignement général.

compress [kəm'pres] vt - **1.** [squeeze, press] comprimer - **2.** [shorten - text] condenser.

compression [kəm'preʃn] n - **1.** [of air] compression f - **2.** [of text] condensation f.

comprise [kəm'praɪz] vt comprendre ; to be ~d of consister en, comprendre.

compromise ['kɒmprəmaɪz] <> n compromis m <> vt compromettre ; to ~ o.s. se compromettre <> vi transiger.

compromising ['kɒmprəmaɪzɪŋ] adj compromettant(e).

compulsion [kəm'pʌlʃn] n - **1.** [strong desire] : to have a ~ to do sthg ne pas pouvoir s'empêcher de faire qqch - **2.** (U) [obligation] obligation f.

compulsive [kəm'pʌlsɪv] adj - **1.** [smoker, liar etc] invétéré(e) - **2.** [book, TV programme] captivant(e).

compulsory [kəm'pʌlsərɪ] adj obligatoire.

compulsory purchase n Br expropriation f (pour cause d'utilité publique).

compunction [kəm'pʌŋkʃn] n (U) scrupule m, remords m.

computation [ˌkɒmpjuː'teɪʃn] n calcul m.

compute [kəm'pjuːt] vt calculer.

computer [kəm'pjuːtə'] <> n ordinateur m

◇ *comp* : ~ **graphics** Infographie® *f* ; ~ **program** programme *m* informatique ; ~ **scientist** programme *m* informatique.

computer dating *n (U)* ≈ rencontres *fpl* par Minitel®.

computer game *n* jeu *m* électronique.

computer-generated [- 'dʒenəreɪtɪd] *adj* créé(e) par ordinateur ; **a ~ image** une image de synthèse.

computerization [kəm,pju:təraɪ'zeɪʃn] *n* informatisation *f*.

computerize, -ise [kəm'pju:təraɪz] *vt* informatiser.

computerized [kəm'pju:təraɪzd] *adj* informatisé(e).

computer language *n* langage *m* de programmation.

computer-literate *adj* qui a des connaissances en informatique.

computer science *n* informatique *f*.

computer scientist *n* informaticien *m*, -enne *f*.

computing [kəm'pju:tɪŋ] *n* informatique *f*.

comrade ['kɒmreɪd] *n* camarade *mf*.

comradeship ['kɒmreɪdʃɪp] *n* camaraderie *f*.

comsat ['kɒmˈsæt] *abbr of* **communications satellite**.

con [kɒn] *(pt & pp -ned ; cont -ning) inf* ◇ *n* - **1.** [trick] escroquerie *f* - **2.** prison sl taulard *m* ◇ *vt* [trick] : **to ~ sb (out of)** escroquer qqn (de) ; **to ~ sb into doing sthg** persuader qqn de faire qqch (en lui mentant).

concave [,kɒn'keɪv] *adj* concave.

conceal [kən'si:l] *vt* cacher, dissimuler ; **to ~ sthg from sb** cacher qqch à qqn.

concede [kən'si:d] ◇ *vt* concéder ◇ *vi* céder.

conceit [kən'si:t] *n* [arrogance] vanité *f*.

conceited [kən'si:tɪd] *adj* vaniteux(euse).

conceivable [kən'si:vəbl] *adj* concevable.

conceivably [kən'si:vəblɪ] *adv* : **they might ~ win** il se peut qu'ils gagnent ; **I can't ~ do that** il n'est pas question que je fasse ça.

conceive [kən'si:v] ◇ *vt* concevoir ◇ *vi* - **1.** MED concevoir - **2.** [imagine] : **to ~ of** concevoir.

concentrate ['kɒnsəntreɪt] ◇ *vt* concentrer ◇ *vi* : **to ~ (on)** se concentrer (sur).

concentrated ['kɒnsəntreɪtɪd] *adj* concentré(e) ; [effort] intense.

concentration [,kɒnsən'treɪʃn] *n* concentration *f*.

concentration camp *n* camp *m* de concentration.

concentric [kən'sentrɪk] *adj* concentrique.

concept ['kɒnsept] *n* concept *m*.

conception [kən'sepʃn] *n* [gen & MED] conception *f*.

conceptualize, -ise [kən'septʃʊəlaɪz] *vt* conceptualiser.

concern [kən'sɜːn] ◇ *n* - **1.** [worry, anxiety] souci *m*, inquiétude *f* ; **to show ~ for** s'inquiéter de - **2.** [matter of interest] : **it's no ~ of mine** cela ne me regarde pas - **3.** COMM [company] affaire *f* ◇ *vt* - **1.** [worry] inquiéter ; **to be ~ed (about)** s'inquiéter (de) - **2.** [involve] concerner, intéresser ; **as far as I'm ~ed** en ce qui me concerne ; **to be ~ed with** [subj : person] s'intéresser à ; **to ~ o.s. with sthg** s'intéresser à, s'occuper de - **3.** [subj : book, film] traiter de.

concerning [kən'sɜːnɪŋ] *prep* en ce qui concerne.

concert ['kɒnsət] *n* concert *m*.

➤ **in concert** *adv* - **1.** MUS à l'unisson - **2.** fml [acting as one] de concert.

concerted [kən'sɜːtɪd] *adj* [effort] concerté(e).

concertgoer ['kɒnsət,gəʊəʳ] *n* amateur *m* de concerts.

concert hall *n* salle *f* de concert.

concertina [,kɒnsə'ti:nə] *(pt & pp -ed ; cont -ing)* ◇ *n* concertina *m* ◇ *vi* [cars] s'écraser en accordéon.

concerto [kən'tʃɜːtəʊ] *(pl -s)* *n* concerto *m*.

concession [kən'seʃn] *n* - **1.** [gen] concession *f* - **2.** [special price] réduction *f*.

concessionaire [kən,seʃə'neəʳ] *n* concessionnaire *mf*.

concessionary [kən'seʃnərɪ] *adj* [fare] à prix réduit.

conciliation [kən,sɪlɪ'eɪʃn] *n* conciliation *f*.

conciliatory [kən'sɪlɪətrɪ] *adj* conciliant(e).

concise [kən'saɪs] *adj* concis(e).

concisely [kən'saɪslɪ] *adv* de façon concise, avec concision.

conclave ['kɒŋkleɪv] *n* conclave *m*.

conclude [kən'klu:d] ◇ *vt* conclure ◇ *vi* [meeting] prendre fin ; [speaker] conclure.

conclusion [kən'klu:ʒn] *n* conclusion *f* ; **it was a foregone ~** c'était à prévoir ; **to jump to the wrong ~** tirer des conclusions trop hâtives.

conclusive [kən'klu:sɪv] *adj* concluant(e).

concoct [kən'kɒkt] *vt* préparer ; fig concocter.

concoction [kən'kɒkʃn] *n* préparation *f*.

concord ['kɒŋkɔːd] *n* [harmony] concorde *f*.

concourse [ˈkɒŋkɔːs] n [hall] hall m.

concrete [ˈkɒŋkriːt] ◇ adj [definite] concret(ète) ◇ n (U) béton m ◇ comp [made of concrete] en béton ◇ vt bétonner.

concrete mixer n bétonnière f.

concubine [ˈkɒŋkjʊbaɪn] n maîtresse f.

concur [kənˈkɜːr] (pt & pp -red ; cont -ring) vi [agree] : **to ~ (with)** être d'accord (avec).

concurrently [kənˈkʌrəntlɪ] adv simultanément.

concussed [kənˈkʌst] adj commotionné(e).

concussion [kənˈkʌʃn] n commotion f.

condemn [kənˈdem] vt condamner.

condemnation [ˌkɒndemˈneɪʃn] n condamnation f.

condemned [kənˈdemd] adj condamné(e).

condensation [ˌkɒndenˈseɪʃn] n condensation f.

condense [kənˈdens] ◇ vt condenser ◇ vi se condenser.

condensed milk [kənˈdenst-] n lait m concentré.

condescend [ˌkɒndɪˈsend] vi - **1.** [talk down] : **to ~ to sb** se montrer condescendant(e) envers qqn - **2.** [deign] : **to ~ to do sthg** daigner faire qqch, condescendre à faire qqch.

condescending [ˌkɒndɪˈsendɪŋ] adj condescendant(e).

condiment [ˈkɒndɪmənt] n condiment m.

condition [kənˈdɪʃn] ◇ n - **1.** [gen] condition f ; **in (a) good/bad ~** en bon/mauvais état ; **out of ~** pas en forme - **2.** MED maladie f ◇ vt - **1.** [gen] conditionner - **2.** [hair] : **to ~ one's hair** mettre de l'après-shampooing.
◆ **conditions** npl conditions fpl.

conditional [kənˈdɪʃənl] adj conditionnel(elle) ; **to be ~ on** OR **upon** dépendre de.

conditionally [kənˈdɪʃnəlɪ] adv conditionnellement.

conditioner [kənˈdɪʃnər] n - **1.** [for hair] après-shampooing m - **2.** [for clothes] assouplissant m.

conditioning [kənˈdɪʃnɪŋ] n PSYCH conditionnement m.

condo [ˈkɒndəʊ] n inf abbr of **condominium**.

condolences [kənˈdəʊlənsɪz] npl condoléances fpl.

condom [ˈkɒndəm] n préservatif m.

condominium [ˌkɒndəˈmɪnɪəm] n Am - **1.** [apartment] appartement m dans un immeuble en copropriété - **2.** [apartment block] immeuble m en copropriété.

condone [kənˈdəʊn] vt excuser.

condor [ˈkɒndɔːr] n condor m.

conducive [kənˈdjuːsɪv] adj : **to be ~ to sthg/ to doing sthg** inciter à qqch/à faire qqch.

conduct [n ˈkɒndʌkt, vb kənˈdʌkt] ◇ n conduite f ◇ vt - **1.** [carry out, transmit] conduire - **2.** [behave] : **to ~ o.s. well/badly** se conduire bien/mal - **3.** MUS diriger ◇ vi MUS diriger.

conducted tour [kənˈdʌktɪd-] n visite f guidée.

conductor [kənˈdʌktər] n - **1.** MUS chef m d'orchestre - **2.** [on bus] receveur m - **3.** Am [on train] chef m de train.

conductress [kənˈdʌktrɪs] n [on bus] receveuse f.

conduit [ˈkɒndɪt] n conduit m.

cone [kəʊn] n - **1.** [shape] cône m - **2.** [for ice cream] cornet m - **3.** [from tree] pomme f de pin.
◆ **cone off** vt sep Br [road, lane] fermer à la circulation.

confectioner [kənˈfekʃnər] n confiseur m ; **~'s (shop)** confiserie f.

confectionery [kənˈfekʃnərɪ] n confiserie f.

confederation [kənˌfedəˈreɪʃn] n confédération f.

Confederation of British Industry n : **the ~** ≃ le conseil du patronat.

confer [kənˈfɜːr] (pt & pp -red ; cont -ring) ◇ vt : **to ~ sthg (on sb)** conférer qqch (à qqn) ◇ vi : **to ~ (with sb on** OR **about sthg)** s'entretenir (avec qqn de qqch).

conference [ˈkɒnfərəns] n conférence f ; **in ~** en conférence.

conference call n audioconférence f.

conference centre n centre m de conférences.

conference hall n salle f de conférence.

conferencing [ˈkɒnfərənsɪŋ] n (U) audioconférence f.

confess [kənˈfes] ◇ vt - **1.** [admit] avouer, confesser - **2.** RELIG confesser ◇ vi : **to ~ (to sthg)** avouer (qqch).

confession [kənˈfeʃn] n confession f ; **I've a ~ to make** j'ai un aveu à vous faire.

confessional [kənˈfeʃənl] n confessionnal m.

confetti [kənˈfetɪ] n (U) confettis mpl.

confidant [ˌkɒnfɪˈdænt] n confident m.

confidante [ˌkɒnfɪˈdænt] n confidente f.

confide [kənˈfaɪd] ◇ vt confier ◇ vi : **to ~ in sb** se confier à qqn.

confidence [ˈkɒnfɪdəns] n - **1.** [self-assurance] confiance f en soi, assurance f - **2.** [trust] confiance f ; **to have ~ in** avoir confiance en

- 3. [secrecy] : **in ~** en confidence **- 4.** [secret] confidence *f*.

confidence trick *n* abus *m* de confiance.

confident ['kɒnfɪdənt] *adj* **- 1.** [self-assured] : **to be ~** avoir confiance en soi **- 2.** [sure] sûr(e).

confidential [ˌkɒnfɪ'denʃl] *adj* confidentiel(elle).

confidentiality ['kɒnfɪˌdenʃɪ'ælətɪ] *n* confidentialité *f*.

confidentially [ˌkɒnfɪ'denʃəlɪ] *adv* confidentiellement.

confidently ['kɒnfɪdəntlɪ] *adv* [speak, predict] avec assurance.

configuration [kənˌfɪgə'reɪʃn] *n* [gen & COMPUT] configuration *f*.

confine [*vb* kən'faɪn, *npl* 'kɒnfaɪnz] *vt* **- 1.** [limit] limiter ; **to ~ o.s. to** se limiter à **- 2.** [shut up] enfermer, confiner.

confined [kən'faɪnd] *adj* [space, area] restreint(e).

confinement [kən'faɪnmənt] *n* **- 1.** [imprisonment] emprisonnement *m* **- 2.** dated & MED couches *fpl*.

confines ['kɒnfaɪnz] *npl* confins *mpl*.

confirm [kən'fɜːm] *vt* confirmer.

confirmation [ˌkɒnfə'meɪʃn] *n* confirmation *f*.

confirmed [kən'fɜːmd] *adj* [habitual] invétéré(e) ; [bachelor, spinster] endurci(e).

confiscate ['kɒnfɪskeɪt] *vt* confisquer.

confiscation [ˌkɒnfɪ'skeɪʃn] *n* confiscation *f*.

conflagration [ˌkɒnflə'greɪʃn] *n* conflagration *f*.

conflict [*n* 'kɒnflɪkt, *vb* kən'flɪkt] <> *n* conflit *m* <> *vi* : **to ~ (with)** s'opposer (à), être en conflit (avec).

conflicting [kən'flɪktɪŋ] *adj* contradictoire.

conform [kən'fɔːm] *vi* : **to ~ (to OR with)** se conformer (à).

conformist [kən'fɔːmɪst] <> *adj* conformiste <> *n* conformiste *mf*.

conformity [kən'fɔːmətɪ] *n* : **~ (to OR with)** conformité *f* (à).

confound [kən'faʊnd] *vt* [confuse, defeat] déconcerter.

confounded [kən'faʊndɪd] *adj* inf sacré(e).

confront [kən'frʌnt] *vt* **- 1.** [problem, enemy] affronter **- 2.** [challenge] : **to ~ sb (with)** confronter qqn (avec).

confrontation [ˌkɒnfrʌn'teɪʃn] *n* affrontement *m*.

confuse [kən'fjuːz] *vt* **- 1.** [disconcert] troubler ;

to ~ the issue brouiller les cartes **- 2.** [mix up] confondre.

confused [kən'fjuːzd] *adj* **- 1.** [not clear] compliqué(e) **- 2.** [disconcerted] troublé(e), désorienté(e) ; **I'm ~** je n'y comprends rien.

confusing [kən'fjuːzɪŋ] *adj* pas clair(e).

confusion [kən'fjuːʒn] *n* confusion *f*.

conga ['kɒŋgə] *n* : **the ~** la conga.

congeal [kən'dʒiːl] *vi* [blood] se coaguler.

congenial [kən'dʒiːnjəl] *adj* sympathique, agréable.

congenital [kən'dʒenɪtl] *adj* MED congénital(e).

conger eel ['kɒŋgər-] *n* congre *m*.

congested [kən'dʒestɪd] *adj* **- 1.** [street, area] encombré(e) **- 2.** MED congestionné(e).

congestion [kən'dʒestʃn] *n* **- 1.** [of traffic] encombrement *m* **- 2.** MED congestion *f*.

conglomerate [ˌkən'glɒmərət] *n* COMM conglomérat *m*.

conglomeration [kənˌglɒmə'reɪʃn] *n* conglomération *f*.

Congo ['kɒŋgəʊ] *n* **- 1.** [country] : **the ~** le Congo ; **in the ~** au Congo **- 2.** [former Zaïre] : **the Democratic Republic of ~** la République démocratique du Congo **- 3.** [river] : **the ~** le fleuve Zaïre.

Congolese [ˌkɒŋgə'liːz] <> *adj* congolais(e) <> *n* Congolais *m*, -e *f*.

congratulate [kən'grætʃʊleɪt] *vt* : **to ~ sb (on sthg/on doing sthg)** féliciter qqn (de qqch/ d'avoir fait qqch).

congratulations [kənˌgrætʃʊ'leɪʃənz] *npl* félicitations *fpl*.

congratulatory [kən'grætʃʊlətrɪ] *adj* de félicitations.

congregate ['kɒŋgrɪgeɪt] *vi* se rassembler.

congregation [ˌkɒŋgrɪ'geɪʃn] *n* assemblée *f* des fidèles.

congress ['kɒŋgres] *n* [meeting] congrès *m*. ◆ **Congress** *n* Am POL le Congrès.

> **CONGRESS**
>
> Le Congrès, organe législatif américain, est constitué du Sénat et de la Chambre des représentants ; une proposition de loi doit obligatoirement être approuvée séparément par ces deux chambres.

congressional [kən'greʃənl] *adj* Am POL du Congrès.

congressman ['kɒŋgresmən] (*pl* **-men** [-mən]) *n* Am POL membre *m* du Congrès.

congresswoman ['kɒŋgresˌwʊmən] (*pl*

-women [-ˌwɪmɪn]) n Am POL membre m (féminin) du Congrès.

conical ['kɒgt·nɪkl] adj conique.

conifer ['kɒnɪfəʳ] n conifère m.

coniferous [kə'nɪfərəs] adj [tree] conifère ; [forest] de conifères.

conjecture [kən'dʒektʃəʳ] <> n conjecture f <> vt & vi conjecturer.

conjugal ['kɒndʒʊgl] adj conjugal(e).

conjugation [ˌkɒndʒʊ'geɪʃn] n GRAMM conjugaison f

conjunction [kən'dʒʌŋkʃn] n - 1. GRAMM conjonction f - 2. [combination] combinaison f, mélange m ; in ~ with conjointement avec.

conjunctivitis [kənˌdʒʌŋktɪ'vaɪtɪs] n conjonctivite f.

conjure [vi 'kʌndʒəʳ, vt sense 2 kən'dʒʊəʳ] <> vt fml supplier <> vi [by magic] faire des tours de prestidigitation.
★ **conjure up** vt sep évoquer.

conjurer ['kʌndʒərəʳ] n prestidigitateur m, -trice f.

conjuring trick ['kʌndʒərɪŋ-] n tour m de prestidigitation.

conjuror ['kʌndʒərəʳ] = conjurer.

conk [kɒŋk] n inf pif m.
★ **conk out** vi inf tomber en panne.

conker ['kɒŋkəʳ] n Br marron m.

conman ['kɒnmæn] (pl -men [-men]) n escroc m.

connect [kə'nekt] <> vt - 1. [join] : to ~ sthg (to) relier qqch (à) - 2. [on telephone] mettre en communication - 3. [associate] associer ; to ~ sb/sthg to, to ~ sb/sthg with associer qqn/qqch à - 4. ELEC [to power supply] : to ~ sthg to brancher qqch à <> vi [train, plane, bus] : to ~ (with) assurer la correspondance (avec).

connected [kə'nektɪd] adj [related] : to be ~ with avoir un rapport avec ; they are not ~ il n'y a aucun rapport entre eux.

Connecticut [kə'netɪkət] n Connecticut m ; in ~ dans le Connecticut.

connecting [kə'nektɪŋ] adj : ~ flight/train correspondance f

connection [kə'nekʃn] n - 1. [relationship] : ~ (between/with) rapport m (entre/avec) ; in ~ with à propos de - 2. ELEC branchement m, connexion f - 3. [on telephone] communication f ; it's a bad ~ la ligne est mauvaise - 4. [plane, train, bus] correspondance f - 5. [professional acquaintance] relation f.

connective tissue [kə'nektɪv-] n tissu m conjonctif.

connexion [kə'nekʃn] Br = connection.

connive [kə'naɪv] vi - 1. [plot] comploter ; to

~ with sb être de connivence avec qqn
- 2. [allow to happen] : to ~ at sthg fermer les yeux sur qqch.

conniving [kə'naɪvɪŋ] adj : you ~ wretch! espèce de sale comploteur!

connoisseur [ˌkɒnə'sɜːʳ] n connaisseur m, -euse f.

connotation [ˌkɒnə'teɪʃn] n connotation f.

conquer ['kɒŋkəʳ] vt - 1. [country etc] conquérir - 2. [fears, inflation etc] vaincre.

conqueror ['kɒŋkərəʳ] n conquérant m, -e f.

conquest ['kɒŋkwest] n conquête f.

cons [kɒnz] npl - 1. Br inf : all mod ~ tout confort - 2. ⊳ pro.

Cons. abbr of Conservative.

conscience ['kɒnʃəns] n conscience f ; to have a guilty ~ avoir mauvaise conscience ; in all ~ en mon/votre etc âme et conscience.

conscientious [ˌkɒnʃɪ'enʃəs] adj consciencieux(euse).

conscientiously [ˌkɒnʃɪ'enʃəslɪ] adv consciencieusement.

conscientiousness [ˌkɒnʃɪ'enʃəsnɪs] n conscience f.

conscientious objector n objecteur m de conscience.

conscious ['kɒnʃəs] adj - 1. [not unconscious] conscient(e) - 2. [aware] : ~ of sthg conscient(e) de qqch ; fashion-~ qui suit la mode ; money-~ qui fait attention à ses dépenses - 3. [intentional - insult] délibéré(e), intentionnel(elle) ; [- effort] conscient(e).

consciously ['kɒnʃəslɪ] adv intentionnellement.

consciousness ['kɒnʃəsnɪs] n conscience f.

conscript [n 'kɒnskrɪpt, vb kən'skrɪpt] MIL <> n conscrit m <> vt appeler sous les drapeaux.

conscription [kən'skrɪpʃn] n conscription f.

consecrate ['kɒnsɪkreɪt] vt consacrer.

consecration [ˌkɒnsɪ'kreɪʃn] n consécration f.

consecutive [kən'sekjʊtɪv] adj consécutif(ive).

consecutively [kən'sekjʊtɪvlɪ] adv consécutivement.

consensus [kən'sensəs] n consensus m.

consent [kən'sent] <> n (U) - 1. [permission] consentement m - 2. [agreement] accord m <> vi : to ~ (to) consentir (à).

consenting [kən'sentɪŋ] adj : ~ adults adultes consentants.

consequence ['kɒnsɪkwəns] n - 1. [result] conséquence f; in ~ par conséquent - **2.** [importance] importance f.

consequent [ˈkɒnsɪkwənt] adj fml consécutif(ive) ; [resulting] résultant(e).

consequently [ˈkɒnsɪkwəntlɪ] adv par conséquent.

conservation [ˌkɒnsəˈveɪʃn] n [of nature] protection f; [of buildings] conservation f; [of energy, water] économie f.

conservation area n secteur m sauvegardé.

conservationist [ˌkɒnsəˈveɪʃənɪst] n écologiste mf.

conservatism [kənˈsɜːvətɪzm] n conservatisme m.

➨ **Conservatism** n POL conservatisme m.

conservative [kənˈsɜːvətɪv] ◇ adj - **1.** [not modern] traditionnel(elle) - **2.** [cautious] prudent(e) ◇ n traditionaliste mf.

➨ **Conservative** POL ◇ adj conservateur(trice) ◇ n conservateur m, -trice f.

Conservative Party n : the ~ le parti conservateur.

conservatory [kənˈsɜːvətrɪ] (pl -ies) n [of house] véranda f.

conserve [n ˈkɒnsɜːv, vb kənˈsɜːv] ◇ n confiture f ◇ vt [energy, supplies] économiser ; [nature, wildlife] protéger.

consider [kənˈsɪdəʳ] vt - **1.** [think about] examiner - **2.** [take into account] prendre en compte ; **all things ~ed** tout compte fait - **3.** [judge] considérer.

considerable [kənˈsɪdrəbl] adj considérable.

considerably [kənˈsɪdrəblɪ] adv considérablement.

considerate [kənˈsɪdərət] adj prévenant(e) ; **that's very ~ of you** c'est très gentil à vous OR de votre part.

consideration [kənˌsɪdəˈreɪʃn] n - **1.** (U) [careful thought] réflexion f; **to take sthg into ~** tenir compte de qqch, prendre qqch en considération ; **under ~** à l'étude - **2.** (U) [care] attention f - **3.** [factor] facteur m.

considered [kənˈsɪdəd] adj : **it's my ~ opinion that ...** après mûre réflexion je pense que ...

considering [kənˈsɪdərɪŋ] ◇ prep étant donné ◇ conj étant donné que.

consign [kənˈsaɪn] vt : **to ~ sb/sthg to** reléguer qqn/qqch à.

consignee [ˌkɒnsaɪˈniː] n destinataire mf.

consignment [kənˈsaɪnmənt] n [load] expédition f.

consignment note n bordereau m d'expédition.

consignor [kənˈsaɪnəʳ] n expéditeur m, -trice f.

consist [kənˈsɪst] ➨ **consist in** vt fus : **to ~ in sthg** consister dans qqch ; **to ~ in doing sthg** consister à faire qqch.

➨ **consist of** vt fus consister en.

consistency [kənˈsɪstənsɪ] (pl -ies) n - **1.** [coherence] cohérence f - **2.** [texture] consistance f.

consistent [kənˈsɪstənt] adj - **1.** [regular - behaviour] conséquent(e) ; [- improvement] régulier(ère) ; [- supporter] constant(e) - **2.** [coherent] cohérent(e) ; **to be ~ with** [with one's position] être compatible avec ; [with the facts] correspondre avec.

consistently [kənˈsɪstəntlɪ] adv - **1.** [without exception] invariablement - **2.** [argue, reason] de manière cohérente.

consolation [ˌkɒnsəˈleɪʃn] n réconfort m.

consolation prize n prix m de consolation.

console [n ˈkɒnsəʊl, vt kənˈsəʊl] ◇ n tableau m de commande ; COMPUT & MUS console f ◇ vt consoler ; **he had to ~ himself with second place** il a dû se contenter de la deuxième place.

consolidate [kənˈsɒlɪdeɪt] ◇ vt - **1.** [strengthen] consolider - **2.** [merge] fusionner ◇ vi fusionner.

consolidation [kənˌsɒlɪˈdeɪʃn] (U) n - **1.** [strengthening] affermissement m - **2.** [merging] fusion f.

consols [ˈkɒnsəlz] npl Br fonds mpl consolidés.

consommé [Br kənˈsɒmeɪ, Am ˌkɒnsəˈmeɪ] n consommé m.

consonant [ˈkɒnsənənt] n consonne f.

consort [vb kənˈsɔːt, n ˈkɒnsɔːt] ◇ vi fml : **to ~ with sb** fréquenter qqn ◇ n : **prince ~** prince m consort.

consortium [kənˈsɔːtjəm] (pl -tiums OR -tia [-tjə]) n consortium m.

conspicuous [kənˈspɪkjʊəs] adj voyant(e), qui se remarque.

conspicuously [kənˈspɪkjʊəslɪ] adv [dressed] de manière voyante ; [wealthy] ostensiblement.

conspiracy [kənˈspɪrəsɪ] (pl -ies) n conspiration f, complot m.

conspirator [kənˈspɪrətəʳ] n conspirateur m, -trice f.

conspiratorial [kənˌspɪrəˈtɔːrɪəl] adj de conspirateur.

conspire [kən'spaɪəʳ] <> vt : **to ~ to do** sthg comploter de faire qqch ; [subj : events] contribuer à faire qqch <> vi : **to ~ against/with** sb conspirer contre/avec qqn.

constable ['kʌnstəbl] n Br [policeman] agent m de police.

constabulary [kən'stæbjʊlərɪ] (pl **-ies**) n police f.

constancy ['kɒnstənsɪ] n constance f.

constant ['kɒnstənt] adj **- 1.** [unvarying] constant(e) **- 2.** [recurring] continuel(elle) **- 3.** literary [faithful] fidèle.

constantly ['kɒnstəntlɪ] adv constamment.

constellation [ˌkɒnstə'leɪʃn] n constellation f.

consternation [ˌkɒnstə'neɪʃn] n consternation f.

constipated ['kɒnstɪpeɪtɪd] adj constipé(e).

constipation [ˌkɒnstɪ'peɪʃn] n constipation f.

constituency [kən'stɪtjʊənsɪ] (pl **-ies**) n [area] circonscription f électorale.

constituency party n Br section f locale du parti.

constituent [kən'stɪtjʊənt] <> adj constituant(e) <> n **- 1.** [voter] électeur m, -trice f **- 2.** [element] composant m.

constitute ['kɒnstɪtjuːt] vt **- 1.** [form, represent] représenter, constituer **- 2.** [establish, set up] constituer.

constitution [ˌkɒnstɪ'tjuːʃn] n constitution f.

➤ **Constitution** n : **the (United States) Constitution** la Constitution américaine.

constitutional [ˌkɒnstɪ'tjuːʃənl] adj constitutionnel(elle).

constrain [kən'streɪn] vt **- 1.** [coerce] forcer, contraindre ; **to ~ sb to do** sthg forcer qqn à faire qqch **- 2.** [restrict] limiter.

constrained [kən'streɪnd] adj [inhibited] contraint(e).

constraint [kən'streɪnt] n **- 1.** [restriction] : **~ (on)** limitation f (à) **- 2.** (U) [self-control] retenue f, réserve f **- 3.** [coercion] contrainte f.

constrict [kən'strɪkt] vt **- 1.** [compress] serrer **- 2.** [limit] limiter.

constricting [kən'strɪktɪŋ] adj **- 1.** [clothes] qui entrave les mouvements **- 2.** [circumstances, lifestyle] contraignant(e).

construct [vb kən'strʌkt , n 'kɒnstrʌkt] <> vt construire <> n fml [concept] concept m.

construction [kən'strʌkʃn] <> n construction f; **under ~** en construction <> comp [worker] du bâtiment ; **~ site** chantier m.

construction industry n industrie f du bâtiment.

constructive [kən'strʌktɪv] adj constructif(ive).

constructively [kən'strʌktɪvlɪ] adv d'une manière constructive.

construe [kən'struː] vt fml [interpret] : **to ~ sthg as** interpréter qqch comme.

consul ['kɒnsəl] n consul m.

consular ['kɒnsjʊləʳ] adj consulaire.

consulate ['kɒnsjʊlət] n consulat m.

consult [kən'sʌlt] <> vt consulter <> vi : **~ with sb** s'entretenir avec qqn.

consultancy [kən'sʌltənsɪ] (pl **-ies**) n [company] cabinet m d'expert-conseil.

consultancy fee n honoraires mpl d'expert.

consultant [kən'sʌltənt] n **- 1.** [expert] expert-conseil m **- 2.** Br [hospital doctor] spécialiste mf.

consultation [ˌkɒnsəl'teɪʃn] n **- 1.** [meeting, discussion] entretien m **- 2.** [reference] consultation f.

consulting room [kən'sʌltɪŋ-] n cabinet m de consultation.

consume [kən'sjuːm] vt **- 1.** [food, fuel etc] consommer **- 2.** literary [fill] : **to be ~d by hatred/passion** être consumé(e) par la haine/la passion.

consumer [kən'sjuːməʳ] <> n consommateur m, -trice f <> comp du consommateur.

consumer credit n (U) crédit m à la consommation.

consumer durables npl biens mpl de consommation durables.

consumer goods npl biens mpl de consommation.

consumerism [kən'sjuːmərɪzm] n (U) **- 1.** [buying] (règne m de la) société f de consommation **- 2.** [protection of rights] consumérisme m.

consumer society n société f de consommation.

consumer spending n (U) dépenses fpl de consommation.

consummate [adj kən'sʌmət , vb 'kɒnsəmeɪt]

◇ *adj* consommé(e) ; [liar] fieffé(e) ◇ *vt* consommer.

consummation [ˌkɒnsə'meɪʃn] *n* **- 1.** [of marriage] consommation *f* **- 2.** [culmination] apogée *m*.

consumption [kən'sʌmpʃn] *n* **- 1.** [use] consommation *f* **- 2.** dated [tuberculosis] phtisie *f*.

cont. *abbr of* continued.

contact ['kɒntækt] ◇ *n* **- 1.** (U) [touch, communication] contact *m ;* **in ~ (with sb)** en rapport OR contact (avec qqn) ; **to lose ~ with sb** perdre le contact avec qqn ; **to make ~ with sb** prendre contact OR entrer en contact avec qqn **- 2.** [person] relation *f*, contact *m* ◇ *vt* contacter, prendre contact avec ; [by phone] joindre, contacter.

contact lens *n* verre *m* de contact, lentille *f* (cornéenne).

contact number *n :* **do you have a ~?** tu as un numéro où on peut te joindre?

contagious [kən'teɪdʒəs] *adj* contagieux(euse).

contain [kən'teɪn] *vt* **- 1.** [hold, include] contenir, renfermer **- 2.** fml [control] contenir ; [epidemic] circonscrire.

contained [kən'teɪnd] *adj* [person] maître (maîtresse) de soi.

container [kən'teɪnəʳ] *n* **- 1.** [box, bottle etc] récipient *m* **- 2.** [for transporting goods] conteneur *m*, container *m*.

containerize, -ise [kən'teɪnəraɪz] *vt* COMM [goods] conteneuriser ; [port] convertir à la conteneurisation.

container ship *n* porte-conteneurs *m inv*.

containment [kən'teɪnmənt] *n* (U) **- 1.** [limitation] : **our efforts at the ~ of this violence** nos efforts pour contenir cette violence **- 2.** POL : **policy of ~** politique *f* d'endiguement.

contaminate [kən'tæmɪneɪt] *vt* contaminer.

contaminated [kən'tæmɪneɪtɪd] *adj* contaminé(e).

contamination [kənˌtæmɪ'neɪʃn] *n* contamination *f*.

cont'd *abbr of* continued.

contemplate ['kɒntempleɪt] ◇ *vt* **- 1.** [consider] envisager ; **to ~ doing sthg** envisager de faire qqch **- 2.** fml [look at] contempler ◇ *vi* [consider] méditer.

contemplation [ˌkɒntem'pleɪʃn] *n* contemplation *f*.

contemplative [kən'templətɪv] *adj* contemplatif(ive).

contemporary [kən'tempərərɪ] (*pl* **-ies**)

◇ *adj* contemporain(e) ◇ *n* contemporain *m*, -e *f*.

contempt [kən'tempt] *n* **- 1.** [scorn] : **~ (for)** mépris *m* (pour) ; **to hold sb in ~** mépriser qqn **- 2.** JUR : **~ (of court)** outrage *m* à la cour.

contemptible [kən'temptəbl] *adj* méprisable.

contemptuous [kən'temptʃuəs] *adj* méprisant(e) ; **~ of sthg** dédaigneux(euse) de qqch.

contend [kən'tend] ◇ *vi* **- 1.** [deal] : **to ~ with sthg** faire face à qqch ; **I've got enough to. ~ with** j'ai assez de problèmes comme ça **- 2.** [compete] : **to ~ for** [subj : several people] se disputer ; [subj : one person] se battre pour ; **to ~ against** lutter contre ◇ *vt* fml [claim] : **to ~ that ...** soutenir OR prétendre que ...

contender [kən'tendəʳ] *n* [in election] candidat *m*, -e *f* ; [in competition] concurrent *m*, -e *f* ; [in boxing etc] prétendant *m*, -e *f*.

content [*n* 'kɒntent, *adj* & *vb* kən'tent] ◇ *adj* : **~ (with)** satisfait(e) (de), content(e) (de) ; **to be ~ to do sthg** ne pas se demander mieux que de faire qqch ◇ *n* **- 1.** [amount] teneur *f* ; **it has a high fibre ~** c'est riche en fibres **- 2.** [subject matter] contenu *m* ◇ *vt* : **to ~ o.s. with sthg/with doing sthg** se contenter de qqch/de faire qqch.

◆ **contents** *npl* **- 1.** [of container, document] contenu *m* **- 2.** [at front of book] table *f* des matières.

contented [kən'tentɪd] *adj* satisfait(e).

contentedly [kən'tentɪdlɪ] *adv* avec contentement.

contention [kən'tenʃn] *n* fml **- 1.** [argument, assertion] assertion *f*, affirmation *f* **- 2.** (U) [disagreement] dispute *f*, contestation *f* **- 3.** [competition] : **to be in ~** être en lice.

contentious [kən'tenʃəs] *adj* contentieux(euse), contesté(e).

contentment [kən'tentmənt] *n* contentement *m*.

contest [*n* 'kɒntest, *vb* kən'test] ◇ *n* **- 1.** [competition] concours *m* **- 2.** [for power, control] combat *m*, lutte *f* ◇ *vt* **- 1.** [compete for] disputer **- 2.** [dispute] contester.

contestant [kən'testənt] *n* concurrent *m*, -e *f*.

context ['kɒntekst] *n* contexte *m ;* **out of ~** [word] hors contexte ; [remark] hors de son contexte.

continent ['kɒntɪnənt] *n* continent *m*.

◆ **Continent** *n* Br : **the Continent** l'Europe *f* continentale.

continental [ˌkɒntɪ'nentl] ◇ *adj* **- 1.** GEOGR continental(e) **- 2.** Br [European - food] d'Europe continentale ; [- holidays] en Europe continentale <> n Br Européen continental m, Européenne continentale f.

continental breakfast n petit déjeuner m (par opposition à 'English breakfast').

> **CONTINENTAL BREAKFAST**
>
> Ce terme désigne un petit déjeuner léger, par opposition à un « English breakfast », beaucoup plus copieux et comportant parfois un plat chaud.

continental climate n climat m continental.

continental quilt n Br couette f.

contingency [kən'tındʒənsɪ] (pl -ies) n éventualité f.

contingency plan n plan m d'urgence.

contingent [kən'tındʒənt] <> adj fml : to be ~ on OR upon dépendre de <> n contingent m.

continual [kən'tınjuəl] adj continuel(elle).

continually [kən'tınjuəlı] adv continuellement.

continuation [kən,tınju'eɪʃn] n - 1. (U) [act] continuation f - 2. [sequel] suite f.

continue [kən'tınju:] <> vt - 1. [carry on] continuer, poursuivre ; to ~ doing OR to do sthg continuer à OR de faire qqch - 2. [after an interruption] reprendre <> vi - 1. [carry on] continuer ; to ~ with sthg poursuivre qqch, continuer qqch - 2. [after an interruption] reprendre, se poursuivre.

continuity [,kɒntı'nju:ətı] n continuité f.

continuous [kən'tınjuəs] adj continu(e).

continuous assessment n contrôle m continu des connaissances.

continuously [kən'tınjuəslı] adv sans arrêt, continuellement.

contort [kən'tɔːt] <> vt tordre <> vi se tordre.

contortion [kən'tɔːʃn] n - 1. (U) [twisting] torsion f - 2. [position] contorsion f.

contour ['kɒn,tuəʳ] <> n - 1. [outline] contour m - 2. [on map] courbe f de niveau <> comp [map] avec courbes de niveau ; ~ line courbe f de niveau.

contraband ['kɒntrəbænd] <> adj de contrebande <> n contrebande f.

contraception [,kɒntrə'sepʃn] n contraception f.

contraceptive [,kɒntrə'septɪv] <> adj [method, device] anticonceptionnel(elle), contraceptif(ive) ; [advice] sur la contraception <> n contraceptif m.

contraceptive pill n pilule f anticonceptionnelle OR contraceptive.

contract [n 'kɒntrækt, vb kən'trækt] <> n contrat m <> vt - 1. [gen] contracter - 2. COMM : to ~ sb (to do sthg) passer un contrat avec qqn (pour faire qqch) ; to ~ to do sthg s'engager par contrat à faire qqch <> vi [decrease in size, length] se contracter.

◆ **contract in** vi esp Br s'engager par contrat.

◆ **contract out** <> vt sep donner en sous-traitance à <> vi esp Br : to ~ out (of) se dégager (de).

contraction [kən'trækʃn] n contraction f.

contractor [kən'træktəʳ] n entrepreneur m.

contractual [kən'træktʃuəl] adj contractuel(elle).

contradict [,kɒntrə'dıkt] vt contredire.

contradiction [,kɒntrə'dıkʃn] n contradiction f ; ~ in terms contradiction dans les termes.

contradictory [,kɒntrə'dıktərı] adj contradictoire ; [behaviour] incohérent(e).

contraflow ['kɒntrəfləu] n circulation f à contre-sens.

contralto [kən'træltəu] (pl -s) n contralto m.

contraption [kən'træpʃn] n machin m, truc m.

contrary ['kɒntrərı, adj sense 2 kən'treərı] <> adj - 1. [opposite] : ~ (to) contraire (à), opposé(e) (à) - 2. [awkward] contrariant(e) <> n contraire m ; on the ~ au contraire ; **evidence to the ~** preuves tendant à démontrer le contraire ; **his statements to the ~** ses propos soutenant le contraire.

◆ **contrary to** prep contrairement à.

contrast [n 'kɒntrɑːst, vb kən'trɑːst] <> n contraste m ; by OR in ~ par contraste ; in ~ with OR to sthg par contraste avec qqch <> vt contraster <> vi : to ~ (with) faire contraste (avec).

contrasting [kən'trɑːstıŋ] adj [colours] contrasté(e) ; [personalities, views] opposé(e), contraire.

contravene [,kɒntrə'viːn] vt enfreindre, transgresser.

contravention [,kɒntrə'venʃn] n infraction f, contravention f.

contribute [kən'trıbjuːt] <> vt - 1. [money] apporter ; [help, advice, ideas] donner, apporter - 2. [write] : to ~ an article to a magazine écrire un article pour un magazine <> vi - 1. [gen] : to ~ (to) contribuer (à) - 2. [write material] : to ~ to collaborer à.

contributing [kən'trɪbjuːtɪŋ] *adj :* **to be a ~ factor in** contribuer à.

contribution [ˌkɒntrɪ'bjuːʃn] *n -* **1.** [of money] : **~ (to)** cotisation *f* (à), contribution *f* (à) **- 2.** [to debate] : **his ~ to the discussion** ce qu'il a apporté à la discussion **- 3.** [article] article *m*.

contributor [kən'trɪbjʊtəʳ] *n -* **1.** [of money] donateur *m*, -trice *f -* **2.** [to magazine, newspaper] collaborateur *m*, -trice *f*.

contributory [kən'trɪbjʊtərɪ] *adj :* **to be a ~ factor in** contribuer à.

contributory pension scheme *n* système *m* de retraite par répartition.

contrite ['kɒntraɪt] *adj* literary contrit(e), pénitent(e).

contrition [kən'trɪʃn] *n* literary contrition *f*, pénitence *f*.

contrivance [kən'traɪvns] *n* [contraption] machine *f*, appareil *m*.

contrive [kən'traɪv] *vt* fml **- 1.** [engineer] combiner **- 2.** [manage] : **to ~ to do sthg** se débrouiller pour faire qqch, trouver moyen de faire qqch.

contrived [kən'traɪvd] *adj* tiré(e) par les cheveux.

control [kən'trəʊl] (*pt & pp* **-led ;** *cont* **-ling**) ◇ *n -* **1.** [gen] contrôle *m ;* [of traffic] régulation *f ;* **to gain** OR **take ~ (of)** prendre le contrôle (de) ; **beyond** OR **outside sb's ~** indépendant de la volonté de qqn ; **to get sb/sthg under ~** maîtriser qqn/qqch ; **to be in ~ of sthg** [subj : boss, government] diriger qqch ; [subj : army] avoir le contrôle de qqch ; [of emotions, situation] maîtriser qqch ; **to get out of ~** [subj : crowd] devenir impossible à contrôler ; **his car went out of ~** il a perdu le contrôle de sa voiture ; **to lose ~** [of emotions] perdre le contrôle **- 2.** [in experiment] témoin *m* ◇ *vt -* **1.** [company, country] être à la tête de, diriger **- 2.** [operate] commander, faire fonctionner **- 3.** [restrict, restrain - disease] enrayer, juguler ; [- inflation] mettre un frein à, contenir ; [- children] tenir ; [- crowd] contenir ; [- traffic] régler ; [- emotions] maîtriser, contenir ; **to ~ o.s.** se maîtriser, se contrôler ◇ *comp* de commande.

➾ **controls** *npl* [of machine, vehicle] commandes *fpl*.

control code *n* COMPUT code *m* de commande.

control group *n* groupe *m* témoin.

control key *n* COMPUT touche *f* « control ».

controlled [kən'trəʊld] *adj -* **1.** [person] maître (maîtresse) de soi **- 2.** ECON dirigé(e).

controller [kən'trəʊləʳ] *n* [person] contrôleur *m*.

controlling [kən'trəʊlɪŋ] *adj* [factor] déterminant(e).

controlling interest *n* participation *f* majoritaire.

control panel *n* tableau *m* de bord.

control tower *n* tour *f* de contrôle.

controversial [ˌkɒntrə'vɜːʃl] *adj* [writer, theory etc] controversé(e) ; **to be ~** donner matière à controverse.

controversy ['kɒntrəvɜːsɪ, Br kən'trɒvəsɪ] (*pl* **-ies**) *n* controverse *f*, polémique *f*.

conundrum [kə'nʌndrəm] (*pl* **-s**) *n* énigme *f*.

conurbation [ˌkɒnɜː'beɪʃn] *n* conurbation *f*.

convalesce [ˌkɒnvə'les] *vi* se remettre d'une maladie, relever de maladie.

convalescence [ˌkɒnvə'lesns] *n* convalescence *f*.

convalescent [ˌkɒnvə'lesnt] ◇ *adj* de convalescence ◇ *n* convalescent *m*, -e *f*.

convection [kən'vekʃn] *n* convection *f*.

convector [kən'vektəʳ] *n* radiateur *m* à convection.

convene [kən'viːn] ◇ *vt* convoquer, réunir ◇ *vi* se réunir, s'assembler.

convener [kən'viːnəʳ] *n* Br président *m*, -e *f* (*d'une commission*).

convenience [kən'viːnjəns] *n -* **1.** [usefulness] commodité *f -* **2.** [personal comfort, advantage] agrément *m*, confort *m ;* **at your earliest ~** fml dès que possible **- 3.** [facility] confort *m*.

convenience food *n* aliment *m* tout préparé.

convenience store *n* Am petit supermarché *de quartier*.

convenient [kən'viːnjənt] *adj -* **1.** [suitable] qui convient **- 2.** [handy] pratique, commode.

conveniently [kən'viːnjəntlɪ] *adv* d'une manière commode ; **~ situated** bien situé.

convent ['kɒnvənt] *n* couvent *m*.

convention [kən'venʃn] *n -* **1.** [agreement, assembly] convention *f -* **2.** [practice] usage *m*, convention *f*.

conventional [kən'venʃənl] *adj* conventionnel(elle) ; **it's ~ to ...** l'usage veut que ...

conventionally [kən'venʃnəlɪ] *adv* d'une manière conventionnelle.

convent school *n* couvent *m*.

converge [kən'vɜːdʒ] *vi :* **to ~ (on)** converger (sur).

conversant [kən'vɜːsənt] *adj* fml : **~ with sthg** familiarisé(e) avec qqch, qui connaît bien qqch.

conversation [ˌkɒnvə'seɪʃn] *n* conversation *f ;* **to make ~** faire la conversation.

conversational [ˌkɒnvəˈseɪʃənl] *adj* de la conversation.

conversationalist [ˌkɒnvəˈseɪʃnəlɪst] *n* causeur *m*, -euse *f*.

converse [*n* & *adj* ˈkɒnvɜːs, *vb* kənˈvɜːs] <> *adj* fml opposé(e), contraire <> *n* [opposite] : **the ~** le contraire, l'inverse *m* <> *vi* fml converser.

conversely [kənˈvɜːslɪ] *adv* fml inversement.

conversion [kənˈvɜːʃn] *n* - **1.** [changing, in religious beliefs] conversion *f* - **2.** [in building] aménagement *m*, transformation *f* - **3.** RUGBY transformation *f*.

conversion table *n* table *f* de conversion.

convert [*vb* kənˈvɜːt, *n* ˈkɒnvɜːt] <> *vt* - **1.** [change] : **to ~ sthg to** OR **into** convertir qqch en ; **to ~ sb to** RELIG convertir qqn (à) - **2.** [building, ship] : **to ~ sthg to** OR **into** transformer qqch en, aménager qqch en - **3.** RUGBY transformer <> *vi* : **to ~ from sthg to sthg** passer de qqch à qqch <> *n* converti *m*, -e *f*.

converted [kənˈvɜːtɪd] *adj* - **1.** [building, ship] aménagé(e) - **2.** RELIG converti(e).

convertible [kənˈvɜːtəbl] <> *adj* - **1.** [bed, sofa] transformable, convertible - **2.** [currency] convertible - **3.** [car] décapotable <> *n* (voiture *f*) décapotable *f*.

convex [kɒnˈveks] *adj* convexe.

convey [kənˈveɪ] *vt* - **1.** fml [transport] transporter - **2.** [express] : **to ~ sthg (to sb)** communiquer qqch (à qqn).

conveyancing [kənˈveɪənsɪŋ] *n (U)* procédure *f* translative de propriété.

conveyer belt [kənˈveɪəʳ-] *n* convoyeur *m*, tapis *m* roulant.

convict [*n* ˈkɒnvɪkt, *vb* kənˈvɪkt] <> *n* détenu *m* <> *vt* : **to ~ sb of sthg** reconnaître qqn coupable de qqch.

convicted [kənˈvɪktɪd] *adj* : **he's a ~ murderer** il a été reconnu coupable d'un meurtre.

conviction [kənˈvɪkʃn] *n* - **1.** [belief, fervour] conviction *f* - **2.** JUR [of criminal] condamnation *f*.

convince [kənˈvɪns] *vt* convaincre, persuader ; **to ~ sb of sthg/to do sthg** convaincre qqn de qqch/de faire qqch, persuader qqn de qqch/de faire qqch.

convinced [kənˈvɪnst] *adj* : **~ (of)** persuadé(e) (de), convaincu(e) (de).

convincing [kənˈvɪnsɪŋ] *adj* - **1.** [persuasive] convaincant(e) - **2.** [resounding - victory] retentissant(e), éclatant(e).

convivial [kənˈvɪvɪəl] *adj* convivial(e), joyeux(euse).

convoluted [ˈkɒnvəluːtɪd] *adj* [tortuous] compliqué(e).

convoy [ˈkɒnvɔɪ] *n* convoi *m* ; **in ~** en convoi.

convulse [kənˈvʌls] *vt* [person] : **to be ~d with** se tordre de.

convulsion [kənˈvʌlʃn] *n* MED convulsion *f*.

convulsive [kənˈvʌlsɪv] *adj* convulsif(ive).

coo [kuː] *vi* roucouler.

cook [kʊk] <> *n* cuisinier *m*, -ère *f* ; **she's a good ~** elle fait bien la cuisine <> *vt* - **1.** [food] faire cuire ; [meal] préparer - **2.** inf [falsify] maquiller <> *vi* [person] cuisiner, faire la cuisine ; [food] cuire.

➤ **cook up** *vt sep* [plan] combiner ; [excuse] inventer.

cookbook [ˈkʊkˌbʊk] = **cookery book.**

cooked [kʊkt] *adj* cuit(e).

cooker [ˈkʊkəʳ] *n* [stove] cuisinière *f*.

cookery [ˈkʊkərɪ] *n* cuisine *f*.

cookery book *n* livre *m* de cuisine.

cookie [ˈkʊkɪ] *n* Am [biscuit] biscuit *m*, gâteau *m* sec.

cooking [ˈkʊkɪŋ] <> *n* cuisine *f* ; **do you like ~?** tu aimes faire la cuisine? <> *comp* de cuisine ; [chocolate] à cuire ; **~ oil** huile *f* de friture.

cooking apple *n* pomme *f* à cuire.

cookout [ˈkʊkaʊt] *n* Am barbecue *m*.

cool [kuːl] <> *adj* - **1.** [not warm] frais (fraîche) ; [dress] léger(ère) - **2.** [calm] calme - **3.** [unfriendly] froid(e) - **4.** inf [excellent] génial(e) ; [trendy] branché(e) <> *vt* faire refroidir <> *vi* - **1.** [become less warm] refroidir - **2.** [abate] se calmer <> *n* [calm] : **to keep/lose one's ~** garder/perdre son sang-froid, garder/perdre son calme.

➤ **cool down** <> *vt sep* - **1.** [make less warm - food etc] faire refroidir ; [- person] rafraîchir - **2.** [make less angry] calmer, apaiser <> *vi* - **1.** [become less warm - food, engine] refroidir ; [- person] se rafraîchir - **2.** [become less angry] se calmer.

➤ **cool off** *vi* - **1.** [become less warm] refroidir ; [person] se rafraîchir - **2.** [become less angry] se calmer.

coolant [ˈkuːlənt] *n* agent *m* de refroidissement.

cool box *n* glacière *f*.

cool-headed [-ˈhedɪd] *adj* calme.

cooling-off period [ˈkuːlɪŋ-] *n* délai *m* de réflexion.

cooling tower [ˈkuːlɪŋ-] *n* refroidisseur *m*.

coolly [ˈkuːlɪ] *adv* - **1.** [calmly] calmement - **2.** [in unfriendly way] froidement.

coolness [ˈkuːlnɪs] n - **1.** [in temperature] fraîcheur f - **2.** [unfriendliness] froideur f.

coop [kuːp] n poulailler m.
◆ **coop up** vt sep inf confiner.

Co-op [ˈkəʊˌɒp] (abbr of co-operative society) n Coop f.

cooperate [kəʊˈɒpəreɪt] vi : **to ~ (with sb/sthg)** coopérer (avec qqn/à qqch), collaborer (avec qqn/à qqch).

cooperation [kəʊˌɒpəˈreɪʃn] n (U) - **1.** [collaboration] coopération f, collaboration f - **2.** [assistance] aide f, concours m.

cooperative [kəʊˈɒpərətɪv] ◇ adj coopératif(ive) ◇ n coopérative f.

co-opt vt : **to ~ sb (into** OR **onto)** coopter qqn (à).

coordinate [n kəʊˈɔːdɪnət, vt kəʊˈɔːdɪneɪt] ◇ n [on map, graph] coordonnée f ◇ vt coordonner.
◆ **coordinates** npl [clothes] coordonnés mpl.

coordination [kəʊˌɔːdɪˈneɪʃn] n coordination f.

co-ownership n copropriété f.

cop [kɒp] (pt & pp -ped ; cont -ping) n inf flic m.
◆ **cop out** vi inf : **to ~ out (of sthg)** se défiler OR se dérober (à qqch).

cope [kəʊp] vi se débrouiller ; **to ~ with** faire face à.

Copenhagen [ˌkəʊpənˈheɪgən] n Copenhague.

copier [ˈkɒpɪəʳ] n copieur m, photocopieur m.

copilot [ˈkəʊˌpaɪlət] n copilote mf.

copious [ˈkəʊpjəs] adj [notes] copieux(euse) ; [supply] abondant(e).

cop-out n inf dérobade f, échappatoire f.

copper [ˈkɒpəʳ] n - **1.** [metal] cuivre m - **2.** Br inf [policeman] flic m.

coppice [ˈkɒpɪs], **copse** [kɒps] n taillis m, hallier m.

copulate [ˈkɒpjʊleɪt] vi : **to ~ (with)** s'accoupler (à OR avec).

copulation [ˌkɒpjʊˈleɪʃn] n copulation f.

copy [ˈkɒpɪ] (pt & pp -ied) ◇ n - **1.** [imitation] copie f, reproduction f - **2.** [duplicate] copie f - **3.** [of book] exemplaire m ; [of magazine] numéro m ◇ vt - **1.** [imitate] copier, imiter - **2.** [photocopy] photocopier ◇ vi copier.
◆ **copy down** vt sep prendre des notes de.
◆ **copy out** vt sep recopier.

copycat [ˈkɒpɪkæt] ◇ n inf copieur m, -euse f ◇ comp inspiré(e) par un autre (une autre).

copy protect vt protéger contre la copie.

copyright [ˈkɒpɪraɪt] n copyright m, droit m d'auteur.

copy typist n Br dactylo f, dactylographe.

copywriter [ˈkɒpɪˌraɪtəʳ] n concepteur-rédacteur publicitaire m, conceptrice-rédactrice publicitaire f.

coral [ˈkɒrəl] ◇ n corail m ◇ comp de corail.

coral reef n récif m de corail.

Coral Sea n : **the ~** la mer de Corail.

cord [kɔːd] ◇ n - **1.** [string] ficelle f ; [rope] corde f - **2.** [electric] fil m, cordon m - **3.** [fabric] velours m côtelé ◇ comp en velours côtelé.
◆ **cords** npl pantalon m en velours côtelé.

cordial [ˈkɔːdjəl] ◇ adj cordial(e), chaleureux(euse) ◇ n cordial m.

cordially [ˈkɔːdɪəlɪ] adv cordialement.

cordless [ˈkɔːdlɪs] adj [telephone] sans fil ; [shaver] à piles.

Cordoba [ˈkɔːdəbə] n Cordoue.

cordon [ˈkɔːdn] n cordon m.
◆ **cordon off** vt sep barrer (par un cordon de police).

cordon bleu [-blɜː] adj cordon bleu.

corduroy [ˈkɔːdərɔɪ] ◇ n velours m côtelé ◇ comp en velours côtelé.

core [kɔːʳ] ◇ n - **1.** [of apple etc] trognon m, cœur m - **2.** [of cable, Earth] noyau m ; [of nuclear reactor] cœur m - **3.** fig [of people] noyau m ; [of problem, policy] essentiel m ◇ vt enlever le cœur de.

CORE [kɔːʳ] (abbr of Congress on Racial Equality) n ligue américaine contre le racisme.

corer [ˈkɔːrəʳ] n vide-pomme m inv.

corespondent [ˌkəʊrɪˈspɒndənt] n JUR codéfendeur m, -eresse f.

core time n Br plage f fixe.

Corfu [kɔːˈfuː] n Corfou ; **in ~** à Corfou.

corgi [ˈkɔːgɪ] (pl -s) n corgi m.

coriander [ˌkɒrɪˈændəʳ] n coriandre f.

cork [kɔːk] n - **1.** [material] liège m - **2.** [stopper] bouchon m.

corkage [ˈkɔːkɪdʒ] n droit de débouchage sur un vin apporté par le consommateur.

corked [kɔːkt] adj [wine] qui a le goût de bouchon.

corkscrew [ˈkɔːkskruː] n tire-bouchon m.

cormorant [ˈkɔːmərənt] n cormoran m.

corn [kɔːn] n - **1.** Br [wheat] grain m ; Am [maize] maïs m ; **~ on the cob** épi m de maïs cuit - **2.** [on foot] cor m ◇ comp : **~ bread** pain m de farine de maïs ; **~ oil** huile f de maïs.

Corn (abbr of Cornwall) comté anglais.

cornea ['kɔːnɪə] (pl -s) n cornée f.

corned beef [kɔːnd-] n corned-beef m inv.

corner ['kɔːnəʳ] ⋄ n - **1.** [angle] coin m, angle m ; **to cut ~s** fig brûler les étapes - **2.** [bend in road] virage m, tournant m - **3.** FTBL corner m ⋄ vt - **1.** [person, animal] acculer - **2.** [market] accaparer.

corner flag n piquet m de coin.

corner kick n FTBL = **corner.**

corner shop n magasin m du coin OR du quartier.

cornerstone ['kɔːnəstəun] n fig pierre f angulaire.

cornet ['kɔːnɪt] n - **1.** [instrument] cornet m à pistons - **2.** Br [ice-cream cone] cornet m de glace.

cornfield ['kɔːnfiːld] n - **1.** Br [of wheat] champ m de blé - **2.** Am [of maize] champ m de maïs.

cornflakes ['kɔːnfleɪks] npl corn-flakes mpl.

cornflour Br ['kɔːnflauəʳ], **cornstarch** Am ['kɔːnstɑːtʃ] n ≃ Maïzena® f, fécule f de maïs.

cornice ['kɔːnɪs] n corniche f.

Cornish ['kɔːnɪʃ] ⋄ adj de Cornouailles, cornouaillais(e) ⋄ npl: **the ~** les Cornouaillais mpl.

Cornishman ['kɔːnɪʃmən] (pl -men [-mən]) n Cornouaillais m.

Cornishwoman ['kɔːnɪʃ,wumən] (pl -women [-,wɪmɪn]) n Cornouaillaise f.

cornstarch ['kɔːnstɑːtʃ] Am = **cornflour.**

cornucopia [,kɔːnjuˈkəupjə] n literary corne f d'abondance.

Cornwall ['kɔːnwɔːl] n Cornouailles f ; **in ~** en Cornouailles.

corny ['kɔːnɪ] (compar -ier ; superl -iest) adj inf [joke] peu original(e) ; [story, film] à l'eau de rose.

corollary [kəˈrɒlərɪ] (pl -ies) n corollaire m.

coronary ['kɒrənrɪ] (pl -ies), **coronary thrombosis** [-θrɒm'bəusɪs] (pl -ses [-siːz]) n infarctus m du myocarde.

coronation [,kɒrə'neɪʃn] n couronnement m.

coroner ['kɒrənəʳ] n coroner m.

Corp. (abbr of **corporation**) Cie.

corpora ['kɔːpərə] pl ⤳ **corpus.**

corporal ['kɔːpərəl] n [gen] caporal m ; [in artillery] brigadier m.

corporal punishment n châtiment m corporel.

corporate ['kɔːpərət] adj - **1.** [business] corporatif(ive), de société - **2.** [collective] collectif(ive).

corporate hospitality n (U) réceptions données par une société pour ses clients.

corporate identity, corporate image n image f de marque de la société.

corporation [,kɔːpə'reɪʃn] n - **1.** [town council] conseil m municipal - **2.** [large company] compagnie f, société f enregistrée.

corporation tax n Br impôt m sur les sociétés.

corps [kɔːʳ] (pl inv) n corps m ; **the press ~** la presse.

corpse [kɔːps] n cadavre m.

corpulent ['kɔːpjulənt] adj corpulent(e).

corpus ['kɔːpəs] (pl **-pora** [-pərə] OR **-puses** [-pəsiːz]) n corpus m, recueil m.

corpuscle ['kɔːpʌsl] n globule m.

corral [kəˈrɑːl] n corral m.

correct [kəˈrekt] ⋄ adj - **1.** [accurate] correct(e), exact(e) ; **you're quite ~** tu as parfaitement raison - **2.** [proper, socially acceptable] correct(e), convenable ⋄ vt corriger.

correction [kəˈrekʃn] n correction f.

correctly [kəˈrektlɪ] adv - **1.** [accurately] correctement, exactement - **2.** [properly, acceptably] correctement, comme il faut.

correlate ['kɒrəleɪt] ⋄ vt mettre en corrélation, corréler ⋄ vi : **to ~ (with)** correspondre (à), être en corrélation (avec).

correlation [,kɒrə'leɪʃn] n corrélation f.

correspond [,kɒrɪ'spɒnd] vi - **1.** [gen] : **to ~ (with OR to)** correspondre (à) - **2.** [write letters] : **to ~ (with sb)** correspondre (avec qqn).

correspondence [,kɒrɪ'spɒndəns] n : **~ (with)** correspondance f (avec).

correspondence course n cours m par correspondance.

correspondent [,kɒrɪ'spɒndənt] n correspondant m, -e f.

corresponding [,kɒrɪ'spɒndɪŋ] adj correspondant(e).

corridor ['kɒrɪdɔːʳ] n [in building] couloir m, corridor m.

corroborate [kəˈrɒbəreɪt] vt corroborer, confirmer.

corroboration [kə,rɒbə'reɪʃən] n corroboration f, confirmation f.

corrode [kəˈrəud] ⋄ vt corroder, attaquer ⋄ vi se corroder.

corrosion [kəˈrəuʒn] n corrosion f.

corrosive [kəˈrəusɪv] adj corrosif(ive).

corrugated ['kɒrəgeɪtɪd] adj ondulé(e).

corrugated iron n tôle f ondulée.

corrupt [kəˈrʌpt] ⋄ adj [gen & COMPUT] corrompu(e) ⋄ vt corrompre, dépraver.

corruption [kə'rʌpʃn] *n* corruption *f*.

corsage [kɔː'sɑːʒ] *n* petit bouquet *m* de fleurs *(porté au corsage)*.

corset ['kɔːsɪt] *n* corset *m*.

Corsica ['kɔːsɪkə] *n* Corse *f* ; **in ~** en Corse.

Corsican ['kɔːsɪkən] <> *adj* corse <> *n* - **1.** [person] Corse *mf* - **2.** [language] corse *m*.

cortege, cortège [kɔː'teɪʒ] *n* cortège *m*.

cortisone ['kɔːtɪzəʊn] *n* cortisone *f*.

cos[1] [kɒz] Br inf = **because.**

cos[2] [kɒz] = **cos lettuce.**

c.o.s. *(abbr of* cash on shipment*)* paiement à l'expédition.

cosh [kɒʃ] <> *n* matraque *f*, gourdin *m* <> *vt* frapper, matraquer.

cosignatory [,kəʊ'sɪgnətrɪ] *(pl* **-ies***)* *n* cosignataire *mf*.

cosine ['kəʊsaɪn] *n* cosinus *m*.

cos lettuce [k gt·s-] *n* Br romaine *f*.

cosmetic [kɒz'metɪk] <> *n* cosmétique *m*, produit *m* de beauté <> *adj* fig superficiel(elle).

cosmetic surgery *n* chirurgie *f* plastique OR esthétique.

cosmic ['kɒzmɪk] *adj* cosmique.

cosmonaut ['kɒzmənɔːt] *n* cosmonaute *mf*.

cosmopolitan [kɒzmə'pɒlɪtn] *adj* cosmopolite.

cosmos ['kɒzmɒs] *n* : **the ~** le cosmos.

Cossack ['kɒsæk] *n* cosaque *m*.

cosset ['kɒsɪt] *vt* dorloter, choyer.

cost [kɒst] *(pt & pp* cost OR **-ed***)* <> *n* lit & fig coût *m* ; **at all ~s** à tout prix, coûte que coûte <> *vt* - **1.** lit & fig coûter ; **it ~ me £10** ça m'a coûté 10 livres ; **it ~ us a lot of time and effort** ça nous a demandé beaucoup de temps et de travail - **2.** COMM [estimate] évaluer le coût de <> *vi* coûter ; **how much does it ~?** combien ça coûte?, combien cela coûte-t-il?

  costs *npl* JUR dépens *mpl*, frais *mpl* judiciaires.

cost accountant *n* responsable *m* de la comptabilité analytique.

co-star ['kəʊ-] <> *n* partenaire *mf* <> *vt* [subj : film] avoir comme vedettes <> *vi* : **to ~ with** partager la vedette avec.

Costa Rica [,kɒstə'riːkə] *n* Costa Rica *m* ; **in ~** au Costa Rica.

Costa Rican [,kɒstə'riːkən] <> *adj* costaricien(enne) <> *n* Costaricien *m*, -enne *f*.

cost-benefit analysis *n* analyse *f* coûts-bénéfices.

cost-effective *adj* rentable.

cost-effectiveness *n* rentabilité *f*.

costing ['kɒstɪŋ] *n* évaluation *f* du coût.

costly ['kɒstlɪ] *(compar* **-ier** ; *superl* **-iest***) adj* lit & fig coûteux(euse).

cost of living *n* : **the ~** le coût de la vie.

cost-of-living index *n* indice *m* du coût de la vie.

cost price *n* prix *m* coûtant.

costume ['kɒstjuːm] *n* - **1.** [gen] costume *m* - **2.** [swimming costume] maillot *m* (de bain).

costume jewellery *n (U)* bijoux *mpl* fantaisie.

cosy Br *(compar* **-ier** ; *superl* **-iest** ; *pl* **-ies***)*, **cozy** Am *(compar* **-ier** ; *superl* **-iest** ; *pl* **-ies***)* ['kəʊzɪ] <> *adj* - **1.** [house, room] douillet(ette) ; [atmosphere] chaleureux(euse) ; **to feel ~** se sentir bien au chaud - **2.** [intimate] intime <> *n* cosy *m*.

cot [kɒt] *n* - **1.** Br [for child] lit *m* d'enfant, petit lit - **2.** Am [folding bed] lit *m* de camp.

cot death *n* mort *f* subite du nourrisson.

cottage ['kɒtɪdʒ] *n* cottage *m*, petite maison *f* (de campagne).

cottage cheese *n* fromage *m* blanc.

cottage hospital *n* Br petit hôpital *m* (en zone rurale).

cottage industry *n* industrie *f* artisanale.

cottage pie *n* Br = hachis *m* Parmentier.

cotton ['kɒtn] <> *n* - **1.** [gen] coton *m* - **2.** [thread] fil *m* de coton <> *comp* de coton.

  cotton on *vi* inf : **to ~ on (to sthg)** piger (qqch), comprendre (qqch).

cotton bud Br, **cotton swab** Am *n* cotontige *m*.

cotton candy *n* Am barbe *f* à papa.

cotton swab Am = **cotton bud.**

cotton wool *n* ouate *f*, coton *m* hydrophile.

couch [kaʊtʃ] <> *n* - **1.** [sofa] canapé *m* - **2.** [in doctor's surgery] lit *m* <> *vt* exprimer, formuler.

couchette [kuː'ʃet] *n* Br couchette *f*.

couch potato *n* inf flemmard *m*, -e *f* (qui passe son temps devant la télé).

cougar ['kuːgəʳ] *(pl inv* OR **-s***)* *n* cougouar *m*, couguar *m*.

cough [kɒf] <> *n* toux *f* ; **I've got a ~** je tousse <> *vi* tousser <> *vt* [blood] cracher (en toussant).

  cough up *vt sep* - **1.** [bring up] cracher (en toussant) - **2.** vinf [pay up] casquer, cracher.

coughing ['kɒfɪŋ] *n (U)* toux *f*.

cough mixture *n* Br sirop *m* pour la toux.

cough sweet *n* Br pastille *f* pour la toux.

cough syrup = cough mixture.

could [kʊd] *pt* ▷ can².

couldn't ['kʊdnt] = could not.

could've ['kʊdəv] = could have.

council ['kaʊnsl] ◇ *n* conseil *m* municipal ◇ *comp* du conseil.

council estate *n* quartier *m* de logements sociaux.

council house *n* Br maison *f* qui appartient à la municipalité, ≃ H.L.M. *m* OR *f*.

councillor ['kaʊnsələr] *n* conseiller municipal *m*, conseillère municipale *f*.

Council of Europe *n* conseil *m* de l'Europe.

council of war *n* conseil *m* de guerre.

council tax *n* Br ≃ impôts *mpl* locaux.

counsel ['kaʊnsəl] (Br *pt* & *pp* -led ; *cont* -ling, Am *pt* & *pp* -ed ; *cont* -ing) ◇ *n* - 1. (U) fml [advice] conseil *m* - 2. [lawyer] avocat *m*, -e *f* ◇ *vt* : to ~ sb to do sthg fml conseiller à qqn de faire qqch.

counselling Br, **counseling** Am ['kaʊnsəlɪŋ] *n* (U) conseils *mpl*.

counsellor Br, **counselor** Am ['kaʊnsələr] *n* - 1. [gen] conseiller *m*, -ère *f* - 2. Am [lawyer] avocat *m*.

count [kaʊnt] ◇ *n* - 1. [total] total *m* ; to keep ~ of tenir le compte de ; to lose ~ of sthg ne plus savoir qqch, ne pas se rappeler qqch - 2. [point] : I disagree with him on two ~s je ne suis pas d'accord avec lui sur deux points - 3. JUR [charge] chef *m* d'accusation - 4. [aristocrat] comte *m* ◇ *vt* - 1. [gen] compter ; there are five people, not ~ing me sans moi, on est cinq - 2. [consider] : to ~ sb as sthg considérer qqn comme qqch ◇ *vi* - 1. [gen] compter ; to ~ (up) to compter jusqu'à - 2. [be considered] : to ~ as être considéré(e) comme.

◆ **count against** *vt fus* jouer contre.

◆ **count in** *vt sep* inf : ~ me in! je suis de la partie!

◆ **count (up)on** *vt fus* - 1. [rely on] compter sur - 2. [expect] s'attendre à, prévoir.

◆ **count out** *vt sep* - 1. [money] compter - 2. inf [leave out] : ~ me out! ne comptez pas sur moi!

◆ **count up** *vt fus* compter.

countdown ['kaʊntdaʊn] *n* compte *m* à rebours.

countenance ['kaʊntənəns] ◇ *n* literary [face] visage *m* ◇ *vt* approuver, admettre.

counter ['kaʊntər] ◇ *n* - 1. [in shop, bank] comptoir *m* - 2. [in board game] pion *m* ◇ *vt* : to ~ sthg (with) [criticism etc] riposter à qqch (par) ; to ~ sthg by doing sthg s'opposer à qqch en faisant qqch ◇ *vi* : to ~ with sthg/by doing sthg riposter par qqch/en faisant qqch.

◆ **counter to** *adv* contrairement à ; to run ~ to aller à l'encontre de.

counteract [,kaʊntə'rækt] *vt* contrebalancer, compenser.

counterattack ['kaʊntərə,tæk] ◇ *n* contreattaque *f* ◇ *vt* & *vi* contre-attaquer.

counterbalance [,kaʊntə'bæləns] *vt* fig contrebalancer, compenser.

counterclaim ['kaʊntəkleɪm] *n* demande *f* reconventionnelle.

counterclockwise [,kaʊntə'klɒkwaɪz] *adj* & *adv* Am dans le sens inverse des aiguilles d'une montre.

counterespionage [,kaʊntər'espɪənɑːʒ] *n* contre-espionnage *m*.

counterfeit ['kaʊntəfɪt] ◇ *adj* faux (fausse) ◇ *vt* contrefaire.

counterfoil ['kaʊntəfɔɪl] *n* talon *m*, souche *f*.

counterintelligence [,kaʊntərɪn'telɪdʒəns] *n* contre-espionnage *m*.

countermand [,kaʊntə'mɑːnd] *vt* annuler.

countermeasure [,kaʊntə'meʒər] *n* contremesure *f*.

counteroffensive [,kaʊntərə'fensɪv] *n* contre-offensive *f*.

counterpane ['kaʊntəpeɪn] *n* couvre-lit *m*, dessus-de-lit *m inv*.

counterpart ['kaʊntəpɑːt] *n* [person] homologue *mf* ; [thing] équivalent *m*, -e *f*.

counterpoint ['kaʊntəpɔɪnt] *n* MUS contrepoint *m*.

counterproductive [,kaʊntəprə'dʌktɪv] *adj* qui a l'effet inverse.

counter-revolution *n* contre-révolution *f*.

countersank ['kaʊntəsæŋk] *pt* ▷ countersink.

countersign ['kaʊntəsaɪn] *vt* contresigner.

countersink ['kaʊntəsɪŋk] (*pt* -sank, *pp* -sunk) *vt* [hole] fraiser ; [screw] noyer.

countess ['kaʊntɪs] *n* comtesse *f*.

countless ['kaʊntlɪs] *adj* innombrable.

countrified ['kʌntrɪfaɪd] *adj* pej campagnard(e), rustique.

country ['kʌntrɪ] (*pl* -ies) ◇ *n* - 1. [nation] pays *m* - 2. [countryside] : the ~ la campagne ; in the ~ à la campagne - 3. [region] région *f* ; [terrain] terrain *m* ◇ *comp* de la campagne, campagnard(e).

country and western ◇ *n* country *m* ◇ *comp* country (*inv*).

country club n club m de loisirs (à la campagne).

country dancing n (U) danse f folklorique.

country house n manoir m.

countryman ['kʌntrɪmən] (pl -men [-mən]) n [from same country] compatriote m.

country music n = country and western.

country park n Br parc m naturel.

countryside ['kʌntrɪsaɪd] n campagne f.

countrywoman ['kʌntrɪ,wʊmən] (pl -women [-,wɪmɪn]) n [from same country] compatriote f.

county ['kaʊntɪ] (pl -ies) n comté m.

county council n Br conseil m général.

county court n Br ≃ tribunal m de grande instance.

county town Br, **county seat** Am n chef-lieu m.

coup [kuː] n - **1.** [rebellion] : ~ (d'état) coup m d'État - **2.** [success] coup m (de maître), beau coup m.

coupé ['kuːpeɪ] n coupé m.

couple ['kʌpl] ⟨> n - **1.** [in relationship] couple m - **2.** [small number] : a ~ (of) [two] deux ; [a few] quelques, deux ou trois ⟨> vt - **1.** [join] : to ~ sthg (to) atteler qqch (à) - **2.** fig [associate] : to ~ sthg with associer qqch à ; ~d with ajouté OR joint à.

couplet ['kʌplɪt] n couplet m.

coupling ['kʌplɪŋ] n RAIL attelage m.

coupon ['kuːpɒn] n - **1.** [voucher] bon m - **2.** [form] coupon m.

courage ['kʌrɪdʒ] n courage m ; to take ~ (from sthg) être encouragé (par qqch) ; to have the ~ of one's convictions avoir le courage de ses opinions.

courageous [kə'reɪdʒəs] adj courageux(euse).

courageously [kə'reɪdʒəslɪ] adv courageusement, avec courage.

courgette [kɔː'ʒet] n Br courgette f.

courier ['kʊrɪə'] n - **1.** [on holiday] guide m, accompagnateur m, -trice f - **2.** [to deliver letters, packages] courrier m, messager m.

course [kɔːs] ⟨> n - **1.** [gen & SCH] cours m ; to take a ~ (in) suivre un cours (de) ; ~ of action ligne f de conduite ; in the ~ of au cours de ; to run OR take its ~ [illness, event] suivre son cours - **2.** MED [of injections] série f ; ~ of treatment traitement m - **3.** [of ship, plane] route f ; to be on ~ suivre le cap fixé ; fig [on target] être dans la bonne voie ; to be off ~ faire

fausse route - **4.** [of meal] plat m - **5.** SPORT terrain m ⟨> vi literary [flow] couler.

➡ **of course** adv - **1.** [inevitably, not surprisingly] évidemment, naturellement - **2.** [certainly] bien sûr ; of ~ not bien sûr que non.

coursebook ['kɔːsbʊk] n livre m de cours.

coursework ['kɔːswɜːk] n (U) travail m personnel.

court [kɔːt] ⟨> n - **1.** [JUR - building, room] cour f, tribunal m ; [- judge, jury etc] : the ~ la justice ; to appear in ~ comparaître devant un tribunal ; to go to ~ aller en justice ; to take sb to ~ faire un procès à qqn - **2.** [SPORT - gen] court m ; [- for basketball, volleyball] terrain m ; on ~ sur le court - **3.** [courtyard, of monarch] cour f ⟨> vt [danger, disaster] braver, aller au-devant de ; [favour] rechercher ⟨> vi dated sortir ensemble, se fréquenter.

court circular n Br bulletin m quotidien de la cour.

courteous ['kɜːtjəs] adj courtois(e), poli(e).

courtesan [,kɔːtɪ'zæn] n courtisane f.

courtesy ['kɜːtɪsɪ] n courtoisie f, politesse f.

➡ **(by) courtesy of** prep avec la permission de.

courtesy car n voiture f mise gratuitement à la disposition du client.

courtesy coach n car m servant au transport des clients.

courthouse ['kɔːthaʊs, pl -haʊzɪz] n Am palais m de justice, tribunal m.

courtier ['kɔːtjə'] n courtisan m.

court-martial (pl court-martials OR courts-martial, Br pt & pp -led ; cont -ling, Am pt & pp -ed ; cont -ing) ⟨> n cour f martiale ⟨> vt traduire en cour f martiale.

court of appeal Br, **court of appeals** Am n cour f d'appel.

court of inquiry n commission f d'enquête.

court of law n tribunal m, cour f de justice.

courtroom ['kɔːtrʊm] n salle f de tribunal.

courtship ['kɔːtʃɪp] n - **1.** [of people] cour f - **2.** [of animals] parade f.

court shoe n escarpin m.

courtyard ['kɔːtjɑːd] n cour f.

cousin ['kʌzn] n cousin m, -e f.

couture [kuː'tʊə'] n haute couture f.

cove [kəʊv] n [bay] crique f.

coven ['kʌvən] n réunion f de sorcières.

covenant ['kʌvənənt] n - **1.** [of money] engagement m contractuel - **2.** [agreement] convention f, contrat m.

Covent Garden [ˌkɒvənt-] *n ancien marché de Londres, aujourd'hui importante galerie marchande.*

COVENT GARDEN

« Covent Garden », jadis le marché aux fruits, légumes et fleurs du centre de Londres, est aujourd'hui une importante galerie marchande ; ce nom désigne également la « Royal Opera House », située près de l'ancien marché.

Coventry [ˈkɒvəntrɪ] *n* : **to send sb to ~** mettre qqn en quarantaine.

cover [ˈkʌvəʳ] ◇ *n* - **1.** [covering - of furniture] housse *f ;* [- of pan] couvercle *m ;* [- of book, magazine] couverture *f* - **2.** [blanket] couverture *f ;* **bed ~** couvre-lit *m* - **3.** [protection, shelter] abri *m ;* **to take ~** s'abriter, se mettre à l'abri ; **under ~** à l'abri, à couvert ; **under ~ of darkness** à la faveur de la nuit ; **to break ~** [person] sortir à découvert *OR* de sa cachette - **4.** [concealment] couverture *f* - **5.** [insurance] couverture *f,* garantie *f* ◇ *vt* - **1.** [gen] : **to ~ sthg (with)** couvrir qqch (de) - **2.** [insure] : **to ~ sb against** couvrir qqn en cas de - **3.** [include] englober, comprendre.

➤ **cover up** *vt sep* - **1.** [person, object, face] couvrir - **2.** fig [scandal etc] dissimuler, cacher.

coverage [ˈkʌvərɪdʒ] *n* [of news] reportage *m.*

coveralls [ˈkʌvərɔːlz] *npl* Am bleu *m* de travail.

cover charge *n* couvert *m.*

cover girl *n* cover-girl *f.*

covering [ˈkʌvərɪŋ] *n* [of floor etc] revêtement *m ;* [of snow, dust] couche *f.*

covering letter Br, **cover letter** Am *n* lettre *f* explicative *OR* d'accompagnement.

cover note *n* Br lettre *f* de couverture, attestation *f* provisoire d'assurance.

cover price *n* [of magazine etc] prix *m.*

covert [ˈkʌvət] *adj* [activity] clandestin(e) ; [look, glance] furtif(ive).

cover-up *n* étouffement *m,* dissimulation *f.*

cover version *n* reprise *f.*

covet [ˈkʌvɪt] *vt* convoiter.

cow [kaʊ] ◇ *n* - **1.** [female type of cattle] vache *f* - **2.** [female elephant etc] femelle *f* - **3.** Br inf pej [woman] vache *f,* chameau *m* ◇ *vt* intimider, effrayer.

coward [ˈkaʊəd] *n* lâche *mf,* poltron *m,* -onne *f.*

cowardice [ˈkaʊədɪs] *n* lâcheté *f.*

cowardly [ˈkaʊədlɪ] *adj* lâche.

cowboy [ˈkaʊbɔɪ] ◇ *n* - **1.** [cattlehand] cow-boy *m* - **2.** Br inf [dishonest workman] fumiste *m* ◇ *comp* de cow-boys.

cower [ˈkaʊəʳ] *vi* se recroqueviller.

cowhide [ˈkaʊhaɪd] *n* peau *f* de vache.

cowl neck [kaʊl-] *n* col *m* capuche.

cowpat [ˈkaʊpæt] *n* bouse *f* de vache.

cowshed [ˈkaʊʃed] *n* étable *f.*

cox [kɒks], **coxswain** [ˈkɒksən] *n* barreur *m.*

coy [kɔɪ] *adj* qui fait le/la timide.

coyly [ˈkɔɪlɪ] *adv* en faisant le/la timide.

coyote [kɔɪˈəʊtɪ] *n* coyote *m.*

cozy Am = **cosy**.

cp. (*abbr of* **compare**) cf.

c/p (*abbr of* **carriage paid**) pp.

CP (*abbr of* **Communist Party**) *n* PC *m.*

CPA *n abbr of* **certified public accountant**.

CPI (*abbr of* **Consumer Price Index**) *n* IPC *m.*

Cpl. (*abbr of* **corporal**) C.

CP/M (*abbr of* **control program for microcomputers**) *n* CP/M *m.*

c.p.s. (*abbr of* **characters per second**) cps.

CPS (*abbr of* **Crown Prosecution Service**) *n* ≃ ministère *m* public.

CPSA (*abbr of* **Civil and Public Services Association**) *n syndicat britannique de la fonction publique.*

CPU *n abbr of* **central processing unit**.

cr. - **1.** *abbr of* **credit** - **2.** *abbr of* **creditor**.

crab [kræb] *n* crabe *m.*

crab apple *n* pomme *f* sauvage.

crack [kræk] ◇ *n* - **1.** [in glass, pottery] fêlure *f ;* [in wall, wood, ground] fissure *f ;* [in skin] gerçure *f* - **2.** [gap - in door] entrebâillement *m ;* [- in curtains] interstice *m ;* **at the ~ of dawn** au point du jour - **3.** [noise - of whip] claquement *m ;* [- of twigs] craquement *m* - **4.** [joke] plaisanterie *f* - **5.** inf [attempt] : **to have a ~ at sthg** tenter qqch, essayer de faire qqch - **6.** drugs sl crack *m* ◇ *adj* [troops etc] de première classe ; **~ shot** tireur *m,* -euse *f* d'élite ◇ *vt* - **1.** [glass, plate] fêler ; [wood, wall] fissurer - **2.** [egg, nut] casser - **3.** [whip] faire claquer - **4.** [bang, hit sharply] : **to ~ one's head** se cogner la tête - **5.** inf [bottle] : **to ~ (open) a bottle** ouvrir une bouteille - **6.** [solve - problem] résoudre ; [- code] déchiffrer - **7.** inf [make - joke] faire ◇ *vi* - **1.** [glass, pottery] se fêler ; [ground, wall] se fissurer ; [skin] se crevasser, se gercer - **2.** [whip] claquer ; [twigs] craquer - **3.** [break down - person] craquer, s'effondrer ; [- system, empire] s'écrouler ; [- resistance] se briser - **4.** Br inf [act quickly] : **to get ~ing** s'y mettre.

crack down *vi* : **to ~ down (on)** sévir (contre).

crack up *vi* craquer.

crackdown [ˈkrækdaʊn] *n* : **~ (on)** mesures *fpl* énergiques (contre).

cracked [ˈkrækt] *adj* - **1.** [vase, glass] fêlé(e) ; [wall] fissuré(e) ; [paint, varnish] craquelé(e) - **2.** [voice] fêlé(e) - **3.** inf [mad] cinglé(e), toqué(e).

cracker [ˈkrækə˞] *n* - **1.** [biscuit] cracker *m*, craquelin *m* - **2.** Br [for Christmas] diablotin *m*.

crackers [ˈkræckəz] *adj* Br inf dingue, cinglé(e).

cracking [ˈkrækɪŋ] *adj* inf : **to walk at a ~ pace** marcher à toute allure.

crackle [ˈkrækl] ⋄ *n* [of fire] crépitement *m* ; [of cooking] grésillement *m* ; [on phone, radio] friture *f* ⋄ *vi* [frying food] grésiller ; [fire] crépiter ; [radio etc] crachoter.

crackling [ˈkræklɪŋ] *n* (U) - **1.** [on phone, radio] friture *f* ; [of fire] crépitement *m* ; [of cooking] grésillement *m* - **2.** [pork skin] couenne *f* rissolée.

crackpot [ˈkrækpɒt] inf ⋄ *adj* fou (folle) ⋄ *n* cinglé *m*, -e *f*, tordu *m*, -e *f*.

Cracow *n* Cracovie.

cradle [ˈkreɪdl] ⋄ *n* berceau *m* ; TECH nacelle *f* ⋄ *vt* [baby] bercer ; [object] tenir délicatement.

craft [krɑːft] (*pl sense 2 inv*) *n* - **1.** [trade, skill] métier *m* - **2.** [boat] embarcation *f*.

craftsman [ˈkrɑːftsmən] (*pl* -men [-mən]) *n* artisan *m*, homme *m* de métier.

craftsmanship [ˈkrɑːftsmənʃɪp] *n* (U) - **1.** [skill] dextérité *f*, art *m* - **2.** [skilled work] travail *m*, exécution *f*.

craftsmen *pl* ▷ craftsman.

crafty [ˈkrɑːftɪ] (*compar* -ier ; *superl* -iest) *adj* rusé(e).

crag [kræg] *n* rocher *m* escarpé

craggy [ˈkrægɪ] (*compar* -ier ; *superl* -iest) *adj* - **1.** [rock] escarpé(e) - **2.** [face] anguleux(euse).

Crakow [ˈkrækaʊ] *n* Cracovie.

cram [kræm] (*pt* & *pp* -med ; *cont* -ming) ⋄ *vt* - **1.** [stuff] fourrer - **2.** [overfill] : **to ~ sthg with** bourrer qqch de ⋄ *vi* bachoter.

cramming [ˈkræmɪŋ] *n* bachotage *m*.

cramp [kræmp] ⋄ *n* crampe *f* ⋄ *vt* gêner, entraver.

cramped [kræmpt] *adj* [room] exigu(ë) ; **it's a bit ~ in here** on est un peu à l'étroit ici.

crampon [ˈkræmpən] *n* crampon *m*.

cranberry [ˈkrænbərɪ] (*pl* -ies) *n* canneberge *f*.

crane [kreɪn] ⋄ *n* grue *f* ⋄ *vt* : **to ~ one's neck** tendre le cou ⋄ *vi* tendre le cou.

crane fly *n* tipule *f*.

cranium [ˈkreɪnjəm] (*pl* -niums OR -nia [-njə]) *n* crâne *m*.

crank [kræŋk] ⋄ *n* - **1.** TECH manivelle *f* - **2.** inf [person] excentrique *mf* ⋄ *vt* - **1.** [wind - handle] tourner ; [- mechanism] remonter (à la manivelle) - **2.** AUT faire démarrer à la manivelle.

crankshaft [ˈkræŋkʃɑːft] *n* vilebrequin *m*.

cranky [ˈkræŋkɪ] (*compar* -ier ; *superl* -iest) *adj* inf - **1.** [odd] excentrique - **2.** Am [bad-tempered] grognon(onne).

cranny [ˈkrænɪ] (*pl* -ies) *n* ▷ nook.

crap [kræp] *n* (U) merde *f* ; **it's a load of ~** tout ça, c'est des conneries.

crappy [ˈkræpɪ] (*compar* -ier ; *superl* -iest) *adj* v inf merdique.

crash [kræʃ] ⋄ *n* - **1.** [accident] accident *m* - **2.** [noise] fracas *m* - **3.** FIN krach *m* ⋄ *vt* : **I ~ed the car** j'ai eu un accident avec la voiture ⋄ *vi* - **1.** [cars, trains] se percuter, se rentrer dedans ; [car, train] avoir un accident ; [plane] s'écraser ; **to ~ into** [wall] rentrer dans, emboutir - **2.** [plate] se fracasser - **3.** [FIN - business, company] faire faillite ; [- stock market] s'effondrer - **4.** COMPUT tomber en panne.

crash barrier *n* glissière *f* de sécurité.

crash course *n* cours *m* intensif.

crash diet *n* régime *m* intensif.

crash-dive *vi* faire une plongée rapide.

crash helmet *n* casque *m* de protection.

crash-land ⋄ *vt* faire atterrir en catastrophe ⋄ *vi* atterrir en catastrophe.

crash landing *n* atterrissage *m* en catastrophe.

crass [kræs] *adj* grossier(ère).

crate [kreɪt] *n* cageot *m*, caisse *f*.

crater [ˈkreɪtə˞] *n* cratère *m*.

cravat [krəˈvæt] *n* cravate *f*.

crave [kreɪv] ⋄ *vt* [affection, luxury] avoir soif de ; [cigarette, chocolate] avoir un besoin fou maladif de ⋄ *vi* : **to ~ for** [affection, luxury] avoir soif de ; [cigarette, chocolate] avoir un besoin fou OR maladif de.

craving [ˈkreɪvɪŋ] *n* : **~ for** [affection, luxury] soif *f* de ; [cigarette, chocolate] besoin *m* fou OR maladif de.

crawl [krɔːl] ⋄ *vi* - **1.** [baby] marcher à quatre pattes ; [person] se traîner - **2.** [insect] ramper - **3.** [vehicle, traffic] avancer au pas - **4.** inf [place, floor] : **to be ~ing with** grouiller de - **5.** inf [grovel] : **to ~ (to sb)** ramper (devant qqn) ⬦ n - **1.** [slow pace] : **at a ~** au pas, au ralenti - **2.** [swimming stroke] : **the ~** le crawl.

crawler lane n Br voie f pour véhicules lents.

crayfish ['kreɪfɪʃ] (pl inv OR -es) n écrevisse f.

crayon ['kreɪɒn] n crayon m de couleur.

craze [kreɪz] n engouement m.

crazed [kreɪzd] adj : **~ (with)** rendu fou (rendue folle) (de).

crazy ['kreɪzɪ] (compar -ier ; superl -iest) adj inf - **1.** [mad] fou (folle) - **2.** [enthusiastic] : **to be ~ about sb/sthg** être fou (folle) de qqn/qqch.

crazy paving n Br dallage m irrégulier.

creak [kriːk] ⬦ n [of door, handle] craquement m ⬦ vi [door, handle] craquer ; [floorboard, bed] grincer.

creaky ['kriːkɪ] (compar -ier ; superl -iest) adj [door, handle] qui craque ; [floorboard, bed] qui grince.

cream [kriːm] ⬦ adj [in colour] crème (inv) ⬦ n - **1.** [gen] crème f - **2.** [colour] crème m ⬦ vt [potatoes] mettre en purée.

➤ **cream off** vt sep fig écrémer.

cream cake n Br gâteau m à la crème.

cream cheese n fromage m frais.

cream cracker n Br biscuit m salé (souvent mangé avec du fromage).

cream of tartar n crème f de tartre.

cream tea n Br goûter se composant de thé et de scones servis avec de la crème et de la confiture.

creamy ['kriːmɪ] (compar -ier ; superl -iest) adj - **1.** [taste, texture] crémeux(euse) - **2.** [colour] crème (inv).

crease [kriːs] ⬦ n [in fabric - deliberate] pli m ; [- accidental] (faux) pli ⬦ vt froisser ⬦ vi - **1.** [fabric] se froisser - **2.** [face, forehead] se plisser.

creased [kriːst] adj - **1.** [fabric] froissé(e) - **2.** [face] plissé(e).

crease-resistant adj infroissable.

create [kriː'eɪt] vt créer.

creation [kriː'eɪʃn] n création f.

creative [kriː'eɪtɪv] adj créatif(ive).

creativity [,kriːeɪ'tɪvətɪ] n créativité f.

creator [kriː'eɪtəʳ] n créateur m, -trice f.

creature ['kriːtʃəʳ] n créature f.

crèche [kreʃ] n Br crèche f.

credence ['kriːdns] n : **to give** OR **lend ~ to sthg** ajouter foi à qqch.

credentials [krɪ'denʃlz] npl - **1.** [papers] pièce f d'identité ; fig [qualifications] capacités fpl - **2.** [references] références fpl.

credibility [,kredə'bɪlətɪ] n crédibilité f.

credible ['kredəbl] adj crédible.

credit ['kredɪt] ⬦ n - **1.** FIN crédit m ; **to be in ~** [person] avoir un compte approvisionné ; [account] être approvisionné ; **on ~** à crédit - **2.** (U) [praise] honneur m, mérite m ; **to be to sb's ~** [successfully completed] être à l'actif de qqn ; [in sb's favour] être à l'honneur de qqn ; **to do sb ~** faire honneur à qqn ; **to give sb ~ for sthg** reconnaître que qqn a fait qqch - **3.** UNIV unité f de valeur ⬦ vt - **1.** FIN : **to ~ £10 to an account, to ~ an account with £10** créditer un compte de 10 livres - **2.** inf [believe] croire - **3.** [give the credit to] : **to ~ sb with sthg** accorder OR attribuer qqch à qqn ; **he's ~ed with inventing ...** il a, dit-on, inventé ...

➤ **credits** npl CINEMA générique m.

creditable ['kredɪtəbl] adj honorable.

credit account n Br compte m créditeur.

credit broker n courtier m en crédits OR en prêts.

credit card n carte f de crédit.

credit control n [on spending] encadrement m du crédit ; [debt recovery] recouvrement m de créances.

credit facilities npl facilités fpl de paiement OR de crédit.

credit limit Br, **credit line** Am n limite f de crédit.

credit note n avoir m ; FIN note f de crédit.

creditor ['kredɪtəʳ] n créancier m, -ère f.

credit rating n degré m de solvabilité.

credit squeeze n restriction f de crédit.

credit transfer n virement m de crédits.

creditworthy ['kredɪt,wɜːðɪ] adj solvable.

credulity [krɪ'djuːlətɪ] n crédulité f.

credulous ['kredjʊləs] adj crédule.

creed [kriːd] n - **1.** [belief] principes mpl - **2.** RELIG croyance f.

creek [kriːk] n - **1.** [inlet] crique f - **2.** Am [stream] ruisseau m.

creep [kriːp] (pt & pp crept) ⬦ vi - **1.** [insect] ramper ; [traffic] avancer au pas - **2.** [move stealthily] se glisser - **3.** inf [grovel] : **to ~ (to sb)** ramper (devant qqn) ⬦ n inf [nasty person] sale type m.

➤ **creeps** npl : **to give sb the ~s** inf donner la chair de poule à qqn.

➤ **creep in** vi [appear] apparaître.

➤ **creep up on** vt surprendre.

creeper ['kriːpəʳ] n [plant] plante f grimpante.

creepers npl chaussures fpl à semelles de crêpe.

creepy ['kriːpɪ] (compar -ier ; superl -iest) adj inf qui donne la chair de poule.

creepy-crawly [-'krɔːlɪ] (pl creepy-crawlies) n inf bestiole f qui rampe.

cremate [krɪ'meɪt] vt incinérer.

cremation [krɪ'meɪʃn] n incinération f.

crematorium Br [ˌkremə'tɔːrɪəm] (pl -riums OR -ria [-rɪə]), **crematory** Am ['kremətrɪ] (pl -ies) n crématorium m.

creosote ['krɪəsəʊt] ◇ n créosote f ◇ vt créosoter.

crepe [kreɪp] n - **1.** [cloth, rubber] crêpe m - **2.** [pancake] crêpe f.

crepe bandage n Br bande f Velpeau®.

crepe paper n (U) papier m crépon.

crepe-soled shoes npl Br chaussures fpl à semelles de crêpe.

crept [krept] pt & pp ▷ creep.

Cres. abbr of Crescent.

crescendo [krɪ'ʃendəʊ] (pl -s) n crescendo m.

crescent ['kresnt] ◇ adj en forme de croissant ; ~ **moon** croissant m de lune ◇ n - **1.** [shape] croissant - **2.** [street] rue f en demi-cercle.

cress [kres] n cresson m.

crest [krest] n - **1.** [of bird, hill] crête f - **2.** [on coat of arms] timbre m.

crestfallen ['krest,fɔːln] adj découragé(e).

Crete [kriːt] n Crète f ; in ~ en Crète.

cretin ['kretɪn] n inf [idiot] crétin m, -e f.

Creutzfeldt-Jakob disease [ˌkrɔɪtsfelt-'jækɒb-] n maladie f de Creutzfeldt-Jakob.

crevasse [krɪ'væs] n crevasse f.

crevice ['krevɪs] n fissure f.

crew [kruː] n - **1.** [of ship, plane] équipage m - **2.** [team] équipe f ; **ambulance ~** ambulanciers mpl.

crew cut n coupe f en brosse.

crewman ['kruːmæn] (pl -men [-men]) n membre m d'équipage.

crew-neck(ed) [-nek(t)] adj ras du cou.

crib [krɪb] (pt & pp -bed ; cont -bing) ◇ n [cot] lit m d'enfant ◇ vt inf [copy] : **to ~ sthg off** OR **from sb** copier qqch sur qqn.

cribbage ['krɪbɪdʒ] n jeu de cartes dans lequel les points sont comptabilisés sur une tablette.

crick [krɪk] ◇ n [in neck] torticolis m ◇ vt : **to ~ one's neck** attraper un torticolis ; **to ~ one's back** se faire un tour de reins.

cricket ['krɪkɪt] ◇ n - **1.** [game] cricket m - **2.** [insect] grillon m ◇ comp de cricket.

cricketer ['krɪkɪtə'] n joueur m de cricket.

crikey ['kraɪkɪ] excl Br inf dated zut alors!

crime [kraɪm] ◇ n crime m ; ~**s against humanity** crimes mpl contre l'humanité ◇ comp : ~ **novel** roman m policier ; ~ **prevention** lutte f contre le crime.

Crimea [kraɪ'mɪə] n : the ~ la Crimée ; in the ~ en Crimée.

crime wave n vague f de criminalité.

criminal ['krɪmɪnl] ◇ adj criminel(elle) ; ~ **lawyer** avocat m pénaliste ◇ n criminel m, -elle f.

criminalize, -ise ['krɪmɪnəlaɪz] vt criminaliser.

criminal law n droit m pénal.

criminology [ˌkrɪmɪ'nɒlədʒɪ] n criminologie f.

crimp [krɪmp] vt [hair] crêper.

crimson ['krɪmzn] ◇ adj [in colour] rouge foncé (inv) ; [with embarrassment] cramoisi(e) ◇ n cramoisi m.

cringe [krɪndʒ] vi - **1.** [in fear] avoir un mouvement de recul (par peur) - **2.** inf [with embarrassment] : **to ~ (at sthg)** ne plus savoir où se mettre (devant qqch).

crinkle ['krɪŋkl] ◇ n [in paper] pli m ; [in cloth] (faux) pli ◇ vt [clothes] froisser ◇ vi [clothes] se froisser.

cripple ['krɪpl] ◇ n dated & offensive infirme mf ◇ vt - **1.** MED [disable] estropier - **2.** [country] paralyser ; [ship, plane] endommager.

crippling ['krɪplɪŋ] adj - **1.** MED [disease] qui rend infirme - **2.** [taxes, debts] écrasant(e).

crisis ['kraɪsɪs] (pl crises ['kraɪsiːz]) n crise f.

crisp [krɪsp] adj - **1.** [pastry] croustillant(e) ; [apple, vegetables] croquant(e) ; [snow] craquant(e) - **2.** [weather, manner] vif (vive).

crisps npl Br chips fpl.

crispbread ['krɪspbred] n pain m suédois.

crispy ['krɪspɪ] (compar -ier ; superl -iest) adj [pastry] croustillant(e) ; [apple, vegetables] croquant(e).

crisscross ['krɪskrɒs] ◇ adj entrecroisé(e) ◇ vt entrecroiser ◇ vi s'entrecroiser.

criterion [kraɪ'tɪərɪən] (pl -rions OR -ria [-rɪə]) n critère m.

critic ['krɪtɪk] n - **1.** [reviewer] critique m - **2.** [detractor] détracteur m, -trice f.

critical ['krɪtɪkl] adj critique ; **to be ~ of sb/sthg** critiquer qqn/qqch.

critically ['krɪtɪklɪ] adv - **1.** [ill] gravement ; ~ **important** d'une importance capitale - **2.** [analytically] de façon critique.

criticism ['krɪtɪsɪzml] n critique f.

criticize, -ise [ˈkrɪtɪsaɪz] *vt* & *vi* critiquer.

critique [krɪˈtiːk] *n* critique *f*.

croak [krəuk] ⇔ *n* - **1.** [of frog] coassement *m ;* [of raven] croassement *m* - **2.** [hoarse voice] voix *f* rauque ⇔ *vi* - **1.** [frog] coasser ; [raven] croasser - **2.** [person] parler d'une voix rauque.

Croat [ˈkrəuæt], **Croatian** [krəuˈeɪʃn] ⇔ *adj* croate ⇔ *n* - **1.** [person] Croate *mf* - **2.** [language] croate *m*.

Croatia [krəuˈeɪʃəl] *n* Croatie *f ;* in ~ en Croatie.

Croatian = Croat.

crochet [ˈkrəuʃeɪ] ⇔ *n* crochet *m* ⇔ *vt* faire au crochet.

crockery [ˈkrɒkərɪ] *n* vaisselle *f*.

crocodile [ˈkrɒkədaɪl] (*pl inv* OR **-s**) *n* crocodile *m*.

crocus [ˈkrəukəs] (*pl* **-es** [-iːzl]) *n* crocus *m*.

croft [krɒft] *n* Br petite ferme *f (particulièrement en Écosse)*.

croissant *n* croissant *m*.

crony [ˈkrəunɪ] (*pl* **-ies**) *n* inf copain *m*, copine *f*.

crook [kruk] ⇔ *n* - **1.** [criminal] escroc *m* - **2.** [of arm, elbow] pliure *f* - **3.** [shepherd's staff] houlette *f* ⇔ *vt* [finger, arm] plier.

crooked [ˈkrukɪd] *adj* - **1.** [bent] courbé(e) - **2.** [teeth, tie] de travers - **3.** inf [dishonest] malhonnête.

croon [kruːn] *vt* & *vi* chantonner.

crop [krɒp] (*pt* & *pp* **-ped** *; cont* **-ping**) ⇔ *n* - **1.** [kind of plant] culture *f* - **2.** [harvested produce] récolte *f* - **3.** [whip] cravache *f* ⇔ *vt* - **1.** [hair] couper très court - **2.** [subj : cows, sheep] brouter.

➣ **crop up** *vi* survenir.

cropper [ˈkrɒpəʳ] *n* inf : to come a ~ [fall over] se casser la figure ; [make mistake] se planter.

crop spraying *n* pulvérisation *f* des cultures.

croquet [ˈkrəukeɪ] *n* croquet *m*.

croquette [krɒˈket] *n* croquette *f*.

cross [krɒs] ⇔ *adj* [person] fâché(e) ; [look] méchant(e) ; to get ~ (with sb) se fâcher (contre qqn) ⇔ *n* - **1.** [gen] croix *f* - **2.** [hybrid] croisement *m* ⇔ *vt* - **1.** [gen] traverser - **2.** [arms, legs] croiser - **3.** RELIG : to ~ o.s. faire le signe de croix, se signer - **4.** Br [cheque] barrer ⇔ *vi* - **1.** [intersect] se croiser - **2.** [traverse - boat] faire la traversée.

➣ **cross off, cross out** *vt sep* rayer.

crossbar [ˈkrɒsbɑːʳ] *n* - **1.** SPORT barre *f* transversale - **2.** [on bicycle] barre *f*.

crossbow [ˈkrɒsbəu] *n* arbalète *f*.

crossbreed [ˈkrɒsbriːd] *n* hybride *m*.

cross-Channel *adj* transManche.

cross-check *n* contre-vérification *f*.

➣ **crosscheck** *vt* faire une contre-vérification de.

cross-country ⇔ *adj* : ~ running cross *m ;* ~ skiing ski *m* de fond ⇔ *adv* à travers champs ⇔ *n* cross-country *m*, cross *m*.

cross-cultural *adj* interculturel(elle).

cross-dressing *n* travestisme *m*.

crossed line *n* TELEC : we've got a ~ il y a des interférences.

cross-examination *n* JUR contre-interrogatoire *m*.

cross-examine *vt* JUR faire subir un contre-interrogatoire à ; fig questionner de près.

cross-eyed [-aɪd] *adj* qui louche.

cross-fertilize *vt* [plants] croiser.

crossfire [ˈkrɒs,faɪəʳ] *n* (U) feu *m* croisé.

crosshead [ˈkrɒs,hed] *adj* : ~ screw vis *m* cruciforme ; ~ screwdriver tournevis *m* cruciforme.

crossing [ˈkrɒsɪŋ] *n* - **1.** [on road] passage *m* clouté ; [on railway line] passage à niveau - **2.** [sea journey] traversée *f*.

cross-legged [-legd] *adv* en tailleur.

crossly [ˈkrɒslɪ] *adv* [say] d'un air fâché.

crossply [ˈkrɒsplaɪ] (*pl* **-ies**) ⇔ *adj* [tyre] à carcasse diagonale ⇔ *n* pneu *m* à carcasse diagonale.

cross-purposes *npl* : to talk at ~ ne pas parler de la même chose ; to be at ~ ne pas être sur la même longueur d'ondes.

cross-question *vt* faire subir un contre-interrogatoire à.

cross-refer *vt* & *vi* renvoyer.

cross-reference *n* renvoi *m*.

crossroads [ˈkrɒsrəudz] (*pl inv*) *n* croisement *m* ; to be at a ~ fig se trouver à un point critique.

cross-section *n* - **1.** [drawing] coupe *f* transversale - **2.** [sample] échantillon *m*.

crosswalk [ˈkrɒswɔːk] *n* Am passage *m* clouté, passage pour piétons.

crossways [ˈkrɒsweɪz] = **crosswise**.

crosswind [ˈkrɒswɪnd] *n* vent *m* de travers.

crosswise [ˈkrɒswaɪz] *adv* en travers.

crossword (puzzle) [ˈkrɒswɜːd-] *n* mots croisés *mpl*.

crotch [krɒtʃ] *n* entrejambe *m*.

crotchet [ˈkrɒtʃɪt] *n* noire *f*.

crotchety [ˈkrɒtʃɪtɪ] *adj* **Br** inf grognon(onne).

crouch [kraʊtʃ] *vi* s'accroupir.

croup [kruːp] *n* - **1.** [illness] croup *m* - **2.** [of horse] croupe *f*.

croupier [ˈkruːpɪə] *n* croupier *m*.

crouton [ˈkruːtɒn] *n* croûton *m*.

crow [krəʊ] <> *n* corbeau *m*; **as the ~ flies** à vol d'oiseau <> *vi* - **1.** [cock] chanter - **2.** inf [person] frimer.

crowbar [ˈkrəʊbɑː] *n* pied-de-biche *m*.

crowd [kraʊd] <> *n* - **1.** [mass of people] foule *f* - **2.** [particular group] bande *f*, groupe *m* <> *vi* s'amasser <> *vt* - **1.** [streets, town] remplir - **2.** [force into small space] entasser.

crowded [ˈkraʊdɪd] *adj* : **~ (with)** bondé(e) (de), plein(e) (de).

crown [kraʊn] <> *n* - **1.** [of king, on tooth] couronne *f* - **2.** [of head, hill] sommet *m*; [of hat] fond *m* <> *vt* couronner.

➡ **Crown** <> *n* : **the Crown** [monarchy] la Couronne <> *comp* de la Couronne.

crown court *n* tribunal *m* de grande instance.

crowning [ˈkraʊnɪŋ] *adj* fig suprême ; **the ~ glory of her career** le couronnement de sa carrière.

crown jewels *npl* joyaux *mpl* de la Couronne.

crown prince *n* prince *m* héritier.

crow's feet *npl* pattes *fpl* d'oie.

crow's nest *n* nid *m* de pie.

crucial [ˈkruːʃl] *adj* crucial(e).

crucially [ˈkruːʃlɪ] *adv* de façon cruciale ; **~ important** d'une importance cruciale.

crucible [ˈkruːsɪbl] *n* creuset *m*.

crucifix [ˈkruːsɪfɪks] *n* crucifix *m*.

Crucifixion [ˌkruːsɪˈfɪkʃn] *n* : **the ~** la Crucifixion.

crucify [ˈkruːsɪfaɪ] (*pt* & *pp* **-ied**) *vt* crucifier.

crude [kruːd] <> *adj* - **1.** [material] brut(e) - **2.** [joke, drawing] grossier(ère) <> *n* (U) : **~ (oil)** brut *m*.

crudely [ˈkruːdlɪ] *adv* - **1.** [joke, remark] grossièrement, crûment - **2.** [draw, sketch] grossièrement, sommairement.

crude oil *n* (U) brut *m*.

cruel [krʊəl] (*compar* **-ler** ; *superl* **-lest**) *adj* cruel(elle).

cruelly [ˈkrʊəlɪ] *adv* cruellement.

cruelty [ˈkrʊəltɪ] *n* (U) cruauté *f*.

cruet [ˈkruːɪt] *n* service *m* à condiments.

cruise [kruːz] <> *n* croisière *f* <> *vi* - **1.** [sail] croiser - **2.** [car] rouler ; [plane] voler.

cruise missile *n* missile *m* de croisière.

cruiser [ˈkruːzə] *n* - **1.** [warship] croiseur *m* - **2.** [cabin cruiser] yacht *m* de croisière.

crumb [krʌm] *n* - **1.** [of food] miette *f* - **2.** fig [of information] bribe *f*.

crumble [ˈkrʌmbl] <> *n* crumble *m* (aux fruits) <> *vt* émietter <> *vi* - **1.** [bread, cheese] s'émietter ; [building, wall] s'écrouler ; [cliff] s'ébouler ; [plaster] s'effriter - **2.** fig [society, relationship] s'effondrer.

crumbly [ˈkrʌmblɪ] (*compar* **-ier** ; *superl* **-iest**) *adj* friable.

crummy [ˈkrʌmɪ] (*compar* **-mier** ; *superl* **-miest**) *adj* inf minable.

crumpet [ˈkrʌmpɪt] *n* CULIN petite crêpe *f* épaisse.

crumple [ˈkrʌmpl] <> *vt* [crease] froisser <> *vi* [clothes] se froisser ; [car, bodywork] se mettre en accordéon.

➡ **crumple up** *vt sep* chiffonner.

crunch [krʌntʃ] <> *n* crissement *m*; **when it comes to the ~** inf au moment crucial OR décisif ; **if it comes to the ~** inf s'il le faut <> *vt* - **1.** [with teeth] croquer - **2.** [underfoot] crisser <> *vi* [feet, tyres] crisser.

crunchy [ˈkrʌntʃɪ] (*compar* **-ier** ; *superl* **-iest**) *adj* - **1.** [food] croquant(e) - **2.** [snow, gravel] qui crisse.

crusade [kruːˈseɪd] <> *n* lit & fig croisade *f* <> *vi* : **to ~ for/against** faire campagne pour/contre.

crusader [kruːˈseɪdə] *n* - **1.** HISTORY croisé *m* - **2.** [campaigner] militant *m*, -e *f*.

crush [krʌʃ] <> *n* - **1.** [crowd] foule *f* - **2.** inf [infatuation] : **to have a ~ on sb** avoir le béguin pour qqn - **3.** Br [drink] : **orange ~** orange *f* pressée <> *vt* - **1.** [gen] écraser ; [seeds, grain] broyer ; [ice] piler - **2.** fig [hopes] anéantir.

crush barrier *n* Br barrière *f* de sécurité.

crushing [ˈkrʌʃɪŋ] *adj* - **1.** [defeat, blow] écrasant(e) - **2.** [remark] humiliant(e).

crust [krʌst] *n* croûte *f*.

crustacean [krʌˈsteɪʃn] *n* crustacé *m*.

crusty [ˈkrʌstɪ] (*compar* **-ier** ; *superl* **-iest**) *adj* - **1.** [food] croustillant(e) - **2.** [person] grincheux(euse).

crutch [krʌtʃ] *n* - **1.** [stick] béquille *f*; fig soutien *m* - **2.** [crotch] entrejambe *m*.

crux [krʌks] *n* nœud *m*.

cry [kraɪ] (*pt* & *pp* **cried**, *pl* **cries**) <> *n* - **1.** [weep] : **to have a good ~** pleurer un bon coup - **2.** [of person, bird] cri *m* ; **a far ~ from** loin de <> *vt* [tears] pleurer ; **to ~ o.s. to sleep** s'endormir à force de pleurer <> *vi* - **1.** [weep] pleurer - **2.** [shout] crier.

cry off *vi* se dédire.

cry out ⇔ *vt* crier ⇔ *vi* crier ; [in pain, dismay] pousser un cri.

cry out for *vt fus* [demand] réclamer à grands cris ; **the room is crying out for ...** la pièce a bien besoin de ...

crybaby [ˈkraɪˌbeɪbɪ] (*pl* -ies) *n* inf pej pleurnicheur *m*, -euse *f*.

crying [ˈkraɪɪŋ] ⇔ *adj* inf : **it's a ~ shame** c'est scandaleux ; **a ~ need for sthg** un grand besoin de qqch, un besoin urgent de qqch ⇔ *n (U)* pleurs *mpl*.

cryogenics [ˌkraɪəˈdʒenɪks] *n (U)* cryogénie *f*.

cryonics [kraɪˈɒnɪks] *n (U)* cryogénisation *f*.

cryopreservation [ˌkraɪəprezəˈveɪʃn] *n (U)* cryoconservation *f*.

crypt [krɪpt] *n* crypte *f*.

cryptic [ˈkrɪptɪk] *adj* mystérieux(euse), énigmatique.

crypto- [krɪptəʊ] *prefix* crypto-.

crystal [ˈkrɪstl] ⇔ *n* cristal *m* ⇔ *comp* en cristal.

crystal ball *n* boule *f* de cristal.

crystal clear *adj* - **1.** [transparent] de cristal - **2.** [obvious] clair(e) comme de l'eau de roche.

crystallize, -ise [ˈkrɪstəlaɪz] ⇔ *vi* lit & fig se cristalliser ⇔ *vt* - **1.** [make clear] cristalliser, concrétiser - **2.** [preserve in sugar] : **~d fruit** fruits *mpl* confits.

CSC (*abbr of* **Civil Service Commission**) *n* commission de recrutement des fonctionnaires.

CSE (*abbr of* **Certificate of Secondary Education**) *n* ancien brevet de l'enseignement secondaire en Grande-Bretagne.

CS gas *n (U)* gaz *m* lacrymogène.

CST (*abbr of* **Central Standard Time**) *n* heure du centre des États-Unis.

CSU (*abbr of* **Civil Service Union**) *n* syndicat de la fonction publique.

ct *abbr of* **carat**.

CT *abbr of* **Connecticut**.

CTC *abbr of* **city technology college**.

cu. *abbr of* **cubic**.

cub [kʌb] *n* - **1.** [young animal] petit *m* - **2.** [boy scout] louveteau *m*.

Cuba [ˈkjuːbə] *n* Cuba ; **in ~** à Cuba.

Cuban [ˈkjuːbən] ⇔ *adj* cubain(e) ⇔ *n* Cubain *m*, -e *f*.

cubbyhole [ˈkʌbɪhəʊl] *n* cagibi *m*.

cube [kjuːb] ⇔ *n* cube *m* ⇔ *vt* MATH élever au cube.

cube root *n* racine *f* cubique.

cubic [ˈkjuːbɪk] *adj* cubique.

cubicle [ˈkjuːbɪkl] *n* cabine *f*.

cubism [ˈkjuːbɪzm] *n* cubisme *m*.

cubist [ˈkjuːbɪst] *n* cubiste *mf*.

cub reporter *n* jeune reporter *m*.

Cub Scout *n* louveteau *m*.

cuckoo [ˈkʊkuː] *n* coucou *m*.

cuckoo clock *n* coucou *m*.

cucumber [ˈkjuːkʌmbər] *n* concombre *m*.

cud [kʌd] *n* : **to chew the ~** lit & fig ruminer.

cuddle [ˈkʌdl] ⇔ *n* caresse *f*, câlin *m* ⇔ *vt* caresser, câliner ⇔ *vi* s'enlacer.

cuddle up *vi* : **to ~ up (to sb)** se pelotonner (contre qqn).

cuddly [ˈkʌdlɪ] (*compar* -ier ; *superl* -iest) *adj* [person] câlin(e).

cuddly toy *n* jouet *m* en peluche.

cudgel [ˈkʌdʒəl] (Br *pt* & *pp* -led ; *cont* -ling, Am *pt* & *pp* -ed ; *cont* -ing) ⇔ *n* trique *f ;* **to take up the ~s for sb/sthg** prendre fait et cause pour qqn/qqch ⇔ *vt* frapper à coups de trique.

cue [kjuː] *n* - **1.** RADIO, THEATRE & TV signal *m ;* **on ~** au bon moment ; **to take one's ~ from sb** emboîter le pas à qqn - **2.** fig [stimulus] signe *m ;* **this could be the ~ for a recovery** cela pourrait marquer le début d'une amélioration - **3.** [in snooker, pool] queue *f* (de billard).

cuff [kʌf] *n* - **1.** [of sleeve] poignet *m ;* **off the ~** au pied levé - **2.** Am [of trouser] revers *m inv* - **3.** [blow] gifle *f* ⇔ *vt* gifler.

cuff link *n* bouton *m* de manchette.

cu. in. *abbr of* **cubic inch(es)**.

cuisine [kwɪˈziːn] *n* cuisine *f*.

cul-de-sac [ˈkʌldəsæk] *n* cul-de-sac *m*.

culinary [ˈkʌlɪnərɪ] *adj* culinaire.

cull [kʌl] ⇔ *n* massacre *m* ⇔ *vt* - **1.** [kill] massacrer - **2.** [gather] recueillir.

culminate [ˈkʌlmɪneɪt] *vi* : **to ~ in sthg** se terminer par qqch, aboutir à qqch.

culmination [ˌkʌlmɪˈneɪʃn] *n (U)* apogée *m*.

culottes [kjuːˈlɒts] *npl* jupe-culotte *f*.

culpable [ˈkʌlpəbl] *adj* coupable.

culprit [ˈkʌlprɪt] *n* coupable *mf*.

cult [kʌlt] ⇔ *n* culte *m* ⇔ *comp* culte.

cultivate [ˈkʌltɪveɪt] *vt* cultiver.

cultivated [ˈkʌltɪveɪtɪd] *adj* cultivé(e).

cultivation [ˌkʌltɪˈveɪʃn] *n (U)* [farming] culture *f*.

cultural [ˈkʌltʃərəl] *adj* culturel(elle).

culture [ˈkʌltʃər] *n* culture *f*.

cultured [ˈkʌltʃəd] *adj* [educated] cultivé(e).

cultured pearl *n* perle *f* de culture.

culture shock *n* choc *m* culturel.

culture vulture *n* inf hum fana *mf* de culture.

culvert ['kʌlvət] *n* conduit *m*.

cumbersome ['kʌmbəsəm] *adj* - **1.** [object] encombrant(e) - **2.** [system] lourd(e).

cumin ['kʌmɪn] *n* cumin *m*.

cumulative ['kju:mjʊlətɪv] *adj* cumulatif(ive).

cunning ['kʌnɪŋ] ◇ *adj* [person] rusé(e) ; [plan, method, device] astucieux(euse) ◇ *n* (*U*) [of person] ruse *f* ; [of plan, method, device] astuce *f*.

cup [kʌp] (*pt* & *pp* -ped ; *cont* -ping) ◇ *n* - **1.** [container, unit of measurement] tasse *f* - **2.** [prize, competition] coupe *f* - **3.** [of bra] bonnet *m* ◇ *vt* [hands] mettre en coupe.

cupboard ['kʌbəd] *n* placard *m*.

Cup Final *n* : **the ~** la finale de la coupe

cup holder *n* SPORT détenteur *m* de la coupe.

cupid ['kju:pɪd] *n* [figure] amour *m*.

cupola ['kju:pələ] (*pl* -s) *n* coupole *f*.

cup tie *n* Br match *m* de coupe.

curable ['kjʊərəbl] *adj* curable, guérissable.

curate ['kjʊərət] *n* vicaire *m*.

curator [ˌkjʊə'reɪtə'] *n* conservateur *m*.

curb [kɜ:b] ◇ *n* - **1.** [control] : **~ (on)** frein *m* (à) - **2.** Am [of road] bord *m* du trottoir ◇ *vt* mettre un frein à.

curd cheese *n* Br ≃ fromage *m* blanc.

curdle ['kɜ:dl] *vi* cailler.

cure [kjʊə'] ◇ *n* : **~ (for)** MED remède *m* (contre) ; fig remède (à) ◇ *vt* - **1.** MED guérir - **2.** [solve - problem] éliminer - **3.** [rid] : **to ~ sb of sthg** guérir qqn de qqch, faire perdre l'habitude de qqch à qqn - **4.** [preserve - by smoking] fumer ; [- by salting] saler ; [- tobacco, hide] sécher.

cure-all *n* panacée *f*.

curfew ['kɜ:fju:] *n* couvre-feu *m*.

curio ['kjʊərɪəʊ] (*pl* -s) *n* bibelot *m*.

curiosity [ˌkjʊərɪ'ɒsətɪ] *n* curiosité *f*.

curious ['kjʊərɪəs] *adj* : **~ (about)** curieux(euse) (à propos de).

curiously ['kjʊərɪəslɪ] *adv* - **1.** [inquisitively] avec curiosité - **2.** [strangely] curieusement ; **~ enough** curieusement, chose curieuse.

curl [kɜ:l] ◇ *n* - **1.** [of hair] boucle *f* - **2.** [of smoke] volute *f* ◇ *vt* - **1.** [hair] boucler - **2.** [roll up] enrouler ◇ *vi* - **1.** [hair] boucler - **2.** [roll up] s'enrouler ; **to ~ into a ball** se mettre en boule.

  ➤ **curl up** *vi* [person, animal] se mettre en boule, se pelotonner.

curler ['kɜ:lə'] *n* bigoudi *m*.

curling ['kɜ:lɪŋ] *n* curling *m*.

curling tongs *npl* fer *m* à friser.

curly ['kɜ:lɪ] (*compar* -ier ; *superl* -iest) *adj* [hair] bouclé(e).

currant ['kʌrənt] *n* [dried grape] raisin *m* de Corinthe, raisin sec.

currency ['kʌrənsɪ] (*pl* -ies) *n* - **1.** [type of money] monnaie *f* - **2.** (*U*) [money] devise *f* - **3.** fml [acceptability] : **to gain ~** s'accréditer.

current ['kʌrənt] ◇ *adj* [price, method] actuel(elle) ; [year, week] en cours ; [boyfriend, girlfriend] du moment ; **~ issue** dernier numéro ◇ *n* - **1.** [of water, air, electricity] courant *m* - **2.** [trend] tendance *f*.

current account *n* Br compte *m* courant.

current affairs *npl* actualité *f*, questions *fpl* d'actualité.

current assets *npl* actif *m* circulant.

current liabilities *npl* passif *m* exigible à court terme.

currently ['kʌrəntlɪ] *adv* actuellement.

curricular [kə'rɪkjələ'] *adj* au programme.

curriculum [kə'rɪkjələm] (*pl* -lums OR -la [-lə]) *n* programme *m* d'études.

curriculum vitae [-'vi:taɪ] (*pl* curricula vitae) *n* curriculum vitae *m*.

curried ['kʌrɪd] *adj* au curry.

curry ['kʌrɪ] (*pl* -ies) *n* curry *m*.

curry powder *n* poudre *f* de curry.

curse [kɜ:s] ◇ *n* - **1.** [evil spell] malédiction *f* ; fig fléau *m* - **2.** [swearword] juron *m* ◇ *vt* maudire ◇ *vi* jurer.

cursor ['kɜ:sə'] *n* COMPUT curseur *m*.

cursory ['kɜ:sərɪ] *adj* superficiel(elle).

curt [kɜ:t] *adj* brusque.

curtail [kɜ:'teɪl] *vt* - **1.** [visit] écourter - **2.** [rights, expenditure] réduire.

curtailment [kɜ:'teɪlmənt] *n* [of rights, expenditure] réduction *f*.

curtain ['kɜ:tn] *n* rideau *m*.

  ➤ **curtain off** *vt sep* [bed] cacher derrière un rideau ; [room] diviser par un rideau.

curtain call *n* rappel *m*.

curtain raiser *n* fig lever *m* de rideau.

curts(e)y ['kɜ:tsɪ] (*pt* & *pp* curtsied) ◇ *n* révérence *f* ◇ *vi* faire une révérence.

curvaceous [kɜ:'veɪʃəs] *adj* inf bien roulé(e).

curvature ['kɜ:vətjə'] *n* courbure *f* ; MED [of spine] déviation *f*.

curve [kɜ:v] ◇ *n* courbe *f* ◇ *vi* faire une courbe.

curved [kɜ:vd] *adj* courbe.

curvy ['kɜ:vɪ] (*compar* -ier ; *superl* -iest) *adj* [line] courbé(e) ; [woman] bien roulée.

cushion ['kʊʃn] ⬦ n coussin m ⬦ vt [fall, blow, effects] amortir ; **to be ~ed against** [inflation, reality] être paré contre.

cushy ['kʊʃɪ] (compar **-ier** ; superl **-iest**) adj inf pépère, peinard(e).

custard ['kʌstəd] n crème f anglaise.

custard pie n tarte f à la crème.

custard powder n crème f anglaise instantanée en poudre.

custodian [kʌ'stəʊdjən] n [of building] gardien m, -enne f; [of museum] conservateur m.

custody ['kʌstədɪ] n - **1.** [of child] garde f - **2.** JUR : **in ~** en garde à vue.

custom ['kʌstəm] n - **1.** [tradition, habit] coutume f - **2.** COMM clientèle f; **thank you for your ~** merci de nous avoir honorés de votre commande.

➡ **customs** n [place] douane f; **to go through ~s** passer (à) la douane.

customary ['kʌstəmrɪ] adj [behaviour] coutumier(ère) ; [way, time] habituel(elle).

custom-built adj fait(e) sur commande OR mesure.

customer ['kʌstəmər] n - **1.** [client] client m, -e f - **2.** inf [person] type m.

customer services npl service m (à la) clientèle.

customize, -ise ['kʌstəmaɪz] vt [make] fabriquer OR assembler sur commande ; [modify] modifier sur commande.

custom-made adj fait(e) sur mesure.

Customs and Excise n Br ≈ service m des contributions indirectes.

customs duty n droit m de douane.

customs officer n douanier m, -ère f.

cut [kʌt] (pt & pp cut ; cont **-ting**) ⬦ n - **1.** [in wood etc] entaille f; [in skin] coupure f - **2.** [of meat] morceau m - **3.** [reduction] : **~ (in)** [taxes, salary, personnel] réduction f (de) ; [film, article] coupure f (dans) - **4.** inf [share] part f - **5.** [of suit, hair] coupe f - **6.** phr : **a ~ above (the rest)** inf supérieur(e) aux autres ⬦ vt - **1.** [gen] couper ; [taxes, costs, workforce] réduire ; **to ~ one's finger** se couper le doigt - **2.** [subj : baby] : **he's cutting a tooth** il fait ses dents - **3.** inf [lecture, class] sécher ⬦ vi - **1.** [gen] couper - **2.** [intersect] se couper.

➡ **cut across** vt fus - **1.** [as short cut] couper à travers - **2.** [transcend] ne pas tenir compte de.

➡ **cut back** ⬦ vt sep - **1.** [prune] tailler - **2.** [reduce] réduire ⬦ vi : **to ~ back on** réduire, diminuer.

➡ **cut down** ⬦ vt sep - **1.** [chop down] couper - **2.** [reduce] réduire, diminuer ⬦ vi : **to ~ down on smoking/eating/spending** fumer/manger/dépenser moins.

➡ **cut in** vi - **1.** [interrupt] : **to ~ in (on sb)** interrompre (qqn) - **2.** AUT & SPORT se rabattre.

➡ **cut off** vt sep - **1.** [piece, crust] couper - **2.** [finger, leg - subj : surgeon] amputer - **3.** [power, telephone, funding] couper - **4.** [separate] : **to be ~ off (from)** [person] être coupé(e) (de) ; [village] être isolé(e) (de).

➡ **cut out** ⬦ vt sep - **1.** [photo, article] découper ; [sewing pattern] couper ; [dress] tailler ; **to be ~ out for sthg** fig [person] être fait pour qqch - **2.** [stop] : **to ~ out smoking/chocolates** arrêter de fumer/de manger des chocolats ; **~ it out!** inf ça suffit! - **3.** [exclude] exclure ⬦ vi [stall] caler.

➡ **cut up** vt sep [chop up] couper, hacher.

cut-and-dried adj tout fait (toute faite).

cut and paste vt & vi COMPUT couper-coller.

cutback ['kʌtbæk] n : **~ (in)** réduction f (de).

cute [kjuːt] adj [appealing] mignon(onne).

cut glass ⬦ n cristal m taillé ⬦ comp en cristal taillé.

cuticle ['kjuːtɪkl] n envie f.

cutlery ['kʌtlərɪ] n (U) couverts mpl.

cutlet ['kʌtlɪt] n côtelette f.

cutoff (point) ['kʌtɒf-] n [limit] point m de limite.

cutout ['kʌtaʊt] n - **1.** [on machine] disjoncteur m - **2.** [shape] découpage m.

cut-price, cut-rate Am adj à prix réduit.

cutter ['kʌtər] n [tool] coupoir m.

cutthroat ['kʌtθrəʊt] adj [ruthless] acharné(e).

cutting ['kʌtɪŋ] ⬦ adj [sarcastic - remark] cinglant(e) ; [- wit] acerbe ⬦ n - **1.** [of plant] bouture f - **2.** [from newspaper] coupure f - **3.** Br [for road, railway] tranchée f.

cuttlefish ['kʌtlfɪʃ] (pl inv) n seiche f.

cut up adj Br inf [upset] affligé(e).

CV (abbr of curriculum vitae) n CV m.

C & W abbr of country and western.

cwo (abbr of cash with order) payable à la commande.

cwt. abbr of hundredweight.

cyanide ['saɪənaɪd] n cyanure m.

cybercafe ['saɪbə,kæfeɪ] n cybercafé m.

cybercrime ['saɪbə,kraɪm] n délinquance f informatique.

cybernaut ['saɪbə,nɔːt] n cybernaute mf.

cybernetics [,saɪbə'netɪks] n (U) cybernétique f.

cyberpet ['saɪbə,pet] n animal m virtuel.

cyberspace ['saɪbəspeɪs] n cyberespace m.

cybersurfer ['saɪbə,sɜːfər] n cybernaute mf.

cyclamen ['sıkləmən] (*pl inv*) *n* cyclamen *m*.

cycle ['saıkl] ⬦ *n* - **1.** [of events, songs] cycle *m* - **2.** [bicycle] bicyclette *f* ⬦ *comp* [path, track] cyclable ; [race] cycliste ; [shop] de cycles ⬦ *vi* faire de la bicyclette.

cyclic(al) ['saıklık(l)] *adj* cyclique.

cycling ['saıklıŋ] *n* cyclisme *m*.

cyclist ['saıklıst] *n* cycliste *mf*.

cyclone ['saıkləʊn] *n* cyclone *m*.

cygnet ['sıgnıt] *n* jeune cygne *m*.

cylinder ['sılındə'] *n* cylindre *m*.

cylinder block *n* bloc-cylindres *m*.

cylinder head *n* culasse *f*.

cylinder-head gasket *n* joint *m* de culasse.

cylindrical [sı'lındrıkl] *adj* cylindrique.

cymbals ['sımblz] *npl* cymbales *fpl*.

cynic ['sınık] *n* cynique *mf*.

cynical ['sınıkl] *adj* cynique.

cynically ['sınıklı] *adv* cyniquement.

cynicism ['sınısızm] *n* cynisme *m*.

CYO (*abbr of* **Catholic Youth Association**) *n* aux États-Unis, association de jeunes catholiques.

cypher ['saıfə'] = **cipher**.

cypress ['saıprəs] *n* cyprès *m*.

Cypriot ['sıprıət] ⬦ *adj* chypriote ⬦ *n* Chypriote *mf;* **Greek/Turkish ~** Chypriote grec (grecque)/turc (turque).

Cyprus ['saıprəs] *n* Chypre *f;* **in ~** à Chypre.

cyst [sıst] *n* kyste *m*.

cystic fibrosis [ˌsıstıkfaı'brəʊsıs] *n* mucoviscidose *f*.

cystitis [sıs'taıtıs] *n* cystite *f*.

cytology [saı'tɒlədʒı] *n* cytologie *f*.

CZ (*abbr of* **canal zone**) *zone du canal de Panama*.

czar [zɑ:'] *n* tsar *m*.

Czech [tʃek] ⬦ *adj* tchèque ⬦ *n* - **1.** [person] Tchèque *mf* - **2.** [language] tchèque *m*.

Czechoslovak [ˌtʃekəs'sləʊvæk] = **Czechoslovakian**.

Czechoslovakia [ˌtʃekəslə'vækıə] *n* Tchécoslovaquie *f;* **in ~** en Tchécoslovaquie.

Czechoslovakian [ˌtʃekəslə'vækıən] ⬦ *adj* tchécoslovaque ⬦ *n* Tchécoslovaque *mf*.

Czech Republic *n* République *f* tchèque.

d¹ (*pl* **d's** OR **ds**), **D** (*pl* **D's** OR **Ds**) [di:] *n* [letter] d *m inv,* D *m inv.*
⬦ **D** ⬦ *n* - **1.** MUS ré *m* - **2.** SCH [mark] D *m inv* ⬦ Am *abbr of* **Democrat, Democratic**.

d² [di:] (*abbr of* **penny**) *symbole du penny anglais jusqu'en 1971.*

d. (*abbr of* **died**) : **~ 1913** mort en 1913.

DA *abbr of* **district attorney**.

dab [dæb] (*pt* & *pp* **-bed** ; *cont* **-bing**) ⬦ *n* [of cream, powder, ointment] petit peu *m;* [of paint] touche *f* ⬦ *vt* - **1.** [skin, wound] tamponner - **2.** [apply - cream, ointment] : **to ~ sthg on** OR **onto** appliquer qqch sur ⬦ *vi* : **to ~ at sthg** tamponner qqch.

dabble ['dæbl] ⬦ *vt* tremper dans l'eau ⬦ *vi* : **to ~ in** toucher un peu à.

dab hand *n* Br : **to be a ~ (at sthg)** être doué(e) (pour qqch).

Dacca ['dækə] *n* Dacca.

dachshund ['dækshʊnd] *n* teckel *m*.

dad [dæd], **daddy** ['dædı] (*pl* **-ies**) *n inf* papa *m*.

daddy longlegs [-'lɒŋlegz] (*pl inv*) *n* faucheur *m*.

daffodil ['dæfədıl] *n* jonquille *f*.

daft [dɑ:ft] *adj inf* stupide, idiot(e).

dagger ['dægə'] *n* poignard *m*.

dahlia ['deıljə] *n* dahlia *m*.

daily ['deılı] (*pl* **-ies**) ⬦ *adj* - **1.** [newspaper, occurrence] quotidien(enne) - **2.** [rate, output] journalier(ère) ⬦ *adv* [happen, write] quotidiennement ; **twice ~** deux fois par jour ⬦ *n* - **1.** [newspaper] quotidien *m* - **2.** esp Br [cleaning woman] femme *f* de ménage.

daintily ['deıntılı] *adv* [made, eat, walk] délicatement ; [dressed] coquettement.

dainty ['deıntı] (*compar* **-ier** ; *superl* **-iest**) *adj* délicat(e).

dairy ['deərı] (*pl* **-ies**) *n* - **1.** [on farm] laiterie *f* - **2.** [shop] crémerie *f*.

dairy cattle *npl* vaches *fpl* laitières.

dairy farm *n* ferme *f* laitière.

dairy products *npl* produits *mpl* laitiers.

dais ['deɪɪs] n estrade f.

daisy ['deɪzɪ] (pl -ies) n [weed] pâquerette f; [cultivated] marguerite f.

daisy wheel n marguerite f.

daisy-wheel printer n imprimante f à marguerite.

Dakar ['dækɑ:] n Dakar.

Dakota [də'kəʊtə] n Dakota m; in ~ dans le Dakota.

dal [dɑ:l] = dhal.

dale [deɪl] n vallée f.

dalmatian [dæl'meɪʃn] n [dog] dalmatien m.

dam [dæm] (pt & pp -med; cont -ming) ⇔ n [across river] barrage m ⇔ vt construire un barrage sur.

◆ **dam up** vt sep endiguer.

damage ['dæmɪdʒ] ⇔ n - 1. [physical harm] dommage m, dégât m - 2. [harmful effect] tort m ⇔ vt - 1. [harm physically] endommager, abîmer - 2. [have harmful effect on] nuire à.

◆ **damages** npl JUR dommages et intérêts mpl.

damaging ['dæmɪdʒɪŋ] adj : ~ (to) préjudiciable (à).

Damascus [də'mæskəs] n Damas.

Dame [deɪm] n Br titre accordé aux femmes titulaires de certaines décorations.

damn [dæm] ⇔ adj inf fichu(e), sacré(e) ⇔ adv inf sacrément ⇔ n inf : **not to give** OR **care a ~ (about sthg)** se ficher pas mal (de qqch) ⇔ vt - 1. RELIG [condemn] damner - 2. inf [curse] : **~ you!** va au diable! ; **~ it!** zut! ⇔ excl inf zut!

damnable ['dæmnəbl] adj dated [appalling] détestable.

damnation [dæm'neɪʃn] n RELIG damnation f.

damned [dæmd] inf ⇔ adj fichu(e), sacré(e) ; **I'm ~ if ...** si tu crois que ... ; **well I'll be** OR **I'm ~!** c'est trop fort!, elle est bien bonne celle-là! ⇔ adv sacrément.

damning ['dæmɪŋ] adj accablant(e).

damp [dæmp] ⇔ adj humide ⇔ n humidité f ⇔ vt [make wet] humecter.

◆ **damp down** vt sep [restrain - unrest, violence] contenir, maîtriser ; [- enthusiasm] refroidir.

damp course n Br couche f d'isolation.

dampen ['dæmpən] vt - 1. [make wet] humecter - 2. fig [emotion] abattre.

damper ['dæmpə'] n - 1. MUS étouffoir m - 2. [for fire] registre m - 3. phr : **to put a ~ on sthg** jeter un froid sur qqch.

dampness ['dæmpnɪs] n humidité f.

damson ['dæmzn] n prune f de Damas.

dance [dɑ:ns] ⇔ n - 1. [gen] danse f - 2. [social event] bal m ⇔ vi danser.

dance floor n piste f de danse.

dancer ['dɑ:nsə'] n danseur m, -euse f.

dancing ['dɑ:nsɪŋ] n (U) danse f.

D and C (abbr of dilation and curettage) n dilatation et curetage.

dandelion ['dændɪlaɪən] n pissenlit m.

dandruff ['dændrʌf] n (U) pellicules fpl.

dandy ['dændɪ] (pl -ies) n dandy m.

Dane [deɪn] n Danois m, -e f.

danger ['deɪndʒə'] n - 1. (U) [possibility of harm] danger m; in ~ en danger ; out of ~ hors de danger - 2. [hazard, risk] : **~ (to)** risque m (pour) ; **to be in ~ of doing sthg** risquer de faire qqch.

danger list n Br : **to be on the ~** être dans un état critique.

danger money n (U) Br prime f de risque.

dangerous ['deɪndʒərəs] adj dangereux(euse).

dangerous driving n JUR conduite f dangereuse.

dangerously ['deɪndʒərəslɪ] adv dangereusement ; **~ ill** gravement malade.

danger zone n zone f dangereuse.

dangle ['dæŋgl] ⇔ vt laisser pendre ⇔ vi pendre.

Danish ['deɪnɪʃ] ⇔ adj danois(e) ⇔ n - 1. [language] danois m - 2. Am = **Danish pastry** ⇔ npl : **the ~** les Danois mpl.

Danish blue n bleu m danois.

Danish pastry n gâteau feuilleté fourré aux fruits.

dank [dæŋk] adj humide et froid(e).

Danube ['dænju:b] n : **the ~** le Danube.

dapper ['dæpə'] adj pimpant(e).

dappled ['dæpld] adj - 1. [light] tacheté(e) - 2. [horse] pommelé(e).

Dardanelles [,dɑːdə'nelz] npl : **the ~** les Dardanelles fpl.

dare [deə'] ⇔ vt - 1. [be brave enough] : **to ~ to do sthg** oser faire qqch - 2. [challenge] : **to ~ sb to do sthg** défier qqn de faire qqch - 3. phr : **I ~ say** je suppose, sans doute ; **how ~ you!** comment osez-vous! ⇔ n défi m ; **to do sthg for a ~** faire qqch par défi.

daredevil ['deə,devl] n casse-cou m inv.

daren't [deənt] = dare not.

Dar es-Salaam [,dɑːressə'lɑːm] n Dar es-Salaam.

daring ['deərɪŋ] ⇔ adj audacieux(euse) ⇔ n audace f.

dark [dɑːk] ⬦ adj - **1.** [room, night] sombre ; **it's getting ~** il commence à faire nuit - **2.** [in colour] foncé(e) - **3.** [dark-haired] brun(e) ; [dark-skinned] basané(e) - **4.** fig [days, thoughts] sombre, triste ; [look] noir(e) ⬦ n - **1.** [darkness] : **the ~** l'obscurité f ; **to be afraid of the ~** avoir peur du noir ; **to be in the ~ about sthg** ignorer tout de qqch - **2.** [night] : **before/after ~** avant/après la tombée de la nuit.

Dark Ages npl : **the ~** le haut Moyen Âge.

darken [ˈdɑːkn] ⬦ vt assombrir ⬦ vi s'assombrir.

dark glasses npl lunettes fpl noires.

dark horse n fig quantité f inconnue.

darkness [ˈdɑːknɪs] n obscurité f.

darkroom [ˈdɑːkrʊm] n chambre f noire.

darling [ˈdɑːlɪŋ] ⬦ adj - **1.** [dear] chéri(e) - **2.** inf [cute] adorable ⬦ n - **1.** [loved person, term of address] chéri m, -e f - **2.** [idol] chouchou m, idole f.

darn [dɑːn] ⬦ n reprise f ⬦ vt repriser ⬦ adj inf sacré(e), satané(e) ⬦ adv inf sacrément ⬦ excl inf zut!

darning [ˈdɑːnɪŋ] n [work] reprisage m.

darning needle n aiguille f à repriser.

dart [dɑːt] ⬦ n - **1.** [arrow] fléchette f - **2.** SEWING pince f ⬦ vt darder ⬦ vi se précipiter.
➡ **darts** n [game] jeu m de fléchettes.

dartboard [ˈdɑːtbɔːd] n cible f de jeu de fléchettes.

dash [dæʃ] ⬦ n - **1.** [of milk, wine] goutte f ; [of cream] soupçon m ; [of salt] pincée f ; [of colour, paint] touche f - **2.** [in punctuation] tiret m - **3.** AUT tableau m de bord - **4.** [rush] : **to make a ~ for** se ruer vers ⬦ vt - **1.** [throw] jeter avec violence - **2.** [hopes] anéantir ⬦ vi se précipiter ; **I must ~!** je dois me sauver!
➡ **dash off** vt sep [write quickly] écrire en vitesse.

dashboard [ˈdæʃbɔːd] n tableau m de bord.

dashing [ˈdæʃɪŋ] adj fringant(e).

dastardly [ˈdæstədlɪ] adj dated lâche.

DAT [dæt] (abbr of **digital audio tape**) n DAT m.

data [ˈdeɪtə] n (U) données fpl.

databank [ˈdeɪtəbæŋk] n banque f de données.

database [ˈdeɪtəbeɪs] n base f de données.

data capture n saisie f de données.

dataglove [ˈdeɪtəglʌv] n gant m numérique.

data processing n traitement m de données.

data protection n COMPUT protection f de l'information.

data transmission n transmission f de données.

date [deɪt] ⬦ n - **1.** [in time] date f ; **to ~** à ce jour - **2.** [appointment] rendez-vous m - **3.** [person] petit ami m, petite amie f - **4.** [fruit] datte f ⬦ vt - **1.** [gen] dater - **2.** [go out with] sortir avec ⬦ vi [go out of fashion] dater.
➡ **date back to, date from** vt fus dater de.

dated [ˈdeɪtɪd] adj qui date.

date line n ligne f de changement de date.

date of birth n date f de naissance.

date stamp n cachet m.

daub [dɔːb] vt : **to ~ sthg with sthg** barbouiller qqch de qqch.

daughter [ˈdɔːtər] n fille f.

daughter-in-law (pl **daughters-in-law**) n belle-fille f.

daunt [dɔːnt] vt intimider.

daunting [ˈdɔːntɪŋ] adj intimidant(e).

dawdle [ˈdɔːdl] vi flâner.

dawn [dɔːn] ⬦ n lit & fig aube f ; **at ~** à l'aube ; **from ~ to dusk** du matin au soir ⬦ vi - **1.** [day] poindre - **2.** [era, period] naître.
➡ **dawn (up)on** vt fus venir à l'esprit de.

dawn chorus n concert m des oiseaux à l'aube.

day [deɪ] n jour m ; [duration] journée f ; **the ~ before** la veille ; **the ~ after** le lendemain ; **the ~ before yesterday** avant-hier ; **the ~ after tomorrow** après-demain ; **any ~ now** d'un jour à l'autre ; **one ~, some ~, one of these ~s** un jour (ou l'autre), un de ces jours ; **~ and night** jour et nuit ; **in my ~** de mon temps ; **in this ~ and age** de nos jours ; **to call it a ~** laisser tomber ; **to make sb's ~** réchauffer le cœur de qqn ; **his ~s are numbered** ses jours sont comptés ; **to save sthg for a rainy ~** garder qqch pour les longues soirées d'hiver ; **to save money for a rainy ~** mettre de l'argent de côté en cas de besoin ; **it's early ~s yet** ce n'est que le début.
➡ **days** adv le jour.

dayboy [ˈdeɪbɔɪ] n Br SCH externe m.

daybreak [ˈdeɪbreɪk] n aube f ; **at ~** à l'aube.

day-care centre n garderie f.

daycentre [ˈdeɪsentər] n Br [for children] garderie f ; [for elderly people] centre de jour pour les personnes du troisième âge.

daydream [ˈdeɪdriːm] ⬦ n rêverie f ⬦ vi rêvasser.

daygirl [ˈdeɪɡɜːl] n Br SCH externe f.

Day-Glo® [ˈdeɪɡləʊ] adj fluorescent(e).

daylight [ˈdeɪlaɪt] n - **1.** [light] lumière f du jour - **2.** [dawn] aube f - **3.** phr : **to scare the (liv-**

ing) ~s out of sb inf faire une peur bleue à qqn.

daylight robbery n : that's ~ inf c'est du vol manifeste.

daylight saving time n heure f d'été.

day nursery n garderie f, crèche f.

day off (pl **days off**) n jour m de congé.

day pupil n Br SCH externe mf.

day release n Br jour de formation.

day return n Br billet aller et retour valable pour une journée.

dayroom ['deɪruːm] n salle f de détente.

day school n externat m.

day shift n équipe f de jour.

daytime ['deɪtaɪm] ◇ n jour m, journée f ◇ comp [television] pendant la journée ; [job, flight] de jour.

day-to-day adj [routine, life] journalier(ère) ; on a ~ basis au jour le jour.

day trip n excursion f d'une journée.

day-tripper n Br excursionniste mf.

daze [deɪz] ◇ n : in a ~ hébété(e), ahuri(e) ◇ vt - **1.** [subj : blow] étourdir - **2.** fig [subj : shock, event] abasourdir, sidérer.

dazed [deɪzd] adj - **1.** [by blow] étourdi(e) - **2.** fig [by shock, event] abasourdi(e), sidéré(e).

dazzle ['dæzl] ◇ n (U) éblouissement m ◇ vt éblouir.

dazzling ['dæzlɪŋ] adj éblouissant(e).

DBE (abbr of **Dame Commander of the Order of the British Empire**) n distinction honorifique britannique pour les femmes.

DBS (abbr of **direct broadcasting by satellite**) n télédiffusion directe par satellite.

DC ◇ n (abbr of **direct current**) courant m continu ◇ abbr of **District of Columbia**.

dd. abbr of **delivered**.

DD (abbr of **Doctor of Divinity**) n docteur en théologie.

D/D abbr of **direct debit**.

D-day ['diːdeɪ] n le jour J.

DDS (abbr of **Doctor of Dental Science**) n docteur en dentisterie.

DDT (abbr of **dichlorodiphenyltrichloro-ethane**) n DDT m.

DE abbr of **Delaware**.

DEA (abbr of **Drug Enforcement Administration**) n agence américaine de lutte contre la drogue.

deacon ['diːkn] n diacre m.

deaconess [ˌdiːkə'nes] n diaconesse f.

deactivate [ˌdiː'æktɪveɪt] vt désamorcer.

dead [ded] ◇ adj - **1.** [not alive, not lively]

mort(e) ; **to shoot sb** ~ abattre qqn ; **he wouldn't be seen** ~ **doing that** il ne ferait cela pour rien au monde - **2.** [numb] engourdi(e) - **3.** [not operating - battery] à plat ; **the telephone's** ~ il n'y a pas de tonalité - **4.** [complete - silence] de mort ; **to come to a** ~ **stop** s'arrêter pile ◇ adv - **1.** [directly, precisely] : ~ **ahead** droit devant soi ; ~ **on time** pile - **2.** [completely] tout à fait ; **to be** ~ **set against sthg** être tout à fait opposé à qqch ; **to be** ~ **set on sthg** vouloir faire qqch à tout prix - **3.** [suddenly] : **to stop** ~ s'arrêter net ◇ n : **in the** ~ **of night/winter** au cœur de la nuit/de l'hiver ◇ npl : **the** ~ les morts mpl.

deadbeat ['dedbiːt] n Am inf flemmard m, -e f.

dead centre n plein milieu m.

dead duck n : **it's a** ~ inf c'est foutu, c'est fichu.

deaden ['dedn] vt [sound] assourdir ; [pain] calmer.

dead end n impasse f.

dead-end job n travail m sans débouchés.

deadhead ['dedhed] vt enlever les fleurs fanées de.

dead heat n arrivée f ex-aequo.

dead letter n fig [rule, law] lettre f morte.

deadline ['dedlaɪn] n dernière limite f.

deadlock ['dedlɒk] n impasse f.

deadlocked ['dedlɒkt] adj dans une impasse.

dead loss n inf : **to be a** ~ [person] être bon (bonne) à rien ; [object] ne rien valoir.

deadly ['dedlɪ] (compar **-ier** ; superl **-iest**) ◇ adj - **1.** [poison, enemy] mortel(elle) - **2.** [accuracy] imparable ◇ adv [boring, serious] tout à fait ; ~ **pale** d'une pâleur mortelle.

deadly nightshade n belladone f.

deadpan ['dedpæn] ◇ adj pince-sans-rire (inv) ◇ adv impassiblement.

Dead Sea n : **the** ~ la mer Morte.

dead wood Br, **deadwood** Am ['dedwʊd] n (U) fig [people] personnes fpl improductives ; [things, material] choses fpl inutiles.

deaf [def] ◇ adj sourd(e) ; **to be** ~ **to sthg** être sourd à qqch ◇ npl : **the** ~ les sourds mpl.

deaf-aid n Br appareil m acoustique.

deaf-and-dumb adj sourd-muet (sourde-muette).

deafen ['defn] vt assourdir.

deafening ['defnɪŋ] adj assourdissant(e).

deaf-mute ◇ adj sourd-muet (sourde-muette) ◇ *n* sourd-muet *m*, sourde-muette *f*.

deafness ['defnıs] *n* surdité *f*.

deal [di:l] (*pt* & *pp* dealt) ◇ *n* - **1.** [quantity] : **a good** OR **great ~** beaucoup ; **a good** OR **great ~ of** beaucoup de, bien de/des - **2.** [business agreement] marché *m*, affaire *f* ; **to do** OR **strike a ~ with sb** conclure un marché avec qqn - **3.** inf [treatment] : **to get a bad ~** ne pas faire une affaire ; **big ~!** et alors!, tu parles! ◇ *vt* - **1.** [strike] : **to ~ sb/sthg a blow, to ~ a blow to sb/sthg** porter un coup à qqn/qqch - **2.** [cards] donner, distribuer ◇ *vi* - **1.** [at cards] donner, distribuer - **2.** [in drugs] faire le trafic (de drogues).

◆ **deal in** *vt fus* COMM faire le commerce de.

◆ **deal out** *vt sep* distribuer.

◆ **deal with** *vt fus* - **1.** [handle] s'occuper de - **2.** [be about] traiter de - **3.** [be faced with] avoir affaire à.

dealer ['di:lə'] *n* - **1.** [trader] négociant *m* ; [in drugs] trafiquant *m* - **2.** [cards] donneur *m*.

dealership ['di:ləʃɪp] *n* concession *f*

dealing ['di:lɪŋ] *n* commerce *m*.

◆ **dealings** *npl* relations *fpl*, rapports *mpl*.

dealt [delt] *pt* & *pp* ▷ **deal**.

dean [di:n] *n* doyen *m*.

dear [dɪə'] ◇ *adj* : **~ (to)** cher (chère) (à) ; **Dear Sir** [in letter] Cher Monsieur ; **Dear Madam** Chère Madame ◇ *n* chéri *m*, -e *f* ◇ *excl* : **oh ~!** mon Dieu!

dearly ['dɪəlɪ] *adv* [love, wish] de tout son cœur.

dearth [dɜ:θ] *n* pénurie *f*.

death [deθ] *n* mort *f* ; **to be put to ~** être mis à mort, être exécuté ; **to frighten sb to ~** faire une peur bleue à qqn ; **to worry sb to ~** rendre qqn fou d'inquiétude ; **to be sick to ~ of sthg/of doing sthg** en avoir marre de qqch/de faire qqch ; **to be at ~'s door** être à l'article de la mort.

deathbed ['deθbed] *n* lit *m* de mort.

death certificate *n* acte *m* de décès.

death duty Br, **death tax** Am *n* droits *mpl* de succession.

death knell *n* glas *m*.

deathly ['deθlı] (*compar* -ier ; *superl* -iest) ◇ *adj* de mort ◇ *adv* comme la mort.

death penalty *n* peine *f* de mort.

death rate *n* taux *m* de mortalité.

death row *n* Am quartier *m* des condamnés à mort.

death sentence *n* condamnation *f* à mort.

death squad *n* escadron *m* de la mort.

death tax Am = **death duty**.

death toll *n* nombre *m* de morts.

death trap *n* inf véhicule *m*/bâtiment *m* dangereux.

Death Valley *n* la Vallée de la Mort.

deathwatch beetle *n* vrillette *f*.

death wish *n* désir *m* de mort.

deb [deb] *n* Br inf débutante *f*.

débâcle [de'bɑ:kl] *n* débâcle *f*.

debar [di:'bɑ:'] (*pt* & *pp* -red ; *cont* -ring) *vt* : **to ~ sb (from)** [place] exclure qqn (de) ; **to ~ sb from doing sthg** interdire à qqn de faire qqch.

debase [dɪ'beɪs] *vt* dégrader ; **to ~ o.s.** s'avilir.

debasement [dɪ'beɪsmənt] *n* dégradation *f* ; [of person] avilissement *m*.

debatable [dɪ'beɪtəbl] *adj* discutable, contestable.

debate [dɪ'beɪt] ◇ *n* débat *m* ; **open to ~** discutable ◇ *vt* débattre, discuter ; **to ~ whether** s'interroger pour savoir si ◇ *vi* débattre.

debating society [dɪ'beɪtɪŋ-] *n* club *m* de débats.

debauched [dɪ'bɔ:tʃt] *adj* débauché(e).

debauchery [dɪ'bɔ:tʃərɪ] *n* débauche *f*.

debenture [dɪ'bentʃə'] *n* obligation *f* (sans garantie).

debenture stock *n* Br capital *m* obligations.

debilitate [dɪ'bɪlɪteɪt] *vt* débiliter, affaiblir.

debilitating [dɪ'bɪlɪteɪtɪŋ] *adj* débilitant(e).

debility [dɪ'bɪlətɪ] *n* débilité *f*, faiblesse *f*.

debit ['debɪt] ◇ *n* débit *m* ◇ *vt* débiter.

debit card *n* carte *f* de paiement à débit immédiat.

debit note *n* note *f* de débit.

debonair [,debə'neə'] *adj* fringant(e).

debrief [,di:'bri:f] *vt* faire faire un compte-rendu de mission à.

debriefing [,di:'bri:fɪŋ] *n* compte-rendu *m* (de mission).

debris ['deɪbri:] *n* (U) débris *mpl*.

debt [det] *n* dette *f* ; **to be in ~** avoir des dettes, être endetté(e) ; **to be in sb's ~** être redevable à qqn.

debt collector *n* agent *m* de recouvrements.

debtor ['detə'] *n* débiteur *m*, -trice *f*.

debug [,di:'bʌg] (*pt* & *pp* -ged ; *cont* -ging) *vt* - **1.** [room] enlever les micros cachés dans - **2.** COMPUT [program] mettre au point, déboguer.

debunk [,diː'bʌŋk] vt démentir.

debut ['deɪbjuː] n débuts mpl.

debutante ['debjutɑːnt] n débutante f.

Dec. (abbr of **December**) déc.

decade ['dekeɪd] n décennie f.

decadence ['dekədəns] n décadence f.

decadent ['dekədənt] adj décadent(e).

decaff ['diːkæf] n inf déca m.

decaffeinated [dɪ'kæfɪneɪtɪd] adj décaféiné(e).

decal ['diːkæl] n Am décalcomanie f.

decamp [dɪ'kæmp] vi inf décamper, filer.

decant [dɪ'kænt] vt décanter.

decanter [dɪ'kæntəʳ] n carafe f.

decapitate [dɪ'kæpɪteɪt] vt décapiter.

decathlete [dɪ'kæθliːt] n décathlonien m.

decathlon [dɪ'kæθlɒn] n décathlon m.

decay [dɪ'keɪ] ⬦ n - **1.** [of body, plant] pourriture f, putréfaction f ; [of tooth] carie f - **2.** fig [of building] délabrement m ; [of society] décadence f ⬦ vi - **1.** [rot] pourrir ; [tooth] se carier - **2.** fig [building] se délabrer, tomber en ruines ; [society] tomber en décadence.

deceased [dɪ'siːst] (pl inv) ⬦ adj décédé(e) ⬦ n : **the ~** le défunt, la défunte.

deceit [dɪ'siːt] n tromperie f, supercherie f.

deceitful [dɪ'siːtfʊl] adj trompeur(euse), fourbe.

deceive [dɪ'siːv] vt [person] tromper, duper ; [subj : memory, eyes] jouer des tours à ; **to ~ o.s.** se leurrer, s'abuser.

decelerate [,diː'seləreɪt] vi ralentir.

December [dɪ'sembəʳ] n décembre m ; see also **September**.

decency ['diːsnsɪ] n décence f, bienséance f ; **to have the ~ to do sthg** avoir la décence de faire qqch.

decent ['diːsnt] adj - **1.** [behaviour, dress] décent(e) - **2.** [wage, meal] correct(e), décent(e) - **3.** [person] gentil(ille), brave.

decently ['diːsntlɪ] adv - **1.** [properly] décemment, convenablement - **2.** [adequately] correctement.

decentralization [diː,sentrəlaɪ'zeɪʃn] n décentralisation f.

decentralize, -ise [,diː'sentrəlaɪz] vt décentraliser.

deception [dɪ'sepʃn] n - **1.** [lie, pretence] tromperie f, duperie f - **2.** (U) [act of lying] supercherie f.

deceptive [dɪ'septɪv] adj trompeur(euse).

deceptively [dɪ'septɪvlɪ] adv en apparence.

decibel ['desɪbel] n décibel m.

decide [dɪ'saɪd] ⬦ vt décider ; **to ~ to do sthg** décider de faire qqch ⬦ vi se décider.
➤ **decide (up)on** vt fus se décider pour, choisir.

decided [dɪ'saɪdɪd] adj - **1.** [definite] certain(e), incontestable - **2.** [resolute] décidé(e), résolu(e).

decidedly [dɪ'saɪdɪdlɪ] adv - **1.** [clearly] manifestement, incontestablement - **2.** [resolutely] résolument.

deciding [dɪ'saɪdɪŋ] adj : **~ vote** vote m décisif.

deciduous [dɪ'sɪdjʊəs] adj à feuilles caduques.

decimal ['desɪml] ⬦ adj décimal(e) ⬦ n décimale f.

decimal currency n monnaie f décimale.

decimalize, -ise ['desɪ.məlaɪz] vt Br décimaliser.

decimal place n décimale f.

decimal point n virgule f.

decimate ['desɪmeɪt] vt décimer.

decimation [,desɪ'meɪʃn] n décimation f.

decipher [dɪ'saɪfəʳ] vt déchiffrer.

decision [dɪ'sɪʒn] n décision f ; **to make a ~** prendre une décision.

decision-making n prise f de décisions.

decisive [dɪ'saɪsɪv] adj - **1.** [person] déterminé(e), résolu(e) - **2.** [factor, event] décisif(ive).

decisively [dɪ'saɪsɪvlɪ] adv - **1.** [speak] d'un ton décidé ; [act] avec décision - **2.** [considerably, definitely] nettement, bien.

decisiveness [dɪ'saɪsɪvnɪs] n fermeté f, résolution f.

deck [dek] ⬦ n - **1.** [of ship] pont m - **2.** [of bus] impériale f - **3.** [of cards] jeu m - **4.** Am [of house] véranda f ⬦ vt [decorate] : **to ~ sthg with** parer OR orner qqch de.
➤ **deck out** vt sep agrémenter, parer.

deckchair ['dektʃeəʳ] n chaise longue f, transat m.

deckhand ['dekhænd] n matelot m.

declaration [,deklə'reɪʃn] n déclaration f.

Declaration of Independence n : **the ~** la Déclaration d'Indépendance des États-Unis d'Amérique (1776).

declare [dɪ'kleəʳ] vt déclarer.

declared [dɪ'kleəd] adj [intention, supporter] avoué(e), déclaré(e).

declassify [,diː'klæsɪfaɪ] (pt & pp **-ied**) vt rayer de la liste des documents secrets.

decline [dɪ'klaɪn] ⬦ n déclin m ; **to be in ~** être en déclin ; **on the ~** en baisse ⬦ vt décliner ; **to ~ to do sthg** refuser de faire qqch

⇔ *vi* - **1.** [deteriorate] décliner - **2.** [refuse] refuser.

declutch [dɪˈklʌtʃ] *vi* débrayer.

decode [ˌdiːˈkəʊd] *vt* décoder.

decoder [ˌdiːˈkəʊdəʳ] *n* décodeur *m*.

decommission [ˌdiːkəˈmɪʃn] *vt* mettre hors service.

decompose [ˌdiːkəmˈpəʊz] *vi* se décomposer.

decomposition [ˌdiːkɒmpəˈzɪʃn] *n* décomposition *f*.

decompression chamber [ˌdiːkəmˈpreʃn-] *n* caisson *m* de décompression.

decompression sickness [ˌdiːkəmˈpreʃn-] *n* maladie *f* des caissons.

decongestant [ˌdiːkənˈdʒestənt] *n* décongestionnant *m*.

decontaminate [ˌdiːkənˈtæmɪneɪt] *vt* décontaminer.

décor [ˈdeɪkɔːʳ] *n* décor *m*.

decorate [ˈdekəreɪt] *vt* décorer.

decoration [ˌdekəˈreɪʃn] *n* décoration *f*.

decorative [ˈdekərətɪv] *adj* décoratif(ive).

decorator [ˈdekəreɪtəʳ] *n* décorateur *m*, -trice *f*.

decorous [ˈdekərəs] *adj* bienséant(e), convenable.

decorum [dɪˈkɔːrəm] *n* décorum *m*.

decoy [*n* ˈdiːkɔɪ, *vt* dɪˈkɔɪ] ⇔ *n* [for hunting] appât *m*, leurre *m* ; [person] compère *m* ⇔ *vt* attirer dans un piège.

decrease [*n* ˈdiːkriːs, *vb* dɪˈkriːs] ⇔ *n* : ~ (in) diminution *f* (de), baisse *f* (de) ⇔ *vt* diminuer, réduire ⇔ *vi* diminuer, décroître.

decreasing [diːˈkriːsɪŋ] *adj* qui diminue, décroissant(e).

decree [dɪˈkriː] ⇔ *n* - **1.** [order, decision] décret *m* - **2.** Am JUR arrêt *m*, jugement *m* ⇔ *vt* décréter, ordonner.

decree absolute (*pl* **decrees absolute**) *n* Br jugement *m* définitif.

decree nisi [-ˈnaɪsaɪ] (*pl* **decrees nisi**) *n* Br jugement *m* provisoire.

decrepit [dɪˈkrepɪt] *adj* [person] décrépit(e) ; [house] délabré(e).

decry [dɪˈkraɪ] (*pt* & *pp* **-ied**) *vt* décrier, dénigrer.

dedicate [ˈdedɪkeɪt] *vt* - **1.** [book etc] dédier - **2.** [life, career] consacrer ; **to ~ o.s. to sthg** se consacrer à qqch.

dedicated [ˈdedɪkeɪtɪd] *adj* - **1.** [person] dévoué(e) - **2.** COMPUT spécialisé(e).

dedication [ˌdedɪˈkeɪʃn] *n* - **1.** [commitment] dévouement *m* - **2.** [in book] dédicace *f*.

deduce [dɪˈdjuːs] *vt* déduire, conclure.

deduct [dɪˈdʌkt] *vt* déduire, retrancher.

deduction [dɪˈdʌkʃn] *n* déduction *f*.

deed [diːd] *n* - **1.** [action] action *f*, acte *m* - **2.** JUR acte *m* notarié.

deed poll (*pl* **deed polls** OR **deeds poll**) *n* Br : **to change one's name by ~** changer de nom légalement OR officiellement.

deem [diːm] *vt* juger, considérer ; **to ~ it wise to do sthg** juger prudent de faire qqch.

deep [diːp] ⇔ *adj* profond(e) ; **to be thrown in at the ~ end** fig recevoir le baptême du feu ⇔ *adv* profondément ; **feelings were running ~** les sentiments se sont exacerbés ; **~ down** [fundamentally] au fond ; **to be ~ in thought** être perdu(e) dans ses pensées.

deepen [ˈdiːpn] ⇔ *vt* [hole, channel] creuser ⇔ *vi* - **1.** [river, sea] devenir profond(e) - **2.** [crisis, recession, feeling] s'aggraver - **3.** [darkness] augmenter.

deepening [ˈdiːpnɪŋ] *adj* [crisis, recession] qui s'aggrave.

deep freeze *n* congélateur *m*.

➤ **deep-freeze** *vt* congeler.

deep fry *vt* faire frire.

deeply [ˈdiːplɪ] *adv* profondément.

deep-rooted *adj* [prejudice] ancré(e), enraciné(e) ; [hatred] vivace, tenace ; [affection] profond(e).

deep-sea *adj* : **~ diving** plongée *f* sous-marine ; **~ fishing** pêche *f* hauturière.

deep-seated [ˈsiːtɪd] *adj* [belief, fear] profond(e), enraciné(e).

deer [dɪəʳ] (*pl inv*) *n* cerf *m*.

deerstalker [ˈdɪəˌstɔːkəʳ] *n* [hat] casquette *f* de chasse.

de-escalate [ˌdiːˈeskəleɪt] ⇔ *vt* faire diminuer ⇔ *vi* diminuer.

deface [dɪˈfeɪs] *vt* barbouiller.

defamation [ˌdefəˈmeɪʃn] *n* diffamation *f*.

defamatory [dɪˈfæmətrɪ] *adj* diffamatoire, diffamant(e).

default [dɪˈfɔːlt] ⇔ *n* - **1.** [failure] défaillance *f* ; **by ~** par défaut - **2.** COMPUT valeur *f* par défaut ⇔ *comp* COMPUT implicite, par défaut ⇔ *vi* manquer à ses engagements ; **to ~ on** manquer à.

defaulter [dɪˈfɔːltəʳ] *n* partie *f* défaillante.

default value *n* COMPUT valeur *f* par défaut.

defeat [dɪˈfiːt] ⇔ *n* défaite *f* ; **to admit ~** s'avouer battu(e) OR vaincu(e) ⇔ *vt*

- **1.** [team, opponent] vaincre, battre - **2.** [motion, proposal] rejeter - **3.** [plans] faire échouer.

defeatism [dɪ'fiːtɪzm] n défaitisme m.

defeatist [dɪ'fiːtɪst] <> adj défaitiste <> n défaitiste mf.

defecate ['defəkeɪt] vi déféquer.

defect [n 'diːfekt, vi dɪ'fekt] <> n défaut m <> vi : **to ~ to** passer à.

defection [dɪ'fekʃn] n défection f.

defective [dɪ'fektɪv] adj défectueux(euse).

defector [dɪ'fektəʳ] n transfuge mf.

defence Br, **defense** Am [dɪ'fens] n - **1.** [gen] défense f - **2.** [protective device, system] protection f - **3.** JUR : **the ~** la défense ; **he said in ~ that** ... il a répondu pour sa défense que ...

➡ **defences** npl [of country] moyens mpl de défense.

defenceless Br, **defenseless** Am [dɪ'fenslɪs] adj sans défense.

defend [dɪ'fend] <> vt défendre ; **to ~ o.s.** se défendre <> vi SPORT défendre.

defendant [dɪ'fendənt] n défendeur m, -eresse f ; [in trial] accusé m, -e f.

defender [dɪ'fendəʳ] n défenseur m.

defense Am = defence.

defenseless Am = defenceless.

defensive [dɪ'fensɪv] <> adj défensif(ive) <> n : **on the ~** sur la défensive.

defer [dɪ'fɜːʳ] (pt & pp -red ; cont -ring) <> vt différer <> vi : **to ~ to sb** s'en remettre à (l'opinion de) qqn.

deference ['defərəns] n déférence f.

deferential [,defə'renʃl] adj respectueux(euse).

defiance [dɪ'faɪəns] n défi m ; **in ~ of** au mépris de.

defiant [dɪ'faɪənt] adj [person] intraitable, intransigeant(e) ; [action] de défi.

defiantly [dɪ'faɪəntlɪ] adv [say] d'un ton de défi.

deficiency [dɪ'fɪʃnsɪ] (pl -ies) n - **1.** [lack] manque m ; [of vitamins etc] carence f - **2.** [inadequacy] imperfection f, défaut m.

deficient [dɪ'fɪʃnt] adj - **1.** [lacking] : **to be ~ in** manquer de - **2.** [inadequate] insuffisant(e), médiocre.

deficit ['defɪsɪt] n déficit m.

defile [dɪ'faɪl] vt souiller, salir.

define [dɪ'faɪn] vt définir.

definite ['defɪnɪt] adj - **1.** [plan] bien déterminé(e) ; [date] certain(e) - **2.** [improvement, difference] net (nette), marqué(e) - **3.** [answer] pré-

cis(e), catégorique - **4.** [confident - person] assuré(e).

definitely ['defɪnɪtlɪ] adv - **1.** [without doubt] sans aucun doute, certainement - **2.** [for emphasis] catégoriquement.

definition [defɪ'nɪʃn] n - **1.** [gen] définition f - **2.** [clarity] clarté f, précision f.

definitive [dɪ'fɪnɪtɪv] adj définitif(ive).

deflate [dɪ'fleɪt] <> vt - **1.** [balloon, tyre] dégonfler - **2.** fig [person] rabaisser, humilier - **3.** ECON provoquer la déflation de <> vi [balloon, tyre] se dégonfler.

deflation [dɪ'fleɪʃn] n ECON déflation f.

deflationary [dɪ'fleɪʃnərɪ] adj [policy] de déflation ; [measure] déflationniste.

deflect [dɪ'flekt] vt [ball, bullet] dévier ; [stream] détourner, dériver ; [criticism] détourner.

deflection [dɪ'flekʃn] n [of ball, bullet] déviation f ; [of stream] dérivation f, détournement m.

defog [,diː'fɒg] vt Am AUT désembuer.

defogger [,diː'fɒgəʳ] n Am AUT dispositif m antibuée.

deforest [,diː'fɒrɪst] vt déboiser.

deforestation [diː,fɒrɪ'steɪʃn] n déforestation f, déboisement m.

deform [dɪ'fɔːm] vt déformer.

deformed [dɪ'fɔːmd] adj difforme.

deformity [dɪ'fɔːmətɪ] (pl -ies) n difformité f, malformation f.

defraud [dɪ'frɔːd] vt [person] escroquer ; [Inland Revenue etc] frauder.

defray [dɪ'freɪ] vt [costs] couvrir ; [expenses] rembourser.

defrost [,diː'frɒst] <> vt - **1.** [fridge] dégivrer ; [frozen food] décongeler - **2.** Am [AUT - de-ice] dégivrer ; [- demist] désembuer <> vi [fridge] dégivrer ; [frozen food] se décongeler.

deft [deft] adj adroit(e).

deftly ['deftlɪ] adv adroitement.

defunct [dɪ'fʌŋkt] adj qui n'existe plus ; [person] défunt(e).

defuse [,diː'fjuːz] vt Br désamorcer.

defy [dɪ'faɪ] (pt & pp -ied) vt - **1.** [gen] défier ; **to ~ sb to do sthg** mettre qqn au défi de faire qqch - **2.** [efforts] résister à, faire échouer.

degenerate [adj & n dɪ'dʒenərət, vb dɪ'dʒenəreɪt] <> adj dégénéré(e) <> n dégénéré m, -e f <> vi : **to ~ (into)** dégénérer (en).

degradation [,degrə'deɪʃn] n [of person] déchéance f ; [of place] dégradation f.

degrade [dɪ'greɪd] vt [person] avilir.

degrading [dɪ'greɪdɪŋ] adj dégradant(e), avilissant(e).

degree [dɪ'gri:] n - **1.** [measurement] degré m - **2.** UNIV diplôme m universitaire ; **to have/ take a ~ (in)** avoir/faire une licence (de) - **3.** [amount] : **to a certain ~** jusqu'à un certain point, dans une certaine mesure ; **a ~ of risk** un certain risque ; **a ~ of truth** une certaine part de vérité ; **by ~s** progressivement, petit à petit.

dehumanize [diː'hjuːmənaɪz], **-ise** vt déshumaniser.

dehydrated [ˌdiːhaɪ'dreɪtɪd] adj déshydraté(e).

dehydration [ˌdiːhaɪ'dreɪʃn] n déshydratation f.

de-ice [diː'aɪs] vt dégivrer.

de-icer [diː'aɪsəʳ] n dégivreur m.

deign [deɪn] vt : **to ~ to do sthg** daigner faire qqch.

deity ['diːɪtɪ] (pl -ies) n dieu m, déesse f, divinité f.

déjà vu [ˌdeʒɑː'vjuː] n déjà vu m.

dejected [dɪ'dʒektɪd] adj abattu(e), découragé(e).

dejection [dɪ'dʒekʃn] n abattement m, découragement m.

del. (abbr of delete) [on keyboard] suppr.

Del. abbr of Delaware.

Delaware ['deləweəʳ] n Delaware m ; **in ~** dans le Delaware.

delay [dɪ'leɪ] ⬦ n retard m, délai m ; **without ~** sans délai ⬦ vt - **1.** [cause to be late] retarder - **2.** [defer] différer ; **to ~ doing sthg** tarder à faire qqch ⬦ vi : **to ~ (in doing sthg)** tarder (à faire qqch).

delayed [dɪ'leɪd] adj : **to be ~** [person, train] être retardé(e).

delayed-action [dɪ'leɪd-] adj [response] après coup ; **~ shutter** PHOT dispositif m à retardement.

delectable [dɪ'lektəbl] adj délicieux(euse).

delegate [n 'delɪgət, vb 'delɪgeɪt] ⬦ n délégué m, -e f ⬦ vt déléguer ; **to ~ sb to do sthg** déléguer qqn pour faire qqch ; **to ~ sthg to sb** déléguer qqch à qqn ⬦ vi déléguer.

delegation [ˌdelɪ'geɪʃn] n délégation f.

delete [dɪ'liːt] vt supprimer, effacer.

deletion [dɪ'liːʃn] n suppression f, effacement m.

Delhi ['delɪ] n Delhi.

deli ['delɪ] n inf abbr of delicatessen.

deliberate [adj dɪ'lɪbərət, vb dɪ'lɪbəreɪt] ⬦ adj - **1.** [intentional] voulu(e), délibéré(e) - **2.** [slow] lent(e), sans hâte ⬦ vi délibérer.

deliberately [dɪ'lɪbərətlɪ] adv - **1.** [on purpose] exprès, à dessein - **2.** [slowly] posément, sans se presser.

deliberation [dɪˌlɪbə'reɪʃn] n - **1.** [consideration] délibération f - **2.** [slowness] mesure f.

⬦ **deliberations** npl délibérations fpl, discussions fpl.

delicacy ['delɪkəsɪ] (pl -ies) n - **1.** [gen] délicatesse f - **2.** [food] mets m délicat.

delicate ['delɪkət] adj délicat(e) ; [movement] gracieux(euse).

delicately ['delɪkətlɪ] adv - **1.** [gen] délicatement ; [move] gracieusement, avec grâce - **2.** [tactfully] avec délicatesse, subtilement.

delicatessen [ˌdelɪkə'tesn] n épicerie f fine.

delicious [dɪ'lɪʃəs] adj délicieux(euse).

delight [dɪ'laɪt] ⬦ n - **1.** [great pleasure] délice m ; **to take ~ in doing sthg** prendre grand plaisir à faire qqch - **2.** [wonderful thing, person] : **she's a ~ to work with** c'est un plaisir de travailler avec elle ; **a ~ to the eyes** un régal pour les yeux ⬦ vt enchanter, charmer ⬦ vi : **to ~ in sthg/in doing sthg** prendre grand plaisir à qqch/à faire qqch.

delighted [dɪ'laɪtɪd] adj : **~ (by OR with)** enchanté(e) (de), ravi(e) (de) ; **to be ~ that** être enchanté OR ravi que ; **to be ~ to do sthg** être enchanté OR ravi de faire qqch.

delightful [dɪ'laɪtfʊl] adj ravissant(e), charmant(e) ; [meal] délicieux(euse).

delightfully [dɪ'laɪtfʊlɪ] adv d'une façon charmante.

delimit [diː'lɪmɪt] vt délimiter.

delineate [dɪ'lɪnɪeɪt] vt exposer, énoncer.

delinquency [dɪ'lɪŋkwənsɪ] n délinquance f.

delinquent [dɪ'lɪŋkwənt] ⬦ adj délinquant(e) ⬦ n délinquant m, -e f.

delirious [dɪ'lɪrɪəs] adj lit & fig délirant(e).

delirium [dɪ'lɪrɪəm] n délire m.

deliver [dɪ'lɪvəʳ] ⬦ vt - **1.** [distribute] : **to ~ sthg (to sb)** [mail, newspaper] distribuer qqch (à qqn) ; COMM livrer qqch (à qqn) - **2.** [speech] faire ; [warning] donner ; [message] remettre ; [blow, kick] donner, porter - **3.** [baby] mettre au monde - **4.** [free] délivrer - **5.** AM POL [votes] obtenir ⬦ vi - **1.** COMM livrer - **2.** [fulfil promise] tenir sa promesse.

deliverance [dɪ'lɪvərəns] n délivrance f.

delivery [dɪ'lɪvərɪ] (pl -ies) n - **1.** COMM livraison f - **2.** [way of speaking] élocution f - **3.** [birth] accouchement m.

delivery note n bulletin m de livraison.

delivery van Br, **delivery truck** Am n camionnette f de livraison.

delphinium [del'fɪnɪəm] (pl -s) n delphinium m, pied-d'alouette m.

delta ['deltə] (*pl* -s) *n* delta *m*.

delude [dɪ'luːd] *vt* tromper, induire en erreur ; **to ~ o.s.** se faire des illusions.

deluge ['deljuːdʒ] <> *n* déluge *m* ; fig avalanche *f* <> *vt* : **to be ~d with** être débordé(e) OR submergé(e) de.

delusion [dɪ'luːʒn] *n* illusion *f* ; **~s of grandeur** folie *f* des grandeurs.

de luxe [də'lʌks] *adj* de luxe.

delve [delv] *vi* : **to ~ into** [past] fouiller ; [bag etc] fouiller dans.

Dem. *abbr of* **Democrat, Democratic**.

demagogue ['demagɒg] *n* démagogue *m*.

demand [dɪ'maːnd] <> *n* - **1.** [claim, firm request] revendication *f*, exigence *f* ; **wage ~** revendication salariale ; **on ~** sur demande - **2.** [need] : **~ (for)** demande *f* (de) ; **in ~** demandé(e), recherché(e) <> *vt* - **1.** [ask for - justice, money] réclamer ; [- explanation, apology] exiger ; **to ~ to do sthg** exiger de faire qqch - **2.** [require] demander, exiger.

demanding [dɪ'maːndɪŋ] *adj* - **1.** [exhausting] astreignant(e) - **2.** [not easily satisfied] exigeant(e).

demarcation [ˌdiːmaː'keɪʃn] *n* démarcation *f*.

demarcation dispute *n* conflit *m* de compétence.

dematerialize, -ise [diːmə'tɪərɪəlaɪz] *vi* se volatiliser.

demean [dɪ'miːn] *vt* avilir, déshonorer ; **to ~ o.s.** s'abaisser.

demeaning [dɪ'miːnɪŋ] *adj* avilissant(e), dégradant(e).

demeanour Br, **demeanor** Am [dɪ'miːnəʳ] *n* (U) fml comportement *m*.

demented [dɪ'mentɪd] *adj* fou (folle), dément(e).

dementia [dɪ'menʃə] *n* démence *f*.

demerara sugar [ˌdemə'reərə-] *n* Br cassonade *f*.

demigod ['demɪgɒd] *n* demi-dieu *m*.

demijohn ['demɪdʒɡt·n] *n* dame-jeanne *f*, bonbonne *f*.

demilitarized zone, demilitarised zone [ˌdiː'mɪlɪtəraɪzd-] *n* zone *f* démilitarisée.

demise [dɪ'maɪz] *n* (U) décès *m* ; fig mort *f*, fin *f*.

demist [ˌdiː'mɪst] *vt* Br désembuer.

demister [ˌdiː'mɪstəʳ] *n* Br dispositif *m* antibuée.

demo ['demǝʊ] (*abbr of* **demonstration**) *n* inf manif *f*.

demobilize, -ise [ˌdiː'mǝʊbɪlaɪz] *vt* démobiliser.

democracy [dɪ'mɒkrǝsɪ] (*pl* -ies) *n* démocratie *f*.

democrat ['deməkræt] *n* démocrate *mf*.
→ **Democrat** *n* Am démocrate *mf*.

democratic [ˌdemə'krætɪk] *adj* démocratique.
→ **Democratic** *adj* Am démocrate.

democratically [ˌdemə'krætɪklɪ] *adv* démocratiquement.

Democratic Party *n* Am : **the ~** le Parti démocrate.

democratize, -ise [dɪ'mɒkrǝtaɪz] *vt* démocratiser.

demographic [ˌdemə'græfɪk] *adj* démographique.

demolish [dɪ'mɒlɪʃ] *vt* - **1.** [destroy] démolir - **2.** inf [eat] engloutir, engouffrer.

demolition [ˌdemə'lɪʃn] *n* démolition *f*.

demon ['diːmən] <> *n* [evil spirit] démon *m* <> *comp* inf : **~ driver/chess player** as du volant/des échecs.

demonstrable [dɪ'mɒnstrəbl] *adj* démontrable.

demonstrably [dɪ'mɒnstrəblɪ] *adv* manifestement.

demonstrate ['demənstreɪt] <> *vt* - **1.** [prove] démontrer, prouver - **2.** [machine, computer] faire une démonstration de <> *vi* : **to ~ (for/against)** manifester (pour/contre).

demonstration [demən'streɪʃn] *n* - **1.** [of machine, emotions] démonstration *f* - **2.** [public meeting] manifestation *f*.

demonstrative [dɪ'mɒnstrətɪv] *adj* expansif(ive), démonstratif(ive).

demonstrator ['demənstreɪtəʳ] *n* - **1.** [in march] manifestant *m*, -e *f* - **2.** [of machine, product] démonstrateur *m*, -trice *f*.

demoralize, -ise [dɪ'mɒrəlaɪz] *vt* démoraliser.

demoralized [dɪ'mɒrəlaɪzd] *adj* démoralisé(e).

demote [ˌdiː'mǝʊt] *vt* rétrograder.

demotion [ˌdiː'mǝʊʃn] *n* rétrogradation *f*.

demotivate [ˌdiː'mǝʊtɪveɪt] *vt* démotiver.

demure [dɪ'mjʊəʳ] *adj* modeste, réservé(e).

demystify [ˌdiː'mɪstɪfaɪ] (*pt* & *pp* -ied) *vt* démystifier.

den [den] *n* [of animal] antre *m*, tanière *f*.

denationalization ['diːˌnæʃnǝlaɪ'zeɪʃn] *n* dénationalisation *f*.

denationalize, -ise [ˌdiː'næʃnǝlaɪz] *vt* dénationaliser.

denial [dɪ'naɪəl] *n* [of rights, facts, truth] dénégation *f*; [of accusation] démenti *m*.
denier ['denɪəʳ] *n* denier *m*.
denigrate ['denɪgreɪt] *vt* dénigrer.
denim ['denɪm] *n* jean *m*.
➤ **denims** *npl* : a pair of ~s un jean.
denim jacket *n* veste *f* en jean.
denizen ['denɪzn] *n* literary OR hum habitant *m*,
-e *f*.
Denmark ['denmɑːk] *n* Danemark *m*; in ~ au
Danemark.
denomination [dɪ,nɒmɪ'neɪʃn] *n* - **1.** RELIG
confession *f* - **2.** [money] valeur *f*.
denominator [dɪ'nɒmɪneɪtəʳ] *n* dénominateur *m*.
denote [dɪ'nəʊt] *vt* dénoter.
denounce [dɪ'naʊns] *vt* dénoncer.
dense [dens] *adj* - **1.** [crowd, forest] dense ; [fog]
dense, épais(aisse) - **2.** inf [stupid] bouché(e).
densely ['denslɪ] *adv* : ~ packed [hall etc] complètement bondé(e) ; ~ populated très peu-
plé(e) ; ~ wooded couvert(e) de forêts
épaisses.
density ['densətɪ] (*pl* -ies) *n* densité *f*.
dent [dent] ◇ *n* bosse *f* ◇ *vt* cabosser.
dental ['dentl] *adj* dentaire ; ~ appointment
rendez-vous *m* chez le dentiste.
dental floss *n* fil *m* dentaire.
dental plate *n* prothèse *f* dentaire.
dental surgeon *n* chirurgien-dentiste *m*.
dental treatment *n* traitement *m* dentaire.
dented ['dentɪd] *adj* cabossé(e).
dentist ['dentɪst] *n* dentiste *mf*.
dentistry ['dentɪstrɪ] *n* dentisterie *f*.
dentures ['dentʃəz] *npl* dentier *m*.
denude [dɪ'njuːd] *vt* fml : to ~ sthg (of) dépouiller qqch (de).
denunciation [dɪ,nʌnsɪ'eɪʃn] *n* dénonciation *f*.
deny [dɪ'naɪ] (*pt & pp* -ied) *vt* - **1.** [refute] nier
- **2.** fml [refuse] nier, refuser ; to ~ sb sthg refuser qqch à qqn.
deodorant [diː'əʊdərənt] *n* déodorant *m*.
depart [dɪ'pɑːt] *vi* fml - **1.** [leave] : to ~ (from)
partir de - **2.** [differ] : to ~ from sthg s'écarter
de qqch.
department [dɪ'pɑːtmənt] *n* - **1.** [in organiza-
tion] service *m* - **2.** [in shop] rayon *m* - **3.** SCH &
UNIV département *m* - **4.** [in government] département *m*, ministère *m*.
departmental [,diːpɑːt'mentl] *adj* de service..

department store *n* grand magasin *m*.
departure [dɪ'pɑːtʃəʳ] *n* - **1.** [leaving] départ *m*
- **2.** [change] nouveau départ *m* ; a ~ from tradition un écart par rapport à la tradition.
departure lounge *n* salle *f* d'embarquement.
depend [dɪ'pend] *vi* : to ~ on [be dependent on]
dépendre de ; [rely on] compter sur ; [emotion-
ally] se reposer sur ; it ~s on you/the weather
cela dépend de vous/du temps ; it ~s cela
dépend ; ~ing on selon.
dependable [dɪ'pendəbl] *adj* [person] sur qui
on peut compter ; [source of income] sûr(e) ;
[car] fiable.
dependant [dɪ'pendənt] *n* personne *f* à
charge.
dependence [dɪ'pendəns] *n* : ~ (on) dépendance *f* (de).
dependent [dɪ'pendənt] *adj* - **1.** [reliant] : ~ (on)
dépendant(e) (de) ; to be ~ on sb/sthg dé-
pendre de qqn/qqch ; the economy is ~ on
oil l'économie repose sur le pétrole - **2.** [ad-
dicted] dépendant(e), accro - **3.** [contingent] : to
be ~ on dépendre de.
depict [dɪ'pɪkt] *vt* - **1.** [show in picture] représenter - **2.** [describe] : to ~ sb/sthg as dépeindre qqn/qqch comme.
depilatory [dɪ'pɪlətrɪ] *adj* dépilatoire.
deplete [dɪ'pliːt] *vt* épuiser.
depletion [dɪ'pliːʃn] *n* épuisement *m*.
deplorable [dɪ'plɔːrəbl] *adj* déplorable.
deplore [dɪ'plɔːʳ] *vt* déplorer.
deploy [dɪ'plɔɪ] *vt* déployer.
deployment [dɪ'plɔɪmənt] *n* déploiement
m.
depopulated [,diː'pɒpjʊleɪtɪd] *adj* dépeu-
plé(e).
depopulation [diː,pɒpjʊ'leɪʃn] *n* dépeuplement *m*.
deport [dɪ'pɔːt] *vt* expulser.
deportation [,diːpɔː'teɪʃn] *n* expulsion *f*.
deportation order *n* arrêt *m* d'expulsion.
depose [dɪ'pəʊz] *vt* déposer.
deposit [dɪ'pɒzɪt] ◇ *n* - **1.** [gen] dépôt *m* ; to
make a ~ [into bank account] déposer de l'argent - **2.** [payment - as guarantee] caution *f* ; [- as
instalment] acompte *m* ; [- on bottle] consigne *f*
◇ *vt* déposer.
deposit account *n* Br compte *m* sur livret.
depositor [də'pɒzɪtəʳ] *n* déposant *m*, -e *f*.
depot ['depəʊ] *n* - **1.** [gen] dépôt *m* - **2.** Am [sta-
tion] gare *f*.
depraved [dɪ'preɪvd] *adj* dépravé(e).

depravity [dɪ'prævətɪ] n dépravation f.
deprecate ['deprɪkeɪt] vt fml désapprouver.
deprecating ['deprɪkeɪtɪŋ] adj désapproba-teur(trice).
depreciate [dɪ'priːʃɪeɪt] vi se déprécier.
depreciation [dɪˌpriːʃɪ'eɪʃn] n dépréciation f.
depress [dɪ'pres] vt - 1. [sadden, discourage] dé-primer - 2. [weaken - economy] affaiblir ; [- pri-ces] faire baisser.
depressant [dɪ'presənt] n dépresseur m.
depressed [dɪ'prest] adj - 1. [sad] déprimé(e) - 2. [run-down - area] en déclin.
depressing [dɪ'presɪŋ] adj déprimant(e).
depression [dɪ'preʃn] n - 1. [gen] dépression f - 2. [sadness] tristesse f.
➤ **Depression** n ECON : **the (Great) Depression** la crise (économique) de 1929.
depressive [dɪ'presɪv] adj dépressif(ive).
deprivation [ˌdeprɪ'veɪʃn] n privation f.
deprive [dɪ'praɪv] vt : **to ~ sb of sthg** priver qqn de qqch.
deprived [dɪ'praɪvd] adj défavorisé(e).
dept. abbr of **department.**
depth [depθ] n profondeur f ; **in ~** [study, ana-lyse] en profondeur ; **to be out of one's ~** [in water] ne pas avoir pied ; fig avoir perdu pied, être dépassé.
➤ **depths** npl : **the ~s** [of seas] les profon-deurs fpl ; [of memory, archives] le fin fond ; **in the ~s of winter** au cœur de l'hiver ; **to be in the ~s of despair** toucher le fond du déses-poir.
depth charge n grenade f sous-marine.
deputation [ˌdepjʊ'teɪʃn] n délégation f.
deputize, -ise ['depjʊtaɪz] vi : **to ~ for sb** as-surer les fonctions de qqn, remplacer qqn.
deputy ['depjʊtɪ] (pl -ies) <> adj adjoint(e) ; **~ chairman** vice-président m ; **~ head** SCH di-recteur m adjoint ; **~ leader** POL vice-président m <> n - 1. [second-in-command] ad-joint m, -e f - 2. Am [deputy sheriff] shérif m adjoint.
derail [dɪ'reɪl] vt [train] faire dérailler.
derailment [dɪ'reɪlmənt] n déraillement m.
deranged [dɪ'reɪndʒd] adj dérangé(e).
derby [Br 'dɑːbɪ, Am 'dɜːbɪ] (pl -ies) n - 1. SPORT derby m - 2. Am [hat] chapeau m melon.
deregulate [ˌdiː'regjʊleɪt] vt déréglemen-ter.
deregulation [ˌdiːregjʊ'leɪʃn] n dérégle-mentation f.
derelict ['derəlɪkt] adj en ruines.
deride [dɪ'raɪd] vt railler.

derision [dɪ'rɪʒn] n dérision f.
derisive [dɪ'raɪsɪv] adj moqueur(euse).
derisory [də'raɪzərɪ] adj - 1. [puny, trivial] déri-soire - 2. [derisive] moqueur(euse).
derivation [ˌderɪ'veɪʃn] n [of word] dérivation f.
derivative [dɪ'rɪvətɪv] <> adj pej pas origi-nal(e) <> n dérivé m.
derive [dɪ'raɪv] <> vt - 1. [draw, gain] : **to ~ sthg from sthg** tirer qqch de qqch - 2. [originate] : **to be ~d from** venir de <> vi : **to ~ from** venir de.
dermatitis [ˌdɜːmə'taɪtɪs] n dermatite f.
dermatologist [ˌdɜːmə'tɒlədʒɪst] n derma-tologue mf.
dermatology [ˌdɜːmə'tɒlədʒɪ] n dermatolo-gie f.
derogatory [dɪ'rɒgətrɪ] adj désobligeant(e).
derrick ['derɪk] n - 1. [crane] mât m de charge - 2. [over oil well] derrick m.
derv [dɜːv] n Br gas-oil m.
desalination [diːˌsælɪ'neɪʃn] n dessalement m, dessalaison f.
descant ['deskænt] n [tune] déchant m.
descend [dɪ'send] <> vt fml [go down] descen-dre <> vi - 1. fml [go down] descendre - 2. [fall] : **to ~ (on)** [enemy] s'abattre (sur) ; [subj : silence, gloom] tomber (sur) - 3. [arrive] : **to ~ on** [a town] arriver en nombre dans, envahir ; [subj : in-laws etc] arriver à l'improviste chez - 4. [stoop] : **to ~ to sthg/to doing sthg** s'abais-ser à qqch/à faire qqch.
descendant [dɪ'sendənt] n descendant m, -e f.
descended [dɪ'sendɪd] adj : **to be ~ from sb** descendre de qqn.
descending [dɪ'sendɪŋ] adj : **in ~ order** en or-dre décroissant.
descent [dɪ'sent] n - 1. [downwards movement] descente f - 2. (U) [origin] origine f.
describe [dɪ'skraɪb] vt décrire.
description [dɪ'skrɪpʃn] n - 1. [account] des-cription f - 2. [type] sorte f, genre m.
descriptive [dɪ'skrɪptɪv] adj descriptif(ive).
desecrate ['desɪkreɪt] vt profaner.
desecration [ˌdesɪ'kreɪʃn] n profanation f.
desegregate [ˌdiː'segrɪgeɪt] vt pratiquer la déségrégation dans.
deselect [ˌdiːsɪ'lekt] vt Br ne pas resélection-ner pour une réélection.
desert [n 'dezət, vb & npl dɪ'zɜːt] <> n désert m <> vt - 1. [place] déserter - 2. [person, group] déserter, abandonner <> vi MIL déserter.

➤ **deserts** *npl* : **to get one's just ~s** recevoir ce que l'on mérite.

deserted [dɪ'zɜːtɪd] *adj* désert(e).

deserter [dɪ'zɜːtəʳ] *n* déserteur *m*.

desertion [dɪ'zɜːʃn] *n* - **1.** MIL désertion *f* - **2.** [of person] abandon *m*.

desert island ['dezət-] *n* île *f* déserte.

deserve [dɪ'zɜːv] *vt* mériter ; **to ~ to do sthg** mériter de faire qqch.

deserved [dɪ'zɜːvd] *adj* mérité(e).

deservedly [dɪ'zɜːvɪdlɪ] *adv* à juste titre.

deserving [dɪ'zɜːvɪŋ] *adj* [person] méritant(e) ; [cause, charity] méritoire ; **to be ~ of** sthg *fml* mériter qqch.

desiccated ['desɪkeɪtɪd] *adj* séché(e).

design [dɪ'zaɪn] ⬦ *n* - **1.** [plan, drawing] plan *m*, étude *f* - **2.** *(U)* [art] design *m* - **3.** [pattern] motif *m*, dessin *m* - **4.** [shape] ligne *f* ; [of dress] style *m* - **5.** *fml* [intention] dessein *m* ; **by ~** à dessein ; **to have ~s on sb/sthg** avoir des desseins sur qqn/qqch ⬦ *vt* - **1.** [draw plans for - building, car] faire les plans de, dessiner ; [- dress] créer - **2.** [plan] concevoir, mettre au point ; **to be ~ed for sthg/to do sthg** être conçu pour qqch/pour faire qqch.

designate [*adj* 'dezɪgnət, *vb* 'dezɪgneɪt] ⬦ *adj* désigné(e) ⬦ *vt* désigner ; **to ~ sb as sthg/to do sthg** désigner qqn à qqch/pour faire qqch.

designation [,dezɪg'neɪʃn] *n fml* [name] appellation *f*.

designer [dɪ'zaɪnəʳ] ⬦ *adj* de marque ⬦ *n* INDUSTRY concepteur *m*, -trice *f* ; ARCHIT dessinateur *m*, -trice *f* ; [of dresses etc] styliste *mf* ; THEATRE décorateur *m*, -trice *f*.

desirable [dɪ'zaɪərəbl] *adj* - **1.** [enviable, attractive] désirable - **2.** *fml* [appropriate] désirable, souhaitable.

desire [dɪ'zaɪəʳ] ⬦ *n* désir *m* ; **~ for sthg/to do sthg** désir de qqch/de faire qqch ⬦ *vt* désirer ; **it leaves a lot to be ~d** ça laisse beaucoup à désirer.

desirous [dɪ'zaɪərəs] *adj fml* : **~ of sthg/of doing sthg** désireux(euse) de qqch/de faire qqch.

desist [dɪ'zɪst] *vi fml* : **to ~ (from doing sthg)** cesser (de faire qqch).

desk [desk] *n* bureau *m* ; **reception ~** réception *f* ; **information ~** bureau *m* de renseignements.

desk clerk *n* Am réceptionniste *mf*.

desk lamp *n* lampe *f* de bureau.

desktop ['desktɒp] *adj* [computer] de bureau.

desktop publishing *n* publication *f* assistée par ordinateur, PAO *f*.

desolate ['desələt] *adj* - **1.** [place] abandonné(e) - **2.** [person] désespéré(e), désolé(e).

desolation [,desə'leɪʃn] *n* désolation *f*.

despair [dɪ'speəʳ] ⬦ *n (U)* désespoir *m* ; **to be in ~** être au désespoir ⬦ *vi* désespérer ; **to ~ of** désespérer de ; **to ~ of doing sthg** désespérer de faire qqch.

despairing [dɪ'speərɪŋ] *adj* de désespoir.

despairingly [dɪ'speərɪŋlɪ] *adv* avec désespoir.

despatch [dɪ'spætʃ] = **dispatch.**

desperate ['desprət] *adj* désespéré(e) ; **to be ~ for sthg** avoir absolument besoin de qqch.

desperately ['desprətlɪ] *adv* désespérément ; **~ ill** gravement malade.

desperation [,despə'reɪʃn] *n* désespoir *m* ; **in ~** de désespoir.

despicable [dɪ'spɪkəbl] *adj* ignoble.

despise [dɪ'spaɪz] *vt* [person] mépriser ; [racism] exécrer.

despite [dɪ'spaɪt] *prep* malgré.

despondent [dɪ'spɒndənt] *adj* découragé(e).

despot ['despɒt] *n* despote *m*.

despotic [de'spɒtɪk] *adj* despotique.

dessert [dɪ'zɜːt] *n* dessert *m*.

dessertspoon [dɪ'zɜːtspuːn] *n* - **1.** [spoon] cuillère *f* à dessert - **2.** [spoonful] cuillerée *f* à dessert.

dessert wine *n* vin *m* doux.

destabilize, -ise [,dɪ'steɪbɪlaɪz] *vt* déstabiliser.

destination [,destɪ'neɪʃn] *n* destination *f*.

destined ['destɪnd] *adj* - **1.** [intended] : **~ for** destiné(e) à ; **~ to do sthg** destiné à faire qqch - **2.** [bound] : **~ for** à destination de.

destiny ['destɪnɪ] *(pl* -**ies)** *n* destinée *f*.

destitute ['destɪtjuːt] *adj* indigent(e).

destroy [dɪ'strɔɪ] *vt* - **1.** [ruin] détruire - **2.** [put down - animal] faire piquer.

destroyer [dɪ'strɔɪəʳ] *n* - **1.** [ship] destroyer *m* - **2.** [person, thing] destructeur *m*, -trice *f*.

destruction [dɪ'strʌkʃn] *n* destruction *f*.

destructive [dɪ'strʌktɪv] *adj* [harmful] destructeur(trice).

destructively [dɪ'strʌktɪvlɪ] *adv* de façon destructrice.

desultory ['desəltrɪ] *adj fml* [conversation] décousu(e) ; [attempt] peu enthousiaste.

Det. *abbr of* **Detective.**

detach [dɪ'tætʃ] *vt* - **1.** [pull off] détacher ; **to ~ sthg from sthg** détacher qqch de qqch - **2.** [dissociate] : **to ~ o.s. from sthg** [from reality] se détacher de qqch ; [from proceedings, discussions] s'écarter de qqch.

detachable [dɪ'tætʃəbl] *adj* détachable, amovible.

detached [dɪ'tætʃt] *adj* [unemotional] détaché(e).

detached house *n* maison *f* individuelle.

detachment [dɪ'tætʃmənt] *n* détachement *m*.

detail ['diːteɪl] ◇ *n* - **1.** [small point] détail *m ;* to go into ~ entrer dans les détails ; in ~ en détail - **2.** MIL détachement *m* ◇ *vt* [list] détailler.

details *npl* [personal information] coordonnées *fpl*.

detailed ['diːteɪld] *adj* détaillé(e).

detain [dɪ'teɪn] *vt* - **1.** [in police station] détenir ; [in hospital] garder - **2.** [delay] retenir.

detainee [,diːteɪ'niː] *n* détenu *m*, -e *f*.

detect [dɪ'tekt] *vt* - **1.** [subj : person] déceler - **2.** [subj : machine] détecter.

detection [dɪ'tekʃn] *n (U)* - **1.** [of crime] dépistage *m* - **2.** [of aircraft, submarine] détection *f*.

detective [dɪ'tektɪv] *n* détective *m*.

detective novel *n* roman *m* policier.

detector [dɪ'tektər] *n* détecteur *m*.

détente [deɪ'tɑːnt] *n* POL détente *f*.

detention [dɪ'tenʃn] *n* - **1.** [of suspect, criminal] détention *f ;* in ~ en détention - **2.** SCH retenue *f ;* in ~ en retenue.

detention centre *n* Br centre *m* de détention.

deter [dɪ'tɜːr] (*pt* & *pp* -red ; *cont* -ring) *vt* dissuader ; to ~ sb from doing sthg dissuader qqn de faire qqch.

detergent [dɪ'tɜːdʒənt] *n* détergent *m*.

deteriorate [dɪ'tɪərɪəreɪt] *vi* se détériorer.

deterioration [dɪ,tɪərɪə'reɪʃn] *n* détérioration *f*.

determination [dɪ,tɜːmɪ'neɪʃn] *n* détermination *f*.

determine [dɪ'tɜːmɪn] *vt* - **1.** [establish, control] déterminer - **2.** fml [decide] : to ~ to do sthg décider de faire qqch.

determined [dɪ'tɜːmɪnd] *adj* - **1.** [person] déterminé(e) ; to do sthg déterminé à faire qqch - **2.** [effort] obstiné(e).

deterrent [dɪ'terənt] ◇ *adj* de dissuasion, dissuasif(ive) ◇ *n* moyen *m* de dissuasion.

detest [dɪ'test] *vt* détester.

detestable [dɪ'testəbl] *adj* détestable.

dethrone [dɪ'θrəʊn] *vt* détrôner.

detonate ['detəneɪt] ◇ *vt* faire détoner ◇ *vi* détoner.

detonator ['detəneɪtər] *n* détonateur *m*.

detour ['diː,tʊər] *n* détour *m*.

detract [dɪ'trækt] *vi :* to ~ from diminuer.

detractor [dɪ'træktər] *n* détracteur *m*, -trice *f*.

detriment ['detrɪmənt] *n :* to the ~ of au détriment de.

detrimental [,detrɪ'mentl] *adj* préjudiciable.

detritus [dɪ'traɪtəs] *n (U)* détritus *m*.

deuce [djuːs] *n* TENNIS égalité *f*.

Deutschmark ['dɔɪtʃ,mɑːk] *n* mark *m* allemand.

devaluation [,diːvæljʊ'eɪʃn] *n* dévaluation *f*.

devalue [,diː'væljuː] *vt* dévaluer.

devastate ['devəsteɪt] *vt* - **1.** [destroy - area, city] dévaster - **2.** fig [person] anéantir.

devastated ['devəsteɪtɪd] *adj* - **1.** [area, city] dévasté(e) - **2.** fig [person] accablé(e).

devastating ['devəsteɪtɪŋ] *adj* - **1.** [hurricane, remark] dévastateur(trice) - **2.** [upsetting] accablant(e) - **3.** [attractive] irrésistible.

devastation [,devə'steɪʃn] *n* dévastation *f*.

develop [dɪ'veləp] ◇ *vt* - **1.** [gen] développer - **2.** [land, area] aménager, développer - **3.** [illness, fault, habit] contracter - **4.** [resources] développer, exploiter ◇ *vi* - **1.** [grow, advance] se développer - **2.** [appear - problem, trouble] se déclarer.

developer [dɪ'veləpər] *n* - **1.** [of land] promoteur *m* immobilier - **2.** [person] : to be an early/a late ~ être en avance/en retard sur son âge - **3.** PHOT [chemical] développateur *m*, révélateur *m*.

developing country [dɪ'veləpɪŋ-] *n* pays *m* en voie de développement.

development [dɪ'veləpmənt] *n* - **1.** [gen] développement *m* - **2.** *(U)* [of land, area] exploitation *f* - **3.** [land being developed] zone *f* d'aménagement ; [developed area] zone aménagée - **4.** *(U)* [of illness, fault] évolution *f*.

development area *n* Br zone *f* d'aménagement.

deviant ['diːvjənt] ◇ *adj* déviant(e) ◇ *n* déviant *m*, -e *f*.

deviate ['diːvɪeɪt] *vi :* to ~ (from) dévier (de), s'écarter (de).

deviation [,diːvɪ'eɪʃn] *n* - **1.** [abnormality] déviance *f* - **2.** [departure - from rule, plan] écart *m ;* pej déviation *f*.

device [dɪ'vaɪs] *n* - **1.** [apparatus] appareil *m*, dispositif *m* - **2.** [plan, method] moyen *m ;* to

leave sb to their own ~s laisser qqn se débrouiller tout seul.

devil ['devl] *n* - **1.** [evil spirit] diable *m* - **2.** inf [person] type *m* ; **poor ~!** pauvre diable! - **3.** [for emphasis] : **who/where/why the ~ ...?** qui/où/pourquoi diable ...?

➤ **Devil** *n* [Satan] : **the Devil** le Diable.

devilish ['devlɪʃ] *adj* diabolique.

devil-may-care *adj* insouciant(e).

devil's advocate *n* avocat *m* du diable.

devious ['di:vjəs] *adj* - **1.** [dishonest - person] retors(e), à l'esprit tortueux ; [- scheme, means] détourné(e) - **2.** [tortuous] tortueux(euse).

deviousness ['di:vjəsnɪs] *n* [dishonesty] sournoiserie *f*.

devise [dɪ'vaɪz] *vt* concevoir.

devoid [dɪ'vɔɪd] *adj* fml : **~ of** dépourvu(e) de, dénué(e) de.

devolution [,di:və'lu:ʃn] *n* POL décentralisation *f*.

devolve [dɪ'vɒlv] *vi* fml : **to ~ on** OR **upon sb** incomber à qqn.

devote [dɪ'vəʊt] *vt* : **to ~ sthg to sthg** consacrer qqch à qqch ; **to ~ o.s. to sthg** se vouer OR se consacrer à qqch.

devoted [dɪ'vəʊtɪd] *adj* dévoué(e) ; **a ~ mother** une mère dévouée à ses enfants.

devotee [,devə'ti:] *n* [fan] passionné *m*, -e *f*.

devotion [dɪ'vəʊʃn] *n* - **1.** [commitment] : **~ (to)** dévouement *m* (à) - **2.** RELIG dévotion *f*.

devour [dɪ'vaʊə^r] *vt* lit & fig dévorer.

devout [dɪ'vaʊt] *adj* dévot(e).

dew [dju:] *n* rosée *f*.

dexterity [dek'sterətɪ] *n* dextérité *f*.

dextrose ['dekstrəʊs] *n* dextrose *m*.

dext(e)rous ['dekstrəs] *adj* habile.

DFE (*abbr of* **Department for Education**) *n* ministère britannique de l'éducation nationale.

dhal [dɑːl] *n* dal *m*.

DHSS (*abbr of* **Department of Health and So-**cial Security) *n* ancien nom du ministère britannique de la santé et de la sécurité sociale.

diabetes [,daɪə'biːtiːz] *n* diabète *m*.

diabetic [,daɪə'betɪk] <> *adj* - **1.** [person] diabétique - **2.** [jam, chocolate] pour diabétiques <> *n* diabétique *mf*.

diabolic(al) [,daɪə'bɒlɪk(l)] *adj* - **1.** [evil] diabolique - **2.** inf [very bad] atroce.

diaeresis Br, **dieresis** Am [daɪ'erɪsɪs] (*pl* -ses [-siːz]) *n* tréma *m*.

diagnose ['daɪəgnəʊz] *vt* diagnostiquer.

diagnosis [,daɪəg'nəʊsɪs] (*pl* -ses [-siːz]) *n* diagnostic *m*.

diagnostic [,daɪəg'nɒstɪk] *adj* diagnostique.

diagonal [daɪ'ægənl] <> *adj* [line] diagonal(e) <> *n* diagonale *f*.

diagonally [daɪ'ægənəlɪ] *adv* en diagonale.

diagram ['daɪəgræm] *n* diagramme *m*.

diagrammatic [,daɪəgrə'mætɪk] *adj* en forme de diagramme.

dial ['daɪəl] (Br *pt* & *pp* **-led** ; *cont* **-ling**, Am *pt* & *pp* **-ed** ; *cont* **-ing**) <> *n* cadran *m* ; [of radio] cadran de fréquences <> *vt* [number] composer.

dialect ['daɪəlekt] *n* dialecte *m*.

dialling code ['daɪəlɪŋ-] *n* Br indicatif *m*.

dialling tone Br ['daɪəlɪŋ-], **dial tone** Am *n* tonalité *f*.

dialogue Br, **dialog** Am ['daɪəlɒg] *n* dialogue *m*.

dial tone Am = dialling tone.

dialysis [daɪ'ælɪsɪs] *n* dialyse *f*.

diamanté [dɪə'mɑːnteɪ] *adj* diamanté(e).

diameter [daɪ'æmɪtə^r] *n* diamètre *m*.

diametrically [,daɪə'metrɪklɪ] *adv* : **~ opposed** diamétralement opposé(e).

diamond ['daɪəmənd] *n* - **1.** [gem] diamant *m* - **2.** [shape] losange *m* - **3.** [playing card] carreau *m*.

➤ **diamonds** *npl* carreau *m* ; **the six of ~s** le six de carreau.

diamond wedding *n* noces *fpl* de diamant.

diaper ['daɪəpə^r] *n* Am couche *f*.

diaphanous [daɪ'æfənəs] *adj* diaphane.

diaphragm ['daɪəfræm] *n* diaphragme *m*.

diarrh(o)ea [,daɪə'rɪə] *n* diarrhée *f*.

diary ['daɪərɪ] (*pl* -ies) *n* - **1.** [appointment book] agenda *m* - **2.** [journal] journal *m*.

diatribe ['daɪətraɪb] *n* diatribe *f*.

dice [daɪs] (*pl inv*) <> *n* [for games] dé *m* ; **no ~** Am inf pas question <> *vt* couper en dés.

dicey [ˈdaɪsɪ] (*compar* **-ier** ; *superl* **-iest**) *adj* esp Br inf risqué(e).

dichotomy [daɪˈkɒtəmɪ] (*pl* **-ies**) *n* dichotomie *f*.

dickens [ˈdɪkɪnz] *n* Br inf dated : **who/what/ where the ~ ...?** qui/que/où diable ...?

Dictaphone® [ˈdɪktəfəʊn] *n* Dictaphone® *m*.

dictate [*vb* dɪkˈteɪt, *n* ˈdɪkteɪt] ⋄ *vt* dicter ; **to ~ sthg to sb** dicter qqch à qqn ⋄ *vi* - **1.** [read aloud] : **to ~ to sb** dicter à qqn - **2.** [give orders] : **to ~ to sb** commander à qqn, donner des ordres à qqn ⋄ *n* ordre *m*.

dictation [dɪkˈteɪʃn] *n* dictée *f*.

dictator [dɪkˈteɪtəʳ] *n* dictateur *m*.

dictatorship [dɪkˈteɪtəʃɪp] *n* dictature *f*.

diction [ˈdɪkʃn] *n* diction *f*.

dictionary [ˈdɪkʃənrɪ] (*pl* **-ies**) *n* dictionnaire *m*.

did [dɪd] *pt* ⊳ do.

didactic [dɪˈdæktɪk] *adj* didactique.

diddle [ˈdɪdl] *vt* inf escroquer, rouler.

didn't [ˈdɪdnt] = did not.

die [daɪ] (*pl sense 2 only* **dice** [daɪs] ; *pt* & *pp* **died** ; *cont* **dying**) ⋄ *vi* mourir ; **to be dying** se mourir ; **to be dying to do sthg** mourir d'envie de faire qqch ; **to be dying for a drink/cigarette** mourir d'envie de boire un verre/de fumer une cigarette ⋄ *n* - **1.** [for shaping metal] matrice *f* - **2.** [dice] dé *m*.

⬦ **die away** *vi* [sound] s'éteindre ; [wind] tomber.

⬦ **die down** *vi* [sound] s'affaiblir ; [wind] tomber ; [fire] baisser.

⬦ **die out** *vi* s'éteindre, disparaître.

diehard [ˈdaɪhɑːd] *n* : **to be a ~** être coriace ; [reactionary] être réactionnaire.

dieresis [daɪˈerɪsɪs] Am = diaeresis.

diesel [ˈdiːzl] *n* diesel *m*.

diesel engine *n* AUT moteur *m* diesel ; RAIL locomotive *f* diesel.

diesel fuel, diesel oil *n* diesel *m*.

diet [ˈdaɪət] ⋄ *n* - **1.** [eating pattern] alimentation *f* - **2.** [to lose weight] régime *m* ; **to be on a ~** être au régime, faire un régime ⋄ *comp* [low-calorie] de régime ⋄ *vi* suivre un régime.

dietary [ˈdaɪətrɪ] *adj* diététique.

dietary fibre *n* (U) fibres *fpl* alimentaires.

dieter [ˈdaɪətəʳ] *n* personne *f* qui suit un régime.

dietician [ˌdaɪəˈtɪʃn] *n* diététicien *m*, -enne *f*.

differ [ˈdɪfəʳ] *vi* - **1.** [be different] être différent(e), différer ; [people] être différent ; **to**

~ from être différent de - **2.** [disagree] : **to ~ with sb (about sthg)** ne pas être d'accord avec qqn (à propos de qqch).

difference [ˈdɪfrəns] *n* différence *f* ; **it doesn't make any ~** cela ne change rien ; **to make all the ~** faire toute la différence.

different [ˈdɪfrənt] *adj* : **~ (from)** différent(e) (de).

differential [ˌdɪfəˈrenʃl] ⋄ *adj* différentiel(elle) ⋄ *n* - **1.** [between pay scales] écart *m* - **2.** TECH différentielle *f*.

differentiate [ˌdɪfəˈrenʃɪeɪt] ⋄ *vt* : **to ~ sthg from sthg** différencier qqch de qqch, faire la différence entre qqch et qqch ⋄ *vi* : **to ~ (between)** faire la différence (entre).

differently [ˈdɪfrəntlɪ] *adv* différemment, autrement ; **to think ~** ne pas être d'accord.

difficult [ˈdɪfɪkəlt] *adj* difficile.

difficulty [ˈdɪfɪkəltɪ] (*pl* **-ies**) *n* difficulté *f* ; **to have ~ in doing sthg** avoir de la difficulté OR du mal à faire qqch.

diffidence [ˈdɪfɪdəns] *n* manque *m* d'assurance.

diffident [ˈdɪfɪdənt] *adj* [person] qui manque d'assurance ; [manner, voice, approach] hésitant(e).

diffuse [*adj* dɪˈfjuːs, *vb* dɪˈfjuːz] ⋄ *adj* - **1.** [vague] diffus(e) - **2.** [spread out - city] étendu(e) ; [- company] éparpillé(e) ⋄ *vt* diffuser, répandre ⋄ *vi* - **1.** [light] se diffuser, se répandre - **2.** [information] se répandre.

diffusion [dɪˈfjuːʒn] *n* diffusion *f*

dig [dɪg] (*pt* & *pp* **dug** ; *cont* **digging**) ⋄ *vi* - **1.** [in ground] creuser - **2.** [subj : belt, strap] : **his elbow was digging into my side** son coude me rentrait dans les côtes ; **to ~ into sb** couper qqn ⋄ *n* - **1.** fig [unkind remark] pique *f* - **2.** ARCHEOL fouilles *fpl* ⋄ *vt* - **1.** [hole] creuser - **2.** [garden] bêcher - **3.** [press] : **to ~ sthg into sthg** enfoncer qqch dans qqch.

⬦ **dig out** *vt sep* - **1.** [rescue] dégager - **2.** [find] dénicher.

⬦ **dig up** *vt sep* - **1.** [from ground] déterrer ; [potatoes] arracher - **2.** inf [information] dénicher.

digest [*n* ˈdaɪdʒest, *vb* dɪˈdʒest] ⋄ *n* résumé *m*, digest *m* ⋄ *vt* lit & fig digérer.

digestible [dɪˈdʒestəbl] *adj* digeste.

digestion [dɪˈdʒestʃn] *n* digestion *f*.

digestive [dɪˈdʒestɪv] *adj* digestif(ive).

digestive biscuit [daɪˈdʒestɪv-] *n* Br ≃ sablé *m* (à la farine complète).

digit [ˈdɪdʒɪt] *n* - **1.** [figure] chiffre *m* - **2.** [finger] doigt *m* ; [toe] orteil *m*.

digital [ˈdɪdʒɪtl] *adj* numérique, digital(e).

digital camera n appareil photo m numérique.

digital recording n enregistrement m numérique.

digital television n télévision f numérique.

digital watch n montre f à affichage digital.

digitize, -ise ['dɪdʒɪtaɪz] vt digitaliser.

dignified ['dɪgnɪfaɪd] adj digne, plein(e) de dignité.

dignify ['dɪgnɪfaɪ] (pt & pp -ied) vt [place, appearance] donner de la grandeur à.

dignitary ['dɪgnɪtrɪ] (pl -ies) n dignitaire m.

dignity ['dɪgnətɪ] n dignité f.

digress [daɪ'gres] vi : to ~ (from) s'écarter (de).

digression [daɪ'greʃn] n digression f.

digs [dɪgz] npl Br inf piaule f.

dike [daɪk] n - 1. [wall, bank] digue f - 2. inf pej [lesbian] gouine f.

diktat ['dɪktɑːt] n diktat m.

dilapidated [dɪ'læpɪdeɪtɪd] adj délabré(e).

dilate [daɪ'leɪt] <> vt dilater <> vi se dilater.

dilated [daɪ'leɪtɪd] adj dilaté(e).

dilemma [dɪ'lemə] n dilemme m.

dilettante [,dɪlɪ'tæntɪ] (pl -tes OR -ti [-tɪ]) n dilettante mf.

diligence ['dɪlɪdʒəns] n application f.

diligent ['dɪlɪdʒənt] adj appliqué(e).

dill [dɪl] n aneth m.

dillydally ['dɪlɪdælɪ] (pt & pp -ied) vi inf lambiner.

dilute [daɪ'luːt] <> adj dilué(e) <> vt : to ~ sthg (with) diluer qqch (avec).

dilution [daɪ'luːʃn] n dilution f.

dim [dɪm] (compar -mer ; superl -mest, pt & pp -med ; cont -ming) <> adj - 1. [dark - light] faible ; [- room] sombre - 2. [indistinct - memory, outline] vague - 3. [weak - eyesight] faible - 4. inf [stupid] borné(e) <> vt & vi baisser.

dime [daɪm] n Am (pièce f de) dix cents mpl ; they're a ~ a **dozen** [common] il y en a à la pelle.

dimension [dɪ'menʃn] n dimension f.

-dimensional [dɪ'menʃənl] suffix -dimensionnel(elle).

diminish [dɪ'mɪnɪʃ] vt & vi diminuer.

diminished [dɪ'mɪnɪʃt] adj réduit(e).

diminished responsibility n JUR responsabilité f atténuée.

diminishing returns npl rendements mpl décroissants.

diminutive [dɪ'mɪnjʊtɪv] fml <> adj minuscule <> n GRAMM diminutif m.

dimly ['dɪmlɪ] adv [lit] faiblement ; [remember] vaguement.

dimmers ['dɪmərz] npl Am [dipped headlights] phares mpl code (inv) ; [parking lights] feux mpl de position.

dimmer (switch) ['dɪmə'-] n variateur m de lumière.

dimple ['dɪmpl] n fossette f.

dimwit ['dɪmwɪt] n inf crétin m, -e f.

dim-witted [-'wɪtɪd] adj inf crétin(o).

din [dɪn] n inf barouf m.

dine [daɪn] vi fml dîner.

➡ **dine out** vi dîner dehors.

diner ['daɪnə'] n - 1. [person] dîneur m, -euse f - 2. Am [café] ≃ resto m routier.

dingdong [,dɪŋ'dɒŋ] <> adj inf [battle, argument] acharné(e) <> n [of bell] ding dong m.

dinghy ['dɪŋgɪ] (pl -ies) n [for sailing] dériveur m ; [for rowing] (petit) canot m.

dingo ['dɪŋgəʊ] (pl -es) n dingo m, chien m sauvage.

dingy ['dɪndʒɪ] (compar -ier ; superl -iest) adj miteux(euse), crasseux(euse).

dining car ['daɪnɪŋ-] n wagon-restaurant m.

dining room ['daɪnɪŋ-] n - 1. [in house] salle f à manger - 2. [in hotel] restaurant m.

dining table ['daɪnɪŋ-] n table f (de salle à manger).

dinner ['dɪnə'] n dîner m.

dinner dance n dîner m dansant.

dinner jacket n smoking m.

dinner party n dîner m (sur invitation).

dinner service n service m de table.

dinner table n table f (de salle à manger).

dinnertime ['dɪnətaɪm] n heure f du dîner.

dinosaur ['daɪnəsɔː'] n dinosaure m.

dint [dɪnt] n fml : by ~ of à force de.

diocese ['daɪəsɪs] n diocèse m.

diode ['daɪəʊd] n diode f.

dioxin [daɪ'ɒksɪn] n dioxine f.

dip [dɪp] (pt & pp -ped ; cont -ping) <> n - 1. [in road, ground] déclivité f - 2. [sauce] sauce f, dip m - 3. [swim] baignade f (rapide) ; to go for a ~ aller se baigner en vitesse, aller faire trempette <> vt - 1. [into liquid] : to ~ sthg in OR into tremper OR plonger qqch dans - 2. Br AUT : to ~ one's headlights se mettre en code <> vi - 1. [sun] baisser, descendre à l'horizon ; [wing] plonger - 2. [road, ground] descendre.

Dip. Br abbr of diploma.

diphtheria [dɪf'θɪərɪə] n diphtérie f.

diphthong ['dɪfθɒŋ] n diphtongue f.

diploma [dɪ'pləʊmə] (pl -s) n diplôme m.

diplomacy [dɪ'pləʊməsɪ] n diplomatie f.

diplomat ['dɪpləmæt] n diplomate m.

diplomatic [,dɪplə'mætɪk] adj - **1.** [service, corps] diplomatique - **2.** [tactful] diplomate.

diplomatic bag n valise f diplomatique.

diplomatic corps n corps m diplomatique.

diplomatic immunity n immunité f diplomatique.

diplomatic relations npl relations fpl diplomatiques.

dipsomaniac [,dɪpsə'meɪnɪæk] n dipsomane mf.

dipstick ['dɪpstɪk] n AUT jauge f (de niveau d'huile).

dipswitch ['dɪpswɪtʃ] n Br AUT manette f des codes.

dire ['daɪəʳ] adj [need, consequences] extrême ; [warning] funeste.

direct [dɪ'rekt] ◇ adj direct(e) ; [challenge] manifeste ◇ vt - **1.** [gen] diriger - **2.** [aim] : to ~ sthg at sb [question, remark] adresser qqch à qqn ; **the campaign is ~ed at teenagers** cette campagne vise les adolescents - **3.** [order] : to ~ sb to do sthg ordonner à qqn de faire qqch ◇ adv directement.

direct action n action f directe.

direct current n courant m continu.

direct debit n Br prélèvement m automatique.

direct dialling n automatique m.

direct hit n coup m au but OR de plein fouet.

direction [dɪ'rekʃn] n direction f ; **under the ~ of** sous la direction de.

◆ **directions** npl - **1.** [to find a place] indications fpl - **2.** [for use] instructions fpl.

directive [dɪ'rektɪv] n directive f.

directly [dɪ'rektlɪ] adv - **1.** [in straight line] directement - **2.** [honestly, clearly] sans détours - **3.** [exactly - behind, above] exactement - **4.** [immediately] immédiatement - **5.** [very soon] tout de suite.

direct mail n publipostage m.

director [dɪ'rektəʳ] n - **1.** [of company] directeur m, -trice f - **2.** THEATRE metteur m en scène ; CINEMA & TV réalisateur m, -trice f.

directorate [dɪ'rektərət] n conseil m d'administration.

director-general (pl **directors-general** OR **director-generals**) n directeur général m.

Director of Public Prosecutions n Br ≃ procureur m général.

directorship [dɪ'rektəʃɪp] n - **1.** [position] poste m de directeur - **2.** [period] direction f.

directory [dɪ'rektərɪ] (pl -ies) n - **1.** [annual publication] annuaire m - **2.** COMPUT répertoire m.

directory enquiries n Br renseignements mpl (téléphoniques).

direct rule n centralisation f de pouvoir.

direct selling n (U) vente f directe.

direct speech n discours m direct.

direct taxation n imposition f directe.

dire straits npl : **in ~** dans une situation désespérée.

dirge [dɜːdʒ] n chant m funèbre.

dirt [dɜːt] n (U) - **1.** [mud, dust] saleté f - **2.** [earth] terre f.

dirt cheap inf ◇ adj très bon marché, donné(e) ◇ adv pour trois fois rien.

dirt track n chemin m de terre.

dirty ['dɜːtɪ] (compar -ier ; superl -iest, pt & pp -ied) ◇ adj - **1.** [not clean, not fair] sale - **2.** [smutty - language, person] grossier(ère) ; [- book, joke] cochon(onne) ◇ vt salir.

disability [,dɪsə'bɪlətɪ] (pl -ies) n infirmité f.

disable [dɪs'eɪbl] vt - **1.** [injure] rendre infirme - **2.** [put out of action - guns, vehicle] mettre hors d'action.

disabled [dɪs'eɪbld] ◇ adj [person] handicapé(e), infirme ◇ npl : **the ~** les handicapés, les infirmes.

disablement [dɪs'eɪblmənt] n invalidité f.

disabuse [,dɪsə'bjuːz] vt fml : to ~ sb (of) détromper qqn (sur).

disadvantage [,dɪsəd'vɑːntɪdʒ] n désavantage m, inconvénient m ; **to be at a ~** être désavantagé ; **to be to sb's ~** être au désavantage de qqn.

disadvantaged [,dɪsəd'vɑːntɪdʒd] adj défavorisé(e).

disadvantageous [,dɪsædvɑːn'teɪdʒəs] adj désavantageux(euse).

disaffected [,dɪsə'fektɪd] adj mécontent(e).

disaffection [,dɪsə'fekʃn] n mécontentement m.

disagree [,dɪsə'griː] vi - **1.** [have different opinions] : **to ~ (with)** ne pas être d'accord (avec) - **2.** [differ] ne pas concorder - **3.** [subj : food, drink] : **to ~ with sb** ne pas réussir à qqn.

disagreeable [,dɪsə'griːəbl] adj désagréable.

disagreement [,dɪsə'griːmənt] n - **1.** [in opinion] désaccord m - **2.** [argument] différend m - **3.** [dissimilarity] différence f.

disallow [ˌdɪsə'laʊ] *vt* - **1.** fml [appeal, claim] rejeter - **2.** [goal] refuser.

disappear [ˌdɪsə'pɪər] *vi* disparaître.

disappearance [ˌdɪsə'pɪərəns] *n* disparition *f*.

disappoint [ˌdɪsə'pɔɪnt] *vt* décevoir.

disappointed [ˌdɪsə'pɔɪntɪd] *adj :* ~ **(in** OR **with)** déçu(e) (par).

disappointing [ˌdɪsə'pɔɪntɪŋ] *adj* décevant(e).

disappointment [ˌdɪsə'pɔɪntmənt] *n* déception *f*.

disapproval [ˌdɪsə'pruːvl] *n* désapprobation *f*.

disapprove [ˌdɪsə'pruːv] *vi :* **to** ~ **of sb/sthg** désapprouver qqn/qqch ; **do you** ~**?** est-ce que tu as quelque chose contre?

disapproving [ˌdɪsə'pruːvɪŋ] *adj* désapprobateur(trice).

disarm [dɪs'ɑːm] *vt* & *vi* lit & fig désarmer.

disarmament [dɪs'ɑːməmənt] *n* désarmement *m*.

disarming [dɪs'ɑːmɪŋ] *adj* désarmant(e).

disarray [ˌdɪsə'reɪ] *n :* **in** ~ en désordre ; [government] en pleine confusion.

disassociate [ˌdɪsə'səʊʃɪeɪt] *vt :* **to** ~ **o.s. from** se dissocier de.

disaster [dɪ'zɑːstər] *n* - **1.** [damaging event] catastrophe *f* - **2.** (U) [misfortune] échec *m*, désastre *m* - **3.** inf [failure] désastre *m*.

disaster area *n* [after natural disaster] zone *f* sinistrée.

disastrous [dɪ'zɑːstrəs] *adj* désastreux(euse).

disastrously [dɪ'zɑːstrəslɪ] *adv* de façon désastreuse.

disband [dɪs'bænd] ⬦ *vt* dissoudre ⬦ *vi* se dissoudre.

disbelief [ˌdɪsbɪ'liːf] *n :* **in** OR **with** ~ avec incrédulité.

disbelieve [ˌdɪsbɪ'liːv] *vt* ne pas croire.

disc Br, **disk** Am [dɪsk] *n* disque *m*.

disc. *abbr of* discount.

discard [dɪ'skɑːd] *vt* mettre au rebut.

discarded [dɪ'skɑːdɪd] *adj* mis(e) au rebut.

disc brake *n* frein *m* à disque.

discern [dɪ'sɜːn] *vt* discerner, distinguer.

discernible [dɪ'sɜːnəbl] *adj* - **1.** [visible] visible - **2.** [noticeable] sensible.

discerning [dɪ'sɜːnɪŋ] *adj* judicieux(euse).

discharge [*n* 'dɪstʃɑːdʒ, *vt* dɪs'tʃɑːdʒ] ⬦ *n* - **1.** [of patient] autorisation *f* de sortie, décharge *f* ; JUR relaxe *f* ; **to get one's** ~ MIL être

rendu à la vie civile - **2.** fml [fulfilment - of duties] accomplissement *m* - **3.** [emission - of smoke] émission *f* ; [- of sewage] déversement *m* ; [- MED] écoulement *m* - **4.** [payment] acquittement *m* ⬦ *vt* - **1.** [allow to leave - patient] signer la décharge de ; [- prisoner, defendant] relaxer ; [- soldier] rendre à la vie civile - **2.** fml [fulfil] assumer - **3.** [emit - smoke] émettre ; [- sewage, chemicals] déverser - **4.** [pay] acquitter, régler.

discharged bankrupt *n* failli *m* réhabilité.

disciple [dɪ'saɪpl] *n* disciple *m*.

disciplinarian [ˌdɪsɪplɪ'neərɪən] *n personne impitoyable en matière de discipline*.

disciplinary ['dɪsɪplɪnərɪ] *adj* disciplinaire ; **to take** ~ **action against sb** prendre des mesures disciplinaires contre qqn.

discipline ['dɪsɪplɪn] ⬦ *n* discipline *f* ⬦ *vt* - **1.** [control] discipliner - **2.** [punish] punir.

disciplined ['dɪsɪplɪnd] *adj* discipliné(e).

disc jockey *n* disc-jockey *m*.

disclaim [dɪs'kleɪm] *vt* fml nier.

disclaimer [dɪs'kleɪmər] *n* dénégation *f*, désaveu *m*.

disclose [dɪs'kləʊz] *vt* révéler, divulguer.

disclosure [dɪs'kləʊʒər] *n* révélation *f*, divulgation *f*.

disco ['dɪskəʊ] (*pl* -**s**) (*abbr of* **discotheque**) *n* discothèque *f*.

discoloration [dɪsˌkʌlə'reɪʃn] *n* décoloration *f*.

discolour Br, **discolor** Am ⬦ *vt* décolorer ; [teeth] jaunir ⬦ *vi* se décolorer ; [teeth] jaunir.

discoloured Br, **discolored** Am *adj* décoloré(e) ; [teeth] jauni(e).

discomfort [dɪs'kʌmfət] *n* - **1.** (U) [physical pain] douleur *f* ; **to be in some** ~ ne pas se sentir très bien ; **to cause sb** ~ gêner qqn - **2.** (U) [anxiety, embarrassment] malaise *m* - **3.** [uncomfortable condition] inconfort *m*.

disconcert [ˌdɪskən'sɜːt] *vt* déconcerter.

disconcerting [ˌdɪskən'sɜːtɪŋ] *adj* déconcertant(e).

disconnect [ˌdɪskə'nekt] *vt* - **1.** [detach] détacher - **2.** [from gas, electricity - appliance] débrancher ; [- house] couper - **3.** TELEC couper.

disconnected [ˌdɪskə'nektɪd] *adj* [thoughts] sans suite ; [events] sans rapport.

disconsolate [dɪs'kɒnsələt] *adj* inconsolable.

discontent [ˌdɪskən'tent] *n :* ~ **(with)** mécontentement *m* (à propos de).

discontented [ˌdɪskən'tentɪd] *adj* mécontent(e).

discontentment [ˌdɪskən'tentmənt] *n* : ~ **(with)** mécontentement *m* (à propos de).

discontinue [ˌdɪskən'tɪnjuːl] *vt* cesser, interrompre.

discontinued line [ˌdɪskən'tɪnjuːd-] *n* COMM fin *f* de série.

discord ['dɪskɔːdl] *n* - **1.** (U) [disagreement] discorde *f*, désaccord *m* - **2.** MUS dissonance *f*.

discordant [dɪ'skɔːdənt] *adj* - **1.** [conflicting] discordant(e) ; [relationship] plein(e) de discordance - **2.** MUS dissonant(e).

discotheque ['dɪskəʊtekl] *n* discothèque *f*.

discount [*n* 'dɪskaʊnt, *vb* Br dɪs'kaʊnt, Am 'dɪskaʊnt] <> *n* remise *f* <> *vt* [report, claim] ne pas tenir compte de.

discount house *n* - **1.** FIN maison *f* d'escompte - **2.** [store] magasin *m* de vente au rabais.

discount rate *n* taux *m* d'escompte.

discount store *n* COMM magasin *m* de vente au rabais.

discourage [dɪs'kʌrɪdʒ] *vt* décourager ; to ~ sb from doing sthg dissuader qqn de faire qqch.

discouraging [dɪ'skʌrɪdʒɪŋ] *adj* décourageant(e).

discourse ['dɪskɔːs] *n fml* : ~ **(on)** discours *m* (sur).

discourteous [dɪs'kɜːtjəs] *adj* discourtois(e).

discourtesy [dɪs'kɜːtɪsɪ] *n* manque *m* de courtoisie.

discover [dɪ'skʌvəʳ] *vt* découvrir.

discoverer [dɪ'skʌvərəʳ] *n* : the ~ of sthg la personne qui a découvert qqch.

discovery [dɪ'skʌvərɪ] (*pl* -ies) *n* découverte *f*.

discredit [dɪs'kredɪt] <> *n* discrédit *m* <> *vt* discréditer.

discredited [dɪs'kredɪtɪd] *adj* discrédité(e).

discreet [dɪ'skriːt] *adj* discret(ète).

discreetly [dɪ'skriːtlɪ] *adv* discrètement.

discrepancy [dɪ'skrepənsɪ] (*pl* -ies) *n* : ~ **(in/between)** divergence *f* (entre).

discrete [dɪs'kriːt] *adj fml* séparé(e), bien distinct(e).

discretion [dɪ'skreʃnl] *n* (U) - **1.** [tact] discrétion *f* - **2.** [judgment] jugement *m*, discernement *m* ; use your own ~ à vous de juger ; at the ~ of avec l'autorisation de.

discretionary [dɪ'skreʃənrɪl] *adj* discrétionnaire.

discriminate [dɪ'skrɪmɪneɪtl] *vi* - **1.** [distinguish] différencier, distinguer ; to ~ between faire la distinction entre - **2.** [be prejudiced] : to ~ against sb faire de la discrimination envers qqn.

discriminating [dɪ'skrɪmɪneɪtɪŋ] *adj* avisé(e).

discrimination [dɪˌskrɪmɪ'neɪʃnl] *n* - **1.** [prejudice] discrimination *f* - **2.** [judgment] discernement *m*, jugement *m*.

discus ['dɪskəsl] (*pl* -es [-iːz]) *n* disque *m*.

discuss [dɪ'skʌsl] *vt* discuter (de) ; to ~ sthg with sb discuter de qqch avec qqn.

discussion [dɪ'skʌʃnl] *n* discussion *f* ; under ~ en discussion.

disdain [dɪs'deɪnl] <> *n* : ~ **(for)** dédain *m* (pour) <> *vt* dédaigner ; to ~ to do sthg dédaigner de faire qqch.

disdainful [dɪs'deɪnfʊl] *adj* dédaigneux(euse).

disease [dɪ'ziːzl] *n* - **1.** [illness] maladie *f* - **2.** fig [unhealthy attitude, habit] mal *m*.

diseased [dɪ'ziːzdl] *adj* [plant, body] malade.

disembark [ˌdɪsɪm'bɑːkl] *vi* débarquer.

disembarkation [ˌdɪsembɑː'keɪʃnl] *n* débarquement *m*.

disembodied [ˌdɪsɪm'bɒdɪdl] *adj* désincarné(e).

disembowel [ˌdɪsɪm'baʊəll] (Br *pt* & *pp* -led ; *cont* -ling, Am *pt* & *pp* -ed ; *cont* -ing) *vt* éviscérer.

disenchanted [ˌdɪsɪn'tʃɑːntɪdl] *adj* : ~ **(with)** désenchanté(e) (de).

disenchantment [ˌdɪsɪn'tʃɑːntmənt] *n* désillusion *f*, désenchantement *m*.

disenfranchise [ˌdɪsɪn'fræntʃaɪzl] = **disfranchise**.

disengage [ˌdɪsɪn'geɪdʒl] *vt* - **1.** [release] : to ~ sthg **(from)** libérer OR dégager qqch (de) ; to ~ o.s. from se libérer OR se dégager de - **2.** TECH déclencher ; to ~ the gears débrayer.

disengagement [ˌdɪsɪn'geɪdʒmənt] *n* désengagement *m*.

disentangle [ˌdɪsɪn'tæŋgll] *vt* : to ~ sthg from enlever qqch de ; to ~ o.s. from se dégager de.

disfavour Br, **disfavor** Am [dɪs'feɪvəʳ] *n* - **1.** [dislike, disapproval] désapprobation *f* - **2.** [state of disapproval] : to be in ~ with sb être mal vu de qqn.

disfigure [dɪs'fɪgəʳl] *vt* défigurer.

disfranchise [ˌdɪs'fræntʃaɪzl] *vt* priver du droit électoral.

disgorge [dɪs'gɔːdʒ] *vt* - **1.** [from stomach] vomir - **2.** [emit] déverser.

disgrace [dɪs'greɪs] ◇ *n* - **1.** [shame] honte *f*; **to bring ~ on sb** jeter la honte sur qqn ; **in ~** en défaveur - **2.** [cause of shame - thing] honte *f*, scandale *m*; [- person] honte *f* ◇ *vt* faire honte à ; **to ~ o.s.** se couvrir de honte.

disgraceful [dɪs'greɪsfʊl] *adj* honteux(euse), scandaleux(euse).

disgruntled [dɪs'grʌntld] *adj* mécontent(e).

disguise [dɪs'gaɪz] ◇ *n* déguisement *m*; **in ~** déguisé(e) ◇ *vt* - **1.** [person, voice] déguiser ; **to ~ o.s. as** se déguiser en - **2.** [hide - fact, feelings] dissimuler.

disgust [dɪs'gʌst] ◇ *n* : **~ (at)** [behaviour, violence etc] dégoût *m* (pour) ; [decision] dégoût (devant) ; **in ~** dégoûté(e), écœuré(e) ◇ *vt* dégoûter, écœurer.

disgusting [dɪs'gʌstɪŋ] *adj* dégoûtant(e).

dish [dɪʃ] *n* plat *m*; Am [plate] assiette *f*.
➤ **dishes** *npl* vaisselle *f*; **to do** OR **wash the ~es** faire la vaisselle.
➤ **dish out** *vt sep inf* distribuer.
➤ **dish up** *vt sep inf* servir.

dish aerial Br, **dish antenna** Am *n* antenne *f* parabolique.

disharmony [ˌdɪs'hɑːmənɪ] *n* désaccord *m*, mésentente *f*.

dishcloth ['dɪʃklɒθ] *n* lavette *f*.

disheartened [dɪs'hɑːtnd] *adj* découragé(e).

disheartening [dɪs'hɑːtnɪŋ] *adj* décourageant(e).

dishevelled Br, **disheveled** Am [dɪ'ʃevəld] *adj* [person] échevelé(e) ; [hair] en désordre.

dishonest [dɪs'ɒnɪst] *adj* malhonnête.

dishonesty [dɪs'ɒnɪstɪ] *n* malhonnêteté *f*.

dishonor *etc* Am = **dishonour** *etc*.

dishonour Br, **dishonor** Am [dɪs'ɒnəʳ] ◇ *n* déshonneur *m* ◇ *vt* déshonorer.

dishonourable Br, **dishonorable** Am [dɪs'ɒnərəbl] *adj* [person] peu honorable ; [behaviour] déshonorant(e).

dish soap *n* Am liquide *m* pour la vaisselle.

dish towel *n* Am torchon *m*.

dishwasher ['dɪʃˌwɒʃəʳ] *n* [machine] lave-vaisselle *m inv*.

dishy ['dɪʃɪ] (*compar* **-ier** ; *superl* **-iest**) *adj* Br inf mignon(onne), sexy (*inv*).

disillusioned [ˌdɪsɪ'luːʒnd] *adj* désillusionné(e), désenchanté(e) ; **to become ~** perdre ses illusions ; **to be ~ with** ne plus avoir d'illusions sur.

disillusionment [ˌdɪsɪ'luːʒnmənt] *n* :

~ (with) désillusion *f* OR désenchantement *m* (en ce qui concerne).

disincentive [ˌdɪsɪn'sentɪv] *n* : **to be a ~** avoir un effet dissuasif ; [in work context] être démotivant(e).

disinclined [ˌdɪsɪn'klaɪnd] *adj* : **to be ~ to do sthg** être peu disposé(e) à faire qqch.

disinfect [ˌdɪsɪn'fekt] *vt* désinfecter.

disinfectant [ˌdɪsɪn'fektənt] *n* désinfectant. *m*.

disinformation [ˌdɪsɪnfə'meɪʃn] *n* désinformation *f*.

disingenuous [ˌdɪsɪn'dʒenjʊəs] *adj* peu sincère.

disinherit [ˌdɪsɪn'herɪt] *vt* déshériter.

disintegrate [dɪs'ɪntɪgreɪt] *vi* - **1.** [object] se désintégrer, se désagréger - **2.** fig [project] s'écrouler ; [marriage] se désagréger.

disintegration [dɪsˌɪntɪ'greɪʃn] *n* - **1.** [of object] désintégration *f*, désagrégation *f* - **2.** fig [of project, marriage] effondrement *m*.

disinterested [ˌdɪs'ɪntrəstɪd] *adj* - **1.** [objective] désintéressé(e) - **2.** inf [uninterested] : **~ (in)** indifférent(e) (à).

disinvestment [ˌdɪsɪn'vestmənt] *n* désinvestissement *m*.

disjointed [dɪs'dʒɔɪntɪd] *adj* décousu(e).

disk [dɪsk] *n* - **1.** COMPUT disque *m*, disquette *f* - **2.** Am = **disc**.

disk drive Br, **diskette drive** Am *n* COMPUT lecteur *m* de disques OR de disquettes.

diskette [dɪs'ket] *n* COMPUT disquette *f*.

diskette drive *n* Am = **disk drive**.

disk operating system *n* COMPUT système *m* d'exploitation (à disques).

dislike [dɪs'laɪk] ◇ *n* : **~ (of)** aversion *f* (pour) ; **her likes and ~s** ce qu'elle aime et ce qu'elle n'aime pas ; **to take a ~ to sb/sthg** prendre qqn/qqch en grippe ◇ *vt* ne pas aimer.

dislocate ['dɪsləkeɪt] *vt* - **1.** MED se démettre - **2.** [disrupt] désorganiser.

dislodge [dɪs'lɒdʒ] *vt* : **to ~ sthg (from)** déplacer qqch (de) ; [free] décoincer qqch (de) ; **to ~ sb from a position** déloger qqn d'un poste.

disloyal [ˌdɪs'lɔɪəl] *adj* : **~ (to)** déloyal(e) (envers).

dismal ['dɪzml] *adj* - **1.** [gloomy, depressing] lugubre - **2.** [unsuccessful - attempt] infructueux(euse) ; [- failure] lamentable.

dismantle [dɪs'mæntl] *vt* démanteler.

dismay [dɪs'meɪ] ◇ *n* consternation *f*; **to sb's ~** à la consternation de qqn ◇ *vt* consterner.

dismember [dɪs'membə'] *vt* démembrer.

dismiss [dɪs'mɪs] *vt* - **1.** [from job] : **to ~ sb (from)** congédier qqn (de) - **2.** [refuse to take seriously - idea, person] écarter ; [- plan, challenge] rejeter - **3.** [allow to leave - class] laisser sortir ; [- troops] faire rompre les rangs à.

dismissal [dɪs'mɪsl] *n* - **1.** [from job] licenciement *m*, renvoi *m* - **2.** [refusal to take seriously] rejet *m*.

dismissive [dɪs'mɪsɪv] *adj* méprisant(e) ; **to be ~ of** ne faire aucun cas de.

dismount [ˌdɪs'maʊnt] *vi* : **to ~ (from)** descendre (de).

disobedience [ˌdɪsə'biːdjəns] *n* désobéissance *f*.

disobedient [ˌdɪsə'biːdjənt] *adj* désobéissant(e).

disobey [ˌdɪsə'beɪ] ◇ *vt* désobéir à ◇ *vi* désobéir.

disorder [dɪs'ɔːdə'] *n* - **1.** [disarray] : **in ~** en désordre - **2.** *(U)* [rioting] troubles *mpl* - **3.** MED trouble *m*.

disordered [dɪs'ɔːdəd] *adj* - **1.** [in disarray] en désordre - **2.** MED : **mentally ~** déséquilibré(e).

disorderly [dɪs'ɔːdəlɪ] *adj* - **1.** [untidy - room] en désordre ; [- appearance] désordonné(e) - **2.** [unruly] indiscipliné(e).

disorderly conduct *n* JUR trouble *m* de l'ordre public.

disorganized, -ised [dɪs'ɔːgənaɪzd] *adj* [person] désorganisé(e), brouillon(onne) ; [system] mal conçu(e).

disorientated Br [dɪs'ɔːrɪənteɪtɪd], **disoriented** Am [dɪs'ɔːrɪəntɪd] *adj* désorienté(e).

disown [dɪs'əʊn] *vt* désavouer.

disparage [dɪ'spærɪdʒ] *vt* dénigrer.

disparaging [dɪ'spærɪdʒɪŋ] *adj* désobligeant(e).

disparate ['dɪspərət] *adj* disparate.

disparity [dɪ'spærətɪ] *(pl* -ies) *n* : **~ (between** OR **in)** disparité *f* (entre).

dispassionate [dɪ'spæʃnət] *adj* impartial(e).

dispatch [dɪ'spætʃ] ◇ *n* [message] dépêche *f* ◇ *vt* [send] envoyer, expédier.

dispatch box *n* Br POL [box] valise *f* officielle ; [in House of Commons] *tribune d'où parlent les membres du gouvernement et leurs homologues du cabinet fantôme.*

dispatch rider *n* MIL estafette *f* ; [courier] coursier *m*.

dispel [dɪ'spel] *(pt & pp* -**led** ; *cont* -**ling***) vt* [feeling] dissiper, chasser.

dispensable [dɪ'spensəbl] *adj* [person] dont on peut se passer ; [expenses, luxury] superflu(e).

dispensary [dɪ'spensərɪ] *(pl* -ies) *n* officine *f*.

dispensation [ˌdɪspen'seɪʃn] *n* [permission] dispense *f*.

dispense [dɪ'spens] *vt* [justice, medicine] administrer.

➠ **dispense with** *vt fus* - **1.** [do without] se passer de - **2.** [make unnecessary] rendre superflu(e) ; **to ~ with the need for sthg** rendre qqch superflu.

dispenser [dɪ'spensə'] *n* distributeur *m*.

dispensing chemist Br, **dispensing pharmacist** Am [dɪ'spensɪŋ-] *n* pharmacien *m*, -enne *f*.

dispersal [dɪ'spɜːsl] *n* dispersion *f*.

disperse [dɪ'spɜːs] ◇ *vt* - **1.** [crowd] disperser - **2.** [knowledge, news] répandre, propager ◇ *vi* se disperser.

dispirited [dɪ'spɪrɪtɪd] *adj* découragé(e), abattu(e).

dispiriting [dɪ'spɪrɪtɪŋ] *adj* décourageant(e).

displace [dɪs'pleɪs] *vt* - **1.** [cause to move] déplacer - **2.** [supplant] supplanter.

displaced person [dɪs'pleɪst-] *n* personne *f* déplacée.

displacement [dɪs'pleɪsmənt] *n* déplacement *m*.

display [dɪ'spleɪ] ◇ *n* - **1.** [arrangement] exposition *f* ; **on ~** exposé - **2.** [demonstration] manifestation *f* - **3.** [public event] spectacle *m* - **4.** [COMPUT - device] écran *m* ; [- information displayed] affichage *m*, visualisation *f* ◇ *vt* - **1.** [arrange] exposer - **2.** [show] faire preuve de, montrer.

display advertising *n (U)* placards *mpl* publicitaires.

displease [dɪs'pliːz] *vt* déplaire à, mécontenter ; **to be ~d with** être mécontent(e) de.

displeasure [dɪs'pleʒə'] *n* mécontentement *m*.

disposable [dɪ'spəʊzəbl] *adj* - **1.** [throw away] jetable - **2.** [income] disponible.

disposal [dɪ'spəʊzl] *n* - **1.** [removal] enlèvement *m* - **2.** [availability] : **at sb's ~** à la disposition de qqn.

dispose [dɪ'spəʊz] ➠ **dispose of** *vt fus* [get rid of] se débarrasser de ; [problem] résoudre.

disposed [dɪ'spəʊzd] *adj* - **1.** [willing] : **to be ~ to do sthg** être disposé(e) à faire qqch - **2.** [friendly] : **to be well ~** OR **towards sb** être bien disposé(e) envers qqn.

disposition [ˌdɪspə'zɪʃn] *n* - **1.** [temperament]

caractère *m*, tempérament *m* - **2.** [tendency] :
~ **to do sthg** tendance *f* à faire qqch.

dispossess [ˌdɪspə'zes] *vt* fml : **to ~ sb of sthg**
déposséder qqn de qqch.

disproportion [ˌdɪsprə'pɔːʃn] *n* disproportion *f*.

disproportionate [ˌdɪsprə'pɔːʃnət] *adj* :
~ **(to)** disproportionné(e) (à)

disprove [ˌdɪs'pruːv] *vt* réfuter.

dispute [dɪ'spjuːt] <> *n* - **1.** [quarrel] dispute *f*
- **2.** (*U*) [disagreement] désaccord *m* ; **in ~** [people]
en désaccord ; [matter] en discussion
- **3.** INDUSTRY conflit *m* <> *vt* contester.

disqualification [dɪsˌkwɒlɪfɪ'keɪʃn] *n* disqualification *f*.

disqualify [ˌdɪs'kwɒlɪfaɪ] (*pt* & *pp* -**ied**) *vt*
- **1.** [subj : authority] : **to ~ sb (from doing sthg)**
interdire à qqn (de faire qqch) ; **to ~ sb from
driving** Br retirer le permis de conduire à
qqn - **2.** [subj : illness, criminal record] : **to ~ sb (from
doing sthg)** rendre qqn incapable (de faire
qqch) - **3.** SPORT disqualifier.

disquiet [dɪs'kwaɪət] *n* inquiétude *f*.

disregard [ˌdɪsrɪ'gɑːd] <> *n* (*U*) : ~ **(for)** [money,
danger] mépris *m* (pour) ; [feelings] indifférence *f* (à) <> *vt* [fact] ignorer ; [danger] mépriser ;
[warning] ne pas tenir compte de.

disrepair [ˌdɪsrɪ'peəʳ] *n* délabrement *m* ; **to
fall into ~** tomber en ruines.

disreputable [dɪs'repjʊtəbl] *adj* peu respectable.

disrepute [ˌdɪsrɪ'pjuːt] *n* : **to bring sthg into ~**
discréditer qqch ; **to fall into ~** acquérir
une mauvaise réputation.

disrespectful [ˌdɪsrɪ'spektfʊl] *adj* irrespec-
tueux(euse).

disrupt [dɪs'rʌpt] *vt* perturber.

disruption [dɪs'rʌpʃn] *n* perturbation *f*.

disruptive [dɪs'rʌptɪv] *adj* perturbateur(trice).

dissatisfaction ['dɪsˌsætɪs'fækʃn] *n* mécontentement *m*.

dissatisfied [ˌdɪs'sætɪsfaɪd] *adj* : ~ **(with)** mé-
content(e) (de), pas satisfait(e) (de).

dissect [dɪ'sekt] *vt* lit & fig disséquer.

dissection [dɪ'sekʃn] *n* lit & fig dissection *f*.

disseminate [dɪ'semɪneɪt] *vt* disséminer.

dissemination [dɪˌsemɪ'neɪʃn] *n* dissémination *f*.

dissension [dɪ'senʃn] *n* discorde *f*, dissension *f*.

dissent [dɪ'sent] <> *n* dissentiment *m* <> *vi* :
to ~ (from) être en désaccord (avec).

dissenter [dɪ'sentəʳ] *n* dissident *m*, -e *f*.

dissenting [dɪ'sentɪŋ] *adj* : ~ **voice** opinion *f*
contraire.

dissertation [ˌdɪsə'teɪʃn] *n* dissertation *f*.

disservice [ˌdɪs'sɜːvɪs] *n* : **to do sb a ~** rendre
un mauvais service à qqn.

dissident ['dɪsɪdənt] *n* dissident *m*, -e *f*.

dissimilar [ˌdɪ'sɪmɪləʳ] *adj* : ~ **(to)** différent(e)
(de).

dissipate ['dɪsɪpeɪt] <> *vt* - **1.** [heat] dissiper
- **2.** [efforts, money] gaspiller <> *vi* se dissiper.

dissipated ['dɪsɪpeɪtɪd] *adj* [person, life] disso-
lu(e).

dissociate [dɪ'səʊʃɪeɪt] *vt* dissocier ; **to ~ o.s.
from** se désolidariser de.

dissolute ['dɪsəluːt] *adj* dissolu(e).

dissolution [ˌdɪsə'luːʃn] *n* dissolution *f*.

dissolve [dɪ'zɒlv] <> *vt* dissoudre <> *vi*
- **1.** [substance] se dissoudre - **2.** fig [disappear]
disparaître.

   dissolve in(to) *vt fus* : **to ~ into tears** fondre en larmes.

dissuade [dɪ'sweɪd] *vt* : **to ~ sb (from)** dissuader qqn (de).

distance ['dɪstəns] <> *n* distance *f* ; **at a ~** assez loin ; **from a ~** de loin ; **in the ~** au loin
<> *vt* : **to ~ o.s. from** se distancier de.

distant ['dɪstənt] *adj* - **1.** [gen] : ~ **(from)** éloi-
gné(e) (de) - **2.** [reserved - person, manner] dis-
tant(e).

distaste [dɪs'teɪst] *n* : ~ **(for)** dégoût *m*
(pour).

distasteful [dɪs'teɪstfʊl] *adj* répugnant(e),
déplaisant(e).

Dist. Atty *abbr* of district attorney.

distemper [dɪ'stempəʳ] *n* (*U*) - **1.** [paint] détrempe *f* - **2.** [disease] maladie *f* de Carré.

distended [dɪ'stendɪd] *adj* [stomach] disten-
du(e).

distil Br (*pt* & *pp* -**led** ; *cont* -**ling**), **distill** Am
[dɪ'stɪl] *vt* - **1.** [liquid] distiller - **2.** fig [information]
tirer.

distiller [dɪ'stɪləʳ] *n* distillateur *m*.

distillery [dɪ'stɪlərɪ] (*pl* -**ies**) *n* distillerie *f*.

distinct [dɪ'stɪŋkt] *adj* - **1.** [different] : ~ **(from)**
distinct(e) (de), différent(e) (de) ; **as ~ from**
par opposition à - **2.** [definite - improvement] net
(nette) ; **a ~ possibility** une forte chance.

distinction [dɪ'stɪŋkʃn] *n* - **1.** [difference] distinction *f*, différence *f* ; **to draw** OR **make a
~ between** faire une distinction entre
- **2.** (*U*) [excellence] distinction *f* - **3.** [exam result]
mention *f* très bien.

distinctive [dɪ'stɪŋktɪv] *adj* caractéristique.

distinctly [dɪ'stɪŋktlɪ] *adv* [see, remember] clairement.

distinguish [dɪ'stɪŋgwɪʃ] *vt* - **1.** [tell apart] : to ~ sthg from sthg distinguer qqch de qqch, faire la différence entre qqch et qqch - **2.** [perceive] distinguer - **3.** [characterize] caractériser - **4.** [excel] : to ~ o.s. se distinguer.

distinguished [dɪ'stɪŋgwɪʃt] *adj* distingué(e).

distinguishing [dɪ'stɪŋgwɪʃɪŋ] *adj* [feature, mark] caractéristique.

distort [dɪ'stɔːt] *vt* déformer.

distorted [dɪ'stɔːtɪd] *adj* déformé(e).

distortion [dɪ'stɔːʃn] *n* déformation *f*.

distract [dɪ'strækt] *vt* : to ~ sb (from) distraire qqn (de).

distracted [dɪ'stræktɪd] *adj* [preoccupied] soucieux(euse).

distraction [dɪ'strækʃn] *n* - **1.** [interruption, diversion] distraction *f* - **2.** [state of mind] confusion *f*; to drive sb to ~ rendre qqn fou.

distraught [dɪ'strɔːt] *adj* éperdu(e).

distress [dɪ'stres] <> *n* [anxiety] détresse *f*; [pain] douleur *f*, souffrance *f* <> *vt* affliger.

distressed [dɪ'strest] *adj* [anxious, upset] affligé(e).

distressing [dɪ'stresɪŋ] *adj* [news, image] pénible.

distress signal *n* signal *m* de détresse.

distribute [dɪ'strɪbjuːt] *vt* - **1.** [gen] distribuer - **2.** [spread out] répartir.

distribution [,dɪstrɪ'bjuːʃn] *n* - **1.** [gen] distribution *f* - **2.** [spreading out] répartition *f*.

distributor [dɪ'strɪbjutəʳ] *n* AUT & COMM distributeur *m*.

district ['dɪstrɪkt] *n* - **1.** [area - of country] région *f*; [- of town] quartier *m* - **2.** ADMIN district *m*.

district attorney *n* Am ≃ procureur *m* de la République.

district council *n* Br ≃ conseil *m* général.

district nurse *n* Br infirmière *f* visiteuse OR à domicile.

District of Columbia *n* district *m* de Columbia ; in the ~ dans le district de Columbia.

distrust [dɪs'trʌst] <> *n* méfiance *f* <> *vt* se méfier de.

distrustful [dɪs'trʌstfʊl] *adj* méfiant(e).

disturb [dɪ'stɜːb] *vt* - **1.** [interrupt] déranger - **2.** [upset, worry] inquiéter - **3.** [sleep, surface] troubler.

disturbance [dɪ'stɜːbəns] *n* - **1.** POL troubles *mpl*; [fight] tapage *m*; ~ of the peace JUR trouble *m* de l'ordre public - **2.** [interruption] dérangement *m* - **3.** [of mind, emotions] trouble *m*.

disturbed [dɪ'stɜːbd] *adj* - **1.** [emotionally, mentally] perturbé(e) - **2.** [worried] inquiet(ète).

disturbing [dɪ'stɜːbɪŋ] *adj* [image] bouleversant(e) ; [news] inquiétant(e).

disunity [,dɪs'juːnətɪ] *n* désunion *f*.

disuse [,dɪs'juːs] *n* : to fall into ~ [factory] être à l'abandon ; [regulation] tomber en désuétude.

disused [,dɪs'juːzd] *adj* désaffecté(e).

ditch [dɪtʃ] <> *n* fossé *m* <> *vt inf* [boyfriend, girlfriend] plaquer ; [old car, clothes] se débarrasser de ; [plan] abandonner.

dither ['dɪðəʳ] *vi* hésiter.

ditto ['dɪtəʊ] *adv* idem.

diuretic [,daɪjʊ'retɪk] *n* diurétique *m*.

diva ['diːvə] (*pl* -s) *n* diva *f*.

divan [dɪ'væn] *n* divan *m*.

divan bed *n* divan-lit *m*.

dive [daɪv] (Br *pt* & *pp* -d, Am *pt* & *pp* -d OR **dove**) <> *vi* plonger ; [bird, plane] piquer ; she ~d into the crowd elle se jeta dans la foule <> *n* - **1.** [gen] plongeon *m* - **2.** [of plane] piqué *m* - **3.** *inf pej* [bar, restaurant] bouge *m*.

dive-bomb *vt* bombarder en piqué.

diver ['daɪvəʳ] *n* plongeur *m*, -euse *f*.

diverge [daɪ'vɜːdʒ] *vi* : to ~ (from) diverger (de).

divergence [daɪ'vɜːdʒəns] *n* divergence *f*.

divergent [daɪ'vɜːdʒənt] *adj* divergent(e).

diverse [daɪ'vɜːs] *adj* divers(e).

diversification [daɪ,vɜːsɪfɪ'keɪʃn] *n* diversification *f*.

diversify [daɪ'vɜːsɪfaɪ] (*pt* & *pp* -ied) <> *vt* diversifier <> *vi* se diversifier.

diversion [daɪ'vɜːʃn] *n* - **1.** [amusement] distraction *f*; [tactical] diversion *f* - **2.** [of traffic] déviation *f* - **3.** [of river, funds] détournement *m*.

diversionary [daɪ'vɜːʃnrɪ] *adj* [tactics] de diversion.

diversity [daɪ'vɜːsətɪ] *n* diversité *f*.

divert [daɪ'vɜːt] *vt* - **1.** [traffic] dévier - **2.** [river, funds] détourner - **3.** [person - amuse] distraire ; [- tactically] détourner.

divest [daɪ'vest] *vt fml* : to ~ sb of dépouiller qqn de ; to ~ o.s. of se défaire de.

divide [dɪ'vaɪd] <> *vt* - **1.** [separate] séparer - **2.** [share out] diviser, partager ; to ~ sthg between OR among partager qqch entre - **3.** [split up] : to ~ sthg (into) diviser qqch (en) - **4.** MATH : 89 ~d by 3 89 divisé par 3 - **5.** [people - in disagreement] diviser ◇ *vi* se diviser ◇ *n* [difference] division *f.*

◆ **divide up** *vt sep* - **1.** [split up] diviser - **2.** [share out] partager.

divided [dɪ'vaɪdɪd] *adj* [nation] divisé(e) ; [opinions, loyalties] partagé(e).

dividend ['dɪvɪdend] *n* dividende *m ;* **to pay ~s** fig porter ses fruits.

dividers [dɪ'vaɪdəz] *npl* compas *m* à pointes sèches.

dividing line [dɪ'vaɪdɪŋ-] *n* ligne *f* de démarcation.

divine [dɪ'vaɪn] ◇ *adj* divin(e) ◇ *vt* - **1.** [truth, meaning] deviner ; [future] prédire - **2.** [water] découvrir, détecter.

diving ['daɪvɪŋ] *n* (U) plongeon *m ;* [with breathing apparatus] plongée *f* (sous-marine).

divingboard ['daɪvɪŋbɔːd] *n* plongeoir *m.*

diving suit *n* combinaison *f* de plongée.

divinity [dɪ'vɪnətɪ] (*pl* -ies) *n* - **1.** [godliness, god] divinité *f* - **2.** [study] théologie *f.*

divisible [dɪ'vɪzəbl] *adj :* **~ (by)** divisible (par).

division [dɪ'vɪʒn] *n* - **1.** [gen] division *f* - **2.** [separation] séparation *f.*

division sign *n* signe *m* de division.

divisive [dɪ'vaɪsɪv] *adj* qui sème la division OR la discorde.

divorce [dɪ'vɔːs] ◇ *n* divorce *m* ◇ *vt* - **1.** [husband, wife] divorcer - **2.** [separate] : **to ~ sthg from** séparer qqch de.

divorced [dɪ'vɔːst] *adj* divorcé(e).

divorcee [dɪvɔː'siː] *n* divorcé *m*, -e *f.*

divulge [daɪ'vʌldʒ] *vt* divulguer.

DIY (*abbr of* **do-it-yourself**) *n* Br bricolage *m.*

dizziness ['dɪzɪnɪs] *n* vertige *m.*

dizzy ['dɪzɪ] (*compar* -ier ; *superl* -iest) *adj* - **1.** [giddy] : **to feel ~** avoir la tête qui tourne - **2.** fig [height] vertigineux(euse).

DJ *n* - **1.** (*abbr of* **disc jockey**) disc-jockey *m* - **2.** (*abbr of* **dinner jacket**) smoking *m.*

Djakarta [dʒə'kɑːtə] = **Jakarta**.

DJIA (*abbr of* **Dow Jones Industrial Average**) *n* Am *indice Dow Jones.*

Djibouti [dʒɪ'buːtɪ] *n* Djibouti ; **in ~** à Djibouti.

dl (*abbr of* **decilitre**) dl.

DLit(t) [ˌdiː'lɪt] (*abbr of* **Doctor of Letters**) *n docteur ès lettres.*

DLO (*abbr of* **dead-letter office**) *n centre de recherche du courrier.*

dm (*abbr of* **decimetre**) dm.

DM (*abbr of* **Deutsche Mark**) DM.

DMA (*abbr of* **direct memory access**) *n accès direct à la mémoire.*

DMus [ˌdiː'mjuːz] (*abbr of* **Doctor of Music**) *n docteur en musique.*

DMZ (*abbr of* **demilitarized zone**) *n zone démilitarisée.*

DNA (*abbr of* **deoxyribonucleic acid**) *n* ADN *m.*

D-notice *n* Br *censure imposée à la presse pour sécurité d'État.*

do¹ [duː] (*pt* did ; *pp* done, *pl* dos OR do's) ◇ *aux vb* - **1.** (in negatives) : **don't leave it there** ne le laisse pas là ; **I didn't want to see him** je ne voulais pas le voir - **2.** (in questions) : **what did he want?** qu'est-ce qu'il voulait? ; **~ you think she'll come?** tu crois qu'elle viendra? - **3.** (referring back to previous verb) : **she reads more than I ~** elle lit plus que moi ; **I like reading — so ~ I** j'aime lire — moi aussi - **4.** (in question tags) : **you know her, don't you?** tu la connais, n'est-ce pas? ; **I upset you, didn't I?** je t'ai fait de la peine, n'est-ce pas? ; **so you think you can dance, ~ you?** alors tu t'imagines que tu sais danser, c'est ça? - **5.** [for emphasis] : **I did tell you but you've forgotten** je te l'avais bien dit, mais tu l'as oublié ; **~ come in** entrez donc ◇ *vt* - **1.** [perform an activity, a service] faire ; **to ~ aerobics/gymnastics** faire de l'aérobic/de la gymnastique ; **they ~ gourmet dinners** ils font OR préparent des repas gastronomiques ; **to ~ the cooking/housework** faire la cuisine/le ménage ; **to ~ one's hair** se coiffer ; **to ~ one's teeth** se laver OR se brosser les dents - **2.** [take action] faire ; **to ~ something about sthg** trouver une solution pour qqch ; **I don't know what to ~ with him!** je ne sais vraiment pas que faire de lui! - **3.** [have particular effect] faire ; **to ~ more harm than good** faire plus de mal que de bien - **4.** [referring to job] : **what do you ~?** qu'est-ce que vous faites dans la vie? - **5.** [study] faire ; **I did physics at school** j'ai fait de la physique à l'école - **6.** [travel at a particular speed] faire, rouler ; **the car can ~ 110 mph** ≃ la voiture peut faire du 180 à l'heure - **7.** [be good enough for] : **that'll ~ me nicely** cela m'ira très bien, cela fera très bien mon affaire ◇ *vi* - **1.** [act] faire ; **~ as I tell you** fais comme je te dis ; **you would ~ well to reconsider** tu ferais bien de reconsidérer la question - **2.** [perform in a particular way] : **they're ~ing really well** leurs affaires marchent bien ; **he could ~ better** il pourrait mieux faire ; **how did you ~ in the exam?** comment ça a marché à l'examen? - **3.** [be good enough, be sufficient] suffire, aller ; **will £6 ~?** est-ce que 6 livres suf-

firont?, 6 livres, ça ira? ; **that will ~** ça suffit
◇ *n* [party] fête *f*, soirée *f*.

◆ **dos** *npl* : **~s and don'ts** ce qu'il faut faire et
ne pas faire.

◆ **do away with** *vt fus* supprimer.

◆ **do down** *vt sep inf* dire du mal de.

◆ **do for** *vt fus inf* : **these kids will ~ for me** ces
gosses vont me tuer ; **I'm done for** je suis fichu OR foutu.

◆ **do in** *vt sep inf* supprimer, assassiner.

◆ **do out of** *vt sep inf* : **to ~ sb out of sthg** escroquer OR carotter qqch à qqn.

◆ **do up** *vt sep* - **1.** [fasten - shoelaces, shoes] attacher ; [- buttons, coat] boutonner ; **your shirt's
not done up** ta chemise est déboutonnée
- **2.** [decorate - room, house] refaire - **3.** [wrap up]
emballer.

◆ **do with** *vt fus* - **1.** [need] avoir besoin de
- **2.** [have connection with] : **that has nothing to
~ with it** ça n'a rien à voir, ça n'a aucun
rapport ; **what's that got to ~ with it?** et
alors, quel rapport?, qu'est-ce que ça a à
voir? ; **I had nothing to ~ with it** je n'y étais
pour rien.

◆ **do without** ◇ *vt fus* se passer de ◇ *vi*
s'en passer.

do² (*abbr of* ditto) do.

DOA (*abbr of* **dead on arrival**) *adj* mort(e)
pendant son transport à l'hôpital.

doable ['duːəbl] *adj inf* faisable.

dob *abbr of* date of birth.

Doberman ['dəʊbəmən] (*pl* -s) *n* : **~ (pinscher)**
doberman *m*.

docile [Br 'dəʊsaɪl, Am 'dɒsəl] *adj* docile.

dock [dɒk] ◇ *n* - **1.** [in harbour] docks *mpl*
- **2.** JUR banc *m* des accusés ◇ *vt* [wages] faire
une retenue sur ◇ *vi* [ship] arriver à quai.

docker ['dɒkər] *n* docker *m*.

docket ['dɒkɪt] *n* Br fiche *f* (descriptive).

docklands ['dɒkləndz] *npl* Br docks *mpl*.

dockworker ['dɒkwɜːkər] = **docker.**

dockyard ['dɒkjɑːd] *n* chantier *m* naval.

doctor ['dɒktər] ◇ *n* - **1.** MED docteur *m*, médecin *m* ; **to go to the ~'s** aller chez le docteur - **2.** UNIV docteur *m* ◇ *vt* - **1.** [results, report]
falsifier ; [text, food] altérer - **2.** Br [cat] châtrer.

doctorate ['dɒktərət], **doctor's degree** *n*
doctorat *m*.

doctrinaire [ˌdɒktrɪ'neər] *adj* doctrinaire.

doctrine ['dɒktrɪn] *n* doctrine *f*.

docudrama [ˌdɒkjʊ'drɑːmə] (*pl* -s) *n* docu-
drame *m*.

document [*n* 'dɒkjʊmənt, *vt* 'dɒkjʊment] ◇ *n*
document *m* ◇ *vt* documenter.

documentary [ˌdɒkjʊ'mentərɪ] (*pl* -ies)
◇ *adj* documentaire ◇ *n* documentaire
m.

documentation [ˌdɒkjʊmen'teɪʃn] *n* documentation *f*.

DOD (*abbr of* **Department of Defense**) *n* ministère américain de la défense.

doddering ['dɒdərɪŋ], **doddery** ['dɒdərɪ]
adj inf branlant(e).

doddle ['dɒdl] *n* Br inf : **it was a ~** c'était du
gâteau.

Dodecanese [ˌdəʊdɪkə'niːz] *npl* : **the ~** le Dodécanèse ; **in the ~** dans le Dodécanèse.

dodge [dɒdʒ] ◇ *n inf* combine *f* ◇ *vt* éviter,
esquiver ◇ *vi* s'esquiver.

Dodgems® ['dɒdʒəmz] *npl* Br autos *fpl* tam-
ponneuses.

dodgy ['dɒdʒɪ] *adj* Br inf [plan, deal] dou-
teux(euse).

doe [dəʊ] *n* - **1.** [deer] biche *f* - **2.** [rabbit] lapine
f.

DOE *n* - **1.** (*abbr of* **Department of the Environment**) *ministère britannique de l'environnement* - **2.** (*abbr of* **Department of Energy**)
ministère américain de l'énergie.

doer ['duːər] *n inf* personne *f* dynamique.

does [*weak form* dəz, *strong form* dʌz] ⯈ **do.**

doesn't ['dʌznt] = **does not.**

dog [dɒg] (*pt* & *pp* -**ged** ; *cont* -**ging**) ◇ *n*
- **1.** [animal] chien *m*, chienne *f* ; **it's a ~'s life**
c'est une vie de chien ; **this country is going
to the ~s** inf ce pays va à vau-l'eau - **2.** Am [hot
dog] hot dog *m* ◇ *vt* - **1.** [subj : person - follow]
suivre de près - **2.** [subj : problems, bad luck]
poursuivre.

dog biscuit *n* biscuit *m* pour chien.

dog collar *n* - **1.** [of dog] collier *m* de chien
- **2.** [of priest] col *m* d'ecclésiastique.

dog-eared [-ɪəd] *adj* écorné(e).

dog-eat-dog *adj* : **it's ~** c'est la loi de la
jungle.

dog-end *n inf* [of cigarette] mégot *m*.

dogfight ['dɒgfaɪt] *n* - **1.** [between dogs] combat *m* de chiens - **2.** [between aircraft] combat *m*
aérien.

dog food *n* nourriture *f* pour chiens.

dogged ['dɒgɪd] *adj* opiniâtre.

doggone ['dɒgɒn], **doggoned** ['dɒgɒnd]
adj Am inf fichu(e).

doggy ['dɒgɪ] (*pl* -ies) *n* toutou *m*.

doggy bag *n* sac *m* en plastique pour emporter
les restes d'un repas.

dogma ['dɒgmə] *n* dogme *m*.

dogmatic [dɒg'mætɪk] *adj* dogmatique.

do-gooder [-'gʊdər] *n* pej bonne âme *f*.

dog paddle *n* nage *f* du chien.

dogsbody ['dɒgz,bɒdɪ] (*pl* -**ies**) *n* Br inf [woman] bonne *f* à tout faire ; [man] factotum *m*.

dog tag *n* MIL plaque *f* d'identification.

doing ['duːɪŋ] *n* : **is this your ~?** c'est toi qui est cause de tout cela?
→ **doings** *npl* actions *fpl*.

do-it-yourself *n* (U) bricolage *m*.

doldrums ['dɒldrəmz] *npl* : **to be in the ~** fig être dans le marasme.

dole [dəʊl] *n* Br [unemployment benefit] allocation *f* de chômage ; **to be on the ~** être au chômage.
→ **dole out** *vt sep* [food, money] distribuer au compte-gouttes.

doleful ['dəʊlfʊl] *adj* morne.

doll [dɒl] *n* poupée *f*.

dollar ['dɒlər] *n* dollar *m*.

dolled up [dɒld-] *adj* inf pomponné(e).

dollhouse Am = **doll's house**.

dollop ['dɒləp] *n* inf bonne cuillerée *f*.

doll's house Br, **dollhouse** [dɒlhaʊs] Am *n* maison *f* de poupée.

dolly ['dɒlɪ] (*pl* -**ies**) *n* - **1.** [doll] poupée *f* - **2.** [for TV or film camera] travelling *m*.

dolly bird *n* Br inf dated poupée *f*.

Dolomites ['dɒləmaɪts] *npl* : **the ~** les Dolomites *fpl*.

dolphin ['dɒlfɪn] *n* dauphin *m*.

domain [də'meɪn] *n* lit & fig domaine *m*.

dome [dəʊm] *n* dôme *m*.

domestic [də'mestɪk] ⟨> *adj* - **1.** [policy, politics, flight] intérieur(e) - **2.** [chores, animal] domestique - **3.** [home-loving] casanier(ère) ⟨> *n* domestique *mf*.

domestic appliance *n* appareil *m* ménager.

domesticated [də'mestɪkeɪtɪd] *adj* - **1.** [animal] domestiqué(e) - **2.** hum [person] popote (inv).

domesticity [,dəʊme'stɪsətɪ] *n* (U) vie *f* de famille.

domicile ['dɒmɪsaɪl] *n* domicile *m*.

dominance ['dɒmɪnəns] *n* prédominance *f* ; [of person] supériorité *f*.

dominant ['dɒmɪnənt] *adj* dominant(e) ; [personality, group] dominateur(trice).

dominate ['dɒmɪneɪt] *vt* dominer.

dominating ['dɒmɪneɪtɪŋ] *adj* [person] dominateur(trice).

domination [,dɒmɪ'neɪʃn] *n* domination *f*.

domineering [,dɒmɪ'nɪərɪŋ] *adj* autoritaire.

Dominica [də'mɪnɪkə] *n* la Dominique ; **in ~** à la Dominique.

Dominican Republic [də'mɪnɪkən-] *n* : **the ~** la République Dominicaine ; **in the ~** en République Dominicaine.

dominion [də'mɪnjən] *n* - **1.** (U) [power] domination *f* - **2.** [land] territoire *m*.

domino ['dɒmɪnəʊ] (*pl* -**es**) *n* domino *m*.
→ **dominoes** *npl* dominos *mpl*.

domino effect *n* réaction *f* en chaîne.

don [dɒn] (*pt* & *pp* -**ned** ; *cont* -**ning**) ⟨> *n* Br UNIV professeur *m* d'université ⟨> *vt* [clothing] revêtir.

donate [də'neɪt] *vt* faire don de.

donation [də'neɪʃn] *n* don *m*.

done [dʌn] ⟨> *pp* ⟩ **do** ⟨> *adj* - **1.** [job, work] achevé(e) ; **I'm nearly ~** j'ai presque fini - **2.** [cooked] cuit(e) - **3.** [socially acceptable] : **that's not the ~ thing** ça ne se fait pas ⟨> *excl* [to conclude deal] tope!

donkey ['dɒŋkɪ] (*pl* -**s**) *n* âne *m*, ânesse *f*.

donkey jacket *n* Br grosse veste *f*.

donkeywork ['dɒŋkɪwɜːk] *n* Br inf : **to do the ~** faire le sale boulot.

donor ['dəʊnər] *n* - **1.** MED donneur *m*, -euse *f* - **2.** [to charity] donateur *m*, -trice *f*.

donor card *n* carte *f* de donneur.

don't [dəʊnt] = **do not**.

doodle ['duːdl] ⟨> *n* griffonnage *m* ⟨> *vi* griffonner.

doom [duːm] *n* [fate] destin *m*.

doomed [duːmd] *adj* condamné(e) ; **they were ~ to die** ils étaient condamnés à mourir ; **the plan was ~ to failure** le plan était voué à l'échec.

door [dɔːr] *n* porte *f* ; [of vehicle] portière *f* ; **to open the ~ to sthg** fig ouvrir la voie à qqch.

doorbell ['dɔːbel] *n* sonnette *f*.

doorhandle ['dɔːhændl] *n* poignée *f* de porte.

doorknob ['dɔːnɒb] *n* bouton *m* de porte.

doorknocker ['dɔː,nɒkər] *n* heurtoir *m*.

doorman ['dɔːmən] (*pl* -**men** [-mən]) *n* portier *m*.

doormat ['dɔːmæt] *n* lit & fig paillasson *m*.

doorstep ['dɔːstep] *n* pas *m* de la porte.

doorstop ['dɔːstɒp] *n* butoir *m* de porte.

door-to-door *adj* [salesman, selling] à domicile.

doorway ['dɔːweɪ] *n* embrasure *f* de la porte.

dope [dəʊp] ⟨> *n* inf - **1.** [drugs] sl dope *f* - **2.** [for athlete, horse] dopant *m* - **3.** inf [fool] imbécile *mf* ⟨> *vt* [horse] doper.

dope test *n* contrôle *m* anti-dopage.

dopey ['dəʊpɪ] (*compar* -**ier** ; *superl* -**iest**) *adj* inf abruti(e).

dormant ['dɔ:mənt] *adj* - **1.** [volcano] endormi(e) - **2.** [law] inappliqué(e).

dormer (window) ['dɔ:məʳ-] *n* lucarne *f*.

dormice ['dɔ:maɪs] *pl* ⊏═ **dormouse**.

dormitory ['dɔ:mətrɪ] (*pl* -**ies**) *n* - **1.** [gen] dortoir *m* - **2.** Am [in university] ≃ cité *f* universitaire.

Dormobile® ['dɔ:məˌbi:l] *n* Br camping-car *m*.

dormouse ['dɔ:maʊs] (*pl* -**mice** [-maɪs]) *n* loir *m*.

Dors (*abbr of* **Dorset**) *comté anglais*.

DOS [dɒs] (*abbr of* **disk operating system**) *n* DOS *m*.

dosage ['dəʊsɪdʒ] *n* dosage *m*.

dose [dəʊs] ⟨⟩ *n* - **1.** MED dose *f* - **2.** fig [amount] : **a ~ of the measles** la rougeole ⟨⟩ *vt* : **to ~ sb with sthg** administrer qqch à qqn.

doss [dɒs] ➡ **doss down** *vi* Br inf crécher.

dosser ['dɒsəʳ] *n* Br inf clochard *m*, -e *f*.

dosshouse ['dɒshaʊs, *pl* -haʊzɪz] *n* Br inf asile *m* de nuit.

dossier ['dɒsɪeɪ] *n* dossier *m*.

dot [dɒt] (*pt* & *pp* -**ted** ; *cont* -**ting**) ⟨⟩ *n* point *m*; **on the ~** à l'heure pile ⟨⟩ *vt* : **dotted with** parsemé(e) de.

DOT (*abbr of* **Department of Transportation**) *n ministère américain du transport*.

dotage ['dəʊtɪdʒ] *n* : **to be in one's ~** être gâteux(euse).

dote [dəʊt] ➡ **dote (up)on** *vt fus* adorer.

doting ['dəʊtɪŋ] *adj* : **she has a ~ grandfather** elle a un grand-père qui l'adore.

dot-matrix printer *n* imprimante *f* matricielle.

dotted line ['dɒtɪd-] *n* ligne *f* pointillée ; **to sign on the ~** fig donner formellement son accord.

dotty ['dɒtɪ] (*compar* -**ier** ; *superl* -**iest**) *adj* inf toqué(e).

double ['dʌbl] ⟨⟩ *adj* double ; **~ doors** porte *f* à deux battants ; **"ally" is spelt "a", ~"l", "y"** « ally » s'écrit « a », deux « l », « y » ⟨⟩ *adv* - **1.** [twice] : **~ the amount** deux fois plus ; **to see ~** voir double - **2.** [in two] en deux ; **to bend ~** se plier en deux ⟨⟩ *n* - **1.** [twice as much] : **I earn ~ what I used to** je gagne le double de ce que je gagnais auparavant - **2.** [drink, look-alike] double *m* - **3.** CINEMA doublure *f* ⟨⟩ *vt* doubler ⟨⟩ *vi* - **1.** [increase twofold]

doubler - **2.** [have second purpose] : **to ~ as** faire office de.

➡ **doubles** *npl* TENNIS double *m*.

➡ **double up** ⟨⟩ *vt sep* : **to be ~d up** être plié(e) en deux ⟨⟩ *vi* [bend over] se plier en deux.

double act *n* duo *m*.

double agent *n* agent *m* double.

double-barrelled Br, **double-barreled** Am [-'bærəld] *adj* - **1.** [shotgun] à deux coups - **2.** [name] à rallonge.

double bass [-beɪs] *n* contrebasse *f*.

double bed *n* lit *m* pour deux personnes, grand lit.

double-breasted [-'brestɪd] *adj* [jacket] croisé(e).

double-check *vt* & *vi* revérifier.

double chin *n* double menton *m*.

double cream *n* Br crème *f* fraîche épaisse.

double-cross *vt* trahir.

double-dealer *n* : **to be a ~** jouer double jeu.

double-decker [-'dekəʳ] *n* [bus] autobus *m* à impériale.

double-declutch [-di:'klʌtʃ] *vi* Br AUT faire un double débrayage.

double-density *adj* COMPUT [disk] doubledensité (*inv*).

double-dutch *n* Br charabia *m*.

double-edged [-'edʒd] *adj* lit & fig à double tranchant.

double entendre [,du:blɑ̃'tɑ̃dr] *n* allusion *f* grivoise.

double figures *npl* : **to be in ~** être audessus de dix.

double-glazing [-'gleɪzɪŋ] *n* double vitrage *m*.

double-jointed [-'dʒɔɪntɪd] *adj* désarticulé(e).

double-park *vi* se garer en double file.

double-quick *adj* & *adv* inf en deux temps trois mouvements.

double room *n* chambre *f* pour deux personnes.

double-sided *adj* COMPUT [disk] double-face.

double standards *npl* : **to have ~** avoir deux poids, deux mesures.

double take *n* : **to do a ~** marquer un temps d'arrêt.

double-talk *n* (U) propos *mpl* ambigus.

double time *n* tarif *m* double.

double vision *n* vue *f* double.

double whammy [-'wæmɪ] *n* double malédiction *f*.

doubly ['dʌblɪ] *adv* doublement.

doubt [daʊt] <> *n* doute *m ;* **there is no ~ that** il n'y a aucun doute que ; **without (a) ~** sans aucun doute ; **beyond all ~** indubitablement ; **to be in ~** [person] ne pas être sûr(e) ; [outcome] être incertain(e) ; **to cast ~ on sthg** mettre qqch en doute ; **no ~** sans aucun doute <> *vt* douter ; **to ~ whether** OR **if** douter que.

doubtful ['daʊtfʊl] *adj* - **1.** [decision, future] incertain(e) - **2.** [unsure] : **to be ~ about** OR **of** douter de - **3.** [person, value] douteux(euse).

doubtless ['daʊtlɪs] *adv* sans aucun doute.

dough [dəʊ] *n (U)* - **1.** CULIN pâte *f* - **2.** *v inf* [money] fric *m*.

doughnut ['dəʊnʌt] *n* beignet *m*.

dour [dʊəʳ] *adj* austère.

douse [daʊs] *vt* - **1.** [fire, flames] éteindre - **2.** [drench] tremper.

dove[1] [dʌv] *n* [bird] colombe *f*.

dove[2] [dəʊv] *Am pt* ⊳ **dive**.

dovecot(e) ['dʌvkɒt] *n* colombier *m*.

Dover ['dəʊvəʳ] *n* Douvres.

dovetail ['dʌvteɪl] *fig* <> *vt* faire coïncider <> *vi* coïncider.

dovetail joint *n* assemblage *m* à queue d'aronde.

dowager ['daʊədʒəʳ] *n* douairière *f*.

dowdy ['daʊdɪ] (*compar* **-ier** ; *superl* **-iest**) *adj* sans chic.

Dow-Jones average [ˌdaʊ'dʒəʊnz-] *n* : **the ~** le Dow-Jones, l'indice *m* Dow-Jones.

down [daʊn] <> *adv* - **1.** [downwards] en bas, vers le bas ; **to bend ~** se pencher ; **to climb ~** descendre ; **to fall ~** tomber (par terre) ; **to pull ~** tirer vers le bas - **2.** [along] : **we went ~ to have a look** on est allé jeter un coup d'œil ; **I'm going ~ to the shop** je vais au magasin - **3.** [southwards] : **we travelled ~ to London** on est descendu à Londres - **4.** [lower in amount] : **prices are coming ~** les prix baissent ; **~ to the last detail** jusqu'au moindre détail - **5.** [in written form] : **to write sthg ~** noter qqch <> *prep* - **1.** [downwards] : **they ran ~ the hill/stairs** ils ont descendu la colline/l'escalier en courant - **2.** [along] : **to walk ~ the street** descendre la rue <> *adj* - **1.** *inf* [depressed] : **to feel ~** avoir le cafard - **2.** [behind] : **they're two goals ~** ils perdent de deux buts - **3.** [lower in amount] : **prices are ~ again** les prix ont encore baissé - **4.** [computer, telephones] en panne <> *n (U)* duvet *m*

<> *vt* - **1.** [knock over] abattre - **2.** [drink] avaler d'un trait.

downs *npl* Br collines *fpl*.

down-and-out <> *adj* indigent(e) <> *n* personne *f* dans le besoin.

down-at-heel *adj* déguenillé(e).

downbeat ['daʊnbiːt] *adj inf* pessimiste.

downcast ['daʊnkɑːst] *adj* - **1.** [sad] démoralisé(e) - **2.** [eyes] baissé(e).

downer ['daʊnəʳ] *n inf* - **1.** [drug] tranquillisant *m* - **2.** [depressing event or person] : **he's/it's a real ~** il est/c'est flippant.

downfall ['daʊnfɔːl] *n (U)* ruine *f*.

downgrade ['daʊngreɪd] *vt* [job] déclasser ; [employee] rétrograder.

downhearted [ˌdaʊn'hɑːtɪd] *adj* découragé(e).

downhill [ˌdaʊn'hɪl] <> *adj* - **1.** [downward] en pente ; **it's ~ all the way now** *fig* ça va être du gâteau maintenant - **2.** SKIING : **~ skier** descendeur *m*, **-euse** *f* <> *n* SKIING [race] descente *f* <> *adv* : **to walk ~** descendre la côte ; **her career is going ~** *fig* sa carrière est sur le déclin.

Downing Street ['daʊnɪŋ-] *n* rue du centre de Londres où réside le premier ministre.

> **DOWNING STREET**
>
> C'est à Downing Street que se trouvent les résidences officielles du Premier ministre, au n° 10, et du ministre des Finances, au n° 11. Le terme « Downing Street » est souvent employé pour désigner le gouvernement.

download [ˌdaʊn'ləʊd] *vt* COMPUT transférer.

down-market *adj* [area] populaire, pas très chic *(inv) ;* [product] bas de gamme *(inv)*.

down payment *n* acompte *m*.

downplay ['daʊnpleɪ] *vt* minimiser.

downpour ['daʊnpɔːʳ] *n* pluie *f* torrentielle.

downright ['daʊnraɪt] <> *adj* franc (franche) ; [lie] effronté(e) <> *adv* franchement.

downside ['daʊnsaɪd] *n* désavantage *m*.

Down's syndrome *n* trisomie *f* 21.

downstairs [ˌdaʊn'steəz] <> *adj* du bas ; [on floor below] à l'étage en-dessous <> *adv* en bas ; [on floor below] à l'étage en-dessous ; **to come** OR **go ~** descendre.

downstream [ˌdaʊn'striːm] *adv* en aval.

downtime ['daʊntaɪm] *n* temps *m* improductif.

down-to-earth *adj* pragmatique, terre-à-terre *(inv)*.

downtown [ˌdaʊn'taʊn] *esp* Am <> *adj :*

~ **New York** le centre de New York ⬦ *adv* en ville.

downtrodden [ˈdaʊnˌtrɒdn] *adj* opprimé(e).

downturn [ˈdaʊntɜːn] *n* : ~ **(in)** baisse *f* (de).

down under *adv* en Australie/Nouvelle-Zélande.

downward [ˈdaʊnwəd] ⬦ *adj* **- 1.** [towards ground] vers le bas **- 2.** [trend] à la baisse ⬦ *adv* Am = **downwards**.

downwards [ˈdaʊnwədz] *adv* **- 1.** [look, move] vers le bas **- 2.** [in hierarchy] : **from the president** ~ du président jusqu'au bas de la hiérarchie.

downwind [ˌdaʊnˈwɪnd] *adv* dans le sens du vent.

dowry [ˈdaʊərɪ] (*pl* -ies) *n* dot *f*.

doz. (*abbr of* **dozen**) douz.

doze [dəʊz] ⬦ *n* somme *m* ⬦ *vi* sommeiller.

◆ **doze off** *vi* s'assoupir.

dozen [ˈdʌzn] ⬦ *num adj* : **a ~ eggs** une douzaine d'œufs ⬦ *n* douzaine *f ;* **50p a ~** 50p la douzaine ; **~s of** inf des centaines de.

dozy [ˈdəʊzɪ] (*compar* -ier ; *superl* -iest) *adj* **- 1.** [sleepy] somnolent(e) **- 2.** Br inf [stupid] lent(e).

DP (*abbr of* **data processing**) *n* informatique *f*.

DPh, DPhil [ˌdiːˈfɪl] (*abbr of* **Doctor of Philosophy**) *n* docteur *en philosophie*.

DPP *abbr of* **Director of Public Prosecutions**.

DPT (*abbr of* **diphtheria, pertussis, tetanus**) *n* DCT *m*.

DPW (*abbr of* **Department of Public Works**) *n* ministère de l'équipement.

dr *abbr of* **debtor**.

Dr. - 1. (*abbr of* **Drive**) av **- 2.** (*abbr of* **Doctor**) Dr.

drab [dræb] (*compar* -ber ; *superl* -best) *adj* terne.

draconian [drəˈkəʊnjən] *adj* draconien(enne).

draft [drɑːft] ⬦ *n* **- 1.** [early version] premier jet *m*, ébauche *f ;* [of letter] brouillon *m* **- 2.** [money order] traite *f* **- 3.** Am MIL : **the ~** la conscription *f* **- 4.** Am = **draught** ⬦ *vt* **- 1.** [speech] ébaucher, faire le plan de ; [letter] faire le brouillon de **- 2.** Am MIL appeler **- 3.** [staff] muter.

draft dodger [-ˌdɒdʒəʳ] *n* Am insoumis *m*.

draftee [ˌdrɑːfˈtiː] *n* Am appelé *m*.

draftsman Am = **draughtsman**.

draftsmanship Am = **draughtsmanship**.

drafty Am = **draughty**.

drag [dræg] (*pt & pp* -ged ; *cont* -ging) ⬦ *vt*

- 1. [gen] traîner **- 2.** [lake, river] draguer ⬦ *vi* **- 1.** [dress, coat] traîner **- 2.** fig [time, action] traîner en longueur ⬦ *n* **- 1.** inf [bore] plaie *f* **- 2.** inf [on cigarette] bouffée *f* **- 3.** [wind resistance] coefficient *m* de pénétration (dans l'air) **- 4.** [cross-dressing] : **in ~** en travesti.

◆ **drag down** *vt sep* fig : **they dragged him down with them** ils l'ont entraîné dans leur chute.

◆ **drag in** *vt sep* [include - person] mêler ; [- subject] faire allusion à.

◆ **drag on** *vi* [meeting, time] s'éterniser, traîner en longueur.

◆ **drag out** *vt sep* **- 1.** [protract] prolonger, faire traîner **- 2.** [facts] tirer, arracher ; **to ~ sthg out of sb** soutirer qqch à qqn.

dragnet [ˈdrægnet] *n* **- 1.** [net] drège *f* **- 2.** fig [to catch criminal] piège *m*.

dragon [ˈdrægən] *n* lit & fig dragon *m*.

dragonfly [ˈdrægnflaɪ] (*pl* -ies) *n* libellule *f*.

dragoon [drəˈguːn] ⬦ *n* dragon *m* ⬦ *vt* : **to ~ sb into doing sthg** contraindre qqn à faire qqch.

drag racing *n* course *f* de dragster.

dragster [ˈdrægstəʳ] *n* dragster *m*.

drain [dreɪn] ⬦ *n* **- 1.** [pipe] égout *m ;* **down the ~** [money] jeté par les fenêtres **- 2.** [depletion - of resources, funds] : **~ on** épuisement *m* de ⬦ *vt* **- 1.** [vegetables] égoutter ; [land] assécher, drainer **- 2.** [strength, resources] épuiser ; **to feel ~ed** être vidé(e) **- 3.** [drink, glass] boire ⬦ *vi* [dishes] égoutter ; **the blood ~ed from his face** il blêmit.

drainage [ˈdreɪnɪdʒ] *n* **- 1.** [pipes, ditches] (système *m* du) tout-à-l'égout *m* **- 2.** [draining - of land] drainage *m*.

draining board Br [ˈdreɪnɪŋ-], **drainboard** Am [ˈdreɪnbɔːrd] *n* égouttoir *m*.

drainpipe [ˈdreɪnpaɪp] *n* tuyau *m* d'écoulement.

drainpipes, drainpipe trousers *npl* Br pantalon-cigarette *m*.

drake [dreɪk] *n* canard *m*.

dram [dræm] *n* goutte *f* (de whisky).

drama [ˈdrɑːmə] ⬦ *n* **- 1.** [play, excitement] drame *m* **- 2.** (U) [art] théâtre *m* ⬦ *comp* [school] d'art dramatique ; [critic] dramatique.

dramatic [drəˈmætɪk] *adj* **- 1.** [gen] dramatique **- 2.** [sudden, noticeable] spectaculaire.

dramatically [drəˈmætɪklɪ] *adv* **- 1.** [noticeably] de façon spectaculaire **- 2.** [theatrically] de façon théâtrale.

dramatist [ˈdræmətɪst] *n* dramaturge *mf*.

dramatization [ˌdræmətaɪˈzeɪʃn] *n* adaptation *f* pour la télévision/la scène/l'écran.

dramatize, -ise ['dræmətaɪz] *vt* - **1.** [rewrite as play, film] adapter pour la télévision/la scène/l'écran - **2.** pej [make exciting] dramatiser.

drank [dræŋk] *pt* ⊳ drink.

drape [dreɪp] *vt* draper ; **to be ~d with** OR **in** être drapé(e) de.
➡ **drapes** *npl* Am rideaux *mpl*.

draper ['dreɪpə'] *n* marchand *m*, -e *f* de tissus.

drastic ['dræstɪk] *adj* - **1.** [measures] drastique, radical(e) - **2.** [improvement, decline] spectaculaire.

drastically ['dræstɪklɪ] *adv* [change, decline] de façon spectaculaire.

draught Br, **draft** Am [drɑːft] *n* - **1.** [air current] courant *m* d'air - **2.** literary [gulp] gorgée *f* - **3.** [from barrel] : **on ~** [beer] à la pression.
➡ **draughts** *n* Br jeu *m* de dames.

draught beer *n* Br bière *f* à la pression.

draughtboard ['drɑːftbɔːd] *n* Br damier *m*.

draughtsman Br (*pl* -men [-mən]), **draftsman** Am (*pl* -men [-mən]) ['drɑːftsmən] *n* dessinateur *m*, -trice *f*.

draughtsmanship Br, **draftsmanship** Am ['drɑːftsmənʃɪp] *n* [skill] talent *m* de dessinateur.

draughty Br (*compar* -ier ; *superl* -iest), **drafty** Am (*compar* -ier ; *superl* -iest) ['drɑːftɪ] *adj* plein(e) de courants d'air.

draw [drɔː] (*pt* **drew** ; *pp* **drawn**) ⟨ *vt* - **1.** [gen] tirer ; **to ~ breath** fig souffler - **2.** [sketch] dessiner - **3.** [comparison, distinction] établir, faire - **4.** [attract] attirer, entraîner ; **to ~ sb's attention to** attirer l'attention de qqn sur ; **to be** OR **feel drawn to** être OR se sentir attiré(e) par ⟨ *vi* - **1.** [sketch] dessiner - **2.** [move] : **to ~ near** [person] s'approcher ; [time] approcher ; **to ~ away** reculer ; **to ~ to an end** OR **a close** tirer à sa fin - **3.** SPORT faire match nul ; **to be ~ing** être à égalité ⟨ *n* - **1.** SPORT [result] match *m* nul - **2.** [lottery] tirage *m* - **3.** [attraction] attraction *f*.
➡ **draw in** *vi* [days] raccourcir.
➡ **draw into** *vt sep* : **to ~ sb into sthg** mêler qqn à qqch.
➡ **draw on** *vt fus* - **1.** = draw upon - **2.** [cigarette] tirer sur.
➡ **draw out** *vt sep* - **1.** [encourage - person] faire sortir de sa coquille - **2.** [prolong] prolonger - **3.** [money] faire un retrait de, retirer.
➡ **draw up** ⟨ *vt sep* [contract, plan] établir, dresser ⟨ *vi* [vehicle] s'arrêter.
➡ **draw upon** *vt fus* [information] utiliser, se servir de ; [reserves, resources] puiser dans.

drawback ['drɔːbæk] *n* inconvénient *m*, désavantage *m*.

drawbridge ['drɔːbrɪdʒ] *n* pont-levis *m*.

drawer [drɔːr] *n* [in desk, chest] tiroir *m*.

drawing ['drɔːɪŋ] *n* dessin *m*.

drawing board *n* planche *f* à dessin ; **back to the ~** inf retour à la case départ.

drawing pin *n* Br punaise *f*.

drawing room *n* salon *m*.

drawl [drɔːl] ⟨ *n* voix *f* traînante ⟨ *vt* dire d'une voix traînante.

drawn [drɔːn] ⟨ *pp* ⊳ draw ⟨ *adj* - **1.** [curtains] tiré(e) - **2.** [face] fatigué(e), tiré(e).

drawn-out *adj* prolongé(e).

drawstring ['drɔːstrɪŋ] *n* cordon *m*.

dread [dred] ⟨ *n* (U) épouvante *f* ⟨ *vt* appréhender ; **to ~ doing sthg** appréhender de faire qqch ; **I ~ to think** je n'ose pas imaginer.

dreaded ['dredɪd] *adj* redouté(e).

dreadful ['dredfʊl] *adj* affreux(euse), épouvantable.

dreadfully ['dredfʊlɪ] *adv* - **1.** [badly] terriblement - **2.** [extremely] extrêmement ; **I'm ~ sorry** je regrette infiniment.

dreadlocks ['dredlɒks] *npl* coiffure *f* rasta.

dream [driːm] (*pt* & *pp* -ed OR dreamt) ⟨ *n* rêve *m* ⟨ *adj* de rêve ⟨ *vt* : **to ~ (that)** ... rêver que ... ; **I never ~ed this would happen** je n'aurais jamais pensé que cela puisse arriver ⟨ *vi* : **to ~ (of** OR **about)** rêver (de) ; **I wouldn't ~ of it** cela ne me viendrait même pas à l'idée.
➡ **dream up** *vt sep* inventer.

dreamer ['driːmə'] *n* [unrealistic person] utopiste *mf*.

dreamily ['driːmɪlɪ] *adv* rêveusement.

dreamlike ['driːmlaɪk] *adj* comme dans un rêve.

dreamt [dremt] *pt* & *pp* ⊳ dream.

dream world *n* monde *m* imaginaire.

dreamy ['driːmɪ] (*compar* -ier ; *superl* -iest) *adj* - **1.** [distracted] rêveur(euse) - **2.** [dreamlike] de rêve.

dreary ['drɪərɪ] (*compar* -ier ; *superl* -iest) *adj* - **1.** [weather] morne - **2.** [dull, boring] ennuyeux(euse).

dredge [dredʒ] *vt* draguer.
➡ **dredge up** *vt sep* - **1.** [with dredger] draguer - **2.** fig [from past] déterrer.

dredger ['dredʒə'] *n* [ship] dragueur *m* ; [machine] drague *f*.

dregs [dregz] *npl* lit & fig lie *f*.

drench [drentʃ] *vt* tremper ; **to be ~ed in** OR **with** être inondé(e) de.

Dresden ['drezdən] *n* Dresde.

dress [dres] ◇ *n* - **1.** [woman's garment] robe *f* - **2.** (U) [clothing] costume *m*, tenue *f* ◇ *vt* - **1.** [clothe] habiller ; **to be ~ed in** être habillé(e) ; **to be ~ed in** être vêtu(e) de ; **to get ~ed** s'habiller - **2.** [bandage] panser - **3.** CULIN [salad] assaisonner ◇ *vi* s'habiller.

➻ **dress up** ◇ *vt sep* [facts] maquiller ◇ *vi* - **1.** [in costume] se déguiser - **2.** [in best clothes] s'habiller (élégamment).

dressage ['dresɑːʒ] *n* dressage *m*.

dress circle *n* premier balcon *m*.

dresser ['dresər] *n* - **1.** [for dishes] vaisselier *m* - **2.** Am [chest of drawers] commode *f* - **3.** [person] : **a smart ~** une personne qui s'habille avec chic.

dressing ['dresɪŋ] *n* - **1.** [bandage] pansement *m* - **2.** [for salad] assaisonnement *m* - **3.** Am [for turkey etc] farce *f*.

dressing gown *n* robe *f* de chambre.

dressing room *n* - **1.** THEATRE loge *f* - **2.** SPORT vestiaire *m*.

dressing table *n* coiffeuse *f*.

dressmaker ['dres,meɪkər] *n* couturier *m*, -ère *f*.

dressmaking ['dres,meɪkɪŋ] *n* couture *f*.

dress rehearsal *n* générale *f*.

dress shirt *n* chemise *f* de soirée.

dressy ['dresɪ] (*compar* -ier ; *superl* -iest) *adj* habillé(e).

drew [druː] *pt* ➥ **draw.**

dribble ['drɪbl] ◇ *n* - **1.** [saliva] bave *f* - **2.** [trickle] traînée *f* ◇ *vt* SPORT dribbler ◇ *vi* - **1.** [drool] baver - **2.** [liquid] tomber goutte à goutte, couler.

dribs [drɪbz] *npl* : **in ~ and drabs** peu à peu, petit à petit.

dried [draɪd] ◇ *pp* ➥ **dry** ◇ *adj* [milk, eggs] en poudre ; [fruit] sec (sèche) ; [flowers] séché(e).

dried fruit *n* (U) fruits *mpl* secs.

dried-up *adj* asséché(e).

drier ['draɪər] = **dryer.**

drift [drɪft] ◇ *n* - **1.** [movement] mouvement *m* ; [direction] direction *f*, sens *m* - **2.** [meaning] sens *m* général ; **I get your ~** je vois ce que vous voulez dire - **3.** [of snow] congère *f* ; [of sand, leaves] amoncellement *m*, entassement *m* ◇ *vi* - **1.** [boat] dériver - **2.** [snow, sand, leaves] s'amasser, s'amonceler - **3.** [person] errer ; **to ~ into sthg** se retrouver dans qqch ; **to ~ apart** se détacher l'un de l'autre.

➻ **drift off** *vi* [person] s'assoupir.

drifter ['drɪftər] *n* [person] personne *f* sans but dans la vie.

driftwood ['drɪftwʊd] *n* bois *m* flottant.

drill [drɪl] ◇ *n* - **1.** [tool] perceuse *f* ; [dentist's] fraise *f* ; [in mine etc] perforatrice *f* - **2.** [exercise, training] exercice *m* ◇ *vt* - **1.** [wood, hole] percer ; [tooth] fraiser ; [well] forer - **2.** [soldiers] entraîner ; **to ~ sthg into sb** faire rentrer qqch dans la tête de qqn ◇ *vi* - **1.** [bore] : **to ~ into** [wood] percer dans ; [tooth] fraiser dans - **2.** [excavate] : **to ~ for oil** forer à la recherche de pétrole.

drilling platform ['drɪlɪŋ-] *n* plate-forme *f* pétrolière OR de forage.

drily ['draɪlɪ] = **dryly.**

drink [drɪŋk] (*pt* **drank** ; *pp* **drunk**) ◇ *n* - **1.** [gen] boisson *f* ; **to have a ~** boire un verre - **2.** (U) [alcohol] alcool *m* ◇ *vt* boire ◇ *vi* boire ; **to ~ to sb/to sb's success** boire à qqn/à la réussite de qqn.

drinkable ['drɪŋkəbl] *adj* - **1.** [water] potable - **2.** [palatable] buvable.

drink-driving Br, **drunk-driving** Am *n* conduite *f* en état d'ivresse.

drinker ['drɪŋkər] *n* buveur *m*, -euse *f*.

drinking ['drɪŋkɪŋ] ◇ *adj* : **I'm not a ~ man** je ne bois pas ◇ *n* (U) boisson *f*.

drinking fountain *n* fontaine *f* d'eau potable.

drinking-up time *n* Br période pendant laquelle les clients d'un pub doivent terminer leur verre avant la fermeture.

drinking water *n* eau *f* potable.

drip [drɪp] (*pt* & *pp* **-ped** ; *cont* **-ping**) ◇ *n* - **1.** [drop] goutte *f* - **2.** MED goutte-à-goutte *m* *inv* - **3.** *inf* [wimp] femmelette *f* ◇ *vt* laisser tomber goutte à goutte ◇ *vi* - **1.** [gen] goutter, tomber goutte à goutte - **2.** [person] : **to be dripping with** lit & fig être ruisselant(e) de.

drip-dry *adj* qui ne se repasse pas.

drip-feed ◇ *n* goutte-à-goutte *m* *inv* ◇ *vt* alimenter par perfusion.

dripping ['drɪpɪŋ] ◇ *adj* : **~ (wet)** dégoulinant(e) ◇ *n* (U) graisse *f*.

drive [draɪv] (*pt* **drove** ; *pp* **driven**) ◇ *n* - **1.** [in car] trajet *m* (en voiture) ; **to go for a ~** faire une promenade (en voiture) - **2.** [urge] désir *m*, besoin *m* - **3.** [campaign] campagne *f* - **4.** (U) [energy] dynamisme *m*, énergie *f* - **5.** [road to house] allée *f* - **6.** SPORT drive *m* ◇ *vt* - **1.** [vehicle, passenger] conduire - **2.** TECH entraîner - **3.** [animals, people] pousser - **4.** [motivate] pousser - **5.** [force] : **to ~ sb to sthg/to do**

sthg pousser qqn à qqch/à faire qqch, conduire qqn à qqch/à faire qqch ; **to ~ sb mad** OR **crazy** rendre qqn fou **- 6.** [nail, stake] enfoncer **- 7.** SPORT driver ◇ *vi* [driver] conduire ; [travel by car] aller en voiture.

➡ **drive at** *vt fus* : **what are you driving at?** où voulez-vous en venir?

drive-in esp Am ◇ *n* drive-in *m* ◇ *adj* drive-in *(inv)*.

drivel ['drɪvl] *n (U)* inf foutaises *fpl*, idioties *fpl*.

driven ['drɪvn] *pp* ▷ **drive.**

driver ['draɪvər] *n* **- 1.** [of vehicle - gen] conducteur *m*, -trice *f*; [- of taxi] chauffeur *m* **- 2.** COMPUT logiciel *m* de commande de périphérique.

driver's license Am = **driving licence.**

drive shaft *n* arbre *m* de transmission.

driveway ['draɪvweɪ] *n* allée *f*.

driving ['draɪvɪŋ] ◇ *adj* [rain] battant(e) ; [wind] cinglant(e) ◇ *n (U)* conduite *f*.

driving force *n* force *f* motrice.

driving instructor *n* moniteur *m*, -trice *f* d'auto-école.

driving lesson *n* leçon *f* de conduite.

driving licence Br, **driver's license** Am *n* permis *m* de conduire.

driving mirror *n* rétroviseur *m*.

driving school *n* auto-école *f*.

driving test *n* (examen *m* du) permis *m* de conduire.

drizzle ['drɪzl] ◇ *n* bruine *f* ◇ *v impers* bruiner.

drizzly ['drɪzlɪ] (*compar* -ier ; *superl* -iest) *adj* bruineux(euse).

droll [drəʊl] *adj* drôle.

dromedary ['drɒmədrɪ] (*pl* -ies) *n* dromadaire *m*.

drone [drəʊn] ◇ *n* **- 1.** [of traffic, voices] ronronnement *m*; [of insect] bourdonnement *m* **- 2.** [male bee] abeille *f* mâle, faux-bourdon *m* ◇ *vi* [engine] ronronner ; [insect] bourdonner.

➡ **drone on** *vi* parler d'une voix monotone ; **to ~ on about sthg** rabâcher qqch.

drool [druːl] *vi* baver ; **to ~ over** fig baver (d'admiration) devant.

droop [druːp] *vi* **- 1.** [head] pencher ; [shoulders, eyelids] tomber **- 2.** fig [spirits] faiblir.

drop [drɒp] (*pt* & *pp* -ped ; *cont* -ping) ◇ *n* **- 1.** [of liquid] goutte *f* **- 2.** [sweet] pastille *f* **- 3.** [decrease] : **~ (in)** baisse *f* (de) **- 4.** [distance down] dénivellation *f*; **sheer ~** à-pic *m inv* ◇ *vt* **- 1.** [let fall] laisser tomber **- 2.** [voice,

speed, price] baisser **- 3.** [abandon] abandonner ; [player] exclure **- 4.** [let out of car] déposer **- 5.** [utter] : **to ~ a hint that** laisser entendre que **- 6.** TENNIS [game, set] perdre **- 7.** [write] : **to ~ sb a note** OR **a line** écrire un petit mot à qqn ◇ *vi* **- 1.** [fall] tomber **- 2.** [temperature, demand] baisser ; [voice, wind] tomber.

➡ **drops** *npl* MED gouttes *fpl*.

➡ **drop by** *vi* inf passer.

➡ **drop in** *vi* inf : **to ~ in (on sb)** passer (chez qqn).

➡ **drop off** ◇ *vt sep* déposer ◇ *vi* **- 1.** [fall asleep] s'endormir **- 2.** [interest, sales] baisser.

➡ **drop out** *vi* : **to ~ out (of** OR **from sthg)** abandonner (qqch) ; **to ~ out of society** vivre en marge de la société.

drop-in centre *n* centre *d'assistance sociale permanente*.

droplet ['drɒplɪt] *n* gouttelette *f*.

dropout ['drɒpaʊt] *n* [from society] marginal *m*, -e *f*; [from college] étudiant *m*, -e *f* qui abandonne ses études.

dropper ['drɒpər] *n* compte-gouttes *m inv*.

droppings ['drɒpɪŋz] *npl* [of bird] fiente *f*; [of animal] crottes *fpl*.

drop shot *n* amorti *m*.

dross [drɒs] *n (U)* déchets *mpl*; fig rebut *m*.

drought [draʊt] *n* sécheresse *f*.

drove [drəʊv] ◇ *pt* ▷ **drive** ◇ *n* [of people] foule *f*.

drown [draʊn] ◇ *vt* **- 1.** [in water] noyer **- 2.** [sound] : **to ~ (out)** couvrir ◇ *vi* se noyer.

drowsy ['draʊzɪ] (*compar* -ier ; *superl* -iest) *adj* assoupi(e), somnolent(e).

drudge [drʌdʒ] *n* homme *m* de peine, femme *f* de peine.

drudgery ['drʌdʒərɪ] *n (U)* corvée *f*.

drug [drʌg] (*pt* & *pp* -ged ; *cont* -ging) ◇ *n* **- 1.** [medicine] médicament *m* **- 2.** [narcotic] drogue *f* ◇ *vt* droguer.

drug abuse *n* usage *m* de stupéfiants.

drug addict *n* drogué *m*, -e *f*.

drug addiction *n* toxicomanie *f*.

druggist ['drʌgɪst] *n* Am pharmacien *m*, -enne *f*.

drug pedlar *n* revendeur *m*, -euse *f* de drogue.

drugstore ['drʌgstɔːr] *n* Am drugstore *m*.

drug test *n* [of athlete, horse] contrôle *m* antidopage.

druid ['druːɪd] *n* druide *m*.

drum [drʌm] (*pt* & *pp* -med ; *cont* -ming) ◇ *n* **- 1.** MUS tambour *m* **- 2.** [container] bidon *m* ◇ *vt* & *vi* tambouriner.

drums *npl* batterie *f*.

drum into *vt sep* : to ~ sthg into sb enfoncer qqch dans la tête de qqn.

drum up *vt sep* [support, business] rechercher, solliciter.

drumbeat ['drʌmbiːt] *n* roulement *m* de tambour.

drum brake *n* frein *m* à tambour.

drummer ['drʌmə'] *n* [gen] (joueur *m*, -euse *f* de) tambour *m* ; [in pop group] batteur *m*, -euse *f*.

drumming ['drʌmɪŋ] *n* [of rain, fingers] tambourinage *m*.

drum roll *n* roulement *m* de tambour.

drumstick ['drʌmstɪk] *n* - **1.** [for drum] baguette *f* de tambour - **2.** [of chicken] pilon *m*.

drunk [drʌŋk] ◇ *pp* ▷ **drink** ◇ *adj* - **1.** [on alcohol] ivre, soûl(e) ; **to get ~** se soûler, s'enivrer ; **~ and disorderly** en état d'ivresse sur la voie publique - **2.** fig [excited, carried away] : **to be ~ with** OR on être enivré(e) OR grisé(e) par ◇ *n* soûlard *m*, -e *f*.

drunkard ['drʌŋkəd] *n* alcoolique *mf*.

drunk-driving Am = **drink-driving**.

drunken ['drʌŋkn] *adj* [person] ivre ; [quarrel] d'ivrognes.

drunken driving = **drink-driving**.

drunkenness ['drʌŋkənɪs] *n* ivresse *f*.

dry [draɪ] (*compar* **-ier** ; *superl* **-iest**, *pt* & *pp* **dried**) ◇ *adj* - **1.** [gen] sec (sèche) ; [day] sans pluie - **2.** [river, earth] asséché(e) - **3.** [wry] pince-sans-rire *(inv)* - **4.** [dull] aride ◇ *vt* [gen] sécher ; [with cloth] essuyer ◇ *vi* sécher.

dry out *vt sep* & *vi* sécher.

dry up ◇ *vt sep* [dishes] essuyer ◇ *vi* - **1.** [river, lake] s'assécher - **2.** [supply] se tarir - **3.** [actor, speaker] avoir un trou, sécher - **4.** [dry dishes] essuyer.

dry battery *n* batterie *f* sèche.

dry-clean *vt* nettoyer à sec.

dry cleaner *n* : ~'s pressing *m*.

dry-cleaning *n* nettoyage *m* à sec.

dry dock *n* cale *f* sèche.

dryer ['draɪə'] *n* [for clothes] séchoir *m*.

dry ginger *n* boisson gazeuse au gingembre.

dry goods *npl* mercerie *f*.

dry ice *n* neige *f* carbonique.

dry land *n* terre *f* ferme.

dryly ['draɪlɪ] *adv* [wryly] sèchement.

dryness ['draɪnɪs] *n* (U) - **1.** [of ground] sécheresse *f* ; [of humour] causticité *f* - **2.** [dullness] aridité *f*.

dry rot *n* pourriture *f* sèche.

dry run *n* répétition *f*.

dry ski slope *n* piste *f* de ski artificielle.

dry-stone wall *n* mur *m* de pierres sèches.

DSc (*abbr of* **Doctor of Science**) *n* docteur ès sciences.

DSS (*abbr of* **Department of Social Security**) *n* ministère britannique de la sécurité sociale.

DST (*abbr of* **daylight saving time**) *heure d'été aux États-Unis*.

DT *abbr of* **data transmission**.

DTI (*abbr of* **Department of Trade and Industry**) *n ministère britannique du commerce et de l'industrie*.

DTP (*abbr of* **desktop publishing**) *n* PAO *f*.

DT's [ˌdiːˈtiːz] (*abbr of* **delirium tremens**) *npl* inf : **to have the ~** avoir une crise de délirium tremens.

dual ['djuːəl] *adj* double.

dual carriageway *n* Br route *f* à quatre voies.

dual control *n* double commande *f*.

dual nationality *n* double nationalité *f*.

dual-purpose *adj* à double emploi.

Dubai [ˌduːˈbaɪ] *n* Dubayy.

dubbed [dʌbd] *adj* - **1.** CINEMA doublé(e) - **2.** [nicknamed] surnommé(e).

dubious ['djuːbjəs] *adj* - **1.** [suspect] douteux(euse) - **2.** [uncertain] hésitant(e), incertain(e) ; **to be ~ about doing sthg** hésiter à faire qqch.

Dublin ['dʌblɪn] *n* Dublin.

Dubliner ['dʌblɪnə'] *n* Dublinois *m*, -e *f*.

duchess ['dʌtʃɪs] *n* duchesse *f*.

duchy ['dʌtʃɪ] (*pl* **-ies**) *n* duché *m*.

duck [dʌk] ◇ *n* canard *m* ; **she took to it like a ~ to water** elle était comme un poisson dans l'eau ◇ *vt* - **1.** [head] baisser - **2.** [responsibility] esquiver, se dérober à - **3.** [submerge] : **to ~ sb** mettre la tête de qqn sous l'eau ◇ *vi* - **1.** [lower head] se baisser - **2.** [dive] : **he ~ed behind the wall** il se cacha derrière le mur.

duck out *vi* : **to ~ out (of sthg)** se soustraire (à qqch).

duckling ['dʌklɪŋ] *n* caneton *m*.

duct [dʌkt] *n* - **1.** [pipe] canalisation *f* - **2.** ANAT canal *m*.

dud [dʌd] ◇ *adj* [bomb] non éclaté(e) ; [cheque] sans provision, en bois ◇ *n* obus *m* non éclaté.

dude [djuːd] *n* Am inf [man] gars *m*, type *m*.

dude ranch n aux États-Unis, ranch qui propose des activités touristiques.

due [dju:] ◇ adj - **1.** [expected] : **the book is ~ out** in May le livre doit sortir en mai ; **she's ~ back shortly** elle devrait rentrer sous peu ; **when is the train ~?** à quelle heure le train doit-il arriver? - **2.** [appropriate] dû (due), qui convient ; **in ~ course** [at the appropriate time] en temps voulu ; [eventually] à la longue - **3.** [owed, owing] dû (due).; **she's ~ a pay rise** elle devrait recevoir une augmentation ◇ adv : **~ west** droit vers l'ouest ◇ n dû m ; **to give him his ~** il faut lui rendre cette justice.

➠ **dues** npl cotisation f.

➠ **due to** prep [owing to] dû à ; [because of] provoqué par, à cause de.

due date n jour m de l'échéance.

duel ['dju:əl] (Br pt & pp -**led** ; cont -**ling**, Am pt & pp -**ed** ; cont -**ing**) ◇ n duel m ◇ vi se battre en duel.

duet [dju:'et] n duo m.

duff [dʌf] adj Br inf [useless] nul (nulle).

➠ **duff up** vt sep Br inf tabasser.

duffel bag ['dʌfl-] n sac m marin.

duffel coat ['dʌfl-] n duffel-coat m.

duffle bag ['dʌfl-] = **duffel bag**.

duffle coat ['dʌfl-] = **duffel coat**.

dug [dʌg] pt & pp ⊳ **dig**.

dugout ['dʌgaʊt] n - **1.** [canoe] pirogue f - **2.** SPORT abri m de touche.

duke [dju:k] n duc m.

dull [dʌl] ◇ adj - **1.** [boring - book, conversation] ennuyeux(euse) ; [- person] terne - **2.** [colour, light] terne - **3.** [weather] maussade - **4.** [sound, ache] sourd(e) ◇ vt - **1.** [pain] atténuer ; [senses] émousser - **2.** [make less bright] ternir.

duly ['dju:lɪ] adv - **1.** [properly] dûment - **2.** [as expected] comme prévu.

dumb [dʌm] adj - **1.** [unable to speak] muet(ette) - **2.** inf [stupid] idiot(e).

dumbbell ['dʌmbell] n [weight] haltère m.

dumbfound [dʌm'faʊnd] vt stupéfier, abasourdir ; **to be ~ed** ne pas en revenir.

dumbstruck ['dʌmstrʌk] adj muet(ette) de stupeur.

dumbwaiter [,dʌm'weɪtər] n [lift] monteplats m inv.

dumdum (bullet) ['dʌmdʌm-] n dum-dum f.

dummy ['dʌmɪ] (pl -**ies**) ◇ adj faux (fausse) ◇ n - **1.** [of tailor] mannequin m - **2.** [copy] maquette f - **3.** Br [for baby] sucette f, tétine f - **4.** SPORT feinte f ◇ vt & vi SPORT feinter.

dummy run n essai m.

dump [dʌmp] ◇ n - **1.** [for rubbish] décharge f - **2.** MIL dépôt m - **3.** inf [ugly place] taudis m ◇ vt - **1.** [put down] déposer - **2.** [dispose of] jeter - **3.** COMPUT vider - **4.** inf [boyfriend, girlfriend] laisser tomber, plaquer.

➠ **dumps** npl : **to be (down) in the ~s** avoir le cafard.

dumper (truck) ['dʌmpər-] Br, **dump truck** Am n tombereau m, dumper m.

dumping ['dʌmpɪŋ] n décharge f ; **'no ~'** 'décharge interdite'.

dumping ground n décharge f.

dumpling ['dʌmplɪŋ] n boulette f de pâte.

dump truck Am = **dumper (truck)**.

dumpy ['dʌmpɪ] (compar -**ier** ; superl -**iest**) adj inf boulot(otte).

dunce [dʌns] n cancre m.

dune [dju:n] n dune f.

dung [dʌŋ] n fumier m.

dungarees [,dʌŋgə'ri:z] npl - **1.** Br [for work] bleu m de travail ; [fashion garment] salopette f - **2.** Am [heavy jeans] jean m épais.

dungeon ['dʌndʒən] n cachot m.

dunk [dʌŋk] vt inf tremper.

Dunkirk [dʌn'kɜ:k] n Dunkerque f.

duo ['dju:əʊ] n duo m.

duodenal ulcer [,dju:əʊ'di:nl-] n ulcère m duodénal.

dupe [dju:p] ◇ n dupe f ◇ vt [trick] duper ; **to ~ sb into doing sthg** amener qqn à faire qqch en le dupant.

duplex ['dju:pleks] n Am - **1.** [apartment] duplex m - **2.** [house] maison f jumelée.

duplicate [adj & n 'dju:plɪkət, vb 'dju:plɪkeɪt] ◇ adj [key, document] en double ◇ n double m ; **in ~** en double ◇ vt - **1.** [copy - gen] faire un double de ; [- on photocopier] photocopier - **2.** [repeat] : **to ~ work** faire double emploi.

duplication [,dju:plɪ'keɪʃn] (U) n - **1.** [copying] copie f - **2.** [repetition] répétition f.

duplicity [dju:'plɪsətɪ] n duplicité f.

Dur (abbr of **Durham**) comté anglais.

durability [,djʊərə'bɪlətɪ] n [of product] solidité f.

durable ['djʊərəbl] adj solide, résistant(e).

duration [djʊ'reɪʃn] n durée f ; **for the ~ of** jusqu'à la fin de.

duress [djʊ'res] n : **under ~** sous la contrainte.

Durex® ['djʊəreks] n préservatif m.

during ['djʊərɪŋ] prep pendant, au cours de.

dusk [dʌsk] n crépuscule m.

dusky ['dʌskɪ] (*compar* -ier ; *superl* -iest) *adj* literary mordoré(e). ·

dust [dʌst] ⬦ *n* (U) poussière *f* ; **to gather ~** [get dusty] se couvrir de poussière ; *fig* tomber dans l'oubli ⬦ *vt* **- 1.** [clean] épousseter **- 2.** [cover with powder] : **to ~ sthg (with)** saupoudrer qqch (de) ⬦ *vi* faire la poussière.

➤ **dust off** *vt sep* épousseter ; *fig* dépoussiérer.

dustbin ['dʌstbɪn] *n* Br poubelle *f*.

dustbowl ['dʌstbəʊl] *n* désert *m* de poussière.

dustcart ['dʌstkɑːt] *n* Br camion *m* des boueux.

dust cover *n* [on book] jaquette *f*.

duster ['dʌstəʳ] *n* **- 1.** [cloth] chiffon *m* (à poussière) **- 2.** Am [overall] blouse *f*, tablier *m*.

dust jacket *n* [on book] jaquette *f*.

dustman ['dʌstmən] (*pl* -men [-mən]) *n* Br éboueur *m*.

dustpan ['dʌstpæn] *n* pelle *f* à poussière.

dustsheet ['dʌstʃiːt] *n* Br housse *f*.

dust storm *n* tempête *f* de poussière. ·

dustup ['dʌstʌp] *n inf* bagarre *f*.

dusty ['dʌstɪ] (*compar* -ier ; *superl* -iest) *adj* poussiéreux(euse).

Dutch [dʌtʃ] ⬦ *adj* néerlandais(e), hollandais(e) ⬦ *n* [language] néerlandais *m*, hollandais *m* ⬦ *npl* : **the ~** les Néerlandais, les Hollandais ⬦ *adv* : **to go ~** partager les frais.

Dutch auction *n* Br enchères *fpl* au rabais.

Dutch barn *n* Br hangar *m* à récoltes.

Dutch cap *n* Br diaphragme *m*.

Dutch courage *n* : **he had a drink to give himself some ~** il but un verre pour se donner du courage.

Dutch elm disease *n* maladie *f* des ormes.

Dutchman ['dʌtʃmən] (*pl* -men [-mən]) *n* Néerlandais *m*, Hollandais *m*.

Dutchwoman ['dʌtʃˌwʊmən] (*pl* -women [-ˌwɪmɪn]) *n* Néerlandaise *f*, Hollandaise *f*.

dutiable ['djuːtjəbl] *adj* [goods] taxable.

dutiful ['djuːtɪfʊl] *adj* obéissant(e)

duty ['djuːtɪ] (*pl* -ies) *n* **- 1.** (U) [responsibility] devoir *m* ; **to do one's ~** faire son devoir **- 2.** [work] : **to be on/off ~** être/ne pas être de service **- 3.** [tax] droit *m*.

➤ **duties** *npl* fonctions *fpl*.

duty bound *adj* : **to be ~ (to do sthg)** être tenu(e) (de faire qqch).

duty-free *adj* hors taxe.

duty-free shop *n* boutique *f* hors taxe.

duty officer *n* préposé *m*, -e *f* de service.

duvet ['duːveɪ] *n* Br couette *f*.

duvet cover *n* Br housse *f* de couette.

DVD (*abbr of* Digital Video or Versatile Disc) *n* DVD *m*.

DVD-ROM (*abbr of* Digital Video or Versatile Disc read only memory) *n* DVD-ROM *m*.

DVLC (*abbr of* Driver and Vehicle Licensing Centre) *n service des immatriculations et des permis de conduire en Grande-Bretagne.*

DVM (*abbr of* Doctor of Veterinary Medicine) *n docteur vétérinaire.*

dwarf [dwɔːf] (*pl* -s OR dwarves [dwɔːvz]) ⬦ *adj* [plant, animal] nain(e) ⬦ *n* nain *m*, -e *f* ⬦ *vt* [tower over] écraser.

dwell [dwell] (*pt* & *pp* dwelt OR -ed) *vi* literary habiter.

➤ **dwell on** *vt fus* s'étendre sur. ·

-dweller ['dweləʳ] *suffix* : **city~** habitant *m*, -e *f* de la ville.

dwelling ['dwelɪŋ] *n* literary habitation *f*.

dwelt [dwelt] *pt* & *pp* ➭ **dwell.**

dwindle ['dwɪndl] *vi* diminuer.

dwindling ['dwɪndlɪŋ] *adj* en diminution.

dye [daɪ] ⬦ *n* teinture *f* ⬦ *vt* teindre.

dyed [daɪd] *adj* teint(e).

dying ['daɪɪŋ] ⬦ *cont* ➭ **die** ⬦ *adj* [person] mourant(e), moribond(e) ; [plant, language, industry] moribond ⬦ *npl* : **the ~** les mourants *mpl*.

dyke [daɪk] = **dike.**

dynamic [daɪ'næmɪk] *adj* dynamique.
➤ **dynamics** *npl* dynamique *f*.

dynamism ['daɪnəmɪzm] *n* dynamisme *m*.

dynamite ['daɪnəmaɪt] ⬦ *n* (U) lit & fig dynamite *f* ⬦ *vt* dynamiter, faire sauter.

dynamo ['daɪnəməʊ] (*pl* -s) *n* dynamo *f*.

dynasty [Br 'dɪnəstɪ, Am 'daɪnəstɪ] (*pl* -ies) *n* dynastie *f*.

dysentery ['dɪsntrɪ] *n* dysenterie *f*.

dyslexia [dɪs'leksɪə] *n* dyslexie *f*.

dyslexic [dɪs'leksɪk] *adj* dyslexique.

dyspepsia [dɪs'pepsɪə] *n* dyspepsie *f*.

dystrophy ['dɪstrəfɪ] *n* ➭ **muscular dystrophy.**

e (*pl* **e's** OR **es**), **E** (*pl* **E's** OR **Es**) [iːl] *n* [letter] e *m inv*, E *m inv*.
◆ **E** *n* - **1.** MUS mi *m* - **2.** (*abbr of* **east**) E.

ea. (*abbr of* **each**) : £3.00 ~ 3 livres pièce.

e-account *n* compte *m* bancaire électronique.

each [iːtʃ] ◇ *adj* chaque ◇ *pron* chacun(e) ; **the books cost £10.99 ~** les livres coûtent 10,99 livres (la) pièce ; **~ other** l'un l'autre (l'une l'autre), les uns les autres (les unes les autres) ; **they love ~ other** ils s'aiment ; **we've known ~ other for years** nous nous connaissons depuis des années.

eager [ˈiːɡəʳ] *adj* passionné(e), avide ; **to be ~ for** être avide de ; **to be ~ to do sthg** être impatient de faire qqch.

eagerly [ˈiːɡəlɪ] *adv* [talk, plan] avec passion, avidement ; [wait] avec impatience.

eagle [ˈiːɡl] *n* [bird] aigle *m*.

eagle-eyed [-aɪd] *adj* qui a des yeux d'aigle.

eaglet [ˈiːɡlɪt] *n* aiglon *m*, -onne *f*.

E and OE (*abbr of* **errors and omissions excepted**) s. e & o.

ear [ɪəʳ] *n* - **1.** [gen] oreille *f* ; **by ~** MUS à l'oreille ; **to have an ~ for** [music, languages] avoir (de) l'oreille pour ; **to go in one ~ and out the other** inf entrer par une oreille et ressortir par l'autre ; **to have** OR **keep one's ~ to the ground** inf être aux écoutes ; **to play it by ~** fig improviser, voir sur le moment - **2.** [of corn] épi *m*.

earache [ˈɪəreɪk] *n* : **to have ~** avoir mal à l'oreille.

eardrum [ˈɪədrʌm] *n* tympan *m*.

earl [ɜːl] *n* comte *m*.

earlier [ˈɜːlɪəʳ] ◇ *adj* [previous] précédent(e) ; [more early] plus tôt ◇ *adv* plus tôt ; **as I mentioned ~** comme je l'ai signalé tout à l'heure ; **~ on** plus tôt.

earliest [ˈɜːlɪəst] ◇ *adj* [first] premier(ère) ; [most early] le plus tôt ◇ *n* : **at the ~** au plus tôt.

earlobe [ˈɪələub] *n* lobe *m* de l'oreille.

early [ˈɜːlɪ] (*compar* **-ier** ; *superl* **-iest**) ◇ *adj* - **1.** [before expected time] en avance - **2.** [in day] de bonne heure ; **the ~ train** le premier train ; **to make an ~ start** partir de bonne heure - **3.** [at beginning] : **in the ~ sixties** au début des années soixante ; **the ~ chapters** les premiers chapitres ◇ *adv* - **1.** [before expected time] en avance ; **I was ten minutes ~** j'étais en avance de dix minutes - **2.** [in day] tôt, de bonne heure ; **as ~ as** dès ; **~ on** tôt - **3.** [at beginning] : **~ in her life** dans sa jeunesse.

early retirement *n* retraite *f* anticipée.

early warning system *n* système *m* de première alerte.

earmark [ˈɪəmɑːk] *vt* : **to be ~ed for** être réservé(e) à.

earmuffs [ˈɪəmʌfs] *npl* cache-oreilles *m inv*.

earn [ɜːn] *vt* - **1.** [as salary] gagner - **2.** COMM rapporter - **3.** *fig* [respect, praise] gagner, mériter.

earned income [ɜːnd-] *n* revenus *mpl* salariaux.

earner [ˈɜːnəʳ] *n* - **1.** [person] salarié *m*, -e *f* - **2.** Br inf [deal] : **a nice little ~** une affaire juteuse.

earnest [ˈɜːnɪst] *adj* sérieux(euse).
◆ **in earnest** ◇ *adj* sérieux(euse) ◇ *adv* pour de bon, sérieusement.

earnestly [ˈɜːnɪstlɪ] *adv* sérieusement.

earnings [ˈɜːnɪŋz] *npl* [of person] salaire *m*, gains *mpl* ; [of company] bénéfices *mpl*.

earnings-related [pension, payment] proportionnel(elle) au salaire.

ear, nose and throat specialist *n* otorhino-laryngologiste *mf*, oto-rhino *mf*.

earphones [ˈɪəfəunz] *npl* casque *m*.

earplugs [ˈɪəplʌgz] *npl* boules *fpl* Quiès®.

earring [ˈɪərɪŋ] *n* boucle *f* d'oreille.

earshot [ˈɪəʃɒt] *n* : **within ~** à portée de voix ; **out of ~** hors de portée de voix.

ear-splitting *adj* assourdissant(e).

earth [ɜːθ] ◇ *n* [gen & ELEC] terre *f* ; **how/what/where/why on ~ ...?** mais comment/que/où/pourquoi donc ...? ; **to cost the ~** Br coûter les yeux de la tête ◇ *vt* Br : **to be ~ed** être à la masse.

earthenware [ˈɜːθnweəʳ] ◇ *adj* en terre cuite ◇ *n* (*U*) poteries *fpl*.

earthling [ˈɜːθlɪŋ] *n* terrien *m*, -enne *f*.

earthly [ˈɜːθlɪ] *adj* terrestre ; **what ~ reason could she have for doing that?** inf pourquoi diable a-t-elle fait ça?

earthquake [ˈɜːθkweɪk] *n* tremblement *m* de terre.

earthshattering ['ɜːˌʃætərɪŋ] *adj* Br inf [news] renversant(e).

earth tremor *n* secousse *f* sismique.

earthward(s) ['ɜːθwəd(z)] *adv* vers la terre.

earthworks ['ɜːθwɜːks] *npl* ARCHEOL fortifications *fpl* en terre.

earthworm ['ɜːθwɜːm] *n* ver *m* de terre.

earthy ['ɜːθɪ] (*compar* -ier ; *superl* -iest) *adj* - **1.** fig [humour, person] truculent(e) - **2.** [taste, smell] de terre, terreux(euse).

earwax ['ɪəwæks] *n* cérumen *m*.

earwig ['ɪəwɪg] *n* perce-oreille *m*.

ease [iːz] ◇ *n (U)* - **1.** [lack of difficulty] facilité *f ;* to do sthg with ~ faire qqch sans difficulté OR facilement - **2.** [comfort] : a life of ~ une vie facile ; at ~ à l'aise ; ill at ~ mal à l'aise ◇ *vt* - **1.** [pain] calmer ; [restrictions] modérer - **2.** [move carefully] : to ~ sthg in/out faire entrer/sortir qqch délicatement ◇ *vi* [problem] s'arranger ; [pain] s'atténuer ; [rain] diminuer.

ease off *vi* [pain] s'atténuer ; [rain] diminuer.

ease up *vi* - **1.** [rain] diminuer - **2.** [relax] se détendre.

easel ['iːzl] *n* chevalet *m*.

easily ['iːzɪlɪ] *adv* - **1.** [without difficulty] facilement - **2.** [without doubt] de loin - **3.** [in a relaxed manner] tranquillement.

easiness ['iːzɪnɪs] *n* [lack of difficulty] facilité *f*.

east [iːst] ◇ *n* - **1.** [direction] est *m* - **2.** [region] : the ~ l'est *m* ◇ *adj* est *(inv)* ; [wind] d'est ◇ *adv* à l'est, vers l'est ; ~ of à l'est de.

East *n* : the East [gen & POL] l'Est *m* ; [Asia] l'Orient *m*.

eastbound ['iːstbaʊnd] *adj* en direction de l'est.

East End *n* : the ~ les quartiers est de Londres.

Easter ['iːstər] *n* Pâques *m*.

Easter egg *n* œuf *m* de Pâques.

Easter Island *n* l'île *f* de Pâques ; in OR on ~ à l'île de Pâques.

easterly ['iːstəlɪ] *adj* à l'est, de l'est ; [wind] de l'est ; in an ~ direction vers l'est.

eastern ['iːstən] *adj* de l'est.

Eastern *adj* [gen & POL] de l'Est ; [from Asia] oriental(e).

Eastern bloc [-blɒk] *n* : the ~ le bloc de l'Est.

Easterner ['iːstənər] *n* personne qui vient de l'est.

Easter Sunday *n* dimanche *m* de Pâques.

East German ◇ *adj* d'Allemagne de l'Est ◇ *n* Allemand *m*, -e *f* de l'Est.

East Germany *n* : (former) ~ (l'ex-) Allemagne *f* de l'Est ; in ~ en Allemagne de l'Est.

eastward ['iːstwəd] ◇ *adj* à l'est, vers l'est ◇ *adv* = eastwards.

eastwards ['iːstwədz] *adv* vers l'est.

easy ['iːzɪ] (*compar* -ier ; *superl* -iest) ◇ *adj* - **1.** [not difficult, comfortable] facile - **2.** [relaxed - manner] naturel(elle) ◇ *adv* : to go ~ on inf y aller doucement avec ; to take it OR things ~ inf ne pas se fatiguer.

easy-care *adj* Br [garment] d'entretien facile.

easy chair *n* fauteuil *m*.

easygoing [ˌiːzɪˈgəʊɪŋ] *adj* [person] facile à vivre ; [manner] complaisant(e).

eat [iːt] (*pt* ate, *pp* eaten) *vt* & *vi* manger.

eat away, eat into *vt fus* - **1.** [subj : acid, rust] ronger - **2.** [deplete] grignoter.

eat out *vi* manger au restaurant.

eat up *vt sep* - **1.** [food] manger - **2.** fig [use up] : to ~ up money revenir très cher ; to ~ up time demander beaucoup de temps.

eatable ['iːtəbl] *adj* [palatable] mangeable.

eaten ['iːtn] *pp* ⊳ eat.

eater ['iːtər] *n* mangeur *m*, -euse *f*.

eatery ['iːtərɪ] *n* Am restaurant *m*.

eating apple ['iːtɪŋ-] *n* pomme *f* à couteau.

eau de cologne [ˌəʊdəkəˈləʊn] *n* eau *f* de Cologne.

eaves ['iːvz] *npl* avant-toit *m*.

eavesdrop ['iːvzdrɒp] (*pt* & *pp* -ped ; *cont* -ping) *vi* : to ~ (on sb) écouter (qqn) de façon indiscrète.

e-banking *n* cyberbanque *f*.

ebb [eb] ◇ *n* reflux *m ;* the ~ and flow fig les hauts et les bas ; to be at a low ~ fig aller mal ◇ *vi* - **1.** [tide, sea] se retirer, refluer - **2.** literary [strength] : to ~ (away) décliner.

ebb tide *n* marée *f* descendante.

ebony ['ebənɪ] ◇ *adj* [colour] noir(e) d'ébène ◇ *n* ébène *f*.

e-book *n* livre *m* électronique.

ebullient [ɪˈbʊljənt] *adj* exubérant(e).

e-business *n* - **1.** [company] cyberentreprise *f* - **2.** *(U)* [trade] cybercommerce *m*, commerce *m* électronique.

EC (*abbr of* European Community) *n* CE *f*.

e-cash *n* argent *m* virtuel OR électronique.

ECB (*abbr of* European Central bank) *n* BCE *f*.

eccentric [ɪkˈsentrɪk] ◇ *adj* [odd] excentrique, bizarre ◇ *n* [person] excentrique *mf*.

eccentricity [ˌeksenˈtrɪsətɪ] (*pl* -ies) *n* [oddity] excentricité *f*, bizarrerie *f*.

ecclesiastic(al) [ɪˌkliːzɪ'æstɪk(l)] *adj* ecclésiastique.

ECG *n* - **1.** (*abbr of* **electrocardiogram**) ECG *m* - **2.** (*abbr of* **electrocardiograph**) ECG *m*.

ECGD (*abbr of* **Export Credits Guarantee Department**) *n organisme d'assurance pour le commerce extérieur,* ≃ COFACE *f*.

ECH Br (*abbr of* **electric central heating**) *chauffage central électrique.*

echelon ['eʃəlɒn] *n* échelon *m*.

echo ['ekəʊ] (*pl* -es, *pt* & *pp* -ed ; *cont* -ing) ⇔ *n* lit & fig écho *m* ⇔ *vt* [words] répéter ; [opinion] faire écho à ⇔ *vi* retentir, résonner.

éclair [eɪ'kleə'] *n* éclair *m*.

eclectic le'klektɪk] *adj* éclectique.

eclipse [ɪ'klɪps] ⇔ *n* lit & fig éclipse *f* ⇔ *vt* fig éclipser.

ECM Am (*abbr of* **European Common Market**) *n Marché commun européen.*

eco- [ˌiːkəʊ-] *prefix* éco-.

eco-friendly *adj* qui respecte l'environnement.

eco-label *n* écolabel *m*.

E-coli [ˌiː'kəʊlaɪ] *n* E-coli *m*, bactérie *f* Escherischia coli.

ecological [ˌiːkə'lɒdʒɪkl] *adj* écologique.

ecologically [ˌiːkə'lɒdʒɪklɪ] *adv* du point de vue écologique.

ecologist [ɪ'kɒlədʒɪst] *n* écologiste *mf*.

ecology [ɪ'kɒlədʒɪ] *n* écologie *f*.

e-commerce *n (U)* commerce *m* électronique, cybercommerce *m*.

economic [ˌiːkə'nɒmɪk] *adj* - **1.** ECON économique - **2.** [profitable] rentable.

economical [ˌiːkə'nɒmɪkl] *adj* - **1.** [cheap] économique - **2.** [person] économe.

Economic and Monetary Union *n* Union *f* économique européenne.

economics [ˌiːkə'nɒmɪks] ⇔ *n (U)* économie *f* (politique), sciences *fpl* économiques ⇔ *npl* [of plan, business] aspect *m* financier.

economist [ɪ'kɒnəmɪst] *n* économiste *mf*.

economize, -ise [ɪ'kɒnəmaɪz] *vi* économiser.

economy [ɪ'kɒnəmɪ] (*pl* -ies) *n* économie *f* ; **economies of scale** économies d'échelle.

economy class *n* classe *f* touriste.

economy drive *n* campagne *f* de restrictions.

economy-size(d) *adj* [pack, jar] taille économique *(inv)*.

ecorefill [ˌiːkəʊ'riːfɪl] *n* écorecharge *f*.

ecosystem ['iːkəʊˌsɪstəm] *n* écosystème *m*.

ecotourism ['iːkəʊˌtʊərɪzm] *n* écotourisme *m*.

ECSC (*abbr of* **European Coal & Steel Community**) *n* CECA *f*.

ecstasy ['ekstəsɪ] (*pl* -ies) *n* - **1.** [pleasure] extase *f*, ravissement *m* ; **to go into ecstasies about sthg** s'extasier sur qqch - **2.** [drug] ecstasy *m* OR *f*.

ecstatic [ek'stætɪk] *adj* [person] en extase ; [feeling] extatique.

ecstatically [ek'stætɪklɪ] *adv* [say, shout] d'un air extasié ; **to be ~ happy** être au comble du bonheur.

ECT (*abbr of* **electroconvulsive therapy**) *n* électrochocs *mpl*.

ectoplasm ['ektəplæzm] *n* ectoplasme *m*.

ECU, Ecu ['ekjuː] (*abbr of* **European Currency Unit**) *n* ECU *m*, écu *m*.

Ecuador ['ekwədɔː'] *n* Équateur *m* ; **in ~** en Équateur.

Ecuadoran [ˌekwə'dɔːrən], **Ecuadorian** [ˌekwə'dɔːrɪən] ⇔ *adj* équatorien(enne) ⇔ *n* Équatorien *m*, -enne *f*.

ecumenical [iːkjuː'menɪkl] *adj* œcuménique.

eczema ['eksɪmə] *n* eczéma *m*.

ed. - **1.** (*abbr of* **edited**) sous la dir. de, coll. - **2.** *abbr of* **edition** - **3.** *abbr of* **editor**.

eddy ['edɪ] (*pl* -ies, *pt* & *pp* -ied) ⇔ *n* tourbillon *m* ⇔ *vi* tourbillonner.

Eden ['iːdn] *n* : **(the Garden of) ~** le jardin *m* d'Éden, l'Éden *m*.

edge [edʒ] ⇔ *n* - **1.** [gen] bord *m* ; [of coin, book] tranche *f* ; [of knife] tranchant *m* ; **to be on the ~ of** fig être à deux doigts de - **2.** [advantage] : **to have an ~ over** OR **the ~ on** avoir un léger avantage sur - **3.** fig [in voice] note *f* tranchante ⇔ *vi* : **to ~ forward** avancer tout doucement.
◆ **on edge** *adj* contracté(e), tendu(e).

edged [edʒd] *adj* : **~ with** bordé(e) de.

edgeways ['edʒweɪz], **edgewise** ['edʒwaɪz] *adv* latéralement, de côté.

edging ['edʒɪŋ] *n* [of cloth] liseré *m* ; [of paper] bordure *f*.

edgy ['edʒɪ] (*compar* -ier ; *superl* -iest) *adj* contracté(e), tendu(e).

edible ['edɪbl] *adj* [safe to eat] comestible.

edict ['iːdɪkt] *n* décret *m*.

edifice ['edɪfɪs] *n* édifice *m*.

edify ['edɪfaɪ] (*pt* & *pp* -ied) *vt* édifier (intellectuellement).

edifying ['edɪfaɪɪŋ] *adj* édifiant(e).

Edinburgh ['edɪnbrə] *n* Édimbourg.

Edinburgh Festival n : the ~ le Festival d'Édimbourg.

EDINBURGH FESTIVAL

Le Festival international d'Édimbourg, créé en 1947, est aujourd'hui un des plus grands festivals de théâtre, de musique et de cinéma au monde ; il se tient chaque année en août et en septembre. Le festival « off » (the Fringe) est une grande rencontre de théâtre expérimental.

edit ['edɪt] vt - **1.** [correct - text] corriger - **2.** CINEMA monter ; RADIO & TV réaliser - **3.** [magazine] diriger ; [newspaper] être le rédacteur en chef de.
➤ **edit out** vt sep couper.

edition [ɪ'dɪʃn] n édition f.

editor ['edɪtər] n - **1.** [of magazine] directeur m, -trice f ; [of newspaper] rédacteur m, -trice f en chef - **2.** [of text] correcteur m, -trice f - **3.** CINEMA monteur m, -euse f ; RADIO & TV réalisateur m, -trice f.

editorial [,edɪ'tɔːrɪəl] <> adj [department, staff] de la rédaction ; [style, policy] éditorial(e) <> n éditorial m.

EDP (abbr of electronic data processing) n traitement électronique de données.

EDT (abbr of Eastern Daylight Time) n heure d'été de l'Est des États-Unis.

educate ['edʒukeɪt] vt - **1.** SCH & UNIV instruire - **2.** [inform] informer, éduquer.

educated ['edʒukeɪtɪd] adj [cultured] cultivé(e).

education [,edʒu'keɪʃn] n - **1.** [gen] éducation f - **2.** [teaching] enseignement m, instruction f.

educational [,edʒu'keɪʃənl] adj - **1.** [establishment, policy] pédagogique - **2.** [toy, experience] éducatif(ive).

educationalist [,edʒu'keɪʃnəlɪst] n pédagogue mf.

educative ['edʒukətɪv] adj éducatif(ive).

educator ['edʒukeɪtər] n éducateur m, -trice f.

edutainment [edʒu'teɪnmənt] n ludo-éducatif m.

Edwardian [ed'wɔːdɪən] adj de l'époque 1900.

EEC (abbr of European Economic Community) n ancien nom de la Communauté Européenne.

EEG n - **1.** (abbr of electroencephalogram) EEG m - **2.** (abbr of electroencephalograph) EEG m.

eel [iːl] n anguille f.

EENT (abbr of eye, ear, nose and throat) n ophtalmologie f et ORL f.

eerie ['ɪərɪ] adj inquiétant(e), sinistre.

EET (abbr of Eastern European Time) n heure d'Europe orientale.

efface [ɪ'feɪs] vt effacer.

effect [ɪ'fekt] <> n - **1.** [gen] effet m ; to have an ~ on avoir OR produire un effet sur ; for ~ pour attirer l'attention, pour se faire remarquer ; to take ~ [law] prendre effet, entrer en vigueur ; to put sthg into ~ [policy, law] mettre qqch en application - **2.** [meaning] : a statement to the ~ that ... une déclaration selon laquelle ... ; or words to that ~ ou quelque chose de ce genre <> vt [repairs, change] effectuer ; [reconciliation] amener.
➤ **effects** npl : (special) ~s effets mpl spéciaux.

effective [ɪ'fektɪv] adj - **1.** [successful] efficace - **2.** [actual, real] effectif(ive).

effectively [ɪ'fektɪvlɪ] adv - **1.** [successfully] efficacement - **2.** [in fact] effectivement.

effectiveness [ɪ'fektɪvnɪs] n efficacité f.

effeminate [ɪ'femɪnət] adj efféminé(e).

effervesce [,efə'ves] vi pétiller.

effervescent [,efə'vesənt] adj [liquid] effervescent(e) ; [drink] gazeux(euse).

effete [ɪ'fiːt] adj [person, gesture] veule.

efficacious [efɪ'keɪʃəs] adj fml efficace.

efficacy ['efɪkəsɪ] n efficacité f.

efficiency [ɪ'fɪʃənsɪ] n [of person, method] efficacité f ; [of factory, system] rendement m.

efficient [ɪ'fɪʃənt] adj efficace.

efficiently [ɪ'fɪʃəntlɪ] adv efficacement.

effigy ['efɪdʒɪ] (pl -ies) n effigie f.

effluent ['efluənt] n effluent m.

effort ['efət] n effort m ; to be worth the ~ valoir la peine ; with ~ avec peine ; to make the ~ to do sthg s'efforcer de faire qqch ; to make an/no ~ to do sthg faire un effort/ne faire aucun effort pour faire qqch.

effortless ['efətlɪs] adj [easy] facile ; [natural] aisé(e).

effortlessly ['efətlɪslɪ] adv sans effort, facilement.

effrontery [ɪ'frʌntərɪ] n effronterie f.

effusive [ɪ'fjuːsɪv] adj [person] démonstratif(ive) ; [welcome] plein(e) d'effusions.

effusively [ɪ'fjuːsɪvlɪ] adv avec effusion.

EFL ['efl] (abbr of English as a foreign language) n anglais langue étrangère.

EFTA ['eftə] (abbr of European Free Trade Association) n AELE f, AEL-E f.

EFTPOS ['eftpɒs] (abbr of electronic funds

transfer at point of sale) *n* transfert électronique de fonds au point de vente.

EFTS [efts] (*abbr of* **electronic funds transfer system**) *n* système électronique de transferts de fonds.

e.g. (*abbr of* **exempli gratia**) *adv* par exemple.

EGA (*abbr of* **enhanced graphics adapter**) *n* adapteur *m* graphique couleur EGA.

egalitarian [ɪ,gælɪ'teərɪən] *adj* égalitaire.

egg [eg] *n* œuf *m*.

egg on *vt sep* pousser, inciter.

eggcup ['egkʌp] *n* coquetier *m*.

eggplant ['egplɑ:nt] *n* Am aubergine *f*.

eggshell ['egʃel] *n* coquille *f* d'œuf.

egg timer *n* [with sand] sablier *m* ; [mechanical] minuteur *m*.

egg whisk *n* fouet *m*.

egg white *n* blanc *m* d'œuf.

egg yolk *n* jaune *m* d'œuf.

ego ['i:gəʊl] (*pl* **-s**) *n* moi *m*.

egocentric [,i:gəʊ'sentrɪk] *adj* égocentrique.

egoism ['i:gəʊɪzm] *n* égoïsme *m*.

egoist ['i:gəʊɪst] *n* égoïste *mf*.

egoistic [,i:gəʊ'ɪstɪk] *adj* égoïste.

egotism ['i:gətɪzm] *n* égotisme *m*.

egotist ['i:gətɪst] *n* égotiste *mf*.

egotistic(al) [,i:gə'tɪstɪk(l)] *adj* égotiste.

ego trip *n* inf : she's just on an ~ c'est par vanité qu'elle le fait.

Egypt ['i:dʒɪpt] *n* Égypte *f* ; in ~ en Égypte.

Egyptian [ɪ'dʒɪpʃn] <> *adj* égyptien(enne) <> *n* Égyptien *m*, -enne *f*.

eh [eɪ] *excl* Br inf hein?

eiderdown ['aɪdədaʊn] *n* esp Br [bed cover] édredon *m*.

eight [eɪt] *num* huit ; *see also* **six**.

eighteen [,eɪ'ti:n] *num* dix-huit ; *see also* **six**.

eighteenth [,eɪ'ti:nθ] *num* dix-huitième ; *see also* **sixth**.

eighth [eɪtθ] *num* huitième ; *see also* **sixth**.

eightieth ['eɪtɪɪθ] *num* quatre-vingtième ; *see also* **sixth**.

eighty ['eɪtɪ] (*pl* **-ies**) *num* quatre-vingts ; *see also* **sixty**.

Eire ['eərə] *n* République *f* d'Irlande.

EIS (*abbr of* **Educational Institute of Scotland**) *n* syndicat écossais d'enseignants.

either ['aɪðə', 'i:ðə'] <> *adj* **- 1.** [one or the other] l'un ou l'autre (l'une ou l'autre) (des deux) ; she couldn't find ~ jumper elle ne trouva ni l'un ni l'autre des pulls ; ~ way de toute façon **- 2.** [each] chaque ; on ~ side de

chaque côté <> *pron :* ~ (of them) l'un ou l'autre *m*, l'une ou l'autre *f* ; I don't like ~ (of them) je n'aime aucun des deux, je n'aime ni l'un ni l'autre <> *adv (in negatives)* non plus ; I don't ~ moi non plus <> *conj :* ~ ... or soit ... soit, ou ... ou ; I'm not fond of ~ him or his wife je ne les aime ni lui ni sa femme.

ejaculate [ɪ'dʒækjʊleɪt] <> *vt* [exclaim] s'écrier <> *vi* [have orgasm] éjaculer.

eject [ɪ'dʒekt] *vt* **- 1.** [object] éjecter, émettre **- 2.** [person] éjecter, expulser.

ejector seat Br [ɪ'dʒektə'-], **ejection seat** Am [ɪ'dʒekʃn-] *n* siège *m* éjectable.

eke [i:k] **eke out** <> *vt sep* [money, food] économiser, faire durer <> *vt fus :* to ~ out a living subsister.

EKG (*abbr of* **electrocardiogram**) *n* Am ECG *m*.

el [el] (*abbr of* **elevated railroad**) *n* Am inf chemin *m* de fer aérien.

elaborate [*adj* ɪ'læbrət, *vb* ɪ'læbəreɪt] <> *adj* [ceremony, procedure] complexe ; [explanation, plan] détaillé(e), minutieux(euse) <> *vi :* to ~ (on) donner des précisions (sur).

elaborately [ɪ'læbərətlɪ] *adv* [planned] minutieusement ; [decorated] avec recherche.

elapse [ɪ'læps] *vi* s'écouler.

elastic [ɪ'læstɪk] <> *adj* lit & fig élastique <> *n* (U) élastique *m*.

elasticated [ɪ'læstɪkeɪtɪd] *adj* élastique.

elastic band *n* Br élastique *m*, caoutchouc *m*.

elasticity [,elæ'stɪsətɪ] *n* élasticité *f*.

elated [ɪ'leɪtɪd] *adj* transporté(e) (de joie).

elation [ɪ'leɪʃn] *n* exultation *f*, joie *f*.

elbow ['elbəʊ] <> *n* coude *m* <> *vt :* to ~ sb aside écarter qqn du coude.

elbow grease *n* inf huile *f* de coude.

elbowroom ['elbəʊrʊm] *n* inf : to have some ~ avoir ses coudées franches.

elder ['eldə'] <> *adj* aîné(e) <> *n* **- 1.** [older person] aîné *m*, -e *f* **- 2.** [of tribe, church] ancien *m* **- 3. :** ~ (tree) sureau *m*.

elderberry ['eldə,berɪ] (*pl* **-ies**) *n* [fruit] baie *f* de sureau ; [tree] sureau *m*.

elderly ['eldəlɪ] <> *adj* âgé(e) <> *npl :* the ~ les personnes *fpl* âgées.

elder statesman *n* vétéran *m* de la politique.

eldest ['eldɪst] *adj* aîné(e).

Eldorado [,eldɔ'rɑ:dəʊ] *n* Eldorado *m*.

elect [ɪ'lekt] <> *adj* élu(e) <> *vt* **- 1.** [by voting] élire **- 2.** fml [choose] : to ~ to do sthg choisir de faire qqch.

elected [ɪ'lektɪd] *adj* élu(e).

election [ɪ'lekʃn] n élection f ; **to have** OR **hold an ~** procéder à une élection ; **local ~s** élections locales.

election campaign n campagne f électorale.

electioneering [ɪ,lekʃə'nɪərɪŋ] n (U) usu pej propagande f électorale.

elective [ɪ'lektɪv] n Am SCH cours m facultatif.

elector [ɪ'lektər] n électeur m, -trice f.

electoral [ɪ'lektərəl] adj électoral(e).

electoral college n collège m électoral.

electoral register, electoral roll n : the **~** la liste électorale.

electorate [ɪ'lektərət] n : the **~** l'électorat m.

electric [ɪ'lektrɪk] adj lit & fig électrique.
➤ **electrics** npl Br inf [in car, machine] installation f électrique.

electrical [ɪ'lektrɪkl] adj électrique.

electrical engineer n ingénieur m électricien.

electrical engineering n électrotechnique f.

electrically [ɪ'lektrɪklɪ] adv [heated] à l'électricité ; [charged, powered] électriquement.

electrical shock Am = electric shock.

electric blanket n couverture f chauffante.

electric chair n : the **~** la chaise électrique.

electric cooker n cuisinière f électrique.

electric current n courant m électrique.

electric fire n radiateur m électrique.

electric guitar n guitare f électrique.

electrician [,ɪlek'trɪʃn] n électricien m, -enne f.

electricity [,ɪlek'trɪsətɪ] n électricité f.

electric light n lumière f électrique.

electric shock Br, **electrical shock** Am n décharge f électrique.

electric shock therapy n (U) électrochocs mpl.

electric storm n orage m magnétique.

electrify [ɪ'lektrɪfaɪ] (pt & pp -ied) vt - 1. TECH électrifier - 2. fig [excite] galvaniser, électriser.

electrifying [ɪ'lektrɪfaɪŋ] adj [exciting] galvanisant(e), électrisant(e).

electro- [ɪ'lektrəʊ] prefix électro-.

electrocardiograph [ɪ,lektrəʊ'kɑːdɪəgrɑːf] n électrocardiographe m.

electrocute [ɪ'lektrəkjuːt] vt électrocuter.

electrode [ɪ'lektrəʊd] n électrode f.

electroencephalograph [ɪ,lektrəʊen'sefələgrɑːf] n électroencéphalographie f.

electrolysis [,ɪlek'trɒləsɪs] n électrolyse f.

electromagnet [ɪ,lektrəʊ'mægnɪt] n électro-aimant m.

electromagnetic [ɪ,lektrəʊmæg'netɪk] adj électromagnétique.

electron [ɪ'lektrɒn] n électron m.

electronic [,ɪlek'trɒnɪk] adj électronique.
➤ **electronics** <> n (U) [technology, science] électronique f <> npl [equipment] (équipement m) électronique f.

electronic data processing n traitement m électronique de données.

electronic mail n courrier m électronique.

electronic mailbox n boîte f aux lettres (électronique).

electronic publishing n (U) édition f électronique.

electron microscope n microscope m électronique.

electroplated [ɪ'lektrəʊpleɪtɪd] adj métallisé(e) par galvanoplastie.

elegance ['elɪgəns] n élégance f.

elegant ['elɪgənt] adj élégant(e).

elegantly ['elɪgəntlɪ] adv élégamment.

elegy ['elɪdʒɪ] (pl -ies) n élégie f.

element ['elɪmənt] n - 1. [gen] élément m ; **an ~ of truth** une part de vérité - 2. [in heater, kettle] résistance f - 3. phr : **to be in one's ~** être dans son élément.
➤ **elements** npl - 1. [basics] rudiments mpl - 2. [weather] : **the ~s** les éléments mpl.

elementary [,elɪ'mentərɪ] adj élémentaire.

elementary school n Am école f primaire.

elephant ['elɪfənt] (pl inv OR -s) n éléphant m

elevate ['elɪveɪt] vt - 1. [give importance to] : **to ~ sb/sthg (to)** élever qqn/qqch (à) - 2. [raise] soulever.

elevated ['elɪveɪtɪd] adj - 1. [important] important(e) - 2. [lofty] élevé(e) - 3. [raised] surélevé(e).

elevation [,elɪ'veɪʃn] n - 1. [promotion] élévation f - 2. [height] hauteur f.

elevator ['elɪveɪtər] n Am ascenseur m.

eleven [ɪ'levn] num onze ; see also **six**.

elevenses [ɪ'levnzɪz] n (U) Br ≃ pause-café f.

eleventh [ɪ'levnθ] num onzième ; see also **sixth**.

eleventh hour n fig : **the ~** la onzième heure, la dernière minute.

elf [elf] (pl **elves** [elvz]) n elfe m, lutin m.

elicit [ɪ'lɪsɪt] *vt* **fml** : **to ~ sthg (from sb)** arracher qqch (à qqn).

eligibility [ˌelɪdʒə'bɪlətɪ] *n* - **1.** [suitability] admissibilité *f* - **2. dated** [of bachelor] acceptabilité *f*.

eligible ['elɪdʒəbl] *adj* - **1.** [suitable, qualified] admissible ; **to be ~ for sthg** avoir droit à qqch ; **to be ~ to do sthg** avoir le droit de faire qqch - **2. dated** [bachelor] : **to be ~** être un bon parti.

eliminate [ɪ'lɪmɪneɪt] *vt* : **to ~ sb/sthg (from)** éliminer qqn/qqch (de).

elimination [ɪˌlɪmɪ'neɪʃn] *n* élimination *f*.

elite [ɪ'liːt] <> *adj* d'élite <> *n* élite *f*.

elitism [ɪ'liːtɪzml] *n* élitisme *m*.

elitist [ɪ'liːtɪst] <> *adj* élitiste <> *n* élitiste *mf*.

elixir [ɪ'lɪksəʳ] *n* - **1.** [magic drink] élixir *m* - **2. fig** [magic cure] panacée *f*.

Elizabethan [ɪˌlɪzə'biːθn] <> *adj* élisabéthain(e) <> *n* Élisabéthain *m*, -e *f*.

elk [elk] (*pl inv* OR **-s**) *n* élan *m*.

ellipse [ɪ'lɪps] *n* ellipse *f*.

elliptical [ɪ'lɪptɪkl] *adj* - **1.** [in shape] en ellipse - **2. fml** [indirect, cryptic] elliptique.

elm [elm] *n* : **~ (tree)** orme *m*.

elocution [ˌelə'kjuːʃn] *n* élocution *f*, diction *f*.

elongated ['iːlɒŋgeɪtɪd] *adj* allongé(e) ; [fingers] long (longue).

elope [ɪ'ləʊp] *vi* : **to ~ (with)** s'enfuir (avec).

elopement [ɪ'ləʊpmənt] *n* fugue *f* (amoureuse).

eloquence ['eləkwəns] *n* éloquence *f*.

eloquent ['eləkwənt] *adj* éloquent(e).

eloquently ['eləkwəntlɪ] *adv* avec éloquence.

El Salvador [ˌel'sælvədɔːʳ] *n* Salvador *m* ; **in ~** au Salvador.

else [els] *adv* : **anything ~** n'importe quoi d'autre ; **anything ~?** [in shop] et avec ça?, ce sera tout? ; **he doesn't need anything ~** il n'a besoin de rien d'autre ; **everyone ~** tous les autres ; **nothing ~** rien d'autre ; **someone ~** quelqu'un d'autre ; **something ~** quelque chose d'autre ; **somewhere ~** autre part ; **who/what ~?** qui/quoi d'autre? ; **where ~?** (à) quel autre endroit?

➤ **or else** *conj* - **1.** [or if not] sinon, sans quoi - **2.** [as threat] ou alors ...!, sinon ...!

elsewhere [els'weəʳ] *adv* ailleurs, autre part.

ELT (*abbr of* **English language teaching**) *n* enseignement de l'anglais.

elucidate [ɪ'luːsɪdeɪt] **fml** <> *vt* élucider <> *vi* s'éclaircir.

elude [ɪ'luːd] *vt* échapper à.

elusive [ɪ'luːsɪv] *adj* insaisissable ; [success] qui échappe.

elves [elvz] *pl* ⊳ **elf.**

'em [əm] *pron inf* = **them.**

emaciated [ɪ'meɪʃieɪtɪd] *adj* [face] émacié(e) ; [person, limb] décharné(e).

e-mail, email (*abbr of* **electronic mail**) *n* e-mail *m*, courrier *m* électronique *f*.

emanate ['eməneɪt] **fml** <> *vt* dégager <> *vi* . **to ~ from** émaner de.

emancipate [ɪ'mænsɪpeɪt] *vt* : **to ~ sb (from)** affranchir OR émanciper qqn (de).

emancipation [ɪˌmænsɪ'peɪʃn] *n* : **~ (from)** affranchissement *m* (de), émancipation *f* (de).

emasculate [ɪ'mæskjʊleɪt] *vt* [weaken] émasculer.

emasculation [ɪˌmæskjʊ'leɪʃn] *n* [weakening] émasculation *f*.

embalm [ɪm'bɑːm] *vt* embaumer.

embankment [ɪm'bæŋkmənt] *n* [of river] berge *f* ; [of railway] remblai *m* ; [of road] banquette *f*.

embargo [em'bɑːgəʊ] (*pl* **-es**, *pt* & *pp* **-ed** ; *cont* **-ing**) <> *n* : **~ (on)** embargo *m* (sur) <> *vt* mettre l'embargo sur.

embark [ɪm'bɑːk] *vi* - **1.** [board ship] : **to ~ (on)** embarquer (sur) - **2.** [start] : **to ~ on** OR **upon sthg** s'embarquer dans qqch.

embarkation [ˌembɑː'keɪʃn] *n* embarquement *m*.

embarkation card *n* **Br** carte *f* d'embarquement.

embarrass [ɪm'bærəs] *vt* embarrasser.

embarrassed [ɪm'bærəst] *adj* embarrassé(e).

embarrassing [ɪm'bærəsɪŋ] *adj* embarrassant(e).

embarrassment [ɪm'bærəsmənt] *n* embarras *m* ; **to be an ~** [person] causer de l'embarras ; [thing] être embarrassant.

embassy ['embəsɪ] (*pl* **-ies**) *n* ambassade *f*.

embattled [ɪm'bætld] *adj* [troubled] en difficulté.

embedded [ɪm'bedɪd] *adj* - **1.** [buried] : **~ in** [in rock, wood] incrusté(e) dans ; [in mud] noyé(e) dans - **2.** [ingrained] enraciné(e).

embellish [ɪm'belɪʃ] *vt* - **1.** [decorate] : **to ~ sthg (with)** [room, house] décorer qqch (de) ; [dress] orner qqch (de) - **2.** [story] enjoliver.

embers ['embəz] *npl* braises *fpl*.

embezzle [ɪm'bezl] *vt* détourner.

embezzlement [ɪm'bezlmənt] *n* détournement *m* de fonds.

embezzler [ɪm'bezlə^r] *n* escroc *m*.

embittered [ɪm'bɪtəd] *adj* aigri(e).

emblazoned [ɪm'bleɪznd] *adj* - **1.** [design, emblem] : ~ **(on)** blasonné(e) (sur) - **2.** [flag, garment] : ~ **with** arborant l'insigne *OR* le blason de.

emblem ['embləm] *n* emblème *m*.

EMBLEMS

La Grande-Bretagne est souvent symbolisée par le personnage de Britannia, une femme en robe longue portant un bouclier au motif de l'Union Jack (drapeau du Royaume-Uni). Les emblèmes de l'Angleterre sont la rose rouge et le lion. Le pays de Galles est traditionnellement représenté par le poireau, ainsi que la jonquille ou le dragon rouge. L'emblème de l'Écosse est le chardon. Le trèfle et la harpe symbolisent l'Irlande.

embodiment [ɪm'bɒdɪmənt] *n* incarnation *f*.

embody [ɪm'bɒdɪ] (*pt* & *pp* **-ied**) *vt* incarner ; **to be embodied in** sthg être exprimé dans qqch.

embolism ['embəlɪzm] *n* embolie *f*.

embossed [ɪm'bɒst] *adj* - **1.** [heading, design] : ~ **(on)** inscrit(e) (sur), gravé(e) en relief (sur) - **2.** [wallpaper] gaufré(e) ; [leather] frappé(e).

embrace [ɪm'breɪs] ◇ *n* étreinte *f* ◇ *vt* embrasser ◇ *vi* s'embrasser, s'étreindre.

embrocation [ˌembrə'keɪʃn] *n* embrocation *f*.

embroider [ɪm'brɔɪdə^r] ◇ *vt* - **1.** SEWING broder - **2.** *pej* [embellish] enjoliver ◇ *vi* SEWING broder.

embroidered [ɪm'brɔɪdəd] *adj* SEWING brodé(e).

embroidery [ɪm'brɔɪdərɪ] *n* (*U*) broderie *f*.

embroil [ɪm'brɔɪl] *vt* : **to be ~ed (in)** être mêlé(e) (à).

embryo ['embrɪəʊ] (*pl* **-s**) *n* embryon *m* ; **in ~ fig** à l'état embryonnaire.

embryonic [ˌembrɪ'ɒnɪk] *adj* embryonnaire.

emcee [ˌem'siː] *Am abbr of* **master of ceremonies**.

emend [ɪ'mend] *vt* corriger.

emerald ['emərəld] ◇ *adj* [colour] émeraude (*inv*) ◇ *n* [stone] émeraude *f*.

emerge [ɪ'mɜːdʒ] ◇ *vi* - **1.** [come out] : **to ~ (from)** émerger (de) - **2.** [from experience, sit-uation] : **to ~ from** sortir de - **3.** [become known] apparaître - **4.** [come into existence - poet, artist] percer ; [- movement, organization] émerger ◇ *vt* : **it ~s that ...** il ressort *OR* il apparaît que ...

emergence [ɪ'mɜːdʒəns] *n* émergence *f*.

emergency [ɪ'mɜːdʒənsɪ] (*pl* **-ies**) ◇ *adj* d'urgence ◇ *n* urgence *f* ; **in an ~, in emergencies** en cas d'urgence.

emergency exit *n* sortie *f* de secours.

emergency landing *n* atterrissage *m* forcé.

emergency services *npl* ≃ police-secours *f*.

emergency stop *n* arrêt *m* d'urgence.

emergent [ɪ'mɜːdʒənt] *adj* qui émerge.

emery board ['emərɪ-] *n* lime *f* à ongles.

emetic [ɪ'metɪk] ◇ *adj* émétique ◇ *n* émétique *m*.

emigrant ['emɪgrənt] *n* émigré *m*, -e *f*.

emigrate ['emɪgreɪt] *vi* : **to ~ (to)** émigrer (en/à).

emigration [ˌemɪ'greɪʃn] *n* émigration *f*.

émigré ['emɪgreɪ] *n* émigré *m*, -e *f*.

eminence ['emɪnəns] *n* (*U*) [prominence] renom *m*.

eminent ['emɪnənt] *adj* éminent(e).

eminently ['emɪnəntlɪ] *adv fml* éminemment.

emir [e'mɪə^r] *n* émir *m*.

emirate ['emərət] *n* émirat *m*.

emissary ['emɪsərɪ] (*pl* **-ies**) *n* émissaire *m*.

emission [ɪ'mɪʃn] *n* émission *f*.

emit [ɪ'mɪt] (*pt* & *pp* **-ted** ; *cont* **-ting**) *vt* émettre.

emollient [ɪ'mɒlɪənt] *n fml* émollient *m*.

emolument [ɪ'mɒljʊmənt] *n fml* émoluments *mpl*.

emotion [ɪ'məʊʃn] *n* - **1.** (*U*) [strength of feeling] émotion *f* - **2.** [particular feeling] sentiment *m*.

emotional [ɪ'məʊʃənl] *adj* - **1.** [sensitive, demonstrative] émotif(ive) - **2.** [moving] émouvant(e) - **3.** [psychological] émotionnel(elle).

emotionally [ɪ'məʊʃnəlɪ] *adv* - **1.** [with strong feeling] avec émotion - **2.** [psychologically] émotionnellement.

emotionless [ɪ'məʊʃnlɪs] *adj* impassible.

emotive [ɪ'məʊtɪv] *adj* qui enflamme l'esprit.

empathy ['empəθɪ] *n* (*U*) : ~ **(with)** empathie *f* (envers), communion *f* de sentiments (avec).

emperor ['empərə^r] *n* empereur *m*.

emphasis ['emfəsɪs] (*pl* **-ses** [-siːz]) *n* : ~ **(on)**

accent *m* (sur) ; **with great ~** avec insistance ; **to lay** OR **place ~ on sthg** insister sur OR souligner qqch.

emphasize, -ise ['emfəsaız] *vt* insister sur.

emphatic [ım'fætık] *adj* [forceful] catégorique.

emphatically [ım'fætıklı] *adv* - **1.** [with emphasis] catégoriquement - **2.** [certainly] absolument.

emphysema [,emfı'si:mə] *n* emphysème *m*.

empire ['empaıə'] *n* empire *m*.

empire building *n* édification *f* d'empires.

empirical [ım'pırıkl] *adj* empirique.

empiricism [ım'pırısızm] *n* empirisme *m*.

employ [ım'plɔı] *vt* employer ; **to be ~ed as** être employé comme ; **to ~ sthg as sthg/to do sthg** employer qqch comme qqch/pour faire qqch.

employable [ım'plɔıəbl] *adj* qui peut être employé(e).

employee [ım'plɔıi:] *n* employé *m*, -e *f*.

employer [ım'plɔıə'] *n* employeur *m*, -euse *f*.

employment [ım'plɔımənt] *n* emploi *m*, travail *m*.

employment agency *n* bureau *m* OR agence *f* de placement.

employment office *n* ≃ Agence *f* Nationale pour l'Emploi.

emporium [em'pɔ:rıəm] *n* [shop] grand magasin *m*.

empower [ım'pauə'] *vt fml* : **to be ~ed to do sthg** être habilité(e) à faire qqch.

empress ['emprıs] *n* impératrice *f*.

emptiness ['emptınıs] *(U) n* vide *m*.

empty ['emptı] *(compar* **-ier** ; *superl* **-iest**, *pt* & *pp* **-ied**, *pl* **-ies**) ◇ *adj* - **1.** [containing nothing] vide - **2.** *pej* [meaningless] vain(e) - **3.** *literary* [tedious] morne ◇ *vt* vider ; **to ~ sthg into/out of** vider qqch dans/de ◇ *vi* se vider ◇ *n inf* bouteille *f* vide.

empty-handed [-'hændıd] *adj* les mains vides.

empty-headed [-'hedıd] *adj* sans cervelle.

EMS (*abbr of* **European Monetary System**) *n* SME *m*.

EMT (*abbr of* **emergency medical technician**) *n technicien médical des services d'urgence.*

emu ['i:mju:] *(pl inv* OR **-s**) *n* émeu *m*.

EMU (*abbr of* **Economic and Monetary Union**) *n* UEM *f*.

emulate ['emjuleıt] *vt* imiter.

emulsion [ı'mʌlʃn] ◇ *n* - **1.** : **~ (paint)** pein-

ture *f* mate OR à émulsion - **2.** PHOT émulsion *f* ◇ *vt* Br peindre.

enable [ı'neıbl] *vt* : **to ~ sb to do sthg** permettre à qqn de faire qqch.

enact [ı'nækt] *vt* - **1.** JUR promulguer - **2.** THEATRE jouer.

enactment [ı'næktmənt] *n* JUR promulgation *f*.

enamel [ı'næml] *n* - **1.** [material] émail *m* - **2.** [paint] peinture *f* laquée.

enamelled Br, **enameled** Am [ı'næmld] *adj* en émail.

enamel paint *n* peinture *f* laquée.

enamoured Br, **enamored** Am [ı'næməd] *adj* : **~ of** amoureux(euse) de.

en bloc [ɒn'blɒk] *adv* en bloc.

enc. - **1.** *abbr of* **enclosure** - **2.** *abbr of* **enclosed.**

encamp [ın'kæmp] *vi* camper.

encampment [ın'kæmpmənt] *n* campement *m*.

encapsulate [ın'kæpsjuleıt] *vt* : **to ~ sthg (in)** résumer qqch (en).

encase [ın'keıs] *vt* : **to be ~d in** [armour] être enfermé(e) dans ; [leather] être bardé(e) de.

encash [ın'kæʃ] *vt* Br encaisser.

enchanted [ın'tʃɑ:ntıd] *adj* : **~ (by/with)** enchanté(e) (par/de).

enchanting [ın'tʃɑ:ntıŋ] *adj* enchanteur(eresse).

encircle [ın'sɜ:kl] *vt* entourer ; [subj : troops] encercler.

enclave ['enkleıv] *n* enclave *f*.

enclose [ın'kləuz] *vt* - **1.** [surround, contain] entourer - **2.** [put in envelope] joindre ; **please find ~d ...** veuillez trouver ci-joint ...

enclosure [ın'kləuʒə'] *n* - **1.** [place] enceinte *f* - **2.** [in letter] pièce *f* jointe.

encompass [ın'kʌmpəs] *vt fml* - **1.** [include] contenir - **2.** [surround] entourer ; [subj : troops] encercler.

encore ['ɒŋkɔ:'] ◇ *n* rappel *m* ◇ *excl* bis !

encounter [ın'kauntə'] ◇ *n* rencontre *f* ◇ *vt fml* rencontrer.

encourage [ın'kʌrıdʒ] *vt* - **1.** [give confidence to] : **to ~ sb (to do sthg)** encourager qqn (à faire qqch) - **2.** [promote] encourager, favoriser.

encouragement [ın'kʌrıdʒmənt] *n* encouragement *m*.

encouraging [ın'kʌrıdʒıŋ] *adj* encourageant(e).

encroach [ın'krəutʃ] *vi* : **to ~ on** OR **upon** empiéter sur.

encrusted [ɪnˈkrʌstɪd] *adj :* ~ **with** incrusté(e) de ; [with mud] encroûté(e) de.

encrypt [enˈkrɪpt] *vt* - **1.** COMPUT crypter - **2.** TV coder.

encryption [enˈkrɪpʃn] *n (U)* - **1.** COMPUT cryptage *m* - **2.** TV codage *m*, encodage *m*.

encumber [ɪnˈkʌmbəʳ] *vt fml :* to be ~ed with être encombré(e) de ; [with debts] être grevé(e) de.

encyclop(a)edia [ɪnˌsaɪkləˈpiːdjə] *n* encyclopédie *f*.

encyclop(a)edic [ɪnˌsaɪkləʊˈpiːdɪk] *adj* encyclopédique.

end [end] ◇ *n* - **1.** [gen] fin *f* ; **at an** ~ terminé, fini ; **to come to an** ~ se terminer, s'arrêter ; **to put an** ~ **to sthg** mettre fin à qqch ; **at the** ~ **of the day** fig en fin de compte ; **in the** ~ [finally] finalement ; **an** ~ **in itself** une fin en soi - **2.** [of rope, path, garden, table etc] bout *m*, extrémité *f* ; [of box] côté *m* ; ~ **to** ~ bout à bout - **3.** [leftover part - of cigarette] mégot *m* ; [- of pencil] bout *m* ◇ *vt* mettre fin à ; [day] finir ; **to** ~ **sthg with** terminer OR finir qqch par ◇ *vi* se terminer ; **to** ~ **in** se terminer par ; **to** ~ **with** se terminer par OR avec.
◆ **on end** *adv* - **1.** [upright] debout - **2.** [continuously] d'affilée.
◆ **no end** *adv inf* [pleased, worried] vachement.
◆ **no end of** *prep inf* énormément de.
◆ **end up** *vi* finir ; **to** ~ **up doing sthg** finir par faire qqch.

endanger [ɪnˈdeɪndʒəʳ] *vt* mettre en danger.

endangered species [ɪnˈdeɪndʒəd-] *n* espèce *f* en voie de disparition.

endear [ɪnˈdɪəʳ] *vt :* **to** ~ **sb to sb** faire aimer OR apprécier qqn de qqn ; **to** ~ **o.s. to sb** se faire aimer de qqn, plaire à qqn.

endearing [ɪnˈdɪərɪŋ] *adj* engageant(e).

endearment [ɪnˈdɪəmənt] *n* paroles *fpl* affectueuses.

endeavour Br, **endeavor** Am [ɪnˈdevəʳ] fml ◇ *n* effort *m*, tentative *f* ◇ *vt :* **to** ~ **to do sthg** s'efforcer OR tenter de faire qqch.

endemic [enˈdemɪk] *adj* endémique.

ending [ˈendɪŋ] *n* fin *f*, dénouement *m*.

endive [ˈendaɪv] *n* - **1.** [salad vegetable] endive *f* - **2.** [chicory] chicorée *f*.

endless [ˈendlɪs] *adj* - **1.** [unending] interminable ; [patience, possibilities] infini(e) ; [resources] inépuisable - **2.** [vast] infini(e).

endlessly [ˈendlɪslɪ] *adv* sans arrêt, continuellement ; [stretch] à perte de vue ; ~ **patient/kind** d'une patience/gentillesse infinie.

endorse [ɪnˈdɔːs] *vt* - **1.** [approve] approuver

- **2.** [cheque] endosser - **3.** Br [driving licence] porter une contravention à.

endorsement [ɪnˈdɔːsmənt] *n* - **1.** [approval] approbation *f* - **2.** [of cheque] endossement *m* - **3.** Br [on driving licence] *contravention portée au permis de conduire.*

endow [ɪnˈdaʊ] *vt* - **1.** [equip] : **to be** ~**ed with sthg** être doté(e) de qqch - **2.** [donate money to] faire des dons à.

endowment [ɪnˈdaʊmənt] *n* - **1.** fml [ability] capacité *f*, qualité *f* - **2.** [donation] don *m*.

endowment insurance *n* assurance *f* à capital différé.

endowment mortgage *n* prêt-logement *lié à une assurance-vie.*

end product *n* produit *m* fini.

end result *n* résultat *m* final.

endurable [ɪnˈdjʊərəbl] *adj* supportable.

endurance [ɪnˈdjʊərəns] *n* endurance *f*.

endurance test *n* épreuve *f* d'endurance.

endure [ɪnˈdjʊəʳ] ◇ *vt* supporter, endurer ◇ *vi* perdurer.

enduring [ɪnˈdjʊərɪŋ] *adj* durable.

end user *n* utilisateur final *m*, utilisatrice finale *f*.

endways Br [ˈendweɪz], **endwise** Am [ˈendwaɪz] *adv* - **1.** [not sideways] en long - **2.** [with ends touching] bout à bout.

enema [ˈenɪmə] *n* lavement *m*.

enemy [ˈenɪmɪ] *(pl* -ies*)* ◇ *n* ennemi *m*, -e *f* ◇ *comp* ennemi(e).

energetic [ˌenəˈdʒetɪk] *adj* énergique ; [person] plein(e) d'entrain.

energy [ˈenədʒɪ] *(pl* -ies*)* *n* énergie *f*.

energy-saving *adj* d'économie d'énergie.

enervate [ˈenəveɪt] *vt fml* affaiblir.

enervating [ˈenəveɪtɪŋ] *adj fml* débilitant(e).

enfold [ɪnˈfəʊld] *vt literary* - **1.** [embrace] : **to** ~ **sb/sthg (in)** envelopper qqn/qqch (dans) ; **to** ~ **sb in one's arms** étreindre qqn - **2.** [engulf] envelopper.

enforce [ɪnˈfɔːs] *vt* appliquer, faire respecter.

enforceable [ɪnˈfɔːsəbl] *adj* applicable.

enforced [ɪnˈfɔːst] *adj* forcé(e).

enforcement [ɪnˈfɔːsmənt] *n* application *f*.

enfranchise [ɪnˈfræntʃaɪz] *vt* - **1.** [give vote to] accorder le droit de vote à - **2.** [set free] affranchir.

engage [ɪnˈgeɪdʒ] ◇ *vt* - **1.** [attention, interest] susciter, éveiller ; **to** ~ **sb in conversation** engager la conversation avec qqn - **2.** TECH engager - **3.** fml [employ] engager ; **to be** ~**d in**

OR **on sthg** prendre part à qqch ◇ *vi* [be involved] : **to ~ in** s'occuper de.

engaged [ɪn'geɪdʒd] *adj* - **1.** [to be married] : **~ (to sb)** fiancé(e) (à qqn) ; **to get ~** se fiancer - **2.** [busy] occupé(e) ; **~ in sthg** engagé dans qqch - **3.** [telephone, toilet] occupé(e).

engaged tone *n* Br tonalité *f* 'occupé'.

engagement [ɪn'geɪdʒmənt] *n* - **1.** [to be married] fiançailles *fpl* - **2.** [appointment] rendez-vous *m inv*.

engagement ring *n* bague *f* de fiançailles.

engaging [ɪn'geɪdʒɪŋ] *adj* engageant(e) ; [personality] attirant(e).

engender [ɪn'dʒendər] *vt fml* engendrer, susciter.

engine ['endʒɪn] *n* - **1.** [of vehicle] moteur *m* - **2.** RAIL locomotive *f*.

engine driver *n* Br mécanicien *m*.

engineer [ˌendʒɪ'nɪər] ◇ *n* - **1.** [of roads] ingénieur *m* ; [of machinery, on ship] mécanicien *m* ; [of electrical equipment] technicien *m* - **2.** Am [engine driver] mécanicien *m* ◇ *vt* - **1.** [construct] construire - **2.** [contrive] manigancer.

engineering [ˌendʒɪ'nɪərɪŋ] *n* ingénierie *f*.

England ['ɪŋglənd] *n* Angleterre *f* ; **in ~** en Angleterre.

English ['ɪŋglɪʃ] ◇ *adj* anglais(e) ◇ *n* [language] anglais *m* ◇ *npl* : **the ~** les Anglais.

English breakfast *n* petit déjeuner *m* anglais traditionnel.

ENGLISH BREAKFAST

Le petit déjeuner anglais traditionnel se compose d'un plat chaud (des œufs au bacon, par exemple), de céréales ou de porridge, et de toasts à la marmelade d'oranges, le tout accompagné de café ou de thé ; aujourd'hui il est généralement remplacé par une collation plus légère.

English Channel *n* : **the ~** la Manche.

Englishman ['ɪŋglɪʃmən] (*pl* -**men** [-mən]) *n* Anglais *m*.

English muffin *n* Am muffin *m*.

Englishwoman ['ɪŋglɪʃˌwʊmən] (*pl* -**women** [-wɪmɪn]) *n* Anglaise *f*.

engrave [ɪn'greɪv] *vt* : **to ~ sthg (on stone/in one's memory)** graver qqch (sur la pierre/dans sa mémoire).

engraver [ɪn'greɪvər] *n* graveur *m*.

engraving [ɪn'greɪvɪŋ] *n* gravure *f*.

engrossed [ɪn'grəʊst] *adj* : **to be ~ (in sthg)** être absorbé(e) (par qqch).

engrossing [ɪn'grəʊsɪŋ] *adj* captivant(e).

engulf [ɪn'gʌlf] *vt* engloutir.

enhance [ɪn'hɑːns] *vt* accroître.

enhancement [ɪn'hɑːnsmənt] *n* amélioration *f*.

enigma [ɪ'nɪgmə] *n* énigme *f*.

enigmatic [ˌenɪg'mætɪk] *adj* énigmatique.

enjoy [ɪn'dʒɔɪ] ◇ *vt* - **1.** [like] aimer ; **to ~ doing sthg** avoir plaisir à OR aimer faire qqch ; **to ~ o.s.** s'amuser - **2.** *fml* [possess] jouir de ◇ *vi* Am : **~!** [enjoy yourself] amuse-toi bien! ; [before meal] bon appétit!

enjoyable [ɪn'dʒɔɪəbl] *adj* agréable.

enjoyment [ɪn'dʒɔɪmənt] *n* - **1.** [gen] plaisir *m* - **2.** *fml* [possession] jouissance *f*.

enlarge [ɪn'lɑːdʒ] *vt* agrandir.

◆ **enlarge (up)on** *vt fus* développer.

enlargement [ɪn'lɑːdʒmənt] *n* - **1.** [expansion] extension *f* - **2.** PHOT agrandissement *m*.

enlighten [ɪn'laɪtn] *vt* éclairer.

enlightened [ɪn'laɪtnd] *adj* éclairé(e).

enlightening [ɪn'laɪtnɪŋ] *adj* édifiant(e).

enlightenment [ɪn'laɪtnmənt] *n* (U) éclaircissement *m*.

◆ **Enlightenment** *n* : **the Enlightenment** le siècle des Lumières.

enlist [ɪn'lɪst] ◇ *vt* - **1.** MIL enrôler - **2.** [recruit] recruter - **3.** [obtain] s'assurer ◇ *vi* MIL : **to ~ (in)** s'enrôler (dans).

enlisted man [ɪn'lɪstɪd-] *n* Am simple soldat *m*.

enliven [ɪn'laɪvn] *vt* animer ; [book, film] égayer.

en masse [ɒn'mæs] *adv* en masse, massivement.

enmeshed [ɪn'meʃt] *adj* : **~ in** empêtré(e) dans.

enmity ['enmətɪ] (*pl* -**ies**) *n* hostilité *f*.

ennoble [ɪ'nəʊbl] *vt* - **1.** [elevate to nobility] anoblir - **2.** [dignify] ennoblir.

enormity [ɪ'nɔːmətɪ] *n* [extent] étendue *f*.

enormous [ɪ'nɔːməs] *adj* énorme ; [patience, success] immense.

enormously [ɪ'nɔːməslɪ] *adv* énormément ; [long, pleased] immensément.

enough [ɪ'nʌf] ◇ *adj* assez de ; **~ money/time** assez d'argent/de temps ◇ *pron* assez ; **more than ~** largement, bien assez ; **~ is ~** trop c'est trop ; **that's ~ (of that)!** ça suffit maintenant! ; **to have had ~ (of sthg)** en avoir assez (de qqch) ◇ *adv* - **1.** [sufficiently] assez ; **big ~ for sthg/to do sthg** assez grand pour qqch/pour faire qqch ; **to be good ~ to do sthg** *fml* être assez gentil pour OR de faire qqch, être assez aimable pour OR de faire qqch - **2.** [rather] plutôt ; **strangely ~** bizarrement, c'est bizarre.

enquire [ɪn'kwaɪəʳ] <> *vt:* to ~ when/whether/how ... demander quand/si/comment ... <> *vi:* to ~ (about) se renseigner (sur).

enquiry [ɪn'kwaɪərɪ] (*pl* -ies) *n* - 1. [question] demande *f* de renseignements ; 'Enquiries' 'renseignements' - 2. [investigation] enquête *f*.

enraged [ɪn'reɪdʒd] *adj* déchaîné(e) ; [animal] enragé(e).

enrich [ɪn'rɪtʃ] *vt* enrichir.

enrol (*pt* & *pp* -led ; *cont* -ling), **enroll** Am [ɪn'rəʊl] <> *vt* inscrire <> *vi:* to ~ (in) s'inscrire (à).

enrolment Br, **enrollment** Am [ɪn'rəʊlmənt] *n* - 1. (U) [registration] inscription *f* - 2. [person enrolled] inscrit *m*.

en route [ɒn'ruːt] *adv:* ~ (to) en route (vers) ; ~ from en provenance de.

ensconced [ɪn'skɒnst] *adj* hum : ~ (in) bien installé(e) (dans).

enshrine [ɪn'ʃraɪn] *vt:* to be ~d in être garanti(e) par.

ensign ['ensaɪn] *n* - 1. [flag] pavillon *m* - 2. Am [sailor] enseigne *m*.

enslave [ɪn'sleɪv] *vt* asservir.

ensue [ɪn'sjuː] *vi* s'ensuivre.

ensuing [ɪn'sjuːɪŋ] *adj* qui s'ensuit.

ensure [ɪn'ʃʊəʳ] *vt* assurer ; to ~ (that) ... s'assurer que ...

ENT (*abbr of* Ear, Nose & Throat) *n* ORL *f*.

entail [ɪn'teɪl] *vt* entraîner ; what does the work ~? en quoi consiste le travail?

entangled [ɪn'tæŋgld] *adj* - 1. [caught] : to be ~ in être emmêlé(e) OR enchevêtré(e) dans - 2. [in problem, difficult situation] : to be ~ in être empêtré(e) dans - 3. fig [with person] : to be ~ with avoir une liaison avec.

entanglement [ɪn'tæŋglmənt] *n* liaison *f* (amoureuse).

enter ['entəʳ] <> *vt* - 1. [room, vehicle] entrer dans - 2. [university, army] entrer à ; [school] s'inscrire à, s'inscrire dans - 3. [competition, race] s'inscrire à ; [politics] se lancer dans - 4. [register] : to ~ sb/sthg for sthg inscrire qqn/qqch à qqch - 5. [write down] inscrire - 6. COMPUT entrer <> *vi* - 1. [come or go in] entrer - 2. [register] : to ~ (for) s'inscrire (à).

➡ **enter into** *vt fus* [negotiations, correspondence] entamer.

enteritis [,entə'raɪtɪs] *n* entérite *f*.

enter key *n* COMPUT (touche *f*) entrée *f*.

enterprise ['entəpraɪz] *n* entreprise *f*.

enterprise culture *n* culture *f* d'entreprise.

enterprise zone *n* Br zone dans une région défavorisée qui bénéficie de subsides de l'État.

enterprising ['entəpraɪzɪŋ] *adj* qui fait preuve d'initiative.

entertain [,entə'teɪn] <> *vt* - 1. [amuse] divertir - 2. [invite - guests] recevoir - 3. fml [thought, proposal] considérer - 4. fml [hopes] nourrir <> *vi* - 1. [amuse] se divertir - 2. [have guests] recevoir.

entertainer [,entə'teɪnəʳ] *n* fantaisiste *mf*.

entertaining [,entə'teɪnɪŋ] <> *adj* divertissant(e) <> *n:* to do a lot of ~ recevoir beaucoup.

entertainment [,entə'teɪnmənt] <> *n* - 1. (U) [amusement] divertissement *m* - 2. [show] spectacle *m* <> *comp* du spectacle.

entertainment allowance *n* frais *mpl* de représentation.

enthral (*pt* & *pp* -led ; *cont* -ling), **enthrall** Am [ɪn'θrɔːl] *vt* captiver.

enthralling [ɪn'θrɔːlɪŋ] *adj* captivant(e).

enthrone [ɪn'θrəʊn] *vt* introniser.

enthuse [ɪn'θjuːz] *vi:* to ~ (about) s'enthousiasmer (pour).

enthusiasm [ɪn'θjuːzɪæzm] *n* - 1. [passion, eagerness] : ~ (for) enthousiasme *m* (pour) - 2. [interest] passion *f*.

enthusiast [ɪn'θjuːzɪæst] *n* amateur *m*, -trice *f*.

enthusiastic [ɪn,θjuːzɪ'æstɪk] *adj* enthousiaste.

enthusiastically [ɪn,θjuːzɪ'æstɪklɪ] *adv* avec enthousiasme.

entice [ɪn'taɪs] *vt* entraîner.

enticing [ɪn'taɪsɪŋ] *adj* alléchant(e) ; [smile] séduisant(e).

entire [ɪn'taɪəʳ] *adj* entier(ère).

entirely [ɪn'taɪəlɪ] *adv* totalement.

entirety [ɪn'taɪrətɪ] *n:* in its ~ en entier.

entitle [ɪn'taɪtl] *vt* [allow] : to ~ sb to sthg donner droit à qqch à qqn ; to ~ sb to do sthg autoriser qqn à faire qqch.

entitled [ɪn'taɪtld] *adj* - 1. [allowed] autorisé(e) ; to be ~ to sthg avoir droit à qqch ; to be ~ to do sthg avoir le droit de faire qqch - 2. [called] intitulé(e).

entitlement [ɪn'taɪtlmənt] *n* droit *m*.

entity ['entətɪ] (*pl* -ies) *n* entité *f*.

entomology [,entə'mɒlədʒɪ] *n* entomologie *f*.

entourage [,ɒntu'rɑːʒ] *n* entourage *m*.

entrails ['entreɪlz] *npl* entrailles *fpl*.

entrance [*n* 'entrəns, *vt* ɪn'trɑːns] <> *n* - 1. [way in] : ~ **(to)** entrée f (de) **- 2.** [arrival] entrée f **- 3.** [entry] : **to gain ~ to** [building] obtenir l'accès à ; [society, university] être admis(e) dans ◇ vt ravir, enivrer.

entrance examination n examen m d'entrée.

entrance fee n **- 1.** [to cinema, museum] droit m d'entrée **- 2.** [for club] droit m d'inscription.

entrancing [ɪn'trɑːnsɪŋ] adj épatant(e).

entrant ['entrənt] n [in race, competition] concurrent m, -e f.

entreat [ɪn'triːt] vt : **to ~ sb (to do sthg)** supplier qqn (de faire qqch)

entreaty [ɪn'triːtɪ] (pl **-ies**) n prière f, supplication f.

entrenched [ɪn'trentʃt] adj ancré(e).

entrepreneur [ˌɒntrəprə'nɜːr] n entrepreneur m.

entrepreneurial [ˌɒntrəprə'nɜːrɪəl] adj [person] qui a l'esprit d'entreprise ; [skill] d'entrepreneur.

entrust [ɪn'trʌst] vt : **to ~ sthg to sb, to ~ sb with sthg** confier qqch à qqn.

entry ['entrɪ] (pl **-ies**) n **- 1.** [gen] entrée f ; **to gain ~ to** avoir accès à ; **'no ~'** 'défense d'entrer' ; AUT 'sens interdit' **- 2.** [in competition] inscription f **- 3.** [in dictionary] entrée f ; [in diary, ledger] inscription f.

entry fee n entrée f.

entry form n formulaire m OR feuille f d'inscription.

entry phone n portier m électronique.

entryway ['entrɪˌweɪ] n Am entrée f.

entwine [ɪn'twaɪn] ◇ vt entrelacer ◇ vi s'entrelacer.

E number n additif m E.

enumerate [ɪ'njuːməreɪt] vt énumérer.

enunciate [ɪ'nʌnsɪeɪt] ◇ vt **- 1.** [word] articuler **- 2.** [idea, plan] énoncer, exposer ◇ vi articuler.

envelop [ɪn'veləp] vt envelopper.

envelope ['envələʊp] n enveloppe f.

enviable ['envɪəbl] adj enviable.

envious ['envɪəs] adj envieux(euse).

enviously ['envɪəslɪ] adv avec envie.

environment [ɪn'vaɪərənmənt] n **- 1.** [surroundings] milieu m, cadre m **- 2.** [natural world] : **the ~** l'environnement m ; **Department of the Environment** Br ≃ ministère m de l'Environnement **- 3.** COMPUT environnement m.

environment agency n agence f pour la protection de l'environnement.

environmental [ɪn,vaɪərən'mentl] adj [pollu-

tion, awareness] de l'environnement ; [impact] sur l'environnement.

environmentalist [ɪn,vaɪərən'mentəlɪst] n écologiste mf, environnementaliste mf.

environmentally [ɪn,vaɪərən'mentəlɪ] adv [damaging] pour l'environnement ; **to be ~ aware** être sensible aux problèmes de l'environnement ; **~ friendly** qui préserve l'environnement.

Environmental Protection Agency n Am ≃ ministère m de l'Environnement.

environs [ɪn'vaɪərənz] npl environs mpl.

envisage [ɪn'vɪzɪdʒ], **envision** Am [ɪn'vɪʒn] vt envisager.

envoy ['envɔɪ] n émissaire m.

envy ['envɪ] (pt & pp **-ied**) ◇ n envie f, jalousie f ; **to be the ~ of** faire envie à ; **to be green with ~** être malade de jalousie ◇ vt envier ; **to ~ sb sthg** envier qqch à qqn.

enzyme ['enzaɪm] n enzyme f.

EOC abbr of **Equal Opportunities Commission.**

eon Am = aeon.

EPA abbr of **Environmental Protection Agency.**

epaulet(te) ['epəlet] n épaulette f.

ephemeral [ɪ'femərəl] adj éphémère.

epic ['epɪk] ◇ adj épique ◇ n épopée f.

epicentre Br, **epicenter** Am ['epɪsentər] n épicentre m.

epidemic [ˌepɪ'demɪk] n épidémie f.

epidural [ˌepɪ'djʊərəl] n péridurale f.

epigram ['epɪgræm] n épigramme f.

epilepsy ['epɪlepsɪ] n épilepsie f.

epileptic [ˌepɪ'leptɪk] ◇ adj épileptique ◇ n épileptique mf.

epilogue Br, **epilog** Am ['epɪlɒg] n épilogue m.

Epiphany [ɪ'pɪfənɪ] n Épiphanie f.

episcopal [ɪ'pɪskəpl] adj épiscopal(e).

episode ['epɪsəʊd] n épisode m.

episodic [ˌepɪ'sɒdɪk] adj [story, play] en épisodes.

epistle [ɪ'pɪsl] n épître f.

epitaph ['epɪtɑːf] n épitaphe f.

epithet ['epɪθet] n épithète f.

epitome [ɪ'pɪtəmɪ] n : **the ~ of** le modèle de.

epitomize, -ise [ɪ'pɪtəmaɪz] vt incarner.

epoch ['iːpɒk] n époque f.

epoch-making [-'meɪkɪŋ] adj qui fait date.

eponymous [ɪ'pɒnɪməs] adj éponyme.

EPOS ['iːpɒs] (abbr of **electronic point of sale**) n point de vente électronique.

equable ['ɛkwəbl] *adj* égal(e), constant(e).

equal ['iːkwəl] (Br *pt* & *pp* -**led** ; *cont* -**ling**, Am *pt* & *pp* -**ed** ; *cont* -**ing**) ◇ *adj* - **1.** [gen] : ~ **(to)** égal(e) (à) ; **on** ~ **terms** d'égal à égal - **2.** [capable] : ~ **to sthg** à la hauteur de qqch ◇ *n* égal *m*, -e *f* ◇ *vt* égaler.

equality [iːˈkwɒlətɪ] *n* égalité *f*.

equalize, -ise ['iːkwəlaɪz] ◇ *vt* niveler ◇ *vi* SPORT égaliser.

equalizer ['iːkwəlaɪzəʳ] *n* SPORT but *m* égalisateur.

equally ['iːkwəlɪ] *adv* - **1.** [important, stupid etc] tout aussi ; **I like them** ~ je les apprécie de la même façon - **2.** [in amount] en parts égales - **3.** [also] en même temps.

equal opportunities *npl* égalité *f* des chances.

Equal Opportunities Commission *n* commission britannique pour l'égalité des chances dans le travail.

equal(s) sign *n* le signe *m* d'égalité.

equanimity [ˌɛkwəˈnɪmətɪ] *n* sérénité *f*, égalité *f* d'âme.

equate [ɪˈkweɪt] *vt* : **to** ~ **sthg with** assimiler qqch à.

equation [ɪˈkweɪʒn] *n* équation *f*.

equator [ɪˈkweɪtəʳ] *n* : **the** ~ l'équateur *m*.

equatorial [ˌɛkwəˈtɔːrɪəl] *adj* équatorial(e).

Equatorial Guinea *n* Guinée *f* équatoriale.

equestrian [ɪˈkwɛstrɪən] *adj* équestre.

equidistant [ˌiːkwɪˈdɪstənt] *adj* : ~ **(from)** équidistant(e) (de).

equilateral triangle [ˌiːkwɪˈlætərəl-] *n* triangle *m* équilatéral.

equilibrium [ˌiːkwɪˈlɪbrɪəm] *n* équilibre *m*.

equine ['ɛkwaɪn] *adj* chevalin(e).

equinox ['iːkwɪnɒks] *n* équinoxe *m*.

equip [ɪˈkwɪp] (*pt* & *pp* -**ped** ; *cont* -**ping**) *vt* équiper ; **to** ~ **sb/sthg with** équiper qqn/ qqch de, munir qqn/qqch de ; **he's well equipped for the job** il est bien préparé pour ce travail.

equipment [ɪˈkwɪpmənt] *n* (U) équipement *m*, matériel *m*.

equitable ['ɛkwɪtəbl] *adj* équitable.

equities ['ɛkwətɪz] *npl* ST EX actions *fpl* ordinaires.

equivalent [ɪˈkwɪvələnt] ◇ *adj* équivalent(e) ; **to be** ~ **to** être équivalent à, équivaloir à ◇ *n* équivalent *m*.

equivocal [ɪˈkwɪvəkl] *adj* équivoque.

equivocate [ɪˈkwɪvəkeɪt] *vi* parler de façon équivoque.

er [ɜːʳ] *excl* euh!

ER (*abbr of* **Elizabeth Regina**) *emblème de la reine Elizabeth*.

era ['ɪərə] (*pl* -**s**) *n* ère *f*, période *f*.

ERA ['ɪərə] (*abbr of* **Equal Rights Amendment**) *n loi américaine sur l'égalité des droits des femmes*.

eradicate [ɪˈrædɪkeɪt] *vt* éradiquer.

eradication [ɪˌrædɪˈkeɪʃn] *n* éradication *f*.

erase [ɪˈreɪz] *vt* - **1.** [rub out] gommer - **2.** fig [memory] effacer ; [hunger, poverty] éliminer.

eraser [ɪˈreɪzəʳ] *n* gomme *f*.

erect [ɪˈrekt] ◇ *adj* - **1.** [person, posture] droit(e) - **2.** [penis] en érection ◇ *vt* - **1.** [statue] ériger ; [building] construire - **2.** [tent] dresser.

erection [ɪˈrekʃn] *n* - **1.** (U) [of statue] érection *f* ; [of building] construction *f* - **2.** [erect penis] érection *f*.

ergonomics [ˌɜːgəˈnɒmɪks] *n* ergonomie *f*.

ERISA [əˈriːsə] (*abbr of* **Employee Retirement Income Security Act**) *n loi américaine sur les pensions de retraite*.

Eritrea [ˌerɪˈtreɪə] *n* Érythrée *f* ; **in** ~ en Érythrée.

Eritrean [ˌerɪˈtreɪən] ◇ *adj* érythréen(enne) ◇ *n* Érythréen *m*, -enne *f*.

ERM (*abbr of* **Exchange Rate Mechanism**) *n* mécanisme *m* des changes (du SME).

ermine ['ɜːmɪn] *n* [fur] hermine *f*.

ERNIE ['ɜːnɪ] (*abbr of* **Electronic Random Number Indicator Equipment**) *n dispositif de tirage des numéros gagnants des 'Premium Bonds'*.

erode [ɪˈrəʊd] ◇ *vt* - **1.** [rock, soil] éroder - **2.** fig [confidence, rights] réduire ◇ *vi* - **1.** [rock, soil] s'éroder - **2.** fig [confidence] diminuer ; [rights] se réduire.

erogenous zone [ɪˈrɒdʒɪnəs-] *n* zone *f* érogène.

erosion [ɪˈrəʊʒn] *n* - **1.** [of rock, soil] érosion *f* - **2.** fig [of confidence] baisse *f* ; [of rights] diminution *f*.

erotic [ɪˈrɒtɪk] *adj* érotique.

eroticism [ɪˈrɒtɪsɪzm] *n* érotisme *m*.

err [ɜːʳ] *vi* se tromper ; **to** ~ **is human** l'erreur est humaine ; **to** ~ **on the side of** pécher par excès de.

errand ['erənd] *n* course *f*, commission *f* ; **to go on** OR **run an** ~ faire une course.

errand boy *n* garçon *m* de courses.

erratic [ɪˈrætɪk] *adj* irrégulier(ère).

erroneous [ɪˈrəʊnjəs] *adj* fml erroné(e).

error ['erəʳ] *n* erreur *f* ; **a spelling/typing** ~ une faute d'orthographe/de frappe ; **an**

~ of judgment une erreur de jugement ; **in ~** par erreur.

error message n COMPUT message m d'erreur.

erstwhile ['ɜ:stwaɪl] adj literary d'autrefois.

erudite ['eru:daɪt] adj savant(e).

erupt [ɪ'rʌpt] vi - 1. [volcano] entrer en éruption - 2. fig [violence, war] éclater.

eruption [ɪ'rʌpʃn] n - 1. [of volcano] éruption f - 2. [of violence] explosion f ; [of war] déclenchement m.

ESA (abbr of European Space Agency) n ESA f, ASE f.

escalate ['eskəleɪt] vi - 1. [conflict] s'intensifier - 2. [costs] monter en flèche.

escalation [,eskə'leɪʃn] n - 1. [of conflict, violence] intensification f - 2. [of costs] montée f en flèche.

escalator ['eskəleɪtəʳ] n escalier m roulant.

escalator clause n clause f d'indexation.

escapade [,eskə'peɪd] n aventure f, exploit m.

escape [ɪ'skeɪp] ◇ n - 1. [gen] fuite f, évasion f ; to make one's ~ s'échapper ; **to have a lucky ~** l'échapper belle - 2. [leakage - of gas, water] fuite f ◇ vt échapper à ; **to ~ notice** échapper à l'attention ◇ vi - 1. [gen] s'échapper, fuir ; [from prison] s'évader ; **to ~ from** [place] s'échapper de ; [danger, person] échapper à - 2. [survive] s'en tirer.

escape clause n clause f échappatoire.

escape key n COMPUT touche f d'échappement.

escape route n - 1. [from prison] moyen m d'évasion - 2. [from fire] itinéraire d'évacuation en cas d'incendie.

escapism [ɪ'skeɪpɪzml] n (U) évasion f (de la réalité).

escapist [ɪ'skeɪpɪst] adj [literature, film] d'évasion.

escapologist [,eskə'pɒlədʒɪst] n virtuose mf de l'évasion.

escarpment [ɪ'skɑ:pmənt] n escarpement m.

eschew [ɪs'tʃu:] vt fml s'abstenir de.

escort [n 'eskɔ:t, vb ɪ'skɔ:t] ◇ n - 1. [guard] escorte f ; **under ~** sous escorte - 2. [companion - male] cavalier m ; [- female] hôtesse f ◇ vt escorter, accompagner.

escort agency n agence f d'hôtesses.

e-shopping n (U) cyberachat m.

Eskimo ['eskɪməʊ] (pl -s) ◇ adj esquimau(aude) ◇ n - 1. [person] Esquimau m, -aude f (attention : le terme 'Eskimo', comme son équivalent français, est souvent considé-

ré comme injurieux en Amérique du Nord. On préférera le terme 'Inuit') - 2. [language] esquimau m.

ESL (abbr of English as a Second Language) n anglais deuxième langue.

esophagus Am = oesophagus.

esoteric [,esə'terɪk] adj ésotérique.

esp. abbr of especially.

ESP n - 1. (abbr of extrasensory perception) perception f extrasensorielle - 2. (abbr of English for special purposes) anglais à usage professionnel.

espadrille [,espə'drɪl] n espadrille f.

especial [ɪ'speʃl] adj spécial(e), particulier(ère).

especially [ɪ'speʃəlɪ] adv - 1. [in particular] surtout - 2. [more than usually] particulièrement - 3. [specifically] spécialement.

Esperanto [,espə'ræntəʊ] n espéranto m.

espionage ['espɪə,nɑ:ʒ] n espionnage m.

esplanade [,esplə'neɪd] n esplanade f.

espouse [ɪ'spaʊz] vt épouser.

espresso [e'spresəʊ] (pl -s) n express m inv.

Esq. abbr of Esquire.

Esquire [ɪ'skwaɪəʳ] n : G. Curry ~ Monsieur G. Curry.

essay ['eseɪ] n - 1. SCH & UNIV dissertation f - 2. LITERATURE essai m.

essayist ['eseɪɪst] n essayiste mf.

essence ['esns] n - 1. [nature] essence f, nature f ; **in ~** par essence - 2. CULIN extrait m.

essential [ɪ'senʃl] adj - 1. [absolutely necessary] : **~ (to OR for)** indispensable (à) - 2. [basic] essentiel(elle), de base.

essentials npl - 1. [basic commodities] produits mpl de première nécessité - 2. [most important elements] essentiel m.

essentially [ɪ'senʃəlɪ] adv fondamentalement, avant tout.

est. - 1. abbr of established - 2. abbr of estimated.

EST (abbr of Eastern Standard Time) n heure d'été de la côte est des États-Unis.

establish [ɪ'stæblɪʃ] vt - 1. [gen] établir ; **to ~ contact with** établir le contact avec - 2. [organization, business] fonder, créer.

established [ɪ'stæblɪʃt] adj - 1. [custom] établi(e) - 2. [business, company] fondé(e).

establishment [ɪ'stæblɪʃmənt] n - 1. [gen] établissement m - 2. [of organization, business] fondation f, création f.

Establishment n [status quo] : **the Establishment** l'ordre m établi, l'Establishment m.

estate [ɪ'steɪt] n - 1. [land, property] propriété f, domaine m - 2. : **(housing) ~** lotissement m

- 3. : (industrial) ~ zone *f* industrielle **- 4.** JUR [inheritance] biens *mpl*.

estate agency *n* Br agence *f* immobilière.

estate agent *n* Br agent *m* immobilier.

estate car *n* Br break *m*.

estd., est'd. *abbr of* established.

esteem [ɪ'stiːm] <> *n* estime *f ;* **to hold sb/ sthg in high ~** tenir qqn/qqch en haute estime <> *vt* estimer.

esthetic *etc* Am = aesthetic *etc*.

estimate [*n* 'estɪmət, *vb* 'estɪmeɪt] <> *n* **- 1.** [calculation, judgment] estimation *f*, évaluation *f* **- 2.** COMM devis *m* <> *vt* estimer, évaluer <> *vi* COMM **: to ~ for** faire OR établir un devis pour.

estimated ['estɪmeɪtɪd] *adj* estimé(e).

estimation [,estɪ'meɪʃn] *n* **- 1.** [opinion] opinion *f* **- 2.** [calculation] estimation *f*, évaluation *f*.

Estonia [e'stəʊnɪə] *n* Estonie *f ;* **in ~** en Estonie.

Estonian [e'stəʊnɪən] <> *adj* estonien(enne) <> *n* **- 1.** [person] Estonien *m*, -enne *f* **- 2.** [language] estonien *m*.

estranged [ɪ'streɪndʒd] *adj* [couple] séparé(e) ; [husband, wife] dont on s'est séparé.

estrogen Am = oestrogen.

estuary ['estjʊərɪ] (*pl* -ies) *n* estuaire *m*.

ETA (*abbr of* estimated time of arrival) *n* HPA *f*.

et al. ['etæl] (*abbr of* et alii) et coll., et al.

etc. (*abbr of* et cetera) etc.

etcetera [ɪt'setərə] *adv* et cetera.

etch [etʃ] *vt* graver à l'eau forte **; to be ~ed on sb's memory** être gravé dans la mémoire de qqn.

etching ['etʃɪŋ] *n* gravure *f* à l'eau forte.

ETD (*abbr of* estimated time of departure) *n* HPD *f*.

eternal [ɪ'tɜːnl] *adj* **- 1.** [life] éternel(elle) **- 2. fig** [complaints, whining] sempiternel(elle) **- 3.** [truth, value] immuable.

eternally [ɪ'tɜːnəlɪ] *adv* éternellement.

eternity [ɪ'tɜːnətɪ] *n* éternité *f*.

eternity ring *n* Br bague *f* de fidélité.

ether ['iːθəʳ] *n* éther *m*.

ethereal [iː'θɪərɪəl] *adj* éthéré(e).

ethic ['eθɪk] *n* éthique *f*, morale *f*.
➥ **ethics** <> *n* (U) [study] éthique *f*, morale *f* <> *npl* [morals] morale *f*.

ethical ['eθɪkl] *adj* moral(e).

Ethiopia [,iːθɪ'əʊpɪə] *n* Éthiopie *f ;* **in ~** en Éthiopie.

Ethiopian [,iːθɪ'əʊpɪən] <> *adj* éthiopien(enne) <> *n* Éthiopien *m*, -enne *f*.

ethnic ['eθnɪk] *adj* **- 1.** [traditions, groups] ethnique **- 2.** [clothes] folklorique.

ethnic cleansing [-'klenzɪŋ] *n* purification *f* ethnique.

ethnic minority *n* minorité *f* ethnique.

ethnology [eθ'nɒlədʒɪ] *n* ethnologie *f*.

ethos ['iːθɒs] *n* génie *m* (d'un peuple/d'une civilisation).

etiquette ['etɪket] *n* convenances *fpl*, étiquette *f*.

e-trade *n* (U) cybercommerce *m*, commerce *m* électronique.

ETU (*abbr of* Electrical Trades Union) *n* syndicat d'électriciens.

ETV (*abbr of* educational television) *n* télévision scolaire.

etymology [,etɪ'mɒlədʒɪ] (*pl* -ies) *n* étymologie *f*.

EU (*abbr of* European Union) *n* UE *f ;* **~ policy** la politique de l'Union Européenne, la politique communautaire.

eucalyptus [,juːkə'lɪptəs] *n* eucalyptus *m*.

eulogize, -ise ['juːlədʒaɪz] *vt* faire le panégyrique de.

eulogy ['juːlədʒɪ] (*pl* -ies) *n* panégyrique *m*.

eunuch ['juːnək] *n* eunuque *m*.

euphemism ['juːfəmɪzm] *n* euphémisme *m*.

euphemistic [,juːfə'mɪstɪk] *adj* euphémique.

euphoria [juː'fɔːrɪə] *n* euphorie *f*.

euphoric [juː'fɒrɪk] *adj* euphorique.

Eurasia [jʊə'reɪʒə] *n* Eurasie *f*.

Eurasian [jʊə'reɪʒən] <> *adj* eurasien(enne) <> *n* Eurasien *m*, -enne *f*.

eureka [jʊə'riːkə] *excl* eurêka!

euro ['jʊərəʊl] *n* euro *m*.

Euro- *prefix* euro-.

euro area *n* zone *f* euro.

Eurocheque ['jʊərəʊ,tʃek] *n* eurochèque *m*.

Eurocrat ['jʊərə,kræt] *n* eurocrate *mf*.

Eurocurrency ['jʊːrəʊ,kʌrənsɪ] (*pl* -ies) *n* eurodevise *f*.

Eurodollar ['jʊːrəʊ,dɒləʳ] *n* eurodollar *m*.

Euro MP *n* député *m* européen.

Europe ['jʊərəpl] *n* Europe *f*.

European [,jʊərə'piːən] <> *adj* européen(enne) <> *n* Européen *m*, -enne *f*.

European Central Bank *n* Banque *f* centrale européenne.

European Commission *n* Commission *f* des communautés européennes.

European Community n : the ~ la Communauté européenne.

European Court of Human Rights n : the ~ la Cour européenne des droits de l'homme.

European Court of Justice n : the ~ la Cour européenne de justice.

European Currency Unit n unité f monétaire européenne.

Europeanism [ˌjuərə'piːənɪzm] n européanisme m.

Europeanize, -ise [ˌjuərə'piːənaɪz] vt européaniser.

European Monetary System n : the ~ le Système monétaire européen.

European Parliament n : the ~ le Parlement européen.

European Union n Union f européenne.

Eurosceptic ['juərəʊˌskeptɪk] n eurosceptique mf.

Eurostar® ['juərəʊstɑːʳ] n Eurostar® m.

euro zone n zone f euro.

euthanasia [ˌjuːθə'neɪzjə] n euthanasie f.

evacuate [ɪ'vækjʊeɪt] vt évacuer.

evacuation [ɪˌvækjʊ'eɪʃn] n évacuation f.

evacuee [ɪˌvækjuː'iː] n évacué m, -e f.

evade [ɪ'veɪd] vt - **1.** [gen] échapper à - **2.** [issue, question] esquiver, éluder.

evaluate [ɪ'væljʊeɪt] vt évaluer.

evaluation [ɪˌvæljʊ'eɪʃn] n évaluation f.

evangelical [ˌiːvæn'dʒelɪkl] adj évangélique.

evangelism [ɪ'vændʒəlɪzm] n évangélisation f.

evangelist [ɪ'vændʒəlɪst] n évangéliste mf.

evangelize, -ise [ɪ'vændʒəlaɪz] vt évangéliser.

evaporate [ɪ'væpəreɪt] vi - **1.** [liquid] s'évaporer - **2.** fig [hopes, fears] s'envoler ; [confidence] disparaître.

evaporated milk [ɪ'væpəreɪtɪd-] n lait m condensé (non sucré).

evaporation [ɪˌvæpə'reɪʃn] n évaporation f.

evasion [ɪ'veɪʒn] n - **1.** [of responsibility] dérobade f ; **tax ~** évasion f fiscale - **2.** [lie] fauxfuyant m.

evasive [ɪ'veɪsɪv] adj évasif(ive) ; **to take ~ action** faire une manœuvre d'évitement.

evasiveness [ɪ'veɪsɪvnɪs] n caractère m évasif.

eve [iːv] n veille f.

even ['iːvn] <> adj - **1.** [speed, rate] régulier(ère) ; [temperature, temperament] égal(e) - **2.** [flat, level] plat(e), régulier(ère)

- **3.** [equal - contest] équilibré(e) ; [- teams, players] de la même force ; [- scores] à égalité ; **to get ~ with sb** se venger de qqn - **4.** [not odd - number] pair(e) <> adv - **1.** [gen] même ; **~ now** encore maintenant ; **~ then** même alors - **2.** [in comparisons] : **~ bigger/better/more stupid** encore plus grand/mieux/plus bête.

▸ **even as** conj au moment même où.

▸ **even if** conj même si.

▸ **even so** adv quand même.

▸ **even though** conj bien que (+ subjunctive).

▸ **even out** <> vt sep égaliser <> vi s'égaliser.

even-handed [-'hændɪd] adj impartial(e).

evening ['iːvnɪŋ] n soir m ; [duration, entertainment] soirée f ; **in the ~** le soir.

▸ **evenings** adv Am le soir.

evening class n cours m du soir.

evening dress n [worn by man] habit m de soirée ; [worn by woman] robe f du soir.

evening star n : the ~ l'étoile f du berger.

evenly ['iːvnlɪ] adv - **1.** [breathe, distributed] régulièrement - **2.** [equally - divided] également ; **to be ~ matched** être de la même force - **3.** [calmly] calmement, sur un ton égal.

evenness ['iːvnnɪs] n - **1.** [of breathing] régularité f - **2.** [equality] bon équilibre m.

evensong ['iːvnsɒŋ] n vêpres fpl.

event [ɪ'vent] n - **1.** [happening] événement m - **2.** SPORT épreuve f - **3.** [case] : **in the ~ of** en cas de ; **in the ~ that** au cas où.

▸ **in any event** adv en tout cas, de toute façon.

▸ **in the event** adv Br en l'occurrence, en réalité.

even-tempered [-'tempəd] adj d'humeur égale.

eventful [ɪ'ventfʊl] adj mouvementé(e).

eventide home ['iːvntaɪd-] n Br euphemism hospice m de vieillards.

eventing [ɪ'ventɪŋ] n Br SPORT : **(three-day) ~** concours m complet.

eventual [ɪ'ventʃʊəl] adj final(e) ; **the ~ winner was X** finalement, le vainqueur a été X.

eventuality [ɪˌventʃʊ'ælətɪ] (pl -ies) n éventualité f.

eventually [ɪ'ventʃʊəlɪ] adv finalement, en fin de compte.

ever ['evəʳ] adv - **1.** [at any time] jamais ; **have you ~ been to Paris?** êtes-vous déjà allé à Paris? ; **I hardly ~ see him** je ne le vois presque jamais ; **if ~** si jamais - **2.** [all the time] toujours ; **as ~** comme toujours ; **for ~** pour toujours - **3.** [for emphasis] : **~ so** tellement ;

~ such vraiment ; **why/how** ~? pourquoi/comment donc?

➡ **ever since** <> adv depuis (ce moment-là) <> conj depuis que <> prep depuis.

Everest ['evərɪst] n l'Everest m.

Everglades ['evə,gleɪdz] npl : **the** ~ les Everglades mpl.

evergreen ['evəgriːn] <> adj à feuilles persistantes <> n arbre m à feuilles persistantes.

everlasting [,evə'lɑːstɪŋ] adj éternel(elle).

every ['evrɪ] adj chaque ; ~ **morning** chaque matin, tous les matins ; **there's** ~ **chance she'll pass the exam** elle a toutes les chances de réussir à son examen.

➡ **every now and then, every so often** adv de temps en temps, de temps à autre.

➡ **every other** adj : ~ **other day** tous les deux jours, un jour sur deux ; ~ **other street** une rue sur deux.

➡ **every which way** adv Am partout, de tous côtés.

everybody ['evrɪ,bɒdɪ] = everyone.

everyday ['evrɪdeɪ] adj quotidien(enne).

everyone ['evrɪwʌn] pron chacun, tout le monde.

everyplace Am = everywhere.

everything ['evrɪθɪŋ] pron tout.

everywhere ['evrɪweəˈ], **everyplace** Am ['evrɪ,pleɪs] adv partout.

evict [ɪ'vɪkt] vt expulser.

eviction [ɪ'vɪkʃn] n expulsion f.

eviction notice n avis m d'expulsion.

evidence ['evɪdəns] n (U) - 1. [proof] preuve f - 2. JUR [of witness] témoignage m ; **to give** ~ témoigner.

➡ **in evidence** adj [noticeable] en évidence.

evident ['evɪdənt] adj évident(e), manifeste.

evidently ['evɪdəntlɪ] adv - 1. [seemingly] apparemment - 2. [obviously] de toute évidence, manifestement.

evil ['iːvl] <> adj [person] mauvais(e), malveillant(e) <> n mal m.

evil-minded [-'maɪndɪd] adj malveillant(e), malintentionné(e).

evince [ɪ'vɪns] vt fml faire montre de.

evocation [,evəʊ'keɪʃn] n évocation f.

evocative [ɪ'vɒkətɪv] adj évocateur(trice).

evoke [ɪ'vəʊk] vt [memory] évoquer ; [emotion, response] susciter.

evolution [,iːvə'luːʃn] n évolution f.

evolve [ɪ'vɒlv] <> vt développer <> vi : **to** ~ **(into/from)** se développer (en/à partir de).

ewe [juː] n brebis f.

ex- [eks] prefix ex-.

exacerbate [ɪg'zæsəbeɪt] vt [feeling] exacerber ; [problems] aggraver.

exact [ɪg'zækt] <> adj exact(e), précis(e) ; **to be** ~ pour être exact OR précis, exactement <> vt : **to** ~ **sthg (from)** exiger qqch (de).

exacting [ɪg'zæktɪŋ] adj [job, standards] astreignant(e) ; [person] exigeant(e).

exactitude [ɪg'zæktɪtjuːd] n exactitude f.

exactly [ɪg'zæktlɪ] <> adv exactement ; **it's not** ~ **what I expected** ce n'est pas tout à fait ce que j'attendais <> excl exactement!, parfaitement!

exaggerate [ɪg'zædʒəreɪt] vt & vi exagérer.

exaggerated [ɪg'zædʒəreɪtɪd] adj [sigh, smile] forcé(e).

exaggeration [ɪg,zædʒə'reɪʃn] n exagération f.

exalted [ɪg'zɔːltɪd] adj haut placé(e).

exam [ɪg'zæm] n examen m ; **to take** OR **sit an** ~ passer un examen.

examination [ɪg,zæmɪ'neɪʃn] n examen m.

examination board n comité m d'examen.

examination paper n Br [test] sujet m (d'examen) ; [answers] copie f.

examine [ɪg'zæmɪn] vt - 1. [gen] examiner ; [passport] contrôler - 2. JUR, SCH & UNIV interroger.

examiner [ɪg'zæmɪnəˈ] n examinateur m, -trice f ; **internal/external** ~ UNIV examinateur m de l'établissement/de l'extérieur.

example [ɪg'zɑːmpl] n exemple m ; **for** ~ par exemple ; **to follow sb's** ~ suivre l'exemple de qqn ; **to make an** ~ **of sb** punir qqn pour l'exemple.

exasperate [ɪg'zæspəreɪt] vt exaspérer.

exasperating [ɪg'zæspəreɪtɪŋ] adj énervant(e), exaspérant(e).

exasperation [ɪg,zæspə'reɪʃn] n exaspération f.

excavate ['ekskəveɪt] vt - 1. [land] creuser - 2. [object] déterrer.

excavation [,ekskə'veɪʃn] n - 1. [gen] excavation f - 2. ARCHEOL fouilles fpl.

excavator ['ekskə,veɪtəˈ] n Br [machine] pelleteuse f.

exceed [ɪk'siːd] vt - 1. [amount, number] excéder - 2. [limit, expectations] dépasser.

exceedingly [ɪk'siːdɪŋlɪ] adv extrêmement.

excel [ɪk'sel] (pt & pp **-led** ; cont **-ling**) vi : ~ **(in** OR **at)** exceller (dans) ; **to** ~ **o.s.** Br se surpasser.

excellence ['eksələns] *n* excellence *f*, supériorité *f*.

Excellency ['eksələnsɪ] (*pl* -ies) *n* Excellence *f*.

excellent ['eksələnt] *adj* excellent(e).

except [ɪk'sept] <> *prep* & *conj* : ~ (for) à part, sauf <> *vt* : to ~ sb (from) exclure qqn (de).

excepted [ɪk'septɪd] *adj* à part, excepté(e).

excepting [ɪk'septɪŋ] *prep* & *conj* = **except**.

exception [ɪk'sepʃn] *n* - **1.** [exclusion] : ~ (to) exception *f* (à) ; **with the ~ of** à l'exception de ; **without ~** sans exception - **2.** [offence] : **to take ~ to** s'offenser de, se froisser de

exceptional [ɪk'sepʃənl] *adj* exceptionnel(elle).

exceptionally [ɪk'sepʃnəlɪ] *adv* exceptionnellement.

excerpt ['eksɜːpt] *n* : ~ (from) extrait *m* (de), passage *m* (de).

excess [ɪk'ses, *before nouns* 'ekses] <> *adj* excédentaire <> *n* excès *m* ; **to be in ~ of** dépasser ; **to ~** à l'excès.

excess baggage *n* excédent *m* de bagages.

excess fare *n* Br supplément *m*.

excessive [ɪk'sesɪv] *adj* excessif(ive).

excess luggage = **excess baggage**.

exchange [ɪks'tʃeɪndʒ] <> *n* - **1.** [gen] échange *m* ; **in ~ (for)** en échange (de) - **2.** TELEC : (telephone) ~ central *m* (téléphonique) <> *vt* [swap] échanger ; **to ~ sthg for sthg** échanger qqch contre qqch ; **to ~ sthg with sb** échanger qqch avec qqn.

exchange rate *n* FIN taux *m* de change.

Exchequer [ɪks'tʃekəʳ] *n* Br : **the ~** ≃ le ministère des Finances.

excise ['eksaɪz] <> *n* (U) contributions *fpl* indirectes <> *vt* fml [tumour] exciser ; [passage from book] supprimer.

excise duties *npl* droits *mpl* de régie.

excitable [ɪk'saɪtəbl] *adj* excitable.

excite [ɪk'saɪt] *vt* exciter.

excited [ɪk'saɪtɪd] *adj* excité(e).

excitement [ɪk'saɪtmənt] *n* - **1.** [state] excitation *f* - **2.** [exciting thing] sensation *f*, émotion *f*.

exciting [ɪk'saɪtɪŋ] *adj* passionnant(e) ; [prospect] excitant(e).

excl. (*abbr of* **excluding**) : ~ **taxes** HT.

exclaim [ɪk'skleɪm] <> *vt* s'écrier <> *vi* s'exclamer.

exclamation [,eksklə'meɪʃn] *n* exclamation *f*.

exclamation mark Br, **exclamation point** Am *n* point *m* d'exclamation.

exclude [ɪk'skluːd] *vt* : **to ~ sb/sthg (from)** exclure qqn/qqch (de).

excluding [ɪk'skluːdɪŋ] *prep* sans compter, à l'exclusion de.

exclusion [ɪk'skluːʒn] *n* : ~ (from) exclusion *f* (de) ; **to the ~ of** à l'exclusion de.

exclusion clause *n* clause *f* d'exclusion.

exclusive [ɪk'skluːsɪv] <> *adj* - **1.** [high-class] fermé(e) - **2.** [unique - use, news story] exclusif(ive) <> *n* PRESS exclusivité *f*.

➨ **exclusive of** *prep* : ~ **of interest** intérêts non compris.

exclusively [ɪk'skluːsɪvlɪ] *adv* exclusivement.

excommunicate [,ekskə'mjuːnɪkeɪt] *vt* excommunier.

excommunication ['ekskə,mjuːnɪ'keɪʃn] *n* excommunication *f*.

excrement ['ekskrɪmənt] *n* excrément *m*.

excrete [ɪk'skriːt] *vt* excréter.

excruciating [ɪk'skruːʃɪeɪtɪŋ] *adj* atroce.

excursion [ɪk'skɜːʃn] *n* [trip] excursion *f*.

excusable [ɪk'skjuːzəbl] *adj* excusable.

excuse [*n* ɪk'skjuːs, *vb* ɪk'skjuːz] <> *n* excuse *f* <> *vt* - **1.** [gen] excuser ; **to ~ sb for sthg/for doing sthg** excuser qqn de qqch/de faire qqch ; **to ~ o.s. (for doing sthg)** s'excuser (de faire qqch) ; ~ **me** [to attract attention] excusez-moi ; [forgive me] pardon, excusez-moi ; Am [sorry] pardon - **2.** [let off] : **to ~ sb (from)** dispenser qqn (de).

ex-directory *adj* Br qui est sur la liste rouge.

exec [ɪg'zek] *abbr of* **executive**.

execrable ['eksɪkrəbl] *adj* exécrable.

execute ['eksɪkjuːt] *vt* exécuter.

execution [,eksɪ'kjuːʃn] *n* exécution *f*.

executioner [,eksɪ'kjuːʃnəʳ] *n* bourreau *m*.

executive [ɪg'zekjutɪv] <> *adj* - **1.** [power, board] exécutif(ive) - **2.** [desk, chair] de cadre, spécial(e) cadre ; [washroom] de la direction <> *n* - **1.** COMM cadre *m* - **2.** [of government] exécutif *m* ; [of political party] comité *m* central, bureau *m*.

executive director *n* cadre *m* supérieur.

executive toy *n* gadget *m* pour cadres.

executor [ɪg'zekjutəʳ] *n* exécuteur *m* testamentaire.

exemplary [ɪg'zemplərɪ] *adj* exemplaire.

exemplify [ɪg'zemplɪfaɪ] (*pt* & *pp* -**ied**) *vt* - **1.** [typify] exemplifier - **2.** [give example of] exemplifier, illustrer.

exempt [ɪg'zempt] <> adj : ~ (from) exempt(e) (de) <> vt : to ~ sb (from) exempter qqn (de).

exemption [ɪg'zempʃn] n exemption f.

exercise ['eksəsaɪz] <> n exercice m ; **to take ~** prendre de l'exercice <> vt - **1.** [gen] exercer - **2.** [trouble] : **to ~ sb's mind** préoccuper qqn <> vi prendre de l'exercice.

exercise bike n vélo m d'appartement.

exercise book n [notebook] cahier m d'exercices ; [published book] livre m d'exercices.

exert [ɪg'zɜːt] vt exercer ; [strength] employer ; **to ~ o.s.** se donner du mal.

exertion [ɪg'zɜːʃn] n effort m.

ex gratia [eks'greɪʃə] adj Br [payment] à titre gracieux.

exhale [eks'heɪl] <> vt exhaler <> vi expirer.

exhaust [ɪg'zɔːst] <> n - **1.** (U) [fumes] gaz mpl d'échappement - **2.** : ~ **(pipe)** pot m d'échappement <> vt épuiser.

exhausted [ɪg'zɔːstɪd] adj épuisé(e).

exhausting [ɪg'zɔːstɪŋ] adj épuisant(e).

exhaustion [ɪg'zɔːstʃn] n épuisement m.

exhaustive [ɪg'zɔːstɪv] adj complet(ète), exhaustif(ive).

exhibit [ɪg'zɪbɪt] <> n - **1.** ART objet m exposé - **2.** JUR pièce f à conviction <> vt - **1.** [demonstrate - feeling] montrer ; [- skill] faire preuve de - **2.** ART exposer <> vi ART exposer.

exhibition [,eksɪ'bɪʃn] n - **1.** ART exposition f - **2.** [of feeling] démonstration f - **3.** phr : **to make an ~ of o.s.** Br se donner en spectacle.

exhibitionist [,eksɪ'bɪʃnɪst] n exhibitionniste mf.

exhibitor [ɪg'zɪbɪtəʳ] n exposant m, -e f.

exhilarating [ɪg'zɪləreɪtɪŋ] adj [experience] grisant(e) ; [walk] vivifiant(e).

exhort [ɪg'zɔːt] vt : **to ~ sb to do sthg** exhorter qqn à faire qqch.

exhume [eks'hjuːm] vt exhumer.

exile ['eksaɪl] <> n - **1.** [condition] exil m ; **in ~** en exil - **2.** [person] exilé m, -e f <> vt : **to ~ sb (from/to)** exiler qqn (de/vers).

exiled ['eksaɪld] adj exilé(e).

exist [ɪg'zɪst] vi exister.

existence [ɪg'zɪstəns] n existence f ; **in ~** qui existe, existant(e) ; **to come into ~** naître.

existentialism [,egzɪ'stenʃəlɪzm] n existentialisme m.

existentialist [,egzɪ'stenʃəlɪst] <> adj existentialiste <> n existentialiste mf.

existing [ɪg'zɪstɪŋ] adj existant(e).

exit ['eksɪt] <> n sortie f ; **to make one's ~** sortir ; THEATRE faire sa sortie <> vi sortir.

exit-poll n Br sondage effectué à la sortie des bureaux de vote.

exit visa n visa m de sortie.

exodus ['eksədəs] n exode m.

ex officio [eksə'fɪʃɪəʊ] adj & adv ex officio.

exonerate [ɪg'zɒnəreɪt] vt : **to ~ sb (from)** disculper qqn (de).

exorbitant [ɪg'zɔːbɪtənt] adj exorbitant(e).

exorcist ['eksɔːsɪst] n exorciste mf.

exorcize, -ise ['eksɔːsaɪz] vt exorciser.

exotic [ɪg'zɒtɪk] adj exotique.

expand [ɪk'spænd] <> vt [production, influence] accroître ; [business, department, area] développer <> vi [population, influence] s'accroître ; [business, department, market] se développer ; [metal] se dilater.

➡ **expand (up)on** vt fus développer.

expanse [ɪk'spæns] n étendue f.

expansion [ɪk'spænʃn] n [of production, population] accroissement m ; [of business, department, area] développement m ; [of metal] dilatation f.

expansion card n COMPUT carte f d'extension.

expansionism [ɪk'spænʃənɪzm] n expansionnisme m.

expansionist [ɪk'spænʃənɪst] adj expansionniste.

expansion slot n COMPUT créneau m pour carte d'extension.

expansive [ɪk'spænsɪv] adj expansif(ive).

expatriate [eks'pætrɪət] <> adj expatrié(e) <> n expatrié m, -e f.

expect [ɪk'spekt] <> vt - **1.** [anticipate] s'attendre à ; [event, letter, baby] attendre ; **when do you ~ it to be ready?** quand pensez-vous que cela sera prêt? ; **to ~ sb to do sthg** s'attendre à ce que qqn fasse qqch - **2.** [count on] compter sur - **3.** [demand] exiger, demander ; **to ~ sb to do sthg** attendre de qqn qu'il fasse qqch ; **to ~ sthg from sb** exiger qqch de qqn - **4.** [suppose] supposer ; **I ~ so** je crois que oui <> vi - **1.** [anticipate] : **to ~ to do sthg** compter faire qqch - **2.** [be pregnant] : **to be ~ing** être enceinte, attendre un bébé.

expectancy ⊳ **life expectancy.**

expectant [ɪk'spektənt] adj qui est dans l'expectative.

expectantly [ɪk'spektəntlɪ] adv dans l'expectative.

expectant mother n femme f enceinte.

expectation [,ekspek'teɪʃn] n - **1.** [hope] espoir m, attente f - **2.** [belief] : **it's my ~ that ...** à mon avis,... ; **against all ~** OR **~s, contrary to all ~** OR **~s** contre toute attente.

expectorant [ɪk'spektərənt] n expectorant m.

expedient [ɪk'spiːdjənt] fml ◇ adj indiqué(e) ◇ n expédient m.

expedite ['ekspɪdaɪt] vt fml accélérer ; [arrival, departure] hâter.

expedition [ˌekspɪ'dɪʃn] n expédition f.

expeditionary force ['ekspɪ'dɪʃnərɪ-] n corps m expéditionnaire.

expel [ɪk'spell] (pt & pp -led ; cont -ling) vt - **1.** [gen] expulser - **2.** SCH renvoyer.

expend [ɪk'spend] vt : to ~ time/money (on) consacrer du temps/de l'argent (à).

expendable [ɪk'spendəbl] adj dont on peut se passer, qui n'est pas indispensable.

expenditure [ɪk'spendɪtʃər] n (U) dépense f.

expense [ɪk'spens] n - **1.** [amount spent] dépense f - **2.** (U) [cost] frais mpl ; **to go to great ~ (to do sthg)** faire beaucoup de frais (pour faire qqch) ; **at the ~ of** au prix de ; **at sb's ~** [financial] aux frais de qqn ; fig aux dépens de qqn.
 ◆ expenses npl COMM frais mpl ; **on ~s** sur la note de frais.

expense account n frais mpl de représentation.

expensive [ɪk'spensɪv] adj - **1.** [financially - gen] cher (chère), coûteux(euse) ; [- tastes] dispendieux(euse) - **2.** [mistake] qui coûte cher.

experience [ɪk'spɪərɪəns] ◇ n expérience f ◇ vt [difficulty] connaître ; [disappointment] éprouver, ressentir ; [loss, change] subir.

experienced [ɪk'spɪərɪənst] adj expérimenté(e) ; **to be ~ at OR in sthg** avoir de l'expérience en OR en matière de qqch.

experiment [ɪk'sperɪmənt] ◇ n expérience f ; **to carry out an ~** faire une expérience ◇ vi : **to ~ (with sthg)** expérimenter (qqch) ; **to ~ on** faire une expérience sur.

experimental [ɪkˌsperɪ'mentl] adj expérimental(e).

expert ['ekspɜːt] ◇ adj expert(e) ; [advice] d'expert ; **~ at sthg/at doing sthg** expert en qqch/à faire qqch ◇ n expert m, -e f.

expertise [ˌekspɜː'tiːz] n (U) compétence f.

expert system n COMPUT système m expert.

expiate ['ekspɪeɪt] vt expier.

expire [ɪk'spaɪər] vi expirer.

expiry [ɪk'spaɪərɪ] n expiration f.

expiry date n date f de péremption.

explain [ɪk'spleɪn] ◇ vt expliquer ; **to ~ sthg to sb** expliquer qqch à qqn ◇ vi s'expliquer ; **to ~ to sb (about sthg)** expliquer (qqch) à qqn.
 ◆ explain away vt sep justifier.

explanation [ˌeksplə'neɪʃn] n : ~ **(for)** explication f (de).

explanatory [ɪk'splænətrɪ] adj explicatif(ive).

expletive [ɪk'spliːtɪv] n fml juron m.

explicit [ɪk'splɪsɪt] adj explicite ; **sexually ~** à teneur sexuelle explicite.

explode [ɪk'spləʊd] ◇ vt - **1.** [bomb] faire exploser - **2.** fig [theory] discréditer ◇ vi lit & fig exploser.

exploit [n 'eksplɔɪt, vb ɪk'splɔɪt] ◇ n exploit m ◇ vt exploiter.

exploitation [ˌeksplɔɪ'teɪʃn] n (U) exploitation f.

exploration [ˌeksplə'reɪʃn] n exploration f.

exploratory [ɪk'splɒrətrɪ] adj exploratoire.

explore [ɪk'splɔːr] vt & vi explorer.

explorer [ɪk'splɔːrər] n explorateur m, -trice f.

explosion [ɪk'spləʊʒn] n explosion f ; [of interest] débordement m.

explosive [ɪk'spləʊsɪv] ◇ adj lit & fig explosif(ive) ◇ n explosif m.

explosive device n engin m explosif.

exponent [ɪk'spəʊnənt] n [of theory] défenseur m.

exponential [ˌekspə'nenʃl] adj exponentiel(elle).

export [n & comp 'ekspɔːt, vb ɪk'spɔːt] ◇ n exportation f ◇ comp d'exportation ◇ vt exporter.
 ◆ exports npl exportations fpl.

exportable [ɪk'spɔːtəbl] adj exportable.

exportation [ˌekspɔː'teɪʃn] n exportation f.

exporter [ek'spɔːtər] n exportateur m, -trice f.

export licence n Br permis m d'exportation.

expose [ɪk'spəʊz] vt - **1.** [uncover] exposer, découvrir ; **to be ~d to sthg** être exposé à qqch - **2.** [unmask - corruption] révéler ; [- person] démasquer.

exposé [eks'pəʊzeɪ] n exposé m.

exposed [ɪk'spəʊzd] adj [land, house, position] exposé(e).

exposition [ˌekspə'zɪʃn] n - **1.** fml [explanation] exposé m - **2.** [exhibition] exposition f.

exposure [ɪk'spəʊʒər] n - **1.** [to light, radiation] exposition f - **2.** MED : **to die of ~** mourir de froid - **3.** [unmasking - of corruption] révélation f ; [- of person] dénonciation f - **4.** [PHOT - time] temps m de pose ; [- photograph] pose f - **5.** (U) [publicity] publicité f ; [coverage] couverture f.

exposure meter n posemètre m.

expound [ɪk'spaʊnd] **fml** ◇ vt exposer ◇ vi :
to ~ on faire un exposé sur.

express [ɪk'spres] ◇ adj - **1.** Br [letter, delivery]
exprès (inv) - **2.** [train, coach] express (inv)
- **3.** fml [specific] exprès(esse) ◇ adv exprès
◇ n [train] rapide m, express m ◇ vt exprimer ; to ~ o.s. s'exprimer.

expression [ɪk'spreʃn] n expression f.

expressionism [ɪk'spreʃənɪzm] n expressionnisme m.

expressionist [ɪk'spreʃənɪst] ◇ adj expressionniste ◇ n expressionniste mf.

expressionless [ɪk'spreʃənlɪs] adj [voice] sans
expression ; [face] impassible.

expressive [ɪk'spresɪv] adj expressif(ive).

expressively [ɪk'spresɪvlɪ] adv de façon expressive.

expressly [ɪk'spreslɪ] adv expressément.

expressway [ɪk'spresweɪ] n Am voie f express.

expropriate [eks'prəʊprɪeɪt] vt exproprier.

expropriation [eks,prəʊprɪ'eɪʃn] n expropriation f.

expulsion [ɪk'spʌlʃn] n - **1.** [gen] expulsion f
- **2.** SCH renvoi m.

exquisite [ɪk'skwɪzɪt] adj exquis(e).

exquisitely [ɪk'skwɪzɪtlɪ] adv de façon exquise.

ex-serviceman n Br ancien combattant m.

ex-servicewoman n Br ancienne combatante f.

ext., extn. (abbr of extension) : ~ 4174 p.
4174.

extant [ek'stænt] adj qui existe encore.

extemporize, -ise [ɪk'stempəraɪz] vi fml improviser.

extend [ɪk'stend] ◇ vt - **1.** [enlarge - building]
agrandir - **2.** [make longer - gen] prolonger ;
[- visa] proroger ; [- deadline] repousser - **3.** [expand - rules, law] étendre (la portée de) ; [- power] accroître - **4.** [stretch out - arm, hand] étendre
- **5.** [offer - help] apporter, offrir ; [- credit] accorder ; to ~ a welcome to sb souhaiter la
bienvenue à qqn ◇ vi - **1.** [stretch - in space]
s'étendre ; [- in time] continuer - **2.** [rule, law] :
to ~ to sb/sthg inclure qqn/qqch.

extendable [ɪk'stendəbl] adj [contract] qui
peut être prolongé(e).

extended-play [ɪk'stendɪd-] adj [record]
double-durée.

extension [ɪk'stenʃn] n - **1.** [to building] agrandissement m - **2.** [lengthening - gen] prolongement m ; [- of visit] prolongation f ; [- of visa]
prorogation f ; [- of deadline] report m - **3.** [of
power] accroissement m ; [of law] élargisse-

ment m - **4.** TELEC poste m - **5.** ELEC prolongateur m - **6.** COMPUT : filename ~ extension m de
nom de fichier.

extension cable n rallonge f.

extensive [ɪk'stensɪv] adj - **1.** [in amount] considérable - **2.** [in area] vaste - **3.** [in range - discussions] approfondi(e) ; [- changes, use] considérable.

extensively [ɪk'stensɪvlɪ] adv - **1.** [in amount]
considérablement - **2.** [in range] abondamment, largement.

extent [ɪk'stent] n - **1.** [of land, area] étendue f,
superficie f ; [of problem, damage] étendue
- **2.** [degree] : to what ~ ...? dans quelle mesure ...? ; to the ~ that [in so far as] dans la mesure où ; [to the point where] au point que ; to a
certain ~ jusqu'à un certain point ; to a large
OR great ~ en grande partie ; to some ~ en
partie.

extenuating circumstances [ɪk'stenjʊeɪtɪŋ-] npl circonstances fpl atténuantes.

exterior [ɪk'stɪərɪə'] ◇ adj extérieur(e) ◇ n
- **1.** [of house, car] extérieur m - **2.** [of person] dehors m, extérieur m.

exterminate [ɪk'stɜːmɪneɪt] vt exterminer.

extermination [ɪk,stɜːmɪ'neɪʃn] n extermination f.

external [ɪk'stɜːnl] adj externe.
➤ **externals** npl apparences fpl.

externally [ɪk'stɜːnəlɪ] adv extérieurement.

extinct [ɪk'stɪŋkt] adj - **1.** [species] disparu(e)
- **2.** [volcano] éteint(e).

extinction [ɪk'stɪŋkʃn] n [of species] extinction
f, disparition f.

extinguish [ɪk'stɪŋgwɪʃ] vt - **1.** [fire, cigarette]
éteindre - **2.** fig [memory, feeling] anéantir.

extinguisher [ɪk'stɪŋgwɪʃə'] n extincteur m.

extn. = ext.

extol (pt & pp **-led** ; cont **-ling**), **extoll** Am
[ɪk'stəʊl] vt louer.

extort [ɪk'stɔːt] vt : to ~ sthg from sb extorquer qqch à qqn.

extortion [ɪk'stɔːʃn] n extorsion f.

extortionate [ɪk'stɔːʃnət] adj exorbitant(e).

extra ['ekstrə] ◇ adj supplémentaire ◇ n
- **1.** [addition] supplément m ; **optional** ~ option f - **2.** CINEMA & THEATRE figurant m, -e f
◇ adv [hard, big etc] extra ; [pay, charge etc] en
plus.

extra- ['ekstrə] prefix extra-.

extract [n 'ekstrækt, vb ɪk'strækt] ◇ n extrait
m ◇ vt - **1.** [take out - tooth] arracher ; to ~ sthg
from sthg tirer qqch de - **2.** [confession, information] :
to ~ sthg (from sb) arracher qqch (à qqn), tirer qqch (de qqn) - **3.** [coal, oil] extraire.

extraction [ɪk'strækʃn] (U) n - **1.** [origin] origine f - **2.** [of coal, tooth] extraction f.

extractor (fan) [ɪk'stræktə^r-] n Br ventilateur m.

extracurricular [ˌekstrəkə'rɪkjʊlə^r] adj en dehors du programme.

extradite ['ekstrədaɪt] vt : **to ~ sb (from/to)** extrader qqn (de/vers).

extradition [ˌekstrə'dɪʃn] <> n extradition f <> comp d'extradition.

extramarital [ˌekstrə'mærɪtl] adj extraconjugal(e).

extramural [ˌekstrə'mjʊərəl] adj UNIV hors faculté.

extraneous [ɪk'streɪnjəs] adj - **1.** [irrelevant] superflu(e) - **2.** [outside] extérieur(e).

extraordinary [ɪk'strɔːdnrɪ] adj extraordinaire.

extraordinary general meeting n assemblée f générale extraordinaire.

extrapolate [ɪk'stræpəleɪt] vt & vi extrapoler.

extrasensory perception [ˌekstrə'sensərɪ-] n perception f extrasensorielle.

extraterrestrial [ˌekstrətə'restrɪəl] adj extraterrestre.

extra time n Br SPORT prolongation f.

extravagance [ɪk'strævəgəns] n - **1.** (U) [excessive spending] gaspillage m, prodigalités fpl - **2.** [luxury] extravagance f, folie f.

extravagant [ɪk'strævəgənt] adj - **1.** [wasteful - person] dépensier(ère) ; [- use, tastes] dispendieux(euse) - **2.** [elaborate, exaggerated] extravagant(e).

extravaganza [ɪkˌstrævə'gænzəl] n folie f, fantaisie f.

extreme [ɪk'striːm] <> adj extrême <> n extrême m ; **to ~s** à l'extrême ; **to take sthg to ~s** mener qqch à l'extrême ; **in the ~** à l'extrême.

extremely [ɪk'striːmlɪ] adv extrêmement.

extremism [ɪk'striːmɪzm] n extrémisme m.

extremist [ɪk'striːmɪst] <> adj extrémiste <> n extrémiste mf.

extremity [ɪk'stremətɪ] (pl -ies) n extrémité f.

extricate ['ekstrɪkeɪt] vt : **to ~ sthg (from)** dégager qqch (de) ; **to ~ o.s. (from)** [from seat belt etc] s'extirper (de) ; [from difficult situation] se tirer (de).

extrovert ['ekstrəvɜːt] <> adj extraverti(e) <> n extraverti m, -e f.

extruded [ɪk'struːdɪd] adj extrudé(e).

exuberance [ɪg'zjuːbərəns] n exubérance f.

exuberant [ɪg'zjuːbərənt] adj exubérant(e).

exude [ɪg'zjuːd] vt - **1.** [liquid, smell] exsuder - **2.** fig [confidence] respirer ; [charm] déborder de.

exult [ɪg'zʌlt] vi exulter ; **to ~ at** OR **in** se réjouir de.

exultant [ɪg'zʌltənt] adj triomphant(e).

eye [aɪ] (cont eyeing OR eying) <> n - **1.** [gen] œil m ; **before my** etc (very) **~s** juste sous mes etc yeux ; **to cast** OR **run one's ~ over sthg** jeter un coup d'œil sur qqch ; **to catch one's ~** attirer le regard ; **to catch sb's ~** attirer l'attention de qqn ; **to clap** OR **lay** OR **set ~s on sb** poser les yeux sur qqn ; **to cry one's ~s out** pleurer toutes les larmes de son corps ; **to feast one's ~s on sthg** se délecter à regarder qqch ; **to have an ~ for sthg** avoir le coup d'œil pour qqch, s'y connaître en qqch ; **to have one's ~ on sb** avoir qqn à l'œil ; **to have one's ~ on sthg** avoir repéré qqch ; **in my** etc **~s** à mes etc yeux ; **to keep one's ~s open** avoir l'œil ; **to keep one's ~s open for sthg** [try to find] essayer de repérer qqch ; **to keep an ~ on sthg** surveiller qqch, garder l'œil sur qqch ; **there is more to this than meets the ~** ce n'est pas aussi simple que cela OR qu'il y paraît ; **to open sb's ~s (to sthg)** ouvrir les yeux de qqn (sur qqch) ; **not to see ~ to ~ with sb** ne pas partager la même opinion que qqn ; **to close** OR **shut one's ~s to sthg** fermer les yeux sur qqch ; **to turn a blind ~ to sthg** ignorer qqch ; **I'm up to my ~s in work** Br j'ai du travail jusque par-dessus la tête - **2.** [of needle] chas m <> vt regarder, reluquer.

➤ **eye up** vt sep Br reluquer.

eyeball ['aɪbɔːl] <> n globe m oculaire <> vt Am inf fixer.

eyebath ['aɪbɑːθ] n œillère f (pour bains d'œil).

eyebrow ['aɪbraʊ] n sourcil m ; **to raise one's ~s** tiquer, sourciller.

eyebrow pencil n crayon m à sourcils.

eye-catching adj voyant(e).

eye contact n : **to make ~ with sb** regarder qqn dans les yeux ; **to avoid ~ with sb** éviter le regard de qqn.

eyedrops ['aɪdrɒps] npl gouttes fpl pour les yeux.

eyelash ['aɪlæʃ] n cil m.

eyelet ['aɪlɪt] n œillet m.

eye-level adj qui est au niveau OR à la hauteur de l'œil.

eyelid ['aɪlɪd] n paupière f ; **she didn't bat an ~** inf elle n'a pas sourcillé OR bronché.

eyeliner ['aɪˌlaɪnə^r] n eye-liner m.

eye-opener *n* inf révélation *f.*

eyepatch ['aɪpætʃ] *n* cache *m.*

eye shadow *n* fard *m* à paupières.

eyesight ['aɪsaɪt] *n* vue *f.*

eyesore ['aɪsɔːʳ] *n* horreur *f.*

eyestrain ['aɪstreɪn] *n* fatigue *f* des yeux.

eyetooth ['aɪtuːθ] (*pl* **-teeth** [-tiːθ]) *n :* **to give one's eyeteeth for sthg/to do sthg** donner n'importe quoi pour qqch/pour faire qqch.

eyewash ['aɪwɒʃ] *n (U)* inf [nonsense] fadaises *fpl.*

eyewitness [ˌaɪ'wɪtnɪs] *n* témoin *m* oculaire.

eyrie ['aɪərɪ] *n* aire *f (d'un aigle).*

e-zine ['iːziːn] *n* magazine *m* électronique.

f (*pl* **f's** OR **fs**), **F** (*pl* **F's** OR **Fs**) [ef] *n* [letter] f *m* inv, F *m* inv.

F *n* **- 1.** MUS fa *m* **- 2.** (*abbr of* **Fahrenheit**) F.

FA (*abbr of* **Football Association**) *n* fédération britannique de football.

FAA (*abbr of* **Federal Aviation Administration**) *n* direction fédérale de l'aviation civile américaine.

fable ['feɪbl] *n* fable *f.*

fabled ['feɪbld] *adj* fabuleux(euse), légendaire.

fabric ['fæbrɪk] *n* **- 1.** [cloth] tissu *m* **- 2.** [of building, society] structure *f.*

fabricate ['fæbrɪkeɪt] *vt* fabriquer.

fabrication [ˌfæbrɪ'keɪʃn] *n* **- 1.** [lie, lying] fabrication *f,* invention *f* **- 2.** [manufacture] fabrication *f.*

fabulous ['fæbjʊləs] *adj* **- 1.** [gen] fabuleux(euse) **- 2.** inf [excellent] sensationnel(elle), fabuleux(euse).

fabulously ['fæbjʊləslɪ] *adv* fabuleusement.

facade [fə'sɑːd] *n* façade *f.*

face [feɪs] *n* **- 1.** [of person] visage *m,* figure *f; ~* **to ~** face à face ; **to look sb in the ~** re-

garder qqn dans les yeux ; **to say sthg to sb's ~** dire qqch à qqn en face ; **to show one's ~** se montrer **- 2.** [expression] visage *m,* mine *f;* **to make** OR **pull a ~** faire la grimace ; **her ~ fell** son visage s'est assombri **- 3.** [of cliff, mountain] face *f,* paroi *f;* [of building] façade *f;* [of clock, watch] cadran *m ;* [of coin, shape] face **- 4.** [surface - of planet] surface *f;* **on the ~ of it** à première vue **- 5.** [respect] : **to save/lose ~** sauver/perdre la face **- 6.** phr : **to fly in the ~ of sthg** être en contradiction avec qqch ; **it flies in the ~ of logic** ce n'est pas logique ⟨> *vt* **- 1.** [look towards - subj : person] faire face à ; **the house ~s the sea/south** la maison donne sur la mer/est orientée vers le sud **- 2.** [decision, crisis] être confronté(e) à ; [problem, danger] faire face à **- 3.** [facts, truth] faire face à, admettre **- 4.** inf [cope with] affronter.

face down *adv* [person] face contre terre ; [object] à l'envers ; [card] face en dessous.

face up *adv* [person] sur le dos ; [object] à l'endroit ; [card] face en dessus.

in the face of *prep* devant.

face up to *vt fus* faire face à.

facecloth ['feɪsklɒθ] *n* Br gant *m* de toilette.

face cream *n* crème *f* pour le visage.

faceless ['feɪslɪs] *adj* anonyme.

face-lift *n* lifting *m ;* fig restauration *f,* rénovation *f.*

face pack *n* masque *m* de beauté.

face powder *n* poudre *f* de riz, poudre pour le visage.

face-saving [-ˌseɪvɪŋ] *adj* qui sauve la face.

facet ['fæsɪt] *n* facette *f.*

facetious [fə'siːʃəs] *adj* facétieux(euse).

facetiously [fə'siːʃəslɪ] *adv* facétieusement.

face-to-face *adj* face à face.

face value *n* [of coin, stamp] valeur *f* nominale ; **to take sthg at ~** prendre qqch au pied de la lettre.

facial ['feɪʃl] ⟨> *adj* facial(e) ⟨> *n* nettoyage *m* de peau.

facile [Br 'fæsaɪl, Am fæsl] *adj* pej facile.

facilitate [fə'sɪlɪteɪt] *vt* faciliter

facility [fə'sɪlətɪ] (*pl* **-ies**) *n* **- 1.** [ability] : **to have a ~ for sthg** avoir de la facilité OR de l'aptitude pour qqch **- 2.** [feature] fonction *f.*

facilities *npl* [amenities] équipement *m,* aménagement *m.*

facing ['feɪsɪŋ] *adj* d'en face ; [sides] opposé(e).

facsimile [fæk'sɪmɪlɪ] *n* **- 1.** [fax] télécopie *f,* fax *m* **- 2.** [copy] fac-similé *m.*

facsimile machine fml = **fax machine**.

fact [fækt] *n* **- 1.** [true piece of information] fait *m ;*

the ~ **is** le fait est ; **the ~ remains that ...** toujours est-il que ... ; **to know sthg for a ~** savoir pertinemment qqch **- 2.** (U) [truth] faits mpl, réalité f.

➤ **in fact** ◇ adv de fait, effectivement ◇ conj en fait.

fact-finding [-'faɪndɪŋ] adj d'enquête.

faction ['fækʃn] n faction f.

factional ['fækʃənl] adj [dispute] de factions.

fact of life n fait m, réalité f ; **the facts of life** euphemism les choses fpl de la vie.

factor ['fæktə'] n facteur m.

factory ['fæktərɪ] (pl -ies) n fabrique f, usine f.

factory farming n élevage m industriel.

factory ship n navire-usine m.

factotum [fæk'təutəm] (pl -s) n factotum m, intendant m, -e f.

fact sheet n Br résumé m, brochure f.

factual ['fæktʃuəl] adj factuel(elle), basé(e) sur les faits.

faculty ['fæklti] (pl -ies) n **- 1.** [gen] faculté f **- 2.** Am [in college] : **the ~** le corps enseignant.

FA Cup n en Angleterre, championnat de football dont la finale se joue à Wembley.

fad [fæd] n engouement m, mode f ; [personal] marotte f.

faddy ['fædɪ] (compar -ier ; superl -iest) adj inf pej capricieux(euse).

fade [feɪd] ◇ vt [jeans, curtains, paint] décolorer ◇ vi **- 1.** [jeans, curtains, paint] se décolorer ; [colour] passer ; [flower] se flétrir, faner **- 2.** [light] baisser, diminuer **- 3.** [sound] diminuer, s'affaiblir **- 4.** [memory] s'effacer ; [feeling, interest] diminuer **- 5.** [smile] s'effacer, s'évanouir.

➤ **fade away, fade out** vi [sound, anger] diminuer ; [image] s'effacer.

faded ['feɪdɪd] adj passé(e).

faeces Br, **feces** Am ['fiːsiːz] npl fèces fpl.

Faeroe, Faroe ['feərəʊ] n : **the ~ Islands, the ~s** les îles fpl Féroé ; **in the ~ Islands** aux îles Féroé.

faff [fæf] ➤ **faff about, faff around** vi Br inf glander.

fag [fæg] n inf **- 1.** Br [cigarette] clope m **- 2.** Br [chore] corvée f **- 3.** Am pej [homosexual] pédé m.

fag end n Br inf mégot m.

fagged out [fægd-] adj Br inf crevé(e).

faggot, fagot Am ['fægət] n **- 1.** Br CULIN crépinette f **- 2.** Am inf pej [homosexual] pédé m.

Fahrenheit ['færənhaɪt] adj Fahrenheit (inv).

fail [feɪl] ◇ vt **- 1.** [exam, test] rater, échouer à **- 2.** [not succeed] : **to ~ to do sthg** ne pas arriver

à faire qqch **- 3.** [neglect] : **to ~ to do sthg** manquer OR omettre de faire qqch **- 4.** [candidate] refuser **- 5.** [subj : courage] manquer à ; [subj : friend, memory] lâcher ◇ vi **- 1.** [not succeed] ne pas réussir OR y arriver **- 2.** [not pass exam] échouer **- 3.** [stop functioning] lâcher **- 4.** [weaken - health, daylight] décliner ; [- eyesight] baisser.

failed [feɪld] adj [singer, writer etc] raté(e).

failing ['feɪlɪŋ] ◇ n [weakness] défaut m, point m faible ◇ prep à moins de ; **~ that** à défaut.

fail-safe adj [device etc] à sûreté intégrée.

failure ['feɪljə'] n **- 1.** [lack of success, unsuccessful thing] échec m ; **her ~ to attend** le fait qu'elle ne soit pas venue **- 2.** [person] raté m, -e f **- 3.** [of engine, brake etc] défaillance f ; [of crop] perte f ; **heart ~** arrêt m cardiaque.

faint [feɪnt] ◇ adj **- 1.** [smell] léger(ère) ; [memory] vague ; [sound, hope] faible **- 2.** [slight - chance] petit(e), faible **- 3.** [dizzy] : **I'm feeling a bit ~** je ne me sens pas bien ◇ vi s'évanouir.

faint-hearted [-'hɑːtɪd] adj timoré(e), timide.

faintly ['feɪntlɪ] adv **- 1.** [recall] vaguement ; [shine] faiblement ; [smile - indifferently] vaguement ; [- sadly] faiblement **- 2.** [rather, slightly] légèrement.

faintness ['feɪntnɪs] n **- 1.** [dizziness] étourdissement m, étourdissements mpl **- 2.** [of image] flou m **- 3.** [of smell, sound, hope] faiblesse f ; [of memory] imprécision f.

fair [feə'] ◇ adj **- 1.** [just] juste, équitable ; **it's not ~!** ce n'est pas juste! ; **to be ~ ...** il faut dire que ... **- 2.** [quite large] grand(e), important(e) **- 3.** [quite good] assez bon (assez bonne) ; **to have a ~ idea of sthg** avoir sa petite idée sur qqch **- 4.** [hair] blond(e) **- 5.** [skin, complexion] clair(e) **- 6.** [weather] beau (belle) ◇ n **- 1.** Br [funfair] fête f foraine **- 2.** [trade fair] foire f ◇ adv [fairly] loyalement.

➤ **fair enough** adv Br inf OK, d'accord.

fair copy n copie f au propre.

fair game n proie f rêvée.

fairground ['feəgraʊnd] n champ m de foire.

fair-haired [-'heəd] adj [person] blond(e).

fairly ['feəlɪ] adv **- 1.** [rather] assez ; **~ certain** presque sûr **- 2.** [justly] équitablement ; [describe] avec impartialité ; [fight, play] loyalement.

fair-minded [-'maɪndɪd] adj impartial(e), équitable.

fairness ['feənɪs] n [justness] équité f ; **in ~ (to sb)** pour être juste (envers qqn).

fair play *n* fair-play *m inv.*

fairway ['feəweɪ] *n* fairway *m*, allée *f* Can.

fairy ['feərɪ] (*pl* -ies) *n* [imaginary creature] fée *f.*

fairy lights *npl* Br guirlande *f* électrique.

fairy tale *n* conte *m* de fées.

fait accompli [ˌfeɪtə'kɒmpliː] (*pl* faits accomplis [ˌfeɪzə'kɒmpliː]) *n* fait *m* accompli.

faith [feɪθ] *n* - **1.** [belief] foi *f*, confiance *f* ; ~ in sb/sthg confiance en qqn/qqch ; in bad ~ de mauvaise foi ; in good ~ en toute bonne foi - **2.** RELIG foi *f.*

faithful ['feɪθfʊl] <> *adj* fidèle <> *npl* RELIG : the ~ les fidèles *mpl.*

faithfully ['feɪθfʊlɪ] *adv* [loyally] fidèlement ; to promise ~ that ... donner sa parole que ... ; Yours ~ Br [in letter] je vous prie d'agréer mes salutations distinguées.

faithfulness ['feɪθfʊlnɪs] *n* - **1.** [loyalty] fidélité *f* - **2.** [truth - of account, translation] exactitude *f.*

faith healer *n* guérisseur *m*, -euse *f.*

faithless ['feɪθlɪs] *adj* déloyal(e).

fake [feɪk] <> *adj* faux (fausse) <> *n* - **1.** [object, painting] faux *m* - **2.** [person] imposteur *m* <> *vt* - **1.** [results] falsifier ; [signature] imiter - **2.** [illness, emotions] simuler <> *vi* [pretend] simuler, faire semblant.

falcon ['fɔːlkən] *n* faucon *m.*

Falkland Islands ['fɔːklənd-], **Falklands** ['fɔːkləndz] *npl* : the ~ les îles *fpl* Falkland, les Malouines *fpl* ; in the ~ aux îles Falkland, aux Malouines.

fall [fɔːl] (*pt* fell, *pp* fallen) <> *vi* - **1.** [gen] tomber ; to ~ flat [joke] tomber à plat - **2.** [decrease] baisser - **3.** [become] : to ~ asleep s'endormir ; to ~ ill tomber malade ; to ~ in love tomber amoureux(euse) ; to ~ open s'ouvrir ; to ~ silent se taire ; to ~ vacant se libérer - **4.** [belong, be classed] : to ~ into two groups se diviser en deux groupes ; the matter ~s under our jurisdiction cette question relève de notre juridiction - **5.** [disintegrate] : to ~ to bits OR pieces tomber en morceaux - **6.** [be captured - city] : to ~ (to sb) tomber (aux mains de qqn) - **7.** Br POL [constituency] : to ~ to sb passer à qqn <> *n* - **1.** [gen] : ~ (in) chute (de) - **2.** Am [autumn] automne *m.*

→ **falls** *npl* chutes *fpl.*

→ **fall about** *vi* Br inf : to ~ about (laughing) se tordre (de rire).

→ **fall apart** *vi* - **1.** [disintegrate - book, chair] tomber en morceaux - **2.** fig [country] tomber en ruine ; [person] s'effondrer.

→ **fall away** *vi* [land] descendre, s'abaisser.

→ **fall back** *vi* [person, crowd] reculer.

→ **fall back on** *vt fus* [resort to] se rabattre sur.

→ **fall behind** *vi* - **1.** [in race] se faire distancer - **2.** [with rent] être en retard ; to ~ behind with one's work avoir du retard dans son travail.

→ **fall down** *vi* [fail] échouer ; the plan ~s down on three points ce plan pèche sur trois points.

→ **fall for** *vt fus* - **1.** inf [fall in love with] tomber amoureux(euse) de - **2.** [trick, lie] se laisser prendre à ; to ~ for it tomber dans le panneau.

→ **fall in** *vi* - **1.** [roof, ceiling] s'écrouler, s'affaisser - **2.** MIL former les rangs.

→ **fall in with** *vt fus* [go along with] accepter.

→ **fall off** *vi* - **1.** [branch, handle] se détacher, tomber - **2.** [demand, numbers] baisser, diminuer.

→ **fall on** *vt fus* - **1.** [subj : eyes, gaze] tomber sur - **2.** [attack] se jeter sur.

→ **fall out** *vi* - **1.** [hair, tooth] tomber - **2.** [friends] se brouiller - **3.** MIL rompre les rangs.

→ **fall over** <> *vt fus* : to ~ over sthg trébucher sur qqch et tomber ; to be ~ing over o.s. to do sthg inf se mettre en quatre pour faire qqch <> *vi* [person, chair etc] tomber.

→ **fall through** *vi* [plan, deal] échouer.

→ **fall to** *vt fus* [subj : duty] incomber à, revenir à ; it ~s to me to ... c'est à moi de ...

fallacious [fə'leɪʃəs] *adj* fml fallacieux(euse).

fallacy ['fæləsɪ] (*pl* -ies) *n* erreur *f*, idée *f* fausse.

fallen ['fɔːln] *pp* ⊳ fall.

fall guy *n* Am inf [scapegoat] bouc *m* émissaire.

fallible ['fæləbl] *adj* faillible.

falling ['fɔːlɪŋ] *adj* [decreasing] en baisse.

fallopian tube [fə'ləupɪən-] *n* trompe *f* de Fallope.

fallout ['fɔːlaʊt] *n* (U) [radiation] retombées *fpl.*

fallout shelter *n* abri *m* antiatomique.

fallow ['fæləʊ] *adj* : to lie ~ être en jachère.

false [fɔːls] *adj* faux (fausse).

false alarm *n* fausse alerte *f.*

falsehood ['fɔːlshʊd] *n* fml - **1.** [lie] mensonge *m* - **2.** (U) [lack of truth] fausseté *f.*

falsely ['fɔːlslɪ] *adv* à tort ; [smile, laugh] faussement.

false start *n* lit & fig faux départ *m.*

false teeth *npl* dentier *m.*

falsetto [fɔːl'setəʊ] (*pl* -s) <> *n* [singer] fausset *m* <> *adv* [sing] en fausset.

falsify ['fɔːlsɪfaɪ] (*pt & pp* -ied) *vt* falsifier.

falter ['fɔːltəʳ] *vi* - **1.** [move unsteadily] chanceler

- **2.** [steps, voice] devenir hésitant(e) - **3.** [hesitate, lose confidence] hésiter.

faltering [ˈfɔːltərɪŋ] *adj* [steps, voice] hésitant(e).

fame [feɪm] *n* gloire *f*, renommée *f*.

familiar [fəˈmɪljəʳ] *adj* familier(ère) ; **~ to sb** connu de qqn ; **~ with sthg** familiarisé(e) avec qqch ; **to be on ~ terms with sb** être en termes familiers avec qqn.

familiarity [fə̩mɪlɪˈærətɪ] *n* (U) - **1.** [knowledge] : **~ with sthg** connaissance *f* de qqch, familiarité *f* avec qqch - **2.** [normality] caractère *m* familier - **3.** pej [excessive informality] familiarité *f*.

familiarize, -ise [fəˈmɪljəraɪz] *vt* : **to ~ o.s. with sthg** se familiariser avec qqch ; **to ~ sb with sthg** familiariser qqn avec qqch.

family [ˈfæmlɪ] (*pl* **-ies**) ◇ *n* famille *f* ◇ *comp* - **1.** [belonging to family] de famille - **2.** [suitable for all ages] familial(e).

family business *n* entreprise *f* familiale.

family credit *n* (U) Br ≃ complément *m* familial.

family doctor *n* médecin *m* de famille.

family life *n* vie *f* de famille.

family planning *n* planning *m* familial ; **~ clinic** centre *m* de planning familial.

family tree *n* arbre *m* généalogique.

famine [ˈfæmɪn] *n* famine *f*.

famished [ˈfæmɪʃt] *adj* inf [very hungry] affamé(e) ; **I'm ~!** je meurs de faim!

famous [ˈfeɪməs] *adj* : **~ (for)** célèbre (pour).

famously [ˈfeɪməslɪ] *adv* dated : **to get on** OR **along ~** s'entendre comme larrons en foire.

fan [fæn] (*pt* & *pp* **-ned** ; *cont* **-ning**) ◇ *n* - **1.** [of paper, silk] éventail *m* - **2.** [electric or mechanical] ventilateur *m* - **3.** [enthusiast] fan *mf* ◇ *vt* - **1.** [face] éventer ; **to ~ o.s.** s'éventer - **2.** [fire, feelings] attiser.

➤ **fan out** *vi* se déployer.

fanatic [fəˈnætɪk] *n* fanatique *mf*.

fanatical [fəˈnætɪkl] *adj* fanatique.

fanaticism [fəˈnætɪsɪzm] *n* fanatisme *m*.

fan belt *n* courroie *f* de ventilateur.

fanciful [ˈfænsɪfʊl] *adj* - **1.** [odd] bizarre, fantasque - **2.** [elaborate] extravagant(e).

fan club *n* fan-club *m*.

fancy [ˈfænsɪ] (*compar* **-ier** ; *superl* **-iest**, *pl* **-ies**, *pt* & *pp* **-ied**) ◇ *adj* - **1.** [elaborate - hat, clothes] extravagant(e) ; [- food, cakes] raffiné(e) - **2.** [expensive - restaurant, hotel] de luxe ; [- prices] fantaisiste ◇ *n* - **1.** [desire, liking] envie *f*, lubie *f* ; **to take a ~ to sb** se prendre d'affec-

tion pour qqn ; **to take a ~ to sthg** se mettre à aimer qqch ; **to take sb's ~** faire envie à qqn, plaire à qqn - **2.** [fantasy] rêve *m* ◇ *vt* - **1.** inf [want] avoir envie de ; **to ~ doing sthg** avoir envie de faire qqch - **2.** inf [like] : **I ~ her** elle me plaît ; **to ~ o.s.** ne pas se prendre pour rien OR n'importe qui ; **to ~ o.s. as sthg** se prendre pour qqch - **3.** [imagine] : **~ meeting you here!** tiens, c'est toi! Je n'aurais jamais pensé te rencontrer ici! ; **~ that!** ça alors! - **4.** dated [think] penser.

fancy dress *n* (U) déguisement *m*.

fancy-dress party *n* bal *m* costumé.

fancy goods *npl* articles *mpl* fantaisie.

fanfare [ˈfænfeəʳ] *n* fanfare *f*.

fang [fæŋ] *n* [of wolf] croc *m* ; [of snake] crochet *m*.

fan heater *n* radiateur *m* soufflant.

fanlight [ˈfænlaɪt] *n* Br imposte *f*.

fan mail *n* courrier *m* de fans.

fanny [ˈfænɪ] *n* Am inf [buttocks] fesses *fpl*.

fanny pack *n* Am banane *f* (sac).

fantasize, -ise [ˈfæntəsaɪz] *vi* : **to ~ (about sthg/about doing sthg)** fantasmer (sur qqch/sur le fait de faire qqch).

fantastic [fænˈtæstɪk] *adj* - **1.** inf [wonderful] fantastique, formidable - **2.** [incredible] extraordinaire, incroyable - **3.** [exotic] fabuleux(euse).

fantastically [fænˈtæstɪklɪ] *adv* - **1.** [extremely] extrêmement - **2.** [exotically] fabuleusement, extraordinairement.

fantasy [ˈfæntəsɪ] (*pl* **-ies**) ◇ *n* - **1.** [dream, imaginary event] rêve *m*, fantasme *m* - **2.** (U) [fiction] fiction *f* - **3.** [imagination] fantaisie *f* ◇ *comp* imaginaire.

fantasy football *n* jeu où chaque participant se constitue une équipe virtuelle avec les noms de footballeurs réels, chaque but marqué par ceux-ci dans la réalité valant un point dans le jeu.

fanzine [ˈfænziːn] *n* fanzine *m*.

fao (*abbr of* **for the attention of**) à l'attention de.

FAO (*abbr of* **Food and Agriculture Organization**) *n* FAO *f*.

FAQ [fak, ˌefeɪˈkjuː] (*abbr of* **frequently asked questions**) *n* COMPUT foire *f* aux questions, FAQ *f*.

far [fɑːʳ] (*compar* **farther** OR **further** ; *superl* **farthest** OR **furthest**) ◇ *adv* - **1.** [in distance] loin ; **how ~ is it?** c'est à quelle distance?, (est-ce que) c'est loin? ; **how far you come ~?** vous venez de loin? ; **~ away** OR **off** loin ; **~ and wide** partout ; **as ~ as** jusqu'à - **2.** [in time] : ~ **away** OR **off** loin ; **as ~ back as** [be founded etc] dès ; [remember, go etc] jusqu'à ; **so ~** jusqu'à maintenant, jusqu'ici - **3.** [in degree or extent] bien ; **I wouldn't trust him very ~** je ne lui ferais pas tellement confiance ; **he's not ~ wrong** OR **out** OR **off** il n'est pas loin ; **as ~ as** autant que ; **as ~ as I'm concerned** en ce qui me concerne ; **as ~ as possible** autant que possible, dans la mesure du possible ; **it's all right as ~ as it goes** pour ce qui est de ça, pas de problème ; **~ and away, by ~** de loin ; **~ from it** loin de là, au contraire ; **so ~ so good** jusqu'ici tout va bien ; **to go so ~ as to do sthg** aller jusqu'à faire qqch ; **to go too ~** aller trop loin ◇ *adj* - **1.** [extreme] : **the ~ end of the street** l'autre bout de la rue ; **the ~ right of the party** l'extrême droite du parti ; **the door on the ~ left** la porte la plus à gauche - **2.** literary [remote] lointain(e).

faraway ['fɑːrəweɪ] *adj* lointain(e).

farce [fɑːs] *n* - **1.** THEATRE farce *f* - **2.** fig [disaster] pagaille *f*, vaste rigolade *f*.

farcical ['fɑːsɪkl] *adj* grotesque.

fare [feəʳ] ◇ *n* - **1.** [payment] prix *m*, tarif *m* - **2.** dated [food] nourriture *f* ◇ *vi* [manage] : **to ~ well/badly** bien/mal se débrouiller.

Far East *n* : **the ~** l'Extrême-Orient *m*.

fare stage *n* Br section *f*.

farewell [ˌfeəˈwel] ◇ *n* adieu *m* ◇ *excl* literary adieu!

farfetched [ˌfɑːˈfetʃt] *adj* tiré(e) par. les cheveux.

farm [fɑːm] ◇ *n* ferme *f* ◇ *vt* cultiver ◇ *vi* être cultivateur.

➤ **farm out** *vt sep* confier en soustraitance.

farmer ['fɑːməʳ] *n* fermier *m*.

farmhand ['fɑːmhænd] *n* ouvrier *m*, -ère *f* agricole.

farmhouse ['fɑːmhaʊs, *pl* -haʊzɪz] *n* ferme *f*.

farming ['fɑːmɪŋ] *n (U)* agriculture *f ;* [of animals] élevage *m*.

farm labourer = farmhand.

farmland ['fɑːmlænd] *n (U)* terres *fpl* cultivées OR arables.

farmstead ['fɑːmsted] *n* Am ferme *f*.

farm worker = farmhand.

farmyard ['fɑːmjɑːd] *n* cour *f* de ferme.

Faroe = Faeroe.

far-off *adj* - **1.** [days] lointain(e) ; [time] reculé(e) - **2.** [in distance] lointain(e).

far-reaching [-'riːtʃɪŋ] *adj* d'une grande portée.

farrier ['færɪəʳ] *n* maréchal *m* ferrant.

farsighted [ˌfɑːˈsaɪtɪd] *adj* - **1.** [person] prévoyant(e) ; [plan] élaboré(e) avec clairvoyance - **2.** Am [longsighted] hypermétrope.

fart [fɑːt] vinf ◇ *n* - **1.** [air] pet *m* - **2.** [person] con *m*, conne *f* ◇ *vi* péter.

farther ['fɑːðəʳ] *compar* ⊳ far.

farthest ['fɑːðəst] *superl* ⊳ far.

FAS (*abbr of* free alongside ship) FLB.

fascia ['feɪʃə] *n* [on shop] enseigne *f ;* [in car] tableau *m* de bord.

fascinate ['fæsɪneɪt] *vt* fasciner.

fascinating ['fæsɪneɪtɪŋ] *adj* [person, country] fascinant(e) ; [job] passionnant(e) ; [idea, thought] très intéressant(e).

fascination [ˌfæsɪˈneɪʃn] *n* fascination *f*.

fascism ['fæʃɪzm] *n* fascisme *m*.

fascist ['fæʃɪst] ◇ *adj* fasciste ◇ *n* fasciste *mf*.

fashion ['fæʃn] ◇ *n* - **1.** [clothing, style] mode *f ;* **to be in/out of ~** être/ne plus être à la mode ; **~ model** mannequin *m* (de mode) - **2.** [manner] manière *f* ◇ *vt* fml façonner, fabriquer.

fashionable ['fæʃnəbl] *adj* à la mode.

fashion-conscious *adj* qui suit la mode.

fashion designer *n* styliste *mf*.

fashion show *n* défilé *m* de mode.

fast [fɑːst] ◇ *adj* - **1.** [rapid] rapide - **2.** [clock, watch] qui avance ◇ *adv* - **1.** [rapidly] vite ; **how ~ does this car go?** à quelle vitesse va cette voiture? - **2.** [firmly] solidement ; **to hold ~ to sthg** lit & fig s'accrocher à qqch ; **~ asleep** profondément endormi ◇ *n* jeûne *m* ◇ *vi* jeûner.

fast breeder reactor *n* surrégénérateur *m*.

fasten ['fɑːsn] ◇ *vt* [jacket, bag] fermer ; [seat belt] attacher ; **to ~ sthg to sthg** attacher qqch à qqch ◇ *vi* : **to ~ on to sb/sthg** se cramponner à qqn/qqch.

fastener ['fɑːsnəʳ] *n* [of bag, necklace] fermoir *m ;* [of dress] fermeture *f*.

fastening ['fɑːsnɪŋ] *n* fermeture *f*.

fast food *n* fast food *m*.

fast-forward ◇ *n* avance *f* rapide ◇ *vt* mettre en avance rapide ◇ *vi* mettre la bande en avance rapide.

fastidious [fəˈstɪdɪəs] *adj* [fussy] méticuleux(euse).

fast lane *n* [on motorway] voie *f* rapide ; **life in the ~** fig la vie à cent à l'heure.

fat [fæt] (*compar* -**ter** ; *superl* -**test**) ◇ *adj* - **1.** [overweight] gros (grosse), gras (grasse) ; **to get ~** grossir - **2.** [not lean - meat] gras (grasse) **- 3.** [thick - file, wallet] gros (grosse), épais(aisse) **- 4.** [large - profit, cheque] gros (grosse) **- 5.** iro [small] : **a ~ lot of good that did you!** ça t'a bien avancé! ⬦ *n* **- 1.** [flesh, on meat, in food] graisse *f* **- 2.** *(U)* [for cooking] matière *f* grasse ; **pork ~** saindoux *m*.

fatal ['feɪtl] *adj* **- 1.** [serious - mistake] fatal(e) ; [- decision, words] fatidique **- 2.** [accident, illness] mortel(elle).

fatalism ['feɪtəlɪzm] *n* fatalisme *m*.

fatalistic [,feɪtə'lɪstɪk] *adj* fataliste.

fatality [fə'tælətɪ] (*pl* -ies) *n* **- 1.** [accident victim] mort *m* **- 2.** = **fatalism**.

fatally ['feɪtəlɪ] *adv* **- 1.** [seriously] sérieusement, gravement **- 2.** [wounded] mortellement ; **~ ill** dans un état désespéré.

fat cat *n* inf richard *m*, huile *f*.

fate [feɪt] *n* **- 1.** [destiny] destin *m ;* **to tempt ~** tenter le diable **- 2.** [result, end] sort *m*.

fated ['feɪtɪd] *adj* fatal(e), marqué(e) par le destin ; **to be ~ to do sthg** être voué OR destiné à faire qqch.

fateful ['feɪtful] *adj* fatidique.

fat-free *adj* sans matières grasses.

fathead ['fæthed] *n* inf imbécile *mf*, patate *f*.

father ['fɑːðəʳ] ⬦ *n* père *m* ⬦ *vt* engendrer.

➤ **Father** *n* **- 1.** [priest] Père *m* **- 2.** [God] Dieu le Père *m ;* **Our Father** notre Père.

Father Christmas *n* Br le Père Noël.

fatherhood ['fɑːðəhud] *n (U)* paternité *f*.

father-in-law (*pl* **fathers-in-law**) *n* beau-père *m*.

fatherly ['fɑːðəlɪ] *adj* paternel(elle).

Father's Day *n* fête *f* des Pères.

fathom ['fæðəm] ⬦ *n* brasse *f* ⬦ *vt :* **to ~ sb/ sthg (out)** comprendre qqn/qqch.

fatigue [fə'tiːg] ⬦ *n* **- 1.** [exhaustion] épuisement *m* **- 2.** [in metal] fatigue *f* ⬦ *vt* épuiser.

➤ **fatigues** *npl* tenue *f* de corvée, treillis *m*.

fatless ['fætlɪs] *adj* sans matières grasses.

fatness ['fætnɪs] *n* [of person] embonpoint *m*.

fatten ['fætn] *vt* engraisser.

➤ **fatten up** *vt sep* engraisser.

fattening ['fætnɪŋ] *adj* qui fait grossir.

fatty ['fætɪ] (*compar* -ier ; *superl* -iest, *pl* -ies) ⬦ *adj* gras (grasse) ⬦ *n* inf pej gros *m*, grosse *f*.

fatuous ['fætjʊəs] *adj* stupide, niais(e).

fatuously ['fætjʊəslɪ] *adv* stupidement, niaisement.

faucet ['fɔːsɪt] *n* Am robinet *m*.

fault ['fɔːlt] ⬦ *n* **- 1.** [responsibility, in tennis] faute *f ;* **it's my ~** c'est de ma faute **- 2.** [mistake, imperfection] défaut *m ;* **to find ~ with sb/sthg** critiquer qqn/qqch ; **at ~** fautif(ive) **- 3.** GEOL faille *f* ⬦ *vt :* **to ~ sb (on sthg)** prendre qqn en défaut (sur qqch).

faultless ['fɔːltlɪs] *adj* impeccable.

faulty ['fɔːltɪ] (*compar* -ier ; *superl* -iest) *adj* défectueux(euse).

fauna ['fɔːnə] *n* faune *f*.

faux pas [,fəʊ'pɑː] (*pl inv*) *n* faux-pas *m*.

favour Br, **favor** Am ['feɪvəʳ] ⬦ *n* **- 1.** [approval] faveur *f*, approbation *f ;* **to look with ~ on sb** considérer qqn favorablement ; **in sb's ~** en faveur de qqn ; **to be in/out of ~ with sb** avoir/ne pas avoir les faveurs de qqn, avoir/ne pas avoir la cote avec qqn ; **to curry ~ with sb** chercher à gagner la faveur de qqn **- 2.** [kind act] service *m ;* **to do sb a ~** rendre (un) service à qqn **- 3.** [favouritism] favoritisme *m* **- 4.** [advantage] : **to rule in sb's ~** décider OR statuer en faveur de qqn ⬦ *vt* **- 1.** [prefer] préférer, privilégier **- 2.** [treat better, help] favoriser **- 3.** iro [honour] : **to ~ sb with sthg** faire à qqn l'honneur de qqch.

➤ **in favour** *adv* [in agreement] pour, d'accord.

➤ **in favour of** *prep* **- 1.** [in preference to] au profit de **- 2.** [in agreement with] : **to be in ~ of sthg/of doing sthg** être partisan(e) de qqch/ de faire qqch.

favourable Br, **favorable** Am ['feɪvrəbl] *adj* [positive] favorable.

favourably Br, **favorably** Am ['feɪvrəblɪ] *adv* favorablement ; [placed] bien.

favoured Br, **favored** Am ['feɪvəd] *adj* favorisé(e).

favourite Br, **favorite** Am ['feɪvrɪt] ⬦ *adj* favori(ite) ⬦ *n* favori *m*, -ite *f*.

favouritism Br, **favoritism** Am ['feɪvrɪtɪzm] *n* favoritisme *m*.

fawn [fɔːn] ⬦ *adj* fauve *(inv)* ⬦ *n* [animal] faon *m* ⬦ *vi :* **to ~ on sb** flatter qqn servilement.

fax [fæks] ⬦ *n* fax *m*, télécopie *f* ⬦ *vt* **- 1.** [person] envoyer un fax à **- 2.** [document] envoyer en fax.

fax machine *n* fax *m*, télécopieur *m*.

fax modem *n* modem *m* fax.

fax number *n* numéro *m* de fax.

faze [feɪz] *vt* inf démonter, déconcerter.

FBI (*abbr of* **Federal Bureau of Investigation**) *n* FBI *m*.

FCC (*abbr of* **Federal Communications Commission**) *n* conseil fédéral de l'audiovisuel aux États-Unis, ≃ CSA *m*.

FCO (*abbr of* **Foreign and Commonwealth**

Office) *n* ministère britannique des affaires étrangères et du Commonwealth.

FD (*abbr of* **Fire Department**) *n* sapeurs-pompiers.

FDA *n* - **1**. (*abbr of* **Food and Drug Administration**) administration délivrant l'autorisation de mise sur le marché des médicaments et des produits alimentaires aux États-Unis - **2**. (*abbr of* **Association of First Division Civil Servants**) syndicat britannique des hauts fonctionnaires.

FE *n abbr of* **Further Education**.

fear [fɪəʳ] <> *n* - **1**. (*U*) [feeling] peur *f* - **2**. [object of fear] crainte *f* - **3**. [risk] risque *m* ; **for ~ of** de peur de (+ *infin*), de peur que (+ *subjunctive*) <> *vt* - **1**. [be afraid of] craindre, avoir peur de - **2**. [anticipate] craindre ; **to ~ (that)** ... craindre que ..., avoir peur que ... <> *vi* [be afraid] : **to ~ for sb/sthg** avoir peur pour qqn/qqch, craindre pour qqn/qqch.

fearful ['fɪəfʊl] *adj* - **1**. *fml* [frightened] peureux(euse) ; **to be ~ of sthg** avoir peur de qqch - **2**. [frightening] effrayant(e).

fearless ['fɪəlɪs] *adj* intrépide.

fearlessly ['fɪəlɪslɪ] *adv* courageusement.

fearsome ['fɪəsəm] *adj* [temper] effroyable.

feasibility [,fi:zə'bɪlətɪ] *n* (*U*) possibilité *f*.

feasibility study *n* étude *f* de faisabilité.

feasible ['fi:zəbl] *adj* faisable, possible.

feast [fi:st] <> *n* [meal] festin *m*, banquet *m* <> *vi* : **to ~ on** *or* **off sthg** se régaler de qqch.

feat [fi:t] *n* exploit *m*, prouesse *f*.

feather ['feðəʳ] *n* plume *f*.

feather bed *n* lit *m* de plume.

featherbrained ['feðəbreɪnd] *adj* [person] écervelé(e) ; [idea, scheme] inconsidéré(e).

featherweight ['feðəweɪt] *n* [boxer] poids *m* plume.

feature ['fi:tʃəʳ] <> *n* - **1**. [characteristic] caractéristique *f* - **2**. GEOGR particularité *f* - **3**. [article] article *m* de fond - **4**. RADIO & TV émission *f* spéciale, spécial *m* - **5**. CINEMA long métrage *m* <> *vt* - **1**. [subj : film, exhibition] mettre en vedette ; **featuring James Dean** avec, dans le rôle principal, James Dean - **2**. [comprise] présenter, comporter <> *vi* : **to ~ (in)** figurer en vedette (dans).

 ◆ **features** *npl* [of face] traits *mpl*.

feature film *n* long métrage *m*.

featureless ['fi:tʃəlɪs] *adj* sans trait distinctif.

Feb. [feb] (*abbr of* **February**) févr.

February ['febrʊərɪ] *n* février *m* ; *see also* **September**.

feces Am = **faeces**.

feckless ['feklɪs] *adj* inepte.

fed [fed] *pt* & *pp* ⊏> **feed**.

Fed [fed] <> *n* inf (*abbr of* **Federal Reserve Board**) organe de contrôle de la Banque centrale américaine <> - **1**. *abbr of* **federal** - **2**. *abbr of* **federation**.

federal ['fedrəl] *adj* fédéral(e).

Federal Bureau of Investigation *n* FBI *m*, ≃ police *f* judiciaire.

federalism ['fedrəlɪzm] *n* fédéralisme *m*.

federation [,fedə'reɪʃn] *n* fédération *f*.

fed up *adj* : **to be ~ (with)** en avoir marre (de).

fee [fi:] *n* [of school] frais *mpl* ; [of doctor] honoraires *mpl* ; [for membership] cotisation *f* ; [for entrance] tarif *m*, prix *m*.

feeble ['fi:bəl] *adj* faible.

feebleminded [,fi:bl'maɪndɪd] *adj* débile.

feebleness ['fi:blnɪs] *n* faiblesse *f*.

feebly ['fi:blɪ] *adv* faiblement.

feed [fi:d] (*pt* & *pp* **fed**) <> *vt* - **1**. [give food to] nourrir - **2**. [fire, fears etc] alimenter - **3**. [put, insert] : **to ~ sthg into sthg** mettre *or* insérer qqch dans qqch <> *vi* - **1**. [take food] : **to ~ (on** *or* **off)** se nourrir (de) - **2**. [be strengthened] : **to ~ on** *or* **off sthg** s'appuyer sur <> *n* - **1**. [for baby] repas *m* - **2**. [animal food] nourriture *f*.

feedback ['fi:dbæk] *n* (*U*) - **1**. [reaction] réactions *fpl* - **2**. ELEC réaction *f*, rétroaction *f*.

feedbag ['fi:dbæg] *n* Am musette *f* (mangeoire).

feeder ['fi:dəʳ] <> *n* [eater] mangeur *m*, -euse *f* <> *comp* [road, railway line] secondaire.

feeding bottle ['fi:dɪŋ-] *n* Br biberon *m*.

feel [fi:l] (*pt* & *pp* **felt**) <> *vt* - **1**. [touch] toucher - **2**. [sense, experience, notice] sentir ; [emotion] ressentir ; **to ~ o.s. doing sthg** se sentir faire qqch - **3**. [believe] : **to ~ (that)** ... croire que ..., penser que ... - **4**. *phr* : **I'm not ~ing myself today** je ne suis pas dans mon assiette aujourd'hui <> *vi* - **1**. [have sensation] : **to ~ cold/hot/sleepy** avoir froid/chaud/sommeil ; **to ~ safe** se sentir en sécurité ; **to ~ like sthg/like doing sthg** [be in mood for] avoir envie de qqch/de faire qqch - **2**. [have emotion] se sentir ; **to ~ angry** être en colère - **3**. [seem] sembler ; **it ~s strange** ça fait drôle ; **it ~s like leather** on dirait du cuir - **4**. [by touch] : **to ~ for sthg** chercher qqch <> *n* - **1**. [sensation, touch] toucher *m*, sensation *f* - **2**. [atmosphere] atmosphère *f* - **3**. *phr* : **to have a ~ for sthg** avoir l'instinct pour qqch.

feeler ['fi:ləʳ] *n* antenne *f*.

feelgood ['fiːlgʊd] adj inf qui donne la pêche ; **the ~ factor** l'optimisme m ambiant.

feeling ['fiːlɪŋ] n - **1.** [emotion] sentiment m ; **I know the ~** je sais ce que c'est ; **bad ~** animosité f, hostilité f - **2.** [physical sensation] sensation f - **3.** [intuition, sense] sentiment m, impression f - **4.** [understanding] sensibilité f ; **to have a ~ for sthg** comprendre OR apprécier qqch.
◆ **feelings** npl sentiments mpl ; **to hurt sb's ~s** blesser (la sensibilité de) qqn ; **no hard ~s!** sans rancune!

fee-paying [-ˌpeɪɪŋ] adj Br [pupil] d'un établissement privé ; [school] privé(e).

feet [fiːt] pl ⊳ **foot.**

feign [feɪn] vt fml feindre.

feint [feɪnt] ◇ n feinte f ◇ vi feinter.

feisty ['faɪstɪ] (compar -ier ; superl -iest) adj inf [lively] plein(e) d'entrain ; [combative] qui a du cran.

felicitous [fɪ'lɪsɪtəs] adj fml heureux(euse).

feline ['fiːlaɪn] ◇ adj félin(e) ◇ n félin m.

fell [fel] ◇ pt ⊳ **fall** ◇ vt [tree, person] abattre.
◆ **fells** npl GEOGR lande f.

fellow ['feləʊ] ◇ n - **1.** dated [man] homme m - **2.** [comrade, peer] camarade m, compagnon m - **3.** [of society, college] membre m, associé m ◇ adj : **one's ~ men** ses semblables ; **~ feeling** sympathie f ; **~ passenger** compagnon m, compagne f (de voyage) ; **~ student** camarade mf (d'études).

fellowship ['feləʊʃɪp] n - **1.** [comradeship] amitié f, camaraderie f - **2.** [society] association f, corporation f - **3.** [of society, college] titre m de membre OR d'associé.

felony ['felənɪ] (pl -ies) n JUR crime m, forfait m.

felt [felt] ◇ pt & pp ⊳ **feel** ◇ n (U) feutre m.

felt-tip pen n stylo-feutre m.

female ['fiːmeɪl] ◇ adj [person] de sexe féminin ; [animal, plant] femelle ; [sex, figure] féminin(e) ; **~ student** étudiante f ; **~ worker** travailleuse f, ouvrière f ◇ n femelle f.

feminine ['femɪnɪn] ◇ adj féminin(e) ◇ n GRAMM féminin m.

femininity [ˌfemɪ'nɪnətɪ] n (U) féminité f.

feminism ['femɪnɪzm] n féminisme m.

feminist ['femɪnɪst] n féministe mf.

fence [fens] ◇ n [barrier] clôture f ; **to sit on the ~** fig ménager la chèvre et le chou ◇ vt clôturer, entourer d'une clôture.
◆ **fence off** vt sep séparer par une clôture

fencing ['fensɪŋ] n - **1.** SPORT escrime f - **2.** [material] clôture f.

fend [fend] vi : **to ~ for o.s.** se débrouiller tout seul.
◆ **fend off** vt sep [blows] parer ; [questions, reporters] écarter.

fender ['fendər] n - **1.** [round fireplace] pare-feu m inv - **2.** [on boat] défense f - **3.** Am [on car] aile f.

fennel ['fenl] n fenouil m.

fens [fenz] npl Br marais mpl.

feral ['fɪərəl] adj sauvage.

ferment [n 'fɜːment, vb fə'ment] ◇ n (U) [unrest] agitation f, effervescence f ; **in ~** en effervescence ◇ vi [wine, beer] fermenter.

fermentation [ˌfɜːmən'teɪʃn] n fermentation f.

fermented [fə'mentɪd] adj fermenté(e).

fern [fɜːn] n fougère f.

ferocious [fə'rəʊʃəs] adj féroce.

ferociously [fə'rəʊʃəslɪ] adv férocement, avec férocité.

ferocity [fə'rɒsətɪ] n férocité f.

ferret ['ferɪt] n furet m.
◆ **ferret about, ferret around** vi inf fureter un peu partout.
◆ **ferret out** vt sep inf dénicher.

ferris wheel ['ferɪs-] n esp Am grande roue f.

ferry ['ferɪ] ◇ n ferry m, ferry-boat m ; [smaller] bac m ◇ vt transporter.

ferryboat ['ferɪbəʊt] n = **ferry.**

ferryman ['ferɪmən] (pl -men [-mən]) n passeur m.

fertile ['fɜːtaɪl] adj - **1.** [land, imagination] fertile, fécond(e) - **2.** [woman] féconde.

fertility [fə'tɪlətɪ] n - **1.** [of land, imagination] fertilité f - **2.** [of woman] fécondité f.

fertility drug n traitement m contre la stérilité.

fertilization [ˌfɜːtɪlaɪ'zeɪʃn] n - **1.** [of soil] fertilisation f - **2.** [of egg] fécondation f.

fertilize, -ise ['fɜːtɪlaɪz] vt - **1.** [soil] fertiliser, amender - **2.** [egg] féconder.

fertilizer ['fɜːtɪlaɪzər] n engrais m.

fervent ['fɜːvənt] adj fervent(e).

fervour Br, **fervor** Am ['fɜːvər] n ferveur f.

fester ['festər] vi - **1.** [wound, sore] suppurer - **2.** [emotion, quarrel] s'aigrir.

festival ['festəvl] n - **1.** [event, celebration] festival m - **2.** [holiday] fête f.

festive ['festɪv] adj de fête.

festive season n : **the ~** la période des fêtes.

festivities [fes'tıvətız] *npl* réjouissances *fpl*.

festoon [fe'stu:n] *vt* décorer de guirlandes ; **to be ~ed with** être décoré de.

fetal ['fi:tl] = **foetal**.

fetch [fetʃ] *vt* - **1.** [go and get] aller chercher - **2.** [raise - money] rapporter.

fetching ['fetʃıŋ] *adj* séduisant(e).

fete, fête [feɪt] ◇ *n* fête *f*, kermesse *f* ◇ *vt* fêter, faire fête à.

> **FETE**
>
> Les « village fêtes » en Grande-Bretagne, où l'on vend en plein air des produits faits maison et où l'on organise des manifestations sportives et des jeux pour enfants, sont généralement destinées à réunir des fonds pour une œuvre de charité.

fetid ['fetɪd] *adj* fétide.

fetish ['fetɪʃ] *n* - **1.** [sexual obsession] objet *m* de fétichisme - **2.** [mania] manie *f*, obsession *f*.

fetishism ['fetɪʃızml] *n* fétichisme *m*.

fetlock ['fetlɒk] *n* boulet *m*.

fetter ['fetəʳ] *vt* [person] enchaîner ; [movements] entraver.

➤ **fetters** *npl* fers *mpl*, chaînes *fpl*.

fettle ['fetl] *n* : **in fine ~** en pleine forme.

fetus ['fi:təs] = **foetus**.

feud [fju:d] ◇ *n* querelle *f* ◇ *vi* se quereller.

feudal ['fju:dl] *adj* féodal(e).

fever ['fi:vəʳ] *n* fièvre *f*.

fevered ['fi:vəd] *adj* fiévreux(euse).

feverish ['fi:vərıʃ] *adj* fiévreux(euse).

fever pitch *n* comble *m*.

few [fju:] ◇ *adj* peu de ; **the first ~ pages** les toutes premières pages ; **quite a ~, a good ~** pas mal de, un bon nombre de ; **~ and far between** rares ◇ *pron* peu ; **a ~** quelques-uns *mpl*, quelques-unes *fpl*.

fewer ['fju:əʳ] ◇ *adj* moins (de) ; **no ~ than** pas moins de ◇ *pron* moins.

fewest ['fju:əst] *adj* le moins (de).

FH Br *abbr of* **fire hydrant**.

FHA (*abbr of* **Federal Housing Administration**) *n organisme de gestion des logements sociaux aux États-Unis*.

fiancé [fı'ɒnseı] *n* fiancé *m*.

fiancée [fı'ɒnseı] *n* fiancée *f*.

fiasco [fı'æskəʊ] (Br *pl* **-s**, Am *pl* **-es**) *n* fiasco *m*.

fib [fıb] (*pt* & *pp* **-bed** ; *cont* **-bing**) inf ◇ *n* bobard *m*, blague *f* ◇ *vi* raconter des bobards OR des blagues.

fibber ['fıbəʳ] *n* inf menteur *m*, -euse *f*.

fibre Br, **fiber** Am ['faıbəʳ] *n* fibre *f*.

fibreboard Br, **fiberboard** Am ['faıbəbɔ:d] *n* (U) panneau *m* de fibres.

fibreglass Br, **fiberglass** Am ['faıbəglɑːs] ◇ *n* (U) fibre *f* de verre ◇ *comp* en fibre de verre.

fibre optics *n* (U) fibre *f* optique.

fibroid ['faıbrɔıd] *n* fibrome *m*.

fibrositis [ˌfaıbrə'saıtıs] *n* fibrosite *f*.

FICA (*abbr of* **Federal Insurance Contributions Act**) *n loi américaine régissant les cotisations sociales*.

fickle ['fıkl] *adj* versatile.

fiction ['fıkʃn] *n* fiction *f*.

fictional ['fıkʃənl] *adj* fictif(ive).

fictionalize, -ise ['fıkʃənəlaız] *vt* romancer.

fictitious [fık'tıʃəs] *adj* [false] fictif(ive).

fiddle ['fıdl] ◇ *vi* [play around] : **to ~ with sthg** tripoter qqch ◇ *vt* Br inf truquer ◇ *n* - **1.** [violin] violon *m* ; **to be (as) fit as a ~** se porter comme un charme ; **to play second ~ (to sb)** jouer un rôle secondaire (auprès de qqn), passer au second plan (auprès de qqn) - **2.** Br inf [fraud] combine *f*, escroquerie *f*.

➤ **fiddle about, fiddle around** *vi* - **1.** [fidget] ne pas se tenir tranquille, s'agiter ; **to ~ about with sthg** tripoter qqch - **2.** [waste time] perdre son temps.

fiddler ['fıdləʳ] *n* joueur *m*, -euse *f* de violon.

fiddly ['fıdlı] (*compar* **-ier** ; *superl* **-iest**) *adj* Br inf délicat(e).

fidelity [fı'delıtı] *n* - **1.** [loyalty] fidélité *f* - **2.** [accuracy - of report] fidélité *f*.

fidget ['fıdʒıt] *vi* remuer.

fidgety ['fıdʒıtı] *adj* inf remuant(e).

fiduciary [fı'dju:ʃıərı] (*pl* **-ies**) ◇ *adj* fiduciaire ◇ *n* fiduciaire *mf*.

field [fi:ld] ◇ *n* - **1.** [gen & COMPUT] champ *m* ; **~ of vision** champ de vision - **2.** [for sports] terrain *m* - **3.** [of knowledge] domaine *m* - **4.** [real environment] : **in the ~** sur le terrain ◇ *vi* tenir le champ.

field day *n* : **to have a ~** s'en donner à cœur joie.

fielder ['fi:ldəʳ] *n* joueur *m* qui tient le champ.

field event *n* compétition *f* d'athlétisme (*hormis la course*).

field glasses *npl* jumelles *fpl*.

field marshal *n* ≃ maréchal *m* (de France).

field mouse *n* mulot *m*.

field trip *n* voyage *m* d'étude.

fieldwork ['fiːldwɜːk] *n (U)* recherches *fpl* sur le terrain.

fieldworker ['fiːldwɜːkəʳ] *n* chercheur *m*, -euse *f* OR enquêteur *m*, -trice *f* sur le terrain.

fiend [fiːnd] *n* - **1.** [cruel person] monstre *m* - **2.** inf [fanatic] fou *m*, folle *f*, mordu *m*, -e *f*.

fiendish ['fiːndɪʃ] *adj* - **1.** [evil] abominable - **2.** inf [very difficult, complex] compliqué(e), complexe.

fierce [fɪəs] *adj* féroce ; [heat] torride ; [storm, temper] violent(e).

fiercely ['fɪəslɪ] *adv* férocement ; [attack] violemment ; [defend] avec acharnement.

fiery ['faɪərɪ] *(compar* -**ier** ; *superl* -**iest)** *adj* - **1.** [burning] ardent(e) - **2.** [spicy] très piquant(e) - **3.** [volatile - speech] enflammé(e) ; [- temper, person] fougueux(euse) - **4.** [bright red] flamboyant(e).

FIFA ['fiːfə] *(abbr of* **Fédération Internationale de Football Association)** *n* FIFA *f*.

fifteen [fɪf'tiːn] *num* quinze ; *see also* **six**.

fifteenth [ˌfɪf'tiːnθ] *num* quinzième ; *see also* **sixth**.

fifth [fɪfθ] *num* cinquième ; *see also* **sixth**.

Fifth Amendment *n* : **the ~** le Cinquième Amendement *(qui garantit les droits des inculpés, aux États-Unis)*.

fifth column *n* cinquième colonne *f*.

fiftieth ['fɪftɪəθ] *num* cinquantième ; *see also* **sixth**.

fifty ['fɪftɪ] *num* cinquante ; *see also* **sixty**.

fifty-fifty <> *adj* moitié-moitié, fifty-fifty ; **to have a ~ chance** avoir cinquante pour cent de chances <> *adv* moitié-moitié, fifty-fifty.

fig [fɪg] *n* figue *f*.

fight [faɪt] *(pt & pp* **fought)** <> *n* - **1.** [physical] bagarre *f* ; **to have a ~ (with sb)** se battre (avec qqn), se bagarrer (avec qqn) ; **to put up a ~** se battre, se défendre - **2.** fig [battle, struggle] lutte *f*, combat *m* - **3.** [argument] dispute *f* ; **to have a ~ (with sb)** se disputer (avec qqn) <> *vt* - **1.** [physically] se battre contre OR avec - **2.** [conduct - war] mener - **3.** [enemy, racism] combattre <> *vi* - **1.** [in war, punch-up] se battre - **2.** fig [struggle] : **to ~ for/against sthg** lutter pour/contre qqch - **3.** [argue] : **to ~ (about OR over)** se battre OR se disputer (à propos de).

 fight back <> *vt fus* refouler <> *vi* riposter.

 fight off *vt sep* - **1.** [attacker] repousser - **2.** [illness, desire] venir à bout de.

 fight out *vt sep :* **leave them to ~ it out** laisse-les se bagarrer et régler cela entre eux.

fighter ['faɪtəʳ] *n* - **1.** [plane] avion *m* de chasse, chasseur *m* - **2.** [soldier] combattant *m* - **3.** [combative person] battant *m*, -e *f*.

fighting ['faɪtɪŋ] *n (U)* [punch-up] bagarres *fpl* ; [in war] conflits *mpl*.

fighting chance *n :* **to have a ~** avoir une petite chance.

figment ['fɪgmənt] *n :* **a ~ of sb's imagination** le fruit de l'imagination de qqn.

figurative ['fɪgərətɪv] *adj* - **1.** [meaning] figuré(e) - **2.** ART figuratif(ive).

figuratively ['fɪgərətɪvlɪ] *adv* au figuré.

figure [Br 'fɪgəʳ, Am 'fɪgjər] <> *n* - **1.** [statistic, number] chiffre *m* ; **to put a ~ on sthg** chiffrer qqch - **2.** [human shape, outline] silhouette *f*, forme *f* - **3.** [personality, diagram] figure *f* - **4.** [shape of body] ligne *f* <> *vt esp Am* [suppose] penser, supposer <> *vi* [feature] figurer, apparaître.

 figure out *vt sep* [understand] comprendre ; [find] trouver.

figurehead ['fɪgəhed] *n* - **1.** [on ship] figure *f* de proue - **2.** fig & pej [leader] homme *m* de paille.

figure of eight Br, **figure eight** Am *n* huit *m inv*.

figure of speech *n* figure *f* de rhétorique.

figure skating *n* patinage *m* artistique.

figurine [Br 'fɪgəriːn, Am ˌfɪgjəˈriːn] *n* figurine *f*.

Fiji ['fiːdʒiː] *n* Fidji *fpl* ; **in ~** à Fidji.

Fijian [ˌfiːˈdʒiːən] <> *adj* fidjien(enne) <> *n* Fidjien *m*, -enne *f*.

filament ['fɪləmənt] *n* [in light bulb] filament *m*.

filch [fɪltʃ] *vt* inf chiper.

file [faɪl] <> *n* - **1.** [folder, report] dossier *m* ; **on ~, on the ~s** répertorié dans les dossiers - **2.** COMPUT fichier *m* - **3.** [tool] lime *f* - **4.** [line] : **in single ~** en file indienne <> *vt* - **1.** [document] classer - **2.** JUR - accusation, complaint] porter, déposer ; [- lawsuit] intenter - **3.** [fingernails, wood] limer <> *vi* - **1.** [walk in single file] marcher en file indienne - **2.** JUR : **to ~ for divorce** demander le divorce.

file clerk Am = **filing clerk**.

filename ['faɪlˌneɪm] *n* COMPUT nom *m* de fichier.

filet Am = **fillet**.

filibuster ['fɪlɪbʌstəʳ] *vi esp Am* POL faire de l'obstruction parlementaire.

filigree ['fɪlɪgriː] <> *adj* en filigrane <> *n* filigrane *m*.

filing cabinet [ˈfaɪlɪŋ-] n classeur m, fichier m.

filing clerk [ˈfaɪlɪŋ-] n Br documentaliste mf.

Filipino [ˌfɪlɪˈpiːnəʊ] (pl -s) ⬦ adj philippin(e) ⬦ n Philippin m, -e f.

fill [fɪl] ⬦ vt - **1.** [gen] remplir ; **to ~ sthg with sthg** remplir qqch de qqch - **2.** [gap, hole] boucher - **3.** [vacancy - subj : employer] pourvoir à ; [- subj : employee] prendre ⬦ n : **to eat one's ~** manger à sa faim ; **to have had one's ~ of sthg** en avoir assez de qqch.
➡ **fill in** ⬦ vt sep - **1.** [form] remplir - **2.** [inform] : **to ~ sb in (on)** mettre qqn au courant (de) ⬦ vt fus : **I'm just ~ing in time** je fais ça en attendant ⬦ vi [substitute] : **to ~ in for sb** remplacer qqn.
➡ **fill out** ⬦ vt sep [form] remplir ⬦ vi [get fatter] prendre de l'embonpoint.
➡ **fill up** ⬦ vt sep remplir ⬦ vi se remplir.

filled [fɪld] adj - **1.** [roll] garni(e) - **2.** [with emotion] : **~ (with)** plein(e) (de).

filler [ˈfɪlər] n [for cracks] mastic m.

filler cap n Br bouchon m du réservoir d'essence.

fillet Br, **filet** Am [ˈfɪlɪt] n filet m.

fillet steak n filet m de bœuf.

fill-in n inf pis-aller m inv.

filling [ˈfɪlɪŋ] ⬦ adj très nourrissant(e) ⬦ n - **1.** [in tooth] plombage m - **2.** [in cake, sandwich] garniture f.

filling station n station-service f.

fillip [ˈfɪlɪp] n coup m de fouet.

filly [ˈfɪlɪ] (pl -ies) n pouliche f.

film [fɪlm] ⬦ n - **1.** [movie] film m - **2.** [layer, for camera] pellicule f - **3.** [footage] images fpl ⬦ vt & vi filmer.

filming [ˈfɪlmɪŋ] n (U) tournage m.

film star n vedette f de cinéma.

filmstrip [ˈfɪlmstrɪp] n film m fixe.

film studio n studio m (de cinéma).

Filofax® [ˈfaɪləʊfæks] n Filofax® m.

filter [ˈfɪltər] ⬦ n filtre m ⬦ vt [coffee] passer ; [water, oil, air] filtrer ⬦ vi [people] : **to ~ in** entrer par petits groupes.
➡ **filter out** vt sep filtrer.
➡ **filter through** vi filtrer.

filter coffee n café m filtre.

filter lane n Br ≃ voie f de droite.

filter paper n papier m filtre.

filter-tipped [-ˈtɪpt] adj à bout filtre.

filth [fɪlθ] n (U) - **1.** [dirt] saleté f, crasse f - **2.** [obscenity] obscénités fpl.

filthy [ˈfɪlθɪ] (compar -ier ; superl -iest) adj - **1.** [very dirty] dégoûtant(e), répugnant(e) - **2.** [obscene] obscène.

filtration plant [fɪlˈtreɪʃn-] n station f d'épuration.

Fimbra [ˈfɪmbrə] (abbr of **Financial Intermediaries, Managers and Brokers Regulatory Association**) n organisme britannique contrôlant les activités des courtiers d'assurances.

fin [fɪn] n - **1.** [of fish] nageoire f - **2.** Am [for swimmer] palme f.

final [ˈfaɪnl] ⬦ adj - **1.** [last] dernier(ère) - **2.** [at end] final(e) - **3.** [definitive] définitif(ive) ⬦ n finale f.
➡ **finals** npl UNIV examens mpl de dernière année.

final demand n dernier avertissement m.

finale [fɪˈnɑːlɪ] n finale m.

finalist [ˈfaɪnəlɪst] n finaliste mf.

finalize, -ise [ˈfaɪnəlaɪz] vt mettre au point.

finally [ˈfaɪnəlɪ] adv enfin.

finance [n ˈfaɪnæns, vb faɪˈnæns] ⬦ n (U) finance f ⬦ vt financer.
➡ **finances** npl finances fpl.

financial [fɪˈnænʃl] adj financier(ère).

financial adviser n conseiller financier m, conseillère financière f.

financially [fɪˈnænʃəlɪ] adv financièrement.

financial services npl services mpl financiers.

financial year Br, **fiscal year** Am n exercice m.

financier [fɪˈnænsɪər] n Br financier m.

finch [fɪntʃ] n fringillidé m.

find [faɪnd] (pt & pp **found**) ⬦ vt - **1.** [gen] trouver ; **to ~ one's way** trouver son chemin - **2.** [realize] : **to ~ (that)** ... s'apercevoir que ... - **3.** JUR : **to be found guilty/not guilty (of)** être déclaré(e) coupable/non coupable (de) ⬦ n trouvaille f.
➡ **find out** ⬦ vi se renseigner ⬦ vt fus - **1.** [information] se renseigner sur - **2.** [truth] découvrir, apprendre ⬦ vt sep démasquer.

findings [ˈfaɪndɪŋz] npl conclusions fpl.

fine [faɪn] ⬦ adj - **1.** [good - work] excellent(e) ; [- building, weather] beau (belle) - **2.** [perfectly satisfactory] très bien ; **I'm ~** ça va bien - **3.** [thin, smooth] fin(e) - **4.** [minute - detail, distinction] subtil(e) ; [- adjustment, tuning] délicat(e) ⬦ adv [very well] très bien ⬦ n amende f ⬦ vt condamner à une amende.

fine arts npl beaux-arts mpl.

finely ['faɪnlɪ] *adv* - **1.** [chopped, ground] fin - **2.** [tuned, balanced] délicatement.

fineness ['faɪnnɪs] *n* finesse *f*.

finery ['faɪnərɪ] *n (U)* parure *f*.

finesse [fɪ'nes] *n* finesse *f*.

fine-tooth comb *n* : to go over sthg with a ~ passer qqch au peigne fin.

fine-tune *vt* [mechanism] régler au quart de tour ; fig régler minutieusement.

finger ['fɪŋgər] ⬦ *n* doigt *m* ; to keep one's ~s crossed croiser les doigts ; she didn't lay a ~ on him elle n'a pas touché un cheveu de sa tête ; he didn't lift a ~ to help il n'a pas levé le petit doigt ; to point a OR the ~ at sb [accuse] accuser qqn ; to put one's ~ on sthg mettre le doigt sur qqch ; to twist sb round one's little ~ faire ce qu'on veut de qqn ⬦ *vt* [feel] palper.

fingermark ['fɪŋgəmɑːk] *n* trace *f* de doigt.

fingernail ['fɪŋgəneɪl] *n* ongle *m* (de la main).

fingerprint ['fɪŋgəprɪnt] *n* empreinte *f* (digitale) ; to take sb's ~s prendre les empreintes de qqn.

fingertip ['fɪŋgətɪp] *n* bout *m* du doigt ; at one's ~s sur le bout des doigts.

finicky ['fɪnɪkɪ] *adj pej* [eater, task] difficile ; [person] tatillon(onne).

finish ['fɪnɪʃ] ⬦ *n* - **1.** [end] fin *f* ; [of race] arrivée *f* - **2.** [texture] finition *f* ⬦ *vt* finir, terminer ; to ~ doing sthg finir OR terminer de faire qqch ⬦ *vi* finir, terminer ; [school, film] se terminer.
➤ **finish off** *vt sep* finir, terminer.
➤ **finish up** *vi* finir.
➤ **finish with** *vt fus* [friend] en finir avec ; [boyfriend, girlfriend] rompre avec.

finished ['fɪnɪʃt] *adj* - **1.** [ready, done, over] fini(e), terminé(e) - **2.** [no longer interested] : to be ~ with sthg en avoir fini avec qqch - **3.** *inf* [done for] fichu(e).

finishing line ['fɪnɪʃɪŋ-] *n* ligne *f* d'arrivée.

finishing school ['fɪnɪʃɪŋ-] *n* école privée pour jeunes filles surtout axée sur l'enseignement des bonnes manières.

finite ['faɪnaɪt] *adj* fini(e).

Finland ['fɪnlənd] *n* Finlande *f* ; in ~ en Finlande.

Finn [fɪn] *n* Finlandais *m*, -e *f*.

Finnish ['fɪnɪʃ] ⬦ *adj* finlandais(e), finnois(e) ⬦ *n* [language] finnois *m*.

fiord [fjɔːd] = fjord.

fir [fɜːr] *n* sapin *m*.

fire ['faɪər] ⬦ *n* - **1.** [gen] feu *m* ; on ~ en feu ;

to catch ~ prendre feu ; to set ~ to sthg mettre le feu à qqch - **2.** [out of control] incendie *m* - **3.** Br [heater] appareil *m* de chauffage - **4.** *(U)* [shooting] coups *mpl* de feu ; to open ~ (on) ouvrir le feu (sur) ⬦ *vt* - **1.** [shoot] tirer - **2.** fig [questions, accusations] lancer - **3.** esp Am [dismiss] renvoyer ⬦ *vi* : to ~ (on OR at) faire feu (sur), tirer (sur).

fire alarm *n* avertisseur *m* d'incendie.

firearm ['faɪərɑːm] *n* arme *f* à feu.

fireball ['faɪəbɔːl] *n* boule *f* de feu.

firebomb ['faɪəbɒm] ⬦ *n* bombe *f* incendiaire ⬦ *vt* lancer des bombes incendiaires à.

firebreak ['faɪəbreɪk] *n* pare-feu *m inv*.

fire brigade Br, **fire department** Am *n* sapeurs-pompiers *mpl*.

fire chief Am = fire master.

firecracker ['faɪəkrækər] *n* pétard *m*.

fire-damaged *adj* endommagé(e) par le feu.

fire department Am = fire brigade.

fire door *n* porte *f* coupe-feu.

fire drill *n* exercice *m* d'évacuation en cas d'incendie.

fire-eater *n* [performer] avaleur *m* de feu.

fire engine *n* voiture *f* de pompiers.

fire escape *n* escalier *m* de secours.

fire extinguisher *n* extincteur *m* d'incendie.

fire fighter *n* pompier *m*.

fireguard ['faɪəgɑːd] *n* garde-feu *m inv*.

fire hazard *n* : to be a ~ présenter un risque d'incendie.

fire hydrant [-'haɪdrənt], **fireplug** Am ['faɪəplʌg] *n* bouche *f* d'incendie.

firelight ['faɪəlaɪt] *n (U)* lueur *f* du feu.

firelighter ['faɪəlaɪtər] *n* allume-feu *m inv*.

fireman ['faɪəmən] (*pl* -men [-mən]) *n* pompier *m*.

fire master Br, **fire chief** Am *n* capitaine *m* des pompiers.

fireplace ['faɪəpleɪs] *n* cheminée *f*.

fireplug Am = fire hydrant.

firepower ['faɪə,paʊər] *n* puissance *f* de feu.

fireproof ['faɪəpruːf] *adj* ignifugé(e).

fire-raiser [-,reɪzər] *n* Br pyromane *mf*.

fire regulations *npl* consignes *fpl* en cas d'incendie.

fire service *n* Br sapeurs-pompiers *mpl*.

fireside ['faɪəsaɪd] *n* : by the ~ au coin du feu.

fire station *n* caserne *f* des pompiers.

firewood ['faɪəwʊd] *n* bois *m* de chauffage.

firework ['faɪəwɜːk] *n* fusée *f* de feu d'artifice.

➤ **fireworks** *npl* [outburst of anger] étincelles *fpl*.

firework display *n* feu *m* d'artifice.

firing ['faɪərɪŋ] *n* (U) MIL tir *m*, fusillade *f*.

firing squad *n* peloton *m* d'exécution.

firm [fɜːm] ◇ *adj* - **1.** [gen] ferme ; **to stand ~** tenir bon - **2.** [support, structure] solide - **3.** [evidence, news] certain(e) ◇ *n* firme *f*, société *f*.
➤ **firm up** ◇ *vt sep* - **1.** [prices, trade] renforcer - **2.** [agreement] rendre définitif(ive) ◇ *vi* [prices, trade] se renforcer.

firmly ['fɜːmlɪ] *adv* fermement.

firmness ['fɜːmnɪs] *n* - **1.** [gen] fermeté *f* - **2.** [discipline] rigueur *f* - **3.** [of beliefs] force *f*.

first [fɜːst] ◇ *adj* premier(ère) ; **for the ~ time** pour la première fois ; **~ thing in the morning** tôt le matin ; **~ things ~** commençons par le plus important ; **I don't know the ~ thing about it** je ne sais absolument rien là-dessus, je n'y connais rien du tout ◇ *adv* - **1.** [before anyone else] en premier - **2.** [before anything else] d'abord ; **~ of all** tout d'abord - **3.** [for the first time] (pour) la première fois ◇ *n* - **1.** [person] premier *m*, -ère *f* - **2.** [unprecedented event] première *f* - **3.** Br UNIV *diplôme universitaire avec mention très bien.*
➤ **at first** *adv* d'abord.
➤ **at first hand** *adv* de première main.

first aid *n* (U) premiers secours *mpl*.

first-aider [-'eɪdəʳ] *n* secouriste *mf*.

first-aid kit *n* trousse *f* de premiers secours.

first-class *adj* - **1.** [excellent] excellent(e) - **2.** Br UNIV avec mention très bien - **3.** [ticket, compartment] de première classe ; [stamp, letter] tarif normal.

first-class mail *n* courrier *m* tarif normal.

first cousin *n* cousin germain *m*, cousine germaine *f*.

first day cover *n* émission *f* du premier jour.

first-degree *adj* - **1.** MED : **~ burn** brûlure *f* au premier degré - **2.** Am JUR : **~ murder** ≃ homicide *m* volontaire.

first floor *n* Br premier étage *m* ; Am rez-de-chaussée *m inv*.

firsthand [fɜːst'hænd] *adj* & *adv* de première main.

first lady *n* première dame *f* du pays, femme *f* du Président.

first language *n* langue *f* maternelle.

first lieutenant *n* lieutenant *m*.

firstly ['fɜːstlɪ] *adv* premièrement.

first mate *n* second *m*.

First Minister *n* [in Scottish Parliament] président *m* du Parlement écossais.

first name *n* prénom *m*.
➤ **first-name** *adj* : **to be on first-name terms with sb** appeler qqn par son prénom.

first night *n* première *f*.

first offender *n* délinquant *m* primaire.

first officer = **first mate.**

first-past-the-post system *n* Br système *m* majoritaire simple.

first-rate *adj* excellent(e).

first refusal *n* priorité *f*.

First Secretary *n* [in Welsh Assembly] président *m* de l'Assemblée galloise.

First World War *n* : **the ~** la Première Guerre Mondiale.

firtree ['fɜːtriː] = **fir.**

FIS (*abbr of Family Income Supplement*) *n* *complément familial en Grande-Bretagne.*

fiscal ['fɪskl] *adj* fiscal(e).

fiscal year Am = **financial year.**

fish [fɪʃ] (*pl inv*) ◇ *n* poisson *m* ◇ *vt* [river, sea] pêcher dans ◇ *vi* - **1.** [fisherman] : **to ~ (for sthg)** pêcher (qqch) - **2.** [try to obtain] : **to ~ for** [compliments] essayer de s'attirer ; [information] essayer d'obtenir.
➤ **fish out** *vt sep* inf sortir, extirper.

fish and chips *npl* Br poisson *m* frit avec frites.

fish and chip shop *n* Br endroit où l'on *vend du poisson frit et des frites.*

fishbowl ['fɪʃbəʊl] *n* bocal *m* (à poissons).

fishcake ['fɪʃkeɪk] *n* croquette *f* de poisson.

fisherman ['fɪʃəmən] (*pl* -men [-mən]) *n* pêcheur *m*.

fishery ['fɪʃərɪ] (*pl* -ies) *n* pêcherie *f*.

fish-eye lens *n* objectif *m* ultra-grand angle.

fish factory *n* usine *f* piscicole.

fish farm *n* centre *m* de pisciculture.

fish fingers Br, **fish sticks** Am *npl* bâtonnets *mpl* de poisson panés.

fishhook ['fɪʃhʊk] *n* hameçon *m*.

fishing ['fɪʃɪŋ] *n* pêche *f* ; **to go ~** aller à la pêche.

fishing boat *n* bateau *m* de pêche.

fishing line *n* ligne *f*.

fishing rod *n* canne *f* à pêche.

fishmonger ['fɪʃ,mʌŋgəʳ] *n* esp Br poissonnier *m*, -ère *f* ; **~'s (shop)** poissonnerie *f*.

fishnet ['fɪʃnet] n - **1.** [for fishing] filet m - **2.** [material] : ~ **stockings/tights** bas mpl/ collant m résille.

fish slice n Br pelle f à poisson.

fish sticks Am = fish fingers.

fishwife ['fɪʃwaɪf] (pl -wives [-waɪvz]) n pej mégère f.

fishy ['fɪʃɪ] (compar -ier; superl -iest) adj - **1.** [smell, taste] de poisson - **2.** [suspicious] louche.

fission ['fɪʃn] n fission f.

fissure ['fɪʃəʳ] n fissure f.

fist [fɪst] n poing m.

fit [fɪt] (pt & pp -ted; cont -ting) ◇ adj - **1.** [suitable] convenable; **to be ~ for** sthg être bon (bonne) à qqch; **to be ~ to do** sthg être apte à faire qqch; **to see** OR **think ~ (to do** sthg) juger bon (de faire qqch) - **2.** [healthy] en forme; **to keep ~** se maintenir en forme ◇ n - **1.** [of clothes, shoes etc] ajustement m; **it's a tight ~** c'est un peu juste; **it's a good ~** c'est la bonne taille - **2.** [epileptic seizure] crise f; **to have a ~** avoir une crise; fig piquer une crise - **3.** [bout - of crying] crise f; [- of rage] accès m; [- of sneezing] suite f; **in ~s and starts** par à-coups ◇ vt - **1.** [be correct size for] aller à - **2.** [place] : **to ~ sthg into** sthg insérer qqch dans qqch - **3.** [provide] : **to ~ sthg with** sthg équiper OR munir qqch de qqch - **4.** [be suitable for] correspondre à - **5.** [for clothes] : **to be fitted for** essayer ◇ vi [be correct size, go] aller; [into container] entrer.
◆ **fit in** ◇ vt sep [accommodate] prendre ◇ vi s'intégrer; **to ~ in with** sthg correspondre à qqch; **to ~ in with** sb s'accorder à qqn.

fitful ['fɪtful] adj [sleep] agité(e); [wind, showers] intermittent(e).

fitment ['fɪtmənt] n meuble m encastré.

fitness ['fɪtnɪs] n (U) - **1.** [health] forme f - **2.** [suitability] : ~ **(for)** aptitude f (pour).

fitted ['fɪtəd] adj - **1.** [suited] : ~ **for** OR **to** apte à; **to be ~ to do** sthg être apte à faire qqch - **2.** [tailored - shirt, jacket] ajusté(e); ~ **sheet** drap-housse m - **3.** Br [built-in] encastré(e).

fitted carpet [ˌfɪtəd-] n moquette f.

fitted kitchen [ˌfɪtəd-] n Br cuisine f intégrée OR équipée.

fitter ['fɪtəʳ] n [mechanic] monteur m.

fitting ['fɪtɪŋ] ◇ adj fml approprié(e) ◇ n - **1.** [part] appareil m - **2.** [for clothing] essayage m.
◆ **fittings** npl installations fpl.

fitting room n cabine f d'essayage.

five [faɪv] num cinq; see also **six**.

five-day week n semaine f de cinq jours.

fiver ['faɪvəʳ] n inf - **1.** Br [amount] cinq livres fpl; [note] billet m de cinq livres - **2.** Am [amount] cinq dollars mpl; [note] billet m de cinq dollars.

five-star adj [hotel] cinq étoiles; [treatment] exceptionnel(elle).

fix [fɪks] ◇ vt - **1.** [gen] fixer; **to ~ sthg to** sthg fixer qqch à qqch - **2.** [in memory] graver - **3.** [repair] réparer - **4.** inf [rig] truquer - **5.** [food, drink] préparer ◇ n - **1.** inf [difficult situation] : **to be in a ~** être dans le pétrin - **2.** drugs sl piqûre f.
◆ **fix up** vt sep - **1.** [provide] : **to ~ sb up with** sthg obtenir qqch pour qqn - **2.** [arrange] arranger.

fixation [fɪk'seɪʃn] n : ~ **(on** OR **about)** obsession f (de).

fixed [fɪkst] adj - **1.** [attached] fixé(e) - **2.** [set, unchanging] fixe; [smile] figé(e).

fixed assets npl immobilisations fpl.

fixture ['fɪkstʃəʳ] n - **1.** [furniture] installation f - **2.** [permanent feature] tradition f bien établie - **3.** SPORT rencontre f (sportive).

fizz [fɪz] ◇ vi [lemonade, champagne] pétiller; [fireworks] crépiter ◇ n [sound] pétillement m.

fizzle ['fɪzl] ◆ **fizzle out** vi [fire] s'éteindre; [firework] se terminer; [interest, enthusiasm] se dissiper.

fizzy ['fɪzɪ] (compar -ier; superl -iest) adj pétillant(e).

fjord [fjɔːd] n fjord m.

FL abbr of Florida.

flab [flæb] n graisse f.

flabbergasted ['flæbəgɑːstɪd] adj sidéré(e).

flabby ['flæbɪ] (compar -ier; superl -iest) adj mou (molle).

flaccid ['flæsɪd] adj flasque.

flag [flæg] (pt & pp -ged; cont -ging) ◇ n drapeau m ◇ vi [person, enthusiasm, energy] faiblir; [conversation] traîner.
◆ **flag down** vt sep [taxi] héler; **to ~ sb down** faire signe à qqn de s'arrêter.

Flag Day n [in US] le 14 juin, jour férié qui commémore la création du drapeau américain.

flag of convenience n pavillon m de complaisance.

flagon ['flægən] n - **1.** [bottle] bonbonne f - **2.** [jug] cruche f.

flagpole ['flægpəʊl] n mât m.

flagrant ['fleɪgrənt] adj flagrant(e).

flagship ['flægʃɪp] n - **1.** [ship] vaisseau m amiral - **2.** fig [product] produit m vedette; [company] fleuron m.

flagstone ['flægstəʊn] n dalle f.

flail [fleɪl] *vi* battre l'air.

flair [fleə'] *n* - **1.** [talent] don *m ;* **to have a ~ for sthg** avoir un don pour qqch - **2.** *(U)* [stylishness] style *m*.

flak [flæk] *n (U)* - **1.** [gunfire] tir *m* antiaérien - **2.** inf [criticism] critiques *fpl* sévères.

flake [fleɪk] ⇔ *n* [of paint, plaster] écaille *f ;* [of snow] flocon *m ;* [of skin] petit lambeau *m* ⇔ *vi* [paint, plaster] s'écailler ; [skin] peler.

➣ **flake out** *vi* inf s'écrouler de fatigue.

flaky ['fleɪkɪ] (*compar* **-ier ;** *superl* **-iest**) *adj* - **1.** [flaking - skin] qui pèle ; [- paintwork] écaillé(e) ; [- texture] floconneux(euse) - **2.** Am inf [person] barjo.

flaky pastry *n (U)* pâte *f* feuilletée.

flambé ['flɑ:mbeɪ] (*pt* & *pp* **-ed ;** *cont* **-ing**) ⇔ *adj* flambé(e) ⇔ *vt* flamber.

flamboyant [flæm'bɔɪənt] *adj* - **1.** [showy, confident] extravagant(e) - **2.** [brightly coloured] flamboyant(e).

flame [fleɪm] ⇔ *n* flamme *f ;* **in ~s** en flammes ; **to burst into ~s** s'enflammer ; **old ~** ancien béguin *m* ⇔ *vi* - **1.** [be on fire] flamber - **2.** [redden] s'empourprer.

flameproof ['fleɪmpru:f] *adj* [dish] allant au feu.

flame-retardant [-rɪ'tɑ:dənt] *adj* qui ralentit la propagation des flammes.

flame-thrower [-ˌθrəʊə'] *n* lance-flammes *m inv*.

flaming ['fleɪmɪŋ] *adj* - **1.** [fire-coloured] flamboyant(e) - **2.** Br [very angry] furibond(e) - **3.** Br inf [expressing annoyance] foutu(e), fichu(e).

flamingo [flə'mɪŋgəʊ] (*pl* **-s** OR **-es**) *n* flamant *m* rose.

flammable ['flæməbl] *adj* inflammable.

flan [flæn] *n* tarte *f*.

Flanders ['flɑ:ndəz] *n* Flandre *f*, Flandres *fpl*.

flange [flændʒ] *n* bride *f*.

flank [flæŋk] ⇔ *n* flanc *m* ⇔ *vt :* **to be ~ed by** être flanqué(e) de.

flannel ['flænl] *n* - **1.** [fabric] flanelle *f* - **2.** Br [facecloth] gant *m* de toilette.

➣ **flannels** *npl* pantalon *m* de flanelle.

flannelette [flænə'let] *n* pilou *m*.

flap [flæp] (*pt* & *pp* **-ped ;** *cont* **-ping**) ⇔ *n* - **1.** [of envelope, pocket] rabat *m ;* [of skin] lambeau *m* - **2.** inf [panic] : **in a ~** paniqué(e) ⇔ *vt* & *vi* battre.

flapjack ['flæpdʒæk] *n* - **1.** Br [biscuit] biscuit *m* à l'avoine - **2.** Am [pancake] crêpe *f* épaisse.

flare [fleə'] ⇔ *n* [distress signal] fusée *f* éclairante ⇔ *vi* - **1.** [burn brightly] : **to ~ (up)** s'embraser - **2.** [intensify] : **to ~ (up)** [war, revolution] s'intensifier soudainement ; [person] s'emporter - **3.** [widen - trousers, skirt] s'évaser ; [- nostrils] se dilater.

➣ **flares** *npl* Br pantalon *m* à pattes d'éléphant.

flared [fleəd] *adj* [trousers] à pattes d'éléphant ; [skirt] évasé(e).

flash [flæʃ] ⇔ *adj* - **1.** PHOT au flash - **2.** inf [expensive-looking] tape-à-l'œil *(inv)* ⇔ *n* - **1.** [of light, colour] éclat *m ;* **~ of lightning** éclair *m* - **2.** PHOT flash *m* - **3.** [sudden moment] éclair *m ;* **in a ~** en un rien de temps ; **quick as a ~** rapide comme l'éclair ⇔ *vt* - **1.** [shine] projeter ; **to ~ one's headlights** faire un appel de phares - **2.** [send out - signal, smile] envoyer ; [- look] jeter - **3.** [show] montrer ⇔ *vi* - **1.** [torch] briller - **2.** [light - on and off] clignoter ; [eyes] jeter des éclairs - **3.** [rush] : **to ~ by** OR **past** passer comme un éclair - **4.** [thought] : **to ~ into one's mind** venir soudainement à l'esprit - **5.** [appear] surgir.

flashback ['flæʃbæk] *n* flash-back *m*, retour *m* en arrière.

flashbulb ['flæʃbʌlb] *n* ampoule *f* de flash.

flash card *n* carte portant un mot, une image etc utilisée comme aide à l'apprentissage.

flashcube ['flæʃkju:b] *n* flash *m* en forme de cube.

flasher ['flæʃə'] *n* - **1.** Br [light] clignotant *m* - **2.** Br inf [man] exhibitionniste *m*.

flash flood *n* crue *f* subite.

flashgun ['flæʃgʌn] *n* flash *m*.

flashlight ['flæʃlaɪt] *n* [torch] lampe *f* électrique.

flash point *n* - **1.** [moment] moment *m* critique - **2.** [place] point *m* chaud.

flashy ['flæʃɪ] (*compar* **-ier ;** *superl* **-iest**) *adj* inf tape-à-l'œil *(inv)*.

flask [flɑ:sk] *n* - **1.** [thermos flask] Thermos® *m* or *f* - **2.** CHEM ballon *m* - **3.** [hip flask] flasque *f*.

flat [flæt] (*compar* **-ter ;** *superl* **-test**) ⇔ *adj* - **1.** [gen] plat(e) - **2.** [tyre] crevé(e) - **3.** [refusal, denial] catégorique - **4.** [business, trade] calme - **5.** [dull - voice, tone] monotone ; [- performance, writing] terne - **6.** [MUS - person] qui chante trop grave ; [- note] bémol - **7.** [fare, price] fixe - **8.** [beer, lemonade] éventé(e) - **9.** [battery] à plat ⇔ *adv* - **1.** [level] à plat - **2.** [absolutely] : **~ broke** complètement fauché(e) - **3.** [exactly] : **two hours ~** deux heures pile - **4.** MUS faux ⇔ *n* - **1.** Br [apartment] appartement *m* - **2.** MUS bémol *m*.

➣ **flat out** *adv* [work] d'arrache-pied ; [travel - subj : vehicle] le plus vite possible.

flat cap *n* Br casquette *f*.

flat-chested [-'tʃestɪd] *adj* plate comme une limande.

flatfish ['flætfɪʃ] (*pl inv*) *n* poisson *m* plat.

flat-footed [-'fʊtɪd] *adj* aux pieds plats.

flatlet ['flætlɪt] *n* Br studio *m*.

flatly ['flætlɪ] *adv* - **1.** [absolutely] catégoriquement - **2.** [dully - say] avec monotonie ; [- perform] de façon terne.

flatmate ['flætmeɪt] *n* Br *personne avec laquelle on partage un appartement.*

flat racing *n (U)* courses *fpl* de plat.

flat rate *n* tarif *m* forfaitaire.

flatten ['flætn] *vt* - **1.** [make flat - steel, paper] aplatir ; [- wrinkles, bumps] aplanir ; **to ~ o.s. against sthg** s'aplatir contre qqch - **2.** [destroy] raser - **3.** inf [knock out] assommer.

➤ **flatten out** ⬦ *vi* s'aplanir ⬦ *vt sep* aplanir.

flatter ['flætər] *vt* flatter ; **to ~ o.s. (that)** se flatter (*de + infin*).

flatterer ['flætərər] *n* flatteur *m*, -euse *f*.

flattering ['flætərɪŋ] *adj* - **1.** [complimentary] flatteur(euse) - **2.** [clothes] seyant(e).

flattery ['flætərɪ] *n* flatterie *f*.

flatulence ['flætjʊləns] *n* flatulence *f*.

flatware ['flætweər] *n (U)* Am couverts *mpl*.

flaunt [flɔːnt] *vt* faire étalage de.

flautist Br ['flɔːtɪst], **flutist** Am ['fluːtɪst] *n* flûtiste *mf*.

flavour Br, **flavor** Am ['fleɪvər] ⬦ *n* - **1.** [of food] goût *m* ; [of ice cream, yoghurt] parfum *m* - **2.** fig [atmosphere] atmosphère *f* ⬦ *vt* parfumer.

flavouring Br, **flavoring** Am ['fleɪvərɪŋ] *n (U)* parfum *m*.

flaw [flɔː] *n* [in material, character] défaut *m* ; [in plan, argument] faille *f*.

flawed [flɔːd] *adj* [material, character] qui présente des défauts ; [plan, argument] qui présente des failles.

flawless ['flɔːlɪs] *adj* parfait(e).

flax [flæks] *n* lin *m*.

flay [fleɪ] *vt* [skin] écorcher.

flea [fliː] *n* puce *f* ; **to send sb away with a ~ in his/her ear** envoyer promener qqn.

flea market *n* marché *m* aux puces.

fleck [flek] ⬦ *n* moucheture *f*, petite tache *f* ⬦ *vt* : **~ed with** moucheté(e) de.

fled [fled] *pt* & *pp* ⬦ **flee**.

fledg(e)ling ['fledʒlɪŋ] ⬦ *adj* [industry] nouveau(elle) ; [doctor, democracy] jeune ⬦ *n* oisillon *m*.

flee [fliː] (*pt* & *pp* **fled**) *vt* & *vi* fuir.

fleece [fliːs] ⬦ *n* toison *f* ⬦ *vt* inf escroquer.

fleet [fliːt] *n* - **1.** [of ships] flotte *f* - **2.** [of cars, buses] parc *m*.

fleeting ['fliːtɪŋ] *adj* [moment] bref (brève) ; [look] fugitif(ive) ; [visit] éclair (*inv*).

Fleet Street *n rue de Londres dont le nom est utilisé pour désigner la presse britannique.*

FLEET STREET

> Cette rue de la City est traditionnellement celle des journaux. Aujourd'hui, beaucoup de journaux ont établi leur siège dans d'autres quartiers, notamment les Docklands. Cependant, le terme « Fleet Street » est encore employé pour désigner la presse et le monde du journalisme.

Fleming ['flemɪŋ] *n* Flamand *m*, -e *f*.

Flemish ['flemɪʃ] ⬦ *adj* flamand(e) ⬦ *n* [language] flamand *m* ⬦ *npl* : **the ~** les Flamands *mpl*.

flesh [fleʃ] *n* chair *f* ; **his/her ~ and blood** [family] les siens ; **in the ~** en chair et en os.

➤ **flesh out** *vt sep* étoffer.

flesh wound *n* blessure *f* superficielle.

fleshy ['fleʃɪ] (*compar* -**ier** ; *superl* -**iest**) *adj* [arms] charnu(e) ; [person] bien en chair ; [cheeks] joufflu(e).

flew [fluː] *pt* ⬦ **fly**.

flex [fleks] ⬦ *n* ELEC fil *m* ⬦ *vt* [bend] fléchir.

flexibility ['fleksə'bɪlətɪ] *n* flexibilité *f*.

flexible ['fleksəbl] *adj* flexible.

flexitime ['fleksɪtaɪm] *n (U)* horaire *m* à la carte OR flexible.

flick [flɪk] ⬦ *n* - **1.** [of whip, towel] petit coup *m* - **2.** [with finger] chiquenaude *f* ⬦ *vt* - **1.** [whip, towel] donner un petit coup de - **2.** [with finger - remove] enlever d'une chiquenaude ; [- throw] envoyer d'une chiquenaude - **3.** [switch] appuyer sur.

➤ **flicks** *npl* inf : **the ~s** le ciné.

➤ **flick through** *vt fus* feuilleter.

flicker ['flɪkər] ⬦ *n* - **1.** [of light, candle] vacillement *m* - **2.** [of hope, interest] lueur *f* ⬦ *vi* - **1.** [candle, light] vaciller - **2.** [shadow] trembler ; [eyelids] ciller.

flick knife *n* Br couteau *m* à cran d'arrêt.

flier ['flaɪər] *n* - **1.** [pilot] aviateur *m*, -trice *f* - **2.** esp Am [advertising leaflet] prospectus *m*.

flight [flaɪt] *n* - **1.** [gen] vol *m* ; **~ of fancy** OR **of the imagination** envolée *f* de l'imagination - **2.** [of steps, stairs] volée *f* - **3.** [escape] fuite *f*.

flight attendant n steward m, hôtesse f de l'air.

flight crew n équipage m.

flight deck n - **1.** [of aircraft carrier] pont m d'envol - **2.** [of plane] cabine f de pilotage.

flight path n trajectoire f.

flight recorder n enregistreur m de vol.

flighty ['flaɪtɪ] (compar -ier ; superl -iest) adj frivole.

flimsy ['flɪmzɪ] (compar -ier ; superl -iest) adj [dress, material] léger(ère) ; [building, bookcase] peu solide ; [excuse] piètre.

flinch [flɪntʃ] vi tressaillir ; **to ~ from sthg/ from doing sthg** reculer devant qqch/à l'idée de faire qqch.

fling [flɪŋ] (pt & pp flung) <> n [affair] aventure f, affaire f <> vt lancer ; **to ~ o.s. into an armchair/onto the ground** se jeter dans un fauteuil/par terre.

flint [flɪnt] n - **1.** [rock] silex m - **2.** [in lighter] pierre f.

flip [flɪp] (pt & pp -ped ; cont -ping) <> vt - **1.** [turn - pancake] faire sauter ; [- record] tourner - **2.** [switch] appuyer sur - **3.** [flick] envoyer d'une chiquenaude ; **to ~ a coin** jouer à pile ou face <> vi [lose control] flipper ; inf [become angry] piquer une colère <> n - **1.** [flick] chiquenaude f - **2.** [somersault] saut m périlleux.

➣ **flip through** vt fus feuilleter.

flip-flop n [shoe] tong f.

flippant ['flɪpənt] adj désinvolte.

flippantly ['flɪpəntlɪ] adv avec désinvolture.

flipper ['flɪpər] n - **1.** [of animal] nageoire f - **2.** [for swimmer, diver] palme f.

flipping ['flɪpɪŋ] Br inf <> adj fichu(e) <> adv sacrément.

flip side n [of record] face f B.

flirt [flɜːt] <> n flirt m <> vi - **1.** [with person] : **~ (with sb)** flirter (avec qqn) - **2.** [with idea] : **to ~ with sthg** caresser qqch.

flirtation [flɜːˈteɪʃn] n - **1.** [gen] flirt m - **2.** [brief interest] : **to have a ~ with sthg** caresser qqch.

flirtatious [flɜːˈteɪʃəs] adj flirteur(euse).

flit [flɪt] (pt & pp -ted ; cont -ting) vi - **1.** [bird] voleter - **2.** [expression, idea] : **to ~ across** traverser.

float [fləʊt] <> n - **1.** [for buoyancy] flotteur m - **2.** [in procession] char m - **3.** [money] petite caisse f <> vt - **1.** [on water] faire flotter - **2.** [idea, project] lancer <> vi [on water] flotter ; [through air] glisser.

floating ['fləʊtɪŋ] adj - **1.** [on water] flottant(e) - **2.** [transitory] instable.

floating voter n Br électeur indécis m, électrice indécise f.

flock [flɒk] <> n - **1.** [of birds] vol m ; [of sheep] troupeau m - **2.** fig [of people] foule f <> vi : **to ~ to** aller en masse à.

floe [fləʊ] n banquise f.

flog [flɒg] (pt & pp -ged ; cont -ging) vt - **1.** [whip] flageller - **2.** Br inf [sell] refiler.

flood [flʌd] <> n - **1.** [of water] inondation f - **2.** [great amount] déluge m, avalanche f <> vt - **1.** [with water, light] inonder - **2.** [overwhelm] : **to ~ sthg (with)** inonder qqch (de) ; **to ~ the market** inonder le marché <> vi - **1.** [river] déborder - **2.** [street, land] être inondé(e) - **3.** [arrive in great amounts] : **applications have ~ed in** on a été inondé de demandes ; **to ~ back** revenir en foule.

➣ **floods** npl - **1.** [of water] inondations fpl - **2.** fig [of tears] torrents mpl.

floodgates ['flʌdgeɪts] npl : **to open the ~** ouvrir les vannes.

flooding ['flʌdɪŋ] n (U) inondations fpl.

floodlight ['flʌdlaɪt] n projecteur m.

floodlit ['flʌdlɪt] adj [match, ground] éclairé(e) (avec des projecteurs) ; [building] illuminé(e).

flood tide n marée f haute.

floor [flɔːr] <> n - **1.** [of room] sol m ; [of club, disco] piste f - **2.** [of valley, sea, forest] fond m - **3.** [storey] étage m - **4.** [at meeting, debate] auditoire m - **5.** ST EX corbeille f <> vt - **1.** [knock down] terrasser - **2.** [baffle] dérouter.

floorboard ['flɔːbɔːd] n plancher m.

floor cloth n Br serpillière f.

flooring ['flɔːrɪŋ] n planchéiage m.

floor lamp n Am lampadaire m.

floor show n spectacle m de cabaret.

floorwalker ['flɔːˌwɔːkər] n surveillant m, -e f de magasin.

floozy ['fluːzɪ] (pl -ies) n dated & pej pouffiasse f.

flop [flɒp] (pt & pp -ped ; cont -ping) inf <> n [failure] fiasco m <> vi - **1.** [fail] être un fiasco - **2.** [fall - subj : person] s'affaler.

floppy ['flɒpɪ] (compar -ier ; superl -iest) adj [flower] flasque ; [collar] lâche.

floppy (disk) n disquette f, disque m souple.

flora ['flɔːrə] n flore f ; **~ and fauna** la flore et la faune.

floral ['flɔːrəl] adj floral(e) ; [pattern, dress] à fleurs.

Florence ['flɒrəns] n Florence.

floret ['flɒrɪt] *n* [of cauliflower, broccoli] bouquet *m*.

florid ['flɒrɪd] *adj* **- 1.** [red] rougeaud(e) **- 2.** [extravagant] fleuri(e).

Florida ['flɒrɪdə] *n* Floride *f* ; **in ~** en Floride.

florist ['flɒrɪst] *n* fleuriste *mf* ; **~'s (shop)** magasin *m* de fleuriste.

floss [flɒs] ◇ *n (U)* **- 1.** [silk] bourre *f* de soie **- 2.** [dental floss] fil *m* dentaire ◇ *vt* : **to ~ one's teeth** se nettoyer les dents au fil dentaire.

flotation [fləʊ'teɪʃn] *n* COMM lancement *m*.

flotilla [flə'tɪlə] *n* flottille *f*.

flotsam ['flɒtsəm] *n (U)* : **~ and jetsam** débris *mpl* ; **fig** épaves *fpl*.

flounce [flaʊns] ◇ *n* volant *m* ◇ *vi* : **to ~ out/off** sortir/partir dans un mouvement d'humeur.

flounder ['flaʊndə'] *(pl inv OR -s)* ◇ *n* flet *m* ◇ *vi* **- 1.** [in water, mud, snow] patauger **- 2.** [in conversation] bredouiller.

flour ['flaʊə'] *n* farine *f*.

flourish ['flʌrɪʃ] ◇ *vi* [plant, flower] bien pousser ; [children] être en pleine santé ; [company, business] prospérer ; [arts] s'épanouir ◇ *vt* brandir ◇ *n* grand geste *m*.

flourishing ['flʌrɪʃɪŋ] *adj* [plant, garden] florissant(e) ; [children] resplendissant(e) de santé ; [company, arts] prospère.

flout [flaʊt] *vt* bafouer.

flow [fləʊ] ◇ *n* **- 1.** [movement - of water, information] circulation *f* ; [- of funds] mouvement *m* ; [- of words] flot *m* **- 2.** [of tide] flux *m* ◇ *vi* **- 1.** [gen] couler **- 2.** [traffic, days, weeks] s'écouler **- 3.** [tide] monter **- 4.** [hair, clothes] flotter **- 5.** [result] : **to ~ from** découler de.

flow chart, flow diagram *n* organigramme *m*.

flower ['flaʊə'] ◇ *n* fleur *f* ◇ *comp* [arrangement, pattern] floral(e) ◇ *vi* **- 1.** [bloom] fleurir **- 2.** fig [flourish] s'épanouir.

flowerbed ['flaʊəbed] *n* parterre *m*.

flowered ['flaʊəd] *adj* à fleurs.

flowering ['flaʊərɪŋ] ◇ *adj* à fleurs ◇ *n* épanouissement *m*.

flowerpot ['flaʊəpɒt] *n* pot *m* de fleurs.

flowery ['flaʊərɪ] *(compar* -ier ; *superl* -iest) *adj* **- 1.** [dress, material] à fleurs **- 2.** pej [style] fleuri(e).

flowing ['fləʊɪŋ] *adj* [water, writing] coulant(e) ; [hair, robes] flottant(e).

flown [fləʊn] *pp* ⊳ **fly.**

fl. oz. *abbr of* **fluid ounce.**

flu [flu:] *n (U)* grippe *f* ; **to have ~** avoir la grippe.

fluctuate ['flʌktʃʊeɪt] *vi* fluctuer.

fluctuation [ˌflʌktʃʊ'eɪʃn] *n* fluctuation *f*.

flue [flu:] *n* conduit *m*, tuyau *m*.

fluency ['flu:ənsɪ] *n* aisance *f* ; **~ in French** aisance à s'exprimer en français.

fluent ['flu:ənt] *adj* **- 1.** [in foreign language] : **to speak ~ French** parler couramment le français ; **to be ~ (in French)** parler couramment (le français) **- 2.** [writing, style] coulant(e), aisé(e).

fluently ['flu:əntlɪ] *adv* **- 1.** [speak - in foreign language] couramment **- 2.** [read, speak, write] avec aisance.

fluff [flʌf] ◇ *n (U)* **- 1.** [down] duvet *m* **- 2.** [dust] moutons *mpl* ◇ *vt* **- 1.** [puff up] faire bouffer **- 2.** inf [do badly] rater.

fluffy ['flʌfɪ] *(compar* -ier ; *superl* -iest) *adj* duveteux(euse) ; [toy] en peluche.

fluid ['flu:ɪd] ◇ *n* fluide *m* ; [in diet, for cleaning] liquide *m* ◇ *adj* **- 1.** [flowing] fluide **- 2.** [unfixed] changeant(e).

fluid ounce *n* = 0,03 litre.

fluke [flu:k] *n* inf [chance] coup *m* de bol.

flummox ['flʌməks] *vt* inf désarçonner.

flung [flʌŋ] *pt* & *pp* ⊳ **fling.**

flunk [flʌŋk] esp Am inf ◇ *vt* **- 1.** [exam, test] rater **- 2.** [student] recaler ◇ *vi* se faire recaler.

fluorescent [flʊə'resənt] *adj* fluorescent(e).

fluorescent light *n* lumière *f* fluorescente.

fluoridate ['flʊərɪdeɪt] *vt* fluorurer.

fluoride ['flʊəraɪd] *n* fluorure *m*.

fluorine ['flʊəri:n] *n* fluor *m*.

flurry ['flʌrɪ] *(pl* -ies) *n* **- 1.** [of snow] rafale *f*, averse *f* **- 2.** fig [of objections] concert *m* ; [of activity, excitement] débordement *m*.

flush [flʌʃ] ◇ *adj* **- 1.** [level] : **~ with** de niveau avec **- 2.** inf [rich] plein(e) aux as ◇ *n* **- 1.** [in lavatory] chasse *f* d'eau **- 2.** [blush] rougeur *f* **- 3.** [sudden feeling] accès *m* ; **in the first ~ of** sthg literary dans la première ivresse de qqch ◇ *vt* **- 1.** [toilet] : **to ~ the toilet** tirer la chasse d'eau ; **to ~ sthg down the toilet** faire partir qqch en tirant la chasse d'eau **- 2.** [force out of hiding] : **to ~ sb out** déloger qqn ◇ *vi* [blush] rougir.

flushed [flʌʃt] *adj* **- 1.** [red-faced] rouge **- 2.** [excited] : **~ with** exalté(e) par.

fluster ['flʌstə'] ◇ *n* trouble *m* ◇ *vt* troubler.

flustered ['flʌstəd] *adj* troublé(e).

flute [flu:t] *n* MUS flûte *f*.

fluted ['flu:tɪd] *adj* cannelé(e).

flutist Am = flautist.

flutter ['flʌtər] ◇ n - **1.** [of wings] battement m - **2.** [of heart] palpitation f - **3.** inf [of excitement] émoi m ◇ vt battre ◇ vi - **1.** [bird, insect] voleter ; [wings] battre - **2.** [flag, dress] flotter - **3.** [heart] palpiter.

flux [flʌks] n [change] : **to be in a state of ~** être en proie à des changements permanents.

fly [flaɪ] (pl **flies**, pt **flew**, pp **flown**) ◇ n - **1.** [insect] mouche f ; **a ~ in the ointment** fig un ennui, un hic - **2.** [of trousers] braguette f ◇ vt - **1.** [kite, plane] faire voler - **2.** [passengers, supplies] transporter par avion - **3.** [flag] faire flotter ◇ vi - **1.** [bird, insect, plane] voler - **2.** [pilot] faire voler un avion - **3.** [passenger] voyager en avion - **4.** [move fast, pass quickly] filer ; **time flies** comme le temps passe - **5.** [rumours, stories] se répandre comme une traînée de poudre - **6.** [attack] : **to ~ at sb** sauter sur qqn - **7.** [flag] flotter.

◆ **fly away** vi s'envoler.

◆ **fly in** ◇ vt sep envoyer par avion ◇ vi [plane] arriver ; [person] arriver par avion.

◆ **fly into** vt fus : **to ~ into a rage/temper** s'emporter.

◆ **fly out** ◇ vt sep envoyer par avion ◇ vi [plane] partir ; [person] partir en avion.

flyby ['flaɪˌbaɪ] Am = flypast.

fly-fishing n pêche f à la mouche.

fly half n Br demi m d'ouverture.

flying ['flaɪɪŋ] ◇ adj volant(e) ◇ n aviation f ; **to like ~** aimer prendre l'avion.

flying colours npl : **to pass (sthg) with ~** réussir (qqch) haut la main.

flying doctor n médecin m volant.

flying officer n Br lieutenant m de l'armée de l'air.

flying picket n piquet m de grève volant.

flying saucer n soucoupe f volante.

flying squad n Br force d'intervention rapide de la police.

flying start n : **to get off to a ~** prendre un départ sur les chapeaux de roue.

flying visit n visite f éclair.

flyleaf ['flaɪliːf] (pl **-leaves** [-liːvz]) n page f de garde.

flyover ['flaɪˌəʊvər] n Br autopont m.

flypast ['flaɪˌpɑːst] n Br défilé m aérien.

flysheet ['flaɪʃiːt] n auvent m.

fly spray n insecticide m.

flyweight ['flaɪweɪt] n poids m mouche.

flywheel ['flaɪwiːl] n volant m.

FM n - **1.** (abbr of **frequency modulation**) FM f - **2.** abbr of **field marshal**.

FMB (abbr of **Federal Maritime Board**) n conseil supérieur de la marine marchande américaine.

FMCS (abbr of **Federal Mediation and Conciliation Services**) n organisme américain de conciliation des conflits du travail.

FO (abbr of **Foreign Office**) n ministère britannique des affaires étrangères.

foal [fəʊl] n poulain m.

foam [fəʊm] ◇ n (U) - **1.** [bubbles] mousse f - **2.** : **~ (rubber)** caoutchouc m Mousse® ◇ vi [water, champagne] mousser.

foamy ['fəʊmɪ] (compar **-ier** ; superl **-iest**) adj [with bubbles] mousseux(euse).

fob [fɒb] (pt & pp **-bed** ; cont **-bing**) ◆ **fob off** vt sep repousser ; **to ~ sthg off on sb** refiler qqch à qqn ; **to ~ sb off with sthg** se débarrasser de qqn à l'aide de qqch.

FOB, f.o.b. (abbr of **free on board**) FOB, F.o.b.

fob watch n montre f de gousset.

foc (abbr of **free of charge**) Fco.

focal ['fəʊkl] adj lit & fig focal(e).

focal point n foyer m ; fig point m central.

focus ['fəʊkəs] (pl **-cuses** [-kəsiːz] OR **-ci** [-kaɪ]) ◇ n - **1.** PHOT mise f au point ; **in ~** net ; **out of ~** flou - **2.** [centre - of rays] foyer m ; [- of earthquake] centre m ; **~ of attention** centre d'attention ◇ vt [lens, camera] mettre au point ; **to ~ sthg on** [lens, camera, eyes] ajuster qqch sur ; [attention] concentrer qqch sur ◇ vi - **1.** [with camera, lens] se fixer ; [eyes] accommoder ; **to ~ on sthg** [with camera, lens] se fixer sur qqch ; [with eyes] fixer qqch - **2.** [attention] : **to ~ on sthg** se concentrer sur qqch.

fodder ['fɒdər] n (U) fourrage m.

foe [fəʊ] n literary ennemi m.

FOE n - **1.** (abbr of **Friends of the Earth**) AT mpl - **2.** (abbr of **Fraternal Order of Eagles**) organisation caritative américaine.

foetal ['fiːtl] adj [position] fœtal(e) ; [death] du fœtus.

foetus ['fiːtəs] n fœtus m.

fog [fɒg] n (U) brouillard m.

fogbound ['fɒgbaʊnd] adj bloqué(e) par le brouillard.

fogey ['fəʊgɪ] = fogy.

foggiest ['fɒgɪəst] n inf : **I haven't the ~** je n'en ai pas la moindre idée.

foggy ['fɒgɪ] (compar **-ier** ; superl **-iest**) adj [misty] brumeux(euse).

foghorn ['fɒghɔːn] n sirène f de brume.

fog lamp n feu m de brouillard.

fogy ['fəʊgɪ] (*pl* **-ies**) *n* inf : **old ~** vieux machin *m*.

foible ['fɔɪbl] *n* marotte *f*.

foil [fɔɪl] ◇ *n* **- 1.** (U) [metal sheet - of tin, silver] feuille *f* ; [- CULIN] papier *m* d'aluminium **- 2.** [contrast] : **to be a ~ to** OR **for** servir de repoussoir *m* à ◇ *vt* déjouer.

foist [fɔɪst] *vt* : **to ~ sthg on sb** imposer qqch à qqn.

fold [fəʊld] ◇ *vt* **- 1.** [bend, close up] plier ; **to ~ one's arms** croiser les bras **- 2.** [wrap] envelopper ◇ *vi* **- 1.** [close up - table, chair] se plier ; [- petals, leaves] se refermer **- 2.** inf [company, project] échouer ; THEATRE quitter l'affiche ◇ *n* **- 1.** [in material, paper] pli *m* **- 2.** [for animals] parc *m* **- 3.** fig [spiritual home] : **the ~** le bercail.
➤ **fold up** ◇ *vt sep* plier ◇ *vi* **- 1.** [close up - table, map] se plier ; [- petals, leaves] se refermer **- 2.** [company, project] échouer.

foldaway ['fəʊldə,weɪ] *adj* pliant(e).

folder ['fəʊldəʳ] *n* **- 1.** [for papers - wallet] chemise *f* ; [- binder] classeur *m* **- 2.** COMPUT classeur *m*.

folding ['fəʊldɪŋ] *adj* [table, umbrella] pliant(e) ; [doors] en accordéon.

foliage ['fəʊlɪɪdʒ] *n* feuillage *m*.

folk [fəʊk] ◇ *adj* [art, dancing] folklorique ; [medicine] populaire ◇ *npl* [people] gens *mpl* ◇ *n* [music] musique *f* folk.
➤ **folks** *npl* inf **- 1.** [relatives] famille *f* **- 2.** [everyone] : **hi there ~s!** bonjour tout le monde !

folklore ['fəʊklɔːʳ] *n* folklore *m*.

folk music *n* musique *f* folk.

folk singer *n* chanteur *m*, -euse *f* folk.

folk song *n* chanson *f* folk.

folksy ['fəʊksɪ] (*compar* **-ier** ; *superl* **-iest**) *adj* Am inf sympa (*inv*), décontract (*inv*).

follicle ['fɒlɪkl] *n* follicule *m*.

follow ['fɒləʊ] ◇ *vt* suivre ; **(to be) ~ed by sthg** (être) suivi de qqch ◇ *vi* **- 1.** [gen] suivre ; **as ~s** comme suit **- 2.** [be logical] tenir debout ; **it ~s that ...** il s'ensuit que ...
➤ **follow up** *vt sep* **- 1.** [pursue - idea, suggestion] prendre en considération ; [- advertisement] donner suite à **- 2.** [complete] : **to ~ sthg up with** faire suivre qqch de.

follower ['fɒləʊəʳ] *n* [believer] disciple *mf*.

following ['fɒləʊɪŋ] ◇ *adj* suivant(e) ◇ *n* groupe *m* d'admirateurs ◇ *prep* après.

follow-up ◇ *adj* complémentaire ◇ *n* suite *f*.

folly ['fɒlɪ] *n* (U) [foolishness] folie *f*.

foment [fəʊ'ment] *vt* fml fomenter.

fond [fɒnd] *adj* **- 1.** [affectionate] affectueux(eu-se) ; **to be ~ of** aimer beaucoup **- 2.** literary [hope, wish] naïf (naïve).

fondle ['fɒndl] *vt* caresser.

fondly ['fɒndlɪ] *adv* **- 1.** [affectionately - gaze, smile] affectueusement ; [- remember] avec tendresse **- 2.** literary [believe, wish] naïvement.

fondness ['fɒndnɪs] *n* [for person] affection *f* ; [for thing] penchant *m*.

fondue ['fɒndjuː] *n* fondue *f*.

font [fɒnt] *n* **- 1.** [in church] fonts *mpl* baptismaux **- 2.** COMPUT & TYPO police *f* (de caractères).

food [fuːd] *n* nourriture *f* ; **that's ~ for thought** cela donne à réfléchir.

food chain *n* chaîne *f* alimentaire.

food mixer *n* mixer *m*.

food poisoning [-,pɔɪznɪŋ] *n* intoxication *f* alimentaire.

food processor [-,prəʊsesəʳ] *n* robot *m* ménager.

food stamp *n* Am bon *m* alimentaire (*accordé aux personnes sans ressources*).

foodstuffs ['fuːdstʌfs] *npl* denrées *fpl* alimentaires.

fool [fuːl] ◇ *n* **- 1.** [idiot] idiot *m*, -e *f* ; **to make a ~ of sb** tourner qqn en ridicule ; **to make a ~ of o.s.** se rendre ridicule ; **to act** OR **play the ~** faire l'imbécile **- 2.** Br [dessert] ≃ mousse *f* ◇ *vt* duper ; **to ~ sb into doing sthg** amener qqn à faire qqch en le dupant ◇ *vi* faire l'imbécile.
➤ **fool about, fool around** *vi* **- 1.** [behave foolishly] faire l'imbécile **- 2.** [be unfaithful] être infidèle

foolhardy ['fuːl,hɑːdɪ] *adj* téméraire.

foolish ['fuːlɪʃ] *adj* idiot(e), stupide.

foolishly ['fuːlɪʃlɪ] *adv* stupidement, bêtement.

foolishness ['fuːlɪʃnɪs] *n* (U) bêtise *f*.

foolproof ['fuːlpruːf] *adj* infaillible.

foolscap ['fuːlzkæp] *n* (U) papier *m* ministre.

foot [fʊt] (*pl sense 1* **feet** [fiːt], *pl sense 2 inv* OR **feet**) ◇ *n* **- 1.** [gen] pied *m* ; [of animal] patte *f* ; [of page, stairs] bas *m* ; **to be on one's feet** être debout ; **to get to one's feet** se mettre debout, se lever ; **on ~** à pied ; **to be back on one's feet** être remis (d'une maladie) ; **to have itchy feet** avoir la bougeotte ; **to put one's ~ down** mettre le holà ; **to put one's ~ in it** mettre les pieds dans le plat ; **to put one's feet up** se reposer ; **to be rushed off one's feet** ne pas avoir le temps de souffler ; **to set ~ in** mettre le pied en ; **to stand on one's own two feet** se débrouiller (par soi-même) - **2.** [unit of measurement] = *30,48 cm*, ≈ pied *m* ⬡ *vt inf* : **to ~ the bill** payer la note.

footage ['fʊtɪdʒ] *n (U)* séquences *fpl*.

foot-and-mouth disease *n* fièvre *f* aphteuse.

football ['fʊtbɔːl] *n* - **1.** [game - soccer] football *m*, foot *m* ; [- American football] football américain - **2.** [ball] ballon *m* de football OR foot.

football club *n* Br club *m* de football.

footballer ['fʊtbɔːlə'] *n* Br joueur *m*, -euse *f* de football, footballeur *m*, -euse *f*.

football field *n* Am terrain *m* de football américain.

football game *n* Am match *m* de football américain.

football ground *n* Br terrain *m* de football.

football match *n* Br match *m* de football.

football player = **footballer.**

football pools *npl* Br ≈ loto *m* sportif.

football supporter *n* supporter *m* (de football).

footbrake ['fʊtbreɪk] *n* frein *m* (à pied).

footbridge ['fʊtbrɪdʒ] *n* passerelle *f*.

foot fault *n* faute *f* de pied.

foothills ['fʊthɪlz] *npl* contreforts *mpl*.

foothold ['fʊthəʊld] *n* prise *f* (de pied) ; **to get a ~** trouver une prise (de pied) ; **fig** prendre pied, s'imposer.

footing ['fʊtɪŋ] *n* - **1.** [foothold] prise *f* ; **to lose one's ~** trébucher - **2.** fig [basis] position *f* ; **on an equal ~ (with)** sur un pied d'égalité (avec).

footlights ['fʊtlaɪts] *npl* rampe *f*.

footling ['fuːtlɪŋ] *adj* dated & pej futile.

footman ['fʊtmən] (*pl* **-men** [-mən]) *n* valet *m* de pied.

footmark ['fʊtmɑːk] = **footprint.**

footnote ['fʊtnəʊt] *n* note *f* en bas de page.

footpath ['fʊtpɑːθ, *pl* -pɑːðz] *n* sentier *m*.

footprint ['fʊtprɪnt] *n* empreinte *f* (de pied), trace *f* (de pas).

footsore ['fʊtsɔː'] *adj* : **to be ~** avoir mal aux pieds.

footstep ['fʊtstep] *n* - **1.** [sound] bruit *m* de pas - **2.** [footprint] empreinte *f* (de pied) ; **to follow in sb's ~s** marcher sur OR suivre les traces de qqn.

footwear ['fʊtweə'] *n (U)* chaussures *fpl*.

footwork ['fʊtwɜːk] *n (U)* SPORT jeu *m* de jambes.

for [fɔː'] ⬡ *prep* - **1.** [referring to intention, destina-tion, purpose] pour ; **this is ~ you** c'est pour vous ; **the plane ~ Paris** l'avion à destination de Paris ; **I'm going ~ the papers** je vais prendre OR acheter les journaux ; **let's meet ~ a drink** retrouvons-nous pour prendre un verre ; **we did it ~ a laugh** OR **~ fun** on l'a fait pour rire ; **what's it ~?** ça sert à quoi? - **2.** [representing, on behalf of] pour ; **the MP ~ Barnsley** le député de Barnsley ; **let me do that ~ you** laissez-moi faire, je vais vous le faire - **3.** [because of] pour, en raison de ; **~ various reasons** pour plusieurs raisons ; **the town is famous ~ its cathedral** la ville est célèbre pour sa cathédrale ; **a prize ~ swimming** un prix de natation ; **~ fear of being ridiculed** de OR par peur d'être ridiculisé - **4.** [with regard to] pour ; **to be ready ~ sthg** être prêt à OR pour qqch ; **it's not ~ me to say** ce n'est pas à moi à le dire ; **to be young ~ one's age** être jeune pour son âge ; **to feel sorry ~ sb** plaindre qqn - **5.** [indicating amount of time, space] **there's no time ~ that** now on n'a pas le temps de faire cela OR de s'occuper de cela maintenant ; **there's room ~ another person** il y a de la place pour encore une personne - **6.** [indicating period of time] **she'll be away ~ a month** elle sera absente (pendant) un mois ; **we talked ~ hours** on a parlé pendant des heures ; **I've lived here ~ 3 years** j'habite ici depuis 3 ans, cela fait 3 ans que j'habite ici ; **I can do it for you ~ tomorrow** je peux vous le faire pour demain - **7.** [indicat-ing distance] pendant, sur ; **~ 50 kilometres** pendant OR sur 50 kilomètres ; **I walked ~ miles** j'ai marché (pendant) des kilomè-tres - **8.** [indicating particular occasion] pour ; **~ Christmas** pour Noël ; **the meeting sched-uled ~ the 30th** la réunion prévue pour le 30 - **9.** [indicating amount of money, price] **they're 50p ~ ten** cela coûte 50p les dix ; **I bought/sold it ~ £10** je l'ai acheté/vendu 10 livres - **10.** [in favour of, in support of] pour ; **to vote ~ sthg** voter pour qqch ; **to be all ~ sthg** être tout à fait pour OR en faveur de qqch - **11.** [in ratios] pour - **12.** [indicating meaning] : **P ~ Peter** P com-me Peter ; **what's the Greek ~ 'mother'?** comment dit-on 'mère' en grec? ⬡ *conj* fml [as, since] car.

⬡ **for all** ⬡ *prep* malgré ; **~ all his money ...** malgré tout son argent ... ⬡ *conj* : **~ all I know** pour autant que je sache ; **~ all I care** pour ce que cela me fait.

FOR (*abbr of* free on rail) franco wagon.

forage ['fɒrɪdʒ] *vi* : **to ~ (for)** fouiller (pour trouver).

foray ['fɒreɪ] *n* : **~ (into)** lit & fig incursion *f* (dans).

forbad [fə'bæd], **forbade** [fə'beɪd] *pt* ▷ forbid.

forbearing [fɔː'beərɪŋ] *adj* tolérant(e).

forbid [fə'bɪd] (*pt* -bade OR -bad, *pp* forbid OR -bidden, *cont* -bidding) *vt* interdire, défendre ; **to ~ sb to do sthg** interdire OR défendre à qqn de faire qqch ; **God** OR **Heaven ~!** pourvu que non!

forbidden [fə'bɪdn] ◇ *pp* ▷ forbid ◇ *adj* interdit(e), défendu(e).

forbidding [fə'bɪdɪŋ] *adj* [severe, unfriendly] austère ; [threatening] sinistre.

force [fɔːs] ◇ *n* - **1.** [gen] force *f ;* **~ of habit** force de l'habitude ; **by ~** de force - **2.** [group] : **sales ~** représentants *mpl* de commerce ; **security ~s** forces *fpl* de sécurité ; **in ~** en force - **3.** [effect] : **to be in/to come into ~** être/entrer en vigueur ◇ *vt* - **1.** [gen] forcer ; **to ~ sb to do sthg** forcer qqn à faire qqch ; **to ~ sthg open** forcer qqch (pour l'ouvrir) ; **to ~ one's way through** se frayer un chemin à travers ; **to ~ one's way into** entrer de force dans - **2.** [press] : **to ~ sthg on sb** imposer qqch à qqn.

➡ **forces** *npl* : **the ~s** les forces *fpl* armées ; **to join ~s** joindre ses efforts.

➡ **by force of** *prep* à force de.

➡ **force back** *vt sep* [crowd etc] repousser ; [emotion, tears] refouler.

➡ **force down** *vt sep* - **1.** [food] se forcer à manger - **2.** [aeroplane] forcer à atterrir.

forced [fɔːst] *adj* forcé(e).

forced landing *n* atterrissage *m* forcé.

force-feed *vt* nourrir de force.

forceful ['fɔːsfʊl] *adj* [person] énergique ; [speech] vigoureux(euse).

forcefully ['fɔːsfʊlɪ] *adv* avec force.

forcemeat ['fɔːsmiːt] *n esp Br* farce *f*.

forceps ['fɔːseps] *npl* forceps *m*.

forcible ['fɔːsəbl] *adj* - **1.** [using physical force] par (la) force - **2.** [powerful] fort(e).

forcibly ['fɔːsəblɪ] *adv* - **1.** [using physical force] de force - **2.** [powerfully] avec vigueur.

ford [fɔːd] ◇ *n* gué *m* ◇ *vt* traverser à gué.

fore [fɔːʳ] ◇ *adj* NAUT à l'avant ◇ *n* : **to come to the ~** s'imposer.

forearm ['fɔːrɑːm] *n* avant-bras *m inv*.

forebears ['fɔːbeəz] *npl* aïeux *mpl*.

foreboding [fɔː'bəʊdɪŋ] *n* pressentiment *m*.

forecast ['fɔːkɑːst] (*pt & pp* forecast OR -ed) ◇ *n* prévision *f ;* **(weather) ~** prévisions météorologiques ◇ *vt* prévoir.

forecaster ['fɔːkɑːstəʳ] *n* - **1.** [analyst] prévi-

sionniste *mf* - **2.** [of weather] présentateur *m*, -trice *f* de la météo.

foreclose [fɔː'kləʊz] ◇ *vt* saisir ◇ *vi* : **to ~ on sb** saisir qqn.

foreclosure [fɔː'kləʊʒəʳ] *n* saisie *f*.

forecourt ['fɔːkɔːt] *n* [of petrol station] devant *m ;* [of building] avant-cour *f*.

forefathers ['fɔːˌfɑːðəz] = forebears.

forefinger ['fɔːˌfɪŋgəʳ] *n* index *m*.

forefront ['fɔːfrʌnt] *n* : **in** OR **at the ~ of** au premier plan de.

forego [fɔː'gəʊ] = forgo.

foregoing [fɔː'gəʊɪŋ] ◇ *adj* précédent(e) ◇ *n fml* : **the ~** ce qui précède.

foregone conclusion ['fɔːgɒn-] *n* : **it's a ~** c'est couru.

foreground ['fɔːgraʊnd] *n* premier plan *m ;* **in the ~** au premier plan.

forehand ['fɔːhænd] *n* TENNIS coup *m* droit.

forehead ['fɔːhed] *n* front *m*.

foreign ['fɒrən] *adj* - **1.** [gen] étranger(ère) ; [correspondent] à l'étranger - **2.** [policy, trade] extérieur(e).

foreign affairs *npl* affaires *fpl* étrangères.

foreign aid *n* aide *f* extérieure.

foreign body *n* corps *m* étranger.

foreign competition *n* concurrence *f* étrangère.

foreign currency *n* (U) devises *fpl* étrangères.

foreigner ['fɒrənəʳ] *n* étranger *m*, -ère *f*.

foreign exchange *n* change *m ;* **~ markets** marchés *mpl* des devises ; **~ rates** taux *mpl* de change.

foreign investment *n* (U) investissement *m* étranger.

foreign minister *n* ministre *m* des Affaires étrangères.

Foreign Office *n Br* : **the ~** ≃ le ministère des Affaires étrangères.

Foreign Secretary *n Br* ≃ ministre *m* des Affaires étrangères.

foreleg ['fɔːleg] *n* [of horse] membre *m* antérieur ; [of other animals] patte *f* de devant.

foreman ['fɔːmən] (*pl* -men [-mən]) *n* - **1.** [of workers] contremaître *m* - **2.** JUR président *m* du jury.

foremost ['fɔːməʊst] ◇ *adj* principal(e) ◇ *adv* : **first and ~** tout d'abord.

forename ['fɔːneɪm] *n* prénom *m*.

forensic [fə'rensɪk] *adj* [department, investigation] médico-légal(e).

forensic medicine, forensic science n médecine f légale.

forerunner ['fɔːˌrʌnəʳ] n précurseur m.

foresee [fɔː'siː] (pt **-saw** [-'sɔː], pp **-seen**) vt prévoir.

foreseeable [fɔː'siːəbl] adj prévisible ; **for the ~ future** pour tous les jours/mois etc à venir ; **in the ~ future** dans un futur proche.

foreseen [fɔː'siːn] pp ⊏➤ foresee.

foreshadow [fɔː'ʃædəʊ] vt présager.

foreshortened [fɔː'ʃɔːtnd] adj raccourci(e).

foresight ['fɔːsaɪt] n (U) prévoyance f.

foreskin ['fɔːskɪn] n prépuce m.

forest ['fɒrɪst] n forêt f.

forestall [fɔː'stɔːl] vt [attempt, discussion] prévenir ; [person] devancer.

forestry ['fɒrɪstrɪ] n sylviculture f.

Forestry Commission n Br : **the ~** ≃ les Eaux fpl et Forêts.

foretaste ['fɔːteɪst] n avant-goût m.

foretell [fɔː'tel] (pt & pp **-told**) vt prédire.

forethought ['fɔːθɔːt] n prévoyance f.

foretold [fɔː'təʊld] pt & pp ⊏➤ foretell.

forever [fə'revəʳ] adv **- 1.** [eternally] (pour) toujours **- 2.** inf [long time] : **don't take ~ about it!** et ne mets pas des heures!

forewarn [fɔː'wɔːn] vt avertir.

foreword ['fɔːwɜːd] n avant-propos m inv.

forfeit ['fɔːfɪt] <> n amende f ; [in game] gage m <> vt perdre.

forgave [fə'geɪv] pt ⊏➤ forgive.

forge [fɔːdʒ] <> n forge f <> vt **- 1.** INDUSTRY & fig forger **- 2.** [signature, money] contrefaire ; [passport] falsifier.

➤ **forge ahead** vi prendre de l'avance.

forger ['fɔːdʒəʳ] n faussaire mf.

forgery ['fɔːdʒərɪ] (pl **-ies**) n **- 1.** (U) [crime] contrefaçon f **- 2.** [forged article] faux m.

forget [fə'get] (pt **-got**, pp **-gotten**, cont **-getting**) <> vt oublier ; **let's ~ the whole business** n'en parlons plus ; **to ~ to do sthg** oublier de faire qqch ; **~ it!** laisse tomber! ; **to ~ o.s.** perdre le contrôle de soi <> vi : **to ~ (about sthg)** oublier (qqch).

forgetful [fə'getfʊl] adj distrait(e), étourdi(e).

forgetfulness [fə'getfʊlnɪs] n étourderie f.

forget-me-not n myosotis m.

forgive [fə'gɪv] (pt **-gave**, pp **-given** [-'gɪvən]) vt pardonner ; **to ~ sb for sthg/for doing sthg** pardonner qqch à qqn/à qqn d'avoir fait qqch.

forgiveness [fə'gɪvnɪs] n (U) pardon m.

forgiving [fə'gɪvɪŋ] adj indulgent(e).

forgo [fɔː'gəʊ] (pt **-went**, pp **-gone** [-'gɒn]) vt renoncer à.

forgot [fə'gɒt] pt ⊏➤ forget.

forgotten [fə'gɒtn] pp ⊏➤ forget.

fork [fɔːk] <> n **- 1.** [for eating] fourchette f **- 2.** [for gardening] fourche f **- 3.** [in road] bifurcation f ; [of river] embranchement m <> vi bifurquer.

➤ **fork out** inf <> vt fus allonger, débourser ; **to ~ out money on** OR **for** allonger OR débourser de l'argent pour <> vi : **to ~ out (for)** casquer (pour).

forklift truck ['fɔːklɪft-] n chariot m élévateur.

forlorn [fə'lɔːn] adj **- 1.** [person, face] malheureux(euse), triste **- 2.** [place, landscape] désolé(e) **- 3.** [hope, attempt] désespéré(e).

form [fɔːm] <> n **- 1.** [shape, fitness, type] forme f ; **on ~** Br, **in ~** Am en forme ; **off ~** pas en forme ; **in the ~ of** sous forme de ; **to take the ~ of** prendre la forme de **- 2.** [questionnaire] formulaire m **- 3.** Br SCH classe f **- 4.** [usual behaviour] : **true to ~** typiquement <> vt former <> vi se former.

formal ['fɔːml] adj **- 1.** [person] formaliste ; [language] soutenu(e) **- 2.** [dinner party, announcement] officiel(elle) ; [dress] de cérémonie.

formality [fɔː'mælətɪ] (pl **-ies**) n formalité f.

formalize, -ise ['fɔːməlaɪz] vt organiser de façon formelle.

formally ['fɔːməlɪ] adv **- 1.** [correctly, seriously] de façon correcte **- 2.** [not casually] : **to be ~ dressed** être en tenue de cérémonie **- 3.** [officially] officiellement.

format ['fɔːmæt] (pt & pp **-ted** ; cont **-ting**) <> n [gen & COMPUT] format m <> vt COMPUT formater.

formation [fɔː'meɪʃn] n **- 1.** [gen] formation f **- 2.** [of idea, plan] élaboration f.

formative ['fɔːmətɪv] adj formateur(trice).

former ['fɔːməʳ] <> adj **- 1.** [previous] ancien(enne) ; **~ husband** ex-mari m ; **~ pupil** ancien élève m, ancienne élève f **- 2.** [first of two] premier(ère) <> n : **the ~** le premier (la première), celui-là (celle-là).

formerly ['fɔːməlɪ] adv autrefois.

form feed n changement m de page.

Formica® [fɔː'maɪkə] n Formica® m.

formidable ['fɔːmɪdəbl] adj impressionnant(e).

formless ['fɔːmlɪs] adj informe.

Formosa [fɔː'məʊsə] *n* Formose ; **in ~** à Formose.

formula ['fɔːmjʊlə] (*pl* **-as** OR **-ae** [-iː]) *n* formule *f*.

formulate ['fɔːmjʊleɪt] *vt* formuler.

formulation [ˌfɔːmjʊ'leɪʃn] *n* formulation *f*.

fornicate ['fɔːnɪkeɪt] *vi* fml forniquer.

forsake [fə'seɪk] (*pt* **forsook**, *pp* **forsaken**) *vt* literary [person] abandonner ; [habit] renoncer à.

forsaken [fə'seɪkn] *adj* abandonné(e).

forsook [fə'sʊk] *pt* ⊳ **forsake**.

forsythia [fɔː'saɪθjə] *n* forsythia *m*.

fort [fɔːt] *n* fort *m* ; **to hold the ~** [at office, shop] garder la boutique.

forte ['fɔːtɪ] *n* point *m* fort.

forth [fɔːθ] *adv* literary en avant ; **from that day ~** dorénavant.

forthcoming [fɔːθ'kʌmɪŋ] *adj* - **1.** [imminent] à venir - **2.** [available] : **no answer was ~** on n'a pas eu de réponse - **3.** [helpful] communicatif(ive).

forthright ['fɔːθraɪt] *adj* franc (franche), direct(e).

forthwith [ˌfɔːθ'wɪθ] *adv* fml aussitôt.

fortieth ['fɔːtɪɪθ] *num* quarantième ; *see also* **sixth**.

fortification [ˌfɔːtɪfɪ'keɪʃn] *n* fortification *f*.

fortified wine ['fɔːtɪfaɪd-] *n* vin *m* de liqueur.

fortify ['fɔːtɪfaɪ] (*pt* & *pp* **-ied**) *vt* - **1.** MIL fortifier - **2.** fig [resolve etc] renforcer.

fortitude ['fɔːtɪtjuːd] *n* courage *m*.

fortnight ['fɔːtnaɪt] *n* quinze jours *mpl*, quinzaine *f*.

fortnightly ['fɔːtˌnaɪtlɪ] ⬦ *adj* bimensuel(elle) ⬦ *adv* tous les quinze jours.

fortress ['fɔːtrɪs] *n* forteresse *f*.

fortuitous [fɔː'tjuːɪtəs] *adj* fortuit(e).

fortunate ['fɔːtʃnət] *adj* heureux(euse) ; **to be ~** avoir de la chance.

fortunately ['fɔːtʃnətlɪ] *adv* heureusement.

fortune ['fɔːtʃuːn] *n* - **1.** [wealth] fortune *f* - **2.** [luck] fortune *f*, chance *f* - **3.** [future] : **to tell sb's ~** dire la bonne aventure à qqn.
➣ **fortunes** *npl* fortune *f*.

fortune-teller [-ˌtelə'] *n* diseuse *f* de bonne aventure.

forty ['fɔːtɪ] *num* quarante ; *see also* **sixty**.

forum ['fɔːrəm] (*pl* **-s**) *n* - **1.** [gén] forum *m*, tribune *f* - **2.** COMPUT forum *m*.

forward ['fɔːwəd] ⬦ *adj* - **1.** [movement] en avant - **2.** [planning] à long terme - **3.** [impu-

dent] effronté(e) ⬦ *adv* - **1.** [ahead] en avant ; **to go** OR **move ~** avancer - **2.** [in time] : **to bring a meeting ~** avancer la date d'une réunion ; **to put a watch ~** avancer une montre ⬦ *n* SPORT avant *m* ⬦ *vt* - **1.** [letter] faire suivre ; [goods] expédier - **2.** [career] faire avancer.

forwarding address ['fɔːwədɪŋ-] *n* adresse *f* où faire suivre le courrier.

forward-looking [-'lʊkɪŋ] *adj* tourné(e) vers le futur.

forwardness ['fɔːwədnɪs] *n* [boldness] effronterie *f*.

forwards ['fɔːwədz] *adv* = **forward**.

forwent [fɔː'went] *pt* ⊳ **forgo**.

fossil ['fɒsl] *n* fossile *m*.

fossil fuel *n* combustible *m* fossile.

fossilized, -ised ['fɒsɪlaɪzd] *adj* fossilisé(e).

foster ['fɒstə'] ⬦ *adj* [family] d'accueil ⬦ *vt* - **1.** [child] accueillir - **2.** fig [nurture] nourrir, entretenir.

foster child *n* enfant *m* placé en famille d'accueil.

foster parent *n* parent *m* nourricier.

fought [fɔːt] *pt* & *pp* ⊳ **fight**.

foul [faʊl] ⬦ *adj* - **1.** [gen] infect(e) ; [water] croupi(e) ; **to fall ~ of sb** se mettre qqn à dos - **2.** [language] ordurier(ère) ⬦ *n* SPORT faute *f* ⬦ *vt* - **1.** [make dirty] souiller, salir - **2.** SPORT commettre une faute contre - **3.** [mechanism, propeller] entraver.
➣ **foul up** *vt sep* inf gâcher.

foul-mouthed [-'maʊðd] *adj* au langage grossier.

foul play *n* (U) - **1.** SPORT antijeu *m* - **2.** [crime] acte *m* malveillant.

found [faʊnd] ⬦ *pt* & *pp* ⊳ **find** ⬦ *vt* - **1.** [hospital, town] fonder - **2.** [base] : **to ~ sthg on** fonder OR baser qqch sur.

foundation [faʊn'deɪʃn] *n* - **1.** [creation, organization] fondation *f* - **2.** [basis] fondement *m*, base *f* - **3.** : **~ (cream)** fond *m* de teint.
➣ **foundations** *npl* CONSTR fondations *fpl*.

foundation stone *n* première pierre *f*.

founder ['faʊndə'] ⬦ *n* fondateur *m*, -trice *f* ⬦ *vi* - **1.** [ship] sombrer - **2.** fig [plan, hopes] s'effondrer, s'écrouler.

founder member *n* membre *m* fondateur.

founding ['faʊndɪŋ] *n* [of hospital etc] fondation *f*, création *f*.

founding father *n* père *m* fondateur.

foundry ['faʊndrɪ] (*pl* **-ies**) *n* fonderie *f*.

fount [faʊnt] *n* [origin] source *f*.

fountain ['faʊntɪn] *n* fontaine *f*.

fountain pen n stylo m à encre.

four [fɔːr] num quatre ; **on all ~s** à quatre pattes ; see also **six**.

four-leaved clover [-liːvd-] n trèfle m à quatre feuilles.

four-letter word n mot m grossier.

four-poster (bed) n lit m à baldaquin.

foursome ['fɔːsəm] n groupe m de quatre.

four-star adj [hotel] quatre étoilès.

fourteen [ˌfɔː'tiːn] num quatorze ; see also **six**.

fourteenth [ˌfɔː'tiːnθ] num quatorzième ; see also **sixth**.

fourth [fɔːθ] num quatrième ; see also **sixth**.

Fourth of July n : the ~ Fête de l'Indépendance américaine, célébrée le 4 juillet.

Fourth World n : the ~ le quart-monde.

four-way stop n Am carrefour m à quatre stops.

four-wheel drive n : **with ~** à quatre roues motrices.

fowl [faʊl] (pl inv OR -s) n volaille f.

fox [fɒks] <> n renard m <> vt laisser perplexe.

foxglove ['fɒksglʌv] n digitale f.

foxhole ['fɒkshəʊl] n terrier m de renard.

foxhound ['fɒkshaʊnd] n fox-hound m.

foxhunt ['fɒkshʌnt] n chasse f au renard.

foxhunting ['fɒksˌhʌntɪŋ] n (U) chasse f au renard.

foxy ['fɒksɪ] adj inf [sexy] sexy (inv).

foyer ['fɔɪeɪ] n - **1.** [of hotel, theatre] foyer m - **2.** Am [of house] hall m d'entrée.

FP n - **1.** abbr of **former pupil** - **2.** abbr of **fireplug**.

FPA (abbr of **Family Planning Association**) n association britannique pour le planning familial.

fr. (abbr of **franc**) F.

Fr. (abbr of **father**) P.

fracas ['frækɑː, Am 'freɪkəs] (Br pl inv, Am pl -ses [-siːz]) n bagarre f.

fraction ['frækʃn] n fraction f ; **a ~ too big** légèrement OR un petit peu trop grand.

fractionally ['frækʃnəlɪ] adv un tout petit peu.

fractious ['frækʃəs] adj grincheux(euse).

fracture ['fræktʃər] <> n fracture f <> vt fracturer.

fragile ['frædʒaɪl] adj fragile.

fragility [frə'dʒɪlətɪ] n fragilité f.

fragment [n 'frægmənt , vb fræg'ment] <> n fragment m <> vi se fragmenter.

fragmentary ['frægməntrɪ] adj fragmentaire.

fragmented [fræg'mentɪd] adj fragmenté(e).

fragrance ['freɪgrəns] n parfum m.

fragrant ['freɪgrənt] adj parfumé(e).

frail [freɪl] adj fragile.

frailty ['freɪltɪ] (pl -ies) n - **1.** [gen] fragilité f - **2.** [moral weakness] faiblesse f.

frame [freɪm] <> n - **1.** [gen] cadre m ; [of glasses] monture f ; [of door, window] encadrement m ; [of boat] carcasse f - **2.** [physique] charpente f <> vt - **1.** [gen] encadrer - **2.** [express] formuler - **3.** inf [set up] monter un coup contre.

frame of mind n état m d'esprit.

framework ['freɪmwɜːk] n - **1.** [structure] armature f, carcasse f - **2.** fig [basis] structure f, cadre m.

France [frɑːns] n France f ; **in ~** en France.

franchise ['fræntʃaɪz] n - **1.** POL droit m de vote - **2.** COMM franchise f.

franchisee [ˌfræntʃaɪ'ziː] n franchisé m.

franchisor ['fræntʃaɪzər] n franchiseur m.

frank [fræŋk] <> adj franc (franche) <> vt affranchir.

Frankfurt ['fræŋkfət] n : ~ **(am Main)** Francfort(-sur-le-Main).

frankfurter ['fræŋkfɜːtər] n saucisse f de Francfort.

frankincense ['fræŋkɪnsens] n encens m.

franking machine ['fræŋkɪŋ-] n machine f à affranchir.

frankly ['fræŋklɪ] adv franchement.

frankness ['fræŋknɪs] n franchise f.

frantic ['fræntɪk] adj frénétique ; **to be ~ (with worry)** être fou (folle) d'inquiétude.

frantically ['fræntɪklɪ] adv frénétiquement, avec frénésie.

fraternal [frə'tɜːnl] adj fraternel(elle).

fraternity [frə'tɜːnətɪ] (pl -ies) n - **1.** [community] confrérie f - **2.** (U) [friendship] fraternité f - **3.** Am [of students] club m d'étudiants.

fraternize, -ise ['frætənaɪz] vi fraterniser.

fraud [frɔːd] n - **1.** (U) [crime] fraude f - **2.** pej [impostor] imposteur m.

fraudulent ['frɔːdjʊlənt] adj frauduleux(euse).

fraught [frɔːt] adj - **1.** [full] : ~ **with** plein(e) de - **2.** Br [person] tendu(e) ; [time, situation] difficile.

fray [freɪ] <> vt fig : **my nerves were ~ed**

j'étais extrêmement tendu(e), j'étais à bout de nerfs ⬦ *vi* [material, sleeves] s'user ; **tempers ~ed** *fig* l'atmosphère était tendue OR électrique ⬦ *n literary* bagarre *f*.

frayed [freɪd] *adj* [jeans, collar] élimé(e).

frazzled ['fræzld] *adj* inf éreinté(e).

FRB (*abbr of* **Federal Reserve Board**) *n organe de contrôle de la Banque centrale américaine*.

FRCP (*abbr of* **Fellow of the Royal College of Physicians**) *membre de l'académie de médecine britannique*.

FRCS (*abbr of* **Fellow of the Royal College of Surgeons**) *membre de l'académie de chirurgie britannique*.

freak [fri:k] ⬦ *adj* bizarre, insolite ⬦ *n* **- 1.** [strange creature] monstre *m*, phénomène *m* **- 2.** [unusual event] accident *m* bizarre **- 3.** inf [fanatic] fana *mf*.
➥ **freak out** inf ⬦ *vi* [get angry] exploser (de colère) ; [panic] paniquer ⬦ *vt sep* : **to ~ sb out** faire sauter qqn au plafond.

freakish ['fri:kɪʃ] *adj* bizarre, insolite.

freckle ['frekl] *n* tache *f* de rousseur.

free [fri:] (*compar* **freer** ; *superl* **freest**, *pt* & *pp* **freed**) ⬦ *adj* **- 1.** [gen] libre ; **to be ~ to do sthg** être libre de faire qqch ; **feel ~!** je t'en prie! ; **to set ~** libérer ; **~ from** OR **of worry** sans souci **- 2.** [not paid for] gratuit(e) ; **~ of charge** gratuitement **- 3.** [generous] : **to be ~ with money** dépenser sans compter ⬦ *adv* **- 1.** [without payment] gratuitement ; **for ~** gratuitement **- 2.** [run, live] librement ⬦ *vt* **- 1.** [gen] libérer **- 2.** [trapped person, object] dégager.

-free [fri:] *suffix* sans.

freebie ['fri:bɪ] *n* inf faveur *f*.

freedom ['fri:dəm] *n* **- 1.** [gen] liberté *f ;* **~ of speech** liberté d'expression **- 2.** [exception] : **~ (from)** exemption *f* (de).

freedom fighter *n* partisan *m*, -e *f*.

free enterprise *n* (*U*) libre entreprise *f*.

free-fall *n* (*U*) chute *f* libre.

Freefone® ['fri:fəʊn] *n* Br (*U*) ≃ numéro *m* vert.

free-for-all *n* mêlée *f* générale.

free gift *n* prime *f*.

freehand ['fri:hænd] *adj* & *adv* à main levée.

freehold ['fri:həʊld] ⬦ *adv* en propriété inaliénable ⬦ *n* propriété *f* foncière inaliénable.

freeholder ['fri:həʊldə'] *n* propriétaire foncier *m*, propriétaire foncière *f*.

free house *n* pub *m* en gérance libre.

free kick *n* coup *m* franc.

freelance ['fri:lɑ:ns] ⬦ *adj* indépendant(e), free-lance *(inv)* ⬦ *adv* en free-lance ⬦ *n* indépendant *m*, -e *f*, free-lance *mf* ⬦ *vi* travailler en indépendant OR en free-lance.

freeloader ['fri:ləʊdə'] *n* inf parasite *m*.

freely ['fri:lɪ] *adv* **- 1.** [gen] librement **- 2.** [generously] sans compter.

freeman ['fri:mən] (*pl* **-men** [-mən]) *n* citoyen *m*, -enne *f* d'honneur.

free-market economy *n* économie *f* de marché.

Freemason ['fri:,meɪsn] *n* franc-maçon *m*.

Freemasonry ['fri:,meɪsnrɪ] *n* franc-maçonnerie *f*.

freemen ['fri:mən] *pl* ⬐ **freeman**.

Freephone® ['fri:fəʊn] = **Freefone**®.

Freepost® ['fri:pəʊst] *n* port *m* payé.

free-range *adj* de ferme.

free sample *n* échantillon *m* gratuit.

freesia ['fri:zjə] *n* freesia *m*.

free speech *n* liberté *f* d'expression.

freestanding [,fri:'stændɪŋ] *adj* [furniture] non-encastré(e).

freestyle ['fri:staɪl] *n* SWIMMING nage *f* libre.

freethinker [fri:'θɪŋkə'] *n* libre-penseur *m*, -euse *f*.

Freetown ['fri:taʊn] *n* Freetown.

free trade *n* (*U*) libre-échange *m*.

freeway ['fri:weɪ] *n* Am autoroute *f*.

freewheel [,fri:'wi:l] *vi* [on bicycle] rouler en roue libre ; [in car] rouler au point mort.

freewheeling [,fri:'wi:lɪŋ] *adj* inf sans contrainte.

free will *n* (*U*) libre arbitre *m ;* **to do sthg of one's own ~** faire qqch de son propre gré

free world *n* : **the ~** les pays *mpl* non-communistes.

freeze [fri:z] (*pt* **froze**, *pp* **frozen**) ⬦ *vt* **- 1.** [gen] geler ; [food] congeler **- 2.** [wages, prices] bloquer ⬦ *vi* **- 1.** [gen] geler **- 2.** [stop moving] s'arrêter ⬦ *n* **- 1.** [cold weather] gel *m* **- 2.** [of wages, prices] blocage *m*.
➥ **freeze over** *vi* geler.
➥ **freeze up** *vi* geler.

freeze-dried [-'draɪd] *adj* lyophilisé(e).

freeze frame *n* [on video] arrêt *m* sur image.

freezer ['fri:zə'] *n* congélateur *m*.

freezing ['fri:zɪŋ] ⬦ *adj* glacé(e) ; **I'm ~** je gèle ⬦ *n* = **freezing point**.

freezing point *n* point *m* de congélation.

freight [freɪt] *n* [goods] fret *m*.

freight train n train m de marchandises.

French [frentʃ] ⇔ adj français(e) ⇔ n [language] français m ⇔ npl : **the ~** les Français mpl.

French bean n haricot m vert.

French bread n (U) baguette f.

French Canadian ⇔ adj canadien français (canadienne française) ⇔ n Canadien français m, Canadienne française f.

French chalk n (U) craie f de tailleur.

French doors = **French windows**.

French dressing n [in UK] vinaigrette f ; [in US] sauce-salade à base de mayonnaise et de ketchup.

French fries npl frites fpl.

Frenchman ['frentʃmən] (pl -men [-mən]) n Français m.

French polish n (U) vernis m à l'alcool.

French Riviera n : **the ~** la Côte d'Azur.

French stick n Br baguette f.

French toast n esp Am pain m perdu.

French windows npl porte-fenêtre f.

Frenchwoman ['frentʃ,wumən] (pl -women [-,wimin]) n Française f.

frenetic [frə'netik] adj frénétique.

frenzied ['frenzɪd] adj [haste, activity] frénétique ; [attack] déchaîné(e) ; [mob] en délire.

frenzy ['frenzɪ] (pl -ies) n frénésie f.

frequency ['fri:kwənsɪ] (pl -ies) n fréquence f.

frequency modulation n modulation f de fréquence.

frequent [adj 'fri:kwənt, vb frɪ'kwent] ⇔ adj fréquent(e) ⇔ vt fréquenter.

frequently ['fri:kwəntlɪ] adv fréquemment.

fresco ['freskəʊ] (pl -es OR -s) n fresque f.

fresh [freʃ] ⇔ adj **- 1.** [gen] frais (fraîche) ; **~ from** [the oven] qui sort de ; [university] frais émoulu (fraîche émoulue) de **- 2.** [not salty] doux (douce) **- 3.** [new - drink, piece of paper] autre ; [- look, approach] nouveau(elle) ; **to make a ~ start** repartir à zéro **- 4.** inf dated [cheeky] familier(ère) ; **to get ~ with sb** se montrer osé avec qqn ⇔ adv : **~-ground/made** qui vient juste d'être moulu/fait ; **to be ~ out of sthg** inf ne plus avoir de qqch.

freshen ['freʃn] ⇔ vt rafraîchir ⇔ vi [wind] devenir plus fort.

➥ **freshen up** ⇔ vt sep **- 1.** [wash] : **to ~ o.s. up** faire un brin de toilette **- 2.** [smarten up] rafraîchir ⇔ vi faire un brin de toilette.

fresher ['freʃə'] n Br inf bleu m, -e f.

freshly ['freʃlɪ] adv [squeezed, ironed] fraîchement.

freshman ['freʃmən] (pl -men [-mən]) n étudiant m, -e f de première année.

freshness ['freʃnɪs] n (U) **- 1.** [gen] fraîcheur f **- 2.** [originality] nouveauté f.

freshwater ['freʃ,wɔːtə'] adj d'eau douce.

fret [fret] (pt & pp -ted ; cont -ting) vi [worry] s'inquiéter.

fretful ['fretful] adj [baby] grognon(onne) ; [night, sleep] agité(e).

fretsaw ['fretsɔː] n scie f à découper.

Freudian slip ['frɔɪdɪən-] n lapsus m.

FRG (abbr of Federal Republic of Germany) n RFA f.

Fri. (abbr of Friday) ven.

friar ['fraɪə'] n frère m.

friction ['frɪkʃn] n (U) friction f.

Friday ['fraɪdɪ] n vendredi m ; see also **Saturday**.

fridge [frɪdʒ] n esp Br frigo m.

fridge-freezer n Br réfrigérateur-congélateur m.

fried [fraɪd] ⇔ pt & pp ⊳ **fry** ⇔ adj frit(e) ; **~ egg** œuf m au plat.

friend [frend] n ami m, -e f ; **to be ~s** être amis ; **to be ~s with sb** être ami avec qqn ; **to make ~s (with sb)** se lier d'amitié (avec qqn).

friendless ['frendlɪs] adj sans amis.

friendly ['frendlɪ] (compar -ier ; superl -iest, pl -ies) ⇔ adj [person, manner, match] amical(e) ; [nation] ami(e) ; [argument] sans conséquence ; **to be ~ with sb** être ami avec qqn ⇔ n esp Br match m amical.

friendly society n Br mutuelle f.

friendship ['frendʃɪp] n amitié f.

fries [fraɪz] = **French fries**.

Friesian (cow) ['fri:zjən-] n (vache f) frisonne f.

frieze [fri:z] n frise f.

frigate ['frɪgət] n frégate f.

fright [fraɪt] n peur f ; **to give sb a ~** faire peur à qqn ; **to take ~** prendre peur.

frighten ['fraɪtn] vt faire peur à, effrayer ; **to ~ sb into doing sthg** forcer qqn à faire qqch sous la menace.

➥ **frighten away** vt sep chasser en faisant peur à.

➥ **frighten off** vt sep chasser en faisant peur à.

frightened ['fraɪtnd] adj apeuré(e) ; **to be ~ of sthg/of doing sthg** avoir peur de qqch/de faire qqch.

frightening ['fraɪtnɪŋ] adj effrayant(e).

frightful ['fraɪtful] adj dated effroyable.

frigid ['frɪdʒɪd] adj [sexually] frigide.

frill [frɪl] n - **1.** [decoration] volant m - **2.** inf [extra] supplément m.

frilly ['frɪlɪ] (compar -ier ; superl -iest) adj à fanfreluches.

fringe [frɪndʒ] ◇ n - **1.** [gen] frange f - **2.** [edge - of village] bordure f ; [- of wood, forest] lisière f ◇ vt [edge] border.

fringe benefit n avantage m extrasalarial.

fringe group n groupe m marginal.

fringe theatre n Br théâtre m d'avant-garde.

Frisbee® ['frɪzbɪ] n Frisbee m inv.

Frisian Islands ['frɪʒən-] npl : the ~ l'archipel m frison.

frisk [frɪsk] ◇ vt fouiller ◇ vi gambader.

frisky ['frɪskɪ] (compar -ier ; superl -iest) adj inf vif (vive).

fritter ['frɪtəʳ] n beignet m.

➡ **fritter away** vt sep gaspiller ; **to ~ money/time away on sthg** gaspiller son argent/son temps en qqch.

frivolity [frɪ'vɒlətɪ] (pl -ies) n frivolité f.

frivolous ['frɪvələs] adj frivole.

frizzy ['frɪzɪ] (compar -ier ; superl -iest) adj crépu(e).

fro [frəʊ] ▷ to.

frock [frɒk] n dated robe f.

frog [frɒg] n [animal] grenouille f ; **to have a ~ in one's throat** avoir un chat dans la gorge.

frogman ['frɒgmən] (pl -men [-mən]) n homme-grenouille m.

frogmarch ['frɒgmɑːtʃ] vt emmener quelqu'un de force en lui tenant les bras dans le dos.

frogmen ['frɒgmən] pl ▷ frogman.

frogspawn ['frɒgspɔːn] n (U) œufs mpl de grenouille.

frolic ['frɒlɪk] (pt & pp -ked ; cont -king) ◇ n ébats mpl ◇ vi folâtrer.

from [weak form frəm, strong form frɒm] prep - **1.** [indicating source, origin, removal] de ; **where are you ~?** d'où venez-vous?, d'où êtes-vous? ; **I got a letter ~ her today** j'ai reçu une lettre d'elle aujourd'hui ; **a flight ~ Paris** un vol en provenance de Paris ; **to translate ~ Spanish into English** traduire d'espagnol en anglais ; **to drink ~ a glass** boire dans un verre ; **he's not back ~ work yet** il n'est pas encore rentré de son travail ; **he took a notebook ~ his pocket** il a sorti un carnet de sa poche ; **to take sthg (away) ~ sb** prendre qqch à qqn - **2.** [indicating a deduction] de ; **to deduct sthg ~ sthg** retrancher qqch de qqch - **3.** [indicating escape, separation] de ; **he ran away ~ home** il a fait une fugue, il s'est sauvé de chez lui - **4.** [indicating position] de ; **seen ~ above/below** vu d'en haut/d'en bas - **5.** [indicating distance] de ; **it's 60 km ~ here** c'est à 60 km d'ici ; **how far is it ~ Paris to Lyons?** combien y a-t-il de Paris à Lyon? - **6.** [indicating material object is made out of] en ; **it's made ~ wood/plastic** c'est en bois/plastique - **7.** [starting at a particular time] de ; **~ 2 pm to** OR **till 6 pm** de 14 h à 18 h ; **~ birth** de naissance ; **~ the moment I saw him** dès que OR dès l'instant où je l'ai vu - **8.** [indicating difference] de ; **to be different ~ sb/sthg** être différent de qqn/qqch - **9.** [indicating change] : **~ ... to ...** de ... à ... ; **the price went up ~ £100 to £150** le prix est passé OR monté de 100 livres à 150 livres - **10.** [because of, as a result of] de ; **to suffer ~ cold/hunger** souffrir du froid/de la faim - **11.** [on the evidence of] d'après, à ; **to speak ~ personal experience** parler par expérience OR d'après son expérience personnelle ; **~ what you're saying ...** d'après ce que vous dites ... - **12.** [indicating lowest amount] depuis, à partir de ; **prices start ~ £50** le premier prix est de 50 livres.

frond [frɒnd] n fronde f.

front [frʌnt] ◇ n - **1.** [most forward part - gen] avant m ; [- of dress, envelope, house] devant m ; [- of class] premier rang m - **2.** METEOR & MIL front m - **3.** [issue, area] plan m ; **on the domestic/employment ~** sur le plan intérieur/du travail - **4.** : **(sea) ~** front m de mer - **5.** [outward appearance - of person] contenance f ; [- of business] pej façade f ◇ adj [tooth, garden] de devant ; [row, page] premier(ère) ; **~ cover** couverture f ◇ vt - **1.** [be opposite] être en face de - **2.** [TV programme] présenter ◇ vi : **to ~ onto sthg** donner sur qqch.

➡ **in front** adv - **1.** [further forward - walk, push] devant ; [- people] à l'avant - **2.** [winning] : **to be in ~** mener.

➡ **in front of** prep devant.

frontage ['frʌntɪdʒ] n [of house] façade f ; [of shop] devanture f.

frontal ['frʌntl] adj - **1.** [attack] de front - **2.** [view] de face.

frontbench [,frʌnt'bentʃ] n à la chambre des Communes, bancs occupés respectivement par les ministres du gouvernement en exercice et ceux du gouvernement fantôme.

front desk n réception f.

front door n porte f d'entrée.

frontier ['frʌn,tɪəʳ, Am frʌn'tɪərl] n [border] frontière f ; fig limite f.

frontispiece ['frʌntɪspiːs] *n* frontispice *m*.

front line *n* : **the ~ le** front.

front man *n* **- 1.** [of company, organization] porte-parole *m inv* **- 2.** TV présentateur *m*.

front-page *adj* [article] de première page.

front room *n* salon *m*.

front-runner *n* favori *m*, -ite *f*.

front-wheel drive *n* traction *f* avant.

frost [frɒst] ◇ *n* gel *m* ◇ *vi* : **to ~ over** OR **up** geler.

frostbite ['frɒstbaɪt] *n (U)* gelure *f*.

frostbitten ['frɒst,bɪtn] *adj* [toe, finger] gelé(e).

frosted ['frɒstɪd] *adj* **- 1.** [glass] dépoli(e) **- 2.** Am CULIN glacé(e).

frosting ['frɒstɪŋ] *n* Am *(U)* glaçage *m*.

frosty ['frɒstɪ] (*compar* **-ier** ; *superl* **-iest**) *adj* **- 1.** [weather, welcome] glacial(e) **- 2.** [field, window] gelé(e).

froth [frɒθ] ◇ *n* [on beer] mousse *f*; [on sea] écume *f* ◇ *vi* [beer] mousser ; [sea] écumer.

frothy ['frɒθɪ] (*compar* **-ier** ; *superl* **-iest**) *adj* [beer] mousseux(euse) ; [sea] écumeux(euse).

frown [fraʊn] ◇ *n* froncement *m* de sourcils ◇ *vi* froncer les sourcils.

➡ **frown (up)on** *vt fus* désapprouver.

froze [frəʊz] *pt* ▷ **freeze**.

frozen [frəʊzn] ◇ *pp* ▷ **freeze** ◇ *adj* gelé(e) ; [food] congelé(e) ; **~ with fear** fig mort(e) de peur.

FRS *n* **- 1.** (*abbr of* **Fellow of the Royal Society**) membre de l'académie des sciences britannique **- 2.** (*abbr of* **Federal Reserve System**) banque centrale américaine.

frugal ['fruːgl] *adj* **- 1.** [meal] frugal(e) **- 2.** [person, life] économe.

fruit [fruːt] (*pl inv* OR **-s**) ◇ *n* fruit *m*; **to bear ~** fig porter ses fruits ◇ *comp* [flan] aux fruits ; **~ tree** arbre *m* fruitier ◇ *vi* donner des fruits.

fruitcake ['fruːtkeɪk] *n* cake *m*.

fruiterer ['fruːtərə'] *n* Br fruitier *m*.

fruitful ['fruːtful] *adj* [successful] fructueux(euse).

fruition [fruː'ɪʃn] *n* : **to come to ~** se réaliser.

fruit juice *n* jus *m* de fruits.

fruitless ['fruːtlɪs] *adj* vain(e).

fruit machine *n* Br machine *f* à sous.

fruit salad *n* salade *f* de fruits.

frumpy ['frʌmpɪ] (*compar* **-ier** ; *superl* **-iest**) *adj* mal attifé(e), mal fagoté(e).

frustrate [frʌ'streɪt] *vt* **- 1.** [annoy, disappoint] frustrer **- 2.** [prevent] faire échouer.

frustrated [frʌ'streɪtɪd] *adj* **- 1.** [person, artist] frustré(e) **- 2.** [effort, love] vain(e).

frustrating [frʌ'streɪtɪŋ] *adj* frustrant(e).

frustration [frʌ'streɪʃn] *n* frustration *f*.

fry [fraɪ] (*pt* & *pp* **fried**) *vt* & *vi* frire.

frying pan ['fraɪɪŋ-] *n* poêle *f* à frire ; **to jump out of the ~ into the fire** tomber de Charybde en Scylla.

ft. *abbr of* **foot, feet.**

FT (*abbr of* **Financial Times**) *n* quotidien britannique d'information financière ; **the ~ index** l'indice *m* boursier du FT, ≃ le Cac 40.

FTC (*abbr of* **Federal Trade Commission**) *n* organisme américain chargé de faire respecter les lois anti-trust.

fuchsia ['fjuːʃə] *n* fuchsia *m*.

fuck [fʌk] vulg ◇ *vt* & *vi* baiser ◇ *excl* putain de merde!

➡ **fuck off** *vi* vulg foutre le camp ; **~ off!** fous le camp!

fucking ['fʌkɪŋ] *adj* vulg putain de.

fuddled ['fʌdld] *adj* confus(e).

fuddy-duddy ['fʌdɪ,dʌdɪ] (*pl* **-ies**) *n* inf personne *f* vieux jeu.

fudge [fʌdʒ] ◇ *n (U)* [sweet] caramel *m* (mou) ◇ *vt* inf [figures] truquer ; [issue] esquiver.

fuel [fjʊəl] (Br *pt* & *pp* **-led** ; *cont* **-ling**, Am *pt* & *pp* **-ed** ; *cont* **-ing**) ◇ *n* combustible *m* ; [for engine] carburant *m* ; **to add ~ to** fig alimenter ◇ *vt* **- 1.** [supply with fuel] alimenter (en combustible/carburant) **- 2.** fig [speculation] nourrir.

fuel pump *n* pompe *f* d'alimentation.

fuel tank *n* réservoir *m* à carburant.

fugitive ['fjuːdʒətɪv] *n* fugitif *m*, -ive *f*.

fugue [fjuːg] *n* fugue *f*.

fulcrum ['fʊlkrəm] (*pl* **-crums** OR **-cra** [-krə]) *n* pivot *m*.

fulfil (*pt* & *pp* **-led** ; *cont* **-ling**), **fulfill** Am [fʊl'fɪl] *vt* **- 1.** [duty, role] remplir ; [hope] répondre à ; [ambition, prophecy] réaliser **- 2.** [satisfy - need] satisfaire ; **to ~ o.s.** s'épanouir.

fulfilling [fʊl'fɪlɪŋ] *adj* épanouissant(e).

fulfilment, fulfillment Am [fʊl'fɪlmənt] *n (U)* **- 1.** [satisfaction] grande satisfaction *f* **- 2.** [of ambition, dream] réalisation *f* ; [of role, promise] exécution *f* ; [of need] satisfaction *f*.

full [fʊl] ◇ *adj* **- 1.** [gen] plein(e) ; [bus, car park] complet(ète) ; [with food] gavé(e), repu(e) **- 2.** [complete - recovery, control] total(e) ; [- explanation, day] entier(ère) ; [- volume] maximum **- 3.** [busy - life] rempli(e) ; [- timetable, day] chargé(e) **- 4.** [flavour] riche **- 5.** [plump - figure] rondelet(ette) ; [- mouth] charnu(e) **- 6.** [skirt, sleeve] ample <> adv - **1.** [directly] : ~ **in the face** en plein (dans le) visage - **2.** [very] : **you know ~ well that ...** tu sais très bien que ... - **3.** [at maximum] au maximum <> n : **in ~** complètement, entièrement ; **to the ~** pleinement.

fullback ['fʊlbæk] n arrière m.

full-blooded [-'blʌdɪd] adj - **1.** [pure-blooded] de race pure - **2.** [strong, complete] robuste.

full-blown [-'bləʊn] adj général(e) ; **to have ~ AIDS** avoir le Sida avéré.

full board n pension f complète.

full-bodied [-'bɒdɪd] adj qui a du corps.

full dress n (U) tenue f de cérémonie.

full-face adj de face.

full-fashioned Am = **fully-fashioned**.

full-fledged Am = **fully-fledged**.

full-frontal adj de face.

full-grown [-'grəʊn] adj adulte.

full house n [at show, event] représentation f à bureaux fermés.

full-length <> adj - **1.** [portrait, mirror] en pied - **2.** [dress, novel] long (longue) ; **~ film** long métrage <> adv de tout son long.

full monty [-'mɒntɪ] n inf : **the ~** la totale.

full moon n pleine lune f.

fullness ['fʊlnɪs] n [of voice] ampleur f ; [of life] richesse f ; **in the ~ of time** avec le temps.

full-page adj sur toute une page.

full-scale adj - **1.** [life-size] grandeur nature (inv) - **2.** [complete] de grande envergure.

full-size(d) adj - **1.** [life-size] grandeur nature (inv) - **2.** [adult] adulte - **3.** Am AUT : **~ car** grande berline.

full stop <> n point m <> adv Br un point c'est tout.

full time n Br SPORT fin f de match.

➡ **full-time** adj & adv [work, worker] à temps plein.

full up adj [bus, train] complet(ète) ; [with food] gavé(e), repu(e).

fully ['fʊlɪ] adv [understand, satisfy] tout à fait ; [trained, describe] entièrement.

fully-fashioned Br, **full-fashioned** Am [-'fæʃnd] adj moulant(e).

fully-fledged Br, **full-fledged** Am [-'fledʒd] adj diplômé(e).

fulness ['fʊlnɪs] = **fullness**.

fulsome ['fʊlsəm] adj excessif(ive).

fumble ['fʌmbl] <> vt [catch] mal attraper <> vi fouiller, tâtonner ; **to ~ for** fouiller pour trouver.

fume [fjuːm] vi [with anger] rager.

➡ **fumes** npl [from paint] émanations fpl ; [from smoke] fumées fpl ; [from car] gaz mpl d'échappement.

fumigate ['fjuːmɪgeɪt] vt fumiger.

fun [fʌn] <> n (U) - **1.** [pleasure, amusement] : **the game is great ~** ce jeu est très amusant ; **to have ~** s'amuser ; **for ~, for the ~ of it** pour s'amuser - **2.** [playfulness] : **to be full of ~** être plein(e) d'entrain - **3.** [ridicule] : **to make ~ of** OR **poke ~ at sb** se moquer de qqn <> adj amusant(e).

function ['fʌŋkʃn] <> n - **1.** [gen] fonction f - **2.** [formal social event] réception f officielle <> vi fonctionner ; **to ~ as** servir de.

functional ['fʌŋkʃnəl] adj - **1.** [practical] fonctionnel(elle) - **2.** [operational] en état de marche.

functionary ['fʌŋkʃnərɪ] (pl -ies) n fonctionnaire mf.

function key n COMPUT touche f de fonction.

fund [fʌnd] <> n fonds m ; fig [of knowledge] puits m <> vt financer.

➡ **funds** npl fonds mpl.

fundamental [ˌfʌndə'mentl] adj : **~ (to)** fondamental(e) (à).

➡ **fundamentals** npl principes mpl de base.

fundamentalism [ˌfʌndə'mentəlɪzm] n fondamentalisme m.

fundamentally [ˌfʌndə'mentəlɪ] adv fondamentalement.

funding ['fʌndɪŋ] n (U) financement m.

fund-raising [-ˌreɪzɪŋ] <> n (U) collecte f de fonds <> comp [event, campaign] organisé(e) pour collecter des fonds.

funeral ['fjuːnərəl] n obsèques fpl.

funeral director n entrepreneur m de pompes funèbres.

funeral parlour n entreprise f de pompes funèbres.

funeral service n service m funèbre.

funereal [fjuː'nɪərɪəl] adj funèbre.

funfair ['fʌnfeəʳ] n fête f foraine.

fungus ['fʌŋgəs] (pl -gi [-gaɪ] OR -guses [-gəsiːz]) n champignon m.

funk [fʌŋk] n (U) - **1.** MUS funk m - **2.** dated [fear] frayeur f.

funky ['fʌŋkɪ] (compar -ier ; superl -iest) adj MUS funky (inv).

funnel ['fʌnl] (Br pt & pp -led ; cont -ling, Am pt & pp -ed ; cont -ing) <> n - **1.** [tube] entonnoir m - **2.** [of ship] cheminée f <> vt [crowd] canaliser ; [money, food] diriger <> vi se diriger.

funnily ['fʌnɪlɪ] adv [strangely] bizarrement ; **~ enough** chose curieuse.

funny [ˈfʌnɪ] (*compar* **-ier** ; *superl* **-iest**) *adj* - **1.** [amusing, odd] drôle - **2.** [ill] tout drôle (toute drôle).

funny bone *n* petit juif *m*.

funny farm *n* inf hum maison *f* de fous.

fun run *n* *course à pied organisée pour collecter des fonds*.

fur [fɜːr] *n* fourrure *f*.

fur coat *n* (manteau *m* de) fourrure *f*.

furious [ˈfjʊərɪəs] *adj* - **1.** [very angry] furieux(euse) - **2.** [wild - effort, battle] acharné(e) ; [- temper] déchaîné(e).

furiously [ˈfjʊərɪəslɪ] *adv* - **1.** [angrily] furieusement - **2.** [wildly - fight, try] avec acharnement ; [- run] à une allure folle.

furled [fɜːld] *adj* [umbrella, flag] roulé(e) ; [sail] serré(e).

furlong [ˈfɜːlɒŋ] *n* = 201,17 mètres.

furnace [ˈfɜːnɪs] *n* [fire] fournaise *f*.

furnish [ˈfɜːnɪʃ] *vt* - **1.** [fit out] meubler - **2.** fml [provide] fournir ; **to ~ sb with sthg** fournir qqch à qqn.

furnished [ˈfɜːnɪʃt] *adj* meublé(e).

furnishings [ˈfɜːnɪʃɪŋz] *npl* mobilier *m*.

furniture [ˈfɜːnɪtʃər] *n* (U) meubles *mpl* ; **a piece of ~** un meuble.

furniture polish *n* encaustique *m*, produit *m* d'entretien des meubles.

furore Br [ˈfjʊərɔːrɪ], **furor** Am [ˈfjʊrɔːr] *n* scandale *m*.

furrier [ˈfʌrɪər] *n* fourreur *m*.

furrow [ˈfʌrəʊ] *n* - **1.** [in field] sillon *m* - **2.** [on forehead] ride *f*.

furrowed [ˈfʌrəʊd] *adj* - **1.** [field, land] labouré(e) - **2.** [brow] ridé(e).

furry [ˈfɜːrɪ] (*compar* **-ier** ; *superl* **-iest**) *adj* - **1.** [animal] à fourrure - **2.** [material] recouvert(e) de fourrure.

further [ˈfɜːðər] ◇ *compar* ⊳ **far** ◇ *adv* - **1.** [gen] plus loin ; **how much ~ is it?** combien de kilomètres y a-t-il? ; **~ on** plus loin ; **this mustn't go any ~** ceci doit rester entre nous - **2.** [more - complicate, develop] davantage ; [- enquire] plus avant - **3.** [in addition] de plus ◇ *adj* nouveau(elle), supplémentaire ; **until ~ notice** jusqu'à nouvel ordre ◇ *vt* [career, aims] faire avancer ; [cause] encourager.

➡ **further to** *prep* fml suite à.

further education *n* Br éducation *f* postscolaire.

furthermore [ˌfɜːðəˈmɔːr] *adv* de plus.

furthermost [ˈfɜːðəməʊst] *adj* le plus éloigné (la plus éloignée).

furthest [ˈfɜːðɪst] ◇ *superl* ⊳ **far** ◇ *adj* le plus éloigné (la plus éloignée) ◇ *adv* le plus loin.

furtive [ˈfɜːtɪv] *adj* [person] sournois(e) ; [glance] furtif(ive).

furtively [ˈfɜːtɪvlɪ] *adv* furtivement.

fury [ˈfjʊərɪ] *n* fureur *f* ; **in a ~** en fureur.

fuse esp Br, **fuze** Am [fjuːz] ◇ *n* - **1.** ELEC fusible *m*, plomb *m* - **2.** [of bomb] détonateur *m* ; [of firework] amorce *f* ◇ *vt* - **1.** [join by heat] réunir par la fusion - **2.** [combine] fusionner ◇ *vi* - **1.** ELEC : **the lights have ~d** les plombs ont sauté - **2.** [join by heat] fondre - **3.** [combine] fusionner.

fuse-box *n* boîte *f* à fusibles.

fused [fjuːzd] *adj* [plug] avec fusible incorporé.

fuselage [ˈfjuːzəlɑːʒ] *n* fuselage *m*.

fuse wire *n* fusible *m*.

fusillade [ˌfjuːzəˈleɪd] *n* fusillade *f*.

fusion [ˈfjuːʒn] *n* fusion *f*.

fuss [fʌs] ◇ *n* - **1.** [excitement, anxiety] agitation *f* ; **to make a ~** faire des histoires - **2.** (U) [complaints] protestations *fpl* - **3.** phr : **to make a ~ of sb** Br être aux petits soins pour qqn ◇ *vi* faire des histoires.

➡ **fuss over** *vt* fus être aux petits soins pour.

fusspot [ˈfʌspɒt] *n* inf tatillon *m*, -onne *f*.

fussy [ˈfʌsɪ] (*compar* **-ier** ; *superl* **-iest**) *adj* - **1.** [fastidious - person] tatillon(onne) ; [- eater] difficile - **2.** [over-decorated] tarabiscoté(e).

fusty [ˈfʌstɪ] (*compar* **-ier** ; *superl* **-iest**) *adj* - **1.** [not fresh] qui sent le renfermé - **2.** [old-fashioned] vieillot(otte).

futile [ˈfjuːtaɪl] *adj* vain(e).

futility [fjuːˈtɪlətɪ] *n* futilité *f*.

futon [ˈfuːtɒn] *n* futon *m*.

future [ˈfjuːtʃər] ◇ *n* - **1.** [gen] avenir *m* ; **in ~** à l'avenir ; **in the ~** dans le futur, à l'avenir - **2.** GRAMM : **~ (tense)** futur *m* ◇ *adj* futur(e).

➡ **futures** *npl* FIN transactions *fpl* à terme.

futuristic [ˌfjuːtʃəˈrɪstɪk] *adj* futuriste.

fuze Am = fuse.

fuzz [fʌz] *n* - **1.** [hair] cheveux *mpl* crépus - **2.** inf [police] : **the ~** les flics *mpl*.

fuzzy [ˈfʌzɪ] (*compar* **-ier** ; *superl* **-iest**) *adj* - **1.** [hair] crépu(e) - **2.** [photo, image] flou(e) - **3.** [thoughts, mind] confus(e).

fwd. *abbr of* forward.

fwy *abbr of* freeway.

FY *n abbr of* fiscal year.

FYI *abbr of* for your information.

G

g¹ (pl g's OR gs), **G** (pl G's OR Gs) [dʒiː] n [letter] g m inv, G m inv.
➡ **G** ◇ n MUS sol m ◇ **- 1.** (abbr of **good**) B **- 2.** (abbr of **general (audience)**) tous publics.
g² **- 1.** (abbr of **gram**) g **- 2.** (abbr of **gravity**) g.
GA abbr of **Georgia**.
gab [gæb] ⊳ **gift**.
gabardine [ˌgæbə'diːn] n gabardine f.
gabble ['gæbl] ◇ vt & vi baragouiner ◇ n charabia m.
gable ['geɪbl] n pignon m.
Gabon [gæ'bɒn] n Gabon m ; in ~ au Gabon.
Gabonese [ˌgæbɒ'niːz] ◇ adj gabonais(e) ◇ npl : **the ~** les Gabonais.
gad [gæd] (pt & pp **-ded** ; cont **-ding**) ➡ **gad about** vi inf partir en vadrouille.
gadget ['gædʒɪt] n gadget m.
gadgetry ['gædʒɪtrɪ] n (U) gadgets mpl.
Gaelic ['geɪlɪk] ◇ adj gaélique ◇ n gaélique m.
gaffe [gæf] n gaffe f.
gaffer ['gæfə'] n Br inf [boss] patron m.
gag [gæg] (pt & pp **-ged** ; cont **-ging**) ◇ n **- 1.** [for mouth] bâillon m **- 2.** inf [joke] blague f, gag m ◇ vt [put gag on] bâillonner ◇ vi [choke] s'étrangler.
gage Am = **gauge**.
gaiety ['geɪətɪ] n gaieté f.
gaily ['geɪlɪ] adv **- 1.** [cheerfully] gaiement **- 2.** [thoughtlessly] allègrement.
gain [geɪn] ◇ n **- 1.** [gen] profit m **- 2.** [improvement] augmentation f ◇ vt **- 1.** [acquire] gagner **- 2.** [increase in - speed, weight] prendre ; [- confidence] gagner en **- 3.** [subj : watch, clock] : **to ~ 10 minutes** avancer de 10 minutes ◇ vi **- 1.** [advance] : **to ~ in sthg** gagner en qqch **- 2.** [benefit] : **to ~ from** OR **by sthg** tirer un avantage de qqch **- 3.** [watch, clock] avancer.
➡ **gain on** vt fus rattraper.
gainful ['geɪnful] adj fml lucratif(ive).
gainfully ['geɪnfulɪ] adv fml lucrativement.
gainsay [ˌgeɪn'seɪ] (pt & pp **-said**) vt fml contredire.

gait [geɪt] n démarche f.
gaiters ['geɪtəz] npl guêtres fpl.
gal. abbr of **gallon**.
gala ['gɑːlə] ◇ n [celebration] gala m ◇ comp de gala.
Galapagos Islands [gə'læpəgəs-] npl : **the ~** les (îles fpl) Galapagos ; **in the ~** aux (îles) Galapagos.
galaxy ['gæləksɪ] (pl **-ies**) n galaxie f.
gale [geɪl] n [wind] grand vent m.
Galicia [gə'lɪʃɪə] n **- 1.** [in Central Europe] Galicie f ; **in ~** en Galicie **- 2.** [in Spain] Galice f ; **in ~** en Galice.
gall [gɔːl] ◇ n [nerve] : **to have the ~ to do sthg** avoir le toupet de faire qqch ◇ vt contrarier.
gall. abbr of **gallon**.
gallant [sense 1 'gælənt, sense 2 gə'lænt, 'gælənt] adj **- 1.** [courageous] courageux(euse) **- 2.** [polite to women] galant.
gallantry ['gæləntrɪ] n **- 1.** [courage] bravoure f **- 2.** [politeness to women] galanterie f.
gall bladder n vésicule f biliaire.
galleon ['gælɪən] n galion m.
gallery ['gælərɪ] (pl **-ies**) n **- 1.** [gen] galerie f **- 2.** [for displaying art] musée m **- 3.** [in theatre] paradis m.
galley ['gælɪ] (pl **-s**) n **- 1.** [ship] galère f **- 2.** [kitchen] coquerie f.
Gallic ['gælɪk] adj français(e).
galling ['gɔːlɪŋ] adj humiliant(e).
gallivant [ˌgælɪ'vænt] vi inf mener une vie de patachon.
gallon ['gælən] n = 4,546 litres, gallon m.
gallop ['gæləp] ◇ n galop m ◇ vi galoper.
galloping ['gæləpɪŋ] adj [inflation] galopant(e).
gallows ['gæləʊz] (pl inv) n gibet m.
gallstone ['gɔːlstəʊn] n calcul m biliaire.
Gallup poll ['gæləp-] n Br sondage m d'opinion.
galore [gə'lɔːr] adj en abondance.
galoshes [gə'lɒʃɪz] npl caoutchoucs mpl, claques fpl Can.
galvanize, -ise ['gælvənaɪz] vt **- 1.** TECH galvaniser **- 2.** [impel] : **to ~ sb into action** pousser qqn à agir.
Gambia ['gæmbɪə] n : **(the) ~** Gambie f ; **in (the) ~** en Gambie.
Gambian ['gæmbɪən] ◇ adj gambien(enne) ◇ n Gambien m, -enne f.
gambit ['gæmbɪt] n entrée f en matière.
gamble ['gæmbl] ◇ n [calculated risk] risque m ;

to take a ~ prendre un risque ◇ *vi* - **1.** [bet] jouer ; **to ~ on** jouer de l'argent sur - **2.** [take risk] : **to ~ on** miser sur.

gambler ['gæmblə^r] *n* joueur *m*, -euse *f*.

gambling ['gæmblɪŋ] *n (U)* jeu *m*.

gambol ['gæmbl] (Br *pt* & *pp* **-led** ; *cont* **-ling**, Am *pt* & *pp* **-ed** ; *cont* **-ing**) *vi* gambader.

game [geɪm] ◇ *n* - **1.** [gen] jeu *m* ; **what's your ~?** inf à quoi joues-tu? - **2.** [match] match *m* - **3.** *(U)* [hunted animals] gibier *m* - **4.** phr : **to beat sb at their own ~** battre qqn sur son propre terrain ; **the ~'s up** tout est perdu ; **to give the ~ away** vendre la mèche ◇ *adj* - **1.** [brave] courageux(euse) - **2.** [willing] : **~ (for sthg/to do sthg)** partant(e) (pour qqch/pour faire qqch).

◆ **games** ◇ *n* SCH éducation *f* physique ◇ *npl* [sporting contest] jeux *mpl*.

gamekeeper ['geɪm,kiːpə^r] *n* garde-chasse *m*.

gamely ['geɪmlɪ] *adv* - **1.** [bravely] courageusement - **2.** [willingly] volontairement.

game plan *n* stratégie *f*, plan *m* d'attaque.

game reserve *n* réserve *f* (de chasse)

games console [geɪmz -] *n* COMPUT console *f* de jeux.

game show *n* jeu *m* télévisé.

gamesmanship ['geɪmzmənʃɪp] *n* art de gagner habilement.

gamma rays ['gæmə-] *npl* rayons *mpl* gamma.

gammon ['gæmən] *n* jambon *m* fumé.

gammy ['gæmɪ] (*compar* **-ier** ; *superl* **-iest**) *adj* Br inf boiteux(euse).

gamut ['gæmət] *n* gamme *f* ; **to run the ~ of** passer par toute la gamme de.

gander ['gændə^r] *n* [male goose] jars *m*.

gang [gæŋ] *n* - **1.** [of criminals] gang *m* - **2.** [of young people] bande *f*.

◆ **gang up** *vi* inf : **to ~ up (on)** se liguer (contre).

Ganges ['gændʒiːz] *n* : **the (River) ~** le Gange.

gangland ['gæŋlænd] *n (U)* milieu *m*.

gangling ['gæŋglɪŋ], **gangly** ['gæŋglɪ] (*compar* **-ier** ; *superl* **-iest**) *adj* dégingandé(e).

gangplank ['gæŋplæŋk] *n* passerelle *f*.

gangrene ['gæŋgriːn] *n* gangrène *f*.

gangrenous ['gæŋgrɪnəs] *adj* gangreneux(euse).

gangster ['gæŋstə^r] *n* gangster *m*.

gangway ['gæŋweɪ] *n* - **1.** Br [aisle] allée *f* - **2.** [gangplank] passerelle *f*.

gannet ['gænɪt] (*pl inv* OR **-s**) *n* [bird] fou *m* (de Bassan).

gantry ['gæntrɪ] (*pl* **-ies**) *n* portique *m*.

GAO (*abbr of* **General Accounting Office**) *n* Cour des comptes américaine.

gaol [dʒeɪl] Br = **jail**.

gap [gæp] *n* - **1.** [empty space] trou *m* ; [in text] blanc *m* ; fig [in knowledge, report] lacune *f* - **2.** [interval of time] période *f* - **3.** fig [great difference] fossé *m*.

gape [geɪp] *vi* - **1.** [person] rester bouche bée - **2.** [hole, shirt] bâiller.

gaping ['geɪpɪŋ] *adj* - **1.** [open-mouthed] bouche bée *(inv)* - **2.** [wide-open] béant(e) ; [shirt] grand ouvert (grande ouverte).

gap year *n* année d'interruption volontaire des études, avant l'entrée à l'université.

garage [Br 'gæraːʒ, 'gærɪdʒ, , Am gə'raːʒ] *n* - **1.** [gen] garage *m* - **2.** Br [for fuel] station-service *f*.

garb [gaːb] *n (U)* fml tenue *f*.

garbage ['gaːbɪdʒ] *n (U)* - **1.** [refuse] détritus *mpl* - **2.** inf [nonsense] idioties *fpl*.

garbage can *n* Am poubelle *f*.

garbage collector *n* Am éboueur *m*.

garbage truck *n* Am camion-poubelle *m*.

garbled ['gaːbld] *adj* confus(e).

garden ['gaːdn] ◇ *n* jardin *m* ◇ *comp* de jardin ◇ *vi* jardiner.

◆ **gardens** *npl* jardins *mpl* (publics).

garden centre *n* jardinerie *f*, garden centre *m*.

garden city *n* Br cité-jardin *f*.

gardener ['gaːdnə^r] *n* [professional] jardinier *m*, -ère *f* ; [amateur] personne *f* qui aime jardiner, amateur *m* de jardinage.

gardenia [gaː'diːnjə] *n* gardénia *m*.

gardening ['gaːdnɪŋ] ◇ *n* jardinage *m* ◇ *comp* [gloves, equipment, book] de jardinage ; [expert] en jardinage.

garden party *n* garden-party *f*.

garden shed *n* abri *m* de jardin.

gargantuan [gaː'gæntjʊən] *adj* gargantuesque.

gargle ['gaːgl] *vi* se gargariser.

gargoyle ['gaːgɔɪl] *n* gargouille *f*.

garish ['geərɪʃ] *adj* criard(e).

garland ['gaːlənd] *n* guirlande *f* de fleurs.

garlic ['gaːlɪk] *n* ail *m*.

garlic bread *n* pain *m* à l'ail.

garlicky ['gaːlɪkɪ] *adj* inf qui sent l'ail.

garment ['gaːmənt] *n* vêtement *m*.

garner ['gaːnə^r] *vt* fml recueillir.

garnet ['gaːnɪt] *n* [red stone] grenat *m*.

garnish ['gɑːnɪʃ] ⬦ n garniture f ⬦ vt garnir.

garret ['gærət] n mansarde f.

garrison ['gærɪsn] ⬦ n [soldiers] garnison f ⬦ vt tenir en garnison.

garrulous ['gærələs] adj volubile.

garter ['gɑːtəʳ] n - **1.** [for socks] supportchaussette m; [for stockings] jarretière f - **2.** Am [suspender] jarretelle f.

gas [gæs] (pl gases OR gasses [gæsiːz], pt & pp -sed; cont -sing) ⬦ n - **1.** [gen] gaz m inv - **2.** Am [for vehicle] essence f ⬦ vt gazer.

gas chamber n chambre f à gaz.

Gascony ['gæskənɪ] n Gascogne f; in ~ en Gascogne.

gas cooker n Br cuisinière f à gaz.

gas cylinder n bouteille f de gaz.

gaseous ['gæsɪəs] adj gazeux(euse).

gas fire n Br appareil m de chauffage à gaz.

gas fitter n ajusteur m gazier.

gas gauge n Am jauge f d'essence.

gash [gæʃ] ⬦ n entaille f ⬦ vt entailler.

gasket ['gæskɪt] n joint m d'étanchéité.

gasman ['gæsmæn] (pl -men [-men]) n [who reads meter] employé m du gaz; [for repairs] installateur m de gaz.

gas mask n masque m à gaz.

gas meter n compteur m à gaz.

gasoline ['gæsəliːn] n Am essence f.

gasometer [gæ'sɒmɪtəʳ] n réservoir m collecteur de gaz.

gas oven n - **1.** [for cooking] four m à gaz - **2.** [gas chamber] chambre f à gaz.

gasp [gɑːsp] ⬦ n halètement m ⬦ vi - **1.** [breathe quickly] haleter - **2.** [in shock, surprise] avoir le souffle coupé.

gas pedal n Am accélérateur m.

gasping ['gɑːspɪŋ] adj Br inf mort(e) de soif.

gas station n Am station-service f.

gas stove = gas cooker.

gassy ['gæsɪ] (compar -ier; superl -iest) adj pej gazeux(euse).

gas tank n Am réservoir m.

gas tap n [for mains supply] robinet m de gaz; [on gas fire] prise f de gaz.

gastric ['gæstrɪk] adj gastrique.

gastric ulcer n ulcère m gastrique.

gastritis [gæs'traɪtɪs] n gastrite f.

gastroenteritis ['gæstrəʊ,entə'raɪtɪs] n gastro-entérite f.

gastronomic [,gæstrə'nɒmɪk] adj gastronomique.

gastronomy [gæs'trɒnəmɪ] n gastronomie f.

gasworks ['gæswɜːks] (pl inv) n usine f à gaz.

gate [geɪt] n [of garden, farm] barrière f; [of town, at airport] porte f; [of park] grille f.

gâteau ['gætəʊ] (pl -x [-z]) n Br gâteau m.

gatecrash ['geɪtkræʃ] vt & vi prendre part à une réunion, une réception sans y avoir été convié.

gatecrasher ['geɪt,kræʃəʳ] n inf intrus m, -e f.

gatehouse ['geɪthaʊs] n loge f du gardien.

gatekeeper ['geɪt,kiːpəʳ] n gardien m, -enne f.

gatepost ['geɪtpəʊst] n montant m de barrière.

gateway ['geɪtweɪ] n - **1.** [entrance] entrée f - **2.** [means of access]: ~ to porte f de; fig clé f de.

gather ['gæðəʳ] ⬦ vt - **1.** [collect] ramasser; [flowers] cueillir; [information] recueillir; [courage, strength] rassembler; to ~ together rassembler - **2.** [increase - speed, force] prendre - **3.** [understand]: to ~ (that) ... croire comprendre que ... - **4.** [cloth - into folds] plisser ⬦ vi [come together] se rassembler; [clouds] s'amonceler.

➤ **gather up** vt sep rassembler.

gathering ['gæðərɪŋ] n [meeting] rassemblement m.

GATT [gæt] (abbr of General Agreement on Tariffs and Trade) n GATT m.

gauche [gəʊʃ] adj gauche.

gaudy ['gɔːdɪ] (compar -ier; superl -iest) adj voyant(e).

gauge, gage Am [geɪdʒ] ⬦ n - **1.** [for rain] pluviomètre m; [for fuel] jauge f (d'essence); [for tyre pressure] manomètre m - **2.** [of gun, wire] calibre m - **3.** RAIL écartement m ⬦ vt - **1.** [measure] mesurer - **2.** [evaluate] jauger.

Gaul [gɔːl] n - **1.** [country] Gaule f - **2.** [person] Gaulois m, -e f.

gaunt [gɔːnt] adj - **1.** [thin] hâve - **2.** [bare, grim] désolé(e).

gauntlet ['gɔːntlɪt] n gant m (de protection); to run the ~ of sthg endurer qqch; to throw down the ~ (to sb) jeter le gant (à qqn).

gauze [gɔːz] n gaze f.

gave [geɪv] pt ➪ give.

gawky ['gɔːkɪ] (compar -ier; superl -iest) adj [person] dégingandé(e); [movement] désordonné(e).

gawp [gɔːp] vi: to ~ (at) rester bouche bée (devant).

gay [geɪ] <> adj - **1.** [gen] gai(e) - **2.** [homosexual] homo (inv), gay (inv) <> n homo mf, gay mf.

Gaza Strip ['gɑːzə-] n : **the ~** la bande de Gaza.

gaze [geɪz] <> n regard m (fixe) <> vi : **to ~ at sb/sthg** regarder qqn/qqch (fixement).

gazebo [gəˈziːbəʊ] (pl inv OR -s) n belvédère m.

gazelle [gəˈzel] (pl inv OR -s) n gazelle f.

gazette [gəˈzet] n [newspaper] gazette f.

gazetteer [ˌgæzɪˈtɪəʳ] n index m géographique.

gazump [gəˈzʌmp] vt Br inf : **to be ~ed** être victime d'une suroffre.

GB (abbr of **Great Britain**) n G-B f.

GBH (abbr of **grievous bodily harm**) n coups mpl et blessures.

GC (abbr of **George Cross**) n distinction honorifique britannique.

GCE (abbr of **General Certificate of Education**) n certificat de fin d'études secondaires en Grande-Bretagne.

GCH Br (abbr of **gas central heating**) chauffage central à gaz.

GCHQ (abbr of **Government Communications Headquarters**) n en Grande-Bretagne, centre d'interception des télécommunications étrangères.

GCSE (abbr of **General Certificate of Secondary Education**) n examen de fin d'études secondaires en Grande-Bretagne.

Gdns abbr of **Gardens**.

GDP (abbr of **gross domestic product**) n PIB m.

GDR (abbr of **German Democratic Republic**) n RDA f.

gear [gɪəʳ] <> n - **1.** TECH [mechanism] embrayage m - **2.** [speed - of car, bicycle] vitesse f ; **to be in/ out of ~** être en prise/au point mort - **3.** (U) [equipment, clothes] équipement m <> vt : **to ~ sthg to sb/sthg** destiner qqch à qqn/qqch.
◆ **gear up** vi : **to ~ up for sthg/to do sthg** se préparer pour qqch/à faire qqch.

gearbox ['gɪəbɒks] n boîte f de vitesses.

gearing ['gɪərɪŋ] n TECH engrenage m.

gear lever, gear stick Br, **gear shift** Am n levier m de changement de vitesse.

gear wheel n pignon m, roue f d'engrenage.

gee [dʒiː] excl - **1.** [to horse] : **~ up!** hue! - **2.** Am inf [expressing surprise, excitement] : **~ (whiz)!** ça alors!

geek ['giːk] n inf débile mf ; **a movie/computer ~** un dingue de cinéma/d'informatique.

geese [giːs] pl ⊳ **goose**.

Geiger counter ['gaɪgəʳ-] n compteur m Geiger.

geisha (girl) ['geɪʃə-] n geisha f.

gel [dʒel] (pt & pp **-led** ; cont **-ling**) <> n [for hair] gel m <> vi - **1.** [thicken] prendre - **2.** fig [take shape] prendre tournure.

gelatin ['dʒelətɪn], **gelatine** [ˌdʒeləˈtiːn] n gélatine f.

gelding ['geldɪŋ] n hongre m.

gelignite ['dʒelɪgnaɪt] n gélignite f.

gem [dʒem] n - **1.** [jewel] pierre f précieuse, gemme f - **2.** fig [person, thing] perle f.

Gemini ['dʒemɪnaɪ] n Gémeaux mpl ; **to be (a) ~** être Gémeaux.

gemstone ['dʒemstəʊn] n pierre f précieuse.

gen [dʒen] (pt & pp **-ned** ; cont **-ning**) n (U) Br inf info f.
◆ **gen up** vi : **to ~ up (on sthg)** se rancarder (sur qqch).

gen. (abbr of **general, generally**) gén.

Gen. (abbr of **General**) Gal.

gender ['dʒendəʳ] n - **1.** [sex] sexe m - **2.** GRAMM genre m.

gene [dʒiːn] n gène m.

genealogist [ˌdʒiːnɪˈælədʒɪst] n généalogiste m f.

genealogy [ˌdʒiːnɪˈælədʒɪ] (pl -ies) n généalogie f.

genera ['dʒenərə] pl ⊳ **genus**.

general ['dʒenərəl] <> adj général(e) <> n général m.
◆ **in general** adv en général.

general anaesthetic n anesthésie f générale.

general delivery n Am poste f restante.

general election n élection f générale.

generality [ˌdʒenəˈrælətɪ] (pl -ies) n généralité f.

generalization [ˌdʒenərəlaɪˈzeɪʃn] n généralisation f.

generalize, -ise ['dʒenərəlaɪz] vi : **to ~ (about)** généraliser (au sujet de OR sur).

general knowledge n culture f générale.

generally ['dʒenərəlɪ] adv - **1.** [usually, in most cases] généralement - **2.** [unspecifically] en général ; [describe] en gros.

general manager n directeur général m, directrice générale f.

general practice n - **1.** [work] médecine f générale - **2.** [place] cabinet m de généraliste.

general practitioner n (médecin m) généraliste m.

general public n : the ~ le grand public.

general-purpose adj polyvalent(e).

general strike n grève f générale.

generate ['dʒenəreɪt] vt [energy, jobs] générer ; [electricity, heat] produire ; [interest, excitement] susciter.

generation [,dʒenə'reɪʃn] n - 1. [gen] génération f ; first/second ~ première/deuxième génération - 2. [creation - of jobs] création f ; [- of interest, excitement] induction f ; [- of electricity] production f.

generation gap n fossé m des générations.

generator ['dʒenəreɪtə'] n générateur m ; ELEC génératrice f, générateur.

generic [dʒɪ'nerɪk] adj générique.

generosity [,dʒenə'rɒsətɪ] n générosité f.

generous ['dʒenərəs] adj généreux(euse).

generously ['dʒenərəslɪ] adv généreusement.

genesis ['dʒenəsɪs] (pl -ses [-siːz]) n [origin] genèse f.

genetic [dʒɪ'netɪk] adj génétique.
➡ **genetics** n (U) génétique f.

genetically [dʒɪ'netɪklɪ] adv génétiquement ; ~ modified génétiquement modifié(e) ; ~ modified organism organisme m génétiquement modifié.

genetic code n code m génétique.

genetic engineering (U) n manipulation f génétique.

genetic fingerprinting [-'fɪŋgəprɪntɪŋ] n empreinte f génétique.

Geneva [dʒɪ'niːvə] n Genève.

Geneva convention [dʒɪ'niːvə] n : the ~ la Convention de Genève.

genial ['dʒiːnjəl] adj affable.

genie ['dʒiːnɪ] (pl genies OR genii ['dʒiːnɪaɪ]) n génie m.

genitals ['dʒenɪtlz] npl organes mpl génitaux.

genius ['dʒiːnjəs] (pl -es [-iːz]) n génie m ; ~ for sthg/for doing sthg génie de qqch/pour faire qqch.

Genoa ['dʒenəuə] n Gênes.

genocide ['dʒenəsaɪd] n génocide m.

genome ['dʒiːnəum] n génome m.

genre ['ʒɑ̃rə] n genre m.

gent [dʒent] n Br inf gentleman m.
➡ **gents** n Br [toilets] toilettes fpl pour hommes ; [sign on door] messieurs.

genteel [dʒen'tiːl] adj raffiné(e).

gentile ['dʒentaɪl] <> adj gentil(ille) <> n gentil m, -ille f.

gentle ['dʒentl] adj doux (douce) ; [hint] discret(ète) ; [telling-off] léger(ère).

gentleman ['dʒentlmən] (pl -men [-mən]) n - 1. [well-behaved man] gentleman m ; ~'s agreement accord m qui repose sur l'honneur - 2. [man] monsieur m.

gentlemanly ['dʒentlmənlɪ] adj courtois(e).

gentleness ['dʒentlnɪs] n douceur f.

gently ['dʒentlɪ] adv [gen] doucement ; [speak, smile] avec douceur.

gentry ['dʒentrɪ] n petite noblesse f.

genuflect ['dʒenjuːflekt] vi fml faire une génuflexion.

genuine ['dʒenjuɪn] adj authentique ; [interest, customer] sérieux(euse) ; [person, concern] sincère.

genuinely ['dʒenjuɪnlɪ] adv réellement.

genus ['dʒiːnəs] (pl genera ['dʒenərəl]) n genre m.

geographer [dʒɪ'ɒgrəfə'] n géographe mf.

geographical [dʒɪə'græfɪkl] adj géographique.

geography [dʒɪ'ɒgrəfɪ] n géographie f.

geological [,dʒɪə'lɒdʒɪkl] adj géologique.

geologist [dʒɪ'ɒlədʒɪst] n géologue mf.

geology [dʒɪ'ɒlədʒɪ] n géologie f.

geometric(al) [,dʒɪə'metrɪk(l)] adj géométrique.

geometry [dʒɪ'ɒmətrɪ] n géométrie f.

geophysics [,dʒiː:əʊ'fɪzɪks] n géophysique f.

Geordie ['dʒɔːdɪ] n personne originaire de Tyneside.

George Cross ['dʒɔːdʒ-] n Br décoration décernée pour actes de bravoure.

Georgia ['dʒɔːdʒə] n [in US, in CIS] Géorgie f ; in ~ en Géorgie.

Georgian ['dʒɔːdʒən] <> adj - 1. Br [house, furniture] ≈ style XVIIIe (siècle) - 2. GEOGR géorgien(enne) <> n Géorgien m, -enne f.

geranium [dʒɪ'reɪnjəm] (pl -s) n géranium m.

gerbil ['dʒɜːbɪl] n gerbille f.

geriatric [,dʒerɪ'ætrɪk] adj - 1. MED gériatrique - 2. pej [person] décrépit(e) ; [object] vétuste.

germ [dʒɜːm] n - 1. [bacterium] germe m - 2. fig [of idea, plan] embryon m.

German ['dʒɜːmən] <> adj allemand(e) <> n - 1. [person] Allemand m, -e f - 2. [language] allemand m.

Germanic [dʒɜː'mænɪk] adj germanique.

German measles n (U) rubéole f.

German shepherd (dog) n berger m allemand.

Germany ['dʒɜːmənɪ] (pl -ies) n Allemagne f ; **in ~** en Allemagne.

germicide ['dʒɜːmɪsaɪd] n germicide m.

germinate ['dʒɜːmɪneɪt] ⟨⟩ vt - **1.** [seed] faire germer - **2.** fig [idea, feeling] faire naître ⟨⟩ vi lit & fig germer.

germination [,dʒɜːmɪ'neɪʃn] n - **1.** [of seed] germination f - **2.** fig [of idea, feeling] développement m.

germ warfare n (U) guerre f bactériologique.

gerrymandering ['dʒerɪmændərɪŋ] (U) n charcutage m électoral.

gerund ['dʒerənd] n gérondif m.

gestation [dʒe'steɪʃn] n gestation f.

gestation period n lit & fig période f de gestation.

gesticulate [dʒes'tɪkjʊleɪt] vi gesticuler.

gesticulation [dʒe,stɪkjʊ'leɪʃn] n gesticulation f.

gesture ['dʒestʃəʳ] ⟨⟩ n geste m ⟨⟩ vi : **to ~ to** OR **towards sb** faire signe à qqn.

get [get] (Br pt & pp got ; cont -ting, Am pt got ; pp gotten ; cont -ting) ⟨⟩ vt - **1.** [cause to do] : **to ~ sb to do sthg** faire faire qqch à qqn ; **I'll ~ my sister to help** je vais demander à ma sœur de nous aider - **2.** [cause to be done] : **to ~ sthg done** faire faire qqch ; **I got the car fixed** j'ai fait réparer la voiture - **3.** [cause to become] : **to ~ sb pregnant** rendre qqn enceinte ; **I can't ~ the car started** je n'arrive pas à mettre la voiture en marche ; **to ~ things going** faire avancer les choses - **4.** [cause to move] : **to ~ sb/sthg through sthg** faire passer qqn/qqch par qqch ; **to ~ sb/sthg out of sthg** faire sortir qqn/qqch de qqch - **5.** [bring, fetch] aller chercher ; **can I ~ you something to eat/drink?** est-ce que je peux vous offrir quelque chose à manger/boire? ; **I'll ~ my coat** je vais chercher mon manteau - **6.** [obtain - gen] obtenir ; [- job, house] trouver - **7.** [receive] recevoir, avoir ; **what did you ~ for your birthday?** qu'est-ce que tu as eu pour ton anniversaire? ; **she ~s a good salary** elle touche un bon traitement ; **when did you ~ the news?** quand as-tu reçu la nouvelle? - **8.** [experience a sensation] avoir ; **do you ~ the feeling he doesn't like us?** tu n'as pas l'impression qu'il ne nous aime pas? ; **I ~ a real thrill out of driving fast** cela me donne des sensations fortes de conduire vite - **9.** [be infected with, suffer from] avoir, attraper ; **to ~ a cold** attraper un rhume - **10.** [under-

stand] comprendre, saisir ; **I don't ~ it** inf je ne comprends pas, je ne saisis pas ; **he didn't seem to ~ the point** il ne semblait pas comprendre OR piger - **11.** [catch - bus, train, plane] prendre - **12.** [capture] prendre, attraper - **13.** inf [annoy] : **what really ~s me is his smugness** c'est sa suffisance qui m'agace OR qui m'énerve - **14.** [find] : **you ~ a lot of artists here** on trouve OR il y a beaucoup d'artistes ici ; see also **have** ⟨⟩ vi - **1.** [become] devenir ; **to ~ suspicious** devenir méfiant ; **I'm getting cold/bored** je commence à avoir froid/à m'ennuyer ; **it's getting late** il se fait tard - **2.** [arrive] arriver ; **he never got there** il n'est jamais arrivé ; **I only got back yesterday** je suis rentré hier seulement - **3.** [eventually succeed in] : **to ~ to do sthg** parvenir à OR finir par faire qqch ; **did you ~ to see him?** est-ce que tu as réussi à le voir? ; **she got to enjoy the classes** elle a fini par aimer les cours ; **I never got to visit Beijing** je n'ai jamais pu aller à Beijing - **4.** [progress] : **how far have you got?** où en es-tu? ; **we got as far as buying the paint** on est allé jusqu'à acheter la peinture ; **I got to the point where I didn't care any more** j'en suis arrivé à m'en ficher complètement ; **now we're getting somewhere** enfin on avance ; **we're getting nowhere** on n'arrive à rien ⟨⟩ aux vb : **to ~ excited** s'exciter ; **to ~ hurt** se faire mal ; **to ~ beaten up** se faire tabasser ; **let's ~ going** OR **moving** allons-y ; see also **have**.

● **get about, get around** vi - **1.** [move from place to place] se déplacer - **2.** [circulate - news, rumour] circuler, se répandre ; see also **get around, get round**.

● **get across** vt sep [idea, policy] communiquer ; **to ~ one's message across** se faire comprendre.

● **get ahead** vi avancer.

● **get along** vi - **1.** [manage] se débrouiller - **2.** [progress] avancer, faire des progrès - **3.** [have a good relationship] s'entendre.

● **get around, get round** ⟨⟩ vt fus [overcome] venir à bout de, surmonter ⟨⟩ vi - **1.** [circulate] circuler, se répandre - **2.** [eventually do] : **to ~ around to (doing) sthg** trouver le temps de faire qqch ; see also **get about**.

● **get at** vt fus - **1.** [reach] parvenir à - **2.** [imply] vouloir dire ; **what are you getting at?** où veux-tu en venir? - **3.** inf [criticize] critiquer, dénigrer.

● **get away** vi - **1.** [leave] partir, s'en aller - **2.** [go on holiday] partir en vacances ; **to ~ away from it all** partir se détendre loin de tout - **3.** [escape] s'échapper, s'évader.

● **get away with** vt fus : **to let sb ~ away with sthg** passer qqch à qqn ; **she just lets** him ~ **away with it** elle le laisse tout faire, elle lui passe tout.

➤ **get back** ◇ vt sep [recover, regain] retrouver, récupérer ◇ vi - **1.** [return] rentrer - **2.** [move away] s'écarter.

➤ **get back to** vt fus - **1.** [return to previous state, activity] revenir à ; **to ~ back to sleep** se rendormir ; **things are getting back to normal** la situation redevient normale ; **to ~ back to work** [after pause] se remettre au travail ; [after illness] reprendre son travail - **2.** inf [phone back] rappeler ; **I'll ~ back to you on that** je te reparlerai de ça plus tard.

➤ **get by** vi se débrouiller, s'en sortir.

➤ **get down** vt sep - **1.** [depress] déprimer - **2.** [fetch from higher level] descendre.

➤ **get down to** vt fus s'attaquer à ; **to ~ down to doing sthg** se mettre à faire qqch ; **to ~ down to work** se mettre au travail.

➤ **get in** ◇ vi - **1.** [enter - gen] entrer ; [- referring to vehicle] monter - **2.** [arrive] arriver ; [arrive home] rentrer - **3.** [be elected] être élu(e) ◇ vt sep - **1.** [bring in] rentrer - **2.** [interject] : **to ~ a word in** placer un mot.

➤ **get in on** vt fus se mêler de, participer à.

➤ **get into** vt fus - **1.** [car] monter dans - **2.** [become involved in] se lancer dans ; **to ~ into an argument with sb** se disputer avec qqn - **3.** [enter into a particular situation, state] : **to ~ into a panic** s'affoler ; **to ~ into trouble** s'attirer des ennuis ; **to ~ into the habit of doing sthg** prendre l'habitude de faire qqch - **4.** [be accepted as a student at] être admis(e) OR accepté(e) à - **5.** inf [affect] : **what's got into you?** qu'est-ce qui te prend?

➤ **get off** ◇ vt sep [remove] enlever ◇ vt fus - **1.** [go away from] partir de - **2.** [train, bus etc] descendre de - **1.** [leave bus, train] descendre - **2.** [escape punishment] s'en tirer ; **he got off lightly** il s'en est tiré à bon compte - **3.** [depart] partir.

➤ **get off with** vt fus Br inf avoir une touche avec.

➤ **get on** ◇ vt sep [put on] mettre ◇ vt fus - **1.** [bus, train, plane] monter dans - **2.** [horse] monter sur ◇ vi - **1.** [enter bus, train] monter - **2.** [have good relationship] s'entendre, s'accorder - **3.** [progress] avancer, progresser ; **how are you getting on?** comment ça va? - **4.** [proceed] : **to ~ on (with sthg)** continuer (qqch), poursuivre (qqch) - **5.** [be successful professionally] réussir - **6.** [grow old] : **to be getting on** se faire vieux (vieille).

➤ **get on for** vt fus inf [be approximately] : **to be getting on for** approcher de ; **there were getting on for 5,000 people at the concert** il y avait près de 5 000 personnes au concert.

➤ **get on to** vt fus - **1.** [talk about] se mettre à parler de - **2.** [contact] contacter.

➤ **get out** ◇ vt sep - **1.** [take out] sortir - **2.** [remove] enlever ◇ vi - **1.** [from car, bus, train] descendre - **2.** [news] s'ébruiter.

➤ **get out of** ◇ vt fus - **1.** [car etc] descendre de - **2.** [escape from] s'évader de, s'échapper de - **3.** [avoid] éviter, se dérober à ; **to ~ out of doing sthg** se dispenser de faire qqch ◇ vt sep [cause to escape from] : **to ~ sb out of jail** faire sortir qqn de prison.

➤ **get over** vt fus - **1.** [recover from] se remettre de - **2.** [overcome] surmonter, venir à bout de - **3.** [communicate] communiquer.

➤ **get over with** vt sep : **to ~ sthg over with** en finir avec qqch.

➤ **get round** = get around.

➤ **get through** ◇ vt fus - **1.** [job, task] arriver au bout de - **2.** [exam] réussir à - **3.** [food, drink] consommer - **4.** [unpleasant situation] endurer, supporter ◇ vi - **1.** [make o.s. understood] : **to ~ through (to sb)** se faire comprendre (de qqn) - **2.** TELEC obtenir la communication.

➤ **get to** vt fus inf [annoy] taper sur les nerfs à.

➤ **get together** ◇ vt sep [organize - team, belongings] rassembler ; [- project, report] préparer ◇ vi se réunir.

➤ **get up** ◇ vi se lever ◇ vt fus [petition, demonstration] organiser.

➤ **get up to** vt fus inf faire ; **I wonder what they're getting up to** je me demande ce qu'ils fabriquent OR ce qu'ils sont en train de faire encore.

getaway ['getəweɪ] n fuite f.

getaway car n voiture qui sert à la fuite des gangsters.

get-together n inf réunion f.

getup ['getʌp] n inf accoutrement m.

get-up-and-go n (U) inf tonus m.

get-well card n carte f de vœux de prompt rétablissement.

geyser ['giːzər] n - **1.** [hot spring] geyser m - **2.** Br [water heater] chauffe-eau m inv.

Ghana ['gɑːnə] n Ghana m ; **in ~** au Ghana.

Ghan(a)ian [gɑː'neɪən] ◇ adj ghanéen(enne) ◇ n Ghanéen m, -enne f.

ghastly ['gɑːstlɪ] (compar -ier ; superl -iest) adj - **1.** inf [very bad, unpleasant] épouvantable ; **to feel/look ~** être dans un état/avoir une mine épouvantable - **2.** [horrifying, macabre] effroyable.

gherkin ['gɜːkɪn] n cornichon m.

ghetto ['getəʊ] (pl -s OR -es) n ghetto m.

ghetto blaster [-ˌblɑːstər] n inf grand radiocassette m portatif.

ghost [gəʊst] ◇ n [spirit] spectre m ; he doesn't have a ~ of a chance il n'a pas l'ombre d'une chance ◇ vt = **ghostwrite.**

ghostly ['gəʊstlɪ] (compar **-ier** ; superl **-iest**) adj spectral(e).

ghost town n ville f fantôme.

ghostwrite ['gəʊstraɪt] (pt **-wrote**, pp **-written**) vt écrire à la place de l'auteur.

ghostwriter ['gəʊst,raɪtəʳ] n nègre m.

ghostwritten ['gəʊst,rɪtn] pp ▷ **ghostwrite.**

ghostwrote ['gəʊstrəʊt] pt ▷ **ghostwrite.**

ghoul [gu:l] n - **1.** [spirit] goule f - **2.** pej [ghoulish person] personne f macabre.

ghoulish ['gu:lɪʃ] adj macabre.

GHQ (abbr of **general headquarters**) n GQG m.

GI (abbr of **government issue**) n GI m.

giant ['dʒaɪənt] ◇ adj géant(e) ◇ n géant m.

giant-size(d) adj géant(e).

gibber ['dʒɪbəʳ] vi bredouiller.

gibberish ['dʒɪbərɪʃ] n (U) charabia m, inepties fpl.

gibbon ['gɪbən] n gibbon m.

gibe [dʒaɪb] ◇ n insulte f ◇ vi : **to ~ at** sb/sthg insulter qqn/qqch.

giblets ['dʒɪblɪts] npl abats mpl.

Gibraltar [dʒɪ'brɔːltəʳ] n Gibraltar m ; **in ~** à Gibraltar ; **the Rock of ~** le rocher de Gibraltar.

giddy ['gɪdɪ] (compar **-ier** ; superl **-iest**) adj [dizzy] : **to feel ~** avoir la tête qui tourne.

gift [gɪft] n - **1.** [present] cadeau m - **2.** [talent] don m ; **to have a ~ for** sthg/for doing sthg avoir un don pour qqch/pour faire qqch ; **the ~ of the gab** le bagou.

GIFT [gɪft] (abbr of **gamete in fallopian transfer**) n fivete f.

gift certificate Am = **gift token.**

gifted ['gɪftɪd] adj doué(e).

gift token, gift voucher n Br chèque-cadeau m.

gift-wrapped [-ræpt] adj sous emballage-cadeau.

gig [gɪg] n inf [concert] concert m.

gigabyte ['gaɪgəbaɪt] n COMPUT giga-octet m.

gigantic [dʒaɪ'gæntɪk] adj énorme, gigantesque.

giggle ['gɪgl] ◇ n - **1.** [laugh] gloussement m - **2.** Br inf [fun] : **to be a ~** être marrant(e) OR tordant(e) ; **to have a ~** bien s'amuser ◇ vi [laugh] glousser.

giggly ['gɪglɪ] (compar **-ier** ; superl **-iest**) adj qui pouffe.

GIGO ['gaɪgəʊ] (abbr of **garbage in, garbage out**) COMPUT qualité à l'entrée = qualité à la sortie.

gigolo ['ʒɪgələʊ] (pl **-s**) n pej gigolo m.

gigot ['ʒiːgəʊ] n gigot m.

gilded ['gɪldɪd] adj = **gilt.**

gill [dʒɪl] n [unit of measurement] = 0,142 litre, quart m de pinte.

gills [gɪlz] npl [of fish] branchies fpl.

gilt [gɪlt] ◇ adj [covered in gold] doré(e) ◇ n (U) [gold layer] dorure f.
⇒ **gilts** npl FIN valeurs fpl de père de famille.

gilt-edged [-edʒd] adj FIN de père de famille.

gimme ['gɪmɪ] inf = **give me.**

gimmick ['gɪmɪk] n pej artifice m.

gin [dʒɪn] n gin m ; **~ and tonic** gin tonic.

ginger ['dʒɪndʒəʳ] ◇ n - **1.** [root] gingembre m - **2.** [powder] gingembre m en poudre ◇ adj Br [colour] roux (rousse).

ginger ale n boisson gazeuse au gingembre.

ginger beer n boisson non-alcoolisée au gingembre.

gingerbread ['dʒɪndʒəbred] n pain m d'épice.

ginger group n Br groupe m de pression.

ginger-haired [-'heəd] adj roux (rousse).

gingerly ['dʒɪndʒəlɪ] adv avec précaution.

gingham ['gɪŋəm] n [cloth] vichy m.

gingivitis [,dʒɪndʒɪ'vaɪtɪs] n gingivite f.

ginseng ['dʒɪnseŋ] n ginseng m

gipsy ['dʒɪpsɪ] (pl **-ies**) ◇ adj gitan(e) ◇ n gitan m, -e f ; Br pej bohémien m, -enne f.

giraffe [dʒɪ'rɑːf] (pl inv OR **-s**) n girafe f.

gird [gɜːd] (pt & pp **-ed** OR **girt**) vt ▷ loin.

girder ['gɜːdəʳ] n poutrelle f.

girdle ['gɜːdl] n [corset] gaine f.

girl [gɜːl] n - **1.** [gen] fille f - **2.** [girlfriend] petite amie f.

girl Friday n aide f.

girlfriend ['gɜːlfrend] n - **1.** [female lover] petite amie f - **2.** [female friend] amie f.

girl guide Br, **girl scout** Am n éclaireuse f, guide f.
⇒ **Girl Guides** n : **the Girl Guides** les Guides fpl.

girlie magazine ['gɜːlɪ] n inf magazine m érotique OR déshabillé.

girlish ['gɜːlɪʃ] adj de petite fille.

girl scout Am = **girl guide.**

giro ['dʒaɪrəʊ] (pl **-s**) n Br - **1.** (U) [system] virement m postal - **2.** : **~ (cheque)** chèque m d'indemnisation f (chômage OR maladie).

girt [gɜːt] pt & pp ▷ **gird.**

girth [gɜːθ] n - **1.** [circumference - of tree] circonférence f ; [- of person] tour m de taille - **2.** [of horse] sangle f.

gist [dʒɪst] n substance f ; **to get the ~ of sthg** comprendre OR saisir l'essentiel de qqch.

give [gɪv] (pt **gave**, pp **given**) ⬦ vt - **1.** [gen] donner ; [message] transmettre ; [attention, time] consacrer ; **to ~ sb/sthg sthg** donner qqch à qqn/qqch ; **to ~ sb pleasure/a fright/a smile** faire plaisir/peur/un sourire à qqn ; **to ~ sb a look** jeter un regard à qqn ; **to ~ a shrug** hausser les épaules ; **to ~ a sigh** pousser un soupir ; **to ~ a speech** faire un discours - **2.** [as present] : **to ~ sb sthg, to ~ sthg to sb** donner qqch à qqn, offrir qqch à qqn - **3.** [pay] : **how much did you ~ for it?** combien l'avez-vous payé? - **4.** phr : **I was given to believe** OR **understand that ...** fml on m'a fait comprendre que ... ; **I'd ~ anything** OR **my right arm to do that** je donnerais n'importe quoi OR très cher pour faire ça ⬦ vi [collapse, break] céder, s'affaisser ⬦ n [elasticity] élasticité f, souplesse f.

⬥ **give or take** prep : **~ or take a day/£10** à un jour/10 livres près.

⬥ **give away** vt sep - **1.** [get rid of] donner - **2.** [reveal] révéler.

⬥ **give back** vt sep [return] rendre.

⬥ **give in** vi - **1.** [admit defeat] abandonner, se rendre - **2.** [agree unwillingly] : **to ~ in to sthg** céder à qqch.

⬥ **give off** vt fus [smell] exhaler ; [smoke] faire ; [heat] produire.

⬥ **give out** ⬦ vt sep [distribute] distribuer ⬦ vi [supplies] s'épuiser ; [car] lâcher.

⬥ **give over** ⬦ vt sep [dedicate] : **to be given over to** [subj : time] être consacré(e) à ; [subj : building] être réservé(e) à ⬦ vi Br inf [stop] : **~ over!** arrête!

⬥ **give up** ⬦ vt sep - **1.** [stop] renoncer à ; **to ~ up drinking/smoking** arrêter de boire/de fumer - **2.** [surrender] : **to ~ o.s. up (to sb)** se rendre (à qqn) ⬦ vi abandonner, se rendre.

⬥ **give up on** vt fus [abandon] laisser tomber.

give-and-take n (U) [compromise] concessions fpl de part et d'autre.

giveaway [ˈgɪvəˌweɪ] ⬦ adj - **1.** [tell-tale] révélateur(trice) - **2.** [very cheap] dérisoire ⬦ n [tell-tale sign] signe m révélateur.

given [ˈgɪvn] ⬦ pp ⊳ **give** ⬦ adj - **1.** [set, fixed] convenu(e), fixé(e) ; **at any ~ time** à un moment donné - **2.** [prone] : **to be ~ to sthg/to doing sthg** être enclin(e) à qqch/à faire qqch ⬦ prep étant donné ; **~ that** étant donné que.

given name n Am prénom m.

giver [ˈgɪvəʳ] n donneur m, -euse f.

glacé cherry [ˈglæseɪ-] n cerise f confite.

glacial [ˈgleɪsjəl] adj - **1.** [of glacier] glaciaire - **2.** [unfriendly] glacial(e).

glacier [ˈglæsjəʳ] n glacier m.

glad [glæd] (compar **-der** ; superl **-dest**) adj - **1.** [happy, pleased] content(e) ; **to be ~ about sthg** être content de qqch ; **to be ~ that** être content que - **2.** [willing] : **to be ~ to do sthg** faire qqch volontiers OR avec plaisir - **3.** [grateful] : **to be ~ of sthg** être content(e) de qqch.

gladden [ˈglædn] vt literary réjouir.

glade [gleɪd] n literary clairière f.

gladiator [ˈglædɪeɪtəʳ] n gladiateur m.

gladioli [ˌglædɪˈəʊlaɪ] npl glaïeuls mpl.

gladly [ˈglædlɪ] adv - **1.** [happily, eagerly] avec joie - **2.** [willingly] avec plaisir.

glamor Am = glamour.

glamorize, -ise [ˈglæməraɪz] vt faire apparaître sous un jour séduisant.

glamorous [ˈglæmərəs] adj [person] séduisant(e) ; [appearance] élégant(e) ; [job, place] prestigieux(euse).

glamour Br, **glamor** Am [ˈglæməʳ] n [of person] charme m ; [of appearance] élégance f, chic m ; [of job, place] prestige m.

glance [glɑːns] ⬦ n [quick look] regard m, coup d'œil m ; **to cast** OR **take a ~ at sthg** jeter un coup d'œil à qqch ; **at a ~** d'un coup d'œil ; **at first ~** au premier coup d'œil ⬦ vi [look quickly] : **to ~ at sb/sthg** jeter un coup d'œil à qqn/qqch ; **to ~ at** OR **through sthg** jeter un coup d'œil à OR sur qqch.

⬥ **glance off** vt fus [subj : ball, bullet] ricocher sur.

glancing [ˈglɑːnsɪŋ] adj de côté, oblique.

gland [glænd] n glande f.

glandular fever [ˌglændjʊlə-] n mononucléose f infectieuse.

glare [gleəʳ] ⬦ n - **1.** [scowl] regard m mauvais - **2.** (U) [of headlights, publicity] lumière f aveuglante ⬦ vi - **1.** [scowl] jeter un regard mauvais ; **to ~ at sb/sthg** regarder qqn/qqch d'un œil mauvais - **2.** [sun, lamp] briller d'une lumière éblouissante.

glaring [ˈgleərɪŋ] adj - **1.** [very obvious] flagrant(e) - **2.** [blazing, dazzling] aveuglant(e).

glasnost [ˈglæznɒst] n glasnost f, transparence f.

glass [glɑːs] ⬦ n - **1.** [gen] verre m - **2.** (U) [glassware] verrerie f ⬦ comp [bottle, jar] en OR de verre ; [door, partition] vitré(e).

⬥ **glasses** npl [spectacles] lunettes fpl.

glassblowing [ˈglɑːsˌbləʊɪŋ] n soufflage m du verre.

glass fibre n (U) Br fibre f de verre.

glasshouse [ˈglɑːshaʊs, pl -haʊzɪz] n Br serre f.

glassware [ˈglɑːsweəʳ] n (U) verrerie f.

glassy [ˈglɑːsɪ] (compar -ier ; superl -iest) adj - **1.** [smooth, shiny] lisse comme un miroir - **2.** [blank, lifeless] vitreux(euse).

Glaswegian [glæzˈwiːdʒjən] ◇ adj de Glasgow ◇ n - **1.** habitant m, -e f de Glasgow - **2.** [dialect] dialecte m de Glasgow.

glaucoma [glɔːˈkəʊmə] n glaucome m.

glaze [gleɪz] ◇ n [on pottery] vernis m ; [on pastry, flan] glaçage m ◇ vt [pottery, tiles, bricks] vernisser ; [pastry, flan] glacer.

◆ **glaze over** vi devenir terne OR vitreux(euse).

glazed [gleɪzd] adj - **1.** [dull, bored] terne, vitreux(euse) - **2.** [covered with shiny layer - pottery] vernissé(e) ; [- pastry, flan] glacé(e) - **3.** [with glass] vitré(e).

glazier [ˈgleɪzjəʳ] n vitrier m.

GLC (abbr of **Greater London Council**) n ancien organe administratif du grand Londres.

gleam [gliːm] ◇ n [of gold] reflet m ; [of fire, sunset, disapproval] lueur f ◇ vi - **1.** [surface, object] luire - **2.** [light, eyes] briller.

gleaming [ˈgliːmɪŋ] adj brillant(e).

glean [gliːn] vt [gather] glaner.

glee [gliː] n (U) [joy] joie f, jubilation f.

gleeful [ˈgliːfʊl] adj joyeux(euse).

glen [glen] n Scot vallée f.

glib [glɪb] (compar -ber ; superl -best) adj pej [salesman, politician] qui a du bagout ; [promise, excuse] facile.

glibly [ˈglɪblɪ] adv pej trop facilement.

glide [glaɪd] vi - **1.** [move smoothly - dancer, boat] glisser sans effort ; [- person] se mouvoir sans effort - **2.** [fly] planer.

glider [ˈglaɪdəʳ] n [plane] planeur m.

gliding [ˈglaɪdɪŋ] n [sport] vol m à voile.

glimmer [ˈglɪməʳ] ◇ n [faint light] faible lueur f ; fig signe m, lueur ; **a ~ of hope** une lueur d'espoir ◇ vi luire OR briller faiblement.

glimpse [glɪmps] ◇ n - **1.** [look, sight] aperçu m ; **to catch a ~ of sb/sthg** apercevoir qqn/qqch, entrevoir qqn/qqch - **2.** [idea, perception] idée f ◇ vt - **1.** [catch sight of] apercevoir, entrevoir - **2.** [perceive] pressentir.

glint [glɪnt] ◇ n - **1.** [flash] reflet m - **2.** [in eyes] éclair m ◇ vi étinceler.

glisten [ˈglɪsn] vi briller.

glitch [glɪtʃ] n Am inf [in plan] pépin m.

glitter [ˈglɪtəʳ] ◇ n (U) scintillement m ◇ vi - **1.** [object, light] scintiller - **2.** [eyes] briller.

glittering [ˈglɪtərɪŋ] adj brillant(e).

glitzy [ˈglɪtsɪ] (compar -ier ; superl -iest) adj inf [glamorous] chic.

gloat [gləʊt] vi : **to ~ (over sthg)** se réjouir (de qqch).

global [ˈgləʊbl] adj [worldwide] mondial(e).

globalization [ˌgləʊbəlaɪˈzeɪʃn] n mondialisation f.

globally [ˈgləʊbəlɪ] adv à l'échelle mondiale, mondialement.

global village n village m planétaire.

global warming [-ˈwɔːmɪŋ] n réchauffement m de la planète.

globe [gləʊb] n - **1.** [Earth] : **the ~** la terre - **2.** [spherical map] globe m terrestre - **3.** [spherical object] globe m.

globetrotter [ˈgləʊbˌtrɒtəʳ] n inf globetrotter m.

globule [ˈglɒbjuːl] n gouttelette f.

gloom [gluːm] n (U) - **1.** [darkness] obscurité f - **2.** [unhappiness] tristesse f.

gloomy [ˈgluːmɪ] (compar -ier ; superl -iest) adj - **1.** [room, sky, prospects] sombre - **2.** [person, atmosphere, mood] triste, lugubre.

glorification [ˌglɔːrɪfɪˈkeɪʃn] n glorification f.

glorified [ˈglɔːrɪfaɪd] adj pej : **it's just a ~ swimming pool** il ne s'agit que d'une vulgaire piscine.

glorify [ˈglɔːrɪfaɪ] (pt & pp -ied) vt exalter.

glorious [ˈglɔːrɪəs] adj - **1.** [beautiful, splendid] splendide - **2.** [very enjoyable] formidable - **3.** [successful, impressive] magnifique.

glory [ˈglɔːrɪ] (pl -ies) n - **1.** (U) [fame, admiration] gloire f - **2.** (U) [beauty] splendeur f - **3.** [best feature] merveille f.

◆ **glories** npl [triumphs] triomphes mpl.

◆ **glory in** vt fus [relish] savourer.

Glos (abbr of **Gloucestershire**) comté anglais.

gloss [glɒs] n - **1.** (U) [shine] brillant m, lustre m - **2.** : **~ (paint)** peinture f brillante.

◆ **gloss over** vt fus passer sur.

glossary [ˈglɒsərɪ] (pl -ies) n glossaire m.

glossy [ˈglɒsɪ] (compar -ier ; superl -iest) adj - **1.** [hair, surface] brillant(e) - **2.** [book, photo] sur papier glacé.

glossy magazine n magazine m de luxe.

glove [glʌv] n gant m.

glove compartment n boîte f à gants.

glove puppet n Br marionnette f (à gaine).

glow [gləʊ] ◇ n (U) - **1.** [of fire, light, sunset] lueur f - **2.** [of skin - because of heat, exercise] rou-

geur *f;* [- because of health] teint *m* rose et frais
- 3. [feeling - of pride] sensation *f;* [- of anger]
élan *m;* [- of shame, pleasure] sentiment *m* <> *vi*
- 1. [shine out - fire] rougeoyer ; [light, stars, eyes]
flamboyer **- 2.** [shine in light] briller **- 3.** [with col-
our] flamboyer **- 4.** [flush] : **to ~ (with)** [heat]
être rouge (de) ; [pleasure, health] rayonner
(de).

glower ['glaʊəʳ] *vi :* **to ~ (at)** lancer des regards noirs (à).

glowing ['glaʊɪŋ] *adj* [very favourable] dithyrambique.

glow-worm *n* ver *m* luisant.

glucose ['glu:kəʊs] *n* glucose *m.*

glue [glu:] (*cont* glueing OR gluing) <> *n* (U)
colle *f* <> *vt* [stick with glue] coller ; **to ~ sthg to
sthg** coller qqch à OR avec qqch ; **to be ~d to
the TV** fig être rivé à la télé.

glue-sniffing [-ˌsnɪfɪŋ] *n* intoxication *f* à la
colle.

glum [glʌm] (*compar* **-mer** ; *superl* **-mest**) *adj*
[unhappy] morne.

glut [glʌt] *n* surplus *m.*

gluten ['glu:tən] *n* gluten *m.*

glutinous ['glu:tɪnəs] *adj* glutineux(euse).

glutton ['glʌtn] *n* [greedy person] glouton *m,*
-onne *f;* **to be a ~ for punishment** être maso,
être masochiste.

gluttony ['glʌtənɪ] *n* gloutonnerie *f.*

glycerin ['glɪsərɪn], **glycerine** ['glɪsəri:n] *n*
glycérine *f.*

gm (*abbr of* gram) g.

GM (*abbr of* genetically modified) *adj* génétiquement modifié(e).

GMAT (*abbr of* Graduate Management Admissions Test) *n* test d'admission aux programmes de MBA.

GMB *n* important syndicat ouvrier britannique.

GMO (*abbr of* genetically modified organism) *n* OGM *m.*

GMT (*abbr of* Greenwich Mean Time) *n* GMT
m.

gnarled [nɑ:ld] *adj* [tree, hands] noueux(euse).

gnash [næʃ] *vt :* **to ~ one's teeth** grincer des
dents.

gnat [næt] *n* moucheron *m.*

gnaw [nɔ:] <> *vt* [chew] ronger <> *vi* [worry] : **to
~ (away) at sb** ronger qqn.

gnome [nəʊm] *n* gnome *m,* lutin *m.*

GNP (*abbr of* gross national product) *n* PNB
m.

gnu [nu:] (*pl inv* OR **-s**) *n* gnou *m.*

GNVQ Br (*abbr of* general national vocational
qualification) *n* diplôme sanctionnant deux
années d'études professionnelles à la fin du
secondaire, ≃ baccalauréat *m* professionnel.

go [gəʊ] (*pt* went, *pp* gone ; *pl* goes) <> *vi*
- 1. [move, travel] aller ; **where are you ~ing?** où
vas-tu? ; **he's gone to Portugal** il est allé au
Portugal ; **we went by bus/train** nous sommes allés en bus/par le train ; **where does
this path ~?** où mène ce chemin? ; **to ~ and
do sthg** aller faire qqch ; **to ~ swimming/
shopping/jogging** aller nager/faire les
courses/faire du jogging ; **to ~ for a walk** aller se promener, faire une promenade ; **to
~ to church/school/university** aller à l'église/
l'école/l'université ; **to ~ to work** aller travailler OR à son travail ; **where do we ~ from
here?** fig qu'est-ce qu'on fait maintenant?
- 2. [depart] partir, s'en aller ; **I must ~, I have
to ~** il faut que je m'en aille ; **what time does
the bus ~?** à quelle heure part le bus? ; **let's
~!** allons-y! **- 3.** [be or remain in a particular state] :
to ~ hungry souffrir de la faim ; **we went in
fear of our lives** nous craignions pour notre
vie ; **to ~ unpunished** rester impuni **- 4.** [be-
come] devenir ; **to ~ grey** grisonner, devenir
gris ; **to ~ mad** devenir fou **- 5.** [pass - time]
passer ; **the time went slowly/quickly** le
temps a passé lentement/a vite passé
- 6. [progress] marcher, se dérouler ; **the conference went very smoothly** la conférence
s'est déroulée sans problème OR s'est très
bien passée ; **to ~ well/badly** aller bien/
mal ; **how's it ~ing?** inf comment ça va?
- 7. [function, work] marcher ; **the clock's stopped ~ing** la pendule s'est arrêtée ; **the car
won't ~** la voiture ne veut pas démarrer
- 8. [indicating intention, expectation] : **to be ~ing to
do sthg** aller faire qqch ; **what are you ~ing
to do now?** qu'est-ce que tu vas faire maintenant? ; **he said he was ~ing to be late** il a
prévenu qu'il allait arriver en retard ;
we're ~ing (to ~) to America in June on va (aller) en Amérique en juin ; **it's ~ing to rain/
snow** il va pleuvoir/neiger ; **she's ~ing to
have a baby** elle attend un bébé ; **it's not
~ing to be easy** cela ne va pas être facile
- 9. [bell, alarm] sonner **- 10.** [be spent] passer,
partir ; **all my money goes on food and rent**
tout mon argent est passé OR parti en
nourriture et en loyer **- 11.** [be given] : **to ~ to**
aller à, être donné(e) à **- 12.** [be disposed of] :
he'll have to ~ il va falloir le congédier OR le
mettre à la porte ; **everything must ~** tout
doit disparaître **- 13.** [stop working, break - light
bulb, fuse] sauter ; [- rope] céder **- 14.** [deterio-
rate - hearing, sight etc] baisser **- 15.** [match, be com-

patible] : **to ~ (with)** aller (avec) ; **this blouse goes well with the skirt** ce chemisier va bien avec la jupe ; **those colours don't really ~** ces couleurs ne vont pas bien ensemble ; **red wine goes well with meat** le vin rouge se marie bien avec la viande - **16.** [fit] aller ; **that goes at the bottom** ça va au fond - **17.** [belong] aller, se mettre ; **the plates ~ in the cupboard** les assiettes vont OR se mettent dans le placard - **18.** [in division] : **three into two won't ~** deux divisé par trois n'y va pas - **19.** [when referring to saying, story or song] : **how does that tune/song ~?** c'est quoi déjà l'air/la chanson? ; **as the saying goes** comme on dit, comme dit le proverbe - **20.** inf [with negative - in giving advice] : **now, don't ~ catching cold** ne va pas attraper froid surtout - **21.** inf [expressing irritation, surprise] : **now what's he gone and done?** qu'est-ce qu'il a fait encore? ; **she's gone and bought a new car!** elle a été s'acheter une nouvelle voiture! ; **you've gone and done it now!** eh bien cette fois-ci, on peut dire que tu en as fait une belle! - **22.** phr : **it just goes to show** c'est bien vrai, vous voyez bien ; **it just goes to show that none of us is perfect** cela prouve bien que personne n'est parfait ◇ vt [make noise of] faire ; **the dog went "woof"** le chien a fait « oua-oua » ◇ n - **1.** [turn] tour m ; **it's my ~** c'est à moi (de jouer) - **2.** inf [attempt] : **to have a ~ (at sthg)** essayer (de faire qqch) ; **have a ~!** tente le coup!, vas-y! - **3.** inf [success] : **to make a ~ of sthg** réussir qqch - **4.** phr : **to have a ~ at sb** inf s'en prendre à qqn, engueuler qqn ; **to be on the ~** inf être sur la brèche.

to go adv - **1.** [remaining] : **there are only three days to ~** il ne reste que trois jours - **2.** Am [to take away] à emporter.

go about ◇ vt fus - **1.** [perform] : **to ~ about one's business** vaquer à ses occupations - **2.** [tackle] : **how do you intend ~ing about it?** comment comptes-tu faire OR t'y prendre? ◇ vi = **go around**.

go after vt fus [person] courir après ; [prize] viser ; [job] essayer d'obtenir.

go against vt fus - **1.** [conflict with] heurter, aller à l'encontre de - **2.** [act contrary to] contrarier, s'opposer à - **3.** [decision, public opinion] être défavorable à.

go ahead vi - **1.** [proceed] : **to ~ ahead with sthg** mettre qqch à exécution ; **~ ahead!** allez-y! - **2.** [take place] avoir lieu.

go along vi [proceed] avancer ; **as you ~ along** au fur et à mesure ; **he makes it up as he goes along** il invente au fur et à mesure.

go along with vt fus [suggestion, idea] appuyer, soutenir ; [person] suivre.

go around vi - **1.** [behave in a certain way] : **she goes around putting everyone's back up** elle n'arrête pas de prendre les gens à rebrousse-poil ; **there's no need to ~ around telling everyone** tu n'as pas besoin d'aller le crier sur les toits - **2.** [frequent] : **to ~ around with sb** fréquenter qqn - **3.** [spread] circuler, courir ; **there's a rumour ~ing around about her** il court un bruit sur elle.

go back on vt fus [one's word, promise] revenir sur.

go back to vt fus - **1.** [return to activity] reprendre, se remettre à ; **to ~ back to sleep** se rendormir - **2.** [return to previous topic] revenir à - **3.** [date from] remonter à, dater de.

go before vi : **her new paintings were unlike anything that had gone before** ses nouveaux tableaux étaient complètement différents de ses précédents ; **we wanted to forget what had gone before** nous voulions oublier ce qui s'était passé avant.

go by ◇ vi [time] s'écouler, passer ◇ vt fus - **1.** [be guided by] suivre - **2.** [judge from] juger d'après.

go down ◇ vi - **1.** [get lower - prices etc] baisser - **2.** [be accepted] être accepté(e) ; **to ~ down well/badly** être bien/mal accueilli - **3.** [sun] se coucher - **4.** [tyre, balloon] se dégonfler ◇ vt fus descendre.

go down with vt fus [illness] attraper.

go for vt fus - **1.** [choose] choisir - **2.** [be attracted to] être attiré(e) par - **3.** [attack] tomber sur, attaquer - **4.** [try to obtain - job, record] essayer d'obtenir - **5.** [be valid] s'appliquer à ; **does that ~ for me too?** est-ce que cela vaut pour OR s'applique à moi aussi?

go in vi entrer.

go in for vt fus - **1.** [competition] prendre part à ; [exam] se présenter à - **2.** [take up as a profession] entrer dans - **3.** [activity - enjoy] aimer ; [- participate in] faire, s'adonner à.

go into vt fus - **1.** [discuss, describe in detail] : **I'd rather not ~ into that now** je préférerais ne pas en parler pour le moment ; **to ~ into detail** OR **details** entrer dans le détail OR les détails - **2.** [investigate] étudier, examiner - **3.** [take up as a profession] entrer dans - **4.** [be put into] : **a lot of hard work went into that book** ce livre a demandé OR nécessité beaucoup de travail - **5.** [begin] : **to ~ into a rage** se mettre en rage ; **to ~ into a spin** [plane] tomber en vrille.

go off ◇ vi - **1.** [explode] exploser - **2.** [alarm] sonner - **3.** [go bad - food] se gâter - **4.** [lights, heating] s'éteindre - **5.** [happen] se passer, se dérouler ◇ vt fus [lose interest in] ne plus aimer.

go off with vt fus prendre.

go on ◇ *vi* - **1.** [take place, happen] se passer - **2.** [heating etc] se mettre en marche - **3.** [continue] : **to ~ on (doing)** continuer (à faire) ; **I can't ~ on!** je n'en peux plus! **; ~ on** [continue talking] allez-y - **4.** [proceed to further activity] : **to ~ on to sthg** passer à qqch ; **to ~ on to do sthg** faire qqch après - **5.** [proceed to another place] : **are you ~ing on to Richard's?** vous allez chez Richard après? - **6.** [go in advance] partir devant - **7.** [talk for too long] parler à n'en plus finir ; **to ~ on about sthg** ne pas arrêter de parler de qqch - **8.** [pass - time] passer ◇ *vt fus* [be guided by] se fonder sur ◇ *excl* allez ; **~ on, treat yourself** allez, fais-toi plaisir.
♦ **go on at** *vt fus* [nag] harceler.
♦ **go out** *vi* - **1.** [leave] sortir - **2.** [for amusement] : **to ~ out (with sb)** sortir (avec qqn) - **3.** [light, fire, cigarette] s'éteindre - **4.** [stop being fashionable] passer de mode.
♦ **go over** *vt fus* - **1.** [examine] examiner, vérifier - **2.** [repeat, review] repasser.
♦ **go over to** *vt fus* - **1.** [change to] adopter, passer à - **2.** [change sides to] passer à ; **to ~ over to the other side** changer de parti - **3.** RADIO & TV passer l'antenne à.
♦ **go round** *vi* - **1.** [be enough for everyone] suffire ; **there's just enough to ~ round** il y en a juste assez pour tout le monde - **2.** [revolve] tourner ; *see also* **go around.**
♦ **go through** ◇ *vt fus* - **1.** [experience] subir, souffrir - **2.** [spend] dépenser - **3.** [study, search through] examiner ; **she went through his pockets** elle lui a fait les poches, elle a fouillé dans ses poches - **4.** [a list - reading] lire ; [- speaking] lire à haute voix ◇ *vi* [be approved] passer, être accepté(e).
♦ **go through with** *vt fus* [action, threat] aller jusqu'au bout de.
♦ **go towards** *vt fus* contribuer à.
♦ **go under** *vi* lit & fig couler.
♦ **go up** ◇ *vi* - **1.** [gen] monter - **2.** [prices] augmenter - **3.** [be built] se construire - **4.** [explode] exploser, sauter - **5.** [burst into flames] : **to ~ up (in flames)** prendre feu, s'enflammer - **6.** [be uttered] : **a cheer went up** on a applaudi ◇ *vt fus* monter.
♦ **go with** *vt fus* aller avec.
♦ **go without** ◇ *vt fus* se passer de ◇ *vi* s'en passer.

goad [gəʊd] *vt* [provoke] talonner ; **to ~ sb into doing sthg** talonner qqn jusqu'à ce qu'il fasse qqch.

go-ahead ◇ *adj* [dynamic] dynamique ◇ *n (U)* [permission] feu *m* vert ; **to give sb the ~ (for sthg)** donner à qqn le feu vert (pour qqch).

goal [gəʊl] *n* but *m* ; **to score a ~** SPORT marquer un but.

goalie ['gəʊlɪ] *n* inf gardien *m* (de but).

goalkeeper ['gəʊl,kiːpər] *n* gardien *m* de but.

goalless ['gəʊllɪs] *adj* : **~ draw** match *m* sans but marqué.

goalmouth ['gəʊlmaʊθ, *pl* -maʊðz] *n* but *m*.

goalpost ['gəʊlpəʊst] *n* poteau *m* de but.

goat [gəʊt] *n* chèvre *f* ; **to act the ~** Br inf faire l'imbécile.

gob [gɒb] (*pt* & *pp* -**bed** ; *cont* -**bing**) v inf ◇ *n* Br [mouth] gueule *f* ◇ *vi* [spit] mollarder.

gobble ['gɒbl] *vt* engloutir.
♦ **gobble down, gobble up** *vt sep* engloutir.

gobbledygook ['gɒbldɪguːk] *n* - **1.** [pompous official language] jargon *m* - **2.** inf [nonsense] charabia *m*.

go-between *n* intermédiaire *mf*.

Gobi ['gəʊbɪ] *n* : **the ~ Desert** le désert de Gobi.

goblet ['gɒblɪt] *n* verre *m* à pied.

goblin ['gɒblɪn] *n* lutin *m*, farfadet *m*.

gobsmacked ['gɒbsmækt] *adj* Br inf bouche bée (*inv*).

go-cart = **go-kart**.

god [gɒd] *n* dieu *m*, divinité *f*.
♦ **God** ◇ *n* Dieu *m* ; **God knows** Dieu seul le sait ; **for God's sake** pour l'amour de Dieu ; **thank God** Dieu merci ◇ *excl* : **(my) God!** mon Dieu!
♦ **gods** *npl* Br inf [in theatre] : **the ~s** le poulailler.

godchild ['gɒdtʃaɪld] (*pl* -**children** [-,tʃɪldrən]) *n* filleul *m*, -e *f*.

goddam(n) ['gɒdæm] esp Am inf ◇ *adj* foutu(e) ◇ *excl* bordel!

goddaughter ['gɒd,dɔːtər] *n* filleule *f*.

goddess ['gɒdɪs] *n* déesse *f*.

godfather ['gɒd,fɑːðər] *n* parrain *m*.

godforsaken ['gɒdfə,seɪkn] *adj* morne, désolé(e).

godmother ['gɒd,mʌðər] *n* marraine *f*.

godparents ['gɒd,peərənts] *npl* parrain et marraine *mpl*.

godsend ['gɒdsend] *n* aubaine *f*.

godson ['gɒdsʌn] *n* filleul *m*.

goes [gəʊz] ▷ **go.**

gofer ['gəʊfər] *n* Am inf larbin *m*.

go-getter [-'getər] *n* battant *m*, -e *f*.

goggle ['gɒgl] *vi* : **to ~ (at sb/sthg)** regarder (qqn/qqch) avec des yeux ronds.

goggles ['gɒglz] *npl* lunettes *fpl*.

go-go dancer *n* danseuse *f* de cabaret.

going ['gəʊɪŋ] <> *n (U)* **- 1.** [rate of advance] allure *f* ; **that was good ~** ça a été vite **- 2.** [travel conditions] conditions *fpl* <> *adj* **- 1.** Br [available] disponible ; **you've got a lot ~ for you** vous avez beaucoup d'atouts **- 2.** [rate, salary] en vigueur.

going concern *n* affaire *f* qui marche.

goings-on *npl* événements *mpl*, histoires *fpl*.

go-kart [-kɑːt] *n* kart *m*.

Golan Heights ['gəʊˌlæn-] *npl* : **the ~** le plateau du Golan.

gold [gəʊld] <> *n* **- 1.** *(U)* [metal, jewellery] or *m* ; **to be as good as ~** être sage comme une image, être mignon tout plein **- 2.** [medal] médaille *f* d'or <> *comp* [made of gold] en or <> *adj* [gold-coloured] doré(e).

golden ['gəʊldən] *adj* **- 1.** [made of gold] en or **- 2.** [gold-coloured] doré(e).

golden age *n* âge *m* d'or.

golden eagle *n* aigle *m* royal.

golden handshake *n* prime *f* de départ.

golden opportunity *n* occasion *f* en or.

golden retriever *n* (golden) retriever *m*.

golden rule *n* règle *f* d'or.

golden wedding *n* noces *fpl* d'or.

goldfish ['gəʊldfɪʃ] *(pl inv)* *n* poisson *m* rouge.

goldfish bowl *n* bocal *m* (à poissons).

gold leaf *n (U)* feuille *f* d'or.

gold medal *n* médaille *f* d'or.

goldmine ['gəʊldmaɪn] *n* lit & fig mine *f* d'or.

gold-plated [-'pleɪtɪd] *adj* plaqué(e) or.

goldsmith ['gəʊldsmɪθ] *n* orfèvre *m*.

gold standard *n* : **the ~** l'étalon-or *m*.

golf [gɒlf] *n* golf *m*.

golf ball *n* **- 1.** [for golf] balle *f* de golf **- 2.** [for typewriter] boule *f*.

golf club *n* [stick, place] club *m* de golf.

golf course *n* terrain *m* de golf.

golfer ['gɒlfə'] *n* golfeur *m*, -euse *f*.

golly ['gɒlɪ] *excl* inf dated mince !

gondola ['gɒndələ] *n* [boat] gondole *f*.

gondolier [ˌgɒndə'lɪə'] *n* gondolier *m*.

gone [gɒn] <> *pp* <> go <> *adj* [no longer here] parti(e) <> *prep* : **it's ~ ten (o'clock)** il est dix heures passées.

gong [gɒŋ] *n* gong *m*.

gonna ['gɒnə] *inf* = **going to**.

gonorrh(o)ea [ˌgɒnə'rɪə] *n* blennorragie *f*.

goo [guː] *n (U)* inf truc *m* poisseux.

good [gʊd] (*compar* **better** ; *superl* **best**) <> *adj* **- 1.** [gen] bon (bonne) ; **it's ~ to see you again**

ça fait plaisir de te revoir ; **it feels ~ to be outside** ça fait du bien d'être dehors ; **to be ~ at sthg** être bon en qqch ; **to be ~ with** [animals, children] savoir y faire avec ; [one's hands] être habile de ; **it's ~ for you** c'est bon pour toi OR pour la santé ; **to feel ~** [person] se sentir bien ; **it's ~ that ...** c'est bien que ... ; **good!** très bien ! **- 2.** [kind - person] gentil(ille) ; **to be ~ to sb** être très attentionné envers qqn ; **to be ~ enough to do sthg** avoir l'amabilité de faire qqch **- 3.** [well-behaved - child] sage ; [- behaviour] correct(e) ; **be ~!** sois sage!, tiens-toi tranquille! **- 4.** [attractive - legs, figure] joli(e) **- 5.** *phr* : **it's a ~ job** OR **thing (that) ...** c'est très bien que ..., c'est une bonne chose que ... ; **~ for you!** très bien ! ; **to give as ~ as one gets** rendre la pareille ; **to make sthg ~** réparer qqch <> *n* **- 1.** *(U)* [benefit] bien *m* ; **for the ~ of** pour le bien de ; **for your own ~** pour ton/votre bien ; **it will do him ~** ça lui fera du bien **- 2.** [use] utilité *f* ; **what's the ~ of doing that?** à quoi bon faire ça? ; **it's no ~** ça ne sert à rien ; **it's no ~ crying/worrying** ça ne sert à rien de pleurer/de s'en faire ; **will this be any ~?** cela peut-il faire l'affaire? **- 3.** *(U)* [morally correct behaviour] bien *m* ; **to be up to no ~** préparer un sale coup.

goods *npl* [merchandise] marchandises *fpl*, articles *mpl* ; **to come up with** OR **deliver the ~s** Br inf tenir ses promesses.

as good as *adv* pratiquement, pour ainsi dire.

for good *adv* [forever] pour de bon, définitivement.

good afternoon *excl* bonjour !

good day *excl* bonjour !

good evening *excl* bonsoir !

good morning *excl* bonjour !

good night *excl* bonsoir ! ; [at bedtime] bonne nuit !

goodbye [ˌgʊd'baɪ] <> *excl* au revoir ! <> *n* au revoir *m*.

good-for-nothing <> *adj* bon (bonne) à rien <> *n* bon *m*, bonne *f* à rien.

Good Friday *n* Vendredi *m* saint.

good-humoured [-'hjuːməd] *adj* [person] de bonne humeur ; [smile, remark, rivalry] bon enfant.

good-looking [-'lʊkɪŋ] *adj* [person] beau (belle).

good-natured [-'neɪtʃəd] *adj* [person] d'un naturel aimable ; [rivalry, argument] bon enfant.

goodness ['gʊdnɪs] <> *n (U)* **- 1.** [kindness] bonté *f* **- 2.** [nutritive quality] valeur *f* nutritive <> *excl* : **(my) ~!** mon Dieu!, Seigneur! ; **for**

~' **sake!** par pitié!, pour l'amour de Dieu! ; **thank** ~! grâce à Dieu!

goods train n Br train m de marchandises.

good-tempered [-'tempəd] adj [meeting, discussion] agréable ; [person] qui a bon caractère.

good turn n : **to do sb a** ~ rendre un service à qqn.

goodwill [,gʊd'wɪl] n bienveillance f.

goody ['gʊdɪ] (pl -ies) inf ⬦ n [person] bon m ⬦ excl chouette!
➡ **goodies** npl Inf - **1.** [delicious food] friandises fpl - **2.** [desirable objects] merveilles fpl, trésors mpl.

gooey ['guːɪ] (compar **gooier** ; superl **gooiest**) adj inf [sticky] qui colle ; pej poisseux(euse).

goof [guːf] Am inf ⬦ n [mistake] gaffe f ⬦ vi faire une gaffe.
➡ **goof off** vi Am inf tirer au flanc.

goofy ['guːfɪ] (compar **-ier** ; superl **-iest**) adj inf [silly] dingue.

goose [guːs] (pl **geese** [giːz]) n [bird] oie f.

gooseberry ['gʊzbərɪ] (pl -ies) n - **1.** [fruit] groseille f à maquereau - **2.** Br inf [third person] : **to play** ~ tenir la chandelle.

gooseflesh ['guːsfleʃ], **goose pimples** Br n, **goosebumps** Am ['guːsbʌmps] npl chair f de poule.

goosestep ['guːs,step] (pt & pp **-ped** ; cont **-ping**) ⬦ n pas m de l'oie ⬦ vi faire le pas de l'oie.

GOP (abbr of **Grand Old Party**) n le parti républicain aux États-Unis.

gopher ['gəʊfəʳ] n geomys m.

gore [gɔːʳ] ⬦ n (U) literary [blood] sang m ⬦ vt encorner.

gorge [gɔːdʒ] ⬦ n gorge f, défilé m ⬦ vt : **to** ~ **o.s. on** OR **with sthg** se bourrer OR se goinfrer de qqch ⬦ vi se goinfrer.

gorgeous ['gɔːdʒəs] adj divin(e) ; inf [good-looking] magnifique, splendide.

gorilla [gə'rɪlə] n gorille m.

gormless ['gɔːmlɪs] adj Br inf bêta (bêtasse).

gorse [gɔːs] n (U) ajonc m.

gory ['gɔːrɪ] (compar **-ier** ; superl **-iest**) adj sanglant(e).

gosh [gɒʃ] excl inf ça alors!

go-slow n Br grève f du zèle.

gospel ['gɒspl] ⬦ n [doctrine] évangile m ; ~ **(truth)** parole f d'évangile ⬦ comp [singer] de gospel ; ~ **songs** OR **music** gospel m.
➡ **Gospel** n Évangile m.

gossamer ['gɒsəməʳ] n (U) - **1.** [spider's thread] fils mpl de la Vierge - **2.** [material] étoffe f légère.

gossip ['gɒsɪp] ⬦ n - **1.** [conversation] bavardage m ; pej commérage m - **2.** [person] commère f ⬦ vi [talk] bavarder, papoter ; pej cancaner.

gossip column n échos mpl.

got [gɒt] pt & pp ⬅ **get.**

Gothic ['gɒθɪk] adj gothique.

gotta ['gɒtə] inf = got to.

gotten ['gɒtn] Am pp ⬅ **get.**

gouge [gaʊdʒ] ➡ **gouge out** vt sep [hole] creuser ; [eyes] arracher.

goulash ['guːlæʃ] n goulache m.

gourd [gʊəd] n gourde f.

gourmet ['gʊəmeɪ] ⬦ n gourmet m ⬦ comp [food, restaurant] gastronomique ; [cook] gastronome.

gout [gaʊt] n (U) goutte f.

govern ['gʌvən] ⬦ vt - **1.** [gen] gouverner - **2.** [control] régir ⬦ vi POL gouverner.

governable ['gʌvnəbl] adj gouvernable.

governess ['gʌvənɪs] n gouvernante f.

governing ['gʌvənɪŋ] adj gouvernant(e).

governing body n conseil m d'administration.

government ['gʌvnmənt] ⬦ n gouvernement m ; **the art of** ~ l'art de gouverner ⬦ comp du gouvernement.

governmental [,gʌvn'mentl] adj gouvernemental(e).

government stock (U) n fonds mpl publics OR d'État.

governor ['gʌvənəʳ] n - **1.** POL gouverneur m - **2.** [of school] ≃ membre m du conseil d'établissement ; [of bank] gouverneur m - **3.** [of prison] directeur m.

governor-general (pl **governor-generals** OR **governors-general**) n gouverneur m général.

govt (abbr of **government**) gvt.

gown [gaʊn] n - **1.** [for woman] robe f - **2.** [for surgeon] blouse f ; [for judge, academic] robe f, toge f.

GP n abbr of **general practitioner.**

GPMU (abbr of **Graphical, Paper and Media Union**) n syndicat britannique des ouvriers du livre.

GPO (abbr of **General Post Office**) n - **1.** [in UK] ancien nom des services postaux britanniques - **2.** [in US] les services postaux américains.

gr. abbr of **gross.**

grab [græb] (pt & pp **-bed** ; cont **-bing**) ⬦ vt

- 1. [seize] saisir **- 2.** inf [sandwich] avaler en vitesse ; **to ~ a few hours' sleep** dormir quelques heures **- 3.** inf [appeal to] emballer ◇ *vi* : **to ~ at sthg** faire un geste pour attraper qqch ◇ *n* : **to make a ~ at** OR **for sthg** faire un geste pour attraper qqch.

grace [greɪs] ◇ *n* **- 1.** [elegance] grâce *f* **- 2.** [graciousness] : **to do sthg with good ~** faire qqch de bonne grâce ; **to have the ~ to do sthg** avoir la bonne grâce de faire qqch **- 3.** *(U)* [extra time] répit *m* **- 4.** [prayer] grâces *fpl* ◇ *vt* fml **- 1.** [honour] honorer de sa présence **- 2.** [decorate] orner, décorer.

graceful ['greɪsfʊl] *adj* gracieux(euse), élégant(e).

graceless ['greɪslɪs] *adj* **- 1.** [ugly] sans attrait **- 2.** [ill-mannered] grossier(ère), peu élégant(e).

gracious ['greɪʃəs] ◇ *adj* **- 1.** [polite] courtois(e) **- 2.** [elegant] élégant(e) ◇ *excl* : **(good) ~!** juste ciel!

graciously ['greɪʃəslɪ] *adv* [politely] poliment.

gradation [grə'deɪʃn] *n* gradation *f*.

grade [greɪd] ◇ *n* **- 1.** [quality - of worker] catégorie *f* ; [- of wool, paper] qualité *f* ; [- of petrol] type *m* ; [- of eggs] calibre *m* ; **to make the ~** y arriver, être à la hauteur **- 2.** Am [class] classe *f* **- 3.** [mark] note *f* ◇ *vt* **- 1.** [classify] classer **- 2.** [mark, assess] noter.

grade crossing *n* Am passage *m* à niveau

grade school *n* Am école *f* primaire.

gradient ['greɪdjənt] *n* pente *f*, inclinaison *f*.

gradual ['grædʒʊəl] *adj* graduel(elle), progressif(ive).

gradually ['grædʒʊəlɪ] *adv* graduellement, petit à petit.

graduate [*n* 'grædʒʊət, *vb* 'grædʒʊeɪt] ◇ *n* **- 1.** [from university] diplômé *m*, -e *f* **- 2.** Am [of high school] ≃ titulaire *mf* du baccalauréat ◇ *comp* Am [postgraduate] de troisième cycle ◇ *vi* **- 1.** [from university] : **to ~ (from)** ≃ obtenir son diplôme (à) **- 2.** Am [from high school] : **to ~ (from)** ≃ obtenir son baccalauréat (à) **- 3.** [progress] : **to ~ from sthg (to sthg)** passer de qqch (à qqch).

graduated ['grædʒʊeɪtɪd] *adj* [ruler etc] gradué(e) ; [tax] progressif(ive) ; **~ pension scheme** régime *m* de retraite proportionnelle.

graduate school *n* Am troisième cycle *m* d'université.

graduation [ˌgrædʒʊ'eɪʃn] *n* *(U)* **- 1.** [ceremony] remise *f* des diplômes **- 2.** [completion of course] obtention *f* de son diplôme.

graffiti [grə'fiːtɪ] *n* *(U)* graffiti *mpl*.

graft [grɑːft] ◇ *n* **- 1.** [from plant] greffe *f*, greffon *m* **- 2.** MED greffe *f* **- 3.** Br [hard work] boulot *m* **- 4.** Am inf [corruption] graissage *m* de patte ◇ *vt* **- 1.** [plant, skin] greffer ; **to ~ sthg onto sthg** greffer qqch sur qqch **- 2.** fig [idea, system] incorporer, intégrer ; **to ~ sthg onto sthg** incorporer qqch à qqch, intégrer qqch dans qqch.

grain [greɪn] *n* **- 1.** [gen] grain *m* **- 2.** *(U)* [crops] céréales *fpl* **- 3.** *(U)* [pattern - in wood] fil *m* ; [- in material] grain *m* ; [- in stone, marble] veines *fpl* ; **it goes against the ~ (for me)** cela va à l'encontre de mes principes.

gram [græm] *n* gramme *m*.

grammar ['græmər] *n* grammaire *f*.

grammar school *n* [in UK] ≃ lycée *m* ; [in US] école *f* primaire.

grammatical [grə'mætɪkl] *adj* grammatical(e).

gramme [græm] Br = **gram**.

gramophone ['græməfəʊn] *n* dated gramophone *m*, phonographe *m*.

gran [græn] *n* Br inf mamie *f*, mémé *f*.

Granada [grə'nɑːdə] *n* Grenade.

granary ['grænərɪ] *(pl* -ies) *n* grenier *m* (à grain).

grand [grænd] ◇ *adj* **- 1.** [impressive] grandiose, imposant(e) **- 2.** [ambitious] grand(e) **- 3.** [important] important(e) ; [socially] distingué(e) **- 4.** inf dated [excellent] sensationnel(elle), formidable ◇ *n* inf [thousand pounds] mille livres *fpl* ; [thousand dollars] mille dollars *mpl*.

grand(d)ad ['grændæd] *n* inf papi *m*, pépé *m*.

Grand Canyon *n* : **the ~** le Grand Canyon.

grandchild ['græntʃaɪld] *(pl* -children [-ˌtʃɪldrən]) *n* [boy] petit-fils *m* ; [girl] petite-fille *f*.

➤ **grandchildren** *npl* petits-enfants *mpl*.

granddaughter ['grænˌdɔːtər] *n* petite-fille *f*.

grand duke *n* grand duc *m*.

grandeur ['grændʒər] *n* **- 1.** [splendour] splendeur *f*, magnificence *f* **- 2.** [status] éminence *f*.

grandfather ['grænd,fɑːðəʳ] n grand-père m.

grandfather clock n horloge f, pendule f de parquet.

grandiose ['grændɪəʊz] adj pej [building] prétentieux(euse) ; [plan] extravagant(e).

grand jury n Am tribunal m d'accusation.

grandma ['grænmɑː] n inf mamie f, mémé f.

grand master n grand maître m.

grandmother ['græn,mʌðəʳ] n grand-mère f.

Grand National n : the ~ la plus importante course d'obstacles de Grande-Bretagne, se déroulant à Aintree dans la banlieue de Liverpool.

grandpa ['grænpɑː] n inf papi m, pépé m.

grandparents ['græn,peərənts] npl grands-parents mpl.

grand piano n piano m à queue.

grand prix [,grɒn'priː] (pl **grands prix** [,grɒn'priː]) n grand prix m.

grand slam n SPORT grand chelem m.

grandson ['grænsʌn] n petit-fils m.

grandstand ['grændstænd] n tribune f.

grand total n somme f globale, total m général.

granite ['grænɪt] n granit m.

granny ['grænɪ] (pl **-ies**) n inf mamie f, mémé f.

granny flat n Br appartement indépendant dans une maison, pour y loger un parent âgé.

granola [grə'nəʊlə] n Am muesli m.

grant [grɑːnt] <> n subvention f ; [for study] bourse f <> vt - **1.** [wish, appeal] accorder ; [request] accéder à - **2.** [admit] admettre, reconnaître ; **I ~ (that)** ... je reconnais OR j'admets que ... - **3.** [give] accorder ; **to take sb for ~ed** [not appreciate sb's help] penser que tout ce que qqn fait va de soi ; [not value sb's presence] penser que qqn fait partie des meubles ; **to take sthg for ~ed** [result, sb's agreement] considérer qqch comme acquis ; **it is taken for ~ed that** ... cela semble aller de soi que ..., cela paraît normal OR tout naturel que ...

grant-maintained [- meɪn'teɪnd] adj SCH subventionné(e) (par l'État).

granulated sugar ['grænjʊleɪtɪd-] n sucre m cristallisé.

granule ['grænjuːl] n granule m ; [of sugar] grain m.

grape [greɪp] n (grain m de) raisin m ; **some ~s** du raisin ; **a bunch of ~s** une grappe de raisin.

grapefruit ['greɪpfruːt] (pl inv OR **-s**) n pamplemousse m.

grape picking [-'pɪkɪŋ] n (U) vendange f, vendanges fpl.

grapevine ['greɪpvaɪn] n vigne f ; **on the ~** fig par le téléphone arabe.

graph [grɑːf] n graphique m.

graphic ['græfɪk] adj - **1.** [vivid] vivant(e) - **2.** ART graphique.

➼ **graphics** npl graphique f ; **computer ~s** infographie f.

graphic design n design m graphique.

graphic designer n graphiste mf.

graphic equalizer n égaliseur m graphique.

graphics card n COMPUT carte f graphique.

graphite ['græfaɪt] n (U) graphite m, mine f de plomb.

graphology [græ'fɒlədʒɪ] n graphologie f.

graph paper n (U) papier m millimétré.

grapple ['græpl] ➼ **grapple with** vt fus - **1.** [person, animal] lutter avec - **2.** [problem] se débattre avec, se colleter avec.

grappling iron ['græplɪŋ-] n grappin m.

grasp [grɑːsp] <> n - **1.** [grip] prise f ; **in** OR **within one's ~** fig à portée de la main - **2.** [understanding] compréhension f ; **to have a good ~ of sthg** avoir une bonne connaissance de qqch <> vt - **1.** [grip, seize] saisir, empoigner - **2.** [understand] saisir, comprendre - **3.** [opportunity] saisir.

grasping ['grɑːspɪŋ] adj pej avide, cupide.

grass [grɑːs] <> n BOT & drugs sl herbe f <> vi Br crime sl moucharder ; **to ~ on sb** dénoncer qqn.

grasshopper ['grɑːs,hɒpəʳ] n sauterelle f.

grassland ['grɑːslænd] n prairie f.

grass roots <> npl fig base f <> comp du peuple.

grass snake n couleuvre f.

grassy ['grɑːsɪ] (compar **-ier** ; superl **-iest**) adj herbeux(euse), herbu(e).

grate [greɪt] <> n grille f de foyer <> vt râper <> vi grincer, crisser ; **to ~ on sb's nerves** taper sur les nerfs de qqn.

grateful ['greɪtfʊl] adj : **to be ~ to sb (for sthg)** être reconnaissant(e) à qqn (de qqch).

gratefully ['greɪtfʊlɪ] adv avec reconnaissance.

grater ['greɪtəʳ] n râpe f.

gratification [,grætɪfɪ'keɪʃn] n - **1.** [pleasure] plaisir m, satisfaction f - **2.** [satisfaction - of wish] assouvissement m, satisfaction f.

gratify ['grætɪfaɪ] (pt & pp **-ied**) vt

- 1. [please - person] : **to be gratified** être content(e), être satisfait(e) **- 2.** [satisfy - wish] satisfaire, assouvir.

gratifying ['grætɪfaɪɪŋ] adj gratifiant(e).

grating ['greɪtɪŋ] ⇔ adj grinçant(e) ; [voix] de crécelle ⇔ n [grille] grille f.

gratitude ['grætɪtjuːd] n (U) : ~ **(to sb for sthg)** gratitude f OR reconnaissance f (envers qqn de qqch).

gratuitous [grə'tjuːɪtəs] adj fml gratuit(e).

gratuity [grə'tjuːɪtɪ] (pl -ies) n fml [tip] pourboire m, gratification f.

grave¹ [greɪv] ⇔ adj grave ; [concern] sérieux(euse) ⇔ n tombe f ; **to turn in one's ~** se retourner dans sa tombe.

grave² [grɑːv] adj LING : **e ~** e m accent grave.

grave accent [grɑːv-] n accent m grave.

gravedigger ['greɪv,dɪgəʳ] n fossoyeur m.

gravel ['grævl] ⇔ n (U) gravier m ⇔ comp de gravier.

gravelled Br, **graveled** Am ['grævld] adj couvert(e) de gravier.

gravestone ['greɪvstəʊn] n pierre f tombale.

graveyard ['greɪvjɑːd] n cimetière m.

gravitate ['grævɪteɪt] vi : **to ~ towards** être attiré(e) par.

gravity ['grævətɪ] n **- 1.** [force] gravité f, pesanteur f **- 2.** [seriousness] gravité f.

gravy ['greɪvɪ] n **- 1.** (U) [meat juice] jus m de viande **- 2.** Am v inf [easy money] bénef m.

gravy boat n saucière f.

gravy train n inf : **the ~** le fromage, l'assiette f au beurre.

gray Am = grey.

grayscale Am = greyscale.

graze [greɪz] ⇔ vt **- 1.** [subj : cows, sheep] brouter, paître **- 2.** [subj : farmer] faire paître **- 3.** [skin] écorcher, égratigner **- 4.** [touch lightly] frôler, effleurer ⇔ vi brouter, paître ⇔ n écorchure f, égratignure f.

grease [griːs] ⇔ n graisse f ; **~ stains** des traces de gras ⇔ vt graisser.

grease gun n pistolet m graisseur.

greasepaint ['griːspeɪnt] n fard m gras.

greaseproof paper [,griːspruːf-] n (U) Br papier m sulfurisé.

greasy ['griːzɪ] (compar -ier ; superl -iest) adj **- 1.** [covered in grease] graisseux(euse) ; [clothes] taché(e) de graisse **- 2.** [food, skin, hair] gras (grasse).

great [greɪt] ⇔ adj **- 1.** [gen] grand(e) ; **~ big** énorme ; **a ~ big coward/layabout** un gros lâche/fainéant **- 2.** inf [splendid] génial(e),

formidable ; **to feel ~** se sentir en pleine forme ; **great!** super!, génial! ⇔ n grand m, -e f.

Great Barrier Reef n : **the ~** la Grande Barrière.

Great Bear n : **the ~** la Grande Ourse.

Great Britain n Grande-Bretagne f ; **in ~** en Grande-Bretagne.

GREAT BRITAIN

Le terme « Great Britain », ou simplement « Britain », au sens strictement géographique, désigne l'île composée de l'Angleterre, de l'Écosse et du pays de Galles. Les « British Isles », elles, incluent la Grande-Bretagne, l'Irlande du Nord et la République d'Irlande, ainsi que l'île de Man, les Orcades, les Shetlands, les îles anglo-normandes et les îles Sorlingues. « The United Kingdom » (Royaume-Uni) désigne l'État créé en 1801 qui comprend l'Angleterre, l'Écosse, le pays de Galles et l'Irlande du Nord.

greatcoat ['greɪtkəʊt] n pardessus m.

Great Dane n danois m.

Greater ['greɪtəʳ] adj : **~ Manchester/New York** l'agglomération f de Manchester/New York.

great-grandchild n [boy] arrière-petit-fils m ; [girl] arrière-petite-fille f.

➥ **great-grandchildren** npl arrière-petits-enfants mpl.

great-grandfather n arrière-grand-père m.

great-grandmother n arrière-grand-mère f.

Great Lakes npl : **the ~** les Grands Lacs mpl.

greatly ['greɪtlɪ] adv beaucoup ; [different] très.

greatness ['greɪtnɪs] n grandeur f.

Great Wall of China n : **the ~** la Grande Muraille (de Chine).

Great War n : **the ~** la Grande Guerre, la guerre de 1914-18.

Grecian ['griːʃn] adj grec (grecque).

Greece [griːs] n Grèce f ; **in ~** en Grèce.

greed [griːd] n (U) **- 1.** [for food] gloutonnerie f **- 2.** fig [for money, power] : **~ (for)** avidité f (de).

greedily ['griːdɪlɪ] adv gloutonnement ; [look at food] avec gourmandise.

greedy ['griːdɪ] (compar -ier ; superl -iest) adj **- 1.** [for food] glouton(onne) **- 2.** [for money, power] : **~ for sthg** avide de qqch.

Greek [griːk] ⇔ adj grec (grecque) ; **the ~ Is-**

lands les îles *fpl* grecques ◇ *n* - **1.** [person] Grec *m*, Grecque *f* - **2.** [language] grec *m*.

green [griːn] ◇ *adj* - **1.** [in colour, unripe] vert(e) - **2.** [ecological - issue, politics] écologique ; [- person] vert(e) - **3.** inf [inexperienced] inexpérimenté(e), jeune - **4.** inf [jealous] : ~ (with envy) malade de jalousie ◇ *n* - **1.** [colour] vert *m* ; in ~ en vert - **2.** GOLF green *m* - **3.** : village ~ pelouse *f* communale.

► **Green** *n* POL vert *m*, -e *f*, écologiste *mf* ; the Greens les Verts, les Écologistes.

► **greens** *npl* [vegetables] légumes *mpl* verts.

greenback ['griːnbæk] *n* Am inf billet *m* vert.

green bean *n* haricot *m* vert.

green belt *n* Br ceinture *f* verte.

Green Beret *n* Am inf : the ~s les bérets *mpl* verts.

green card *n* - **1.** Br [for vehicle] carte *f* verte - **2.** Am [residence permit] carte *f* de séjour.

Green Cross Code *n* Br *code de sécurité routière destiné aux enfants.*

greenery ['griːnərɪ] *n* verdure *f*.

greenfinch ['griːnfɪntʃ] *n* verdier *m*.

green fingers *npl* Br : to have ~ avoir la main verte.

greenfly ['griːnflaɪ] (*pl inv* OR **-ies**) *n* puceron *m*.

greengage ['griːngeɪdʒ] *n* reine-claude *f*.

greengrocer ['griːngrəʊsər] *n* marchand *m*, -e *f* de légumes ; ~'s (shop) magasin *m* de fruits et légumes.

greenhorn ['griːnhɔːn] *n* Am - **1.** [newcomer] immigrant *m*, -e *f* - **2.** [novice] novice *mf*.

greenhouse ['griːnhaʊs, *pl* -haʊzɪz] *n* serre *f*.

greenhouse effect *n* : the ~ l'effet *m* de serre.

greening ['griːnɪŋ] *n* prise *f* de conscience écologique.

greenish ['griːnɪʃ] *adj* verdâtre, qui tire sur le vert.

greenkeeper ['griːnˌkiːpər] *n personne chargée de l'entretien d'un terrain de golf ou de bowling.*

Greenland ['griːnlənd] *n* Groenland *m* ; in ~ au Groenland.

Greenlander ['griːnləndər] *n* Groenlandais *m*, -e *f*.

green light *n* fig : to give sb/sthg the ~ donner le feu vert à qqn/qqch.

green paper *n* POL ≃ livre *m* blanc.

Green Party *n* : the ~ le Parti écologiste.

green salad *n* salade *f* verte.

green thumb *n* Am : to have a ~ avoir la main verte.

greet [griːt] *vt* - **1.** [say hello to] saluer - **2.** [receive] accueillir - **3.** [subj : sight, smell] s'offrir à.

greeting ['griːtɪŋ] *n* salutation *f*, salut *m*.

► **greetings** *npl* : Christmas/birthday ~s vœux *mpl* de Noël/d'anniversaire.

greetings card Br, **greeting card** Am *n* carte *f* de vœux.

gregarious [grɪ'geərɪəs] *adj* sociable.

gremlin ['gremlɪn] *n* inf lutin *m*.

Grenada [grə'neɪdə] *n* Grenade *f* ; in ~ à la Grenade.

grenade [grə'neɪd] *n* : (hand) ~ grenade *f* (à main).

Grenadian [grə'neɪdɪən] ◇ *adj* grenadin(e) ◇ *n* Grenadin *m*, -e *f*.

grenadier [ˌgrenə'dɪər] *n* grenadier *m*.

grenadine ['grenədiːn] *n* grenadine *f*.

grew [gruː] *pt* ▷ **grow**.

grey Br, **gray** Am [greɪ] ◇ *adj* - **1.** [in colour] gris(e) - **2.** [grey-haired] : to go ~ grisonner - **3.** [unhealthily pale] blême - **4.** [dull, gloomy] morne, triste ◇ *n* gris *m* ; in ~ en gris.

grey area *n* zone *f* d'ombre.

grey-haired [-'heəd] *adj* aux cheveux gris.

greyhound ['greɪhaʊnd] *n* lévrier *m*.

greying Br, **graying** Am ['greɪɪŋ] *adj* grisonnant(e).

grey matter *n* matière *f* grise.

greyscale Br, **grayscale** Am ['greɪskeɪl] *n* COMPUT échelle *f* de gris.

grey squirrel *n* écureuil *m* gris.

grid [grɪd] *n* - **1.** [grating] grille *f* - **2.** [system of squares] quadrillage *m*.

griddle ['grɪdl] *n* plaque *f* à cuire.

gridiron ['grɪdˌaɪən] *n* - **1.** [in cooking] gril *m* - **2.** Am [game] football *m* américain ; [field] terrain *m* de football américain.

gridlock ['grɪdlɒk] *n* Am embouteillage *m*.

grief [griːf] *n* (*U*) - **1.** [sorrow] chagrin *m*, peine *f* - **2.** inf [trouble] ennuis *mpl* - **3.** phr : to come to ~ [person] avoir de gros problèmes ; [project] échouer, tomber à l'eau ; good ~! Dieu du ciel!, mon Dieu!

grief-stricken *adj* accablé(e) de douleur.

grievance ['griːvns] *n* grief *m*, doléance *f*.

grieve [griːv] ◇ *vt* fml : it ~s me to ... cela me peine OR me consterne de ... ◇ *vi* [at death] être en deuil ; to ~ for sb/sthg pleurer qqn/qqch.

grieving ['griːvɪŋ] *n* deuil *m*.

grievous ['griːvəs] *adj* fml grave ; [shock] cruel(elle).

grievous bodily harm *n* (*U*) coups *mpl* et blessures *fpl*.

grievously ['griːvəslɪ] *adv* **fml** gravement ; [wounded] grièvement.

grill [grɪl] <> *n* - **1.** [on cooker, fire] gril *m* - **2.** [food] grillade *f* <> *vt* - **1.** [cook on grill] griller, faire griller - **2.** inf [interrogate] cuisiner.

grille [grɪl] *n* grille *f*.

grim [grɪm] (*compar* **-mer** ; *superl* **-mest**) *adj* - **1.** [stern - face, expression] sévère ; [- determination] inflexible - **2.** [cheerless - truth, news] sinistre ; [- room, walls] lugubre ; [- day] morne, triste.

grimace [grɪ'meɪs] <> *n* grimace *f* <> *vi* grimacer, faire la grimace.

grime [graɪm] *n* (*U*) crasse *f*, saleté *f*.

grimly ['grɪmlɪ] *adv* sévèrement.

grimy ['graɪmɪ] (*compar* **-ier** ; *superl* **-iest**) *adj* sale, encrassé(e).

grin [grɪn] (*pt* & *pp* **-ned** ; *cont* **-ning**) <> *n* (large) sourire *m* <> *vi* : **to** ~ **(at sb/sthg)** adresser un large sourire (à qqn/qqch) ; **to** ~ **and bear it** en prendre son parti.

grind [graɪnd] (*pt* & *pp* **ground**) <> *vt* - **1.** [crush] moudre - **2.** [press] : **to** ~ **sthg into sthg** enfoncer qqch dans qqch ; [ash, cigarette] écraser qqch dans qqch <> *vi* [scrape] grincer <> *n* - **1.** [hard, boring work] corvée *f* ; **the daily** ~ le train-train quotidien - **2.** Am inf [hard worker] bûcheur *m*, -euse *f*, bosseur *m*, -euse *f*.

◆ **grind down** *vt sep* [oppress] opprimer.

◆ **grind up** *vt sep* pulvériser.

grinder ['graɪndər] *n* moulin *m*.

grinding ['graɪndɪŋ] *adj* écrasant(e) ; ~ **poverty** misère *f* noire.

grinning ['grɪnɪŋ] *adj* souriant(e).

grip [grɪp] (*pt* & *pp* **-ped** ; *cont* **-ping**) <> *n* - **1.** [grasp, hold] prise *f* ; **to release one's** ~ **on sb/sthg** lâcher qqn/qqch ; **to have a good** ~ **on sb/sthg** bien tenir qqn/qqch - **2.** [control] contrôle *m* ; **he's got a good** ~ **on the situation** il a la situation bien en main ; **in the** ~ **of sthg** en proie à qqch ; **to get to** ~**s with sthg** s'attaquer à qqch ; **to get a** ~ **on o.s.** se ressaisir ; **to lose one's** ~ fig perdre les pédales - **3.** [adhesion] adhérence *f* - **4.** [handle] poignée *f* - **5.** [bag] sac *m* (de voyage) <> *vt* - **1.** [grasp] saisir ; [subj : tyres] adhérer à - **2.** fig [imagination, country] captiver.

gripe [graɪp] inf <> *n* [complaint] plainte *f* <> *vi* : **to** ~ **(about sthg)** râler OR rouspéter (contre qqch).

gripping ['grɪpɪŋ] *adj* passionnant(e).

grisly ['grɪzlɪ] (*compar* **-ier** ; *superl* **-iest**) *adj* [horrible, macabre] macabre.

grist [grɪst] *n* : **it's all** ~ **to the mill for him** cela apporte de l'eau à son moulin.

gristle ['grɪsl] *n* (*U*) nerfs *mpl*.

gristly ['grɪslɪ] (*compar* **-ier** ; *superl* **-iest**) *adj* nerveux(euse).

grit [grɪt] (*pt* & *pp* **-ted** ; *cont* **-ting**) <> *n* - **1.** [stones] gravillon *m* ; [in eye] poussière *f* - **2.** inf [courage] cran *m* <> *vt* sabler.

◆ **grits** *npl* Am gruau *m* de maïs.

gritter ['grɪtər] *n* camion *m* de sablage.

gritty ['grɪtɪ] (*compar* **-ier** ; *superl* **-iest**) *adj* - **1.** [stony] couvert(e) de gravillon - **2.** inf [brave - person] qui a du cran ; [- performance, determination] courageux(euse).

grizzled ['grɪzld] *adj* grisonnant(e).

grizzly ['grɪzlɪ] (*pl* **-ies**) *n* : ~ **(bear)** ours *m* gris, grizzli *m*.

groan [grəʊn] <> *n* gémissement *m* <> *vi* - **1.** [moan] gémir - **2.** [creak] grincer, gémir.

grocer ['grəʊsər] *n* épicier *m*, -ère *f* ; ~**'s (shop)** épicerie *f*.

groceries ['grəʊsərɪz] *npl* [foods] provisions *fpl*.

grocery ['grəʊsərɪ] (*pl* **-ies**) *n* [shop] épicerie *f*.

groggy ['grɒgɪ] (*compar* **-ier** ; *superl* **-iest**) *adj* groggy (*inv*).

groin [grɔɪn] *n* aine *f*.

groom [gruːm] <> *n* - **1.** [of horses] palefrenier *m*, garçon *m* d'écurie - **2.** [bridegroom] marié *m* <> *vt* - **1.** [brush] panser - **2.** fig [prepare] : **to** ~ **sb (for sthg)** préparer OR former qqn (pour qqch).

groove [gruːv] *n* [in metal, wood] rainure *f* ; [in record] sillon *m*.

groovy ['gruːvɪ] *adj* inf - **1.** [excellent] super, génial(e) - **2.** [fashionable] branché(e).

grope [grəʊp] <> *vt* - **1.** [woman] peloter - **2.** [try to find] : **to** ~ **one's way** avancer à tâtons <> *vi* : **to** ~ **(about) for sthg** chercher qqch à tâtons.

gross [grəʊs] (*pl inv* OR **-es** [-iːz]) <> *adj* - **1.** [total] brut(e) - **2.** fml [serious - negligence] coupable ; [- misconduct] choquant(e) ; [- inequality] flagrant(e) - **3.** [coarse, vulgar] grossier(ère) - **4.** inf [obese] obèse, énorme <> *n* grosse *f*, douze douzaines *fpl* <> *vt* gagner brut, faire une recette brute de.

gross domestic product *n* produit *m* intérieur brut.

grossly ['grəʊslɪ] *adv* [seriously] extrêmement, énormément ; ~ **overweight** obèse ; ~ **unjust** d'une injustice criante.

gross national product *n* produit *m* national brut.

gross profit n bénéfice m brut.

grotesque [grəʊˈtesk] adj grotesque.

grotto [ˈgrɒtəʊ] (pl -es OR -s) n grotte f.

grotty [ˈgrɒtɪ] (compar -ier ; superl -iest) adj Br inf minable.

grouchy [ˈgraʊtʃɪ] (compar -ier ; superl -iest) adj inf grognon(onne), maussade.

ground [graʊnd] ⟨> pt & pp ⊳ **grind** ⟨> n - **1.** (U) [surface of earth] sol m, terre f ; above ~ en surface ; below ~ sous terre ; on the ~ par terre, au sol ; to be thin on the ~ être rare ; to get sthg off the ~ fig faire démarrer qqch ; to break fresh OR new ~ fig innover, faire œuvre de pionnier - **2.** (U) [area of land] terrain m - **3.** [for sport etc] terrain m - **4.** [advantage] : to gain/lose ~ gagner/perdre du terrain - **5.** phr : to cut the ~ from under sb's feet couper l'herbe sous les pieds de qqn ; to go to ~ se terrer ; to run sb/sthg to ~ traquer qqn/qqch ; to stand one's ~ tenir bon, rester sur ses positions ⟨> vt - **1.** [base] : to be ~ed on OR in sthg être fondé(e) sur qqch - **2.** [aircraft, pilot] interdire de vol - **3.** esp Am inf [child] priver de sortie - **4.** Am ELEC : to be ~ed être à la masse.

➤ **grounds** npl - **1.** [reason] motif m, raison f ; on the ~s of pour raison de ; on the ~s that en raison du fait que ; ~s for sthg motifs de qqch ; ~s for doing sthg raisons de faire qqch - **2.** [land round building] parc m - **3.** [of coffee] marc m - **4.** [area] : hunting ~s terrain m de chasse ; fishing ~s lieux mpl de pêche.

ground control n contrôle m au sol.

ground cover n (U) sous-bois mpl.

ground crew n personnel m au sol.

ground floor n rez-de-chaussée m inv.

ground-in adj [dirt] incrusté(e).

grounding [ˈgraʊndɪŋ] n : ~ (in) connaissances fpl de base (en).

groundless [ˈgraʊndlɪs] adj sans fondement.

ground level n : at ~ au rez-de-chaussée, au niveau du sol.

groundnut [ˈgraʊndnʌt] n arachide f.

ground plan n [of building] plan m horizontal.

ground rent n redevance f foncière.

ground rules npl règles fpl de base.

groundsheet [ˈgraʊndʃiːt] n tapis m de sol.

groundsman [ˈgraʊndzmən] (pl -men [-mən]) n Br personne chargée de l'entretien d'un terrain de sport.

ground staff n - **1.** [at sports ground] personnel m d'entretien (d'un terrain de sport) - **2.** Br = ground crew.

groundswell [ˈgraʊndswel] n vague f de fond.

groundwork [ˈgraʊndwɜːk] n (U) travail m préparatoire.

group [gruːp] ⟨> n groupe m ⟨> vt grouper, réunir ⟨> vi : to ~ (together) se grouper.

group captain n Br colonel m de l'armée de l'air.

groupie [ˈgruːpɪ] n inf groupie f.

group practice n cabinet m de groupe.

group therapy n thérapie f de groupe.

grouse [graʊs] (pl inv OR -s) ⟨> n - **1.** [bird] grouse f, coq m de bruyère - **2.** inf [complaint] plainte f ⟨> vi inf râler, rouspéter.

grove [grəʊv] n [group of trees] bosquet m ; orange ~ orangerie f.

grovel [ˈgrɒvl] (Br pt & pp -led ; cont -ling, Am pt & pp -ed ; cont -ing) vi : to ~ (to sb) ramper (devant qqn).

grow [grəʊ] (pt grew ; pp grown) ⟨> vi - **1.** [gen] pousser ; [person, animal] grandir ; [company, city] s'agrandir ; [fears, influence, traffic] augmenter, s'accroître ; [problem, idea, plan] prendre de l'ampleur ; [economy] se développer - **2.** [become] devenir ; to ~ old vieillir ; to ~ tired of sthg se fatiguer de qqch - **3.** [do eventually] : to ~ to like sb/sthg finir par aimer qqn/qqch ; to ~ to hate sb/sthg finir par détester qqn/qqch ⟨> vt - **1.** [plants] faire pousser - **2.** [hair, beard] laisser pousser.

➤ **grow apart** vi [friends] s'éloigner ; [family] se défaire.

➤ **grow into** vt fus [clothes, shoes] devenir assez grand pour mettre.

➤ **grow on** vt fus inf plaire de plus en plus à ; it'll ~ on you cela finira par te plaire.

➤ **grow out** vi [perm, dye] disparaître.

➤ **grow out of** vt fus - **1.** [clothes, shoes] devenir trop grand pour - **2.** [habit] perdre.

➤ **grow up** vi - **1.** [become adult] grandir, devenir adulte ; ~ up! ne fais pas l'enfant! - **2.** [develop] se développer.

grower [ˈgrəʊəʳ] n cultivateur m, -trice f.

growl [graʊl] ⟨> n [of animal, engine] grondement m ; [of person] grognement m ⟨> vi [animal] grogner, gronder ; [engine] vrombir, gronder ; [person] grogner.

grown [grəʊn] ⟨> pp ⊳ **grow** ⟨> adj adulte.

grown-up ⟨> adj - **1.** [fully grown] adulte, grand(e) - **2.** [mature] mûr(e) ⟨> n adulte mf, grande personne f.

growth [grəʊθ] n - **1.** [increase - gen] croissance f ; [- of opposition, company] développement m ; [- of population] augmentation f, accroissement *m* - **2.** MED [lump] tumeur *f*, excroissance *f*.

growth rate *n* taux *m* de croissance.

GRSM (*abbr of* Graduate of the Royal Schools of Music) *n* diplôme *m* du conservatoire de musique britannique.

grub [grʌb] *n* - **1.** [insect] larve *f* - **2.** inf [food] bouffe *f*.

grubby ['grʌbɪ] (*compar* -**ier** ; *superl* -**iest**) *adj* sale, malpropre.

grudge [grʌdʒ] <> *n* rancune *f* ; **to bear sb a ~**, **to bear a ~ against sb** garder rancune à qqn <> *vt* : **to ~ sb sthg** donner qqch à qqn à contrecœur ; [success] en vouloir à qqn à cause de qqch ; **to ~ doing sthg** faire qqch à contrecœur.

grudging ['grʌdʒɪŋ] *adj* peu enthousiaste.

grudgingly ['grʌdʒɪŋlɪ] *adv* à contrecœur, de mauvaise grâce.

gruelling Br, **grueling** Am ['grʊəlɪŋ] *adj* épuisant(e), exténuant(e).

gruesome ['gru:səm] *adj* horrible, effroyable.

gruff [grʌf] *adj* - **1.** [hoarse] gros (grosse) - **2.** [rough, unfriendly] brusque, bourru(e).

grumble ['grʌmbl] <> *n* - **1.** [complaint] ronchonnement *m*, grognement *m* - **2.** [rumble - of thunder, train] grondement *m* ; [- of stomach] gargouillement *m* <> *vi* - **1.** [complain] : **to ~ about sthg** rouspéter OR grommeler contre qqch - **2.** [rumble - thunder, train] gronder ; [- stomach] gargouiller.

grumbling ['grʌmblɪŋ] *n* - **1.** [complaining] rouspétance *f* - **2.** [rumbling] grondement *m*.

grumpy ['grʌmpɪ] (*compar* -**ier** ; *superl* -**iest**) *adj* inf renfrogné(e).

grunge [grʌndʒ] *n* - **1.** inf [dirt] crasse *f* - **2.** [music, fashion] grunge *m*.

grunt [grʌnt] <> *n* grognement *m* <> *vi* grogner.

G-string *n* cache-sexe *m inv*.

GU *abbr of* Guam.

Guadeloupe [ˌgwɑːdəˈluːp] *n* la Guadeloupe *f* ; **in ~** à la Guadeloupe.

Guam [gwɑːm] *n* Guam *f*.

guarantee [ˌgærənˈtiː] <> *n* garantie *f* ; **there's no ~ that he'll arrive on time** ce n'est pas sûr OR certain qu'il arrivera à l'heure ; **under ~** sous garantie <> *vt* garantir.

guarantor [ˌgærənˈtɔːr] *n* garant *m*, -e *f*, caution *f*.

guard [gɑːd] <> *n* - **1.** [person] garde *m* ; [in prison] gardien *m* - **2.** [group of guards] garde *f* - **3.** [defensive operation] garde *f* ; **to stand ~** monter la garde ; **to be on ~** être de garde

OR de faction ; **to be on (one's) ~ (against)** se tenir OR être sur ses gardes (contre) ; **to catch sb off ~** prendre qqn au dépourvu - **4.** Br RAIL chef *m* de train - **5.** [protective device - for body] protection *f* ; [- for fire] garde-feu *m inv* <> *vt* - **1.** [protect - building] protéger, garder ; [- person] protéger - **2.** [prisoner] garder, surveiller - **3.** [hide - secret] garder.

➥ **guard against** *vt fus* se protéger contre.

guard dog *n* chien *m* de garde.

guarded ['gɑːdɪd] *adj* prudent(e) ; **he's always very ~** il surveille toujours ses paroles.

guardian ['gɑːdjən] *n* - **1.** [of child] tuteur *m*, -trice *f* - **2.** [protector] gardien *m*, -enne *f*, protecteur *m*, -trice *f*.

guardian angel *n* ange *m* gardien.

guardianship ['gɑːdjənʃɪp] *n* tutelle *f*.

guardrail ['gɑːdreɪl] *n* Am [on road] barrière *f* de sécurité.

guardsman ['gɑːdzmən] (*pl* -**men** [-mən]) *n* soldat *m* de la garde royale.

guard's van *n* Br wagon *m* du chef de train.

Guatemala [ˌgwɑːtəˈmɑːlə] *n* Guatemala *m* ; **in ~** au Guatemala.

Guatemalan [ˌgwɑːtəˈmɑːlən] <> *adj* guatémaltèque <> *n* Guatémaltèque *mf*.

guava ['gwɑːvə] [fruit] goyave *f* ; [tree] goyavier *m*.

guerilla [gəˈrɪlə] = **guerrilla**.

Guernsey ['gɜːnzɪ] *n* - **1.** [place] Guernesey *f* ; **in ~** à Guernesey - **2.** [sweater] jersey *m* - **3.** [cow] vache *f* de Guernesey.

guerrilla [gəˈrɪlə] *n* guérillero *m* ; **urban ~** guérillero *m* des villes.

guerrilla warfare *n* (*U*) guérilla *f*.

guess [ges] <> *n* conjecture *f* ; **to take a ~** essayer de deviner ; **it's anybody's ~** Dieu seul le sait, qui sait? <> *vt* deviner ; **~ what?** tu sais quoi? <> *vi* - **1.** [conjecture] deviner ; **to ~ at sthg** deviner qqch ; **to keep sb ~ing** laisser qqn dans l'ignorance - **2.** [suppose] : **I ~ (so)** je suppose (que oui).

guesstimate ['gestɪmət] *n* inf calcul *m* au pif.

guesswork ['geswɜːk] *n* (*U*) conjectures *fpl*, hypothèses *fpl*.

guest [gest] *n* - **1.** [gen] invité *m*, -e *f* - **2.** [at hotel] client *m*, -e *f* - **3.** *phr* : **be my ~!** je t'en prie!

guesthouse ['gesthaʊs, *pl* -haʊzɪz] *n* pension *f* de famille.

guest of honour *n* invité *m*, -e *f* d'honneur.

guestroom ['gestrʊm] *n* chambre *f* d'amis.

guest star n invité-vedette m, invitée-vedette f.

guffaw [gʌ'fɔ:] ⬦ n gros rire m ⬦ vi rire bruyamment.

Guiana [gaɪ'ænə] n Guyane f.

guidance ['gaɪdəns] n (U) - **1.** [help] conseils mpl - **2.** [leadership] direction f ; under the ~ of sous la houlette de.

guide [gaɪd] ⬦ n - **1.** [person, book] guide m - **2.** [indication] indication f ⬦ vt - **1.** [show by leading] guider - **2.** [control] diriger - **3.** [influence] : to be ~d by sb/sthg se laisser guider par qqn/qqch.
◆ **Guide** n = **Girl Guide**.

guide book n guide m.

guided missile ['gaɪdɪd-] n missile m guidé.

guide dog n chien m d'aveugle.

guidelines ['gaɪdlaɪnz] npl directives fpl, lignes fpl directrices.

guiding ['gaɪdɪŋ] adj qui sert de guide ; [principle] directeur(trice).

guild [gɪld] n - **1.** HISTORY corporation f, guilde f - **2.** [association] association f

guildhall ['gɪldhɔ:l] n salle f de réunion d'une corporation.

guile [gaɪl] n (U) literary ruse f, astuce f.

guileless ['gaɪllɪs] adj literary franc (franche).

guillemot ['gɪlɪmɒt] n guillemot m.

guillotine ['gɪlə,ti:n] ⬦ n - **1.** [for executions] guillotine f - **2.** [for paper] massicot m - **3.** Br POL limite de temps fixée pour le vote d'une loi au Parlement ⬦ vt [execute] guillotiner.

guilt [gɪlt] n culpabilité f.

guiltily ['gɪltɪlɪ] adv d'un air coupable ; [behave] d'une façon coupable.

guilty ['gɪltɪ] (compar -ier ; superl -iest) adj coupable ; to be ~ of sthg être coupable de qqch ; to be found ~/not ~ JUR être reconnu coupable/non coupable ; to have a ~ conscience avoir mauvaise conscience.

guinea ['gɪnɪ] n guinée f.

Guinea ['gɪnɪ] n Guinée f ; in ~ en Guinée.

Guinea-Bissau [-bɪ'saʊ] n Guinée-Bissau f.

guinea fowl n pintade f.

guinea pig ['gɪnɪ-] n cobaye m.

guise [gaɪz] n fml apparence f.

guitar [gɪ'tɑ:r] n guitare f.

guitarist [gɪ'tɑ:rɪst] n guitariste mf.

gulch [gʌltʃ] n Am ravin m.

gulf [gʌlf] n - **1.** [sea] golfe m - **2.** [breach, chasm] : ~ (between) abîme m (entre).
◆ **Gulf** n : the Gulf le Golfe.

Gulf States npl : the ~ [in US] les États du gol-

fe du Mexique ; [around Persian Gulf] les États du Golfe.

Gulf Stream n : the ~ le Gulf Stream.

gull [gʌl] n mouette f.

gullet ['gʌlɪt] n œsophage m ; [of bird] gosier m.

gullible ['gʌləbl] adj crédule.

gully ['gʌlɪ] (pl -ies) n - **1.** [valley] ravine f - **2.** [ditch] rigole f.

gulp [gʌlp] ⬦ n [of drink] grande gorgée f ; [of food] grosse bouchée f ⬦ vt avaler ⬦ vi avoir la gorge nouée.
◆ **gulp down** vt sep avaler.

gum [gʌm] (pt & pp -med ; cont -ming) ⬦ n - **1.** [chewing gum] chewing-gum m - **2.** [adhesive] colle f, gomme f - **3.** ANAT gencive f ⬦ vt coller.

gumboil ['gʌmbɔɪl] n abcès m à la gencive.

gumboots ['gʌmbu:ts] npl Br bottes fpl de caoutchouc.

gumption ['gʌmpʃn] n inf - **1.** [common sense] jugeote f - **2.** [determination] cran m.

gumshoe ['gʌmʃu:] n Am crime sl privé m.

gun [gʌn] (pt & pp -ned ; cont -ning) ⬦ n - **1.** [weapon - small] revolver m ; [- rifle] fusil m ; [- large] canon m ; to stick to one's ~s tenir bon, ne pas en démordre - **2.** [starting pistol] pistolet m ; to jump the ~ agir prématurément - **3.** [tool] pistolet m ; [for staples] agrafeuse f.
◆ **gun down** vt sep abattre.

gunboat ['gʌnbəʊt] n canonnière f.

gundog ['gʌndɒg] n chien m de chasse.

gunfire ['gʌnfaɪər] n (U) coups mpl de feu.

gunge [gʌndʒ] n (U) Br inf matière f poisseuse.

gung-ho [,gʌŋ'həʊ] adj inf trop enthousiaste.

gunk [gʌŋk] n inf matière f poisseuse.

gunman ['gʌnmən] (pl -men [-mən]) n personne f armée.

gunner ['gʌnər] n artilleur m.

gunpoint ['gʌnpɔɪnt] n : at ~ sous la menace d'un fusil OR pistolet.

gunpowder ['gʌn,paʊdər] n poudre f à canon.

gunrunning ['gʌn,rʌnɪŋ] n trafic m d'armes.

gunshot ['gʌnʃɒt] n [firing of gun] coup m de feu.

gunsmith ['gʌnsmɪθ] n armurier m.

gurgle ['gɜ:gl] ⬦ vi - **1.** [water] glouglouter - **2.** [baby] gazouiller ⬦ n - **1.** [of water] glouglou m - **2.** [of baby] gazouillis m.

guru ['gʊru:] n gourou m, guru m.

gush [gʌʃ] ◇ n jaillissement m ◇ vt [blood] répandre ; [oil] cracher ◇ vi - **1.** [flow out] jaillir - **2.** pej [enthuse] s'exprimer de façon exubérante.

gushing ['gʌʃɪŋ] adj pej trop exubérant(e).

gusset ['gʌsɪt] n gousset m.

gust [gʌst] ◇ n rafale f, coup m de vent ◇ vi souffler par rafales.

gusto ['gʌstəʊ] n : with ~ avec enthousiasme.

gusty ['gʌstɪ] (compar -ier ; superl -iest) adj venteux(euse), de grand vent ; [wind] qui souffle par rafales.

gut [gʌt] (pt & pp -ted ; cont -ting) ◇ n MED intestin m ◇ vt - **1.** [remove organs from] vider - **2.** [destroy] éventrer.

◆ **guts** npl inf - **1.** [intestines] intestins mpl ; to hate sb's ~s ne pas pouvoir piffer qqn, ne pas pouvoir voir qqn en peinture - **2.** [courage] cran m ; to have ~s avoir du cran.

gut reaction n réaction f viscérale.

gutter ['gʌtə'] n - **1.** [ditch] rigole f - **2.** [on roof] gouttière f.

guttering ['gʌtərɪŋ] n (U) gouttières fpl.

gutter press n presse f à sensation.

guttural ['gʌtərəl] adj guttural(e).

guv [gʌv] n Br inf chef m.

guy [gaɪ] n - **1.** inf [man] type m - **2.** [person] copain m, copine f - **3.** Br [dummy] effigie de Guy Fawkes.

Guyana [gaɪ'ænə] n Guyana m ; in ~ au Guyana.

Guy Fawkes' Night [-'fɔːks-] n fête célébrée le 5 novembre en Grande-Bretagne.

GUY FAWKES' NIGHT

Cette fête familiale se déroule en plein air autour d'un grand feu de joie sur lequel on brûle une effigie (« le Guy ») censée représenter Guy Fawkes, l'instigateur de la Conspiration des Poudres. C'est également l'occasion d'un feu d'artifice.

guy rope n corde f de tente.

guzzle ['gʌzl] ◇ vt bâfrer ; [drink] lamper ◇ vi s'empiffrer.

gym [dʒɪm] n inf - **1.** [gymnasium] gymnase m - **2.** [exercises] gym f.

gymkhana [dʒɪm'kɑːnə] n gymkhana m.

gymnasium [dʒɪm'neɪzjəm] (pl -iums OR -ia [-jə]) n gymnase m.

gymnast ['dʒɪmnæst] n gymnaste mf.

gymnastics [dʒɪm'næstɪks] n (U) gymnastique f.

gym shoes npl (chaussures fpl de) tennis mpl.

gymslip ['dʒɪm,slɪp] n Br tunique f.

gynaecological Br, **gynecological** Am [,gaɪnəkə'lɒdʒɪkl] adj gynécologique.

gynaecologist Br, **gynecologist** Am [,gaɪnə'kɒlədʒɪst] n gynécologue mf.

gynaecology Br, **gynecology** Am [,gaɪnə'kɒlədʒɪ] n gynécologie f.

gyp [dʒɪp] Am ◇ vt escroquer ◇ n escroc.

gypsy ['dʒɪpsɪ] (pl -ies) = gipsy.

gyrate [dʒaɪ'reɪt] vi tournoyer.

gyration [dʒaɪ'reɪʃn] n mouvement m giratoire.

gyroscope ['dʒaɪrəskəʊp] n gyroscope m.

H

h (pl **h's** OR **hs**), **H** (pl **H's** OR **Hs**) [eɪtʃ] n [letter] h m inv, H m inv.

ha [hɑː] excl ha!

habeas corpus [,heɪbjəs'kɔːpəs] n habeas corpus m.

haberdashery ['hæbədæʃərɪ] (pl -ies) n mercerie f.

habit ['hæbɪt] n - **1.** [customary practice] habitude f ; out of ~ par habitude ; to be in/get into the ~ of doing sthg avoir/prendre l'habitude de faire qqch ; to make a ~ of doing sthg avoir l'habitude de faire qqch - **2.** [garment] habit m.

habitable ['hæbɪtəbl] adj habitable.

habitat ['hæbɪtæt] n habitat m.

habitation [hæbɪ'teɪʃn] n habitation f.

habit-forming [-,fɔːmɪŋ] adj qui crée une accoutumance.

habitual [hə'bɪtʃʊəl] adj - **1.** [usual, characteristic] habituel(elle) - **2.** [regular] invétéré(e).

habitually [hə'bɪtʃʊəlɪ] adv habituellement.

hack [hæk] ◇ n - **1.** [writer] écrivailleur m, -euse f - **2.** Am inf [taxi] taxi m ◇ vt - **1.** [cut] tailler - **2.** COMPUT pirater ◇ vi [cut] taillader.

hack into vt fus COMPUT pirater.

hack through vt fus : **to ~ through sthg** se frayer un chemin dans qqch à coups de hache.

hacker ['hækə'] n : **(computer) ~** pirate m informatique.

hackie ['hækɪ] n Am inf chauffeur m de taxi.

hacking ['hækɪŋ] n COMPUT piratage f informatique.

hacking cough n toux f sèche et douloureuse.

hackles ['hæklz] npl [on animal] plumes fpl du cou ; **to make sb's ~ rise** hérisser qqn.

hackney cab, hackney carriage ['hæknɪ-] n fml [taxi] taxi m.

hackneyed ['hæknɪd] adj rebattu(e).

hacksaw ['hæksɔː] n scie f à métaux.

had [weak form həd, strong form hæd] pt & pp ▷ **have**.

haddock ['hædək] (pl inv) n églefin m, aiglefin m.

hadn't ['hædnt] = **had not**.

haematology [ˌhiːmə'tɒlədʒɪ] = **hematology**.

haemoglobin [ˌhiːmə'gləʊbɪn] = **hemoglobin**.

haemophilia [ˌhiːmə'fɪlɪə] = **hemophilia**.

haemophiliac [ˌhiːmə'fɪlɪæk] = **hemophiliac**.

haemorrhage ['hemərɪdʒ] = **hemorrhage**.

haemorrhoids ['hemərɔɪdz] = **hemorrhoids**.

hag [hæg] n vieille sorcière f.

haggard ['hægəd] adj [face] défait(e) ; [person] abattu(e).

haggis ['hægɪs] n plat typique écossais fait d'une panse de brebis farcie, le plus souvent servie avec des navets et des pommes de terre.

haggle ['hægl] vi marchander ; **to ~ over** OR **about sthg** marchander qqch ; **to ~ with sb** marchander avec qqn.

haggling ['hæglɪŋ] n marchandage m.

Hague [heɪg] n : **The ~** La Haye.

hail [heɪl] ◇ n grêle f ; fig pluie f ◇ vt - **1.** [call] héler - **2.** [acclaim] : **to ~ sb/sthg as sthg** acclamer qqn/qqch comme qqch ◇ v impers grêler.

hailstone ['heɪlstəʊn] n grêlon m.

hair [heə'] n - **1.** (U) [on human head] cheveux mpl ; **to do one's ~** se coiffer ; **to let one's ~ down** se défouler ; **to make sb's ~ stand on end** faire dresser les cheveux sur la tête à qqn - **2.** (U) [on animal, human skin] poils mpl - **3.** [individual hair - on head] cheveu m ; [- on skin] poil m ; **to split ~s** couper les cheveux en quatre.

hairbrush ['heəbrʌʃ] n brosse f à cheveux.

haircut ['heəkʌt] n coupe f de cheveux.

hairdo ['heəduː] (pl -s) n inf coiffure f.

hairdresser ['heəˌdresə'] n coiffeur m, -euse f ; **~'s (salon)** salon m de coiffure.

hairdressing ['heəˌdresɪŋ] ◇ n coiffure f ◇ comp de coiffure.

hairdryer ['heəˌdraɪə'] n [handheld] sèche-cheveux m inv ; [with hood] casque m.

hair gel n gel m coiffant.

hairgrip ['heəgrɪp] n Br pince f à cheveux.

hairline ['heəlaɪn] n naissance f des cheveux.

hairline fracture n fêlure f.

hairnet ['heənet] n filet m à cheveux.

hairpiece ['heəpiːs] n postiche m.

hairpin ['heəpɪn] n épingle f à cheveux.

hairpin bend n virage m en épingle à cheveux.

hair-raising [-ˌreɪzɪŋ] adj à faire dresser les cheveux sur la tête ; [journey] effrayant(e).

hair remover [-rɪˌmuːvə'] n (crème f) dépilatoire m.

hair-restorer n lotion f capillaire régénératrice.

hair's breadth n : **by a ~** d'un cheveu, de justesse.

hair slide n Br barrette f.

hair-splitting n ergotage m.

hairspray ['heəspreɪ] n laque f.

hairstyle ['heəstaɪl] n coiffure f.

hairstylist ['heəˌstaɪlɪst] n coiffeur m, -euse f.

hairy ['heərɪ] (compar -ier ; superl -iest) adj - **1.** [covered in hair] velu(e), poilu(e) - **2.** inf [frightening] à faire dresser les cheveux sur la tête.

Haiti ['heɪtɪ] n Haïti f ; **in ~** à Haïti.

Haitian ['heɪʃn] ◇ adj haïtien(enne) ◇ n Haïtien m, -enne f.

hake [heɪk] (pl inv OR -s) n colin m, merluche f.

halal [hə'lɑːl] ◇ adj hallal (inv) ◇ n viande f hallal.

halcyon ['hælsɪən] adj paradisiaque.

hale [heɪl] adj : **~ and hearty** en pleine forme.

half [Br hɑːf, Am hæf] (pl senses 1 and 2 **halves** [Br hɑːvz, Am hævz], pl senses 3, 4 and 5 **halves** OR **halfs**) ◇ adj demi(e) ; **~ a dozen** une demi-douzaine ; **~ an hour** une demi-heure ; **~ a pound** une demi-livre ; **~ English** à moitié anglais ; **my ~ life** la moitié de ma vie ◇ adv - **1.** [gen] à moitié ; **~-and-~** moitié-moitié ; **not ~!** Br inf tu parles! - **2.** [by half] de moitié **- 3.** [in telling the time] : **~ past ten** Br, **~ after ten** Am dix heures et demie ; **it's ~ past** il est la demie ⬦ *n* **- 1.** [gen] moitié *f* ; **by ~** de moitié ; **in ~** en deux ; **to be too clever by ~** être un peu trop malin ; **he doesn't do things by halves** il ne fait pas les choses à moitié ; **to go halves (with sb)** partager (avec qqn) **- 2.** SPORT [of match] mi-temps *f* **- 3.** SPORT [halfback] demi *m* **- 4.** [of beer] demi *m* **- 5.** [child's ticket] demi-tarif *m*, tarif *m* enfant ⬦ *pron* la moitié ; **~ of them** la moitié d'entre eux ; **I wrote ~ of it** j'en ai écrit la moitié.

halfback [ˈhɑːfbæk] *n* demi *m*.

half-baked [-ˈbeɪkt] *adj* à la noix.

half board *n* esp Br demi-pension *f*.

half-breed ⬦ *adj* métis(isse) ⬦ *n* métis *m*, -isse *f* *(attention : le terme 'half-breed' est considéré comme raciste)*.

half-brother *n* demi-frère *m*.

half-caste [-kɑːst] ⬦ *adj* métis(isse) ⬦ *n* métis *m*, -isse *f* *(attention : le terme 'half-caste' est considéré raciste)*.

half cock *n* : **to go off (at) ~** mal partir.

half-day *n* demi-journée *f*.

half-hearted [-ˈhɑːtɪd] *adj* sans enthousiasme.

half-heartedly [-ˈhɑːtɪdlɪ] *adv* sans enthousiasme.

half hour *n* demi-heure *f*.
◆ **half-hour** *adj* = **half-hourly**.

half-hourly *adj* (de) toutes les demi-heures.

half-length *adj* [coat, jacket] court(e).

half-light *n* pénombre *f*.

half-mast *n* : **at ~** [flag] en berne.

half measure *n* demi-mesure *f*.

half moon *n* demi-lune *f*.

half note *n* Am MUS blanche *f*.

halfpenny [ˈheɪpnɪ] *(pl* -pennies OR -pence [-pens]) *n* demi-penny *m*.

half-price *adj* à moitié prix.
◆ **half price** *adv* moitié prix.

half-sister *n* demi-sœur *f*.

half step *n* Am MUS demi-ton *m*.

half term *n* Br congé *m* de mi-trimestre.

half time *n* (U) mi-temps *f*.

half tone *n* Am MUS demi-ton *m*.

half-truth *n* demi-vérité *f*.

halfway [hɑːfˈweɪ] ⬦ *adj* à mi-chemin ⬦ *adv* **- 1.** [in space] à mi-chemin **- 2.** [in time] à la moitié **- 3.** *phr* : **to meet sb ~** arriver à un compromis avec qqn.

half-wit *n* faible *mf* d'esprit.

half-yearly *adj* semestriel(elle).

◆ **half yearly** *adv* tous les six mois.

halibut [ˈhælɪbət] *(pl inv* OR **-s**) *n* flétan *m*.

halitosis [ˌhælɪˈtəʊsɪs] *n* mauvaise haleine *f*.

hall [hɔːl] *n* **- 1.** [in house] vestibule *m*, entrée *f* **- 2.** [meeting room, building] salle *f* **- 3.** Br UNIV [hall of residence] résidence *f* universitaire ; **to live in ~** loger en cité universitaire **- 4.** [country house] manoir *m*.

halleluja [ˌhælɪˈluːjə] *excl* alléluia!

hallmark [ˈhɔːlmɑːk] *n* **- 1.** [typical feature] marque *f* **- 2.** [on metal] poinçon *m*.

hallo [həˈləʊ] = **hello.**

hall of residence *(pl* **halls of residence)** *n* Br UNIV résidence *f* universitaire.

hallowed [ˈhæləʊd] *adj* [respected] consacré(e).

Hallowe'en [ˌhæləʊˈiːn] *n* Halloween *f* *(fête des sorcières et des fantômes)*.

HALLOWE'EN

Fête célébrée le 31 octobre au cours de laquelle les enfants déguisés en sorcières et en fantômes présentent des paniers pour qu'on y dépose des friandises.

hallucinate [həˈluːsɪneɪt] *vi* avoir des hallucinations.

hallucination [ˌhəluːsɪˈneɪʃn] *n* hallucination *f*.

hallucinogenic [həˌluːsɪnəˈdʒenɪk] *adj* hallucinogène.

hallway [ˈhɔːlweɪ] *n* vestibule *m*.

halo [ˈheɪləʊ] *(pl* **-es** OR **-s**) *n* nimbe *m* ; ASTRON halo *m*.

halogen [ˈhælədʒen] ⬦ *n* halogène *m* ⬦ *comp* halogène.

halt [hɔːlt] ⬦ *n* [stop] : **to come to a ~** [vehicle] s'arrêter, s'immobiliser ; [activity] s'interrompre ; **to grind to a ~** [stop moving] s'arrêter ; [stop working] péricliter ; **to call a ~ to sthg** mettre fin à qqch ⬦ *vt* arrêter ⬦ *vi* s'arrêter.

halter [ˈhɔːltəʳ] *n* [for horse] licou *m*.

halterneck [ˈhɔːltənek] *adj* dos nu *(inv)*.

halting [ˈhɔːltɪŋ] *adj* hésitant(e).

halve [Br hɑːv, Am hæv] *vt* **- 1.** [reduce by half] réduire de moitié **- 2.** [divide] couper en deux.

halves [Br hɑːvz, Am hævz] *pl* ⬦ **half.**

ham [hæm] *(pt & pp* **-med** ; *cont* **-ming)** ⬦ *n* **- 1.** [meat] jambon *m* **- 2.** pej [actor] cabotin *m* **- 3.** [radio fanatic] : **(radio) ~** radioamateur *m* ⬦ *comp* au jambon ⬦ *vt* : **to ~ it up** cabotiner.

Hamburg [ˈhæmbɜːg] *n* Hambourg.

hamburger ['hæmbɜːgəʳ] n - **1.** [burger] hamburger m - **2.** (U) Am [mince] viande f hachée.
ham-fisted [-'fɪstɪd] adj maladroit(e).
hamlet ['hæmlɪt] n hameau m.
hammer ['hæməʳ] ◇ n marteau m ◇ vt - **1.** [with tool] marteler ; [nail] enfoncer à coups de marteau - **2.** [with fist] marteler du poing - **3.** fig : **to ~ sthg into sb** faire entrer qqch dans la tête de qqn - **4.** inf [defeat] battre à plates coutures ◇ vi - **1.** [with tool] frapper au marteau - **2.** [with fist] : **to ~ (on)** cogner du poing (à) - **3.** fig : **to ~ away at** [task] s'acharner à.
➡ **hammer into** vt sep : **to ~ sthg into sb** faire entrer qqch dans la tête de qqn.
➡ **hammer out** ◇ vt fus [agreement, solution] parvenir finalement à ◇ vt sep [dent] enlever à coups de marteau.
hammock ['hæmək] n hamac m.
hammy ['hæmɪ] (compar **-ier** ; superl **-iest**) adj inf cabotin(e).
hamper ['hæmpəʳ] ◇ n - **1.** [for food] panier m d'osier - **2.** Am [for laundry] coffre m à linge ◇ vt gêner.
hamster ['hæmstəʳ] n hamster m.
hamstring ['hæmstrɪŋ] ◇ n tendon m du jarret ◇ vt paralyser.
hand [hænd] ◇ n - **1.** [part of body] main f ; **to hold ~s** se tenir la main ; **~ in ~** [people] main dans la main ; **~s up!** haut les mains! ; **by ~** à la main ; **at the ~s of** aux mains de ; **with one's bare ~s** à mains nues ; **to change ~s** [car, house etc] changer de propriétaire ; **to force sb's ~** forcer la main à qqn ; **to get OR lay one's ~s on** mettre la main sur ; **to get out of ~** échapper à tout contrôle ; **to give sb a free ~** donner carte blanche à qqn ; **to go ~ in ~** [things] aller de pair ; **to have a ~ in sthg** être impliqué dans qqch ; **to have a ~ in doing sthg** contribuer à faire qqch ; **to have a situation in ~** avoir une situation en main ; **to have one's ~s full** avoir du pain sur la planche ; **to have time in ~** avoir du temps libre ; **to take sb in ~** prendre qqn en main ; **to try one's ~ at sthg** s'essayer à qqch ; **to wait on sb ~ and foot** être aux petits soins pour qqn ; **to wash one's ~s of sthg** se laver les mains de qqch - **2.** [help] coup m de main ; **to give OR lend sb a ~ (with sthg)** donner un coup de main à qqn (pour faire qqch) - **3.** [worker] ouvrier m, -ère f - **4.** [of clock, watch] aiguille f - **5.** [handwriting] écriture f - **6.** [of cards] jeu m, main f ; **to overplay one's ~** fig trop présumer de ses capacités ◇ vt : **to ~ sthg to sb, to ~ sb sthg** passer qqch à qqn.
➡ **(close) at hand** adv proche.

➡ **on hand** adv disponible.
➡ **on the other hand** conj d'autre part.
➡ **out of hand** adv [completely] d'emblée.
➡ **to hand** adv à portée de la main, sous la main.
➡ **hand down** vt sep transmettre.
➡ **hand in** vt sep remettre.
➡ **hand on** vt sep transmettre.
➡ **hand out** vt sep distribuer.
➡ **hand over** ◇ vt sep - **1.** [baton, money] remettre - **2.** [responsibility, power] transmettre ◇ vi : **to ~ over (to)** passer le relais (à).
handbag ['hændbæg] n sac m à main.
handball ['hændbɔːl] n [game] handball m.
handbill ['hændbɪl] n prospectus m.
handbook ['hændbʊk] n manuel m ; [for tourist] guide m.
handbrake ['hændbreɪk] n frein m à main.
handclap ['hændklæp] n : **to give the slow ~** taper des mains lentement pour manifester sa désapprobation.
handcrafted ['hændkrɑːftɪd] adj fait(e) (à la) main.
handcuff ['hændkʌf] vt mettre OR passer les menottes à.
handcuffs ['hændkʌfs] npl menottes fpl.
handful ['hændfʊl] n - **1.** [of sand, grass, people] poignée f - **2.** inf [person] : **to be a ~** être difficile.
handgun ['hændgʌn] n revolver m, pistolet m.
handicap ['hændɪkæp] (pt & pp **-ped** ; cont **-ping**) ◇ n handicap m ◇ vt handicaper ; [progress, work] entraver.
handicapped ['hændɪkæpt] ◇ adj handicapé(e) ◇ npl : **the ~** les handicapés mpl.
handicraft ['hændɪkrɑːft] n activité f artisanale.
handiwork ['hændɪwɜːk] n (U) ouvrage m.
handkerchief ['hæŋkətʃɪf] (pl **-chiefs** OR **-chieves** [-tʃiːvz]) n mouchoir m.
handle ['hændl] ◇ n poignée f ; [of jug, cup] anse f ; [of knife, pan] manche m ; **to fly off the ~** sortir de ses gonds ◇ vt - **1.** [with hands] manipuler ; [without permission] toucher à - **2.** [deal with, be responsible for] s'occuper de ; [difficult situation] faire face à - **3.** [treat] traiter, s'y prendre avec ◇ vi [car] : **to ~ well/badly** être maniable/peu maniable.
handlebars ['hændlbɑːz] npl guidon m.
handler ['hændləʳ] n - **1.** [of dog] maître-chien m - **2.** [at airport] : **(baggage) ~** bagagiste m.
handling charges ['hændlɪŋ-] npl [at bank] frais mpl de gestion.
hand lotion n lotion f pour les mains.

hand luggage n (U) Br bagages mpl à main.
handmade [,hænd'meɪd] adj fait(e) (à la) main.
hand-me-down n inf vêtement m usagé.
handout [ˈhændaʊt] n - **1.** [gift] don m - **2.** [leaflet] prospectus m.
handover [ˈhændəʊvəʳ] n remise f; [of power] passation f; [in relay race] passage m.
handpicked [,hænd'pɪkt] adj trié(e) sur le volet.
handrail [ˈhændreɪl] n rampe f.
handset [ˈhændset] n combiné m.
handshake [ˈhændʃeɪk] n serrement m OR poignée f de main.
hands-off adj non-interventionniste.
handsome [ˈhænsəm] adj - **1.** [good-looking] beau (belle) - **2.** [reward, profit] beau (belle) ; [gift] généreux(euse).
handsomely [ˈhænsəmlɪ] adv généreusement.
hands-on adj [training] pratique ; [manager] qui s'implique.
handstand [ˈhændstænd] n équilibre m (sur les mains).
hand-to-mouth adj précaire.
➤ **hand to mouth** adv au jour le jour.
handwriting [ˈhænd,raɪtɪŋ] n écriture f.
handwritten [ˈhænd,rɪtn] adj écrit(e) à la main, manuscrit(e).
handy [ˈhændɪ] (compar -ier ; superl -iest) adj inf - **1.** [useful] pratique ; **to come in ~** être utile - **2.** [skilful] adroit(e) - **3.** [near] tout près, à deux pas ; **to keep sthg ~** garder qqch à portée de la main.
handyman [ˈhændɪmæn] (pl -men [-men]) n bricoleur m.
hang [hæŋ] (pt & pp sense 1 hung ; pt & pp sense 2 hung OR hanged) <> vt - **1.** [fasten] suspendre - **2.** [execute] pendre <> vi - **1.** [be fastened] pendre, être accroché(e) - **2.** [be executed] être pendu(e) <> n : **to get the ~ of sthg** inf saisir le truc OR attraper le coup pour faire qqch.
➤ **hang about, hang around** vi traîner.
➤ **hang on** <> vt fus [depend on] dépendre de <> vi - **1.** [keep hold] : **to ~ on (to)** s'accrocher OR se cramponner (à) - **2.** inf [continue waiting] attendre - **3.** [persevere] tenir bon.
➤ **hang onto** vt fus - **1.** [keep hold of] se cramponner à, s'accrocher à - **2.** [keep] garder.
➤ **hang out** <> vt sep [washing] étendre <> vi inf [spend time] traîner.
➤ **hang round** = hang about.
➤ **hang together** vi [alibi, argument] se tenir.
➤ **hang up** <> vt sep pendre <> vi - **1.** [on tele-

phone] raccrocher - **2.** [hang] être accroché(e), pendre.
➤ **hang up on** vt fus TELEC raccrocher au nez de.
hangar [ˈhæŋəʳ] n hangar m.
hangdog [ˈhæŋdɒg] adj de chien battu.
hanger [ˈhæŋəʳ] n cintre m.
hanger-on (pl hangers-on) n parasite m.
hang glider n [apparatus] deltaplane m.
hang gliding n deltaplane m, vol m libre.
hanging [ˈhæŋɪŋ] n - **1.** [execution] pendaison f - **2.** [drapery] tenture f.
hangman [ˈhæŋmən] (pl -men [-mən]) n bourreau m.
hangover [ˈhæŋ,əʊvəʳ] n - **1.** [from drinking] gueule f de bois - **2.** [from past] : **~ (from)** reliquat m (de).
hang-up n inf complexe m.
hank [hæŋk] n écheveau m.
hanker [ˈhæŋkəʳ] ➤ **hanker after, hanker for** vt fus convoiter.
hankering [ˈhæŋkərɪŋ] n : **~ after OR for** envie f de.
hankie, hanky [ˈhæŋkɪ] (pl -ies) (abbr of handkerchief) n inf mouchoir m.
Hanoi [hæˈnɔɪ] n Hanoi.
Hansard [ˈhænsɑːd] n compte-rendu officiel des débats parlementaires en Grande-Bretagne.
Hants [hænts] (abbr of Hampshire) comté anglais.
haphazard [,hæp'hæzəd] adj fait(e) au hasard.
haphazardly [,hæp'hæzədlɪ] adv au hasard.
hapless [ˈhæplɪs] adj literary infortuné(e).
happen [ˈhæpən] vi - **1.** [occur] arriver, se passer ; **to ~ to sb** arriver à qqn - **2.** [chance] : **I just ~ed to meet him** je l'ai rencontré par hasard ; **it ~s to be right** il se trouve que c'est juste ; **as it ~s** en fait.
happening [ˈhæpənɪŋ] n événement m.
happily [ˈhæpɪlɪ] adv - **1.** [with pleasure] de bon cœur - **2.** [contentedly] : **to be ~ doing sthg** être bien tranquille en train de faire qqch - **3.** [fortunately] heureusement.
happiness [ˈhæpɪnɪs] n bonheur m.
happy [ˈhæpɪ] (compar -ier ; superl -iest) adj - **1.** [gen] heureux(euse) ; **to be ~ to do sthg** être heureux de faire qqch ; **~ Christmas/birthday!** joyeux Noël/anniversaire! ; **~ New Year!** bonne année! - **2.** [satisfied] heureux(euse), content(e) ; **to be ~ with OR about sthg** être heureux de qqch.
happy event n heureux événement m.

happy-go-lucky *adj* décontracté(e).

happy hour *n* inf *moment dans la journée où les boissons sont vendues moins cher dans les bars.*

happy medium *n* juste milieu *m*.

harangue [həˈræŋ] ◇ *n* harangue *f* ◇ *vt* haranguer.

Harare [həˈrɑːrɪ] *n* Harare.

harass [ˈhærəs] *vt* harceler.

harassed [ˈhærəst] *adj* harcelé(e), tourmenté(e).

harassment [ˈhærəsmənt] *n* harcèlement *m*.

harbinger [ˈhɑːbɪndʒər] *n* literary signe *m* avant-coureur.

harbour Br, **harbor** Am [ˈhɑːbər] ◇ *n* port *m* ◇ *vt* - **1.** [feeling] entretenir ; [doubt, grudge] garder - **2.** [person] héberger.

harbour master *n* capitaine *m* de port.

hard [hɑːd] ◇ *adj* - **1.** [gen] dur(e) ; **to be ~ on sb/sthg** être dur avec qqn/pour qqch - **2.** [winter, frost] rude - **3.** [water] calcaire - **4.** [fact] concret(ète) ; [news] sûr(e), vérifié(e) - **5.** Br POL : **~ left/right** extrême gauche/droite ◇ *adv* - **1.** [strenuously - work] dur ; [- listen, concentrate] avec effort ; **to try ~ (to do sthg)** faire de son mieux (pour faire qqch) - **2.** [forcefully] fort - **3.** [heavily - rain] à verse ; [- snow] dru - **4.** phr : **to be ~ pushed** OR **put** OR **pressed to do sthg** avoir bien de la peine à faire qqch ; **to feel ~ done by** avoir l'impression d'avoir été traité injustement.

hard-and-fast *adj* [rule] absolu(e).

hardback [ˈhɑːdbæk] ◇ *adj* relié(e) ◇ *n* livre *m* relié.

hard-bitten *adj* dur(e) à cuire.

hardboard [ˈhɑːdbɔːd] *n* panneau *m* de fibres.

hard-boiled *adj* - **1.** CULIN : **~ egg** œuf *m* dur - **2.** [person] dur(e) à cuire.

hard cash *n* (U) espèces *fpl*.

hard cider *n* Am cidre *m*.

hard copy *n* COMPUT sortie *f* papier.

hard-core *adj* - **1.** [criminal] endurci(e) - **2.** [pornography] hard *(inv)*.
◈ **hard core** *n* [of group] noyau *m* (dur).

hard court *n* court *m* en dur.

hard currency *n* devise *f* forte.

hard disk *n* COMPUT disque *m* dur.

hard drugs *npl* drogues *fpl* dures.

harden [ˈhɑːdn] ◇ *vt* durcir ; [steel] tremper ◇ *vi* - **1.** [glue, concrete] durcir - **2.** [person] s'endurcir - **3.** [attitude, opposition] se durcir.

hardened [ˈhɑːdnd] *adj* [criminal] endurci(e).

hardening [ˈhɑːdnɪŋ] *n* durcissement *m*.

hard hat *n* casque *m*.

hard-headed [-ˈhedɪd] *adj* [decision] pragmatique ; **to be ~** [person] avoir la tête froide.

hard-hearted [-ˈhɑːtɪd] *adj* insensible, impitoyable.

hard-hitting [-ˈhɪtɪŋ] *adj* [report] sans indulgence.

hard labour *n* (U) travaux *mpl* forcés.

hard line *n* : **to take a ~ on sthg** adopter une position ferme vis-à-vis de qqch.
◈ **hard-line** *adj* convaincu(e).
◈ **hard lines** *npl* Br inf : **~s!** pas de chance !

hard-liner *n* partisan *m* de la manière forte.

hardly [ˈhɑːdlɪ] *adv* - **1.** [scarcely] à peine, ne ... guère ; **this is ~ the time for complaints** ce n'est guère le moment de se plaindre ; **~ ever/anything** presque jamais/rien ; **I can ~ move/wait** je peux à peine bouger/attendre - **2.** [only just] à peine.

hardness [ˈhɑːdnɪs] *n* - **1.** [firmness] dureté *f* - **2.** [difficulty] difficulté *f*.

hard-nosed [-nəʊzd] *adj* [businessman] à la tête froide ; [approach] pragmatique.

hard sell *n* vente *f* agressive ; **to give sb the ~** y aller à la vente agressive avec qqn.

hardship [ˈhɑːdʃɪp] *n* - **1.** (U) [difficult conditions] épreuves *fpl* - **2.** [difficult circumstance] épreuve *f*.

hard shoulder *n* Br AUT bande *f* d'arrêt d'urgence.

hard up *adj* inf fauché(e) ; **~ for sthg** à court de qqch.

hardware [ˈhɑːdweər] *n* (U) - **1.** [tools, equipment] quincaillerie *f* - **2.** COMPUT hardware *m*, matériel *m*.

hardware shop *n* quincaillerie *f*.

hardwearing [ˌhɑːdˈweərɪŋ] *adj* Br résistant(e).

hardwood [ˈhɑːdwʊd] *n* bois *m* dur.

hardworking [ˌhɑːdˈwɜːkɪŋ] *adj* travailleur(euse).

hardy [ˈhɑːdɪ] *(compar* -ier ; *superl* -iest*) adj* - **1.** [person, animal] vigoureux(euse), robuste - **2.** [plant] résistant(e), vivace.

hare [heər] ◇ *n* lièvre *m* ◇ *vi* Br inf : **to ~ off** partir à fond de train.

harebrained [ˈheəˌbreɪnd] *adj* inf [person] écervelé(e) ; [scheme, idea] insensé(e).

harelip [ˌheəˈlɪp] *n* bec-de-lièvre *m*.

harem [Br hɑːˈriːm, Am ˈhærəm] *n* harem *m*.

haricot (bean) [ˈhærɪkəʊ-] *n* haricot *m* blanc.

hark [hɑːk] ➠ **hark back** vi : **to ~ back to** revenir à.

harlequin ['hɑːləkwɪn] n arlequin m.

Harley Street ['hɑːlɪ-] n rue du centre de Londres célèbre pour ses spécialistes en médecine.

harm [hɑːm] ◇ n - **1.** [injury] mal m - **2.** [damage - to clothes, plant] dommage m ; [- to reputation] tort m ; **to do ~ to sb, to do sb ~** faire du tort à qqn ; **to do ~ to sthg, to do sthg ~** endommager qqch ; **to mean no ~ by sthg** ne pas faire qqch méchamment ; **there's no ~ in it** il n'y a pas de mal à cela ; **to be out of ~'s way** [person] être en sûreté or en lieu sûr ; [thing] être en lieu sûr ; **she/it came to no ~** il ne lui est rien arrivé ◇ vt - **1.** [injure] faire du mal à - **2.** [damage - clothes, plant] endommager ; [- reputation] faire du tort à.

harmful ['hɑːmfʊl] adj nuisible, nocif(ive).

harmless ['hɑːmlɪs] adj - **1.** [not dangerous] inoffensif(ive) - **2.** [inoffensive] innocent(e).

harmlessly ['hɑːmlɪslɪ] adv sans faire de mal ; [explode] sans faire de dégâts.

harmonic [hɑːˈmɒnɪk] adj harmonique.

harmonica [hɑːˈmɒnɪkə] n harmonica m.

harmonious [hɑːˈməʊnjəs] adj harmonieux(euse).

harmonium [hɑːˈməʊnjəm] (pl -s) n harmonium m.

harmonize, -ise ['hɑːmənaɪz] ◇ vt harmoniser ◇ vi s'harmoniser.

harmony ['hɑːmənɪ] (pl -ies) n harmonie f ; **in ~ with** [in agreement] en harmonie or en accord avec.

harness ['hɑːnɪs] ◇ n [for horse, child] harnais m ◇ vt - **1.** [horse] harnacher - **2.** [energy, resources] exploiter.

harp [hɑːp] n harpe f.

➠ **harp on** vi : **to ~ on (about sthg)** rabâcher (qqch).

harpist ['hɑːpɪst] n harpiste mf.

harpoon [hɑːˈpuːn] ◇ n harpon m ◇ vt harponner.

harpsichord ['hɑːpsɪkɔːd] n clavecin m.

harrowing ['hærəʊɪŋ] adj [experience] éprouvant(e) ; [report, film] déchirant(e).

harry ['hærɪ] (pt & pp -ied) vt : **to ~ sb (for sthg)** harceler qqn (pour obtenir qqch).

harsh [hɑːʃ] adj - **1.** [life, conditions] rude ; [criticism, treatment] sévère - **2.** [to senses - sound] discordant(e) ; [- light, voice] criard(e) ; [- surface] rugueux(euse), rêche ; [- taste] âpre.

harshly ['hɑːʃlɪ] adv - **1.** [punish, treat, criticize] sévèrement ; [speak] durement - **2.** [to senses - shine] de façon criarde.

harshness ['hɑːʃnɪs] n - **1.** [of life, conditions] rigueur f ; [of criticism, treatment] sévérité f, dureté f - **2.** [to senses - of sound] discordance f ; [- of texture] rugosité f, dureté f ; [- of light, colour] aspect m criard.

harvest ['hɑːvɪst] ◇ n [of cereal crops] moisson f ; [of fruit] récolte f ; [of grapes] vendange f, vendanges fpl ◇ vt [cereals] moissonner ; [fruit] récolter ; [grapes] vendanger.

harvest festival n fête f de la moisson.

has [weak form həz, strong form hæz] ⊳ **have**.

has-been n inf pej ringard m, -e f.

hash [hæʃ] n - **1.** [meat] hachis m - **2.** inf [mess] : **to make a ~ of sthg** faire un beau gâchis de qqch - **3.** drugs sl hasch m.

➠ **hash up** vt sep Br inf faire un beau gâchis de.

hash browns npl Am pommes de terre fpl sautées.

hashish ['hæʃiːʃ] n haschich m.

hasn't ['hæznt] = has not.

hassle ['hæsl] inf ◇ n [annoyance] tracas m, embêtement m ; **it can be a real ~** ça peut être vraiment l'horreur ◇ vt tracasser.

haste [heɪst] n hâte f ; **to do sthg in ~** faire qqch à la hâte ; **to make ~** dated se hâter.

hasten ['heɪsn] fml ◇ vt hâter, accélérer ◇ vi se hâter, se dépêcher ; **to ~ to do sthg** s'empresser de faire qqch.

hastily ['heɪstɪlɪ] adv - **1.** [quickly] à la hâte - **2.** [rashly] sans réfléchir.

hasty ['heɪstɪ] (compar -ier ; superl -iest) adj - **1.** [quick] hâtif(ive) - **2.** [rash] irréfléchi(e).

hat [hæt] n chapeau m ; **keep it under your ~** gardez-le pour vous ; **to be talking through one's ~** dire n'importe quoi ; **old ~** vieux jeu, dépassé.

hatbox ['hætbɒks] n carton m à chapeau.

hatch [hætʃ] ◇ vt - **1.** [chick] faire éclore ; [egg] couver - **2.** fig [scheme, plot] tramer ◇ vi [chick, egg] éclore ◇ n [for serving food] passe-plats m inv.

hatchback ['hætʃˌbæk] n voiture f avec hayon.

hatchet ['hætʃɪt] n hachette f ; **to bury the ~** enterrer la hache de guerre.

hatchet job n inf : **to do a ~ on sb** démolir qqn.

hatchway ['hætʃˌweɪ] n passe-plats m inv, guichet m.

hate [heɪt] ◇ n (U) haine f ◇ vt - **1.** [detest] haïr - **2.** [dislike] détester ; **I ~ to bother you, but ...** je suis désolé de vous déranger, mais ... ; **to ~ doing sthg** avoir horreur de faire qqch.

hateful ['heɪtfʊl] *adj* odieux(euse).

hatred ['heɪtrɪd] *n (U)* haine *f*.

hat trick *n* SPORT : **to score a ~** marquer trois buts.

haughty ['hɔːtɪ] (*compar* **-ier** ; *superl* **-iest**) *adj* hautain(e).

haul [hɔːl] ⬦ *n* - **1.** [of drugs, stolen goods] prise *f*, butin *m* - **2.** [distance] : **long ~** long voyage *m* OR trajet *m* ⬦ *vt* - **1.** [pull] traîner, tirer - **2.** [transport by lorry] camionner.

haulage ['hɔːlɪdʒ] *n* transport *m* routier, camionnage *m*.

haulage contractor *n* entrepreneur *m* de transports routiers.

haulier Br ['hɔːlɪər], **hauler** Am ['hɔːlər] *n* entrepreneur *m* de transports routiers.

haunch [hɔːntʃ] *n* [of person] hanche *f* ; [of animal] derrière *m*, arrière-train *m* ; **a ~ of venison** un cuissot de chevreuil.

haunt [hɔːnt] ⬦ *n* repaire *m* ⬦ *vt* hanter.

haunted ['hɔːntɪd] *adj* - **1.** [house, castle] hanté(e) - **2.** [look] égaré(e).

haunting ['hɔːntɪŋ] *adj* obsédant(e).

Havana [hə'vænə] *n* La Havane.

have [hæv] (*pt* & *pp* **had**) ⬦ *aux vb (to form perfect tenses - gen)* : (*- with many intransitive verbs*) être ; **to ~ eaten** avoir mangé ; **to ~ left** être parti(e) ; **I've been on holiday** j'étais en vacances ; **she hasn't gone yet, has she?** elle n'est pas encore partie, si ? ; **no, she hasn't** non ; **yes, she has** oui ; **I was out of breath, having run all the way** j'étais essoufflé d'avoir couru tout le long du chemin ⬦ *vt* - **1.** [possess, receive] : **to ~ (got)** avoir ; **I ~ no money, I haven't got any money** je n'ai pas d'argent ; **she's got loads of imagination** elle a plein d'imagination ; **I've got things to do** j'ai (des choses) à faire - **2.** [experience illness] avoir ; **to ~ flu** avoir la grippe - **3.** (*referring to an action, instead of another verb*) : **to ~ a read** lire ; **to ~ a swim** nager ; **to ~ a bath/ shower** prendre un bain/une douche ; **to ~ a cigarette** fumer une cigarette ; **to ~ a meeting** tenir une réunion ; **to ~ a bad day** passer une mauvaise journée - **4.** [give birth to] avoir ; **to ~ a baby** avoir un bébé - **5.** [cause to be done] : **to ~ sb do sthg** faire faire qqch à qqn ; **to ~ sthg done** faire faire qqch ; **I'm having the house decorated** je fais décorer la maison ; **to ~ one's hair cut** se faire couper les cheveux - **6.** [be treated in a certain way] : **I had my car stolen** je me suis fait voler ma voiture, on m'a volé ma voiture - **7.** inf [cheat] : **to be had** se faire avoir - **8.** *phr* : **to ~ it in for sb** en avoir après qqn, en vouloir à qqn ; **to ~ had it** [car, machine, clothes] avoir fait son

temps ; **I've had it!** je n'en peux plus! ⬦ *modal vb* [be obliged] : **to ~ (got) to do sthg** devoir faire qqch, être obligé(e) de faire qqch ; **do you ~ to go?, ~ you got to go?** est-ce que tu dois partir?, est-ce que tu es obligé de partir? ; **I've got to go to work** il faut que j'aille travailler.

➤ **haves** *npl* : **the ~s and the ~ nots** les riches et les pauvres.

➤ **have on** *vt sep* - **1.** [be wearing] porter ; **to ~ nothing on** être tout nu - **2.** [tease] faire marcher - **3.** [have to do] : **to ~ (got) a lot on** être très pris(e).

➤ **have out** *vt sep* - **1.** [have removed] : **to ~ one's appendix/tonsils out** se faire opérer de l'appendicite/des amygdales ; **to ~ a tooth out** se faire arracher une dent - **2.** [discuss frankly] : **to ~ it out with sb** s'expliquer avec qqn.

➤ **have up** *vt sep* Br inf : **to ~ sb up for sthg** traduire qqn en justice pour qqch.

haven ['heɪvn] *n* havre *m*.

haven't ['hævnt] **= have not**.

haversack ['hævəsæk] *n* sac *m* à dos.

havoc ['hævək] *n (U)* dégâts *mpl* ; **to play ~ with** [gen] abîmer ; [with health] détraquer ; [with plans] ruiner.

Hawaii [hə'waɪiː] *n* Hawaii *m* ; **in ~** à Hawaii.

Hawaiian [hə'waɪjən] ⬦ *adj* hawaiien(enne) ⬦ *n* Hawaiien *m*, -enne *f*.

hawk [hɔːk] ⬦ *n* faucon *m* ; **to watch sb like a ~** ne pas lâcher qqn des yeux ⬦ *vt* colporter.

hawker ['hɔːkər] *n* colporteur *m*.

hawthorn ['hɔːθɔːn] *n* aubépine *f*.

hay [heɪ] *n* foin *m*.

hay fever *n (U)* rhume *m* des foins.

haymaking ['heɪˌmeɪkɪŋ] *n* fenaison *f*.

haystack ['heɪˌstæk] *n* meule *f* de foin.

haywire ['heɪˌwaɪər] *adj* inf : **to go ~** [person] perdre la tête ; [machine] se détraquer.

hazard ['hæzəd] ⬦ *n* hasard *m* ⬦ *vt* hasarder.

hazardous ['hæzədəs] *adj* hasardeux(euse).

hazard warning lights *npl* Br AUT feux *mpl* de détresse.

haze [heɪz] *n* brume *f*.

hazel ['heɪzl] ⬦ *adj* noisette (*inv*) ⬦ *n* [tree] noisetier *m*.

hazelnut ['heɪzlˌnʌt] *n* noisette *f*.

hazy ['heɪzɪ] (*compar* **-ier** ; *superl* **-iest**) *adj* - **1.** [misty] brumeux(euse) - **2.** [memory, ideas] flou(e), vague.

H-bomb *n* bombe *f* H.

h & c *abbr of* **hot and cold (water)**.

he [hiː] ⬦ *pers pron* - **1.** *(unstressed)* il ; ~'s tall il est grand ; ~ **who** *fml* (celui) qui ; **there** ~ **is** le voilà - **2.** *(stressed)* lui ; **HE can't do it** lui ne peut pas le faire ⬦ *n inf* [referring to animal, baby] : **it's a** ~ [animal] c'est un mâle ; [baby] c'est un garçon ⬦ *comp* mâle ; **~-goat** bouc *m*.

HE - 1. *abbr of* **high explosive - 2.** *(abbr of* **His (or Her) Excellency)** S.Exc., S.E.

head [hed] ⬦ *n* - **1.** [of person, animal] tête *f ; a* OR *per* ~ par tête, par personne ; **off the top of my** ~, **I'd say** ... comme ça je dirais ... ; **I couldn't make** ~ **nor tail of it** je n'y comprenais rien ; **on your own** ~ **be it** à vos risques et périls ; **I'm banging my** ~ **against a brick wall** je me tape la tête contre les murs ; **to bite** OR **snap sb's** ~ **off** rembarrer qqn ; **to laugh one's** ~ **off** rire à gorge déployée ; **to sing/shout one's** ~ **off** chanter/crier à tue-tête ; **to be off one's** ~ Br, **to be out of one's** ~ Am être dingue ; **to be soft in the** ~ être débile ; **to go to one's** ~ [alcohol, praise] monter à la tête ; **to keep one's** ~ **off** garder son sang-froid ; **to lose one's** ~ perdre la tête ; **we put our ~s together** nous avons conjugué nos efforts - **2.** [of table, bed, hammer] tête *f* ; [of stairs, page] haut *m* - **3.** [of flower] tête *f* ; [of cabbage] pomme *f* - **4.** [leader] chef *m* ; ~ **of state** chef *m* d'État - **5.** [head teacher] directeur *m*, -trice *f* - **6.** *phr* : **to come to a** ~ atteindre un point critique ⬦ *vt* - **1.** [procession, list] être en tête de - **2.** [be in charge of] être à la tête de - **3.** FTBL : **to** ~ **the ball** faire une tête ⬦ *vi* : **where are you ~ing?** où allez-vous?

➤ **heads** *npl* [on coin] face *f* ; **~s or tails?** pile ou face?

➤ **head for** *vt fus* - **1.** [place] se diriger vers - **2.** *fig* [trouble, disaster] aller au devant de.

➤ **head off** *vt sep* - **1.** [intercept] intercepter - **2.** *fig* [threat, disaster] parer à.

headache [ˈhedeɪk] *n* mal *m* de tête ; **to have a** ~ avoir mal à la tête.

headband [ˈhedbænd] *n* bandeau *m*.

headboard [ˈhedˌbɔːd] *n* dosseret *m*.

head boy *n* Br *élève chargé de la discipline et qui siège aux conseils de son école.*

head cold *n* rhume *m* de cerveau.

head count *n* compte *m*.

headdress [ˈhedˌdres] *n* coiffe *f*.

header [ˈhedəʳ] *n* FTBL tête *f*.

headfirst [ˌhedˈfɜːst] *adv* (la) tête la première.

headgear [ˈhedˌɡɪəʳ] *n (U)* couvre-chef *m*.

head girl *n* Br *élève chargée de la discipline et qui siège aux conseils de son école.*

headhunt [ˈhedhʌnt] *vt* recruter (chez la concurrence).

headhunter [ˈhedˌhʌntəʳ] *n* chasseur *m* de têtes.

heading [ˈhedɪŋ] *n* titre *m*, intitulé *m*.

headlamp [ˈhedlæmp] *n* Br phare *m*.

headland [ˈhedlənd] *n* cap *m*.

headlight [ˈhedlaɪt] *n* phare *m*.

headline [ˈhedlaɪn] *n* [in newspaper] gros titre *m ;* TV & RADIO grand titre *m*.

headlong [ˈhedlɒŋ] ⬦ *adv* - **1.** [quickly] à toute allure - **2.** [unthinkingly] tête baissée - **3.** [head-first] (la) tête la première ⬦ *adj* [unthinking] irréfléchi(e).

headmaster [ˌhedˈmɑːstəʳ] *n* directeur *m* (d'une école).

headmistress [ˌhedˈmɪstrɪs] *n* directrice *f* (d'une école).

head office *n* siège *m* social.

head-on ⬦ *adj* [collision] de plein fouet ; [confrontation] de front ⬦ *adv* de plein fouet.

headphones [ˈhedfəʊnz] *npl* casque *m*.

headquarters [ˌhedˈkwɔːtəz] *npl* [of business, organization] siège *m ;* [of armed forces] quartier *m* général.

headrest [ˈhedrest] *n* appui-tête *m*.

headroom [ˈhedrʊm] *n (U)* hauteur *f*.

headscarf [ˈhedskɑːf] *(pl* **-scarves** [-skɑːvz] OR **-scarfs**) *n* foulard *m*.

headset [ˈhedset] *n* casque *m*.

headship [ˈhedʃɪp] *n* direction *f* (d'une école).

headstand [ˈhedstænd] *n* poirier *m*.

head start *n* avantage *m* au départ ; ~ **on** OR **over** avantage sur.

headstone [ˈhedstəʊn] *n* pierre *f* tombale.

headstrong [ˈhedstrɒŋ] *adj* volontaire, têtu(e).

head teacher *n* directeur *m*, -trice *f* (d'une école).

head waiter *n* maître *m* d'hôtel.

headway [ˈhedweɪ] *n :* **to make** ~ faire des progrès.

headwind [ˈhedwɪnd] *n* vent *m* contraire.

heady [ˈhedɪ] *(compar* **-ier** *; superl* **-iest)** *adj* - **1.** [exciting] grisant(e) - **2.** [causing giddiness] capiteux(euse).

heal [hiːl] ⬦ *vt* - **1.** [cure] guérir - **2.** *fig* [troubles, discord] apaiser ⬦ *vi* se guérir.

➤ **heal up** *vi* se cicatriser, se refermer.

healing [ˈhiːlɪŋ] ⬦ *adj* curatif(ive) ⬦ *n (U)* guérison *f*.

health [helθ] *n* santé *f* ; **to be in good/poor** ~ être en bonne/mauvaise santé ; **to drink (to) sb's** ~ boire à la santé de qqn.

health centre n ≃ centre m médico-social.

health-conscious adj soucieux(euse) de sa santé.

health farm n établissement m de cure.

health food n produits mpl diététiques OR naturels.

health food shop n magasin m de produits diététiques.

health hazard n danger m OR risque m pour la santé.

health service n ≃ sécurité f sociale.

health visitor n Br infirmière f visiteuse.

healthy ['helθɪ] (compar **-ier** ; superl **-iest**) adj - **1.** [gen] sain(e) - **2.** [well] en bonne santé, bien portant(e) - **3.** fig [economy, company] qui se porte bien - **4.** [profit] bon (bonne).

heap [hiːp] ◇ n tas m ; **in a** ~ en tas ◇ vt - **1.** [pile up] entasser - **2.** fig [give] : **to** ~ **gifts on sb** couvrir qqn de cadeaux ; **to** ~ **praise on sb** combler qqn d'éloges ; **to** ~ **scorn on sb** accabler qqn de mépris.

➡ **heaps** npl inf : ~**s of** [people, objects] des tas de ; [time, money] énormément de.

hear [hɪəʳ] (pt & pp **heard** [hɜːd]) ◇ vt - **1.** [gen & JUR] entendre - **2.** [learn of] apprendre ; **to** ~ **(that)** ... apprendre que ... ◇ vi - **1.** [perceive sound] entendre - **2.** [know] : **to** ~ **about** entendre parler de ; **did you** ~ **about her husband?** tu es au courant, pour son mari? - **3.** [receive news] : **to** ~ **about** avoir des nouvelles de ; **have you heard about your blood test yet?** as-tu déjà reçu des nouvelles à propos de ta prise de sang? ; **to** ~ **from sb** recevoir des nouvelles de qqn - **4.** phr : **to have heard of** avoir entendu parler de ; **I won't** ~ **of it!** je ne veux pas en entendre parler!

➡ **hear out** vt sep écouter jusqu'au bout.

hearing ['hɪərɪŋ] n - **1.** [sense] ouïe f ; **Joe was in** OR **within Jim's** ~ Jim était à portée de voix de Joe ; **hard of** ~ dur(e) d'oreille - **2.** [trial] audience f ; **to get a fair** ~ pouvoir défendre sa cause ; JUR être jugé équitablement.

hearing aid n audiophone m.

hearsay ['hɪəseɪ] n ouï-dire m.

hearse [hɜːs] n corbillard m.

heart [hɑːt] n lit & fig cœur m ; **from the** ~ du fond du cœur ; **to lose** ~ perdre courage ; **my** ~ **leapt** j'ai bondi de joie ; **my** ~ **sank** je me suis senti abattu ; **it's a subject close to my** ~ c'est un sujet qui me tient à cœur ; **from the bottom of my** ~ du fond du cœur ; **his** ~ **isn't in it** il n'a pas le cœur à cela ; **in one's** ~ **of** ~**s** au plus profond de son cœur ;

to do sthg to one's ~**'s content** faire qqch à souhait ; **to break sb's** ~ briser le cœur à qqn ; **to set one's** ~ **on sthg/on doing sthg** désirer absolument qqch/faire qqch, vouloir à tout prix qqch/faire qqch ; **to take sthg to** ~ prendre qqch à cœur ; **to have a** ~ **of gold** avoir un cœur d'or.

➡ **hearts** npl cœur m ; **the six of** ~**s** le six de cœur.

➡ **at heart** adv au fond (de soi).

➡ **by heart** adv par cœur.

heartache ['hɑːteɪk] n peine f de cœur.

heart attack n crise f cardiaque.

heartbeat ['hɑːtbiːt] n battement m de cœur.

heartbreaking ['hɑːtˌbreɪkɪŋ] adj à fendre le cœur.

heartbroken ['hɑːtˌbrəʊkn] adj qui a le cœur brisé.

heartburn ['hɑːtbɜːn] n (U) brûlures fpl d'estomac.

heart disease n maladie f de cœur.

heartening ['hɑːtnɪŋ] adj encourageant(e).

heart failure n arrêt m cardiaque.

heartfelt ['hɑːtfelt] adj sincère.

hearth [hɑːθ] n foyer m.

heartland ['hɑːtlænd] n centre m, cœur m.

heartless ['hɑːtlɪs] adj sans cœur.

heartrending ['hɑːtˌrendɪŋ] adj déchirant(e), qui fend le cœur.

heart-searching n : **after a lot of** ~ après s'être beaucoup interrogé.

heartthrob ['hɑːtθrɒb] n inf idole f, coqueluche f.

heart-to-heart ◇ adj à cœur ouvert ◇ n conversation f à cœur ouvert.

heart transplant n greffe f du cœur.

heartwarming ['hɑːtˌwɔːmɪŋ] adj réconfortant(e).

hearty ['hɑːtɪ] (compar **-ier** ; superl **-iest**) adj - **1.** [greeting, person] cordial(e) - **2.** [substantial - meal] copieux(euse) ; [- appetite] gros (grosse).

heat [hiːt] ◇ n - **1.** (U) [warmth] chaleur f - **2.** (U) fig [pressure] pression f - **3.** [eliminating round] éliminatoire f - **4.** ZOOL : **on** Br OR **in** ~ en chaleur ◇ vt chauffer.

➡ **heat up** ◇ vt sep réchauffer ◇ vi chauffer.

heated ['hiːtɪd] adj [argument, discussion, person] animé(e) ; [issue] chaud(e).

heater ['hiːtəʳ] n appareil m de chauffage.

heath [hiːθ] n lande f.

heathen ['hi:ðn] ◇ *adj* païen(enne) ◇ *n* païen *m*, -enne *f*.

heather ['heðə^r] *n* bruyère *f*.

heating ['hi:tɪŋ] *n* chauffage *m*.

heat rash *n* boutons *mpl* de chaleur.

heat-resistant *adj* résistant(e) à la chaleur.

heat-seeking [-,si:kɪŋ] *adj* guidé(e) par la chaleur.

heatstroke ['hi:tstrəʊk] *n (U)* coup *m* de chaleur.

heat wave *n* canicule *f*, vague *f* de chaleur.

heave [hi:v] ◇ *vt* - **1.** [pull] tirer (avec effort) ; [push] pousser (avec effort) - **2.** inf [throw] lancer ◇ *vi* - **1.** [pull] tirer - **2.** [rise and fall] se soulever - **3.** [retch] avoir des haut-le-cœur ◇ *n* : to give sthg a ~ [pull] tirer qqch (avec effort) ; [push] pousser qqch (avec effort).

heaven ['hevn] *n* paradis *m* ; it was ~ fig c'était divin OR merveilleux ; ~ (alone) knows! Dieu seul le sait!

➤ **heavens** ◇ *npl* : the ~s literary les cieux *mpl* ◇ *excl* : (good) ~s! juste ciel!

heavenly ['hevnlɪ] *adj* - **1.** inf [delightful] délicieux(euse), merveilleux(euse) - **2.** literary [of the skies] céleste.

heavily ['hevɪlɪ] *adv* - **1.** [booked, in debt] lourdement ; [rain, smoke, drink] énormément - **2.** [solidly - built] solidement - **3.** [breathe, sigh] péniblement, bruyamment - **4.** [fall, sit down] lourdement.

heaviness ['hevɪnɪs] *n* - **1.** [gen] lourdeur *f* - **2.** [intensity] intensité *f*.

heavy ['hevɪ] (compar **-ier** ; superl **-iest**) *adj* - **1.** [gen] lourd(e) ; how ~ is it? ça pèse combien? ; with a ~ heart [sad] le cœur gros - **2.** [traffic] dense ; [rain] battant(e) ; [fighting] acharné(e) ; [casualties, corrections] nombreux(euses) ; [smoker, drinker] gros (grosse) ; to be ~ on petrol consommer beaucoup (d'essence) - **3.** [noisy - breathing] bruyant(e) - **4.** [schedule] chargé(e) - **5.** [physically exacting - work, job] pénible.

heavy cream *n* Am crème *f* fraîche épaisse.

heavy-duty *adj* solide, robuste.

heavy goods vehicle *n* Br poids lourd *m*.

heavy-handed [-'hændɪd] *adj* maladroit(e).

heavy industry *n* industrie *f* lourde.

heavy metal *n* MUS heavy metal *m*.

heavyweight ['hevɪweɪt] SPORT ◇ *adj* poids lourd ◇ *n* poids lourd *m*.

Hebrew ['hi:bru:] ◇ *adj* hébreu, hébraïque ◇ *n* - **1.** [person] Hébreu *m*, Israélite *mf* - **2.** [language] hébreu *m*.

Hebrides ['hebrɪdi:z] *npl* : the ~ les (îles *fpl*) Hébrides ; in the ~ aux Hébrides.

heck [hek] *excl* inf : what/where/why the ~ ...? que/où/pourquoi diable ...? ; a ~ of a nice guy un type vachement sympa ; a ~ of a lot of people un tas de gens.

heckle ['hekl] ◇ *vt* interpeller, interrompre ◇ *vi* interrompre bruyamment.

heckler ['heklə^r] *n* perturbateur *m*, -trice *f*.

hectare ['hekteə^r] *n* hectare *m*.

hectic ['hektɪk] *adj* [meeting, day] agité(e), mouvementé(e).

hector ['hektə^r] ◇ *vt* rudoyer ◇ *vi* agir de façon autoritaire.

he'd [hi:d] = he had, he would.

hedge [hedʒ] ◇ *n* haie *f* ◇ *vi* [prevaricate] répondre de façon détournée.

hedgehog ['hedʒhɒg] *n* hérisson *m*.

hedgerow ['hedʒrəʊ] *n* bordure *f* d'arbres.

hedonism ['hi:dənɪzm] *n* hédonisme *m*.

hedonist ['hi:dənɪst] *n* hédoniste *mf*

heed [hi:d] ◇ *n* : to pay ~ to sb prêter attention à qqn ; to take ~ of sthg tenir compte de qqch ◇ *vt* fml tenir compte de.

heedless ['hi:dlɪs] *adj* : ~ of sthg qui ne tient pas compte de qqch.

heel [hi:l] *n* talon *m* ; to dig one's ~s in fig se buter ; to follow hard on the ~s of sb être sur les talons de qqn ; to follow hard on the ~s of sthg arriver immédiatement après qqch ; to take to one's ~s prendre ses jambes à son cou ; to turn on one's ~ tourner les talons.

hefty ['heftɪ] (compar **-ier** ; superl **-iest**) *adj* - **1.** [well-built] costaud(e) - **2.** [large] gros (grosse).

heifer ['hefə^r] *n* génisse *f*.

height [haɪt] *n* - **1.** [of building, mountain] hauteur *f* ; [of person] taille *f* ; 5 metres in ~ 5 mètres de haut ; what ~ is it? ça fait quelle hauteur? ; what ~ are you? combien mesurez-vous? - **2.** [above ground - of aircraft] altitude *f* ; to gain/lose ~ gagner/perdre de l'altitude ; at shoulder ~ à hauteur de l'épaule - **3.** [zenith] : at the ~ of the summer/season au cœur de l'été/de la saison ; at the ~ of his fame au sommet de sa gloire.

➤ **heights** *npl* [high places] hauteurs *fpl* ; to be afraid of ~s avoir le vertige.

heighten ['haɪtn] *vt* & *vi* augmenter.

heinous ['heɪnəs] *adj* fml odieux(euse).

heir [eə^r] *n* héritier *m*.

heir apparent (*pl* **heirs apparent**) *n* héritier *m* présomptif.

heiress ['eərɪs] n héritière f.

heirloom ['eəlu:m] n meuble m/bijou m de famille.

heist [haɪst] n inf casse m.

held [held] pt & pp ⊳ hold.

helices ['helɪsi:z] pl ⊳ helix.

helicopter ['helɪkɒptər] n hélicoptère m.

heliport ['helɪpɔ:t] n héliport m.

helium ['hi:lɪəm] n hélium m.

helix ['hi:lɪks] (pl -lixes [-lɪksi:z] OR -lices [-lɪsi:z]) n hélice f.

hell [hel] ⊳ n - **1.** lit & fig enfer m - **2.** inf [for emphasis] : **he's a ~ of a nice guy** c'est un type vachement sympa ; **what/where/why the ~ ...?** que/où/pourquoi ..., bon sang? ; **a ~ of a mess** un sacré bazar ; **to hurt like ~** faire vachement mal ; **like ~ you will!** il n'y a pas de danger! ; **to get the ~ out (of)** foutre le camp (de) - **3.** phr : **all ~ broke loose** inf il y a eu de l'orage ; **to do sthg for the ~ of it** inf faire qqch pour le plaisir, faire qqch juste comme ça ; **to give sb ~** inf [verbally] engueuler qqn ; **go to ~!** v inf va te faire foutre! ; **to play ~ with sthg** inf foutre qqch en l'air ; **to ~ with him!** inf il peut aller se faire voir! ; **to ~ with the expense!** inf au diable l'avarice! ⊳ excl inf merde!, zut!

he'll [hi:l] = he will.

hell-bent adj : **to be ~ on sthg/on doing sthg** vouloir à tout prix qqch/faire qqch.

hellish ['helɪʃ] adj inf infernal(e).

hello [hə'ləu] excl - **1.** [as greeting] bonjour! ; [on phone] allô! - **2.** [to attract attention] hé!

helm [helm] n lit & fig barre f ; **at the ~** à la barre.

helmet ['helmɪt] n casque m.

helmsman ['helmzmən] (pl -men [-mən]) n NAUT timonier m.

help [help] ⊳ n - **1.** (U) [assistance] aide f ; **he gave me a lot of ~** il m'a beaucoup aidé ; **with the ~ of sthg** à l'aide de qqch ; **with sb's ~ avec l'aide de qqn ; to be of ~** rendre service - **2.** (U) [emergency aid] secours m - **3.** [useful person or object] : **to be a ~** aider, rendre service ⊳ vi aider ⊳ vt - **1.** [assist] aider ; **to ~ sb (to) do sthg** aider qqn à faire qqch ; **to ~ sb with sthg** aider qqn à faire qqch ; **can I ~ you?** que désirez-vous? - **2.** [avoid] : **I can't ~ it** je n'y peux rien ; **I can't ~ feeling sad about it** je n'y peux rien, cela me rend triste ; **I couldn't ~ laughing** je ne pouvais pas m'empêcher de rire - **3.** phr : **to ~ o.s. (to sthg)** se servir (de qqch) ⊳ excl au secours!, à l'aide!

➤ **help out** vt sep & vi aider.

help desk n service m d'assistance technique, help-desk m.

helper ['helpər] n - **1.** [gen] aide mf - **2.** Am [to do housework] femme f de ménage.

helpful ['helpful] adj - **1.** [person] serviable ; **you've been very ~** vous (nous) avez bien rendu service - **2.** [advice, suggestion] utile.

helping ['helpɪŋ] n portion f ; [of cake, tart] part f.

helping hand n coup m de main.

helpless ['helplɪs] adj impuissant(e) ; [look, gesture] d'impuissance.

helplessly ['helplɪslɪ] adv - **1.** [stand by, watch] sans rien pouvoir faire - **2.** [uncontrollably] : **to laugh ~** avoir le fou rire.

helpline ['helplaɪn] n ligne f d'assistance téléphonique.

Helsinki [hel'sɪŋkɪ] n Helsinki.

helter-skelter ['heltə'skeltər] Br ⊳ n toboggan m ⊳ adv pêle-mêle.

hem [hem] (pt & pp -med ; cont -ming) ⊳ n ourlet m ⊳ vt ourler.

➤ **hem in** vt sep encercler.

he-man n inf hum vrai mâle m.

hematology [,hi:mə'tɒlədʒɪ] n hématologie f.

hemisphere ['hemɪ,sfɪər] n hémisphère m.

hemline ['hemlaɪn] n ourlet m.

hemoglobin [,hi:mə'gləubɪn] n hémoglobine f.

hemophilia [,hi:mə'fɪlɪə] n hémophilie f.

hemophiliac [,hi:mə'fɪlɪæk] n hémophile mf.

hemorrhage ['hemərɪdʒ] ⊳ n hémorragie f ⊳ vi faire une hémorragie.

hemorrhoids ['hemərɔɪdz] npl hémorroïdes fpl.

hemp [hemp] n [plant, fibre] chanvre m.

hen [hen] n - **1.** [female chicken] poule f - **2.** [female bird] femelle f.

hence [hens] adv fml - **1.** [therefore] d'où - **2.** [from now] d'ici.

henceforth [,hens'fɔ:θ] adv fml dorénavant.

henchman ['hentʃmən] (pl -men [-mən]) n pej acolyte m.

henna ['henə] ⊳ n henné m ⊳ vt [hair] appliquer du henné sur.

hen party n soirée f entre femmes ; [before wedding] soirée où une future mariée enterre sa vie de célibataire avec ses amies.

henpecked ['henpekt] adj pej dominé par sa femme.

hepatitis [,hepə'taɪtɪs] n hépatite f.

her [hɜ:r] ⊳ pers pron - **1.** (direct - unstressed)

la, l' *(+ vowel or silent 'h')* ; *(- stressed)* elle ; **I know/like ~** je la connais/l'aime ; **it's ~** c'est elle ; **if I were** OR **was ~** si j'étais elle, à sa place ; **you can't expect HER to do it** tu ne peux pas exiger que ce soit elle qui le fasse - **2.** *(referring to animal, car, ship etc) follow the gender of your translation* - **3.** *(indirect)* lui ; **we spoke to ~** nous lui avons parlé ; **he sent ~ a letter** il lui a envoyé une lettre - **4.** *(after prep, in comparisons etc)* elle ; **I'm shorter than ~** je suis plus petit qu'elle ◇ *poss adj* son (sa), ses *(pl)* ; **~ coat** son manteau ; **~ bedroom** sa chambre ; **~ children** ses enfants ; **~ name is Sarah** elle s'appelle Sarah ; **it was HER fault** c'était de sa faute à elle.

herald ['herəld] ◇ *vt fml* annoncer ◇ *n* - **1.** [messenger] héraut *m* - **2.** [sign] signe *m*.

heraldry ['herəldrɪ] *n* héraldique *f*.

herb [hɜːb] *n* herbe *f*.

herbaceous [hɜːˈbeɪʃəs] *adj* herbacé(e).

herbal ['hɜːbl] *adj* à base de plantes.

herbicide ['hɜːbɪsaɪd] *n* herbicide *m*.

herbivore ['hɜːbɪvɔːʳ] *n* herbivore *m*.

herb tea *n* tisane *f*.

herd [hɜːd] ◇ *n* troupeau *m* ◇ *vt* - **1.** [cattle, sheep] mener - **2.** *fig* [people] conduire, mener ; [into confined space] parquer.

herdsman ['hɜːdzmən] *(pl* -men [-mən]) *n* gardien *m* de troupeau.

here [hɪəʳ] *adv* - **1.** [in this place] ici ; **~ he is/they are** le/les voici ; **~ it is** le/la voici ; **~ is/are** voici ; **~ and there** çà et là - **2.** [present] là ; **he's not ~ today** il n'est pas là aujourd'hui - **3.** [in toasts] : **~'s to** à la santé de.

hereabouts Br [,hɪərəˈbauts], **hereabout** Am [,hɪərəˈbaut] *adv* par ici.

hereafter [,hɪərˈɑːftəʳ] ◇ *adv fml* ci-après ◇ *n* : **the ~** l'au-delà *m*.

hereby [,hɪəˈbaɪ] *adv fml* par la présente.

hereditary [hɪˈredɪtrɪ] *adj* héréditaire.

heredity [hɪˈredətɪ] *n* hérédité *f*.

heresy ['herəsɪ] *(pl* -ies) *n* hérésie *f*.

heretic ['herətɪk] *n* hérétique *mf*.

herewith [,hɪəˈwɪð] *adv fml* [with letter] ci-joint, ci-inclus.

heritage ['herɪtɪdʒ] *n* héritage *m*, patrimoine *m*.

heritage centre *n* musée *m*.

hermaphrodite [hɜːˈmæfrədaɪt] ◇ *adj* hermaphrodite ◇ *n* hermaphrodite *m*.

hermetic [hɜːˈmetɪk] *adj* hermétique.

hermetically [hɜːˈmetɪklɪ] *adv* : **~ sealed** fermé(e) hermétiquement.

hermit ['hɜːmɪt] *n* ermite *m*.

hernia ['hɜːnjə] *n* hernie *f*.

hero ['hɪərəʊ] *(pl* -es) *n* héros *m*.

heroic [hɪˈrəʊɪk] *adj* héroïque.

heroin ['herəʊɪn] *n* héroïne *f*.

heroine ['herəʊɪn] *n* héroïne *f*.

heroism ['herəʊɪzm] *n* héroïsme *m*.

heron ['herən] *(pl inv* OR -s) *n* héron *m*.

hero worship *n* culte *m* du héros.

herpes ['hɜːpiːz] *n* herpès *m*.

herring ['herɪŋ] *(pl inv* OR -s) *n* hareng *m*.

herringbone ['herɪŋbəʊn] *n* [pattern] chevrons *mpl*.

hers [hɜːz] *poss pron* le sien (la sienne), les siens (les siennes) *(pl)* ; **that money is ~** cet argent est à elle OR est le sien ; **it wasn't his fault, it was HERS** ce n'était pas de sa faute à lui, c'était de sa faute à elle ; **a friend of ~** un ami à elle, un de ses amis.

herself [hɜːˈself] *pron* - **1.** *(reflexive)* se ; *(after prep)* elle ; **2.** *(for emphasis)* elle-même ; **she did it ~** elle l'a fait toute seule.

Herts [hɑːts] *(abbr of* **Hertfordshire)** *comté anglais.*

he's [hiːz] = he is, he has.

hesitant ['hezɪtənt] *adj* hésitant(e) ; **to be ~ about doing sthg** hésiter à faire qqch.

hesitate ['hezɪteɪt] *vi* hésiter ; **to ~ to do sthg** hésiter à faire qqch.

hesitation [,hezɪˈteɪʃn] *n* hésitation *f* ; **to have no ~ in doing sthg** ne pas hésiter à faire qqch.

hessian ['hesɪən] *n* Br jute *m*.

heterogeneous [,hetərəˈdʒiːnjəs] *adj fml* hétérogène.

heterosexual [,hetərəʊˈsekʃʊəl] ◇ *adj* hétérosexuel(elle) ◇ *n* hétérosexuel *m*, -elle *f*.

het up [het-] *adj* excité(e), énervé(e).

hew [hjuː] *(pt* -ed ; *pp* -ed OR hewn [hjuːn]) *vt literary* [stone] tailler ; [wood] couper.

HEW *(abbr of* **(Department of) Health, Education and Welfare)** *n ministère américain de l'éducation et de la santé publique.*

hex [heks] *n* [curse] sort *m*.

hexagon ['heksəgən] *n* hexagone *m*.

hexagonal [hek'sægənl] *adj* hexagonal(e).

hey [heɪ] *excl* hé!

heyday ['heɪdeɪ] *n* âge *m* d'or.

hey presto [-'prestəʊ] *excl* passez muscade!

HF *(abbr of* **high frequency)** HF.

HGV *(abbr of* **heavy goods vehicle)** *n* PL *m* ; **an ~ licence** un permis PL.

hi [haɪ] *excl inf* salut!

HI *abbr of* **Hawaii.**

hiatus [haɪˈeɪtəs] *(pl* -es [-iːz]) *n fml* pause *f*.

hiatus hernia n hernie f hiatale.
hibernate ['haɪbəneɪt] vi hiberner.
hibernation [ˌhaɪbə'neɪʃn] n hibernation f.
hiccough, hiccup ['hɪkʌp] (pt & pp -ped ; cont -ping) ⬦ n hoquet m ; fig [difficulty] accroc m ; **to have ~s** avoir le hoquet ⬦ vi hoqueter.
hick [hɪk] n esp Am inf pej péquenaud m, -e f.
hid [hɪd] pt ⟹ hide.
hidden ['hɪdn] ⬦ pp ⟹ hide ⬦ adj caché(e).
hide [haɪd] (pt hid ; pp hidden) ⬦ vt : **to ~ sthg (from sb)** cacher qqch (à qqn) ; [information] taire qqch (à qqn) ⬦ vi se cacher ⬦ n - **1.** [animal skin] peau f - **2.** [for watching birds, animals] cachette f.
hide-and-seek n cache-cache m.
hideaway ['haɪdəweɪ] n cachette f.
hidebound ['haɪdbaʊnd] adj pej [person] borné(e) ; [institution] rigide.
hideous ['hɪdɪəs] adj hideux(euse) ; [error, conditions] abominable.
hideout ['haɪdaʊt] n cachette f.
hiding ['haɪdɪŋ] n - **1.** [concealment] : **to be in ~** se tenir caché(e) - **2.** inf [beating] : **to give sb a (good) ~** donner une (bonne) raclée OR correction à qqn.
hiding place n cachette f.
hierarchical [ˌhaɪə'rɑːkɪkl] adj hiérarchique.
hierarchy ['haɪərɑːkɪ] (pl -ies) n hiérarchie f.
hieroglyphics [ˌhaɪərə'glɪfɪks] npl hiéroglyphes mpl.
hi-fi ['haɪfaɪ] n hi-fi f inv.
higgledy-piggledy [ˌhɪgldɪ'pɪgldɪ] inf ⬦ adj pêle-mêle (inv) ⬦ adv pêle-mêle.
high [haɪ] ⬦ adj - **1.** [gen] haut(e) ; **it's 3 feet/6 metres ~** cela fait 3 pieds/6 mètres de haut ; **how ~ is it?** cela fait combien de haut? ; **to have a ~ opinion of sb/sthg** avoir une haute opinion de qqn/qqch - **2.** [speed, figure, altitude, office] élevé(e) - **3.** [high-pitched] aigu(uë) - **4.** drugs sl qui plane, défoncé(e) - **5.** inf [drunk] bourré(e) ⬦ adv haut ⬦ n [highest point] maximum m ; **to reach a new ~** atteindre un nouveau record OR maximum.
highball ['haɪbɔːl] n Am whisky m à l'eau avec de la glace.
highbrow ['haɪbraʊ] adj intellectuel(elle).
high chair n chaise f haute (d'enfant).
high-class adj de premier ordre ; [hotel, restaurant] de grande classe.

high command n haut commandement m.
high commissioner n haut commissaire m.
High Court n Br JUR Cour f suprême.
high-density adj COMPUT haute densité (inv).
higher ['haɪəʳ] adj [exam, qualification] supérieur(e).
➡ **Higher** n : **Higher (Grade)** SCH examen de fin d'études secondaires en Écosse.
higher education n (U) études fpl supérieures.
high explosive n explosif m puissant.
high-fidelity adj haute-fidélité (inv).
high-flier n ambitieux m, -euse f.
high-flying adj [ambitious] ambitieux(euse).
high-handed [-'hændɪd] adj despotique.
high-heeled [-hiːld] adj à talons hauts.
high horse n inf : **to get on one's ~** monter sur ses grands chevaux.
high jump n saut m en hauteur ; **to be for the ~** Br inf être bon pour une engueulade.
Highland Games ['haɪlənd-] npl jeux mpl écossais.

Highlands ['haɪləndz] npl : **the ~** les Highlands fpl (région montagneuse du nord de l'Écosse).
high-level adj [talks, discussions] à haut niveau ; [diplomats, officials] de haut niveau.
high life n : **the ~** la grande vie.
highlight ['haɪlaɪt] ⬦ n [of event, occasion] moment m OR point m fort ⬦ vt souligner ; [with highlighter] surligner.
➡ **highlights** npl [in hair] reflets mpl, mèches fpl.
highlighter (pen) ['haɪlaɪtəʳ-] n surligneur m.
highly ['haɪlɪ] adv - **1.** [very] extrêmement, très - **2.** [in important position] : **~ placed** haut placé(e) - **3.** [favourably] : **to think ~ of sb/sthg** penser du bien de qqn/qqch ; **to speak ~ of sb/sthg** dire du bien de qqn/qqch.
highly-strung adj nerveux(euse).
high mass n grand-messe f.

high-minded [-'maɪndɪd] *adj* au caractère noble.

Highness ['haɪnɪs] *n* : **His/Her/Your (Royal) ~** Son/Votre Altesse (Royale) ; **their (Royal) ~es** leurs Altesses (Royales).

high-octane *adj* à indice d'octane élevé.

high-pitched [-'pɪtʃt] *adj* aigu(uë).

high point *n* [of occasion] point *m* fort.

high-powered [-'paʊəd] *adj* - **1.** [powerful] de forte puissance - **2.** [prestigious - activity, place] de haut niveau ; [- job, person] très important(e).

high-pressure *adj* - **1.** [air, gas] à haute pression ; **~ area** METEOR zone *f* de hautes pressions - **2.** [selling] agressif(ive).

high priest *n* RELIG grand prêtre *m*.

high-ranking [-'ræŋkɪŋ] *adj* de haut rang.

high resolution *n* COMPUT haute résolution *f*.

high-rise *adj* : **~ block of flats** tour *f*.

high-risk *adj* à haut risque.

high school *n* Br lycée *m* ; Am établissement *m* d'enseignement supérieur.

high seas *npl* : **the ~** la haute mer *f*.

high season *n* haute saison *f*.

high-speed *adj* - **1.** [train] à grande vitesse - **2.** PHOT à obturation rapide.

high-spirited *adj* [person] plein(e) d'entrain.

high spot *n* point *m* fort.

high street *n* Br rue *f* principale.

hightail ['haɪteɪl] *vt esp Am inf* : **to ~ it** filer.

high tea *n* Br repas tenant lieu de goûter et de dîner, pris en fin d'après-midi.

high-tech [-'tek] *adj* [method, industry] de pointe.

high technology *n* technologie *f* de pointe.

high-tension *adj* à haute tension.

high tide *n* marée *f* haute.

high treason *n* haute trahison *f*.

high water *n* (U) marée *f* haute.

highway ['haɪweɪ] *n* - **1.** Am [motorway] autoroute *f* - **2.** [main road] grande route *f*.

Highway Code *n* Br : **the ~** le code de la route.

high wire *n* corde *f* raide.

hijack ['haɪdʒæk] ◇ *n* détournement *m* ◇ *vt* détourner.

hijacker ['haɪdʒækə'] *n* [of aircraft] pirate *m* de l'air ; [of vehicle] pirate *m* de la route.

hike [haɪk] ◇ *n* [long walk] randonnée *f* ◇ *vi* faire une randonnée.

hiker ['haɪkə'] *n* randonneur *m*, -euse *f*.

hiking ['haɪkɪŋ] *n* marche *f*.

hilarious [hɪ'leərɪəs] *adj* hilarant(e).

hilarity [hɪ'lærətɪ] *n* hilarité *f*.

hill [hɪl] *n* - **1.** [mound] colline *f* - **2.** [slope] côte *f*.

hillbilly ['hɪl,bɪlɪ] (*pl* -ies) *n* Am inf pej péquenaud *m*, -e *f*.

hillock ['hɪlək] *n* petite colline *f* ; [smaller] petite élévation *f*.

hillside ['hɪlsaɪd] *n* coteau *m*.

hill start *n* démarrage *m* en côte.

hilltop ['hɪltɒp] ◇ *adj* au sommet de la colline ◇ *n* sommet *m*.

hilly ['hɪlɪ] (*compar* -ier ; *superl* -iest) *adj* vallonné(e).

hilt [hɪlt] *n* garde *f* ; **to the ~** jusqu'au cou ; **to support/defend sb to the ~** soutenir/défendre qqn à fond.

him [hɪm] *pers pron* - **1.** (*direct - unstressed*) le, l' (+ vowel or silent 'h') ; (- stressed) lui ; **I know/like ~** je le connais/l'aime ; **it's ~** c'est lui ; **if I were** OR **was ~** si j'étais lui, à sa place ; **you can't expect HIM to do it** tu ne peux pas exiger que ce soit lui qui le fasse - **2.** (*indirect*) lui ; **we spoke to ~** nous lui avons parlé ; **she sent ~ a letter** elle lui a envoyé une lettre - **3.** (*after prep, in comparisons etc*) lui ; **I'm shorter than ~** je suis plus petit que lui.

Himalayan [,hɪmə'leɪən] *adj* himalayen(enne).

Himalayas [,hɪmə'leɪəz] *npl* : **the ~** l'Himalaya *m* ; **in the ~** dans l'Himalaya.

himself [hɪm'self] *pron* - **1.** (*reflexive*) se ; (*after prep*) lui - **2.** (*for emphasis*) lui-même ; **he did it ~** il l'a fait tout seul.

hind [haɪnd] (*pl inv* OR -s) ◇ *adj* de derrière ◇ *n* biche *f*.

hinder ['hɪndə'] *vt* gêner, entraver.

Hindi ['hɪndɪ] *n* hindi *m*.

hindmost ['haɪndməʊst] *adj* arrière.

hindquarters ['haɪndkwɔːtəz] *npl* arrière-train *m*.

hindrance ['hɪndrəns] *n* obstacle *m*.

hindsight ['haɪndsaɪt] *n* : **with the benefit of ~** avec du recul.

Hindu ['hɪnduː] (*pl* -s) ◇ *adj* hindou(e) ◇ *n* Hindou *m*, -e *f*.

Hinduism ['hɪnduːɪzm] *n* hindouisme *m*.

hinge [hɪndʒ] (*cont* hingeing) *n* [whole fitting] charnière *f* ; [pin] gond *m*.

➤ **hinge (up)on** *vt fus* [depend on] dépendre de.

hint [hɪnt] ◇ *n* - **1.** [indication] allusion *f* ; **to drop a ~** faire une allusion ; **to take the ~**

saisir l'allusion - **2.** [piece of advice] conseil *m*, indication *f* - **3.** [small amount] soupçon *m* ◇ *vi* : **to ~ at sthg** faire allusion à qqch ◇ *vt* : **to ~ that ...** insinuer que ...

hinterland ['hɪntəlænd] *n* arrière-pays *m*.

hip [hɪp] *n* hanche *f*.

hipbath ['hɪpbɑːθ] *n* bain *m* de siège.

hipbone ['hɪpbəʊn] *n* os *m* de la hanche, os *m* iliaque.

hip flask *n* flasque *f*.

hip-hop *n* [music] hip-hop *m*.

hippie ['hɪpɪ] = **hippy**.

hippo ['hɪpəʊ] (*pl* **-s**) *n* hippopotame *m*.

hippopotamus [ˌhɪpə'pɒtəməs] (*pl* **-muses** [-məsiːz] OR **-mi** [-maɪ]) *n* hippopotame *m*.

hippy ['hɪpɪ] (*pl* **-ies**) *n* hippie *mf*.

hire ['haɪəʳ] ◇ *n* (U) [of car, equipment] location *f* ; **for ~** [bicycles etc] à louer ; [taxi] libre ; **on ~** en location ◇ *vt* - **1.** [rent] louer - **2.** [employ] employer les services de.
◆ **hire out** *vt sep* louer.

hire car *n* Br voiture *f* de location.

hire purchase *n* (U) Br achat *m* à crédit OR à tempérament ; **to buy sthg on ~** acheter qqch à crédit OR à tempérament.

his [hɪz] ◇ *poss adj* son (sa), ses (*pl*) ; **~ house** sa maison ; **~ money** son argent ; **~ children** ses enfants ; **~ name is Joe** il s'appelle Joe ; **it wasn't HIS fault** ce n'était pas de sa faute à lui ◇ *poss pron* le sien (la sienne), les siens (les siennes) (*pl*) ; **that money is ~** cet argent est à lui OR est le sien ; **it wasn't HER fault, it was HIS** ce n'était pas de sa faute à elle, c'était de sa faute à lui ; **a friend of ~** un ami à lui, un de ses amis.

Hispanic [hɪ'spænɪk] ◇ *adj* hispanique ◇ *n* esp Am Hispano-américain *m*, -e *f*.

hiss [hɪs] ◇ *n* [of animal, gas etc] sifflement *m* ; [of crowd] sifflet *m* ◇ *vt* [speaker, speech] siffler ◇ *vi* [animal, gas etc] siffler.

histogram ['hɪstəgræm] *n* histogramme *m*.

historian [hɪ'stɔːrɪən] *n* historien *m*, -enne *f*.

historic [hɪ'stɒrɪk] *adj* historique.

historical [hɪ'stɒrɪkəl] *adj* historique.

history ['hɪstərɪ] (*pl* **-ies**) *n* - **1.** [gen] histoire *f* ; **to go down in ~** entrer dans l'histoire ; **to make ~** faire l'histoire - **2.** [past record] antécédents *mpl* ; **medical ~** passé *m* médical.

histrionics [ˌhɪstrɪ'ɒnɪks] *npl* pej drame *m*.

hit [hɪt] (*pt* & *pp* hit, *cont* -ting) ◇ *n* - **1.** [blow] coup *m* - **2.** [successful strike] coup *m* OR tir *m* réussi ; [in fencing] touche *f* ; **to score a ~ on** sthg toucher qqch - **3.** [success] succès *m* ; **to be a ~ with** plaire à - **4.** COMPUT visite *f* (d'un site Internet) ◇ *comp* à succès ◇ *vt*

- **1.** [strike] frapper ; [nail] taper sur - **2.** [crash into] heurter, percuter - **3.** [reach] atteindre - **4.** [affect badly] toucher, affecter - **5.** phr : **to ~ it off (with sb)** bien s'entendre (avec qqn).
◆ **hit back** *vi* : **to ~ back (at)** répondre (à).
◆ **hit on** *vt fus* - **1.** = hit upon - **2.** Am inf [chat up] draguer.
◆ **hit out** *vi* : **to ~ out at** [physically] envoyer un coup à ; [criticize] attaquer.
◆ **hit upon** *vt fus* [think of] trouver.

hit-and-miss = **hit-or-miss**.

hit-and-run *adj* [accident] avec délit de fuite ; **~ driver** chauffard *m* (*qui a commis un délit de fuite*).

hitch [hɪtʃ] ◇ *n* [problem, snag] ennui *m* ◇ *vt* - **1.** [catch] : **to ~ a lift** faire du stop - **2.** [fasten] : **to ~ sthg on** OR **onto** accrocher OR attacher qqch à ◇ *vi* [hitchhike] faire du stop.
◆ **hitch up** *vt sep* [pull up] remonter.

hitchhike ['hɪtʃhaɪk] *vi* faire de l'auto-stop.

hitchhiker ['hɪtʃhaɪkəʳ] *n* auto-stoppeur *m*, -euse *f*.

hi-tech [ˌhaɪ'tek] = **high-tech**.

hither ['hɪðəʳ] *adv* literary ici ; **~ and thither** çà et là.

hitherto [ˌhɪðə'tuː] *adv* fml jusqu'ici.

hit list *n* liste *f* noire.

hit man *n* tueur *m* (*à gages*).

hit-or-miss *adj* aléatoire.

hit parade *n* dated hit-parade *m*.

HIV (*abbr of* human immunodeficiency virus) *n* VIH *m*, HIV *m* ; **to be ~-positive** être séropositif.

hive [haɪv] *n* ruche *f* ; **a ~ of activity** une véritable ruche.
◆ **hive off** *vt sep* [assets] séparer.

hl (*abbr of* hectolitre) hl.

HM (*abbr of* His (or Her) Majesty) SM.

HMG (*abbr of* His (or Her) Majesty's Government) *expression utilisée sur des documents officiels en Grande-Bretagne.*

HMI (*abbr of* His (or Her) Majesty's Inspector) *n inspecteur de l'éducation nationale en Grande-Bretagne.*

HMO (*abbr of* health maintenance organization) *n organisme américain pour la santé publique.*

HMS (*abbr of* His (or Her) Majesty's Ship) *expression précédant le nom d'un bâtiment de la marine britannique.*

HMSO (*abbr of* His (or Her) Majesty's Stationery Office) *n service officiel des publications en Grande-Bretagne,* ≃ Imprimerie *f* nationale.

HNC (*abbr of* **Higher National Certificate**) *n* brevet de technicien en Grande-Bretagne.

HND (*abbr of* **Higher National Diploma**) *n* brevet de technicien supérieur en Grande-Bretagne.

hoard [hɔːd] ⬦ *n* [store] réserves *fpl ;* [of useless items] tas *m* ⬦ *vt* amasser ; [food, petrol] faire des provisions de.

hoarding ['hɔːdɪŋ] *n* Br [for advertisements] panneau *m* d'affichage publicitaire.

hoarfrost ['hɔːfrɒst] *n* gelée *f* blanche.

hoarse [hɔːs] *adj* [person, voice] enroué(e) ; [shout, whisper] rauque.

hoax [həʊks] *n* canular *m.*

hoaxer ['həʊksəʳ] *n* mauvais plaisant *m.*

hob [hɒb] *n* Br [on cooker] rond *m*, plaque *f.*

hobble ['hɒbl] *vi* [limp] boitiller.

hobby ['hɒbɪ] (*pl* **-ies**) *n* passe-temps *m inv*, hobby *m.*

hobbyhorse ['hɒbɪhɔːs] *n* - **1.** [toy] cheval *m* à bascule - **2.** fig [favourite topic] dada *m.*

hobnob ['hɒbnɒb] (*pt & pp* **-bed** ; *cont* **-bing**) *vi :* to ~ with sb frayer avec qqn.

hobo ['həʊbəʊ] (*pl* **-es** OR **-s**) *n* Am clochard *m*, -e *f.*

Ho Chi Minh City ['həʊˌtʃiː'mɪn-] *n* Hô Chi Minh-Ville.

hock [hɒk] *n* [wine] vin *m* du Rhin.

hockey ['hɒkɪ] *n* - **1.** [on grass] hockey *m* - **2.** Am [ice hockey] hockey *m* sur glace.

hocus-pocus ['həʊkəs'pəʊkəs] *n* [trickery] supercherie *f*, tromperie *f.*

hod [hɒd] *n* hotte *f.*

hodgepodge Am = hotchpotch.

hoe [həʊ] ⬦ *n* houe *f* ⬦ *vt* biner.

hog [hɒg] (*pt & pp* **-ged** ; *cont* **-ging**) ⬦ *n* - **1.** Am [pig] cochon *m* - **2.** inf [greedy person] goinfre *m* - **3.** phr : **to go the whole ~** aller jusqu'au bout ⬦ *vt* inf [monopolize] accaparer, monopoliser.

Hogmanay ['hɒgməneɪ] *n* la Saint-Sylvestre en Écosse.

hoist [hɔɪst] ⬦ *n* [device] treuil *m* ⬦ *vt* hisser.

hokum ['həʊkəm] *n* (U) Am inf niaiseries *fpl*.

hold [həʊld] (*pt & pp* **held**) ⬦ *vt* - **1.** [gen] tenir - **2.** [keep in position] maintenir - **3.** [as prisoner] détenir ; **to ~ sb prisoner/hostage** détenir qqn prisonnier/comme otage - **4.** [have, possess] avoir - **5.** fml [consider] considérer, estimer ; **to ~ (that)** ... considérer que ..., estimer que ... ; **to ~ sb responsible for sthg** rendre qqn responsable de qqch, tenir qqn pour responsable de qqch ; **to ~ sthg dear** tenir à qqch - **6.** [on telephone] : **please ~ the line** ne quittez pas, je vous prie

- **7.** [keep, maintain] retenir - **8.** [sustain, support] supporter - **9.** [contain] contenir ; **the main hall ~s 500** on peut tenir à 500 dans la grande salle ; **what does the future ~ for him?** que lui réserve l'avenir? - **10.** phr : **~ it!, ~ everything!** attendez!, arrêtez! ; **to ~ one's own** se défendre ⬦ *vi* - **1.** [remain unchanged - gen] tenir ; [- luck] persister ; [- weather] se maintenir ; **to ~ still** OR **steady** ne pas bouger, rester tranquille - **2.** [on phone] attendre ⬦ *n* - **1.** [grasp, grip] prise *f*, étreinte *f* ; **to take** OR **lay ~ of sthg** saisir qqch ; **to get ~ of sthg** [obtain] se procurer qqch ; **to get ~ of sb** [find] joindre - **2.** [of ship, aircraft] cale *f* - **3.** [control, influence] prise *f* ; **to take ~** [fire] prendre.

➧ **hold against** *vt sep :* **to ~ sthg against sb** fig en vouloir à qqn de qqch.

➧ **hold back** ⬦ *vi* [hesitate] se retenir ; **to ~ back from doing sthg** se retenir de faire qqch ⬦ *vt sep* - **1.** [restrain, prevent] retenir ; [anger] réprimer ; **to ~ sb back from doing sthg** retenir qqn de faire qqch - **2.** [keep secret] cacher.

➧ **hold down** *vt sep* [job] garder.

➧ **hold off** *vt sep* [fend off] tenir à distance ⬦ *vi :* **the rain held off** il n'a pas plu.

➧ **hold on** *vi* - **1.** [wait] attendre ; [on phone] ne pas quitter - **2.** [grip] : **to ~ on (to sthg)** se tenir (à qqch).

➧ **hold onto** *vt fus* [power, job] garder.

➧ **hold out** ⬦ *vt sep* [hand, arms] tendre ⬦ *vi* - **1.** [last] durer - **2.** [resist] : **to ~ out (against sb/ sthg)** résister (à qqn/qqch).

➧ **hold out for** *vt fus* continuer à réclamer.

➧ **hold up** *vt sep* - **1.** [raise] lever - **2.** [delay] retarder - **3.** inf [rob] faire un hold-up dans.

➧ **hold with** *vt fus* [approve of] approuver.

holdall ['həʊldɔːl] *n* Br fourre-tout *m inv.*

holder ['həʊldəʳ] *n* - **1.** [for cigarette] porte-cigarettes *m inv* - **2.** [owner] détenteur *m*, -trice *f* ; [of position, title] titulaire *mf.*

holding ['həʊldɪŋ] ⬦ *n* - **1.** [investment] effets *mpl* en portefeuille - **2.** [farm] ferme *f* ⬦ *adj* [action, operation] mené en vue de maintenir le statu quo.

holding company *n* holding *m.*

holdup ['həʊldʌp] *n* - **1.** [robbery] hold-up *m* - **2.** [delay] retard *m.*

hole [həʊl] *n* - **1.** [gen] trou *m* ; **~ in one** GOLF trou réussi en un coup ; **to pick ~s in sthg** [criticize] trouver à redire à qqch - **2.** inf [predicament] pétrin *m.*

➧ **hole up** *vi* [hide, take shelter] se terrer.

holiday ['hɒlɪdeɪ] *n* - **1.** [vacation] vacances *fpl* ; **to be/go on ~** être/partir en vacances - **2.** [public holiday] jour *m* férié.

holiday camp n Br camp m de vacances.

holidaymaker [ˈhɒlɪdɪˌmeɪkəʳ] n Br vacancier m, -ère f.

holiday pay n Br salaire payé pendant les vacances.

holiday resort n Br lieu m de vacances.

holiday season n Br période f des vacances.

holiness [ˈhəʊlɪnɪs] n [holy quality] sainteté f.
 Holiness n [in titles] : **His/Your Holiness** Sa/Votre Sainteté.

hollstic [həʊˈlɪstɪk] adj holistique.

Holland [ˈhɒlənd] n Hollande f ; **in ~** en Hollande.

hollandaise sauce [ˌhɒlənˈdeɪz-] n sauce f hollandaise.

holler [ˈhɒləʳ] vi & vt inf gueuler, brailler.

hollow [ˈhɒləʊ] ⬦ adj creux (creuse) ; [eyes] cave ; [promise, victory] faux (fausse) ; [laugh] qui sonne faux ⬦ n creux m.
 hollow out vt sep creuser, évider.

holly [ˈhɒlɪ] n houx m.

Hollywood [ˈhɒlɪwʊd] ⬦ n [film industry] Hollywood ⬦ comp hollywoodien(enne).

holocaust [ˈhɒləkɔːst] n [destruction] destruction f, holocauste m.
 Holocaust n : **the Holocaust** l'holocauste m.

hologram [ˈhɒləgræm] n hologramme m.

hols [hɒlz] npl Br inf vacances fpl.

holster [ˈhəʊlstəʳ] n étui m.

holy [ˈhəʊlɪ] (compar -ier ; superl -iest) adj saint(e) ; [ground] sacré(e).

Holy Communion n Sainte Communion f.

Holy Ghost n : **the ~** le Saint-Esprit.

Holy Grail [-ˈɡreɪl] n : **the ~** le Saint-Graal.

Holy Land n : **the ~** la Terre sainte.

holy orders npl ordres mpl sacrés.

Holy Spirit n : **the ~** le Saint-Esprit.

homage [ˈhɒmɪdʒ] (U) fml n hommage m ; **to pay ~ to sb/sthg** rendre hommage à qqn/qqch.

home [həʊm] ⬦ n - **1.** [house, institution] maison f ; **to make one's ~** s'établir, s'installer ; **it's a ~ from ~** Br OR **~ away from ~** Am on est ici comme chez soi - **2.** [own country] patrie f ; [city] ville f natale - **3.** [one's family] foyer m ; **to leave ~** quitter la maison - **4.** fig [place of origin] berceau m ⬦ adj - **1.** [not foreign - gen] intérieur(e) ; [- product] national(e) - **2.** [in one's own home - cooking] familial(e) ; [- life] de famille ; [- improvements] domestique - **3.** [SPORT - game] sur son propre terrain ; [- team] qui re-

çoit ⬦ adv - **1.** [to or at one's house] chez soi, à la maison - **2.** phr : **to bring sthg ~ (to sb)** faire prendre conscience de qqch (à qqn) ; **to drive** OR **hammer sthg ~ to sb** enfoncer OR faire rentrer qqch dans la tête de qqn.
 at home adv - **1.** [in one's house, flat] chez soi, à la maison - **2.** [comfortable] à l'aise ; **at ~ with sthg** à l'aise dans qqch ; **to make o.s. at ~** faire comme chez soi - **3.** [in one's own country] chez nous - **4.** SPORT : **to play at ~** jouer sur son propre terrain.
 home in vi : **to ~ in on sthg** viser qqch, se diriger vers qqch ; fig pointer sur qqch.

home address n adresse f du domicile.

home banking n opérations bancaires effectuées à domicile par ordinateur.

home brew n (U) [beer] bière f faite à la maison.

homecoming [ˈhəʊmˌkʌmɪŋ] n - **1.** [return] retour m au foyer OR à la maison - **2.** Am SCH & UNIV fête donnée en l'honneur de l'équipe de football et à laquelle sont invités les anciens élèves.

home computer n ordinateur m domestique.

Home Counties npl : **the ~** les comtés entourant Londres.

home economics n (U) économie f domestique.

home fries npl Am pommes de terre fpl sautées.

home ground n - **1.** [familiar territory] : **to be on ~** lit & fig être sur son terrain - **2.** SPORT terrain m du club.

homegrown [ˌhəʊmˈɡrəʊn] adj du jardin.

home help n Br aide f ménagère.

homeland [ˈhəʊmlænd] n - **1.** [country of birth] patrie f - **2.** [in South Africa] homeland m, bantoustan m.

homeless [ˈhəʊmlɪs] ⬦ adj sans abri ⬦ npl : **the ~** les sans-abri mpl.

homelessness [ˈhəʊmlɪsnəs] n fait d'être sans abri.

home loan n prêt m d'accession à la propriété.

homely [ˈhəʊmlɪ] adj - **1.** [simple] simple - **2.** [unattractive] ordinaire.

homemade [ˌhəʊmˈmeɪd] adj fait(e) (à la) maison.

home movie n film m amateur.

Home Office n Br : **the ~** ≃ le ministère de l'Intérieur.

homeopathic [ˌhəʊmɪəʊˈpæθɪk] adj homéopathique.

homeopathy [ˌhəʊmɪ'ɒpəθɪ] n homéopathie f.

homeowner ['həʊmˌəʊnəʳ] n propriétaire mf (d'une maison/d'un appartement).

home page n COMPUT page f d'accueil.

home rule n autonomie f.

home run n Am inf coup m de circuit.

Home Secretary n Br ≈ ministre m de l'Intérieur.

homesick ['həʊmsɪk] adj qui a le mal du pays.

homesickness ['həʊmˌsɪknɪs] n mal m du pays.

homespun ['həʊmspʌn] adj fig simple.

homestead ['həʊmsted] n Am ferme f (avec dépendances).

home straight n : the ~ [of race] la dernière ligne droite ; [of task] le dernier stade.

hometown ['həʊmtaʊn] n ville f natale.

home truth n : to tell sb a few ~s dire ses quatre vérités à qqn.

homeward ['həʊmwəd] ⟨⟩ adj de retour ⟨⟩ adv = **homewards.**

homewards ['həʊmwədz] adv vers la maison.

homework ['həʊmwɜːk] n (U) - **1.** SCH devoirs mpl - **2.** inf [preparation] boulot m.

homey, homy ['həʊmɪ] adj Am confortable, agréable.

homicidal ['hɒmɪsaɪdl] adj homicide.

homicide ['hɒmɪsaɪd] n homicide m.

homily ['hɒmɪlɪ] (pl -ies) n [lecture] homélie f.

homing ['həʊmɪŋ] adj de retour au gîte ; MIL : ~ **device** tête f chercheuse.

homing pigeon n pigeon m voyageur.

homoeopathy etc [ˌhəʊmɪ'ɒpəθɪ] = **homeopathy** etc.

homogeneous [ˌhɒmə'dʒiːnjəs] adj homogène.

homogenize, -ise [hə'mɒdʒənaɪz] vt Br homogénéiser.

homosexual [ˌhɒmə'sekʃʊəl] ⟨⟩ adj homosexuel(elle) ⟨⟩ n homosexuel m, -elle f.

homosexuality [ˌhɒməˌseksjʊ'ælətɪ] n homosexualité f.

homy = **homey.**

Hon. - 1. abbr of **Honourable - 2.** abbr of **Honorary.**

Honduran [hɒn'djʊərən] ⟨⟩ adj hondurien(enne) ⟨⟩ n Hondurien m, -enne f.

Honduras [hɒn'djʊərəs] n Honduras m ; in ~ au Honduras.

hone [həʊn] vt aiguiser.

honest ['ɒnɪst] ⟨⟩ adj - **1.** [trustworthy] honnête, probe - **2.** [frank] franc (franche), sincère ; **to be** ~ ... pour dire la vérité ..., à dire vrai ... - **3.** [legal] légitime ⟨⟩ adv inf = **honestly 2.**

honestly ['ɒnɪstlɪ] ⟨⟩ adv - **1.** [truthfully] honnêtement - **2.** [expressing sincerity] je vous assure ⟨⟩ excl [expressing impatience, disapproval] franchement!

honesty ['ɒnɪstɪ] n honnêteté f, probité f.

honey ['hʌnɪ] n - **1.** [food] miel m - **2.** [dear] chéri m, -e f.

honeybee ['hʌnɪbiː] n abeille f.

honeycomb ['hʌnɪkəʊm] n gâteau m de miel.

honeymoon ['hʌnɪmuːn] ⟨⟩ n lit & fig lune f de miel ⟨⟩ vi aller en voyage de noces, passer sa lune de miel.

honeysuckle ['hʌnɪˌsʌkl] n chèvrefeuille m.

Hong Kong [ˌhɒŋ'kɒŋ] n Hong Kong, Hongkong ; **in** ~ à Hongkong.

honk [hɒŋk] ⟨⟩ vi - **1.** [motorist] klaxonner - **2.** [goose] cacarder ⟨⟩ vt : **to** ~ **the horn** klaxonner ⟨⟩ n - **1.** [of horn] coup m de Klaxon® - **2.** [of goose] cri m.

honky ['hɒŋkɪ] (pl -ies) n Am v inf terme injurieux désignant un Blanc.

Honolulu [ˌhɒnə'luːluː] n Honolulu.

honor etc Am = **honour** etc.

honorary [Br 'ɒnərərɪ, Am ɒnə'reərɪ] adj honoraire.

honor roll n Am tableau m d'honneur.

honour Br, **honor** Am ['ɒnəʳ] ⟨⟩ n honneur m ; **in** ~ **of sb/sthg** en l'honneur de qqn/qqch ⟨⟩ vt honorer.

➤ **Honour** n : **His/Your Honour** Son/Votre Honneur.

➤ **honours** npl - **1.** [tokens of respect] honneurs mpl - **2.** [of university degree] ≈ licence f - **3.** phr : **to do the ~s** [serve food] servir ; [introduce people] faire les présentations.

honourable Br, **honorable** Am ['ɒnrəbl] adj honorable.

➤ **Honourable** adj [in titles] : **the Honourable** ... l'honorable ...

honourably Br, **honorably** Am ['ɒnərəblɪ] adv honorablement.

honour bound adj : **to be** ~ **to do sthg** être tenu(e) par l'honneur de faire qqch.

honours list n Br liste des personnes qui doivent recevoir des titres honorifiques (conférés par la reine).

Hons. (abbr of **honours degree**) licence.

hooch [huːtʃ] n inf [drink] gnôle f.

hood [hʊd] n - **1.** [on cloak, jacket] capuchon m

- 2. [of cooker] hotte f **- 3.** [of pram, convertible car] capote f **- 4.** Am [car bonnet] capot m.

hooded ['hʊdɪd] adj **- 1.** [wearing a hood] encapuchonné(e) **- 2.** [eyes] aux paupières tombantes.

hoodlum ['hu:dləm] n Am inf gangster m, truand m.

hoodwink ['hʊdwɪŋk] vt tromper, berner.

hooey ['hu:ɪ] n (U) Am inf salades fpl.

hoof [hu:f, hʊf] (pl -s OR hooves [hu:vz]) n sabot m.

hook [hʊk] ◇ n **- 1.** [for hanging things on] crochet m **- 2.** [for catching fish] hameçon m **- 3.** [fastener] agrafe f **- 4.** [of telephone] : off the ~ décroché **- 5.** phr : to get sb off the ~ tirer qqn d'affaire ◇ vt **- 1.** [attach with hook] accrocher **- 2.** [catch with hook] prendre **- 3.** [arm, leg] : to ~ one's arm round sthg passer son bras autour de qqch.

◆ **hook up** vt sep : to ~ sthg up to sthg connecter qqch à qqch.

hook and eye (pl hooks and eyes) n agrafe f.

hooked [hʊkt] adj **- 1.** [shaped like a hook] crochu(e) **- 2.** inf [addicted] : to be ~ (on) être accro (à) ; [music, art] être mordu(e) (de).

hooker ['hʊkəʳ] n Am inf putain f.

hook(e)y ['hʊkɪ] n Am inf : to play ~ faire l'école buissonnière.

hooligan ['hu:lɪgən] n hooligan m, vandale m.

hooliganism ['hu:lɪgənɪzm] n hooliganisme m, vandalisme m.

hoop [hu:p] n **- 1.** [circular band] cercle m **- 2.** [toy] cerceau m.

hoop-la ['hu:plɑ:] n (U) [game] jeu m d'anneaux.

hooray [hʊ'reɪ] = hurray.

hoot [hu:t] ◇ n **- 1.** [of owl] hululement m **- 2.** [of horn] coup m de Klaxon® **- 3.** [of person] : a ~ of laughter un hurlement de rire **- 4.** Br inf [something amusing] : to be a ~ être tordant(e) ◇ vi **- 1.** [owl] hululer **- 2.** [horn] klaxonner **- 3.** inf [person] : to ~ with laughter hurler de rire, rire aux éclats ◇ vt : to ~ the horn klaxonner.

hooter ['hu:təʳ] n **- 1.** [horn] Klaxon® m **- 2.** Br inf [nose] pif m.

Hoover® Br ['hu:vəʳ] n aspirateur m.

◆ **hoover** ◇ vt [room] passer l'aspirateur dans ; [carpet] passer à l'aspirateur ◇ vi passer l'aspirateur.

hooves [hu:vz] pl ▷ hoof.

hop [hɒp] (pt & pp -ped ; cont -ping) ◇ n saut m ; [on one leg] saut à cloche-pied ◇ vi sauter ; [on one leg] sauter à cloche-pied ; [bird] sautiller ◇ vt Am inf [bus, train] sauter dans.

◆ **hops** npl houblon m.

hope [həʊp] ◇ vi espérer ; to ~ for sthg espérer qqch ; I ~ so j'espère bien ; I ~ not j'espère bien que non ; to ~ for the best espérer que tout aille pour le mieux ◇ vt : to ~ (that) espérer que ; to ~ to do sthg espérer faire qqch ◇ n espoir m ; in the ~ of dans l'espoir de ; I don't hold out much ~ je n'ai pas beaucoup d'espoir, je n'y compte pas trop ; to pin one's ~s on sthg mettre tous ses espoirs dans qqch ; to raise sb's ~s donner de l'espoir à qqn.

hope chest n Am trousseau m.

hopeful ['həʊpfʊl] ◇ adj **- 1.** [optimistic] plein(e) d'espoir ; to be ~ of doing sthg avoir l'espoir de faire qqch ; to be ~ of sthg espérer qqch **- 2.** [promising] encourageant(e), qui promet ◇ n espoir m.

hopefully ['həʊpfəlɪ] adv **- 1.** [in a hopeful way] avec bon espoir, avec optimisme **- 2.** [with luck] : ~,... espérons que ...

hopeless ['həʊplɪs] adj **- 1.** [gen] désespéré(e) ; [tears] de désespoir **- 2.** inf [useless] nul (nulle).

hopelessly ['həʊplɪslɪ] adv **- 1.** [despairingly] avec désespoir **- 2.** [completely] complètement.

hopper ['hɒpəʳ] n [funnel] trémie f.

hopping ['hɒpɪŋ] adv : to be ~ mad être fou (folle) de colère.

hopscotch ['hɒpskɒtʃ] n marelle f.

horde [hɔ:d] n horde f, foule f.

◆ **hordes** npl : ~s of une foule de.

horizon [hə'raɪzn] n horizon m ; on the ~ lit & fig à l'horizon.

◆ **horizons** npl horizons mpl.

horizontal [ˌhɒrɪ'zɒntl] ◇ adj horizontal(e) ◇ n : the ~ l'horizontale f.

hormone ['hɔ:məʊn] n hormone f.

hormone replacement therapy n traitement m hormonal substitutif.

horn [hɔ:n] n **- 1.** [of animal] corne f **- 2.** MUS [instrument] cor m **- 3.** [on car] Klaxon® m ; [on ship] sirène f.

hornet ['hɔ:nɪt] n frelon m.

horn-rimmed [-'rɪmd] adj à monture d'écaille.

horny ['hɔ:nɪ] (compar -ier ; superl -iest) adj **- 1.** [hard] corné(e) ; [hand] calleux(euse) **- 2.** v inf [sexually excited] excité(e) (sexuellement).

horoscope ['hɒrəskəʊp] n horoscope m.

horrendous [hɒ'rendəs] adj horrible.

horrible ['hɒrəbl] *adj* horrible.

horribly ['hɒrəblɪ] *adv* horriblement.

horrid ['hɒrɪd] *adj* [unpleasant] horrible.

horrific [hɒ'rɪfɪk] *adj* horrible.

horrify ['hɒrɪfaɪ] (*pt* & *pp* **-ied**) *vt* horrifier.

horrifying ['hɒrɪfaɪɪŋ] *adj* horrifiant(e).

horror ['hɒrə*r*] *n* horreur *f* ; **to have a ~ of sthg** avoir horreur de qqch ; **to my/his ~** à ma/sa grande horreur.

horror film *n* film *m* d'épouvante.

horror-struck *adj* frappé(e) d'horreur.

hors d'oeuvre [ɔː'dɜːvr] (*pl* **hors d'oeuvres** [ɔː'dɜːvr]) *n* hors-d'œuvre *m inv*.

horse [hɔːs] *n* [animal] cheval *m*.

horseback ['hɔːsbæk] <> *adj* à cheval ; **~ riding** Am équitation *f* <> *n* : **on ~** à cheval.

horsebox Br ['hɔːsbɒks], **horsecar** Am ['hɔːskɑːr] *n* van *m*.

horse chestnut *n* [nut] marron *m* d'Inde ; **~ (tree)** marronnier *m* d'Inde.

horse-drawn *adj* tiré(e) par des chevaux.

horsefly ['hɔːsflaɪ] (*pl* **-flies**) *n* taon *m*.

horsehair ['hɔːsheə*r*] *n* crin *m*.

horseman ['hɔːsmən] (*pl* **-men** [-mən]) *n* cavalier *m*.

horse opera *n* Am hum western *m*.

horseplay ['hɔːspleɪ] *n* chahut *m*.

horsepower ['hɔːs,pauə*r*] *n* puissance *f* en chevaux.

horse racing *n (U)* courses *fpl* de chevaux.

horseradish ['hɔːs,rædɪʃ] *n* [plant] raifort *m*.

horse riding *n* équitation *f*.

horseshoe ['hɔːsʃuː] *n* fer *m* à cheval.

horse show *n* concours *m* hippique.

horse-trading *n* fig & pej maquignonnage *m*.

horse trials *npl* concours *m* hippique.

horsewhip ['hɔːswɪp] (*pt* & *pp* **-ped** ; *cont* **-ping**) *vt* cravacher.

horsewoman ['hɔːs,wumən] (*pl* **-women** [-,wɪmɪn]) *n* cavalière *f*.

horticultural [,hɔːtɪ'kʌltʃərəl] *adj* d'horticulture.

horticulture ['hɔːtɪkʌltʃə*r*] *n* horticulture *f*.

hose [həuz] <> *n* [hosepipe] tuyau *m* <> *vt* arroser au jet.

hose down *vt sep* laver au jet.

hosepipe ['həuzpaɪp] *n* = **hose**.

hosiery ['həuzɪərɪ] *n* bonneterie *f*.

hospice ['hɒspɪs] *n* hospice *m*.

hospitable [hɒ'spɪtəbl] *adj* hospitalier(ère), accueillant(e).

hospital ['hɒspɪtl] *n* hôpital *m*.

hospitality [,hɒspɪ'tælətɪ] *n* hospitalité *f*.

hospitality suite *n* salon privé où sont offerts des rafraîchissements (lors d'une conférence etc).

hospitalize, -ise ['hɒspɪtəlaɪz] *vt* hospitaliser.

host [həust] <> *n* - **1.** [gen] hôte *m* ; **~ city/country** ville *f*/pays *m* d'accueil - **2.** [compere] animateur *m*, -trice *f* - **3.** [large number] : **a ~ of** une foule de <> *vt* présenter, animer.

hostage ['hɒstɪdʒ] *n* otage *m* ; **to be taken ~** être pris en otage ; **to be held ~** être détenu comme otage.

hostel ['hɒstl] *n* - **1.** [basic accommodation] foyer *m* - **2.** [youth hostel] auberge *f* de jeunesse.

hostelry ['hɒstəlrɪ] (*pl* **-ries**) *n* hum hostellerie *f*.

hostess ['həustes] *n* hôtesse *f*.

host family *n* famille *f* d'accueil.

hostile [Br 'hɒstaɪl, Am 'hɒstl] *adj* : **~ (to)** hostile (à).

hostility [hɒ'stɪlətɪ] *n* [antagonism, unfriendliness] hostilité *f*.

hostilities *npl* hostilités *fpl*.

hot [hɒt] (*compar* **-ter** ; *superl* **-test** ; *pt* & *pp* **-ted** ; *cont* **-ting**) *adj* - **1.** [gen] chaud(e) ; **I'm ~** j'ai chaud ; **it's ~** il fait chaud - **2.** [spicy] épicé(e) - **3.** inf [expert] fort(e), calé(e) ; **to be ~ on** OR **at sthg** être fort OR calé en qqch - **4.** [recent] de dernière heure OR minute - **5.** [temper] colérique.

hot up *vi* inf chauffer.

hot-air balloon *n* montgolfière *f*.

hotbed ['hɒtbed] *n* foyer *m*.

hotchpotch Br ['hɒtʃpɒtʃ], **hodgepodge** Am ['hɒdʒpɒdʒ] *n* inf fouillis *m*, méli-mélo *m*.

hot-cross bun *n* petit pain sucré que l'on mange le vendredi saint.

hot dog *n* hot dog *m*.

hotel [həu'tel] <> *n* hôtel *m* <> *comp* d'hôtel.

hotelier [həu'telɪə*r*] *n* hôtelier *m*, -ère *f*.

hot flush Br, **hot flash** Am *n* bouffée *f* de chaleur.

hotfoot ['hɒt,fut] *adv* à toute vitesse.

hotheaded [,hɒt'hedɪd] *adj* impulsif(ive).

hothouse ['hɒthaus, *pl* -hauzɪz] <> *n* [greenhouse] serre *f* <> *comp* de serre.

hot line *n* - **1.** [between government heads] téléphone *m* rouge - **2.** [special line] hot line *f*.

hotly ['hɒtlɪ] *adv* - **1.** [passionately] avec véhémence - **2.** [closely] de près.

hotplate ['hɒtpleɪt] *n* plaque *f* chauffante.

hotpot ['hɒtpɒt] *n* Br type de ragoût.

hot potato *n* inf fig affaire *f* brûlante.

hot rod n voiture f gonflée.

hot seat n inf : **to be in the ~** être sur la sellette.

hot spot n - **1.** [exciting place] endroit m à la mode - **2.** [politically unsettled area] point m chaud.

hot-tempered [-'tempəd] adj colérique.

hot water n fig : **to get into ~** s'attirer des ennuis ; **to be in ~** être dans le pétrin.

hot-water bottle n bouillotte f.

hot-wire vt inf faire démarrer en court-circuitant l'allumage.

hound [haʊnd] ◇ n [dog] chien m ◇ vt - **1.** [persecute] poursuivre, pourchasser - **2.** [drive] : **to ~ sb out (of)** chasser qqn (de).

hour ['aʊər] n heure f ; **half an ~** une demi-heure ; **70 miles per** OR **an ~** 110 km à l'heure ; **on the ~** à l'heure juste ; **in the small ~s** au petit matin OR jour.

➤ **hours** npl - **1.** [of business] heures fpl d'ouverture ; **after ~s** après l'heure de fermeture, après la fermeture - **2.** [routine] : **to keep late ~s** se coucher très tard ; **to keep regular ~s** avoir une vie réglée.

hourly ['aʊəli] ◇ adj - **1.** [happening every hour] toutes les heures - **2.** [per hour] à l'heure ◇ adv - **1.** [every hour] toutes les heures - **2.** [per hour] à l'heure - **3.** fig [constantly] sans cesse, constamment.

house [n & adj haʊs, pl 'haʊzɪz, vb haʊz] ◇ n - **1.** [gen] maison f ; **on the ~** aux frais de la maison ; **to put** OR **set one's ~ in order** balayer devant sa porte - **2.** POL chambre f - **3.** [in debates] assistance f - **4.** THEATRE [audience] auditoire m, salle f ; **to bring the ~ down** inf faire crouler la salle sous les applaudissements - **5.** MUS = **house music** ◇ vt [accommodate] loger, héberger ; [department, store] abriter ◇ adj - **1.** [within business] d'entreprise ; [style] de la maison - **2.** [wine] maison (inv).

house arrest n : **under ~** en résidence surveillée.

houseboat ['haʊsbəʊt] n péniche f aménagée.

housebound ['haʊsbaʊnd] adj confiné(e) chez soi.

housebreaking ['haʊs,breɪkɪŋ] n (U) cambriolage m.

housebroken ['haʊs,brəʊkn] adj Am [pet] propre.

housecoat ['haʊskəʊt] n peignoir m.

household ['haʊshəʊld] ◇ adj - **1.** [domestic] ménager(ère) - **2.** [word, name] connu(e) de tous ◇ n maison f, ménage m.

householder ['haʊs,həʊldər] n propriétaire mf (d'une maison).

househunting ['haʊs,hʌntɪŋ] n recherche f d'une maison (à acheter OR louer).

house husband n homme m au foyer.

housekeeper ['haʊs,kiːpər] n gouvernante f.

housekeeping ['haʊs,kiːpɪŋ] n (U) - **1.** [work] ménage m - **2.** : **~ (money)** argent m du ménage.

houseman ['haʊsmən] (pl -men [-mən]) n Br ≃ interne m.

housemen ['haʊsmən] pl ➭ houseman.

house music, house n house music f.

House of Commons n Br : **the ~** la Chambre des communes.

HOUSE OF COMMONS

La Chambre des communes est composée de 650 députés (« MPs ») élus pour 5 ans et qui siègent environ 175 jours par an.

House of Lords n Br : **the ~** la Chambre des lords.

HOUSE OF LORDS

La Chambre des lords est composée de pairs et d'hommes d'Église. Il s'agit de la plus haute cour au Royaume-Uni (en excluant l'Écosse). Elle a le pouvoir d'amender certains projets de loi qui ont été votés par la Chambre des communes.

House of Representatives n Am : **the ~** la Chambre des représentants.

HOUSE OF REPRESENTATIVES

La Chambre des représentants constitue, avec le Sénat, l'organe législatif américain ; ses membres sont élus par le peuple, en proportion de la population de chaque État.

house-owner n propriétaire mf d'une maison.

houseplant ['haʊsplɑːnt] n plante f d'appartement.

house-proud adj qui a la manie d'astiquer.

Houses of Parliament npl : **the ~** le Parlement britannique (où se réunissent la Chambre des communes et la Chambre des lords).

house-to-house adj de porte en porte, maison par maison.

house-train vt Br [animal] dresser à être propre.

housewarming (party) [ˈhaʊsˌwɔːmɪŋ-] *n* pendaison *f* de crémaillère.

housewife [ˈhaʊswaɪf] (*pl* **-wives** [-waɪvz]) *n* femme *f* au foyer.

housework [ˈhaʊswɜːk] *n (U)* ménage *m*.

housing [ˈhaʊzɪŋ] ◇ *n* - **1.** *(U)* [accommodation] logement *m* - **2.** [TECH - gen] boîtier *m* ; [- of engine] coquille *f* ◇ *comp* [policy] du logement ; [conditions] de logement ; [shortage] de logements.

housing association *n* Br association *f* d'aide au logement.

housing benefit *n (U)* Br allocation *f* logement.

housing development *n* ensemble *m* immobilier.

housing estate Br, **housing project** Am *n* cité *f*.

hovel [ˈhɒvl] *n* masure *f*, taudis *m*.

hover [ˈhɒvəʳ] *vi* - **1.** [fly] planer - **2.** [person] : to ~ **round sb** tourner OR rôder autour de qqn - **3.** [hesitate] hésiter.

hovercraft [ˈhɒvəkrɑːft] (*pl inv* OR **-s**) *n* aéroglisseur *m*, hovercraft *m*.

hoverport [ˈhɒvəpɔːt] *n* hoverport *m*.

how [haʊ] *adv* - **1.** [gen] comment ; ~ **do you do it?** comment fait-on? ; ~ **are you?** comment allez-vous? ; ~ **do you do?** enchanté(e) (de faire votre connaissance) - **2.** [referring to degree, amount] : ~ **high is it?** combien cela fait-il de haut?, quelle en est la hauteur? ; ~ **long have you been waiting?** cela fait combien de temps que vous attendez? ; ~ **many people came?** combien de personnes sont venues? ; ~ **old are you?** quel âge as-tu? - **3.** [in exclamations] : ~ **nice!** que c'est bien! ; ~ **awful!** quelle horreur! ; ~ **pretty you look!** que tu es jolie! - **4.** [expressing surprise] : ~ **can you be so rude?** comment peux-tu être aussi grossier?

◆ **how about** *adv :* ~ **about a drink?** si on prenait un verre? ; ~ **about you?** et toi?

◆ **how much** ◇ *pron* combien ; ~ **much does it cost?** combien ça coûte? ◇ *adj* combien de ; ~ **much bread?** combien de pain?

howdy [ˈhaʊdɪ] *excl* Am inf salut!

however [haʊˈevəʳ] ◇ *adv* - **1.** [nevertheless] cependant, toutefois - **2.** [no matter how] quelque ... que (*+ subjunctive*), si ... que (*+ subjunctive*) ; ~ **many/much** peu importe la quantité de - **3.** [how] comment ◇ *conj* [in whatever way] de quelque manière que (*+ subjunctive*).

howl [haʊl] ◇ *n* hurlement *m ;* [of laughter] éclat *m* ◇ *vi* hurler ; [with laughter] rire aux éclats.

howler [ˈhaʊləʳ] *n* inf bourde *f*, gaffe *f*.

howling [ˈhaʊlɪŋ] *adj* inf [success] fou (folle).

hp (*abbr of* **horsepower**) *n* CV *m*.

HP *n* - **1.** Br (*abbr of* **hire purchase**) : to buy sthg on ~ acheter qqch à crédit - **2.** = hp.

HQ (*abbr of* **headquarters**) *n* QG *m*.

hr (*abbr of* **hour**) h.

HRH (*abbr of* **His (or Her) Royal Highness**) SAR.

HS *abbr of* **high school**.

HST (*abbr of* **Hawaiian Standard Time**) *heure de Hawaii.*

ht (*abbr of* **height**) haut.

HT (*abbr of* **high tension**) HT.

HTML (*abbr of* **hypertext markup language**) *n* COMPUT HTML.

hub [hʌb] *n* - **1.** [of wheel] moyeu *m* - **2.** [of activity] centre *m*.

hub airport *n* Am aéroport *m* important.

hubbub [ˈhʌbʌb] *n* vacarme *m*, brouhaha *m*.

hubcap [ˈhʌbkæp] *n* enjoliveur *m*.

HUD (*abbr of* **Department of Housing and Urban Development**) *n* ancien ministère américain de l'urbanisme et du logement.

huddle [ˈhʌdl] ◇ *vi* se blottir ◇ *n* petit groupe *m*.

hue [hjuː] *n* [colour] teinte *f*, nuance *f*.

huff [hʌf] ◇ *n :* in a ~ froissé(e) ◇ *vi :* to ~ **and puff** souffler et haleter.

huffy [ˈhʌfɪ] (*compar* **-ier** ; *superl* **-iest**) *adj* inf - **1.** [offended] froissé(e) - **2.** [touchy] susceptible.

hug [hʌg] (*pt* & *pp* **-ged** ; *cont* **-ging**) ◇ *n* étreinte *f ;* **to give sb a** ~ serrer qqn dans ses bras ◇ *vt* - **1.** [embrace] étreindre, serrer dans ses bras - **2.** [hold] tenir ; **to** ~ **sthg to o.s.** serrer qqch contre soi - **3.** [stay close to] serrer.

huge [hjuːdʒ] *adj* énorme ; [subject] vaste ; [success] fou (folle).

huh [hʌ] *excl* - **1.** [gen] hein? - **2.** [expressing scorn] berk!

hulk [hʌlk] *n* - **1.** [of ship] carcasse *f* - **2.** [person] malabar *m*, mastodonte *m*.

hulking [ˈhʌlkɪŋ] *adj* énorme.

hull [hʌl] *n* coque *f*.

hullabaloo [ˌhʌləbəˈluː] *n* inf tintamarre *m*, raffut *m*.

hullo [həˈləʊ] *excl* = hello.

hum [hʌm] (*pt* & *pp* **-med** ; *cont* **-ming**) ◇ *vi* - **1.** [buzz] bourdonner ; [machine] vrombir, ronfler - **2.** [sing] fredonner, chantonner - **3.** [be busy] être en pleine activité - **4.** phr : to ~ **and haw** bredouiller, bafouiller ◇ *vt* fredonner, chantonner ◇ *n (U)* bourdon-

nement *m ;* [of machine] vrombissement *m,*
ronflement *m ;* [of conversation] brouhaha *m.*

human ['hju:mən] ⋄ *adj* humain(e) ⋄ *n :*
~ (being) être *m* humain.

humane [hju:'meɪn] *adj* humain(e).

humanely [hju:'meɪnlɪ] *adv* humainement.

human error *n* erreur *f* humaine.

humanist ['hju:mənɪst] *n* humaniste *mf.*

humanitarian [hju:,mænɪ'teərɪən] ⋄ *adj*
humanitaire ⋄ *n* humanitaire *mf.*

humanity [hju:'mænətɪ] *n* humanité *f.*
➡ **humanities** *npl :* the humanities les humanités *fpl,* les sciences *fpl* humaines.

humanly ['hju:mənlɪ] *adv :* ~ possible humainement possible.

human nature *n* nature *f* humaine

human race *n :* the ~ la race humaine.

human resources *npl* ressources *fpl* humaines.

human rights *npl* droits *mpl* de l'homme.

humble ['hʌmbl] ⋄ *adj* humble ; [origins, employee] modeste ⋄ *vt* humilier ; to ~ o.s.
s'abaisser, s'humilier.

humbly ['hʌmblɪ] *adv* - 1. [not proudly] humblement - 2. [live, begin] modestement.

humbug ['hʌmbʌg] *n* - 1. dated [hypocrisy] hypocrisie *f* - 2. Br [sweet] *type de bonbon dur.*

humdrum ['hʌmdrʌm] *adj* monotone.

humid ['hju:mɪd] *adj* humide.

humidity [hju:'mɪdətɪ] *n* humidité *f.*

humiliate [hju:'mɪlɪeɪt] *vt* humilier.

humiliating [hju:'mɪlɪeɪtɪŋ] *adj* humiliant(e).

humiliation [hju:,mɪlɪ'eɪʃn] *n* humiliation *f.*

humility [hju:'mɪlətɪ] *n* humilité *f.*

hummingbird ['hʌmɪŋbɜ:d] *n* colibri *m,*
oiseau-mouche *m.*

humor Am = humour.

humorist ['hju:mərɪst] *n* humoriste *mf.*

humorous ['hju:mərəs] *adj* humoristique ;
[person] plein(e) d'humour.

humour Br, **humor** Am ['hju:məʳ] ⋄ *n*
- 1. [sense of fun] humour *m* - 2. [of situation, remark] côté *m* comique - 3. dated [mood] humeur *f* ⋄ *vt* se montrer conciliant(e) envers.

hump [hʌmp] ⋄ *n* bosse *f* ⋄ *vt* inf [carry] porter, coltiner.

humpbacked bridge ['hʌmpbækt-] *n* pont
m en dos d'âne.

humus ['hju:məs] *n* humus *m.*

hunch [hʌntʃ] ⋄ *n* inf pressentiment *m,* intuition *f* ⋄ *vt* voûter ⋄ *vi* se pencher.

hunchback ['hʌntʃbæk] *n* bossu *m,* -e *f ;*
about a ~ pupils une centaine d'élèves.

hunched [hʌntʃt] *adj* voûté(e).

hundred ['hʌndrəd] *num* cent ; a OR one ~
cent ; *see also* six.
➡ **hundreds** *npl* des centaines.

hundredth ['hʌndrətθ] *num* centième ; *see
also* sixth.

hundredweight ['hʌndrədweɪt] *n* [in UK]
poids *m* de 112 livres, = 50,8 kg ; [in US] poids
m de 100 livres, = 45,3 kg.

hung [hʌŋ] ⋄ *pt* & *pp* ➡ **hang** ⋄ *adj* [parliament, jury] sans majorité.

Hungarian [hʌŋ'geərɪən] ⋄ *adj* hongrois(e)
⋄ *n* - 1. [person] Hongrois *m,* -e *f* - 2. [language]
hongrois *m.*

Hungary ['hʌŋgərɪ] *n* Hongrie *f ;* in ~ en Hongrie.

hunger ['hʌŋgəʳ] *n* - 1. [gen] faim *f* - 2. [strong
desire] soif *f.*
➡ **hunger after, hunger for** *vt fus* avoir
faim de, avoir soif de.

hunger strike *n* grève *f* de la faim.

hung over *adj* inf : to be ~ avoir la gueule de
bois.

hungry ['hʌŋgrɪ] (*compar* -ier ; *superl* -iest) *adj*
- 1. [for food] : to be ~ avoir faim ; [starving] être
affamé(e) ; to go ~ souffrir de la faim
- 2. [eager] : to be ~ for être avide de.

hung up *adj* inf : to be ~ (on OR about) être
obsédé(e) (par).

hunk [hʌŋk] *n* - 1. [large piece] gros morceau *m*
- 2. inf [man] beau mec *m.*

hunky-dory [,hʌŋkɪ'dɔ:rɪ] *adj* inf au poil.

hunt [hʌnt] ⋄ *n* chasse *f ;* [for missing person] recherches *fpl* ⋄ *vi* - 1. [chase animals, birds]
chasser - 2. Br [chase foxes] chasser le renard
- 3. [search] : to ~ (for sthg) chercher partout
(qqch) ⋄ *vt* - 1. [animals, birds] chasser - 2. [person] poursuivre, pourchasser.
➡ **hunt down** *vt sep* traquer.

hunter ['hʌntəʳ] *n* - 1. [of animals, birds] chasseur *m* - 2. [of things] : bargain ~ dénicheur *m,*
-euse *f* d'occasions ; autograph ~ collectionneur *m,* -euse *f* d'autographes.

hunting ['hʌntɪŋ] ⋄ *n* - 1. [of animals] chasse *f*
- 2. Br [of foxes] chasse *f* au renard ⋄ *comp*
de chasse.

huntsman ['hʌntsmən] (*pl* -men [-mən]) *n*
chasseur *m.*

hurdle ['hɜ:dl] ⋄ *n* - 1. [in race] haie *f* - 2. [obstacle] obstacle *m* ⋄ *vt* [jump over] sauter.

hurl [hɜ:l] *vt* - 1. [throw] lancer avec violence
- 2. [shout] lancer.

hurrah [hʊ'rɑ:] *excl* dated hourra !

hurray [hʊ'reɪ] *excl* hourra!

hurricane ['hʌrɪkən] *n* ouragan *m*.

hurried ['hʌrɪd] *adj* [hasty] précipité(e).

hurriedly ['hʌrɪdlɪ] *adv* précipitamment ; [eat, write] vite, en toute hâte.

hurry ['hʌrɪ] (*pt* & *pp* **-ied**) ⋄ *vt* [person] faire se dépêcher ; [process] hâter ; **to ~ to do sthg** se dépêcher *OR* se presser de faire qqch ⋄ *vi* se dépêcher, se presser ⋄ *n* hâte *f*, précipitation *f* ; **to be in a ~** être pressé ; **to do sthg in a ~** faire qqch à la hâte ; **to be in no ~ to do sthg** [unwilling] ne pas être pressé de faire qqch.

➡ **hurry up** ⋄ *vi* se dépêcher ⋄ *vt sep* faire se dépêcher.

hurt [hɜːt] (*pt* & *pp* **hurt**) ⋄ *vt* **- 1.** [physically, emotionally] blesser ; [one's leg, arm] se faire mal à ; **to ~ o.s.** se faire mal **- 2.** *fig* [harm] faire du mal à ⋄ *vi* **- 1.** [gen] faire mal ; **my leg ~s** ma jambe me fait mal **- 2.** *fig* [do harm] faire du mal ⋄ *adj* blessé(e) ; [voice] offensé(e) ⋄ *n* (*U*) [emotional pain] peine *f*.

hurtful ['hɜːtfʊl] *adj* blessant(e).

hurtle ['hɜːtl] *vi* aller à toute allure.

husband ['hʌzbənd] *n* mari *m*.

husbandry ['hʌzbəndrɪ] *n* *fml* agriculture *f*.

hush [hʌʃ] ⋄ *n* silence *m* ⋄ *excl* silence!, chut!

hush money *n* (*U*) *inf* pot-de-vin *m* (*pour acheter le silence de qqn*).

husk [hʌsk] *n* [of seed, grain] enveloppe *f*.

husky ['hʌskɪ] (*compar* **-ier** ; *superl* **-iest**) ⋄ *adj* [hoarse] rauque ⋄ *n* husky *m*.

hustings ['hʌstɪŋz] *npl* Br plate-forme *f* électorale.

hustle ['hʌsl] ⋄ *vt* **- 1.** [hurry] pousser, bousculer **- 2.** Am [persuade] : **to ~ sb into doing sthg** forcer la main à qqn pour qu'il fasse qqch ⋄ *n* agitation *f*.

hut [hʌt] *n* **- 1.** [rough house] hutte *f* **- 2.** [shed] cabane *f*.

hutch [hʌtʃ] *n* clapier *m*.

hyacinth ['haɪəsɪnθ] *n* jacinthe *f*.

hybrid ['haɪbrɪd] ⋄ *adj* hybride ⋄ *n* **- 1.** [plant, animal] hybride *m* **- 2.** [mixture] entité *f* hybride.

hydrangea [haɪ'dreɪndʒə] *n* hortensia *m*.

hydrant ['haɪdrənt] *n* bouche *f* d'incendie.

hydraulic [haɪ'drɔːlɪk] *adj* hydraulique.

➡ **hydraulics** *n* hydraulique *f*.

hydrocarbon [,haɪdrə'kɑːbən] *n* hydrocarbure *m*.

hydrochloric acid [,haɪdrə'klɔːrɪk-] *n* acide *m* chlorhydrique.

hydroelectric [,haɪdrəʊ'lektrɪk] *adj* hydroélectrique.

hydroelectricity [,haɪdrəʊlek'trɪsətɪ] *n* hydro-électricité *f*.

hydrofoil ['haɪdrəfɔɪl] *n* hydrofoil *m*.

hydrogen ['haɪdrədʒən] *n* hydrogène *m*.

hydrogen bomb *n* bombe *f* à hydrogène.

hydrophobia [,haɪdrə'fəʊbjə] *n* hydrophobie *f*.

hydroplane ['haɪdrəpleɪn] *n* **- 1.** [speedboat] hydroglisseur *m* **- 2.** [hydrofoil] hydrofoil *m*.

hyena [haɪ'iːnə] *n* hyène *f*.

hygiene ['haɪdʒiːn] *n* hygiène *f*.

hygienic [haɪ'dʒiːnɪk] *adj* hygiénique.

hygienist [haɪ'dʒiːnɪst] *n* personne qui se charge du détartrage des dents.

hymn [hɪm] *n* hymne *m*, cantique *m*.

hymn book *n* livre *m* de cantiques.

hype [haɪp] *inf* ⋄ *n* (*U*) battage *m* publicitaire ⋄ *vt* faire un battage publicitaire autour de.

hyped up [haɪpt-] *adj* *inf* [person] excité(e).

hyper ['haɪpə'] *adj* *inf* qui a la bougeotte.

hyperactive [,haɪpər'æktɪv] *adj* hyperactif(ive).

hyperbole [haɪ'pɜːbəlɪ] *n* hyperbole *f*.

hyperinflation [,haɪpərɪn'fleɪʃn] *n* hyperinflation *f*.

hyperlink ['haɪpəlɪŋk] *n* lien *m* hypertexte, hyperlien *m*.

hypermarket ['haɪpə,mɑːkɪt] *n* hypermarché *m*.

hypersensitive [,haɪpə'sensɪtɪv] *adj* hypersensible.

hypertension [,haɪpə'tenʃn] *n* hypertension *f*.

hypertext ['haɪpətekst] COMPUT ⋄ *n* hypertexte *m* ⋄ *comp* : **~ link** lien *m* hypertexte.

hyperventilate [,haɪpə'ventɪleɪt] *vi* faire de l'hyperventilation.

hyphen ['haɪfn] *n* trait *m* d'union.

hyphenate ['haɪfəneɪt] *vt* mettre un trait d'union à.

hypnosis [hɪp'nəʊsɪs] *n* hypnose *f* ; **under ~** sous hypnose, en état d'hypnose.

hypnotic [hɪp'nɒtɪk] *adj* hypnotique.

hypnotism ['hɪpnətɪzm] *n* hypnotisme *m*.

hypnotist ['hɪpnətɪst] *n* hypnotiseur *m*.

hypnotize, -ise ['hɪpnətaɪz] *vt* hypnotiser.

hypoallergenic ['haɪpəʊ,ælə'dʒenɪk] *adj* hypoallergénique.

hypochondriac [,haɪpə'kɒndrɪæk] *n* hypochondriaque *mf*.

hypocrisy [hɪ'pɒkrəsɪl] *n* hypocrisie *f*.
hypocrite ['hɪpəkrɪt] *n* hypocrite *mf*.
hypocritical [ˌhɪpə'krɪtɪkl] *adj* hypocrite.
hypodermic needle [ˌhaɪpə'dɜːmɪk-] *n* aiguille *f* hypodermique.
hypodermic syringe [ˌhaɪpə'dɜːmɪk-] *n* seringue *f* hypodermique.
hypothermia [ˌhaɪpəʊ'θɜːmɪə] *n* hypothermie *f*.
hypothesis [haɪ'pɒθɪsɪs] (*pl* **-theses** [-θɪsiːz]) *n* hypothèse *f*.
hypothesize, -ise [haɪ'pɒθɪsaɪz] ⟷ *vt* émettre une hypothèse OR des hypothèses sur ⟷ *vi* émettre une hypothèse OR des hypothèses.
hypothetical [ˌhaɪpə'θetɪkl] *adj* hypothétique.
hysterectomy [ˌhɪstə'rektəmɪ] (*pl* **-ies**) *n* hystérectomie *f*.
hysteria [hɪs'tɪərɪə] *n* hystérie *f*.
hysterical [hɪs'terɪkl] *adj* **- 1.** [gen] hystérique **- 2.** inf [very funny] désopilant(e).
hysterics [hɪs'terɪks] *npl* **- 1.** [panic, excitement] crise *f* de nerfs **- 2.** inf [laughter] fou rire *m*.
HZ (*abbr of* **hertz**) Hz.

i (*pl* **i's** OR **is**), **I** (*pl* **I's** OR **Is**) [aɪ] *n* [letter] i *m inv*, I *m inv*.
I¹ [aɪ] *pers pron* **- 1.** (*unstressed*) je, j' (*before vowel or silent 'h'*) ; **he and I are leaving for Paris** lui et moi (nous) partons pour Paris ; **it is I** fml c'est moi **- 2.** (*stressed*) moi ; **I can't do it** moi je ne peux pas le faire.
I² *abbr of* **Island, Isle.**
IA *abbr of* **Iowa.**
IAEA (*abbr of* **International Atomic Energy Agency**) *n* AIEA *f*.
IBA (*abbr of* **Independent Broadcasting Authority**) *n organisme d'agrément et de coordination des stations de radio et chaînes de télévision du secteur privé en Grande-Bretagne.*
Iberian [aɪ'bɪərɪən] ⟷ *adj* ibérique ⟷ *n* Ibère *mf*.
Iberian peninsula *n* : **the ~** la péninsule Ibérique.
ibid (*abbr of* **ibidem**) ibid.
i/c *abbr of* **in charge.**
ICA (*abbr of* **Institute of Contemporary Art**) *n centre d'art moderne à Londres.*
ICBM (*abbr of* **intercontinental ballistic missile**) *n* ICBM *m*.
ICC *n* **- 1.** (*abbr of* **International Chamber of Commerce**) CCI *f* **- 2.** (*abbr of* **Interstate Commerce Commission**) *commission fédérale américaine réglementant le commerce entre les États.*
ice [aɪs] ⟷ *n* **- 1.** [frozen water, ice cream] glace *f* ; **to break the ~** fig rompre OR briser la glace **- 2.** (U) [on road] verglas *m* **- 3.** (U) [ice cubes] glaçons *mpl* ⟷ *vt* Br glacer.
➤ **ice over, ice up** *vi* [lake, pond] geler ; [window, windscreen] givrer ; [road] se couvrir de verglas.
ice age *n* période *f* glaciaire.
iceberg ['aɪsbɜːg] *n* iceberg *m*.
iceberg lettuce *n* laitue *f* iceberg.
icebox ['aɪsbɒks] *n* **- 1.** Br [in refrigerator] freezer *m* **- 2.** Am [refrigerator] réfrigérateur *m*.
icebreaker ['aɪsˌbreɪkər] *n* [ship] brise-glace *m*, brise-glaces *m*.
ice bucket *n* seau *m* à glace.
ice cap *n* calotte *f* glaciaire.
ice-cold *adj* glacé(e).
ice cream *n* glace *f*.
ice cream van *n* Br camionnette *f* de vendeur de glaces.

ICE CREAM VAN

La petite camionnette du vendeur de glaces est très caractéristique ; elle se reconnaît au carillon qui annonce son arrivée dans un quartier.

ice cube *n* glaçon *m*.
iced [aɪst] *adj* glacé(e).
ice floe *n* banc *m* de glace, glaciel *m* Can.
ice hockey *n* hockey *m* sur glace.
Iceland ['aɪslənd] *n* Islande *f* ; **in ~** en Islande.
Icelander ['aɪsləndər] *n* Islandais *m*, -e *f*.
Icelandic [aɪs'lændɪk] ⟷ *adj* islandais(e) ⟷ *n* [language] islandais *m*.
ice lolly *n* Br sucette *f* glacée.

ice pick *n* pic *m* à glace.
ice rink *n* patinoire *f*.
ice skate *n* patin *m* à glace.
➡ **ice-skate** *vi* faire du patin (à glace).
ice-skater *n* patineur *m*, -euse *f*.
ice-skating *n* patinage *m* (sur glace).
icicle ['aɪsɪkl] *n* glaçon *m* (naturel).
icily ['aɪsɪlɪ] *adv* [in unfriendly way] d'une manière glaciale ; [say, reply] d'un ton glacial.
icing ['aɪsɪŋ] *n* (U) glaçage *m*, glace *f* ; **the ~ on
the cake** fig un plus, la cerise sur le gâteau.
icing sugar *n* Br sucre *m* glace.
ICJ (*abbr of* **International Court of Justice**) *n*
CIJ *f*.
icon ['aɪkɒn] *n* [gen & COMPUT] icône *f*.
iconoclast [aɪ'kɒnəklæst] *n* iconoclaste *mf*.
ICR (*abbr of* **Institute for Cancer Research**) *n*
institut de recherche contre le cancer.
ICU (*abbr of* **intensive care unit**) *n unité de réanimation*.
icy ['aɪsɪ] (*compar* **-ier** ; *superl* **-iest**) *adj*
- **1.** [weather, manner] glacial(e) - **2.** [covered in ice]
verglacé(e).
id [ɪd] *n* ça *m*.
I'd [aɪd] = I would, I had.
ID ◇ *n* (U) (*abbr of* **identification**) papiers *mpl*
◇ *abbr of* **Idaho**.
Idaho ['aɪdə,həʊ] *n* Idaho *m ;* **in ~** dans l'Idaho.
ID card = identity card.
IDD (*abbr of* **international direct dialling**) *n*
automatique *m* international.
idea [aɪ'dɪə] *n* idée *f ;* [intention] intention *f ;* **to
have an ~ of** avoir une idée de ; **to have an
~ (that) ...** avoir idée que ... ; **to have no ~**
n'avoir aucune idée ; **to get the ~** inf piger ;
don't get the ~ (that) ... ne va pas croire OR
t'imaginer que ... ; **the ~ is to ...** l'idée est de
..., l'intention est de ...
ideal [aɪ'dɪəl] ◇ *adj* idéal(e) ; **to be ~ for** être
idéal OR parfait pour ◇ *n* idéal *m*.
idealism [aɪ'dɪəlɪzml] *n* idéalisme *m*.
idealist [aɪ'dɪəlɪst] *n* idéaliste *mf*.
idealize, -ise [aɪ'dɪəlaɪz] *vt* idéaliser.
ideally [aɪ'dɪəlɪ] *adv* idéalement ; [suited] parfaitement.
identical [aɪ'dentɪkl] *adj* identique.
identical twins *npl* vrais jumeaux *mpl*,
vraies jumelles *fpl*.
identifiable [aɪ'dentɪfaɪəbl] *adj* identifiable,
reconnaissable.
identification [aɪ,dentɪfɪ'keɪʃn] *n* (U)
- **1.** [gen] : **~ (with)** identification *f*(à) - **2.** [docu-
mentation] pièce *f* d'identité.

identify [aɪ'dentɪfaɪ] (*pt* & *pp* **-ied**) ◇ *vt*
- **1.** [recognize] identifier - **2.** [subj : document,
card] permettre de reconnaître - **3.** [associ-
ate] : **to ~ sb with sthg** associer qqn à qqch
◇ *vi* [empathize] : **to ~ with** s'identifier à.
Identikit picture® [aɪ'dentɪkɪt-] *n* portrait-
robot *m*.
identity [aɪ'dentətɪ] (*pl* **-ies**) *n* identité *f*.
identity card *n* carte *f* d'identité.
identity parade *n séance d'identification
d'un suspect dans un échantillon de plusieurs
personnes*.
ideological [,aɪdɪə'lɒdʒɪkl] *adj* idéologique.
ideology [,aɪdɪ'ɒlədʒɪ] (*pl* **-ies**) *n* idéologie *f*.
idiom ['ɪdɪəm] *n* - **1.** [phrase] expression *f* idiomatique - **2.** fml [style] langue *f*.
idiomatic [,ɪdɪə'mætɪk] *adj* idiomatique.
idiosyncrasy [,ɪdɪə'sɪŋkrəsɪ] (*pl* **-ies**) *n* particularité *f*, caractéristique *f*.
idiot ['ɪdɪət] *n* idiot *m*, -e *f*, imbécile *mf*.
idiotic [,ɪdɪ'ɒtɪk] *adj* idiot(e).
idle ['aɪdl] ◇ *adj* - **1.** [lazy] oisif(ive), désœu-
vré(e) - **2.** [not working - machine, factory] arrê-
té(e) ; [- worker] qui chôme, en chômage
- **3.** [threat] vain(e) - **4.** [curiosity] simple, pur(e)
◇ *vi* tourner au ralenti.
➡ **idle away** *vt sep* [time] perdre à ne rien
faire.
idleness ['aɪdlnɪs] *n* oisiveté *f*, désœuvrement *m*.
idler ['aɪdlər] *n* paresseux *m*, -euse *f*.
idly ['aɪdlɪ] *adv* - **1.** [lazily] paresseusement
- **2.** [without purpose] négligemment.
idol ['aɪdl] *n* idole *f*.
idolize, -ise ['aɪdəlaɪz] *vt* idolâtrer, adorer.
idyl(l) ['ɪdɪl] *n* idylle *f*.
idyllic [ɪ'dɪlɪk] *adj* idyllique.
i.e. (*abbr of* **id est**) c-à-d.
if [ɪf] ◇ *conj* - **1.** [gen] si ; **~ I were you** à ta place, si j'étais toi - **2.** [though] bien que - **3.** [that]
que ◇ *n* : **~s and buts** les si et les mais *mpl*.
➡ **if not** *conj* sinon.
➡ **if only** ◇ *conj* - **1.** [naming a reason] ne
serait-ce que - **2.** [expressing regret] si seulement ◇ *excl* si seulement !
iffy ['ɪfɪ] (*compar* **-ier** ; *superl* **-iest**) *adj* inf in-
certain(e).
igloo ['ɪgluː] (*pl* **-s**) *n* igloo *m*, iglou *m*.
ignite [ɪg'naɪt] ◇ *vt* mettre le feu à, enflammer ; [firework] tirer ◇ *vi* prendre feu, s'enflammer.
ignition [ɪg'nɪʃn] *n* - **1.** [act of igniting] ignition *f*
- **2.** AUT allumage *m ;* **to switch on the ~** mettre le contact.

ignition key n clef f de contact.
ignoble [ɪgˈnəʊbl] adj fml infâme.
ignominious [ˌɪgnəˈmɪnɪəs] adj ignominieux(euse).
ignominy [ˈɪgnəmɪnɪ] n ignominie f.
ignoramus [ˌɪgnəˈreɪməs] (pl -es [-iːz]) n ignare mf.
ignorance [ˈɪgnərəns] n ignorance f.
ignorant [ˈɪgnərənt] adj - **1.** [uneducated, unaware] ignorant(e) ; **to be ~ of sthg** être ignorant de qqch - **2.** [rude] mal élevé(e).
ignore [ɪgˈnɔːʳ] vt [advice, facts] ne pas tenir compte de ; [person] faire semblant de ne pas voir.
iguana [ɪˈgwɑːnə] (pl inv OR -s) n iguane m.
ikon [ˈaɪkɒn] = **icon**.
IL abbr of **Illinois**.
ILEA [ˈɪlɪə] (abbr of **Inner London Education Authority**) n anciens services londoniens de l'enseignement.
ileum [ˈɪlɪəm] (pl **ilea** [ˈɪlɪə]) n iléon m.
ilk [ɪlk] n : **of that ~** [of that sort] de cet acabit, de ce genre.
ill [ɪl] <> adj - **1.** [unwell] malade ; **to feel ~** se sentir malade OR souffrant ; **to be taken ~, to fall ~** tomber malade - **2.** [bad] mauvais(e) ; **~ luck** malchance f <> adv mal ; **to speak/think ~ of sb** dire/penser du mal de qqn.
➟ **ills** npl maux mpl, malheurs mpl.
ill. (abbr of **illustration**) ill.
I'll [aɪl] = **I will, I shall**.
ill-advised [-ədˈvaɪzd] adj [remark, action] peu judicieux(euse) ; [person] malavisé(e) ; **to be ~ to do sthg** être malavisé de faire qqch.
ill at ease adj mal à l'aise.
ill-bred adj mal élevé(e).
ill-considered adj irréfléchi(e).
ill-disposed adj : **to be ~ towards sb** être mal disposé(e) OR malintentionné(e) envers qqn.
illegal [ɪˈliːgl] adj illégal(e) ; [immigrant] en situation irrégulière.
illegally [ɪˈliːgəlɪ] adv illégalement, d'une manière illégale.
illegible [ɪˈledʒəbl] adj illisible.
illegitimate [ˌɪlɪˈdʒɪtɪmət] adj illégitime.
ill-equipped [-ɪˈkwɪpt] adj : **to be ~ to do sthg** être mal placé(e) pour faire qqch.
ill-fated [-ˈfeɪtɪd] adj fatal(e), funeste.
ill feeling n animosité f.
ill-founded [-ˈfaʊndɪd] adj [confidence, trust] mal fondé(e) ; [doubts] sans fondement.

ill-gotten gains [-ˈgɒtən-] npl hum biens mpl mal acquis.
ill health n mauvaise santé f.
illicit [ɪˈlɪsɪt] adj illicite.
illicitly [ɪˈlɪsɪtlɪ] adv illicitement.
ill-informed adj mal renseigné(e).
Illinois [ˌɪlɪˈnɔɪ] n Illinois m ; **in ~** dans l'Illinois.
illiteracy [ɪˈlɪtərəsɪ] n analphabétisme m, illettrisme m.
illiterate [ɪˈlɪtərət] <> adj analphabète, illettré(e) <> n analphabète mf, illettré m, -e f.
ill-mannered adj mal élevé(e) ; [behaviour] grossier(ère).
illness [ˈɪlnɪs] n maladie f.
illogical [ɪˈlɒdʒɪkl] adj illogique.
ill-suited adj mal assorti(e) ; **to be ~ for sthg** être inapte à qqch.
ill-tempered adj qui a mauvais caractère.
ill-timed [-ˈtaɪmd] adj déplacé(e), mal à propos.
ill-treat vt maltraiter.
ill-treatment n mauvais traitement m.
illuminate [ɪˈluːmɪneɪt] vt éclairer.
illuminated [ɪˈluːmɪneɪtɪd] adj - **1.** [lit up] lumineux(euse) - **2.** [book, manuscript] enluminé(e).
illuminating [ɪˈluːmɪneɪtɪŋ] adj éclairant(e).
illumination [ɪˌluːmɪˈneɪʃn] n [lighting] éclairage m.
➟ **illuminations** npl Br illuminations fpl.
illusion [ɪˈluːʒn] n illusion f ; **to have no ~s about** ne se faire OR n'avoir aucune illusion sur ; **to be under the ~ that** croire OR s'imaginer que, avoir l'illusion que.
illusionist [ɪˈluːʒənɪst] n prestidigitateur m, -euse f, illusionniste mf.
illusory [ɪˈluːsərɪ] adj illusoire.
illustrate [ˈɪləstreɪt] vt illustrer.
illustration [ˌɪləˈstreɪʃn] n illustration f.
illustrator [ˈɪləstreɪtəʳ] n illustrateur m, -trice f.
illustrious [ɪˈlʌstrɪəs] adj illustre, célèbre.
ill will n animosité f.
ill wind n : **it's an ~ (that blows nobody any good)** proverb à quelque chose malheur est bon.
ILO (abbr of **International Labour Organization**) n OIT f.
ILWU (abbr of **International Longshoremen's and Warehousemen's Union**) n syndicat international de dockers et de magasiniers.
I'm [aɪm] = **I am**.

image ['ɪmɪdʒ] *n* - **1.** [gen] image *f ;* **to be the ~ of sb** *fig* être tout le portrait de qqn, être qqn tout craché - **2.** [of company, politician] image *f* de marque.

imagery ['ɪmɪdʒrɪ] *n (U)* images *fpl.*

imaginable [ɪ'mædʒɪnəbl] *adj* imaginable.

imaginary [ɪ'mædʒɪnrɪ] *adj* imaginaire.

imagination [ɪ,mædʒɪ'neɪʃn] *n* - **1.** [ability] imagination *f* - **2.** [fantasy] invention *f.*

imaginative [ɪ'mædʒɪnətɪv] *adj* imaginatif(ive) ; [solution] plein(e) d'imagination.

imagine [ɪ'mædʒɪn] *vt* imaginer ; **to ~ doing sthg** s'imaginer *OR* se voir faisant qqch ; **~ (that)!** tu t'imagines!

imaginings [ɪ'mædʒɪnɪŋz] *npl* imaginations *fpl.*

imbalance [,ɪm'bæləns] *n* déséquilibre *m.*

imbecile ['ɪmbɪsiːl] *n* imbécile *mf*, idiot *m*, -e *f.*

imbue [ɪm'bju:] *vt :* **to be ~d with** être imbu(e) de.

IMF (*abbr of* **International Monetary Fund**) *n* FMI *m.*

imitate ['ɪmɪteɪt] *vt* imiter.

imitation [,ɪmɪ'teɪʃn] <> *n* imitation *f* <> *adj* [leather] imitation *(before n) ;* [jewellery] en toc.

imitator ['ɪmɪteɪtə'] *n* imitateur *m*, -trice *f.*

immaculate [ɪ'mækjʊlət] *adj* impeccable.

immaculately [ɪ'mækjʊlətlɪ] *adv* impeccablement.

immaterial [,ɪmə'tɪərɪəl] *adj* [unimportant] sans importance.

immature [,ɪmə'tjʊə'] *adj* - **1.** [lacking judgment] qui manque de maturité - **2.** [not fully grown] jeune, immature.

immaturity [,ɪmə'tjʊərətɪ] *n* immaturité *f.*

immeasurable [ɪ'meʒrəbl] *adj* incommensurable.

immediacy [ɪ'mi:djəsɪ] *n* caractère *m* immédiat.

immediate [ɪ'mi:djət] *adj* - **1.** [urgent] immédiat(e) ; [problem, meeting] urgent(e) - **2.** [very near] immédiat(e) ; [family] le plus proche.

immediately [ɪ'mi:djətlɪ] <> *adv* - **1.** [at once] immédiatement - **2.** [directly] directement <> *conj* dès que.

immemorial [,ɪmɪ'mɔ:rɪəl] *adj* immémorial(e) ; **from time ~** de temps immémorial.

immense [ɪ'mens] *adj* immense ; [improvement, change] énorme.

immensely [ɪ'menslɪ] *adv* extrêmement, immensément.

immensity [ɪ'mensətɪ] *n* immensité *f.*

immerse [ɪ'mɜ:s] *vt :* **to ~ sthg in sthg** immerger *OR* plonger qqch dans qqch ; **to ~ o.s. in sthg** *fig* se plonger dans qqch.

immersion heater [ɪ'mɜ:ʃn-] *n* chauffe-eau *m* électrique.

immigrant ['ɪmɪgrənt] <> *n* immigré *m*, -e *f* <> *comp* d'immigrés.

immigration [,ɪmɪ'greɪʃn] <> *n* immigration *f* <> *comp* de l'immigration.

imminence ['ɪmɪnəns] *n* imminence *f.*

imminent ['ɪmɪnənt] *adj* imminent(e).

immobile [ɪ'məʊbaɪl] *adj* immobile.

immobilization [ɪ,məʊbɪlaɪ'zeɪʃn] *n* immobilisation *f.*

immobilize, -ise [ɪ'məʊbɪlaɪz] *vt* immobiliser.

immobilizer [ɪ'məʊbɪlaɪzə'] *n* AUT système *m* antidémarrage.

immodest [ɪ'mɒdɪst] *adj* - **1.** [vain] vaniteux(euse), présomptueux(euse) - **2.** [indecent] impudique.

immoral [ɪ'mɒrəl] *adj* immoral(e).

immorality [,ɪmə'rælətɪ] *n* immoralité *f.*

immortal [ɪ'mɔ:tl] <> *adj* immortel(elle) <> *n* immortel *m*, -elle *f.*

immortality [,ɪmɔ:'tælətɪ] *n* immortalité *f.*

immortalize, -ise [ɪ'mɔ:təlaɪz] *vt* immortaliser.

immovable [ɪ'mu:vəbl] *adj* - **1.** [fixed] fixe - **2.** [determined] inébranlable.

immune [ɪ'mju:n] *adj* - **1.** MED : **~ (to)** immunisé(e) (contre) - **2.** *fig* [protected] : **to be ~ to** *OR* **from** être à l'abri de.

immune system *n* système *m* immunitaire.

immunity [ɪ'mju:nətɪ] *n* - **1.** MED : **~ (to)** immunité *f* (contre) - **2.** *fig* [protection] : **~ to** *OR* **from** immunité *f* contre.

immunization [,ɪmjuː:naɪ'zeɪʃn] *n* immunisation *f.*

immunize, -ise ['ɪmjuː:naɪz] *vt :* **to ~ sb (against)** immuniser qqn (contre).

immunodeficiency [,ɪmjuː:nəʊdɪ'fɪʃənsɪ] *n* immunodéficience *f.*

immunology [,ɪmjuː:'nɒlədʒɪ] *n* immunologie *f.*

immutable [ɪ'mjuː:təbl] *adj* immuable.

imp [ɪmp] *n* - **1.** [creature] lutin *m* - **2.** [naughty child] petit diable *m*, coquin *m*, -e *f.*

impact [*n* 'ɪmpækt, *vb* ɪm'pækt] <> *n* impact *m ;* **to make an ~ on** *OR* **upon sb** faire une forte impression sur qqn ; **to make an ~ on** *OR* **upon sthg** avoir un impact sur qqch ; **on ~** au moment de l'impact <> *vt* - **1.** [collide with] entrer en collision avec - **2.** [influence] avoir un impact sur.

impair [ɪm'peəʳ] vt affaiblir, abîmer ; [efficiency] réduire.

impaired [ɪm'peəd] adj affaibli(e) ; [efficiency] réduit(e).

impale [ɪm'peɪl] vt : **to ~ sb/sthg (on)** empaler qqn/qqch (sur).

impart [ɪm'pɑːt] vt fml - **1.** [information] : **to ~ sthg (to sb)** communiquer OR transmettre qqch (à qqn) - **2.** [feeling, quality] : **to ~ sthg (to)** donner qqch (à).

impartial [ɪm'pɑːʃl] adj impartial(e).

impartiality [ɪm,pɑːʃɪ'ælətɪ] n impartialité f.

impassable [ɪm'pɑːsəbl] adj impraticable.

impasse [æm'pɑːs] n impasse f ; **to reach an ~** aboutir à une impasse.

impassioned [ɪm'pæʃnd] adj passionné(e).

impassive [ɪm'pæsɪv] adj impassible.

impatience [ɪm'peɪʃns] n - **1.** [gen] impatience f - **2.** [irritability] irritation f.

impatient [ɪm'peɪʃnt] adj - **1.** [gen] impatient(e) ; **to be ~ to do sthg** être impatient de faire qqch ; **to be ~ for sthg** attendre qqch avec impatience - **2.** [irritable] : **to become** OR **get ~** s'impatienter.

impatiently [ɪm'peɪʃntlɪ] adv avec impatience.

impeach [ɪm'piːtʃ] vt [official] mettre en accusation ; [president] entamer la procédure d'impeachment contre.

impeachment [ɪm'piːtʃmənt] n [of president] procédure f d'impeachment.

impeccable [ɪm'pekəbl] adj impeccable.

impeccably [ɪm'pekəblɪ] adv impeccablement.

impecunious [,ɪmpɪ'kjuːnjəs] adj impécunieux(euse).

impede [ɪm'piːd] vt entraver, empêcher ; [person] gêner.

impediment [ɪm'pedɪmənt] n - **1.** [obstacle] obstacle m - **2.** [disability] défaut m.

impel [ɪm'pel] (pt & pp **-led** ; cont **-ling**) vt : **to ~ sb to do sthg** inciter qqn à faire qqch.

impending [ɪm'pendɪŋ] adj imminent(e).

impenetrable [ɪm'penɪtrəbl] adj impénétrable.

imperative [ɪm'perətɪv] <> adj [essential] impératif(ive), essentiel(elle) <> n impératif m.

imperceptible [,ɪmpə'septəbl] adj imperceptible.

imperfect [ɪm'pɜːfɪkt] <> adj imparfait(e) <> n GRAMM : **~ (tense)** imparfait m.

imperfection [,ɪmpə'fekʃn] n - **1.** [gen] imperfection f - **2.** [failing] défaut m.

imperial [ɪm'pɪərɪəl] adj - **1.** [of empire] impérial(e) - **2.** [system of measurement] qui a cours légal dans le Royaume-Uni.

imperialism [ɪm'pɪərɪəlɪzml] n impérialisme m.

imperialist [ɪm'pɪərɪəlɪst] <> adj impérialiste <> n impérialiste mf.

imperil [ɪm'perɪl] (Br pt & pp **-led** ; cont **-ling**, Am pt & pp **-ed** ; cont **-ing**) vt mettre en péril OR en danger ; [project] compromettre.

imperious [ɪm'pɪərɪəs] adj impérieux(euse)

impersonal [ɪm'pɜːsnl] adj impersonnel(elle).

impersonate [ɪm'pɜːsəneɪt] vt se faire passer pour.

impersonation [ɪm,pɜːsə'neɪʃn] n usurpation f d'identité ; [by mimic] imitation f.

impersonator [ɪm'pɜːsəneɪtəʳ] n imitateur m, -trice f.

impertinence [ɪm'pɜːtɪnəns] n impertinence f.

impertinent [ɪm'pɜːtɪnənt] adj impertinent(e).

imperturbable [,ɪmpə'tɜːbəbl] adj imperturbable.

impervious [ɪm'pɜːvjəs] adj [not influenced] : **~ to** indifférent(e) à.

impetuous [ɪm'petʃʊəs] adj impétueux(euse).

impetus ['ɪmpɪtəs] n (U) - **1.** [momentum] élan m - **2.** [stimulus] impulsion f.

impinge [ɪm'pɪndʒ] vi : **to ~ on sb/sthg** affecter qqn/qqch.

impish ['ɪmpɪʃ] adj espiègle.

implacable [ɪm'plækəbl] adj implacable.

implant [n 'ɪmplɑːnt, vb ɪm'plɑːnt] <> n implant m <> vt : **to ~ sthg in** OR **into sb** implanter qqch dans qqn.

implausible [ɪm'plɔːzəbl] adj peu plausible.

implement [n 'ɪmplɪmənt, vb 'ɪmplɪment] <> n outil m, instrument m <> vt exécuter, appliquer.

implementation [,ɪmplɪmen'teɪʃn] n application f, exécution f.

implicate ['ɪmplɪkeɪt] vt : **to ~ sb in sthg** impliquer qqn dans qqch.

implication [,ɪmplɪ'keɪʃn] n implication f ; **by ~** par voie de conséquence.

implicit [ɪm'plɪsɪt] adj - **1.** [inferred] implicite - **2.** [belief, faith] absolu(e).

implicitly [ɪm'plɪsɪtlɪ] *adv* - **1.** [by inference] implicitement - **2.** [believe] absolument.

implied [ɪm'plaɪd] *adj* implicite.

implode [ɪm'pləʊd] *vi* imploser.

implore [ɪm'plɔːʳ] *vt :* **to ~ sb (to do sthg)** implorer qqn (de faire qqch).

imply [ɪm'plaɪ] (*pt & pp* -ied) *vt* - **1.** [suggest] sous-entendre, laisser supposer OR entendre - **2.** [involve] impliquer.

impolite [ˌɪmpə'laɪt] *adj* impoli(e).

imponderable [ɪm'pɒndrəbl] *adj* impondérable.

➡ **imponderables** *npl* impondérables *mpl*.

import [*n* 'ɪmpɔːt, *vb* ɪm'pɔːt] ◇ *n* - **1.** [product, action] importation *f* - **2.** fml [meaning] teneur *f* - **3.** fml [importance] importance *f* ◇ *vt* [gen & COMPUT] importer.

importance [ɪm'pɔːtns] *n* importance *f*.

important [ɪm'pɔːtnt] *adj* important(e) ; **to be ~ to sb** importer à qqn.

importantly [ɪm'pɔːtntlɪ] *adv :* **more ~** ce qui est plus important.

importation [ˌɪmpɔː'teɪʃn] *n* importation *f*.

imported [ɪm'pɔːtɪd] *adj* importé(e).

importer [ɪm'pɔːtəʳ] *n* importateur *m*, -trice *f*.

impose [ɪm'pəʊz] ◇ *vt* [force] : **to ~ sthg (on)** imposer qqch (à) ◇ *vi* [cause trouble] : **to ~ (on sb)** abuser (de la gentillesse de qqn).

imposing [ɪm'pəʊzɪŋ] *adj* imposant(e).

imposition [ˌɪmpə'zɪʃn] *n* - **1.** [of tax, limitations etc] imposition *f* - **2.** [cause of trouble] : **it's an ~** c'est abuser de ma/notre gentillesse.

impossibility [ɪm,pɒsə'bɪlətɪ] (*pl* -ies) *n* impossibilité *f*.

impossible [ɪm'pɒsəbl] ◇ *adj* impossible ◇ *n :* **to do the ~** faire l'impossible.

impostor, imposter Am [ɪm'pɒstəʳ] *n* imposteur *m*.

impotence ['ɪmpətəns] *n* impuissance *f*.

impotent ['ɪmpətənt] *adj* impuissant(e).

impound [ɪm'paʊnd] *vt* confisquer.

impoverished [ɪm'pɒvərɪʃt] *adj* appauvri(e).

impracticable [ɪm'præktɪkəbl] *adj* irréalisable.

impractical [ɪm'præktɪkl] *adj* pas pratique.

imprecation [ˌɪmprɪ'keɪʃn] *n* imprécation *f*.

imprecise [ˌɪmprɪ'saɪs] *adj* imprécis(e).

impregnable [ɪm'pregnəbl] *adj* - **1.** [fortress, defences] imprenable - **2.** fig [person] inattaquable.

impregnate ['ɪmpregneɪt] *vt* - **1.** [introduce substance into] : **to ~ sthg with** imprégner qqch de - **2.** fml [fertilize] féconder.

impresario [ˌɪmprɪ'sɑːrɪəʊ] (*pl* -s) *n* impresario *m*.

impress [ɪm'pres] *vt* - **1.** [person] impressionner - **2.** [stress] : **to ~ sthg on sb** faire bien comprendre qqch à qqn.

impression [ɪm'preʃn] *n* - **1.** [gen] impression *f;* **to be under the ~ (that) ...** avoir l'impression que ... ; **to make an ~** faire impression - **2.** [by mimic] imitation *f* - **3.** [of stamp, book] impression *f*, empreinte *f*.

impressionable [ɪm'preʃnəbl] *adj* impressionnable.

Impressionism [ɪm'preʃənɪzm] *n* impressionnisme *m*.

impressionist [ɪm'preʃənɪst] *n* imitateur *m*, -trice *f*.

➡ **Impressionist** ◇ *adj* impressionniste ◇ *n* impressionniste *mf*.

impressive [ɪm'presɪv] *adj* impressionnant(e).

imprint [*n* 'ɪmprɪnt , *vt* ɪm'prɪnt] *n* - **1.** [mark] empreinte *f* - **2.** [publisher's name] nom *m* de l'éditeur.

imprinted [ɪm'prɪntɪd] *adj* imprimé(e).

imprison [ɪm'prɪzn] *vt* emprisonner.

imprisonment [ɪm'prɪznmənt] *n* emprisonnement *m*.

improbable [ɪm'prɒbəbl] *adj* - **1.** [story, excuse] improbable - **2.** [hat, contraption] bizarre.

impromptu [ɪm'prɒmptjuː] *adj* impromptu(e).

improper [ɪm'prɒpəʳ] *adj* - **1.** [unsuitable] impropre - **2.** [incorrect, illegal] incorrect(e) - **3.** [rude] indécent(e).

impropriety [ˌɪmprə'praɪətɪ] *n* inconvenance *f*.

improve [ɪm'pruːv] ◇ *vi* s'améliorer ; [patient] aller mieux ; **to ~ on OR upon sthg** améliorer qqch ◇ *vt* améliorer.

improved [ɪm'pruːvd] *adj* amélioré(e).

improvement [ɪm'pruːvmənt] *n :* **~ (in/on)** amélioration *f* (de/par rapport à).

improvisation [ˌɪmprəvaɪ'zeɪʃn] *n* improvisation *f*.

improvise ['ɪmprəvaɪz] *vt & vi* improviser.

imprudent [ɪm'pruːdənt] *adj* imprudent(e).

impudent ['ɪmpjʊdənt] *adj* impudent(e).

impugn [ɪm'pjuːn] *vt* fml contester.

impulse ['ɪmpʌls] *n* impulsion *f;* **on ~** par impulsion.

impulse buying [-'baɪɪŋ] *n (U)* achats *mpl* impulsifs.

impulsive [ɪm'pʌlsɪv] *adj* impulsif(ive).

impunity [ɪm'pjuːnətɪ] *n* : **with ~** avec impunité.

impure [ɪm'pjʊəʳ] *adj* impur(e).

impurity [ɪm'pjʊərətɪ] (*pl* -**ies**) *n* impureté *f*.

IMRO ['ɪmrəʊ] (*abbr of* **Investment Management Regulatory Organization**) *organisme britannique contrôlant les activités de banques d'affaires et de gestionnaires de fonds de retraite.*

in [ɪn] ⟨⟩ *prep* - **1.** [indicating place, position] dans ; **~ a box/bag/drawer** dans une boîte/un sac/un tiroir ; **~ the room/garden/lake** dans la pièce/le jardin/le lac ; **~ Paris** à Paris ; **~ Belgium** en Belgique ; **~ Canada** au Canada ; **~ the United States** aux États-Unis ; **~ the country** à la campagne ; **to be ~ hospital/prison** être à l'hôpital/en prison ; **~ here** ici ; **~ there** là - **2.** [wearing] en ; **she was still ~ her nightclothes** elle était encore en chemise de nuit ; **dressed ~ a suit** vêtu d'un costume - **3.** [appearing in, included in] dans ; **there's a mistake ~ this paragraph** il y a une erreur dans ce paragraphe ; **~ chapter six** au sixième chapitre - **4.** [at a particular time, season] : **~ 1994** en 1994 ; **~ April** en avril ; **~ (the) spring** au printemps ; **~ (the) winter** en hiver ; **at two o'clock ~ the afternoon** à deux heures de l'après-midi - **5.** [period of time - within] en ; [- after] dans ; **he learned to type ~ two weeks** il a appris à taper à la machine en deux semaines ; **I'll be ready ~ five minutes** je serai prêt dans 5 minutes - **6.** [during] : **it's my first decent meal ~ weeks** c'est mon premier repas correct depuis des semaines - **7.** [indicating situation, circumstances] : **~ the sun** au soleil ; **~ the rain** sous la pluie ; **~ these circumstances** dans ces circonstances, en de telles circonstances ; **a rise ~ prices** une augmentation des prix ; **to live/die ~ poverty** vivre/mourir dans la misère ; **~ danger/difficulty** en danger/difficulté - **8.** [indicating manner, condition] : **~ a loud/soft voice** d'une voix forte/douce ; **to write ~ pencil/ink** écrire au crayon/à l'encre ; **to speak ~ English/French** parler (en) anglais/français - **9.** [indicating emotional state] : **~ anger** sous le coup de la colère ; **~ joy/delight** avec joie/plaisir ; **he looked at me ~ amazement/horror** il me regarda stupéfait/horrifié - **10.** [specifying area of activity] dans ; **he's ~ computers** il est dans l'informatique ; **advances ~ science** des progrès en science - **11.** [referring to quantity, numbers, age] : **~ large/small quantities** en grande/petite quantité ; **~ (their) thousands** par milliers ; **she's ~ her sixties** elle a la soixantaine

- **12.** [describing arrangement] : **~ twos** par deux ; **~ a line/row/circle** en ligne/rang/cercle - **13.** [as regards] : **to be three metres ~ length/width** faire trois mètres de long/large ; **a change ~ direction** un changement de direction - **14.** [in ratios] : **5 pence ~ the pound** 5 pence par livre sterling ; **one ~ ten** un sur dix - **15.** (*after superl*) de ; **the longest river ~ the world** le fleuve le plus long du monde - **16.** (+ *present participle*) : **~ doing sthg** en faisant qqch ⟨⟩ *adv* - **1.** [inside] dedans, à l'intérieur ; **put the clothes ~** mets les vêtements dedans ; **do come ~!** entrez donc! - **2.** [at home, work] là ; **I'm staying ~ tonight** je reste à la maison OR chez moi ce soir ; **is Judith ~?** est-ce que Judith est là? - **3.** [of train, boat, plane] : **to be ~** être arrivé(e) - **4.** [of tide] : **the tide's ~** c'est la marée haute - **5.** *phr* : **we're ~ for some bad weather** nous allons avoir du mauvais temps ; **you're ~ for a shock** tu vas avoir un choc ; **to be ~ on sthg** être au courant de qqch ⟨⟩ *adj* inf à la mode ; **short skirts are ~ this year** les jupes courtes sont à la mode cette année.

➡ **ins** *npl* : **the ~s and outs** les tenants et les aboutissants *mpl*.

➡ **in that** *conj* étant donné que.

in. *abbr of* **inch**.

IN *abbr of* **Indiana**.

inability [ˌɪnə'bɪlətɪ] *n* : **~ (to do sthg)** incapacité *f* (à faire qqch).

inaccessible [ˌɪnək'sesəbl] *adj* inaccessible.

inaccuracy [ɪn'ækjʊrəsɪ] (*pl* -**ies**) *n* inexactitude *f*.

inaccurate [ɪn'ækjʊrət] *adj* inexact(e).

inaction [ɪn'ækʃn] *n* inaction *f*.

inactive [ɪn'æktɪv] *adj* inactif(ive).

inactivity [ˌɪnæk'tɪvətɪ] *n* inactivité *f*.

inadequacy [ɪn'ædɪkwəsɪ] (*pl* -**ies**) *n* insuffisance *f*.

inadequate [ɪn'ædɪkwət] *adj* insuffisant(e).

inadmissible [ˌɪnəd'mɪsəbl] *adj* inadmissible ; [evidence] irrecevable.

inadvertent [ˌɪnəd'vɜːtnt] *adj* commis(e) par inadvertance.

inadvertently [ˌɪnəd'vɜːtəntlɪ] *adv* par inadvertance.

inadvisable [ˌɪnəd'vaɪzəbl] *adj* déconseillé(e).

inalienable [ɪn'eɪljənəbl] *adj* inaliénable.

inane [ɪ'neɪn] *adj* inepte ; [person] stupide.

inanely [ɪ'neɪnlɪ] *adv* stupidement.

inanimate [ɪn'ænɪmət] *adj* inanimé(e).

inanity [ɪ'nænətɪ] *n* ineptie *f* ; [of person] stupidité *f*.

inapplicable [ɪnˈæplɪkəbl] *adj* inapplicable.

inappropriate [ɪnəˈprəʊprɪət] *adj* inopportun(e) ; [expression, word] impropre ; [clothing] peu approprié(e).

inarticulate [ˌɪnɑːˈtɪkjʊlət] *adj* inarticulé(e), indistinct(e) ; [person] qui s'exprime avec difficulté ; [explanation] mal exprimé(e).

inasmuch [ˌɪnəzˈmʌtʃ] ➠ **inasmuch as** *conj* fml attendu que.

inattention [ˌɪnəˈtenʃn] *n :* ~ **(to)** inattention *f* (à).

inattentive [ˌɪnəˈtentɪv] *adj :* ~ **(to)** inattentif(ive) (à).

inaudible [ɪˈnɔːdɪbl] *adj* inaudible.

inaugural [ɪˈnɔːgjʊrəl] *adj* inaugural(e).

inaugurate [ɪˈnɔːgjʊreɪt] *vt* [leader, president] investir ; [building, system] inaugurer.

inauguration [ɪˌnɔːgjʊˈreɪʃn] *n* [of leader, president] investiture *f ;* [of building, system] inauguration *f.*

inauspicious [ˌɪnɔːˈspɪʃəs] *adj* peu propice.

in-between *adj* intermédiaire.

inboard [ˈɪnbɔːd] *adj* in-bord *(inv)*.

inborn [ˌɪnˈbɔːn] *adj* inné(e).

inbound [ˈɪnbaʊnd] *adj* Am qui arrive.

inbred [ˌɪnˈbred] *adj* - **1.** [closely related] consanguin(e) ; [animal] croisé(e) - **2.** [inborn] inné(e).

inbreeding [ˈɪnˌbriːdɪŋ] *n* consanguinité *f ;* [of animals] croisement *m.*

inbuilt [ˌɪnˈbɪlt] *adj* [inborn] inné(e).

inc. *(abbr of* **inclusive)** : **12-15 April** ~ du 12 au 15 avril inclus.

Inc. [ɪŋk] *(abbr of* **incorporated)** ≃ SARL.

Inca [ˈɪŋkə] *n* Inca *mf.*

incalculable [ɪnˈkælkjʊləbl] *adj* incalculable.

incandescent [ˌɪnkænˈdesnt] *adj* incandescent(e).

incantation [ˌɪnkænˈteɪʃn] *n* incantation *f.*

incapable [ɪnˈkeɪpəbl] *adj* incapable ; **to be** ~ **of sthg/of doing sthg** être incapable de qqch/de faire qqch.

incapacitate [ˌɪnkəˈpæsɪteɪt] *vt* rendre inapte physiquement.

incapacitated [ˌɪnkəˈpæsɪteɪtɪd] *adj* inapte physiquement ; ~ **for work** mis(e) dans l'incapacité de travailler.

incapacity [ˌɪnkəˈpæsətɪ] *n :* ~ **(for)** incapacité *f* (eu égard à).

incarcerate [ɪnˈkɑːsəreɪt] *vt* incarcérer.

incarceration [ɪnˌkɑːsəˈreɪʃn] *n* incarcération *f.*

incarnate [ɪnˈkɑːneɪt] *adj* incarné(e).

incarnation [ˌɪnkɑːˈneɪʃn] *n* incarnation *f.*

incendiary device [ɪnˈsendjərɪ-] *n* dispositif *m* incendiaire.

incense [*n* ˈɪnsens, *vb* ɪnˈsens] ◇ *n* encens *m* ◇ *vt* [anger] mettre en colère.

incentive [ɪnˈsentɪv] *n -* **1.** [encouragement] motivation *f -* **2.** COMM récompense *f*, prime *f.*

incentive scheme *n* programme *m* d'encouragement.

inception [ɪnˈsepʃn] *n* fml commencement *m.*

incessant [ɪnˈsesnt] *adj* incessant(e).

incessantly [ɪnˈsesntlɪ] *adv* sans cesse.

incest [ˈɪnsest] *n* inceste *m.*

incestuous [ɪnˈsestjʊəs] *adj -* **1.** [sexual] incestueux(euse) - **2.** fig [too close] très fermé(e) ; [relationship] en vase clos.

inch [ɪntʃ] ◇ *n =* 2,5 *cm*, ≃ pouce *m* ◇ *vi :* **to** ~ **forward** avancer petit à petit.

incidence [ˈɪnsɪdəns] *n* [of disease, theft] fréquence *f.*

incident [ˈɪnsɪdənt] *n* incident *m.*

incidental [ˌɪnsɪˈdentl] *adj* accessoire.

incidentally [ˌɪnsɪˈdentəlɪ] *adv* à propos.

incidental music *n* musique *f* de fond.

incinerate [ɪnˈsɪnəreɪt] *vt* incinérer.

incinerator [ɪnˈsɪnəreɪtəʳ] *n* incinérateur *m.*

incipient [ɪnˈsɪpɪənt] *adj* fml naissant(e).

incision [ɪnˈsɪʒn] *n* incision *f.*

incisive [ɪnˈsaɪsɪv] *adj* incisif(ive).

incisor [ɪnˈsaɪzəʳ] *n* incisive *f.*

incite [ɪnˈsaɪt] *vt* inciter ; **to** ~ **sb to do sthg** inciter qqn à faire qqch.

incitement [ɪnˈsaɪtmənt] *n (U) :* ~ **(to sthg/to do sthg)** incitation *f* (à qqch/à faire qqch).

incl. - **1.** abbr of **including** - **2.** abbr of **inclusive.**

inclement [ɪnˈklemənt] *adj* inclément(e).

inclination [ˌɪnklɪˈneɪʃn] *n -* **1.** (*U*) [liking, preference] inclination *f*, goût *m -* **2.** [tendency] : ~ **to do sthg** inclination *f* à faire qqch.

incline [*n* ˈɪnklaɪn, *vb* ɪnˈklaɪn] ◇ *n* inclinaison *f* ◇ *vt* [head] incliner.

inclined [ɪnˈklaɪnd] *adj -* **1.** [tending] : **to be** ~ **to sthg/to do sthg** avoir tendance à qqch/à faire qqch - **2.** [wanting] : **to be** ~ **to do sthg** être enclin(e) à faire qqch - **3.** [sloping] incliné(e).

include [ɪnˈkluːd] *vt* inclure.

included [ɪnˈkluːdɪd] *adj* inclus(e).

including [ɪnˈkluːdɪŋ] *prep* y compris.

inclusion [ɪnˈkluːʒn] *n* inclusion *f.*

inclusive [ɪnˈkluːsɪv] *adj* inclus(e) ; [including all costs] tout compris ; ~ **of VAT** TVA incluse OR comprise.

incognito [,ɪnkɒg'niːtəʊ] *adv* incognito.

incoherent [,ɪnkəʊ'hɪərənt] *adj* incohérent(e).

income ['ɪŋkʌm] *n* revenu *m*.

incomes policy *n* Br politique *f* des revenus OR salariale.

income support *n* Br *allocations supplémentaires accordées aux personnes ayant un faible revenu.*

income tax *n* impôt *m* sur le revenu.

incoming ['ɪn,kʌmɪŋ] *adj* - **1.** [tide, wave] montant(e) - **2.** [plane, passengers, mail] qui arrive ; [phone call] de l'extérieur - **3.** [government, official] nouveau (nouvelle).

incommunicado [,ɪnkəmjuːnɪ'kɑːdəʊl] *adv :* to be held ~ être tenu(e) au secret.

incomparable [ɪn'kɒmpərəbl] *adj* incomparable.

incompatible [,ɪnkəm'pætɪbl] *adj :* ~ (with) incompatible (avec).

incompetence [ɪn'kɒmpɪtəns] *n* incompétence *f*.

incompetent [ɪn'kɒmpɪtənt] *adj* incompétent(e).

incomplete [,ɪnkəm'pliːt] *adj* incomplet(ète).

incomprehensible [ɪn,kɒmprɪ'hensəbl] *adj* incompréhensible.

inconceivable [,ɪnkən'siːvəbl] *adj* inconcevable.

inconclusive [,ɪnkən'kluːsɪv] *adj* peu concluant(e).

incongruous [ɪn'kɒŋgrʊəs] *adj* incongru(e).

inconsequential [,ɪnkɒnsɪ'kwenʃl] *adj* sans importance.

inconsiderable [,ɪnkən'sɪdərəbl] *adj :* not ~ non négligeable.

inconsiderate [,ɪnkən'sɪdərət] *adj* inconsidéré(e) ; [person] qui manque de considération.

inconsistency [,ɪnkən'sɪstənsɪ] *(pl* -ies*) n* inconsistance *f*.

inconsistent [,ɪnkən'sɪstənt] *adj* - **1.** [not agreeing, contradictory] contradictoire ; [person] inconséquent(e) ; ~ with sthg en contradiction avec qqch - **2.** [erratic] inconsistant(e).

inconsolable [,ɪnkən'səʊləbl] *adj* inconsolable.

inconspicuous [,ɪnkən'spɪkjʊəs] *adj* qui passe inaperçu(e).

incontinence [ɪn'kɒntɪnəns] *n* incontinence *f*.

incontinent [ɪn'kɒntɪnənt] *adj* incontinent(e).

incontrovertible [,ɪnkɒntrə'vɜːtəbl] *adj* indéniable, irréfutable.

inconvenience [,ɪnkən'viːnjəns] <> *n* désagrément *m* <> *vt* déranger.

inconvenient [,ɪnkən'viːnjənt] *adj* inopportun(e).

incorporate [ɪn'kɔːpəreɪt] *vt* - **1.** [integrate] : to ~ sb/sthg (into) incorporer qqn/qqch (dans) - **2.** [comprise] contenir, comprendre.

incorporated [ɪn'kɔːpəreɪtɪd] *adj* COMM constitué(e) en société commerciale.

incorporation [ɪn,kɔːpə'reɪʃn] *n* - **1.** [integration] incorporation *f* - **2.** COMM [of company] constitution *f* en société commerciale.

incorrect [,ɪnkə'rekt] *adj* incorrect(e).

incorrigible [ɪn'kɒrɪdʒəbl] *adj* incorrigible.

incorruptible [,ɪnkə'rʌptəbl] *adj* incorruptible.

increase [*n* 'ɪnkriːs, *vb* ɪn'kriːs] <> *n :* ~ (in) augmentation *f* (de) ; to be on the ~ aller en augmentant <> *vt* & *vi* augmenter.

increased [ɪn'kriːst] *adj* accru(e).

increasing [ɪn'kriːsɪŋ] *adj* croissant(e).

increasingly [ɪn'kriːsɪŋlɪ] *adv* de plus en plus.

incredible [ɪn'kredəbl] *adj* incroyable.

incredulous [ɪn'kredjʊləs] *adj* incrédule.

increment ['ɪnkrɪmənt] *n* augmentation *f*.

incriminate [ɪn'krɪmɪneɪt] *vt* incriminer ; to ~ o.s. se compromettre.

incriminating [ɪn'krɪmɪneɪtɪŋ] *adj* compromettant(e).

incrusted [ɪn'krʌst] = encrusted.

incubate ['ɪnkjʊbeɪt] <> *vt* incuber <> *vi* être en incubation.

incubation [,ɪnkjʊ'beɪʃn] *n* incubation *f*.

incubator ['ɪnkjʊbeɪtər] *n* [for baby] incubateur *m*, couveuse *f*.

inculcate ['ɪnkʌlkeɪt] *vt :* to ~ sthg in OR into sb inculquer qqch à qqn.

incumbent [ɪn'kʌmbənt] *fml* <> *adj :* to be ~ on OR upon sb to do sthg incomber à qqn de faire qqch <> *n* [of post] titulaire *m*.

incur [ɪn'kɜːr] *(pt* & *pp* -red ; *cont* -ring*) vt* encourir.

incurable [ɪn'kjʊərəbl] *adj* [disease] incurable.

incursion [Br ɪn'kɜːʃn, Am ɪn'kɜːʒn] *n* incursion *f*.

indebted [ɪn'detɪd] *adj* [grateful] : ~ to sb redevable à qqn.

indecency [ɪn'diːsnsɪ] *n* indécence *f*.

indecent [ɪn'diːsnt] *adj* - **1.** [improper] indécent(e) - **2.** [unreasonable] malséant(e).

indecent assault n attentat m à la pudeur.

indecent exposure n outrage m public à la pudeur.

indecipherable [ˌɪndɪˈsaɪfərəbl] adj indéchiffrable.

indecision [ˌɪndɪˈsɪʒn] n indécision f.

indecisive [ˌɪndɪˈsaɪsɪv] adj indécis(e).

indeed [ɪnˈdiːd] adv - **1.** [certainly, to express surprise] vraiment ; ~ I am, yes ~ certainement - **2.** [in fact] en effet - **3.** [for emphasis] : very big/bad ~ extrêmement grand/mauvais, vraiment grand/mauvais.

indefatigable [ˌɪndɪˈfætɪɡəbl] adj infatigable.

indefensible [ˌɪndɪˈfensəbl] adj indéfendable.

indefinable [ˌɪndɪˈfaɪnəbl] adj indéfinissable.

indefinite [ɪnˈdefɪnɪt] adj - **1.** [not fixed] indéfini(e) - **2.** [imprecise] vague.

indefinitely [ɪnˈdefɪnətlɪ] adv - **1.** [for unfixed period] indéfiniment - **2.** [imprecisely] vaguement.

indelible [ɪnˈdeləbl] adj indélébile.

indelicate [ɪnˈdelɪkət] adj indélicat(e).

indemnify [ɪnˈdemnɪfaɪ] (pt & pp -ied) vt : to ~ sb for OR against sthg indemniser qqn de qqch.

indemnity [ɪnˈdemnətɪ] n indemnité f.

indent [ɪnˈdent] vt - **1.** [dent] entailler - **2.** [text] mettre en retrait.

indentation [ˌɪndenˈteɪʃn] n - **1.** [dent] découpure f, entaille f - **2.** [in text] alinéa m.

indenture [ɪnˈdentʃəʳ] n contrat m d'apprentissage.

independence [ˌɪndɪˈpendəns] n indépendance f.

Independence Day n fête de l'indépendance américaine, le 4 juillet.

independent [ˌɪndɪˈpendənt] adj : ~ (of) indépendant(e) (de).

independently [ˌɪndɪˈpendəntlɪ] adv de façon indépendante ; ~ of sb/sthg indépendamment de qqn/qqch.

independent school n Br école f privée.

in-depth adj approfondi(e).

indescribable [ˌɪndɪˈskraɪbəbl] adj indescriptible.

indestructible [ˌɪndɪˈstrʌktəbl] adj indestructible.

indeterminate [ˌɪndɪˈtɜːmɪnət] adj indéterminé(e).

index [ˈɪndeks] (pl senses 1 and 2 **-dexes** [-deksiːz] ; sense 3 **-dexes** OR **-dices** [-dɪsiːz]) <> n - **1.** [of book] index m - **2.** [in library] répertoire m, fichier m - **3.** ECON indice m <> vt [book] faire l'index de.

index card n fiche f.

index finger n index m.

index-linked [-ˌlɪŋkt] adj indexé(e).

India [ˈɪndjə] n Inde f ; in ~ en Inde.

India ink Am = Indian ink.

Indian [ˈɪndjən] <> adj indien(enne) <> n Indien m, -enne f.

Indiana [ˌɪndɪˈænə] n Indiana m ; in ~ dans l'Indiana.

Indian ink Br, **India ink** Am n encre f de Chine.

Indian Ocean n : the ~ l'océan m Indien.

Indian summer n été m indien.

india rubber n caoutchouc m.

indicate [ˈɪndɪkeɪt] <> vt indiquer <> vi AUT mettre son clignotant.

indication [ˌɪndɪˈkeɪʃn] n - **1.** [suggestion] indication f - **2.** [sign] signe m.

indicative [ɪnˈdɪkətɪv] <> adj : ~ of indicatif(ive) de <> n GRAMM indicatif m.

indicator [ˈɪndɪkeɪtəʳ] n - **1.** [sign] indicateur m - **2.** AUT clignotant m.

indices [ˈɪndɪsiːz] pl ⊏> **index.**

indict [ɪnˈdaɪt] vt : to ~ sb (for) accuser qqn (de), mettre qqn en examen (pour).

indictable [ɪnˈdaɪtəbl] adj [person] qui peut être traduit(e) en justice ; [offence] punissable.

indictment [ɪnˈdaɪtmənt] n [JUR - bill] acte m d'accusation ; [- process] mise f en examen.

indie [ˈɪndɪ] adj Br inf indépendant(e).

indifference [ɪnˈdɪfrəns] n indifférence f.

indifferent [ɪnˈdɪfrənt] adj - **1.** [uninterested] : ~ (to) indifférent(e) (à) - **2.** [mediocre] médiocre.

indigenous [ɪnˈdɪdʒɪnəs] adj indigène.

indigestible [ˌɪndɪˈdʒestəbl] adj indigeste.

indigestion [ˌɪndɪˈdʒestʃn] n (U) indigestion f.

indignant [ɪnˈdɪɡnənt] adj : ~ (at) indigné(e) (de).

indignantly [ɪnˈdɪɡnəntlɪ] adv avec indignation.

indignation [ˌɪndɪɡˈneɪʃn] n indignation f.

indignity [ɪnˈdɪɡnətɪ] (pl -ies) n indignité f.

indigo [ˈɪndɪɡəʊ] <> adj indigo (inv) <> n indigo m.

indirect [ˌɪndɪˈrekt] adj indirect(e).

indirect costs npl frais mpl généraux.

indirect lighting n éclairage m indirect.
indirectly [,ındı'rektlı] adv indirectement.
indirect speech n discours m indirect.
indirect taxation n (U) contributions fpl indirectes, impôts mpl indirects.
indiscreet [,ındı'skri:t] adj indiscret(ète).
indiscretion [,ındı'skreʃn] n indiscrétion f.
indiscriminate [,ındı'skrımınət] adj [person] qui manque de discernement ; [treatment] sans distinction ; [killing] commis au hasard.
indiscriminately [,ındı'skrımınətlı] adv [admire] aveuglément ; [treat] sans faire de distinction ; [kill] au hasard.
indispensable [,ındı'spensəbl] adj indispensable.
indisposed [,ındı'spəuzd] adj fml [unwell] indisposé(e).
indisputable [,ındı'spju:təbl] adj indiscutable.
indistinct [,ındı'stıŋkt] adj indistinct(e) ; [memory] vague.
indistinguishable [,ındı'stıŋgwıʃəbl] adj : ~ (from) que l'on ne peut distinguer (de).
individual [,ındı'vıdʒuəl] ◇ adj - **1.** [separate, for one person] individuel(elle) - **2.** [distinctive] personnel(elle) ◇ n individu m.
individualist [,ındı'vıdʒuəlıst] n individualiste mf.
individualistic ['ındı,vıdʒuə'lıstık] adj individualiste.
individuality ['ındı,vıdʒu'ælətı] n individualité f.
individually [,ındı'vıdʒuəlı] adv individuellement.
indivisible [,ındı'vızəbl] adj indivisible.
Indochina [,ındəu'tʃaınəə] n Indochine f ; in ~ en Indochine.
indoctrinate [ın'dɒktrıneıt] vt endoctriner.
indoctrination [ın,dɒktrı'neıʃn] n endoctrinement m.
indolent ['ındələnt] adj indolent(e).
indomitable [ın'dɒmıtəbl] adj indomptable.
Indonesia [,ındə'ni:zjə] n Indonésie f ; in ~ en Indonésie.
Indonesian [,ındə'ni:zjən] ◇ adj indonésien(enne) ◇ n - **1.** [person] Indonésien m, -enne f - **2.** [language] indonésien m.
indoor ['ındɔ:r] adj d'intérieur ; [swimming pool] couvert(e) ; [sports] en salle.
indoors [,ın'dɔ:z] adv à l'intérieur.
indubitably [ın'dju:bıtəblı] adv indubitablement.
induce [ın'dju:s] vt - **1.** [persuade] : **to ~ sb to do**

sthg inciter OR pousser qqn à faire qqch - **2.** MED [labour] provoquer ; [woman] provoquer l'accouchement de - **3.** [bring about] provoquer.
inducement [ın'dju:smənt] n [incentive] incitation f, encouragement m.
induction [ın'dʌkʃn] n - **1.** [into official position] : ~ **(into)** installation f (à) - **2.** [introduction to job] introduction f - **3.** ELEC induction f.
induction course n stage m d'initiation.
indulge [ın'dʌldʒ] ◇ vt - **1.** [whim, passion] céder à - **2.** [child, person] gâter ; **to ~ o.s.** se faire plaisir ◇ vi : **to ~ in** sthg se permettre qqch.
indulgence [ın'dʌldʒəns] n - **1.** [act of indulging] indulgence f - **2.** [special treat] gâterie f.
indulgent [ın'dʌldʒənt] adj indulgent(e).
Indus ['ındəs] n : **the (River)** ~ l'Indus m.
industrial [ın'dʌstrıəl] adj industriel(elle).
industrial action n : **to take ~** se mettre en grève.
industrial estate Br, **industrial park** Am n zone f industrielle.
industrial injury n accident m du travail.
industrialist [ın'dʌstrıəlıst] n industriel m.
industrialization [ın,dʌstrıəlaı'zeıʃn] n industrialisation f.
industrialize, -ise [ın'dʌstrıəlaız] ◇ vt industrialiser ◇ vi s'industrialiser.
industrial park Am = industrial estate.
industrial relations npl relations fpl patronat-syndicats.
industrial revolution n révolution f industrielle.
industrial tribunal n ≃ conseil m de prud'hommes.
industrious [ın'dʌstrıəs] adj industrieux(euse).
industry ['ındəstrı] (pl -ies) n - **1.** [gen] industrie f - **2.** (U) [hard work] assiduité f, application f.
inebriated [ı'ni:brıeıtıd] adj fml ivre.
inedible [ın'edıbl] adj - **1.** [meal, food] immangeable - **2.** [plant, mushroom] non comestible.
ineffective [,ını'fektıv] adj inefficace.
ineffectual [,ını'fektʃuəl] adj inefficace ; [person] incapable, incompétent(e).
inefficiency [,ını'fıʃnsı] n inefficacité f ; [of person] incapacité f, incompétence f.
inefficient [,ını'fıʃnt] adj inefficace ; [person] incapable, incompétent(e).
inelegant [ın'elıgənt] adj inélégant(e), sans élégance.

ineligible [ɪn'elɪdʒəbl] adj inéligible ; **to be ~ for sthg** ne pas avoir droit à qqch.

inept [ɪ'nept] adj inepte ; [person] stupide.

ineptitude [ɪ'neptɪtjuːd] n ineptie f ; [of person] stupidité f.

inequality [,ɪnɪ'kwɒlətɪ] (pl -ies) n inégalité f.

inequitable [ɪn'ekwɪtəbl] adj fml inéquitable.

ineradicable [,ɪnɪ'rædɪkəbl] adj fml tenace, dont on ne peut se débarrasser.

inert [ɪ'nɜːt] adj inerte

inertia [ɪ'nɜːʃə] n inertie f.

inertia-reel seat belt n ceinture f de sécurité à enrouleur.

inescapable [,ɪnɪ'skeɪpəbl] adj inéluctable.

inessential [,ɪnɪ'senʃl] adj superflu(e).

inestimable [ɪn'estɪməbl] adj inestimable.

inevitable [ɪn'evɪtəbl] ◇ adj inévitable ◇ n : **the ~** l'inévitable m.

inevitably [ɪn'evɪtəblɪ] adv inévitablement.

inexact [,ɪnɪg'zækt] adj inexact(e).

inexcusable [,ɪnɪk'skjuːzəbl] adj inexcusable, impardonnable.

inexhaustible [,ɪnɪg'zɔːstəbl] adj inépuisable.

inexorable [ɪn'eksərəbl] adj inexorable.

inexorably [ɪn'eksərəblɪ] adv inexorablement.

inexpensive [,ɪnɪk'spensɪv] adj bon marché (inv), pas cher (chère).

inexperience [,ɪnɪk'spɪərɪəns] n inexpérience f.

inexperienced [,ɪnɪk'spɪərɪənst] adj inexpérimenté(e), qui manque d'expérience.

inexpert [ɪn'ekspɜːt] adj inexpert(e).

inexplicable [,ɪnɪk'splɪkəbl] adj inexplicable.

inexplicably [,ɪnɪk'splɪkəblɪ] adv inexplicablement.

inextricably [ɪn'ekstrɪkəblɪ] adv inextricablement.

infallible [ɪn'fæləbl] adj infaillible.

infamous ['ɪnfəməs] adj infâme.

infamy ['ɪnfəmɪ] n infamie f.

infancy ['ɪnfənsɪ] n petite enfance f ; **in its ~** fig à ses débuts.

infant ['ɪnfənt] n - **1.** [baby] nouveau-né m, nouveau-née f, nourrisson m - **2.** [young child] enfant mf en bas âge.

infantile ['ɪnfəntaɪl] adj lit & pej infantile.

infant mortality n mortalité f infantile.

infantry ['ɪnfəntrɪ] n infanterie f.

infantryman ['ɪnfəntrɪmən] (pl -men [-mən]) n fantassin m.

infant school n Br école f maternelle (de 5 à 7 ans).

infatuated [ɪn'fætjʊeɪtɪd] adj : **~ (with)** entiché(e) (de).

infatuation [ɪn,fætjʊ'eɪʃn] n : **~ (with)** béguin m (pour).

infect [ɪn'fekt] vt - **1.** MED infecter - **2.** fig [subj : enthusiasm etc] se propager à.

infected [ɪn'fektɪd] adj : **~ (with)** infecté(e) (par).

infection [ɪn'fekʃn] n infection f.

infectious [ɪn'fekʃəs] adj - **1.** [disease] infectieux(euse) - **2.** fig [feeling, laugh] contagieux(euse).

infer [ɪn'fɜːr] (pt & pp -red ; cont -ring) vt [deduce] : **to ~ sthg (from)** déduire qqch (de).

inference ['ɪnfrəns] n - **1.** [conclusion] conclusion f - **2.** [process of deduction] : **by ~** par déduction.

inferior [ɪn'fɪərɪər] ◇ adj - **1.** [in status] inférieur(e) - **2.** [product] de qualité inférieure ; [work] médiocre ◇ n [in status] subalterne mf.

inferiority [ɪn,fɪərɪ'ɒrətɪ] n infériorité f.

inferiority complex n complexe m d'infériorité.

infernal [ɪn'fɜːnl] adj inf dated infernal(e).

inferno [ɪn'fɜːnəʊ] (pl -s) n brasier m.

infertile [ɪn'fɜːtaɪl] adj - **1.** [woman] stérile - **2.** [soil] infertile.

infertility [,ɪnfə'tɪlətɪ] n - **1.** [of woman] stérilité f - **2.** [of soil] infertilité f.

infestation [,ɪnfe'steɪʃn] n infestation f.

infested [ɪn'festɪd] adj : **~ with** infesté(e) de.

infidelity [,ɪnfɪ'delətɪ] n infidélité f.

infighting ['ɪn,faɪtɪŋ] n (U) querelles fpl intestines.

infiltrate ['ɪnfɪltreɪt] ◇ vt infiltrer ◇ vi : **to ~ into** s'infiltrer dans.

infinite ['ɪnfɪnət] adj infini(e).

infinitely ['ɪnfɪnətlɪ] adv infiniment.

infinitesimal [,ɪnfɪnɪ'tesɪml] adj infinitésimal(e).

infinitive [ɪn'fɪnɪtɪv] n infinitif m.

infinity [ɪn'fɪnətɪ] n infini m.

infirm [ɪn'fɜːm] ◇ adj infirme ◇ npl : **the ~** les infirmes mpl.

infirmary [ɪn'fɜːmərɪ] (pl -ies) n [hospital] hôpital m.

infirmity [ɪn'fɜːmətɪ] (pl -ies) n infirmité f.

inflamed [ɪn'fleɪmd] adj MED enflammé(e).

inflammable [ɪn'flæməbl] adj inflammable.

inflammation [ˌɪnfləˈmeɪʃn] n MED inflammation f.

inflammatory [ɪnˈflæmətrɪ] adj inflammatoire.

inflatable [ɪnˈfleɪtəbl] adj gonflable.

inflate [ɪnˈfleɪt] vt **- 1.** [tyre, life jacket etc] gonfler **- 2.** ECON [prices, salaries] hausser, gonfler.

inflated [ɪnˈfleɪtɪd] adj **- 1.** [tyre, life jacket etc] gonflé(e) **- 2.** pej [exaggerated] : **he has an ~ opinion of himself** il a une haute opinion de lui-même **- 3.** ECON [salary, prices] exagéré(e), gonflé(o).

inflation [ɪnˈfleɪʃn] n ECON inflation f.

inflationary [ɪnˈfleɪʃnrɪ] adj ECON inflationniste.

inflationary spiral n spirale f inflationniste.

inflation-proof adj protégé(e) contre les effets de l'inflation.

inflexible [ɪnˈfleksəbl] adj **- 1.** [material] rigide **- 2.** [person, arrangement] inflexible.

inflict [ɪnˈflɪkt] vt : **to ~ sthg on sb** infliger qqch à qqn.

in-flight adj en vol (inv).

inflow [ˈɪnfləʊ] n afflux m.

influence [ˈɪnfluəns] ◇ n influence f ; **under the ~ of** [person, group] sous l'influence de ; [alcohol, drugs] sous l'effet OR l'empire de ◇ vt influencer.

influential [ˌɪnfluˈenʃl] adj influent(e).

influenza [ˌɪnfluˈenzə] n (U) grippe f.

influx [ˈɪnflʌks] n afflux m.

info [ˈɪnfəʊ] n (U) inf info f.

inform [ɪnˈfɔːm] vt : **to ~ sb (of)** informer qqn (de) ; **to ~ sb about** renseigner qqn sur.

➣ **inform on** vt fus dénoncer.

informal [ɪnˈfɔːml] adj **- 1.** [party, person] simple ; [clothes] de tous les jours **- 2.** [negotiations, visit] officieux(euse) ; [meeting] informel(elle).

informally [ɪnˈfɔːməlɪ] adv **- 1.** [talk, dress] simplement **- 2.** [meet, agree] officieusement.

informant [ɪnˈfɔːmənt] n informateur m, -trice f.

information [ˌɪnfəˈmeɪʃn] n (U) : **~ (on** OR **about)** renseignements mpl OR informations fpl (sur) ; **a piece of ~** un renseignement ; **for your ~** fml à titre d'information.

information desk n bureau m de renseignements.

information highway, information superhighway n autoroute f de l'information.

information office n bureau m de renseignements.

information retrieval n recherche f documentaire sur ordinateur.

information scientist n informaticien m, -enne f.

information superhighway = **information highway**.

information technology n informatique f.

informative [ɪnˈfɔːmətɪv] adj informatif(ive).

informed [ɪnˈfɔːmd] adj : **well/badly ~** bien/mal renseigné(e) ; **he made an ~ guess** il a essayé de deviner en s'aidant de ce qu'il savait.

informer [ɪnˈfɔːməʳ] n indicateur m, -trice f.

infra dig [ˌɪnfrə-] adj dégradant(e).

infrared [ˌɪnfrəˈred] adj infrarouge.

infrastructure [ˈɪnfrəˌstrʌktʃəʳ] n infrastructure f.

infrequent [ɪnˈfriːkwənt] adj peu fréquent(e).

infringe [ɪnˈfrɪndʒ] (cont **infringeing**) ◇ vt **- 1.** [right] empiéter sur **- 2.** [law, agreement] enfreindre ◇ vi **- 1.** [on right] : **to ~ on** empiéter sur **- 2.** [on law, agreement] : **to ~ on** enfreindre.

infringement [ɪnˈfrɪndʒmənt] n **- 1.** [of right] : **~ (of)** atteinte f (à) **- 2.** [of law, agreement] transgression f.

infuriate [ɪnˈfjʊərɪeɪt] vt rendre furieux(euse).

infuriating [ɪnˈfjʊərɪeɪtɪŋ] adj exaspérant(e).

infuse [ɪnˈfjuːz] ◇ vt : **to ~ sb with sthg** fig insuffler qqch à qqn ◇ vi [tea] infuser.

infusion [ɪnˈfjuːʒn] n **- 1.** [of enthusiasm, ideas] fait m d'insuffler ; [of money] injection f **- 2.** [of tea, herbs] infusion f.

ingenious [ɪnˈdʒiːnjəs] adj ingénieux(euse).

ingenuity [ˌɪndʒɪˈnjuːətɪ] n ingéniosité f.

ingenuous [ɪnˈdʒenjʊəs] adj ingénu(e), naïf (naïve).

ingest [ɪnˈdʒest] vt ingérer.

ingot [ˈɪŋgət] n lingot m.

ingrained [ˌɪnˈgreɪnd] adj **- 1.** [dirt] incrusté(e) **- 2.** fig [belief, hatred] enraciné(e).

ingratiate [ɪnˈgreɪʃɪeɪt] vt : **to ~ o.s. with sb** se faire bien voir de qqn.

ingratiating [ɪnˈgreɪʃɪeɪtɪŋ] adj doucereux(euse), mielleux(euse).

ingratitude [ɪnˈgrætɪtjuːd] n ingratitude f.

ingredient [ɪnˈgriːdjənt] n ingrédient m ; fig élément m.

ingrowing [ˈɪnˌgrəʊɪŋ], **ingrown** [ˈɪnˌgrəʊn] adj : **~ toenail** ongle m incarné.

inhabit [ɪn'hæbɪt] *vt* habiter.
inhabitant [ɪn'hæbɪtənt] *n* habitant *m*, -e *f*.
inhalation [ˌɪnhə'leɪʃn] *n* inhalation *f*.
inhale [ɪn'heɪl] ⬦ *vt* inhaler, respirer ⬦ *vi* [breathe in] respirer.
inhaler [ɪn'heɪləʳ] *n* MED inhalateur *m*.
inherent [ɪn'hɪərənt, ɪn'herənt] *adj :* ~ (in) inhérent(e) (à).
inherently [ɪn'hɪərəntlɪ, ɪn'herəntlɪ] *adv* fondamentalement, en soi.
inherit [ɪn'herɪt] ⬦ *vt :* to ~ sthg (from sb) hériter qqch (de qqn) ⬦ *vi* hériter.
inheritance [ɪn'herɪtəns] *n* héritage *m*.
inheritor [ɪn'herɪtəʳ] *n* héritier *m*, -ère *f*.
inhibit [ɪn'hɪbɪt] *vt* - **1.** [prevent] empêcher - **2.** PSYCH inhiber.
inhibited [ɪn'hɪbɪtɪd] *adj* [person] inhibé(e).
inhibition [ˌɪnhɪ'bɪʃn] *n* inhibition *f*.
inhospitable [ˌɪnhɒ'spɪtəbl] *adj* inhospitalier(ère).
in-house ⬦ *adj* interne ; [staff] de la maison ⬦ *adv* [produce, work] sur place.
inhuman [ɪn'hjuːmən] *adj* inhumain(e).
inhumane [ˌɪnhjuː'meɪn] *adj* inhumain(e).
inimitable [ɪ'nɪmɪtəbl] *adj* inimitable.
iniquitous [ɪ'nɪkwɪtəs] *adj* inique.
iniquity [ɪ'nɪkwətɪ] (*pl* -ies) *n* iniquité *f*.
initial [ɪ'nɪʃl] (Br *pt* & *pp* -led ; *cont* -ling, Am *pt* & *pp* -ed ; *cont* -ing) ⬦ *adj* initial(e), premier(ère) ; ~ letter initiale *f* ⬦ *vt* parapher.
➡ **initials** *npl* initiales *fpl*.
initialize, -ise [ɪ'nɪʃəlaɪz] *vt* COMPUT initialiser.
initially [ɪ'nɪʃəlɪ] *adv* initialement, au début.
initiate [ɪ'nɪʃɪeɪt] ⬦ *vt* - **1.** [talks] engager ; [scheme] ébaucher, inaugurer - **2.** [teach] : to ~ sb into sthg initier qqn à qqch ⬦ *n* initié *m*, -e *f*.
initiation [ɪˌnɪʃɪ'eɪʃn] *n* - **1.** [of talks] commencement *m*, début *m* ; [of scheme] ébauche *f*, inauguration *f* - **2.** [teaching] initiation *f*.
initiative [ɪ'nɪʃətɪv] *n* - **1.** [gen] initiative *f* ; on one's own ~ de sa propre initiative ; to take the ~ prendre l'initiative ; to use one's ~ faire preuve d'initiative - **2.** [advantage] : to have the ~ avoir l'avantage *m*.
inject [ɪn'dʒekt] *vt* - **1.** MED : to ~ sb with sthg, to ~ sthg into sb injecter qqch à qqn - **2.** fig [excitement] insuffler ; [money] injecter.
injection [ɪn'dʒekʃn] *n* lit & fig injection *f*.
injudicious [ˌɪndʒuː'dɪʃəs] *adj* peu judicieux(euse).

injunction [ɪn'dʒʌŋkʃn] *n* JUR injonction *f*.
injure ['ɪndʒəʳ] *vt* - **1.** [limb, person] blesser ; to ~ o.s. se blesser ; to ~ one's arm se blesser au bras - **2.** fig [reputation, chances] compromettre.
injured ['ɪndʒəd] ⬦ *adj* - **1.** [limb, person] blessé(e) - **2.** fig [reputation] compromis(e) ; [pride] froissé(e) ⬦ *npl :* the ~ les blessés *mpl*.
injurious [ɪn'dʒʊərɪəs] *adj* fml : ~ (to) nuisible (à), néfaste (à).
injury ['ɪndʒərɪ] (*pl* -ies) *n* - **1.** [to limb, person] blessure *f* ; to do o.s. an ~ se blesser - **2.** fig [to reputation] coup *m*, atteinte *f*.
injury time *n* (U) arrêts *mpl* de jeu.
injustice [ɪn'dʒʌstɪs] *n* injustice *f* ; to do sb an ~ se montrer injuste envers qqn.
ink [ɪŋk] ⬦ *n* encre *f* ⬦ *comp* [pen] à encre ; [stain, blot] d'encre.
➡ **ink in** *vt sep* repasser à l'encre.
ink-jet printer *n* COMPUT imprimante *f* à jet d'encre.
inkling ['ɪŋklɪŋ] *n :* to have an ~ of avoir une petite idée de.
inkpad ['ɪŋkpæd] *n* tampon *m* encreur.
inkwell ['ɪŋkwel] *n* encrier *m*.
inlaid [ˌɪn'leɪd] *adj :* ~ (with) incrusté(e) (de).
inland [*adj* 'ɪnlənd, *adv* ɪn'lænd] ⬦ *adj* intérieur(e) ⬦ *adv* à l'intérieur.
Inland Revenue *n* Br : the ~ ≃ le fisc.
in-laws *npl* inf [parents-in-law] beaux-parents *mpl* ; [others] belle-famille *f*.
inlet ['ɪnlet] *n* - **1.** [of lake, sea] avancée *f* - **2.** TECH arrivée *f*.
inmate ['ɪnmeɪt] *n* [of prison] détenu *m*, -e *f* ; [of mental hospital] interné *m*, -e *f*.
inmost ['ɪnməʊst] *adj* literary [secrets, thoughts] le plus profond (la plus profonde), le plus secret (la plus secrète).
inn [ɪn] *n* auberge *f*.
innards ['ɪnədz] *npl* entrailles *fpl*.
innate [ɪ'neɪt] *adj* inné(e).
inner ['ɪnəʳ] *adj* - **1.** [on inside] interne, intérieur(e) - **2.** [feelings] intime.
inner city ⬦ *n :* the ~ les quartiers *mpl* pauvres ⬦ *comp* des quartiers pauvres.
innermost ['ɪnəməʊst] *adj* = inmost.
inner tube *n* chambre *f* à air.
innings ['ɪnɪŋz] (*pl inv*) *n* Br CRICKET tour *m* de batte ; to have had a good ~ fig avoir bien profité de l'existence.
innocence ['ɪnəsəns] *n* innocence *f*.
innocent ['ɪnəsənt] ⬦ *adj* innocent(e) ; ~ of [crime] non coupable de ⬦ *n* innocent *m*, -e *f*.

innocuous [ɪ'nɒkjʊəs] adj inoffensif(ive).

innovation [ˌɪnə'veɪʃn] n innovation f.

innovative ['ɪnəvətɪv] adj - **1.** [idea, design] innovateur(trice) - **2.** [person, company] novateur(trice).

innovator ['ɪnəveɪtəʳ] n innovateur m, -trice f.

innuendo [ˌɪnjuː'endəʊ] (pl -es OR -s) n insinuation f.

innumerable [ɪ'njuːmərəbl] adj innombrable.

inoculate [ɪ'nɒkjʊleɪt] vt : to ~ sb (with sthg) inoculer (qqch à) qqn ; to ~ sb (against) vacciner qqn (contre).

inoculation [ɪˌnɒkjʊ'leɪʃn] n inoculation f.

inoffensive [ˌɪnə'fensɪv] adj inoffensif(ive).

inoperable [ɪn'ɒprəbl] adj - **1.** MED inopérable - **2.** [method] impossible à mettre en œuvre.

inoperative [ɪn'ɒprətɪv] adj - **1.** [rule, tax] inopérant(e) - **2.** [machine] qui ne marche pas.

inopportune [ɪn'ɒpətjuːn] adj inopportun(e).

inordinate [ɪ'nɔːdɪnət] adj excessif(ive), démesuré(e).

inordinately [ɪ'nɔːdɪnətlɪ] adv excessivement.

inorganic [ˌɪnɔː'gænɪk] adj inorganique.

in-patient n malade hospitalisé m, malade hospitalisée f.

input ['ɪnpʊt] (pt & pp input OR -ted, cont -ting) ⬦ n - **1.** [contribution] contribution f, concours m - **2.** COMPUT & ELEC entrée f ⬦ vt COMPUT entrer.

input/output n COMPUT entrée-sortie f.

inquest ['ɪnkwest] n enquête f.

inquire [ɪn'kwaɪəʳ] ⬦ vt : to ~ when/whether/how ... demander quand/si/comment ... ⬦ vi : to ~ (about) se renseigner (sur).
➤ **inquire after** vt fus s'enquérir de.
➤ **inquire into** vt fus enquêter sur.

inquiring [ɪn'kwaɪərɪŋ] adj - **1.** [person, mind] curieux(euse) - **2.** [look, tone] interrogateur(trice).

inquiry [ɪn'kwaɪərɪ] (pl -ies) n - **1.** [question] demande f de renseignements ; 'Inquiries' 'renseignements' - **2.** [investigation] enquête f.

inquiry desk n bureau m de renseignements.

inquisition [ˌɪnkwɪ'zɪʃn] n inquisition f.
➤ **Inquisition** n : the Inquisition l'Inquisition f.

inquisitive [ɪn'kwɪzətɪv] adj inquisiteur(trice).

inroads ['ɪnrəʊdz] npl : to make ~ into [savings] entamer.

insane [ɪn'seɪn] ⬦ adj fou (folle) ⬦ npl : the ~ les malades mpl mentaux.

insanitary [ɪn'sænɪtrɪ] adj insalubre.

insanity [ɪn'sænətɪ] n folie f.

insatiable [ɪn'seɪʃəbl] adj insatiable.

inscribe [ɪn'skraɪb] vt - **1.** [engrave] graver - **2.** [write] inscrire.

inscription [ɪn'skrɪpʃn] n - **1.** [engraved] inscription f - **2.** [written] dédicace f.

inscrutable [ɪn'skruːtəbl] adj impénétrable.

insect ['ɪnsekt] n insecte m.

insect bite n piqûre f d'insecte.

insecticide [ɪn'sektɪsaɪd] n insecticide m.

insect repellent n lotion f anti-moustiques.

insecure [ˌɪnsɪ'kjʊəʳ] adj - **1.** [person] anxieux(euse) - **2.** [job, investment] incertain(e).

insecurity [ˌɪnsɪ'kjʊərətɪ] n insécurité f.

insensible [ɪn'sensəbl] adj - **1.** [unconscious] inconscient(e) - **2.** [unaware, not feeling] : ~ of/to insensible à.

insensitive [ɪn'sensətɪv] adj : ~ (to) insensible (à).

insensitivity [ɪnˌsensə'tɪvətɪ] n insensibilité f.

inseparable [ɪn'seprəbl] adj inséparable.

insert [vb ɪn'sɜːt, n 'ɪnsɜːt] ⬦ vt : to ~ sthg (in OR into) insérer qqch (dans) ⬦ n [in newspaper] encart m.

insertion [ɪn'sɜːʃn] n insertion f.

in-service training n Br formation f en cours d'emploi.

inset ['ɪnset] n encadré m.

inshore [adj 'ɪnʃɔːʳ, adv ɪn'ʃɔːʳ] ⬦ adj côtier(ère) ⬦ adv [be situated] près de la côte ; [move] vers la côte.

inside [ɪn'saɪd] ⬦ prep - **1.** [building, object] à l'intérieur de, dans ; [group, organization] au sein de - **2.** [time] : ~ three weeks en moins de trois semaines ⬦ adv - **1.** [gen] dedans, à l'intérieur ; to go ~ entrer ; come ~! entrez! - **2.** prison sl en taule ⬦ adj intérieur(e) ⬦ n - **1.** [interior] : the ~ l'intérieur m ; ~ out [clothes] à l'envers ; to know sthg ~ out connaître qqch à fond - **2.** AUT : the ~ [in UK] la gauche ; [in Europe, US etc] la droite.
➤ **insides** npl inf tripes fpl.
➤ **inside of** prep Am [building, object] à l'intérieur de, dans.

inside information n (U) renseignements mpl obtenus à la source.

inside job n inf coup m monté de l'intérieur.

inside lane n AUT [in UK] voie f de gauche ; [in Europe, US etc] voie de droite.

insider [,ɪn'saɪdəʳ] n initié m, -e f.

insider dealing, insider trading n (U) délits mpl d'initiés.

inside story n : I got the ~ from his wife j'ai appris la vérité sur cette affaire par sa femme.

insidious [ɪn'sɪdɪəs] adj insidieux(euse).

insight ['ɪnsaɪt] n - **1.** [wisdom] sagacité f, perspicacité f - **2.** [glimpse] : ~ (into) aperçu m (de).

insignia [ɪn'sɪgnɪə] (pl inv) n insigne m.

insignificance [,ɪnsɪg'nɪfɪkəns] n insignifiance f.

insignificant [,ɪnsɪg'nɪfɪkənt] adj insignifiant(e).

insincere [,ɪnsɪn'sɪəʳ] adj pas sincère.

insincerity [,ɪnsɪn'serətɪ] n manque m de sincérité.

insinuate [ɪn'sɪnjʊeɪt] vt insinuer, laisser entendre.

insinuation [ɪn,sɪnjʊ'eɪʃn] n insinuation f.

insipid [ɪn'sɪpɪd] adj insipide.

insist [ɪn'sɪst] ⋄ vt - **1.** [claim] : to ~ (that) ... insister sur le fait que ... - **2.** [demand] : to ~ (that) ... insister pour que (+ subjunctive) ... ⋄ vi : to ~ (on sthg) exiger (qqch) ; to ~ on doing sthg tenir à faire qqch, vouloir absolument faire qqch.

insistence [ɪn'sɪstəns] n : ~ (on) insistance f (à).

insistent [ɪn'sɪstənt] adj - **1.** [determined] insistant(e) ; to be ~ on insister sur - **2.** [continual] incessant(e).

in situ [,ɪn'sɪtjuː] adv in situ.

insofar [,ɪnsəʊ'fɑːʳ] ▸ insofar as conj dans la mesure où.

insole ['ɪnsəʊl] n semelle f intérieure.

insolence ['ɪnsələns] n insolence f.

insolent ['ɪnsələnt] adj insolent(e).

insoluble Br [ɪn'sɒljʊbl], **insolvable** Am [ɪn'sɒlvəbl] adj insoluble.

insolvency [ɪn'sɒlvənsɪ] n insolvabilité f.

insolvent [ɪn'sɒlvənt] adj insolvable.

insomnia [ɪn'sɒmnɪə] n insomnie f.

insomniac [ɪn'sɒmnɪæk] n insomniaque mf.

insomuch [,ɪnsəʊ'mʌtʃ] ▸ insomuch as conj d'autant que.

inspect [ɪn'spekt] vt - **1.** [letter, person] examiner - **2.** [factory, troops etc] inspecter.

inspection [ɪn'spekʃn] n - **1.** [investigation] examen m - **2.** [official check] inspection f.

inspector [ɪn'spektəʳ] n inspecteur m, -trice f.

inspector of taxes n inspecteur m, -trice f des impôts.

inspiration [,ɪnspə'reɪʃn] n inspiration f.

inspire [ɪn'spaɪəʳ] vt : to ~ sb to do sthg pousser OR encourager qqn à faire qqch ; to ~ sb with sthg, to ~ sthg in sb inspirer qqch à qqn.

inspired [ɪn'spaɪəd] adj - **1.** [artist, performance] inspiré(e) - **2.** [guess, idea] brillant(e).

inspiring [ɪn'spaɪərɪŋ] adj qui inspire.

inst. (abbr of instant) : on the 4th ~ le 4 courant.

instability [,ɪnstə'bɪlətɪ] n instabilité f.

install Br, **instal** Am [ɪn'stɔːl] vt - **1.** [fit] installer - **2.** [appoint] : to ~ sb (as sthg) nommer qqn (qqch) - **3.** [settle] : to ~ o.s. s'installer.

installation [,ɪnstə'leɪʃn] n installation f.

installment Am = instalment.

installment plan n Am achat m à crédit.

instalment Br, **installment** Am [ɪn'stɔːlmənt] n - **1.** [payment] acompte m ; in ~s par acomptes - **2.** [episode] épisode m.

instance ['ɪnstəns] n exemple m ; for ~ par exemple ; in the first ~ en premier lieu.

instant ['ɪnstənt] ⋄ adj - **1.** [immediate] instantané(e), immédiat(e) - **2.** [coffee] soluble ; [food] à préparation rapide ⋄ n instant m ; the ~ (that) ... dès OR aussitôt que ... ; this ~ tout de suite, immédiatement.

instantaneous [,ɪnstən'teɪnjəs] adj instantané(e).

instantly ['ɪnstəntlɪ] adv immédiatement.

instead [ɪn'sted] adv au lieu de cela.
▸ **instead of** prep au lieu de ; ~ of him à sa place.

instep ['ɪnstep] n cou-de-pied m.

instigate ['ɪnstɪgeɪt] vt être à l'origine de, entreprendre.

instigation [,ɪnstɪ'geɪʃn] n : at the ~ of à l'instigation f de.

instigator ['ɪnstɪgeɪtəʳ] n instigateur m, -trice f.

instil Br (pt & pp -led ; cont -ling), **instill** Am (pt & pp -ed ; cont -ing) [ɪn'stɪl] vt : to ~ sthg in OR into sb instiller qqch à qqn.

instinct ['ɪnstɪŋkt] n - **1.** [intuition] instinct m - **2.** [impulse] réaction f, mouvement m.

instinctive [ɪn'stɪŋktɪv] adj instinctif(ive).

instinctively [ɪn'stɪŋktɪvlɪ] *adv* instinctive-ment.

institute ['ɪnstɪtjuːt] ⬦ *n* institut *m* ⬦ *vt* instituer.

institution [ˌɪnstɪ'tjuːʃn] *n* institution *f*.

institutional [ˌɪnstɪ'tjuːʃənl] *adj* institution-nel(elle) ; **pej** [food] d'internat.

institutionalized, -ised [ˌɪnstɪ'tjuː-ʃnəˌlaɪzd] *adj* - **1.** **pej** [person] influencé(e) par la vie en collectivité - **2.** [established] institu-tionnalisé(e).

instruct [ɪn'strʌkt] *vt* - **1.** [tell, order] : **to ~ sb to do sthg** charger qqn de faire qqch - **2.** [teach] instruire ; **to ~ sb in sthg** enseigner qqch à qqn.

instruction [ɪn'strʌkʃn] *n* instruction *f*.
➡ **instructions** *npl* mode *m* d'emploi, ins-tructions *fpl*.

instruction manual *n* manuel *m*.

instructive [ɪn'strʌktɪv] *adj* instructif(ive).

instructor [ɪn'strʌktəʳ] *n* - **1.** [gen] instruc-teur *m*, -trice *f*, moniteur *m*, -trice *f* - **2.** Am **SCH** enseignant *m*, -e *f*.

instructress [ɪn'strʌktrɪs] *n* instructrice *f*, monitrice *f*.

instrument ['ɪnstrʊmənt] *n* lit & fig instru-ment *m*.

instrumental [ˌɪnstrʊ'mentl] ⬦ *adj* - **1.** [im-portant, helpful] : **to be ~ in** contribuer à - **2.** [mu-sic] instrumental(e) ⬦ *n* morceau *m* instru-mental.

instrumentalist [ˌɪnstrʊ'mentəlɪst] *n* ins-trumentiste *mf*.

instrument panel *n* tableau *m* de bord.

insubordinate [ˌɪnsə'bɔːdɪnət] *adj* insubor-donné(e).

insubordination ['ɪnsəˌbɔːdɪ'neɪʃn] *n* insu-bordination *f*.

insubstantial [ˌɪnsəb'stænʃl] *adj* [structure] peu solide ; [meal] peu substantiel(elle).

insufferable [ɪn'sʌfərəbl] *adj* **fml** insuppor-table.

insufficient [ˌɪnsə'fɪʃnt] *adj* **fml** insuffi-sant(e)

insular ['ɪnsjʊləʳ] *adj* [outlook] borné(e) ; [person] à l'esprit étroit.

insulate ['ɪnsjʊleɪt] *vt* - **1.** [loft, cable] isoler ; [hot water tank] calorifuger - **2.** [protect] : **to ~ sb against OR from sthg** protéger qqn de qqch.

insulating tape ['ɪnsjʊleɪtɪŋ-] *n* Br chatter-ton *m*.

insulation [ˌɪnsjʊ'leɪʃn] *n* isolation *f*.

insulin ['ɪnsjʊlɪn] *n* insuline *f*.

insult [*vt* ɪn'sʌlt, *n* 'ɪnsʌlt] ⬦ *vt* insulter, inju-

rier ⬦ *n* insulte *f*, injure *f* ; **to add ~ to injury** aggraver les choses.

insulting [ɪn'sʌltɪŋ] *adj* insultant(e), inju-rieux(euse).

insuperable [ɪn'suːprəbl] *adj* **fml** insurmon-table.

insurance [ɪn'ʃʊərəns] ⬦ *n* - **1.** [against fire, ac-cident, theft] assurance *f* - **2.** fig [safeguard, protec-tion] protection *f*, garantie *f* ⬦ *comp* [compa-ny, agent] d'assurances ; [certificate] d'assu-rance.

insurance broker *n* courtier *m* d'assu-rances.

insurance policy *n* police *f* d'assurance.

insurance premium *n* prime *f* d'assu-rance.

insure [ɪn'ʃʊəʳ] ⬦ *vt* - **1.** [against fire, accident, theft] : **to ~ sb/sthg against sthg** assurer qqn/qqch contre qqch - **2.** Am [make certain] s'assu-rer ⬦ *vi* [prevent] : **to ~ against** se protéger de.

insured [ɪn'ʃʊəd] ⬦ *adj* - **1.** [against fire, accident, theft] : **~ (against OR for sthg)** assuré(e) (con-tre qqch) - **2.** Am [certain] certain(e), sûr(e) ⬦ *n* : **the ~** l'assuré *f*.

insurer [ɪn'ʃʊərəʳ] *n* assureur *m*.

insurgent [ɪn'sɜːdʒənt] *n* insurgé *m*, -e *f*.

insurmountable [ˌɪnsə'maʊntəbl] *adj* **fml** in-surmontable.

insurrection [ˌɪnsə'rekʃn] *n* insurrection *f*.

intact [ɪn'tækt] *adj* intact(e).

intake ['ɪnteɪk] *n* - **1.** [amount consumed] con-sommation *f* - **2.** [people recruited] admission *f* - **3.** [inlet] prise *f*, arrivée *f*.

intangible [ɪn'tændʒəbl] *adj* intangible, im-palpable ; [proof] non tangible.

integral ['ɪntɪgrəl] *adj* intégral(e) ; **to be ~ to sthg** faire partie intégrante de qqch.

integrate ['ɪntɪgreɪt] ⬦ *vi* s'intégrer ; **to ~ with OR into sthg** s'intégrer dans qqch ⬦ *vt* intégrer ; **to ~ sb/sthg with sthg, to ~ sb/sthg into sthg** intégrer qqn/qqch dans qqch.

integrated ['ɪntɪgreɪtɪd] *adj* intégré(e).

integrated circuit *n* circuit *m* intégré.

integration [ˌɪntɪ'greɪʃn] *n* : **~ (with/into)** in-tégration *f* (à/dans).

integrity [ɪn'tegrətɪ] *ṅ* - **1.** [honour] intégrité *f*, honnêteté *f* - **2.** **fml** [wholeness] intégrité *f*, to-talité *f*.

intellect ['ɪntəlekt] *n* - **1.** [ability to think] intel-lect *m* - **2.** [cleverness] intelligence *f*.

intellectual [ˌɪntə'lektjʊəl] ⬦ *adj* intellec-tuel(elle) ⬦ *n* intellectuel *m*, -elle *f*.

intellectualize

intellectualize, -ise [ˌɪntə'lektjuəlaɪz] *vt* intellectualiser.

intelligence [ɪn'telɪdʒəns] *n* (U) - **1.** [ability to think] intelligence *f* - **2.** [information service] service *m* de renseignements - **3.** [information] informations *fpl*, renseignements *mpl*.

intelligence quotient *n* quotient *m* intellectuel.

intelligence test *n* test *m* d'aptitude intellectuelle.

intelligent [ɪn'telɪdʒənt] *adj* intelligent(e).

intelligent card *n* carte *f* à puce OR à mémoire.

intelligently [ɪn'telɪdʒəntlɪ] *adv* intelligemment, avec intelligence.

intelligentsia [ɪn,telɪ'dʒentsɪə] *n* : **the ~** l'intelligentsia *f*.

intelligible [ɪn'telɪdʒəbl] *adj* intelligible.

intemperate [ɪn'tempərət] *adj* fml immodéré(e).

intend [ɪn'tend] *vt* [mean] avoir l'intention de ; **it was ~ed as advice** je voulais/il voulait juste donner des conseils ; **it wasn't ~ed as criticism** je n'ai pas/il n'a pas dit pour critiquer ; **to be ~ed for** être destiné à ; **to be ~ed to do sthg** être destiné à faire qqch, viser à faire qqch ; **to ~ doing** OR **to do sthg** avoir l'intention de faire qqch.

intended [ɪn'tendɪd] *adj* [result] voulu(e) ; [victim] visé(e).

intense [ɪn'tens] *adj* - **1.** [gen] intense - **2.** [serious - person] sérieux(euse).

intensely [ɪn'tenslɪ] *adv* - **1.** [irritating, boring] extrêmement ; [suffer] énormément - **2.** [look] intensément.

intensify [ɪn'tensɪfaɪ] (*pt & pp* -**ied**) ⇔ *vt* intensifier, augmenter ⇔ *vi* s'intensifier.

intensity [ɪn'tensətɪ] *n* intensité *f*.

intensive [ɪn'tensɪv] *adj* intensif(ive).

intensive care *n* : **to be in ~** être en réanimation.

intensive care unit *n* service *m* de réanimation, unité *f* de soins intensifs.

intent [ɪn'tent] ⇔ *adj* - **1.** [absorbed] absorbé(e) - **2.** [determined] : **to be ~ on** OR **upon doing sthg** être résolu(e) OR décidé(e) à faire qqch ⇔ *n* fml intention *f*, dessein *m* ; **to all ~s and purposes** pratiquement, virtuellement.

intention [ɪn'tenʃn] *n* intention *f*.

intentional [ɪn'tenʃənl] *adj* intentionnel(elle), voulu(e).

intentionally [ɪn'tenʃənəlɪ] *adv* intentionnellement ; **I didn't do it ~** je ne l'ai pas fait exprès.

intently [ɪn'tentlɪ] *adv* avec attention, attentivement.

inter [ɪn'tɜːʳ] (*pt & pp* -**red** ; *cont* -**ring**) *vt* fml enterrer.

interact [ˌɪntər'ækt] *vi* - **1.** [communicate, work together] : **to ~ (with sb)** communiquer (avec qqn) - **2.** [react] : **to ~ (with sthg)** interagir (avec qqch).

interaction [ˌɪntər'ækʃn] *n* interaction *f*.

interactive [ˌɪntər'æktɪv] *adj* COMPUT interactif(ive).

intercede [ˌɪntə'siːd] *vi* fml : **to ~ (with sb)** intercéder (auprès de qqn).

intercept [ˌɪntə'sept] *vt* intercepter.

interception [ˌɪntə'sepʃn] *n* interception *f*.

interchange [*n* 'ɪntətʃeɪndʒ, *vb* ˌɪntə'tʃeɪndʒ] ⇔ *n* - **1.** [exchange] échange *m* - **2.** [road junction] échangeur *m* ⇔ *vt* échanger.

interchangeable [ˌɪntə'tʃeɪndʒəbl] *adj* : **~ (with)** interchangeable (avec).

intercity [ˌɪntə'sɪtɪ] ⇔ *adj* Br interurbain(e) ⇔ *n* système de trains rapides reliant les grandes villes en Grande-Bretagne ; **Intercity 125**® train rapide pouvant rouler à 125 miles (200 km) à l'heure.

intercom ['ɪntəkɒm] *n* Interphone® *m* ; **on** OR **over the ~** à l'Interphone®.

interconnect [ˌɪntəkə'nekt] *vi* : **to ~ (with)** être relié(e) (à), être connecté(e) (à).

intercontinental ['ɪntə,kɒntɪ'nentl] *adj* intercontinental(e).

intercontinental ballistic missile *n* missile *m* balistique intercontinental.

intercourse ['ɪntəkɔːs] *n* (U) [sexual] rapports *mpl* (sexuels).

interdenominational ['ɪntədɪ,nɒmɪ'neɪʃənl] *adj* interconfessionnel(elle).

interdepartmental ['ɪntə,diːpɑːt'mentl] *adj* entre services ; [in government] entre départements.

interdependent [ˌɪntədɪ'pendənt] *adj* interdépendant(e).

interdict ['ɪntədɪkt] *n* - **1.** JUR interdiction *f* - **2.** RELIG interdit *m*.

interest ['ɪntrəst] ⇔ *n* - **1.** [gen] intérêt *m* ; **to have an ~ in** s'intéresser à ; **to lose ~** se désintéresser ; **in the ~s of** dans l'intérêt de - **2.** [hobby] centre *m* d'intérêt - **3.** (U) FIN intérêt *m*, intérêts *mpl* ⇔ *vt* intéresser ; **to ~ sb in sthg** [arouse interest] intéresser qqn à qqch ; **can I ~ you in a drink?** je peux vous offrir un verre?

interested ['ɪntrəstɪd] *adj* intéressé(e) ; **to be ~ in** s'intéresser à ; **I'm not ~ in that** cela ne m'intéresse pas ; **to be ~ in doing sthg** avoir envie de faire qqch.

interest-free *adj* FIN sans intérêt.

interesting ['ɪntrəstɪŋ] *adj* intéressant(e).

interest rate *n* taux *m* d'intérêt.

interface [*n* 'ɪntəfeɪs , *vb* ,ɪntə'feɪs] ◇ *n* - **1.** COMPUT interface *f* - **2.** fig [junction] rapports *mpl*, relations *fpl* ◇ *vt* COMPUT interfacer.

interfere [,ɪntə'fɪə'] *vi* - **1.** [meddle] : **to ~ in sthg** s'immiscer dans qqch, se mêler de qqch ; **don't ~!** ne t'en mêle pas! - **2.** [damage] : **to ~ with sthg** gêner OR contrarier qqch ; [routine] déranger qqch.

interference [,ɪntə'fɪərəns] *n (U)* - **1.** [meddling] : **~ (with** OR **in)** ingérence *f* (dans), intrusion *f* (dans) - **2.** TELEC parasites *mpl*.

interfering [,ɪntə'fɪərɪŋ] *adj* pej qui se mêle de tout.

intergalactic [,ɪntəgə'læktɪk] *adj* intergalactique.

interim ['ɪntərɪm] ◇ *adj* provisoire ◇ *n* : **in the ~** dans l'intérim, entre-temps.

interior [ɪn'tɪərɪə'] ◇ *adj* - **1.** [inner] intérieur(e) - **2.** POL de l'Intérieur ◇ *n* intérieur *m*.

interior decorator *n* décorateur *m*, -trice *f*.

interior designer *n* architecte *mf* d'intérieur.

interject [,ɪntə'dʒekt] ◇ *vt* - **1.** [add] lancer - **2.** [interrupt] interrompre ◇ *vi* interrompre, lancer une remarque.

interjection [,ɪntə'dʒekʃn] *n* - **1.** [remark] interruption *f* - **2.** GRAMM interjection *f*.

interleave [,ɪntə'liːv] *vt* : **to ~ sthg with sthg** interfolier qqch avec qqch.

interlock [,ɪntə'lɒk] ◇ *vi* [gears] s'enclencher, s'engrener ; [fingers] s'entrelacer ◇ *vt* [gears] enclencher, engrener ; [fingers] entrelacer.

interloper ['ɪntələʊpə'] *n* intrus *m*, -e *f*.

interlude ['ɪntəluːd] *n* - **1.** [pause] intervalle *m* - **2.** [interval] interlude *m*.

intermarry [,ɪntə'mærɪ] (*pt* & *pp* -**ied**) *vi* : **to ~ (with)** se marier (avec).

intermediary [,ɪntə'miːdjərɪ] (*pl* -ies) *n* intermédiaire *mf*.

intermediate [,ɪntə'miːdjət] *adj* - **1.** [transitional] intermédiaire - **2.** [post-beginner - level] moyen(enne) ; [- student, group] de niveau moyen.

interminable [ɪn'tɜːmɪnəbl] *adj* interminable, sans fin.

intermingle [,ɪntə'mɪŋgl] *vi* : **to ~ with sb** se

mêler à qqn ; **to ~ with sthg** se mélanger avec qqch.

intermission [,ɪntə'mɪʃn] *n* entracte *m*.

intermittent [,ɪntə'mɪtənt] *adj* intermittent(e).

intern [*vb* ɪn'tɜːn, *n* 'ɪntɜːn] ◇ *vt* interner ◇ *n* Am [gen] stagiaire *mf* ; MED interne *mf*.

internal [ɪn'tɜːnl] *adj* - **1.** [gen] interne - **2.** [within country] intérieur(e).

internal-combustion engine *n* moteur *m* à combustion interne.

internally [ɪn'tɜːnəlɪ] *adv* - **1.** [within the body] : **to bleed ~** faire une hémorragie interne - **2.** [within country] à l'intérieur - **3.** [within organization] intérieurement.

Internal Revenue *n* Am : **the ~** ≃ le fisc.

international [,ɪntə'næʃənl] ◇ *adj* international(e) ◇ *n* Br SPORT - **1.** [match] match *m* international - **2.** [player] international *m*, -e *f*.

international date line *n* : **the ~** la ligne de changement de date.

internationally [,ɪntə'næʃnəlɪ] *adv* dans le monde entier.

International Monetary Fund *n* : **the ~** le Fonds monétaire international.

international relations *npl* relations *fpl* internationales.

internecine [Br ,ɪntə'niːsaɪn, Am ɪntər'niːsn] *adj* fml intestin(e).

internee [,ɪntɜː'niː] *n* interné *m*, -e *f* politique.

internet, Internet ['ɪntənet] *n* : **the ~** l'Internet *m*.

internet café, Internet café *n* cybercafé *m*.

Internet Service Provider *n* fournisseur *m* d'accès.

internment [ɪn'tɜːnmənt] *n* internement *m* politique.

interpersonal [,ɪntə'pɜːsənl] *adj* de personne à personne, entre personnes ; [skills] de communication.

interplay ['ɪntəpleɪ] *n* : **~ (of/between)** interaction *f* (de/entre).

Interpol ['ɪntəpɒl] *n* Interpol *m*.

interpolate [ɪn'tɜːpəleɪt] *vt* fml - **1.** [add] : **to ~ sthg (into)** ajouter qqch (à) - **2.** [interrupt] interrompre.

interpose [,ɪntə'pəʊz] *vt* fml - **1.** [add] ajouter - **2.** [interrupt] interrompre.

interpret [ɪn'tɜːprɪt] ◇ *vt* : **to ~ sthg (as)** interpréter qqch (comme) ◇ *vi* [translate] faire l'interprète.

interpretation [ɪnˌtɜːprɪ'teɪʃn] n interprétation f.

interpreter [ɪn'tɜːprɪtəʳ] n interprète mf.

interpreting [ɪn'tɜːprɪtɪŋ] n [occupation] interprétariat m.

interracial [ˌɪntə'reɪʃl] adj entre des races différentes, racial(e).

interrelate [ˌɪntərɪ'leɪt] ◇ vt mettre en corrélation ◇ vi : to ~ (with) être lié(e) (à), être en corrélation (avec).

interrogate [ɪn'terəgeɪt] vt interroger.

interrogation [ɪnˌterə'geɪʃn] n interrogatoire m.

interrogation mark n Am point m d'interrogation.

interrogative [ˌɪntə'rɒgətɪv] GRAMM ◇ adj interrogatif(ive) ◇ n interrogatif m.

interrogator [ɪn'terəgeɪtəʳ] n interrogateur m, -trice f.

interrupt [ˌɪntə'rʌpt] ◇ vt interrompre ; [calm] rompre ◇ vi interrompre.

interruption [ˌɪntə'rʌpʃn] n interruption f.

intersect [ˌɪntə'sekt] ◇ vi s'entrecroiser, s'entrecouper ◇ vt croiser, couper.

intersection [ˌɪntə'sekʃn] n [in road] croisement m, carrefour m.

intersperse [ˌɪntə'spɜːs] vt : to be ~d with être émaillé(e) de, être entremêlé(e) de.

interstate (highway) ['ɪntəsteɪt-] n Am autoroute f.

interval ['ɪntəvl] n - 1. [gen] intervalle m ; at ~s par intervalles ; at monthly/yearly ~s tous les mois/ans - 2. Br [at play, concert] entracte m.

intervene [ˌɪntə'viːn] vi - 1. [person, police] : to ~ (in) intervenir (dans), s'interposer (dans) - 2. [event, war, strike] survenir - 3. [time] s'écouler.

intervening [ˌɪntə'viːnɪŋ] adj [period] qui s'est écoulé(e).

intervention [ˌɪntə'venʃn] n intervention f.

interventionist [ˌɪntə'venʃənɪst] ◇ adj interventionniste ◇ n interventionniste mf.

interview ['ɪntəvjuː] ◇ n - 1. [for job] entrevue f, entretien m - 2. PRESS interview f ◇ vt - 1. [for job] faire passer une entrevue OR un entretien à - 2. PRESS interviewer.

interviewee [ˌɪntəvjuː'iː] n - 1. [for job] candidat m, -e f - 2. PRESS interviewé m, -e f.

interviewer ['ɪntəvjuːəʳ] n - 1. [for job] personne f qui fait passer une entrevue - 2. PRESS interviewer m.

interweave [ˌɪntə'wiːv] (pt -wove ; pp -woven) fig ◇ vt entremêler ◇ vi s'entremêler.

intestate [ɪn'testeɪt] adj : to die ~ mourir intestat.

intestine [ɪn'testɪn] n intestin m.
➡ **intestines** npl intestins mpl.

intimacy ['ɪntɪməsɪ] (pl -ies) n - 1. [closeness] : ~ (between/with) intimité f (entre/avec) - 2. [intimate remark] familiarité f.

intimate [adj n 'ɪntɪmət, vb 'ɪntɪmeɪt] ◇ adj - 1. [gen] intime - 2. fml [sexually] : to be ~ with sb avoir des rapports intimes avec qqn - 3. [detailed - knowledge] approfondi(e) ◇ n fml intime mf ◇ vt fml faire savoir, faire connaître.

intimately ['ɪntɪmətlɪ] adv - 1. [very closely] étroitement - 2. [as close friends] intimement - 3. [in detail] à fond.

intimation [ˌɪntɪ'meɪʃn] n fml signe m, indication f.

intimidate [ɪn'tɪmɪdeɪt] vt intimider.

intimidation [ɪnˌtɪmɪ'deɪʃn] n intimidation f.

into ['ɪntʊ] prep - 1. [inside] dans - 2. [against] : to bump ~ sthg se cogner contre qqch ; to crash ~ rentrer dans - 3. [referring to change in state] en ; to translate sthg ~ Spanish traduire qqch en espagnol - 4. [concerning] : research/investigation ~ recherche/enquête sur - 5. MATH : 3 ~ 2 2 divisé par 3 - 6. inf [interested in] : to be ~ sthg être passionné(e) par qqch.

intolerable [ɪn'tɒlrəbl] adj intolérable, insupportable.

intolerance [ɪn'tɒlərəns] n intolérance f.

intolerant [ɪn'tɒlərənt] adj intolérant(e) ; to be ~ of faire preuve d'intolérance à l'égard de.

intonation [ˌɪntə'neɪʃn] n intonation f.

intone [ɪn'təʊn] vt psalmodier.

intoxicated [ɪn'tɒksɪkeɪtɪd] adj - 1. [drunk] ivre - 2. fig [excited] : to be ~ with sthg être grisé(e) OR enivré(e) par qqch.

intoxicating [ɪn'tɒksɪkeɪtɪŋ] adj - 1. [alcoholic] alcoolisé(e) - 2. fig [exciting] grisant(e), enivrant(e).

intoxication [ɪnˌtɒksɪ'keɪʃn] n - 1. [drunkenness] ivresse f - 2. [excitement] griserie f, ivresse f.

intractable [ɪn'træktəbl] adj - 1. [stubborn] intraitable - 2. [insoluble] insoluble.

intranet, Intranet ['ɪntrənet] n intranet m.

intransigent [ɪn'trænzɪdʒənt] adj intransigeant(e).

intransitive [ɪn'trænzətɪv] adj intransitif(ive).

intrauterine device [ˌɪntrə'juːtəraɪn] n stérilet *m*, dispositif *m* anticonceptionnel intra-utérin.

intravenous [ˌɪntrə'viːnəs] *adj* intraveineux(euse).

in-tray *n* casier *m* des affaires à traiter.

intrepid [ɪn'trepɪd] *adj* intrépide.

intricacy ['ɪntrɪkəsɪ] (*pl* **-ies**) *n* complexité *f*.

intricate ['ɪntrɪkət] *adj* compliqué(e).

intrigue [ɪn'triːg] ⬦ *n* intrigue *f* ⬦ *vt* intriguer, exciter la curiosité de ⬦ *vi*: **to ~ against** intriguer OR comploter contre.

intriguing [ɪn'triːgɪŋ] *adj* fascinant(e).

intrinsic [ɪn'trɪnsɪk] *adj* intrinsèque.

intro ['ɪntrəʊ] (*pl* **-s**) *n* inf introduction *f*.

introduce [ˌɪntrə'djuːs] *vt* - **1.** [present] présenter ; **to ~ sb to sb** présenter qqn à qqn - **2.** [bring in] : **to ~ sthg (to** OR **into)** introduire qqch (dans) - **3.** [allow to experience] : **to ~ sb to sthg** initier qqn à qqch, faire découvrir qqch à qqn - **4.** [signal beginning of] annoncer.

introduction [ˌɪntrə'dʌkʃn] *n* - **1.** [in book, of new method etc] introduction *f* - **2.** [first experience] : **~ to sthg** premier contact *m* avec qqch - **3.** [of people] : **~ (to sb)** présentation *f* (à qqn).

introductory [ˌɪntrə'dʌktrɪ] *adj* d'introduction, préliminaire.

introspective [ˌɪntrə'spektɪv] *adj* introspectif(ive).

introvert ['ɪntrəvɜːt] *n* introverti *m*, -e *f*.

introverted ['ɪntrəvɜːtɪd] *adj* introverti(e).

intrude [ɪn'truːd] *vi* faire intrusion ; **to ~ on sb** déranger qqn.

intruder [ɪn'truːdə'] *n* intrus *m*, -e *f*.

intrusion [ɪn'truːʒn] *n* intrusion *f*.

intrusive [ɪn'truːsɪv] *adj* gênant(e), importun(e).

intuition [ˌɪntjuː'ɪʃn] *n* intuition *f*.

intuitive [ɪn'tjuːɪtɪv] *adj* intuitif(ive).

Inuit ['ɪnʊɪt] ⬦ *adj* inuit (*inv*) ⬦ *n* Inuit *mf* *inv*.

inundate ['ɪnʌndeɪt] *vt* - **1.** fml [flood] inonder - **2.** [overwhelm] : **to be ~d with** être submergé(e) de.

inured [ɪ'njʊəd] *adj* fml : **to be ~ to sthg** être aguerri(e) à qqch, être endurci(e) à qqch ; **to become ~ to sthg** s'aguerrir à qqch, s'endurcir à qqch.

invade [ɪn'veɪd] *vt* - **1.** MIL & fig envahir - **2.** [disturb - privacy etc] violer.

invader [ɪn'veɪdə'] *n* envahisseur *m*, -euse *f*.

invading [ɪn'veɪdɪŋ] *adj* [troops] d'invasion.

invalid [*adj* ɪn'vælɪd, *n vb* 'ɪnvəlɪd] ⬦ *adj* - **1.** [illegal, unacceptable] non valide, non valable - **2.** [not reasonable] non valable ⬦ *n* invalide *mf*.

⬦ **invalid out** *vt sep* : **to be ~ed out of the army** être réformé(e) pour raisons de santé.

invalidate [ɪn'vælɪdeɪt] *vt* invalider, annuler.

invalid chair ['ɪnvəlɪd-] *n* fauteuil *m* roulant.

invaluable [ɪn'væljʊəbl] *adj* : **~ (to)** [help, advice, person] précieux(euse) (pour) ; [experience, information] inestimable (pour).

invariable [ɪn'veərɪəbl] *adj* invariable.

invariably [ɪn'veərɪəblɪ] *adv* invariablement, toujours.

invasion [ɪn'veɪʒn] *n* lit & fig invasion *f*.

invective [ɪn'vektɪv] *n* (U) invectives *fpl*.

inveigle [ɪn'veɪgl] *vt* : **to ~ sb into sthg** attirer qqn dans qqch par la ruse ; **to ~ sb into doing sthg** amener qqn à faire qqch (par la ruse), persuader qqn de faire qqch (par la ruse).

invent [ɪn'vent] *vt* inventer.

invention [ɪn'venʃn] *n* invention *f*.

inventive [ɪn'ventɪv] *adj* inventif(ive).

inventor [ɪn'ventə'] *n* inventeur *m*, -trice *f*.

inventory ['ɪnvəntrɪ] (*pl* **-ies**) *n* - **1.** [list] inventaire *m* - **2.** Am [goods] stock *m*.

inventory control *n* gestion *f* du stock.

inverse [ɪn'vɜːs] ⬦ *adj* inverse ⬦ *n* inverse *m*, contraire *m*.

invert [ɪn'vɜːt] *vt* retourner.

invertebrate [ɪn'vɜːtɪbreɪt] *n* invertébré *m*.

inverted commas [ɪnˌvɜːtɪd-] *npl* Br guillemets *mpl*.

inverted snob [ɪn'vɜːtɪd-] *n* snob *mf* à l'envers, personne *f* qui fait du snobisme à l'envers.

invest [ɪn'vest] ⬦ *vt* - **1.** [money] : **to ~ sthg (in)** investir qqch (dans) - **2.** [time, energy] : **to ~ sthg in sthg/in doing sthg** consacrer qqch à qqch/à faire qqch, employer qqch à qqch/à faire qqch - **3.** fml [endow] : **to ~ sb with sthg** investir qqn de qqch ⬦ *vi* - **1.** FIN : **to ~ (in sthg)** investir (dans qqch) - **2.** fig [buy] : **to ~ in sthg** se payer qqch, s'acheter qqch.

investigate [ɪn'vestɪgeɪt] ⬦ *vt* enquêter sur, faire une enquête sur ; [subj : scientist] faire des recherches sur ⬦ *vi* faire une enquête.

investigation [ɪnˌvestɪ'geɪʃn] *n* - **1.** [enquiry] : **~ (into)** enquête *f* (sur) ; [scientific] recherches *fpl* (sur) - **2.** (U) [investigating] investigation *f*.

investigative [ɪn'vestɪgətɪv] *adj* d'investigation ; ~ **journalism** journalisme *m* d'enquête OR d'investigation.

investigator [ɪn'vestɪgeɪtəʳ] *n* investigateur *m*, -trice *f*.

investiture [ɪn'vestɪtʃəʳ] *n* investiture *f*.

investment [ɪn'vestmənt] *n* - **1.** FIN investissement *m*, placement *m* - **2.** [of energy] dépense *f*.

investment analyst *n* analyste *mf* en placements.

investment trust *n* société *f* d'investissement.

investor [ɪn'vestəʳ] *n* investisseur *m*.

inveterate [ɪn'vetərət] *adj* invétéré(e).

invidious [ɪn'vɪdɪəs] *adj* [task] ingrat(e) ; [comparison] injuste.

invigilate [ɪn'vɪdʒɪleɪt] Br ◇ *vi* surveiller les candidats (à un examen) ◇ *vt* surveiller.

invigilator [ɪn'vɪdʒɪleɪtəʳ] *n* Br surveillant *m*, -e *f*.

invigorating [ɪn'vɪgəreɪtɪŋ] *adj* tonifiant(e), vivifiant(e).

invincible [ɪn'vɪnsɪbl] *adj* [army, champion] invincible ; [record] imbattable.

inviolate [ɪn'vaɪələt] *adj* literary inviolé(e).

invisible [ɪn'vɪzɪbl] *adj* invisible.

invisible assets *npl* biens *mpl* incorporels.

invisible earnings *npl* revenus *mpl* invisibles.

invisible ink *n* encre *f* sympathique.

invitation [ˌɪnvɪ'teɪʃn] *n* - **1.** [request] invitation *f* - **2.** [encouragement] : **an ~ to sthg/to do sthg** une incitation à qqch/à faire qqch, une invite à qqch/à faire qqch.

invite [ɪn'vaɪt] *vt* - **1.** [ask to come] : **to ~ sb (to)** inviter qqn (à) - **2.** [ask politely] : **to ~ sb to do sthg** inviter qqn à faire qqch - **3.** [ask for] : **the chairman ~d questions** le président a invité l'assistance à poser des questions - **4.** [encourage] : **to ~ trouble** aller au devant des ennuis ; **to ~ gossip** faire causer.

inviting [ɪn'vaɪtɪŋ] *adj* attrayant(e), agréable ; [food] appétissant(e).

in vitro fertilization [ˌɪn'viːtrəʊ-] *n* fécondation *f* in vitro.

invoice ['ɪnvɔɪs] ◇ *n* facture *f* ◇ *vt* - **1.** [client] envoyer la facture à - **2.** [goods] facturer.

invoke [ɪn'vəʊk] *vt* - **1.** fml [law, act] invoquer - **2.** [feelings] susciter, faire naître ; [help] demander, implorer.

involuntary [ɪn'vɒləntrɪ] *adj* involontaire.

involve [ɪn'vɒlv] *vt* - **1.** [entail] nécessiter ; **what's ~d?** de quoi s'agit-il? ; **to ~ doing sthg**

nécessiter de faire qqch - **2.** [concern, affect] toucher ; **to be ~d in an accident** avoir un accident - **3.** [person] : **to ~ sb in sthg** impliquer qqn dans qqch ; **to ~ o.s. in sthg** s'impliquer dans qqch, prendre part à qqch.

involved [ɪn'vɒlvd] *adj* - **1.** [complex] complexe, compliqué(e) - **2.** [participating] : **to be ~ in sthg** participer OR prendre part à qqch - **3.** [in relationship] : **to be ~ with sb** avoir des relations intimes avec qqn ; **he doesn't want to get ~** il ne veut pas s'attacher.

involvement [ɪn'vɒlvmənt] *n* - **1.** [participation] : **~ (in)** participation *f* (à) - **2.** [concern, enthusiasm] : **~ (in)** engagement *m* (dans).

invulnerable [ɪn'vʌlnərəbl] *adj* : **~ (to)** invulnérable (à).

inward ['ɪnwəd] ◇ *adj* - **1.** [inner] intérieur(e) - **2.** [towards the inside] vers l'intérieur ◇ *adv* Am = **inwards**.

inwardly ['ɪnwədlɪ] *adv* intérieurement.

inwards ['ɪnwədz] *adv* vers l'intérieur.

I/O (*abbr of* **input/output**) E/S.

IOC (*abbr of* **International Olympic Committee**) *n* CIO *m*.

iodine [Br 'aɪədiːn, Am 'aɪədaɪn] *n* iode *m*.

IOM *abbr of* **Isle of Man**.

ion ['aɪən] *n* ion *m*.

Ionian Sea [aɪ'əʊnjən-] *n* : **the ~** la mer Ionienne.

iota [aɪ'əʊtə] *n* brin *m*, grain *m*.

IOU (*abbr of* **I owe you**) *n* reconnaissance *f* de dette.

IOW *abbr of* **Isle of Wight**.

Iowa ['aɪəʊə] *n* Iowa *m* ; **in ~** dans l'Iowa.

IPA (*abbr of* **International Phonetic Alphabet**) *n* API *m*.

IQ (*abbr of* **intelligence quotient**) *n* QI *m*.

IRA *n* - **1.** (*abbr of* **Irish Republican Army**) IRA *f* - **2.** (*abbr of* **individual retirement account**) *aux États-Unis, compte d'épargne retraite (à avantages fiscaux)*.

Iran [ɪ'rɑːn] *n* Iran *m* ; **in ~** en Iran.

Iranian [ɪ'reɪnjən] ◇ *adj* iranien(enne) ◇ *n* Iranien *m*, -enne *f*.

Iraq [ɪ'rɑːk] *n* Iraq *m*, Irak *m* ; **in ~** en Iraq.

Iraqi [ɪ'rɑːkɪ] ◇ *adj* iraquien(enne), irakien(enne) ◇ *n* Iraquien *m*, -enne *f*, Irakien *m*, -enne *f*.

irascible [ɪ'ræsəbl] *adj* irascible, coléreux(euse).

irate [aɪ'reɪt] *adj* furieux(euse).

Ireland ['aɪələnd] *n* Irlande *f* ; **in ~** en Irlande ; **the Republic of ~** la République d'Irlande.

iridescent [ˌɪrɪ'desənt] *adj* literary irisé(e) ; [silk] chatoyant(e).

iris ['aɪərɪs] (*pl* -es [-iːzl) *n* iris *m*.

Irish ['aɪrɪʃ] ⬦ *adj* irlandais(e) ⬦ *n* [language] irlandais *m* ⬦ *npl* : **the ~** les Irlandais.

Irish coffee *n* Irish coffee *m*.

Irishman ['aɪrɪʃmən] (*pl* -**men** [-mən]) *n* Irlandais *m*.

Irish Sea *n* : **the ~** la mer d'Irlande.

Irish stew *n* ragoût *m* de viande à l'irlandaise.

Irishwoman ['aɪrɪʃˌwumən] (*pl* -**women** [-ˌwɪmɪn]) *n* Irlandaise *f*.

irk [ɜːk] *vt* ennuyer, contrarier.

irksome ['ɜːksəm] *adj* ennuyeux(euse), assommant(e).

IRN (*abbr of* **Independent Radio News**) *n* agence de presse radiophonique.

IRO (*abbr of* **International Refugee Organization**) *n* organisation humanitaire américaine pour les réfugiés.

iron ['aɪən] ⬦ *adj* - **1.** [made of iron] de OR en fer - **2.** fig [very strict] de fer ⬦ *n* - **1.** [metal, golf club] fer *m* - **2.** [for clothes] fer *m* à repasser ⬦ *vt* repasser.
➡ **iron out** *vt sep* fig [difficulties] aplanir ; [problems] résoudre.

Iron Age *n* : **the ~** l'âge de fer ⬦ *comp* de l'âge de fer.

Iron Curtain *n* : **the ~** le rideau de fer.

ironic(al) [aɪ'rɒnɪk(l)] *adj* ironique.

ironically [aɪ'rɒnɪklɪ] *adv* ironiquement.

ironing ['aɪənɪŋ] *n* repassage *m* ; **to do the ~** faire le repassage.

ironing board *n* planche *f* OR table *f* à repasser.

iron lung *n* poumon *m* d'acier.

ironmonger ['aɪənˌmʌŋgəʳ] *n* Br quincaillier *m* ; **~'s (shop)** quincaillerie *f*.

ironworks ['aɪənwɜːks] (*pl inv*) *n* usine *f* sidérurgique.

irony ['aɪrənɪ] (*pl* -ies) *n* ironie *f*.

irradiate [ɪ'reɪdɪeɪt] *vt* irradier.

irrational [ɪ'ræʃənl] *adj* irrationnel(elle), déraisonnable ; [person] non rationnel(elle).

irreconcilable [ɪˌrekən'saɪləbl] *adj* inconciliable.

irredeemable [ˌɪrɪ'diːməbl] *adj* fml - **1.** [irreplaceable] irréparable - **2.** [hopeless] irrémédiable.

irrefutable [ɪ'refjʊtəbl] *adj* irréfutable.

irregular [ɪ'regjʊləʳ] *adj* irrégulier(ère).

irregularity [ɪˌregjʊ'lærətɪ] (*pl* -ies) *n* irrégularité *f*.

irregularly [ɪ'regjʊləlɪ] *adv* irrégulièrement.

irrelevance [ɪ'reləvəns], **irrelevancy** [ɪ'reləvənsɪ] (*pl* -ies) *n* manque *m* de pertinence.

irrelevant [ɪ'reləvənt] *adj* sans rapport.

irreligious [ˌɪrɪ'lɪdʒəs] *adj* irréligieux(euse).

irremediable [ˌɪrɪ'miːdjəbl] *adj* fml irrémédiable.

irreparable [ɪ'repərəbl] *adj* irréparable.

irreplaceable [ˌɪrɪ'pleɪsəbl] *adj* irremplaçable.

irrepressible [ˌɪrɪ'presəbl] *adj* [enthusiasm] que rien ne peut entamer ; **he's ~** il est d'une bonne humeur à toute épreuve.

irreproachable [ˌɪrɪ'prəʊtʃəbl] *adj* irréprochable.

irresistible [ˌɪrɪ'zɪstəbl] *adj* irrésistible.

irresolute [ɪ'rezəluːt] *adj* irrésolu(e), indécis(e).

irrespective [ˌɪrɪ'spektɪv] ➡ **irrespective of** *prep* sans tenir compte de.

irresponsible [ˌɪrɪ'spɒnsəbl] *adj* irresponsable.

irretrievable [ˌɪrɪ'triːvəbl] *adj* irréparable, irrémédiable.

irreverent [ɪ'revərənt] *adj* irrévérencieux(euse).

irreversible [ˌɪrɪ'vɜːsəbl] *adj* [judgement, decision] irrévocable ; [change, damage] irréversible.

irrevocable [ɪ'revəkəbl] *adj* irrévocable.

irrigate ['ɪrɪgeɪt] *vt* irriguer.

irrigation [ˌɪrɪ'geɪʃn] ⬦ *n* irrigation *f* ⬦ *comp* d'irrigation.

irritable ['ɪrɪtəbl] *adj* irritable.

irritant ['ɪrɪtənt] ⬦ *adj* irritant(e) ⬦ *n* - **1.** [irritating situation] source *f* d'irritation - **2.** [substance] irritant *m*.

irritate ['ɪrɪteɪt] *vt* irriter.

irritating ['ɪrɪteɪtɪŋ] *adj* irritant(e).

irritation [ɪrɪ'teɪʃn] *n* - **1.** [anger, soreness] irritation *f* - **2.** [cause of anger] source *f* d'irritation.

IRS (*abbr of* **Internal Revenue Service**) *n* Am : **the ~** = le fisc.

is [ɪz] ➡ **be**.

ISBN (*abbr of* **International Standard Book Number**) *n* ISBN *m*.

Islam ['ɪzlɑːm] *n* islam *m*.

Islamabad [ɪz'lɑːməbæd] *n* Islamabad.

Islamic [ɪz'læmɪk] *adj* islamique.

island ['aɪlənd] *n* - **1.** [isle] île *f* - **2.** AUT refuge *m* pour piétons.

islander [ˈaɪləndəʳ] n habitant m, -e f d'une île.

isle [aɪl] n île f.

Isle of Man n : the ~ l'île f de Man ; in OR on the ~ à l'île de Man.

Isle of Wight [-waɪt] n : the ~ l'île f de Wight ; on the ~ à l'île de Wight.

isn't [ˈɪznt] = is not.

isobar [ˈaɪsəbɑːʳ] n isobare f.

isolate [ˈaɪsəleɪt] vt : to ~ sb/sthg (from) isoler qqn/qqch (de).

isolated [ˈaɪsəleɪtɪd] adj isolé(e).

isolation [aɪsəˈleɪʃn] n isolement m ; in ~ [alone] dans l'isolement ; [separately] isolément.

isolationism [ˌaɪsəˈleɪʃənɪzm] n isolationnisme m.

isosceles triangle [aɪˈsɒsɪliːz-] n triangle m isocèle.

isotope [ˈaɪsətəʊp] n isotope m.

ISP n abbr of Internet Service Provider.

Israel [ˈɪzreɪəl] n Israël m ; in ~ en Israël.

Israeli [ɪzˈreɪlɪ] <> adj israélien(enne) <> n Israélien m, -enne f.

Israelite [ˈɪzˌrɪəlaɪt] <> adj israélite <> n Israélite mf.

issue [ˈɪʃuː] <> n - 1. [important subject] question f, problème m ; to make an ~ of sthg faire toute une affaire de qqch ; at ~ en question, en cause - 2. [edition] numéro m - 3. [bringing out - of banknotes, shares] émission f <> vt - 1. [make public - decree, statement] faire ; [- warning] lancer - 2. [bring out - banknotes, shares] émettre ; [- book] publier - 3. [passport etc] délivrer ; to ~ sthg to sb, to ~ sb with sthg fournir qqch à qqn <> vi - 1. [smoke, steam] : to ~ from sortir de, s'échapper de - 2. [problems] : to ~ from découler de.

Istanbul [ˌɪstænˈbʊl] n Istanbul.

ISTC (abbr of Iron and Steels Confederation) n syndicat britannique des ouvriers de la sidérurgie.

isthmus [ˈɪsməs] n isthme m.

it [ɪt] pron - 1. [referring to specific person or thing - subj] il (elle) ; [- direct object] le (la), l' (+ vowel or silent 'h') ; [- indirect object] lui ; did you find ~? tu l'as trouvé(e)? ; give ~ to me at once donne-moi ça tout de suite ; give ~ a shake secoue-le - 2. [with prepositions] : in/to/at ~ y ; put the vegetables in ~ mettez-y les légumes ; on ~ dessus ; about ~ en ; under ~ dessous ; beside ~ à côté ; from/of ~ en ; he's very proud of ~ il en est très fier - 3. [impersonal use] il, ce ; ~ is cold today il fait froid aujourd'hui ; ~'s two o'clock il est deux heu-

res ; who is ~? - ~'s Mary/me qui est-ce? - c'est Mary/moi ; ~'s the children who worry me most ce sont les enfants qui m'inquiètent le plus.

IT n abbr of information technology

Italian [ɪˈtæljən] <> adj italien(enne) <> n - 1. [person] Italien m, -enne f - 2. [language] italien m.

italic [ɪˈtælɪk] adj italique.

➡ **italics** npl italiques fpl.

Italy [ˈɪtəlɪ] n Italie f ; in ~ en Italie.

itch [ɪtʃ] <> n démangeaison f <> vi - 1. [be itchy] : my arm ~es mon bras me démange - 2. fig [be impatient] : to be ~ing to do sthg mourir d'envie de faire qqch.

itchy [ˈɪtʃɪ] (compar -ier ; superl -iest) adj qui démange.

it'd [ˈɪtəd] = it would, it had.

item [ˈaɪtəm] n - 1. [gen] chose f, article m ; [on agenda] question f, point m - 2. PRESS article m.

itemize, -ise [ˈaɪtəmaɪz] vt détailler.

itemized bill [ˈaɪtəmaɪzd-] n facture f détaillée.

itinerant [ɪˈtɪnərənt] adj [salesperson] ambulant(e) ; [preacher] itinérant(e).

itinerary [aɪˈtɪnərərɪ] (pl -ies) n itinéraire m.

it'll [ɪtl] = it will.

ITN (abbr of Independent Television News) n service britannique d'actualités télévisées pour les chaînes relevant de l'IBA.

its [ɪts] poss adj son (sa), ses (pl).

it's [ɪts] = it is, it has.

itself [ɪtˈself] pron - 1. (reflexive) se ; (after prep) soi - 2. (for emphasis) lui-même (elle-même) ; in ~ en soi.

ITV (abbr of Independent Television) n sigle désignant les programmes diffusés par les chaînes relevant de l'IBA.

IUCD (abbr of intrauterine contraceptive device) n stérilet m.

IUD (abbr of intrauterine device) n stérilet m.

I've [aɪv] = I have.

IVF (abbr of in vitro fertilization) n FIV f.

ivory [ˈaɪvərɪ] <> adj [ivory-coloured] ivoire (inv) <> n ivoire m <> comp [made of ivory] en ivoire, d'ivoire.

Ivory Coast n : the ~ la Côte-d'Ivoire ; in the ~ en Côte-d'Ivoire.

ivory tower n fig tour f d'ivoire.

ivy [ˈaɪvɪ] n lierre m.

Ivy League n Am les huit grandes universités de l'est des États-Unis.

j (pl **j's** OR **js**), **J** (pl **J's** OR **Js**) [dʒeɪl] n [letter] j m inv, J m inv.

J/A abbr of **joint account**.

jab [dʒæb] (pt & pp **-bed** ; cont **-bing**) ◇ n - **1.** Br inf [injection] piqûre f - **2.** BOXING direct m ◇ vt : **to ~ sthg into** planter OR enfoncer qqch dans ◇ vi : **to ~ at** BOXING envoyer un direct à.

jabber ['dʒæbəʳ] vt & vi baragouiner.

jack [dʒæk] n - **1.** [device] cric m - **2.** [playing card] valet m.

jack in vt sep Br inf laisser tomber, plaquer.

jack up vt sep - **1.** [car] soulever avec un cric - **2.** fig [prices] faire grimper.

jackal ['dʒækəl] n chacal m.

jackdaw ['dʒækdɔːl] n choucas m.

jacket ['dʒækɪt] n - **1.** [garment] veste f - **2.** [of potato] peau f, pelure f - **3.** [of book] jaquette f - **4.** Am [of record] pochette f.

jacket potato n pomme de terre f en robe de chambre.

jackhammer ['dʒæk.hæməʳ] n Am marteau-piqueur m.

jack-in-the-box n diable m qui sort de sa boîte.

jack knife n canif m.

jack-knife vi [lorry] se mettre en travers de la route.

jack-of-all-trades (pl **jacks-of-all-trades**) n touche-à-tout m.

jack plug n jack m.

jackpot ['dʒækpɒt] n gros lot m.

Jacobean [,dʒækə'bɪən] adj de l'époque de Jacques Iᵉʳ.

Jacobite ['dʒækəbaɪt] ◇ adj jacobite ◇ n jacobite mf.

Jacuzzi® [dʒə'kuːzɪ] n Jacuzzi® m, bain m à remous.

jade [dʒeɪd] ◇ adj [jade-coloured] vert (de) jade (inv) ◇ n - **1.** [stone] jade m - **2.** [colour] vert m jade ◇ comp [made of jade] de jade (inv).

jaded ['dʒeɪdɪd] adj blasé(e).

jagged ['dʒægɪd] adj déchiqueté(e), dentelé(e).

jaguar ['dʒægjʊəʳ] n jaguar m.

jail [dʒeɪl] ◇ n prison f ◇ vt emprisonner, mettre en prison.

jailbird ['dʒeɪlbɜːd] n inf taulard m, -e f.

jailbreak ['dʒeɪlbreɪk] n évasion f de prison.

jailer ['dʒeɪləʳ] n geôlier m, -ère f.

Jakarta [dʒə'kɑːtə] n Djakarta, Jakarta.

jam [dʒæm] (pt & pp **-med** ; cont **-ming**) ◇ n - **1.** [preserve] confiture f - **2.** [of traffic] embouteillage m, bouchon m - **3.** inf [difficult situation] : **to get into/be in a ~** se mettre/être dans le pétrin ◇ vt - **1.** [mechanism, door] bloquer, coincer - **2.** [push tightly] : **to ~ sthg into** entasser OR tasser qqch dans ; **to ~ sthg onto** enfoncer qqch sur - **3.** [block - streets] embouteiller ; [- switchboard] surcharger - **4.** RADIO brouiller ◇ vi [lever, door] se coincer ; [brakes] se bloquer.

Jamaica [dʒə'meɪkə] n la Jamaïque ; **in ~** à la Jamaïque.

Jamaican [dʒə'meɪkn] ◇ adj jamaïcain(e), jamaïquain(e) ◇ n Jamaïcain m, -e f, Jamaïquain m, -e f.

jamb [dʒæm] n chambranle m, montant m.

jamboree [,dʒæmbə'riː] n - **1.** [celebration] fête f, festivités fpl - **2.** [gathering of scouts] jamboree m.

jamming ['dʒæmɪŋ] n RADIO brouillage m.

jam-packed [-'pækt] adj inf plein(e) à craquer.

jam session n bœuf m, jam-session f.

Jan. ['dʒæn] (abbr of **January**) janv.

jangle ['dʒæŋgl] ◇ n [of keys] cliquetis m ; [of bells] tintamarre m ◇ vt [keys] faire cliqueter ; [bells] faire retentir ◇ vi [keys] cliqueter ; [bells] retentir.

janitor ['dʒænɪtəʳ] n Am & Scot concierge mf.

January ['dʒænjʊərɪ] n janvier m ; see also **September**.

Japan [dʒə'pæn] n Japon m ; **in ~** au Japon.

Japanese [,dʒæpə'niːz] (pl inv) ◇ adj japonais(e) ◇ n [language] japonais m ◇ npl [people] : **the ~** les Japonais mpl.

jape [dʒeɪp] n dated tour m, farce f.

jar [dʒɑːʳ] (pt & pp **-red** ; cont **-ring**) ◇ n pot m ◇ vt [shake] secouer ◇ vi - **1.** [noise, voice] : **to ~ (on sb)** irriter (qqn), agacer (qqn) - **2.** [colours] jurer.

jargon ['dʒɑːgən] n jargon m.

jarring ['dʒɑːrɪŋ] adj [noise, colours] discordant(e).

Jas. (abbr of **James**) Jacques.

jasmine ['dʒæzmɪn] *n* jasmin *m*.

jaundice ['dʒɔ:ndɪs] *n* jaunisse *f*.

jaundiced ['dʒɔ:ndɪst] *adj fig* [attitude, view] aigri(e).

jaunt [dʒɔ:nt] *n* balade *f*.

jaunty ['dʒɔ:ntɪ] (*compar* **-ier** ; *superl* **-iest**) *adj* désinvolte, insouciant(e).

Java ['dʒɑ:və] *n* Java ; **in ~ à** Java.

javelin ['dʒævlɪn] *n* javelot *m*.

jaw [dʒɔ:] ◇ *n* mâchoire *f* ◇ *vi inf* tailler une bavette.

jawbone ['dʒɔ:bəʊn] *n* (os *m*) maxillaire *m*.

jay [dʒeɪ] *n* geai *m*.

jaywalk ['dʒeɪwɔ:k] *vi* traverser en dehors des clous.

jaywalker ['dʒeɪwɔ:kər] *n* piéton *m* qui traverse en dehors des clous.

jazz [dʒæz] *n* **- 1.** MUS jazz *m* **- 2.** *Am inf* [insincere talk] baratin *m*.

◆ **jazz up** *vt sep inf* égayer.

jazz band *n* orchestre *m* de jazz.

jazz singer *n* chanteur *m*, -euse *f* de jazz.

jazzy ['dʒæzɪ] (*compar* **-ier** ; *superl* **-iest**) *adj* [bright] voyant(e).

JCR (*abbr of* **junior common room**) *n* salle des étudiants.

JCS *n abbr of* **Joint Chiefs of Staff**.

JD (*abbr of* **Justice Department**) *n* ministère américain de la Justice.

jealous ['dʒeləs] *adj* jaloux(ouse).

jealously ['dʒeləslɪ] *adv* jalousement.

jealousy ['dʒeləsɪ] *n* jalousie *f*.

jeans [dʒi:nz] *npl* jean *m*, blue-jean *m*.

Jedda ['dʒedə] *n* Djedda.

Jeep® [dʒi:p] *n* Jeep® *f*.

jeer [dʒɪər] ◇ *vt* huer, conspuer ◇ *vi* : **to ~ (at sb)** huer (qqn), conspuer (qqn).

◆ **jeers** *npl* huées *fpl*.

jeering ['dʒɪərɪŋ] *adj* moqueur(euse), railleur(euse).

Jehovah's Witness [dʒɪ,həʊvəz-] *n* témoin *m* de Jéhovah.

Jello® ['dʒeləʊ] *n Am* gelée *f*.

jelly ['dʒelɪ] (*pl* **-ies**) *n* gelée *f*.

jelly baby *n Br* bonbon *à la gélatine en forme de bébé*.

jelly bean *n* bonbon *à la gélatine couvert de sucre*.

jellyfish ['dʒelɪfɪʃ] (*pl inv* OR **-es** [-i:z]) *n* méduse *f*.

jelly roll *n Am* gâteau *m* roulé.

jemmy *Br* ['dʒemɪ], **jimmy** *Am* ['dʒɪmɪ] (*pl* **-ies**) *n* pince-monseigneur *f*.

jeopardize, -ise ['dʒepədaɪz] *vt* compromettre, mettre en danger.

jeopardy ['dʒepədɪ] *n* : **in ~** en péril OR danger, menacé(e).

jerk [dʒɜ:k] ◇ *n* **- 1.** [movement] secousse *f*, saccade *f* **- 2.** *v inf* [fool] abruti *m*, -e *f* ◇ *vt* : **he ~ed his head round** il tourna la tête brusquement ; **he ~ed the door open** il ouvrit la porte d'un coup sec ◇ *vi* [person] sursauter ; [vehicle] cahoter.

jerkily ['dʒɜ:kɪlɪ] *adv* par à-coups, par saccades.

jerkin ['dʒɜ:kɪn] *n* blouson *m*.

jerky ['dʒɜ:kɪ] (*compar* **-ier** ; *superl* **-iest**) *adj* saccadé(e).

jerry-built ['dʒerɪ-] *adj* construit(e) à la va-vite.

jersey ['dʒɜ:zɪ] (*pl* **-s**) *n* **- 1.** [sweater] pull *m* **- 2.** [cloth] jersey *m*.

Jersey ['dʒɜ:zɪ] *n* Jersey *f* ; **in ~** à Jersey.

Jerusalem [dʒə'ru:sələm] *n* Jérusalem.

jest [dʒest] *n* plaisanterie *f* ; **in ~** pour rire.

jester ['dʒestər] *n* bouffon *m*.

Jesuit ['dʒezjʊɪt] ◇ *adj* jésuite ◇ *n* jésuite *m*.

Jesus (Christ) ['dʒi:zəs-] *n* Jésus *m*, Jésus-Christ *m*.

jet [dʒet] (*pt* & *pp* **-ted** ; *cont* **-ting**) ◇ *n* **- 1.** [plane] jet *m*, avion *m* à réaction **- 2.** [of fluid] jet *m* **- 3.** [nozzle, outlet] ajutage *m* ◇ *vi* [travel by jet] voyager en jet OR en avion.

jet-black *adj* noir(e) comme (du) jais.

jet engine *n* moteur *m* à réaction.

jetfoil ['dʒetfɔɪl] *n* hydroglisseur *m*.

jet lag *n* fatigue *f* due au décalage horaire.

jet-propelled [-prə'peld] *adj* à réaction.

jetsam ['dʒetsəm] ▷ **flotsam**.

jet set *n* : **the ~** la jet-set.

jettison ['dʒetɪsən] *vt* **- 1.** [cargo] jeter, larguer **- 2.** *fig* [ideas] abandonner, renoncer à.

jetty ['dʒetɪ] (*pl* **-ies**) *n* jetée *f*.

Jew [dʒu:] *n* Juif *m*, -ive *f*.

jewel ['dʒu:əl] ◇ *n* bijou *m* ; [in watch] rubis *m* ◇ *comp* [box, chest] à bijoux.

jeweller *Br*, **jeweler** *Am* ['dʒu:ələr] *n* bijoutier *m* ; **~'s (shop)** bijouterie *f*.

jewellery *Br*, **jewelry** *Am* ['dʒu:əlrɪ] *n* (U) bijoux *mpl*.

Jewess ['dʒu:ɪs] *n* juive *f*.

Jewish ['dʒu:ɪʃ] *adj* juif(ive).

JFK (*abbr of* **John Fitzgerald Kennedy International Airport**) *n* aéroport de New York.

jib [dʒɪb] (*pt* & *pp* **-bed** ; *cont* **-bing**) ◇ *n* **- 1.** [of crane] flèche *f* - **2.** [sail] foc *m* ⬦ *vi* : **to ~ at** rechigner à.

jibe [dʒaɪb] *n* sarcasme *m*, moquerie *f*.

Jidda ['dʒɪdə] = **Jedda.**

jiffy ['dʒɪfɪ] *n* inf : **in a ~** en un clin d'œil.

Jiffy bag® *n* enveloppe *f* matelassée.

jig [dʒɪg] (*pt* & *pp* **-ged** ; *cont* **-ging**) ⬦ *n* gigue *f* ⬦ *vi* danser la gigue ; **to ~ about** se trémousser.

jiggle ['dʒɪgl] *vt* secouer.

jigsaw (puzzle) ['dʒɪgsɔ:-] *n* puzzle *m*.

jihad [dʒɪ'hɑːd] *n* djihad *m*.

jilt [dʒɪlt] *vt* laisser tomber.

jimmy Am = **jemmy.**

jingle ['dʒɪŋgl] ⬦ *n* - **1.** [sound] cliquetis *m* - **2.** [song] jingle *m*, indicatif *m* ⬦ *vi* [bell] tinter ; [coins, bracelets] cliqueter.

jingoism ['dʒɪŋgəʊɪzm] *n* chauvinisme *m*.

jinx [dʒɪŋks] *n* poisse *f*.

jinxed [dʒɪŋkst] *adj* qui a la poisse.

jitters ['dʒɪtəz] *npl* inf : **the ~** le trac.

jittery ['dʒɪtərɪ] *adj* inf nerveux(euse).

jive [dʒaɪv] ⬦ *n* - **1.** [dance] rock *m* - **2.** Am inf [glib talk] baratin *m* ⬦ *vi* danser le rock.

job [dʒɒb] *n* - **1.** [employment] emploi *m* - **2.** [task] travail *m*, tâche *f* ; **to do a good ~** faire du bon travail ; **to make a good ~ of sthg** faire bien *OR* réussir qqch ; **it's not my ~ to ...** ce n'est pas à moi de ... - **3.** [difficult task] : **to have a ~ doing sthg** avoir du mal à faire qqch - **4.** inf [plastic surgery] : **to have a nose ~** se faire refaire le nez - **5.** phr : **that's just the ~** Br inf c'est exactement *OR* tout à fait ce qu'il faut.

jobbing ['dʒɒbɪŋ] *adj* Br qui travaille à la tâche.

job centre *n* Br agence *f* pour l'emploi.

job creation scheme *n* plan *m* de création d'emplois.

job description *n* profil *m* du poste.

jobless ['dʒɒblɪs] ⬦ *adj* au chômage ⬦ *npl* : **the ~** les chômeurs *mpl*.

job lot *n* lot *m* de marchandises.

job satisfaction *n* satisfaction *f* dans le travail.

job security *n* sécurité *f* de l'emploi.

job seeker *n* demandeur *m* d'emploi.

Job Seekers Allowance *n* Br indemnité *f* de chômage.

jobsharing ['dʒɒbʃeərɪŋ] *n* partage *m* de l'emploi.

Joburg, Jo'burg ['dʒəʊbɜːg] *n* inf Johannesburg.

jockey ['dʒɒkɪ] (*pl* **-s**) ⬦ *n* jockey *m* ⬦ *vi* : **to**

~ for position manœuvrer pour devancer ses concurrents.

jockstrap ['dʒɒkstræp] *n* suspensoir *m*.

jocular ['dʒɒkjʊlə'] *adj* - **1.** [cheerful] enjoué(e), jovial(e) - **2.** [funny] amusant(e).

jodhpurs ['dʒɒdpəz] *npl* jodhpurs *mpl*, culotte *f* de cheval.

Joe Public [dʒəʊ-] *n* l'homme *m* de la rue.

jog [dʒɒg] (*pt* & *pp* **-ged** ; *cont* **-ging**) ⬦ *n* : **to go for a ~** faire du jogging ⬦ *vt* pousser ; **to ~ sb's memory** rafraîchir la mémoire de qqn ⬦ *vi* faire du jogging, jogger.

jogger ['dʒɒgə'] *n* joggeur *m*, -euse *f*.

jogging ['dʒɒgɪŋ] *n* jogging *m*.

joggle ['dʒɒgl] *vt* secouer.

Johannesburg [dʒə'hænɪsbɜːg] *n* Johannesburg.

john [dʒɒn] *n* Am inf petit coin *m*, cabinets *mpl*.

John Hancock [-'hænkɒk] *n* Am inf signature *f*.

join [dʒɔɪn] ⬦ *n* raccord *m*, joint *m* ⬦ *vt* - **1.** [connect - gen] unir, joindre ; [- towns etc] relier~ **2.** [get together with] rejoindre, retrouver - **3.** [political party] devenir membre de ; [club] s'inscrire à ; [army] s'engager dans ; **to ~ a queue** Br, **to ~ a line** Am prendre la queue ⬦ *vi* - **1.** [connect] se joindre - **2.** [become a member - gen] devenir membre ; [- of club] s'inscrire.

join in ⬦ *vt fus* prendre part à, participer à ⬦ *vi* participer.

join up *vi* MIL s'engager dans l'armée.

joiner ['dʒɔɪnə'] *n* menuisier *m*.

joinery ['dʒɔɪnərɪ] *n* menuiserie *f*.

joint [dʒɔɪnt] ⬦ *adj* [effort] conjugué(e) ; [responsibility] collectif(ive) ⬦ *n* - **1.** [gen & TECH] joint *m* - **2.** ANAT articulation *f* - **3.** Br [of meat] rôti *m* - **4.** inf [place] bouge *m* - **5.** drugs sl joint *m*.

joint account *n* compte *m* joint.

Joint Chiefs of Staff *npl* : **the ~** *l'organe consultatif du ministère américain de la Défense, composé des chefs d'état-major des trois armées.*

jointed ['dʒɔɪntɪd] *adj* articulé(e).

jointly ['dʒɔɪntlɪ] *adv* conjointement.

joint ownership *n* copropriété *f*.

joint-stock company *n* société *f* anonyme par actions.

joint venture *n* joint-venture *m*.

joist [dʒɔɪst] *n* poutre *f*, solive *f*.

jojoba [hə'həʊbəl] *n* jojoba *m*.

joke [dʒəʊk] ⬦ *n* blague *f*, plaisanterie *f* ; **he's just a ~** il est un objet de risée ; **to play a**

~ **on sb** faire une blague à qqn, jouer un tour à qqn ; **it's gone beyond a ~** ça commence à bien faire ; **it's no ~ inf** [not easy] ce n'est pas de la tarte ◇ *vi* plaisanter, blaguer ; **to ~ about sthg** plaisanter sur qqch, se moquer de qqch.

joker ['dʒəʊkəʳ] *n* - **1.** [person] blagueur *m*, -euse *f* - **2.** [playing card] joker *m*.

jollity ['dʒɒlətɪ] *n* jovialité *f*, gaieté *f*.

jolly ['dʒɒlɪ] (*compar* -ier ; *superl* -iest) ◇ *adj* [person] jovial(e), enjoué(e) ; [time, party] agréable ◇ *adv* **Br inf** drôlement, rudement.

jolt [dʒəʊlt] ◇ *n* - **1.** [jerk] secousse *f*, soubresaut *m* - **2.** [shock] choc *m* ◇ *vt* secouer ; **to ~ sb into doing sthg** inciter fortement qqn à faire qqch ◇ *vi* cahoter.

Joneses ['dʒəʊnzɪz] *npl* : **to keep up with the ~** essayer d'avoir le même standing que ses voisins.

Jordan ['dʒɔ:dn] *n* Jordanie *f* ; **in ~** en Jordanie ; **the (River) ~** le Jourdain.

Jordanian [dʒɔ:'deɪnjən] ◇ *adj* jordanien(enne) ◇ *n* Jordanien *m*, -enne *f*.

joss stick [dʒɒs-] *n* bâton *m* d'encens.

jostle ['dʒɒsl] ◇ *vt* bousculer ◇ *vi* se bousculer.

jot [dʒɒt] (*pt & pp* -ted ; *cont* -ting) *n* [of truth] grain *m*, brin *m*.
➤ **jot down** *vt sep* noter, prendre note de.

jotter ['dʒɒtəʳ] *n* [notepad] bloc-notes *m*.

jottings ['dʒɒtɪŋz] *npl* notes *fpl*.

journal ['dʒɜ:nl] *n* - **1.** [magazine] revue *f* - **2.** [diary] journal *m*.

journalese [,dʒɜ:nə'li:z] *n* **pej** jargon *m* journalistique.

journalism ['dʒɜ:nəlɪzm] *n* journalisme *m*.

journalist ['dʒɜ:nəlɪst] *n* journaliste *mf*.

journey ['dʒɜ:nɪ] (*pl* -s) *n* voyage *m*.

joust [dʒaʊst] *vi* jouter.

jovial ['dʒəʊvjəl] *adj* jovial(e).

jowls [dʒaʊlz] *npl* bajoues *fpl*.

joy [dʒɔɪ] *n* joie *f*.

joyful ['dʒɔɪfʊl] *adj* joyeux(euse).

joyfully ['dʒɔɪfʊlɪ] *adv* joyeusement, avec joie.

joyous ['dʒɔɪəs] *adj* joyeux(euse).

joyously ['dʒɔɪəslɪ] *adv* avec joie, joyeusement.

joyride ['dʒɔɪraɪd] (*pt* -rode ; *pp* -ridden) *vi* faire une virée dans une voiture volée.

joyrider ['dʒɔɪraɪdəʳ] *n* personne qui vole une voiture pour aller faire une virée.

joyrode ['dʒɔɪrəʊd] *pt* ⊳ **joyride**.

joystick ['dʒɔɪstɪk] *n* **AERON** manche *m* (à balai) ; **COMPUT** manette *f*.

JP *n abbr of* **Justice of the Peace.**

Jr. (*abbr of* **Junior**) Jr.

JSA *n* **Br** *abbr of* **Job Seekers Allowance.**

JTPA (*abbr of* **Job Training Partnership Act**) *n* *programme gouvernemental américain de formation.*

jubilant ['dʒu:bɪlənt] *adj* [person] débordant(e) de joie, qui jubile ; [shout] de joie.

jubilation [,dʒu:bɪ'leɪʃn] *n* joie *f*, jubilation *f*.

jubilee ['dʒu:bɪli:] *n* jubilé *m*.

Judaism [dʒu:'deɪɪzml *n* judaïsme *m*.

judder ['dʒʌdəʳ] *vi* **Br** trembler violemment.

judge [dʒʌdʒ] ◇ *n* juge *m* ◇ *vt* - **1.** [gen] juger - **2.** [estimate] évaluer, juger ◇ *vi* juger ; **to ~ from** OR **by, judging from** OR **by** à en juger par.

judg(e)ment ['dʒʌdʒmənt] *n* jugement *m* ; **to pass ~ (on)** **JUR** prononcer OR rendre un jugement (sur) ; **fig** [on person, situation] porter un jugement (sur) ; **to reserve ~** s'abstenir de donner son avis OR de porter un jugement ; **against my better ~** sachant pertinemment que j'avais tort.

judg(e)mental [dʒʌdʒ'mentl] *adj* **pej** qui critique, qui porte des jugements.

judicial [dʒu:'dɪʃl] *adj* judiciaire.

judiciary [dʒu:'dɪʃərɪ] *n* : **the ~** la magistrature.

judicious [dʒu:'dɪʃəs] *adj* judicieux(euse).

judo ['dʒu:dəʊ] *n* judo *m*.

jug [dʒʌg] *n* pot *m*, pichet *m*.

juggernaut ['dʒʌgənɔ:t] *n* poids *m* lourd.

juggle ['dʒʌgl] ◇ *vt* **lit & fig** jongler avec ◇ *vi* jongler.

juggler ['dʒʌgləʳ] *n* jongleur *m*, -euse *f*.

jugular (vein) ['dʒʌgjʊləʳ-] *n* (veine *f*) jugulaire *f*.

juice [dʒu:s] *n* jus *m*.
➤ **juices** *npl* [in stomach] sucs *mpl*.

juicy ['dʒu:sɪ] (*compar* -ier ; *superl* -iest) *adj* - **1.** [fruit] juteux(euse) - **2.** **inf** [story] croustillant(e) - **3.** [role] séduisant(e), tentant(e).

jujitsu [dʒu:'dʒɪtsu:] *n* jiu-jitsu *m*.

jukebox ['dʒu:kbɒks] *n* juke-box *m*.

Jul. (*abbr of* **July**) juill.

July [dʒu:'laɪ] *n* juillet *m* ; *see also* **September.**

jumble ['dʒʌmbl] ◇ *n* [mixture] mélange *m*, fatras *m* ◇ *vt* : **to ~ (up)** mélanger, embrouiller.

jumble sale *n* **Br** vente *f* de charité *(où sont vendus des articles d'occasion).*

jumbo jet ['dʒʌmbəʊ-] *n* jumbo-jet *m*.

jumbo-sized [-saɪzd] *adj* géant(e), énorme.

jump [dʒʌmp] ⬦ *n* - **1.** [leap] saut *m*, bond *m* - **2.** [fence] obstacle *m* - **3.** [rapid increase] flambée *f*, hausse *f* brutale - **4.** *phr* : **to keep one ~ ahead of sb** avoir une longueur d'avance sur qqn ⬦ *vt* - **1.** [fence, stream etc] sauter, franchir d'un bond - **2.** *inf* [attack] sauter sur, tomber sur - **3.** Am [train, bus] prendre sans payer ⬦ *vi* - **1.** [gen] sauter, bondir ; [in surprise] sursauter ; **to ~ across sthg** traverser qqch d'un bond - **2.** [increase rapidly] grimper en flèche, faire un bond.

➡ **jump at** *vt fus fig* sauter sur.

jumped-up [ˈdʒʌmpt-] *adj* Br *inf pej* prétentieux(euse).

jumper [ˈdʒʌmpəʳ] *n* - **1.** Br [pullover] pull *m* - **2.** Am [dress] robe *f* chasuble.

jump jet *n* avion *m* à décollage vertical.

jump leads *npl* câbles *mpl* de démarrage.

jump-start *vt* : **to ~ a car** faire démarrer une voiture en la poussant.

jumpsuit [ˈdʒʌmpsuːt] *n* combinaison-pantalon *f*.

jumpy [ˈdʒʌmpɪ] (*compar* -**ier** ; *superl* -**iest**) *adj* nerveux(euse).

Jun. - **1.** *abbr of* **June** - **2.** = **Junr**.

junction [ˈdʒʌŋkʃn] *n* [of roads] carrefour *m* ; RAIL embranchement *m*.

junction box *n* ELEC boîte *f* d'accouplement.

juncture [ˈdʒʌŋktʃəʳ] *n fml* : **at this ~** à ce moment même.

June [dʒuːn] *n* juin *m* ; *see also* **September**.

jungle [ˈdʒʌŋgl] *n* lit & fig jungle *f*.

jungle gym *n* Am [in playground] cage *f* d'écureuil.

junior [ˈdʒuːnjəʳ] ⬦ *adj* - **1.** [gen] jeune - **2.** Am [after name] junior ⬦ *n* - **1.** [in rank] subalterne *mf* - **2.** [in age] cadet *m*, -ette *f* - **3.** Am SCH ≃ élève *mf* de première ; UNIV ≃ étudiant *m*, -e *f* de deuxième année.

junior college *n* Am *établissement d'enseignement supérieur où l'on obtient un diplôme en deux ans*.

junior doctor *n* interne *mf*.

junior high school *n* Am ≃ collège *m* d'enseignement secondaire.

junior minister *n* Br secrétaire *mf* d'État.

junior school *n* Br école *f* primaire.

juniper [ˈdʒuːnɪpəʳ] *n* genièvre *m*.

junk [dʒʌŋk] ⬦ *n* [unwanted objects] bric-à-brac *m* ⬦ *vt* balancer, se débarrasser de.

junket [ˈdʒʌŋkɪt] *n* - **1.** [pudding] lait *m* caillé - **2.** *inf pej* [trip] voyage *m* aux frais de la princesse.

junk food *n* (U) *pej* : **to eat ~** manger des cochonneries.

junkie [ˈdʒʌŋkɪ] *n* drugs sl drogué *m*, -e *f*.

junk mail *n* (U) *pej* prospectus *mpl* publicitaires envoyés par la poste.

junk shop *n* boutique *f* de brocanteur.

Junr (*abbr of* **Junior**) Jr.

junta [Br ˈdʒʌntə, Am ˈhʊntə] *n* junte *f*.

Jupiter [ˈdʒuːpɪtəʳ] *n* [planet] Jupiter *f*.

jurisdiction [ˌdʒʊərɪsˈdɪkʃn] *n* juridiction *f*.

jurisprudence [ˌdʒʊərɪsˈpruːdəns] *n* jurisprudence *f*.

juror [ˈdʒʊərəʳ] *n* juré *m*, -e *f*.

jury [ˈdʒʊərɪ] (*pl* -**ies**) *n* jury *m*.

jury box *n* banc *m* des jurés.

jury service *n* participation *f* à un jury.

just [dʒʌst] ⬦ *adv* - **1.** [recently] : **he's ~ left** il vient de partir - **2.** [at that moment] : **I was ~ about to go** j'allais juste partir, j'étais sur le point de partir ; **I'm ~ going to do it now** je vais le faire tout de suite OR à l'instant ; **she arrived ~ as I was leaving** elle est arrivée au moment même où je partais OR juste comme je partais - **3.** [only, simply] : **it's ~ a rumour** ce n'est qu'une rumeur ; **~ add water** vous n'avez plus qu'à ajouter de l'eau ; **~ a minute** OR **moment** OR **second!** un (petit) instant! - **4.** [almost not] tout juste, à peine ; **I only ~ missed the train** j'ai manqué le train de peu ; **we have ~ enough time** on a juste assez de temps - **5.** [for emphasis] : **the coast is ~ marvellous** la côte est vraiment magnifique ; **~ look at this mess!** non, mais regarde un peu ce désordre! - **6.** [exactly, precisely] tout à fait, exactement ; **it's ~ what I need** c'est tout à fait ce qu'il me faut - **7.** [in requests] : **could you ~ move over please?** pourriez-vous vous pousser un peu s'il vous plaît? ⬦ *adj* juste, équitable.

➡ **just about** *adv* à peu près, plus ou moins.

➡ **just as** *adv* [in comparison] tout aussi ; **you're ~ as clever as he is** tu es tout aussi intelligent que lui.

➡ **just now** *adv* - **1.** [a short time ago] il y a un moment, tout à l'heure - **2.** [at this moment] en ce moment.

justice [ˈdʒʌstɪs] *n* - **1.** [gen] justice *f* - **2.** [of claim, cause] bien-fondé *m* - **3.** *phr* : **to do ~ to sthg** [job] faire bien qqch, faire qqch comme il faut ; **to do ~ to a meal** faire honneur à un repas.

Justice of the Peace (*pl* **Justices of the Peace**) *n* juge *m* de paix.

justifiable [ˈdʒʌstɪfaɪəbl] *adj* justifiable, défendable.

justifiable homicide *n* homicide *m* par légitime défense.

justifiably ['dʒʌstɪfaɪəblɪ] *adv* à juste titre.

justification [ˌdʒʌstɪfɪ'keɪʃn] *n* justification *f*.

justify ['dʒʌstɪfaɪ] (*pt* & *pp* -ied) *vt* [give reasons for] justifier.

justly ['dʒʌstlɪ] *adv* [act] avec justice ; [deserved] à juste titre.

justness ['dʒʌstnɪs] *n* bien-fondé *m*.

jut [dʒʌt] (*pt* & *pp* -ted ; *cont* -ting) *vi* : to ~ (out) faire saillie, avancer.

jute [dʒuːt] *n* jute *m*.

juvenile ['dʒuːvənaɪl] <> *adj* - **1.** JUR mineur(e), juvénile - **2.** [childish] puéril(e) <> *n* JUR mineur *m*, -e *f*.

juvenile court *n* tribunal *m* pour enfants.

juvenile delinquent *n* jeune délinquant *m*, -e *f*.

juxtapose [ˌdʒʌkstə'pəʊz] *vt* juxtaposer.

juxtaposition [ˌdʒʌkstəpə'zɪʃn] *n* juxtaposition *f*.

K

k (*pl* **k's** OR **ks**), **K** (*pl* **K's** OR **Ks**) [keɪ] *n* [letter] k *m* inv, K *m inv*.

K - 1. (*abbr of* **kilobyte**) Ko - **2.** *abbr of* **Knight** - **3.** (*abbr of* **thousand**) K.

Kabul ['kɑːbl] *n* Kaboul.

kaftan ['kæftæn] *n* cafetan *m*.

Kalahari Desert [ˌkælə'hɑːrɪ-] *n* : the ~ le (désert du) Kalahari.

kale [keɪl] *n* chou *m* frisé.

kaleidoscope [kə'laɪdəskəʊp] *n* kaléidoscope *m*.

kamikaze [ˌkæmɪ'kɑːzɪ] *n* kamikaze *m*.

Kampala [kæm'pɑːlə] *n* Kampala.

Kampuchea [ˌkæmpuː'tʃɪə] *n* Kampuchéa *m* ; in ~ au Kampuchéa.

Kampuchean [ˌkæmpuː'tʃɪən] <> *adj* cambodgien(enne) <> *n* Cambodgien *m*, -enne *f*.

kangaroo [ˌkæŋgə'ruː] *n* kangourou *m*.

Kansas ['kænzəs] *n* Kansas *m* ; in ~ dans le Kansas.

kaolin ['keɪəlɪn] *n* kaolin *m*.

kaput [kə'pʊt] *adj* inf fichu(e), foutu(e).

karat ['kærət] *n* Am carat *m*.

karate [kə'rɑːtɪ] *n* karaté *m*.

Kashmir [kæʃ'mɪəʳ] *n* Cachemire *m* ; in ~ au Cachemire.

Katar [kæ'tɑːʳ] = **Qatar**.

Katmandu [ˌkætmæn'duː] *n* Katmandou, Katmandu.

kayak ['kaɪæk] *n* kayak *m*.

Kazakhstan [ˌkæzæk'stɑːn] *n* Kazakhstan *m* ; in ~ au Kazakhstan.

KB (*abbr of* **kilobyte(s)**) *n* COMPUT Ko *m*.

KC (*abbr of* **King's Counsel**) *n* ≃ bâtonnier *m* de l'ordre.

kcal (*abbr of* **kilocalorie**) Kcal.

kd (*abbr of* **knocked down**) *livré en kit, à monter soi-même*.

kebab [kɪ'bæb] *n* brochette *f*.

kedgeree [ˌkedʒə'riː] *n* Br *plat de riz, poisson et œufs durs mélangés*.

keel [kiːl] *n* quille *f* ; on an even ~ stable.

→ **keel over** *vi* [ship] chavirer ; [person] tomber dans les pommes.

keen [kiːn] *adj* - **1.** [enthusiastic] enthousiaste, passionné(e) ; to be ~ on sthg avoir la passion de qqch ; he's ~ on her elle lui plaît ; to be ~ to do OR on doing sthg tenir à faire qqch - **2.** [interest, desire, mind] vif (vive) ; [competition] âpre, acharné(e) - **3.** [sense of smell] fin(e) ; [eyesight] perçant(e).

keenly ['kiːnlɪ] *adv* - **1.** [contested, interested] vivement - **2.** [listen, watch] attentivement.

keenness ['kiːnnɪs] *n* - **1.** [enthusiasm] enthousiasme *m* - **2.** [of competition] intensité *f* - **3.** [of eyesight] acuité *f* ; [of hearing] finesse *f*.

keep [kiːp] (*pt* & *pp* **kept**) <> *vt* - **1.** [retain, store] garder ; ~ the change! gardez la monnaie! ; to ~ sthg warm garder OR tenir qqch au chaud - **2.** [prevent] : to keep sb/sthg from doing sthg empêcher qqn/qqch de faire qqch - **3.** [detain] retenir ; [prisoner] détenir ; I don't want to ~ you je ne voudrais pas vous retenir ; what kept you? qu'est-ce qui t'a retardé? ; to ~ sb waiting faire attendre qqn - **4.** [promise] tenir ; [appointment] aller à ; [vow] être fidèle à - **5.** [not disclose] : to ~ sthg from sb cacher qqch à qqn ; to ~ sthg to o.s. garder qqch pour soi - **6.** [diary, record, notes] tenir - **7.** [own - sheep, pigs etc] élever ; [- shop] tenir ;

[- car] avoir, posséder - **8.** phr : **they ~ them-selves to themselves** ils restent entre eux, ils se tiennent à l'écart ◇ vi - **1.** [remain] : **to ~ warm** se tenir au chaud ; **to ~ quiet** garder le silence ; **~ quiet!** taisez-vous! - **2.** [continue] : **he ~s interrupting me** il n'arrête pas de m'interrompre ; **to ~ talking/walking** continuer à parler/à marcher - **3.** [continue moving] : **to ~ left/right** garder sa gauche/sa droite ; **to ~ north/south** continuer vers le nord/le sud - **4.** [food] se conserver - **5.** Br [in health] : **how are you ~ing?** comment allez-vous? ; **she's ~ing well** elle va bien ◇ n : **to earn one's ~** gagner sa vie.

◆ **keeps** n : **for ~s** pour toujours.

◆ **keep at** vt fus : **to ~ at it** [work hard] travailler d'arrache-pied.

◆ **keep back** vt sep [information] cacher, ne pas divulguer ; [money] retenir.

◆ **keep down** vt sep [prices] empêcher de monter ; [numbers, costs] restreindre, limiter.

◆ **keep off** vt fus : **'~ off the grass'** (il est) interdit de marcher sur la pelouse'.

◆ **keep on** vi - **1.** [continue] : **to ~ on (doing sthg)** [without stopping] continuer (de OR à faire qqch) ; [repeatedly] ne pas arrêter (de faire qqch) - **2.** [talk incessantly] : **to ~ on (about sthg)** ne pas arrêter de parler (de qqch).

◆ **keep on at** vt fus Br harceler.

◆ **keep out** ◇ vt sep empêcher d'entrer ◇ vi : **'~ out'** 'défense d'entrer'.

◆ **keep to** ◇ vt fus [rules, deadline] respecter, observer ◇ vt sep [limit] : **we must ~ spending to a minimum** il faut limiter les dépenses au minimum.

◆ **keep up** ◇ vt sep [continue to do] continuer ; [maintain] maintenir ; **to ~ up appearances** sauver les apparences ◇ vi - **1.** [maintain pace, level etc] : **to ~ up (with sb)** aller aussi vite (que qqn) ; **to ~ up with the news** suivre l'actualité - **2.** [remain in contact] : **to ~ up with sb** rester en contact avec qqn.

keeper ['ki:pə'] n gardien m, -enne f.

keep-fit ◇ n (U) Br gymnastique f ◇ comp de gymnastique.

keeping ['ki:pɪŋ] n - **1.** [care] garde f - **2.** [conformity, harmony] : **to be in/out of ~ with** [rules etc] être/ne pas être conforme à ; [subj : clothes, furniture] aller/ne pas aller avec

keepsake ['ki:pseɪk] n souvenir m.

keg [keg] n tonnelet m, baril m.

kelp [kelp] n varech m.

ken [ken] n : **it's beyond my ~** ça dépasse mes compétences.

kennel ['kenl] n - **1.** [shelter for dog] niche f - **2.** Am = kennels.

◆ **kennels** npl Br chenil m.

Kentucky [ken'tʌkɪ] n Kentucky m ; **in ~** dans le Kentucky.

Kenya ['kenjə] n Kenya m ; **in ~** au Kenya.

Kenyan ['kenjən] ◇ adj kenyan(e) ◇ n Kenyan m, -e f.

kept [kept] pt & pp ▷ **keep.**

kerb [kɜ:b] n Br bordure f du trottoir.

kerb crawler [-ˌkrɔːlə'] n Br homme en voiture qui accoste les prostituées.

kerbstone ['kɜ:bstəʊn] n Br (pierre f de) bordure de trottoir.

kerfuffle [kə'fʌfl] n Br inf : **what a ~!** quelle histoire!

kernel ['kɜ:nl] n amande f.

kerosene ['kerəsi:n] n kérosène m.

kestrel ['kestrəl] n crécerelle f.

ketch [ketʃ] n ketch m.

ketchup ['ketʃəp] n ketchup m.

kettle ['ketl] n bouilloire f.

kettledrum ['ketldrʌm] n timbale f.

key [ki:] ◇ n - **1.** [gen & MUS] clef f, clé f ; **the ~ (to sthg)** fig la clé (de qqch) - **2.** [of typewriter, computer, piano] touche f - **3.** [of map] légende f ◇ adj clé (after n).

◆ **key in** vt sep [text, data] saisir ; [code] composer.

keyboard ['ki:bɔ:d] ◇ n [gen & COMPUT] clavier m ◇ vt COMPUT [text, data] saisir.

keyboarder ['ki:bɔ:də'] n COMPUT claviste mf.

keyed up [ˌki:d-] adj tendu(e), énervé(e).

keyhole ['ki:həʊl] n trou m de serrure.

keynote ['ki:nəʊt] ◇ n note f dominante ◇ comp : **~ speech** discours-programme m.

keypad ['ki:pæd] n COMPUT pavé m numérique.

keypunch ['ki:pʌntʃ] n Am perforatrice f à clavier.

key ring n porte-clés m inv.

keystone ['ki:stəʊn] n lit & fig clef f de voûte.

keystroke ['ki:strəʊk] n COMPUT frappe f d'une touche.

kg (abbr of **kilogram**) kg.

KGB n KGB m.

khaki ['kɑ:kɪ] ◇ adj kaki (inv) ◇ n - **1.** [colour] kaki m - **2.** [cloth] toile f kaki.

Khmer [kmeə'] ◇ adj khmer (khmère) ◇ n - **1.** [person] Khmer m, -ère f ; **~ Rouge** Khmer rouge - **2.** [language] khmer m.

kibbutz [kɪ'bʊts] (pl **kibbutzim** [kɪbʊ'tsi:m] OR -es [-i:z]) n kibboutz m.

kick [kɪk] ◇ n - **1.** [with foot] coup m de pied - **2.** inf [excitement] : **to get a ~ from sthg** trouver qqch excitant ; **to do sthg for ~s** faire qqch pour le plaisir ◇ vt - **1.** [with foot] donner un coup de pied à ; **to ~ o.s.** fig se don-

ner des gifles OR des claques **- 2.** inf [give up] :
to ~ the habit arrêter ◇ *vi* **- 1.** [person - repeatedly] donner des coups de pied ; [- once] donner un coup de pied **- 2.** [baby] gigoter **- 3.** [animal] ruer.

◆ **kick about, kick around** *vi* Br inf traîner.

◆ **kick off** *vi* **- 1.** FTBL donner le coup d'envoi **- 2.** inf fig [start] démarrer.

◆ **kick out** *vt sep* inf vider, jeter dehors.

◆ **kick up** *vt fus* inf : **to ~ up a fuss/row** faire toute une histoire.

kickoff ['kɪkɒf] *n* engagement *m*.

kick-start *vt* faire démarrer à l'aide du pied OR au kick.

kid [kɪd] (*pt & pp* **-ded** ; *cont* **-ding**) ◇ *n* **- 1.** [child] gosse *mf*, gamin *m*, -e *f* **- 2.** inf [young person] petit jeune *m*, petite jeune *f* **- 3.** [goat, leather] chevreau *m* ◇ *comp* inf [brother, sister] petit(e) ◇ *vt* inf **- 1.** [tease] faire marcher **- 2.** [delude] : **to ~ o.s.** se faire des illusions ◇ *vi* inf : **to be kidding** plaisanter ; **no kidding!** sans blague!

kiddie, kiddy ['kɪdɪ] (*pl* **-ies**) *n* inf gosse *mf*, gamin *m*, -e *f*.

kid gloves *npl* : **to treat** OR **handle sb with ~** prendre des gants avec qqn.

kidnap ['kɪdnæp] (Br *pt & pp* **-ped** ; *cont* **-ping**, Am *pt & pp* **-ed** ; *cont* **-ing**) *vt* kidnapper, enlever.

kidnapper Br, **kidnaper** Am ['kɪdnæpəʳ] *n* kidnappeur *m*, -euse *f*, ravisseur *m*, -euse *f*.

kidnapping Br, **kidnaping** Am ['kɪdnæpɪŋ] *n* enlèvement *m*.

kidney ['kɪdnɪ] (*pl* **-s**) *n* **- 1.** ANAT rein *m* **- 2.** CULIN rognon *m*.

kidney bean *n* haricot *m* rouge.

kidney machine *n* rein *m* artificiel.

Kilimanjaro [,kɪlɪmən'dʒɑːrəʊ] *n* Kilimandjaro *m*.

kill [kɪl] ◇ *vt* **- 1.** [cause death of] tuer ; **my feet are killing me** fig j'ai horriblement mal aux pieds ; **to ~ time** tuer le temps **- 2.** fig [hope, chances] mettre fin à ; [pain] supprimer ◇ *vi* tuer ◇ *n* mise *f* à mort.

◆ **kill off** *vt sep* **- 1.** [species, animal] exterminer **- 2.** fig [hope, chances] mettre fin à.

killer ['kɪləʳ] *n* [person] meurtrier *m*, -ère *f* ; [animal] tueur *m*, -euse *f*.

killer whale *n* épaulard *m*, orque *f*.

killing ['kɪlɪŋ] ◇ *adj* inf [very funny] tordant(e) ◇ *n* meurtre *m* ; **to make a ~** inf faire une bonne affaire, réussir un beau coup.

killjoy ['kɪldʒɔɪ] *n* rabat-joie *m inv*.

kiln [kɪln] *n* four *m*.

kilo ['kiːləʊ] (*pl* **-s**) (*abbr of* **kilogram**) *n* kilo *m*.

kilo- ['kɪlə] *prefix* kilo-.

kilobyte ['kɪləbaɪt] *n* COMPUT kilo-octet *m*.

kilocalorie ['kɪlə,kæləʳɪ] *n* kilocalorie *f*.

kilogram(me) ['kɪləgræm] *n* kilogramme *m*.

kilohertz ['kɪləhɜːtz] (*pl inv*) *n* kilohertz *m*.

kilojoule ['kɪlədʒuːl] *n* kilojoule *m*.

kilometre Br ['kɪlə,miːtəʳ], **kilometer** Am [kɪ'lɒmɪtər] *n* kilomètre *m*.

kilowatt ['kɪləwɒt] *n* kilowatt *m*.

kilt [kɪlt] *n* kilt *m*.

kimono [kɪ'məʊnəʊ] (*pl* **-s**) *n* kimono *m*.

kin [kɪn] *n* ▷ **kith**.

kind [kaɪnd] ◇ *adj* gentil(ille), aimable ; **would you be so ~ as to ...?** voulez-vous avoir la gentillesse OR l'amabilité de ...? ◇ *n* genre *m*, sorte *f* ; **an agreement of a ~** une sorte d'accord ; **they're two of a ~** ils se ressemblent ; **in ~** [payment] en nature ; **a ~ of** une espèce de, une sorte de ; **~ of** Am inf un peu.

kindergarten ['kɪndə,gɑːtn] *n* jardin *m* d'enfants.

kind-hearted [-'hɑːtɪd] *adj* qui a bon cœur, bon (bonne).

kindle ['kɪndl] *vt* **- 1.** [fire] allumer **- 2.** fig [feeling] susciter.

kindling ['kɪndlɪŋ] *n* (U) petit bois *m*.

kindly ['kaɪndlɪ] (*compar* **-ier** ; *superl* **-iest**) ◇ *adj* **- 1.** [person] plein(e) de bonté, bienveillant(e) **- 2.** [gesture] plein(e) de gentillesse ◇ *adv* **- 1.** [speak, smile etc] avec gentillesse ; **to look ~ on** fig être favorable à **- 2.** [please] : **~ leave the room!** veuillez sortir, s'il vous plaît! ; **will you ~ ...?** veuillez ..., je vous prie de ... **- 3.** phr : **not to take ~ to sthg** mal prendre qqch.

kindness ['kaɪndnɪs] *n* gentillesse *f*.

kindred ['kɪndrɪd] *adj* [similar] semblable, similaire ; **~ spirit** âme *f* sœur.

kinetic [kɪ'netɪk] *adj* cinétique.

kinfolk(s) ['kɪnfəʊk(s)] Am = **kinsfolk**.

king [kɪŋ] *n* roi *m*.

kingdom ['kɪŋdəm] *n* **- 1.** [country] royaume *m* **- 2.** [of animals, plants] règne *m*.

kingfisher ['kɪŋ,fɪʃəʳ] *n* martin-pêcheur *m*.

kingpin ['kɪŋpɪn] *n* **- 1.** AUT pivot *m* de l'essieu avant **- 2.** fig [person] pilier *m*, cheville *f* ouvrière.

king-size(d) [-saɪz(d)] *adj* [cigarette] long (longue) ; [pack] géant(e) ; **a ~ bed** un grand lit (de 195 cm).

kink [kɪŋk] *n* [in rope] entortillement *m*.

kinky ['kɪŋkɪ] (*compar* -ier ; *superl* -iest) *adj* inf vicieux(euse).

kinsfolk ['kɪnzfəʊk] *npl* famille *f*.

kinship ['kɪnʃɪp] *n* (*U*) - **1.** [family relationship] parenté *f* - **2.** [closeness] affinités *fpl*.

kiosk ['kiːɒsk] *n* - **1.** [small shop] kiosque *m* - **2.** Br [telephone box] cabine *f* (téléphonique).

kip [kɪp] (*pt* & *pp* -ped ; *cont* -ping) Br inf <> *n* somme *m*, roupillon *m* <> *vi* faire OR piquer un petit somme.

kipper ['kɪpə'] *n* hareng *m* fumé OR saur.

Kirk [kɜːk] *n* Scot : **the ~** l'Église *f* (presbytérienne) d'Écosse.

kirsch [kɪəʃ] *n* kirsch *m*.

kiss [kɪs] <> *n* baiser *m* ; **to give sb a ~** embrasser qqn, donner un baiser à qqn <> *vt* embrasser ; **to ~ sb's cheek** embrasser qqn sur la joue ; **to ~ sb goodbye** dire au revoir à qqn en l'embrassant <> *vi* s'embrasser.

kissagram ['kɪsəgræm] *n* *service de « télégramme parlé » comprenant un baiser, à l'occasion d'un anniversaire, par exemple*.

kiss curl *n* Br accroche-cœur *m*.

kiss of life *n* : **the ~** le bouche-à-bouche.

kit [kɪt] (*pt* & *pp* -ted ; *cont* -ting) *n* - **1.** [set] trousse *f* - **2.** (*U*) SPORT affaires *fpl*, équipement *m* - **3.** [to be assembled] kit *m*.
    kit out *vt sep* Br équiper.

kit bag *n* sac *m* de marin.

kitchen ['kɪtʃɪn] *n* cuisine *f*.

kitchenette [ˌkɪtʃɪ'net] *n* kitchenette *f*.

kitchen garden *n* (jardin *m*) potager *m*.

kitchen sink *n* évier *m*.

kitchen unit *n* élément *m* de cuisine.

kitchenware ['kɪtʃɪnweə'] *n* (*U*) ustensiles *mpl* de cuisine.

kite [kaɪt] *n* - **1.** [toy] cerf-volant *m* - **2.** [bird] milan *m*.

Kite mark *n* Br ≃ NF (*conforme aux normes françaises de sécurité*).

kith [kɪθ] *n* : **~ and kin** parents et amis *mpl*.

kitsch [kɪtʃ] *n* kitsch *m inv*.

kitten ['kɪtn] *n* chaton *m*.

kitty ['kɪtɪ] (*pl* -ies) *n* [shared fund] cagnotte *f*.

kiwi ['kiːwiː] *n* - **1.** [bird] kiwi *m*, aptéryx *m* - **2.** inf [New Zealander] Néo-Zélandais *m*, -e *f*.

kiwi fruit *n* kiwi *m*.

KKK *abbr of* **Ku Klux Klan**.

klaxon ['klæksn] *n* sirène *f*.

Kleenex® ['kliːneks] *n* Kleenex® *m*.

kleptomaniac [ˌkleptə'meɪnɪæk] *n* kleptomane *mf*.

km (*abbr of* **kilometre**) km.

km/h (*abbr of* **kilometres per hour**) km/h.

knack [næk] *n* : **to have a** OR **the ~ (for doing sthg)** avoir le coup (pour faire qqch).

knacker ['nækə'] Br <> *n* [horse slaughterer] équarrisseur *m* <> *vt* v inf épuiser.

knackered ['nækəd] *adj* Br v inf crevé(e), claqué(e).

knapsack ['næpsæk] *n* sac *m* à dos.

knave [neɪv] *n* [in cards] valet *m*.

knead [niːd] *vt* pétrir.

knee [niː] *n* genou *m* ; **to be on one's ~s** être à genoux ; fig être sur les genoux ; **to bring sb to their ~s** fig faire capituler qqn.

kneecap ['niːkæp] *n* rotule *f*.

knee-deep *adj* : **we were ~ in snow/water** la neige/l'eau nous arrivait jusqu'aux genoux.

knee-high *adj* à hauteur de genou.

kneel [niːl] (Br *pt* & *pp* knelt, Am *pt* & *pp* knelt OR -ed) *vi* se mettre à genoux, s'agenouiller.
    kneel down *vi* se mettre à genoux, s'agenouiller.

knee-length *adj* [skirt] qui arrive aux genoux ; [boots] qui montent jusqu'aux genoux.

knees-up *n* Br inf fête *f*.

knell [nel] *n* glas *m*.

knelt [nelt] *pt* & *pp* ▷ **kneel**.

knew [njuː] *pt* ▷ **know**.

knickers ['nɪkəz] *npl* - **1.** Br [underwear] culotte *f* - **2.** Am [knickerbockers] pantalon *m* de golf.

knick-knack ['nɪknæk] *n* babiole *f*, bibelot *m*.

knife [naɪf] (*pl* knives [naɪvz]) <> *n* couteau *m* <> *vt* donner un coup de couteau à, poignarder.

knifing ['naɪfɪŋ] *n* bagarre *f* au couteau.

knight [naɪt] <> *n* - **1.** [in history, member of nobility] chevalier *m* - **2.** [in chess] cavalier *m* <> *vt* faire chevalier.

knighthood ['naɪthʊd] *n* titre *m* de chevalier.

knit [nɪt] (*pt* & *pp* knit OR -ted, *cont* -ting) <> *adj* : **closely** OR **tightly ~** fig très uni(e) <> *vt* tricoter <> *vi* - **1.** [with wool] tricoter - **2.** [broken bones] se souder.

knitted ['nɪtɪd] *adj* tricoté(e).

knitting ['nɪtɪŋ] *n* (*U*) tricot *m*.

knitting machine *n* machine *f* à tricoter.

knitting needle *n* aiguille *f* à tricoter.

knitting pattern *n* modèle *m* (de tricot).

knitwear ['nɪtweə'] *n* (*U*) tricots *mpl*.

knives [naɪvz] *pl* ▷ **knife**.

knob [nɒb] *n* - **1.** [on door] poignée *f*, bouton

m ; [on drawer] poignée ; [on bedstead] pomme *f*
- 2. [on TV, radio etc] bouton *m.*

knobbly Br [ˈnɒblɪ] (*compar* **-ier** ; *superl* **-iest**),
knobby Am [ˈnɒbɪ] (*compar* **-ier** ; *superl* **-iest**)
adj noueux(euse).

knock [nɒk] ⬦ *n* **- 1.** [hit] coup *m* **- 2.** inf [piece
of bad luck] coup *m* dur ⬦ *vt* **- 1.** [hit] frapper,
cogner ; **to ~ a hole in a wall** faire un trou
dans un mur ; **to ~ a nail into a wall** enfoncer
un clou dans un mur ; **to ~ sb/sthg over** renverser qqn/qqch **- 2.** inf [criticize] critiquer,
dire du mal de ⬦ *vi* **- 1.** [on door] : **to ~ (at** OR
on) frapper (à) **- 2.** [car engine] cogner, avoir
des ratés.

◆ **knock about, knock around** inf ⬦ *vt*
sep tabasser ⬦ *vi* **- 1.** [travel] bourlinguer
- 2. [spend time] : **to ~ about with sb** fréquenter
qqn.

◆ **knock back** *vt sep* inf [drink] s'enfiler.

◆ **knock down** *vt sep* **- 1.** [subj : car, driver] renverser **- 2.** [building] démolir **- 3.** [price] (faire)
baisser.

◆ **knock off** ⬦ *vt sep* **- 1.** [money] : **to ~ £5 off**
faire un rabais de 5 livres **- 2.** Br inf [steal] chiper, piquer ⬦ *vi* inf [stop working] finir son
travail OR sa journée.

◆ **knock out** *vt sep* **- 1.** [make unconscious] assommer **- 2.** [from competition] éliminer.

◆ **knock up** ⬦ *vt sep* [meal, report] préparer
OR faire en vitesse ; [structure] construire à la
va-vite ⬦ *vi* TENNIS faire des balles.

knocker [ˈnɒkə'] *n* [on door] heurtoir *m.*

knocking [ˈnɒkɪŋ] *n* (U) **- 1.** [on door etc] coups
mpl **- 2.** inf [criticism] critique *f*, critiques *fpl.*

knock-kneed [-ˈniːd] *adj* cagneux(euse),
qui a les genoux cagneux.

knock-on effect *n* Br réaction *f* en chaîne.

knockout [ˈnɒkaʊt] *n* knock-out *m*, K.-O. *m.*

knockout competition *n* Br compétition
f avec éliminatoires.

knock-up *n* TENNIS : **to have a ~** faire des balles.

knot [nɒt] (*pt* & *pp* **-ted** ; *cont* **-ting**) ⬦ *n*
- 1. [gen] nœud *m ;* **to tie/untie a ~** faire/
défaire un nœud **- 2.** [of people] petit attroupement *m* ⬦ *vt* nouer, faire un nœud à.

knotted [ˈnɒtɪd] *adj* noué(e).

knotty [ˈnɒtɪ] (*compar* **-ier** ; *superl* **-iest**) *adj* fig
épineux(euse).

know [nəʊ] (*pt* **knew** ; *pp* **known**) ⬦ *vt*
- 1. [gen] savoir ; [language] savoir parler ; **to
~ (that)** ... savoir que ... ; **to let sb ~ (about
sthg)** faire savoir (qqch) à qqn, informer
qqn (de qqch) ; **to ~ how to do sthg** savoir
faire qqch ; **to get to ~ sthg** apprendre qqch
- 2. [person, place] connaître ; **to get to ~ sb** ap-

prendre à mieux connaître qqn ⬦ *vi* sa-
voir ; **to ~ of sthg** connaître qqch ; **to ~ about**
[be aware of] être au courant de ; [be expert in]
s'y connaître en ; **God** OR **Heaven ~s!** Dieu
seul le sait! ; **he ought to have known better**
il aurait dû réfléchir ⬦ *n* : **to be in the ~**
être au courant.

know-all *n* Br (monsieur) je-sais-tout *m*,
(madame) je-sais-tout *f.*

know-how *n* savoir-faire *m*, technique *f.*

knowing [ˈnəʊɪŋ] *adj* [smile, look] entendu(e).

knowingly [ˈnəʊɪŋlɪ] *adv* **- 1.** [smile, look] d'un
air entendu **- 2.** [intentionally] sciemment.

know-it-all = **know-all.**

knowledge [ˈnɒlɪdʒ] *n* (U) **- 1.** [gen] connaissance *f ;* **it's common ~ that** ... tout le monde
sait que ... ; **without my ~** à mon insu ; **to my
~** à ma connaissance ; **to the best of my ~** à
ma connaissance, autant que je sache
- 2. [learning, understanding] savoir *m*, connaissances *fpl.*

knowledgeable [ˈnɒlɪdʒəbl] *adj* bien infor-
mé(e).

known [nəʊn] ⬦ *pp* ▷ **know** ⬦ *adj* con-
nu(e).

knuckle [ˈnʌkl] *n* **- 1.** ANAT articulation *f* OR
jointure *f* du doigt **- 2.** [of meat] jarret *m.*

◆ **knuckle down** *vi* s'y mettre, se mettre
au travail ; **to ~ down to sthg/to doing sthg**
se mettre sérieusement à qqch/à faire
qqch.

◆ **knuckle under** *vi* céder, capituler.

knuckle-duster *n* coup-de-poing *m* américain.

KO (*abbr of* **knock-out**) *n* K.-O. *m.*

koala (bear) [kəʊˈɑːlə-] *n* koala *m.*

kook [kuːk] *n* Am inf fou *m*, folle *f*, dingue *mf.*

kooky [ˈkuːkɪ] (*compar* **-ier** ; *superl* **-iest**) *adj* Am
inf fêlé(e), dingue.

Koran [kɒˈrɑːn] *n* : **the ~** le Coran.

Korea [kəˈrɪə] *n* Corée *f* ; **in ~** en Corée.

Korean [kəˈrɪən] ⬦ *adj* coréen(enne) ⬦ *n*
- 1. [person] Coréen *m*, -enne *f* **- 2.** [language]
coréen *m.*

kosher [ˈkəʊʃə'] *adj* **- 1.** [meat] kasher (*inv*)
- 2. inf [reputable] O.K. (*inv*), régло (*inv*).

Kosovar [kɔsɔvaˈr] *n* kosovar *mf.*

Kosovo [kɔsɔvɔ] *n* Kosovo *m.*

Koweit = **Kuwait.**

kowtow [ˌkaʊˈtaʊ] *vi* : **to ~ (to sb)** faire des
courbettes (à OR devant qqn).

Krakow = **Cracow.**

Kremlin [ˈkremlɪn] *n* : **the ~** le Kremlin.

KS *abbr of* **Kansas.**

KT *abbr of* **Knight.**

Kuala Lumpur [ˌkwɑːləˈlʊmˌpʊəʳ] *n* Kuala Lumpur.

kudos [ˈkjuːdɒs] *n* prestige *m*, gloire *f*.

Ku Klux Klan [kuːklʌksˈklæn] *n* : **the ~** le Ku Klux Klan.

kumquat [ˈkʌmkwɒt] *n* kumquat *m*.

kung fu [ˌkʌŋˈfuː] *n* kung-fu *m*.

Kurd [kɜːd] *n* Kurde *mf*.

Kurdish [ˈkɜːdɪʃ] *adj* kurde.

Kurdistan [ˌkɜːdɪˈstɑːn] *n* Kurdistan *m* ; **in ~** au Kurdistan.

Kuwait [kʊˈweɪt], **Koweit** [kəʊˈweɪt] *n* - **1.** [country] Koweït *m* ; **in ~** au Koweït - **2.** [city] Koweït City.

Kuwaiti [kʊˈweɪtɪ] ◇ *adj* koweïtien(enne) ◇ *n* Koweïtien *m*, -enne *f*.

kW (*abbr of* **kilowatt**) kW.

KY *abbr of* **Kentucky.**

l¹ (*pl* **l's** OR **ls**), **L** (*pl* **L's** OR **Ls**) [el] *n* [letter] l *m inv*, L *m inv*.

◆ **L** - **1.** *abbr of* **lake** - **2.** *abbr of* **large** - **3.** (*abbr of* **left**) g - **4.** *abbr of* **learner.**

> **L**
> En Grande-Bretagne, la lettre « L » apposée sur l'arrière d'un véhicule indique que le conducteur n'a pas encore son permis mais qu'il est en conduite accompagnée.

l² (*abbr of* **litre**) l.

la [lɑː] *n* MUS la *m*.

La *abbr of* **Louisiana.**

LA - **1.** *abbr of* **Los Angeles** - **2.** *abbr of* **Louisiana.**

L.A. (*abbr of* **Los Angeles**) *n* Los Angeles.

lab [læb] *n inf* labo *m*.

label [ˈleɪbl] (Br *pt* & *pp* **-led** ; *cont* **-ling**, Am *pt* & *pp* **-ed** ; *cont* **-ing**) ◇ *n* - **1.** [identification] étiquette *f* - **2.** [of record] label *m*, maison *f* de

disques ◇ *vt* - **1.** [fix label to] étiqueter - **2.** [describe] : **to ~ sb (as)** cataloguer OR étiqueter qqn (comme).

labor *etc* Am = **labour** *etc*.

laboratory [Br ləˈbɒrətrɪ, Am ˈlæbrəˌtɔːrɪ] (*pl* **-ies**) ◇ *n* laboratoire *m* ◇ *comp* de laboratoire.

Labor Day *n* fête *du travail américaine* (*premier lundi de septembre*).

laborious [ləˈbɔːrɪəs] *adj* laborieux(euse).

labor union *n* Am syndicat *m*.

labour Br, **labor** Am [ˈleɪbəʳ] ◇ *n* - **1.** [gen & MED] travail *m* ; **she went into ~** MED le travail a commencé - **2.** [workers, work carried out] main d'œuvre *f* ◇ *vt* : **there's no need to ~ the point** pas besoin de s'appesantir là-dessus ◇ *vi* travailler dur ; **to ~ at** OR **over** peiner sur ; **to ~ under a delusion** se faire des illusions OR des idées ; **to ~ under a misapprehension** être dans l'erreur.

◆ **Labour** POL ◇ *adj* travailliste ◇ *n* (U) Br les travaillistes *mpl*.

labour camp *n* camp *m* de travaux forcés.

labour costs *npl* coûts *mpl* de la main-d'œuvre.

laboured Br, **labored** Am [ˈleɪbəd] *adj* [breathing] pénible ; [style] lourd(e), laborieux(euse).

labourer Br, **laborer** Am [ˈleɪbərəʳ] *n* travailleur manuel *m*, travailleuse manuelle *f* ; [agricultural] ouvrier agricole *m*, ouvrière agricole *f*.

labour force *n* main-d'œuvre *f*.

labour-intensive *adj* à forte main d'œuvre.

labour market *n* marché *m* du travail.

labour of love *n* tâche *f* effectuée par plaisir.

labour pains *npl* douleurs *fpl* de l'accouchement.

Labour Party *n* Br : **the ~** le parti travailliste.

labour relations *npl* relations *fpl* entre employeurs et employés.

laboursaving Br, **laborsaving** Am [ˈleɪbəˌseɪvɪŋ] *adj* : **~ device** appareil *m* ménager.

Labrador [ˈlæbrədɔːʳ] *n* - **1.** [dog] labrador *m* - **2.** GEOGR Labrador *m*.

labyrinth [ˈlæbərɪnθ] *n* labyrinthe *m*.

lace [leɪs] ◇ *n* - **1.** [fabric] dentelle *f* - **2.** [of shoe etc] lacet *m* ◇ *comp* en OR de dentelle ◇ *vt* - **1.** [shoe etc] lacer - **2.** [drink] verser de l'alcool dans.

◆ **lace up** *vt sep* lacer.

lacemaking ['leɪsˌmeɪkɪŋ] n fabrication f de (la) dentelle.

laceration [ˌlæsə'reɪʃn] n lacération f.

lace-up ◇ adj [shoes] à lacets ◇ n Br chaussure f à lacets.

lack [læk] ◇ n manque m ; **for** OR **through ~ of** par manque de ; **no ~ of** bien assez de ◇ vt manquer de ◇ vi : **to be ~ing in sthg** manquer de qqch ; **to be ~ing** manquer, faire défaut.

lackadaisical [ˌlækə'deɪzɪkl] adj pej nonchalant(e).

lackey ['lækɪ] (pl -s) n pej larbin m.

lacklustre Br, **lackluster** Am ['lækˌlʌstər] adj terne.

laconic [lə'kɒnɪk] adj laconique.

lacquer ['lækər] ◇ n [for wood] vernis m, laque f ; [for hair] laque f ◇ vt laquer.

lacrosse [lə'krɒs] n crosse f.

lactic acid ['læktɪk-] n acide m lactique.

lacy ['leɪsɪ] (compar -ier ; superl -iest) adj de OR en dentelle.

lad [læd] n - **1.** inf [boy] garçon m, gars m - **2.** Br [stable boy] lad m.

ladder ['lædər] ◇ n - **1.** [for climbing] échelle f - **2.** Br [in tights] maille f filée, estafilade f ◇ vt & vi Br [tights] filer.

laden ['leɪdn] adj : **~ (with)** chargé(e) (de).

la-di-da [ˌlɑːdɪ'dɑː] adj inf pej maniéré(e).

ladies Br ['leɪdɪz], **ladies' room** Am n toilettes fpl (pour dames).

lading ['leɪdɪŋ] ▷ **bill of lading**.

ladle ['leɪdl] ◇ n louche f ◇ vt servir (à la louche).

lady ['leɪdɪ] (pl -ies) ◇ n - **1.** [gen] dame f - **2.** Am inf [to address woman] ma petite dame ◇ comp : **a ~ doctor** une femme docteur.

➤ **Lady** n Lady f ; **Our Lady** Notre-Dame f.

ladybird Br ['leɪdɪbɜːd], **ladybug** Am ['leɪdɪbʌg] n coccinelle f.

lady-in-waiting [-'weɪtɪŋ] (pl **ladies-in-waiting**) n dame f d'honneur.

lady-killer n inf bourreau m des cœurs, don Juan m.

ladylike ['leɪdɪlaɪk] adj distingué(e).

Ladyship ['leɪdɪʃɪp] n : **her/your ~** Madame la baronne/la duchesse etc.

lag [læg] (pt & pp **-ged** ; cont **-ging**) ◇ vi : **to ~ (behind)** [person, runner] traîner ; [economy, development] être en retard, avoir du retard ◇ vt [roof, pipe] calorifuger ◇ n [timelag] décalage m.

lager ['lɑːgər] n (bière f) blonde f.

lager lout n Br jeune qui, sous l'influence de l'alcool, cherche la bagarre ou commet des actes de vandalisme.

lagging ['lægɪŋ] n calorifuge m.

lagoon [lə'guːn] n lagune f.

Lagos ['leɪgɒs] n Lagos.

lah-di-dah = **la-di-da**.

laid [leɪd] pt & pp ▷ **lay**.

laid-back adj inf relaxe, décontracté(e).

lain [leɪn] pp ▷ **lie**.

lair [leər] n repaire m, antre m.

laissez-faire ['leɪseɪ'feər] ◇ adj non-interventionniste ◇ n non-interventionnisme m.

laity ['leɪətɪ] n RELIG : **the ~** les laïcs mpl.

lake [leɪk] n lac m.

Lake District n : **the ~** la région des lacs (au nord-ouest de l'Angleterre).

Lake Geneva n le lac Léman OR de Genève.

lakeside ['leɪksaɪd] adj au bord de l'eau.

lama ['lɑːmə] (pl -s) n lama m.

lamb [læm] n agneau m.

lambast [læm'bæst], **lambaste** [læm'beɪst] vt démolir.

lamb chop n côtelette f d'agneau.

lambing ['læmɪŋ] n agnelage m.

lambskin ['læmskɪn] n agneau m, peau f d'agneau.

lambswool ['læmzwʊl] ◇ n lambswool m ◇ comp en lambswool, en laine d'agneau.

lame [leɪm] adj lit & fig boiteux(euse).

lamé ['lɑːmeɪ] n lamé m.

lame duck n - **1.** fig [person, business] canard m boiteux - **2.** Am [President] président non réélu, pendant la période séparant l'élection de l'investiture de son successeur.

lamely ['leɪmlɪ] adv [argue, lie etc] maladroitement.

lament [lə'ment] ◇ n lamentation f ◇ vt se lamenter sur.

lamentable ['læməntəbl] adj lamentable.

laminated ['læmɪneɪtɪd] adj [wood] stratifié(e) ; [glass] feuilleté(e) ; [steel] laminé(e).

lamp [læmp] n lampe f.

lamplight ['læmplaɪt] n lumière f de la lampe.

lampoon [læm'puːn] ◇ n satire f ◇ vt faire la satire de.

lamppost ['læmppəʊst] n réverbère m.

lampshade ['læmpʃeɪd] n abat-jour m.

lance [lɑːns] ◇ n lance f ◇ vt [boil] percer.

lance corporal n caporal m.

lancet ['lɑːnsɪt] n bistouri m, lancette f.

Lancs [lænks] (*abbr of* **Lancashire**) *comté anglais.*

land [lænd] <> *n* **- 1.** [solid ground] terre *f* (ferme) ; [farming ground] terre, terrain *m* **- 2.** [property] terres *fpl*, propriété *f* **- 3.** [nation] pays *m* <> *vt* **- 1.** [from ship, plane] débarquer **- 2.** [catch - fish] prendre **- 3.** [plane] atterrir **- 4.** inf [obtain] décrocher **- 5.** inf [place] : **to ~ sb in trouble** attirer des ennuis à qqn ; **to be ~ed with sthg** se coltiner qqch <> *vi* **- 1.** [plane] atterrir **- 2.** [fall] tomber **- 3.** [from ship] débarquer.

land up *vi* inf atterrir.

landed gentry [ˈlændɪd-] *npl* noblesse *f* de province

landing [ˈlændɪŋ] *n* **- 1.** [of stairs] palier *m* **- 2.** AERON atterrissage *m* **- 3.** [of goods from ship] débarquement *m*.

landing card *n* carte *f* de débarquement.

landing craft *n* péniche *f* de débarquement.

landing gear *n* (U) train *m* d'atterrissage.

landing stage *n* débarcadère *m*.

landing strip *n* piste *f* d'atterrissage.

landlady [ˈlændˌleɪdɪ] (*pl* -ies) *n* [living in] logeuse *f* ; [owner] propriétaire *f*.

landlocked [ˈlændlɒkt] *adj* sans accès à la mer.

landlord [ˈlændlɔːd] *n* **- 1.** [of rented property] propriétaire *m* **- 2.** [of pub] patron *m*.

landmark [ˈlændmɑːk] *n* point *m* de repère ; fig événement *m* marquant.

landmine [ˈlændmaɪn] *n* mine *f* (terrestre).

landowner [ˈlændˌəʊnəʳ] *n* propriétaire foncier *m*, propriétaire foncière *f*.

Land Rover® [ˈ-rəʊvəʳ] *n* Land Rover® *f*.

landscape [ˈlændskeɪp] <> *n* paysage *m* <> *vt* concevoir les plans de, aménager.

landscape gardener *n* (jardinier *m*) paysagiste *mf*.

landslide [ˈlændslaɪd] *n* **- 1.** [of earth] glissement *m* de terrain ; [of rocks] éboulement *m* **- 2.** fig [election victory] victoire *f* écrasante.

landslip [ˈlændslɪp] *n* glissement *m* de terrain.

lane [leɪn] *n* **- 1.** [in country] petite route *f*, chemin *m* **- 2.** [in town] ruelle *f* **- 3.** [for traffic] voie *f ;* 'keep in ~' 'ne changez pas de file' **- 4.** AERON & SPORT couloir *m* **- 5.** [for shipping] route *f* de navigation.

language [ˈlæŋgwɪdʒ] *n* **- 1.** [of people, country] langue *f* **- 2.** [terminology, ability to speak] langage *m*.

language laboratory *n* laboratoire *m* de langues.

languid [ˈlæŋgwɪd] *adj* indolent(e).

languish [ˈlæŋgwɪʃ] *vi* languir.

languorous [ˈlæŋgərəs] *adj* literary langoureux(euse).

lank [læŋk] *adj* terne.

lanky [ˈlæŋkɪ] (*compar* -ier ; *superl* -iest) *adj* dégingandé(e).

lanolin(e) [ˈlænəlɪn] *n* lanoline *f*.

lantern [ˈlæntən] *n* lanterne *f*.

Laos [laʊs] *n* Laos *m ;* in ~ au Laos.

Laotian [ˈlaʊʃn] <> *adj* laotien(enne) <> *n* **- 1.** [person] Laotien *m*, -enne *f* **- 2.** [language] laotien *m*.

lap [læp] (*pt* & *pp* -ped ; *cont* -ping) <> *n* **- 1.** [of person] : **on sb's ~** sur les genoux de qqn **- 2.** [of race] tour *m* de piste <> *vt* **- 1.** [subj : animal] laper **- 2.** [in race] prendre un tour d'avance sur <> *vi* [water, waves] clapoter.

lap up *vt sep* **- 1.** [drink] laper **- 2.** fig [compliments] se gargariser de ; [lies] gober, avaler.

laparoscopy [ˌlæpəˈrɒskəpɪ] (*pl* -ies) *n* laparoscopie *f*.

La Paz [læˈpæz] *n* La Paz.

lapdog [ˈlæpdɒg] *n* petit chien *m* d'appartement ; fig [person] toutou *m*, caniche *m*.

lapel [ləˈpel] *n* revers *m*.

Lapland [ˈlæplænd] *n* Laponie *f ;* in ~ en Laponie.

Lapp [læp] <> *adj* lapon(e) <> *n* **- 1.** [person] Lapon *m*, -e *f* **- 2.** [language] lapon *m*.

lapse [læps] <> *n* **- 1.** [failing] défaillance *f* **- 2.** [in behaviour] écart *m* de conduite **- 3.** [of time] intervalle *m*, laps *m* de temps <> *vi* **- 1.** [passport] être périmé(e) ; [membership] prendre fin ; [tradition] se perdre **- 2.** [person] : **to ~ into bad habits** prendre de mauvaises habitudes ; **to ~ into silence** se taire.

lapsed [læpst] *adj* [Catholic etc] qui ne pratique plus.

laptop computer *n* (ordinateur *m*) portable *m*.

larceny [ˈlɑːsənɪ] *n* (U) vol *m* (simple).

larch [lɑːtʃ] *n* mélèze *m*.

lard [lɑːd] *n* saindoux *m*.

larder [ˈlɑːdəʳ] *n* garde-manger *m*.

large [lɑːdʒ] *adj* grand(e) ; [person, animal, book] gros (grosse).

at large *adv* **- 1.** [as a whole] dans son ensemble **- 2.** [prisoner, animal] en liberté.

by and large *adv* dans l'ensemble.

largely [ˈlɑːdʒlɪ] *adv* en grande partie.

larger-than-life [ˈlɑːdʒəʳ-] *adj* [character] exubérant(e).

large-scale *adj* à grande échelle.

largesse, largess Am [lɑːˈdʒes] n (U) largesses fpl.

lark [lɑːk] n - **1.** [bird] alouette f - **2.** inf [joke] blague f ; **for a** ~ pour rigoler.
◆ **lark about** vi s'amuser.

larva [ˈlɑːvə] (pl -**vae** [-viː]) n larve f.

laryngitis [ˌlærɪnˈdʒaɪtɪs] n (U) laryngite f.

larynx [ˈlærɪŋks] (pl **larynges** [ˈlærɪndʒiːz] OR **larynxes** [ˈlærɪŋksiːz]) n larynx m.

lasagna, lasagne [ləˈzænjə] n (U) lasagnes fpl.

lascivious [ləˈsɪvɪəs] adj lascif(ive).

laser [ˈleɪzəʳ] n laser m.

laser beam n rayon m laser.

laser printer n imprimante f (à) laser.

laser show n spectacle m laser.

lash [læʃ] ◇ n - **1.** [eyelash] cil m - **2.** [with whip] coup m de fouet ◇ vt - **1.** [gen] fouetter - **2.** [tie] attacher.
◆ **lash out** vi - **1.** [physically] : **to ~ out (at** OR **against)** envoyer un coup (à) - **2.** Br inf [spend money] : **to ~ out (on sthg)** faire une folie (en s'achetant qqch).

lass [læs] n jeune fille f.

lasso [læˈsuː] (pl -**s**, pt & pp -**ed** ; cont -**ing**) ◇ n lasso m ◇ vt attraper au lasso.

last [lɑːst] ◇ adj dernier(ère) ; ~ **week/year** la semaine/l'année dernière, la semaine/l'année passée ; ~ **night** hier soir ; ~ **but one** avant-dernier (avant-dernière) ; **down to the** ~ **detail/penny** jusqu'au moindre détail/dernier sou ◇ adv - **1.** [most recently] la dernière fois - **2.** [finally] en dernier, le dernier (la dernière) ◇ pron : **the Saturday before** ~ pas samedi dernier, mais le samedi d'avant ; **the year before** ~ il y a deux ans ; **the** ~ **but one** l'avant-dernier m, l'avant-dernière f ; **to leave sthg till** ~ faire qqch en dernier ◇ n : **the** ~ **I saw of him** la dernière fois que je l'ai vu ◇ vi durer ; [food] se garder, se conserver ; [feeling] persister.
◆ **at (long) last** adv enfin.

last-ditch adj ultime, désespéré(e).

lasting [ˈlɑːstɪŋ] adj durable.

lastly [ˈlɑːstlɪ] adv pour terminer, finalement.

last-minute adj de dernière minute.

last name n nom m de famille.

last post n Br - **1.** [postal collection] dernière levée f - **2.** MIL extinction f des feux.

last rites npl derniers sacrements mpl.

last straw n : **it was the** ~ cela a été la goutte (d'eau) qui fait déborder le vase.

Last Supper n : **the** ~ la Cène.

last word n : **to have the** ~ avoir le dernier mot.

Las Vegas [ˌlæsˈveɪgəs] n Las Vegas.

latch [lætʃ] ◇ n loquet m ; **on the** ~ qui n'est pas fermé à clef ◇ vt fermer au loquet.
◆ **latch onto** vt fus inf s'accrocher à.

latchkey [ˈlætʃkiː] (pl -**s**) n clef f de la porte d'entrée.

late [leɪt] ◇ adj - **1.** [not on time] : **to be** ~ **(for sthg)** être en retard (pour qqch) - **2.** [near end of] : **in** ~ **December** vers la fin décembre - **3.** [later than normal] tardif(ive) - **4.** [former] ancien(enne) - **5.** [dead] feu(e) ◇ adv - **1.** [not on time] en retard ; **to arrive 20 minutes** ~ arriver avec 20 minutes de retard - **2.** [later than normal] tard ; **to work/go to bed** ~ travailler/se coucher tard.
◆ **of late** adv récemment, dernièrement.

latecomer [ˈleɪtˌkʌməʳ] n retardataire mf.

lately [ˈleɪtlɪ] adv ces derniers temps, dernièrement.

lateness [ˈleɪtnɪs] n (U) - **1.** [of person, train] retard m - **2.** [of meeting, event] heure f tardive.

late-night adj [TV programme] programmé(e) à une heure tardive ; [shop] ouvert(e) en nocturne.

latent [ˈleɪtənt] adj latent(e).

later [ˈleɪtəʳ] ◇ adj [date] ultérieur(e) ; [edition] postérieur(e) ; **in** ~ **life** plus tard (dans la vie) ◇ adv : ~ **(on)** plus tard.

lateral [ˈlætərəl] adj latéral(e).

latest [ˈleɪtɪst] ◇ adj dernier(ère) ◇ n : **at the** ~ au plus tard.

latex [ˈleɪteks] ◇ n latex m ◇ comp en latex.

lath [lɑːθ] n latte f.

lathe [leɪð] n tour m.

lather [ˈlɑːðəʳ] ◇ n mousse f (de savon) ◇ vt savonner ◇ vi mousser.

Latin [ˈlætɪn] ◇ adj latin(e) ◇ n [language] latin m.

Latin America n Amérique f latine ; **in** ~ en Amérique latine.

Latin American ◇ adj latino-américain(e) ◇ n [person] Latino-Américain m, -e f.

latitude [ˈlætɪtjuːd] n latitude f.

latrine [ləˈtriːn] n latrines fpl.

latter [ˈlætəʳ] ◇ adj - **1.** [later] dernier(ère) - **2.** [second] deuxième ◇ n : **the** ~ celui-ci (celle-ci), ce dernier (cette dernière).

latter-day adj moderne.

latterly [ˈlætəlɪ] adv récemment.

lattice [ˈlætɪs] n treillis m, treillage m.

lattice window n fenêtre f treillagée.

Latvia ['lætvɪə] n Lettonie f ; **in ~** en Lettonie.
Latvian ['lætvɪən] <> adj letton(onne) <> n
- **1.** [person] Letton m, -onne f- **2.** [language] letton m.
laudable ['lɔːdəbl] adj louable.
laugh [lɑːf] <> n rire m ; **we had a good ~** inf
on a bien rigolé, on s'est bien amusé ; **to do
sthg for ~s** OR **a ~** inf faire qqch pour rire OR
rigoler ; **they had the last ~** finalement, ce
sont eux qui ont bien ri <> vi rire.
➤ **laugh at** vt fus [mock] se moquer de, rire
de.
➤ **laugh off** vt sep tourner en plaisanterie.
laughable ['lɑːfəbl] adj ridicule, risible.
laughing gas ['lɑːfɪŋ-] n gaz m hilarant.
laughingstock ['lɑːfɪŋstɒk] n risée f.
laughter ['lɑːftəʳ] n (U) rire m, rires mpl.
launch [lɔːntʃ] <> n - **1.** [gen] lancement m
- **2.** [boat] chaloupe f <> vt lancer.
➤ **launch into** vt fus se lancer dans.
launching ['lɔːntʃɪŋ] n lancement m.
launch(ing) pad ['lɔːntʃ(ɪŋ)-] n pas m de tir.
launder ['lɔːndəʳ] vt lit & fig blanchir.
laund(e)rette [lɔːn'dret], **Laundromat**®
Am ['lɔːndrəmæt] n laverie f automatique.
laundry ['lɔːndrɪ] (pl -ies) n - **1.** (U) [clothes] lessive f - **2.** [business] blanchisserie f - **3.** [room]
buanderie f.
laundry basket n panier m à linge.
laureate ['lɔːrɪət] ➪ **poet laureate.**
laurel ['lɒrəl] n laurier m.
laurels ['lɒrəlz] npl : **to rest on one's ~** se reposer sur ses lauriers.
Lautro ['lautrəʊ] (abbr of **Life Assurance and
Unit Trust Regulatory Organization**) n organisme britannique contrôlant les activités de
compagnies d'assurance-vie et de SICAV.
lava ['lɑːvə] n lave f.
lavatory ['lævətrɪ] (pl -ies) n toilettes fpl.
lavatory paper n Br papier m hygiénique.
lavender ['lævəndəʳ] <> adj [colour] (bleu) lavande (inv) <> n [plant] lavande f.
lavish ['lævɪʃ] <> adj - **1.** [generous] géné-
reux(euse) ; **to be ~ with** être prodigue de
- **2.** [sumptuous] somptueux(euse) <> vt : **to
~ sthg on sb** prodiguer qqch à qqn.
lavishly ['lævɪʃlɪ] adv - **1.** [generously] généreusement - **2.** [sumptuously] somptueusement.
law [lɔː] <> n - **1.** [gen] loi f ; **against the ~** contraire à la loi, illégal(e) ; **to break the ~** enfreindre OR transgresser la loi ; **~ and order**
ordre m public ; **to lay down the ~** pej faire la
loi ; **the ~ of the jungle** la loi de la jungle

- **2.** JUR droit m - **3.** inf [police] : **the ~** les flics
mpl <> comp [student, degree] en droit.
law-abiding [-ə,baɪdɪŋ] adj respec-
tueux(euse) des lois.
law-breaker n personne f qui enfreint OR
transgresse les lois.
law court n tribunal m, cour f de justice.
lawful ['lɔːfʊl] adj légal(e), licite.
lawfully ['lɔːfʊlɪ] adv légalement.
lawless ['lɔːlɪs] adj - **1.** [illegal] contraire à la
loi, illégal(e) - **2.** [without laws] sans loi.
Law Lords npl Br JUR : **the ~** les juges mpl de
la Chambre des Lords.
lawmaker ['lɔː,meɪkəʳ] n législateur m, -tri-
ce f.
lawn [lɔːn] n pelouse f, gazon m.
lawnmower ['lɔːn,məʊəʳ] n tondeuse f à
gazon.
lawn party n Am garden-party f.
lawn tennis n tennis m.
law school n faculté f de droit.
lawsuit ['lɔːsuːt] n procès m.
lawyer ['lɔːjəʳ] n [in court] avocat m ; [of company]
conseiller m juridique ; [for wills, sales] notaire
m.
lax [læks] adj relâché(e).
laxative ['læksətɪv] n laxatif m.
laxity ['læksɪtɪ], **laxness** ['læksnɪs] n relâchement m.
lay [leɪ] (pt & pp **laid**) <> pt ➪ **lie** <> vt
- **1.** [gen] poser, mettre ; fig : **to ~ the blame
for sthg on sb** rejeter la responsabilité de
qqch sur qqn - **2.** [trap, snare] tendre, dresser ; [plans] faire ; **to ~ the table** mettre la table OR le couvert - **3.** [egg] pondre <> adj
- **1.** RELIG laïque - **2.** [untrained] profane.
➤ **lay aside** vt sep mettre de côté.
➤ **lay before** vt sep : **to ~ sthg before sb** [pro-
posal] présenter OR soumettre qqch à qqn.
➤ **lay down** vt sep - **1.** [guidelines, rules] imposer, stipuler - **2.** [put down] déposer.
➤ **lay into** vt fus inf attaquer.
➤ **lay off** <> vt sep [make redundant] licencier
<> vt fus inf - **1.** [leave alone] fiche la paix à
- **2.** [give up] arrêter.
➤ **lay on** vt sep Br [provide, supply] organiser.
➤ **lay out** vt sep - **1.** [arrange] arranger, disposer - **2.** [design] concevoir.
➤ **lay over** vi Am faire escale.
layabout ['leɪəbaʊt] n Br inf fainéant m, -e f.
lay-by (pl lay-bys) n Br aire f de stationnement.
lay days npl starie f, jours mpl de planche.
layer ['leɪəʳ] n couche f ; fig [level] niveau m.

layette [leɪˈet] n layette f.

layman [ˈleɪmən] (pl -men [-mən]) n - **1.** [untrained person] profane m - **2.** RELIG laïc m.

lay-off n licenciement m.

layout [ˈleɪaʊt] n [of office, building] agencement m ; [of garden] plan m ; [of page] mise f en page.

layover [ˈleɪəʊvər] n Am escale f.

laze [leɪz] vi : **to ~ (about** OR **around)** paresser.

lazily [ˈleɪzɪlɪ] adv paresseusement, avec nonchalance.

laziness [ˈleɪzɪnɪs] n paresse f.

lazy [ˈleɪzɪ] (compar -ier ; superl -iest) adj [person] paresseux(euse), fainéant(e) ; [action] nonchalant(e).

lazybones [ˈleɪzɪbəʊnz] (pl inv) n paresseux m, -euse f, fainéant m, -e f.

lb (abbr of pound) livre (unité de poids).

LB abbr of Labrador.

lbw (abbr of leg before wicket) au cricket, faute d'un joueur qui met une jambe devant le guichet.

lc (abbr of lower case) bdc.

L/C abbr of letter of credit.

LCD (abbr of liquid crystal display) n affichage à cristaux liquides.

Ld abbr of Lord.

L-driver n Br conducteur m débutant, conductrice débutante f (qui n'a pas encore son permis).

LDS n (abbr of Licentiate in Dental Surgery) diplômé en chirurgie dentaire.

LEA (abbr of local education authority) n services régionaux de l'enseignement en Grande-Bretagne.

lead¹ [liːd] (pt & pp led) <> n - **1.** [winning position] : **to be in** OR **have the ~** mener, être en tête - **2.** [amount ahead] : **to have a ~ of ...** devancer de ... - **3.** [initiative, example] initiative f, exemple m ; **to take the ~** montrer l'exemple - **4.** THEATRE : **the ~** le rôle principal - **5.** [clue] indice m - **6.** [for dog] laisse f - **7.** [wire, cable] câble m, fil m <> adj [role etc] principal(e) ; **~ singer** chanteur m, -euse f <> vt - **1.** [be at front of] mener, être à la tête de - **2.** [guide] guider, conduire - **3.** [be in charge of] être à la tête de, diriger - **4.** [organize - protest etc] mener, organiser ; **to ~ the way** lit & fig ouvrir la marche - **5.** [life] mener - **6.** [cause] : **to ~ sb to do sthg** inciter OR pousser qqn à faire qqch <> vi - **1.** [path, cable etc] mener, conduire - **2.** [give access] : **to ~ to/into** donner sur, donner accès à - **3.** [in race, match] mener - **4.** [result in] : **to ~ to sthg** aboutir à qqch, causer qqch.

➤ **lead off** <> vt fus [subj : door, room] donner sur <> vi - **1.** [road, corridor] : **to ~ off (from)** partir (de) - **2.** [begin] commencer.

➤ **lead up to** vt fus - **1.** [precede] conduire à, aboutir à - **2.** [build up to] amener.

lead² [led] <> n plomb m ; [in pencil] mine f <> comp en OR de plomb.

leaded [ˈledɪd] adj [petrol] au plomb ; [window] à petits carreaux.

leaden [ˈledn] adj - **1.** literary [sky] de plomb - **2.** fig [very dull] mortellement ennuyeux(euse).

leader [ˈliːdər] n - **1.** [head, chief] chef m ; POL leader m - **2.** [in race, competition] premier m, -ère f - **3.** Br PRESS éditorial m.

leadership [ˈliːdəʃɪp] n - **1.** [people in charge] : **the ~** les dirigeants mpl - **2.** [position of leader] direction f - **3.** [qualities of leader] qualités fpl de chef.

lead-free [led-] adj sans plomb.

leading [ˈliːdɪŋ] adj - **1.** [most important] principal(e) - **2.** [main] : **~ part** OR **role** THEATRE rôle m principal ; fig rôle prépondérant - **3.** [at front] de tête.

leading article n Br éditorial m.

leading lady n vedette f, premier rôle m féminin.

leading light n personnage m très important OR influent.

leading man n premier rôle m masculin.

leading question n question f insidieuse.

lead pencil [led-] n crayon m à mine de plomb OR à papier.

lead poisoning [led-] n saturnisme m.

lead time [liːd-] n COMM délai m de livraison.

leaf [liːf] (pl leaves [liːvz]) n - **1.** [of tree, plant] feuille f - **2.** [of table - hinged] abattant m ; [- pullout] rallonge f - **3.** [of book] feuille f, page f.

➤ **leaf through** vt fus [magazine etc] parcourir, feuilleter.

leaflet [ˈliːflɪt] <> n prospectus m <> vt [area] distribuer des prospectus dans.

leafy [ˈliːfɪ] (compar -ier ; superl -iest) adj feuillu(e) ; [suburb, lane] planté(e) d'arbres.

league [liːg] n ligue f ; SPORT championnat m ; **to be in ~ with** être de connivence avec.

league table n classement m du championnat.

leak [liːk] <> n lit & fig fuite f <> vt fig [secret, information] divulguer <> vi fuir.

➤ **leak out** vi - **1.** [liquid] fuir - **2.** fig [secret, information] transpirer, être divulgué(e).

leakage [ˈliːkɪdʒ] n fuite f.

leaky ['li:kɪ] (*compar* -**ier** ; *superl* -**iest**) *adj* qui fuit.

lean [li:n] (*pt* & *pp* **leant** OR -**ed**) ◇ *adj* - **1.** [slim] mince - **2.** [meat] maigre - **3.** fig [month, time] mauvais(e) ◇ *vt* [rest] : **to ~ sthg against** appuyer qqch contre, adosser qqch à ◇ *vi* - **1.** [bend, slope] se pencher - **2.** [rest] : **to ~ on/against** s'appuyer sur/contre.

leaning ['li:nɪŋ] *n* : **~ (towards)** penchant *m* (pour).

leant [lent] *pt* & *pp* ⊳ **lean**.

lean-to (*pl* **lean-tos**) *n* appentis *m*.

leap [li:p] (*pt* & *pp* **leapt** OR -**ed**) ◇ *n* lit & fig bond *m* ◇ *vi* - **1.** [gen] bondir - **2.** fig [increase] faire un bond.

◆ **leap at** *vt fus* fig [opportunity] sauter sur.

leapfrog ['li:pfrɒg] (*pt* & *pp* -**ged** ; *cont* -**ging**) ◇ *n* saute-mouton *m* ◇ *vt* dépasser (d'un bond) ◇ *vi* : **to ~ over** sauter par-dessus.

leapt [lept] *pt* & *pp* ⊳ **leap**.

leap year *n* année *f* bissextile.

learn [lɜ:n] (*pt* & *pp* -**ed** OR **learnt**) ◇ *vt* : **to ~ (that)** ... apprendre que ... ; **to ~ (how) to do sthg** apprendre à faire qqch ◇ *vi* : **to ~ (of** OR **about sthg)** apprendre (qqch).

learned ['lɜ:nɪd] *adj* savant(e).

learner ['lɜ:nəʳ] *n* débutant *m*, -e *f*.

learner (driver) *n* conducteur débutant *m*, conductrice débutante *f* (*qui n'a pas encore son permis*).

learning ['lɜ:nɪŋ] *n* savoir *m*, érudition *f*.

learning curve *n* courbe *f* d'apprentissage.

learnt [lɜ:nt] *pt* & *pp* ⊳ **learn**.

lease [li:s] ◇ *n* bail *m* ; **a new ~ of life** Br, **a new ~ on life** Am une seconde jeunesse ◇ *vt* louer ; **to ~ sthg from sb** louer qqch à qqn ; **to ~ sthg to sb** louer qqch à qqn.

leaseback ['li:sbæk] *n* cession *f* de bail, cession-bail *f*.

leasehold ['li:shəʊld] ◇ *adj* loué(e) à bail, tenu(e) à bail ◇ *adv* à bail.

leaseholder ['li:s,həʊldəʳ] *n* locataire *mf*.

leash [li:ʃ] *n* laisse *f*.

least [li:st] (*superl of* **little**) ◇ *adj* : **the ~ le** moindre (la moindre), le plus petit (la plus petite) ; **he earns the ~ money of any of us** de nous tous, c'est lui qui gagne le moins ◇ *pron* [smallest amount] : **the ~** le moins ; **it's the ~ (that) he can do** c'est la moindre des choses qu'il puisse faire ; **not in the ~** pas du tout, pas le moins du monde ; **to say the ~** c'est le moins qu'on puisse dire ◇ *adv* : **(the) ~** le moins (la moins).

◆ **at least** *adv* au moins ; [to correct] du moins.

◆ **least of all** *adv* surtout pas, encore moins.

◆ **not least** *adv* fml notamment.

leather ['leðəʳ] ◇ *n* cuir *m* ◇ *comp* en cuir.

leatherette [,leðə'ret] *n* similicuir *m*.

leave [li:v] (*pt* & *pp* **left**) ◇ *vt* - **1.** [gen] laisser ; **to ~ sb alone** laisser qqn tranquille ; **it ~s me cold** ça me laisse froid - **2.** [go away from] quitter - **3.** [bequeath] : **to ~ sb sthg, to ~ sthg to sb** léguer OR laisser qqch à qqn ; *see also* **left** ◇ *vi* partir ◇ *n* congé *m* ; **to be on ~** [from work] être en congé ; [from army] être en permission.

◆ **leave behind** *vt sep* - **1.** [abandon] abandonner, laisser - **2.** [forget] oublier, laisser.

◆ **leave off** ◇ *vt sep* - **1.** [omit] : **to ~ sthg off (sthg)** omettre qqch (de qqch) - **2.** [stop] : **to ~ off doing sthg** s'arrêter de faire qqch ◇ *vi* s'arrêter.

◆ **leave out** *vt sep* omettre, exclure ; **to feel left out** se sentir de trop, se sentir exclu.

leave of absence *n* congé *m*.

leaves [li:vz] *pl* ⊳ **leaf**.

Lebanese [,lebə'ni:z] (*pl inv*) ◇ *adj* libanais(e) ◇ *n* [person] Libanais *m*, -e *f*.

Lebanon ['lebənən] *n* Liban *m* ; **in (the) ~** au Liban.

lecherous ['letʃərəs] *adj* lubrique, libidineux(euse).

lechery ['letʃərɪ] *n* lubricité *f*.

lectern ['lektən] *n* lutrin *m*.

lecture ['lektʃəʳ] ◇ *n* - **1.** [talk - gen] conférence *f* ; [- UNIV] cours *m* magistral ; **to give a ~ (on sthg)** faire une conférence (sur qqch), UNIV faire un cours (sur qqch) - **2.** [scolding] : **to give sb a ~** réprimander qqn, sermonner qqn ◇ *vt* [scold] réprimander, sermonner ◇ *vi* : **to ~ on sthg** faire un cours sur qqch ; **to ~ in sthg** être professeur de qqch.

lecture hall *n* amphithéâtre *m*.

lecturer ['lektʃərəʳ] *n* [speaker] conférencier *m*, -ère *f* ; UNIV maître assistant *m*.

lecture theatre *n* amphithéâtre *m*.

led [led] *pt* & *pp* ⊳ **lead**[1].

LED (*abbr of* **light-emitting diode**) *n* LED *f*.

ledge [ledʒ] *n* - **1.** [of window] rebord *m* - **2.** [of mountain] corniche *f*.

ledger ['ledʒəʳ] *n* grand livre *m*.

lee [li:] *n* : **in the ~ of** à l'abri de.

leech [li:tʃ] *n* lit & fig sangsue *f*.

leek [li:k] *n* poireau *m*.

leer [lɪəʳ] ◇ *n* regard *m* libidineux ◇ *vi* : **to ~ at** reluquer.

Leeward Islands ['li:wəd-] *npl* : **the ~** les îles *fpl* Sous-le-Vent.

leeway ['li:weɪ] *n* - **1.** [room to manoeuvre] marge *f* de manœuvre - **2.** [time lost] : **to make up ~** rattraper son retard.

left [left] ⋄ *pt* & *pp* ⊳ leave ⋄ *adj* - **1.** [remaining] : **to be ~** rester ; **have you any money ~?** il te reste de l'argent? - **2.** [not right] gauche ⋄ *adv* à gauche ⋄ *n* : **on** OR **to the ~** à gauche ; **keep to the ~** gardez votre gauche.

◆ Left *n* POL : **the Left** la Gauche.

left-hand *adj* de gauche ; **~ side** gauche *f*, côté *m* gauche.

left-hand drive ⋄ *adj* [car] avec la conduite à gauche ⋄ *n* conduite *f* à gauche.

left-handed [-'hændɪd] ⋄ *adj* - **1.** [person] gaucher(ère) - **2.** [implement] pour gaucher - **3.** Am [compliment] faux (fausse) ⋄ *adv* de la main gauche.

left-hander [-'hændəʳ] *n* gaucher *m*, -ère *f*.

Leftist ['leftɪst] POL ⋄ *adj* de gauche, gauchiste ⋄ *n* gauchiste *mf*.

left luggage (office) *n* Br consigne *f*.

leftover ['leftəʊvəʳ] *adj* qui reste, en surplus.

◆ leftovers *npl* restes *mpl*.

left wing *n* POL gauche *f*.

◆ left-wing *adj* POL de gauche.

left-winger *n* POL homme *m*, femme *f* de gauche.

lefty ['leftɪ] (*pl* -ies) *n* - **1.** Br inf POL gauchiste *mf*, gaucho *m* - **2.** Am [left-handed person] gaucher *m*, -ère *f*.

leg [leg] *n* - **1.** [of person, trousers] jambe *f* ; [of animal] patte *f* ; **to be on one's last ~s** être à bout de souffle ; **you don't have a ~ to stand on!** ça ne tient pas debout! ; **to pull sb's ~** faire marcher qqn - **2.** CULIN [of lamb] gigot *m* ; [of pork, chicken] cuisse *f* - **3.** [of furniture] pied *m* - **4.** [of journey, match] étape *f* ; **away ~** FTBL match *m* à l'extérieur OR sur terrain adverse.

legacy ['legəsɪ] (*pl* -ies) *n* lit & fig legs *m*, héritage *m*.

legal ['li:gl] *adj* - **1.** [concerning the law] juridique - **2.** [lawful] légal(e).

legal action *n* : **to take ~ against sb** intenter un procès à qqn, engager des poursuites contre qqn.

legal aid *n* assistance *f* judiciaire.

legality [li:'gælətɪ] *n* légalité *f*.

legalize, -ise ['li:gəlaɪz] *vt* légaliser, rendre légal.

legally ['li:gəlɪ] *adv* légalement ; **~ binding** qui oblige en droit.

legal tender *n* monnaie *f* légale.

legation [lɪ'geɪʃn] *n* légation *f*.

legend ['ledʒənd] *n* lit & fig légende *f*.

legendary ['ledʒəndrɪ] *adj* lit & fig légendaire.

leggings ['legɪŋz] *npl* jambières *fpl*, leggings *mpl* OR *fpl*.

leggy ['legɪ] (*compar* -ier ; *superl* -iest) *adj* [woman] qui a des jambes interminables.

legible ['ledʒəbl] *adj* lisible.

legibly ['ledʒəblɪ] *adv* lisiblement.

legion ['li:dʒən] ⋄ *n* lit & fig légion *f* ⋄ *adj* fml : **to be ~** être légion (*inv*).

legionnaire's disease [,li:dʒə'neəz-] *n* maladie *f* du légionnaire.

legislate ['ledʒɪsleɪt] *vi* : **to ~ (for/against)** faire des lois (pour/contre).

legislation [,ledʒɪs'leɪʃn] *n* législation *f*.

legislative ['ledʒɪslətɪv] *adj* législatif(ive).

legislator ['ledʒɪsleɪtəʳ] *n* législateur *m*, -trice *f*.

legislature ['ledʒɪsleɪtʃəʳ] *n* corps *m* législatif.

legitimacy [lɪ'dʒɪtɪməsɪ] *n* légitimité *f*.

legitimate [lɪ'dʒɪtɪmət] *adj* légitime.

legitimately [lɪ'dʒɪtɪmətlɪ] *adv* légitimement.

legitimize, -ise [lɪ'dʒɪtəmaɪz] *vt* légitimer.

legless ['leglɪs] *adj* Br inf [drunk] bourré(e), rond(e).

legroom ['legrʊm] *n (U)* place *f* pour les jambes.

leg-warmers [-,wɔ:məz] *npl* jambières *fpl*.

legwork ['legwɜ:k] *n* : **I had to do the ~** inf j'ai dû beaucoup me déplacer.

Leics (*abbr of* Leicestershire) *comté anglais*.

leisure [Br 'leʒəʳ, Am 'li:ʒəʳ] *n* loisir *m*, temps *m* libre ; **at (one's) ~** à loisir, tout à loisir.

leisure centre *n* centre *m* de loisirs.

leisurely [Br 'leʒəlɪ, Am 'li:ʒərlɪ] ⋄ *adj* [pace] lent(e), tranquille ⋄ *adv* [walk] sans se presser.

leisure time *n (U)* temps *m* libre, loisirs *mpl*.

lemming ['lemɪŋ] *n* lemming *m* ; **like ~s** fig comme les moutons de Panurge.

lemon ['lemən] *n* [fruit] citron *m*.

lemonade [,lemə'neɪd] *n* - **1.** Br [fizzy] limonade *f* - **2.** [still] citronnade *f*.

lemon curd *n* Br crème *f* au citron.

lemon juice *n* jus *m* de citron.

lemon sole *n* limande-sole *f*.

lemon squash *n* Br citronnade *f*

lemon squeezer [-'skwiːzəʳ] *n* presse-citron *m inv*.

lemon tea *n* thé *m* (au) citron.

lend [lend] (*pt* & *pp* lent) *vt* - **1.** [loan] prêter ; **to ~ sb sthg, to ~ sthg to sb** prêter qqch à qqn - **2.** [offer] : **to ~ support (to sb)** offrir son soutien (à qqn) ; **to ~ assistance (to sb)** prêter assistance (à qqn) - **3.** [add] : **to ~ sthg to sthg** [quality etc] ajouter qqch à qqch.

lender ['lendəʳ] *n* prêteur *m*, -euse *f*.

lending library ['lendɪŋ-] *n* bibliothèque *f* de prêt.

lending rate ['lendɪŋ-] *n* taux *m* de crédit.

length [leŋθ] *n* - **1.** [gen] longueur *f* ; **what ~ is it?** ça fait quelle longueur? ; **it's five metres in ~** cela fait cinq mètres de long ; **the ~ and breadth of** partout dans, dans tout - **2.** [piece - of string, wood] morceau *m*, bout *m* ; [- of cloth] coupon *m* - **3.** [duration] durée *f* - **4.** phr : **to go to great ~s to do sthg** tout faire pour faire qqch.

➤ **at length** *adv* - **1.** [eventually] enfin - **2.** [in detail] à fond.

lengthen ['leŋθən] *vt* [dress etc] rallonger ; [life] prolonger *vi* allonger.

lengthways ['leŋθweɪz] *adv* dans le sens de la longueur.

lengthy ['leŋθɪ] (*compar* -ier ; *superl* -iest) *adj* très long (longue).

leniency ['liːnjənsɪ] *n* clémence *f*, indulgence *f*.

lenient ['liːnjənt] *adj* [person] indulgent(e) ; [laws] clément(e).

lens [lenz] *n* - **1.** [of camera] objectif *m* ; [of glasses] verre *m* - **2.** [contact lens] verre *m* de contact, lentille *f* (cornéenne).

lent [lent] *pt* & *pp* ▷ **lend.**

Lent [lent] *n* Carême *m*.

lentil ['lentɪl] *n* lentille *f*.

Leo ['liːəʊ] *n* Lion ; **to be (a) ~** être Lion.

leopard ['lepəd] *n* léopard *m*.

leopardess ['lepədɪs] *n* léopard *m* femelle.

leotard ['liːətɑːd] *n* collant *m*.

leper ['lepəʳ] *n* lépreux *m*, -euse *f*.

leprechaun ['leprəkɔːn] *n* lutin *m* (irlandais).

leprosy ['leprəsɪ] *n* lèpre *f*.

lesbian ['lezbɪən] *adj* lesbien(enne) *n* lesbienne *f*.

lesbianism ['lezbɪənɪzml] *n* lesbianisme *m*.

lesion ['liːʒn] *n* lésion *f*.

Lesotho [lə'suːtuː] *n* Lesotho *m*.

less [les] (*compar of little*) *adj* moins de ; **~ money/time than me** moins d'argent/de temps que moi *pron* moins ; **it costs ~ than you think** ça coûte moins cher que tu ne le crois ; **no ~ than £50** pas moins de 50 livres ; **the ~ ... the ~ ...** moins ... moins ... *adv* moins ; **~ than five** moins de cinq ; **~ and ~** de moins en moins *prep* [minus] moins.

lessee [le'siː] *n* preneur *m*, -euse *f*, locataire *mf*.

lessen ['lesn] *vt* [risk, chance] diminuer, réduire ; [pain] atténuer *vi* [gen] diminuer ; [pain] s'atténuer.

lesser ['lesəʳ] *adj* moindre ; **to a ~ extent** OR **degree** à un degré moindre.

lesson ['lesn] *n* leçon *f*, cours *m* ; **to give/take ~s (in)** donner/prendre des leçons (de) ; **to teach sb a ~** *fig* donner une (bonne) leçon à qqn.

lessor [le'sɔːʳ] *n* bailleur *m*, -eresse *f*.

lest [lest] *conj fml* de crainte que.

let [let] (*pt* & *pp* let, *cont* -ting) *vt* - **1.** [allow] : **to ~ sb do sthg** laisser qqn faire qqch ; **she ~ her hair grow** elle s'est laissé pousser les cheveux ; **we can't ~ this happen** on ne peut pas laisser faire ça ; **to ~ sb know sthg** dire qqch à qqn ; **to ~ go of sb/sthg** lâcher qqn/qqch ; **to ~ sb go** [gen] laisser (partir) qqn ; [prisoner] libérer qqn - **2.** [in verb forms] : **~ them wait** qu'ils attendent ; **~'s go!** allons-y! ; **~'s see** voyons - **3.** [rent out] louer ; '**to ~**' 'à louer'.

➤ **let alone** *conj* encore moins, sans parler de.

➤ **let down** *vt sep* - **1.** [deflate] dégonfler - **2.** [disappoint] décevoir.

➤ **let in** *vt sep* [admit] laisser OR faire entrer.

➤ **let in for** *vt sep* : **you don't know what you're letting yourself in for** tu ne sais pas à quoi tu t'engages.

➤ **let in on** *vt sep* : **to ~ sb in on sthg** mettre qqn au courant de qqch.

➤ **let off** *vt sep* - **1.** [excuse] : **to ~ sb off sthg** dispenser qqn de qqch - **2.** [not punish] ne pas punir - **3.** [bomb] faire éclater ; [gun, firework] faire partir.

➤ **let on** *vi* : **don't ~ on!** ne dis rien (à personne)!

➤ **let out** *vt sep* - **1.** [allow to go out] laisser sortir ; **to ~ air out of sthg** dégonfler qqch - **2.** [laugh, scream] laisser échapper.

➤ **let up** *vi* - **1.** [rain] diminuer - **2.** [person] s'arrêter.

letdown ['letdaʊn] *n inf* déception *f*.

lethal ['liːθl] *adj* mortel(elle), fatal(e).

lethargic [lə'θɑːdʒɪk] *adj* léthargique.

lethargy ['leθədʒɪ] *n* léthargie *f*.

Letraset® ['letrəset] *n* Letraset®.

let's [lets] = **let us.**

letter ['letə'] n lettre f.

letter bomb n lettre f piégée.

letterbox ['letəbɒks] n Br boîte f aux OR à lettres.

letterhead ['letəhed] n en-tête m.

lettering ['letərɪŋ] n (U) caractères mpl.

letter of credit n lettre f de crédit.

letter opener n coupe-papier m inv.

letter-perfect adj Am absolument parfait(e).

letter quality n COMPUT qualité f courrier.

letters patent npl lettres fpl patentes.

lettuce ['letɪs] n laitue f, salade f.

letup ['letʌp] n [in fighting] répit m ; [in work] relâchement m.

leuk(a)emia [luːˈkiːmɪə] n leucémie f.

levee ['levɪ] n Am [embankment] digue f.

level ['levl] (Br pt & pp -led ; cont -ling, Am pt & pp -ed ; cont -ing) <> adj - 1. [equal in height] à la même hauteur ; [horizontal] horizontal(e) ; **to be ~ with** être au niveau de - 2. [equal in standard] à égalité - 3. [flat] plat(e), plan(e) <> adv : **to draw ~ with sb** arriver à la même hauteur que qqn, rejoindre qqn <> n - 1. [gen] niveau m ; **to be on a ~ (with)** être du même niveau (que) ; **to be on the ~ inf** être réglo - 2. Am [spirit level] niveau m à bulle <> vt - 1. [make flat] niveler, aplanir - 2. [demolish] raser - 3. [aim] : **to ~ a gun at** pointer OR braquer un fusil sur ; **to ~ an accusation at** OR **against sb** lancer une accusation contre qqn.

➤ **level off, level out** vi - 1. [inflation etc] se stabiliser - 2. [aeroplane] se mettre en palier.

➤ **level with** vt fus inf être franc (franche) OR honnête avec.

level crossing n Br passage m à niveau.

level-headed [-ˈhedɪd] adj raisonnable.

level pegging [-ˈpegɪŋ] adj Br : **to be ~** être à égalité.

lever [Br ˈliːvəʳ, Am ˈlevərl] n levier m.

leverage [Br ˈliːvərɪdʒ, Am ˈlevərɪdʒ] n (U) - 1. [force] : **to get ~ on sthg** avoir une prise sur qqch - 2. fig [influence] influence f.

leviathan [lɪˈvaɪəθn] n fig colosse m.

levitation [ˌlevɪˈteɪʃn] n lévitation f.

levity ['levətɪ] n légèreté f.

levy ['levɪ] (pt & pp -ied) <> n prélèvement m, impôt m <> vt prélever, percevoir.

lewd [ljuːd] adj obscène.

lexical ['leksɪkl] adj lexical(e).

LI abbr of **Long Island.**

liability [ˌlaɪəˈbɪlətɪ] (pl -ies) n responsabilité f ; fig [person] danger m public.

➤ **liabilities** npl FIN dettes fpl, passif m.

liable ['laɪəbl] adj - 1. [likely] : **to be ~ to do sthg** risquer de faire qqch, être susceptible de faire qqch - 2. [prone] : **to be ~ to sthg** être sujet(ette) à qqch - 3. JUR : **to be ~ (for)** être responsable (de) ; **to be ~ to** être passible de.

liaise [lɪˈeɪz] vi : **to ~ with** assurer la liaison avec.

liaison [lɪˈeɪzɒn] n liaison f.

liar ['laɪəʳ] n menteur m, -euse f.

Lib. [lɪb] abbr of **Liberal.**

libel ['laɪbl] (Br pt & pp -led ; cont -ling, Am pt & pp -ed ; cont -ing) <> n diffamation f <> vt diffamer.

libellous Br, **libelous** Am ['laɪbələs] adj diffamatoire.

liberal ['lɪbərəl] <> adj - 1. [tolerant] libéral(e) - 2. [generous] généreux(euse) <> n libéral m, -e f.

➤ **Liberal** POL <> adj libéral(e) <> n libéral m, -e f.

liberal arts npl esp Am arts mpl libéraux.

Liberal Democrat n adhérent du principal parti centriste britannique.

liberalize, -ise ['lɪbərəlaɪz] vt libéraliser.

liberal-minded [-ˈmaɪndɪd] adj large d'esprit.

Liberal Party n : **the ~** le parti libéral.

liberate ['lɪbəreɪt] vt libérer.

liberation [ˌlɪbəˈreɪʃn] n libération f.

liberator ['lɪbəreɪtəʳ] n libérateur m, -trice f.

Liberia [laɪˈbɪərɪə] n Liberia m ; **in ~** au Liberia.

Liberian [laɪˈbɪərɪən] <> adj libérien(enne) <> n Libérien m, -enne f.

libertine ['lɪbətiːn] n libertin m.

liberty ['lɪbətɪ] (pl -ies) n liberté f ; **at ~** en liberté ; **to be at ~ to do sthg** être libre de faire qqch ; **to take liberties (with sb)** prendre des libertés (avec qqn).

libido [lɪˈbiːdəʊ] (pl -s) n libido f.

Libra ['liːbrə] n Balance f ; **to be (a) ~** être Balance.

librarian [laɪˈbreərɪən] n bibliothécaire mf.

librarianship [laɪˈbreərɪənʃɪp] n : **diploma in ~** diplôme de bibliothécaire.

library ['laɪbrərɪ] (pl -ies) n bibliothèque f.

library book n livre m de bibliothèque.

libretto [lɪˈbretəʊ] (pl -s) n livret m.

Libya ['lɪbɪə] n Libye f ; **in ~** en Libye.

Libyan ['lɪbɪən] <> adj libyen(enne) <> n Libyen m, -enne f.

lice [laɪs] *pl* ⊏▷ **louse.**

licence ['laɪsəns] ⟨⟩ *n* - **1.** [gen] permis *m*, autorisation *f*; **driving ~** permis *m* de conduire; **TV ~** redevance *f* télé - **2.** COMM licence *f*; **under ~** sous licence ⟨⟩ *vt* Am = **license.**

license ['laɪsəns] ⟨⟩ *vt* autoriser ⟨⟩ *n* Am = **licence.**

licensed ['laɪsənst] *adj* - **1.** [person] : **to be ~ to do sthg** avoir un permis pour OR l'autorisation de faire qqch - **2.** Br [premises] qui détient une licence de débit de boissons.

licensee [,laɪsən'siː] *n* [of pub] gérant *m*, -e *f*.

license plate *n* Am plaque *f* d'immatriculation.

licensing hours ['laɪsənsɪŋ-] *npl* Br *heures d'ouverture des débits de boissons.*

> **LICENSING HOURS**
>
> Traditionnellement, les heures d'ouverture des pubs répondaient à une réglementation très stricte (liée à la législation sur la vente des boissons alcoolisées), mais celle-ci a été assouplie en 1988. Au lieu d'ouvrir uniquement de 11h 30 à 14h 30 et de 18h à 23h, les pubs restent ouverts de 11h à 23h, sauf le dimanche (de 11h à 15h et de 19h à 22h 30).

licensing laws ['laɪsənsɪŋ-] *npl* Br *lois réglementant la vente d'alcool.*

licentious [laɪ'senʃəs] *adj* licencieux(euse).

lichen ['laɪkən] *n* lichen *m*.

lick [lɪk] ⟨⟩ *n* - **1.** [act of licking] : **to give sthg a ~** lécher qqch - **2.** inf [small amount] : **a ~ of paint** un petit coup de peinture ⟨⟩ *vt* - **1.** [gen] lécher ; **to ~ one's lips** se lécher les lèvres ; *fig* se frotter les mains - **2.** inf [defeat] écraser, battre à plates coutures.

licorice ['lɪkərɪs] = **liquorice.**

lid [lɪd] *n* - **1.** [cover] couvercle *m* - **2.** [eyelid] paupière *f*.

lido ['liːdəʊ] (*pl* -**s**) *n* - **1.** Br [swimming pool] piscine *f* en plein air - **2.** [beach] plage *f*.

lie [laɪ] (*pt sense 1* **lied** ; *pt senses 2-6* **lay** ; *pp sense 1* **lied** ; *pp senses 2-6* **lain** ; *cont all senses* **lying**) ⟨⟩ *n* mensonge *m* ; **to tell ~s** mentir, dire des mensonges ⟨⟩ *vi* - **1.** [tell lie] : **to ~ (to sb)** mentir (à qqn) - **2.** [be horizontal] être allongé(e), être couché(e) - **3.** [lie down] s'allonger, se coucher - **4.** [be situated] se trouver, être - **5.** [difficulty, solution etc] résider - **6.** *phr* : **to ~ low** se planquer, se tapir.

➤ **lie about, lie around** *vi* traîner.

➤ **lie down** *vi* s'allonger, se coucher ; **he won't take it lying down** il ne va pas accepter ça sans rien dire.

➤ **lie in** *vi* Br rester au lit, faire la grasse matinée.

Liechtenstein ['lɪktənstaɪn] *n* Liechtenstein *m* ; **in ~** au Liechtenstein.

lie detector *n* détecteur *m* de mensonges.

lie-down *n* Br : **to have a ~** faire une sieste OR un petit somme.

lie-in *n* Br : **to have a ~** faire la grasse matinée.

lieu [ljuː, luː] ➤ **in lieu** *adv* à la place ; **in ~ of** au lieu de, à la place de.

Lieut. (*abbr of* **lieutenant**) lieut.

lieutenant [Br lef'tenənt, Am luː'tenənt] *n* lieutenant *m*.

lieutenant colonel *n* lieutenant-colonel *m*.

life [laɪf] (*pl* **lives** [laɪvz]) ⟨⟩ *n* - **1.** [gen] vie *f* ; **that's ~!** c'est la vie! ; **for ~** à vie ; **I can't for the ~ of me remember ...** rien à faire, je n'arrive pas à me rappeler ... ; **to breathe ~ into** donner vie à ; **to come to ~** s'éveiller, s'animer ; **to lay down one's ~** donner sa vie ; **to risk ~ and limb** risquer sa peau ; **to scare the ~ out of sb** faire une peur bleue à qqn ; **to take sb's ~** tuer qqn ; **to take one's own ~** se donner la mort - **2.** (U) inf [life imprisonment] emprisonnement *m* à perpétuité ⟨⟩ *comp* [member etc] à vie.

life-and-death *adj* extrêmement grave OR critique.

life annuity *n* rente *f* viagère.

life assurance = **life insurance.**

life belt *n* bouée *f* de sauvetage.

lifeblood ['laɪfblʌd] *n* *fig* élément *m* vital, âme *f*.

lifeboat ['laɪfbəʊt] *n* canot *m* de sauvetage.

lifeboatman ['laɪfbəʊtmən] (*pl* -**men** [-mən]) *n* sauveteur *m* en mer.

life buoy *n* bouée *f* de sauvetage.

life expectancy [-ɪk'spektənsɪ] *n* espérance *f* de vie.

lifeguard ['laɪfgɑːd] *n* [at swimming pool] maître-nageur sauveteur *m* ; [at beach] gardien *m* de plage.

life imprisonment [-ɪm'prɪznmənt] *n* emprisonnement *m* à perpétuité.

life insurance *n* assurance-vie *f*.

life jacket *n* gilet *m* de sauvetage.

lifeless ['laɪflɪs] *adj* - **1.** [dead] sans vie, inanimé(e) - **2.** [listless - performance] qui manque de vie ; [- voice] monotone.

lifelike ['laɪflaɪk] *adj* - **1.** [statue, doll] qui semble vivant(e) - **2.** [portrait] ressemblant(e).

lifeline ['laɪflaɪn] *n* corde *f* (de sauvetage) ; fig lien *m* vital (avec l'extérieur).

lifelong ['laɪflɒŋ] *adj* de toujours.

life peer *n* Br pair *m* à vie.

life preserver [-prɪˌzɜːvər] *n* Am [life belt] bouée *f* de sauvetage ; [life jacket] gilet *m* de sauvetage.

life raft *n* canot *m* pneumatique (de sauvetage).

lifesaver ['laɪfˌseɪvər] *n* [person] maître-nageur sauveteur *m*.

life sentence *n* condamnation *f* à perpétuité.

life-size(d) [-saɪz(d)] *adj* grandeur nature *(inv)*.

lifespan ['laɪfspæn] *n* - **1.** [of person, animal] espérance *f* de vie - **2.** [of product, machine] durée *f* de vie.

lifestyle ['laɪfstaɪl] *n* style *m* de vie.

life-support system *n* respirateur *m* artificiel.

lifetime ['laɪftaɪm] *n* vie *f ;* in my ~ de mon vivant.

lift [lɪft] ⟨> *n* - **1.** [in car] : to give sb a ~ emmener OR prendre qqn en voiture - **2.** Br [elevator] ascenseur *m* ⟨> *vt* - **1.** [gen] lever ; [weight] soulever - **2.** [plagiarize] plagier - **3.** inf [steal] voler ⟨> *vi* - **1.** [lid etc] s'ouvrir - **2.** [fog etc] se lever.

lift-off *n* décollage *m*.

ligament ['lɪgəmənt] *n* ligament *m*.

light [laɪt] (*pt* & *pp* lit OR -ed) ⟨> *adj* - **1.** [not dark] clair(e) ; ~ blue/green bleu/vert clair *(inv)* - **2.** [not heavy] léger(ère) - **3.** [not strong] : to be a ~ sleeper avoir le sommeil léger - **3.** [traffic] fluide ; [corrections] peu nombreux(euses) - **4.** [work] facile ⟨> *n* - **1.** (U) [brightness] lumière *f* - **2.** [device] lampe *f* - **3.** [AUT - gen] feu *m ;* [- headlamp] phare *m* - **4.** [for cigarette etc] feu *m ;* have you got a ~? vous avez du feu? ; to set ~ to sthg mettre le feu à qqch - **5.** [perspective] : in the ~ of Br, in ~ of Am à la lumière de ; to see sb/sthg in a different ~ voir qqn/qqch sous un jour nouveau - **6.** phr : to come to ~ être découvert(e) OR dévoilé(e) ; to see the ~ [understand] comprendre ; to throw OR cast OR shed ~ on sthg clarifier qqch ⟨> *vt* - **1.** [fire, cigarette] allumer - **2.** [room, stage] éclairer ⟨> *adv* : to travel ~ voyager léger.

➤ **light out** *vi* Am inf se tirer.

➤ **light up** ⟨> *vt sep* - **1.** [illuminate] éclairer - **2.** [cigarette etc] allumer ⟨> *vi* - **1.** [face] s'éclairer - **2.** inf [start smoking] allumer une cigarette.

light aircraft *n* avion *m* léger.

light ale *n* Br bière blonde légère.

light bulb *n* ampoule *f*.

light cream *n* Am crème *f* liquide.

lighted ['laɪtɪd] *adj* [room] éclairé(e).

light-emitting diode [-ɪ'mɪtɪŋ-] *n* diode *f* électroluminescente.

lighten ['laɪtn] ⟨> *vt* - **1.** [give light to] éclairer ; [make less dark] éclaircir - **2.** [make less heavy] alléger ⟨> *vi* [brighten] s'éclaircir.

➤ **lighten up** *vi* inf se dérider.

lighter ['laɪtər] *n* [cigarette lighter] briquet *m*.

light-fingered [-'fɪŋgəd] *adj* inf chapardeur(euse).

light-headed [-'hedɪd] *adj* : to feel ~ avoir la tête qui tourne.

light-hearted [-'hɑːtɪd] *adj* - **1.** [cheerful] joyeux(euse), gai(e) - **2.** [amusing] amusant(e).

lighthouse ['laɪthaʊs, *pl* -haʊzɪz] *n* phare *m*.

light industry *n* industrie *f* légère.

lighting ['laɪtɪŋ] *n* éclairage *m*.

lighting-up time *n* heure où les véhicules doivent allumer leurs phares.

lightly ['laɪtlɪ] *adv* - **1.** [gen] légèrement - **2.** [frivolously] à la légère.

light meter *n* posemètre *m*, cellule *f* photoélectrique.

lightning ['laɪtnɪŋ] *n* (U) éclair *m*, foudre *f*.

lightning conductor Br, **lightning rod** Am *n* paratonnerre *m*.

lightning strike *n* Br grève *f* surprise.

light opera *n* opérette *f*.

light pen *n* crayon *m* optique, photostyle *m*.

lightship ['laɪtʃɪp] *n* bateau-feu *m*, bateau-phare *m*.

lights-out *n* extinction *f* des feux.

lightweight ['laɪtweɪt] ⟨> *adj* - **1.** [object] léger(ère) - **2.** fig & pej [person] insignifiant(e) ⟨> *n* - **1.** [boxer] poids *m* léger - **2.** fig & pej [person] personne *f* insignifiante.

light year *n* année-lumière *f*.

likable ['laɪkəbl] *adj* sympathique.

like [laɪk] ⟨> *prep* - **1.** [gen] comme ; to look ~ sb/sthg ressembler à qqn/qqch ; to taste ~ sthg avoir un goût de qqch ; ~ this/that comme ci/ça - **2.** [typical of] : that's just ~ him! c'est bien de lui!, ça lui ressemble! - **3.** [such as] tel que, comme ⟨> *vt* - **1.** [gen] aimer ; I ~ her elle me plaît ; to ~ doing OR to do sthg aimer faire qqch - **2.** [expressing a wish] : would you ~ some more cake? vous prendrez encore du gâteau? ; I'd ~ to go je voudrais bien OR j'aimerais y aller ; I'd ~ you to come je

voudrais bien OR j'aimerais que vous veniez ; **if you ~** si vous voulez ◇ adj : **people
of ~ mind** des gens qui pensent comme lui/
moi etc ◇ n : **the ~** une chose pareille ; **and
the ~** et d'autres choses du même genre.
➤ **likes** npl : **~s and dislikes** goûts mpl.

likeable ['laɪkəbl] = likable.

likelihood ['laɪklɪhʊd] n (U) chances fpl, probabilité f ; **in all ~** selon toute probabilité.

likely ['laɪklɪ] adj - **1.** [probable] probable ; **he's
~ to get angry** il risque de se fâcher ; **they're
~ to win** ils vont sûrement gagner ; **a
~ story!** iro à d'autres ! - **2.** [candidate] prometteur(euse).

like-minded [-'maɪndɪd] adj de même opinion.

liken ['laɪkn] vt : **to ~ sb/sthg to** assimiler
qqn/qqch à.

likeness ['laɪknɪs] n - **1.** [resemblance] : **~ (to)**
ressemblance f (avec) - **2.** [portrait] portrait
m.

likewise ['laɪkwaɪz] adv [similarly] de même ; **to
do ~** faire pareil OR de même.

liking ['laɪkɪŋ] n [for person] affection f, sympathie f ; [for food, music] goût m, penchant m ; **to
have a ~ for sthg** avoir le goût de qqch ; **to be
to sb's ~** être du goût de qqn, plaire à qqn.

lilac ['laɪlək] ◇ adj [colour] lilas (inv) ◇ n lilas
m.

Lilo® ['laɪləʊ] (pl -s) n Br matelas m pneumatique.

lilt [lɪlt] n rythme m, cadence f.

lilting ['lɪltɪŋ] adj [voice] mélodieux(euse),
chantant(e).

lily ['lɪlɪ] (pl -ies) n lis m.

lily of the valley (pl lilies of the valley) n
muguet m.

Lima ['liːmə] n Lima.

limb [lɪm] n - **1.** [of body] membre m - **2.** [of tree]
branche f - **3. phr : to be out on a ~** être en
mauvaise posture.

limber ['lɪmbə'] ➤ **limber up** vi s'échauffer.

limbo ['lɪmbəʊ] (pl -s) n - **1.** (U) [uncertain state] :
to be in ~ être dans les limbes - **2.** [dance] :
the ~ le limbo.

lime [laɪm] n - **1.** [fruit] citron m vert - **2.** [drink] :
~ (juice) jus m de citron vert - **3.** [linden tree]
tilleul m - **4.** [substance] chaux f.

lime cordial n sirop m de citron vert.

lime-green adj vert jaune (inv).

limelight ['laɪmlaɪt] n : **to be in the ~** être au
premier plan.

limerick ['lɪmərɪk] n poème humoristique en
cinq vers.

limestone ['laɪmstəʊn] n (U) pierre f à
chaux, calcaire m.

limey ['laɪmɪ] (pl -s) n Am inf terme péjoratif
désignant un Anglais.

limit ['lɪmɪt] ◇ n limite f ; **he's/she's the ~!** inf
il/elle dépasse les bornes! ; **off ~s** esp Am
d'accès interdit ; **within ~s** [to an extent] dans
une certaine mesure ◇ vt limiter, restreindre ; **to ~ o.s. to sthg** se limiter à qqch.

limitation [ˌlɪmɪ'teɪʃn] n limitation f, restriction f ; **to know one's ~s** connaître ses
limites.

limited ['lɪmɪtɪd] adj limité(e), restreint(e).

limited edition n [of book] édition f à tirage
limité.

limited (liability) company n société f
anonyme.

limitless ['lɪmɪtlɪs] adj illimité(e).

limo ['lɪməʊ] n inf abbr of limousine.

limousine ['lɪməziːn] n limousine f.

limp [lɪmp] ◇ adj mou (molle) ◇ n : **to have
a ~** boiter ◇ vi boiter.

limpet ['lɪmpɪt] n patelle f, bernique f.

limpid ['lɪmpɪd] adj literary limpide.

limply ['lɪmplɪ] adv mollement.

linchpin ['lɪntʃpɪn] n fig cheville f ouvrière.

Lincs. [lɪŋks] (abbr of Lincolnshire) comté anglais.

linctus ['lɪŋktəs] n Br sirop m pour la toux.

line [laɪn] ◇ n - **1.** [gen] ligne f ; **to walk in a
straight ~** marcher en ligne droite - **2.** [row]
rangée f - **3.** [queue] file f, queue f ; **to stand
OR wait in ~** faire la queue ; **he's in ~ for promotion** il devrait être promu bientôt
- **4.** [RAIL - track] voie f ; [- route] ligne f - **5.** NAUT :
shipping ~ compagnie f de navigation
- **6.** [of poem, song] vers m - **7.** [wrinkle] ride f
- **8.** [string, wire etc] corde f ; **a fishing ~** une ligne - **9.** TELEC ligne f ; **hold the ~!** ne quittez
pas! - **10.** inf [short letter] : **to drop sb a ~** écrire
un (petit) mot à qqn - **11.** [course of action] :
what ~ did you take? quelle stratégie as-tu
adoptée? ; **to think along the same ~s** partager la même opinion ; **~ of argument** raisonnement m - **12.** inf [work] : **~ of business**
branche f - **13.** [borderline] frontière f - **14.** [lineage] lignée f - **15.** COMM gamme f - **16. phr : to
be on the right ~s** être sur la bonne voie ; **to
read between the ~s** lire entre les lignes ; **to
draw the ~ at sthg** refuser de faire OR d'aller
jusqu'à faire qqch ; **to step out of ~** faire cavalier seul ◇ vt - **1.** [form rows along] : **trees ~d
the streets** les rues étaient bordées d'arbres - **2.** [drawer, box] tapisser ; [clothes] doubler.

➤ **lines** *npl* - **1.** SCH : to be given 100 ~s avoir 100 lignes à faire - **2.** THEATRE texte *m.*

➤ **on the line** *adv* : to put sthg/to be on the ~ mettre qqch/être en jeu.

➤ **out of line** *adj* [remark, behaviour] déplacé(e).

➤ **line up** ◇ *vt sep* - **1.** [in rows] aligner - **2.** [organize] prévoir ◇ *vi* [in row] s'aligner ; [in queue] faire la queue.

lineage ['lɪnɪɪdʒ] *n* lignée *f.*

linear ['lɪnɪə'] *adj* linéaire.

lined [laɪnd] *adj* - **1.** [paper] réglé(e) - **2.** [wrinkled] ridé(e).

line drawing *n* dessin *m* au trait.

line feed *n* saut *m* de ligne.

linen ['lɪnɪn] ◇ *n (U)* - **1.** [cloth] lin *m* - **2.** [tablecloths, sheets] linge *m* (de maison) ◇ *comp* - **1.** [suit etc] de OR en lin - **2.** [cupboard] à linge.

linen basket *n* panier *m* à linge.

line printer *n* imprimante *f* ligne par ligne.

liner ['laɪnə'] *n* [ship] paquebot *m.*

linesman ['laɪnzmən] (*pl* -men [-mən]) *n* TENNIS juge *m* de ligne ; FTBL juge de touche.

lineup ['laɪnʌp] *n* - **1.** SPORT équipe *f* - **2.** Am [identification parade] rangée *f* de suspects *(pour identification par un témoin).*

linger ['lɪŋgə'] *vi* - **1.** [person] s'attarder - **2.** [doubt, pain] persister.

lingerie ['læɲʒərɪ] *n (U)* lingerie *f.*

lingering ['lɪŋgrɪŋ] *adj* [doubt] persistant(e) ; [hope] faible ; [illness] long (longue).

lingo ['lɪŋgəʊ] (*pl* -es) *n* inf jargon *m.*

linguist ['lɪŋgwɪst] *n* linguiste *mf.*

linguistic [lɪŋ'gwɪstɪk] *adj* linguistique.

linguistics [lɪŋ'gwɪstɪks] *n (U)* linguistique *f.*

liniment ['lɪnɪmənt] *n* liniment *m.*

lining ['laɪnɪŋ] *n* - **1.** [of coat, curtains, box] doublure *f* - **2.** [of stomach] muqueuse *f* - **3.** AUT [of brakes] garniture *f.*

link [lɪŋk] ◇ *n* - **1.** [of chain] maillon *m* - **2.** [connection] : ~ (between/with) lien *m* (entre/avec) ; a rail/telephone ~ une liaison ferroviaire/téléphonique ◇ *vt* [cities, parts] relier ; [events etc] lier ; to ~ arms se donner le bras.

➤ **link up** *vt sep* relier ; to ~ sthg up with sthg relier qqch up OR à qqch.

linkage ['lɪŋkɪdʒ] *n (U)* [relationship] lien *m*, relation *f.*

linked [lɪŋkt] *adj* lié(e).

links [lɪŋks] (*pl inv*) *n* terrain *m* de golf *(au bord de la mer).*

linkup ['lɪŋkʌp] *n* liaison *f.*

lino ['laɪnəʊ], **linoleum** [lɪ'nəʊlɪəm] *n* lino *m*, linoléum *m.*

linseed oil ['lɪnsiːd-] *n* huile *f* de lin.

lint [lɪnt] *n (U)* - **1.** [dressing] compresse *f* - **2.** Am [fluff] peluches *fpl.*

lintel ['lɪntl] *n* linteau *m.*

lion ['laɪən] *n* lion *m.*

lion cub *n* lionceau *m.*

lioness ['laɪənes] *n* lionne *f.*

lionize, -ise ['laɪənaɪz] *vt* porter aux nues.

lip [lɪp] *n* - **1.** [of mouth] lèvre *f ;* my ~s are sealed je ne dirai rien - **2.** [of container] bord *m.*

lip-read *vi* lire sur les lèvres.

lip-reading *n* lecture *f* sur les lèvres.

lip salve [-sælv] *n* Br pommade *f* pour les lèvres.

lip service *n :* to pay ~ to sthg approuver qqch pour la forme.

lipstick ['lɪpstɪk] *n* rouge *m* à lèvres.

liquefy ['lɪkwɪfaɪ] (*pt* & *pp* -ied) ◇ *vt* liquéfier ◇ *vi* se liquéfier.

liqueur [lɪ'kjʊə'] *n* liqueur *f.*

liquid ['lɪkwɪd] ◇ *adj* liquide ◇ *n* liquide *m.*

liquid assets *npl* liquidités *fpl.*

liquidate ['lɪkwɪdeɪt] *vt* liquider.

liquidation [ˌlɪkwɪ'deɪʃn] *n* liquidation *f.*

liquidator ['lɪkwɪdeɪtə'] *n* liquidateur *m*, -trice *f.*

liquid crystal display *n* affichage *m* à cristaux liquides.

liquidity [lɪ'kwɪdətɪ] *n* liquidité *f.*

liquidize, -ise ['lɪkwɪdaɪz] *vt* Br CULIN passer au mixer.

liquidizer ['lɪkwɪdaɪzə'] *n* Br mixer *m.*

liquor ['lɪkə'] *n (U)* alcool *m*, spiritueux *mpl.*

liquorice ['lɪkərɪs] *n* réglisse *f.*

liquor store *n* Am magasin *m* de vins et d'alcools.

lira ['lɪərə] *n* lire *f.*

Lisbon ['lɪzbən] *n* Lisbonne.

lisp [lɪsp] ◇ *n* zézaiement *m* ◇ *vi* zézayer.

lissom(e) ['lɪsəm] *adj* gracile.

list [lɪst] ◇ *n* liste *f* ◇ *vt* [in writing] faire la liste de ; [in speech] énumérer ◇ *vi* NAUT donner de la bande, gîter.

listed building [ˌlɪstɪd-] *n* Br monument *m* classé.

listed company ['lɪstɪd-] *n* Br société *f* cotée en Bourse.

listen ['lɪsn] *vi :* to ~ to (sb/sthg) écouter (qqn/qqch) ; to ~ for sthg guetter qqch.

➤ **listen in** *vi* - **1.** RADIO être à l'écoute, écouter - **2.** [eavesdrop] : **to ~ in (on sthg)** écouter (qqch).

➤ **listen up** *vi* Am inf écouter.

listener ['lɪsnəʳ] *n* auditeur *m*, -trice *f*.

listing ['lɪstɪŋ] *n* [COMPUT - action] listage *m* ; [- result] listing *m*.

➤ **listings** *npl* : **the ~s** le calendrier des spectacles.

listless ['lɪstlɪs] *adj* apathique, mou (molle).

list price *n* prix *m* de catalogue.

lit [lɪt] *pt & pp* ⊳ **light**.

litany ['lɪtənɪ] (*pl* -ies) *n* litanie *f*.

liter Am = **litre**.

literacy ['lɪtərəsɪ] *n* fait *m* de savoir lire et écrire.

literal ['lɪtərəl] *adj* littéral(e).

literally ['lɪtərəlɪ] *adv* littéralement ; **to take sthg ~** prendre qqch au pied de la lettre.

literary ['lɪtərərɪ] *adj* littéraire.

literate ['lɪtərət] *adj* - **1.** [able to read and write] qui sait lire et écrire - **2.** [well-read] cultivé(e).

literature ['lɪtrətʃəʳ] *n* littérature *f* ; [printed information] documentation *f*.

lithe [laɪð] *adj* souple, agile.

lithograph ['lɪθəɡrɑːf] *n* lithographie *f*.

lithography [lɪ'θɒɡrəfɪ] *n* lithographie *f*.

Lithuania [ˌlɪθjʊ'eɪnɪə] *n* Lituanie *f* ; **in ~** en Lituanie.

Lithuanian [ˌlɪθjʊ'eɪnɪən] ⟨ *adj* lituanien (enne) ⟨ *n* - **1.** [person] Lituanien *m*, -enne *f* - **2.** [language] lituanien *m*.

litigant ['lɪtɪɡənt] *n* plaideur *m*, -euse *f*.

litigate ['lɪtɪɡeɪt] *vi* plaider.

litigation [ˌlɪtɪ'ɡeɪʃn] *n* litige *m* ; **to go to ~** aller en justice.

litmus paper ['lɪtməs-] *n* papier *m* de tournesol.

litre Br, **liter** Am ['liːtəʳ] *n* litre *m*.

litter ['lɪtəʳ] ⟨ *n* - **1.** (U) [rubbish] ordures *fpl*, détritus *mpl* - **2.** [of animals] portée *f* ⟨ *vt* : **to be ~ed with** être couvert(e) de.

litterbin ['lɪtəˌbɪn] *n* Br boîte *f* à ordures.

litterlout Br ['lɪtəlaʊt], **litterbug** ['lɪtəbʌɡ] *n* *personne qui jette des ordures n'importe où.*

litter tray *n* caisse *f* (pour litière).

little ['lɪtl] (*compar sense 2* **less** ; *superl sense 2* **least**) ⟨ *adj* - **1.** [not big] petit(e) ; **a ~ chat** un brin de causette ; **a ~ while** un petit moment - **2.** [not much] peu de ; **~ money** peu d'argent ; **a ~ money** un peu d'argent ⟨ *pron* : **~ of the money was left** il ne restait pas beaucoup d'argent, il restait peu d'argent ; **I understood ~ of what was said** je n'ai

pas compris grand-chose à ce qu'ils ont dit ; **I see very ~ of him now** je ne le vois plus beaucoup, je ne le vois guère ; **a ~** un peu ⟨ *adv* peu, pas beaucoup ; **~ by ~** peu à peu.

little finger *n* petit doigt *m*, auriculaire *m*.

little-known *adj* peu connu(e).

liturgy ['lɪtədʒɪ] (*pl* -ies) *n* liturgie *f*.

live[1] [lɪv] ⟨ *vi* - **1.** [gen] vivre ; **long ~ the Queen!** vive la reine! - **2.** [have one's home] habiter, vivre ; **to ~ in Paris** habiter (à) Paris ⟨ *vt* : **to ~ a quiet life** mener une vie tranquille ; **to ~ it up** inf faire la noce.

➤ **live down** *vt sep* faire oublier.

➤ **live for** *vt fus* vivre pour.

➤ **live in** *vi* [student] être interne.

➤ **live off** *vt fus* [savings, the land] vivre de ; [family] vivre aux dépens de.

➤ **live on** ⟨ *vt fus* vivre de ⟨ *vi* [memory, feeling] rester, survivre.

➤ **live out** ⟨ *vt fus* passer ⟨ *vi* [student] être externe.

➤ **live together** *vi* vivre ensemble.

➤ **live up to** *vt fus* : **to ~ up to sb's expectations** répondre à l'attente de qqn ; **to ~ up to one's reputation** faire honneur à sa réputation.

➤ **live with** *vt fus* - **1.** [cohabit with] vivre avec - **2.** inf [accept] se faire à, accepter.

live[2] [laɪv] ⟨ *adj* - **1.** [living] vivant(e) - **2.** [coal] ardent(e) - **3.** [bullet, bomb] non explosé(e) ; **~ ammunition** munitions *fpl* de combat - **4.** ELEC sous tension - **5.** RADIO & TV en direct ; [performance] en public ⟨ *adv* RADIO & TV en direct ; [perform] en public.

live-in [lɪv-] *adj* [housekeeper] logé(e) et nourri(e) ; **a ~ boyfriend/girlfriend** un petit ami/ une petite amie avec qui on vit.

livelihood ['laɪvlɪhʊd] *n* gagne-pain *m*.

liveliness ['laɪvlɪnɪs] *n* vivacité *f*.

lively ['laɪvlɪ] (*compar* -**ier** ; *superl* -**iest**) *adj* - **1.** [person] plein(e) d'entrain - **2.** [debate, meeting] animé(e) - **3.** [mind] vif (vive).

liven ['laɪvn] ➤ **liven up** ⟨ *vt sep* [person] égayer ; [place] animer ⟨ *vi* s'animer.

liver ['lɪvəʳ] *n* foie *m*.

Liverpudlian ⟨ *adj* de Liverpool ⟨ *n* habitant *m*, -e *f* de Liverpool.

liver sausage Br, **liverwurst** Am ['lɪvəwɜːst] *n* saucisse *f* (au pâté) de foie.

livery ['lɪvərɪ] (*pl* -ies) *n* livrée *f*.

lives [laɪvz] *pl* ⊳ **life**.

livestock ['laɪvstɒk] *n* (U) bétail *m*.

live wire [laɪv-] *n* fil *m* sous tension ; inf fig boute-en-train *m inv*.

livid ['lɪvɪd] *adj* - **1.** [angry] furieux(euse) - **2.** [bruise] violacé(e).

living ['lɪvɪŋ] ⬦ *adj* vivant(e), en vie ⬦ *n :* **to earn** OR **make a ~** gagner sa vie ; **what do you do for a ~?** qu'est-ce que vous faites dans la vie?

living conditions *npl* conditions *fpl* de vie.

living expenses *npl* frais *mpl* de subsistance.

living room *n* salle *f* de séjour, living *m*.

living standards *npl* niveau *m* de vie.

living wage *n* minimum *m* vital.

lizard ['lɪzəd] *n* lézard *m*.

llama ['lɑːmə] (*pl inv* OR **-s**) *n* lama *m*.

LLB (*abbr of* **Bachelor of Laws**) *n* (*titulaire d'une*) *licence de droit.*

LLD (*abbr of* **Doctor of Laws**) *n* docteur en droit.

LMT (*abbr of* **Local Mean Time**) *n heure locale aux États-Unis.*

lo [ləʊ] *excl :* **~ and behold** et comme par miracle.

load [ləʊd] ⬦ *n* - **1.** [something carried] chargement *m*, charge *f* - **2.** [large amount] : **~s of, a ~ of** inf des tas de, plein de ; **a ~ of rubbish** inf de la foutaise ⬦ *vt* [gen & COMPUT] charger ; [video recorder] mettre une vidéo-cassette dans ; **to ~ sb/sthg with** charger qqn/qqch de ; **to ~ a gun/camera (with)** charger un fusil/un appareil (avec).
➤ **load up** *vt sep* & *vi* charger.

loaded ['ləʊdɪd] *adj* - **1.** [question] insidieux(euse) - **2.** inf [rich] plein(e) aux as.

loading bay ['ləʊdɪŋ-] *n* aire *f* de chargement.

loaf [ləʊf] (*pl* **loaves** [ləʊvz]) *n :* **a ~ (of bread)** un pain.

loafer ['ləʊfə'] *n* [shoe] mocassin *m*.

loam [ləʊm] *n* terreau *m*.

loan [ləʊn] ⬦ *n* prêt *m ;* **on ~** prêté(e) ⬦ *vt* prêter ; **to ~ sthg to sb, to ~ sb sthg** prêter qqch à qqn.

loan account *n* compte *m* d'avances.

loan capital *n* capital-obligations *m*.

loan shark *n* inf pej usurier *m*.

loath [ləʊθ] *adj :* **to be ~ to do sthg** ne pas vouloir faire qqch, hésiter à faire qqch.

loathe [ləʊð] *vt* détester ; **to ~ doing sthg** avoir horreur de OR détester faire qqch.

loathing ['ləʊðɪŋ] *n* dégoût *m*, répugnance *f*.

loathsome ['ləʊðsəm] *adj* dégoûtant(e), répugnant(e).

loaves [ləʊvz] *pl* ➤ **loaf.**

lob [lɒb] (*pt* & *pp* **-bed** ; *cont* **-bing**) ⬦ *n* TENNIS lob *m* ⬦ *vt* - **1.** [throw] lancer - **2.** TENNIS : **to ~ a ball** lober, faire un lob.

lobby ['lɒbɪ] (*pl* **-ies**, *pt* & *pp* **-ied**) ⬦ *n* - **1.** [of hotel] hall *m* - **2.** [pressure group] lobby *m*, groupe *m* de pression ⬦ *vt* faire pression sur.

lobbyist ['lɒbɪɪst] *n* membre *m* d'un groupe de pression.

lobe [ləʊb] *n* lobe *m*.

lobelia [lə'biːljə] *n* lobélie *f*.

lobotomy [lə'bɒtəmɪ] (*pl* **-ies**) *n* lobotomie *f*.

lobster ['lɒbstə'] *n* homard *m*.

local ['ləʊkl] ⬦ *adj* local(e) ⬦ *n* inf - **1.** [person] : **the ~s** les gens *mpl* du coin OR du pays - **2.** Br [pub] café *m* OR bistro *m* du coin - **3.** Am [bus, train] omnibus *m*.

local anaesthetic *n* anesthésie *f* locale.

local area network *n* COMPUT réseau *m* local.

local authority *n* Br autorités *fpl* locales.

local call *n* communication *f* urbaine.

local colour *n* couleur *f* locale.

local derby *n* Br derby *m*.

locale [ləʊ'kɑːl] *n* fml lieu *m*, endroit *m*.

local government *n* administration *f* municipale.

locality [ləʊ'kælətɪ] (*pl* **-ies**) *n* endroit *m*.

localized, -ised ['ləʊkəlaɪzd] *adj* localisé(e).

locally ['ləʊkəlɪ] *adv* - **1.** [on local basis] localement - **2.** [nearby] dans les environs, à proximité.

local time *n* heure *f* locale.

locate [Br ləʊ'keɪt, Am 'ləʊkeɪt] ⬦ *vt* - **1.** [find - position] trouver, repérer ; [- source, problem] localiser - **2.** [situate - business, factory] implanter, établir ; **to be ~d** être situé ⬦ *vi* Am [settle] s'installer.

location [ləʊ'keɪʃn] *n* - **1.** [place] emplacement *m* - **2.** CINEMA : **on ~** en extérieur.

loc. cit. (*abbr of* **loco citato**) loc. cit.

loch [lɒk, lɒx] *n* Scot loch *m*, lac *m*.

lock [lɒk] ⬦ *n* - **1.** [of door etc] serrure *f ;* **under ~ and key** [object] sous clef ; [person] sous les verrous - **2.** [on canal] écluse *f* - **3.** AUT [steering lock] angle *m* de braquage - **4.** [of hair] mèche *f* - **5.** *phr :* **~, stock and barrel** en bloc ⬦ *vt* - **1.** [door, car, drawer] fermer à clef ; [bicycle] cadenasser - **2.** [immobilize] bloquer - **3.** [hold firmly] : **to be ~ed in an embrace** être étroitement enlacés ⬦ *vi* - **1.** [door, suitcase] fermer à clef - **2.** [become immobilized] se bloquer.
➤ **locks** *npl* literary chevelure *f*, cheveux *mpl*.

lock in *vt sep* enfermer (à clef).

lock out *vt sep* - **1.** [accidentally] enfermer dehors, laisser dehors ; **to ~ o.s. out** s'enfermer dehors - **2.** [deliberately] empêcher d'entrer, mettre à la porte.

lock up ⬥ *vt sep* - **1.** [person - in prison] mettre en prison OR sous les verrous ; [- in asylum] enfermer - **2.** [house] fermer à clef - **3.** [valuables] enfermer, mettre sous clef ⬥ *vi* fermer (à clef).

lockable ['lɒkəbl] *adj* qu'on peut fermer à clef.

locker ['lɒkəʳ] *n* casier *m*.

locker room *n* Am vestiaire *m*.

locket ['lɒkɪt] *n* médaillon *m*.

lockjaw ['lɒkdʒɔ:] *n* tétanos *m*.

lockout ['lɒkaʊt] *n* lock-out *m inv*.

locksmith ['lɒksmɪθ] *n* serrurier *m*.

lockup ['lɒkʌp] *n* - **1.** [prison] prison *f* - **2.** Br [garage] garage *m*, box *m*.

loco ['ləʊkəʊ] (*pl* -s) *inf* ⬥ *adj* Am timbré(e) ⬥ *n* Br locomotive.

locomotive ['ləʊkə,məʊtɪv] *n* locomotive *f*.

locum ['ləʊkəm] (*pl* -s) *n* remplaçant *m*, -e *f*.

locust ['ləʊkəst] *n* sauterelle *f*, locuste *f*.

lodge [lɒdʒ] ⬥ *n* - **1.** [of caretaker, freemasons] loge *f* - **2.** [of manor house] pavillon *m* (de gardien) - **3.** [for hunting] pavillon *m* de chasse ⬥ *vi* - **1.** [stay] : **to ~ with sb** loger chez qqn - **2.** [become stuck] se loger, se coincer - **3.** fig [in mind] s'enraciner, s'ancrer ⬥ *vt* [complaint] déposer ; **to ~ an appeal** interjeter OR faire appel.

lodger ['lɒdʒəʳ] *n* locataire *mf*.

lodging ['lɒdʒɪŋ] *n* ⊳ **board**.

lodgings *npl* chambre *f* meublée.

loft [lɒft] *n* grenier *m*.

lofty ['lɒftɪ] (*compar* -ier ; *superl* -iest) *adj* - **1.** [noble] noble - **2.** pej [haughty] hautain(e), arrogant(e) - **3.** literary [high] haut(e), élevé(e).

log [lɒg] (*pt* & *pp* **-ged** ; *cont* **-ging**) ⬥ *n* - **1.** [of wood] bûche *f* - **2.** [of ship] journal *m* de bord ; [of plane] carnet *m* de vol ⬥ *vt* consigner, enregistrer.

log in *vi* COMPUT ouvrir une session.

log on *vi* COMPUT ouvrir une session.

log off *vi* COMPUT fermer une session.

log out *vi* COMPUT fermer une session.

loganberry ['ləʊgənbərɪ] (*pl* -ies) *n* sorte de framboise.

logarithm ['lɒgərɪðm] *n* logarithme *m*.

logbook ['lɒgbʊk] *n* - **1.** [of ship] journal *m* de bord ; [of plane] carnet *m* de vol - **2.** [of car] ≃ carte *f* grise.

log cabin *n* cabane *f* en rondins.

log fire *n* feu *m* de bois.

loggerheads ['lɒgəhedz] *n* : **at ~** en désaccord.

logic ['lɒdʒɪk] *n* logique *f*.

logical ['lɒdʒɪkl] *adj* logique.

logically ['lɒdʒɪklɪ] *adv* logiquement.

logistical [lə'dʒɪstɪkl] *adj* logistique.

logistics [lə'dʒɪstɪks] ⬥ *n* (U) MIL logistique *f* ⬥ *npl* fig organisation *f*.

logjam ['lɒgdʒæm] *n* esp Am impasse *f*.

logo ['ləʊgəʊ] (*pl* -s) *n* logo *m*.

logrolling ['lɒgrəʊlɪŋ] *n* (U) Am échange *m* de faveurs.

logy ['ləʊgɪ] *adj* Am inf patraque.

loin [lɔɪn] *n* filet *m*.

loins *npl* reins *mpl* ; **to gird one's ~s** prendre son courage à deux mains.

loincloth ['lɔɪnklɒθ] *n* pagne *m*.

loiter ['lɔɪtəʳ] *vi* traîner.

loll [lɒl] *vi* - **1.** [sit, lie about] se prélasser - **2.** [hang down - head, tongue] pendre.

lollipop ['lɒlɪpɒp] *n* sucette *f*.

lollipop lady *n* Br dame qui fait traverser la rue aux enfants à la sortie des écoles.

lollipop man *n* Br monsieur qui fait traverser la rue aux enfants à la sortie des écoles.

lolly ['lɒlɪ] (*pl* -ies) *n* inf - **1.** [lollipop] sucette *f* - **2.** Br [ice lolly] sucette *f* glacée - **3.** Br [money] fric *m*, blé *m*.

London ['lʌndən] *n* Londres.

Londoner ['lʌndənəʳ] *n* Londonien *m*, -enne *f*.

lone [ləʊn] *adj* solitaire.

loneliness ['ləʊnlɪnɪs] *n* [of person] solitude *f* ; [of place] isolement *m*.

lonely ['ləʊnlɪ] (*compar* -ier ; *superl* -iest) *adj* - **1.** [person] solitaire, seul(e) ; **to feel ~** se sentir seul - **2.** [childhood] solitaire - **3.** [place] isolé(e).

lone parent *n* Br père *m*/mère *f* célibataire.

loner ['ləʊnəʳ] *n* solitaire *mf*.

lonesome ['ləʊnsəm] *adj* Am inf - **1.** [person] solitaire, seul(e) - **2.** [place] isolé(e).

long [lɒŋ] ⬥ *adj* long (longue) ; **two days/years ~** de deux jours/ans, qui dure deux jours/ans ; **10 metres/miles ~** long de 10 mètres/miles, de 10 mètres/miles (de long) ; **a ~ memory** une bonne mémoire ⬥ *adv* longtemps ; **how ~ will it take?** combien de temps cela va-t-il prendre? ; **how ~ will you be?** tu en as pour combien de temps? ; **how ~ is the book?** le livre fait combien de pages? ; **I no ~er like him** je ne l'aime plus ; **I can't wait any ~er** je ne peux pas attendre plus longtemps ; **so ~!** inf au revoir!, salut! ; **before ~** sous peu ; **for ~** pour longtemps ◇ *n* : **the ~ and the short of it is that ...** le fin mot de l'histoire, c'est que ..., enfin bref ... ◇ *vt* : **to ~ to do sthg** avoir très envie de faire qqch.

◆ **as long as, so long as** *conj* tant que.

◆ **long for** *vt fus* [peace and quiet] désirer ardemment ; [holidays] attendre avec impatience.

long. (*abbr of* **longitude**) long.

long-awaited [-ə'weɪtɪd] *adj* tant attendu(e).

long-distance *adj* [runner, race] de fond ; **~ lorry driver** routier *m*.

long-distance call *n* communication *f* interurbaine.

long division *n* division *f* par écrit.

long-drawn-out *adj* interminable, qui n'en finit pas.

long drink *n* long drink *m*.

longevity [lɒn'dʒevətɪ] *n* longévité *f*.

long-haired *adj* [person] aux cheveux longs ; [animal] à longs poils.

longhand ['lɒŋhænd] *n* écriture *f* normale.

long-haul *adj* long-courrier.

longing ['lɒŋɪŋ] ◇ *adj* plein(e) de convoitise ◇ *n* **- 1.** [desire] envie *f*, convoitise *f*; **a ~ for** un grand désir *or* une grande envie de **- 2.** [nostalgia] nostalgie *f*, regret *m*.

longingly ['lɒŋɪŋlɪ] *adv* [with desire] avec envie ; [nostalgically] avec nostalgie.

Long Island *n* Long Island ; **in ~** à Long Island.

longitude ['lɒndʒɪtjuːd] *n* longitude *f*.

long johns *npl* caleçon *m* long.

long jump *n* saut *m* en longueur.

long-lasting *adj* qui dure longtemps, durable.

long-life *adj* [milk] longue conservation (*inv*) ; [battery] longue durée (*inv*).

long-lost *adj* [artefact] perdu(e) depuis longtemps ; [relative] perdu(e) de vue depuis longtemps.

long-playing record [-'pleɪɪŋ-] *n* 33 tours *m*.

long-range *adj* **- 1.** [missile, bomber] à longue portée **- 2.** [plan, forecast] à long terme.

long-running *adj* [TV programme] diffusé(e) depuis de nombreuses années ; [play] qui tient depuis longtemps l'affiche ; [dispute] qui dure depuis longtemps.

longshoreman ['lɒŋʃɔːmən] (*pl* **-men** [-mən]) *n* Am docker *m*.

long shot *n* [guess] coup *m* à tenter (*sans grand espoir de succès*).

longsighted [,lɒŋ'saɪtɪd] *adj* presbyte.

long-standing *adj* de longue date.

longsuffering [,lɒŋ'sʌfərɪŋ] *adj* [person] à la patience infinie.

long term *n* : **in the ~** à long terme.

◆ **long-term** *adj* à long terme.

long vacation *n* Br grandes vacances *fpl*.

long wave *n* (U) grandes ondes *fpl*.

longways ['lɒŋweɪz] *adv* dans le sens de la longueur.

longwearing [,lɒŋ'weərɪŋ] *adj* Am solide, résistant(e).

long weekend *n* long week-end *m*.

longwinded [,lɒŋ'wɪndɪd] *adj* [person] prolixe, verbeux(euse) ; [speech] interminable, qui n'en finit pas.

loo [luː] (*pl* **-s**) *n* Br inf cabinets *mpl*, petit coin *m*.

loofa(h) ['luːfə] *n* luffa *m*, éponge *f*.

look [lʊk] ◇ *n* **- 1.** [with eyes] regard *m* ; **to take** *or* **have a ~ (at sthg)** regarder (qqch), jeter un coup d'œil (à qqch) ; **to give sb a ~** jeter un regard à qqn, regarder qqn de travers **- 2.** [search] : **to have a ~ (for sthg)** chercher (qqch) **- 3.** [appearance] aspect *m*, air *m* ; **by the ~** *or* **~s of it, by the ~** *or* **~s of things** vraisemblablement, selon toute probabilité ◇ *vi* **- 1.** [with eyes] regarder **- 2.** [search] chercher **- 3.** [building, window] : **to ~ (out) onto** donner sur **- 4.** [seem] avoir l'air, sembler ; **he ~s as if he hasn't slept** il a l'air d'avoir mal dormi ; **it ~s like rain** *or* **as if it will rain** on dirait qu'il va pleuvoir ; **she ~s like her mother** elle ressemble à sa mère ◇ *vt* **- 1.** [look at] : **~ what you've done!** regarde ce que tu as fait! **- 2.** [appear] : **to ~ one's age** faire *or* porter son âge ; **to ~ one's best** être *or* paraître à son avantage ◇ *excl* : **~!, ~ here!** dites donc!

◆ **looks** *npl* [attractiveness] beauté *f*.

◆ **look after** *vt fus* s'occuper de.

◆ **look at** *vt fus* **- 1.** [see, glance at] regarder ; [examine] examiner **- 2.** [judge] considérer.

◆ **look back** *vi* [reminisce] penser au passé, évoquer le passé ; **she's never ~ed back** depuis, elle a accumulé les succès.

◆ **look down on** *vt fus* [condescend to] mépriser.

◆ **look for** *vt fus* chercher.

◆ **look forward to** *vt fus* attendre avec impatience.

◆ **look into** *vt fus* examiner, étudier.

look on ⬦ vt fus = **look upon** ⬦ vi regarder.

look out vi prendre garde, faire attention ; **~ out!** attention!

look out for vt fus [person] guetter ; [new book] être à l'affût de, essayer de repérer.

look round ⬦ vt fus [house, shop, town] faire le tour de ⬦ vi **- 1.** [turn] se retourner **- 2.** [browse] regarder.

look through vt fus [gen] examiner ; [newspaper] parcourir.

look to vt fus **- 1.** [depend on] compter sur **- 2.** [future] songer à.

look up ⬦ vt sep **- 1.** [in book] chercher **- 2.** [visit - person] aller OR passer voir ⬦ vi [improve - business] reprendre ; **things are ~ing up** ça va mieux, la situation s'améliore.

look upon vt fus : **to ~ upon sb/sthg as** considérer qqn/qqch comme.

look up to vt fus admirer.

look-alike n sosie m.

look-in n Br inf : **I didn't get a ~** je n'avais aucune chance ; [in conversation] je n'ai pas pu en placer une.

lookout ['lʊkaʊt] n **- 1.** [place] poste m de guet **- 2.** [person] guetteur m **- 3.** [search] : **to be on the ~ for** être à la recherche de.

look-up table n COMPUT table f de recherche.

loom [lu:m] ⬦ n métier m à tisser ⬦ vi [building, person] se dresser ; fig [date, threat] être imminent(e) ; **to ~ large** être un sujet d'inquiétude OR de préoccupation.

loom up vi surgir.

LOOM (abbr of Loyal Order of the Moose) n association caritative américaine.

looming ['lu:mɪŋ] adj imminent(e).

loony ['lu:nɪ] (compar -ier ; superl -iest, pl -ies) inf ⬦ adj cinglé(e), timbré(e) ⬦ n cinglé m, -e f, fou m, folle f.

loop [lu:p] ⬦ n **- 1.** [gen & COMPUT] boucle f **- 2.** [contraceptive] stérilet m ⬦ vt faire une boucle à ⬦ vi faire une boucle.

loophole ['lu:phəʊl] n faille f, échappatoire f.

loo roll n Br inf rouleau m de papier hygiénique.

loose [lu:s] ⬦ adj **- 1.** [not firm - joint] desserré(e) ; [- handle, post] branlant(e) ; [- tooth] qui bouge OR branle ; [- knot] défait(e) **- 2.** [unpackaged - sweets, nails] en vrac, au poids **- 3.** [clothes] ample, large **- 4.** [not restrained - hair] dénoué(e) ; [- animal] en liberté, détaché(e) **- 5.** pej & dated [woman] facile ; [living] dissolu(e) **- 6.** [inexact - translation] approximatif(ive)

- 7. Am inf [relaxed] : **to stay ~** rester cool ⬦ n : **on the ~** en liberté.

loose change n petite OR menue monnaie f.

loose end n détail m inexpliqué ; **to be at a ~** Br, **to be at ~s** Am être désœuvré, n'avoir rien à faire.

loose-fitting adj ample.

loose-leaf binder n classeur m.

loosely ['lu:slɪ] adv **- 1.** [not firmly] sans serrer **- 2.** [inexactly] approximativement.

loosen ['lu:sn] ⬦ vt desserrer, défaire ⬦ vi se desserrer.

loosen up vi **- 1.** [before game, race] s'échauffer **- 2.** inf [relax] se détendre.

loot [lu:t] ⬦ n butin m ⬦ vt piller.

looter ['lu:tər] n pillard m, -e f.

looting ['lu:tɪŋ] n pillage m.

lop [lɒp] (pt & pp **-ped** ; cont **-ping**) vt élaguer, émonder.

lop off vt sep couper.

lope [ləʊp] vi courir en faisant des bonds.

lop-sided [-'saɪdɪd] adj **- 1.** [table] bancal(e), boiteux(euse) ; [picture] de travers **- 2.** fig [biased] tendancieux(euse).

lord [lɔ:d] n Br seigneur m.

Lord n **- 1.** RELIG : **the Lord** [God] le Seigneur ; **good Lord!** Br Seigneur!, mon Dieu! **- 2.** [in titles] Lord m ; [as form of address] : **my Lord** Monsieur le duc/comte etc.

Lords npl Br POL : **the (House of) Lords** la Chambre des lords.

Lord Chancellor n Br Lord Chancelier m.

lordly ['lɔ:dlɪ] (compar -ier ; superl -iest) adj **- 1.** [noble] noble **- 2.** pej [arrogant] arrogant(e), hautain(e).

Lord Mayor n Br Lord-Maire m.

Lordship ['lɔ:dʃɪp] n : **your/his ~** Monsieur le duc/comte etc.

Lord's Prayer n : **the ~** le Notre Père.

lore [lɔ:r] n (U) traditions fpl.

lorry ['lɒrɪ] (pl -ies) n Br camion m.

lorry driver n Br camionneur m, conducteur m de poids lourd.

lose [lu:z] (pt & pp lost) ⬦ vt **- 1.** [gen] perdre ; **to ~ sight of** lit & fig perdre de vue ; **to ~ one's way** se perdre, perdre son chemin ; fig être un peu perdu **- 2.** [subj : clock, watch] retarder de ; **to ~ time** retarder **- 3.** [pursuers] semer ⬦ vi perdre.

lose out vi être perdant(e) ; **to ~ out on a deal** être perdant dans une affaire.

loser ['lu:zər] n **- 1.** [gen] perdant m, -e f ; **a good/bad ~** un bon/mauvais joueur m, une bonne/mauvaise joueuse f - **2. inf pej** [unsuccessful person] raté m, -e f.

losing ['luːzɪŋ] adj perdant(e).

loss [lɒs] n - **1.** [gen] perte f - **2.** COMM : **to make a ~** perdre de l'argent - **3.** phr : **to be at a ~** être perplexe, être embarrassé(e) ; **I'm at a ~ to explain what happened** je n'arrive pas à expliquer comment cela a pu se produire ; **to cut one's ~es** faire la part du feu.

loss adjuster [-ə'dʒʌstər] n responsable m de l'évaluation des sinistres.

loss leader n COMM article vendu à perte dans le but d'attirer la clientèle.

lost [lɒst] <> pt & pp |> **lose** <> adj - **1.** [gen] perdu(e) ; **to get ~** se perdre ; **get ~!** inf fous/foutez le camp! - **2.** [ineffective] : **to be ~ on sb** [advice, warning] être sans effet sur qqn, n'avoir aucun effet sur qqn - **3.** [opportunity] perdu(e), manqué(e).

lost-and-found office n Am bureau m des objets trouvés.

lost cause n cause f perdue.

lost property n (U) objets mpl trouvés.

lost property office n Br bureau m des objets trouvés.

lot [lɒt] n - **1.** [large amount] : **a ~ (of), ~s (of)** beaucoup (de) ; [entire amount] : **the ~** le tout - **2.** [at auction] lot m - **3.** inf [group of people] : **they're a strange ~** ce sont des gens bizarres - **4.** [destiny] sort m - **5.** Am [of land] terrain m ; [car park] parking m - **6.** phr : **to draw ~s** tirer au sort.

➡ **a lot** adv beaucoup.

loth [ləʊθ] = **loath.**

lotion ['ləʊʃn] n lotion f.

lottery ['lɒtərɪ] (pl -ies) n lit & fig loterie f.

lotus position ['ləʊtəs-] n position f du lotus.

loud [laʊd] <> adj - **1.** [not quiet, noisy - gen] fort(e) ; [- person] bruyant(e) - **2.** [colour, clothes] voyant(e) <> adv fort ; **~ and clear** clairement ; **out ~** tout haut.

loudhailer [,laʊd'heɪlər] n Br mégaphone m, porte-voix m.

loudly ['laʊdlɪ] adv - **1.** [noisily] fort - **2.** [gaudily] de façon voyante.

loudmouth ['laʊdmaʊθ, pl -maʊðz] n inf grande gueule f.

loudness ['laʊdnɪs] n force f, intensité f ; [of TV, radio] bruit m.

loudspeaker [,laʊd'spiːkər] n haut-parleur m.

Louisiana [luːˌiːzɪ'ænə] n Louisiane f ; **in ~** en Louisiane.

lounge [laʊndʒ] (cont **loungeing**) <> n - **1.** [in house] salon m - **2.** [in airport] hall m, salle f - **3.** Br = **lounge bar** <> vi se prélasser.

➡ **lounge about, lounge around** vi flemmarder, traîner.

lounge bar n Br l'une des deux salles d'un bar, la plus confortable.

lounge suit n Br complet m, complet-veston m.

louse [laʊs] (pl sense 1 **lice** [laɪs] ; pl sense 2 -**s**) n - **1.** [insect] pou m - **2.** inf pej [person] salaud m.

➡ **louse up** vt sep Am v inf foutre en l'air.

lousy ['laʊzɪ] (compar -ier ; superl -iest) adj inf minable, nul(le) ; [weather] pourri(e) ; **to feel ~** être mal fichu.

lout [laʊt] n rustre m.

louvre Br, **louver** Am ['luːvər] n persienne f.

lovable ['lʌvəbl] adj adorable.

love [lʌv] <> n - **1.** [gen] amour m ; **a ~ of** OR **for** football une passion pour le football ; **to be in ~** être amoureux(euse) ; **to fall in ~** tomber amoureux(euse) ; **to make ~** faire l'amour ; **give her my ~** embrasse-la pour moi ; **~ from** [at end of letter] affectueusement, grosses bises ; **a ~-hate relationship** des rapports mpl d'attraction-répulsion - **2.** inf [form of address] mon chéri (ma chérie) - **3.** TENNIS zéro m <> vt aimer ; **to ~ to do sthg** OR **doing sthg** aimer OR adorer faire qqch.

love affair n liaison f.

lovebite ['lʌvbaɪt] n suçon m.

loveless ['lʌvlɪs] adj sans amour.

love letter n lettre f d'amour.

love life n vie f amoureuse.

lovely ['lʌvlɪ] (compar -ier ; superl -iest) adj - **1.** [beautiful] très joli(e) - **2.** [pleasant] très agréable, excellent(e).

lovemaking ['lʌv,meɪkɪŋ] n (U) amour m, rapports mpl.

lover ['lʌvər] n - **1.** [sexual partner] amant m, -e f - **2.** [enthusiast] passionné m, -e f, amoureux m, -euse f.

lovesick ['lʌvsɪk] adj qui languit d'amour.

love song n chanson f d'amour.

love story n histoire f d'amour.

loving ['lʌvɪŋ] adj [person, relationship] affectueux(euse) ; [care] tendre.

lovingly ['lʌvɪŋlɪ] adv avec amour.

low [ləʊ] <> adj - **1.** [not high - gen] bas (basse) ; [- wall, building] peu élevé(e) ; [- standard, quality] mauvais(e) ; [- intelligence] faible ; [- neckline] décolleté(e) ; **to have a ~ opinion of sb** avoir mauvaise opinion de qqn ; **to cook sthg over a ~ heat** faire cuire qqch à petit feu - **2.** [little remaining] presque épuisé(e) ; **to be ~ on sthg** manquer de qqch - **3.** [not loud - voice] bas (basse) ; [- whisper, moan] faible - **4.** [depressed] déprimé(e) - **5.** [not respectable] bas (basse) ◇ *adv* - **1.** [not high] bas ; **to fly ~** [plane] voler à basse altitude - **2.** [not loudly - speak] à voix basse ; [- whisper] faiblement ◇ *n* - **1.** [low point] niveau *m* OR point *m* bas - **2.** METEOR dépression *f*.

low-alcohol *adj* à faible teneur en alcool.

lowbrow ['ləʊbraʊ] *adj* peu intellectuel(elle).

low-calorie *adj* à basses calories.

Low Church *n* Basse Église *f*.

Low Countries *npl* : **the ~** les Pays-Bas *mpl*.

low-cut *adj* décolleté(e).

low-down inf ◇ *adj* méprisable ◇ *n* : **to give sb the ~ (on sthg)** mettre qqn au parfum (de qqch).

lower[1] ['ləʊər] ◇ *adj* inférieur(e) ◇ *vt* - **1.** [gen] baisser ; [flag] abaisser - **2.** [reduce - price, level] baisser ; [- age of consent] abaisser ; [- resistance] diminuer.

lower[2] ['laʊər] *vi* - **1.** [sky] se faire menaçant(e) - **2.** [person] : **to ~ at sb** regarder qqn d'un air menaçant.

Lower Chamber ['ləʊər-] *n* POL Chambre *f* basse OR des communes.

lower class ['ləʊər-] *n* : **the ~** OR **~es** les classes populaires *fpl*.

Lower House ['ləʊər-] *n* = Lower Chamber.

lowest common denominator ['ləʊɪst-] *n* : **the ~** le plus petit dénominateur commun.

low-fat *adj* [yoghurt, crisps] allégé(e) ; [milk] demi-écrémé(e).

low-flying *adj* volant à basse altitude.

low frequency *n* basse fréquence *f*.

low gear *n* Am première (vitesse) *f*.

low-key *adj* discret(ète).

Lowlands ['ləʊləndz] *npl* : **the ~** [of Scotland] les Basses Terres *fpl* (d'Écosse).

low-level language *n* COMPUT langage *m* de bas niveau.

low-loader [-'ləʊdər] *n* Br - **1.** AUT semi-remorque *m* à plate-forme surbaissée - **2.** RAIL wagon *m* à plate-forme surbaissée.

lowly ['ləʊlɪ] (*compar* -**ier** ; *superl* -**iest**) *adj* modeste, humble.

low-lying *adj* bas (basse).

Low Mass *n* messe *f* basse.

low-necked [-'nekt] *adj* décolleté(e).

low-paid *adj* mal payé(e).

low-rise *adj* bas (basse).

low season *n* basse saison *f*.

low-tech [-'tek] *adj* rudimentaire.

low tide *n* marée *f* basse.

loyal ['lɔɪəl] *adj* loyal(e).

loyalist ['lɔɪəlɪst] *n* loyaliste *mf*.

loyalty ['lɔɪəltɪ] (*pl* -**ies**) *n* loyauté *f*.

lozenge ['lɒzɪndʒ] *n* - **1.** [tablet] pastille *f* - **2.** [shape] losange *m*.

LP (*abbr of* **long-playing record**) *n* 33 tours *m*.

L-plate *n* Br plaque signalant que le conducteur du véhicule est en conduite accompagnée.

LPN (*abbr of* **licensed practical nurse**) *n* aide infirmière diplômée.

LRAM (*abbr of* **Licentiate of the Royal Academy of Music**) *n* membre de l'Académie de musique britannique.

LSAT (*abbr of* **Law School Admissions Test**) *n* aux États-Unis, test d'admission aux études de droit.

LSD[1] (*abbr of* **lysergic acid diethylamide**) *n* LSD *m*.

LSD[2], **L.S.D.**, **£.s.d.**, **l.s.d.** (*abbr of* **pounds, shillings and pence - librae, solidi, denarii**) *n* système monétaire en usage en Grande-Bretagne jusqu'en 1971.

LSE (*abbr of* **London School of Economics**) *n* grande école de sciences économiques et politiques à Londres.

LSO (*abbr of* **London Symphony Orchestra**) *n* orchestre symphonique de Londres.

Lt. (*abbr of* **lieutenant**) Lieut.

LT (*abbr of* **low tension**) *n* BT.

Ltd, **ltd** (*abbr of* **limited**) ≃ SARL ; **Smith and Sons, ~** ≃ Smith & Fils, SARL.

lubricant ['luːbrɪkənt] *n* lubrifiant *m*.

lubricate ['luːbrɪkeɪt] *vt* lubrifier.

lubrication [,luːbrɪ'keɪʃn] *n* lubrification *f*.

lucid ['luːsɪd] *adj* lucide.

lucidly ['luːsɪdlɪ] *adv* lucidement.

luck [lʌk] *n* chance *f* ; **good ~** chance ; **good ~!** bonne chance! ; **bad ~** malchance *f* ; **bad** OR **hard ~!** pas de chance! ; **to be in ~** avoir de la chance ; **to try one's ~ at sthg** tenter sa chance à qqch ; **with (any) ~** avec un peu de chance.

◆ **luck out** *vi* Am inf avoir un coup de pot.

luckily ['lʌkɪlɪ] *adv* heureusement.

luckless ['lʌklɪs] *adj* malchanceux(euse).

lucky ['lʌkɪ] (*compar* -**ier** ; *superl* -**iest**) *adj* - **1.** [fortunate - person] qui a de la chance ; [- event] heureux(euse) ; **to have a ~ escape** l'échapper belle - **2.** [bringing good luck] porte-bonheur (*inv*).

lucky dip n Br sac rempli de cadeaux, dans lequel on pioche sans regarder.

lucrative ['lu:krətɪv] adj lucratif(ive).

ludicrous ['lu:dɪkrəs] adj ridicule.

ludo ['lu:dəʊ] n Br jeu m des petits chevaux.

lug [lʌg] (pt & pp **-ged** ; cont **-ging**) vt inf traîner.

luggage ['lʌgɪdʒ] n (U) Br bagages mpl.

luggage rack n Br porte-bagages m inv.

luggage van n Br fourgon m.

lugubrious [lu:'gu:brɪəs] adj lugubre.

lukewarm ['lu:kwɔ:m] adj lit & fig tiède.

lull [lʌl] ◇ n : ~ (in) [storm] accalmie f (de) ; [fighting, conversation] arrêt m (de) ; **the ~ before the storm** fig le calme avant la tempête ◇ vt : **to ~ sb to sleep** endormir qqn en le berçant ; **to ~ sb into a false sense of security** endormir les soupçons de qqn.

lullaby ['lʌləbaɪ] (pl **-ies**) n berceuse f.

lumbago [lʌm'beɪgəʊ] n (U) lumbago m.

lumber ['lʌmbə^r] ◇ n (U) **- 1.** Am [timber] bois m de charpente **- 2.** Br [bric-a-brac] bric-à-brac m inv ◇ vi se traîner d'un pas lourd.

◆ **lumber with** vt sep Br inf : **to ~ sb with sthg** coller qqch à qqn.

lumbering ['lʌmbərɪŋ] adj lourd(e), pesant (e).

lumberjack ['lʌmbədʒæk] n bûcheron m, -onne f.

lumbermill ['lʌmbə,mɪl] n Am scierie f.

lumber-room n Br débarras m.

lumberyard ['lʌmbəjɑ:d] n chantier m de bois.

luminous ['lu:mɪnəs] adj [dial] lumineux(euse) ; [paint, armband] phosphorescent(e).

lump [lʌmp] ◇ n **- 1.** [gen] morceau m ; [of earth, clay] motte f ; [in sauce] grumeau m **- 2.** [on body] grosseur f ◇ vt : **to ~ sthg together** réunir qqch ; **to ~ it** inf faire avec, s'en accommoder.

lumpectomy [,lʌm'pektəmɪ] (pl **-ies**) n ablation f d'une tumeur au sein.

lump sum n somme f globale.

lumpy ['lʌmpɪ] (compar **-ier** ; superl **-iest**) adj [sauce] plein(e) de grumeaux ; [mattress] défoncé(e).

lunacy ['lu:nəsɪ] n folie f.

lunar ['lu:nə^r] adj lunaire.

lunatic ['lu:nətɪk] ◇ adj pej dément(e), démentiel(elle) ◇ n **- 1.** pej [fool] fou m, folle f **- 2.** [insane person] fou m, folle f, aliéné m, -e f.

lunatic asylum n asile m d'aliénés.

lunatic fringe n éléments mpl extrémistes.

lunch [lʌntʃ] ◇ n déjeuner m ◇ vi déjeuner.

luncheon ['lʌntʃən] n fml déjeuner m.

luncheonette [,lʌntʃə'net] n Am ≃ cafétéria f.

luncheon meat n sorte de saucisson.

luncheon voucher n Br ticket-restaurant m.

lunch hour n pause f de midi.

lunchtime ['lʌntʃtaɪm] n heure f du déjeuner.

lung [lʌŋ] n poumon m.

lung cancer n cancer m du poumon.

lunge [lʌndʒ] (cont **lungeing**) vi faire un brusque mouvement (du bras) en avant ; **to ~ at sb** s'élancer sur qqn.

lupin Br ['lu:pɪn], **lupine** Am ['lu:paɪn] n lupin m.

lurch [lɜ:tʃ] ◇ n [of person] écart m brusque ; [of car] embardée f ; **to leave sb in the ~** laisser qqn dans le pétrin ◇ vi [person] tituber ; [car] faire une embardée.

lure [ljʊə^r] ◇ n charme m trompeur ◇ vt attirer OR persuader par la ruse.

lurid ['ljʊərɪd] adj **- 1.** [outfit] aux couleurs criardes **- 2.** [story, details] affreux(euse).

lurk [lɜ:k] vi **- 1.** [person] se cacher, se dissimuler **- 2.** [memory, danger, fear] subsister.

lurking ['lɜ:kɪŋ] adj [doubts, fear] vague.

Lusaka [lu:'sɑ:kə] n Lusaka.

luscious ['lʌʃəs] adj **- 1.** [delicious] succulent(e) **- 2.** fig [woman] appétissant(e).

lush [lʌʃ] ◇ adj **- 1.** [luxuriant] luxuriant(e) **- 2.** [rich] luxueux(euse) ◇ n Am inf [drunkard] alcolo mf.

lust [lʌst] n **- 1.** [sexual desire] désir m **- 2.** fig : ~ **for sthg** soif de qqch ; ~ **for life** fureur de vivre.

◆ **lust after, lust for** vt fus **- 1.** [wealth, power etc] être assoiffé(e) de **- 2.** [person] désirer.

luster Am = lustre.

lustful ['lʌstfʊl] adj lubrique.

lustre Br, **luster** Am ['lʌstə^r] n lustre m.

lusty ['lʌstɪ] (compar **-ier** ; superl **-iest**) adj vigoureux(euse).

lute [lu:t] n luth m.

luv [lʌv] n Br inf chéri m, -e f.

luvvie ['lʌvɪ] n inf théâtreux m prétentieux, théâtreuse prétentieuse f.

Luxembourg ['lʌksəmbɜ:g] n **- 1.** [country] Luxembourg m ; **in ~** au Luxembourg **- 2.** [city] Luxembourg.

luxuriant [lʌg'ʒʊərɪənt] adj luxuriant(e).

luxuriate [lʌg'ʒʊərɪeɪt] *vi* : **to ~ in** s'abandonner aux plaisirs de.

luxurious [lʌg'ʒʊərɪəs] *adj* - **1.** [expensive] luxueux(euse) - **2.** [pleasurable] voluptueux(euse).

luxury ['lʌkʃərɪ] (*pl* -**ies**) <> *n* luxe *m* <> *comp* de luxe.

luxury goods *npl* produits *mpl* de luxe.

LV *abbr of* **luncheon voucher.**

LW (*abbr of* **long wave**) GO.

lychee [ˌlaɪ'tʃiː] *n* litchi *m*.

Lycra® ['laɪkrə] <> *n* Lycra® *m* <> *comp* en Lycra®.

lying ['laɪɪŋ] <> *adj* [person] menteur(euse) <> *n (U)* mensonges *mpl*.

lymph gland [lɪmf-] *n* ganglion *m* lymphatique.

lynch [lɪntʃ] *vt* lyncher.

lynx [lɪŋks] (*pl inv* OR -**es** [-iːz]) *n* lynx *m inv*.

Lyons ['laɪənz] *n* Lyon *m*.

lyre ['laɪəʳ] *n* lyre *f*.

lyric ['lɪrɪk] *adj* lyrique.

lyrical ['lɪrɪkl] *adj* lyrique.

lyrics ['lɪrɪks] *npl* paroles *fpl*.

M

m¹ (*pl* **m's** OR **ms**), **M** (*pl* **M's** OR **Ms**) [em] *n* [letter] m *m inv*, M *m inv*.
➡ **M - 1.** Br *abbr of* **motorway - 2.** (*abbr of* **medium**) M.

m² - 1. (*abbr of* **metre**) m - **2.** (*abbr of* **million**) M - **3.** *abbr of* **mile.**

ma [mɑː] *n esp* Am *inf* maman *f*.

MA <> *n abbr of* **Master of Arts** <> *abbr of* **Massachusetts.**

ma'am [mæm] *n* madame *f*.

mac [mæk] (*abbr of* **mackintosh**) *n* Br *inf* [coat] imper *m*.

macabre [mə'kɑːbrə] *adj* macabre.

Macao [mə'kaʊ] *n* Macao *m* ; **in ~** à Macao.

macaroni [ˌmækə'rəʊnɪ] *n (U)* macaronis *mpl*.

macaroni cheese *n* macaronis *mpl* au gratin.

macaroon [ˌmækə'ruːn] *n* macaron *m*.

mace [meɪs] *n* - **1.** [ornamental rod] masse *f* - **2.** [spice] macis *m*.

Macedonia [ˌmæsɪ'dəʊnjə] *n* Macédoine *f* ; **in ~** en Macédoine.

Macedonian [ˌmæsɪ'dəʊnjən] <> *adj* macédonien(enne) <> *n* Macédonien *m*, -enne *f*.

machete [mə'ʃetɪ] *n* machette *f*.

Machiavellian [ˌmækɪə'velɪən] *adj* machiavélique.

machinations [ˌmækɪ'neɪʃnz] *npl* machinations *fpl*.

machine [mə'ʃiːn] <> *n* lit & fig machine *f* <> *vt* - **1.** SEWING coudre à la machine - **2.** TECH usiner.

machine code *n* COMPUT code *m* machine.

machinegun [mə'ʃiːngʌn] (*pt* & *pp* -**ned** ; *cont* -**ning**) <> *n* mitrailleuse *f* <> *vt* mitrailler.

machine language *n* COMPUT langage *m* machine.

machine-readable *adj* COMPUT en langage machine.

machinery [mə'ʃiːnərɪ] *n (U)* machines *fpl* ; fig mécanisme *m*.

machine shop *n* atelier *m* d'usinage.

machine tool *n* machine-outil *f*.

machine-washable *adj* lavable en machine.

machinist [mə'ʃiːnɪst] *n* - **1.** SEWING mécanicienne *f* - **2.** TECH machiniste *mf*, opérateur *m*, -trice *f*.

machismo [mə'tʃɪzməʊ] *n* machisme *m*.

macho ['mætʃəʊ] *adj* macho (*inv*).

mackerel ['mækrəl] (*pl inv* OR -**s**) *n* maquereau *m*.

mackintosh ['mækɪntɒʃ] *n* Br imperméable *m*.

macramé [mə'krɑːmɪ] *n* macramé *m*.

macro ['mækrəʊ] (*abbr of* **macroinstruction**) *n* COMPUT macro-instruction *f*.

macrobiotic [ˌmækrəʊbaɪ'ɒtɪk] *adj* macrobiotique.

macrocosm ['mækrəʊkɒzm] *n* macrocosme *m*.

macroeconomics ['mækrəʊˌiːkə'nɒmɪks] *n (U)* macroéconomie *f*.

mad [mæd] (*compar* -**der** ; *superl* -**dest**) *adj* - **1.** [insane] fou (folle) ; **to go ~** devenir fou - **2.** [foolish] insensé(e) - **3.** [furious] furieux(euse) - **4.** [hectic - rush, pace] fou (folle) ; **like ~** *inf* comme un fou - **5.** [very enthusiastic] : **to be ~ about** sb/sthg être fou (folle) de qqn/qqch.

Madagascan [ˌmædə'gæskn] <> *adj* malgache <> *n* - **1.** [person] Malgache *mf* - **2.** [language] malgache *m*.

Madagascar [ˌmædə'gæskəʳ] *n* Madagascar *m*; **in ~ à** Madagascar.

madam ['mædəm] *n* madame *f*.

madcap ['mædkæp] *adj* risqué(e), insensé(e).

mad cow disease *n* inf maladie *f* de la vache folle.

madden ['mædn] *vt* exaspérer.

maddening ['mædnɪŋ] *adj* exaspérant(e).

made [meɪd] *pt* & *pp* ⊳ **make**.

-made [meɪd] *suffix* fait(e) ; **factory ~** fait OR fabriqué en usine ; **French~** de fabrication française.

Madeira [mə'dɪərə] *n* - **1.** [wine] madère *m* - **2.** GEOGR Madère *f*; **in ~ à** Madère.

made-to-measure *adj* fait(e) sur mesure.

made-up *adj* - **1.** [with make-up] maquillé(e) - **2.** [prepared] préparé(e) - **3.** [invented] fabriqué(e).

madhouse ['mædhaus] *n* fig maison *f* de fous.

madly ['mædlɪ] *adv* [frantically] comme un fou ; **~ in love** follement amoureux.

madman ['mædmən] (*pl* **-men** [-mən]) *n* fou *m*.

madness ['mædnɪs] *n* lit & fig folie *f*, démence *f*.

Madonna [mə'dɒnə] *n* Madone *f*.

Madrid [mə'drɪd] *n* Madrid.

madrigal ['mædrɪgl] *n* madrigal *m*.

madwoman ['mædˌwumən] (*pl* **-women** [-ˌwɪmɪn]) *n* folle *f*.

maestro ['maɪstrəu] (*pl* **-tros** OR **-tri** [-trɪ]) *n* maestro *m*.

Mafia ['mæfɪə] *n* : **the ~** la Mafia.

mag [mæg] (*abbr of* **magazine**) *n* inf revue *f*, magazine *m*.

magazine [ˌmægə'ziːn] *n* - **1.** PRESS revue *f*, magazine *m*; RADIO & TV magazine - **2.** [of gun] magasin *m*.

magenta [mə'dʒentə] <> *adj* magenta *(inv)* <> *n* magenta *m*.

maggot ['mægət] *n* ver *m*, asticot *m*.

Maghreb ['mɑːgrəb] *n* : **the ~** le Maghreb.

magic ['mædʒɪk] <> *adj* magique <> *n* magie *f*.

magical ['mædʒɪkl] *adj* magique.

magic carpet *n* tapis *m* volant.

magic eye *n* Br cellule *f* photo-électrique, œil *m* électrique.

magician [mə'dʒɪʃn] *n* magicien *m*.

magic wand *n* baguette *f* magique.

magisterial [ˌmædʒɪ'stɪərɪəl] *adj* - **1.** [behaviour, manner] magistral(e) - **2.** JUR de magistrat.

magistrate ['mædʒɪstreɪt] *n* magistrat *m*, juge *m*.

magistrates' court *n* Br ≃ tribunal *m* d'instance.

Magna Carta ['mægnə'kɑːtə] *n* : **the ~** La Grande Charte d'Angleterre.

magnanimous [mæg'nænɪməs] *adj* magnanime.

magnate ['mægneɪt] *n* magnat *m*.

magnesium [mæg'niːzɪəm] *n* magnésium *m*.

magnet ['mægnɪt] *n* aimant *m*.

magnetic [mæg'netɪk] *adj* lit & fig magnétique.

magnetic disk *n* disque *m* magnétique.

magnetic field *n* champ *m* magnétique.

magnetic tape *n* bande *f* magnétique.

magnetism ['mægnɪtɪzm] *n* lit & fig magnétisme *m*.

magnification [ˌmægnɪfɪ'keɪʃn] *n* grossissement *m*.

magnificence [mæg'nɪfɪsəns] *n* splendeur *f*.

magnificent [mæg'nɪfɪsənt] *adj* magnifique, superbe.

magnify ['mægnɪfaɪ] (*pt* & *pp* **-ied**) *vt* [in vision] grossir ; [sound] amplifier ; fig exagérer.

magnifying glass ['mægnɪfaɪɪŋ-] *n* loupe *f*.

magnitude ['mægnɪtjuːd] *n* envergure *f*, ampleur *f*.

magnolia [mæg'nəuljə] *n* - **1.** [tree] magnolia *m* - **2.** [flower] fleur *f* de magnolia.

magnum ['mægnəm] (*pl* **-s**) *n* magnum *m*.

magpie ['mægpaɪ] *n* pie *f*.

maharaja(h) [ˌmɑːhə'rɑːdʒə] *n* maharaja *m*, maharajah *m*.

mahogany [mə'hɒgənɪ] *n* acajou *m*.

maid [meɪd] *n* [servant] domestique *f*.

maiden ['meɪdn] <> *adj* [flight, voyage] premier(ère) <> *n* literary jeune fille *f*.

maiden aunt *n* tante *f* célibataire.

maiden name *n* nom *m* de jeune fille.

maiden speech *n* POL premier discours *m*.

mail [meɪl] <> *n* - **1.** [letters, parcels] courrier *m* - **2.** [system] poste *f* <> *vt* esp Am poster.

mailbag ['meɪlbæg] *n* sac *m* postal.

mailbox ['meɪlbɒks] *n* Am boîte *f* à OR aux lettres.

mailing list ['meɪlɪŋ-] *n* liste *f* d'adresses.

mailman ['meɪlmən] (*pl* **-men** [-mən]) *n* Am facteur *m*.

mail order *n* vente *f* par correspondance.

mailshot ['meɪlʃɒt] *n* publipostage *m*.

mail train *n* train *m* postal.

mail truck *n* Am fourgonnette *f* des postes.

mail van *n* Br **- 1.** AUT fourgonnette *f* des postes **- 2.** RAIL wagon-poste *m*.

maim [meɪm] *vt* estropier.

main [meɪn] ⬦ *adj* principal(e) ⬦ *n* [pipe] conduite *f*.
➤ **mains** *npl* : **the ~s** le secteur.
➤ **In the main** *adv* dans l'ensemble.

main course *n* plat *m* principal.

Maine [meɪn] *n* le Maine ; **in ~** dans le Maine.

mainframe (computer) ['meɪnfreɪm-] *n* ordinateur *m* central.

mainland ['meɪnlənd] ⬦ *adj* continental(e) ⬦ *n* : **the ~** le continent.

main line *n* RAIL grande ligne *f*.
➤ **mainline** ⬦ *adj* RAIL de grande ligne ⬦ *vt drugs sl* shooter ⬦ *vi drugs sl* shooter.

mainly ['meɪnlɪ] *adv* principalement.

main road *n* route *f* à grande circulation.

mainsail ['meɪnseɪl, 'meɪnsəl] *n* grand-voile *f*.

mainstay ['meɪnsteɪ] *n* pilier *m*, élément *m* principal.

mainstream ['meɪnstriːm] ⬦ *adj* dominant(e) ⬦ *n* : **the ~** la tendance générale.

maintain [meɪn'teɪn] *vt* **- 1.** [preserve, keep constant] maintenir **- 2.** [provide for, look after] entretenir **- 3.** [assert] : **to ~ (that)** ... maintenir que ..., soutenir que ...

maintenance ['meɪntənəns] *n* **- 1.** [of public order] maintien *m* **- 2.** [care] entretien *m*, maintenance *f* **- 3.** JUR pension *f* alimentaire.

maintenance order *n* Br JUR obligation *f* alimentaire.

maisonette [,meɪzə'net] *n* duplex *m*.

maize [meɪz] *n* maïs *m*.

Maj. (*abbr of* **Major**) ≃ Cdt.

majestic [mə'dʒestɪk] *adj* majestueux(euse).

majestically [mə'dʒestɪklɪ] *adv* majestueusement.

majesty ['mædʒəstɪ] (*pl* **-ies**) *n* [grandeur] majesté *f*.
➤ **Majesty** *n* : **His/Her Majesty** Sa Majesté le roi/la reine.

major ['meɪdʒər] ⬦ *adj* **- 1.** [important] majeur(e) **- 2.** [main] principal(e) **- 3.** MUS majeur(e) ⬦ *n* **- 1.** [in army] ≃ chef *m* de bataillon ; [in air force] commandant *m* **- 2.** UNIV

[subject] matière *f* ⬦ *vi* : **to ~ in** se spécialiser en.

Majorca [mə'dʒɔːkə, mə'jɔːkə] *n* Majorque *f* ; **in ~** à Majorque.

Majorcan [mə'dʒɔːkn, mə'jɔːkn] ⬦ *adj* majorquin(e) ⬦ *n* Majorquin *m*, -e *f*.

majorette [,meɪdʒə'ret] *n* majorette *f*.

major general *n* général *m* de division.

majority [mə'dʒɒrətɪ] (*pl* **-ies**) *n* majorité *f* ; **in a** OR **the ~** dans la majorité.

majority shareholder *n* actionnaire *mf* majoritaire.

make [meɪk] (*pt* & *pp* **made**) ⬦ *vt* **- 1.** [gen - produce] faire ; [- manufacture] faire, fabriquer ; **to ~ a meal** préparer un repas ; **to ~ a film** tourner OR réaliser un film **- 2.** [perform an action] faire ; **to ~ a decision** prendre une décision ; **to ~ a mistake** faire une erreur, se tromper **- 3.** [cause to be] rendre ; **to ~ sb happy/sad** rendre qqn heureux/triste ; **he made her a manager** il l'a nommée directrice ; **to ~ o.s. heard** se faire entendre **- 4.** [force, cause to do] : **to ~ sb do sthg** faire faire qqch à qqn, obliger qqn à faire qqch ; **you made me jump** tu m'as fait sursauter ; **we were made to wait in the hall** on nous a fait attendre dans le vestibule ; **to ~ sb laugh** faire rire qqn **- 5.** [be constructed] : **to be made of** être en ; **it's made of wood/metal/wool** c'est en bois/métal/laine ; **what's it made of?** c'est en quoi? **- 6.** [add up to] faire ; **2 and 2 ~ 4** 2 et 2 font 4 **- 7.** [calculate] : **I ~ it 50** d'après moi il y en a 50, j'en ai compté 50 ; **what time do you ~ it?** quelle heure as-tu? ; **I ~ it 6 o'clock** il est 6 heures (à ma montre) **- 8.** [earn] gagner, se faire ; **she ~s £30,000 a year** elle se fait OR elle gagne 30 000 livres par an ; **to ~ a profit** faire des bénéfices ; **to ~ a loss** essuyer des pertes **- 9.** [have the right qualities for] : **she'd ~ a good dancer** elle ferait une bonne danseuse ; **books ~ excellent presents** les livres constituent de très beaux cadeaux **- 10.** [reach] arriver à **- 11.** [cause to be a success] assurer OR faire le succès de ; **she really ~s the play/film** c'est elle qui fait le succès de la pièce/du film **- 12.** [gain - friend, enemy] se faire ; **to ~ friends (with sb)** se lier d'amitié (avec qqn) **- 13.** phr : **to ~ it** [reach in time] arriver à temps ; [be a success] réussir, arriver ; [be able to attend] se libérer, pouvoir venir ; **to have it made** avoir trouvé le filon ; **to ~ do with** se contenter de ⬦ *n* **- 1.** [brand] marque *f* ; **what ~ is your car?** de quelle marque est votre voiture? **- 2.** *inf pej* : **to be on the ~** [act dishonestly, selfishly] être intéressé(e).
➤ **make for** *vt fus* **- 1.** [move towards] se diriger

vers **- 2.** [contribute to, be conducive to] rendre probable, favoriser.

👈 **make of** *vt sep* **- 1.** [understand] comprendre **- 2.** [have opinion of] penser de.

👈 **make off** *vi* filer.

👈 **make off with** *vt fus* filer avec.

👈 **make out** ⬦ *vt sep* **- 1.** [see, hear] discerner ; [understand] comprendre **- 2.** [fill out - cheque] libeller ; [- bill, receipt] faire ; [- form] remplir ⬦ *vt fus* [pretend, claim] : **to ~ out (that)** ... prétendre que ...

👈 **make up** ⬦ *vt sep* **- 1.** [compose, constitute] composer, constituer **- 2.** [story, excuse] inventer **- 3.** [apply cosmetics to] maquiller ; **to ~ o.s. up** se maquiller **- 4.** [prepare - gen] faire ; [- prescription] préparer, exécuter **- 5.** [make complete] compléter **- 6.** [resolve - quarrel] : **to ~ it up (with sb)** se réconcilier (avec qqn) ⬦ *vi* [become friends again] se réconcilier.

👈 **make up for** *vt fus* compenser ; **to ~ up for lost time** rattraper le temps perdu.

👈 **make up to** *vt sep* : **to ~ it up to sb (for sthg)** se racheter auprès de qqn (pour qqch).

make-believe *n* : **it's all ~** c'est (de la) pure fantaisie.

makeover ['meɪkəʊvə'] *n* transformation *f*.

maker ['meɪkə'] *n* [of product] fabricant *m*, -e *f* ; [of film] réalisateur *m*, -trice *f*.

makeshift ['meɪkʃɪft] *adj* de fortune.

make-up *n* **- 1.** [cosmetics] maquillage *m* ; **~ bag** trousse *f* de maquillage ; **~ remover** démaquillant *m* **- 2.** [person's character] caractère *m* **- 3.** [of team, group, object] constitution *f*.

makeweight ['meɪkweɪt] *n* complément *m* de poids.

making ['meɪkɪŋ] *n* fabrication *f* ; **to be the ~ of sb/sthg** être l'origine de la réussite de qqn/qqch ; **his problems are of his own ~** ses problèmes sont de sa faute ; **in the ~** en formation ; **history in the ~** l'histoire en train de se faire ; **to have the ~s of** avoir l'étoffe de.

maladjusted [,mælə'dʒʌstɪd] *adj* inadapté(e).

malaise [mə'leɪz] *n fml* malaise *m*.

malaria [mə'leərɪə] *n* malaria *f*.

Malawi [mə'lɑːwɪ] *n* Malawi *m* ; **in ~** au Malawi.

Malawian [mə'lɑːwɪən] ⬦ *adj* malawite ⬦ *n* Malawite *mf*.

Malay [mə'leɪ] ⬦ *adj* malais(e) ⬦ *n* **- 1.** [person] Malais *m*, -e *f* **- 2.** [language] malais *m*.

Malaya [mə'leɪə] *n* Malaisie *f*, Malaysia *f* occidentale ; **in ~** en Malaisie.

Malayan [mə'leɪən] ⬦ *adj* malais(e) ⬦ *n* Malais *m*, -e *f*.

Malaysia [mə'leɪzɪə] *n* Malaysia *f* ; **in ~** en Malaysia.

Malaysian [mə'leɪzɪən] ⬦ *adj* malaysien(enne) ⬦ *n* Malaysien *m*, -enne *f*.

malcontent ['mælkən,tent] *n fml* mécontent *m*, -e *f*.

Maldives ['mɔːldaɪvz] *npl* : **the ~** les (îles *fpl*) Maldives ; **in the ~** aux Maldives.

male [meɪl] ⬦ *adj* [gen] mâle ; [sex] masculin(e) ⬦ *n* mâle *m*.

male chauvinist (pig) *n pej* phallocrate *m*.

male nurse *n* infirmier *m*.

malevolent [mə'levələnt] *adj* malveillant(e).

malformed [mæl'fɔːmd] *adj* difforme.

malfunction [mæl'fʌŋkʃn] ⬦ *n* mauvais fonctionnement *m* ⬦ *vi* mal fonctionner.

Mali ['mɑːlɪ] *n* Mali *m* ; **in ~** au Mali.

malice ['mælɪs] *n* méchanceté *f*.

malicious [mə'lɪʃəs] *adj* malveillant(e).

malign [mə'laɪn] ⬦ *adj* pernicieux(euse) ⬦ *vt* calomnier.

malignant [mə'lɪgnənt] *adj* MED malin(igne).

malinger [mə'lɪŋgə'] *vi pej* simuler une maladie.

malingerer [mə'lɪŋgərə'] *n pej* simulateur *m*, -trice *f*.

mall [mɔːl] *n esp Am* : **(shopping) ~** centre *m* commercial.

malleable ['mælɪəbl] *adj lit* & *fig* malléable.

mallet ['mælɪt] *n* maillet *m*.

malnourished [,mæl'nʌrɪʃt] *adj* sous-alimenté(e).

malnutrition [,mælnjuː'trɪʃn] *n* malnutrition *f*.

malpractice [,mæl'præktɪs] *n (U)* JUR faute *f* professionnelle.

malt [mɔːlt] *n* malt *m*.

Malta ['mɔːltə] *n* Malte *f* ; **in ~** à Malte.

Maltese [,mɔːl'tiːz] *(pl inv)* ⬦ *adj* maltais(e) ⬦ *n* **- 1.** [person] Maltais *m*, -e *f* **- 2.** [language] maltais *m*.

maltreat [,mæl'triːt] *vt* maltraiter.

maltreatment [,mæl'triːtmənt] *n* mauvais traitement *m*.

malt whisky *n* whisky *m* pur, malt *m inv*.

mammal ['mæml] *n* mammifère *m*.

mammogram ['mæməgræm] *n* mammographie *f*.

Mammon ['mæmən] *n* le Veau d'or.

mammoth ['mæməθ] <> adj gigantesque <> n mammouth m.

man [mæn] (pl men [men], pt & pp -ned ; cont -ning) <> n - **1.** homme m ; **the ~ in the street** l'homme de la rue ; **to talk ~ to ~** parler d'homme à homme ; **to be ~ enough to do sthg** avoir le courage de faire qqch - **2.** [as form of address] mon vieux <> vt [ship, spaceship] fournir du personnel pour ; [telephone] répondre au ; [switchboard] assurer le service de.

manacles ['mænəklz] npl [round wrists] menottes fpl ; [round legs] chaînes fpl.

manage ['mænɪdʒ] <> vi - **1.** [cope] se débrouiller, y arriver - **2.** [survive, get by] s'en sortir <> vt - **1.** [succeed] : **to ~ to do sthg** arriver à faire qqch - **2.** [be responsible for, control] gérer.

manageable ['mænɪdʒəbl] adj maniable.

management ['mænɪdʒmənt] n - **1.** [control, running] gestion f - **2.** [people in control] direction f.

management consultant n conseiller m, -ère f en gestion.

manager ['mænɪdʒər] n [of organization] directeur m, -trice f ; [of shop, restaurant, hotel] gérant m, -e f ; [of football team, pop star] manager m.

manageress [,mænɪdʒə'res] n Br [of organization] directrice f ; [of shop, restaurant, hotel] gérante f.

managerial [,mænɪ'dʒɪərɪəl] adj directorial(e).

managing director ['mænɪdʒɪŋ-] n directeur général m, directrice générale f.

Managua [mə'nægwəl n Managua.

Mancunian [mæŋ'kjuːnjən] <> adj de Manchester <> n [person] habitant m, -e f de Manchester.

mandarin ['mændərɪn] n - **1.** [fruit] mandarine f - **2.** [civil servant] mandarin m.

mandate ['mændeɪt] n mandat m

mandatory ['mændətrɪ] adj obligatoire.

mandolin [mændə'lɪn] n mandoline f.

mane [meɪn] n crinière f.

man-eating [-,iːtɪŋ] adj mangeur d'hommes.

maneuver Am = manoeuvre.

manfully ['mænfʊlɪ] adv courageusement, vaillamment.

manganese ['mæŋgəniːz] n manganèse m.

mange [meɪndʒ] n gale f.

manger ['meɪndʒər] n mangeoire f.

mangetout (pea) [,mɑ̃ʒ'tuː-] n Br mangetout m inv.

mangle ['mæŋgl] vt mutiler, déchirer.

mango ['mæŋgəʊ] (pl -es OR -s) n mangue f.

mangrove ['mæŋgrəʊv] n palétuvier m.

mangy ['meɪndʒɪ] (compar -ier ; superl -iest) adj galeux(euse).

manhandle ['mæn,hændl] vt malmener.

manhole ['mænhəʊl] n regard m, trou m d'homme.

manhood ['mænhʊd] n : **to reach ~** devenir un homme.

manhour ['mæn,aʊər] n heure-homme f.

manhunt ['mænhʌnt] n chasse f à l'homme.

mania ['meɪnjə] n : **~ (for)** manie f (de).

maniac ['meɪnɪæk] n fou m, folle f ; **a sex ~** un obsédé sexuel (une obsédée sexuelle).

manic ['mænɪk] adj fig [person] surexcité(e) ; [behaviour] de fou.

manic-depressive <> adj maniaco-dépressif (maniaco-dépressive) <> n maniaco-dépressif m, maniaco-dépressive f.

manicure ['mænɪ,kjʊər] <> n manucure f <> vt [person] faire une manucure à ; **to ~ one's nails** se faire les ongles.

manifest ['mænɪfest] fml <> adj manifeste, évident(e) <> vt manifester.

manifestation [,mænɪfes'teɪʃn] n fml manifestation f.

manifestly ['mænɪfestlɪ] adv fml manifestement.

manifesto [,mænɪ'festəʊl (pl -s OR -es) n manifeste m.

manifold ['mænɪfəʊld] <> adj literary nombreux(euse), multiple <> n AUT tubulure f, collecteur m.

Manila [mə'nɪlə] n Manille.

manil(l)a [mə'nɪlə] adj en papier kraft.

manipulate [mə'nɪpjʊleɪt] vt lit & fig manipuler.

manipulation [mə,nɪpjʊ'leɪʃn] n lit & fig manipulation f.

manipulative [mə'nɪpjʊlətɪv] adj [person] rusé(e) ; [behaviour] habile, subtil(e).

Manitoba [,mænɪ'təʊbə] n Manitoba m ; **in ~** dans le Manitoba.

mankind [mæn'kaɪnd] n humanité f, genre m humain.

manly ['mænlɪ] (compar -ier ; superl -iest) adj viril(e).

man-made adj [fabric, fibre] synthétique ; [environment] artificiel(elle) ; [problem] causé(e) par l'homme.

manna ['mænə] n manne f.

manned [mænd] *adj* [vehicle] doté(e) d'un équipage ; [flight] habité(e).

mannequin ['mænɪkɪn] *n* mannequin *m*.

manner ['mænəʳ] *n* - **1.** [method] manière *f*, façon *f ;* **in a ~ of speaking** pour ainsi dire - **2.** [attitude] attitude *f*, comportement *m* - **3.** [type, sort] : **all ~ of** toutes sortes de.
➤ **manners** *npl* manières *fpl*.

mannered ['mænəd] *adj fml* maniéré(e), affecté(e).

mannerism ['mænərɪzm] *n* tic *m*, manie *f*.

mannish ['mænɪʃ] *adj* masculin(e).

manoeuvrable Br, **maneuverable** Am [mə'nuːvrəbl] *adj* facile à manœuvrer, maniable.

manoeuvre Br, **maneuver** Am [mə'nuːvəʳ] ◇ *n* manœuvre *f* ◇ *vt* & *vi* manœuvrer.
➤ **manoeuvres** *npl* MIL manœuvres *fpl*.

manor ['mænəʳ] *n* manoir *m*.

manpower ['mæn,paʊəʳ] *n* main-d'œuvre *f*.

manservant ['mænsɜːvənt] (*pl* **menservants** [men-]) *n* dated valet *m* de chambre.

mansion ['mænʃn] *n* château *m*.

man-size(d) *adj* grand(e), de grande personne.

manslaughter ['mæn,slɔːtəʳ] *n* homicide *m* involontaire.

mantelpiece ['mæntlpiːs] *n* (dessus *m* de) cheminée *f*.

mantle ['mæntl] *n* - **1.** literary [of snow] manteau *m* - **2.** [of leadership, high office] responsabilité *f*.

man-to-man *adj* d'homme à homme.

manual ['mænjʊəl] ◇ *adj* manuel(elle) ◇ *n* manuel *m*.

manually ['mænjʊəlɪ] *adv* à la main, manuellement.

manual worker *n* travailleur manuel *m*, travailleuse manuelle *f*.

manufacture [,mænjʊ'fæktʃəʳ] ◇ *n* fabrication *f ;* [of cars] construction *f* ◇ *vt* fabriquer ; [cars] construire.

manufacturer [,mænjʊ'fæktʃərəʳ] *n* fabricant *m ;* [of cars] constructeur *m*.

manufacturing [,mænjʊ'fæktʃərɪŋ] *n* fabrication *f*.

manufacturing industries *npl* industries *fpl* de fabrication.

manure [mə'njʊəʳ] *n* fumier *m*.

manuscript ['mænjʊskrɪpt] *n* manuscrit *m*.

Manx [mæŋks] ◇ *adj* de l'île de Man, manxois(e) ◇ *n* [language] manx *m*.

many ['menɪ] (*compar* **more ;** *superl* **most**) ◇ *adj* beaucoup de ; **how ~ ...?** combien de

...? ; **too ~** trop de ; **as ~ ... as** autant de ... que ; **so ~** autant de ; **a good** OR **great ~** un grand nombre de ◇ *pron* [a lot, plenty] beaucoup.

Maori ['maʊrɪ] ◇ *adj* maori(e) ◇ *n* Maori *m*, -e *f*.

map [mæp] (*pt* & *pp* -**ped ;** *cont* -**ping**) *n* carte *f*.
➤ **map out** *vt sep* [plan] élaborer ; [timetable] établir ; [task] définir.

maple ['meɪpl] *n* érable *m*.

maple leaf *n* feuille *f* d'érable.

maple syrup *n* sirop *m* d'érable.

Maputo [mə'puːtəʊ] *n* Maputo.

mar [maːʳ] (*pt* & *pp* -**red ;** *cont* -**ring**) *vt* gâter, gâcher.

Mar. *abbr of* March.

marathon ['mærəθn] ◇ *adj* marathon *(inv)* ◇ *n* marathon *m*.

marathon runner *n* marathonien *m*, -enne *f*.

marauder [mə'rɔːdəʳ] *n* maraudeur *m*, -euse *f*.

marauding [mə'rɔːdɪŋ] *adj* maraudeur (euse).

marble ['maːbl] *n* - **1.** [stone] marbre *m* - **2.** [for game] bille *f*.
➤ **marbles** *n (U)* [game] billes *fpl*.

march [maːtʃ] ◇ *n* marche *f* ◇ *vi* - **1.** [soldiers etc] marcher au pas - **2.** [demonstrators] manifester, faire une marche de protestation - **3.** [quickly] : **to ~ up to sb** s'approcher de qqn d'un pas décidé ◇ *vt* : **to ~ sb out the door** faire sortir qqn.

March [maːtʃ] *n* mars *m ; see also* **September.**

marcher ['maːtʃəʳ] *n* [protester] marcheur *m*, -euse *f*.

marching orders ['maːtʃɪŋ-] *npl* : **to get one's ~** se faire mettre à la porte.

marchioness ['maːʃənes] *n* marquise *f*.

march-past *n* défilé *m*.

Mardi Gras [,maːdɪ'graː] *n* mardi gras, carnaval *m*.

mare [meəʳ] *n* jument *f*.

marg. [maːdʒ] *n* inf abbr of **margarine.**

margarine [,maːdʒə'riːn, ,maːgə'riːn] *n* margarine *f*.

marge [maːdʒ] *n* inf margarine *f*.

margin ['maːdʒɪn] *n* - **1.** [gen] marge *f ;* **to win by a narrow ~** gagner de peu OR de justesse - **2.** [edge - of an area] bord *m*.

marginal ['maːdʒɪnl] *adj* - **1.** [unimportant] marginal(e), secondaire - **2.** Br POL : **~ seat** cir-

conscription électorale où la majorité passe facilement d'un parti à un autre.

marginally [ˈmɑːdʒɪnəlɪ] *adv* très peu.

marigold [ˈmærɪɡəʊld] *n* souci *m*.

marihuana, marijuana [ˌmærɪˈwɑːnə] *n* marihuana *f*.

marina [məˈriːnə] *n* marina *f*.

marinade [ˌmærɪˈneɪd] ◇ *n* marinade *f* ◇ *vt* & *vi* mariner.

marinate [ˈmærɪneɪt] *vt* & *vi* mariner.

marine [məˈriːn] ◇ *adj* marin(e) ◇ *n* marine *m*.

marionette [ˌmærɪəˈnet] *n* marionnette *f*.

marital [ˈmærɪtl] *adj* [sex, happiness] conjugal(e) ; [problems] matrimonial(e).

marital status *n* situation *f* de famille.

maritime [ˈmærɪtaɪm] *adj* maritime.

Maritime Provinces, Maritimes *npl* : the ~ les Provinces *fpl* Maritimes.

marjoram [ˈmɑːdʒərəm] *n* marjolaine *f*.

mark [mɑːk] ◇ *n* - **1.** [stain] tache *f*, marque *f* - **2.** [sign, written symbol] marque *f* - **3.** [in exam] note *f*, point *m* - **4.** [stage, level] barre *f* - **5.** [currency] mark *m* - **6.** *phr* : to make one's ~ se faire un nom, réussir ; to be quick off the ~ in doing sthg faire qqch sans perdre de temps ; wide of the ~ à côté de la question ◇ *vt* - **1.** [gen] marquer - **2.** [stain] marquer, tacher - **3.** [exam, essay] noter, corriger.

➡ **mark down** *vt sep* - **1.** [COMM - prices] baisser ; [- goods] baisser le prix de, démarquer - **2.** [downgrade] baisser la note de.

➡ **mark off** *vt sep* [cross off] cocher.

➡ **mark up** *vt sep* [COMM - prices] augmenter ; [- goods] augmenter le prix de.

marked [mɑːkt] *adj* [change, difference] marqué(e) ; [improvement, deterioration] sensible.

markedly [ˈmɑːkɪdlɪ] *adv* [different] d'une façon marquée ; [worse, better] sensiblement, manifestement.

marker [ˈmɑːkəʳ] *n* [sign] repère *m*.

marker pen *n* marqueur *m*.

market [ˈmɑːkɪt] ◇ *n* marché *m* ; to be on the ~ être sur le marché OR en vente ◇ *vt* commercialiser ◇ *vi* Am [shop] : to go ~ing aller faire ses courses.

marketable [ˈmɑːkɪtəbl] *adj* commercialisable.

market analysis *n* analyse *f* de marché.

market day *n* jour *m* de marché.

market forces *npl* forces *fpl* OR tendances *fpl* du marché.

market garden *n* esp Br jardin *m* maraîcher.

marketing [ˈmɑːkɪtɪŋ] *n* marketing *m*.

marketplace [ˈmɑːkɪtpleɪs] *n* - **1.** [in a town] place *f* du marché - **2.** COMM marché *m*.

market price *n* prix *m* du marché.

market research *n* étude *f* de marché.

market town *n* marché *m*.

market value *n* valeur *f* marchande.

marking [ˈmɑːkɪŋ] *n* SCH correction *f*.

➡ **markings** *npl* [on animal, flower] taches *fpl*, marques *fpl* ; [on road] signalisation *f* horizontale.

marksman [ˈmɑːksmən] (*pl* -men [-mən]) *n* tireur *m* d'élite.

marksmanship [ˈmɑːksmənʃɪp] *n* adresse *f* au tir.

markup [ˈmɑːkʌp] *n* majoration *f*.

marmalade [ˈmɑːməleɪd] *n* confiture *f* d'oranges amères.

maroon [məˈruːn] *adj* bordeaux *(inv)*.

marooned [məˈruːnd] *adj* abandonné(e).

marquee [mɑːˈkiː] *n* grande tente *f*.

marquess [ˈmɑːkwɪs] = **marquis**.

marquetry [ˈmɑːkɪtrɪ] *n* marqueterie *f*.

marquis [ˈmɑːkwɪs] *n* marquis *m*.

marriage [ˈmærɪdʒ] *n* mariage *m*.

marriage bureau *n* Br agence *f* matrimoniale.

marriage certificate *n* acte *m* de mariage.

marriage guidance *n* conseil *m* conjugal.

marriage guidance counsellor *n* conseiller conjugal *m*, conseillère conjugale *f*.

married [ˈmærɪd] *adj* - **1.** [person] marié(e) ; to get ~ se marier - **2.** [life] conjugal(e).

marrow [ˈmærəʊ] *n* - **1.** Br [vegetable] courge *f* - **2.** [in bones] moelle *f*.

marry [ˈmærɪ] (*pt* & *pp* -ied) ◇ *vt* - **1.** [become spouse of] épouser, se marier avec - **2.** [subj : priest, registrar] marier ◇ *vi* se marier.

Mars [mɑːz] *n* [planet] Mars *f*.

Marseilles [mɑːˈseɪlz] *n* Marseille.

marsh [mɑːʃ] *n* marais *m*, marécage *m*.

marshal [ˈmɑːʃl] (Br *pt* & *pp* -led ; *cont* -ling, Am *pt* & *pp* -ed ; *cont* -ing) ◇ *n* - **1.** MIL maréchal *m* - **2.** [steward] membre *m* du service d'ordre - **3.** Am [law officer] officier *m* de police fédérale ◇ *vt* lit & fig rassembler.

marshalling yard [ˈmɑːʃlɪŋ-] *n* gare *f* de triage.

marshland [ˈmɑːʃlænd] *n* terrain *m* marécageux.

marshmallow [Br ˌmɑːʃˈmæləʊ, Am ˈmɑːrʃˌmeləʊ] *n* guimauve *f*.

marshy ['mɑːʃɪ] (*compar* -ier ; *superl* -iest) *adj* marécageux(euse).

marsupial [mɑːˈsuːpjəl] *n* marsupial *m*.

martial ['mɑːʃl] *adj* martial(e).

martial arts *npl* arts *mpl* martiaux.

martial law *n* loi *f* martiale.

Martian ['mɑːʃn] ◇ *adj* martien(enne) ◇ *n* Martien *m*, -enne *f*.

martin ['mɑːtɪn] *n* martinet *m*.

martini [mɑːˈtiːnɪ] *n* [cocktail] martini *m*.

Martinique [ˌmɑːtɪˈniːk] *n* la Martinique *f* ; **in ~** à la Martinique.

martyr ['mɑːtəʳ] *n* martyr *m*, -e *f*.

martyrdom ['mɑːtədəm] *n* martyre *m*.

martyred ['mɑːtəd] *adj* de martyr.

marvel ['mɑːvl] (Br *pt* & *pp* -led ; *cont* -ling, Am *pt* & *pp* -ed ; *cont* -ing) ◇ *n* merveille *f* ; **it's a ~ that ...** c'est un miracle que ... (+ *subjunctive*) ◇ *vt* : **to ~ that** s'étonner de ce que ◇ *vi* : **to ~ (at)** s'émerveiller (de), s'étonner (de).

marvellous Br, **marvelous** Am ['mɑːvələs] *adj* merveilleux(euse).

Marxism ['mɑːksɪzml] *n* marxisme *m*.

Marxist ['mɑːksɪst] ◇ *adj* marxiste ◇ *n* marxiste *mf*.

Maryland ['meərɪlænd] *n* Maryland *m* ; **in ~** dans le Maryland.

marzipan ['mɑːzɪpæn] *n* (U) pâte *f* d'amandes.

mascara [mæsˈkɑːrə] *n* mascara *m*.

mascot ['mæskət] *n* mascotte *f*.

masculine ['mæskjulɪn] *adj* masculin(e).

masculinity [ˌmæskjʊˈlɪnətɪ] *n* masculinité *f*.

mash [mæʃ] *vt* faire une purée de.

MASH [mæʃ] (*abbr of* **mobile army surgical hospital**) *n* hôpital *militaire de campagne*.

mashed potatoes [mæʃt-] *npl* purée *f* de pommes de terre.

mask [mɑːsk] lit & fig ◇ *n* masque *m* ◇ *vt* masquer.

masked [mɑːskt] *adj* masqué(e).

masking tape ['mɑːskɪŋ-] *n* papier *m* cache.

masochism ['mæsəkɪzm] *n* masochisme *m*.

masochist ['mæsəkɪst] *n* masochiste *mf*.

masochistic [ˌmæsəˈkɪstɪk] *adj* masochiste.

mason ['meɪsn] *n* - **1.** [stonemason] maçon *m* - **2.** [freemason] franc-maçon *m*.

masonic [məˈsɒnɪk] *adj* maçonnique.

masonry ['meɪsnrɪ] *n* [stones] maçonnerie *f*.

masquerade [ˌmæskəˈreɪd] *vi* : **to ~ as** se faire passer pour ; **to ~ under an assumed name** se cacher sous un faux nom.

mass [mæs] ◇ *n* [gen & PHYSICS] masse *f* ◇ *adj* [protest, meeting] en masse, en nombre ; [unemployment, support] massif(ive) ◇ *vt* masser ◇ *vi* se masser.
➤ **Mass** *n* RELIG messe *f*.
➤ **masses** *npl* - **1.** inf [lots] : **~es (of)** des masses (de) ; [food] des tonnes (de) - **2.** [workers] : **the ~es** les masses *fpl*.

Massachusetts [ˌmæsəˈtʃuːsɪts] *n* Massachusetts *m* ; **in ~** dans le Massachusetts.

massacre ['mæsəkəʳ] ◇ *n* massacre *m* ◇ *vt* massacrer.

massage [Br 'mæsɑːʒ, Am məˈsɑːʒ] ◇ *n* massage *m* ◇ *vt* masser.

massage parlour *n* institut *m* de massage.

masseur [mæˈsɜːʳ] *n* masseur *m*.

masseuse [mæˈsɜːz] *n* masseuse *f*.

massive ['mæsɪv] *adj* massif(ive), énorme.

massively ['mæsɪvlɪ] *adv* massivement.

mass-market *adj* grand public (inv).

mass media *n* & *npl* : **the ~** les (mass) media *mpl*.

mass-produce *vt* fabriquer en série.

mass production *n* fabrication *f* OR production *f* en série.

mast [mɑːst] *n* - **1.** [on boat] mât *m* - **2.** RADIO & TV pylône *m*.

mastectomy [mæsˈtektəmɪ] (*pl* -ies) *n* mastectomie *f*.

master ['mɑːstəʳ] ◇ *n* - **1.** [gen] maître *m* - **2.** Br [SCH - in primary school] instituteur *m*, maître *m* ; [- in secondary school] professeur *m* ◇ *adj* maître ◇ *vt* maîtriser ; [difficulty] surmonter, vaincre ; [situation] se rendre maître de.

master bedroom *n* chambre *f* principale.

master disk *n* COMPUT disque *m* d'exploitation.

masterful ['mɑːstəfʊl] *adj* autoritaire.

master key *n* passe *m*, passe-partout *m*.

masterly ['mɑːstəlɪ] *adj* magistral(e).

mastermind ['mɑːstəmaɪnd] ◇ *n* cerveau *m* ◇ *vt* organiser, diriger.

Master of Arts (*pl* **Masters of Arts**) *n* - **1.** [degree] maîtrise *f* ès lettres - **2.** [person] titulaire *mf* d'une maîtrise ès lettres.

master of ceremonies (*pl* **masters of ceremonies**) *n* maître *m* de cérémonie.

Master of Science (*pl* **Masters of Science**)

n - **1.** [degree] maîtrise *f* ès sciences - **2.** [person] titulaire *mf* d'une maîtrise ès sciences.

masterpiece ['mɑːstəpiːs] *n* chef-d'œuvre *m*.

master plan *n* stratégie *f* globale.

master's degree *n* ≃ maîtrise *f*.

masterstroke ['mɑːstəstrəʊk] *n* coup *m* magistral OR de maître.

master switch *n* interrupteur *m* général OR principal.

masterwork ['mɑːstəwɜːk] *n* chef-d'œuvre *m*.

mastery ['mɑːstərɪ] *n* maîtrise *f*.

mastic ['mæstɪk] *n* mastic *m*.

masticate ['mæstɪkeɪt] *vt* & *vi* fml mastiquer, mâcher.

mastiff ['mæstɪf] *n* mastiff *m*.

masturbate ['mæstəbeɪt] *vi* se masturber.

masturbation [,mæstə'beɪʃn] *n* masturbation *f*.

mat [mæt] *n* - **1.** [on floor] petit tapis *m* ; [at door] paillasson *m* - **2.** [on table] set *m* de table ; [coaster] dessous *m* de verre.

match [mætʃ] ◇ *n* - **1.** [game] match *m* - **2.** [for lighting] allumette *f* - **3.** [equal] : **to be no ~ for sb** ne pas être de taille à lutter contre qqn ◇ *vt* - **1.** [be the same as] correspondre à, s'accorder avec - **2.** [pair off] faire correspondre - **3.** [be equal with] égaler, rivaliser avec ◇ *vi* - **1.** [be the same] correspondre - **2.** [go together well] être assorti(e).

matchbox ['mætʃbɒks] *n* boîte *f* à allumettes.

matched [mætʃt] *adj* : **to be well ~** [well suited] être bien assortis(es) ; [equal in strength] être de force égale.

matching ['mætʃɪŋ] *adj* assorti(e).

matchless ['mætʃlɪs] *adj* sans pareil, incomparable.

matchmaker ['mætʃ,meɪkə'] *n* marieur *m*, -euse *f*.

match play *n* GOLF match-play *m*.

match point *n* TENNIS balle *f* de match.

matchstick ['mætʃstɪk] *n* allumette *f*.

mate [meɪt] ◇ *n* - **1.** inf [friend] copain *m*, copine *f*, pote *m* - **2.** Br inf [term of address] mon vieux - **3.** [of female animal] mâle *m* ; [of male animal] femelle *f* - **4.** NAUT : **(first) ~** second *m* ◇ *vi* s'accoupler.

material [mə'tɪərɪəl] ◇ *adj* - **1.** [goods, benefits, world] matériel(elle) - **2.** [important] important(e), essentiel(elle) ◇ *n* - **1.** [substance] matière *f*, substance *f* ; [type of substance] matériau *m*, matière - **2.** [fabric] tissu *m*, étoffe

f ; [type of fabric] tissu - **3.** (*U*) [information - for book, article etc] matériaux *mpl*.

➡ **materials** *npl* matériaux *mpl*.

materialism [mə'tɪərɪəlɪzm] *n* matérialisme *m*.

materialist [mə'tɪərɪəlɪst] *n* matérialiste *mf*.

materialistic [mə,tɪərɪə'lɪstɪk] *adj* matérialiste.

materialize, -ise [mə'tɪərɪəlaɪz] *vi* - **1.** [offer, threat] se concrétiser, se réaliser - **2.** [person, object] apparaître.

materially [mə'tɪərɪəlɪ] *adv* - **1.** [benefit, suffer] matériellement - **2.** [different] essentiellement.

maternal [mə'tɜːnl] *adj* maternel(elle).

maternity [mə'tɜːnətɪ] *n* maternité *f*.

maternity benefit *n* (*U*) allocations *fpl* (de) maternité.

maternity dress *n* robe *f* de grossesse.

maternity hospital *n* maternité *f*.

math Am = maths.

mathematical [,mæθə'mætɪkl] *adj* mathématique.

mathematician [,mæθəmə'tɪʃn] *n* mathématicien *m*, -enne *f*.

mathematics [,mæθə'mætɪks] *n* (*U*) mathématiques *fpl*.

maths Br [mæθs], **math** Am [mæθ] (*abbr of* **mathematics**) inf ◇ *n* (*U*) maths *fpl* ◇ *comp* de maths.

maths coprocessor [-,kəʊ'prəʊsesə'] *n* COMPUT coprocesseur *m* mathématique.

matinée ['mætɪneɪ] *n* matinée *f*.

matinée jacket *n* Br veste *f* de bébé.

mating call ['meɪtɪŋ-] *n* appel *m* du mâle.

mating season ['meɪtɪŋ-] *n* saison *f* des amours.

matriarch ['meɪtrɪɑːk] *n* - **1.** [of society] femme ayant une autorité matriarcale - **2.** literary [of family] aïeule *f*, doyenne *f*.

matrices ['meɪtrɪsiːz] *pl* ▷ **matrix**.

matriculate [mə'trɪkjʊleɪt] *vi* s'inscrire.

matriculation [mə,trɪkjʊ'leɪʃn] *n* inscription *f*.

matrimonial [,mætrɪ'məʊnjəl] *adj* matrimonial(e), conjugal(e).

matrimony ['mætrɪmənɪ] *n* (*U*) mariage *m*.

matrix ['meɪtrɪks] (*pl* **matrices** ['meɪtrɪsiːz] OR **-es** [-iːz]) *n* - **1.** [context, framework] contexte *m*, structure *f* - **2.** MATH & TECH matrice *f*.

matron ['meɪtrən] *n* - **1.** Br [in hospital] infirmière *f* en chef - **2.** [in school] infirmière *f* - **3.** Am [in prison] gardienne *f*.

matronly ['meɪtrənlɪ] *adj* euphemism [woman]

qui a l'allure d'une matrone ; [figure] de matrone.

matt Br, **matte** Am [mæt] *adj* mat(e).

matted ['mætɪd] *adj* emmêlé(e).

matter ['mætəʳ] <> *n* - **1.** [question, situation] question *f*, affaire *f* ; a ~ of life and death une question de vie ou de mort ; the fact OR truth of the ~ is ... la vérité c'est que ..., le fait est que ... ; that's another OR a different ~ c'est tout autre chose, c'est une autre histoire ; as a ~ of course automatiquement ; to make ~s worse aggraver la situation ; and to make ~s worse ... pour tout arranger ... ; as a ~ of principle par principe ; within a ~ of hours en l'affaire de quelques heures ; that's a ~ of opinion c'est (une) affaire OR question d'opinion ; a ~ of time une question de temps - **2.** [trouble, cause of pain] : there's something the ~ with my radio il y a quelque chose qui cloche OR ne va pas dans ma radio ; what's the ~? qu'est-ce qu'il y a? ; what's the ~ with him? qu'est-ce qu'il a? - **3.** PHYSICS matière *f* - **4.** (U) [material] matière *f* ; reading ~ choses *fpl* à lire ; printed ~ imprimés *mpl* <> *vi* [be important] importer, avoir de l'importance ; it doesn't ~ cela n'a pas d'importance.

➤ **as a matter of fact** *adv* en fait, à vrai dire.

➤ **for that matter** *adv* d'ailleurs.

➤ **no matter** *adv :* no ~ what coûte que coûte, à tout prix ; no ~ how hard I try to explain ... j'ai beau essayer de lui expliquer ...

Matterhorn ['mætə,hɔːn] *n :* the ~ le mont Cervin.

matter-of-fact *adj* terre-à-terre, neutre.

matting ['mætɪŋ] *n* natte *f*.

mattress ['mætrɪs] *n* matelas *m*.

mature [mə'tjuəʳ] <> *adj* - **1.** [person, attitude] mûr(e) - **2.** [cheese] fait(e) ; [wine] arrivé(e) à maturité <> *vi* - **1.** [person] mûrir - **2.** [cheese, wine] se faire.

mature student *n* Br UNIV *étudiant qui a commencé ses études sur le tard*.

maturity [mə'tjuərətɪ] *n* maturité *f*.

maudlin ['mɔːdlɪn] *adj* larmoyant(e).

maul [mɔːl] *vt* mutiler.

Mauritania [,mɒrɪ'teɪnjə] *n* Mauritanie *f* ; in ~ en Mauritanie.

Mauritanian [,mɒrɪ'teɪnjən] <> *adj* mauritanien(enne) <> *n* Mauritanien *m*, -enne *f*.

Mauritian [mə'rɪʃn] <> *adj* mauricien(enne) <> *n* Mauricien *m*, -enne *f*.

Mauritius [mə'rɪʃəs] *n* l'île *f* Maurice ; in ~ à l'île Maurice.

mausoleum [,mɔːsə'lɪəm] (*pl* -s) *n* mausolée *m*.

mauve [məuv] <> *adj* mauve <> *n* mauve *m*.

maverick ['mævərɪk] *n* non-conformiste *mf*.

mawkish ['mɔːkɪʃ] *adj* d'une sentimentalité excessive.

max. [mæks] (*abbr of* maximum) max.

maxim ['mæksɪm] (*pl* -s) *n* maxime *f*.

maxima ['mæksɪmə] *pl* ▷ **maximum**.

maximize, -ise ['mæksɪmaɪz] *vt* maximiser, porter au maximum.

maximum ['mæksɪməm] (*pl* **maxima** ['mæksɪmə] OR **-s**) <> *adj* maximum *(inv)* <> *n* maximum *m*.

may [meɪ] *modal vb* - **1.** [expressing possibility] : it ~ rain il se peut qu'il pleuve, il va peut-être pleuvoir ; be that as it ~ quoi qu'il en soit - **2.** [can] pouvoir ; on a clear day the coast ~ be seen on peut voir la côte par temps clair - **3.** [asking permission] : ~ I come in? puis-je entrer? - **4.** [as contrast] : it ~ be expensive but ... c'est peut-être cher, mais ... - **5.** *fml* [expressing wish, hope] : ~ they be happy! qu'ils soient heureux! ; *see also* **might**.

May [meɪ] *n* mai *m* ; *see also* **September**.

Maya ['maɪə] *n :* the ~ les Mayas *mpl*.

Mayan ['maɪən] *adj* maya.

maybe ['meɪbiː] *adv* peut-être ; ~ I'll come je viendrai peut-être.

mayday ['meɪdeɪ] *n* S.O.S. *m*.

May Day *n* le Premier mai.

mayfly ['meɪflaɪ] (*pl* -flies) *n* éphémère *m*.

mayhem ['meɪhem] *n* pagaille *f*.

mayn't [meɪnt] = **may not**.

mayonnaise [,meɪə'neɪz] *n* mayonnaise *f*.

mayor [meəʳ] *n* maire *m*.

mayoress ['meərɪs] *n* - **1.** [female mayor] femme *f* maire - **2.** [mayor's wife] femme *f* du maire.

maypole ['meɪpəʊl] *n* ≈ mai *m*.

may've ['meɪəv] = **may have**.

maze [meɪz] *n* lit & fig labyrinthe *m*, dédale *m*.

MB - **1.** (*abbr of* megabyte) Mo - **2.** *abbr of* Manitoba.

MBA (*abbr of* Master of Business Administration) *n* *(titulaire d'une) formation supérieure au management*.

MBBS (*abbr of* Bachelor of Medicine and Surgery) *n* *(titulaire d'une) licence de médecine et de chirurgie*.

MBE (*abbr of* Member of the Order of the British Empire) *n* *distinction honorifique britannique*.

MC *abbr of* **master of ceremonies.**

MCAT (*abbr of* **Medical College Admissions Test**) *n* test d'admission aux études de médecine.

MCC (*abbr of* **Marylebone Cricket Club**) *n* célèbre club de cricket de Londres.

McCarthyism [mə'ka:θιιzml] *n* Maccartisme *m*, Maccarthysme *m*.

McCoy [mə'kɔı] *n* inf : **the real ~** de l'authentique, du vrai de vrai.

MCP (*abbr of* **male chauvinist pig**) *n* inf phallo *m*.

MD ⬦ *n* **- 1.** *abbr of* **Doctor of Medicine - 2.** *abbr of* **managing director** ⬦ *abbr of* **Maryland.**

MDT (*abbr of* **Mountain Daylight Time**) *n* heure d'été des montagnes Rocheuses.

me [mi:] *pers pron* **- 1.** [direct, indirect] me, m' (+ vowel or silent 'h') ; **can you see/hear ~?** tu me vois/m'entends? ; **it's ~** c'est moi ; **they spoke to ~** ils m'ont parlé ; **she gave it to ~** elle me l'a donné **- 2.** [stressed, after prep, in comparisons etc] moi ; **you can't expect ME to do it** tu ne peux pas exiger que ce soit moi qui le fasse ; **she's shorter than ~** elle est plus petite que moi.

ME ⬦ *n* (*abbr of* **myalgic encephalomyelitis**) myélo-encéphalite *f* ⬦ *abbr of* **Maine.**

meadow ['medəʊ] *n* prairie *f*, pré *m*.

meagre Br, **meager** Am ['mi:gə'] *adj* maigre.

meal [mi:l] *n* repas *m* ; **to make a ~ of sthg** Br fig & pej faire toute une histoire OR tout un plat de qqch.

meals on wheels *npl* Br repas *mpl* à domicile (pour personnes âgées ou handicapées).

mealtime ['mi:ltaɪm] *n* heure *f* du repas ; **at ~s** aux heures des repas.

mealy-mouthed ['mi:lɪ'maʊðd] *adj* pej mielleux(euse), patelin(e).

mean [mi:n] (*pt & pp* **meant**) ⬦ *vt* **- 1.** [signify] signifier, vouloir dire ; **money ~s nothing to him** l'argent ne compte pas pour lui **- 2.** [intend] : **to ~ to do sthg** vouloir faire qqch, avoir l'intention de faire qqch ; **I didn't ~ to drop it** je n'ai pas fait exprès de le laisser tomber ; **to be meant for sb/sthg** être destiné(e) à qqn/qqch ; **to be meant to do sthg** être censé(e) faire qqch ; **to ~ well** agir dans une bonne intention **- 3.** [be serious about] : **I ~ it** je suis sérieux(euse) **- 4.** [entail] occasionner, entraîner **- 5.** phr : **I ~** [as explanation] c'est vrai ; [as correction] je veux dire ⬦ *adj* **- 1.** [miserly] radin(e), chiche ; **to be ~ with sthg** être avare de qqch **- 2.** [unkind] mesquin(e), méchant(e) ; **to be ~ to sb** être mesquin envers qqn **- 3.** [average] moyen(en-

ne) **- 4.** iro : **she's no ~ singer** elle a de la voix ; **that's no ~ feat** c'est un véritable exploit ⬦ *n* [average] moyenne *f; see also* **means.**

meander [mɪ'ændə'] *vi* [river, road] serpenter ; [person] errer.

meaning ['mi:nɪŋ] *n* sens *m*, signification *f.*

meaningful ['mi:nɪŋfʊl] *adj* [look] significatif(ive) ; [relationship, discussion] important(e).

meaningless ['mi:nɪŋlɪs] *adj* [gesture, word] dénué(e) OR vide de sens ; [proposal, discussion] sans importance.

meanness ['mi:nnɪs] *n* **- 1.** [stinginess] avarice *f* **- 2.** [unkindness] mesquinerie *f*, méchanceté *f.*

means [mi:nz] ⬦ *n* [method, way] moyen *m ;* **a ~ to an end** un moyen d'arriver à ses fins ; **by ~ of** au moyen de ⬦ *npl* [money] moyens *mpl*, ressources *fpl.*

➤ **by all means** *adv* mais certainement, bien sûr.

➤ **by no means** *adv* fml nullement, en aucune façon.

means test *n* esp Br enquête sur les ressources d'une personne (qui demande une aide financière à l'État).

meant [ment] *pt & pp* ➤ **mean.**

meantime ['mi:n,taɪm] *n* : **in the ~** en attendant.

meanwhile ['mi:n,waɪl] *adv* **- 1.** [at the same time] pendant ce temps **- 2.** [between two events] en attendant.

measles ['mi:zlz] *n* : **(the) ~** la rougeole.

measly ['mi:zlɪ] (*compar* **-ier** ; *superl* **-iest**) *adj* inf misérable, minable.

measurable ['meʒərəbl] *adj* [improvement, deterioration] sensible.

measurably ['meʒərəblɪ] *adv* sensiblement.

measure ['meʒə'] ⬦ *n* **- 1.** [gen] mesure *f* **- 2.** [amount] : **to achieve a ~ of independence** parvenir à une certaine indépendance ; **for good ~** pour faire bonne mesure **- 3.** [indication] : **it is a ~ of her success that ...** la preuve de son succès, c'est que ... ⬦ *vt & vi* mesurer.

➤ **measure up** *vi* : **to ~ up (to)** être à la hauteur (de).

measured ['meʒəd] *adj* [steps, tone] mesuré(e).

measurement ['meʒəmənt] *n* mesure *f*

measuring tape ['meʒərɪŋ-] *n* mètre *m* (à ruban) ; [in dressmaking] centimètre *m.*

meat [mi:t] *n* viande *f.*

meatball ['mi:tbɔ:l] *n* boulette *f* de viande.

meat pie *n* Br tourte *f* à la viande.

meaty ['mi:tɪ] (compar -ier ; superl -iest) adj fig important(e).

Mecca ['mekə] n La Mecque ; **a ~ for** la Mecque de.

mechanic [mɪ'kænɪk] n mécanicien m, -enne f.

➤ **mechanics** ◇ n (U) [study] mécanique f ◇ npl fig mécanisme m.

mechanical [mɪ'kænɪkl] adj - **1.** [device] mécanique - **2.** [person, mind] fort(e) en mécanique - **3.** [routine, automatic] machinâl(e).

mechanical engineering n génie m mécanique.

mechanism ['mekənɪzm] n lit & fig mécanisme m.

mechanization [,mekənaɪ'zeɪʃn] n mécanisation f.

mechanize, -ise ['mekənaɪz] vt & vi mécaniser.

MEd [,em'ed] (abbr of Master of Education) n (titulaire d'une) maîtrise en sciences de l'éducation.

medal ['medl] n médaille f.

medallion [mɪ'dæljən] n médaillon m.

medallist Br, **medalist** Am ['medəlɪst] n médaillé m, -e f.

meddle ['medl] vi : **to ~ in** se mêler de.

meddlesome ['medlsəm] adj [person] qui met son nez partout.

media ['mi:djə] ◇ pl ⊳ **medium** ◇ n & npl : **the ~** les médias mpl.

mediaeval [,medɪ'i:vl] = medieval.

media event n événement m médiatique.

median ['mi:djən] ◇ adj MATH médian(e) ◇ n Am [of road] bande f médiane (qui sépare les deux côtés d'une grande route).

mediate ['mi:dɪeɪt] ◇ vt négocier ◇ vi : **to ~ (for/between)** servir de médiateur (pour/entre).

mediation [,mi:dɪ'eɪʃn] n médiation f.

mediator ['mi:dɪeɪtəʳ] n médiateur m, -trice f.

medic ['medɪk] n inf - **1.** [medical student] carabin m - **2.** [doctor] toubib m.

Medicaid ['medɪkeɪd] n Am assistance médicale aux personnes sans ressources.

medical ['medɪkl] ◇ adj médical(e) ◇ n examen m médical.

medical certificate n certificat m médical.

medical insurance n assurance f maladie.

medical officer n [in factory etc] médecin m du travail ; MIL médecin militaire.

medical student n étudiant m, -e f en médecine.

medicament ['medɪkəmənt] n médicament m.

Medicare ['medɪkeəʳ] n Am programme fédéral d'assistance médicale pour personnes âgées.

medicated ['medɪkeɪtɪd] adj traitant(e).

medication [,medɪ'keɪʃn] n - **1.** [use of medicines] médication f - **2.** [medicine] médicament m.

medicinal [me'dɪsɪnl] adj médicinal(e).

medicine ['medsɪn] n - **1.** [subject, treatment] médecine f ; **Doctor of Medicine** UNIV docteur m en médecine - **2.** [substance] médicament m.

medicine man n sorcier m.

medieval [,medɪ'i:vl] adj médiéval(e).

mediocre [,mi:dɪ'əʊkəʳ] adj médiocre.

mediocrity [,mi:dɪ'ɒkrətɪ] n médiocrité f.

meditate ['medɪteɪt] vi : **to ~ (on OR upon)** méditer (sur).

meditation [,medɪ'teɪʃn] n méditation f.

Mediterranean [,medɪtə'reɪnjən] ◇ n - **1.** [sea] : **the ~ (Sea)** la (mer) Méditerranée - **2.** [person] Méditerranéen m, -enne f ◇ adj méditerranéen(enne).

medium ['mi:djəm] (pl sense 1 media ['mi:djə] ; pl sense 2 mediums) ◇ adj moyen(enne) ◇ n - **1.** [way of communicating] moyen m - **2.** [spiritualist] médium m.

medium-dry adj demi-sec.

medium-size(d) [-saɪz(d)] adj de taille moyenne.

medium wave n onde f moyenne.

medley ['medlɪ] (pl -s) n - **1.** [mixture] mélange m - **2.** MUS pot-pourri m.

meek [mi:k] adj docile.

meekly ['mi:klɪ] adv docilement.

meet [mi:t] (pt & pp met) ◇ vt - **1.** [gen] rencontrer ; [by arrangement] retrouver - **2.** [go to meet - person] aller/venir attendre, aller/venir chercher ; [- train, plane] aller attendre - **3.** [need, requirement] satisfaire, répondre à - **4.** [problem] résoudre ; [challenge] répondre à - **5.** [costs] payer - **6.** [join] rejoindre ◇ vi - **1.** [gen] se rencontrer ; [by arrangement] se retrouver ; [for a purpose] se réunir - **2.** [join] se joindre ◇ n Am [meeting] meeting m.

➤ **meet up** vi se retrouver ; **to ~ up with sb** rencontrer qqn, retrouver qqn.

➤ **meet with** vt fus - **1.** [encounter - disapproval] être accueilli(e) par ; [- success] remporter ; [- failure] essuyer - **2.** Am [by arrangement] retrouver.

meeting ['miːtɪŋ] *n* - **1.** [for discussions, business] réunion *f* - **2.** [by chance] rencontre *f ;* [by arrangement] entrevue *f* - **3.** [people at meeting] : **the ~** l'assemblée *f.*

meeting place *n* lieu *m* de réunion.

mega- ['megə] *prefix* méga-.

megabit ['megəbɪt] *n* COMPUT méga-bit *m.*

megabyte ['megəbaɪt] *n* COMPUT méga-octet *m.*

megahertz ['megəhɜːts] *n* mégahertz *m.*

megalomania [ˌmegələ'meɪnjə] *n* mégalomanie *f.*

megalomaniac [ˌmegələ'meɪnɪæk] *n* mégalomane *mf.*

megaphone ['megəfəʊn] *n* mégaphone *m,* porte-voix *m.*

megaton ['megətʌn] *n* mégatonne *f.*

megawatt ['megəwɒt] *n* mégawatt *m.*

melamine ['meləmiːn] *n* mélamine *f.*

melancholy ['melənkəlɪ] <> *adj* [person] mélancolique ; [news, facts] triste <> *n* mélancolie *f.*

mellow ['meləʊ] <> *adj* [light, voice] doux (douce) ; [taste, wine] moelleux(euse) <> *vt* : **to be ~ed by age** s'assagir avec l'âge <> *vi* s'adoucir.

melodic [mɪ'lɒdɪk] *adj* mélodique.

melodious [mɪ'ləʊdjəs] *adj* mélodieux(euse).

melodrama ['melədrɑːmə] *n* mélodrame *m.*

melodramatic [ˌmelədrə'mætɪk] *adj* mélodramatique.

melody ['melədɪ] (*pl* -**ies**) *n* mélodie *f.*

melon ['melən] *n* melon *m.*

melt [melt] <> *vt* faire fondre <> *vi* - **1.** [become liquid] fondre - **2.** fig : **his heart ~ed at the sight** il fut tout attendri devant ce spectacle - **3.** [disappear] : **to ~ (away)** fondre ; **to ~ into the background** s'effacer.

◆ **melt down** *vt sep* fondre.

meltdown ['meltdaʊn] *n* fusion *f* du cœur (du réacteur).

melting point ['meltɪŋ-] *n* point *m* de fusion.

melting pot ['meltɪŋ-] *n* fig creuset *m.*

member ['membəʳ] <> *n* membre *m ;* [of club] adhérent *m,* -e *f* <> *comp* membre.

Member of Congress (*pl* **Members of Congress**) *n* Am membre *m* du Congrès.

Member of Parliament (*pl* **Members of Parliament**) *n* Br ≃ député *m.*

Member of the Scottish Parliament *n* membre *m* du Parlement écossais.

membership ['membəʃɪp] *n* - **1.** [of organiza-

tion] adhésion *f* - **2.** [number of members] nombre *m* d'adhérents - **3.** [members] : **the ~** les membres *mpl.*

membership card *n* carte *f* d'adhésion.

membrane ['membreɪn] *n* membrane *f.*

memento [mɪ'mentəʊ] (*pl* -**s**) *n* souvenir *m.*

memo ['meməʊ] (*pl* -**s**) *n* note *f* de service.

memoirs ['memwɑːz] *npl* mémoires *mpl.*

memo pad *n* bloc-notes *m.*

memorabilia [ˌmemərə'bɪlɪə] *npl* souvenirs *mpl.*

memorable ['memərəbl] *adj* mémorable.

memorandum [ˌmemə'rændəm] (*pl* -**da** [-də] OR -**dums**) *n* note *f* de service.

memorial [mɪ'mɔːrɪəl] <> *adj* commémoratif(ive) <> *n* monument *m.*

memorize, -ise ['meməraɪz] *vt* [phone number, list] retenir ; [poem] apprendre par cœur.

memory ['memərɪ] (*pl* -**ies**) *n* - **1.** [gen & COMPUT] mémoire *f ;* **from ~** de mémoire ; **to lose one's ~** perdre la mémoire ; **within living ~** de mémoire d'homme - **2.** [event, experience] souvenir *m ;* **I have no ~ of it** je n'en ai aucun souvenir ; **in ~ of** en souvenir de.

memory card *n* COMPUT carte *f* d'extension mémoire.

men [men] *pl* ▷ **man.**

menace ['menəs] <> *n* - **1.** [gen] menace *f* - **2.** inf [nuisance] plaie *f* <> *vt* menacer.

menacing ['menəsɪŋ] *adj* menaçant(e).

menacingly ['menəsɪŋlɪ] *adv* [speak] d'un ton menaçant ; [look] d'un air menaçant.

menagerie [mɪ'nædʒərɪ] *n* ménagerie *f.*

mend [mend] <> *n* inf : **to be on the ~** aller mieux <> *vt* réparer ; [clothes] raccommoder ; [sock, pullover] repriser ; **to ~ one's ways** s'amender.

mending ['mendɪŋ] *n* : **to do the ~** faire le raccommodage.

menfolk ['menfəʊk] *npl* hommes *mpl.*

menial ['miːnjəl] *adj* avilissant(e).

meningitis [ˌmenɪn'dʒaɪtɪs] *n* (*U*) méningite *f.*

menopause ['menəpɔːz] *n* : **the ~** la ménopause.

menservants ['mensɜːvənts] *pl* ▷ **manservant.**

men's room *n* Am : **the ~** les toilettes *fpl* pour hommes.

menstrual ['menstruəl] *adj* menstruel(elle).

menstruate ['menstrueɪt] *vi* avoir ses règles.

menstruation [ˌmenstrʊ'eɪʃn] *n* menstruation *f.*

menswear ['menzweə'] n (U) vêtements mpl pour hommes.

mental ['mentl] adj mental(e) ; [image, picture] dans la tête.

mental age n âge m mental.

mental block n blocage m (psychologique).

mental hospital n hôpital m psychiatrique.

mentality [men'tælətı] n mentalité f.

mentally ['mentəlı] adv mentalement ; **to be ~ ill** être malade mental ; **to be ~ retarded** être arriéré mental.

mentally handicapped npl : **the ~** les handicapés mpl mentaux.

◆ **mentally-handicapped** adj : **to be mentally-handicapped** être handicapé mental (handicapée mentale).

mental note n : **to make a ~ to do sthg** prendre note mentalement de faire qqch.

menthol ['menθɒl] n menthol m.

mentholated ['menθəleɪtɪd] adj mentholé (e).

mention ['menʃn] <> vt mentionner, signaler ; **not to ~** sans parler de ; **don't ~ it!** je vous en prie! <> n mention f.

mentor ['mentɔ:'] n mentor m.

menu ['menju:] n [gen & COMPUT] menu m.

menu bar n COMPUT barre f de menu.

menu-driven adj COMPUT dirigé(e) par menu.

meow Am = miaow.

MEP (abbr of Member of the European Parliament) n parlementaire m européen.

mercantile ['mɜːkəntaɪl] adj commercial(e).

mercenary ['mɜːsɪnrɪ] (pl -ies) <> adj mercenaire <> n mercenaire m.

merchandise ['mɜːtʃəndaɪz] n (U) marchandises fpl.

merchant ['mɜːtʃənt] <> adj marchand(e) <> n marchand m, -e f, commerçant m, -e f.

merchant bank n Br banque f d'affaires.

merchant navy Br, **merchant marine** Am n marine f marchande.

merciful ['mɜːsɪfʊl] adj - **1.** [person] clément(e) - **2.** [death, release] qui est une délivrance.

mercifully ['mɜːsɪfʊlɪ] adv [fortunately] par bonheur, heureusement.

merciless ['mɜːsɪlɪs] adj impitoyable.

mercilessly ['mɜːsɪlɪslɪ] adv impitoyablement.

mercurial [mɜː'kjʊərɪəl] adj literary [tempera-ment] changeant(e), inégal(e) ; [person] d'humeur changeante.

mercury ['mɜːkjʊrɪ] n mercure m.

Mercury ['mɜːkjʊrɪ] n [planet] Mercure f.

mercy ['mɜːsɪ] (pl -ies) n - **1.** [kindness, pity] pitié f ; **at the ~ of** fig à la merci de - **2.** [blessing] : **what a ~ that ...** quelle chance que ...

mercy killing n euthanasie f.

mere [mɪə'] adj seul(e) ; **she's a ~ child** ce n'est qu'une enfant ; **it cost a ~ £10** cela n'a coûté que 10 livres.

merely ['mɪəlɪ] adv seulement, simplement.

meretricious [,merɪ'trɪʃəs] adj factice.

merge [mɜːdʒ] <> vt COMM & COMPUT fusionner <> vi - **1.** COMM : **to ~ (with)** fusionner (avec) - **2.** [roads, lines] : **to ~ (with)** se joindre (à) - **3.** [colours] se fondre <> n COMPUT fusion f.

merger ['mɜːdʒə'] n fusion f.

meridian [mə'rɪdɪən] n méridien m.

meringue [mə'ræŋ] n meringue f.

merino [mə'riːnəʊ] adj de mérinos.

merit ['merɪt] <> n [value] mérite m, valeur f <> vt mériter.

◆ **merits** npl [advantages] qualités fpl ; **to judge sthg on its ~s** juger qqch selon ses qualités.

meritocracy [,merɪ'tɒkrəsɪ] (pl -ies) n méritocratie f.

mermaid ['mɜːmeɪd] n sirène f.

merrily ['merɪlɪ] adv joyeusement ; iro allègrement.

merriment ['merɪmənt] n hilarité f.

merry ['merɪ] (compar -ier ; superl -iest) adj - **1.** literary [happy] joyeux(euse) ; **Merry Christmas!** joyeux Noël! - **2.** inf [tipsy] gai(e), éméché(e).

merry-go-round n manège m.

merrymaking ['merɪ,meɪkɪŋ] n (U) réjouissances fpl.

mesh [meʃ] <> n maille f (du filet) ; **wire ~** grillage m <> vi [gears] s'engrener.

mesmerize, -ise ['mezməraɪz] vt : **to be ~d by** être fasciné(e) par.

mess [mes] n - **1.** [untidy state] désordre m ; fig gâchis m ; **to be (in) a ~** [room] être en désordre ; [hair] être ébouriffé ; fig [life] être sens dessus dessous - **2.** MIL mess m.

◆ **mess about, mess around** inf <> vt sep : **to ~ sb about** traiter qqn par-dessus OR par-dessous la jambe <> vi - **1.** [fool around] perdre OR gaspiller son temps - **2.** [interfere] : **to ~ about with sthg** s'immiscer dans qqch.

◆ **mess up** vt sep inf - **1.** [room] mettre en désordre ; [clothes] salir - **2.** fig [spoil] gâcher.

mess with *vt fus* inf : **don't ~ with them** tiens-toi à l'écart.

message ['mesɪdʒ] *n* message *m* ; **to get the ~** inf piger.

messenger ['mesɪndʒəʳ] *n* messager *m*, -ère *f* ; **by ~** par porteur.

Messiah [mɪ'saɪə] *n* : **the ~** le Messie.

Messrs, Messrs. ['mesəz] (*abbr of* **messieurs**) MM.

messy ['mesɪ] (*compar* **-ier** ; *superl* **-iest**) *adj* - **1.** [dirty] sale ; [untidy] désordonné(e) ; **a ~ job** un travail salissant - **2.** inf [divorce] difficile ; [situation] embrouillé(e).

met [met] *pt* & *pp* ▷ **meet**.

Met [met] (*abbr of* **Metropolitan Opera**) *n* : **the ~** l'opéra *m* de New-York.

metabolism [mɪ'tæbəlɪzm] *n* métabolisme *m*.

metal ['metl] ◇ *n* métal *m* ◇ *comp* en OR de métal.

metallic [mɪ'tælɪk] *adj* - **1.** [sound, ore] métallique - **2.** [paint, finish] métallisé(e).

metallurgist [me'tælədʒɪst] *n* métallurgiste *m*.

metallurgy [me'tælədʒɪ] *n* métallurgie *f*.

metalwork ['metəlwɜːk] *n* [craft] ferronnerie *f*.

metalworker ['metəl,wɜːkəʳ] *n* [craftsman] ferronnier *m* ; [in industry] métallurgiste *m*.

metamorphose [,metə'mɔːfəʊz] *vi* : **to ~ (into)** se métamorphoser (en).

metamorphosis [,metə'mɔːfəsɪs, ,metəmɔː'fəʊsɪs] (*pl* **-phoses** [-'fəʊsiːz]) *n* métamorphose *f*.

metaphor ['metəfəʳ] *n* métaphore *f*.

metaphorical [,metə'fɒrɪkl] *adj* métaphorique.

metaphysical [,metə'fɪzɪkl] *adj* métaphysique.

metaphysics [,metə'fɪzɪks] *n* métaphysique *f*.

mete [miːt] ◆ **mete out** *vt sep* [punishment] infliger.

meteor ['miːtɪəʳ] *n* météore *m*.

meteoric [miːtɪ'ɒrɪk] *adj* météorique.

meteorite ['miːtjəraɪt] *n* météorite *m* or *f*.

meteorological [,miːtjərə'lɒdʒɪkl] *adj* météorologique.

meteorologist [miːtjə'rɒlədʒɪst] *n* météorologue *mf*, météorologiste *mf*.

meteorology [miːtjə'rɒlədʒɪ] *n* météorologie *f*.

meter ['miːtəʳ] ◇ *n* - **1.** [device] compteur *m* ;

parking ~ parcmètre *m* - **2.** Am = **metre** ◇ *vt* [gas, electricity] établir la consommation de.

methadone ['meθədəʊn] *n* méthadone *f*.

methane ['miːθeɪn] *n* méthane *m*.

method ['meθəd] *n* méthode *f*.

methodical [mɪ'θɒdɪkl] *adj* méthodique.

methodically [mɪ'θɒdɪklɪ] *adv* méthodiquement.

Methodist ['meθədɪst] ◇ *adj* méthodiste ◇ *n* méthodiste *mf*.

methodology [,meθə'dɒlədʒɪ] (*pl* **-ies**) *n* méthodologie *f*.

meths [meθs] *n* Br inf alcool *m* à brûler.

methylated spirits ['meθɪleɪtɪd-] *n* alcool *m* à brûler.

meticulous [mɪ'tɪkjʊləs] *adj* méticuleux(euse).

meticulously [mɪ'tɪkjʊləslɪ] *adv* méticuleusement.

Met Office (*abbr of* **Meteorological Office**) *n* la météo britannique.

metre Br, **meter** Am ['miːtəʳ] *n* mètre *m*.

metric ['metrɪk] *adj* métrique.

metrication [,metrɪ'keɪʃn] *n* Br adoption *f* du système métrique.

metric system *n* : **the ~** le système métrique.

metric ton *n* tonne *f*.

metro ['metrəʊ] (*pl* **-s**) *n* métro *m*.

metronome ['metrənəʊm] *n* métronome *m*.

metropolis [mɪ'trɒpəlɪs] (*pl* **-es** [-iːz]) *n* métropole *f*.

metropolitan [,metrə'pɒlɪtn] *adj* métropolitain(e).

Metropolitan Police *npl* : **the ~** la police de Londres.

mettle ['metl] *n* : **to be on one's ~** être d'attaque ; **to show** OR **prove one's ~** montrer ce dont on est capable.

mew [mjuː] = **miaow**.

mews [mjuːz] (*pl inv*) *n* Br ruelle *f*.

Mexican ['meksɪkn] ◇ *adj* mexicain(e) ◇ *n* Mexicain *m*, -e *f*.

Mexico ['meksɪkəʊ] *n* Mexique *m* ; **in ~** au Mexique.

Mexico City *n* Mexico.

mezzanine ['metsəniːn] *n* - **1.** [floor] mezzanine *f* - **2.** Am [in theatre] corbeille *f*.

MFA (*abbr of* **Master of Fine Arts**) *n* (*titulaire d'une*) *maîtrise en beaux-arts*.

mfr *abbr of* **manufacturer**.

mg (*abbr of* **milligram**) mg.

Mgr - **1.** (*abbr of* **Monseigneur, Monsignor**) Mgr - **2.** *abbr of* **manager.**

MHR *abbr of* **Member of the House of Representatives.**

MHz (*abbr of* **megahertz**) MHz.

MI *abbr of* **Michigan.**

MI5 (*abbr of* **Military Intelligence 5**) *n service de contre-espionnage britannique.*

MI6 (*abbr of* **Military Intelligence 6**) *n service de renseignements britannique.*

MIA (*abbr of* **missing in action**) *expression indiquant qu'une personne a disparu lors d'un combat.*

miaow Br [miːˈaʊ], **meow** Am [mɪˈaʊ] ◇ *n* miaulement *m*, miaou *m* ◇ *vi* miauler.

mice [maɪs] *pl* ▷ **mouse.**

Mich. *abbr of* **Michigan.**

Michigan [ˈmɪʃɪɡən] *n* Michigan *m ;* **in ~** dans le Michigan.

mickey [ˈmɪkɪ] *n :* **to take the ~ out of sb** Br inf se payer la tête de qqn, faire marcher qqn.

MICR (*abbr of* **magnetic ink character recognition**) *n reconnaissance magnétique de caractères.*

micro [ˈmaɪkrəʊ] (*pl* **-s**) *n* micro *m*.

micro- [ˈmaɪkrəʊ] *prefix* micro-.

microbe [ˈmaɪkrəʊb] *n* microbe *m*.

microbiologist [ˌmaɪkrəʊbaɪˈɒlədʒɪst] *n* microbiologiste *mf*.

microbiology [ˌmaɪkrəʊbaɪˈɒlədʒɪ] *n* microbiologie *f*.

microchip [ˈmaɪkrəʊtʃɪp] *n* COMPUT puce *f*.

microcircuit [ˈmaɪkrəʊˌsɜːkɪt] *n* microcircuit *m*.

microcomputer [ˌmaɪkrəʊkəmˈpjuːtəʳ] *n* micro-ordinateur *m*.

microcosm [ˈmaɪkrəkɒzm] *n* microcosme *m*.

microfiche [ˈmaɪkrəʊfiːʃ] (*pl inv* OR **-s**) *n* microfiche *f*.

microfilm [ˈmaɪkrəʊfɪlm] *n* microfilm *m*.

microlight [ˈmaɪkrəlaɪt] *n* ULM *m*.

micromesh [ˈmaɪkrəʊmeʃ] *n* maille *f* superfine.

micron [ˈmaɪkrɒn] *n* micron *m*.

microorganism [ˌmaɪkrəʊˈɔːɡənɪzm] *n* micro-organisme *m*.

microphone [ˈmaɪkrəfəʊn] *n* microphone *m*, micro *m*.

microprocessor [ˈmaɪkrəʊˌprəʊsesəʳ] *n* COMPUT microprocesseur *m*.

microscope [ˈmaɪkrəskəʊp] *n* microscope *m*.

microscopic [ˌmaɪkrəˈskɒpɪk] *adj* microscopique.

microsecond [ˈmaɪkrəʊˌsekənd] *n* microseconde *m*.

microsurgery [ˌmaɪkrəˈsɜːdʒərɪ] *n* microchirurgie *f*.

microwave (oven) [ˈmaɪkrəweɪv-] *n* (four *m* à) micro-ondes *m*.

mid- [mɪd] *prefix :* **~height** mi-hauteur ; **~morning** milieu de la matinée ; **~winter** plein hiver.

midair [mɪdˈeəʳ] ◇ *adj* en plein ciel ◇ *n :* **in ~** en plein ciel.

midday [mɪdˈdeɪ] *n* midi *m*.

middle [ˈmɪdl] ◇ *adj* - **1.** [centre] du milieu, du centre - **2.** [in time] : **she was in her ~ twenties** elle avait dans les 25 ans ◇ *n* - **1.** [centre] milieu *m*, centre *m ;* **in the ~ (of)** au milieu (de) ; **in the ~ of nowhere** en pleine cambrousse - **2.** [in time] milieu *m ;* **to be in the ~ of doing sthg** être en train de faire qqch ; **to be in the ~ of a meeting** être en pleine réunion ; **in the ~ of the night** au milieu de la nuit, en pleine nuit - **3.** [waist] taille *f*.

middle age *n* âge *m* mûr.

middle-aged *adj* d'une cinquantaine d'années.

Middle Ages *npl :* **the ~** le Moyen Âge.

middle-class *adj* bourgeois(e).

middle classes *npl :* **the ~** la bourgeoisie.

middle distance *n :* **in the ~** au second plan.

Middle East *n :* **the ~** le Moyen-Orient.

Middle Eastern *adj* du Moyen-Orient.

middleman [ˈmɪdlmæn] (*pl* **-men** [-men]) *n* intermédiaire *mf*.

middle management *n* (U) cadres *mpl* moyens.

middle name *n* second prénom *m*.

middle-of-the-road *adj* modéré(e).

middle school *n* Br ≃ premier cycle *m* du secondaire.

middleweight [ˈmɪdlweɪt] *n* poids *m* moyen.

middling [ˈmɪdlɪŋ] *adj* moyen(enne).

Middx (*abbr of* **Middlesex**) *ancien comté anglais.*

Mideast [ˌmɪdˈiːst] *n* Am : **the ~** le Moyen-Orient.

midfield [ˌmɪdˈfiːld] *n* FTBL milieu *m* de terrain.

midge [mɪdʒ] *n* moucheron *m*.

midget [ˈmɪdʒɪt] *n* nain *m*, -e *f*.

midi system [ˈmɪdɪ-] *n* chaîne *f* midi.

Midlands [ˈmɪdləndz] *npl :* **the ~** *les comtés du centre de l'Angleterre.*

midnight ['mɪdnaɪt] ◇ n minuit m ◇ comp de minuit.

midriff ['mɪdrɪf] n diaphragme m.

midst [mɪdst] n - **1.** [in space] : **in the ~ of** au milieu de ; **in our ~** parmi nous - **2.** [in time] : **to be in the ~ of doing sthg** être en train de faire qqch.

midstream [mɪd'striːm] n : **in ~** [in river] au milieu du courant ; fig [when talking] en plein milieu.

midsummer ['mɪd,sʌmə'] n cœur m de l'été.

Midsummer Day n la Saint-Jean.

midway [,mɪd'weɪ] adv - **1.** [in space] : **~ (between)** à mi-chemin (entre) - **2.** [in time] : **~ through the meeting** en pleine réunion.

midweek [adj 'mɪdwiːk, adv mɪd'wiːk] ◇ adj du milieu de la semaine ◇ adv en milieu de semaine.

Midwest [,mɪd'west] n : **the ~** le Midwest.

Midwestern [,mɪd'westən] adj du Midwest.

midwife ['mɪdwaɪf] (pl **-wives** [-waɪvz]) n sage-femme f.

midwifery ['mɪd,wɪfərɪ] n obstétrique f.

miffed [mɪft] adj inf vexé(e).

might [maɪt] ◇ modal vb - **1.** [expressing possibility] : **the criminal ~ be armed** il est possible que le criminel soit armé - **2.** [expressing suggestion] : **it ~ be better to wait** il vaut peut-être mieux attendre - **3.** fml [asking permission] : **he asked if he ~ leave the room** il demanda s'il pouvait sortir de la pièce - **4.** [expressing concession] : **you ~ well be right** vous avez peut-être raison - **5.** phr : **I ~ have known OR guessed** j'aurais dû m'en douter ◇ n (U) force f.

mightn't ['maɪtənt] = might not.

might've ['maɪtəv] = might have.

mighty ['maɪtɪ] (compar **-ier** ; superl **-iest**) ◇ adj - **1.** [powerful] puissant(e) - **2.** [very large] imposant(e) ◇ adv Am inf drôlement, vachement.

migraine ['miːɡreɪn, 'maɪɡreɪn] n migraine f.

migrant ['maɪɡrənt] ◇ adj - **1.** [bird, animal] migrateur(trice) - **2.** [workers] émigré(e) ◇ n - **1.** [bird, animal] migrateur m - **2.** [person] émigré m, -e f.

migrate [Br maɪ'ɡreɪt, Am 'maɪɡreɪt] vi - **1.** [bird, animal] migrer - **2.** [person] émigrer.

migration [maɪ'ɡreɪʃn] n migration f.

migratory ['maɪɡrətrɪ] adj [bird] migrateur(trice) ; [journey] migratoire.

mike [maɪk] (abbr of microphone) n inf micro m.

mild [maɪld] ◇ adj - **1.** [disinfectant, reproach] lé-

ger(ère) - **2.** [tone, weather] doux (douce) - **3.** [illness] bénin(igne) ◇ n bière anglaise légère.

mildew ['mɪldjuː] n (U) moisissure f.

mildly ['maɪldlɪ] adv - **1.** [gently] doucement ; **that's putting it ~** c'est le moins qu'on puisse dire - **2.** [not strongly] légèrement - **3.** [slightly] un peu.

mild-mannered adj mesuré(e), calme.

mildness ['maɪldnɪs] n (U) douceur f.

mile [maɪl] n mile m ; NAUT mille m ; **to see for ~s** voir sur des kilomètres ; **to walk for ~s** marcher pendant des kilomètres ; **this is ~s better** c'est cent fois mieux ; **to be ~s away** fig être très loin.

mileage ['maɪlɪdʒ] n distance f en miles, ≃ kilométrage m.

mileage allowance n ≃ indemnité f kilométrique.

mileometer [maɪ'lɒmɪtə'] n compteur m de miles, ≃ compteur kilométrique.

milestone ['maɪlstəʊn] n [marker stone] borne f ; fig événement m marquant OR important.

milieu [Br 'miːljɜː, Am miːl'juː] (pl **-s** OR **-x** [-z]) n milieu m.

militant ['mɪlɪtənt] ◇ adj militant(e) ◇ n militant m, -e f.

militarism ['mɪlɪtərɪzml] n militarisme m.

militarist ['mɪlɪtərɪst] n militariste mf.

militarized zone, militarised zone ['mɪlɪtəraɪzd-] n zone f militarisée.

military ['mɪlɪtrɪ] ◇ adj militaire ◇ n : **the ~** les militaires mpl, l'armée f.

military police n police f militaire.

militate ['mɪlɪteɪt] vi : **to ~ against** militer contre.

militia [mɪ'lɪʃə] n milice f.

milk [mɪlk] ◇ n lait m ◇ vt - **1.** [cow] traire - **2.** fig [use to own ends] exploiter.

milk chocolate ◇ n chocolat m au lait ◇ comp au chocolat au lait.

milk float Br, **milk truck** Am n voiture f de laitier.

milking ['mɪlkɪŋ] n traite f.

milkman ['mɪlkmən] (pl **-men** [-mən]) n laitier m.

milk round n Br [by milkman] tournée f du laitier.

milk shake n milk-shake m.

milk tooth n dent f de lait.

milk truck Am = milk float.

milky ['mɪlkɪ] (compar **-ier** ; superl **-iest**) adj

- 1. Br [coffee] avec beaucoup de lait **- 2.** [pale white] laiteux(euse).

Milky Way *n* : the ~ la Voie lactée.

mill [mɪl] <> *n* **- 1.** [flour-mill, grinder] moulin *m* **- 2.** [factory] usine *f* <> *vt* moudre.

◆ **mill about, mill around** *vi* grouiller.

millennium [mɪ'lenɪəm] (*pl* **millennia** [mɪ'lenɪə]) *n* millénaire *m*.

miller ['mɪlə^r] *n* meunier *m*.

millet ['mɪlɪt] *n* millet *m*.

milli- ['mɪlɪ] *prefix* milli-.

millibar ['mɪlɪbɑ:^r] *n* millibar *m*.

milligram(me) ['mɪlɪgræm] *n* milligramme *m*.

millilitre Br, **milliliter** Am ['mɪlɪ,li:tə^r] *n* millilitre *m*.

millimetre Br, **millimeter** Am ['mɪlɪ,mi:tə^r] *n* millimètre *m*.

millinery ['mɪlɪnrɪ] *n* chapellerie *f* féminine

million ['mɪljən] *n* million *m* ; **a ~, ~s of** fig des milliers de, un million de.

millionaire [,mɪljə'neə^r] *n* millionnaire *mf*.

millionairess [,mɪljə'neərɪs] *n* millionnaire *f*.

millipede ['mɪlɪpi:d] *n* mille-pattes *m inv*.

millisecond ['mɪlɪ,sekənd] *n* millième *m* de seconde.

millstone ['mɪlstəʊn] *n* meule *f* ; **he's like a ~ round my neck** c'est un boulet que je traîne.

millwheel ['mɪlwi:l] *n* roue *f* de moulin.

milometer [maɪ'lɒmɪtə^r] = **mileometer.**

mime [maɪm] <> *n* mime *m* <> *vt* & *vi* mimer.

mimic ['mɪmɪk] (*pt* & *pp* **-ked** ; *cont* **-king**) <> *n* imitateur *m*, -trice *f* <> *vt* imiter.

mimicry ['mɪmɪkrɪ] *n* imitation *f*.

mimosa [mɪ'məʊzə] *n* mimosa *m*.

min. [mɪn] **- 1.** (*abbr of* **minute**) mn, min **- 2.** (*abbr of* **minimum**) min.

Min. *abbr of* **ministry.**

mince [mɪns] <> *n* Br viande *f* hachée <> *vt* [meat] hacher <> *vi* marcher à petits pas maniérés.

mincemeat ['mɪnsmi:t] *n* **- 1.** [fruit] *mélange de pommes, raisins secs et épices utilisé en pâtisserie* **- 2.** Am [meat] viande *f* hachée.

mince pie *n* tartelette *f* de Noël.

mincer ['mɪnsə^r] *n* hachoir *m*.

mind [maɪnd] <> *n* **- 1.** [gen] esprit *m* ; **state of ~** état d'esprit ; **to bear sthg in ~** ne pas oublier qqch ; **to call sthg to ~** se rappeler qqch ; **to cast one's ~ back to sthg** repenser à qqch ; **to come into/cross sb's ~** venir à/

traverser l'esprit de qqn ; **to have sthg on one's ~** avoir l'esprit préoccupé, être préoccupé par qqch ; **to keep an open ~** réserver son jugement ; **the trip took her ~ off her worries** ce petit voyage lui a changé les idées ; **that's a load** OR **weight off my ~!** je me sens soulagé, quel soulagement! ; **to have a ~ to do sthg** avoir bien envie de faire qqch ; **to have sthg in ~** avoir qqch dans l'idée ; **to broaden one's ~** enrichir l'esprit ; **to make one's ~ up** se décider ; **to put** OR **set sb's ~ at rest** rassurer qqn **- 2.** [attention] : **to put one's ~ to sthg** s'appliquer à qqch ; **to keep one's ~ on sthg** se concentrer sur qqch ; **to slip one's ~** sortir de l'esprit **- 3.** [opinion] : **to change one's ~** changer d'avis ; **to my ~** à mon avis ; **to speak one's ~** parler franchement ; **to be in two ~s (about sthg)** se tâter OR être indécis (à propos de qqch) **- 4.** [person] cerveau *m* ; **great ~s think alike** <> *vi* **- 1.** [be bothered] : **I don't ~** ça m'est égal ; **I hope you don't ~** j'espère que vous n'y voyez pas d'inconvénient ; **never ~** [don't worry] ne t'en fais pas ; [it's not important] ça ne fait rien **- 2.** [be careful] : **~ out!** Br attention! <> *vt* **- 1.** [be bothered about, dislike] : **I don't ~ waiting** ça ne me gêne OR dérange pas d'attendre ; **do you ~ if ...?** cela ne vous ennuie pas si ...? ; **I wouldn't ~ a beer** je prendrais bien une bière **- 2.** [pay attention to] faire attention à, prendre garde à **- 3.** [take care of - luggage] garder, surveiller ; [- shop] tenir.

◆ **mind you** *adv* remarquez.

mind-bending [-,bendɪŋ] *adj* inf hallucinant(e).

minder ['maɪndə^r] *n* Br inf [bodyguard] ange *m* gardien.

mindful ['maɪndfʊl] *adj* : **~ of** [risks] attentif(ive) à ; [responsibility] soucieux(euse) de.

mindless ['maɪndlɪs] *adj* stupide, idiot(e).

mind reader *n* : **I'm not a ~** hum je ne suis pas devin.

mindset ['maɪndset] *n* façon *f* de voir les choses.

mind's eye *n* : **in my ~** dans mon imagination.

mine[1] [maɪn] *poss pron* le mien (la mienne), les miens (les miennes) (*pl*) ; **that money is ~** cet argent est à moi ; **it wasn't your fault, it was MINE** ce n'était pas de votre faute, c'était de la mienne OR de ma faute à moi ; **a friend of ~** un ami à moi, un de mes amis.

mine[2] [maɪn] <> *n* mine *f* ; **a ~ of information** fig une mine de renseignements <> *vt* **- 1.** [coal, gold] extraire **- 2.** [road, beach, sea] miner.

mine detector n détecteur m de mines.

minefield ['maɪnfiːld] n champ m de mines ; fig situation f explosive.

minelayer ['maɪn,leɪəʳ] n mouilleur m de mines.

miner ['maɪnəʳ] n mineur m.

mineral ['mɪnərəl] ◇ adj minéral(e) ◇ n minéral m.

mineralogy [,mɪnə'rælədʒɪ] n minéralogie f.

mineral water n eau f minérale.

minestrone [,mɪnɪ'strəʊnɪ] n minestrone m.

minesweeper ['maɪn,swiːpəʳ] n dragueur m de mines.

mingle ['mɪŋgl] ◇ vt : to ~ sthg with sthg mélanger qqch à qqch ◇ vi : to ~ (with) [sounds, fragrances] se mélanger (à) ; [people] se mêler (à).

mini ['mɪnɪ] n [skirt] minijupe f.

miniature ['mɪnətʃəʳ] ◇ adj miniature ◇ n - **1.** [painting] miniature f - **2.** [of alcohol] bouteille f miniature - **3.** [small scale] : **in ~** en miniature.

minibus ['mɪnɪbʌs] (pl -es) n minibus m.

minicab ['mɪnɪkæb] n Br radiotaxi m.

minicomputer [,mɪnɪkəm'pjuːtəʳ] n miniordinateur m.

minim ['mɪnɪm] n MUS blanche f.

minima ['mɪnɪmə] pl ⊏▷ **minimum**.

minimal ['mɪnɪml] adj [cost] insignifiant(e) ; [damage] minime.

minimize, -ise ['mɪnɪ,maɪz] vt minimiser.

minimum ['mɪnɪməm] (pl **minima** ['mɪnɪmə] OR **-s**) ◇ adj minimum (inv) ◇ n minimum m.

minimum lending rate [-'lendɪŋ-] n taux m de crédit minimum.

minimum wage n salaire m minimum.

mining ['maɪnɪŋ] ◇ n exploitation f minière ◇ adj minier(ère) ; **~ engineer** ingénieur m des mines.

minion ['mɪnjən] n larbin m, laquais m.

miniseries ['mɪnɪsɪərɪz] (pl inv) n mini-série f télévisée.

miniskirt ['mɪnɪskɜːt] n minijupe f.

minister ['mɪnɪstəʳ] n - **1.** POL ministre m - **2.** RELIG pasteur m.

➠ **minister to** vt fus [person] donner OR prodiguer ses soins à ; [needs] pourvoir à.

ministerial [,mɪnɪ'stɪərɪəl] adj ministériel(elle).

minister of state n secrétaire mf d'État.

ministry ['mɪnɪstrɪ] (pl -ies) n - **1.** POL ministère m ; **Ministry of Defence** ministère m de la Défense - **2.** RELIG : **the ~** le saint ministère.

mink [mɪŋk] (pl inv) n vison m.

mink coat n manteau m de vison.

Minnesota [,mɪnɪ'səʊtə] n Minnesota m ; **in ~** dans le Minnesota.

minnow ['mɪnəʊ] n vairon m.

minor ['maɪnəʳ] ◇ adj [gen & MUS] mineur(e) ; [detail] petit(e) ; [role] secondaire ◇ n mineur m, -e f.

minority [maɪ'nɒrətɪ] (pl -ies) n minorité f ; **to be in a** OR **the ~** être en minorité.

minority government n gouvernement m minoritaire.

minster ['mɪnstəʳ] n cathédrale f.

minstrel ['mɪnstrəl] n ménestrel m.

mint [mɪnt] ◇ n - **1.** [herb] menthe f - **2.** [sweet] bonbon m à la menthe - **3.** [for coins] : **the Mint** l'hôtel de la Monnaie ; **in ~ condition** en parfait état ◇ vt [coins] battre.

mint sauce n sauce f à la menthe.

minuet [,mɪnjʊ'et] n menuet m.

minus ['maɪnəs] (pl -es [-iːz]) ◇ prep moins ◇ adj [answer, quantity] négatif(ive) ◇ n - **1.** MATH signe m moins - **2.** [disadvantage] handicap m.

minuscule ['mɪnəskjuːl] adj minuscule.

minus sign n signe m moins.

minute[1] ['mɪnɪt] n minute f ; **at any ~** à tout moment, d'une minute à l'autre ; **at the last ~** au dernier moment, à la dernière minute ; **stop that this ~!** arrête tout de suite OR immédiatement ! ; **up to the ~** [news] de dernière heure ; [design] dernier cri (inv) ; **wait a ~!** attendez une minute OR un instant !

➠ **minutes** npl procès-verbal m, compte rendu m.

minute[2] [maɪ'njuːt] adj minuscule ; **in ~ detail** par le menu.

minutiae [maɪ'njuːʃɪaɪ] npl menus détails mpl.

miracle ['mɪrəkl] n miracle m.

miraculous [mɪ'rækjʊləs] adj miraculeux(euse).

miraculously [mɪ'rækjʊləslɪ] adv miraculeusement, par miracle.

mirage [mɪ'rɑːʒ] n lit & fig mirage m.

mire [maɪəʳ] n fange f, boue f.

mirror ['mɪrəʳ] ◇ n miroir m, glace f ◇ vt refléter.

mirror image n image f inversée.

mirth [mɜːθ] n hilarité f, gaieté f.

misadventure [,mɪsəd'ventʃəʳ] n : **death by ~** JUR mort f accidentelle.

misanthropist [mɪ'sænθrəpɪst] *n* misanthrope *mf*.

misapplication ['mɪsˌæplɪ'keɪʃn] *n* mauvaise application *f*, application erronée.

misapprehension ['mɪsˌæprɪ'henʃn] *n* idée *f* fausse.

misappropriate [ˌmɪsə'prəʊprɪeɪt] *vt* détourner.

misappropriation ['mɪsəˌprəʊprɪ'eɪʃn] *n* détournement *m*.

misbehave [ˌmɪsbɪ'heɪv] *vi* se conduire mal.

misbehaviour Br, **misbehavior** Am [ˌmɪsbɪ'heɪvjər] *n* mauvaise conduite *f*.

misc [mɪsk] *abbr of* miscellaneous.

miscalculate [ˌmɪs'kælkjʊleɪt] <> *vt* mal calculer <> *vi* se tromper.

miscalculation [ˌmɪskælkjʊ'leɪʃn] *n* mauvais calcul *m*, erreur *f* de calcul.

miscarriage [ˌmɪs'kærɪdʒ] *n* MED fausse couche *f*; **to have a ~** faire une fausse couche.

miscarriage of justice *n* erreur *f* judiciaire.

miscarry [ˌmɪs'kærɪ] (*pt* & *pp* -**ied**) *vi* - **1.** [woman] faire une fausse couche - **2.** [plan] échouer.

miscellaneous [ˌmɪsə'leɪnjəs] *adj* varié(e), divers(e).

miscellany [Br mɪ'selənɪ, Am 'mɪsəleɪnɪ] (*pl* -**ies**) *n* recueil *m*.

mischance [ˌmɪs'tʃɑːns] *n* malchance *f*; **by ~** par malheur.

mischief ['mɪstʃɪf] *n* (*U*) - **1.** [playfulness] malice *f*, espièglerie *f* - **2.** [naughty behaviour] sottises *fpl*, bêtises *fpl* - **3.** [harm] dégât *m*.

mischievous ['mɪstʃɪvəs] *adj* - **1.** [playful] malicieux(euse) - **2.** [naughty] espiègle, coquin(e).

misconceived [ˌmɪskən'siːvd] *adj* [idea] mal conçu(e).

misconception [ˌmɪskən'sepʃn] *n* idée *f* fausse.

misconduct [ˌmɪs'kɒndʌkt] *n* inconduite *f*.

misconstrue [ˌmɪskən'struː] *vt fml* mal interpréter.

miscount [ˌmɪs'kaʊnt] *vt* & *vi* mal compter.

misdeed [ˌmɪs'diːd] *n* méfait *m*.

misdemeanour Br, **misdemeanor** Am [ˌmɪsdɪ'miːnər] *n* JUR délit *m*.

misdirected [ˌmɪsdɪ'rektɪd] *adj* [letter] mal adressé(e) ; [efforts, energy] mal dirigé(e).

miser ['maɪzər] *n* avare *mf*.

miserable ['mɪzrəbl] *adj* - **1.** [person] malheureux(euse), triste - **2.** [conditions, life] misé-

rable ; [pay] dérisoire ; [weather] maussade - **3.** [failure] pitoyable, lamentable.

miserably ['mɪzrəblɪ] *adv* - **1.** [reply, cry] pitoyablement - **2.** [live] misérablement - **3.** [fail] pitoyablement, lamentablement.

miserly ['maɪzəlɪ] *adj* avare.

misery ['mɪzərɪ] (*pl* -**ies**) *n* - **1.** [of person] tristesse *f* - **2.** [of conditions, life] misère *f*.

misfire [ˌmɪs'faɪər] *vi* - **1.** [gun, plan] rater - **2.** [car engine] avoir des ratés.

misfit ['mɪsfɪt] *n* inadapté *m*, -e *f*.

misfortune [mɪs'fɔːtʃuːn] *n* - **1.** [bad luck] malchance *f* - **2.** [piece of bad luck] malheur *m*.

misgivings [mɪs'gɪvɪŋz] *npl* craintes *fpl*, doutes *mpl*.

misguided [ˌmɪs'gaɪdɪd] *adj* [person] malavisé(e) ; [attempt] malencontreux(euse) ; [opinion] peu judicieux(euse).

mishandle [ˌmɪs'hændl] *vt* - **1.** [person, animal] manier sans précaution - **2.** [negotiations] mal mener ; [business] mal gérer.

mishap ['mɪshæp] *n* mésaventure *f*; **without ~** sans encombre OR incident.

mishear [ˌmɪs'hɪər] (*pt* & *pp* -**heard** [-'hɜːd]) *vt* & *vi* mal entendre.

mishmash ['mɪʃmæʃ] *n* inf méli-mélo *m*.

misinform [ˌmɪsɪn'fɔːm] *vt* mal renseigner, mal informer.

misinformation [ˌmɪsɪnfə'meɪʃn] *n* POL désinformation *f*.

misinterpret [ˌmɪsɪn'tɜːprɪt] *vt* mal interpréter.

misjudge [ˌmɪs'dʒʌdʒ] *vt* - **1.** [distance, time] mal évaluer - **2.** [person, mood] méjuger, se méprendre sur.

misjudg(e)ment [ˌmɪs'dʒʌdʒmənt] *n* : **to make a ~** faire une erreur de jugement.

mislay [ˌmɪs'leɪ] (*pt* & *pp* -**laid** [-'leɪd]) *vt* égarer.

mislead [ˌmɪs'liːd] (*pt* & *pp* -**led**) *vt* induire en erreur.

misleading [ˌmɪs'liːdɪŋ] *adj* trompeur(euse).

misled [ˌmɪs'led] *pt* & *pp* ⊳ **mislead**.

mismanage [ˌmɪs'mænɪdʒ] *vt* mal gérer, mal administrer.

mismanagement [ˌmɪs'mænɪdʒmənt] *n* mauvaise gestion *f* OR administration *f*.

mismatch [ˌmɪs'mætʃ] *vt* : **to be ~ed** être mal assorti(e).

misnomer [ˌmɪs'nəʊmər] *n* nom *m* mal approprié.

misogynist [mɪ'sɒdʒɪnɪst] *n* misogyne *mf*.

misplace [ˌmɪs'pleɪs] *vt* égarer.

misplaced [ˌmɪs'pleɪst] *adj* mal placé(e), déplacé(e).

misprint ['mɪsprɪnt] *n* faute *f* d'impression.

mispronounce [ˌmɪsprə'naʊns] *vt* mal prononcer.

misquote [ˌmɪs'kwəʊt] *vt* citer de façon inexacte.

misread [ˌmɪs'riːd] (*pt* & *pp* **-read** [-'red]) *vt* **- 1.** [read wrongly] mal lire **- 2.** [misinterpret] mal interpréter.

misrepresent ['mɪsˌreprɪ'zent] *vt* dénaturer.

misrepresentation ['mɪsˌreprɪzen'teɪʃn] *n* **- 1.** (*U*) [wrong interpretation] mauvaise interprétation *f* **- 2.** [false account] déformation *f*.

misrule [ˌmɪs'ruːl] *n* mauvais gouvernement *m*, mauvaise administration *f*.

miss [mɪs] ⋄ *vt* **- 1.** [gen] rater, manquer **- 2.** [home, person] : **I ~ my family/her** ma famille/elle me manque **- 3.** [avoid, escape] échapper à ; **I just ~ed being run over** j'ai failli me faire écraser ⋄ *vi* rater ⋄ *n* : **to give sthg a ~ inf** ne pas aller à qqch.
➡ **miss out** ⋄ *vt sep* [omit - by accident] oublier ; [- deliberately] omettre ⋄ *vi* : **to ~ out on sthg** ne pas pouvoir profiter de qqch.

Miss [mɪs] *n* Mademoiselle *f*.

misshapen [ˌmɪs'ʃeɪpn] *adj* difforme.

missile [Br 'mɪsaɪl, Am 'mɪsəl] *n* **- 1.** [weapon] missile *m* **- 2.** [thrown object] projectile *m*.

missile launcher [-ˌlɔːntʃər] *n* lance-missiles *m inv*.

missing ['mɪsɪŋ] *adj* **- 1.** [lost] perdu(e), égaré(e) **- 2.** [not present] manquant(e), qui manque.

missing link *n* maillon *m* qui manque à la chaîne.

missing person *n* personne *f* disparue.

mission ['mɪʃn] *n* mission *f*.

missionary ['mɪʃənrɪ] (*pl* **-ies**) *n* missionnaire *mf*.

Mississippi [ˌmɪsɪ'sɪpɪ] **- 1.** [river] : **the ~ (River)** le Mississippi **- 2.** [state] Mississippi *m* ; **in ~** dans le Mississippi.

missive ['mɪsɪv] *n* missive *f*.

Missouri [mɪ'zʊərɪ] *n* Missouri *m* ; **in ~** dans le Missouri.

misspell [ˌmɪs'spel] (*pt* & *pp* **-spelt** OR **-spelled**) *vt* mal orthographier.

misspelling [ˌmɪs'spelɪŋ] *n* faute *f* d'orthographe.

misspelt [ˌmɪs'spelt] *pt* & *pp* ➡ **misspell**.

misspend [ˌmɪs'spend] (*pt* & *pp* **-spent** [-'spent]) *vt* gaspiller.

mist [mɪst] *n* brume *f*.
➡ **mist over, mist up** *vi* s'embuer.

mistake [mɪ'steɪk] (*pt* **-took** ; *pp* **-taken**) ⋄ *n* erreur *f* ; **by ~** par erreur ; **to make a ~** faire une erreur, se tromper ⋄ *vt* **- 1.** [misunderstand - meaning] mal comprendre ; [- intention] se méprendre sur **- 2.** [fail to recognize] : **to ~ sb/sthg for** prendre qqn/qqch pour, confondre qqn/qqch avec ; **there's no mistaking ...** il est impossible de ne pas reconnaître ...

mistaken [mɪ'steɪkn] ⋄ *pp* ➡ **mistake** ⋄ *adj* **- 1.** [person] : **to be ~ (about)** se tromper (en ce qui concerne OR sur) **- 2.** [belief, idea] erroné(e), faux (fausse).

mistaken identity *n* : **a case of ~** une erreur sur la personne.

mistakenly [mɪ'steɪknlɪ] *adv* par erreur.

mister ['mɪstər] *n inf* monsieur *m*.
➡ **Mister** *n* Monsieur *m*.

mistime [ˌmɪs'taɪm] *vt* [tackle, shot] mal calculer ; [announcement] faire au mauvais moment.

mistletoe ['mɪsltəʊ] *n* gui *m*.

mistook [mɪ'stʊk] *pt* ➡ **mistake**.

mistranslation [ˌmɪstræns'leɪʃn] *n* erreur *f* de traduction.

mistreat [ˌmɪs'triːt] *vt* maltraiter.

mistreatment [ˌmɪs'triːtmənt] *n* mauvais traitement *m*.

mistress ['mɪstrɪs] *n* maîtresse *f*.

mistrial ['mɪstraɪəl] *n* [in UK] erreur *f* judiciaire ; [in US] *procès annulé par manque d'unanimité parmi les jurés*.

mistrust [ˌmɪs'trʌst] ⋄ *n* méfiance *f* ⋄ *vt* se méfier de.

mistrustful [ˌmɪs'trʌstfʊl] *adj* : **~ (of)** méfiant(e) (à l'égard de).

misty ['mɪstɪ] (*compar* **-ier** ; *superl* **-iest**) *adj* brumeux(euse).

misunderstand [ˌmɪsʌndə'stænd] (*pt* & *pp* **-stood**) *vt* & *vi* mal comprendre.

misunderstanding [ˌmɪsʌndə'stændɪŋ] *n* malentendu *m*.

misunderstood [ˌmɪsʌndə'stʊd] *pt* & *pp* ➡ **misunderstand**.

misuse [*n* ˌmɪs'juːs, *vb* ˌmɪs'juːz] ⋄ *n* **- 1.** [of one's time, resources] mauvais emploi *m* **- 2.** [of power] abus *m* ; [of funds] détournement *m* ⋄ *vt* **- 1.** [one's time, resources] mal employer **- 2.** [power] abuser de ; [funds] détourner.

MIT (*abbr of* **Massachusetts Institute of Technology**) *n l'institut de technologie du Massachusetts*.

mite [maɪt] *n* **- 1.** [insect] mite *f* **- 2.** inf [small amount] : **a ~** un brin, un tantinet **- 3.** [small child] petit *m*, -e *f*.

miter Am = mitre.

mitigate ['mɪtɪgeɪt] *vt* atténuer, mitiger.

mitigating ['mɪtɪgeɪtɪŋ] *adj* : **~ circumstances** circonstances *fpl* atténuantes.

mitigation [,mɪtɪ'geɪʃn] *n* atténuation *f*.

mitre Br, **miter** Am ['maɪtəʳ] *n* **- 1.** [hat] mitre *f* **- 2.** [joint] onglet *m*.

mitt [mɪt] *n* **- 1.** = **mitten - 2.** [in baseball] gant *m*.

mitten ['mɪtn] *n* moufle *f*.

mix [mɪks] ◇ *vt* **- 1.** [gen] mélanger **- 2.** [activities] : **to ~ sthg with sthg** combiner OR associer qqch et qqch **- 3.** [drink] préparer ; [cement] malaxer ◇ *vi* **- 1.** [gen] se mélanger **- 2.** [socially] : **to ~ with** fréquenter ◇ *n* **- 1.** [gen] mélange *m* **- 2.** MUS mixage *m*.

➤ **mix up** *vt sep* **- 1.** [confuse] confondre **- 2.** [disorganize] mélanger.

mixed [mɪkst] *adj* **- 1.** [assorted] assortis(ies) ; **to have ~ feelings** être partagé **- 2.** [education] mixte.

mixed-ability *adj* Br [class] tous niveaux confondus.

mixed blessing *n* quelque chose qui a du bon et du mauvais.

mixed doubles *n* double *m* mixte.

mixed economy *n* économie *f* mixte.

mixed grill *n* assortiment *m* de grillades.

mixed marriage *n* mariage *m* mixte.

mixed up *adj* **- 1.** [confused - person] qui ne sait plus où il en est, paumé(e) ; [- mind] embrouillé(e) **- 2.** [involved] : **to be ~ in sthg** être mêlé(e) à qqch.

mixer ['mɪksəʳ] *n* [for food] mixer *m*.

mixer tap *n* Br (robinet *m*) mélangeur *m*.

mixing bowl ['mɪksɪŋ-] *n* grand bol *m* de cuisine.

mixture ['mɪkstʃəʳ] *n* **- 1.** [gen] mélange *m* **- 2.** MED préparation *f*.

mix-up *n inf* confusion *f*.

mk, MK *abbr of* **mark**.

mkt *abbr of* **market**.

MLitt [em'lɪt] (*abbr of* **Master of Literature, Master of Letters**) *n* (*titulaire d'une*) *maîtrise de lettres*.

MLR *abbr of* **minimum lending rate**.

mm (*abbr of* **millimetre**) mm.

MN ◇ *n abbr of* **Merchant Navy** ◇ *abbr of* **Minnesota**.

mnemonic [nɪ'mɒnɪk] *n* mnémotechnique *f*.

m.o. *abbr of* **money order**.

MO ◇ *n abbr of* **medical officer** ◇ *abbr of* **Missouri**.

moan [məʊn] ◇ *n* **- 1.** [of pain, sadness] gémissement *m* **- 2.** inf [complaint] plainte *f* ◇ *vi* **- 1.** [in pain, sadness] gémir **- 2.** inf [complain] : **to ~ (about)** rouspéter OR râler (à propos de).

moaning ['məʊnɪŋ] *n (U)* [complaining] plaintes *fpl*, jérémiades *fpl*.

moat [məʊt] *n* douves *fpl*.

mob [mɒb] (*pt & pp* **-bed** ; *cont* **-bing**) ◇ *n* foule *f* ◇ *vt* assaillir.

mobile ['məʊbaɪl] ◇ *adj* **- 1.** [gen] mobile **- 2.** [able to travel] motorisé(e) ◇ *n* mobile *m*.

mobile home *n* auto-caravane *f*.

mobile library *n* bibliobus *m*.

mobile phone *n* téléphone *m* portatif.

mobile shop *n* marchand *m* ambulant.

mobility [mə'bɪlətɪ] *n* mobilité *f*.

mobility allowance *n* Br allocation *f* de transport.

mobilization [,məʊbɪlaɪ'zeɪʃn] *n* mobilisation *f*.

mobilize, -ise ['məʊbɪlaɪz] *vt & vi* mobiliser.

moccasin ['mɒkəsɪn] *n* mocassin *m*.

mock [mɒk] ◇ *adj* faux (fausse) ; **~ exam** examen blanc ◇ *vt* se moquer de ◇ *vi* se moquer.

mockery ['mɒkərɪ] *n* moquerie *f ;* **to make a ~ of sthg** tourner qqch en dérision.

mocking ['mɒkɪŋ] *adj* moqueur(euse).

mockingbird ['mɒkɪŋbɜːd] *n* moqueur *m*.

mock-up *n* maquette *f*.

mod [mɒd] *n* en Angleterre, membre d'un groupe de jeunes des années 60 qui s'opposaient aux rockers.

MoD *n abbr of* **Ministry of Defence**.

mod cons [,mɒd-] (*abbr of* **modern conveniences**) *npl* Br inf : **all ~** tout confort, tt. conf.

mode [məʊd] *n* mode *m*.

model ['mɒdl] (Br *pt & pp* **-led** ; *cont* **-ling**, Am *pt & pp* **-ed** ; *cont* **-ing**) ◇ *n* **- 1.** [gen] modèle *m* **- 2.** [fashion model] mannequin *m* ◇ *adj* **- 1.** [perfect] modèle **- 2.** [reduced-scale] (en) modèle réduit ◇ *vt* **- 1.** [clay] modeler **- 2.** [clothes] : **to ~ a dress** présenter un modèle de robe **- 3.** [copy] : **to ~ o.s. on sb** prendre modèle OR exemple sur qqn, se modeler sur qqn ◇ *vi* être mannequin.

modem ['məʊdem] *n* COMPUT modem *m*.

moderate [*adj & n* 'mɒdərət, *vb* 'mɒdəreɪt] ◇ *adj* modéré(e) ◇ *n* POL modéré *m*, -e *f* ◇ *vt* modérer ◇ *vi* se modérer.

moderately ['mɒdərətlɪ] *adv* [not very] pas très, plus ou moins.

moderation [ˌmɒdə'reɪʃn] n modération f ; **in ~** avec modération.

moderator ['mɒdəreɪtəʳ] n [of exam] examinateur m, -trice f.

modern ['mɒdən] adj moderne.

modern-day adj moderne, d'aujourd'hui.

modernism ['mɒdənɪzml] n modernisme m.

modernization [ˌmɒdənaɪ'zeɪʃn] n modernisation f.

modernize, -ise ['mɒdənaɪz] <> vt moderniser <> vi se moderniser.

modern languages npl langues fpl vivantes.

modest ['mɒdɪst] adj modeste.

modestly ['mɒdɪstlɪ] adv modestement.

modesty ['mɒdɪstɪ] n modestie f.

modicum ['mɒdɪkəm] n minimum m.

modification [ˌmɒdɪfɪ'keɪʃn] n modification f.

modify ['mɒdɪfaɪ] (pt & pp -ied) vt modifier.

modular ['mɒdjʊləʳ] adj modulaire.

modulated ['mɒdjʊleɪtɪd] adj modulé(e).

modulation [ˌmɒdjʊ'leɪʃn] n modulation f.

module ['mɒdju:l] n module m.

Mogadishu [ˌmɒgə'dɪʃu:] n Mogadishu.

moggy ['mɒgɪ] (pl -ies) n Br inf minou m.

mogul ['məʊgl] n fig magnat m.

MOH (abbr of **Medical Officer of Health**) n en Grande-Bretagne, direction de la santé publique.

mohair ['məʊheəʳ] <> n mohair m <> comp en mohair.

Mohammedan [mə'hæmɪdn] <> adj mahométan(e), musulman(e) <> n Mahométan m, -e f.

Mohican [məʊ'hi:kən, 'məʊɪkən] n Mohican m.

moist [mɔɪst] adj [soil, climate] humide ; [cake] moelleux(euse).

moisten ['mɔɪsn] vt humecter.

moisture ['mɔɪstʃəʳ] n humidité f.

moisturize, -ise ['mɔɪstʃəraɪz] vt hydrater.

moisturizer ['mɔɪstʃəraɪzəʳ] n crème f hydratante, lait m hydratant.

molar ['məʊləʳ] n molaire f.

molasses [mə'læsɪz] n (U) mélasse f.

mold etc Am = **mould**.

Moldavia [mɒl'deɪvjə] n Moldavie f ; **in ~** en Moldavie.

mole [məʊl] n - **1.** [animal, spy] taupe f - **2.** [on skin] grain m de beauté.

molecular [mə'lekjʊləʳ] adj moléculaire.

molecule ['mɒlɪkju:l] n molécule f.

molehill ['məʊlhɪl] n taupinière f.

molest [mə'lest] vt - **1.** [attack sexually] attenter à la pudeur de - **2.** [attack] molester.

molester [mə'lestəʳ] n : **child ~** personne qui est coupable d'attentat à la pudeur sur des enfants.

mollify ['mɒlɪfaɪ] (pt & pp -ied) vt apaiser, calmer.

mollusc, mollusk Am ['mɒləsk] n mollusque m.

mollycoddle ['mɒlɪˌkɒdl] vt inf chouchouter.

Molotov cocktail ['mɒlətɒf-] n cocktail m Molotov.

molt Am = **moult**.

molten ['məʊltn] adj en fusion.

mom [mɒm] n Am inf maman f.

moment ['məʊmənt] n moment m, instant m ; **to choose the right ~** choisir son moment ; **~ of truth** minute f de vérité ; **at any ~** d'un moment à l'autre ; **at the ~** en ce moment ; **at the last ~** au dernier moment ; **for the ~** pour le moment ; **for one ~** pendant un instant.

momentarily ['məʊməntərɪlɪ] adv - **1.** [for a short time] momentanément - **2.** Am [soon] très bientôt.

momentary ['məʊməntrɪ] adj momentané(e), passager(ère).

momentous [mə'mentəs] adj capital(e), très important(e).

momentum [mə'mentəm] n (U) - **1.** PHYSICS moment m - **2.** fig [speed, force] vitesse f ; **to gather ~** prendre de la vitesse.

momma ['mɒmə], **mommy** ['mɒmɪ] n Am maman f.

Mon. (abbr of **Monday**) lun.

Monaco ['mɒnəkəʊ] n Monaco.

monarch ['mɒnək] n monarque m.

monarchist ['mɒnəkɪst] n monarchiste mf.

monarchy ['mɒnəkɪ] (pl -ies) n monarchie f.

monastery ['mɒnəstrɪ] (pl -ies) n monastère m.

monastic [mə'næstɪk] adj monastique.

Monday ['mʌndɪ] n lundi m ; see also **Saturday**.

monetarism ['mʌnɪtərɪzml] n monétarisme m.

monetarist ['mʌnɪtərɪst] n monétariste mf.

monetary ['mʌnɪtrɪ] adj monétaire.

money ['mʌnɪ] n argent m ; **to make ~** gagner de l'argent ; **to get one's ~'s worth** en avoir pour son argent.

moneybox ['mʌnɪbɒks] n tirelire f.

moneyed ['mʌnɪd] *adj* riche, cossu(e).

moneylender ['mʌnɪ,lendəʳ] *n* prêteur *m*, -euse *f* sur gages.

moneymaker ['mʌnɪ,meɪkəʳ] *n* affaire *f* lucrative.

moneymaking ['mʌnɪ,meɪkɪŋ] *adj* lucratif(ive).

money market *n* marché *m* monétaire.

money order *n* mandat *m* postal.

money-spinner [-,spɪnəʳ] *n esp Br inf* mine *f* d'or.

money supply *n* masse *f* monétaire.

mongol ['mɒŋgəl] **dated** & **offensive** ◇ *adj* mongolien(enne) ◇ *n* mongolien *m*, -ienne *f*.

➤ **Mongol** = Mongolian.

Mongolia [mɒŋ'gəʊlɪə] *n* Mongolie *f*; **in ~** en Mongolie.

Mongolian [mɒŋ'gəʊlɪən] ◇ *adj* mongol(e) ◇ *n* - **1.** [person] Mongol *m*, -e *f* - **2.** [language] mongol *m*.

mongoose ['mɒŋguːs] (*pl* -s) *n* mangouste *f*.

mongrel ['mʌŋgrəl] *n* [dog] bâtard *m*.

monitor ['mɒnɪtəʳ] ◇ *n* COMPUT, MED & TV moniteur *m* ◇ *vt* - **1.** [check] contrôler, suivre de près - **2.** [broadcasts, messages] être à l'écoute de.

monk [mʌŋk] *n* moine *m*.

monkey ['mʌŋkɪ] (*pl* -s) *n* singe *m*.

monkey nut *n* cacahuète *f*.

monkey wrench *n* clef *f* à molette.

mono ['mɒnəʊ] ◇ *adj* mono (*inv*) ◇ *n* - **1.** [sound] monophonie *f* - **2.** *Am inf* [glandular fever] mononucléose *f* (infectieuse).

monochrome ['mɒnəkrəʊm] *adj* monochrome.

monocle ['mɒnəkl] *n* monocle *m*.

monogamous [mɒ'nɒgəməs] *adj* monogame.

monogamy [mɒ'nɒgəmɪ] *n* monogamie *f*.

monogrammed ['mɒnəgræmd] *adj* marqué(e) d'un monogramme.

monolingual [,mɒnə'lɪŋgwəl] *adj* monolingue.

monolithic [,mɒnə'lɪθɪk] *adj* monolithique.

monologue, monolog *Am* ['mɒnəlɒg] *n* monologue *m*.

mononucleosis ['mɒnəʊ,njuːklɪ'əʊsɪs] *n Am* mononucléose *f* (infectieuse).

monoplane ['mɒnəpleɪn] *n* monoplan *m*.

monopolize, -ise [mə'nɒpəlaɪz] *vt* monopoliser.

monopoly [mə'nɒpəlɪ] (*pl* -ies) *n* : **~ (on OR of)**

monopole *m* (de) ; **the Monopolies and Mergers Commission** *Br* organisme chargé de contrôler le fusionnement des entreprises.

monorail ['mɒnəreɪl] *n* monorail *m*.

monosodium glutamate [,mɒnə'səʊdjəm'gluːtəmeɪt] *n* glutamate *m* (de sodium).

monosyllabic [,mɒnəsɪ'læbɪk] *adj* monosyllabique.

monosyllable ['mɒnə,sɪləbl] *n* monosyllabe *m*.

monotone ['mɒnətəʊn] *n* ton *m* monocorde.

monotonous [mə'nɒtənəs] *adj* monotone.

monotonously [mə'nɒtənəslɪ] *adv* de façon monotone.

monotony [mə'nɒtənɪ] *n* monotonie *f*.

monoxide [mɒ'nɒksaɪd] *n* monoxyde *m*.

Monrovia [mən'rəʊvɪə] *n* Monrovia.

Monsignor [,mɒn'siːnjəʳ] *n* monsignor *m*.

monsoon [mɒn'suːn] *n* mousson *f*.

monster ['mɒnstəʳ] ◇ *n* - **1.** [creature, cruel person] monstre *m* - **2.** [huge thing, person] colosse *m* ◇ *adj* géant(e), monstre.

monstrosity [mɒn'strɒsətɪ] (*pl* -ies) *n* monstruosité *f*.

monstrous ['mɒnstrəs] *adj* monstrueux(euse).

montage ['mɒntɑːʒ] *n* montage *m*.

Montana [mɒn'tænə] *n* Montana *m*; **in ~** dans le Montana.

Mont Blanc [,mɔ̃'blɑ̃] *n* le mont Blanc.

Montenegro [,mɒntɪ'niːgrəʊ] *n* Monténégro *m*.

Montevideo [,mɒntɪvɪ'deɪəʊ] *n* Montevideo.

month [mʌnθ] *n* mois *m*.

monthly ['mʌnθlɪ] (*pl* -ies) ◇ *adj* mensuel(elle) ◇ *adv* mensuellement ◇ *n* [publication] mensuel *m*.

Montreal [,mɒntrɪ'ɔːl] *n* Montréal.

monument ['mɒnjʊmənt] *n* monument *m*.

monumental [,mɒnjʊ'mentl] *adj* monumental(e).

moo [muː] (*pl* -s) ◇ *n* meuglement *m*, beuglement *m* ◇ *vi* meugler, beugler.

mooch [muːtʃ] ➤ **mooch about, mooch around** *vi inf* traîner.

mood [muːd] *n* humeur *f*; **in a (bad) ~** de mauvaise humeur ; **in a good ~** de bonne humeur.

moody ['muːdɪ] (*compar* -ier ; *superl* -iest) *adj pej* - **1.** [changeable] lunatique - **2.** [bad-tempered] de mauvaise humeur, mal luné(e).

moon [muːn] *n* lune *f*; **to be over the ~** *inf* être aux anges.

moonbeam ['muːnbiːm] n rayon m de lune.
moonlight ['muːnlaɪt] (pt & pp -ed) ◇ n clair m de lune ◇ vi travailler au noir.
moonlighting ['muːnlaɪtɪŋ] n (U) travail m au noir.
moonlit ['muːnlɪt] adj [countryside] éclairé(e) par la lune ; [night] de lune.
moonscape ['muːnskeɪp] n paysage m lunaire.
moon shot n tir m lunaire.
moonstone ['muːnstəʊn] n pierre f de lune.
moonstruck ['muːnstrʌk] adj inf fêlé(e).
moony ['muːnɪ] (compar -ier ; superl -iest) adj Br inf rêveur(euse).
moor [mɔːʳ] ◇ n esp Br lande f ◇ vt amarrer ◇ vi mouiller.
Moor [mɔːʳ] n Maure m, Mauresque f.
moorings ['mɔːrɪŋz] npl [ropes, chains] amarres fpl ; [place] mouillage m.
Moorish ['mɔːrɪʃ] adj mauresque.
moorland ['mɔːlənd] n esp Br lande f.
moose [muːs] (pl inv) n [North American] orignal m.
moot [muːt] vt [question] soulever.
moot point n point m discutable.
mop [mɒp] (pt & pp -ped ; cont -ping) ◇ n - 1. [for cleaning] balai m à laver - 2. inf [hair] tignasse f ◇ vt - 1. [floor] laver - 2. [sweat] essuyer ; **to ~ one's face** s'essuyer le visage.
◆ **mop up** vt sep [clean up] éponger.
mope [məʊp] vi broyer du noir.
◆ **mope about, mope around** vi traîner.
moped ['məʊped] n vélomoteur m.
moral ['mɒrəl] ◇ adj moral(e) ; **~ support** soutien m moral ◇ n [lesson] morale f.
◆ **morals** npl moralité f.
morale [mə'rɑːl] n (U) moral m.
moralistic [,mɒrə'lɪstɪk] adj pej moralisateur(trice).
morality [mə'rælətɪ] (pl -ies) n moralité f.
moralize, -ise ['mɒrəlaɪz] vi pej : **to ~ (about** OR **on)** moraliser (sur).
morally ['mɒrəlɪ] adv moralement.
Moral Majority n groupe de pression américain ultra-conservateur lié aux églises fondamentalistes.
morass [mə'ræs] n fig [of detail, paperwork] fatras m.
moratorium [,mɒrə'tɔːrɪəm] (pl -ria [-rɪə]) n moratoire m.
morbid ['mɔːbɪd] adj morbide.
more [mɔːʳ] ◇ adv - 1. (with adjectives and adverbs) plus ; **~ important (than)** plus important (que) ; **~ often/quickly (than)** plus souvent/rapidement (que) - 2. [to a greater degree] plus, davantage ; **she's ~ like a mother to me than a sister** elle est davantage une mère qu'une sœur pour moi ; **we were ~ hurt than angry** nous étions plus offensés que fâchés, nous étions offensés plutôt que fâchés - 3. [another time] : **once/twice ~** une fois/deux fois de plus, encore une fois/deux fois ◇ adj - 1. [larger number, amount of] plus de, davantage de ; **there are ~ trains in the morning** il y a plus de trains le matin ; **~ than 70 people died** plus de 70 personnes ont péri - 2. [an extra amount of] encore (de) ; **have some ~ tea** prends encore du thé ; **I finished two ~ chapters today** j'ai fini deux autres OR encore deux chapitres aujourd'hui ; **we need ~ money/time** il nous faut plus d'argent/de temps, il nous faut davantage d'argent/de temps ◇ pron plus, davantage ; **~ than five** plus de cinq ; **he's got ~ than I have** il en a plus que moi ; **there's ~ if you want it** il y en a encore si vous en voulez ; **there's no ~ (left)** il n'y en a plus, il n'en reste plus ; **what ~ do you want?** qu'est-ce que tu veux de plus? ; **(and) what's ~** de plus, qui plus est.
◆ **any more** adv : **not ... any ~** ne ... plus.
◆ **more and more** adv & pron de plus en plus ; **~ and ~ depressed** de plus en plus déprimé ◇ adj de plus en plus de ; **there are ~ and ~ cars on the roads** il y a de plus en plus de voitures sur les routes.
◆ **more or less** adv - 1. [almost] plus ou moins - 2. [approximately] environ, à peu près.
moreover [mɔː'rəʊvəʳ] adv de plus.
morgue [mɔːg] n morgue f.
MORI ['mɒrɪ] (abbr of **Market & Opinion Research Institute**) n institut de sondage.
moribund ['mɒrɪbʌnd] adj moribond(e).
Mormon ['mɔːmən] n mormon m, -e f.
morning ['mɔːnɪŋ] n matin m ; [duration] matinée f ; **I work in the ~** je travaille le matin ; **I'll do it tomorrow ~** OR **in the ~** je le ferai demain.
◆ **mornings** adv Am le matin.
morning-after pill n pilule f du lendemain.
morning dress n esp Br habit m, frac m.
morning sickness n (U) nausées fpl (matinales).
Moroccan [mə'rɒkən] ◇ adj marocain(e) ◇ n Marocain m, -e f.
Morocco [mə'rɒkəʊ] n Maroc m ; **in ~** au Maroc.

moron ['mɔːrɒn] n inf idiot m, -e f, crétin m, -e f.

moronic [mə'rɒnɪk] adj idiot(e), crétin(e).

morose [mə'rəʊs] adj morose.

morphine ['mɔːfiːn] n morphine f.

morris dancing ['mɒrɪs-] n (U) danse folklorique anglaise.

Morse (code) [mɔːs-] n morse m.

morsel ['mɔːsl] n bout m, morceau m.

mortal ['mɔːtl] <> adj mortel(elle) <> n mortel m, -elle f.

mortality [mɔː'tælətɪ] n mortalité f.

mortality rate n taux m de mortalité.

mortally ['mɔːtəlɪ] adv mortellement.

mortar ['mɔːtər] n mortier m.

mortarboard ['mɔːtəbɔːd] n mortier m (chapeau).

mortgage ['mɔːgɪdʒ] <> n emprunt-logement m <> vt hypothéquer.

mortgagee [,mɔːgɪ'dʒiː] n créancier m, -ère f hypothécaire.

mortgagor [,mɔːgɪ'dʒɔːr] n débiteur m, -trice f hypothécaire.

mortician [mɔː'tɪʃn] n Am entrepreneur m de pompes funèbres.

mortified ['mɔːtɪfaɪd] adj mortifié(e).

mortise lock ['mɔːtɪs-] n serrure f encastrée.

mortuary ['mɔːtʃʊərɪ] (pl -ies) n morgue f.

mosaic [mə'zeɪɪk] n mosaïque f.

Moscow ['mɒskəʊ] n Moscou.

Moslem ['mɒzləm] = Muslim.

mosque [mɒsk] n mosquée f.

mosquito [mə'skiːtəʊ] (pl -es OR -s) n moustique m.

mosquito net n moustiquaire f.

moss [mɒs] n mousse f.

mossy ['mɒsɪ] (compar -ier ; superl -iest) adj moussu(e), couvert(e) de mousse.

most [məʊst] (superl of many) <> adj - 1. [the majority of] la plupart de ; ~ **tourists here are German** la plupart des touristes ici sont allemands - 2. [largest amount of] : **(the)** ~ le plus de ; **she's got (the)** ~ **money/sweets** c'est elle qui a le plus d'argent/de bonbons <> pron - 1. [the majority] la plupart ; ~ **of the tourists here are German** la plupart des touristes ici sont allemands ; ~ **of them** la plupart d'entre eux - 2. [largest amount] : **(the)** ~ le plus ; **at** ~ au maximum, tout au plus - 3. phr : **to make the** ~ **of sthg** profiter de qqch au maximum <> adv - 1. [to greatest extent] : **(the)** ~ le plus - 2. fml [very] très, fort - 3. Am [almost] presque.

mostly ['məʊstlɪ] adv principalement, surtout.

MOT <> n (abbr of Ministry of Transport (test)) contrôle technique annuel obligatoire pour les véhicules de plus de trois ans <> vt : **to have one's car ~'d** soumettre sa voiture au contrôle technique.

motel [məʊ'tel] n motel m.

moth [mɒθ] n papillon m de nuit ; [in clothes] mite f.

mothball ['mɒθbɔːl] n boule f de naphtaline.

moth-eaten adj mité(e).

mother ['mʌðər] <> n mère f <> vt [child] materner, dorloter.

motherboard ['mʌðəbɔːd] n COMPUT carte f mère.

motherhood ['mʌðəhʊd] n maternité f.

Mothering Sunday ['mʌðərɪŋ-] n fête f des Mères.

mother-in-law (pl **mothers-in-law**) n belle-mère f.

motherland ['mʌðəlænd] n mère patrie f.

motherless ['mʌðəlɪs] adj orphelin(e) de mère.

motherly ['mʌðəlɪ] adj maternel(elle).

Mother Nature n la nature.

mother-of-pearl <> n nacre f <> comp de nacre.

Mother's day n fête f des Mères.

mother ship n ravitailleur m.

mother superior n mère f supérieure.

mother-to-be (pl **mothers-to-be**) n future maman f.

mother tongue n langue f maternelle.

motif [məʊ'tiːf] n motif m.

motion ['məʊʃn] <> n - 1. [gen] mouvement m ; **to set sthg in** ~ mettre qqch en branle ; **to go through the ~s** [act insincerely] faire semblant de faire quelque chose - 2. [in debate] motion f <> vt : **to** ~ **sb to do sthg** faire signe à qqn de faire qqch <> vi : **to** ~ **to sb** faire signe à qqn.

motionless ['məʊʃənlɪs] adj immobile.

motion picture n Am film m.

motivate ['məʊtɪveɪt] vt - 1. [act, decision] motiver - 2. [student, workforce] : **to** ~ **sb (to do sthg)** pousser qqn (à faire qqch).

motivated ['məʊtɪveɪtɪd] adj motivé(e).

motivation [,məʊtɪ'veɪʃn] n motivation f.

motive ['məʊtɪv] n motif m.

motley ['mɒtlɪ] adj pej hétéroclite.

motocross ['məʊtəkrɒs] n motocross m.

motor ['məʊtər] ⟨> adj Br automobile ⟨> n [engine] moteur m ⟨> vi dated aller en automobile.

Motorail® ['məʊtəreɪl] n Br train m autocouchette OR autos-couchettes.

motorbike ['məʊtəbaɪk] n inf moto f.

motorboat ['məʊtəbəʊt] n canot m automobile.

motorcade ['məʊtəkeɪd] n cortège m de voitures.

motorcar ['məʊtəkɑːr] n Br automobile f, voiture f.

motorcycle ['məʊtəˌsaɪkl] n moto f.

motorcyclist ['məʊtəˌsaɪklɪst] n motocycliste mf.

motoring ['məʊtərɪŋ] ⟨> adj Br [magazine, correspondent] automobile ; **a ~ offence** une infraction au code de la route ⟨> n tourisme m automobile.

motorist ['məʊtərɪst] n automobiliste mf.

motorize, -ise ['məʊtəraɪz] vt motoriser.

motor lodge n Am motel m.

motor racing n (U) course f automobile.

motor scooter n scooter m.

motor vehicle n véhicule m automobile.

motorway ['məʊtəweɪ] Br ⟨> n autoroute f ⟨> comp d'autoroute.

mottled ['mɒtld] adj [leaf] tacheté(e) ; [skin] marbré(e).

motto ['mɒtəʊ] (pl -s OR -es) n devise f.

mould, mold Am [məʊld] ⟨> n - **1.** [growth] moisissure f - **2.** [shape] moule m ⟨> vt - **1.** [shape] mouler, modeler - **2.** fig [influence] former, façonner.

moulding, molding Am ['məʊldɪŋ] n - **1.** [decoration] moulure f - **2.** [moulded object] moulage m.

mouldy, moldy Am ['məʊldɪ] (compar -ier ; superl -iest) adj moisi(e).

moult, molt Am [məʊlt] ⟨> vt perdre ⟨> vi muer.

mound [maʊnd] n - **1.** [small hill] tertre m, butte f - **2.** [pile] tas m, monceau m.

mount [maʊnt] ⟨> n - **1.** [support - for jewel] monture f ; [- for photograph] carton m de montage ; [- for machine] support m - **2.** [horse] monture f - **3.** [mountain] mont m ⟨> vt monter ; **to ~ a horse** monter sur un cheval ; **to ~ a bike** monter sur OR enfourcher un vélo ; **to ~ guard over** monter la garde auprès de ⟨> vi - **1.** [increase] monter, augmenter - **2.** [climb on horse] se mettre en selle.

mountain ['maʊntɪn] n lit & fig montagne f ;

don't make a ~ out of a mohehill n'en fais pas une montagne.

mountain bike n VTT m.

mountaineer [ˌmaʊntɪ'nɪər] n alpiniste mf.

mountaineering [ˌmaʊntɪ'nɪərɪŋ] n alpinisme m.

mountainous ['maʊntɪnəs] adj [region] montagneux(euse).

mountain range n chaîne f de montagnes.

mountain rescue n secours m en montagne.

mounted ['maʊntɪd] adj monté(e), à cheval.

mounted police n : **the ~** la police montée.

Mountie ['maʊntɪ] n inf membre de la police montée canadienne.

mourn [mɔːn] ⟨> vt pleurer ⟨> vi : **to ~ (for sb)** pleurer (qqn).

mourner ['mɔːnər] n [related] parent m du défunt ; [unrelated] ami m, -e f du défunt.

mournful ['mɔːnfʊl] adj [face] triste ; [sound] lugubre.

mourning ['mɔːnɪŋ] n deuil m ; **in ~** en deuil.

mouse [maʊs] (pl **mice** [maɪs]) n COMPUT & ZOOL souris f.

mouse mat n COMPUT tapis m de souris.

mousetrap ['maʊstræp] n souricière f.

moussaka [muː'sɑːkə] n moussaka f.

mousse [muːs] n mousse f.

moustache Br [mə'stɑːʃ], **mustache** Am ['mʌstæʃ] n moustache f.

mouth [n maʊθ, vt maʊð] ⟨> n - **1.** [of person, animal] bouche f ; [of dog, cat, lion] gueule f ; **to keep one's ~ shut** inf se taire - **2.** [of cave] entrée f ; [of river] embouchure f ⟨> vt [words] former silencieusement (avec la bouche).

mouthful ['maʊθfʊl] n - **1.** [of food] bouchée f ; [of drink] gorgée f - **2.** inf [difficult name] nom m à coucher dehors.

mouthorgan ['maʊθˌɔːgən] n harmonica m.

mouthpiece ['maʊθpiːs] n - **1.** [of telephone] microphone m ; [of musical instrument] bec m - **2.** [spokesperson] porte-parole m inv.

mouth-to-mouth adj : **~ resuscitation** bouche-à-bouche m inv.

mouthwash ['maʊθwɒʃ] n eau f dentifrice.

mouth-watering [-ˌwɔːtərɪŋ] adj alléchant (e).

movable ['muːvəbl] adj mobile.

move [muːv] ⟨> n - **1.** [movement] mouvement m ; **to be on the ~** [person] être en déplacement ; [troops] être en marche ; **to get a ~ on** inf se remuer, se grouiller - **2.** [change - of house] déménagement *m* ; [- of job] changement *m* d'emploi **- 3.** [in game - action] coup *m* ; [- turn to play] tour *m* ; fig démarche *f* ◇ *vt* **- 1.** [shift] déplacer, bouger **- 2.** [change - job, office] changer de ; **to ~ house** déménager **- 3.** [cause] : **to ~ sb to do sthg** inciter qqn à faire qqch **- 4.** [emotionally] émouvoir **- 5.** [propose] : **to ~ sthg/that ...** proposer qqch/que ... ◇ *vi* **- 1.** [shift] bouger **- 2.** [act] agir **- 3.** [to new house] déménager ; [to new job] changer d'emploi.

◆ **move about** *vi* **- 1.** [fidget] remuer **- 2.** [travel] voyager.

◆ **move along** ◇ *vt sep* faire avancer ◇ *vi* se déplacer ; **the police asked him to ~ along** la police lui a demandé de circuler.

◆ **move around** = **move about**.

◆ **move away** *vi* [leave] partir.

◆ **move in** ◇ *vt sep* [troops] faire intervenir ◇ *vi* [to house] emménager.

◆ **move off** *vi* [train, car] partir, s'ébranler.

◆ **move on** ◇ *vt sep* faire circuler ◇ *vi* **- 1.** [after stopping] se remettre en route **- 2.** [in discussion] changer de sujet.

◆ **move out** ◇ *vt sep* [troops] retirer ◇ *vi* [from house] déménager.

◆ **move over** *vi* s'écarter, se pousser.

◆ **move up** *vi* [on bench etc] se déplacer.

moveable ['mu:vəbl] = **movable**.

movement ['mu:vmənt] *n* mouvement *m*.

movie ['mu:vɪ] *n esp Am* film *m*.

movie camera *n* caméra *f*.

moviegoer ['mu:vɪ,gəʊəʳ] *n Am* cinéphile *mf*.

movie star *n Am* star *f*, vedette *f* de cinéma.

movie theater *n Am* cinéma *m*.

moving ['mu:vɪŋ] *adj* **- 1.** [emotionally] émouvant(e), touchant(e) **- 2.** [not fixed] mobile.

moving staircase *n* escalier *m* roulant.

mow [məʊ] (*pt* **-ed** ; *pp* **-ed** OR **mown**) *vt* faucher ; [lawn] tondre.

◆ **mow down** *vt sep* faucher.

mower ['məʊəʳ] *n* tondeuse *f* à gazon.

mown [məʊn] *pp* ▷ **mow**.

Mozambican [,məʊzæm'bi:kn] ◇ *adj* mozambicain(e) ◇ *n* Mozambicain *m*, -e *f*.

Mozambique [,məʊzæm'bi:k] *n* Mozambique *m* ; **in ~** au Mozambique.

MP *n* **- 1.** (*abbr of* **Military Police**) PM **- 2.** *Br* (*abbr of* **Member of Parliament**) ≃ député *m* **- 3.** *Can abbr of* **Mounted Police**.

mpg (*abbr of* **miles per gallon**) *n* miles au gallon.

mph (*abbr of* **miles per hour**) *n* miles à l'heure.

MPhil [,em'fɪl] (*abbr of* **Master of Philosophy**) *n* (titulaire d'une) maîtrise de lettres.

MPS (*abbr of* **Member of the Pharmaceutical Society**) *n* membre de l'Académie de pharmacie britannique.

Mr ['mɪstəʳ] *n* Monsieur *m* ; [on letter] M.

MRC (*abbr of* **Medical Research Council**) *n* conseil de la recherche médicale en Grande-Bretagne.

MRCP (*abbr of* **Member of the Royal College of Physicians**) *n* membre de l'Académie de médecine britannique.

MRCS (*abbr of* **Member of the Royal College of Surgeons**) *n* membre de l'Académie de chirurgie britannique.

MRCVS (*abbr of* **Member of the Royal College of Veterinary Surgeons**) *n* membre de l'Académie de chirurgie vétérinaire britannique.

Mrs ['mɪsɪz] *n* Madame *f* ; [on letter] Mme.

ms. (*abbr of* **manuscript**) *n* ms.

Ms [mɪz] *n* titre que les femmes peuvent utiliser au lieu de madame ou mademoiselle pour éviter la distinction entre les femmes mariées et les célibataires.

MS ◇ *n* **- 1.** (*abbr of* **manuscript**) ms **- 2.** (*abbr of* **Master of Science**) (titulaire d'une) maîtrise de sciences américaine **- 3.** (*abbr of* **multiple sclerosis**) SEP *f* ◇ *abbr of* **Mississippi**.

MSA (*abbr of* **Master of Science in Agriculture**) *n* (titulaire d'une) maîtrise en sciences agricoles.

MSB (*abbr of* **most significant bit/byte**) *n* bit/octet de poids fort.

MSc (*abbr of* **Master of Science**) *n* (titulaire d'une) maîtrise de sciences.

MSC (*abbr of* **Manpower Services Commission**) *n* agence nationale britannique pour l'emploi.

MSF (*abbr of* **Manufacturing Science and Finance**) *n* confédération syndicale britannique.

MSG *abbr of* **monosodium glutamate**.

Msgr (*abbr of* **Monsignor**) Mgr.

MSP *n abbr of* **Member of the Scottish Parliament**.

MSt (*abbr of* **Mountain Standard Time**) *n* heure d'hiver des montagnes Rocheuses.

MSW (*abbr of* **Master of Social Work**) *n* (titulaire d'une) maîtrise en travail social.

Mt (*abbr of* **mount**) Mt.

MT ◇ *n* (*abbr of* **machine translation**) TA *f* ◇ *abbr of* **Montana**.

much [mʌtʃ] (*compar* **more** ; *superl* **most**) ◇ *adj* beaucoup de ; **there isn't ~ rice left** il ne reste pas beaucoup de riz ; **as ~ money as ...** autant d'argent que ... ; **too ~** trop de ; **how ~ ...?** combien de ...? ; **how ~ money do you earn?** tu gagnes combien? ⟨> *pron'* beaucoup ; **I don't think ~ of his new house** sa nouvelle maison ne me plaît pas trop ; **as ~ as** autant que ; **too ~** trop ; **how ~?** combien? ; **I'm not ~ of a cook** je suis un piètre cuisinier ; **so ~ for all my hard work** tout ce travail pour rien ; **I thought as ~** c'est bien ce que je pensais ; **it's not up to ~** inf ça ne vaut pas grand-chose ⟨> *adv* beaucoup ; **I don't go out ~** je ne sors pas beaucoup OR souvent ; **as ~ as** autant que ; **thank you very ~** merci beaucoup ; **without so ~ as ...** sans même ...

◆ **much as** conj bien que (+ subjunctive).

muchness ['mʌtʃnɪs] n : **to be much of a ~** être blanc bonnet et bonnet blanc.

muck [mʌk] inf n (U) - **1.** [dirt] saletés fpl - **2.** [manure] fumier m.

◆ **muck about, muck around** Br inf ⟨> vt sep : **to ~ sb about** traiter qqn par-dessus OR par-dessous la jambe ⟨> vi traîner.

◆ **muck in** vi Br inf donner un coup de main.

◆ **muck out** vt sep nettoyer.

◆ **muck up** vt sep Br inf gâcher.

muckraking ['mʌkreɪkɪŋ] n fig mise f au jour de scandales.

mucky ['mʌkɪ] (compar **-ier** ; superl **-iest**) adj sale.

mucus ['mju:kəs] n mucus m.

mud [mʌd] n boue f.

muddle ['mʌdl] ⟨> n désordre m, fouillis m ; **to be in a ~** [room, finances] être en désordre ; [person] ne plus s'y retrouver ⟨> vt - **1.** [papers] mélanger - **2.** [person] embrouiller.

◆ **muddle along** vi se débrouiller tant bien que mal.

◆ **muddle through** vi se tirer d'affaire, s'en sortir tant bien que mal.

◆ **muddle up** vt sep mélanger.

muddle-headed [-,hedɪd] adj [thinking] confus(e) ; [person] brouillon(onne).

muddy ['mʌdɪ] (compar **-ier** ; superl **-iest**, pt & pp **-ied**) ⟨> adj boueux(euse) ⟨> vt fig embrouiller.

mudflap ['mʌdflæp] n pare-boue m inv.

mudflat ['mʌdflæt] n laisse f.

mudguard ['mʌdgɑːd] n garde-boue m inv.

mudpack ['mʌdpæk] n masque m de beauté.

mudslinging ['mʌd,slɪŋɪŋ] n (U) fig attaques fpl.

muesli ['mju:zlɪ] n Br muesli m.

muff [mʌf] ⟨> n manchon m ⟨> vt inf louper.

muffin ['mʌfɪn] n muffin m.

muffle ['mʌfl] vt étouffer.

muffled ['mʌfld] adj - **1.** [sound] sourd(e), étouffé(e) - **2.** [person] : **~ (up)** emmitouflé(e).

muffler ['mʌflər] n Am [for car] silencieux m.

mug [mʌg] (pt & pp **-ged** ; cont **-ging**) ⟨> n - **1.** [cup] (grande) tasse f - **2.** inf [fool] andouille f ⟨> vt [attack] agresser.

mugger ['mʌgər] n agresseur m.

mugging ['mʌgɪŋ] n agression f.

muggy ['mʌgɪ] (compar **-ier** ; superl **-iest**) adj lourd(e), moite.

mugshot ['mʌgʃɒt] n inf photo f (de criminel).

mujaheddin [,mu:dʒəhe'di:n] npl moudjahiddin mpl.

mulatto [mju:'lætəʊ] (pl **-s** OR **-es**) n mulâtre m, mulâtresse f.

mulberry ['mʌlbərɪ] (pl **-ies**) n - **1.** [tree] mûrier m - **2.** [fruit] mûre f.

mule [mju:l] n mule f.

mull [mʌl] ◆ **mull over** vt sep ruminer, réfléchir à.

mullah ['mʌlə] n mollah m.

mulled [mʌld] adj : **~ wine** vin m chaud.

mullet ['mʌlɪt] (pl inv OR **-s**) n mulet m.

mulligatawny [,mʌlɪgə'tɔːnɪ] n soupe indienne au curry.

mullioned ['mʌlɪənd] adj [window] à meneaux.

multi- ['mʌltɪ] prefix multi-.

multicoloured Br, **multicolored** Am ['mʌltɪ,kʌləd] adj multicolore.

multicultural [,mʌltɪ'kʌltʃərəl] adj multiculturel(elle).

multifarious [,mʌltɪ'feərɪəs] adj divers, très varié(e).

multigym ['mʌltɪdʒɪm] n appareil m de musculation.

multilateral [,mʌltɪ'lætərəl] adj multilatéral(e).

multimedia [,mʌltɪ'miːdjə] adj multimédia (inv).

multimillionaire ['mʌltɪ,mɪljə'neər] n multimillionnaire mf.

multinational [,mʌltɪ'næʃənl] ⟨> adj multinational(e) ⟨> n multinationale f.

multiparty ['mʌltɪ,pɑːtɪ] adj multipartite ; **the ~ system** le pluripartisme.

multiple ['mʌltɪpl] ⟨> adj multiple ⟨> n multiple m.

multiple-choice adj à choix multiple.

multiple crash n carambolage m.

multiple injuries npl lésions fpl multiples.

multiple sclerosis [-sklɪ'rəʊsɪs] n sclérose f en plaques.

multiplex cinema ['mʌltɪpleks-] n complexe m multisalles.

multiplication [ˌmʌltɪplɪ'keɪʃn] n multiplication f.

multiplication sign n signe m de multiplication.

multiplication table n table f de multiplication.

multiplicity [ˌmʌltɪ'plɪsətɪ] n multiplicité f.

multiply ['mʌltɪplaɪ] (pt & pp -ied) ◇ vt multiplier ◇ vi se multiplier.

multipurpose [ˌmʌltɪ'pɜːpəs] adj polyvalent(e), à usages multiples.

multiracial [ˌmʌltɪ'reɪʃl] adj multiracial(e).

multistorey Br, **multistory** Am [ˌmʌltɪ'stɔːrɪ] ◇ adj à étages ◇ n [car park] parking m à étages.

multitude ['mʌltɪtjuːd] n multitude f.

multi-user adj COMPUT [system] multi-utilisateurs (inv).

multivitamin [Br 'mʌltɪvɪtəmɪn, Am 'mʌltɪvaɪtəmɪn] n multivitamine f.

mum [mʌm] Br inf ◇ n maman f ◇ adj : **to keep ~** ne pas piper mot.

mumble ['mʌmbl] vt & vi marmotter.

mumbo jumbo ['mʌmbəʊ'dʒʌmbəʊ] n charabia m.

mummify ['mʌmɪfaɪ] (pt & pp -ied) vt momifier.

mummy ['mʌmɪ] (pl -ies) n - **1.** Br inf [mother] maman f - **2.** [preserved body] momie f.

mumps [mʌmps] n (U) oreillons mpl.

munch [mʌntʃ] vt & vi croquer.

mundane [mʌn'deɪn] adj banal(e), ordinaire.

mung bean [mʌŋ-] n mungo m.

municipal [mjuː'nɪsɪpl] adj municipal(e).

municipality [mjuːˌnɪsɪ'pælətɪ] (pl -ies) n municipalité f.

munificent [mjuː'nɪfɪsənt] adj munificent(e).

munitions [mjuː'nɪʃnz] npl munitions fpl.

mural ['mjuːərəl] n peinture f murale.

murder ['mɜːdər] ◇ n meurtre m; **to get away with ~** fig pouvoir faire n'importe quoi impunément ◇ vt assassiner.

murderer ['mɜːdərər] n meurtrier m, assassin m.

murderess ['mɜːdərɪs] n meurtrière f.

murderous ['mɜːdərəs] adj meurtrier(ère).

murky ['mɜːkɪ] (compar -ier ; superl -iest) adj - **1.** [place] sombre - **2.** [water, past] trouble.

murmur ['mɜːmər] ◇ n murmure m; MED souffle m au cœur ◇ vt & vi murmurer.

MusB [mjuːz'biː], **MusBac** [mjuːz'bæk] (abbr of Bachelor of Music) n (titulaire d'un) diplôme d'études musicales.

muscle ['mʌsl] n muscle m; fig [power] poids m, impact m.
➤ **muscle in** vi intervenir, s'immiscer.

muscleman ['mʌslmən] (pl -men [-men]) n hercule m.

Muscovite ['mʌskəvaɪt] ◇ adj moscovite ◇ n Moscovite mf.

muscular ['mʌskjʊlər] adj - **1.** [spasm, pain] musculaire - **2.** [person] musclé(e).

muscular dystrophy [-'dɪstrəfɪ] n myopathie f primitive progressive, dystrophie f musculaire.

MusD [mjuːz'diː], **MusDoc** [mjuːz'dɒk] (abbr of Doctor of Music) n (titulaire d'un) doctorat d'études musicales.

muse [mjuːz] ◇ n muse f ◇ vi méditer, réfléchir.

museum [mjuː'ziːəm] n musée m.

mush [mʌʃ] n - **1.** [gunge] bouillie f - **2.** inf [sentimentality] sentimentalité f.

mushroom ['mʌʃrʊm] ◇ n champignon m ◇ vi [organization, party] se développer, grandir ; [houses] proliférer.

mushroom cloud n champignon m atomique.

mushy ['mʌʃɪ] (compar -ier ; superl -iest) adj - **1.** [food] en bouillie - **2.** inf [over-sentimental] à l'eau de rose, à la guimauve.

music ['mjuːzɪk] n musique f.

musical ['mjuːzɪkl] ◇ adj - **1.** [event, voice] musical(e) - **2.** [child] doué(e) pour la musique, musicien(enne) ◇ n comédie f musicale.

musical box Br, **music box** Am n boîte f à musique.

musical chairs n (U) chaises fpl musicales.

musical instrument n instrument m de musique.

music box Am = musical box.

music centre n chaîne f compacte.

music hall n Br music-hall m.

musician [mjuː'zɪʃn] n musicien m, -enne f.

music stand n pupitre m à musique.

musk [mʌsk] n musc m.

musket ['mʌskɪt] n mousquet m.

muskrat ['mʌskræt] *n* rat *m* musqué, onda- tra *m*.

Muslim ['muzlɪm] ⟨⟩ *adj* musulman(e) ⟨⟩ *n* Musulman *m*, -e *f*.

muslin ['mʌzlɪn] *n* mousseline *f*.

musquash ['mʌskwɒʃ] *n* rat *m* musqué, on- datra *m*.

muss [mʌs] *vt* Am : **to ~ (up)** [clothes] chiffon- ner, froisser ; [hair] déranger.

mussel ['mʌsl] *n* moule *f*.

must [mʌst] ⟨⟩ *modal vb* - **1.** [expressing obliga- tion] devoir ; **I ~ go** il faut que je m'en aille, je dois partir ; **you ~ come and visit** il faut ab- solument que tu viennes nous voir - **2.** [ex- pressing likelihood] : **they ~ have known** ils de- vaient le savoir ⟨⟩ *n inf* : **a ~** un must, un impératif ; **the film is a ~** c'est un film à voir absolument.

mustache Am = **moustache**.

mustard ['mʌstəd] *n* moutarde *f* ; **~ and cress** Br moutarde blanche et cresson alénois.

mustard gas *n* gaz *m* moutarde.

muster ['mʌstə^r] ⟨⟩ *vt* rassembler ⟨⟩ *vi* se réunir, se rassembler.

➡ **muster up** *vt fus* rassembler.

mustn't [mʌsnt] = **must not**.

must've ['mʌstəv] = **must have**.

musty ['mʌstɪ] (*compar* -**ier** ; *superl* -**iest**) *adj* [smell] de moisi ; [room] qui sent le renfermé OR le moisi.

mutant ['mjuːtənt] ⟨⟩ *adj* mutant(e) ⟨⟩ *n* mutant *m*.

mutate [mjuː'teɪt] *vi* subir une mutation, muter ; **to ~ into sthg** se changer en qqch, se transformer en qqch.

mutation [mjuː'teɪʃn] *n* mutation *f*.

mute [mjuːt] ⟨⟩ *adj* muet(ette) ⟨⟩ *n* muet *m*, -ette *f* ⟨⟩ *vt* étouffer, assourdir.

muted ['mjuːtɪd] *adj* - **1.** [colour] sourd(e) - **2.** [reaction] peu marqué(e) ; [protest] voilé(e).

mutilate ['mjuːtɪleɪt] *vt* mutiler.

mutilation [ˌmjuːtɪ'leɪʃn] *n* mutilation *f*.

mutineer [ˌmjuːtɪ'nɪə^r] *n* mutiné *m*, mutin *m*.

mutinous ['mjuːtɪnəs] *adj* [crew, soldiers] muti- né(e) ; [person, attitude] rebelle.

mutiny ['mjuːtɪnɪ] (*pl* -**ies**, *pt* & *pp* -**ied**) ⟨⟩ *n* mutinerie *f* ⟨⟩ *vi* se mutiner.

mutt [mʌt] *n inf* - **1.** [fool] andouille *f*, crétin *m*, -e *f* - **2.** Am [dog] clébard *m*.

mutter ['mʌtə^r] ⟨⟩ *vt* [threat, curse] marmon- ner ⟨⟩ *vi* marmotter, marmonner ; **to ~ to o.s.** marmotter, parler dans sa barbe.

muttering ['mʌtərɪŋ] *n* - **1.** [remark] marmon-

nement *m*, marmottement *m* - **2.** [sound] murmure *m*.

mutton ['mʌtn] *n* mouton *m* ; **she's ~ dressed as lamb** Br c'est une vieille coquette.

mutual ['mjuːtʃʊəl] *adj* - **1.** [feeling, help] réci- proque, mutuel(elle) - **2.** [friend, interest] com- mun(e).

mutual fund *n* Am fonds *m* commun de placement.

mutually ['mjuːtʃʊəlɪ] *adv* mutuellement, réciproquement ; **~ exclusive** qui s'ex- cluent l'un l'autre.

Muzak® ['mjuːzæk] *n* musique *f* d'ambiance.

muzzle ['mʌzl] ⟨⟩ *n* - **1.** [of dog - mouth] mu- seau *m* ; [- guard] muselière *f* - **2.** [of gun] gueule *f* ⟨⟩ *vt lit* & *fig* museler.

muzzy ['mʌzɪ] (*compar* -**ier** ; *superl* -**iest**) *adj* embrouillé(e), confus(e).

MVP (*abbr of* **most valuable player**) *n* Am titre de meilleur joueur décerné dans une équipe à celui qui a réalisé la meilleure performance lors d'un match, d'une saison etc.

MW (*abbr of* **medium wave**) PO.

my [maɪ] *poss adj* - **1.** [referring to oneself] mon (ma), mes (*pl*) ; **~ dog** mon chien ; **~ house** ma maison ; **~ children** mes enfants ; **~ name is Joe/Sarah** je m'appelle Joe/ Sarah ; **it wasn't MY fault** ce n'était pas de ma faute à moi - **2.** [in titles] : **yes, ~ Lord** oui, monsieur le comte/duc *etc*.

mynah (bird) ['maɪnə-] *n* mainate *m*.

myopic [maɪ'ɒpɪk] *adj* myope.

myriad ['mɪrɪəd] *literary* ⟨⟩ *adj* innombrable ⟨⟩ *n* myriade *f*.

myrrh [mɜː^r] *n* myrrhe *f*.

myrtle ['mɜːtl] *n* myrte *m*.

myself [maɪ'self] *pron* - **1.** (*reflexive*) me ; (*after prep*) moi - **2.** (*for emphasis*) moi-même ; **I did it ~** je l'ai fait tout seul.

mysterious [mɪ'stɪərɪəs] *adj* mystérieux(eu- se) ; **to be ~ about sthg** faire (un) mystère de qqch.

mysteriously [mɪ'stɪərɪəslɪ] *adv* mystérieu- sement.

mystery ['mɪstərɪ] (*pl* -**ies**) ⟨⟩ *n* mystère *m* ⟨⟩ *comp* mystérieux(euse).

mystery story *n* histoire *f* à suspense.

mystery tour *n* voyage *m* surprise (*dont la destination est inconnue*).

mystic ['mɪstɪk] ⟨⟩ *adj* [power] occulte ; [rite] mystique, ésotérique ⟨⟩ *n* mystique *mf*.

mystical ['mɪstɪkl] *adj* mystique.

mysticism ['mɪstɪsɪzm] *n* mysticisme *m*.

mystified ['mɪstɪfaɪd] *adj* perplexe.

mystifying [ˈmɪstɪfaɪɪŋ] adj inexplicable, déconcertant(e).

mystique [mɪˈstiːk] n mystique f.

myth [mɪθ] n mythe m.

mythic [ˈmɪθɪk] adj légendaire.

mythical [ˈmɪθɪkl] adj mythique.

mythological [ˌmɪθəˈlɒdʒɪkl] adj mythologique.

mythology [mɪˈθɒlədʒɪ] (pl -ies) n mythologie f.

myxomatosis [ˌmɪksəməˈtəʊsɪs] n myxomatose f.

n (pl **n's** OR **ns**), **N** (pl **N's** OR **Ns**) [en] n [letter] n m inv, N m inv.
➤ **N** (abbr of **north**) N.

n/a, N/A (abbr of **not applicable**) s.o.

NA (abbr of **Narcotics Anonymous**) n association américaine d'aide aux toxicomanes.

NAACP (abbr of **National Association for the Advancement of Colored People**) n association nationale américaine pour la promotion de gens de couleur.

NAAFI [ˈnæfɪ] (abbr of **Navy, Army & Air Force Institute**) n organisme approvisionnant les forces armées britanniques en biens de consommation.

nab [næb] (pt & pp **-bed**; cont **-bing**) vt inf - **1.** [arrest] pincer - **2.** [get quickly] attraper, accaparer.

NACU (abbr of **National Association of Colleges and Universities**) n association des établissements d'enseignement supérieur américains.

nadir [ˈneɪˌdɪəʳ] n ASTRON nadir m; to be at/reach a ~ fig être/tomber au plus bas.

naff [næf] adj Br inf nul (nulle).

nag [næg] (pt & pp **-ged**; cont **-ging**) ⇔ vt harceler ⇔ vi : to ~ at sb harceler qqn ; stop nagging! arrête de me casser les pieds!

⇔ n inf - **1.** [person] enquiquineur m, -euse f - **2.** [horse] canasson m.

nagging [ˈnægɪŋ] adj - **1.** [doubt] persistant(e), tenace - **2.** [husband, wife] enquiquineur(euse).

nail [neɪl] ⇔ n - **1.** [for fastening] clou m; to hit the ~ on the head mettre le doigt dessus - **2.** [of finger, toe] ongle m ⇔ vt clouer.
➤ **nail down** vt sep - **1.** [lid] clouer - **2.** fig [person] : to ~ sb down to sthg faire préciser qqch à qqn.
➤ **nail up** vt sep [notice] fixer avec des clous, clouer.

nail-biting adj plein(e) de suspense.

nailbrush [ˈneɪlbrʌʃ] n brosse f à ongles.

nail file n lime f à ongles.

nail polish n vernis m à ongles.

nail scissors npl ciseaux mpl à ongles.

nail varnish n vernis m à ongles.

nail varnish remover [-rɪˈmuːvəʳ] n dissolvant m.

Nairobi [naɪˈrəʊbɪ] n Nairobi.

naive, naïve [naɪˈiːv] adj naïf(ïve).

naivety, naïvety [naɪˈiːvtɪ] n naïveté f.

naked [ˈneɪkɪd] adj - **1.** [body, flame] nu(e) ; with the ~ eye à l'œil nu - **2.** [emotions] manifeste, évident(e) ; [aggression] non déguisé(e) ; the ~ truth la vérité toute nue.

NALGO [ˈnælgəʊ] (abbr of **National and Local Government Officers' Association**) n ancien syndicat britannique de la fonction publique.

Nam [næm] (abbr of **Vietnam**) n Am Vietnam m.

NAM (abbr of **National Association of Manufacturers**) n organisation patronale américaine.

name [neɪm] ⇔ n - **1.** [identification] nom m; what's your ~? comment vous appelez-vous?; to know sb by ~ connaître qqn de nom ; by the ~ of qui répond au nom de ; in my/his ~ à mon/son nom ; in the ~ of peace au nom de la paix ; in ~ only de nom seulement ; to call sb ~s traiter qqn de tous les noms, injurier qqn - **2.** [reputation] réputation f; to make a ~ for o.s. se faire un nom - **3.** [famous person] grand nom m, célébrité f ⇔ vt - **1.** [gen] nommer ; to ~ sb/sthg after Br, to ~ sb/sthg for Am donner à qqn/à qqch le nom de - **2.** [date, price] fixer.

namedropping [ˈneɪmdrɒpɪŋ] n : I hate ~ je déteste les gens qui veulent donner l'impression de connaître tous les grands de ce monde.

nameless [ˈneɪmlɪs] adj inconnu(e), sans nom ; [author] anonyme.

namely ['neɪmlɪ] *adv* à savoir, c'est-à-dire.
nameplate ['neɪmpleɪt] *n* plaque *f*.
namesake ['neɪmseɪk] *n* homonyme *m*.
Namibia [nɑː'mɪbɪə] *n* Namibie *f* ; **in ~** en Namibie.
Namibian [nɑː'mɪbɪən] ◇ *adj* namibien(enne) ◇ *n* Namibien *m*, -enne *f*.
nan(a) [næn(ə)] *n* Br inf mamie *f*, mémé *f*.
nan bread *n* (*U*) pain *m* nan.
nanny ['nænɪ] (*pl* -ies) *n* nurse *f*, bonne *f* d'enfants.
nanny goat *n* chèvre *f*, bique *f*.
nap [næp] (*pt* & *pp* -ped ; *cont* -ping) ◇ *n* : **to have** OR **take a ~** faire un petit somme ◇ *vi* faire un petit somme ; **to be caught napping** inf fig être pris au dépourvu.
NAPA (*abbr of* **National Association of Performing Artists**) *n* syndicat américain des gens du spectacle.
napalm ['neɪpɑːm] *n* napalm *m*.
nape [neɪp] *n* nuque *f*.
napkin ['næpkɪn] *n* serviette *f*.
nappy ['næpɪ] (*pl* -ies) *n* Br couche *f*.
nappy liner *n* change *m* (jetable).
narcissi [nɑː'sɪsaɪ] *pl* ⊳ **narcissus**.
narcissism ['nɑːsɪsɪzm] *n* narcissisme *m*.
narcissistic [ˌnɑːsɪ'sɪstɪk] *adj* narcissique.
narcissus [nɑː'sɪsəs] (*pl* -cissuses OR -cissi [-sɪsaɪ]) *n* narcisse *m*.
narcotic [nɑː'kɒtɪk] *n* stupéfiant *m*, narcotique *m*.
nark [nɑːk] Br inf ◇ *n* police sl mouchard *m*, indic *m* ◇ *vt* mettre en rogne.
narky ['nɑːkɪ] (*compar* -ier ; *superl* -iest) *adj* Br inf de mauvais poil.
narrate [Br nə'reɪt, Am 'næreɪt] *vt* raconter, narrer.
narration [Br nə'reɪʃn, Am næ'reɪʃn] *n* narration *f*.
narrative ['nærətɪv] ◇ *adj* narratif(ive) ◇ *n*
- **1.** [story] récit *m*, narration *f* - **2.** [skill] art *m* de la narration.
narrator [Br nə'reɪtə', Am 'næreɪtər] *n* narrateur *m*, -trice *f*.
narrow ['nærəʊ] ◇ *adj* - **1.** [gen] étroit(e) ; **to have a ~ escape** l'échapper belle - **2.** [victory, majority] de justesse ◇ *vt* - **1.** [reduce] réduire, limiter - **2.** [eyes] fermer à demi, plisser ◇ *vi* lit & fig se rétrécir.
➡ **narrow down** *vt sep* réduire, limiter.
narrow-gauge *adj* RAIL : **~ track** voie *f* étroite.
narrowly ['nærəʊlɪ] *adv* - **1.** [win, lose] de justesse - **2.** [miss] de peu.

narrow-minded [-'maɪndɪd] *adj* [person] à l'esprit étroit, borné(e) ; [attitude] étroit(e), borné(e).
NAS (*abbr of* **National Academy of Sciences**) *n* académie américaine des sciences.
NASA ['næsə] (*abbr of* **National Aeronautics and Space Administration**) *n* NASA *f*.
nasal ['neɪzl] *adj* nasal(e).
nascent ['neɪsənt] *adj* fml naissant(e).
NASDAQ [næzdæk] (*abbr of* **National Association of Securities Dealers Automated Quotation**) *n* [in US] NASDAQ *m*.
nastily ['nɑːstɪlɪ] *adv* - **1.** [unkindly] méchamment - **2.** [painfully] : **to fall ~** faire une mauvaise chute.
nastiness ['nɑːstɪnɪs] *n* [unkindness] méchanceté *f*.
nasturtium [nəs'tɜːʃəm] (*pl* -s) *n* capucine *f*.
nasty ['nɑːstɪ] (*compar* -ier ; *superl* -iest) *adj*
- **1.** [unpleasant - smell, feeling] mauvais(e) ;
[- weather] vilain(e), mauvais(e) - **2.** [unkind] méchant(e) - **3.** [problem] difficile, délicat(e)
- **4.** [injury] vilain(e) ; [accident] grave ; [fall] mauvais(e).
NAS/UWT (*abbr of* **National Association of Schoolmasters/Union of Women Teachers**) *n* syndicat d'enseignants et de chefs d'établissement en Grande-Bretagne.
Natal [nə'tæl] *n* Natal *m* ; **in ~** au Natal.
nation ['neɪʃn] *n* nation *f*.
national ['næʃənl] ◇ *adj* national(e) ; [campaign, strike] à l'échelon national ; [custom] du pays, de la nation ◇ *n* ressortissant *m*, -e *f*.
national anthem *n* hymne *m* national.
national debt *n* dette *f* publique.
national dress *n* costume *m* national.
national grid *n* Br réseau *m* électrique national.
National Guard *n* : **the ~** la Garde Nationale (armée nationale américaine composée de volontaires).
National Health Service *n* : **the ~** le service national de santé britannique.
National Heritage Minister *n* ministre britannique de la culture et des sports.
National Insurance Br *n* (*U*) - **1.** [system] système de sécurité sociale (maladie, retraite) et d'assurance chômage - **2.** [payment] ≈ contributions *fpl* à la Sécurité sociale.
nationalism ['næʃnəlɪzm] *n* nationalisme *m*.
nationalist ['næʃnəlɪst] ◇ *adj* nationaliste ◇ *n* nationaliste *mf*.
nationality [ˌnæʃə'nælətɪ] (*pl* -ies) *n* nationalité *f*.

nationalization [ˌnæʃnəlaɪˈzeɪʃn] n nationalisation f.

nationalize, -ise [ˈnæʃnəlaɪz] vt nationaliser.

nationalized [ˈnæʃnəlaɪzd] adj nationalisé(e).

national park n parc m national.

national service n Br MIL service m national OR militaire.

National Trust n Br : the ~ organisme non gouvernemental assurant la conservation de certains sites et monuments historiques.

nation state n nation f.

nationwide [ˈneɪʃənwaɪd] ◇ adj dans tout le pays ; [campaign, strike] à l'échelon national ◇ adv à travers tout le pays.

native [ˈneɪtɪv] ◇ adj - **1.** [country, area] natal(e) - **2.** [language] maternel(elle) ; **an English ~ speaker** une personne de langue maternelle anglaise - **3.** [plant, animal] indigène ; **~ to** originaire de ◇ n autochtone mf ; [of colony] indigène mf.

Native American n Indien m, -enne f d'Amérique, Amérindien m, -enne f.

Nativity [nəˈtɪvətɪ] n : the **~** la Nativité.

nativity play n mystère m de la Nativité.

NATO [ˈneɪtəʊ] (abbr of **North Atlantic Treaty Organization**) n OTAN f.

natter [ˈnætəʳ] Br inf ◇ n : **to have a ~** tailler une bavette, bavarder ◇ vi bavarder.

natty [ˈnætɪ] (compar **-ier** ; superl **-iest**) adj inf [smart] chic (inv).

natural [ˈnætʃrəl] ◇ adj - **1.** [gen] naturel(elle) ; **to die of ~ causes** mourir de mort naturelle - **2.** [instinct, talent] inné(e) - **3.** [footballer, musician] né(e) - **4.** [parent] vrai(e) ◇ n : **she's a ~ at dancing** c'est une danseuse née.

natural childbirth n accouchement m sans douleur.

natural gas n gaz m naturel.

natural history n histoire f naturelle.

naturalist [ˈnætʃrəlɪst] n naturaliste mf.

naturalize, -ise [ˈnætʃrəlaɪz] vt naturaliser ; **to be ~d** se faire naturaliser.

naturally [ˈnætʃrəlɪ] adv - **1.** [gen] naturellement ; **to come ~ to sb** être naturel chez qqn - **2.** [unaffectedly] sans affectation, avec naturel.

naturalness [ˈnætʃrəlnɪs] n naturel m.

natural resources npl ressources fpl naturelles.

natural science n sciences fpl naturelles.

natural wastage n (U) départs mpl volontaires.

nature [ˈneɪtʃəʳ] n nature f ; **by ~** [basically] par essence ; [by disposition] de nature, naturellement.

nature reserve n réserve f naturelle.

nature trail n sentier m signalisé pour amateurs de la nature.

naturist [ˈneɪtʃərɪst] n naturiste mf.

naturopathy [ˌneɪtʃəˈrɒpəθɪ] n naturopathie f.

naughty [ˈnɔːtɪ] (compar **-ier** ; superl **-iest**) adj - **1.** [badly behaved] vilain(e), méchant(e) - **2.** [rude] grivois(e).

nausea [ˈnɔːzjə] n nausée f.

nauseam [ˈnɔːzɪæm] ▷ **ad nauseam.**

nauseate [ˈnɔːsɪeɪt] vt lit & fig écœurer.

nauseating [ˈnɔːsɪeɪtɪŋ] adj lit & fig écœurant(e).

nauseous [ˈnɔːsjəs] adj - **1.** MED : **to feel ~** avoir mal au cœur, avoir des nausées - **2.** fig [revolting] écœurant(e), dégoutant(e).

nautical [ˈnɔːtɪkl] adj nautique.

nautical mile n mille m marin.

naval [ˈneɪvl] adj naval(e).

naval officer n officier m de marine.

nave [neɪv] n nef f.

navel [ˈneɪvl] n nombril m.

navigable [ˈnævɪɡəbl] adj navigable.

navigate [ˈnævɪɡeɪt] ◇ vt - **1.** [plane] piloter ; [ship] gouverner - **2.** [seas, river] naviguer sur ◇ vi AERON & NAUT naviguer ; AUT lire la carte.

navigation [ˌnævɪˈɡeɪʃn] n navigation f.

navigator [ˈnævɪɡeɪtəʳ] n navigateur m.

navvy [ˈnævɪ] (pl **-ies**) n Br inf terrassier m.

navy [ˈneɪvɪ] (pl **-ies**) ◇ n marine f ◇ adj [in colour] bleu marine (inv).

navy blue ◇ adj bleu marine (inv) ◇ n bleu m marine.

Nazareth [ˈnæzərɪθ] n Nazareth.

Nazi [ˈnɑːtsɪ] (pl **-s**) ◇ adj nazi(e) ◇ n Nazi m, -e f.

NB - 1. (abbr of **nota bene**) NB - **2.** abbr of **New Brunswick**.

NBA n - **1.** (abbr of **National Basketball Association**) fédération américaine de basket-ball - **2.** (abbr of **National Boxing Association**) fédération américaine de boxe.

NBC (abbr of **National Broadcasting Company**) n chaîne de télévision américaine.

NBS (abbr of **National Bureau of Standards**) n service américain des poids et mesures.

NC - 1. abbr of **no charge - 2.** abbr of **North Carolina**.

NCC (abbr of **Nature Conservancy Council**) n

organisme britannique de protection de la nature.

NCCL (*abbr of* **National Council for Civil Liberties**) *n* ligue britannique de défense des libertés civiles.

NCO *n abbr of* **noncommissioned officer.**

NCU (*abbr of* **National Communications Union**) *n* syndicat britannique des communications.

ND *abbr of* **North Dakota.**

NE - 1. *abbr of* **Nebraska - 2.** *abbr of* **New England - 3.** (*abbr of* **north-east**) N.E.

Neanderthal [nɪ'ændətɑːl] ◇ *adj :* ~ **man** homme *m* de Néandertal ◇ *n* homme *m* de Néandertal.

neap tide [niːp-] *n* (marée *f* de) morte-eau *f*.

near [nɪəʳ] ◇ *adj* proche ; **a** ~ **disaster** une catastrophe évitée de justesse OR de peu ; **in the** ~ **future** dans un proche avenir, dans un avenir prochain ; **it was a** ~ **thing** il était moins cinq ◇ *adv* **- 1.** [close] près ; **Christmas is drawing** ~ Noël approche **- 2.** [almost] : ~ **impossible** presque impossible ; **nowhere** ~ **ready/enough** loin d'être prêt/assez ◇ *prep :* ~ **(to)** [in space] près de ; [in time] près de, vers ; ~ **to tears** au bord des larmes ; ~ **(to) death** sur le point de mourir ; ~ **(to) the truth** proche de la vérité ◇ *vt* approcher de ; **to** ~ **completion** être près d'être fini ◇ *vi* approcher.

nearby [nɪə'baɪ] ◇ *adj* proche ◇ *adv* tout près, à proximité.

Near East *n :* **the** ~ le Proche-Orient.

nearly ['nɪəlɪ] *adv* presque ; **I** ~ **fell** j'ai failli tomber ; **I** ~ **cried** j'étais sur le point de pleurer ; **not** ~ **enough/as good** loin d'être suffisant/aussi bon.

near miss *n* **- 1.** SPORT coup *m* qui a raté de peu **- 2.** [between planes, vehicles] quasi-collision *f*, collision *f* évitée de justesse.

nearness ['nɪənɪs] *n* proximité *f*.

nearside ['nɪəsaɪd] ◇ *adj* [right-hand drive] de gauche ; [left-hand drive] de droite ◇ *n* [right-hand drive] côté *m* gauche ; [left-hand drive] côté *m* droit.

nearsighted [,nɪə'saɪtɪd] *adj* Am myope.

neat [niːt] *adj* **- 1.** [room, house] bien tenu(e), en ordre ; [work] soigné(e) ; [handwriting] net (nette) ; [appearance] soigné(e), net (nette) **- 2.** [solution, manoeuvre] habile, ingénieux(euse) **- 3.** [alcohol] pur(e), sans eau **- 4.** Am inf [very good] chouette, super (inv).

neatly ['niːtlɪ] *adv* **- 1.** [arrange] avec ordre ; [write] soigneusement ; [dress] avec soin **- 2.** [skilfully] habilement, adroitement.

neatness ['niːtnɪs] *n* [of room] bon ordre *m* ; [of handwriting] netteté *f* ; [of appearance] mise *f* soignée.

Nebraska [nɪ'bræskə] *n* Nebraska *m* ; **in** ~ dans le Nebraska.

nebulous ['nebjʊləs] *adj* nébuleux(euse).

NEC (*abbr of* **National Exhibition Centre**) *n* parc d'expositions près de Birmingham en Angleterre.

necessarily [Br 'nesəsrəlɪ, ,nesə'serɪlɪ] *adv* forcément, nécessairement.

necessary ['nesəsrɪ] *adj* **- 1.** [required] nécessaire, indispensable ; **to make the** ~ **arrangements** faire le nécessaire **- 2.** [inevitable] inévitable, inéluctable.

necessitate [nɪ'sesɪteɪt] *vt* nécessiter, rendre nécessaire.

necessity [nɪ'sesətɪ] (*pl* **-ies**) *n* nécessité *f* ; **of** ~ inévitablement, fatalement.

neck [nek] ◇ *n* **- 1.** ANAT cou *m* ; **to be up to one's** ~ **(in sthg)** fig être (dans qqch) jusqu'au cou ; **to breathe down sb's** ~ fig talonner qqn, être sur le dos de qqn ; **to stick one's** ~ **out** fig prendre des risques, se mouiller **- 2.** [of shirt, dress] encolure *f* **- 3.** [of bottle] col *m*, goulot *m* ◇ *vi* inf se bécoter.

neckerchief ['nekətʃɪf] (*pl* **-chiefs** OR **-chieves** [-tʃiːvz]) *n* foulard *m*.

necklace ['neklɪs] *n* collier *m*.

neckline ['neklaɪn] *n* encolure *f*.

necktie ['nektaɪ] *n* Am cravate *f*.

nectar ['nektəʳ] *n* nectar *m*.

nectarine ['nektərɪn] *n* brugnon *m*, nectarine *f*.

NEDC (*abbr of* **National Economic Development Council**) *n* agence nationale britannique de développement économique.

Neddy ['nedɪ] *n* inf surnom de la NEDC.

née [neɪ] *adj* née.

need [niːd] ◇ *n* besoin *m* ; **there's no** ~ **to get up** ce n'est pas la peine de te lever ; **there's no** ~ **for such language** tu n'as pas besoin d'être grossier ; ~ **for sthg/to do sthg** besoin de qqch/de faire qqch ; **to be in** OR **have** ~ **of sthg** avoir besoin de qqch ; **if** ~ **be** si besoin est, si nécessaire ; **in** ~ dans le besoin ◇ *vt* **- 1.** [require] : **to** ~ **sthg/to do sthg** avoir besoin de qqch/de faire qqch ; **I** ~ **to go to the doctor** il faut que j'aille chez le médecin **- 2.** [be obliged] : **to** ~ **to do sthg** être obligé(e) de faire qqch ◇ *modal vb :* ~ **we go?** faut-il qu'on y aille? ; **it** ~ **not happen** cela ne doit pas forcément se produire.

◂ **needs** *adv :* **if** ~**s must** s'il le faut.

needle ['niːdl] ◇ *n* **- 1.** [gen] aiguille *f* ; **it's like**

looking for a ~ in a haystack c'est comme chercher une aiguille dans une botte de foin - **2.** [stylus] saphir *m* ◇ *vt* inf [annoy] asticoter, lancer des piques à.

needlecord ['niːdlkɔːd] *n* velours *m* milleraies.

needlepoint ['niːdlpɔɪnt] *n* dentelle *f* à l'aiguille.

needless ['niːdlɪs] *adj* [risk, waste] inutile ; [remark] déplacé(e) ; **~ to say** ... bien entendu ...

needlessly ['niːdlɪslɪ] *adv* inutilement, sans raison.

needlework ['niːdlwɜːk] *n* - **1.** [embroidery] travail *m* d'aiguille - **2.** *(U)* [activity] couture *f*.

needn't ['niːdnt] = **need not.**

needy ['niːdɪ] *(compar* -ier *; superl* -iest) ◇ *adj* nécessiteux(euse), indigent(e) ◇ *npl :* **the ~** les nécessiteux *mpl.*

nefarious [nɪ'feərɪəs] *adj* fml odieux(euse), abominable.

negate [nɪ'geɪt] *vt* fml [efforts, achievements] annuler, détruire.

negation [nɪ'geɪʃn] *n* fml [of efforts, achievements] destruction *f.*

negative ['negətɪv] ◇ *adj* négatif(ive) ◇ *n* - **1.** PHOT négatif *m* - **2.** LING négation *f;* **to answer in the ~** répondre négativement OR par la négative.

neglect [nɪ'glekt] ◇ *n* [of garden] mauvais entretien *m ;* [of children] manque *m* de soins ; [of duty] manquement *m* ◇ *vt* négliger ; [garden] laisser à l'abandon ; **to ~ to do sthg** négliger OR omettre de faire qqch.

neglected [nɪ'glektɪd] *adj* [child] délaissé(e), abandonné(e) ; [garden] laissé(e) à l'abandon.

neglectful [nɪ'glektfʊl] *adj* négligent(e) ; **to be ~ of sb/sthg** négliger qqn/qqch.

negligee ['neglɪʒeɪ] *n* déshabillé *m*, négligé *m.*

negligence ['neglɪdʒəns] *n* négligence *f.*

negligent ['neglɪdʒənt] *adj* négligent(e).

negligently ['neglɪdʒəntlɪ] *adv* avec négligence.

negligible ['neglɪdʒəbl] *adj* négligeable.

negotiable [nɪ'gəʊʃjəbl] *adj* négociable ; [price, conditions] à débattre.

negotiate [nɪ'gəʊʃɪeɪt] ◇ *vt* - **1.** COMM & POL négocier - **2.** [obstacle] franchir ; [bend] prendre, négocier ◇ *vi* négocier ; **to ~ with sb (for sthg)** engager des négociations avec qqn (pour obtenir qqch).

negotiation [nɪ,gəʊʃɪ'eɪʃn] *n* négociation *f.*

negotiator [nɪ'gəʊʃɪeɪtəʳ] *n* négociateur *m*, -trice *f.*

Negress ['niːgrɪs] *n* négresse *f (attention : le terme 'Negress' est considéré raciste).*

Negro ['niːgrəʊ] *(pl* -es) ◇ *adj* noir(e) ◇ *n* Noir *m (attention : le terme 'Negro' est considéré raciste).*

neigh [neɪ] *vi* [horse] hennir.

neighbour Br, **neighbor** Am ['neɪbəʳ] *n* voisin *m*, -e *f.*

neighbourhood Br, **neighborhood** Am ['neɪbəhʊd] *n* - **1.** [of town] voisinage *m*, quartier *m ;* **in the ~** à proximité - **2.** [approximate figure] : **in the ~ of** £300 environ 300 livres, dans les 300 livres.

neighbourhood watch *n* Br *système de surveillance d'un quartier par tous ses habitants (pour prévenir les cambriolages et autres crimes).*

neighbouring Br, **neighboring** Am ['neɪbərɪŋ] *adj* avoisinant(e).

neighbourly Br, **neighborly** Am ['neɪbəlɪ] *adj* bon voisin (bonne voisine).

neither ['naɪðəʳ, 'niːðəʳ] ◇ *adv :* **~ good nor bad** ni bon ni mauvais ; **that's ~ here nor there** cela n'a rien à voir ◇ *pron* & *adj* **ni l'un ni l'autre** (ni l'une ni l'autre) ◇ *conj :* **~ do I** moi non plus.

neo- ['niːəʊ] *prefix* néo-.

neoclassical [,niːəʊ'klæsɪkl] *adj* néo-classique.

neolithic [,niːə'lɪθɪk] *adj* néolithique.

neologism [niː'ɒlədʒɪzm] *n* néologisme *m.*

neon ['niːɒn] *n* néon *m.*

neon light *n* néon *m*, lumière *f* au néon.

neon sign *n* enseigne *f* lumineuse au néon.

Nepal [nɪ'pɔːl] *n* Népal *m ;* **in ~** au Népal.

Nepalese [,nepə'liːz] *(pl inv)* ◇ *adj* népalais(e) ◇ *n* Népalais *m*, -e *f.*

Nepali [nɪ'pɔːlɪ] *n* [language] népalais *m*, népali *m.*

nephew ['nefjuː] *n* neveu *m.*

nepotism ['nepətɪzm] *n* népotisme *m.*

Neptune ['neptjuːn] *n* [planet] Neptune *f.*

nerve [nɜːv] *n* - **1.** ANAT nerf *m* - **2.** [courage] courage *m*, sang-froid *m ;* **to lose one's ~** se dégonfler, flancher - **3.** [cheek] culot *m*, toupet *m ;* **to have the ~ to do sthg** avoir le culot OR le toupet de faire qqch.

➤ **nerves** *npl* nerfs *mpl ;* **to get on sb's ~s** taper sur les nerfs OR le système de qqn.

nerve centre *n* lit & fig centre *m* nerveux.

nerve gas *n* gaz *m* neurotoxique.

nerve-racking [-,rækɪŋ] *adj* angoissant(e), éprouvant(e).

nervous ['nɜːvəs] *adj* - **1.** [gen] nerveux(euse) - **2.** [apprehensive - smile, person etc] inquiet(ète) ; [- performer] qui a le trac ; **to be ~ about sthg** appréhender qqch.

nervous breakdown *n* dépression *f* nerveuse.

nervously ['nɜːvəslɪ] *adv* - **1.** [gen] nerveusement - **2.** [apprehensively] avec inquiétude.

nervousness ['nɜːvəsnɪs] *n (U)* - **1.** [apprehension - of voice etc] inquiétude *f* ; [- of performer] trac *m* - **2.** [tenseness] nervosité *f*, tension *f*.

nervous system *n* système *m* nerveux.

nervous wreck *n* : **to be a ~** être à bout de nerfs.

nervy ['nɜːvɪ] (*compar* -ier ; *superl* -iest) *adj* - **1.** inf [nervous] énervé(e) - **2.** Am [cheeky] culotté(e).

nest [nest] ◇ *n* nid *m* ; **~ of tables** table *f* gigogne ◇ *vi* [bird] faire son nid, nicher.

nest egg *n* pécule *m*, bas *m* de laine.

nestle ['nesl] *vi* se blottir.

nestling ['neslɪŋ] *n* oisillon *m*.

net[1] [net] (*pt & pp* -ted ; *cont* -ting) ◇ *adj* net (nette) ; **~ result** résultat final ◇ *n* - **1.** [gen] filet *m* - **2.** [fabric] voile *m*, tulle *m* ◇ *vt* - **1.** [fish] prendre au filet - **2.** [money - subj : person] toucher net, gagner net ; [- subj : deal] rapporter net.

net[2], **Net** [net] *n* : **the ~** le Net ; **to surf the ~** surfer sur le Net.

netball ['netbɔːl] *n* netball *m*.

net curtains *npl* voilage *m*.

nethead ['nethed] *n* inf accro *mf* d'Internet.

Netherlands ['neðələndz] *npl* : **the ~** les Pays-Bas *mpl* ; **in the ~** aux Pays-Bas.

netiquette ['netiket] *n* nétiquette *f*.

net profit *n* bénéfice *m* net.

net revenue *n* Am chiffre *m* d'affaires.

net surfer *n* internaute *mf*.

nett [net] *adj* = **net**[1].

netting ['netɪŋ] *n* - **1.** [metal, plastic] grillage *m* - **2.** [fabric] voile *m*, tulle *m*.

nettle ['netl] ◇ *n* ortie *f* ◇ *vt* piquer OR toucher au vif.

network ['netwɜːk] ◇ *n* réseau *m* ◇ *vt* - **1.** RADIO & TV diffuser - **2.** COMPUT interconnecter.

neuralgia [njʊəˈrældʒəl] *n* névralgie *f*.

neurological [ˌnjʊərəˈlɒdʒɪkl] *adj* neurologique.

neurologist [njʊəˈrɒlədʒɪst] *n* neurologue *mf*

neurology [ˌnjʊəˈrɒlədʒɪl] *n* neurologie *f*.

neurosis [ˌnjʊəˈrəʊsɪs] (*pl* -ses [-siːz]) *n* névrose *f*.

neurosurgery [ˌnjʊərəʊˈsɜːdʒərɪ] *n* neurochirurgie *f*.

neurotic [ˌnjʊəˈrɒtɪk] ◇ *adj* névrosé(e) ◇ *n* névrosé *m*, -e *f*.

neuter ['njuːtəʳ] ◇ *adj* neutre ◇ *vt* [cat] châtrer.

neutral ['njuːtrəl] ◇ *adj* - **1.** [gen] neutre - **2.** [face, eyes etc] inexpressif(ive), sans expression ◇ *n* - **1.** AUT point *m* mort - **2.** [country] état *m* OR pays *m* neutre ; [person] personne *f* neutre.

neutrality [njuːˈtrælətɪ] *n* neutralité *f*.

neutralize, -ise ['njuːtrəlaɪz] *vt* neutraliser.

neutron ['njuːtrɒn] *n* neutron *m*.

neutron bomb *n* bombe *f* à neutrons.

Nevada [nɪˈvɑːdə] *n* Nevada *m* ; **in ~** dans le Nevada.

never ['nevəʳ] *adv* jamais ... ne, ne ... jamais ; **~ ever** jamais, au grand jamais ; **well I ~!** ça par exemple!

never-ending *adj* interminable.

never-never *n* Br inf : **on the ~** à crédit, à tempérament.

nevertheless [ˌnevəðəˈles] *adv* néanmoins, pourtant.

new [*adj* njuː, *n* njuːz] *adj* - **1.** [gen] nouveau(elle) ; **to be ~ to** [place] être nouveau dans ; [job] être neuf dans - **2.** [not used] neuf (neuve) ; **as good as ~** comme neuf.

➧ **news** *n (U)* - **1.** [information] nouvelle *f* ; **a piece of ~s** une nouvelle ; **that's ~s to me** première nouvelle ; **to break the ~s to sb** annoncer OR apprendre la nouvelle à qqn - **2.** RADIO informations *fpl* - **3.** TV journal *m* télévisé, actualités *fpl*.

New Age *n* New Age *m*.

New Age travel(l)er *n* voyageur *m* New Age.

new blood *n* fig sang *m* neuf OR frais.

newborn ['njuːbɔːn] *adj* nouveau-né(e).

New Brunswick [-'brʌnzwɪk] *n* Nouveau-Brunswick *m* ; **in ~** dans le Nouveau-Brunswick.

New Caledonia [-ˌkælɪˈdəʊnjə] *n* Nouvelle-Calédonie *f* ; **in ~** en Nouvelle-Calédonie.

New Caledonian [-ˌkælɪˈdəʊnjən] ◇ *adj* néo-calédonien(enne) ◇ *n* Néo-Calédonien *m*, -enne *f*.

newcomer ['njuːˌkʌməʳ] *n* : **~ (to sthg)** nouveau-venu *m*, nouvelle-venue *f* (dans qqch).

New Delhi *n* New Delhi.

New England n Nouvelle-Angleterre f ; **in ~** en Nouvelle-Angleterre.

newfangled [,nju:'fæŋgld] adj inf pej ultramoderne, trop moderne.

new-found adj récent(e), de fraîche date.

Newfoundland ['nju:fəndlənd] n Terre-Neuve f ; **in ~** à Terre-Neuve.

New Guinea n Nouvelle-Guinée f ; **in ~** en Nouvelle-Guinée.

New Hampshire [-'hæmpʃər] n New Hampshire m ; **in ~** dans le New Hampshire.

New Hebrides npl Nouvelles-Hébrides fpl ; **in the ~** aux Nouvelles-Hébrides.

New Jersey n le New Jersey ; **in ~** dans le New Jersey.

newly ['nju:lɪ] adv récemment, fraîchement.

newlyweds ['nju:lɪwedz] npl nouveaux OR jeunes mariés mpl.

New Mexico n Nouveau-Mexique m ; **in ~** au Nouveau-Mexique.

new moon n nouvelle lune f.

New Orleans [-'ɔːlɪənz] n La Nouvelle-Orléans.

New Quebec n Nouveau-Québec m ; **in ~** au Nouveau-Québec.

news agency n agence f de presse.

newsagent Br ['nju:zeɪdʒənt], **newsdealer** Am ['nju:zdi:lər] n marchand m de journaux.

news bulletin n bulletin m d'informations.

newscast ['nju:zkɑːst] n **- 1.** RADIO informations fpl **- 2.** TV actualités fpl.

newscaster ['nju:zkɑːstər] n présentateur m, -trice f.

news conference n conférence f de presse.

newsdealer Am = newsagent.

newsflash ['nju:zflæʃ] n flash m d'information.

newsgroup ['nju:zgru:p] n COMPUT [on Internet] newsgroup m, groupe m de discussion.

newshound ['nju:zhaʊnd] n reporter m.

newsletter ['nju:z,letər] n bulletin m.

newsman ['nju:zmæn] (pl -men [-mən]) n journaliste m, reporter m.

New South Wales n Nouvelle-Galles du Sud f ; **in ~** en Nouvelle-Galles du Sud.

newspaper ['nju:z,peɪpər] n journal m.

newspaperman ['nju:z,peɪpəmæn] (pl -men [-men]) n journaliste m.

newsprint ['nju:zprɪnt] n papier m journal.

newsreader ['nju:z,ri:dər] n présentateur m, -trice f.

newsreel ['nju:zri:l] n actualités fpl filmées.

newsroom ['nju:zru:m] n **- 1.** PRESS salle f de rédaction **- 2.** RADIO & TV studio m.

newssheet ['nju:zʃi:t] n feuille f d'informations.

newsstand ['nju:zstænd] n kiosque m à journaux.

newsworthy ['nju:z,wɜːðɪ] adj qui vaut la peine d'être publié OR qu'on en parle.

newt [nju:t] n triton m.

new technology n nouvelle technologie f, technologie de pointe.

New Testament n : **the ~** le Nouveau Testament.

new town n Br ville f nouvelle.

new wave n nouvelle vague f.

New World n : **the ~** le Nouveau Monde.

New Year n nouvel an m, nouvelle année f ; **Happy ~!** bonne année!

New Year's Day n jour m de l'an, premier m de l'an.

New Year's Eve n la Saint-Sylvestre.

New York [-'jɔːk] n **- 1.** [city] : **~ (City)** New York **- 2.** [state] : **~ (State)** l'État m de New York ; **in (the State of) ~**, **in ~ (State)** dans l'État de New York.

New Yorker [-'jɔːkər] n New-Yorkais m, -e f.

New Zealand [-'zi:lənd] n Nouvelle-Zélande f ; **in ~** en Nouvelle-Zélande.

New Zealander [-'zi:ləndər] n Néo-Zélandais m, -e f.

next [nekst] ◇ adj prochain(e) ; [room] d'à côté ; [page] suivant(e) ; **~ Tuesday** mardi prochain ; **~ time** la prochaine fois ; **~ week** la semaine prochaine ; **the ~ week** la semaine suivante OR d'après ; **~ year** l'année prochaine ; **~, please!** au suivant! ; **the day after ~** le surlendemain ; **the week after ~** dans deux semaines ◇ adv **- 1.** [afterwards] ensuite, après **- 2.** [again] la prochaine fois **- 3.** (with superlatives) : **he's the ~ biggest after Dan** c'est le plus grand après OR à part Dan ◇ prep Am à côté de.
◆ **next to** prep à côté de ; **it cost ~ to nothing** cela a coûté une bagatelle OR trois fois rien ; **I know ~ to nothing** je ne sais presque OR pratiquement rien.

next door adv à côté.
◆ **next-door** adj : **next-door neighbour** voisin m, -e f d'à côté.

next of kin n plus proche parent m.

NF ◇ *n* (*abbr of* **National Front**) ≃ FN *m*
◇ *abbr of* **Newfoundland**.

NFL (*abbr of* **National Football League**) *n fédération nationale de football américain*.

NFU (*abbr of* **National Farmers' Union**) *n syndicat britannique d'exploitants agricoles*.

NG *abbr of* **National Guard**.

NGO (*abbr of* **non-governmental organization**) *n* ONG *f*.

NH *abbr of* **New Hampshire**.

NHL (*abbr of* **National Hockey League**) *n fédération nationale américaine de hockey sur glace*.

NHS (*abbr of* **National Health Service**) *n service national de santé en Grande-Bretagne*, ≃ sécurité sociale *f*.

NI ◇ *n abbr of* **National Insurance** ◇ *abbr of* **Northern Ireland**.

Niagara [naɪˈægrə] *n* : **~ Falls** les chutes *fpl* du Niagara.

nib [nɪb] *n* plume *f*.

nibble [ˈnɪbl] ◇ *vt* grignoter, mordiller ◇ *vi* : **to ~ at sthg** grignoter qqch.

Nicaragua [ˌnɪkəˈrægjʊə] *n* Nicaragua *m ;* **in ~** au Nicaragua.

Nicaraguan [ˌnɪkəˈrægjʊən] ◇ *adj* nicaraguayen(enne) ◇ *n* Nicaraguayen *m*, -enne *f*.

nice [naɪs] *adj* - **1.** [holiday, food] bon (bonne) ; [day, picture] beau (belle) ; [dress] joli(e) - **2.** [person] gentil(ille), sympathique ; **to be ~ to sb** être gentil OR aimable avec qqn.

nice-looking [-ˈlʊkɪŋ] *adj* joli(e), beau (belle).

nicely [ˈnaɪslɪ] *adv* - **1.** [made, manage etc] bien ; [dressed] joliment ; **that will do ~** cela fera très bien l'affaire - **2.** [politely - ask] poliment, gentiment ; [- behave] bien.

nicety [ˈnaɪsətɪ] (*pl* **-ies**) *n* délicatesse *f*, subtilité *f*.

niche [niːʃ] *n* [in wall] niche *f ; fig* bonne situation *f*, voie *f*.

nick [nɪk] ◇ *n* - **1.** [cut] entaille *f*, coupure *f* - **2.** Br prison sl [jail] : **the ~** la taule OR tôle - **3.** Br inf [condition] : **in good/bad ~** en bon/mauvais état - **4.** phr : **in the ~ of time** juste à temps ◇ *vt* - **1.** [cut] couper, entailler - **2.** Br inf [steal] piquer, faucher - **3.** Br inf [arrest] pincer, choper.

nickel [ˈnɪkl] *n* - **1.** [metal] nickel *m* - **2.** Am [coin] pièce *f* de cinq cents.

nickname [ˈnɪkneɪm] ◇ *n* sobriquet *m*, surnom *m* ◇ *vt* surnommer.

Nicosia [ˌnɪkəˈsiːə] *n* Nicosie.

nicotine [ˈnɪkətiːn] *n* nicotine *f*.

niece [niːs] *n* nièce *f*.

nifty [ˈnɪftɪ] (*compar* **-ier** ; *superl* **-iest**) *adj* inf génial(e), super (*inv*).

Niger [ˈnaɪdʒəʳ] *n* - **1.** [country] Niger *m ;* **in ~** au Niger - **2.** [river] : **the (River) ~** le Niger.

Nigeria [naɪˈdʒɪərɪə] *n* Nigeria *m ;* **in ~** au Nigeria.

Nigerian [naɪˈdʒɪərɪən] ◇ *adj* nigérian(e) ◇ *n* Nigérian *m*, -e *f*.

Nigerien [naɪˈdʒɪərɪən] ◇ *adj* nigérien(enne) ◇ *n* Nigérien *m*, -enne *f*.

niggardly [ˈnɪgədlɪ] *adj* [person] pingre, avare ; [gift, amount] mesquin(e), chiche.

niggle [ˈnɪgl] ◇ *n* [worry] souci *m*, tracas *m* ◇ *vt* Br - **1.** [worry] tracasser - **2.** [criticize] faire des réflexions à, critiquer ◇ *vi* - **1.** [worry] : **to ~ at sb** tracasser qqn - **2.** [criticize] faire des réflexions, critiquer.

nigh [naɪ] *adv literary* près, proche ; **well ~** presque.

night [naɪt] *n* - **1.** [not day] nuit *f ;* **at ~** la nuit ; **~ and day, day and ~** nuit et jour - **2.** [evening] soir *m ;* **at ~** le soir - **3.** phr : **to have an early ~** se coucher de bonne heure ; **to have a late ~** veiller, se coucher tard.

➤ **nights** *adv* - **1.** Am [at night] la nuit - **2.** Br [nightshift] : **to work ~s** travailler OR être de nuit.

nightcap [ˈnaɪtkæp] *n* - **1.** [drink] *boisson alcoolisée prise avant de se coucher* - **2.** [hat] bonnet *m* de nuit.

nightclothes [ˈnaɪtkləʊðz] *npl* vêtements *mpl* de nuit.

nightclub [ˈnaɪtklʌb] *n* boîte *f* de nuit, nightclub *m*.

nightdress [ˈnaɪtdres] *n* chemise *f* de nuit.

nightfall [ˈnaɪtfɔːl] *n* tombée *f* de la nuit OR du jour.

nightgown [ˈnaɪtgaʊn] *n* chemise *f* de nuit.

nightie [ˈnaɪtɪ] *n* inf chemise *f* de nuit.

nightingale [ˈnaɪtɪŋgeɪl] *n* rossignol *m*.

nightlife [ˈnaɪtlaɪf] *n* vie *f* nocturne, activités *fpl* nocturnes.

nightlight [ˈnaɪtlaɪt] *n* veilleuse *f*.

nightly [ˈnaɪtlɪ] ◇ *adj* (de) toutes les nuits OR tous les soirs ◇ *adv* toutes les nuits, tous les soirs.

nightmare [ˈnaɪtmeəʳ] *n lit* & *fig* cauchemar *m*.

nightmarish [ˈnaɪtmeərɪʃ] *adj* cauchemardesque, de cauchemar.

night owl *n fig* couche-tard *m inv*, noctambule *mf*.

night porter *n* veilleur *m* de nuit.

night safe n coffre m de nuit.

night school n (U) cours mpl du soir.

night shift n [period] poste m de nuit.

nightshirt ['naɪtʃɜːt] n chemise f de nuit d'homme.

nightspot ['naɪtˌspɒt] n boîte f de nuit, night-club m.

nightstick ['naɪtˌstɪk] n Am matraque f.

nighttime ['naɪttaɪm] n nuit f.

night watchman n gardien m de nuit.

nightwear ['naɪtweəʳ] n (U) vêtements mpl de nuit.

nihilism ['naɪəlɪzm] n nihilisme m.

nil [nɪl] n néant m ; Br SPORT zéro m.

Nile [naɪl] n : the ~ le Nil.

nimble ['nɪmbl] adj agile, leste ; fig [mind] vif (vive).

nimbly ['nɪmblɪ] adv agilement, lestement.

nine [naɪn] num neuf ; see also **six**.

nineteen [ˌnaɪn'tiːn] num dix-neuf ; see also **six**.

nineteenth [naɪn'tiːnθ] num dix-neuvième ; see also **sixth**.

ninetieth ['naɪntɪəθ] num quatre-vingt-dixième ; see also **sixth**.

ninety ['naɪntɪ] num quatre-vingt-dix ; see also **sixty**.

ninny ['nɪnɪ] (pl -ies) n inf nigaud m, -e f.

ninth [naɪnθ] num neuvième ; see also **sixth**.

nip [nɪp] (pt & pp -ped ; cont -ping) ◇ n - 1. [pinch] pinçon m ; [bite] morsure f - 2. [of drink] goutte f, doigt m ◇ vt [pinch] pincer ; [bite] mordre ◇ vi Br inf : to ~ down the pub faire un saut au pub.

nipper ['nɪpəʳ] n Br inf gamin m, -e f, gosse mf.

nipple ['nɪpl] n - 1. ANAT bout m de sein, mamelon m - 2. [of bottle] tétine f.

nippy ['nɪpɪ] (compar -ier ; superl -iest) adj inf - 1. [cold] froid(e), frisquet(ette) - 2. [quick - person] vif (vive) ; [- car] nerveux(euse).

Nissen hut ['nɪsn-] n hutte f préfabriquée en tôle.

nit [nɪt] n - 1. [in hair] lente f - 2. Br inf [idiot] idiot m, -e f, crétin m, -e f.

nitpicking ['nɪtpɪkɪŋ] n inf ergotage m, pinaillage m.

nitrate ['naɪtreɪt] n nitrate m.

nitric acid ['naɪtrɪk-] n acide m nitrique.

nitrogen ['naɪtrədʒən] n azote m.

nitroglycerin(e) [ˌnaɪtrəʊ'glɪsəriːn] n nitroglycérine f.

nitty-gritty [ˌnɪtɪ'grɪtɪ] n inf : to get down to the ~ en venir à l'essentiel OR aux choses sérieuses.

nitwit ['nɪtwɪt] n inf imbécile mf, idiot m, -e f.

nix [nɪks] Am ◇ n [nothing] rien ◇ adv non ◇ vt [say no to] mettre son veto à.

NJ abbr of New Jersey.

NLF (abbr of National Liberation Front) n FLN m.

NLQ (abbr of near letter quality) qualité quasi-courrier.

NLRB (abbr of National Labor Relations Board) n commission américaine d'arbitrage en matière d'emploi.

NM abbr of New Mexico.

no [nəʊ] (pl noes [nəʊz]) ◇ adv - 1. [gen] non ; [expressing disagreement] mais non - 2. [not any] : ~ bigger/smaller pas plus grand/petit ; ~ better pas mieux ◇ adj aucun(e), pas de ; there's ~ telling what will happen impossible de dire ce qui va se passer ; he's ~ friend of mine je ne le compte pas parmi mes amis ◇ n non m ; she won't take ~ for an answer elle n'accepte pas de refus OR qu'on lui dise non.

No., no. (abbr of number) No, no.

Noah's ark ['nəʊəz-] n l'arche f de Noé.

nobble ['nɒbl] vt Br inf - 1. [racehorse] droguer - 2. [bribe] soudoyer, acheter - 3. [detain - person] accrocher.

Nobel prize [nəʊ'bel-] n prix m Nobel.

nobility [nə'bɪlətɪ] n noblesse f.

noble ['nəʊbl] ◇ adj noble ◇ n noble m.

nobleman ['nəʊblmən] (pl -men [-mən]) n noble m, aristocrate m.

noblewoman ['nəʊblˌwʊmən] (pl -women [-ˌwɪmɪn]) n (femme) noble f, aristocrate f.

nobly ['nəʊblɪ] adv noblement.

nobody ['nəʊbədɪ] (pl -ies) ◇ pron personne, aucun(e) ◇ n pej rien-du-tout mf, moins que rien mf.

no-claim bonus n bonus m.

nocturnal [nɒk'tɜːnl] adj nocturne.

nod [nɒd] (pt & pp -ded ; cont -ding) ◇ n signe m OR inclination f de la tête ◇ vt : to ~ one's head incliner la tête, faire un signe de tête ◇ vi - 1. [in agreement] faire un signe de tête affirmatif, faire signe que oui - 2. [to indicate sthg] faire un signe de tête - 3. [as greeting] : to ~ to sb saluer qqn d'un signe de tête.

nod off vi somnoler, s'assoupir.

node [nəʊd] n nœud m.

nodule ['nɒdjuːl] n nodule m.

no-frills [-'frɪlz] adj [service] minimum ; [airline] à bas prix.

no-go area n Br zone f interdite.

noise [nɔɪz] *n* bruit *m*.

noiseless ['nɔɪzlɪs] *adj* silencieux(euse).

noiselessly ['nɔɪzlɪslɪ] *adv* sans bruit, silencieusement.

noisily ['nɔɪzɪlɪ] *adv* bruyamment.

noisy ['nɔɪzɪ] (*compar* **-ier** ; *superl* **-iest**) *adj* bruyant(e).

nomad ['nəʊmæd] *n* nomade *mf*.

nomadic [nə'mædɪk] *adj* nomade.

no-man's-land *n* no man's land *m*.

nominal ['nɒmɪnl] *adj* - **1.** [in name only] de nom seulement, nominal(e) - **2.** [very small] nominal(e), insignifiant(e).

nominally ['nɒmɪnəlɪ] *adv* nominalement, de nom.

nominate ['nɒmɪneɪt] *vt* - **1.** [propose] : **to ~ sb (for/as sthg)** proposer qqn (pour/comme qqch) - **2.** [appoint] : **to ~ sb (as sthg)** nommer qqn (qqch) ; **to ~ sb (to sthg)** nominer qqn (à qqch).

nomination [ˌnɒmɪ'neɪʃn] *n* nomination *f*.

nominee [ˌnɒmɪ'niː] *n* personne *f* nommée OR désignée.

non- [nɒn] *prefix* non-.

nonaddictive [ˌnɒnə'dɪktɪv] *adj* qui ne provoque pas d'accoutumance OR de dépendance.

nonaggression [ˌnɒnə'greʃn] *n* non-agression *f*.

nonalcoholic [ˌnɒnælkə'hɒlɪk] *adj* non-alcoolisé(e).

nonaligned [ˌnɒnə'laɪnd] *adj* non-aligné(e).

nonbeliever [ˌnɒnbɪ'liːvə'] *n* incroyant *m*, -e *f*, athée *mf*.

nonchalant [Br 'nɒnʃələnt, Am ˌnɒnʃə'lɑːnt] *adj* nonchalant(e).

nonchalantly [Br 'nɒnʃələntlɪ, Am ˌnɒnʃə'lɑːntlɪ] *adv* nonchalamment.

noncombatant [Br ˌnɒn'kɒmbətənt, Am ˌnɒnkəm'bætənt] *n* non-combattant *m*, -e *f*.

noncommissioned officer [ˌnɒnkə'mɪʃənd-] *n* sous-officier *m*.

noncommittal [ˌnɒnkə'mɪtl] *adj* évasif(ive).

noncompetitive [ˌnɒnkəm'petɪtɪv] *adj* qui n'est pas basé(e) sur la compétition.

non compos mentis [-ˌkɒmpəs'mentɪs] *adj* : **to be ~** ne pas avoir toute sa raison.

nonconformist [ˌnɒnkən'fɔːmɪst] ⬦ *adj* non-conformiste ⬦ *n* non-conformiste *mf*.

nonconformity [ˌnɒnkən'fɔːmətɪ] *n* non-conformité *f*.

noncontributory [ˌnɒnkən'trɪbjʊtərɪ] *adj* sans versements de la part des bénéficiaires.

noncooperation ['nɒnkəʊˌɒpə'reɪʃn] *n* refus *m* de coopération.

nondescript [Br 'nɒndɪskrɪpt, Am ˌnɒndɪ'skrɪpt] *adj* quelconque, terne.

nondrinker [ˌnɒn'drɪŋkə'] *n* personne *f* qui ne boit pas d'alcool.

nondrip [ˌnɒn'drɪp] *adj* qui ne coule pas.

nondriver [ˌnɒn'draɪvə'] *n* personne f qui n'a pas le permis de conduire.

none [nʌn] ⬦ *pron* - **1.** [gen] aucun(e) ; **there was ~ left** il n'y en avait plus, il n'en restait plus ; **I'll have ~ of your nonsense** je ne tolérerai pas de bêtises de ta part - **2.** [nobody] personne, nul (nulle) ⬦ *adv* : **~ the worse/wiser** pas plus mal/avancé ; **~ the better** pas mieux.

➡ **none too** *adv* pas tellement OR trop.

nonentity [nɒ'nentətɪ] (*pl* **-ies**) *n* nullité *f*, zéro *m*.

nonessential [ˌnɒnɪ'senʃl] *adj* non-essentiel(elle), peu important(e).

nonetheless [ˌnʌnðə'les] *adv* néanmoins, pourtant.

non-event *n* événement *m* raté OR décevant.

nonexecutive director [ˌnɒnɪgsekjətɪv-] *n* administrateur *m*; -trice *f*.

nonexistent [ˌnɒnɪg'zɪstənt] *adj* inexistant(e).

nonfattening [ˌnɒn'fætnɪŋ] *adj* qui ne fait pas grossir.

nonfiction [ˌnɒn'fɪkʃn] *n* (*U*) ouvrages *mpl* généraux.

nonflammable [ˌnɒn'flæməbl] *adj* ininflammable.

noninfectious [ˌnɒnɪn'fekʃəs] *adj* qui n'est pas infectieux(euse).

noninflammable [ˌnɒnɪn'flæməbl] = **nonflammable**.

noninterference [ˌnɒnɪntə'fɪərəns], **nonintervention** [ˌnɒnɪntə'venʃn] *n* non-ingérence *f*, non-intervention *f*.

non-iron *adj* qui ne se repasse pas.

nonmalignant [ˌnɒnmə'lɪgnənt] *adj* bénin(igne).

non-member *n* [of club] personne *f* qui n'est pas membre.

non-negotiable *adj* qu'on ne peut pas négocier OR débattre.

no-no *n* inf : it's a ~ c'est interdit OR défendu.

no-nonsense *adj* direct(e), sérieux(euse).

nonoperational [ˌnɒnɒpə'reɪʃənl] *adj* non-opérationnel(elle).

nonparticipation [ˌnɒnpɑːtɪsəˈpeɪʃən] *n* non-participation *f*.

nonpayment [ˌnɒnˈpeɪmənt] *n* non-paiement *m*.

nonplussed, nonplused Am [ˌnɒnˈplʌst] *adj* déconcerté(e), perplexe.

non-profit-making Br, **non-profit** Am *adj* à but non lucratif.

nonproliferation [ˈnɒnprəˌlɪfəˈreɪʃn] *n* non-prolifération *f*.

nonrenewable [ˌnɒnrɪˈnjuːəbl] *adj* non renouvelable.

nonresident [ˌnɒnˈrezɪdənt] *n* - **1.** [of country] non-résident *m*, -e *f* - **2.** [of hotel] client *m*, -e *f* de passage.

nonreturnable [ˌnɒnrɪˈtɜːnəbl] *adj* [bottle] non consigné(e).

nonsense [ˈnɒnsəns] ⟨⟩ *n (U)* - **1.** [meaningless words] charabia *m* - **2.** [foolish idea] : **it was ~ to suggest ...** il était absurde de suggérer ... - **3.** [foolish behaviour] bêtises *fpl*, idioties *fpl ;* **to make (a) ~ of sthg** gâcher OR saboter qqch ⟨⟩ *excl* quelles bêtises OR foutaises!

nonsensical [nɒnˈsensɪkl] *adj* absurde, qui n'a pas de sens.

non sequitur [-ˈsekwɪtər] *n* remarque *f* qui manque de suite.

nonshrink [ˌnɒnˈʃrɪŋk] *adj* irrétrécissable.

nonskid [ˌnɒnˈskɪd] *adj* [tyre] antidérapant(e).

nonslip [ˌnɒnˈslɪp] *adj* antidérapant(e).

nonsmoker [ˌnɒnˈsmoʊkər] *n* non-fumeur *m*, -euse *f*, personne *f* qui ne fume pas.

nonstarter [ˌnɒnˈstɑːtər] *n* - **1.** Br inf [plan etc] : **this is a ~** ceci n'a aucune chance de réussir - **2.** [in race] non-partant *m*.

nonstick [ˌnɒnˈstɪk] *adj* qui n'attache pas, téflonisé(e).

nonstop [ˌnɒnˈstɒp] ⟨⟩ *adj* [flight] direct(e), sans escale ; [activity] continu(e) ; [rain] continuel(elle) ⟨⟩ *adv* [talk, work] sans arrêt ; [rain] sans discontinuer.

nontaxable [ˌnɒnˈtæksəbl] *adj* non imposable.

nontoxic [ˌnɒnˈtɒksɪk] *adj* non toxique.

nontransferable [ˌnɒntrænzˈfɜːrəbl] *adj* non transmissible.

non-U *adj* Br dated qui n'est pas très distingué(e), vulgaire.

nonviolence [ˌnɒnˈvaɪələns] *n* non-violence *f*.

nonvoter [ˌnɒnˈvoʊtər] *n* abstentionniste *mf*, personne *f* qui ne vote pas.

nonvoting [ˌnɒnˈvoʊtɪŋ] *adj* - **1.** [person] abstentionniste, qui ne vote pas - **2.** FIN [shares] sans droit de vote.

nonwhite [ˌnɒnˈwaɪt] ⟨⟩ *adj* de couleur ⟨⟩ *n* personne *f* de couleur.

noodles [ˈnuːdlz] *npl* nouilles *fpl*.

nook [nʊk] *n* [of room] coin *m*, recoin *m ;* **every ~ and cranny** tous les coins, les coins et les recoins.

noon [nuːn] ⟨⟩ *n* midi *m* ⟨⟩ *comp* de midi.

noonday [ˈnuːndeɪ] *literary* = **noon**.

no one *pron* = **nobody**.

noose [nuːs] *n* nœud *m* coulant.

no-place Am = **nowhere**.

nor [nɔːr] *conj* : **~ do I** moi non plus ⊳ **neither**.

Nordic [ˈnɔːdɪk] *adj* nordique.

Norf (*abbr of* **Norfolk**) *comté anglais*.

norm [nɔːm] *n* norme *f*.

normal [ˈnɔːml] *adj* normal(e).

normality [nɔːˈmælɪtɪ], **normalcy** Am [ˈnɔːmlsɪ] *n* normalité *f*.

normalize, -ise [ˈnɔːməlaɪz] ⟨⟩ *vt* normaliser ⟨⟩ *vi* se normaliser, redevenir normal.

normally [ˈnɔːməlɪ] *adv* normalement.

Norman [ˈnɔːmən] ⟨⟩ *adj* normand(e) ⟨⟩ *n* Normand *m*, -e *f*.

Normandy [ˈnɔːməndɪ] *n* Normandie *f ;* **in ~** en Normandie.

Norse [nɔːs] *adj* nordique, scandinave.

north [nɔːθ] ⟨⟩ *n* - **1.** [direction] nord *m* - **2.** [region] : **the ~** le nord ⟨⟩ *adj* nord *(inv) ;* [wind] du nord ⟨⟩ *adv* au nord, vers le nord ; **~ of** au nord de.

North Africa *n* Afrique *f* du Nord ; **in ~** en Afrique du Nord.

North America *n* Amérique *f* du Nord.

North American ⟨⟩ *adj* nord-américain(e) ⟨⟩ *n* Nord-Américain *m*, -e *f*.

Northants [nɔːˈθænts] (*abbr of* **Northamptonshire**) *comté anglais*.

northbound [ˈnɔːθbaʊnd] *adj* en direction du nord ; **~ carriageway** chaussée (du) nord.

North Carolina [-ˌkærəˈlaɪnə] *n* Caroline *f* du Nord ; **in ~** en Caroline du Nord.

North Country *n :* **the ~** le Nord de l'Angleterre.

Northd (*abbr of* **Northumberland**) *comté anglais*.

North Dakota [-dəˈkəʊtəl] *n* Dakota *m* du Nord ; **in ~** dans le Dakota du Nord.

northeast [ˌnɔːθˈiːst] ⟨⟩ *n* - **1.** [direction] nord-est *m* - **2.** [region] : **the ~** le nord-est ⟨⟩ *adj* nord-est *(inv) ;* [wind] du nord-est ⟨⟩ *adv* au nord-est, vers le nord-est ; **~ of** au nord-est de.

northeasterly [ˌnɔ:θ'i:stəlɪ] *adj* au nord-est, du nord-est ; **in a ~ direction** vers le nord-est.

northerly ['nɔ:ðəlɪ] *adj* du nord ; **in a ~ direction** vers le nord, en direction du nord.

northern ['nɔ:ðən] *adj* du nord, nord *(inv)*.

Northerner ['nɔ:ðənə'] *n* habitant *m*, -e *f* du Nord.

Northern Ireland *n* Irlande *f* du Nord ; **in ~** en Irlande du Nord.

Northern Lights *npl* : **the ~** l'aurore *f* boréale.

northernmost ['nɔ:ðənməust] *adj* le plus au nord (la plus au nord), à l'extrême nord.

Northern Territory *n* Territoire *m* du Nord ; **in ~** dans le Territoire du Nord.

North Korea *n* Corée *f* du Nord.

North Korean ◇ *adj* nord-coréen(enne) ◇ *n* Nord-Coréen *m*, -enne *f*.

North Pole *n* : **the ~** le pôle Nord.

North Sea ◇ *n* : **the ~** la mer du Nord ◇ *comp* de la mer du Nord.

North Star *n* : **the ~** l'étoile *f* polaire.

North Vietnam *n* Nord Viêt-Nam *m* ; **in ~** au Nord Viêt-Nam.

North Vietnamese ◇ *adj* nord-vietnamien(enne) ◇ *n* Nord-Vietnamien *m*, -enne *f*.

northward ['nɔ:θwəd] ◇ *adj* au nord ; **in a ~ direction** vers le nord ◇ *adv* = **northwards**.

northwards ['nɔ:θwədz] *adv* au nord, vers le nord.

northwest [ˌnɔ:θ'west] ◇ *n* - **1.** [direction] nord-ouest *m* - **2.** [region] : **the ~** le nord-ouest ◇ *adj* nord-ouest *(inv)* ; [wind] du nord-ouest ◇ *adv* au nord-ouest, vers le nord-ouest ; **~ of** au nord-ouest de.

northwesterly [ˌnɔ:θ'westəlɪ] *adj* au nord-ouest, du nord-ouest ; **in a ~ direction** vers le nord-ouest.

Northwest Territories *npl* Can : **the ~** les Territoires *mpl* du Nord-Ouest.

North Yemen *n* Yemen *m* du Nord ; **in ~** au Yemen du Nord.

Norway ['nɔ:weɪ] *n* Norvège *f* ; **in ~** en Norvège.

Norwegian [nɔ:'wi:dʒən] ◇ *adj* norvégien(enne) ◇ *n* - **1.** [person] Norvégien *m*, -enne *f* - **2.** [language] norvégien *m*.

Nos., nos. *(abbr of* **numbers***)* no.

nose [nəuz] *n* nez *m* ; **under one's ~** sous le nez ; **you're just cutting your ~ off to spite your face** c'est toi qui en pâtis ; **to have a ~ for sthg** flairer qqch, savoir reconnaître

qqch ; **he gets up my ~** inf il me tape sur les nerfs ; **keep your ~ out of my business** occupe-toi OR mêle-toi de tes affaires, occupe-toi OR mêle-toi de tes oignons ; **to look down one's ~ at sb** fig traiter qqn de haut ; **to look down one's ~ at sthg** fig considérer qqch avec mépris ; **to pay through the ~** payer les yeux de la tête ; **to poke** OR **stick one's ~ into sthg** mettre OR fourrer son nez dans qqch ; **to turn up one's ~ at sthg** dédaigner qqch.

➤ **nose about, nose around** *vi* fouiner, fureter.

nosebag ['nəuzbæg] *n* musette *f* (mangeoire).

nosebleed ['nəuzbli:d] *n* : **to have a ~** saigner du nez.

nosecone ['nəuzkəun] *n* [of rocket] coiffe *f* ; [of plane] nez *m*.

nosedive ['nəuzdaɪv] ◇ *n* [of plane] piqué *m* ◇ *vi* - **1.** [plane] descendre en piqué, piquer du nez - **2.** fig [prices] dégringoler ; [hopes] s'écrouler.

nosey ['nəuzɪ] = **nosy**.

nosh [nɒʃ] *n* Br inf [food] bouffe *f*.

nosh-up *n* Br inf gueuleton *m*, bouffe *f*.

nostalgia [nɒ'stældʒə] *n* : **~ (for sthg)** nostalgie *f* (de qqch).

nostalgic [nɒ'stældʒɪk] *adj* nostalgique.

nostril ['nɒstrəl] *n* narine *f*.

nosy ['nəuzɪ] *(compar* **-ier** ; *superl* **-iest***) adj* curieux(euse), fouinard(e).

not [nɒt] *adv* ne pas, pas ; **I think ~** je ne crois pas ; **I'm afraid ~** je crains que non ; **~ always** pas toujours ; **~ that ...** ce n'est pas que ..., non pas que ... ; **~ at all** [no] pas du tout ; [to acknowledge thanks] de rien, je vous en prie.

notable ['nəutəbl] ◇ *adj* notable, remarquable ; **to be ~ for sthg** être célèbre pour qqch ◇ *n* notable *m*.

notably ['nəutəblɪ] *adv* - **1.** [in particular] notamment, particulièrement - **2.** [noticeably] sensiblement, nettement.

notary ['nəutərɪ] *(pl* **-ies***) n* : **~ (public)** notaire *m*.

notation [nəu'teɪʃn] *n* notation *f*.

notch [nɒtʃ] *n* - **1.** [cut] entaille *f*, encoche *f* - **2.** fig [on scale] cran *m*.

➤ **notch up** *vt fus* marquer.

note [nəut] ◇ *n* - **1.** [gen & MUS] note *f* ; [short letter] mot *m* ; **to take ~ of sthg** prendre note de qqch ; **to compare ~s** échanger ses impressions OR ses vues - **2.** [money] billet *m* (de banque) - **3.** [importance] : **of ~** de marque, éminent(e) ◇ *vt* - **1.** [notice] remarquer, constater - **2.** [mention] mentionner, signaler.

➤ **notes** *npl* [in book] notes *fpl*.

➤ **note down** *vt sep* noter, inscrire.

notebook ['nəʊtbʊk] *n* - **1.** [for notes] carnet *m*, calepin *m* - **2.** COMPUT ordinateur *m* portable compact.

noted ['nəʊtɪd] *adj* célèbre, éminent(e).

notepad ['nəʊtpæd] *n* bloc-notes *m*.

notepaper ['nəʊtpeɪpəʳ] *n* papier *m* à lettres.

noteworthy ['nəʊt,wɜːðɪ] (*compar* -**ier** ; *superl* -**iest**) *adj* remarquable, notable.

nothing ['nʌθɪŋ] ⬦ *pron* rien ; **I've got ~ to do** je n'ai rien à faire ; **there's ~ in it** ce n'est pas vrai du tout, il n'y a pas un brin de vérité là-dedans ; **there's ~ to it** c'est facile comme tout OR simple comme bonjour ; **for ~** pour rien ; **~ if not** avant tout, surtout ; **~ but** ne ... que, rien que ; **there's ~ for it (but to do sthg)** Br il n'y a rien d'autre à faire (que de faire qqch) ⬦ *adv* : **you're ~ like your brother** tu ne ressembles pas du tout OR en rien à ton frère ; **I'm ~ like finished** je suis loin d'avoir fini.

nothingness ['nʌθɪŋnɪs] *n* néant *m*.

notice ['nəʊtɪs] ⬦ *n* - **1.** [written announcement] affiche *f*, placard *m* - **2.** [attention] : **it has come to my ~ that ...** mon attention a été attirée par le fait que ... ; **it escaped my ~** je ne l'ai pas remarqué, je ne m'en suis pas aperçu ; **to take ~ (of sb/sthg)** faire OR prêter attention (à qqn/qqch) ; **to take no ~ (of sb/sthg)** ne pas faire attention (à qqn/qqch) ; **he didn't take a blind bit of ~** il n'y a tenu aucun compte - **3.** [warning] avis *m*, avertissement *m* ; **at short ~** dans un bref délai ; **until further ~** jusqu'à nouvel ordre - **4.** [at work] : **to be given one's ~** recevoir son congé, être renvoyé(e) ; **to hand in one's ~** donner sa démission, demander son congé ⬦ *vt* remarquer, s'apercevoir de.

noticeable ['nəʊtɪsəbl] *adj* sensible, perceptible.

noticeably ['nəʊtɪsəblɪ] *adv* sensiblement, nettement.

notice board *n* panneau *m* d'affichage.

notification [,nəʊtɪfɪ'keɪʃn] *n* notification *f*, avis *m*.

notify ['nəʊtɪfaɪ] (*pt* & *pp* -**ied**) *vt* : **to ~ sb (of sthg)** avertir OR aviser qqn (de qqch).

notion ['nəʊʃn] *n* idée *f*, notion *f*.

➤ **notions** *npl* Am mercerie *f*.

notional ['nəʊʃənl] *adj* imaginaire, fictif(ive).

notoriety [,nəʊtə'raɪətɪ] *n* mauvaise OR triste réputation *f*.

notorious [nəʊ'tɔːrɪəs] *adj* [criminal] notoire ; [place] mal famé(e) ; **to be ~ for sthg** être réputé pour qqch.

notoriously [nəʊ'tɔːrɪəslɪ] *adv* notoirement.

Notts [nɒts] (*abbr of* **Nottinghamshire**) comté anglais.

notwithstanding [,nɒtwɪð'stændɪŋ] *fml* ⬦ *prep* malgré, en dépit de ⬦ *adv* néanmoins, malgré tout.

nougat ['nuːgɑː] *n* nougat *m*.

nought [nɔːt] *num* zéro *m* ; **~s and crosses** morpion *m*.

noun [naʊn] *n* nom *m*.

nourish ['nʌrɪʃ] *vt* nourrir.

nourishing ['nʌrɪʃɪŋ] *adj* nourrissant(e).

nourishment ['nʌrɪʃmənt] *n* (U) nourriture *f*, aliments *mpl*.

Nov. (*abbr of* **November**) nov.

Nova Scotia [,nəʊvə'skəʊʃə] *n* Nouvelle-Écosse *f* ; **in ~** en Nouvelle-Écosse.

Nova Scotian [,nəʊvə'skəʊʃn] ⬦ *n* Néo-Écossais *m*, -e *f* ⬦ *adj* néo-écossais(e).

novel ['nɒvl] ⬦ *adj* nouveau (nouvelle), original(e) ⬦ *n* roman *m*.

novelist ['nɒvəlɪst] *n* romancier *m*, -ère *f*.

novelty ['nɒvltɪ] (*pl* -**ies**) *n* - **1.** [gen] nouveauté *f* - **2.** [cheap object] gadget *m*.

November [nə'vembəʳ] *n* novembre *m* ; *see also* **September**.

novice ['nɒvɪs] *n* novice *mf*.

Novocaine® ['nəʊvəkeɪn] *n* novocaïne® *f*.

now [naʊ] ⬦ *adv* - **1.** [at this time, at once] maintenant ; **any day/time ~** d'un jour/moment à l'autre ; **~ and then** OR **again** de temps en temps, de temps à autre - **2.** [in past] à ce moment-là, alors - **3.** [to introduce statement] : **~ let's just calm down** bon, on se calme maintenant ⬦ *conj* : **~ (that)** maintenant que ⬦ *n* : **for ~** pour le présent ; **from ~ on** à partir de maintenant, désormais ; **up until ~** jusqu'à présent ; **by ~** déjà.

NOW [naʊ] (*abbr of* **National Organization for Women**) *n* organisation féministe américaine.

nowadays ['naʊədeɪz] *adv* actuellement, aujourd'hui.

nowhere Br ['nəʊweəʳ], **no-place** Am *adv* nulle part ; **to appear out of** OR **from ~** apparaître tout d'un coup ; **~ near** loin de ; **we're getting ~** on n'avance pas, on n'arrive à rien ; **this is getting us ~** cela ne nous avance à rien.

no-win situation *n* impasse *f*.

noxious ['nɒkʃəs] *adj* toxique.

nozzle [ˈnɒzl] n ajutage m, buse f.

NP abbr of notary public.

NS abbr of Nova Scotia.

NSC (abbr of National Security Council) n conseil national américain de sécurité.

NSF ◇ n (abbr of National Science Foundation) fondation nationale américaine pour la science ◇ abbr of not sufficient funds.

NSPCC (abbr of National Society for the Prevention of Cruelty to Children) n association britannique de protection de l'enfance.

NSU (abbr of nonspecific urethritis) n urétrite f non spécifique.

NSW abbr of New South Wales.

NT n - 1. (abbr of New Testament) NT m - 2. abbr of National Trust.

nth [enθ] adj inf énième.

nuance [ˈnjuːɒns] n nuance f.

nub [nʌb] n nœud m, fond m.

Nubian Desert [ˈnjuːbjən-] n : the ~ le désert de Nubie.

nubile [Br ˈnjuːbaɪl, Am ˈnuːbəl] adj nubile.

nuclear [ˈnjuːklɪəʳ] adj nucléaire.

nuclear bomb n bombe f nucléaire.

nuclear disarmament n désarmement m nucléaire.

nuclear energy n énergie f nucléaire.

nuclear family n famille f nucléaire.

nuclear fission n fission f nucléaire.

nuclear-free zone n zone f antinucléaire.

nuclear fusion n fusion f nucléaire.

nuclear physics n physique f nucléaire.

nuclear power n énergie f nucléaire.

nuclear reactor n réacteur m nucléaire.

nuclear winter n hiver m nucléaire.

nucleus [ˈnjuːklɪəs] (pl -lei [-lɪaɪ]) n lit & fig noyau m.

NUCPS (abbr of National Union of Civil and Public Servants) n syndicat britannique des employés de la fonction publique.

nude [njuːd] ◇ adj nu(e) ◇ n nu m ; in the ~ nu(e).

nudge [nʌdʒ] ◇ n coup m de coude ; fig encouragement m, incitation f ◇ vt pousser du coude ; fig encourager, pousser.

nudist [ˈnjuːdɪst] ◇ adj nudiste ◇ n nudiste mf.

nudity [ˈnjuːdətɪ] n nudité f.

nugget [ˈnʌɡɪt] n pépite f ; ~ of information fig information f précieuse.

nuisance [ˈnjuːsns] n ennui m, embêtement m ; he's such a ~ il est vraiment casse-pieds ; to make a ~ of o.s. embêter le monde ; what a ~! quelle plaie!

NUJ (abbr of National Union of Journalists) n syndicat britannique des journalistes.

nuke [njuːk] inf ◇ n bombe f nucléaire ◇ vt atomiser.

null [nʌl] adj : ~ and void nul et non avenu.

nullify [ˈnʌlɪfaɪ] (pt & pp -ied) vt annuler.

NUM (abbr of National Union of Mineworkers) n syndicat britannique des mineurs.

numb [nʌm] ◇ adj engourdi(e) ; to be ~ with [fear] être paralysé par ; [cold] être transi de ◇ vt engourdir.

number [ˈnʌmbəʳ] ◇ n - 1. [numeral] chiffre m - 2. [of telephone, house, car] numéro m - 3. [quantity] nombre m ; a ~ of un certain nombre de, plusieurs ; any ~ of un grand nombre de, bon nombre de - 4. [song] chanson f ◇ vt - 1. [amount to, include] compter ; to ~ among compter parmi - 2. [give number to] numéroter.

number-crunching [-ˌkrʌntʃɪŋ] n inf calcul m numérique.

numberless [ˈnʌmbəlɪs] adj sans nombre, innombrable.

number one ◇ adj premier(ère), principal(e) ◇ n - 1. [priority] priorité f - 2. inf [oneself] soi, sa pomme.

numberplate [ˈnʌmbəpleɪt] n Br plaque f d'immatriculation.

Number Ten n la résidence officielle du premier ministre britannique.

numbness [ˈnʌmnɪs] n engourdissement m.

numbskull [ˈnʌmskʌl] = numskull.

numeracy [ˈnjuːmərəsɪ] n Br compétence f en calcul.

numeral [ˈnjuːmərəl] n chiffre m.

numerate [ˈnjuːmərət] adj Br [person] qui sait compter.

numerical [njuːˈmerɪkl] adj numérique.

numerous [ˈnjuːmərəs] adj nombreux(euse).

numskull [ˈnʌmskʌl] n inf crétin(e), imbécile mf.

nun [nʌn] n religieuse f, sœur f.

NUPE [ˈnjuːpɪ] (abbr of National Union of Public Employees) n ancien syndicat britannique des employés de la fonction publique.

nuptial [ˈnʌpʃl] adj fml nuptial(e).

NURMTW (abbr of National Union of Rail, Maritime and Transport Workers) n syndicat britannique des transports.

nurse [nɜːs] ◇ n infirmière f ; (male) ~ infirmier m ◇ vt - 1. [patient, cold] soigner - 2. fig [desires, hopes] nourrir **- 3.** [subj : mother] allaiter.

nursemaid ['nɜːsmeɪd] *n* gouvernante *f*, nurse *f*.

nursery ['nɜːsərɪ] (*pl* **-ies**) ◇ *adj* de maternelle ◇ *n* **- 1.** [for children] garderie *f* **- 2.** [for plants] pépinière *f*.

nursery nurse *n* Br puéricultrice *f*.

nursery rhyme *n* comptine *f*.

nursery school *n* (école *f*) maternelle *f*.

nursery slopes *npl* pistes *fpl* pour débutants.

nursing ['nɜːsɪŋ] *n* métier *m* d'infirmière.

nursing home *n* [for old people] maison *f* de retraite privée ; [for childbirth] maternité *f* privée.

nurture ['nɜːtʃər] *vt* **- 1.** [children] élever ; [plants] soigner **- 2.** fig [hopes etc] nourrir.

NUS (*abbr of* **National Union of Students**) *n* union nationale des étudiants de Grande-Bretagne.

nut [nʌt] *n* **- 1.** [to eat] *terme générique désignant les fruits tels que les noix, noisettes etc* **- 2.** [of metal] écrou *m* ; **~s and bolts** fig rudiments *mpl* **- 3.** inf [mad person] cinglé *m*, -e *f* **- 4.** inf [enthusiast] fana *mf*, mordu *m*, -e *f* **- 5.** inf [head] caboche *f*.

◆ **nuts** ◇ *adj* inf : **to be ~s** être dingue ◇ *excl* Am inf zut!

NUT (*abbr of* **National Union of Teachers**) *n* syndicat britannique d'enseignants.

nutcase ['nʌtkeɪs] *n* inf cinglé *m*, -e *f*.

nutcrackers ['nʌtˌkrækəz] *npl* casse-noix *m inv*, casse-noisettes *m inv*.

nutmeg ['nʌtmeg] *n* noix *f* (de) muscade.

nutrient ['njuːtrɪənt] *n* élément *m* nutritif.

nutrition [njuːˈtrɪʃn] *n* nutrition *f*.

nutritional [njuːˈtrɪʃənl] *adj* nutritif(ive).

nutritionist [njuːˈtrɪʃənɪst] *n* nutritionniste *mf*.

nutritious [njuːˈtrɪʃəs] *adj* nourrissant(e).

nutshell ['nʌtˌʃel] *n* : **in a ~** en un mot.

nutter ['nʌtər] *n* Br inf cinglé *m*, -e *f*.

nuzzle ['nʌzl] ◇ *vt* frotter son nez contre ◇ *vi* : **to ~ (up) against** se frotter contre, frotter son nez contre.

NV *abbr of* **Nevada**.

NVQ (*abbr of* **National Vocational Qualification**) *n* examen sanctionnant une formation professionnelle.

NW (*abbr of* **north-west**) N.O.

NWT *abbr of* **Northwest Territories**.

NY *abbr of* **New York**.

Nyasaland [naɪˈæsəlænd] *n* Nyassaland *m*.

NYC *abbr of* **New York City**.

nylon ['naɪlɒn] ◇ *n* Nylon® *m* ◇ *comp* en Nylon®.

◆ **nylons** *npl* dated [stockings] bas *mpl* nylon.

nymph [nɪmf] *n* nymphe *f*.

nymphomaniac [ˌnɪmfəˈmeɪnɪæk] *n* nymphomane *f*.

NYSE (*abbr of* **New York Stock Exchange**) *n* la bourse de New York.

NZ *abbr of* **New Zealand**.

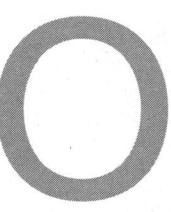

o (*pl* **o's** OR **os**), **O** (*pl* **O's** OR **Os**) [əʊ] *n* **- 1.** [letter] o *m inv*, O *m inv* **- 2.** [zero] zéro *m*.

oaf [əʊf] *n* butor *m*.

oak [əʊk] ◇ *n* chêne *m* ◇ *comp* de OR en chêne.

OAP (*abbr of* **old age pensioner**) *n* retraité *m*, -e *f*.

oar [ɔːr] *n* rame *f*, aviron *m* ; **to put** OR **stick one's ~ in** mettre son grain de sel.

oarlock ['ɔːlɒk] *n* Am [rowlock] dame *f* de nage.

oarsman ['ɔːzmən] (*pl* **-men** [-mən]) *n* rameur *m*.

oarswoman ['ɔːzˌwʊmən] (*pl* **-women** [-ˌwɪmɪn]) *n* rameuse *f*.

OAS (*abbr of* **Organization of American States**) *n* OEA *f*.

oasis [əʊˈeɪsɪs] (*pl* **oases** [əʊˈeɪsiːz]) *n* oasis *f*.

oatcake ['əʊtkeɪk] *n* galette *f* d'avoine.

oath [əʊθ] *n* **- 1.** [promise] serment *m* ; **on** OR **under ~** sous serment **- 2.** [swearword] juron *m*.

oatmeal ['əʊtmiːl] ◇ *n* (U) flocons *mpl* d'avoine ◇ *comp* d'avoine.

oats [əʊts] *npl* [grain] avoine *f*.

OAU (*abbr of* **Organization of African Unity**) *n* OUA *f*.

OB *abbr of* **outside broadcast**.

obdurate ['ɒbdjʊrət] *adj* fml opiniâtre.

OBE (*abbr of* **Order of the British Empire**) *n* distinction honorifique britannique.

obedience [ə'biːdjəns] n obéissance f.

obedient [ə'biːdjənt] adj obéissant(e), docile.

obediently [ə'biːdjəntlɪ] adv docilement.

obelisk ['ɒbəlɪsk] n obélisque m.

obese [əʊ'biːs] adj fml obèse.

obesity [əʊ'biːsətɪ] n obésité f.

obey [ə'beɪ] <> vt obéir à <> vi obéir.

obfuscate ['ɒbfʌskeɪt] vt fml obscurcir.

obituary [ə'bɪtjʊərɪ] (pl -ies) n nécrologie f.

object [n 'ɒbdʒɪkt, vb ɒb'dʒekt] <> n - **1.** [gen] objet m - **2.** [aim] objectif m, but m - **3.** GRAMM complément m d'objet <> vt objecter <> vi protester ; **to ~ to sthg** faire objection à qqch, s'opposer à qqch ; **to ~ to doing sthg** se refuser à faire qqch.

objection [əb'dʒekʃn] n objection f ; **to have no ~ to sthg/to doing sthg** ne voir aucune objection à qqch/à faire qqch.

objectionable [əb'dʒekʃənəbl] adj [person, behaviour] désagréable ; [language] choquant(e).

objective [əb'dʒektɪv] <> adj objectif(ive) <> n objectif m.

objectively [əb'dʒektɪvlɪ] adv d'une manière objective.

objectivity [,ɒbdʒek'tɪvətɪ] n objectivité f.

object lesson ['ɒbdʒɪkt-] n : **an ~ in sthg** une illustration de qqch.

objector [əb'dʒektər] n opposant m, -e f.

obligate ['ɒblɪgeɪt] vt fml obliger.

obligation [,ɒblɪ'geɪʃn] n obligation f.

obligatory [ə'blɪgətrɪ] adj obligatoire.

oblige [ə'blaɪdʒ] <> vt - **1.** [force] : **to ~ sb to do sthg** forcer OR obliger qqn à faire qqch - **2.** fml [do a favour to] obliger <> vi rendre service.

obliging [ə'blaɪdʒɪŋ] adj obligeant(e).

oblique [ə'bliːk] <> adj oblique ; [reference, hint] indirect(e) <> n TYPO barre f oblique.

obliquely [ə'bliːklɪ] adv indirectement.

obliterate [ə'blɪtəreɪt] vt [destroy] détruire, raser.

obliteration [ə,blɪtə'reɪʃn] n destruction f.

oblivion [ə'blɪvɪən] n oubli m.

oblivious [ə'blɪvɪəs] adj : **to be ~ to** OR **of** être inconscient(e) de.

oblong ['ɒblɒŋ] <> adj rectangulaire <> n rectangle m.

obnoxious [əb'nɒkʃəs] adj [person] odieux (euse) ; [smell] infect(e), fétide ; [comment] désobligeant(e).

o.b.o. (abbr of or best offer) à déb.

oboe ['əʊbəʊ] n hautbois m.

oboist ['əʊbəʊɪst] n hautboïste mf.

obscene [əb'siːn] adj obscène.

obscenity [əb'senətɪ] (pl -ies) n obscénité f.

obscure [əb'skjʊər] <> adj obscur(e) <> vt - **1.** [gen] obscurcir - **2.** [view] masquer.

obscurity [əb'skjʊərətɪ] n obscurité f.

obsequious [əb'siːkwɪəs] adj fml & pej obséquieux(euse).

observable [əb'zɜːvəbl] adj [appreciable] notable, sensible ; [visible] qu'on peut observer.

observably [əb'zɜːvəblɪ] adv sensiblement.

observance [əb'zɜːvəns] n observation f.

observant [əb'zɜːvnt] adj observateur(trice).

observation [,ɒbzə'veɪʃn] n observation f.

observation post n poste m d'observation.

observatory [əb'zɜːvətrɪ] (pl -ies) n observatoire m.

observe [əb'zɜːv] vt - **1.** [gen] observer - **2.** [remark] remarquer, faire observer.

observer [əb'zɜːvər] n observateur m, -trice f.

obsess [əb'ses] vt obséder ; **to be ~ed by** OR **with sb/sthg** être obsédé par qqn/qqch.

obsession [əb'seʃn] n obsession f.

obsessional [əb'seʃənl] adj obsessionnel(elle).

obsessive [əb'sesɪv] adj [person] obsessionnel(elle) ; [need etc] qui est une obsession.

obsolescence [,ɒbsə'lesns] n obsolescence f.

obsolescent [,ɒbsə'lesnt] adj [system] qui tombe en désuétude ; [machine] obsolescent(e).

obsolete ['ɒbsəliːt] adj obsolète.

obstacle ['ɒbstəkl] n obstacle m.

obstacle race n course f d'obstacles.

obstetrician [,ɒbstə'trɪʃn] n obstétricien m, -enne f.

obstetrics [ɒb'stetrɪks] n obstétrique f.

obstinacy ['ɒbstɪnəsɪ] n obstination f.

obstinate ['ɒbstənət] adj - **1.** [stubborn] obstiné(e) - **2.** [cough] persistant(e) ; [stain, resistance] tenace.

obstinately ['ɒbstənətlɪ] adv obstinément.

obstreperous [əb'strepərəs] adj turbulent(e).

obstruct [əb'strʌkt] vt - **1.** [block] obstruer - **2.** [hinder] entraver, gêner.

obstruction [əb'strʌkʃn] n - **1.** [in road] encombrement m ; [in pipe] engorgement m - **2.** SPORT obstruction f.

obstructive [əb'strʌktɪv] *adj* [tactics] d'obstruction ; [person] contrariant(e).

obtain [əb'teɪn] *vt* obtenir.

obtainable [əb'teɪnəbl] *adj* que l'on peut obtenir.

obtrusive [əb'truːsɪv] *adj* [behaviour] qui attire l'attention ; [smell] fort(e).

obtrusively [əb'truːsɪvlɪ] *adv* de façon indiscrète.

obtuse [əb'tjuːs] *adj* obtus(e).

obverse ['ɒbvɜːs] *n* - **1.** [of coin] : **the ~** la face - **2.** [opposite] inverse *m*.

obviate ['ɒbvɪeɪt] *vt* fml parer à.

obvious ['ɒbvɪəs] <> *adj* évident(e) <> *n* : **to state the ~** enfoncer des portes ouvertes.

obviously ['ɒbvɪəslɪ] *adv* - **1.** [of course] bien sûr - **2.** [clearly] manifestement.

obviousness ['ɒbvɪəsnɪs] *n* évidence *f*.

OCAS (*abbr of* **Organization of Central American States**) *n* ODEAC *f*.

occasion [ə'keɪʒn] <> *n* - **1.** [gen] occasion *f* ; **on ~** fml de temps en temps, quelquefois - **2.** [important event] événement *m* ; **to rise to the ~** se montrer à la hauteur de la situation <> *vt* [cause] provoquer, occasionner.

occasional [ə'keɪʒənl] *adj* [showers] passager(ère) ; [visit] occasionnel(elle) ; **I have the ~ drink/cigarette** je bois un verre/je fume une cigarette de temps à autre.

occasionally [ə'keɪʒnəlɪ] *adv* de temps en temps, quelquefois.

occasional table *n* table *f* basse.

occluded front [ə'kluːdɪd-] *n* METEOR front *m* occlus.

occult [ɒ'kʌlt] <> *adj* occulte <> *n* : **the ~** le surnaturel.

occupancy ['ɒkjʊpənsɪ] *n* occupation *f*.

occupant ['ɒkjʊpənt] *n* occupant *m*, -e *f* ; [of vehicle] passager *m*.

occupation [ˌɒkjʊ'peɪʃn] *n* - **1.** [job] profession *f* - **2.** [pastime, by army] occupation *f*.

occupational [ˌɒkjʊ'peɪʃənl] *adj* [accident, injury] du travail ; [pension] professionnel(elle).

occupational hazard *n* risque *m* du métier.

occupational therapist *n* ergothérapeute *mf*.

occupational therapy *n* thérapeutique *f* occupationnelle, ergothérapie *f*.

occupied ['ɒkjʊpaɪd] *adj* occupé(e).

occupier ['ɒkjʊpaɪəʳ] *n* occupant *m*, -e *f*.

occupy ['ɒkjʊpaɪ] (*pt & pp* -**ied**) *vt* occuper ; **to ~ o.s.** s'occuper.

occur [ə'kɜːʳ] (*pt & pp* -**red** ; *cont* -**ring**) *vi* - **1.** [happen - gen] avoir lieu, se produire ; [- difficulty] se présenter - **2.** [be present] se trouver, être présent(e) - **3.** [thought, idea] : **~ to sb** venir à l'esprit de qqn.

occurrence [ə'kʌrəns] *n* [event] événement *m*, circonstance *f*.

ocean ['əʊʃn] *n* océan *m* ; Am [sea] mer *f*.

oceangoing ['əʊʃn,gəʊɪŋ] *adj* au long cours.

Oceania [ˌəʊʃɪ'eɪnɪə] *n* Océanie *f* ; **in ~** en Océanie.

Oceanian [ˌəʊʃɪ'eɪnɪən] <> *adj* océanien(enne) <> *n* Océanien *m*, -enne *f*.

ochre Br, **ocher** Am ['əʊkəʳ] *adj* ocre (*inv*).

o'clock [ə'klɒk] *adv* : **two ~** deux heures.

OCR *n* - **1.** *abbr of* **optical character reader** - **2.** *abbr of* **optical character recognition**.

Oct. (*abbr of* **October**) oct.

octagon ['ɒktəgən] *n* octogone *m*.

octagonal [ɒk'tægənl] *adj* octogonal(e).

octane ['ɒkteɪn] *n* octane *m*.

octane number, octane rating *n* indice *m* d'octane.

octave ['ɒktɪv] *n* octave *f*.

octet [ɒk'tet] *n* octuor *m*.

October [ɒk'təʊbəʳ] *n* octobre *m* ; see also **September**.

octogenarian [ˌɒktəʊdʒɪ'neərɪən] *n* octogénaire *mf*.

octopus ['ɒktəpəs] (*pl* -**puses** OR -**pi** [-paɪ]) *n* pieuvre *f*.

OD - **1.** *abbr of* **overdose** - **2.** *abbr of* **overdrawn**.

odd [ɒd] *adj* - **1.** [strange] bizarre, étrange - **2.** [leftover] qui reste - **3.** [occasional] : **I play the ~ game of tennis** je joue au tennis de temps en temps - **4.** [not part of pair] dépareillé(e) - **5.** [number] impair(e) - **6.** phr : **twenty ~ years** une vingtaine d'années.

➡ **odds** *npl* : **the ~s** les chances *fpl* ; **the ~s are that ...** il y a des chances pour que ... (+ *subjunctive*), il est probable que ... ; **against the ~s** envers et contre tout ; **~s and ends** petites choses *fpl*, petits bouts *mpl* ; **to be at ~s with sb** être en désaccord avec qqn ; **to be at ~s with sthg** ne pas concorder avec qqch.

oddball ['ɒdbɔːl] *n* inf excentrique *mf*.

oddity ['ɒdɪtɪ] (*pl* -**ies**) *n* - **1.** [person] personne *f* bizarre ; [thing] chose *f* bizarre - **2.** [strangeness] étrangeté *f*.

odd-job man Br, **odd jobber** Am *n* homme *m* à tout faire.

odd jobs *npl* petits travaux *mpl*.

oddly ['ɒdlɪ] *adv* curieusement ; ~ **enough** chose curieuse.

oddments ['ɒdmənts] *npl* fins *fpl* de série.

odds-on ['ɒdz-] *adj inf* : ~ **favourite** grand favori.

ode [əʊd] *n* ode f.

odious ['əʊdjəs] *adj* odieux(euse).

odometer [əʊ'dɒmɪtər] *n* odomètre *m*.

odorless Am = odourless.

odour Br, **odor** Am ['əʊdər] *n* odeur f.

odourless Br, **odorless** Am ['əʊdəlɪs] *adj* inodore.

odyssey ['ɒdɪsɪ] *n* odyssée f.

OECD (*abbr of* **Organization for Economic Cooperation and Development**) *n* OCDE f.

oesophagus Br, **esophagus** Am [ɪ'sɒfəgəs] *n* œsophage *m*.

oestrogen Br, **estrogen** Am ['iːstrədʒən] *n* œstrogène *m*.

of [*unstressed* əv, *stressed* ɒv] *prep* - **1.** [gen] de ; **the cover** ~ **a book** la couverture d'un livre ; **the King** ~ **England** le roi d'Angleterre ; **to die** ~ **cancer** mourir d'un cancer - **2.** [expressing quantity, amount, age etc] de ; **thousands** ~ **people** des milliers de gens ; **a piece** ~ **cake** un morceau de gâteau ; **a pound** ~ **tomatoes** une livre de tomates ; **a gang** ~ **criminals** une bande de malfaiteurs ; **a child** ~ **five** un enfant de cinq ans ; **a cup** ~ **coffee** une tasse de café - **3.** [made from] en ; **to be made** ~ **sthg** être en qqch - **4.** [with dates, periods of time] : **the 12th** ~ **February** le 12 février ; **the night** ~ **the disaster** la nuit de la catastrophe.

off [ɒf] <> *adv* - **1.** [at a distance, away] : **10 miles** ~ à 16 kilomètres ; **two days** ~ dans deux jours ; **a long time** ~ encore loin ; **far** ~ au loin ; **to keep** ~ se tenir éloigné(e) ; **to be** ~ partir, s'en aller - **2.** [so as to remove] : **to take** ~ enlever ; **to cut sthg** ~ couper qqch ; **could you help me** ~ **with my coat?** pouvez-vous m'aider à enlever mon manteau? - **3.** [so as to complete] : **to finish** ~ terminer ; **to kill** ~ achever - **4.** [not at work etc] : **a day/week** ~ un jour/une semaine de congé - **5.** [so as to separate] : **to fence/curtain sthg** ~ séparer qqch par une clôture/un rideau - **6.** [discounted] : **£10** ~ 10 livres de remise OR réduction - **7.** [financially] : **to be well** ~ être aisé(e) OR riche ; **to be badly** ~ être pauvre <> *prep* - **1.** [at a distance from, away from] de ; **to get** ~ **a bus** descendre d'un bus ; **to jump** ~ **a wall** sauter d'un mur ; **to take a book** ~ **a shelf** prendre un livre sur une étagère ; ~ **the coast** près de la côte - **2.** [so as to remove from] : **to cut a branch** ~ **a tree** couper une branche d'un arbre - **3.** [not attending] : **to be** ~ **work** ne

pas travailler ; ~ **school** absent de l'école - **4.** [no longer liking] : **she's** ~ **her food** elle n'a pas d'appétit - **5.** [deducted from] sur - **6.** inf [from] : **to buy sthg** ~ **sb** acheter qqch à qqn <> *adj* - **1.** [food] avarié(e), gâté(e) ; [milk] tourné(e) - **2.** [TV, light] éteint(e) ; [engine] coupé(e) - **3.** [cancelled] annulé(e) - **4.** [not at work etc] absent(e) ; **I'll be** ~ **next week** je serai absent la semaine prochaine - **5.** inf [offhand] : **he was a bit** ~ **with me** il n'a pas été sympa avec moi.

offal ['ɒfl] *n* (*U*) abats *mpl*.

off-balance *adv* : **to throw/push sb** ~ faire perdre l'équilibre à qqn.

offbeat ['ɒfbiːt] *adj inf* original(e), excentrique.

off-centre <> *adj* décentré(e), décalé(e) <> *adv* de côté.

off-chance *n* : **on the** ~ **that ...** au cas où ...

off colour *adj* [ill] patraque.

offcut ['ɒfkʌt] *n* chute f.

off-day *n inf* : **I'm having an** ~ **today** je ne suis pas dans mon assiette aujourd'hui.

off duty *adj* qui n'est pas de service ; [doctor, nurse] qui n'est pas de garde.

offence Br, **offense** Am [ə'fens] *n* - **1.** [crime] délit *m* - **2.** [upset] : **to cause sb** ~ vexer qqn ; **to take** ~ se vexer.

offend [ə'fend] <> *vt* offenser <> *vi* commettre un délit ; **to** ~ **against** enfreindre.

offended [ə'fendɪd] *adj* offensé(e), froissé(e).

offender [ə'fendər] *n* - **1.** [criminal] criminel *m*, -elle f - **2.** [culprit] coupable *mf*.

offending [ə'fendɪŋ] *adj* qui est la cause OR à l'origine du problème.

offense [*sense 2* 'ɒfens] *n* Am - **1.** = offence - **2.** SPORT attaque f.

offensive [ə'fensɪv] <> *adj* - **1.** [behaviour, comment] blessant(e) - **2.** [weapon, action] offensif(ive) <> *n* offensive f ; **to go on** OR **take the** ~ passer à OR prendre l'offensive.

offensiveness [ə'fensɪvnɪs] *n* caractère *m* choquant.

offer ['ɒfər] <> *n* - **1.** [gen] offre f, proposition f - **2.** [price, bid] offre f - **3.** [in shop] promotion f ; **on** ~ [available] en vente ; [at a special price] en réclame, en promotion <> *vt* - **1.** [gen] offrir ; **to** ~ **sthg to sb, to** ~ **sb sthg** offrir qqch à qqn ; **to** ~ **to do sthg** proposer OR offrir de faire qqch - **2.** [provide - services etc] proposer ; [- hope] donner <> *vi* s'offrir.

OFFER ['ɒfər] (*abbr of* **Office of Electricity Regulation**) *n organisme britannique chargé de*

contrôler les activités des compagnies régionales de la distribution d'électricité.
offering ['ɒfərɪŋ] *n* RELIG offrande *f*.
off-guard *adv* au dépourvu.
offhand [ˌɒf'hænd] <> *adj* cavalier(ère) <> *adv* tout de suite.
office ['ɒfɪs] *n* - **1.** [place, staff] bureau *m* - **2.** [department] département *m*, service *m* - **3.** [position] fonction *f*, poste *m* ; **in ~** en fonction ; **to take ~** entrer en fonction.
office automation *n* bureautique *f*.
office block *n* immeuble *m* de bureaux.
office boy *n* garçon *m* de bureau.
officeholder ['ɒfɪsˌhəʊldər] *n* fonctionnaire *mf*.
office hours *npl* heures *fpl* de bureau.
office junior *n* Br employé *m*, -e *f* subalterne.
Office of Fair Trading *n organisme de défense des consommateurs.*
officer ['ɒfɪsər] *n* - **1.** [in armed forces] officier *m* - **2.** [in organization] agent *m*, fonctionnaire *mf* - **3.** [in police force] officier *m* (de police).
office work *n* travail *m* de bureau.
office worker *n* employé *m*, -e *f* de bureau.
official [ə'fɪʃl] <> *adj* officiel(elle) <> *n* fonctionnaire *mf*.
officialdom [ə'fɪʃəldəm] *n* bureaucratie *f*.
officially [ə'fɪʃəlɪ] *adv* - **1.** [formally] officiellement - **2.** [supposedly] en principe.
official receiver *n* syndic *m* de faillite.
officiate [ə'fɪʃɪeɪt] *vi* officier ; **to ~ at a wedding** célébrer un mariage.
officious [ə'fɪʃəs] *adj* pej trop zélé(e).
offing ['ɒfɪŋ] *n* : **in the ~** en vue, en perspective.
off-key <> *adj* faux (fausse) <> *adv* faux.
off-licence *n* Br *magasin autorisé à vendre des boissons alcoolisées à emporter.*
off limits *adj* esp Am interdit(e).
off-line *adj* COMPUT non connecté(e).
offload [ɒf'ləʊd] *vt* inf : **to ~ sthg (onto sb)** se décharger de qqch (sur qqn).
off-peak <> *adj* [electricity] utilisé(e) aux heures creuses ; [fare] réduit(e) aux heures creuses <> *adv* [travel] aux heures creuses.
off-putting [-ˌpʊtɪŋ] *adj* désagréable, rébarbatif(ive).
off sales *npl* Br vente *f* de boissons alcoolisées à emporter.
off season *n* : **the ~** la morte-saison.
off-season *adj* hors saison.

offset [ˌɒf'set] (*pt* & *pp* offset, *cont* -ting) *vt* [losses] compenser.
offshoot ['ɒfʃuːt] *n* : **to be an ~ of sthg** être né(e) OR provenir de qqch.
offshore ['ɒfʃɔːr] <> *adj* [oil rig] offshore *(inv)* ; [island] proche de la côte ; [fishing] côtier(ère) <> *adv* au large.
offside [*adj* & *adv* ˌɒf'saɪd, *n* 'ɒfsaɪd] <> *adj* - **1.** [right-hand drive] de droite ; [left-hand drive] de gauche - **2.** SPORT hors-jeu *(inv)* <> *adv* SPORT hors-jeu <> *n* [right-hand drive] côté *m* droit ; [left-hand drive] côté gauche.
offspring ['ɒfsprɪŋ] (*pl* inv) *n* rejeton *m*.
offstage [ˌɒf'steɪdʒ] *adj* & *adv* dans les coulisses.
off-the-peg *adj* Br de prêt-à-porter.
off-the-record <> *adj* officieux(euse) <> *adv* confidentiellement.
off-the-wall *adj* inf loufoque.
off-white *adj* blanc cassé *(inv)*.
OFGAS ['ɒfgæs] (*abbr of* Office of Gas Supply) *n organisme britannique chargé de contrôler les activités des compagnies régionales de la distribution du gaz.*
OFLOT ['ɒflɒt] (*abbr of* Office of the National Lottery) *n organisme britannique chargé de contrôler la loterie nationale.*
OFSTED ['ɒfsted] (*abbr of* Office for Standards in Education) *n organisme britannique chargé de contrôler les établissements scolaires.*
OFT *abbr of* Office of Fair Trading.
OFTEL ['ɒftel] (*abbr of* Office of Telecommunications) *n organisme britannique chargé de contrôler les activités des compagnies de télécommunications.*
often ['ɒfn, 'ɒftn] *adv* souvent, fréquemment ; **how ~ do you visit her?** vous la voyez tous les combien? ; **as ~ as not** assez souvent ; **every so ~** de temps en temps ; **more ~ than not** le plus souvent, la plupart du temps.
OFWAT ['ɒfwɒt] (*abbr of* Office of Water Supply) *n organisme britannique chargé de contrôler les activités des compagnies régionales de la distribution de l'eau.*
ogle ['əʊgl] *vt* reluquer.
ogre ['əʊgər] *n* ogre *m*.
oh [əʊ] *excl* oh! ; [expressing hesitation] euh!
OH *abbr of* Ohio.
Ohio [əʊ'haɪəʊ] *n* Ohio *m* ; **in ~** dans l'Ohio.
ohm [əʊm] *n* ohm *m*.
OHMS (*abbr of* On His (or Her) Majesty's Service) *expression indiquant le caractère officiel d'un document en Grande-Bretagne.*

oil [ɔɪl] <> *n* - **1.** [gen] huile *f* - **2.** [for heating] mazout *m* - **3.** [petroleum] pétrole *m* <> *vt* graisser, lubrifier.
    oils *npl* ART huiles *fpl*.

oilcan [ˈɔɪlkæn] *n* burette *f* d'huile.

oil change *n* vidange *f*.

oilcloth [ˈɔɪlklɒθ] *n* toile *f* cirée.

oilfield [ˈɔɪlfiːld] *n* gisement *m* pétrolifère.

oil filter *n* filtre *m* à huile.

oil-fired [-ˌfaɪəd] *adj* au mazout.

oil industry *n* : the ~ l'industrie *f* pétrolière.

oilman [ˈɔɪlmən] (*pl* -**men** [-mən]) *n* pétrolier *m*.

oil paint *n* peinture *f* à l'huile (*produit*).

oil painting *n* peinture *f* à l'huile.

oilrig [ˈɔɪlrɪg] *n* [at sea] plate-forme *f* de forage *or* pétrolière ; [on land] derrick *m*.

oilskins [ˈɔɪlskɪnz] *npl* ciré *m*.

oil slick *n* marée *f* noire.

oil tanker *n* - **1.** [ship] pétrolier *m*, tanker *m* - **2.** [lorry] camion-citerne *m*.

oil well *n* puits *m* de pétrole.

oily [ˈɔɪlɪ] (*compar* -**ier** ; *superl* -**iest**) *adj* - **1.** [rag etc] graisseux(euse) ; [food] gras (grasse) - **2.** pej [smarmy] onctueux(euse), mielleux(euse).

ointment [ˈɔɪntmənt] *n* pommade *f*.

oiro (*abbr of* **offers in the region of**) : ~ £100 100 livres à débattre.

OK¹ (*pl* OKs, *pt* & *pp* OKed ; *cont* OKing), **okay** [ˌəʊˈkeɪ] inf <> *adj* : is it ~ with *or* by you? ça vous va?, vous êtes d'accord? ; are you ~? ça va? <> *n* : to give (sb) the ~ donner le feu vert (à qqn) <> *excl* - **1.** [expressing agreement] d'accord, O.K. - **2.** [to introduce new topic] : ~, can we start now? bon, on commence? <> *vt* approuver, donner le feu vert à.

OK² *abbr of* **Oklahoma**.

Oklahoma [ˌəʊkləˈhəʊmə] *n* Oklahoma *m* ; in ~ dans l'Oklahoma.

okra [ˈəʊkrə] *n* gombo *m*.

old [əʊld] <> *adj* - **1.** [gen] vieux (vieille), âgé(e) ; I'm 20 years ~ j'ai 20 ans ; how ~ are you? quel âge as-tu? - **2.** [former] ancien(enne) ; in the ~ days dans le temps, autrefois - **3.** inf [as intensifier] : any ~ n'importe quel (n'importe quelle) <> *npl* : the ~ les personnes *fpl* âgées.

old age *n* vieillesse *f*.

old age pension *n* Br pension *f* de vieillesse.

old age pensioner *n* Br retraité *m*, -e *f*.

Old Bailey [-ˈbeɪlɪ] *n* : the ~ la Cour d'assises de Londres.

olden [ˈəʊldn] *adj* literary : in the ~ days au temps jadis.

old-fashioned [-ˈfæʃnd] *adj* - **1.** [outmoded] démodé(e), passé(e) de mode - **2.** [traditional] vieux jeu (*inv*).

old flame *n* fig ancien flirt *m*.

old hat *adj* inf pej dépassé(e).

old maid *n* pej vieille fille *f*.

old master *n* - **1.** [painter] maître *m* - **2.** [painting] tableau *m* de maître.

old people's home *n* hospice *m* de vieillards.

Old Testament *n* : the ~ l'Ancien Testament *m*.

old-time *adj* d'autrefois.

old-timer *n* - **1.** [veteran] vieux routier *m*, vétéran *m* - **2.** esp Am [old man] vieillard *m*.

old wives' tale *n* histoires *fpl* de bonne femme.

Old World *n* : the ~ l'Ancien monde *m*.

O level *n* Br examen optionnel destiné, jusqu'en 1988, aux élèves de niveau seconde ayant obtenu de bons résultats.

oligarchy [ˈɒlɪgɑːkɪ] (*pl* -**ies**) *n* oligarchie *f*.

olive [ˈɒlɪv] <> *adj* olive (*inv*) <> *n* olive *f* ; ~ (tree) olivier *m*.

olive green *adj* vert olive (*inv*).

olive oil *n* huile *f* d'olive.

Olympic [əˈlɪmpɪk] *adj* olympique.
    Olympics *npl* : the ~s les Jeux *mpl* Olympiques.

Olympic Games *npl* : the ~ les Jeux *mpl* Olympiques.

OM (*abbr of* **Order of Merit**) *n* distinction honorifique britannique.

O & M (*abbr of* **organization and method**) *n* O et M.

Oman [əʊˈmɑːn] *n* Oman *m* ; in ~ à Oman.

OMB (*abbr of* **Office of Management and Budget**) *n* organisme fédéral américain chargé de préparer le budget.

ombudsman [ˈɒmbʊdzmən] (*pl* -**men** [-mən]) *n* ombudsman *m*.

omelet(te) [ˈɒmlɪt] *n* omelette *f* ; mushroom ~ omelette aux champignons.

omen [ˈəʊmen] *n* augure *m*, présage *m*.

ominous [ˈɒmɪnəs] *adj* [event, situation] de mauvais augure ; [sign] inquiétant(e) ; [look, silence] menaçant(e).

ominously [ˈɒmɪnəslɪ] *adv* [speak] d'un ton menaçant ; [happen, change] de façon inquiétante.

omission [ə'mɪʃn] n omission f.

omit [ə'mɪt] (pt & pp **-ted** ; cont **-ting**) vt omettre ; **to ~ to do sthg** oublier de faire qqch.

omnibus ['ɒmnɪbəs] n - **1.** [book] recueil m - **2.** Br RADIO & TV diffusion groupée des épisodes de la semaine.

omnipotence [ɒm'nɪpətəns] n omnipotence f.

omnipotent [ɒm'nɪpətənt] adj tout-puissant (toute-puissante), omnipotent(e).

omnipresent [ˌɒmnɪ'prezənt] adj omniprésent(e).

omniscient [ɒm'nɪsɪənt] adj omniscient(e).

omnivorous [ɒm'nɪvərəs] adj omnivore.

on [ɒn] <> prep - **1.** [indicating position, location] sur ; **~ a chair/the wall** sur une chaise/le mur ; **to stand ~ one leg** se tenir sur une jambe ; **~ the ceiling** au plafond ; **the information is ~ disk** l'information est sur disquette ; **she had a strange look ~ her face** elle avait une drôle d'expression ; **~the left/right** à gauche/droite - **2.** [indicating means] : **the car runs ~ petrol** la voiture marche à l'essence ; **to be shown ~ TV** passer à la télé ; **~ the radio** à la radio ; **~ the telephone** au téléphone ; **to live ~ fruit** vivre OR se nourrir de fruits ; **to hurt o.s. ~ sthg** se faire mal avec qqch - **3.** [indicating mode of transport] : **to travel ~ a bus/train/ship** voyager en bus/par le train/en bateau ; **I was ~ the bus** j'étais dans le bus ; **~ foot** à pied - **4.** [concerning] sur ; **a book ~ astronomy** un livre sur l'astronomie - **5.** [indicating time, activity] : **~ Thursday** jeudi ; **~ the 10th of February** le 10 février ; **~ my birthday** le jour de mon anniversaire ; **~ my return, ~ returning** à mon retour ; **~ holiday** en vacances ; **to be ~ night shift** être de nuit - **6.** [indicating influence] sur ; **the impact ~ the environment** l'impact sur l'environnement - **7.** [indicating membership] : **to be ~ a committee** faire partie OR être membre d'un comité - **8.** [using, supported by] : **to be ~ social security** recevoir l'aide sociale ; **he's ~ tranquillizers** il prend des tranquillisants ; **to be ~ drugs** se droguer - **9.** [earning] : **to be ~ £25,000 a year** gagner 25 000 livres par an ; **to be ~ a low income** avoir un faible revenu - **10.** [obtained from] : **interest ~ investments** intérêts de placements ; **a tax ~ alcohol** une taxe sur l'alcool - **11.** [referring to musical instrument] à ; **to play sthg ~ the violin/flute/guitar** jouer qqch au violon/à la flûte/à la guitare - **12.** inf [paid by] : **the drinks are ~ me** c'est moi qui régale, c'est ma tournée <> adv - **1.** [indicating covering, clothing] : **put the lid ~** mettez le couvercle ; **to put a sweater ~** mettre un pull ; **what did she have ~?** qu'est-ce qu'elle portait? ; **he had nothing ~** il était tout nu - **2.** [taking place] : **when the war was ~** quand c'était la guerre, pendant la guerre - **3.** [being shown] : **what's ~ at the Ritz?** qu'est-ce qu'on joue OR donne au Ritz? - **4.** [working - radio, TV, light] allumé(e) ; [- machine] en marche ; [- tap] ouvert(e) ; **turn ~ the power** mets le courant - **5.** [indicating continuing action] : **to work ~** continuer à travailler ; **we talked ~ into the night** nous avons parlé jusque tard dans la nuit ; **he kept ~ walking** il continua à marcher - **6.** [forward] : **send my mail ~ (to me)** faites suivre mon courrier ; **later ~** plus tard ; **earlier ~** plus tôt - **7.** [of transport] : **the train stopped and we all got ~** le train s'est arrêté et nous sommes tous montés - **8.** [referring to behaviour] : **it's just not ~!** cela ne se fait pas! - **9.** inf : **to be** OR **go ~ at sb (to do sthg)** harceler qqn (pour qu'il fasse qqch).

➤ **from ... on** adv : **from now ~** dorénavant, désormais ; **from then ~** à partir de ce moment-là.

➤ **on and on** adv : **to go ~ and ~ (about)** parler sans arrêt (de) ; **the list goes ~ and ~** la liste n'en finit plus.

➤ **on and off** adv de temps en temps ; **it happened ~ and off throughout the day** cela s'est produit par intervalles OR intermittence toute la journée.

➤ **on to, onto** prep (only written as onto for senses 4 and 5) - **1.** [to a position on top of] sur ; **she jumped ~ to the chair** elle a sauté sur la chaise - **2.** [to a position on a vehicle] dans ; **she got ~ to the bus** elle est montée dans le bus ; **he jumped ~ to his bicycle** il a sauté sur sa bicyclette - **3.** [to a position attached to] : **stick the photo ~ to the page with glue** colle la photo sur la page - **4.** [aware of wrongdoing] : **to be onto sb** être sur la piste de qqn - **5.** [in contact with] : **get onto the factory** contactez l'usine.

ON abbr of **Ontario.**

ONC (abbr of **Ordinary National Certificate**) n brevet de technicien en Grande-Bretagne.

once [wʌns] <> adv - **1.** [on one occasion] une fois ; **~ a day** une fois par jour ; **~ again** OR **more** encore une fois ; **~ and for all** une fois pour toutes ; **~ in a while** de temps en temps ; **~ or twice** une ou deux fois ; **for ~** pour une fois - **2.** [previously] autrefois, jadis ; **~ upon a time** il était une fois <> conj dès que.

➤ **at once** adv - **1.** [immediately] immédiate-

ment - **2.** [at the same time] en même temps ;
all at ~ tout d'un coup.

once-over n inf : **to give sb the ~** jauger qqn
d'un coup d'œil ; **to give sthg the ~** jeter un
coup d'œil à qqch.

oncoming [ˈɒnˌkʌmɪŋ] adj [traffic] venant en
sens inverse ; [danger] imminent(e).

OND (abbr of **Ordinary National Diploma**) n
brevet de technicien supérieur en Grande-
Bretagne.

one [wʌn] ◇ num [the number 1] un (une) ;
~ hundred cent ; **~ thousand** mille ; **page ~**
page un ; **~ of my friends** l'un de mes amis,
un ami à moi ; **~ fifth** un cinquième ; **in ~s
and twos** par petits groupes ◇ adj - **1.** [only]
seul(e), unique ; **it's her ~ ambition/love**
c'est son unique ambition/son seul amour
- **2.** [indefinite] : **~ day we went to Athens** un
jour nous sommes allés à Athènes ; **~ of
these days** un de ces jours - **3.** inf [a] : **I've got
~ awful hangover!** j'ai une de ces gueules
de bois! ; **~ hell of a bang** une détonation de
tous les diables ◇ pron - **1.** [referring to a particular thing or person] : **which ~ do you want?** lequel
voulez-vous? ; **this ~** celui-ci ; **that ~** celui-
là ; **the ~ I told you about** c'est celle
dont je vous ai parlé ; **I'm not** OR **I've never
been ~ to gossip but ...** je ne suis pas du genre à cancaner, mais ... - **2.** inf [blow] coup m ;
she really thumped him ~ elle lui a flanqué
un de ces coups - **3.** fml [you, anyone] on ; **to do
~'s duty** faire son devoir.
◆ **at one** adv : **to be at ~ with sb/sthg** être
d'accord avec qqn/en accord avec qqch.
◆ **for one** adv pour ma/sa etc part ; **I for
~ remain unconvinced** pour ma part je ne
suis pas convaincu.
◆ **one up on** adv : **to be** OR **have ~ up on sb**
avoir l'avantage sur qqn.

one-armed bandit n machine f à sous.

one-liner n bon mot m.

one-man adj [business] dirigé(e) par un seul
homme ; **~ show** one-man show m inv,
spectacle solo m.

one-man band n - **1.** [musician] homme-
orchestre m - **2.** fig [business] entreprise f dirigée par un seul homme.

oneness [ˈwʌnnɪs] n (U) [harmony] accord m,
harmonie f.

one-night stand n - **1.** THEATRE représentation f unique - **2.** inf [sexual relationship] aventure f d'un soir.

one-off inf ◇ adj [offer, event, product] unique
◇ n : **a ~** [product] un exemplaire unique ;
[event] un événement unique.

one-on-one Am = one-to-one.

one-parent family n famille f monoparentale.

one-piece adj [swimsuit] une pièce (inv).

onerous [ˈɔːnərəs] adj [task] pénible ; [responsi-
bility] lourd(e), pesant(e).

oneself [wʌnˈself] pron - **1.** (reflexive) se ;
(after prep) soi - **2.** (emphatic) soi-même.

one-sided [-ˈsaɪdɪd] adj - **1.** [unequal] inégal(e)
- **2.** [biased] partial(e).

onetime [ˈwʌntaɪm] adj ancien(enne).

one-to-one Br, **one-on-one** Am adj [discus-
sion] en tête à tête ; **~ tuition** cours mpl particuliers.

one-upmanship [ˌwʌnˈʌpmənʃɪp] n art m
de faire toujours mieux que les autres.

one-way adj - **1.** [street] à sens unique
- **2.** [ticket] simple.

ongoing [ˈɒnˌɡəʊɪŋ] adj en cours, conti-
nu(e).

onion [ˈʌnjən] n oignon m.

online [ˈɒnlaɪn] adj & adv COMPUT en ligne,
connecté(e).

onlooker [ˈɒnˌlʊkəʳ] n spectateur m, -trice f.

only [ˈəʊnlɪ] ◇ adj seul(e), unique ; **an ~ child**
un enfant unique ◇ adv - **1.** [gen] ne ... que,
seulement ; **he ~ reads science fiction** il ne lit
que de la science fiction ; **it's ~ a scratch**
c'est juste une égratignure ; **he left ~ a few
minutes ago** il est parti il n'y a pas deux minutes - **2.** [for emphasis] : **I ~ wish I could** je voudrais bien ; **it's ~ natural (that) ...** c'est tout à
fait normal que ... ; **I was ~ too willing to help**
je ne demandais qu'à aider ; **not ~ ... but
also** non seulement ... mais encore ; **I ~ just
caught the train** j'ai eu le train de justesse
◇ conj seulement, mais ; **he looks like his
brother, ~ smaller** il ressemble à son frère,
mais en plus petit.

o.n.o., ono (abbr of **or near(est) offer**) à
déb.

onrush [ˈɒnrʌʃ] n [of emotion] vague f, montée
f.

on-screen adj & adv COMPUT à l'écran.

onset [ˈɒnset] n début m, commencement m.

onshore [ˈɒnʃɔːʳ] adj & adv [from sea] du large ; [on land] à terre.

onside [ɒnˈsaɪd] adj & adv SPORT en jeu.

onslaught [ˈɒnslɔːt] n attaque f.

Ont. abbr of **Ontario.**

Ontario [ɒnˈteərɪəʊ] n Ontario m ; **in ~** dans
l'Ontario.

on-the-job adj [training] sur le tas.

on-the-spot adj [interview] sur place.

onto [unstressed before consonant ˈɒntə , un-

stressed before vowel 'ɒntʊ , *stressed* 'ɒntu:]
= **on to.**

onus ['ɔunəs] *n* responsabilité *f*, charge *f*.

onward ['ɒnwəd] *adj* & *adv* en avant.

onwards ['ɒnwədz] *adv* en avant ; **from now ~** dorénavant, désormais ; **from then ~** à partir de ce moment-là.

onyx ['ɒnɪks] *n* onyx *m*.

oodles ['u:dlz] *npl* *inf* : **~ of** plein de, un tas de.

oof [ʊf] *excl inf* ouïe!, ouille!, aïe!

ooh [u:] *excl inf* oh!

oops [ʊps, u:ps] *excl inf* houp!, hop là!

ooze [u:z] ◇ *vt fig* [charm, confidence] respirer ◇ *vi* : **to ~ from** OR **out of sthg** suinter de qqch ◇ *n* vase *f*.

opacity [ə'pæsətɪ] *n* opacité *f* ; *fig* obscurité *f*.

opal ['ɔupl] *n* [gem] opale *f*.

opaque [ɔu'peɪk] *adj* opaque ; *fig* obscur(e).

OPEC ['ɔupek] (*abbr of* **Organization of Petroleum Exporting Countries**) *n* OPEP *f*.

open ['ɔupn] ◇ *adj* - **1.** [gen] ouvert(e) - **2.** [receptive] : **to be ~ (to)** être réceptif(ive) (à) ; **to lay o.s. ~ to criticism** s'exposer aux critiques - **3.** [view, road, space] dégagé(e) - **4.** [uncovered - car] découvert(e) ; **an ~ fire** un feu de cheminée - **5.** [meeting] public(ique) ; [competition] ouvert(e) à tous - **6.** [disbelief, honesty] manifeste, évident(e) - **7.** [unresolved] non résolu(e) ◇ *n* : **in the ~** [sleep] à la belle étoile ; [eat] au grand air ; **to bring sthg out into the ~** divulguer qqch, exposer qqch au grand jour ◇ *vt* - **1.** [gen] ouvrir - **2.** [inaugurate] inaugurer ◇ *vi* - **1.** [door, flower] s'ouvrir - **2.** [shop, library etc] ouvrir - **3.** [meeting, play etc] commencer.

➤ **open on to** *vt fus* [subj : room, door] donner sur.

➤ **open out** *vi* [road, river] s'élargir.

➤ **open up** ◇ *vt sep* [develop] exploiter, développer ◇ *vi* - **1.** [possibilities etc] s'offrir, se présenter - **2.** [unlock door] ouvrir.

open-air *adj* en plein air.

open-and-shut *adj* clair(e), évident(e).

opencast ['ɔupnkɑ:st] *adj* [mining] à ciel ouvert.

open day *n* journée *f* portes ouvertes.

open-ended [-'endɪd] *adj* [meeting] sans limite de durée.

opener ['ɔupnə'] *n* [for cans] ouvre-boîtes *m inv* ; [for bottles] ouvre-bouteilles *m inv*, décapsuleur *m*.

open-handed [-'hændɪd] *adj* généreux(euse).

openhearted [,ɔupn'hɑ:tɪd] *adj* franc (franche).

open-heart surgery *n* chirurgie *f* à cœur ouvert.

opening ['ɔupnɪŋ] ◇ *adj* [first] premier(ère) ; [remarks] préliminaire ◇ *n* - **1.** [beginning] commencement *m*, début *m* - **2.** [in fence] trou *m*, percée *f* ; [in clouds] trouée *f*, déchirure *f* - **3.** [opportunity - gen] occasion *f* ; [- COMM] débouché *m* - **4.** [job vacancy] poste *m*.

opening hours *npl* heures *fpl* d'ouverture.

opening night *n* première *f*.

opening time *n* Br [of pub] heure *f* d'ouverture.

open letter *n* lettre *f* ouverte.

openly ['ɔupnlɪ] *adv* ouvertement, franchement.

open market *n* marché *m* libre.

open marriage *n* mariage *m* moderne (*où chacun est libre d'avoir des aventures*).

open-minded [-'maɪndɪd] *adj* [person] qui a l'esprit large ; [attitude] large.

open-mouthed [-'maʊðd] *adj* & *adv* bouche bée (*inv*).

open-necked [-'nekt] *adj* à col ouvert.

openness ['ɔupnnɪs] *n* [frankness] franchise *f*.

open-plan *adj* non cloisonné(e).

open prison *n* prison *f* ouverte.

open sandwich *n* canapé *m*.

open season *n* saison *f* de la chasse.

open shop *n* *absence de monopole syndical*.

Open University *n* Br : **the ~** ≃ centre *m* national d'enseignement à distance.

open verdict *n* JUR *jugement qui enregistre un décès sans en préciser la cause*.

opera ['ɒpərə] *n* opéra *m*.

opera glasses *npl* jumelles *fpl* de théâtre.

opera house *n* opéra *m*.

opera singer *n* chanteur *m*, -euse *f* d'opéra.

operate ['ɒpəreɪt] ◇ *vt* - **1.** [machine] faire marcher, faire fonctionner - **2.** COMM diriger ◇ *vi* - **1.** [rule, law, system] jouer, être appliqué(e) ; [machine] fonctionner, marcher - **2.** COMM opérer, travailler - **3.** MED opérer ; **to ~ on sb/sthg** opérer qqn/de qqch.

operatic [,ɒpə'rætɪk] *adj* d'opéra.

operating room ['ɒpəreɪtɪŋ-] *n* Am salle *f* d'opération.

operating system ['ɒpəreɪtɪŋ-] *n* COMPUT système *m* d'exploitation.

operating theatre Br, **operating room** Am ['ɒpəreɪtɪŋ-] *n* salle *f* d'opération.

operation [ˌɒpə'reɪʃn] n - **1.** [gen & MED] opération f; **to have an ~ (for)** se faire opérer (de) - **2.** [of machine] marche f, fonctionnement m; **to be in ~** [machine] être en marche OR en service ; [law, system] être en vigueur - **3.** [COMM - company] exploitation f; [- management] administration f, gestion f.

operational [ˌɒpə'reɪʃənl] adj - **1.** [machine] en état de marche - **2.** [difficulty, costs] d'exploitation.

operative ['ɒprətɪv] ⇔ adj en vigueur ⇔ n ouvrier m, -ère f.

operator ['ɒpəreɪtəʳ] n - **1.** TELEC standardiste mf - **2.** [of machine] opérateur m, -trice f - **3.** COMM directeur m, -trice f.

operetta [ˌɒpə'retə] n opérette f.

ophthalmic optician [ɒf'θælmɪk-] n opticien m, -enne f.

ophthalmologist [ˌɒfθæl'mɒlədʒɪst] n ophtalmologue mf, ophtalmologiste mf.

opinion [ə'pɪnjən] n opinion f, avis m; **to be of the ~ that** être d'avis que, estimer que ; **in my ~** à mon avis.

opinionated [ə'pɪnjəneɪtɪd] adj pej dogmatique.

opinion poll n sondage m d'opinion.

opium ['əʊpjəm] n opium m.

opponent [ə'pəʊnənt] n adversaire mf.

opportune ['ɒpətjuːn] adj opportun(e).

opportunism [ˌɒpə'tjuːnɪzm] n opportunisme m.

opportunist [ˌɒpə'tjuːnɪst] n opportuniste mf.

opportunity [ˌɒpə'tjuːnətɪ] (pl -ies) n occasion f; **to take the ~ to do** OR **of doing sthg** profiter de l'occasion pour faire qqch ; **to get the ~** avoir l'occasion.

oppose [ə'pəʊz] vt s'opposer à.

opposed [ə'pəʊzd] adj opposé(e) ; **to be ~ to** être contre, être opposé à ; **as ~ to** par opposition à.

opposing [ə'pəʊzɪŋ] adj opposé(e).

opposite ['ɒpəzɪt] ⇔ adj opposé(e) ; [house] d'en face ⇔ adv en face ⇔ prep en face de ⇔ n contraire m.

opposite number n homologue mf.

opposite sex n : **the ~** le sexe opposé.

opposition [ˌɒpə'zɪʃn] n - **1.** [gen] opposition f - **2.** [opposing team] adversaire mf.
➤ **Opposition** n Br POL : **the Opposition** l'opposition.

oppress [ə'pres] vt - **1.** [persecute] opprimer - **2.** [depress] oppresser.

oppressed [ə'prest] ⇔ adj opprimé(e) ⇔ npl : **the ~** les opprimés mpl.

oppression [ə'preʃn] n oppression f.

oppressive [ə'presɪv] adj - **1.** [unjust] oppressif(ive) - **2.** [weather, heat] étouffant(e), lourd(e) - **3.** [silence] oppressant(e).

oppressor [ə'presəʳ] n oppresseur m.

opprobrium [ə'prəʊbrɪəm] n opprobre m.

opt [ɒpt] ⇔ vt : **to ~ to do sthg** choisir de faire qqch ⇔ vi : **to ~ for** opter pour.
➤ **opt in** vi : **to ~ in (to)** choisir de participer (à).
➤ **opt out** vi : **to ~ out (of)** [gen] choisir de ne pas participer (à) ; [of responsibility] se dérober (à) ; [of NHS] ne plus faire partie (de).

optic ['ɒptɪk] adj optique.

optical ['ɒptɪkl] adj optique.

optical character reader n COMPUT lecteur m optique de caractères.

optical character recognition n COMPUT reconnaissance f optique de caractères.

optical fibre n TELEC fibre f optique.

optical illusion n illusion f d'optique.

optician [ɒp'tɪʃn] n - **1.** [who sells glasses] opticien m, -enne f - **2.** [ophthalmologist] ophtalmologiste mf.

optics ['ɒptɪks] n (U) optique f.

optimism ['ɒptɪmɪzm] n optimisme m.

optimist ['ɒptɪmɪst] n optimiste mf.

optimistic [ˌɒptɪ'mɪstɪk] adj optimiste ; **to be ~ about** être optimiste pour.

optimize, -ise ['ɒptɪmaɪz] vt optimaliser.

optimum ['ɒptɪməm] adj optimum.

option ['ɒpʃn] n option f, choix m; **she had no ~ but to pay up** elle n'a pas pu faire autrement que de payer ; **to have the ~ to do** OR **of doing sthg** pouvoir faire qqch, avoir la possibilité de faire qqch.

optional ['ɒpʃənl] adj facultatif(ive) ; **an ~ extra** un accessoire.

opulence ['ɒpjʊləns] n - **1.** [wealth] opulence f - **2.** [sumptuousness] magnificence f.

opulent ['ɒpjʊlənt] adj - **1.** [wealthy] opulent(e) - **2.** [sumptuous] magnifique.

opus ['əʊpəs] (pl -es [-iːz] OR **opera** ['ɒpərə]) n MUS opus m.

or [ɔːʳ] conj - **1.** [gen] ou - **2.** [after negative] : **he can't read ~ write** il ne sait ni lire ni écrire - **3.** [otherwise] sinon - **4.** [as correction] ou plutôt.

OR abbr of Oregon.

oracle ['ɒrəkl] n [prophet] oracle m.

oral ['ɔːrəl] ⇔ adj - **1.** [spoken] oral(e) - **2.** [MED - medicine] par voie orale, par la bouche ; [- hygiene] buccal(e) ◇ n oral m, épreuve f orale.

orally ['ɔːrəlɪ] adv - **1.** [in spoken form] oralement - **2.** MED par voie orale.

orange ['ɒrɪndʒ] ◇ adj orange (inv) ◇ n - **1.** [fruit] orange f - **2.** [colour] orange m.

orangeade [,ɒrɪndʒ'eɪd] n orangeade f.

orange blossom n (U) fleur f d'oranger.

Orangeman ['ɒrɪndʒmən] (pl -men [-mən]) n Br orangiste m.

orangutang [ɔː,ræŋuː'tæŋ] n orang-outang m.

oration [ɔː'reɪʃn] n fml discours m.

orator ['ɒrətər] n orateur m, -trice f.

oratorio [,ɒrə'tɔːrɪəʊ] (pl -s) n oratorio m.

oratory ['ɒrətrɪ] n art m oratoire, éloquence f.

orb [ɔːb] n globe m.

orbit ['ɔːbɪt] ◇ n orbite f ; to be in/go into ~ (around) être/entrer sur orbite (autour de), être/entrer en orbite (autour de) ◇ vt décrire une orbite autour de.

orchard ['ɔːtʃəd] n verger m ; apple ~ champ m de pommiers, pommeraie f.

orchestra ['ɔːkɪstrə] n orchestre m.

orchestral [ɔː'kestrəl] adj orchestral(e).

orchestra pit n fosse f d'orchestre.

orchestrate ['ɔːkɪstreɪt] vt lit & fig orchestrer.

orchestration [,ɔːke'streɪʃn] n lit & fig orchestration f.

orchid ['ɔːkɪd] n orchidée f.

ordain [ɔː'deɪn] vt - **1.** [decree] ordonner, décréter - **2.** RELIG : to be ~ed être ordonné prêtre.

ordeal [ɔː'diːl] n épreuve f.

order ['ɔːdər] ◇ n - **1.** [gen] ordre m ; to be under ~s to do sthg avoir (reçu) l'ordre de faire qqch - **2.** COMM commande f ; to place an ~ with sb for sthg passer une commande de qqch à qqn ; on ~ commandé ; to ~ sur commande - **3.** [sequence] ordre m ; in ~ dans l'ordre ; in ~ of importance par ordre d'importance - **4.** [fitness for use] : in working ~ en état de marche ; out of ~ [machine] en panne ; [behaviour] déplacé(e) ; in ~ [correct] en ordre - **5.** (U) [discipline - gen] ordre m ; [- in classroom] discipline f ; to keep ~ maintenir l'ordre - **6.** Am [portion] part f ◇ vt - **1.** [command] ordonner ; to ~ sb to do sthg ordonner à qqn de faire qqch ; to ~ that ordonner que - **2.** COMM commander ◇ vi commander.
◆ **orders** npl RELIG : to take holy ~s entrer dans les ordres.

◆ **in the order of** Br, **on the order of** Am adv environ, de l'ordre de.

◆ **in order that** conj pour que, afin que (+ subjunctive).

◆ **in order to** conj pour, afin de.

◆ **order about, order around** vt sep commander.

order book n carnet m de commandes.

order form n bulletin m de commande.

orderly ['ɔːdəlɪ] (pl -ies) ◇ adj [person] ordonné(e) ; [crowd] discipliné(e) ; [office, room] en ordre ◇ n [in hospital] garçon m de salle.

order number n numéro m de commande.

ordinal ['ɔːdɪnl] ◇ adj ordinal(e) ◇ n nombre m ordinal.

ordinarily ['ɔːdənrəlɪ] adv d'habitude, d'ordinaire.

ordinary ['ɔːdənrɪ] ◇ adj - **1.** [normal] ordinaire - **2.** pej [unexceptional] ordinaire, quelconque ◇ n : out of the ~ qui sort de l'ordinaire, exceptionnel(elle).

ordinary level n Br ≃ brevet m des collèges.

ordinary seaman n Br simple matelot m.

ordinary shares npl Br FIN actions fpl ordinaires.

ordination [,ɔːdɪ'neɪʃn] n ordination f.

ordnance ['ɔːdnəns] n (U) - **1.** [supplies] matériel m militaire - **2.** [artillery] artillerie f.

Ordnance Survey n service cartographique national en Grande-Bretagne, ≃ IGN m.

ore [ɔːr] n minerai m.

oregano [,ɒrɪ'gɑːnəʊ] n origan m.

Oregon ['ɒrɪgən] n Oregon m ; in ~ dans l'Oregon.

organ ['ɔːgən] n - **1.** [gen] organe m - **2.** MUS orgue m.

organic [ɔː'gænɪk] adj - **1.** [of animals, plants] organique - **2.** [farming, food] biologique - **3.** fig [development] naturel(elle).

organically [ɔː'gænɪklɪ] adv [farm, grow] sans engrais chimiques.

organic chemistry n chimie f organique.

organism ['ɔːgənɪzm] n organisme m.

organist ['ɔːgənɪst] n organiste mf.

organization [,ɔːgənaɪ'zeɪʃn] n organisation f.

organizational [,ɔːgənaɪ'zeɪʃnl] adj - **1.** [structure, links] organisationnel(elle) - **2.** [skill] d'organisation.

organization chart n organigramme m.

organize, -ise ['ɔːgənaɪz] ◇ vt organiser ◇ vi [workers] se syndiquer.

organized ['ɔːgənaɪzd] *adj* organisé(e).

organized crime *n* crime *m* organisé.

organized labour *n* main d'œuvre *f* syndiquée.

organizer ['ɔːgənaɪzə'] *n* - **1.** [person] organisateur *m*, -trice *f* - **2.** [diary] organiseur *m*.

organza [ɔː'gænzə] *n* organza *m*.

orgasm ['ɔːgæzm] *n* orgasme *m*.

orgy ['ɔːdʒɪ] (*pl* -**ies**) *n* lit & fig orgie *f*.

orient ['ɔːrɪənt] = **orientate**.

Orient ['ɔːrɪənt] *n :* the ~ l'Orient *m*.

oriental [ˌɔːrɪ'entl] ⬦ *adj* oriental(e) ⬦ *n* Oriental *m*, -e *f* (*attention : le terme 'oriental' est considéré raciste*).

orientate ['ɔːrɪenteɪt] *vt :* to be ~d towards viser, s'adresser à ; **to ~ o.s.** s'orienter.

orientation [ˌɔːrɪen'teɪʃn] *n* orientation *f*.

orienteering [ˌɔːrɪən'tɪərɪŋ] *n (U)* course *f* d'orientation.

orifice ['ɒrɪfɪs] *n* orifice *m*.

origami [ˌɒrɪ'gɑːmɪ] *n* origami *m*.

origin ['ɒrɪdʒɪn] *n* - **1.** [of river] source *f;* [of word, conflict] origine *f* - **2.** [birth] : **country of ~** pays *m* d'origine.

➡ **origins** *npl* origines *fpl*.

original [ə'rɪdʒənl] ⬦ *adj* original(e) ; [owner] premier(ère) ⬦ *n* original *m*.

originality [əˌrɪdʒə'nælətɪ] *n* originalité *f*.

originally [ə'rɪdʒənəlɪ] *adv* à l'origine, au départ.

original sin *n* péché *m* originel.

originate [ə'rɪdʒəneɪt] ⬦ *vt* être l'auteur de, être à l'origine de ⬦ *vi* [belief, custom] : **to ~ (in)** prendre naissance (dans) ; **to ~ from** provenir de.

origination [əˌrɪdʒə'neɪʃn] *n (U)* origine *f*.

originator [ə'rɪdʒəneɪtə'] *n* auteur *m*, initiateur *m*, -trice *f*.

Orinoco [ˌɒrɪ'nəʊkəʊ] *n :* the (River) ~ l'Orénoque *m*.

Orkney Islands ['ɔːknɪ-], **Orkneys** ['ɔːknɪz] *npl :* the ~ les Orcades *fpl ;* in the ~s dans les Orcades.

ornament ['ɔːnəmənt] *n* - **1.** [object] bibelot *m* - **2.** *(U)* [decoration] ornement *m*.

ornamental [ˌɔːnə'mentl] *adj* [garden, pond] d'agrément ; [design] décoratif(ive).

ornamentation [ˌɔːnəmen'teɪʃn] *n* décoration *f*.

ornate [ɔː'neɪt] *adj* orné(e).

ornately [ɔː'neɪtlɪ] *adv* avec beaucoup d'ornements.

ornery ['ɔːnərɪ] *adj* Am inf désagréable.

ornithologist [ˌɔːnɪ'θɒlədʒɪst] *n* ornithologue *mf*, ornithologiste *mf*.

ornithology [ˌɔːnɪ'θɒlədʒɪ] *n* ornithologie *f*.

orphan ['ɔːfn] ⬦ *n* orphelin *m*, -e *f* ⬦ *vt :* **to be ~ed** devenir orphelin(e).

orphanage ['ɔːfənɪdʒ] *n* orphelinat *m*.

orthodontist [ˌɔːθə'dɒntɪst] *n* orthodontiste *mf*.

orthodox ['ɔːθədɒks] *adj* - **1.** [conventional] orthodoxe - **2.** RELIG [traditional] traditionaliste.

Orthodox Church *n :* the ~ l'Église *f* orthodoxe.

orthodoxy ['ɔːθədɒksɪ] *n* orthodoxie *f*.

orthopaedic [ˌɔːθə'piːdɪk] *adj* orthopédique.

orthopaedics [ˌɔːθə'piːdɪks] *n (U)* orthopédie *f*.

orthopaedist [ˌɔːθə'piːdɪst] *n* orthopédiste *mf*.

orthopedic *etc* [ˌɔːθə'piːdɪk] = **orthopaedic** *etc*.

OS ⬦ *n* (*abbr of* **Ordnance Survey**) ≃ IGN *m* ⬦ *abbr of* **outsize**.

O/S *abbr of* **out of stock**.

Oscar ['ɒskə'] *n* CINEMA Oscar *m*.

oscillate ['ɒsɪleɪt] *vi* lit & fig osciller.

oscilloscope [ɒ'sɪləskəʊp] *n* oscilloscope *m*.

OSD (*abbr of* **optical scanning device**) *n* lecteur optique.

OSHA (*abbr of* **Occupational Safety and Health Administration**) *n* direction de la sécurité et de l'hygiène au travail aux États-Unis.

Oslo ['ɒzləʊ] *n* Oslo.

osmosis [ɒz'məʊsɪs] *n* osmose *f*.

osprey ['ɒsprɪ] (*pl* -**s**) *n* balbuzard *m*.

Ostend [ɒs'tend] *n* Ostende.

ostensible [ɒ'stensəbl] *adj* prétendu(e).

ostensibly [ɒ'stensəblɪ] *adv* en apparence, soi-disant.

ostentation [ˌɒstən'teɪʃn] *n* ostentation *f*.

ostentatious [ˌɒstən'teɪʃəs] *adj* ostentatoire.

osteoarthritis [ˌɒstɪəʊɑː'θraɪtɪs] *n (U)* ostéoarthrose *f*.

osteopath ['ɒstɪəpæθ] *n* ostéopathe *mf*.

osteopathy [ˌɒstɪ'ɒpəθɪ] *n* ostéopathie *f*.

osteoporosis [ˌɒstɪəpɔː'rəʊsɪs] *n* ostéoporose *f*.

ostracize, -ise ['ɒstrəsaɪz] *vt* frapper d'ostracisme, mettre au ban.

ostrich ['ɒstrɪtʃ] *n* autruche *f*.

OT *n* - **1.** (*abbr of* Old Testament) AT *m* - **2.** *abbr of* occupational therapy.

OTC (*abbr of* Officer Training Corps) *n* section de formation des officiers en Grande-Bretagne.

other [ˈʌðəʳ] ◇ *adj* autre ; **the ~ one** l'autre ; **the ~ day/week** l'autre jour/semaine ◇ *adv :* **there was nothing to do ~ than confess** il ne pouvait faire autrement que d'avouer ; **~ than John** John à part ◇ *pron :* **~s** d'autres ; **the ~ l**'autre ; **the ~s** les autres ; **one after the ~** l'un après l'autre (l'une après l'autre) ; **one or ~ of you** l'un (l'une) de vous deux ; **none ~ than** nul (nulle) autre que.

➡ **something or other** *pron* quelque chose, je ne sais quoi.

➡ **somehow or other** *adv* d'une manière ou d'une autre.

otherwise [ˈʌðəwaɪz] ◇ *adv* autrement ; **or ~** [or not] ou non ◇ *conj* sinon.

other world *n :* **the ~** l'au-delà *m*.

otherworldly [ˌʌðəˈwɜːldlɪ] *adj* détaché(e) des biens de ce monde.

OTT (*abbr of* over the top) *adj* Br *inf :* **it's a bit ~** c'est un peu trop.

Ottawa [ˈɒtəwə] *n* Ottawa.

otter [ˈɒtəʳ] *n* loutre *f*.

OU *abbr of* Open University.

ouch [aʊtʃ] *excl* aïe!, ouïe!

ought [ɔːt] *aux vb* - **1.** [sensibly] : **I really ~ to go** il faut absolument que je m'en aille ; **you ~ to see a doctor** tu devrais aller chez le docteur - **2.** [morally] : **you ~ not to have done that** tu n'aurais pas dû faire cela ; **you ~ to look after your children better** tu devrais t'occuper un peu mieux de tes enfants - **3.** [expressing probability] : **she ~ to pass her exam** elle devrait réussir à son examen.

oughtn't [ˈɔːtnt] = ought not.

Ouija board® [ˈwiːdʒə-] *n* oui-ja *m*.

ounce [aʊns] *n* = 28,35 g, once *f*.

our [aʊəʳ] *poss adj* notre, nos *(pl)* ; **~ money/house** notre argent/maison ; **~ children** nos enfants ; **it wasn't OUR fault** ce n'était pas de notre faute à nous

ours [aʊəz] *poss pron* le nôtre (la nôtre), les nôtres *(pl)* ; **that money is ~** cet argent est à nous OR est le nôtre ; **it wasn't their fault, it was OURS** ce n'était pas de leur faute, c'était de notre faute à nous OR de la nôtre ; **a friend of ~** un ami à nous, un de nos amis.

ourselves [aʊəˈselvz] *pron pl* - **1.** (*reflexive*) nous - **2.** (*for emphasis*) nous-mêmes ; **we did it by ~** nous l'avons fait tout seuls.

oust [aʊst] *vt :* **to ~ sb (from)** évincer qqn (de).

ouster [ˈaʊstəʳ] *n* Am [from country] expulsion *f ;* [from office] renvoi *m*.

out [aʊt] *adv* - **1.** [not inside, out of doors] dehors ; **we all got ~** [of car] nous sommes tous sortis ; **I'm going ~ for a walk** je sors me promener ; **to run ~** sortir en courant ; **~ here** ici ; **~ there** là-bas ; **~ you go!** sors!, file! - **2.** [away from home, office, published] sorti(e) ; **John's ~ at the moment** John est sorti, John n'est pas là en ce moment ; **don't stay ~ too late** ne rentre pas trop tard ; **an afternoon ~** une sortie l'après-midi ; **let's have an evening ~** et si on sortait ce soir? - **3.** [extinguished] éteint(e) ; **the lights went ~** les lumières se sont éteintes - **4.** [of tides] : **the tide is ~** la marée est basse - **5.** [out of fashion] démodé(e), passé(e) de mode - **6.** [in flower] en fleur ; **the crocuses are ~** les crocus sont sortis - **7.** [visible - moon] levé(e) ; **the sun is ~** il fait du soleil ; **the stars are ~** les étoiles brillent - **8.** *inf* [on strike] en grève - **9.** [not possible] : **sorry, that's ~** désolé, cela ne va pas OR n'est pas possible - **10.** [determined] : **to be ~ to do sthg** être résolu(e) OR décidé(e) à faire qqch.

➡ **out of** *prep* - **1.** [outside] en dehors de ; **to go ~ of the room** sortir de la pièce ; **to be ~ of the country** être à l'étranger - **2.** [indicating cause] par ; **~ of spite/love/boredom** par dépit/amour/ennui - **3.** [indicating origin, source] de, dans ; **a page ~ of a book** une page d'un livre ; **to drink ~ of a glass** boire dans un verre ; **to get information ~ of sb** arracher OR soutirer des renseignements à qqn ; **it's made ~ of plastic** c'est en plastique ; **we can pay for it ~ of petty cash** on peut le payer avec l'argent des dépenses courantes - **4.** [without] sans ; **~ of petrol/money** à court d'essence/d'argent ; **we're ~ of sugar** nous n'avons plus de sucre - **5.** [sheltered from] à l'abri de ; **we're ~ of the wind here** nous sommes à l'abri du vent ici - **6.** [to indicate proportion] sur ; **one ~ of ten people** une personne sur dix ; **ten ~ of ten** dix sur dix.

out-and-out *adj* [liar] fieffé(e) ; [disgrace] complet(ète).

outback [ˈaʊtbæk] *n :* **the ~** l'intérieur *m* du pays (*en Australie*).

outbid [aʊtˈbɪd] (*pt & pp* outbid ; *cont* -ding) *vt :* **to ~ sb (for)** enchérir sur qqn (pour).

outboard (motor) [ˈaʊtbɔːd-] *n* (moteur *m*) hors-bord *m*.

outbound [ˈaʊtbaʊnd] *adj* [train, flight] en partance.

outbreak ['aʊtbreɪk] n [of war, crime] début m, déclenchement m ; [of spots etc] éruption f.

outbuildings ['aʊtbɪldɪŋz] npl dépendances fpl.

outburst ['aʊtbɜːst] n explosion f.

outcast ['aʊtkɑːst] n paria m.

outclass [ˌaʊt'klɑːs] vt surclasser.

outcome ['aʊtkʌm] n issue f, résultat m.

outcrop ['aʊtkrɒp] n affleurement m.

outcry ['aʊtkraɪ] (pl -ies) n tollé m.

outdated [ˌaʊt'deɪtɪd] adj démodé(e), vieilli(e).

outdid [ˌaʊt'dɪd] pt ▷ outdo.

outdistance [ˌaʊt'dɪstəns] vt lit & fig distancer.

outdo [ˌaʊt'duː] (pt -did ; pp -done [-'dʌn]) vt surpasser.

outdoor ['aʊtdɔːr] adj [life, swimming pool] en plein air ; [activities] de plein air.

outdoors [aʊt'dɔːz] adv dehors.

outer ['aʊtər] adj extérieur(e) ; **Outer London** la grande banlieue de Londres.

Outer Mongolia n Mongolie-Extérieure f.

outermost ['aʊtəməʊst] adj [area] le plus éloigné (la plus éloignée) ; [layer] le plus (la plus) à l'extérieur.

outer space n cosmos m.

outfit ['aʊtfɪt] n - **1.** [clothes] tenue f - **2.** inf [organization] équipe f.

outfitters ['aʊtˌfɪtəz] n Br dated [for clothes] magasin m spécialisé de confection pour hommes.

outflank [ˌaʊt'flæŋk] vt MIL déborder, prendre à revers ; fig déjouer les manœuvres de.

outgoing ['aʊtˌgəʊɪŋ] adj - **1.** [chairman etc] sortant(e) ; [mail] à expédier ; [train] en partance - **2.** [friendly, sociable] ouvert(e).

→ **outgoings** npl Br dépenses fpl.

outgrow [ˌaʊt'grəʊ] (pt -grew ; pp -grown) vt - **1.** [clothes] devenir trop grand(e) pour - **2.** [habit] se défaire de.

outhouse ['aʊthaʊs, pl -haʊzɪz] n appentis m.

outing ['aʊtɪŋ] n - **1.** [trip] sortie f - **2.** [of homosexuals] campagne, menée par des militants homosexuels, destinée à dévoiler l'homosexualité d'une personne publique.

outlandish [aʊt'lændɪʃ] adj bizarre.

outlast [ˌaʊt'lɑːst] vt survivre à.

outlaw ['aʊtlɔː] ◇ n hors-la-loi m inv ◇ vt - **1.** [practice] proscrire - **2.** [person] mettre hors la loi.

outlay ['aʊtleɪ] n dépenses fpl.

outlet ['aʊtlet] n - **1.** [for emotion] exutoire m - **2.** [hole, pipe] sortie f - **3.** [shop] : retail ~ point m de vente - **4.** Am ELEC prise f (de courant).

outline ['aʊtlaɪn] ◇ n - **1.** [brief description] grandes lignes fpl ; in ~ en gros - **2.** [silhouette] silhouette f ◇ vt - **1.** [describe briefly] exposer les grandes lignes de - **2.** [silhouette] : to be ~d against se dessiner OR se découper sur.

outlive [ˌaʊt'lɪv] vt - **1.** [subj : person] survivre à - **2.** [subj : idea, object] : it's ~d its usefulness cela a fait son temps.

outlook ['aʊtlʊk] n - **1.** [disposition] attitude f, conception f - **2.** [prospect] perspective f.

outlying ['aʊtˌlaɪŋ] adj [village] reculé(e) ; [suburbs] écarté(e).

outmanoeuvre Br, **outmaneuver** Am [ˌaʊtmə'nuːvər] vt [competitor, rival] l'emporter sur.

outmoded [ˌaʊt'məʊdɪd] adj démodé(e).

outnumber [ˌaʊt'nʌmbər] vt surpasser en nombre.

out-of-date adj [passport] périmé(e) ; [clothes] démodé(e) ; [belief] dépassé(e).

out of doors adv dehors.

out-of-the-way adj [village] perdu(e) ; [pub] peu fréquenté(e).

outpace [ˌaʊt'peɪs] vt - **1.** [subj : person] devancer - **2.** fig [subj : technology] dépasser.

outpatient ['aʊtˌpeɪʃnt] n malade mf en consultation externe.

outplay [ˌaʊt'pleɪ] vt SPORT dominer.

outpost ['aʊtpəʊst] n avant-poste m.

outpouring [ˌaʊt'pɔːrɪŋ] n literary [of emotion] effusion f.

output ['aʊtpʊt] ◇ n - **1.** [production] production f - **2.** COMPUT sortie f ◇ vt COMPUT sortir.

outrage ['aʊtreɪdʒ] ◇ n - **1.** [emotion] indignation f - **2.** [act] atrocité f ◇ vt outrager.

outraged ['aʊtreɪdʒd] adj outré(e).

outrageous [aʊt'reɪdʒəs] adj - **1.** [offensive, shocking] scandaleux(euse), monstrueux(euse) - **2.** [very unusual] choquant(e).

outran [ˌaʊt'ræn] pt ▷ outrun.

outrank [aʊt'ræŋk] vt être le supérieur de ; MIL avoir un grade supérieur à.

outrider ['aʊtˌraɪdər] n [on motorcycle] motocycliste m d'escorte.

outright [adj 'aʊtraɪt, adv ˌaʊt'raɪt] ◇ adj absolu(e), total(e) ◇ adv - **1.** [deny] carrément, franchement - **2.** [win, fail] complètement, totalement ; to be killed ~ être tué sur le coup.

outrun [ˌaʊt'rʌn] (pt -ran ; pp -run ; cont -ning) vt distancer.

outsell [,aʊt'sel] (*pt* & *pp* -**sold**) *vt* dépasser les ventes de.

outset ['aʊtset] *n* : **at the ~** au commencement, au début ; **from the ~** depuis le commencement *OR* début.

outshine [,aʊt'ʃaɪn] (*pt* & *pp* -**shone** [-'ʃɒn]) *vt fig* éclipser, surpasser.

outside [*adv* ,aʊt'saɪd, *adj, prep* & *n* 'aʊtsaɪd] ◇ *adj* - **1.** [gen] extérieur(e) ; **an ~ opinion** une opinion indépendante - **2.** [unlikely - chance, possibility] faible ◇ *adv* à l'extérieur ; **to go/run/look ~** aller/courir/regarder dehors ◇ *prep* - **1.** [not inside] à l'extérieur de, en dehors de - **2.** [beyond] : **~ office hours** en dehors des heures de bureau ◇ *n* extérieur *m* ; **at the ~** *fig* au plus, au maximum.

➥ **outside of** *prep* Am [apart from] à part.

outside broadcast *n* Br RADIO & TV émission *f* réalisée à l'extérieur.

outside lane *n* AUT [in UK] voie *f* de droite ; [in Europe, US] voie *f* de gauche.

outside line *n* TELEC ligne *f* extérieure.

outsider [,aʊt'saɪdə'] *n* - **1.** [in race] outsider *m* - **2.** [from society] étranger *m*, -ère *f*.

outsize ['aʊtsaɪz] *adj* - **1.** [bigger than usual] énorme, colossal(e) - **2.** [clothes] grande taille *(inv)*.

outsized ['aʊtsaɪzd] *adj* énorme, colossal(e).

outskirts ['aʊtskɜːts] *npl* : **the ~** la banlieue.

outsmart [,aʊt'smɑːt] *vt* être plus malin(igne) que.

outsold [,aʊt'səʊld] *pt* & *pp* ▷ **outsell**.

outspoken [,aʊt'spəʊkn] *adj* franc (franche).

outspread [,aʊt'spred] *adj* [arms, legs] écarté(e) ; [wings, newspaper] déployé(e).

outstanding [,aʊt'stændɪŋ] *adj* - **1.** [excellent] exceptionnel(elle), remarquable - **2.** [example] marquant(e) - **3.** [not paid] impayé(e) - **4.** [unfinished - work, problem] en suspens.

outstay [,aʊt'steɪ] *vt* : **I don't want to ~ my welcome** je ne veux pas abuser de votre hospitalité.

outstretched [,aʊt'stretʃt] *adj* [arms, hands] tendu(e) ; [wings] déployé(e).

outstrip [,aʊt'strɪp] (*pt* & *pp* -**ped** ; *cont* -**ping**) *vt* devancer.

out-take *n* CINEMA & TV prise *f* ratée.

out-tray *n* corbeille *f* pour le courrier à expédier.

outvote [,aʊt'vəʊt] *vt* : **to be ~d** ne pas obtenir la majorité.

outward ['aʊtwəd] ◇ *adj* - **1.** [going away] : **~ journey** aller *m* - **2.** [apparent, visible] extérieur(e) ◇ *adv* Am = **outwards**.

outwardly ['aʊtwədlɪ] *adv* [apparently] en apparence.

outwards Br ['aʊtwədz], **outward** Am *adv* vers l'extérieur.

outweigh [,aʊt'weɪ] *vt fig* primer sur.

outwit [,aʊt'wɪt] (*pt* & *pp* -**ted** ; *cont* -**ting**) *vt* se montrer plus malin(igne) que.

outworker ['aʊt,wɜːkə'] *n* travailleur *m*, -euse *f* à domicile.

oval ['əʊvl] ◇ *adj* ovale ◇ *n* ovale *m*.

Oval Office *n* : **the ~** *bureau du président des États-Unis à la Maison-Blanche*.

ovarian [əʊ'veərɪən] *adj* ovarien(enne).

ovary ['əʊvərɪ] (*pl* -**ies**) *n* ovaire *m*.

ovation [əʊ'veɪʃn] *n* ovation *f* ; **the audience gave her a standing ~** le public l'a ovationnée.

oven ['ʌvn] *n* [for cooking] four *m*.

oven glove *n* gant *m* de cuisine.

ovenproof ['ʌvnpruːf] *adj* qui va au four.

oven-ready *adj* prêt(e) à cuire.

ovenware ['ʌvnweə'] *n (U)* plats *mpl* qui vont au four.

over ['əʊvə'] ◇ *prep* - **1.** [above] au-dessus de - **2.** [on top of] sur - **3.** [on other side of] de l'autre côté de ; **they live ~ the road** ils habitent en face - **4.** [to other side of] par-dessus ; **to go ~ the border** franchir la frontière - **5.** [more than] plus de ; **~ and above** en plus de - **6.** [senior to] : **he's ~ me at work** il occupe un poste plus élevé que le mien - **7.** [concerning] à propos de, au sujet de - **8.** [during] pendant ◇ *adv* - **1.** [distance away] : **~ here** ici ; **~ there** là-bas - **2.** [across] : **they flew ~ to America** ils se sont envolés pour les États-Unis ; **we invited them ~** nous les avons invités chez nous - **3.** [to the ground] : **to lean ~** se pencher ; **she pushed the pile of books ~** elle a renversé la pile de livres - **4.** [more] plus - **5.** [remaining] : **there's nothing (left) ~** il ne restera rien - **6.** RADIO : **~ and out!** à vous ! - **7.** [involving repetitions] : **(all) ~ again** (tout) au début ; **~ and ~ again** à maintes reprises, maintes fois ◇ *adj* [finished] fini(e), terminé(e) ◇ *n* over *m*.

➥ **all over** ◇ *prep* - **1.** [covering] : **the child had chocolate all ~ her face** l'enfant avait du chocolat sur toute la figure - **2.** [throughout] partout, dans tout ; **all ~ the world** dans le monde entier ◇ *adv* [everywhere] partout ◇ *adj* [finished] fini(e).

over- ['əʊvə'] *prefix* sur-.

overabundance [,əʊvərə'bʌndəns] *n* surabondance *f*.

overact [,əʊvər'ækt] *vi pej* THEATRE en faire trop.

overactive [,əʊvər'æktɪv] *adj* trop actif(ive).

overall [*adj* & *n* 'əʊvərɔːl, *adv* ,əʊvər'ɔːl] ◇ *adj* [general] d'ensemble ◇ *adv* en général ◇ *n* - **1.** [gen] tablier *m* - **2.** Am [for work] bleu *m* de travail.

➠ **overalls** *npl* - **1.** [for work] bleu *m* de travail - **2.** Am [dungarees] salopette *f*.

overambitious [,əʊvəræm'bɪʃəs] *adj* trop ambitieux(euse).

overanxious [,əʊvər'æŋkʃəs] *adj* trop inquiet(ète), trop anxieux(euse).

overarm ['əʊvərɑːm] *adj* & *adv* par en-dessus.

overate [,əʊvər'et] *pt* ▷ **overeat.**

overawe [,əʊvər'ɔː] *vt* impressionner.

overbalance [,əʊvə'bæləns] *vi* basculer.

overbearing [,əʊvə'beərɪŋ] *adj* autoritaire.

overblown [,əʊvə'bləʊn] *adj* pej exagéré(e).

overboard ['əʊvəbɔːd] *adv* : **to fall ~** tomber par-dessus bord ; **to go ~** inf fig en faire trop ; **to go ~ about** inf fig s'enthousiasmer pour.

overbook [,əʊvə'bʊk] *vi* surréserver.

overburden [,əʊvə'bɜːdn] *vt* : **to be ~ed with** sthg être surchargé(e) de qqch.

overcame [,əʊvə'keɪm] *pt* ▷ **overcome.**

overcapitalize, -ise [,əʊvə'kæpɪtəlaɪz] *vt* & *vi* FIN surcapitaliser.

overcast [,əʊvə'kɑːst] *adj* couvert(e).

overcharge [,əʊvə'tʃɑːdʒ] ◇ *vt* : **to ~ sb (for** sthg) faire payer (qqch) trop cher à qqn ◇ *vi* : **to ~ (for** sthg) demander un prix excessif (pour qqch).

overcoat ['əʊvəkəʊt] *n* pardessus *m*.

overcome [,əʊvə'kʌm] (*pt* -**came** ; *pp* -**come**) *vt* - **1.** [fears, difficulties] surmonter - **2.** [overwhelm] : **to be ~ (by** OR with**)** [emotion] être submergé(e) (de) ; [grief] être accablé(e) (de).

overcompensate [,əʊvə'kɒmpənseɪt] *vi* : **to ~ (for** sthg) surcompenser (qqch).

overconfident [,əʊvə'kɒnfɪdənt] *adj* [too certain] trop sûr(e) de soi ; [arrogant] suffisant(e).

overcook [,əʊvə'kʊk] *vt* faire trop cuire.

overcrowded [,əʊvə'kraʊdɪd] *adj* bondé(e).

overcrowding [,əʊvə'kraʊdɪŋ] *n* surpeuplement *m*.

overdeveloped [,əʊvədɪ'veləpt] *adj* PHOT & fig trop développé(e).

overdo [,əʊvə'duː] (*pt* -**did** [-'dɪd] ; *pp* -**done**) *vt* - **1.** [exaggerate] exagérer - **2.** [do too much] trop faire ; **to ~ it** se surmener - **3.** [overcook] trop cuire.

overdone [,əʊvə'dʌn] ◇ *pp* ▷ **overdo** ◇ *adj* [food] trop cuit(e).

overdose [*n* 'əʊvədəʊs , *vb* ,əʊvə'dəʊs] ◇ *n* overdose *f* ◇ *vi* : **to ~ on** prendre une dose excessive de.

overdraft ['əʊvədrɑːft] *n* découvert *m*.

overdrawn [,əʊvə'drɔːn] *adj* à découvert.

overdress [,əʊvə'dres] *vi* être trop bien habillé(e) (pour l'occasion).

overdrive ['əʊvədraɪv] *n* fig : **to go into ~** mettre les bouchées doubles.

overdue [,əʊvə'djuː] *adj* - **1.** [late] : **~ (for)** en retard (pour) - **2.** [change, reform] : **(long) ~** attendu(e) (depuis longtemps) - **3.** [unpaid] arriéré(e), impayé(e).

overeager [,əʊvər'iːgəʳ] *adj* trop zélé(e).

overeat [,əʊvər'iːt] (*pt* -**ate** ; *pp* -**eaten**) *vi* trop manger.

overemphasize, -ise [,əʊvər'emfəsaɪz] *vt* donner trop d'importance à.

overenthusiastic ['əʊvərɪn,θjuːzɪ'æstɪk] *adj* trop enthousiaste.

overestimate [,əʊvər'estɪmeɪt] *vt* surestimer.

overexcited [,əʊvərɪk'saɪtɪd] *adj* surexcité(e).

overexpose [,əʊvərɪk'spəʊz] *vt* PHOT surexposer.

overfeed [,əʊvə'fiːd] (*pt* & *pp* -**fed** [-fedl]) *vt* suralimenter.

overfill [,əʊvə'fɪl] *vt* trop remplir.

overflow [*vb* ,əʊvə'fləʊ, *n* 'əʊvəfləʊl] ◇ *vi* - **1.** [gen] déborder - **2.** [streets, box] : **to be ~ing (with)** regorger (de) ; **full to ~ing** plein à craquer ◇ *vt* déborder de ◇ *n* [pipe, hole] trop-plein *m*.

overgrown [,əʊvə'grəʊn] *adj* [garden] envahi(e) par les mauvaises herbes.

overhang [*n* 'əʊvəhæŋ, *vb* ,əʊvə'hæŋl] (*pt* & *pp* -**hung**) ◇ *n* surplomb *m* ◇ *vt* surplomber ◇ *vi* être en surplomb.

overhaul [*n* 'əʊvəhɔːl, *vb* ,əʊvə'hɔːl] ◇ *n* - **1.** [of car, machine] révision *f* - **2.** fig [of system] refonte *f*, remaniement *m* ◇ *vt* - **1.** [car, machine] réviser - **2.** fig [system] refondre, remanier.

overhead [*adv* ,əʊvə'hed, *adj* & *n* 'əʊvəhed] ◇ *adj* aérien(enne) ◇ *adv* au-dessus ◇ *n* (U) Am frais *mpl* généraux.

➠ **overheads** *npl* Br frais *mpl* généraux.

overhead projector *n* rétroprojecteur *m*.

overhear [,əʊvə'hɪəʳ] (*pt* & *pp* -**heard** [-'hɜːd]) *vt* entendre par hasard.

overheat [,əʊvə'hiːt] ◇ *vt* surchauffer ◇ *vi* [engine] chauffer.

overhung [ˌəʊvə'hʌŋ] *pt* & *pp* ⊳ overhang.

overindulge [ˌəʊvərɪn'dʌldʒ] <> *vt* trop gâter <> *vi :* **to ~ (in)** abuser (de).

overjoyed [ˌəʊvə'dʒɔɪd] *adj :* **~ (at)** transporté(e) de joie (à).

overkill ['əʊvəkɪl] *n* [excess] : **that would be ~** ce serait de trop.

overladen [ˌəʊvə'leɪdn] <> *pp* ⊳ overload <> *adj* surchargé(e).

overlaid [ˌəʊvə'leɪd] *pt* & *pp* ⊳ overlay.

overland ['əʊvəlænd] *adj* & *adv* par voie de terre.

overlap [*n* 'əʊvəlæp , *vb* ˌəʊvə'læp] (*pt* & *pp* -ped ; *cont* -ping) <> *n* lit & fig chevauchement *m* <> *vt* [edge] dépasser de <> *vi* lit & fig se chevaucher.

overlay [ˌəʊvə'leɪ] (*pt* & *pp* -laid) *vt :* **to be overlaid with** être recouvert(e) de.

overleaf [ˌəʊvə'liːf] *adv* au verso, au dos.

overload [ˌəʊvə'ləʊd] (*pp* -loaded OR -laden) *vt* surcharger.

overlong [ˌəʊvə'lɒŋ] <> *adj* long (trop longue) <> *adv* trop longtemps.

overlook [ˌəʊvə'lʊk] *vt* - **1.** [subj : building, room] donner sur - **2.** [disregard, miss] oublier, négliger - **3.** [excuse] passer sur, fermer les yeux sur.

overlord ['əʊvəlɔːd] *n* suzerain *m*.

overly ['əʊvəlɪ] *adv* trop.

overmanning [ˌəʊvə'mænɪŋ] *n (U)* sureffectifs *mpl*.

overnight [*adj* 'əʊvənaɪt, *adv* ˌəʊvə'naɪt] <> *adj* - **1.** [journey, parking] de nuit ; [stay] d'une nuit - **2.** fig [sudden] : **~ success** succès *m* immédiat <> *adv* - **1.** [stay, leave] la nuit - **2.** [suddenly] du jour au lendemain.

overpaid [ˌəʊvə'peɪd] <> *pt* & *pp* ⊳ overpay <> *adj* trop payé(e), surpayé(e).

overpass ['əʊvəpɑːs] *n* Am ≃ Toboggan® *m*.

overpay [ˌəʊvə'peɪ] (*pt* & *pp* -paid) *vt* trop payer.

overplay [ˌəʊvə'pleɪ] *vt* [exaggerate] exagérer.

overpopulated [ˌəʊvə'pɒpjʊleɪtɪd] *adj* surpeuplé(e).

overpower [ˌəʊvə'paʊəʳ] *vt* - **1.** [in fight] vaincre - **2.** fig [overwhelm] accabler, terrasser.

overpowering [ˌəʊvə'paʊərɪŋ] *adj* [desire] irrésistible ; [smell] entêtant(e).

overpriced [ˌəʊvə'praɪst] *adj* pej excessivement cher (chère).

overproduction [ˌəʊvəprə'dʌkʃn] *n* surproduction *f*.

overprotective [ˌəʊvəprə'tektɪv] *adj* protecteur(trice) à l'excès.

overran [ˌəʊvə'ræn] *pt* ⊳ overrun.

overrated [ˌəʊvə'reɪtɪd] *adj* surfait(e).

overreach [ˌəʊvə'riːtʃ] *vt :* **to ~ o.s.** trop entreprendre.

overreact [ˌəʊvərɪ'ækt] *vi :* **to ~ (to sthg)** réagir (à qqch) de façon excessive.

override [ˌəʊvə'raɪd] (*pt* -rode ; *pp* -ridden) *vt* - **1.** [be more important than] l'emporter sur, prévaloir sur - **2.** [overrule - decision] annuler.

overriding [ˌəʊvə'raɪdɪŋ] *adj* [need, importance] primordial(e).

overripe [ˌəʊvə'raɪp] *adj* trop mûr(e).

overrode [ˌəʊvə'rəʊd] *pt* ⊳ override.

overrule [ˌəʊvə'ruːl] *vt* [person] prévaloir contre ; [decision] annuler ; [objection] rejeter.

overrun [ˌəʊvə'rʌn] (*pt* -ran ; *pp* -run ; *cont* -running) <> *vt* - **1.** MIL [occupy] occuper - **2.** fig [cover, fill] : **to be ~ with** [weeds] être envahi(e) de ; [rats] être infesté(e) de <> *vi* dépasser (le temps alloué).

oversaw [ˌəʊvə'sɔː] *pt* ⊳ oversee.

overseas [*adj* 'əʊvəsiːz, *adv* ˌəʊvə'siːz] <> *adj* [sales, company] à l'étranger ; [market] extérieur(e) ; [visitor, student] étranger(ère) ; **~ aid** aide *f* aux pays étrangers <> *adv* à l'étranger.

oversee [ˌəʊvə'siː] (*pt* -saw ; *pp* -seen [-'siːn]) *vt* surveiller.

overseer ['əʊvəˌsiːəʳ] *n* contremaître *m*.

overshadow [ˌəʊvə'ʃædəʊ] *vt* [subj : building, tree] dominer ; fig éclipser.

overshoot [ˌəʊvə'ʃuːt] (*pt* & *pp* -shot) *vt* dépasser, rater.

oversight ['əʊvəsaɪt] *n* oubli *m* ; **through ~** par mégarde.

oversimplification ['əʊvəˌsɪmplɪfɪ'keɪʃn] *n* simplification *f* excessive.

oversimplify [ˌəʊvə'sɪmplɪfaɪ] (*pt* & *pp* -ied) *vt* & *vi* trop simplifier.

oversleep [ˌəʊvə'sliːp] (*pt* & *pp* -slept [-'slept]) *vi* ne pas se réveiller à temps.

overspend [ˌəʊvə'spend] (*pt* & *pp* -spent [-'spent]) *vi* trop dépenser.

overspill ['əʊvəspɪl] *n* [of population] excédent *m*.

overstaffed [ˌəʊvə'stɑːft] *adj :* **to be ~** avoir un excédent de personnel.

overstate [ˌəʊvə'steɪt] *vt* exagérer.

overstay [ˌəʊvə'steɪ] *vt :* **I don't want to ~ my welcome** je ne veux pas abuser de votre hospitalité.

overstep [ˌəʊvə'step] (*pt* & *pp* -ped ; *cont*

-ping) *vt* dépasser ; **to ~ the mark** dépasser la mesure.

overstock [ˌəʊvəˈstɒk] *vt* stocker à l'excès.

overstrike [ˈəʊvəstraɪk] COMPUT ◇ *n* surimpression *f* ◇ *vt* surimprimer.

oversubscribed [ˌəʊvəsʌbˈskraɪbd] *adj :* **the share offer was ~** la demande d'achats a dépassé le nombre de titres émis.

overt [ˈəʊvɜːt] *adj* déclaré(e), non déguisé(e).

overtake [ˌəʊvəˈteɪk] (*pt* **-took** ; *pp* **-taken** [-ˈteɪkn]) ◇ *vt* - **1.** AUT doubler, dépasser - **2.** [subj : misfortune, emotion] frapper ◇ *vi* AUT doubler.

overtaking [ˌəʊvəˈteɪkɪŋ] *n* dépassement *m* ; **'no ~'** 'défense de doubler'.

overthrow [*n* ˈəʊvəθrəʊ, *vb* ˌəʊvəˈθrəʊ] (*pt* **-threw** [-ˈθruː] ; *pp* **-thrown** [-ˈθrəʊn]) ◇ *n* [of government] coup *m* d'État ◇ *vt* - **1.** [government] renverser - **2.** [idea] rejeter, écarter.

overtime [ˈəʊvətaɪm] ◇ *n* (*U*) - **1.** [extra work] heures *fpl* supplémentaires - **2.** Am SPORT prolongations *fpl* ◇ *adv :* **to work ~** faire des heures supplémentaires.

overtly [əʊˈvɜːtlɪ] *adv* ouvertement.

overtones [ˈəʊvətəʊnz] *npl* notes *fpl*, accents *mpl*.

overtook [ˌəʊvəˈtʊk] *pt* ▷ **overtake.**

overture [ˈəʊvəˌtjʊəʳ] *n* MUS ouverture *f*.

◆ **overtures** *npl :* **to make ~s to sb** faire des ouvertures à qqn.

overturn [ˌəʊvəˈtɜːn] ◇ *vt* - **1.** [gen] renverser - **2.** [decision] annuler ◇ *vi* [vehicle] se renverser ; [boat] chavirer.

overuse [ˌəʊvəˈjuːz] *vt* abuser de.

overview [ˈəʊvəvjuː] *n* vue *f* d'ensemble.

overweening [ˌəʊvəˈwiːnɪŋ] *adj* démesuré(e).

overweight [ˌəʊvəˈweɪt] *adj* trop gros (grosse).

overwhelm [ˌəʊvəˈwelm] *vt* - **1.** [subj : grief, despair] accabler ; **to be ~ed with joy** être au comble de la joie - **2.** MIL [gain control of] écraser.

overwhelming [ˌəʊvəˈwelmɪŋ] *adj* - **1.** [overpowering] irrésistible, irrépressible - **2.** [defeat, majority] écrasant(e).

overwhelmingly [ˌəʊvəˈwelmɪŋlɪ] *adv* - **1.** [generous, happy] immensément - **2.** [in large numbers] en masse.

overwork [ˌəʊvəˈwɜːk] ◇ *n* surmenage *m* ◇ *vt* - **1.** [person, staff] surmener - **2.** fig [idea] exploiter ◇ *vi* se surmener.

overwrought [ˌəʊvəˈrɔːt] *adj* excédé(e), à bout.

ovulate [ˈɒvjʊleɪt] *vi* ovuler.

ovulation [ˌɒvjʊˈleɪʃn] *n* ovulation *f*.

ow [aʊ] *excl* aïe!

owe [əʊ] *vt :* **to ~ sthg to sb, to ~ sb sthg** devoir qqch à qqn.

owing [ˈəʊɪŋ] *adj* dû (due).

◆ **owing to** *prep* à cause de, en raison de.

owl [aʊl] *n* hibou *m*.

own [əʊn] ◇ *adj* propre ; **my ~ car** ma propre voiture ; **she has her ~ style** elle a son style à elle ◇ *pron :* **I've got my ~** j'ai le mien ; **he has a house of his ~** il a une maison à lui, il a sa propre maison ; **on one's ~** tout seul (toute seule) ; **to get one's ~ back** inf prendre sa revanche ◇ *vt* posséder.

◆ **own up** *vi :* **to ~ up (to sthg)** avouer OR confesser (qqch).

own brand *n* COMM produit qui porte la marque de la maison.

owner [ˈəʊnəʳ] *n* propriétaire *mf*.

owner-occupier *n* esp Br occupant *m* propriétaire.

ownership [ˈəʊnəʃɪp] *n* propriété *f*.

own goal *n* esp Br - **1.** FTBL : **to score an ~** marquer contre son camp - **2.** Br fig [foolish mistake] gaffe *f*.

ox [ɒks] (*pl* **oxen** [ˈɒksn]) *n* bœuf *m*.

Oxbridge [ˈɒksbrɪdʒ] *n* désignation collective des universités d'Oxford et de Cambridge.

oxen [ˈɒksn] *pl* ▷ **ox.**

Oxfam [ˈɒksfæm] *n* association humanitaire contre la faim.

oxide [ˈɒksaɪd] *n* oxyde *m*.

oxidize, -ise [ˈɒksɪdaɪz] *vi* s'oxyder.

Oxon (*abbr of* **Oxfordshire**) *comté anglais*.

Oxon. (*abbr of* **Oxoniensis**) *de l'université d'Oxford*.

oxtail soup [ˈɒksteɪl-] *n* soupe *f* à la queue de bœuf.

ox tongue *n* langue *f* de bœuf.

oxyacetylene [ˌɒksɪəˈsetɪliːn] ◇ *n* mélange *m* d'oxygène et d'acétylène ◇ *comp* [torch] oxyacétylénique.

oxygen [ˈɒksɪdʒən] *n* oxygène *m*.

oxygenate [ˈɒksɪdʒəneɪt] *vt* oxygéner.

oxygen mask *n* masque *m* à oxygène.

oxygen tent *n* tente *f* à oxygène.

oyster [ˈɔɪstəʳ] *n* huître *f*.

oz. *abbr of* **ounce.**

ozone [ˈəʊzəʊn] *n* ozone *m*.

ozone-friendly *adj* qui préserve la couche d'ozone.

ozone layer *n* couche *f* d'ozone.

P

p¹ (*pl* **p's** OR **ps**), **P** (*pl* **P's** OR **Ps**) [piː] *n* [letter] p *m inv*, P *m inv*.
◆ **P - 1.** *abbr of* **president - 2.** (*abbr of* **prince**) Pce.

p² **- 1.** (*abbr of* **page**) p **- 2.** *abbr of* **penny, pence.**

pa [pɑː] *n inf esp* Am papa *m*.

p.a. (*abbr of* **per annum**) p.a.

PA ◇ *n* **- 1.** Br *abbr of* **personal assistant - 2.** (*abbr of* **public address system**) sono *f* **- 3.** (*abbr of* **Press Association**) *agence de presse britannique* ◇ *abbr of* **Pennsylvania.**

PABX (*abbr of* **private automatic branch exchange**) *n* autocommutateur *m* privé.

PAC (*abbr of* **political action committee**) *n comité américain de promotion du recours à l'action politique.*

pace [peɪs] ◇ *n* **- 1.** [speed, rate] vitesse *f*, allure *f* ; **at one's own ~** à son propre rythme ; **to keep ~ (with sb)** marcher à la même allure (que qqn) ; **to keep ~ (with sthg)** se maintenir au même niveau (que qqch) **- 2.** [step] pas *m* ◇ *vt* [room etc] arpenter ◇ *vi* : **to ~ (up and down)** faire les cent pas.

pacemaker ['peɪsˌmeɪkər] *n* **- 1.** MED stimulateur *m* cardiaque, pacemaker *m* **- 2.** SPORT meneur *m*, -euse *f*.

pacesetter ['peɪsˌsetər] *n* Am SPORT meneur *m*, -euse *f*.

pachyderm ['pækɪdɜːm] *n* pachyderme *m*.

Pacific [pə'sɪfɪk] ◇ *adj* du Pacifique ◇ *n* : **the ~ (Ocean)** l'océan *m* Pacifique, le Pacifique.

pacification [ˌpæsɪfɪ'keɪʃn] *n* **- 1.** [of person, baby] apaisement *m* **- 2.** [of country] pacification *f*.

pacifier ['pæsɪfaɪər] *n* Am [for child] tétine *f*, sucette *f*.

pacifism ['pæsɪfɪzml] *n* pacifisme *m*.

pacifist ['pæsɪfɪst] *n* pacifiste *mf*.

pacify ['pæsɪfaɪ] (*pt & pp* **-ied**) *vt* **- 1.** [person, baby] apaiser **- 2.** [country] pacifier.

pack [pæk] ◇ *n* **- 1.** [bag] sac *m* **- 2.** esp Am [packet] paquet *m* **- 3.** [of cards] jeu *m* **- 4.** [of dogs] meute *f* ; [of wolves, thieves] bande *f* **- 5.** RUGBY pack *m* ◇ *vt* **- 1.** [clothes, belongings] emballer ; **to ~ one's bags** faire ses bagages **- 2.** [fill] remplir ; **to be ~ed into** être entassé dans ◇ *vi* [for journey] faire ses bagages OR sa valise.
◆ **pack in** ◇ *vt sep* Br *inf* [stop] plaquer ; **~ it in!** [stop annoying me] arrête!, ça suffit maintenant! ; [shut up] la ferme! ◇ *vi* tomber en panne.
◆ **pack off** *vt sep inf* [send away] expédier.
◆ **pack up** ◇ *vt* [clothes, belongings] mettre dans une valise ◇ *vi* **- 1.** [for journey] faire sa valise **- 2.** *inf* [finish work] se casser **- 3.** Br *inf* [car, washing machine] tomber en panne.

package ['pækɪdʒ] ◇ *n* **- 1.** [of books, goods] paquet *m* **- 2.** *fig* [of proposals etc] ensemble *m*, série *f* **- 3.** COMPUT progiciel *m* ◇ *vt* [wrap up] conditionner.

package deal *n* contrat *m* global.

package holiday *n* vacances *fpl* organisées.

packager ['pækɪdʒər] *n* **- 1.** [person] emballeur *m*, -euse *f* **- 2.** COMM maison d'édition qui crée des livres sur commande pour d'autres maisons.

package tour *n* vacances *fpl* organisées.

packaging ['pækɪdʒɪŋ] *n* conditionnement *m*.

packed [pækt] *adj* : **~ (with)** bourré(e) (de).

packed lunch *n* Br panier-repas *m*.

packed-out *adj* Br *inf* bourré(e).

packet ['pækɪt] *n* **- 1.** [gen] paquet *m* **- 2.** Br *inf* [lot of money] : **their new car cost a ~** leur nouvelle voiture leur a coûté un paquet OR très cher.

packhorse ['pækhɔːs] *n* cheval *m* de charge.

pack ice *n* pack *m*.

packing ['pækɪŋ] *n* [material] emballage *m*.

packing case *n* caisse *f* d'emballage.

pact [pækt] *n* pacte *m*.

pad [pæd] (*pt & pp* **-ded** ; *cont* **-ding**) ◇ *n* **- 1.** [of cotton wool etc] morceau *m* ; **shin ~** FTBL protège-tibia *m* ; **shoulder ~s** épaulettes *fpl* **- 2.** [of paper] bloc *m* **- 3.** SPACE : **(launch) ~** pas *m* de tir **- 4.** [of cat, dog] coussinet *m* **- 5.** *inf* [home] pénates *mpl* ◇ *vt* [furniture, jacket] rembourrer ; [wound] tamponner ◇ *vi* [walk softly] marcher à pas feutrés.
◆ **pad out** *vt sep fig* [speech, letter] délayer.

padded ['pædɪd] *adj* rembourré(e).

padded cell *n* cellule *f* matelassée.

padding ['pædɪŋ] *n* **- 1.** [material] rembourrage *m* **- 2.** *fig* [in speech, letter] délayage *m*.

paddle ['pædl] ◇ *n* **- 1.** [for canoe etc] pagaie *f*

- 2. [in sea] : **to have a ~** faire trempette **- 3.** [table-tennis bat] raquette *f* (de ping-pong) ⟨⟩ *vi* **- 1.** [in canoe etc] avancer en pagayant **- 2.** [duck] barboter **- 3.** [in sea] faire trempette.

paddle boat, paddle steamer *n* bateau *m* à aubes.

paddling pool ['pædlɪŋ-] *n* **Br - 1.** [in park etc] pataugeoire *f* **- 2.** [inflatable] piscine *f* gonflable.

paddock ['pædək] *n* **- 1.** [small field] enclos *m* **- 2.** [at racecourse] paddock *m*.

paddy field ['pædɪ-] *n* rizière *f*.

paddy wagon ['pædɪ-] *n* **Am** [Black Maria] panier *m* à salade.

padlock ['pædlɒk] ⟨⟩ *n* cadenas *m* ⟨⟩ *vt* cadenasser.

paederast ['pedəræst] = **pederast.**

paediatric [ˌpiːdɪ'ætrɪk] = **pediatric.**

paediatrician [ˌpiːdɪə'trɪʃn] = **pediatrician.**

paediatrics [ˌpiːdɪ'ætrɪks] = **pediatrics.**

paedophile ['piːdəfaɪl] = **pedophile.**

paella [paɪ'elə] *n* paella *f*.

paeony = **peony.**

pagan ['peɪɡən] ⟨⟩ *adj* païen(enne) ⟨⟩ *n* païen *m*, -enne *f*.

paganism ['peɪɡənɪzm] *n* paganisme *m*.

page [peɪdʒ] ⟨⟩ *n* **- 1.** [of book] page *f* **- 2.** [sheet of paper] feuille *f* ⟨⟩ *vt* **- 1.** [using a pager] biper **- 2.** [in airport] appeler au micro.

pageant ['pædʒənt] *n* [show] spectacle *m* historique.

pageantry ['pædʒəntrɪ] *n* apparat *m*.

page boy *n* **- 1.** **Br** [at wedding] garçon *m* d'honneur **- 2.** [hairstyle] coiffure *f* à la page.

pager ['peɪdʒər] *n* récepteur *m* de poche.

pagination [ˌpædʒɪ'neɪʃn] *n* pagination *f*.

pagoda [pə'ɡəʊdə] *n* pagode *f*.

paid [peɪd] ⟨⟩ *pt* & *pp* ⊳ **pay** ⟨⟩ *adj* [work, holiday, staff] rémunéré(e), payé(e) ; **badly/ well ~** mal/bien payé

paid-up *adj* **Br** qui a payé sa cotisation.

pail [peɪl] *n* seau *m*.

pain [peɪn] ⟨⟩ *n* **- 1.** [hurt] douleur *f* ; **to be in ~** souffrir ; **a ~ in the neck** inf un enquiquineur (une enquiquineuse), un casse-pieds *m inv* **- 2.** inf [annoyance] : **it's/he is such a ~** c'est/il est vraiment assommant ⟨⟩ *vt* : **it ~s me (to do sthg)** je suis peiné (de faire qqch).

➡ **pains** *npl* [effort, care] : **to be at ~s to do sthg** vouloir absolument faire qqch ; **to take ~s to do sthg** se donner beaucoup de mal OR peine pour faire qqch ; **for one's ~s** pour sa peine.

pained [peɪnd] *adj* peiné(e).

painful ['peɪnfʊl] *adj* **- 1.** [physically] douloureux(euse) **- 2.** [emotionally] pénible.

painfully ['peɪnfʊlɪ] *adv* **- 1.** [fall, hit] douloureusement **- 2.** [remember, feel] péniblement.

painkiller ['peɪnˌkɪlər] *n* calmant *m*, analgésique *m*.

painless ['peɪnlɪs] *adj* **- 1.** [without hurt] indolore, sans douleur **- 2.** fig [changeover] sans heurt.

painlessly ['peɪnlɪslɪ] *adv* sans douleur.

painstaking ['peɪnzˌteɪkɪŋ] *adj* [worker] assidu(e) ; [detail, work] soigné(e).

painstakingly ['peɪnzˌteɪkɪŋlɪ] *adv* assidûment, avec soin.

paint [peɪnt] ⟨⟩ *n* peinture *f* ⟨⟩ *vt* **- 1.** [gen] peindre **- 2.** [with make-up] : **to ~ one's nails** se vernir les ongles.

paintbox ['peɪntbɒks] *n* **ART** boîte *f* de couleurs.

paintbrush ['peɪntbrʌʃ] *n* pinceau *m*.

painted ['peɪntɪd] *adj* peint(e).

painter ['peɪntər] *n* peintre *m*.

painting ['peɪntɪŋ] *n* **- 1.** (U) [gen] peinture *f* **- 2.** [picture] toile *f*, tableau *m*.

paint stripper *n* décapant *m*.

paintwork ['peɪntwɜːk] *n* (U) surfaces *fpl* peintes.

pair [peər] *n* **- 1.** [of shoes, wings etc] paire *f* ; **a ~ of trousers** un pantalon ; **a ~ of compasses** un compas **- 2.** [couple] couple *m*.

➡ **pair off** ⟨⟩ *vt sep* mettre par paires OR deux ⟨⟩ *vi* se mettre par paires OR deux par deux.

paisley (pattern) ['peɪzlɪ-] ⟨⟩ *n* (U) (motif *m*) cachemire *m* ⟨⟩ *comp* cachemire.

pajamas [pə'dʒɑːməz] *esp* **Am** = **pyjamas.**

Paki *v* inf ['pækɪ] *n* **Br** terme raciste désignant un Pakistanais.

Pakistan [**Br** ˌpɑːkɪ'stɑːn, **Am** ˌpækɪ'stæn] *n* Pakistan *m* ; **in ~** au Pakistan.

Pakistani [**Br** ˌpɑːkɪ'stɑːnɪ, **Am** 'pækɪstænɪ] ⟨⟩ *adj* pakistanais(e) ⟨⟩ *n* Pakistanais *m*, -e *f*.

pal [pæl] *n* inf **- 1.** [friend] copain *m*, copine *f* **- 2.** [as term of address] mon vieux *m*.

PAL (*abbr of* **phase alternation line**) *n* PAL *m*.

palace ['pælɪs] *n* palais *m*.

palaeontology **Br**, **paleontology** **Am** [ˌpælɪɒn'tɒlədʒɪ] *n* paléontologie *f*.

palatable ['pælətəbl] *adj* **- 1.** [food] agréable au goût **- 2.** fig [idea] acceptable, agréable.

palate ['pælət] *n* palais *m*.

palatial [pə'leɪʃl] *adj* pareil(eille) à un palais.

palaver [pə'lɑːvəʳ] *n (U)* inf - **1.** [talk] palabres *fpl* - **2.** [fuss] histoire *f*, affaire *f*.

pale [peɪl] ◇ *adj* pâle ◇ *vi : to ~ into insignificance (beside)* n'être rien (à côté de).

pale ale *n* Br pale-ale *f*.

paleness ['peɪlnɪs] *n* pâleur *f*.

Palestine ['pæləˌstaɪn] *n* Palestine *f*.

Palestinian [ˌpælə'stɪnɪən] ◇ *adj* palestinien(enne) ◇ *n* Palestinien *m*, -enne *f*.

palette ['pælət] *n* palette *f*.

palette knife *n* ART couteau *m* à palette ; CULIN spatule *f* (en métal).

palimony ['pælɪmənɪ] *n* pension alimentaire versée à un concubin.

palindrome ['pælɪndrəʊm] *n* palindrome *m*.

palings ['peɪlɪŋz] *npl* palissade *f*.

pall [pɔːl] ◇ *n* - **1.** [of smoke] voile *m* - **2.** Am [coffin] cercueil *m* ◇ *vi* perdre de son charme.

pallbearer ['pɔːlˌbeərəʳ] *n* porteur *m* de cercueil.

pallet ['pælɪt] *n* palette *f*.

palliative ['pælɪətɪv] *n* palliatif *m*.

pallid ['pælɪd] *adj literary* pâle, blafard(e).

pallor ['pæləʳ] *n literary* pâleur *f*.

palm [pɑːm] *n* - **1.** [tree] palmier *m* - **2.** [of hand] paume *f*.

➤ **palm off** *vt sep* inf : *to ~ sthg off on sb* refiler qqch à qqn ; *to ~ sb off with sthg* se débarrasser de qqn avec qqch ; *to ~ sthg off as* faire passer qqch pour.

palmistry ['pɑːmɪstrɪ] *n* chiromancie *f*.

palm oil *n* huile *f* de palme.

Palm Sunday *n* dimanche *m* des Rameaux.

palmtop *n* COMPUT ordinateur *m* de poche.

palm tree *n* palmier *m*.

palomino [ˌpælə'miːnəʊ] (*pl* -s) *n* cheval doré à crinière et queue blanches.

palpable ['pælpəbl] *adj* évident(e), manifeste.

palpably ['pælpəblɪ] *adv* de façon évidente, manifestement.

palpitate ['pælpɪteɪt] *vi* palpiter.

palpitations [ˌpælpɪ'teɪʃənz] *npl* palpitations *fpl*.

palsy ['pɔːlzɪ] *n* paralysie *f*.

paltry ['pɔːltrɪ] (*compar* -ier ; *superl* -iest) *adj* dérisoire.

pampas ['pæmpəz] *n : the ~* la pampa.

pampas grass *n* herbe *f* de la pampa.

pamper ['pæmpəʳ] *vt* choyer, dorloter.

pamphlet ['pæmflɪt] ◇ *n* brochure *f* ◇ *vi* distribuer des brochures.

pamphleteer [ˌpæmflə'tɪəʳ] *n* POL pamphlétaire *mf*.

pan [pæn] (*pt* & *pp* -ned ; *cont* -ning) ◇ *n* - **1.** [gen] casserole *f* - **2.** Am [for bread, cakes etc] moule *m* ◇ *vt* inf [criticize] démolir ◇ *vi* - **1.** [prospect] : *to ~ for gold* laver l'or - **2.** CINEMA faire un panoramique.

panacea [ˌpænə'sɪə] *n* panacée *f*.

panache [pə'næʃ] *n* panache *m*.

panama [ˌpænə'mɑː] *n : ~ (hat)* panama *m*.

Panama ['pænəmɑː] *n* Panama *m ;* in ~ au Panama.

Panama Canal *n : the ~* le canal de Panama.

Panama City *n* Panama.

Panamanian [ˌpænə'meɪnjən] ◇ *adj* panaméen(enne) ◇ *n* Panaméen *m*, -enne *f*.

pan-American *adj* panaméricain(e).

pancake ['pænkeɪk] *n* crêpe *f*.

Pancake Day *n* Br mardi gras *m*.

pancake roll *n* rouleau *m* de printemps.

Pancake Tuesday *n* mardi gras *m*.

pancreas ['pæŋkrɪəs] *n* pancréas *m*.

panda ['pændə] (*pl* inv OR -s) *n* panda *m*.

Panda car *n* Br voiture *f* de patrouille.

pandemonium [ˌpændɪ'məʊnjəm] *n* tohubohu *m* inv.

pander ['pændəʳ] *vi : to ~ to sb* se prêter aux exigences de qqn ; *to ~ to sthg* se plier à qqch.

pane [peɪn] *n* vitre *f*, carreau *m*.

panel ['pænl] *n* - **1.** TV & RADIO invités *mpl ;* [of experts] comité *m* - **2.** [of wood] panneau *m* - **3.** [of machine] tableau *m* de bord.

panel game *n* Br jeu télévisé où rivalisent des équipes d'invités célèbres.

panelling Br, **paneling** Am ['pænəlɪŋ] *n (U)* lambris *m*.

panellist Br, **panelist** Am ['pænəlɪst] *n* invité *m*, -e *f*.

panel pin *n* Br clou *m* sans tête.

pang [pæŋ] *n* tiraillement *m*.

panic ['pænɪk] (*pt* & *pp* -ked ; *cont* -king) ◇ *n* panique *f* ◇ *vi* paniquer.

panicky ['pænɪkɪ] *adj* [person] paniqué(e) ; [feeling] de panique.

panic stations *n* inf : *it was ~* c'était la panique générale.

panic-stricken *adj* affolé(e), pris(e) de panique.

pannier [ˈpænɪəʳ] *n* [on horse] bât *m* ; [on bicycle] sacoche *f*.

panoply [ˈpænəplɪ] *n* panoplie *f*.

panorama [ˌpænəˈrɑːmə] *n* panorama *m*.

panoramic [ˌpænəˈræmɪk] *adj* panoramique.

pansy [ˈpænzɪ] (*pl* **-ies**) *n* **- 1.** [flower] pensée *f* **- 2.** inf pej [man] tante *f*, tapette *f*.

pant [pænt] *vi* haleter.

panther [ˈpænθəʳ] (*pl inv* OR **-s**) *n* panthère *f*.

panties [ˈpæntɪz] *npl* inf culotte *f*.

pantihose [ˈpæntɪhəʊz] = **panty hose**.

panto [ˈpæntəʊ] (*pl* **-s**) *n* Br inf genre théâtral pour enfants.

pantomime [ˈpæntəmaɪm] *n* Br spectacle de Noël pour enfants, généralement inspiré de contes de fée ; ~ **dame** rôle travesti outré et ridicule dans la 'pantomime'.

PANTOMIME

Le genre typiquement britannique de la « pantomime » est très conventionnel ; certains personnages-types (« pantomime dame », « principal boy ») et certaines rengaines (« look behind you! », « oh yes he is! - oh no he isn't! ») apparaissent dans toutes les pièces. Ces pièces, qui se jouent au moment des fêtes de fin d'année, sont généralement inspirées d'un conte de fées.

pantry [ˈpæntrɪ] (*pl* **-ies**) *n* garde-manger *m* inv.

pants [pænts] *npl* **- 1.** Br [underpants - for men] slip *m* ; [- for women] culotte *f*, slip **- 2.** Am [trousers] pantalon *m*.

panty hose [ˈpæntɪhəʊz] *npl* Am collant *m*.

papa [Br pəˈpɑː, Am ˈpæpə] *n* papa *m*.

papacy [ˈpeɪpəsɪ] (*pl* **-ies**) *n* : **the ~** la papauté.

papadum [ˈpæpədəm] = **popadum**.

papal [ˈpeɪpl] *adj* papal(e).

paparazzi [ˌpæpəˈrætsɪ] *npl* usu pej paparazzi *mpl*.

papaya [pəˈpaɪə] *n* papaye *f*.

paper [ˈpeɪpəʳ] ⋄ *n* **- 1.** (U) [for writing on] papier *m* ; **a piece of ~** [sheet] une feuille de papier ; [scrap] un bout de papier ; **on ~** [written down] par écrit ; [in theory] sur le papier **- 2.** [newspaper] journal *m* **- 3.** [in exam - test] épreuve *f* ; [- answers] copie *f* **- 4.** [essay] : **~ (on)** essai *m* (sur) ⋄ *adj* [hat, bag etc] en papier ; fig [profits] théorique ⋄ *vt* tapisser.

⬥ **papers** *npl* [official documents] papiers *mpl*.

⬥ **paper over** *vt fus* fig dissimuler.

paperback [ˈpeɪpəbæk] *n* : **~ (book)** livre *m* de poche ; **in ~** en poche.

paperboy [ˈpeɪpəbɔɪ] *n* livreur *m* de journaux.

paper clip *n* trombone *m*.

papergirl [ˈpeɪpəgɜːl] *n* livreuse *f* de journaux.

paper handkerchief *n* mouchoir *m* en papier.

paper knife *n* coupe-papier *m* inv.

paper money *n* (U) papier-monnaie *m*.

paper shop *n* Br marchand *m* de journaux.

paperweight [ˈpeɪpəweɪt] *n* presse-papiers *m* inv.

paperwork [ˈpeɪpəwɜːk] *n* paperasserie *f*.

papier-mâché [ˌpæpjeɪˈmæʃeɪ] ⋄ *n* papier mâché *m* ⋄ *comp* en papier mâché.

papist [ˈpeɪpɪst] *n* pej papiste *mf*.

paprika [ˈpæprɪkə] *n* paprika *m*.

Papua [ˈpæpjʊə] *n* Papouasie *f*.

Papuan [ˈpæpjʊən] ⋄ *adj* papou(e) ⋄ *n* Papou *m*, -e *f*.

Papua New Guinea *n* Papouasie-Nouvelle-Guinée *f* ; **in ~** en Papouasie-Nouvelle-Guinée.

par [pɑːʳ] *n* **- 1.** [parity] : **on a ~ with** à égalité avec **- 2.** GOLF par *m*, normale *f* Can ; **under/over ~** en-dessous/en-dessus du par **- 3.** [good health] : **below** OR **under ~** pas en forme.

para [ˈpærə] *n* Br inf para *m*.

parable [ˈpærəbl] *n* parabole *f*.

parabola [pəˈræbələ] *n* parabole *f*.

paracetamol [ˌpærəˈsiːtəmɒl] *n* paracétamol *m*.

parachute [ˈpærəʃuːt] ⋄ *n* parachute *m* ⋄ *vi* sauter en parachute.

parade [pəˈreɪd] ⋄ *n* **- 1.** [celebratory] parade *f*, revue *f* **- 2.** MIL défilé *m* ; **to be on ~** défiler **- 3.** Br [street of shops] : **shopping ~** rue *f* commerçante ⋄ *vt* **- 1.** [people] faire défiler **- 2.** [object] montrer **- 3.** fig [flaunt] afficher ⋄ *vi* défiler.

parade ground *n* terrain *m* de manœuvres.

paradigm [ˈpærədaɪm] *n* paradigme *m*.

paradigmatic [ˌpærədɪgˈmætɪk] *adj* paradigmatique.

paradise [ˈpærədaɪs] *n* paradis *m*.
⬥ **Paradise** *n* Paradis *m*.

paradox [ˈpærədɒks] *n* paradoxe *m*.

paradoxical [ˌpærəˈdɒksɪkl] *adj* paradoxal(e).

paradoxically [ˌpærəˈdɒksɪklɪ] *adv* paradoxalement.

paraffin [ˈpærəfɪn] *n* paraffine *f*.

paraffin wax *n* paraffine *f*.

paragliding ['pærə,glaıdıŋ] n parapente m.

paragon ['pærəgən] n modèle m, parangon m.

paragraph ['pærəgrɑːf] n paragraphe m.

Paraguay ['pærəgwaı] n Paraguay m ; **in ~** au Paraguay.

Paraguayan [,pærə'gwaıən] <> adj paraguayen(enne) <> n Paraguayen m ; -enne f.

parakeet ['pærəkiːt] n perruche f.

parallel ['pærəlel] <> adj lit & fig : **~ (to** OR **with)** parallèle (à) <> n - **1.** GEOM parallèle f - **2.** [similarity & GEOGR] parallèle m - **3.** fig [similar person, object] équivalent m ; **to have no ~** ne pas avoir d'équivalent <> vt fig être semblable à.

parallel bars npl barres fpl parallèles.

paralyse Br, **paralyze** Am ['pærəlaız] vt lit & fig paralyser.

paralysed Br, **paralyzed** Am ['pærəlaızd] adj lit & fig paralysé(e).

paralysis [pə'rælısıs] (pl -lyses [-lısiːz]) n paralysie f.

paralytic [,pærə'lıtık] <> adj - **1.** MED paralytique - **2.** Br inf [drunk] ivre mort(e) <> n paralytique mf.

paramedic [,pærə'medık] n esp Am auxiliaire médical m, auxiliaire médicale f.

paramedical [,pærə'medıkl] adj esp Am paramédical(e).

parameter [pə'ræmıtəʳ] n paramètre m.

paramilitary [,pærə'mılıtrı] adj paramilitaire.

paramount ['pærəmaʊnt] adj primordial (e) ; **of ~ importance** d'une importance suprême.

paranoia [,pærə'nɔıə] n paranoïa f.

paranoiac [,pærə'nɔıæk] <> adj paranoïaque <> n paranoïaque mf.

paranoid ['pærənɔıd] adj paranoïaque.

paranormal [,pærə'nɔːml] adj paranormal(e).

parapet ['pærəpıt] n parapet m.

paraphernalia [,pærəfə'neıljə] n (U) attirail m, bazar m.

paraphrase ['pærəfreız] <> n paraphrase f <> vt paraphraser <> vi faire une paraphrase.

paraplegia [,pærə'pliːdʒə] n paraplégie f.

paraplegic [,pærə'pliːdʒık] <> adj paraplégique <> n paraplégique mf.

parapsychology [,pærəsaı'kɒlədʒı] n parapsychologie f.

Paraquat® ['pærəkwɒt] n Paraquat® m.

parasite ['pærəsaıt] n lit & fig parasite m.

parasitic [,pærə'sıtık] adj lit & fig parasite.

parasol ['pærəsɒl] n [above table] parasol m ; [hand-held] ombrelle f.

paratrooper ['pærətruːpəʳ] n parachutiste mf.

parboil ['pɑːbɔıl] vt faire bouillir OR cuire à demi.

parcel ['pɑːsl] (Br pt & pp **-led** ; cont **-ling**, Am pt & pp **-ed** ; cont **-ing**) n paquet m.
➤ **parcel up** vt sep empaqueter.

parcel post n : **to send sthg ~** envoyer qqch par colis postal.

parched [pɑːtʃt] adj - **1.** [gen] desséché(e) - **2.** inf [very thirsty] assoiffé(e), mort(e) de soif.

parchment ['pɑːtʃmənt] n parchemin m.

pardon ['pɑːdn] <> n - **1.** JUR grâce f - **2.** (U) [forgiveness] pardon m ; **I beg your ~?** [showing surprise, asking for repetition] comment?, pardon? ; **I beg your ~!** [to apologize] je vous demande pardon! <> vt - **1.** [forgive] pardonner ; **to ~ sb for sthg** pardonner qqch à qqn ; **~ me!** pardon!, excusez-moi! - **2.** JUR gracier <> excl comment?

pardonable ['pɑːdnəbl] adj pardonnable.

pare [peəʳ] vt [apple] peler, éplucher ; [fingernails] couper.
➤ **pare down** vt sep - **1.** [stick, fingernails] couper - **2.** fig [reduce] réduire.

parent ['peərənt] n père m, mère f.
➤ **parents** npl parents mpl.

parentage ['peərəntıdʒ] n (U) naissance f.

parental [pə'rentl] adj parental(e).

parent company n société f mère.

parenthesis [pə'renθısıs] (pl -theses [-θısiːz]) n parenthèse f.

parenthetical [,pærən'θetıkl] adj entre parenthèses.

parenthood ['peərənthʊd] n condition f de parent.

parenting ['peərəntıŋ] n l'art m d'être parent.

parent-teacher association n association f des parents d'élèves et des professeurs.

pariah [pə'raıə] n paria m.

Paris ['pærıs] n Paris.

parish ['pærıʃ] n - **1.** RELIG paroisse f - **2.** Br [area of local government] commune f.

parish council n Br conseil m municipal.

parishioner [pə'rıʃənəʳ] n paroissien m, -enne f.

Parisian [pə'rızjən] <> adj parisien(enne) <> n Parisien m, -enne f.

parity ['pærətı] n égalité f.

park [pɑːk] ◇ *n* parc *m*, jardin *m* public ◇ *vt* garer. ◇ *vi* se garer, stationner.

parka ['pɑːkə] *n* parka *f*.

parking ['pɑːkɪŋ] *n* stationnement *m* ; 'no ~' 'défense de stationner' ,' stationnement interdit'.

parking garage *n* Am parking *m* couvert.

parking light *n* Am feu *m* de position.

parking lot *n* Am parking *m*.

parking meter *n* parcmètre *m*.

parking place *n* place *f* de stationnement.

parking ticket *n* contravention *f*, PV *m*.

Parkinson's disease ['pɑːkɪnsnz-] *n* maladie *f* de Parkinson.

park keeper *n* Br gardien *m*, -enne *f* de parc.

parkland ['pɑːklænd] *n* (U) parc *m*.

parkway ['pɑːkweɪ] *n* Am *large route divisée ou bordée d'arbres.*

parky ['pɑːkɪ] (*compar* -ier ; *superl* -iest) *adj* Br *inf* : it's ~ il fait frisquet.

parlance ['pɑːləns] *n* : in **common/legal** *etc* ~ en langage courant/juridique *etc.*

parliament ['pɑːləmənt] *n* parlement *m*.

parliamentarian [,pɑːləmən'teərɪən] *n* parlementaire *mf*.

parliamentary [,pɑːlə'mentərɪ] *adj* parlementaire.

parlour Br, **parlor** Am ['pɑːləʳ] *n* dated salon *m*.

parlour game *n* jeu *m* de salon.

parlous ['pɑːləs] *adj* fml précaire.

Parmesan (cheese) [,pɑːmɪ'zæn-] *n* parmesan *m*.

parochial [pə'rəʊkjəl] *adj* pej de clocher.

parody ['pærədɪ] (*pl* -ies, *pt* & *pp* -ied) ◇ *n* parodie *f* ◇ *vt* parodier.

parole [pə'rəʊl] ◇ *n* (U) parole *f* ; **on** ~ en liberté conditionnelle ◇ *vt* mettre en liberté conditionnelle.

paroxysm ['pærəksɪzm] *n* [of rage] accès *m* ; **a** ~ **of laughter** un fou rire.

parquet ['pɑːkeɪ] *n* parquet *m*.

parrot ['pærət] *n* perroquet *m*.

parrot fashion *adv* comme un perroquet.

parry ['pærɪ] (*pt* & *pp* -ied) *vt* - **1.** [blow] parer - **2.** [question] éluder.

parsimonious [,pɑːsɪ'məʊnjəs] *adj* fml & pej parcimonieux(euse).

parsley ['pɑːslɪ] *n* persil *m*.

parsnip ['pɑːsnɪp] *n* panais *m*.

parson ['pɑːsn] *n* pasteur *m*.

parson's nose *n* Br croupion *m*.

part [pɑːt] ◇ *n* - **1.** [gen] partie *f* ; **the best** OR **better** ~ **of** la plus grande partie de ; **for the most** ~ dans l'ensemble ; **in** ~ en partie ; ~ **and parcel of** partie intégrante de - **2.** [of TV serial etc] épisode *m* - **3.** [component] pièce *f* - **4.** [in proportions] mesure *f* - **5.** THEATRE rôle *m* - **6.** [involvement] : ~ **in** participation *f* à ; **to play an important** ~ **in** jouer un rôle important dans ; **to take** ~ **in** participer à ; **to want no** ~ **in** ne pas vouloir se mêler de ; **for my** ~ en ce qui me concerne ; **on my/his** *etc* ~ de ma/sa *etc part* - **7.** Am [hair parting] raie *f* ◇ *adv* en partie ◇ *vt* : **to** ~ **one's hair** se faire une raie ◇ *vi* - **1.** [couple] se séparer - **2.** [curtains] s'écarter, s'ouvrir.

◆ **parts** *npl* : **in these** ~**s** dans cette région.

◆ **part with** *vt fus* [money] débourser ; [possession] se défaire de.

partake [pɑː'teɪk] (*pt* -took ; *pp* -taken) *vi* fml : **to** ~ **of** prendre.

part exchange *n* reprise *f* ; **to take sthg in** ~ reprendre qqch.

partial ['pɑːʃl] *adj* - **1.** [incomplete] partiel(elle) - **2.** [biased] partial(e) - **3.** [fond] : **to be** ~ **to** avoir un penchant pour.

partiality [,pɑːʃɪ'ælətɪ] *n* - **1.** [bias] partialité *f* - **2.** [fondness] : ~ **for** prédilection *f* OR penchant *m* pour.

partially ['pɑːʃəlɪ] *adv* partiellement.

participant [pɑː'tɪsɪpənt] *n* participant *m*, -e *f*.

participate [pɑː'tɪsɪpeɪt] *vi* : **to** ~ **(in)** participer (à).

participation [pɑː,tɪsɪ'peɪʃn] *n* participation *f*.

participle ['pɑːtɪsɪpl] *n* participe *m*.

particle ['pɑːtɪkl] *n* particule *f*.

parti-coloured ['pɑːtɪ-] *adj* bariolé(e).

particular [pə'tɪkjʊləʳ] *adj* - **1.** [gen] particulier(ère) - **2.** [fussy] pointilleux(euse) ; ~ **about** exigeant(e) à propos de.

◆ **particulars** *npl* renseignements *mpl*.

◆ **in particular** *adv* en particulier.

particularity [pə,tɪkjʊ'lærətɪ] (*pl* -ies) *n* particularité *f*.

particularly [pə'tɪkjʊləlɪ] *adv* particulièrement.

parting ['pɑːtɪŋ] *n* - **1.** [separation] séparation *f* - **2.** Br [in hair] raie *f*.

parting shot *n* flèche *f* du Parthe.

partisan [,pɑːtɪ'zæn] ◇ *adj* partisan(e) ◇ *n* partisan *m*, -e *f*.

partition [pɑː'tɪʃn] ◇ *n* - **1.** [wall, screen] cloison *f* - **2.** [of country] partition *f* ◇ *vt* - **1.** [room] cloisonner - **2.** [country] partager.

partly ['pɑːtlɪ] *adv* partiellement, en partie.
partner ['pɑːtnəʳ] ⟨⟩ *n* - **1.** [in game dance] partenaire *mf* ; [spouse] conjoint *m*, -e *f* ; [not married] compagnon *m*, compagne *f* - **2.** [in a business, crime] associé *m*, -e *f* ⟨⟩ *vt* être le partenaire de.
partnership ['pɑːtnəʃɪp] *n* association *f* ; **to enter into ~ (with)** s'associer (avec).
partook [pɑː'tʊk] *pt* ⊏⟩ **partake**.
partridge ['pɑːtrɪdʒ] *n* perdrix *f*.
part-time *adj* & *adv* à temps partiel.
part-timer *n* travailleur *m*, -euse *f* à temps partiel.
party ['pɑːtɪ] (*pl* **-ies**) ⟨⟩ *n* - **1.** POL parti *m* - **2.** [social gathering] fête *f*, réception *f* ; **to have** OR **throw a ~** donner une fête - **3.** [group] groupe *m* - **4.** JUR partie *f* ; **to be a ~ to** être complice de ⟨⟩ *vi* inf faire la fête.
party line *n* - **1.** POL ligne *f* du parti - **2.** TELEC ligne *f* commune à deux abonnés.
party piece *n* inf numéro *m* habituel.
party political broadcast *n* Br *moment d'antenne réservé à un parti politique.*
party politics *n* (U) politique *f* politicienne.
party wall *n* mur *m* mitoyen.
parvenu(e) ['pɑːvənjuː] *n* pej parvenu *m*, -e *f*.
pass [pɑːs] ⟨⟩ *n* - **1.** SPORT passe *f* - **2.** [document - for security] laissez-passer *m inv* ; [- for travel] carte *f* d'abonnement - **3.** Br [in exam] mention *f* passable - **4.** [between mountains] col *m* - **5.** phr : **to make a ~ at sb** faire du plat à qqn ⟨⟩ *vt* - **1.** [object, time] passer ; **to ~ sthg to sb, to ~ sb sthg** passer qqch à qqn - **2.** [person in street etc] croiser - **3.** [place] passer devant - **4.** AUT dépasser, doubler - **5.** [exceed] dépasser - **6.** [exam] réussir (à) ; [driving test] passer - **7.** [candidate] recevoir, admettre - **8.** [law, motion] voter - **9.** [opinion] émettre ; [judgment] rendre, prononcer ⟨⟩ *vi* - **1.** [gen] passer - **2.** AUT doubler, dépasser - **3.** SPORT faire une passe - **4.** [in exam] réussir, être reçu(e) - **5.** [occur] se dérouler, avoir lieu.
◆ **pass around** = **pass round**.
◆ **pass as** *vt fus* passer pour.
◆ **pass away** *vi* s'éteindre.
◆ **pass by** ⟨⟩ *vt sep* : **the news ~ed him by** la nouvelle ne l'a pas affecté ⟨⟩ *vi* passer à côté.
◆ **pass for** = **pass as**.
◆ **pass off** *vt sep* : **to ~ sb/sthg off as** faire passer qqn/qqch pour.
◆ **pass on** ⟨⟩ *vt sep* : **to ~ sthg on (to)** [object] faire passer qqch (à) ; [tradition, information]

transmettre qqch (à) ⟨⟩ *vi* - **1.** [move on] continuer son chemin - **2.** = **pass away**.
◆ **pass out** *vi* - **1.** [faint] s'évanouir - **2.** Br MIL finir OR terminer ses classes.
◆ **pass over** *vt fus* [problem, topic] passer sous silence.
◆ **pass round** *vt sep* faire passer.
◆ **pass to** *vt fus* passer à, revenir à.
◆ **pass up** *vt sep* [opportunity, invitation] laisser passer.
passable ['pɑːsəbl] *adj* - **1.** [satisfactory] passable - **2.** [road] praticable ; [river] franchissable.
passably ['pɑːsəblɪ] *adv* passablement.
passage ['pæsɪdʒ] *n* - **1.** [gen] passage *m* - **2.** [between rooms] couloir *m* - **3.** [sea journey] traversée *f*.
passageway ['pæsɪdʒweɪ] *n* [between houses] passage *m* ; [between rooms] couloir *m*.
passbook ['pɑːsbʊk] *n* livret *m* (d'épargne).
passé [pæ'seɪ] *adj* pej démodé(e).
passenger ['pæsɪndʒəʳ] *n* passager *m*, -ère *f*.
passerby [,pɑːsə'baɪ] (*pl* **passersby** [,pɑːsəz'baɪ]) *n* passant *m*, -e *f*.
passing ['pɑːsɪŋ] ⟨⟩ *adj* [remark] en passant ; [trend] passager(ère) ⟨⟩ *n* : **with the ~ of time** avec le temps.
◆ **in passing** *adv* en passant.
passion ['pæʃn] *n* passion *f* ; **to have a ~ for** avoir la passion de.
◆ **Passion** *n* : **the Passion** la Passion.
passionate ['pæʃənət] *adj* passionné(e).
passionately ['pæʃənətlɪ] *adv* avec passion.
passionfruit ['pæʃənfruːt] *n* fruit *m* de la passion.
passive ['pæsɪv] ⟨⟩ *adj* passif(ive) ⟨⟩ *n* GRAMM : **the ~** le passif.
passively ['pæsɪvlɪ] *adv* passivement.
passive resistance *n* résistance *f* passive.
passive smoking *n* tabagisme *m* passif.
passivity [pæ'sɪvətɪ] *n* passivité *f*.
passkey ['pɑːskiː] *n* passe *m*.
Passover ['pɑːs,əʊvəʳ] *n* : **(the) ~** la Pâque juive.
passport ['pɑːspɔːt] *n* - **1.** [document] passeport *m* - **2.** fig [means] : **~ to** clef *f* de.
passport control *n* contrôle *m* des passeports.
password ['pɑːswɜːd] *n* mot *m* de passe.
past [pɑːst] ⟨⟩ *adj* - **1.** [former] passé(e) ; **for the ~ five years** ces cinq dernières années ; **the ~ week** la semaine passée OR dernière - **2.** [finished] fini(e) ⟨⟩ *adv* - **1.** [in times] : **it's ten**

~ il est dix - **2.** [in front] : **to drive** ~ passer (devant) en voiture ; **to run** ~ passer (devant) en courant ◇ *n* passé *m* ; **in the** ~ dans le temps ◇ *prep* - **1.** [in times] : **it's half** ~ **eight** il est huit heures et demie ; **it's five** ~ **nine** il est neuf heures cinq - **2.** [in front of] devant ; **we drove** ~ **them** nous les avons dépassés en voiture - **3.** [beyond] après, au-delà de ; **to be** ~ **it** inf être trop vieux pour ça ; **I wouldn't put it** ~ **him** inf pej cela ne m'étonnerait pas de lui.

pasta ['pæstə] *n (U)* pâtes *fpl.*

paste [peist] ◇ *n* - **1.** [gen] pâte *f* - **2.** CULIN pâté *m* - **3.** *(U)* [glue] colle *f* - **4.** *(U)* [jewellery] strass *m* ◇ *vt* coller.

pastel ['pæstl] ◇ *adj* pastel *(inv)* ◇ *n* pastel *m.*

paste-up *n* TYPO collage *m.*

pasteurize, -ise ['pɑːstʃəraɪz] *vt* pasteuriser.

pastiche [pæ'stiːʃ] *n* pastiche *m.*

pastille ['pæstɪl] *n* pastille *f.*

pastime ['pɑːstaɪm] *n* passe-temps *m inv.*

pasting ['peɪstɪŋ] *n* inf [beating] rossée *f.*

pastor ['pɑːstə'] *n* pasteur *m.*

pastoral ['pɑːstərəl] *adj* pastoral(e)

past participle *n* participe *m* passé.

pastrami [pə'strɑːmɪ] *n viande de bœuf fumée et épicée.*

pastry ['peɪstrɪ] *(pl* **-ies**) *n* - **1.** [mixture] pâte *f* - **2.** [cake] pâtisserie *f.*

past tense *n* passé *m.*

pasture ['pɑːstʃə'] *n* pâturage *m,* pré *m.*

pastureland ['pɑːstʃələænd] *n* pâturage *m,* herbage *m.*

pasty[1] ['peɪstɪ] *(compar* **-ier** ; *superl* **-iest**) *adj* blafard(e), terreux(euse).

pasty[2] ['pæstɪ] *(pl* **-ies**) *n* Br petit pâté *m,* friand *m.*

pasty-faced ['peɪstɪ,feɪst] *adj* au teint blafard OR terreux.

pat [pæt] *(compar* **-ter** ; *superl* **-test**, *pt & pp* **-ted** ; *cont* **-ting**) ◇ *adj* tout prêt (toute prête), tout fait (toute faite) ◇ *n* - **1.** [light stroke] petite tape *f* ; [to animal] caresse *f* - **2.** [of butter] noix *f,* noisette *f* ◇ *vt* [person] tapoter, donner une tape à ; [animal] caresser.

Patagonia [,pætə'gəʊnjə] *n* Patagonie *f* ; **in** ~ en Patagonie.

Patagonian [,pætə'gəʊnjən] ◇ *adj* patagon(onne) ◇ *n* Patagon *m,* -onne *f.*

patch [pætʃ] ◇ *n* - **1.** [piece of material] pièce *f* ; [to cover eye] bandeau *m* - **2.** [small area - of snow, ice] plaque *f* - **3.** [of land] parcelle *f,* lopin *m* ;

vegetable ~ carré *m* de légumes - **4.** MED patch *m* - **5.** [period of time] : **a difficult** ~ une mauvaise passe - **6.** phr : **not to be a** ~ **on sb** inf ne pas arriver OR venir à la cheville de qqn ; **not to be a** ~ **on sthg** inf ne pas valoir qqch ◇ *vt* rapiécer.

◆ **patch together** *vt sep* faire à la va-vite.

◆ **patch up** *vt sep* - **1.** [mend] rafistoler, bricoler - **2.** fig [quarrel] régler, arranger ; **to** ~ **up a relationship** se raccommoder.

patchwork ['pætʃwɜːk] ◇ *adj* en patchwork ◇ *n* patchwork *m.*

patchy ['pætʃɪ] *(compar* **-ier** ; *superl* **-iest**) *adj* [gen] inégal(e) ; [knowledge] insuffisant(e), imparfait(e).

pâté ['pæteɪ] *n* pâté *m.*

patent [Br 'peɪtənt, Am 'pætənt] ◇ *adj* [obvious] évident(e), manifeste ◇ *n* brevet *m* (d'invention) ◇ *vt* faire breveter.

patented [Br 'peɪtəntɪd, Am 'pætəntɪd] *adj* breveté(e).

patentee [Br ,peɪtən'tiː, Am ,pætən'tiː] *n* titulaire *m* d'un brevet.

patent leather *n* cuir *m* verni.

patently [Br 'peɪtəntlɪ, Am 'pætəntlɪ] *adv* manifestement.

Patent Office *n* bureau *m* des brevets.

paternal [pə'tɜːnl] *adj* paternel(elle).

paternalistic [pə,tɜːnə'lɪstɪk] *adj* pej paternaliste.

paternity [pə'tɜːnətɪ] *n* paternité *f.*

paternity leave *n* congé *m* parental *(pour pères).*

paternity suit *n* JUR action *f* en recherche de paternité.

path [pɑːθ, *pl* pɑːðz] *n* - **1.** [track] chemin *m,* sentier *m* - **2.** [way ahead, course of action] voie *f,* chemin *m* - **3.** [trajectory] trajectoire *f* - **4.** phr : **our ~s had crossed before** nos chemins s'étaient déjà croisés.

pathetic [pə'θetɪk] *adj* - **1.** [causing pity] pitoyable, attendrissant(e) - **2.** [useless - efforts, person] pitoyable, minable.

pathetically [pə'θetɪklɪ] *adv* - **1.** [cry, whimper] pitoyablement - **2.** [inadequate, feeble] lamentablement.

pathological [,pæθə'lɒdʒɪkl] *adj* pathologique.

pathologist [pə'θɒlədʒɪst] *n* pathologiste *mf.*

pathology [pə'θɒlədʒɪ] *n* pathologie *f.*

pathos ['peɪθɒs] *n* pathétique *m.*

pathway ['pɑːθweɪ] *n* chemin *m,* sentier *m.*

patience ['peɪʃns] *n* - **1.** [of person] patience *f* ;

to try sb's ~ mettre la patience de qqn à l'épreuve, éprouver la patience de qqn - **2.** [card game] réussite f.

patient ['peɪʃnt] ⬦ adj patient(e) ⬦ n [in hospital] patient m, -e f, malade mf ; [of doctor] patient.

patiently ['peɪʃntlɪ] adv patiemment.

patina ['pætɪnə] n patine f.

patio ['pætɪəʊ] (pl -s) n patio m.

patio doors npl portes vitrées coulissantes.

Patna rice ['pætnə-] n riz m Patna (à grains longs).

patois ['pætwɑ:] (pl inv) n patois m.

patriarch ['peɪtrɪɑ:k] n patriarche m.

patriarchy ['peɪtrɪɑ:kɪ] (pl -ies) n patriarcat m.

patrimony [Br 'pætrɪmənɪ, Am 'pætrɪməʊnɪ] n fml patrimoine m, héritage m.

patriot [Br 'pætrɪət, Am 'peɪtrɪət] n patriote mf.

patriotic [Br ˌpætrɪ'ɒtɪk, Am ˌpeɪtrɪ'ɒtɪk] adj [gen] patriotique ; [person] patriote.

patriotism [Br 'pætrɪətɪzm, Am 'peɪtrɪətɪzm] n patriotisme m.

patrol [pə'trəʊl] (pt & pp -led ; cont -ling) ⬦ n patrouille f ; **to be on** ~ être de patrouille ; **to go on** ~ aller en patrouille ⬦ vt patrouiller dans, faire une patrouille dans.

patrol car n voiture f de police.

patrolman [pə'trəʊlmən] (pl -men [-mən]) n Am agent m de police.

patrol wagon n Am fourgon m cellulaire.

patrolwoman [pə'trəʊlˌwʊmən] (pl -women [-ˌwɪmɪn]) n Am femme f agent de police.

patron ['peɪtrən] n - **1.** [of arts] mécène m, protecteur m, -trice f - **2.** Br [of charity] patron m, -onne f - **3.** fml [customer] client m, -e f.

patronage ['peɪtrənɪdʒ] n patronage m.

patronize, -ise ['pætrənaɪz] vt - **1.** [talk down to] traiter avec condescendance - **2.** fml [back financially] patronner, protéger.

patronizing ['pætrənaɪzɪŋ] adj condescendant(e).

patron saint n saint patron m, sainte patronne f.

patter ['pætər] ⬦ n - **1.** [sound - of rain] crépitement m - **2.** [talk] baratin m, bavardage m ⬦ vi [feet, paws] trottiner ; [rain] frapper, fouetter.

pattern ['pætən] n - **1.** [design] motif m, dessin m - **2.** [of distribution, population] schéma m ; [of life, behaviour] mode m - **3.** [diagram] : **(sewing)** ~ patron m - **4.** [model] modèle m.

patterned ['pætənd] adj à motifs.

patty ['pætɪ] (pl -ies) n petit pâté m.

paucity ['pɔ:sətɪ] n indigence f.

paunch [pɔ:ntʃ] n bedaine f.

paunchy ['pɔ:ntʃɪ] (compar -ier ; superl -iest) adj ventru(e), ventripotent(e).

pauper ['pɔ:pər] n indigent m, -e f, nécessiteux m, -euse f.

pause [pɔ:z] ⬦ n - **1.** [short silence] pause f, silence m - **2.** [break] pause f, arrêt m ⬦ vi - **1.** [stop speaking] marquer un temps - **2.** [stop moving, doing] faire une pause, s'arrêter.

pave [peɪv] vt paver ; **to** ~ **the way for sb/sthg** ouvrir la voie à qqn/qqch.

paved [peɪvd] adj pavé(e).

pavement ['peɪvmənt] n - **1.** Br [at side of road] trottoir m - **2.** Am [roadway] chaussée f.

pavement artist n Br artiste mf des rues.

pavilion [pə'vɪljən] n pavillon m.

paving ['peɪvɪŋ] n (U) pavé m.

paving stone n pavé m.

paw [pɔ:] ⬦ n patte f ⬦ vt - **1.** [subj : animal] donner des coups de patte à - **2.** pej [subj : person] tripoter, peloter.

pawn [pɔ:n] ⬦ n lit & fig pion m ⬦ vt mettre en gage.

pawnbroker ['pɔ:nˌbrəʊkər] n prêteur m, -euse f sur gages.

pawnshop ['pɔ:nʃɒp] n boutique f de prêteur sur gages.

pay [peɪ] (pt & pp paid) ⬦ vt - **1.** [gen] payer ; **to** ~ **sb for sthg** payer qqn pour qqch, payer qqch à qqn ; **I paid £20 for that shirt** j'ai payé cette chemise 20 livres ; **to** ~ **money into an account** Br verser de l'argent sur un compte ; **to** ~ **a cheque into an account** déposer un chèque sur un compte ; **to** ~ **one's way** payer sa part - **2.** [be profitable to] rapporter à ; **it will** ~ **you not to say anything** fig tu as intérêt OR tu gagneras à ne rien dire - **3.** [give, make] : **to** ~ **attention (to sb/sthg)** prêter attention (à qqn/qqch) ; **to** ~ **sb a compliment** faire un compliment à qqn ; **to** ~ **sb a visit** rendre visite à qqn ⬦ vi payer ; **to** ~ **dearly for sthg** fig payer qqch cher ⬦ n salaire m, traitement m.

◆ **pay back** vt sep - **1.** [return loan of money] rembourser - **2.** [revenge oneself on] revaloir ; **I'll** ~ **you back for that** tu me le paieras, je te le revaudrai.

◆ **pay off** ⬦ vt sep - **1.** [repay - debt] s'acquitter de, régler ; [- loan] rembourser - **2.** [dismiss] licencier, congédier - **3.** [bribe] soudoyer, acheter ⬦ vi [course of action] être payant(e).

◆ **pay out** ⬦ vt sep - **1.** [money] dépenser,

débourser **- 2.** [rope] laisser filer, lâcher ◇ *vi* dépenser, débourser.

pay up *vi* payer.

payable ['peɪəbl] *adj* **- 1.** [gen] payable **- 2.** [on cheque] : ~ **to** à l'ordre de.

paybed ['peɪbed] *n* Br lit *m* privé.

paycheck ['peɪtʃek] *n* Am paie *f*.

payday ['peɪdeɪ] *n* jour *m* de paie.

PAYE (*abbr of* **pay as you earn**) *n en Grande-Bretagne, système de retenue à la source des impôts sur le revenu*.

payee [peɪ'iː] *n* bénéficiaire *mf*.

pay envelope *n* Am salaire *m*.

payer ['peɪə'] *n* payeur *m*, -euse *f*.

paying guest ['peɪɪŋ-] *n* hôte *m* payant.

paying-in book ['peɪɪŋ-] *n* Br carnet *m* de versements.

payload ['peɪləʊd] *n* charge *f* utile.

paymaster ['peɪˌmɑːstə'] *n* intendant *m*.

paymaster general *n* trésorier-payeur *m*.

payment ['peɪmənt] *n* paiement *m*.

payoff ['peɪɒf] *n* **- 1.** [result] résultat *m* **- 2.** Br [redundancy payment] indemnité *f* de licenciement.

payola [peɪ'əʊlə] *n* inf esp Am pot-de-vin *m*, dessous *m* de table.

pay packet *n* Br **- 1.** [envelope] enveloppe *f* de paie **- 2.** [wages] paie *f*.

pay-per-view *adj* [television, distributor] à péage.

pay phone, pay station Am *n* téléphone *m* public, cabine *f* téléphonique.

payroll ['peɪrəʊl] *n* registre *m* du personnel ; **they have 100 people on the** ~ ils ont 100 employés OR salariés.

payslip ['peɪslɪp] *n* Br feuille *f* OR bulletin *m* de paie.

pay station Am = **pay phone**.

pay television, pay TV *n* chaîne *f* à péage.

PBS (*abbr of* **Public Broadcasting Service**) *n société américaine de production télévisuelle*.

PBX (*abbr of* **private branch exchange**) *n* autocommutateur *m* privé.

pc ◇ *n abbr of* **postcard** ◇ (*abbr of* **per cent**) p. cent.

p/c *abbr of* **petty cash**.

PC ◇ *n* **- 1.** (*abbr of* **personal computer**) PC *m*,. micro *m* **- 2.** *abbr of* **police constable - 3.** (*abbr of* **privy councillor**) *membre du conseil privé* ◇ *adj abbr of* **politically correct**.

PCB (*abbr of* **printed circuit board**) *n* plaquette *f* à circuits imprimés.

PCV (*abbr of* **passenger carrying vehicle**) *n véhicule de transport en commun* (en Grande-Bretagne).

pd *abbr of* **paid**.

PD *abbr of* **police department**.

pdq (*abbr of* **pretty damn quick**) *adv* inf illico presto.

PDSA (*abbr of* **People's Dispensary for Sick Animals**) *n association britannique de soins aux animaux malades*.

PDT (*abbr of* **Pacific Daylight Time**) *n heure d'été du Pacifique*.

PE (*abbr of* **physical education**) *n* EPS *f*.

pea [piː] *n* pois *m*.

peace [piːs] *n (U)* paix *f* ; [quiet, calm] calme *m*, tranquillité *f* ; **to be at** ~ **with sthg/sb/o.s.** être en paix avec qqch/qqn/soi-même, être en accord avec qqch/qqn/soi-même ; **to make (one's)** ~ **with sb** faire la paix avec qqn.

peaceable ['piːsəbl] *adj* paisible, pacifique.

peaceably ['piːsəblɪ] *adv* paisiblement, pacifiquement.

Peace Corps *n organisation américaine de coopération avec les Pays en Voie de Développement*.

peaceful ['piːsful] *adj* **- 1.** [quiet, calm] paisible, calme **- 2.** [not aggressive - person] pacifique ; [- demonstration] non-violent(e).

peacefully ['piːsfulɪ] *adv* paisiblement.

peacefulness ['piːsfulnɪs] *n* paix *f*, calme *m*.

peacekeeping force ['piːsˌkiːpɪŋ-] *n* force *f* de maintien de la paix.

peacemaker ['piːsˌmeɪkə'] *n* pacificateur *m*, -trice *f*.

peace offering *n* inf gage *m* de paix, cadeau *m* (pour faire la paix).

peacetime ['piːstaɪm] *n* temps *m* de paix.

peach [piːtʃ] ◇ *adj* couleur pêche *(inv)* ◇ *n* pêche *f*.

Peach Melba [-'melbə] *n* pêche *f* Melba.

peacock ['piːkɒk] *n* paon *m*.

peahen ['piːhen] *n* paonne *f*.

peak [piːk] ◇ *n* **- 1.** [mountain top] sommet *m*, cime *f* **- 2.** fig [of career, success] apogée *m*, sommet *m* **- 3.** [of cap] visière *f* ◇ *adj* [condition] optimum ◇ *vi* atteindre un niveau maximum.

peaked [piːkt] *adj* [cap] à visière.

peak hours *npl* heures *fpl* d'affluence OR de pointe.

peak period *n* période *f* de pointe.

peak rate *n* tarif *m* normal.

peaky ['piːkɪ] (*compar* -ier ; *superl* -iest) *adj* Br inf souffrant(e), fatigué(e).

peal [piːl] ◇ *n* [of bells] carillonnement *m* ; [of laughter] éclat *m* ; [of thunder] coup *m* ◇ *vi* [bells] carillonner.

peanut ['piːnʌt] *n* cacahuète *f*.

peanut butter *n* beurre *m* de cacahuètes.

pear [peə'] *n* poire *f*.

pearl [pɜːl] *n* perle *f*.

pearly ['pɜːlɪ] (*compar* -ier ; *superl* -iest) *adj* nacré(e).

peasant ['peznt] *n* - **1.** [in countryside] paysan *m*, -anne *f* - **2.** pej [ignorant person] péquenaud *m*, -e *f*.

peasantry ['pezntrɪ] *n* : **the ~** la paysannerie, les paysans *mpl*.

peashooter ['piːˌʃuːtə'] *n* sarbacane *f*.

peat [piːt] *n* tourbe *f*.

peaty ['piːtɪ] (*compar* -ier ; *superl* -iest) *adj* tourbeux(euse).

pebble ['pebl] *n* galet *m*, caillou *m*.

pebbledash [ˌpebl'dæʃ] *n* Br crépi *m*.

pecan (nut) [pɪ'kæn-] *n* noix *f* de pecan OR pacane.

peck [pek] ◇ *n* - **1.** [with beak] coup *m* de bec - **2.** [kiss] bise *f* ◇ *vt* - **1.** [with beak] picoter, becqueter - **2.** [kiss] : **to ~ sb on the cheek** faire une bise à qqn.

pecking order ['pekɪŋ-] *n* hiérarchie *f*.

peckish ['pekɪʃ] *adj* Br inf : **to feel ~** avoir un petit creux.

pectin ['pektɪn] *n* pectine *f*.

pectoral ['pektərəl] *adj* pectoral(e).

peculiar [pɪ'kjuːljə'] *adj* - **1.** [odd] bizarre, curieux(euse) - **2.** [slightly ill] : **to feel ~** se sentir tout drôle (toute drôle) OR tout chose (toute chose) - **3.** [characteristic] : **~ to** propre à, particulier(ère) à.

peculiarity [pɪˌkjuːlɪ'ærətɪ] (*pl* -ies) *n* - **1.** [oddness] bizarrerie *f*, singularité *f* - **2.** [characteristic] particularité *f*, caractéristique *f*.

peculiarly [pɪ'kjuːljəlɪ] *adv* - **1.** [especially] particulièrement - **2.** [oddly] curieusement, bizarrement - **3.** [characteristically] typiquement.

pecuniary [pɪ'kjuːnjərɪ] *adj* pécuniaire.

pedagogical [ˌpedə'gɒdʒɪkl] *adj* pédagogique.

pedagogy ['pedəgɒdʒɪ] *n* pédagogie *f*.

pedal ['pedl] (Br *pt* & *pp* -led ; *cont* -ling, Am *pt* & *pp* -ed ; *cont* -ing), ◇ *n* pédale *f* ◇ *vi* pédaler.

pedal bin *n* poubelle *f* à pédale.

pedalo ['pedələʊ] *n* Br pédalo *m*.

pedant ['pedənt] *n* pédant *m*, -e *f*.

pedantic [pɪ'dæntɪk] *adj* pej pédant(e).

pedantry ['pedəntrɪ] *n* pej pédantisme *m*, pédanterie *f*.

peddle ['pedl] *vt* - **1.** [drugs] faire le trafic de - **2.** [gossip, rumour] colporter, répandre.

peddler ['pedlə'] *n* - **1.** [drug dealer] trafiquant *m* de drogue - **2.** Am = **pedlar**.

pederast ['pedəræst] *n* pédéraste *m*.

pedestal ['pedɪstl] *n* piédestal *m* ; **to put sb on a ~** mettre qqn sur un piédestal.

pedestrian [pɪ'destrɪən] ◇ *adj* pej médiocre, dépourvu(e) d'intérêt ◇ *n* piéton *m*.

pedestrian crossing *n* Br passage *m* pour piétons, passage clouté.

pedestrianize, -ise [pɪ'destrɪənaɪz] *vt* transformer en zone piétonne.

pedestrian precinct Br, **pedestrian zone** Am *n* zone *f* piétonne.

pediatric [ˌpiːdɪ'ætrɪk] *adj* de pédiatrie.

pediatrician [ˌpiːdɪə'trɪʃn] *n* pédiatre *mf*.

pediatrics [ˌpiːdɪ'ætrɪks] *n* pédiatrie *f*.

pedicure ['pedɪˌkjʊə'] *n* pédicurie *f*.

pedigree ['pedɪgriː] ◇ *adj* [animal] de race ◇ *n* - **1.** [of animal] pedigree *m* - **2.** [of person] ascendance *f*, généalogie *f*.

pedlar Br, **peddler** Am ['pedlə'] *n* colporteur *m*.

pedophile ['piːdəfaɪl] *n* pédophile *m*.

pee [piː] inf ◇ *n* pipi *m*, pisse *f* ; **to go for a ~** aller pisser un coup ◇ *vi* faire pipi, pisser.

peek [piːk] inf ◇ *n* coup *m* d'œil furtif ◇ *vi* jeter un coup d'œil furtif.

peel [piːl] ◇ *n* [of apple, potato] peau *f* ; [of orange, lemon] écorce *f* ◇ *vt* éplucher, peler ◇ *vi* - **1.** [paint] s'écailler - **2.** [wallpaper] se décoller - **3.** [skin] peler.

➤ **peel off** *vt sep* [gen] enlever ; [label] décoller, détacher.

peeler ['piːlə'] *n* couteau-éplucheur *m*.

peelings ['piːlɪŋz] *npl* épluchures *fpl*.

peep [piːp] ◇ *n* - **1.** [look] coup *m* d'œil OR regard *m* furtif - **2.** inf [sound] bruit *m* ◇ *vi* jeter un coup d'œil furtif.

➤ **peep out** *vi* apparaître, se montrer.

peephole ['piːphəʊl] *n* judas *m*.

peeping Tom [ˌpiːpɪŋ'tɒm] *n* voyeur *m*.

peep show *n* visionneuse *f*.

peer [pɪə'] ◇ *n* pair *m* ◇ *vi* scruter, regarder attentivement.

peerage ['pɪərɪdʒ] *n* [rank] pairie *f* ; **the ~** les pairs *mpl*.

peeress ['pɪərɪs] *n* pairesse *f*.

peer group *n* pairs *mpl*.

peer pressure n influence f de ses pairs.
peeved [piːvd] adj inf fâché(e), irrité(e).
peevish ['piːvɪʃ] adj grincheux(euse).
peg [peg] (pt & pp **-ged** ; cont **-ging**) ◇ n
- **1.** [hook] cheville f - **2.** [for clothes] pince f à
linge - **3.** [for tent] piquet m ◇ vt fig [prices] bloquer.
➤ **peg out** vi Br inf casser sa pipe.
pegboard ['pegbɔːd] n tableau m à trous.
PEI abbr of **Prince Edward Island.**
pejorative [pɪ'dʒɒrətɪv] adj péjoratif(ive).
pekinese [,piːkə'niːz], **pekingese** [,piːkɪŋ-
'iːz] (pl inv) n [dog] pékinois m.
➤ **Pekinese, Pekingese** ◇ adj pékinois(e)
◇ n Pékinois m, -e f.
Peking [piː'kɪŋ] n Pékin.
pekingese = **pekinese.**
pelican ['pelɪkən] (pl inv OR **-s**) n pélican m.
pelican crossing n Br passage pour piétons
avec feux de circulation.
pellet ['pelɪt] n - **1.** [small ball] boulette f - **2.** [for
gun] plomb m.
pell-mell [,pel'mel] adv à la débandade.
pelmet ['pelmɪt] n Br lambrequin m.
Peloponnese [,peləpə'niːz] npl : **the ~** le Pé-
loponnèse.
pelt [pelt] ◇ n - **1.** [animal skin] peau f, fourrure f - **2.** [speed] : **at full ~** à fond de train, à toute vitesse ◇ vt : **to ~ sb (with sthg)** bombarder qqn (de qqch) ◇ vi [run fast] : **to ~ along**
courir ventre à terre ; **to ~ down the stairs**
dévaler l'escalier.
➤ **pelt down** v impers [rain] : **it's ~ing down** il
pleut à verse.
pelvic ['pelvɪk] adj pelvien(enne).
pelvis ['pelvɪs] (pl **-vises** OR **-ves** [-viːz]) n pelvis m, bassin m.
pen [pen] (pt & pp **-ned** ; cont **-ning**) ◇ n
- **1.** [for writing] stylo m - **2.** [enclosure] parc m,
enclos m ◇ vt - **1.** literary [write] écrire - **2.** [en-
close] parquer.
penal ['piːnl] adj pénal(e).
penalize, -ise ['piːnəlaɪz] vt - **1.** [gen] pénaliser - **2.** [put at a disadvantage] désavantager.
penal settlement n colonie f pénitentiaire.
penalty ['penltɪ] (pl **-ies**) n - **1.** [punishment] pénalité f ; **to pay the ~ (for sthg)** fig supporter
OR subir les conséquences (de qqch)
- **2.** [fine] amende f - **3.** HOCKEY pénalité f ;
~ (kick) FTBL penalty m ; RUGBY (coup m de pied
de) pénalité f.
penalty area n Br FTBL surface f de réparation.

penalty box n - **1.** Br FTBL = **penalty area**
- **2.** ICE HOCKEY banc m des pénalités.
penalty clause n clause f pénale.
penalty goal n RUGBY but m de pénalité.
penalty kick ▷ **penalty.**
penance ['penəns] n - **1.** RELIG pénitence f
- **2.** fig [punishment] corvée f, pensum m.
pen-and-ink adj à la plume.
pence [pens] Br pl ▷ **penny.**
penchant [Br pɑ̃ʃɑ̃, Am 'pentʃənt] n : **to have a
~ for sthg** avoir un faible pour qqch ; **to have
a ~ for doing sthg** avoir tendance à OR bien
aimer faire qqch.
pencil ['pensl] (Br pt & pp **-led** ; cont **-ling**, Am
pt & pp **-ed** ; cont **-ing**) ◇ n crayon m ; **in ~**
au crayon ◇ vt griffonner au crayon,
crayonner.
pencil case n trousse f (d'écolier).
pencil sharpener n taille-crayon m.
pendant ['pendənt] n [jewel on chain] pendentif
m.
pending ['pendɪŋ] fml ◇ adj - **1.** [imminent] im-
minent(e) - **2.** [court case] en instance ◇ prep
en attendant.
pending tray n Br (corbeille f des) affaires
fpl en attente OR à traiter.
pendulum ['pendjʊləm] (pl **-s**) n balancier m.
penetrate ['penɪtreɪt] ◇ vt - **1.** [gen] pénétrer dans ; [subj : light] percer ; [subj : rain] s'infiltrer dans - **2.** [subj : spy] infiltrer ◇ vi inf [be
understood] : **it didn't ~** c'est resté sans effet
sur lui/elle etc.
penetrating ['penɪtreɪtɪŋ] adj pénétrant(e) ;
[scream, voice] perçant(e).
penetration [,penɪ'treɪʃn] n pénétration f.
pen friend n correspondant m, -e f.
penguin ['peŋgwɪn] n manchot m.
penicillin [,penɪ'sɪlɪn] n pénicilline f.
peninsula [pə'nɪnsjʊlə] (pl **-s**) n péninsule f.
penis ['piːnɪs] (pl **penises** [-ɪz]) n pénis m.
penitent ['penɪtənt] adj repentant(e), con-
trit(e).
penitentiary [,penɪ'tenʃərɪ] (pl **-ies**) n Am prison f.
penknife ['pennaɪf] (pl **-knives** [-naɪvz]) n canif m.
pen name n pseudonyme m.
pennant ['penənt] n fanion m, flamme f.
penniless ['penɪlɪs] adj sans le sou.
Pennines ['penaɪnz] npl : **the ~** les Pennines,
la chaîne Pennine.

Pennsylvania [ˌpensɪl'veɪnjə] n Pennsylvanie f; **in ~** en Pennsylvanie.

penny ['penɪ] (pl sense 1 -ies ; pl sense 2 **pence** [pens]) n - **1.** [coin] Br penny m; Am cent m - **2.** Br [value] pence m - **3.** phr : **a ~ for your thoughts** à quoi penses-tu? ; **the ~ dropped** Br inf j'ai compris OR pigé, ça a fait tilt ; **to spend a ~** Br aller au petit coin ; **they are two** OR **ten a ~** Br inf il y en a à la pelle.

penny-pinching [-ˌpɪntʃɪŋ] ⬦ adj [person] radin(e), pingre ; [attitude] mesquin(e) ⬦ n (U) économies fpl de bouts de chandelle.

pen pal n inf correspondant m, -e f.

pension ['penʃn] n - **1.** Br [on retirement] retraite f - **2.** [from disability] pension f.

⬥ **pension off** vt sep mettre à la retraite.

pensionable ['penʃənəbl] adj : **to be of ~ age** avoir l'âge de la retraite.

pension book n Br livret m de retraite.

pensioner ['penʃənər] n Br : **(old-age) ~** retraité m, -e f.

pension fund n caisse f de retraite.

pension plan, pension scheme n plan m OR régime m de retraite.

pensive ['pensɪv] adj songeur(euse).

pentagon ['pentəgən] n pentagone m.

⬥ **Pentagon** n Am : **the Pentagon** le Pentagone (siège du ministère américain de la Défense).

PENTAGON

Le Pentagone, immense bâtiment à cinq façades situé à Washington, abrite le ministère américain de la Défense ; plus généralement, ce terme désigne le pouvoir militaire américain.

pentathlon [pen'tæθlən] (pl -s) n pentathlon m.

Pentecost ['pentɪkɒst] n Pentecôte f.

penthouse ['penthaʊs, pl -haʊzɪz] n appartement m de luxe (au dernier étage).

pent up ['pent-] adj [emotions] refoulé(e) ; [energy] contenu(e).

penultimate [pe'nʌltɪmət] adj avant-dernier(ère).

penury ['penjʊrɪ] n indigence f, misère f.

peony ['pɪənɪ] (pl -ies) n pivoine f.

people ['piːpl] ⬦ n [nation, race] nation f, peuple m ⬦ npl - **1.** [persons] personnes fpl ; **few/a lot of ~** peu/beaucoup de monde, peu/beaucoup de gens ; **there were a lot of ~ present** il y avait beaucoup de monde - **2.** [in general] gens mpl ; **~ say that ...** on dit que ... - **3.** [inhabitants] habitants mpl - **4.** POL :

the ~ le peuple ⬦ vt : **to be ~d by** OR **with** être peuplé(e) de.

people carrier n monospace m.

pep [pep] (pt & pp **-ped** ; cont **-ping**) n (U) inf entrain m, pep m.

⬥ **pep up** vt sep inf - **1.** [person] remonter, requinquer - **2.** [party, event] animer.

PEP (abbr of personal equity plan) n en Grande-Bretagne, plan d'épargne en actions exonéré d'impôt.

pepper ['pepər] n - **1.** [spice] poivre m ; **black/white ~** poivre noir/blanc - **2.** [vegetable] poivron m ; **red/green ~** poivron rouge/vert.

pepperbox n Am = pepper pot.

peppercorn ['pepəkɔːn] n grain m de poivre.

peppered ['pepəd] adj - **1.** [essay, speech] : **~ (with)** truffé(e) (de) - **2.** [walls] : **~ (with)** criblé(e) (de).

pepper mill n moulin m à poivre.

peppermint ['pepəmɪnt] n - **1.** [sweet] bonbon m à la menthe - **2.** [herb] menthe f poivrée.

pepper pot Br, **pepperbox** Am ['pepəbɒks] n poivrier m.

peppery ['pepərɪ] adj poivré(e).

pep talk n inf paroles fpl OR discours m d'encouragement.

peptic ulcer ['peptɪk-] n ulcère m gastroduodénal.

per [pɜːr] prep : **~ person** par personne ; **to be paid £10 ~ hour** être payé 10 livres de l'heure ; **~ kilo** le kilo ; **as ~ instructions** conformément aux instructions.

per annum adv par an.

P-E ratio (abbr of price-earnings ratio) n indice de rentabilité d'une valeur.

per capita [pə'kæpɪtə] adj & adv par habitant OR tête.

perceive [pə'siːv] vt - **1.** [notice] percevoir - **2.** [understand, realize] remarquer, s'apercevoir de - **3.** [consider] : **to ~ sb/sthg as** considérer qqn/qqch comme.

percent adv pour cent.

percentage [pə'sentɪdʒ] n pourcentage m.

perceptible [pə'septəbl] adj sensible.

perception [pə'sepʃn] n - **1.** [aural, visual] perception f - **2.** [insight] perspicacité f, intuition f - **3.** [opinion] opinion f.

perceptive [pə'septɪv] adj perspicace.

perceptively [pə'septɪvlɪ] adv de manière perspicace.

perch [pɜːtʃ] (pl sense 2 only, inv OR -es) ⬦ n - **1.** lit & fig [position] perchoir m - **2.** [fish] perche f ⬦ vi se percher.

percolate [ˈpɜːkəleɪt] vi **- 1.** [coffee] passer **- 2.** fig [news] s'infiltrer, filtrer.

percolator [ˈpɜːkəleɪtəʳ] n cafetière f à pression.

percussion [pəˈkʌʃn] n MUS percussion f; **the ~ (section)** la batterie, la percussion.

percussionist [pəˈkʌʃənɪst] n percussionniste mf.

peremptory [pəˈremptərɪ] adj péremptoire.

perennial [pəˈrenjəl] ◇ adj permanent(e), perpétuel(elle) ; BOT vivace ◇ n BOT plante f vivace.

perestroika [ˌperəˈstrɔɪkə] n perestroïka f.

perfect [adj & n ˈpɜːfɪkt, vb pəˈfekt] ◇ adj parfait(e) ; **he's a ~ nuisance** il est absolument insupportable ◇ n GRAMM : **~ (tense)** parfait m ◇ vt parfaire, mettre au point.

perfect competition [ˈpɜːfɪkt-] n ECON concurrence f parfaite.

perfection [pəˈfekʃn] n perfection f; **to ~** parfaitement (bien).

perfectionist [pəˈfekʃənɪst] n perfectionniste mf.

perfectly [ˈpɜːfɪktlɪ] adv parfaitement ; **you know ~ well** tu sais très bien.

perforate [ˈpɜːfəreɪt] vt perforer.

perforations [ˌpɜːfəˈreɪʃnz] npl [in paper] pointillés mpl.

perform [pəˈfɔːm] ◇ vt **- 1.** [carry out - gen] exécuter ; [- function] remplir ; **to ~ an operation** [- MED] opérer **- 2.** [play, concert] jouer ◇ vi **- 1.** [machine] marcher, fonctionner ; [team, person] : **to ~ well/badly** avoir de bons/mauvais résultats **- 2.** [actor] jouer ; [singer] chanter.

performance [pəˈfɔːməns] n **- 1.** [carrying out] exécution f **- 2.** [show] représentation f **- 3.** [by actor, singer etc] interprétation f **- 4.** [of car, engine] performance f.

performance art n art m de représentation.

performance car n voiture f à hautes performances OR très performante.

performer [pəˈfɔːməʳ] n artiste mf, interprète mf.

performing arts [pəˈfɔːmɪŋ-] npl : **the ~** les arts mpl du spectacle.

perfume [ˈpɜːfjuːm] n parfum m.

perfumed [Br ˈpɜːfjuːmd, Am pərˈfjuːmd] adj parfumé(e).

perfunctory [pəˈfʌŋktərɪ] adj rapide, superficiel(elle).

perhaps [pəˈhæps] adv peut-être ; **~ so/not** peut-être que oui/non.

peril [ˈperɪl] n danger m, péril m ; **at one's ~** à ses risques et périls.

perilous [ˈperələs] adj dangereux(euse), périlleux(euse).

perilously [ˈperələslɪ] adv dangereusement.

perimeter [pəˈrɪmɪtəʳ] n périmètre m ; **~ fence** clôture f ; **~ wall** mur m d'enceinte.

period [ˈpɪərɪəd] ◇ n **- 1.** [gen] période f **- 2.** SCH ≃ heure f **- 3.** [menstruation] règles fpl **- 4.** Am [full stop] point m ◇ comp [dress, house] d'époque.

periodic [ˌpɪərɪˈɒdɪk] adj périodique

periodical [ˌpɪərɪˈɒdɪkl] ◇ adj = **periodic** ◇ n [magazine] périodique m.

periodic table n tableau m de Mendéleïev.

period pains npl règles fpl douloureuses.

period piece n [furniture] meuble m d'époque.

peripatetic [ˌperɪpəˈtetɪk] adj [salesman] itinérant(e) ; [teacher] qui enseigne dans plusieurs écoles.

peripheral [pəˈrɪfərəl] ◇ adj **- 1.** [unimportant] secondaire **- 2.** [at edge] périphérique ◇ n COMPUT périphérique m.

periphery [pəˈrɪfərɪ] (pl -ies) n [edge] périphérie f.

periscope [ˈperɪskəʊp] n périscope m.

perish [ˈperɪʃ] vi **- 1.** [die] périr, mourir **- 2.** [food] pourrir, se gâter ; [rubber] se détériorer.

perishable [ˈperɪʃəbl] adj périssable.
◆ **perishables** npl denrées fpl périssables.

perishing [ˈperɪʃɪŋ] adj Br inf **- 1.** [cold] très froid(e) **- 2.** [damn] sacré(e).

peritonitis [ˌperɪtəˈnaɪtɪs] n (U) péritonite f.

perjure [ˈpɜːdʒəʳ] vt JUR : **to ~ o.s.** se parjurer.

perjury [ˈpɜːdʒərɪ] n (U) JUR parjure m, faux serment m.

perk [pɜːk] n inf à-côté m, avantage m.
◆ **perk up** vi se ragaillardir.

perky [ˈpɜːkɪ] (compar -ier ; superl -iest) adj inf [cheerful] guilleret(ette) ; [lively] plein(e) d'entrain.

perm [pɜːm] ◇ n permanente f ◇ vt : **to have one's hair ~ed** se faire faire une permanente.

permanence [ˈpɜːmənəns] n permanence f.

permanent [ˈpɜːmənənt] ◇ adj permanent(e) ◇ n Am [perm] permanente f.

permanently [ˈpɜːmənəntlɪ] adv **- 1.** [blind, damaged] définitivement, de manière permanente **- 2.** [closed, available] en permanence.

permeable ['pɜːmjəbl] *adj* perméable.

permeate ['pɜːmɪeɪt] *vt* - **1.** [subj: liquid, smell] s'infiltrer dans, pénétrer - **2.** [subj: feeling, idea] se répandre dans.

permissible [pə'mɪsəbl] *adj* acceptable, admissible.

permission [pə'mɪʃn] *n* permission *f*, autorisation *f*; **to give sb ~ to do sthg** donner à qqn la permission de faire qqch.

permissive [pə'mɪsɪv] *adj* permissif(ive).

permissiveness [pə'mɪsɪvnɪs] *n* permissivité *f*.

permit [*vb* pə'mɪt, *n* 'pɜːmɪt] (*pt* & *pp* **-ted**; *cont* **-ting**) <> *vt* permettre; **to ~ sb to do sthg** permettre à qqn de faire qqch, autoriser qqn à faire qqch; **to ~ sb sthg** permettre qqch à qqn; **weather permitting** si le temps le permet <> *n* permis *m*.

permutation [,pɜːmjuː'teɪʃn] *n* permutation *f*.

pernicious [pə'nɪʃəs] *adj* fml [harmful] pernicieux(euse).

pernickety [pə'nɪkətɪ] *adj* inf [fussy] tatillon(onne), pointilleux(euse).

peroxide [pə'rɒksaɪd] *n* peroxyde *m*.

peroxide blonde *n* blonde *f* décolorée.

perpendicular [,pɜːpən'dɪkjələʳ] <> *adj* perpendiculaire <> *n* perpendiculaire *f*.

perpetrate ['pɜːpɪtreɪt] *vt* perpétrer, commettre.

perpetration [,pɜːpɪ'treɪʃn] *n* perpétration *f*.

perpetrator ['pɜːpɪtreɪtəʳ] *n* auteur *m*.

perpetual [pə'petʃʊəl] *adj* - **1.** pej [continuous] continuel(elle), incessant(e) - **2.** [long-lasting] perpétuel(elle).

perpetually [pə'petʃʊəlɪ] *adv* - **1.** pej [continuously] sans cesse, continuellement - **2.** [for ever] toujours, constamment.

perpetual motion *n* mouvement *m* perpétuel.

perpetuate [pə'petʃʊeɪt] *vt* perpétuer.

perpetuation [pə,petʃʊ'eɪʃn] *n* perpétuation *f*.

perpetuity [,pɜːpɪ'tjuːətɪ] *n*: **in ~** fml à perpétuité.

perplex [pə'pleks] *vt* rendre perplexe.

perplexed [pə'plekst] *adj* perplexe.

perplexing [pə'pleksɪŋ] *adj* déroutant(e), déconcertant(e).

perplexity [pə'pleksətɪ] *n* perplexité *f*.

perquisite ['pɜːkwɪzɪt] *n* fml à-côté *m*, avantage *m*.

per se [pɜː'seɪ] *adv* en tant que tel (telle), en soi.

persecute ['pɜːsɪkjuːt] *vt* persécuter, tourmenter.

persecution [,pɜːsɪ'kjuːʃn] *n* persécution *f*.

persecutor ['pɜːsɪkjuːtəʳ] *n* persécuteur *m*, -trice *f*.

perseverance [,pɜːsɪ'vɪərəns] *n* persévérance *f*, ténacité *f*.

persevere [,pɜːsɪ'vɪəʳ] *vi* - **1.** [with difficulty] persévérer, persister; **to ~ with** persévérer *OR* persister dans - **2.** [with determination]: **to ~ in doing sthg** persister à faire qqch.

Persia ['pɜːʃə] *n* Perse *f*; **in ~** en Perse.

Persian ['pɜːʃn] <> *adj* persan(e); HIST perse <> *n* - **1.** [person] Persan *m*, -e *f*; HIST Perse *mf* - **2.** [language] persan *m*.

Persian cat *n* chat *m* persan.

Persian Gulf *n*: **the ~** le golfe Persique.

persist [pə'sɪst] *vi*: **to ~ (in doing sthg)** persister *OR* s'obstiner (à faire qqch).

persistence [pə'sɪstəns] *n* persistance *f*.

persistent [pə'sɪstənt] *adj* - **1.** [noise, rain] continuel(elle); [problem] constant(e) - **2.** [determined] tenace, obstiné(e).

persistently [pə'sɪstəntlɪ] *adv* - **1.** [constantly] continuellement, constamment - **2.** [determinedly] obstinément, avec persévérance.

persnickety [pə'snɪkɪtɪ] *adj* Am tatillon(onne), pointilleux(euse).

person ['pɜːsn] (*pl* **people** ['piːpl] *OR* **persons** *fml*) *n* - **1.** [man or woman] personne *f*; **in ~** en personne; **in the ~ of** en la personne de - **2.** fml [body]: **about one's ~** sur soi.

persona [pə'səʊnə] (*pl* **-s** *OR* **-ae** [-iː]) *n* personnage *m*.

personable ['pɜːsnəbl] *adj* sympathique, agréable.

personage ['pɜːsənɪdʒ] *n* personnage *m*.

personal ['pɜːsənl] <> *adj* - **1.** [gen] personnel(elle) - **2.** pej [rude] désobligeant(e) <> *n* Am petite annonce *f* (pour rencontres).

personal account *n* compte *m* personnel.

personal allowance *n* TAX abattement *m*.

personal assistant *n* secrétaire *mf* de direction.

personal call *n* communication *f* téléphonique privée.

personal column *n* petites annonces *fpl*.

personal computer *n* ordinateur *m* personnel *OR* individuel.

personal estate *n* (U) biens *mpl* personnels.

personal hygiene *n* hygiène *f* corporelle.

personality [ˌpɜːsə'nælətɪ] (*pl* -ies) *n* personnalité *f*.

personalize, -ise ['pɜːsənəlaɪz] *vt* - **1.** [mark with name] personnaliser - **2.** [make too personal] rendre trop personnel(elle).

personalized ['pɜːsənəlaɪzd] *adj* - **1.** [marked with name] personnalisé(e) - **2.** [for one person] personnel(elle).

personally ['pɜːsnəlɪ] *adv* personnellement ; **to take sthg ~** se sentir visé par qqch.

personal organizer *n* organiseur *m*.

personal pension plan *n* retraite *f* personnelle.

personal pronoun *n* pronom *m* personnel.

personal property *n (U)* JUR biens *mpl* personnels.

personal stereo *n* baladeur *m*, Walkman® *m*.

persona non grata [-'grɑːtə] (*pl* **personae non gratae** [-'grɑːtiː]) *n* persona non grata.

personify [pə'sɒnɪfaɪ] (*pt* & *pp* -ied) *vt* personnifier.

personnel [ˌpɜːsə'nel] ⬦ *n (U)* [department] service *m* du personnel ⬦ *npl* [staff] personnel *m*.

personnel department *n* service *m* du personnel.

personnel officer *n* responsable *mf* du personnel.

person-to-person *adj esp* Am avec préavis.

perspective [pə'spektɪv] *n* - **1.** ART perspective *f ;* **to get sthg in ~** *fig* mettre qqch dans son contexte - **2.** [view, judgment] point *m* de vue, optique *f*.

Perspex® ['pɜːspeks] *n* Br ≃ Plexiglas® *m*.

perspicacious [ˌpɜːspɪ'keɪʃəs] *adj* perspicace.

perspiration [ˌpɜːspə'reɪʃn] *n* - **1.** [sweat] sueur *f* - **2.** [act of perspiring] transpiration *f*.

perspire [pə'spaɪəʳ] *vi* transpirer, suer.

persuade [pə'sweɪd] *vt :* **to ~ sb to do sthg** persuader OR convaincre qqn de faire qqch ; **to ~ sb that** convaincre qqn que ; **to ~ sb of** convaincre qqn de.

persuasion [pə'sweɪʒn] *n* - **1.** [act of persuading] persuasion *f* - **2.** [belief - religious] confession *f ;* [- political] opinion *f*, conviction *f*.

persuasive [pə'sweɪsɪv] *adj* [person] persuasif(ive) ; [argument] convaincant(e).

persuasively [pə'sweɪsɪvlɪ] *adv* d'un ton persuasif, d'une manière convaincante.

pert [pɜːt] *adj* mutin(e), coquin(e).

pertain [pə'teɪn] *vi fml :* **~ing to** concernant, relatif(ive) à.

pertinence ['pɜːtɪnəns] *n* pertinence *f*.

pertinent ['pɜːtɪnənt] *adj* pertinent(e), approprié(e).

perturb [pə'tɜːb] *vt* inquiéter, troubler.

perturbed [pə'tɜːbd] *adj fml* inquiet(ète), troublé(e).

Peru [pə'ruː] *n* Pérou *m ;* **in ~** au Pérou.

perusal [pə'ruːzl] *n* lecture *f* attentive.

peruse [pə'ruːz] *vt* lire attentivement.

Peruvian [pə'ruːvjən] ⬦ *adj* péruvien(enne) ⬦ *n* [person] Péruvien *m*, -enne *f*.

pervade [pə'veɪd] *vt* [subj : smell] se répandre dans ; [subj : feeling, influence] envahir.

pervasive [pə'veɪsɪv] *adj* pénétrant(e), envahissant(e).

perverse [pə'vɜːs] *adj* [contrary - person] contrariant(e) ; [- enjoyment] malin(igne).

perversely [pə'vɜːslɪ] *adv* [contrarily] par esprit de contradiction.

perversion [Br pə'vɜːʃn, Am pə'vɜːrʒn] *n* - **1.** [sexual] perversion *f* - **2.** [of truth] travestissement *m*.

perversity [pə'vɜːsətɪ] *n* [contrariness] caractère *m* contrariant, esprit *m* de contradiction.

pervert [*n* 'pɜːvɜːt, *vb* pə'vɜːt] ⬦ *n* pervers *m*, -e *f* ⬦ *vt* - **1.** [truth, meaning] travestir, déformer ; [course of justice] entraver - **2.** [sexually] pervertir.

perverted [pə'vɜːtɪd] *adj* - **1.** [sexually] pervers(e) - **2.** [reasoning] tordu(e).

peseta [pə'seɪtə] *n* peseta *f*.

peso ['peɪsəʊ] (*pl* -s) *n* peso *m*.

pessary ['pesərɪ] (*pl* -ies) *n* [medicine] ovule *m*.

pessimism ['pesɪmɪzm] *n* pessimisme *m*.

pessimist ['pesɪmɪst] *n* pessimiste *mf*.

pessimistic [ˌpesɪ'mɪstɪk] *adj* pessimiste.

pest [pest] *n* - **1.** [insect] insecte *m* nuisible ; [animal] animal *m* nuisible - **2.** *inf* [nuisance] casse-pieds *mf inv*.

pester ['pestəʳ] *vt* harceler, importuner.

pesticide ['pestɪsaɪd] *n* pesticide *m*.

pestle ['pesl] *n* pilon *m*.

pet [pet] (*pt* & *pp* -ted ; *cont* -ting) ⬦ *adj* [favourite] : **~ subject** dada *m ;* **~ hate** bête *f* noire ⬦ *n* - **1.** [animal] animal *m* (familier) - **2.** [favourite person] chouchou *m*, -oute *f* ⬦ *vt* caresser, câliner ⬦ *vi* se peloter, se caresser.

petal ['petl] *n* pétale *m*.

peter ['piːtəʳ] ➝ **peter out** vi [path] s'arrêter, se perdre ; [interest] diminuer, décliner.

pethidine ['peθidiːn] n péthidine f.

petit bourgeois [pə,tiː'buəʒwaː] (pl **petits bourgeois** [pə,tiː'buəʒwaː]) ◇ adj petit-bourgeois (petite-bourgeoise) ◇ n petit-bourgeois m, petite-bourgeoise f.

petite [pə'tiːt] adj menu(e).

petit four [,peti'fɔː] (pl **petits fours** [peti'fɔːz]) n petit-four m.

petition [pɪ'tɪʃn] ◇ n pétition f ◇ vt adresser une pétition à ◇ vi - **1.** [campaign] : **to ~ for/against** faire une pétition en faveur de/contre - **2.** JUR : **to ~ for divorce** faire une demande en divorce.

petitioner [pɪ'tɪʃənəʳ] n pétitionnaire mf.

pet name n petit nom m.

petrified ['petrɪfaɪd] adj [terrified] paralysé(e) OR pétrifié(e) de peur.

petrify ['petrɪfaɪ] (pt & pp **-ied**) vt [terrify] paralyser OR pétrifier de peur.

petrochemical [,petrəʊ'kemɪkl] adj pétrochimique.

petrodollar ['petrəʊ,dɒləʳ] n FIN pétrodollar m.

petrol ['petrəl] n Br essence f.

petrolatum [,petrə'leɪtəm] n Am vaseline f.

petrol bomb n Br cocktail m Molotov.

petrol can n Br bidon m à essence.

petroleum [pɪ'trəʊljəm] n pétrole m.

petroleum jelly n Br vaseline f.

petrol pump n Br pompe f à essence.

petrol station n Br station-service f.

petrol tank n Br réservoir m d'essence.

pet shop n animalerie f.

petticoat ['petɪkəʊt] n jupon m.

pettiness ['petɪnɪs] n [small-mindedness] mesquinerie f, étroitesse f d'esprit.

petty ['petɪ] (compar **-ier** ; superl **-iest**) adj - **1.** [small-minded] mesquin(e) - **2.** [trivial] insignifiant(e), sans importance.

petty cash n (U) caisse f des dépenses courantes.

petty officer n second maître m.

petulant ['petjʊlənt] adj irritable.

pew [pjuː] n banc m d'église.

pewter ['pjuːtəʳ] n étain m.

PG (abbr of **parental guidance**) en Grande-Bretagne, désigne un film pour lequel l'avis des parents est recommandé.

PGA (abbr of **Professional Golfers' Association**) n association de joueurs de golf professionnels.

p & h (abbr of **postage and handling**) n Am frais de port.

PH (abbr of **Purple Heart**) n distinction militaire américaine.

PHA (abbr of **Public Housing Administration**) n services du logement social aux États-Unis.

phallic ['fælɪk] adj phallique ; **~ symbol** symbole m phallique.

phallus ['fæləs] (pl **-es** [-iːz] OR **phalli** ['fælaɪ]) n phallus m.

phantom ['fæntəm] ◇ adj fantomatique, spectral(e) ◇ n [ghost] fantôme m.

phantom pregnancy n grossesse f nerveuse, fausse grossesse.

pharaoh ['feərəʊ] n pharaon m.

Pharisee ['færɪsiː] n Pharisien m, -enne f.

pharmaceutical [,faːmə'sjuːtɪkl] adj pharmaceutique.

➝ **pharmaceuticals** npl produits mpl pharmaceutiques.

pharmacist ['faːməsɪst] n pharmacien m, -enne f.

pharmacology [,faːmə'kɒlədʒɪ] n pharmacologie f.

pharmacy ['faːməsɪ] (pl **-ies**) n pharmacie f.

phase [feɪz] ◇ n phase f ◇ vt faire progressivement.

➝ **phase in** vt sep introduire progressivement.

➝ **phase out** vt sep supprimer progressivement.

PhD (abbr of **Doctor of Philosophy**) n (titulaire d'un) doctorat de 3e cycle.

pheasant ['feznt] (pl inv OR **-s**) n faisan m.

phenobarbitone Br [,fiːnəʊ'baːbɪtəʊn], **phenobarbitol** Am [,fiːnəʊ'baːbɪtl] n phénobarbital m.

phenomena [fɪ'nɒmɪnə] pl ⊳ **phenomenon**.

phenomenal [fɪ'nɒmɪnl] adj phénoménal(e), extraordinaire.

phenomenon [fɪ'nɒmɪnən] (pl **-mena** [-mɪnə]) n phénomène m.

phew [fjuː] excl ouf!

phial ['faɪəl] n fiole f.

Philadelphia [,fɪlə'delfjə] n Philadelphie ; **in ~** à Philadelphie.

philanderer [fɪ'lændərəʳ] n coureur m, don Juan m.

philanthropic [,fɪlən'θrɒpɪk] adj philanthropique.

philanthropist [fɪ'lænθrəpɪst] n philanthrope mf.

philately [fɪ'lætəlɪ] n philatélie f.

philharmonic [ˌfɪlɑː'mɒnɪk] *adj* philharmonique.

Philippine ['fɪlɪpiːn] *adj* philippin(e) ; **the ~ Islands** les Philippines *fpl.*

➼ **Philippines** *npl* : **the ~s** les Philippines *fpl.*

philistine [Br 'fɪlɪstaɪn, Am 'fɪlɪstiːn] *n* philistin *m*, béotien *m*, -enne *f.*

Phillips® ['fɪlɪps] *comp* : **~ screw** vis *f* cruciforme ; **~ screwdriver** tournevis *m* cruciforme.

philosopher [fɪ'lɒsəfəʳ] *n* philosophe *mf.*

philosophical [ˌfɪlə'sɒfɪkl] *adj* **- 1.** [gen] philosophique **- 2.** [stoical] philosophe.

philosophize, -ise [fɪ'lɒsəfaɪz] *vi* philosopher.

philosophy [fɪ'lɒsəfɪ] (*pl* **-ies**) *n* philosophie *f.*

phlegm [flem] *n* flegme *m.*

phlegmatic [fleg'mætɪk] *adj* flegmatique.

Phnom Penh [ˌnɒm'pen] *n* Phnom Penh.

phobia ['fəʊbjə] *n* phobie *f* ; **to have a ~ about** avoir la phobie de.

phoenix ['fiːnɪks] *n* phénix *m.*

phone [fəʊn] <> *n* téléphone *m* ; **to be on the ~** [speaking] être au téléphone ; Br [connected to network] avoir le téléphone <> *comp* téléphonique <> *vt* téléphoner à, appeler <> *vi* téléphoner.

➼ **phone up** *vt sep* & *vi* téléphoner.

phone book *n* annuaire *m* (du téléphone).

phone booth *n* cabine *f* téléphonique.

phone box *n* Br cabine *f* téléphonique.

phone call *n* coup *m* de téléphone OR fil ; **to make a ~** passer OR donner un coup de fil.

phonecard ['fəʊnkɑːd] *n* ≃ Télécarte® *f.*

phone-in *n* RADIO & TV programme *m* à ligne ouverte.

phone line *n* **- 1.** [wire] câble *m* téléphonique **- 2.** [connection] ligne *f* téléphonique.

phone number *n* numéro *m* de téléphone.

phone-tapping [-ˌtæpɪŋ] *n* écoute *f* téléphonique.

phonetics [fə'netɪks] *n* (U) phonétique *f.*

phoney Br, **phony** Am ['fəʊnɪ] (*compar* **-ier** ; *superl* **-iest**, *pl* **-ies**) inf <> *adj* **- 1.** [passport, address] bidon *(inv)* **- 2.** [person] hypocrite, pas franc (pas franche) <> *n* poseur *m*, -euse *f.*

phoney war *n* drôle de guerre *f.*

phony Am = **phoney**.

phosphate ['fɒsfeɪt] *n* phosphate *m.*

phosphorus ['fɒsfərəs] *n* phosphore *m.*

photo ['fəʊtəʊ] *n* photo *f* ; **to take a ~ of sb/ sthg** photographier qqn/qqch, prendre qqn/qqch en photo.

photocall ['fəʊtəʊkɔːl] *n* séance *f* de photos.

photocopier ['fəʊtəʊˌkɒpɪəʳ] *n* photocopieur *m*, copieur *m.*

photocopy ['fəʊtəʊˌkɒpɪ] (*pt* & *pp* **-ied**, *pl* **-ies**) <> *n* photocopie *f* <> *vt* photocopier.

photoelectric cell [ˌfəʊtəʊɪ'lektrɪk-] *n* cellule *f* photoélectrique.

photo finish *n* SPORT photo-finish *f.*

Photofit® ['fəʊtəʊfɪt] *n* : **~ (picture)** portrait-robot *m*, photo-robot *f.*

photogenic [ˌfəʊtəʊ'dʒenɪk] *adj* photogénique.

photograph ['fəʊtəgrɑːf] <> *n* photographie *f* ; **to take a ~ (of sb/sthg)** prendre (qqn/qqch) en photo, photographier (qqn/qqch) <> *vt* photographier, prendre en photo.

photographer [fə'tɒgrəfəʳ] *n* photographe *mf.*

photographic [ˌfəʊtə'græfɪk] *adj* photographique.

photographic memory *n* mémoire *f* photographique.

photography [fə'tɒgrəfɪ] *n* photographie *f.*

photojournalism [ˌfəʊtəʊ'dʒɜːnəlɪzm] *n* photojournalisme *m.*

photon ['fəʊtɒn] *n* photon *m.*

photo opportunity *n* séance *f* photoprotocolaire.

photosensitive [ˌfəʊtəʊ'sensɪtɪv] *adj* photosensible.

Photostat® ['fəʊtəstæt] (*pt* & *pp* **-ted** ; *cont* **-ting**) *n* photostat *m*, photocopie *f.*

➼ **photostat** *vt* photocopier, faire un photostat de.

photosynthesis [ˌfəʊtəʊ'sɪnθəsɪs] *n* photosynthèse *f.*

phrasal verb ['freɪzl-] *n* verbe *m* à postposition.

phrase [freɪz] <> *n* expression *f* <> *vt* exprimer, tourner.

phrasebook ['freɪzbʊk] *n* guide *m* de conversation *(pour touristes).*

phraseology [ˌfreɪzɪ'ɒlədʒɪ] *n* phraséologie *f.*

physical ['fɪzɪkl] <> *adj* **- 1.** [gen] physique **- 2.** [world, objects] matériel(elle) <> *n* [examination] visite *f* médicale.

physical chemistry *n* chimie *f* physique.

physical education *n* éducation *f* physique.

physical examination n visite f médicale.

physical geography n géographie f physique.

physical jerks npl Br hum exercices mpl, gymnastique f.

physically ['fɪzɪklɪ] adv physiquement.

physically handicapped ◇ adj : **to be ~** être handicapé(e) physique ◇ npl : **the ~** les handicapés mpl physiques.

physical science n science f physique.

physical training n éducation f physique.

physician [fɪ'zɪʃn] n médecin m.

physicist ['fɪzɪsɪst] n physicien m, -enne f.

physics ['fɪzɪks] n (U) physique f.

physio ['fɪzɪəʊ] (pl -s) n Br inf - **1.** (abbr of **physiotherapist**) kiné mf - **2.** (abbr of **physiotherapy**) kiné f.

physiognomy [ˌfɪzɪ'ɒnəmɪ] (pl -ies) n physionomie f.

physiology [ˌfɪzɪ'ɒlədʒɪ] n physiologie f.

physiotherapist [ˌfɪzɪəʊ'θerəpɪst] n kinésithérapeute mf.

physiotherapy [ˌfɪzɪəʊ'θerəpɪ] n kinésithérapie f.

physique [fɪ'ziːk] n physique m.

pianist ['pɪənɪst] n pianiste mf.

piano [pɪ'ænəʊ] (pl -s) n piano m.

piano accordion n accordéon m à clavier.

Picardy ['pɪkədɪ] n Picardie f ; **in ~** en Picardie.

piccalilli [ˌpɪkə'lɪlɪ] n piccalilli f.

piccolo ['pɪkələʊ] (pl -s) n piccolo m.

pick [pɪk] ◇ n - **1.** [tool] pioche f, pic m - **2.** [selection] : **to take one's ~** choisir, faire son choix - **3.** [best] : **the ~ of** le meilleur (la meilleure) de ◇ vt - **1.** [select, choose] choisir, sélectionner ; **to ~ one's way across** OR **through sthg** traverser avec précaution - **2.** [gather] cueillir - **3.** [remove] enlever - **4.** [nose] : **to ~ one's nose** se décrotter le nez ; **to ~ one's teeth** se curer les dents - **5.** [fight, quarrel] chercher ; **to ~ a fight (with sb)** chercher la bagarre (à qqn) - **6.** [lock] crocheter ◇ vi : **to ~ and choose** faire le/la difficile.
➤ **pick at** vt fus [food] picorer.
➤ **pick on** vt fus s'en prendre à, être sur le dos de.
➤ **pick out** vt sep - **1.** [recognize] repérer, reconnaître - **2.** [select, choose] choisir, désigner.
➤ **pick up** ◇ vt sep - **1.** [lift up] ramasser ; **to ~ up the pieces** fig recoller les morceaux, recommencer comme avant - **2.** [collect] aller chercher, passer prendre - **3.** [collect in car] prendre, chercher - **4.** [skill, language] apprendre ; [habit] prendre ; [bargain] découvrir ; **to ~ up speed** prendre de la vitesse - **5.** [subj : police] : **to ~ sb up for sthg** arrêter OR cueillir qqn pour qqch - **6.** inf [sexually - woman, man] draguer - **7.** RADIO & TELEC [detect, receive] capter, recevoir - **8.** [conversation, work] reprendre, continuer ◇ vi [improve, start again] reprendre.

pickaxe Br, **pickax** Am ['pɪkæks] n pioche f, pic m.

picker ['pɪkər] n cueilleur m, -euse f.

picket ['pɪkɪt] ◇ n piquet m de grève ◇ vt mettre un piquet de grève devant.

picketing ['pɪkətɪŋ] n (U) piquets mpl de grève.

picket line n piquet m de grève.

pickings ['pɪkɪŋz] npl : **there are rich ~ to be had** ça peut rapporter beaucoup d'argent.

pickle ['pɪkl] ◇ n pickles mpl ; **to be in a ~** être dans le pétrin ◇ vt conserver dans du vinaigre, de la saumure etc.

pickled ['pɪkld] adj - **1.** [food] au vinaigre - **2.** inf [drunk] rond(e), pompette.

pick-me-up n inf remontant m.

pickpocket ['pɪkˌpɒkɪt] n pickpocket m, voleur m à la tire.

pick-up n - **1.** [of record player] pick-up m - **2.** [truck] camionnette f.

pick-up truck n camionnette f.

picky ['pɪkɪ] (compar -ier ; superl -iest) adj difficile.

picnic ['pɪknɪk] (pt & pp -ked ; cont -king) ◇ n pique-nique m ◇ vi pique-niquer.

picnicker ['pɪknɪkər] n pique-niqueur m, -euse f.

Pict [pɪkt] n : **the ~s** les Pictes mpl.

pictorial [pɪk'tɔːrɪəl] adj illustré(e).

picture ['pɪktʃər] ◇ n - **1.** [painting] tableau m, peinture f ; [drawing] dessin m - **2.** [photograph] photo f, photographie f - **3.** TV image f - **4.** CINEMA film m - **5.** [in mind] tableau m, image f - **6.** fig [situation] tableau m - **7.** [epitome] : **she's the ~ of health** elle respire la santé - **8.** phr : **to get the ~** inf piger ; **to be in/out of the ~** être/ne pas être au courant ; **to put sb in the ~** mettre qqn au courant ◇ vt - **1.** [in mind] imaginer, s'imaginer, se représenter - **2.** [in photo] photographier - **3.** [in painting] représenter, peindre.
➤ **pictures** npl Br : **the ~s** le cinéma.

picture book n livre m d'images.

picture rail n cimaise f.

picturesque [ˌpɪktʃə'resk] adj pittoresque.

picture window n fenêtre f panoramique.

piddling ['pɪdlɪŋ] adj inf pej dérisoire, insignifiant(e).

pidgin ['pɪdʒɪn] <> n pidgin m <> comp : ~ **English** pidgin english m ; ~ **French** petit nègre m.

pie [paɪ] n [savoury] tourte f ; [sweet] tarte f ; **it's just ~ in the sky** ce ne sont que des projets en l'air.

piebald ['paɪbɔ:ld] adj pie (inv).

piece [pi:s] n - **1.** [gen] morceau m ; [of string] bout m ; **a ~ of furniture** un meuble ; **a ~ of clothing** un vêtement ; **a ~ of advice** un conseil ; **a ~ of information** un renseignement ; **a ~ of work** un travail ; **to fall to ~s** tomber en morceaux ; **to be smashed to ~s** être cassé en mille morceaux ; **to take sthg to ~s** démonter qqch ; **in ~s** en morceaux ; **in one ~** [intact] intact(e) ; [unharmed] sain et sauf (saine et sauve) ; **to go to ~s** fig s'effondrer, craquer - **2.** [coin, item, in chess] pièce f ; [in draughts] pion m - **3.** PRESS article m.

 piece together vt sep [facts] coordonner.

pièce de résistance [ˌpjesdərezɪsˈtɑ̃:s] (pl **pièces de résistance** [ˌpjesdərezɪsˈtɑ̃:s]) n pièce f de résistance.

piecemeal ['pi:smi:l] <> adj fait(e) petit à petit <> adv petit à petit, peu à peu.

piecework ['pi:swɜ:k] n (U) travail m à la pièce OR aux pièces.

pie chart n camembert m, graphique m rond.

pied-à-terre [ˌpɪeɪdæ'teəʳ] (pl **pieds-a-terre** [ˌpɪeɪdæ'teəʳ]) n pied-à-terre m inv.

pie-eyed [-'aɪd] adj inf rond(e), gris(e).

pie plate n Am plat allant au four.

pier [pɪəʳ] n [at seaside] jetée f.

pierce [pɪəs] vt percer, transpercer ; **to have one's ears ~d** se faire percer les oreilles.

pierced [pɪəst] adj percé(e).

piercing ['pɪəsɪŋ] adj - **1.** [sound, look] perçant(e) - **2.** [wind] pénétrant(e).

piety ['paɪətɪ] n piété f.

piffle ['pɪfl] n (U) inf bêtises fpl, balivernes fpl.

piffling ['pɪflɪŋ] adj inf insignifiant(e).

pig [pɪg] (pt & pp -ged ; cont -ging) n - **1.** [animal] porc m, cochon m - **2.** inf pej [greedy eater] goinfre m, glouton m ; **to make a ~ of o.s.** se goinfrer - **3.** inf pej [unkind person] sale type m.
 pig out vi inf s'empiffrer.

pigeon ['pɪdʒɪn] (pl inv OR -s) n pigeon m.

pigeon-chested [-ˌtʃestɪd] adj à la poitrine bombée.

pigeonhole ['pɪdʒɪnhəʊl] <> n [compartment] casier m <> vt [classify] étiqueter, cataloguer.

pigeon-toed [-ˌtəʊd] adj qui a les pieds en dedans.

piggish ['pɪgɪʃ] adj inf cochon(onne), dégoûtant(e).

piggy ['pɪgɪ] (compar -ier ; superl -iest, pl -ies) <> adj de cochon <> n inf cochon m.

piggyback ['pɪgɪbæk] n : **to give sb a ~** porter qqn sur son dos.

piggybank ['pɪgɪbæŋk] n tirelire f.

pigheaded [ˌpɪg'hedɪd] adj têtu(e).

piglet ['pɪglɪt] n porcelet m.

pigment ['pɪgmənt] n pigment m.

pigmentation [ˌpɪgmən'teɪʃn] n pigmentation f.

pigmy ['pɪgmɪ] (pl -ies) = pygmy.

pigpen Am = pigsty.

pigskin ['pɪgskɪn] <> n (peau f de) porc m <> comp en peau de porc.

pigsty ['pɪgstaɪ] (pl -ies), **pigpen** Am ['pɪgpen] n lit & fig porcherie f.

pigswill ['pɪgswɪl] n lit & fig pâtée f pour les porcs.

pigtail ['pɪgteɪl] n natte f.

pike [paɪk] (pl sense 1 only, inv OR -s) n - **1.** [fish] brochet m - **2.** [spear] pique f.

pikestaff ['paɪkstɑ:f] n manche m d'une pique.

pilaster [pɪ'læstəʳ] n pilastre m.

pilchard ['pɪltʃəd] n pilchard m.

pile [paɪl] <> n - **1.** [heap] tas m ; **a ~ of, ~s of** un tas OR des tas de - **2.** [neat stack] pile f - **3.** [of carpet] poil m <> vt empiler.
 piles npl MED hémorroïdes fpl.
 pile in vi inf s'empiler.
 pile into vt fus inf s'entasser dans, s'empiler dans.
 pile out vi inf sortir en se bousculant.
 pile up <> vt sep empiler, entasser <> vi - **1.** [form a heap] s'entasser - **2.** fig [work, debts] s'accumuler.

pile driver n sonnette f.

pileup ['paɪlʌp] n AUT carambolage m.

pilfer ['pɪlfəʳ] <> vt chaparder <> vi : **to ~ (from)** faire du chapardage (dans).

pilgrim ['pɪlgrɪm] n pèlerin m.

pilgrimage ['pɪlgrɪmɪdʒ] n pèlerinage m.

pill [pɪl] n - **1.** [gen] pilule f - **2.** [contraceptive] : **the ~** la pilule ; **to be on the ~** prendre la pilule.

pillage ['pɪlɪdʒ] <> n pillage m <> vt piller.

pillar ['pɪlə'] n lit & fig pilier m.

pillar box n Br boîte f aux lettres.

pillbox ['pɪlbɒks] n - **1.** [box for pills] boîte f à pilules - **2.** MIL casemate f.

pillion ['pɪljən] n siège m arrière ; **to ride ~** monter derrière.

pillock ['pɪlək] n Br inf imbécile mf.

pillory ['pɪlərɪ] (pl -ies, pt & pp -ied) <> n pilori m <> vt : **to be pilloried** être mis(e) au pilori.

pillow ['pɪləʊ] n - **1.** [for bed] oreiller m - **2.** Am [on sofa, chair] coussin m.

pillowcase ['pɪləʊkeɪs], **pillowslip** ['pɪləʊslɪp] n taie f d'oreiller.

pilot ['paɪlət] <> n - **1.** AERON & NAUT pilote m - **2.** TV émission f pilote <> comp pilote <> vt piloter.

pilot burner, pilot light n veilleuse f.

pilot scheme n projet-pilote m.

pilot study n étude f pilote OR expérimentale.

pimento [pɪ'mentəʊ] (pl inv OR -s) n piment m.

pimp [pɪmp] n inf maquereau m, souteneur m.

pimple ['pɪmpl] n bouton m.

pimply ['pɪmplɪ] (compar -ier ; superl -iest) adj boutonneux(euse).

pin [pɪn] (pt & pp -ned ; cont -ning) <> n - **1.** [for sewing] épingle f ; **to have ~s and needles** avoir des fourmis ; **to be on ~s and needles** Am être sur des charbons ardents - **2.** [drawing pin] punaise f - **3.** [safety pin] épingle f de nourrice OR de sûreté - **4.** [of plug] fiche f - **5.** TECH goupille f, cheville f - **6.** [in grenade] goupille f - **7.** GOLF : **the ~** le drapeau de trou <> vt : **to ~ sthg to/on sthg** épingler qqch à/sur qqch ; **to ~ sb against OR to sb** clouer qqn contre ; **to ~ sthg on sb** [blame] mettre OR coller qqch sur le dos de qqn ; **to ~ one's hopes on sb/sthg** mettre tous ses espoirs en qqn/dans qqch.

◆ **pin down** vt sep - **1.** [identify] définir, identifier - **2.** [force to make a decision] : **to ~ sb down** obliger qqn à prendre une décision.

◆ **pin up** vt sep épingler.

PIN [pɪn] (abbr of **personal identification number**) n code m confidentiel.

pinafore ['pɪnəfɔː'] n - **1.** [apron] tablier m - **2.** Br [dress] chasuble f.

pinball ['pɪnbɔːl] n flipper m.

pinball machine n flipper m.

pincer movement ['pɪnsə'-] n mouvement m de tenailles.

pincers ['pɪnsəz] npl - **1.** [tool] tenailles fpl - **2.** [of crab] pinces fpl.

pinch [pɪntʃ] <> n - **1.** [nip] pincement m ; **to feel the ~** tirer le diable par la queue - **2.** [of salt] pincée f <> vt - **1.** [nip] pincer - **2.** [subj : shoes] serrer - **3.** inf [steal] piquer, faucher.

◆ **at a pinch** Br, **in a pinch** Am adv à la rigueur.

pinched [pɪntʃt] adj [features] tiré(e) ; **to be ~ for time/money** être à court de temps/d'argent ; **~ with cold** transi de froid.

pincushion ['pɪn,kʊʃn] n pelote f à épingles.

pine [paɪn] <> n pin m <> comp en pin <> vi : **to ~ for** désirer ardemment.

◆ **pine away** vi languir.

pineapple ['paɪnæpl] n ananas m.

pinecone ['paɪnkəʊn] n pomme f de pin.

pine needle n aiguille f de pin.

pinetree ['paɪntriː] n pin m.

pinewood ['paɪnwʊd] n - **1.** [forest] pinède f - **2.** (U) [material] bois m de pin.

ping [pɪŋ] <> n [of bell] tintement m ; [of metal] bruit m métallique <> vi [bell] tinter ; [metal] faire un bruit métallique.

Ping-Pong® [-pɒŋ] n ping-pong m.

pinhole ['pɪnhəʊl] n trou m d'épingle.

pinion ['pɪnjən] <> n pignon m <> vt [person] clouer.

pink [pɪŋk] <> adj rose ; **to go** OR **turn ~** rosir, rougir <> n - **1.** [colour] rose m ; **in ~** en rose - **2.** [flower] mignardise f.

pink gin n Br boisson alcoolisée contenant du gin et de l'angusture.

pinkie ['pɪŋkɪ] n Am & Scot petit doigt m.

pinking ['pɪŋkɪŋ] n Br AUT cliquettement m.

pinking scissors, pinking shears npl ciseaux mpl à cranter.

pin money n argent m de poche.

pinnacle ['pɪnəkl] n - **1.** [mountain peak, spire] pic m, cime f - **2.** fig [high point] apogée m.

pinny ['pɪnɪ] (pl -ies) n inf tablier m.

pinpoint ['pɪnpɔɪnt] vt - **1.** [cause, problem] définir, mettre le doigt sur - **2.** [position] localiser.

pinprick ['pɪnprɪk] n piqûre f d'épingle ; fig petit désagrément m.

pin-striped [-,straɪpt] adj à très fines rayures.

pint [paɪnt] n - **1.** Br [unit of measurement] = 0,568 litre, ≃ demi-litre m - **2.** Am [unit of measurement] = 0,473 litre, ≃ demi-litre m - **3.** Br [beer] ≃ demi m.

pintable ['pɪnteɪbl] n Br flipper m.

pinto ['pɪntəʊ] (pl -s OR -es) Am ⬦ adj pie (inv) ⬦ n cheval m pie.

pint-size(d) adj inf minuscule.

pinup ['pɪnʌp] n pin-up f inv.

pioneer [,paɪə'nɪər] ⬦ n lit & fig pionnier m ⬦ vt : **to ~ sthg** être un des premiers (une des premières) à faire qqch.

pioneering [,paɪə'nɪərɪŋ] adj [work, research] de pionnier.

pious ['paɪəs] adj - **1.** RELIG pieux (pieuse) - **2.** pej [sanctimonious] moralisateur(trice).

piously ['paɪəslɪ] adv pieusement.

pip [pɪp] n - **1.** [seed] pépin m - **2.** Br RADIO top m.

pipe [paɪp] ⬦ n - **1.** [for gas, water] tuyau m - **2.** [for smoking] pipe f ⬦ vt acheminer par tuyau.
➤ **pipes** npl MUS cornemuse f.
➤ **pipe down** vi inf se taire, la fermer.
➤ **pipe up** vi inf se faire entendre.

pipe cleaner n cure-pipe m.

piped music n Br musique f de fond.

pipe dream n projet m chimérique.

pipeline ['paɪplaɪn] n [for gas] gazoduc m ; [for oil] oléoduc m, pipeline m ; **to be in the ~** fig être imminent OR proche.

piper ['paɪpər] n joueur m, -euse f de cornemuse.

piping hot ['paɪpɪŋ-] adj bouillant(e).

pipsqueak ['pɪpskwiːk] n pej moins m que rien.

piquant ['piːkənt] adj piquant(e).

pique [piːk] n dépit m ; **a fit of ~** un accès de dépit.

piracy ['paɪrəsɪ] n - **1.** [at sea] piraterie f - **2.** [of video, program] piratage m.

piranha [pɪ'rɑːnə] n piranha m.

pirate ['paɪrət] ⬦ adj [video, program] pirate ⬦ n pirate m ⬦ vt [video, program] pirater.

pirate radio n Br radio f pirate.

pirouette [,pɪru'et] ⬦ n pirouette f ⬦ vi pirouetter.

Pisces ['paɪsiːz] n Poissons mpl ; **to be (a) ~** être Poissons.

piss [pɪs] vulg ⬦ n - **1.** [urine] pisse f ; **to have a ~** pisser - **2.** phr : **to take the ~ out of** se foutre de ⬦ vi pisser.
➤ **piss down** v impers Br vulg pleuvoir comme vache qui pisse.
➤ **piss off** vulg ⬦ vt sep emmerder ⬦ vi Br foutre le camp ; **~ off!** fous le camp!

pissed [pɪst] adj vulg - **1.** Br [drunk] bourré(e) - **2.** Am [annoyed] en boule.

pissed off adj vulg qui en a plein le cul.

pistachio [pɪ'stɑːʃɪəʊ] (pl -s) n pistache f.

pistol ['pɪstl] n pistolet m.

pistol-whip vt Am frapper avec un pistolet.

piston ['pɪstən] n piston m.

pit [pɪt] (pt & pp -ted ; cont -ting) ⬦ n - **1.** [hole] trou m ; [in road] petit trou ; [on face] marque f - **2.** [for orchestra] fosse f - **3.** [mine] mine f - **4.** [quarry] carrière f - **5.** Am [of fruit] noyau m - **6.** phr : **the ~ of one's stomach** le creux de l'estomac ⬦ vt : **to ~ sb against sb** opposer qqn à qqn ; **to ~ one's wits against sb** se mesurer avec qqn.
➤ **pits** npl - **1.** [in motor racing] : **the ~s** les stands mpl - **2.** inf [awful] : **the ~s** l'horreur f complète OR totale.

pit bull (terrier) n pitbull m, pit-bull m.

pitch [pɪtʃ] ⬦ n - **1.** SPORT terrain m - **2.** MUS ton m - **3.** [level, degree] degré m - **4.** [selling place] place f - **5.** inf [sales talk] baratin m - **6.** AERON & NAUT tangage m - **7.** [throw] lancement m ⬦ vt - **1.** [throw] lancer ; **to be ~ed into sthg** être catapulté dans qqch - **2.** [set - price] fixer ; [- speech] adapter - **3.** [tent] dresser ; [camp] établir ⬦ vi - **1.** [ball] rebondir - **2.** [fall] : **to ~ forward** être projeté(e) en avant - **3.** AERON & NAUT tanguer.
➤ **pitch in** vi s'y mettre.

pitch-black adj : **it's ~ in here** il fait noir comme dans un four.

pitched [pɪtʃt] adj [sloping] penché(e).

pitched battle [,pɪtʃt-] n bataille f rangée.

pitcher ['pɪtʃər] n Am - **1.** [jug] cruche f - **2.** [in baseball] lanceur m.

pitchfork ['pɪtʃfɔːk] n fourche f.

piteous ['pɪtɪəs] adj pitoyable.

piteously ['pɪtɪəslɪ] adv pitoyablement.

pitfall ['pɪtfɔːl] n piège m.

pith [pɪθ] n - **1.** [in plant] moelle f - **2.** [of fruit] peau f blanche - **3.** fig [crux] essence f.

pithead ['pɪthed] n carreau m de mine.

pith helmet n casque m colonial.

pithy ['pɪθɪ] (compar -ier ; superl -iest) adj [brief] concis(e) ; [terse] piquant(e).

pitiable ['pɪtɪəbl] adj pitoyable.

pitiful ['pɪtɪfʊl] adj [condition] pitoyable ; [excuse, effort] lamentable.

pitifully ['pɪtɪfʊlɪ] adv [look, cry] pitoyablement ; [poor] lamentablement.

pitiless ['pɪtɪlɪs] adj sans pitié, impitoyable.

pitman ['pɪtmən] (pl -men [-mən]) n mineur m de fond.

pit pony n Br cheval m de mine.

pit prop n poteau m de mine.

pit stop n [in motor racing] arrêt m aux stands.

pitta bread ['pɪtə-] n pain m grec, pita m.

pittance ['pɪtəns] n [wage] salaire m de misère.

pitted ['pɪtɪd] adj : ~ (with) [face] grêlé(e) (par) ; [metal] piqué(e) (de).

pitter-patter ['pɪtə,pætə'] n [of rain] crépitement m.

pituitary [pɪ'tjʊɪtrɪ] (pl -ies) n : ~ (gland) glande f pituitaire.

pity ['pɪtɪ] (pt & pp -ied) ◇ n pitié f ; what a ~! quel dommage! ; it's a ~ c'est dommage ; to take OR have ~ on sb prendre qqn en pitié, avoir pitié de qqn ◇ vt plaindre.

pitying ['pɪtɪɪŋ] adj compatissant(e).

pivot ['pɪvət] ◇ n lit & fig pivot m ◇ vi : to ~ (on) pivoter (sur).

pixel ['pɪksl] n COMPUT pixel m.

pixie, pixy ['pɪksɪ] (pl -ies) n lutin m.

pizza ['pi:tsə] n pizza f.

pizzazz [pɪ'zæz] n inf vitalité f, énergie f.

Pl. (abbr of **Place**) rue.

P & L (abbr of **profit and loss**) n pertes et profits.

placard ['plækɑ:d] n placard m, affiche f.

placate [plə'keɪt] vt calmer, apaiser.

placatory [plə'keɪtərɪ] adj apaisant(e).

place [pleɪs] ◇ n - **1.** [location] endroit m, lieu m ; ~ of birth lieu de naissance - **2.** [proper position, seat, vacancy, rank] place f ; everything fell into ~ fig tout s'éclaircit ; to put sb in their ~ remettre qqn à sa place - **3.** [home] : at/to my ~ chez moi - **4.** [in book] : to lose one's ~ perdre sa page - **5.** MATH : decimal ~ décimale f - **6.** [instance] : in the first ~ tout de suite ; in the first ~ ... and in the second ~ ... premièrement ... et deuxièmement ... - **7.** phr : to take ~ avoir lieu ; to take the ~ of prendre la place de, remplacer ◇ vt - **1.** [position, put] placer, mettre - **2.** [apportion] : to ~ the responsibility for sthg on sb tenir qqn pour responsable de qqch - **3.** [identify] remettre - **4.** [an order] passer ; to ~ a bet parier - **5.** [in race] : to be ~d être placé(e).

◆ **all over the place** adv [everywhere] partout.

◆ **in place** adv - **1.** [in proper position] à sa place - **2.** [established] mis en place.

◆ **in place of** prep à la place de.

◆ **out of place** adv pas à sa place ; fig déplacé(e).

placebo [plə'si:bəʊ] (pl -s OR -es) n placebo m.

place card n carte f marque-place.

placed [pleɪst] adj : how are we ~ for time? est-ce qu'on a assez de temps? ; how are you ~ for money? qu'est-ce que tu as comme argent?

placekick ['pleɪskɪk] n coup m de pied placé.

place mat n set m (de table).

placement ['pleɪsmənt] n placement m.

placenta [plə'sentə] (pl -s OR -tae [-ti:]) n placenta m.

place setting n couvert m.

placid ['plæsɪd] adj - **1.** [person] placide - **2.** [sea, place] calme.

placidly ['plæsɪdlɪ] adv avec placidité.

plagiarism ['pleɪdʒərɪzm] n plagiat m.

plagiarist ['pleɪdʒərɪst] n plagiaire mf.

plagiarize, -ise ['pleɪdʒəraɪz] vt plagier.

plague [pleɪg] ◇ n - **1.** MED peste f ; to avoid sb/sthg like the ~ fuir qqn/qqch comme la peste - **2.** fig [nuisance] fléau m ◇ vt : to be ~d by [bad luck] être poursuivi(e) par ; [doubt] être rongé(e) par ; to ~ sb with questions harceler qqn de questions.

plaice [pleɪs] (pl inv) n carrelet m.

plaid [plæd] n plaid m.

Plaid Cymru [,plaɪd'kʌmrɪ] n parti nationaliste gallois.

plain [pleɪn] ◇ adj - **1.** [not patterned] uni(e) - **2.** [simple] simple - **3.** [clear] clair(e), évident(e) ; to make sthg ~ to sb (bien) faire comprendre qqch à qqn - **4.** [blunt] carré(e), franc (franche) - **5.** [absolute] pur(e) (et simple) - **6.** [not pretty] quelconque, ordinaire ◇ adv inf complètement ◇ n GEOGR plaine f.

plain chocolate n Br chocolat m à croquer.

plain-clothes adj en civil.

plain flour n Br farine f (sans levure).

plainly ['pleɪnlɪ] adv - **1.** [obviously] manifestement - **2.** [distinctly] clairement - **3.** [frankly] carrément, sans détours - **4.** [simply] simplement.

plain sailing n : it should be ~ from now on ça devrait aller comme sur des roulettes maintenant.

plainspoken [,pleɪn'spəʊkən] adj au franc-parler.

plaintiff ['pleɪntɪf] n demandeur m, -eresse f.

plaintive ['pleɪntɪv] adj plaintif(ive).

plait [plæt] ◇ n natte f ◇ vt natter, tresser.

plan [plæn] (pt & pp -ned ; cont -ning) ◇ n plan m, projet m ; to go according to ~ se passer OR aller comme prévu ◇ vt - **1.** [organize] préparer - **2.** [propose] : to ~ to do sthg projeter de faire qqch, avoir l'intention de faire qqch **- 3.** [design] concevoir ⬦ *vi :* **to ~ (for sthg)** faire des projets (pour qqch).

➤ **plans** *npl* plans *mpl*, projets *mpl ;* **have you any ~s for tonight?** avez-vous prévu quelque chose pour ce soir?

➤ **plan on** *vt fus :* **to ~ on doing sthg** prévoir de faire qqch.

➤ **plan out** *vt sep* préparer dans le détail.

plane [pleɪn] ⬦ *adj* plan(e) ⬦ *n* **- 1.** [aircraft] avion *m* **- 2.** GEOM plan *m* **- 3.** fig [level] niveau *m* **- 4.** [tool] rabot *m* **- 5.** [tree] platane *m* ⬦ *vt* raboter.

planet [ˈplænɪt] *n* planète *f*.

planetarium [ˌplænɪˈteərɪəm] (*pl* **-riums** OR **-ria** [-rɪə]) *n* planétarium *m*.

planetary [ˈplænɪtrɪ] *adj* planétaire.

plane tree *n* platane *m*.

plangent [ˈplændʒənt] *adj* literary retentissant(e).

plank [plæŋk] *n* **- 1.** [of wood] planche *f* **- 2.** POL [policy] point *m*.

plankton [ˈplæŋktən] *n* plancton *m*.

planned [plænd] *adj* [crime] prémédité(e) ; [economy] planifié(e), dirigé(e).

planner [ˈplænər] *n* **- 1.** [designer] : **town ~** urbaniste *mf* **- 2.** [strategist] planificateur *m*, -trice *f*.

planning [ˈplænɪŋ] *n* **- 1.** [designing] planification *f* **- 2.** [preparation] préparation *f*, organisation *f*.

planning permission *n* permis *m* de construire.

plan of action *n* plan *m* d'action.

plant [plɑːnt] ⬦ *n* **- 1.** BOT plante *f* **- 2.** [factory] usine *f* **- 3.** (U) [heavy machinery] matériel *m* ⬦ *vt* **- 1.** [gen] planter **- 2.** [bomb] poser ; **to ~ sthg on sb** cacher qqch sur qqn.

➤ **plant out** *vt sep* repiquer.

plantain [ˈplæntɪn] *n* plantain *m*.

plantation [plænˈteɪʃn] *n* plantation *f*.

planter [ˈplɑːntər] *n* [farmer] planteur *m*, -euse *f*.

plant pot *n* pot *m* de fleurs.

plaque [plɑːk] *n* **- 1.** [commemorative sign] plaque *f* **- 2.** (U) [on teeth] plaque *f* dentaire.

plasma [ˈplæzmə] *n* plasma *m*.

plaster [ˈplɑːstər] ⬦ *n* **- 1.** [material] plâtre *m ;* **in ~** dans le plâtre **- 2.** Br [bandage] pansement *m* adhésif ⬦ *vt* **- 1.** [wall, ceiling] plâtrer **- 2.** [cover] : **to ~ sthg (with)** couvrir qqch (de).

plasterboard [ˈplɑːstəbɔːd] *n* placoplâtre® *m*.

plaster cast *n* **- 1.** [for broken bones] plâtre *m* **- 2.** [model, statue] moule *m*.

plastered [ˈplɑːstəd] *adj* inf [drunk] bourré(e).

plasterer [ˈplɑːstərər] *n* plâtrier *m*.

plastering [ˈplɑːstərɪŋ] *n* plâtrage *m*.

plaster of Paris *n* plâtre *m* de moulage.

plastic [ˈplæstɪk] ⬦ *adj* plastique ⬦ *n* plastique *m*.

plastic bullet *n* balle *f* de plastique.

plastic explosive *n* plastic *m*.

Plasticine® Br [ˈplæstɪsiːn] *n* pâte *f* à modeler.

plasticize, -ise [ˈplæstɪsaɪz] *vt* plastifier.

plastic money *n* (U) cartes *fpl* de crédit.

plastic surgeon *n* spécialiste *mf* en chirurgie esthétique.

plastic surgery *n* chirurgie *f* esthétique OR plastique.

plate [pleɪt] ⬦ *n* **- 1.** [dish] assiette *f ;* **to have a lot on one's ~** fig avoir du pain sur la planche ; **you can't expect everything to be handed to you on a ~** fig on ne peut pas tout t'apporter sur un plateau **- 2.** [sheet of metal, plaque] tôle *f* **- 3.** (U) [metal covering] : **gold/silver ~** plaqué *m* or/argent **- 4.** [in book] planche *f* **- 5.** [in dentistry] dentier *m* ⬦ *vt :* **to be ~d (with)** être plaqué(e) (de).

Plate *n :* **the River ~** le Rio de la Plata.

plateau [ˈplætəʊ] (*pl* **-s** OR **-x** [-z]) *n* plateau *m ;* fig phase *f* OR période *f* de stabilité.

plateful [ˈpleɪtfʊl] *n* assiettée *f*.

plate-glass *adj* vitré(e).

plate rack *n* égouttoir *m*.

platform [ˈplætfɔːm] *n* **- 1.** [stage] estrade *f ;* [for speaker] tribune *f* **- 2.** [raised structure, of bus, of political party] plate-forme *f* **- 3.** RAIL quai *m*.

platform ticket *n* Br ticket *m* de quai.

plating [ˈpleɪtɪŋ] *n* placage *m*.

platinum [ˈplætɪnəm] ⬦ *adj* [hair] platiné(e) ⬦ *n* platine *m* ⬦ *comp* en platine.

platinum blonde *n* blonde *f* platinée.

platitude [ˈplætɪtjuːd] *n* platitude *f*.

platonic [pləˈtɒnɪk] *adj* platonique.

platoon [pləˈtuːn] *n* section *f*.

platter [ˈplætər] *n* [dish] plat *m*.

platypus [ˈplætɪpəs] (*pl* **-es** [-iːz]) *n* ornithorynque *m*.

plaudits [ˈplɔːdɪts] *npl* louanges *fpl*, éloges *mpl*.

plausible [ˈplɔːzəbl] *adj* plausible.

plausibly [ˈplɔːzəblɪ] *adv* de façon plausible.

play [pleɪ] ⬦ *n* **- 1.** (U) [amusement] jeu *m*, amusement *m* **- 2.** THEATRE pièce *f* (de théâtre) ; **a**

radio ~ une pièce radiophonique - **3.** SPORT : **in/out of** ~ en/hors jeu - **4.** [consideration] : **to come into** ~ fig entrer en jeu - **5.** [game] : **~ on words** jeu m de mots - **6.** TECH jeu m ◇ vt - **1.** [gen] jouer ; **to ~ a part** OR **role in** fig jouer un rôle dans - **2.** [game, sport] jouer à - **3.** [team, opponent] jouer contre - **4.** MUS [instrument] jouer de - **5.** phr : **to ~ it safe** ne pas prendre de risques ◇ vi jouer.

◆ **play along** vi : **to ~ along (with sb)** entrer dans le jeu (de qqn).

◆ **play at** vt fus jouer à ; **what's he ~ing at?** inf à quoi joue-t-il?

◆ **play back** vt sep [tape] réécouter ; [film] repasser.

◆ **play down** vt sep minimiser.

◆ **play off** ◇ vt sep : **to ~ sb/sthg off against** monter qqn/qqch contre ◇ vi SPORT jouer la belle.

◆ **play (up)on** vt fus jouer sur.

◆ **play up** ◇ vt sep [emphasize] insister sur ◇ vi - **1.** [machine] faire des siennes - **2.** [child] ne pas être sage.

playable ['pleɪəbl] adj [pitch] praticable.

play-act vi jouer la comédie.

playbill ['pleɪbɪl] n affiche f.

playboy ['pleɪbɔɪ] n playboy m.

play dough Am pâte f à modeler.

player ['pleɪər] n - **1.** [gen] joueur m, -euse f - **2.** THEATRE acteur m, -trice f.

playfellow ['pleɪˌfeləʊ] n camarade mf.

playful ['pleɪfʊl] adj - **1.** [person, mood] taquin(e) - **2.** [kitten, puppy] joueur(euse).

playfully ['pleɪfʊlɪ] adv en badinant.

playgoer ['pleɪˌgəʊər] n amateur m de théâtre.

playground ['pleɪgraʊnd] n cour f de récréation.

playgroup ['pleɪgruːp] n jardin m d'enfants.

playhouse ['pleɪhaʊs, pl -haʊzɪz] n Am maison f en modèle réduit (pour jouer).

playing card ['pleɪɪŋ-] n carte f à jouer.

playing field ['pleɪɪŋ-] n terrain m de sport.

playlist ['pleɪlɪst] n Br liste f de disques à passer (à la radio).

playmate ['pleɪmeɪt] n camarade mf.

play-off n SPORT belle f.

playpen ['pleɪpen] n parc m.

playroom ['pleɪrʊm] n salle f de jeu.

playschool ['pleɪskuːl] n jardin m d'enfants.

plaything ['pleɪθɪŋ] n lit & fig jouet m.

playtime ['pleɪtaɪm] n récréation f.

playwright ['pleɪraɪt] n dramaturge m.

plaza ['plɑːzəl] n [square] place f ; **shopping ~** centre m commercial.

plc abbr of **public limited company.**

plea [pliː] n - **1.** [for forgiveness, mercy] supplication f ; [for help, quiet] appel m - **2.** JUR : **to enter a ~ of not guilty** plaider non coupable.

plea bargaining n possibilité pour un inculpé de se voir notifier un chef d'inculpation moins grave s'il accepte de plaider coupable.

plead [pliːd] (pt & pp **-ed** OR **pled**) ◇ vt - **1.** JUR plaider - **2.** [give as excuse] invoquer ◇ vi - **1.** [beg] : **to ~ with sb (to do sthg)** supplier qqn (de faire qqch) ; **to ~ for sthg** implorer qqch - **2.** JUR plaider.

pleading ['pliːdɪŋ] ◇ adj suppliant(e) ◇ n (U) supplications fpl.

pleasant ['plezntl] adj agréable.

pleasantly ['plezntlɪ] adv [smile, speak] aimablement ; [surprised] agréablement.

pleasantry ['plezntrɪ] (pl **-ies**) n : **to exchange pleasantries** échanger des propos aimables.

please [pliːz] ◇ vt plaire à, faire plaisir à ; **to ~ o.s.** faire comme on veut ; **~ yourself!** comme vous voulez! ◇ vi plaire, faire plaisir ; **to do as one ~s** faire comme on veut ; **if you ~** s'il vous plaît ◇ adv s'il vous plaît.

pleased [pliːzd] adj - **1.** [satisfied] : **to be ~ (with)** être content(e) (de) - **2.** [happy] : **to be ~ (about)** être heureux(euse) (de) ; **~ to meet you!** enchanté(e)!

pleasing ['pliːzɪŋ] adj plaisant(e).

pleasingly ['pliːzɪŋlɪ] adv agréablement.

pleasurable ['pleʒərəbl] adj agréable.

pleasure ['pleʒər] n plaisir m ; **with ~** avec plaisir, volontiers ; **it's a ~, my ~** je vous en prie.

pleat [pliːt] ◇ n pli m ◇ vt plisser.

pleated ['pliːtɪd] adj plissé(e).

plebiscite ['plebɪsaɪt] n plébiscite m.

plectrum ['plektrəm] (pl **-s**) n plectre m.

pled [pled] pt & pp ⊳ **plead.**

pledge [pledʒ] ◇ n - **1.** [promise] promesse f - **2.** [token] gage m ◇ vt - **1.** [promise] promettre - **2.** [make promise] : **to ~ o.s. to** s'engager à ; **to ~ sb to secrecy** faire promettre le secret à qqn - **3.** [pawn] mettre en gage.

plenary session ['pliːnərɪ-] n séance f plénière.

plenitude ['plenɪtjuːd] n plénitude f.

plentiful ['plentɪfʊl] adj abondant(e).

plenty ['plentɪ] ◇ n (U) abondance f ◇ pron : **~ of** beaucoup de ; **we've got ~ of**

time nous avons largement le temps ◇ *adv* Am [very] très.

plethora ['pleθərə] *n* pléthore *f*.

pleurisy ['pluərəsɪ] *n* pleurésie *f*.

Plexiglas® ['pleksɪglɑːs] *n* Am plexiglas® *m*.

pliable ['plaɪəbl], **pliant** ['plaɪənt] *adj* - **1.** [material] pliable, souple - **2.** fig [person] docile.

pliers ['plaɪəz] *npl* tenailles *fpl*, pinces *fpl*.

plight [plaɪt] *n* condition *f* critique.

plimsoll ['plɪmsəl] *n* Br tennis *m*.

Plimsoll line *n* ligne *f* de flottaison en charge.

plinth [plɪnθ] *n* socle *m*

PLO (*abbr of* **Palestine Liberation Organization**) *n* OLP *f*.

plod [plɒd] (*pt* & *pp* **-ded**; *cont* **-ding**) *vi* - **1.** [walk slowly] marcher lentement OR péniblement - **2.** [work slowly] peiner.

plodder ['plɒdə'] *n* pej bûcheur *m*, -euse *f*.

plonk [plɒŋk] *n* (U) Br inf [wine] pinard *m*, vin *m* ordinaire.

◆ **plonk down** *vt sep* inf poser brutalement.

plop [plɒp] (*pt* & *pp* **-ped**; *cont* **-ping**) ◇ *n* ploc *m* ◇ *vi* faire ploc.

plot [plɒt] (*pt* & *pp* **-ted**; *cont* **-ting**) ◇ *n* - **1.** [plan] complot *m*, conspiration *f* - **2.** [story] intrigue *f* - **3.** [of land] (parcelle *f* de) terrain *m*, lopin *m* - **4.** Am [house plan] plan *m* ◇ *vt* - **1.** [plan] comploter ; **to ~ to do sthg** comploter de faire qqch - **2.** [chart] déterminer, marquer - **3.** MATH tracer, marquer ◇ *vi* comploter.

plotter ['plɒtə'] *n* [schemer] conspirateur *m*, -trice *f*.

plough Br, **plow** Am [plaʊ] ◇ *n* charrue *f* ◇ *vt* [field] labourer.

◆ **plough into** ◇ *vt sep* [money] investir ◇ *vt fus* [subj : car] rentrer dans.

◆ **plough on** *vi* continuer péniblement OR laborieusement.

◆ **plough up** *vt sep* [field] labourer.

ploughman's ['plaʊmənz] (*pl inv*) *n* Br : **~ (lunch)** repas de pain, fromage et pickles.

ploughshare Br, **plowshare** Am ['plaʊʃeə'] *n* soc *m* de charrue.

plow *etc* Am = **plough** *etc*.

ploy [plɔɪ] *n* stratagème *m*, ruse *f*.

PLR (*abbr of* **Public Lending Right**) *n* droit d'auteur versé pour les ouvrages prêtés par les bibliothèques.

pluck [plʌk] ◇ *vt* - **1.** [flower, fruit] cueillir - **2.** [pull sharply] arracher - **3.** [chicken, turkey] plumer - **4.** [eyebrows] épiler - **5.** MUS pincer ◇ *n* (U) dated courage *m*, cran *m*.

◆ **pluck up** *vt fus* : **to ~ up the courage to do sthg** rassembler son courage pour faire qqch.

plucky ['plʌkɪ] (*compar* **-ier** ; *superl* **-iest**) *adj* dated qui a du cran, courageux(euse).

plug [plʌg] (*pt* & *pp* **-ged** ; *cont* **-ging**) ◇ *n* - **1.** ELEC prise *f* de courant - **2.** [for bath, sink] bonde *f* - **3.** inf [for new book, film etc] pub *f*, publicité *f* ◇ *vt* - **1.** [hole] boucher, obturer - **2.** inf [new book, film etc] faire de la publicité pour.

◆ **plug in** *vt sep* brancher.

plughole ['plʌghəʊl] *n* bonde *f*, trou *m* d'écoulement.

plum [plʌm] ◇ *adj* - **1.** [colour] prune (*inv*) - **2.** [very good] : **a ~ job** un poste en or ◇ *n* [fruit] prune *f*.

plumage ['pluːmɪdʒ] *n* plumage *m*.

plumb [plʌm] ◇ *adv* - **1.** Br [exactly] exactement, en plein - **2.** Am [completely] complètement ◇ *vt* : **to ~ the depths of** toucher le fond de.

◆ **plumb in** *vt sep* Br raccorder.

plumber ['plʌmə'] *n* plombier *m*.

plumbing ['plʌmɪŋ] *n* (U) - **1.** [fittings] plomberie *f*, tuyauterie *f* - **2.** [work] plomberie *f*.

plumb line *n* fil *m* à plomb.

plume [pluːm] *n* - **1.** [feather] plume *f* - **2.** [on hat] panache *m* - **3.** [column] : **a ~ of smoke** un panache de fumée.

plummet ['plʌmɪt] *vi* - **1.** [bird, plane] plonger - **2.** fig [decrease] dégringoler.

plummy ['plʌmɪ] (*compar* **-ier** ; *superl* **-iest**) *adj* Br pej [voice] de la haute, snob.

plump [plʌmp] *adj* bien en chair, grassouillet(ette).

◆ **plump for** *vt fus* opter pour, choisir.

◆ **plump up** *vt sep* [cushion] secouer.

plumpness ['plʌmpnɪs] *n* corpulence *f*, embonpoint *m*.

plum pudding *n* pudding *m* de Noël.

plunder ['plʌndə'] ◇ *n* (U) - **1.** [stealing, raiding] pillage *m* - **2.** [stolen goods] butin *m* ◇ *vt* piller.

plunge [plʌndʒ] ◇ *n* - **1.** [dive] plongeon *m* ; **to take the ~** se jeter à l'eau - **2.** fig [decrease] dégringolade *f*, chute *f* ◇ *vt* : **to ~ sthg into** plonger qqch dans ◇ *vi* - **1.** [dive] plonger, tomber - **2.** fig [decrease] dégringoler.

plunger ['plʌndʒə'] *n* débouchoir *m* à ventouse.

plunging ['plʌndʒɪŋ] *adj* [neckline] plongeant(e).

pluperfect [ˌpluːˈpɜːfɪkt] *n* : **~ (tense)** plus-que-parfait *m*.

plural ['pluərəl] <> adj - **1.** GRAMM pluriel(elle) - **2.** [not individual] collectif(ive) - **3.** [multicultural] multiculturel(elle) <> n pluriel m.

pluralistic [,pluərə'lıstık] adj pluraliste.

plurality [plu'rælətı] n - **1.** [large number] : a ~ of une multiplicité de - **2.** Am [majority] majorité f.

plus [plʌs] (pl **pluses** OR **plusses** [plʌsiːz]) <> adj : 30 ~ 30 ou plus <> n - **1.** MATH signe m plus - **2.** inf [bonus] plus m, atout m <> prep et <> conj [moreover] de plus.

plus fours npl pantalon m de golf.

plush [plʌʃ] adj luxueux(euse), somptueux(euse).

plus sign n signe m plus.

Pluto ['pluːtəu] n [planet] Pluton f.

plutocrat ['pluːtəkræt] n ploutocrate m.

plutonium [pluː'təunıəm] n plutonium m.

ply [plaı] (pt & pp **plied**) <> adj : **four** ~ [wool] à quatre fils ; [wood] à quatre plis <> n [of wool] fil m ; [of wood] pli m <> vt - **1.** [trade] exercer - **2.** [supply] : **to** ~ **sb with drink** ne pas arrêter de remplir le verre de qqn <> vi [ship etc] faire la navette.

plywood ['plaıwud] n contreplaqué m.

p.m., pm (abbr of **post meridiem**) : **at 3** ~ à 15 h.

PM abbr of **prime minister**.

PMS abbr of **premenstrual syndrome**.

PMT abbr of **premenstrual tension**.

pneumatic [njuː'mætık] adj pneumatique.

pneumatic drill n marteau piqueur m.

pneumonia [njuː'məunjə] n (U) pneumonie f.

po = PO².

Po [pəu] n : **the (River)** ~ le Pô.

PO¹ abbr of **Post Office**.

PO², po abbr of **postal order**.

POA (abbr of **Prison Officers' Association**) n syndicat des agents pénitentiaires en Grande-Bretagne.

poach [pəutʃ] <> vt - **1.** [fish] pêcher sans permis ; [deer etc] chasser sans permis - **2.** fig [idea] voler - **3.** CULIN pocher <> vi braconner.

poacher ['pəutʃəʳ] n braconnier m.

poaching ['pəutʃıŋ] n braconnage m.

PO Box (abbr of **Post Office Box**) n BP f.

pocket ['pɒkıt] <> n lit & fig poche f ; **to be out of** ~ en être de sa poche ; **to live in each other's** ~s être trop ensemble ; **to pick sb's** ~ faire les poches à qqn <> adj de poche <> vt empocher.

pocketbook ['pɒkıtbuk] n - **1.** [notebook] carnet m - **2.** Am [handbag] sac m à main.

pocket calculator n calculatrice f de poche, calculette f.

pocketful ['pɒkıtful] n pleine poche f.

pocket-handkerchief n mouchoir m de poche.

pocketknife ['pɒkıtnaıf] (pl **-knives** [-naıvz]) n canif m.

pocket money n argent m de poche.

pocket-size(d) adj de poche.

pockmark ['pɒkmɑːk] n marque f de la petite vérole.

pod [pɒd] n - **1.** [of plants] cosse f - **2.** [of spacecraft] nacelle f.

podgy ['pɒdʒı] (compar **-ier** ; superl **-iest**) adj inf boulot(otte), rondelet(ette).

podiatrist [pə'daıətrıst] n Am pédicure mf.

podium ['pəudıəm] (pl **-diums** OR **-dia** [-dıə]) n podium m.

POE (abbr of **port of entry**) n port d'arrivée.

poem ['pəuım] n poème m.

poet ['pəuıt] n poète m.

poetic [pəu'etık] adj poétique.

poetic justice n justice f immanente.

poet laureate n poète m lauréat.

poetry ['pəuıtrı] n poésie f.

pogo stick ['pəugəu-] n échasse f à ressort.

pogrom ['pɒgrəm] n pogrom m, pogrome m.

poignancy ['pɔınjənsı] n caractère m poignant.

poignant ['pɔınjənt] adj poignant(e).

poinsettia [pɔın'setıə] n poinsettia m.

point [pɔınt] <> n - **1.** [tip] pointe f - **2.** [place] endroit m, point m - **3.** [time] stade m, moment m ; ~ **of no return** point m de non-retour - **4.** [detail, argument] question f, détail m ; **you have a** ~ il y a du vrai dans ce que vous dites ; **to make a** ~ faire une remarque ; **to make one's** ~ dire ce qu'on a à dire, dire son mot ; **it's a sore** ~ **with her** fig elle est très sensible sur ce point - **5.** [main idea] point m essentiel ; **to get** OR **come to the** ~ en venir au fait ; **to miss the** ~ ne pas comprendre ; **beside the** ~ à côté de la question ; **to the** ~ pertinent(e), approprié(e) - **6.** [feature] : **good** ~ qualité f ; **bad** ~ défaut m - **7.** [purpose] : **what's the** ~ **in buying a new car?** à quoi bon acheter une nouvelle voiture? ; **there's no** ~ **in having a meeting** cela ne sert à rien d'avoir une réunion - **8.** [on scale, in scores] point m - **9.** MATH : **two** ~ **six** deux virgule six - **10.** [of compass] aire f du vent - **11.** Br ELEC prise f (de courant) - **12.** Am [full stop] point m (final) - **13.** phr : **to make a** ~ **of doing sthg** ne pas manquer de faire qqch <> vt : **to** ~ **sthg (at)** [gun, camera] braquer qqch (sur) ; [finger, hose].pointer qqch (sur) ⬦ *vi* - **1.** [indicate with finger] : **to ~ (at sb/sthg), to ~ (to sb/sthg)** montrer (qqn/qqch) du doigt, indiquer (qqn/qqch) du doigt - **2.** [face] : **to ~ north/south** indiquer le nord/le sud - **3.** fig [suggest] : **to ~ to sthg** suggérer qqch, laisser supposer qqch.

➤ **points** *npl* Br RAIL aiguillage *m*.

➤ **up to a point** *adv* jusqu'à un certain point, dans une certaine mesure.

➤ **on the point of** *prep* sur le point de.

➤ **point out** *vt sep* [person, place] montrer, indiquer ; [fact, mistake] signaler.

point-blank ⬦ *adj* [refusal] catégorique ; [question] de but en blanc ; **at ~ range** à bout portant ⬦ *adv* - **1.** [refuse] catégoriquement ; [ask] de but en blanc - **2.** [shoot] à bout portant.

point duty *n* Br service *m* de la circulation.

pointed ['pɔɪntɪd] *adj* - **1.** [sharp] pointu(e) - **2.** fig [remark] mordant(e), incisif(ive).

pointedly ['pɔɪntɪdlɪ] *adv* d'un ton mordant.

pointer ['pɔɪntə'] *n* - **1.** [piece of advice] tuyau *m*, conseil *m* - **2.** [needle] aiguille *f* - **3.** [stick] baguette *f* - **4.** COMPUT pointeur *m*.

pointing ['pɔɪntɪŋ] *n* [on wall] jointoiement *m*.

pointless ['pɔɪntlɪs] *adj* inutile, vain(e).

point of order (*pl* points of order) *n* question *f* de procédure OR de droit.

point of sale (*pl* points of sale) *n* point *m* de vente.

point of view (*pl* points of view) *n* point *m* de vue.

point-to-point *n* Br steeple-chase *m* pour cavaliers amateurs.

poise [pɔɪz] *n* fig calme *m*, sang-froid *m*.

poised [pɔɪzd] *adj* - **1.** [ready] : **~ (for)** prêt(e) (pour) ; **to be ~ to do sthg** se tenir prêt à faire qqch - **2.** fig [calm] calme, posé(e).

poison ['pɔɪzn] ⬦ *n* poison *m* ⬦ *vt* - **1.** [gen] empoisonner - **2.** [pollute] polluer.

poisoning ['pɔɪznɪŋ] *n* empoisonnement *m* ; **food ~** intoxication *f* alimentaire.

poisonous ['pɔɪznəs] *adj* - **1.** [fumes] toxique ; [plant] vénéneux(euse) - **2.** [snake] venimeux (euse) - **3.** fig [rumours, influence] pernicieux (euse).

poison-pen letter *n* lettre *f* anonyme venimeuse.

poke [pəʊk] ⬦ *n* [prod, jab] coup *m* ⬦ *vt* - **1.** [prod] pousser, donner un coup de coude à - **2.** [put] fourrer - **3.** [fire] attiser, tisonner - **4.** [stretch] : **he ~d his head round the door** il a passé la tête dans l'embrasure de la porte ⬦ *vi* [protrude] sortir, dépasser.

➤ **poke about, poke around** *vi* inf fouiller, fourrager.

➤ **poke at** *vt fus* [with finger] pousser (du doigt) ; [with stick] pousser (avec un bâton).

poker ['pəʊkə'] *n* - **1.** [game] poker *m* - **2.** [for fire] tisonnier *m*.

poker-faced [-,feɪst] *adj* au visage impassible.

poky ['pəʊkɪ] (*compar* -ier ; *superl* -iest) *adj* pej [room] exigu(ë), minuscule.

Poland ['pəʊlənd] *n* Pologne *f ;* **in ~** en Pologne.

polar ['pəʊlə'] *adj* polaire.

polar bear *n* ours *m* polaire OR blanc.

polarity [pəʊ'lærətɪ] *n* polarité *f*.

polarization [,pəʊləraɪ'zeɪʃn] *n* polarisation *f*.

polarize, -ise ['pəʊləraɪz] *vt* polariser.

Polaroid® ['pəʊlərɔɪd] *n* - **1.** [camera] Polaroïd® *m* - **2.** [photograph] photo *f* polaroïd.

Polaroids® ['pəʊlərɔɪdz] *npl* lunettes *fpl* polaroïd.

pole [pəʊl] *n* - **1.** [rod, post] perche *f*, mât *m* - **2.** ELEC & GEOGR pôle *m ;* **~s apart** aux antipodes (l'un de l'autre).

Pole [pəʊl] *n* Polonais *m*, -e *f*.

poleaxed ['pəʊlækst] *adj* assommé(e).

polecat ['pəʊlkæt] *n* putois *m*.

polemic [pə'lemɪk] *n* polémique *f*.

pole position *n* pole position *f*.

Pole Star *n* : **the ~** l'Étoile *f* Polaire.

pole vault *n* : **the ~** le saut à la perche.

➤ **pole-vault** *vi* sauter à la perche.

pole-vaulter [-,vɔːltə'] *n* sauteur *m*, -euse *f* à la perche.

police [pə'liːs] ⬦ *npl* - **1.** [police force] : **the ~** la police - **2.** [policemen] agents *mpl* de police ⬦ *vt* maintenir l'ordre dans.

police car *n* voiture *f* de police.

police constable *n* Br agent *m* de police.

police department *n* Am service *m* de police.

police dog *n* chien *m* policier.

police force *n* police *f*.

policeman [pə'liːsmən] (*pl* -men [-mən]) *n* agent *m* de police.

police officer *n* policier *m*.

police record *n* casier *m* judiciaire.

police state *n* état *m* policier.

police station *n* commissariat *m* (de police).

policewoman [pə'liːs,wʊmən] (*pl* -women [-,wɪmɪn]) *n* femme *f* agent de police.

policy ['pɒləsɪ] (*pl* -ies) *n* - **1.** [plan] politique *f*
- **2.** [document] police *f*.
policy-holder *n* assuré *m*, -e *f*.
polio ['pəʊlɪəʊ] *n* polio *f*.
polish ['pɒlɪʃ] ◇ *n* - **1.** [for shoes] cirage *m* ; [for
floor] cire *f*, encaustique *f* - **2.** [shine] brillant
m, lustre *m* - **3.** fig [refinement] raffinement *m*
◇ *vt* [shoes, floor] cirer ; [car] astiquer ; [cutlery,
glasses] faire briller.
◆ **polish off** *vt sep* inf expédier.
◆ **polish up** *vt sep* [maths, language] perfectionner ; [travail] peaufiner.
Polish ['pəʊlɪʃ] ◇ *adj* polonais(e) ◇ *n* [lan-
guage] polonais *m* ◇ *npl* : **the ~** les Polonais
mpl.
polished ['pɒlɪʃt] *adj* - **1.** [refined] raffiné(e)
- **2.** [accomplished] accompli(e), parfait(e).
polite [pə'laɪt] *adj* - **1.** [courteous] poli(e) - **2.** [re-
fined] bien élevé(e), qui a du savoir-vivre.
politely [pə'laɪtlɪ] *adv* poliment.
politeness [pə'laɪtnɪs] *n* (U) politesse *f*.
politic ['pɒlətɪk] *adj* politique.
political [pə'lɪtɪkl] *adj* politique.
political asylum *n* droit *m* d'asile (politique).
political football *n* : **the abortion issue has
become a ~** les partis politiques se ren-
voient la balle au sujet de l'avortement.
political geography *n* géographie *f* politique.
politically [pə'lɪtɪklɪ] *adv* politiquement.
politically correct [pə,lɪtɪklɪ-] *adj* conforme
au mouvement qui préconise le remplacement de termes jugés discriminants par d'autres 'politiquement corrects'.

POLITICALLY CORRECT

Le mouvement « PC » est un mouvement
intellectuel, surtout américain, qui vise à
établir une nouvelle éthique, notamment
en bannissant de la langue certains termes
jugés discriminants. Ce mouvement prône
de remplacer par exemple « American Indian » par « Native American », « Black »
par « African American », « short » par
« vertically challenged ».

political prisoner *n* prisonnier *m* politique.
political science *n* (U) sciences *fpl* politiques.
politician [,pɒlɪ'tɪʃn] *n* homme *m* politique,
femme *f* politique.
politicize, -ise [pə'lɪtɪsaɪz] *vt* politiser.
politics ['pɒlətɪks] ◇ *n* (U) politique *f* ◇ *npl*

- **1.** [personal beliefs] : **what are his ~?** de quel
bord est-il? - **2.** [of group, area] politique *f*.
polka ['pɒlkə] *n* polka *f*.
polka dot *n* pois *m*.
poll [pəʊl] ◇ *n* vote *m*, scrutin *m* ◇ *vt*
- **1.** [people] interroger, sonder - **2.** [votes] obtenir.
◆ **polls** *npl* : **to go to the ~s** aller aux urnes.
pollen ['pɒlən] *n* pollen *m*.
pollen count *n* taux *m* de pollen.
pollinate ['pɒləneɪt] *vt* féconder avec du
pollen.
pollination [,pɒlɪ'neɪʃn] *n* pollinisation *f*.
polling ['pəʊlɪŋ] *n* (U) élections *fpl*.
polling booth *n* isoloir *m*.
polling day *n* Br jour *m* du scrutin OR des
élections.
polling station *n* bureau *m* de vote.
pollster ['pəʊlstər] *n* enquêteur *m*, -euse *f*.
poll tax *n* Br ≈ impôts *mpl* locaux.
pollutant [pə'luːtnt] *n* polluant *m*.
pollute [pə'luːt] *vt* polluer.
pollution [pə'luːʃn] *n* pollution *f*.
polo ['pəʊləʊ] *n* polo *m*.
polo neck *n* Br - **1.** [neck] col *m* roulé
- **2.** [jumper] pull *m* à col roulé.
◆ **polo-neck** *adj* Br à col roulé.
poltergeist ['pɒltəgaɪst] *n* esprit *m* frap-
peur.
poly ['pɒlɪ] (*pl* -s) *n* inf abbr of polytechnic.
polyanthus [,pɒlɪ'ænθəs] (*pl* -thuses [-θəsiːz]
OR -thi [-θaɪ]) *n* primevère *f*.
poly bag *n* Br inf sac *m* en plastique.
polyester [,pɒlɪ'estər] *n* polyester *m*.
polyethylene Am = polythene.
polygamist [pə'lɪgəmɪst] *n* polygame *mf*.
polygamy [pə'lɪgəmɪ] *n* polygamie *f*.
polygon ['pɒlɪgɒn] *n* polygone *m*.
polymer ['pɒlɪmər] *n* polymère *m*.
Polynesia [,pɒlɪ'niːzjə] *n* Polynésie *f* ; **in ~** en
Polynésie ; **French ~** Polynésie française.
Polynesian [,pɒlɪ'niːzjən] ◇ *adj* polyné-
sien(enne) ◇ *n* - **1.** [person] Polynésien *m*,
-enne *f* - **2.** [language] polynésien *m*.
polyp ['pɒlɪp] *n* polype *m*.
polyphony [pə'lɪfənɪ] *n* fml polyphonie *f*.
polystyrene [,pɒlɪ'staɪriːn] *n* polystyrène *m*.
polytechnic [,pɒlɪ'teknɪk] *n* Br établissement
d'enseignement supérieur ; en 1993, les 'polytechnics' ont été transformés en universités.
polythene ['pɒlɪθiːn], **polyethylene** Am
[,pɒlɪ'eθɪliːn] *n* polyéthylène *m*.
polythene bag *n* Br sac *m* en plastique.

polyunsaturated [ˌpɒlɪʌn'sætʃəreɪtɪd] *adj* polyinsaturé(e).

polyurethane [ˌpɒlɪ'jʊərəθeɪn] *n* polyuréthane *m*.

pom [pɒm] *n* Austr inf *terme péjoratif désignant un Anglais.*

pomander [pə'mændə'] *n* diffuseur *m* de parfum.

pomegranate ['pɒmɪˌɡrænɪt] *n* grenade *f*.

pommel ['pɒml] *n* pommeau *m*.

pomp [pɒmp] *n* pompe *f*, faste *m*.

pompom ['pɒmpɒm] *n* pompon *m*.

pompous ['pɒmpəs] *adj* - **1.** [person] fat, suffisant(e) - **2.** [style, speech] pompeux(euse).

ponce [pɒns] *n* Br v inf pej - **1.** [effeminate man] homme *m* efféminé - **2.** [pimp] maquereau *m*.

poncho ['pɒntʃəʊ] (*pl* -**s**) *n* poncho *m*.

pond [pɒnd] *n* étang *m*, mare *f*.

ponder ['pɒndə'] ⬦ *vt* considérer, peser ⬦ *vi* : **to ~** (**on** OR **over**) réfléchir (sur).

ponderous ['pɒndərəs] *adj* - **1.** [dull] lourd(e) - **2.** [large, heavy] pesant(e).

pong [pɒŋ] Br inf ⬦ *n* puanteur *f* ⬦ *vi* puer, schlinguer.

pontiff ['pɒntɪf] *n* souverain *m* pontife.

pontificate [pɒn'tɪfɪkeɪt] *vi* pej : **to ~** (**on**) pontifier (sur).

pontoon [pɒn'tuːn] *n* - **1.** [bridge] ponton *m* - **2.** Br [game] vingt-et-un *m*.

pony ['pəʊnɪ] (*pl* -**ies**) *n* poney *m*.

ponytail ['pəʊnɪteɪl] *n* queue-de-cheval *f*.

pony-trekking [-ˌtrekɪŋ] *n* randonnée *f* à cheval OR en poney.

poodle ['puːdl] *n* caniche *m*.

poof [pʊf] *n* Br v inf pej tapette *f*, pédé *m*.

pooh [puː] *excl* berk!, pouah!

pooh-pooh *vt* inf dédaigner.

pool [puːl] ⬦ *n* - **1.** [pond, of blood] mare *f* ; [of rain, light] flaque *f* - **2.** [swimming pool] piscine *f* - **3.** SPORT billard *m* américain ⬦ *vt* [resources etc] mettre en commun.

➠ **pools** *npl* Br : **the ~s** ≈ le loto sportif.

pooped [puːpt] *adj* inf crevé(e).

poor [pɔː'] ⬦ *adj* - **1.** [gen] pauvre - **2.** [not very good] médiocre, mauvais(e) ⬦ *npl* : **the ~** les pauvres *mpl*.

poorhouse ['pɔːhaʊs, *pl* -haʊzɪz] *n* hospice *m* des pauvres.

poorly ['pɔːlɪ] ⬦ *adj* Br souffrant(e) ⬦ *adv* mal, médiocrement.

poorness ['pɔːnɪs] *n* médiocrité *f*.

poor relation *n* fig parent *m* pauvre.

pop [pɒp] (*pt* & *pp* -**ped** ; *cont* -**ping**) ⬦ *n* - **1.** (U) [music] pop *m* - **2.** (U) inf [fizzy drink] boisson *f* gazeuse - **3.** esp Am inf [father] papa *m* - **4.** [sound] pan *m* ⬦ *vt* - **1.** [burst] faire éclater, crever - **2.** [put quickly] mettre, fourrer ⬦ *vi* - **1.** [balloon] éclater, crever ; [cork, button] sauter - **2.** [eyes] : **his eyes popped** il a écarquillé les yeux - **3.** [go quickly] : **I'm just popping to the newsagent's** je fais un saut chez le marchand de journaux.

➠ **pop in** *vi* faire une petite visite.

➠ **pop up** *vi* surgir.

popadum ['pɒpədəm] *n* poppadum *m*.

pop art *n* pop art *m*.

pop concert *n* concert *m* pop.

popcorn ['pɒpkɔːn] *n* pop-corn *m*.

pope [pəʊp] *n* pape *m*.

pop group *n* groupe *m* pop.

poplar ['pɒplə'] *n* peuplier *m*.

poplin ['pɒplɪn] *n* popeline *f*.

popper ['pɒpə'] *n* Br pression *f*.

poppy ['pɒpɪ] (*pl* -**ies**) *n* coquelicot *m*, pavot *m*.

poppycock ['pɒpɪkɒk] *n* (U) inf pej idioties *fpl*, bêtises *fpl*.

Poppy Day *n* Br anniversaire *m* de l'armistice.

POPPY DAY

> Journée de commémoration pendant laquelle on porte un coquelicot en papier en souvenir des soldats britanniques morts lors des guerres mondiales.

Popsicle® ['pɒpsɪkl] *n* Am sucette *f* glacée.

pop singer *n* chanteur *m*, -euse *f* pop.

populace ['pɒpjʊləs] *n* : **the ~** le peuple.

popular ['pɒpjʊlə'] *adj* - **1.** [gen] populaire - **2.** [name, holiday resort] à la mode.

popularity [ˌpɒpjʊ'lærətɪ] *n* popularité *f*.

popularize, -ise ['pɒpjʊləraɪz] *vt* - **1.** [make popular] populariser - **2.** [simplify] vulgariser.

popularly ['pɒpjʊləlɪ] *adv* communément.

populate ['pɒpjʊleɪt] *vt* peupler.

populated ['pɒpjʊleɪtɪd] *adj* peuplé(e).

population [ˌpɒpjʊ'leɪʃn] *n* population *f*.

population explosion *n* explosion *f* démographique.

populist ['pɒpjʊlɪst] *n* populiste *mf*.

pop-up *adj* - **1.** [toaster] automatique - **2.** [book] dont les images se déplient.

porcelain ['pɔːsəlɪn] *n* porcelaine *f*.

porch [pɔːtʃ] *n* - **1.** [entrance] porche *m* - **2.** Am [verandah] véranda *f*.

porcupine ['pɔːkjʊpaɪn] *n* porc-épic *m*.

pore [pɔːʳ] *n* pore *m*.
➡ **pore over** *vt fus* examiner de près.
pork [pɔːk] *n* porc *m*.
pork chop *n* côtelette *f* de porc.
pork pie *n* pâté *m* de porc en croûte.
porn [pɔːn] (*abbr of* **pornography**) *n* (U) inf porno *m ;* **hard ~** porno *m* hard, hard *m ;* **soft ~** porno *m* soft, soft *m*.
pornographic [ˌpɔːnəˈgræfɪk] *adj* pornographique.
pornography [pɔːˈnɒgrəfɪ] *n* pornographie *f*.
porous [ˈpɔːrəs] *adj* poreux(euse).
porpoise [ˈpɔːpəs] *n* marsouin *m*.
porridge [ˈpɒrɪdʒ] *n* porridge *m*.
port [pɔːt] <> *n* - **1.** [town, harbour] port *m* - **2.** NAUT [left-hand side] bâbord *m ;* **to ~** à bâbord - **3.** [drink] porto *m* - **4.** COMPUT port *m* <> *comp* - **1.** [of a port] portuaire, du port - **2.** NAUT [left-hand] de bâbord.
portable [ˈpɔːtəbl] *adj* portatif(ive).
Portacrib® [ˈpɔːtəˌkrɪb] *n* Am moïse *m*, porte-bébé *m*.
portal [ˈpɔːtl] *n* literary portail *m*.
Port-au-Prince [ˌpɔːtəʊˈprɪns] *n* Port-au-Prince.
portcullis [ˌpɔːtˈkʌlɪs] *n* herse *f*.
portend [pɔːˈtend] *vt* présager, augurer.
portent [ˈpɔːtənt] *n* présage *m*.
porter [ˈpɔːtəʳ] *n* - **1.** Br [doorman] concierge *m*, portier *m* - **2.** [for luggage] porteur *m* - **3.** Am [on train] employé *m*, -e *f* des wagons-lits.
portfolio [ˌpɔːtˈfəʊljəʊ] (*pl* -s) *n* - **1.** [case] serviette *f* - **2.** [sample of work] portfolio *m* - **3.** FIN portefeuille *m*.
porthole [ˈpɔːthəʊl] *n* hublot *m*.
portion [ˈpɔːʃn] *n* - **1.** [section] portion *f*, part *f* - **2.** [of food] portion *f*.
portly [ˈpɔːtlɪ] (*compar* -ier ; *superl* -iest) *adj* corpulent(e).
port of call *n* - **1.** NAUT port *m* d'escale - **2.** fig [on journey] endroit *m*.
Port of Spain *n* Port of Spain.
portrait [ˈpɔːtreɪt] *n* portrait *m*.
portraitist [ˈpɔːtreɪtɪst] *n* portraitiste *mf*.
portray [pɔːˈtreɪ] *vt* - **1.** CINEMA & THEATRE jouer, interpréter - **2.** [describe] dépeindre - **3.** [paint] faire le portrait de.
portrayal [pɔːˈtreɪəl] *n* - **1.** CINEMA & THEATRE interprétation *f* - **2.** [painting, photograph] portrait *m* - **3.** [description] description *f*.
Portugal [ˈpɔːtʃʊgl] *n* Portugal *m ;* **in ~** au Portugal.
Portuguese [ˌpɔːtʃʊˈgiːz] <> *adj* portu-

gais(e) <> *n* [language] portugais *m* <> *npl :* **the ~** les Portugais *mpl*.
Portuguese man-of-war *n* galère *f*.
pose [pəʊz] <> *n* - **1.** [stance] pose *f* - **2.** pej [affectation] pose *f*, affectation *f* <> *vt* - **1.** [danger] présenter - **2.** [problem, question] poser <> *vi* - **1.** ART & pej poser - **2.** [pretend to be] : **to ~ as** se faire passer pour.
poser [ˈpəʊzəʳ] *n* - **1.** pej [person] poseur *m*, -euse *f* - **2.** inf [hard question] question *f* difficile, colle *f*.
poseur [pəʊˈzɜːʳ] *n* pej poseur *m*, -euse *f*.
posh [pɒʃ] *adj* inf - **1.** [hotel, clothes etc] chic *(inv)* - **2.** Br [accent, person] de la haute.
posit [ˈpɒzɪt] *vt* fml énoncer, poser en principe.
position [pəˈzɪʃn] <> *n* - **1.** [gen] position *f ;* **in ~** en place, en position - **2.** [job] poste *m*, emploi *m* - **3.** [state] situation *f ;* **to be in a/no ~ to do sthg** être/ne pas être à même de faire qqch <> *vt* placer, mettre en position ; **to ~ o.s.** se placer, se mettre.
positive [ˈpɒzətɪv] *adj* - **1.** [gen] positif(ive) - **2.** [sure] sûr(e), certain(e) ; **to be ~ about sthg** être sûr de qqch - **3.** [optimistic] positif(ive), optimiste ; **to be ~ about sthg** avoir une attitude positive au sujet de qqch - **4.** [definite] formel(elle), précis(e) - **5.** [evidence] irréfutable, indéniable - **6.** [downright] véritable.
positive discrimination *n* discrimination *f* positive.
positively [ˈpɒzətɪvlɪ] *adv* - **1.** [optimistically] avec optimisme, de façon positive - **2.** [definitely] formellement - **3.** [favourably] favorablement - **4.** [irrefutably] d'une manière irréfutable - **5.** [completely] absolument, complètement.
positive vetting *n* Br enquête sur une personne pour des raisons de sécurité.
positivism [ˈpɒzɪtɪvɪzm] *n* positivisme *m*.
posse [ˈpɒsɪ] *n* Am détachement *m*, troupe *f*.
possess [pəˈzes] *vt* posséder.
possessed [pəˈzest] *adj* [mad] possédé(e).
possession [pəˈzeʃn] *n* possession *f*.
➡ **possessions** *npl* possessions *fpl*, biens *mpl*.
possessive [pəˈzesɪv] <> *adj* possessif(ive) <> *n* GRAMM possessif *m*.
possessively [pəˈzesɪvlɪ] *adv* d'une manière possessive.
possessor [pəˈzesəʳ] *n* possesseur *m*, propriétaire *mf*.
possibility [ˌpɒsəˈbɪlətɪ] (*pl* -ies) *n* - **1.** [chance, likelihood] possibilité *f*, chances *fpl ;* **there is a**

~ **that** ... il se peut que ... *(+ subjunctive)*
- **2.** [option] possibilité *f*, option *f*.

possible ['pɒsəbl] ⬦ *adj* possible ; **as much as** ~ autant que possible ; **as soon as** ~ dès que possible ; **the best/worst** ~ le meilleur/pire possible ⬦ *n* possible *m*.

possibly ['pɒsəblɪ] *adv* - **1.** [perhaps] peut-être - **2.** [within one's power] : **I'll do all I** ~ **can** je ferai tout mon possible - **3.** [expressing surprise] : **how could he** ~ **have known?** mais comment a-t-il pu le savoir? - **4.** [for emphasis] : **I can't** ~ **accept your money** je ne peux vraiment pas accepter cet argent.

possum ['pɒsəm] *(pl inv* OR **-s)** *n* Am opossum *m*.

post [pəʊst] ⬦ *n* - **1.** [service] : **the** ~ la poste ; **the letter is in the** ~ la lettre a été postée ; **by** ~ par la poste - **2.** [letters, delivery] courrier *m* - **3.** Br [collection] levée *f* - **4.** [pole] poteau *m* - **5.** [position, job] poste *m*, emploi *m* - **6.** MIL poste *m* - **7.** *phr* : **to pip sb at the** ~ coiffer qqn au poteau ⬦ *vt* - **1.** [by mail] poster, mettre à la poste - **2.** [employee] muter - **3.** COMPUT [message, question, advertisement] envoyer sur Internet - **4.** *phr* : **to keep sb ~ed** tenir qqn au courant.

post- [pəʊst] *prefix* post-.

postage ['pəʊstɪdʒ] *n* affranchissement *m* ; ~ **and packing** frais *mpl* de port et d'emballage.

postage stamp *n* timbre-poste *m*.

postal ['pəʊstl] *adj* postal(e).

postal order *n* mandat *m* postal.

postbag ['pəʊstbæg] *n* - **1.** Br [bag] sac *m* postal - **2.** inf [letters received] courrier *m*, lettres *fpl*.

postbox ['pəʊstbɒks] *n* Br boîte *f* aux lettres.

postcard ['pəʊstkɑːd] *n* carte *f* postale.

postcode ['pəʊstkəʊd] *n* Br code *m* postal

postdate [,pəʊst'deɪt] *vt* postdater.

poster ['pəʊstər] *n* [for advertising] affiche *f* ; [for decoration] poster *m*.

poste restante [,pəʊst'restɑːnt] *n* poste *f* restante.

posterior [pɒ'stɪərɪər] ⬦ *adj* postérieur(e) ⬦ *n* hum postérieur *m*, derrière *m*.

posterity [pɒ'sterətɪ] *n* postérité *f*.

poster paint *n* gouache *f*.

post-free *adj* esp Br franco (de port) *(inv)*.

postgraduate [,pəʊst'grædʒʊət] ⬦ *adj* de troisième cycle ⬦ *n* étudiant *m*, -e *f* de troisième cycle.

posthaste [,pəʊst'heɪst] *adv* très vite, en toute hâte.

posthumous ['pɒstjʊməs] *adj* posthume.

posthumously ['pɒstjʊməslɪ] *adv* à titre posthume.

post-industrial *adj* post-industriel(elle).

posting ['pəʊstɪŋ] *n* [assignment] affectation *f*.

Post-it (note)® *n* Post-it® *m*.

postman ['pəʊstmən] *(pl* **-men** [-mən]) *n* facteur *m*.

postmark ['pəʊstmɑːk] ⬦ *n* cachet *m* de la poste ⬦ *vt* timbrer, tamponner.

postmaster ['pəʊst,mɑːstər] *n* receveur *m* des postes.

Postmaster General *(pl* **Postmasters General)** *n* ≃ ministre *m* des Postes et Télécommunications.

postmistress ['pəʊst,mɪstrɪs] *n* receveuse *f* des postes.

postmortem [,pəʊst'mɔːtəm] ⬦ *adj* : ~ **examination** autopsie *f* ⬦ *n* lit & fig autopsie *f*.

postnatal [,pəʊst'neɪtl] *adj* post-natal(e).

post office *n* - **1.** [organization] : **the Post Office** les Postes et Télécommunications *fpl* - **2.** [building] (bureau *m* de) poste *f*.

post office box *n* boîte *f* postale.

postoperative [,pəʊst'ɒpərətɪv] *adj* postopératoire *f*.

postpaid [,pəʊst'peɪd] *adj* port payé.

postpone [,pəʊst'pəʊn] *vt* reporter, remettre.

postponement [,pəʊst'pəʊnmənt] *n* renvoi *m*, report *m*.

postscript ['pəʊstskrɪpt] *n* post-scriptum *m inv* ; fig supplément *m*, addenda *m inv*.

postulate [*n* 'pɒstjʊlət, *vb* 'pɒstjʊleɪt] ⬦ *n* postulat *m* ⬦ *vt* [theory] avancer.

posture ['pɒstʃər] ⬦ *n* - **1.** *(U)* [pose] position *f*, posture *f* - **2.** fig [attitude] attitude *f* ⬦ *vi* poser, prendre des attitudes.

posturing ['pɒstʃərɪŋ] *n* pose *f*, affectation *f*.

postviral syndrome [,pəʊst'vaɪərl-] *n* syndrome *m* de fatigue chronique.

postwar [,pəʊst'wɔːr] *adj* d'après-guerre.

posy ['pəʊzɪ] *(pl* **-ies)** *n* petit bouquet *m* de fleurs.

pot [pɒt] *(pt* & *pp* **-ted** ; *cont* **-ting)** ⬦ *n* - **1.** [for cooking] marmite *f*, casserole *f* - **2.** [for tea] théière *f* ; [for coffee] cafetière *f* - **3.** [for paint, jam, plant] pot *m* - **4.** *(U)* inf [cannabis] herbe *f* ⬦ *vt* [plant] mettre en pot.

potash ['pɒtæʃ] *n* potasse *f*.

potassium [pə'tæsɪəm] *n* potassium *m*.

potato [pə'teɪtəʊ] *(pl* **-es)** *n* pomme *f* de terre.

potato crisps Br, **potato chips** Am *npl* (pommes *fpl*) chips *fpl*.

potato peeler [-,pi:lə'] n (couteau m) éplucheur m.

pot-bellied [-,belɪd] adj [from overeating] ventru(e) ; [from malnutrition] au ventre gonflé.

potboiler ['pɒt,bɔɪlə'] n fig œuvre f alimentaire.

potbound ['pɒtbaʊnd] adj : a ~ plant une plante qui est devenue trop grande pour son pot.

potency ['pəʊtənsɪ] (U) n - 1. [power, influence] puissance f - 2. [of drink] teneur f en alcool - 3. [of man] virilité f.

potent ['pəʊtənt] adj - 1. [powerful, influential] puissant(e) - 2. [drink] fort(e) - 3. [man] viril.

potentate ['pəʊtənteɪt] n potentat m.

potential [pə'tenʃl] <> adj [energy, success] potentiel(elle) ; [uses, danger] possible ; [enemy] en puissance <> n (U) [of person] capacités fpl latentes ; **to have** ~ [person] promettre ; [company] avoir de l'avenir ; [scheme] offrir des possibilités.

potentially [pə'tenʃəlɪ] adv potentiellement.

pothole ['pɒthəʊl] n - 1. [in road] nid-de-poule m - 2. [underground] caverne f, grotte f.

potholer ['pɒt,həʊlə'] n Br spéléologue mf.

potholing ['pɒt,həʊlɪŋ] n Br spéléologie f; **to go** ~ faire de la spéléologie.

potion ['pəʊʃn] n [magic] breuvage m ; **love** ~ philtre m.

potluck [,pɒt'lʌk] n : **to take** ~ [gen] choisir au hasard ; [at meal] manger à la fortune du pot.

pot plant n plante f d'appartement.

potpourri [,pəʊ'pʊərɪ] n (U) [dried flowers] fleurs fpl séchées.

pot roast n rôti m braisé.

potshot ['pɒt,ʃɒt] n : **to take a** ~ (**at sthg**) tirer (sur qqch) sans viser.

potted ['pɒtɪd] adj - 1. [plant] : ~ **plant** plante f d'appartement - 2. [food] conservé(e) en pot - 3. Br fig [condensed] condensé(e), abrégé(e).

potter ['pɒtə'] n potier m.

➤ **potter about, potter around** vi Br bricoler.

Potteries ['pɒtərɪz] npl : **the** ~ la région des poteries dans le Staffordshire (en Angleterre).

potter's wheel n tour m de potier.

pottery ['pɒtərɪ] (pl -ies) n poterie f; **a piece of** ~ une poterie.

potting compost ['pɒtɪŋ-] n terreau m.

potty ['pɒtɪ] (compar -ier ; superl -iest, pl -ies) Br inf <> adj : ~ (**about**) toqué(e) (de) <> n pot m (de chambre).

potty-trained adj propre.

pouch [paʊtʃ] n - 1. [small bag] petit sac m ; **tobacco** ~ blague f à tabac - 2. [of kangaroo] poche f ventrale.

pouffe [pu:f] n Br [seat] pouf m.

poultice ['pəʊltɪs] n cataplasme m.

poultry ['pəʊltrɪ] <> n (U) [meat] volaille f <> npl [birds] volailles fpl.

pounce [paʊns] vi : **to** ~ (**on**) [bird] fondre (sur) ; [person] se jeter (sur) ; **to** ~ **on** fig sauter sur.

pound [paʊnd] <> n - 1. Br [money] livre f - 2. [weight] = 453,6 grammes, ≃ livre f - 3. [for cars, dogs] fourrière f <> vt - 1. [strike loudly] marteler, piler, broyer <> - 1. [strike loudly] : **to** ~ **on** donner de grands coups à - 2. [heart] battre fort ; **my head is** ~**ing** j'ai des élancements dans la tête.

pounding ['paʊndɪŋ] n (U) - 1. [of fists] martèlement m - 2. [of heart] battement m violent ; **to get** OR **take a** ~ [city] être pilonné ; [team] être battu à plate couture OR à plates coutures.

pound sterling n livre f sterling.

pour [pɔ:'] <> vt verser ; **shall I** ~ **you a drink?** je te sers quelque chose à boire? ; **to** ~ **money into sthg** fig investir beaucoup d'argent dans qqch <> vi - 1. [liquid] couler à flots - 2. fig [rush] : **to** ~ **in/out** entrer/sortir en foule <> v impers [rain hard] pleuvoir à verse.

➤ **pour in** vi [letters, news] affluer.

➤ **pour out** vt sep - 1. [empty] vider - 2. [serve - drink] verser, servir - 3. fig [emotions] épancher.

pouring ['pɔ:rɪŋ] adj [rain] torrentiel(elle).

pout [paʊt] <> n moue f <> vi faire la moue.

poverty ['pɒvətɪ] n pauvreté f; fig [of ideas] indigence f, manque m.

poverty line n seuil m de pauvreté.

poverty-stricken adj [person] dans la misère ; [area] misérable, très pauvre.

poverty trap n Br situation dans laquelle, du fait d'une augmentation d'un revenu faible, on ne peut plus toucher les prestations sociales.

pow [paʊ] excl inf pan!, paf!

POW abbr of **prisoner of war**.

powder ['paʊdə'] <> n poudre f <> vt [face, body] poudrer.

powder compact n poudrier m.

powdered ['paʊdəd] adj - 1. [milk, eggs] en poudre - 2. [face] poudré(e).

powder puff n houppette f.

powder room n toilettes fpl pour dames.

powdery ['paʊdərɪ] *adj* [snow etc] poudreux(euse).

power ['paʊəʳ] ⬦ *n* **- 1.** *(U)* [authority, ability] pouvoir *m ;* **to have ~ over sb** avoir de l'autorité sur qqn ; **to take ~** prendre le pouvoir ; **to come to ~** parvenir au pouvoir ; **to be in ~** être au pouvoir ; **to be in** OR **within one's ~ to do sthg** être en son pouvoir de faire qqch ; **~ of speech** parole *f ;* **the ~s that be** les autorités *fpl* **- 2.** [strength, powerful person] puissance *f,* force *f* **- 3.** *(U)* [energy] énergie *f* **- 4.** [electricity] courant *m,* électricité *f* ⬦ *vt* faire marcher, actionner.

power base *n* support *m* politique.

powerboat ['paʊəbəʊt] *n* hors-bord *m inv.*

power broker *n* négociateur *m,* -trice *f.*

power cut *n* coupure *f* de courant.

power failure *n* panne *f* de courant.

powerful ['paʊəfʊl] *adj* **- 1.** [gen] puissant(e) **- 2.** [smell, voice] fort(e) **- 3.** [speech, novel] émouvant(e).

powerhouse ['paʊəhaʊs, *pl* -haʊzɪz] *n* fig personne *f* dynamique OR énergique.

powerless ['paʊəlɪs] *adj* impuissant(e) ; **to be ~ to do sthg** être dans l'impossibilité de faire qqch, ne pas pouvoir faire qqch.

power line *n* ligne *f* à haute tension.

power of attorney *n* procuration *f.*

power plant *n* centrale *f* électrique.

power point *n* Br prise *f* de courant.

power-sharing [-ˌʃeərɪŋ] *n* partage *m* du pouvoir.

power station *n* centrale *f* électrique.

power steering *n* direction *f* assistée.

power worker *n* employé *m,* -e *f* de l'électricité.

pp (*abbr of* per procurationem) pp.

p & p *abbr of* **postage and packing.**

PPE (*abbr of* **philosophy, politics and economics**) *n* philosophie, science politique et science économique (cours à l'université).

ppm (*abbr of* **parts per million**) ppm.

PPS ⬦ *n* (*abbr of* **parliamentary private secretary**) parlementaire britannique assurant la liaison entre un ministre et les députés de son parti ⬦ (*abbr of* **post postscriptum**) PPS.

PQ *abbr of* **Province of Quebec.**

Pr. (*abbr of* **Prince**) Pce.

PR ⬦ *n* **- 1.** *abbr of* **proportional representation - 2.** *abbr of* **public relations** ⬦ *n abbr of* **Puerto Rico.**

practicable ['præktɪkəbl] *adj* réalisable, faisable.

practical ['præktɪkl] ⬦ *adj* **- 1.** [gen] pratique

- 2. [plan, solution] réalisable ⬦ *n* épreuve *f* pratique.

practicality [ˌpræktɪ'kælətɪ] *n (U)* aspect *m* pratique.

➡ **practicalities** *npl* détails *mpl* pratiques.

practical joke *n* farce *f.*

practically ['præktɪklɪ] *adv* **- 1.** [in a practical way] d'une manière pratique **- 2.** [almost] presque, pratiquement.

practice, practise Am ['præktɪs] *n* **- 1.** *(U)* [at sport] entraînement *m ;* [at music etc] répétition *f ;* **to be out of ~** être rouillé(e) **- 2.** [training session - at sport] séance *f* d'entrainement ; [-at music etc] répétition *f* **- 3.** [act of doing] : **to put sthg into ~** mettre qqch en pratique ; **in ~** [in fact] en réalité, en fait **- 4.** [habit] pratique *f,* coutume *f* **- 5.** *(U)* [of profession] exercice *m* **- 6.** [of doctor] cabinet *m ;* [of lawyer] étude *f.*

practiced Am = **practised.**

practicing Am = **practising.**

practise, practice Am ['præktɪs] ⬦ *vt* **- 1.** [sport] s'entraîner à ; [piano etc] s'exercer à **- 2.** [custom] suivre, pratiquer ; [religion] pratiquer ; **to ~ what one preaches** prêcher par l'exemple **- 3.** [profession] exercer ⬦ *vi* **- 1.** SPORT s'entraîner ; MUS s'exercer **- 2.** [doctor, lawyer] exercer.

practised, practiced Am ['præktɪst] *adj* [teacher, nurse] expérimenté(e) ; [liar] fieffé(e) ; **to be ~ at doing sthg** être expert à faire qqch ; **a ~ eye** un œil exercé.

practising, practicing Am ['præktɪsɪŋ] *adj* [doctor, lawyer] en exercice ; [Christian etc] pratiquant(e) ; [homosexual] déclaré(e).

practitioner [præk'tɪʃnəʳ] *n* praticien *m,* -enne *f ;* **medical ~** médecin *m.*

pragmatic [præg'mætɪk] *adj* pragmatique.

pragmatism ['prægmətɪzm] *n* pragmatisme *m.*

pragmatist ['prægmətɪst] *n* pragmatiste *mf.*

Prague [prɑːg] *n* Prague.

prairie ['preərɪ] *n* prairie *f.*

praise [preɪz] ⬦ *n (U)* louange *f,* louanges *fpl,* éloge *m,* éloges *mpl ;* **to sing sb's ~s** chanter les louanges de qqn ⬦ *vt* louer, faire l'éloge de.

praiseworthy ['preɪzˌwɜːðɪ] *adj* louable, méritoire.

praline ['prɑːliːn] *n* praline *f.*

pram [præm] *n* Br landau *m.*

PRAM [præm] (*abbr of* **programmable random access memory**) *n* RAM *f* programmable.

prance [prɑːns] *vi* **- 1.** [person] se pavaner **- 2.** [horse] caracoler.

prang [præŋ] Br inf dated ◇ n [of car] accrochage m ; [of plane] collision f ◇ vt emboutir, bousiller.

prank [præŋk] n tour m, niche f.

prat [præt] n Br v inf pej crétin m, -e f.

prattle ['prætl] pej ◇ n (U) bavardage m, babillage m ◇ vi babiller ; **to ~ on** about sthg parler sans fin de qqch.

prawn [prɔːn] n crevette f rose.

prawn cocktail n crevettes fpl mayonnaise.

prawn cracker n genre de chips au goût de crevette.

pray [preɪ] vi : **to ~ (to sb)** prier (qqn) ; **to ~ for rain** prier pour qu'il pleuve.

prayer [preə^r] n lit & fig prière f ; **to say one's ~s** faire sa prière.
➤ **prayers** npl [service] office m.

prayer book n livre m de messe.

prayer meeting n réunion f pour dire des prières.

pre- [priː] prefix pré-.

preach [priːtʃ] ◇ vt [gen] prêcher ; [sermon] prononcer ◇ vi **- 1.** RELIG : **to ~ (to sb)** prêcher (qqn) **- 2.** pej [pontificate] : **to ~ (at sb)** sermonner (qqn).

preacher ['priːtʃə^r] n prédicateur m, pasteur m.

preamble [priː'æmbl] n préambule m, avant-propos m inv.

prearrange [ˌpriːə'reɪndʒ] vt organiser OR fixer à l'avance.

precarious [prɪ'keərɪəs] adj précaire.

precariously [prɪ'keərɪəslɪ] adv d'une manière précaire.

precast [ˌpriː'kɑːst] adj : **~ concrete** béton m précoulé.

precaution [prɪ'kɔːʃn] n précaution f ; **as a ~ (against)** par précaution (contre).

precautionary [prɪ'kɔːʃənərɪ] adj de précaution, préventif(ive).

precede [prɪ'siːd] vt précéder.

precedence ['presɪdəns] n : **to take ~ over** sthg avoir la priorité sur qqch ; **to have** OR **take ~ over sb** avoir la préséance sur qqn.

precedent ['presɪdənt] n précédent m.

preceding [prɪ'siːdɪŋ] adj précédent(e).

precept ['priːsept] n précepte m.

precinct ['priːsɪŋkt] n **- 1.** Br [area] : **pedestrian ~** zone f piétonne ; **shopping ~** centre m commercial **- 2.** Am [district] circonscription f (administrative).
➤ **precincts** npl [of institution] enceinte f.

precious ['preʃəs] adj **- 1.** [gen] précieux(eu-

se) **- 2.** inf iro [damned] sacré(e) ; **~ little** très peu, bien peu **- 3.** [affected] affecté(e).

precious metal n métal m précieux.

precious stone n pierre f précieuse.

precipice ['presɪpɪs] n précipice m, paroi f à pic.

precipitate [adj prɪ'sɪpɪtət, vb prɪ'sɪpɪteɪt] fml ◇ adj hâtif(ive) ◇ vt [hasten] hâter, précipiter.

precipitation [prɪˌsɪpɪ'teɪʃn] n précipitation f.

precipitous [prɪ'sɪpɪtəs] adj **- 1.** [very steep] escarpé(e), à pic **- 2.** [hasty] hâtif(ive).

précis [Br 'preɪsiː, Am 'presiː] n résumé m.

precise [prɪ'saɪs] adj précis(e) ; [measurement, date] exact(e) ; **49.5 to be ~** 49,5 pour être exact.

precisely [prɪ'saɪslɪ] adv précisément, exactement.

precision [prɪ'sɪʒn] ◇ n précision f, exactitude f ◇ comp de précision.

preclude [prɪ'kluːd] vt fml empêcher ; [possibility] écarter ; **to ~ sb from doing sthg** empêcher qqn de faire qqch.

precocious [prɪ'kəʊʃəs] adj précoce.

precocity [prɪ'kɒsɪtɪ] n précocité f.

precognition [ˌpriːkɒg'nɪʃn] n connaissance f anticipée.

preconceived [ˌpriːkən'siːvd] adj préconçu(e).

preconception [ˌpriːkən'sepʃn] n préjugé m, idée f préconçue.

precondition [ˌpriːkən'dɪʃn] n fml condition f sine qua non.

precooked [ˌpriː'kʊkt] adj précuit(e).

precursor [ˌpriː'kɜːsə^r] n fml précurseur m.

predate [ˌpriː'deɪt] vt précéder.

predator ['predətə^r] n **- 1.** [animal, bird] prédateur m, rapace m **- 2.** fig [person] corbeau m.

predatory ['predətrɪ] adj **- 1.** [animal, bird] prédateur(trice) **- 2.** fig [person] rapace.

predecease [ˌpriːdɪ'siːs] vt décéder avant.

predecessor ['priːdɪsesə^r] n **- 1.** [person] prédécesseur m **- 2.** [thing] précédent m, -e f.

predestination [priːˌdestɪ'neɪʃn] n prédestination f.

predestine [ˌpriː'destɪn] vt : **to be ~d to sthg/ to do sthg** être prédestiné(e) à qqch/à faire qqch.

predetermine [ˌpriːdɪ'tɜːmɪn] vt **- 1.** [predestine] déterminer d'avance **- 2.** [prearrange] organiser OR fixer à l'avance.

predetermined [ˌpriːdɪ'tɜːmɪnd] adj **- 1.** [predestined] déterminé(e) d'avance **- 2.** [prearranged] organisé(e) or fixé(e) à l'avance.

predicament [prɪˈdɪkəmənt] *n* situation *f* difficile ; **to be in a ~** être dans de beaux draps.

predict [prɪˈdɪkt] *vt* prédire.

predictable [prɪˈdɪktəbl] *adj* prévisible.

predictably [prɪˈdɪktəblɪ] *adv* [react, behave] d'une manière prévisible ; **~, he was late** comme c'était à prévoir, il est arrivé en retard.

prediction [prɪˈdɪkʃn] *n* prédiction *f*.

predictor [prɪˈdɪktəʳ] *n* indicateur *m*.

predigest [ˌpriːdaɪˈdʒest] *vt* fig prédigérer.

predilection [ˌpriːdɪˈlekʃn] *n* : **~ for sthg** prédilection *f* pour qqch.

predispose [ˌpriːdɪsˈpəʊz] *vt* : **to be ~d to sthg/to do sthg** être prédisposé(e) à qqch/à faire qqch.

predisposition [ˈpriːˌdɪspəˈzɪʃn] *n* : **~ to sthg/to do sthg, ~ towards sthg/towards doing sthg** prédisposition *f* à qqch/à faire qqch.

predominance [prɪˈdɒmɪnəns] *n* prédominance *f*.

predominant [prɪˈdɒmɪnənt] *adj* prédominant(e).

predominantly [prɪˈdɒmɪnəntlɪ] *adv* principalement, surtout.

predominate [prɪˈdɒmɪneɪt] *vi* prédominer.

preeminent [priːˈemɪnənt] *adj* le plus en vue (la plus en vue).

preempt [ˌpriːˈempt] *vt* **- 1.** [action, decision] devancer, prévenir **- 2.** [land] acquérir par droit de préemption.

preemptive [ˌpriːˈemptɪv] *adj* préventif(ive).

preemptive strike *n* attaque *f* préventive.

preen [priːn] *vt* **- 1.** [subj : bird] lisser, nettoyer **- 2.** fig [subj : person] : **to ~ o.s.** se faire beau (belle).

preexist [ˌpriːɪgˈzɪst] *vi* préexister.

prefab [ˈpriːfæb] *n* inf maison *f* préfabriquée.

prefabricate [ˌpriːˈfæbrɪkeɪt] *vt* préfabriquer.

preface [ˈprefɪs] <> *n* : **~ (to)** préface *f* (de), préambule *m* (de) <> *vt* : **to ~ sthg with sthg** faire précéder qqch de qqch.

prefect [ˈpriːfekt] *n* Br [pupil] *élève de terminale qui aide les professeurs à maintenir la discipline.*

prefer [prɪˈfɜːʳ] (*pt* & *pp* **-red** ; *cont* **-ring**) *vt*

préférer ; **to ~ sthg to sthg** préférer qqch à qqch, aimer mieux qqch que qqch ; **to ~ to do sthg** préférer faire qqch, aimer mieux faire qqch.

preferable [ˈprefrəbl] *adj* : **~ (to)** préférable (à).

preferably [ˈprefrəblɪ] *adv* de préférence.

preference [ˈprefərəns] *n* préférence *f*.

preference shares Br *npl*, **preferred stock** Am *n (U)* actions *fpl* privilégiées or de priorité.

preferential [ˌprefəˈrenʃl] *adj* préférentiel(elle).

preferred [prɪˈfɜːd] *adj* préféré(e).

preferred stock Am = preference shares.

prefigure [priːˈfɪgəʳ] *vt* annoncer, préfigurer.

prefix [ˈpriːfɪks] *n* préfixe *m*.

pregnancy [ˈpregnənsɪ] (*pl* **-ies**) *n* grossesse *f*.

pregnancy test *n* test *m* de grossesse.

pregnant [ˈpregnənt] *adj* **- 1.** [woman] enceinte ; [animal] pleine, gravide **- 2.** fig [pause] lourd(e) de sens.

preheated [ˌpriːˈhiːtɪd] *adj* préchauffé(e).

prehistoric [ˌpriːhɪˈstɒrɪk] *adj* préhistorique.

prehistory [ˌpriːˈhɪstərɪ] *n* préhistoire *f*.

pre-industrial *adj* pré-industriel(elle).

prejudge [ˌpriːˈdʒʌdʒ] *vt* [situation, issue] préjuger de ; [person] juger d'avance.

prejudice [ˈpredʒʊdɪs] <> *n* **- 1.** [biased view] : **~ (in favour of/against)** préjugé *m* (en faveur de/contre), préjugés *mpl* (en faveur de/contre) **- 2.** *(U)* [harm] préjudice *m*, tort *m* <> *vt* **- 1.** [bias] : **to ~ sb (in favour of/against)** prévenir qqn (en faveur de/contre), influencer qqn (en faveur de/contre) **- 2.** [harm] porter préjudice à.

prejudiced [ˈpredʒʊdɪst] *adj* [person] qui a des préjugés ; [opinion] préconçu(e) ; **to be ~ in favour of/against** avoir des préjugés en faveur de/contre.

prejudicial [ˌpredʒʊˈdɪʃl] *adj* : **~ (to)** préjudiciable (à), nuisible (à).

prelate [ˈprelɪt] *n* prélat *m*.

preliminary [prɪˈlɪmɪnərɪ] (*pl* **-ies**) *adj* préliminaire.

➤ **preliminaries** *npl* préliminaires *mpl*.

prelims [ˈpriːlɪmz] *npl* Br [exams] examens *mpl* préliminaires.

prelude [ˈpreljuːd] *n* [event] : **~ to sthg** prélude *m* de qqch.

premarital [ˌpriːˈmærɪtl] *adj* avant le mariage.

premature [ˈpremətjʊəʳ] *adj* prématuré(e).

prematurely [ˈpremətjʊəlɪ] *adv* prématurément.

premeditated [ˌpriːˈmedɪteɪtɪd] *adj* prémédité(e).

premenstrual syndrome, premenstrual tension [priːˈmenstrʊəl-] *n* syndrome *m* prémenstruel.

premier [ˈpremjəʳ] ◇ *adj* primordial(e), premier(ère) ◇ *n* premier ministre *m*.

premiere [ˈpremɪeəʳ] *n* première *f*.

Premier League *n* en Angleterre, ligue indépendante regroupant les meilleurs clubs de football.

premiership [ˈpremɪəʃɪp] *n* fonction *f* de premier ministre.

premise [ˈpremɪs] *n* prémisse *f* ; **on the ~ that** en partant du principe que.

➡ **premises** *npl* local *m*, locaux *mpl* ; **on the ~s** sur place, sur les lieux.

premium [ˈpriːmjəm] *n* prime *f* ; **at a ~** [above usual value] à prix d'or ; [in great demand] très recherché OR demandé ; **to put** OR **place a high ~ on sthg** accorder OR attacher beaucoup d'importance à qqch.

premium bond *n* Br ≃ billet *m* de loterie.

premonition [ˌpreməˈnɪʃn] *n* prémonition *f*, pressentiment *m*.

prenatal [ˌpriːˈneɪtl] *adj* Am prénatal(e).

preoccupation [priːˌɒkjʊˈpeɪʃn] *n* préoccupation *f* ; **~ with sthg** souci de qqch.

preoccupied [priːˈɒkjʊpaɪd] *adj* : **~ (with)** préoccupé(e) (de).

preoccupy [priːˈɒkjʊpaɪ] (*pt* & *pp* -ied) *vt* préoccuper.

preordain [ˌpriːɔːˈdeɪn] *vt* décider OR déterminer d'avance ; **to be ~ed to do sthg** être prédestiné à faire qqch.

prep [prep] *n* (*U*) Br inf devoirs *mpl*.

prepacked [ˌpriːˈpækt] *adj* préconditionné(e).

prepaid [ˈpriːpeɪd] *adj* payé(e) d'avance ; [envelope] affranchi(e).

preparation [ˌprepəˈreɪʃn] *n* préparation *f* ; **in ~ for** en vue de.

➡ **preparations** *npl* préparatifs *mpl* ; **to make ~s for** faire des préparatifs pour, prendre ses dispositions pour.

preparatory [prɪˈpærətrɪ] *adj* [work, classes] préparatoire ; [actions, measures] préliminaire.

preparatory school *n* [in UK] école *f* primaire privée ; [in US] école privée qui prépare à l'enseignement supérieur.

prepare [prɪˈpeəʳ] ◇ *vt* préparer ◇ *vi* : **to ~ for sthg/to do sthg** se préparer à qqch/à faire qqch.

prepared [prɪˈpeəd] *adj* - **1.** [done beforehand] préparé(e) d'avance - **2.** [willing] : **to be ~ to do sthg** être prêt(e) OR disposé(e) à faire qqch - **3.** [ready] : **to be ~ for sthg** être prêt(e) pour qqch.

preponderance [prɪˈpɒndərəns] *n* majorité *f*.

preponderantly [prɪˈpɒndərəntlɪ] *adv* surtout, pour la plupart.

preposition [ˌprepəˈzɪʃn] *n* préposition *f*.

prepossessing [ˌpriːpəˈzesɪŋ] *adj* fml agréable, attrayant(e).

preposterous [prɪˈpɒstərəs] *adj* ridicule, absurde.

preppy [ˈprepɪ] (*pl* -ies) Am inf ◇ *adj* bon chic bon genre ◇ *n* personne *f* bon chic bon genre.

prep school *abbr of* **preparatory school**.

Pre-Raphaelite [ˌpriːˈræfəlaɪt] ◇ *adj* préraphaélite ◇ *n* préraphaélite *mf*.

prerecorded [ˌpriːrɪˈkɔːdɪd] *adj* enregistré(e) à l'avance, préenregistré(e).

prerequisite [ˌpriːˈrekwɪzɪt] *n* condition *f* préalable.

prerogative [prɪˈrɒɡətɪv] *n* prérogative *f*, privilège *m*.

presage [ˈpresɪdʒ] *vt* présager.

Presbyterian [ˌprezbɪˈtɪərɪən] ◇ *adj* presbytérien(enne) ◇ *n* presbytérien *m*, -enne *f*.

presbytery [ˈprezbɪtrɪ] *n* [residence] presbytère *m*.

preschool [ˌpriːˈskuːl] ◇ *adj* préscolaire ◇ *n* Am école *f* maternelle.

prescient [ˈpresɪənt] *adj* prescient(e).

prescribe [prɪˈskraɪb] *vt* - **1.** MED prescrire - **2.** [order] ordonner, imposer.

prescription [prɪˈskrɪpʃn] *n* [MED - written form] ordonnance *f* ; [- medicine] médicament *m* ; **on ~** sur ordonnance.

prescription charge *n* Br prix (fixe) à payer pour chaque médicament figurant sur une ordonnance.

prescriptive [prɪˈskrɪptɪv] *adj* normatif(ive).

presence [ˈprezns] *n* présence *f* ; **to be in sb's ~ in the ~ of sb** être en présence de qqn ; **to have ~** avoir de la présence.

presence of mind *n* présence *f* d'esprit.

present [*adj* & *n* ˈpreznt, *vb* prɪˈzent] ◇ *adj* - **1.** [current] actuel(elle) - **2.** [in attendance] présent(e) ; **to be ~ at** assister à $\diamond$ *n* - **1.** [current time] : **the ~** le présent ; **at ~** actuellement, en ce moment ; **for the ~** pour le moment - **2.** [gift] cadeau *m* - **3.** GRAMM : **~ (tense)** présent *m* $\diamond$ *vt* - **1.** [gen] présenter ; [opportunity] donner - **2.** [give] donner, remettre ; **to ~ sb with sthg, to ~ sthg to sb** donner OR remettre qqch à qqn - **3.** [portray] représenter, décrire - **4.** [arrive] : **to ~ o.s.** se présenter.

presentable [prɪ'zentəbl] *adj* présentable.

presentation [,prezn'teɪʃn] *n* - **1.** [gen] présentation *f* - **2.** [ceremony] remise *f* (de récompense/prix) - **3.** [talk] exposé *m* - **4.** [of play] représentation *f*.

presentation copy *n* exemplaire *m* offert gracieusement.

present day *n* : **the ~** aujourd'hui.

➤ **present-day** *adj* d'aujourd'hui, contemporain(e).

presenter [prɪ'zentə'] *n* Br présentateur *m*, -trice *f*.

presentiment [prɪ'zentɪmənt] *n* pressentiment *m*.

presently ['prezəntlɪ] *adv* - **1.** [soon] bientôt, tout à l'heure - **2.** [at present] actuellement, en ce moment.

preservation [,prezə'veɪʃn] *n (U)* - **1.** [maintenance] maintien *m* - **2.** [protection] protection *f*, conservation *f*.

preservation order *n* esp Br décret ordonnant la conservation d'un monument, édifice etc.

preservative [prɪ'zɜ:vətɪv] *n* conservateur *m*.

preserve [prɪ'zɜ:v] $\diamond$ *vt* - **1.** [maintain] maintenir - **2.** [protect] conserver - **3.** [food] conserver, mettre en conserve $\diamond$ *n* [jam] confiture *f*.

➤ **preserves** *npl* [jam] confiture *f* ; [vegetables] pickles *mpl*, condiments *mpl*.

preserved [prɪ'zɜ:vd] *adj* conservé(e).

preset [,pri:'set] (*pt & pp* preset, *cont* -ting) *vt* prérégler.

preshrunk [,pri:'ʃrʌŋk] *adj* irrétrécissable.

preside [prɪ'zaɪd] *vi* : **to ~ (over** OR **at sthg)** présider (qqch).

presidency ['prezɪdənsɪ] (*pl* -ies) *n* présidence *f*.

president ['prezɪdənt] *n* - **1.** [gen] président *m* - **2.** Am [company chairman] P-DG *m*.

president-elect *n* titre du président des États-Unis nouvellement élu (en novembre) jusqu'à la cérémonie d'investiture présidentielle (le 20 janvier).

presidential [,prezɪ'denʃl] *adj* présidentiel(elle).

press [pres] $\diamond$ *n* - **1.** [push] pression *f* - **2.** [journalism] : **the ~** [newspapers] la presse, les journaux *mpl* ; [reporters] les journalistes *mpl* ; **to get a good/bad ~** avoir bonne/mauvaise presse - **3.** [printing machine] presse *f* ; [for wine] pressoir *m* $\diamond$ *vt* - **1.** [push] appuyer sur ; **to ~ sthg against sthg** appuyer qqch sur qqch - **2.** [squeeze] serrer - **3.** [iron] repasser, donner un coup de fer à - **4.** [urge] : **to ~ sb (to do sthg** OR **into doing sthg)** presser qqn (de faire qqch) ; **to ~ sb for sthg** demander qqch à qqn avec insistance - **5.** [force] : **to ~ sthg on** OR **upon sb** offrir qqch à qqn avec insistance - **6.** [pursue - claim] insister sur - **7.** JUR : **to ~ charges (against sb)** porter plainte (contre qqn) $\diamond$ *vi* - **1.** [push] : **to ~ (on sthg)** appuyer (sur qqch) - **2.** [squeeze] : **to ~ (on sthg)** serrer (qqch) - **3.** [crowd] se presser.

➤ **press for** *vt fus* demander avec insistance.

➤ **press on** *vi* [continue] : **to ~ on (with sthg)** continuer (qqch), ne pas abandonner (qqch).

press agency *n* agence *f* de presse.

press agent *n* agent *m* de publicité.

press baron *n* Br baron *m* OR magnat *m* de la presse.

press box *n* tribune *f* de la presse.

press conference *n* conférence *f* de presse.

press corps *n* Am journalistes *mpl*.

press cutting *n* Br coupure *f* de journal.

pressed [prest] *adj* : **to be ~ for time/money** être à court de temps/d'argent.

press fastener *n* Br pression *f*.

press gallery *n* tribune *f* de la presse.

pressgang ['presgæŋ] $\diamond$ *n* enrôleurs *mpl*, racoleurs *mpl* $\diamond$ *vt* Br : **to ~ sb into doing sthg** forcer la main à qqn pour qu'il fasse qqch.

pressing ['presɪŋ] *adj* urgent(e).

pressman ['presmæn] (*pl* -men [-men]) *n* Br journaliste *m*.

press officer *n* attaché *m* de presse.

press release *n* communiqué *m* de presse.

press-stud *n* Br pression *f*

press-up *n* Br pompe *f*, traction *f*.

pressure ['preʃə'] $\diamond$ *n (U)* - **1.** [gen] pression *f* ; **to put ~ on sb (to do sthg)** faire pression sur qqn (pour qu'il fasse qqch) - **2.** [stress] tension *f* $\diamond$ *vt* : **to ~ sb to do** OR **into doing sthg** forcer qqn à faire qqch.

pressure cooker *n* Cocotte-Minute® *f*, autocuiseur *m*.

pressure gauge *n* manomètre *m*.

pressure group *n* groupe *m* de pression.

pressurize, -ise ['preʃəraɪz] *vt* - **1.** TECH pressuriser - **2.** Br [force] : **to ~ sb to do** OR **into doing sthg** forcer qqn à faire qqch.

Prestel® ['prestel] *n* Br ≃ Télétel® *m*.

prestige [pre'stiːʒ] ◇ *n* prestige *m* ◇ *comp* de prestige.

prestigious [pre'stɪdʒəs] *adj* prestigieux(euse).

prestressed concrete [ˌpriː'strest-] *n* béton *m* précontraint.

presumably [prɪ'zjuːməblɪ] *adv* vraisemblablement.

presume [prɪ'zjuːm] *vt* présumer ; **to ~ (that)** ... supposer que ...

presumption [prɪ'zʌmpʃn] *n* - **1.** [assumption] supposition *f*, présomption *f* - **2.** *(U)* [audacity] présomption *f*.

presumptuous [prɪ'zʌmptʃuəs] *adj* présomptueux(euse).

presuppose [ˌpriːsə'pəuz] *vt* présupposer.

pretax [ˌpriː'tæks] *adj* avant impôts.

pretence, pretense Am [prɪ'tens] *n* prétention *f* ; **to make a ~ of doing sthg** faire semblant de faire qqch ; **under false ~s** sous des prétextes fallacieux.

pretend [prɪ'tend] ◇ *vt* : **to ~ to do sthg** faire semblant de faire qqch ◇ *vi* faire semblant.

pretense Am = **pretence**.

pretension [prɪ'tenʃn] *n* prétention *f* ; **to have ~s to sthg** avoir des prétentions à qqch.

pretentious [prɪ'tenʃəs] *adj* prétentieux(euse).

pretentiously [prɪ'tenʃəslɪ] *adv* de façon prétentieuse.

pretentiousness [prɪ'tenʃəsnɪs] *n* *(U)* prétention *f*.

preterite ['pretərət] *n* prétérit *m*.

pretext ['priːtekst] *n* prétexte *m* ; **on** OR **under the ~ that** ... sous prétexte que ... ; **on** OR **under the ~ of doing sthg** sous prétexte de faire qqch.

Pretoria [prɪ'tɔːrɪə] *n* Pretoria.

prettify ['prɪtɪfaɪ] (*pt* & *pp* **-ied**) *vt* enjoliver.

prettily ['prɪtɪlɪ] *adv* joliment.

pretty ['prɪtɪ] (*compar* **-ier** ; *superl* **-iest**) ◇ *adj* joli(e) ◇ *adv* [quite] plutôt ; **~ much** OR **well** pratiquement, presque.

pretzel ['pretsl] *n* bretzel *m*.

prevail [prɪ'veɪl] *vi* - **1.** [be widespread] avoir cours, régner - **2.** [triumph] : **to ~ (over)** prévaloir (sur), l'emporter (sur) - **3.** [persuade] : **to ~ on** OR **upon sb to do sthg** persuader qqn de faire qqch.

prevailing [prɪ'veɪlɪŋ] *adj* - **1.** [current] actuel(elle) - **2.** [wind] dominant(e).

prevalence ['prevələns] *n* *(U)* fréquence *f*.

prevalent ['prevələnt] *adj* courant(e), répandu(e).

prevaricate [prɪ'værɪkeɪt] *vi* tergiverser.

prevent [prɪ'vent] *vt* : **to ~ sb/sthg (from doing sthg)** empêcher qqn/qqch (de faire qqch).

preventable [prɪ'ventəbl] *adj* qui peut être évité(e).

preventative [prɪ'ventətɪv] = **preventive**.

prevention [prɪ'venʃn] *n* *(U)* prévention *f*.

preventive [prɪ'ventɪv] *adj* préventif(ive).

preview ['priːvjuː] *n* avant-première *f*.

previous ['priːvjəs] *adj* - **1.** [earlier] antérieur(e) - **2.** [preceding] précédent(e).

previously ['priːvjəslɪ] *adv* avant, auparavant.

prewar [ˌpriː'wɔː'] *adj* d'avant-guerre.

prey [preɪ] *n* proie *f* ; **to fall ~ to** devenir la proie de.

➤ **prey on** *vt fus* - **1.** [live off] faire sa proie de - **2.** [trouble] : **to ~ on sb's mind** ronger qqn, tracasser qqn.

price [praɪs] ◇ *n* - **1.** [cost] prix *m* ; **at any ~** à tout prix ; **she achieved fame, but at a ~** elle est devenue célèbre, mais ça lui a coûté cher - **2.** [penalty] : **to pay the ~ for sthg** payer le prix pour qqch ◇ *vt* fixer le prix de.

price-cutting *n* *(U)* réductions *fpl* de prix.

price-fixing [-fɪksɪŋ] *n* *(U)* contrôle *m* des prix.

priceless ['praɪslɪs] *adj* sans prix, inestimable.

price list *n* tarif *m*.

price tag *n* [label] étiquette *f*.

price war *n* guerre *f* des prix.

pricey ['praɪsɪ] (*compar* **-ier** ; *superl* **-iest**) *adj* chérot.

prick [prɪk] ◇ *n* - **1.** [scratch, wound] piqûre *f* - **2.** vulg [stupid person] con *m*, conne *f* ◇ *vt* piquer.

➤ **prick up** *vt fus* : **to ~ up one's ears** [animal] dresser les oreilles ; [person] dresser OR tendre l'oreille.

prickle ['prɪkl] ⬦ n - **1.** [thorn] épine f - **2.** [sensation on skin] picotement m ⬦ vi picoter.

prickly ['prɪklɪ] (compar -ier ; superl -iest) adj - **1.** [plant, bush] épineux(euse) - **2.** fig [person] irritable.

prickly heat n (U) boutons mpl de chaleur.

pride [praɪd] ⬦ n (U) - **1.** [satisfaction] fierté f ; **to take ~ in sthg/in doing sthg** être fier de qqch/de faire qqch ; **it was his ~ and joy** c'était sa fierté ; **to have ~ of place** avoir la place d'honneur - **2.** [self-esteem] orgueil m, amour-propre m ; **to swallow one's ~** ravaler son orgueil - **3.** pej [arrogance] orgueil m ⬦ vt : **to ~ o.s. on sthg** être fier (fière) de qqch.

priest [priːst] n prêtre m.

priestess ['priːstɪs] n prêtresse f.

priesthood ['priːsthʊd] n - **1.** [position, office] : **the ~** le sacerdoce - **2.** [priests] : **the ~** le clergé.

prig [prɪg] n petit saint m, petite sainte f.

prim [prɪm] (compar -mer ; superl -mest) adj guindé(e).

primacy ['praɪməsɪ] n primauté f.

prima donna [ˌpriːmə'dɒnə] (pl -s) n prima donna f inv ; **to be a ~** fig & pej se prendre pour le nombril du monde.

primaeval [praɪ'miːvl] = primeval.

prima facie [ˌpraɪmə'feɪʃiː] adj : **~ evidence** commencement m de preuve ; **~ case** affaire f qui, de prime abord, paraît fondée.

primal ['praɪml] adj - **1.** [original] primitif(ive) - **2.** [most important] primordial(e).

primarily ['praɪmərɪlɪ] adv principalement.

primary ['praɪmərɪ] (pl -ies) ⬦ adj - **1.** [main] premier(ère), principal(e) - **2.** SCH primaire ⬦ n Am POL primaire f.

PRIMARIES

Les primaires américaines sont des élections (directes ou indirectes selon les États) aboutissant à la sélection des candidats qui seront en lice pour représenter les deux partis nationaux à l'élection présidentielle.

primary colour n couleur f primaire.

primary election n Am primaire f.

primary school n école f primaire.

primate ['praɪmeɪt] n - **1.** ZOOL primate m - **2.** RELIG primat m.

prime [praɪm] ⬦ adj - **1.** [main] principal(e), primordial(e) - **2.** [excellent] excellent(e) ; **~ quality** première qualité ; **~ cut of meat** morceau de premier choix ⬦ n : **to be in one's ~** être dans la fleur de l'âge ; **to be**

past one's ~ être sur le retour ⬦ vt - **1.** [gun, pump] amorcer - **2.** [paint] apprêter - **3.** [inform] : **to ~ sb about sthg** mettre qqn au courant de qqch.

prime minister n premier ministre m.

prime mover [-'muːvəʳ] n fig instigateur m, -trice f.

prime number n nombre m premier.

primer ['praɪməʳ] n - **1.** [paint] apprêt m - **2.** [textbook] introduction f.

prime time n (U) RADIO & TV heures fpl de grande écoute.
➤ **prime-time** adj aux heures de grande écoute.

primeval [praɪ'miːvl] adj [ancient] primitif(ive).

primitive ['prɪmɪtɪv] adj primitif(ive).

primordial [praɪ'mɔːdjəl] adj primordial(e).

primrose ['prɪmrəʊz] n primevère f.

Primus stove® ['praɪməs-] n réchaud m de camping.

prince [prɪns] n prince m.
➤ **Prince** n : **Prince of Wales** Prince de Galles.

Prince Charming n hum prince m charmant.

Prince Edward Island [-'edwəd-] n l'île f du Prince-Édouard.

princely ['prɪnslɪ] (compar -ier ; superl -iest) adj princier(ère).

princess [prɪn'ses] n princesse f.
➤ **Princess** n : **Princess Royal** princesse royale.

principal ['prɪnsəpl] ⬦ adj principal(e) ⬦ n SCH directeur m, -trice f ; UNIV doyen m, -enne f.

principality [ˌprɪnsɪ'pælətɪ] (pl -ies) n principauté f.

principally ['prɪnsəplɪ] adv principalement.

principle ['prɪnsəpl] n principe m ; **on ~, as a matter of ~** par principe.
➤ **in principle** adv en principe.

principled ['prɪnsəpld] adj [behaviour] dicté(e) par des principes ; [person] qui a des principes.

print [prɪnt] ⬦ n - **1.** (U) [type] caractères mpl ; **to be in ~** être disponible ; **to be out of ~** être épuisé - **2.** ART gravure f - **3.** [photograph] épreuve f - **4.** [fabric] imprimé m - **5.** [mark] empreinte f ⬦ vt - **1.** [produce by printing] imprimer - **2.** [publish] publier - **3.** [write in block letters] écrire en caractères d'imprimerie ⬦ vi [printer] imprimer.
➤ **print out** vt sep COMPUT imprimer.

printed circuit ['prɪntɪd-] n circuit m imprimé.

printed matter ['prɪntɪd-] n (U) imprimés mpl.

printer ['prɪntəʳ] n - **1.** [person, firm] imprimeur m - **2.** COMPUT imprimante f.

printing ['prɪntɪŋ] n (U) - **1.** [act of printing] impression f - **2.** [trade] imprimerie f.

printing press n presse f typographique.

printout ['prɪntaʊt] n COMPUT sortie f d'imprimante, listing m.

prior ['praɪəʳ] <> adj antérieur(e), précédent(e) <> n [monk] prieur m.
◆ **prior to** prep avant ; ~ **to doing sthg** avant de faire qqch.

prioritize, -ise [praɪ'ɒrɪtaɪz] vt donner la priorité à.

priority [praɪ'ɒrətɪ] (pl -ies) <> adj prioritaire <> n priorité f ; **to have** OR **take ~ (over)** avoir la priorité (sur).
◆ **priorities** npl priorités fpl.

priory ['praɪərɪ] (pl -ies) n prieuré m.

prise [praɪz] vt : **to ~ sthg away from sb** arracher qqch à qqn ; **to ~ sthg open** forcer qqch.

prism ['prɪzm] n prisme m.

prison ['prɪzn] n prison f.

prison camp n camp m de prisonniers.

prisoner ['prɪznəʳ] n prisonnier m, -ère f ; **to be taken ~** être fait prisonnier.

prisoner of war (pl **prisoners of war**) n prisonnier m, -ère f de guerre.

prissy ['prɪsɪ] (compar -ier ; superl -iest) adj prude, guindé(e).

pristine ['prɪstiːn] adj [condition] parfait(e) ; [clean] immaculé(e).

privacy [Br 'prɪvəsɪ, Am 'praɪvəsɪ] n intimité f.

private ['praɪvɪt] <> adj - **1.** [not public] privé(e) - **2.** [confidential] confidentiel(elle) - **3.** [personal] personnel(elle) - **4.** [unsociable - person] secret(ète) <> n - **1.** [soldier] (simple) soldat m - **2.** [secrecy] : **in ~** en privé.
◆ **privates** npl inf parties fpl.

private company n société f privée.

private detective n détective m privé.

private enterprise n (U) entreprise f privée.

private eye n détective m privé.

private income n Br revenu m personnel.

private investigator n détective m privé.

privately ['praɪvɪtlɪ] adv - **1.** [not by the state] : **~ owned** du secteur privé - **2.** [confidentially]

en privé - **3.** [personally] intérieurement, dans son for intérieur.

private member n Br simple député m.

private parts npl inf parties fpl.

private practice n (U) Br cabinet m de médecin non conventionné.

private property n propriété f privée.

private school n école f privée.

private sector n : **the ~** le secteur privé.

privation [praɪ'veɪʃn] n privation f.

privatization [ˌpraɪvɪtaɪ'zeɪʃn] n privatisation f.

privatize, -ise ['praɪvɪtaɪz] vt privatiser.

privet ['prɪvɪt] n troène m.

privilege ['prɪvɪlɪdʒ] n privilège m.

privileged ['prɪvɪlɪdʒd] adj privilégié(e).

privy ['prɪvɪ] adj : **to be ~ to sthg** être dans le secret de qqch.

Privy Council n Br : **the ~** le Conseil privé.

PRIVY COUNCIL

En font partie tous les ministres du gouvernement ainsi que d'autres personnalités du Commonwealth. Le « Privy Council » compte environ 400 membres, mais ils ne se réunissent en plénière que dans des circonstances exceptionnelles.

Privy Purse n : **the ~** la cassette du souverain.

prize [praɪz] <> adj [possession] très précieux(euse) ; [animal] primé(e) ; [idiot, example] parfait(e) <> n prix m <> vt priser.

prize day n Br jour m de la distribution des prix.

prizefight ['praɪzfaɪt] n combat m professionnel.

prize-giving [-ˌgɪvɪŋ] n Br distribution f des prix.

prizewinner ['praɪzˌwɪnəʳ] n gagnant m, -e f.

pro [prəʊ] (pl -s) n - **1.** inf [professional] pro mf - **2.** [advantage] : **the ~s and cons** le pour et le contre.

pro- [prəʊ] prefix pro-.

PRO (abbr of **public relations officer**) n responsable des relations publiques.

pro-am ['prəʊˈæm] <> adj pro-am <> n tournoi m pro-am.

probability [ˌprɒbə'bɪlətɪ] (pl -ies) n probabilité f ; **in all ~** selon toute probabilité.

probable ['prɒbəbl] adj probable.

probably ['prɒbəblɪ] adv probablement.

probate ['prəʊbeɪt] JUR <> n homologation f <> vt Am homologuer.

probation [prə'beɪʃn] n (U) - **1.** JUR mise f à l'épreuve ; **to put sb on ~** mettre qqn en sursis avec mise à l'épreuve - **2.** [trial period] essai m ; **to be on ~** être à l'essai.

probationary [prə'beɪʃnrɪ] adj [teacher, nurse] à l'essai ; [period, year] d'essai.

probationer [prə'beɪʃnə'] n - **1.** [employee] stagiaire mf - **2.** JUR sursitaire mf avec mise à l'épreuve.

probation officer n agent m de probation.

probe [prəʊb] ⬦ n - **1.** [investigation] : **~ (into)** enquête f (sur) - **2.** MED & TECH sonde f ⬦ vt sonder ⬦ vi : **to ~ for** OR **into sthg** chercher à découvrir qqch.

probing ['prəʊbɪŋ] adj [question] pénétrant (e) ; [look] inquisiteur(trice).

probity ['prəʊbətɪ] n probité f.

problem ['prɒbləm] ⬦ n problème m ; **no ~!** inf pas de problème! ⬦ comp difficile.

problematic(al) [,prɒblə'mætɪk(l)] adj problématique.

procedural [prə'si:dʒərəl] adj de procédure.

procedure [prə'si:dʒə'] n procédure f.

proceed [vb prə'si:d, npl 'prəʊsi:dz] ⬦ vt [do subsequently] : **to ~ to do sthg** se mettre à faire qqch ⬦ vi - **1.** [continue] : **to ~ (with sthg)** continuer (qqch), poursuivre (qqch) - **2.** fml [advance] avancer.
➡ **proceeds** npl recette f.

proceedings [prə'si:dɪŋz] npl - **1.** [of meeting] débats mpl - **2.** JUR poursuites fpl.

process ['prəʊses] ⬦ n - **1.** [series of actions] processus m ; **in the ~** ce faisant ; **to be in the ~ of doing sthg** être en train de faire qqch - **2.** [method] procédé m ⬦ vt [raw materials, food, data] traiter, transformer ; [application] s'occuper de.

processed cheese ['prəʊsest-] n fromage en minces lamelles préemballé.

processing ['prəʊsesɪŋ] n traitement m, transformation f.

procession [prə'seʃn] n cortège m, procession f.

processor ['prəʊsesə'] n - **1.** COMPUT processeur m - **2.** CULIN robot m ménager OR de cuisine.

pro-choice adj pour le droit d'avortement.

proclaim [prə'kleɪm] vt [declare] proclamer.

proclamation [,prɒklə'meɪʃn] n proclamation f.

proclivity [prə'klɪvətɪ] (pl -ies) n fml : **~ to** OR **towards sthg** propension f à qqch.

procrastinate [prə'kræstɪneɪt] vi faire traîner les choses.

procrastination [prə,kræstɪ'neɪʃn] n procrastination f.

procreate ['prəʊkrɪeɪt] vi procréer.

procreation [,prəʊkrɪ'eɪʃn] n procréation f.

procurator fiscal ['prɒkjʊreɪtə'-] n Scot ≃ procureur m.

procure [prə'kjʊə'] vt [for oneself] se procurer ; [for someone else] procurer ; [release] obtenir.

procurement [prə'kjʊəmənt] n obtention f.

prod [prɒd] (pt & pp **-ded** ; cont **-ding**) ⬦ n petit coup m ; fig faire rappeler à qqn ⬦ vt - **1.** [push, poke] pousser doucement - **2.** [remind, prompt] : **to ~ sb (into doing sthg)** pousser OR inciter qqn (à faire qqch).

prodigal ['prɒdɪgl] adj prodigue.

prodigious [prə'dɪdʒəs] adj prodigieux(euse).

prodigy ['prɒdɪdʒɪ] (pl -ies) n prodige m.

produce [n 'prɒdju:s, vb prə'dju:s] ⬦ n (U) produits mpl ⬦ vt - **1.** [gen] produire - **2.** [cause] provoquer, causer - **3.** [show] présenter - **4.** THEATRE mettre en scène.

producer [prə'dju:sə'] n - **1.** [of film, manufacturer] producteur m, -trice f - **2.** THEATRE metteur m en scène.

product ['prɒdʌkt] n produit m ; **to be a ~ of sthg** être le produit OR le résultat de qqch.

production [prə'dʌkʃn] n - **1.** (U) [manufacture, of film] production f ; **to go into ~** entrer en production ; **to put sthg into ~** entreprendre la fabrication de qqch - **2.** (U) [output] rendement m - **3.** (U) THEATRE [of play] mise f en scène - **4.** [show - gen] production f ; [- THEATRE] pièce f.

production line n chaîne f de fabrication.

production manager n directeur m, -trice f de la production.

productive [prə'dʌktɪv] adj - **1.** [land, business, workers] productif(ive) - **2.** [meeting, experience] fructueux(euse).

productively [prə'dʌktɪvlɪ] adv - **1.** [operate, use] de façon productive - **2.** [spend time] de façon fructueuse.

productivity [,prɒdʌk'tɪvətɪ] n productivité f.

productivity deal n accord m de productivité.

Prof. (abbr of **Professor**) Pr.

profane [prə'feɪn] adj impie.

profanity [prə'fænətɪ] (pl -ies) n impiété f.

profess [prə'fes] vt professer ; **to ~ to do/be** prétendre faire/être.

professed [prə'fest] *adj* déclaré(e).

profession [prə'feʃn] *n* profession *f ; by ~* de son métier.

professional [prə'feʃənl] <> *adj* **- 1.** [gen] professionnel(elle) **- 2.** [of high standard] de (haute) qualité <> *n* professionnel *m*, -elle *f.*

professional foul *n* faute *f* délibérée.

professionalism [prə'feʃnəlɪzm] *n* professionnalisme *m.*

professionally [prə'feʃnəlɪ] *adv* **- 1.** [as professional] en professionnel ; ~ **qualified** diplômé(e) **- 2.** [skilfully] de façon professionnelle.

professor [prə'fesəʳ] *n* **- 1.** Br UNIV professeur *m* (de faculté) **- 2.** Am & Can [teacher] professeur *m.*

professorship [prə'fesəʃɪp] *n* chaire *f.*

proffer ['prɒfəʳ] *vt :* **to ~ sthg (to sb)** offrir qqch (à qqn) ; **to ~ one's hand (to sb)** tendre la main (à qqn).

proficiency [prə'fɪʃənsɪ] *n : ~* **(in)** compétence *f* (en).

proficient [prə'fɪʃənt] *adj : ~* **(in OR at sthg)** compétent(e) (en qqch).

profile ['prəʊfaɪl] *n* profil *m ;* **in ~** de profil ; **to keep a low ~** adopter un profil bas.

profit ['prɒfɪt] <> *n* **- 1.** [financial] bénéfice *m*, profit *m ;* **to make a ~** faire un bénéfice ; **to sell sthg at a ~** vendre qqch à profit **- 2.** [advantage] profit *m* <> *vi* [financially] être le bénéficiaire ; [gain advantage] tirer avantage OR profit.

profitability [,prɒfɪtə'bɪlətɪ] *n* rentabilité *f.*

profitable ['prɒfɪtəbl] *adj* **- 1.** [financially] rentable, lucratif(ive) **- 2.** [beneficial] fructueux(euse), profitable.

profitably ['prɒfɪtəblɪ] *adv* **- 1.** [at a profit] de façon rentable **- 2.** [spend time] utilement.

profiteering [,prɒfɪ'tɪərɪŋ] *n* affairisme *m*, mercantilisme *m.*

profit-making <> *adj* à but lucratif <> *n* réalisation *f* de bénéfices.

profit margin *n* marge *f* bénéficiaire.

profit sharing [-,ʃeərɪŋ] *n* participation *f* aux bénéfices.

profligate ['prɒflɪgɪt] *adj* **- 1.** [extravagant] prodigue **- 2.** [immoral] débauché(e).

pro forma [-'fɔːmə] *adj* pro forma.

profound [prə'faʊnd] *adj* profond(e).

profoundly [prə'faʊndlɪ] *adv* profondément.

profuse [prə'fjuːs] *adj* [apologies, praise] profus(e) ; [bleeding] abondant(e).

profusely [prə'fjuːslɪ] *adv* [sweat, bleed] abon-

damment ; **to apologize ~** se confondre en excuses.

profusion [prə'fjuːʒn] *n* profusion *f.*

progeny ['prɒdʒənɪ] *(pl* **-ies)** *n* progéniture *f.*

progesterone [prə'dʒestərəʊn] *n* progestérone *f.*

prognosis [prɒg'nəʊsɪs] *(pl* **-ses** [-siːz]*) n* pronostic *m.*

prognostication [prɒg,nɒstɪ'keɪʃn] *n* pronostic *m.*

program ['prəʊgræm] *(pt & pp* **-med** OR **-ed ;** *cont* **-ming** OR **-ing)** <> *n* **- 1.** COMPUT programme *m* **- 2.** Am = programme <> *vt* **- 1.** COMPUT programmer **- 2.** Am = programme.

programer Am = programmer.

programmable [prəʊ'græməbl] *adj* programmable.

programme Br, **program** Am ['prəʊgræm] <> *n* **- 1.** [schedule, booklet] programme *m* **- 2.** RADIO & TV émission *f* <> *vt* programmer ; **to ~ sthg to do sthg** programmer qqch pour faire qqch.

programmer Br, **programer** Am ['prəʊgræməʳ] *n* COMPUT programmeur *m*, -euse *f.*

programming ['prəʊgræmɪŋ] *n* programmation *f.*

programming language *n* langage *m* de programmation.

progress [*n* 'prəʊgres, *vb* prə'gres] <> *n* progrès *m ;* **to make ~** [improve] faire des progrès ; **to make ~ in sthg** avancer dans qqch ; **in ~** en cours <> *vi* **- 1.** [improve - gen] progresser, avancer ; [- person] faire des progrès **- 2.** [continue] avancer **- 3.** [move on]**:** **to ~ to sthg** passer à qqch.

progression [prə'greʃn] *n* progression *f.*

progressive [prə'gresɪv] *adj* **- 1.** [enlightened] progressiste **- 2.** [gradual] progressif(ive).

progressively [prə'gresɪvlɪ] *adv* progressivement.

progress report *n* [on patient] bulletin *m* de santé ; [on student] bulletin scolaire ; [on work] compte-rendu *m.*

prohibit [prə'hɪbɪt] *vt* prohiber ; **to ~ sb from doing sthg** interdire OR défendre à qqn de faire qqch.

prohibition [,prəʊɪ'bɪʃn] *n* **- 1.** [law, rule] prohibition *f* **- 2.** *(U)* [act of prohibiting] interdiction *f*, défense *f.*

prohibitive [prə'hɪbətɪv] *adj* prohibitif(ive).

project [*n* 'prɒdʒekt, *vb* prə'dʒekt] <> *n* **- 1.** [plan, idea] projet *m*, plan *m* **- 2.** SCH [study]**:** *~* **(on)** dossier *m* (sur), projet *m* (sur) <> *vt*

- 1. [gen] projeter **- 2.** [estimate] prévoir ◇ *vi* [jut out] faire saillie.

projectile [prə'dʒektaɪl] *n* projectile *m.*

projection [prə'dʒekʃn] *n* **- 1.** [estimate] prévision *f* **- 2.** [protrusion] saillie *f* **- 3.** *(U)* [display, showing] projection *f.*

projectionist [prə'dʒekʃənɪst] *n* projectionniste *mf.*

projection room *n* cabine *f* de projection.

projector [prə'dʒektəʳ] *n* projecteur *m.*

proletarian [,prəʊlɪ'teərɪən] *adj* prolétarien(enne).

proletariat [,prəʊlɪ'teərɪət] *n* prolétariat *m.*

pro-life *adj* pour le respect de la vie.

proliferate [prə'lɪfəreɪt] *vi* proliférer.

prolific [prə'lɪfɪk] *adj* prolifique.

prologue, prolog Am ['prəʊlɒg] *n* lit & fig prologue *m.*

prolong [prə'lɒŋ] *vt* prolonger.

prom [prɒm] *n* **- 1.** Br inf (*abbr of* **promenade**) promenade *f*, front *m* de mer **- 2.** Am [ball] bal *m* d'étudiants **- 3.** Br inf (*abbr of* **promenade concert**) concert *m* promenade.

promenade [,prɒmə'nɑːd] *n* Br [road by sea] promenade *f*, front *m* de mer.

promenade concert *n* Br concert *m* promenade.

prominence ['prɒmɪnəns] *n* **- 1.** [importance] importance *f* **- 2.** [conspicuousness] proéminence *f.*

prominent ['prɒmɪnənt] *adj* **- 1.** [important] important(e) **- 2.** [noticeable] proéminent(e).

prominently ['prɒmɪnəntlɪ] *adv* au premier plan, bien en vue.

promiscuity [,prɒmɪs'kjuːətɪ] *n* promiscuité *f.*

promiscuous [prɒ'mɪskjʊəs] *adj* [person] aux mœurs légères ; [behaviour] immoral(e).

promise ['prɒmɪs] ◇ *n* promesse *f* ; **to make (sb) a** ~ faire une promesse (à qqn) ; **to show** ~ avoir de l'avenir, promettre ◇ *vt* : **to** ~ **(sb) to do sthg** promettre (à qqn) de faire qqch ; **to** ~ **sb sthg** promettre qqch à qqn ◇ *vi* promettre.

promising ['prɒmɪsɪŋ] *adj* prometteur(euse).

promissory note ['prɒmɪsərɪ-] *n* billet *m* à ordre.

promo ['prəʊməʊ] (*pl* **-s**) (*abbr of* **promotion**) *n* inf promo *f.*

promontory ['prɒməntrɪ] (*pl* **-ies**) *n* promontoire *m.*

promote [prə'məʊt] *vt* **- 1.** [foster] promouvoir **- 2.** [push, advertise] promouvoir, lancer **- 3.** [in job] promouvoir.

promoter [prə'məʊtəʳ] *n* **- 1.** [organizer] organisateur *m*, -trice *f* **- 2.** [supporter] promoteur *m*, -trice *f.*

promotion [prə'məʊʃn] *n* promotion *f*, avancement *m* ; **to get** OR **be given** ~ être promu, obtenir de l'avancement.

prompt [prɒmpt] ◇ *adj* rapide, prompt(e) ◇ *adv* : **at nine o'clock** ~ à neuf heures précises OR tapantes ◇ *vt* **- 1.** [motivate, encourage] : **to** ~ **sb (to do sthg)** pousser OR inciter qqn (à faire qqch) **- 2.** THEATRE souffler sa réplique à ◇ *n* THEATRE réplique *f.*

prompter ['prɒmptəʳ] *n* THEATRE souffleur *m*, -euse *f.*

promptly ['prɒmptlɪ] *adv* **- 1.** [immediately] rapidement, promptement **- 2.** [punctually] ponctuellement.

promptness ['prɒmptnɪs] *n* **- 1.** [speediness] promptitude *f* **- 2.** [punctuality] ponctualité *f.*

promulgate ['prɒmlgeɪt] *vt* promulguer.

prone [prəʊn] *adj* **- 1.** [susceptible] : **to be** ~ **to sthg** être sujet(ette) à qqch ; **to be** ~ **to do sthg** avoir tendance à faire qqch **- 2.** [lying flat] étendu(e) face contre terre.

prong [prɒŋ] *n* [of fork] dent *f.*

pronoun ['prəʊnaʊn] *n* pronom *m.*

pronounce [prə'naʊns] ◇ *vt* prononcer ◇ *vi* : **to** ~ **on** se prononcer sur.

pronounced [prə'naʊnst] *adj* prononcé(e).

pronouncement [prə'naʊnsmənt] *n* déclaration *f.*

pronunciation [prə,nʌnsɪ'eɪʃn] *n* prononciation *f.*

proof [pruːf] *n* **- 1.** [evidence] preuve *f* **- 2.** [of book etc] épreuve *f* **- 3.** [of alcohol] teneur *f* en alcool.

proofread ['pruːfriːd] (*pt* & *pp* **-read** [-red]) *vt* corriger les épreuves de.

proofreader ['pruːf,riːdəʳ] *n* correcteur *m*, -trice *f* d'épreuves.

prop [prɒp] (*pt* & *pp* **-ped** ; *cont* **-ping**) ◇ *n* **- 1.** [physical support] support *m*, étai *m* **- 2.** fig [supporting thing, person] soutien *m* **- 3.** RUGBY pilier *m* ◇ *vt* : **to** ~ **sthg against** appuyer qqch contre OR à.
➧ **props** *npl* accessoires *mpl.*
➧ **prop up** *vt sep* **- 1.** [physically support] soutenir, étayer **- 2.** fig [sustain] soutenir.

Prop. *abbr of* **proprietor.**

propaganda [,prɒpə'gændə] *n* propagande *f.*

propagate [ˈprɒpəgeɪt] ⬦ vt propager ⬦ vi se propager.

propagation [ˌprɒpəˈgeɪʃn] n propagation f.

propane [ˈprəʊpeɪn] n propane m.

propel [prəˈpel] (pt & pp **-led** ; cont **-ling**) vt propulser ; **fig** pousser.

propeller [prəˈpelər] n hélice f.

propelling pencil [prəˈpelɪŋ-] n **Br** portemine m inv.

propensity [prəˈpensətɪ] (pl **-ies**) n : ~ **(for** OR **to)** propension f (à).

proper [ˈprɒpər] adj - **1.** [real] vrai(e) - **2.** [correct] correct(e), bon (bonne) - **3.** [decent - behaviour etc] convenable - **4.** inf [for emphasis] : **he's a ~ idiot!** c'est un imbécile fini!

properly [ˈprɒpəlɪ] adv - **1.** [satisfactorily, correctly] correctement, comme il faut - **2.** [decently] convenablement, comme il faut.

proper noun n nom m propre.

property [ˈprɒpətɪ] (pl **-ies**) n - **1.** (U) [possessions] biens mpl, propriété f - **2.** [building] bien m immobilier ; [land] terres fpl - **3.** [quality] propriété f.

property developer n promoteur m immobilier.

property owner n propriétaire m (foncier).

property tax n impôt m foncier.

prophecy [ˈprɒfɪsɪ] (pl **-ies**) n prophétie f.

prophesy [ˈprɒfɪsaɪ] (pt & pp **-ied**) vt prédire.

prophet [ˈprɒfɪt] n prophète m.

prophetic [prəˈfetɪk] adj prophétique

propitious [prəˈpɪʃəs] adj **fml** propice, favorable.

proponent [prəˈpəʊnənt] n adepte m f, partisan m, -e f.

proportion [prəˈpɔːʃn] n - **1.** [part] part f, partie f - **2.** [ratio] rapport m, proportion f ; **in ~ to** proportionnellement à ; **out of all ~ to** sans commune mesure avec - **3.** ART : **in ~** proportionné(e) ; **out of ~** mal proportionné ; **to get sthg out of ~** fig exagérer qqch ; **a sense of ~** fig le sens de la mesure.

proportional [prəˈpɔːʃənl] adj proportionnel(elle).

proportional representation n représentation f proportionnelle.

proportionate [prəˈpɔːʃnət] adj proportionnel(elle).

proposal [prəˈpəʊzl] n - **1.** [suggestion] proposition f, offre f - **2.** [offer of marriage] demande f en mariage.

propose [prəˈpəʊz] ⬦ vt - **1.** [suggest] proposer - **2.** [intend] : **to ~ to do** OR **doing sthg** avoir l'intention de faire qqch, se proposer de faire qqch - **3.** [toast] porter ⬦ vi faire une demande en mariage ; **to ~ to sb** demander qqn en mariage.

proposed [prəˈpəʊzd] adj proposé(e).

proposition [ˌprɒpəˈzɪʃn] ⬦ n proposition f ; **to make sb a ~** faire une proposition à qqn ⬦ vt faire des propositions à.

propound [prəˈpaʊnd] vt **fml** soumettre, proposer.

proprietary [prəˈpraɪətrɪ] adj de marque déposée ; **~ brand** marque f déposée.

proprietor [prəˈpraɪətər] n propriétaire mf.

propriety [prəˈpraɪətɪ] **fml** n (U) [moral correctness] bienséance f.

propulsion [prəˈpʌlʃn] n propulsion f.

pro rata [-ˈrɑːtə] ⬦ adj proportionnel(elle) ⬦ adv au prorata.

prosaic [prəʊˈzeɪɪk] adj prosaïque, banal(e).

Pros. Atty (abbr of **prosecuting attorney**) avocat général.

proscenium [prəˈsiːnjəm] (pl **-niums** OR **-nia** [-njə]) n : ~ **(arch)** proscenium m.

proscribe [prəʊˈskraɪb] vt proscrire.

prose [prəʊz] ⬦ n (U) prose f ⬦ comp en prose.

prosecute [ˈprɒsɪkjuːt] ⬦ vt poursuivre (en justice) ⬦ vi [police] engager des poursuites judiciaires ; [lawyer] représenter la partie plaignante.

prosecution [ˌprɒsɪˈkjuːʃn] n poursuites fpl judiciaires, accusation f ; **the ~** la partie plaignante ; [in Crown case] ≈ le ministère public.

prosecutor [ˈprɒsɪkjuːtər] n esp **Am** plaignant m, -e f.

prospect [n ˈprɒspekt, vb prəˈspekt] ⬦ n - **1.** [hope] possibilité f, chances fpl - **2.** [probability] perspective f ⬦ vi : **to ~ (for sthg)** prospecter (pour chercher qqch).
➡ **prospects** npl : **~s (for)** chances fpl (de), perspectives fpl (de).

prospecting [prəˈspektɪŋ] n prospection f.

prospective [prəˈspektɪv] adj éventuel(elle).

prospector [prəˈspektər] n prospecteur m, -trice f.

prospectus [prəˈspektəs] (pl **-es**) n prospectus m.

prosper [ˈprɒspər] vi prospérer.

prosperity [prɒˈsperətɪ] n prospérité f.

prosperous [ˈprɒspərəs] adj prospère.

prostate (gland) ['prɒsteɪt-] *n* prostate *f.*

prosthesis [prɒs'θiːsɪs] (*pl* **-ses** [-siːz]) *n* prothèse *f.*

prostitute ['prɒstɪtjuːt] *n* prostituée *f; male* ~ prostitué *m.*

prostitution [,prɒstɪ'tjuːʃn] *n* prostitution *f.*

prostrate [*adj* 'prɒstreɪt, *vb* prɒ'streɪt] <> *adj* - **1.** [lying down] à plat ventre - **2.** [with grief etc] prostré(e) <> *vt :* **to ~ o.s. (before sb)** se prosterner (devant qqn).

protagonist [prə'tægənɪst] *n* protagoniste *mf.*

protect [prə'tekt] *vt :* **to ~ sb/sthg (against), to ~ sb/sthg (from)** protéger qqn/qqch (contre), protéger qqn/qqch (de).

protection [prə'tekʃn] *n :* ~ **(from** OR **against)** protection *f* (contre), défense *f* (contre).

protectionism [prə'tekʃənɪzm] *n* protectionnisme *m.*

protectionist [prə'tekʃənɪst] *adj* protectionniste.

protection money *n* argent versé par les victimes d'un racket.

protective [prə'tektɪv] *adj* - **1.** [layer, clothing] de protection - **2.** [person, feelings] protecteur(trice) ; **to feel ~ towards sb** se montrer protecteur envers qqn.

protective custody *n* détention d'une personne pour sa propre sécurité.

protectiveness [prə'tektɪvnɪs] *n* attitude *f* protectrice.

protector [prə'tektə'] *n* - **1.** [person] protecteur *m*, -trice *f* - **2.** [object] dispositif *m* de protection.

protectorate [prə'tektərət] *n* protectorat *m.*

protégé ['prɒteʒeɪ] *n* protégé *m.*

protégée ['prɒteʒeɪ] *n* protégée *f.*

protein ['prəutiːn] *n* protéine *f.*

protest [*n* 'prəutest, *vb* prə'test] <> *n* protestation *f* <> *vt* - **1.** [state] protester de - **2.** Am [protest against] protester contre <> *vi :* **to ~ (about/against)** protester (à propos de/contre).

Protestant ['prɒtɪstənt] <> *adj* protestant(e) <> *n* protestant *m*, -e *f.*

Protestantism ['prɒtɪstəntɪzm] *n* protestantisme *m.*

protestation [,prɒte'steɪʃn] *n* protestation *f.*

protester [prə'testə'] *n* [on march, at demonstration] manifestant *m*, -e *f.*

protest march *n* manifestation *f*, marche *f* de protestation.

protocol ['prəutəkɒl] *n* protocole *m.*

proton ['prəutɒn] *n* proton *m.*

prototype ['prəutətaɪp] *n* prototype *m.*

protracted [prə'træktɪd] *adj* prolongé(e).

protractor [prə'træktə'] *n* rapporteur *m.*

protrude [prə'truːd] *vi* avancer, dépasser.

protrusion [prə'truːʒn] *n* avancée *f*, saillie *f.*

protuberance [prə'tjuːbərəns] *n* protubérance *f.*

proud [praud] *adj* - **1.** [satisfied, dignified] fier (fière) ; **to be ~ to do sthg** être fier de faire qqch - **2.** pej [arrogant] orgueilleux(euse), fier (fière).

proudly ['praudlɪ] *adv* - **1.** [with satisfaction, dignity] fièrement, avec fierté - **2.** pej [arrogantly] orgueilleusement.

provable ['pruːvəbl] *adj* qui peut être prouvé(e), prouvable.

prove [pruːv] (*pp* **-d** OR **proven**) *vt* - **1.** [show to be true] prouver - **2.** [turn out] : **to ~ (to be) false/ useful** s'avérer faux/utile ; **to ~ o.s. to be** sthg se révéler être qqch.

proven ['pruːvn, 'prəuvn] <> *pp* ⊳ **prove** <> *adj* [fact] avéré(e), établi(e) ; [liar] fieffé(e).

Provençal [,prɒvɒn'saːl] <> *adj* provençal(e) <> *n* - **1.** [person] Provençal *m*, -e *f* - **2.** [language] Provençal *m.*

Provence [prɒ'vɑːns] *n* Provence *f; in* ~ en Provence. ·

proverb ['prɒvɜːb] *n* proverbe *m.*

proverbial [prə'vɜːbjəl] *adj* proverbial(e).

provide [prə'vaɪd] *vt* fournir ; **to ~ sb with sthg** fournir qqch à qqn ; **to ~ sthg for sb** fournir qqch à qqn.

➡ **provide for** *vt fus* - **1.** [support] subvenir aux besoins de - **2.** fml [make arrangements for] prévoir.

provided [prə'vaɪdɪd] ➡ **provided (that)** *conj* à condition que *(+ subjunctive)*, pourvu que *(+ subjunctive).*

providence ['prɒvɪdəns] *n* providence *f.*

providential [,prɒvɪ'denʃl] *adj* providentiel(elle).

provider [prə'vaɪdə'] *n* pourvoyeur *m*, -euse *f.*

providing [prə'vaɪdɪŋ] ➡ **providing (that)** *conj* à condition que *(+ subjunctive)*, pourvu que *(+ subjunctive).*

province ['prɒvɪns] *n* - **1.** [part of country] province *f* - **2.** [speciality] domaine *m*, compétence *f.*

➡ **provinces** *npl :* **the ~s** la province.

provincial [prə'vɪnʃl] *adj* - **1.** [town, newspaper] de province - **2.** pej [narrow-minded] provincial(e).

provision [prə'vɪʒn] n - **1.** (U) [act of supplying] : ~ **(of)** approvisionnement m (en), fourniture f (de) - **2.** [supply] provision f, réserve f - **3.** (U) [arrangements] : **to make ~ for** [the future] prendre des mesures pour ; [one's family] pourvoir aux besoins de - **4.** [in agreement, law] clause f, disposition f.

➡ **provisions** npl [supplies] provisions fpl.

provisional [prə'vɪʒənl] adj provisoire.

Provisional IRA n branche de l'IRA qui pratique le terrorisme.

provisional licence n Br permis m de conduire provisoire (jusqu'à l'obtention du permis de conduire).

provisionally [prə'vɪʒnəlɪ] adv provisoirement, à titre provisoire.

proviso [prə'vaɪzəʊ] (pl -s) n condition f, stipulation f; **with the ~ that** à (la) condition que (+ subjunctive).

Provo ['prəʊvəʊ] (pl -s) (abbr of **Provisional**) n inf membre de la branche de l'IRA pratiquant le terrorisme.

provocation [ˌprɒvə'keɪʃn] n provocation f.

provocative [prə'vɒkətɪv] adj provocant(e).

provocatively [prə'vɒkətɪvlɪ] adv d'une manière provocante.

provoke [prə'vəʊk] vt - **1.** [annoy] agacer, contrarier - **2.** [cause - fight, argument] provoquer ; [- reaction] susciter.

provoking [prə'vəʊkɪŋ] adj agaçant(e), énervant(e).

provost ['prɒvəst] n - **1.** Br UNIV doyen m - **2.** Scot [head of town council] maire m.

prow [praʊ] n proue f.

prowess ['praʊɪs] n prouesse f.

prowl [praʊl] <> n : **to be on the ~** rôder <> vt [streets etc] rôder dans <> vi rôder.

prowl car n Am voiture f de police en patrouille.

prowler ['praʊlə'] n rôdeur m, -euse f.

proximity [prɒk'sɪmətɪ] n : ~ **(to)** proximité f (de) ; **in the ~ of** à proximité de.

proxy ['prɒksɪ] (pl -ies) n : **by ~** par procuration.

prude [pruːd] n prude f.

prudence ['pruːdns] n prudence f.

prudent ['pruːdnt] adj prudent(e).

prudently ['pruːdntlɪ] adv prudemment, avec prudence.

prudish ['pruːdɪʃ] adj prude, pudibond(e).

prune [pruːn] <> n [fruit] pruneau m <> vt [tree, bush] tailler.

prurient ['prʊərɪənt] adj lascif(ive).

Prussian ['prʌʃn] <> adj prussien(enne) <> n Prussien m, -enne f.

pry [praɪ] (pt & pp pried) vi se mêler de ce qui ne vous regarde pas ; **to ~ into sthg** chercher à découvrir qqch.

PS (abbr of postscript) n PS m.

psalm [sɑːm] n psaume m.

PSBR (abbr of public sector borrowing requirement) n partie du budget de l'État non couverte par les impôts en Grande-Bretagne.

pseud [sjuːd] n Br inf frimeur m, -euse f.

pseudo- [ˌsjuːdəʊ] prefix pseudo-.

pseudonym ['sjuːdənɪm] n pseudonyme m.

psi (abbr of pounds per square inch) livres au pouce carré (mesure de pression).

psoriasis [sɒ'raɪəsɪs] n psoriasis m.

psst [pst] excl psitt!

PST (abbr of Pacific Standard Time) n heure du Pacifique.

psych [saɪk] ➡ **psych up** vt sep inf préparer psychologiquement ; **to ~ o.s. up** se préparer psychologiquement.

psyche ['saɪkɪ] n psyché f.

psychedelic [ˌsaɪkɪ'delɪk] adj psychédélique.

psychiatric [ˌsaɪkɪ'ætrɪk] adj psychiatrique.

psychiatric nurse n infirmière f en psychiatrie.

psychiatrist [saɪ'kaɪətrɪst] n psychiatre mf.

psychiatry [saɪ'kaɪətrɪ] n psychiatrie f.

psychic ['saɪkɪk] <> adj - **1.** [clairvoyant - person] doué(e) de seconde vue ; [- powers] parapsychique - **2.** MED psychique <> n médium m.

psychoanalyse, -yze Am [ˌsaɪkəʊ'ænəlaɪz] vt psychanalyser.

psychoanalysis [ˌsaɪkəʊə'næləsɪs] n psychanalyse f.

psychoanalyst [ˌsaɪkəʊ'ænəlɪst] n psychanalyste mf.

psychological [ˌsaɪkə'lɒdʒɪkl] adj psychologique.

psychological warfare n (U) guerre f psychologique.

psychologist [saɪ'kɒlədʒɪst] n psychologue mf.

psychology [saɪ'kɒlədʒɪ] n psychologie f.

psychopath ['saɪkəpæθ] n psychopathe mf.

psychosis [saɪ'kəʊsɪs] (pl -ses [-siːz]) n psychose f.

psychosomatic [ˌsaɪkəʊsə'mætɪk] adj psychosomatique.

psychotherapy [ˌsaɪkəʊ'θerəpɪ] n psychothérapie f.

psychotic [saɪˈkɒtɪk] ◇ *adj* psychotique ◇ *n* psychotique *mf*.

pt - 1. *abbr of* **pint - 2.** *abbr of* **point.**

Pt. (*abbr of* **Point**) [on map] Pte.

PT (*abbr of* **physical training**) *n* EPS *f*.

PTA (*abbr of* **parent-teacher association**) *n* association de parents d'élèves et de professeurs.

Pte. *abbr of* **Private.**

PTO ◇ *n* (*abbr of* **parent-teacher organization**) *aux États-Unis, association de parents d'élèves et de professeurs* ◇ (*abbr of* **please turn over**) TSVP.

PTV *n* **- 1.** (*abbr of* **pay television**) *télévision payante* **- 2.** (*abbr of* **public television**) *programmes télévisés éducatifs.*

pub [pʌb] *n* pub *m*.

> **PUB**
>
> Dans l'ensemble des îles britanniques, le pub est un des grands foyers de la vie sociale. Ces établissements - interdits aux personnes non accompagnées de moins de 16 ans - étaient soumis à des horaires stricts, mais ceux-ci se sont beaucoup assouplis récemment (voir « licensing hours »). De simple débit de boissons, qu'il était souvent, de plus en plus le pub évolue vers une sorte de brasserie servant des repas légers.

pub. *abbr of* **published.**

pub-crawl *n* Br : **to go on a ~** faire la tournée des pubs.

puberty [ˈpjuːbətɪ] *n* puberté *f*.

pubescent [pjuːˈbesnt] *adj* pubescent(e).

pubic [ˈpjuːbɪk] *adj* du pubis.

public [ˈpʌblɪk] ◇ *adj* public(ique) ; [library] municipal(e) ; **it's ~ knowledge that ...** tout le monde sait que ..., il est de notoriété publique que ... ; **to make sthg ~** rendre qqch public ; **to go ~** COMM émettre des actions dans le public ◇ *n* : **the ~** le public ; **in ~** en public.

public-address system *n* système *m* de sonorisation.

publican [ˈpʌblɪkən] *n* Br gérant *m*, -e *f* d'un pub.

publication [ˌpʌblɪˈkeɪʃn] *n* publication *f*.

public bar *n* Br bar *m*.

public company *n* société *f* anonyme (*cotée en Bourse*).

public convenience *n* Br toilettes *fpl* publiques.

public domain *n* : **in the ~** dans le domaine public.

public holiday *n* jour *m* férié.

public house *n* Br pub *m*.

publicist [ˈpʌblɪsɪst] *n* agent *m* de publicité.

publicity [pʌbˈlɪsɪtɪ] ◇ *n* (U) publicité *f* ◇ *comp* de publicité.

publicity stunt *n* coup *m* publicitaire.

publicize, -ise [ˈpʌblɪsaɪz] *vt* faire connaître au public.

public limited company *n* société *f* anonyme (*cotée en Bourse*).

publicly [ˈpʌblɪklɪ] *adv* publiquement, en public.

public office *n* fonctions *fpl* officielles.

public opinion *n* (U) opinion *f* publique.

public ownership *n* nationalisation *f*.

public prosecutor *n* ≃ procureur *m* de la République.

public relations ◇ *n* (U) relations *fpl* publiques ◇ *npl* relations *fpl* publiques.

public relations officer *n* responsable *m f* des relations publiques.

public school *n* **- 1.** Br [private school] école *f* privée **- 2.** Am [state school] école *f* publique.

> **PUBLIC SCHOOL**
>
> En Angleterre et au pays de Galles, le terme « public school » désigne une école privée de type traditionnel ; certaines de ces écoles (Eton et Harrow, par exemple) sont très réputées et recherchées. La « public school » est censée former l'élite de la nation. Aux États-Unis et parfois en Écosse, le terme désigne une école publique.

public sector *n* secteur *m* public.

public servant *n* fonctionnaire *m f*.

public service vehicle *n* Br autobus *m*.

public-spirited *adj* qui fait preuve de civisme.

public transport *n* (U) transports *mpl* en commun.

public utility *n* service *m* public.

public works *npl* travaux *mpl* publics.

publish [ˈpʌblɪʃ] *vt* publier.

publisher [ˈpʌblɪʃəʳ] *n* éditeur *m*, -trice *f*.

publishing [ˈpʌblɪʃɪŋ] *n* (U) [industry] édition *f*.

publishing company, publishing house *n* société *f* OR maison *f* d'édition.

pub lunch *n* repas de midi servi dans un pub.

puce [pjuːs] *adj* puce (*inv*).

puck [pʌk] *n* ICE HOCKEY palet *m*, rondelle *f* Can.

pucker [ˈpʌkəʳ] ◇ *vt* plisser ◇ *vi* se plisser.

pudding [ˈpʊdɪŋ] *n* **- 1.** [food - sweet] entremets *m* ; [- savoury] pudding *m* - **2.** *(U)* Br [course] dessert *m*.

puddle ['pʌdl] *n* flaque *f*.

pudgy ['pʌdʒɪ] = **podgy**.

puerile ['pjʊəraɪl] *adj* puéril(e).

Puerto Rican [,pwɜ:təʊ'ri:kən] ◇ *adj* portoricain(e) ◇ *n* Portoricain *m*, -e *f*.

Puerto Rico [,pwɜ:təʊ'ri:kəʊ] *n* Porto Rico, Puerto Rico.

puff [pʌf] ◇ *n* - **1.** [of cigarette, smoke] bouffée *f* - **2.** [gasp] souffle *m* ◇ *vt* [cigarette etc] tirer sur ◇ *vi* - **1.** [smoke] : **to ~ at** OR **on sthg** fumer qqch - **2.** [pant] haleter.

◆ **puff out** *vt sep* [cheeks, chest] gonfler.

◆ **puff up** *vi* se gonfler.

puffed [pʌft] *adj* - **1.** [swollen] : **~ (up)** gonflé(e) - **2.** Br inf [out of breath] : **~ (out)** essoufflé(e).

puffed sleeve *n* manche *f* ballon.

puffin ['pʌfɪn] *n* macareux *m*.

puffiness ['pʌfɪnɪs] *n* gonflement *m*, bouffissure *f*.

puff pastry, puff paste Am *n.* *(U)* pâte *f* feuilletée.

puffy ['pʌfɪ] (*compar* -ier ; *superl* -iest) *adj* gonflé(e), bouffi(e).

pug [pʌg] *n* carlin *m*.

pugnacious [pʌg'neɪʃəs] *adj* fml querelleur(euse), batailleur(euse).

puke [pju:k] *vi* inf dégobiller.

Pulitzer Prize [pʊlɪtsə-] *n* [in US] prix *m* Pulitzer.

pull [pʊl] ◇ *vt* - **1.** [gen] tirer - **2.** [strain - muscle, hamstring] se froisser - **3.** [tooth] arracher - **4.** [attract] attirer - **5.** [gun] sortir ◇ *vi* tirer ◇ *n* - **1.** [tug with hand] : **to give sthg a ~** tirer sur qqch - **2.** *(U)* [influence] influence *f*.

◆ **pull ahead** *vi* : **to ~ ahead (of)** prendre la tête (devant).

◆ **pull apart** *vt sep* [separate] séparer.

◆ **pull at** *vt fus* tirer sur.

◆ **pull away** *vi* - **1.** AUT démarrer - **2.** [in race] prendre de l'avance.

◆ **pull back** *vi* reculer.

◆ **pull down** *vt sep* [building] démolir.

◆ **pull in** *vi* AUT se ranger.

◆ **pull off** *vt sep* - **1.** [take off] enlever, ôter - **2.** [succeed in] réussir.

◆ **pull on** *vt sep* [clothes] mettre, enfiler.

◆ **pull out** ◇ *vt sep* [troops etc] retirer ◇ *vi* - **1.** RAIL partir, démarrer - **2.** AUT déboîter - **3.** [withdraw] se retirer.

◆ **pull over** *vi* AUT se ranger.

◆ **pull through** ◇ *vi* s'en sortir, s'en tirer ◇ *vt sep* tirer d'affaire.

◆ **pull together** *vt sep* : **to ~ o.s. together** se ressaisir, se reprendre ◇ *vi* fig faire un effort.

◆ **pull up** ◇ *vt sep* - **1.** [raise] remonter - **2.** [chair] avancer - **3.** [stop] : **to ~ sb up short** arrêter qqn court ◇ *vi* s'arrêter.

pull-down menu *n* COMPUT menu *m* déroulant.

pulley ['pʊlɪ] (*pl* -s) *n* poulie *f*.

pullout ['pʊlaʊt] *n* supplément *m* détachable.

pullover ['pʊl,əʊvə'] *n* pull *m*.

pulp [pʌlp] ◇ *adj* [fiction, novel] de quatre sous ◇ *n* - **1.** [for paper] pâte *f* à papier - **2.** [of fruit] pulpe *f* ◇ *vt* [food] réduire en pulpe.

pulpit ['pʊlpɪt] *n* chaire *f*.

pulsar ['pʌlsɑː'] *n* pulsar *m*.

pulsate [pʌl'seɪt] *vi* [heart] battre fort ; [air, music] vibrer.

pulse [pʌls] ◇ *n* - **1.** MED pouls *m* ; **to take sb's ~** prendre le pouls de qqn - **2.** TECH impulsion *f* ◇ *vi* battre, palpiter.

◆ **pulses** *npl* [food] légumes *mpl* secs.

pulverize, -ise ['pʌlvəraɪz] *vt* - **1.** [crush] pulvériser - **2.** fig [destroy - town] détruire ; [- person] démolir.

puma ['pju:mə] (*pl inv* OR -s) *n* puma *m*.

pumice (stone) ['pʌmɪs-] *n* pierre *f* ponce.

pummel ['pʌml] (Br *pt* & *pp* -led ; *cont* -ling, Am *pt* & *pp* -ed ; *cont* -ing) *vt* bourrer de coups.

pump [pʌmp] ◇ *n* pompe *f* ◇ *vt* - **1.** [water, gas etc] pomper - **2.** inf [invest] : **to ~ money into sthg** injecter des capitaux dans qqch - **3.** inf [interrogate] essayer de tirer les vers du nez à ◇ *vi* [heart] battre fort.

◆ **pumps** *npl* [shoes] escarpins *mpl*.

pumpernickel ['pʌmpənɪkl] *n* pain *m* de seigle noir.

pumpkin ['pʌmpkɪn] *n* potiron *m*.

pumpkin pie *n* tarte *f* au potiron *(dessert achevant traditionnellement le dîner de Thanksgiving)*.

pun [pʌn] *n* jeu *m* de mots, calembour *m*.

punch [pʌntʃ] ◇ *n* - **1.** [blow] coup *m* de poing

- 2. [tool] poinçonneuse f **- 3.** [drink] punch m ⬦ vt **- 1.** [hit - once] donner un coup de poing à ; [- repeatedly] donner des coups de poing à ; **to ~ a hole in sthg** faire un trou dans qqch **- 2.** [ticket] poinçonner ; [paper] perforer.

➤ **punch in** vi Am pointer (en arrivant).

➤ **punch out** vi Am pointer (en partant).

Punch-and-Judy show [-'dʒuːdɪ-] n guignol m.

punch bag, punch ball, punching bag Am ['pʌntʃɪŋ-] n punching-ball m.

punch bowl n coupe f à punch.

punch-drunk adj sonné(e), groggy (inv).

punch(ed) card [pʌntʃ(t)-] n carte f perforée.

punching bag Am = **punch bag**.

punch line n chute f.

punch-up n Br inf bagarre f.

punchy ['pʌntʃɪ] (compar **-ier** ; superl **-iest**) adj inf [style] incisif(ive).

punctilious [pʌŋk'tɪlɪəs] adj pointilleux(euse).

punctual ['pʌŋktʃʊəl] adj ponctuel(elle).

punctually ['pʌŋktʃʊəlɪ] adv à l'heure.

punctuate ['pʌŋktʃʊət] vt ponctuer.

punctuation [,pʌŋktʃʊ'eɪʃn] n ponctuation f.

punctuation mark n signe m de ponctuation.

puncture ['pʌŋktʃər] ⬦ n crevaison f ⬦ vt [tyre, ball] crever ; [skin] piquer.

pundit ['pʌndɪt] n pontife m.

pungent ['pʌndʒənt] adj **- 1.** [smell] âcre ; [taste] piquant(e) **- 2.** fig [criticism] caustique, acerbe.

punish ['pʌnɪʃ] vt punir ; **to ~ sb for sthg/for doing sthg** punir qqn pour qqch/pour avoir fait qqch.

punishable ['pʌnɪʃəbl] adj punissable.

punishing ['pʌnɪʃɪŋ] adj [schedule, work] épuisant(e), éreintant(e) ; [defeat] cuisant(e).

punishment ['pʌnɪʃmənt] n punition f, châtiment m ; **to take a lot of ~** [car, furniture] être malmené.

punitive ['pjuːnətɪv] adj [action] punitif(ive) ; [tax] très lourd(e).

Punjab [,pʌn'dʒɑːb] n : **the ~** le Pendjab ; **in the ~** au Pendjab.

Punjabi [,pʌn'dʒɑːbɪ] ⬦ adj du Pendjab ⬦ n **- 1.** [person] habitant m, -e f du Pendjab **- 2.** [language] pendjabi m.

punk [pʌŋk] ⬦ adj punk (inv) ⬦ n **- 1.** (U) [music] : **~ (rock)** punk m **- 2. : ~ (rocker)** punk mf **- 3.** Am inf [lout] loubard m.

punnet ['pʌnɪt] n Br barquette f.

punt [pʌnt] ⬦ n [boat] bateau m à fond plat ⬦ vi [in boat] se promener en bateau à fond plat.

punter ['pʌntər] n Br **- 1.** [gambler] parieur m, -euse f **- 2.** inf [customer] client m, -e f.

puny ['pjuːnɪ] (compar **-ier** ; superl **-iest**) adj chétif(ive).

pup [pʌp] n **- 1.** [young dog] chiot m **- 2.** [young seal] bébé phoque m.

pupil ['pjuːpl] n **- 1.** [student] élève mf **- 2.** [of eye] pupille f.

puppet ['pʌpɪt] n **- 1.** [toy] marionnette f **- 2.** pej [person, country] fantoche m, pantin m.

puppet government n gouvernement m fantoche.

puppet show n spectacle m de marionnettes.

puppy ['pʌpɪ] (pl **-ies**) n chiot m.

puppy fat n (U) inf rondeurs fpl d'adolescence.

purchase ['pɜːtʃəs] ⬦ n achat m ⬦ vt acheter.

purchase order n bon m de commande OR d'achat.

purchase price n prix m d'achat.

purchaser ['pɜːtʃəsər] n acheteur m, -euse f.

purchase tax n Br taxe f à l'achat.

purchasing power ['pɜːtʃəsɪŋ-] n pouvoir m d'achat.

purdah ['pɜːdə] n système qui oblige les femmes musulmanes à vivre à l'écart du monde.

pure [pjʊər] adj pur(e).

purebred ['pjʊəbred] adj de race.

puree ['pjʊəreɪ] ⬦ n purée f ⬦ vt écraser en purée.

purely ['pjʊəlɪ] adv purement.

pureness ['pjʊənɪs] n pureté f.

purgative ['pɜːgətɪv] n purgatif m.

purgatory ['pɜːgətrɪ] (U) n hum [suffering] purgatoire m.

➤ **Purgatory** n [place] purgatoire m.

purge [pɜːdʒ] ⬦ n POL purge f ⬦ vt **- 1.** POL purger **- 2.** [rid] débarrasser, purger.

purification [,pjʊərɪfɪ'keɪʃn] n purification f, épuration f.

purifier ['pjʊərɪfaɪər] n épurateur m.

purify ['pjʊərɪfaɪ] (pt & pp **-ied**) vt purifier, épurer.

purist ['pjʊərɪst] n puriste mf.

puritan ['pjʊərɪtən] ◇ adj puritain(e) ◇ n puritain m, -e f.

puritanical [,pjʊərɪ'tænɪkl] adj pej puritain (e).

purity ['pjʊərətɪ] n pureté f.

purl [pɜ:l] ◇ n maille f à l'envers ◇ vt tricoter à l'envers.

purloin [pɜ:'lɔɪn] vt fml OR hum voler, dérober.

purple ['pɜ:pl] ◇ adj violet(ette) ◇ n violet m.

purport [pə'pɔ:t] vi fml : to ~ to do/be sthg prétendre faire/être qqch.

purpose ['pɜ:pəs] n - **1.** [reason] raison f, motif m - **2.** [aim] but m, objet m ; **to no ~** en vain, pour rien - **3.** [determination] détermination f.
➤ **on purpose** adv exprès.

purpose-built adj construit(e) spécialement.

purposeful ['pɜ:pəsfʊl] adj résolu(e), déterminé(e).

purposely ['pɜ:pəslɪ] adv exprès.

purr [pɜ:ʳ] ◇ n ronronnement m ◇ vi ronronner.

purse [pɜ:s] ◇ n - **1.** [for money] portemonnaie m inv, bourse f - **2.** Am [handbag] sac m à main ◇ vt [lips] pincer.

purser ['pɜ:səʳ] n commissaire m de bord.

purse snatcher [-,snætʃəʳ] n Am voleur m, -euse f à la tire.

purse strings npl : **to hold the ~** tenir les cordons de la bourse.

pursue [pə'sju:] vt - **1.** [follow] poursuivre, pourchasser - **2.** [policy, aim] poursuivre ; [question] continuer à débattre ; [matter] approfondir ; [project] donner suite à ; **to ~ an interest in sthg** se livrer à qqch.

pursuer [pə'sju:əʳ] n poursuivant m, -e f.

pursuit [pə'sju:t] n - **1.** (U) fml [attempt to obtain] recherche f, poursuite f - **2.** [chase, in sport] poursuite f ; **in ~ of** à la poursuite de ; **in hot ~ aux trousses** - **3.** [occupation] occupation f, activité f.

purveyor [pə'veɪəʳ] n fml fournisseur m.

pus [pʌs] n pus m.

push [pʊʃ] ◇ vt - **1.** [press, move - gen] pousser ; [- button] appuyer - **2.** [encourage] : **to ~ sb (to do sthg)** inciter OR pousser qqn (à faire qqch) - **3.** [force] : **to ~ sb (into doing sthg)** forcer OR obliger qqn (à faire qqch) - **4.** inf [promote] faire de la réclame pour - **5.** drugs sl vendre, fournir ◇ vi - **1.** [gen] pousser ; [on button] appuyer - **2.** [campaign] : **to ~ for sthg** faire pression pour obtenir qqch ◇ n

- **1.** [with hand] poussée f - **2.** [forceful effort] effort m - **3.** phr : **to give sb the ~** Br inf [end relationship] plaquer qqn ; [dismiss] ficher qqn à la porte.
➤ **push ahead** vi continuer, persévérer ; **to ~ ahead with sthg** persévérer dans qqch, continuer (à faire) qqch.
➤ **push around** vt sep inf fig marcher sur les pieds de.
➤ **push in** vi [in queue] resquiller.
➤ **push off** vi inf filer, se sauver.
➤ **push on** vi continuer.
➤ **push over** vt sep faire tomber.
➤ **push through** vt sep [law, reform] faire accepter.

pushbike ['pʊʃbaɪk] n Br vélo m.

push-button adj à touches.

pushcart ['pʊʃkɑ:t] n charrette f à bras.

pushchair ['pʊʃtʃeəʳ] n Br poussette f.

pushed [pʊʃt] adj inf : **to be ~ for sthg** être à court de qqch ; **to be hard ~ to do sthg** avoir du mal OR de la peine à faire qqch.

pusher ['pʊʃəʳ] n drugs sl dealer m.

pushing ['pʊʃɪŋ] prep inf : **he's ~ 40** il frise la quarantaine.

pushover ['pʊʃ,əʊvəʳ] n inf : **it's a ~** c'est un jeu d'enfant.

push-start vt faire démarrer en poussant.

push-up n pompe f, traction f.

pushy ['pʊʃɪ] (compar -ier ; superl -iest) adj pej qui se met toujours en avant.

puss [pʊs], **pussy (cat)** ['pʊsɪ-] n inf minet m, minou m

pussy willow n saule m.

put [pʊt] (pt & pp **put**, cont **-ting**) vt - **1.** [gen] mettre ; **to ~ responsibility on sb** donner des responsabilités à qqn - **2.** [place] mettre, poser, placer ; **to ~ the children to bed** coucher les enfants - **3.** [express] dire, exprimer - **4.** [question] poser ; **to ~ it to sb that ...** suggérer à qqn que ... - **5.** [estimate] estimer, évaluer - **6.** [invest] : **to ~ money into** investir l'argent dans ; **I've ~ a lot of time into this work** j'ai passé beaucoup de temps à faire ce travail.
➤ **put across** vt sep [ideas] faire comprendre.
➤ **put aside** vt sep - **1.** [place on one side] mettre de côté, poser - **2.** fig [money] mettre de côté ; [differences] ne pas tenir compte de.
➤ **put away** vt sep - **1.** [tidy away] ranger - **2.** inf [lock up] enfermer.
➤ **put back** vt sep - **1.** [replace] remettre (à sa place OR en place) - **2.** [postpone] remettre - **3.** [clock, watch] retarder.

put by *vt sep* [money] mettre de côté.

put down *vt sep* - **1.** [lay down] poser, déposer - **2.** [quell - rebellion] réprimer - **3.** inf [criticize] humilier - **4.** [write down] inscrire, noter - **5.** Br [kill] : **to have a dog/cat ~ down** faire piquer un chien/chat.

put down to *vt sep* attribuer à.

put forward *vt sep* - **1.** [propose] proposer, avancer - **2.** [meeting, clock, watch] avancer.

put in *vt sep* - **1.** [spend - time] passer - **2.** [submit] présenter.

put off *vt sep* - **1.** [postpone] remettre (à plus tard) - **2.** [cause to wait] décommander - **3.** [discourage] dissuader - **4.** [disturb] déconcerter, troubler - **5.** [cause to dislike] dégoûter - **6.** [switch off - radio, TV] éteindre.

put on *vt sep* - **1.** [clothes] mettre, enfiler - **2.** [arrange - exhibition etc] organiser ; [- play] monter - **3.** [gain] : **to ~ on weight** prendre du poids, grossir - **4.** [switch on - radio, TV] allumer, mettre ; **to ~ the light on** allumer (la lumière) ; **to ~ the brake on** freiner - **5.** [record, CD, tape] passer, mettre - **6.** [start cooking] mettre à cuire - **7.** [pretend - gen] feindre ; [- accent etc] prendre - **8.** [bet] parier, miser - **9.** [add] ajouter - **10.** inf [tease] faire marcher.

put onto *vt sep* : **to ~ sb onto sb/sthg** indiquer qqn/qqch à qqn.

put out *vt sep* - **1.** [place outside] mettre dehors - **2.** [book, statement] publier ; [record] sortir - **3.** [fire, cigarette] éteindre ; **to ~ the light out** éteindre (la lumière) - **4.** [extend - hand] tendre - **5.** inf [injure] : **to ~ one's back/hip out** se démettre le dos/la hanche - **6.** [annoy, upset] : **to be ~ out** être contrarié(e) - **7.** [inconvenience] déranger ; **to ~ o.s. out** se donner du mal.

put over *vt sep* [ideas] faire comprendre.

put through *vt sep* TELEC passer.

put together *vt sep* - **1.** [assemble - machine, furniture] monter, assembler ; [- team] réunir ; [- report] composer - **2.** [combine] mettre ensemble ; **more than all the others ~ together** plus que tous les autres réunis - **3.** [organize] monter, organiser.

put up $\diamond$ *vt sep* - **1.** [build - gen] ériger ; [- tent] dresser - **2.** [umbrella] ouvrir ; [flag] hisser - **3.** [fix to wall] accrocher - **4.** [provide - money] fournir - **5.** [propose - candidate] proposer - **6.** [increase] augmenter - **7.** [provide accommodation for] loger, héberger $\diamond$ *vt fus* : **to ~ up a fight** se défendre.

put upon *vt fus* Br : **to be ~ upon** se laisser faire.

put up to *vt sep* : **to ~ sb up to sthg** pousser OR inciter qqn à faire qqch.

put up with *vt fus* supporter.

putative ['pju:tətɪv] *adj* putatif(ive).

put-down *n* inf rebuffade *f*.

putrefaction [,pju:trɪ'fækʃn] *n* putréfaction *f*.

putrefy ['pju:trɪfaɪ] (*pt* & *pp* -**ied**) *vi* se putréfier.

putrid ['pju:trɪd] *adj* putride.

putsch [pʊtʃ] *n* putsch *m*.

putt [pʌt] $\diamond$ *n* putt *m* $\diamond$ *vt* & *vi* putter.

putter ['pʌtə^r] *n* [club] putter *m*.

putter about, putter around *vi* Am bricoler.

putting green ['pʌtɪŋ-] *n* green *m*.

putty ['pʌtɪ] *n* mastic *m*.

put-up job *n* inf coup *m* monté.

put-upon *adj* inf qui se laisse marcher sur les pieds.

puzzle ['pʌzl] $\diamond$ *n* - **1.** [toy] puzzle *m* ; [mental] devinette *f* - **2.** [mystery] mystère *m*, énigme *f* $\diamond$ *vt* rendre perplexe $\diamond$ *vi* : **to ~ over sthg** essayer de comprendre qqch.

puzzle out *vt sep* comprendre.

puzzled ['pʌzld] *adj* perplexe.

puzzling ['pʌzlɪŋ] *adj* curieux(euse).

PVC (*abbr of* **polyvinyl chloride**) *n* PVC *m*.

Pvt. *abbr of* **Private**.

pw (*abbr of* **per week**) p.sem.

PWR (*abbr of* **pressurized-water reactor**) *n* REP *m*.

PX (*abbr of* **post exchange**) *n* magasin de l'armée.

pygmy ['pɪgmɪ] (*pl* -**ies**) *n* pygmée *m*.

pyjama [pə'dʒɑːmə] *comp* de pyjama.

pyjamas [pə'dʒɑːməz] *npl* pyjama *m* ; **a pair of ~** un pyjama.

pylon ['paɪlən] *n* pylône *m*.

pyramid ['pɪrəmɪd] *n* pyramide *f*.

pyramid selling *n* vente *f* en pyramide.

pyre ['paɪə^r] *n* bûcher *m* funéraire.

Pyrenean [,pɪrə'niːən] *adj* pyrénéen(enne).

Pyrenees [,pɪrə'niːz] *npl* : **the ~** les Pyrénées *fpl*.

Pyrex® ['paɪreks] $\diamond$ *n* Pyrex® *m* $\diamond$ *comp* en Pyrex®.

pyromaniac [,paɪrə'meɪnɪæk] *n* pyromane *mf*.

pyrotechnics [,paɪrəʊ'teknɪks] $\diamond$ *n* (U) pyrotechnie *f* $\diamond$ *npl* fig [skill] feu *m* d'artifice.

python ['paɪθn] (*pl inv* OR -**s**) *n* python *m*.

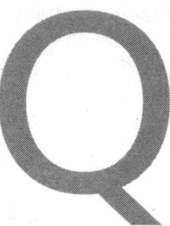

q (*pl* **q's** OR **qs**), **Q** (*pl* **Q's** OR **Qs**) [kjuː] *n* [letter] q *m inv*, Q *m inv*.

Qatar [kæ'tɑːʳ] Qatar *m*, Katar *m* ; **in ~** au Qatar.

QC (*abbr of* **Queen's Counsel**) *n* ≃ bâtonnier *m* de l'ordre.

QED (*abbr of* **quod erat demonstrandum**) CQFD.

QM *abbr of* **quartermaster.**

q.t., QT (*abbr of* **quiet**) *inf* : **on the ~** en douce.

qty (*abbr of* **quantity**) qté.

quack [kwæk] <> *n* - **1.** [noise] coin-coin *m inv* - **2.** *inf pej* [doctor] charlatan *m* <> *vi* faire coin-coin.

quad [kwɒd] - **1.** *abbr of* **quadruple** - **2.** *abbr of* **quadrangle.**

quadrangle ['kwɒdræŋgl] *n* - **1.** [figure] quadrilatère *m* - **2.** [courtyard] cour *f*.

quadrant ['kwɒdrənt] *n* quadrant *m*.

quadraphonic [ˌkwɒdrə'fɒnɪk] *adj* quadriphonique.

quadrilateral [ˌkwɒdrɪ'lætərəl] <> *adj* quadrilatéral(e) <> *n* quadrilatère *m*.

quadruped ['kwɒdruped] *n* quadrupède *m*.

quadruple [kwɒ'druːpl] <> *adj* quadruple <> *vt* & *vi* quadrupler.

quadruplets ['kwɒdruplɪts] *npl* quadruplés *mpl*.

quads [kwɒdz] *npl inf* quadruplés *mpl*.

quaff [kwɒf] *vt dated* boire (à longs traits).

quagmire ['kwægmaɪəʳ] *n* bourbier *m*.

quail [kweɪl] (*pl inv* OR **-s**) <> *n* caille *f* <> *vi* literary reculer.

quaint [kweɪnt] *adj* pittoresque.

quaintness ['kweɪntnɪs] *n* pittoresque *m*.

quake [kweɪk] <> *n* (*abbr of* **earthquake**) *inf* tremblement *m* de terre <> *vi* trembler.

Quaker ['kweɪkəʳ] *n* quaker *m*, -eresse *f*.

qualification [ˌkwɒlɪfɪ'keɪʃn] *n* - **1.** [certificate] diplôme *m* - **2.** [quality, skill] compétence *f* - **3.** [qualifying statement] réserve *f*.

qualified ['kwɒlɪfaɪd] *adj* - **1.** [trained] diplô-mé(e) - **2.** [able] : **to be ~ to do sthg** avoir la compétence nécessaire pour faire qqch - **3.** [limited] restreint(e), modéré(e).

qualify ['kwɒlɪfaɪ] (*pt* & *pp* **-ied**) <> *vt* - **1.** [modify] apporter des réserves à - **2.** [entitle] : **to ~ sb to do sthg** qualifier qqn pour faire qqch <> *vi* - **1.** [pass exams] obtenir un diplôme - **2.** [be entitled] : **to ~ (for sthg)** avoir droit (à qqch), remplir les conditions requises (pour qqch) - **3.** SPORT se qualifier.

qualifying ['kwɒlɪfaɪɪŋ] *adj* - **1.** [modifying] nuancé(e) - **2.** [entitling] : **~ exam** examen *m* d'entrée - **3.** SPORT [time] qui permet de se qualifier ; **~ round** série *f* éliminatoire.

qualitative ['kwɒlɪtətɪv] *adj* qualitatif(ive).

quality ['kwɒlətɪ] (*pl* **-ies**) <> *n* qualité *f* <> *comp* de qualité.

quality control *n* contrôle *m* de qualité.

quality press *n* Br : **the ~** la presse sérieuse.

qualms [kwɑːmz] *npl* doutes *mpl*.

quandary ['kwɒndərɪ] (*pl* **-ies**) *n* embarras *m* ; **to be in a ~ about** OR **over sthg** être bien embarrassé à propos de qqch.

quango ['kwæŋgəʊ] (*pl* **-s**) *n* (*abbr of* **quasiautonomous non-governmental organization**) Br usu pej commission indépendante financée par l'État.

quantifiable [kwɒntɪ'faɪəbl] *adj* quantifiable.

quantify ['kwɒntɪfaɪ] (*pt* & *pp* **-ied**) *vt* quantifier.

quantitative ['kwɒntɪtətɪv] *adj* quantitatif(ive).

quantity ['kwɒntətɪ] (*pl* **-ies**) *n* quantité *f* ; **in ~** en quantité ; **an unknown ~** une inconnue.

quantity surveyor *n* métreur *m*, -euse *f*.

quantum leap ['kwɒntəm-] *n* fig bond *m* en avant.

quantum theory ['kwɒntəm-] *n* théorie *f* des quanta.

quarantine ['kwɒrəntiːn] <> *n* quarantaine *f* ; **to be in ~** être en quarantaine <> *vt* mettre en quarantaine.

quark [kwɑːk] *n* quark *m*.

quarrel ['kwɒrəl] (Br *pt* & *pp* **-led** ; cont **-ling** ; Am *pt* & *pp* **-ed** ; cont **-ing**) <> *n* querelle *f*, dispute *f* ; **I have no ~ with her** je n'ai rien contre elle <> *vi* : **to ~ (with)** se quereller (avec), se disputer (avec).

quarrelsome ['kwɒrəlsəm] *adj* querelleur (euse).

quarry ['kwɒrɪ] (*pl* **-ies**, *pt* & *pp* **-ied**) <> *n*

- 1. [place] carrière f **- 2.** [prey] proie f ◇ vt extraire.

quarry tile n carreau m.

quart [kwɔːt] n = 1,136 litre Br, = 0,946 litre Am, ≃ litre m.

quarter ['kwɔːtəʳ] n **- 1.** [fraction, weight] quart m ; a ~ past two Br, a ~ after two Am deux heures et quart ; a ~ to two Br, a ~ of two Am deux heures moins le quart **- 2.** [of year] trimestre m **- 3.** Am [coin] pièce f de 25 cents **- 4.** [area in town] quartier m **- 5.** [direction] : from all ~s de tous côtés.
◆ **quarters** npl [rooms] quartiers mpl.
◆ **at close quarters** adv de près.

quarterback ['kwɔːtəbæk] n SPORT quarterback m, quart-arrière mf Can.

quarterdeck ['kwɔːtədek] n gaillard m d'arrière.

quarterfinal [ˌkwɔːtə'faɪnl] n quart m de finale.

quarter-hour adj [intervals] d'un quart d'heure.

quarter light n Br AUT déflecteur m.

quarterly ['kwɔːtəlɪ] (pl **-ies**) ◇ adj trimestriel(elle) ◇ adv trimestriellement ◇ n publication f trimestrielle.

quartermaster ['kwɔːtəˌmɑːstəʳ] n MIL intendant m.

quarter note n Am MUS noire f.

quarter sessions npl [in UK] tribunal m de grande instance ; [in US] dans certains États, tribunal local à compétence criminelle, pouvant avoir des fonctions administratives.

quartet [kwɔː'tet] n quatuor m.

quarto ['kwɔːtəʊ] (pl **-s**) n in-quarto m inv.

quartz [kwɔːts] n quartz m.

quartz watch n montre f à quartz.

quasar ['kweɪzɑːʳ] n quasar m.

quash [kwɒʃ] vt **- 1.** [sentence] annuler, casser **- 2.** [rebellion] réprimer.

quasi- ['kweɪzaɪ] prefix quasi-.

quaver ['kweɪvəʳ] ◇ n **- 1.** MUS croche f **- 2.** [in voice] tremblement m, chevrotement m ◇ vi trembler, chevroter.

quavering ['kweɪvərɪŋ] adj tremblant(e), chevrotant(e).

quay [kiː] n quai m.

quayside ['kiːsaɪd] n bord m du quai.

queasy ['kwiːzɪ] (compar **-ier** ; superl **-iest**) adj : to feel ~ avoir mal au cœur.

Quebec [kwɪ'bek] n **- 1.** [province] Québec m ; in ~ au Québec **- 2.** [city] Québec.

Quebecer, Quebecker [kwɪ'bekəʳ] n Québécois m, -e f.

queen [kwiːn] n **- 1.** [gen] reine f **- 2.** [playing card] dame f.

Queen Mother n : the ~ la reine mère.

Queen's Counsel n Br avocat m de la Couronne.

Queen's English n Br : the ~ l'anglais m correct.

queen's evidence n Br : to turn ~ témoigner contre ses complices.

queer [kwɪəʳ] ◇ adj [odd] étrange, bizarre ; I'm feeling a bit ~ je ne me sens pas très bien ◇ n inf pej pédé m, homosexuel m.

quell [kwel] vt réprimer, étouffer.

quench [kwentʃ] vt : to ~ one's thirst se désaltérer.

querulous ['kwerʊləs] adj [child] ronchonneur(euse) ; [voice] plaintif(ive).

query ['kwɪərɪ] (pl **-ies**, pt & pp **-ied**) ◇ n question f ◇ vt mettre en doute, douter de.

quest [kwest] n literary : ~ (for) quête f (de).

question ['kwestʃn] ◇ n **- 1.** [gen] question f ; to ask (sb) a ~ poser une question (à qqn) **- 2.** [doubt] doute m ; to call OR bring sthg into ~ mettre qqch en doute ; it's open to ~ whether... on peut se demander si... ; without ~ incontestablement, sans aucun doute ; beyond ~ [know] sans aucun doute **- 3.** phr : there's no ~ of ... il n'est pas question de ... ◇ vt **- 1.** [interrogate] questionner **- 2.** [express doubt about] mettre en question OR doute.
◆ **in question** adv : the ... in ~ le/la/les ... en question.
◆ **out of the question** adv hors de question.

questionable ['kwestʃənəbl] adj **- 1.** [uncertain] discutable **- 2.** [not right, not honest] douteux(euse).

questioner ['kwestʃənəʳ] n personne f qui pose une question.

questioning ['kwestʃənɪŋ] ◇ adj interrogateur(trice) ◇ n (U) interrogation f.

question mark n point m d'interrogation.

question master esp Br, **quizmaster** esp Am ['kwɪzˌmɑːstəʳ] n meneur m de jeu.

questionnaire [ˌkwestʃə'neəʳ] n questionnaire m.

question time n Br POL heure réservée aux questions des députés.

queue [kjuː] Br ◇ n queue f, file f ; to jump the ~ resquiller, passer avant son tour ◇ vi faire la queue.

queue-jump *vi* Br resquiller.

quibble ['kwɪbl] **pej** ⟨⟩ *n* chicane *f* ⟨⟩ *vi* : **to ~ (over** OR **about)** chicaner (à propos de).

quiche [kiːʃ] *n* quiche *f*.

quick [kwɪk] ⟨⟩ *adj* **- 1.** [gen] rapide **- 2.** [response, decision] prompt(e), rapide ⟨⟩ *adv* vite, rapidement.

quicken ['kwɪkn] ⟨⟩ *vt* accélérer, presser ⟨⟩ *vi* s'accélérer.

quickly ['kwɪklɪ] *adv* **- 1.** [rapidly] vite, rapidement **- 2.** [without delay] promptement, immédiatement.

quickness ['kwɪknɪs] *n* [speed] rapidité *f*.

quicksand ['kwɪksænd] *n* sables *mpl* mouvants.

quicksilver ['kwɪkˌsɪlvəʳ] *n* vif-argent *m*, mercure *m*.

quickstep ['kwɪkstep] *n* : **the ~** le fox-trot.

quick-tempered *adj* emporté(e).

quick-witted [-'wɪtɪd] *adj* [person] à l'esprit vif.

quid [kwɪd] (*pl inv*) *n* Br inf livre *f*.

quid pro quo [-'kwəʊ] (*pl* quid pro quos [-'kwəʊz]) *n* contrepartie *f*.

quiescent [kwaɪ'esnt] *adj* fml immobile.

quiet ['kwaɪət] ⟨⟩ *adj* **- 1.** [not noisy] tranquille ; [voice] bas (basse) ; [engine] silencieux(euse) ; **be ~!** taisez-vous! **- 2.** [not busy] calme **- 3.** [silent] silencieux(euse) ; **to keep ~ about sthg** ne rien dire à propos de qqch, garder qqch secret **- 4.** [intimate] intime ; **to have a ~ word with sb** dire deux mots en particulier à qqn **- 5.** [colour] discret(ète), sobre ⟨⟩ *n* tranquillité *f ;* **on the ~** inf en douce ⟨⟩ *vt* Am calmer, apaiser.

🔹 **quiet down** ⟨⟩ *vt sep* calmer, apaiser ⟨⟩ *vi* se calmer.

quieten ['kwaɪətn] *vt* calmer, apaiser.

🔹 **quieten down** ⟨⟩ *vt sep* calmer, apaiser ⟨⟩ *vi* se calmer.

quietly ['kwaɪətlɪ] *adv* **- 1.** [without noise] sans faire de bruit, silencieusement ; [say] doucement **- 2.** [without excitement] tranquillement, calmement **- 3.** [without fuss - leave] discrètement.

quietness ['kwaɪətnɪs] *(U) n* **- 1.** [silence] silence *m* **- 2.** [peacefulness] calme *m*, tranquillité *f*.

quiff [kwɪf] *n* Br mèche *f*.

quill (pen) [kwɪl-] *n* plume *f* d'oie.

quilt [kwɪlt] *n* [padded] édredon *m ;* **(continental) ~** couette *f*.

quilted ['kwɪltɪd] *adj* matelassé(e).

quince [kwɪns] *n* coing *m*.

quinine [kwɪ'niːn] *n* quinine *f*.

quins Br [kwɪnz], **quints** Am [kwɪnts] *npl* inf quintuplés *mpl*.

quintessential [kwɪntə'senʃl] *adj* typique.

quintet [kwɪn'tet] *n* quintette *m*.

quints Am = quins.

quintuplets [kwɪn'tjuːplɪts] *npl* quintuplés *mpl*.

quip [kwɪp] (*pt* & *pp* **-ped** ; *cont* **-ping**) ⟨⟩ *n* raillerie *f* ⟨⟩ *vi* railler.

quire ['kwaɪəʳ] *n* cahier *m*.

quirk [kwɜːk] *n* bizarrerie *f ;* **a ~ of fate** un caprice du sort.

quirky ['kwɜːkɪ] (*compar* **-ier** ; *superl* **-iest**) *adj* étrange, bizarre.

quit [kwɪt] (Br *pt* & *pp* quit OR **-ted**, *cont* **-ting**, Am *pt* & *pp* quit, *cont* **-ting**) ⟨⟩ *vt* **- 1.** [resign from] quitter **- 2.** [stop] : **to ~ smoking** arrêter de fumer ⟨⟩ *vi* **- 1.** [resign] démissionner **- 2.** [give up] abandonner.

quite [kwaɪt] *adv* **- 1.** [completely] tout à fait, complètement ; **I ~ agree** je suis entièrement d'accord ; **not ~** pas tout à fait ; **I don't ~ understand** je ne comprends pas bien **- 2.** [fairly] assez, plutôt **- 3.** [for emphasis] : **she's ~ a singer** c'est une chanteuse formidable ; **it was ~ a surprise** c'était une drôle de surprise **- 4.** [to express agreement] : **~ (so)!** exactement!

Quito ['kiːtəʊ] *n* Quito.

quits [kwɪts] *adj* inf : **to be ~ (with sb)** être quitte (envers qqn) ; **to call it ~** en rester là.

quitter ['kwɪtəʳ] *n* inf pej dégonflé *m*, -e *f*.

quiver ['kwɪvəʳ] ⟨⟩ *n* **- 1.** [shiver] frisson *m* **- 2.** [for arrows] carquois *m* ⟨⟩ *vi* frissonner.

quivering ['kwɪvərɪŋ] *adj* frissonnant(e).

quixotic [kwɪk'sɒtɪk] *adj* chevaleresque.

quiz [kwɪz] (*pl* quizzes, *pt* & *pp* **-zed**, *cont* **-zing**) ⟨⟩ *n* **- 1.** [gen] quiz *m*, jeu-concours *m* **- 2.** Am SCH interrogation *f* ⟨⟩ *vt* : **to ~ sb (about sthg)** interroger qqn (au sujet de qqch).

quizmaster esp Am = question master.

quizzical ['kwɪzɪkl] *adj* narquois(e), moqueur(euse).

quoits [kwɔɪts] *n* (U) jeu *m* de palet.

Quonset hut ['kwɒnsɪt-] *n* Am hutte *f* préfabriquée en tôle.

quorate ['kwɔːreɪt] *adj* Br dont le quorum est atteint.

quorum ['kwɔːrəm] *n* quorum *m*.

quota ['kwəʊtə] *n* quota *m*.

quotation [kwəʊ'teɪʃn] *n* **- 1.** [citation] citation *f* **- 2.** COMM devis *m*.

quotation marks *npl* guillemets *mpl* ; in ~ entre guillemets.

quote [kwəʊt] ◇ *n* - **1.** [citation] citation *f* - **2.** COMM devis *m* ◇ *vt* - **1.** [cite] citer - **2.** COMM indiquer, spécifier ◇ *vi* - **1.** [cite] : **to ~ (from sthg)** citer (qqch) - **2.** COMM : **to ~ for sthg** établir un devis pour qqch.

~ **quotes** *npl* inf guillemets *mpl*.

quoted company [ˈkwəʊtɪd-] *n* Br société *f* cotée en Bourse.

quotient [ˈkwəʊʃnt] *n* quotient *m*.

qv (*abbr of* quod vide) *expression renvoyant le lecteur à une autre entrée dans une encyclopédie.*

qwerty keyboard [ˈkwɜːtɪ-] *n* Br clavier *m* QWERTY.

r (*pl* **r's** OR **rs**), **R** (*pl* **R's** OR **Rs**) [ɑːʳ] *n* [letter] r *m inv*, R *m inv*.

~ **R** - **1.** (*abbr of* right) dr. - **2.** *abbr of* **River** - **3.** (*abbr of* Réaumur) R - **4.** (*abbr of* restricted) *aux États-Unis, indique qu'un film est interdit aux moins de 17 ans* - **5.** Am *abbr of* Republican - **6.** Br (*abbr of* Rex) *suit le nom d'un roi* - **7.** Br (*abbr of* Regina) *suit le nom d'une reine.*

RA (*abbr of* Royal Academy) *n académie britannique des beaux-arts* (*organisant notamment un salon annuel*).

RAAF (*abbr of* Royal Australian Air Force) *n armée de l'air australienne.*

Rabat [rəˈbɑːt] *n* Rabat.

rabbi [ˈræbaɪ] *n* rabbin *m*.

rabbit [ˈræbɪt] *n* lapin *m*.

rabbit hole *n* terrier *m*.

rabbit hutch *n* clapier *m*.

rabbit warren *n* garenne *f*.

rabble [ˈræbl] *n* cohue *f*.

rabble-rousing *adj* [speech] qui incite à la violence.

rabid [ˈræbɪd, ˈreɪbɪd] *adj* lit & fig enragé(e).

rabies [ˈreɪbiːz] *n* rage *f*.

RAC (*abbr of* Royal Automobile Club) *n club automobile britannique,* ≃ TCF *m*, ≃ ACF *m*.

raccoon [rəˈkuːn] *n* raton *m* laveur, chat *m* sauvage Can.

race [reɪs] ◇ *n* - **1.** [competition] course *f* - **2.** [people, ethnic background] race *f* ◇ *vt* - **1.** [compete against] faire la course avec - **2.** [horse] faire courir ◇ *vi* - **1.** [compete] courir ; **to ~ against sb** faire la course avec qqn - **2.** [rush] : **to ~ in/out** entrer/sortir à toute allure - **3.** [pulse] être très rapide - **4.** [engine] s'emballer.

race car Am = racing car.

racecourse [ˈreɪskɔːs] *n* champ *m* de courses.

race driver Am = racing driver.

racehorse [ˈreɪshɔːs] *n* cheval *m* de course.

race meeting *n* courses *fpl*.

race relations *npl* relations *fpl* interraciales.

race riot *n* émeute *f* raciale.

racetrack [ˈreɪstræk] *n* piste *f*.

racial discrimination [ˈreɪʃl-] *n* discrimination *f* raciale.

racialism *etc* [ˈreɪʃəlɪzm] = racism *etc*.

racing [ˈreɪsɪŋ] *n* (U) : (horse) ~ les courses *fpl*.

racing car Br, **race car** Am *n* voiture *f* de course.

racing driver Br, **race driver** Am *n* coureur *m* automobile, pilote *m* de course.

racism [ˈreɪsɪzm] *n* racisme *m*.

racist [ˈreɪsɪst] ◇ *adj* raciste ◇ *n* raciste *mf*.

rack [ræk] ◇ *n* [for bottles] casier *m* ; [for luggage] porte-bagages *m inv* ; [for plates] égouttoir *m* ; **toast ~** porte-toasts *m inv* ◇ *vt* literary : **to be ~ed by** OR **with sthg** être tenaillé(e) par qqch.

racket [ˈrækɪt] *n* - **1.** [noise] boucan *m* - **2.** [illegal activity] racket *m* - **3.** SPORT raquette *f*.

racketeering [ˌrækəˈtɪərɪŋ] *n* racket *m*.

raconteur [ˌrækɒnˈtɜːʳ] *n* conteur *m*, -euse *f*.

racquet [ˈrækɪt] *n* raquette *f*.

racy [ˈreɪsɪ] (*compar* -**ier** ; *superl* -**iest**) *adj* [novel, style] osé(e).

RADA [ˈrɑːdə] (*abbr of* Royal Academy of Dramatic Art) *n conservatoire britannique d'art dramatique.*

radar [ˈreɪdɑːʳ] *n* radar *m*.

radar trap *n* piège *m* radar.

radial (tyre) [ˈreɪdjəl-] *n* pneu *m* à carcasse radiale.

radian [ˈreɪdjən] *n* radian *m*.

radiance ['reɪdjəns] n (U) rayonnement m, éclat m.

radiant ['reɪdjənt] adj - **1.** [happy] radieux(euse) - **2.** literary [brilliant] rayonnant(e) - **3.** TECH radiant(e).

radiate ['reɪdɪeɪt] ⋄ vt - **1.** [heat, light] émettre, dégager - **2.** fig [confidence, health] respirer ⋄ vi - **1.** [heat, light] irradier - **2.** [roads, lines] rayonner.

radiation [,reɪdɪ'eɪʃn] n [radioactive] radiation f.

radiation sickness n mal m des rayons.

radiator ['reɪdɪeɪtə'] n radiateur m.

radiator grille n calandre f.

radical ['rædɪkl] ⋄ adj radical(e) ⋄ n POL radical m, -e f.

radically ['rædɪklɪ] adv radicalement.

radii ['reɪdɪaɪ] pl ⊳ radius.

radio ['reɪdɪəʊ] (pl -s) ⋄ n radio f ; on the ~ à la radio ⋄ comp de radio ⋄ vt [person] appeler par radio ; [information] envoyer par radio.

radioactive [,reɪdɪəʊ'æktɪv] adj radioactif(ive).

radioactive waste n (U) déchets mpl radioactifs.

radioactivity [,reɪdɪəʊæk'tɪvətɪ] n radioactivité f.

radio alarm n radio-réveil m.

radio-controlled [-kən'trəʊld] adj téléguidé(e).

radio frequency n radiofréquence f.

radiogram ['reɪdɪəʊ,græm] n [message] radiogramme m.

radiographer [,reɪdɪ'ɒgrəfə'] n radiologue mf.

radiography [,reɪdɪ'ɒgrəfɪ] n radiographie f.

radiology [,reɪdɪ'ɒlədʒɪ] n radiologie f.

radiopaging ['reɪdɪəʊ,peɪdʒɪŋ] n système d'appel par récepteur de poche.

radiotelephone [,reɪdɪəʊ'telɪfəʊn] n radiotéléphone m.

radiotherapist [,reɪdɪəʊ'θerəpɪst] n radiothérapeute mf.

radiotherapy [,reɪdɪəʊ'θerəpɪ] n radiothérapie f.

radish ['rædɪʃ] n radis m.

radium ['reɪdɪəm] n radium m.

radius ['reɪdɪəs] (pl radii ['reɪdɪaɪ]) n - **1.** MATH rayon m - **2.** ANAT radius m.

radon ['reɪdɒn] n radon m.

RAF [ɑːreɪ'ef, ræf] n abbr of Royal Air Force.

raffia ['ræfɪə] n raphia m.

raffish ['ræfɪʃ] adj dissolu(e).

raffle ['ræfl] ⋄ n tombola f ⋄ vt mettre en tombola.

raft [rɑːft] n - **1.** [of wood] radeau m - **2.** [large number] tas m ; a ~ of policies POL un train de mesures.

rafter ['rɑːftə'] n chevron m.

rag [ræg] n - **1.** [piece of cloth] chiffon m ; it's like a red ~ to a bull c'est comme la couleur rouge pour le taureau - **2.** pej [newspaper] torchon m.
➡ **rags** npl [clothes] guenilles fpl ; from ~s to riches de la misère à la richesse.

ragamuffin ['rægə,mʌfɪn] n galopin m.

rag-and-bone man n chiffonnier m.

ragbag ['rægbæg] n fig ramassis m.

rag doll n poupée f de chiffon.

rage [reɪdʒ] ⋄ n - **1.** [fury] rage f, fureur f - **2.** inf [fashion] : to be (all) the ~ faire fureur ⋄ vi - **1.** [person] être furieux(euse) - **2.** [storm, argument] faire rage.

ragged ['rægɪd] adj - **1.** [person] en haillons ; [clothes] en lambeaux - **2.** [line, edge, performance] inégal(e).

raging ['reɪdʒɪŋ] adj [thirst, headache] atroce ; [storm] déchaîné(e).

ragout ['rægu:] n ragoût m.

ragtime ['rægtaɪm] n ragtime m.

rag trade n inf : the ~ la confection.

rag week n Br semaine de carnaval organisée par des étudiants afin de collecter des fonds pour des œuvres charitables.

raid [reɪd] ⋄ n - **1.** MIL raid m - **2.** [by criminals] hold-up m inv ; [by police] descente f ⋄ vt - **1.** MIL faire un raid sur - **2.** [subj : criminals] faire un hold-up dans ; [subj : police] faire une descente dans.

raider ['reɪdə'] n - **1.** [attacker] agresseur m - **2.** [thief] braqueur m.

rail [reɪl] ⋄ n - **1.** [on ship] bastingage m ; [on staircase] rampe f ; [on walkway] garde-fou m - **2.** [bar] barre f - **3.** RAIL rail m ; by ~ en train ⋄ comp [transport, travel] par le train ; [strike] des cheminots.

railcard ['reɪlkɑːd] n Br carte donnant droit à des tarifs préférentiels sur les chemins de fer.

railing ['reɪlɪŋ] n [fence] grille f ; [on ship] bastingage m ; [on staircase] rampe f ; [on walkway] garde-fou m.

railway Br ['reɪlweɪ], **railroad** Am ['reɪlrəʊd] n [system, company] chemin m de fer ; [track] voie f ferrée.

railway engine n locomotive f.

railway line n [route] ligne f de chemin de fer ; [track] voie f ferrée.

railwayman ['reɪlweɪmən] (pl -men [-mən]) n Br cheminot m.

railway station n gare f.

railway track n voie f ferrée.

rain [reɪn] ◇ n pluie f ◇ v impers METEOR pleuvoir ; **it's ~ing** il pleut ◇ vi [fall like rain] pleuvoir.

◆ **rain down** vi pleuvoir.

◆ **rain off** Br, **rain out** Am vt sep annuler à cause de la pluie.

rainbow ['reɪnbəʊ] n arc-en-ciel m.

rain check n Am : **I'll take a ~ (on that)** une autre fois peut-être.

raincoat ['reɪnkəʊt] n imperméable m.

raindrop ['reɪndrɒp] n goutte f de pluie.

rainfall ['reɪnfɔːl] n [shower] chute f de pluie ; [amount] précipitations fpl.

rain forest n forêt f tropicale humide.

rain gauge n pluviomètre m.

rainproof ['reɪnpruːf] adj imperméable.

rainstorm ['reɪnstɔːm] n trombe f d'eau, pluie f torrentielle.

rainwater ['reɪn,wɔːtəʳ] n eau f de pluie.

rainy ['reɪnɪ] (compar -ier ; superl -iest) adj pluvieux(euse).

raise [reɪz] ◇ vt - **1.** [lift up] lever ; **to ~ o.s.** se lever - **2.** [increase - gen] augmenter ; [- standards] élever ; **to ~ one's voice** élever la voix - **3.** [obtain] : **to ~ money** [from donations] collecter des fonds ; [by selling, borrowing] se procurer de l'argent - **4.** [subject, doubt] soulever ; [memories] évoquer - **5.** [children, cattle] élever - **6.** [crops] cultiver - **7.** [build] ériger, élever ◇ n Am augmentation f (de salaire).

raisin ['reɪzn] n raisin m sec.

Raj [rɑːdʒ] n : **the ~** l'empire britannique aux Indes.

rajah ['rɑːdʒə] n raja m, rajah m.

rake [reɪk] ◇ n - **1.** [implement] râteau m - **2.** dated & literary [immoral man] débauché m ◇ vt [path, lawn] ratisser ; [leaves] râteler.

◆ **rake in** vt sep inf amasser.

◆ **rake up** vt sep [past] fouiller dans.

rake-off n inf pourcentage m, commission f.

rakish ['reɪkɪʃ] adj - **1.** [dissolute] dissolu(e) - **2.** [jaunty] désinvolte.

rally ['rælɪ] (pl -ies, pt & pp -ied) ◇ n - **1.** [meeting] rassemblement m - **2.** [car race] rallye m - **3.** SPORT [exchange of shots] échange m ◇ vt rallier ◇ vi - **1.** [supporters] se rallier - **2.** [patient] aller mieux ; [prices] remonter.

◆ **rally round** ◇ vt fus apporter son soutien à ◇ vi inf venir en aide.

rallying ['rælɪɪŋ] n (U) rallye m.

rallying cry n cri m de ralliement.

rallying point n point m de rassemblement

ram [ræm] (pt & pp -med ; cont -ming) ◇ n bélier m ◇ vt - **1.** [crash into] percuter contre, emboutir - **2.** [force] tasser - **3.** phr : **to ~ sthg home** beaucoup insister sur qqch.

RAM [ræm] (abbr of random access memory) n RAM f.

Ramadan [,ræmə'dæn] n ramadan m.

ramble ['ræmbl] ◇ n randonnée f, promenade f à pied ◇ vi - **1.** [walk] faire une promenade à pied - **2.** pej [talk] radoter.

◆ **ramble on** vi pej radoter.

rambler ['ræmbləʳ] n [walker] randonneur m, -euse f.

rambling ['ræmblɪŋ] adj - **1.** [house] plein(e) de coins et recoins - **2.** [speech] décousu(e).

RAMC (abbr of Royal Army Medical Corps) n service de santé des armées britanniques.

ramekin ['ræmɪkɪn] n ramequin m.

ramification [,ræmɪfɪ'keɪʃn] n ramification f.

ramp [ræmp] n - **1.** [slope] rampe f - **2.** AUT [to slow traffic down] ralentisseur m ; 'ramp' 'dénivellation'.

rampage [ræm'peɪdʒ] ◇ n : **to go on the ~** tout saccager ◇ vi se déchaîner.

rampant ['ræmpənt] adj qui sévit.

ramparts ['ræmpɑːts] npl rempart m.

ramshackle ['ræm,ʃækl] adj branlant(e).

ran [ræn] pt ▷ run.

RAN (abbr of Royal Australian Navy) n marine de guerre australienne.

ranch [rɑːntʃ] n ranch m.

rancher ['rɑːntʃəʳ] n propriétaire mf de ranch.

ranch house n Am ranch m.

rancid ['rænsɪd] adj rance.

rancour Br, **rancor** Am ['ræŋkəʳ] n rancœur f.

random ['rændəm] ◇ adj fait(e) au hasard ; [number] aléatoire ◇ n : **at ~** au hasard.

random access memory n COMPUT mémoire f vive.

randomly ['rændəmlɪ] adv au hasard.

R and R (abbr of rest and recreation) n Am permission f.

randy ['rændɪ] (compar -ier ; superl -iest) adj inf excité(e).

rang [ræŋ] pt ▷ ring.

range [reɪndʒ] (cont **rangeing**) ◇ n - **1.** [of plane, telescope etc] portée f; **at close ~** à bout portant ; **to be out of ~** être hors de portée ; **to be within ~** of être à portée de - **2.** [of subjects, goods] gamme f; **price ~** éventail m des prix - **3.** [of mountains] chaîne f - **4.** [shooting area] champ m de tir - **5.** MUS [of voice] tessiture f ◇ vt [place in row] mettre en rang ◇ vi - **1.** [vary] : **to ~ between ... and ...** varier entre ... et ... ; **to ~ from ... to ...** varier de ... à ... - **2.** [include] : **to ~ over sthg** couvrir qqch.

ranger ['reɪndʒəʳ] n garde m forestier.

Rangoon [ræŋ'guːn] n Rangoon.

rangy ['reɪndʒɪ] (compar **-ier** ; superl **-iest**) adj élancé(e).

rank [ræŋk] ◇ adj - **1.** [absolute - disgrace, stupidity] complet(ète) ; [- injustice] flagrant(e) ; **he's a ~ outsider** il n'a aucune chance - **2.** [smell] fétide ◇ n - **1.** [in army, police etc] grade m; **to pull ~** user de sa supériorité hiérarchique (pour faire faire qqch à qqn) - **2.** [social class] rang m - **3.** [row] rangée f; **taxi ~ station** f de taxis ; **to close ~s** serrer les rangs - **4.** phr : **the ~ and file** la masse ; [of union] la base ◇ vt - **1.** [classify] classer - **2.** Am [outrank] avoir un grade supérieur à ◇ vi : **to ~ among** compter parmi ; **to ~ as** être aux rangs de.

▶ **ranks** npl - **1.** MIL : **the ~s** le rang - **2.** fig [members] rangs mpl.

ranking ['ræŋkɪŋ] ◇ n [rating] classement m ◇ adj Am [high-ranking] du plus haut rang.

rankle ['ræŋkl] vi : **it ~d with him** ça lui est resté sur l'estomac OR le cœur.

ransack ['rænsæk] vt [search through] mettre tout sens dessus dessous dans ; [damage] saccager.

ransom ['rænsəm] n rançon f; **to hold sb to ~** [keep prisoner] mettre qqn à rançon ; fig exercer un chantage sur qqn.

rant [rænt] vi déblatérer.

ranting ['ræntɪŋ] n (U) invectives fpl.

rap [ræp] (pt & pp **-ped** ; cont **-ping**) ◇ n - **1.** [knock] coup m sec - **2.** MUS rap m - **3.** phr : **to take the ~** inf trinquer, payer les pots cassés ◇ vt [table] frapper sur ; [knuckles] taper sur ◇ vi - **1.** [knock] : **to ~ on** [door] frapper à ; [table] frapper sur - **2.** MUS rapper.

rapacious [rə'peɪʃəs] adj rapace.

rapacity [rə'pæsətɪ] n rapacité f.

rape [reɪp] ◇ n - **1.** [crime, attack] viol m - **2.** fig [of countryside etc] destruction f - **3.** [plant] colza m ◇ vt violer.

rapeseed ['reɪpsiːd] n graine f de colza.

rapid ['ræpɪd] adj rapide.

▶ **rapids** npl rapides mpl.

rapid-fire adj [gun] à tir rapide ; **~ questions** un feu roulant de questions.

rapidity [rə'pɪdətɪ] n rapidité f.

rapidly ['ræpɪdlɪ] adv rapidement.

rapidness ['ræpɪdnɪs] = **rapidity**.

rapist ['reɪpɪst] n violeur m.

rapper ['ræpəʳ] n rappeur m, -euse f.

rapport [ræ'pɔːʳ] n rapport m.

rapprochement [ræ'prɒʃmɑ̃] n rapprochement m.

rapt [ræpt] adj [interest, attention] profond(e) ; **to be ~ in thought** être plongé dans ses pensées.

rapture ['ræptʃəʳ] n ravissement m; **to go into ~s over** OR **about** s'extasier sur.

rapturous ['ræptʃərəs] adj [applause, welcome] enthousiaste.

rare [reəʳ] adj - **1.** [gen] rare - **2.** [meat] saignant(e).

rarefied ['reərɪfaɪd] adj - **1.** [air] raréfié(e) - **2.** fig [place, atmosphere] raffiné(e).

rarely ['reəlɪ] adv rarement.

rareness ['reənɪs] n rareté f.

raring ['reərɪŋ] adj : **to be ~ to go** être impatient(e) de commencer.

rarity ['reərətɪ] (pl **-ies**) n rareté f.

rascal ['rɑːskl] n polisson m, -onne f.

rash [ræʃ] ◇ adj irréfléchi(e), imprudent(e) ◇ n - **1.** MED éruption f - **2.** [spate] succession f, série f.

rasher ['ræʃəʳ] n tranche f.

rashly ['ræʃlɪ] adv sans réfléchir.

rashness ['ræʃnɪs] n imprudence f.

rasp [rɑːsp] ◇ n [harsh sound] grincement m ◇ vi dire d'une voix âpre.

raspberry ['rɑːzbərɪ] (pl **-ies**) n - **1.** [fruit] framboise f - **2.** [rude sound] : **to blow a ~** faire pfft.

rasping ['rɑːspɪŋ] adj [voiced] âpre ; [sound] grinçant(e).

rasta ['ræstə] n inf rasta mf.

rastafarian [ˌræstə'feərɪən] n rastafari mf.

rat [ræt] n - **1.** [animal] rat m; **to smell a ~** soupçonner anguille sous roche - **2.** inf pej [person] ordure f, salaud m.

ratbag ['rætbæg] n Br inf pej salope f.

ratchet ['rætʃɪt] n rochet m.

rate [reɪt] ◇ n - **1.** [speed] vitesse f; [of pulse] fréquence f; **~ of flow** débit m; **at this ~** à ce train-là - **2.** [ratio, proportion] taux m - **3.** [price] tarif m ◇ vt - **1.** [consider] : **I ~ her very highly** je la tiens en haute estime ; **to ~ sb/sthg as**

considérer qqn/qqch comme ; **to ~** sb/sthg among classer qqn/qqch parmi - **2.** [deserve] mériter.
➠ **rates** npl Br impôts mpl locaux.
➠ **at any rate** adv en tout cas.

rateable value ['reɪtəbl-] n Br valeur f locative imposable.

rate of exchange n taux m OR cours m du change.

ratepayer ['reɪt,peɪəʳ] n Br contribuable mf.

rather ['rɑːðəʳ] adv - **1.** [somewhat, more exactly] plutôt - **2.** [to small extent] un peu - **3.** [preferably] : **I'd ~ wait** je préférerais attendre ; **she'd ~ not go** elle préférerait ne pas y aller - **4.** [on the contrary] : **(but) ~ ...** au contraire ...
➠ **rather than** conj plutôt que.

ratification [,rætɪfɪ'keɪʃn] n ratification f.

ratify ['rætɪfaɪ] (pt & pp -ied) vt ratifier, approuver.

rating ['reɪtɪŋ] n - **1.** [of popularity etc] cote f - **2.** Br [sailor] matelot m.
➠ **ratings** npl RADIO & TV indice m d'écoute.

ratio ['reɪʃɪəʊ] (pl -s) n rapport m.

ration ['ræʃn] <> n ration f <> vt rationner.
➠ **rations** npl vivres mpl.

rational ['ræʃənl] adj rationnel(elle).

rationale [,ræʃə'nɑːl] n logique f.

rationalization [,ræʃənəlaɪ'zeɪʃn] n rationalisation f.

rationalize, -ise ['ræʃənəlaɪz] vt rationaliser.

rationing ['ræʃənɪŋ] n rationnement m.

rat race n jungle f.

rattle ['rætl] <> n - **1.** [of bottles, typewriter keys] cliquetis m ; [of engine] bruit m de ferraille - **2.** [toy] hochet m <> vt - **1.** [bottles] faire s'entrechoquer ; [keys] faire cliqueter - **2.** [unsettle] secouer <> vi [bottles] s'entrechoquer ; [keys, machine] cliqueter ; [engine] faire un bruit de ferraille.
➠ **rattle off** vt sep réciter à toute vitesse.
➠ **rattle on** vi : **to ~ on (about sthg)** parler sans arrêt (de qqch).
➠ **rattle through** vt fus [work] expédier ; [speech, list] lire à toute allure.

rattlesnake ['rætlsneɪk], **rattler** Am ['rætləʳ] n serpent m à sonnettes.

ratty ['rætɪ] (compar -ier ; superl -iest) adj inf - **1.** Br [in bad mood] de mauvais poil - **2.** Am [in bad condition] pourri(e).

raucous ['rɔːkəs] adj [voice, laughter] rauque ; [behaviour] bruyant(e).

raunchy ['rɔːntʃɪ] (compar -ier ; superl -iest) adj d'un sensualité brute.

ravage ['rævɪdʒ] vt ravager.
➠ **ravages** npl ravages mpl.

rave [reɪv] <> adj [review] élogieux(euse) <> n Br inf [party] rave f <> vi - **1.** [talk angrily] : **to ~ at** OR **against** tempêter OR fulminer contre - **2.** [talk enthusiastically] : **to ~ about** parler avec enthousiasme de.

raven ['reɪvn] <> adj [hair] de jais <> n corbeau m.

ravenous ['rævənəs] adj [person] affamé(e) ; [animal, appetite] vorace.

raver ['reɪvəʳ] n Br inf : **she's a ~** elle fait faire la fête.

rave-up n Br inf fête f.

ravine [rə'viːn] n ravin m.

raving ['reɪvɪŋ] adj : **~ lunatic** fou furieux (folle furieuse).
➠ **ravings** npl délire m.

ravioli [,rævɪ'əʊlɪ] n (U) ravioli mpl.

ravish ['rævɪʃ] vt [delight] ravir, enchanter.

ravishing ['rævɪʃɪŋ] adj ravissant(e), enchanteur(eresse).

raw [rɔː] adj - **1.** [uncooked] cru(e) - **2.** [untreated] brut(e) - **3.** [painful] à vif - **4.** [inexperienced] novice ; **~ recruit** bleu m - **5.** [weather] froid(e) ; [wind] âpre.

raw deal n : **to get a ~** être défavorisé(e).

raw material n matière f première.

ray [reɪ] n [beam] rayon m ; fig [of hope] lueur f.

rayon ['reɪɒn] n rayonne f.

raze [reɪz] vt raser.

razor ['reɪzəʳ] n rasoir m.

razor blade n lame f de rasoir.

razor-sharp adj coupant(e) comme un rasoir ; fig [person, mind] vif (vive).

razzle ['ræzl] n Br inf : **to go on the ~** faire les quatre cents coups.

razzmatazz ['ræzmətæz] n inf tape-à-l'œil m inv.

R & B (abbr of rhythm and blues) n R & B m.

RC abbr of Roman Catholic.

RCA (abbr of Royal College of Art) n école de beaux-arts à Londres.

RCAF (abbr of Royal Canadian Air Force) n armée de l'air canadienne.

RCMP (abbr of Royal Canadian Mounted Police) n police montée canadienne.

RCN n - **1.** (abbr of Royal College of Nursing) syndicat britannique des infirmières et des infirmiers - **2.** (abbr of Royal Canadian Navy) marine de guerre canadienne.

Rd abbr of Road.

R & D (*abbr of* research and development) *n* R-D *f*.

RDC (*abbr of* rural district council) *n municipalité en zone rurale en Grande-Bretagne*.

re [riː] *prep* concernant.

RE *n* - **1.** (*abbr of* religious education) instruction *f* religieuse - **2.** (*abbr of* Royal Engineers) *le génie militaire britannique*.

reach [riːtʃ] ⬦ *vt* - **1.** [gen] atteindre ; [place, destination] arriver à ; [agreement, decision] parvenir à - **2.** [contact] joindre, contacter ⬦ *vi* [land] s'étendre ; **to ~ out** tendre le bras ; **to ~ down to pick sthg up** se pencher pour ramasser qqch ⬦ *n* [of arm, boxer] allonge *f ;* **within ~** [object] à portée ; [place] à proximité ; **out of** OR **beyond sb's ~** [object] hors de portée ; [place] d'accès difficile, difficilement accessible.

◆ **reaches** *npl* étendue *f*.

reachable [ˈriːtʃəbl] *adj* - **1.** [place] accessible ; [object] à portée - **2.** [contactable] joignable.

react [rɪˈækt] *vi* - **1.** [gen] réagir - **2.** MED : **to ~ to sthg** avoir une réaction à qqch.

reaction [rɪˈækʃn] *n* réaction *f*.

reactionary [rɪˈækʃənrɪ] ⬦ *adj* réactionnaire ⬦ *n* réactionnaire *mf*.

reactivate [rɪˈæktɪveɪt] *vt* réactiver.

reactor [rɪˈæktəʳ] *n* réacteur *m*.

read [riːd] (*pt & pp* read [red]) ⬦ *vt* - **1.** [gen] lire - **2.** [subj : sign, letter] dire - **3.** [interpret, judge] interpréter - **4.** [subj : meter, thermometer etc] indiquer - **5.** Br UNIV étudier ⬦ *vi* lire ; **the book ~s well** le livre se lit bien ⬦ *n* : **to be a good ~** être un bon livre, être d'une lecture agréable.

◆ **read into** *vt sep* : **to ~ a lot into sthg** attacher beaucoup d'importance à qqch.

◆ **read out** *vt sep* lire à haute voix.

◆ **read up on** *vt fus* étudier.

readable [ˈriːdəbl] *adj* agréable à lire.

readdress [ˌriːəˈdres] *vt* faire suivre.

reader [ˈriːdəʳ] *n* [of book, newspaper] lecteur *m*, -trice *f*.

readership [ˈriːdəʃɪp] *n* [of newspaper] nombre *m* de lecteurs.

readily [ˈredɪlɪ] *adv* - **1.** [willingly] volontiers - **2.** [easily] facilement.

readiness [ˈredɪnɪs] *n* - **1.** [preparation] : **to be in ~** être prêt(e) - **2.** [willingness] empressement *m*.

reading [ˈriːdɪŋ] *n* - **1.** (U) [gen] lecture *f* - **2.** [interpretation] interprétation *f* - **3.** [on thermometer, meter etc] indications *fpl*.

reading lamp *n* lampe *f* de lecture OR de bureau.

reading room *n* salle *f* de lecture.

readjust [ˌriːəˈdʒʌst] ⬦ *vt* [instrument] régler (de nouveau) ; [mirror] rajuster ; [policy] rectifier ⬦ *vi* [person] : **to ~ (to)** se réadapter (à).

readmit [ˌriːədˈmɪt] *vt* réadmettre.

readout [ˈriːdaʊt] *n* COMPUT affichage *m*.

read-through [riːd-] *n :* **to have a ~ of sthg** parcourir qqch.

ready [ˈredɪ] (*pt & pp* -ied) ⬦ *adj* - **1.** [prepared] prêt(e) ; **to be ~ to do sthg** être prêt à faire qqch ; **to get ~** se préparer ; **to get sthg ~** préparer qqch - **2.** [willing] : **to be ~ to do sthg** être prêt(e) OR disposé(e) à faire qqch ⬦ *vt* préparer.

ready cash *n* liquide *m*.

ready-made *adj* lit & fig tout fait (toute faite).

ready meal *n* plat *m* préparé.

ready money *n* liquide *m*.

ready-to-wear *adj* prêt-à-porter.

reaffirm [ˌriːəˈfɜːm] *vt* réaffirmer.

reafforest [ˌriːəˈfɒrɪst] *vt* reboiser.

reafforestation [ˈriːəˌfɒrɪˈsteɪʃn] *n* reboisement *m*.

real [rɪəl] ⬦ *adj* - **1.** [gen] vrai(e), véritable ; **~ life** life ; **for ~** pour de vrai ; **this is the ~ thing** [object] c'est de l'authentique ; [situation] c'est pour de vrai OR de bon - **2.** [actual] réel(elle) ; **in ~ terms** dans la pratique ⬦ *adv* Am très.

real ale *n* Br ale *f* véritable.

real estate *n* (U) biens *mpl* immobiliers.

realign [ˌriːəˈlaɪn] *vt* POL regrouper.

realignment [ˌriːəˈlaɪnmənt] *n* POL regroupement *m*.

realism [ˈrɪəlɪzm] *n* réalisme *m*.

realist [ˈrɪəlɪst] *n* réaliste *mf*.

realistic [ˌrɪəˈlɪstɪk] *adj* réaliste.

realistically [ˌrɪəˈlɪstɪklɪ] *adv* d'une manière réaliste, avec réalisme.

reality [rɪˈælətɪ] (*pl* -ies) *n* réalité *f ;* **in ~** en réalité.

realization [ˌrɪəlaɪˈzeɪʃn] *n* réalisation *f*.

realize, -ise [ˈrɪəlaɪz] *vt* - **1.** [understand] se rendre compte de, réaliser - **2.** [sum of money, idea, ambition] réaliser.

reallocate [ˌriːˈæləkeɪt] *vt* réattribuer.

really [ˈrɪəlɪ] ⬦ *adv* - **1.** [gen] vraiment - **2.** [in fact] en réalité ⬦ *excl* - **1.** [expressing doubt] vraiment? - **2.** [expressing surprise] pas possible! **- 3.** [expressing disapproval] franchement!, ça alors!

realm [relm] *n* **- 1. fig** [subject area] domaine *m* **- 2.** [kingdom] royaume *m*.

real-time *adj* COMPUT en temps réel.

realtor ['rɪəltər] *n* **Am** agent *m* immobilier.

ream [riːm] *n* [of papers] rame *f*.
➡ **reams** *npl* des pages et des pages.

reap [riːp] *vt* **- 1.** [harvest] moissonner **- 2. fig** [obtain] récolter.

reappear [ˌriːə'pɪər] *vi* réapparaître, reparaître.

reappearance [ˌriːə'pɪərəns] *n* réapparition *f*.

reapply [ˌriːə'plaɪ] (*pt* & *pp* **-ied**) *vi* : **to ~ (for a job)** postuler de nouveau (à un emploi).

reappraisal [ˌriːə'preɪzl] *n* réévaluation *f*.

reappraise [ˌriːə'preɪz] *vt* réévaluer.

rear [rɪər] <> *adj* arrière (*inv*), de derrière <> *n* **- 1.** [back] arrière *m* ; **to bring up the ~** fermer la marche **- 2.** inf [bottom] derrière *m* <> *vt* [children, animals] élever <> *vi* [horse] : **to ~ (up)** se cabrer.

rear admiral *n* vice-amiral *m*.

rearguard action ['rɪəgɑːd-] *n* combat *m* d'arrière-garde.

rear light *n* feu *m* arrière.

rearm [riːˈɑːm] *vt* & *vi* réarmer.

rearmament [riːˈɑːməmənt] *n* réarmement *m*.

rearmost ['rɪəməʊst] *adj* dernier(ère).

rearrange [ˌriːəˈreɪndʒ] *vt* **- 1.** [furniture, room] réarranger ; [plans] changer **- 2.** [meeting - to new time] changer l'heure de ; [- to new date] changer la date de.

rearrangement [ˌriːəˈreɪndʒmənt] *n* **- 1.** [of furniture etc] réarrangement *m* **- 2.** [of meeting - to new time] changement *m* de l'heure ; [- to new date] changement de la date.

rearview mirror ['rɪəvjuː-] *n* rétroviseur *m*.

reason ['riːzn] <> *n* **- 1.** [cause] : **~ (for)** raison *f* (de) ; **by ~ of** fml en raison de ; **for some ~** pour une raison ou pour une autre **- 2.** (U) [justification] : **to have ~ to do sthg** avoir de bonnes raisons de faire qqch ; **I have ~ to believe (that)** ... j'ai lieu de croire que ... **- 3.** [common sense] bon sens *m* ; **he won't listen to ~** on ne peut pas lui faire entendre raison ; **it stands to ~** c'est logique <> *vt* déduire <> *vi* raisonner.
➡ **reason with** *vt fus* raisonner (avec).

reasonable ['riːznəbl] *adj* raisonnable.

reasonably ['riːznəblɪ] *adv* **- 1.** [quite] assez **- 2.** [sensibly] raisonnablement.

reasoned ['riːznd] *adj* raisonné(e).

reasoning ['riːznɪŋ] *n* raisonnement *m*.

reassemble [ˌriːə'sembl] <> *vt* **- 1.** [reconstruct] remonter **- 2.** [regroup] rassembler <> *vi* se rassembler.

reassess [ˌriːə'ses] *vt* réexaminer.

reassessment [ˌriːə'sesmənt] *n* réexamen *m*.

reassurance [ˌriːə'ʃʊərəns] *n* **- 1.** [comfort] réconfort *m* **- 2.** [promise] assurance *f*.

reassure [ˌriːə'ʃʊər] *vt* rassurer.

reassuring [ˌriːə'ʃʊərɪŋ] *adj* rassurant(e).

reawaken [ˌriːə'weɪkn] *vt* [interest] faire renaître.

rebate ['riːbeɪt] *n* [on product] rabais *m* ; **tax ~** ≃ dégrèvement *m* fiscal.

rebel [*n* 'rebl, *vb* rɪ'bel] (*pt* & *pp* **-led** ; *cont* **-ling**) <> *n* rebelle *mf* <> *vi* : **to ~ (against)** se rebeller (contre).

rebellion [rɪ'beljən] *n* rébellion *f*.

rebellious [rɪ'beljəs] *adj* rebelle.

rebirth [ˌriː'bɜːθ] *n* renaissance *f*.

rebound [*n* 'riːbaʊnd, *vb* rɪ'baʊnd] <> *n* [of ball] rebond *m* ; **to be on the ~** [person] être sous le coup d'une déception sentimentale <> *vi* **- 1.** [ball] rebondir **- 2. fig** [action, joke] : **to ~ on** OR **upon sb** se retourner contre qqn.

rebuff [rɪ'bʌf] <> *n* rebuffade *f* <> *vt* repousser.

rebuild [ˌriː'bɪld] (*pt* & *pp* **rebuilt** [ˌriː'bɪlt]) *vt* reconstruire.

rebuke [rɪ'bjuːk] <> *n* réprimande *f* <> *vt* réprimander.

rebut [riː'bʌt] (*pt* & *pp* **-ted** ; *cont* **-ting**) *vt* réfuter.

rebuttal [riː'bʌtl] *n* réfutation *f*.

rec. *abbr of* **received.**

recalcitrant [rɪ'kælsɪtrənt] *adj* récalcitrant(e).

recall [rɪ'kɔːl] <> *n* **- 1.** [memory] rappel *m* **- 2.** [change] : **beyond ~** irrévocable <> *vt* **- 1.** [remember] se rappeler, se souvenir de **- 2.** [summon back] rappeler ; **to ~ Parliament** convoquer le Parlement.

recant [rɪ'kænt] <> *vt* [statement] rétracter ; RELIG abjurer <> *vi* se rétracter ; RELIG abjurer.

recap ['riːkæp] (*pt* & *pp* **-ped** ; *cont* **-ping**) <> *n* récapitulation *f* <> *vt* **- 1.** [summarize] récapituler **- 2.** **Am** [tyre] rechaper <> *vi* récapituler.

recapitulate [ˌriːkə'pɪtjʊleɪt] *vt* & *vi* récapituler.

recapture [,ri:'kæptʃə^r] ⬦ n reprise f ⬦ vt - **1.** [feeling] retrouver - **2.** [territory, prisoner] reprendre.

recd, rec'd abbr of **received**.

recede [ri:'si:d] vi - **1.** [person, car etc] s'éloigner ; [hopes] s'envoler - **2.** [hair] : **his hair is receding** son front se dégarnit.

receding [rɪ'si:dɪŋ] adj [hairline] dégarni(e) ; [chin, forehead] fuyant(e).

receipt [rɪ'si:t] n - **1.** [piece of paper] reçu m - **2.** (U) [act of receiving] réception f.
➡ **receipts** npl recettes fpl.

receivable [rɪ'si:vəbl] adj - **1.** [able to be received] recevable - **2.** FIN à recevoir.

receive [rɪ'si:v] ⬦ vt - **1.** [gen] recevoir ; [news] apprendre - **2.** [welcome] accueillir, recevoir ; **to be well/badly ~d** [film, speech etc] être bien/mal accueilli ⬦ vi [in tennis etc] recevoir le service.

receiver [rɪ'si:və^r] n - **1.** [of telephone] récepteur m, combiné m - **2.** [radio, TV set] récepteur m - **3.** [criminal] receleur m, -euse f - **4.** FIN [official] administrateur m, -trice f judiciaire.

receivership [rɪ'si:vəʃɪp] n : **to go into ~** être mis(e) en liquidation.

receiving end [rɪ'si:vɪŋ-] n : **to be on the ~ (of sthg)** faire les frais de (qqch).

recent ['ri:snt] adj récent(e).

recently ['ri:sntlɪ] adv récemment ; **until ~** jusqu'à ces derniers temps.

receptacle [rɪ'septəkl] n récipient m.

reception [rɪ'sepʃn] n - **1.** [gen] réception f - **2.** [welcome] accueil m, réception f.

reception centre n centre m d'accueil.

reception class n Br cours m préparatoire.

reception desk n réception f.

receptionist [rɪ'sepʃənɪst] n réceptionniste mf.

reception room n salon m.

receptive [rɪ'septɪv] adj réceptif(ive).

receptiveness [rɪ'septɪvnɪs] n réceptivité f.

recess ['ri:ses, rɪ'ses] n - **1.** [alcove] niche f - **2.** [secret place] recoin m - **3.** POL : **to be in ~** être en vacances - **4.** Am SCH récréation f.

recessed ['ri:sest, rɪ'sest] adj [window] dans un renfoncement ; [door handle, light] encastré(e).

recession [rɪ'seʃn] n récession f.

recessionary [rɪ'seʃənrɪ] adj de récession.

recessive [rɪ'sesɪv] adj BIOL récessif(ive).

recharge [,ri:'tʃɑ:dʒ] vt recharger.

rechargeable [,ri:'tʃɑ:dʒəbl] adj rechargeable.

recipe ['resɪpɪ] n lit & fig recette f.

recipient [rɪ'sɪpɪənt] n [of letter] destinataire mf ; [of cheque] bénéficiaire mf ; [of award] récipiendaire mf.

reciprocal [rɪ'sɪprəkl] adj réciproque.

reciprocate [rɪ'sɪprəkeɪt] ⬦ vt rendre, retourner ⬦ vi en faire autant.

recital [rɪ'saɪtl] n récital m.

recitation [,resɪ'teɪʃn] n récitation f.

recite [rɪ'saɪt] vt - **1.** [say aloud] réciter - **2.** [list] énumérer.

reckless ['reklɪs] adj imprudent(e).

recklessness ['reklɪsnɪs] n imprudence f.

reckon ['rekn] vt - **1.** inf [think] penser - **2.** [consider, judge] considérer - **3.** [expect] : **to ~ to do sthg** compter faire qqch - **4.** [calculate] calculer.
➡ **reckon on** vt fus compter sur.
➡ **reckon with** vt fus [expect] s'attendre à ; **he's a person to be ~ed with** il faut compter avec lui.
➡ **reckon without** vt fus compter sans.

reckoning ['rekənɪŋ] n (U) [calculation] calculs mpl ; **day of ~** jour m de vérité.

reclaim [rɪ'kleɪm] vt - **1.** [claim back] réclamer - **2.** [land] assécher.

reclamation [,reklə'meɪʃn] n [of land] assèchement m.

recline [rɪ'klaɪn] vi [person] être allongé(e).

reclining [rɪ'klaɪnɪŋ] adj [chair] à dossier réglable.

recluse [rɪ'klu:s] n reclus m, -e f.

reclusive [rɪ'klu:sɪv] adj reclus(e).

recognition [,rekəg'nɪʃn] n reconnaissance f ; **in ~ of** en reconnaissance de ; **the town has changed beyond** OR **out of all ~** la ville est méconnaissable.

recognizable ['rekəgnaɪzəbl] adj reconnaissable.

recognize, -ise ['rekəgnaɪz] vt reconnaître.

recoil [vb rɪ'kɔɪl, n 'ri:kɔɪl] ⬦ vi : **to ~ (from)** reculer (devant) ⬦ n [of gun] recul m.

recollect [,rekə'lekt] vt se rappeler.

recollection [,rekə'lekʃn] n souvenir m.

recommence [,ri:kə'mens] vt & vi recommencer.

recommend [,rekə'mend] vt - **1.** [commend] : **to ~ sb/sthg (to sb)** recommander qqn/qqch (à qqn) - **2.** [advise] conseiller, recommander.

recommendation [,rekəmen'deɪʃn] n recommandation f.

recommended retail price [,rekə'mendɪd-] n prix m de vente conseillé.

recompense ['rekəmpens] ◇ *n* dédommagement *m* ◇ *vt* dédommager.

reconcile ['rekənsaıl] *vt* - **1.** [beliefs, ideas] concilier - **2.** [people] réconcilier ; **to be ~d with sb** se réconcilier avec qqn - **3.** [accept] : **to ~ o.s. to sthg** se faire à l'idée de qqch.

reconciliation [,rekənsılı'eıʃn] *n* - **1.** [of beliefs, ideas] conciliation *f* - **2.** [of people] réconciliation *f*.

recondite ['rekəndaıt] *adj fml* obscur(e).

reconditioned [,ri:kən'dıʃnd] *adj* remis(e) en état.

reconnaissance [rı'kɒnısəns] *n* reconnaissance *f*.

reconnect [,ri:kə'nekt] *vt* rebrancher.

reconnoitre Br, **reconnoiter** Am [,rekə'nɔıtə'] ◇ *vt* reconnaître ◇ *vi* aller en reconnaissance.

reconsider [,ri:kən'sıdə'] ◇ *vt* reconsidérer ◇ *vi* reconsidérer la question.

reconstitute [,ri:'kɒnstıtju:t] *vt* reconstituer.

reconstruct [,ri:kən'strʌkt] *vt* - **1.** [gen] reconstruire - **2.** [crime, event] reconstituer.

reconstruction [,ri:kən'strʌkʃn] *n* - **1.** [gen] reconstruction *f* - **2.** [of crime, event] reconstitution *f*.

reconvene [,ri:kən'vi:n] *vt* convoquer de nouveau.

record [*n* & *adj* 'rekɔ:d, *vb* rı'kɔ:d] ◇ *n* - **1.** [written account] rapport *m* ; [file] dossier *m* ; **to keep sthg on ~** archiver qqch ; **to go on ~ as saying (that)** ... déclarer publiquement que ... ; (police) **~** casier *m* judiciaire ; **off the ~** non officiel ; **to set** OR **put the ~ straight** mettre les choses au clair - **2.** [vinyl disc] disque *m* - **3.** [best achievement] record *m* ◇ *adj* record *(inv)* ◇ *vt* - **1.** [write down] noter - **2.** [put on tape] enregistrer.

record-breaker *n* personne *f* qui bat le record.

record-breaking *adj* qui bat tous les records.

recorded delivery [rı'kɔ:dıd-] *n* : **to send sthg by ~** envoyer qqch en recommandé.

recorder [rı'kɔ:də'] *n* [musical instrument] flûte *f* à bec.

record holder *n* détenteur *m*, -trice *f* du record.

recording [rı'kɔ:dıŋ] *n* enregistrement *m*.

recording studio *n* studio *m* d'enregistrement.

record library *n* discothèque *f*.

record player *n* tourne-disque *m*.

recount [*n* 'ri:kaunt, *vt sense 1* rı'kaunt, *sense 2* ,ri:'kaunt] ◇ *n* [of vote] deuxième dépouillement *m* du scrutin ◇ *vt* - **1.** [narrate] raconter - **2.** [count again] recompter.

recoup [rı'ku:p] *vt* récupérer.

recourse [rı'kɔ:s] *n* : **to have ~ to** avoir recours à.

recover [rı'kʌvə'] ◇ *vt* - **1.** [retrieve] récupérer ; **to ~ sthg from sb** reprendre qqch à qqn - **2.** [one's balance] retrouver ; [consciousness] reprendre ; **to ~ o.s.** se ressaisir ◇ *vi* - **1.** [from illness] se rétablir ; [from shock, divorce] se remettre - **2.** fig [economy] se redresser ; [trade] reprendre.

recoverable [rı'kʌvrəbl] *adj* FIN récupérable.

recovery [rı'kʌvərı] (*pl* -**ies**) *n* - **1.** [from illness] guérison *f*, rétablissement *m* - **2.** fig [of economy] redressement *m*, reprise *f* - **3.** [retrieval] récupération *f*.

recovery vehicle *n* Br dépanneuse *f*.

recreate [,ri:krı'eıt] *vt* recréer.

recreation [,rekrı'eıʃn] *n (U)* [leisure] récréation *f*, loisirs *mpl*.

recreational [,rekrı'eıʃənl] *adj* de récréation.

recreation room *n* salle *f* de récréation ; Am [in house] salle de jeu.

recrimination [rı,krımı'neıʃn] *n* récrimination *f*.

recrudescence [,ri:kru:'desns] *n* recrudescence *f*.

recruit [rı'kru:t] ◇ *n* recrue *f* ◇ *vt* recruter ; **to ~ sb to do sthg** fig embaucher qqn pour faire qqch ◇ *vi* recruter.

recruitment [rı'kru:tmənt] *n* recrutement *m*.

rectangle ['rek,tæŋgl] *n* rectangle *m*.

rectangular [rek'tæŋgjolə'] *adj* rectangulaire.

rectification [,rektıfı'keıʃn] *n* rectification *f*.

rectify ['rektıfaı] (*pt* & *pp* -**ied**) *vt* [mistake] rectifier.

rectitude ['rektıtju:d] *n* rectitude *f*.

rector ['rektə'] *n* - **1.** [priest] pasteur *m* - **2.** Scot [head - of school] directeur *m* ; [- of college, university] président élu par les étudiants.

rectory ['rektərı] (*pl* -**ies**) *n* presbytère *m*.

rectum ['rektəm] *n* rectum *m*.

recuperate [rı'ku:pəreıt] *vi* se rétablir.

recuperation [rı,ku:pə'reıʃn] *n* rétablissement *m*.

recur [rı'kɜ:'] (*pt* & *pp* -**red** ; *cont* -**ring**) *vi* [error, problem] se reproduire ; [dream] revenir ; [pain] réapparaître.

recurrence [rɪ'kʌrəns] n répétition f.

recurrent [rɪ'kʌrənt] adj [error, problem] qui se reproduit souvent ; [dream] qui revient souvent.

recurring [rɪ'kɜːrɪŋ] adj - **1.** [error, problem] qui se reproduit souvent ; [dream] qui revient souvent - **2.** MATH périodique.

recyclable [ˌriː'saɪkləbl] adj recyclable.

recycle [ˌriː'saɪkl] vt recycler.

recycling [ˌriː'saɪklɪŋ] n recyclage m.

red [red] (compar **-der** ; superl **-dest**) ⬦ adj rouge ; [hair] roux (rousse) ⬦ n rouge m ; **to be in the ~** inf être à découvert ; **to see ~** voir rouge.
➤ **Red** pej ⬦ adj rouge ⬦ n rouge m f.

red alert n alerte f maximale ; **to be on ~** être en état d'alerte maximale.

red blood cell n globule m rouge.

red-blooded [-'blʌdɪd] adj hum viril(e).

red-brick adj Br [building] en brique rouge.
➤ **redbrick** adj Br : **redbrick university** université f moderne.

red card n FTBL : **to be shown the ~, to get a ~** recevoir un carton rouge.

red carpet n : **to roll out the ~ for sb** dérouler le tapis rouge pour qqn.
➤ **red-carpet** adj : **to give sb the red-carpet treatment** recevoir qqn en grande pompe.

Red Crescent n : **the ~** le Croissant Rouge.

Red Cross n : **the ~** la Croix-Rouge.

redcurrant ['red,kʌrənt] n [fruit] groseille f ; [bush] groseillier m.

red deer n cerf m.

redden ['redn] vt & vi rougir.

redecorate [ˌriː'dekəreɪt] ⬦ vt repeindre et retapisser ⬦ vi refaire la peinture et les papiers peints.

redeem [rɪ'diːm] vt - **1.** [save, rescue] racheter ; **to ~ o.s.** se racheter - **2.** [from pawnbroker] dégager.

redeeming [rɪ'diːmɪŋ] adj qui rachète (les défauts).

redefine [ˌriːdɪ'faɪn] vt redéfinir.

redemption [rɪ'dempʃn] n rédemption f ; **beyond** OR **past ~** fig irrémédiable.

redeploy [ˌriːdɪ'plɔɪ] vt MIL redéployer ; [staff] réorganiser, réaffecter.

redeployment [ˌriːdɪ'plɔɪmənt] n MIL redéploiement m ; [of staff] réorganisation f, réaffectation f.

redesign [ˌriːdɪ'zaɪn] vt [room] redessiner ; [system] réorganiser.

redevelop [ˌriːdɪ'veləp] vt réaménager.

redevelopment [ˌriːdɪ'veləpmənt] n réaménagement m.

red-faced [-'feɪst] adj rougeaud(e), rubicond(e) ; [with embarrassment] rouge de confusion.

red-haired [-'heəd] adj roux (rousse).

red-handed [-'hændɪd] adj : **to catch sb ~** prendre qqn en flagrant délit OR la main dans le sac.

redhead ['redhed] n roux m, rousse f.

red herring n fig fausse piste f.

red-hot adj - **1.** [extremely hot] brûlant(e) ; [metal] chauffé(e) au rouge - **2.** [very enthusiastic] ardent(e).

redid [ˌriː'dɪd] pt ⊳ **redo**.

Red Indian ⬦ adj de Peau-Rouge ⬦ n Peau-Rouge mf (attention : le terme 'Red Indian' est considéré comme raciste).

redirect [ˌriːdɪ'rekt] vt - **1.** [energy, money] réorienter - **2.** [traffic] détourner - **3.** [letters] faire suivre.

rediscover [ˌriːdɪ'skʌvəʳ] vt redécouvrir.

redistribute [ˌriːdɪ'strɪbjuːt] vt redistribuer.

red-letter day n jour m mémorable, jour à marquer d'une pierre blanche.

red light n [traffic signal] feu m rouge.

red-light district n quartier m chaud.

red meat n viande f rouge.

redness ['rednɪs] n rougeur f.

redo [ˌriː'duː] (pt **-did** ; pp **-done**) vt refaire.

redolent ['redələnt] adj literary - **1.** [reminiscent] : **~ of** qui rappelle, évocateur(trice) de - **2.** [smelling] : **~ of** qui sent.

redone [ˌriː'dʌn] pp ⊳ **redo**.

redouble [ˌriː'dʌbl] vt : **to ~ one's efforts (to do sthg)** redoubler d'efforts (pour faire qqch).

redoubtable [rɪ'daʊtəbl] adj redoutable, formidable.

redraft [ˌriː'drɑːft] vt rédiger à nouveau.

redraw [ˌriː'drɔː] (pt **-drew** ; pp **-drawn**) vt dessiner à nouveau.

redress [rɪ'dres] ⬦ n (U) fml réparation f ⬦ vt : **to ~ the balance** rétablir l'équilibre.

redrew [ˌriː'druː] pt ⊳ **redraw**.

Red Sea n : **the ~** la mer Rouge.

Red Square n la place Rouge.

red squirrel n écureuil m.

red tape n fig paperasserie f administrative.

reduce [rɪ'djuːs] ⬦ vt réduire ; **to be ~d to**

doing sthg en être réduit à faire qqch ; **to ~ sb to tears** faire pleurer qqn ⬦ *vi* Am [diet] suivre un régime amaigrissant.

reduced [rɪ'dju:st] *adj* réduit(e) ; **in ~ circumstances** dans la gêne.

reduction [rɪ'dʌkʃn] *n* - **1.** [decrease] : **~ (in)** réduction *f* (de), baisse *f* (de) - **2.** [discount] rabais *m*, réduction *f*.

redundancy [rɪ'dʌndənsɪ] (*pl* -ies) *n* Br [dismissal] licenciement *m* ; [unemployment] chômage *m*.

redundancy payment *n* Br indemnité *f* de licenciement.

redundant [rɪ'dʌndənt] *adj* - **1.** Br [jobless] : **to be made ~** être licencié(e) - **2.** [not required] superflu(e).

redwood ['redwʊd] *n* : **~ (tree)** séquoia *m*.

reecho [,ri:'ekəʊ] ⬦ *vt* [repeat] répéter ⬦ *vi* [echo again] retentir.

reed [ri:d] ⬦ *n* - **1.** [plant] roseau *m* - **2.** MUS anche *f* ⬦ *comp* [basket etc] en roseau.

reeducate [,ri:'edjʊkeɪt] *vt* rééduquer.

reedy ['ri:dɪ] (*compar* -**ier** ; *superl* -**iest**) *adj* [voice] flûté(e), aigu(ë).

reef [ri:f] *n* récif *m*, écueil *m*.

reek [ri:k] ⬦ *n* relent *m* ⬦ *vi* : **to ~ (of sthg)** puer (qqch), empester (qqch).

reel [ri:l] ⬦ *n* - **1.** [roll] bobine *f* - **2.** [on fishing rod] moulinet *m* ⬦ *vi* - **1.** [stagger] chanceler - **2.** [whirl] : **my mind was ~ing** j'avais la tête qui tournait.

reel in *vt sep* remonter.

reel off *vt sep* [list] débiter.

reelect [,ri:ɪ'lekt] *vt* : **to ~ sb (as) sthg** réélire qqn qqch.

reelection [,ri:ɪ'lekʃn] *n* réélection *f*.

reemphasize [,ri:'emfəsaɪz] *vt* souligner de nouveau.

reenact [,ri:ɪ'nækt] *vt* [play] reproduire ; [event] reconstituer.

reenter [,ri:'entəʳ] *vt* [room, earth's atmosphere] rentrer dans ; [country] retourner dans.

reentry [,ri:'entrɪ] *n* [into earth's atmosphere] rentrée *f* ; [into country] retour *m*.

reexamine [,ri:ɪg'zæmɪn] *vt* examiner de nouveau.

reexport [,ri:'ekspɔ:t] COMM ⬦ *n* réexportation *f* ⬦ *vt* réexporter.

ref [ref] *n* - **1.** inf (*abbr of* **referee**) arbitre *m* - **2.** (*abbr of* **reference**) ADMIN réf. *f*.

refectory [rɪ'fektərɪ] (*pl* -ies) *n* réfectoire *m*.

refer [rɪ'fɜːʳ] (*pt* & *pp* -**red** ; *cont* -**ring**) *vt* - **1.** [person] : **to ~ sb to** [hospital] envoyer qqn à ; [specialist] adresser qqn à ; ADMIN renvoyer qqn

à - **2.** [report, case, decision] : **to ~ sthg to** soumettre qqch à.

refer to *vt fus* - **1.** [speak about] parler de, faire allusion à OR mention de - **2.** [apply to] s'appliquer à, concerner - **3.** [consult] se référer à, se reporter à.

referee [,refə'ri:] ⬦ *n* - **1.** SPORT arbitre *m* - **2.** Br [for job application] répondant *m*, -e *f* ⬦ *vt* SPORT arbitrer ⬦ *vi* SPORT être arbitre.

reference ['refrəns] *n* - **1.** [mention] : **~ (to)** allusion *f* (à), mention *f* (de) ; **with ~ to** comme suite à - **2.** (*U*) [for advice, information] : **~ (to)** consultation *f* (de), référence *f* (à) ; **for future ~** à titre d'information - **3.** COMM référence *f* - **4.** [in book] renvoi *m* ; **map ~** coordonnées *fpl* - **5.** [for job application - letter] référence *f* ; [- person] répondant *m*, -e *f*.

reference book *n* ouvrage *m* de référence.

reference library *n* bibliothèque *f* d'ouvrages à consulter.

reference number *n* numéro *m* de référence.

referendum [,refə'rendəm] (*pl* -s OR -**da** [-də]) *n* référendum *m*.

referral [rɪ'fɜːrəl] *n* fml - **1.** (*U*) [act of referring] envoi *m* - **2.** [patient referred] malade envoyé *m*, malade envoyée *f*.

refill [*n* 'ri:fɪl, *vb* ,ri:'fɪl] ⬦ *n* - **1.** [for pen] recharge *f* - **2.** inf [drink] : **would you like a ~?** vous voulez encore un verre? ⬦ *vt* remplir à nouveau.

refillable [,ri:'fɪləbl] *adj* [pen] rechargeable ; [bottle] qu'on peut faire remplir à nouveau.

refine [rɪ'faɪn] *vt* raffiner ; fig peaufiner.

refined [rɪ'faɪnd] *adj* raffiné(e) ; [system, theory] perfectionné(e).

refinement [rɪ'faɪnmənt] *n* - **1.** [improvement] perfectionnement *m* - **2.** (*U*) [gentility] raffinement *m*.

refinery [rɪ'faɪnərɪ] (*pl* -ies) *n* raffinerie *f*.

refit [*n* 'ri:fɪt, *vb* ,ri:'fɪt] (*pt* & *pp* -**ted** ; *cont* -**ting**) ⬦ *n* [of ship] réparation *f*, remise *f* en état ⬦ *vt* [ship] réparer, remettre en état.

reflate [,ri:'fleɪt] ECON ⬦ *vt* relancer ⬦ *vi* effectuer une relance (de l'économie).

reflation [,ri:'fleɪʃn] *n* ECON relance *f*.

reflationary [rɪ'fleɪʃənrɪ] *adj* ECON de relance.

reflect [rɪ'flekt] ⬦ *vt* - **1.** [be a sign of] refléter - **2.** [light, image] réfléchir, refléter ; [heat] réverbérer ; **to be ~ed in** se refléter dans - **3.** [think] : **to ~ that ...** se dire que ... ⬦ *vi* [think] : **to ~ (on OR upon)** réfléchir (sur), penser (à).

reflection [rɪˈflekʃn] n - **1.** [sign] indication f, signe m - **2.** [criticism] : ~ **on** critique f de - **3.** [image] reflet m - **4.** (U) [of light, heat] réflexion f - **5.** [thought] réflexion f; **on** ~ réflexion faite.

reflective [rɪˈflektɪv] adj - **1.** [surface, material] réfléchissant(e) - **2.** [thoughtful] pensif(ive).

reflector [rɪˈflektəʳ] n réflecteur m.

reflex [ˈriːfleks] n : ~ **(action)** réflexe m.
➡ **reflexes** npl réflexes mpl.

reflex camera n appareil m reflex.

reflexive [rɪˈfleksɪv] adj GRAMM [pronoun] réfléchi(e) ; ~ **verb** verbe m pronominal réfléchi.

reflexology [ˌriːflekˈsɒlədʒɪ] n réflexothérapie f.

reforest [ˌriːˈfɒrɪst] = **reafforest**.

reforestation [riːˌfɒrɪˈsteɪʃn] = **reafforestation**.

reform [rɪˈfɔːm] <> n réforme f <> vt [gen] réformer ; [person] corriger <> vi [behave better] se corriger, s'amender.

reformat [ˌriːˈfɔːmæt] (pt & pp **-ted** ; cont **-ting**) vt COMPUT reformater.

Reformation [ˌrefəˈmeɪʃn] n : **the** ~ la Réforme.

reformatory [rɪˈfɔːmətrɪ] n Am centre m d'éducation surveillée (pour jeunes délinquants).

reformed [rɪˈfɔːmd] adj [better behaved] qui s'est corrigé(e) OR amendé(e).

reformer [rɪˈfɔːməʳ] n réformateur m, -trice f.

reformist [rɪˈfɔːmɪst] <> adj réformiste <> n réformiste m f.

refract [rɪˈfrækt] <> vt réfracter <> vi se réfracter.

refrain [rɪˈfreɪn] <> n refrain m <> vi : **to** ~ **from doing sthg** s'abstenir de faire qqch.

refresh [rɪˈfreʃ] vt rafraîchir, revigorer ; **to** ~ **sb's memory** rafraîchir la mémoire de qqn.

refreshed [rɪˈfreʃt] adj reposé(e).

refresher course [rɪˈfreʃəʳ-] n cours m de recyclage OR remise à niveau.

refreshing [rɪˈfreʃɪŋ] adj - **1.** [pleasantly different] agréable, réconfortant(e) - **2.** [drink, swim] rafraîchissant(e).

refreshments [rɪˈfreʃmənts] npl rafraîchissements mpl.

refrigerate [rɪˈfrɪdʒəreɪt] vt réfrigérer.

refrigeration [rɪˌfrɪdʒəˈreɪʃn] n réfrigération f.

refrigerator [rɪˈfrɪdʒəreɪtəʳ] n réfrigérateur m, Frigidaire® m.

refuel [ˌriːˈfjʊəl] (Br pt & pp **-led** ; cont **-ling**, Am pt & pp **-ed** ; cont **-ing**) <> vt ravitailler <> vi se ravitailler en carburant.

refuge [ˈrefjuːdʒ] n lit & fig refuge m, abri m ; **to take** ~ **in** se réfugier dans.

refugee [ˌrefjʊˈdʒiː] n réfugié m, -e f.

refugee camp n camp m de réfugiés.

refund [n ˈriːfʌnd, vb rɪˈfʌnd] <> n remboursement m <> vt : **to** ~ **sthg to sb, to** ~ **sb sthg** rembourser qqch à qqn.

refurbish [ˌriːˈfɜːbɪʃ] vt remettre à neuf, rénover.

refurbishment [ˌriːˈfɜːbɪʃmənt] n rénovation f.

refurnish [ˌriːˈfɜːnɪʃ] vt remeubler.

refusal [rɪˈfjuːzl] n : ~ **(to do sthg)** refus m (de faire qqch).

refuse¹ [rɪˈfjuːz] <> vt refuser ; **to** ~ **to do sthg** refuser de faire qqch <> vi refuser.

refuse² [ˈrefjuːs] n (U) [rubbish] ordures fpl, détritus mpl.

refuse collection [ˈrefjuːs-] n enlèvement m des ordures ménagères.

refuse collector [ˈrefjuːs-] n éboueur m.

refuse dump [ˈrefjuːs-] n décharge f (publique).

refute [rɪˈfjuːt] vt réfuter.

reg., regd. (abbr of **registered**) : ~ **trademark** marque f déposée.

regain [rɪˈgeɪn] vt [composure, health] retrouver ; [leadership] reprendre.

regal [ˈriːgl] adj majestueux(euse), royal(e).

regale [rɪˈgeɪl] vt : **to** ~ **sb with sthg** divertir qqn en lui racontant qqch.

regalia [rɪˈgeɪljə] n (U) insignes mpl.

regard [rɪˈgɑːd] <> n - **1.** (U) [respect] estime f, respect m - **2.** [aspect] : **in this/that** ~ à cet égard <> vt considérer ; **to** ~ **o.s. as** se considérer comme ; **to be highly ~ed** être tenu(e) en haute estime.
➡ **regards** npl : (**with best**) ~**s** bien amicalement ; **give her my** ~**s** faites-lui mes amitiés.
➡ **as regards** prep en ce qui concerne.
➡ **in regard to, with regard to** prep en ce qui concerne, relativement à.

regarding [rɪˈgɑːdɪŋ] prep concernant, en ce qui concerne.

regardless [rɪˈgɑːdlɪs] adv quand même.
➡ **regardless of** prep sans tenir compte de, sans se soucier de.

regatta [rɪˈgætə] n régate f.

regd. = reg.

Regency ['ri:dʒənsɪ] *adj* Régence (anglaise).

regenerate [rɪ'dʒenəreɪt] *vt* [economy, project] relancer.

regeneration [rɪ,dʒenə'reɪʃn] *n* [of economy, project] relance *f*.

regent ['ri:dʒənt] *n* régent *m*, -e *f*.

reggae ['regeɪ] *n* reggae *m*.

regime [reɪ'ʒi:m] *n* régime *m*.

regiment ['redʒɪmənt] *n* régiment *m*.

regimental [,redʒɪ'mentl] *adj* du régiment.

regimented ['redʒɪmentɪd] *adj* [organization] trop rigide ; [life] strict(e).

region ['ri:dʒən] *n* région *f*; **in the ~ of** environ.

regional ['ri:dʒənl] *adj* régional(e).

register ['redʒɪstər] <> *n* [record] registre *m* <> *vt* - **1.** [record officially] déclarer - **2.** [show, measure] indiquer, montrer - **3.** [express] exprimer <> *vi* - **1.** [on official list] s'inscrire, se faire inscrire - **2.** [at hotel] signer le registre - **3.** inf [advice, fact] : **it didn't ~** je n'ai pas compris.

registered ['redʒɪstəd] *adj* - **1.** [person] inscrit(e) ; [car] immatriculé(e) ; [charity] agréé(e) par le gouvernement - **2.** [letter, parcel] recommandé(e).

registered nurse *n* infirmier diplômé d'État *m*, infirmière diplômée d'État *f*.

registered post Br, **registered mail** Am *n* : **to send sthg by ~** envoyer qqch en recommandé.

registered trademark *n* marque *f* déposée.

registrar [,redʒɪ'strɑ:r] *n* - **1.** [keeper of records] officier *m* de l'état civil - **2.** UNIV secrétaire *m* général - **3.** Br [doctor] chef *m* de clinique.

registration [,redʒɪ'streɪʃn] *n* - **1.** [gen] enregistrement *m*, inscription *f* - **2.** AUT = **registration number.**

registration document *n* ≃ carte *f* grise.

registration number *n* AUT numéro *m* d'immatriculation.

registry ['redʒɪstrɪ] (*pl* **-ies**) *n* bureau *m* de l'enregistrement.

registry office *n* bureau *m* de l'état civil.

regress [rɪ'gres] *vi* : **to ~ (to)** régresser (au stade de).

regression [rɪ'greʃn] *n* régression *f*.

regressive [rɪ'gresɪv] *adj* régressif(ive).

regret [rɪ'gret] (*pt* & *pp* **-ted** ; *cont* **-ting**) <> *n* regret *m* <> *vt* [be sorry about] : **to ~ sthg/doing sthg** regretter qqch/d'avoir fait qqch ; **we** **~ to announce ...** nous sommes au regret d'annoncer ...

regretful [rɪ'gretfʊl] *adj* [person] plein(e) de regrets ; [look] de regret.

regretfully [rɪ'gretfʊlɪ] *adv* à regret.

regrettable [rɪ'gretəbl] *adj* regrettable, fâcheux(euse).

regrettably [rɪ'gretəblɪ] *adv* malheureusement.

regroup [,ri:'gru:p] *vi* se regrouper.

regt *abbr of* **regiment.**

regular ['regjʊlər] <> *adj* - **1.** [gen] régulier(ère) ; [customer] fidèle - **2.** [usual] habituel(elle) - **3.** Am [normal - size] standard (*inv*) - **4.** Am [pleasant] sympa (*inv*) <> *n* [at pub] habitué *m*, -e *f* ; [at shop] client *m*, -e *f* fidèle.

regular army *n* armée *f* de métier.

regularity [,regjʊ'lærətɪ] *n* régularité *f*.

regularly ['regjʊləlɪ] *adv* régulièrement.

regulate ['regjʊleɪt] *vt* régler.

regulation [,regjʊ'leɪʃn] <> *adj* [standard] réglementaire <> *n* - **1.** [rule] règlement *m* - **2.** (U) [control] réglementation *f*.

regurgitate [rɪ'gɜ:dʒɪteɪt] *vt* régurgiter ; fig & pej ressortir, répéter.

rehabilitate [,ri:ə'bɪlɪteɪt] *vt* [criminal] réinsérer, réhabiliter ; [patient] rééduquer.

rehabilitation ['ri:ə,bɪlɪ'teɪʃn] *n* [of criminal] réinsertion *f*, réhabilitation *f*; [of patient] rééducation *f*.

rehash [,ri:'hæʃ] *vt* inf pej remanier.

rehearsal [rɪ'hɜ:sl] *n* répétition *f*.

rehearse [rɪ'hɜ:s] *vt* & *vi* répéter.

rehouse [,ri:'haʊz] *vt* reloger.

reign [reɪn] <> *n* règne *m* <> *vi* : **to ~ (over)** lit & fig régner (sur).

reigning ['reɪnɪŋ] *adj* [champion] actuel(elle).

reimburse [,ri:ɪm'bɜ:s] *vt* : **to ~ sb (for)** rembourser qqn (de).

reimbursement [,ri:ɪm'bɜ:smənt] *n* remboursement *m*.

Reims [ri:mz] *n* Reims.

rein [reɪn] *n* fig : **to give (a) free ~ to sb, to give sb free ~** laisser la bride sur le cou à qqn ; **to keep a tight ~ on sb** tenir la bride haute à qqn ; **to keep a tight ~ on sthg** contrôler étroitement qqch.

➡ **reins** *npl* - **1.** [for horse] rênes *fpl* - **2.** [for child] laisse *f*.

➡ **rein in** *vt sep* [horse] serrer la bride à ; fig modérer.

reincarnation [,ri:ɪnkɑ:'neɪʃn] *n* réincarnation *f*.

reindeer ['reɪnˌdɪəʳ] (pl inv) n renne m.

reinforce [ˌriːɪn'fɔːs] vt - **1.** [strengthen] renforcer - **2.** [back up, confirm] appuyer, étayer.

reinforced concrete [ˌriːɪn'fɔːst-] n béton m armé.

reinforcement [ˌriːɪn'fɔːsmənt] n - **1.** (U) [strengthening] renforcement m - **2.** [strengthener] renfort m.

➠ **reinforcements** npl renforts mpl.

reinstate [ˌriːɪn'steɪt] vt [employee] rétablir dans ses fonctions, réintégrer ; [policy, method] rétablir.

reinstatement [ˌriːɪn'steɪtmənt] n réintégration f, rétablissement m.

reinterpret [ˌriːɪn'tɜːprɪt] vt interpréter de nouveau (différemment).

reintroduce ['riːˌɪntrə'djuːs] vt réintroduire.

reintroduction [ˌriːɪntrə'dʌkʃn] n réintroduction f.

reissue [riː'ɪʃuː] ⬦ n [of book] réédition f ⬦ vt [book] rééditer ; [film, record] ressortir.

reiterate [riː'ɪtəreɪt] vt réitérer, répéter.

reiteration [riːˌɪtə'reɪʃn] n réitération f.

reject [n 'riːdʒekt, vb rɪ'dʒekt] ⬦ n [product] article m de rebut ⬦ vt - **1.** [not accept] rejeter - **2.** [candidate, coin] refuser.

rejection [rɪ'dʒekʃn] n - **1.** [non-acceptance] rejet m - **2.** [of candidate] refus m.

rejig [ˌriː'dʒɪg] (pt & pp -ged ; cont -ging) vt Br inf réorganiser.

rejoice [rɪ'dʒɔɪs] vi : to ~ (at OR in) se réjouir (de).

rejoicing [rɪ'dʒɔɪsɪŋ] n (U) réjouissance f.

rejoin¹ [ˌriː'dʒɔɪn] vt rejoindre ; [club] adhérer de nouveau à.

rejoin² [rɪ'dʒɔɪn] vt [reply] répondre, répliquer.

rejoinder [rɪ'dʒɔɪndəʳ] n réplique f, riposte f.

rejuvenate [rɪ'dʒuːvəneɪt] vt rajeunir.

rejuvenation [rɪˌdʒuːvə'neɪʃn] n rajeunissement m.

rekindle [ˌriː'kɪndl] vt fig ranimer, raviver.

relapse [rɪ'læps] ⬦ n rechute f ; to have a ~ faire une rechute, rechuter ⬦ vi : to ~ into retomber dans.

relate [rɪ'leɪt] ⬦ vt - **1.** [connect] : to ~ sthg to sthg établir un lien OR rapport entre qqch et qqch - **2.** [tell] raconter ⬦ vi - **1.** [be connected] : to ~ to avoir un rapport avec - **2.** [concern] : to ~ to se rapporter à - **3.** [empathize] : to ~ (to sb) s'entendre (avec qqn).

➠ **relating to** prep concernant.

related [rɪ'leɪtɪd] adj - **1.** [people] apparenté(e) - **2.** [issues, problems etc] lié(e).

relation [rɪ'leɪʃn] n - **1.** [connection] : ~ (to/ between) rapport m (avec/entre) ; in ~ to par rapport à - **2.** [person] parent m, -e f.

➠ **relations** npl [relationship] relations fpl, rapports mpl.

relational [rɪ'leɪʃənl] adj COMPUT relationnel(elle).

relationship [rɪ'leɪʃnʃɪp] n - **1.** [between people, countries] relations fpl, rapports mpl ; [romantic] liaison f - **2.** [connection] rapport m, lien m.

relative ['relətɪv] ⬦ adj relatif(ive) ⬦ n parent m, -e f.

➠ **relative to** prep [compared with] relativement à ; [connected with] se rapportant à, relatif(ive) à.

relatively ['relətɪvlɪ] adv relativement.

relativity [ˌrelə'tɪvətɪ] n relativité f.

relax [rɪ'læks] ⬦ vt - **1.** [person] détendre, relaxer - **2.** [muscle, body] décontracter, relâcher ; [one's grip] desserrer - **3.** [rule] relâcher ⬦ vi - **1.** [person] se détendre, se décontracter - **2.** [muscle, body] se relâcher, se décontracter - **3.** [one's grip] se desserrer.

relaxation [ˌriːlæk'seɪʃn] n - **1.** [of person] relaxation f, détente f - **2.** [of rule] relâchement m.

relaxed [rɪ'lækst] adj détendu(e), décontracté(e).

relaxing [rɪ'læksɪŋ] adj relaxant(e), qui détend.

relay ['riːleɪ] (pt & pp senses 1 & 2 -ed ; pt & pp sense 3 relaid) ⬦ n - **1.** SPORT : ~ (race) course f de relais ; in ~s fig en se relayant - **2.** RADIO & TV [broadcast] retransmission f ⬦ vt - **1.** RADIO & TV [broadcast] relayer - **2.** [message, information] transmettre, communiquer - **3.** [carpet, tiles] poser à nouveau, reposer.

release [rɪ'liːs] ⬦ n - **1.** [from prison, cage] libération f - **2.** [from pain, misery] délivrance f - **3.** [statement] communiqué m - **4.** [of gas, heat] échappement m - **5.** (U) [of film, record] sortie f ; to be on ~ CINEMA passer dans les salles de cinéma - **6.** [film] nouveau film m ; [record] nouveau disque m ⬦ vt - **1.** [set free] libérer - **2.** [lift restriction on] : to ~ sb from dégager qqn de - **3.** [make available - supplies] libérer ; [- funds] débloquer - **4.** [let go of] lâcher - **5.** [TECH - brake, handle] desserrer ; [- mechanism] déclencher - **6.** [gas, heat] : to be ~d (from/into) se dégager (de/dans), s'échapper (de/dans) - **7.** [film, record] sortir ; [statement, report] publier.

relegate ['relɪgeɪt] vt reléguer ; to be ~d Br SPORT être relégué à la division inférieure.

relegation [ˌrelɪ'geɪʃn] n relégation f.

relent [rɪ'lent] *vi* [person] se laisser fléchir ; [wind, storm] se calmer.

relentless [rɪ'lentlɪs] *adj* implacable.

relentlessly [rɪ'lentlɪslɪ] *adv* implacablement.

relevance ['reləvəns] (*U*) *n* - **1.** [connection] : ~ **(to)** rapport *m* (avec) - **2.** [significance] : ~ **(to)** importance *f* (pour).

relevant ['reləvənt] *adj* - **1.** [connected] : ~ **(to)** qui a un rapport (avec) - **2.** [significant] : ~ **(to)** important(e) (pour) - **3.** [appropriate - information] utile ; [- document] justificatif(ive).

reliability [rɪ,laɪə'bɪlətɪ] *n* fiabilité *f*.

reliable [rɪ'laɪəbl] *adj* [person] sur qui on peut compter, fiable ; [device] fiable ; [company, information] sérieux(euse).

reliably [rɪ'laɪəblɪ] *adv* de façon fiable ; **to be ~ informed (that)** ... savoir de source sûre que ...

reliance [rɪ'laɪəns] *n :* ~ **(on)** dépendance *f* (de).

reliant [rɪ'laɪənt] *adj :* **to be ~ on** être dépendant(e) de.

relic ['relɪk] *n* relique *f* ; [of past] vestige *m*.

relief [rɪ'liːf] *n* - **1.** [comfort] soulagement *m* - **2.** [for poor, refugees] aide *f*, assistance *f* - **3.** Am [social security] aide *f* sociale.

relief map *n* carte *f* en relief.

relief road *n* Br route *f* de délestage.

relieve [rɪ'liːv] *vt* - **1.** [pain, anxiety] soulager ; **to ~ sb of sthg** [take away from] délivrer qqn de qqch - **2.** [take over from] relayer - **3.** [give help to] secourir, venir en aide à.

relieved [rɪ'liːvd] *adj* soulagé(e).

religion [rɪ'lɪdʒn] *n* religion *f*.

religious [rɪ'lɪdʒəs] *adj* religieux(euse) ; [book] de piété.

reline [,riː'laɪn] *vt* [clothes, bag] redoubler ; [brakes] changer les garnitures de.

relinquish [rɪ'lɪŋkwɪʃ] *vt* [power] abandonner ; [claim, plan] renoncer à ; [post] quitter.

relish ['relɪʃ] ⇔ *n* - **1.** [enjoyment] : **with (great) ~** avec délectation - **2.** [pickle] condiment *m* ⇔ *vt* [enjoy] prendre plaisir à ; **I don't ~ the thought** OR **idea** OR **prospect of seeing him** la perspective de le voir ne m'enchante OR ne me sourit guère.

relive [,riː'lɪv] *vt* revivre.

relocate [,riː'ləʊ'keɪt] ⇔ *vt* installer ailleurs, transférer ⇔ *vi* s'installer ailleurs, déménager.

relocation [,rɪləʊ'keɪʃn] *n* transfert *m*, déménagement *m*.

relocation expenses *npl* frais *mpl* de déménagement.

reluctance [rɪ'lʌktəns] *n* répugnance *f*.

reluctant [rɪ'lʌktənt] *adj* peu enthousiaste ; **to be ~ to do sthg** rechigner à faire qqch, être peu disposé à faire qqch.

reluctantly [rɪ'lʌktəntlɪ] *adv* à contrecœur, avec répugnance.

rely [rɪ'laɪ] (*pt & pp* **-ied**) ➠ **rely on** *vt fus* - **1.** [count on] compter sur ; **to ~ on sb to do sthg** compter sur qqn OR faire confiance à qqn pour faire qqch - **2.** [be dependent on] dépendre de.

REM (*abbr of* **rapid eye movement**) *n* activité *oculaire intense durant le sommeil para-doxal.*

remain [rɪ'meɪn] ⇔ *vt* rester ; **to ~ to be done** rester à faire ; **it ~s to be seen** ... reste à savoir ... ⇔ *vi* rester.

➠ **remains** *npl* - **1.** [remnants] restes *mpl* - **2.** [antiquities] ruines *fpl*, vestiges *mpl*.

remainder [rɪ'meɪndəʳ] *n* reste *m*.

remaining [rɪ'meɪnɪŋ] *adj* qui reste ; **last ~** dernier(ère).

remake [*n* 'riːmeɪk, *vb* ,riː'meɪk] CINEMA ⇔ *n* remake *m* ⇔ *vt* refaire.

remand [rɪ'mɑːnd] JUR ⇔ *n* : **on ~** en détention préventive ⇔ *vt :* **to ~ sb (in custody)** placer qqn en détention préventive.

remand centre *n* Br maison *f* de détention préventive.

remark [rɪ'mɑːk] ⇔ *n* [comment] remarque *f*, observation *f* ⇔ *vt* [comment] : **to ~ that** ... faire remarquer que ... ⇔ *vi :* **to ~ on** faire des remarques sur.

remarkable [rɪ'mɑːkəbl] *adj* remarquable.

remarkably [rɪ'mɑːkəblɪ] *adv* remarquablement.

remarry [,riː'mærɪ] (*pt & pp* **-ied**) *vi* se remarier.

remedial [rɪ'miːdjəl] *adj* - **1.** [pupil, class] de rattrapage - **2.** [exercise] correctif(ive) ; [action] de rectification.

remedy ['remədɪ] (*pl* **-ies**, *pt & pp* **-ied**) ⇔ *n :* ~ **(for)** MED remède *m* (pour OR contre) ; fig remède (à OR contre) ⇔ *vt* remédier à.

remember [rɪ'membəʳ] ⇔ *vt* - **1.** [gen] se souvenir de, se rappeler ; **to ~ to do sthg** ne pas oublier de faire qqch, penser à faire qqch ; **to ~ doing sthg** se souvenir d'avoir fait qqch, se rappeler avoir fait qqch - **2.** [as greeting] : **to ~ sb to sb** rappeler qqn au bon souvenir de qqn ⇔ *vi* se souvenir, se rappeler.

remembrance [rɪ'membrəns] *n :* in ~ of en souvenir OR mémoire de.

Remembrance Day *n* l'Armistice *m*.

remind [rɪ'maɪnd] *vt :* to ~ sb of OR about sthg rappeler qqch à qqn ; to ~ sb to do sthg rappeler à qqn de faire qqch, faire penser à qqn à faire qqch.

reminder [rɪ'maɪndə'] *n* - **1.** [to jog memory] : to give sb a ~ (to do sthg) faire penser à qqn (à faire qqch) - **2.** [letter, note] rappel *m*.

reminisce [ˌremɪ'nɪs] *vi* évoquer des souvenirs ; to ~ about sthg évoquer qqch.

reminiscences [ˌremɪ'nɪsənsɪz] *npl* souvenirs *mpl*.

reminiscent [ˌremɪ'nɪsnt] *adj :* ~ of qui rappelle, qui fait penser à.

remiss [rɪ'mɪs] *adj* négligent(e).

remission [rɪ'mɪʃn] *n* (U) - **1.** JUR remise *f* - **2.** MED rémission *f*.

remit[1] [rɪ'mɪt] (*pt & pp* -ted ; *cont* -ting) *vt* [money] envoyer, verser.

remit[2] ['riːmɪt] *n* Br [responsibility] attributions *fpl*.

remittance [rɪ'mɪtns] *n* - **1.** [amount of money] versement *m* - **2.** COMM règlement *m*, paiement *m*.

remnant ['remnənt] *n* - **1.** [remaining part] reste *m*, restant *m* - **2.** [of cloth] coupon *m*.

remodel [ˌriː'mɒdl] (Br *pt & pp* -led ; *cont* -ling, Am *pt & pp* -ed ; *cont* -ing) *vt* remodeler.

remold Am = remould.

remonstrate ['remənstreɪt] *vi :* to ~ (with sb about sthg) faire des remontrances (à qqn au sujet de qqch).

remorse [rɪ'mɔːs] *n* (U) remords *m*.

remorseful [rɪ'mɔːsfʊl] *adj* plein(e) de remords.

remorseless [rɪ'mɔːslɪs] *adj* implacable.

remorselessly [rɪ'mɔːslɪslɪ] *adv* implacablement.

remote [rɪ'məʊt] *adj* - **1.** [far-off - place] éloigné(e) ; [- time] lointain(e) - **2.** [person] distant(e) - **3.** [possibility, chance] vague.

remote control *n* télécommande *f*.

remote-controlled [-kən'trəʊld] *adj* télécommandé(e).

remotely [rɪ'məʊtlɪ] *adv* - **1.** [in the slightest] : not ~ pas le moins du monde, absolument pas - **2.** [far off] au loin.

remoteness [rɪ'məʊtnɪs] *n* - **1.** [of place] éloignement *m*, isolement *m* - **2.** [of person] attitude *f* distante.

remould Br, **remold** Am ['riːməʊld] *n* pneu *m* rechapé.

removable [rɪ'muːvəbl] *adj* [detachable] détachable, amovible.

removal [rɪ'muːvl] *n* - **1.** (U) [act of removing] enlèvement *m* - **2.** Br [change of house] déménagement *m*.

removal man *n* Br déménageur *m*.

removal van *n* Br camion *m* de déménagement.

remove [rɪ'muːv] *vt* - **1.** [take away - gen] enlever ; [- stain] faire partir, enlever ; [- problem] résoudre ; [- suspicion] dissiper - **2.** [clothes] ôter, enlever - **3.** [employee] renvoyer.

removed [rɪ'muːvd] *adj :* to be far ~ from être très éloigné(e) OR différent(e) de.

remover [rɪ'muːvə'] *n* [for paint] décapant *m ;* [for stains] détachant *m ;* [for nail-varnish] dissolvant *m*.

remuneration [rɪˌmjuːnə'reɪʃn] *n* rémunération *f*.

Renaissance [rə'neɪsəns] ◇ *n :* the ~ la Renaissance ◇ *comp* (de la) Renaissance.

rename [ˌriː'neɪm] *vt* rebaptiser.

rend [rend] (*pt & pp* rent) *vt* déchirer.

render ['rendə'] *vt* rendre ; [assistance] porter ; FIN [account] présenter.

rendering ['rendərɪŋ] *n* [of play, music etc] interprétation *f*.

rendezvous ['rɒndɪvuː] (*pl inv*) *n* rendezvous *m inv*.

rendition [ren'dɪʃn] *n* interprétation *f*.

renegade ['renɪgeɪd] *n* renégat *m*, -e *f*.

renege [rɪ'niːg] *vi :* to ~ on manquer à, revenir sur.

renegotiate [ˌriːnɪ'gəʊʃɪeɪt] ◇ *vt* renégocier ◇ *vi* négocier à nouveau.

renew [rɪ'njuː] *vt* - **1.** [gen] renouveler ; [negotiations, strength] reprendre ; [interest] faire renaître ; to ~ acquaintance with sb renouer connaissance avec qqn - **2.** [replace] remplacer.

renewable [rɪ'njuːəbl] *adj* renouvelable.

renewal [rɪ'njuːəl] *n* - **1.** [of activity] reprise *f* - **2.** [of contract, licence etc] renouvellement *m*.

rennet ['renɪt] *n* présure *f*.

renounce [rɪ'naʊns] *vt* [reject] renoncer à.

renovate ['renəveɪt] *vt* rénover.

renovation [ˌrenə'veɪʃn] *n* rénovation *f*.

renown [rɪ'naʊn] *n* renommée *f*, renom *m*.

renowned [rɪ'naʊnd] *adj :* ~ (for) renommé(e) (pour).

rent [rent] ⬦ *pt* & *pp* ⊳ **rend** ⬦ *n* [for house] loyer *m* ⬦ *vt* louer.
➤ **rent out** *vt sep* louer.

rental ['rentl] ⬦ *adj* de location ⬦ *n* [for car, television, video] prix *m* de location ; [for house] loyer *m*.

rent book *n* carnet *m* de quittances de loyer.

rent boy *n* Br inf jeune garçon *m* qui se prostitue.

rented ['rentɪd] *adj* loué(e).

rent-free ⬦ *adj* gratuit(e) ⬦ *adv* sans payer de loyer.

renumber [,riː'nʌmbəʳ] *vt* renuméroter.

renunciation [rɪ,nʌnsɪ'eɪʃn] *n* renonciation *f.*

reoccurrence [,riːə'kʌrəns] *n* : if there's a ~ ... si cela se reproduit ...

reopen [,riː'əupn] ⬦ *vt* rouvrir ; [negotiations] reprendre ⬦ *vi* rouvrir ; [negotiations] reprendre ; [wound] se rouvrir.

reorganization ['riː,ɔːgənaɪ'zeɪʃn] *n* réorganisation *f.*

reorganize, -ise [,riː'ɔːgənaɪz] ⬦ *vt* réorganiser ⬦ *vi* se réorganiser.

rep [rep] *n* - **1.** (*abbr of* **representative**) VRP *m* - **2.** *abbr of* **repertory** - **3.** *abbr of* **repertory company.**

Rep. Am - **1.** *abbr of* **Representative** - **2.** *abbr of* **Republican.**

repaid [riː'peɪd] *pt* & *pp* ⊳ **repay.**

repaint [,riː'peɪnt] *vt* repeindre.

repair [rɪ'peəʳ] ⬦ *n* réparation *f* ; in good/bad ~ en bon/mauvais état ⬦ *vt* réparer.

repair kit *n* trousse *f* à outils.

repaper [,riː'peɪpəʳ] *vt* retapisser.

reparations [,repə'reɪʃnz] *npl* réparations *fpl.*

repartee [,repɑː'tiː] *n* repartie *f.*

repatriate [,riː'pætrɪeɪt] *vt* rapatrier.

repay [riː'peɪ] (*pt* & *pp* **repaid**) *vt* - **1.** [money] : to ~ sb sthg, to ~ sthg to sb rembourser qqch à qqn - **2.** [favour] payer de retour, récompenser ; to ~ sb for sthg récompenser qqn de OR pour qqch.

repayment [riː'peɪmənt] *n* remboursement *m.*

repeal [rɪ'piːl] ⬦ *n* abrogation *f* ⬦ *vt* abroger.

repeat [rɪ'piːt] ⬦ *vt* - **1.** [gen] répéter ; to ~ o.s. se répéter - **2.** RADIO & TV rediffuser ⬦ *n* RADIO & TV reprise *f*, rediffusion *f.*

repeated [rɪ'piːtɪd] *adj* répété(e).

repeatedly [rɪ'piːtɪdlɪ] *adv* à maintes reprises, très souvent.

repel [rɪ'pel] (*pt* & *pp* **-led** ; *cont* **-ling**) *vt* repousser.

repellent [rɪ'pelənt] ⬦ *adj* répugnant(e), repoussant(e) ⬦ *n* : insect ~ crème *f* anti-insecte.

repent [rɪ'pent] ⬦ *vt* se repentir de ⬦ *vi* : to ~ (of) se repentir (de).

repentance [rɪ'pentəns] *n* (U) repentir *m.*

repentant [rɪ'pentənt] *adj* repentant(e).

repercussions [,riːpə'kʌʃnz] *npl* répercussions *fpl.*

repertoire ['repətwɑːʳ] *n* répertoire *m.*

repertory ['repətrɪ] *n* répertoire *m.*

repertory company *n* compagnie *f* OR troupe *f* de répertoire.

repetition [,repɪ'tɪʃn] *n* répétition *f.*

repetitious [,repɪ'tɪʃəs], **repetitive** [rɪ'petɪtɪv] *adj* [action, job] répétitif(ive) ; [article, speech] qui a des redites.

rephrase [,riː'freɪz] *vt* réécrire, tourner autrement.

replace [rɪ'pleɪs] *vt* - **1.** [gen] remplacer - **2.** [put back] remettre (à sa place).

replacement [rɪ'pleɪsmənt] *n* - **1.** [substituting] remplacement *m* ; [putting back] replacement *m* - **2.** [new person] : ~ (for sb) remplaçant *m*, -e *f* (de qqn).

replacement part *n* pièce *f* de rechange.

replay [*n* 'riːpleɪ, *vb* ,riː'pleɪ] ⬦ *n* match *m* rejoué ⬦ *vt* - **1.** [match, game] rejouer - **2.** [film, tape] repasser.

replenish [rɪ'plenɪʃ] *vt* : to ~ one's supply of sthg se réapprovisionner en qqch.

replete [rɪ'pliːt] *adj fml* rempli(e) ; [person] rassasié(e).

replica ['replɪkə] *n* copie *f* exacte, réplique *f.*

replicate ['replɪkeɪt] *vt fml* reproduire.

replication [,replɪ'keɪʃn] *n fml* reproduction *f.*

reply [rɪ'plaɪ] (*pl* **-ies** ; *pt* & *pp* **-ied**) ⬦ *n* : ~ (to) réponse *f* (à) ; in ~ (to) en réponse (à) ⬦ *vt* & *vi* répondre.

reply coupon *n* coupon-réponse *m.*

reply-paid *adj* réponse payée.

report [rɪ'pɔːt] ⬦ *n* - **1.** [account] rapport *m*, compte *m* rendu ; PRESS reportage *m* - **2.** Br SCH bulletin *m* ⬦ *vt* - **1.** [news, crime] rapporter, signaler - **2.** [make known] : to ~ that ... annoncer que ... - **3.** [complain about] : to ~ sb (to) dénoncer qqn (à) ⬦ *vi* - **1.** [give account] : to ~ (on) faire un rapport (sur) ; PRESS faire un reportage (sur) - **2.** [present oneself] : to ~ (to

sb/for sthg) se présenter (à qqn/pour qqch).

report back vi : to ~ back (to) présenter son rapport (à).

reportage [,repɔː'tɑːʒ] (U) n reportage m.

report card n bulletin m scolaire.

reportedly [rɪ'pɔːtɪdlɪ] adv à ce qu'il paraît.

reported speech [rɪ'pɔːtɪd-] n style m indirect.

reporter [rɪ'pɔːtəʳ] n reporter m.

repose [rɪ'pəʊz] n literary repos m.

repository [rɪ'pɒzɪtrɪ] (pl -ies) n dépôt m.

repossess [,riːpə'zes] vt saisir.

repossession [,riːpə'zeʃn] n saisie f.

repossession order n ordre m de saisie.

reprehensible [,reprɪ'hensəbl] adj répréhensible.

represent [,reprɪ'zent] vt - **1.** [gen] représenter ; to be well OR strongly ~ed être bien représenté - **2.** [describe] : to ~ sb/sthg as décrire qqn/qqch comme.

representation [,reprɪzen'teɪʃn] n [gen] représentation f.

representations npl : to make ~s to sb faire une démarche auprès de qqn.

representative [,reprɪ'zentətɪv] <> adj représentatif(ive) <> n représentant m, -e f.

repress [rɪ'pres] vt réprimer.

repressed [rɪ'prest] adj - **1.** [person - sexually] refoulé(e) - **2.** [feelings] réprimé(e), contenu(e).

repression [rɪ'preʃn] n répression f ; [sexual] refoulement m.

repressive [rɪ'presɪv] adj répressif(ive).

reprieve [rɪ'priːv] <> n - **1.** fig [delay] sursis m, répit m - **2.** JUR sursis m <> vt accorder un sursis à.

reprimand ['reprɪmɑːnd] <> n réprimande f <> vt réprimander.

reprint [n 'riːprɪnt, vb ,riː'prɪnt] <> n réimpression f <> vt réimprimer.

reprisal [rɪ'praɪzl] n représailles fpl.

reproach [rɪ'prəʊtʃ] <> n reproche m <> vt : to ~ sb for OR with sthg reprocher qqch à qqn.

reproachful [rɪ'prəʊtʃfʊl] adj [look, words] de reproche.

reprobate ['reprəbeɪt] n hum dépravé m, -e f.

reproduce [,riːprə'djuːs] <> vt reproduire <> vi se reproduire.

reproduction [,riːprə'dʌkʃn] n reproduction f.

reproductive [,riːprə'dʌktɪv] adj reproducteur(trice).

reprogram [,riː'prəʊɡræm] (pt & pp -ed OR -med ; cont -ing OR -ming) vt reprogrammer.

reproof [rɪ'pruːf] n reproche m, blâme m.

reprove [rɪ'pruːv] vt : to ~ sb (for) blâmer qqn (pour OR de), réprimander qqn (pour).

reproving [rɪ'pruːvɪŋ] adj réprobateur(trice).

reptile ['reptaɪl] n reptile m.

Repub. Am abbr of Republican.

republic [rɪ'pʌblɪk] n république f.

republican [rɪ'pʌblɪkən] <> adj républicain(e) <> n républicain m, -e f.

Republican <> adj républicain(e) ; the Republican Party Am le parti républicain <> n républicain m, -e f.

repudiate [rɪ'pjuːdɪeɪt] vt fml [offer, suggestion] rejeter ; [friend] renier.

repudiation [rɪ,pjuːdɪ'eɪʃn] n fml [of offer, suggestion] rejet m ; [of friend] reniement m.

repugnant [rɪ'pʌgnənt] adj répugnant(e).

repulse [rɪ'pʌls] vt repousser.

repulsion [rɪ'pʌlʃn] n répulsion f.

repulsive [rɪ'pʌlsɪv] adj repoussant(e).

reputable ['repjʊtəbl] adj de bonne réputation.

reputation [,repjʊ'teɪʃn] n réputation f ; to have a ~ for sthg être réputé pour qqch ; to have a ~ for being ... avoir la réputation d'être ...

repute [rɪ'pjuːt] n : of ~ de renom ; of good ~ de bonne réputation.

reputed [rɪ'pjuːtɪd] adj réputé(e) ; to be ~ to be sthg être réputé pour être qqch, avoir la réputation d'être qqch.

reputedly [rɪ'pjuːtɪdlɪ] adv à OR d'après ce qu'on dit.

reqd abbr of required.

request [rɪ'kwest] <> n : ~ (for) demande f (de) ; on ~ sur demande ; at sb's ~ sur OR à la demande de qqn <> vt demander ; to ~ sb to do sthg demander à qqn de faire qqch.

request stop n Br arrêt m facultatif.

requiem (mass) ['rekwɪəm-] n messe f de requiem.

require [rɪ'kwaɪəʳ] vt [subj : person] avoir besoin de ; [subj : situation] nécessiter ; to ~ sb to do sthg exiger de qqn qu'il fasse qqch.

required [rɪ'kwaɪəd] adj exigé(e), requis(e).

requirement [rɪ'kwaɪəmənt] n besoin m.

requisite ['rekwɪzɪt] adj fml requis(e).

requisition [,rekwɪ'zɪʃn] vt réquisitionner.

reran [,riː'ræn] pt ▷ rerun.

reread [,ri:'ri:d] (pt & pp **reread** [,ri:'redl) vt relire.

rerecord [,ri:'rɪkɔːd] vt réenregistrer.

reroute [,ri:'ruːt] vt dérouter.

rerun [n 'riːrʌn, vb ,riː'rʌn] (pt -ran ; pp -run, cont -ning) ⇔ n [of TV programme] rediffusion f, reprise f; fig répétition f ⇔ vt - **1.** [race] réorganiser - **2.** [TV programme] rediffuser ; [tape] passer à nouveau, repasser.

resale price maintenance ['riːseɪl-] n Br prix imposé aux distributeurs par le fabricant.

resat [,ri:'sæt] pt & pp ⊳ resit.

reschedule [Br ,ri:'ʃedjʊl, Am ,ri:'skedʒʊl] vt [to new date] changer la date de ; [to new time] changer l'heure de ; FIN rééchelonner.

rescind [rɪ'sɪnd] vt [contract] annuler ; [law] abroger.

rescue ['reskjuː] ⇔ n - **1.** (U) [help] secours mpl ; **to go/come to sb's ~** aller/venir au secours de qqn - **2.** [successful attempt] sauvetage m ⇔ vt sauver, secourir.

rescue operation n opération f de sauvetage.

rescuer ['reskjʊər] n sauveteur m.

reseal [,ri:'si:l] vt [letter] recacheter.

resealable [,ri:'si:ləbl] adj [envelope] qui peut être recacheté(e).

research [rɪ'sɜːtʃ] ⇔ n (U) : **~ (on** OR **into)** recherche f (sur), recherches fpl (sur) ; **~ and development** recherche et développement ⇔ vt faire des recherches sur ⇔ vi : **to ~ (into)** faire des recherches (sur).

researcher [rɪ'sɜːtʃər] n chercheur m, -euse f.

research work n (U) recherches fpl.

resell [,ri:'sell] (pt & pp **resold**) vt revendre.

resemblance [rɪ'zembləns] n : **~ (to)** ressemblance f (avec).

resemble [rɪ'zembl] vt ressembler à.

resent [rɪ'zent] vt être indigné(e) par ; **I ~ that!** je n'apprécie pas (ça) du tout !

resentful [rɪ'zentfʊl] adj plein(e) de ressentiment.

resentfully [rɪ'zentfʊlɪ] adv avec ressentiment.

resentment [rɪ'zentmənt] n ressentiment m.

reservation [,rezə'veɪʃn] n - **1.** [booking] réservation f - **2.** [uncertainty] : **without ~** sans réserve - **3.** Am [for Native Americans] réserve f indienne.

➡ **reservations** npl [doubts] réserves fpl.

reserve [rɪ'zɜːv] ⇔ n - **1.** [gen] réserve f ; **in ~**

en réserve - **2.** SPORT remplaçant m, -e f ⇔ vt - **1.** [save] garder, réserver - **2.** [book] réserver - **3.** [retain] : **to ~ the right to do sthg** se réserver le droit de faire qqch.

reserve bank n Am banque f de réserve.

reserve currency n monnaie f de réserve.

reserved [rɪ'zɜːvd] adj réservé(e).

reserve price n Br prix m minimum.

reserve team n Br deuxième équipe f.

reservist [rɪ'zɜːvɪst] n réserviste m.

reservoir ['rezəvwɑːr] n réservoir m.

reset [,ri:'set] (pt & pp **reset**, cont -ting) ⇔ vt - **1.** [clock, watch] remettre à l'heure ; [meter, controls] remettre à zéro - **2.** [bone] remettre - **3.** COMPUT ré-initialiser ⇔ vi COMPUT ré-initialiser.

resettle [,ri:'setl] ⇔ vt [land] repeupler ; [people] établir, implanter ⇔ vi [people] se fixer (ailleurs), s'établir (ailleurs).

resettlement [,ri:'setlmənt] n [of land] repeuplement m ; [of people] établissement m, implantation f.

reshape [,ri:'ʃeɪp] vt [policy, thinking] réorganiser.

reshuffle [,ri:'ʃʌfl] ⇔ n remaniement m ; **cabinet ~** remaniement ministériel ⇔ vt remanier.

reside [rɪ'zaɪd] vi fml résider.

residence ['rezɪdəns] n résidence f ; **in ~** en résidence ; **to take up ~** s'installer.

residence permit n permis m de séjour.

resident ['rezɪdənt] ⇔ adj résidant(e) ; [chaplain, doctor] à demeure ⇔ n résident m, -e f.

residential [,rezɪ'denʃl] adj : **~ course** stage ou formation avec logement sur place ; **~ institution** internat m.

residential area n quartier m résidentiel.

residents' association n association f de quartier.

residual [rɪ'zɪdjʊəl] adj restant(e) ; CHEM résiduel(elle).

residue ['rezɪdjuː] n reste m ; CHEM résidu m.

resign [rɪ'zaɪn] ⇔ vt - **1.** [job] démissionner de - **2.** [accept calmly] : **to ~ o.s. to** se résigner à ⇔ vi : **to ~ (from)** démissionner (de).

resignation [,rezɪg'neɪʃn] n - **1.** [from job] démission f - **2.** [calm acceptance] résignation f.

resigned [rɪ'zaɪnd] adj : **~ (to)** résigné(e) (à).

resilience [rɪ'zɪlɪəns] n [of material] élasticité f ; [of person] ressort m.

resilient [rɪ'zɪlɪənt] adj [material] élastique ; [person] qui a du ressort.

resin ['rezɪn] n résine f.

resist [rɪ'zɪst] *vt* résister à.
resistance [rɪ'zɪstəns] *n* résistance *f*.
resistant [rɪ'zɪstənt] *adj* - **1.** [opposed] : **to be ~ to** [gen] résister à ; [change] s'opposer à - **2.** [immune] : **~ (to)** rebelle (à).
resistor [rɪ'zɪstə'] *n* ELEC résistance *f*.
resit [*n* 'riːsɪt, *vb* ,riː'sɪt] (*pt* & *pp* **-sat**, *cont* **-ting**) Br ◇ *n* deuxième session *f* ◇ *vt* repasser, se représenter à.
resold [,riː'səʊld] *pt* & *pp* ▷ **resell**.
resolute ['rezəluːt] *adj* résolu(e).
resolutely ['rezəluːtlɪ] *adv* résolument.
resolution [,rezə'luːʃn] *n* résolution *f*.
resolve [rɪ'zɒlv] ◇ *n* (U) [determination] résolution *f* ◇ *vt* - **1.** [decide] : **to ~ (that)** ... décider que ... ; **to ~ to do sthg** résoudre OR décider de faire qqch - **2.** [solve] résoudre.
resonance ['rezənəns] *n* résonance *f*.
resonant ['rezənənt] *adj* résonnant(e).
resonate ['rezəneɪt] *vi* résonner.
resort [rɪ'zɔːt] *n* - **1.** [for holidays] lieu *m* de vacances - **2.** [recourse] recours *m* ; **as a last ~, in the last ~** en dernier ressort OR recours.
◆ **resort to** *vt fus* recourir à, avoir recours à.
resound [rɪ'zaʊnd] *vi* - **1.** [noise] résonner - **2.** [place] : **to ~ with** retentir de.
resounding [rɪ'zaʊndɪŋ] *adj* retentissant(e).
resource [rɪ'sɔːs] *n* ressource *f*.
resourceful [rɪ'sɔːsfʊl] *adj* plein(e) de ressources, débrouillard(e).
resourcefulness [rɪ'sɔːsfʊlnɪs] *n* (U) ressource *f*.
respect [rɪ'spekt] ◇ *n* - **1.** [gen] : **~ (for)** respect *m* (pour) ; **to have ~ for sb** avoir du respect à OR pour qqn ; **to show ~ for sb** témoigner du respect à OR pour qqn ; **with ~** avec respect ; **with ~,...** sauf votre respect,... - **2.** [aspect] : **in this** OR **that ~** à cet égard ; **in every ~** à tous égards ; **in some ~s** à certains égards ◇ *vt* respecter ; **to ~ sb for sthg** respecter qqn pour qqch.
◆ **respects** *npl* respects *mpl*, hommages *mpl* ; **to pay one's last ~s to sb** rendre un dernier hommage à qqn.
◆ **with respect to** *prep* en ce qui concerne, quant à.
respectability [rɪ,spektə'bɪlətɪ] *n* respectabilité *f*.
respectable [rɪ'spektəbl] *adj* - **1.** [morally correct] respectable - **2.** [adequate] raisonnable, honorable.
respectably [rɪ'spektəblɪ] *adv* [correctly] convenablement.

respectful [rɪ'spektfʊl] *adj* respectueux(euse).
respectfully [rɪ'spektfʊlɪ] *adv* avec respect, respectueusement.
respective [rɪ'spektɪv] *adj* respectif(ive).
respectively [rɪ'spektɪvlɪ] *adv* respectivement.
respiration [,respə'reɪʃn] *n* respiration *f*.
respirator ['respəreɪtə'] *n* respirateur *m*.
respiratory [Br rɪ'spɪrətrɪ, Am 'respərətɔːrɪ] *adj* respiratoire.
respire [rɪ'spaɪə'] *vi* respirer.
respite ['respaɪt] *n* répit *m*.
resplendent [rɪ'splendənt] *adj* resplendissant(e).
respond [rɪ'spɒnd] ◇ *vt* répondre ◇ *vi* : **to ~ (to)** répondre (à).
response [rɪ'spɒns] *n* réponse *f* ; **in ~** en réponse.
responsibility [rɪ,spɒnsə'bɪlətɪ] (*pl* **-ies**) *n* : **~ (for)** responsabilité *f* (de) ; **to accept** OR **take ~ for sthg** prendre OR accepter la responsabilité de qqch.
responsible [rɪ'spɒnsəbl] *adj* - **1.** [gen] : **~ (for sthg)** responsable (de qqch) ; **to be ~ to sb** être responsable devant qqn - **2.** [job, position] qui comporte des responsabilités.
responsibly [rɪ'spɒnsəblɪ] *adv* de façon responsable.
responsive [rɪ'spɒnsɪv] *adj* - **1.** [quick to react] qui réagit bien - **2.** [aware] : **~ (to)** attentif(ive) (à).
respray [*n* 'riːspreɪ, *vb* ,riː'spreɪ] ◇ *n* : **to give a car a ~** repeindre une voiture ◇ *vt* repeindre.
rest [rest] ◇ *n* - **1.** [remainder] : **the ~ (of)** le reste (de) ; **the ~ (of them)** les autres *mfpl* - **2.** [relaxation, break] repos *m* ; **to have a ~** se reposer - **3.** [support] support *m*, appui *m* - **4.** *phr* : **to come to a ~** s'arrêter ◇ *vt* - **1.** [relax] faire OR laisser reposer - **2.** [support] : **to ~ sthg on/against** appuyer qqch sur/contre - **3.** *phr* : **~ assured** soyez certain(e) ◇ *vi* - **1.** [relax] se reposer - **2.** [be supported] : **to ~ on/against** s'appuyer sur/contre - **3.** fig [argument, result] : **to ~ on** reposer sur ; **the responsibility ~s with you** c'est vous qui êtes responsable ; **the decision ~s with you** il vous appartient de décider.
rest area *n* Am & Austr aire *f* de repos.
restart [,riː'stɑːt] ◇ *vt* [engine] remettre en marche ; [work] reprendre, recommencer ◇ *vi* - **1.** [play, film] reprendre - **2.** [engine] se remettre en marche.
restate [,riː'steɪt] *vt* répéter.

restaurant ['restərɒnt] *n* restaurant *m*.

restaurant car *n* Br wagon-restaurant *m*.

rest cure *n* cure *f* de repos.

rested ['restɪd] *adj* reposé(e).

restful ['restfʊl] *adj* reposant(e).

rest home *n* maison *f* de repos.

resting place ['restɪŋ-] *n* lieu *m* de repos.

restitution [ˌrestɪ'tjuːʃn] *n* [returning] restitution *f* ; [compensation] réparation *f*.

restive ['restɪv] *adj* agité(e).

restless ['restlɪs] *adj* agité(e).

restlessly ['restlɪslɪ] *adv* avec agitation.

restock [ˌriː'stɒk] ⬦ *vt* réapprovisionner ⬦ *vi* se réapprovisionner.

restoration [ˌrestə'reɪʃn] *n* - **1.** [of law and order, monarchy] rétablissement *m* - **2.** [renovation] restauration *f*.

restorative [rɪ'stɒrətɪv] *adj* fortifiant(e).

restore [rɪ'stɔːr] *vt* - **1.** [law and order, monarchy] rétablir ; [confidence] redonner - **2.** [renovate] restaurer - **3.** [give back] rendre, restituer.

restorer [rɪ'stɔːrər] *n* [person] restaurateur *m*, -trice *f*.

restrain [rɪ'streɪn] *vt* [person, crowd] contenir, retenir ; [emotions] maîtriser, contenir ; **to ~ o.s. from doing sthg** se retenir de faire qqch.

restrained [rɪ'streɪnd] *adj* [tone] mesuré(e) ; [person] qui se domine.

restraint [rɪ'streɪnt] *n* - **1.** [restriction] restriction *f*, entrave *f* - **2.** (U) [self-control] mesure *f*, retenue *f*.

restrict [rɪ'strɪkt] *vt* restreindre, limiter ; **to ~ o.s. to** se limiter à.

restricted [rɪ'strɪktɪd] *adj* - **1.** [limited, small] limité(e) - **2.** [not public - document] confidentiel(elle) ; [- area] interdit(e).

restriction [rɪ'strɪkʃn] *n* restriction *f*, limitation *f* ; **to place ~s on sthg** apporter des restrictions à qqch.

restrictive [rɪ'strɪktɪv] *adj* restrictif(ive).

restrictive practices *npl* pratiques *fpl* restrictives.

rest room *n* Am toilettes *fpl*.

restructure [ˌriː'strʌktʃər] *vt* restructurer.

result [rɪ'zʌlt] ⬦ *n* résultat *m* ; **as a ~** en conséquence ; **as a ~ of** [as a consequence of] à la suite de ; [because of] à cause de ⬦ *vi* - **1.** [cause] : **to ~ in** aboutir à - **2.** [be caused] : **to ~ (from)** résulter (de).

resultant [rɪ'zʌltənt] *adj* fml qui (en) résulte.

resume [rɪ'zjuːm] *vt & vi* reprendre.

résumé ['rezjuːmeɪ] *n* - **1.** [summary] résumé *m*

➤ **2.** Am [curriculum vitae] curriculum vitae *m inv*, CV *m*.

resumption [rɪ'zʌmpʃn] *n* reprise *f*.

resurface [ˌriː'sɜːfɪs] ⬦ *vt* [road] regoudronner ⬦ *vi* [rivalries, problems] réapparaître.

resurgence [rɪ'sɜːdʒəns] *n* réapparition *f*.

resurrect [ˌrezə'rekt] *vt* fig ressusciter.

resurrection [ˌrezə'rekʃn] *n* fig résurrection *f*.

➤ **Resurrection** *n* : **the Resurrection** la Résurrection.

resuscitate [rɪ'sʌsɪteɪt] *vt* réanimer.

resuscitation [rɪˌsʌsɪ'teɪʃn] *n* réanimation *f*.

retail ['riːteɪl] ⬦ *n* (U) détail *m* ⬦ *adv* au détail.

retailer ['riːteɪlər] *n* détaillant *m*, -e *f*.

retail outlet *n* magasin *m* de détail.

retail price *n* prix *m* de détail.

retail price index *n* Br indice *m* des prix.

retain [rɪ'teɪn] *vt* conserver.

retainer [rɪ'teɪnər] *n* - **1.** [fee] provision *f* - **2.** [servant] serviteur *m*.

retaining wall [rɪ'teɪnɪŋ-] *n* mur *m* de soutènement.

retaliate [rɪ'tælɪeɪt] *vi* rendre la pareille, se venger.

retaliation [rɪˌtælɪ'eɪʃn] *n* (U) vengeance *f*, représailles *fpl*.

retarded [rɪ'tɑːdɪd] *adj* retardé(e).

retch [retʃ] *vi* avoir des haut-le-cœur.

retention [rɪ'tenʃn] *n* maintien *m*, conservation *f* ; MED rétention *f*.

retentive [rɪ'tentɪv] *adj* [memory] fidèle.

rethink [*n* 'riːθɪŋk, *vb* ˌriː'θɪŋk] (*pt & pp* **-thought** [-'θɔːt]) ⬦ *n* : **to have a ~ (on OR about sthg)** repenser (qqch) ⬦ *vt & vi* repenser.

reticence ['retɪsəns] *n* réticence *f*.

reticent ['retɪsənt] *adj* peu communicatif(ive) ; **to be ~ about sthg** ne pas beaucoup parler de qqch.

retina ['retɪnə] (*pl* **-nas** OR **-nae** [-niː]) *n* rétine *f*.

retinue ['retɪnjuː] *n* suite *f*.

retire [rɪ'taɪər] *vi* - **1.** [from work] prendre sa retraite - **2.** [withdraw] se retirer - **3.** [to bed] (aller) se coucher.

retired [rɪ'taɪəd] *adj* à la retraite, retraité(e).

retirement [rɪ'taɪəmənt] *n* retraite *f*.

retirement age *n* âge *m* de la retraite.

retirement pension *n* retraite *f*.

retiring [rɪ'taɪərɪŋ] *adj* - **1.** [shy] réservé(e)

- 2. [from work] sur le point de prendre sa retraite.

retort [rɪ'tɔːt] ⟷ n [sharp reply] riposte f ⟷ vt riposter.

retouch [,riː'tʌtʃ] vt retoucher.

retrace [rɪ'treɪs] vt : **to ~ one's steps** revenir sur ses pas.

retract [rɪ'trækt] ⟷ vt - **1.** [statement] rétracter - **2.** [undercarriage] rentrer, escamoter ; [claws] rentrer ⟷ vi [undercarriage] rentrer, s'escamoter.

retractable [rɪ'træktəbl] adj escamotable.

retraction [rɪ'trækʃn] n [of statement] rétractation f.

retrain [,riː'treɪn] ⟷ vt recycler ⟷ vi se recycler.

retraining [,riː'treɪnɪŋ] n recyclage m.

retread [n 'riːtred , vb ,riː'tred] ⟷ n pneu m rechapé ⟷ vt rechaper.

retreat [rɪ'triːt] ⟷ n retraite f ; **to beat a hasty ~** partir en vitesse ⟷ vi [move away] se retirer ; MIL battre en retraite.

retrenchment [rɪ'trentʃmənt] n [of spending] réduction f.

retrial [,riː'traɪəl] n nouveau procès m

retribution [,retrɪ'bjuːʃn] n châtiment m.

retrieval [rɪ'triːvl] n (U) COMPUT recherche f et extraction f.

retrieve [rɪ'triːv] vt - **1.** [get back] récupérer - **2.** COMPUT rechercher et extraire - **3.** [situation] sauver.

retriever [rɪ'triːvəʳ] n [dog] retriever m.

retroactive [,retrəʊ'æktɪv] adj rétroactif(ive).

retrograde ['retrəgreɪd] adj rétrograde.

retrogressive [,retrə'gresɪv] adj rétrograde.

retrospect ['retrəspekt] n : **in ~** après coup.

retrospective [,retrə'spektɪv] ⟷ adj - **1.** [mood, look] rétrospectif(ive) - **2.** JUR [law, pay rise] rétroactif(ive) ⟷ n rétrospective f.

retrospectively [,retrə'spektɪvlɪ] adv - **1.** [looking back] rétrospectivement - **2.** JUR rétroactivement.

return [rɪ'tɜːn] ⟷ n - **1.** (U) [arrival back, giving back] retour m - **2.** TENNIS renvoi m - **3.** Br [ticket] aller et retour m - **4.** [profit] rapport m, rendement m ⟷ comp [journey] de retour ⟷ vt - **1.** [gen] rendre ; [a loan] rembourser ; [library book] rapporter - **2.** [send back] renvoyer - **3.** [replace] remettre - **4.** POL élire ⟷ vi [come back] revenir ; [go back] retourner.

➡ **returns** npl COMM recettes fpl ; **many happy ~s (of the day)!** bon anniversaire!

➡ **in return** adv en retour, en échange.

➡ **in return for** prep en échange de.

returnable [rɪ'tɜːnəbl] adj [bottle] consigné(e).

returning officer [rɪ'tɜːnɪŋ-] n Br responsable mf du scrutin.

return key n COMPUT touche f entrée.

return match n match m retour.

return ticket n Br aller et retour m.

reunification [,riːjuːnɪfɪ'keɪʃn] n réunification f.

reunion [,riː'juːnjən] n réunion f.

Reunion [,riː'juːnjən] n : **~ (Island)** (l'île f de) la Réunion ; **in ~** à la Réunion.

reunite [,riːjuː'naɪt] vt : **to be ~d with sb** retrouver qqn.

reupholster [,riːʌp'həʊlstəʳ] vt recouvrir.

reusable [riː'juːzəbl] adj réutilisable.

reuse [n ,riː'juːs, vb ,riː'juːz] ⟷ n réutilisation f ⟷ vt réutiliser.

rev [rev] (pt & pp -ved ; cont -ving) inf ⟷ n (abbr of **revolution**) tour m ⟷ vt : **to ~ the engine (up)** emballer le moteur ⟷ vi : **to ~ (up)** s'emballer.

revalue [,riː'væljuː] vt FIN réévaluer.

revamp [,riː'væmp] vt inf [system, department] réorganiser ; [house] retaper.

rev counter n compte-tours m inv.

reveal [rɪ'viːl] vt révéler.

revealing [rɪ'viːlɪŋ] adj - **1.** [clothes - low-cut] décolleté(e) ; [- transparent] qui laisse deviner le corps - **2.** [comment] révélateur(trice).

reveille [Br rɪ'vælɪ, Am 'revəlɪ] n réveil m.

revel ['revl] (Br pt & pp -led ; cont -ling, Am pt & pp -ed ; cont -ing) vi : **to ~ in sthg** se délecter de qqch.

revelation [,revə'leɪʃn] n révélation f.

reveller Br, **reveler** Am ['revələʳ] n fêtard m, -e f.

revelry ['revəlrɪ] n (U) festivités fpl.

revenge [rɪ'vendʒ] ⟷ n vengeance f ; **to take ~ (on sb)** se venger (de qqn) ⟷ comp [killing, attack] suscité(e) par la vengeance ⟷ vt venger ; **to ~ o.s. on sb** se venger de qqn.

revenue ['revənjuː] n revenu m.

reverberate [rɪ'vɜːbəreɪt] vi retentir, se répercuter ; fig avoir des répercussions.

reverberations [rɪ,vɜːbə'reɪʃnz] npl réverbérations fpl ; fig répercussions fpl.

revere [rɪ'vɪəʳ] vt révérer, vénérer.

reverence ['revərəns] n révérence f, vénération f.

Reverend ['revərənd] n révérend m.

Reverend Mother n révérende mère f.

reverent ['revərənt] adj respectueux(euse).

reverential [,revə'renʃl] adj révérencieux(euse).

reverie ['revərı] n rêverie f.

revers [rı'vıə] (pl inv) n revers m.

reversal [rı'vɜːsl] n - **1.** [of policy, decision] revirement m - **2.** [ill fortune] revers m de fortune.

reverse [rı'vɜːs] <> adj [order, process] inverse <> n - **1.** AUT : ~ (gear) marche f arrière ; to be in ~ être en marche arrière ; to go into ~ faire marche arrière - **2.** [opposite] : the ~ le contraire - **3.** [back] : the ~ [of paper] le verso, le dos ; [of coin] le revers <> vt - **1.** [order, positions] inverser ; [decision, trend] renverser - **2.** [turn over] retourner - **3.** Br TELEC : to ~ the charges téléphoner en PCV <> vi AUT faire marche arrière ; to ~ into a wall rentrer dans un mur en faisant marche arrière.

reverse-charge call n Br appel m en PCV.

reversible [rı'vɜːsəbl] adj réversible.

reversing light [rı'vɜːsıŋ-] n Br feu m de marche arrière.

reversion [rı'vɜːʃn] n (U) retour m.

revert [rı'vɜːt] vi : to ~ to retourner à.

review [rı'vjuː] <> n - **1.** [of salary, spending] révision f ; [of situation] examen m ; salaries come up for ~ in December les salaires doivent être révisés en décembre ; the situation is under ~ on est en train d'examiner la situation - **2.** [of book, play etc] critique f, compte rendu m <> vt - **1.** [salary] réviser ; [situation] examiner - **2.** [book, play etc] faire la critique de - **3.** [troops] passer en revue - **4.** Am [study again] réviser.

reviewer [rı'vjuːəʳ] n critique mf.

revile [rı'vaıl] vt injurier.

revise [rı'vaız] <> vt - **1.** [reconsider] modifier - **2.** [rewrite] corriger - **3.** Br [study again] réviser <> vi Br : to ~ (for) réviser (pour).

revised [rı'vaızd] adj [estimate, figure] nouveau(elle) ; [version] revu(e) et corrigé(e).

revision [rı'vıʒn] n révision f.

revisionist [rı'vıʒnıst] <> adj révisionniste <> n révisionniste mf.

revisit [,riː'vızıt] vt visiter de nouveau.

revitalize, -ise [,riː'vaıtəlaız] vt revitaliser.

revival [rı'vaıvl] n [of economy, trade] reprise f ; [of interest] regain m.

revive [rı'vaıv] <> vt - **1.** [person] ranimer - **2.** fig [economy] relancer ; [interest] faire renaître ; [tradition] rétablir ; [musical, play] reprendre ; [memories] ranimer, raviver <> vi - **1.** [person] reprendre connaissance - **2.** fig

[economy] repartir, reprendre ; [hopes] renaître.

revoke [rı'vəuk] vt [law] abroger ; [order] annuler ; [licence] retirer.

revolt [rı'vəult] <> n révolte f <> vt révolter, dégoûter <> vi se révolter.

revolting [rı'vəultıŋ] adj dégoûtant(e) ; [smell] infect(e).

revolution [,revə'luːʃn] n - **1.** [gen] révolution f - **2.** TECH tour m, révolution f.

revolutionary [,revə'luːʃnərı] (pl -ies) <> adj révolutionnaire <> n révolutionnaire mf.

revolutionize, -ise [,revə'luːʃənaız] vt révolutionner.

revolve [rı'vɒlv] vi : to ~ (around) tourner (autour de).

revolver [rı'vɒlvəʳ] n revolver m.

revolving [rı'vɒlvıŋ] adj tournant(e) ; [chair] pivotant(e).

revolving door n tambour m.

revue [rı'vjuː] n revue f.

revulsion [rı'vʌlʃn] n répugnance f.

reward [rı'wɔːd] <> n récompense f <> vt : to ~ sb (for/with sthg) récompenser qqn (de/par qqch).

rewarding [rı'wɔːdıŋ] adj [job] qui donne de grandes satisfactions ; [book] qui vaut la peine d'être lu(e).

rewind [,riː'waınd] (pt & pp rewound) vt [tape] rembobiner.

rewire [,riː'waıəʳ] vt [house] refaire l'installation électrique de.

reword [,riː'wɜːd] vt reformuler.

rework [,riː'wɜːk] vt retravailler.

rewound [,riː'waund] pt & pp ⊳ rewind.

rewrite [,riː'raıt] (pt rewrote [,riː'rəut] ; pp rewritten [,riː'rıtnl] vt récrire.

REX (abbr of real-time executive routine) n superviseur en temps réel.

Reykjavik ['rekjəvık] n Reykjavik.

RFC (abbr of Rugby Football Club) n fédération de rugby.

RGN (abbr of registered general nurse) n en Grande-Bretagne, infirmier ou infirmière diplômé(e) d'État.

Rh (abbr of rhesus) Rh.

rhapsody ['ræpsədı] (pl -ies) n rhapsodie f ; to go into rhapsodies about sthg s'extasier sur qqch.

Rheims = Reims.

Rhesus ['riːsəs] n : ~ positive/negative rhésus m positif/négatif.

rhetoric ['retərık] n rhétorique f.

rhetorical question [rɪ'tɒrɪkl-] *n* question *f* pour la forme.

rheumatic [ru:'mætɪk] *adj* [pain, joint] rhumatismal(e) ; [person] rhumatisant(e).

rheumatism ['ru:mətɪzm] *n (U)* rhumatisme *m*.

rheumatoid arthritis ['ru:mətɔɪd-] *n* polyarthrite *f* rhumatoïde.

Rhine [raɪn] *n* : **the ~** le Rhin.

Rhineland ['raɪnlænd] *n* Rhénanie *f*.

rhinestone ['raɪnstəʊn] *n* faux diamant *m*.

rhino ['raɪnəʊ] *(pl inv OR* **-s)**, **rhinoceros** [raɪ'nɒsərəs] *(pl inv OR* **-es)** *n* rhinocéros *m*.

Rhode Island [rəʊd-] *n* Rhode Island *m* ; **in ~** dans le Rhode Island.

Rhodes [rəʊdz] *n* Rhodes.

Rhodesia [rəʊ'di:ʃə] *n* Rhodésie *f* ; **in ~** en Rhodésie.

Rhodesian [rəʊ'di:ʃn] <> *adj* rhodésien(enne) <> *n* Rhodésien *m*, -enne *f*.

rhododendron [,rəʊdə'dendrən] *n* rhododendron *m*.

Rhône [rəʊn] *n* : **the (River) ~** le Rhône.

rhubarb ['ru:bɑ:b] *n* rhubarbe *f*.

rhyme [raɪm] <> *n* - **1.** [word, technique] rime *f* ; **in ~** en vers - **2.** [poem] poème *m* <> *vi* : **to ~ (with)** rimer (avec).

rhyming slang ['raɪmɪŋ-] *n* Br sorte d'argot traditionnellement employé par les Cockneys qui consiste à remplacer un mot par un groupe de mots choisis pour la rime.

rhythm ['rɪðm] *n* rythme *m*.

rhythm and blues *n* rhythm and blues *m*.

rhythmic(al) ['rɪðmɪk(l)] *adj* rythmique.

RI <> *n (abbr of* **religious instruction)** instruction *f* religieuse <> *abbr of* **Rhode Island.**

rib [rɪb] *n* - **1.** ANAT côte *f* - **2.** [of umbrella] baleine *f* ; [of structure] membrure *f*.

ribald ['rɪbəld] *adj* paillard(e).

ribbed [rɪbd] *adj* [jumper, fabric] à côtes.

ribbon ['rɪbən] *n* ruban *m*.

rib cage *n* cage *f* thoracique.

rice [raɪs] *n* riz *m*.

rice field *n* rizière *f*.

rice paper *n* papier *m* de riz.

rice pudding *n* riz *m* au lait.

rich [rɪtʃ] <> *adj* riche ; [clothes, fabrics] somptueux(euse) ; **to be ~ in** être riche en <> *npl* : **the ~** les riches *mpl*.

➤ **riches** *npl* richesses *fpl*, richesse *f*.

richly ['rɪtʃlɪ] *adv* - **1.** [rewarded] largement ; [provided] très bien ; **~ deserved** bien mérité - **2.** [sumptuously] richement.

richness ['rɪtʃnɪs] *n (U)* richesse *f*.

Richter scale ['rɪktə'-] *n* : **the ~** l'échelle *f* de Richter.

rickets ['rɪkɪts] *n (U)* rachitisme *m*.

rickety ['rɪkətɪ] *adj* branlant(e).

rickshaw ['rɪkʃɔ:] *n* pousse-pousse *m inv.*

ricochet ['rɪkəʃeɪ] *(pt & pp* **-ed** OR **-ted** ; *cont* **-ing** OR **-ting)** <> *n* ricochet *m* <> *vi* : **to ~ (off)** ricocher (sur).

rid [rɪd] *(pt* rid OR **-ded** ; *pp* rid, *cont* **-ding)** <> *adj* : **to be ~ of** être débarrassé(e) de <> *vt* : **to ~ sb/sthg of** débarrasser qqn/qqch de ; **to get ~ of** se débarrasser de.

riddance ['rɪdəns] *n inf* : **good ~!** bon débarras!

ridden ['rɪdn] *pp* ▷ ride.

riddle ['rɪdl] *n* énigme *f*.

riddled ['rɪdld] *adj* : **to be ~ with** être criblé(e) de.

ride [raɪd] *(pt* rode ; *pp* ridden) <> *n* promenade *f*, tour *m* ; **to go for a ~** [on horse] faire une promenade à cheval ; [on bike] faire une promenade à vélo ; [in car] faire un tour en voiture ; **to take sb for a ~** inf fig faire marcher qqn <> *vt* - **1.** [travel on] : **to ~ a horse/a bicycle** monter à cheval/à bicyclette - **2.** Am [travel in - bus, train, elevator] prendre - **3.** [distance] parcourir, faire <> *vi* [on horseback] monter à cheval, faire du cheval ; [on bicycle] faire de la bicyclette OR du vélo ; **to ~ in a car/bus** aller en voiture/bus.

➤ **ride up** *vi* remonter.

rider ['raɪdə'] *n* [of horse] cavalier *m*, -ère *f* ; [of bicycle] cycliste *mf* ; [of motorbike] motocycliste *mf*.

ridge [rɪdʒ] *n* - **1.** [of mountain, roof] crête *f*, arête *f* - **2.** [on surface] strie *f*.

ridicule ['rɪdɪkju:l] <> *n* ridicule *m* <> *vt* ridiculiser.

ridiculous [rɪ'dɪkjʊləs] *adj* ridicule.

ridiculously [rɪ'dɪkjʊləslɪ] *adv* ridiculement.

riding ['raɪdɪŋ] <> *n* équitation *f* ; **to go ~** faire de l'équitation OR du cheval <> *comp* d'équitation.

riding crop *n* cravache *f*.

riding habit *n* habit *m* d'amazone.

riding school *n* école *f* d'équitation.

rife [raɪf] *adj* répandu(e) ; **the city was ~ with rumours** des bruits couraient dans toute la ville.

riffraff ['rɪfræf] *n* racaille *f*.

rifle ['raɪfl] <> *n* fusil *m* <> *vt* [drawer, bag] vider.

rifle through vt fus fouiller dans.

rifle range n [indoor] stand m de tir ; [outdoor] champ m de tir.

rift [rɪft] n - **1.** GEOL fissure f - **2.** [quarrel] désaccord m.

Rift Valley n : the ~ le Rift Valley.

rig [rɪg] (pt & pp -ged ; cont -ging) ⟨> n : (oil) ~ [on land] derrick m ; [at sea] plate-forme f de forage ⟨> vt [match, election] truquer.

rig up vt sep installer avec les moyens du bord.

rigging ['rɪgɪŋ] n [of ship] gréement m.

right [raɪt] ⟨> adj - **1.** [correct - answer, time] juste, exact(e) ; [- decision, direction, idea] bon (bonne) ; **to be ~ (about)** avoir raison (au sujet de) ; **to get a question ~** donner la bonne réponse ; **to get one's facts ~** être sûr de ce qu'on avance ; [morally correct] bien (inv) ; **to be ~ to do sthg** avoir raison de faire qqch - **3.** [appropriate] qui convient - **4.** [not left] droit(e) - **5.** Br inf [complete] véritable ⟨> n - **1.** (U) [moral correctness] bien m ; **to be in the ~** avoir raison - **2.** [entitlement, claim] droit m ; **by ~s** en toute justice ; **in one's own ~** soi-même - **3.** [not left] droite f ⟨> adv - **1.** [correctly] correctement - **2.** [not left] à droite - **3.** [emphatic use] : **~ down/up** tout en bas/en haut ; **~ here** ici (même) ; **~ in the middle** en plein milieu ; **go ~ to the end of the street** allez tout au bout de la rue ; **to turn ~ round** se retourner ; **~ after Christmas** tout de suite après Noël ; **~ now** tout de suite ; **~ away** immédiatement ⟨> vt - **1.** [injustice, wrong] réparer - **2.** [ship] redresser ⟨> excl bon !

Right n POL : the Right la droite.

right angle n angle m droit ; **to be at ~s (to)** faire un angle droit (avec).

righteous ['raɪtʃəs] adj [person] droit(e) ; [indignation] justifié(e).

righteousness ['raɪtʃəsnɪs] n vertu f.

rightful ['raɪtfʊl] adj légitime.

rightfully ['raɪtfʊlɪ] adv légitimement.

right-hand adj de droite ; **~ side** droite f, côté m droit.

right-hand drive adj avec conduite à droite.

right-handed [-'hændɪd] adj [person] droitier(ère).

right-hand man n bras m droit.

rightly ['raɪtlɪ] adv - **1.** [answer, believe] correctement - **2.** [behave] bien - **3.** [angry, worried etc] à juste titre.

right-minded [-'maɪndɪd] adj sensé(e).

rightness ['raɪtnɪs] n - **1.** [correctness] justesse f - **2.** [moral correctness] droiture f.

righto ['raɪtəʊ] excl inf d'accord !

right of way n - **1.** AUT priorité f - **2.** [access] droit m de passage.

right-on adj inf branché(e).

rights issue n émission f de droits de souscription.

right-thinking [-'θɪŋkɪŋ] adj sensé(e).

right wing n : the ~ la droite.

right-wing adj de droite.

right-winger n POL personne f qui est de droite.

rigid ['rɪdʒɪd] adj - **1.** [gen] rigide - **2.** [harsh] strict(e).

rigidity [rɪ'dʒɪdətɪ] n rigidité f.

rigidly ['rɪdʒɪdlɪ] adv - **1.** [gen] rigidement - **2.** [harshly] strictement.

rigmarole ['rɪgmərəʊl] n pej - **1.** [process] comédie f - **2.** [story] galimatias m.

rigor Am = rigour.

rigor mortis [-'mɔːtɪs] n rigidité f cadavérique.

rigorous ['rɪgərəs] adj rigoureux(euse).

rigorously ['rɪgərəslɪ] adv rigoureusement.

rigour Br, **rigor** Am ['rɪgər] n rigueur f.

rig-out n Br inf accoutrement m.

rile [raɪl] vt agacer.

rim [rɪm] n [of container] bord m ; [of wheel] jante f ; [of spectacles] monture f.

rind [raɪnd] n [of fruit] peau f ; [of cheese] croûte f ; [of bacon] couenne f.

ring [rɪŋ] (pt rang ; pp vt senses 1 & 2 & vi rung, pt & pp vt sense 3 only ringed) ⟨> n - **1.** [telephone call] : **to give sb a ~** donner OR passer un coup de téléphone à qqn - **2.** [sound of bell] sonnerie f ; **the name has a familiar ~** ce nom me dit quelque chose - **3.** [circular object] anneau m ; [on finger] bague f ; [for napkin] rond m - **4.** [of people, trees etc] cercle m - **5.** [for boxing] ring m - **6.** [of criminals, spies] réseau m ⟨> vt - **1.** Br [make phone call to] téléphoner à, appeler - **2.** [bell] (faire) sonner ; **to ~ the doorbell** sonner à la porte - **3.** [draw a circle round, surround] entourer ⟨> vi - **1.** Br [make phone call] téléphoner - **2.** [bell, telephone, person] sonner ; **to ~ for sb** sonner qqn - **3.** [resound] : **to ~ with** résonner de - **4.** phr : **to ~ true** sonner juste.

ring back vt sep & vi Br rappeler.

ring off vi Br raccrocher.

ring out vi - **1.** [sound] retentir - **2.** Br TELEC téléphoner à l'extérieur.

ring up vt sep Br téléphoner à, appeler.

ring binder n classeur m à anneaux.

ringer ['rɪŋər] n : **to be a dead ~ for sb** être le sosie de qqn.

ring finger n annulaire m.

ringing ['rɪŋɪŋ] <> adj retentissant(e) <> n [of bell] sonnerie f ; [in ears] tintement m.

ringing tone n sonnerie f.

ringleader ['rɪŋ,li:dər] n chef m.

ringlet ['rɪŋlɪt] n anglaise f.

ringmaster ['rɪŋ,mɑ:stər] n présentateur m.

ring road n Br (route f) périphérique m.

ringside ['rɪŋsaɪd] <> n : the ~ le premier rang <> comp [seat] au premier rang.

ringway ['rɪŋweɪ] n Br (route f) périphérique m.

ringworm ['rɪŋwɜ:m] n teigne f.

rink [rɪŋk] n [for ice skating] patinoire f ; [for roller-skating] skating m.

rinse [rɪns] <> n : to give sthg a ~ rincer qqch <> vt rincer ; to ~ one's mouth out se rincer la bouche.

Rio (de Janeiro) [,ri:əʊ(dədʒə'nɪərəʊ)] n Rio de Janeiro.

Rio Grande [,ri:əʊ'grændɪ] n : the ~ le Rio Grande.

Rio Negro [,ri:əʊ'neɪɡrəʊ] n : the ~ le Rio Negro.

riot ['raɪət] <> n émeute f ; to run ~ se déchaîner <> vi participer à une émeute.

rioter ['raɪətər] n émeutier m, -ère f.

rioting ['raɪətɪŋ] n (U) émeutes fpl.

riotous ['raɪətəs] adj [crowd] tapageur(euse) ; [behaviour] séditieux(euse) ; [party] bruyant(e).

riot police npl ≃ CRS mpl.

riot shield n bouclier m anti-émeute.

rip [rɪp] (pt & pp -ped ; cont -ping) <> n déchirure f, accroc m <> vt - 1. [tear] déchirer - 2. [remove violently] arracher <> vi se déchirer.

➤ **rip off** vt sep inf - 1. [person] arnaquer - 2. [product, idea] copier.

➤ **rip up** vt sep déchirer.

RIP (abbr of rest in peace) qu' il/elle repose en paix.

ripcord ['rɪpkɔ:d] n poignée f d'ouverture.

ripe [raɪp] adj mûr(e).

ripen ['raɪpn] vt & vi mûrir.

ripeness ['raɪpnɪs] n maturité f.

rip-off n inf : that's a ~! c'est de l'escroquerie OR de l'arnaque!

ripple ['rɪpl] <> n ondulation f, ride f ; a ~ of applause des applaudissements discrets <> vt rider.

rip-roaring adj inf [party] de tous les diables ; [success] monstre.

rise [raɪz] (pt rose ; pp risen ['rɪzn]) <> n - 1. Br [increase] augmentation f, hausse f ; [in temperature] élévation f, hausse - 2. Br [increase in salary] augmentation f (de salaire) - 3. [to power, fame] ascension f - 4. [slope] côte f, pente f - 5. phr : to give ~ to donner lieu à <> vi - 1. [move upwards] s'élever, monter ; to ~ to power arriver au pouvoir ; to ~ to fame devenir célèbre ; to ~ to a challenge/to the occasion se montrer à la hauteur d'un défi/de la situation - 2. [from chair, bed] se lever - 3. [increase - gen] monter, augmenter ; [- voice, level] s'élever - 4. [rebel] se soulever.

➤ **rise above** vt fus [problem] surmonter ; [argument] ne pas faire cas de.

riser ['raɪzər] n : early ~ lève-tôt mf inv ; late ~ lève-tard mf inv.

risible ['rɪzəbl] adj risible.

rising ['raɪzɪŋ] <> adj - 1. [ground, tide] montant(e) - 2. [prices, inflation, temperature] en hausse - 3. [star, politician etc] à l'avenir prometteur <> n [revolt] soulèvement m.

rising damp n humidité f (qui monte du sol).

risk [rɪsk] <> n risque m, danger m ; at one's own ~ à ses risques et périls ; to run the ~ of doing sthg courir le risque de faire qqch ; to take a ~ prendre un risque ; at ~ en danger ; at the ~ of au risque de <> vt [health, life etc] risquer ; to ~ doing sthg courir le risque de faire qqch ; to ~ it tenter le coup.

risk capital n capital m à risque.

risk-taking n (U) le fait de prendre des risques.

risky ['rɪskɪ] (compar -ier ; superl -iest) adj risqué(e).

risotto [rɪ'zɒtəʊ] (pl -s) n risotto m.

risqué ['ri:skeɪ] adj risqué(e), osé(e).

rissole ['rɪsəʊl] n Br rissole f.

rite [raɪt] n rite m.

ritual ['rɪtʃʊəl] <> adj rituel(elle) <> n rituel m.

rival ['raɪvl] (Br pt & pp -led ; cont -ling, Am pt & pp -ed ; cont -ing) <> adj rival(e), concurrent(e) <> n rival m, -e f <> vt rivaliser avec.

rivalry ['raɪvlrɪ] n rivalité f.

river ['rɪvər] n rivière f, fleuve m.

river bank n berge f, rive f.

riverbed ['rɪvəbed] n lit m (de rivière OR de fleuve).

riverside ['rɪvəsaɪd] n : the ~ le bord de la rivière OR du fleuve.

rivet ['rɪvɪt] <> n rivet m <> vt - 1. [fasten with rivets] river, riveter - 2. fig [fascinate] : to be ~ed by être fasciné(e) par.

riveting ['rɪvɪtɪŋ] *adj* fig fascinant(e).

Riviera [,rɪvɪ'eərə] *n :* **the French ~** la Côte d'Azur ; **the Italian ~** la Riviera italienne.

Riyadh ['riːæd] *n* Riyad, Riad.

RN *n* - **1.** *abbr of* Royal Navy - **2.** *abbr of* registered nurse.

RNA (*abbr of* ribonucleic acid) *n* ARN *m*.

RNLI (*abbr of* Royal National Lifeboat Institution) *n* société britannique de sauvetage en mer.

RNZAF (*abbr of* Royal New Zealand Air Force) *n* armée de l'air néo-zélandaise.

RNZN (*abbr of* Royal New Zealand Navy) *n* marine de guerre néo-zélandaise.

roach [rəʊtʃ] *n* Am [cockroach] cafard *m*.

road [rəʊd] *n* route *f* ; [small] chemin *m* ; [in town] rue *f* ; **by ~** par la route ; **on the ~ to** fig sur le chemin de ; **on the ~** sur la route ; **we've been on the ~ for two days** on voyage depuis deux jours.

road atlas *n* atlas *m* routier.

roadblock ['rəʊdblɒk] *n* barrage *m* routier.

road-fund licence *n* Br ≃ vignette *f*.

road hog *n* inf pej chauffard *m*.

roadholding ['rəʊd,həʊldɪŋ] *n* AUT tenue *f* de route.

roadie ['rəʊdɪ] *n* inf membre de l'équipe technique d'un groupe en tournée.

road map *n* carte *f* routière.

road rage *n* accès de colère de la part d'un automobiliste, se traduisant parfois par un acte de violence.

road roller [-,rəʊləʳl] *n* rouleau *m* compresseur.

road safety *n* sécurité *f* routière.

road sense *n* [of driver] notion *f* de la conduite.

roadshow ['rəʊdʃəʊ] *n* spectacle *m* de tournée.

roadside ['rəʊdsaɪd] *n :* **the ~** le bord de la route *n comp* au bord de la route.

road sign *n* panneau *m* routier OR de signalisation.

roadsweeper ['rəʊd,swiːpəʳ] *n* [vehicle] balayeuse *f*.

road tax *n* ≃ vignette *f*.

road test *n* essai *m* sur route.
road-test *vt* essayer sur route.

road transport *n* transport *m* routier.

roadway ['rəʊdweɪ] *n* chaussée *f*.

road works [-wɜːks] *npl* travaux *mpl* (de réfection des routes).

roadworthy ['rəʊd,wɜːðɪ] *adj* en bon état de marche.

roam [rəʊm] ◇ *vt* errer dans ◇ *vi* errer.

roar [rɔːʳ] ◇ *vi* [person, lion] rugir ; [wind] hurler ; [car] gronder ; [plane] vrombir ; **to ~ with laughter** se tordre de rire ◇ *vt* hurler ◇ *n* [of person, lion] rugissement *m* ; [of traffic] grondement *m* ; [of plane, engine] vrombissement *m*.

roaring ['rɔːrɪŋ] *adj :* **a ~ fire** une belle flambée ; **~ drunk** complètement saoul(e) ; **a ~ success** un succès monstre OR fou ; **to do a ~ trade** faire des affaires en or.

roast [rəʊst] ◇ *adj* rôti(e) ◇ *n* rôti *m* ◇ *vt* - **1.** [meat, potatoes] rôtir - **2.** [coffee, nuts etc] griller.

roast beef *n* rôti *m* de bœuf, rosbif *m*.

roasting ['rəʊstɪŋ] inf ◇ *adj* torride ◇ *adv :* **a ~ hot day** une journée torride.

roasting tin *n* plat *m* à rôtir.

rob [rɒb] (*pt* & *pp* -bed ; *cont* -bing) *vt* [person] voler ; [bank] dévaliser ; **to ~ sb of sthg** [money, goods] voler OR dérober qqch à qqn ; [opportunity, glory] enlever qqch à qqn.

robber ['rɒbəʳ] *n* voleur *m*, -euse *f*.

robbery ['rɒbərɪ] (*pl* -ies) *n* vol *m*.

robe [rəʊb] *n* - **1.** [gen] robe *f* - **2.** Am [dressing gown] peignoir *m*.

robin ['rɒbɪn] *n* rouge-gorge *m*.

robot ['rəʊbɒt] *n* robot *m*.

robotics [rəʊ'bɒtɪks] *n* (U) robotique *f*.

robust [rəʊ'bʌst] *adj* robuste.

robustly [rəʊ'bʌstlɪ] *adv* robustement.

rock [rɒk] ◇ *n* - **1.** (U) [substance] roche *f* - **2.** [boulder] rocher *m* - **3.** Am [pebble] caillou *m* - **4.** [music] rock *m* - **5.** Br [sweet] sucre *m* d'orge ◇ *comp* [music, band] de rock ◇ *vt* - **1.** [baby] bercer ; [cradle, boat] balancer - **2.** [shock] secouer ◇ *vi* (se) balancer.
on the rocks *adv* - **1.** [drink] avec de la glace OR des glaçons - **2.** [marriage, relationship] près de la rupture.

rock and roll *n* rock *m*, rock and roll *m*.

rock bottom *n :* **at ~** au plus bas ; **to hit ~** toucher le fond.
rock-bottom *adj* [price] sacrifié(e).

rock cake *n* Br rocher *m*.

rock climber *n* varappeur *m*, -euse *f*.

rock-climbing *n* varappe *f* ; **to go ~** faire de la varappe.

rock dash *n* Am crépi *m*.

rocker ['rɒkəʳ] *n* - **1.** [chair] fauteuil *m* à bascule, rocking-chair *m* - **2.** phr : **to be off one's ~** inf être fêlé.

rockery ['rɒkərɪ] (pl -ies) n rocaille f.
rocket ['rɒkɪt] ◇ n - **1.** [gen] fusée f - **2.** MIL fusée f, roquette f ◇ vi monter en flèche.
rocket launcher [-ˌlɔːntʃərˈ] n lance-fusées m inv, lance-roquettes m inv.
rock face n paroi f rocheuse.
rockfall ['rɒkfɔːll n chute f de pierres.
rock-hard adj dur(e) comme de la pierre.
Rockies ['rɒkɪz] npl : the ~ les Rocheuses fpl.
rocking chair ['rɒkɪŋ-] n fauteuil m à bascule, rocking-chair m.
rocking horse ['rɒkɪŋ-] n cheval m à bascule.
rock music n rock m.
rock'n'roll [ˌrɒkən'rəʊl] = rock and roll.
rock pool n mare f dans les rochers.
rock salt n sel m gemme.
rocky ['rɒkɪ] (compar -ier ; superl -iest) adj - **1.** [ground, road] rocailleux(euse), caillouteux(euse) - **2.** fig [economy, marriage] précaire.
Rocky Mountains npl : the ~ les montagnes fpl Rocheuses.
rococo [rə'kəʊkəʊ] adj rococo (inv).
rod [rɒd] n [metal] tige f ; [wooden] baguette f ; (fishing) ~ canne f à pêche.
rode [rəʊd] pt ⊳ ride.
rodent ['rəʊdənt] n rongeur m.
rodeo ['rəʊdɪəʊ] (pl -s) n rodéo m.
roe [rəʊ] n (U) œufs mpl de poisson.
roe deer n chevreuil m.
rogue [rəʊg] ◇ adj - **1.** [animal] solitaire - **2.** fig [person] dissident(e) ◇ n - **1.** [likeable rascal] coquin m - **2.** dated [dishonest person] filou m, crapule f.
roguish ['rəʊgɪʃ] adj espiègle.
role [rəʊl] n rôle m.
roll [rəʊl] ◇ n - **1.** [of material, paper etc] rouleau m - **2.** [of bread] petit pain m - **3.** [list] liste f - **4.** [of drums, thunder] roulement m ◇ vt rouler ; [log, ball etc] faire rouler ; **to ~ one's eyes** [in fear, despair] rouler les yeux ; **~ed into one** tout à la fois ◇ vi rouler.
➤ **roll about, roll around** vi [person] se rouler ; [object] rouler çà et là.
➤ **roll back** vt sep Am [prices] baisser.
➤ **roll in** vi inf [money] couler à flots.
➤ **roll over** vi se retourner.
➤ **roll up** ◇ vt sep - **1.** [carpet, paper etc] rouler - **2.** [sleeves] retrousser ◇ vi inf [arrive] s'amener, se pointer.
roll bar n arceau m de sécurité.
roll call n appel m.
rolled gold [rəʊld-] n plaqué m or.

roller ['rəʊlərˈ] n rouleau m.
Rollerblades® ['rəʊləbleɪd] n rollers mpl, patins mpl en ligne.
rollerblading ['rəʊləbleɪdɪŋ] n roller m ; **to go ~** faire du roller.
roller blind n store m.
roller coaster n montagnes fpl russes.
roller skate n patin m à roulettes.
➤ **roller-skate** vi faire du patin à roulettes.
roller towel n essuie-main m à rouleau.
rollicking ['rɒlɪkɪŋ] adj : **we had a ~ good time** on s'est amusé comme des (petits) fous.
rolling ['rəʊlɪŋ] adj - **1.** [hills] onduleux(euse) - **2.** phr : **to be ~ in it** inf rouler sur l'or.
rolling mill n laminoir m.
rolling pin n rouleau m à pâtisserie.
rolling stock n matériel m roulant.
rollneck ['rəʊlnek] adj à col roulé.
roll of honour n liste f des combattants morts au champ d'honneur.
roll-on adj [deodorant] à bille.
roll-on roll-off adj Br : ~ **ferry** roll on-roll off m inv, roulier m.
roly-poly [ˌrəʊlɪ'pəʊlɪ] (pl -ies) n Br : ~ **(pudding)** roulé m à la confiture.
ROM [rɒm] (abbr of **read only memory**) n ROM f.
romaine lettuce [rəʊ'meɪn-] n Am romaine f (laitue).
Roman ['rəʊmən] ◇ adj romain(e) ◇ n Romain m, -e f.
Roman candle n chandelle f romaine.
Roman Catholic ◇ adj catholique ◇ n catholique mf.
romance [rəʊ'mæns] n - **1.** (U) [romantic quality] charme m - **2.** [love affair] idylle f - **3.** [book] roman m (d'amour).
Romanesque [ˌrəʊmə'nesk] adj roman(e).
Romani ['rəʊmənɪ] = Romany.
Romania [ruː'meɪnjə] n Roumanie f ; **in ~** en Roumanie.
Romanian [ruː'meɪnjən] ◇ adj roumain(e) ◇ n - **1.** [person] Roumain m, -e f - **2.** [language] roumain m.
Roman numerals npl chiffres mpl romains.
romantic [rəʊ'mæntɪk] adj romantique.
romanticism [rəʊ'mæntɪsɪzm] n romantisme m.
romanticize, -ise [rəʊ'mæntɪsaɪz] vt & vi romancer.
Romany ['rəʊmənɪ] (pl -ies) ◇ adj de bohé-

·mien ◇ n - **1.** [person] bohémien m, -enne f - **2.** [language] romani m.

Rome [rəʊm] n Rome.

romp [rɒmp] ◇ n ébats mpl ◇ vi s'ébattre.

rompers ['rɒmpəz] npl, **romper suit** ['rɒmpə'-] n barboteuse f.

roof [ru:f] n toit m ; [of cave, tunnel] plafond m ; the ~ of the mouth la voûte du palais ; to have a ~ over one's head avoir OR posséder un toit ; to go through OR hit the ~ fig exploser.

roof garden n jardin m sur le toit.

roofing ['ru:fɪŋ] n toiture f.

roof rack n galerie f.

rooftop ['ru:ftɒp] n toit m.

rook [rʊk] n - **1.** [bird] freux m - **2.** [chess piece] tour f.

rookie ['rʊkɪ] n Am inf bleu m.

room [ru:m, rʊm] n - **1.** [in building] pièce f - **2.** [bedroom] chambre f - **3.** (U) [space] place f ; there is ~ for improvement on peut faire mieux ; ~ to OR for manoeuvre marge f de manœuvre.

rooming house ['ru:mɪŋ-] n Am maison f de rapport.

roommate ['ru:mmeɪt] n camarade mf de chambre.

room service n service m dans les chambres.

room temperature n température f ambiante.

roomy ['ru:mɪ] (compar -ier ; superl -iest) adj spacieux(euse).

roost [ru:st] ◇ n perchoir m, juchoir m ; to rule the ~ faire la loi ◇ vi se percher, se jucher.

rooster ['ru:stə'] n coq m.

root [ru:t] ◇ adj [fundamental] principal(e), fondamental(e) ◇ n racine f ; fig [of problem] origine f ; to take ~ lit & fig prendre racine ; to put down ~s [person] s'enraciner ◇ vi : to ~ through fouiller dans.

➡ **roots** npl racines fpl.

➡ **root for** vt fus Am inf encourager.

➡ **root out** vt sep [eradicate] extirper.

root beer n Am boisson gazeuse à base de racines de plantes.

root crop n racine f.

rooted ['ru:tɪd] adj : to be ~ to the spot être cloué(e) sur place.

rootless ['ru:tlɪs] adj sans racines.

root vegetable n racine f.

rope [rəʊp] ◇ n corde f ; to know the ~s connaître son affaire, être au courant ◇ vt corder ; [climbers] encorder.

➡ **rope in** vt sep inf fig enrôler.

➡ **rope off** vt sep délimiter par une corde.

rop(e)y ['rəʊpɪ] (compar -ier ; superl -iest) adj Br inf - **1.** [poor-quality] pas fameux(euse), pas brillant(e) - **2.** [unwell] : I feel a bit ~ today je me sens un peu patraque aujourd'hui.

rosary ['rəʊzərɪ] (pl -ies) n rosaire m.

rose [rəʊz] ◇ pt ▷ **rise** ◇ adj [pink] rose ◇ n [flower] rose f.

rosé ['rəʊzeɪ] n rosé m.

rosebed ['rəʊzbed] n massif m de rosiers.

rosebud ['rəʊzbʌd] n bouton m de rose.

rose bush n rosier m.

rose hip n gratte-cul m.

rosemary ['rəʊzmərɪ] n romarin m.

rosette [rəʊ'zet] n rosette f.

rosewater ['rəʊz,wɔ:tə'] n eau f de rose.

rosewood ['rəʊzwʊd] n bois m de rose.

ROSPA ['rɒspə] (abbr of **Royal Society for the Prevention of Accidents**) n association britannique pour la prévention des accidents.

roster ['rɒstə'] n liste f, tableau m.

rostrum ['rɒstrəm] (pl -trums OR -tra [-trə]) n tribune f.

rosy ['rəʊzɪ] (compar -ier ; superl -iest) adj rose.

rot [rɒt] (pt & pp -ted ; cont -ting) ◇ n (U) - **1.** [decay] pourriture f - **2.** Br dated [nonsense] bêtises fpl, balivernes fpl ◇ vt & vi pourrir.

rota ['rəʊtə] n liste f, tableau m.

rotary ['rəʊtərɪ] ◇ adj rotatif(ive) ◇ n Am [roundabout] rond-point m.

Rotary Club n : the ~ le Rotary Club.

rotate [rəʊ'teɪt] ◇ vt - **1.** [turn] faire tourner - **2.** [alternate - jobs] faire à tour de rôle ; [- crops] alterner ◇ vi [turn] tourner.

rotation [rəʊ'teɪʃn] n - **1.** [turning movement] rotation f - **2.** [alternation] alternance f ; in ~ à tour de rôle.

rote [rəʊt] n : by ~ de façon machinale, par cœur.

rote learning n apprentissage m machinal OR par cœur.

rotor ['rəʊtə'] n rotor m.

rotten ['rɒtn] adj - **1.** [decayed] pourri(e) - **2.** inf [bad] moche - **3.** inf [unwell] : to feel ~ se sentir mal fichu(e) - **4.** [unhappy] : I feel ~ about it ça me contrarie.

rotund [rəʊ'tʌnd] adj rondelet(ette).

rouble ['ru:bl] n rouble m.

rouge [ru:ʒ] n rouge m à joues.

rough [rʌf] ⬦ adj - **1.** [not smooth - surface] rugueux(euse), rêche ; [- road] accidenté(e) ; [- sea] agité(e), houleux(euse) ; [-, crossing] mauvais(e) - **2.** [person, treatment] brutal(e) ; [manners, conditions] rude ; [area] mal fréquenté(e) - **3.** [guess] approximatif(ive) ; ~ **copy**, ~ **draft** brouillon m ; ~ **sketch** ébauche f - **4.** [harsh - voice, wine] âpre ; [- life] dur(e) ; **to have a** ~ **time** en baver - **5.** [tired, ill] mal fichu(e) ⬦ adv : **to sleep** ~ coucher à la dure ⬦ n - **1.** GOLF rough m - **2.** [undetailed form] : **in** ~ au brouillon ⬦ vt phr : **to** ~ **it** vivre à la dure.

➥ **rough out** vt sep ébaucher.

roughage [ˈrʌfɪdʒ] n (U) fibres fpl alimentaires.

rough and ready adj rudimentaire.

rough-and-tumble n (U) bagarre f.

roughcast [ˈrʌfkɑːst] n crépi m.

rough diamond n Br fig : **he's a** ~ sous ses dehors frustes, il a beaucoup de qualités.

roughen [ˈrʌfn] vt rendre rugueux(euse) OR rêche.

rough justice n justice f sommaire.

roughly [ˈrʌflɪ] adv - **1.** [approximately] approximativement - **2.** [handle, treat] brutalement - **3.** [built, made] grossièrement.

roughneck [ˈrʌfnek] n - **1.** [oil-rig worker] personne travaillant sur une plate-forme pétrolière - **2.** Am inf [ruffian] dur m.

roughness [ˈrʌfnɪs] n - **1.** [of skin, surface] rugosité f - **2.** [of treatment, person] brutalité f.

roughshod [ˈrʌfʃɒd] adv : **to ride** ~ **over sthg** passer outre à qqch ; **to ride** ~ **over sb** traiter qqn cavalièrement.

roulette [ruːˈlet] n roulette f.

round [raʊnd] ⬦ adj rond(e) ⬦ prep autour de ; ~ **here** par ici ; **all** ~ **the country** dans tout le pays ; **just** ~ **the corner** au coin de la rue ; fig tout près ; **to go** ~ **sthg** [obstacle] contourner qqch ; **to go** ~ **a museum** visiter un musée ⬦ adv - **1.** [surrounding] : **all** ~ tout autour - **2.** [near] : ~ **about** dans le coin - **3.** [in measurements] : **10 metres** ~ 10 mètres de diamètre - **4.** [to other side] : **to go** ~ faire le tour ; **to turn** ~ se retourner ; **to look** ~ se retourner (pour regarder) - **5.** [at or to nearby place] : **come** ~ **and see us** venez OR passez nous voir ; **he's** ~ **at her house** il est chez elle ; **I'm just going** ~ **to the shop** je vais juste faire une course - **6.** [approximately] : ~ **(about)** vers, environ ⬦ n - **1.** [of talks etc] série f ; **a** ~ **of applause** une salve d'applaudissements - **2.** [of competition] manche f - **3.** [of doctor] visites fpl ; [of postman, milkman] tournée f - **4.** [of ammunition] cartouche f - **5.** [of drinks] tournée

f - **6.** BOXING reprise f, round m - **7.** GOLF partie f ⬦ vt [corner] tourner ; [bend] prendre.

➥ **rounds** npl [of doctor] visites fpl ; **to do** OR **go the** ~**s** [story, joke] circuler ; [illness] faire des ravages.

➥ **round off** vt sep terminer, conclure.

➥ **round up** vt sep - **1.** [gather together] rassembler - **2.** MATH arrondir.

roundabout [ˈraʊndəbaʊt] ⬦ adj détourné(e) ⬦ n Br - **1.** [on road] rond-point m - **2.** [at fairground] manège m - **3.** [at playground] tourniquet m.

rounded [ˈraʊndɪd] adj arrondi(e).

rounders [ˈraʊndəz] n Br sorte de baseball.

Roundhead [ˈraʊndhed] n Tête f ronde.

roundly [ˈraʊndlɪ] adv [beaten] complètement ; [condemned etc] franchement, carrément.

round-shouldered [-ˈʃəʊldəd] adj voûté(e).

round-table adj : ~ **talks** table f ronde.

round the clock adv vingt-quatre heures sur vingt-quatre.

➥ **round-the-clock** adj vingt-quatre heures sur vingt-quatre.

round trip ⬦ adj Am aller-retour ⬦ n aller et retour m.

roundup [ˈraʊndʌp] n [summary] résumé m.

rouse [raʊz] vt - **1.** [wake up] réveiller - **2.** [impel] : **to** ~ **o.s. to do sthg** se forcer à faire qqch ; **to** ~ **sb to action** pousser OR inciter qqn à agir - **3.** [emotions] susciter, provoquer.

rousing [ˈraʊzɪŋ] adj [speech] vibrant(e), passionné(e) ; [welcome] enthousiaste.

rout [raʊt] ⬦ n déroute f ⬦ vt mettre en déroute.

route [ruːt] ⬦ n - **1.** [gen] itinéraire m - **2.** fig [way] chemin m, voie f ⬦ vt [goods] acheminer.

route map n [for journey] croquis m d'itinéraire ; [for buses, trains] carte f du réseau.

route march n marche f d'entraînement.

routine [ruːˈtiːn] ⬦ adj - **1.** [normal] habituel(elle), de routine - **2.** pej [uninteresting] de routine ⬦ n routine f.

routinely [ruːˈtiːnlɪ] adv de façon systématique.

rove [rəʊv] literary ⬦ vt errer dans ⬦ vi : **to** ~ **around** errer.

roving [ˈrəʊvɪŋ] adj itinérant(e).

row[1] [rəʊ] ⬦ n - **1.** [line] rangée f ; [of seats] rang m - **2.** fig [of defeats, victories] série f ; **in a** ~ d'affilée, de suite ⬦ vt [boat] faire aller à la rame ; [person] transporter en canot OR bateau ⋄ *vi* ramer.

row² [rau] ⋄ *n* - **1.** [quarrel] dispute *f*, querelle *f* - **2.** inf [noise] vacarme *m*, raffut *m* ⋄ *vi* [quarrel] se disputer, se quereller.

rowboat ['rəubəut] *n* Am canot *m*.

rowdiness ['raudinis] *n* chahut *m*, tapage *m*.

rowdy ['raudi] (*compar* -ier ; *superl* -iest) *adj* chahuteur(euse), tapageur(euse).

rower ['rəuər] *n* rameur *m*, -euse *f*.

row house [rəu-] *n* Am maison attenante aux maisons voisines.

rowing ['rəuiŋ] *n* SPORT aviron *m*.

rowing boat *n* Br canot *m*.

rowing machine *n* machine *f* à ramer.

royal ['rɔiəl] ⋄ *adj* royal(e) ⋄ *n* inf membre *m* de la famille royale.

Royal Air Force *n* : the ~ l'armée *f* de l'air britannique.

royal blue *adj* bleu roi (inv).

royal family *n* famille *f* royale.

royalist ['rɔiəlist] *n* royaliste *mf*.

royal jelly *n* gelée *f* royale.

Royal Mail *n* Br : the ~ ≃ la Poste.

Royal Marines *n* Br : the ~ les Marines *mpl*.

Royal Navy *n* : the ~ la marine de guerre britannique.

royalty ['rɔiəlti] *n* royauté *f*.
➤ **royalties** *npl* droits *mpl* d'auteur.

RP (abbr of received pronunciation) *n* prononciation standard de l'anglais britannique.

RPI (abbr of retail price index) *n* IPC *m*.

rpm *npl* (abbr of revolutions per minute) tours *mpl* par minute, tr/min.

RR abbr of railroad.

RRP *n* abbr of recommended retail price.

RSA (abbr of Royal Society of Arts) *n* société britannique pour la promotion des arts, de l'industrie et du commerce.

RSC (abbr of Royal Shakespeare Company) *n* compagnie de théâtre britannique.

RSI (abbr of repetitive strain injury) *n* douleur de poignet provoquée par les mouvements effectués au clavier d'un ordinateur.

RSPB (abbr of Royal Society for the Protection of Birds) *n* ligue britannique pour la protection des oiseaux.

RSPCA (abbr of Royal Society for the Prevention of Cruelty to Animals) *n* société britannique protectrice des animaux, ≃ SPA *f*.

RST (abbr of Royal Shakespeare Theatre) *n* célèbre théâtre à Stratford-upon-Avon.

RSVP (abbr of répondez s'il vous plaît) RSVP.

Rt Hon (abbr of Right Honourable) expression utilisée pour des titres nobiliaires.

Rt Rev (abbr of Right Reverend) expression utilisée pour un évêque de l'Église anglicane.

rub [rʌb] (*pt & pp* -bed ; *cont* -bing) ⋄ *vt* frotter ; **to ~ sthg in** [cream etc] faire pénétrer qqch (en frottant) ; **to ~ one's eyes/hands** se frotter les yeux/les mains ; **to ~ it in** inf fig remuer le couteau dans la plaie ; **to ~ sb up the wrong way** Br, **to ~ sb the wrong way** Am fig prendre qqn à rebrousse-poil ⋄ *vi* frotter.
➤ **rub off on** *vt fus* [subj . quality] déteindre sur.
➤ **rub out** *vt sep* [erase] effacer.

rubber ['rʌbər] ⋄ *adj* en caoutchouc ⋄ *n* - **1.** [substance] caoutchouc *m* - **2.** Br [eraser] gomme *f* - **3.** Am inf [condom] préservatif *m* - **4.** [in bridge] robre *m*, rob *m* - **5.** Am [overshoe] caoutchouc *m*.

rubber band *n* élastique *m*.

rubber plant *n* caoutchouc *m*.

rubber boot *n* Am botte *f* de caoutchouc.

rubber dinghy *n* canot *m* pneumatique.

rubberize, -ise ['rʌbəraiz] *vt* caoutchouter.

rubberneck ['rʌbənek] *vi* Am inf faire le badaud.

rubber ring *n* anneau *m* en caoutchouc ; [for swimmer] bouée *f*.

rubber stamp *n* tampon *m*.
➤ **rubber-stamp** *vt* fig approuver sans discussion.

rubber tree *n* hévéa *m*.

rubbery ['rʌbəri] *adj* caoutchouteux(euse).

rubbing ['rʌbiŋ] *n* [of brass] décalque *m*.

rubbish ['rʌbiʃ] ⋄ *n* (U) - **1.** [refuse] détritus *mpl*, ordures *fpl* - **2.** inf fig [worthless objects] camelote *f* ; **the play was ~** la pièce était nulle - **3.** inf [nonsense] bêtises *fpl*, inepties *fpl* ⋄ *vt* inf débiner.

rubbish bin *n* Br poubelle *f*.

rubbish dump *n* Br dépotoir *m*.

rubbishy ['rʌbiʃi] *adj* inf qui ne vaut rien, nul (nulle).

rubble ['rʌbl] *n* (U) décombres *mpl*.

rubella [ru:'belə] *n* rubéole *f*.

ruby ['ru:bi] (*pl* -ies) *n* rubis *m*.

RUC (abbr of Royal Ulster Constabulary) *n* corps de police d'Irlande du Nord.

ruched [ru:ʃt] *adj* garni(e) d'un ruché.

ruck [rʌk] *n* - **1.** inf [fight] bagarre *f* - **2.** RUGBY mêlée *f* ouverte.

rucksack ['rʌksæk] *n* sac *m* à dos.

ructions ['rʌkʃnz] *npl* inf grabuge *m*.

rudder ['rʌdəʳ] n gouvernail m.

ruddy ['rʌdɪ] (compar -ier ; superl -iest) adj - **1.** [complexion, face] coloré(e) - **2.** Br inf dated [damned] sacré(e).

rude [ruːd] adj - **1.** [impolite - gen] impoli(e) ; [- word] grossier(ère) ; [- noise] incongru(e) - **2.** [sudden] : **it was a ~ awakening** le réveil fut pénible - **3.** literary [primitive] grossier(ère), rudimentaire.

rudely ['ruːdlɪ] adv - **1.** [impolitely] impoliment - **2.** [suddenly] brusquement.

rudeness ['ruːdnɪs] n [impoliteness] impolitesse f ; [of joke] grossièreté f.

rudimentary [ˌruːdɪ'mentərɪ] adj rudimentaire.

rudiments ['ruːdɪmənts] npl rudiments mpl.

rue [ruː] vt regretter (amèrement).

rueful ['ruːfʊl] adj triste.

ruff [rʌf] n fraise f.

ruffian ['rʌfjən] n voyou m.

ruffle ['rʌfl] vt - **1.** [hair] ébouriffer ; [water] troubler - **2.** [person] froisser ; [composure] faire perdre.

rug [rʌg] n - **1.** [carpet] tapis m - **2.** [blanket] couverture f.

rugby ['rʌgbɪ] n rugby m.

Rugby League n rugby m à treize.

Rugby Union n rugby m à quinze.

rugged ['rʌgɪd] adj - **1.** [landscape] accidenté(e) ; [features] rude - **2.** [vehicle etc] robuste.

ruggedness ['rʌgɪdnɪs] n [of landscape] aspect m accidenté.

rugger ['rʌgəʳ] n Br inf rugby m.

ruin ['ruːɪn] <> n ruine f <> vt ruiner ; [clothes, shoes] abîmer.

➡ **in ruin(s)** adv lit & fig en ruine.

ruination [ˌruːɪ'neɪʃn] n ruine f.

ruinous ['ruːɪnəs] adj [expensive] ruineux(euse).

rule [ruːl] <> n - **1.** [gen] règle f ; **as a ~** en règle générale - **2.** [regulation] règlement m ; **to bend the ~s** faire une entorse au règlement - **3.** (U) [control] autorité f <> vt - **1.** [control] dominer - **2.** [govern] gouverner - **3.** [decide] : **to ~ (that)** ... décider que ... <> vi - **1.** [give decision - gen] décider ; [- JUR] statuer - **2.** fml [be paramount] prévaloir - **3.** [king, queen] régner ; POL gouverner.

➡ **rule out** vt sep exclure, écarter.

rulebook ['ruːlbʊk] n : **the ~** le règlement.

ruled [ruːld] adj [paper] réglé(e).

ruler ['ruːləʳ] n - **1.** [for measurement] règle f - **2.** [leader] chef m d'État.

ruling ['ruːlɪŋ] <> adj au pouvoir <> n décision f.

rum [rʌm] (compar -mer ; superl -mest) <> n rhum m <> adj Br dated bizarre.

Rumania [ruː'meɪnjə] = **Romania**.

Rumanian [ruː'meɪnjən] = **Romanian**.

rumba ['rʌmbə] n rumba f.

rumble ['rʌmbl] <> n - **1.** [of thunder, traffic] grondement m ; [in stomach] gargouillement m - **2.** Am inf [fight] bagarre f <> vt Br inf dated : **to ~ sb** voir clair dans le jeu de qqn <> vi [thunder, traffic] gronder ; [stomach] gargouiller.

rumbustious [rʌm'bʌstɪəs] adj Br bruyant(e).

ruminate ['ruːmɪneɪt] vi : **to ~ (about OR on sthg)** ruminer (qqch).

rummage ['rʌmɪdʒ] vi fouiller.

rummage sale n Am vente f de charité.

rummy ['rʌmɪ] n rami m.

rumour Br, **rumor** Am ['ruːməʳ] n rumeur f.

rumoured Br, **rumored** Am ['ruːməd] adj : **he is ~ to be very wealthy** le bruit court OR on dit qu'il est très riche.

rump [rʌmp] n - **1.** [of animal] croupe f - **2.** inf [of person] derrière m - **3.** POL restant m.

rumple ['rʌmpl] vt froisser, chiffonner.

rump steak n romsteck m.

rumpus ['rʌmpəs] n inf chahut m.

rumpus room n Am salle f de jeu.

run [rʌn] (pt ran, pp run, cont -ning) <> n - **1.** [on foot] course f ; **to go for a ~** faire un petit peu de course à pied ; **to break into a ~** se mettre à courir ; **on the ~** en fuite, en cavale ; **to make a ~ for it** se sauver - **2.** [in car - for pleasure] tour m ; [- journey] trajet m - **3.** [series] suite f, série f ; **a ~ of bad luck** une période de déveine ; **in the short/long ~** à court/long terme - **4.** THEATRE : **to have a long ~** tenir longtemps l'affiche - **5.** [great demand] : **~ on** ruée f sur - **6.** [in tights] échelle f - **7.** [in cricket, baseball] point m - **8.** [track - for skiing, bobsleigh] piste f <> vt - **1.** [race, distance] courir ; **to ~ errands (for sb)** faire des courses OR commissions (pour qqn) - **2.** [manage - business] diriger ; [- shop, hotel] tenir ; [- course] organiser - **3.** [operate] faire marcher - **4.** [car] avoir, entretenir - **5.** [water, bath] faire couler - **6.** [publish] publier - **7.** inf [drive] : **can you ~ me to the station?** tu peux m'amener OR me conduire à la gare? - **8.** [move] : **to ~ sthg along/over sthg** passer qqch le long de/sur qqch <> vi - **1.** [on foot] courir ; **to ~ for it** se sauver - **2.** [pass - road, river, pipe] passer ; **to ~ through sthg** traverser qqch - **3.** Am [in election] : **to ~ (for)** être candidat (à) **- 4.** [operate - machine, factory] marcher ; [- engine] tourner ; **everything is running smoothly** tout va comme sur des roulettes, tout va bien ; **to ~ on sthg** marcher à qqch ; **to ~ off sthg** marcher sur qqch **- 5.** [bus, train] faire le service ; **trains ~ every hour** il y a un train toutes les heures ; **to be running late** [person] être en retard ; [bus, train] avoir du retard **- 6.** [flow] couler ; **my nose is running** j'ai le nez qui coule ; **to ~ dry** se tarir **- 7.** [colour] déteindre ; [ink] baver **- 8.** [continue - contract, insurance policy] être valide ; [- THEATRE] se jouer ; **output is running at 100 units a day** la production est de 100 unités par jour.

➤ **run across** *vt fus* [meet] tomber sur.

➤ **run along** *vi* dated : **~ along now!** filez maintenant!

➤ **run away** *vi* **- 1.** [flee] : **to ~ away (from)** s'enfuir (de) ; **to ~ away from home** faire une fugue **- 2.** fig [avoid] : **to ~ away from sthg** éviter qqch.

➤ **run away with** *vt fus* : **don't let your enthusiasm ~ away with you!** ne t'emballe pas trop!

➤ **run down** ◇ *vt sep* **- 1.** [in vehicle] renverser **- 2.** [criticize] dénigrer **- 3.** [production] restreindre ; [industry] réduire l'activité de ◇ *vi* [clock] s'arrêter ; [battery] se décharger.

➤ **run into** *vt fus* **- 1.** [encounter - problem] se heurter à ; [- person] tomber sur ; **to ~ into debt** s'endetter, faire des dettes **- 2.** [in vehicle] rentrer dans **- 3.** [amount to] se monter à, s'élever à.

➤ **run off** ◇ *vt sep* [a copy] tirer ◇ *vi* : **to ~ off (with)** s'enfuir (avec).

➤ **run on** *vi* [meeting] durer ; **time is running on** le temps passe.

➤ **run out** *vi* **- 1.** [food, supplies] s'épuiser ; **time is running out** il ne reste plus beaucoup de temps **- 2.** [licence, contract] expirer.

➤ **run out of** *vt fus* manquer de ; **to ~ out of petrol** tomber en panne d'essence, tomber en panne sèche.

➤ **run over** *vt sep* renverser.

➤ **run through** *vt fus* **- 1.** [practise] répéter **- 2.** [read through] parcourir.

➤ **run to** *vt fus* **- 1.** [amount to] monter à, s'élever à **- 2.** [afford] : **I think I could ~ to a new suit** je crois bien que je pourrais me payer OR m'offrir un nouveau costume.

➤ **run up** *vt fus* [bill, debt] laisser accumuler.

➤ **run up against** *vt fus* se heurter à.

run-around *n* inf : **to give sb the ~** faire des réponses de Normand à qqn.

runaway ['rʌnəweɪ] ◇ *adj* [train, lorry] fou (folle) ; [horse] emballé(e) ; [victory] haut la main ; [inflation] galopant(e) ◇ *n* fuyard *m*, fugitif *m*, -ive *f*.

rundown ['rʌndaʊn] *n* **- 1.** [report] bref résumé *m* **- 2.** [of industry] réduction *f* délibérée.

➤ **run-down** *adj* **- 1.** [building] délabré(e) **- 2.** [person] épuisé(e).

rung [rʌŋ] ◇ *pp* ▷ ring ◇ *n* échelon *m*, barreau *m*.

run-in *n* inf prise *f* de bec.

runnel ['rʌnl] *n* ruisseau *m*.

runner ['rʌnər] *n* **- 1.** [athlete] coureur *m*, -euse *f* **- 2.** [of guns, drugs] contrebandier *m* **- 3.** [of sledge] patin *m* ; [for car seat] glissière *f* ; [for drawer] coulisseau *m*.

runner bean *n* Br haricot *m* à rames.

runner-up (*pl* runners-up) *n* second *m*, -e *f*.

running ['rʌnɪŋ] ◇ *adj* **- 1.** [argument, battle] continu(e) **- 2.** [consecutive] : **three weeks ~** trois semaines de suite **- 3.** [water] courant(e) ◇ *n* **- 1.** (U) SPORT course *f* ; **to go ~** faire de la course **- 2.** [management] direction *f*, administration *f* **- 3.** [of machine] marche *f*, fonctionnement *m* **- 4.** phr : **to be in the ~ (for)** avoir des chances de réussir (dans) ; **to be out of the ~ (for)** n'avoir aucune chance de réussir (dans) ; **to make the ~** [in race] mener la course ; [in relationship] prendre l'initiative ◇ *comp* de course.

running commentary *n* commentaire *m* suivi.

running costs *npl* frais *mpl* d'exploitation.

running mate *n* Am candidat *m* à la vice-présidence.

running repairs *npl* réparations *fpl* courantes.

runny ['rʌnɪ] (*compar* **-ier** ; *superl* **-iest**) *adj* **- 1.** [food] liquide **- 2.** [nose] qui coule.

run-of-the-mill *adj* banal(e), ordinaire.

runt [rʌnt] *n* avorton *m*.

run-through *n* répétition *f*.

run-up *n* **- 1.** [preceding time] : **in the ~ to sthg** dans la période qui précède qqch **- 2.** SPORT course *f* d'élan.

runway ['rʌnweɪ] *n* piste *f*.

rupture ['rʌptʃər] *n* rupture *f*.

rural ['rʊərəl] *adj* rural(e).

ruse [ruːz] *n* ruse *f*.

rush [rʌʃ] ◇ *n* **- 1.** [hurry] hâte *f* ; **there's no ~** ça ne presse pas, ce n'est pas pressé **- 2.** [surge] ruée *f*, bousculade *f* ; **to make a ~ for sthg** se ruer OR se précipiter vers qqch ; **a ~ of air** une bouffée d'air ; **a ~ of blood to the head** un coup de sang **- 3.** [demand] : **~ (on OR for)** ruée *f* (sur) ◇ *vt* **- 1.** [hurrywork] faire à la hâte ; [- person] bousculer ; [- meal] expédier ; **to ~ sb into doing sthg** forcer qqn à faire qqch à la hâte **- 2.** [send quickly] transporter OR envoyer d'urgence - **3.** [attack suddenly] prendre d'assaut ◇ vi - **1.** [hurry] se dépêcher ; **to ~ into sthg** faire qqch sans réfléchir - **2.** [move quickly, suddenly] se précipiter, se ruer ; **the blood ~ed to her head** le sang lui monta à la tête.

➤ **rushes** npl - **1.** BOT joncs mpl - **2.** CINEMA épreuves fpl de tournage, rushes mpl.

rushed [rʌʃt] adj [person] pressé(e) ; [work] fait(e) à la hâte.

rush hour n heures fpl de pointe OR d'affluence.

rush job n travail m d'urgence.

rusk [rʌsk] n biscotte f.

russet ['rʌsɪt] adj feuille-morte (inv).

Russia ['rʌʃə] n Russie f ; **in ~** en Russie.

Russian ['rʌʃn] ◇ adj russe ◇ n - **1.** [person] Russe mf - **2.** [language] russe m.

Russian roulette n roulette f russe.

rust [rʌst] ◇ n rouille f ◇ vi se rouiller.

rustic ['rʌstɪk] adj rustique.

rustle ['rʌsl] ◇ n [of leaves] bruissement m ; [of papers] froissement m ◇ vt - **1.** [paper] froisser - **2.** Am [cattle] voler ◇ vi [leaves] bruire ; [papers] produire un froissement.

rustproof ['rʌstpruːf] adj inoxydable.

rusty ['rʌstɪ] (compar -ier ; superl -iest) adj lit & fig rouillé(e).

rut [rʌt] n ornière f ; **to get into a ~** s'encroûter ; **to be in a ~** être prisonnier de la routine.

rutabaga [ˌruːtəˈbeɪɡə] n Am rutabaga m.

ruthless ['ruːθlɪs] adj impitoyable.

ruthlessly ['ruːθlɪslɪ] adv de façon impitoyable.

ruthlessness ['ruːθlɪsnɪs] n caractère m impitoyable.

RV n - **1.** (abbr of revised version) traduction de la Bible de 1611 révisée entre 1881 et 1895 - **2.** Am (abbr of recreational vehicle) camping-car m.

Rwanda [rʊˈændə] n Ruanda m, Rwanda m ; **in ~** au Ruanda.

Rwandan [rʊˈændən] ◇ adj ruandais(e) ◇ n Ruandais m, -e f.

rye [raɪ] n - **1.** [grain] seigle m - **2.** [bread] pain m de seigle.

rye bread n pain m de seigle.

rye grass n ivraie f.

rye whiskey n whisky m à base de seigle.

S

s (pl ss OR s's), **S** (pl Ss OR S's) [es] n [letter] s m inv, S m inv.

➤ **S** (abbr of south) S.

SA - **1.** abbr of South Africa - **2.** abbr of South America.

Saar [sɑːr] n : **the ~** la Sarre.

Sabbath ['sæbəθ] n : **the ~** le sabbat.

sabbatical [səˈbætɪkl] n année f sabbatique ; **to be on ~** faire une année sabbatique.

saber Am = sabre.

sabotage ['sæbətɑːʒ] ◇ n sabotage m ◇ vt saboter.

saboteur [ˌsæbəˈtɜːr] n saboteur m.

sabre Br, **saber** Am ['seɪbər] n sabre m.

saccharin(e) ['sækərɪn] n saccharine f.

sachet ['sæʃeɪ] n sachet m.

sack [sæk] ◇ n - **1.** [bag] sac m - **2.** Br inf [dismissal] : **to get** OR **be given the ~** être renvoyé(e), se faire virer ◇ vt Br inf [dismiss] renvoyer, virer.

sackful ['sækful] n sac m.

sacking ['sækɪŋ] n [fabric] toile f à sac.

sacrament ['sækrəmənt] n sacrement m.

sacred ['seɪkrɪd] adj sacré(e).

sacrifice ['sækrɪfaɪs] lit & fig ◇ n sacrifice m ◇ vt sacrifier.

sacrilege ['sækrɪlɪdʒ] n lit & fig sacrilège m.

sacrilegious [ˌsækrɪˈlɪdʒəs] adj sacrilège.

sacrosanct ['sækrəʊsæŋkt] adj sacro-saint (e).

sad [sæd] (compar -der ; superl -dest) adj triste.

sadden ['sædn] vt attrister, affliger.

saddle ['sædl] ◇ n selle f ◇ vt - **1.** [horse] seller - **2.** fig [burden] : **to ~ sb with sthg** coller qqch à qqn.

➤ **saddle up** ◇ vt fus seller ◇ vi seller son cheval.

saddlebag ['sædlbæg] n sacoche f (de selle ou de bicyclette).

saddler ['sædlər] n sellier m.

sadism ['seɪdɪzm] n sadisme m.

sadist ['seɪdɪst] n sadique mf.

sadistic [səˈdɪstɪk] adj sadique.

sadly ['sædlɪ] *adv* - **1.** [unhappily] tristement - **2.** [unfortunately] malheureusement.

sadness ['sædnɪs] *n* tristesse *f*.

s.a.e., sae *abbr of* stamped addressed envelope.

safari [sə'fɑːrɪ] *n* safari *m* ; **to go on ~** aller en safari.

safari park *n* réserve *f*.

safe [seɪf] <> *adj* - **1.** [not dangerous - gen] sans danger ; [- driver, play, guess] prudent(e) ; **it's not ~** c'est dangereux ; **it's ~ to say (that)** ... on peut dire à coup sûr que ... ; **in ~ hands** en bonnes mains - **2.** [not in danger] hors de danger, en sécurité ; **your secret is ~ with me** je saurai garder votre secret ; **~ and sound** sain et sauf (saine et sauve) - **3.** [not risky - bet, method] sans risque ; [- investment] sûr(e) ; **to be on the ~ side** par précaution <> *n* coffre-fort *m*.

safebreaker ['seɪf,breɪkəʳ] *n* perceur *m* de coffre-fort.

safe-conduct *n* sauf-conduit *m*.

safe-deposit box *n* coffre-fort *m*.

safeguard ['seɪfgɑːd] <> *n* : **~ (against)** sauvegarde *f* (contre) <> *vt* : **to ~ sb/sthg (against)** sauvegarder qqn/qqch (contre), protéger qqn/qqch (contre).

safe house *n* lieu *m* sûr.

safekeeping [,seɪf'kiːpɪŋ] *n* bonne garde *f*.

safely ['seɪflɪ] *adv* - **1.** [not dangerously] sans danger - **2.** [not in danger] en toute sécurité, à l'abri du danger - **3.** [arrive - person] à bon port, sain et sauf (saine et sauve) ; [- parcel] à bon port - **4.** [for certain] : **I can ~ say (that)** ... je peux dire à coup sûr que ...

safe sex *n* sexe *m* sans risques, S.S.R. *m*.

safety ['seɪftɪ] <> *n* sécurité *f* <> *comp* de sécurité.

safety belt *n* ceinture *f* de sécurité.

safety catch *n* cran *m* de sûreté.

safety curtain *n* rideau *m* de fer.

safety-deposit box = safe-deposit box.

safety island *n* Am refuge *m*.

safety match *n* allumette *f* de sûreté.

safety net *n* filet *m* (de protection).

safety pin *n* épingle *f* de sûreté OR de nourrice.

safety valve *n* soupape *f* de sûreté.

saffron ['sæfrən] *n* safran *m*.

sag [sæg] (*pt & pp* -**ged** ; *cont* -**ging**) *vi* - **1.** [sink downwards] s'affaisser, fléchir - **2.** fig [decrease] baisser.

saga ['sɑːgə] *n* saga *f* ; fig & pej histoire *f*.

sage [seɪdʒ] <> *adj* sage <> *n* - **1.** (U) [herb] sauge *f* - **2.** [wise man] sage *m*.

saggy ['sægɪ] (*compar* -**gier** ; *superl* -**giest**) *adj* [bed] affaissé(e) ; [breasts] pendant(e).

Sagittarius [,sædʒɪ'teərɪəs] *n* Sagittaire *m* ; **to be (a) ~** être Sagittaire.

Sahara [sə'hɑːrə] *n* : **the ~ (Desert)** le (désert du) Sahara.

Saharan [sə'hɑːrən] *adj* saharien(enne).

said [sed] *pt & pp* ⊳ say.

sail [seɪl] <> *n* - **1.** [of boat] voile *f* ; **to set ~** faire voile, prendre la mer - **2.** [journey] tour *m* en bateau <> *vt* - **1.** [boat] piloter, manœuvrer - **2.** [sea] parcourir <> *vi* - **1.** [person - move] aller en bateau ; [- sport] faire de la voile - **2.** [boat - move] naviguer ; [- leave] partir, prendre la mer ; **the ship ~ed into harbour** le bateau est entré au port - **3.** fig [through air] voler.

◆ **sail through** *vt fus* fig réussir les doigts dans le nez.

sailboard ['seɪlbɔːd] *n* planche *f* à voile.

sailboat Am = sailing boat.

sailcloth ['seɪlklɒθ] *n* toile *f* à voile.

sailing ['seɪlɪŋ] *n* - **1.** (U) sport voile *f* ; **to go ~** faire de la voile - **2.** [departure] départ *m*.

sailing boat Br, **sailboat** Am ['seɪlbəʊt] *n* bateau *m* à voiles, voilier *m*.

sailing ship *n* voilier *m*.

sailor ['seɪləʳ] *n* marin *m*, matelot *m* ; **to be a good ~** avoir le pied marin.

saint [seɪnt] *n* saint *m*, -e *f*.

Saint Helena [-ɪ'liːnə] *n* Sainte-Hélène *f* ; **on ~** à Sainte-Hélène.

Saint Lawrence [-'lɒrəns] *n* : **the ~ (River)** le Saint-Laurent.

Saint Lucia [-'luːʃə] *n* Sainte-Lucie.

saintly ['seɪntlɪ] (*compar* -**ier** ; *superl* -**iest**) *adj* [person] saint(e) ; [life] de saint.

Saint Patrick's Day [-'pætrɪks-] *n* la Saint-Patrick.

SAINT PATRICK'S DAY

La Saint-Patrick (17 mars) est une fête célébrée par les Irlandais et descendants d'Irlandais du monde entier. De grands défilés se tiennent dans les rues de Dublin, New York et Sydney. La coutume veut que chacun arbore une feuille de trèfle à la boutonnière, ou porte un vêtement de couleur verte, le vert symbolisant l'Irlande. À cette occasion, certains bars américains servent même de la bière verte.

sake [seɪk] *n* : **for the ~ of sb** par égard pour qqn, pour (l'amour de) qqn ; **for the chil-**

dren's ~ pour les enfants ; for the ~ of my health pour ma santé ; for the ~ of argument à titre d'exemple ; to do sthg for its own ~ faire qqch pour le plaisir ; for God's OR heaven's ~ pour l'amour de Dieu OR du ciel.

salad ['sæləd] n salade f.

salad bowl n saladier m.

salad cream n Br sorte de mayonnaise douce.

salad dressing n vinaigrette f.

salad oil n huile f de table.

salamander ['sælə,mændə'] n salamandre f.

salami [sə'lɑːmɪ] n salami m.

salaried ['sælərɪd] adj salarié(e).

salary ['sælərɪ] (pl -ies) n salaire m, traitement m.

salary scale n échelle f des salaires.

sale [seɪl] n - 1. [gen] vente f ; on ~ en vente ; (up) for ~ à vendre - 2. [at reduced prices] soldes mpl ; the shop is having a ~ le magasin fait des soldes ; in a ~ en solde.

➡ **sales** <> npl - 1. [quantity sold] ventes fpl - 2. [at reduced prices] the ~s les soldes mpl <> comp [figures, department] des ventes ; ~s manager directeur commercial m, directrice commerciale f.

saleroom Br ['seɪlrʊm], **salesroom** Am ['seɪlzrʊm] n salle f des ventes.

sales assistant ['seɪlz-], **salesclerk** ['seɪlzklɑːrk] Am n vendeur m, -euse f.

sales conference n conférence f du personnel des ventes.

sales drive n campagne f de vente.

sales force n force f de vente.

salesman ['seɪlzmən] (pl -men [-mən]) n [in shop] vendeur m ; [travelling] représentant m de commerce.

sales pitch n boniment m.

sales rep n inf représentant m de commerce.

sales representative n réprésentant m de commerce.

salesroom Am = saleroom.

sales slip n Am [receipt] ticket m de caisse.

sales tax n taxe f à l'achat.

sales team n équipe f de vente.

saleswoman ['seɪlz,wʊmən] (pl -women [-,wɪmɪn]) n [in shop] vendeuse f ; [travelling] représentante f de commerce.

salient ['seɪljənt] adj fml qui ressort.

saline ['seɪlaɪn] adj salin(e) ; ~ drip perfusion f de sérum artificiel.

saliva [sə'laɪvə] n salive f.

salivate ['sælɪveɪt] vi saliver.

sallow ['sæləʊ] adj cireux(euse).

sally ['sælɪ] (pl -ies, pt & pp -ied) n [sortie] sortie f.

➡ **sally forth** vi hum OR literary sortir.

salmon ['sæmən] (pl inv OR -s) n saumon m.

salmonella [,sælmə'nelə] n salmonelle f.

salmon pink <> adj rose saumon (inv) <> n rose m saumon.

salon ['sælɒn] n salon m.

saloon [sə'luːn] n - 1. Br [car] berline f - 2. Am [bar] saloon m - 3. Br [in pub] : ~ (bar) bar m - 4. [in ship] salon m.

salopettes [,sælə'pets] npl combinaison f de ski.

salt [sɔːlt, splt] <> n sel m ; the ~ of the earth le sel de la terre ; to rub ~ into sb's wounds remuer OR retourner le couteau dans la plaie ; take what he says with a pinch of ~ ne prenez pas ce qu'il dit au pied de la lettre <> comp [food] salé(e) <> vt [food] saler ; [roads] mettre du sel sur.

➡ **salt away** vt sep mettre de côté.

SALT [sɔːlt] (abbr of Strategic Arms Limitation Talks/Treaty) n SALT m, négociations américano-soviétiques sur la limitation des armes stratégiques.

saltcellar Br, **salt shaker** Am [-,ʃeɪkə'] n salière f.

salted ['sɔːltɪd] adj salé(e).

saltpetre Br, **saltpeter** Am [,sɔːlt'piːtə'] n salpêtre m.

salt shaker Am = saltcellar.

saltwater ['sɔːlt,wɔːtə'] <> n eau f de mer <> adj de mer.

salty ['sɔːltɪ] (compar -ier ; superl -iest) adj [food] salé(e) ; [water] saumâtre.

salubrious [sə'luːbrɪəs] adj salubre.

salutary ['sæljʊtrɪ] adj salutaire.

salute [sə'luːt] <> n salut m <> vt saluer <> vi faire un salut.

Salvadorean, Salvadorian [,sælvə'dɔːrɪən] <> adj salvadorien(enne) <> n Salvadorien m, -enne f.

salvage ['sælvɪdʒ] <> n (U) - 1. [rescue of ship] sauvetage m - 2. [property rescued] biens mpl sauvés <> vt sauver.

salvage vessel n bateau m de sauvetage.

salvation [sæl'veɪʃn] n salut m.

Salvation Army n : the ~ l'Armée f du Salut.

salve [sælv] vt : to do sthg to ~ one's conscience faire qqch pour avoir la conscience en paix.

salver ['sælvə'] n plateau m.

salvo ['sælvəʊ] (pl -s OR -es) n salve f.

Samaritan [sə'mærɪtn] n : good ~ bon Samaritain m.

samba ['sæmbə] n samba f.

same [seɪm] ⬦ adj même ; she was wearing the ~ jumper as I was elle portait le même pull que moi ; at the ~ time en même temps ; one and the ~ un seul et même (une seule et même) ⬦ pron : the ~ le même (la même), les mêmes (pl) ; I'll have the ~ as you je prendrai la même chose que toi ; she earns the ~ as I do elle gagne autant que moi ; to do the ~ faire de même, en faire autant ; all OR just the ~ [anyway] quand même, tout de même ; it's all the ~ to me ça m'est égal ; it's not the ~ ce n'est pas pareil ⬦ adv : the ~ [treat, spelled] de la même manière.

sameness ['seɪmnɪs] n pej monotonie f.

Samoa [sə'məʊə] n Samoa m ; in ~ à Samoa ; American ~ les Samoa américaines fpl.

Samoan [sə'məʊən] ⬦ adj samoan(e) ⬦ n Samoan m, -e f.

samosa [sə'məʊsə] n genre de brick indien aux légumes.

sample ['sɑːmpl] ⬦ n échantillon m ⬦ vt - 1. [taste] goûter - 2. MUS faire le sampling de.

sampler ['sɑːmplə'] n SEWING modèle m de broderie.

sanatorium, sanitorium Am [ˌsænə'tɔːrɪəm] (pl -riums OR -ria [-rɪəl] n sanatorium m.

sanctify ['sæŋktɪfaɪ] (pt & pp -ied) vt sanctifier.

sanctimonious [ˌsæŋktɪ'məʊnjəs] adj moralisateur(trice).

sanction ['sæŋkʃn] ⬦ n sanction f ⬦ vt sanctionner.

➤ **sanctions** npl sanctions fpl.

sanctity ['sæŋktətɪ] n sainteté f.

sanctuary ['sæŋktʃʊərɪ] (pl -ies) n - 1. [for birds, wildlife] réserve f - 2. [refuge] asile m - 3. [holy place] sanctuaire m.

sanctum ['sæŋktəm] (pl -s) n fig [private place] retraite f.

sand [sænd] ⬦ n sable m ⬦ vt [wood] poncer.

➤ **sands** npl plage f de sable.

sandal ['sændl] n sandale f.

sandalwood ['sændlwʊd] n (bois m de) santal m.

sandbag ['sændbæg] n sac m de sable.

sandbank ['sændbæŋk] n banc m de sable.

sandblast ['sændblɑːst] vt décaper à la sableuse, sabler.

sandbox Am = sandpit.

sandcastle ['sænd,kɑːsl] n château m de sable.

sand dune n dune f.

sander ['sændə'] n ponceuse f.

sandpaper ['sænd,peɪpə'] ⬦ n (U) papier m de verre ⬦ vt poncer (au papier de verre).

sandpit Br ['sændpɪt], **sandbox** Am ['sændbɒks] n bac m à sable.

sandstone ['sændstəʊn] n grès m.

sandstorm ['sændstɔːm] n tempête f de sable.

sand trap n Am & Can GOLF bunker m, fosse f de sable Can.

sandwich ['sænwɪdʒ] ⬦ n sandwich m ⬦ vt fig : to be ~ed between être (pris(e)) en sandwich entre.

sandwich board n panneau m publicitaire (d'homme sandwich ou posé comme un tréteau).

sandwich course n Br stage m de formation professionnelle.

sandy ['sændɪ] (compar -ier ; superl -iest) adj - 1. [beach] de sable ; [earth] sableux(euse) - 2. [sand-coloured] sable (inv).

sane [seɪn] adj - 1. [not mad] sain(e) d'esprit - 2. [sensible] raisonnable, sensé(e).

sang [sæŋ] pt ⊳ sing.

sanguine ['sæŋgwɪn] adj optimiste.

sanitary ['sænɪtrɪ] adj - 1. [method, system] sanitaire - 2. [clean] hygiénique, salubre.

sanitary towel, sanitary napkin Am n serviette f hygiénique.

sanitation [ˌsænɪ'teɪʃn] n (U) [in house] installations fpl sanitaires.

sanitation worker n Am éboueur m.

sanitize, -ise ['sænɪtaɪz] vt fig expurger.

sanitorium Am = sanatorium.

sanity ['sænɪtɪ] n (U) - 1. [saneness] santé f mentale, raison f - 2. [good sense] bon sens m.

sank [sæŋk] pt ⊳ sink.

San Marino [ˌsænmə'riːnəʊ] n Saint-Marin m ; in ~ à Saint-Marin.

San Salvador [ˌsæn'sælvədɔː'] n San Salvador.

Sanskrit ['sænskrɪt] n sanskrit m, sanscrit m.

Santa (Claus) ['sæntə(ˌklɔːz)] n le père Noël.

São Paulo [ˌsaʊ'paʊləʊ] n - 1. [city] São Paulo - 2. [state] : ~ **(State)** São Paulo m, l'État m de São Paulo ; in ~ dans le São Paulo.

sap [sæp] (pt & pp -ped ; cont -ping) ⬦ n - 1. [of plant] sève f - 2. Am inf [gullible person] nigaud m, -e f ⬦ vt [weaken] saper.

sapling ['sæplɪŋ] n jeune arbre m.

sapphire ['sæfaɪəʳ] n saphir m.

Sarajevo [,særə'jeɪvəʊ] n Sarajevo.

sarcasm ['sɑːkæzm] n sarcasme m.

sarcastic [sɑː'kæstɪk] adj sarcastique.

sarcophagus [sɑː'kɒfəgəs] (pl -gi [-gaɪ] OR -guses [-gəsiːz]) n sarcophage m.

sardine [sɑː'diːn] n sardine f.

Sardinia [sɑː'dɪnjə] n Sardaigne f; in ~ en Sardaigne.

sardonic [sɑː'dɒnɪk] adj sardonique.

Sargasso Sea [sɑː'gæsəʊ-] n : the ~ la mer des Sargasses.

sari ['sɑːrɪ] n sari m.

sarong [sə'rɒŋ] n sarong m.

sarsaparilla [,sɑːspə'rɪlə] n salsepareille f.

sartorial [sɑː'tɔːrɪəl] adj fml vestimentaire.

SAS (abbr of Special Air Service) n commando d'intervention spéciale de l'armée britannique.

SASE abbr of self-addressed stamped envelope.

sash [sæʃ] n [of cloth] écharpe f.

sash window n fenêtre f à guillotine.

Saskatchewan [,sæs'kætʃɪ,wən] n Saskatchewan m.

sassy ['sæsɪ] adj Am inf culotté(e).

sat [sæt] pt & pp ⊏⊐ sit.

Sat. (abbr of Saturday) sam.

SAT [sæt] n - 1. (abbr of Standard Assessment Test) examen national en Grande-Bretagne pour les élèves de 7 ans, 11 ans et 14 ans - 2. (abbr of Scholastic Aptitude Test) examen d'entrée à l'université aux États-Unis.

Satan ['seɪtn] n Satan m.

satanic [sə'tænɪk] adj satanique.

satchel ['sætʃəl] n cartable m.

sated ['seɪtɪd] adj [person, hunger] : ~ (with) rassasié(e) (de).

satellite ['sætəlaɪt] <> n satellite m <> comp - 1. [link] par satellite ; ~ dish antenne f parabolique - 2. [country, company] satellite.

satellite TV n télévision f par satellite.

satiate ['seɪʃɪeɪt] vt [person, hunger] rassasier.

satin ['sætɪn] <> n satin m <> comp [sheets, pyjamas] de OR en satin ; [wallpaper, finish] satiné(e).

satire ['sætaɪəʳ] n satire f.

satirical [sə'tɪrɪkl] adj satirique.

satirist ['sætərɪst] n satiriste mf.

satirize, -ise ['sætəraɪz] vt faire la satire de.

satisfaction [,sætɪs'fækʃn] n satisfaction f.

satisfactory [,sætɪs'fæktərɪ] adj satisfaisant(e).

satisfied ['sætɪsfaɪd] adj - 1. [happy] : ~ (with) satisfait(e) (de) - 2. [convinced] : to be ~ that être sûr(e) que.

satisfy ['sætɪsfaɪ] (pt & pp -ied) vt - 1. [gen] satisfaire - 2. [convince] convaincre, persuader ; to ~ sb that convaincre qqn que ; to ~ o.s. that s'assurer que.

satisfying ['sætɪsfaɪɪŋ] adj satisfaisant(e).

satsuma [,sæt'suːmə] n satsuma f.

saturate ['sætʃəreɪt] vt : to ~ sthg (with) saturer qqch (de).

saturated fat ['sætʃəreɪtɪd-] n matière f grasse saturée.

saturation [,sætʃə'reɪʃn] <> n saturation f <> comp [bombing] en masse.

saturation point n : to reach ~ arriver à saturation f.

Saturday ['sætədɪ] <> n samedi m ; it's ~ on est samedi ; are you going ~? inf tu y vas samedi? ; see you ~! inf à samedi! ; on ~ samedi ; on ~s le samedi ; last ~ samedi dernier ; this ~ ce samedi ; next ~ samedi prochain ; every ~ tous les samedis ; every other ~ un samedi sur deux ; the ~ before l'autre samedi ; the ~ before last pas samedi dernier, mais le samedi d'avant ; the ~ after next, ~ week, a week on ~ samedi en huit ; to work ~s travailler le samedi <> comp [paper] du OR de samedi ; I have a ~ appointment j'ai un rendez-vous samedi ; ~ morning/afternoon/evening samedi matin/après-midi/soir ; a ~ job un petit boulot (le samedi pour gagner de l'argent de poche).

Saturn ['sætən] n [planet] Saturne f.

sauce [sɔːs] n - 1. CULIN sauce f - 2. Br inf [cheek] toupet m.

sauce boat n saucière f.

saucepan ['sɔːspən] n casserole f.

saucer ['sɔːsəʳ] n sous-tasse f, soucoupe f.

saucy ['sɔːsɪ] (compar -ier ; superl -iest) adj inf coquin(e).

Saudi Arabia ['saʊdɪ-] n Arabie f Saoudite ; in ~ en Arabie Saoudite.

Saudi (Arabian) ['saʊdɪ-] <> adj saoudien(enne) <> n [person] Saoudien m, -enne f.

sauna ['sɔːnə] n sauna m.

saunter ['sɔːntəʳ] vi flâner.

sausage ['sɒsɪdʒ] n saucisse f.

sausage roll n Br feuilleté m à la saucisse.

sauté [Br 'səʊteɪ, Am sɔː'teɪ] (pt & pp sautéed OR sautéd) <> adj sauté(e) <> vt [potatoes] faire sauter ; [onions] faire revenir.

savage [ˈsævɪdʒ] ◇ *adj* [fierce] féroce ◇ *n* sauvage *mf* ◇ *vt* attaquer avec férocité.

savageness [ˈsævɪdʒnɪs], **savagery** [ˈsævɪdʒrɪ] *n* férocité *f*.

savanna(h) [səˈvænə] *n* savane *f*.

save [seɪv] ◇ *vt* - **1.** [rescue] sauver ; **to ~ sb's life** sauver la vie à *or* de qqn - **2.** [money - set aside] mettre de côté ; [- spend less] économiser ; **we ~d £10 by buying in bulk** on a économisé 10 livres en achetant en grosses quantités - **3.** [time] gagner ; [strength] économiser ; [food] garder - **4.** [avoid] éviter, épargner ; **to ~ sb sthg** épargner qqch à qqn ; **to ~ sb from doing sthg** éviter à qqn de faire qqch - **5.** SPORT arrêter - **6.** COMPUT sauvegarder ◇ *vi* [save money] mettre de l'argent de côté ◇ *n* SPORT arrêt *m* ◇ *prep* fml : **~ (for)** sauf, à l'exception de.

➤ **save up** *vi* mettre de l'argent de côté.

save as you earn *n* Br plan d'épargne national par prélèvements mensuels.

saveloy [ˈsævəlɔɪ] *n* Br cervelas *m*.

saver [ˈseɪvəʳ] *n* - **1.** [object] : **it's a money ~** ça me fait économiser de l'argent - **2.** FIN épargnant *m*, -e *f*.

saving grace [ˈseɪvɪŋ-] *n* : **its ~ was ...** ce qui le rachetait, c'était ...

savings [ˈseɪvɪŋz] *npl* économies *fpl*.

savings account *n* Am compte *m* d'épargne.

savings and loan association *n* Am société *f* de crédit immobilier.

savings bank *n* caisse *f* d'épargne.

saviour Br, **savior** Am [ˈseɪvjəʳ] *n* sauveur *m*.

➤ **Saviour** *n* : **the Saviour** le Sauveur.

savoir-faire [ˌsævwɑːˈfeəʳ] *n* savoir-vivre *m*.

savour Br, **savor** Am [ˈseɪvəʳ] *vt* lit & fig savourer.

savoury Br, **savory** Am [ˈseɪvərɪ] (*pl* -ies) ◇ *adj* - **1.** [food] salé(e) - **2.** [respectable] recommandable ◇ *n* petit plat *m* salé.

Savoy [səˈvɔɪ] *n* Savoie *f* ; **in ~** en Savoie.

saw [sɔː] (Br *pt* -ed ; *pp* sawn, Am *pt*. & *pp* -ed) ◇ *pt* ⟁ see ◇ *n* scie *f* ◇ *vt* scier.

sawdust [ˈsɔːdʌst] *n* sciure *f* (de bois).

sawed-off shotgun Am = sawn-off shotgun.

sawmill [ˈsɔːmɪl] *n* scierie *f*, moulin *m* à scie Can.

sawn [sɔːn] Br *pp* ⟁ saw.

sawn-off shotgun Br, **sawed-off shotgun** [ˈsɔːd-] Am *n* carabine *f* à canon scié.

sax [sæks] *n* inf saxo *m*.

Saxon [ˈsæksn] ◇ *adj* saxon(onne) ◇ *n* Saxon *m*, -onne *f*.

saxophone [ˈsæksəfəʊn] *n* saxophone *m*.

saxophonist [Br sækˈsɒfənɪst, Am ˈsæksəfəʊnɪst] *n* saxophoniste *mf*.

say [seɪ] (*pt* & *pp* said) ◇ *vt* - **1.** [gen] dire ; **could you ~ that again?** vous pouvez répéter ce que vous venez de dire? ; **(let's) ~ you won a lottery ...** supposons que tu gagnes le gros lot ... ; **it ~s a lot about him** cela en dit long sur lui ; **she's said to be ...** on dit qu'elle est ... ; **to ~ to o.s.** se dire ; **to ~ nothing of** sans parler de ; **that goes without ~ing** cela va sans dire ; **I'll ~ this for him ...** je dois lui rendre cette justice que ... ; **it has a lot to be said for it** cela a beaucoup d'avantages ; **she didn't have much to ~ for herself** *inf* elle n'avait pas grand-chose à dire - **2.** [subj : clock, watch] indiquer ◇ *n* : **to have a/no ~** avoir/ne pas avoir voix au chapitre ; **to have a ~ in sthg** avoir son mot à dire sur qqch ; **to have one's ~** dire ce que l'on a à dire, dire son mot.

➤ **that is to say** *adv* c'est-à-dire.

SAYE *n* abbr of save as you earn.

saying [ˈseɪɪŋ] *n* dicton *m*.

say-so *n* inf [permission] autorisation *f*.

SBA (abbr of **Small Business Administration**) *n* organisme fédéral américain d'aide aux petites entreprises.

s/c abbr of self-contained.

SC ◇ *n* abbr of **supreme court** ◇ abbr of **South Carolina**.

scab [skæb] *n* - **1.** [of wound] croûte *f* - **2.** inf pej [non-striker] jaune *m*.

scabby [ˈskæbɪ] (*compar* -ier ; *superl* -iest) *adj* couvert(e) de croûtes.

scabies [ˈskeɪbiːz] *n* (U) gale *f*.

scaffold [ˈskæfəʊld] *n* échafaud *m*.

scaffolding [ˈskæfəldɪŋ] *n* échafaudage *m*.

scalawag Am = scallywag.

scald [skɔːld] ◇ *n* brûlure *f* ◇ *vt* ébouillanter ; **to ~ one's arm** s'ébouillanter le bras.

scalding [ˈskɔːldɪŋ] *adj* bouillant(e).

scale [skeɪl] ◇ *n* - **1.** [gen] échelle *f* ; **to ~** [map, drawing] à l'échelle - **2.** [of ruler, thermometer] graduation *f* - **3.** MUS gamme *f* - **4.** [of fish, snake] écaille *f* - **5.** Am = scales ◇ *vt* - **1.** [cliff, mountain, fence] escalader - **2.** [fish] écailler.

➤ **scales** *npl* balance *f*.

➤ **scale down** *vt fus* réduire.

scale diagram *n* plan *m* à l'échelle.

scale model *n* modèle *m* réduit.

scallion [ˈskæljən] *n* Am [spring onion] ciboule *f*.

scallop [ˈskɒləp] ◇ *n* [shellfish] coquille *f*

Saint-Jacques ⬦ *vt* [edge, garment] feston-
ner.

scallywag Br ['skælɪwæg], **scalawag** Am
['skæləwæg] *n inf* polisson *m*, -onne *f*.

scalp [skælp] ⬦ *n* - **1.** ANAT cuir *m* chevelu
- **2.** [trophy] scalp *m* ⬦ *vt* scalper.

scalpel ['skælpəl] *n* scalpel *m*.

scalper ['skælpər] *n* Am [tout] revendeur *m* de
billets.

scam [skæm] *n inf* arnaque *f*.

scamp [skæmp] *n inf* coquin *m*, -e *f*.

scamper ['skæmpər] *vi* trottiner.

scampi ['skæmpɪ] *n* (U) scampi *mpl*.

scan [skæn] (*pt & pp* -ned ; *cont* -ning) ⬦ *n* MED
scanographie *f* ; [during pregnancy] échographie *f* ⬦ *vt* - **1.** [examine carefully] scruter
- **2.** [glance at] parcourir - **3.** TECH balayer
- **4.** COMPUT faire un scannage de ⬦ *vi* - **1.** LIT-
ERATURE se scander - **2.** COMPUT scanner.

scandal ['skændl] *n* - **1.** [gen] scandale *m*
- **2.** [gossip] médisance *f*.

scandalize, -ise ['skændəlaɪz] *vt* scandaliser.

scandalous ['skændələs] *adj* scanda-
leux(euse).

Scandinavia [,skændɪ'neɪvjə] *n* Scandinavie
f ; in ~ en Scandinavie.

Scandinavian [,skændɪ'neɪvjən] ⬦ *adj*
scandinave ⬦ *n* [person] Scandinave *mf*.

scanner ['skænər] *n* [gen & COMPUT] scanner *m*.

scant [skænt] *adj* insuffisant(e).

scanty ['skæntɪ] (*compar* -ier ; *superl* -iest) *adj*
[amount, resources] insuffisant(e) ; [income] maigre ; [dress] minuscule.

scapegoat ['skeɪpgəʊt] *n* bouc *m* émissaire.

scar [skɑːr] (*pt & pp* -red ; *cont* -ring) ⬦ *n* cicatrice *f* ⬦ *vt* - **1.** [skin, face] marquer d'une
cicatrice ; [landscape] défigurer - **2.** fig [mental-
ly] marquer.

scarce ['skeəs] *adj* rare, peu abondant(e) ; to
make o.s. ~ s'esquiver.

scarcely ['skeəslɪ] *adv* à peine ; ~ anyone
presque personne ; I ~ ever go there now je
n'y vais presque OR pratiquement plus jamais.

scarcity ['skeəsətɪ] *n* manque *m*.

scare [skeər] ⬦ *n* - **1.** [sudden fear] : to give sb a
~ faire peur à qqn - **2.** [public fear] panique *f* ;
bomb ~ alerte *f* à la bombe ⬦ *vt* faire peur
à, effrayer.

➤ **scare away, scare off** *vt sep* faire fuir.

scarecrow ['skeəkrəʊ] *n* épouvantail *m*.

scared ['skeəd] *adj* apeuré(e) ; to be ~ avoir

peur ; to be ~ stiff OR to death être mort de
peur.

scarey ['skeərɪ] = scary.

scarf [skɑːf] (*pl* -s OR scarves [skɑːvz]) *n* [wool]
écharpe *f* ; [silk etc] foulard *m*.

scarlet ['skɑːlət] ⬦ *adj* écarlate ⬦ *n* écarlate *f*.

scarlet fever *n* scarlatine *f*.

scarves [skɑːvz] *pl* ⊏⟶ scarf.

scary [skeərɪ] (*compar* -ier ; *superl* -iest) *adj inf*
qui fait peur.

scathing ['skeɪðɪŋ] *adj* [criticism] acerbe ; [reply]
cinglant(e) ; to be ~ about sb/sthg critiquer
qqn/qqch de manière acerbe.

scatter ['skætər] ⬦ *vt* [clothes, paper etc] éparpiller ; [seeds] semer à la volée ⬦ *vi* se disperser.

scatterbrained ['skætəbreɪnd] *adj inf* écer-
velé(e).

scattered ['skætəd] *adj* [wreckage, population]
dispersé(e) ; [paper] éparpillé(e) ; [showers] in-
termittent(e).

scattering ['skætərɪŋ] *n* [small number] petit
nombre *m* ; [small amount] petite quantité *f*.

scatty ['skætɪ] (*compar* -ier ; *superl* -iest) *adj* Br
inf écervelé(e).

scavenge ['skævɪndʒ] ⬦ *vt* [object] récupérer
⬦ *vi* [person] : to ~ for sthg faire les poubelles
pour trouver qqch.

scavenger ['skævɪndʒər] *n* - **1.** [animal] animal
m nécrophage - **2.** [person] personne *f* qui
fait les poubelles.

SCE (*abbr of* **Scottish Certificate of Education**)
*n certificat de fin d'études secondaires en
Écosse.*

scenario [sɪ'nɑːrɪəʊ] (*pl* -s) *n* - **1.** [possible situ-
ation] hypothèse *f*, scénario *m* - **2.** [of film, play]
scénario *m*.

scene [siːn] *n* - **1.** [in play, film, book] scène *f* ; to
make a ~ fig faire une scène ; behind the ~s
dans les coulisses - **2.** [sight] spectacle *m*,
vue *f* ; [picture] tableau *m* - **3.** [location] lieu *m*,
endroit *m* ; on the ~ sur les lieux ; a change
of ~ un changement de décor - **4.** [area of ac-
tivity] : the political ~ la scène politique ; the
music ~ le monde de la musique ; it's not my
~ inf ce n'est pas mon truc - **5.** *phr* : to set the
~ for sb mettre qqn au courant de la situation ; to set the ~ for sthg préparer la voie à
qqch.

scenery ['siːnərɪ] *n* (U) - **1.** [of countryside] paysage *m* - **2.** THEATRE décor *m*, décors *mpl*.

scenic ['siːnɪk] *adj* [tour] touristique ; a ~ view
un beau panorama.

scenic route *n* route *f* touristique.

scent [sent] ⟨> *n* - **1.** [smell - of flowers] senteur *f*, parfum *m* ; [- of animal] odeur *f*, fumet *m* - **2.** fig [track] piste *f* - **3.** *(U)* [perfume] parfum *m* ⟨> *vt* lit & fig sentir.

scented ['sentɪd] *adj* parfumé(e).

scepter Am = sceptre.

sceptic Br, **skeptic** Am ['skeptɪk] *n* sceptique *mf*.

sceptical Br, **skeptical** Am ['skeptɪkl] *adj* : ~ (about) sceptique (sur).

scepticism Br, **skepticism** Am ['skeptɪsɪzm] *n* scepticisme *m*.

sceptre Br, **scepter** Am ['septə'] *n* sceptre *m*.

SCF (*abbr of* Save the Children Fund) *n* association caritative britannique s'occupant des enfants.

schedule [Br 'ʃedjuːl, Am 'skedʒʊl] ⟨> *n* - **1.** [plan] programme *m*, plan *m* ; **(according) to** ~ selon le programme, comme prévu ; **on** ~ [at expected time] à l'heure (prévue) ; [on expected day] à la date prévue ; **ahead of/behind** ~ en avance/en retard (sur le programme) - **2.** [list - of times] horaire *m* ; [- of prices] tarif *m* ⟨> *vt* : **to** ~ **sthg (for)** prévoir qqch (pour).

scheduled flight [Br 'ʃedjuːld-, Am 'skedʒʊld-] *n* vol *m* régulier.

schematic [skɪ'mætɪk] *adj* schématique.

scheme [skiːm] ⟨> *n* - **1.** [plan] plan *m*, projet *m* - **2.** pej [dishonest plan] combine *f* - **3.** [arrangement] arrangement *m* ; **colour** ~ combinaison *f* de couleurs ; **the** ~ **of things** l'ordre des choses ⟨> *vt* pej : **to** ~ **to do sthg** conspirer pour faire qqch ⟨> *vi* pej conspirer.

scheming ['skiːmɪŋ] *adj* intrigant(e).

schism ['sɪzm, 'skɪzm] *n* schisme *m*

schizophrenia [ˌskɪtsə'friːnjə] *n* schizophrénie *f*.

schizophrenic [ˌskɪtsə'frenɪk] ⟨> *adj* schizophrène ⟨> *n* schizophrène *mf*.

schlepp [ʃlep] Am inf ⟨> *vt* trimbaler ⟨> *vi* : **to** ~ **(around)** se trimbaler.

schmal(t)z [ʃmɔːlts] *n* inf sentimentalité *f* à la guimauve.

schmuck [ʃmʌk] *n* Am inf rigolo *m*.

scholar ['skɒlə'] *n* - **1.** [expert] érudit *m*, -e *f*, savant *m*, -e *f* - **2.** dated [student] écolier *m*, -ère *f*, élève *mf* - **3.** [holder of scholarship] boursier *m*, -ère *f*.

scholarship ['skɒləʃɪp] *n* - **1.** [grant] bourse *f* (d'études) - **2.** [learning] érudition *f*.

scholastic [skə'læstɪk] *adj* fml scolaire.

school [skuːl] *n* - **1.** [gen] école *f* ; [secondary school] lycée *m*, collège *m* - **2.** [university department] faculté *f* - **3.** Am [university] université *f* - **4.** [of fish] banc *m*.

school age *n* âge *m* scolaire.

schoolbook ['skuːlbʊk] *n* livre *m* scolaire OR de classe.

schoolboy ['skuːlbɔɪ] *n* écolier *m*, élève *m*.

schoolchild ['skuːltʃaɪld] (*pl* -children [-tʃɪldrən]) *n* écolier *m*, -ère *f*, élève *mf*.

schooldays ['skuːldeɪz] *npl* années *fpl* d'école.

school dinner *n* déjeuner *m* à la cantine (*de l'école*).

school district *n* Am *aux États-Unis, autorité locale décisionnaire dans le domaine de l'enseignement primaire et secondaire.*

school friend *n* camarade *mf* d'école.

schoolgirl ['skuːlɡɜːl] *n* écolière *f*, élève *f*.

schooling ['skuːlɪŋ] *n* instruction *f*.

schoolkid ['skuːlkɪd] *n* inf écolier *m*, -ère *f*, élève *mf*.

school-leaver [-ˌliːvə'] *n* Br *élève qui a fini ses études secondaires.*

school-leaving age [-'liːvɪŋ-] *n* Br âge *m* de fin de scolarité.

schoolmarm ['skuːlmɑːm] *n* Am institutrice *f*.

schoolmaster ['skuːlˌmɑːstə'] *n* [primary] instituteur *m*, maître *m* d'école ; [secondary] professeur *m*.

schoolmistress ['skuːlˌmɪstrɪs] *n* [primary] institutrice *f*, maîtresse *f* d'école ; [secondary] professeur *m*.

school of thought *n* école *f* (de pensée).

school report *n* bulletin *m*.

schoolroom ['skuːlrʊm] *n* salle *f* de classe.

schoolteacher ['skuːlˌtiːtʃə'] *n* [primary] instituteur *m*, -trice *f* ; [secondary] professeur *m*.

school uniform *n* uniforme *m* scolaire.

schoolwork ['skuːlwɜːk] *n (U)* travail *m* scolaire OR de classe.

school year *n* année *f* scolaire.

schooner ['skuːnə'] *n* - **1.** [ship] schooner *m*, goélette *f* - **2.** Br [sherry glass] grand verre *m* à xérès.

sciatica [saɪ'ætɪkə] *n* sciatique *f*.

science ['saɪəns] ⟨> *n* science *f* ⟨> *comp* [student] en sciences ; [degree] de OR ès sciences ; [course] de sciences.

science fiction *n* science-fiction *f*.

science park *n* parc *m* scientifique.

scientific [ˌsaɪən'tɪfɪk] *adj* scientifique.

scientist ['saɪəntɪst] *n* scientifique *mf*.

sci-fi [ˌsaɪ'faɪ] (*abbr of* science fiction) *n* inf science-fiction *f*, S.F. *f*.

Scilly Isles ['sɪlɪ-], **Scillies** ['sɪlɪz] *npl* : **the** ~

les îles *fpl* Sorlingues ; **in the ~** aux îles Sorlingues.

scintillating ['sɪntɪleɪtɪŋ] *adj* brillant(e).

scissors ['sɪzəz] *npl* ciseaux *mpl* ; **a pair of ~** une paire de ciseaux.

sclerosis [sklɪ'rəʊsɪs] ⊳ **multiple sclerosis.**

scoff [skɒf] ⬦ *vt* Br *inf* bouffer, boulotter ⬦ *vi* : **to ~ (at)** se moquer (de).

scold [skəʊld] *vt* gronder, réprimander.

scone [skɒn] *n* scone *m*.

scoop [sku:p] ⬦ *n* - **1.** [for sugar] pelle *f* à main ; [for ice cream] cuiller *f* à glace - **2.** [of ice cream] boule *f* - **3.** [news report] exclusivité *f*, scoop *m* ⬦ *vt* [with hands] prendre avec les mains ; [with scoop] prendre avec une pelle à main.

➤ **scoop out** *vt sep* évider.

scoot [sku:t] *vi inf* filer.

scooter ['sku:tə'] *n* - **1.** [toy] trottinette *f* - **2.** [motorcycle] scooter *m*.

scope [skəʊp] *n (U)* - **1.** [opportunity] occasion *f*, possibilité *f* - **2.** [of report, inquiry] étendue *f*, portée *f*.

scorch [skɔ:tʃ] ⬦ *vt* [clothes] brûler légèrement, roussir ; [skin] brûler ; [land, grass] dessécher ⬦ *vi* roussir.

scorched earth policy [skɔ:tʃt-] *n* politique *f* de la terre brûlée.

scorcher ['skɔ:tʃə'] *n inf* [day] journée *f* torride.

scorching ['skɔ:tʃɪŋ] *adj inf* [day] torride ; [sun] brûlant(e).

score [skɔ:'] ⬦ *n* - **1.** SPORT score *m* - **2.** [in test] note *f* - **3.** dated [twenty] vingt - **4.** MUS partition *f* - **5.** [subject] : **on that ~** à ce sujet, sur ce point ⬦ *vt* - **1.** [goal, point etc] marquer ; **to ~ 100%** avoir 100 sur 100 - **2.** [success, victory] remporter - **3.** [cut] entailler ⬦ *vi* - **1.** SPORT marquer (un but/point *etc*) - **2.** [in an argument] : **to ~ over sb** marquer un point contre qqn.

➤ **scores** *npl* : **~s of** des tas de, plein de.

➤ **score out** *vt sep* Br barrer, rayer.

scoreboard ['skɔ:bɔ:d] *n* tableau *m*.

scorecard ['skɔ:ka:d] *n* carte *f* de score.

scorer ['skɔ:rə'] *n* marqueur *m*.

scorn [skɔ:n] ⬦ *n (U)* mépris *m*, dédain *m* ; **to pour ~ on sb** accabler qqn de mépris ⬦ *vt* - **1.** [person, attitude] mépriser - **2.** [help, offer] rejeter, dédaigner.

scornful ['skɔ:nfʊl] *adj* méprisant(e) ; **to be ~ of sthg** mépriser qqch, dédaigner qqch.

Scorpio ['skɔ:pɪəʊ] *(pl -s) n* Scorpion *m* ; **to be (a) ~** être Scorpion.

scorpion ['skɔ:pjən] *n* scorpion *m*.

Scot [skɒt] *n* Écossais *m*, -e *f*.

scotch [skɒtʃ] *vt* [rumour] étouffer ; [plan] faire échouer.

Scotch [skɒtʃ] ⬦ *adj* écossais(e) ⬦ *n* scotch *m*, whisky *m*.

Scotch egg *n* Br œuf dur enrobé de chair à saucisse et recouvert de chapelure.

Scotch (tape)® *n* Am Scotch® *m*.

scot-free *adj inf* : **to get off ~** s'en tirer sans être puni(e).

Scotland ['skɒtlənd] *n* Écosse *f* ; **in ~** en Écosse.

Scotland Yard *n* ancien nom du siège de la police à Londres (aujourd'hui New Scotland Yard).

Scots [skɒts] ⬦ *adj* écossais(e) ⬦ *n* [dialect] écossais *m*.

Scotsman ['skɒtsmən] *(pl -men* [-mən]*) n* Écossais *m*.

Scotswoman ['skɒtswʊmən] *(pl -women* [-ˌwɪmɪn]*) n* Écossaise *f*.

Scottish ['skɒtɪʃ] *adj* écossais(e).

Scottish National Party *n* parti nationaliste écossais.

Scottish Parliament *n* Parlement *m* écossais.

THE SCOTTISH PARLIAMENT

Le Parlement écossais fut inauguré officiellement le 1er juillet 1999. Siégeant à Édimbourg, il est constitué de 129 membres (« Members of the Scottish Parliament » ou « MSPs. ») dirigés par le président du Parlement (First Minister). Il est chargé de voter la plupart des lois en matière de politique intérieure, notamment celles concernant les impôts. En revanche, les lois concernant la politique étrangère, l'économie, la défense et les affaires européennes demeurent sous le contrôle du gouvernement britannique à Londres.

scoundrel ['skaʊndrəl] *n* dated gredin *m*.

scour [skaʊə'] *vt* - **1.** [clean] récurer - **2.** [search - town etc] parcourir ; [- countryside] battre.

scourer ['skaʊərə'] *n* [pad] tampon *m* à récurer ; [powder] poudre *f* à récurer.

scourge [skɜ:dʒ] *n* fléau *m*.

Scouse [skaʊs] *n inf* - **1.** [person] habitant *m*, -e *f* de Liverpool - **2.** [accent] accent *m* de Liverpool.

scout [skaʊt] *n* MIL éclaireur *m*.

➤ **Scout** *n* [boy scout] Scout *m*.

➤ **scout around** *vi* : **to ~ around (for)** aller à la recherche (de).

scoutmaster ['skaʊt,mɑːstər] n chef m scout.

scowl [skaʊl] ⋄ n regard m noir, air m renfrogné ⋄ vi se renfrogner, froncer les sourcils ; **to ~ at sb** jeter des regards noirs à qqn.

SCR (abbr of **senior common room**) n Br salle des étudiants de 3ᵉ cycle.

scrabble ['skræbl] vi - **1.** [scrape] : **to ~ at sthg** gratter qqch - **2.** [feel around] : **to ~ around for sthg** tâtonner pour trouver qqch.

Scrabble® ['skræbl] n Scrabble® m.

scraggy ['skrægɪ] (compar -ier ; superl -iest) adj décharné(e), maigre.

scram [skræm] (pt & pp -med ; cont -ming) vi inf filer, ficher le camp.

scramble ['skræmbl] ⋄ n [rush] bousculade f, ruée f ⋄ vi - **1.** [climb] : **to ~ up a hill** grimper une colline en s'aidant des mains OR à quatre pattes - **2.** [compete] : **to ~ for sthg** se disputer qqch.

scrambled eggs ['skræmbld-] npl œufs mpl brouillés.

scrambler ['skræmblər] n COMPUT brouilleur m.

scrap [skræp] (pt & pp -ped ; cont -ping) ⋄ n - **1.** [of paper, material] bout m ; [of information] fragment m ; [of conversation] bribe f ; **it won't make a ~ of difference** cela ne changera absolument rien - **2.** [metal] ferraille f - **3.** inf [fight, quarrel] bagarre f ⋄ vt [car] mettre à la ferraille ; [plan, system] abandonner, laisser tomber.

➤ **scraps** npl [food] restes mpl.

scrapbook ['skræpbʊk] n album m (de coupures de journaux etc).

scrap dealer n ferrailleur m, marchand m de ferraille.

scrape [skreɪp] ⋄ n - **1.** [scraping noise] raclement m, grattement m - **2.** dated [difficult situation] : **to get into a ~** se fourrer dans le pétrin ⋄ vt - **1.** [clean, rub] gratter, racler ; **to ~ sthg off sthg** enlever qqch de qqch en grattant OR raclant - **2.** [surface, car, skin] érafler ⋄ vi gratter.

➤ **scrape through** vt fus réussir de justesse.

➤ **scrape together, scrape up** vt sep : **to ~ some money together** réunir de l'argent en raclant les fonds de tiroirs.

scraper ['skreɪpər] n grattoir m, racloir m.

scrap heap n tas m de ferraille ; **on the ~** fig au rebut, au placard.

scrapings ['skreɪpɪŋz] npl raclures fpl.

scrap merchant n Br ferrailleur m, marchand m de ferraille.

scrap metal n ferraille f.

scrap paper Br, **scratch paper** Am n (papier m) brouillon m.

scrappy ['skræpɪ] (compar -ier ; superl -iest) adj [work, speech] décousu(e).

scrapyard ['skræpjɑːd] n parc m à ferraille.

scratch [skrætʃ] ⋄ n - **1.** [wound] égratignure f, éraflure f - **2.** [on glass, paint etc] éraflure f - **3.** phr : **to be up to ~** être à la hauteur ; **to do sthg from ~** faire qqch à partir de rien ⋄ vt - **1.** [wound] écorcher, égratigner - **2.** [mark - paint, glass etc] rayer, érafler - **3.** [rub] gratter ; **to ~ o.s.** se gratter ⋄ vi gratter ; [person] se gratter.

scratch card n carte f à gratter.

scratchpad ['skrætʃpæd] n Am bloc-notes m.

scratch paper Am = **scrap paper**.

scratchy ['skrætʃɪ] (compar -ier ; superl -iest) adj - **1.** [record] qui grésille, qui craque - **2.** [material] qui gratte.

scrawl [skrɔːl] ⋄ n griffonnage m, gribouillage m ⋄ vt griffonner, gribouiller.

scrawny ['skrɔːnɪ] (compar -ier ; superl -iest) adj [person] efflanqué(e) ; [body, animal] décharné(e).

scream [skriːm] ⋄ n - **1.** [cry] cri m perçant, hurlement m ; [of laughter] éclat m - **2.** inf [funny person] : **he's a ~** il est tordant ⋄ vt hurler ⋄ vi [cry out] crier, hurler.

scree [skriː] n éboulis m.

screech [skriːtʃ] ⋄ n - **1.** [cry] cri m perçant - **2.** [of tyres] crissement m ⋄ vt hurler ⋄ vi - **1.** [cry out] pousser des cris perçants - **2.** [tyres] crisser.

screen [skriːn] ⋄ n - **1.** [gen] écran m - **2.** [panel] paravent m ⋄ vt - **1.** CINEMA projeter, passer ; TV téléviser, passer - **2.** [hide] cacher, masquer - **3.** [shield] protéger - **4.** [candidate, employee] passer au crible, filtrer - **5.** MED : **to ~ sb for sthg** faire subir à qqn un test de dépistage pour qqch.

➤ **screen off** vt sep séparer par un paravent.

screen door n porte f avec moustiquaire.

screen dump n COMPUT vidage m d'écran.

screening ['skriːnɪŋ] n - **1.** CINEMA projection f ; TV passage m à la télévision - **2.** [for security] sélection f, tri m - **3.** MED dépistage m.

screenplay ['skriːnpleɪ] n scénario m.

screen print n sérigraphie f.

screen saver n COMPUT économiseur m (d'écran).

screen test n bout m d'essai.

screenwriter ['skriːn,raɪtər] n scénariste mf.

screw [skruː] ⋄ n [for fastening] vis f ⋄ vt - **1.** [fix with screws] : **to ~ sthg to sthg** visser

qqch à OR sur qqch - **2.** [twist] visser - **3. vulg**
[woman] baiser $\diamond$ *vi* [bolt, lid] se visser.

➼ **screw up** *vt sep* - **1.** [crumple up] froisser,
chiffonner - **2.** [eyes] plisser ; [face] tordre
- **3. vinf** [ruin] gâcher, bousiller.

screwball ['skru:bɔ:l] *n* **Am inf** [person] cinglé
m, -e *f*.

screwdriver ['skru:,draɪvəʳ] *n* [tool] tournevis
m.

screwtop jar ['skru:tɒp-] *n* pot *m* à couvercle à pas de vis.

screwy ['skru:ɪ] *adj* **Am inf** fou (folle), cin-
glé(e).

scribble ['skrɪbl] $\diamond$ *n* gribouillage *m*, griffonnage *m* $\diamond$ *vt & vi* gribouiller, griffonner.

scribe [skraɪb] *n* scribe *m*.

scrimp [skrɪmp] *vi* : **to ~ and save** économiser
OR lésiner sur tout.

script [skrɪpt] *n* - **1.** [of play, film etc] scénario *m*,
script *m* - **2.** [writing system] écriture *f*
- **3.** [handwriting] (écriture *f*) script *m*.

scripted ['skrɪptɪd] *adj* préparé(e) à l'avance.

Scriptures ['skrɪptʃəz] *npl* : **the ~** les (sain-
tes) Écritures *fpl*.

scriptwriter ['skrɪpt,raɪtəʳ] *n* scénariste *mf*.

scroll [skrəʊl] $\diamond$ *n* rouleau *m* $\diamond$ *vt* COMPUT faire défiler.

➼ **scroll down** *vi* COMPUT défiler vers le bas.
➼ **scroll up** *vi* COMPUT défiler vers le haut.

scroll bar *n* COMPUT barre *f* de défilement.

scrooge [skru:dʒ] *n inf pej* grippe-sou *m*.

scrotum ['skrəʊtəm] (*pl* **-ta** [-tə] OR **-tums**) *n*
scrotum *m*.

scrounge [skraʊndʒ] *inf* $\diamond$ *vt* : **to ~ money off**
sb taper qqn ; **can I ~ a cigarette off you?** je
peux te piquer une cigarette? $\diamond$ *vi* faire le
parasite ; **to ~ off sb Br** vivre aux crochets
de qqn.

scrounger ['skraʊndʒəʳ] *n inf* parasite *m*.

scrub [skrʌb] (*pt & pp* **-bed** ; *cont* **-bing**) $\diamond$ *n*
- **1.** [rub] : **to give sthg a ~** nettoyer qqch à la
brosse - **2.** (*U*) [undergrowth] broussailles *fpl*
$\diamond$ *vt* [floor, clothes etc] laver OR nettoyer à la
brosse ; [hands, back] frotter ; [saucepan] récurer.

scrubbing brush Br ['skrʌbɪŋ-], **scrub**
brush Am *n* brosse *f* dure.

scruff [skrʌf] *n* : **by the ~ of the neck** par la
peau du cou.

scruffy ['skrʌfɪ] (*compar* **-ier** ; *superl* **-iest**) *adj*
mal soigné(e), débraillé(e).

scrum(mage) ['skrʌm(ɪdʒ)] *n* RUGBY mêlée *f*.

scrumptious ['skrʌmpʃəs] *adj* **inf** déli-
cieux(euse), fameux(euse).

scrunch [skrʌntʃ] $\diamond$ *vt* écraser, faire craquer $\diamond$ *vi* craquer, crisser.

scrunchie, scrunchy ['skrʌntʃɪ] *n* chouchou *m*.

scruples ['skru:plz] *npl* scrupules *mpl*.

scrupulous ['skru:pjʊləs] *adj* scrupu-
leux(euse).

scrupulously ['skru:pjʊləslɪ] *adv* scrupuleusement ; **~ clean** d'une propreté méticu-
leuse ; **~ honest** d'une honnêteté scrupu-
leuse.

scrutinize, -ise ['skru:tɪnaɪz] *vt* scruter,
examiner attentivement.

scrutiny ['skru:tɪnɪ] *n* (*U*) examen *m* attentif.

scuba diving ['sku:bə-] *n* plongée *f* sous-
marine (*avec bouteilles*).

scud [skʌd] (*pt & pp* **-ded** ; *cont* **-ding**) *vi* literary [clouds] courir.

scuff [skʌf] *vt* - **1.** [damage] érafler - **2.** [drag] : **to**
~ one's feet traîner les pieds.

scuffle ['skʌfl] $\diamond$ *n* bagarre *f*, échauffourée
f $\diamond$ *vi* se bagarrer, se battre.

scull [skʌl] $\diamond$ *n* aviron *m* $\diamond$ *vi* ramer.

scullery ['skʌlərɪ] (*pl* **-ies**) *n* arrière-cuisine *f*.

sculpt [skʌlpt] *vt* sculpter.

sculptor ['skʌlptəʳ] *n* sculpteur *m*.

sculpture ['skʌlptʃəʳ] $\diamond$ *n* sculpture *f* $\diamond$ *vt*
sculpter.

scum [skʌm] *n* - **1.** (*U*) [froth] écume *f*, mousse
f - **2. v inf pej** [person] salaud *m* - **3.** (*U*) **v inf pej**
[people] déchets *mpl*.

scupper ['skʌpəʳ] *vt* - **1.** NAUT couler - **2. Br fig**
[plan] saboter, faire tomber à l'eau.

scurf [skɜ:f] *n* (*U*) pellicules *fpl*.

scurrilous ['skʌrələs] *adj* calomnieux(euse).

scurry ['skʌrɪ] (*pt & pp* **-ied**) *vi* se précipiter ;
to ~ away OR **off** se sauver, détaler.

scurvy ['skɜ:vɪ] *n* scorbut *m*.

scuttle ['skʌtl] $\diamond$ *n* seau *m* à charbon $\diamond$ *vi*
courir précipitamment OR à pas précipi-
tés.

scythe [saɪð] $\diamond$ *n* faux *f* $\diamond$ *vt* faucher.

SD *abbr of* **South Dakota.**

SDI (*abbr of* **Strategic Defense Initiative**) *n*
IDS *f*.

SDLP (*abbr of* **Social Democratic and Labour**
Party) *n parti travailliste d'Irlande du Nord.*

SDP (*abbr of* **Social Democratic Party**) *n parti*
social-démocrate en Grande-Bretagne.

SE (*abbr of* **south-east**) S-E.

sea [si:] $\diamond$ *n* - **1.** [gen] mer *f* ; **at ~** en mer ; **by**

~ par mer ; **by the ~** au bord de la mer ; **out to ~** au large - **2. phr : to be all at ~** nager complètement - **3. fig** [large number] multitude f <> **comp** [voyage] en mer ; [animal] marin(e), de mer.

➥ **seas** npl : **the ~s** les mers fpl.

sea air n air m marin OR de la mer.

sea anemone n anémone f de mer.

seabed ['si:bed] n : **the ~** le fond de la mer.

seabird ['si:bɜ:d] n oiseau m marin OR de mer.

seaboard ['si:bɔ:d] n littoral m, côte f.

sea breeze n brise f de mer.

seafaring ['si:ˌfeərɪŋ] adj [nation] maritime ; **a ~ man** un marin.

seafood ['si:fu:d] n (U) fruits mpl de mer.

seafront ['si:frʌnt] n front m de mer.

seagoing ['si:ˌɡəʊɪŋ] adj [boat] de mer.

seagull ['si:ɡʌl] n mouette f.

seahorse ['si:hɔ:s] n hippocampe m.

seal [si:l] (pl inv OR **-s**) <> n - **1.** [animal] phoque m - **2.** [official mark] cachet m, sceau m ; **~ of approval** approbation f ; **to put** OR **set the ~ on sthg** sceller qqch - **3.** [official fastening] cachet m - **4.** [TECH - device] joint m d'étanchéité ; [- join] joint m étanche <> vt - **1.** [envelope] coller, fermer - **2.** [document, letter] sceller, cacheter - **3.** [block off] obturer, boucher.

➥ **seal off** vt sep [area, entrance] interdire l'accès de.

sealable ['si:ləbl] adj qui peut être fermé(e) hermétiquement.

sea lane n couloir m maritime.

sealant ['si:lənt] n enduit m étanche.

sea level n niveau m de la mer.

sealing wax ['si:lɪŋ-] n cire f à cacheter.

sea lion (pl inv OR **-s**) n otarie f.

sealskin ['si:lskɪn] n peau f de phoque.

seam [si:m] n - **1.** SEWING couture f ; **to be bursting at the ~s** fig être plein à craquer - **2.** [of coal] couche f, veine f.

seaman ['si:mən] (pl **-men** [-mən]) n marin m.

seamanship ['si:mənʃɪp] n habileté f de marin.

sea mist n brume f de mer.

seamless ['si:mlɪs] adj - **1.** SEWING sans coutures - **2.** fig [faultless] parfait(e), irréprochable.

seamstress ['semstrɪs] n couturière f.

seamy ['si:mɪ] (compar **-ier** ; superl **-iest**) adj sordide.

séance ['seɪɒns] n séance f de spiritisme.

seaplane ['si:pleɪn] n hydravion m.

seaport ['si:pɔ:t] n port m de mer.

search [sɜ:tʃ] <> n [of person, luggage, house] fouille f ; [for lost person, thing] recherche f, recherches fpl ; **~ for** recherche de ; **in ~ of** à la recherche de <> vt [house, area, person] fouiller ; [memory, mind, drawer] fouiller dans ; **to ~ one's bag/pocket for sthg** fouiller dans son sac/sa poche pour essayer de retrouver qqch ; **to ~ a house/an area for sthg** fouiller une maison/un quartier pour essayer de retrouver qqch <> vi : **to ~ (for sb/sthg)** chercher (qqn/qqch).

➥ **search out** vt sep découvrir.

search engine n COMPUT moteur m de recherche.

searcher ['sɜ:tʃər] n chercheur m, -euse f.

searching ['sɜ:tʃɪŋ] adj [question] poussé(e), approfondi(e) ; [look] pénétrant(e) ; [review, examination] minutieux(euse).

searchlight ['sɜ:tʃlaɪt] n projecteur m.

search party n équipe f de secours.

search warrant n mandat m de perquisition.

searing ['sɪərɪŋ] adj - **1.** [pain] fulgurant(e) ; [heat] torride - **2.** fig [exposure, attack] virulent(e).

sea salt n sel m marin OR de mer.

seashell ['si:ʃel] n coquillage m.

seashore ['si:ʃɔ:r] n : **the ~** le rivage, la plage.

seasick ['si:sɪk] adj : **to be** OR **feel ~** avoir le mal de mer.

seaside ['si:saɪd] n : **the ~** le bord de la mer.

seaside resort n station f balnéaire.

season ['si:zn] <> n - **1.** [gen] saison f ; **in ~** [food] de saison ; **out of ~** [holiday] hors saison ; [food] hors de saison - **2.** [of films] cycle m <> vt assaisonner, relever.

seasonal ['si:zənl] adj saisonnier(ère).

seasoned ['si:znd] adj [traveller, campaigner] chevronné(e), expérimenté(e) ; [soldier] aguerri(e).

seasoning ['si:znɪŋ] n assaisonnement m.

season ticket n carte f d'abonnement.

seat [si:t] <> n - **1.** [gen] siège m ; [in theatre] fauteuil m ; **take a ~!** asseyez-vous! - **2.** [place to sit - in bus, train] place f - **3.** [of trousers] fond m <> vt - **1.** [sit down] faire asseoir, placer ; **please be ~ed** veuillez vous asseoir ; **to ~ o.s.** s'asseoir - **2.** [have room for] : **the car ~s five** on tient à cinq dans cette voiture ; **the hall ~s 200** il y a 200 places assises dans cette salle.

seat belt n ceinture f de sécurité.

seated ['si:tɪd] adj assis(e).

-seater ['si:tə'] *suffix :* a two~ (car) une voiture à deux places.

seating ['si:tɪŋ] <> *n (U)* [capacity] sièges *mpl*, places *fpl* (assises) <> *comp* [plan] de table ; ~ **capacity** nombre *m* de places assises.

SEATO ['si:təʊ] (*abbr of* Southeast Asia Treaty Organization) *n* OTASE *f*.

sea urchin *n* oursin *m*.

seawall [,si:'wɔ:l] *n* digue *f*.

seawater ['si:,wɔ:tə'] *n* eau *f* de mer.

seaweed ['si:wi:d] *n (U)* algue *f*.

seaworthy ['si:,wɜ:ðɪ] *adj* en bon état de navigabilité.

sebaceous [sɪ'beɪʃəs] *adj* sébacé(e).

sec. *abbr of* second.

SEC (*abbr of* Securities and Exchange Commission) *n* commission américaine des opérations de Bourse, ≃ COB *f*.

secateurs [,sekə'tɜ:z] *npl* Br sécateur *m*.

secede [sɪ'si:d] *vi* fml : to ~ (from) se séparer (de), faire sécession (de).

secession [sɪ'seʃn] *n* fml sécession *f*.

secluded [sɪ'klu:dɪd] *adj* retiré(e), écarté(e).

seclusion [sɪ'klu:ʒn] *n* solitude *f*, retraite *f*.

second[1] ['sekənd] <> *n* - **1.** [gen] seconde *f ;* wait a ~! une seconde!, (attendez) un instant! ; ~ (gear) seconde *f*. - **2.** Br UNIV ≃ licence *f* avec mention assez bien <> *num* deuxième, second(e) ; his score was ~ only to hers il n'y a qu'elle qui ait fait mieux que lui OR qui l'ait surpassé ; *see also* **sixth** <> *vt* [proposal, motion] appuyer.
➡ **seconds** *npl* - **1.** COMM articles *mpl* de second choix - **2.** [of food] rabiot *m*.

second[2] [sɪ'kɒnd] *vt* Br [employee] affecter temporairement.

secondary ['sekəndrɪ] *adj* secondaire ; to be ~ to être moins important(e) que.

secondary modern *n* Br ≃ collège *m*.

secondary picketing *n (U)* piquets *mpl* de grève de solidarité.

secondary school *n* école *f* secondaire, lycée *m*.

second best ['sekənd-] *adj* deuxième ; to come off ~ se faire battre, perdre ; don't settle for ~ ne choisis que ce qu'il y a de mieux.

second-class ['sekənd-] *adj* - **1.** pej [citizen] de deuxième zone ; [product] de second choix - **2.** [ticket] de seconde OR deuxième classe - **3.** [stamp] à tarif réduit - **4.** Br UNIV [degree] ≃ avec mention assez bien.

second cousin ['sekənd-] *n* petit cousin *m*, petite cousine *f*.

second-degree burn ['sekənd-] *n* brûlure *f* du deuxième degré.

seconder ['sekəndə'] *n* personne qui appuie une proposition.

second floor ['sekənd-] *n* Br troisième étage *m ;* Am deuxième étage.

second-guess ['sekənd-] *vt* esp Am inf - **1.** [with hindsight] juger avec le recul - **2.** [predict] anticiper, prévoir.

second-hand ['sekənd-] <> *adj* - **1.** [goods, shop] d'occasion - **2.** fig [information] de seconde main <> *adv* - **1.** [not new] d'occasion - **2.** fig [indirectly] : to hear sthg ~ apprendre qqch de seconde main OR indirectement.

second hand ['sekənd-] *n* [of clock] trotteuse *f*.

second-in-command ['sekənd-] *n* commandant *m* en second.

secondly ['sekəndlɪ] *adv* deuxièmement, en second lieu.

secondment [sɪ'kɒndmənt] *n* Br affectation *f* temporaire.

second nature ['sekənd-] *n* seconde nature *f*.

second-rate ['sekənd-] *adj* pej de deuxième ordre, médiocre.

second thought ['sekənd-] *n :* to have ~s about sthg avoir des doutes sur qqch ; on ~s Br, on ~ Am réflexion faite, tout bien réfléchi.

secrecy ['si:krəsɪ] *n (U)* secret *m*.

secret ['si:krɪt] <> *adj* secret(ète) <> *n* secret *m ;* in ~ en secret.

secret agent *n* agent *m* secret.

secretarial [,sekrə'teərɪəl] *adj* [course, training] de secrétariat, de secrétaire ; ~ **staff** secrétaires *mpl*.

secretariat [,sekrə'teərɪət] *n* secrétariat *m*.

secretary [Br 'sekrətrɪ, Am 'sekrə,terɪ] (*pl* -ies) *n* - **1.** [gen] secrétaire *mf* - **2.** POL [minister] ministre *m*.

secretary-general (*pl* secretaries-general) *n* secrétaire *m* général.

Secretary of State *n* - **1.** Br : ~ (for) ministre *m* (de) - **2.** Am ≃ ministre *m* des Affaires étrangères.

secrete [sɪ'kri:t] *vt* - **1.** [produce] sécréter - **2.** fml [hide] cacher.

secretion [sɪ'kri:ʃn] *n* sécrétion *f*.

secretive ['si:krətɪv] *adj* secret(ète), dissimulé(e).

secretly ['si:krɪtlɪ] *adv* secrètement.

secret police *n* police *f* secrète.

secret service *n* [in UK] ≃ Deuxième Bureau m ; [in US] service de protection du président, du vice-président et de leur famille.

sect [sekt] n secte f.

sectarian [sek'teəriən] adj [killing, violence] d'ordre religieux.

section ['sekʃn] ◇ n - **1.** [portion - gen] section f, partie f ; [- of road, pipe] tronçon m ; [- of document, law] article m ; **the sports** ◇ [- PRESS] la rubrique des sports - **2.** GEOM coupe f, section f ◇ vt sectionner.

sector ['sektəʳ] n secteur m.

secular ['sekjələʳ] adj [life] séculier(ère) ; [education] laïque ; [music] profane.

secure [sɪ'kjʊəʳ] ◇ adj - **1.** [fixed - gen] fixe ; [- windows, building] bien fermé(e) - **2.** [safe - job, future] sûr(e) ; [- valuable object] en sécurité, en lieu sûr - **3.** [free of anxiety - childhood] sécurisant(e) ; [- marriage] solide ; **to feel ~** se sentir en sécurité ◇ vt - **1.** [obtain] obtenir - **2.** [fasten - gen] attacher ; [- door, window] bien fermer - **3.** [make safe] assurer la sécurité de.

securely [sɪ'kjʊəlɪ] adv [fixed, locked] solidement, bien.

security [sɪ'kjʊərətɪ] (pl -ies) ◇ n sécurité f ◇ comp de sécurité.

securities npl FIN titres mpl, valeurs fpl.

security blanket n doudou m.

Security Council n : **the ~** le Conseil de Sécurité.

security forces npl forces fpl de sécurité.

security guard n garde m de sécurité.

security risk n personne qui présente un risque pour la sécurité nationale ou d'une organisation.

secy (abbr of secretary) secr.

sedan [sɪ'dæn] n Am berline f.

sedan chair n chaise f à porteurs.

sedate [sɪ'deɪt] ◇ adj posé(e), calme ◇ vt donner un sédatif à.

sedation [sɪ'deɪʃn] n (U) sédation f ; **under ~** sous calmants.

sedative ['sedətɪv] ◇ adj sédatif(ive) ◇ n sédatif m, calmant m.

sedentary ['sedntrɪ] adj sédentaire.

sediment ['sedɪmənt] n sédiment m, dépôt m.

sedition [sɪ'dɪʃn] n sédition f.

seditious [sɪ'dɪʃəs] adj séditieux(euse).

seduce [sɪ'djuːs] vt séduire ; **to ~ sb into doing sthg** amener OR entraîner qqn à faire qqch.

seduction [sɪ'dʌkʃn] n séduction f.

seductive [sɪ'dʌktɪv] adj séduisant(e).

see [siː] (pt saw ; pp seen) ◇ vt - **1.** [gen] voir ;

~ you! au revoir! ; **~ you soon/later/tomorrow!** etc à bientôt/tout à l'heure/demain! etc ; **I'll ~ what I can do** je vais voir ce que je peux faire - **2.** [accompany] : **I saw her to the door** je l'ai accompagnée OR reconduite jusqu'à la porte ; **I saw her onto the train** je l'ai accompagnée au train - **3.** [like] : **what do you ~ in him?** qu'est-ce que tu lui trouves? - **4.** [make sure] : **to ~ (that)** ... s'assurer que ... ◇ vi voir ; **you ~,...** voyez-vous,... ; **I ~** je vois, je comprends ; **let's ~,** let me ~ voyons, voyons voir.

seeing as, seeing that conj inf vu que, étant donné que.

see about vt fus [arrange] s'occuper de.

see off vt sep - **1.** [say goodbye to] accompagner (pour dire au revoir) - **2.** Br [chase away] faire partir OR fuir.

see through ◇ vt fus [scheme] voir clair dans ; **to ~ through sb** voir dans le jeu de qqn ◇ vt sep [deal, project] mener à terme, mener à bien.

see to vt fus s'occuper de, se charger de.

seed [siːd] n - **1.** [of plant] graine f - **2.** SPORT fifth ~ joueur classé cinquième m, joueuse classée cinquième f.

seeds npl fig germes mpl, semences fpl.

seedless ['siːdlɪs] adj sans pépins.

seedling ['siːdlɪŋ] n jeune plant m, semis m.

seedy ['siːdɪ] (compar -ier ; superl -iest) adj miteux(euse).

seek [siːk] (pt & pp sought) vt - **1.** [gen] chercher ; [peace, happiness] rechercher ; **to ~ to do sthg** chercher à faire qqch ; **to ~ revenge** chercher à se venger - **2.** [advice, help] demander.

seek out vt sep chercher.

seem [siːm] ◇ vi sembler, paraître ; **to ~ bored** avoir l'air de s'ennuyer ; **to ~ sad/tired** avoir l'air triste/fatigué ; **I ~ to remember ...** je crois me rappeler ... ◇ v impers : **it ~s (that)** ... il semble OR paraît que ...

seeming ['siːmɪŋ] adj fml apparent(e).

seemingly ['siːmɪŋlɪ] adv apparemment.

seemly ['siːmlɪ] (compar -ier ; superl -iest) adj dated & literary convenable.

seen [siːn] pp ▷ see.

seep [siːp] vi suinter

seersucker ['sɪə,sʌkəʳ] n crépon m de coton.

seesaw ['siːsɔː] n bascule f.

seethe [siːð] vi - **1.** [person] bouillir, être furieux(euse) - **2.** [place] : **to be seething with** grouiller de.

seething ['siːðɪŋ] adj [furious] furieux(euse).

see-through adj transparent(e).

segment ['segmənt] *n* - **1.** [section] partie *f*, section *f* - **2.** [of fruit] quartier *m*.

segregate ['segrɪgeɪt] *vt* séparer.

segregation [,segrɪ'geɪʃn] *n* ségrégation *f*.

Seine [seɪn] *n* : **the (River)** ~ la Seine.

seismic ['saɪzmɪk] *adj* sismique.

seize [si:z] *vt* - **1.** [grab] saisir, attraper - **2.** [capture] s'emparer de, prendre - **3.** [arrest] arrêter - **4.** fig [opportunity, chance] saisir, sauter sur.

➤ **seize (up)on** *vt fus* saisir, sauter sur.

➤ **seize up** *vi* - **1.** [body] s'ankyloser - **2.** [engine, part] se gripper.

seizure ['si:ʒəʳ] *n* - **1.** MED crise *f*, attaque *f* - **2.** (U) [of town] capture *f ;* [of power] prise *f*.

seldom ['seldəm] *adv* peu souvent, rarement.

select [sɪ'lekt] <> *adj* - **1.** [carefully chosen] choisi(e) - **2.** [exclusive] de premier ordre, d'élite <> *vt* sélectionner, choisir.

select committee *n* commission *f* d'enquête.

selected [sɪ'lektɪd] *adj* choisi(e).

selection [sɪ'lekʃn] *n* sélection *f*, choix *m*.

selective [sɪ'lektɪv] *adj* sélectif(ive) ; [person] difficile.

selector [sɪ'lektəʳ] *n* [person] sélectionneur *m*, -euse *f*.

self [self] (*pl* **selves** [selvz]) *n* moi *m ;* **she's her old** ~ **again** elle est redevenue elle-même.

self- [self] *prefix* auto-.

self-addressed envelope [-ə'drest-] *n* enveloppe *f* portant ses propres nom et adresse.

self-addressed stamped envelope [-ə'drest-] *n* Am enveloppe *f* affranchie pour la réponse.

self-adhesive *adj* autocollant(e).

self-appointed [-ə'pɔɪntɪd] *adj* pej : **she's the** ~ **leader** elle se pose en chef.

self-assembly *adj* Br qu'on monte OR assemble soi-même.

self-assertive *adj* qui sait s'affirmer.

self-assurance *n* confiance *f* en soi, assurance *f*.

self-assured *adj* sûr(e) de soi, plein(e) d'assurance.

self-catering *adj* [holiday - in house] en maison louée ; [- in flat] en appartement loué.

self-centred [-'sentəd] *adj* égocentrique.

self-cleaning *adj* autonettoyant(e).

self-coloured *adj* Br uni(e).

self-confessed [-kən'fest] *adj* de son propre aveu.

self-confident *adj* sûr(e) de soi, plein(e) d'assurance.

self-conscious *adj* timide, embarrassé(e).

self-contained [-kən'teɪnd] *adj* [flat] indépendant(e), avec entrée particulière ; [person] qui se suffit à soi-même.

self-control *n* maîtrise *f* de soi.

self-controlled *adj* maître (maîtresse) de soi.

self-defence *n* autodéfense *f ;* **in** ~ JUR en légitime défense ; [reply] pour sa défense.

self-denial *n* abnégation *f*.

self-destruct [-dɪs'trʌkt] <> *adj* autodestructeur(trice) <> *vi* s'autodétruire.

self-determination *n* autodétermination *f*.

self-discipline *n* autodiscipline *f*.

self-doubt *n* manque *m* de confiance en soi.

self-drive *adj* Br sans chauffeur.

self-educated *adj* autodidacte.

self-effacing [-ɪ'feɪsɪŋ] *adj* qui cherche à s'effacer.

self-employed [-ɪm'plɔɪd] *adj* qui travaille à son propre compte.

self-esteem *n* respect *m* de soi, estime *f* de soi.

self-evident *adj* qui va de soi, évident(e).

self-explanatory *adj* évident(e), qui ne nécessite pas d'explication.

self-expression *n* libre expression *f*.

self-focusing [-'fəʊkəsɪŋ] *adj* autofocus (inv), à mise au point automatique.

self-government *n* autonomie *f*.

self-help *n* (U) initiative *f* personnelle.

self-important *adj* suffisant(e).

self-imposed [-ɪm'pəʊzd] *adj* que l'on s'impose à soi-même.

self-indulgent *adj* pej [person] qui ne se refuse rien ; [film, book, writer] nombriliste.

self-inflicted [-ɪn'flɪktɪd] *adj* que l'on s'inflige à soi-même, volontaire.

self-interest *n* (U) pej intérêt *m* personnel.

selfish ['selfɪʃ] *adj* égoïste.

selfishness ['selfɪʃnɪs] *n* égoïsme *m*.

selfless ['selflɪs] *adj* désintéressé(e).

self-locking [-'lɒkɪŋ] *adj* à fermeture automatique.

self-made *adj* : ~ **man** self-made-man *m*.

self-medication *n* automédication *f*.

self-opinionated *adj* opiniâtre.

self-perpetuating [-pə'petʃʊeɪtɪŋ] *adj* qui se perpétue indéfiniment.

self-pity *n* apitoiement *m* sur soi-même.

self-portrait *n* autoportrait *m*.

self-possessed *adj* maître (maîtresse) de soi.

self-proclaimed [-prə'kleɪmd] *adj* **pej** soi-disant *(inv)*, prétendu(e).

self-raising flour **Br** [-ˌreɪzɪŋ-], **self-rising flour** **Am** *n* farine *f* avec levure incorporée.

self-regard *(U)* *n* - **1.** **pej** [self-interest] intérêt *m* personnel - **2.** [self-respect] respect *m* de soi.

self-regulating [-'regjuleɪtɪŋ] *adj* qui se réglemente soi-même.

self-reliant *adj* indépendant(e), qui ne compte que sur soi.

self-respect *n* respect *m* de soi.

self-respecting [-rɪs'pektɪŋ] *adj* qui se respecte.

self-restraint *n (U)* retenue *f*, mesure *f*.

self-righteous *adj* satisfait(e) de soi.

self-rising flour **Am** = self-raising flour.

self-rule *n* autonomie *f*.

self-sacrifice *n* abnégation *f*.

selfsame ['selfseɪm] *adj* exactement le même (exactement la même).

self-satisfied *adj* suffisant(e), content(e) de soi.

self-sealing [-'si:lɪŋ] *adj* [envelope] autocollant(e).

self-seeking [-'si:kɪŋ] *adj* égoïste.

self-service ◇ *n* libre-service *m*, self-service *m* ◇ *comp* libre-service, self-service.

self-starter *n* **AUT** démarreur *m* automatique.

self-styled [-'staɪld] *adj* **pej** soi-disant *(inv)*, prétendu(e).

self-sufficient *adj* autosuffisant(e) ; **to be ~ in** satisfaire à ses besoins en.

self-supporting [-sə'pɔːtɪŋ] *adj* [business, industry] financièrement indépendant(e).

self-taught *adj* autodidacte.

self-test *vi* **COMPUT** faire un autotest.

self-will *n* obstination *f*.

sell [sel] *(pt & pp* **sold**) ◇ *vt* - **1.** [gen] vendre ; **to ~ sthg for £100** vendre qqch 100 livres ; **to ~ sthg to sb, to ~ sb sthg** vendre qqch à qqn - **2.** **fig** [make acceptable] : **to ~ sthg to sb, to ~ sb sthg** faire accepter qqch à qqn ; **to ~ o.s.** se faire valoir ◇ *vi* - **1.** [person] vendre - **2.** [product] se vendre ; **it ~s for OR at £10** il se vend 10 livres.

➤ **sell off** *vt sep* vendre, liquider.

➤ **sell out** ◇ *vt sep* : **the performance is sold out** il ne reste plus de places, tous les billets ont été vendus ◇ *vi* - **1.** [shop] : **we've sold out** on n'en a plus - **2.** [betray one's principles] être infidèle à ses principes.

➤ **sell up** *vi* vendre son affaire.

sell-by date *n* **Br** date *f* limite de vente.

seller ['selə'] *n* vendeur *m*, -euse *f*.

seller's market *n* marché *m* à la hausse.

selling ['selɪŋ] *n (U)* vente *f*.

selling price *n* prix *m* de vente.

Sellotape® ['seləteɪp] *n* **Br** ≃ Scotch® *m*, ruban *m* adhésif.

➤ **sellotape** *vt* scotcher.

sell-out *n* : **the match was a ~** on a joué à guichets fermés.

seltzer ['seltsə'] *n* **Am** eau *f* de seltz.

selves [selvz] *pl* ▷ self.

semantic [sɪ'mæntɪk] *adj* sémantique.

semantics [sɪ'mæntɪks] *n (U)* sémantique *f*.

semaphore ['seməfɔː'] *n (U)* signaux *mpl* à bras.

semblance ['sembləns] *n* semblant *m*.

semen ['si:men] *n (U)* sperme *m*, semence *f*.

semester [sɪ'mestə'] *n* semestre *m*.

semi ['semɪ] *n* - **1.** **Br** **inf** (*abbr of* **semidetached house**) maison *f* jumelée - **2.** **Am** *abbr of* **semitrailer**.

semi- [ˌsemɪ] *prefix* semi-, demi-.

semiautomatic [ˌsemɪˌɔːtə'mætɪk] *adj* semi-automatique.

semicircle ['semɪˌsɜːkl] *n* demi-cercle *m*.

semicircular [ˌsemɪ'sɜːkjulə'] *adj* semi-circulaire, demi-circulaire.

semicolon [ˌsemɪ'kəulən] *n* point-virgule *m*.

semiconscious [ˌsemɪ'kɒnʃəs] *adj* à demi conscient(e).

semidetached [ˌsemɪdɪ'tætʃt] ◇ *adj* jumelé(e) ◇ *n* **Br** maison *f* jumelée.

semifinal [ˌsemɪ'faɪnl] *n* demi-finale *f*.

semifinalist [ˌsemɪ'faɪnəlɪst] *n* demi-finaliste *mf*.

seminal ['semɪnl] *adj* - **1.** [of semen] séminal(e) - **2.** [influential] qui fait école.

seminar ['semɪnɑː'] *n* séminaire *m*.

seminary ['semɪnərɪ] (*pl* **-ies**) *n* **RELIG** séminaire *m*.

semiotics [ˌsemɪ'ɒtɪks] *n (U)* sémiotique *f*.

semiprecious ['semɪˌpreʃəs] *adj* semi-précieux(euse).

semiskilled [ˌsemɪ'skɪld] *adj* spécialisé(e).

semi-skimmed [-skɪmd] *adj* [milk] demi-écrémé.

semitrailer [ˌsemɪ'treɪləʳ] n - **1.** [trailer] semi-remorque f - **2.** Am [lorry] semi-remorque m.

semolina [ˌseməˈliːnə] n semoule f.

Sen. - 1. abbr of senator - **2.** abbr of Senior.

SEN (abbr of State Enrolled Nurse) n en Grande-Bretagne, infirmier ou infirmière diplômé(e) d'État.

Senate ['senɪt] n POL : **the ~** le sénat ; **the United States ~** le Sénat américain.

senator ['senətəʳ] n sénateur m.

send [send] (pt & pp sent) vt - **1.** [gen] envoyer ; [letter] expédier, envoyer ; **to ~ sb sthg, to ~ sthg to sb** envoyer qqch à qqn ; **~ her my love** embrasse-la pour moi ; **to ~ sb for sthg** envoyer qqn chercher qqch ; **to ~ sb home** renvoyer qqn (chez lui) ; **to ~ sb to the doctor's/to prison** envoyer qqn chez le médecin/en prison - **2.** [cause to move] : **the explosion sent glass everywhere** l'explosion a projeté des débris de verre partout.

➤ **send down** vt sep [send to prison] coffrer.

➤ **send for** vt fus - **1.** [person] appeler, faire venir - **2.** [by post] commander par correspondance.

➤ **send in** vt sep [report, application] envoyer, soumettre.

➤ **send off** vt sep - **1.** [by post] expédier - **2.** SPORT expulser.

➤ **send off for** vt fus commander par correspondance.

➤ **send up** vt sep - **1.** Br inf [imitate] parodier, ridiculiser - **2.** Am [send to prison] coffrer.

sender ['sendəʳ] n expéditeur m, -trice f.

send-off n fête f d'adieu.

send-up n Br inf parodie f.

Senegal [ˌsenɪ'gɔːl] n Sénégal m ; **in ~** au Sénégal.

Senegalese [ˌsenɪgə'liːz] <> adj sénégalais(e) <> npl : **the ~** les Sénégalais mpl.

senile ['siːnaɪl] adj sénile.

senile dementia n démence f sénile.

senility [sɪ'nɪlətɪ] n sénilité f.

senior ['siːnjəʳ] <> adj - **1.** [highest-ranking] plus haut placé(e) - **2.** [higher-ranking] : **~ to sb** d'un rang plus élevé que qqn - **3.** SCH [pupils, classes] grand(e) ; **~ year** Am dernière année <> n - **1.** [older person] aîné m, -e f - **2.** SCH grand m, -e f.

senior citizen n personne f âgée OR du troisième âge.

senior high school n Am ≃ lycée m.

seniority [ˌsiːnɪ'ɒrətɪ] n [in rank] supériorité f, ancienneté f.

sensation [sen'seɪʃn] n sensation f.

sensational [sen'seɪʃənl] adj - **1.** [gen] sensationnel(elle) - **2.** [pej & PRESS] à sensation.

sensationalist [sen'seɪʃnəlɪst] adj pej à sensation.

sense [sens] <> n - **1.** [ability, meaning] sens m ; **to make ~** [have meaning] avoir un sens ; **to make ~ of sthg** comprendre qqch ; **~ of humour** sens de l'humour ; **~ of smell** odorat m - **2.** [feeling] sentiment m - **3.** [wisdom] bon sens m, intelligence f ; **to make ~** [be sensible] être logique ; **to talk ~** parler raison ; **there's no ~ in arguing/fighting** cela ne sert à rien de discuter/se battre - **4.** phr : **to come to one's ~s** [be sensible again] revenir à la raison ; [regain consciousness] reprendre connaissance <> vt [feel] sentir.

➤ **in a sense** adv dans un sens.

senseless ['senslɪs] adj - **1.** [stupid] stupide - **2.** [unconscious] sans connaissance.

sensibilities [ˌsensɪ'bɪlətɪz] npl susceptibilité f.

sensible ['sensəbl] adj [reasonable] raisonnable, judicieux(euse).

sensibly ['sensəblɪ] adv raisonnablement, judicieusement.

sensitive ['sensɪtɪv] adj - **1.** [gen] : **~ (to)** sensible (à) - **2.** [subject] délicat(e) - **3.** [easily offended] : **~ (about)** susceptible (en ce qui concerne).

sensitivity [ˌsensɪ'tɪvətɪ] n sensibilité f.

sensor ['sensəʳ] n détecteur m.

sensual ['sensjʊəl] adj sensuel(elle).

sensuous ['sensjʊəs] adj qui affecte les sens.

sent [sent] pt & pp ▷ **send**.

sentence ['sentəns] <> n - **1.** GRAMM phrase f - **2.** JUR condamnation f, sentence f <> vt : **to ~ sb (to)** condamner qqn (à).

sententious [sen'tenʃəs] adj sentencieux(euse).

sentiment ['sentɪmənt] n - **1.** [feeling] sentiment m - **2.** [opinion] opinion f, avis m - **3.** pej [sentimentality] sentimentalité f, sensiblerie f.

sentimental [ˌsentɪ'mentl] adj sentimental(e).

sentimentality [ˌsentɪmen'tælətɪ] n pej sentimentalité f, sensiblerie f.

sentinel ['sentɪnl] n sentinelle f.

sentry ['sentrɪ] (pl -ies) n sentinelle f.

Seoul [saʊl] n Séoul.

separable ['seprəbl] adj : ~ **(from)** séparable (de).

separate [adj & n 'seprət, vb 'sepəreɪt] <> adj - **1.** [not joined] : ~ **(from)** séparé(e) (de) - **2.** [individual, distinct] distinct(e) <> vt - **1.** [gen] : **to ~ sb/sthg (from)** séparer qqn/qqch (de) ; **to ~ sthg into** diviser OR séparer qqch en - **2.** [distinguish] : **to ~ sb/sthg (from)** distinguer qqn/qqch (de) <> vi se séparer ; **to ~ into** se diviser OR se séparer en.

➡ **separates** npl Br coordonnés mpl.

separated ['sepəreɪtɪd] adj [not living together] séparé(e).

separately ['seprətlɪ] adv séparément.

separation [,sepə'reɪʃn] n séparation f.

separatist ['seprətɪst] n séparatiste mf.

sepia ['siːpjə] adj sépia (inv).

Sept. (abbr of **September**) sept.

September [sep'tembəʳ] <> n septembre m ; **when are you going?** — ~ quand partez-vous? — en septembre ; **one of the hottest ~s on record** un des mois de septembre les plus chauds qu'on ait connus ; **in ~** en septembre ; **last ~** en septembre dernier ; **this ~** en septembre de cette année ; **next ~** en septembre prochain ; **by ~** en septembre, d'ici septembre ; **every ~** tous les ans en septembre ; **during ~** pendant le mois de septembre ; **at the beginning of ~** au début du mois de septembre, début septembre ; **at the end of ~** à la fin du mois de septembre, fin septembre ; **in the middle of ~** au milieu du mois de septembre, à la mi-septembre <> comp (du mois de) septembre ; [election] au mois de septembre, en septembre.

septet [sep'tet] n septuor m.

septic ['septɪk] adj infecté(e).

septicaemia Br, **septicemia** Am [,septɪ'siːmɪə] n septicémie f.

septic tank n fosse f septique.

sepulchre Br ['sepəlkəʳ], **sepulcher** Am ['sepəlkərʳ] n literary sépulcre m, tombeau m.

sequel ['siːkwəl] n - **1.** [book, film] : ~ **(to)** suite f (de) - **2.** [consequence] : ~ **(to)** conséquence f (de).

sequence ['siːkwəns] n - **1.** [series] suite f, succession f - **2.** [order] ordre m ; **in ~** par ordre - **3.** [of film] séquence f.

sequester [sɪ'kwestəʳ], **sequestrate** [sɪ'kwestreɪt] vt séquestrer, mettre sous séquestre.

sequin ['siːkwɪn] n paillette f.

Serb = **Serbian.**

Serbia ['sɜːbjə] n Serbie f ; **in ~** en Serbie.

Serbian ['sɜːbjən], **Serb** [sɜːb] <> adj serbe <> n - **1.** [person] Serbe mf - **2.** [dialect] serbe m.

Serbo-Croat [,sɜːbəʊ'krəʊæt], **Serbo-Croatian** [,sɜːbəʊkrəʊ'eɪʃn] <> adj serbo-croate <> n [language] serbo-croate m.

serenade [,serə'neɪd] <> n sérénade f <> vt donner la sérénade à.

serene [sɪ'riːn] adj [calm] serein(e), tranquille.

serenely [sɪ'riːnlɪ] adv sereinement, avec sérénité.

serenity [sɪ'renətɪ] n sérénité f, tranquillité f.

serf [sɜːf] n serf m, serve f.

serge [sɜːdʒ] n serge f.

sergeant ['sɑːdʒənt] n - **1.** MIL sergent m - **2.** [in police] brigadier m.

sergeant major n sergent-major m.

serial ['sɪərɪəl] n feuilleton m.

serialize, -ise ['sɪərɪəlaɪz] vt [on TV] diffuser en feuilleton ; [in newspaper etc] publier en feuilleton.

serial killer n meurtrier m en série.

serial number n numéro m de série.

series ['sɪəriːz] (pl inv) n série f.

serious ['sɪərɪəs] adj sérieux(euse) ; [illness, accident, trouble] grave ; **to be ~ about doing sthg** songer sérieusement à faire qqch.

seriously ['sɪərɪəslɪ] adv sérieusement ; [ill] gravement ; [wounded] grièvement, gravement ; **to take sb/sthg ~** prendre qqn/qqch au sérieux.

seriousness ['sɪərɪəsnɪs] n - **1.** [of mistake, illness] gravité f ; **in all ~** en toute sincérité - **2.** [of person, speech] sérieux m.

sermon ['sɜːmən] n sermon m.

serpent ['sɜːpənt] n literary serpent m.

serrated [sɪ'reɪtɪd] adj en dents de scie.

serum ['sɪərəm] (pl -s) n sérum m.

servant ['sɜːvənt] n domestique mf.

serve [sɜːv] <> vt - **1.** [work for] servir - **2.** [have effect] : **to ~ to do sthg** servir à faire qqch ; **to ~ a purpose** [subj : device etc] servir à un usage ; **it ~s my purpose** cela fait l'affaire - **3.** [provide for] desservir - **4.** [meal, drink, customer] servir ; **to ~ sthg to sb, to ~ sb sthg** servir qqch à qqn - **5.** JUR : **to ~ sb with a summons/writ, to ~ a summons/writ on sb** signifier une assignation/une citation à qqn, notifier une assignation/une citation à qqn - **6.** [prison sentence] purger, faire ; [apprenticeship] faire - **7.** SPORT servir - **8.** phr : **it ~s him/you right** c'est bien fait pour lui/toi <> vi servir ; **to ~ as** servir de ; **to ~ on a committee** être membre d'un comité ⇔ n SPORT service m.

● **serve out, serve up** vt sep [food] servir.

server ['sɜːvəʳ] n COMPUT serveur m.

service ['sɜːvɪs] ⇔ n - **1.** [gen] service m ; **in/out of ~** en/hors service ; **to be of ~ (to sb)** être utile (à qqn), rendre service (à qqn) - **2.** [of car] révision f ; [of machine] entretien m ⇔ vt - **1.** [car] réviser ; [machine] assurer l'entretien de - **2.** FIN [debt] rembourser.

● **services** npl - **1.** [on motorway] aire f de services - **2.** [armed forces] : **the ~s** les forces fpl armées - **3.** [help] service m.

serviceable ['sɜːvɪsəbl] adj pratique.

service area n aire f de services.

service charge n service m.

service industries npl : **the ~** le secteur tertiaire.

serviceman ['sɜːvɪsmən] (pl -men [-mən]) n soldat m, militaire m.

service provider n COMPUT fournisseur m d'accès, provider m.

service station n station-service f.

servicewoman ['sɜːvɪsˌwʊmən] (pl -women [-ˌwɪmɪn]) n femme f soldat.

serviette [ˌsɜːvɪˈet] n serviette f (de table).

servile ['sɜːvaɪl] adj servile, obséquieux(euse).

servility [sɜːˈvɪlətɪ] n servilité f.

serving ['sɜːvɪŋ] ⇔ adj [spoon, dish] de service ⇔ n [of food] portion f.

sesame ['sesəmɪ] n sésame m.

session ['seʃn] n - **1.** [gen] séance f ; **in ~** en séance - **2.** Am [school term] trimestre m.

set [set] (pt & pp set ; cont -ting) ⇔ adj - **1.** [fixed - gen] fixe ; [- phrase] figé(e) - **2.** Br SCH [book] au programme - **3.** [ready] : **~ (for sthg/to do sthg)** prêt(e) (à qqch/à faire qqch) - **4.** [determined] : **to be ~ on sthg** vouloir absolument qqch ; **to be ~ on doing sthg** être résolu(e) à faire qqch ; **to be dead ~ against sthg** s'opposer formellement à qqch - **5.** phr : **to be ~ in one's ways** tenir à ses habitudes ⇔ n - **1.** [of keys, tools, golf clubs etc] jeu m ; [of stamps, books] collection f ; [of saucepans] série f ; [of tyres] train m ; **a ~ of teeth** [natural] une dentition, une denture ; [false] un dentier - **2.** [television, radio] poste m - **3.** CINEMA plateau m ; THEATRE scène f - **4.** TENNIS manche f, set m ⇔ vt - **1.** [place] placer, poser, mettre ; [jewel] sertir, monter ; **to be ~ back from sthg** être en retrait de qqch - **2.** [cause to be] : **to ~ sb free** libérer qqn, mettre qqn en liberté ; **to ~ sthg in motion** mettre qqch en branle OR en route ; **to ~ sb's mind at rest** tran-

quilliser qqn ; **to ~ sthg on fire** mettre le feu à qqch - **3.** [prepare - trap] tendre ; [- table] mettre - **4.** [adjust] régler - **5.** [fix - date, deadline, target] fixer - **6.** [establish - example] donner ; [- trend] lancer ; [- record] établir - **7.** [homework, task] donner ; [problem] poser - **8.** MED [bone, leg] remettre - **9.** [arrange] : **to ~ sthg to music** mettre qqch en musique - **10.** [story] : **to be ~** se passer, se dérouler ⇔ vi - **1.** [sun] se coucher - **2.** [jelly] prendre ; [glue, cement] durcir.

● **set about** vt fus [start] entreprendre, se mettre à ; **to ~ about doing sthg** se mettre à faire qqch.

● **set against** vt sep - **1.** [compare] mettre en balance ; **to ~ expenses against tax** déduire les dépenses des impôts - **2.** [cause to oppose] : **to ~ sb against sb** monter qqn contre qqn.

● **set ahead** vt sep [clock] avancer.

● **set apart** vt sep [distinguish] distinguer.

● **set aside** vt sep - **1.** [save] mettre de côté - **2.** [not consider] rejeter, écarter.

● **set back** vt sep - **1.** [delay] retarder - **2.** inf [cost] : **it ~ me back £300** cela m'a coûté 300 livres.

● **set down** vt sep - **1.** [write down] : **to ~ sthg down (in writing)** coucher qqch par écrit - **2.** [put down] déposer.

● **set in** vi [weather, feeling] commencer, s'installer ; [infection] se déclarer.

● **set off** ⇔ vt sep - **1.** [cause] déclencher, provoquer - **2.** [bomb] faire exploser ; [firework] faire partir ⇔ vi se mettre en route, partir.

● **set on** vt sep : **to ~ a dog on sb** lâcher un chien contre OR sur qqn.

● **set out** ⇔ vt sep - **1.** [arrange] disposer - **2.** [explain] présenter, exposer ⇔ vt fus [intend] : **to ~ out to do sthg** entreprendre OR tenter de faire qqch ⇔ vi [on journey] se mettre en route, partir.

● **set up** ⇔ vt sep - **1.** [organization] créer, fonder ; [committee, procedure] constituer, mettre en place ; [meeting] arranger, organiser ; **to ~ o.s. up** s'établir à son compte ; **to ~ up house** OR **home** s'installer - **2.** [statue, monument] dresser, ériger ; [roadblock] placer, installer - **3.** [equipment] préparer, installer - **4.** inf [make appear guilty] monter un coup contre ⇔ vi [in business] s'établir.

setback ['setbæk] n contretemps m, revers m.

set menu n menu m fixe.

set piece n ART & LITERATURE morceau m traditionnel.

setsquare ['setskweəʳ] n Br équerre f.

settee [se'tiː] n canapé m.

setter ['setəʳ] n [dog] setter m.

setting ['setɪŋ] *n* - **1.** [surroundings] décor *m*, cadre *m* - **2.** [of dial, machine] réglage *m*.

settle ['setl] ⟡ *vt* - **1.** [argument] régler ; **that's ~d then** (c'est) entendu - **2.** [bill, account] régler, payer - **3.** [calm - nerves] calmer ; **to ~ one's stomach** calmer les douleurs d'estomac - **4.** [make comfortable] installer ; **to ~ o.s.** s'installer ⟡ *vi* - **1.** [make one's home] s'installer, se fixer - **2.** [make oneself comfortable] s'installer - **3.** [dust] retomber ; [sediment] se déposer - **4.** [bird, insect] se poser.

settle down *vi* - **1.** [give one's attention] : **to ~ down to sthg/to doing sthg** se mettre à qqch/à faire qqch - **2.** [make oneself comfortable] s'installer - **3.** [become respectable] se ranger - **4.** [become calm] se calmer.

settle for *vt fus* accepter, se contenter de.

settle in *vi* s'adapter.

settle on *vt fus* [choose] fixer son choix sur, se décider pour.

settle up *vi* : **to ~ up (with sb)** régler (qqn).

settled ['setld] *adj* [weather] au beau fixe.

settlement ['setlmənt] *n* - **1.** [agreement] accord *m* - **2.** [colony] colonie *f* - **3.** [payment] règlement *m*.

settler ['setlə'] *n* colon *m*.

set-to *n inf* bagarre *f*.

set-top box *n* boîtier *m* électronique.

set-up *n inf* - **1.** [system] : **what's the ~?** comment est-ce que c'est organisé? - **2.** [deception to incriminate] coup *m* monté.

seven ['sevn] *num* sept ; *see also* **six**.

seventeen [,sevn'tiːn] *num* dix-sept ; *see also* **six**.

seventeenth [,sevn'tiːnθ] *num* dix-septième ; *see also* **sixth**.

seventh ['sevnθ] *num* septième ; *see also* **sixth**.

seventh heaven *n* : **to be in (one's) ~** être au septième ciel.

seventieth ['sevntjəθ] *num* soixante-dixième ; *see also* **sixth**.

seventy ['sevntɪ] *num* soixante-dix ; *see also* **sixty**.

sever ['sevə'] *vt* - **1.** [cut through] couper - **2.** fig [relationship, ties] rompre.

several ['sevrəl] ⟡ *adj* plusieurs ⟡ *pron* plusieurs *mfpl*.

severance ['sevrəns] *n* [of relations] rupture *f*.

severance pay *n* indemnité *f* de licenciement.

severe [sɪ'vɪə'] *adj* - **1.** [weather] rude, rigoureux(euse) ; [shock] gros (grosse), dur(e) ; [pain] violent(e) ; [illness, injury] grave - **2.** [person, criticism] sévère.

severely [sɪ'vɪəlɪ] *adv* - **1.** [injured] grièvement ; [damaged] sérieusement - **2.** [sternly] sévèrement.

severity [sɪ'verətɪ] *n* - **1.** [of storm] violence *f*; [of problem, illness] gravité *f* - **2.** [sternness] sévérité *f*.

sew [səʊ] (Br *pp* **sewn**, Am *pp* **sewed** OR **sewn**) *vt & vi* coudre.

sew up *vt sep* - **1.** [join] recoudre - **2.** inf [deal] : **it's (all) sewn up!** c'est dans la poche!

sewage ['suːɪdʒ] *n (U)* eaux *fpl* d'égout, eaux usées.

sewage farm *n* champs *mpl* d'épandage.

sewer ['suə'] *n* égout *m*.

sewerage ['suərɪdʒ] *n* système *m* d'égouts.

sewing ['səʊɪŋ] *n (U)* - **1.** [activity] couture *f* - **2.** [work] ouvrage *m*.

sewing machine *n* machine *f* à coudre.

sewn [səʊn] *pp* ⟡ **sew**.

sex [seks] *n* - **1.** [gender] sexe *m* - **2.** *(U)* [sexual intercourse] rapports *mpl* (sexuels) ; **to have ~ with** avoir des rapports (sexuels) avec.

sex appeal *n* sex-appeal *m*.

sex education *n* éducation *f* sexuelle.

sexism ['seksɪzm] *n* sexisme *m*.

sexist ['seksɪst] ⟡ *adj* sexiste ⟡ *n* sexiste *mf*.

sex life *n* vie *f* sexuelle.

sex object *n* objet *m* sexuel.

sex shop *n* sex-shop *m*.

sextet [seks'tet] *n* sextuor *m*.

sextuplet [seks'tjuːplɪt] *n* sextuplé *m*, -e *f*.

sexual ['sekʃʊəl] *adj* sexuel(elle).

sexual assault *n* agression *f* sexuelle, tentative *f* de viol.

sexual harassment *n* harcèlement *m* sexuel.

sexual intercourse *n (U)* rapports *mpl* (sexuels).

sexuality [,sekʃʊ'ælətɪ] *n* sexualité *f*.

sexy ['seksɪ] (*compar* **-ier** ; *superl* **-iest**) *adj* inf sexy (inv).

Seychelles [seɪ'ʃelz] *npl* : **the ~** les Seychelles *fpl* ; **in the ~** aux Seychelles.

SF, sf (*abbr of* **science fiction**) *n* SF *f*.

SFO (*abbr of* **Serious Fraud Office**) *n service britannique de la répression des fraudes*.

SG (*abbr of* **Surgeon General**) *n directeur fédéral américain de la santé publique*.

Sgt (*abbr of* **sergeant**) Sgt.

sh [ʃ] *excl* chut!

shabby ['ʃæbɪ] (*compar* -**ier** ; *superl* -**iest**) *adj*
- **1.** [clothes] élimé(e), râpé(e) ; [furniture] minable ; [person, street] miteux(euse) - **2.** [behaviour]
moche, méprisable.

shack [ʃæk] *n* cabane *f*, hutte *f*.

shackle ['ʃækl] *vt* enchaîner ; fig entraver.
➧ **shackles** *npl* fers *mpl* ; fig entraves *fpl*.

shade [ʃeɪd] <> *n* - **1.** (U) [shadow] ombre *f*
- **2.** [lampshade] abat-jour *m inv* - **3.** [colour]
nuance *f*, ton *m* - **4.** [of meaning, opinion] nuance *f* <> *vt* [from light] abriter ; **to ~ one's eyes**
s'abriter les yeux <> *vi* : **to ~ into** se fondre
en.
➧ **shades** *npl* inf [sunglasses] lunettes *fpl* de soleil.

shading ['ʃeɪdɪŋ] (U) *n* ombres *fpl*.

shadow ['ʃædəʊ] <> *adj* Br POL fantôme, de
l'opposition <> *n* ombre *f* ; **to be a ~ of one's
former self** n'être plus que l'ombre de soi-
même ; **there's not a OR the ~ of a doubt** il n'y
a pas l'ombre d'un doute.

shadow cabinet *n* cabinet *m* fantôme.

shadowy ['ʃædəʊɪ] *adj* - **1.** [dark] ombreux(euse) - **2.** [hard to see] indistinct(e)
- **3.** [sinister] mystérieux(euse).

shady ['ʃeɪdɪ] (*compar* -**ier** ; *superl* -**iest**) *adj*
- **1.** [garden, street etc] ombragé(e) ; [tree] qui
donne de l'ombre - **2.** inf [dishonest] louche.

shaft [ʃɑːft] <> *n* - **1.** [vertical passage] puits *m* ;
[of lift] cage *f* - **2.** TECH arbre *m* - **3.** [of light]
rayon *m* - **4.** [of tool, golf club] manche *m* <> *vt*
vinf - **1.** [dupe] avoir, baiser - **2.** Am [treat unfairly]
s'en prendre à.

shaggy ['ʃægɪ] (*compar* -**ier** ; *superl* -**iest**) *adj*
hirsute.

shaggy-dog story *n* histoire *f* farfelue OR
à dormir debout.

shake [ʃeɪk] (*pt* **shook** ; *pp* **shaken**) <> *vt*
- **1.** [move vigorously - gen] secouer ; [- bottle] agiter ; **to ~ sb's hand** serrer la main de OR à
qqn ; **to ~ hands** se serrer la main ; **to
~ one's head** secouer la tête ; [to say no] faire
non de la tête - **2.** [shock] ébranler, secouer
<> *vi* trembler <> *n* [tremble] tremblement
m ; **to give sthg a ~** secouer qqch.
➧ **shake down** *vt sep* Am inf - **1.** [rob] racketter - **2.** [search] fouiller.
➧ **shake off** *vt sep* [police, pursuers] semer ; [ill-
ness] se débarrasser de.

shakedown ['ʃeɪkdaʊn] *n* Am inf - **1.** [extortion]
racket *m* - **2.** [search] fouille *f*.

shaken ['ʃeɪkn] *pp* ⊳ **shake.**

shakeout ['ʃeɪkaʊt] *n* FIN récession *f*.

Shakespearean [ʃeɪk'spɪərɪən] *adj* shakes-
pearien(enne).

shake-up *n* inf remaniement *m*.

shaky ['ʃeɪkɪ] (*compar* -**ier** ; *superl* -**iest**) *adj*
[building, table] branlant(e) ; [hand] trem-
blant(e) ; [person] faible ; [argument, start] incer-
tain(e).

shale [ʃeɪl] *n* schiste *m*.

shall [weak form ʃəl, strong form ʃæl] *aux vb*
- **1.** (1st person sg & 1st person pl) (to express
future tense) : **I ~ be ...** je serai ... - **2.** (esp 1st
person sg & 1st person pl) (in questions) : **~ we
have lunch now?** tu veux qu'on déjeune
maintenant? ; **where ~ I put this?** où est-ce
qu'il faut mettre ça? - **3.** [will definitely] : **we
~ succeed** nous réussirons - **4.** (in orders) :
you ~ tell me! tu vas OR dois me le dire!

shallot [ʃə'lɒt] *n* échalote *f*.

shallow ['ʃæləʊ] *adj* - **1.** [water, dish, hole] peu
profond(e) - **2.** pej [superficial] superficiel(elle).
➧ **shallows** *npl* bas-fond *m*.

sham [ʃæm] (*pt* & *pp* -**med** ; *cont* -**ming**)
<> *adj* feint(e), simulé(e) <> *n* comédie *f*
<> *vi* faire semblant, jouer la comédie

shambles ['ʃæmblz] *n* désordre *m*, pagaille
f.

shame [ʃeɪm] <> *n* - **1.** (U) [remorse, humiliation]
honte *f* ; **to bring ~ on OR upon sb** faire la
honte de qqn - **2.** [pity] : **it's a ~ (that ...)** c'est
dommage (que ... (+ subjunctive)) ; **what a ~!**
quel dommage! <> *vt* faire honte à, mortifier ; **to ~ sb into doing sthg** obliger qqn à faire qqch en lui faisant honte.

shamefaced [,ʃeɪm'feɪst] *adj* honteux(euse), penaud(e).

shameful ['ʃeɪmfʊl] *adj* honteux(euse),
scandaleux(euse).

shameless ['ʃeɪmlɪs] *adj* effronté(e), éhon-
té(e).

shammy ['ʃæmɪ] (*pl* -**ies**) *n* : **~ (leather)** peau *f*
de chamois.

shampoo [ʃæm'puː] (*pl* -**s**, *pt* & *pp* -**ed** ; *cont*
-**ing**) <> *n* shampooing *m* <> *vt* : **to ~ sb** OR
sb's hair faire un shampooing à qqn.

shamrock ['ʃæmrɒk] *n* trèfle *m*.

shandy ['ʃændɪ] (*pl* -**ies**) *n* panaché *m*.

shan't [ʃɑːnt] = shall not.

shantytown ['ʃæntɪtaʊn] *n* bidonville *m*.

shape [ʃeɪp] <> *n* - **1.** [gen] forme *f* ; **in the ~ of
a T** en forme de T ; **to take ~** prendre forme
OR tournure - **2.** [guise] : **in the ~ of** sous forme de ; **in any ~ or form** de n'importe quelle
sorte - **3.** [health] : **to be in good/bad ~** être en
bonne/mauvaise forme ; **to lick OR knock sb
into ~** dresser qqn <> *vt* - **1.** [pastry, clay etc] : **to**

~ **sthg (into)** façonner OR modeler qqch (en) - **2.** [ideas, project, character] former.

🔹 **shape up** vi [person, plans] se développer, progresser ; [job, events] prendre tournure OR forme.

SHAPE [ʃeɪp] (abbr of **Supreme Headquarters Allied Powers, Europe**) n quartier général des forces alliées en Europe.

-shaped ['ʃeɪpt] suffix : **egg~** en forme d'œuf ; **L~** en forme de L.

shapeless ['ʃeɪplɪs] adj informe.

shapely ['ʃeɪplɪ] (compar -ier ; superl -iest) adj bien fait(e).

shard [ʃɑːd] n tesson m.

share [ʃeəʳ] ◇ n [portion, contribution] part f ; **to have a ~ in the profits** participer aux bénéfices ◇ vt partager ; **to ~ the news with sb** faire part d'une nouvelle à qqn ◇ vi : **to ~ (in sthg)** partager (qqch).

🔹 **shares** npl actions fpl.

🔹 **share out** vt sep partager, répartir.

share capital n capital m actions.

share certificate n titre m OR certificat m d'actions.

shareholder ['ʃeə,həʊldəʳ] n actionnaire mf.

share index n indice m des valeurs boursières.

share-out n partage m, répartition f.

shareware ['ʃeəweəʳ] n COMPUT shareware m.

shark [ʃɑːk] (pl inv OR -s) n - **1.** [fish] requin m - **2.** fig [dishonest person] escroc m, pirate m.

sharp [ʃɑːp] ◇ adj - **1.** [knife, razor] tranchant(e), affilé(e) ; [needle, pencil, teeth] pointu(e) - **2.** [image, outline, contrast] net (nette) - **3.** [person, mind] vif (vive) ; [eyesight] perçant(e) - **4.** [sudden - change, rise] brusque, soudain(e) ; [- hit, tap] sec (sèche) - **5.** [words, order, voice] cinglant(e) - **6.** [cry, sound] perçant(e) ; [pain, cold] vif (vive) ; [taste] piquant(e) - **7.** MUS : **C/D ~** do/ré dièse ◇ adv - **1.** [punctually] : **at 8 o'clock ~** à 8 heures pile OR tapantes - **2.** [immediately] : **~ left/right** tout à fait à gauche/droite ◇ n MUS dièse m.

sharpen ['ʃɑːpn] ◇ vt - **1.** [knife, tool] aiguiser ; [pencil] tailler - **2.** fig [senses] aiguiser ; [mind] affiner ; [disagreement, conflict] aviver, envenimer ◇ vi [senses] s'aiguiser.

sharp end n Br fig : **to be at the ~** être en première ligne.

sharpener ['ʃɑːpnəʳ] n [for pencil] taille-crayon m ; [for knife] aiguisoir m (pour couteaux).

sharp-eyed [-'aɪd] adj : **she's very ~** elle remarque tout, rien ne lui échappe.

sharply ['ʃɑːplɪ] adv - **1.** [distinctly] nettement

- **2.** [suddenly] brusquement - **3.** [harshly] sévèrement, durement.

sharpness ['ʃɑːpnɪs] n - **1.** [of image, outline] netteté f - **2.** [of mind] vivacité f - **3.** [of remarks, criticism] dureté f, sévérité f.

sharpshooter ['ʃɑːp,ʃuːtəʳ] n tireur m d'élite.

sharp-tongued [-'tʌŋd] adj qui a la langue acérée.

sharp-witted [-'wɪtɪd] adj à l'esprit vif.

shat [ʃæt] pt & pp ⊳ shit.

shatter ['ʃætəʳ] ◇ vt - **1.** [window, glass] briser, fracasser - **2.** fig [hopes, dreams] détruire - **3.** fig [upset] : **to be ~ed (by)** être bouleversé(e) (par) ◇ vi se fracasser, voler en éclats.

shattered ['ʃætəd] adj - **1.** [upset] bouleversé(e) - **2.** Br inf [very tired] flapi(e).

shattering ['ʃætərɪŋ] adj - **1.** [upsetting] bouleversant(e) - **2.** Br [tiring] crevant(e), épuisant(e).

shatterproof ['ʃætəpruːf] adj anti-éclats.

shave [ʃeɪv] ◇ n : **to have a ~** se raser ; **that was a close ~** fig on l'a échappé belle, il était moins cinq ◇ vt - **1.** [remove hair from] raser ; **to ~ one's legs** se raser les jambes - **2.** [wood] planer, raboter ◇ vi se raser.

🔹 **shave off** vt sep [beard, hair] se raser.

shaven ['ʃeɪvn] adj rasé(e).

shaver ['ʃeɪvəʳ] n rasoir m électrique.

shaving brush ['ʃeɪvɪŋ-] n blaireau m.

shaving cream ['ʃeɪvɪŋ-] n crème f à raser.

shaving foam ['ʃeɪvɪŋ-] n mousse f à raser.

shavings ['ʃeɪvɪŋz] npl [of wood, metal] copeaux mpl.

shaving soap ['ʃeɪvɪŋ-] n savon m à barbe.

shawl [ʃɔːl] n châle m.

she [ʃiː] ◇ pers pron - **1.** [referring to woman, girl, animal] elle ; **~'s tall** elle est grande ; **SHE can't do it** elle, elle ne peut pas le faire ; **there ~ is** la voilà ; **if I were** OR **was ~** fml si j'étais elle, à sa place - **2.** [referring to boat, car, country] follow the gender of your translation ◇ n : **it's a ~** [animal] c'est une femelle ; [baby] c'est une fille ◇ comp : **~-elephant** éléphant m femelle ; **~-wolf** louve f.

sheaf [ʃiːf] (pl **sheaves** [ʃiːvz]) n - **1.** [of papers, letters] liasse f - **2.** [of corn, grain] gerbe f.

shear [ʃɪəʳ] (pt **-ed** ; pp **-ed** OR **shorn**) vt [sheep] tondre.

🔹 **shears** npl - **1.** [for garden] sécateur m, cisaille f - **2.** [for dressmaking] ciseaux mpl.

🔹 **shear off** ◇ vt sep [branch] couper ; [piece of metal] cisailler ◇ vi se détacher.

sheath [ʃiːθ] (*pl* sheaths [ʃiːðz]) *n* - **1.** [for knife, cable] gaine *f* - **2.** Br [condom] préservatif *m*.

sheathe *vt* - **1.** [knife] engainer, rengainer - **2.** [cover - gen] recouvrir ; [- cable] gainer.

sheath knife *n* couteau *m* à gaine.

sheaves [ʃiːvz] *pl* ⊳ sheaf.

shed [ʃed] (*pt* & *pp* shed, *cont* -ding) ◇ *n* [small] remise *f*, cabane *f ;* [larger] hangar *m* ◇ *vt* - **1.** [hair, skin, leaves] perdre - **2.** [tears] verser, répandre ; **to ~ blood** verser le sang - **3.** [employees] se défaire de, congédier - **4.** [load - subj : lorry] déverser, perdre.

she'd [*weak form* ʃid, *strong form* ʃiːd] = she had, she would.

sheen [ʃiːn] *n* lustre *m*, éclat *m*.

sheep [ʃiːp] (*pl inv*) *n* mouton *m*.

sheepdog [ʃiːpdɒg] *n* chien *m* de berger.

sheepfold [ʃiːpfəʊld] *n* parc *m* à moutons.

sheepish [ʃiːpɪʃ] *adj* penaud(e).

sheepishly [ʃiːpɪʃlɪ] *adv* d'un air penaud.

sheepskin [ʃiːpskɪn] *n* peau *f* de mouton.

sheepskin jacket *n* veste *f* en mouton.

sheepskin rug *n* (petit tapis *m* en) peau *f* de mouton.

sheer [ʃɪəʳ] *adj* - **1.** [absolute] pur(e) - **2.** [very steep] à pic, abrupt(e) - **3.** [material] fin(e).

sheet [ʃiːt] *n* - **1.** [for bed] drap *m ;* **as white as a ~** blanc (blanche) comme un linge - **2.** [of paper, glass, wood] feuille *f ;* [of metal] plaque *f*.

sheet feed *n* COMPUT alimentation *f* feuille à feuille.

sheet ice *n* verglas *m*.

sheeting [ʃiːtɪŋ] *n* (U) [metal] tôles *fpl ;* [plastic etc] feuilles *fpl*.

sheet lightning *n* (U) éclair *m* diffus.

sheet metal *n* (U) tôle *f*.

sheet music *n* (U) partition *f*.

sheik(h) [ʃeɪk] *n* cheik *m*.

shelf [ʃelf] (*pl* shelves [ʃelvz]) *n* [for storage] rayon *m*, étagère *f*.

shelf life *n* durée *f* de conservation.

shell [ʃel] ◇ *n* - **1.** [of egg, nut, snail] coquille *f* - **2.** [of tortoise, crab] carapace *f* - **3.** [on beach] coquillage *m* - **4.** [of building, car] carcasse *f* - **5.** MIL obus *m* ◇ *vt* - **1.** [peas] écosser ; [nuts, prawns] décortiquer ; [eggs] enlever la coquille de, écaler - **2.** MIL bombarder.

➡ **shell out** inf ◇ *vt sep* débourser ◇ *vi :* **to ~ out (for)** casquer (pour).

she'll [ʃiːl] = she will, she shall.

shellfish [ʃelfɪʃ] (*pl inv*) *n* - **1.** [creature] crustacé *m*, coquillage *m* - **2.** (U) [food] fruits *mpl* de mer.

shelling [ʃelɪŋ] *n* MIL bombardement *m*.

shellshock [ʃelʃɒk] *n* (U) psychose *f* traumatique.

shell suit *n* Br survêtement *m* (*en Nylon*® *imperméabilisé*).

shelter [ʃeltəʳ] ◇ *n* abri *m* ◇ *vt* - **1.** [protect] abriter, protéger - **2.** [refugee, homeless person] offrir un asile à ; [criminal, fugitive] cacher ◇ *vi* s'abriter, se mettre à l'abri.

sheltered [ʃeltəd] *adj* - **1.** [from weather] abrité(e) - **2.** [life, childhood] protégé(e), sans souci ; **~ housing** foyers-logements *mpl* (*pour personnes âgées ou handicapées*).

shelve [ʃelv] ◇ *vt* fig mettre au Frigidaire®, mettre en sommeil ◇ *vi* descendre en pente.

shelves [ʃelvz] *pl* ⊳ shelf.

shelving [ʃelvɪŋ] *n* (U) étagères *fpl*, rayonnages *mpl*.

shenanigans [ʃɪˈnænɪgənz] *npl* inf [trickery] micmacs *mpl*, manigances *fpl*.

shepherd [ʃepəd] ◇ *n* berger *m* ◇ *vt* fig conduire.

shepherd's pie [ʃepədz-] *n* ≃ hachis *m* Parmentier.

sherbet [ʃɜːbət] *n* - **1.** Br [sweet powder] poudre *f* aromatisée - **2.** Am [sorbet] sorbet *m*.

sheriff [ʃerɪf] *n* Am shérif *m*.

sherry [ʃerɪ] (*pl* -ies) *n* xérès *m*, sherry *m*.

she's [ʃiːz] = she is, she has.

Shetland [ʃetlənd] *n :* **(the) ~ (Islands)** les (îles) Shetland *fpl ;* **in (the) ~ (Islands)** dans les Shetland.

sh(h) [ʃ] *excl* chut!

shield [ʃiːld] ◇ *n* - **1.** [armour] bouclier *m* - **2.** Br [sports trophy] plaque *f* ◇ *vt :* **to ~ sb (from)** protéger qqn (de OR contre).

shift [ʃɪft] ◇ *n* - **1.** [change] changement *m*, modification *f* - **2.** [period of work] poste *m ;* [workers] équipe *f* ◇ *vt* - **1.** [move] déplacer, changer de place ; **to ~ the blame onto sb** rejeter la responsabilité sur qqn - **2.** [change] changer, modifier ◇ *vi* - **1.** [move - gen] changer de place ; [- wind] tourner, changer - **2.** [change] changer, se modifier - **3.** Am AUT changer de vitesse.

shift key *n* [on typewriter] touche *f* de majuscules.

shiftless [ʃɪftlɪs] *adj* fainéant(e), paresseux(euse).

shift stick *n* Am levier *m* de vitesse.

shifty [ʃɪftɪ] (*compar* -ier ; *superl* -iest) *adj* inf sournois(e), louche.

Shiite [ʃiːaɪt] ◇ *adj* chiite ◇ *n* Chiite *mf*.

shilling [ʃɪlɪŋ] *n* shilling *m*.

shilly-shally [ˈʃɪlɪˌʃælɪ] (*pt* & *pp* -ied) *vi* hésiter, être indécis(e).

shimmer [ˈʃɪməʳ] ◇ *n* reflet *m*, miroitement *m* ◇ *vi* miroiter.

shin [ʃɪn] (*pt* & *pp* -ned ; *cont* -ning) *n* tibia *m*.
➡ **shin up** Br, **shinny up** Am *vt fus* grimper à.

shinbone [ˈʃɪnbəʊn] *n* tibia *m*.

shine [ʃaɪn] (*pt* & *pp* shone) ◇ *n* brillant *m* ◇ *vt* - **1.** [direct] : **to ~ a torch on sthg** éclairer qqch - **2.** [polish] faire briller, astiquer ◇ *vi* briller ; **to ~ at sthg** fig briller dans qqch.

shingle [ˈʃɪŋgl] *n (U)* [on beach] galets *mpl.*
➡ **shingles** *n (U)* zona *m.*

shining [ˈʃaɪnɪŋ] *adj* - **1.** [gleaming] brillant(e), luisant(e) - **2.** [achievement] extraordinaire ; **to be a ~ example of sthg** être un modèle de qqch.

shinny [ˈʃɪnɪ] Am ➡ **shinny up** = **shin up.**

shiny [ˈʃaɪnɪ] (*compar* -ier ; *superl* -iest) *adj* brillant(e).

ship [ʃɪp] (*pt* & *pp* -ped ; *cont* -ping) ◇ *n* bateau *m* ; [larger] navire *m* ◇ *vt* [goods] expédier ; [troops, passengers] transporter.

shipbuilder [ˈʃɪpˌbɪldəʳ] *n* constructeur *m* de navires.

shipbuilding [ˈʃɪpˌbɪldɪŋ] *n* construction *f* navale.

ship canal *n* canal *m* maritime.

shipment [ˈʃɪpmənt] *n* [cargo] cargaison *f*, chargement *m.*

shipper [ˈʃɪpəʳ] *n* affréteur *m*, chargeur *m.*

shipping [ˈʃɪpɪŋ] *n (U)* - **1.** [transport] transport *m* maritime - **2.** [ships] navires *mpl.*

shipping agent *n* agent *m* maritime.

shipping company *n* compagnie *f* de navigation.

shipping forecast *n* météo *f* marine.

shipping lane *n* voie *f* de navigation.

shipshape [ˈʃɪpʃeɪp] *adj* bien rangé(e), en ordre.

shipwreck [ˈʃɪprek] ◇ *n* - **1.** [destruction of ship] naufrage *m* - **2.** [wrecked ship] épave *f* ◇ *vt* : **to be ~ed** faire naufrage.

shipwrecked [ˈʃɪprekt] *adj* naufragé(e).

shipyard [ˈʃɪpjɑːd] *n* chantier *m* naval.

shire [ʃaɪəʳ] *n* [county] comté *m.*
➡ **Shire** *n* : **the Shires** les *Comtés du centre de l'Angleterre.*

shire horse *n* cheval *m* de gros trait.

shirk [ʃɜːk] *vt* se dérober à.

shirker [ˈʃɜːkəʳ] *n* tire-au-flanc *m.*

shirt [ʃɜːt] *n* chemise *f.*

shirtsleeves [ˈʃɜːtsliːvz] *npl* : **to be in (one's) ~** être en manches OR en bras de chemise.

shirttail [ˈʃɜːtteɪl] *n* pan *m* de chemise.

shirty [ˈʃɜːtɪ] (*compar* -ier ; *superl* -iest) *adj* Br inf de mauvais poil, de mauvaise humeur.

shit [ʃɪt] (*pt* & *pp* -ted OR shat, *cont* -ting) vulg ◇ *n* - **1.** [excrement] merde *f* - **2.** *(U)* [nonsense] conneries *fpl* - **3.** [person] salaud *m* ◇ *vi* chier ◇ *excl* merde!

shiver [ˈʃɪvəʳ] ◇ *n* frisson *m* ; **to give sb the ~s** fig donner le frisson OR la chair de poule à qqn ◇ *vi* : **to ~ (with)** trembler (de), frissonner (de).

shoal [ʃəʊl] *n* [of fish] banc *m.*

shock [ʃɒk] ◇ *n* - **1.** [surprise] choc *m*, coup *m* - **2.** *(U)* MED : **to be suffering from ~**, **to be in (a state of) ~** être en état de choc - **3.** [impact] choc *m*, heurt *m* - **4.** ELEC décharge *f* électrique ◇ *vt* - **1.** [upset] bouleverser - **2.** [offend] choquer, scandaliser.

shock absorber [-əbˌzɔːbəʳ] *n* amortisseur *m.*

shocked [ʃɒkt] *adj* - **1.** [upset] bouleversé(e) - **2.** [offended] choqué(e), scandalisé(e).

shocking [ˈʃɒkɪŋ] *adj* - **1.** [very bad] épouvantable, terrible - **2.** [outrageous] scandaleux(euse).

shockproof [ˈʃɒkpruːf] *adj* antichoc *(inv).*

shock tactics *npl* tactique *f* de choc.

shock therapy, shock treatment *n* traitement *m* par électrochocs.

shock troops *npl* troupes *fpl* de choc.

shock wave *n* onde *f* de choc.

shod [ʃɒd] ◇ *pt* & *pp* ▷ shoe ◇ *adj* chaussé(e).

shoddy [ˈʃɒdɪ] (*compar* -ier ; *superl* -iest) *adj* [goods, work] de mauvaise qualité ; [treatment] indigne, méprisable.

shoe [ʃuː] (*pt* & *pp* -ed OR shod, *cont* -ing) ◇ *n* chaussure *f*, soulier *m* ◇ *vt* [horse] ferrer.

shoebrush [ˈʃuːbrʌʃ] *n* brosse *f* à chaussures.

shoe cleaner *n* produit *m* pour chaussures.

shoehorn [ˈʃuːhɔːn] *n* chausse-pied *m.*

shoelace [ˈʃuːleɪs] *n* lacet *m* de soulier.

shoemaker [ˈʃuːˌmeɪkəʳ] *n* [repairer] cordonnier *m* ; [manufacturer] fabricant *m* de chaussures.

shoe polish *n* cirage *m.*

shoe repairer [-rɪˌpeərəʳ] *n* cordonnier *m.*

shoe shop *n* magasin *m* de chaussures.

shoestring [ˈʃuːstrɪŋ] ◇ adj [budget] étroit(e) ◇ n fig : **on a ~** à peu de frais.

shoetree [ˈʃuːtriː] n embauchoir m.

shone [ʃɒn] pt & pp ▷ **shine**.

shoo [ʃuː] ◇ vt chasser ◇ excl ouste!

shook [ʃʊk] pt ▷ **shake**.

shoot [ʃuːt] (pt & pp **shot**) ◇ vt - **1.** [kill with gun] tuer d'un coup de feu ; [wound with gun] blesser d'un coup de feu ; **to ~ o.s.** [kill o.s.] se tuer avec une arme à feu - **2.** Br [hunt] chasser - **3.** [arrow] décocher, tirer - **4.** [direct - glance, look] lancer, décocher ; **to ~ questions at sb** bombarder qqn de questions - **5.** CINEMA tourner - **6.** Am [play - pool] jouer à ◇ vi - **1.** [fire gun] : **to ~ (at)** tirer (sur) - **2.** Br [hunt] chasser - **3.** [move quickly] : **to ~ in/out/past** entrer/sortir/passer en trombe, entrer/sortir/passer comme un bolide - **4.** CINEMA tourner - **5.** SPORT tirer, shooter ◇ n - **1.** Br [hunting expedition] partie f de chasse - **2.** [of plant] pousse f ◇ excl Am inf - **1.** [go ahead] vas-y! - **2.** [damn] zut!

◆ **shoot down** vt sep - **1.** [aeroplane] descendre, abattre - **2.** [person] abattre - **3.** fig [proposal] démolir ; [person] descendre en flammes.

◆ **shoot up** vi - **1.** [child, plant] pousser vite - **2.** [price, inflation] monter en flèche - **3.** drugs sl se shooter.

shooting [ˈʃuːtɪŋ] n - **1.** [killing] meurtre m - **2.** (U) [hunting] chasse f.

shooting range n champ m de tir.

shooting star n étoile f filante.

shooting stick n canne-siège f.

shoot-out n fusillade f.

shop [ʃɒp] (pt & pp **-ped** ; cont **-ping**) ◇ n - **1.** [store] magasin m, boutique f ; **to talk ~** parler métier OR boutique - **2.** [workshop] atelier m ◇ vi faire ses courses ; **to go shopping** aller faire ses courses OR commissions.

◆ **shop around** vi comparer les prix.

shop assistant n Br vendeur m, -euse f.

shop floor n : **the ~ fig** les ouvriers mpl.

shopkeeper [ˈʃɒpˌkiːpəʳ] n commerçant m, -e f.

shoplifter [ˈʃɒpˌlɪftəʳ] n voleur m, -euse f à l'étalage.

shoplifting [ˈʃɒpˌlɪftɪŋ] n (U) vol m à l'étalage.

shopper [ˈʃɒpəʳ] n personne f qui fait ses courses.

shopping [ˈʃɒpɪŋ] n (U) [purchases] achats mpl.

shopping bag n sac m à provisions.

shopping centre Br, **shopping mall** Am,

shopping plaza Am [-ˌplɑːzəl] n centre m commercial.

shopping list n liste f des commissions.

shopping mall Am, **shopping plaza** Am = **shopping centre**.

shopsoiled Br [ˈʃɒpsɔɪld], **shopworn** Am [ˈʃɒpwɔːn] adj qui a fait l'étalage, abîmé(e) (en magasin).

shop steward n délégué syndical m, déléguée syndicale f.

shopwalker [ˈʃɒpˌwɔːkəʳ] n Br surveillant m, -e f de magasin.

shopwindow [ˌʃɒpˈwɪndəʊ] n vitrine f.

shopworn Am = **shopsoiled**.

shore [ʃɔːʳ] n rivage m, bord m ; **on ~** à terre.

◆ **shore up** vt sep étayer, étançonner ; fig consolider.

shore leave n permission f à terre.

shoreline [ˈʃɔːlaɪn] n côte f.

shorn [ʃɔːn] ◇ pp ▷ **shear** ◇ adj tondu(e).

short [ʃɔːt] ◇ adj - **1.** [not long - in time] court(e), bref (brève) ; [- in space] court - **2.** [not tall] petit(e) - **3.** [curt] brusque, sec (sèche) - **4.** [lacking] : **time/money is ~** nous manquons de temps/d'argent ; **we're £10 ~** il nous manque 10 livres ; **to be ~ of** manquer de ; **to be ~ of breath** être essoufflé(e) - **5.** [abbreviated] : **to be ~ for** être le diminutif de ◇ adv : **to be running ~ of** [running out of] commencer à manquer de, commencer à être à court de ; **to cut sthg ~** [visit, speech] écourter qqch ; [discussion] couper court à qqch ; **to stop ~** s'arrêter net ; **to bring** OR **pull sb up ~** arrêter qqn net ◇ n - **1.** Br [alcoholic drink] alcool m fort - **2.** [film] court métrage m.

◆ **shorts** npl - **1.** [gen] short m - **2.** Am [underwear] caleçon m.

◆ **for short** adv : **he's called Bob for ~** Bob est son diminutif.

◆ **in short** adv [enfin] bref.

◆ **nothing short of** prep rien moins que, pratiquement.

◆ **short of** prep [unless, without] : **~ of doing sthg** à moins de faire qqch, à part faire qqch.

shortage [ˈʃɔːtɪdʒ] n manque m, insuffisance f.

short back and sides n Br coupe f bien dégagée.

shortbread [ˈʃɔːtbred] n sablé m.

short-change vt - **1.** [subj : shopkeeper] : **to ~ sb** ne pas rendre assez à qqn - **2.** fig [cheat] tromper, rouler.

short circuit n court-circuit m.

short-circuit ⟨⟩ *vt* court-circuiter ⟨⟩ *vi* se mettre en court-circuit.

shortcomings [ˈʃɔːtˌkʌmɪŋz] *npl* défauts *mpl*.

shortcrust pastry [ˈʃɔːtkrʌst-] *n* pâte *f* brisée.

short cut *n* - **1.** [quick route] raccourci *m* - **2.** [quick method] solution *f* miracle.

shorten [ˈʃɔːtn] ⟨⟩ *vt* - **1.** [holiday, time] écourter - **2.** [skirt, rope etc] raccourcir ⟨⟩ *vi* [days] raccourcir.

shortening [ˈʃɔːtnɪŋ] *n* (U) CULIN matière *f* grasse.

shortfall [ˈʃɔːtfɔːl] *n* déficit *m*.

shorthand [ˈʃɔːthænd] *n* (U) - **1.** [writing system] sténographie *f* - **2.** [abbreviation] forme *f* abrégée.

shorthanded [ˌʃɔːtˈhændɪd] *adj* : to be ~ manquer de personnel.

shorthand typist *n* Br sténodactylo *f*.

short-haul *adj* court-courrier *(inv)*.

short list *n* Br liste *f* des candidats sélectionnés.

short-list *vt* Br : to be short-listed (for) être au nombre des candidats sélectionnés (pour).

short-lived [-ˈlɪvd] *adj* de courte durée.

shortly [ˈʃɔːtlɪ] *adv* - **1.** [soon] bientôt - **2.** [curtly] d'une manière brusque, sèchement.

shortness [ˈʃɔːtnɪs] *n* - **1.** [of visit etc] brièveté *f* - **2.** [of person] petite taille *f* ; [of skirt, hair] peu *m* de longueur.

short-range *adj* à courte portée.

short shrift [-ˈʃrɪft] *n* : to give sb ~ envoyer promener qqn.

shortsighted [ˌʃɔːtˈsaɪtɪd] *adj* myope ; fig imprévoyant(e).

short-staffed [-ˈstɑːft] *adj* : to be ~ manquer de personnel.

short story *n* nouvelle *f*.

short-tempered [-ˈtempəd] *adj* emporté(e), irascible.

short-term *adj* [effects, solution] à court terme ; [problem] de courte durée.

short time *n* Br : on ~ en chômage partiel.

short wave *n* (U) ondes *fpl* courtes.

shot [ʃɒt] ⟨⟩ *pt* & *pp* ⊳ **shoot** ⟨⟩ *n* - **1.** [gunshot] coup *m* de feu ; **like a ~** sans hésiter - **2.** [marksman] tireur *m* - **3.** SPORT coup *m* - **4.** [photograph] photo *f* ; CINEMA plan *m* - **5.** inf [attempt] : **to have a ~ at sthg** essayer de faire qqch - **6.** [injection] piqûre *f* - **7.** [of alcohol] coup *m*.

shotgun [ˈʃɒtgʌn] *n* fusil *m* de chasse.

shot put *n* [event] lancer *m* du poids ; [object] poids *m*.

should [ʃʊd] *aux vb* - **1.** [indicating duty] : **we ~ leave now** il faudrait partir maintenant - **2.** [seeking advice, permission] : **~ I go too?** est-ce que je devrais y aller aussi? - **3.** [as suggestion] : **I ~ deny everything** moi, je nierais tout - **4.** [indicating probability] : **she ~ be home soon** elle devrait être de retour bientôt, elle va bientôt rentrer - **5.** [was or were expected] : **they ~ have won the match** ils auraient dû gagner le match - **6.** [indicating intention, wish] : **I ~ like to come with you** j'aimerais bien venir avec vous - **7.** (as conditional) : **you ~ go if you're invited** tu devrais y aller si tu es invité - **8.** (in subordinate clauses) : **we decided that you ~ meet him** nous avons décidé que ce serait toi qui irais le chercher - **9.** [expressing uncertain opinion] : **I ~ think he's about 50 (years old)** je pense qu'il doit avoir dans les 50 ans.

shoulder [ˈʃəʊldə] ⟨⟩ *n* épaule *f* ; **to look over one's ~** se retourner ; **he needed a ~ to cry on** il avait besoin de réconfort ; **to rub ~s with sb** fig côtoyer qqn ⟨⟩ *vt* - **1.** [carry] porter - **2.** [responsibility] endosser.

shoulder bag *n* sac *m* en bandoulière.

shoulder blade *n* omoplate *f*.

shoulder-length *adj* : ~ **hair** cheveux milongs.

shoulder strap *n* - **1.** [on dress] bretelle *f* - **2.** [on bag] bandoulière *f*.

shouldn't [ˈʃʊdnt] = should not.

should've [ˈʃʊdəv] = should have.

shout [ʃaʊt] ⟨⟩ *n* [cry] cri *m* ⟨⟩ *vt* & *vi* crier.

shout down *vt sep* huer, conspuer.

shout out *vt sep* crier.

shouting [ˈʃaʊtɪŋ] *n* (U) cris *mpl*.

shove [ʃʌv] ⟨⟩ *n* : **to give sb/sthg a ~** pousser qqn/qqch ⟨⟩ *vt* pousser ; **to ~ sb about** bousculer qqn ; **to ~ clothes into a bag** fourrer des vêtements dans un sac.

shove off *vi* - **1.** [in boat] pousser au large - **2.** inf [go away] ficher le camp, filer.

shovel [ˈʃʌvl] (Br *pt* & *pp* -**led** ; *cont* -**ling**, Am *pt* & *pp* -**ed** ; *cont* -**ing**) ⟨⟩ *n* [tool] pelle *f* ⟨⟩ *vt* enlever à la pelle, pelleter.

show [ʃəʊ] (*pt* -**ed** ; *pp* **shown** OR -**ed**) ⟨⟩ *n* - **1.** [display] démonstration *f*, manifestation *f* - **2.** [at theatre] spectacle *m* ; [on radio, TV] émission *f* - **3.** CINEMA séance *f* - **4.** [exhibition] exposition *f* ; **on ~** exposé(e) ; **for ~** pour (faire de) l'effet ; **flower ~** floralies *fpl* ⟨⟩ *vt* - **1.** [gen] montrer ; [profit, loss] indiquer ; [respect] témoigner ; [courage, mercy] faire preuve de ; **he has nothing to ~ for all his hard work**

tout son travail n'a rien donné ; **to ~ sb sthg, to ~ sthg to sb** montrer qqch à qqn ; **to ~ sb how to do sthg** montrer OR faire voir à qqn comment faire qqch ; **it just goes to ~ that ...** cela prouve que ... - **2.** [escort] : **to ~ sb to his seat/table** conduire qqn à sa place/sa table - **3.** [film] projeter, passer ; [TV programme] donner, passer ⬦ vi - **1.** [indicate] indiquer, montrer - **2.** [be visible] se voir, être visible - **3.** CINEMA : **what's ~ing tonight?** qu'est-ce qu'on joue comme film ce soir?

➡ **show around** = **show round.**

➡ **show off** ⬦ vt sep exhiber ⬦ vi faire l'intéressant(e).

➡ **show round** vt sep : **to ~ sb round a town/a house** faire visiter une ville/une maison à qqn.

➡ **show up** ⬦ vt sep [embarrass] embarrasser, faire honte à ⬦ vi - **1.** [stand out] se voir, ressortir - **2.** [arrive] s'amener, rappliquer.

showbiz ['ʃəʊbɪz] n inf show-biz m.

show business n (U) monde m du spectacle, show-business m.

showcase ['ʃəʊkeɪs] n lit & fig vitrine f.

showdown ['ʃəʊdaʊn] n : **to have a ~ with sb** s'expliquer avec qqn, mettre les choses au point avec qqn.

shower ['ʃaʊə'] ⬦ n - **1.** [device, act] douche f ; **to have** OR **take a ~** prendre une douche, se doucher - **2.** [of rain] averse f - **3.** fig [of questions, confetti] avalanche f, déluge m - **4.** Am [party] fête organisée en l'honneur d'une femme qui va se marier, par exemple, et à laquelle chacun des invités offre un petit cadeau ⬦ vt : **to ~ sb with** couvrir qqn de ⬦ vi [wash] prendre une douche, se doucher.

shower cap n bonnet m de douche.

showerproof ['ʃaʊəpruːf] adj imperméable.

shower room n salle f d'eau.

showery ['ʃaʊərɪ] adj pluvieux(euse).

showing ['ʃəʊɪŋ] n CINEMA projection f.

show jumping [-,dʒʌmpɪŋ] n jumping m.

showman ['ʃəʊmən] (pl -men [-mən]) n - **1.** [at fair, circus] forain m - **2.** fig [publicity-seeker] : **he's a real ~** il a le sens du spectacle.

showmanship ['ʃəʊmənʃɪp] n sens m du spectacle.

shown [ʃəʊn] pp ⬅ **show.**

show-off n inf m'as-tu-vu m, -e f.

show of hands n : **to have a ~** voter à main levée.

showpiece ['ʃəʊpiːs] n [main attraction] joyau m, trésor m.

showroom ['ʃəʊrʊm] n salle f OR magasin m

d'exposition ; [for cars] salle de démonstration.

showy ['ʃəʊɪ] (compar -ier ; superl -iest) adj voyant(e) ; [person] prétentieux(euse).

shrank [ʃræŋk] pt ⬅ **shrink.**

shrapnel ['ʃræpnl] n (U) éclats mpl d'obus.

shred [ʃred] (pt & pp -ded ; cont -ding) ⬦ n - **1.** [of material, paper] lambeau m, brin m - **2.** fig [of evidence] parcelle f ; [of truth] once f, grain m ⬦ vt [food] râper ; [paper] déchirer en lambeaux.

shredder ['ʃredə'] n [machine] destructeur m de documents.

shrew [ʃruː] n [animal] musaraigne f.

shrewd [ʃruːd] adj fin(e), astucieux(euse).

shrewdness ['ʃruːdnɪs] n finesse f, perspicacité f.

shriek [ʃriːk] ⬦ n cri m perçant, hurlement m ; [of laughter] éclat m ⬦ vt hurler, crier ⬦ vi pousser un cri perçant ; **to ~ with laughter** éclater de rire.

shrill [ʃrɪl] adj [sound, voice] aigu(ë) ; [whistle] strident(e).

shrimp [ʃrɪmp] n crevette f.

shrine [ʃraɪn] n [place of worship] lieu m saint.

shrink [ʃrɪŋk] (pt shrank ; pp shrunk) ⬦ vt rétrécir ⬦ vi - **1.** [cloth, garment] rétrécir ; [person] rapetisser ; fig [income, popularity etc] baisser, diminuer - **2.** [recoil] : **to ~ away from sthg** reculer devant qqch ; **to ~ from doing sthg** rechigner OR répugner à faire qqch.

shrinkage ['ʃrɪŋkɪdʒ] n rétrécissement m ; fig diminution f, baisse f.

shrink-wrap vt emballer sous film plastique.

shrivel ['ʃrɪvl] (Br pt & pp -led ; cont -ling, Am pt & pp -ed ; cont -ing) ⬦ vt : **to ~ (up)** rider, flétrir ⬦ vi : **to ~ (up)** se rider, se flétrir.

shroud [ʃraʊd] ⬦ n [cloth] linceul m ⬦ vt : **to be ~ed in** [darkness, fog] être enseveli(e) sous ; [mystery] être enveloppé(e) de.

Shrove Tuesday ['ʃrəʊv-] n Mardi m gras.

shrub [ʃrʌb] n arbuste m.

shrubbery ['ʃrʌbərɪ] n massif m d'arbustes.

shrug [ʃrʌg] (pt & pp -ged ; cont -ging) ⬦ n haussement m d'épaules ⬦ vt : **to ~ one's shoulders** hausser les épaules ⬦ vi hausser les épaules.

➡ **shrug off** vt sep ignorer.

shrunk [ʃrʌŋk] pp ⬅ **shrink.**

shrunken ['ʃrʌŋkən] adj [person] ratatiné(e).

shucks [ʃʌks] excl Am inf - **1.** [it was nothing] de rien! - **2.** [damn] zut!

shudder ['ʃʌdə'] ⬦ n frisson m, frémissement *m* ⬦ *vi* **- 1.** [tremble] : **to ~ (with)** frémir (de), frissonner (de) ; **I ~ to think** je n'ose pas y penser **- 2.** [shake] vibrer, trembler.

shuffle [ˈʃʌfl] ⬦ *n* **- 1.** [of feet] marche *f* traînante **- 2.** [of cards] : **to give the cards a ~** battre les cartes ⬦ *vt* **- 1.** [drag] : **to ~ one's feet** traîner les pieds **- 2.** [cards] mélanger, battre ⬦ *vi* **- 1.** [walk] : **to ~ in/out** entrer/sortir en traînant les pieds **- 2.** [fidget] remuer.

shun [ʃʌn] (*pt & pp* **-ned** ; *cont* **-ning**) *vt* fuir, éviter.

shunt [ʃʌnt] *vt* **- 1.** RAIL aiguiller **- 2.** fig [move] transférer, déplacer.

shunter [ˈʃʌntəʳ] *n* RAIL [engine] locomotive *f* de manœuvre.

shush [ʃʊʃ] *excl* chut!

shut [ʃʌt] (*pt & pp* shut, *cont* **-ting**) ⬦ *adj* [closed] fermé(e) ⬦ *vt* fermer ; **~ your mouth** OR **face! v** inf ta gueule!, la ferme! ⬦ *vi* **- 1.** [door, window] se fermer **- 2.** [shop] fermer.

➡ **shut away** *vt sep* [valuables, papers] mettre sous clef ; **to ~ o.s. away** s'enfermer.

➡ **shut down** *vt sep & vi* fermer.

➡ **shut in** *vt sep* enfermer ; **to ~ o.s. in** s'enfermer.

➡ **shut out** *vt sep* **- 1.** [noise] supprimer ; [light] ne pas laisser entrer ; **to ~ sb out** laisser qqn à la porte **- 2.** [feelings, thoughts] chasser.

➡ **shut up** inf ⬦ *vt sep* [silence] faire taire ⬦ *vi* se taire.

shutdown [ˈʃʌtdaʊn] *n* fermeture *f*

shutter [ˈʃʌtəʳ] *n* **- 1.** [on window] volet *m* **- 2.** [in camera] obturateur *m*.

shuttle [ˈʃʌtl] ⬦ *adj* : **~ service** (service *m* de) navette *f* ⬦ *n* [train, bus, plane] navette *f* ⬦ *vi* faire la navette.

shuttlecock [ˈʃʌtlkɒk] *n* volant *m*.

shy [ʃaɪ] (*pt & pp* shied) ⬦ *adj* **- 1.** [timid] timide **- 2.** [wary] : **to be ~ of doing sthg** avoir peur de faire qqch, hésiter à faire qqch ⬦ *vi* [horse] s'effaroucher.

➡ **shy away from** *vt fus* : **to ~ away from sthg** reculer devant qqch ; **to ~ away from doing sthg** répugner à faire qqch.

shyly [ˈʃaɪlɪ] *adv* timidement.

shyness [ˈʃaɪnɪs] *n* timidité *f*.

Siam [ˌsaɪˈæm] *n* Siam *m* ; **in ~** au Siam.

Siamese [ˌsaɪəˈmiːz] (*pl inv*) ⬦ *adj* siamois(e) ⬦ *n* **- 1.** [person] Siamois *m*, -e *f* **- 2.** : **~ (cat)** chat *m* siamois.

Siamese twins *npl* [brothers] frères *mpl* siamois ; [sisters] sœurs *fpl* siamoises.

SIB (*abbr of* **Securities and Investment Board**) *n organisme britannique qui fait appliquer la*

réglementation concernant les investissements.

Siberia [saɪˈbɪərɪə] *n* Sibérie *f* ; **in ~** en Sibérie.

Siberian [saɪˈbɪərɪən] ⬦ *adj* sibérien(enne) ⬦ *n* Sibérien *m*, -enne *f*.

sibling [ˈsɪblɪŋ] *n* [brother] frère *m* ; [sister] sœur *f*.

Sicilian [sɪˈsɪljən] ⬦ *adj* sicilien(enne) ⬦ *n* [person] Sicilien *m*, -enne *f*.

Sicily [ˈsɪsɪlɪ] *n* Sicile *f* ; **in ~** en Sicile.

sick [sɪk] *adj* **- 1.** [ill] malade **- 2.** [nauseous] : **to feel ~** avoir envie de vomir, avoir mal au cœur ; **to be ~** Br [vomit] vomir ; **to make sb ~** fig écœurer qqn, dégoûter qqn **- 3.** [fed up] : **to be ~ of** en avoir assez OR marre de **- 4.** [joke, humour] macabre.

sickbay [ˈsɪkbeɪ] *n* infirmerie *f*.

sickbed [ˈsɪkbed] *n* lit *m* de malade.

sicken [ˈsɪkn] ⬦ *vt* écœurer, dégoûter ⬦ *vi* Br : **to be ~ing for sthg** couver qqch.

sickening [ˈsɪknɪŋ] *adj* [disgusting] écœurant(e), dégoûtant(e).

sickle [ˈsɪkl] *n* faucille *f*.

sick leave *n* (*U*) congé *m* de maladie.

sickly [ˈsɪklɪ] (*compar* **-ier** ; *superl* **-iest**) *adj* **- 1.** [unhealthy] maladif(ive), souffreteux(euse) **- 2.** [smell, taste] écœurant(e).

sickness [ˈsɪknɪs] *n* **- 1.** [illness] maladie *f* **- 2.** Br (*U*) [nausea] nausée *f*, nausées *fpl* ; [vomiting] vomissement *m*, vomissements *mpl*.

sickness benefit *n* (*U*) prestations *fpl* en cas de maladie.

sick pay *n* (*U*) indemnité *f* OR allocation *f* de maladie.

sickroom [ˈsɪkruːm] *n* chambre *f* de malade.

side [saɪd] ⬦ *n* **- 1.** [gen] côté *m* ; **at** OR **by my/her** *etc* **~** à mes/ses *etc* côtés ; **to stand to one ~** se tenir sur le côté ; **on every ~, on all ~s** de tous côtés ; **from ~ to ~** d'un côté à l'autre ; **by ~** côte à côte ; **to put sthg to** OR **on one ~** mettre qqch de côté **- 2.** [of table, river] bord *m* **- 3.** [of hill, valley] versant *m*, flanc *m* **- 4.** [in war, debate] camp *m*, côté *m* ; SPORT équipe *f*, camp ; [of argument] point *m* de vue ; **to be on sb's ~** être avec qqn, soutenir qqn ; **to take sb's ~** prendre le parti de qqn **- 5.** [aspect - gen] aspect *m* ; [- of character] facette *f* ; **to be on the safe ~** pour plus de sûreté, par précaution **- 6.** phr : **on the large/small ~** plutôt grand/petit, un peu trop grand/petit ; **to do sthg on the ~** faire qqch en plus ; **to keep** OR **stay on the right ~ of sb** se faire bien voir de qqn ⬦ *adj* [situated on side] latéral(e).

side with vt fus prendre le parti de, se ranger du côté de.

sideboard ['saɪdbɔːd] n [cupboard] buffet m.

sideboards Br ['saɪdbɔːdz], **sideburns** Am ['saɪdbɜːnz] npl favoris mpl, rouflaquettes fpl.

sidecar ['saɪdkɑːr] n side-car m.

side dish n accompagnement m, garniture f.

side effect n - **1.** MED effet m secondaire OR indésirable - **2.** [unplanned result] effet m secondaire, répercussion f.

sidekick ['saɪdkɪk] n inf [friend] copain m, copine f ; pej acolyte mf.

sidelight ['saɪdlaɪt] n AUT feu m de position.

sideline ['saɪdlaɪn] n - **1.** [extra business] activité f secondaire - **2.** SPORT ligne f de touche ; **on the ~** fig dans la coulisse.

sidelong ['saɪdlɒŋ] adj & adv de côté.

side-on adj & adv de côté.

side plate n assiette f à pain, petite assiette.

side road n [not main road] route f secondaire ; [off main road] route transversale.

sidesaddle ['saɪd,sædl] adv : **to ride ~** monter en amazone.

sideshow ['saɪdʃəʊ] n spectacle m forain.

sidestep ['saɪdstep] (pt & pp -ped ; cont -ping) vt faire un pas de côté pour éviter OR esquiver ; fig éviter.

side street n [not main street] petite rue f ; [off main street] rue transversale.

sidetrack ['saɪdtræk] vt : **to be ~ed** se laisser distraire.

sidewalk ['saɪdwɔːk] n Am trottoir m.

sideways ['saɪdweɪz] adj & adv de côté.

siding ['saɪdɪŋ] n voie f de garage.

sidle ['saɪdl] **sidle up** vi : **to ~ up to sb** se glisser vers qqn.

SIDS (abbr of **sudden infant death syndrome**) n mort subite du nourrisson.

siege [siːdʒ] n siège m.

Sierra Leone [sɪ'erəlɪ'əʊn] n Sierra Leone f ; **in ~** en Sierra Leone.

Sierra Leonean [sɪ'erəlɪ'əʊnjən] adj de la Sierra Leone n habitant m, -e f de la Sierra Leone.

sieve [sɪv] n [for flour, sand etc] tamis m ; [for liquids] passoire f ; **I've got a head** OR **memory like a ~** ma mémoire est une passoire vt [flour etc] tamiser ; [liquid] passer.

sift [sɪft] vt - **1.** [flour, sand] tamiser - **2.** fig [evidence] passer au crible vi : **to ~ through** examiner, éplucher.

sigh [saɪ] n soupir m ; **to heave a ~ of relief** pousser un soupir de soulagement vi [person] soupirer, pousser un soupir.

sight [saɪt] n - **1.** [seeing] vue f ; **in ~** en vue ; **in/out of ~** en/hors de vue ; **to catch ~ of** apercevoir qqn de vue ; **to know sb by ~** connaître qqn de vue ; **to lose ~ of** perdre de vue ; **to shoot on ~** tirer à vue ; **at first ~** à première vue, au premier abord - **2.** [spectacle] spectacle m - **3.** [on gun] mire f ; **to set one's ~s on sthg** décider d'obtenir qqch, viser qqch ; **to set one's ~s on doing sthg** décider de faire qqch - **4.** [a lot] : **a ~ better/worse** bien mieux/pire vt apercevoir.

sights npl [of city] attractions fpl touristiques.

sighting ['saɪtɪŋ] n : **there has been a ~ of the escaped criminal** on a vu le fugitif.

sightseeing ['saɪt,siːɪŋ] n tourisme m ; **to go ~** faire du tourisme.

sightseer ['saɪt,siːər] n touriste mf.

sign [saɪn] n - **1.** [gen] signe m ; **no ~ of** aucune trace de ; **there's no ~ of him yet** il n'est pas encore arrivé - **2.** [notice] enseigne f ; AUT panneau m vt signer ; **to ~ one's name** signer.

sign away vt sep signer la renonciation à.

sign for vt fus - **1.** [letter, parcel] signer à la réception de - **2.** SPORT [team] signer un contrat avec.

sign in vi signer à l'arrivée OR en arrivant.

sign on vi - **1.** [enrol - MIL] s'engager ; [- for course] s'inscrire - **2.** [register as unemployed] s'inscrire au chômage.

sign out vi signer à la sortie OR en sortant.

sign up vt sep [worker] embaucher ; [soldier] engager vi MIL s'engager ; [for course] s'inscrire.

signal ['sɪgnl] (Br pp & pt -led ; cont -ling, Am pp & pt -ed ; cont -ing) n signal m adj fml remarquable vt - **1.** [indicate] indiquer - **2.** [gesture to] : **to ~ sb (to do sthg)** faire signe à qqn (de faire qqch) vi - **1.** AUT clignoter, mettre son clignotant - **2.** [gesture] : **to ~ to sb (to do sthg)** faire signe à qqn (de faire qqch).

signal box Br, **signal tower** Am n poste m d'aiguillage.

signally ['sɪgnəlɪ] adv fml remarquablement, singulièrement.

signalman ['sɪgnlmən] (pl -men [-mən]) n RAIL aiguilleur m.

signal tower Am = signal box.

signatory ['sɪgnətrɪ] (pl -ies) n signataire mf.

signature ['sɪgnətʃəʳ] n [name] signature f.

signature tune n indicatif m.

signet ring ['sɪgnɪt-] n chevalière f.

significance [sɪg'nɪfɪkəns] n - **1.** [importance] importance f, portée f - **2.** [meaning] signification f.

significant [sɪg'nɪfɪkənt] adj - **1.** [considerable] considérable - **2.** [important] important(e) - **3.** [meaningful] significatif(ive).

significantly [sɪg'nɪfɪkəntlɪ] adv - **1.** [considerably] considérablement, énormément - **2.** [meaningfully] d'une manière significative.

signify ['sɪgnɪfaɪ] (pt & pp -ied) vt signifier, indiquer.

signing ['saɪnɪŋ] n Br SPORT footballeur etc qui a signé un contrat avec un club.

sign language n langage m des signes.

signpost ['saɪnpəʊst] n poteau m indicateur.

Sikh [siːk] ◇ adj sikh (inv) ◇ n [person] Sikh mf.

Sikhism ['siːkɪzm] n sikhisme m.

silage ['saɪlɪdʒ] n fourrage m ensilé.

silence ['saɪləns] ◇ n silence m ◇ vt réduire au silence, faire taire.

silencer ['saɪlənsəʳ] n silencieux m.

silent ['saɪlənt] adj - **1.** [person, place] silencieux(euse) ; **to be ~ about** sthg garder le silence sur qqch - **2.** CINEMA & LING muet(ette).

silently ['saɪləntlɪ] adv silencieusement.

silent partner n Am (associé m) commanditaire m, bailleur m de fonds.

silhouette [ˌsɪluː'et] ◇ n silhouette f ◇ vt : **to be ~d against** se profiler sur, se silhouetter sur.

silicon ['sɪlɪkən] n silicium m.

silicon chip [ˌsɪlɪkən-] n puce f, pastille f de silicium.

silicone ['sɪlɪkəʊn] n silicone f.

Silicon Valley n Silicon Valley f (centre de l'industrie électronique américaine).

silk [sɪlk] ◇ n soie f ◇ comp en OR de soie.

silk screen printing n sérigraphie f.

silkworm ['sɪlkwɜːm] n ver m à soie.

silky ['sɪlkɪ] (compar -ier ; superl -iest) adj soyeux(euse).

sill [sɪl] n [of window] rebord m.

silliness ['sɪlɪnɪs] n (U) stupidité f, bêtise f.

silly ['sɪlɪ] (compar -ier ; superl -iest) adj stupide, bête.

silo ['saɪləʊ] (pl -s) n silo m.

silt [sɪlt] n vase f, limon m.
◆ **silt up** vi s'envaser.

silver ['sɪlvəʳ] ◇ adj [colour] argenté(e) ◇ n (U) - **1.** [metal] argent m - **2.** [coins] pièces fpl d'argent - **3.** [silverware] argenterie f ◇ comp en argent, d'argent.

silver foil, silver paper n (U) papier m d'argent OR d'étain.

silver-plated [-'pleɪtɪd] adj plaqué(e) argent.

silver screen n inf : **the ~** le grand écran.

silversmith ['sɪlvəsmɪθ] n orfèvre mf.

silverware ['sɪlvəweəʳ] n (U) - **1.** [dishes, spoons, etc] argenterie f - **2.** Am [cutlery] couverts mpl.

silver wedding n noces fpl d'argent.

similar ['sɪmɪləʳ] adj : **~ (to)** semblable (à), similaire (à).

similarity [ˌsɪmɪ'lærətɪ] (pl -ies) n : **~ (between/ to)** similitude f (entre/avec), ressemblance f (entre/avec).

similarly ['sɪmɪləlɪ] adv de la même manière, pareillement.

simile ['sɪmɪlɪ] n comparaison f.

simmer ['sɪməʳ] ◇ vt faire cuire à feu doux, mijoter ◇ vi cuire à feu doux, mijoter.
◆ **simmer down** vi inf se calmer.

simper ['sɪmpəʳ] ◇ n sourire m affecté ◇ vi minauder.

simpering ['sɪmpərɪŋ] adj affecté(e).

simple ['sɪmpl] adj - **1.** [gen] simple - **2.** dated [mentally retarded] simplet(ette), simple d'esprit.

simple-minded [-'maɪndɪd] adj simplet(ette), simple d'esprit.

simpleton ['sɪmpltən] n dated niais m, -e f.

simplicity [sɪm'plɪsətɪ] n simplicité f.

simplification [ˌsɪmplɪfɪ'keɪʃn] n simplification f.

simplify ['sɪmplɪfaɪ] (pt & pp -ied) vt simplifier.

simplistic [sɪm'plɪstɪk] adj simpliste.

simply ['sɪmplɪ] adv - **1.** [gen] simplement - **2.** [for emphasis] absolument ; **quite ~** tout simplement.

simulate ['sɪmjʊleɪt] vt simuler.

simulation [ˌsɪmjʊ'leɪʃn] n simulation f.

simulator ['sɪmjʊleɪtəʳ] n simulateur m.

simultaneous [Br ˌsɪmʊl'teɪnjəs, Am ˌsaɪməl-'teɪnjəs] adj simultané(e).

simultaneously [Br ˌsɪmʊl'teɪnjəslɪ, Am ˌsaɪməl'teɪnjəslɪ] adv simultanément, en même temps.

sin [sɪn] (pt & pp -ned ; cont -ning) ◇ n péché m ; **to live in ~** vivre en concubinage ◇ vi : **to ~ (against)** pécher (contre).

sin bin n inf ICE HOCKEY prison f.

since [sɪns] ⬦ adv depuis ; **long** ~ il y a long-temps ⬦ prep depuis ⬦ conj - **1.** [in time] depuis que - **2.** [because] comme, puisque.

sincere [sɪn'sɪə^r] adj sincère.

sincerely [sɪn'sɪəlɪ] adv sincèrement ; **Yours** ~ [at end of letter] veuillez agréer, Monsieur/Madame, l'expression de mes sentiments les meilleurs.

sincerity [sɪn'serətɪ] n sincérité f.

sinecure ['saɪnɪˌkjʊə^r] n sinécure f.

sinew ['sɪnjuː] n tendon m.

sinewy ['sɪnjuːɪ] adj musclé(e).

sinful ['sɪnfʊl] adj [thought] mauvais(e) ; [desire, act] coupable ; ~ **person** pécheur m, -eresse f.

sing [sɪŋ] (pt **sang** ; pp **sung**) vt & vi chanter.

Singapore [ˌsɪŋə'pɔː^r] n Singapour m.

Singaporean [ˌsɪŋə'pɔːrɪən] ⬦ adj singapourien(enne) ⬦ n [person] Singapourien m, -enne f.

singe [sɪndʒ] (cont **singeing**) ⬦ n légère brûlure f ⬦ vt brûler légèrement ; [cloth] roussir.

singer ['sɪŋə^r] n chanteur m, -euse f.

Singhalese [ˌsɪŋhə'liːz] ⬦ adj cingalais(e), ceylanais(e) ⬦ n - **1.** [person] Cingalais m, -e f, Ceylanais m, -e f - **2.** [language] cingalais m.

singing ['sɪŋɪŋ] ⬦ adj [lesson, teacher] de chant ⬦ n (U) chant m.

singing telegram n télégramme m chanté.

single ['sɪŋgl] ⬦ adj - **1.** [only one] seul(e), unique ; **every** ~ chaque - **2.** [unmarried] célibataire - **3.** Br [ticket] simple ⬦ n - **1.** Br [one-way ticket] billet m simple, aller m (simple) - **2.** MUS (disque m) 45 tours m.
⬦ **singles** npl TENNIS simples mpl.
⬦ **single out** vt sep : **to** ~ **sb out (for)** choisir qqn (pour).

single bed n lit m à une place.

single-breasted [-'brestɪd] adj [jacket] droit (e).

single cream n Br crème f liquide.

single currency n monnaie f unique.

single-decker (bus) [-'dekə^r-] n Br bus m sans impériale.

Single European Market n : **the** ~ le Marché unique.

single file n : **in** ~ en file indienne, à la file.

single-handed [-'hændɪd] adv tout seul (toute seule).

single-minded [-'maɪndɪd] adj résolu(e) ; **to be** ~ **about sthg** concentrer toute son attention sur qqch.

single parent n père m OR mère f célibataire.

single-parent family n famille f monoparentale.

single quotes npl guillemets mpl.

single room n chambre f pour une personne OR à un lit.

singles bar n club m pour célibataires.

singlet ['sɪŋglɪt] n Br tricot m de peau ; SPORT maillot m.

single ticket n Br billet m simple, aller m (simple).

singsong ['sɪŋsɒŋ] ⬦ adj [voice] chantant(e) ⬦ n Br inf : **to have a** ~ chanter en chœur.

singular ['sɪŋgjʊlə^r] ⬦ adj singulier(ère) ⬦ n singulier m.

singularly ['sɪŋgjʊləlɪ] adv singulièrement.

Sinhalese ['sɪnəliːz] = **Singhalese.**

sinister ['sɪnɪstə^r] adj sinistre.

sink [sɪŋk] (pt **sank** ; pp **sunk**) ⬦ n [in kitchen] évier m ; [in bathroom] lavabo m ⬦ vt - **1.** [ship] couler - **2.** [teeth, claws] : **to** ~ **sthg into** enfoncer qqch dans ⬦ vi - **1.** [in water - ship] couler, sombrer ; [- person, object] couler - **2.** [ground] s'affaisser ; [sun] baisser ; **his spirits sank** il a été pris de découragement ; **to** ~ **into a chair** se laisser tomber dans un fauteuil ; **to** ~ **to one's knees** tomber à genoux ; **to** ~ **into poverty/despair** sombrer dans la misère/le désespoir - **3.** [value, amount] baisser, diminuer ; [voice] faiblir.
⬦ **sink in** vi : **it hasn't sunk in yet** je n'ai pas encore réalisé.

·sink board n Am égouttoir m.

sinking ['sɪŋkɪŋ] n naufrage m.

sinking fund n fonds m OR caisse f d'amortissement.

sink unit n bloc-évier m.

sinner ['sɪnə^r] n pécheur m, -eresse f.

Sinn Féin [ˌʃɪn'feɪn] n Sinn Féin m.

sinuous ['sɪnjʊəs] adj sinueux(euse).

sinus ['saɪnəs] (pl **-es** [-iːz]) n sinus m inv.

sip [sɪp] (pt & pp **-ped** ; cont **-ping**) ⬦ n petite gorgée f ⬦ vt siroter, boire à petits coups.

siphon ['saɪfn] ⬦ n siphon m ⬦ vt - **1.** [liquid] siphonner - **2.** fig [money] canaliser.
⬦ **siphon off** vt sep - **1.** [liquid] siphonner - **2.** fig [money] canaliser.

sir [sɜː^r] n - **1.** [form of address] monsieur m - **2.** [in titles] : **Sir Phillip Holden** sir Phillip Holden.

siren ['saɪərən] n sirène f.

sirloin (steak) ['sɜːlɔɪn-] n bifteck m dans l'aloyau OR d'aloyau.

sissy ['sɪsɪ] (*pl* -ies) *n* inf poule *f* mouillée, dégonflé *m*, -e *f*.

sister ['sɪstər] ⬦ *adj* [organization] sœur ; ~ ship sister-ship *m* ⬦ *n* - **1.** [sibling] sœur *f* - **2.** [nun] sœur *f*, religieuse *f* - **3.** Br [senior nurse] infirmière *f* chef.

sisterhood ['sɪstəhʊd] *n* RELIG communauté *f* religieuse.

sister-in-law (*pl* sisters-in-law) *n* belle-sœur *f*.

sisterly ['sɪstəlɪ] *adj* de sœur, fraternel(elle).

sit [sɪt] (*pt* & *pp* sat, *cont* -ting) ⬦ *vt* Br [exam] passer ⬦ *vi* - **1.** [person] s'asseoir ; to be sitting être assis(e) ; to ~ on a committee faire partie OR être membre d'un comité - **2.** [court, parliament] siéger, être en séance - **3.** [be situated] se trouver, être - **4.** phr : to ~ tight ne pas bouger.

⬧ **sit about, sit around** *vi* rester assis(e) à ne rien faire.

⬧ **sit back** *vi* [relax] se détendre ; to ~ back in a chair se caler dans un fauteuil ; we can't just ~ back and do nothing! il faut que nous fassions quelque chose!

⬧ **sit down** ⬦ *vt sep* asseoir ⬦ *vi* s'asseoir.

⬧ **sit in on** *vt fus* assister à.

⬧ **sit out** *vt sep* - **1.** [meeting, play etc] rester jusqu'à la fin de - **2.** [dance] : to ~ out a dance ne pas danser.

⬧ **sit through** *vt fus* rester jusqu'à la fin de.

⬧ **sit up** *vi* - **1.** [sit upright] se redresser, s'asseoir - **2.** [stay up] veiller.

sitcom ['sɪtkɒm] *n* inf sitcom *f*.

sit-down ⬦ *adj* [meal] servi(e) à la table ; [protest] sur le tas ⬦ *n* Br inf : to have a ~ (s'asseoir pour) se reposer.

site [saɪt] ⬦ *n* [of town, building] emplacement *m* ; [archaeological] site *m* ; CONSTR chantier *m* ⬦ *vt* situer, placer.

sit-in *n* sit-in *m*, occupation *f* des locaux.

sitter ['sɪtər] *n* - **1.** ART modèle *m* - **2.** [babysitter] baby-sitter *mf*.

sitting ['sɪtɪŋ] *n* - **1.** [of meal] service *m* - **2.** [of court, parliament] séance *f*.

sitting duck *n* inf cible *f* OR proie *f* facile.

sitting room *n* salon *m*.

sitting tenant *n* Br locataire *mf* en possession des lieux.

situate ['sɪtjʊeɪt] *vt* situer.

situated ['sɪtjʊeɪtɪd] *adj* : to be ~ être situé(e), se trouver.

situation [,sɪtjʊ'eɪʃn] *n* - **1.** [gen] situation *f* - **2.** [job] situation *f*, emploi *m* ; '~s vacant' Br 'offres d'emploi'.

situation comedy *n* sitcom *f*.

sit-up *n* redressement *m* assis.

six [sɪks] ⬦ *num adj* six (*inv*) ; she's ~ (years old) elle a six ans ⬦ *num pron* six *mfpl* ; I want ~ j'en veux six ; ~ of us went six d'entre nous sont allés ; there were ~ of us nous étions six ⬦ *num n* - **1.** [gen] six *m inv* ; two hundred and ~ deux cent six ; we sell them in ~es on les vend par paquets de six - **2.** [six o'clock] : it's ~ il est six heures ; we arrived at ~ nous sommes arrivés à six heures - **3.** [six degrees] : it's ~ below il fait moins six.

six-shooter [-'ʃuːtər] *n* Am revolver *m* à six coups.

sixteen [sɪks'tiːn] *num* seize ; *see also* six.

sixteenth [sɪks'tiːnθ] *num* seizième ; *see also* sixth.

sixth [sɪksθ] ⬦ *num adj* sixième ⬦ *num adv* - **1.** [in race, competition] sixième, en sixième place - **2.** [in list] sixièmement ⬦ *num pron* sixième *mf* ⬦ *n* - **1.** [fraction] sixième *m* - **2.** [in dates] : the ~ (of September) le six (septembre).

sixth form *n* Br SCH ≃ (classe *f*) terminale *f*.

sixth form college *n* Br établissement préparant aux A-levels.

sixth sense *n* sixième sens *m*.

sixtieth ['sɪkstɪəθ] *num* soixantième ; *see also* sixth.

sixty ['sɪkstɪ] (*pl* -ies) *num* soixante ; *see also* six.

⬧ **sixties** *npl* - **1.** [decade] : the sixties les années *fpl* soixante - **2.** [in ages] : to be in one's sixties être sexagénaire - **3.** [in temperatures] : in the sixties ≃ entre 15 et 20 degrés.

size [saɪz] *n* [of person, clothes, company] taille *f* ; [of building] grandeur *f*, dimensions *fpl* ; [of problem] ampleur *f*, taille ; [of shoes] pointure *f* ; to cut sb down to ~ rabattre le caquet à qqn.

⬧ **size up** *vt sep* [person] jauger ; [situation] apprécier, peser.

sizeable ['saɪzəbl] *adj* assez important(e).

-sized [-saɪzd] *suffix* : medium~ de taille moyenne.

sizzle ['sɪzl] *vi* grésiller.

SK *abbr of* Saskatchewan.

skate [skeɪt] (*pl sense 2 only, inv* OR -s) ⬦ *n* - **1.** [ice skate, roller skate] patin *m* - **2.** [fish] raie *f* ⬦ *vi* [on ice skates] faire du patin à glace, patiner ; [on roller skates] faire du patin à roulettes.

⬧ **skate over, skate round** *vt fus* [problem] éluder, éviter.

skateboard ['skeɪtbɔːd] *n* planche *f* à roulettes, skateboard *m*, skate *m*.

skateboarder ['skeɪtbɔːdəʳ] *n* personne *f* qui fait du skateboard OR du skate OR de la planche à roulettes.

skater ['skeɪtəʳ] *n* [on ice] patineur *m*, -euse *f*; [on roller skates] patineur à roulettes.

skating ['skeɪtɪŋ] *n* [on ice] patinage *m*; [on roller skates] patinage à roulettes.

skating rink *n* patinoire *f*.

skein [skeɪn] *n* [of thread] écheveau *m*.

skeletal ['skelɪtl] *adj* [emaciated] squelettique.

skeleton ['skelɪtn] <> *adj* [crew, service] squelettique, réduit(e) <> *n* squelette *m*; **to have a ~ in the cupboard** fig avoir un secret honteux.

skeleton key *n* passe *m*, passe-partout *m* inv.

skeleton staff *n* personnel *m* réduit.

skeptic *etc* Am = **sceptic** *etc*.

sketch [sketʃ] <> *n* - **1.** [drawing] croquis *m*, esquisse *f* - **2.** [description] aperçu *m*, résumé *m* - **3.** [by comedian] sketch *m* <> *vt* - **1.** [draw] dessiner, faire un croquis de - **2.** [describe] donner un aperçu de, décrire à grands traits <> *vi* dessiner.

◆ **sketch in** *vt sep* [details] ajouter, donner.

◆ **sketch out** *vt sep* esquisser, décrire à grands traits.

sketchbook ['sketʃbʊk] *n* carnet *m* à dessins.

sketchpad ['sketʃpæd] *n* bloc *m* à dessins.

sketchy ['sketʃɪ] (*compar* -**ier**; *superl* -**iest**) *adj* incomplet(ète).

skew [skjuː] <> *n* Br : **on the ~** de travers, en biais <> *vt* [distort] fausser.

skewer ['skjʊəʳ] <> *n* brochette *f*, broche *f* <> *vt* embrocher.

skew-whiff [ˌskjuːˈwɪf] *adj* Br inf de guingois, de traviole.

ski [skiː] (*pt & pp* **skied**; *cont* **skiing**) <> *n* ski *m* <> *comp* de ski <> *vi* skier, faire du ski.

ski boots *npl* chaussures *fpl* de ski.

skid [skɪd] (*pt & pp* -**ded**; *cont* -**ding**) <> *n* dérapage *m*; **to go into a ~** déraper <> *vi* déraper.

skid mark *n* trace *f* de frein OR dérapage.

skid row *n* Am inf : **to be on ~** être sur le pavé.

skier ['skiːəʳ] *n* skieur *m*, -euse *f*.

skies [skaɪz] *pl* ▷ **sky**.

skiing ['skiːɪŋ] <> *n* (U) ski *m*; **to go ~** faire du ski <> *comp* de ski.

ski instructor *n* moniteur *m*, -trice *f* de ski.

ski jump *n* [slope] tremplin *m*; [event] saut *m* à OR en skis.

skilful, skillful Am ['skɪlfʊl] *adj* habile, adroit(e).

skilfully, skillfully Am ['skɪlfʊlɪ] *adv* habilement, adroitement.

ski lift *n* remonte-pente *m*.

skill [skɪl] *n* - **1.** (U) [ability] habileté *f*, adresse *f* - **2.** [technique] technique *f*, art *m*.

skilled [skɪld] *adj* - **1.** [skilful] : **~ (in** OR **at doing sthg)** habile OR adroit(e) (pour faire qqch) - **2.** [trained] qualifié(e).

skillet ['skɪlɪt] *n* Am poêle *f* à frire.

skillful *etc* Am = **skilful** *etc*.

skim [skɪm] (*pt & pp* -**med**; *cont* -**ming**) <> *vt* - **1.** [cream] écrémer; [soup] écumer - **2.** [move above] effleurer, raser - **3.** [newspaper, book] parcourir <> *vi* : **to ~ through sthg** [newspaper, book] parcourir qqch.

skim(med) milk [skɪm(d)-] *n* lait *m* écrémé.

skimp [skɪmp] <> *vt* lésiner sur <> *vi* : **to ~ on** lésiner sur.

skimpy ['skɪmpɪ] (*compar* -**ier**; *superl* -**iest**) *adj* [meal] maigre; [clothes] étriqué(e); [facts] insuffisant(e).

skin [skɪn] (*pt & pp* -**ned**; *cont* -**ning**) <> *n* peau *f*; **by the ~ of one's teeth** de justesse; **to jump out of one's ~** Br sursauter, sauter au plafond; **to make sb's ~ crawl** donner la chair de poule à qqn; **to save** OR **protect one's own ~** sauver sa peau <> *vt* - **1.** [dead animal] écorcher, dépouiller; [fruit] éplucher, peler - **2.** [graze] : **to ~ one's knee** s'érafler OR s'écorcher le genou.

skincare ['skɪnkeəʳ] *n* (U) soins *mpl* pour la peau.

skin-deep *adj* superficiel(elle).

skin diver *n* plongeur sous-marin *m*, plongeuse sous-marine *f*.

skin diving *n* plongée *f* sous-marine.

skinflint ['skɪnflɪnt] *n* inf grippe-sou *m*, avare *mf*.

skin graft *n* greffe *f* de la peau.

skinhead ['skɪnhed] *n* Br skinhead *m*, skin *m*.

skinny ['skɪnɪ] (*compar* -**ier**; *superl* -**iest**) *adj* maigre.

skint [skɪnt] *adj* Br v inf fauché(e), à sec.

skin test *n* cuti *f*, cutiréaction *f*.

skin-tight *adj* moulant(e), collant(e).

skip [skɪp] (*pt & pp* -**ped**; *cont* -**ping**) <> *n* - **1.** [jump] petit saut *m* - **2.** Br [container] benne *f* ◇ *vt* [page, class, meal] sauter ◇ *vi* **- 1.** [gen] sauter, sautiller **- 2.** Br [over rope] sauter à la corde.

ski pants *npl* fuseau *m*.

ski pole *n* bâton *m* de ski.

skipper ['skɪpəʳ] *n* NAUT & SPORT capitaine *m*.

skipping ['skɪpɪŋ] *n* Br (U) saut *m* à la corde.

skipping rope *n* Br corde *f* à sauter.

ski resort *n* station *f* de ski.

skirmish ['skɜːmɪʃ] ◇ *n* escarmouche *f* ◇ *vi* s'engager dans une escarmouche ; fig avoir une escarmouche.

skirt [skɜːt] ◇ *n* [garment] jupe *f* ◇ *vt* **- 1.** [town, obstacle] contourner **- 2.** [problem] éviter.

➡ **skirt round** *vt fus* **- 1.** [town, obstacle] contourner **- 2.** [problem] éviter.

skirting board ['skɜːtɪŋ-] *n* Br plinthe *f*.

ski stick *n* bâton *m* de ski.

skit [skɪt] *n* sketch *m*.

skittish ['skɪtɪʃ] *adj* [person] frivole ; [animal] ombrageux(euse).

skittle ['skɪtl] *n* Br quille *f*.

➡ **skittles** *n* (U) [game] quilles *fpl*.

skive [skaɪv] *vi* Br inf : **to ~ (off)** s'esquiver, tirer au flanc.

skivvy ['skɪvɪ] (*pl* -ies, *pt* & *pp* -ied) Br inf ◇ *n* boniche *f*, bonne *f* à tout faire ◇ *vi* faire la boniche.

skulduggery [skʌl'dʌgərɪ] *n* (U) magouilles *fpl*.

skulk [skʌlk] *vi* [hide] se cacher ; [prowl] rôder.

skull [skʌl] *n* crâne *m*.

skullcap ['skʌlkæp] *n* calotte *f*.

skunk [skʌŋk] *n* [animal] mouffette *f*.

sky [skaɪ] (*pl* skies) *n* ciel *m*.

skycap ['skaɪkæp] *n* Am porteur *m* (dans un aéroport).

skydiver ['skaɪ,daɪvəʳ] *n* parachutiste *mf* qui fait de la chute libre.

skydiving ['skaɪ,daɪvɪŋ] *n* parachutisme *m* en chute libre.

sky-high inf ◇ *adj* [prices] astronomique, exorbitant(e) ◇ *adv* : **to blow sthg ~** [building etc] faire sauter qqch ; [argument, theory] démolir qqch ; **to go ~** [prices] monter en flèche.

skylark ['skaɪlɑːk] *n* alouette *f*.

skylight ['skaɪlaɪt] *n* lucarne *f*.

skyline ['skaɪlaɪn] *n* ligne *f* d'horizon

skyscraper ['skaɪ,skreɪpəʳ] *n* gratte-ciel *m* inv.

slab [slæb] *n* [of concrete] dalle *f* ; [of stone] bloc *m* ; [of cake] pavé *m*.

slack [slæk] ◇ *adj* **- 1.** [not tight] lâche **- 2.** [not busy] calme **- 3.** [person] négligent(e), pas sérieux(euse) ◇ *n* [in rope] mou *m*.

➡ **slacks** *npl* pantalon *m*.

slacken ['slækn] ◇ *vt* [speed, pace] ralentir ; [rope] relâcher ◇ *vi* [speed, pace] ralentir.

slag [slæg] *n* (U) [waste material] scories *fpl*.

slagheap ['slæghiːp] *n* terril *m*.

slain [sleɪn] *pp* ➡ slay.

slalom ['slɑːləm] *n* slalom *m*.

slam [slæm] (*pt* & *pp* -med ; *cont* -ming) ◇ *vt* **- 1.** [shut] claquer **- 2.** [criticize] éreinter **- 3.** [place with force] : **to ~ sthg on OR onto** jeter qqch brutalement sur, flanquer qqch sur ◇ *vi* claquer.

slander ['slɑːndəʳ] ◇ *n* calomnie *f* ; JUR diffamation *f* ◇ *vt* calomnier ; JUR diffamer.

slanderous ['slɑːndrəs] *adj* calomnieux(euse) ; JUR diffamatoire.

slang [slæŋ] ◇ *adj* argotique ◇ *n* (U) argot *m*.

slant [slɑːnt] ◇ *n* **- 1.** [angle] inclinaison *f* ; **on OR at a ~** de biais **- 2.** [perspective] point *m* de vue, perspective *f* ◇ *vt* [bias] présenter d'une manière tendancieuse ◇ *vi* [slope] être incliné(e), pencher.

slanting ['slɑːntɪŋ] *adj* [roof] en pente.

slap [slæp] (*pt* & *pp* -ped ; *cont* -ping) ◇ *n* claque *f*, tape *f* ; [on face] gifle *f* ; **a ~ in the face** fig une gifle ◇ *vt* **- 1.** [person, face] gifler ; [back] donner une claque OR une tape à **- 2.** [place with force] : **to ~ sthg on OR onto** jeter qqch brutalement sur, flanquer qqch sur ◇ *adv* inf [directly] en plein.

slapdash ['slæpdæʃ], **slaphappy** ['slæp,hæpɪ] *adj* inf [work] bâclé(e) ; [person, attitude] insouciant(e).

slapstick ['slæpstɪk] *n* (U) grosse farce *f*.

slap-up *adj* Br inf [meal] fameux(euse).

slash [slæʃ] ◇ *n* **- 1.** [long cut] entaille *f* **- 2.** esp Am [oblique stroke] barre *f* oblique ◇ *vt* **- 1.** [cut] entailler **- 2.** inf [prices] casser ; [budget, unemployment] réduire considérablement.

slat [slæt] *n* lame *f* ; [wooden] latte *f*.

slate [sleɪt] ◇ *n* ardoise *f* ◇ *vt* inf [criticize] descendre en flammes.

slatted ['slætɪd] *adj* à lames ; [wooden] en lattes de bois.

slaughter ['slɔːtəʳ] ◇ *n* **- 1.** [of animals] abattage *m* **- 2.** [of people] massacre *m*, carnage *m* ◇ *vt* **- 1.** [animals] abattre **- 2.** [people] massacrer.

slaughterhouse ['slɔːtəhaʊs, *pl* -haʊzɪz] *n* abattoir *m*.

Slav [slɑːv] ◇ *adj* slave ◇ *n* Slave *mf*.

slave [sleɪv] ⬦ n esclave mf ; **to be a ~ to sthg** fig être esclave de qqch ⬦ vi travailler comme un nègre ; **to ~ over sthg** peiner sur qqch.

slaver ['sleɪvəʳ] vi [salivate] baver.

slavery ['sleɪvərɪ] n esclavage m.

slave trade n : **the ~** la traite des noirs.

Slavic ['slɑːvɪk] ⬦ adj slave ⬦ n [language] slave m ; HISTORY slavon m.

slavish ['sleɪvɪʃ] adj servile.

Slavonic [slə'vɒnɪk] = **Slavic**.

slay [sleɪ] (pt **slew** ; pp **slain**) vt literary tuer.

sleazy ['sliːzɪ] (compar -ier ; superl -iest) adj [disreputable] mal famé(e).

sledge [sledʒ], **sled** Am [sled] n luge f ; [larger] traîneau m.

sledgehammer ['sledʒˌhæməʳ] n masse f.

sleek [sliːk] adj - 1. [hair, fur] lisse, luisant(e) - 2. [shape] aux lignes pures.

sleep [sliːp] (pt & pp **slept**) ⬦ n sommeil m ; **to go to ~** s'endormir ; **my foot has gone to ~** j'ai le pied engourdi OR endormi ; **to put an animal to ~** euphemism piquer un animal ⬦ vi - 1. [be asleep] dormir - 2. [spend night] coucher.

◆ **sleep around** vi inf pej coucher à droite et à gauche.

◆ **sleep in** vi faire la grasse matinée.

◆ **sleep off** vt sep dormir pour faire passer.

◆ **sleep through** vt fus : **I slept through the alarm** je n'ai pas entendu le réveil.

◆ **sleep together** vi euphemism coucher ensemble.

◆ **sleep with** vt fus euphemism coucher avec.

sleeper ['sliːpəʳ] n - 1. [person] : **to be a heavy/light ~** avoir le sommeil lourd/léger - 2. [RAIL - berth] couchette f ; [- carriage] wagon-lit m ; [- train] train-couchettes m - 3. Br [on railway track] traverse f.

sleepily ['sliːpɪlɪ] adv d'un air endormi.

sleeping bag ['sliːpɪŋ-] n sac m de couchage.

sleeping car ['sliːpɪŋ-] n wagon-lit m.

sleeping partner ['sliːpɪŋ-] n Br (associé m) commanditaire m, bailleur m de fonds.

sleeping pill ['sliːpɪŋ-] n somnifère m.

sleeping policeman ['sliːpɪŋ-] n Br inf ralentisseur m.

sleeping tablet ['sliːpɪŋ-] n somnifère m.

sleepless ['sliːplɪs] adj : **to have a ~ night** passer une nuit blanche.

sleeplessness ['sliːplɪsnɪs] n insomnie f.

sleep mode n COMPUT mode m veille.

sleepwalk ['sliːpwɔːk] vi être somnambule.

sleepy ['sliːpɪ] (compar -ier ; superl -iest) adj - 1. [person] qui a envie de dormir - 2. [place] endormi(e).

sleet [sliːt] ⬦ n neige f fondue ⬦ v impers : **it's ~ing** il tombe de la neige fondue.

sleeve [sliːv] n - 1. [of garment] manche f ; **to have sthg up one's ~** fig avoir qqch en réserve - 2. [for record] pochette f.

sleeveless ['sliːvlɪs] adj sans manches.

sleigh [sleɪ] n traîneau m.

sleight of hand [ˌslaɪt-] n (U) - 1. [skill] habileté f - 2. [trick] tour m de passe-passe.

slender ['slendəʳ] adj - 1. [thin] mince - 2. fig [resources, income] modeste, maigre ; [hope, chance] faible.

slept [slept] pt & pp ▷ **sleep**.

sleuth [sluːθ] n inf hum limier m.

S level (abbr of **Special level**) n [in UK] examen optionnel de niveau supérieur au A level, sanctionnant la fin des études secondaires.

slew [sluː] ⬦ pt ▷ **slay** ⬦ vi [car] déraper.

slice [slaɪs] ⬦ n - 1. [thin piece] tranche f - 2. fig [of profits, glory] part f - 3. SPORT slice m ⬦ vt - 1. [cut into slices] couper en tranches - 2. [cut cleanly] trancher - 3. SPORT slicer ⬦ vi : **to ~ through sthg** trancher qqch.

sliced bread [slaɪst-] n (U) pain m en tranches.

slick [slɪk] ⬦ adj - 1. [skilful] bien mené(e), habile - 2. pej [superficial - talk] facile ; [- person] rusé(e) ⬦ n nappe f de pétrole, marée f noire.

slicker ['slɪkəʳ] n Am [raincoat] ciré m.

slide [slaɪd] (pt & pp **slid** [slɪd]) ⬦ n - 1. [in playground] toboggan m - 2. PHOT diapositive f, diapo f - 3. [for microscope] porte-objet m - 4. Br [for hair] barrette f - 5. [decline] déclin m ; [in prices] baisse f ⬦ vt faire glisser ⬦ vi glisser ; **to let things ~** fig laisser les choses aller à vau-l'eau.

slide projector n projecteur m de diapositives.

slide rule n règle f à calcul.

sliding door [ˌslaɪdɪŋ-] n porte f coulissante.

sliding scale [ˌslaɪdɪŋ-] n échelle f mobile.

slight [slaɪt] ⬦ adj - 1. [minor] léger(ère) ; **the ~est** le moindre (la moindre) ; **not in the ~est** pas du tout - 2. [thin] mince ⬦ n affront m ⬦ vt offenser, faire un affront à.

slightly ['slaɪtlɪ] adv - 1. [to small extent] légèrement - 2. [slenderly] : ~ **built** mince.

slim [slɪm] (compar -**mer** ; superl -**mest**, pt & pp -**med** ; cont -**ming**) ⬦ adj - 1. [person, object] mince - **2.** [chance, possibility] faible ◇ *vi* maigrir ; [diet] suivre un régime amaigrissant.

slime [slaɪm] *n (U)* substance *f* visqueuse ; [of snail] bave *f*.

slimmer ['slɪmə'] *n* personne *f* suivant un régime amaigrissant.

slimming ['slɪmɪŋ] ◇ *n* amaigrissement *m* ◇ *adj* [product] amaigrissant(e), pour maigrir.

slimness ['slɪmnɪs] *n* minceur *f*.

slimy ['slaɪmɪ] (*compar* -ier ; *superl* -iest) *adj* lit & fig visqueux(euse).

sling [slɪŋ] (*pt* & *pp* slung) ◇ *n* - **1.** [for arm] écharpe *f* - **2.** NAUT [for loads] élingue *f* ◇ *vt* - **1.** [hammock etc] suspendre ; **to ~ a bag over one's shoulder** mettre son sac en bandoulière - **2.** inf [throw] lancer.

slingback ['slɪŋbæk] *n* chaussure *f* à talon ouvert.

slingshot ['slɪŋʃɒt] *n* Am lance-pierres *m inv*.

slink [slɪŋk] (*pt* & *pp* slunk) *vi* : **to ~ away** OR **off** s'en aller furtivement.

slip [slɪp] (*pt* & *pp* -ped ; *cont* -ping) ◇ *n* - **1.** [mistake] erreur *f* ; **a ~ of the pen** un lapsus ; **a ~ of the tongue** un lapsus - **2.** [of paper - gen] morceau *m* ; [- strip] bande *f* - **3.** [underwear] combinaison *f* - **4.** phr : **to give sb the ~** inf fausser compagnie à qqn ◇ *vt* glisser ; **to ~ sthg on** enfiler qqch ◇ *vi* - **1.** [slide] glisser ; **to ~ into** sthg se glisser dans qqch - **2.** [decline] décliner ; **to let things ~** laisser les choses aller à vau-l'eau - **3.** phr : **to let** sthg **~** laisser échapper qqch.
➤ **slip up** *vi* fig faire une erreur.

slip-on *adj* : **~ shoes** mocassins *mpl*.
➤ **slip-ons** *npl* mocassins *mpl*.

slippage ['slɪpɪdʒ] *n* baisse *f*.

slipped disc [ˌslɪpt-] *n* hernie *f* discale.

slipper ['slɪpə'] *n* pantoufle *f*, chausson *m*.

slippery ['slɪpərɪ] *adj* glissant(e).

slip road *n* Br bretelle *f*.

slipshod ['slɪpʃɒd] *adj* peu soigné(e).

slipstream ['slɪpstriːm] *n* sillage *m*.

slip-up *n* inf gaffe *f*.

slipway ['slɪpweɪ] *n* cale *f* de lancement.

slit [slɪt] (*pt* & *pp* slit, *cont* -ting) ◇ *n* [opening] fente *f* ; [cut] incision *f* ◇ *vt* [make opening in] faire une fente dans, fendre ; [cut] inciser.

slither ['slɪðə'] *vi* [person] glisser ; [snake] onduler.

sliver ['slɪvə'] *n* [of glass, wood] éclat *m* ; [of meat, cheese] lamelle *f*.

slob [slɒb] *n* inf [in habits] saligaud *m* ; [in appearance] gros lard *m*.

slobber ['slɒbə'] *vi* baver.

slog [slɒg] (*pt* & *pp* -ged ; *cont* -ging) inf ◇ *n* - **1.** [tiring work] corvée *f* - **2.** [tiring journey] voyage *m* pénible ◇ *vi* - **1.** [work] travailler comme un bœuf OR un nègre - **2.** [move] avancer péniblement.

slogan ['sləʊgən] *n* slogan *m*.

sloop [sluːp] *n* sloop *m*.

slop [slɒp] (*pt* & *pp* -ped ; *cont* -ping) ◇ *vt* renverser ◇ *vi* déborder.

slope [sləʊp] ◇ *n* pente *f* ; **to be on a slippery ~** fig être sur une pente savonneuse ◇ *vi* [land] être en pente ; [handwriting, table] pencher.

sloping ['sləʊpɪŋ] *adj* [land, shelf] en pente ; [handwriting] penché(e).

sloppy ['slɒpɪ] (*compar* -ier ; *superl* -iest) *adj* - **1.** [careless] peu soigné(e) - **2.** inf [sentimental] sentimental(e), à l'eau de rose.

slosh [slɒʃ] ◇ *vt* renverser ◇ *vi* : **to ~ about** [liquid] clapoter ; [person] patauger.

sloshed [slɒʃt] *adj* inf bourré(e).

slot [slɒt] (*pt* & *pp* -ted ; *cont* -ting) *n* - **1.** [opening] fente *f* - **2.** [groove] rainure *f* - **3.** [in schedule] créneau *m*.
➤ **slot in** ◇ *vt sep* [part] insérer ◇ *vi* [part] s'emboîter.

sloth [sləʊθ] *n* - **1.** [animal] paresseux *m* - **2.** literary [laziness] paresse *f*.

slot machine *n* - **1.** [vending machine] distributeur *m* automatique - **2.** [for gambling] machine *f* à sous.

slot meter *n* Br compteur *m* à pièces.

slouch [slaʊtʃ] ◇ *n* [posture] allure *f* avachie ◇ *vi* être avachi(e).

slough [slaʊ] ➤ **slough off** *vt sep* - **1.** [skin] : **to ~ off one's skin** muer - **2.** fig [get rid of] se débarrasser de.

Slovak ['sləʊvæk] ◇ *adj* slovaque ◇ *n* - **1.** [person] Slovaque *mf* - **2.** [language] slovaque *m*.

Slovakia [slə'vækɪə] *n* Slovaquie *f* ; **in ~** en Slovaquie.

Slovakian [slə'vækɪən] ◇ *adj* slovaque ◇ *n* Slovaque *mf*.

Slovenia [slə'viːnjə] *n* Slovénie *f* ; **in ~** en Slovénie.

Slovenian [slə'viːnjən] ◇ *adj* slovène ◇ *n* Slovène *mf*.

slovenly ['slʌvnlɪ] *adj* négligé(e).

slow [sləʊ] ◇ *adj* - **1.** [gen] lent(e) - **2.** [clock, watch] : **to be ~** retarder - **3.** [not busy] calme ◇ *adv* lentement ; **to go ~** [driver] aller lentement ; [workers] faire la grève perlée ◇ *vt* & *vi* ralentir.

➤ **slow down, slow up** *vt sep* & *vi* ralentir.

slow-acting *adj* à action lente.

slowcoach ['sləʊkəʊtʃ], **slow-poke** Am *n* inf lambin *m*, -e *f*.

slowdown ['sləʊdaʊn] *n* ralentissement *m*.

slow handclap *n* applaudissements *mpl* rythmés *(pour montrer sa désapprobation).*

slowly ['sləʊlı] *adv* lentement ; ~ **but surely** lentement mais sûrement.

slow motion *n* : in ~ au ralenti *m*.

➤ **slow-motion** *adj* au ralenti.

slow-poke ['sləʊpəʊk] Am = slowcoach.

SLR (*abbr of* **single-lens reflex**) *n* reflex *m*.

sludge [slʌdʒ] *n* boue *f*.

slug [slʌg] (*pt* & *pp* **-ged** ; *cont* **-ging**) ⬦ *n* - **1.** [animal] limace *f* - **2.** inf [of alcohol] rasade *f* - **3.** Am inf [bullet] balle *f* ⬦ *vt* inf donner un coup de poing violent à.

sluggish ['slʌgıʃ] *adj* [person] apathique ; [movement, growth] lent(e) ; [business] calme, stagnant(e).

sluice [slu:s] ⬦ *n* écluse *f* ⬦ *vt* : **to ~ sthg down** OR **out** laver qqch à grande eau.

slum [slʌm] (*pt* & *pp* **-med** ; *cont* **-ming**) ⬦ *n* [area] quartier *m* pauvre ⬦ *vt* : **to ~ it** inf hum s'encanailler.

slumber ['slʌmbəʳ] literary ⬦ *n* sommeil *m* ⬦ *vi* dormir paisiblement.

slump [slʌmp] ⬦ *n* - **1.** [decline] : **~ (in)** baisse *f* (de) - **2.** [period of poverty] crise *f* (économique) ⬦ *vi* lit & fig s'effondrer.

slung [slʌŋ] *pt* & *pp* ⊳ **sling**.

slunk [slʌŋk] *pt* & *pp* ⊳ **slink**.

slur [slɜ:ʳ] (*pt* & *pp* **-red** ; *cont* **-ring**) ⬦ *n* - **1.** [of voice] : **to speak with a ~** mal articuler - **2.** [slight] : **~ (on)** atteinte *f* (à) - **3.** [insult] affront *m*, insulte *f* ⬦ *vt* mal articuler.

slurp [slɜ:p] *vt* boire avec bruit.

slurred [slɜ:d] *adj* mal articulé(e).

slurry ['slʌrı] *n* AGR purin *m*.

slush [slʌʃ] *n* [snow] neige *f* fondue, sloche *f* Can.

slush fund, slush money Am *n* fonds *mpl* secrets, caisse *f* noire.

slut [slʌt] *n* - **1.** inf [dirty, untidy] souillon *f* - **2.** v inf [sexually immoral] salope *f*.

sly [slaɪ] (*compar* **slyer** OR **slier** ; *superl* **slyest** OR **sliest**) ⬦ *adj* - **1.** [look, smile] entendu(e) - **2.** [person] rusé(e), sournois(e) ⬦ *n* : **on the ~** en cachette.

slyness ['slaınıs] *n* (U) ruse *f*.

smack [smæk] ⬦ *n* - **1.** [slap] claque *f* ; [on face] gifle *f* - **2.** [impact] claquement *m* ⬦ *vt* - **1.** [slap] donner une claque à ; [face] gifler

- **2.** [place violently] poser violemment - **3.** phr : **to ~ one's lips** se lécher les babines ⬦ *adv* inf [directly] en plein ; ~ **in the middle** en plein milieu.

small [smɔ:l] ⬦ *adj* - **1.** [gen] petit(e) - **2.** [trivial] petit, insignifiant(e) ⬦ *n* : **the ~ of the back** le creux OR le bas des reins.

➤ **smalls** *npl* Br inf dated dessous *mpl*.

small ads [-ædz] *npl* Br petites annonces *fpl*.

small arms *npl* armes *fpl* (à feu) portatives.

small change *n* petite monnaie *f*.

small fry *n* menu fretin *m*.

smallholder ['smɔ:l,həʊldəʳ] *n* Br petit cultivateur *m*, petit exploitant *m* agricole.

smallholding ['smɔ:l,həʊldıŋ] *n* Br petite exploitation *f* agricole.

small hours *npl* : in the ~ au petit jour OR matin.

smallness ['smɔ:lnıs] *n* [of building, person] petite taille *f* ; [of amount, income] modicité *f*, petitesse *f*.

smallpox ['smɔ:lpɒks] *n* variole *f*, petite vérole *f*.

small print *n* : the ~ les clauses *fpl* écrites en petits caractères.

small-scale *adj* [activity, organization] peu important(e).

small talk *n* (U) papotage *m*, bavardage *m*.

small-time *adj* de second ordre.

smarmy ['smɑ:mı] (*compar* **-ier** ; *superl* **-iest**) *adj* mielleux(euse).

smart [smɑ:t] ⬦ *adj* - **1.** [stylish - person, clothes, car] élégant(e) - **2.** esp Am [clever] intelligent(e) - **3.** [fashionable - club, society, hotel] à la mode, in *(inv)* - **4.** [quick - answer, tap] vif (vive), rapide ⬦ *vi* - **1.** [eyes, skin] brûler, piquer - **2.** [person] être blessé(e).

smart card *n* carte *f* à mémoire.

smart drug *n* médicament agissant comme un stimulant mental, nootrope *m*.

smarten ['smɑ:tn] ➤ **smarten up** *vt sep* [room] arranger ; **to ~ o.s. up** se faire beau (belle).

smash [smæʃ] ⬦ *n* - **1.** [sound] fracas *m* - **2.** inf [car crash] collision *f*, accident *m* - **3.** inf [success] succès *m* fou - **4.** SPORT smash *m* ⬦ *vt* - **1.** [glass, plate etc] casser, briser - **2.** fig [defeat] détruire ⬦ *vi* - **1.** [glass, plate etc] se briser - **2.** [crash] : **to ~ through sthg** défoncer qqch ; **to ~ into sthg** s'écraser contre qqch.

➤ **smash up** *vt sep* casser, briser ; [car] bousiller.

smash-and-grab (raid) *n* Br *vol effectué après avoir brisé une vitrine.*

smashed [smæʃt] *adj* inf bourré(e).

smash hit n succès m fou.

smashing ['smæʃɪŋ] adj inf super (inv).

smash-up n collision f, accident m.

smattering ['smætərɪŋ] n : to have a ~ of German savoir quelques mots d'allemand.

SME (abbr of small and medium-sized enterprise) n PME f.

smear [smɪəʳ] ◇ n - 1. [dirty mark] tache f - 2. [slander] diffamation f ◇ vt - 1. [smudge] barbouiller, maculer - 2. [spread] : to ~ sthg onto sthg étaler qqch sur qqch ; to ~ sthg with sthg enduire qqch de qqch - 3. [slander] calomnier.

smear campaign n campagne f de diffamation.

smear test n frottis m.

smell [smel] (pt & pp **-ed** OR **smelt**) ◇ n - 1. [odour] odeur f - 2. [sense of smell] odorat m ◇ vt sentir ◇ vi - 1. I can't ~ je ne sens rien du tout ; to ~ of sthg sentir qqch ; to ~ good/bad sentir bon/mauvais - 2. [smell unpleasantly] sentir (mauvais), puer.

smelly ['smelɪ] (compar **-ier** ; superl **-iest**) adj qui sent mauvais, qui pue.

smelt [smelt] ◇ pt & pp ⊳ **smell** ◇ vt [metal] extraire par fusion ; [ore] fondre.

smile [smaɪl] ◇ n sourire m ◇ vi sourire ◇ vt : to ~ one's agreement acquiescer d'un sourire.

smiley ['smaɪlɪ] n smiley.

smiling ['smaɪlɪŋ] adj souriant(e).

smirk [smɜːk] ◇ n sourire m narquois ◇ vi sourire d'un air narquois.

smith [smɪθ] n forgeron m.

smithereens [ˌsmɪðə'riːnz] npl inf : to be smashed to ~ être brisé(e) en mille morceaux.

smithy ['smɪðɪ] (pl **-ies**) n forge f.

smitten ['smɪtn] adj hum : to be ~ (with) être fou (folle) (de).

smock [smɒk] n blouse f.

smog [smɒg] n smog m.

smoke [sməʊk] ◇ n - 1. (U) [from fire] fumée f - 2. [act of smoking] : to have a ~ [cigarette] fumer une cigarette ; [cigar] fumer un cigare ◇ vt & vi fumer.

smoked [sməʊkt] adj [food] fumé(e).

smokeless fuel ['sməʊklɪs-] n combustible qui ne produit pas de fumée.

smokeless zone ['sməʊklɪs-] n zone où la combustion de matériaux est réglementée.

smoker ['sməʊkəʳ] n - 1. [person] fumeur m, -euse f - 2. RAIL compartiment m fumeurs.

smokescreen ['sməʊkskriːn] n fig couverture f.

smoke shop n Am bureau m de tabac.

smokestack ['sməʊkstæk] n cheminée f.

smokestack industry n Am industrie f lourde.

smoking ['sməʊkɪŋ] n tabagisme m ; 'no ~' 'défense de fumer'.

smoking compartment Br, **smoking car** Am n compartiment m fumeurs.

smoky ['sməʊkɪ] (compar **-ier** ; superl **-iest**) adj - 1. [room, air] enfumé(e) - 2. [taste] fumé(e).

smolder Am = smoulder.

smooch [smuːtʃ] vi inf se bécoter et se peloter.

smooth [smuːð] ◇ adj - 1. [surface] lisse - 2. [sauce] homogène, onctueux(euse) - 3. [movement] régulier(ère) - 4. [taste] moelleux(euse) - 5. [flight, ride] confortable ; [landing, take-off] en douceur - 6. pej [person, manner] doucereux(euse), mielleux(euse) - 7. [operation, progress] sans problèmes ◇ vt [hair] lisser ; [clothes, tablecloth] défroisser ; to ~ the way aplanir les difficultés OR les obstacles.
➤ **smooth out** vt sep défroisser.
➤ **smooth over** vt fus [difficulties] aplanir ; [disagreements] arranger.

smoothly ['smuːðlɪ] adv - 1. [move] sans heurt - 2. pej [suavely] d'un ton doucereux - 3. [without problems] sans problèmes.

smoothness ['smuːðnɪs] (U) n - 1. [of surface] aspect m lisse - 2. [of mixture] onctuosité f - 3. [of movement] régularité f - 4. [of flight, ride] confort m - 5. pej [of person] caractère m doucereux.

smooth-talking [-ˌtɔːkɪŋ] adj doucereux(euse), mielleux(euse).

smother ['smʌðəʳ] vt - 1. [cover thickly] : to ~ sb/sthg with couvrir qqn/qqch de - 2. [person, fire] étouffer - 3. fig [emotions] cacher, étouffer.

smoulder Br, **smolder** Am ['sməʊldəʳ] vi lit & fig couver.

smudge [smʌdʒ] ◇ n tache f ; [of ink] bavure f ◇ vt [drawing, painting] maculer ; [paper] faire une marque OR trace sur ; [face] salir.

smug [smʌg] (compar **-ger** ; superl **-gest**) adj suffisant(e).

smuggle ['smʌgl] vt - 1. [across frontiers] faire passer en contrebande - 2. [against rules] : to ~ sthg in/out faire entrer/sortir qqch clandestinement.

smuggler ['smʌgləʳ] n contrebandier m, -ère f.

smuggling ['smʌglɪŋ] n (U) contrebande f.

smugness ['smʌgnɪs] n suffisance f.

smut [smʌt] n - **1.** [dirty mark] tache f de suie - **2.** (U) pej [books, talk etc] obscénités fpl.

smutty ['smʌtɪ] (compar -ier ; superl -iest) adj pej [book, language] cochon(onne).

snack [snæk] ⟨⟩ n casse-croûte m inv ⟨⟩ vi Am manger un morceau.

snack bar n snack m, snack-bar m.

snag [snæg] (pt & pp -ged ; cont -ging) ⟨⟩ n [problem] inconvénient m, écueil m ⟨⟩ vt accrocher ⟨⟩ vi : to ~ (on) s'accrocher (à).

snail [sneɪl] n escargot m.

snake [sneɪk] ⟨⟩ n serpent m ⟨⟩ vi serpenter.

snap [snæp] (pt & pp -ped ; cont -ping) ⟨⟩ adj [decision, election] subit(e) ; [judgment] irréfléchi(e) ⟨⟩ n - **1.** [of branch] craquement m ; [of fingers] claquement m - **2.** [photograph] photo f - **3.** [card game] ≃ bataille f ⟨⟩ vt - **1.** [break] casser net - **2.** [move] : to ~ sthg open/shut ouvrir/fermer qqch avec un bruit sec ; to ~ one's fingers claquer des doigts - **3.** [speak sharply] dire d'un ton sec ⟨⟩ vi - **1.** [break] se casser net - **2.** [move] : to ~ into place s'emboîter avec un bruit sec - **3.** [dog] : to ~ at essayer de mordre - **4.** [speak sharply] : to ~ (at sb) parler (à qqn) d'un ton sec - **5.** phr : to ~ out of it inf réagir, se secouer.

➤ **snap up** vt sep [bargain] sauter sur.

snap fastener n esp Am pression f.

snappish ['snæpɪʃ] adj hargneux(euse).

snappy ['snæpɪ] (compar -ier ; superl -iest) adj inf - **1.** [stylish] chic - **2.** [quick] prompt(e) ; make it ~! dépêche-toi!, et que ça saute!

snapshot ['snæpʃɒt] n photo f.

snare [sneəʳ] ⟨⟩ n piège m, collet m ⟨⟩ vt prendre au piège, attraper.

snarl [snɑːl] ⟨⟩ n grondement m ⟨⟩ vi gronder.

snarl-up n enchevêtrement m ; [of traffic] embouteillage m.

snatch [snætʃ] ⟨⟩ n [of conversation] bribe f ; [of song] extrait m ⟨⟩ vt - **1.** [grab] saisir - **2.** fig [time] réussir à avoir ; [opportunity] saisir ; to ~ a look at sthg regarder qqch à la dérobée ⟨⟩ vi : to ~ at sthg essayer de saisir qqch.

snazzy ['snæzɪ] (compar -ier ; superl -iest) adj inf [clothes, car] beau (belle), super (inv) ; [dresser] qui s'habille chic.

sneak [sniːk] (Am pt snuck) ⟨⟩ n Br inf rapporteur m, -euse f ⟨⟩ vt : to ~ a look at sb/sthg regarder qqn/qqch à la dérobée ⟨⟩ vi [move quietly] se glisser ; to ~ up on sb s'approcher de qqn sans faire de bruit.

sneakers ['sniːkəz] npl Am tennis mpl, baskets fpl.

sneaking ['sniːkɪŋ] adj secret(ète).

sneak preview n avant-première f.

sneaky ['sniːkɪ] (compar -ier ; superl -iest) adj inf sournois(e).

sneer [snɪəʳ] ⟨⟩ n [smile] sourire m dédaigneux ; [laugh] ricanement m ⟨⟩ vi - **1.** [smile] sourire dédaigneusement - **2.** [ridicule] : ~ at sthg tourner qqch en ridicule.

sneeze [sniːz] ⟨⟩ n éternuement m ⟨⟩ vi éternuer ; it's not to be ~d at! inf il ne faut pas cracher dessus!

snicker ['snɪkəʳ] vi Am ricaner.

snide [snaɪd] adj sournois(e).

sniff [snɪf] ⟨⟩ n reniflement m ⟨⟩ vt - **1.** [smell] renifler - **2.** [inhale - drug] sniffer ⟨⟩ vi - **1.** [to clear nose] renifler - **2.** [to show disapproval] faire la grimace.

➤ **sniff out** vt sep - **1.** [detect by sniffing] flairer - **2.** inf [seek out] rechercher.

sniffer dog ['snɪfəʳ-] n chien m renifleur.

sniffle ['snɪfl] vi renifler.

snigger ['snɪgəʳ] ⟨⟩ n rire m en dessous ⟨⟩ vi ricaner.

snip [snɪp] (pt & pp -ped ; cont -ping) ⟨⟩ n inf [bargain] bonne affaire f ⟨⟩ vt couper.

snipe [snaɪp] vi - **1.** [shoot] : to ~ at sb/sthg canarder qqn/qqch - **2.** [criticize] : to ~ at sb critiquer qqn sournoisement.

sniper ['snaɪpəʳ] n tireur m isolé.

snippet ['snɪpɪt] n fragment m.

snivel ['snɪvl] (Br pt & pp -led ; cont -ling, Am pt & pp -ed ; cont -ing) vi geindre.

snob [snɒb] n snob mf.

snobbery ['snɒbərɪ] n snobisme m.

snobbish ['snɒbɪʃ], **snobby** ['snɒbɪ] (compar -ier ; superl -iest) adj snob (inv).

snooker ['snuːkəʳ] ⟨⟩ n [game] ≃ jeu m de billard ⟨⟩ vt Br inf fig : to be ~ed être coincé(e).

snoop [snuːp] vi inf fureter.

snooper ['snuːpəʳ] n inf fouineur m, -euse f.

snooty ['snuːtɪ] (compar -ier ; superl -iest) adj inf prétentieux(euse).

snooze [snuːz] ⟨⟩ n petit somme m ⟨⟩ vi faire un petit somme.

snore [snɔːʳ] ⟨⟩ n ronflement m ⟨⟩ vi ronfler.

snoring ['snɔːrɪŋ] n (U) ronflement m, ronflements mpl.

snorkel ['snɔːkl] n tuba m.

snorkelling Br, **snorkeling** Am ['snɔːklɪŋ] n : to go ~ faire de la plongée avec un tuba.

snort [snɔːt] ⟨⟩ n [of person] grognement m ;

[of horse, bull] ébrouement *m* ⬦ *vi* [person] grogner ; [horse] s'ébrouer ⬦ *vt* **drugs sl** sniffer.

snotty ['snɒtɪ] (*compar* -**ier** ; *superl* -**iest**) *adj* inf - **1.** [snooty] prétentieux(euse) - **2.** [face, child] morveux(euse).

snout [snaʊt] *n* groin *m*.

snow [snəʊ] ⬦ *n* neige *f* ⬦ *v impers* neiger.
➤ **snow in** *vt sep* : **to be ~ed in** être bloqué(e) par la neige.
➤ **snow under** *vt sep* fig : **to be ~ed under (with)** être submergé(e) (de).

snowball ['snəʊbɔːl] ⬦ *n* boule *f* de neige ⬦ *vi* fig faire boule de neige.

snowbank ['snəʊbæŋk] *n* congère *f*, banc *m* de neige **Can**.

snow blindness *n* cécité *f* des neiges.

snowboard ['snəʊ,bɔːd] *n* surf *m* des neiges.

snowboarding ['snəʊ,bɔːdɪŋ] *n* surf *m* (des neiges).

snowbound ['snəʊbaʊnd] *adj* bloqué(e) par la neige.

snow-capped [-kæpt] *adj* couronné(e) de neige.

snowdrift ['snəʊdrɪft] *n* congère *f*.

snowdrop ['snəʊdrɒp] *n* perce-neige *m inv*.

snowfall ['snəʊfɔːl] *n* chute *f* de neige.

snowflake ['snəʊfleɪk] *n* flocon *m* de neige.

snowman ['snəʊmæn] (*pl* -**men** [-men]) *n* bonhomme *m* de neige.

snowmobile ['snəʊməbiːl] *n* scooter *m* des neiges, motoneige *f* **Can**.

snow pea *n* **Am** mange-tout *m inv*.

snowplough Br, **snowplow Am** ['snəʊplaʊ] *n* chasse-neige *m inv*.

snowshoe ['snəʊʃuː] *n* raquette *f*.

snowstorm ['snəʊstɔːm] *n* tempête *f* de neige.

snowy ['snəʊɪ] (*compar* -**ier** ; *superl* -**iest**) *adj* neigeux(euse).

SNP (*abbr of* **Scottish National Party**) *n* parti nationaliste écossais.

Snr, snr *abbr of* **senior**.

snub [snʌb] (*pt* & *pp* -**bed** ; *cont* -**bing**) ⬦ *n* rebuffade *f* ⬦ *vt* snober, ignorer.

snuck [snʌk] **Am** *pt* ⟐ **sneak**.

snuff [snʌf] *n* tabac *m* à priser.

snuffle ['snʌfl] *vi* renifler.

snuff movie *n* film porno où l'acteur est tué à la fin.

snug [snʌg] (*compar* -**ger** ; *superl* -**gest**) *adj* - **1.** [person] à l'aise, confortable ; [in bed] bien au chaud - **2.** [place] douillet(ette) - **3.** [close-fitting] bien ajusté(e).

snuggle ['snʌgl] *vi* se blottir.

so [səʊ] ⬦ *adv* - **1.** [to such a degree] si, tellement ; ~ **difficult (that)** ... si *or* tellement difficile que ... ; **don't be ~ stupid!** ne sois pas si bête! ; **he's not ~ stupid as he looks** il n'est pas si *or* aussi bête qu'il en a l'air ; **we're ~ glad you could come** nous sommes si contents que vous ayez pu venir ; **he's ~ sweet/ kind** il est tellement mignon/gentil ; **we had ~ much work!** nous avions tant de travail! ; **I've never seen ~ much money/many cars** je n'ai jamais vu autant d'argent/de voitures - **2.** [in referring back to previous statement, event etc] : ~ **what's the point then?** alors à quoi bon? ; ~ **you knew already?** alors tu le savais déjà? ; **I don't think ~** je ne crois pas ; **I'm afraid ~** je crains bien que oui ; **if ~** si oui ; **is that ~?** vraiment? - **3.** [also] aussi ; ~ **can/do/would** *etc* **I** moi aussi ; **she speaks French and ~ does her husband** elle parle français et son mari aussi ; **as with ...,~ with** il en va pour ... comme pour ; **just as some people like family holidays, ~ others prefer to holiday alone** de même que certains aiment les vacances en famille, de même d'autres préfèrent passer leurs vacances tout seuls - **4.** [in this way] : **(like)** ~ comme cela *or* ça, de cette façon ; **hold your arm out,** ~ étendez votre bras, comme cela *or* ça - **5.** [in expressing agreement] : ~ **there is** en effet, c'est vrai ; ~ **I see** c'est ce que je vois - **6.** [unspecified amount, limit] : **they pay us** ~ **much a week** ils nous payent tant par semaine ; **not** ~ **much ... as** pas tant ... que ; **it's not** ~ **much the money as the time involved** ce n'est pas tant l'argent que le temps que ça demande ; **or** ~ environ, à peu près ; **a year/ week or** ~ **ago** il y a environ un an/une semaine ⬦ *conj* alors ; **he said yes and** ~ **we got married** il a dit oui, alors on s'est mariés ; **I'm away next week** ~ **I won't be there** je suis en voyage la semaine prochaine donc *or* par conséquent je ne serai pas là ; ~ **what have you been up to?** alors, qu'est-ce que vous devenez? ; ~ **what?** inf et alors?, et après? ; ~ **there!** inf là!, et voilà!
➤ **so as** *conj* afin de, pour ; **we didn't knock** ~ **as not to disturb them** nous n'avons pas frappé pour ne pas les déranger.
➤ **so that** *conj* [for the purpose that] pour que (+ *subjunctive*) ; **he lied** ~ **that she would go free** il a menti pour qu'elle soit relâchée.

SO *abbr of* **standing order**.

soak [səʊk] ⬦ *vt* laisser *or* faire tremper ⬦ *vi* - **1.** [become thoroughly wet] : **to leave sthg to ~, to let sthg ~** laisser *or* faire tremper qqch - **2.** [spread] : **to ~ into sthg** tremper

dans qqch ; **to ~ through (sthg)** traverser (qqch).
➤ **soak up** *vt sep* absorber.
soaked [səʊkt] *adj* trempé(e) ; **to be ~ through** être trempé (jusqu'aux os).
soaking ['səʊkɪŋ] *adj* trempé(e).
so-and-so *n inf* - **1.** [to replace a name] : **Mr ~** Monsieur Untel - **2.** [annoying person] enquiquineur *m*, -euse *f*.
soap [səʊp] <> *n* - **1.** (*U*) [for washing] savon *m* - **2.** TV soap opera *m* <> *vt* savonner.
soap bubble *n* bulle *f* de savon.
soap flakes *npl* savon *m* en paillettes.
soap opera *n* soap opera *m*.
soap powder *n* lessive *f*.
soapsuds ['səʊpsʌdz] *npl* mousse *f* de savon.
soapy ['səʊpɪ] (*compar* -ier ; *superl* -iest) *adj* [water] savonneux(euse) ; [taste] de savon.
soar [sɔːʳ] *vi* - **1.** [bird] planer - **2.** [balloon, kite] monter - **3.** [prices, temperature] monter en flèche - **4.** [building, tree, mountain] s'élever, s'élancer - **5.** [music, voice] monter.
soaring ['sɔːrɪŋ] *adj* - **1.** [prices, temperature] qui monte en flèche - **2.** [building, tree, mountain] qui s'élève - **3.** [music, voice] qui monte.
sob [sɒb] (*pt & pp* -**bed** ; *cont* -**bing**) <> *n* sanglot *m* <> *vt* dire en sanglotant <> *vi* sangloter.
sobbing ['sɒbɪŋ] *n* (*U*) sanglots *mpl*.
sober ['səʊbəʳ] *adj* - **1.** [not drunk] qui n'est pas ivre - **2.** [serious] sérieux(euse) - **3.** [plain - clothes, colours] sobre.
➤ **sober up** *vi* dessoûler.
sobering ['səʊbərɪŋ] *adj* qui donne à réfléchir.
sobriety [səʊ'braɪətɪ] *n fml* [seriousness] sérieux *m*.
Soc. *abbr of* **Society.**
so-called [-kɔːld] *adj* - **1.** [misleadingly named] soi-disant (*inv*) - **2.** [widely known as] ainsi appelé(e).
soccer ['sɒkəʳ] *n* football *m*.
sociable ['səʊʃəbl] *adj* sociable.
social ['səʊʃl] *adj* social(e).
social climber *n pej* arriviste *mf*.
social club *n* club *m*.
social conscience *n* conscience *f* sociale.
social democracy *n* social-démocratie *f*.
social event *n* événement *m* social.
social fund *n* fonds *m* d'entraide.
socialism ['səʊʃəlɪzm] *n* socialisme *m*.
socialist ['səʊʃəlɪst] <> *adj* socialiste <> *n* socialiste *mf*.

socialite ['səʊʃəlaɪt] *n* mondain *m*, -e *f*.
socialize, -ise ['səʊʃəlaɪz] *vi* fréquenter des gens ; **to ~ with sb** fréquenter qqn, frayer avec qqn.
socialized medicine ['səʊʃəlaɪzd-] *n* Am soins médicaux payés par les impôts.
social life *n* vie *f* sociale.
socially ['səʊʃəlɪ] *adv* - **1.** [in society] socialement, en société - **2.** [outside business] en dehors du travail.
social order *n* ordre *m* social.
social science *n* sciences *fpl* humaines.
social security *n* aide *f* sociale.
social services *npl* services *mpl* sociaux.
social studies *n* sciences *fpl* sociales.
social work *n* (*U*) assistance *f* sociale.
social worker *n* assistant social *m*, assistante sociale *f*.
society [sə'saɪətɪ] (*pl* -ies) *n* - **1.** [gen] société *f* - **2.** [club] association *f*, club *m*.
socioeconomic ['səʊsɪəʊ,iːkə'nɒmɪk] *adj* socio-économique.
sociological [,səʊsjə'lɒdʒɪkl] *adj* sociologique.
sociologist [,səʊsɪ'ɒlədʒɪst] *n* sociologue *mf*.
sociology [,səʊsɪ'ɒlədʒɪ] *n* sociologie *f*.
sock [sɒk] *n* chaussette *f* ; **to pull one's ~s up** *inf fig* se secouer.
socket ['sɒkɪt] *n* - **1.** [for light bulb] douille *f* ; [for plug] prise *f* de courant - **2.** [of eye] orbite *f* ; [for bone] cavité *f* articulaire.
sod [sɒd] *n* - **1.** [of turf] motte *f* de gazon - **2.** v *inf* [person] con *m*.
soda ['səʊdə] *n* - **1.** CHEM soude *f* - **2.** [soda water] eau *f* de Seltz - **3.** Am [fizzy drink] soda *m*.
soda syphon *n* siphon *m* d'eau de Seltz.
soda water *n* eau *f* de Seltz.
sodden ['sɒdn] *adj* trempé(e), détrempé(e).
sodium ['səʊdɪəm] *n* sodium *m*.
sofa ['səʊfə] *n* canapé *m*.
sofa bed *n* canapé-lit *m*.
Sofia ['səʊfjə] *n* Sofia.
soft [sɒft] *adj* - **1.** [not hard] doux (douce), mou (molle) - **2.** [smooth, not loud, not bright] doux (douce) - **3.** [without force] léger(ère) - **4.** [caring] tendre - **5.** [lenient] faible, indulgent(e).
soft-boiled *adj* à la coque.
soft drink *n* boisson *f* non alcoolisée.
soft drugs *npl* drogues *fpl* douces.
soften ['sɒfn] <> *vt* - **1.** [fabric] assouplir ; [substance] ramollir ; [skin] adoucir - **2.** [shock, blow] atténuer, adoucir - **3.** [attitude] modérer,

adoucir ⇔ vi **- 1.** [substance] se ramollir **- 2.** [attitude, person] s'adoucir, se radoucir.

➡ **soften up** vt sep inf [persuade] amadouer.

softener ['sɒfnə'] n [for washing] adoucissant m.

soft focus n flou m ; **in ~** en flou.

soft furnishings npl Br tissus mpl d'ameublement.

softhearted [ˌsɒft'hɑːtɪd] adj au cœur tendre.

softly ['sɒftlɪ] adv **- 1.** [gently, quietly] doucement **- 2.** [not brightly] faiblement **- 3.** [leniently] avec indulgence.

softness ['sɒftnɪs] n **- 1.** [of bed, ground, substance] mollesse f, moelleux m **- 2.** [of skin, sound, light] douceur f **- 3.** [lenience] indulgence f.

soft-pedal vi inf y aller doucement.

soft sell n inf méthode f de vente discrète or non agressive.

soft-spoken adj à la voix douce.

soft toy n jouet m en peluche.

software ['sɒftweə'] n (U) COMPUT logiciel m.

software package n COMPUT logiciel m, progiciel m.

softwood ['sɒftwʊd] n bois m tendre.

softy ['sɒftɪ] (pl -ies) n inf **- 1.** pej [weak person] mauviette f, poule f mouillée **- 2.** [sensitive person] : **he's a big ~** c'est un tendre.

soggy ['sɒgɪ] (compar -ier ; superl -iest) adj trempé(e), détrempé(e).

soil [sɔɪl] ⇔ n (U) **- 1.** [earth] sol m, terre f **- 2.** fig [territory] sol m, territoire m ⇔ vt souiller, salir.

soiled [sɔɪld] adj sale.

solace ['sɒləs] n literary consolation f, réconfort m.

solar ['səʊlə'] adj solaire.

solarium [sə'leərɪəm] (pl -riums or -ria [-rɪə]) n solarium m.

solar panel n panneau m solaire.

solar plexus [-'pleksəs] n plexus m solaire.

solar system n système m solaire.

sold [səʊld] pt & pp ⊳ **sell.**

solder ['səʊldə'] ⇔ n (U) soudure f ⇔ vt souder.

soldering iron ['səʊldərɪŋ-] n fer m à souder.

soldier ['səʊldʒə'] n soldat m.

➡ **soldier on** vi Br persévérer.

sold-out adj [tickets] qui ont tous été vendus ; [play, concert] qui joue à guichets fermés.

sole [səʊl] (pl sense 2 only, inv or -s) ⇔ adj **- 1.** [only] seul(e), unique **- 2.** [exclusive] exclu-

sif(ive) ⇔ n **- 1.** [of foot] semelle f **- 2.** [fish] sole f.

solely ['səʊllɪ] adv seulement, uniquement ; **~ responsible** seul or entièrement responsable.

solemn ['sɒləm] adj solennel(elle) ; [person] sérieux(euse).

solemnly ['sɒləmlɪ] adv **- 1.** [speak, behave] avec solennité, sérieusement **- 2.** [promise, swear] solennellement.

sole trader n Br COMM entreprise f unipersonnelle or individuelle.

solicit [sə'lɪsɪt] ⇔ vt [request] solliciter ⇔ vi [prostitute] racoler.

solicitor [sə'lɪsɪtə'] n Br JUR notaire m.

solicitous [sə'lɪsɪtəs] adj **- 1.** [caring] plein(e) de sollicitude **- 2.** [anxious] : **~ about** or **for** préoccupé(e) de, soucieux(euse) de.

solid ['sɒlɪd] ⇔ adj **- 1.** [not fluid, sturdy, reliable] solide **- 2.** [not hollow - tyres] plein(e) ; [- wood, rock, gold] massif(ive) **- 3.** [without interruption] : **two hours ~** deux heures d'affilée ⇔ n solide m.

solidarity [ˌsɒlɪ'dærətɪ] n solidarité f.

solid fuel n combustible m solide.

solidify [sə'lɪdɪfaɪ] (pt & pp -ied) vi se solidifier.

solidly ['sɒlɪdlɪ] adv **- 1.** [sturdily] solidement **- 2.** [completely] tout à fait, absolument **- 3.** [without interruption] sans s'arrêter, sans interruption.

soliloquy [sə'lɪləkwɪ] (pl -ies) n soliloque m.

solitaire [ˌsɒlɪ'teə'] n **- 1.** [jewel, board game] solitaire m **- 2.** Am [card game] réussite f, patience f.

solitary ['sɒlɪtrɪ] adj **- 1.** [lonely, alone] solitaire **- 2.** [just one] seul(e).

solitary confinement n isolement m cellulaire.

solitude ['sɒlɪtjuːd] n solitude f.

solo ['səʊləʊ] (pl -s) ⇔ adj solo (inv) ⇔ n solo m ⇔ adv en solo.

soloist ['səʊləʊɪst] n soliste mf.

Solomon Islands ['sɒləmən-] npl : **the ~** les îles fpl Salomon ; **in the ~** dans les îles Salomon.

solstice ['sɒlstɪs] n solstice m.

soluble ['sɒljʊbl] adj soluble.

solution [sə'luːʃn] n **- 1.** [to problem] : **~ (to)** solution f (de) **- 2.** [liquid] solution f.

solve [sɒlv] vt résoudre.

solvency ['sɒlvənsɪ] n solvabilité f.

solvent ['sɒlvənt] ⇔ adj FIN solvable ⇔ n dissolvant m, solvant m.

solvent abuse *n* usage *m* de solvants.

Som. *(abbr of* **Somerset)** *comté anglais.*

Somali [sə'mɑːlɪ] ◇ *adj* somali(e), somalien(enne) ◇ *n* - **1.** [person] Somali *m*, -e *f*, Somalien *m*, -enne *f* - **2.** [language] somali *m*.

Somalia [sə'mɑːlɪə] *n* Somalie *f*; **in ~** en Somalie.

sombre Br, **somber** Am ['sɒmbə'] *adj* sombre.

some [sʌm] ◇ *adj* - **1.** [a certain amount, number of] : **~ meat** de la viande ; **~ money** de l'argent ; **~ coffee** du café ; **~ sweets** des bonbons - **2.** [fairly large number or quantity of] quelque ; **I had ~ difficulty getting here** j'ai eu quelque mal à venir ici ; **I've known him for ~ years** je le connais depuis plusieurs années OR pas mal d'années ; **we haven't seen them for ~ time** ça fait quelque temps qu'on ne les a pas vus - **3.** *(contrastive use)* [certain] : **~ jobs are better paid than others** certains boulots sont mieux rémunérés que d'autres ; **~ people like his music** il y en a qui aiment sa musique - **4.** [in imprecise statements] quelque, quelconque ; **she married ~ writer or other** elle a épousé un écrivain quelconque OR quelque écrivain ; **there must be ~ mistake** il doit y avoir erreur - **5.** inf [very good] : **that was ~ party!** c'était une soirée formidable!, quelle soirée! - **6.** inf iro [not very good] : **~ party that was!** tu parles d'une soirée! ; **~ help you are!** tu parles d'une aide!, beaucoup tu m'aides! ◇ *pron* - **1.** [a certain amount] : **can I have ~?** [money, milk, coffee etc] est-ce que je peux en prendre? ; **~ of it is mine** une partie est à moi - **2.** [a certain number] quelques-uns (quelques-unes), certains (certaines) ; **can I have ~?** [books, pens, potatoes etc] est-ce que je peux en prendre (quelques-uns)? ; **~ (of them) left early** quelques-uns d'entre eux sont partis tôt ; **~ say he lied** certains disent OR il y en a qui disent qu'il a menti ◇ *adv* quelque, environ ; **there were ~ 7,000 people there** il y avait quelque OR environ 7 000 personnes.

somebody ['sʌmbədɪ] ◇ *pron* quelqu'un ◇ *n* : **he really thinks he's ~** il se prend pour OR se croit quelqu'un.

someday ['sʌmdeɪ] *adv* un jour, un de ces jours.

somehow ['sʌmhaʊ], **someway** Am ['sʌmweɪ] *adv* - **1.** [by some action] d'une manière ou d'une autre - **2.** [for some reason] pour une raison ou pour une autre.

someone ['sʌmwʌn] *pron* quelqu'un.

someplace Am = **somewhere.**

somersault ['sʌməsɔːlt] ◇ *n* cabriole *f*, culbute *f* ◇ *vi* faire une cabriole OR culbute.

something ['sʌmθɪŋ] ◇ *pron* - **1.** [unknown thing] quelque chose ; **~ odd/interesting** quelque chose de bizarre/d'intéressant ; **or ~** inf ou quelque chose comme ça - **2.** [useful thing] : **(at least) that's ~** c'est déjà quelque chose ; **there's ~ in what you say** il y a du vrai dans ce que vous dites - **3.** phr : **that's really ~!** ce n'est pas rien! ; **she's ~ of a cook** elle est assez bonne cuisinière ◇ *adv* : **~ like, ~ in the region of** environ, à peu près.

sometime ['sʌmtaɪm] ◇ *adj* ancien(enne) ◇ *adv* un de ces jours ; **~ last week** la semaine dernière.

sometimes ['sʌmtaɪmz] *adv* quelquefois, parfois.

someway Am = **somehow.**

somewhat ['sʌmwɒt] *adv* quelque peu.

somewhere Br ['sʌmweə'], **someplace** Am ['sʌmpleɪs] *adv* - **1.** [unknown place] quelque part ; **~ else** ailleurs ; **~ near here** près d'ici - **2.** [used in approximations] environ, à peu près - **3.** phr : **to be getting ~** avancer, faire des progrès.

son [sʌn] *n* fils *m*.

sonar ['səʊnɑː'] *n* sonar *m*.

sonata [sə'nɑːtə] *n* sonate *f*.

song [sɒŋ] *n* chanson *f*; [of bird] chant *m*, ramage *m*; **for a ~** inf [cheaply] pour une bouchée de pain ; **to make a ~ and dance about sthg** inf faire toute une histoire OR tout un plat à propos de qqch.

songbook ['sɒŋbʊk] *n* recueil *m* de chansons.

sonic ['sɒnɪk] *adj* sonique.

sonic boom *n* bang *m*.

son-in-law *(pl* **sons-in-law)** *n* gendre *m*, beau-fils *m*.

sonnet ['sɒnɪt] *n* sonnet *m*.

sonny ['sʌnɪ] *n* inf fiston *m*.

soon [suːn] *adv* - **1.** [before long] bientôt ; **~ after** peu après - **2.** [early] tôt ; **write back ~** réponds-moi vite ; **how ~ will it be ready?** ce sera prêt quand?, dans combien de temps est-ce que ce sera prêt? ; **as ~ as** dès que, aussitôt que - **3.** phr : **I'd just as ~ ...** je préférerais ..., j'aimerais autant ...

sooner ['suːnə'] *adv* - **1.** [in time] plus tôt ; **no ~ ... than ...** à peine ... que ... ; **~ or later** tôt ou tard ; **the ~ the better** le plus tôt sera le mieux - **2.** [expressing preference] : **I would ~ ...** je préférerais ..., j'aimerais mieux ...

soot [sʊt] *n* suie *f*.

soothe [suːð] vt calmer, apaiser.

soothing ['suːðɪŋ] adj - **1.** [pain-relieving] lénifiant(e); lénitif(ive) - **2.** [music, words] apaisant(e).

sooty ['sʊtɪ] (compar -ier ; superl -iest) adj couvert(e) de suie.

sop [sɒp] n pej : ~ (to) concession f (à).

SOP (abbr of standard operating procedure) n marche à suivre normale.

sophisticated [sə'fɪstɪkeɪtɪd] adj - **1.** [stylish] raffiné(e), sophistiqué(e) - **2.** [intelligent] averti(e) - **3.** [complicated] sophistiqué(e), très perfectionné(e).

sophistication [sə,fɪstɪ'keɪʃn] n - **1.** [stylishness] raffinement m, sophistication f - **2.** [intelligence] intelligence f - **3.** [complexity] sophistication f, perfectionnement m.

sophomore ['sɒfəmɔːr] n Am étudiant m, -e f de seconde année.

soporific [,sɒpə'rɪfɪk] adj soporifique.

sopping ['sɒpɪŋ] adj : ~ (wet) tout trempé (toute trempée).

soppy ['sɒpɪ] (compar -ier ; superl -iest) adj inf - **1.** [sentimental - book, film] à l'eau de rose ; [- person] sentimental(e) - **2.** [silly] bêta(asse), bête.

soprano [sə'prɑːnəʊ] (pl -s) n [person] soprano mf ; [voice] soprano m.

sorbet ['sɔːbeɪ] n sorbet m.

sorcerer ['sɔːsərər] n sorcier m.

sordid ['sɔːdɪd] adj sordide.

sore [sɔːr] ⬦ adj - **1.** [painful] douloureux(euse) ; to have a ~ throat avoir mal à la gorge - **2.** Am [upset] fâché(e), contrarié(e) - **3.** literary [great] : to be in ~ need of sthg avoir grandement besoin de qqch ⬦ n plaie f.

sorely ['sɔːlɪ] adv literary [needed] grandement.

sorority [sə'rɒrətɪ] n Am club m d'étudiantes.

sorrel ['sɒrəl] n oseille f.

sorrow ['sɒrəʊ] n peine f, chagrin m.

sorrowful ['sɒrəʊfʊl] adj triste, affligé(e).

sorry ['sɒrɪ] (compar -ier ; superl -iest) ⬦ adj - **1.** [expressing apology, disappointment, sympathy] désolé(e) ; to be ~ about sthg s'excuser pour qqch ; to be ~ for sthg regretter qqch ; to be ~ to do sthg être désolé OR regretter de faire qqch ; to be OR feel ~ for sb plaindre qqn ; to be OR feel ~ for o.s. s'apitoyer sur son sort - **2.** [poor] : in a ~ state en piteux état, dans un triste état ⬦ excl - **1.** [expressing apology] pardon!, excusez-moi! ; ~, we're sold out désolé, on n'en a plus - **2.** [asking for repetition] pardon?, comment? - **3.** [to correct oneself] non, pardon OR je veux dire.

sort [sɔːt] ⬦ n genre m, sorte f, espèce f ; what ~ of car have you got? qu'est-ce que tu as comme voiture? ; ~ of [rather] plutôt, quelque peu ; a ~ of une espèce OR sorte de ⬦ vt trier, classer.

➠ **sorts** npl : of ~s si on veut, si on peut dire ; to be out of ~s ne pas être dans son assiette, être patraque.

➠ **sort out** vt sep - **1.** [classify] ranger, classer - **2.** [solve] résoudre.

sortie ['sɔːtiː] n sortie f.

sorting office ['sɔːtɪŋ-] n centre m de tri.

sort-out n Br inf : to have a ~ faire du rangement.

SOS (abbr of save our souls) n SOS m.

so-so inf ⬦ adj quelconque ⬦ adv comme ci comme ça.

soufflé ['suːfleɪ] n soufflé m.

sought [sɔːt] pt & pp ⮑ seek.

sought-after adj recherché(e), demandé(e).

soul [səʊl] n - **1.** [gen] âme f ; I didn't see a ~ je n'ai pas vu âme qui vive - **2.** [music] soul m.

soul-destroying [-dɪ,strɔɪɪŋ] adj abrutissant(e).

soulful ['səʊlfʊl] adj [look] expressif(ive) ; [song etc] sentimental(e).

soulless ['səʊllɪs] adj [job] abrutissant(e) ; [place] sans âme.

soul mate n âme f sœur.

soul music n soul m.

soul-searching n (U) examen m de conscience.

sound [saʊnd] ⬦ adj - **1.** [healthy - body] sain(e), en bonne santé ; [- mind] sain - **2.** [sturdy] solide - **3.** [reliable - advice] judicieux(euse), sage ; [- investment] sûr(e) ⬦ adv : to be ~ asleep dormir à poings fermés, dormir d'un sommeil profond ⬦ n son m ; [particular sound] bruit m, son m ; I don't like the ~ of that fig cela ne me dit rien qui vaille ; by the ~ of it ... d'après ce que j'ai compris ... ⬦ vt [alarm, bell] sonner ; to ~ one's horn klaxonner ⬦ vi - **1.** [make a noise] sonner, retentir ; to ~ like sthg ressembler à qqch - **2.** [seem] sembler, avoir l'air ; to ~ like sthg avoir l'air de qqch, sembler être qqch.

➠ **sound out** vt sep : to ~ sb out (on OR about) sonder qqn (sur).

sound barrier n mur m du son.

sound bite n petite phrase f (prononcée par un homme politique etc à la radio ou à la télévision pour frapper les esprits).

soundcard ['saʊndkɑːd] n COMPUT carte f son.

sound effects *npl* bruitage *m*, effets *mpl* sonores.

sounding ['saʊndɪŋ] *n* NAUT & fig sondage *m*.

sounding board *n* - **1.** THEATRE abat-voix *m* inv - **2.** fig [person] *personne sur laquelle on peut essayer une nouvelle idée.*

soundly ['saʊndlɪ] *adv* - **1.** [beaten] à plates coutures - **2.** [sleep] profondément.

soundness ['saʊndnɪs] *n* [of argument] solidité *f*, validité *f* ; [of theory, method] fiabilité *f*.

soundproof ['saʊndpruːf] *adj* insonorisé(e).

soundtrack ['saʊndtræk] *n* bande-son *f*.

sound wave *n* onde *f* sonore.

soup [suːp] *n* soupe *f*, potage *m*.
◆ **soup up** *vt sep* inf [car] gonfler le moteur de.

soup kitchen *n* soupe *f* populaire.

soup plate *n* assiette *f* creuse OR à soupe.

soup spoon *n* cuiller *f* à soupe.

sour ['saʊə'] ◇ *adj* - **1.** [taste, fruit] acide, aigre - **2.** [milk] aigre ; **to go** OR **turn ~** tourner à l'aigre ; fig [relationship] mal tourner, tourner au vinaigre - **3.** [ill-tempered] aigre, acerbe ◇ *vt* fig faire tourner au vinaigre, faire mal tourner ◇ *vi* tourner au vinaigre, mal tourner.

source [sɔːs] *n* - **1.** [gen] source *f* - **2.** [cause] origine *f*, cause *f*.

sour cream *n* crème *f* aigre.

sour grapes *n* (U) inf : **what he said was just ~** il a dit ça par dépit.

sourness ['saʊənɪs] *n* - **1.** [of taste, fruit] aigreur *f*, acidité *f* - **2.** [of milk, person] aigreur *f*.

south [saʊθ] ◇ *n* - **1.** [direction] sud *m* - **2.** [region] : **the ~** le sud ; **the South of France** le Sud de la France, le Midi (de la France) ◇ *adj* sud *(inv)* ; [wind] du sud ◇ *adv* au sud, vers le sud ; **~ of** au sud de.

South Africa *n* Afrique *f* du Sud ; **in ~** en Afrique du Sud ; **the Republic of ~** la République d'Afrique du Sud.

South African ◇ *adj* sud-africain(e) ◇ *n* [person] Sud-Africain *m*, -e *f*.

South America *n* Amérique *f* du Sud ; **in ~** en Amérique du Sud.

South American ◇ *adj* sud-américain(e) ◇ *n* [person] Sud-Américain *m*, -e *f*.

southbound ['saʊθbaʊnd] *adj* qui se dirige vers le sud ; [carriageway] sud *(inv)*.

South Carolina [-,kærə'laɪnə] *n* Caroline *f* du Sud ; **in ~** en Caroline du Sud.

South Dakota [-də'kəʊtə] *n* Dakota *m* du Sud ; **in ~** dans le Dakota du Sud.

southeast [,saʊθ'iːst] ◇ *n* - **1.** [direction] sud-est *m* - **2.** [region] : **the ~** le sud-est ◇ *adj* au sud-est, du sud-est ; [wind] du sud-est ◇ *adv* au sud-est, vers le sud-est ; **~ of** au sud-est de.

Southeast Asia *n* Asie *f* du Sud-Est ; **in ~** en Asie du Sud-Est.

southeasterly [,saʊθ'iːstəlɪ] *adj* au sud-est, du sud-est ; [wind] du sud-est ; **in a ~ direction** vers le sud-est.

southeastern [,saʊθ'iːstən] *adj* du sud-est, au sud-est.

southerly ['sʌðəlɪ] *adj* au sud, du sud ; [wind] du sud ; **in a ~ direction** vers le sud.

southern ['sʌðən] *adj* du sud ; [France] du Midi.

Southern Africa *n* Afrique *f* australe ; **in ~** en Afrique australe.

Southerner ['sʌðənə'] *n* habitant *m*, -e *f* du Sud.

South Korea *n* Corée *f* du Sud ; **in ~** en Corée du Sud.

South Korean ◇ *adj* sud-coréen(enne) ◇ *n* Sud-Coréen *m*, -enne *f*.

South Pole *n* : **the ~** le pôle Sud.

South Vietnam *n* Sud Viêt-Nam *m* ; **in ~** au Sud Viêt-Nam.

South Vietnamese ◇ *adj* sud-vietnamien(enne) ◇ *n* Sud-Vietnamien *m*, -enne *f*.

southward ['saʊθwəd] ◇ *adj* au sud, du sud ◇ *adv* = **southwards**.

southwards ['saʊθwədz] *adv* vers le sud.

southwest [,saʊθ'west] ◇ *n* - **1.** [direction] sud-ouest *m* - **2.** [region] : **the ~** le sud-ouest ◇ *adj* au sud-ouest, du sud-ouest ; [wind] du sud-ouest ◇ *adv* au sud-ouest, vers le sud-ouest ; **~ of** au sud-ouest de.

southwesterly [,saʊθ'westəlɪ] *adj* au sud-ouest, du sud-ouest ; [wind] du sud-ouest ; **in a ~ direction** vers le sud-ouest.

southwestern [,saʊθ'westən] *adj* au sud-ouest, du sud-ouest.

South Yemen *n* Yémen *m* du Sud ; **in ~** au Yémen du Sud.

souvenir [,suːvə'nɪə'] *n* souvenir *m*.

sou'wester [saʊ'westə'] *n* [hat] suroît *m*.

sovereign ['sɒvrɪn] ◇ *adj* souverain(e) ◇ *n* - **1.** [ruler] souverain *m*, -e *f* - **2.** [coin] souverain *m*.

sovereignty ['sɒvrɪntɪ] *n* souveraineté *f*.

soviet ['səʊvɪət] *n* soviet *m*.
◆ **Soviet** ◇ *adj* soviétique ◇ *n* [person] Soviétique *mf*.

Soviet Union n : the (former) ~ l'(ex-)Union f soviétique.

sow[1] [səʊ] (pt -ed ; pp sown OR -ed) vt lit & fig semer.

sow[2] [saʊ] n truie f.

sown [səʊn] pp ⊳ sow[1].

sox [sɒks] ⊳ bobby sox.

soya ['sɔɪə] n soja m.

soy(a) bean ['sɔɪ(ə)-] n graine f de soja.

soy sauce [sɔɪ-] n sauce f au soja.

sozzled ['sɒzld] adj Br inf rond(e), pompette.

spa [spɑ:] n station f thermale.

spa bath n Jacuzzi® m.

space [speɪs] ⬦ n - **1.** [gap, roominess, outer space] espace m ; [on form] blanc m, espace ; **to stare into** ~ regarder dans le vide - **2.** [room] place f - **3.** [of time] : **within** OR **in the** ~ **of ten minutes** en l'espace de dix minutes ; ~ **of time** laps m de temps ⬦ comp spatial(e) ⬦ vt espacer.

◆ **space out** vt sep espacer.

space age n : **the** ~ l'ère f spatiale.

◆ **space-age** adj de l'ère f spatiale.

space bar n barre f d'espacement.

space capsule n capsule f spatiale.

spacecraft ['speɪskrɑ:ft] (pl inv) n vaisseau m spatial.

spaceman ['speɪsmæn] (pl -men [-men]) n astronaute m, cosmonaute m.

space probe n sonde f spatiale.

spaceship ['speɪsʃɪp] n vaisseau m spatial.

space shuttle n navette f spatiale.

space station n station f orbitale OR spatiale.

spacesuit ['speɪssu:t] n combinaison f spatiale.

spacewoman ['speɪs,wʊmən] (pl -women [-,wɪmɪn]) n astronaute f, cosmonaute f.

spacing ['speɪsɪŋ] n TYPO espacement m.

spacious ['speɪʃəs] adj spacieux(euse).

spade [speɪd] n - **1.** [tool] pelle f - **2.** [playing card] pique m.

◆ **spades** npl pique m ; **the six of** ~**s** le six de pique.

spadework ['speɪdwɜ:k] n inf gros m du travail.

spaghetti [spə'getɪ] n (U) spaghettis mpl.

Spain [speɪn] n Espagne f ; **in** ~ en Espagne.

span [spæn] (pt & pp -ned ; cont -ning) ⬦ pt ⊳ spin ⬦ n - **1.** [in time] espace m de temps, durée f - **2.** [range] éventail m, gamme f - **3.** [of bird, plane] envergure f - **4.** [of bridge] travée f ; [of arch] ouverture f ⬦ vt

- **1.** [in time] embrasser, couvrir - **2.** [subj : bridge] franchir.

spandex ['spændeks] n Am textile proche du Lycra®.

spangled ['spæŋgld] adj : ~ **(with)** pailleté(e) (de).

Spaniard ['spænjəd] n Espagnol m, -e f.

spaniel ['spænjəl] n épagneul m.

Spanish ['spænɪʃ] ⬦ adj espagnol(e) ⬦ n [language] espagnol m ⬦ npl : **the** ~ les Espagnols.

Spanish America n Amérique f hispanophone.

Spanish American ⬦ adj - **1.** [in US] hispanique - **2.** [in Latin America] hispano-américain(e) ⬦ n - **1.** [in US] Hispanique mf - **2.** [in Latin America] Hispano-Américain m, -e f.

spank [spæŋk] ⬦ n fessée f ⬦ vt donner une fessée à, fesser.

spanner ['spænə'] n clé f à écrous.

spar [spɑ:'] (pt & pp -red ; cont -ring) ⬦ n espar m ⬦ vi - **1.** BOXING s'entraîner à la boxe - **2.** [verbally] : **to** ~ **(with)** se disputer (avec).

spare [speə'] ⬦ adj - **1.** [surplus] de trop ; [component, clothing etc] de réserve, de rechange ; ~ **bed** lit m d'appoint - **2.** [available - seat, time, tickets] disponible ⬦ n - **1.** [tyre] pneu m de rechange OR de secours - **2.** [part] pièce f détachée OR de rechange ⬦ vt - **1.** [make available - staff, money] se passer de ; [- time] disposer de ; **to have an hour to** ~ avoir une heure de battement OR de libre ; **with a minute to** ~ avec une minute d'avance ; **with £2 to** ~ et il nous/lui etc reste encore deux livres - **2.** [not harm] épargner - **3.** [not use] épargner, ménager ; **to** ~ **no expense** ne pas regarder à la dépense - **4.** [save from] : **to** ~ **sb sthg** épargner qqch à qqn, éviter qqch à qqn.

spare part n pièce f détachée OR de rechange.

spare room n chambre f d'amis.

spare time n (U) temps m libre, loisirs mpl.

spare tyre n - **1.** AUT pneu m de rechange OR de secours - **2.** hum [fat waist] bourrelet m (de graisse).

spare wheel n roue f de secours.

sparing ['speərɪŋ] adj : **to be** ~ **with** OR **of sthg** être économe de qqch, ménager qqch.

sparingly ['speərɪŋlɪ] adv [use] avec modération ; [spend] avec parcimonie.

spark [spɑ:k] ⬦ n lit & fig étincelle f ⬦ vt [interest] susciter, éveiller ; [scandal] provoquer ; [debate] déclencher.

sparking plug ['spɑ:kɪŋ-] Br = spark plug.

sparkle ['spɑːkl] ◇ n (U) [of eyes, jewel] éclat m ; [of stars] scintillement m ◇ vi étinceler, scintiller.

sparkler ['spɑːklər] n [firework] cierge m merveilleux.

sparkling wine ['spɑːklɪŋ-] n vin m mousseux.

spark plug n bougie f.

sparrow ['spærəʊ] n moineau m.

sparse ['spɑːs] adj clairsemé(e), épars(e).

spartan ['spɑːtn] adj austère, de spartiate.

spasm ['spæzm] n - **1.** MED spasme m ; [of coughing] quinte f - **2.** [of emotion] accès m.

spasmodic [spæz'mɒdɪk] adj spasmodique.

spastic ['spæstɪk] MED ◇ adj handicapé(e) moteur ◇ n handicapé m, -e f moteur.

spat [spæt] pt & pp ⊏⊐ spit.

spate [speɪt] n [of attacks etc] série f.

spatial ['speɪʃl] adj spatial(e).

spatter ['spætər] ◇ vt éclabousser ◇ vi gicler.

spatula ['spætjʊlə] n spatule f.

spawn [spɔːn] ◇ n (U) frai m, œufs mpl ◇ vt fig donner naissance à, engendrer ◇ vi [fish, frog] frayer.

spay [speɪ] vt châtrer.

SPCA (abbr of **Society for the Prevention of Cruelty to Animals**) n société américaine protectrice des animaux, ≃ SPA f.

SPCC (abbr of **Society for the Prevention of Cruelty to Children**) n société américaine pour la protection de l'enfance.

speak [spiːk] (pt **spoke** ; pp **spoken**) ◇ vt - **1.** [say] dire ; **to ~ ill of sb** dire du mal de qqn - **2.** [language] parler ◇ vi parler ; **to ~ to OR with sb** parler à qqn ; **to ~ to sb about sthg** parler de qqch à qqn ; **to ~ about sb/sthg** parler de qqn/qqch ; **to ~ well/highly of sb** dire du bien/beaucoup de bien de, qqn ; **nobody to ~ of** pas grand-monde ; **nothing to ~ of** pas grand-chose.
- **so to speak** adv pour ainsi dire.
- **speak for** vt fus [represent] parler pour, parler au nom de ; **~ for yourself!** parle pour toi! ; **it ~s for itself** cela tombe sous le sens, c'est évident.
- **speak out** vi oser prendre la parole ; **to ~ out against** s'élever contre, se dresser contre.
- **speak up** vi - **1.** [support] : **to ~ up for sb/sthg** parler en faveur de qqn/qqch, soutenir qqn/qqch - **2.** [speak louder] parler plus fort.

speaker ['spiːkər] n - **1.** [person talking] personne f qui parle - **2.** [person making speech] orateur m - **3.** [of language] : **a German ~** une personne qui parle allemand - **4.** [loudspeaker] haut-parleur m.

speaking ['spiːkɪŋ] ◇ adv : **politically ~** politiquement parlant ; **~ as** [in the position of] en tant que ; **~ of** [on the subject of] à propos de ◇ n (U) discours m, parole f.

speaking clock n Br horloge f parlante.

spear [spɪər] ◇ n lance f ◇ vt transpercer d'un coup de lance.

spearhead ['spɪəhed] ◇ n fer m de lance ◇ vt [campaign] mener ; [attack] être le fer de lance de.

spec [spek] n Br inf : **on ~** à tout hasard.

special ['speʃl] ◇ adj - **1.** [gen] spécial(e) - **2.** [needs, effort, attention] particulier(ère) ◇ n - **1.** [on menu] plat m du jour - **2.** TV émission f spéciale.

special agent n [spy] agent m secret.

special constable n Br auxiliaire m de police.

special correspondent n envoyé m spécial.

special delivery n (U) [service] exprès m, envoi m par exprès ; **by ~** en exprès.

special effects npl effets mpl spéciaux.

specialist ['speʃəlɪst] ◇ adj spécialisé(e) ◇ n spécialiste mf.

speciality [ˌspeʃɪ'ælətɪ] (pl -ies), **specialty** Am ['speʃltɪ] (pl -ies) n spécialité f.

specialize, -ise ['speʃəlaɪz] vi : **to ~ (in)** se spécialiser (dans).

specially ['speʃəlɪ] adv - **1.** [specifically] spécialement ; [on purpose] exprès - **2.** [particularly] particulièrement.

special needs [- niːdz] n : **~ children** enfants ayant des difficultés scolaires ; **~ teacher** enseignant spécialisé s'occupant d'enfants ayant des difficultés scolaires.

special offer n promotion f.

special school n école f pour enfants handicapés, établissement m spécialisé.

specialty n Am = speciality.

species ['spiːʃiːz] (pl inv) n espèce f.

specific [spə'sɪfɪk] adj - **1.** [particular] particulier(ère), précis(e) - **2.** [precise] précis(e) - **3.** [unique] : **~ to** propre à.
- **specifics** npl détails mpl.

specifically [spə'sɪfɪklɪ] adv - **1.** [particularly] particulièrement, spécialement - **2.** [precisely] précisément.

specification [ˌspesɪfɪ'keɪʃn] n stipulation f.
- **specifications** npl TECH caractéristiques fpl techniques, spécification f.

specify ['spesɪfaɪ] (*pt* & *pp* **-ied**) *vt* préciser, spécifier.

specimen ['spesɪmən] *n* - **1.** [example] exemple *m*, spécimen *m* - **2.** [of blood] prélèvement *m* ; [of urine] échantillon *m*.

specimen copy *n* spécimen *m*.

specimen signature *n* spécimen *m* de signature

speck [spek] *n* - **1.** [small stain] toute petite tache *f* - **2.** [of dust] grain *m*.

speckled ['spekld] *adj* : ~ **(with)** tacheté(e) de.

specs [speks] *npl* inf [glasses] lunettes *fpl*.

spectacle ['spektəkl] *n* spectacle *m*.
➣ **spectacles** *npl* Br [glasses] lunettes *fpl*.

spectacular [spek'tækjʊlər] ◇ *adj* spectaculaire ◇ *n* pièce *f* OR revue *f* à grand spectacle.

spectate [spek'teɪt] *vi* regarder, être là en tant que spectateur.

spectator [spek'teɪtər] *n* spectateur *m*, -trice *f*.

spectator sport *n* sport *m* que l'on regarde en tant que spectateur.

spectre Br, **specter** Am ['spektər] *n* spectre *m*.

spectrum ['spektrəm] (*pl* **-tra** [-trə]) *n* - **1.** PHYSICS spectre *m* - **2.** fig [variety] gamme *f*.

speculate ['spekjʊleɪt] ◇ *vt* : **to ~ that ...** émettre l'hypothèse que ... ◇ *vi* - **1.** [wonder] faire des conjectures - **2.** FIN spéculer.

speculation [ˌspekjʊ'leɪʃn] *n* - **1.** [gen] spéculation *f* - **2.** [conjecture] conjectures *fpl*.

speculative ['spekjʊlətɪv] *adj* spéculatif(ive).

speculator ['spekjʊleɪtər] *n* FIN spéculateur *m*, -trice *f*.

sped [sped] *pt* & *pp* ▷ **speed.**

speech [spiːtʃ] *n* - **1.** *(U)* [ability] parole *f* - **2.** [formal talk] discours *m* ; **to give** OR **make a ~** faire un discours - **3.** THEATRE texte *m* - **4.** [manner of speaking] façon *f* de parler - **5.** [dialect] parler *m*.

speech day *n* Br distribution *f* des prix.

speech impediment *n* défaut *m* d'élocution.

speechless ['spiːtʃlɪs] *adj* : ~ **(with)** muet(ette) (de).

speech processing *n* traitement *m* de la parole.

speech recognition *n* COMPUT reconnaissance *f* de la parole.

speech therapist *n* orthophoniste *mf*.

speech therapy *n* orthophonie *f*.

speed [spiːd] (*pt* & *pp* **-ed** OR **sped**) ◇ *n* vitesse *f* ; [of reply, action] vitesse, rapidité *f* ◇ *vi* - **1.** [move fast] : **to ~ along** aller à toute allure OR vitesse ; **to ~ away** démarrer à toute allure - **2.** AUT [go too fast] rouler trop vite, faire un excès de vitesse.
➣ **speed up** ◇ *vt sep* [person] faire aller plus vite ; [work, production] accélérer ◇ *vi* aller plus vite ; [car] accélérer.

speedboat ['spiːdbəʊt] *n* hors-bord *m inv*.

speed bump *n* dos-d'âne *m inv*.

speeding ['spiːdɪŋ] *n (U)* excès *m* de vitesse.

speed limit *n* limitation *f* de vitesse.

speedo ['spiːdəʊ] (*pl* **-s**) *n* Br inf compteur *m* (de vitesse).

speedometer [spɪ'dɒmɪtər] *n* compteur *m* (de vitesse).

speed trap *n* radar *m* de contrôle.

speedway ['spiːdweɪ] *n* - **1.** *(U)* SPORT course *f* de motos - **2.** Am [road] voie *f* express.

speedy ['spiːdɪ] (*compar* **-ier** ; *superl* **-iest**) *adj* rapide.

speleology [ˌspiːlɪ'ɒlədʒɪ] *n* spéléologie *f*.

spell [spel] (Br *pt* & *pp* **spelt** OR **-ed**, Am *pt* & *pp* **-ed**) ◇ *n* - **1.** [period of time] période *f* - **2.** [enchantment] charme *m* ; [words] formule *f* magique ; **to cast** OR **put a ~ on sb** jeter un sort à qqn, envoûter qqn ◇ *vt* - **1.** [word, name] écrire - **2.** fig [signify] signifier ◇ *vi* épeler.
➣ **spell out** *vt sep* - **1.** [read aloud] épeler - **2.** [explain] : **to ~ sthg out (for** OR **to sb)** expliquer qqch clairement (à qqn).

spellbound ['spelbaʊnd] *adj* subjugué(e).

spell-check ◇ *vt* [text, file, document] vérifier l'orthographe de ◇ *n* vérification *f* orthographique.

spell-checker [-tʃekər] *n* correcteur *m* OR vérificateur *m* orthographique.

spelling ['spelɪŋ] *n* orthographe *f*.

spelt [spelt] Br *pt* & *pp* ▷ **spell.**

spend [spend] (*pt* & *pp* **spent**) *vt* - **1.** [pay out] : **to ~ money (on)** dépenser de l'argent (pour) - **2.** [time, life] passer ; [effort] consacrer.

spender ['spendər] *n* : **to be a big ~** être très dépensier(ère), dépenser beaucoup.

spending ['spendɪŋ] *n (U)* dépenses *fpl*.

spending money *n* argent *m* de poche.

spending power *n (U)* pouvoir *m* d'achat.

spendthrift ['spendθrɪft] *n* dépensier *m*, -ère *f*.

spent [spent] ◇ *pt* & *pp* ▷ **spend** ◇ *adj*

[fuel, match, ammunition] utilisé(e) ; [patience, energy] épuisé(e).

sperm [spɜːm] (*pl inv* OR -**s**) *n* sperme *m*.

spermicidal cream [ˌspɜːmɪˈsaɪdl-] *n* crème *f* spermicide.

sperm whale *n* cachalot *m*.

spew [spjuː] *vt* & *vi* vomir.

sphere [sfɪəʳ] *n* sphère *f*.

spherical [ˈsferɪkl] *adj* sphérique.

sphincter [ˈsfɪŋktəʳ] *n* sphincter *m*.

sphinx [sfɪŋks] (*pl* -**es** [-iːz]) *n* sphinx *m*.

spice [spaɪs] ⬦ *n* - **1.** CULIN épice *f* - **2.** *(U)* fig [excitement] piment *m* ⬦ *vt* - **1.** CULIN épicer - **2.** fig [add excitement to] pimenter, relever.

spick-and-span [ˌspɪkənˈspæn] *adj* impeccable, nickel (*inv*).

spicy [ˈspaɪsɪ] (*compar* -**ier** ; *superl* -**iest**) *adj* - **1.** CULIN épicé(e) - **2.** fig [story] pimenté(e), piquant(e).

spider [ˈspaɪdəʳ] *n* araignée *f*.

spider's web, spiderweb Am [ˈspaɪdə-web] *n* toile *f* d'araignée.

spidery [ˈspaɪdərɪ] *adj* en pattes d'araignée.

spiel [ʃpiːl] *n* inf baratin *m*.

spike [spaɪk] *n* [metal] pointe *f*, lance *f* ; [of plant] piquant *m* ; [of hair] épi *m*.
⬧ **spikes** *npl* Br chaussures *fpl* à pointes.

spiky [ˈspaɪkɪ] (*compar* -**ier** ; *superl* -**iest**) *adj* [branch, plant] hérissé(e) de piquants ; [hair] en épi.

spill [spɪl] (Br *pt* & *pp* **spilt** OR -**ed**, Am *pt* & *pp* -**ed**) ⬦ *vt* renverser ⬦ *vi* - **1.** [liquid] se répandre - **2.** [people] : **to ~ out of a building** sortir d'un bâtiment en masse.

spillage [ˈspɪlɪdʒ] *n* [of oil] déversement *m*.

spilt [spɪlt] Br *pt* & *pp* ⟼ **spill**.

spin [spɪn] (*pt* **span** OR **spun** ; *pp* **spun**, *cont* -**ning**) ⬦ *n* - **1.** [turn] : **to give sthg a ~** faire tourner qqch - **2.** AERON vrille *f* - **3.** inf [in car] tour *m* - **4.** SPORT effet *m* ⬦ *vt* - **1.** [wheel] faire tourner ; **to ~ a coin** jouer à pile ou face - **2.** [washing] essorer - **3.** [thread, wool, cloth] filer - **4.** SPORT [ball] donner de l'effet à ⬦ *vi* tourner, tournoyer ; **my head is spinning** j'ai la tête qui tourne.
⬧ **spin out** *vt sep* [money, story] faire durer.

spina bifida [ˌspaɪnəˈbɪfɪdə] *n* spina-bifida *m*.

spinach [ˈspɪnɪdʒ] *n (U)* épinards *mpl*.

spinal column [ˈspaɪnl-] *n* colonne *f* vertébrale.

spinal cord [ˈspaɪnl-] *n* moelle *f* épinière.

spindle [ˈspɪndl] *n* - **1.** TECH broche *f*, axe *m* - **2.** [for textiles] fuseau *m*.

spindly [ˈspɪndlɪ] (*compar* -**ier** ; *superl* -**iest**) *adj* grêle, chétif(ive).

spin doctor *n* pej *expression désignant la personne qui au sein d'un parti politique est chargée de promouvoir l'image de celui-ci.*

spin-dry *vt* Br essorer.

spin-dryer *n* Br essoreuse *f*.

spine [spaɪn] *n* - **1.** ANAT colonne *f* vertébrale - **2.** [of book] dos *m* - **3.** [of plant, hedgehog] piquant *m*.

spine-chilling *adj* qui glace le sang.

spineless [ˈspaɪnlɪs] *adj* [feeble] faible, qui manque de cran.

spinner [ˈspɪnəʳ] *n* [of thread] fileur *m*, -euse *f*.

spinning [ˈspɪnɪŋ] *n* [of thread] filage *m*.

spinning top *n* toupie *f*.

spin-off *n* [by-product] dérivé *m*.

spinster [ˈspɪnstəʳ] *n* célibataire *f* ; pej vieille fille *f*.

spiral [ˈspaɪərəl] (Br *pt* & *pp* -**led** ; *cont* -**ling**, Am *pt* & *pp* -**ed** ; *cont* -**ing**) ⬦ *adj* spiral(e) ⬦ *n* spirale *f* ⬦ *vi* - **1.** [staircase, smoke] monter en spirale - **2.** [amount, prices] monter en flèche ; **to ~ downwards** descendre en flèche.

spiral staircase *n* escalier *m* en colimaçon.

spire [spaɪəʳ] *n* flèche *f*.

spirit [ˈspɪrɪt] ⬦ *n* - **1.** [gen] esprit *m* ; **to enter into the ~ of sthg** participer à qqch de bon cœur - **2.** *(U)* [determination] caractère *m*, courage *m* ⬦ *vt* : **to ~ sb out of a building** faire sortir qqn d'un bâtiment de façon secrète.
⬧ **spirits** *npl* - **1.** [mood] humeur *f* ; **to be in high ~s** être gai(e) ; **to be in low ~s** être déprimé(e) - **2.** [alcohol] spiritueux *mpl*.

spirited [ˈspɪrɪtɪd] *adj* fougueux(euse) ; [performance] interprété(e) avec brio.

spirit level *n* niveau *m* à bulle d'air.

spiritual [ˈspɪrɪtʃuəl] *adj* spirituel(elle).

spiritualism [ˈspɪrɪtʃuəlɪzm] *n* spiritisme *m*.

spiritualist [ˈspɪrɪtʃuəlɪst] *n* spirite *mf*.

spit [spɪt] (Br *pt* & *pp* **spat**, *cont* -**ting**, Am *pt* & *pp* **spit**, *cont* -**ting**) ⬦ *n* - **1.** *(U)* [spittle] crachat *m* ; [saliva] salive *f* - **2.** [skewer] broche *f* ⬦ *vi* cracher ⬦ *v impers* Br : **it's spitting** il tombe quelques gouttes.
⬧ **spit out** *vt sep* cracher ; **~ it out!** inf accouche!

spite [spaɪt] ⬦ *n* rancune *f* ; **to do sthg out of** OR **from ~** faire qqch par malice ⬦ *vt* contrarier.
⬧ **in spite of** *prep* en dépit de, malgré ; **to do sthg in ~ of o.s.** faire qqch malgré soi.

spiteful ['spaɪtfʊl] *adj* malveillant(e).
spitting image ['spɪtɪŋ-] *n* : **to be the ~ of sb** être le portrait (tout) craché de qqn.
spittle ['spɪtl] *n (U)* crachat *m*.
splash [splæʃ] ◇ *n* - **1.** [sound] plouf *m* - **2.** [small quantity] goutte *f* - **3.** [of colour, light] tache *f* ◇ *vt* éclabousser ◇ *vi* - **1.** [person] : **to ~ about** *OR* **around** barboter - **2.** [liquid] jaillir.
◆ **splash out** **inf** ◇ *vt sep* [money] claquer ◇ *vi* : **to ~ out (on)** dépenser une fortune (pour).
splashdown ['splæʃdaʊn] *n* amerrissage *m*.
splashguard ['splæʃgɑːd] *n* **Am** garde-boue *m inv*.
splay [spleɪ] ◇ *vt* écarter ◇ *vi* : **to ~ (out)** s'écarter.
spleen [spliːn] *n* - **1.** ANAT rate *f* - **2.** *(U)* **fig** [anger] mauvaise humeur *f*.
splendid ['splendɪd] *adj* splendide ; [work, holiday, idea] excellent(e).
splendidly ['splendɪdlɪ] *adv* - **1.** [marvellously] de façon splendide, splendidement - **2.** [magnificently] magnifiquement.
splendour Br, **splendor Am** ['splendəʳ] *n* splendeur *f*.
splice [splaɪs] *vt* [join - gen] coller ; [- rope] épisser.
splint [splɪnt] *n* attelle *f*.
splinter ['splɪntəʳ] ◇ *n* éclat *m* ◇ *vt* [wood] fendre en éclats ; [glass] briser en éclats ◇ *vi* [wood] se fendre en éclats ; [glass] se briser en éclats.
splinter group *n* groupe *m* dissident.
split [splɪt] (*pt* & *pp* **split** ; *cont* **-ting**) ◇ *n* - **1.** [in wood] fente *f* - **2.** [in garment - tear] déchirure *f* ; [- by design] échancrure *f* - **3.** POL : **~ (in)** division *f OR* scission *f* (au sein de) - **4.** [difference] : **~ between** écart *m* entre ◇ *vt* - **1.** [wood] fendre ; [clothes] déchirer - **2.** POL diviser - **3.** [share] partager ; **to ~ the difference fig** couper la poire en deux ◇ *vi* - **1.** [wood] se fendre ; [clothes] se déchirer - **2.** POL se diviser ; [road, path] se séparer - **3. Am inf** [leave] se casser.
◆ **splits** *npl* : **to do the ~s** faire le grand écart.
◆ **split off** ◇ *vt sep* : **to ~ sthg off (from)** enlever *OR* détacher qqch (de) ◇ *vi* : **to ~ off (from)** se détacher (de).
◆ **split up** ◇ *vt sep* : **to ~ sthg up (into)** diviser *OR* séparer qqch (en) ◇ *vi* [group, couple] se séparer.
split end *n* [in hair] fourche *f*.
split-level *adj* [house] à deux niveaux.
split pea *n* pois *m* cassé.
split personality *n* : **to have a ~** souffrir d'un dédoublement de la personnalité.
split screen *n* écran *m* divisé.
split second *n* fraction *f* de seconde.
splitting ['splɪtɪŋ] *adj* : **I've got a ~ headache** j'ai un mal de tête épouvantable *OR* atroce.
splutter ['splʌtəʳ] ◇ *n* [of person] bafouillage *m* ◇ *vi* [person] bredouiller, bafouiller ; [engine] tousser ; [fire] crépiter.
spoil [spɔɪl] (*pt* & *pp* **-ed** OR **spoilt**) *vt* - **1.** [ruin - holiday] gâcher, gâter ; [- view] gâter ; [- food] gâter, abîmer - **2.** [over-indulge, treat well] gâter ; **to ~ o.s.** s'offrir une gâterie, se faire plaisir.
◆ **spoils** *npl* butin *m*.
spoiled [spɔɪld] *adj* = **spoilt**.
spoilsport ['spɔɪlspɔːt] *n* trouble-fête *mf inv*.
spoilt [spɔɪlt] ◇ *pt* & *pp* ▷ **spoil** ◇ *adj* [child] gâté(e).
spoke [spəʊk] ◇ *pt* ▷ **speak** ◇ *n* rayon *m*.
spoken ['spəʊkn] *pp* ▷ **speak**.
spokesman ['spəʊksmən] (*pl* **-men** [-mən]) *n* porte-parole *m inv*.
spokesperson ['spəʊks,pɜːsn] *n* porte-parole *m inv*.
spokeswoman ['spəʊks,wʊmən] (*pl* **-women** [-,wɪmɪn]) *n* porte-parole *m inv*.
sponge [spʌndʒ] (**Br** *cont* **spongeing**, **Am** *cont* **sponging**) ◇ *n* - **1.** [for cleaning, washing] éponge *f* - **2.** [cake] gâteau *m OR* biscuit *m* de Savoie ◇ *vt* éponger ◇ *vi* **inf** : **to ~ off sb** taper qqn.
sponge bag *n* **Br** trousse *f* de toilette.
sponge cake *n* gâteau *m OR* biscuit *m* de Savoie.
sponge pudding *n* **Br** pudding *m*.
sponger ['spʌndʒəʳ] *n* **inf pej** parasite *m*.
spongy ['spʌndʒɪ] (*compar* **-ier** ; *superl* **-iest**) *adj* spongieux(euse).
sponsor ['spɒnsəʳ] ◇ *n* sponsor *m* ◇ *vt* - **1.** [finance, for charity] sponsoriser, parrainer - **2.** [support] soutenir.
sponsored walk [,spɒnsəd-] *n* *marche organisée pour recueillir des fonds.*

SPONSORED WALK

Les « sponsored walks » sont destinées à rassembler des fonds, chaque marcheur établissant une liste de personnes ayant accepté de donner une certaine somme d'argent par kilomètre parcouru. Le terme « sponsored » s'applique également à d'autres activités, sportives ou non : « sponsored swim », « sponsored parachute jump », etc.

sponsorship [ˈspɒnsəʃɪp] n sponsoring m, parrainage m.

spontaneity [ˌspɒntəˈneɪətɪ] n spontanéité f.

spontaneous [spɒnˈteɪnjəs] adj spontané(e).

spontaneously [spɒnˈteɪnjəslɪ] adv spontanément.

spoof [spuːf] n : ~ (of OR on) parodie f (de).

spook [spuːk] vt Am faire peur à.

spooky [ˈspuːkɪ] (compar -ier ; superl -iest) adj inf qui donne la chair de poule.

spool [spuːl] ◇ n [gen & COMPUT] bobine f ◇ vi faire un spooling.

spoon [spuːn] ◇ n cuillère f, cuiller f ◇ vt : to ~ sthg onto a plate verser qqch dans une assiette avec une cuillère.

spoon-feed vt nourrir à la cuillère ; to ~ sb fig mâcher le travail à qqn.

spoonful [ˈspuːnfʊl] (pl -s OR spoonsful [ˈspuːnsfʊl]) n cuillerée f.

sporadic [spəˈrædɪk] adj sporadique.

sport [spɔːt] ◇ n - 1. [game] sport m - 2. dated [cheerful person] chic type m/fille f ◇ vt arborer, exhiber.

◆ **sports** ◇ npl Br [sports day] réunion f sportive scolaire ◇ comp de sport.

sporting [ˈspɔːtɪŋ] adj - 1. [relating to sport] sportif(ive) - 2. [generous, fair] chic (inv) ; to have a ~ chance of doing sthg avoir des chances de faire qqch.

sports car [ˈspɔːts-] n voiture f de sport.

sports day n Br réunion f sportive scolaire.

sports jacket [ˈspɔːts-] n veste f sport.

sportsman [ˈspɔːtsmən] (pl -men [-mən]) n sportif m.

sportsmanship [ˈspɔːtsmənʃɪp] n sportivité f, esprit m sportif.

sports pages npl pages fpl des sports.

sports personality n personnalité f sportive.

sportswear [ˈspɔːtsweəʳ] n (U) vêtements mpl de sport.

sportswoman [ˈspɔːtsˌwʊmən] (pl -women [-ˌwɪmɪn]) n sportive f.

sporty [ˈspɔːtɪ] (compar -ier ; superl -iest) adj inf - 1. [person] sportif(ive) - 2. [car, clothes etc] chic (inv).

spot [spɒt] (pt & pp -ted ; cont -ting) ◇ n - 1. [mark, dot] tache f - 2. [pimple] bouton m - 3. [drop] goutte f - 4. inf [small amount] : to have a ~ of lunch manger un morceau ; to have a ~ of bother avoir quelques ennuis - 5. [place] endroit m ; on the ~ sur place ; to do sthg on the ~ faire qqch immédiatement OR sur-le-

champ - 6. RADIO & TV numéro m - 7. phr : to have a soft ~ for sb avoir un faible pour qqn ; to put sb on the ~ embarrasser qqn par des questions ◇ vt [notice] apercevoir.

spot check n contrôle m au hasard OR intermittent.

spotless [ˈspɒtlɪs] adj [clean] impeccable.

spotlight [ˈspɒtlaɪt] n [in theatre] projecteur m, spot m ; [in home] spot m ; to be in the ~ fig être en vedette.

spot-on adj Br inf absolument exact(e) OR juste, dans le mille.

spot price n prix m comptant.

spotted [ˈspɒtɪd] adj [pattern, material] à pois.

spotty [ˈspɒtɪ] (compar -ier ; superl -iest) adj - 1. Br [skin] boutonneux(euse) - 2. Am [patchy] irrégulier(ère).

spouse [spaʊs] n époux m, épouse f.

spout [spaʊt] ◇ n bec m ◇ vt pej débiter ◇ vi : to ~ from OR out of jaillir de.

sprain [spreɪn] ◇ n entorse f ◇ vt : to ~ one's ankle/wrist se faire une entorse à la cheville/au poignet, se fouler la cheville/le poignet.

sprang [spræŋ] pt ▷ spring.

sprat [spræt] n sprat m.

sprawl [sprɔːl] ◇ n (U) étendue f ◇ vi - 1. [person] être affalé(e) - 2. [city] s'étaler.

sprawling [ˈsprɔːlɪŋ] adj [city] tentaculaire.

spray [spreɪ] ◇ n - 1. (U) [of water] gouttelettes fpl ; [from sea] embruns mpl - 2. [container] bombe f, pulvérisateur m - 3. [of flowers] gerbe f ◇ vt [product] pulvériser ; [plants, crops] pulvériser de l'insecticide sur ◇ vi : to ~ over sb/sthg asperger qqn/qqch.

spray can n bombe f.

spray paint n peinture f en bombe.

spread [spred] (pt & pp spread) ◇ n - 1. (U) [food] pâte f à tartiner - 2. [of fire, disease] propagation f - 3. [of opinions] gamme f - 4. PRESS double page f ◇ vt - 1. [map, rug] étaler, étendre ; [fingers, arms, legs] écarter - 2. [butter, jam etc] : to ~ sthg (over) étaler qqch (sur) - 3. [disease, rumour, germs] répandre, propager - 4. [in time] : to be ~ over s'étaler sur - 5. [wealth, work] distribuer, répartir ◇ vi - 1. [disease, rumour] se propager, se répandre - 2. [water, cloud] s'étaler.

◆ **spread out** ◇ vt sep - 1. [distribute] : to be ~ out [people, houses etc] être dispersé(e) ; [city, forest] être étendu(e) - 2. [map, rug] étaler, étendre - 3. [fingers, arms, legs] écarter ◇ vi se disperser.

spread-eagled [-ˌiːgld] adj affalé(e).

spreadsheet [ˈspredʃiːt] n COMPUT tableur m.

spree [spriː] n : to go on a spending OR shopping ~ faire des folies.

sprig [sprɪg] n brin m.

sprightly ['spraɪtlɪ] (compar -ier ; superl -iest) adj alerte, fringant(e).

spring [sprɪŋ] (pt sprang ; pp sprung) ⬦ n - **1.** [season] printemps m ; **in** ~ au printemps - **2.** [coil] ressort m - **3.** [jump] saut m, bond m - **4.** [water source] source f ⬦ comp de printemps ⬦ vt - **1.** [make known suddenly] : **to** ~ **sthg on sb** annoncer qqch à qqn de but en blanc ; **to** ~ **a surprise on sb** surprendre qqn - **2.** [develop] : **to** ~ **a leak** faire eau ⬦ vi - **1.** [jump] sauter, bondir - **2.** [move suddenly] : **to** ~ **to one's feet** se lever d'un bond ; **to** ~ **into action** passer à l'action ; **to** ~ **to life** se mettre en marche - **3.** [originate] : **to** ~ **from** provenir de.

➡ **spring up** vi [problem] surgir, se présenter ; [friendship] naître ; [wind] se lever.

springboard ['sprɪŋbɔːd] n lit & fig tremplin m.

spring-clean ⬦ vt nettoyer de fond en comble ⬦ vi faire le nettoyage de printemps.

spring onion n Br ciboule f.

spring roll n Br rouleau m de printemps.

spring tide n marée f de vive-eau.

springtime ['sprɪŋtaɪm] n : **in (the)** ~ au printemps.

springy ['sprɪŋɪ] (compar -ier ; superl -iest) adj [carpet] moelleux(euse) ; [mattress, rubber] élastique.

sprinkle ['sprɪŋkl] vt : **to** ~ **water over** OR **on sthg, to** ~ **sthg with water** asperger qqch d'eau ; **to** ~ **salt** etc **over** OR **on sthg, to** ~ **sthg with salt** etc saupoudrer qqch de sel etc.

sprinkler ['sprɪŋklər] n [for water] arroseur m.

sprinkling ['sprɪŋklɪŋ] n [of water] quelques gouttes fpl ; [of sand] couche f légère ; **a** ~ **of people** quelques personnes.

sprint [sprɪnt] ⬦ n sprint m ⬦ vi sprinter.

sprinter ['sprɪntər] n sprinter m.

sprite [spraɪt] n lutin m.

spritzer ['sprɪtsər] n : **a white wine** ~ du vin blanc additionné d'eau de Seltz.

sprocket ['sprɒkɪt] n pignon m.

sprout [spraut] ⬦ n - **1.** [vegetable] : **(Brussels)** ~**s** choux mpl de Bruxelles - **2.** [shoot] pousse f ⬦ vt [leaves] produire ; **to** ~ **shoots** germer ⬦ vi - **1.** [grow] pousser - **2.** fig [buildings] : **to** ~ **(up)** surgir.

spruce [spruːs] ⬦ adj net (nette), pimpant(e) ⬦ n épicéa m.

➡ **spruce up** vt sep astiquer, briquer ; **to** ~ **o.s. up** se faire tout beau.

sprung [sprʌŋ] pp ▷ **spring.**

spry [spraɪ] (compar -ier ; superl -iest) adj vif (vive).

SPUC (abbr of **Society for the Protection of the Unborn Child**) n ligue contre l'avortement.

spud [spʌd] n inf patate f.

spun [spʌn] pt & pp ▷ **spin.**

spunk [spʌŋk] n (U) inf [courage] cran m.

spur [spɜːr] (pt & pp **-red** ; cont **-ring**) ⬦ n - **1.** [incentive] incitation f - **2.** [on rider's boot] éperon m ⬦ vt - **1.** [encourage] : **to** ~ **sb to do sthg** encourager OR inciter qqn à faire qqch - **2.** [bring about] provoquer.

➡ **on the spur of the moment** adv sur un coup de tête, sous l'impulsion du moment.

➡ **spur on** vt sep encourager.

spurious ['spuərɪəs] adj - **1.** [affection, interest] feint(e) - **2.** [argument, logic] faux (fausse).

spurn [spɜːn] vt repousser.

spurt [spɜːt] ⬦ n - **1.** [gush] jaillissement m - **2.** [of activity, energy] sursaut m - **3.** [burst of speed] accélération f ; **to put on a** ~ sprinter ⬦ vi - **1.** [gush] : **to** ~ **(out of** OR **from)** jaillir (de) - **2.** [run] foncer, sprinter.

sputter ['spʌtər] vi [engine] tousser, bafouiller ; [fire] crépiter.

spy [spaɪ] (pl spies, pt & pp spied) ⬦ n espion m ⬦ vt inf apercevoir ⬦ vi espionner, faire de l'espionnage ; **to** ~ **on sb** espionner qqn.

spying ['spaɪɪŋ] n (U) espionnage m.

spy satellite n satellite m espion.

Sq., sq. abbr of **square.**

squabble ['skwɒbl] ⬦ n querelle f ⬦ vi : **to** ~ **(about** OR **over)** se quereller (à propos de).

squad [skwɒd] n - **1.** [of police] brigade f - **2.** MIL peloton m - **3.** SPORT [group of players] équipe f (parmi laquelle la sélection sera faite).

squad car n voiture f de police.

squadron ['skwɒdrən] n escadron m.

squadron leader n Br commandant m.

squalid ['skwɒlɪd] adj sordide, ignoble.

squall [skwɔːl] n [storm] bourrasque f.

squalor ['skwɒlər] n (U) conditions fpl sordides.

squander ['skwɒndər] vt gaspiller.

square [skweər] ⬦ adj - **1.** [in shape] carré(e) ; **one** ~ **metre** Br un mètre carré ; **three metres** ~ trois mètres sur trois - **2.** [not owing money] : **to be** ~ être quitte - **3.** inf [unfashionable] vieux jeu (inv) ⬦ n - **1.** [shape] carré m - **2.** [in town] place f - **3.** inf [unfashionable person] : **he's a** ~ il est vieux jeu - **4. phr : to be back to ~ one** se retrouver au point de départ ◇ *vt* - **1.** MATH élever au carré - **2.** [reconcile] accorder.

➤ **square up** *vi* - **1.** [settle up] : **to ~ up with sb** régler ses comptes avec qqn - **2.** [for fight] : **to ~ up to sb** se mettre en posture de combat face à qqn ; **to ~ up to a problem** faire face à un problème.

squared ['skweəd] *adj* quadrillé(e).

square dance *n* quadrille *m*.

square deal *n* arrangement *m* équitable.

squarely ['skweəlɪ] *adv* - **1.** [directly] carrément - **2.** [honestly] honnêtement.

square meal *n* bon repas *m*.

square root *n* racine *f* carrée.

squash [skwɒʃ] ◇ *n* - **1.** SPORT squash *m* - **2.** Br [drink] : **orange ~** orangeade *f* - **3.** Am [vegetable] courge *f* ◇ *vt* écraser.

squat [skwɒt] (*compar* -**ter** ; *superl* -**test**, *pt* & *pp* -**ted** ; *cont* -**ting**) ◇ *adj* courtaud(e), ramassé(e) ◇ *n* Br [building] squat *m* ◇ *vi* - **1.** [crouch] : **to ~ (down)** s'accroupir - **2.** [in building] squatter.

squatter ['skwɒtəʳ] *n* Br squatter *m*.

squawk [skwɔːk] ◇ *n* cri *m* strident OR perçant ◇ *vi* pousser un cri strident OR perçant.

squeak [skwiːk] ◇ *n* - **1.** [of animal] petit cri *m* aigu - **2.** [of door, hinge] grincement *m* ◇ *vi* - **1.** [mouse] pousser un petit cri aigu - **2.** [door, hinge] grincer.

squeaky ['skwiːkɪ] (*compar* -**ier** ; *superl* -**iest**) *adj* [voice, door] grinçant(e) ; [shoes] qui craquent.

squeal [skwiːl] ◇ *n* - **1.** [of person, animal] cri *m* aigu - **2.** [of brakes] grincement *m ;* [of tyres] crissement *m* ◇ *vi* - **1.** [person, animal] pousser des cris aigus - **2.** [brakes] grincer ; [tyres] crisser.

squeamish ['skwiːmɪʃ] *adj* facilement dégoûté(e).

squeeze [skwiːz] ◇ *n* - **1.** [pressure] pression *f* - **2.** *inf* [squash] : **it was a ~** on était serrés comme des sardines ◇ *vt* - **1.** [press firmly] presser - **2.** [liquid, toothpaste] exprimer ; **to ~ information out of sb** soutirer OR arracher des informations à qqn - **3.** [cram] : **to ~ sthg into sthg** entasser qqch dans qqch ◇ *vi* : **to ~ into/under** se glisser dans/sous.

squeezebox ['skwiːzbɒks] *n* Br accordéon *m*.

squeezer ['skwiːzəʳ] *n :* **orange/lemon ~** presse-citron *m inv*.

squelch [skweltʃ] *vi* : **to ~ through mud** patauger dans la boue.

squib [skwɪb] *n* [firework] pétard *m ;* **it was a damp ~** ça a été une déception.

squid [skwɪd] (*pl inv* OR -**s**) *n* calmar *m*.

squiffy ['skwɪfɪ] (*compar* -**ier** ; *superl* -**iest**) *adj* Br *inf dated* pompette.

squiggle ['skwɪɡl] *n* gribouillis *m*.

squint [skwɪnt] ◇ *n* : **to have a ~** loucher, être atteint(e) de strabisme ◇ *vi* : **to ~ at sthg** regarder qqch en plissant les yeux.

squire ['skwaɪəʳ] *n* [landowner] propriétaire *m*.

squirm [skwɜːm] *vi* - **1.** [wriggle] se tortiller - **2.** *fig* [wince] avoir des haut-le-cœur ; **to ~ with embarrassment** ne plus savoir où se mettre.

squirrel [Br 'skwɪrəl, Am 'skwɜːrəl] *n* écureuil *m*.

squirt [skwɜːt] ◇ *vt* [water, oil] faire jaillir, faire gicler ; **to ~ sb/sthg with sthg** asperger qqn/qqch de qqch ◇ *vi* : **to ~ (out of)** jaillir (de), gicler (de).

Sr - **1.** *abbr of* **senior** - **2.** *abbr of* **sister**.

SRC *n* - **1.** (*abbr of* **Students' Representative Council**) *comité étudiant* - **2.** (*abbr of* **Science Research Council**) *conseil britannique de la recherche scientifique*.

Sri Lanka [ˌsriːˈlæŋkə] *n* Sri Lanka *m ;* **in ~** au Sri Lanka.

Sri Lankan [ˌsriːˈlæŋkn] ◇ *adj* sri lankais(e) ◇ *n* [person] Sri Lankais *m*, -e *f*.

SRN (*abbr of* **State Registered Nurse**) *n* en Grande-Bretagne, infirmier ou infirmière diplômé(e) d'État.

SS (*abbr of* **steamship**) SS.

SSA (*abbr of* **Social Security Administration**) *n* sécurité sociale américaine.

ssh [ʃ] *excl* chut!

SSSI (*abbr of* **Site of Special Scientific Interest**) *n* en Grande-Bretagne, site déclaré d'intérêt scientifique.

St - **1.** (*abbr of* **saint**) St, Ste - **2.** *abbr of* **Street**.

ST (*abbr of* **Standard Time**) *n heure légale*.

stab [stæb] (*pt* & *pp* -**bed** ; *cont* -**bing**) ◇ *n* - **1.** [with knife] coup *m* de couteau - **2.** *inf* [attempt] : **to have a ~ (at sthg)** essayer (qqch), tenter (qqch) - **3.** [twinge] : **~ of pain** élancement *m ;* **~ of guilt** remords *m* ◇ *vt* - **1.** [person] poignarder ; **to ~ sb to death** tuer qqn d'un coup/à coups de poignard - **2.** [food] piquer ◇ *vi* : **to ~ at sthg** frapper qqch.

stabbing ['stæbɪŋ] ◇ *adj* [pain] lancinant(e) ◇ *n* agression *f* à coups de couteau.

stability [stəˈbɪlətɪ] *n* stabilité *f*.

stabilize, -ise ['steɪbəlaɪz] ◇ *vt* stabiliser ◇ *vi* se stabiliser.

stabilizer ['steɪbəlaɪzəʳ] *n* stabilisateur *m*.

stable ['steɪbl] ◇ adj stable ◇ n écurie f.

stable lad n garçon m d'écurie.

staccato [stə'kɑːtəʊ] adj [note] piqué(e) ; [sound, voice] saccadé(e).

stack [stæk] ◇ n - **1.** [pile] pile f - **2.** inf [large amount] : ~s OR a ~ of des tas de, un tas de ◇ vt - **1.** [pile up] empiler - **2.** [fill] : **to be ~ed with** être encombré de.

◆ **stack up** vi Am inf être à la hauteur.

stadium ['steɪdjəm] (pl -diums OR -dia [-djə]) n stade m.

staff [stɑːf] ◇ n [employees] personnel m ; [of school] personnel enseignant, professeurs mpl ◇ vt pourvoir en personnel.

staffing ['stɑːfɪŋ] n dotation f en personnel ; ~ levels les besoins mpl en personnel.

staff nurse n Br infirmier m, -ère f.

staff room n salle f des professeurs.

Staffs [stæfs] (abbr of **Staffordshire**) comté anglais.

stag [stæg] (pl inv OR -s) n cerf m.

stage [steɪdʒ] ◇ n - **1.** [phase] étape f, phase f, stade m - **2.** [platform] scène f ; on ~ sur scène ; **to set the ~ for sthg** préparer la voie à qqch - **3.** [acting profession] : **the ~** le théâtre ◇ vt - **1.** THEATRE monter, mettre en scène - **2.** [organize] organiser.

stagecoach ['steɪdʒkəʊtʃ] n diligence f.

stage door n entrée f des artistes.

stage fright n trac m.

stagehand ['steɪdʒhænd] n machiniste m.

stage-manage vt lit & fig mettre en scène.

stage name n nom m de scène.

stagflation [stæg'fleɪʃn] n stagflation f.

stagger ['stægər] ◇ vt - **1.** [astound] stupéfier - **2.** [working hours] échelonner ; [holidays] étaler ◇ vi tituber.

staggering ['stægərɪŋ] adj stupéfiant(e).

staging ['steɪdʒɪŋ] n mise f en scène.

stagnant ['stægnənt] adj stagnant(e).

stagnate [stæg'neɪt] vi stagner.

stagnation [stæg'neɪʃn] n stagnation f.

stag party n soirée f entre hommes ; [before wedding] soirée où un futur marié enterre sa vie de garçon avec ses amis.

staid [steɪd] adj guindé(e), collet monté.

stain [steɪn] ◇ n [mark] tache f ◇ vt [discolour] tacher.

stained [steɪnd] adj - **1.** [marked] taché(e) - **2.** [coloured] coloré(e).

stained glass [ˌsteɪnd-] n (U) [windows] vitraux mpl.

stainless steel ['steɪnlɪs-] n acier m inoxydable, Inox® m.

stain remover [-ˌrɪmuːvər] n détachant m.

stair [steər] n marche f.

◆ **stairs** npl escalier m.

staircase ['steəkeɪs] n escalier m.

stairway ['steəweɪ] n escalier m.

stairwell ['steəwel] n cage f d'escalier.

stake [steɪk] ◇ n - **1.** [share] : **to have a ~ in sthg** avoir des intérêts dans qqch - **2.** [wooden post] poteau m - **3.** [in gambling] enjeu m ◇ vt : **to ~ money (on** OR **upon)** jouer OR miser de l'argent (sur) ; **to ~ one's reputation (on)** jouer OR risquer sa réputation (sur) ; **to ~ a claim to sthg** revendiquer qqch.

◆ **stakes** npl enjeux mpl.

◆ **at stake** adv en jeu.

stakeout ['steɪkaʊt] n esp Am [police surveillance] surveillance f.

stalactite ['stæləktaɪt] n stalactite f.

stalagmite ['stæləgmaɪt] n stalagmite f.

stale [steɪl] adj - **1.** [food, water] pas frais (fraîche) ; [bread] rassis(e) ; [air] qui sent le renfermé - **2.** [person] qui manque d'entrain.

stalemate ['steɪlmeɪt] n - **1.** [deadlock] impasse f - **2.** CHESS pat m.

staleness ['steɪlnɪs] n [of food] manque m de fraîcheur.

stalk [stɔːk] ◇ n - **1.** [of flower, plant] tige f - **2.** [of leaf, fruit] queue f ◇ vt [hunt] traquer ◇ vi : **to ~ in/out** entrer/sortir d'un air hautain.

stall [stɔːl] ◇ n - **1.** [in street, market] éventaire m, étal m ; [at exhibition] stand m - **2.** [in stable] stalle f ◇ vt - **1.** AUT caler - **2.** [delay - person] faire patienter ◇ vi - **1.** AUT caler - **2.** [delay] essayer de gagner du temps.

◆ **stalls** npl Br [in cinema, theatre] orchestre m.

stallholder ['stɔːlˌhəʊldər] n Br marchand m qui possède un éventaire.

stallion ['stæljən] n étalon m.

stalwart ['stɔːlwət] ◇ adj [loyal] fidèle ◇ n pilier m.

stamen ['steɪmən] n étamine f.

stamina ['stæmɪnə] n (U) résistance f.

stammer ['stæmər] ◇ n bégaiement m ◇ vi bégayer.

stamp [stæmp] ◇ n - **1.** [for letter] timbre m - **2.** [tool] tampon m - **3.** fig [of authority etc] marque f ◇ vt - **1.** [mark by stamping] tamponner - **2.** [stomp] : **to ~ one's foot** taper du pied - **3.** [envelope, postcard] timbrer, affranchir ◇ vi - **1.** [stomp] taper du pied - **2.** [tread heavily] : **to ~ on sthg** marcher sur qqch.

◆ **stamp out** vt sep [fire] éteindre en piétinant ; [opposition] éliminer ; [corruption, crime] supprimer ; [disease] éradiquer.

stamp album *n* album *m* de timbres.

stamp-collecting [-kə,lektɪŋ] *n* philatélie *f*.

stamp collector *n* collectionneur *m*, -euse *f* de timbres, philatéliste *mf*.

stamp duty *n* Br droit *m* de timbre

stamped addressed envelope ['stæmptə,drest-] *n* Br enveloppe *f* affranchie pour la réponse.

stampede [stæm'piːd] ⬦ *n* débandade *f* ⬦ *vi* s'enfuir à la débandade.

stamp machine *n* distributeur *m* de timbres-poste.

stance [stæns] *n* lit & fig position *f*.

stand [stænd] (*pt* & *pp* stood) ⬦ *n* - 1. [stall] stand *m*; [selling newspapers] kiosque *m* - 2. [supporting object] : umbrella ~ porte-parapluies *m inv*; hat ~ porte-chapeaux *m inv* - 3. SPORT tribune *f* - 4. MIL résistance *f*; to make a ~ résister - 5. [public position] position *f*; to take a ~ on sthg prendre position sur qqch - 6. Am JUR barre *f*; to take the ~ comparaître à la barre ⬦ *vt* - 1. [place] mettre (debout), poser (debout) - 2. [withstand, tolerate] supporter - 3. [treat] : to ~ sb a meal/a drink payer à déjeuner/à boire à qqn - 4. JUR : to ~ trial comparaître en jugement - 5. [be likely] : to ~ to do sthg risquer de faire qqch ⬦ *vi* - 1. [be upright - person] être OR se tenir debout ; [- object] se trouver ; [- building] se dresser ; ~ still! ne bouge pas!, reste tranquille! - 2. [stand up] se lever - 3. [liquid] reposer - 4. [offer] tenir toujours ; [decision] demeurer valable - 5. [be in particular state] : as things ~ ... vu l'état actuel des choses ... ; unemployment/production ~s at ... le nombre de chômeurs/la production est de ... - 6. [have opinion] : where do you ~ on ...? quelle est votre position sur ...? - 7. Br POL se présenter - 8. Am [park car] : 'no ~ing' 'stationnement interdit'.

⬦ **stand aside** *vi* s'écarter.

⬦ **stand back** *vi* reculer.

⬦ **stand by** ⬦ *vt fus* - 1. [person] soutenir - 2. [statement, decision] s'en tenir à ⬦ *vi* - 1. [in readiness] : to ~ by (for sthg/to do sthg) être prêt(e) (pour qqch/pour faire qqch) - 2. [remain inactive] rester là.

⬦ **stand down** *vi* [resign] démissionner.

⬦ **stand for** *vt fus* - 1. [signify] représenter - 2. [tolerate] supporter, tolérer.

⬦ **stand in** *vi* : to ~ in for sb remplacer qqn.

⬦ **stand out** *vi* ressortir.

⬦ **stand up** ⬦ *vt sep* inf [boyfriend, girlfriend] poser un lapin à ⬦ *vi* - 1. [rise from seat] se lever ; ~ up! debout! - 2. [claim, evidence] être accepté(e).

⬦ **stand up for** *vt fus* défendre.

⬦ **stand up to** *vt fus* - 1. [weather, heat etc] résister à - 2. [person, boss] tenir tête à.

standard ['stændəd] ⬦ *adj* - 1. [normal - gen] normal(e) ; [- size] standard (*inv*) - 2. [accepted] correct(e) - 3. [basic] de base ⬦ *n* - 1. [level] niveau *m* - 2. [point of reference] critère *m*; TECH norme *f* - 3. [flag] étendard *m*.

⬦ **standards** *npl* [principles] valeurs *fpl*.

standard-bearer *n* fig porte-drapeau *m*.

standardize, -ise ['stændədaɪz] *vt* standardiser.

standard lamp *n* Br lampadaire *m*.

standard of living (*pl* standards of living) *n* niveau *m* de vie.

standard time *n* heure *f* légale.

standby ['stændbaɪ] (*pl* -s) ⬦ *n* [person] remplaçant *m*, -e *f*; on ~ prêt à intervenir ⬦ *comp* [ticket, flight] stand-by (*inv*).

stand-in *n* remplaçant *m*, -e *f*.

standing ['stændɪŋ] ⬦ *adj* [invitation, army] permanent(e) ; [joke] continuel(elle) ⬦ *n* - 1. [reputation] importance *f*, réputation *f* - 2. [duration] : of long ~ de longue date ; we're friends of 20 years' ~ nous sommes amis depuis 20 ans.

standing committee *n* comité *m* permanent.

standing order *n* prélèvement *m* automatique.

standing ovation *n* : to give sb a ~ se lever pour applaudir qqn.

standing room *n* (*U*) places *fpl* debout.

standoffish [,stænd'ɒfɪʃ] *adj* distant(e).

standpipe ['stændpaɪp] *n* colonne *f* d'alimentation.

standpoint ['stændpɔɪnt] *n* point *m* de vue.

standstill ['stændstɪl] *n* : at a ~ [traffic, train] à l'arrêt ; [negotiations, work] paralysé(e) ; to come to a ~ [traffic, train] s'immobiliser ; [negotiations, work] cesser.

stank [stæŋk] *pt* ⬦ stink.

stanza ['stænzə] *n* strophe *f*.

staple ['steɪpl] ⬦ *adj* [principal] principal(e), de base ⬦ *n* - 1. [for paper] agrafe *f* - 2. [principal commodity] produit *m* de base ⬦ *vt* agrafer.

staple diet *n* nourriture *f* de base.

staple gun *n* agrafeuse *f* (professionnelle).

stapler ['steɪplə'] *n* agrafeuse *f*.

star [stɑːr] (*pt* & *pp* -red ; *cont* -ring) ⬦ *n* - 1. [gen] étoile *f* - 2. [celebrity] vedette *f*, star *f* - 3. [asterisk] astérisque *m* ⬦ *comp* [quality] de star ; ~ performer vedette *f* ⬦ *vt* CINEMA &

THEATRE avoir pour vedette ⬦ *vi* : **to ~ (in)** être la vedette (de).
➡ **stars** *npl* horoscope *m*.

star attraction *n* attraction *f* principale, clou *m*.

starboard [ˈstɑːbəd] ⬦ *adj* de tribord ⬦ *n* : **to ~** à tribord.

starch [stɑːtʃ] *n* amidon *m*.

starched [stɑːtʃt] *adj* amidonné(e).

starchy [ˈstɑːtʃɪ] (*compar* -**ier** ; *superl* -**iest**) *adj* [food] féculent(e).

stardom [ˈstɑːdəm] *n* (U) célébrité *f*.

stare [steəʳ] ⬦ *n* regard *m* fixe ⬦ *vi* : **to ~ at sb/sthg** fixer qqn/qqch du regard.

starfish [ˈstɑːfɪʃ] (*pl inv* OR -**es** [-iːz]) *n* étoile *f* de mer.

stark [stɑːk] ⬦ *adj* - **1.** [room, decoration] austère ; [landscape] désolé(e) - **2.** [reality, fact] à l'état brut ; [contrast] dur(e) ⬦ *adv* : **~ naked** tout nu (toute nue), à poil.

starlight [ˈstɑːlaɪt] *n* lumière *f* des étoiles.

starling [ˈstɑːlɪŋ] *n* étourneau *m*.

starlit [ˈstɑːlɪt] *adj* [night] étoilé(e) ; [countryside] illuminé(e) par les étoiles.

starry [ˈstɑːrɪ] (*compar* -**ier** ; *superl* -**iest**) *adj* étoilé(e).

starry-eyed [-ˈaɪd] *adj* innocent(e).

Stars and Stripes *n* : **the ~** le drapeau des États-Unis, la bannière étoilée.

THE STARS AND STRIPES

Ceci n'est que l'une des nombreuses appellations populaires du drapeau américain, au même titre que « Old Glory » ou « Stars and Bars ». Les 50 étoiles représentent les 50 États actuels, alors que les rayures rouges et blanches symbolisent les 13 États fondateurs de l'Union. Les Américains sont très fiers de leur bannière étoilée et il n'est pas rare de la voir flotter devant les maisons particulières.

---

star sign *n* signe *m* du zodiaque.

star-studded *adj* avec de nombreuses vedettes.

start [stɑːt] ⬦ *n* - **1.** [beginning] début *m* ; **to make a good/bad ~** bien/mal commencer ; **for a ~** pour commencer, d'abord - **2.** [jump] sursaut *m* - **3.** [starting place] départ *m* - **4.** [time advantage] avance *f* ⬦ *vt* - **1.** [begin] commencer ; **to ~ doing** OR **to do sthg** commencer à faire qqch - **2.** [turn on - machine] mettre en marche ; [- engine, vehicle] démarrer, mettre en marche - **3.** [set up - business, band] créer ⬦ *vi* - **1.** [begin] commencer, débuter ; **to ~ with** pour commencer, d'abord - **2.** [func-

tion - machine] se mettre en marche ; [- car] démarrer - **3.** [begin journey] partir - **4.** [jump] sursauter - **5.** *inf* [be annoying] : **don't (you) ~!** ne commence pas, toi!

➡ **start off** ⬦ *vt sep* [meeting] ouvrir, commencer ; [rumour] faire naître ; [discussion] entamer, commencer ⬦ *vi* - **1.** [begin] commencer ; [begin job] débuter - **2.** [leave on journey] partir.

➡ **start on** *vt fus* entamer.

➡ **start out** *vi* - **1.** [in job] débuter - **2.** [leave on journey] partir.

➡ **start up** ⬦ *vt sep* - **1.** [business] créer ; [shop] ouvrir - **2.** [car, engine] mettre en marche ⬦ *vi* - **1.** [begin] commencer - **2.** [machine] se mettre en route ; [car, engine] démarrer.

starter [ˈstɑːtəʳ] *n* - **1.** Br [of meal] hors-d'œuvre *m inv* - **2.** AUT démarreur *m* - **3.** [to begin race] starter *m*.

starter motor *n* démarreur *m*.

starter pack *n* [information] *informations de base nécessaires pour commencer une activité* ; [equipment] kit *m* de base.

starting block [ˈstɑːtɪŋ-] *n* starting-block *m*, bloc *m* de départ.

starting point [ˈstɑːtɪŋ-] *n* point *m* de départ.

starting price [ˈstɑːtɪŋ-] *n* cote *f* de départ.

startle [ˈstɑːtl] *vt* faire sursauter.

startling [ˈstɑːtlɪŋ] *adj* surprenant(e).

start-up *n* (U) - **1.** [launch] création *f* (d'entreprise) ; **~ costs** frais *mpl* de création d'une entreprise - **2.** [new company] start-up *f*.

starvation [stɑːˈveɪʃn] *n* faim *f*.

starve [stɑːv] ⬦ *vt* - **1.** [deprive of food] affamer - **2.** *fig* [deprive] : **to ~ sb of sthg** priver qqn de qqch ⬦ *vi* - **1.** [have no food] être affamé(e) ; **to ~ to death** mourir de faim - **2.** *inf* [be hungry] avoir très faim, crever OR mourir de faim.

Star Wars *n* la Guerre des Étoiles (*nom populaire de l'Initiative de Défense Stratégique, programme militaire spatial du Président Reagan*).

state [steɪt] ⬦ *n* état *m* ; **he's not in a fit ~ to drive** il n'est pas en état de conduire ; **to be in a ~** être dans tous ses états ⬦ *comp* d'État ⬦ *vt* - **1.** [express - reason] donner ; [- name and address] décliner ; **to ~ that ...** déclarer que ... - **2.** [specify] préciser.

➡ **State** *n* : **the State** l'État *m*.

➡ **States** *npl* : **the States** les États-Unis *mpl*.

state-controlled *adj* étatisé(e), sous contrôle de l'État.

State Department *n* Am ≃ ministère *m* des Affaires étrangères.

state education n Br enseignement m public.

stateless ['steɪtlɪs] adj apatride.

stately ['steɪtlɪ] (compar -ier ; superl -iest) adj majestueux(euse).

stately home n Br château m.

statement ['steɪtmənt] n - 1. [declaration] déclaration f - 2. JUR déposition f - 3. [from bank] relevé m de compte.

state of affairs n état m des choses.

state of emergency n état m d'urgence.

state of mind (pl states of mind) n humeur f.

state-of-the-art adj tout dernier (toute dernière) ; [technology] de pointe.

state-owned [-'əʊnd] adj national(e), d'État.

state school n école f publique.

state secret n secret m d'État.

state's evidence n Am : to turn ~ témoigner contre ses complices.

stateside ['steɪtsaɪd] Am <> adj des États-Unis <> adv aux États-Unis.

statesman ['steɪtsmən] (pl -men [-mən]) n homme m d'État.

statesmanship ['steɪtsmənʃɪp] n (U) habileté f politique.

static ['stætɪk] <> adj statique <> n (U) parasites mpl.

static electricity n électricité f statique.

station ['steɪʃn] <> n - 1. RAIL gare f ; [for buses, coaches] gare routière - 2. RADIO station f - 3. [building] poste m - 4. fml [rank] rang m <> vt - 1. [position] placer, poster - 2. MIL poster.

stationary ['steɪʃnərɪ] adj immobile.

stationer ['steɪʃnər] n papetier m, -ère f ; ~'s (shop) papeterie f.

stationery ['steɪʃnərɪ] n (U) [equipment] fournitures fpl de bureau ; [paper] papier m à lettres.

station house n Am poste m de police.

stationmaster ['steɪʃn,mɑːstər] n chef m de gare.

station wagon n Am break m.

statistic [stə'tɪstɪk] n statistique f.
statistics n (U) [science] statistique f.

statistical [stə'tɪstɪkl] adj statistique ; [expert] en statistiques ; [report] de statistiques.

statistician [,stætɪ'stɪʃn] n statisticien m, -enne f.

statue ['stætʃuː] n statue f.

statuesque [,stætʃʊ'esk] adj sculptural(e).

statuette [,stætʃʊ'et] n statuette f.

stature ['stætʃər] n - 1. [height, size] stature f, taille f - 2. [importance] envergure f.

status ['steɪtəs] n (U) - 1. [legal or social position] statut m - 2. [prestige] prestige m.

status quo [-'kwəʊ] n : the ~ le statu quo.

status symbol n signe m extérieur de richesse.

statute ['stætjuːt] n loi f.

statute book n : the ~ ≃ le code, les textes mpl de loi.

statutory ['stætjʊtrɪ] adj statutaire.

staunch [stɔːntʃ] <> adj loyal(e) <> vt [flow] arrêter ; [blood] étancher.

stave [steɪv] (pt & pp -d OR stove) n MUS portée f.
stave off vt sep [disaster, defeat] éviter ; [hunger] tromper.

stay [steɪ] <> vi - 1. [not move away] rester ; to ~ put ne pas bouger - 2. [as visitor - with friends] passer quelques jours ; [- in town, country] séjourner ; to ~ in a hotel descendre à l'hôtel - 3. [continue, remain] rester, demeurer ; to ~ away from sb ne pas s'approcher de qqn ; to ~ away from a place ne pas aller à un endroit ; to ~ out of sthg ne pas se mêler de qqch - 4. Scot [reside] habiter <> n [visit] séjour m.
stay in vi rester chez soi, ne pas sortir.
stay on vi rester (plus longtemps).
stay out vi - 1. [from home] ne pas rentrer - 2. [strikers] rester en grève.
stay up vi ne pas se coucher, veiller ; to ~ up late se coucher tard.

stayer ['steɪər] n Br [horse] stayer m ; [person] personne f qui a de l'endurance.

staying power ['steɪɪŋ-] n endurance f.

St Bernard [Br -'bɜːnəd, Am -bər'nɑːrd] n saint-bernard m inv.

STD n - 1. (abbr of subscriber trunk dialling) téléphone interurbain - 2. (abbr of sexually transmitted disease) MST f.

stead [sted] n : to stand sb in good ~ être utile à qqn.

steadfast ['stedfɑːst] adj ferme, résolu(e) ; [supporter] loyal(e).

steadily ['stedɪlɪ] adv - 1. [gradually] progressivement - 2. [regularly - breathe] régulièrement ; [- move] sans arrêt - 3. [calmly] de manière imperturbable.

steady ['stedɪ] (compar -ier ; superl -iest, pt & pp -ied) <> adj - 1. [gradual] progressif(ive) - 2. [regular] régulier(ère) - 3. [not shaking] ferme ; to hold sthg ~ tenir qqch bien OR sans bouger - 4. [calm - voice] calme ; [- stare] imperturbable - 5. [stable - job, relationship] stable

- **6.** [sensible] sérieux(euse) ⬦ *vt* - **1.** [stop from shaking] empêcher de bouger ; **to ~ o.s.** se remettre d'aplomb - **2.** [control - nerves] calmer ; **to ~ o.s.** retrouver son calme.

steak [steɪk] *n* steak *m*, bifteck *m* ; [of fish] darne *f*.

steakhouse ['steɪkhaʊs, *pl* -haʊzɪz] *n* grill *m*, grill-room *m*.

steal [stiːl] (*pt* stole ; *pp* stolen) ⬦ *vt* voler, dérober ; **to ~ a look at** jeter un regard furtif à ⬦ *vi* - **1.** [take illegally] voler - **2.** [move secretly] se glisser.

stealing ['stiːlɪŋ] *n (U)* vol *m*.

stealth [stelθ] *n :* **by ~** en secret, discrètement.

stealthy ['stelθɪ] (*compar* -ier ; *superl* -iest) *adj* furtif(ive).

steam [stiːm] ⬦ *n (U)* vapeur *f* ; **to let off ~** fig se défouler ; **to run out of ~** fig s'essouffler ⬦ *comp* à vapeur ⬦ *vt* CULIN cuire à la vapeur ⬦ *vi* - **1.** [give off steam] fumer - **2.** [ship] avancer.

➤ **steam up** ⬦ *vt sep* - **1.** [mist up] embuer - **2.** fig [get angry] : **to get ~ed up (about)** s'énerver (pour) ⬦ *vi* se couvrir de buée.

steamboat ['stiːmbəʊt] *n* (bateau *m* à) vapeur *m*.

steam engine *n* locomotive *f* à vapeur.

steamer ['stiːmər] *n* - **1.** [ship] (bateau *m* à) vapeur *m* - **2.** CULIN cuiseur-vapeur *m*.

steam iron *n* fer *m* à vapeur.

steamroller ['stiːmˌrəʊlər] *n* rouleau *m* compresseur.

steam shovel *n* Am bulldozer *m*.

steamy ['stiːmɪ] (*compar* -ier ; *superl* -iest) *adj* - **1.** [full of steam] embué(e) - **2.** inf [erotic] érotique.

steel [stiːl] ⬦ *n (U)* acier *m* ⬦ *comp* en acier, d'acier ⬦ *vt* : **to ~ o.s. (for)** s'armer de courage (pour).

steel industry *n* industrie *f* sidérurgique, sidérurgie *f*.

steel wool *n* paille *f* de fer.

steelworker ['stiːlˌwɜːkər] *n* sidérurgiste *mf*.

steelworks ['stiːlwɜːks] (*pl inv*) *n* aciérie *f*.

steely ['stiːlɪ] (*compar* -ier ; *superl* -iest) *adj* - **1.** [steel-coloured] acier (*inv*) - **2.** [strong - person] dur(e) ; [- determination, will] de fer.

steep [stiːp] *adj* - **1.** [hill, road] raide, abrupt(e) - **2.** [increase, decline] énorme - **3.** inf [expensive] excessif(ive).

steeped [stiːpt] *adj* fig : **~ in** imprégné(e) de.

steeple ['stiːpl] *n* clocher *m*, flèche *f*.

steeplechase ['stiːpltʃeɪs] *n* - **1.** [horse race] steeple-chase *m* - **2.** [athletics race] steeple *m*.

steeplejack ['stiːpldʒæk] *n* réparateur *m* de cheminées industrielles et de clochers.

steeply ['stiːplɪ] *adv* - **1.** [at steep angle] en pente raide - **2.** [considerably] en flèche.

steer ['stɪər] ⬦ *n* bœuf *m* ⬦ *vt* - **1.** [ship] gouverner ; [car, aeroplane] conduire, diriger - **2.** [person] diriger, guider ⬦ *vi* : **to ~ well** [ship] gouverner bien ; [car] être facile à manœuvrer ; **to ~ clear of sb/sthg** éviter qqn/qqch.

steering ['stɪərɪŋ] *n (U)* direction *f*.

steering column *n* colonne *f* de direction.

steering committee *n* comité *m* d'organisation.

steering lock *n* rayon *m* de braquage.

steering wheel *n* volant *m*.

stellar ['stelər] *adj* stellaire.

stem [stem] (*pt & pp* -med ; *cont* -ming) ⬦ *n* - **1.** [of plant] tige *f* - **2.** [of glass] pied *m* - **3.** [of pipe] tuyau *m* - **4.** GRAMM radical *m* ⬦ *vt* [stop] arrêter.

➤ **stem from** *vt fus* provenir de.

stench [stentʃ] *n* puanteur *f*.

stencil ['stensl] (Br *pt & pp* -led ; *cont* -ling ; Am *pt & pp* -ed ; *cont* -ing) ⬦ *n* pochoir *m* ⬦ *vt* faire au pochoir.

stenographer [stə'nɒgrəfər] *n* Am sténographe *mf*.

stenography [stə'nɒgrəfɪ] *n* Am sténographie *f*.

step [step] (*pt & pp* -ped ; *cont* -ping) ⬦ *n* - **1.** [pace] pas *m* ; **in/out of ~ with** fig en accord/désaccord avec ; **to watch one's ~** faire attention où l'on marche ; fig faire attention à ce que l'on fait - **2.** [action] mesure *f* - **3.** [stage] étape *f* ; **~ by ~** petit à petit, progressivement - **4.** [stair] marche *f* - **5.** [of ladder] barreau *m*, échelon *m* - **6.** Am MUS ton *m* ⬦ *vi* - **1.** [move foot] : **to ~ forward** avancer ; **to ~ off** OR **down from sthg** descendre de qqch ; **to ~ back** reculer - **2.** [tread] : **to ~ on/in sthg** marcher sur/dans qqch.

➤ **steps** *npl* - **1.** [stairs] marches *fpl* - **2.** Br [stepladder] escabeau *m*.

➤ **step aside** *vi* - **1.** [move away] s'écarter - **2.** [leave job] démissionner.

➤ **step back** *vi* [pause to reflect] prendre du recul.

➤ **step down** *vi* [leave job] démissionner.

➤ **step in** *vi* intervenir.

➤ **step up** *vt sep* intensifier.

stepbrother ['step,brʌðər] *n* demi-frère *m*.

stepchild ['steptʃaild] (*pl* -children [-,tʃildrən]) *n* beau-fils *m*, belle-fille *f*.

stepdaughter ['step,dɔ:tə'] *n* belle-fille *f*.

stepfather ['step,fɑ:ðə'] *n* beau-père *m*.

stepladder ['step,lædə'] *n* escabeau *m*.

stepmother ['step,mʌðə'] *n* belle-mère *f*.

stepping-stone ['stepɪŋ-] *n* pierre *f* de gué ; *fig* tremplin *m*.

stepsister ['step,sistə'] *n* demi-sœur *f*.

stepson ['stepsʌn] *n* beau-fils *m*.

stereo ['steriəʊ] (*pl* -s) ⟨⟩ *adj* stéréo (inv) ⟨⟩ *n* - 1. [appliance] chaîne *f* stéréo - 2. [sound] : **in** ~ en stéréo.

stereophonic [,steriə'fɒnɪk] *adj* stéréophonique.

stereotype ['steriətaɪp] ⟨⟩ *n* stéréotype *m* ⟨⟩ *vt* stéréotyper.

sterile ['steraɪl] *adj* stérile.

sterility [ste'rɪlətɪ] *n* stérilité *f*.

sterilization [,steralaɪ'zeɪʃn] *n* stérilisation *f*.

sterilize, -ise ['steralaɪz] *vt* stériliser.

sterilized milk ['steralaɪzd-] *n* lait *m* stérilisé.

sterling ['stɜ:lɪŋ] ⟨⟩ *adj* - 1. [of British money] sterling (inv) - 2. [excellent] exceptionnel(elle) ⟨⟩ *n* (U) livre *f* sterling ⟨⟩ *comp* [traveller's cheques] en livres sterling.

sterling silver *n* argent *m* fin.

stern [stɜ:n] ⟨⟩ *adj* sévère ⟨⟩ *n* NAUT arrière *m*.

sternly ['stɜ:nlɪ] *adv* sévèrement.

steroid ['stɪərɔɪd] *n* stéroïde *m*.

stethoscope ['steθəskəʊp] *n* stéthoscope *m*.

stetson ['stetsn] *n* chapeau *m* de cow-boy.

stevedore ['sti:vədɔ:'] *n* Am docker *m*.

stew [stju:] ⟨⟩ *n* ragoût *m* ⟨⟩ *vt* [meat] cuire en ragoût ; [fruit] faire cuire ⟨⟩ *vi* : **to let sb** ~ *fig* laisser mariner qqn.

steward ['stjʊəd] *n* - 1. [on plane, ship, train] steward *m* - 2. Br [at demonstration, meeting] membre *m* du service d'ordre.

stewardess ['stjʊədɪs] *n* hôtesse *f*.

stewing steak Br ['stju:ɪŋ-], **stewbeef** Am ['stju:bi:f] *n* (U) bœuf *m* à braiser.

St. Ex. *abbr of* stock exchange.

stg *abbr of* sterling.

stick [stɪk] (*pt & pp* stuck) ⟨⟩ *n* - 1. [of wood, dynamite, candy] bâton *m* - 2. [walking stick] canne *f* - 3. SPORT crosse *f* - 4. *phr* : **to get the wrong end of the** ~ mal comprendre ⟨⟩ *vt* - 1. [push] : **to** ~ **sthg in** OR **into** planter qqch dans ; **to** ~ **sthg through sthg** transpercer qqch avec qqch - 2. [with glue, adhesive tape] : **to**

~ **sthg (on** OR **to)** coller qqch (sur) - 3. *inf* [put] mettre - 4. Br *inf* [tolerate] supporter ; **to** ~ **it** tenir le coup ⟨⟩ *vi* - 1. [adhere] : **to** ~ **(to)** coller (à) - 2. [jam] se coincer - 3. [remain] : **to** ~ **in sb's mind** marquer qqn.

➤ **stick around** *vi inf* rester dans les parages.

➤ **stick at** *vt fus* [activity] persévérer dans ; **to** ~ **at a job** rester dans un emploi.

➤ **stick by** *vt fus* [statement] s'en tenir à ; [person] ne pas abandonner.

➤ **stick out** ⟨⟩ *vt sep* - 1. [head] sortir ; [hand] lever ; [tongue] tirer - 2. *inf* [endure] : **to** ~ **it out** tenir le coup ⟨⟩ *vi* - 1. [protrude] dépasser - 2. *inf* [be noticeable] se remarquer.

➤ **stick out for** *vt fus* Br exiger.

➤ **stick to** *vt fus* - 1. [follow closely] suivre - 2. [principles] rester fidèle à ; [decision] s'en tenir à ; [promise] tenir.

➤ **stick together** *vi* rester ensemble ; *fig* se serrer les coudes.

➤ **stick up** ⟨⟩ *vt sep* - 1. [poster, notice] afficher - 2. [with gun] attaquer à main armée ⟨⟩ *vi* dépasser.

➤ **stick up for** *vt fus* défendre.

➤ **stick with** *vt fus* - 1. [decision, choice] s'en tenir à - 2. [follow closely] rester avec.

sticker ['stɪkə'] *n* [label] autocollant *m*.

sticking plaster ['stɪkɪŋ-] *n* sparadrap *m*.

stick insect *n* phasme *m*.

stick-in-the-mud *n inf* réac *mf*.

stickleback ['stɪklbæk] *n* épinoche *f*.

stickler ['stɪklə'] *n* : **to be a** ~ **for** être à cheval sur.

stick-on *adj* autocollant(e), adhésif(ive).

stickpin ['stɪkpɪn] *n* Am épingle *f* de cravate.

stick shift *n* Am levier *m* de vitesses.

stick-up *n inf* vol *m* à main armée.

sticky ['stɪkɪ] (*compar* -ier ; *superl* -iest) *adj* - 1. [hands, sweets] poisseux(euse) ; [label, tape] adhésif(ive) - 2. *inf* [awkward] délicat(e) - 3. [humid] humide.

stiff [stɪf] ⟨⟩ *adj* - 1. [rod, paper, material] rigide ; [shoes, brush] dur(e) ; [fabric] raide - 2. [door, drawer, window] dur(e) (à ouvrir/fermer) ; [joint] ankylosé(e) ; **to have a** ~ **back** avoir des courbatures dans le dos ; **to have a** ~ **neck** avoir le torticolis - 3. [formal] guindé(e) - 4. [severe - penalty] sévère ; [- competition] serré(e) - 5. [difficult - task] difficile - 6. [drink] bien tassé(e) ; [wind] fort(e) ⟨⟩ *adv inf* : **to be bored** ~ s'ennuyer à mourir ; **to be frozen/scared** ~ mourir de froid/peur.

stiffen ['stɪfn] ⟨⟩ *vt* - 1. [material] raidir ; [with starch] empeser - 2. [resolve] renforcer ⟨⟩ *vi*

- 1. [body] se raidir ; [joints] s'ankyloser **- 2.** [competition, resistance] s'intensifier **- 3.** [wind] devenir plus fort, fraîchir.

stiffener ['stɪfnər] n **- 1.** [starch] amidon m **- 2.** TECH raidisseur m.

stiffness ['stɪfnɪs] (U) n **- 1.** [inflexibility] raideur f, rigidité f **- 2.** [of body, joint] ankylose f **- 3.** [formality] froideur f.

stifle ['staɪfl] vt & vi étouffer.

stifling ['staɪflɪŋ] adj étouffant(e).

stigma ['stɪgmə] n **- 1.** [disgrace] honte f, stigmate m **- 2.** BOT stigmate m.

stigmatize, -ise ['stɪgmətaɪz] vt stigmatiser.

stile [staɪl] n échalier m.

stiletto heel [stɪ'letəu-] n Br talon m aiguille.

still [stɪl] ◇ adv **- 1.** [up to now, up to then] encore, toujours ; **I've ~ got £5 left** il me reste encore 5 livres **- 2.** [even now] encore **- 3.** [nevertheless] tout de même **- 4.** (with comparatives) : **~ bigger/more important** encore plus grand/plus important ◇ adj **- 1.** [not moving] immobile **- 2.** [calm] calme, tranquille **- 3.** [not windy] sans vent **- 4.** [not fizzy - gen] non gazeux(euse) ; [- mineral water] plat(e) ◇ n **- 1.** PHOT photo f **- 2.** [for making alcohol] alambic m.

stillborn ['stɪlbɔːn] adj mort-né(e).

still life (pl -s) n nature f morte.

stillness ['stɪlnɪs] n [calmness] tranquillité f.

stilted ['stɪltɪd] adj emprunté(e), qui manque de naturel.

stilts ['stɪlts] npl **- 1.** [for person] échasses fpl **- 2.** [for building] pilotis mpl.

stimulant ['stɪmjʊlənt] n stimulant m.

stimulate ['stɪmjʊleɪt] vt stimuler.

stimulating ['stɪmjʊleɪtɪŋ] adj stimulant(e).

stimulation [ˌstɪmjʊ'leɪʃn] n stimulation f.

stimulus ['stɪmjʊləs] (pl -li [-laɪ]) n **- 1.** [encouragement] stimulant m **- 2.** BIOL & PSYCH stimulus m.

sting [stɪŋ] (pt & pp stung) ◇ n **- 1.** [by bee] piqûre f ; [of bee] dard m **- 2.** [sharp pain] brûlure f ; **to take the ~ out of sthg** adoucir OR atténuer qqch ◇ vt **- 1.** [gen] piquer **- 2.** [subj : criticism] blesser ◇ vi piquer.

stinging nettle ['stɪŋɪŋ-] n Br ortie f.

stingray ['stɪŋreɪ] n pastenague f.

stingy ['stɪndʒɪ] (compar -ier ; superl -iest) adj inf radin(e).

stink [stɪŋk] (pt stank OR stunk ; pp stunk) ◇ n puanteur f ◇ vi **- 1.** [smell] puer, empester **- 2.** inf fig [be worthless] ne rien valoir.

stink-bomb n boule f puante.

stinking ['stɪŋkɪŋ] inf ◇ adj [cold] gros (grosse) ; [weather] pourri(e) ; [place] infect(e) ◇ adv : **to be ~ rich** être plein(e) aux as.

stint [stɪnt] ◇ n [period of work] part f de travail ◇ vi : **to ~ on** lésiner sur.

stipend ['staɪpend] n traitement m, salaire m.

stipulate ['stɪpjʊleɪt] vt stipuler.

stipulation [ˌstɪpjʊ'leɪʃn] n **- 1.** [statement] stipulation f **- 2.** [condition] condition f.

stir [stɜːr] (pt & pp **-red** ; cont **-ring**) ◇ n **- 1.** [act of stirring] : **to give sthg a ~** remuer qqch **- 2.** [public excitement] sensation f ◇ vt **- 1.** [mix] remuer **- 2.** [move gently] agiter **- 3.** [move emotionally] émouvoir **- 4.** [move] : **to ~ o.s.** se remuer ◇ vi bouger, remuer.

➡ **stir up** vt sep **- 1.** [dust] soulever **- 2.** [trouble] provoquer ; [resentment, dissatisfaction] susciter ; [rumour] faire naître.

stir-fry vt faire sauter à feu très vif.

stirring ['stɜːrɪŋ] ◇ adj excitant(e), émouvant(e) ◇ n [of interest, emotion] éveil m.

stirrup ['stɪrəp] n étrier m.

stitch [stɪtʃ] ◇ n **- 1.** SEWING point m ; [in knitting] maille f **- 2.** MED point m de suture **- 3.** [stomach pain] : **to be in ~es** être plié(e) en deux (de rire), se tenir les côtes ◇ vt **- 1.** SEWING coudre **- 2.** MED suturer.

stitching ['stɪtʃɪŋ] n (U) points mpl, piqûres fpl.

stoat [stəʊt] n hermine f.

stock [stɒk] ◇ n **- 1.** [supply] réserve f **- 2.** (U) COMM stock m, réserve f ; **in ~** en stock ; **out of ~** épuisé(e) **- 3.** FIN valeurs fpl ; **~s and shares** titres mpl **- 4.** [ancestry] souche f **- 5.** CULIN bouillon m **- 6.** [livestock] cheptel m **- 7.** phr : **to take ~ (of)** faire le point (de) ◇ adj classique ◇ vt **- 1.** COMM vendre, avoir en stock **- 2.** [fill - shelves] garnir ; [- lake] empoissonner.

➡ **stock up** vi : **to ~ up (with)** faire des provisions (de).

stockade [stɒ'keɪd] n palissade f.

stockbroker ['stɒkˌbrəʊkər] n agent m de change.

stockbroking ['stɒkˌbrəʊkɪŋ] n commerce m des valeurs en Bourse.

stockcar ['stɒkkɑːr] n stock-car m.

stock company n Am société f anonyme par actions.

stock control n contrôle m des stocks.

stock cube n Br bouillon-cube m.

stock exchange n Bourse f.

stockholder ['stɒkˌhəʊldər] n Am actionnaire mf.

Stockholm ['stɒkhəʊm] *n* Stockholm.

stocking ['stɒkɪŋ] *n* [for woman] bas *m*.

stock-in-trade *n* rudiments *mpl* du métier.

stockist ['stɒkɪst] *n* Br dépositaire *m*, stockiste *m*.

stock market *n* Bourse *f*.

stock phrase *n* cliché *m*.

stockpile ['stɒkpaɪl] ⬦ *n* stock *m* ⬦ *vt* [weapons] amasser ; [food] stocker.

stockroom ['stɒkrʊm] *n* réserve *f*.

stock-still *adv* sans bouger.

stocktaking ['stɒk,teɪkɪŋ] *n* (U) inventaire *m*.

stocky ['stɒkɪ] (*compar* -ier ; *superl* -iest) *adj* trapu(e).

stodgy ['stɒdʒɪ] (*compar* -ier ; *superl* -iest) *adj* - **1.** [food] lourd(e) (à digérer) - **2.** pej [book] indigeste.

stoic ['stəʊɪk] ⬦ *adj* stoïque ⬦ *n* stoïque *mf*.

stoical ['stəʊɪkl] *adj* stoïque.

stoicism ['stəʊɪsɪzm] *n* stoïcisme *m*.

stoke [stəʊk] *vt* [fire] entretenir.

stole [stəʊl] ⬦ *pt* ⊳ steal. ⬦ *n* étole *f*.

stolen ['stəʊln] *pp* ⊳ steal.

stolid ['stɒlɪd] *adj* impassible.

stomach ['stʌmək] ⬦ *n* [organ] estomac *m* ; [abdomen] ventre *m* ⬦ *vt* [tolerate] encaisser, supporter.

stomachache ['stʌməkeɪk] *n* : **to have ~** avoir mal au ventre.

stomach pump *n* pompe *f* stomacale.

stomach ulcer *n* ulcère *m* de l'estomac.

stomach upset *n* embarras *m* gastrique.

stomp [stɒmp] *vi* : **to ~ in/out** entrer/sortir d'un pas bruyant, entrer/sortir d'un pas lourd.

stone [stəʊn] (*pl sense 3 only, inv* OR -s) ⬦ *n* - **1.** [rock] pierre *f* ; [smaller] caillou *m* ; **a ~'s throw from** à deux pas de - **2.** [seed] noyau *m* - **3.** Br [unit of measurement] = *6,348 kg* ⬦ *comp* de OR en pierre ⬦ *vt* [person, car etc] jeter des pierres sur.

Stone Age *n* : **the ~** l'âge *m* de pierre.

stone-cold *adj* complètement froid(e) OR glacé(e).

stoned [stəʊnd] *adj* inf - **1.** drugs sl défoncé(e) - **2.** [drunk] soûl(e), bourré(e).

stonemason ['stəʊn,meɪsn] *n* tailleur *m* de pierre OR pierres.

stonewall [,stəʊn'wɔːl] *vi* être évasif(ive).

stoneware ['stəʊnweəʳ] *n* poterie *f* en grès.

stonewashed ['stəʊnwɒʃt] *adj* délavé(e).

stonework ['stəʊnwɜːk] *n* maçonnerie *f*.

stony ['stəʊnɪ] (*compar* -ier ; *superl* -iest) *adj* - **1.** [ground] pierreux(euse) - **2.** [unfriendly] froid(e).

stood [stʊd] *pt* & *pp* ⊳ stand.

stooge [stuːdʒ] *n* [in comedy act] comparse *m* ; fig pantin *m*, fantoche *m*.

stool [stuːl] *n* [seat] tabouret *m*.

stoop [stuːp] ⬦ *n* - **1.** [bent back] : **to walk with a ~** marcher le dos voûté - **2.** Am [of house] porche *m* ⬦ *vi* - **1.** [bend down] se pencher - **2.** [hunch shoulders] être voûté(e) - **3.** fig [debase oneself] : **to ~ to doing sthg** s'abaisser jusqu'à faire qqch.

stop [stɒp] (*pt* & *pp* -ped ; *cont* -ping) ⬦ *n* - **1.** [gen] arrêt *m* ; **to come to a ~** [car, train etc] s'arrêter ; [production, growth] cesser ; **to put a ~ to sthg** mettre un terme à qqch - **2.** [full stop] point *m* ⬦ *vt* - **1.** [gen] arrêter ; [end] mettre fin à ; **to ~ doing sthg** arrêter de faire qqch ; **to ~ work** arrêter de travailler, cesser le travail - **2.** [prevent] : **to ~ sb/sthg (from doing sthg)** empêcher qqn/qqch (de faire qqch) - **3.** [wages] retenir ; [cheque] faire opposition à - **4.** [block] boucher ⬦ *vi* s'arrêter, cesser ; **to ~ at nothing (to do sthg)** ne reculer devant rien (pour faire qqch).

➡ **stop off** *vi* s'arrêter, faire halte.

➡ **stop over** *vi* s'arrêter un jour/quelques jours.

➡ **stop up** ⬦ *vt sep* [block] boucher ⬦ *vi* Br veiller.

stopcock ['stɒpkɒk] *n* robinet *m* d'arrêt

stopgap ['stɒpgæp] *n* bouche-trou *m*.

stopover ['stɒp,əʊvəʳ] *n* halte *f*.

stoppage ['stɒpɪdʒ] *n* - **1.** [strike] grève *f* - **2.** Br [deduction] retenue *f*.

stopper ['stɒpəʳ] *n* bouchon *m*.

stopping ['stɒpɪŋ] *adj* Br : **~ train** train *m* omnibus.

stop press *n* nouvelles *fpl* de dernière heure.

stopwatch ['stɒpwɒtʃ] *n* chronomètre *m*.

storage ['stɔːrɪdʒ] *n* - **1.** [of goods] entreposage *m*, emmagasinage *m* ; [of household objects] rangement *m* - **2.** COMPUT stockage *m*, mémorisation *f*.

storage heater *n* Br radiateur *m* à accumulation.

store [stɔːʳ] ⬦ *n* - **1.** esp Am [shop] magasin *m* - **2.** [supply] provision *f* - **3.** [place of storage] réserve *f* - **4.** phr : **to set great ~ by** OR **on** accorder OR attacher beaucoup d'importance à, faire grand cas de ⬦ *vt* - **1.** [save] mettre en réserve ; [goods] entreposer, emmagasiner **- 2.** COMPUT stocker, mémoriser.

➤ **in store** adv : **who knows what the future holds in ~?** qui sait ce que nous réserve l'avenir? ; **there's a shock in ~ for him** un choc l'attend.

➤ **store up** vt sep [provisions] mettre en réserve ; [goods] emmagasiner ; [information] mettre en mémoire, noter.

store detective n surveillant m, -e f de magasin.

storehouse ['stɔ:haʊs, pl -haʊzɪz] n entrepôt m ; fig mine f.

storekeeper ['stɔ:ˌki:pəʳ] n Am commerçant m, -e f.

storeroom ['stɔ:rʊm] n magasin m.

storey Br (pl -s), **story** Am (pl -ies) ['stɔ:rɪ] n étage m.

stork [stɔ:k] n cigogne f.

storm [stɔ:m] <> n **- 1.** [bad weather] orage m ; a **~ in a teacup** une tempête dans un verre d'eau **- 2.** fig [of abuse] torrent m ; [of applause] tempête f <> vt MIL prendre d'assaut <> vi **- 1.** [go angrily] : **to ~ in/out** entrer/sortir comme un ouragan **- 2.** [speak angrily] fulminer.

storm cloud n nuage m orageux.

storming ['stɔ:mɪŋ] n prise f d'assaut.

stormy ['stɔ:mɪ] (compar **-ier** ; superl **-iest**) adj lit & fig orageux(euse).

story ['stɔ:rɪ] (pl **-ies**) n **- 1.** [gen] histoire f ; **it's the (same) old ~** c'est toujours la même histoire, c'est toujours pareil ; **to cut a long ~ short** (enfin) bref **- 2.** PRESS article m ; RADIO & TV nouvelle f **- 3.** Am = storey.

storybook ['stɔ:rɪbʊk] adj [romance etc] de conte de fées.

storyteller ['stɔ:rɪˌteləʳ] n **- 1.** [narrator] conteur m, -euse f **- 2.** euphemism [liar] menteur m, -euse f.

stout [staʊt] <> adj **- 1.** [rather fat] corpulent(e) **- 2.** [strong] solide **- 3.** [resolute] ferme, résolu(e) <> n (U) stout m, bière f brune.

stoutness ['staʊtnɪs] n [fatness] corpulence f.

stove [stəʊv] <> pt & pp ⊳ **stave** <> n [for cooking] cuisinière f ; [for heating] poêle m, calorifère m Can.

stow [stəʊ] vt : **to ~ sthg (away)** ranger qqch.

➤ **stow away** vi embarquer clandestinement.

stowaway ['stəʊəweɪ] n passager m clandestin.

straddle ['strædl] vt enjamber ; [chair] s'asseoir à califourchon sur.

strafe [strɑ:f] vt MIL mitrailler.

straggle ['strægl] vi **- 1.** [buildings] s'étendre, s'étaler ; [hair] être en désordre **- 2.** [person] traîner, lambiner.

straggler ['stræɡləʳ] n traînard m, -e f.

straggly ['stræɡlɪ] (compar **-ier** ; superl **-iest**) adj [hair] en désordre.

straight [streɪt] <> adj **- 1.** [not bent] droit(e) ; [hair] raide **- 2.** [frank] franc (franche), honnête **- 3.** [tidy] en ordre **- 4.** [choice, exchange] simple **- 5.** [alcoholic drink] sec, sans eau **- 6.** inf [conventional] normal(e) **- 7.** gay sl hétéro (inv) **- 8.** phr : **let's get this ~** entendons-nous bien <> adv **- 1.** [in a straight line] droit **- 2.** [directly, immediately] droit, tout de suite **- 3.** [frankly] carrément, franchement **- 4.** [undiluted] sec, sans eau **- 5.** phr : **to go ~** [criminal] rester dans le droit chemin <> n SPORT : **the ~** la ligne droite.

➤ **straight off** adv tout de suite, sur-le-champ.

➤ **straight out** adv sans mâcher ses mots.

straightaway [ˌstreɪtə'weɪ] adv tout de suite, immédiatement.

straighten ['streɪtn] <> vt **- 1.** [tidy - hair, dress] arranger ; [- room] mettre de l'ordre dans **- 2.** [make straight - horizontally] rendre droit(e) ; [- vertically] redresser <> vi [person] : **to ~ (up)** se redresser.

➤ **straighten out** vt sep [problem] résoudre ; **to ~ things out** arranger les choses.

straight face n : **to keep a ~** garder son sérieux.

straightforward [ˌstreɪt'fɔ:wəd] adj **- 1.** [easy] simple **- 2.** [frank] honnête, franc (franche).

strain [streɪn] <> n **- 1.** [mental] tension f, stress m **- 2.** MED foulure f ; **back ~** tour m de reins **- 3.** TECH contrainte f, effort m **- 4.** [type of plant] variété f ; [- of virus] souche f <> vt **- 1.** [work hard - eyes] plisser fort ; **to ~ one's ears** tendre l'oreille **- 2.** [MED - muscle] se froisser ; [- eyes] se fatiguer ; **to ~ one's back** se faire un tour de reins **- 3.** [patience] mettre à rude épreuve ; [budget] grever **- 4.** [drain] passer **- 5.** TECH exercer une contrainte sur <> vi [try very hard] : **to ~ to do sthg** faire un gros effort pour faire qqch, se donner du mal pour faire qqch.

➤ **strains** npl [of music] accords mpl, airs mpl.

strained [streɪnd] adj **- 1.** [worried] contracté(e), tendu(e) **- 2.** [relations, relationship] tendu(e) **- 3.** [unnatural] forcé(e).

strainer ['streɪnəʳ] n passoire f.

strait [streɪt] n détroit m.

➤ **straits** npl : **in dire** OR **desperate ~s** dans une situation désespérée.

straitened ['streɪtnd] *adj* fml : **in ~ circum-stances** dans la gêne, dans le besoin.

straitjacket ['streɪt,dʒækɪt] *n* camisole *f* de force.

straitlaced [,streɪt'leɪst] *adj* collet monté *(inv)*.

Strait of Gibraltar *n* : **the ~** le détroit de Gibraltar.

Strait of Hormuz [,hɔː'muːh] *n* : **the ~** le détroit d'Hormuz OR Ormuz.

strand [strænd] *n* - **1.** [of cotton, wool] brin *m*, fil *m* ; [of hair] mèche *f* - **2.** [theme] fil *m*.

stranded ['strændɪd] *adj* [boat] échoué(e) ; [people] abandonné(e), en rade.

strange [streɪndʒ] *adj* - **1.** [odd] étrange, bizarre - **2.** [unfamiliar] inconnu(e).

strangely ['streɪndʒlɪ] *adv* étrangement, bizarrement ; **~ (enough)** chose curieuse.

stranger ['streɪndʒəʳ] *n* - **1.** [unfamiliar person] inconnu *m*, -e *f* ; **to be a ~ to sthg** ne pas connaître qqch ; **to be no ~ to sthg** bien connaître qqch - **2.** [from another place] étranger *m*, -ère *f*.

strangle ['stræŋgl] *vt* étrangler ; *fig* étouffer.

stranglehold ['stræŋglhəʊld] *n* - **1.** [round neck] étranglement *m* - **2.** *fig* [control] : **~ (on)** domination *f* (de).

strangulation [,stræŋgjʊ'leɪʃn] *n* strangulation *f*.

strap [stræp] (*pt* & *pp* **-ped** ; *cont* **-ping**) ⬦ *n* [for fastening] sangle *f*, courroie *f* ; [of bag] bandoulière *f* ; [of rifle, dress, bra] bretelle *f* ; [of watch] bracelet *m* ⬦ *vt* [fasten] attacher.

strapless ['stræplɪs] *adj* sans bretelles.

strapping ['stræpɪŋ] *adj* bien bâti(e), robuste.

Strasbourg ['stræzbɜːg] *n* Strasbourg.

strata ['strɑːtə] *pl* ⬦ **stratum**.

stratagem ['strætədʒəm] *n* stratagème *m*.

strategic [strə'tiːdʒɪk] *adj* stratégique.

strategist ['strætɪdʒɪst] *n* stratège *m*.

strategy ['strætɪdʒɪ] (*pl* **-ies**) *n* stratégie *f*.

stratified ['strætɪfaɪd] *adj* - **1.** GEOL stratifié(e) - **2.** *fig* [society] divisé(e) en différentes couches sociales.

stratosphere ['strætə,sfɪəʳ] *n* : **the ~** la stratosphère.

stratum ['strɑːtəm] (*pl* **-ta** [-tə]) *n* - **1.** GEOL strate *f*, couche *f* - **2.** *fig* [of society] couche *f*.

straw [strɔː] ⬦ *n* paille *f* ; **to clutch at ~s** se raccrocher à n'importe quoi ; **the last ~** la goutte qui fait déborder le vase ; **that's the last ~!** ça c'est le comble! ⬦ *comp* de OR en paille.

strawberry ['strɔːbərɪ] (*pl* **-ies**) ⬦ *n* [fruit] fraise *f* ⬦ *comp* [tart, yoghurt] aux fraises ; [jam] de fraises.

straw poll *n* sondage *m* d'opinion.

stray [streɪ] ⬦ *adj* - **1.** [animal] errant(e), perdu(e) - **2.** [bullet] perdu(e) ; [example] isolé(e) ⬦ *n* [animal] animal *m* errant ⬦ *vi* - **1.** [person, animal] errer, s'égarer - **2.** [thoughts] vagabonder, errer.

streak [striːk] ⬦ *n* - **1.** [line] bande *f*, marque *f* ; **~ of lightning** éclair *m* - **2.** [in character] côté *m* ; **a ~ of cruelty** une propension à la cruauté - **3.** [period] : **a winning/losing ~** une période de succès/d'échecs, une série de succès/d'échecs ⬦ *vi* [move quickly] se déplacer comme un éclair.

streaked [striːkt] *adj* [marked] : **to be ~ with** être maculé(e) de, porter des traces de.

streaky ['striːkɪ] (*compar* **-ier** ; *superl* **-iest**) *adj* [paint] qui n'est pas uniforme ; [surface] couvert(e) de traces.

streaky bacon *n* Br bacon *m* assez gras.

stream [striːm] ⬦ *n* - **1.** [small river] ruisseau *m* - **2.** [of liquid, light] flot *m*, jet *m* - **3.** [of people, cars] flot *m* ; [of complaints, abuse] torrent *m* - **4.** Br SCH classe *f* de niveau ⬦ *vi* - **1.** [liquid] couler à flots, ruisseler ; [light] entrer à flots - **2.** [people, cars] affluer ; **to ~ past** passer à flots ⬦ *vt* Br SCH répartir par niveau.

streamer ['striːməʳ] *n* [for party] serpentin *m*.

streamline ['striːmlaɪn] *vt* - **1.** [make aerodynamic] caréner, donner un profil aérodynamique à - **2.** [make efficient] rationaliser.

streamlined ['striːmlaɪnd] *adj* - **1.** [aerodynamic] au profil aérodynamique - **2.** [efficient] rationalisé(e).

street [striːt] *n* rue *f* ; **it's right up his ~** Br *inf* c'est son rayon ; **to be ~s ahead of sb** Br devancer OR dépasser qqn de loin.

streetcar ['striːtkɑːʳ] *n* Am tramway *m*.

street-credibility *n* (*U*) *inf* image *f* (de marque).

street lamp, street light *n* réverbère *m*.

street lighting *n* éclairage *m* des rues.

street map *n* plan *m*.

street market *n* marché *m* en plein air.

street plan *n* plan *m*.

street value *n* [of drugs] valeur *f* à la revente.

streetwise ['striːtwaɪz] *adj* *inf* averti(e), futé(e).

strength [streŋθ] *n* - **1.** [gen] force *f* ; **on the ~ of** [evidence] sur la foi de ; [advice] s'appuyant sur, en vertu de - **2.** [power, influence] puissance *f* ; **to go from ~ to ~** connaître un succès de plus en plus éclatant, prospérer - **3.** [solidity, of currency] solidité f - **4.** [number] effectif m ; in ~ en force, en grand nombre ; at full ~ au (grand) complet ; to be below ~ avoir un effectif insuffisant.

strengthen ['streŋθn] <> vt - **1.** [structure, team, argument] renforcer - **2.** [economy, currency, friendship] consolider - **3.** [resolve, dislike] fortifier, affermir - **4.** [person] enhardir <> vi - **1.** [sales, economy] s'améliorer - **2.** [opposition] s'affermir, se renforcer - **3.** [friendship] se cimenter, se consolider - **4.** [currency] se raffermir.

strenuous ['strenjʊəs] adj [exercise, activity] fatigant(e), dur(e) ; [effort] vigoureux(euse), acharné(e).

stress [stres] <> n - **1.** [emphasis] : ~ **(on)** accent m (sur) - **2.** [mental] stress m, tension f ; to be under ~ être stressé(e) - **3.** TECH : ~ **(on)** contrainte f (sur), effort m (sur) - **4.** LING accent m <> vt - **1.** [emphasize] souligner, insister sur - **2.** LING accentuer.

stressed [strest] adj [tense] stressé(e).

stressful ['stresfʊl] adj stressant(e).

stretch [stretʃ] <> n - **1.** [of land, water] étendue f ; [of road, river] partie f, section f - **2.** [of time] période f - **3.** [effort] : by no ~ of the imagination même avec beaucoup d'imagination <> vt - **1.** [arms] allonger ; [legs] se dégourdir ; [muscles] distendre - **2.** [pull taut] tendre, étirer - **3.** [overwork - person] surmener ; [- resources, budget] grever - **4.** [challenge] : to ~ sb pousser qqn à la limite de ses capacités <> vi - **1.** [area] : to ~ over s'étendre sur ; to ~ from ... to s'étendre de ... à - **2.** [person, animal] s'étirer - **3.** [material, elastic] se tendre, s'étirer <> adj extensible.

➤ **at a stretch** adv d'affilée, sans interruption.

➤ **stretch out** <> vt sep [arm, leg, hand] tendre <> vi [lie down] s'étendre, s'allonger.

stretcher ['stretʃəʳ] n brancard m, civière f.

stretcher party n équipe f de brancardiers.

stretchmarks ['stretʃmɑːks] npl vergetures fpl.

stretchy ['stretʃɪ] (compar -ier ; superl -iest) adj extensible, élastique.

strew [struː] (pt -ed ; pp strewn [struːn] OR -ed) vt : to be strewn on OR over être éparpillé(e) sur ; to be strewn with être jonché(e) de.

stricken ['strɪkn] adj : to be ~ by OR with panic être pris(e) de panique ; to be ~ by an illness souffrir OR être atteint(e) d'une maladie.

strict [strɪkt] adj - **1.** [gen] strict(e) - **2.** [faithful] :

she's a ~ **Catholic** elle observe rigoureusement la foi catholique.

strictly ['strɪktlɪ] adv - **1.** [gen] strictement ; ~ **speaking** à proprement parler - **2.** [severely] d'une manière stricte, sévèrement.

strictness ['strɪktnɪs] n sévérité f.

stride [straɪd] (pt strode ; pp stridden ['strɪdn]) <> n - **1.** [long step] grand pas m, enjambée f - **2.** phr : to take sthg in one's ~ ne pas se laisser démonter par qqch <> vi marcher à grandes enjambées OR à grands pas.

➤ **strides** npl [progress] : to make (great) ~s faire des progrès rapides.

strident ['straɪdnt] adj - **1.** [voice, sound] strident(e) - **2.** [demand, attack] véhément(e), bruyant(e).

strife [straɪf] n (U) conflit m, lutte f.

strike [straɪk] (pt & pp struck) <> n - **1.** [by workers] grève f ; to be (out) on ~ être en grève ; to go on ~ faire grève, se mettre en grève - **2.** MIL raid m - **3.** [of oil, gold] découverte f <> comp de grève <> vt - **1.** [hit - deliberately] frapper ; [- accidentally] heurter - **2.** [subj : thought] venir à l'esprit de ; she ~s me as (being) very capable elle me fait l'impression d'être très capable, elle me paraît très capable - **3.** [impress] : to be struck by OR with être frappé(e) par - **4.** [conclude - deal, bargain] conclure - **5.** [light - match] frotter - **6.** [find] découvrir, trouver ; to ~ a balance (between) trouver le juste milieu (entre) ; to ~ a serious/happy etc note adopter un ton sérieux/gai etc - **7.** phr : to be struck blind être frappé(e) de cécité, devenir aveugle ; to be struck dumb rester muet ; to ~ fear OR terror into sb frapper qqn de terreur ; to ~ (it) lucky avoir de la veine ; to ~ it rich trouver le filon <> vi - **1.** [workers] faire grève - **2.** [hit] frapper - **3.** [attack] attaquer - **4.** [chime] sonner.

➤ **strike back** vi se venger, exercer des représailles.

➤ **strike down** vt sep terrasser.

➤ **strike off** vt sep : to be struck off être radié(e) OR rayé(e).

➤ **strike out** <> vt sep rayer, barrer <> vi [head out] se mettre en route, partir ; to ~ out on one's own [in business] se mettre à son compte.

➤ **strike up** <> vt fus - **1.** [conversation] commencer, engager ; to ~ up a friendship (with) se lier d'amitié (avec) - **2.** [music] commencer à jouer <> vi commencer à jouer.

strikebound ['straɪkbaʊnd] adj paralysé(e) par la grève.

strikebreaker ['straɪkˌbreɪkəʳ] n briseur m de grève.

strike pay *n* (U) allocation *f* de grève, allocation-gréviste *f*.

striker ['straɪkə'] *n* - **1.** [person on strike] gréviste *mf* - **2.** FTBL buteur *m*.

striking ['straɪkɪŋ] *adj* - **1.** [noticeable] frappant(e), saisissant(e) - **2.** [attractive] d'une beauté frappante.

striking distance *n :* to be within ~ (of) être à deux pas (de) ; **to be within ~ of doing sthg** fig être à deux doigts de faire qqch.

string [strɪŋ] (*pt* & *pp* **strung**) ◇ *n* - **1.** (U) [thin rope] ficelle *f* - **2.** [piece of thin rope] bout *m* de ficelle ; **(with) no ~s attached** sans conditions ; **to pull ~s** faire jouer le piston - **3.** [of beads, pearls] rang *m* - **4.** [series] série *f*, suite *f* - **5.** [of musical instrument] corde *f* ◇ *comp* : **~ vest** tricot *m* de peau à grosses mailles ; **~ bag** filet *m* à provisions.

⮞ **strings** *npl* MUS : **the ~s** les cordes *fpl*.

⮞ **string along** *vt sep* inf [deceive] faire marcher, tromper.

⮞ **string out** *vt fus* échelonner.

⮞ **string together** *vt sep* fig aligner.

⮞ **string up** *vt sep* inf [kill by hanging] pendre.

string bean *n* haricot *m* vert.

stringed instrument [ˌstrɪŋd-] *n* instrument *m* à cordes.

stringent ['strɪndʒənt] *adj* strict(e), rigoureux(euse).

string quartet *n* quatuor *m* à cordes.

strip [strɪp] (*pt* & *pp* **-ped** ; *cont* **-ping**) ◇ *n* - **1.** [narrow piece] bande *f* ; **to tear a ~ off sb, to tear sb off a ~** Br passer un bon savon à qqn, sonner les cloches à qqn - **2.** Br SPORT tenue *f* ◇ *vt* - **1.** [undress] déshabiller, dévêtir - **2.** [paint, wallpaper] enlever - **3.** [take away from] : **to ~ sb of sthg** dépouiller qqn de qqch ◇ *vi* - **1.** [undress] se déshabiller, se dévêtir - **2.** [do a striptease] faire un strip-tease.

⮞ **strip off** ◇ *vt sep* enlever, ôter ◇ *vi* se déshabiller, se dévêtir.

strip cartoon *n* Br bande *f* dessinée.

stripe [straɪp] *n* - **1.** [band of colour] rayure *f* - **2.** [sign of rank] galon *m*.

striped [straɪpt] *adj* à rayures, rayé(e).

strip lighting *n* éclairage *m* au néon.

stripper ['strɪpə'] *n* - **1.** [performer of striptease] strip-teaseuse *f*, effeuilleuse *f* - **2.** [for paint] décapant *m*.

strip-search ◇ *n* fouille *f* d'une personne dévêtue ◇ *vt* : **to ~ sb** obliger qqn à se déshabiller pour le fouiller.

strip show *n* (spectacle *m* de) strip-tease *m*.

striptease ['striptiːz] *n* strip-tease *m*.

stripy ['straɪpɪ] (*compar* **-ier** ; *superl* **-iest**) *adj* à rayures, rayé(e).

strive [straɪv] (*pt* **strove** ; *pp* **striven** ['strɪvn]) *vi* : **to ~ for sthg** essayer d'obtenir qqch ; **to ~ to do sthg** s'efforcer de faire qqch.

strobe (light) ['strəʊb-] *n* lumière *f* stroboscopique.

strode [strəʊd] *pt* ⮕ **stride**.

stroke [strəʊk] ◇ *n* - **1.** MED attaque *f* cérébrale - **2.** [of pen, brush] trait *m* - **3.** [in swimming - movement] mouvement *m* des bras ; [- style] nage *f* - **4.** [in rowing] coup *m* d'aviron - **5.** [in golf, tennis etc] coup *m* - **6.** [of clock] : **on the third ~** ≃ au quatrième top ; **at the ~ of 12** sur le coup de minuit - **7.** Br TYPO [oblique] barre *f* - **8.** [piece] : **a ~ of genius** un trait de génie ; **a ~ of luck** un coup de chance OR de veine ; **not to do a ~ of work** ne pas en ficher une datte OR rame, ne rien faire ; **at a ~** d'un seul coup ◇ *vt* caresser.

stroll [strəʊl] ◇ *n* petite promenade *f*, petit tour *m* ◇ *vi* se promener, flâner.

stroller ['strəʊlə'] *n* Am [for baby] poussette *f*.

strong [strɒŋ] *adj* - **1.** [gen] fort(e) ; **to be ~ at sthg** être fort en qqch ; **~ point** point *m* fort - **2.** [structure, argument, friendship] solide - **3.** [healthy] robuste, vigoureux(euse) ; **to be still going ~** [person, group] être toujours d'attaque, être solide au poste ; [machine] marcher toujours bien - **4.** [policy, measures] énergique - **5.** [in numbers] : **the crowd was 2,000 ~** il y avait une foule de 2 000 personnes - **6.** [team, candidate] sérieux(euse), qui a des chances de gagner.

strongarm ['strɒŋɑːm] *adj* : **~ tactics** la méthode forte.

strongbox ['strɒŋbɒks] *n* coffre-fort *m*.

stronghold ['strɒŋhəʊld] *n* fig bastion *m*.

strong language *n* (U) euphemism grossièretés *fpl*.

strongly ['strɒŋlɪ] *adv* - **1.** [gen] fortement - **2.** [solidly] solidement.

strong man *n* [in circus] homme *m* fort, hercule *m*.

strong-minded [-'maɪndɪd] *adj* résolu(e).

strong room *n* chambre *f* forte.

strong-willed [-'wɪld] *adj* têtu(e), volontaire.

stroppy ['strɒpɪ] (*compar* **-ier** ; *superl* **-iest**) *adj* Br inf difficile.

strove [strəʊv] *pt* ⮕ **strive**.

struck [strʌk] *pt* & *pp* ⮕ **strike**.

structural ['strʌktʃərəl] *adj* de construction.

structurally ['strʌktʃərəlɪ] *adv* du point de vue de la construction.

structure ['strʌktʃəʳ] <> n - **1.** [organization] structure f - **2.** [building] construction f <> vt structurer.

struggle ['strʌgl] <> n - **1.** [great effort] : **~ (for sthg/to do sthg)** lutte f (pour qqch/pour faire qqch) - **2.** [fight] bagarre f <> vi - **1.** [make great effort] : **to ~ (for)** lutter (pour) ; **to ~ to do sthg** s'efforcer de faire qqch - **2.** [to free oneself] se débattre ; [fight] se battre - **3.** [move with difficulty] : **to ~ to one's feet** se lever avec difficulté.

◆ **struggle on** vi : **to ~ on (with)** persévérer (dans).

struggling ['strʌglɪŋ] adj qui a du mal OR des difficultés.

strum [strʌm] (pt & pp -med ; cont -ming) vt [guitar] gratter de ; [tune] jouer.

strung [strʌŋ] pt & pp ▷ string.

strut [strʌt] (pt & pp -ted ; cont -ting) <> n - **1.** CONSTR étai m, support m - **2.** AERON pilier m <> vi se pavaner.

strychnine ['strɪkniːn] n strychnine f.

stub [stʌb] (pt & pp -bed ; cont -bing) <> n - **1.** [of cigarette] mégot m ; [of pencil] morceau m - **2.** [of ticket, cheque] talon m <> vt : **to ~ one's toe** se cogner le doigt de pied.

◆ **stub out** vt sep écraser.

stubble ['stʌbl] n (U) - **1.** [in field] chaume m - **2.** [on chin] barbe f de plusieurs jours.

stubborn ['stʌbən] adj - **1.** [person] têtu(e), obstiné(e) - **2.** [stain] qui ne veut pas partir, rebelle.

stubbornly ['stʌbənlɪ] adv obstinément.

stubby ['stʌbɪ] (compar -ier ; superl -iest) adj boudiné(e).

stucco ['stʌkəʊ] n stuc m.

stuck [stʌk] <> pt & pp ▷ stick <> adj - **1.** [jammed, trapped] coincé(e) - **2.** [stumped] : **to be ~** sécher - **3.** [stranded] bloqué(e), en rade.

stuck-up adj inf pej bêcheur(euse).

stud [stʌd] n - **1.** [metal decoration] clou m décoratif - **2.** [earring] clou m d'oreille - **3.** Br [on boot, shoe] clou m ; [on sports boots] crampon m - **4.** [of horses] haras m ; **to be put out to ~** être utilisé comme étalon.

studded ['stʌdɪd] adj : **~ (with)** parsemé(e) (de), constellé(e) (de).

student ['stjuːdnt] <> n étudiant m, -e f <> comp [life] estudiantin(e) ; [politics] des étudiants ; [disco] pour étudiants ; **~ nurse** élève-infirmière f ; **~ teacher** professeur m stagiaire.

students' union n - **1.** [organization] union f des étudiants - **2.** [building] club m (des étudiants).

stud farm n haras m.

studied ['stʌdɪd] adj étudié(e), calculé(e).

studio ['stjuːdɪəʊ] (pl -s) n studio m ; [of artist] atelier m.

studio apartment n Am = studio flat.

studio audience n public m invité.

studio flat Br, **studio apartment** Am n studio m.

studious ['stjuːdjəs] adj studieux(euse).

studiously ['stjuːdjəslɪ] adv studieusement.

study ['stʌdɪ] (pl -ies, pt & pp -ied) <> n - **1.** [gen] étude f - **2.** [room] bureau m <> vt - **1.** [learn] étudier, faire des études de - **2.** [examine] examiner, étudier <> vi étudier, faire ses études.

stuff [stʌf] <> n (U) - **1.** inf [things] choses fpl ; **and all that ~** et tout ça ; **to know one's ~** s'y connaître - **2.** [substance] substance f - **3.** inf [belongings] affaires fpl <> vt - **1.** [push] fourrer - **2.** [fill] : **to ~ sthg (with)** remplir OR bourrer qqch (de) - **3.** inf [with food] : **to ~ o.s. (with** OR **on)** se gaver (de), s'empiffrer (de) - **4.** CULIN farcir.

stuffed [stʌft] adj - **1.** [filled] : **~ with** bourré(e) de - **2.** inf [with food] gavé(e) - **3.** CULIN farci(e) - **4.** [toy] en peluche ; **he loves ~ animals** il adore les peluches - **5.** [preserved - animal] empaillé(e) - **6.** phr : **get ~!** Br inf va te faire foutre!

stuffing ['stʌfɪŋ] n (U) - **1.** [filling] bourre f, rembourrage m - **2.** CULIN farce f.

stuffy ['stʌfɪ] (compar -ier ; superl -iest) adj - **1.** [room] mal aéré(e), qui manque d'air - **2.** [person, club] vieux jeu (inv).

stumble ['stʌmbl] vi trébucher.

◆ **stumble across, stumble on** vt fus tomber sur.

stumbling block ['stʌmblɪŋ-] n pierre f d'achoppement.

stump [stʌmp] <> n [of tree] souche f ; [of arm, leg] moignon m <> vt [subj : question, problem] dérouter, rendre perplexe <> vi : **to ~ in/out** entrer/sortir à pas lourds.

◆ **stumps** npl CRICKET piquets mpl.

◆ **stump up** vt fus Br inf cracher, payer.

stun [stʌn] (pt & pp -ned ; cont -ning) vt - **1.** [knock unconscious] étourdir, assommer - **2.** [surprise] stupéfier, renverser.

stung [stʌŋ] pt & pp ▷ sting.

stun grenade n grenade f cataplexiante.

stunk [stʌŋk] pt & pp ▷ stink.

stunning ['stʌnɪŋ] adj - **1.** [very beautiful] ravissant(e) ; [scenery] merveilleux(euse) - **2.** [surprising] stupéfiant(e), renversant(e).

stunt [stʌnt] ◇ n - **1.** [for publicity] coup m - **2.** CINEMA cascade f ◇ vt retarder, arrêter.

stunted ['stʌntɪd] adj rabougri(e).

stunt man n cascadeur m.

stupefy ['stjuːpɪfaɪ] (pt & pp -ied) vt - **1.** [tire] abrutir - **2.** [surprise] stupéfier, abasourdir.

stupendous [stjuː'pendəs] adj extraordinaire, prodigieux(euse).

stupid ['stjuːpɪd] adj - **1.** [foolish] stupide, bête - **2.** inf [annoying] fichu(e).

stupidity [stjuː'pɪdətɪ] n (U) bêtise f, stupidité f.

stupidly ['stjuːpɪdlɪ] adv stupidement.

stupor ['stjuːpəʳ] n stupeur f, hébétude f.

sturdy ['stɜːdɪ] (compar -ier ; superl -iest) adj [person] robuste ; [furniture, structure] solide.

sturgeon ['stɜːdʒən] (pl inv) n esturgeon m.

stutter ['stʌtəʳ] ◇ n bégaiement m ◇ vi bégayer.

sty [staɪ] (pl sties) n [pigsty] porcherie f.

stye [staɪ] n orgelet m, compère-loriot m.

style [staɪl] ◇ n - **1.** [characteristic manner] style m - **2.** (U) [elegance] chic m, élégance f - **3.** [design] genre m, modèle m ◇ vt [hair] coiffer.

styling mousse ['staɪlɪŋ-] n mousse f coiffante.

stylish ['staɪlɪʃ] adj chic (inv), élégant(e).

stylist ['staɪlɪst] n [hairdresser] coiffeur m, -euse f.

stylized, -ised ['staɪlaɪzd] adj stylisé(e).

stylus ['staɪləs] (pl -es) n [on record player] pointe f de lecture, saphir m.

stymie ['staɪmɪ] vt inf [plan] contrarier, contrecarrer ; **to be ~d** [person] être coincé(e).

styrofoam® ['staɪrəfəʊm] n Am polystyrène m.

suave [swɑːv] adj doucereux(euse).

sub [sʌb] n inf - **1.** SPORT (abbr of substitute) remplaçant m, -e f - **2.** (abbr of submarine) sous-marin m - **3.** Br (abbr of subscription) cotisation f - **4.** Am [sandwich] sandwich m (de baguette).

sub- [sʌb] prefix sous-, sub-.

subcommittee ['sʌbkə,mɪtɪ] n sous-comité m.

subconscious [,sʌb'kɒnʃəs] ◇ adj inconscient(e) ◇ n : **the ~** l'inconscient m.

subconsciously [,sʌb'kɒnʃəslɪ] adv inconsciemment.

subcontinent [,sʌb'kɒntɪnənt] n sous-continent m.

subcontract [,sʌbkən'trækt] vt sous-traiter.

subculture ['sʌb,kʌltʃəʳ] n sous-culture f.

subdivide [,sʌbdɪ'vaɪd] vt subdiviser.

subdue [səb'djuː] vt - **1.** [control - rioters, enemy] soumettre, subjuguer ; [- temper, anger] maîtriser, réprimer - **2.** [light, colour] adoucir, atténuer.

subdued [səb'djuːd] adj - **1.** [person] abattu(e) - **2.** [anger, emotion] contenu(e) - **3.** [colour] doux (douce) ; [light] tamisé(e).

subeditor [,sʌb'edɪtəʳ] n secrétaire mf de rédaction.

subgroup ['sʌbgruːp] n sous-groupe m.

subheading ['sʌb,hedɪŋ] n sous-titre m.

subhuman [,sʌb'hjuːmən] adj pej [crime] brutal(e), bestial(e).

subject [adj, n & prep 'sʌbdʒekt, vt səb'dʒekt] ◇ adj soumis(e) ; **to be ~ to** [tax, law] être soumis à ; [disease, headaches] être sujet (sujette) à ◇ n - **1.** [gen] sujet m - **2.** SCH & UNIV matière f ◇ vt - **1.** [control] soumettre, assujettir - **2.** [force to experience] : **to ~ sb to sthg** exposer OR soumettre qqn à qqch.

➤ **subject to** prep sous réserve de.

subjection [səb'dʒekʃn] n sujétion f, soumission f.

subjective [səb'dʒektɪv] adj subjectif(ive).

subjectively [səb'dʒektɪvlɪ] adv subjectivement.

subject matter n (U) sujet m.

sub judice [-'dʒuːdɪsɪ] adj JUR en train de passer devant le tribunal.

subjugate ['sʌbdʒugeɪt] vt [people, country] conquérir, subjuguer.

subjunctive [səb'dʒʌŋktɪv] n GRAMM : **~ (mood)** (mode m) subjonctif m.

sublet [,sʌb'let] (pt & pp sublet, cont -ting) vt sous-louer.

sublime [sə'blaɪm] adj sublime ; **from the ~ to the ridiculous** du sublime au ridicule OR grotesque.

sublimely [sə'blaɪmlɪ] adv suprêmement, souverainement.

subliminal [,sʌb'lɪmɪnl] adj subliminal(e).

submachine gun [,sʌbmə'ʃiːn-] n mitraillette f.

submarine [,sʌbmə'riːn] n sous-marin m.

submenu ['sʌb,menjuː] n COMPUT sous-menu m.

submerge [səb'mɜːdʒ] ◇ vt immerger, plonger ; **to ~ o.s. in sthg** fig se plonger dans qqch ◇ vi s'immerger, plonger.

submission [səb'mɪʃn] n - **1.** [obedience] soumission f - **2.** [presentation] présentation f, soumission f.

submissive [səb'mɪsɪv] adj soumis(e), docile.

submit [səb'mɪt] (pt & pp -ted ; cont -ting)

◇ *vt* soumettre ◇ *vi* : **to ~ (to)** se soumettre (à).

subnormal [ˌsʌb'nɔːml] *adj* arriéré(e), attardé(e).

subordinate [*adj & n* sə'bɔːdɪnət , *vt* sə'bɔːdɪneɪt] ◇ *adj* fml [less important] : **~ (to)** subordonné(e) (à), moins important(e) (que) ◇ *n* subordonné *m*, -e *f* ◇ *vt* subordonner, faire passer après.

subordinate clause [sə'bɔːdɪnət-] *n* proposition *f* subordonnée.

subordination [səˌbɔːdɪ'neɪʃn] *n* subordination *f*.

subpoena [sə'piːnə] (*pt & pp* **-ed**) JUR ◇ *n* citation *f*, assignation *f* ◇ *vt* citer OR assigner à comparaître.

sub-post office *n* Br petit bureau *m* de poste.

subroutine ['sʌbruːˌtiːn] *n* COMPUT sousprogramme *m*.

subscribe [səb'skraɪb] ◇ *vi* - **1.** [to magazine, newspaper] s'abonner, être abonné(e) - **2.** [to view, belief] : **to ~ to** être d'accord avec, approuver ◇ *vt* [money] donner.

subscriber [səb'skraɪbəʳ] *n* - **1.** [to magazine, service] abonné *m*, -e *f* - **2.** [to charity, campaign] souscripteur *m*, -trice *f*.

subscription [səb'skrɪpʃn] *n* - **1.** [to magazine] abonnement *m* - **2.** [to charity, campaign] souscription *f* - **3.** [to club] cotisation *f*.

subsection ['sʌbˌsekʃn] *n* subdivision *f*, paragraphe *m*.

subsequent ['sʌbsɪkwənt] *adj* ultérieur(e), suivant(e).

subsequently ['sʌbsɪkwəntlɪ] *adv* par la suite, plus tard.

subservient [səb'sɜːvjənt] *adj* [servile] : **~ (to)** servile (vis-à-vis de), obséquieux(euse) (envers).

subset ['sʌbset] *n* MATH sous-ensemble *m*.

subside [səb'saɪd] *vi* - **1.** [pain, anger] se calmer, s'atténuer ; [noise] diminuer - **2.** [CONSTR - building] s'affaisser ; [- ground] se tasser.

subsidence [səb'saɪdns, 'sʌbsɪdns] *n* [CONSTR - of building] affaissement *m* ; [- of ground] tassement *m*.

subsidiarity [sʌbsɪdɪ'ærɪtɪ] *n* subsidiarité *f*.

subsidiary [səb'sɪdjərɪ] (*pl* **-ies**) ◇ *adj* subsidiaire ◇ *n* : **~ (company)** filiale *f*.

subsidize, -ise ['sʌbsɪdaɪz] *vt* subventionner.

subsidy ['sʌbsɪdɪ] (*pl* **-ies**) *n* subvention *f*, subside *m*.

subsist [səb'sɪst] *vi* : **to ~ (on)** vivre (de).

subsistence [səb'sɪstəns] *n* subsistance *f*, existence *f*.

subsistence allowance *n (U)* Br frais *mpl* de subsistance.

subsistence farming *n* agriculture *f* d'autoconsommation.

subsistence level *n* minimum *m* vital.

substance ['sʌbstəns] *n* - **1.** [gen] substance *f* - **2.** [importance] importance *f*.

substandard [ˌsʌb'stændəd] *adj* de qualité inférieure.

substantial [səb'stænʃl] *adj* - **1.** [considerable] considérable, important(e) ; [meal] substantiel(elle) - **2.** [solid, well-built] solide.

substantially [səb'stænʃəlɪ] *adv* - **1.** [considerably] considérablement ; **~ better** bien mieux ; **~ bigger** beaucoup plus grand - **2.** [mainly] en grande partie.

substantiate [səb'stænʃɪeɪt] *vt* fml prouver, établir.

substantive [sʌb'stæntɪv] *adj* fml [meaningful] positif(ive), constructif(ive).

substitute ['sʌbstɪtjuːt] ◇ *n* - **1.** [replacement] : **~ (for)** [person] remplaçant *m*, -e *f* (de) ; [thing] succédané *m* (de) ; **to be no ~ for sthg** ne pas pouvoir remplacer qqch - **2.** SPORT remplaçant *m*, -e *f* ◇ *vt* : **to ~ A for B** substituer A à B, remplacer B par A ◇ *vi* : **to ~ for sb/sthg** remplacer qqn/qqch.

substitute teacher *n* Am suppléant *m*, -e *f*.

substitution [ˌsʌbstɪ'tjuːʃn] *n* substitution *f*, remplacement *m*.

subterfuge ['sʌbtəfjuːdʒ] *n* subterfuge *m*.

subterranean [ˌsʌbtə'reɪnjən] *adj* souterrain(e).

subtitle ['sʌbˌtaɪtl] *n* sous-titre *m*.

subtle ['sʌtl] *adj* subtil(e).

subtlety ['sʌtltɪ] *n* subtilité *f*.

subtly ['sʌtlɪ] *adv* subtilement.

subtotal ['sʌbˌtəʊtl] *n* total *m* partiel.

subtract [səb'trækt] *vt* : **to ~ sthg (from)** soustraire qqch (de).

subtraction [səb'trækʃn] *n* soustraction *f*.

subtropical [ˌsʌb'trɒpɪkl] *adj* subtropical(e).

suburb ['sʌbɜːb] *n* faubourg *m*.
  ➡ **suburbs** *npl* : **the ~s** la banlieue.

suburban [sə'bɜːbn] *adj* - **1.** [of suburbs] de banlieue - **2.** pej [life] étriqué(e) ; [person] à l'esprit étroit.

suburbia [sə'bɜːbɪə] *n (U)* la banlieue.

subversion [səb'vɜːʃn] *n* subversion *f*.

subversive [səb'vɜːsɪv] ◇ *adj* subversif(ive) <> *n* personne *f* qui agit de façon subversive.

subvert [səb'vɜ:t] *vt* subvertir, renverser.

subway ['sʌbweɪ] *n* - **1.** Br [underground walkway] passage *m* souterrain - **2.** Am [underground railway] métro *m*.

sub-zero *adj* au-dessous de zéro.

succeed [sək'si:d] <> *vt* succéder à <> *vi* réussir ; **to ~ in doing sthg** réussir à faire qqch.

succeeding [sək'si:dɪŋ] *adj* fml [in future] à venir ; [in past] suivant(e).

success [sək'ses] *n* succès *m*, réussite *f*.

successful [sək'sesfʊl] *adj* - **1.** [attempt] couronné(e) de succès - **2.** [film, book etc] à succès ; [person] qui a du succès.

successfully [sək'sesfʊlɪ] *adv* avec succès.

succession [sək'seʃn] *n* succession *f* ; **in (quick** OR **close) ~** coup sur soup.

successive [sək'sesɪv] *adj* successif(ive).

successor [sək'sesər] *n* successeur *m*.

success story *n* réussite *f*.

succinct [sək'sɪŋkt] *adj* succinct(e).

succinctly [sək'sɪŋktlɪ] *adv* succinctement, de façon succincte.

succour Br, **succor** Am ['sʌkər] *n* (U) literary secours *m*.

succulent ['sʌkjʊlənt] *adj* succulent(e).

succumb [sə'kʌm] *vi* : **to ~ (to)** succomber (à).

such [sʌtʃ] <> *adj* tel (telle), pareil(eille) ; **~ nonsense** de telles inepties ; **do you have ~ a thing as a tin-opener?** est-ce que tu aurais un ouvre-boîtes par hasard? ; **~ money/books as I have** le peu d'argent/de livres que j'ai ; **~ ... that** tel ... que <> *adv* - **1.** [for emphasis] si, tellement ; **it's ~ a horrible day!** quelle journée épouvantable! ; **~ a lot of books** tellement de livres ; **~ a long time** si OR tellement longtemps - **2.** [in comparisons] aussi <> *pron* : **and ~ (like)** et autres choses de ce genre ; **this is my car, ~ as it is** voilà ma voiture, pour ce qu'elle vaut ; **have some wine, ~ as there is** prenez un peu de vin, il en reste un petit fond.
➤ **as such** *adv* en tant que tel (telle), en soi.
➤ **such and such** *adj* tel et tel (telle et telle).

suchlike ['sʌtʃlaɪk] <> *adj* de ce genre, de la sorte <> *pron* : **and ~** [people] et autres gens de ce genre ; [things] et autres choses de ce genre.

suck [sʌk] *vt* - **1.** [with mouth] sucer - **2.** [draw in] aspirer - **3.** fig [involve] : **to be ~ed into sthg** être impliqué(e) dans qqch.

➤ **suck up** *vi* inf : **to ~ up (to sb)** faire de la lèche (à qqn).

sucker ['sʌkər] *n* - **1.** [suction pad] ventouse *f* - **2.** inf [gullible person] poire *f*.

suckle ['sʌkl] <> *vt* allaiter <> *vi* téter.

sucrose ['su:krəʊz] *n* saccharose *m*.

suction ['sʌkʃn] *n* succion *f*.

suction pump *n* pompe *f* aspirante.

Sudan [su:'dɑ:n] *n* Soudan *m* ; **in (the) ~** au Soudan.

Sudanese [ˌsu:də'ni:z] <> *adj* soudanais(e) <> *npl* : **the ~** les Soudanais *mpl*.

sudden ['sʌdn] *adj* soudain(e), brusque ; **all of a ~** tout d'un coup, soudain.

sudden death *n* SPORT jeu pour départager les ex aequo (le premier point perdu entraîne l'élimination immédiate).

suddenly ['sʌdnlɪ] *adv* soudainement, tout d'un coup.

suddenness ['sʌdnnɪs] *n* soudaineté *f*.

suds [sʌdz] *npl* mousse *f* de savon.

sue [su:] *vt* : **to ~ sb (for)** poursuivre qqn en justice (pour).

suede [sweɪd] <> *n* daim *m* <> *comp* en daim.

suet ['sʊɪt] *n* graisse *f* de rognon.

Suez ['su:ɪz] *n* Suez.

Suez Canal *n* : **the ~** le canal de Suez.

suffer ['sʌfər] <> *vt* - **1.** [pain, injury] souffrir de - **2.** [consequences, setback, loss] subir <> *vi* souffrir ; **to ~ from** MED souffrir de.

sufferance ['sʌfrəns] *n* : **on ~** par tolérance.

sufferer ['sʌfrər] *n* MED malade *mf*.

suffering ['sʌfrɪŋ] *n* souffrance *f*.

suffice [sə'faɪs] *vi* fml suffire.

sufficient [sə'fɪʃnt] *adj* suffisant(e).

sufficiently [sə'fɪʃntlɪ] *adv* suffisamment.

suffix ['sʌfɪks] *n* suffixe *m*.

suffocate ['sʌfəkeɪt] *vt* & *vi* suffoquer.

suffocation [ˌsʌfə'keɪʃn] *n* suffocation *f*.

suffrage ['sʌfrɪdʒ] *n* suffrage *m*.

suffuse [sə'fju:z] *vt* baigner.

sugar ['ʃʊgər] <> *n* sucre *m* <> *vt* sucrer.

sugar beet *n* betterave *f* à sucre.

sugar bowl *n* sucrier *m*.

sugarcane ['ʃʊgəkeɪn] *n* (U) canne *f* à sucre.

sugar-coated [-'kəʊtɪd] *adj* dragéifié(e).

sugared ['ʃʊgəd] *adj* sucré(e).

sugar lump *n* morceau *m* de sucre.

sugar refinery *n* raffinerie *f* de sucre.

sugary ['ʃʊgərɪ] *adj* - **1.** [food] sucré(e) - **2.** pej [sentimental] doucereux(euse).

suggest [sə'dʒest] *vt* - **1.** [propose] proposer, suggérer - **2.** [imply] suggérer.

suggestion [sə'dʒestʃn] *n* - **1.** [proposal] pro-position *f*, suggestion *f* - **2.** *(U)* [implication] suggestion *f*.

suggestive [sə'dʒestɪv] *adj* suggestif(ive) ; **to be ~ of** sthg suggérer qqch.

suicidal [sʊɪ'saɪdl] *adj* suicidaire.

suicide ['sʊɪsaɪd] *n* suicide *m ;* **to commit ~** se suicider.

suicide attempt *n* tentative *f* de suicide.

suit [suːt] ⬦ *n* - **1.** [for man] costume *m*, com-plet *m ;* [for woman] tailleur *m* - **2.** [outfit] : **ski/diving ~** combinaison *f* de ski/de plongée - **3.** [in cards] couleur *f* - **4.** JUR procès *m*, action *f* - **5.** *phr* : **to follow ~** *fig* faire de même ⬦ *vt* - **1.** [subj : clothes, hairstyle] aller à - **2.** [be con-venient, appropriate to] convenir à ; **to ~ o.s.** faire comme on veut ⬦ *vi* convenir, aller.

suitability [ˌsuːtə'bɪlətɪ] *n* convenance *f ;* [of candidate] aptitude *f*.

suitable ['suːtəbl] *adj* qui convient, qui va.

suitably ['suːtəblɪ] *adv* convenablement ; **~ impressed** favorablement impressionné.

suitcase ['suːtkeɪs] *n* valise *f*.

suite [swiːt] *n* - **1.** [of rooms] suite *f* - **2.** [of furni-ture] ensemble *m*.

suited ['suːtɪd] *adj* - **1.** [suitable] : **to be ~ to/for** convenir à/pour, aller à/pour - **2.** [couple] : **well ~** très bien assortis ; **ideally ~** faits l'un pour l'autre.

suitor ['suːtər] *n* dated soupirant *m*.

sulfate Am = **sulphate**.

sulfur Am = **sulphur**.

sulfuric acid Am = **sulphuric acid**.

sulk [sʌlk] ⬦ *n* bouderie *f* ⬦ *vi* bouder.

sulky ['sʌlkɪ] *(compar* -ier ; *superl* -iest) *adj* boudeur(euse).

sullen ['sʌlən] *adj* maussade.

sulphate Br, **sulfate** Am ['sʌlfeɪt] *n* sulfate *m*.

sulphur Br, **sulfur** Am ['sʌlfər] *n* soufre *m*.

sulphuric acid Br, **sulfuric acid** Am [sʌl'fjʊərɪk-] *n* acide *m* sulfurique.

sultan ['sʌltən] *n* sultan *m*.

sultana [səl'tɑːnə] *n* Br [dried grape] raisin *m* sec.

sultry ['sʌltrɪ] *(compar* -ier ; *superl* -iest) *adj* - **1.** [weather] lourd(e) - **2.** [sexual] sensuel(el-le).

sum [sʌm] *(pt* & *pp* -**med** ; *cont* -**ming**) *n* - **1.** [amount of money] somme *f* - **2.** [calculation] calcul *m*.

➡ **sum up** ⬦ *vt sep* [summarize] résumer ⬦ *vi* récapituler.

Sumatra [sʊ'mɑːtrə] *n* Sumatra *f ;* **in ~** à Su-matra.

Sumatran [sʊ'mɑːtrən] ⬦ *adj* sumatra-nais(e) ⬦ *n* Sumatranais *m*, -e *f*.

summarily ['sʌmərəlɪ] *adv* sommairement.

summarize, -ise ['sʌməraɪz] ⬦ *vt* résumer ⬦ *vi* récapituler.

summary ['sʌmərɪ] *(pl* -ies) ⬦ *adj* sommaire ⬦ *n* résumé *m*.

summation [sʌ'meɪʃn] *n* - **1.** [total] addition *f* - **2.** [summary] résumé *m*.

summer ['sʌmər] ⬦ *n* été *m ;* **in ~** en été ⬦ *comp* d'été ; **the ~ holidays** les grandes vacances *fpl*.

summer camp *n* Am colonie *f* de vacances.

summerhouse ['sʌməhaʊs, *pl* -haʊzɪz] *n* pa-villon *m* (de verdure).

summer school *n* université *f* d'été.

summertime ['sʌmətaɪm] ⬦ *adj* d'été ⬦ *n* été *m*.

Summer Time *n* Br heure *f* d'été.

summery ['sʌmərɪ] *adj* estival(e).

summing-up [ˌsʌmɪŋ-] *(pl* **summings-up** [ˌsʌmɪŋz-]) *n* JUR résumé *m*.

summit ['sʌmɪt] *n* sommet *m*.

summon ['sʌmən] *vt* appeler, convoquer.

➡ **summon up** *vt sep* rassembler.

summons ['sʌmənz] *(pl* -es [-iːz]) JUR ⬦ *n* as-signation *f* ⬦ *vt* assigner.

sumo (wrestling) ['suːməʊ-] *n* sumo *m*.

sump [sʌmp] *n* carter *m*.

sumptuous ['sʌmptʃʊəs] *adj* somp-tueux(euse).

sum total *n* somme *f* totale.

sun [sʌn] *(pt* & *pp* -**ned** ; *cont* -**ning**) ⬦ *n* so-leil *m ;* **in the ~** au soleil ⬦ *vt* : **to ~ o.s.** se chauffer au soleil.

Sun. *(abbr of* **Sunday**) dim.

sunbathe ['sʌnbeɪð] *vi* prendre un bain de soleil.

sunbather ['sʌnbeɪðər] *n* personne *f* qui prend un bain de soleil.

sunbeam ['sʌnbiːm] *n* rayon *m* de soleil.

sunbed ['sʌnbed] *n* lit *m* à ultra-violets.

sunburn ['sʌnbɜːn] *n (U)* coup *m* de soleil.

sunburned ['sʌnbɜːnd], **sunburnt** ['sʌn-bɜːnt] *adj* brûlé(e) par le soleil, qui a attrapé un coup de soleil.

sun cream *n* crème *f* solaire.

sundae ['sʌndeɪ] *n* coupe *f* de glace aux fruits et à la Chantilly.

Sunday ['sʌndɪ] *n* dimanche *m ;* **~ lunch** dé-jeuner *m* du dimanche OR dominical ; *see also* **Saturday**.

Sunday paper n Br *journal hebdomadaire paraissant le dimanche.*

Sunday school n catéchisme m.

sundial ['sʌndaɪəl] n cadran m solaire.

sundown ['sʌndaʊn] n coucher m du soleil.

sundries ['sʌndrɪz] npl fml articles mpl divers, objets mpl divers.

sundry ['sʌndrɪ] adj fml divers ; **all and ~** tout le monde, n'importe qui.

sunflower ['sʌn,flaʊəʳ] n tournesol m.

sung [sʌŋ] pp ▷ sing.

sunglasses ['sʌn,glɑːsɪz] npl lunettes fpl de soleil.

sunhat ['sʌnhæt] n chapeau m de soleil.

sunk [sʌŋk] pp ▷ sink.

sunken ['sʌŋkən] adj - **1.** [in water] coulé(e), submergé(e) - **2.** [garden] en contrebas ; [cheeks, eyes] creux(euse).

sunlamp ['sʌnlæmp] n lampe f à ultra-violets.

sunlight ['sʌnlaɪt] n lumière f du soleil.

Sunni ['sʊnɪ] (pl -s) n Sunnite mf.

sunny ['sʌnɪ] (compar -ier ; superl -iest) adj - **1.** [day, place] ensoleillé(e) ; **it's ~** il fait beau, il fait (du) soleil - **2.** [cheerful] radieux(euse), heureux(euse) - **3.** phr : **~ side up** Am [egg] sur le plat.

sunray lamp n lampe f à ultra-violets.

sunrise ['sʌnraɪz] n lever m du soleil.

sunroof ['sʌnruːf] n toit m ouvrant.

sunscreen ['sʌnskriːn] n écran m OR filtre m solaire.

sunset ['sʌnset] n coucher m du soleil.

sunshade ['sʌnʃeɪd] n parasol m.

sunshine ['sʌnʃaɪn] n lumière f du soleil.

sunspot ['sʌnspɒt] n tache f solaire.

sunstroke ['sʌnstrəʊk] n (U) insolation f.

suntan ['sʌntæn] ◇ n bronzage m ◇ comp [lotion, cream] solaire.

suntanned ['sʌntænd] adj bronzé(e).

suntrap ['sʌntræp] n endroit très ensoleillé.

sunup ['sʌnʌp] n Am inf lever m du soleil.

super ['suːpəʳ] adj inf génial(e), super (inv).

superabundance [,suːpərə'bʌndəns] n surabondance f.

superannuation ['suːpə,rænjʊ'eɪʃn] n (U) pension f de retraite.

superb [suː'pɜːb] adj superbe.

superbly [suː'pɜːblɪ] adv superbement.

Super Bowl n Am : **the ~** le Super Bowl ; finale du championnat des États-Unis de football américain.

superbug ['suːpəbʌg] n germe résistant aux traitements antibiotiques.

supercilious [,suːpə'sɪlɪəs] adj hautain(e).

supercomputer [,suːpəkəm'pjuːtəʳ] n superordinateur m, supercalculateur m.

superficial [,suːpə'fɪʃl] adj superficiel(elle).

superfluous [suː'pɜːflʊəs] adj superflu(e).

superglue ['suːpəgluː] n colle f forte.

superhero ['suːpə,hɪərəʊ] n superman m, surhomme m.

superhighway ['suːpə,haɪweɪ] n - **1.** Am autoroute f - **2.** = information highway.

superhuman [,suːpə'hjuːmən] adj surhumain(e).

superimpose [,suːpərɪm'pəʊz] vt : **to ~ sthg (on)** superposer qqch (à).

superintend [,suːpərɪn'tend] vt diriger.

superintendent [,suːpərɪn'tendənt] n - **1.** Br [of police] ≃ commissaire m - **2.** [of department] directeur m, -trice f.

superior [suː'pɪərɪəʳ] ◇ adj - **1.** [gen] : **~ (to)** supérieur(e) (à) - **2.** [goods, craftsmanship] de qualité supérieure ◇ n supérieur m, -e f.

superiority [suː,pɪərɪ'ɒrətɪ] n supériorité f.

superlative [suː'pɜːlətɪv] ◇ adj exceptionnel(elle), sans pareil(eille) ◇ n GRAMM superlatif m.

supermarket ['suːpə,mɑːkɪt] n supermarché m.

supernatural [ˌsuːpəˈnætʃrəl] ◇ adj surnaturel(elle) ◇ n : **the ~** le surnaturel m.

superpower [ˈsuːpəˌpauəʳ] n superpuissance f.

superscript [ˈsuːpəskrɪpt] adj écrit(e)/imprimé(e) au-dessus de la ligne.

supersede [ˌsuːpəˈsiːd] vt remplacer.

supersonic [ˌsuːpəˈsɒnɪk] adj supersonique.

superstar [ˈsuːpəstɑːʳ] n superstar f.

superstition [ˌsuːpəˈstɪʃn] n superstition f.

superstitious [ˌsuːpəˈstɪʃəs] adj superstitieux(euse).

superstore [ˈsuːpəstɔːʳ] n hypermarché m.

superstructure [ˈsuːpəˌstrʌktʃəʳ] n superstructure f.

supertanker [ˈsuːpəˌtæŋkəʳ] n supertanker m.

supertax [ˈsuːpətæks] n tranche f supérieure de l'impôt.

supervise [ˈsuːpəvaɪz] vt surveiller ; [work] superviser.

supervision [ˌsuːpəˈvɪʒn] n surveillance f; [of work] supervision f.

supervisor [ˈsuːpəvaɪzəʳ] n surveillant m, -e f.

supper [ˈsʌpəʳ] n - **1.** [evening meal] dîner m - **2.** [before bedtime] collation f.

supplant [səˈplɑːnt] vt supplanter.

supple [ˈsʌpl] adj souple.

supplement [n ˈsʌplɪmənt, vb ˈsʌplɪment] ◇ n supplément m ◇ vt compléter.

supplementary [ˌsʌplɪˈmentərɪ] adj supplémentaire.

supplementary benefit n Br ancien nom des allocations supplémentaires accordées aux personnes ayant un faible revenu.

supplier [səˈplaɪəʳ] n fournisseur m.

supply [səˈplaɪ] (pl -ies ; pt & pp -ied) ◇ n - **1.** [store] réserve f, provision f; **to be in short ~** manquer - **2.** [system] alimentation f - **3.** (U) ECON offre f ◇ vt - **1.** [provide] : **to ~ sthg (to sb)** fournir qqch (à qqn) - **2.** [provide to] : **to ~ sb (with)** fournir qqn (en), approvisionner qqn (en) ; **to ~ sthg with sthg** alimenter qqch en qqch.

➻ **supplies** npl [food] vivres mpl ; MIL approvisionnements mpl ; **office supplies** fournitures fpl de bureau.

supply teacher n Br suppléant m, -e f.

support [səˈpɔːt] ◇ n - **1.** (U) [physical help] appui m - **2.** (U) [emotional, financial help] soutien m - **3.** [object] support m, appui m ◇ vt - **1.** [physically] soutenir, supporter ; [weight] supporter - **2.** [emotionally] soutenir - **3.** [financially] subvenir aux besoins de ; **to ~ o.s.** subvenir

à ses propres besoins - **4.** [theory] être en faveur de, être partisan de ; [political party, candidate] appuyer ; SPORT être un supporter de.

supporter [səˈpɔːtəʳ] n - **1.** [of person, plan] partisan m, -e f - **2.** SPORT supporter m.

supportive [səˈpɔːtɪv] adj qui est d'un grand secours, qui soutient.

suppose [səˈpəʊz] ◇ vt supposer ; **I don't ~ you could ...?** [in polite requests] vous ne pourriez pas ... par hasard? ; **you don't ~ ...?** [asking opinion] vous ne pensez pas que ...? ◇ vi supposer ; **I ~ (so)** je suppose que oui ; **I ~ not** je suppose que non ◇ conj et si, à supposer que (+ subjunctive).

supposed [səˈpəʊzd] adj - **1.** [doubtful] supposé(e) - **2.** [reputed, intended] : **to be ~ to be** être censé(e) être.

supposedly [səˈpəʊzɪdlɪ] adv soi-disant.

supposing [səˈpəʊzɪŋ] conj et si, à supposer que (+ subjunctive).

supposition [ˌsʌpəˈzɪʃn] n supposition f.

suppository [səˈpɒzɪtrɪ] (pl -ies) n suppositoire m.

suppress [səˈpres] vt - **1.** [uprising] réprimer - **2.** [information] supprimer - **3.** [emotions] réprimer, étouffer.

suppression [səˈpreʃn] n - **1.** [of uprising, emotions] répression f - **2.** [of information] suppression f.

suppressor [səˈpresəʳ] n ELEC dispositif m antiparasite.

supranational [ˌsuːprəˈnæʃənl] adj supranational(e).

supremacy [sʊˈpreməsɪ] n suprématie f.

supreme [sʊˈpriːm] adj suprême.

Supreme Court n [in US] : **the ~** la Cour suprême.

SUPREME COURT

> La Cour suprême, organe supérieur du pouvoir judiciaire, est composée de membres nommés par le président des États-Unis ; elle détient le pouvoir de décision finale ainsi que le droit d'interpréter la Constitution.

supremely [sʊˈpriːmlɪ] adv suprêmement.

supremo [sʊˈpriːməʊ] (pl -s) n Br inf grand chef m.

Supt. abbr of **superintendent**.

surcharge [ˈsɜːtʃɑːdʒ] ◇ n [extra payment] surcharge f; [extra tax] surtaxe f ◇ vt surcharger.

sure [ʃʊəʳ] ◇ adj - **1.** [gen] sûr(e) ; **to be ~ of o.s.** être sûr de soi - **2.** [certain] : **to be ~ (of sthg/of doing sthg)** être sûr(e) (de qqch/de

faire qqch), être certain(e) (de qqch/de faire qqch) ; **to make ~ (that)** ... s'assurer OR vérifier que ... - **3. phr : to be ~ to do sthg** [remember] s'assurer de faire qqch ; **I am** OR **I'm ~ (that)** ... je suis bien certain que ..., je ne doute pas que ... ◇ adv - **1.** inf [yes] bien sûr - **2.** Am [really] vraiment.
➠ **for sure** adv sans aucun doute.
➠ **sure enough** adv en effet, effectivement.

surefire ['ʃʊəfaɪəʳ] adj inf certain(e), infaillible.

surefooted ['ʃʊə,fʊtɪd] adj d'un pied sûr.

surely ['ʃʊəlɪ] adv sûrement.

sure thing excl Am inf d'accord!

surety ['ʃʊərətɪ] n (U) caution f.

surf [sɜːf] ◇ n ressac m ◇ vi surfer.

surface ['sɜːfɪs] ◇ n surface f ; **on the ~** fig à première vue, vu de l'extérieur ; **below** OR **beneath the ~** fig au fond ; **to scratch the ~** fig [of problem] effleurer le problème ; [of subject] effleurer le sujet ◇ vi - **1.** [diver] remonter à la surface ; [submarine] faire surface - **2.** [problem, rumour] apparaître OR s'étaler au grand jour - **3.** inf hum [after absence] refaire surface.

surface mail n courrier m par voie de terre/de mer.

surface-to-air adj sol-air (inv).

surfboard ['sɜːfbɔːd] n planche f de surf.

surfeit ['sɜːfɪt] n fml excès m.

surfer ['sɜːfəʳ] n surfeur m, -euse f.

surfing ['sɜːfɪŋ] n surf m.

surge [sɜːdʒ] ◇ n - **1.** [of people, vehicles] déferlement m ; ELEC surtension f - **2.** [of emotion, interest] vague f, montée f ; [of anger] bouffée f ; [of sales, applications] afflux m ◇ vi - **1.** [people, vehicles] déferler - **2.** [emotion] monter.

surgeon ['sɜːdʒən] n chirurgien m.

surgery ['sɜːdʒərɪ] (pl -ies) n - **1.** (U) MED [performing operations] chirurgie f - **2.** Br MED [place] cabinet m de consultation - **3.** Br MED & POL [consulting period] consultation f.

surgical ['sɜːdʒɪkl] adj chirurgical(e) ; **~ stocking** bas m orthopédique.

surgical spirit n Br alcool m à 90°.

Surinam [,sʊərɪ'næm] n Surinam m, Suriname m ; **in ~** au Surinam.

surly ['sɜːlɪ] (compar -ier ; superl -iest) adj revêche, renfrogné(e).

surmise [sɜː'maɪz] vt fml présumer.

surmount [sɜː'maʊnt] vt surmonter.

surname ['sɜːneɪm] n nom m de famille.

surpass [sə'pɑːs] vt fml dépasser.

surplus ['sɜːpləs] ◇ adj en surplus ◇ n surplus m.

surprise [sə'praɪz] ◇ n surprise f ; **to take sb by ~** prendre qqn au dépourvu ◇ vt surprendre.

surprised [sə'praɪzd] adj surpris(e) ; **I wouldn't be ~ (if ...)** ça ne m'étonnerait pas (que ...).

surprising [sə'praɪzɪŋ] adj surprenant(e).

surprisingly [sə'praɪzɪŋlɪ] adv étonnamment.

surreal [sə'rɪəl] adj surréaliste.

surrealism [sə'rɪəlɪzm] n surréalisme m.

surrealist [sə'rɪəlɪst] ◇ adj surréaliste ◇ n surréaliste m f.

surrender [sə'rendəʳ] ◇ n reddition f, capitulation f ◇ vt fml [weapons, passport] rendre ; [claim, rights] renoncer à ◇ vi - **1.** [stop fighting] : **to ~ (to)** se rendre (à) - **2.** fig [give in] : **to ~ (to)** se laisser aller (à), se livrer (à).

surreptitious [,sʌrəp'tɪʃəs] adj subreptice.

surrogate ['sʌrəgeɪt] ◇ adj de substitution ◇ n substitut m.

surrogate mother n mère f porteuse.

surround [sə'raʊnd] ◇ n bordure f ◇ vt entourer ; [subj : police, army] cerner.

surrounding [sə'raʊndɪŋ] adj environnant(e).

surroundings [sə'raʊndɪŋz] npl environnement m.

surtax ['sɜːtæks] n surtaxe f.

surveillance [sɜː'veɪləns] n surveillance f.

survey [n 'sɜːveɪ, vb sə'veɪ] ◇ n - **1.** [investigation] étude f ; [of public opinion] sondage m - **2.** [of land] levé m ; [of building] inspection f ◇ vt - **1.** [contemplate] passer en revue - **2.** [investigate] faire une étude de, enquêter sur - **3.** [land] faire le levé de ; [building] inspecter.

surveyor [sə'veɪəʳ] n [of building] expert m ; [of land] géomètre m.

survival [sə'vaɪvl] n - **1.** [continuing to live] survie f - **2.** [relic] vestige m.

survive [sə'vaɪv] ◇ vt survivre à ◇ vi survivre.
➠ **survive on** vt fus vivre de.

survivor [sə'vaɪvəʳ] n survivant m, -e f ; fig battant m, -e f.

susceptible [sə'septəbl] adj : **~ (to)** sensible (à).

suspect [adj & n 'sʌspekt, vb sə'spekt] ◇ adj suspect(e) ◇ n suspect m, -e f ◇ vt - **1.** [distrust] douter de - **2.** [think likely, consider guilty] soupçonner ; **to ~ sb of sthg** soupçonner qqn de qqch.

suspend [sə'spend] vt - **1.** [gen] suspendre - **2.** [from school] renvoyer temporairement.

suspended animation [sə'spendɪd-] *n* hibernation *f*.

suspended sentence [sə'spendɪd-] *n* condamnation *f* avec sursis.

suspender belt [sə'spendəʳ-] *n* Br portejarretelles *m inv*.

suspenders [sə'spendəz] *npl* - **1.** Br [for stockings] jarretelles *fpl* - **2.** Am [for trousers] bretelles *fpl*.

suspense [sə'spens] *n* suspense *m ;* **to keep sb in ~** tenir qqn en suspens.

suspension [sə'spenʃn] *n* - **1.** [gen & AUT] suspension *f* - **2.** [from school] renvoi *m* temporaire.

suspension bridge *n* pont *m* suspendu.

suspicion [sə'spɪʃn] *n* soupçon *m ;* **to be under ~** être considéré comme suspect ; **to have one's ~s (about)** avoir des soupçons OR des doutes (sur).

suspicious [sə'spɪʃəs] *adj* - **1.** [having suspicions] soupçonneux(euse) - **2.** [causing suspicion] suspect(e), louche.

suspiciously [sə'spɪʃəslɪ] *adv* - **1.** [with suspicious attitude] de façon soupçonneuse, avec méfiance - **2.** [causing suspicion] de façon suspecte OR louche.

suss [sʌs] ➡ **suss out** *vt sep* Br *inf* piger, comprendre.

sustain [sə'steɪn] *vt* - **1.** [maintain] soutenir - **2.** [nourish] nourrir - **3.** *fml* [suffer - damage] subir ; [- injury] recevoir - **4.** *fml* [weight] supporter.

sustenance ['sʌstɪnəns] *n (U) fml* nourriture *f*.

suture ['suːtʃəʳ] *n* suture *f*.

svelte [sveltl] *adj* svelte.

SW - **1.** (*abbr of* **short wave**) OC - **2.** (*abbr of* **south-west**) S-O.

swab [swɒb] *n* MED tampon *m*.

swagger ['swægəʳ] ◇ *n* air *m* de parade ◇ *vi* parader.

Swahili [swɑː'hiːlɪ] ◇ *adj* swahili(e) ◇ *n* [language] swahili *m*.

swallow ['swɒləʊ] ◇ *n* - **1.** [bird] hirondelle *f* - **2.** [of food] bouchée *f*; [of drink] gorgée *f* ◇ *vt* avaler ; *fig* [anger, tears] ravaler ◇ *vi* avaler.

swam [swæm] *pt* ⊏▷ **swim**.

swamp [swɒmp] ◇ *n* marais *m* ◇ *vt* - **1.** [flood] submerger - **2.** [overwhelm] déborder, submerger.

swan [swɒn] *n* cygne *m*.

swap [swɒp] (*pt & pp* **-ped** ; *cont* **-ping**) ◇ *n* [exchange] échange *m* ◇ *vt* : **to ~ sthg (with sb/ for sthg)** échanger qqch (avec qqn/contre qqch) ◇ *vi* échanger.

swap meet *n* Am foire *f* au troc.

SWAPO ['swɑːpəʊ] (*abbr of* **South West Africa People's Organization**) *n* SWAPO *f*.

swarm [swɔːm] ◇ *n* essaim *m* ◇ *vi* - **1.** [bees] essaimer - **2.** *fig* [people] grouiller ; **to be ~ing (with)** [place] grouiller (de).

swarthy ['swɔːðɪ] (*compar* **-ier** ; *superl* **-iest**) *adj* basané(e).

swashbuckling ['swɒʃˌbʌklɪŋ] *adj* de cape et d'épée.

swastika ['swɒstɪkə] *n* croix *f* gammée.

swat [swɒt] (*pt & pp* **-ted** ; *cont* **-ting**) *vt* écraser.

swatch [swɒtʃ] *n* échantillon *m*.

swathe [sweɪð] ◇ *n* [large area] étendue *f* ◇ *vt literary* emmailloter, envelopper.

swathed [sweɪðd] *adj literary* : **~ (in)** emmailloté(e) (de), enveloppé(e) (de).

swatter ['swɒtəʳ] *n* tapette *f*.

sway [sweɪ] ◇ *vt* - **1.** [cause to swing] balancer - **2.** [influence] influencer ◇ *vi* se balancer ◇ *n fml* : **to hold ~ over sb** tenir qqn sous son empire ; **to come under the ~ of** se laisser influencer par.

Swazi ['swɑːzɪ] *n* Swazi *mf*.

Swaziland ['swɑːzɪlænd] *n* Swaziland *m ;* **in ~** au Swaziland.

swear [sweəʳ] (*pt* **swore** ; *pp* **sworn**) ◇ *vt* jurer ; **to ~ to do sthg** jurer de faire qqch ; **to ~ an oath** prêter serment ◇ *vi* jurer.

➡ **swear by** *vt fus* [have confidence in] jurer par.

➡ **swear in** *vt sep* JUR assermenter.

swearword ['sweəwɜːd] *n* juron *m*, gros mot *m*.

sweat [swet] ◇ *n* - **1.** [perspiration] transpiration *f*, sueur *f*; **to be in a cold ~** avoir des sueurs froides - **2.** *(U)* *inf* [hard work] corvée *f* ◇ *vi* - **1.** [perspire] transpirer, suer - **2.** *inf* [worry] se faire du mouron.

sweatband ['swetbænd] *n* SPORT bandeau *m ;* [of hat] cuir *m* intérieur.

sweater ['swetəʳ] *n* pullover *m*.

sweat pants *n* Am pantalon *m* de jogging OR survêtement.

sweatshirt ['swetʃɜːt] *n* sweat-shirt *m*.

sweatshop ['swetʃɒp] *n* ≃ atelier *m* clandestin.

sweatsuit [swetsjuːt] *n* jogging *m*, survêtement *m*.

sweaty ['swetɪ] (*compar* **-ier** ; *superl* **-iest**) *adj* - **1.** [skin, clothes] mouillé(e) de sueur - **2.** [place] chaud(e) et humide ; [activity] qui fait transpirer.

swede [swiːd] *n* Br rutabaga *m*.

Swede [swi:d] n Suédois m, -e f.

Sweden ['swi:dn] n Suède f ; **in ~ en** Suède.

Swedish ['swi:dɪʃ] <> adj suédois(e) <> n [language] suédois m <> npl : **the ~ les** Suédois mpl.

sweep [swi:p] (pt & pp swept) <> n
- **1.** [sweeping movement] grand geste m - **2.** [with brush] : **to give sthg a ~ donner un coup de** balai à qqch, balayer qqch - **3.** [electronic] balayage m - **4.** [chimney sweep] ramoneur m <> vt - **1.** [gen] balayer ; [scan with eyes] parcourir des yeux - **2.** [move] : **to ~ sthg off sthg en-** lever qqch de qqch d'un grand geste ; **to be** swept out to sea être emporté vers le large <> vi - **1.** [wind] s'engouffrer - **2.** [emotion] : **to** ~ **through sb** s'emparer de qqn - **3.** [person] : **to ~ along/in** avancer/entrer rapidement.

◆ **sweep aside** vt sep écarter, rejeter.

◆ **sweep away** vt sep [destroy] emporter, entraîner.

◆ **sweep up** <> vt sep [with brush] balayer <> vi balayer.

sweeper ['swi:pə'] n FTBL libero m.

sweeping ['swi:pɪŋ] adj - **1.** [effect, change] radical(e) - **2.** [statement] hâtif(ive) - **3.** [curve] large

sweepstake ['swi:psteɪk] n sweepstake m.

sweet [swi:t] <> adj - **1.** [gen] doux (douce) ; [cake, flavour, pudding] sucré(e) - **2.** [kind] gentil(ille) - **3.** [attractive] adorable, mignon(onne) <> n Br - **1.** [candy] bonbon m - **2.** [dessert] dessert m.

sweet-and-sour adj aigre-doux (aigre-douce).

sweet corn n maïs m.

sweeten ['swi:tn] vt sucrer.

sweetener ['swi:tnə'] n - **1.** [substance] édulcorant m - **2.** inf [bribe] pot-de-vin m.

sweetheart ['swi:thɑ:t] n - **1.** [term of endearment] chéri m, -e f, mon cœur m - **2.** [boyfriend, girlfriend] petit ami m, petite amie f.

sweetness ['swi:tnɪs] n - **1.** [gen] douceur f ; [of taste] goût m sucré, douceur - **2.** [attractiveness] charme m.

sweet pea n pois m de senteur.

sweet potato n patate f douce.

sweet shop n Br confiserie f.

sweet tooth n : **to have a ~ aimer les su-** creries.

swell [swel] (pt -ed ; pp swollen OR -ed) <> vi
- **1.** [leg, face etc] enfler ; [lungs, balloon] se gonfler ; **to ~ with pride** se gonfler d'orgueil
- **2.** [crowd, population etc] grossir, augmenter ; [sound] grossir, s'enfler <> vt grossir, aug-

menter <> n [of sea] houle f <> adj Am inf chouette, épatant(e).

swelling ['swelɪŋ] n enflure f.

sweltering ['sweltərɪŋ] adj étouffant(e), suffocant(e).

swept [swept] pt & pp ▷ sweep.

swerve [swɜːv] vi faire une embardée.

swift [swɪft] <> adj - **1.** [fast] rapide
- **2.** [prompt] prompt(e) <> n [bird] martinet m.

swiftly ['swɪftlɪ] adv - **1.** [quickly] rapidement, vite - **2.** [promptly] promptement.

swiftness ['swɪftnɪs] n - **1.** [quickness] rapidité f - **2.** [promptness] promptitude f.

swig [swɪg] (pt & pp -ged ; cont -ging) inf <> vt lamper <> n lampée f.

swill [swɪl] <> n (U) [pig food] pâtée f <> vt Br [wash] laver à grande eau.

swim [swɪm] (pt swam ; pp swum, cont -ming) <> n : **to have a ~ nager ; to go for a ~ aller se** baigner, aller nager <> vi - **1.** [person, fish, animal] nager - **2.** [room] tourner ; **my head was** swimming j'avais la tête qui tournait, la tête me tournait.

swimmer ['swɪmə'] n nageur m, -euse f.

swimming ['swɪmɪŋ] <> n natation f ; **to go** ~ **aller nager** <> comp [club, competition] de natation.

swimming baths npl Br piscine f.

swimming cap n bonnet m de bain.

swimming costume n Br maillot m de bain.

swimming pool n piscine f.

swimming trunks npl maillot m OR slip m de bain.

swimsuit ['swɪmsu:t] n maillot m de bain.

swindle ['swɪndl] <> n escroquerie f <> vt escroquer, rouler ; **to ~ sb out of sthg** escroquer qqch à qqn.

swine [swaɪn] n inf [person] salaud m.

swing [swɪŋ] (pt & pp swung) <> n - **1.** [child's toy] balançoire f - **2.** [change - of opinion] revirement m ; [- of mood] changement m, saute f
- **3.** [sway] balancement m - **4.** inf [blow] : **to** take a ~ **at sb** lancer OR envoyer un coup de poing à qqn - **5.** phr : **to be in full ~ battre son** plein ; **to get into the ~ of things** se mettre dans le bain <> vt - **1.** [move back and forth] balancer - **2.** [move in a curve] faire virer <> vi
- **1.** [move back and forth] se balancer
- **2.** [turn - vehicle] virer, tourner ; **to ~ round** [person] se retourner - **3.** [hit out] : **to ~ at sb** lancer OR envoyer un coup de poing à qqn
- **4.** [change] changer.

swing bridge n pont m tournant.

swing door n porte f battante.

swingeing ['swɪndʒɪŋ] *adj esp* Br très sévère.

swinging ['swɪŋɪŋ] *adj inf* - **1.** [lively] animé(e), plein(e) d'entrain - **2.** [uninhibited] dans le vent.

swipe [swaɪp] ◇ *n* : **to take a ~ at** envoyer OR donner un coup à ◇ *vt inf* [steal] faucher, piquer ◇ *vi* : **to ~ at** envoyer OR donner un coup à.

swipe card *n* carte *f* magnétique.

swirl [swɜːl] ◇ *n* tourbillon *m* ◇ *vt* agiter, remuer ◇ *vi* tourbillonner, tournoyer.

swish [swɪʃ] ◇ *n* [of tail] battement *m* ; [of dress] froufrou *m* ◇ *vt* [tail] battre l'air de ◇ *vi* bruire, froufrouter.

Swiss [swɪs] ◇ *adj* suisse ◇ *n* [person] Suisse *mf* ◇ *npl* : **the ~** les Suisses *mpl*.

swiss roll *n* Br gâteau *m* roulé.

switch [swɪtʃ] ◇ *n* - **1.** [control device] interrupteur *m*, commutateur *m* ; [on radio, stereo etc] bouton *m* - **2.** [change] changement *m* - **3.** Am RAIL aiguillage *m* ◇ *vt* [swap] échanger ; [jobs] changer de ◇ *vi* : **to ~ to/from** passer à/de.
➥ **switch off** ◇ *vt sep* éteindre ◇ *vi inf fig* décrocher.
➥ **switch on** *vt sep* allumer.

Switch® *n système de paiement non différé par carte bancaire.*

switchblade ['swɪtʃbleɪd] *n* Am couteau *m* à cran d'arrêt.

switchboard ['swɪtʃbɔːd] *n* standard *m*.

switchboard operator *n* standardiste *mf*.

switched-on [ˌswɪtʃt-] *adj inf* branché(e).

Switzerland ['swɪtsələnd] *n* Suisse *f* ; **in ~** en Suisse.

swivel ['swɪvl] (Br *pt & pp* -**led** ; *cont* -**ling**, Am *pt & pp* -**ed** ; *cont* -**ing**) ◇ *vt* [chair] faire pivoter ; [head, eyes] faire tourner ◇ *vi* [chair] pivoter ; [head, eyes] tourner.

swivel chair *n* fauteuil *m* pivotant OR tournant.

swollen ['swəʊln] ◇ *pp* ► swell ◇ *adj* [ankle, face] enflé(e) ; [river] en crue.

swoon [swuːn] *vi literary* s'évanouir ; *hum* se pâmer.

swoop [swuːp] ◇ *n* - **1.** [downward flight] descente *f* en piqué ; **in one fell ~** d'un seul coup - **2.** [raid] descente *f* ◇ *vi* - **1.** [bird, plane] piquer - **2.** [police, army] faire une descente.

swop [swɒp] = swap.

sword [sɔːd] *n* épée *f* ; **to cross ~s (with sb)** croiser le fer (avec qqn).

swordfish ['sɔːdfɪʃ] (*pl inv* OR -**es** [-iːz]) *n* espadon *m*.

swordsman ['sɔːdzmən] (*pl* -**men** [-mən]) *n* tireur *m* d'épée.

swore [swɔːʳ] *pt* ► swear.

sworn [swɔːn] ◇ *pp* ► swear ◇ *adj* - **1.** [committed] : **to be ~ enemies** être ennemis jurés - **2.** JUR sous serment.

swot [swɒt] (*pt & pp* -**ted** ; *cont* -**ting**) Br *inf* ◇ *n pej* bûcheur *m*, -euse *f* ◇ *vi* : **to ~ (for)** bûcher (pour).
➥ **swot up** *vt sep & vi inf* potasser, bûcher.

swum [swʌm] *pp* ► swim.

swung [swʌŋ] *pt & pp* ► swing.

sycamore ['sɪkəmɔːʳ] *n* sycomore *m*.

Sydney ['sɪdnɪ] *n* Sydney.

syllable ['sɪləbl] *n* syllabe *f*.

syllabub ['sɪləbʌb] *n* ≃ sabayon *m*.

syllabus ['sɪləbəs] (*pl* -**buses** [-bəsiːz] OR -**bi** [-baɪ]) *n* programme *m*.

symbol ['sɪmbl] *n* symbole *m*.

symbolic [sɪm'bɒlɪk] *adj* symbolique ; **to be ~ of** être le symbole de.

symbolism ['sɪmbəlɪzm] *n* symbolisme *m*.

symbolize, -ise ['sɪmbəlaɪz] *vt* symboliser.

symmetrical [sɪ'metrɪkl] *adj* symétrique.

symmetry ['sɪmətrɪ] *n* symétrie *f*.

sympathetic [ˌsɪmpə'θetɪk] *adj* - **1.** [understanding] compatissant(e), compréhensif(ive) - **2.** [willing to support] : **~ (to)** bien disposé(e) (à l'égard de) - **3.** [likable] sympathique.

sympathize, -ise ['sɪmpəθaɪz] *vi* - **1.** [feel sorry] compatir ; **to ~ with sb** plaindre qqn ; [in grief] compatir à la douleur de qqn - **2.** [understand] : **to ~ with sthg** comprendre qqch - **3.** [support] : **to ~ with sthg** approuver qqch, soutenir qqch.

sympathizer, -iser ['sɪmpəθaɪzəʳ] *n* sympathisant *m*, -e *f*.

sympathy ['sɪmpəθɪ] *n* (*U*) - **1.** [understanding] : **~ (for)** compassion *f* (pour), sympathie *f* (pour) - **2.** [agreement] approbation *f*, sympathie *f* ; **to be in ~ (with sthg)** être d'accord (avec qqch) - **3.** [support] : **in ~ (with sb)** en solidarité (avec qqn).
➥ **sympathies** *npl* - **1.** [support] soutien *m*, loyauté *f* - **2.** [to bereaved person] condoléances *fpl*.

symphonic [sɪm'fɒnɪk] *adj* symphonique.

symphony ['sɪmfənɪ] (*pl* -**ies**) *n* symphonie *f*.

symphony orchestra *n* orchestre *m* symphonique.

symposium [sɪm'pəʊzjəm] (*pl* -**siums** OR -**sia** [-zjə]) *n* symposium *m*.

symptom ['sɪmptəm] *n* symptôme *m*.

symptomatic [ˌsɪmptə'mætɪk] *adj* symptomatique.

synagogue ['sɪnəgɒg] *n* synagogue *f*.

sync [sɪŋk] *n inf* : out of ~ mal synchronisé(e) ; in ~ bïen synchronisé.

synchromesh gearbox ['sɪŋkrəʊmeʃ-] *n* boîte *f* de vitesses synchronisées.

synchronize, -ise ['sɪŋkrənaɪz] <> *vt* synchroniser <> *vi* être synchronisés(es).

synchronized swimming ['sɪŋkrənaɪzd-] *n* natation *f* synchronisée.

syncopated ['sɪŋkəpeɪtɪd] *adj* syncopé(e).

syncopation [ˌsɪŋkə'peɪʃn] *n* syncope *f*.

syndicate [*n* 'sɪndɪkət, *vb* 'sɪndɪkeɪt] <> *n* syndicat *m*, consortium *m* <> *vt* PRESS publier dans plusieurs journaux.

syndrome ['sɪndrəʊm] *n* syndrome *m*.

synod ['sɪnəd] *n* synode *m*.

synonym ['sɪnənɪm] *n* : ~ (for OR of) synonyme *m* (de).

synonymous [sɪ'nɒnɪməs] *adj* : ~ (with) synonyme (de).

synopsis [sɪ'nɒpsɪs] (*pl* -ses [-siːz]) *n* résumé *m* ; [film] synopsis *m*.

syntax ['sɪntæks] *n* syntaxe *f*.

synthesis ['sɪnθəsɪs] (*pl* -ses [-siːz]) *n* synthèse *f*.

synthesize, -ise ['sɪnθəsaɪz] *vt* synthétiser ; CHEM faire la synthèse de.

synthesizer ['sɪnθəsaɪzəʳ] *n* MUS synthétiseur *m*.

synthetic [sɪn'θetɪk] *adj* - **1.** [man-made] synthétique - **2.** pej [insincere] artificiel(elle), forcé(e).

syphilis ['sɪfɪlɪs] *n* syphilis *f*.

syphon ['saɪfn] = **siphon**.

Syria ['sɪrɪə] *n* Syrie *f* ; in ~ en Syrie.

Syrian ['sɪrɪən] <> *adj* syrien(enne) <> *n* [person] Syrien *m*, -enne *f*.

syringe [sɪ'rɪndʒ] (*cont* syringeing) <> *n* seringue *f* <> *vt* [wound] seringuer ; [ear] nettoyer à l'aide d'une seringue.

syrup ['sɪrəp] *n (U)* - **1.** [sugar and water] sirop *m* - **2.** Br [golden syrup] mélasse *f* raffinée.

system ['sɪstəm] *n* - **1.** [gen] système *m* ; road/railway ~ réseau *m* routier/de chemins de fer ; transport ~ réseau *m* des transports ; digestive ~ appareil *m* digestif - **2.** [equipment - gen] installation *f* ; [- electric, electronic] appareil *m* - **3.** *(U)* [methodical approach] système *m*, méthode *f* - **4.** phr : to get sthg out of one's ~ inf laisser OR donner libre cours à qqch ; to get it out of one's ~ inf se défouler.

systematic [ˌsɪstə'mætɪk] *adj* systématique.

systematize, -ise ['sɪstəmətaɪz] *vt* systématiser.

system disk *n* COMPUT disque *m* système.

systems analyst ['sɪstəmz-] *n* COMPUT analyste fonctionnel *m*, analyste fonctionnelle *f*.

systems engineer ['sɪstəmz-] *n* COMPUT ingénieur *m* de système.

system software *n (U)* COMPUT logiciel *m* d'exploitation.

T

t (*pl* t's OR ts), **T** (*pl* T's OR Ts) [tiː] *n* [letter] t *m inv*, T *m inv*.

ta [tɑː] *excl Br inf* merci!

TA (*abbr of* Territorial Army) *n* armée de réserve britannique.

tab [tæb] *n* - **1.** [of cloth] étiquette *f* - **2.** [of metal] languette *f* - **3.** Am [bill] addition *f* - **4.** (*abbr of* tabulator) [on typewriter] tabulateur *m* - **5.** phr : to keep ~s on sb tenir OR avoir qqn à l'œil, surveiller qqn.

Tabasco sauce® [tə'bæskəʊ-] *n* sauce *f* Tabasco.

tabby ['tæbɪ] (*pl* -ies) *n* : ~ (cat) chat tigré *m*, chatte tigrée *f*.

tabernacle ['tæbənækl] *n* tabernacle *m*.

tab key *n* touche *f* de tabulation.

table ['teɪbl] <> *n* table *f* ; to turn the ~s on sb fig renverser les rôles, retourner la situation <> *vt* - **1.** Br [propose] présenter, proposer - **2.** Am [postpone] ajourner la discussion de.

tableau ['tæbləʊ] (*pl* -x [-z] OR -s) *n* tableau *m* vivant.

tablecloth ['teɪblklɒθ] *n* nappe *f*.

table d'hôte ['tɑːbl,dəʊt] *n* : the ~ le menu à prix fixe.

table lamp *n* lampe *f*.

table licence *n* licence autorisant la vente de boissons alcoolisées seulement aux repas.

table linen *n* linge *m* de table.

table manners *npl* : **to have good/bad ~** savoir/ne pas savoir se tenir à table.

tablemat ['teɪblmæt] *n* dessous-de-plat *m inv.*

table salt *n* sel *m* fin.

tablespoon ['teɪblspuːn] *n* - **1.** [spoon] cuiller *f* de service - **2.** [spoonful] cuillerée *f* à soupe.

tablet ['tæblɪt] *n* - **1.** [pill] comprimé *m*, cachet *m* - **2.** [of stone] plaque *f* commémorative - **3.** [of soap] savonnette *f*, pain *m* de savon.

table tennis *n* ping-pong *m*, tennis *m* de table.

tableware ['teɪblweəʳ] *n* vaisselle *f*.

table wine *n* vin *m* de table.

tabloid ['tæblɔɪd] *n* : **~ (newspaper)** tabloïd *m*, tabloïde *m* ; **the ~ press** la presse populaire.

TABLOID

Dans les pays anglo-saxons, le format tabloïde est caractéristique des journaux populaires. Les principaux journaux populaires britanniques sont : the Daily Express, the Daily Mail, the Daily Mirror, The Star, The Sun et Today.

---

taboo [tə'buː] (*pl* **-s**) ◇ *adj* tabou(e) ◇ *n* tabou *m*.

tabulate ['tæbjʊleɪt] *vt* présenter sous forme de tableau.

tachograph ['tækəgrɑːf] *n* tachygraphe *m*.

tachometer [tæ'kɒmɪtəʳ] *n* tachymètre *m*.

tacit ['tæsɪt] *adj* tacite.

taciturn ['tæsɪtɜːn] *adj* taciturne.

tack [tæk] ◇ *n* - **1.** [nail] clou *m* - **2.** NAUT bord *m*, bordée *f* - **3.** fig [course of action] tactique *f*, méthode *f* ; **to change ~** changer de tactique ◇ *vt* - **1.** [fasten with nail - gen] clouer ; [- notice] punaiser - **2.** SEWING faufiler ◇ *vi* NAUT tirer une bordée.

◆ **tack on** *vt sep* inf ajouter, rajouter.

tackle ['tækl] ◇ *n* - **1.** FTBL tacle *m* ; RUGBY plaquage *m* - **2.** [equipment] équipement *m*, matériel *m* - **3.** [for lifting] palan *m*, appareil *m* de levage ◇ *vt* - **1.** [deal with] s'attaquer à - **2.** FTBL tacler ; RUGBY plaquer - **3.** [attack] empoigner - **4.** [talk to] : **to ~ sb about** OR **on sthg** parler franchement à qqn de qqch, entreprendre qqn sur qqch.

tacky ['tækɪ] (*compar* **-ier** ; *superl* **-iest**) *adj* - **1.** inf [film, remark] d'un goût douteux ; [jewellery] de pacotille - **2.** [sticky] collant(e), pas encore sec (sèche).

taco ['tækəʊ] (*pl* **-s**) *n* galette de maïs fourrée à la viande et au fromage.

tact [tækt] *n* (U) tact *m*, délicatesse *f*.

tactful ['tæktfʊl] *adj* [remark] plein(e) de tact ; [person] qui a du tact OR de la délicatesse.

tactfully ['tæktfʊlɪ] *adv* avec tact, avec délicatesse.

tactic ['tæktɪk] *n* tactique *f*.

◆ **tactics** *n* (U) MIL tactique *f*.

tactical ['tæktɪkl] *adj* tactique.

tactical voting *n* Br vote *m* tactique.

tactless ['tæktlɪs] *adj* qui manque de tact OR délicatesse.

tactlessly ['tæktlɪslɪ] *adv* sans tact, sans délicatesse.

tadpole ['tædpəʊl] *n* têtard *m*.

Tadzhikistan [tɑːˌdʒɪkɪ'stɑːn] *n* Tadjikistan *m* ; **in ~** au Tadjikistan.

taffeta ['tæfɪtə] *n* (U) taffetas *m*.

taffy ['tæfɪ] (*pl* **-ies**) *n* Am caramel *m*.

tag [tæg] (*pt* & *pp* **-ged** ; *cont* **-ging**) ◇ *n* - **1.** [of cloth] marque *f* - **2.** [of paper] étiquette *f* - **3.** (U) [game] jeu *m* du chat - **4.** COMPUT balise *f* ◇ *vt* marquer, étiqueter.

◆ **tag along** *vi* inf suivre.

Tagus ['teɪgəs] *n* : **the ~** le Tage.

Tahiti [tɑː'hiːtɪ] *n* Tahiti *m* ; **in ~** à Tahiti.

Tahitian [tɑː'hiːʃn] ◇ *adj* tahitien(enne) ◇ *n* Tahitien *m*, -enne *f*.

tail [teɪl] ◇ *n* - **1.** [gen] queue *f* ; **with one's ~ between one's legs** fig la queue entre les jambes - **2.** [of coat] basque *f*, pan *m* ; [of shirt] pan ◇ *comp* arrière ◇ *vt* inf [follow] filer.

◆ **tails** ◇ *n* [side of coin] pile *f* ◇ *npl* [formal dress] queue-de-pie *f*, habit *m*.

◆ **tail off** *vi* - **1.** [voice] s'affaiblir ; [noise] diminuer - **2.** [figures, sales] diminuer, baisser.

tailback ['teɪlbæk] *n* Br bouchon *m*.

tailcoat [ˌteɪl'kəʊt] *n* habit *m*, queue-de-pie *f*.

tail end *n* fin *f*.

tailgate ['teɪlgeɪt] *n* AUT hayon *m*.

taillight ['teɪllaɪt] *n* feu *m* arrière.

tailor ['teɪləʳ] ◇ *n* tailleur *m* ◇ *vt* fig adapter.

tailored ['teɪləd] *adj* ajusté(e), cintré(e).

tailor-made *adj* fig sur mesure.

tail pipe *n* Am tuyau *m* d'échappement.

tailplane ['teɪlpleɪn] *n* plan *m* fixe horizontal.

tailwind ['teɪlwɪnd] *n* vent *m* arrière.

taint [teɪnt] ◇ *n* souillure *f* ◇ *vt* [reputation] souiller, entacher.

tainted [ˈteɪntɪd] *adj* - **1.** [reputation] souillé(e), entaché(e) - **2.** Am [food] avarié(e).

Taiwan [ˌtaɪˈwɑːn] *n* Taiwan ; **in ~** à Taiwan.

Taiwanese [ˌtaɪwəˈniːz] <> *adj* taiwanais(e) <> *n* Taiwanais *m*, -e *f*.

take [teɪk] (*pt* **took** ; *pp* **taken**) <> *vt* - **1.** [gen] prendre ; **to ~ a seat** prendre un siège, s'asseoir ; **to ~ control/command** prendre le contrôle/le commandement ; **to ~ an exam** passer un examen ; **to ~ a walk** se promener, faire une promenade ; **to ~ a bath/ photo** prendre un bain/une photo ; **to ~ a lot of criticism** être très critiqué(e) ; **to ~ pity on sb** prendre qqn en pitié, avoir pitié de qqn ; **to ~ offence** se vexer, s'offenser ; **to ~ an interest in** s'intéresser à - **2.** [lead, drive] emmener - **3.** [accept] accepter - **4.** [contain] contenir, avoir une capacité de - **5.** [tolerate] supporter - **6.** [require] demander ; **how long will it ~?** combien de temps cela va-t-il prendre? - **7.** [wear] : **what size do you ~?** [clothes] quelle taille faites-vous? ; [shoes] vous chaussez du combien? - **8.** [assume] : **I ~ it (that)** ... je suppose que ..., je pense que ... - **9.** [rent] prendre, louer <> *vi* [dye, vaccine, fire] prendre <> *n* CINEMA prise *f* de vues.

◆ **take aback** *vt sep* surprendre, décontenancer ; **to be taken aback** être décontenancé(e) OR surpris(e).

◆ **take after** *vt fus* tenir de, ressembler à.

◆ **take apart** *vt sep* [dismantle] démonter.

◆ **take away** *vt sep* - **1.** [remove] enlever - **2.** [deduct] retrancher, soustraire.

◆ **take back** *vt sep* - **1.** [return] rendre, rapporter - **2.** [accept] reprendre - **3.** [statement, accusation] retirer.

◆ **take down** *vt sep* - **1.** [dismantle] démonter - **2.** [write down] prendre - **3.** [lower] baisser.

◆ **take in** *vt sep* - **1.** [deceive] rouler, tromper - **2.** [understand] comprendre - **3.** [include] englober, couvrir - **4.** [provide accommodation for] recueillir.

◆ **take off** <> *vt sep* - **1.** [remove] enlever, ôter - **2.** [have as holiday] : **to ~ a week/day off** prendre une semaine/un jour de congé ; **to ~ time off** prendre un congé - **3.** Br [imitate] imiter - **4.** [go away suddenly] : **to ~ o.s. off** s'en aller, partir <> *vi* - **1.** [plane] décoller - **2.** [go away suddenly] partir - **3.** [be successful] démarrer.

◆ **take on** <> *vt sep* - **1.** [accept] accepter, prendre - **2.** [employ] embaucher, prendre - **3.** [confront] s'attaquer à ; [competitor] faire concurrence à ; SPORT jouer contre <> *vt fus* [assume] prendre.

◆ **take out** *vt sep* - **1.** [from container] sortir ; [from pocket] prendre - **2.** [delete] enlever, sup-

primer - **3.** [go out with] emmener, sortir avec ; **to ~ it** OR **a lot out of sb** *inf* épuiser qqn, vider qqn.

◆ **take out on** *vt sep* : **to ~ sthg out on sb** passer qqch sur qqn ; **don't ~ it out on me!** ne t'en prends pas à moi!

◆ **take over** <> *vt sep* - **1.** [take control of] reprendre, prendre la direction de - **2.** [job] : **to ~ over sb's job** remplacer qqn, prendre la suite de qqn <> *vi* - **1.** [take control] prendre le pouvoir - **2.** [in job] prendre la relève.

◆ **take to** *vt fus* - **1.** [person] éprouver de la sympathie pour, sympathiser avec ; [activity] prendre goût à - **2.** [begin] : **to ~ to doing sthg** se mettre à faire qqch.

◆ **take up** *vt sep* - **1.** [begin - job] prendre ; **to ~ up singing** se mettre au chant - **2.** [continue - story] reprendre, continuer - **3.** [discuss] : **to ~ an issue up with sb** aborder une question avec qqn - **4.** [use up] prendre, occuper.

◆ **take up on** *vt sep* - **1.** [accept] : **to ~ sb up on an offer** accepter l'offre de qqn - **2.** [ask to explain] : **to ~ sb up on sthg** demander à qqn d'expliquer qqch.

◆ **take upon** *vt sep* : **to ~ it upon o.s. to do sthg** prendre sur soi de faire qqch.

takeaway Br [ˈteɪkəˌweɪ], **takeout** Am [ˈteɪkaʊt] *n* - **1.** [shop] restaurant *m* qui fait des plats à emporter - **2.** [food] plat *m* à emporter.

take-home pay *n* salaire *m* net (après déductions).

taken [ˈteɪkn] <> *pp* ⊳ **take** <> *adj* : **she was very ~ with him/the idea** il/l'idée lui plaisait beaucoup.

takeoff [ˈteɪkɒf] *n* [of plane] décollage *m*.

takeout Am = **takeaway**.

takeover [ˈteɪkˌəʊvər] *n* - **1.** [of company] prise *f* de contrôle, rachat *m* - **2.** [of government] prise *f* de pouvoir.

takeover bid *n* offre *f* publique d'achat, OPA *f*.

taker [ˈteɪkər] *n* preneur *m*, -euse *f*.

takeup [ˈteɪkʌp] *n* [of shares] souscription *f*.

takings [ˈteɪkɪŋz] *npl* recette *f*.

talc [tælk], **talcum (powder)** [ˈtælkəm-] *n* talc *m*.

tale [teɪl] *n* - **1.** [fictional story] histoire *f*, conte *m* - **2.** [anecdote] récit *m*, histoire *f*.

talent [ˈtælənt] *n* : **~ (for)** talent *m* (pour).

talented [ˈtæləntɪd] *adj* qui a du talent, talentueux(euse).

talent scout *n* dénicheur *m*, -euse *f* de talents.

talisman [ˈtælɪzmən] (*pl* **-s**) *n* talisman *m*.

talk [tɔːk] ◇ *n* - **1.** [conversation] discussion *f*, conversation *f* - **2.** (U) [gossip] bavardages *mpl*, racontars *mpl* - **3.** [lecture] conférence *f*, causerie *f* ◇ *vi* - **1.** [speak] : **to ~ (to sb)** parler (à qqn) ; **to ~ about** parler de ; **~ing of Lucy,...** à propos de Lucy,.... ; **to ~ big** se vanter - **2.** [gossip] bavarder, jaser - **3.** [make a speech] faire un discours, parler ; **to ~ on** OR **about** parler de ◇ *vt* parler.

➤ **talks** *npl* entretiens *mpl*, pourparlers *mpl*.

➤ **talk down to** *vt fus* parler avec condescendance à.

➤ **talk into** *vt sep* : **to ~ sb into doing sthg** persuader qqn de faire qqch.

➤ **talk out of** *vt sep* : **to ~ sb out of doing sthg** dissuader qqn de faire qqch.

➤ **talk over** *vt sep* discuter de.

talkative ['tɔːkətɪv] *adj* bavard(e), loquace.

talker ['tɔːkəʳ] *n* causeur *m*, -euse *f*, bavard *m*, -e *f*.

talking point ['tɔːkɪŋ-] *n* sujet *m* de conversation OR discussion.

talking-to ['tɔːkɪŋ-] *n* inf savon *m*, réprimande *f* ; **to give sb a good ~** passer un bon savon à qqn.

talk show *n* Am talk-show *m*, causerie *f*.

tall [tɔːl] *adj* grand(e) ; **how ~ are you?** combien mesurez-vous? ; **she's 5 feet ~** elle mesure 1,50 m.

tallboy ['tɔːlbɔɪ] *n* commode *f*.

tall order *n* : **that's a ~** c'est demander beaucoup, cela va être difficile.

tall story *n* histoire *f* à dormir debout.

tally ['tælɪ] (*pl* **-ies**, *pt* & *pp* **-ied**) ◇ *n* compte *m* ◇ *vi* correspondre, concorder.

talon ['tælən] *n* serre *f*, griffe *f*.

tambourine [,tæmbə'riːn] *n* tambourin *m*.

tame [teɪm] ◇ *adj* - **1.** [animal, bird] apprivoisé(e) - **2.** pej [person] docile ; [party, story, life] terne, morne ◇ *vt* - **1.** [animal, bird] apprivoiser - **2.** [people] mater, dresser.

tamely ['teɪmlɪ] *adv* [accept, agree] docilement.

tamer ['teɪməʳ] *n* dompteur *m*, -euse *f*.

Tamil ['tæmɪl] ◇ *adj* tamoul(e), tamil(e) ◇ *n* - **1.** [person] Tamoul *m*, -e *f*, Tamil *m*, -e *f* - **2.** [language] tamoul *m*, tamil *m*.

tamper ['tæmpəʳ] ➤ **tamper with** *vt fus* [machine] toucher à ; [records, file] altérer, falsifier ; [lock] essayer de crocheter.

tampon ['tæmpɒn] *n* tampon *m*.

tan [tæn] (*pt* & *pp* **-ned** ; *cont* **-ning**) ◇ *adj* brun clair (inv) ◇ *n* bronzage *m*, hâle *m* ◇ *vi* bronzer.

tandem ['tændəm] *n* [bicycle] tandem *m* ; **in ~** en tandem.

tandoori [tæn'dʊərɪ] ◇ *n* tandouri *m*, tandoori *m* ◇ *comp* tandouri, tandoori.

tang [tæŋ] *n* [taste] saveur *f* forte OR piquante ; [smell] odeur *f* forte OR piquante.

tangent ['tændʒənt] *n* GEOM tangente *f* ; **to go off at a ~** fig changer de sujet, faire une digression.

tangerine [,tændʒə'riːn] *n* mandarine *f*.

tangible ['tændʒəbl] *adj* tangible.

Tangier [tæn'dʒɪəʳ] *n* Tanger.

tangle ['tæŋgl] ◇ *n* - **1.** [mass] enchevêtrement *m*, emmêlement *m* - **2.** fig [confusion] embrouillamini *m* ; **to get into a ~** s'empêtrer, s'embrouiller ◇ *vt* : **to get ~d (up)** s'emmêler ◇ *vi* s'emmêler, s'enchevêtrer.

➤ **tangle with** *vt fus* inf se frotter à.

tangled ['tæŋgld] *adj* emmêlé(e) ; fig embrouillé(e).

tango ['tæŋgəʊ] (*pl* **-es**) ◇ *n* tango *m* ◇ *vi* danser le tango.

tangy ['tæŋɪ] (*compar* **-ier** ; *superl* **-iest**) *adj* piquant(e), fort(e).

tank [tæŋk] *n* - **1.** [container] réservoir *m* ; **fish ~** aquarium *m* - **2.** MIL tank *m*, char *m* (d'assaut).

tankard ['tæŋkəd] *n* chope *f*.

tanker ['tæŋkəʳ] *n* - **1.** [ship - for oil] pétrolier *m* - **2.** [truck] camion-citerne *m* - **3.** [train] wagon-citerne *m*.

tankful ['tæŋkfʊl] *n* [of petrol] réservoir *m* plein d'essence.

tanned [tænd] *adj* bronzé(e), hâlé(e).

tannin ['tænɪn] *n* tannin *m*, tanin *m*.

Tannoy® ['tænɔɪ] *n* système *m* de haut-parleurs.

tantalize, -ise ['tæntəlaɪz] *vt* mettre au supplice.

tantalizing ['tæntəlaɪzɪŋ] *adj* [smell] très appétissant(e) ; [possibility, thought] très tentant(e).

tantamount ['tæntəmaʊnt] *adj* : **~ to** équivalent(e) à.

tantrum ['tæntrəm] (*pl* **-s**) *n* crise *f* de colère ; **to have** OR **throw a ~** faire OR piquer une colère.

Tanzania [,tænzə'nɪə] *n* Tanzanie *f* ; **in ~** en Tanzanie.

Tanzanian [,tænzə'nɪən] ◇ *adj* tanzanien(enne) ◇ *n* Tanzanien *m*, -enne *f*.

tap [tæp] (*pt* & *pp* **-ped** ; *cont* **-ping**) ◇ *n* - **1.** [device] robinet *m* - **2.** [light blow] petite tape *f*, petit coup *m* ◇ *vt* - **1.** [hit] tapoter, taper - **2.** [resources, energy] exploiter, utiliser - **3.** [telephone, wire] mettre sur écoute ◇ *vi* taper, frapper.

tap dance *n* claquettes *fpl*.

tap dancer *n* danseur *m*, -euse *f* de claquettes.

tape [teɪp] ◇ *n* - **1.** [magnetic tape] bande *f* magnétique ; [cassette] cassette *f* - **2.** [strip of cloth, adhesive material] ruban *m* - **3.** SPORT bande *f* d'arrivée ◇ *vt* - **1.** [record] enregistrer ; [on video] magnétoscoper, enregistrer au magnétoscope - **2.** [stick] scotcher - **3.** Am [bandage] bander.

tape deck *n* dérouleur *m* de bande magnétique.

tape measure *n* centimètre *m*, mètre *m*.

taper ['teɪpəʳ] ◇ *n* [candle] bougie *f* fine ◇ *vi* s'effiler ; [trousers] se terminer en fuseau.

➡ **taper off** *vi* diminuer.

tape-record [-rɪˌkɔːd] *vt* enregistrer (au magnétophone).

tape recorder *n* magnétophone *m*.

tape recording *n* enregistrement *m* (au magnétophone).

tapered ['teɪpəd] *adj* [fingers] effilé(e), fuselé(e) ; [trousers] en fuseau.

tapestry ['tæpɪstrɪ] (*pl* -**ies**) *n* tapisserie *f*.

tapeworm ['teɪpwɜːm] *n* ténia *m*.

tapioca [ˌtæpɪ'əʊkə] *n* tapioca *m*.

tapir ['teɪpəʳ] (*pl inv* OR -**s**) *n* tapir *m*.

tappet ['tæpɪt] *n* poussoir *m*.

tar [tɑːʳ] *n* (*U*) goudron *m*.

tarantula [tə'ræntjʊlə] *n* tarentule *f*.

target ['tɑːgɪt] ◇ *n* - **1.** [of missile, bomb] objectif *m* ; [for archery, shooting] cible *f* - **2.** fig [for criticism] cible *f* - **3.** fig [goal] objectif *m* ; **on** ~ dans les temps ◇ *vt* - **1.** [city, building] viser - **2.** fig [subj : policy] s'adresser à, viser ; [subj : advertising] cibler.

tariff ['tærɪf] *n* - **1.** [tax] tarif *m* douanier - **2.** [list] tableau *m* OR liste *f* des prix.

Tarmac® ['tɑːmæk] *n* [material] macadam *m*.

➡ **tarmac** *n* AERON : **the tarmac** la piste.

tarnish ['tɑːnɪʃ] ◇ *vt* lit & fig ternir ◇ *vi* se ternir.

tarnished ['tɑːnɪʃt] *adj* lit & fig terni(e).

tarot ['tærəʊ] *n* : **the** ~ le tarot, les tarots *mpl*.

tarot card *n* tarot *m*.

tarpaulin [tɑː'pɔːlɪn] *n* [material] toile *f* goudronnée ; [sheet] bâche *f*.

tarragon ['tærəgən] *n* estragon *m*.

tart [tɑːt] ◇ *adj* - **1.** [bitter] acide - **2.** [sarcastic]

acide, acerbe ◇ *n* - **1.** CULIN tarte *f* - **2.** *v* inf [prostitute] pute *f*, grue *f*.

➡ **tart up** *vt sep* Br inf pej [room] retaper, rénover ; **to** ~ **o.s. up** se faire beau (belle).

tartan ['tɑːtn] ◇ *n* tartan *m* ◇ *comp* écossais(e).

tartar(e) sauce ['tɑːtəʳ-] *n* sauce *f* tartare.

tartness ['tɑːtnɪs] *n* acidité *f*.

task [tɑːsk] *n* tâche *f*, besogne *f*.

task force *n* MIL corps *m* expéditionnaire.

taskmaster ['tɑːskˌmɑːstəʳ] *n* : **hard** ~ tyran *m*.

Tasmania [tæz'meɪnjə] *n* Tasmanie *f*.

Tasmanian [tæz'meɪnjən] ◇ *adj* tasmanien(enne) ◇ *n* Tasmanien *m*, -enne *f*.

tassel ['tæsl] *n* pompon *m*, gland *m*.

taste [teɪst] ◇ *n* - **1.** [gen] goût *m* ; **have a** ~! goûte! ; **in good/bad** ~ de bon/mauvais goût - **2.** fig [liking] : ~ **(for)** penchant *m* (pour), goût *m* (pour) - **3.** fig [experience] aperçu *m* ; **to have had a** ~ **of sthg** avoir tâté OR goûté de qqch ◇ *vt* - **1.** [sense - food] sentir - **2.** [test, try] déguster, goûter - **3.** fig [experience] tâter de, goûter de ◇ *vi* : **to** ~ **of/like** avoir le goût de ; **to** ~ **good/odd** *etc* avoir bon goût/un drôle de goût *etc*.

taste bud *n* papille *f* gustative.

tasteful ['teɪstfʊl] *adj* de bon goût.

tastefully ['teɪstfʊlɪ] *adv* avec goût.

tasteless ['teɪstlɪs] *adj* - **1.** [object, decor, remark] de mauvais goût - **2.** [food] qui n'a aucun goût, fade.

taster ['teɪstəʳ] *n* dégustateur *m*, -trice *f*.

tasty ['teɪstɪ] (*compar* -**ier** ; *superl* -**iest**) *adj* [delicious] délicieux(euse), succulent(e).

tat [tæt] *n* (*U*) Br inf pej camelote *f*.

tattered ['tætəd] *adj* en lambeaux.

tatters ['tætəz] *npl* : **in** ~ [clothes] en lambeaux ; [confidence] brisé(e) ; [reputation] ruiné(e).

tattoo [tə'tuː] (*pl* -**s**) ◇ *n* - **1.** [design] tatouage *m* - **2.** Br [military display] parade *f* OR défilé *m* militaire ◇ *vt* tatouer.

tattooist [tə'tuːɪst] *n* tatoueur *m*.

tatty ['tætɪ] (*compar* -**ier** ; *superl* -**iest**) *adj* Br inf pej [clothes] défraîchi(e), usé(e) ; [flat, area] miteux(euse), minable.

taught [tɔːt] *pt* & *pp* ⊳ **teach.**

taunt [tɔːnt] ◇ *vt* railler, se moquer de ◇ *n* raillerie *f*, moquerie *f*

Taurus ['tɔːrəs] *n* Taureau *m* ; **to be (a)** ~ être Taureau.

taut [tɔːt] *adj* tendu(e).

tauten ['tɔːtn] ◇ *vt* tendre ◇ *vi* se tendre.

tautology [tɔːˈtɒlədʒɪ] n tautologie f.

tavern [ˈtævn] n taverne f.

tawdry [ˈtɔːdrɪ] (compar -ier ; superl -iest) adj pej [jewellery] clinquant(e) ; [clothes] voyant(e), criard(e).

tawny [ˈtɔːnɪ] adj fauve.

tax [tæks] <> n taxe f, impôt m <> vt - **1.** [goods] taxer - **2.** [profits, business, person] imposer - **3.** [strain] mettre à l'épreuve.

taxable [ˈtæksəbl] adj imposable.

tax allowance n abattement m fiscal.

taxation [tækˈseɪʃn] n (U) - **1.** [system] imposition f - **2.** [amount] impôts mpl.

tax avoidance [-əˈvɔɪdəns] n évasion f fiscale.

tax collector n percepteur m.

tax cut n baisse f de l'impôt.

tax-deductible [-dɪˈdʌktəbl] adj déductible des impôts.

tax disc n Br vignette f.

tax evasion n fraude f fiscale.

tax-exempt Am = tax-free.

tax exemption n exonération f d'impôt.

tax exile n Br personne qui vit à l'étranger pour échapper au fisc.

tax-free Br, **tax-exempt** Am adj exonéré(e) (d'impôt).

tax haven n paradis m fiscal.

taxi [ˈtæksɪ] <> n taxi m <> vi [plane] rouler au sol.

taxicab [ˈtæksɪkæb] n taxi m.

taxidermist [ˈtæksɪdɜːmɪst] n taxidermiste mf.

taxi driver n chauffeur m de taxi.

taximeter [ˈtæksɪˌmiːtər] n taximètre m.

taxing [ˈtæksɪŋ] adj éprouvant(e).

tax inspector n inspecteur m des impôts.

taxi rank Br, **taxi stand** n station f de taxis.

taxman [ˈtæksmæn] (pl -men [-men]) n percepteur m.

taxpayer [ˈtæksˌpeɪər] n contribuable mf.

tax relief n allègement m OR dégrèvement m fiscal.

tax return n déclaration f d'impôts.

tax year n année f fiscale.

TB n abbr of tuberculosis.

T-bone steak n steak m dans l'aloyau.

tbs., tbsp. (abbr of tablespoon(ful)) cs.

TD n - **1.** (abbr of Treasury Department) ministère américain de l'Économie et des Finances - **2.** abbr of touchdown.

tea [tiː] n - **1.** [drink, leaves] thé m - **2.** Br [afternoon meal] goûter m ; [evening meal] dîner m.

teabag [ˈtiːbæg] n sachet m de thé.

tea ball n Am boule f à thé.

tea break n Br pause pour prendre le thé, ≃ pause-café f.

tea caddy [-ˌkædɪ] n boîte f à thé.

teacake [ˈtiːkeɪk] n Br petit pain rond avec des raisins secs.

teach [tiːtʃ] (pt & pp taught) <> vt - **1.** [instruct] apprendre ; to ~ sb sthg, to ~ sthg to sb apprendre qqch à qqn ; to ~ sb to do sthg apprendre à qqn à faire qqch ; to ~ (sb) that ... apprendre (à qqn) que ... - **2.** [subj : teacher] enseigner ; to ~ sb sthg, to ~ sthg to sb enseigner qqch à qqn <> vi enseigner.

teacher [ˈtiːtʃər] n [in primary school] instituteur m, -trice f, maître m, maîtresse f ; [in secondary school] professeur m.

teachers college Am = teacher training college.

teacher's pet n pej chouchou m, chouchoute f.

teacher training college Br, **teachers college** Am n ≃ institut m universitaire de formation des maîtres, ≃ IUFM m.

teaching [ˈtiːtʃɪŋ] n enseignement m.

teaching aid n support m pédagogique.

teaching hospital n Br centre m hospitalo-universitaire, C.H.U. m.

teaching practice n (U) stage m de formation.

teaching staff npl enseignants mpl.

tea cloth n Br - **1.** [tablecloth] nappe f - **2.** [tea towel] torchon m.

tea cosy Br, **tea cozy** Am n couvre-théière m inv, cosy m.

teacup [ˈtiːkʌp] n tasse f à thé.

teak [tiːk] <> n teck m <> comp en teck.

tea leaves npl feuilles fpl de thé.

team [tiːm] n équipe f.

➡ **team up** vi : to ~ up (with sb) faire équipe (avec qqn).

team games npl jeux mpl d'équipe.

teammate [ˈtiːmmeɪt] n co-équipier m, -ère f.

team spirit n esprit m d'équipe.

teamster [ˈtiːmstər] n Am routier m, camionneur m.

teamwork [ˈtiːmwɜːk] n (U) travail m d'équipe, collaboration f.

tea party n thé m.

teapot [ˈtiːpɒt] n théière f.

tear[1] [tɪər] n larme f ; in ~s en larmes.

tear[2] [teər] (pt tore ; pp torn) <> vt - **1.** [rip] déchirer ; **to ~ sthg open** ouvrir qqch (en le déchirant) ; **to ~ sb/sthg to pieces** fig éreinter qqn/qqch - **2.** [remove roughly] arracher - **3. phr : to be torn between** être tiraillé(e) entre ⬦ vi - **1.** [rip] se déchirer - **2.** [move quickly] foncer, aller à toute allure - **3. phr : to ~ loose** s'échapper ⬦ n déchirure f, accroc m.

➤ **tear apart** vt sep - **1.** [rip up] déchirer, mettre en morceaux - **2.** fig [country, company] diviser ; [person] déchirer.

➤ **tear at** vt fus déchirer.

➤ **tear away** vt sep : **to ~ o.s. away (from)** s'arracher (de OR à).

➤ **tear down** vt sep [building] démolir ; [poster] arracher.

➤ **tear off** vt sep [clothes] enlever à la hâte.

➤ **tear up** vt sep déchirer.

tearaway ['teərə,weı] n Br inf casse-cou mf inv.

teardrop ['tıədrɒp] n larme f.

tearful ['tıəfʊl] adj - **1.** [person] en larmes - **2.** [event] larmoyant(e).

tear gas [tıəʳ-] n (U) gaz m lacrymogène.

tearing ['teərıŋ] adj inf terrible, fou (folle).

tearjerker ['tıə,dʒɜːkəʳ] n hum roman m OR film m qui fait pleurer dans les chaumières.

tearoom ['tiːrʊm] n salon m de thé.

tease [tiːz] ⬦ n taquin m, -e f ⬦ vt [mock] : **to ~ sb (about sthg)** taquiner qqn (à propos de qqch).

tea service, tea set n service m à thé.

tea shop n salon m de thé.

teasing ['tiːzıŋ] adj taquin(e).

Teasmaid® ['tiːzmeıd] n Br théière f automatique avec horloge incorporée.

teaspoon ['tiːspuːn] n - **1.** [utensil] petite cuillère f, cuillère à café - **2.** [amount] cuillerée f à café.

tea strainer n passoire f.

teat [tiːt] n tétine f.

teatime ['tiːtaım] n Br l'heure f du thé.

tea towel n torchon m.

tea urn n fontaine f à thé.

technical ['teknıkl] adj technique.

technical college n Br collège m technique.

technical drawing n (U) dessin m industriel.

technicality [,teknı'kælətı] (pl -ies) n - **1.** [intricacy] technicité f - **2.** [detail] détail m technique.

technically ['teknıklı] adv - **1.** [gen] techniquement - **2.** [theoretically] en théorie.

technician [tek'nıʃn] n technicien m, -enne f.

Technicolor® ['teknı,kʌləʳ] n (U) Technicolor® m.

technique [tek'niːk] n technique f.

techno ['teknəʊ] n MUS techno f.

technobabble ['teknəʊ,bæbl] n inf jargon m technique.

technocrat ['teknəkræt] n technocrate mf.

technological [,teknə'lɒdʒıkl] adj technologique.

technologist [tek'nɒlədʒıst] n technologue mf.

technology [tek'nɒlədʒı] (pl -ies) n technologie f.

technophobe ['teknəfəʊb] n technophobe.

teddy ['tedı] (pl -ies) n : **~ (bear)** ours m en peluche, nounours m.

tedious ['tiːdjəs] adj ennuyeux(euse).

tedium ['tiːdjəm] n fml ennui m.

tee [tiː] n GOLF tee m.

➤ **tee off** vi GOLF partir du tee.

teem [tiːm] vi - **1.** [rain] pleuvoir à verse - **2.** [place] : **to be ~ing with** grouiller de.

teen [tiːn] adj inf [fashion] pour ados ; [music, problems] d'ados.

teenage ['tiːneıdʒ] adj adolescent(e).

teenager ['tiːn,eıdʒəʳ] n adolescent m, -e f.

teens [tiːnz] npl adolescence f.

teeny (weeny) [,tiːnı('wiːnı)], **teensy (weensy)** [,tiːnzı('wiːnzı)] adj inf minuscule, tout petit (toute petite).

tee shirt n tee-shirt m.

teeter ['tiːtəʳ] vi vaciller ; **to ~ on the brink of** fig être au bord de.

teeter-totter n Am bascule f.

teeth [tiːθ] pl ➪ **tooth**.

teethe [tiːð] vi [baby] percer ses dents.

teething ring ['tiːðıŋ-] n anneau m de dentition.

teething troubles ['tiːðıŋ-] npl fig difficultés fpl initiales.

teetotal [tiː'təʊtl] adj qui ne boit jamais d'alcool.

teetotaller Br, **teetotaler** Am [tiː'təʊtləʳ] n personne f qui ne boit jamais d'alcool.

TEFL ['tefl] (abbr of teaching of English as a foreign language) n enseignement de l'anglais langue étrangère.

Teflon® ['teflɒn] ⬦ n Téflon® m ⬦ comp en Téflon®.

Tehran, Teheran [,teə'rɑːn] n Téhéran.

tel. (abbr of telephone) tél.

Tel-Aviv [ˌteləˈviːv] *n :* ~(-Jaffa) Tel-Aviv(-Jaffa).

tele- [ˈtelɪ] *prefix* télé-.

telebanking [ˈtelɪˌbæŋkɪŋ] *n* télébanque *f*.

telecast [ˈtelɪkɑːst] *n* émission *f* de télévision.

telecom [ˈtelɪkɒm] *n*, **telecoms** [ˈtelɪkɒmz] *npl* Br inf télécommunications *fpl*.

telecommunications [ˈtelɪkəˌmjuːnɪˈkeɪʃnz] *npl* télécommunications *fpl*.

teleconference [ˈtelɪˌkɒnfərəns] *n* téléconférence *f*.

telegram [ˈtelɪɡræm] *n* télégramme *m*.

telegraph [ˈtelɪɡrɑːf] ◇ *n* télégraphe *m* ◇ *vt* télégraphier.

telegraph pole, telegraph post Br *n* poteau *m* télégraphique.

telepathic [ˌtelɪˈpæθɪk] *adj* télépathique.

telepathy [tɪˈlepəθɪ] *n* télépathie *f*.

telephone [ˈtelɪfəʊn] ◇ *n* téléphone *m ;* **to be on the ~** Br [connected] avoir le téléphone ; [speaking] être au téléphone ◇ *vt* téléphoner à ◇ *vi* téléphoner.

telephone book *n* annuaire *m*.

telephone booth *n* cabine *f* téléphonique.

telephone box *n* Br cabine *f* téléphonique.

telephone call *n* appel *m* téléphonique, coup *m* de téléphone.

telephone directory *n* annuaire *m*.

telephone exchange *n* central *m* téléphonique.

telephone kiosk *n* Br cabine *f* téléphonique.

telephone number *n* numéro *m* de téléphone.

telephone operator *n* standardiste *mf*.

telephone tapping [-ˈtæpɪŋ] *n* mise *f* sur écoute.

telephonist [tɪˈlefənɪst] *n* Br téléphoniste *mf*.

telephoto lens [ˌtelɪˈfəʊtəʊ-] *n* téléobjectif *m*.

teleprinter [ˈtelɪˌprɪntəʳ], **teletypewriter** Am [ˌtelɪˈtaɪpˌraɪtəʳ] *n* téléscripteur *m*.

Teleprompter® [ˌtelɪˈprɒmptəʳ] *n* téléprompteur *m*.

telesales [ˈtelɪseɪlz] *npl* vente *f* par téléphone.

telescope [ˈtelɪskəʊp] *n* télescope *m*.

telescopic [ˌtelɪˈskɒpɪk] *adj* télescopique.

teleshopping [ˌtelɪˈʃɒpɪŋ] *n* téléachat *m*.

teletext [ˈtelɪtekst] *n* télétexte *m*.

telethon [ˈtelɪθɒn] *n* téléthon *m*.

teletypewriter Am = **teleprinter**.

televise [ˈtelɪvaɪz] *vt* téléviser.

television [ˈtelɪˌvɪʒn] *n* **- 1.** *(U)* [medium, industry] télévision *f ;* **on ~** à la télévision **- 2.** [apparatus] (poste *m* de) télévision *f*, téléviseur *m*.

television licence *n* Br redevance *f*.

television programme *n* émission *f* de télévision.

television set *n* poste *m* de télévision, téléviseur *m*.

teleworker [ˈtelɪˌwɜːkəʳ] *n* télétravailleur *m*, -euse *f*.

teleworking [ˈtelɪˌwɜːkɪŋ] *n* télétravail *m*.

telex [ˈteleks] ◇ *n* télex *m* ◇ *vt* [message] envoyer par télex, télexer ; [person] envoyer un télex à.

tell [tel] (*pt* & *pp* **told**) ◇ *vt* **- 1.** [gen] dire ; [story] raconter ; **to ~ sb (that)** ... dire à qqn que ... ; **to ~ sb sthg, to ~ sthg to sb** dire qqch à qqn ; **to ~ sb to do sthg** dire or ordonner à qqn de faire qqch ; **I told you so!** je te l'avais bien dit! **- 2.** [judge, recognize] savoir, voir ; **he can't ~ the time** il ne sait pas lire l'heure ; **could you ~ me the time?** tu peux me dire l'heure (qu'il est)? ; **there's no ~ing** ... on ne peut pas savoir ... ◇ *vi* **- 1.** [speak] parler **- 2.** [judge] savoir **- 3.** [have effect] se faire sentir.

◆ **tell apart** *vt sep* distinguer.

◆ **tell off** *vt sep* gronder.

teller [ˈteləʳ] *n* **- 1.** [of votes] scrutateur *m*, -trice *f* **- 2.** Esp am [in bank] caissier *m*, -ère *f*.

telling [ˈtelɪŋ] *adj* [remark] révélateur(trice).

telling-off (*pl* **tellings-off**) *n* réprimande *f*.

telltale [ˈtelteɪl] ◇ *adj* révélateur(trice) ◇ *n* rapporteur *m*, -euse *f*, mouchard *m*, -e *f*.

telly [ˈtelɪ] (*pl* **-ies**) (*abbr of* **television**) *n* Br inf télé *f ;* **on ~** à la télé.

temerity [tɪˈmerətɪ] *n* témérité *f*.

temp [temp] inf ◇ *n* (*abbr of* **temporary (employee)**) intérimaire *mf* ◇ *vi* travailler comme intérimaire.

temp. (*abbr of* **temperature**) temp.

temper [ˈtempəʳ] ◇ *n* **- 1.** [angry state] : **to be in a ~** être en colère ; **to lose one's ~** se mettre en colère ; **to have a short ~** être emporté **- 2.** [mood] humeur *f* **- 3.** [temperament] tempérament *m* ◇ *vt* [moderate] tempérer.

temperament [ˈtemprəmənt] *n* tempérament *m*.

temperamental [ˌtemprə'mentl] adj [volatile, unreliable] capricieux(euse).

temperance ['temprəns] (U) n [moderation] modération f ; [from alcohol] tempérance f.

temperate ['temprət] adj tempéré(e).

temperature ['temprətʃəʳ] n température f ; **to take sb's ~** prendre la température de qqn ; **to have a ~** avoir de la température OR de la fièvre.

tempered ['tempəd] adj - **1.** [steel] trempé(e) - **2.** [moderated] tempéré(e), modéré(e).

tempest ['tempɪst] n literary tempête f.

tempestuous [tem'pestjʊəs] adj lit & fig orageux(euse).

tempi ['tempiː] pl ⊳ **tempo**.

template ['templɪt] n gabarit m.

temple ['templ] n - **1.** RELIG temple m - **2.** ANAT tempe f.

templet ['templɪt] = **template**.

tempo ['tempəʊ] (pl -**pos** OR -**pi** [-piː]) n tempo m.

temporarily [ˌtempə'rerəlɪ] adv temporairement, provisoirement.

temporary ['tempərərɪ] adj temporaire, provisoire.

tempt [tempt] vt tenter ; **to ~ sb to do sthg** donner à qqn l'envie de faire qqch ; **to be** OR **feel ~ed to do sthg** être tenté OR avoir envie de faire qqch.

temptation [temp'teɪʃn] n tentation f.

tempting ['temptɪŋ] adj tentant(e).

ten [ten] num dix ; see also **six**.

tenable ['tenəbl] adj - **1.** [argument, position] défendable - **2.** [job, post] : **~ for** auquel on est nommé(e) pour.

tenacious [tɪ'neɪʃəs] adj tenace.

tenacity [tɪ'næsətɪ] n (U) ténacité f.

tenancy ['tenənsɪ] (pl -**ies**) n location f.

tenant ['tenənt] n locataire mf.

Ten Commandments npl : **the ~** les dix commandements mpl.

tend [tend] vt - **1.** [have tendency] : **to ~ to do sthg** avoir tendance à faire qqch ; **I ~ to think (that)** ... j'ai tendance à penser que ... - **2.** [look after] s'occuper de, garder.

tendency ['tendənsɪ] (pl -**ies**) n : **~ (to do sthg)** tendance f (à faire qqch) ; **a ~ towards fascism** une tendance fasciste.

tender ['tendəʳ] ⊳ adj tendre ; [bruise, part of body] sensible, douloureux(euse) ⊳ n COMM soumission f ⊳ vt fml [apology, money] offrir ; [resignation] donner.

tenderize, -ise ['tendəraɪz] vt attendrir.

tenderly ['tendəlɪ] adv [caringly] tendrement.

tenderness ['tendənɪs] (U) n - **1.** [compassion] tendresse f - **2.** [soreness] sensibilité f.

tendon ['tendən] n tendon m.

tendril ['tendrəl] n vrille f.

tenement ['tenəmənt] n immeuble m.

Tenerife [ˌtenə'riːf] n Tenerife ; **in ~** à Tenerife.

tenet ['tenɪt] n fml principe m.

tenner ['tenəʳ] n Br inf [amount] dix livres ; [note] billet m de dix livres.

Tennessee [ˌtenə'siː] n Tennessee m ; **in ~** dans le Tennessee.

tennis ['tenɪs] ⊳ n (U) tennis m ⊳ comp de tennis.

tennis ball n balle f de tennis.

tennis court n court m de tennis.

tennis racket n raquette f de tennis.

tenor ['tenəʳ] ⊳ adj [saxophone, recorder] ténor (inv) ; [voice] de ténor ⊳ n - **1.** [singer] ténor m - **2.** fml [meaning] sens m, substance f.

tenpin bowling Br ['tenpɪn-], **tenpins** Am ['tenpɪnz] n (U) bowling m (à dix quilles).

tense [tens] ⊳ adj tendu(e) ⊳ n temps m ⊳ vt tendre ⊳ vi se contracter.

tensed up [tenst-] adj contracté(e), tendu(e).

tension ['tenʃn] n tension f.

ten-spot n Am billet m de dix dollars.

tent [tent] n tente f.

tentacle ['tentəkl] n tentacule m.

tentative ['tentətɪv] adj - **1.** [hesitant] hésitant(e) - **2.** [not final] provisoire.

tentatively ['tentətɪvlɪ] adv - **1.** [hesitantly] de façon hésitante - **2.** [not finally] provisoirement.

tenterhooks ['tentəhʊks] npl : **to be on ~** être sur les charbons ardents.

tenth [tenθ] num dixième ; see also **sixth**.

tent peg n piquet m de tente.

tent pole n montant m OR mât m de tente.

tenuous ['tenjʊəs] adj ténu(e).

tenuously ['tenjʊəslɪ] adv de façon ténue.

tenure ['tenjəʳ] n (U) fml - **1.** [of property] bail m - **2.** [of job] : **to have ~** être titulaire.

tepee ['tiːpiː] n tipi m.

tepid ['tepɪd] adj tiède.

tequila [tɪ'kiːlə] n tequila f.

Ter., Terr. abbr of **Terrace**.

term [tɜːm] ⊳ n - **1.** [word, expression] terme m - **2.** SCH & UNIV trimestre m - **3.** [period of time] durée f, période f ; **a ~ in prison** une peine de prison ; **in the long/short ~** à long/court terme ⊳ vt appeler.

terms *npl* - **1.** [of contract, agreement] conditions *fpl* - **2.** [basis] : **in international/real ~s** en termes internationaux/réels ; **on equal** OR **the same ~s** d'égal à égal ; **to be on good ~s (with sb)** être en bons termes (avec qqn) ; **to be on speaking ~s** s'adresser la parole, se parler ; **to be on speaking ~s with sb** adresser la parole à qqn, parler à qqn ; **to come to ~s with sthg** accepter qqch - **3.** *phr* : **to think in ~s of doing sthg** envisager de OR penser faire qqch.

in terms of *prep* sur le plan de, en termes de.

terminal ['tɜ:mɪnl] ◇ *adj* MED en phase terminale ◇ *n* - **1.** AERON, COMPUT & RAIL terminal *m* - **2.** ELEC borne *f*.

terminally ['tɜ:mɪnəlɪ] *adv* : **to be ~ ill** être en phase terminale.

terminate ['tɜ:mɪneɪt] ◇ *vt* - **1.** fml [end - gen] terminer, mettre fin à ; [- contract] résilier - **2.** [pregnancy] interrompre ◇ *vi* - **1.** [bus, train] s'arrêter - **2.** [contract] se terminer.

termination [,tɜ:mɪ'neɪʃn] *n* - **1.** (U) fml [ending - gen] conclusion *f* ; [- of contract] résiliation *f* - **2.** [of pregnancy] interruption *f* (volontaire) de grossesse.

termini ['tɜ:mɪnaɪ] *pl* ⊳ **terminus.**

terminology [,tɜ:mɪ'nɒlədʒɪ] *n* terminologie *f*.

terminus ['tɜ:mɪnəs] (*pl* **-ni** [-naɪ] OR **-nuses** [-nəsi:z]) *n* terminus *m*.

termite ['tɜ:maɪt] *n* termite *m*.

Terr. = Ter.

terrace ['terəs] *n* - **1.** [patio, on hillside] terrasse *f* - **2.** Br [of houses] rangée *f* de maisons.

terraces *npl* FTBL : **the ~s** les gradins *mpl*.

terraced ['terəst] *adj* [hillside] en terrasses.

terraced house *n* Br *maison attenante aux maisons voisines*.

terracotta [,terə'kɒtə] *n* terre *f* cuite.

terrain [te'reɪn] *n* terrain *m*.

terrapin ['terəpɪn] (*pl inv* OR **-s**) *n* tortue *f* d'eau douce.

terrestrial [tə'restrɪəl] *adj* fml terrestre.

terrible ['terəbl] *adj* terrible ; [holiday, headache, weather] affreux(euse), épouvantable.

terribly ['terəblɪ] *adv* terriblement ; [sing, write, organized] affreusement mal ; [injured] affreusement.

terrier ['terɪə'] *n* terrier *m*.

terrific [tə'rɪfɪk] *adj* - **1.** [wonderful] fantastique, formidable - **2.** [enormous] énorme, fantastique.

terrified ['terɪfaɪd] *adj* terrifié(e) ; **to be ~ of** avoir une terreur folle OR peur folle de.

terrify ['terɪfaɪ] (*pt* & *pp* **-ied**) *vt* terrifier.

terrifying ['terɪfaɪɪŋ] *adj* terrifiant(e).

terrine [te'ri:n] *n* terrine *f*.

territorial [,terɪ'tɔ:rɪəl] *adj* territorial(e).

Territorial Army *n* Br : **the ~** l'armée territoriale.

territorial waters *npl* eaux *fpl* territoriales.

territory ['terətrɪ] (*pl* **-ies**) *n* territoire *m*.

terror ['terə'] *n* terreur *f*.

terrorism ['terərɪzml] *n* terrorisme *m*.

terrorist ['terərɪst] *n* terroriste *mf*.

terrorize, -ise ['terəraɪz] *vt* terroriser.

terror-stricken *adj* épouvanté(e).

terry(cloth) ['terɪ(klɒθ)] *n* tissu *m* éponge.

terse [tɜ:s] *adj* brusque.

tersely ['tɜ:slɪ] *adv* avec brusquerie.

tertiary ['tɜ:ʃərɪ] *adj* tertiaire.

tertiary education *n* enseignement *m* supérieur.

Terylene® ['terəli:n] *n* Térylène® *m*.

TESL ['tesl] (*abbr of* **teaching of English as a second language**) *n* enseignement de l'anglais seconde langue.

TESSA ['tesə] (*abbr of* **tax-exempt special savings account**) *n* en Grande-Bretagne, plan d'épargne exonéré d'impôt.

test [test] ◇ *n* - **1.** [trial] essai *m* ; [of friendship, courage] épreuve *f* ; **to put sb/sthg to the ~** mettre qqn/qqch à l'épreuve - **2.** [examination - of aptitude, psychological] test *m* ; SCH & UNIV interrogation *f* écrite/orale ; [- of driving] (examen *m* du) permis *m* de conduire - **3.** [MED - of blood, urine] analyse *f* ; [- of eyes] examen *m* ◇ *vt* - **1.** [try] essayer ; [determination, friendship] mettre à l'épreuve - **2.** SCH & UNIV faire faire une interrogation écrite/orale à ; **to ~ sb on sthg** interroger qqn sur qqch - **3.** [MED - blood, urine] analyser ; [- eyes, reflexes] faire un examen de.

testament ['testəmənt] *n* - **1.** [will] testament *m* - **2.** [proof] : **~ to** témoignage *m* de.

test ban *n* interdiction *f* d'essais nucléaires.

test card *n* Br mire *f*.

test case *n* JUR affaire-test *f*.

test-drive *vt* essayer.

tester ['testə'] *n* - **1.** [person] contrôleur *m*, -euse *f* - **2.** [sample] échantillon *m*.

test flight *n* vol *m* d'essai.

testicles ['testɪklz] *npl* testicules *mpl*.

testify ['testɪfaɪ] (*pt* & *pp* **-ied**) ◇ *vt* : **to ~ that ...** témoigner que ... ◇ *vi* - **1.** JUR témoigner - **2.** [be proof] : **to ~ to sthg** témoigner de qqch.

testimonial [ˌtestɪ'məʊnjəl] *n* - **1.** [character reference] recommandation *f* - **2.** [tribute] témoignage *m* d'estime.

testimony [Br 'testɪmənɪ, Am 'testəməʊnɪ] *n* témoignage *m*.

testing ['testɪŋ] *adj* éprouvant(e).

testing ground *n* banc *m* d'essai.

test match *n* Br match *m* international.

test paper *n* - **1.** SCH interrogation *f* écrite - **2.** CHEM papier *m* réactif.

test pattern *n* Am mire *f*.

test pilot *n* pilote *m* d'essai.

test tube *n* éprouvette *f*.

test-tube baby *n* bébé-éprouvette *m*.

testy ['testɪ] (*compar* **-ier** ; *superl* **-iest**) *adj* [person] irritable ; [remark] désobligeant(e).

tetanus ['tetənəs] *n* tétanos *m*.

tetchy ['tetʃɪ] (*compar* **-ier** ; *superl* **-iest**) *adj* ombrageux(euse), qui prend ombrage facilement.

tête-à-tête [ˌteɪtɑː'teɪt] *n* tête-à-tête *m inv.*

tether ['teðər] ◇ *vt* attacher ◇ *n :* **to be at the end of one's ~** être au bout du rouleau.

Texan ['teksn] *n* Texan *m*, -e *f.*

Texas ['teksəs] *n* Texas *m ;* **in ~** au Texas.

Tex-Mex [ˌteks'meks] *adj* Tex-Mex *(inv).*

text [tekst] *n* texte *m.*

textbook ['tekstbʊk] *n* livre *m* OR manuel *m* scolaire.

textile ['tekstaɪl] ◇ *n* textile *m* ◇ *comp* textile.

➡ **textiles** *npl* [industry] textile *m.*

texture ['tekstʃər] *n* texture *f ;* [of paper, wood] grain *m.*

TGIF inf (*abbr of* **thank God it's Friday!**) *encore une semaine de tirée!*

TGWU (*abbr of* **Transport and General Workers' Union**) *n* le plus grand syndicat interprofessionnel britannique.

Thai [taɪ] ◇ *adj* thaïlandais(e) ◇ *n* - **1.** [person] Thaïlandais *m*, -e *f* - **2.** [language] thaï *m.*

Thailand ['taɪlænd] *n* Thaïlande *f ;* **in ~** en Thaïlande.

thalidomide [θə'lɪdəmaɪd] *n* thalidomide *f.*

Thames [temz] *n :* **the ~** la Tamise.

than [weak form ðən, strong form ðæn] *conj* que ; **Sarah is younger ~ her sister** Sarah est plus jeune que sa sœur ; **more ~ three days/50 people** plus de trois jours/50 personnes.

thank [θæŋk] *vt :* **to ~ sb (for)** remercier qqn

(pour OR de) ; **~ God** OR **goodness** OR **heavens! Dieu merci!**

➡ **thanks** ◇ *npl* remerciements *mpl* ◇ *excl* merci!

➡ **thanks to** *prep* grâce à.

thankful ['θæŋkfʊl] *adj* - **1.** [grateful] : **~ (for)** reconnaissant(e) (de) - **2.** [relieved] soulagé(e).

thankfully ['θæŋkfʊlɪ] *adv* - **1.** [with relief] avec soulagement - **2.** [with gratitude] avec reconnaissance.

thankless ['θæŋklɪs] *adj* ingrat(e).

thanksgiving ['θæŋks,gɪvɪŋ] *n* action *f* de grâce.

➡ **Thanksgiving (Day)** *n* fête nationale américaine commémorant l'installation des premiers colons en Amérique.

thank you *excl :* **~ (for)** merci (pour OR de).

➡ **thankyou** *n* merci *m.*

that [ðæt, weak form of pron sense 2 & conj ðət] (*pl* **those** [ðəʊz]) ◇ *pron* - **1.** (*demonstrative use : pl 'those'*) ce, cela, ça ; (*as opposed to 'this'*) celui-là (celle-là) ; **who's ~?** qui est-ce? ; **is ~ Maureen?** c'est Maureen? ; **what's ~?** qu'est-ce que c'est que ça? ; **~'s a shame** c'est dommage ; **I had never seen ~ before** je n'avais jamais vu cela OR ça auparavant ; **which shoes are you going to wear, these or those?** quelles chaussures vas-tu mettre, celles-ci ou celles-là? ; **those who** ceux (celles) qui - **2.** (*to introduce relative clauses - subject*) qui ; (*- object*) que ; (*- with prep*) lequel (laquelle), lesquels (lesquelles) *(pl) ;* **we came to a path ~ led into the woods** nous arrivâmes à un sentier qui menait dans les bois ; **show me the book ~ you bought** montre-moi le livre que tu as acheté ; **on the day ~ we left** le jour où nous sommes partis ◇ *adj* (*demonstrative : pl 'those'*) ce (cette), cet (*before vowel or silent 'h'*), ces (*pl*) ; (*as opposed to 'this'*) ce (cette) ...-là, ces ...-là (*pl*) ; **those chocolates are delicious** ces chocolats sont délicieux ; **later ~ day** plus tard ce jour-là ; **I prefer ~ book** je préfère ce livre-là ; **I'll have ~ one** je prendrai celui-là ◇ *adv* aussi, si ; **it wasn't ~ bad/good** ce

n'était pas si mal/bien que ça ⬥ *conj* que ;
tell him ~ the children aren't coming dites-lui
que les enfants ne viennent pas ; **he recommended ~ I phone you** il m'a conseillé de
vous appeler.

➤ **at that** *adv* en plus, par surcroît.

➤ **that is (to say)** *adv* c'est-à-dire.

➤ **that's it** *adv* [that's all] c'est tout ; **~'s it, I'm
leaving** ça y est, je m'en vais.

➤ **that's that** *adv* : **and ~'s ~** un point c'est
tout.

thatched [θætʃt] *adj* de chaume.

Thatcherism [ˈθætʃərɪzm] *n* thatcherisme
m.

that's [ðæts] = **that is**.

thaw [θɔː] ⬥ *vt* [ice] faire fondre *OR* dégeler ;
[frozen food] décongeler ⬥ *vi* - **1.** [ice] dégeler,
fondre ; [frozen food] décongeler - **2.** fig [peo-
ple, relations] se dégeler ⬥ *n* dégel *m*.

the [weak form ðə, before vowel ðɪ, strong form
ðiː] *def art* - **1.** [gen] le (la), l' (+ vowel or silent
'h'), les (pl) ; **~ book** le livre ; **~ sea** la mer ;
~ man l'homme ; **~ boys/girls** les garçons/
filles ; **~ highest mountain in ~ world** la montagne la plus haute du monde ; **has ~ postman been?** est-ce que le facteur est passé? ;
~ monkey is a primate le singe est un primate ; **~ Joneses are coming to supper** les Jones
viennent dîner ; **you're not THE John Smith,
are you?** vous n'êtes pas le célèbre John
Smith, si? ; **it's THE place to go to in Paris** c'est
l'endroit à la mode *OR* l'endroit chic de Paris (où il faut aller) ; **to play ~ piano** jouer du
piano - **2.** (with an adjective to form a noun) :
~ British les Britanniques ; **~ old/young** les
vieux/jeunes ; **~ impossible** l'impossible
- **3.** [in dates] : **~ twelfth of May** le douze mai ;
~ forties les années quarante - **4.** [in compari-
sons] : **~ more ... ~ less** plus ... moins ; **~ sooner
~ better** le plus tôt sera le mieux - **5.** [in ti-
tles] : **Alexander ~ Great** Alexandre le
Grand ; **George ~ First** Georges Premier.

theatre, theater Am [ˈθɪətər] *n* - **1.** THEATRE
théâtre *m* - **2.** Br MED salle *f* d'opération
- **3.** Am [cinema] cinéma *m*.

theatregoer, theatergoer Am [ˈθɪətə-
ˌgəʊəʳ] *n* habitué *m*, -e *f* du théâtre.

theatrical [θɪˈætrɪkl] *adj* théâtral(e) ; [compa-
ny] de théâtre.

theft [θeft] *n* vol *m*.

their [ðeəʳ] *poss adj* leur, leurs (pl) ; **~ house**
leur maison ; **~ children** leurs enfants ; **it
wasn't THEIR fault** ce n'était pas de leur faute à eux.

theirs [ðeəz] *poss pron* le leur (la leur), les
leurs (pl) ; **that house is ~** cette maison est la

leur, cette maison est à eux/elles ; **it wasn't
our fault, it was THEIRS** ce n'était pas de notre faute, c'était de la leur ; **a friend of ~** un
de leurs amis, un ami à eux/elles.

them [weak form ðəm, strong form ðem] *pers
pron pl* - **1.** (direct) les ; **I know ~** je les connais ; **if I were OR was ~** si j'étais eux/elles, à
leur place - **2.** (indirect) leur ; **we spoke to ~**
nous leur avons parlé ; **she sent ~ a letter** elle leur a envoyé une lettre ; **I gave it to ~** je
le leur ai donné - **3.** (stressed, after prep, in
comparisons etc) eux (elles) ; **you can't expect
THEM to do it** tu ne peux pas exiger que ce
soit eux qui le fassent ; **with ~** avec eux/
elles ; **without ~** sans eux/elles ; **we're not
as wealthy as ~** nous ne sommes pas aussi
riches qu'eux/qu'elles.

thematic [θɪˈmætɪk] *adj* thématique.

theme [θiːm] *n* - **1.** [topic, motif] thème *m*, sujet
m - **2.** MUS thème *m* ; [signature tune] indicatif *m*.

theme park *n* parc *m* à thème.

theme song *n* chanson *f* principale, thème *m* principal.

theme tune *n* chanson *f* principale, thème *m* principal.

themselves [ðemˈselvz] *pron* - **1.** (reflexive)
se ; (after prep) eux (elles) - **2.** (for emphasis)
eux-mêmes *mpl*, elles-mêmes *fpl* ; **they did
it ~** ils l'ont fait tout seuls.

then [ðen] *adv* - **1.** [not now] alors, à cette époque - **2.** [next] puis, ensuite - **3.** [in that case]
alors, dans ce cas - **4.** [therefore] donc - **5.** [al-
so] d'ailleurs, et puis.

thence [ðens] *adv fml & literary* de là.

theologian [θɪəˈləʊdʒən] *n* théologien *m*.

theology [θɪˈɒlədʒɪ] *n* théologie *f*.

theorem [ˈθɪərəm] *n* théorème *m*.

theoretical [θɪəˈretɪkl] *adj* théorique.

theoretically [θɪəˈretɪklɪ] *adv* théoriquement.

theorist [ˈθɪərɪst] *n* théoricien *m*, -enne *f*.

theorize, -ise [ˈθɪəraɪz] *vi* : **to ~ (about)**
émettre une théorie (sur), théoriser (sur).

theory [ˈθɪərɪ] (pl **-ies**) *n* théorie *f* ; **in ~** en
théorie.

therapeutic [ˌθerəˈpjuːtɪk] *adj* thérapeutique.

therapist [ˈθerəpɪst] *n* thérapeute *mf*, psychothérapeute *mf*.

therapy [ˈθerəpɪ] *n* (U) thérapie *f*.

there [ðeəʳ] ⬥ *pron* - **1.** [indicating existence of
sthg] : **~ is/are** il y a ; **~'s someone at the door** il
y a quelqu'un à la porte ; **~ must be some
mistake** il doit y avoir erreur - **2.** fml (with
vb) : **~ followed an ominous silence** un silen-

ce lourd de menaces suivit ⬦ *adv* - **1.** [in existence, available] y, là ; **is anybody ~?** il y a quelqu'un? ; **is John ~, please?** [when telephoning] est-ce que John est là, s'il vous plaît? - **2.** [referring to place] y, là ; **I'm going ~ next week** j'y vais la semaine prochaine ; **~ it is** c'est là ; **~ he is!** le voilà! ; **over ~** là-bas ; **it's six kilometres ~ and back** cela fait six kilomètres aller-retour - **3.** [point in conversation, particular stage] là ; **can I stop you ~?** est-ce que je peux vous arrêter là? ; **we're getting ~** on y arrive - **4.** inf phr : **all/not all ~** qui a/n'a plus toute sa tête ⬦ *excl :* **~, I knew he'd turn up** tiens OR voilà, je savais bien qu'il s'amènerait ; **~, ~** allons, allons.

➡ **there and then, then and there** *adv* immédiatement, sur-le-champ.

➡ **there you are** *adv* - **1.** [handing over something] voilà - **2.** [emphasizing that one is right] vous voyez bien ; **~ you are, what did I tell you!** tu vois, qu'est-ce que je t'avais dit! - **3.** [expressing reluctant acceptance] c'est comme ça, que voulez-vous?

thereabouts [ðeərə'bauts], **thereabout** Am [ðeərə'baut] *adv :* **or ~** [nearby] par là ; [approximately] environ.

thereafter [ˌðeər'ɑːftə'] *adv* fml après cela, par la suite.

thereby [ˌðeər'baɪ] *adv* fml ainsi, de cette façon.

therefore ['ðeəfɔː'] *adv* donc, par conséquent.

therein [ˌðeər'ɪn] *adv* fml [inside] dedans ; [in that matter] en cela.

there's [ðeəz] = **there is**.

thereupon [ˌðeərə'pɒn] *adv* fml sur ce, sur quoi.

thermal ['θɜːml] *adj* thermique ; [clothes] en Thermolactyl®.

thermal reactor *n* réacteur *m* thermique.

thermal underwear *n* (U) sous-vêtements *mpl* en thermolactyl.

thermodynamics [ˌθɜːməʊdaɪ'næmɪks] *n* (U) thermodynamique *f*.

thermoelectric [ˌθɜːməʊɪ'lektrɪk] *adj* thermoélectrique.

thermometer [θə'mɒmɪtə'] *n* thermomètre *m*.

thermonuclear [ˌθɜːməʊ'njuːklɪə'] *adj* thermonucléaire.

thermoplastic [ˌθɜːməʊ'plæstɪk] ⬦ *adj* thermoplastique ⬦ *n* thermoplastique *m*, thermoplaste *m*.

Thermos (flask)® ['θɜːməs-] *n* (bouteille *f*) Thermos® *m* or *f*.

thermostat ['θɜːməstæt] *n* thermostat *m*.

thesaurus [θɪ'sɔːrəs] (*pl* **-es** [-iːz]) *n* dictionnaire *m* de synonymes.

these [ðiːz] *pl* ⬦ **this**.

thesis ['θiːsɪs] (*pl* **theses** ['θiːsiːz]) *n* thèse *f*.

they [ðeɪ] *pers pron pl* - **1.** [people, things, animals - unstressed] ils (elles) ; [- stressed] eux (elles) ; **~'re pleased** ils sont contents (elles sont contentes) ; **~'re pretty earrings** ce sont de jolies boucles d'oreille ; **THEY can't do it** eux (elles), ils (elles) ne peuvent pas le faire ; **there ~ are** les voilà - **2.** [unspecified people] on, ils ; **~ say it's going to snow** on dit qu'il va neiger ; **~'re going to put up petrol prices** ils vont augmenter le prix de l'essence.

they'd [ðeɪd] = **they had**, **they would**.

they'll [ðeɪl] = **they shall**, **they will**.

they're [ðeə'] = **they are**.

they've [ðeɪv] = **they have**.

thick [θɪk] ⬦ *adj* - **1.** [gen] épais (épaisse) ; [forest, hedge, fog] dense ; [voice] indistinct(e) ; **to be 6 inches ~** avoir 15 cm d'épaisseur - **2.** inf [stupid] bouché(e) - **3.** [full, covered] : **to be ~ with** [dust] être couvert(e) de ; [people] être plein(e) de ; **~ with smoke** [from cigarettes] enfumé(e) ; [from fire] plein d'une fumée épaisse ⬦ *n :* **in the ~ of** au plus fort de, en plein OR au beau milieu de.

➡ **thick and fast** *adv :* **questions came ~ and fast** les questions pleuvaient.

➡ **through thick and thin** *adv* envers et contre tout, quoi qu'il advienne.

thicken ['θɪkn] ⬦ *vt* épaissir ⬦ *vi* s'épaissir.

thickening ['θɪknɪŋ] *n* épaississant *m*.

thicket ['θɪkɪt] *n* fourré *m*.

thickly ['θɪklɪ] *adv* - **1.** [not thinly - spread] en couche épaisse ; [- cut] en tranches épaisses - **2.** [densely - wooded, populated] très - **3.** [speak, say] d'une voix indistincte.

thickness ['θɪknɪs] *n* épaisseur *f*.

thickset [ˌθɪk'set] *adj* trapu(e).

thick-skinned [-'skɪnd] *adj* qui a la peau dure.

thief [θiːf] (*pl* **thieves** [θiːvz]) *n* voleur *m*, -euse *f*.

thieve [θiːv] *vt* & *vi* voler.

thieves [θiːvz] *pl* ⬦ **thief**.

thieving ['θiːvɪŋ] ⬦ *adj* voleur(euse) ⬦ *n* (U) vol *m*.

thigh [θaɪ] *n* cuisse *f*.

thighbone ['θaɪbəʊn] *n* fémur *m*.

thimble ['θɪmbl] *n* dé *m* (à coudre).

thin [θɪn] (*compar* **-ner** ; *superl* **-nest**, *pt* & *pp*

-ned ; *cont* -ning⟩ ⟷ *adj* - **1.** [slice, layer, paper]
mince ; [cloth] léger(ère) ; [person] maigre
- **2.** [liquid, sauce] clair(e), peu épais (peu
épaisse) - **3.** [sparse - crowd] épars(e) ; [- vegetation, hair] clairsemé(e) ; **to be ~ on top** [person]
se dégarnir ⟷ *adv :* **to be wearing ~** [joke]
n'être plus amusant(e) ; **my patience is
wearing ~** je suis à bout de patience ⟷ *vi*
[hair] : **to be thinning** s'éclaircir, se dégarnir.

◄ **thin down** *vt sep* [liquid, paint] délayer, diluer ; [sauce] éclaircir.

thin air *n :* **to appear out of ~** apparaître
tout d'un coup ; **to disappear into ~** disparaître complètement, se volatiliser.

thing [θɪŋ] *n* - **1.** [gen] chose *f ;* **the (best) ~ to
do would be ...** le mieux serait de ... ; **for one
~** en premier lieu, pour commencer ;
(what) with one ~ and another au bout du
compte ; **the ~ is ...** le problème, c'est que
... ; **it's just one of those ~s** inf c'est comme
ça, ce sont des choses qui arrivent ; **to have
a ~ about sb/sthg** inf [like] adorer qqn/qqch,
être fou de qqn/qqch ; [dislike] avoir qqn/
qqch en horreur ; **to make a ~ (out) of** inf faire tout un plat *OR* toute une histoire de
- **2.** [anything] : **I don't know a ~** je n'y connais
absolument rien - **3.** [object] chose *f*, objet *m*
- **4.** [person] : **the ~** la mode.

◄ **things** *npl* - **1.** [clothes, possessions] affaires
fpl - **2.** inf [life] : **how are ~s?** comment ça va?

thingamabob [ˈθɪŋəməˌbɒb], **thingamajig** [ˈθɪŋəmədʒɪg], **thingummy (jig)** Br
[ˈθɪŋəmɪ-], **thingie** Br, **thingy** Br [ˈθɪŋɪ] *n*
inf truc *m*, machin *m*.

think [θɪŋk] (*pt* & *pp* thought) ⟷ *vt* - **1.** [be-
lieve] : **to ~ (that)** croire que, penser que ; **I
~ so/not** je crois que oui/non, je pense que
oui/non - **2.** [have in mind] penser à - **3.** [imag-
ine] s'imaginer ; **I can't ~ why you agreed to
do it** je ne comprends pas *OR* je me demande bien pourquoi tu as accepté de le faire
- **4.** [remember] : **did you ~ to bring any money?**
avez-vous pensé à apporter de l'argent?
- **5.** [in polite requests] : **do you ~ you could help
me?** tu pourrais m'aider? ⟷ *vi* - **1.** [gen]
réfléchir, penser - **2.** [have stated opinion] :
what do you ~ of *OR* **about his new film?** que
pensez-vous de son dernier film? ; **to ~ a
lot of sb/sthg** penser beaucoup de bien de
qqn/qqch - **3.** *phr* : **to ~ better of sthg/of doing sthg** décider après tout de ne pas faire
qqch ; **to ~ nothing of doing sthg** trouver
tout à fait normal *OR* tout naturel de faire
qqch ; **to ~ twice** y réfléchir à deux fois ⟷ *n*
inf : **to have a ~ (about sthg)** réfléchir (à
qqch).

◄ **think about** *vt fus :* **to ~ about sb/sthg**
songer à *OR* penser à qqn/qqch ; **to ~ about
doing sthg** songer à faire qqch ; **I'll ~ about it**
je vais y réfléchir.

◄ **think back** *vi :* **to ~ back (to)** repenser (à).

◄ **think of** *vt fus* - **1.** [consider] = **think about**
- **2.** [remember] se rappeler - **3.** [conceive] penser à, avoir l'idée de ; **to ~ of doing sthg**
avoir l'idée de faire qqch - **4.** [show consideration for] penser à.

◄ **think out, think through** *vt sep* bien
étudier, bien considérer.

◄ **think over** *vt sep* réfléchir à

◄ **think up** *vt sep* imaginer.

thinker [ˈθɪŋkəʳ] *n* penseur *m*.

thinking [ˈθɪŋkɪŋ] ⟷ *adj* qui pense, qui ré-
fléchit ⟷ *n* (U) opinion *f*, pensée *f ;* **to do
some ~** réfléchir ; **to my way of ~** à mon avis.

think tank *n* comité *m* d'experts.

thinly [ˈθɪnlɪ] *adv* - **1.** [not thickly - spread] en couche mince ; [- cut] en tranches minces
- **2.** [sparsely - wooded, populated] peu.

thinner [ˈθɪnəʳ] *n* diluant *m*.

thinness [ˈθɪnnɪs] *n* (U) [of slice, layer, paper] minceur *f ;* [of person] maigreur *f ;* [of cloth] légèreté *f*.

thin-skinned [-ˈskɪnd] *adj* susceptible, très
sensible.

third [θɜːd] ⟷ *num* troisième ; *see also* sixth
⟷ *n* UNIV ≃ licence *f* mention passable.

third-class *adj* Br UNIV : **~ degree** ≃ licence *f*
mention passable.

third-degree burns *npl* brûlures *fpl* du
troisième degré.

thirdly [ˈθɜːdlɪ] *adv* troisièmement, tertio.

third party *n* tiers *m*, tierce personne *f*.

third party insurance *n* assurance *f* de
responsabilité civile.

third-rate *adj* pej de dernier *OR* troisième
ordre.

Third World *n :* **the ~** le tiers-monde.

thirst [θɜːst] *n* soif *f ;* **~ for** fig soif de.

thirsty [ˈθɜːstɪ] (*compar* -ier ; *superl* -iest) *adj*
- **1.** [person] : **to be** *OR* **feel ~** avoir soif - **2.** [work]
qui donne soif.

thirteen [ˌθɜːˈtiːn] *num* treize ; *see also* six.

thirteenth [ˌθɜːˈtiːnθ] *num* treizième ; *see also* sixth.

thirtieth [ˈθɜːtɪəθ] *num* trentième ; *see also*
sixth.

thirty [ˈθɜːtɪ] (*pl* -ies) *num* trente ; *see also* sixty.

thirty-something *adj* caractéristique de
certaines personnes ayant la trentaine et issues d'un milieu aisé.

this [ðɪs] (*pl* **these** [ðiːz]) ⬦ *pron (demonstrative use)* ce, ceci ; *(as opposed to 'that')* celui-ci (celle-ci) ; **~ is for you** c'est pour vous ; **who's ~?** qui est-ce? ; **what's ~?** qu'est-ce que c'est? ; **which sweets does she prefer, these or those?** quels bonbons préfère-t-elle, ceux-ci ou ceux-là? ; **~ is Daphne Logan** [introducing another person] je vous présente Daphne Logan ; [introducing oneself on phone] ici Daphne Logan, Daphne Logan à l'appareil ; **to talk about ~ and that** parler de choses et d'autres ; **to do ~ and that** faire toutes sortes de choses ⬦ *adj* **- 1.** *(demonstrative use)* ce (cette), cet *(before vowel or silent 'h')*, ces *(pl)* ; *(as opposed to 'that')* ce (cette) ...-ci, ces ...-ci *(pl)* ; **these chocolates are delicious** ces chocolats sont délicieux ; **I prefer ~ book** je préfère ce livre-ci ; **I'll have ~ one** je prendrai celui-ci ; **~ afternoon** cet après-midi ; **~ morning** ce matin ; **~ week** cette semaine **- 2.** inf [a certain] un certain (une certaine) ⬦ *adv* aussi ; **it was ~ big** c'était aussi grand que ça ; **you'll need about ~ much** il vous en faudra à peu près comme ceci.

thistle [ˈθɪsl] *n* chardon *m*.

thither [ˈðɪðəʳ] ⊳ **hither.**

tho' [ðəʊ] = **though.**

thong [θɒŋ] *n* **- 1.** [of leather] lanière *f* **- 2. Am** [flip-flop] tong *f.*

thorn [θɔːn] *n* épine *f ;* **to be a ~ in sb's flesh** OR **side** être une source continuelle d'exaspération pour qqn.

thorny [ˈθɔːnɪ] (*compar* **-ier ;** *superl* **-iest**) *adj* lit & fig épineux(euse).

thorough [ˈθʌrə] *adj* **- 1.** [exhaustive - search, inspection] minutieux(euse) ; [- investigation, knowledge] approfondi(e) **- 2.** [meticulous] méticuleux(euse) **- 3.** [complete, utter] complet(ète), absolu(e).

thoroughbred [ˈθʌrəbred] *n* pur-sang *m* inv.

thoroughfare [ˈθʌrəfeəʳ] *n* fml rue *f*, voie *f* publique.

thoroughly [ˈθʌrəlɪ] *adv* **- 1.** [fully, in detail] à fond **- 2.** [completely, utterly] absolument, complètement.

thoroughness [ˈθʌrənɪs] (*U*) *n* **- 1.** [exhaustiveness] minutie *f* **- 2.** [meticulousness] soin *m* méticuleux.

those [ðəʊz] *pl* ⊳ **that.**

though [ðəʊ] ⬦ *conj* bien que *(+ subjunctive)*, quoique *(+ subjunctive)* ⬦ *adv* pourtant, cependant.

thought [θɔːt] ⬦ *pt* & *pp* ⊳ **think** ⬦ *n* **- 1.** [gen] pensée *f* ; [idea] idée *f*, pensée ; **after**

much ~ après avoir mûrement réfléchi **- 2.** [intention] intention *f.*

thoughts *npl* **- 1.** [reflections] pensées *fpl*, réflexions *fpl ;* **to collect one's ~s** rassembler ses idées **- 2.** [views] opinions *fpl*, idées *fpl.*

thoughtful [ˈθɔːtfʊl] *adj* **- 1.** [pensive] pensif(ive) **- 2.** [considerate - person] prévenant(e), attentionné(e) ; [- remark, act] plein(e) de gentillesse.

thoughtfulness [ˈθɔːtfʊlnɪs] (*U*) *n* **- 1.** [pensiveness] air *m* pensif **- 2.** [considerateness - of person] prévenance *f* ; [- of remark, act] délicatesse *f.*

thoughtless [ˈθɔːtlɪs] *adj* [person] qui manque d'égards (pour les autres) ; [remark, behaviour] irréfléchi(e).

thoughtlessness [ˈθɔːtlɪsnɪs] *n* (*U*) manque *m* d'égards OR de prévenance.

thousand [ˈθaʊznd] *num* mille ; **a** OR **one ~** mille ; **~s of** des milliers de ; *see also* **six.**

thousandth [ˈθaʊzntθ] *num* millième ; *see also* **sixth.**

thrash [θræʃ] *vt* **- 1.** [hit] battre, rosser **- 2.** inf [defeat] écraser, battre à plates coutures.

➤ **thrash about, thrash around** *vi* s'agiter.

➤ **thrash out** *vt sep* [problem] débrouiller, démêler ; [idea] débattre, discuter.

thrashing [ˈθræʃɪŋ] *n* **- 1.** [hitting] rossée *f*, correction *f* **- 2.** inf [defeat] défaite *f.*

thread [θred] ⬦ *n* **- 1.** [gen] fil *m* **- 2.** [of screw] filet *m*, pas *m* ⬦ *vt* **- 1.** [needle] enfiler **- 2.** [move] : **to ~ one's way through the crowd** se faufiler parmi la foule.

threadbare [ˈθredbeəʳ] *adj* usé(e) jusqu'à la corde.

threat [θret] *n* : **~ (to)** menace *f* (pour).

threaten [ˈθretn] ⬦ *vt* : **to ~ sb (with)** menacer qqn (de) ; **to ~ to do sthg** menacer de faire qqch ⬦ *vi* menacer.

threatening [ˈθretnɪŋ] *adj* menaçant(e) ; [letter] de menace.

three [θriː] *num* trois ; *see also* **six.**

three-D *adj* [film, picture] en relief.

three-day event *n* concours *m* complet d'équitation.

three-dimensional [-dɪˈmenʃənl] *adj* [film, picture] en relief ; [object] à trois dimensions.

threefold [ˈθriːfəʊld] ⬦ *adj* triple ⬦ *adv* : **to increase ~** tripler.

three-legged race [-ˈlegɪd-] *n* course *f* à trois pieds.

three-piece *adj* : **~ suit** (costume *m*) trois

pièces *m* ; ~ **suite** canapé *m* et deux fauteuils assortis.

three-ply *adj* [wool] à trois fils.

three-point turn *n* Br demi-tour *m* en trois manœuvres.

three-quarters *npl* [fraction] trois quarts *mpl.*

threesome ['θri:səml] *n* trio *m*, groupe *m* de trois personnes.

three-star *adj* trois étoiles.

three-wheeler [-'wi:lə'] *n* voiture *f* à trois roues.

thresh [θreʃ] *vt* battre.

threshing machine ['θreʃɪŋ-] *n* batteuse *f.*

threshold ['θreʃhəʊld] *n* seuil *m* ; **to be on the ~ of** fig être au bord OR seuil de.

threshold agreement *n* accord *m* d'indexation des salaires sur le coût de la vie.

threw [θru:] *pt* ⤇ **throw**.

thrift [θrɪft] *n* - **1.** [gen] *(U)* économie *f*, épargne *f* - **2.** Am [savings bank] = **thrift institution**.

thrift institution *n* Am caisse *f* d'épargne.

thrift shop, thrift store *n* Am *magasin vendant des articles d'occasion au profit d'œuvres charitables.*

thrifty ['θrɪftɪ] (*compar* **-ier** ; *superl* **-iest**) *adj* économe.

thrill [θrɪl] ⟨⟩ *n* - **1.** [sudden feeling] frisson *m*, sensation *f* - **2.** [enjoyable experience] plaisir *m* ⟨⟩ *vt* transporter, exciter ⟨⟩ *vi* : **to ~ to a story/the music** être transporté(e) par une histoire/la musique.

thrilled [θrɪld] *adj* : ~ **(with sthg/to do sthg)** ravi(e) (de qqch/de faire qqch), enchanté(e) (de qqch/de faire qqch).

thriller ['θrɪlə'] *n* thriller *m*.

thrilling ['θrɪlɪŋ] *adj* saisissant(e), palpitant(e).

thrive [θraɪv] (*pt* **-d** OR **throve** ; *pp* **-d**) *vi* [person] bien se porter ; [plant] pousser bien ; [business] prospérer.

thriving ['θraɪvɪŋ] *adj* [person] bien portant(e) ; [plant] qui pousse bien ; [business] prospère.

throat [θrəʊt] *n* gorge *f* ; **to ram** OR **force sthg down sb's ~** fig rebattre les oreilles de qqn avec qqch ; **it stuck in my ~** fig ça m'est resté en travers de la gorge ; **to be at each other's ~s** se disputer, se battre.

throaty ['θrəʊtɪ] (*compar* **-ier** ; *superl* **-iest**) *adj* guttural(e).

throb [θrɒb] (*pt* & *pp* **-bed** ; *cont* **-bing**) ⟨⟩ *n* [of drums] battement *m* ; [of pulse] pulsation *f* ; [of engine] vibration *f* ⟨⟩ *vi* [heart] palpiter, battre fort ; [engine] vibrer ; [music] taper ; **my head is throbbing** j'ai des élancements dans la tête.

throes [θrəʊz] *npl* : **to be in the ~ of** [war, disease] être en proie à ; **to be in the ~ of an argument** être en pleine dispute.

thrombosis [θrɒm'bəʊsɪs] (*pl* **-boses** [-'bəʊsi:z]) *n* thrombose *f.*

throne [θrəʊn] *n* trône *m*.

throng [θrɒŋ] ⟨⟩ *n* foule *f*, multitude *f* ⟨⟩ *vt* remplir, encombrer ⟨⟩ *vi* affluer.

throttle ['θrɒtl] ⟨⟩ *n* [valve] papillon *m* des gaz ; [lever] commande *f* des gaz ⟨⟩ *vt* [strangle] étrangler.

through [θru:] ⟨⟩ *adj* [finished] : **are you ~?** tu as fini ? ; **to be ~ with sthg** avoir fini qqch ⟨⟩ *adv* : **to let sb ~** laisser passer qqn ; **to read sthg ~** lire qqch jusqu'au bout ; **to sleep ~ till ten** dormir jusqu'à dix heures ⟨⟩ *prep* - **1.** [relating to place, position] à travers ; **to travel ~ sthg** traverser qqch ; **to cut ~ sthg** couper qqch - **2.** [during] pendant - **3.** [because of] à cause de - **4.** [by means of] par l'intermédiaire de, par l'entremise de - **5.** Am [up till and including] : **Monday ~ Friday** du lundi au vendredi.

◆ **through and through** *adv* [completely] jusqu'au bout des ongles ; [thoroughly] par cœur, à fond.

throughout [θru:'aʊt] ⟨⟩ *prep* - **1.** [during] pendant, durant ; **~ the meeting** pendant toute la réunion - **2.** [everywhere in] partout dans ⟨⟩ *adv* - **1.** [all the time] tout le temps - **2.** [everywhere] partout.

throve [θrəʊv] *pt* ⤇ **thrive**.

throw [θrəʊ] (*pt* **threw** ; *pp* **thrown**) ⟨⟩ *vt* - **1.** [gen] jeter ; [ball, javelin] lancer ; **to ~ one's arms around sb** jeter ses bras autour de qqn ; **to ~ o.s. into sthg** fig se jeter à corps perdu dans qqch - **2.** [rider] désarçonner - **3.** [have suddenly - tantrum, fit] piquer - **4.** fig [confuse] déconcerter, décontenancer ⟨⟩ *n* lancement *m*, jet *m*.

◆ **throw away** *vt sep* - **1.** [discard] jeter - **2.** fig [money] gaspiller ; [opportunity] perdre.

◆ **throw in** *vt sep* [include] donner en plus OR en prime.

◆ **throw out** *vt sep* - **1.** [discard] jeter - **2.** fig [reject] rejeter - **3.** [from house] mettre à la porte ; [from army, school] expulser, renvoyer.

◆ **throw up** ⟨⟩ *vt sep* [dust, water] jeter, projeter ⟨⟩ *vi* inf [vomit] dégobiller, vomir.

throwaway ['θrəʊə,weɪl] *adj* - **1.** [disposable] jetable, à jeter - **2.** [remark] désinvolte.

throwback ['θrəʊbæk] *n* : ~ **(to)** retour *m* (à).

throw-in n Br FTBL rentrée f en touche, remise f en jeu.

thrown [θrəʊn] pp ⊳ throw.

thru [θruː] Am inf = through.

thrush [θrʌʃ] n - **1.** [bird] grive f - **2.** MED muguet m.

thrust [θrʌst] ◇ n - **1.** [forward movement] poussée f; [of knife] coup m - **2.** [main aspect] idée f principale, aspect m principal ◇ vt - **1.** [shove] enfoncer, fourrer - **2.** [jostle] : **to ~ one's way** se frayer un passage.

◆ **thrust upon** vt sep : **to ~ sthg upon sb** imposer qqch à qqn.

thrusting [ˈθrʌstɪŋ] adj [person] qui se met en avant.

thruway [ˈθruːweɪ] n Am voie f express.

thud [θʌd] (pt & pp **-ded**; cont **-ding**) ◇ n bruit m sourd ◇ vi tomber en faisant un bruit sourd.

thug [θʌg] n brute f, voyou m.

thumb [θʌm] ◇ n pouce m; **to twiddle one's ~s** se tourner les pouces ◇ vt inf [hitch] : **to ~ a lift** faire du stop OR de l'auto-stop.

◆ **thumb through** vt fus feuilleter, parcourir.

thumb index n répertoire m à onglets.

thumbnail [ˈθʌmneɪl] ◇ adj bref (brève), concis(e) ◇ n ongle m du pouce.

thumbnail sketch n croquis m rapide.

thumbs down [ˌθʌmz-] n : **to get** OR **be given the ~** être rejeté(e).

thumbs up [ˌθʌmz-] n [go-ahead] : **to give sb the ~** donner le feu vert à qqn.

thumbtack [ˈθʌmtæk] n Am punaise f.

thump [θʌmp] ◇ n - **1.** [blow] grand coup m - **2.** [thud] bruit m sourd ◇ vt - **1.** [hit] cogner, taper sur - **2.** [place heavily] poser violemment ◇ vi - **1.** [move heavily] : **to ~ in/out** entrer/sortir à pas pesants - **2.** [heart] battre fort.

thunder [ˈθʌndər] ◇ n (U) - **1.** METEOR tonnerre m - **2.** fig [of traffic] vacarme m; [of applause] tonnerre m ◇ vt tonner, tonitruer ◇ v impers METEOR tonner ◇ vi fig [traffic] tonner, gronder.

thunderbolt [ˈθʌndəbəʊlt] n coup m de foudre.

thunderclap [ˈθʌndəklæp] n coup m de tonnerre.

thundercloud [ˈθʌndəklaʊd] n nuage m orageux.

thundering [ˈθʌndərɪŋ] adj Br inf & dated terrible, monstre.

thunderous [ˈθʌndərəs] adj [noise] assourdissant(e) ; **~ applause** un tonnerre d'applaudissements.

thunderstorm [ˈθʌndəstɔːm] n orage m.

thunderstruck [ˈθʌndəstrʌk] adj fig stupéfait(e), sidéré(e).

thundery [ˈθʌndərɪ] adj orageux(euse).

Thur, Thurs (abbr of Thursday) jeu.

Thursday [ˈθɜːzdɪ] n jeudi m; see also **Saturday**.

thus [ðʌs] adv fml - **1.** [therefore] par conséquent, donc, ainsi - **2.** [in this way] ainsi, de cette façon, comme ceci.

thwart [θwɔːt] vt contrecarrer, contrarier.

thyme [taɪm] n thym m.

thyroid [ˈθaɪrɔɪd] n thyroïde f.

tiara [tɪˈɑːrə] n [worn by woman] diadème m.

Tiber [ˈtaɪbər] n : **the (River) ~** le Tibre.

Tibet [tɪˈbet] n Tibet m; **in ~** au Tibet.

Tibetan [tɪˈbetn] ◇ adj tibétain(e) ◇ n - **1.** [person] Tibétain m, -e f - **2.** [language] tibétain m.

tibia [ˈtɪbɪə] (pl **-biae** [-bɪiː] OR **-s**) n tibia m.

tic [tɪk] n tic m.

tick [tɪk] ◇ n - **1.** [written mark] coche f; **to put a ~ beside sthg** cocher qqch - **2.** [sound] tic-tac m - **3.** [insect] tique f ◇ vt cocher ◇ vi faire tic-tac ; **what makes him ~?** fig je me demande comment il fonctionne.

◆ **tick away, tick by** vi passer.

◆ **tick off** vt sep - **1.** [mark off] cocher - **2.** [tell off] passer un savon à, enguirlander.

◆ **tick over** vi [engine, business] tourner au ralenti.

ticked [tɪkt] adj Am en rogne.

tickertape [ˈtɪkəteɪp] n (U) bande f de téléimprimeur.

ticket [ˈtɪkɪt] n - **1.** [for access, train, plane] billet m; [for bus] ticket m; [for library] carte f; [label on product] étiquette f - **2.** [for traffic offence] P.-V. m, papillon m - **3.** POL liste f.

ticket agency n billetterie f.

ticket collector n Br contrôleur m, -euse f.

ticket holder n personne f munie d'un billet.

ticket inspector n Br contrôleur m, -euse f.

ticket machine n distributeur m de billets.

ticket office n bureau m de vente des billets.

ticking off [ˈtɪkɪŋ-] (pl **tickings off** [ˈtɪkɪŋz-]) n : **to give sb a ~** passer un savon à qqn, enguirlander qqn ; **to get a ~** recevoir un savon, se faire enguirlander.

tickle [ˈtɪkl] ◇ vt - **1.** [touch lightly] chatouiller - **2.** fig [amuse] amuser ◇ vi chatouiller.

ticklish ['tɪklɪʃ] adj - **1.** [person] qui craint les chatouilles, chatouilleux(euse) - **2.** fig [delicate] délicat(e), difficile.

tick-tack-toe n Am [game] ≃ morpion m.

tidal ['taɪdl] adj [force] de la marée ; [river] à marées ; [barrier] contre la marée.

tidal wave n raz-de-marée m inv.

tidbit Am = titbit.

tiddler ['tɪdlər] n Br [fish] petit poisson m.

tiddly ['tɪdlɪ] (compar -ier ; superl -iest) adj Br inf - **1.** [tipsy] pompette, gai(e) - **2.** [tiny] minuscule.

tiddlywinks ['tɪdlɪwɪŋks], **tiddledywinks** Am ['tɪdldɪwɪŋks] n jeu m de puce.

tide [taɪd] n - **1.** [of sea] marée f - **2.** fig [of opinion, fashion] courant m, tendance f ; [of protest] vague f.
◆ **tide over** vt sep dépanner.

tidemark ['taɪdmɑːk] n - **1.** [of sea] ligne f de marée haute - **2.** Br [round bath, neck] ligne f de crasse.

tidily ['taɪdɪlɪ] adv soigneusement, avec ordre.

tidiness ['taɪdɪnɪs] n (U) ordre m.

tidings ['taɪdɪŋz] npl literary nouvelles fpl.

tidy ['taɪdɪ] (compar -ier ; superl -iest, pt & pp -ied) ◇ adj - **1.** [room, desk] en ordre, bien rangé(e) ; [hair, dress] soigné(e) - **2.** [person - in habits] ordonné(e) ; [- in appearance] soigné(e) - **3.** inf [sizeable] coquet(ette), rondelet(ette) ◇ vt ranger, mettre de l'ordre dans.
◆ **tidy away** vt sep ranger.
◆ **tidy up** ◇ vt sep ranger, mettre de l'ordre dans ◇ vi ranger.

tie [taɪ] (pt & pp tied ; cont tying) ◇ n - **1.** [necktie] cravate f - **2.** [string, cord] cordon m - **3.** fig [link] lien m - **4.** [in game, competition] égalité f de points - **5.** Am RAIL traverse f ◇ vt - **1.** [fasten] attacher - **2.** [shoelaces] nouer, attacher ; **to ~ a knot** faire un nœud - **3.** fig [link] : **to be ~d to** être lié(e) à - **4.** fig [restricted] : **to be ~d to** être cloué(e) à ◇ vi [draw] être à égalité.
◆ **tie down** vt sep fig [restrict] restreindre la liberté de.
◆ **tie in with** vt fus concorder avec, coïncider avec.
◆ **tie up** vt sep - **1.** [with string, rope] attacher - **2.** [shoelaces] nouer, attacher - **3.** fig [money, resources] immobiliser - **4.** fig [link] : **to be ~d up with** être lié(e) à.

tiebreak(er) ['taɪbreɪk(ər)] n - **1.** TENNIS tiebreak m - **2.** [in game, competition] question f subsidiaire.

tied [taɪd] adj SPORT : **a ~ match** un match nul.

tied cottage n Br logement m de fonction (mis à la disposition d'un employé agricole etc).

tied up adj [busy] occupé(e), pris(e).

tie-dye vt nouer et teindre.

tie-in n - **1.** [link] lien m, rapport m - **2.** [product] : **the book is a ~ with the TV series** le livre est tiré de la série télévisée.

tiepin ['taɪpɪn] n épingle f de cravate.

tier [tɪər] n [of seats] gradin m ; [of cake] étage m.

Tierra del Fuego [tɪˌerədel'fweɪɡəʊ] n Terre de Feu f ; **in ~** en Terre de Feu.

tie-up n - **1.** [link] lien m, rapport m - **2.** Am [interruption] interruption f, arrêt m.

tiff [tɪf] n bisbille f, petite querelle f.

tiger ['taɪɡər] n tigre m.

tiger cub n petit m du tigre.

tight [taɪt] ◇ adj - **1.** [clothes, group, competition, knot] serré(e) ; **the dress was a ~ fit** la robe était un peu juste - **2.** [taut] tendu(e) - **3.** [painful - chest] oppressé(e) ; [- stomach] noué(e) - **4.** [schedule] serré(e), minuté(e) - **5.** [strict] strict(e), sévère - **6.** [corner, bend] raide - **7.** inf [drunk] soûl(e), rond(e) - **8.** inf [miserly] radin(e), avare ◇ adv - **1.** [firmly, securely] bien, fort ; **to hold ~** tenir bien ; **hold ~!** tiens bon! ; **to shut** OR **close sthg ~** bien fermer qqch - **2.** [tautly] à fond.
◆ **tights** npl collant m, collants mpl.

tighten ['taɪtn] ◇ vt - **1.** [belt, knot, screw] resserrer ; **to ~ one's hold** OR **grip on** resserrer sa prise sur - **2.** [pull tauter] tendre - **3.** [make stricter] renforcer ◇ vi - **1.** [rope] se tendre - **2.** [grip, hold] se resserrer.
◆ **tighten up** vt sep - **1.** [belt, screw] resserrer - **2.** [make stricter] renforcer.

tightfisted [ˌtaɪt'fɪstɪd] adj pej radin(e), pingre.

tightknit [ˌtaɪt'nɪt] adj [family, community] uni(e).

tight-lipped [-'lɪpt] adj - **1.** [in anger] les lèvres serrées - **2.** [silent] qui ne dit rien, qui garde le silence.

tightly ['taɪtlɪ] adv - **1.** [closely] : **to fit ~** être juste ; **to pack ~** entasser, tasser - **2.** [firmly] bien, fort - **3.** [tautly] à fond.

tightness ['taɪtnɪs] n - **1.** [of clothes] étroitesse f - **2.** [in chest] oppression f - **3.** [strictness] sévérité f, rigueur f.

tightrope ['taɪtrəʊp] n corde f raide ; **to be on** OR **walking a ~** fig être sur la corde raide.

tightrope walker n funambule mf.

Tigré ['tiːɡreɪ] n Tigré m ; **in ~** dans le Tigré.

tigress ['taɪɡrɪs] n tigresse f.

Tigris ['taɪɡrɪs] n : **the (River) ~** le Tigre.

tilde [ˈtɪldə] *n* tilde *m*.

tile [taɪl] *n* [on roof] tuile *f* ; [on floor, wall] carreau *m*.

tiled [taɪld] *adj* [floor, wall] carrelé(e) ; [roof] couvert de tuiles.

tiling [ˈtaɪlɪŋ] *n* [of floor, wall] carrelage *m* ; [of roof - action] pose *f* de tuiles ; [- tuiles] tuiles *fpl*.

till [tɪl] ◇ *prep* jusqu'à ; **from six ~ ten o'clock** de six heures à dix heures ◇ *conj* jusqu'à ce que *(+ subjunctive)* ; **wait ~ I come back** attends que je revienne ; *(after negative)* avant que *(+ subjunctive)* ; **it won't be ready ~ tomorrow** ça ne sera pas prêt avant demain ◇ *n* tiroir-caisse *m*.

tiller [ˈtɪləʳ] *n* NAUT barre *f*.

tilt [tɪlt] ◇ *n* inclinaison *f* ◇ *vt* incliner, pencher ◇ *vi* s'incliner, pencher.

timber [ˈtɪmbəʳ] *n* **- 1.** *(U)* [wood] bois *m* de charpente OR de construction **- 2.** [beam] poutre *f*, madrier *m*.

timbered [ˈtɪmbəd] *adj* en bois.

time [taɪm] ◇ *n* **- 1.** [gen] temps *m* ; **a long ~** longtemps ; **in a short ~** dans peu de temps, sous peu ; **to take ~** prendre du temps ; **to be ~ for sthg** être l'heure de qqch ; **to get the ~ to do sthg** prendre le temps de faire qqch ; **it's a good ~ to do sthg** c'est le moment de faire qqch ; **to have a good ~** s'amuser bien ; **to have a hard ~ doing sthg** avoir du mal à faire qqch ; **in good ~** de bonne heure ; **ahead of ~** en avance, avant l'heure ; **on ~** à l'heure ; **it's high ~ (that)** ... il est grand temps que ... ; **~ and a half** une fois et demie le tarif normal ; **to have no ~ for sb/sthg** ne pas supporter qqn/qqch ; **to make good ~** [on journey] bien rouler OR marcher ; [in schedule] bien avancer ; **to pass the ~** passer le temps ; **to play for ~** essayer de gagner du temps ; **to take one's ~ (doing sthg)** prendre son temps (pour faire qqch) **- 2.** [as measured by clock] heure *f* ; **what's the ~?** quelle heure est-il? ; **in a week's/year's ~** dans une semaine/un an ; **to keep ~** être toujours à l'heure ; **to lose ~** retarder **- 3.** [point in time in past] époque *f* ; **to be ahead of one's ~** être en avance sur son temps ; **before my ~** avant que j'arrive ici **- 4.** [occasion] fois *f* ; **from ~ to ~** de temps en temps, de temps à autre ; **~ after ~, ~ and again** à maintes reprises, maintes et maintes fois ; **at the best of ~s** même quand tout va bien **- 5.** MUS mesure *f* ◇ *vt* **- 1.** [schedule] fixer, prévoir **- 2.** [race, runner] chronométrer **- 3.** [arrival, remark] choisir le moment de.

➤ **times** ◇ *npl* fois *fpl* ; **four ~s as much as me** quatre fois plus que moi ◇ *prep* MATH fois.

➤ **at a time** *adv* d'affilée ; **one at a ~** un par un, un seul à la fois ; **months at a ~** des mois et des mois.

➤ **at (any) one time** *adv* à la fois.

➤ **at times** *adv* quelquefois, parfois.

➤ **at the same time** *adv* en même temps.

➤ **about time** *adv* : **it's about ~ (that)** ... il est grand temps que ... ; **about ~ too!** ce n'est pas trop tôt!

➤ **for the time being** *adv* pour le moment.

➤ **in time** *adv* **- 1.** [not late] : **in ~ (for)** à l'heure (pour) **- 2.** [eventually] à la fin, à la longue ; [after a while] avec le temps, à la longue.

time-and-motion study *n* étude *f* de productivité *(axée sur l'efficacité des employés)*.

time bomb *n* lit & fig bombe *f* à retardement.

time-consuming [-kənˌsjuːmɪŋ] *adj* qui prend beaucoup de temps.

timed [taɪmd] *adj* [race, test] chronométré(e) ; **well ~** opportun(e) ; **badly ~** inopportun(e).

time difference *n* décalage *m* horaire.

time-honoured [-ˌɒnəd] *adj* consacré(e).

timekeeping [ˈtaɪmˌkiːpɪŋ] *n* ponctualité *f*.

time lag *n* décalage *m*.

time-lapse *adj* : **~ photography** accéléré *m*.

timeless [ˈtaɪmlɪs] *adj* éternel(elle).

time limit *n* délai *m*.

timely [ˈtaɪmlɪ] *(compar* -ier ; *superl* -iest) *adj* opportun(e).

time machine *n* machine *f* à voyager dans le temps.

time off *n* temps *m* libre.

time out *n* **- 1.** SPORT temps *m* mort **- 2.** [break] : **to take ~ to do sthg** trouver le temps de faire qqch.

timepiece [ˈtaɪmpiːs] *n* dated [watch] montre *f* ; [clock] horloge *f*.

timer [ˈtaɪməʳ] *n* minuteur *m*.

timesaving [ˈtaɪmˌseɪvɪŋ] *adj* qui fait gagner du temps.

time scale *n* période *f* ; [of project] délai *m*.

time-share *n* Br logement *m* en multipropriété.

time-sharing [-ˈʃeərɪŋ] *n* **- 1.** [in holiday home] multipropriété *f* **- 2.** COMPUT (travail *m* en) temps *m* partagé.

time sheet *n* feuille *f* de présence.

time signal *n* top *m* horaire.

time switch *n* minuterie *f*.

timetable [ˈtaɪmˌteɪbl] *n* **- 1.** SCH emploi *m* du

temps - **2.** [of buses, trains] horaire *m* - **3.** [schedule] calendrier *m*.

time zone *n* fuseau *m* horaire.

timid ['tɪmɪd] *adj* timide.

timidly ['tɪmɪdlɪ] *adv* timidement.

timing ['taɪmɪŋ] *n (U)* - **1.** [of remark] à-propos *m* - **2.** [scheduling] : **the ~ of the election** le moment choisi pour l'élection - **3.** [measuring] chronométrage *m*.

timing device *n* mouvement *m* d'horlogerie.

timpani ['tɪmpənɪ] *npl* timbales *fpl*.

tin [tɪn] ◇ *n* - **1.** *(U)* [metal] étain *m* ; [in sheets] fer-blanc *m* - **2.** Br [can] boîte *f* de conserve - **3.** [small container] boîte *f* ; **cake ~** [for baking] moule *m* à gâteau ; [for storing] boîte *f* à gâteaux ◇ *comp* en étain, d'étain.

tin can *n* boîte *f* de conserve.

tinder ['tɪndə'] *n* petit bois *m*.

tinfoil ['tɪnfɔɪl] *n (U)* papier *m* (d')aluminium.

tinge [tɪndʒ] *n* - **1.** [of colour] teinte *f*, nuance *f* - **2.** [of feeling] nuance *f*.

tinged [tɪndʒd] *adj* : **~ with** teinté(e) de.

tingle ['tɪŋgl] *vi* picoter ; **to ~ with** brûler de.

tingling ['tɪŋglɪŋ] *n (U)* picotement *m*.

tinker ['tɪŋkə'] ◇ *n* Br - **1.** pej [gypsy] romanichel *m*, -elle *f* - **2.** [rascal] polisson *m*, -onne *f* ◇ *vi* : **to ~ (with sthg)** bricoler (qqch).

tinkle ['tɪŋkl] ◇ *n* - **1.** [sound] tintement *m* - **2.** Br inf [phone call] : **to give sb a ~** passer un coup de fil à qqn ◇ *vi* [ring] tinter.

tin mine *n* mine *f* d'étain.

tinned [tɪnd] *adj* Br en boîte.

tinnitus [tɪ'naɪtəs] *n* acouphène *m*.

tinny ['tɪnɪ] (*compar* -ier ; *superl* -iest) *adj* - **1.** [sound] métallique - **2.** inf pej [badly made] : **a ~ car** un tas de ferraille, une vraie casserole.

tin opener *n* Br ouvre-boîtes *m inv*.

tin-pot *adj* Br inf pej [country, dictator] de rien du tout.

tinsel ['tɪnsl] *n (U)* guirlandes *fpl* de Noël.

tint [tɪnt] ◇ *n* teinte *f*, nuance *f* ; [in hair] rinçage *m* ◇ *vt* teinter.

tinted ['tɪntɪd] *adj* [glasses, windows] teinté(e).

tiny ['taɪnɪ] (*compar* -ier ; *superl* -iest) *adj* minuscule.

tip [tɪp] (*pt* & *pp* **-ped** ; *cont* **-ping**) ◇ *n* - **1.** [end] bout *m* ; **it's on the ~ of my tongue** je l'ai sur le bout de la langue - **2.** Br [dump] décharge *f* - **3.** [to waiter etc] pourboire *m* ◇ *vt* - **1.** [tilt] faire basculer - **2.** [spill] renverser - **3.** [waiter etc]

donner un pourboire à ◇ *vi* - **1.** [tilt] basculer - **2.** [spill] se renverser - **3.** [give money to waiter etc] laisser un pourboire.

▸ **tip off** *vt sep* prévenir.

▸ **tip over** ◇ *vt sep* renverser ◇ *vi* se renverser.

tip-off *n* tuyau *m* ; [to police] dénonciation *f*.

tipped ['tɪpt] *adj* [cigarette] qui a un embout, à bout filtre.

Tipp-Ex® ['tɪpeks] Br ◇ *n* Tipp-ex® *m* ◇ *vt* effacer avec du Tipp-Ex®.

tipple ['tɪpl] *n* inf : **what's your ~?** qu'est-ce que tu aimes boire d'habitude?

tipsy ['tɪpsɪ] (*compar* -ier ; *superl* -iest) *adj* inf gai(e).

tiptoe ['tɪptəʊ] ◇ *n* : **on ~** sur la pointe des pieds ◇ *vi* marcher sur la pointe des pieds.

tip-top *adj* inf dated excellent(e).

TIR (*abbr of* Transports Internationaux Routiers) TIR.

tirade [taɪ'reɪd] *n* diatribe *f*.

Tirana, Tiranë [tɪ'rɑːnə] *n* Tirana.

tire ['taɪə'] ◇ *n* Am = tyre ◇ *vt* fatiguer ◇ *vi* - **1.** [get tired] se fatiguer - **2.** [get fed up] : **to ~ of** se lasser de.

▸ **tire out** *vt sep* épuiser.

tired ['taɪəd] *adj* - **1.** [sleepy] fatigué(e), las (lasse) - **2.** [fed up] : **to be ~ of sthg/of doing sthg** en avoir assez de qqch/de faire qqch.

tiredness ['taɪədnɪs] *n* fatigue *f*.

tireless ['taɪəlɪs] *adj* infatigable.

tiresome ['taɪəsəm] *adj* ennuyeux(euse).

tiring ['taɪərɪŋ] *adj* fatigant(e).

Tirol = **Tyrol**.

tissue ['tɪʃuː] *n* - **1.** [paper handkerchief] mouchoir *m* en papier - **2.** *(U)* BIOL tissu *m* - **3.** phr : **a ~ of lies** un tissu de mensonges.

tissue paper *n (U)* papier *m* de soie.

tit [tɪt] *n* - **1.** [bird] mésange *f* - **2.** vulg [breast] nichon *m*, néné *m*.

titbit Br ['tɪtbɪt], **tidbit** Am ['tɪdbɪt] *n* - **1.** [of food] bon morceau *m* - **2.** fig [of news] petite nouvelle *f* ; **a ~ of gossip** un petit potin.

tit for tat [-'tæt] *n* un prêté pour un rendu.

titillate ['tɪtɪleɪt] ◇ *vt* titiller ◇ *vi* titiller les sens.

titivate ['tɪtɪveɪt] *vt* pomponner.

title ['taɪtl] *n* titre *m*.

titled ['taɪtld] *adj* titré(e).

title deed *n* titre *m* de propriété.

titleholder ['taɪtl,həʊldə'] *n* SPORT tenant *m*, -e *f* du titre.

title page *n* page *f* de titre.

title role n rôle m principal.

titter ['tɪtə'] vi rire bêtement.

tittle-tattle ['tɪtl,tatl] n (U) inf pej ragots mpl, cancans mpl.

titular ['tɪtjulə'] adj nominal(e).

T-junction n intersection f en T.

TLS (abbr of Times Literary Supplement) n édition littéraire du Times.

TM ◇ n (abbr of transcendental meditation) MT f ◇ abbr of trademark.

TN abbr of Tennessee.

TNT (abbr of trinitrotoluene) n TNT m.

to [unstressed before consonant tə, unstressed before vowel tu, stressed tu:] ◇ prep - **1.** [indicating place, direction] à ; **to go ~ Liverpool/Spain/ school** aller à Liverpool/en Espagne/à l'école ; **to go ~ the butcher's** aller chez le boucher ; **~ the left/right** à gauche/droite - **2.** (to express indirect object) à ; **to give sthg ~ sb** donner qqch à qqn ; **we were listening ~ the radio** nous écoutions la radio ; **he refused to give an answer ~ my question** il refusa de répondre à ma question - **3.** [indicating reaction, effect] à ; **~ my delight/surprise** à ma grande joie/surprise ; **it worked ~ our advantage** cela a tourné à notre avantage ; **to be ~ sb's liking** être au goût de qqn - **4.** [in stating opinion] : **~ me,...** à mon avis,... ; **it seemed quite unnecessary ~ me/him** etc cela me/lui etc semblait tout à fait inutile - **5.** [indicating state, process] : **to drive sb ~ drink** pousser qqn à boire ; **to shoot ~ fame** devenir célèbre du jour au lendemain ; **it could lead ~ trouble** cela pourrait causer des ennuis - **6.** [as far as] à, jusqu'à ; **to count ~ 10** compter jusqu'à 10 ; **we work from 9 ~ 5** nous travaillons de 9 heures à 17 heures - **7.** [in expressions of time] moins ; **it's ten ~ three/quarter ~ one** il est trois heures moins dix/une heure moins le quart - **8.** [per] à ; **40 miles ~ the gallon** ≃ 7 litres aux cent (km) - **9.** [accompanied by] : **a poem set ~ music** un poème mis en musique ; **we danced ~ the sound of guitars** on a dansé au son des guitares - **10.** [of, for] de ; **the key ~ the car** la clef de la voiture ; **a letter ~ my daughter** une lettre à ma fille ◇ adv [shut] : **push the door ~** fermez la porte ◇ with infinitive - **1.** (forming simple infinitive) : **~ walk** marcher ; **~ laugh** rire - **2.** (following another verb) : **to begin ~ do sthg** commencer à faire qqch ; **to try ~ do sthg** essayer de faire qqch ; **to want ~ do sthg** vouloir faire qqch - **3.** (following an adjective) : **difficult ~ do** difficile à faire ; **ready ~ go** prêt à partir - **4.** (indicating purpose) pour ; **he worked hard ~ pass his exam** il a travaillé dur pour réussir son examen - **5.** (substituting for a relative clause) : **I have a lot ~ do** j'ai beaucoup à faire ; **he told me ~ leave** il m'a dit de partir - **6.** (to avoid repetition of infinitive) : **I meant to call him but I forgot ~** je voulais l'appeler, mais j'ai oublié - **7.** [in comments] : **~ be honest ...** en toute franchise ... ; **~ sum up,...** en résumé,..., pour récapituler,....

toad [təʊd] n crapaud m.

toadstool ['təʊdstu:l] n champignon m vénéneux.

toady ['təʊdɪ] (pl -ies, pt & pp -ied) pej ◇ n lèche-bottes m f inv ◇ vi : **to ~ (to sb)** lécher les bottes (de qqn).

to and fro adv : **to go ~** aller et venir ; **to walk ~** marcher de long en large.
◆ **to-and-fro** adj de va-et-vient.

toast [təʊst] ◇ n - **1.** (U) [bread] pain m grillé, toast m - **2.** [drink] toast m ; **to drink a ~ to sb/ sthg** lever son verre en l'honneur de qqn/à qqch ◇ vt - **1.** [bread] (faire) griller - **2.** [person] porter un toast à.

toasted sandwich [,təʊstɪd-] n sandwich m grillé.

toaster ['təʊstə'] n grille-pain m inv.

toast rack n porte-toasts m inv.

tobacco [tə'bækəʊ] n (U) tabac m.

tobacconist [tə'bækənɪst] n buraliste mf ; **~'s (shop)** bureau m de tabac.

Tobago [tə'beɪgəʊ] ▷ **Trinidad and Tobago.**

toboggan [tə'bɒgən] ◇ n luge f, traîne f sauvage Can ◇ vi faire de la luge, faire de la traîne sauvage Can.

today [tə'deɪ] ◇ n aujourd'hui m ◇ adv aujourd'hui.

toddle ['tɒdl] vi [child] marcher d'un pas hésitant.

toddler ['tɒdlə'] n tout-petit m (qui commence à marcher).

toddy ['tɒdɪ] (pl -ies) n grog m.

to-do (pl -s) n inf dated histoire f.

toe [təʊ] ◇ n [of foot] orteil m, doigt m de pied ; [of sock, shoe] bout m ◇ vt : **to ~ the line** se plier.

TOEFL ['tɒfl] (abbr of Test of English as a Foreign Language) n test d'anglais passé par les étudiants étrangers désirant faire des études dans une université américaine.

toehold ['təʊhəʊld] n prise f ; **to have a ~ in a market** fig avoir un pied dans un marché.

toenail ['təʊneɪl] n ongle m d'orteil.

toffee ['tɒfɪ] n caramel m.

toffee apple n Br pomme f caramélisée.

tofu [ˈtəʊfuː] n tofu m.

toga [ˈtəʊɡə] n toge f.

together [təˈɡeðəʳ] ◇ adv - **1.** [gen] ensemble - **2.** [at the same time] en même temps ◇ adj inf équilibré(e).

➡ **together with** prep ainsi que.

togetherness [təˈɡeðənɪs] n (U) unité f.

toggle [ˈtɒɡl] n bouton m de duffle-coat.

toggle switch n ELECTRON & COMPUT interrupteur m à bascule.

Togo [ˈtəʊɡəʊ] n Togo m ; **in ~** au Togo.

Togolese [ˌtɒɡəˈliːz] ◇ adj togolais(e) ◇ n Togolais m, -e f.

togs [tɒɡz] npl inf fringues fpl.

toil [tɔɪl] literary ◇ n labeur m ◇ vi travailler dur.

➡ **toil away** vi : **to ~ away (at sthg)** travailler dur (à qqch).

toilet [ˈtɔɪlɪt] n [lavatory] toilettes fpl, cabinets mpl ; **to go to the ~** aller aux toilettes OR aux cabinets.

toilet bag n trousse f de toilette.

toilet paper n (U) papier m hygiénique.

toiletries [ˈtɔɪlɪtrɪz] npl articles mpl de toilette.

toilet roll n rouleau m de papier hygiénique.

toilet soap n savonnette f.

toilet tissue n (U) papier m hygiénique.

toilet-trained [-ˌtreɪnd] adj propre.

toilet water n eau f de toilette.

to-ing and fro-ing [ˌtuːɪŋənˈfrəʊɪŋ] n (U) allées fpl et venues.

token [ˈtəʊkn] ◇ adj symbolique ◇ n - **1.** [voucher] bon m - **2.** [symbol] marque f.

➡ **by the same token** adv de même.

Tokyo [ˈtəʊkjəʊ] n Tokyo.

told [təʊld] pt & pp ▷ **tell**.

tolerable [ˈtɒlərəbl] adj passable.

tolerably [ˈtɒlərəblɪ] adv passablement.

tolerance [ˈtɒlərəns] n tolérance f.

tolerant [ˈtɒlərənt] adj tolérant(e).

tolerate [ˈtɒləreɪt] vt - **1.** [put up with] supporter - **2.** [permit] tolérer.

toleration [ˌtɒləˈreɪʃn] n (U) tolérance f.

toll [təʊl] ◇ n - **1.** [number] nombre m - **2.** [fee] péage m - **3.** phr : **to take its ~** se faire sentir ◇ vt & vi sonner.

tollbooth [ˈtəʊlbuːθ] n poste m de péage.

toll bridge n pont m à péage.

toll-free Am ◇ adj : **~ number** numéro m vert ◇ adv : **to call ~** appeler un numéro vert.

tomato [Br təˈmɑːtəʊ, Am təˈmeɪtəʊ] (pl -es) n tomate f.

tomb [tuːm] n tombe f.

tombola [tɒmˈbəʊlə] n esp Br tombola f.

tomboy [ˈtɒmbɔɪ] n garçon m manqué.

tombstone [ˈtuːmstəʊn] n pierre f tombale.

tomcat [ˈtɒmkæt] n matou m.

tomfoolery [tɒmˈfuːlərɪ] n (U) bêtises fpl.

tomorrow [təˈmɒrəʊ] ◇ n demain m ◇ adv demain.

ton [tʌn] (pl inv OR -s) n - **1.** [imperial] = 1016 kg Br, = 907,2 kg Am, ≃ tonne f - **2.** [metric] = 1000 kg, tonne f - **3.** phr : **to weigh a ~** inf peser une tonne ; **to come down on sb like a ~ of bricks** tomber sur qqn à bras raccourcis.

➡ **tons** npl inf : **~s (of)** des tas (de), plein (de).

tonal [ˈtəʊnl] adj tonal(e).

tone [təʊn] n - **1.** [gen] ton m - **2.** [on phone] tonalité f ; [on answering machine] bip m sonore - **3.** phr : **to lower the ~ (of)** rabaisser le ton (de).

➡ **tone down** vt sep modérer.

➡ **tone in** vi : **to ~ in (with)** s'harmoniser (avec).

➡ **tone up** vt sep tonifier.

tone-deaf adj qui n'a aucune oreille.

toner [ˈtəʊnəʳ] n - **1.** [for photocopier, printer] toner m - **2.** [cosmetic] astringent m, lotion f tonique.

Tonga [ˈtɒŋɡə] n Tonga ; **in ~** à Tonga.

tongs [tɒŋz] npl pinces fpl ; [for hair] fer m à friser.

tongue [tʌŋ] n - **1.** [gen] langue f ; **to have a sharp ~** avoir la langue bien acérée OR affilée ; **to have one's ~ in one's cheek** inf ne pas être sérieux ; **to hold one's ~** fig tenir sa langue ; **~s will wag** on va jaser - **2.** [of shoe] languette f.

tongue-in-cheek adj ironique.

tongue-tied [-ˌtaɪd] adj muet(ette).

tongue twister [-ˌtwɪstəʳ] n phrase f difficile à dire.

tonic [ˈtɒnɪk] n - **1.** [tonic water] Schweppes® m - **2.** [medicine] tonique m ; **the holiday was a real ~** fig ces vacances m'ont fait beaucoup de bien.

tonic water n Schweppes® m.

tonight [təˈnaɪt] ◇ n ce soir m ; [late] cette nuit f ◇ adv ce soir ; [late] cette nuit.

tonnage [ˈtʌnɪdʒ] n tonnage m.

tonne [tʌn] (pl inv OR -s) n tonne f.

tonsil [ˈtɒnsl] n amygdale f.

tonsil(l)itis [ˌtɒnsɪˈlaɪtɪs] n (U) amygdalite f.

too [tuː] adv - **1.** [also] aussi - **2.** [excessively] trop ; ~ **many people** tróp de gens ; **it was over all ~ soon** ça s'était terminé bien trop tôt ; **I'd be only ~ happy to help** je serais trop heureux de vous aider ; **I wasn't ~ impressed** ça ne m'a pas impressionné outre mesure.

took [tʊk] *pt* ⊳ take.

tool [tu:l] *n* lit & fig outil *m ;* **to down ~s** Br cesser le travail ; **the ~s of sb's trade** les outils du métier de qqn.

⊳ **tool around** *vi* Am inf traîner.

tool bar *n* COMPUT barre *f* d'outils.

tool box *n* boîte *f* à outils.

tool kit *n* trousse *f* à outils.

toot [tu:t] ⊳ *n* coup *m* de Klaxon® ⊳ *vt :* **to ~ one's horn** klaxonner ⊳ *vi* klaxonner.

tooth [tu:θ] (*pl* **teeth** [ti:θ]) *n* dent *f ;* **to be long in the ~** Br pej n'être plus tout jeune ; **to be fed up to the back teeth with** Br inf en avoir ras le bol de ; **to grit one's teeth** serrer les dents ; **to lie through one's teeth** mentir comme un arracheur de dents.

⊳ **teeth** *npl* fig [power] : **to have no teeth** être impuissant.

toothache ['tu:θeɪk] *n* mal *m* OR rage *f* de dents ; **to have ~** avoir mal aux dents.

toothbrush ['tu:θbrʌʃ] *n* brosse *f* à dents.

toothless ['tu:θlɪs] *adj* édenté(e).

toothpaste ['tu:θpeɪst] *n* (pâte *f)* dentifrice *m.*

toothpick ['tu:θpɪk] *n* cure-dents *m inv.*

tooth powder *n* poudre *f* dentifrice.

tootle ['tu:tl] *vi* inf : **to ~ off** se sauver.

top [tɒp] (*pt* & *pp* **-ped ;** *cont* **-ping**) ⊳ *adj* **- 1.** [highest] du haut **- 2.** [most important, successful - officials] important(e) ; [- executives] supérieur(e) ; [- pop singer] fameux(euse) ; [- sportsman, sportswoman] meilleur(e) ; [- in exam] premier(ère) **- 3.** [maximum] maximum ; **at ~ speed** à toute vitesse ⊳ *n* **- 1.** [highest point - of hill] sommet *m ;* [- of page, pile] haut *m ;* [- of tree] cime *f ;* [- of list] début *m,* tête *f ;* **at the ~ of the stairs/the street** en haut de l'escalier/la rue ; **on ~** dessus ; **to go over the ~** Br en faire un peu trop ; **at the ~ of one's voice** à tue-tête **- 2.** [lid - of bottle, tube] bouchon *m ;* [- of pen] capuchon *m ;* [- of jar] couvercle *m* **- 3.** [of table, box] dessus *m* **- 4.** [clothing] haut *m* **- 5.** [toy] toupie *f* **- 6.** [highest rank - in league] tête *f ;* [- in scale] haut *m ;* [- SCH] premier *m,* -ère *f* ⊳ *vt* **- 1.** [be first in] être en tête de **- 2.** [better] surpasser ; **to ~ an offer** surenchérir **- 3.** [exceed] dépasser.

⊳ **on top of** *prep* **- 1.** [in space] sur **- 2.** [in addition to] en plus de **- 3.** [in control of] : **to be on ~ of one's work** avoir son travail bien en main

- 4. phr : **my work is getting on ~ of me** je me suis laissé dépasser par mon travail ; **things are getting on ~ of me** je suis complètement dépassé.

⊳ **top up** Br, **top off** Am *vt sep* remplir.

topaz ['təʊpæz] *n* topaze *f.*

top brass *n (U)* inf : **the ~** les gros bonnets *mpl.*

topcoat ['tɒpkəʊt] *n* **- 1.** [item of clothing] manteau *m* **- 2.** [paint] dernière couche *f.*

top dog *n* inf chef *m.*

top-flight *adj* de premier ordre.

top floor *n* dernier étage *m.*

top gear *n* quatrième/cinquième vitesse *f.*

top hat *n* haut-de-forme *m.*

top-heavy *adj* mal équilibré(e).

topic ['tɒpɪk] *n* sujet *m.*

topical ['tɒpɪkl] *adj* d'actualité.

topknot ['tɒpnɒt] *n* [in hair] houppe *f.*

topless ['tɒplɪs] *adj* [woman] aux seins nus ; **~ swimsuit** monokini *m.*

top-level *adj* au plus haut niveau.

topmost ['tɒpməʊst] *adj* le plus haut (la plus haute).

top-notch *adj* inf de premier choix.

topographer [tə'pɒɡrəfər] *n* topographe *mf.*

topography [tə'pɒɡrəfɪ] *n* topographie *f.*

topped [tɒpt] *adj :* **~ by** OR **with** recouvert(e) de.

topping ['tɒpɪŋ] *n* garniture *f.*

topple ['tɒpl] ⊳ *vt* renverser ⊳ *vi* basculer.

⊳ **topple over** *vi* tomber.

top-ranking [-'ræŋkɪŋ] *adj* [official] haut placé(e) ; [player] haut classé(e).

TOPS [tɒps] (*abbr of* **Training Opportunities Scheme**) *n* programme de recyclage professionnel en Grande-Bretagne.

top-secret *adj* top secret (top secrète).

top-security *adj* de haute surveillance.

topsoil ['tɒpsɔɪl] *n* terre *f.*

topspin ['tɒpspɪn] *n* lift *m.*

topsy-turvy [,tɒpsɪ'tɜ:vɪ] ⊳ *adj* **- 1.** [messy] sens dessus dessous **- 2.** [confused] : **to be ~** ne pas tourner rond ⊳ *adv* [messily] sens dessus dessous.

tor [tɔ:r] *n* esp Br [hill] colline *f* rocheuse.

torch [tɔ:tʃ] *n* **- 1.** Br [electric] lampe *f* électrique **- 2.** [burning] torche *f.*

tore [tɔ:r] *pt* ⊳ tear².

torment [*n* 'tɔ:ment, *vb* tɔ:'ment] ⊳ *n* tourment *m* ⊳ *vt* tourmenter.

tormentor [tɔːˈmentəʳ] n bourreau m.

torn [tɔːn] pp ⊳ tear ².

tornado [tɔːˈneɪdəʊ] (pl -es OR -s) n tornade f.

Toronto [təˈrɒntəʊ] n Toronto.

torpedo [tɔːˈpiːdəʊ] (pl -es) ◇ n torpille f ◇ vt torpiller.

torpedo boat n torpilleur m.

torpor [ˈtɔːpəʳ] n torpeur f.

torque [tɔːk] n couple m (de torsion).

torrent [ˈtɒrənt] n torrent m.

torrential [təˈrenʃl] adj torrentiel(elle).

torrid [ˈtɒrɪd] adj - **1.** [hot] torride - **2.** fig [passionate] ardent(e).

torso [ˈtɔːsəʊ] (pl -s) n torse m.

tortoise [ˈtɔːtəs] n tortue f.

tortoiseshell [ˈtɔːtəʃel] ◇ adj : ~ **cat** chat m roux tigré ◇ n (U) [material] écaille f ◇ comp en écaille.

tortuous [ˈtɔːtʃʊəs] adj - **1.** [winding] tortueux(euse) - **2.** [over-complicated] alambiqué(e).

torture [ˈtɔːtʃəʳ] ◇ n torture f ◇ vt torturer.

torturer [ˈtɔːtʃərəʳ] n tortionnaire mf.

Tory [ˈtɔːrɪ] (pl -ies) ◇ adj tory, conservateur(trice) ◇ n tory mf, conservateur m, -trice f.

toss [tɒs] ◇ vt - **1.** [throw] jeter ; **to ~ a coin** jouer à pile ou face ; **to ~ one's head** rejeter la tête en arrière - **2.** [salad] remuer ; [pancake] faire sauter - **3.** [throw about] ballotter ◇ vi - **1.** [with coin] jouer à pile ou face - **2.** [move about] : **to ~ and turn** se tourner et se retourner ◇ n - **1.** [of coin] coup m de pile ou face - **2.** [of head] mouvement m brusque.
➤ **toss up** vi jouer à pile ou face.

toss-up n inf : **it was a ~ who'd win** il était impossible de savoir qui allait gagner.

tot [tɒt] (pt & pp -ted ; cont -ting) n - **1.** inf [small child] tout-petit m - **2.** [of drink] larme f, goutte f.
➤ **tot up** vt sep inf additionner.

total [ˈtəʊtl] (Br pt & pp -led ; cont -ling, Am pt & pp -ed ; cont -ing) ◇ adj total(e) ; [disgrace, failure] complet(ète) ; **a ~ fool** un abruti fini ◇ n total m ; **in ~** au total ◇ vt - **1.** [add up] additionner - **2.** [amount to] s'élever à - **3.** Am inf [wreck] bousiller, détruire.

totalitarian [ˌtəʊtælɪˈteərɪən] adj totalitaire.

totality [təʊˈtælətɪ] n totalité f.

totally [ˈtəʊtəlɪ] adv totalement ; **I ~ agree** je suis entièrement d'accord.

tote bag [təʊt-] n Am sac m (à provisions).

totem pole [ˈtəʊtəm-] n mât m totémique.

toto [ˈtəʊtəʊ] ➤ **in toto** adv fml entièrement, complètement.

totter [ˈtɒtəʳ] vi lit & fig chanceler.

toucan [ˈtuːkən] n toucan m.

touch [tʌtʃ] ◇ n - **1.** (U) [sense] toucher m - **2.** [detail] touche f ; **to put the finishing ~es to sthg** mettre la dernière main à qqch - **3.** (U) [skill] marque f, note f - **4.** [contact] : **to keep in ~ (with sb)** rester en contact (avec qqn) ; **to get in ~ with sb** entrer en contact avec qqn ; **to lose ~** [friends] se perdre de vue ; **to lose ~ with sb** perdre qqn de vue ; **to be out of ~ with** ne plus être au courant de - **5.** SPORT : **in ~** en touche - **6.** [small amount] : **a ~** un petit peu - **7.** phr : **it was ~ and go** c'était tangent ; **it was ~ and go whether ...** il n'était pas sûr que ... ; **he's a soft ~** [for money] on peut le taper facilement ◇ vt toucher ◇ vi - **1.** [with fingers etc] toucher - **2.** [be in contact] se toucher.
➤ **a touch** adv [loud, bright] un peu trop.
➤ **touch down** vi [plane] atterrir.
➤ **touch on** vt fus effleurer.

touch-and-go adj incertain(e).

touchdown [ˈtʌtʃdaʊn] n - **1.** [of plane] atterrissage m - **2.** [in American football] but m.

touched [tʌtʃt] adj - **1.** [grateful] touché(e) - **2.** inf [slightly mad] fêlé(e).

touching [ˈtʌtʃɪŋ] adj touchant(e).

touch judge n RUGBY juge m de touche.

touchline [ˈtʌtʃlaɪn] n ligne f de touche.

touchpaper [ˈtʌtʃˌpeɪpəʳ] n papier m nitraté.

touch screen n écran m tactile.

touch-type vi taper au toucher.

touchy [ˈtʌtʃɪ] (compar -ier ; superl -iest) adj - **1.** [person] susceptible ; **to be ~ about sthg** ne pas aimer parler de qqch - **2.** [subject, question] délicat(e).

tough [tʌf] adj - **1.** [material, vehicle, person] solide ; [character, life] dur(e) - **2.** [meat] dur(e) - **3.** [decision, problem, task] difficile - **4.** [rough - area of town] dangereux(euse) - **5.** [strict] sévère - **6.** inf [unfortunate] : **~ luck!** pas de veine! ; **that's ~!** c'est vache!, c'est dur!

toughen [ˈtʌfn] vt - **1.** [character] endurcir - **2.** [material] renforcer.

toughened [ˈtʌfnd] adj [glass] trempé(e).

toughness [ˈtʌfnɪs] (U) n - **1.** [resilience] dureté f - **2.** [of material] solidité f - **3.** [of decision, problem, task] difficulté f - **4.** [strictness] sévérité f.

toupee [ˈtuːpeɪ] n postiche m.

tour [tʊəʳ] ◇ n - **1.** [journey] voyage m ; [by pop group etc] tournée f - **2.** [of town, museum] visite f, tour *m* ◇ *vt* visiter ◇ *vi* : **to ~ round a country** visiter un pays.

tourer ['tʊərər] *n* voiture *f* de tourisme.

touring ['tʊərɪŋ] ◇ *adj* [show, theatre group] en tournée ; [exhibition] ambulant(e) ◇ *n* tourisme *m* ; **to go ~** faire du tourisme.

tourism ['tʊərɪzm] *n* tourisme *m*.

tourist ['tʊərɪst] *n* touriste *mf*.

tourist class *n* classe *f* touriste.

tourist (information) office *n* office *m* de tourisme.

touristy ['tʊərɪstɪ] *adj* pej touristique.

tournament ['tɔːnəmənt] *n* tournoi *m*.

tourniquet ['tʊənɪkeɪ] *n* tourniquet *m*.

tour operator *n* voyagiste *m*.

tousle ['taʊzl] *vt* ébouriffer.

tout [taʊt] ◇ *n* revendeur *m* de billets ◇ *vt* [tickets] revendre ; [goods] vendre ◇ *vi* : **to ~ for trade** racoler les clients.

tow [təʊ] ◇ *n* : **to give sb a ~** remorquer qqn ; **'on ~'** Br 'véhicule en remorque' ; **with sb in ~** à la suite de qqn ◇ *vt* remorquer.

towards Br [tə'wɔːdz], **toward** Am [tə'wɔːd] *prep* - **1.** [gen] vers ; [movement] vers, en direction de - **2.** [in attitude] envers - **3.** [for the purpose of] pour.

towaway zone ['təʊəweɪ-] *n* Am *zone de stationnement interdit sous peine de mise à la fourrière.*

towbar ['təʊbɑː] *n* barre *f* de remorquage.

towel ['taʊəl] *n* serviette *f* ; [tea towel] torchon *m*.

towelling Br, **toweling** Am ['taʊəlɪŋ] ◇ *n* (U) tissu *m* éponge ◇ *comp* en tissu éponge.

towel rail *n* porte-serviettes *m inv*.

tower ['taʊər] ◇ *n* tour *f* ; **a ~ of strength** Br un appui solide ◇ *vi* s'élever ; **to ~ over sb/sthg** dominer qqn/qqch.

tower block *n* Br tour *f*.

towering ['taʊərɪŋ] *adj* imposant(e).

town [taʊn] *n* ville *f* ; **to go out on the ~** faire la tournée des grands ducs ; **to go to ~ on sthg** fig ne pas lésiner sur qqch.

town centre *n* centre-ville *m*.

town clerk *n* ≃ secrétaire *mf* de mairie.

town council *n* conseil *m* municipal.

town hall *n* mairie *f*.

town house *n* [fashionable house] hôtel *m* particulier

town plan *n* plan *m* de ville.

town planner *n* urbaniste *mf*.

town planning *n* urbanisme *m*.

townsfolk ['taʊnzfəʊk], **townspeople** ['taʊnz,piːpl] *npl* citadins *mpl*.

township ['taʊnʃɪp] *n* - **1.** [in South Africa] township *f* - **2.** [in US] ≃ canton *m*.

towpath ['təʊpɑːθ, *pl* -pɑːðz] *n* chemin *m* de halage.

towrope ['təʊrəʊp] *n* câble *m* de remorquage.

tow truck *n* Am dépanneuse *f*.

toxic ['tɒksɪk] *adj* toxique.

toxin ['tɒksɪn] *n* toxine *f*.

toy [tɔɪ] *n* jouet *m*.

➡ **toy with** *vt fus* - **1.** [idea] caresser - **2.** [coin etc] jouer avec ; **to ~ with one's food** manger du bout des dents.

toy boy *n* inf étalon *m*, *jeune amant d'une femme plus âgée.*

toy shop *n* magasin *m* de jouets.

trace [treɪs] ◇ *n* trace *f* ; **without ~** sans laisser de traces ◇ *vt* - **1.** [relatives, criminal] retrouver ; [development, progress] suivre ; [history, life] retracer - **2.** [on paper] tracer.

trace element *n* oligo-élément *m*.

tracer bullet ['treɪsər-] *n* balle *f* traçante.

tracing ['treɪsɪŋ] *n* [copy] calque *m*.

tracing paper ['treɪsɪŋ-] *n* (U) papier-calque *m*.

track [træk] ◇ *n* - **1.** [path] chemin *m* ; **off the beaten ~** hors des sentiers battus - **2.** SPORT piste *f* - **3.** RAIL voie *f* ferrée - **4.** [of animal, person] trace *f* ; **to hide** OR **cover one's ~s** brouiller les pistes ; **to stop dead in one's ~s** s'arrêter net - **5.** [on record, tape] piste *f* - **6.** phr : **to keep ~ of sb** rester en contact avec qqn ; **to keep ~ of** [events] suivre ; **to lose ~ of sb** perdre contact avec qqn ; **to lose ~ of** [events] ne plus suivre ; **to lose ~ of time** perdre la notion du temps ; **to be on the right ~** être sur la bonne voie ; **to be on the wrong ~** être sur la mauvaise piste ◇ *vt* suivre la trace de ◇ *vi* [camera] faire un travelling.

➡ **track down** *vt sep* [criminal, animal] dépister ; [object, address etc] retrouver.

trackball ['trækbɔːl] *n* COMPUT boule *f* de commande.

tracker dog ['trækər-] *n* chien *m* policier.

track event *n* épreuve *f* sur piste.

tracking station ['trækɪŋ-] *n* station *f* d'observation.

track record *n* palmarès *m*.

track shoes *npl* chaussures *fpl* à pointes.

tracksuit ['træksuːt] *n* survêtement *m*.

tract [trækt] *n* - **1.** [pamphlet] tract *m* - **2.** [of land, forest] étendue *f* - **3.** MED appareil *m*, système *m*.

traction ['trækʃn] *n (U)* - **1.** PHYSICS traction *f* - **2.** MED extension *f*; in ~ en extension.

traction engine *n* locomobile *f*.

tractor ['træktəʳ] *n* tracteur *m*.

tractor-trailer *n* Am semi-remorque *m*.

trade [treɪd] ⋄ *n* - **1.** *(U)* [commerce] commerce *m* - **2.** [job] métier *m*; by ~ de son état ⋄ *vt* [exchange] : **to ~ sthg (for)** échanger qqch (contre) ⋄ *vi* - **1.** COMM : **to ~ (with sb)** commercer (avec qqn) - **2.** Am [shop] : **to ~ at** OR **with** faire ses courses à OR chez.

➡ **trade in** *vt sep* [exchange] échanger, faire reprendre.

trade barrier *n* barrière *f* douanière.

trade deficit *n* déficit *m* commercial.

trade discount *n* remise *f* confraternelle OR à la profession.

trade fair *n* exposition *f* commerciale.

trade gap *n* déficit *m* commercial.

trade-in *n* reprise *f*.

trademark ['treɪdmɑːk] *n* - **1.** COMM marque *f* de fabrique - **2.** fig [characteristic] marque *f*.

trade name *n* nom *m* de marque.

trade-off *n* compromis *m*.

trade price *n* prix *m* de gros.

trader ['treɪdəʳ] *n* marchand *m*, -e *f*, commerçant *m*, -e *f*.

trade route *n* route *f* commerciale.

trade secret *n* secret *m* de fabrication.

tradesman ['treɪdzmən] *(pl* **-men** [-mən]) *n* commerçant *m*.

tradespeople ['treɪdz,piːpl] *npl* commerçants *mpl*.

trade(s) union *n* Br syndicat *m*.

Trades Union Congress *n* Br : **the ~** la Confédération des syndicats britanniques.

trade(s) unionist [-'juːnjənɪst] *n* Br syndicaliste *mf*.

trade wind *n* alizé *m*.

trading ['treɪdɪŋ] *n (U)* commerce *m*.

trading estate *n* Br zone *f* industrielle.

trading stamp *n* timbre-prime *m*.

tradition [trə'dɪʃn] *n* tradition *f*.

traditional [trə'dɪʃənl] *adj* traditionnel(elle).

traditionally [trə'dɪʃnəlɪ] *adv* traditionnellement.

traffic ['træfɪk] *(pt & pp* **-ked**; *cont* **-king)** ⋄ *n (U)* - **1.** [vehicles] circulation *f* - **2.** [illegal trade] : **~ (in)** trafic *m* (de) ⋄ *vi* : **to ~ in** faire le trafic de.

traffic circle *n* Am rond-point *m*.

traffic island *n* refuge *m*.

traffic jam *n* embouteillage *m*.

trafficker ['træfɪkəʳ] *n* : **~ (in)** trafiquant *m*, -e *f* (de).

traffic lights *npl* feux *mpl* de signalisation.

traffic offence Br, **traffic violation** Am *n* infraction *f* au code de la route.

traffic sign *n* panneau *m* de signalisation.

traffic violation Am = traffic offence.

traffic warden *n* Br contractuel *m*, -elle *f*.

tragedy ['trædʒədɪ] *(pl* **-ies)** *n* tragédie *f*.

tragic ['trædʒɪk] *adj* tragique.

tragically ['trædʒɪklɪ] *adv* tragiquement, de façon tragique.

trail [treɪl] ⋄ *n* - **1.** [path] sentier *m*; **to blaze a ~** fig faire œuvre de pionnier - **2.** [trace] piste *f*; **on the ~ of** sur la piste de ⋄ *vt* - **1.** [drag] traîner - **2.** [follow] suivre ⋄ *vi* - **1.** [drag, move slowly] traîner - **2.** SPORT [lose] : **to be ~ing** être mené(e).

➡ **trail away**, **trail off** *vi* s'estomper.

trailblazing ['treɪl,bleɪzɪŋ] *adj* de pionnier.

trailer ['treɪləʳ] *n* - **1.** [vehicle - for luggage] remorque *f* ; [- for living in] caravane *f* - **2.** CINEMA bande-annonce *f*.

trailer park *n* Am *terrain aménagé pour les camping-cars.*

train [treɪn] ⋄ *n* - **1.** RAIL train *m* - **2.** [of dress] traîne *f* ⋄ *vt* - **1.** [teach] : **to ~ sb to do sthg** apprendre à qqn à faire qqch - **2.** [for job] former ; **to ~ sb as/in** former qqn comme/dans - **3.** SPORT : **to ~ sb (for)** entraîner qqn (pour) - **4.** [plant] faire grimper - **5.** [gun, camera] braquer ⋄ *vi* - **1.** [for job] : **to ~ (as)** recevoir OR faire une formation (de) - **2.** SPORT : **to ~ (for)** s'entraîner (pour).

trained [treɪnd] *adj* formé(e).

trainee [treɪ'niː] ⋄ *adj* stagiaire, apprenti(e) ⋄ *n* stagiaire *mf*.

trainer ['treɪnəʳ] *n* - **1.** [of animals] dresseur *m*, -euse *f* - **2.** SPORT entraîneur *m*.

➡ **trainers** *npl* Br chaussures *fpl* de sport.

training ['treɪnɪŋ] *n (U)* - **1.** [for job] : **~ (in)** formation *f* (de) - **2.** SPORT entraînement *m*.

training college *n* Br école *f* professionnelle.

training course *n* cours *m* OR stage *m* de formation.

training shoes *npl* Br chaussures *fpl* de sport.

train of thought *n* : **my/his ~** le fil de mes/ses pensées.

train set *n* train *m* électrique.

train-spotter [-spɒtə^r] *n* - **1.** Br passionné *m*, -e *f* de trains - **2.** inf [nerd] crétin *m*, -e *f*.

train station *n* Am gare *f*.

traipse [treɪps] *vi* traîner.

trait [treɪt] *n* trait *m*.

traitor ['treɪtə^r] *n* traître *m*.

trajectory [trə'dʒektərɪ] (*pl* -ies) *n* trajectoire *f*.

tram [træm], **tramcar** ['træmkɑ:^r] *n* Br tram *m*, tramway *m*.

tramlines ['træmlaɪnz] *npl* Br - **1.** [for trams] voies *fpl* de tram - **2.** TENNIS lignes *fpl* de côté.

tramp [træmp] ⬦ *n* - **1.** [homeless person] clochard *m*, -e *f* - **2.** Am inf [woman] traînée *f* ⬦ *vt* [countryside] parcourir, battre ; **to ~ the streets** battre le pavé ⬦ *vi* marcher d'un pas lourd.

trample ['træmpl] ⬦ *vt* piétiner ⬦ *vi* : **to ~ on sthg** piétiner qqch ; **to ~ on sb** fig bafouer qqn.

trampoline ['træmpəli:n] *n* trampoline *m*.

trance [trɑ:ns] *n* transe *f* ; **in a ~** en transe.

tranquil ['træŋkwɪl] *adj* tranquille.

tranquility Am = tranquillity.

tranquilize Am = tranquillize.

tranquilizer Am = tranquillizer.

tranquillity Br, **tranquility** Am [træŋ'kwɪlətɪ] *n* tranquillité *f*.

tranquillize, -ise Br, **tranquilize** Am ['træŋkwɪlaɪz] *vt* mettre sous tranquillisants OR calmants.

tranquillizer Br, **tranquilizer** Am ['træŋkwɪlaɪzə^r] *n* tranquillisant *m*, calmant *m*.

transact [træn'zækt] *vt* traiter, régler.

transaction [træn'zækʃn] *n* transaction *f*.

transatlantic [,trænzət'læntɪk] *adj* [flight, crossing] transatlantique ; [politics] d'outre-Atlantique.

transceiver [træn'si:və^r] *n* émetteur-récepteur *m*.

transcend [træn'send] *vt* transcender.

transcendental meditation [,trænsen-'dentl-] *n* méditation *f* transcendantale.

transcribe [træn'skraɪb] *vt* transcrire.

transcript ['trænskrɪpt] *n* transcription *f*.

transept ['trænsept] *n* transept *m*.

transfer [*n* 'trænsfɜ:^r, *vb* træns'fɜ:^r] (*pt* & *pp* -red ; *cont* -ring) ⬦ *n* - **1.** [gen] transfert *m* ; [of power] passation *f* ; [of money] virement *m* - **2.** [design] décalcomanie *f* - **3.** Am [ticket] *ticket permettant de changer de train ou de bus sans payer de supplément* ⬦ *vt* - **1.** [gen]

transférer ; [power, control] faire passer ; [money] virer - **2.** [employee] transférer, muter ⬦ *vi* être transféré.

transferable [træns'fɜ:rəbl] *adj* transférable, transmissible ; **not ~** [ticket] non cessible.

transference ['trænsfərəns] *n* [of power] passation *f*.

transfer fee *n* Br SPORT prix *m* d'un transfert.

transfigure [træns'fɪgə^r] *vt* transfigurer.

transfix [træns'fɪks] *vt* : **to be ~ed with fear** être paralysé(e) par la peur.

transform [træns'fɔ:ml] *vt* : **to ~ sb/sthg (into)** transformer qqn/qqch (en).

transformation [,trænsfə'meɪʃn] *n* transformation *f*.

transformer [træns'fɔ:mə^r] *n* ELEC transformateur *m*.

transfusion [træns'fju:ʒn] *n* transfusion *f*.

transgenic [trænz'dʒenɪk] *adj* transgénique.

transgress [træns'gres] fml ⬦ *vt* transgresser ⬦ *vi* pécher.

transgression [træns'greʃn] *n* fml - **1.** [fault] faute *f* - **2.** (U) [doing wrong] transgression *f*.

transient ['trænzɪənt] ⬦ *adj* passager(ère) ⬦ *n* Am [person] voyageur *m*, -euse *f* en transit.

transistor [træn'zɪstə^r] *n* transistor *m*.

transistor radio *n* transistor *m*.

transit ['trænsɪt] *n* : **in ~** en transit.

transit camp *n* camp *m* volant.

transition [træn'zɪʃn] *n* transition *f* ; **in ~** en transition.

transitional [træn'zɪʃənl] *adj* de transition.

transitive ['trænzɪtɪv] *adj* GRAMM transitif(ive).

transit lounge *n* salle *f* de transit.

transitory ['trænzɪtrɪ] *adj* transitoire.

translate [træns'leɪt] ⬦ *vt* traduire ⬦ *vi* [person] traduire ; [expression, word] se traduire.

translation [træns'leɪʃn] *n* traduction *f*.

translator [træns'leɪtə^r] *n* traducteur *m*, -trice *f*.

translucent [trænz'lu:snt] *adj* translucide.

transmission [trænz'mɪʃn] *n* - **1.** [gen] transmission *f* - **2.** RADIO & TV [programme] émission *f*.

transmit [trænz'mɪt] (*pt* & *pp* -ted ; *cont* -ting) *vt* transmettre.

transmitter [trænz'mɪtə^r] *n* émetteur *m*.

transparency [trans'pærənsɪ] (*pl* -ies) *n* - **1.** PHOT diapositive *f* ; [for overhead projector]

transparent m - **2.** *(U)* [quality] transparence f.

transparent [træns'pærənt] *adj* transparent(e).

transpire [træn'spaɪəʳ] *fml* <> *vt* : **it ~s that ...** on a appris que ... <> *vi* [happen] se passer, arriver.

transplant [*n* 'trænsplɑːnt, *vb* træns'plɑːnt] <> *n* MED greffe f, transplantation f <> *vt* - **1.** MED greffer, transplanter - **2.** [seedlings] repiquer - **3.** [move] transplanter.

transport [*n* 'trænspɔːt, *vb* træn'spɔːt] <> *n* transport m <> *vt* transporter.

transportable [træn'spɔːtəbl] *adj* transportable.

transportation [ˌtrænspɔː'teɪʃn] *n* esp Am transport m.

transport cafe *n* Br restaurant m de routiers, routier m.

transporter [træn'spɔːtəʳ] *n* [for cars] transporteur m de voitures.

transpose [træns'pəʊz] *vt* transposer.

transsexual [træns'sekʃʊəl] *n* transsexuel(elle).

transvestite [trænz'vestaɪt] *n* travesti m, -e f.

trap [træp] (*pt & pp* -**ped**; *cont* -**ping**) <> *n* piège m <> *vt* prendre au piège ; **to be trapped** être coincé ; **to be trapped in a relationship** être piégé dans une relation.

trapdoor [ˌtræp'dɔːʳ] *n* trappe f.

trapeze [trə'piːz] *n* trapèze m.

trapper ['træpəʳ] *n* trappeur m.

trappings ['træpɪŋz] *npl* signes *mpl* extérieurs.

trash [træʃ] *n (U)* - **1.** Am [refuse] ordures *fpl* - **2.** inf pej [poor-quality thing] camelote f.

trashcan ['træʃkæn] *n* Am poubelle f.

trashy ['træʃi] (*compar* -**ier**; *superl* -**iest**) *adj* inf qui ne vaut rien, nul (nulle).

trauma ['trɔːmə] *n* MED trauma m ; fig traumatisme m.

traumatic [trɔː'mætɪk] *adj* traumatisant(e).

traumatize, -ise ['trɔːmətaɪz] *vt* traumatiser.

travel ['trævl] (Br *pt & pp* -**led** ; *cont* -**ling**, Am *pt & pp* -**ed** ; *cont* -**ing**) <> *n (U)* voyage m, voyages *mpl* <> *vi* parcourir <> *vi* - **1.** [make journey] voyager - **2.** [move - current, signal] aller, passer ; [- news] se répandre, circuler.

➨ **travels** *npl* voyages *mpl*.

travel agency *n* agence f de voyages.

travel agent *n* agent m de voyages ; **to/at the ~'s** à l'agence f de voyages.

travel brochure *n* dépliant m touristique.

traveler etc Am = **traveller** etc.

travelled Br, **traveled** Am ['trævld] *adj* - **1.** [person] qui a beaucoup voyagé - **2.** [road, route] : **much ~** très fréquenté(e).

traveller Br, **traveler** Am ['trævləʳ] *n* - **1.** [person on journey] voyageur m, -euse f - **2.** [sales representative] représentant m - **3.** = **New Age travel(l)er.**

traveller's cheque *n* chèque m de voyage.

travelling Br, **traveling** Am ['trævlɪŋ] *adj* - **1.** [theatre, circus] ambulant(e) - **2.** [clock, bag etc] de voyage ; [allowance] de déplacement ; **~ time** durée f du voyage.

travelling expenses *npl* frais *mpl* de déplacement.

travelling salesman *n* représentant m.

travelogue, travelog Am ['trævəlɒg] *n* - **1.** [talk] compte-rendu m OR récit m de voyage - **2.** [film] documentaire m.

travelsick ['trævəlsɪk] *adj* : **to be ~** avoir le mal de la route/de l'air/de mer.

traverse ['trævəs, ˌtrə'vɜːs] *vt* fml traverser.

travesty ['trævəstɪ] (*pl* -**ies**) *n* parodie f.

trawl [trɔːl] <> *n* [fishing net] chalut m <> *vt* [area of sea] pêcher au chalut dans <> *vi* : **to ~ for cod/mackerel** pêcher la morue/le hareng au chalut.

trawler ['trɔːləʳ] *n* chalutier m.

tray [treɪ] *n* plateau m.

treacherous ['tretʃərəs] *adj* traître (traîtresse).

treachery ['tretʃərɪ] *n* traîtrise f.

treacle ['triːkl] *n* Br mélasse f.

tread [tred] (*pt* trod ; *pp* trodden) <> *n* - **1.** [on tyre] bande f de roulement ; [of shoe] semelle f - **2.** [way of walking] pas m ; [sound] bruit m de pas <> *vt* [crush] : **to ~ sthg into** écraser qqch dans <> *vi* : **to ~ (on)** marcher (sur) ; **to ~ carefully** fig y aller doucement.

treadle ['tredl] *n* pédale f.

treadmill ['tredmɪl] *n* - **1.** [wheel] trépigneuse f - **2.** fig [dull routine] routine f, train-train m.

treas. (*abbr of* **treasurer**) trés.

treason ['triːzn] *n* trahison f.

treasure ['treʒəʳ] <> *n* trésor m <> *vt* [object] garder précieusement ; [memory] chérir.

treasure hunt *n* chasse f au trésor.

treasurer ['treʒərəʳ] *n* trésorier m, -ère f.

treasure trove *n* JUR trésor m, *objets de valeur trouvés et que personne n'a réclamés.*

treasury ['treʒərɪ] (*pl* -**ies**) *n* [room] trésorerie f.

Treasury n : the Treasury le ministère des Finances.

treasury bill n bon m du Trésor.

treat [tri:t] ◇ vt - **1.** [gen] traiter ; **to ~ sb like a child** traiter qqn en enfant ; **to ~ sthg as a joke** prendre qqch à la rigolade - **2.** [on special occasion] : **to ~ sb to sthg** offrir OR payer qqch à qqn ; **to ~ o.s. to sthg** s'offrir qqch, se payer qqch ◇ n - **1.** [gift] cadeau m ; **to give sb a ~** faire plaisir à qqn ; **this is my ~** [pay for meal, drink] c'est moi qui régale - **2.** [delight] plaisir m.

treatise ['tri:tɪz] n : ~ **(on)** traité m (de).

treatment ['tri:tmənt] n traitement m.

treaty ['tri:tɪ] (pl -ies) n traité m.

treble ['trebl] ◇ adj - **1.** [MUS - voice] de soprano ; [- recorder] aigu (aiguë) - **2.** [triple] triple ◇ n [on stereo control] aigu m ; [boy singer] soprano m ◇ vt & vi tripler.

treble clef n clef f de sol.

tree [tri:] n - **1.** [gen] arbre m ; **to be barking up the wrong ~** fig se tromper d'adresse - **2.** COMPUT arbre m, arborescence f.

tree-lined adj bordé(e) d'arbres.

tree surgeon n arboriculteur m, -trice f.

treetop ['tri:tɒp] n cime f.

tree-trunk n tronc m d'arbre.

trek [trek] (pt & pp -ked ; cont -king) ◇ n randonnée f ◇ vi faire une randonnée ; fig se traîner.

trellis ['trelɪs] n treillis m.

tremble ['trembl] vi trembler.

tremendous [trɪ'mendəs] adj - **1.** [size, success, difference] énorme ; [noise] terrible - **2.** inf [really good] formidable.

tremendously [trɪ'mendəslɪ] adv [exciting, expensive, big] extrêmement ; [loud] terriblement.

tremor ['tremə'] n tremblement m.

tremulous ['tremjuləs] adj literary [voice] tremblant(e) ; [smile] timide.

trench [trentʃ] n tranchée f.

trenchant ['trentʃənt] adj mordant(e), incisif(ive).

trench coat n trench-coat m.

trench warfare n (U) guerre f de tranchées.

trend [trend] n [tendency] tendance f.

trendsetter ['trend,setə'] n personne f qui lance une mode.

trendy ['trendɪ] (compar -ier ; superl -iest, pl -ies) inf ◇ adj branché(e), à la mode ◇ n personne f branchée.

trepidation [,trepɪ'deɪʃn] n fml : **in** OR **with ~** avec inquiétude.

trespass ['trespəs] vi [on land] entrer sans permission ; **'no ~ing'** 'défense d'entrer'.

trespasser ['trespəsə'] n intrus m, -e f ; **'~s will be prosecuted'** 'défense d'entrer sous peine de poursuites'.

trestle ['tresl] n tréteau m.

trestle table n table f à tréteaux.

trial ['traɪəl] n - **1.** JUR procès m ; **to be on ~ (for)** passer en justice (pour) - **2.** [test, experiment] essai m ; **on ~** à l'essai ; **by ~ and error** en tâtonnant - **3.** [unpleasant experience] épreuve f ; **~s and tribulations** tribulations fpl.

trial basis n : **on a ~** à l'essai.

trial period n période f d'essai.

trial run n essai m.

trial-size(d) adj [pack, box] d'essai.

triangle ['traɪæŋgl] n - **1.** [gen] triangle m - **2.** Am [set square] équerre f.

triangular [traɪ'æŋgjʊlə'] adj triangulaire.

triathlon [traɪ'æθlɒn] (pl -s) n triathlon m.

tribal ['traɪbl] adj tribal(e).

tribe [traɪb] n tribu f.

tribulation [,trɪbjʊ'leɪʃn] n ⊏⊐ **trial.**

tribunal [traɪ'bju:nl] n tribunal m.

tribune ['trɪbju:n] n HISTORY tribun m.

tributary ['trɪbjʊtrɪ] (pl -ies) n affluent m.

tribute ['trɪbju:t] n tribut m, hommage m ; **to pay ~** to payer tribut à, rendre hommage à ; **to be a ~ to sthg** témoigner de qqch.

trice [traɪs] n : **in a ~** en un clin d'œil.

triceps ['traɪseps] (pl inv OR **-es** [-i:zl) n triceps m.

trick [trɪk] ◇ n - **1.** [to deceive] tour m, farce f ; **to play a ~ on sb** jouer un tour à qqn - **2.** [to entertain] tour m - **3.** [knack] truc m ; **that will do the ~** inf ça fera l'affaire ◇ comp [knife, moustache etc] truqué(e), faux (fausse) ◇ vt attraper, rouler ; **to ~ sb into doing sthg** amener qqn à faire qqch (par la ruse).

trickery ['trɪkərɪ] n (U) ruse f.

trickle ['trɪkl] ◇ n [of liquid] filet m ; **a ~ of people/letters** quelques personnes/lettres ◇ vi [liquid] dégouliner ; **to ~ in/out** [people] entrer/sortir par petits groupes.

trick or treat n une gâterie ou une farce (phrase rituelle des enfants déguisés qui font la quête le soir de Halloween).

trick question n question-piège f.

tricky ['trɪkɪ] (compar -ier ; superl -iest) adj [difficult] difficile.

tricycle ['traɪsɪkl] n tricycle m.

trident ['traɪdnt] n trident m.

tried [traɪd] ⟷ pt & pp ⊳ try ⟷ adj : ~ and tested [method, system] qui a fait ses preuves.

trier ['traɪə'] n : to be a ~ être persévérant(e).

trifle ['traɪfl] n - 1. Br CULIN ≃ diplomate m - 2. [unimportant thing] bagatelle f.
➡ a **trifle** adv un peu, un tantinet.
➡ **trifle with** vt fus badiner avec ; [sb's affections] se jouer de.

trifling ['traɪflɪŋ] adj insignifiant(e).

trigger ['trɪgə'] ⟷ n [on gun] détente f, gâchette f ⟷ vt déclencher, provoquer.
➡ **trigger off** vt sep déclencher, provoquer.

trigonometry [ˌtrɪgə'nɒmətrɪ] n trigonométrie f.

trilby ['trɪlbɪ] (pl -ies) n Br feutre m.

trill [trɪl] ⟷ n trille m ⟷ vi triller.

trillions ['trɪljənz] npl inf : ~ (of) tout un tas (de), plein (de).

trilogy ['trɪlədʒɪ] (pl -ies) n trilogie f.

trim [trɪm] (compar -mer ; superl -mest, pt & pp -med ; cont -ming) ⟷ adj - 1. [neat and tidy] net (nette) - 2. [slim] svelte ⟷ n - 1. [of hair] coupe f - 2. [on clothes] garniture f ; [inside car] garniture intérieure ⟷ vt - 1. [cut - gen] couper ; [- hedge] tailler - 2. [decorate] : to ~ sthg (with) garnir OR orner qqch (de).
➡ **trim away, trim off** vt sep couper.

trimmed [trɪmd] adj : ~ with [clothes] orné(e) de.

trimming ['trɪmɪŋ] n - 1. [on clothing] parement m - 2. CULIN garniture f.

Trinidad and Tobago ['trɪnɪdæd-] n Trinité-et-Tobago f; in ~ à Trinité-et-Tobago.

Trinidadian [ˌtrɪnɪ'dædɪən] ⟷ adj trinidadien(enne) ⟷ n Trinidadien m, -enne f.

Trinity ['trɪnətɪ] n RELIG : the ~ la Trinité.

trinket ['trɪŋkɪt] n bibelot m.

trio ['triːəʊ] (pl -s) n trio m.

trip [trɪp] (pt & pp -ped ; cont -ping) ⟷ n - 1. [journey] voyage m - 2. drugs sl trip m ⟷ vt [make stumble] faire un croche-pied à ⟷ vi [stumble] : to ~ (over) trébucher (sur).
➡ **trip up** vt sep - 1. [make stumble] faire un croche-pied à - 2. [catch out] prendre en défaut.

tripartite [ˌtraɪ'pɑːtaɪt] adj triparti(e), tripartite.

tripe [traɪp] n (U) - 1. CULIN tripe f - 2. inf [nonsense] bêtises fpl, idioties fpl.

triple ['trɪpl] ⟷ adj triple ⟷ vt & vi tripler.

triple jump n : the ~ le triple saut.

triplets ['trɪplɪts] npl triplés mpl, triplées fpl.

triplicate ['trɪplɪkət] ⟷ adj en trois exemplaires ⟷ n : in ~ en trois exemplaires.

tripod ['traɪpɒd] n trépied m.

Tripoli [ˈtrɪpəlɪ] n Tripoli.

tripper ['trɪpə'] n Br excursionniste mf.

tripwire ['trɪpwaɪə'] n fil m de détente.

trite [traɪt] adj pej banal(e).

triumph ['traɪəmf] ⟷ n triomphe m ⟷ vi : to ~ (over) triompher (de).

triumphal [traɪ'ʌmfl] adj triomphal(e).

triumphant [traɪ'ʌmfənt] adj [exultant] triomphant(e).

triumphantly [trɪ'ʌmfəntlɪ] adv de façon triomphante, triomphalement.

triumvirate [traɪ'ʌmvɪrət] n HIST triumvirat m.

trivet ['trɪvɪt] n - 1. [over fire] trépied m - 2. [to protect table] dessous-de-plat m inv.

trivia ['trɪvɪə] n (U) [trifles] vétilles fpl, riens mpl.

trivial ['trɪvɪəl] adj insignifiant(e).

triviality [ˌtrɪvɪ'ælətɪ] (pl -ies) n banalité f.

trivialize, -ise ['trɪvɪəlaɪz] vt banaliser.

trod [trɒd] pt ⊳ tread.

trodden ['trɒdn] pp ⊳ tread.

Trojan ['trəʊdʒən] ⟷ adj troyen(enne) ⟷ n Troyen m, -enne f ; to work like a ~ travailler comme un nègre OR une bête de somme.

troll [trəʊl] n troll m.

trolley ['trɒlɪ] (pl -s) n - 1. Br [for shopping, luggage] chariot m, caddie® m - 2. Br [for food, drinks] chariot m, table f roulante - 3. Am [tram] tramway m, tram m.

trolleybus ['trɒlɪbʌs] n trolleybus m.

trombone [trɒm'bəʊn] n MUS trombone m.

troop [truːp] ⟷ n bande f, troupe f ⟷ vi : to ~ in/out/off entrer/sortir/partir en groupe.
➡ **troops** npl troupes fpl.

trooper ['truːpə'] n - 1. MIL soldat m - 2. Am [policeman] policier m (appartenant à la police d'un État).

troopship ['truːpʃɪp] n transport m.

trophy ['trəʊfɪ] (pl -ies) n trophée m.

tropical ['trɒpɪkl] adj tropical(e).

Tropic of Cancer ['trɒpɪk-] n : the ~ le tropique du Cancer.

Tropic of Capricorn ['trɒpɪk-] n : the ~ le tropique du Capricorne.

tropics ['trɒpɪks] npl : the ~ les tropiques mpl.

trot [trɒt] (*pt* & *pp* **-ted** ; *cont* **-ting**) ⬦ *n* [of horse] trot *m* ⬦ *vi* trotter.
➤ **on the trot** *adv inf* de suite, d'affilée.
➤ **trot out** *vt sep pej* débiter.

Trotskyism ['trɒtskɪɪzm] *n* trotskisme *m*.

trotter ['trɒtə'] *n* [pig's foot] pied *m* de porc.

trouble ['trʌbl] ⬦ *n* (U) - **1.** [difficulty] problème *m*, difficulté *f*; **to be in ~** avoir des ennuis ; **to get into ~** s'attirer des ennuis ; **the ~ (with sb/sthg) is** ... l'ennui (avec qqn/qqch), c'est que ... - **2.** [bother] peine *f*, mal *m*; **to take the ~ to do sthg** se donner la peine de faire qqch ; **it's no ~!** ça ne me dérange pas! ; **to be asking for ~** chercher les ennuis - **3.** [pain, illness] mal *m*, ennui *m* - **4.** [fighting] bagarre *f*; POL troubles *mpl*, conflits *mpl* ⬦ *vt* - **1.** [worry, upset] peiner, troubler - **2.** [bother] déranger - **3.** [give pain to] faire mal à.
➤ **troubles** *npl* - **1.** [worries] ennuis *mpl* - **2.** POL troubles *mpl*, conflits *mpl*.

troubled ['trʌbld] *adj* - **1.** [worried] inquiet(iète) - **2.** [disturbed - period] de troubles, agité(e) ; [- country] qui connaît une période de troubles.

trouble-free *adj* sans problèmes.

troublemaker ['trʌbl,meɪkə'] *n* fauteur *m*, -trice *f* de troubles.

troubleshooter ['trʌbl,ʃuːtə'] *n* expert *m*, spécialiste *m*.

troublesome ['trʌblsəm] *adj* [job] pénible ; [cold] gênant(e) ; [back, knee] qui fait souffrir.

trouble spot *n* point *m* chaud.

trough [trɒf] *n* - **1.** [for animals - with water] abreuvoir *m*; [- with food] auge *f* - **2.** [low point - of wave] creux *m*; fig point *m* bas - **3.** METEOR dépression *f*.

trounce [traʊns] *vt inf* écraser.

troupe [truːp] *n* troupe *f*.

trouser press ['traʊzə'-] *n* presse *f* à pantalons.

trousers ['traʊzəz] *npl* pantalon *m*.

trouser suit ['traʊzə'-] *n* Br tailleur-pantalon *m*.

trousseau ['truːsəʊ] (*pl* **-x** [-z] OR **-s**) *n* trousseau *m*.

trout [traʊt] (*pl inv* OR **-s**) *n* truite *f*.

trove [trəʊv] ⊳ **treasure trove**.

trowel ['traʊəl] *n* [for gardening] déplantoir *m*; [for cement, plaster] truelle *f*.

truancy ['truːənsɪ] *n* absentéisme *m*.

truant ['truːənt] *n* [child] élève *mf* absentéiste ; **to play ~** faire l'école buissonnière.

truce [truːs] *n* trêve *f*.

truck [trʌk] ⬦ *n* - **1.** Esp am [lorry] camion *m* - **2.** RAIL wagon *m* à plate-forme ⬦ *vt* Am transporter par camion.

truck driver *n* esp Am routier *m*.

trucker ['trʌkə'] *n* Am routier *m*.

truck farm *n* Am jardin *m* maraîcher.

trucking ['trʌkɪŋ] *n* Am camionnage *m*.

truck stop *n* Am relais *m* routier.

truculent ['trʌkjʊlənt] *adj* agressif(ive).

trudge [trʌdʒ] ⬦ *n* marche *f* pénible ⬦ *vi* marcher péniblement.

true ['truː] *adj* - **1.** [factual] vrai(e) ; **to come ~** se réaliser - **2.** [genuine] vrai(e), authentique ; **~ love** le grand amour - **3.** [exact] exact(e) - **4.** [faithful] fidèle, loyal(e) - **5.** TECH droit(e) ; [wheel] dans l'axe.

true-life *adj* vrai(e), vécu(e).

truffle ['trʌfl] *n* truffe *f*.

truism ['truːɪzm] *n* truisme *m*.

truly ['truːlɪ] *adv* - **1.** [gen] vraiment - **2.** [sincerely] vraiment, sincèrement - **3.** *phr* : **yours ~** [at end of letter] je vous prie de croire à l'expression de mes sentiments distingués.

trump [trʌmp] ⬦ *n* atout *m* ⬦ *vt* couper.

trump card *n* fig atout *m*.

trumped-up ['trʌmpt-] *adj pej* inventé(e) de toutes pièces.

trumpet ['trʌmpɪt] ⬦ *n* trompette *f* ⬦ *vi* [elephant] barrir.

trumpeter ['trʌmpɪtə'] *n* trompettiste *mf*.

truncate [trʌŋ'keɪt] *vt* tronquer.

truncheon ['trʌntʃən] *n* matraque *f*.

trundle ['trʌndl] ⬦ *vt* [cart, wheelbarrow] pousser lentement ⬦ *vi* aller lentement.

trunk [trʌŋk] *n* - **1.** [of tree, person] tronc *m* - **2.** [of elephant] trompe *f* - **3.** [box] malle *f* - **4.** Am [of car] coffre *m*.
➤ **trunks** *npl* maillot *m* de bain.

trunk call *n* Br communication *f* interurbaine.

trunk road *n* (route *f*) nationale *f*.

truss [trʌs] *n* - **1.** MED bandage *m* herniaire - **2.** CONSTR ferme *f*.

trust [trʌst] ⬦ *vt* - **1.** [have confidence in] avoir confiance en, se fier à ; **to ~ sb to do sthg** compter sur qqn pour faire qqch - **2.** [entrust] : **to ~ sb with sthg** confier qqch à qqn - **3.** *fml* [hope] : **to ~ (that)** ... espérer que ... ⬦ *n* - **1.** (U) [faith] : **~ (in sb/sthg)** confiance *f* (en qqn/dans qqch) ; **to take sthg on ~** accepter qqch les yeux fermés ; **to put** OR **place one's ~ in sb** faire confiance à qqn - **2.** (U) [responsibility] responsabilité *f*; **a posi-**

tion of ~ un poste de confiance - **3.** FIN : in ~ en dépôt - **4.** COMM trust *m*.

trust company *n* société *f* fiduciaire.

trusted ['trʌstɪd] *adj* [person] de confiance ; [method] qui a fait ses preuves.

trustee [trʌs'tiː] *n* FIN & JUR fidéicommissaire *mf* ; [of institution] administrateur *m*, -trice *f*.

trusteeship [ˌtrʌs'tiːʃɪp] *n* FIN & JUR fidéicommis *m* ; [of institution] fonction *f* d'administrateur.

trust fund *n* fonds *m* en fidéicommis.

trusting ['trʌstɪŋ] *adj* confiant(e).

trustworthy ['trʌstˌwɜːðɪ] *adj* digne de confiance.

trusty ['trʌstɪ] (*compar* -**ier** ; *superl* -**iest**) *adj* hum fidèle.

truth [truːθ] *n* vérité *f* ; in (all) ~ à dire vrai, en vérité.

truth drug *n* sérum *m* de vérité.

truthful ['truːθfʊl] *adj* [person, reply] honnête ; [story] véridique.

try [traɪ] (*pt* & *pp* -**ied**, *pl* -**ies**) ◇ *vt* - **1.** [attempt, test] essayer ; [food, drink] goûter ; to ~ to do sthg essayer de faire qqch - **2.** JUR juger - **3.** [put to the test] éprouver, mettre à l'épreuve ◇ *vi* essayer ; to ~ for sthg essayer d'obtenir qqch ◇ *n* - **1.** [attempt] essai *m*, tentative *f* ; to have a ~ at sthg essayer de faire qqch ; to give sthg a ~ essayer qqch - **2.** RUGBY essai *m*.

➤ **try on** *vt sep* [clothes] essayer.

➤ **try out** *vt sep* essayer.

trying ['traɪɪŋ] *adj* pénible, éprouvant(e).

try-out *n* inf essai *m*.

tsar [zɑːʳ] *n* tsar *m*.

T-shirt *n* tee-shirt *m*.

tsp. (*abbr of* teaspoon) cc.

T-square *n* té *m*.

TT *abbr of* teetotal.

Tuareg ['twɑːreg] *n* [person] Touareg *m*, -ègue *f*.

tub [tʌb] *n* - **1.** [of ice cream - large] boîte *f* ; [- small] petit pot *m* ; [of margarine] barquette *f* - **2.** [bath] baignoire *f*.

tuba ['tjuːbə] *n* tuba *m*.

tubby ['tʌbɪ] (*compar* -**ier** ; *superl* -**iest**) *adj* inf rondouillard(e), boulot(otte).

tube [tjuːb] *n* - **1.** [cylinder, container] tube *m* - **2.** ANAT : bronchial ~s bronches *fpl* - **3.** Br [underground train] métro *m* ; the ~ [system] le métro ; by ~ en métro.

tubeless ['tjuːblɪs] *adj* [tyre] sans chambre à air.

tuber ['tjuːbəʳ] *n* tubercule *m*.

tuberculosis [tjuːˌbɜːkjʊ'ləʊsɪs] *n* tuberculose *f*.

tube station *n* Br station *f* de métro.

tubing ['tjuːbɪŋ] *n* (U) tubes *mpl*, tuyaux *mpl*.

tubular ['tjuːbjʊləʳ] *adj* tubulaire.

TUC *n abbr of* Trades Union Congress.

tuck [tʌk] ◇ *n* SEWING rempli *m* ◇ *vt* [place neatly] ranger.

➤ **tuck away** *vt sep* [store] mettre de côté OR en lieu sûr ; to be ~ed away [village, house] être caché(e) OR blotti(e).

➤ **tuck in** ◇ *vt* - **1.** [child, patient] border - **2.** [clothes] rentrer ◇ *vi* inf boulotter ; ~ in! allez-y, mangez!

➤ **tuck up** *vt sep* [child, patient] border.

tuck shop *n* Br [at school] petite boutique qui vend des bonbons et des gâteaux.

Tudor ['tjuːdəʳ] *adj* - **1.** HISTORY des Tudors - **2.** ARCHIT Tudor (*inv*).

Tue., Tues. (*abbr of* Tuesday) mar.

Tuesday ['tjuːzdɪ] *n* mardi *m* ; *see also* Saturday.

tuft [tʌft] *n* touffe *f*.

tug [tʌg] (*pt* & *pp* -**ged** ; *cont* -**ging**) ◇ *n* - **1.** [pull] : to give sthg a ~ tirer sur qqch - **2.** [boat] remorqueur *m* ◇ *vt* tirer ◇ *vi* : to ~ (at) tirer (sur).

tugboat ['tʌgbəʊt] *n* remorqueur *m*.

tug-of-love *n* Br inf conflit entre des parents pour obtenir la garde des enfants.

tug-of-war *n* lutte *f* de traction à la corde ; fig lutte acharnée.

tuition [tjuː'ɪʃn] *n* (U) cours *mpl*.

tulip ['tjuːlɪp] *n* tulipe *f*.

tulle [tjuːl] *n* tulle *m*.

tumble ['tʌmbl] ◇ *vi* - **1.** [person] tomber, faire une chute ; [water] tomber en cascades - **2.** fig [prices] tomber, chuter ◇ *n* chute *f*, culbute *f*.

➤ **tumble to** *vt fus* Br inf piger.

tumbledown ['tʌmbldaʊn] *adj* délabré(e), qui tombe en ruines.

tumble-dry *vt* faire sécher en machine.

tumble-dryer [-ˌdraɪəʳ] *n* sèche-linge *m inv*.

tumbler ['tʌmbləʳ] *n* [glass] verre *m* (droit).

tummy ['tʌmɪ] (*pl* -**ies**) *n* inf ventre *m*.

tumour Br, **tumor** Am ['tjuːməʳ] *n* tumeur *f*.

tumult ['tjuːmʌlt] *n* tumulte *m*.

tumultuous ['tjuːmʌltjʊəs] *adj* tumultueux(euse) ; [applause] frénétique.

tuna [Br 'tjuːnə, Am 'tuːnə] (*pl inv* OR -**s**) *n* thon *m*.

tundra ['tʌndrə] *n* toundra *f*.

tune [tjuːn] ◇ *n* - **1.** [song, melody] air *m*

- 2. [harmony] : **in ~** [instrument] accordé(e), juste ; [play, sing] juste ; **out of ~** [instrument] mal accordé(e) ; [play, sing] faux ; **to the ~ of** fig d'un montant de ; **to be in/out of ~ (with)** fig être en accord/désaccord (avec) ; **to change one's ~** inf changer de ton ◇ *vt* **- 1.** MUS accorder **- 2.** RADIO & TV régler **- 3.** [engine] régler ◇ *vi* RADIO & TV : **to ~ to a channel** se mettre sur une chaîne.

◆ **tune in** *vi* RADIO & TV être à l'écoute ; **to ~ in to** se mettre sur.

◆ **tune up** *vi* MUS accorder son instrument.

tuneful ['tjuːnfʊl] *adj* mélodieux(euse).

tuneless ['tjuːnlɪs] *adj* discordant(e).

tuner ['tjuːnəʳ] *n* **- 1.** RADIO & TV syntoniseur *m*, tuner *m* **- 2.** MUS [person] accordeur *m*.

tuner amplifier *n* ampli-tuner *m*.

tungsten ['tʌŋstən] ◇ *n* tungstène *m* ◇ *comp* au tungstène.

tunic ['tjuːnɪk] *n* tunique *f*.

tuning fork ['tjuːnɪŋ-] *n* diapason *m*.

Tunis ['tjuːnɪs] *n* Tunis.

Tunisia [tjuːˈnɪzɪə] *n* Tunisie *f* ; **in ~** en Tunisie.

Tunisian [tjuːˈnɪzɪən] ◇ *adj* tunisien(enne) ◇ *n* [person] Tunisien *m*, -enne *f*.

tunnel ['tʌnl] (Br *pt & pp* **-led** ; *cont* **-ling**, Am *pt & pp* **-ed** ; *cont* **-ing**) ◇ *n* tunnel *m* ◇ *vi* faire OR creuser un tunnel.

tunnel vision *n* rétrécissement *m* du champ visuel ; fig & pej vues *fpl* étroites.

tunny ['tʌnɪ] (*pl inv* OR **-ies**) *n* thon *m*.

tuppence ['tʌpəns] *n* Br dated deux pence *mpl*.

turban ['tɜːbən] *n* turban *m*.

turbid ['tɜːbɪd] *adj* trouble.

turbine ['tɜːbaɪn] *n* turbine *f*.

turbo ['tɜːbəʊ] (*pl* **-s**) *n* turbo *m*.

turbocharged ['tɜːbəʊtʃɑːdʒd] *adj* turbo (inv).

turbojet [ˌtɜːbəʊˈdʒet] *n* [engine] turboréacteur *m* ; [plane] avion *m* à turboréacteur.

turboprop [ˌtɜːbəʊˈprɒp] *n* [engine] turbopropulseur *m* ; [plane] avion *m* à turbopropulseur.

turbot ['tɜːbət] (*pl inv* OR **-s**) *n* turbot *m*.

turbulence ['tɜːbjʊləns] *n (U)* **- 1.** [in air, water] turbulence *f* **- 2.** fig [unrest] agitation *f*.

turbulent ['tɜːbjʊlənt] *adj* **- 1.** [air, water] agité(e) **- 2.** fig [disorderly] tumultueux(euse), agité(e).

tureen [təˈriːn] *n* soupière *f*.

turf [tɜːf] (*pl* **-s** OR **turves** [tɜːvz]) ◇ *n* [grass surface] gazon *m* ; [clod] motte *f* de gazon ◇ *vt* gazonner.

◆ **turf out** *vt sep* Br inf [person] virer ; [old clothes] balancer, bazarder.

turf accountant *n* Br bookmaker *m*.

turgid ['tɜːdʒɪd] *adj* fml [style, writing] pompeux(euse), ampoulé(e).

Turk [tɜːk] *n* Turc *m*, Turque *f*.

Turkestan, Turkistan [ˌtɜːkɪˈstɑːn] *n* Turkistan *m* ; **in ~** au Turkistan.

turkey ['tɜːkɪ] (*pl* **-s**) *n* dinde *f*.

Turkey ['tɜːkɪ] *n* Turquie *f* ; **in ~** en Turquie.

Turkish ['tɜːkɪʃ] ◇ *adj* turc (turque) ◇ *n* [language] turc *m* ◇ *npl* : **the ~** les Turcs *mpl*.

Turkish bath *n* bain *m* turc.

Turkish delight *n* loukoum *m*.

Turkmenian [ˌtɜːkˈmeniən] *adj* turkmène.

Turkmenistan [ˌtɜːkmenɪˈstɑːn] *n* Turkménistan *m*.

turmeric ['tɜːmərɪk] *n* curcuma *m*.

turmoil ['tɜːmɔɪl] *n* agitation *f*, trouble *m*.

turn [tɜːn] ◇ *n* **- 1.** [in road] virage *m*, tournant *m* ; [in river] méandre *m* **- 2.** [revolution, twist] tour *m* **- 3.** [change] tournure *f*, tour *m* **- 4.** [in game] tour *m* ; **it's my ~** c'est (à) mon tour ; **in ~** tour à tour, chacun (à) son tour ; **to take (it in) ~s to do sthg** faire qqch à tour de rôle **- 5.** [end - of year, century] fin *f* **- 6.** [performance] numéro *m* **- 7.** MED crise *f*, attaque *f* **- 8.** phr : **to do sb a good ~** rendre (un) service à qqn ◇ *vt* **- 1.** [gen] tourner ; [omelette, steak etc] retourner ; **to ~ sthg inside out** retourner qqch ; **to ~ one's thoughts/attention to sthg** tourner ses pensées/son attention vers qqch **- 2.** [change] : **to ~ sthg into** changer qqch en **- 3.** [become] : **to ~ red** rougir ; **his hair is ~ing grey** ses cheveux grisonnent ; **the demonstration ~ed nasty** la manifestation a mal tourné ◇ *vi* **- 1.** [gen] tourner ; [person] se tourner, se retourner **- 2.** [in book] : **to ~ to a page** se reporter OR aller à une page **- 3.** [for consolation] : **to ~ to sb/sthg** se tourner vers qqn/qqch **- 4.** [change] : **to ~ into** se changer en, se transformer en.

◆ **turn against** *vt fus* se retourner contre.

◆ **turn around** = turn round.

◆ **turn away** ◇ *vt sep* [refuse entry to] refuser ◇ *vi* se détourner.

◆ **turn back** ◇ *vt sep* [sheets] replier ; [person, vehicle] refouler ◇ *vi* rebrousser chemin.

◆ **turn down** *vt sep* **- 1.** [reject] rejeter, refuser **- 2.** [radio, volume, gas] baisser.

◆ **turn in** *vi inf* [go to bed] se pieuter.

◆ **turn off** ◇ *vt fus* [road, path] quitter ◇ *vt sep* [radio, TV, engine, gas] éteindre ; [tap] fermer ◇ *vi* [leave path, road] tourner.

turn on ⬦ *vt sep* - **1.** [radio, TV, engine, gas] allumer ; [tap] ouvrir ; **to ~ the light on** allumer la lumière - **2.** *inf* [excite sexually] exciter ⬦ *vt fus* [attack] attaquer.

turn out ⬦ *vt sep* - **1.** [light, gas fire] éteindre - **2.** [produce] produire - **3.** [eject - person] mettre dehors - **4.** [empty - pocket, bag] retourner, vider ⬦ *vt fus* : **to ~ out to be** s'avérer ; **it ~ed out to be a success** en fin de compte, cela a été une réussite ; **it ~s out that ...** il s'avère OR se trouve que ... ⬦ *vi* - **1.** [end up] finir - **2.** [arrive - person] venir.

turn over ⬦ *vt sep* - **1.** [playing card, stone] retourner ; [page] tourner - **2.** [consider] retourner dans sa tête - **3.** [hand over] rendre, remettre ⬦ *vi* - **1.** [roll over] se retourner - **2.** Br TV changer de chaîne.

turn round ⬦ *vt sep* - **1.** [reverse] retourner - **2.** [wheel, words] tourner ⬦ *vi* [person] se retourner.

turn up ⬦ *vt sep* [TV, radio] mettre plus fort ; [gas] monter ⬦ *vi* - **1.** [arrive - person] se pointer - **2.** [be found - person, object] être retrouvé ; [- opportunity] se présenter.

turnabout ['tɜ:nəbaʊt] *n* [of situation] revirement *m* ; [of policy] changement *m*.

turnaround Am = turnround.

turncoat ['tɜ:nkəʊt] *n pej* renégat *m*.

turning ['tɜ:nɪŋ] *n* [off road] route *f* latérale ; **take the first ~ on the left** prenez la première à gauche.

turning circle *n* rayon *m* de braquage.

turning point *n* tournant *m*, moment *m* décisif.

turnip ['tɜ:nɪp] *n* navet *m*.

turnout ['tɜ:naʊt] *n* [at election] taux *m* de participation ; [at meeting] assistance *f*.

turnover ['tɜ:n,əʊvəʳ] *n* (U) - **1.** [of personnel] renouvellement *m* - **2.** FIN chiffre *m* d'affaires.

turnpike ['tɜ:npaɪk] *n* Am autoroute *f* à péage.

turnround Br ['tɜ:nraʊnd], **turnaround** Am ['tɜ:nəraʊnd] *n* - **1.** COMM : **~ (time)** délai *m* - **2.** [change] retournement *m*.

turn signal lever *n* Am (manette *f* de) clignotant *m*.

turnstile ['tɜ:nstaɪl] *n* tourniquet *m*.

turntable ['tɜ:n,teɪbl] *n* platine *f*.

turn-up *n* Br [on trousers] revers *m inv* ; **a ~ for the books** *inf* une sacrée surprise.

turpentine ['tɜ:pəntaɪn] *n* térébenthine *f*.

turps [tɜ:ps] *n* Br *inf* térébenthine *f*.

turquoise ['tɜ:kwɔɪz] ⬦ *adj* turquoise *(inv)* ⬦ *n* - **1.** [mineral, gem] turquoise *f* - **2.** [colour] turquoise *m*.

turret ['tʌrɪt] *n* tourelle *f*.

turtle ['tɜ:tl] *(pl inv* OR **-s)** *n* tortue *f* de mer.

turtledove ['tɜ:tldʌv] *n* tourterelle *f*.

turtleneck ['tɜ:tlnek] *n* [garment] pull *m* à col montant ; [neck] col *m* montant.

turves [tɜ:vz] Br *pl* ⮊ **turf.**

tusk [tʌsk] *n* défense *f*.

tussle ['tʌsl] ⬦ *n* lutte *f* ⬦ *vi* se battre ; **to ~ over sthg** se disputer qqch.

tut [tʌt] *excl* mais non!, allons donc!

tutor ['tju:təʳ] ⬦ *n* - **1.** [private] professeur *m* particulier - **2.** UNIV directeur *m*, -trice *f* d'études ⬦ *vt* : **to ~ sb (in sthg)** donner à qqn des cours particuliers (de qqch).

tutorial [tju:'tɔ:rɪəl] ⬦ *adj* [group, class] de travaux dirigés ⬦ *n* travaux *mpl* dirigés.

tutu ['tu:tu:] *n* tutu *m*.

tux [tʌks] *n inf* smoking *m*.

tuxedo [tʌk'si:dəʊ] *(pl* **-s)** *n* smoking *m*.

TV *(abbr of* **television)** ⬦ *n* - **1.** (U) [medium, industry] télé *f* ; **on ~** à la télé - **2.** [apparatus] (poste *m* de) télé *f* ⬦ *comp* de télé.

TV dinner *n* repas *m* surgelé *(sur un plateau)*.

TV movie *n* téléfilm *m*.

twaddle ['twɒdl] *n* (U) *inf* bêtises *fpl*, fadaises *fpl*.

twang [twæŋ] ⬦ *n* - **1.** [sound] bruit *m* de pincement - **2.** [accent] nasillement *m* ⬦ *vt* [guitar] pincer ⬦ *vi* [wire, string] vibrer.

tweak [twi:k] *vt inf* [ear] tirer ; [nose] tordre.

twee [twi:] *adj* Br *pej* mièvre.

tweed [twi:d] ⬦ *n* tweed *m* ⬦ *comp* de OR en tweed.

tweet [twi:t] *vi* gazouiller.

tweezers ['twi:zəz] *npl* pince *f* à épiler.

twelfth [twelfθ] *num* douzième ; *see also* **sixth.**

Twelfth Night *n* la fête des Rois.

twelve [twelv] *num* douze ; *see also* **six.**

twentieth ['twentɪəθ] *num* vingtième ; *see also* **sixth.**

twenty ['twentɪ] *(pl* **-ies)** *num* vingt ; *see also* **six.**

twenty-twenty vision *n* vision *f* de dix dixièmes à chaque œil.

twerp [twɜ:p] *n inf* crétin *m*, -e *f*, andouille *f*.

twice [twaɪs] *adv* deux fois ; **~ a day** deux fois par jour ; **he earns ~ as much as me** il gagne deux fois plus que moi ; **~ as big** deux fois plus grand ; **~ my size/age** le double de ma taille/mon âge.

twiddle ['twɪdl] ⬦ vt jouer avec ⬦ vi : **to ~ with** sthg jouer avec qqch.

twig [twɪg] n brindille f, petite branche f.

twilight ['twaɪlaɪt] n crépuscule m.

twill [twɪl] n sergé m.

twin [twɪn] ⬦ adj jumeau (jumelle) ; [town] jumelé(e) ; **~ beds** lits mpl jumeaux ⬦ n jumeau m, jumelle f.

twin-bedded [-'bedɪd] adj à deux lits.

twin carburettor n carburateur m double-corps.

twine [twaɪn] ⬦ n (U) ficelle f ⬦ vt : **to ~** sthg **round** sthg enrouler qqch autour de qqch.

twin-engined [-'endʒɪnd] adj bimoteur.

twinge [twɪndʒ] n [of pain] élancement m ; **a ~ of guilt** un remords.

twinkie ['twɪŋkɪ] n Am [cake] petit gâteau fourré à la crème.

twinkle ['twɪŋkl] ⬦ n [of stars, lights] scintillement m ; [in eyes] pétillement m ⬦ vi [star, lights] scintiller ; [eyes] briller, pétiller.

twin room n chambre f à deux lits.

twin set n Br twin-set m.

twin town n ville f jumelée.

twin tub n machine f à double tambour.

twirl [twɜ:l] ⬦ vt faire tourner ⬦ vi tournoyer.

twist [twɪst] ⬦ n - **1.** [in road] zigzag m, tournant m ; [in river] méandre m, coude m ; [in rope] entortillement m - **2.** [turn] : **to give the lid a ~** [to open] dévisser le couvercle ; [to close] visser le couvercle - **3.** fig [in plot] tour m ⬦ vt - **1.** [wind, curl] entortiller - **2.** [contort] tordre - **3.** [turn] tourner ; [lid - to open] dévisser ; [- to close] visser - **4.** [sprain] : **to ~ one's ankle** se tordre OR se fouler la cheville - **5.** [words, meaning] déformer ⬦ vi - **1.** [river, path] zigzaguer - **2.** [be contorted] se tordre - **3.** [turn] : **to ~ round** se retourner.

twisted ['twɪstɪd] adj pej tordu(e).

twister ['twɪstər] n Am tornade f.

twisty ['twɪstɪ] (compar **-ier** ; superl **-iest**) adj inf sinueux(euse), en zigzag.

twit [twɪt] n Br inf crétin m, -e f.

twitch [twɪtʃ] ⬦ n tic m ⬦ vt [rope] tirer d'un coup sec ; [ears - subj : animal] remuer ⬦ vi [muscle, eye, face] se contracter.

twitter ['twɪtər] vi - **1.** [bird] gazouiller - **2.** pej [person] jacasser.

two [tu:] num deux ; **in ~** en deux ; see also **six**.

two-bit adj pej de pacotille.

two-dimensional adj à deux dimensions ; pej superficiel(elle), simpliste.

two-door adj [car] à deux portes.

twofaced [,tu:'feɪst] adj pej fourbe.

twofold ['tu:fəʊld] ⬦ adj double ⬦ adv doublement ; **to increase ~** doubler.

two-handed [-'hændɪd] adj à deux poignées.

two-piece adj : **~ swimsuit** deux-pièces m inv ; **~ suit** [for man] costume m (deux-pièces).

two-ply adj [yarn] à deux fils ; [wood] à deux épaisseurs.

two-seater n [car] voiture f à deux places ; [plane] biplace m.

twosome ['tu:səm] n inf couple m.

two-stroke ⬦ adj à deux temps ⬦ n deux-temps m inv.

two-time vt inf tromper.

two-tone adj de deux tons.

two-way adj [traffic, trade] dans les deux sens ; **~ radio** poste m émetteur-récepteur.

TX abbr of **Texas.**

tycoon [taɪ'ku:n] n magnat m.

type [taɪp] ⬦ n - **1.** [sort, kind] genre m, sorte f ; [model] modèle m ; [in classification] type m - **2.** [person] : **he's not the marrying ~** il n'est pas du genre à se marier ; **he's/she's not my ~** inf lui/elle, ce n'est pas mon genre OR type - **3.** (U) TYPO caractères mpl ⬦ vt [letter, reply] taper (à la machine) ; **to ~ data into a computer** introduire des données dans un ordinateur ⬦ vi taper (à la machine).

➭ **type up** vt sep taper.

typecast ['taɪpkɑ:st] (pt & pp **typecast**) vt : **to be ~ as** être cantonné dans le rôle de ; **to be ~** être cantonné aux mêmes rôles.

typeface ['taɪpfeɪs] n TYPO œil m de caractère.

typescript ['taɪpskrɪpt] n texte m dactylographié.

typeset ['taɪpset] (pt & pp **typeset**, cont **-ting**) vt composer.

typewriter ['taɪp,raɪtər] n machine f à écrire.

typhoid (fever) ['taɪfɔɪd-] n typhoïde f.

typhoon [taɪ'fu:n] n typhon m.

typhus ['taɪfəs] n typhus m.

typical ['tɪpɪkl] adj : **~ (of)** typique (de), caractéristique (de) ; **that's ~ (of him/her)!** c'est bien de lui/d'elle !

typically ['tɪpɪklɪ] adv typiquement.

typify ['tɪpɪfaɪ] (pt & pp **-ied**) vt - **1.** [characterize] être caractéristique de - **2.** [represent] représenter.

typing ['taɪpɪŋ] n dactylo f, dactylographie f.

typing error *n* faute *f* de frappe.

typing pool *n* bureau *m* OR pool *m* des dactylos.

typist ['taɪpɪst] *n* dactylo *mf*, dactylographe *mf*.

typo ['taɪpəʊ] *n* inf coquille *f*.

typographic(al) error [ˌtaɪpə'græfɪk(l)-] *n* faute *f* typographique.

typography [taɪ'pɒgrəfɪ] *n* typographie *f*.

tyrannical [tɪ'rænɪkl] *adj* tyrannique.

tyranny ['tɪrənɪ] *n* tyrannie *f*.

tyrant ['taɪrənt] *n* tyran *m*.

tyre Br, **tire** Am ['taɪəʳ] *n* pneu *m*.

tyre pressure *n* pression *f* (de gonflage).

Tyrol, Tirol ['tɪrɒl] *n* Tyrol *m*.

Tyrolean [tɪrə'liːən], **Tyrolese** [ˌtɪrə'liːz] ◇ *adj* tyrolien(enne) ◇ *n* Tyrolien *m*, -enne *f*.

Tyrrhenian Sea [tɪ'riːnɪən-] *n* : **the ~** la mer Tyrrhénienne.

tzar [zɑːʳ] = tsar.

u (*pl* **u's** OR **us**), **U** (*pl* **U's** OR **Us**) [juː] *n* [letter] u *m inv*, U *m inv*.

➤ **U** (*abbr of* **universal**) *en Grande-Bretagne, désigne un film tous publics*.

UAW (*abbr of* **United Automobile Workers**) *n* syndicat américain de l'industrie automobile.

UB40 (*abbr of* **unemployment benefit form 40**) *n* en Grande-Bretagne, carte de pointage pour bénéficier de l'allocation de chômage.

U-bend *n* siphon *m*.

ubiquitous [juː'bɪkwɪtəs] *adj* omniprésent(e).

UCAS ['juːkas] (*abbr of* **Universities and Colleges Admissions Service**) *n* organisme gérant les inscriptions dans les universités au Royaume-Uni.

UCATT [juːkæt] (*abbr of* **Union of Construc-**

tion, Allied Trades and Technicians) *n* syndicat britannique des employés du bâtiment.

UCCA ['ʌkə] (*abbr of* **Universities Central Council on Admissions**) *n* ancien organisme centralisant les demandes d'inscription dans les universités britanniques, maintenant remplacé par l'UCAS.

UCL (*abbr of* **University College, London**) *n* université londonienne.

UCW (*abbr of* **The Union of Communication Workers**) *n* syndicat britannique des communications.

UDA (*abbr of* **Ulster Defence Association**) *n* ancienne organisation paramilitaire protestante en Irlande du Nord.

UDC (*abbr of* **Urban District Council**) *n* conseil d'une communauté urbaine.

udder ['ʌdəʳ] *n* mamelle *f*.

UDI (*abbr of* **unilateral declaration of independence**) *n* déclaration unilatérale d'indépendance.

UDR (*abbr of* **Ulster Defence Regiment**) *n* régiment de réservistes en Irlande du Nord.

UEFA [juː'eɪfə] (*abbr of* **Union of European Football Associations**) *n* UEFA *f*.

UFC (*abbr of* **Universities Funding Council**) *n* organisme répartissant les crédits entre les universités en Grande-Bretagne.

UFO (*abbr of* **unidentified flying object**) *n* OVNI *m*, ovni *m*.

Uganda [juː'gændə] *n* Ouganda *m* ; **in ~** en Ouganda.

Ugandan [juː'gændən] ◇ *adj* ougandais(e) ◇ *n* [person] Ougandais *m*, -e *f*.

ugh [ʌg] *excl* pouah!, beurk!

ugliness ['ʌglɪnɪs] (*U*) *n* - **1.** [unattractiveness] laideur *f* - **2.** fig [unpleasantness] caractère *m* pénible OR désagréable.

ugly ['ʌglɪ] (*compar* **-ier** ; *superl* **-iest**) *adj* - **1.** [unattractive] laid(e) - **2.** fig [unpleasant] pénible, désagréable.

UHF (*abbr of* **ultra-high frequency**) *n* UHF.

UHT (*abbr of* **ultra-heat treated**) UHT.

UK (*abbr of* **United Kingdom**) *n* Royaume-Uni *m*, R.U. *m*.

Ukraine [juː'kreɪn] *n* : **the ~** l'Ukraine *f* ; **in the ~** en Ukraine.

Ukrainian [juː'kreɪnjən] ◇ *adj* ukrainien(enne) ◇ *n* - **1.** [person] Ukrainien *m*, -enne *f* - **2.** [language] ukrainien *m*.

ukulele [ˌjuːkə'leɪlɪ] *n* guitare *f* hawaïenne, ukulélé *m*.

Ulan Bator [uˈlɑːnˈbɑːtəl] *n* Oulan-Bator.

ulcer ['ʌlsəʳ] *n* ulcère *m*.

ulcerated ['ʌlsəreɪtɪd] *adj* ulcéré(e).

Ulster [ˈʌlstəʳ] n Ulster m ; in ~ dans l'Ulster.

Ulsterman [ˈʌlstəmən] (pl -men [-mən]) n habitant m OR natif m de l'Ulster.

Ulster Unionist Party n parti politique essentiellement protestant favorable au maintien de l'Ulster au sein du Royaume-Uni.

ulterior [ʌlˈtɪərɪəʳ] adj : ~ motive arrière-pensée f.

ultimata [ˌʌltɪˈmeɪtə] pl ⊏ ultimatum.

ultimate [ˈʌltɪmət] ◇ adj - **1.** [final] final(e), ultime - **2.** [most powerful] ultime, suprême ◇ n : the ~ in le fin du fin dans.

ultimately [ˈʌltɪmətlɪ] adv [finally] finalement.

ultimatum [ˌʌltɪˈmeɪtəm] (pl -tums OR -ta [-tə]) n ultimatum m.

ultra- [ˈʌltrə] prefix ultra-.

ultramarine [ˌʌltrəməˈriːn] adj (bleu) outremer (inv).

ultrasonic [ˌʌltrəˈsɒnɪk] adj ultrasonique.

ultrasound [ˈʌltrəsaʊnd] n (U) ultrasons mpl.

ultraviolet [ˌʌltrəˈvaɪələt] adj ultraviolet(ette).

um [ʌm] excl heu!

umbilical cord [ʌmˈbɪlɪkl-] n cordon m ombilical.

umbrage [ˈʌmbrɪdʒ] n : to take ~ (at) prendre ombrage (de).

umbrella [ʌmˈbrelə] ◇ n [portable] parapluie m ; [fixed] parasol m ◇ adj [organization] qui en regroupe plusieurs autres.

UMIST [ˈjuːmɪst] (abbr of University of Manchester Institute of Science and Technology) n institut de science et de technologie de l'université de Manchester.

umpire [ˈʌmpaɪəʳ] ◇ n arbitre m ◇ vt arbitrer ◇ vi être l'arbitre.

umpteen [ˌʌmpˈtiːn] num adj inf je ne sais combien de.

umpteenth [ˌʌmpˈtiːnθ] num adj inf énième.

UMW (abbr of United Mineworkers of America) n syndicat américain de mineurs.

UN (abbr of United Nations) n : the ~ l'ONU f, l'Onu f.

unabashed [ˌʌnəˈbæʃt] adj nullement décontenancé(e).

unabated [ˌʌnəˈbeɪtɪd] adj : the rain continued ~ la pluie continua de tomber sans répit.

unable [ʌnˈeɪbl] adj : to be ~ to do sthg ne pas pouvoir faire qqch, être incapable de faire qqch.

unabridged [ˌʌnəˈbrɪdʒd] adj intégral(e).

unacceptable [ˌʌnəkˈseptəbl] adj inacceptable.

unaccompanied [ˌʌnəˈkʌmpənɪd] adj - **1.** [child] non accompagné(e) ; [luggage] sans surveillance - **2.** [song] a cappella, sans accompagnement.

unaccountable [ˌʌnəˈkaʊntəbl] adj - **1.** [inexplicable] inexplicable - **2.** [not responsible] : to be ~ for sthg ne pas être responsable de qqch ; to be ~ to sb ne pas être responsable envers OR devant qqn.

unaccountably [ˌʌnəˈkaʊntəblɪ] adv [inexplicably] de façon inexplicable, inexplicablement.

unaccounted [ˌʌnəˈkaʊntɪd] adj : to be ~ for manquer.

unaccustomed [ˌʌnəˈkʌstəmd] adj - **1.** [unused] : to be ~ to sthg/to doing sthg ne pas être habitué(e) à qqch/à faire qqch - **2.** [not usual] inaccoutumé(e), inhabituel(elle).

unacquainted [ˌʌnəˈkweɪntɪd] adj : to be ~ with sb/sthg ne pas connaître qqn/qqch.

unadulterated [ˌʌnəˈdʌltəreɪtɪd] adj - **1.** [unspoilt - wine] non frelaté(e) ; [- food] naturel(elle) - **2.** [absolute - joy] sans mélange ; [- nonsense, truth] pur et simple (pure et simple).

unadventurous [ˌʌnədˈventʃərəs] adj qui manque d'audace.

unaffected [ˌʌnəˈfektɪd] adj - **1.** [unchanged] : ~ (by) non affecté(e) (par) - **2.** [natural] naturel(elle).

unafraid [ˌʌnəˈfreɪd] adj sans crainte, sans peur.

unaided [ˌʌnˈeɪdɪd] adj sans aide.

unambiguous [ˌʌnæmˈbɪgjʊəs] adj non équivoque.

un-American [ˈʌn-] adj anti-américain(e).

unanimity [ˌjuːnəˈnɪmətɪ] n unanimité f.

unanimous [juːˈnænɪməs] adj unanime.

unanimously [juːˈnænɪməslɪ] adv à l'unanimité.

unannounced [ˌʌnəˈnaʊnst] adj sans tambour ni trompette.

unanswered [ˌʌnˈɑːnsəd] adj qui reste sans réponse.

unappealing [ˌʌnəˈpiːlɪŋ] adj peu attirant(e).

unappetizing, -ising [ˌʌnˈæpɪtaɪzɪŋ] adj peu appétissant(e).

unappreciated [ˌʌnəˈpriːʃɪeɪtɪd] adj peu apprécié(e).

unappreciative [ˌʌnəˈpriːʃɪətɪv] adj : ~ (of) indifférent(e) (à).

unapproachable [ˌʌnəˈprəʊtʃəbl] adj inabordable, d'un abord difficile.

unarmed [ˌʌnˈɑːmd] *adj* non armé(e).

unarmed combat *n* combat *m* sans armes.

unashamed [ˌʌnəˈʃeɪmd] *adj* [luxury] insolent(e) ; [liar, lie] effronté(e), éhonté(e).

unassisted [ˌʌnəˈsɪstɪd] *adj* sans aide.

unassuming [ˌʌnəˈsjuːmɪŋ] *adj* modeste, effacé(e).

unattached [ˌʌnəˈtætʃt] *adj* - **1.** [not fastened, linked] : ~ **(to)** indépendant(e) (de) - **2.** [without partner] libre, sans attaches.

unattainable [ˌʌnəˈteɪnəbl] *adj* inaccessible.

unattended [ˌʌnəˈtendɪd] *adj* [luggage, shop] sans surveillance ; [child] seul(e).

unattractive [ˌʌnəˈtræktɪv] *adj* - **1.** [not beautiful] peu attrayant(e), peu séduisant(e) - **2.** [not pleasant] déplaisant(e).

unauthorized, -ised [ˌʌnˈɔːθəraɪzd] *adj* non autorisé(e).

unavailable [ˌʌnəˈveɪləbl] *adj* qui n'est pas disponible, indisponible.

unavoidable [ˌʌnəˈvɔɪdəbl] *adj* inévitable.

unavoidably [ˌʌnəˈvɔɪdəblɪ] *adj* inévitablement ; **to be ~ detained** être retardé pour des raisons indépendantes de sa volonté.

unaware [ˌʌnəˈweəʳ] *adj* ignorant(e), inconscient(e) ; **to be ~ of sthg** ne pas avoir conscience de qqch, ignorer qqch.

unawares [ˌʌnəˈweəz] *adv* : **to catch** OR **take sb ~** prendre qqn au dépourvu.

unbalanced [ˌʌnˈbælənst] *adj* - **1.** [biased] tendancieux(euse), partial(e) - **2.** [deranged] déséquilibré(e).

unbearable [ʌnˈbeərəbl] *adj* insupportable.

unbearably [ʌnˈbeərəblɪ] *adv* insupportablement ; **it's ~ hot** il fait une chaleur insupportable.

unbeatable [ʌnˈbiːtəbl] *adj* imbattable.

unbecoming [ˌʌnbɪˈkʌmɪŋ] *adj* [unattractive] peu seyant(e).

unbeknown(st) [ˌʌnbɪˈnəʊn(st)] *adv* : **~ to** à l'insu de.

unbelievable [ˌʌnbɪˈliːvəbl] *adj* incroyable.

unbelievably [ˌʌnbɪˈliːvəblɪ] *adv* incroyablement ; **to be ~ stupid** être d'une bêtise incroyable.

unbend [ˌʌnˈbend] (*pt* & *pp* **unbent**) *vi* [relax] se détendre.

unbending [ˌʌnˈbendɪŋ] *adj* inflexible, intransigeant(e).

unbent [ˌʌnˈbent] *pt* & *pp* ▷ **unbend**.

unbia(s)sed [ˌʌnˈbaɪəst] *adj* impartial(e).

unblemished [ˌʌnˈblemɪʃt] *adj* fig sans tache.

unblock [ˌʌnˈblɒk] *vt* déboucher.

unbolt [ˌʌnˈbəʊlt] *vt* déverrouiller.

unborn [ˌʌnˈbɔːn] *adj* [child] qui n'est pas encore né(e).

unbreakable [ˌʌnˈbreɪkəbl] *adj* incassable.

unbridled [ˌʌnˈbraɪdld] *adj* effréné(e), débridé(e).

unbuckle [ˌʌnˈbʌkl] *vt* déboucler.

unbutton [ˌʌnˈbʌtn] *vt* déboutonner.

uncalled-for [ˌʌnˈkɔːld-] *adj* [remark] déplacé(e) ; [criticism] injustifié(e).

uncanny [ʌnˈkænɪ] (*compar* **-ier** ; *superl* **-iest**) *adj* étrange, mystérieux(euse) ; [resemblance] troublant(e).

uncared-for [ˌʌnˈkeəd-] *adj* délaissé(e), négligé(e).

uncaring [ˌʌnˈkeərɪŋ] *adj* qui ne se soucie pas des autres.

unceasing [ˌʌnˈsiːsɪŋ] *adj* fml incessant(e), continuel(elle).

unceremonious [ˈʌnˌserɪˈməʊnjəs] *adj* brusque.

unceremoniously [ˈʌnˌserɪˈməʊnjəslɪ] *adj* brusquement.

uncertain [ʌnˈsɜːtn] *adj* incertain(e) ; **in no ~ terms** sans mâcher ses mots.

unchain [ˌʌnˈtʃeɪn] *vt* désenchaîner.

unchallenged [ˌʌnˈtʃælɪndʒd] *adj* incontesté(e), indiscuté(e).

unchanged [ˌʌnˈtʃeɪndʒd] *adj* inchangé(e).

unchanging [ˌʌnˈtʃeɪndʒɪŋ] *adj* invariable, immuable.

uncharacteristic [ˈʌnˌkærəktəˈrɪstɪk] *adj* inhabituel(elle).

uncharitable [ˌʌnˈtʃærɪtəbl] *adj* peu charitable.

uncharted [ˌʌnˈtʃɑːtɪd] *adj* [land, sea] qui n'est pas sur la carte ; **~ territory** fig domaine inexploré.

unchecked [ˌʌnˈtʃekt] *adj* non maîtrisé(e), sans frein.

uncivilized, -ised [ˌʌnˈsɪvɪlaɪzd] *adj* non civilisé(e), barbare.

unclassified [ˌʌnˈklæsɪfaɪd] *adj* [documents] non classé(e) ; [information] non secret(ète).

uncle [ˈʌŋkl] *n* oncle *m*.

unclean [ˌʌnˈkliːn] *adj* - **1.** [dirty] sale - **2.** RELIG impur(e).

unclear [ˌʌnˈklɪəʳ] *adj* - **1.** [message, meaning, motive] qui n'est pas clair(e) - **2.** [uncertain - person, future] incertain(e).

Uncle Sam l'Oncle Sam (*personnage repré-*

sentant les États-Unis dans la propagande pour l'armée).

unclothed [ˌʌn'kləʊðd] *adj* nu(e), sans vêtements.

uncomfortable [ˌʌn'kʌmftəbl] *adj* - **1.** [shoes, chair, clothes etc] inconfortable ; *fig* [fact, truth] désagréable - **2.** [person - physically] qui n'est pas à l'aise ; [- ill at ease] mal à l'aise.

uncomfortably [ˌʌn'kʌmftəblɪ] *adv* - **1.** [in physical discomfort] inconfortablement - **2.** *fig* [uneasily] avec gêne.

uncommitted [ˌʌnkə'mɪtɪd] *adj* non engagé(e).

uncommon [ʌn'kɒmən] *adj* - **1.** [rare] rare - **2.** *fml* [extreme] extraordinaire.

uncommonly [ʌn'kɒmənlɪ] *adv fml* extraordinairement.

uncommunicative [ˌʌnkə'mjuːnɪkətɪv] *adj* peu expansif(ive), peu communicatif(ive).

uncomplicated [ˌʌn'kɒmplɪkeɪtɪd] *adj* simple, peu compliqué(e).

uncomprehending ['ʌnˌkɒmprɪ'hendɪŋ] *adj* qui ne comprend pas.

uncompromising [ˌʌn'kɒmprəmaɪzɪŋ] *adj* intransigeant(e).

unconcerned [ˌʌnkən'sɜːnd] *adj* [not anxious] qui ne s'inquiète pas.

unconditional [ˌʌnkən'dɪʃənl] *adj* inconditionnel(elle).

uncongenial [ˌʌnkən'dʒiːnjəl] *adj fml* peu agréable.

unconnected [ˌʌnkə'nektɪd] *adj* [facts, events] sans rapport.

unconquered [ˌʌn'kɒŋkəd] *adj* qui n'a pas été conquis(e).

unconscious [ʌn'kɒnʃəs] ◇ *adj* - **1.** [having lost consciousness] sans connaissance - **2.** *fig* [unaware] : **to be ~ of** ne pas avoir conscience de, ne pas se rendre compte de - **3.** [unnoticed - desires, feelings] inconscient(e) ◇ *n* PSYCH inconscient *m*.

unconsciously [ʌn'kɒnʃəslɪ] *adv* inconsciemment.

unconstitutional ['ʌnˌkɒnstɪ't juːʃənl] *adj* inconstitutionnel(elle), anticonstitutionnel(elle).

uncontested [ˌʌnkən'testɪd] *adj* incontesté(e) ; [election] sans opposition.

uncontrollable [ˌʌnkən'trəʊləbl] *adj* - **1.** [unrestrainable - emotion, urge] irrépressible, irrésistible ; [- increase, epidemic] qui ne peut être enrayé(e) - **2.** [unmanageable - person] impossible, difficile.

uncontrolled [ˌʌnkən'trəʊld] *adj* [emotion,

urge] non contenu(e) ; [increase] effréné(e) ; [inflation, epidemic] galopant(e).

unconventional [ˌʌnkən'venʃənl] *adj* peu conventionnel(elle), original(e).

unconvinced [ˌʌnkən'vɪnst] *adj* qui n'est pas convaincu(e), sceptique.

unconvincing [ˌʌnkən'vɪnsɪŋ] *adj* peu convaincant(e).

uncooked [ˌʌn'kʊkt] *adj* non cuit(e), cru(e).

uncooperative [ˌʌnkəʊ'ɒpərətɪv] *adj* peu coopératif(ive).

uncork [ˌʌn'kɔːk] *vt* déboucher.

uncorroborated [ˌʌnkə'rɒbəreɪtɪd] *adj* non corroboré(e).

uncouth [ʌn'kuːθ] *adj* grossier(ère).

uncover [ʌn'kʌvər] *vt* découvrir.

uncurl [ˌʌn'kɜːl] *vi* [hair] se défriser, se déboucler ; [wire, snake] se dérouler.

uncut [ˌʌn'kʌt] *adj* - **1.** [film] intégral(e), sans coupures - **2.** [jewel] brut(e), non taillé(e).

undamaged [ˌʌn'dæmɪdʒd] *adj* non endommagé(e), intact(e).

undaunted [ˌʌn'dɔːntɪd] *adj* non découragé(e).

undecided [ˌʌndɪ'saɪdɪd] *adj* [person] indécis(e), irrésolu(e) ; [issue] indécis(e).

undemanding [ˌʌndɪ'mɑːndɪŋ] *adj* [task] peu astreignant(e), peu exigeant(e) ; [person] peu exigeant(e).

undemonstrative [ˌʌndɪ'mɒnstrətɪv] *adj* peu expansif(ive), peu démonstratif(ive).

undeniable [ˌʌndɪ'naɪəbl] *adj* indéniable, incontestable.

under ['ʌndər] ◇ *prep* - **1.** [gen] sous - **2.** [less than] moins de ; **children ~ five** les enfants de moins de cinq ans - **3.** [subject to - effect, influence] sous ; **~ the circumstances** dans ces circonstances, étant donné les circonstances ; **to be ~ an obligation to sb** être redevable à qqn, avoir une dette de reconnaissance envers qqn ; **to be ~ the impression that ...** avoir l'impression que ... - **4.** [undergoing] : **~ discussion** en discussion ; **~ consideration** à l'étude, à l'examen ; **~ review** qui doit être révisé - **5.** [according to] selon, conformément à ◇ *adv* - **1.** [underneath] dessous ; [underwater] sous l'eau ; **to go ~** [company] couler, faire faillite - **2.** [less] au-dessous.

under- ['ʌndər] *prefix* sous-.

underachiever [ˌʌndərə'tʃiːvər] *n* personne dont les résultats ne correspondent pas à ses possibilités.

underage [ˌʌndər'eɪdʒ] *adj* mineur(e) ; **~ drinking** consommation *f* d'alcool par les mineurs ; ~ **sex** rapports *mpl* sexuels entre des mineurs.

underarm [ˈʌndərɑːm] ◇ *adj* [deodorant] pour les aisselles ◇ *adv* [throw, bowl] par en-dessous.

underbrush [ˈʌndəbrʌʃ] *n (U)* Am sous-bois *m inv.*

undercarriage [ˈʌndəˌkærɪdʒ] *n* train *m* d'atterrissage.

undercharge [ˌʌndəˈtʃɑːdʒ] *vt* faire payer insuffisamment à.

underclothes [ˈʌndəkləʊðz] *npl* sous-vêtements *mpl.*

undercoat [ˈʌndəkəʊt] *n* [of paint] couche *f* de fond.

undercook [ˌʌndəˈkʊk] *vt* ne pas assez cui-re.

undercover [ˈʌndəˌkʌvəʳ] ◇ *adj* secret(ète) ◇ *adv* clandestinement.

undercurrent [ˈʌndəˌkʌrənt] *n* fig [tendency] courant *m* sous-jacent.

undercut [ˌʌndəˈkʌt] (*pt* & *pp* **undercut**, *cont* -ting) *vt* [in price] vendre moins cher que.

underdeveloped [ˌʌndədɪˈveləpt] *adj* [coun-try] sous-développé(e) ; [person] qui n'est pas complètement développé(e) OR formé(e).

underdog [ˈʌndədɒg] *n* : **the ~** l'opprimé *m ;* SPORT celui (celle) que l'on donne per-dant(e).

underdone [ˌʌndəˈdʌn] *adj* [food] pas assez cuit(e) ; [steak] saignant(e).

underemployment [ˌʌndərɪmˈplɔɪmənt] *n* sous-emploi *m.*

underestimate [*n* ˌʌndərˈestɪmət , *vb* ˌʌndərˈestɪmeɪt] ◇ *n* sous-estimation *f* ◇ *vt* sous-estimer.

underexposed [ˌʌndərɪkˈspəʊzd] *adj* PHOT sous-exposé(e).

underfinanced [ˌʌndəˈfaɪnænst] *adj* insuffi-samment financé(e).

underfoot [ˌʌndəˈfʊt] *adv* sous les pieds ; **to trample sthg ~** fouler qqch aux pieds ; **the ground ~** le sol.

undergo [ˌʌndəˈgəʊ] (*pt* -went ; *pp* -gone [-ˈgɒn]) *vt* subir ; [pain, difficulties] éprouver.

undergraduate [ˌʌndəˈgrædjʊət] ◇ *adj* [course, studies] pour étudiants de licence ◇ *n* étudiant *m*, -e *f* qui prépare la licence.

underground [*adj* & *n* ˈʌndəgraʊnd, *adv* ˌʌndəˈgraʊnd] ◇ *adj* - **1.** [below the ground] sou-terrain(e) - **2.** fig [secret] clandestin(e) ◇ *adv* : **to go/be forced ~** entrer dans la clandestinité ◇ *n* - **1.** Br [subway] métro *m* - **2.** [activist movement] résistance *f.*

undergrowth [ˈʌndəgrəʊθ] *n (U)* sous-bois *m inv.*

underhand [ˌʌndəˈhænd] *adj* sournois(e), en dessous.

underinsured [ˌʌndərɪnˈʃʊəd] *adj* sous-assuré(e).

underlay [ˈʌndəleɪ] *n* [for carpet] thibaude *f.*

underline [ˌʌndəˈlaɪn] *vt* souligner.

underlying [ˌʌndəˈlaɪɪŋ] *adj* sous-jacent(e).

undermanned [ˌʌndəˈmænd] *adj* à court de personnel OR de main d'œuvre.

undermentioned [ˌʌndəˈmenʃnd] *adj* fml (cité(e)) ci-dessous.

undermine [ˌʌndəˈmaɪn] *vt* fig [weaken] saper, ébranler.

underneath [ˌʌndəˈniːθ] ◇ *prep* - **1.** [beneath] sous, au-dessous de - **2.** [in movements] sous ◇ *adv* - **1.** [beneath] en dessous, dessous - **2.** fig [fundamentally] au fond ◇ *adj* inf d'en dessous ◇ *n* [underside] : **the ~** le dessous.

undernourished [ˌʌndəˈnʌrɪʃt] *adj* sous-alimenté(e).

underpaid [*pt* & *pp* ˌʌndəˈpeɪd, *adj* ˈʌndəpeɪd] ◇ *pt* & *pp* ▷ **underpay** ◇ *adj* sous-payé(e).

underpants [ˈʌndəpænts] *npl* slip *m.*

underpass [ˈʌndəpɑːs] *n* [for cars] passage *m* inférieur ; [for pedestrians] passage *m* souter-rain.

underpay [ˌʌndəˈpeɪ] (*pt* & *pp* -paid) *vt* sous-payer.

underpin [ˌʌndəˈpɪn] (*pt* & *pp* -ned ; *cont* -ning) *vt* étayer.

underplay [ˌʌndəˈpleɪ] *vt* réduire l'impor-tance de, minimiser.

underprice [ˌʌndəˈpraɪs] *vt* mettre un prix trop bas à.

underprivileged [ˌʌndəˈprɪvɪlɪdʒd] *adj* dé-favorisé(e), déshérité(e).

underproduction [ˌʌndəprəˈdʌkʃn] *n* sous-production *f.*

underrated [ˌʌndəˈreɪtɪd] *adj* sous-estimé(e).

underscore [ˌʌndəˈskɔːʳ] *vt* lit & fig souli-gner.

undersea [ˈʌndəsiː] *adj* sous-marin(e).

undersecretary [ˌʌndəˈsekrətərɪ] (*pl* -ies) *n* sous-secrétaire *m.*

undersell [ˌʌndəˈsell] (*pt* & *pp* -sold) *vt* COMM vendre moins cher que ; **to ~ o.s.** fig ne pas se mettre assez en valeur.

undershirt [ˈʌndəʃɜːt] *n* Am maillot *m* de corps.

underside [ˈʌndəsaɪd] *n :* **the ~** le dessous.

undersigned [ˈʌndəsaɪnd] n fml : **I, the ~** je soussigné(e).

undersize(d) [ˌʌndəˈsaɪz(d)] adj trop petit(e).

underskirt [ˈʌndəskɜːt] n jupon m.

undersold [ˌʌndəˈsəʊld] pt & pp ➾ **undersell.**

understaffed [ˌʌndəˈstɑːft] adj à court de personnel.

understand [ˌʌndəˈstænd] (pt & pp **-stood**) ⟷ vt - **1.** [gen] comprendre ; **to make o.s. understood** se faire comprendre - **2.** fml [be informed] : **I ~ (that)** ... je crois comprendre que ..., il paraît que ... ⟷ vi comprendre.

understandable [ˌʌndəˈstændəbl] adj compréhensible.

understandably [ˌʌndəˈstændəblɪ] adv - **1.** [speak] de façon compréhensible - **2.** [naturally] naturellement.

understanding [ˌʌndəˈstændɪŋ] ⟷ n - **1.** [knowledge, sympathy] compréhension f ; **it was my ~ that** ... j'avais compris que ... - **2.** [agreement] accord m, arrangement m ; **to come to an ~ (over)** s'entendre (sur) ; **on the ~ that** ... à condition que ... (+ subjunctive) ⟷ adj [sympathetic] compréhensif(ive).

understate [ˌʌndəˈsteɪt] vt réduire l'importance de, minimiser.

understatement [ˌʌndəˈsteɪtmənt] n - **1.** [inadequate statement] affirmation f en dessous de la vérité - **2.** (U) [quality of understating] euphémisme m.

understood [ˌʌndəˈstʊd] pt & pp ➾ **understand.**

understudy [ˈʌndəˌstʌdɪ] (pl **-ies**) n doublure f.

undertake [ˌʌndəˈteɪk] (pt **-took** ; pp **-taken** [-ˈteɪkn]) vt - **1.** [take on - gen] entreprendre ; [- responsibility] assumer - **2.** [promise] : **to ~ to do sthg** promettre de faire qqch, s'engager à faire qqch.

undertaker [ˈʌndəˌteɪkə'] n entrepreneur m des pompes funèbres.

undertaking [ˌʌndəˈteɪkɪŋ] n - **1.** [task] entreprise f - **2.** [promise] promesse f.

undertone [ˈʌndətəʊn] n - **1.** [quiet voice] voix f basse - **2.** [vague feeling] courant m.

undertook [ˌʌndəˈtʊk] pt ➾ **undertake.**

undertow [ˈʌndətəʊ] n courant m sousmarin.

undervalue [ˌʌndəˈvæljuː] vt [house, antique etc] sous-évaluer ; [person] sous-estimer, mésestimer.

underwater [ˌʌndəˈwɔːtə'] ⟷ adj sousmarin(e) ⟷ adv sous l'eau.

underwear [ˈʌndəweə'] n (U) sousvêtements mpl.

underweight [ˌʌndəˈweɪt] adj qui ne pèse pas assez, qui est trop maigre.

underwent [ˌʌndəˈwent] pt ➾ **undergo.**

underworld [ˈʌndəˌwɜːld] n [criminal society] : **the ~** le milieu, la pègre.

underwrite [ˈʌndəraɪt] (pt **-wrote** ; pp **-written**) vt - **1.** FIN garantir - **2.** [in insurance] garantir, assurer contre.

underwriter [ˈʌndəˌraɪtə'] n assureur m.

underwritten [ˈʌndəˌrɪtn] pp ➾ **underwrite.**

underwrote [ˈʌndərəʊt] pt ➾ **underwrite.**

undeserved [ˌʌndɪˈzɜːvd] adj immérité(e).

undesirable [ˌʌndɪˈzaɪərəbl] adj indésirable.

undeveloped [ˌʌndɪˈveləpt] adj [land] non exploité(e), inexploité(e).

undid [ˌʌnˈdɪd] pt ➾ **undo.**

undies [ˈʌndɪz] npl inf dessous mpl, lingerie f.

undignified [ʌnˈdɪgnɪfaɪd] adj peu digne, qui manque de dignité.

undiluted [ˌʌndaɪˈljuːtɪd] adj - **1.** [quality, emotion] sans mélange - **2.** [liquid] non dilué(e).

undiplomatic [ˌʌndɪpləˈmætɪk] adj peu diplomate.

undischarged [ˌʌndɪsˈtʃɑːdʒd] adj [debt] non acquitté(e), non liquidé(e) ; **~ bankrupt** [person] failli m non réhabilité.

undisciplined [ʌnˈdɪsɪplɪnd] adj indiscipliné(e).

undiscovered [ˌʌndɪsˈkʌvəd] adj non découvert(e).

undisputed [ˌʌndɪsˈpjuːtɪd] adj incontesté(e).

undistinguished [ˌʌndɪsˈtɪŋgwɪʃt] adj médiocre, quelconque.

undivided [ˌʌndɪˈvaɪdɪd] adj indivisé(e), entier(ère).

undo [ˌʌnˈduː] (pt **-did** ; pp **-done**) vt - **1.** [unfasten] défaire - **2.** [nullify] annuler, détruire.

undoing [ˌʌnˈduːɪŋ] n (U) fml perte f, ruine f.

undone [ˌʌnˈdʌn] ⟷ pp ➾ **undo** ⟷ adj - **1.** [unfastened] défait(e) - **2.** [task] non accompli(e).

undoubted [ʌnˈdaʊtɪd] adj indubitable, certain(e).

undoubtedly [ʌnˈdaʊtɪdlɪ] adv sans aucun doute.

undreamed-of [ʌnˈdriːmdɒv], **undreamt-of** [ʌnˈdremtɒv] adj inimaginable.

undress [ˌʌnˈdres] ⟷ vt déshabiller ⟷ vi se déshabiller.

undressed [ˌʌnˈdrest] *adj* déshabillé(e) ; **to get ~** se déshabiller.

undrinkable [ˌʌnˈdrɪŋkəbl] *adj* [unfit to drink] non potable ; [disgusting] imbuvable.

undue [ˌʌnˈdjuː] *adj fml* excessif(ive).

undulate [ˈʌndjʊleɪt] *vi* onduler.

unduly [ˌʌnˈdjuːlɪ] *adv fml* trop, excessivement.

undying [ʌnˈdaɪɪŋ] *adj literary* éternel(elle).

unearned income [ˌʌnɜːnd-] *n (U)* rentes *fpl*.

unearth [ˌʌnˈɜːθ] *vt* - **1.** [dig up] déterrer - **2.** fig [discover] découvrir, dénicher.

unearthly [ʌnˈɜːθlɪ] *adj* - **1.** [ghostly] mystérieux(euse) - **2.** inf [uncivilized - time of day] indu(e), impossible.

unease [ʌnˈiːz] *n (U)* malaise *m*.

uneasy [ʌnˈiːzɪ] (*compar* -**ier** ; *superl* -**iest**) *adj* [person, feeling] mal à l'aise, gêné(e) ; [peace] troublé(e), incertain(e) ; [silence] gêné(e).

uneatable [ˌʌnˈiːtəbl] *adj* [not fit to eat] non comestible ; [disgusting] immangeable.

uneaten [ˌʌnˈiːtn] *adj* non mangé(e).

uneconomic [ˈʌnˌiːkəˈnɒmɪk] *adj* peu économique, peu rentable.

uneducated [ˌʌnˈedjʊkeɪtɪd] *adj* [person] sans instruction.

unemotional [ˌʌnɪˈməʊʃənl] *adj* qui ne montre OR trahit aucune émotion.

unemployable [ˌʌnɪmˈplɔɪəbl] *adj* inapte au travail.

unemployed [ˌʌnɪmˈplɔɪd] ⟨⟩ *adj* au chômage, sans travail ⟨⟩ *npl* : **the ~** les chômeurs *mpl*.

unemployment [ˌʌnɪmˈplɔɪmənt] *n* chômage *m*.

unemployment benefit Br, **unemployment compensation** Am *n* allocation *f* de chômage.

unenviable [ˌʌnˈenvɪəbl] *adj* peu enviable.

unequal [ˌʌnˈiːkwəl] *adj* - **1.** [different] inégal(e) - **2.** [unfair] injuste.

unequalled Br, **unequaled** Am [ˌʌnˈiːkwəld] *adj* inégalé(e).

unequivocal [ˌʌnɪˈkwɪvəkl] *adj* sans équivoque.

unerring [ˌʌnˈɜːrɪŋ] *adj* sûr(e), infaillible.

UNESCO [juːˈneskəʊ] (*abbr of* United Nations Educational, Scientific and Cultural Organization) *n* UNESCO *f*, Unesco *f*.

unethical [ʌnˈeθɪkl] *adj* immoral(e).

uneven [ˌʌnˈiːvn] *adj* - **1.** [not flat - surface] inégal(e) ; [- ground] accidenté(e) - **2.** [inconsistent] inégal(e) - **3.** [unfair] injuste.

uneventful [ˌʌnɪˈventfʊl] *adj* sans incidents.

unexceptional [ˌʌnɪkˈsepʃənl] *adj* qui n'a rien d'exceptionnel.

unexpected [ˌʌnɪkˈspektɪd] *adj* inattendu(e), imprévu(e).

unexpectedly [ˌʌnɪkˈspektɪdlɪ] *adv* subitement, d'une manière imprévue.

unexplained [ˌʌnɪkˈspleɪnd] *adj* inexpliqué(e).

unexploded [ˌʌnɪkˈspləʊdɪd] *adj* [bomb] non explosé(e), non éclaté(e).

unexpurgated [ʌnˈekspɜːgeɪtɪd] *adj* non expurgé(e), intégral(e).

unfailing [ʌnˈfeɪlɪŋ] *adj* qui ne se dément pas, constant(e).

unfair [ˌʌnˈfeəʳ] *adj* injuste.

unfair dismissal *n* licenciement *m* injuste OR abusif.

unfairness [ˌʌnˈfeənɪs] *n* injustice *f*.

unfaithful [ˌʌnˈfeɪθfʊl] *adj* infidèle.

unfamiliar [ˌʌnfəˈmɪljəʳ] *adj* - **1.** [not well-known] peu familier(ère), peu connu(e) - **2.** [not acquainted] : **to be ~ with sb/sthg** mal connaître qqn/qqch, ne pas connaître qqn/qqch.

unfashionable [ˌʌnˈfæʃnəbl] *adj* démodé(e), passé(e) de mode ; [person] qui n'est plus à la mode.

unfasten [ˌʌnˈfɑːsn] *vt* défaire.

unfavourable Br, **unfavorable** Am [ˌʌnˈfeɪvrəbl] *adj* défavorable.

unfazed [ʌnˈfeɪzd] *adj* inf imperturbable, impassible.

unfeeling [ʌnˈfiːlɪŋ] *adj* impitoyable, insensible.

unfinished [ˌʌnˈfɪnɪʃt] *adj* inachevé(e).

unfit [ˌʌnˈfɪt] *adj* - **1.** [not in good health] qui n'est pas en forme - **2.** [not suitable] : **~ (for)** impropre (à) ; [person] inapte (à).

unflagging [ˌʌnˈflægɪŋ] *adj* inlassable, infatigable.

unflappable [ˌʌnˈflæpəbl] *adj* esp Br imperturbable, flegmatique.

unflattering [ˌʌnˈflætərɪŋ] *adj* peu flatteur(euse).

unflinching [ʌnˈflɪntʃɪŋ] *adj* inébranlable.

unfold [ʌnˈfəʊld] ⟨⟩ *vt* - **1.** [map, newspaper] déplier - **2.** [explain - plan, proposal] exposer ⟨⟩ *vi* [become clear] se dérouler.

unforeseeable [ˌʌnfɔːˈsiːəbl] *adj* imprévisible.

unforeseen [ˌʌnfɔːˈsiːn] *adj* imprévu(e).

unforgettable [ˌʌnfə'getəbl] *adj* inoubliable.

unforgivable [ˌʌnfə'gɪvəbl] *adj* impardonnable.

unformatted [ˌʌn'fɔːmætɪd] *adj* COMPUT non formaté(e).

unfortunate [ʌn'fɔːtʃnət] *adj* - **1.** [unlucky] malheureux(euse), malchanceux(euse) - **2.** [regrettable] regrettable, fâcheux(euse).

unfortunately [ʌn'fɔːtʃnətlɪ] *adv* malheureusement.

unfounded [ˌʌn'faundɪd] *adj* sans fondement, dénué(e) de tout fondement.

unfriendly [ˌʌn'frendlɪ] (*compar* -ier ; *superl* -iest) *adj* hostile, malveillant(e).

unfulfilled [ˌʌnfʊl'fɪld] *adj* - **1.** [ambition, potential, prophecy] non réalisé(e), inaccompli(e) ; [promise] non tenu(e) - **2.** [person, life] insatisfait(e), frustré(e).

unfurl [ˌʌn'fɜːl] *vt* déployer.

unfurnished [ˌʌn'fɜːnɪʃt] *adj* non meublé(e).

ungainly [ʌn'geɪnlɪ] *adj* gauche.

ungenerous [ˌʌn'dʒenərəs] *adj* - **1.** [mean - person] peu généreux(euse) ; [- amount] mesquin(e) - **2.** [unkind] peu charitable, mesquin(e).

ungodly [ˌʌn'gɒdlɪ] *adj* - **1.** [irreligious] impie, irréligieux(euse) - **2.** *inf* [unreasonable] indu(e), impossible.

ungrateful [ʌn'greɪtful] *adj* ingrat(e), peu reconnaissant(e).

ungratefulness [ʌn'greɪtfulnɪs] *n* ingratitude *f*.

unguarded [ˌʌn'gɑːdɪd] *adj* - **1.** [house, camp etc] sans surveillance - **2.** [careless] : **in an ~ moment** dans un moment d'inattention.

unhappily [ʌn'hæpɪlɪ] *adv* - **1.** [sadly] tristement - **2.** [unfortunately] malheureusement.

unhappiness [ʌn'hæpɪnɪs] *n* (U) tristesse *f*, chagrin *m*.

unhappy [ʌn'hæpɪ] (*compar* -ier ; *superl* -iest) *adj* - **1.** [sad] triste, malheureux(euse) - **2.** [uneasy] : **to be ~ (with** OR **about)** être inquiet(ète) (au sujet de) - **3.** [unfortunate] malheureux(euse), regrettable.

unharmed [ˌʌn'hɑːmd] *adj* indemne, sain et sauf (saine et sauve).

UNHCR (*abbr of* United Nations High Commission for Refugees) *n* HCR *m*.

unhealthy [ʌn'helθɪ] (*compar* -ier ; *superl* -iest) *adj* - **1.** [person, skin] maladif(ive) ; [conditions, place] insalubre, malsain(e) ; [habit] malsain - **2.** *fig* [undesirable] malsain(e).

unheard [ˌʌn'hɜːd] *adj* : **her warning went ~**

on n'a pas tenu compte de son avertissement.

unheard-of [ʌn'hɜːdɒv] *adj* - **1.** [unknown] inconnu(e) - **2.** [unprecedented] sans précédent, inouï(e).

unheeded [ˌʌn'hiːdɪd] *adj* : **his advice went ~** on n'a pas suivi OR écouté ses conseils.

unhelpful [ˌʌn'helpful] *adj* - **1.** [person, attitude] peu serviable, peu obligeant(e) - **2.** [advice, book] qui n'aide en rien, peu utile.

unhindered [ˌʌn'hɪndəd] *adj* sans obstacles, sans encombre.

unhook [ˌʌn'huk] *vt* - **1.** [dress, bra] dégrafer - **2.** [coat, picture, trailer] décrocher.

unhurt [ˌʌn'hɜːt] *adj* indemne, sain et sauf (saine et sauve).

unhygienic [ˌʌnhaɪ'dʒiːnɪk] *adj* non hygiénique.

UNICEF ['juːnɪˌsef] (*abbr of* United Nations International Children's Emergency Fund) *n* UNICEF *m*, Unicef *m*.

unicorn ['juːnɪkɔːn] *n* licorne *f*.

unicycle ['juːnɪsaɪkl] *n* monocyle *m*.

unidentified *adj* non identifié(e).

unidentified flying object [ˌʌnaɪ'dentɪfaɪd-] *n* objet *m* volant non identifié.

unification [ˌjuːnɪfɪ'keɪʃn] *n* unification *f*.

uniform ['juːnɪfɔːm] <> *adj* [rate, colour] uniforme ; [size] même <> *n* uniforme *m*.

uniformity [ˌjuːnɪ'fɔːmətɪ] *n* uniformité *f*.

uniformly ['juːnɪfɔːmlɪ] *adv* uniformément.

unify ['juːnɪfaɪ] (*pt* & *pp* -ied) *vt* unifier.

unifying ['juːnɪfaɪɪŋ] *adj* qui unifie, unificateur(trice).

unilateral [ˌjuːnɪ'lætərəl] *adj* unilatéral(e).

unimaginable [ˌʌnɪ'mædʒɪnəbl] *adj* inimaginable, inconcevable.

unimaginative [ˌʌnɪ'mædʒɪnətɪv] *adj* qui manque d'imagination, peu imaginatif(ive).

unimpaired [ˌʌnɪm'peəd] *adj* intact(e).

unimpeded [ˌʌnɪm'piːdɪd] *adj* sans entrave.

unimportant [ˌʌnɪm'pɔːtənt] *adj* sans importance, peu important(e).

unimpressed [ˌʌnɪm'prest] *adj* qui n'est pas impressionné(e).

uninhabited [ˌʌnɪn'hæbɪtɪd] *adj* inhabité(e).

uninhibited [ˌʌnɪn'hɪbɪtɪd] *adj* sans inhibitions, qui n'a pas d'inhibitions.

uninitiated [ˌʌnɪ'nɪʃɪeɪtɪd] *npl* : **the ~** les non-initiés, les profanes.

uninjured [ˌʌn'ɪndʒəd] *adj* qui n'est pas blessé(e), indemne.

uninspiring [ˌʌnɪnˈspaɪrɪŋ] *adj* qui n'a rien d'inspirant.

unintelligent [ˌʌnɪnˈtelɪdʒənt] *adj* inintelligent(e).

unintentional [ˌʌnɪnˈtenʃənl] *adj* involontaire, non intentionnel(elle).

uninterested [ˌʌnˈɪntrəstɪd] *adj* indifférent(e).

uninterrupted [ˈʌnˌɪntəˈrʌptɪd] *adj* ininterrompu(e), continu(e).

uninvited [ˌʌnɪnˈvaɪtɪd] *adj* qui n'a pas été invité(e).

union [ˈjuːnjən] <> *n* - **1.** [trade union] syndicat *m* - **2.** [alliance] union *f* <> *comp* syndical(e).

Unionist [ˈjuːnjənɪst] *n* Br POL unioniste *mf*.

unionize, -ise [ˈjuːnjənaɪz] *vt* syndiquer.

Union Jack *n* : the ~ l'Union Jack *m*, le drapeau britannique.

THE UNION JACK

Le drapeau du Royaume-Uni est composé de trois éléments. Il rassemble en effet la croix de Saint-Georges anglaise (rouge sur fond blanc), la croix de Saint-André écossaise (blanche sur fond bleu) et la croix de Saint-Patrick irlandaise (rouge). Le drapeau gallois, avec son dragon rouge sur fond vert, ne fait pas partie de l'Union Jack.

union shop *n* Am atelier *m* d'ouvriers syndiqués.

unique [juːˈniːk] *adj* - **1.** [exceptional] unique, exceptionnel(elle) - **2.** [exclusive] : ~ **to** propre à - **3.** [very special] unique.

uniquely [juːˈniːklɪ] *adv* - **1.** [exclusively] uniquement - **2.** [exceptionally] exceptionnellement.

unisex [ˈjuːnɪseks] *adj* unisexe.

unison [ˈjuːnɪzn] *n* unisson *m ;* **in** ~ à l'unisson ; [say] en chœur, en même temps.

UNISON [ˈjuːnɪzn] *n* « super-syndicat » britannique des services publics.

unit [ˈjuːnɪt] *n* - **1.** [gen] unité *f* - **2.** [machine part] élément *m*, bloc *m* - **3.** [of furniture] élément *m ;* **storage** ~ meuble *m* de rangement - **4.** [department] service *m* - **5.** [chapter] chapitre *m*.

unit cost *n* prix *m* de revient unitaire.

unite [juːˈnaɪt] <> *vt* unifier <> *vi* s'unir.

united [juːˈnaɪtɪd] *adj* - **1.** [in harmony] uni(e) ; **to be** ~ **in** sthg être uni dans qqch - **2.** [unified] unifié(e).

United Arab Emirates *npl :* the ~ les Émirats *mpl* arabes unis.

united front *n :* **to present a** ~ montrer un front uni.

United Kingdom *n :* the ~ le Royaume-Uni.

United Nations *n :* the ~ les Nations *fpl* Unies.

United States *n :* the ~ **(of America)** les États-Unis *mpl* (d'Amérique) ; **in the** ~ aux États-Unis.

unit price *n* prix *m* unitaire.

unit trust *n* Br société *f* d'investissement à capital variable.

unity [ˈjuːnətɪ] *n* (U) unité *f*.

Univ. *abbr of* **University**.

universal [ˌjuːnɪˈvɜːsl] *adj* universel(elle).

universal joint *n* joint *m* universel OR de cardan.

universe [ˈjuːnɪvɜːs] *n* univers *m*.

university [ˌjuːnɪˈvɜːsətɪ] *(pl* **-ies)** <> *n* université *f* <> *comp* universitaire ; [lecturer] d'université ; ~ **student** étudiant *m*, -e *f* à l'université.

unjust [ˌʌnˈdʒʌst] *adj* injuste.

unjustifiable [ʌnˈdʒʌstɪfaɪəbl] *adj* injustifiable.

unjustified [ʌnˈdʒʌstɪfaɪd] *adj* injustifié(e).

unkempt [ˌʌnˈkempt] *adj* [clothes, person] négligé(e), débraillé(e) ; [hair] mal peigné(e).

unkind [ʌnˈkaɪnd] *adj* - **1.** [uncharitable] méchant(e), pas gentil(ille) - **2.** fig [weather, climate] rude, rigoureux(euse).

unkindly [ʌnˈkaɪndlɪ] *adv* méchamment.

unknown [ˌʌnˈnəʊn] <> *adj* inconnu(e) <> *n* [person] inconnu *m*, -e *f* ; **the** ~ l'inconnu *m*.

unlace [ˌʌnˈleɪs] *vt* défaire, délacer.

unladen [ˌʌnˈleɪdn] *adj* sans charge ; ~ **weight** poids *m* à vide.

unlawful [ˌʌnˈlɔːfʊl] *adj* illégal(e).

unleaded [ˌʌnˈledɪd] <> *adj* sans plomb <> *n* essence *f* sans plomb.

unleash [ˌʌnˈliːʃ] *vt* literary déchaîner.

unleavened [ˌʌnˈlevnd] *adj* sans levain, azyme.

unless [ənˈles] *conj* à moins que (+ *subjunctive)* ; ~ **I'm mistaken** à moins que je (ne) me trompe ; ~ **otherwise informed** sauf avis contraire.

unlicensed, unlicenced Am [ˌʌnˈlaɪsənst] *adj* [person] qui ne détient pas de licence ; [activity] non autorisé(e), illicite ; [vehicle] sans vignette ; [restaurant, premises] qui ne détient pas de licence de débit de boissons.

unlike [ˌʌnˈlaɪk] *prep* - **1.** [different from] différent(e) de - **2.** [in contrast to] contrairement à, à la différence de - **3.** [not typical of] : **it's** ~ **you**

to complain cela ne te ressemble pas de te plaindre.

unlikely [ʌn'laɪklɪ] *adj* - **1.** [event, result] peu probable, improbable ; [story] invraisemblable. - **2.** [bizarre - clothes etc] invraisemblable

unlimited [ʌn'lɪmɪtɪd] *adj* illimité(e).

unlisted [ʌn'lɪstɪd] *adj* Am [phone number] qui est sur la liste rouge.

unlit [ˌʌn'lɪt] *adj* - **1.** [lamp, fire, cigarette] non allumé(e) - **2.** [street, building] non éclairé(e).

unload [ˌʌn'ləʊd] *vt* décharger ; **to ~ sthg on** OR **onto sb** fig se décharger de qqch sur qqn.

unlock [ˌʌn'lɒk] *vt* ouvrir.

unloved [ˌʌn'lʌvd] *adj* qui n'est pas aimé(e) ; **to feel ~** ne pas se sentir aimé.

unluckily [ʌn'lʌkɪlɪ] *adv* malheureusement.

unlucky [ʌn'lʌkɪ] (*compar* -**ier** ; *superl* -**iest**) *adj* - **1.** [unfortunate - person] malchanceux(euse), qui n'a pas de chance ; [- experience, choice] malheureux(euse) - **2.** [object, number etc] qui porte malheur.

unmanageable [ʌn'mænɪdʒəbl] *adj* [vehicle, parcel] peu maniable ; [hair] difficiles à coiffer.

unmanly [ˌʌn'mænlɪ] (*compar* -**ier** ; *superl* -**iest**) *adj* qui n'est pas viril.

unmanned [ˌʌn'mænd] *adj* sans équipage.

unmarked [ˌʌn'mɑːkt] *adj* - **1.** [uninjured - body, face] sans marque - **2.** [unidentified - box, suitcase] sans marque d'identification ; [- police car] banalisé(e).

unmarried [ˌʌn'mærɪd] *adj* célibataire, qui n'est pas marié(e).

unmask [ˌʌn'mɑːsk] *vt* démasquer ; [truth, hypocrisy] dévoiler.

unmatched [ˌʌn'mætʃt] *adj* sans pareil(eille).

unmentionable [ʌn'menʃnəbl] *adj* [subject] dont il ne faut pas parler ; [word] qu'il ne faut pas dire.

unmistakable [ˌʌnmɪ'steɪkəbl] *adj* facilement reconnaissable.

unmitigated [ʌn'mɪtɪgeɪtɪd] *adj* [disaster] total(e) ; [evil] non mitigé(e).

unmoved [ˌʌn'muːvd] *adj :* **~ (by)** indifférent(e) (à).

unnamed [ˌʌn'neɪmd] *adj* [person] anonyme ; [object] sans dénomination.

unnatural [ʌn'nætʃrəl] *adj* - **1.** [unusual] anormal(e), qui n'est pas naturel(elle) - **2.** [affected] peu naturel(elle) ; [smile] forcé(e).

unnecessary [ʌn'nesəsərɪ] *adj* [remark, expense, delay] inutile ; **it's ~ to do sthg** ce n'est pas la peine de faire qqch.

unnerving [ˌʌn'nɜːvɪŋ] *adj* troublant(e).

unnoticed [ˌʌn'nəʊtɪst] *adj* inaperçu(e).

UNO (*abbr of* **United Nations Organization**) *n* ONU *m*, Onu *m*.

unobserved [ˌʌnəb'zɜːvd] *adj* inaperçu(e).

unobtainable [ˌʌnəb'teɪnəbl] *adj* impossible à obtenir.

unobtrusive [ˌʌnəb'truːsɪv] *adj* [person] effacé(e) ; [object] discret(ète) ; [building] que l'on remarque à peine.

unoccupied [ˌʌn'ɒkjʊpaɪd] *adj* [house] inhabité(e) ; [seat] libre.

unofficial [ˌʌnə'fɪʃl] *adj* non officiel(elle).

unopened [ˌʌn'əʊpənd] *adj* non ouvert(e), qui n'a pas été ouvert(e).

unorthodox [ˌʌn'ɔːθədɒks] *adj* peu orthodoxe.

unpack [ˌʌn'pæk] <> *vt* [suitcase] défaire ; [box] vider ; [clothes] déballer <> *vi* défaire ses bagages.

unpaid [ˌʌn'peɪd] *adj* - **1.** [person] bénévole ; [work] sans rémunération, bénévole - **2.** [rent] non acquitté(e) ; [bill] impayé(e).

unpalatable [ʌn'pælətəbl] *adj* d'un goût désagréable ; fig dur(e) à avaler.

unparalleled [ʌn'pærəleld] *adj* [success, crisis] sans précédent ; [beauty] sans égal.

unpatriotic ['ʌnˌpætrɪ'ɒtɪk] *adj* [person] peu patriote ; [act] antipatriotique.

unpick [ˌʌn'pɪk] *vt* découdre.

unpin [ˌʌn'pɪn] (*pt* & *pp* -**ned** ; *cont* -**ning**) *vt* [sewing, hair] retirer les épingles de.

unplanned [ˌʌn'plænd] *adj* imprévu(e) ; [pregnancy] accidentel(elle).

unpleasant [ʌn'pleznt] *adj* désagréable.

unpleasantness [ʌn'plezntnɪs] *n* caractère *m* désagréable.

unplug [ʌn'plʌg] (*pt* & *pp* -**ged** ; *cont* -**ging**) *vt* débrancher.

unpolished [ˌʌn'pɒlɪʃt] *adj* - **1.** [not shined - floor] non poli(e) ; [- furniture, shoes] non ciré(e) - **2.** [not accomplished] peu raffiné(e).

unpolluted [ˌʌnpə'luːtɪd] *adj* non pollué(e).

unpopular [ˌʌn'pɒpjʊləʳ] *adj* impopulaire.

unprecedented [ʌn'presɪdəntɪd] *adj* sans précédent.

unpredictable [ˌʌnprɪ'dɪktəbl] *adj* imprévisible.

unprejudiced [ˌʌn'predʒʊdɪst] *adj* sans préjugés.

unprepared [ˌʌnprɪ'peəd] *adj* non préparé(e) ; **to be ~ for sthg** ne pas s'attendre à qqch.

unprepossessing ['ʌnˌpriːpə'zesɪŋ] *adj* peu avenant(e).

unpretentious [ˌʌnprɪ'tenʃəs] *adj* sans prétention.

unprincipled [ʌn'prɪnsəpld] *adj* sans scrupules.

unprintable [ˌʌn'prɪntəbl] *adj* **fig** qu'on ne peut pas répéter, grossier(ère).

unproductive [ˌʌnprə'dʌktɪv] *adj* improductif(ive).

unprofessional [ˌʌnprə'feʃənl] *adj* [person, work] peu professionnel(elle) ; [attitude] contraire à l'éthique de la profession.

unprofitable [ˌʌn'prɒfɪtəbl] *adj* peu rentable.

UNPROFOR ['ʌnprəfɔː] (*abbr of* **United Nations Protection Force**) *n* FORPRONU *f*.

unprompted [ˌʌn'prɒmptɪd] *adj* spontané(e).

unpronounceable [ˌʌnprə'naʊnsəbl] *adj* imprononçable.

unprotected [ˌʌnprə'tektɪd] *adj* sans protection.

unprovoked [ˌʌnprə'vəʊkt] *adj* sans provocation.

unpublished [ˌʌn'pʌblɪʃt] *adj* inédit(e).

unpunished [ˌʌn'pʌnɪʃt] *adj* : **to go ~** rester impuni(e).

unqualified [ˌʌn'kwɒlɪfaɪd] *adj* - **1.** [person] non qualifié(e) ; [teacher, doctor] non diplômé(e) - **2.** [success] formidable ; [support] inconditionnel(elle).

unquestionable [ʌn'kwestʃənəbl] *adj* [fact] incontestable ; [honesty] certain(e).

unquestioning [ʌn'kwestʃənɪŋ] *adj* aveugle, absolu(e).

unravel [ʌn'rævl] (**Br** *pt* & *pp* **-led** ; *cont* **-ling**, **Am** *pt* & *pp* **-ed** ; *cont* **-ing**) *vt* - **1.** [undo - knitting] défaire ; [- fabric] effiler ; [- threads] démêler - **2. fig** [solve] éclaircir.

unreadable [ˌʌn'riːdəbl] *adj* illisible.

unreal [ˌʌn'rɪəl] *adj* [strange] irréel(elle).

unrealistic [ˌʌnrɪə'lɪstɪk] *adj* irréaliste.

unreasonable [ʌn'riːznəbl] *adj* qui n'est pas raisonnable, déraisonnable.

unrecognizable [ˌʌn'rekəgnaɪzəbl] *adj* méconnaissable.

unrecognized [ˌʌn'rekəgnaɪzd] *adj* - **1.** [person] non reconnu(e) - **2.** [achievement, talent] méconnu(e).

unrecorded [ˌʌnrɪ'kɔːdɪd] *adj* non enregistré(e).

unrefined [ˌʌnrɪ'faɪnd] *adj* - **1.** [not processed] non raffiné(e), brut(e) - **2.** [vulgar] peu raffiné(e).

unrehearsed [ˌʌnrɪ'hɜːst] *adj* [performance] sans répétition ; [speech, response] improvisé(e).

unrelated [ˌʌnrɪ'leɪtɪd] *adj* : **to be ~ (to)** n'avoir aucun rapport (avec).

unrelenting [ˌʌnrɪ'lentɪŋ] *adj* implacable.

unreliable [ˌʌnrɪ'laɪəbl] *adj* [machine, method] peu fiable ; [person] sur qui on ne peut pas compter.

unrelieved [ˌʌnrɪ'liːvd] *adj* [pain, gloom] constant(e).

unremarkable [ˌʌnrɪ'mɑːkəbl] *adj* quelconque.

unremitting [ˌʌnrɪ'mɪtɪŋ] *adj* inlassable.

unrepeatable [ˌʌnrɪ'piːtəbl] *adj* [comment] qu'on ne peut pas répéter.

unrepentant [ˌʌnrɪ'pentənt] *adj* impénitent(e).

unrepresentative [ˌʌnreprɪ'zentətɪv] *adj* : **~ (of)** peu représentatif(ive) (de).

unrequited [ˌʌnrɪ'kwaɪtɪd] *adj* non partagé(e).

unreserved [ˌʌnrɪ'zɜːvd] *adj* - **1.** [support, admiration] sans réserve - **2.** [seat] non réservé(e).

unresolved [ˌʌnrɪ'zɒlvd] *adj* non résolu(e).

unresponsive [ˌʌnrɪ'spɒnsɪv] *adj* : **to be ~ to** ne pas réagir à.

unrest [ˌʌn'rest] *n (U)* troubles *mpl*.

unrestrained [ˌʌnrɪ'streɪnd] *adj* effréné(e).

unrestricted [ˌʌnrɪ'strɪktɪd] *adj* sans restriction, illimité(e).

unrewarding [ˌʌnrɪ'wɔːdɪŋ] *adj* ingrat(e).

unripe [ˌʌn'raɪp] *adj* qui n'est pas mûr(e).

unrivalled Br, unrivaled Am [ʌn'raɪvld] *adj* sans égal(e).

unroll [ˌʌn'rəʊl] *vt* dérouler.

unruffled [ˌʌn'rʌfld] *adj* [person] imperturbable.

unruly [ʌn'ruːlɪ] (*compar* **-ier** ; *superl* **-iest**) *adj* [crowd, child] turbulent(e) ; [hair] indisciplinés.

unsafe [ˌʌn'seɪf] *adj* - **1.** [dangerous] dangereux(euse) - **2.** [in danger] : **to feel ~** ne pas se sentir en sécurité.

unsaid [ˌʌn'sed] *adj* : **to leave sthg ~** passer qqch sous silence.

unsaleable, unsalable Am [ˌʌn'seɪləbl] *adj* invendable.

unsatisfactory ['ʌnˌsætɪs'fæktərɪ] *adj* qui laisse à désirer, peu satisfaisant(e).

unsavoury Br, unsavory Am [ˌʌn'seɪvərɪ] *adj* [person] peu recommandable ; [district] mal famé(e).

unscathed [ˌʌn'skeɪðd] *adj* indemne.

unscheduled [**Br** ˌʌn'ʃedjuːld, **Am** ˌʌn'skedʒʊld] *adj* non prévu(e).

unscientific [ˈʌnˌsaɪənˈtɪfɪk] *adj* peu scientifique.

unscrew [ˌʌnˈskruːl] *vt* dévisser.

unscripted [ˌʌnˈskrɪptɪd] *adj* improvisé(e).

unscrupulous [ʌnˈskruːpjʊləs] *adj* sans scrupules.

unseat [ˌʌnˈsiːt] *vt* - **1.** [rider] désarçonner - **2.** fig [MP] faire perdre son siège à ; [leader] faire perdre sa position à.

unseeded [ˌʌnˈsiːdɪd] *adj* qui n'est pas classé(e) en tête de série.

unseemly [ʌnˈsiːmlɪ] (*compar* -**ier** ; *superl* -**iest**) *adj* inconvenant(e).

unseen [ˌʌnˈsiːn] *adj* [not observed] inaperçu(e).

unselfish [ˌʌnˈselfɪʃ] *adj* désintéressé(e).

unselfishly [ˌʌnˈselfɪʃlɪ] *adv* de manière désintéressée.

unsettle [ˌʌnˈsetl] *vt* perturber.

unsettled [ˌʌnˈsetld] *adj* - **1.** [person] perturbé(e), troublé(e) - **2.** [weather] variable, incertain(e) - **3.** [argument] qui n'a pas été résolu(e) ; [situation] incertain(e).

unsettling [ˌʌnˈsetlɪŋ] *adj* inquiétant(e).

unshak(e)able [ʌnˈʃeɪkəbl] *adj* inébranlable.

unshaven [ˌʌnˈʃeɪvn] *adj* non rasé(e).

unsheathe [ˌʌnˈʃiːð] *vt* dégainer.

unsightly [ʌnˈsaɪtlɪ] *adj* laid(e).

unskilled [ˌʌnˈskɪld] *adj* non qualifié(e).

unsociable [ʌnˈsəʊʃəbl] *adj* sauvage.

unsocial [ˌʌnˈsəʊʃl] *adj* : **to work ~ hours** travailler en dehors des heures normales.

unsold [ˌʌnˈsəʊld] *adj* invendu(e).

unsolicited [ˌʌnsəˈlɪsɪtɪd] *adj* non sollicité(e).

unsolved [ˌʌnˈsɒlvd] *adj* non résolu(e).

unsophisticated [ˌʌnsəˈfɪstɪkeɪtɪd] *adj* simple.

unsound [ˌʌnˈsaʊnd] *adj* - **1.** [theory] mal fondé(e) ; [decision] peu judicieux(euse) - **2.** [building, structure] en mauvais état.

unspeakable [ʌnˈspiːkəbl] *adj* indescriptible.

unspeakably [ʌnˈspiːkəblɪ] *adv* indescriptiblement.

unspecified [ˌʌnˈspesɪfaɪd] *adj* non spécifié(e).

unspoiled [ˌʌnˈspɔɪld], **unspoilt** [ˌʌnˈspɔɪlt] *adj* intact(e) ; [countryside] qui n'a pas été défiguré(e).

unspoken [ˌʌnˈspəʊkən] *adj* [thought, wish] inexprimé(e) ; [agreement] tacite.

unsporting [ˌʌnˈspɔːtɪŋ] *adj* qui n'est pas fair-play.

unstable [ˌʌnˈsteɪbl] *adj* instable.

unstated [ˌʌnˈsteɪtɪd] *adj* non déclaré(e).

unsteady [ˌʌnˈstedɪ] (*compar* -**ier** ; *superl* -**iest**) *adj* [hand] tremblant(e) ; [table, ladder] instable.

unstinting [ˌʌnˈstɪntɪŋ] *adj* [praise, support] sans réserve ; [person] généreux(euse), prodigue.

unstoppable [ˌʌnˈstɒpəbl] *adj* qu'on ne peut pas arrêter.

unstrap [ˌʌnˈstræp] (*pt* & *pp* -**ped** ; *cont* -**ping**) *vt* défaire les attaches de.

unstructured [ˌʌnˈstrʌktʃəd] *adj* non structuré(e).

unstuck [ˌʌnˈstʌk] *adj* : **to come ~** [notice, stamp, label] se décoller ; fig [plan, system] s'effondrer ; fig [person] essuyer un échec.

unsubstantiated [ˌʌnsəbˈstænʃɪeɪtɪd] *adj* sans fondement.

unsuccessful [ˌʌnsəkˈsesfʊl] *adj* [attempt] vain(e) ; [meeting] infructueux(euse) ; [candidate] refusé(e).

unsuccessfully [ˌʌnsəkˈsesfʊlɪ] *adv* en vain, sans succès.

unsuitable [ˌʌnˈsuːtəbl] *adj* qui ne convient pas ; [clothes] peu approprié(e) ; **to be ~ for** ne pas convenir à.

unsuited [ˌʌnˈsuːtɪd] *adj* - **1.** [not appropriate] : **to be ~ to/for** ne pas convenir à/pour - **2.** [not compatible] : **to be ~ (to each other)** ne pas aller ensemble.

unsung [ˌʌnˈsʌŋ] *adj* [hero] méconnu(e).

unsure [ˌʌnˈʃɔːʳ] *adj* - **1.** [not certain] : **to be ~ (about/of)** ne pas être sûr(e) (de) - **2.** [not confident] : **to be ~ (of o.s.)** ne pas être sûr(e) de soi.

unsurpassed [ˌʌnsəˈpɑːst] *adj* non surpassé(e).

unsuspecting [ˌʌnsəˈspektɪŋ] *adj* qui ne se doute de rien.

unsweetened [ˌʌnˈswiːtnd] *adj* non sucré(e).

unswerving [ʌnˈswɜːvɪŋ] *adj* [loyalty, determination] inébranlable.

unsympathetic [ˈʌnˌsɪmpəˈθetɪk] *adj* [unfeeling] indifférent(e).

untamed [ˌʌnˈteɪmd] *adj* [animal] sauvage ; fig [person] farouche.

untangle [ˌʌnˈtæŋgl] *vt* [string, hair] démêler.

untapped [ˌʌnˈtæpt] *adj* inexploité(e).

untaxed [ˌʌnˈtækst] *adj* non imposé(e).

untenable [ˌʌnˈtenəbl] *adj* indéfendable.

unthinkable [ʌnˈθɪŋkəbl] *adj* impensable.

unthinkingly [ʌn'θɪŋkɪŋlɪ] *adv* sans réflé-chir.

untidy [ʌn'taɪdɪ] (*compar* **-ier** ; *superl* **-iest**) *adj* [room, desk] en désordre ; [work, handwriting] brouillon (*inv*) ; [person, appearance] négligé(e).

untie [ˌʌn'taɪ] (*cont* **untying**) *vt* [knot, parcel, shoelaces] défaire ; [prisoner] détacher.

until [ən'tɪl] <> *prep* **- 1.** [gen] jusqu'à ; **~ now** jusqu'ici **- 2.** (*after negative*) avant ; **not ~ to-morrow** pas avant demain ; **we weren't told the news ~ four o'clock** on ne nous a appris la nouvelle qu'à quatre heures <> *conj* **- 1.** [gen] jusqu'à ce que (+ *subjunctive*) **- 2.** (*after negative*) avant que (+ *subjunctive*) ; **don't sign ~ you've checked everything** ne signe rien avant d'avoir tout vérifié.

untimely [ʌn'taɪmlɪ] *adj* [death] prématu-ré(e) ; [arrival] intempestif(ive) ; [remark] mal à propos ; [moment] mal choisi(e).

untiring [ʌn'taɪərɪŋ] *adj* infatigable.

untold [ˌʌn'təʊld] *adj* [amount, wealth] incalcu-lable ; [suffering, joy] indescriptible.

untouched [ˌʌn'tʌtʃt] *adj* **- 1.** [unharmed - per-son] indemne ; [- thing] intact(e) **- 2.** [uneat-en - meal] auquel on n'a pas touché.

untoward [ˌʌntə'wɔːd] *adj* malencon-treux(euse).

untrained [ˌʌn'treɪnd] *adj* **- 1.** [person, worker] sans formation **- 2.** [voice] non travaillé(e) ; [mind] non formé(e).

untrammelled Br, **untrammeled** Am [ʌn'træməld] *adj fml* libre.

untreated [ˌʌn'triːtɪd] *adj* **- 1.** MED non soi-gné(e) **- 2.** [sewage, chemical] non traité(e).

untried [ˌʌn'traɪd] *adj* [method] qui n'a pas été mis(e) à l'épreuve ; [product] qui n'a pas été essayé(e).

untroubled [ˌʌn'trʌbld] *adj* [undisturbed] : **to be ~ by sthg** rester impassible devant qqch.

untrue [ˌʌn'truː] *adj* **- 1.** [not accurate] faux (fausse), qui n'est pas vrai(e) **- 2.** [unfaithful] : **to be ~ to sb** être infidèle à qqn.

untrustworthy [ˌʌn'trʌst,wɜːðɪ] *adj* [person] qui n'est pas digne de confiance.

untruth [ˌʌn'truːθ] *n* mensonge *m*.

untruthful [ˌʌn'truːθʊl] *adj* [person] men-teur(euse) ; [statement] mensonger(ère).

untutored [ˌʌn'tjuːtəd] *adj* [person] peu ins-truit(e).

unusable [ˌʌn'juːzəbl] *adj* inutilisable.

unused [*sense 1* ˌʌn'juːzd, *sense 2* ʌn'juːst] *adj* **- 1.** [clothes] neuf (neuve) ; [machine] qui n'a ja-mais servi ; [land] qui n'est pas exploité

- 2. [unaccustomed] : **to be ~ to sthg/to doing sthg** ne pas avoir l'habitude de qqch/de faire qqch.

unusual [ʌn'juːʒl] *adj* rare, inhabituel(elle).

unusually [ʌn'juːʒəlɪ] *adv* exceptionnelle-ment.

unvarnished [ʌn'vɑːnɪʃt] *adj fig* [truth] tout nu (toute nue) ; [account] sans embellisse-ment.

unveil [ˌʌn'veɪl] *vt lit* & *fig* dévoiler.

unwaged [ˌʌn'weɪdʒd] *adj* Br non salarié(e).

unwanted [ˌʌn'wɒntɪd] *adj* [object] dont on ne se sert pas ; [child] non désiré(e) ; **to feel ~** se sentir mal-aimé(e).

unwarranted [ʌn'wɒrəntɪd] *adj* injusti-fié(e).

unwavering [ʌn'weɪvərɪŋ] *adj* [determination] inébranlable.

unwelcome [ʌn'welkəm] *adj* [news, situation] fâcheux(euse) ; [visitor] importun(e) ; **to make sb feel ~** faire sentir à qqn qu'il dé-range.

unwell [ˌʌn'wel] *adj* : **to be/feel ~** ne pas être/se sentir bien.

unwholesome [ˌʌn'həʊlsəm] *adj* mal-sain(e).

unwieldy [ʌn'wiːldɪ] (*compar* **-ier** ; *superl* **-iest**) *adj* **- 1.** [cumbersome] peu maniable **- 2.** fig [system] lourd(e) ; [method] trop com-plexe.

unwilling [ˌʌn'wɪlɪŋ] *adj* : **to be ~ to do sthg** ne pas vouloir faire qqch ; **to be an ~ helper** aider à contrecœur.

unwind [ˌʌn'waɪnd] (*pt* & *pp* **-wound**) <> *vt* dérouler <> *vi fig* [person] se détendre.

unwise [ˌʌn'waɪz] *adj* imprudent(e), peu sa-ge.

unwitting [ˌʌn'wɪtɪŋ] *adj fml* involontaire.

unwittingly [ʌn'wɪtɪŋlɪ] *adv fml* involontai-rement.

unworkable [ˌʌn'wɜːkəbl] *adj* impraticable.

unworldly [ˌʌn'wɜːldlɪ] *adj* détaché(e) de ce monde.

unworthy [ʌn'wɜːðɪ] (*compar* **-ier** ; *superl* **-iest**) *adj* [undeserving] : **~ (of)** indigne (de).

unwound [ˌʌn'waʊnd] *pt* & *pp* ⊳ **unwind**.

unwrap [ˌʌn'ræp] (*pt* & *pp* **-ped** ; *cont* **-ping**) *vt* défaire.

unwritten law [ˌʌnrɪtn-] *n* droit *m* coutu-mier.

unyielding [ʌn'jiːldɪŋ] *adj* inflexible.

unzip [ˌʌn'zɪp] (*pt* & *pp* **-ped** ; *cont* **-ping**) *vt* ouvrir la fermeture éclair de.

up [ʌp] (*pt* & *pp* **-ped** ; *cont* **-ping**) <> *adv*

- 1. [towards or in a higher position] en haut ; **she's ~ in her bedroom** elle est en haut dans sa chambre ; **we walked ~ to the top** on est montés jusqu'en haut ; **a house ~ in the mountains** une maison à la montagne ; **pick it ~!** ramasse-le! ; **the sun came ~** le soleil s'est levé ; **prices are going ~** les prix augmentent ; **~ there** là-haut **- 2.** [into an upright position] **to stand ~** se lever ; **to sit ~** s'asseoir (bien droit) ; **~ you get!** allez, lève-toi! **- 3.** [northwards] : **I'm coming ~ to York next week** je viens à York la semaine prochaine ; **~ north** dans le nord **- 4.** [along a road, river] : **their house is a little further ~** leur maison est un peu plus loin **- 5.** [close up, towards] : **to come ~ to sb** s'approcher de qqn ◇ *prep* **- 1.** [towards or in a higher position] en haut de ; **~ a hill/mountain** en haut d'une colline/d'une montagne ; **~ a ladder** sur une échelle ; **I went ~ the stairs** j'ai monté l'escalier **- 2.** [at far end of] : **they live ~ the road from us** ils habitent un peu plus haut *OR* loin que nous (dans la même rue) ; **her flat is just ~ the corridor** son appartement est juste au bout du couloir **- 3.** [against current of river] : **to sail ~ the Amazon** remonter l'Amazone en bateau ◇ *adj* **- 1.** [out of bed] levé(e) ; **I was ~ at six today** je me suis levé à six heures aujourd'hui **- 2.** [at an end] : **the five weeks are ~ next Monday** les cinq semaines finissent *OR* se terminent lundi prochain ; **time's ~** c'est l'heure **- 3.** [under repair] : '**road ~**' 'attention travaux' **- 4.** inf [wrong] : **is something ~?** il y a quelque chose qui ne va pas? ; **what's ~?** qu'est-ce qui ne va pas?, qu'est-ce qu'il y a? ◇ *n* : **~s and downs** hauts et bas *mpl* ◇ *vt* inf [price, cost] augmenter.

➤ **up against** *prep* : **we came ~ against a lot of opposition** nous nous sommes heurtés à une forte opposition ; **to be ~ against it** avoir beaucoup de mal (à s'en sortir).

➤ **up and down** ◇ *adv* : **to jump ~ and down** sauter ; **to walk ~ and down** faire les cent pas ◇ *prep* : **she's ~ and down the stairs all day** elle n'arrête pas de monter et descendre l'escalier toute la journée ; **she looked ~ and down the ranks of soldiers** elle passa les troupes en revue ; **we walked ~ and down the avenue** nous avons arpenté l'avenue.

➤ **up to** *prep* **- 1.** [as far as] jusqu'à **- 2.** [indicating level] jusqu'à ; **it could take ~ to six weeks** cela peut prendre jusqu'à six semaines ; **it's not ~ to standard** ce n'est pas de la qualité voulue, ceci n'a pas le niveau requis **- 3.** [well or able enough for] : **to be ~ to doing sthg** [able to] être capable de faire qqch ; [well enough for] être en état de faire qqch ; **my French isn't**

~ to much mon français ne vaut pas grand-chose *OR* n'est pas fameux **- 4.** inf [secretly doing something] : **what are you ~ to?** qu'est-ce que tu fabriques? ; **they're ~ to something** ils mijotent quelque chose, ils préparent un coup **- 5.** [indicating responsibility] : **it's not ~ to me to decide** ce n'est pas moi qui décide, il ne m'appartient pas de décider ; **it's ~ to you** c'est à vous de voir.

➤ **up until** *prep* jusqu'à.

up-and-coming *adj* à l'avenir prometteur.

up-and-up *n* : **to be on the ~** Br [improving] aller de mieux en mieux ; **on the ~** Am [honest] honnête.

upbeat ['ʌpbiːt] *adj* optimiste.

upbraid [ʌp'breɪd] *vt* : **to ~ sb (for sthg/for doing sthg)** réprimander qqn (pour qqch/pour avoir fait qqch).

upbringing ['ʌp,brɪŋɪŋ] *n* éducation *f*.

update [,ʌp'deɪt] *vt* mettre à jour.

upend [ʌp'end] *vt* [object] mettre debout.

upfront [,ʌp'frʌnt] ◇ *adj* : **~ (about)** franc (franche) (au sujet de) ◇ *adv* [in advance] d'avance.

upgrade [,ʌp'greɪd] *vt* [facilities] améliorer ; [employee] promouvoir ; [pay] augmenter.

upheaval [ʌp'hiːvl] *n* bouleversement *m*.

upheld [ʌp'held] *pt* & *pp* ▷ **uphold**.

uphill [,ʌp'hɪl] ◇ *adj* **- 1.** [slope, path] qui monte **- 2.** fig [task] ardu(e) ◇ *adv* : **to go ~** monter.

uphold [ʌp'həʊld] (*pt* & *pp* **-held**) *vt* [law] maintenir ; [decision, system] soutenir.

upholster [ʌp'həʊlstəʳ] *vt* rembourrer.

upholstery [ʌp'həʊlstərɪ] *n* rembourrage *m* ; [of car] garniture *f* intérieure.

upkeep ['ʌpkiːp] *n* entretien *m*.

upland ['ʌplənd] *adj* des hautes terres.

➤ **uplands** *npl* hautes terres *fpl*.

uplift [ʌp'lɪft] *vt* élever ; [person] élever l'âme de.

uplifting [ʌp'lɪftɪŋ] *adj* édifiant(e).

uplighter ['ʌplaɪtəʳ] *n* applique *qui diffuse une lumière dirigée vers le haut*.

up-market *adj* haut de gamme *(inv)*.

upon [ə'pɒn] *prep* fml sur ; **~ hearing the news ...** à ces nouvelles ... ; **summer/the weekend is ~ us** l'été/le week-end approche.

upper ['ʌpəʳ] ◇ *adj* supérieur(e) ◇ *n* [of shoe] empeigne *f*.

upper class *n* : **the ~** la haute société.

➤ **upper-class** *adj* [accent, person] aristocratique.

uppercut [ˈʌpəkʌt] *n* uppercut *m*.

upper hand *n* : **to have the ~** avoir le dessus ; **to gain** OR **get the ~** prendre le dessus.

uppermost [ˈʌpəməʊst] *adj* le plus haut (la plus haute) ; **it was ~ in his mind** c'était sa préoccupation majeure.

Upper Volta [-ˈvɒltə] *n* Haute-Volta *f ;* **in ~** en Haute-Volta.

uppity [ˈʌpətɪ] *adj* inf prétentieux(euse).

upright [*adj sense 1 & adv* ˌʌpˈraɪt, *adj sense 2 & n* ˈʌpraɪt] ⬦ *adj* - **1.** [person] droit(e) ; [structure] vertical(e) ; [chair] à dossier droit ; **~ freezer** congélateur *m* armoire ; **~ vacuum cleaner** aspirateur *m* balai - **2.** fig [honest] droit(e) ⬦ *adv* [stand, sit] droit ⬦ *n* montant *m*.

upright piano *n* piano *m* droit.

uprising [ˈʌpˌraɪzɪŋ] *n* soulèvement *m*.

uproar [ˈʌprɔːʳ] *n* - **1.** *(U)* [commotion] tumulte *m* - **2.** [protest] protestations *fpl*.

uproarious [ʌpˈrɔːrɪəs] *adj* - **1.** [noisy] tumultueux(euse) - **2.** [amusing] tordant(e).

uproot [ʌpˈruːt] *vt* lit & fig déraciner.

upset [ʌpˈset] (*pt & pp* **upset**, *cont* **-ting**) ⬦ *adj* - **1.** [distressed] peiné(e), triste ; [offended] vexé(e) - **2.** MED : **to have an ~ stomach** avoir l'estomac dérangé ⬦ *n :* **to have a stomach ~** avoir l'estomac dérangé ⬦ *vt* - **1.** [distress] faire de la peine à - **2.** [plan, operation] déranger - **3.** [over-turn] renverser.

upsetting [ʌpˈsetɪŋ] *adj* [distressing] bouleversant(e).

upshot [ˈʌpʃɒt] *n* résultat *m*.

upside down [ˌʌpsaɪd-] ⬦ *adj* à l'envers ⬦ *adv* à l'envers ; **to turn sthg ~** fig mettre qqch sens dessus dessous.

upstage [ˌʌpˈsteɪdʒ] *vt* éclipser.

upstairs [ˌʌpˈsteəz] ⬦ *adj* d'en haut, du dessus ⬦ *adv* en haut ⬦ *n* étage *m*.

upstanding [ˌʌpˈstændɪŋ] *adj* droit(e).

upstart [ˈʌpstaːt] *n* parvenu *m*, -e *f*.

upstate [ˌʌpˈsteɪt] Am ⬦ *adj :* **~ New York** la partie nord de l'État de New York ⬦ *adv* dans/vers le nord de l'État.

upstream [ˌʌpˈstriːm] ⬦ *adj* d'amont ; **to be ~ (from)** être en amont (de) ⬦ *adv* vers l'amont ; [swim] contre le courant.

upsurge [ˈʌpsɜːdʒ] *n :* **~ (of/in)** recrudescence *f* (de).

upswing [ˈʌpswɪŋ] *n :* **~ (in)** [popularity] remontée *f* (de) ; **an ~ in economic activity** une reprise de l'activité économique.

uptake [ˈʌpteɪk] *n :* **to be quick on the ~** saisir vite ; **to be slow on the ~** être lent(e) à comprendre.

uptight [ʌpˈtaɪt] *adj* inf tendu(e).

up-to-date *adj* - **1.** [modern] moderne - **2.** [most recent - news] tout dernier (toute dernière) - **3.** [informed] : **to keep ~ with** se tenir au courant de.

up-to-the-minute *adj* de dernière minute.

uptown [ˌʌpˈtaʊn] Am ⬦ *adj* [area] résidentiel(elle) ⬦ *adv* dans/vers les quartiers résidentiels.

upturn [ˈʌptɜːn] *n :* **~ (in)** reprise *f* (de).

upturned [ʌpˈtɜːnd] *adj* [car, cup] renversé(e) ; [nose] retroussé(e).

upward [ˈʌpwəd] ⬦ *adj* [movement] ascendant(e) ; [look, rise] vers le haut ⬦ *adv* Am = **upwards**.

upwardly-mobile [ˈʌpwədlɪ-] *adj* susceptible de promotion sociale.

upwards [ˈʌpwədz] *adv* vers le haut.
➡ **upwards of** *prep* plus de.

upwind [ˌʌpˈwɪnd] *adj :* **to be ~ of sthg** être dans le vent OR au vent par rapport à qqch.

URA (*abbr of* **Urban Renewal Administration**) *n* administration américaine des rénovations urbaines.

Urals [ˈjʊərəlz] *npl :* **the ~** l'Oural *m ;* **in the ~** dans l'Oural.

uranium [jʊˈreɪnjəm] *n* uranium *m*.

Uranus [ˈjʊərənəs] *n* [planet] Uranus *f*.

urban [ˈɜːbən] *adj* urbain(e).

urbane [ɜːˈbeɪn] *adj* courtois(e).

urbanize, -ise [ˈɜːbənaɪz] *vt* urbaniser.

urban renewal *n* réaménagement *m* des zones urbaines.

urchin [ˈɜːtʃɪn] *n* dated gamin *m*, -e *f*.

Urdu [ˈʊəduː] *n* ourdou *m*.

urge [ɜːdʒ] ⬦ *n* forte envie *f ;* **to have an ~ to do sthg** avoir une forte envie de faire qqch ⬦ *vt* - **1.** [try to persuade] : **to ~ sb to do sthg** pousser qqn à faire qqch, presser qqn de faire qqch - **2.** [advocate] conseiller.

urgency [ˈɜːdʒənsɪ] *n (U)* urgence *f*.

urgent [ˈɜːdʒənt] *adj* [letter, case, request] urgent(e) ; [plea, voice, need] pressant(e).

urgently [ˈɜːdʒəntlɪ] *adv* d'urgence ; [appeal] d'une manière pressante.

urinal [ˌjʊəˈraɪnl] *n* urinoir *m*.

urinary [ˈjʊərɪnərɪ] *adj* urinaire.

urinate [ˈjʊərɪneɪt] *vi* uriner.

urine [ˈjʊərɪn] *n* urine *f*.

URL (*abbr of* **uniform resource locator**) *n* COMPUT URL *m* (*adresse électronique*).

urn [ɜːn] *n* - **1.** [for ashes] urne *f* - **2.** [for tea] : **tea ~** fontaine *f* à thé.

Uruguay ['jʊərəgwaɪ] *n* Uruguay *m ;* in ~ en Uruguay.

Uruguayan [ˌjʊərəˈgwaɪən] ◇ *adj* uruguayen(enne) ◇ *n* Uruguayen *m*, -enne *f*.

us [ʌs] *pers pron* nous ; **can you see/hear~?** vous nous voyez/entendez? ; **it's ~** c'est nous ; **you can't expect us to do it** vous ne pouvez pas exiger que ce soit nous qui le fassions ; **she gave it to ~** elle nous l'a donné ; **with/without ~** avec/sans nous ; **they are more wealthy than ~** ils sont plus riches que nous ; **some of ~** quelques-uns d'entre nous.

US *n abbr of* United States.

USA *n* - **1.** *abbr of* United States of America - **2.** (*abbr of* United States Army) *armée de terre américaine.*

usable ['juːzəbl] *adj* utilisable.

USAF (*abbr of* United States Air Force) *n armée de l'air américaine.*

usage ['juːzɪdʒ] *n* - **1.** LING usage *m* - **2.** *(U)* [handling, treatment] traitement *m*.

USCG (*abbr of* United States Coast Guard) *n service de surveillance côtière américain.*

USDA (*abbr of* United States Department of Agriculture) *n ministère américain de l'Agriculture.*

USDAW ['ʌzdɔː] (*abbr of* Union of Shop, Distributive and Allied Workers) *n syndicat britannique des personnels de la distribution.*

USDI (*abbr of* United States Department of the Interior) *n ministère américain de l'Intérieur.*

use [*n* & *aux vb* juːs, *vt* juːz] ◇ *n* - **1.** [act of using] utilisation *f*, emploi *m ;* **to be in ~** être utilisé ; **to be out of ~** être hors d'usage ; **to make ~ of sthg** utiliser qqch - **2.** [ability to use] usage *m ;* **to let sb have the ~ of sthg** prêter qqch à qqn - **3.** [usefulness] : **to be of ~** être utile ; **it's no ~** ça ne sert à rien ; **what's the ~ (of doing sthg)?** à quoi bon (faire qqch)? ◇ *aux vb* : **I ~d to live in London** avant j'habitais à Londres ; **he didn't ~ to be so fat** il n'était pas si gros avant ; **there ~d to be a tree here** (autrefois) il y avait un arbre ici ◇ *vt* - **1.** [gen] utiliser, se servir de, employer - **2.** pej [exploit] se servir de.

➤ **use up** *vt sep* [supply] épuiser ; [food] finir ; [money] dépenser.

used [*senses 1 and 2* juːzd, *sense 3* juːst] *adj* - **1.** [handkerchief, towel] sale - **2.** [car] d'occasion - **3.** [accustomed] : **to be ~ to sthg/to doing sthg** avoir l'habitude de qqch/de faire qqch ; **to get ~ to sthg** s'habituer à qqch.

useful ['juːsfʊl] *adj* utile ; **to cóme in ~** être utile.

usefulness ['juːsfʊlnɪs] *n (U)* utilité *f*.

useless ['juːslɪs] *adj* - **1.** [gen] inutile - **2.** inf [person] incompétent(e), nul (nulle).

uselessness ['juːslɪsnɪs] *n (U)* inutilité *f*.

Usenet® ['juːznet] *n* Usenet® *m*, forum *m* électronique.

user ['juːzə^r] *n* [of product, machine] utilisateur *m*, -trice *f ;* [of service] usager *m*.

user-friendly *adj* convivial(e), facile à utiliser.

USES (*abbr of* United States Employment Service) *n services américains de l'emploi.*

usher ['ʌʃə^r] ◇ *n* placeur *m* ◇ *vt* : **to ~ sb in/out** faire entrer/sortir qqn.

usherette [ˌʌʃəˈret] *n* ouvreuse *f*.

USIA (*abbr of* United States Information Agency) *n agence américaine de renseignements.*

USM *n* - **1.** (*abbr of* United States Mail) ≃ la Poste - **2.** (*abbr of* United States Mint) ≃ la Monnaie.

USN (*abbr of* United States Navy) *n marine de guerre américaine.*

USPHS (*abbr of* United States Public Health Service) *n aux États-Unis, Direction des affaires sanitaires et sociales.*

USS (*abbr of* United States Ship) *expression précédant le nom d'un bâtiment de la marine américaine.*

USSR (*abbr of* Union of Soviet Socialist Republics) *n* : **the (former) ~** l'(ex-)URSS *f ;* **in the ~** en URSS.

usu. *abbr of* usually.

usual ['juːʒəl] *adj* habituel(elle) ; **as ~** comme d'habitude.

usually ['juːʒəlɪ] *adv* d'habitude, d'ordinaire.

usurp [juːˈzɜːp] *vt* usurper.

usury ['juːʒʊrɪ] *n (U)* usure *f*.

UT *abbr of* Utah.

Utah ['juːtɑː] *n* Utah *m ;* **in ~** dans l'Utah.

utensil [juːˈtensl] *n* ustensile *m*.

uterus ['juːtərəs] (*pl* -ri [-raɪ] OR -ruses [-rəsiːz]) *n* utérus *m*.

utilitarian [ˌjuːtɪlɪˈteərɪən] *adj* utilitaire.

utility [juːˈtɪlətɪ] (*pl* -ies) *n* - **1.** *(U)* [usefulness] utilité *f* - **2.** [public service] service *m* public - **3.** COMPUT utilitaire *m*.

utility room *n* buanderie *f*.

utilize, -ise ['juːtəlaɪz] *vt* utiliser ; [resources] exploiter, utiliser.

utmost ['ʌtməʊst] ◇ *adj* le plus grand (la plus grande) ◇ *n* : **to do one's ~** faire tout son possible, faire l'impossible ; **to the ~** au plus haut point.

utopia [juːˈtəupjəl] n utopie f.

utter [ˈʌtəʳ] ◇ adj total(e), complet(ète) ◇ vt prononcer ; [cry] pousser.

utterly [ˈʌtəlɪ] adv complètement.

U-turn n demi-tour m ; fig revirement m.

UV (abbr of ultra-violet) UV.

UV-A, UVA (abbr of ultra-violet-A) UVA.

UV-B, UVB (abbr of ultra-violet-B) UVB.

UWIST [ˈjuːwɪst] (abbr of University of Wales Institute of Science and Technology) n institut de science et de technologie de l'université du pays de Galles.

Uzbek [ˈuzbek] ◇ adj ouzbek ◇ n - **1.** [person] Ouzbek mf - **2.** [language] ouzbek m.

Uzbekistan [uzˌbekɪˈstɑːn] n Ouzbékistan m ; **in ~** en Ouzbékistan.

v¹ (pl **v's** OR **vs**), **V** (pl **V's** OR **Vs**) [viː] n [letter] v m inv, V m inv.

v² - **1.** (abbr of verse) v. - **2.** (abbr of vide) [cross-reference] v. - **3.** abbr of versus - **4.** (abbr of volt) v.

VA abbr of Virginia.

vac (abbr of vacation) n Br inf vacances fpl.

vacancy [ˈveɪkənsɪ] (pl -ies) n - **1.** [job] poste m vacant - **2.** [room available] chambre f à louer ; 'vacancies' 'chambres à louer' ; 'no vacancies' 'complet'.

vacant [ˈveɪkənt] adj - **1.** [room] inoccupé(e) ; [chair, toilet] libre - **2.** [job, post] vacant(e) - **3.** [look, expression] distrait(e).

vacant lot n terrain m inoccupé ; [for sale] terrain m à vendre.

vacantly [ˈveɪkəntlɪ] adv d'un air distrait.

vacate [vəˈkeɪt] vt quitter.

vacation [vəˈkeɪʃn] n Am vacances fpl.

vacationer [vəˈkeɪʃənəʳ] n Am vacancier m, -ère f.

vacation resort n Am camp m de vacances.

vaccinate [ˈvæksɪneɪt] vt vacciner.

vaccination [ˌvæksɪˈneɪʃn] n vaccination f.

vaccine [Br ˈvæksiːn, Am vækˈsiːn] n vaccin m.

vacillate [ˈvæsəleɪt] vi hésiter.

vacuum [ˈvækjuəm] ◇ n - **1.** TECH & fig vide m - **2.** [cleaner] aspirateur m ◇ vt [room] passer l'aspirateur dans ; [carpet] passer à l'aspirateur.

vacuum cleaner n aspirateur m.

vacuum-packed adj emballé(e) sous vide.

vacuum pump n pompe f à vide.

vagabond [ˈvægəbɒnd] n literary vagabond m, -e f.

vagaries [ˈveɪgərɪz] npl caprices mpl.

vagina [vəˈdʒaɪnə] n vagin m.

vagrancy [ˈveɪgrənsɪ] n vagabondage m.

vagrant [ˈveɪgrənt] n vagabond m, -e f.

vague [veɪg] adj - **1.** [gen] vague, imprécis(e) - **2.** [absent-minded] distrait(e).

vaguely [ˈveɪglɪ] adv vaguement.

vain [veɪn] adj - **1.** [futile, worthless] vain(e) - **2.** pej [conceited] vaniteux(euse).
➡ **in vain** adv en vain, vainement.

vainly [ˈveɪnlɪ] adv - **1.** [in vain] en vain, vainement - **2.** [conceitedly] avec vanité.

valance [ˈvæləns] n - **1.** [on bed] tour m de lit - **2.** Am [over window] cantonnière f.

vale [veɪl] n literary val m.

valedictory [ˌvælɪˈdɪktərɪ] adj fml d'adieu.

valentine card [ˈvæləntaɪn-] n carte f de la Saint-Valentin.

Valentine's Day [ˈvæləntaɪnz-] n : **(St) ~** la Saint-Valentin.

valet [ˈvæleɪ, ˈvælɪt] n valet m de chambre.

valet parking n : '~' 'voiturier'.

valet service n - **1.** [for clothes] service m pressing - **2.** [for cars] nettoyage m complet.

Valetta, Valleta [vəˈletə] n la Valette.

valiant [ˈvæljənt] adj vaillant(e).

valid [ˈvælɪd] adj - **1.** [reasonable] valable - **2.** [legally usable] valide.

validate [ˈvælɪdeɪt] vt valider.

validity [vəˈlɪdətɪ] n validité f.

Valium® [ˈvælɪəm] n Valium® m.

Valletta = Valetta.

valley [ˈvælɪ] (pl -s) n vallée f.

valour Br, **valor** Am [ˈvæləʳ] n (U) fml & literary bravoure f.

valuable [ˈvæljuəbl] adj - **1.** [advice, time, information] précieux(euse) - **2.** [object, jewel] de valeur.

◆ **valuables** *npl* objets *mpl* de valeur.

valuation [ˌvælju'eɪʃn] *n* - **1.** *(U)* [pricing] estimation *f*, expertise *f* - **2.** [estimated price] valeur *f* estimée - **3.** [opinion] opinion *f*.

value ['vælju:] ◇ *n* valeur *f*; **to be good ~** être d'un bon rapport qualité-prix ; **to place a high ~ on sthg** accorder beaucoup de valeur à qqch ; **to get ~ for money** en avoir pour son argent ; **to take sb/sthg at face ~** prendre qqn/qqch au pied de la lettre ◇ *vt* - **1.** [estimate price of] expertiser - **2.** [cherish] apprécier.

◆ **values** *npl* [morals] valeurs *fpl*.

value-added tax [-ædɪd-] *n* taxe *f* sur la valeur ajoutée.

valued ['vælju:d] *adj* précieux(euse).

value judg(e)ment *n* jugement *m* de valeur.

valuer ['væljuə'] *n* expert *m*.

valve [vælv] *n* [on tyre] valve *f*; TECH soupape *f*.

vamoose [və'mu:s] *vi* inf s'éclipser.

vampire ['væmpaɪə'] *n* vampire *m*.

van [væn] *n* - **1.** AUT camionnette *f* - **2.** Br RAIL fourgon *m*.

V and A (*abbr of* **Victoria and Albert Museum**) *n* grand musée londonien des arts décoratifs.

vandal ['vændl] *n* vandale *mf*.

vandalism ['vændəlɪzm] *n* vandalisme *m*.

vandalize, -ise ['vændəlaɪz] *vt* saccager.

vanguard ['vænɡɑ:d] *n* avant-garde *f*; **in the ~ of** à l'avant-garde de.

vanilla [və'nɪlə] ◇ *n* vanille *f* ◇ *comp* [ice cream, yoghurt] à la vanille.

vanish ['vænɪʃ] *vi* disparaître.

vanishing point ['vænɪʃɪŋ-] *n* point *m* de fuite.

vanity ['vænətɪ] *n* *(U)* pej vanité *f*.

vanity unit *n* élément de salle de bains avec lavabo encastré.

vanquish ['væŋkwɪʃ] *vt* literary vaincre.

vantagepoint ['vɑ:ntɪdʒ,pɔɪnt] *n* [for view] bon endroit *m* ; fig position *f* avantageuse.

vapour Br, **vapor** Am ['veɪpə'] *n* *(U)* vapeur *f* ; [condensation] buée *f*.

vapour trail *n* traînée *f* de vapeur.

variable ['veərɪəbl] ◇ *adj* variable ; [mood] changeant(e) ◇ *n* variable *f*.

variance ['veərɪəns] *n* fml : **at ~ (with)** en désaccord (avec).

variant ['veərɪənt] ◇ *adj* différent(e) ◇ *n* variante *f*.

variation [ˌveərɪ'eɪʃn] *n* : **~ (in)** variation *f* (de).

varicose veins ['værɪkəus-] *npl* varices *fpl*.

varied ['veərɪd] *adj* varié(e).

variety [və'raɪətɪ] (*pl* **-ies**) *n* - **1.** [gen] variété *f* - **2.** [type] variété *f*, sorte *f*.

variety show *n* spectacle *m* de variétés.

various ['veərɪəs] *adj* - **1.** [several] plusieurs - **2.** [different] divers.

varnish ['vɑ:nɪʃ] ◇ *n* vernis *m* ◇ *vt* vernir.

varnished ['vɑ:nɪʃt] *adj* verni(e).

vary ['veərɪ] (*pt* & *pt* **-ied**) ◇ *vt* varier ◇ *vi* : **to ~ (in/with)** varier (en/selon), changer (en/selon).

varying ['veərɪŋ] *adj* qui varie, variable.

vascular ['væskjulə'] *adj* vasculaire.

vase [Br vɑ:z, Am veɪz] *n* vase *m*.

vasectomy [və'sektəmɪ] (*pl* **-ies**) *n* vasectomie *f*.

Vaseline® ['væsəli:n] *n* vaseline *f*.

vast [vɑ:st] *adj* vaste, immense.

vastly ['vɑ:stlɪ] *adv* extrêmement, infiniment.

vastness ['vɑ:stnɪs] *n* immensité *f*.

vat [væt] *n* cuve *f*.

VAT [væt, ˌvi:eɪ'ti:] (*abbr of* **value added tax**) *n* TVA *f*.

Vatican ['vætɪkən] *n* : **the ~** le Vatican.

Vatican City *n* l'État *m* de la cité du Vatican, le Vatican ; **in ~** au Vatican.

vault [vɔ:lt] ◇ *n* - **1.** [in bank] chambre *f* forte - **2.** [roof] voûte *f* - **3.** [jump] saut *m* - **4.** [in church] caveau *m* ◇ *vt* sauter ◇ *vi* : **to ~ over sthg** sauter (par-dessus) qqch.

vaulted ['vɔ:ltɪd] *adj* voûté(e).

vaulting horse ['vɔ:ltɪŋ-] *n* cheval-d'arçons *m inv*.

vaunted ['vɔ:ntɪd] *adj* fml : **much ~** tant vanté(e).

VC *n* - **1.** (*abbr of* **vice-chairman**) vice-président *m* - **2.** (*abbr of* **Victoria·Cross**) la plus haute distinction militaire britannique.

VCR (*abbr of* **video cassette recorder**) *n* magnétoscope *m*.

VD (*abbr of* **venereal disease**) *n* *(U)* MST *f*.

VDU (*abbr of* **visual display unit**) *n* moniteur *m*.

veal [vi:l] *n* *(U)* veau *m*.

veer [vɪə'] *vi* virer.

veg [vedʒ] *n* inf - **1.** (*abbr of* **vegetable**) légume *m* - **2.** (*U*) (*abbr of* **vegetables**) légumes *mpl*.

vegan ['vi:gən] <> *adj* végétalien(enne) <> *n* végétalien *m*, -enne *f*.

vegetable ['vedʒtəbl] <> *n* légume *m* <> *adj* [matter, protein] végétal(e) ; [soup, casserole] de OR aux légumes.

vegetable garden *n* jardin *m* potager.

vegetable knife *n* couteau *m* à légumes.

vegetable oil *n* huile *f* végétale.

vegetarian [,vedʒɪ'teəriən] <> *adj* végétarien(enne) <> *n* végétarien *m*, -enne *f*.

vegetarianism [,vedʒɪ'teəriənɪzm] *n* végétarisme *m*.

vegetate ['vedʒteɪt] *vi pej* végéter.

vegetation [,vedʒɪ'teɪʃn] *n* (*U*) végétation *f*.

veggie ['vedʒɪ] (*abbr of* **vegetarian**) Br *inf* <> *adj* végétarien(enne) <> *n* végétarien *m*, -enne *f*.

vehement ['vi:ɪmənt] *adj* véhément(e).

vehemently ['vi:ɪməntlɪ] *adv* avec véhémence.

vehicle ['vi:ɪkl] *n lit* & *fig* véhicule *m*.

vehicular [vɪ'hɪkjʊləʳ] *adj fml* [transport] de véhicules ; ~ **traffic** circulation *f*.

veil [veɪl] *n lit* & *fig* voile *m*.

veiled [veɪld] *adj* [threat, reference] voilé(e).

vein [veɪn] *n* - **1.** ANAT veine *f* - **2.** [of leaf] nervure *f* - **3.** [of mineral] filon *m* - **4.** [mood] : **in the same** ~ dans le même style.

Velcro® ['velkrəʊ] *n* Velcro® *m*.

vellum ['veləm] *n* vélin *m*.

velocity [vɪ'lɒsətɪ] (*pl* **-ies**) *n* vélocité *f*.

velour [və'lʊəʳ] *n* velours *m*.

velvet ['velvɪt] <> *n* velours *m* <> *comp* de OR en velours.

vend [vend] *vt fml* & JUR vendre.

vendetta [ven'detə] *n* vendetta *f*.

vending machine ['vendɪŋ-] *n* distributeur *m* automatique.

vendor ['vendəʳ] *n* - **1.** *fml* [salesperson] marchand *m*, -e *f* - **2.** JUR vendeur *m*, -eresse *f*.

veneer [və'nɪəʳ] *n* placage *m* ; *fig* apparence *f*.

venerable ['venərəbl] *adj* vénérable.

venerate ['venəreɪt] *vt* vénérer.

venereal disease [vɪ'nɪərɪəl-] *n* maladie *f* vénérienne.

Venetian [vɪ'ni:ʃn] <> *adj* vénitien(enne) <> *n* Vénitien *m*, -enne *f*.

venetian blind [vɪ,ni:ʃn-] *n* store *m* vénitien.

Venezuela [,veniz'weilə] *n* Venezuela *m* ; **in** ~ au Venezuela.

Venezuelan [,veniz'weilən] <> *adj* vénézuélien(enne) <> *n* Vénézuélien *m*, -enne *f*.

vengeance ['vendʒəns] *n* vengeance *f* ; **it began raining with a** ~ il a commencé à pleuvoir très fort ; **she's back with a** ~ elle fait un retour en force.

vengeful ['vendʒfʊl] *adj* vengeur(eresse).

Venice ['venɪs] *n* Venise.

venison ['venɪzn] *n* venaison *f*.

venom ['venəm] *n lit* & *fig* venin *m*.

venomous ['venəməs] *adj lit* & *fig* venimeux(euse).

vent [vent] <> *n* [pipe] tuyau *m* ; [opening] orifice *m* ; **to give** ~ **to** donner libre cours à <> *vt* [anger, feelings] donner libre cours à ; **to** ~ **sthg on sb** décharger qqch sur qqn.

ventilate ['ventɪleɪt] *vt* ventiler.

ventilation [,ventɪ'leɪʃn] *n* ventilation *f*.

ventilator ['ventɪleɪtəʳ] *n* ventilateur *m*.

Ventimiglia [ventɪ'mɪljə] *n* Vintimille.

ventriloquist [ven'trɪləkwɪst] *n* ventriloque *mf*.

venture ['ventʃəʳ] <> *n* entreprise *f* <> *vt* risquer ; **to** ~ **to do sthg** se permettre de faire qqch <> *vi* s'aventurer.

venture capital *n* capital-risque *m*.

venturesome ['ventʃəsəm] *adj* - **1.** [person] téméraire - **2.** [action] risqué(e).

venue ['venju:] *n* lieu *m*.

Venus ['vi:nəs] *n* [planet] Vénus *f*.

veracity [və'ræsətɪ] *n* véracité *f*.

veranda(h) [və'rændə] *n* véranda *f*.

verb [vɜ:b] *n* verbe *m*.

verbal ['vɜ:bl] *adj* verbal(e).

verbally ['vɜ:bəlɪ] *adv* verbalement.

verbatim [vɜ:'beɪtɪm] *adj* & *adv* mot pour mot.

verbose [vɜ:'bəʊs] *adj* verbeux(euse).

verdict ['vɜ:dɪkt] *n* - **1.** JUR verdict *m* - **2.** [opinion] : ~ **(on)** avis *m* (sur).

verge [vɜ:dʒ] *n* - **1.** [of lawn] bordure *f* ; [of road] bas-côté *m*, accotement *m* - **2.** [brink] : **on the** ~ **of sthg** au bord de qqch ; **on the** ~ **of doing sthg** sur le point de faire qqch.
➡ **verge (up)on** *vt fus* friser, approcher de.

verger ['vɜ:dʒəʳ] *n* bedeau *m*.

verification [,verɪfɪ'keɪʃn] *n* vérification *f*.

verify ['verɪfaɪ] (*pt* & *pp* **-ied**) *vt* vérifier.

veritable ['verɪtəbl] *adj hum* or *fml* véritable.

vermilion [vəˈmɪljən] ◇ adj vermillon (inv) ◇ n vermillon m.

vermin [ˈvɜːmɪn] npl vermine f.

Vermont [vɜːˈmɒnt] n Vermont m ; **in** ~ dans le Vermont.

vermouth [ˈvɜːməθ] n vermouth m.

vernacular [vəˈnækjʊləʳ] ◇ adj vernaculaire ◇ n dialecte m.

verruca [vəˈruːkə] (pl **-cas** OR **-cae** [-kaɪ]) n verrue f plantaire.

versa ▷ vice versa.

versatile [ˈvɜːsətaɪl] adj [person, player] aux talents multiples ; [machine, tool, food] souple d'emploi.

versatility [ˌvɜːsəˈtɪlətɪ] n [of person] variété f de talents ; [of machine, tool] souplesse f d'emploi.

verse [vɜːs] n - **1.** (U) [poetry] vers mpl - **2.** [stanza] strophe f - **3.** [in Bible] verset m.

versed [vɜːst] adj : **to be well** ~ **in sthg** être versé(e) dans qqch.

version [ˈvɜːʃn] n version f.

versus [ˈvɜːsəs] prep - **1.** SPORT contre - **2.** [as opposed to] par opposition à.

vertebra [ˈvɜːtɪbrə] (pl **-brae** [-briː]) n vertèbre f.

vertebrate [ˈvɜːtɪbreɪt] n vertébré m.

vertical [ˈvɜːtɪkl] adj vertical(e).

vertical integration n FIN intégration f verticale.

vertically [ˈvɜːtɪklɪ] adv verticalement.

vertigo [ˈvɜːtɪɡəʊ] n (U) vertige m ; **to suffer from** ~ avoir le vertige.

verve [vɜːv] n verve f.

very [ˈverɪ] ◇ adv - **1.** [as intensifier] très ; ~ **much** beaucoup - **2.** [as euphemism] : **not** ~ pas très ◇ adj : **the** ~ **room/book** la pièce/le livre même ; **the** ~ **man/thing I've been looking for** juste l'homme/la chose que je cherchais ; **at the** ~ **least** tout au moins ; ~ **last/first** tout dernier/premier ; **of one's** ~ **own** bien à soi.

➤ **very well** adv très bien ; **I can't** ~ **well tell him ...** je ne peux tout de même pas lui dire que ...

vespers [ˈvespəz] n (U) vêpres fpl.

vessel [ˈvesl] n fml - **1.** [boat] vaisseau m - **2.** [container] récipient m.

vest [vest] n - **1.** Br [undershirt] maillot m de corps - **2.** Am [waistcoat] gilet m.

vested interest [ˈvestɪd-] n : ~ **(in)** intérêt m particulier (à).

vestibule [ˈvestɪbjuːl] n - **1.** fml [entrance hall] vestibule m - **2.** Am [on train] sas m.

vestige [ˈvestɪdʒ] n vestige m.

vestry [ˈvestrɪ] (pl **-ies**) n sacristie f.

Vesuvius [vɪˈsuːvjəs] n le Vésuve.

vet [vet] (pt & pp **-ted** ; cont **-ting**) ◇ n - **1.** (abbr of **veterinary surgeon**) vétérinaire mf - **2.** Am (abbr of **veteran**) ancien combattant m, vétéran m ◇ vt [candidates] examiner avec soin.

veteran [ˈvetrən] ◇ adj [experienced] chevronné(e) ◇ n - **1.** MIL ancien combattant m, vétéran m - **2.** [experienced person] vétéran m.

veteran car n Br voiture f d'époque (construite avant 1905).

Veteran's Day n aux États-Unis, fête nationale en l'honneur des anciens combattants (le 11 novembre).

veterinarian [ˌvetərɪˈneərɪən] n Am vétérinaire mf.

veterinary science [ˈvetərɪnrɪ-] n science f vétérinaire.

veterinary surgeon [ˈvetərɪnrɪ-] n Br fml vétérinaire mf.

veto [ˈviːtəʊ] (pl **-es**, pt & pp **-ed** ; cont **-ing**) ◇ n veto m ◇ vt opposer son veto à.

vetting [ˈvetɪŋ] n (U) [of candidates] examen m minutieux.

vex [veks] vt contrarier.

vexed question [ˌvekst-] n question f controversée.

VFD (abbr of **voluntary fire department**) n pompiers bénévoles aux États-Unis.

vg (abbr of **very good**) tb.

vgc (abbr of **very good condition**) TBE, tbe.

VHF (abbr of **very high frequency**) VHF.

VHS (abbr of **video home system**) n VHS m.

VI abbr of **Virgin Islands**.

via [ˈvaɪə] prep - **1.** [travelling through] via, par - **2.** [by means of] au moyen de.

viability [ˌvaɪəˈbɪlətɪ] n viabilité f.

viable [ˈvaɪəbl] adj viable.

viaduct [ˈvaɪədʌkt] n viaduc m.

vibrant [ˈvaɪbrənt] adj vibrant(e).

vibrate [vaɪˈbreɪt] vi vibrer.

vibration [vaɪˈbreɪʃn] n vibration f.

vicar [ˈvɪkəʳ] n [in Church of England] pasteur m.

vicarage [ˈvɪkərɪdʒ] n presbytère m.

vicarious [vɪˈkeərɪəs] adj : **to take a** ~ **pleasure in sthg** retirer du plaisir indirectement de qqch.

vice [vaɪs] *n* - **1.** [immorality, fault] vice *m* - **2.** [tool] étau *m*.

vice- [vaɪs] *prefix* vice-.

vice-admiral *n* vice-amiral *m*.

vice-chairman *n* vice-président *m*, -e *f*.

vice-chancellor *n* UNIV président *m*, -e *f*.

vice-president *n* vice-président *m*, -e *f*.

vice squad *n* brigade *f* des mœurs.

vice versa [ˌvaɪsɪ'vɜːsə] *adv* vice versa.

vicinity [vɪ'sɪnətɪ] *n* : in the ~ (of) aux alentours (de), dans les environs (de).

vicious [ˈvɪʃəs] *adj* violent(e), brutal(e).

vicious circle *n* cercle *m* vicieux.

viciousness [ˈvɪʃəsnɪs] *n* violence *f*, brutalité *f*.

vicissitudes [vɪ'sɪsɪtjuːdz] *npl* fml vicissitudes *fpl*.

victim [ˈvɪktɪm] *n* victime *f*.

victimize, -ise [ˈvɪktɪmaɪz] *vt* faire une victime de.

victor [ˈvɪktəʳ] *n* vainqueur *m*.

Victoria Cross [vɪk'tɔːrɪə-] *n* Croix *f* de Victoria.

Victoria Falls [vɪk'tɔːrɪə-] *npl* les chutes *fpl* Victoria.

Victorian [vɪk'tɔːrɪən] *adj* victorien(enne).

Victoriana [ˌvɪktɔːrɪ'ɑːnə] *n* (U) objets *mpl* de l'époque victorienne.

victorious [vɪk'tɔːrɪəs] *adj* victorieux(euse).

victory [ˈvɪktərɪ] (*pl* -ies) *n* : ~ (over) victoire *f* (sur).

video [ˈvɪdɪəʊ] (*pl* -s, *pt* & *pp* -ed ; *cont* -ing) ◇ *n* - **1.** [medium, recording] vidéo *f* - **2.** [machine] magnétoscope *m* - **3.** [cassette] vidéocassette *f* ◇ *comp* vidéo (*inv*) ◇ *vt* - **1.** [using video recorder] enregistrer sur magnétoscope - **2.** [using camera] faire une vidéo de, filmer.

video camera *n* caméra *f* vidéo.

video cassette *n* vidéocassette *f*.

videoconference [ˈvɪdɪəʊˈkɒnfərəns] *n* vidéoconférence *f*.

videodisc Br, **videodisk** Am [ˈvɪdɪəʊdɪsk] *n* vidéodisque *m*.

video game *n* jeu *m* vidéo.

video machine *n* magnétoscope *m*.

video-on-demand *n* service de location de vidéos par câble.

videophone [ˈvɪdɪəʊfəʊn] *n* vidéophone *m*, visiophone *m*.

videorecorder [ˈvɪdɪəʊrɪˌkɔːdəʳ] *n* magnétoscope *m*.

video recording *n* enregistrement *m* vidéo.

video shop *n* vidéoclub *m*.

videotape [ˈvɪdɪəʊteɪp] *n* - **1.** [cassette] vidéocassette *f* - **2.** (U) [ribbon] bande *f* vidéo.

vie [vaɪ] (*pt* & *pp* vied ; *cont* vying) *vi* : to ~ for sthg lutter pour qqch ; to ~ with sb (for sthg/to do sthg) rivaliser avec qqn (pour qqch/pour faire qqch).

Vienna [vɪ'enə] *n* Vienne.

Viennese [ˌvɪə'niːz] ◇ *adj* viennois(e) ◇ *n* Viennois *m*, -e *f*.

Vietnam [Br ˌvjet'næm, Am ˌvjet'nɑːm] *n* Viêt-nam *m* ; in ~ au Viêt-nam.

Vietnamese [ˌvjetnə'miːz] ◇ *adj* vietnamien(enne) ◇ *n* [language] vietnamien *m* ◇ *npl* : the ~ les Vietnamiens.

view [vjuː] ◇ *n* - **1.** [opinion] opinion *f*, avis *m* ; ~ on sthg opinion sur qqch ; in my ~ à mon avis ; to take the ~ that ... être d'avis que ... - **2.** [scene, ability to see] vue *f* ; to come into ~ apparaître ◇ *vt* - **1.** [consider] considérer - **2.** [examine - gen] examiner ; [- house] visiter.

➡ **in view of** *prep* vu, étant donné.

➡ **with a view to** *conj* dans l'intention de, avec l'idée de.

viewdata [ˈvjuːˌdeɪtə] *n* vidéotex *m*.

viewer [ˈvjuːəʳ] *n* - **1.** TV téléspectateur *m*, -trice *f* - **2.** [for slides] visionneuse *f*.

viewfinder [ˈvjuːˌfaɪndəʳ] *n* viseur *m*.

viewpoint [ˈvjuːpɔɪnt] *n* point *m* de vue.

vigil [ˈvɪdʒɪl] *n* veille *f* ; RELIG vigile *f*.

vigilance [ˈvɪdʒɪləns] *n* vigilance *f*.

vigilant [ˈvɪdʒɪlənt] *adj* vigilant(e).

vigilante [ˌvɪdʒɪ'læntɪ] *n* membre *m* d'un groupe d'autodéfense.

vigor Am = vigour.

vigorous [ˈvɪɡərəs] *adj* vigoureux(euse).

vigour Br, **vigor** Am [ˈvɪɡəʳ] *n* vigueur *f*.

Viking [ˈvaɪkɪŋ] ◇ *adj* viking (*inv*) ◇ *n* Viking *mf*.

vile [vaɪl] *adj* [mood] massacrant(e), exécrable ; [person, act] vil(e), ignoble ; [food] infect(e), exécrable.

vilify [ˈvɪlɪfaɪ] (*pt* & *pp* -ied) *vt* calomnier.

villa [ˈvɪlə] *n* villa *f* ; [bungalow] pavillon *m*.

village [ˈvɪlɪdʒ] *n* village *m*.

villager [ˈvɪlɪdʒəʳ] *n* villageois *m*, -e *f*.

villain [ˈvɪlən] *n* - **1.** [of film, book] méchant *m*, -e *f* ; [of play] traître *m* - **2.** [criminal] bandit *m*.

Vilnius [ˈvɪlnɪəs] *n* Vilnious.

VIN (*abbr of* vehicle identification number) *n* numéro d'immatriculation.

vinaigrette [,vɪnɪ'gret] n vinaigrette f.

vindicate ['vɪndɪkeɪt] vt justifier.

vindication [,vɪndɪ'keɪʃn] n justification f.

vindictive [vɪn'dɪktɪv] adj vindicatif(ive).

vine [vaɪn] n vigne f.

vinegar ['vɪnɪgəʳ] n vinaigre m.

vine leaf n feuille f de vigne.

vineyard ['vɪnjəd] n vignoble m.

vintage ['vɪntɪdʒ] <> adj - **1.** [wine] de grand cru - **2.** [classic] typique <> n année f, millésime m.

vintage car n Br voiture f d'époque (construite entre 1919 et 1930).

vintage wine n vin m de grand cru.

vintner ['vɪntnəʳ] n négociant m en vins.

vinyl ['vaɪnɪl] <> n vinyle m <> comp de or en vinyle.

viola [vɪ'əʊlə] n alto m.

violate ['vaɪəleɪt] vt violer.

violation [,vaɪə'leɪʃn] n violation f.

violence ['vaɪələns] n violence f.

violent ['vaɪələnt] adj - **1.** [gen] violent(e) - **2.** [colour] criard(e).

violently ['vaɪələntlɪ] adv violemment ; [die] de mort violente.

violet ['vaɪələt] <> adj violet(ette) <> n - **1.** [flower] violette f - **2.** [colour] violet m.

violin [,vaɪə'lɪn] n violon m.

violinist [,vaɪə'lɪnɪst] n violoniste mf.

VIP (abbr of very important person) n VIP mf.

viper ['vaɪpəʳ] n vipère f.

viral ['vaɪrəl] adj viral(e).

virgin ['vɜːdʒɪn] <> adj literary [land, forest, soil] vierge <> n [woman] vierge f ; [man] garçon m/ homme m vierge.

Virginia [və'dʒɪnjə] n Virginie f ; in ~ en Virginie.

Virgin Islands n : the ~ les îles fpl Vierges ; in the ~ dans les îles Vierges.

virginity [və'dʒɪnətɪ] n virginité f.

Virgo ['vɜːgəʊ] (pl -s) n Vierge f ; to be (a) ~ être Vierge.

virile ['vɪraɪl] adj viril(e).

virility [vɪ'rɪlətɪ] n virilité f.

virtual ['vɜːtʃʊəl] adj virtuel(elle) ; it's a ~ certainty c'est quasiment or pratiquement certain.

virtually ['vɜːtʃʊəlɪ] adv virtuellement, pratiquement.

virtual memory n COMPUT mémoire f virtuelle.

virtual reality n réalité f virtuelle.

virtue ['vɜːtjuː] n - **1.** [good quality] vertu f - **2.** [benefit] : ~ (in doing sthg) mérite m (à faire qqch).
  by virtue of prep fml en vertu de.

virtuoso [,vɜːtjʊ'əʊzəʊ] (pl -sos OR -si [-siː]) n virtuose m.

virtuous ['vɜːtʃʊəs] adj vertueux(euse).

virulent ['vɪrʊlənt] adj virulent(e).

virus ['vaɪrəs] n COMPUT & MED virus m.

visa ['viːzə] n visa m.

vis-à-vis [,viːzɑː'viː] prep fml par rapport à.

viscose ['vɪskəʊs] n viscose f.

viscosity [vɪ'skɒsətɪ] n viscosité f.

viscount ['vaɪkaʊnt] n vicomte m.

viscous ['vɪskəs] adj visqueux(euse).

vise [vaɪs] n Am étau m.

visibility [,vɪzɪ'bɪlətɪ] n visibilité f.

visible ['vɪzəbl] adj visible.

visibly ['vɪzəblɪ] adv visiblement.

vision ['vɪʒn] n - **1.** (U) [ability to see] vue f - **2.** [foresight, dream] vision f - **3.** (U) TV image f.

visionary ['vɪʒənrɪ] (pl -ies) <> adj visionnaire <> n visionnaire mf.

visit ['vɪzɪt] <> n visite f ; on a ~ en visite <> vt [person] rendre visite à ; [place] visiter.
  visit with vt fus Am - **1.** [go and see] aller voir - **2.** [chat to] parler avec.

visiting card ['vɪzɪtɪŋ-] n carte f de visite.

visiting hours ['vɪzɪtɪŋ-] npl heures fpl de visite.

visitor ['vɪzɪtəʳ] n [to person] invité m, -e f ; [to place] visiteur m, -euse f ; [to hotel] client m, -e f.

visitors' book n livre m d'or ; [in hotel] registre m.

visitor's passport n Br passeport m temporaire.

visor ['vaɪzəʳ] n visière f.

vista ['vɪstə] n [view] vue f.

VISTA ['vɪstə] (abbr of Volunteers in Service to America) n programme américain d'aide aux personnes les plus défavorisées.

visual ['vɪʒʊəl] adj visuel(elle).

visual aids npl supports mpl visuels.

visual display unit n écran m de visualisation.

visualize, -ise ['vɪʒʊəlaɪz] vt se représenter, s'imaginer.

visually ['vɪʒʊəlɪ] adv visuellement ; ~ handicapped malvoyant(e).

vital ['vaɪtl] *adj* - **1.** [essential] essentiel(elle) - **2.** [full of life] plein(e) d'entrain.

vitality [vaɪ'tælətɪ] *n* vitalité *f*.

vitally ['vaɪtəlɪ] *adv* absolument.

vital statistics *npl* inf [of woman] mensurations *fpl*.

vitamin [Br 'vɪtəmɪn, Am 'vaɪtəmɪn] *n* vitamine *f*.

vitriolic [,vɪtrɪ'ɒlɪk] *adj* au vitriol.

viva ['vaɪvə] = **viva voce**.

vivacious [vɪ'veɪʃəs] *adj* enjoué(e).

vivacity [vɪ'væsətɪ] *n* vivacité *f*.

viva voce [,vaɪvə'vəʊsɪ] *n* examen *m* oral.

vivid ['vɪvɪd] *adj* - **1.** [bright] vif (vive) - **2.** [clear - description] vivant(e) ; [- memory] net (nette), précis(e).

vividly ['vɪvɪdlɪ] *adv* [describe] d'une manière vivante ; [remember] clairement.

vivisection [,vɪvɪ'sekʃn] *n* vivisection *f*.

vixen ['vɪksn] *n* [fox] renarde *f*.

viz [vɪz] (*abbr of* vide licet) c.-à-d.

VLF (*abbr of* very low frequency) *n* très basse fréquence.

V-neck *n* [neck] décolleté *m* en V ; [sweater] pull *m* à décolleté en V.

VOA (*abbr of* Voice of America) *n* station radiophonique américaine à destination de l'étranger.

vocabulary [və'kæbjʊlərɪ] (*pl* -ies) *n* vocabulaire *m*.

vocal ['vəʊkl] *adj* - **1.** [outspoken] qui se fait entendre - **2.** [of the voice] vocal(e).

➤ **vocals** *npl* chant *m*.

vocal cords *npl* cordes *fpl* vocales.

vocalist ['vəʊkəlɪst] *n* chanteur *m*, -euse *f* (*dans un groupe*).

vocation [vəʊ'keɪʃn] *n* vocation *f*.

vocational [vəʊ'keɪʃənl] *adj* professionnel(elle).

vociferous [və'sɪfərəs] *adj* bruyant(e).

vodka ['vɒdkə] *n* vodka *f*.

vogue [vəʊg] *adj* en vogue, à la mode ◇ *n* vogue *f*, mode *f* ; **in ~** en vogue, à la mode

voice [vɔɪs] ◇ *n* - **1.** [gen] voix *f* ; **to raise/lower one's ~** élever/baisser la voix ; **to keep one's ~ down** parler bas - **2.** [influence] : **to have a ~ in** avoir son mot à dire dans ◇ *vt* [opinion, emotion] exprimer.

voice box *n* larynx *m*.

voice mail *n* COMPUT messagerie *f* vocale ; **to send/receive ~** envoyer/recevoir un message sur une boîte vocale.

voice-over *n* voix *f* off.

void [vɔɪd] ◇ *adj* - **1.** [invalid] nul (nulle) ➭ **null** - **2.** fml [empty] : **~ of** dépourvu(e) de, dénué(e) de ◇ *n* vide *m*.

voile [vɔɪl] *n* (U) voile *m*.

vol. (*abbr of* volume) vol.

volatile [Br 'vɒlətaɪl, Am 'vɒlətl] *adj* [situation] explosif(ive) ; [person] lunatique, versatile ; [market] instable.

vol-au-vent ['vɒləʊvɒ̃] *n* vol-au-vent *m inv*.

volcanic [vɒl'kænɪk] *adj* volcanique.

volcano [vɒl'keɪnəʊ] (*pl* -es OR -s) *n* volcan *m*.

vole [vəʊl] *n* campagnol *m*.

Volga ['vɒlgə] *n* : **the (River) ~** la Volga.

volition [və'lɪʃn] *n* fml : **of one's own ~** de son propre gré.

volley ['vɒlɪ] (*pl* -s) ◇ *n* - **1.** [of gunfire] salve *f* - **2.** fig [of questions, curses] torrent *m* ; [of blows] volée *f*, pluie *f* - **3.** SPORT volée *f* ◇ *vt* frapper à la volée, reprendre de volée.

volleyball ['vɒlɪbɔːl] *n* volley-ball *m*.

volt [vəʊlt] *n* volt *m*.

Volta ['vɒltə] *n* Volta *f*.

voltage ['vəʊltɪdʒ] *n* voltage *m*, tension *f*.

voluble ['vɒljʊbl] *adj* volubile, loquace.

volume ['vɒljuːm] *n* - **1.** [gen] volume *m* - **2.** [of work, letters] quantité *f* ; [of traffic] densité *f*.

volume control *n* réglage *m* du volume.

voluminous [və'luːmɪnəs] *adj* fml - **1.** [garment] immense - **2.** [container] volumineux(euse).

voluntarily [Br 'vɒləntrɪlɪ, Am ,vɒlən'terəlɪ] *adv* volontairement.

voluntary ['vɒləntrɪ] *adj* - **1.** [not obligatory] volontaire - **2.** [unpaid] bénévole.

voluntary liquidation *n* liquidation *f* volontaire.

voluntary redundancy *n* Br départ *m* volontaire.

volunteer [,vɒlən'tɪər] ◇ *n* - **1.** [gen & MIL] volontaire *mf* - **2.** [unpaid worker] bénévole *mf* ◇ *vt* - **1.** [offer] : **to ~ to do sthg** se proposer OR se porter volontaire pour faire qqch - **2.** [information, advice] donner spontanément ◇ *vi* - **1.** [offer one's services] : **to ~ (for)** se porter volontaire (pour), proposer ses services (pour) - **2.** MIL s'engager comme volontaire.

voluptuous [və'lʌptʃʊəs] *adj* voluptueux(euse).

vomit ['vɒmɪt] ◇ *n* vomi *m* ◇ *vi* vomir.

voracious [və'reɪʃəs] *adj* vorace.

vortex ['vɔːteks] (*pl* -texes [-teksɪːz] OR -tices [-tɪsɪːz]) *n* vortex *m* ; fig [of events] tourbillon *m*.

vote [vəʊt] ◇ *n* - **1.** [individual decision] : **~ (for/against)** vote *m* (pour/contre), voix *f* (pour/contre) - **2.** [ballot] vote *m* ; **to put sthg to the ~** procéder à un vote sur qqch - **3.** [right to vote] droit *m* de vote ◇ *vt* - **1.** [declare] élire - **2.** [choose] : **to ~ to do sthg** voter OR se prononcer pour faire qqch ; **they ~d to return to work** ils ont voté le retour au travail ◇ *vi* : **to ~ (for/against)** voter (pour/contre).
◆ **vote in** *vt sep* élire.
◆ **vote out** *vt sep* évincer par un vote.

vote of confidence (*pl* **votes of confidence**) *n* vote *m* de confiance.

vote of no confidence (*pl* **votes of no confidence**) *n* motion *f* de censure.

vote of thanks (*pl* **votes of thanks**) *n* discours *m* de remerciement.

voter [ˈvəʊtəʳ] *n* électeur *m*, -trice *f*.

voting [ˈvəʊtɪŋ] *n* scrutin *m*.

vouch [vaʊtʃ] ◆ **vouch for** *vt fus* répondre de, se porter garant de.

voucher [ˈvaʊtʃəʳ] *n* bon *m*, coupon *m*.

vow [vaʊ] ◇ *n* vœu *m*, serment *m* ◇ *vt* : **to ~ to do sthg** jurer de faire qqch ; **to ~ (that)** ... jurer que ...

vowel [ˈvaʊəl] *n* voyelle *f*.

voyage [ˈvɔɪɪdʒ] *n* voyage *m* en mer ; [in space] vol *m*.

voyeur [vwɑːˈjɜːʳ] *n* voyeur *m*, -euse *f*.

voyeurism [vwɑːˈjɜːrɪzm] *n* voyeurisme *m*.

VP *n abbr of* **vice-president.**

vs *abbr of* **versus.**

VSO (*abbr of* **Voluntary Service Overseas**) *n* *organisation britannique envoyant des travailleurs bénévoles dans des pays en voie de développement pour contribuer à leur développement technique.*

VSOP (*abbr of* **very special old pale**) *appellation réservée à certains cognacs et armagnacs.*

VT *abbr of* **Vermont.**

VTOL [ˈviːtɒl] (*abbr of* **vertical takeoff and landing**) *n* ADAV *m*.

VTR (*abbr of* **video tape recorder**) *n* magnétoscope *m*.

vulgar [ˈvʌlgəʳ] *adj* - **1.** [in bad taste] vulgaire - **2.** [offensive] grossier(ère).

vulgarity [vʌlˈgærətɪ] *(U)* *n* - **1.** [poor taste] vulgarité *f* - **2.** [offensiveness] grossièreté *f*.

vulnerability [ˌvʌlnərəˈbɪlətɪ] *n* vulnérabilité *f*.

vulnerable [ˈvʌlnərəbl] *adj* vulnérable ; **~ to** [attack] exposé(e) à ; [colds] sensible à.

vulture [ˈvʌltʃəʳ] *n* **lit** & **fig** vautour *m*.

W

w (*pl* **w's** OR **ws**), **W** (*pl* **W's** OR **Ws**) [ˈdʌbljuː] *n* [letter] w *m inv*, W *m inv*.
◆ **W** - **1.** (*abbr of* **west**) O, W - **2.** (*abbr of* **watt**) w.

WA *abbr of* **Washington.**

wacky [ˈwækɪ] (*compar* **-ier** ; *superl* **-iest**) *adj* **inf** farfelu(e).

wad [wɒd] *n* - **1.** [of cotton wool, paper] tampon *m* - **2.** [of banknotes, documents] liasse *f* - **3.** [of tobacco] chique *f* ; [of chewing-gum] boulette *f*.

wadding [ˈwɒdɪŋ] *n* rembourrage *m*, capitonnage *m*.

waddle [ˈwɒdl] *vi* se dandiner.

wade [weɪd] *vi* patauger.
◆ **wade through** *vt fus* **fig** se taper.

wadge [wɒdʒ] *n* **Br inf** morceau *m* ; [of papers] tas *m*.

wading pool [ˈweɪdɪŋ-] *n* **Am** pataugeoire *f*.

wafer [ˈweɪfəʳ] *n* [thin biscuit] gaufrette *f*.

wafer-thin *adj* mince comme du papier à cigarette OR une pelure d'oignon.

waffle [ˈwɒfl] ◇ *n* - **1.** CULIN gaufre *f* - **2.** **Br inf** [vague talk] verbiage *m* ◇ *vi* parler pour ne rien dire.

waft [wɑːft, wɒft] *vi* flotter.

wag [wæg] (*pt* & *pp* **-ged** ; *cont* **-ging**) ◇ *vt* remuer, agiter ◇ *vi* [tail] remuer.

wage [weɪdʒ] ◇ *n* salaire *m*, paie *f*, paye *f* ◇ *vt* : **to ~ war against** faire la guerre à.
◆ **wages** *npl* salaire *m*.

wage claim *n* revendication *f* salariale.

wage differential *n* écart *m* des salaires.

wage earner [-ˌɜːnəʳ] *n* salarié *m*, -e *f*.

wage freeze *n* blocage *m* des salaires.

wage packet *n* **Br** - **1.** [envelope] enveloppe *f* de paye - **2.** **fig** [pay] paie *f*, paye *f*.

wager [ˈweɪdʒəʳ] *n* pari *m*.

wage rise *n* **Br** augmentation *f* de salaire.

waggish [ˈwægɪʃ] *adj* **inf** facétieux(euse), plaisant(e).

waggle [ˈwægl] **inf** ◇ *vt* agiter, remuer ; [ears] remuer ◇ *vi* remuer.

waggon ['wægən] **Br** = **wagon**.

wagon ['wægən] n - **1.** [horse-drawn] chariot m, charrette f - **2. Br RAIL** wagon m.

waif [weɪf] n enfant abandonné m, enfant abandonnée f.

wail [weɪl] ◇ n gémissement m ◇ vi gémir.

wailing ['weɪlɪŋ] n (U) gémissements mpl, plaintes fpl.

waist [weɪst] n taille f.

waistband ['weɪstbænd] n ceinture f.

waistcoat ['weɪskəʊt] n esp Br gilet m.

waistline ['weɪstlaɪn] n taille f.

wait [weɪt] ◇ n attente f ; **to have a long ~** attendre longtemps ◇ vi attendre ; **I can't ~ to see you** je brûle d'impatience de te voir ; **(just) you ~!** tu ne perds rien pour attendre! ; **~ and see!** tu vas bien voir! ; **~ a minute OR second OR moment!** [interrupting person] minute (papillon)! ; [interrupting oneself] attends voir! ◇ vt Am [delay] retarder.

➤ **wait about, wait around** vi attendre ; [waste time] perdre son temps à attendre.

➤ **wait for** vt fus attendre ; **to ~ for sb to do sthg** attendre que qqn fasse qqch.

➤ **wait on** vt fus [serve food to] servir.

➤ **wait up** vi veiller, ne pas se coucher.

waiter ['weɪtəʳ] n garçon m, serveur m.

waiting game ['weɪtɪŋ-] n politique f d'attente.

waiting list ['weɪtɪŋ-] n liste f d'attente.

waiting room ['weɪtɪŋ-] n salle f d'attente.

waitress ['weɪtrɪs] n serveuse f.

waive [weɪv] vt [fee] renoncer à ; [rule] prévoir une dérogation à.

waiver ['weɪvəʳ] n JUR dérogation f.

wake [weɪk] (pt woke OR -d ; pp woken OR -d) ◇ n [of ship] sillage m ; **in one's ~** fig dans son sillage ; **in the ~ of** fig à la suite de ◇ vt réveiller ◇ vi se réveiller.

➤ **wake up** ◇ vt sep réveiller ◇ vi - **1.** [wake] se réveiller - **2.** fig [become aware] : **to ~ up (to sthg)** prendre conscience (de qqch), se sensibiliser (à qqch).

waken ['weɪkən] fml ◇ vt réveiller ◇ vi se réveiller.

waking hours ['weɪkɪŋ-] npl heures fpl de veille.

Wales [weɪlz] n pays m de Galles ; **in ~** au pays de Galles.

walk [wɔːk] ◇ n - **1.** [way of walking] démarche f, façon f de marcher - **2.** [journey - for pleasure] promenade f ; [- long distance] marche f ; **it's a long ~** c'est loin à pied ; **to go for a ~** aller se promener, aller faire une promenade

- **3.** [route] promenade f ◇ vt - **1.** [accompany - person] accompagner ; [- dog] promener - **2.** [distance] faire à pied ; **to ~ the streets** [homeless] être sur le pavé ; [in search] arpenter la ville ; [prostitute] faire le trottoir ◇ vi - **1.** [gen] marcher - **2.** [for pleasure] se promener.

➤ **walk away with** vt fus inf fig gagner OR remporter haut la main.

➤ **walk in on** vt fus [interrupt] déranger ; [in embarrassing situation] prendre en flagrant délit.

➤ **walk off** vt sep [headache, cramp] faire une promenade pour se débarrasser de.

➤ **walk off with** vt fus inf - **1.** [steal] faucher - **2.** [win easily] gagner OR remporter haut la main.

➤ **walk out** vi - **1.** [leave suddenly] partir - **2.** [go on strike] se mettre en grève, faire grève.

➤ **walk out on** vt fus quitter.

walkabout ['wɔːkəˌbaʊt] n Br [by president etc] bain m de foule.

walker ['wɔːkəʳ] n [for pleasure] promeneur m, -euse f ; [long-distance] marcheur m, -euse f.

walkie-talkie [ˌwɔːkɪ'tɔːkɪ] n talkie-walkie m.

walk-in adj - **1.** [cupboard] assez grand(e) pour qu'on puisse y entrer - **2.** Am [easy] facile.

walking ['wɔːkɪŋ] n (U) marche f à pied, promenade f.

walking shoes npl chaussures fpl de marche.

walking stick n canne f.

Walkman® ['wɔːkmən] n baladeur m, Walkman® m.

walk of life (pl walks of life) n milieu m.

walk-on adj [part, role] de figurant(e).

walkout ['wɔːkaʊt] n [strike] grève f, débrayage m.

walkover ['wɔːkˌəʊvəʳ] n victoire f facile.

walkway ['wɔːkweɪ] n passage m ; [between buildings] passerelle f.

wall [wɔːl] n - **1.** [of room, building] mur m ; [of rock, cave] paroi f ; **to come up against a brick ~** se heurter à un mur ; **to drive sb up the ~** rendre qqn fou, taper sur le système de qqn - **2.** ANAT paroi f.

wallchart ['wɔːltʃɑːt] n planche f murale.

wall cupboard n placard m mural.

walled [wɔːld] adj fortifié(e).

wallet ['wɒlɪt] n portefeuille m.

wallflower ['wɔːlˌflaʊəʳ] n - **1.** [plant] giroflée f - **2.** inf fig [person] : **to be a ~** faire tapisserie.

Walloon [wɒˈluːn] ⋄ *adj* wallon(onne) ⋄ *n*
- **1.** [person] Wallon *m*, -onne *f* - **2.** [language]
wallon *m*.

wallop [ˈwɒləp] *inf* ⋄ *n* gros coup *m* ⋄ *vt*
[person] flanquer un coup à ; [ball] taper fort
dans.

wallow [ˈwɒləʊ] *vi* - **1.** [in liquid] se vautrer
- **2.** [in emotion] : **to ~ in** se complaire dans.

wall painting *n* peinture *f* murale.

wallpaper [ˈwɔːlˌpeɪpəʳ] ⋄ *n* papier *m* peint
⋄ *vt* tapisser.

Wall Street *n* Wall Street *m (quartier financier de New York).*

wall-to-wall *adj* : **~ carpet** moquette *f*.

wally [ˈwɒlɪ] *(pl* **-ies)** *n* Br *inf* idiot *m*, -e *f*, andouille *f*.

walnut [ˈwɔːlnʌt] *n* - **1.** [nut] noix *f* - **2.** [tree,
wood] noyer *m*.

walrus [ˈwɔːlrəs] *(pl inv* OR **-es** [-iːz]) *n* morse
m.

waltz [wɔːls] ⋄ *n* valse *f* ⋄ *vi* - **1.** [dance] valser, danser la valse - **2.** *inf* [walk confidently]
marcher d'un air dégagé OR de façon désinvolte.

wan [wɒn] *(compar* **-ner** ; *superl* **-nest**) *adj* pâle,
blême.

wand [wɒnd] *n* baguette *f*.

wander [ˈwɒndəʳ] *vi* - **1.** [person] errer
- **2.** [mind] divaguer ; [thoughts] vagabonder.

wanderer [ˈwɒndərəʳ] *n* vagabond *m*, -e *f*.

wandering [ˈwɒndərɪŋ] *adj* ambulant(e).

wanderlust [ˈwɒndəlʌst] *n* bougeotte *f*, envie *f* de voyager.

wane [weɪn] ⋄ *n* : **on the ~** en déclin ; [power,
interest] faiblissant(e) ⋄ *vi* - **1.** [influence, inter-
est] diminuer, faiblir - **2.** [moon] décroître.

wangle [ˈwæŋgl] *vt inf* se débrouiller pour
obtenir.

wanna [ˈwɒnə] *esp* Am = **want a, want to.**

want [wɒnt] ⋄ *n* - **1.** [need] besoin *m* - **2.** [lack]
manque *m* ; **for ~ of** faute de, par manque
de - **3.** [deprivation] pauvreté *f*, besoin *m* ⋄ *vt*
- **1.** [desire] vouloir ; **to ~ to do sthg** vouloir
faire qqch ; **to ~ sb to do sthg** vouloir que
qqn fasse qqch - **2.** *inf* [need] avoir besoin de ;
you ~ to be more careful tu devrais être plus
prudent.

want ad *n* Am *inf* petite annonce *f*.

wanted [ˈwɒntɪd] *adj* : **to be ~ (by the police)**
être recherché(e) (par la police).

wanting [ˈwɒntɪŋ] *adj* : **to be ~ in** manquer
de ; **to be found ~** ne pas être à la hauteur ;
not to be found ~ être à la hauteur.

wanton [ˈwɒntən] *adj* [destruction, neglect] gra-
tuit(e).

war [wɔːʳ] *(pt* & *pp* **-red** ; *cont* **-ring**) ⋄ *n*
guerre *f* ; **to go to ~** entrer OR se mettre en
guerre ; **to have been in the ~s** Br être dans
un sale état ⋄ *vi* se battre.

War., Warks. (*abbr of* **Warwickshire**) *comté
anglais.*

warble [ˈwɔːbl] *vi* [bird] gazouiller.

war crime *n* crime *m* de guerre.

war criminal *n* criminel *m* de guerre.

war cry *n* cri *m* de guerre.

ward [wɔːd] *n* - **1.** [in hospital] salle *f* - **2.** Br POL
circonscription *f* électorale - **3.** JUR pupille
mf.

➤ **ward off** *vt fus* [danger] écarter ; [disease,
blow] éviter ; [evil spirits] éloigner.

war dance *n* danse *f* guerrière.

warden [ˈwɔːdn] *n* - **1.** [of park etc] gardien *m*,
-enne *f* - **2.** Br [of youth hostel, hall of residence] directeur *m*, -trice *f* - **3.** Am [of prison] directeur
m, -trice *f*.

warder [ˈwɔːdəʳ] *n* [in prison] gardien *m*, -enne
f.

ward of court *n* pupille *mf* sous tutelle judiciaire.

wardrobe [ˈwɔːdrəʊb] *n* garde-robe *f*.

wardrobe mistress *n* Br costumière *f*.

warehouse [ˈweəhaʊs, *pl* -haʊzɪz] *n* entrepôt
m, magasin *m*.

wares [weəz] *npl* marchandises *fpl*.

warfare [ˈwɔːfeəʳ] *n (U)* guerre *f*.

war game *n* - **1.** [military exercise] manœuvres
fpl militaires - **2.** [game of strategy] jeu *m* de
stratégie militaire.

warhead [ˈwɔːhed] *n* ogive *f*, tête *f*.

warily [ˈweərəlɪ] *adv* avec précaution OR circonspection.

warlike [ˈwɔːlaɪk] *adj* belliqueux(euse).

warm [wɔːm] ⋄ *adj* - **1.** [gen] chaud(e) ; **are
you ~ enough?** tu as assez chaud ? ; **it's ~ today** il fait chaud aujourd'hui - **2.** [friendly]
chaleureux(euse) ⋄ *vt* chauffer.

➤ **warm over** *vt sep* Am *lit* & *fig* resservir.

➤ **warm to** *vt fus* [person] se prendre de sympathie pour ; [idea, place] se mettre à aimer.

➤ **warm up** ⋄ *vt sep* réchauffer ⋄ *vi*
- **1.** [person, room] se réchauffer - **2.** [machine,
engine] chauffer - **3.** SPORT s'échauffer.

warm-blooded [-'blʌdɪd] *adj* à sang chaud.

war memorial *n* monument *m* aux morts.

warm front *n* METEOR front *m* chaud.

warm-hearted [-'hɑːtɪd] *adj* chaleureux(euse), affectueux(euse).

warmly ['wɔːmlɪ] *adv* - **1.** [in warm clothes] : **to dress ~** s'habiller chaudement - **2.** [in a friendly way] chaleureusement.

warmness ['wɔːmnɪs] *n* chaleur *f.*

warmonger ['wɔː,mʌŋgəʳ] *n* belliciste *mf.*

warmth [wɔːmθ] *n* chaleur *f.*

warm-up *n* SPORT échauffement *m.*

warn [wɔːn] ⋄ *vt* avertir, prévenir ; **to ~ sb of sthg** avertir qqn de qqch ; **to ~ sb not to do sthg** conseiller à qqn de ne pas faire qqch, déconseiller à qqn de faire qqch ⋄ *vi* : **to ~ of sthg** annoncer un risque de qqch.

warning ['wɔːnɪŋ] ⋄ *adj* d'avertissement ⋄ *n* avertissement *m.*

warning light *n* voyant *m*, avertisseur *m* lumineux.

warning triangle *n* Br triangle *m* de signalisation.

warp [wɔːp] ⋄ *vt* - **1.** [wood] gauchir, voiler - **2.** [personality] fausser, pervertir ⋄ *vi* [wood] gauchir, se voiler ⋄ *n* [of cloth] chaîne *f.*

warpath ['wɔːpɑːθ] *n* : **to be on the ~** fig être sur le sentier de la guerre.

warped [wɔːpt] *adj* - **1.** [wood] gauchi(e) - **2.** [personality, idea] perverti(e).

warrant ['wɒrənt] ⋄ *n* JUR mandat *m* ⋄ *vt* - **1.** [justify] justifier - **2.** [guarantee] garantir.

warrant officer *n* adjudant *m.*

warranty ['wɒrəntɪ] (*pl* **-ies**) *n* garantie *f.*

warren ['wɒrən] *n* terrier *m.*

warring ['wɔːrɪŋ] *adj* en guerre.

warrior ['wɒrɪəʳ] *n* guerrier *m*, -ère *f.*

Warsaw ['wɔːsɔː] *n* Varsovie ; **the ~ Pact** le pacte de Varsovie.

warship ['wɔːʃɪp] *n* navire *m* de guerre.

wart [wɔːt] *n* verrue *f.*

wartime ['wɔːtaɪm] ⋄ *adj* de guerre ⋄ *n* : **in ~** en temps de guerre.

war-torn *adj* déchiré(e) par la guerre.

war widow *n* veuve *f* de guerre.

wary ['weərɪ] (*compar* **-ier** ; *superl* **-iest**) *adj* prudent(e), circonspect(e) ; **to be ~ of** se méfier de ; **to be ~ of doing sthg** hésiter à faire qqch.

was [weak form wəz, strong form wɒz] *pt* ⊳ be.

wash [wɒʃ] ⋄ *n* - **1.** [act] lavage *m* ; **to have a ~** se laver ; **to give sthg a ~** laver qqch

- **2.** [clothes] lessive *f* - **3.** [from boat] remous *m* ⋄ *vt* - **1.** [clean] laver ; **to ~ one's hands** se laver les mains - **2.** [carry] : **the waves ~ed the oil/body onto the beach** les vagues ont rejeté le pétrole/corps sur la plage ⋄ *vi* se laver.

➤ **wash away** *vt sep* emporter.

➤ **wash down** *vt sep* - **1.** [food] arroser - **2.** [clean] laver à grande eau.

➤ **wash out** *vt sep* - **1.** [stain, dye] faire partir, enlever - **2.** [container] laver.

➤ **wash up** ⋄ *vt sep* - **1.** Br [dishes] : **to ~ the dishes up** faire OR laver la vaisselle - **2.** [subj : sea, river] rejeter ⋄ *vi* - **1.** Br [wash dishes] faire OR laver la vaisselle - **2.** Am [wash oneself] se laver.

washable ['wɒʃəbl] *adj* lavable.

wash-and-wear *adj* qui ne nécessite aucun repassage.

washbasin Br ['wɒʃ,beɪsn], **washbowl** Am ['wɒʃbəʊl] *n* lavabo *m.*

washcloth ['wɒʃ,klɒθ] *n* Am gant *m* de toilette.

washed-out [,wɒʃt-] *adj* - **1.** [pale] délavé(e) - **2.** [exhausted] lessivé(e).

washed-up [,wɒʃt-] *adj* inf [person] fini(e) ; [project] fichu(e).

washer ['wɒʃəʳ] *n* - **1.** TECH rondelle *f* - **2.** [washing machine] machine *f* à laver.

washer-dryer *n* machine *f* à laver séchante.

washing ['wɒʃɪŋ] *n* (U) - **1.** [action] lessive *f* - **2.** [clothes] linge *m*, lessive *f.*

washing line *n* corde *f* à linge.

washing machine *n* machine *f* à laver.

washing powder *n* Br lessive *f*, détergent *m.*

Washington ['wɒʃɪŋtən] *n* - **1.** [state] : **~ State** l'État *m* de Washington - **2.** [city] : **~ D.C.** Washington.

washing-up *n* Br vaisselle *f.*

washing-up liquid *n* Br liquide *m* pour la vaisselle.

washout ['wɒʃaʊt] *n* inf fiasco *m.*

washroom ['wɒʃrʊm] *n* Am toilettes *fpl.*

wasn't [wɒznt] = was not.

wasp [wɒsp] *n* guêpe *f.*

Wasp, WASP [wɒsp] (*abbr of* **White Anglo-Saxon Protestant**) *n* inf *personne de race blanche, d'origine anglo-saxonne et protestante.*

waspish ['wɒspɪʃ] *adj* revêche, grincheux(euse).

wastage ['weɪstɪdʒ] *n* gaspillage *m.*

waste [weɪst] ◇ *adj* [material] de rebut ; [fuel] perdu(e) ; [area of land] en friche ◇ *n* - **1.** [misuse] gaspillage *m* ; **it's a ~ of money** [extravagance] c'est du gaspillage ; [bad investment] c'est de l'argent perdu ; **to go to ~** [gen] être gaspillé ; [food] se perdre ; [work] ne servir à rien ; **a ~ of time** une perte de temps - **2.** *(U)* [refuse] déchets *mpl*, ordures *fpl* ◇ *vt* [money, food, energy] gaspiller ; [time, opportunity] perdre.

◆ **wastes** *npl literary* étendues *fpl* désertes.

wastebasket Am = **wastepaper basket**.

waste disposal unit *n* broyeur *m* d'ordures.

wasteful ['weɪstfʊl] *adj* [person] gaspilleur(euse) ; [activity] peu économique.

waste ground *n* *(U)* terrain *m* vague.

wasteland ['weɪst,lænd] *n* [in country] terre *f* à l'abandon ; [in city] terrain *m* vague.

waste paper *n* papier *m* de rebut.

wastepaper basket, **wastepaper bin** [,weɪst'peɪpəˈ-], **wastebasket** Am ['weɪst,bɑːskɪt] *n* corbeille *f* à papier.

watch [wɒtʃ] ◇ *n* - **1.** [timepiece] montre *f* - **2.** [act of watching] : **to keep ~** faire le guet, monter la garde ; **to keep ~ on sb/sthg** surveiller qqn/qqch - **3.** [guard] garde *f* ; NAUT [shift] quart *m* ◇ *vt* - **1.** [look at] regarder - **2.** [spy on, guard] surveiller - **3.** [be careful about] faire attention à ; **~ your language!** surveille ton langage! ; **~ it!** *inf* attention! ◇ *vi* regarder.

◆ **watch out** *vi* faire attention, prendre garde.

◆ **watch over** *vt fus* veiller sur.

watchdog ['wɒtʃdɒg] *n* - **1.** [dog] chien *m* de garde - **2.** *fig* [organization] organisation *f* de contrôle.

watchful ['wɒtʃfʊl] *adj* vigilant(e).

watchmaker ['wɒtʃ,meɪkəˈ] *n* horloger *m*.

watchman ['wɒtʃmən] (*pl* -**men** [-mən]) *n* gardien *m*.

watchword ['wɒtʃwɜːd] *n* mot *m* d'ordre.

water ['wɔːtəˈ] ◇ *n* - **1.** [liquid] eau *f* ; **to pour** OR **throw cold ~ on sthg** *fig* se montrer négatif à l'égard de qqch ; **to tread ~** flotter ; **that's all ~ under the bridge** tout ça, c'est du passé - **2.** [urine] : **to pass ~** uriner ◇ *vt* arroser ◇ *vi* - **1.** [eyes] pleurer, larmoyer - **2.** [mouth] : **my mouth is ~ing** j'en avais l'eau à la bouche ; **it made my mouth ~** cela m'a fait venir l'eau à la bouche.

◆ **waters** *npl* [sea] eaux *fpl*.

◆ **water down** *vt sep* - **1.** [dilute] diluer ; [alcohol] couper d'eau - **2.** *usu pej* [plan, demand] atténuer, modérer ; [play, novel] édulcorer.

water bed *n* lit *m* d'eau.

water bird *n* oiseau *m* aquatique.

water biscuit *n* cracker *m*, craquelin *m*.

waterborne ['wɔːtəbɔːn] *adj* [disease] d'origine hydrique.

water bottle *n* gourde *f*, bidon *m* (à eau).

water buffalo *n* karbau *m*, kérabau *m*.

water cannon *n* canon *m* à eau.

water chestnut *n* châtaigne *f* d'eau.

water closet *n dated* toilettes *fpl*, waters *mpl*.

watercolour ['wɔːtə,kʌləˈ] *n* - **1.** [picture] aquarelle *f* - **2.** [paint] peinture *f* à l'eau, couleur *f* pour aquarelle.

water-cooled [-,kuːld] *adj* à refroidissement par eau.

watercourse ['wɔːtəkɔːs] *n* cours *m* d'eau.

watercress ['wɔːtəkres] *n* cresson *m*.

watered-down [,wɔːtəd-] *adj usu pej* modéré(e), atténué(e) ; [version] édulcoré(e).

waterfall ['wɔːtəfɔːl] *n* chute *f* d'eau, cascade *f*.

waterfront ['wɔːtəfrʌnt] *n* quais *mpl*.

water heater *n* chauffe-eau *m inv*.

waterhole ['wɔːtəhəʊl] *n* mare *f*, point *m* d'eau.

watering can ['wɔːtərɪŋ-] *n* arrosoir *m*.

water jump *n* brook *m*.

water level *n* niveau *m* de l'eau.

water lily *n* nénuphar *m*.

waterline ['wɔːtəlaɪn] *n* NAUT ligne *f* de flottaison.

waterlogged ['wɔːtəlɒgd] *adj* - **1.** [land] détrempé(e) - **2.** [vessel] plein(e) d'eau.

water main *n* conduite *f* principale d'eau.

watermark ['wɔːtəmɑːk] *n* - **1.** [in paper] filigrane *m* - **2.** [showing water level] laisse *f*.

watermelon ['wɔːtə,melən] *n* pastèque *f*.

water pipe *n* conduite *f* d'eau.

water pistol *n* pistolet *m* à eau.

water polo *n* water-polo *m*.

waterproof ['wɔːtəpruːf] ◇ *adj* imperméable ◇ *n* imperméable *m* ◇ *vt* imperméabiliser.

water rates *npl* Br taxe *f* sur l'eau.

water-resistant *adj* qui résiste à l'eau.

watershed ['wɔːtəʃed] *n fig* [turning point] tournant *m*, moment *m* critique.

waterside ['wɔːtəsaɪd] ◇ *adj* au bord de l'eau ◇ *n* : **the ~** le bord de l'eau.

water skiing *n* ski *m* nautique.

water softener *n* adoucisseur *m* d'eau.

water-soluble *adj* soluble dans l'eau.

waterspout ['wɔːtəspaut] *n* trombe *f.*

water supply *n* alimentation *f* en eau, approvisionnement *m* d'eau.

water table *n* niveau *m* hydrostatique.

water tank *n* réservoir *m* d'eau, citerne *f.*

watertight ['wɔːtətaɪt] *adj* - **1.** [waterproof] étanche - **2.** *fig* [excuse, contract] parfait(e) ; [argument] irréfutable ; [plan] infaillible.

water tower *n* château *m* d'eau.

waterway ['wɔːtəweɪ] *n* voie *f* navigable.

waterworks ['wɔːtəwɜːks] (*pl inv*) *n* [building] installation *f* hydraulique, usine *f* de distribution d'eau.

watery ['wɔːtərɪ] *adj* - **1.** [food, drink] trop dilué(e) ; [tea, coffee] pas assez fort(e) - **2.** [pale] pâle.

watt [wɒt] *n* watt *m.*

wattage ['wɒtɪdʒ] *n* puissance *f* OR consommation *f* en watts.

wave [weɪv] ◇ *n* - **1.** [of hand] geste *m*, signe *m* - **2.** [of water, emotion, nausea] vague *f* - **3.** [of light, sound] onde *f* ; [of heat] bouffée *f* - **4.** [in hair] cran *m*, ondulation *f* ◇ *vt* - **1.** [arm, handkerchief] agiter ; [flag, stick] brandir - **2.** [signal to] : **he ~d the car on** il a fait signe à la voiture d'avancer ◇ *vi* - **1.** [with hand] faire signe de la main ; **to ~ at** OR **to sb** faire signe à qqn, saluer qqn de la main - **2.** [flags, trees] flotter.

➤ **wave aside** *vt sep fig* [dismiss] écarter, rejeter.

➤ **wave down** *vt sep* : **to ~ down a vehicle** faire signe à un véhicule de s'arrêter.

wave band *n* bande *f* de fréquences, gamme *f* d'ondes.

wavelength ['weɪvleŋθ] *n* longueur *f* d'ondes ; **to be on the same ~** *fig* être sur la même longueur d'ondes.

waver ['weɪvər] *vi* - **1.** [falter] vaciller, chanceler - **2.** [hesitate] hésiter, vaciller - **3.** [fluctuate] fluctuer, varier.

wavy ['weɪvɪ] (*compar* -**ier** ; *superl* -**iest**) *adj* [hair] ondulé(e) ; [line] onduleux(euse).

wax [wæks] ◇ *n* (U) - **1.** [in candles, polish] cire *f* ; [for skis] fart *m* - **2.** [in ears] cérumen *m* ◇ *vt* cirer ; [skis] farter ◇ *vi* - **1.** *dated or hum* [become] devenir ; **to ~ and wane** connaître des hauts et des bas - **2.** [moon] croître.

waxen ['wæksən] *adj* cireux(euse).

wax paper *n* Am papier *m* sulfurisé.

waxworks ['wækswɜːks] (*pl inv*) *n* [museum] musée *m* de cire.

way [weɪ] ◇ *n* - **1.** [means, method] façon *f* ; **~s and means** moyens *mpl* ; **to get** OR **have one's ~** obtenir ce qu'on veut ; **she expects to have everything her own ~** elle s'attend à ce qu'on lui fasse ses quatre volontés - **2.** [manner, style] façon *f*, manière *f* ; **in the same ~** de la même manière OR façon ; **this/ that ~** comme ça, de cette façon ; **in a ~** d'une certaine manière, en quelque sorte ; **in a big/small ~** à un haut/moindre degré - **3.** [skill] : **to have a ~ with** savoir comment s'y prendre avec ; **to have a ~ of doing sthg** avoir le chic pour faire qqch - **4.** [route, path] chemin *m* ; **~ in** entrée *f* ; **~ out** sortie *f* ; **to be out of one's ~** [place] ne pas être sur sa route ; **on the** OR **one's ~** sur la OR son chemin ; **across** OR **over the ~** juste en face ; **to be under ~** [ship] faire route ; *fig* [meeting] être en cours ; **to get under ~** [ship] se mettre en route ; *fig* [meeting] démarrer ; **'give ~'** Br AUT 'vous n'avez pas la priorité' ; **to be in the ~** gêner ; **to be out of the ~** [finished] être fini ; [not blocking] ne pas gêner ; **to go out of one's ~ to do sthg** se donner du mal pour faire qqch ; **to keep out of sb's ~** éviter qqn ; **keep out of the ~!** restez à l'écart ! ; **to make one's ~** aller ; **to make one's ~ towards** se diriger vers ; **to make ~ for** faire place à ; **to stand in sb's ~** *fig* [subj : obstacle] gêner qqn ; [subj : person] s'opposer à la volonté de qqn ; **to work one's ~** progresser - **5.** [direction] : **to go/look/come this ~** aller/regarder/venir par ici ; **the right/ wrong ~ round** [in sequence] dans le bon/ mauvais ordre ; **she had her hat on the wrong ~ round** elle avait mis son chapeau à l'envers ; **the right/wrong ~ up** dans le bon/ mauvais sens - **6.** [distance] : **all the ~** tout le trajet ; *fig* [support etc] jusqu'au bout ; **most of the ~** presque tout le trajet OR chemin ; **a long ~** loin ; **to go a long ~ towards doing sthg** *fig* contribuer largement à faire qqch - **7.** *phr* : **to give ~** [under weight, pressure] céder ; **no ~!** pas question ! ◇ *adv inf* [a lot] largement ; **~ better** bien mieux.

➤ **ways** *npl* [customs, habits] coutumes *fpl.*

➤ **by the way** *adv* au fait.

➤ **by way of** *prep* - **1.** [via] par - **2.** [as a sort of] en guise de.

➤ **in the way of** *prep* comme.

waylay [ˌweɪˈleɪ] (*pt* & *pp* -**laid** [-ˈleɪd]) *vt* arrêter (au passage).

way of life *n* façon *f* de vivre.

way-out *adj* inf excentrique.

wayside ['weɪsaɪd] *n* [roadside] bord *m* (de la route) ; **to fall by the ~** *fig* tomber à l'eau.

wayward ['weɪwəd] *adj* qui n'en fait qu'à sa tête ; [behaviour] capricieux(euse).

WC (*abbr of* **water closet**) *n* W.-C. *mpl.*

WCC (*abbr of* **World Council of Churches**) *n* assemblée mondiale des Églises.

we [wiː] *pers pron* nous ; **WE can't do it** nous, nous ne pouvons pas le faire ; **as ~ say in France** comme on dit en France ; **~ British** nous autres Britanniques.

weak [wiːk] *adj* - **1.** [gen] faible - **2.** [delicate] fragile - **3.** [unconvincing] peu convaincant(e) - **4.** [drink] léger(ère).

weaken ['wiːkn] ◇ *vt* - **1.** [undermine] affaiblir - **2.** [reduce] diminuer - **3.** [physically - person] affaiblir ; [- structure] fragiliser ◇ *vi* faiblir.

weak-kneed [-niːd] *adj* inf pej lâche.

weakling ['wiːklɪŋ] *n* pej mauviette *f.*

weakly ['wiːklɪ] *adv* faiblement.

weak-minded [-'maɪndɪd] *adj* [weak-willed] faible de caractère.

weakness ['wiːknɪs] *n* - **1.** (U) [physical - of person] faiblesse *f ;* [- of structure] fragilité *f* - **2.** [liking] : **to have a ~ for sthg** avoir un faible pour qqch - **3.** [imperfect point] point *m* faible, faiblesse *f.*

weal [wiːl] *n* marque *f.*

wealth [welθ] *n* - **1.** (U) [riches] richesse *f* - **2.** [abundance] : **a ~ of** une profusion de.

wealth tax *n* Br impôt *m* sur la fortune.

wealthy ['welθɪ] (*compar* -ier ; *superl* -iest) *adj* riche.

wean [wiːn] *vt* - **1.** [baby, lamb] sevrer - **2.** [discourage] : **to ~ sb from** OR **off sthg** [interest, habit] faire perdre qqch à qqn ; [drugs, alcohol] détourner qqn de qqch.

weapon ['wepən] *n* arme *f.*

weaponry ['wepənrɪ] *n* (U) armement *m.*

wear [weəʳ] (*pt* wore ; *pp* worn) ◇ *n* (U) - **1.** [type of clothes] tenue *f* - **2.** [damage] usure *f ;* **~ and tear** usure - **3.** [use] : **these shoes have had a lot of ~** ces chaussures ont fait beaucoup d'usage ; **to be the worse for ~** être fatigué ; [drunk] être mûr ◇ *vt* - **1.** [clothes, hair] porter ; **she ~s her hair in a bun** elle porte un chignon - **2.** [damage] user ◇ *vi* - **1.** [deteriorate] s'user - **2.** [last] : **to ~ well** durer longtemps, faire de l'usage ; **to ~ badly** ne pas durer longtemps - **3.** *phr* : **to ~ thin** [excuse] ne plus marcher.

➤ **wear away** ◇ *vt sep* [rock, wood] user ; [grass] abîmer ◇ *vi* [rock, wood] s'user ; [grass] s'abîmer.

➤ **wear down** ◇ *vt sep* - **1.** [material] user - **2.** [person, resistance] épuiser ◇ *vi* s'user.

➤ **wear off** *vi* disparaître.

➤ **wear on** *vi* [time] passer lentement ; [evening, afternoon] se traîner ; [discussion] traîner en longueur.

➤ **wear out** ◇ *vt sep* - **1.** [shoes, clothes] user - **2.** [person] épuiser ◇ *vi* s'user.

wearable ['weərəbl] *adj* mettable.

wearily ['wɪərɪlɪ] *adv* péniblement ; **to sigh ~** pousser un soupir de lassitude.

weariness ['wɪərɪnɪs] *n* lassitude *f.*

wearing ['weərɪŋ] *adj* [exhausting] épuisant(e).

weary ['wɪərɪ] (*compar* -ier ; *superl* -iest) *adj* - **1.** [exhausted] las (lasse) ; [sigh] de lassitude - **2.** [fed up] : **to be ~ of sthg/of doing sthg** être las de qqch/de faire qqch.

weasel ['wiːzl] *n* belette *f.*

weather ['weðəʳ] ◇ *n* temps *m ;* **what's the ~ like?** quel temps fait-il? ; **good ~** beau temps ; **to make heavy ~ of it** se compliquer la tâche ; **to be under the ~** être patraque ◇ *vt* [crisis, problem] surmonter ◇ *vi* [rock] s'éroder ; [wood] s'user.

weather-beaten [-ˌbiːtn] *adj* - **1.** [face, skin] tanné(e) - **2.** [building, stone] abîmé(e) par les intempéries.

weathercock ['weðəkɒk] *n* girouette *f.*

weathered ['weðəd] *adj* [stone] érodé(e) ; [building, wood] qui a souffert des intempéries.

weather forecast *n* météo *f,* prévisions *fpl* météorologiques.

weatherman ['weðəmæn] (*pl* -men [-men]) *n* météorologue *m.*

weather map *n* carte *f* météorologique.

weatherproof ['weðəpruːf] *adj* [clothing] imperméable ; [building] à l'épreuve des intempéries.

weather report *n* bulletin *m* météorologique.

weather ship *n* navire *m* météo.

weather vane [-veɪn] *n* girouette *f.*

weave [wiːv] (*pt* wove ; *pp* woven) ◇ *n* tissage *m* ◇ *vt* - **1.** [using loom] tisser - **2.** [move] : **to ~ one's way** se faufiler ◇ *vi* [move] se faufiler.

weaver ['wiːvəʳ] *n* tisserand *m,* -e *f.*

web, Web [web] *n* - **1.** [cobweb] toile *f* (d'araignée) - **2.** COMPUT : **the ~** le Web, la Toile - **3.** *fig* [of lies] tissu *m.*

webbed [webd] *adj* palmé(e).

webbing ['webɪŋ] *n* (U) sangles *fpl.*

web-footed [-'fʊtɪd] *adj* aux pieds palmés.

webmaster ['web,mɑːstəʳ] *n* webmaster *m,* webmestre *m.*

web page, Web page *n* page *f* Web.

website, Web site *n* COMPUT site *m* Internet OR Web.

wed [wed] (*pt* & *pp* wed OR -ded) *literary* ◇ *vt* épouser ◇ *vi* se marier.

we'd [wiːd] = we had, we would.

Wed. (*abbr of* **Wednesday**) mer.

wedded ['wedɪd] *adj* [committed] : ~ **to** dévoué(e) à.

wedding ['wedɪŋ] *n* mariage *m*.

wedding anniversary *n* anniversaire *m* de mariage.

wedding cake *n* pièce *f* montée.

wedding dress *n* robe *f* de mariée.

wedding reception *n* réception *f* de mariage.

wedding ring *n* alliance *f*.

wedge [wedʒ] ⬦ *n* - **1.** [for steadying] cale *f* - **2.** [for splitting] coin *m* ; **to drive a ~ between** fig semer la discorde entre ; **the thin end of the ~** fig le commencement de la fin - **3.** [of cake, cheese] morceau *m* ⬦ *vt* caler.

wedlock ['wedlɒk] *n* (U) literary mariage *m*.

Wednesday ['wenzdɪ] *n* mercredi *m* ; *see also* **Saturday**.

wee [wi:] ⬦ *adj* Scot petit(e) ⬦ *n* inf pipi *m* ⬦ *vi* inf faire pipi.

weed [wi:d] ⬦ *n* - **1.** [plant] mauvaise herbe *f* - **2.** Br inf [feeble person] mauviette *f* ⬦ *vt* désherber.

⬤ **weed out** *vt sep* éliminer.

weeding ['wi:dɪŋ] *n* désherbage *m*.

weedkiller ['wi:d,kɪlər] *n* désherbant *m*.

weedy ['wi:dɪ] (*compar* -**ier** ; *superl* -**iest**) *adj* Br inf [feeble] qui agit comme une mauviette.

week [wi:k] *n* semaine *f* ; **Saturday ~, a ~ on Saturday** samedi en huit.

weekday ['wi:kdeɪ] *n* jour *m* de semaine.

weekend [,wi:k'end] *n* week-end *m* ; **on** OR **at the ~** le week-end.

weekend bag *n* sac *m* de voyage.

weekly ['wi:klɪ] ⬦ *adj* hebdomadaire ⬦ *adv* chaque semaine ⬦ *n* hebdomadaire *m*.

weeny ['wi:nɪ] *adj* Br inf tout petit (toute petite).

weep [wi:p] (*pt & pp* **wept**) ⬦ *n* : **to have a ~** pleurer ⬦ *vt & vi* pleurer.

weeping willow [,wi:pɪŋ-] *n* saule *m* pleureur.

weepy ['wi:pɪ] (*compar* -**ier** ; *superl* -**iest**) *adj* [person] pleurnicheur(euse) ; [film] sentimental(e).

wee-wee *n & vi* = **wee**.

weft [weft] *n* trame *f*.

weigh [weɪ] *vt* - **1.** [gen] peser - **2.** NAUT : **to ~ anchor** lever l'ancre.

⬤ **weigh down** *vt sep* - **1.** [physically] : **to be ~ed down with sthg** plier sous le poids de

qqch - **2.** [mentally] : **to be ~ed down by** OR **with sthg** être accablé par qqch.

⬤ **weigh (up)on** *vt fus* peser à.

⬤ **weigh out** *vt sep* peser.

⬤ **weigh up** *vt sep* - **1.** [consider carefully] examiner ; **to ~ up the pros and cons** peser le pour et le contre - **2.** [size up] juger, évaluer.

weighbridge ['weɪbrɪdʒ] *n* Br pont-bascule *m*.

weighing machine ['weɪŋ-] *n* balance *f*.

weight [weɪt] *n* lit & fig poids *m* ; **to put on** OR **gain ~** prendre du poids, grossir ; **to lose ~** perdre du poids, maigrir ; **to pull one's ~** faire sa part du travail, participer à la tâche ; **to take the ~ off one's feet** se reposer, s'asseoir ; **to throw one's ~ about** faire l'important ; **to carry ~** avoir du poids ⬦ *vt* : **to ~ sthg (down)** [hold in place] maintenir qqch avec un poids ; [make heavier] alourdir qqch.

weighted ['weɪtɪd] *adj* : **to be ~ in favour of/against** être favorable/défavorable à.

weighting ['weɪtɪŋ] *n* indemnité *f*.

weightlessness ['weɪtlɪsnɪs] *n* apesanteur *f*.

weightlifter ['weɪt,lɪftər] *n* haltérophile *m*.

weightlifting ['weɪt,lɪftɪŋ] *n* haltérophilie *f*.

weight training *n* musculation *f*.

weighty ['weɪtɪ] (*compar* -**ier** ; *superl* -**iest**) *adj* [serious] important(e), de poids.

weir [wɪər] *n* barrage *m*.

weird [wɪəd] *adj* bizarre.

weirdo ['wɪədəʊ] (*pl* -**s**) *n* inf drôle de type *m*.

welcome ['welkəm] ⬦ *adj* - **1.** [guest, help etc] bienvenu(e) ; **to make sb ~** faire bon accueil à qqn - **2.** [free] : **you're ~ to ...** n'hésitez pas à ... - **3.** [in reply to thanks] : **you're ~** pas de quoi, de rien ⬦ *n* accueil *m* ⬦ *vt* - **1.** [receive] accueillir - **2.** [approve of] se réjouir de ⬦ *excl* bienvenue!

welcoming ['welkəmɪŋ] *adj* accueillant(e).

weld [weld] ⬦ *n* soudure *f* ⬦ *vt* souder.

welder ['weldər] *n* soudeur *m*.

welfare ['welfeər] ⬦ *adj* social(e) ⬦ *n* - **1.** [well-being] bien-être *m* - **2.** Am [income support] assistance *f* publique.

welfare state *n* État-providence *m*.

well [wel] (*compar* **better** ; *superl* **best**) ⬦ *adj* bien ; **I'm very ~, thanks** je vais très bien, merci ; **all is ~** tout va bien ; **(all) ~ and good** très bien ; **just as ~** aussi bien ⬦ *adv* bien ; **the team was ~ beaten** l'équipe a été battue à plates coutures ; **to go ~** aller bien ; **~ done!** bravo! ; **~ and truly** bel et bien ; **to be ~ in with sb** inf être bien avec qqn ; **you're**

~ out of it inf c'est mieux comme ça pour toi <> n [for water, oil] puits m <> excl - **1.** [in hesitation] heu!, eh bien! - **2.** [to correct oneself] bon!, enfin! - **3.** [to express resignation] : oh ~! eh bien! - **4.** [in surprise] tiens!

➡ **as well** adv - **1.** [in addition] aussi, également - **2.** [with same result] : l/you etc may OR might as ~ (do sthg) je/tu etc ferais aussi bien (de faire qqch).

➡ **as well as** conj en plus de, aussi bien que.

➡ **well up** vi : tears ~ed up in her eyes les larmes lui montaient aux yeux.

we'll [wiːl] = we shall, we will.

well-adjusted adj bien dans sa peau.

well-advised [-əd'vaɪzd] adj sage ; **you would be ~ to do sthg** tu ferais bien de faire qqch.

well-appointed [-ə'pɔɪntɪd] adj bien équipé(e).

well-balanced adj (bien) équilibré(e).

well-behaved [-bɪ'heɪvd] adj sage.

wellbeing [ˌwel'biːɪŋ] n bien-être m.

well-bred [-'bred] adj bien élevé(e).

well-built adj bien bâti(e).

well-chosen adj bien choisi(e).

well-disposed adj : **to be ~ to** OR **towards sb** être bien disposé(e) envers qqn ; **to be ~ towards sthg** être favorable à qqch.

well-done adj CULIN bien cuit(e).

well-dressed [-'drest] adj bien habillé(e).

well-earned [-ɜːnd] adj bien mérité(e).

well-established adj bien établi(e).

well-fed adj bien nourri(e).

well-groomed [-'gruːmd] adj soigné(e).

wellhead ['welhed] n source f.

well-heeled [-'hiːld] adj inf nanti(e).

wellies ['weliz] npl Br inf = wellington boots.

well-informed adj : **to be ~ (about/on)** être bien informé(e) (sur).

Wellington ['welɪŋtən] n Wellington.

wellington boots ['welɪŋtən-], **wellingtons** ['welɪŋtənz] npl bottes fpl de caoutchouc.

well-intentioned [-ɪn'tenʃnd] adj bien intentionné(e).

well-kept adj - **1.** [building, garden] bien tenu(e) - **2.** [secret] bien gardé(e).

well-known adj bien connu(e).

well-mannered [-'mænəd] adj bien élevé(e).

well-meaning adj bien intentionné(e).

well-nigh [-naɪ] adv presque, pratiquement.

well-off adj - **1.** [rich] riche - **2.** [well-provided] : **to be ~ for sthg** être bien pourvu(e) en qqch ; **he doesn't know when he is ~** inf il ne connaît pas son bonheur.

well-paid adj bien payé(e).

well-preserved adj fig bien conservé(e).

well-proportioned [-prə'pɔːʃnd] adj bien proportionné(e).

well-read [-'red] adj cultivé(e).

well-rounded [-'raʊndɪd] adj [education, background] complet(ète).

well-spoken adj qui parle bien.

well-thought-of adj qui a une bonne réputation.

well-thought-out adj bien conçu(e).

well-timed [-'taɪmd] adj bien calculé(e), qui vient à point nommé.

well-to-do adj riche.

wellwisher ['wel,wɪʃər] n admirateur m, -trice f.

well-woman clinic n Br centre m de santé pour femmes.

Welsh [welʃ] <> adj gallois(e) <> n [language] gallois m <> npl : **the ~** les Gallois mpl.

Welsh Assembly n Assemblée f galloise.

THE WELSH ASSEMBLY

L'Assemblée galloise, qui siège à Cardiff, est constituée de 60 membres (Members of Parliament ou MPs) dirigés par le président de l'Assemblée (First Secretary). Elle est chargée de voter la plupart des lois en matière de politique intérieure, mais, contrairement au Parlement écossais, elle n'est pas compétente dans le domaine des impôts. La politique étrangère, l'économie, la défense et les affaires européennes demeurent sous le contrôle du gouvernement britannique à Londres.

Welshman ['welʃmən] (pl -men [-mən]) n Gallois m.

Welsh rarebit [-'reəbɪt] n toast m au fromage chaud.

Welshwoman ['welʃ,wʊmən] (pl -women [-,wɪmɪn]) n Galloise f.

welter ['weltər] n [of ideas, emotions] confusion f.

welterweight ['weltəweɪt] n poids m welter.

wend [wend] vt literary : **to ~ one's way homewards** [set off] se mettre en route pour rentrer à la maison ; [be on one's way] être sur le chemin de la maison.

wendy house ['wendɪ-] n Br maison f en modèle réduit (pour jouer).

went [went] pt ▷ go.

wept [wept] *pt & pp* ⊳ **weep.**

were [wɜːʳ] ⊳ **be.**

we're [wɪəʳ] = **we are.**

weren't [wɜːnt] = **were not.**

werewolf ['wɪəwʊlf] (*pl* **-wolves** [-wʊlvz]) *n* loup-garou *m*.

west [west] ⊳ *n* - **1.** [direction] ouest *m* - **2.** [region] : **the ~** l'ouest *m* ⊳ *adj* ouest (*inv*) ; [wind] d'ouest ⊳ *adv* de l'ouest, vers l'ouest ; **~ of** à l'ouest de.
◆ **West** *n* POL : **the West** l'Occident *m*.

West Bank *n* : **the ~** la Cisjordanie ; **on the ~** en Cisjordanie.

westbound ['westbaʊnd] *adj* en direction de l'ouest.

West Country *n* Br : **the ~** le sud-ouest de l'Angleterre.

West End *n* Br : **the ~** le West-End (*quartier des grands magasins et des théâtres, à Londres*).

westerly ['westəlɪ] *adj* à l'ouest ; [wind] de l'ouest ; **in a ~ direction** vers l'ouest.

western ['westən] ⊳ *adj* - **1.** [gen] de l'ouest - **2.** POL occidental(e) ⊳ *n* [book, film] western *m*.

Westerner ['westənəʳ] *n* - **1.** POL Occidental *m*, -e *f* - **2.** [inhabitant of west of country] personne *f* de l'ouest.

westernize, -ise ['westənaɪz] *vt* occidentaliser.

Western Samoa *n* Samoa *fpl* occidentales ; **in ~** dans les Samoa occidentales.

West German ⊳ *adj* ouest-allemand(e) ⊳ *n* Allemand *m*, -e *f* de l'Ouest.

West Germany *n* : **(former) ~** (ex-) Allemagne *f* de l'Ouest ; **in ~** en Allemagne de l'Ouest.

West Indian ⊳ *adj* antillais(e) ⊳ *n* Antillais *m*, -e *f*.

West Indies [-'ɪndɪːz] *npl* : **the ~** les Antilles *fpl* ; **in the ~** aux Antilles.

Westminster ['westmɪnstəʳ] *n* quartier de Londres où se situe le Parlement britannique.

WESTMINSTER

C'est dans ce quartier que se trouvent le Parlement et le palais de Buckingham. Le nom « Westminster » est également employé pour désigner le Parlement lui-même.

West Virginia *n* Virginie-Occidentale *f* ; **in ~** en Virginie-Occidentale.

westward ['westwəd] *adj & adv* vers l'ouest.

westwards ['westwədz] *adv* vers l'ouest.

wet [wet] (*compar* **-ter** ; *superl* **-test**, *pt & pp*

wet OR **-ted**, *cont* **-ting**) ⊳ *adj* - **1.** [damp, soaked] mouillé(e) - **2.** [rainy] pluvieux(euse) - **3.** [not dry - paint, cement] frais (fraîche) - **4.** Br *inf pej* [weak, feeble] ramolli(e) ⊳ *n inf* POL modéré *m*, -e *f* ⊳ *vt* mouiller ; **to ~ o.s.** [child] mouiller sa culotte ; *inf* [be terrified] pisser dans son froc.

wet blanket *n inf pej* rabat-joie *m inv*.

wet-look *adj* brillant(e).

wetness ['wetnɪs] *n* - **1.** [dampness] humidité *f* - **2.** Br *inf pej* [feebleness] faiblesse *f*.

wet nurse *n* nourrice *f*.

wet rot *n* pourriture *f* humide.

wet suit *n* combinaison *f* de plongée.

WEU (*abbr of* **Western European Union**) *n* UEO *f*.

we've [wiːv] = **we have.**

whack [wæk] *inf* ⊳ *n* - **1.** [share] part *f* - **2.** [hit] grand coup *m* ⊳ *vt* donner un grand coup à, frapper fort.

whacked [wækt] *adj* Br *inf* [exhausted] crevé(e).

whacky ['wækɪ] *adj* = **wacky.**

whale [weɪl] *n* baleine *f* ; **to have a ~ of a time** *inf* drôlement bien s'amuser.

whaling ['weɪlɪŋ] *n* pêche *f* à la baleine.

wham [wæm] *excl* inf vlan!

wharf [wɔːf] (*pl* **-s** OR **wharves** [wɔːvz]) *n* quai *m*.

what [wɒt] ⊳ *adj* - **1.** (in direct, indirect questions) quel (quelle), quels (quelles) (*pl*) ; **~ colour is it?** c'est de quelle couleur? ; **he asked me ~ colour it was** il m'a demandé de quelle couleur c'était - **2.** (in exclamations) quel (quelle), quels (quelles) (*pl*) ; **~ a surprise!** quelle surprise! ; **~ an idiot I am!** que je peux être bête! ⊳ *pron* - **1.** (interrogative - subject) qu'est-ce qui ; (- object) qu'est-ce que, que ; (- after prep) quoi ; **~ are they doing?** qu'est-ce qu'ils font?, que font-ils? ; **~ is going on?** qu'est-ce qui se passe? ; **~ are they talking about?** de quoi parlent-ils? ; **~ about another drink/going out for a meal?** et si on prenait un autre verre/allait manger au restaurant? ; **~ about the rest of us?** et nous alors? ; **~ if ...?** et si ...? - **2.** (relative - subject) ce qui ; (- object) ce que ; **I saw ~ happened/fell** j'ai vu ce qui s'était passé/était tombé ; **you can't have ~ you want** tu ne peux pas avoir ce que tu veux ⊳ *excl* [expressing disbelief] comment!, quoi!

whatever [wɒt'evəʳ] ⊳ *adj* quel (quelle) que soit ; **any book ~** n'importe quel livre ; **no chance ~** pas la moindre chance ; **nothing ~** rien du tout ⊳ *pron* quoi que (+ subjunctive) ; **I'll do ~ I can** je ferai tout ce que je peux ; ~ **can this be?** qu'est-ce que cela peut-il bien être? ; ~ **that may mean** quoi que cela puisse bien vouloir dire ; **or** ~ ou n'importe quoi d'autre.

whatnot ['wɒtnɒt] *n inf* - **1.** [thing] machin *m* - **2.** [other things] : **and** ~ et d'autres bricoles.

whatsoever [ˌwɒtsəʊ'evəʳ] *adj* : **I had no interest** ~ je n'éprouvais pas le moindre intérêt ; **nothing** ~ rien du tout.

wheat [wiːt] *n* blé *m*.

wheat germ *n* germe *m* de blé.

wheatmeal ['wiːtmiːl] *n* farine *f* de blé.

wheedle ['wiːdl] *vt* : **to** ~ **sb into doing sthg** enjôler qqn pour qu'il fasse qqch ; **to** ~ **sthg out of sb** enjôler qqn pour obtenir qqch.

wheel [wiːl] ◇ *n* - **1.** [gen] roue *f* - **2.** [steering wheel] volant *m* ◇ *vt* pousser ◇ *vi* : **to** ~ **(round)** se retourner brusquement.

wheelbarrow ['wiːlˌbærəʊ] *n* brouette *f*.

wheelbase ['wiːlbeɪs] *n* empattement *m*.

wheelchair ['wiːlˌtʃeəʳ] *n* fauteuil *m* roulant.

wheelclamp ['wiːlˌklæmp] ◇ *n* sabot *m* de Denver ◇ *vt* : **my car was** ~**ed** on a mis un sabot à ma voiture.

wheeler-dealer ['wiːləʳ-] *n pej* combinard *m*.

wheeling and dealing ['wiːlɪŋ-] *n (U) pej* combines *fpl*.

wheeze [wiːz] ◇ *n* [sound] respiration *f* sifflante ◇ *vi* respirer avec un bruit sifflant.

wheezy ['wiːzɪ] (*compar* **-ier** ; *superl* **-iest**) *adj* [person] poussif(ive) ; [cough] sifflant(e) ; [voice, chest] d'asthmatique.

whelk [welk] *n* bulot *m*, buccin *m*.

when [wen] ◇ *adv* (*in direct, indirect questions*) quand ; ~ **does the plane arrive?** quand *OR* à quelle heure arrive l'avion? ; **he asked me** ~ **I would be in London** il m'a demandé quand je serais à Londres ◇ *conj* - **1.** [referring to time] quand, lorsque ; **he came to see me** ~ **I was abroad** il est venu me voir quand j'étais à l'étranger ; **one day** ~ **I was on my own** un jour que *OR* où j'étais tout seul ; **on the day** ~ **it happened** le jour où cela s'est passé - **2.** [whereas, considering that] alors que.

whenever [wen'evəʳ] ◇ *conj* quand ; [each time that] chaque fois que ◇ *adv* n'importe quand.

where [weəʳ] ◇ *adv* (*in direct, indirect questions*) où ; ~ **do you live?** où habitez-vous? ; **do you know** ~ **he lives?** est-ce que vous savez où il habite? ◇ *conj* - **1.** [referring to place, situation] où ; **this is** ~ ... c'est là que ... - **2.** [whereas] alors que.

whereabouts [*adv* ˌweərə'baʊts, *n* 'weərəbaʊts] ◇ *adv* où ◇ *npl* : **their** ~ **are still unknown** on ne sait toujours pas où ils se trouvent.

whereas [weər'æz] *conj* alors que.

whereby [weə'baɪ] *conj fml* par lequel (laquelle), au moyen duquel (de laquelle).

wheresoever [ˌweəsəʊ'evəʳ] *conj* = **wherever**.

whereupon [ˌweərə'pɒn] *conj fml* après quoi, sur quoi.

wherever [weər'evəʳ] ◇ *conj* où que (+ *subjunctive*) ◇ *adv* - **1.** [no matter where] n'importe où - **2.** [where] où donc ; ~ **did you hear that?** mais où donc as-tu entendu dire cela?

wherewithal ['weəwɪðɔːl] *n fml* : **to have the** ~ **to do sthg** avoir les moyens de faire qqch.

whet [wet] (*pt* & *pp* **-ted** ; *cont* **-ting**) *vt* : **to** ~ **sb's appetite for sthg** donner à qqn envie de qqch.

whether ['weðəʳ] *conj* - **1.** [indicating choice, doubt] si - **2.** [no matter if] : ~ **I want to or not** que je le veuille ou non.

whew [hwjuː] *excl* ouf!

whey [weɪ] *n* petit-lait *m*.

which [wɪtʃ] ◇ *adj* - **1.** (*in direct, indirect questions*) quel (quelle), quels (quelles) (*pl*) ; ~ **house is yours?** quelle maison est la tienne? ; ~ **one?** lequel (laquelle)? - **2.** [to refer back to sthg] : **in** ~ **case** auquel cas ◇ *pron* - **1.** (*in direct, indirect questions*) lequel (laquelle), lesquels (lesquelles) (*pl*) ; ~ **do you prefer?** lequel préférez-vous? ; **I can't decide** ~ **to have** je ne sais vraiment pas lequel prendre - **2.** (*in relative clauses - subject*) qui ; (- *object*) que ; (- *after prep*) lequel (laquelle), lesquels (lesquelles) (*pl*) ; **take the slice** ~ **is nearer to you** prends la tranche qui est la plus près de toi ; **the television** ~ **we bought** le téléviseur que nous avons acheté ; **the settee on** ~ **I am sitting** le canapé sur lequel je suis assis ; **the film of** ~ **you spoke** le film dont vous avez parlé - **3.** (*referring back - subject*) ce qui ; (- *object*) ce que ; **why did you say you were ill,** ~ **nobody believed?** pourquoi as-tu dit que tu étais malade, ce que personne n'a cru?

whichever [wɪtʃ'evəʳ] ◇ *adj* quel (quelle) que soit ; **choose** ~ **colour you prefer** choisissez la couleur que vous préférez, n'importe laquelle ◇ *pron* n'importe lequel (laquelle).

whiff [wɪf] *n* - **1.** [of perfume, smoke] bouffée *f* ; [of food] odeur *f* - **2.** *fig* [sign] signe *m*.

while [waɪl] ◇ *n* moment *m* ; **let's stay here**

for a ~ restons ici un moment ; **we've been waiting for a** ~ nous attendons depuis un moment ; **for a long** ~ longtemps ; **after a** ~ après quelque temps ; **to be worth one's** ~ valoir la peine ◇ *conj* - **1.** [during the time that] pendant que - **2.** [as long as] tant que - **3.** [whereas] alors que.
◆ **while away** *vt sep* passer.

whilst [waɪlst] *conj* = **while**.

whim [wɪm] *n* lubie *f*.

whimper ['wɪmpəʳ] ◇ *n* gémissement *m* ◇ *vt* & *vi* gémir.

whimsical ['wɪmzɪkl] *adj* saugrenu(e).

whine [waɪn] ◇ *n* gémissement *m*, longue plainte *f* ◇ *vi* - **1.** [make sound] gémir - **2.** [complain] : **to** ~ **(about)** se plaindre (de).

whinge [wɪndʒ] (*cont* **whingeing**) *vi* Br : **to** ~ **(about)** se plaindre (de).

whip [wɪp] (*pt* & *pp* **-ped** ; *cont* **-ping**) ◇ *n* - **1.** [for hitting] fouet *m* - **2.** Br POL chef *m* de file (*d'un groupe parlementaire*) ◇ *vt* - **1.** [gen] fouetter - **2.** [take quickly] : **to** ~ **sthg out** sortir qqch brusquement ; **to** ~ **sthg off** ôter OR enlever qqch brusquement.
◆ **whip up** *vt sep* [provoke] stimuler, attiser.

whiplash injury ['wɪplæʃ-] *n* coup *m* du lapin.

whipped cream [wɪpt-] *n* crème *f* fouettée.

whippet ['wɪpɪt] *n* whippet *m*.

whip-round *n* Br inf : **to have a** ~ faire une collecte.

whirl [wɜːl] ◇ *n* - **1.** lit & fig tourbillon *m* ; **I/my mind was in a** ~ tout tourbillonnait en moi/dans ma tête - **2.** phr : **let's give it a** ~ inf tentons le coup ◇ *vt* : **to** ~ **sb/sthg round** [spin round] faire tourbillonner qqn/qqch ◇ *vi* tourbillonner ; fig [head, mind] tourner.

whirlpool ['wɜːlpuːl] *n* tourbillon *m*.

whirlpool bath *n* = spa bath.

whirlwind ['wɜːlwɪnd] ◇ *adj* fig éclair (*inv*) ◇ *n* tornade *f*.

whirr [wɜːʳ] ◇ *n* [of engine] ronronnement *m* ◇ *vi* [engine] ronronner.

whisk [wɪsk] ◇ *n* CULIN fouet *m*, batteur *m* (à œufs) ◇ *vt* - **1.** [move quickly] emmener OR emporter rapidement - **2.** CULIN battre.

whisker ['wɪskəʳ] *n* moustache *f*.
◆ **whiskers** *npl* favoris *mpl*.

whisky Br (*pl* **-ies**), **whiskey** Am & Irish (*pl* **-s**) ['wɪskɪ] *n* whisky *m*.

whisper ['wɪspəʳ] ◇ *n* murmure *m* ◇ *vt* murmurer, chuchoter ◇ *vi* chuchoter.

whispering ['wɪspərɪŋ] *n* chuchotement *m*.

whist [wɪst] *n* whist *m*.

whistle ['wɪsl] ◇ *n* - **1.** [sound] sifflement *m* - **2.** [device] sifflet *m* ◇ *vt* & *vi* siffler.

whistle-stop tour *n* : **to make a** ~ **of** [subj : politician] faire une tournée éclair dans.

whit [wɪt] *n* brin *m*.

Whit [wɪt] *n* Br Pentecôte *f*.

white [waɪt] ◇ *adj* - **1.** [in colour] blanc (blanche) ; **to go** OR **turn** ~ [hair] blanchir ; [face] pâlir - **2.** [coffee, tea] au lait ◇ *n* - **1.** [colour, of egg, eye] blanc *m* - **2.** [person] Blanc *m*, Blanche *f*.
◆ **whites** *npl* - **1.** SPORT tenue *f* blanche - **2.** [washing] linge *m* blanc.

white blood cell *n* globule *m* blanc.

whiteboard ['waɪtbɔːd] *n* tableau *m* blanc.

white Christmas *n* Noël *m* blanc.

white-collar *adj* de bureau.

white elephant *n* fig objet *m* coûteux et inutile.

white goods *npl* - **1.** [linen] articles *mpl* de blanc - **2.** [household machines] électroménager *m*.

white-haired [-'heəd] *adj* aux cheveux blancs.

Whitehall ['waɪthɔːl] *n rue de Londres, centre administratif du gouvernement britannique.*

white horses *npl* Br [of waves] moutons *mpl*.

white-hot *adj* chauffé(e) à blanc.

White House *n* : **the** ~ la Maison-Blanche.

white knight *n* chevalier *m* blanc.

white lie *n* pieux mensonge *m*.

white light *n* lumière *f* blanche.

white magic *n* magie *f* blanche.

white meat *n* viande *f* blanche.

whiten ['waɪtn] *vt* & *vi* blanchir.

whitener ['waɪtnəʳ] *n* agent *m* blanchissant.

whiteness ['waɪtnɪs] *n* blancheur *f*.

white noise *n* son *m* blanc.

whiteout ['waɪtaʊt] *n* jour *m* blanc.

white paper *n* POL livre *m* blanc

white sauce *n* sauce *f* blanche.

White Sea *n* : **the** ~ la mer Blanche.

white spirit *n* Br white-spirit *m*.

white-tie *adj* [dinner] en habit.

whitewash ['waɪtwɒʃ] ◇ *n* - **1.** (U) [paint] chaux *f* - **2.** pej [cover-up] : **a government** ~ une combine du gouvernement pour étouffer l'affaire ◇ vt - **1.** [paint] blanchir à la chaux - **2.** pej [cover up] blanchir.

whitewater rafting [ˈwaɪtˌwɔːtəʳ-] n raft m, rafting m.

white wedding n mariage m en blanc.

white wine n vin m blanc.

whiting [ˈwaɪtɪŋ] (pl inv OR -s) n merlan m.

Whit Monday [wɪt-] n le lundi m de Pentecôte.

Whitsun [ˈwɪtsn] n Pentecôte f.

whittle [ˈwɪtl] vt [reduce] : **to ~ sthg away** OR **down** réduire qqch.

whiz (pt & pp -**zed** ; cont -**zing**), **whizz** [wɪz] ◇ n inf : **to be a ~ at sthg** être un as de qqch ◇ vi [go fast] aller à toute allure.

whiz(z) kid n inf petit prodige m.

who [huː] pron - **1.** (in direct, indirect questions) qui ; **~ are you?** qui êtes-vous? ; **I didn't know ~ she was** je ne savais pas qui c'était - **2.** (in relative clauses) qui ; **he's the doctor ~ treated me** c'est le médecin qui m'a soigné ; **I don't know the person ~ came to see you** je ne connais pas la personne qui est venue vous voir.

WHO (abbr of **World Health Organization**) n OMS f.

who'd [huːd] = who had, who would.

whodu(n)nit [ˌhuːˈdʌnɪt] n inf polar m.

whoever [huːˈevəʳ] pron - **1.** [unknown person] quiconque - **2.** [indicating surprise, astonishment] qui donc - **3.** [no matter who] qui que (+ subjunctive) ; **~ you are** qui que vous soyez ; **~ wins** qui que ce soit qui gagne.

whole [həʊl] ◇ adj - **1.** [entire, complete] entier(ère) - **2.** [for emphasis] : **a ~ lot of questions** toute une série de questions ; **a ~ lot bigger** bien plus gros ; **a ~ new idea** une idée tout à fait nouvelle ◇ n - **1.** [all] : **the ~ of the school** toute l'école ; **the ~ of the summer** tout l'été - **2.** [unit, complete thing] tout m.
➥ **as a whole** adv dans son ensemble.
➥ **on the whole** adv dans l'ensemble.

wholefood [ˈhəʊlfuːd] n Br aliments mpl complets.

whole-hearted [-ˈhɑːtɪd] adj sans réserve, total(e).

wholemeal [ˈhəʊlmiːl] Br, **whole wheat** Am adj complet(ète).

wholemeal bread n Br (U) pain m complet.

whole note n Am ronde f.

wholesale [ˈhəʊlseɪl] ◇ adj - **1.** [buying, selling] en gros ; [price] de gros - **2.** pej [excessive] en

masse ◇ adv - **1.** [in bulk] en gros - **2.** pej [excessively] en masse.

wholesaler [ˈhəʊlˌseɪləʳ] n marchand m de gros, grossiste mf.

wholesome [ˈhəʊlsəm] adj sain(e).

whole wheat Am = wholemeal.

who'll [huːl] = who will.

wholly [ˈhəʊlɪ] adv totalement.

whom [huːm] pron fml - **1.** (in direct, indirect questions) qui ; **~ did you phone?** qui avez-vous appelé au téléphone? ; **for/of/to ~** pour/de/à qui - **2.** (in relative clauses) que ; **the girl ~ he married** la jeune fille qu'il a épousée ; **the man of ~ you speak** l'homme dont vous parlez ; **the man to ~ you were speaking** l'homme à qui vous parliez.

whoop [wuːp] ◇ n cri m ◇ vi pousser des cris (de joie/de triomphe).

whoopee [wʊˈpiː] excl youpi!

whooping cough [ˈhuːpɪŋ-] n coqueluche f.

whoops [wʊps] excl oups!

whoosh [wʊʃ] inf ◇ n [of water, air] jet m ◇ vi [water] jaillir.

whop [wɒp] vt inf battre à plates coutures.

whopper [ˈwɒpəʳ] n inf - **1.** [something big] : **it's a real ~** c'est absolument énorme - **2.** [lie] mensonge m énorme.

whopping [ˈwɒpɪŋ] inf ◇ adj énorme ◇ adv : **a ~ great lorry/lie** un camion/mensonge absolument énorme.

whore [hɔːʳ] n offensive putain f.

who're [ˈhuːəʳ] = who are.

whose [huːz] ◇ pron (in direct, indirect questions) à qui ; **~ is this?** à qui est ceci? ◇ adj - **1.** à qui ; **~ car is that?** à qui est cette voiture? ; **~ son is he?** de qui est-il le fils? - **2.** (in relative clauses) dont ; **that's the boy ~ father's an MP** c'est le garçon dont le père est député ; **the girl ~ mother you phoned yesterday** la fille à la mère de qui OR de laquelle tu as téléphoné hier.

whosoever [ˌhuːsəʊˈevəʳ] pron dated quiconque.

who's who [huːz-] n [book] Bottin® m mondain.

who've [huːv] = who have.

why [waɪ] ◇ adv (in direct questions) pourquoi ; **~ did you lie to me?** pourquoi m'as-tu menti? ; **~ don't you all come?** pourquoi ne pas tous venir?, pourquoi est-ce que vous ne viendriez pas tous? ; **~ not?** pourquoi pas? ◇ conj pourquoi ; **I don't know ~ he said that** je ne sais pas pourquoi il a dit cela

◇ *pron* : there are several reasons ~ he left il est parti pour plusieurs raisons, les raisons pour lesquelles il est parti sont nombreuses ; **I don't know the reason ~** je ne sais pas pourquoi ◇ *excl* tiens!

➤ **why ever** *adv* pourquoi donc.

WI ◇ *n abbr of* **Women's Institute** ◇ **- 1.** *abbr of* **West Indies - 2.** *abbr of* **Wisconsin.**

wick [wɪk] *n* **- 1.** [of candle, lighter] mèche *f* **- 2.** *phr* : **to get on sb's ~** Br *inf* taper sur les nerfs de qqn.

wicked ['wɪkɪd] *adj* **- 1.** [evil] mauvais(e) **- 2.** [mischievous, devilish] malicieux(euse) **- 3.** *inf* [very good] génial(e), super *(inv)*.

wicker ['wɪkə'] *adj* en osier.

wickerwork ['wɪkəwɜːk] ◇ *n* vannerie *f* ◇ *comp* en osier.

wicket ['wɪkɪt] *n* CRICKET **- 1.** [stumps, dismissal] guichet *m* **- 2.** [pitch] terrain *m* entre les guichets.

wicket keeper *n* CRICKET gardien *m* de guichet.

wide [waɪd] ◇ *adj* **- 1.** [gen] large ; **how ~ is the room?** quelle est la largeur de la pièce? ; **to be six metres ~** faire six mètres de large OR de largeur **- 2.** [gap, difference] grand(e) **- 3.** [experience, knowledge, issue] vaste **- 4.** [eyes] écarquillé(e) **- 5.** [off-target] qui passe à côté ◇ *adv* **- 1.** [broadly] largement ; **open ~!** ouvrez grand! **- 2.** [off-target] : **the shot went ~** le coup est passé loin du but OR à côté.

wide-angle lens *n* PHOT objectif *m* grand angle.

wide-awake *adj* tout à fait réveillé(e).

wide boy *n* Br *inf* pej escroc *m*.

wide-eyed [-'aɪd] *adj* **- 1.** [surprised, frightened] aux yeux écarquillés **- 2.** [innocent] aux yeux grands ouverts.

widely ['waɪdlɪ] *adv* **- 1.** [smile, vary] largement **- 2.** [extensively] beaucoup ; **to be ~ read** avoir beaucoup lu ; **it is ~ believed that ...** beaucoup pensent que ..., nombreux sont ceux qui pensent que ... ; **~ known** largement OR bien connu, largement OR bien connue.

widen ['waɪdn] ◇ *vt* **- 1.** [make broader] élargir **- 2.** [gap, difference] agrandir, élargir ◇ *vi* **- 1.** [become broader] s'élargir **- 2.** [gap, difference] s'agrandir, s'élargir **- 3.** [eyes] s'agrandir.

wide open *adj* grand ouvert (grande ouverte) ; **the ~ spaces** les grands espaces.

wide-ranging [-'reɪndʒɪŋ] *adj* varié(e) ; [consequences] de grande envergure.

wide screen *n* TV & CIN écran *m* 16/9.

wide-screen *adj* [television, film, format] 16/9.

widespread ['waɪdspred] *adj* très répandu(e).

widow ['wɪdəʊ] *n* veuve *f*.

widowed ['wɪdəʊd] *adj* veuf (veuve).

widower ['wɪdəʊə'] *n* veuf *m*.

width [wɪdθ] *n* largeur *f* ; **in ~** de large.

widthways ['wɪdθweɪz] *adv* en largeur.

wield [wiːld] *vt* **- 1.** [weapon] manier **- 2.** [power] exercer.

wife [waɪf] (*pl* **wives** [waɪvz]) *n* femme *f*, épouse *f*.

wig [wɪg] *n* perruque *f*.

wiggle ['wɪgl] *inf* ◇ *n* **- 1.** [movement] tortillement *m* **- 2.** [wavy line] ondulation *f* ◇ *vt* remuer ◇ *vi* se tortiller.

wiggly ['wɪglɪ] (*compar* **-ier** ; *superl* **-iest**) *adj inf* [line] ondulé(e).

wigwam ['wɪgwæm] *n* wigwam *m*.

wild [waɪld] ◇ *adj* **- 1.** [animal, attack, scenery, flower] sauvage **- 2.** [weather, sea] déchaîné(e) **- 3.** [laughter, hope, plan] fou (folle) ; **the crowd went ~** la foule s'est déchaînée ; **to run ~** être déchaîné **- 4.** [eyes] de fou (de folle) ; [hair] en bataille **- 5.** [random - estimate] fantaisiste ; **I made a ~ guess** j'ai dit ça au hasard **- 6.** *inf* [very enthusiastic] : **to be ~ about** être dingue de ◇ *n* : **in the ~** dans la nature.

➤ **wilds** *npl* : **the ~s of** le fin fond de ; **to live in the ~s** habiter en pleine nature.

wild card *n* COMPUT caractère *m* joker.

wildcat ['waɪldkæt] *n* [animal] chat *m* sauvage.

wildcat strike *n* grève *f* sauvage.

wildebeest ['wɪldɪbiːst] (*pl inv* OR **-s**) *n* gnou *m*.

wilderness ['wɪldənɪs] *n* étendue *f* sauvage ; **to be in the ~** *fig* faire une traversée du désert.

wildfire ['waɪld,faɪə'] *n* : **to spread like ~** se répandre comme une traînée de poudre.

wild flower *n* fleur *f* sauvage.

wild-goose chase *n inf* : **it turned out to be a ~** ça s'est révélé être totalement inutile.

wildlife ['waɪldlaɪf] *n* (U) faune *f* et flore *f*.

wildly ['waɪldlɪ] *adv* **- 1.** [enthusiastically, fanatically] frénétiquement **- 2.** [guess, suggest] au hasard ; [shoot] dans tous les sens **- 3.** [very - different, impractical] tout à fait **- 4.** [menacingly] farouchement.

wild rice *n* riz *m* sauvage.

wild West *n inf* : **the ~** le Far West.

wiles [waɪlz] *npl* artifices *mpl*.

wilful Br, **willful** Am ['wɪlfʊl] *adj* - **1.** [determined] obstiné(e) - **2.** [deliberate] délibéré(e).

will¹ [wɪl] ⬦ *n* - **1.** [mental] volonté *f*; against one's ~ contre son gré ; at ~ à volonté - **2.** [document] testament *m* ⬦ *vt* : to ~ sthg to happen prier de toutes ses forces pour que qqch se passe ; to ~ sb to do sthg concentrer toute sa volonté sur qqn pour qu'il fasse qqch.

will² [wɪl] *modal vb* - **1.** (*to express future tense*) : I ~ see you next week je te verrai la semaine prochaine ; when ~ you have finished it? quand est-ce que vous l'aurez fini? ; I'll be arriving at six j'arriverai à six heures ; ~ you be here next week? — yes I ~/no I won't est-ce que tu seras là la semaine prochaine? — oui/non - **2.** [indicating willingness] : ~ you have some more tea? voulez-vous encore du thé? ; I won't do it je refuse de le faire, je ne veux pas le faire - **3.** [in commands, requests] : you ~ leave this house at once tu vas quitter cette maison tout de suite ; close that window, ~ you? ferme cette fenêtre, veux-tu? ; ~ you be quiet! veux-tu te taire!, tu vas te taire! - **4.** [indicating possibility, what usually happens] : the hall ~ hold up to 1000 people la salle peut abriter jusqu'à 1000 personnes ; this ~ stop any draughts ceci supprimera tous les courants d'air ; pensions ~ be paid monthly les pensions sont payées tous les mois - **5.** [expressing an assumption] : that'll be your father cela doit être ton père - **6.** [indicating irritation] : well, if you ~ leave your toys everywhere ... que veux-tu, si tu t'obstines à laisser traîner tes jouets partout ... ; she ~ keep phoning me elle n'arrête pas de me téléphoner.

willful Am = **wilful**.

willing ['wɪlɪŋ] *adj* - **1.** [prepared] : if you're ~ si vous voulez bien ; to be ~ to do sthg être disposé(e) OR prêt(e) à faire qqch - **2.** [eager] enthousiaste.

willingly ['wɪlɪŋlɪ] *adv* volontiers.

willingness ['wɪlɪŋnɪs] *n* - **1.** [preparedness] : ~ to do sthg bonne volonté *f* à faire qqch - **2.** [keenness] enthousiasme *m*.

willow (tree) ['wɪləʊ-] *n* saule *m*.

willowy ['wɪləʊɪ] *adj* svelte.

willpower ['wɪl,paʊəʳ] *n* volonté *f*.

willy ['wɪlɪ] (*pl* -ies) *n* Br inf zizi *m*.

willy-nilly [,wɪlɪ'nɪlɪ] *adv* - **1.** [at random] n'importe comment - **2.** [wanting to or not] bon gré mal gré.

wilt [wɪlt] *vi* [plant] se faner ; fig [person] dépérir.

Wilts [wɪlts] (*abbr of* **Wiltshire**) *comté anglais*.

wily ['waɪlɪ] (*compar* -ier ; *superl* -iest) *adj* rusé(e).

wimp [wɪmp] *n pej inf* mauviette *f*.

win [wɪn] (*pt & pp* won, *cont* -ning) ⬦ *n* victoire *f* ⬦ *vt* - **1.** [game, prize, competition] gagner - **2.** [support, approval] obtenir ; [love, friendship] gagner ⬦ *vi* gagner ; you/I etc can't ~ il n'y a rien à faire.
➤ **win over, win round** *vt sep* convaincre, gagner à sa cause.

wince [wɪns] ⬦ *vi* : to ~ (at/with) [with body] tressaillir (à/de) ; [with face] grimacer (à/de) ⬦ *n* tressaillement *m*.

winch [wɪntʃ] ⬦ *n* treuil *m* ⬦ *vt* hisser à l'aide d'un treuil.

Winchester disk ['wɪntʃestəʳ-] *n* disque *m* (dur) Winchester.

wind¹ [wɪnd] *n* - **1.** METEOR vent *m* - **2.** [breath] souffle *m* - **3.** (*U*) [in stomach] gaz *mpl* ; to break ~ euphemism lâcher un vent - **4.** [in orchestra] : the ~ les instruments *mpl* à vent - **5.** phr : to get ~ of sthg inf avoir vent de qqch ⬦ *vt* - **1.** [knock breath out of] couper le souffle à - **2.** Br [baby] faire faire son rot à.

wind² [waɪnd] (*pt & pp* wound) ⬦ *vt* - **1.** [string, thread] enrouler - **2.** [clock] remonter - **3.** phr : to ~ its way [river, road] serpenter ⬦ *vi* [river, road] serpenter.
➤ **wind back** *vt sep* [tape] rembobiner.
➤ **wind down** ⬦ *vt sep* - **1.** [car window] baisser - **2.** [business] cesser graduellement ⬦ *vi* - **1.** [clock] ralentir - **2.** [relax] se détendre.
➤ **wind forward** *vt sep* [tape] embobiner.
➤ **wind up** ⬦ *vt sep* - **1.** [finish - meeting] clôturer ; [- business] liquider - **2.** [clock, car window] remonter - **3.** Br inf [deliberately annoy] faire marcher - **4.** inf [end up] : to ~ up doing sthg finir par faire qqch ⬦ *vi* inf [end up] finir.

windbreak ['wɪndbreɪk] *n* pare-vent *m inv*.

windcheater Br ['wɪnd,tʃiːtəʳ], **windbreaker** Am ['wɪnd,breɪkəʳ] *n* coupe-vent *m inv*.

windchill factor ['wɪndtʃɪl-] *n* facteur d'abaissement de la température provoqué par le vent, facteur *m* vent Can, indice *m* de refroidissement Can.

winded ['wɪndɪd] *adj* essoufflé(e).

windfall ['wɪndfɔːl] *n* - **1.** [fruit] fruit *m* que le vent a fait tomber - **2.** [unexpected gift] aubaine *f*.

winding ['waɪndɪŋ] *adj* sinueux(euse).

wind instrument [wɪnd-] *n* instrument *m* à vent.

windmill ['wɪndmɪl] *n* moulin *m* à vent.

window ['wɪndəʊ] *n* - **1.** [gen & COMPUT] fenêtre *f* - **2.** [pane of glass, in car] vitre *f* - **3.** [of shop] vitrine *f*.

window box *n* jardinière *f*.

window cleaner *n* laveur *m*, -euse *f* de vitres.

window dressing *n (U)* - **1.** [in shop] étalage *m* - **2.** fig [non-essentials] façade *f*.

window envelope *n* enveloppe *f* à fenêtre.

window frame *n* châssis *m* de fenêtre.

window ledge *n* rebord *m* de fenêtre.

windowpane *n* vitre *f*

window shade *n* Am store *m*.

window-shopping *n* lèche-vitrines *m ;* to go ~ (aller) faire du lèche-vitrines.

windowsill ['wɪndəʊsɪl] *n* [outside] rebord *m* de fenêtre ; [inside] appui *m* de fenêtre.

windpipe ['wɪndpaɪp] *n* trachée *f*.

windscreen Br ['wɪndskriːn], **windshield** Am ['wɪndʃiːld] *n* pare-brise *m inv*.

windscreen washer *n* lave-glace *m*.

windscreen wiper [-ˌwaɪpəʳ] *n* essuie-glace *m*.

windshield Am = **windscreen**.

windsock ['wɪndsɒk] *n* manche *f* à air.

windsurfer ['wɪndˌsɜːfəʳ] *n* - **1.** [person] véliplanchiste *mf* - **2.** [board] planche *f* à voile.

windsurfing ['wɪndˌsɜːfɪŋ] *n :* to go ~ faire de la planche à voile.

windswept ['wɪndswept] *adj* - **1.** [scenery] balayé(e) par les vents - **2.** [person] échevelé(e) ; [hair] ébouriffé(e).

wind tunnel [wɪnd-] *n* soufflerie *f*, tunnel *m* aérodynamique.

Windward Islands ['wɪndwəd-] *n :* the ~ les îles *fpl* du Vent.

windy ['wɪndɪ] (*compar* -**ier** ; *superl* -**iest**) *adj* venteux(euse) ; it's ~ il fait OR il y a du vent.

wine [waɪn] *n* vin *m*.

wine bar *n* Br bar *m* à vin.

wine bottle *n* bouteille *f* à vin.

wine box *n* Cubitainer® *m*.

wine cellar *n* cave *f* (à vin).

wineglass ['waɪnglɑːs] *n* verre *m* à vin.

wine list *n* carte *f* des vins.

wine merchant *n* Br marchand *m* de vins.

winepress ['waɪnpres] *n* pressoir *m*.

wine tasting [-ˌteɪstɪŋ] *n* dégustation *f* (de vins).

wine waiter *n* sommelier *m*.

wing [wɪŋ] *n* aile *f*.

wings *npl* - **1.** THEATRE : the ~s les coulisses *fpl* - **2.** [pilot's badge] galons *mpl*.

wing commander *n* Br lieutenant-colonel *m*.

winger ['wɪŋəʳ] *n* SPORT ailier *m*.

wing nut *n* vis *f* à ailettes.

wingspan ['wɪŋspæn] *n* envergure *f*.

wink [wɪŋk] ◇ *n* clin *m* d'œil ; to have forty ~s inf faire un petit roupillon ; not to sleep a ~, not to get a ~ of sleep inf ne pas fermer l'œil ◇ *vi* - **1.** [with eyes] : to ~ (at sb) faire un clin d'œil (à qqn) - **2.** literary [lights] clignoter.

winkle ['wɪŋkl] *n* bigorneau *m*.

winkle out *vt sep* extirper ; to ~ sthg out of sb arracher qqch à qqn.

winner ['wɪnəʳ] *n* [person] gagnant *m*, -e *f*.

winning ['wɪnɪŋ] *adj* - **1.** [victorious, successful] gagnant(e) - **2.** [pleasing] charmeur(euse).

winnings *npl* gains *mpl*.

winning post *n* poteau *m* d'arrivée.

Winnipeg ['wɪnɪˌpeg] *n* Winnipeg.

winsome ['wɪnsəm] *adj* literary séduisant(e).

winter ['wɪntəʳ] ◇ *n* hiver *m* ; in ~ en hiver ◇ *comp* d'hiver.

winter sports *npl* sports *mpl* d'hiver.

wintertime ['wɪntətaɪm] *n (U)* hiver *m* ; in ~ en hiver.

wint(e)ry ['wɪntrɪ] *adj* d'hiver.

wipe [waɪp] ◇ *n* - **1.** [action of wiping] : to give sthg a ~ essuyer qqch, donner un coup de torchon à qqch - **2.** [cloth] lingette *f* ◇ *vt* essuyer.

wipe away *vt sep* [tears] essuyer.

wipe out *vt sep* - **1.** [erase] effacer - **2.** [eradicate] anéantir.

wipe up *vt sep* & *vi* essuyer.

wiper ['waɪpəʳ] *n* [windscreen wiper] essuie-glace *m*.

wire ['waɪəʳ] ◇ *n* - **1.** *(U)* [metal] fil *m* de fer - **2.** [cable etc] fil *m* - **3.** esp Am [telegram] télégramme *m* ◇ *comp* en fil de fer ◇ *vt* - **1.** [fasten, connect] : to ~ sthg to sthg relier qqch à qqch avec du fil de fer - **2.** [ELEC - plug] installer ; [- house] faire l'installation électrique de - **3.** esp Am [send telegram to] télégraphier à.

wire brush *n* brosse *f* métallique.

wire cutters *npl* cisaille *f*.

wireless ['waɪəlɪs] *n* dated T.S.F. *f*.

wire netting *n (U)* grillage *m*.

wire-tapping [-ˌtæpɪŋ] *n (U)* écoute *f* téléphonique.

wire wool *n* Br paille *f* de fer.

wiring ['waɪərɪŋ] *n (U)* installation *f* électrique.

wiry ['waɪərɪ] (*compar* **-ier ;** *superl* **-iest**) *adj* **- 1.** [hair] crépu(e) **- 2.** [body, man] noueux(euse).

Wisconsin [wɪs'kɒnsɪn] *n* Wisconsin *m ;* **in ~** dans le Wisconsin.

wisdom ['wɪzdəm] *n* sagesse *f.*

wisdom tooth *n* dent *f* de sagesse.

wise [waɪz] *adj* sage ; **to get ~ to sthg** *inf* piger qqch ; **to be no ~r, to be none the ~r** ne pas en savoir plus (pour autant), ne pas être plus avancé.

➭ **wise up** *vi esp* Am piger.

wisecrack ['waɪzkræk] *n pej* vanne *f.*

wish [wɪʃ] ◇ *n* **- 1.** [desire] souhait *m*, désir *m ;* **~ for sthg/to do sthg** désir de qqch/de faire qqch **- 2.** [magic request] vœu *m* ◇ *vt* **- 1.** [want] : **to ~ to do sthg** souhaiter faire qqch ; **I ~ (that) he'd come** j'aimerais bien qu'il vienne ; **I ~ I could** si seulement je pouvais **- 2.** [expressing hope] : **to ~ sb sthg** souhaiter qqch à qqn ◇ *vi* [by magic] : **to ~ for sthg** souhaiter qqch.

➭ **wishes** *npl* : **best ~es** meilleurs vœux ; **(with) best ~es** [at end of letter] bien amicalement.

➭ **wish on** *vt sep* : **to ~ sthg on sb** souhaiter qqch à qqn.

wishbone ['wɪʃbəʊn] *n* bréchet *m.*

wishful thinking [,wɪʃful-] *n* : **that's just ~** c'est prendre mes/ses *etc* désirs pour des réalités.

wishy-washy ['wɪʃɪ,wɒʃɪ] *adj inf pej* [person] sans personnalité ; [ideas] vague.

wisp [wɪsp] *n* **- 1.** [tuft] mèche *f* **- 2.** [small cloud] mince filet *m* OR volute *f.*

wispy ['wɪspɪ] (*compar* **-ier ;** *superl* **-iest**) *adj* [hair] fin(e).

wistful ['wɪstfʊl] *adj* nostalgique.

wit [wɪt] *n* **- 1.** [humour] esprit *m* **- 2.** [funny person] homme *m* d'esprit, femme *f* d'esprit **- 3.** [intelligence] : **to have the ~ to do sthg** avoir l'intelligence de faire qqch.

➭ **wits** *npl* : **to have** OR **keep one's ~s about one** être attentif(ive) OR sur ses gardes ; **to be scared out of one's ~s** *inf* avoir une peur bleue ; **to be at one's ~s' end** ne plus savoir que faire.

witch [wɪtʃ] *n* sorcière *f.*

witchcraft ['wɪtʃkrɑːft] *n* sorcellerie *f.*

witchdoctor ['wɪtʃ,dɒktəʳ] *n* sorcier *m.*

witch-hazel *n* hamamélis *m.*

witch-hunt *n pej* chasse *f* aux sorcières.

with [wɪð] *prep* **- 1.** [in company of] avec ; **I play tennis ~ his wife** je joue au tennis avec sa femme ; **we stayed ~ them for a week** nous avons passé une semaine chez eux ; **you can leave it ~ me** je m'en occupe, laissez-moi faire **- 2.** [indicating opposition] avec ; **to argue ~ sb** discuter avec qqn ; **the war ~ Germany** la guerre avec OR contre l'Allemagne **- 3.** [indicating means, manner, feelings] avec ; **I washed it ~ detergent** je l'ai lavé avec un détergent ; **the room was hung ~ balloons** la pièce était ornée de ballons ; **"All right", she said ~ a smile** « Très bien », dit-elle en souriant OR avec un sourire ; **she was trembling ~ fright** elle tremblait de peur ; **~ care** avec soin **- 4.** [having] avec ; **a man ~ a beard** un homme avec une barbe, un barbu ; **the man ~ the moustache** l'homme à la moustache ; **a city ~ many churches** une ville qui a de nombreuses églises ; **the computer comes ~ a printer** l'ordinateur est vendu avec une imprimante **- 5.** [regarding] : **he's very mean ~ money** il est très près de ses sous, il est très avare ; **what will you do ~ the house?** qu'est-ce que tu vas faire de la maison? ; **the trouble ~ her is that ...** l'ennui avec elle OR ce qu'il y a avec elle c'est que ... **- 6.** [indicating simultaneity] : **I can't do it ~ you watching me** je ne peux pas le faire quand OR pendant que tu me regardes **- 7.** [because of] : **~ the weather as it is, we've decided to stay at home** vu le temps qu'il fait OR étant donné le temps, nous avons décidé de rester à la maison ; **~ my luck, I'll probably lose** avec ma chance habituelle, je suis sûr de perdre **- 8.** *phr* : **I'm ~ you** [I understand] je vous suis ; [I'm on your side] je suis des vôtres ; [I agree] je suis d'accord avec vous.

withdraw [wɪð'drɔː] (*pt* **-drew ;** *pp* **-drawn**) ◇ *vt* **- 1.** *fml* [remove] : **to ~ sthg (from)** enlever qqch (de) **- 2.** [money, troops, remark] retirer ◇ *vi* **- 1.** *fml* [leave] : **to ~ (from)** se retirer (de) **- 2.** MIL se replier ; **to ~ from** évacuer ; **to ~ to safety** se mettre à l'abri **- 3.** [quit, give up] : **to ~ (from)** se retirer (de).

withdrawal [wɪð'drɔːəl] *n* **- 1.** [gen] : **~ (from)** retrait *m* (de) **- 2.** MIL repli *m* **- 3.** MED manque *m.*

withdrawal symptoms *npl* crise *f* de manque.

withdrawn [wɪð'drɔːn] ◇ *pp* ▷ **withdraw** ◇ *adj* [shy, quiet] renfermé(e).

withdrew [wɪð'druː] *pt* ▷ **withdraw.**

wither ['wɪðəʳ] ◇ *vt* flétrir ◇ *vi* **- 1.** [dry up] se flétrir **- 2.** [weaken] mourir.

withered ['wɪðəd] *adj* flétri(e).

withering ['wɪðərɪŋ] *adj* [look] foudroyant(e).

withhold [wɪð'həʊldl (*pt* & *pp* **-held** [-'held]) *vt* [services] refuser ; [information] cacher ; [salary] retenir.

within [wɪ'ðɪn] ◇ *prep* - **1.** [inside] à l'intérieur de, dans ; ~ **her** en elle, à l'intérieur d'elle-même - **2.** [budget, comprehension] dans les limites de ; [limits] dans - **3.** [less than - distance] à moins de ; [- time] d'ici, en moins de ; ~ **the week** avant la fin de la semaine ◇ *adv* à l'intérieur.

without [wɪð'aʊt] ◇ *prep* sans ; ~ **a coat** sans manteau ; **I left** ~ **seeing him** je suis parti sans l'avoir vu ; **I left** ~ **him seeing me** je suis parti sans qu'il m'ait vu ; **to go** ~ **sthg** se passer de qqch ◇ *adv* : **to go** OR **do** ~ s'en passer.

withstand [wɪð'stænd] (*pt* & *pp* **-stood** [-'stʊd]) *vt* résister à.

witness ['wɪtnɪs] ◇ *n* - **1.** [gen] témoin *m* ; **to be** ~ **to sthg** être témoin de qqch - **2.** [testimony] : **to bear** ~ **to sthg** témoigner de qqch ◇ *vt* - **1.** [accident, crime] être témoin de - **2.** fig [changes, rise in birth rate] assister à - **3.** [countersign] contresigner.

witness box Br, **witness stand** Am *n* barre *f* des témoins.

witter ['wɪtər] *vi* Br inf pej radoter, parler pour ne rien dire.

witticism ['wɪtɪsɪzm] *n* mot *m* d'esprit.

witty ['wɪtɪ] (*compar* **-ier** ; *superl* **-iest**) *adj* plein(e) d'esprit, spirituel(elle).

wives [waɪvz] *pl* ⊳ **wife**.

wizard ['wɪzəd] *n* magicien *m* ; fig as *m*, champion *m*, -onne *f*.

wizened ['wɪznd] *adj* ratatiné(e).

wk (*abbr of* **week**) sem.

Wm. (*abbr of* **William**) Guillaume.

WO *n abbr of* **warrant officer**.

wobble ['wɒbl] *vi* [hand, wings] trembler ; [chair, table] branler.

wobbly ['wɒblɪ] (*compar* **-ier** ; *superl* **-iest**) *adj* inf [jelly] tremblant(e) ; [table] branlant(e).

woe [wəʊ] *n literary* malheur *m*.

wok [wɒk] *n* wok *m*.

woke [wəʊk] *pt* ⊳ **wake**.

woken ['wəʊkn] *pp* ⊳ **wake**.

wolf [wʊlf] (*pl* **wolves** ['wʊlvz]) *n* [animal] loup *m*.

⬥ **wolf down** *vt sep* inf engloutir.

wolf whistle *n* sifflement *m* admiratif (*à l'adresse d'une femme*).

wolves ['wʊlvz] *pl* ⊳ **wolf**.

woman ['wʊmən] (*pl* **women**) ◇ *n* femme *f*

◇ *comp* : ~ **doctor** femme *f* médecin ; ~ **footballer** footballeuse *f* ; ~ **taxi driver** femme *f* chauffeur de taxi ; ~ **teacher** professeur *m* femme.

womanhood ['wʊmənhʊd] *n* (U) - **1.** [adult life] : **to reach** ~ devenir une femme - **2.** [women] femmes *fpl*.

womanize, -ise ['wʊmənaɪz] *vi* pej courir les femmes.

womanly ['wʊmənlɪ] *adj* féminin(e).

womb [wuːm] *n* utérus *m*.

wombat ['wɒmbæt] *n* wombat *m*.

women ['wɪmɪn] *pl* ⊳ **woman**.

women's group *n* groupe *m* féministe.

Women's Institute *n* Br : **the** ~ l'association locale des femmes.

women's lib *n* libération *f* de la femme.

women's liberation *n* libération *f* de la femme.

won [wʌn] *pt* & *pp* ⊳ **win**.

wonder ['wʌndər] ◇ *n* - **1.** (U) [amazement] étonnement *m* - **2.** [cause for surprise] : **it's a** ~ **(that)** ... c'est un miracle que ... ; **it's no** OR **little** OR **small** ~ **(that)** ... il n'est pas étonnant que ... - **3.** [amazing thing, person] merveille *f* ; **to work** OR **do** ~s faire des merveilles ◇ *vt* - **1.** [speculate] : **to** ~ (**if** OR **whether)** se demander (si) - **2.** [in polite requests] : **I** ~ **whether you would mind shutting the window?** est-ce que cela ne vous ennuierait pas de fermer la fenêtre ? ◇ *vi* - **1.** [speculate] se demander ; **to** ~ **about sthg** s'interroger sur qqch - **2.** literary [be amazed] : **to** ~ **at sthg** s'étonner de qqch.

wonderful ['wʌndəfʊl] *adj* merveilleux(euse).

wonderfully ['wʌndəfʊlɪ] *adv* - **1.** [very well] merveilleusement, à merveille - **2.** [for emphasis] extrêmement.

wonderland ['wʌndələænd] *n* pays *m* merveilleux.

wonky ['wɒŋkɪ] (*compar* **-ier** ; *superl* **-iest**) *adj* Br inf bancal(e).

wont [wəʊnt] ◇ *adj* : **to be** ~ **to do sthg** avoir l'habitude de faire qqch ◇ *n* dated or literary : **as is one's** ~ comme à son habitude OR à l'accoutumée.

won't [wəʊnt] = **will not**.

woo [wuː] *vt* - **1.** literary [court] courtiser - **2.** [try to win over] chercher à rallier (à soi OR à sa cause).

wood [wʊd] ◇ *n* bois *m* ; **touch** ~! touchons du bois ! ; **you can't see the** ~ **for the trees** Br ce sont les arbres qui cachent la forêt ◇ *comp* en bois.

➥ **woods** *npl* bois *mpl*.

wooded ['wʊdɪd] *adj* boisé(e).

wooden ['wʊdn] *adj* - **1.** [of wood] en bois - **2.** pej [actor] gauche.

wooden spoon *n* cuillère *f* de bois ; **to win** OR **get the ~** Br fig être classé dernier.

woodland ['wʊdlənd] *n* région *f* boisée.

woodpecker ['wʊd,pekə'] *n* pivert *m*.

wood pigeon *n* ramier *m*.

woodshed ['wʊdʃed] *n* bûcher *m*.

woodwind ['wʊdwɪnd] *n* : **the ~** les bois *mpl*.

woodwork ['wʊdwɜːk] *n* menuiserie *f*.

woodworm ['wʊdwɜːm] *n* ver *m* du bois ; **to have ~** être piqué par les vers.

woof [wʊf] ◇ *n* aboiement *m* ◇ *excl* ouah!

wool [wʊl] *n* laine *f ;* **to pull the ~ over sb's eyes** inf rouler qqn (dans la farine).

woollen Br, **woolen** Am ['wʊlən] *adj* en laine, de laine.

➥ **woollens** *npl* lainages *mpl*.

woolly ['wʊlɪ] (*compar* -**ier** ; *superl* -**iest**) ◇ *adj* - **1.** [woollen] en laine, de laine - **2.** inf [idea, thinking] confus(e) ◇ *n* inf lainage *m*.

woolly-headed [-'hedɪd] *adj* inf pej confus(e).

woozy ['wuːzɪ] (*compar* -**ier** ; *superl* -**iest**) *adj* inf sonné(e).

Worcester sauce ['wʊstə'-] *n* (U) *sauce épicée à base de soja et de vinaigre.*

Worcs (*abbr of* **Worcestershire**) *ancien comté anglais.*

word [wɜːd] ◇ *n* - **1.** LING mot *m ;* **in your own ~s** dans vos mots à vous ; **too stupid for ~s** vraiment trop bête ; **~ for ~** [repeat, copy] mot pour mot ; [translate] mot à mot ; **in other ~s** en d'autres termes OR termes ; **not in so many ~s** pas exactement ; **in a ~** en un mot ; **by ~ of mouth** de bouche à oreille ; **to put in a (good) ~ for sb** glisser un mot en faveur de qqn ; **just say the ~** vous n'avez qu'un mot à dire ; **to have a ~ (with sb)** parler (à qqn) ; **to have ~s with sb** inf avoir des mots avec qqn ; **to have the last ~** avoir le dernier mot ; **she doesn't mince her ~s** elle ne mâche pas ses mots ; **to weigh one's ~s** peser ses mots ; **I couldn't get a ~ in edgeways** je n'ai pas réussi à placer un seul mot - **2.** (U) [news] nouvelles *fpl* - **3.** [promise] parole *f ;* **to give sb one's ~** donner sa parole à qqn ; **to be as good as one's ~, to be true to one's ~** tenir (sa) parole ◇ *vt* [letter, reply] rédiger.

word game *n* jeu *m* de lettres.

wording ['wɜːdɪŋ] *n* (U) termes *mpl*.

word-perfect *adj* : he had his lines ~ il connaissait ses répliques au mot près.

wordplay ['wɜːdpleɪ] *n* (U) jeux *mpl* de mots.

word processing *n* (U) COMPUT traitement *m* de texte.

word processor [-,prəʊsesə'] *n* COMPUT machine *f* à traitement de texte.

wordwrap ['wɜːdræp] *n* COMPUT retour *m* à la ligne automatique.

wordy ['wɜːdɪ] (*compar* -**ier** ; *superl* -**iest**)' *adj* pej verbeux(euse).

wore [wɔː'] *pt* ⊳ wear.

work [wɜːk] ◇ *n* - **1.** (U) [employment] travail *m*, emploi *m ;* **to be in ~** avoir un emploi ; **out of ~** sans emploi, au chômage ; **at ~** au travail - **2.** [activity, tasks] travail *m ;* **at ~** au travail ; **to have one's ~ cut out doing sthg** OR **to do sthg** avoir du mal OR de la peine à faire qqch - **3.** ART & LITERATURE œuvre *f* - **4.** phr : **he's a nasty piece of ~** inf c'est un salaud ◇ *vt* - **1.** [person, staff] faire travailler - **2.** [machine] faire marcher - **3.** [wood, metal, land] travailler - **4.** [cause to become] : **to ~ o.s. into a rage** se mettre en rage - **5.** [make] : **to ~ one's way through a crowd** se frayer un chemin à travers une foule ; **to ~ one's way along** avancer petit à petit ; **he ~ed his way to the top** il est parvenu au sommet à la force du poignet ◇ *vi* - **1.** [do a job] travailler ; **to ~ on sthg** travailler à qqch - **2.** [function] fonctionner, marcher - **3.** [succeed] marcher - **4.** [have effect] : **to ~ against sb** jouer contre qqn ; **to ~ against sthg** aller à l'encontre de qqch - **5.** [become] : **to ~ loose** se desserrer.

➥ **works** ◇ *n* [factory] usine *f* ◇ *npl* - **1.** [mechanism] mécanisme *m* - **2.** [digging, building] travaux *mpl* - **3.** inf [everything] : **the ~s** tout le tralala.

➥ **work off** *vt sep* [anger etc] passer.

➥ **work on** *vt fus* - **1.** [pay attention to] travailler à - **2.** [take as basis] se baser sur.

➥ **work out** ◇ *vt sep* - **1.** [plan, schedule] mettre au point - **2.** [total, answer] trouver ◇ *vi* - **1.** [figure, total] : **to ~ out at** se monter à - **2.** [turn out] se dérouler - **3.** [be successful] (bien) marcher - **4.** [train, exercise] s'entraîner.

➥ **work up** *vt sep* - **1.** [excite] : **to ~ o.s. up into** se mettre dans - **2.** [generate] : **to ~ up an appetite** s'ouvrir l'appétit ; **to ~ up enthusiasm** s'enthousiasmer ; **to ~ up courage** trouver du courage.

workable ['wɜːkəbl] *adj* [plan] réalisable ; [system] fonctionnel(elle).

workaday [ˈwɜːkədeɪ] *adj* pej ordinaire, commun(e).

workaholic [ˌwɜːkəˈhɒlɪk] *n* bourreau *m* de travail.

workbasket [ˈwɜːkˌbɑːskɪt] *n* corbeille *f* à ouvrage.

workbench [ˈwɜːkbentʃ] *n* établi *m*.

workbook [ˈwɜːkbʊk] *n* cahier *m* d'exercices.

workday [ˈwɜːkdeɪ] *n* - **1.** [day's work] journée *f* de travail - **2.** [not weekend] jour *m* ouvrable.

worked up [ˌwɜːkt-] *adj* dans tous ses états.

worker [ˈwɜːkəʳ] *n* travailleur *m*, -euse *f*, ouvrier *m*, -ère *f* ; **to be a hard/fast ~** travailler dur/vite ; **to be a good ~** bien travailler.

workforce [ˈwɜːkfɔːs] *n* main *f* d'œuvre.

workhouse [ˈwɜːkhaʊs] *n* - **1.** Br [poorhouse] hospice *m* - **2.** Am [prison] maison *f* de correction.

working [ˈwɜːkɪŋ] *adj* - **1.** [in operation] qui marche - **2.** [having employment] qui travaille - **3.** [conditions, clothes, hours] de travail.

➡ **workings** *npl* [of system, machine] mécanisme *m* ; **I'll never understand the ~s of his mind** *fig* je ne comprendrai jamais ce qui se passe dans sa tête.

working capital *n (U)* - **1.** [assets minus liabilities] fonds *mpl* de roulement - **2.** [available money] capital *m* d'exploitation.

working class *n* : **the ~** la classe ouvrière.
➡ **working-class** *adj* ouvrier(ère)

working day *n* = workday.

working group *n* groupe *m* de travail.

working knowledge *n* connaissance *f* pratique.

working man *n* ouvrier *m*.

working model *n* modèle *m* opérationnel.

working order *n* : **in ~** en état de marche.

working party *n* groupe *m* de travail.

working week *n* semaine *f* de travail.

work-in-progress *n* travail *m* en cours.

workload [ˈwɜːkləʊd] *n* quantité *f* de travail.

workman [ˈwɜːkmən] (*pl* **-men** [-mən]) *n* ouvrier *m*.

workmanship [ˈwɜːkmənʃɪp] *n (U)* travail *m*.

workmate [ˈwɜːkmeɪt] *n* camarade *mf* OR collègue *mf* de travail.

work of art *n* lit & fig œuvre *f* d'art.

workout [ˈwɜːkaʊt] *n* séance *f* d'entraînement.

work permit [-ˌpɜːmɪt] *n* permis *m* de travail.

workplace [ˈwɜːkpleɪs] *n* lieu *m* de travail.

workroom [ˈwɜːkrʊm] *n* salle *f* de travail.

works council *n* comité *m* d'entreprise.

workshop [ˈwɜːkʃɒp] *n* atelier *m*.

workshy [ˈwɜːkʃaɪ] *adj* Br fainéant(e).

workstation [ˈwɜːkˌsteɪʃn] *n* COMPUT poste *m* de travail.

work surface *n* plan *m* de travail.

worktable [ˈwɜːkˌteɪbl] *n* table *f* de travail.

worktop [ˈwɜːktɒp] *n* Br plan *m* de travail.

work-to-rule *n* Br grève *f* du zèle.

world [wɜːld] ◇ *n* - **1.** [gen] monde *m* ; **what/where in the ~ ...?** que/où diable ...? ; **the ~** over dans le monde entier - **2.** loc : **to be dead to the ~** dormir profondément ; **to get the best of both ~s** gagner sur tous les plans ; **to think the ~ of sb** admirer qqn énormément, ne jurer que par qqn ; **to do sb the ~ of good** faire un bien fou à qqn, faire énormément de bien à qqn ; **a ~ of difference** une énorme différence ◇ *comp* [power] mondial(e) ; [language] universel(elle) ; [tour] du monde.

World Bank *n* : **the ~** la Banque mondiale.

world-class *adj* de niveau international.

World Cup ◇ *n* : **the ~** la Coupe du monde ◇ *comp* de Coupe du monde.

world-famous *adj* de renommée mondiale ; **to become ~** acquérir une renommée mondiale.

worldly [ˈwɜːldlɪ] *adj* de ce monde, matériel(elle) ; **~ goods** literary biens *mpl*.

world music *n* world music *f*.

world power *n* puissance *f* mondiale.

World Series *n* Am : **the ~** le championnat américain de baseball.

World Trade Organization *n* Organisation *f* mondiale du commerce.

World War I *n* la Première Guerre mondiale.

World War II *n* la Deuxième Guerre mondiale.

world-weary *adj* [person] las (lasse) du monde ; [cynicism, sigh] blasé(e).

worldwide [ˈwɜːldwaɪd] ◇ *adj* mondial(e) ◇ *adv* dans le monde entier.

World Wide Web *n* : **the ~** le World Wide Web.

worm [wɜːm] ◇ *n* [animal] ver *m* ◇ *vt* : **to ~ one's way** [move] avancer à plat ventre OR en rampant ; **to ~ one's way into sb's affec-**

tions gagner insidieusement l'affection de qqn.

➤ **worms** npl [parasites] vers mpl.

➤ **worm out** vt sep : **to ~ sthg out of sb** soutirer qqch à qqn.

worn [wɔːn] ◇ pp ▷ **wear** ◇ adj - **1.** [threadbare] usé(e) - **2.** [tired] las (lasse).

worn-out adj - **1.** [old, threadbare] usé(e) - **2.** [tired] épuisé(e).

worried ['wʌrɪd] adj soucieux(euse), inquiet(ète) ; **you really had me ~** vous m'avez fait faire bien du souci ; **to be ~ (about)** se faire du souci (à propos de) ; **to be ~ sick** se faire un sang d'encre.

worrier ['wʌrɪəʳ] n anxieux m, -euse f.

worry ['wʌrɪ] (pl -ies, pt & pp -ied) ◇ n - **1.** [feeling] souci m - **2.** [problem] souci m, ennui m ◇ vt inquiéter, tracasser ◇ vi s'inquiéter ; **to ~ about** se faire du souci au sujet de ; **don't worry!, not to ~!** ne vous en faites pas!

worrying ['wʌrɪɪŋ] adj inquiétant(e).

worse [wɜːs] ◇ adj - **1.** [not as good] pire ; **to get ~** [situation] empirer - **2.** [more ill] : **he's ~ today** il va plus mal aujourd'hui ◇ adv plus mal ; **they're even ~ off** c'est encore pire pour eux ; **~ off** [financially] plus pauvre ◇ n pire m ; **for the ~** pour le pire ; **a change for the ~** une détérioration.

worsen ['wɜːsn] vt & vi empirer.

worsening ['wɜːsnɪŋ] adj qui va en empirant.

worship ['wɜːʃɪp] (Br pt & pp -ped ; cont -ping, Am pt & pp -ed ; cont -ing) ◇ vt adorer ◇ n - **1.** (U) RELIG culte m - **2.** [adoration] adoration f.

➤ **Worship** n : **Your/Her/His Worship** Votre/Son Honneur m.

worshipper Br, **worshiper** Am ['wɜːʃɪpəʳ] n - **1.** RELIG fidèle mf - **2.** [admirer] adorateur m, -trice f.

worst [wɜːst] ◇ adj : **the ~** le pire (la pire), le plus mauvais (la plus mauvaise) ; **his ~ enemy** son pire ennemi ◇ adv le plus mal ; **the ~ affected area** la zone la plus touchée ◇ n : **the ~** le pire ; **to get the ~ of it** [in fight] avoir le dessous ; **if the ~ comes to the ~** au pire.

➤ **at (the) worst** adv au pire.

worsted ['wʊstɪd] n laine f peignée.

worth [wɜːθ] ◇ prep - **1.** [in value] : **to be ~ sthg** valoir qqch ; **how much is it ~?** combien cela vaut-il? - **2.** [deserving of] : **it's ~ a visit** cela vaut une visite ; **it's/she is ~ it** cela/elle en vaut la peine ; **to be ~ doing sthg** valoir la peine de faire qqch ◇ n valeur f ; **a week's/**

£20 **~ of groceries** pour une semaine/20 livres d'épicerie.

worthless ['wɜːθlɪs] adj - **1.** [object] sans valeur, qui ne vaut rien - **2.** [person] qui n'est bon à rien.

worthwhile [,wɜːθ'waɪl] adj [job, visit] qui en vaut la peine ; [charity] louable.

worthy ['wɜːðɪ] (compar -ier ; superl -iest) adj - **1.** [deserving of respect] digne - **2.** [deserving] : **to be ~ of sthg** mériter qqch - **3.** pej [good but unexciting] méritant(e).

would [wʊd] modal vb - **1.** (in reported speech) : **she said she ~ come** elle a dit qu'elle viendrait - **2.** [indicating likelihood] : **what ~ you do?** que ferais-tu? ; **what ~ you have done?** qu'aurais-tu fait? ; **I ~ be most grateful** je vous en serais très reconnaissant - **3.** [indicating willingness] : **she ~n't go** elle ne voulait pas y aller ; **he ~ do anything for her** il ferait n'importe quoi pour elle - **4.** (in polite questions) : **~ you like a drink?** voulez-vous OR voudriez-vous à boire? ; **~ you mind closing the window?** cela vous ennuierait de fermer la fenêtre? - **5.** [indicating inevitability] : **he ~ say that** j'étais sûr qu'il allait dire ça, ça ne m'étonne pas de lui - **6.** [giving advice] : **I ~ report it if I were you** si j'étais vous je préviendrais les autorités - **7.** [expressing opinions] : **I ~ prefer** je préférerais ; **I ~ have thought (that)** ... j'aurais pensé que ... - **8.** [indicating habit] : **he ~ smoke a cigar after dinner** il fumait un cigare après le dîner ; **she ~ often complain about the neighbours** elle se plaignait souvent des voisins.

would-be adj prétendu(e).

wouldn't ['wʊdnt] = **would not**.

would've ['wʊdəv] = **would have**.

wound[1] [wuːnd] ◇ n blessure f ; **to lick one's ~s** fig panser ses plaies ◇ vt blesser.

wound[2] [waʊnd] pt & pp ▷ **wind**[2].

wounded ['wuːndɪd] ◇ adj blessé(e) ◇ npl : **the ~** les blessés mpl.

wounding ['wuːndɪŋ] adj blessant(e).

wove [wəʊv] pt ▷ **weave**.

woven ['wəʊvn] pp ▷ **weave**.

wow [waʊ] excl inf oh là là!

WP ◇ n (abbr of **word processing, word processor**) TTX m ◇ (abbr of **weather permitting**) si le temps le permet.

WPC (abbr of **woman police constable**) n Br femme agent de police ; **~ Roberts** l'agent Roberts.

wpm (abbr of **words per minute**) mots/min.

WRAC [ræk] (abbr of **Women's Royal Army**

Corps) *n* section féminine de l'armée de terre britannique.

WRAF [ræf] (*abbr of* **Women's Royal Air Force**) *n* section féminine de l'armée de l'air britannique.

wrangle ['ræŋgl] ⬦ *n* dispute *f* ⬦ *vi* : to ~ **(with sb over sthg)** se disputer (avec qqn à propos de qqch).

wrap [ræp] (*pt & pp* -**ped** ; *cont* -**ping**) ⬦ *vt* - **1.** [cover in paper, cloth] : **to ~ sthg (in)** envelopper OR emballer qqch (dans) ; **to ~ sthg around** OR **round sthg** enrouler qqch autour de qqch - **2.** [encircle] : **to ~ one's hands around** OR **round sthg** entourer qqch de ses mains ; **to wrap one's fingers around** OR **round sthg** entourer qqch de ses doigts ; **to ~ one's arms around** OR **round sb** enlacer qqn ⬦ *n* [garment] châle *m*.

⬦ **wrap up** ⬦ *vt sep* - **1.** [cover in paper or cloth] envelopper, emballer - **2.** *inf* [complete] conclure, régler ⬦ *vi* [put warm clothes on] : ~ **up well** OR **warmly!** couvrez-vous bien !

wrapped up [ræpt-] *adj inf* : **to be ~ in sthg** être absorbé(e) par qqch ; **to be ~ in sb** ne penser qu'à qqn.

wrapper ['ræpər] *n* papier *m* ; Br [of book] jaquette *f*, couverture *f*.

wrapping ['ræpɪŋ] *n* emballage *m*.

wrapping paper *n (U)* papier *m* d'emballage.

wrath [rɒθ] *n (U) literary* courroux *m*.

wreak [ri:k] *vt* [destruction, havoc] entraîner.

wreath [ri:θ] *n* couronne *f*.

wreathe [ri:ð] *vt literary* couronner.

wreck [rek] ⬦ *n* - **1.** [car, plane, ship] épave *f* - **2.** *inf* [person] loque *f* ; **I feel a ~** je me sens épuisé ; **I look a ~** j'ai l'air d'une véritable loque ⬦ *vt* - **1.** [destroy] détruire - **2.** NAUT provoquer le naufrage de ; **to be ~ed** s'échouer - **3.** [spoil - holiday] gâcher ; [- health, hopes, plan] ruiner.

wreckage ['rekɪdʒ] *n (U)* débris *mpl*.

wrecker ['rekər] *n Am* [vehicle] dépanneuse *f*.

wren [ren] *n* roitelet *m*.

wrench [rentʃ] ⬦ *n* - **1.** [tool] clef *f* anglaise - **2.** [injury] entorse *f* - **3.** [emotional] déchirement *m* ⬦ *vt* - **1.** [pull violently] tirer violemment ; **to ~ sthg off** arracher qqch - **2.** [arm, leg, knee] se tordre.

wrest [rest] *vt literary* : **to ~ sthg from sb** arracher violemment qqch à qqn.

wrestle ['resl] ⬦ *vt* lutter ⬦ *vi* - **1.** [fight] : **to ~ (with sb)** lutter (contre qqn) - **2.** *fig* [struggle] : **to ~ with sthg** se débattre OR lutter contre qqch.

wrestler ['reslər] *n* lutteur *m*, -euse *f*.

wrestling ['reslɪŋ] *n* lutte *f*.

wretch [retʃ] *n* pauvre diable *m*.

wretched ['retʃɪd] *adj* - **1.** [miserable] misérable - **2.** *inf* [damned] fichu(e), maudit(e).

wriggle ['rɪgl] ⬦ *vt* remuer, tortiller ⬦ *vi* remuer, se tortiller.

⬦ **wriggle out of** *vt fus* : **to ~ out of sthg** se tirer de qqch ; **to ~ out of doing sthg** éviter de faire qqch.

wring [rɪŋ] (*pt & pp* **wrung**) *vt* - **1.** [washing] essorer, tordre - **2.** [hands, neck] tordro.

⬦ **wring out** *vt sep* essorer, tordre.

wringing ['rɪŋɪŋ] *adj* : ~ **(wet)** [person] trempé(e) ; [clothes] mouillé(e), à tordre.

wrinkle ['rɪŋkl] ⬦ *n* - **1.** [on skin] ride *f* - **2.** [in cloth] pli *m* ⬦ *vt* plisser ⬦ *vi* se plisser, faire des plis.

wrinkled ['rɪŋkld], **wrinkly** ['rɪŋklɪ] *adj* - **1.** [skin] ridée(e) - **2.** [cloth] froissé(e).

wrist [rɪst] *n* poignet *m*.

wristband ['rɪstbænd] *n* [of watch] bracelet *m*.

wristwatch ['rɪstwɒtʃ] *n* montre-bracelet *f*.

writ [rɪt] *n* acte *m* judiciaire.

write [raɪt] (*pt* **wrote** ; *pp* **written**) ⬦ *vt* - **1.** [gen & COMPUT] écrire ; **to ~ sb a letter** écrire une lettre à qqn - **2.** *Am* [person] écrire à - **3.** [cheque, prescription] faire ⬦ *vi* [gen & COMPUT] écrire ; **to ~ to sb** Br écrire à qqn.

⬦ **write back** ⬦ *vt sep* : **to ~ a letter back** répondre par une lettre ⬦ *vi* répondre.

⬦ **write down** *vt sep* écrire, noter.

⬦ **write in** *vi* écrire.

⬦ **write into** *vt sep* : **to ~ a clause into a contract** insérer une clause dans un contrat.

⬦ **write off** ⬦ *vt sep* - **1.** [project] considérer comme fichu - **2.** [debt, investment] passer aux profits et pertes - **3.** [person] considérer comme fini - **4.** Br *inf* [vehicle] bousiller ⬦ *vi* écrire pour demander des renseignements ; **to ~ off to sb** écrire à qqn ; **to ~ off for sthg** écrire pour demander qqch.

⬦ **write up** *vt sep* [notes] mettre au propre.

write-off *n* [vehicle] : **to be a ~** être complètement démoli(e).

write-protect *vt* COMPUT protéger en écriture.

writer ['raɪtər] *n* - **1.** [as profession] écrivain *m* - **2.** [of letter, article, story] auteur *m*.

write-up *n inf* critique *f*.

writhe [raɪð] *vi* se tordre.

writing ['raɪtɪŋ] *n (U)* - **1.** [handwriting, activity] écriture *f* ; **in** ~ par écrit - **2.** [something written] écrit *m*.

⬦ **writings** *npl* écrits *mpl*.

writing case *n* Br nécessaire *m* de correspondance.

writing desk *n* secrétaire *m*.

writing paper *n (U)* papier *m* à lettres.

written ['rɪtn] ⬦ *pp* ▷ **write** ⬦ *adj* écrit(e).

WRNS (*abbr of* **Women's Royal Naval Service**) *n* section féminine de la marine de guerre britannique.

wrong [rɒŋ] ⬦ *adj* - **1.** [not normal, not satisfactory] qui ne va pas ; **is something ~?** y a-t-il quelque chose qui ne va pas? ; **what's ~?** qu'est-ce qui ne va pas? ; **there's something ~ with the switch** l'interrupteur ne marche pas bien - **2.** [not suitable] qui ne convient pas - **3.** [not correct - answer, address] faux (fausse), mauvais(e) ; [- decision] mauvais ; **to be ~** [person] avoir tort ; **to be ~ to do sthg** avoir tort de faire qqch - **4.** [morally bad] : **it's ~ to ...** c'est mal de ... ⬦ *adv* [incorrectly] mal ; **to get sthg ~** se tromper à propos de qqch ; **to go ~** [make a mistake] se tromper, faire une erreur ; [stop functioning] se détraquer ; **don't get me ~** *inf* comprenez-moi bien ⬦ *n* mal *m ;* **to be in the ~** être dans son tort ⬦ *vt* faire du tort à.

wrong-foot Br *vt* - **1.** SPORT prendre à contre-pied - **2.** fig [surprise] prendre par surprise OR au dépourvu.

wrongful ['rɒŋfʊl] *adj* [unfair] injuste ; [arrest, dismissal] injustifié(e).

wrongly ['rɒŋlɪ] *adv* - **1.** [unsuitably] mal - **2.** [mistakenly] à tort.

wrong number *n* faux numéro *m*.

wrote [rəʊt] *pt* ▷ **write.**

wrought iron [rɔːt-] *n* fer *m* forgé.

wrung [rʌŋ] *pt* & *pp* ▷ **wring.**

WRVS (*abbr of* **Women's Royal Voluntary Service**) *n* association de femmes au service des déshérités.

wry [raɪ] *adj* - **1.** [amused - smile, look] amusé(e) ; [- humour] ironique - **2.** [displeased] désabusé(e).

wt. (*abbr of* **weight**) pds.

WTO (*abbr of* **World Trade Organization**) *n* OMC *f*.

WV *abbr of* **West Virginia.**

WW *abbr of* **world war.**

WWW (*abbr of* **World Wide Web**) *n* WWW *m*.

WY *abbr of* **Wyoming.**

Wyoming [waɪ'əʊmɪŋ] *n* Wyoming *m ;* **in ~** dans le Wyoming.

WYSIWYG ['wɪzɪwɪg] (*abbr of* **what you see is what you get**) WYSIWYG, tel écran, tel écrit.

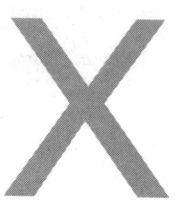

x (*pl* **x's** OR **xs**), **X** (*pl* **X's** OR **Xs**) [eks] *n* - **1.** [letter] x *m inv*, X *m inv* - **2.** [unknown thing] x *m inv* - **3.** [to mark place] croix *f* - **4.** [at end of letter] : **XXX** grosses bises.

xenophobia [,zenə'fəʊbjə] *n* xénophobie *f*.

Xerox® ['zɪərɒks] ⬦ *n* - **1.** [machine] photocopieuse *f* - **2.** [copy] photocopie *f* ⬦ *vt* photocopier.

Xmas ['eksməs] ⬦ *n* Noël *m* ⬦ *comp* de Noël.

X-ray ⬦ *n* - **1.** [ray] rayon *m* X - **2.** [picture] radiographie *f*, radio *f* ⬦ *vt* radiographier.

xylophone ['zaɪləfəʊn] *n* xylophone *m*.

y (*pl* **y's** OR **ys**), **Y** (*pl* **Y's** OR **Ys**) [waɪ] *n* - **1.** [letter] y *m inv*, Y *m inv* - **2.** MATH y *m inv*.

Y2K (*abbr of* **the year 2000**) *n* - **1.** [year] l'an 2000 - **2.** COMPUT le bogue de l'an 2000.

yacht [jɒt] *n* yacht *m*.

yachting ['jɒtɪŋ] *n* yachting *m*.

yachtsman ['jɒtsmən] (*pl* **-men** [-mən]) *n* yachtman *m*.

yachtswoman ['jɒts,wʊmən] (*pl* **-women** [-,wɪmɪn]) *n* yachtwoman *f*.

yahoo [jɑː'huː] *n* rustre *m*.

yak [jæk] *n* yack *m*.

Yale lock® [jeɪl-] *n* serrure *f* à barillet.

yam [jæm] *n* igname *f*.

Yangtze ['jæŋtsɪ] *n :* **the ~** le Yang-tseu-kiang, le Yangzi Jiang *m*.

yank [jæŋk] *vt* tirer d'un coup sec.

Yank [jæŋk] *n* Br inf *terme péjoratif désignant un Américain,* Amerloque *mf.*

Yankee ['jæŋkɪ] *n* - **1.** Br inf [American] *terme péjoratif désignant un Américain,* Amerloque *mf* - **2.** Am [citizen] Yankee *mf.*

yap [jæp] (*pt* & *pp* -**ped** ; *cont* -**ping**) *vi* - **1.** [dog] japper - **2.** pej [person] jacasser.

yard [jɑːd] *n* - **1.** [unit of measurement] = 91,44 *cm,* yard *m* - **2.** [walled area] cour *f* - **3.** [area of work] chantier *m* - **4.** Am [attached to house] jardin *m.*

yardstick ['jɑːdstɪk] *n* mesure *f.*

yarn [jɑːn] *n* - **1.** [thread] fil *m* - **2.** inf [story] histoire *f ;* **to spin sb a ~** raconter une histoire à qqn.

yashmak ['jæʃmæk] *n* litham *m.*

yawn [jɔːn] ⟨⟩ *n* - **1.** [when tired] bâillement *m ;* **to give a ~** bâiller - **2.** Br inf [boring event] : **it was a real ~** c'était vraiment ennuyeux ⟨⟩ *vi* - **1.** [when tired] bâiller - **2.** [gape] s'ouvrir, béer.

yd *abbr of* yard.

yeah [jeə] *adv* inf ouais.

year [jɪəʳ] *n* - **1.** [calendar year] année *f ;* **all (the) ~ round** toute l'année ; **~ in ~ out** année après année - **2.** [period of 12 months] année *f,* an *m ;* **to be 21 ~s old** avoir 21 ans - **3.** [financial year] année *f ;* **the ~ 1992-93** l'exercice 1992-93.

➤ **years** *npl* [long time] années *fpl.*

yearbook ['jɪəbʊk] *n* annuaire *m,* almanach *m.*

yearling ['jɪəlɪŋ] *n* yearling *m.*

yearly ['jɪəlɪ] ⟨⟩ *adj* annuel(elle) ⟨⟩ *adv* - **1.** [once a year] annuellement - **2.** [every year] chaque année ; **twice ~** deux fois par an.

yearn [jɜːn] *vi :* **to ~ for sthg/to do sthg** aspirer à qqch/à faire qqch.

yearning ['jɜːnɪŋ] *n :* **~ (for sb/sthg)** désir *m* ardent (pour qqn/de qqch).

yeast [jiːst] *n* levure *f.*

yell [jel] ⟨⟩ *n* hurlement *m* ⟨⟩ *vi* & *vt* hurler.

yellow ['jeləʊ] ⟨⟩ *adj* - **1.** [colour] jaune - **2.** [cowardly] lâche ⟨⟩ *n* jaune *m* ⟨⟩ *vi* jaunir.

yellow card *n* FTBL carton *m* jaune.

yellow fever *n* fièvre *f* jaune.

yellow lines *n* bandes *fpl* jaunes.

> ▓ **YELLOW LINES** ▓
>
> En Grande-Bretagne, une ligne jaune parallèle au trottoir signifie « arrêt autorisé réglementé » ; une double ligne jaune signifie « stationnement interdit ».

yellowness ['jeləʊnɪs] *n (U)* couleur *f* jaune.

Yellow Pages® *n :* **the ~** les pages *fpl* jaunes.

Yellow River *n :* **the ~** le fleuve Jaune.

Yellow Sea *n :* **the ~** la mer Jaune.

yelp [jelp] ⟨⟩ *n* jappement *m* ⟨⟩ *vi* japper.

Yemen ['jemən] *n* Yémen *m ;* **in ~** au Yémen.

Yemeni ['jemənɪ] ⟨⟩ *adj* yéménite ⟨⟩ *n* Yéménite *mf.*

yen [jen] (*pl sense 1 inv ; pl sense 2* -**s**) *n* - **1.** [Japanese currency] yen *m* - **2.** [longing] : **to have a ~ for sthg/to do sthg** avoir une forte envie de qqch/de faire qqch.

yeoman of the guard ['jəʊmən-] (*pl* yeomen of the guard ['jəʊmən-]) *n* hallebardier *m* de la garde royale.

yep [jep] *adv* inf ouais.

yes [jes] ⟨⟩ *adv* - **1.** [gen] oui ; **~, please** oui, s'il te/vous plaît - **2.** [expressing disagreement] si ⟨⟩ *n* oui *m inv.*

yes-man *n* pej béni-oui-oui *m inv.*

yesterday ['jestədɪ] ⟨⟩ *n* hier *m ;* **the day before ~** avant-hier ⟨⟩ *adv* hier.

yet [jet] ⟨⟩ *adv* - **1.** [gen] encore ; **~ faster** encore plus vite ; **not ~** pas encore ; **~ again** encore une fois ; **as ~** jusqu'ici - **2.** déjà ; **have they finished ~?** est-ce qu'ils ont déjà fini? ⟨⟩ *conj* et cependant, mais.

yeti ['jetɪ] *n* yéti *m.*

yew [juː] *n* if *m.*

Y-fronts *npl* Br slip *m.*

YHA (*abbr of* **Youth Hostels Association**) *n* association britannique des auberges de jeunesse.

Yiddish ['jɪdɪʃ] ⟨⟩ *adj* yiddish (*inv*) ⟨⟩ *n* [language] yiddish *m.*

yield [jiːld] ⟨⟩ *n* rendement *m* ⟨⟩ *vt* - **1.** [produce] produire - **2.** [give up] céder ⟨⟩ *vi* - **1.** [gen] : **to ~ (to)** céder (à) - **2.** Am AUT [give way] : '**~**' 'cédez le passage'.

yippee [Br jɪˈpiː, Am ˈjɪpɪ] *excl* hourra!

YMCA (*abbr of* **Young Men's Christian Association**) *n* union chrétienne de jeunes gens (*proposant notamment des services d'hébergement*).

yo [jəʊ] *excl* inf salut!

yob(bo) ['jɒb(əʊ)] *n* Br inf voyou *m,* loubard *m.*

yodel ['jəʊdl] (Br *pt* & *pp* -**led** ; *cont* -**ling**, Am *pt* & *pp* -**ed** ; *cont* -**ing**) *vi* iodler, jodler.

yoga ['jəʊgə] *n* yoga *m.*

yoghurt, yoghurt, yogurt [Br ˈjɒgət, Am ˈjəʊgərt] *n* yaourt *m.*

yoke [jəʊk] *n* lit & fig joug *m.*

yokel ['jəʊkl] *n* pej péquenaud *m,* -e *f.*

yolk [jəʊk] n jaune m (d'œuf).

yonder ['jɒndər] adv literary là-bas.

Yorks. [jɔːks] (abbr of Yorkshire) comté anglais.

Yorkshire pudding ['jɔːkʃər-] n pâte à choux cuite qui accompagne le rosbif.

Yorkshire terrier ['jɔːkʃər-] n Yorkshire-terrier m.

you [juː] pers pron - **1.** (subject - sg) tu ; (- polite form, pl) vous ; **~'re a good cook** tu es/vous êtes bonne cuisinière ; **are ~ French?** tu es/vous êtes français? ; **~ French** vous autres Français ; **~ idiot!** espèce d'idiot! ; **if I were** OR **was ~** si j'étais toi/vous, à ta/votre place ; **there ~ are** [you've appeared] te/vous voilà ; [have this] voilà, tiens/tenez ; **that jacket really isn't ~** cette veste n'est pas vraiment ton/votre style - **2.** (object - unstressed, sg) te ; (- polite form, pl) vous ; **I can see ~** je te/vous vois ; **I gave it to ~** je te/vous l'ai donné - **3.** (object - stressed, sg) toi ; (- polite form, pl) vous ; **I don't expect YOU to do it** je n'exige pas que ce soit toi qui le fasses/vous qui le fassiez - **4.** (after prep, in comparisons etc, sg) toi ; (- polite form, pl) vous ; **we shall go without ~** nous irons sans toi/vous ; **I'm shorter than ~** je suis plus petit que toi/vous - **5.** [anyone, one] on ; **~ have to be careful** on doit faire attention ; **exercise is good for ~** l'exercice est bon pour la santé.

you'd [juːd] = you had, you would.

you'll [juːl] = you will.

young [jʌŋ] ◇ adj jeune ◇ npl - **1.** [young people] : **the ~** les jeunes mpl - **2.** [baby animals] les petits mpl.

younger ['jʌŋgər] adj plus jeune.

youngish ['jʌŋɪʃ] adj assez jeune.

young man n jeune homme m.

youngster ['jʌŋstər] n jeune m.

young woman n jeune femme f.

your [jɔːr] poss adj - **1.** (referring to one person) ton (ta), tes (pl) ; (polite form, pl) votre, vos (pl) ; **~ dog** ton/votre chien ; **~ house** ta/votre maison ; **~ children** tes/vos enfants ; **what's ~ name?** comment t'appelles-tu/vous appelez-vous? ; **it wasn't YOUR fault** ce n'était pas de ta faute à toi/de votre faute à vous - **2.** (impersonal - one's) son (sa), ses (pl) ; **~ attitude changes as you get older** on change sa manière de voir en vieillissant ; **it's good for ~ teeth/hair** c'est bon pour les dents/les cheveux ; **~ average Englishman** l'Anglais moyen.

you're [jɔːr] = you are.

yours [jɔːz] poss pron (referring to one person) le tien (la tienne), les tiens (les tiennes) (pl) ; (polite form, pl) le vôtre (la vôtre), les vôtres (pl) ; **that desk is ~** ce bureau est à toi/à vous, ce bureau est le tien/le vôtre ; **it wasn't her fault, it was YOURS** ce n'était pas de sa faute, c'était de ta faute à toi/de votre faute à vous ; **a friend of ~** un ami à toi/vous, un de tes/vos amis.

➤ **Yours** adv [in letter] ▷ **faithfully, sincerely** etc.

yourself [jɔːˈself] (pl **-selves** [-ˈselvz]) pron - **1.** (reflexive - sg) te ; (- polite form, pl) vous ; (after preposition - sg) toi ; (- polite form, pl) vous - **2.** (for emphasis - sg) toi-même ; (- polite form) vous-même ; (- pl) vous-mêmes ; **did you do it ~?** tu l'as/vous l'avez fait tout seul?

youth [juːθ] n - **1.** (U) [period, quality] jeunesse f - **2.** [young man] jeune homme m - **3.** (U) [young people] jeunesse f, jeunes mpl.

youth club n centre m de jeunes.

youthful ['juːθfʊl] adj - **1.** [eager, innocent] de jeunesse, juvénile - **2.** [young] jeune.

youthfulness ['juːθfʊlnɪs] n jeunesse f.

youth hostel n auberge f de jeunesse.

youth hostelling [-ˈhɒstəlɪŋ] n Br : **to go ~** voyager en dormant dans des auberges de jeunesse.

you've [juːv] = you have.

yowl [jaʊl] ◇ n [of dog, person] hurlement m ; [of cat] miaulement m ◇ vi [dog, person] hurler ; [cat] miauler.

yo-yo ['jəʊjəʊ] n yo-yo m.

yr abbr of year.

YTS (abbr of Youth Training Scheme) n programme gouvernemental britannique d'insertion des jeunes dans la vie professionnelle.

Yucatan [ˌjʌkəˈtɑːn] n Yucatán m.

yuck [jʌk] excl inf berk!

Yugoslav = Yugoslavian.

Yugoslavia [ˌjuːgəˈslɑːvɪə] n Yougoslavie f ; **in ~** en Yougoslavie ; **the former ~** l'ex-Yougoslavie.

Yugoslavian [ˌjuːgəˈslɑːvɪən], **Yugoslav** [ˌjuːgəˈslɑːv] ◇ adj yougoslave ◇ n Yougoslave mf.

yule log [juːl-] n - **1.** [piece of wood] bûche f - **2.** [cake] bûche f de Noël.

yuletide ['juːltaɪd] n (U) literary époque f de Noël.

yummy ['jʌmɪ] (compar **-ier** ; superl **-iest**) adj inf délicieux(euse).

yuppie, yuppy ['jʌpɪ] (pl **-ies**) n inf yuppie mf.

YWCA (*abbr of* Young Women's Christian Association) *n* union chrétienne de jeunes filles (*proposant notamment des services d'hébergement*).

z (*pl* **z's** OR **zs**), **Z** (*pl* **Z's** OR **Zs**) [Br zed, Am zi:] *n* [letter] z *m inv*, Z *m inv*.

Zagreb ['zɑːgreb] *n* Zagreb.

Zaïre [zɑː'ɪəʳ] *n* Zaïre *m* ; **in** ~ au Zaïre.

Zaïrese [zɑː'ɪəriːz] ◇ *adj* zaïrois(e) ◇ *n* Zaïrois *m*, -e *f*.

Zambesi, Zambezi [zæm'biːzɪ] *n* : **the** ~ le Zambèze.

Zambia ['zæmbɪə] *n* Zambie *f* ; **in** ~ en Zambie.

Zambian ['zæmbɪən] ◇ *adj* zambien(enne) ◇ *n* Zambien *m*, -enne *f*.

zany ['zeɪnɪ] (*compar* **-ier** ; *superl* **-iest**) *adj* inf dingue.

Zanzibar [ˌzænzɪ'bɑː] *n* Zanzibar *m*.

zap [zæp] (*pt* & *pp* **-ped** ; *cont* **-ping**) ◇ *vt* [kill] descendre, tuer ◇ *vi* inf : **to** ~ **(off)** somewhere foncer quelque part.

zeal [ziːl] *n* zèle *m*.

zealot ['zelət] *n* fml fanatique *mf*.

zealous ['zeləs] *adj* zélé(e).

zebra [Br 'zebrə, Am 'ziːbrə] (*pl inv* OR **-s**) *n* zèbre *m*.

zebra crossing *n* Br passage *m* pour piétons.

Zen (Buddhism) [zen-] *n* bouddhisme *m* zen.

zenith [Br 'zenɪθ, Am 'ziːnəθ] *n* lit & fig zénith *m*.

zeppelin ['zepəlɪn] *n* zeppelin *m*.

zero [Br 'zɪərəʊ, Am 'ziːrəʊ] (*pl inv* OR **-es**) ◇ *adj* zéro, aucun(e) ◇ *n* zéro *m*.

◆ **zero in on** *vt fus* **- 1.** [subj : weapon] se diri-ger droit sur **- 2.** [subj : person] s'attaquer (d'entrée de jeu) à.

zero-rated [-ˌreɪtɪd] *adj* Br exempt(e) de TVA.

zest [zest] *n* (U) **- 1.** [excitement] piquant *m* **- 2.** [eagerness] entrain *m* **- 3.** [of orange, lemon] zeste *m*.

zigzag ['zɪgzæg] (*pt* & *pp* **-ged** ; *cont* **-ging**) ◇ *n* zigzag *m* ◇ *vi* zigzaguer.

zilch [zɪltʃ] *n* Am inf zéro *m*, que dalle.

Zimbabwe [zɪm'bɑːbwɪ] *n* Zimbabwe *m* ; **in** ~ au Zimbabwe.

Zimbabwean [zɪm'bɑːbwɪən] ◇ *adj* zim-babwéen(enne) ◇ *n* Zimbabwéen *m*, -en-ne *f*.

Zimmer frame® ['zɪməʳ-] *n* déambulateur *m*.

zinc [zɪŋk] *n* zinc *m*.

Zionism ['zaɪənɪzm] *n* sionisme *m*.

Zionist ['zaɪənɪst] ◇ *adj* sioniste ◇ *n* Sio-niste *mf*.

zip [zɪp] (*pt* & *pp* **-ped** ; *cont* **-ping**) *n* Br [fastener] fermeture *f* Éclair®.

◆ **zip up** *vt sep* [jacket] remonter la fermetu-re Éclair® de ; [bag] fermer la fermeture Éclair® de.

zip code *n* Am code *m* postal.

zip fastener *n* Br = **zip**.

zipper ['zɪpəʳ] *n* Am = **zip**.

zit [zɪt] *n* esp Am inf bouton *m*.

zither ['zɪðəʳ] *n* cithare *f*.

zodiac ['zəʊdɪæk] *n* : **the** ~ le zodiaque ; **sign of the** ~ signe *m* du zodiaque.

zombie ['zɒmbɪ] *n* fig & pej zombi *m*.

zone [zəʊn] *n* zone *f*.

zoo [zuː] *n* zoo *m*.

zoological [ˌzəʊə'lɒdʒɪkl] *adj* zoologique.

zoologist [zəʊ'ɒlədʒɪst] *n* zoologiste *mf*.

zoology [zəʊ'ɒlədʒɪl] *n* zoologie *f*.

zoom [zuːm] ◇ *vi* inf **- 1.** [move quickly] aller en trombe **- 2.** [rise rapidly] monter en flèche ◇ *n* PHOT zoom *m*.

◆ **zoom in** *vi* CINEMA : **to** ~ **in (on)** faire un zoom (sur).

◆ **zoom off** *vi* inf partir en trombe.

zoom lens *n* zoom *m*.

zucchini [zuː'kiːnɪ] (*pl inv*) *n* Am courgette *f*.

Zulu ['zuːluː] ◇ *adj* zoulou(e) ◇ *n* **- 1.** [person] Zoulou *m*, -e *f* **- 2.** [language] zoulou *m*.

Zürich ['zjʊərɪk] *n* Zurich.

CONJUGAISONS

	1 avoir	**2 être**	**3 chanter**
Indicatif présent	j'ai tu as il, elle a nous avons vous avez ils, elles ont	je suis tu es il, elle est nous sommes vous êtes ils, elles sont	je chante tu chantes il, elle chante nous chantons vous chantez ils, elles chantent
Indicatif imparfait	il, elle avait	il, elle était	il, elle chantait
Indicatif passé simple	il, elle eut ils, elles eurent	il, elle fut ils, elles furent	il, elle chanta ils, elles chantèrent
Indicatif futur	j'aurai il, elle aura	je serai il, elle sera	je chanterai il, elle chantera
Conditionnel présent	j'aurais il, elle aurait	je serais il, elle serait	je chanterais il, elle chanterait
Subjonctif présent	que j'aie qu'il, elle ait que nous ayons qu'ils, elles aient	que je sois qu'il, elle soit que nous soyons qu'ils, elles soient	que je chante qu'il, elle chante que nous chantions qu'ils, elles chantent
Subjonctif imparfait	qu'il, elle eût qu'ils, elles eussent	qu'il, elle fût qu'ils, elles fussent	qu'il, elle chantât qu'ils, elles chantassent
Impératif	aie ayons, ayez	sois soyons, soyez	chante chantons, chantez
Participe présent	ayant	étant	chantant
Participe passé	eu, eue	été	chanté, e

	4 baisser	**5 pleurer**	**6 jouer**
Indicatif présent	je baisse tu baisses il, elle baisse nous baissons vous baissez ils, elles baissent	je pleure tu pleures il, elle pleure nous pleurons vous pleurez ils, elles pleurent	je joue tu joues il, elle joue nous jouons vous jouez ils, elles jouent
Indicatif imparfait	il, elle baissait	il, elle pleurait	il, elle jouait
Indicatif passé simple	il, elle baissa ils, elles baissèrent	il, elle pleura ils, elles pleurèrent	il, elle joua ils, elles jouèrent
Indicatif futur	je baisserai il, elle baissera	je pleurerai il, elle pleurera	je jouerai il, elle jouera
Conditionnel présent	je baisserais il, elle baisserait	je pleurerais il, elle pleurerait	je jouerais il, elle jouerait
Subjonctif présent	que je baisse qu'il, elle baisse que nous baissions qu'ils, elles baissent	que je pleure qu'il, elle pleure que nous pleurions qu'ils, elles pleurent	que je joue qu'il, elle joue que nous jouions qu'ils, elles jouent
Subjonctif imparfait	qu'il, elle baissât qu'ils, elles baissassent	qu'il, elle pleurât qu'ils, elles pleurassent	qu'il, elle jouât qu'ils, elles jouassent
Impératif	baisse baissons, baissez	pleure pleurons, pleurez	joue jouons, jouez
Participe présent	baissant	pleurant	jouant
Participe passé	baissé, e	pleuré, e	joué, e

	7 saluer	8 arguer	9 copier
Indicatif présent	je salue tu salues il, elle salue nous saluons vous saluez ils, elles saluent	j'argue, arguë tu argues, arguës il, elle argue, arguë nous arguons vous arguez ils, elles arguent, arguënt	je copie tu copies il, elle copie nous copions vous copiez ils, elles copient
Indicatif imparfait	il, elle saluait	il, elle arguait	il, elle copiait
Indicatif passé simple	il, elle salua ils, elles saluèrent	il, elle argua ils, elles arguèrent	il, elle copia ils, elles copièrent
Indicatif futur	je saluerai il, elle saluera	j'arguerai, arguërai il, elle arguera, arguëra	je copierai il, elle copiera
Conditionnel présent	je saluerais il, elle saluerait	j'arguerais, arguërais il, elle arguerait, arguërait	je copierais il, elle copierait
Subjonctif présent	que je salue qu'il, elle salue que nous saluions qu'ils, elles saluent	que j'argue, arguë qu'il, elle argue, arguë que nous arguions qu'ils, elles arguent, arguënt	que je copie qu'il, elle copie que nous copiions qu'ils, elles copient
Subjonctif imparfait	qu'il, elle saluât qu'ils, elles saluassent	qu'il, elle arguât qu'ils, elles arguassent	qu'il, elle copiât qu'ils, elles copiassent
Impératif	salue saluons, saluez	argue, arguë arguons, arguez	copie copions, copiez
Participe présent	saluant	arguant	copiant
Participe passé	salué, e	argué, e	copié, e

	10 prier	11 payer	12 grasseyer
Indicatif présent	je prie tu pries il, elle prie nous prions vous priez ils, elles prient	je paie, paye tu paies, payes il, elle paie, paye nous payons vous payez ils, elles paient, payent	je grasseye tu grasseyes il, elle grasseye nous grasseyons vous grasseyez ils, elles grasseyent
Indicatif imparfait	il, elle priait	il, elle payait	il, elle grasseyait
Indicatif passé simple	il, elle pria ils, elles prièrent	il, elle paya ils, elles payèrent	il, elle grasseya ils, elles grasseyèrent
Indicatif futur	je prierai il, elle priera	je paierai, payerai il, elle paiera, payera	je grasseyerai il, elle grasseyera
Conditionnel présent	je prierais il, elle prierait	je paierais, payerais il, elle paierait, payerait	je grasseyerais il, elle grasseyerait
Subjonctif présent	que je prie qu'il, elle prie que nous priions qu'ils, elles prient	que je paie, paye qu'il, elle paie, paye que nous payions qu'ils, elles paient, payent	que je grasseye qu'il, elle grasseye que nous grasseyions qu'ils, elles grasseyent
Subjonctif imparfait	qu'il, elle priât qu'ils, elles priassent	qu'il, elle payât qu'ils, elles payassent	qu'il, elle grasseyât qu'ils, elles grasseyassent
Impératif	prie prions, priez	paie, paye payons, payez	grasseye grasseyons, grasseyez
Participe présent	priant	payant	grasseyant
Participe passé	prié, e	payé, e	grasseyé, e

	13 ployer	**14 essuyer**	**15 créer**
Indicatif présent	je ploie tu ploies il, elle ploie nous ployons vous ployez ils, elles ploient	j'essuie tu essuies il, elle essuie nous essuyons vous essuyez ils, elles essuient	je crée tu crées il, elle crée nous créons vous créez ils, elles créent
Indicatif imparfait	il, elle ployait	il, elle essuyait	il, elle créait
Indicatif passé simple	il, elle ploya ils, elles ployèrent	il, elle essuya ils, elles essuyèrent	il, elle créa ils, elles créèrent
Indicatif futur	je ploierai il, elle ploiera	j'essuierai il, elle essuiera	je créerai il, elle créera
Conditionnel présent	je ploierais il, elle ploierait	j'essuierais il, elle essuierait	je créerais il, elle créerait
Subjonctif présent	que je ploie qu'il, elle ploie que nous ployions qu'ils, elles ploient	que j'essuie qu'il, elle essuie que nous essuyions qu'ils, elles essuient	que je crée qu'il, elle crée que nous créions qu'ils, elles créent
Subjonctif imparfait	qu'il, elle ployât qu'ils, elles ployassent	qu'il, elle essuyât qu'ils, elles essuyassent	qu'il, elle créât qu'ils, elles créassent
Impératif	ploie ployons, ployez	essuie essuyons, essuyez	crée créons, créez
Participe présent	ployant	essuyant	créant
Participe passé	ployé, e	essuyé, e	créé, e

	16 avancer	**17 manger**	**18 céder**
Indicatif présent	j'avance tu avances il, elle avance nous avançons vous avancez ils, elles avancent	je mange tu manges il, elle mange nous mangeons vous mangez ils, elles mangent	je cède tu cèdes il, elle cède nous cédons vous cédez ils, elles cèdent
Indicatif imparfait	il, elle avançait	il, elle mangeait	il, elle cédait
Indicatif passé simple	il, elle avança ils, elles avancèrent	il, elle mangea ils, elles mangèrent	il, elle céda ils, elles cédèrent
Indicatif futur	j'avancerai il, elle avancera	je mangerai il, elle mangera	je céderai, cèderai il, elle cédera, cèdera
Conditionnel présent	j'avancerais il, elle avancerait	je mangerais il, elle mangerait	je céderais, cèderais il, elle céderait, cèderait
Subjonctif présent	que j'avance qu'il, elle avance que nous avancions qu'ils, elles avancent	que je mange qu'il, elle mange que nous mangions qu'ils, elles mangent	que je cède qu'il, elle cède que nous cédions qu'ils, elles cèdent
Subjonctif imparfait	qu'il, elle avançât qu'ils, elles avançassent	qu'il, elle mangeât qu'ils, elles mangeassent	qu'il, elle cédât qu'ils, elles cédassent
Impératif	avance avançons, avancez	mange mangeons, mangez	cède cédons, cédez
Participe présent	avançant	mangeant	cédant
Participe passé	avancé, e	mangé, e	cédé, e

	19 semer	20 rapiécer	21 acquiescer
Indicatif présent	je sème tu sèmes il, elle sème nous semons vous semez ils, elles sèment	je rapièce tu rapièces il, elle rapièce nous rapiéçons vous rapiécez ils, elles rapiècent	j'acquiesce tu acquiesces il, elle acquiesce nous acquiesçons vous acquiescez ils, elles acquiescent
Indicatif imparfait	il, elle semait	il, elle rapiéçait	il, elle acquiesçait
Indicatif passé simple	il, elle sema ils, elles semèrent	il, elle rapiéça ils, elles rapiécèrent	il, elle acquiesça ils, elles acquiescèrent
Indicatif futur	je sèmerai il, elle sèmera	je rapiécerai, rapiècerai il, elle rapiécera, rapiècera	j'acquiescerai il, elle acquiescera
Conditionnel présent	je sèmerais il, elle sèmerait	je rapiécerais, rapiècerais il, elle rapiécerait, rapiècerait	j'acquiescerais il, elle acquiescerait
Subjonctif présent	que je sème qu'il, elle sème que nous semions qu'ils, elles sèment	que je rapièce qu'il, elle rapièce que nous rapiécions qu'ils, elles rapiècent	que j'acquiesce qu'il, elle acquiesce que nous acquiescions qu'ils, elles acquiescent
Subjonctif imparfait	qu'il, elle semât qu'ils, elles semassent	qu'il, elle rapiéçât qu'ils, elles rapiéçassent	qu'il, elle acquiesçât qu'ils, elles acquiesçassent
Impératif	sème semons, semez	rapièce rapiéçons, rapiécez	acquiesce acquiesçons, acquiescez
Participe présent	semant	rapiéçant	acquiesçant
Participe passé	semé, e	rapiécé, e	acquiescé

	22 siéger	23 déneiger	24 appeler
Indicatif présent	je siège tu sièges il, elle siège nous siégeons vous siégez ils, elles siègent	je déneige tu déneiges il, elle déneige nous déneigeons vous déneigez ils, elles déneigent	j'appelle tu appelles il, elle appelle nous appelons vous appelez ils, elles appellent
Indicatif imparfait	il, elle siégeait	il, elle déneigeait	il, elle appelait
Indicatif passé simple	il, elle siégea ils, elles siégèrent	il, elle déneigea ils, elles déneigèrent	il, elle appela ils, elles appelèrent
Indicatif futur	je siégerai, siègerai il, elle siégera, siègera	je déneigerai il, elle déneigera	j'appellerai il, elle appellera
Conditionnel présent	je siégerais, siègerais il, elle siégerait, siègerait	je déneigerais il, elle déneigerait	j'appellerais il, elle appellerait
Subjonctif présent	que je siège qu'il, elle siège que nous siégions qu'ils, elles siègent	que je déneige qu'il, elle déneige que nous déneigions qu'ils, elles déneigent	que j'appelle qu'il, elle appelle que nous appelions qu'ils, elles appellent
Subjonctif imparfait	qu'il, elle siégeât qu'ils, elles siégeassent	qu'il, elle déneigeât qu'ils, elles déneigeassent	qu'il, elle appelât qu'ils, elles appelassent
Impératif	siège siégeons, siégez	déneige déneigeons, déneigez	appelle appelons, appelez
Participe présent	siégeant	déneigeant	appelant
Participe passé	siégé	déneigé, e	appelé, e

	25 peler	26 interpeller	27 jeter
Indicatif présent	je pèle tu pèles il, elle pèle nous pelons vous pelez ils, elles pèlent	j'interpelle tu interpelles il, elle interpelle nous interpellons vous interpellez ils, elles interpellent	je jette tu jettes il, elle jette nous jetons vous jetez ils, elles jettent
Indicatif imparfait	il, elle pelait	il, elle interpellait	il, elle jetait
Indicatif passé simple	il, elle pela ils, elles pelèrent	il, elle interpella ils, elles interpellèrent	il, elle jeta ils, elles jetèrent
Indicatif futur	je pèlerai il, elle pèlera	j'interpellerai il, elle interpellera	je jetterai il, elle jettera
Conditionnel présent	je pèlerais il, elle pèlerait	j'interpellerais il, elle interpellerait	je jetterais il, elle jetterait
Subjonctif présent	que je pèle qu'il, elle pèle que nous pelions qu'ils, elles pèlent	que j'interpelle qu'il, elle interpelle que nous interpellions qu'ils, elles interpellent	que je jette qu'il, elle jette que nous jetions qu'ils, elles jettent
Subjonctif imparfait	qu'il, elle pelât qu'ils, elles pelassent	qu'il, elle interpellât qu'ils, elles interpellassent	qu'il, elle jetât qu'ils, elles jetassent
Impératif	pèle pelons, pelez	interpelle interpellons, interpellez	jette jetons, jetez
Participe présent	pelant	interpellant	jetant
Participe passé	pelé, e	interpellé, e	jeté, e

	28 acheter	29 dépecer	30 envoyer
Indicatif présent	j'achète tu achètes il, elle achète nous achetons vous achetez ils, elles achètent	je dépèce tu dépèces il, elle dépèce nous dépeçons vous dépecez ils, elles dépècent	j'envoie tu envoies il, elle envoie nous envoyons vous envoyez ils, elles envoient
Indicatif imparfait	il, elle achetait	il, elle dépeçait	il, elle envoyait
Indicatif passé simple	il, elle acheta ils, elles achetèrent	il, elle dépeça ils, elles dépecèrent	il, elle envoya ils, elles envoyèrent
Indicatif futur	j'achèterai il, elle achètera	je dépècerai il, elle dépècera	j'enverrai il, elle enverra
Conditionnel présent	j'achèterais il, elle achèterait	je dépècerais il, elle dépècerait	j'enverrais il, elle enverrait
Subjonctif présent	que j'achète qu'il, elle achète que nous achetions qu'ils, elles achètent	que je dépèce qu'il, elle dépèce que nous dépecions qu'ils, elles dépècent	que j'envoie qu'il, elle envoie que nous envoyions qu'ils, elles envoient
Subjonctif imparfait	qu'il, elle achetât qu'ils, elles achetassent	qu'il, elle dépeçât qu'ils, elles dépeçassent	qu'il, elle envoyât qu'ils, elles envoyassent
Impératif	achète achetons, achetez	dépèce dépeçons, dépecez	envoie envoyons, envoyez
Participe présent	achetant	depeçant	envoyant
Participe passé	acheté, e	dépecé, e	envoyé, e

	31 aller	32 finir	33 haïr
Indicatif présent	je vais tu vas il, elle va nous allons vous allez ils, elles vont	je finis tu finis il, elle finit nous finissons vous finissez ils, elles finissent	je hais tu hais il, elle hait nous haïssons vous haïssez ils, elles haïssent
Indicatif imparfait	il, elle allait	il, elle finissait	il, elle haïssait
Indicatif passé simple	il, elle alla ils, elles allèrent	il, elle finit ils, elles finirent	il, elle haït ils, elles haïrent
Indicatif futur	j'irai il, elle ira	je finirai il, elle finira	je haïrai il, elle haïra
Conditionnel présent	j'irais il, elle irait	je finirais il, elle finirait	je haïrais il, elle haïrait
Subjonctif présent	que j'aille qu'il, elle aille que nous allions qu'ils, elles aillent	que je finisse qu'il, elle finisse que nous finissions qu'ils, elles finissent	que je haïsse qu'il, elle haïsse que nous haïssions qu'ils, elles haïssent
Subjonctif imparfait	qu'il, elle allât qu'ils, elles allassent	qu'il, elle finît qu'ils, elles finissent	qu'il, elle haït qu'ils, elles haïssent
Impératif	va allons, allez	finis finissons, finissez	hais haïssons, haïssez
Participe présent	allant	finissant	haïssant
Participe passé	allé, e	fini, e	haï, e

	34 ouvrir	35 fuir	36 dormir
Indicatif présent	j'ouvre tu ouvres il, elle ouvre nous ouvrons vous ouvrez ils, elles ouvrent	je fuis tu fuis il, elle fuit nous fuyons vous fuyez ils, elles fuient	je dors tu dors il, elle dort nous dormons vous dormez ils, elles dorment
Indicatif imparfait	il, elle ouvrait	il, elle fuyait	il, elle dormait
Indicatif passé simple	il, elle ouvrit ils, elles ouvrirent	il, elle fuit ils, elles fuirent	il, elle dormit ils, elles dormirent
Indicatif futur	j'ouvrirai il, elle ouvrira	je fuirai il, elle fuira	je dormirai il, elle dormira
Conditionnel présent	j'ouvrirais il, elle ouvrirait	je fuirais il, elle fuirait	je dormirais il, elle dormirait
Subjonctif présent	que j'ouvre qu'il, elle ouvre que nous ouvrions qu'ils, elles ouvrent	que je fuie qu'il, elle fuie que nous fuyions qu'ils, elles fuient	que je dorme qu'il, elle dorme que nous dormions qu'ils, elles dorment
Subjonctif imparfait	qu'il, elle ouvrît qu'ils, elles ouvrissent	qu'il, elle fuît qu'ils, elles fuissent	qu'il, elle dormît qu'ils, elles dormissent
Impératif	ouvre ouvrons, ouvrez	fuis fuyons, fuyez	dors dormons, dormez
Participe présent	ouvrant	fuyant	dormant
Participe passé	ouvert, e	fui, e	dormi

	37 mentir	**38 servir**	**39 acquérir**
Indicatif présent	je mens	je sers	j'acquiers
	tu mens	tu sers	tu acquiers
	il, elle ment	il, elle sert	il, elle acquiert
	nous mentons	nous servons	nous acquérons
	vous mentez	vous servez	vous acquérez
	ils, elles mentent	ils, elles servent	ils, elles acquièrent
Indicatif imparfait	il, elle mentait	il, elle servait	il, elle acquérait
Indicatif passé simple	il, elle mentit	il, elle servit	il, elle acquit
	ils, elles mentirent	ils, elles servirent	ils, elles acquirent
Indicatif futur	je mentirai	je servirai	j'acquerrai
	il, elle mentira	il, elle servira	il, elle acquerra
Conditionnel présent	je mentirais	je servirais	j'acquerrais
	il, elle mentirait	il, elle servirait	il, elle acquerrait
Subjonctif présent	que je mente	que je serve	que j'acquière
	qu'il, elle mente	qu'il, elle serve	qu'il, elle acquière
	que nous mentions	que nous servions	que nous acquérions
	qu'ils, elles mentent	qu'ils, elles servent	qu'ils, elles acquièrent
Subjonctif imparfait	qu'il, elle mentît	qu'il, elle servît	qu'il, elle acquît
	qu'ils, elles mentissent	qu'ils, elles servissent	qu'ils, elles acquissent
Impératif	mens	sers	acquiers
	mentons, mentez	servons, servez	acquérons, acquérez
Participe présent	mentant	servant	acquérant
Participe passé	menti	servi, e	acquis, e

	40 venir	**41 cueillir**	**42 mourir**
Indicatif présent	je viens	je cueille	je meurs
	tu viens	tu cueilles	tu meurs
	il, elle vient	il, elle cueille	il, elle meurt
	nous venons	nous cueillons	nous mourons
	vous venez	vous cueillez	vous mourez
	ils, elles viennent	ils, elles cueillent	ils, elles meurent
Indicatif imparfait	il, elle venait	il, elle cueillait	il, elle mourait
Indicatif passé simple	il, elle vint	il, elle cueillit	il, elle mourut
	ils, elles vinrent	ils, elles cueillirent	ils, elles moururent
Indicatif futur	je viendrai	je cueillerai	je mourrai
	il, elle viendra	il, elle cueillera	il, elle mourra
Conditionnel présent	je viendrais	je cueillerais	je mourrais
	il, elle viendrait	il, elle cueillerait	il, elle mourrait
Subjonctif présent	que je vienne	que je cueille	que je meure
	qu'il, elle vienne	qu'il, elle cueille	qu'il, elle meure
	que nous venions	que nous cueillions	que nous mourions
	qu'ils, elles viennent	qu'ils, elles cueillent	qu'ils, elles meurent
Subjonctif imparfait	qu'il, elle vînt	qu'il, elle cueillît	qu'il, elle mourût
	qu'ils, elles vinssent	qu'ils, elles cueillissent	qu'ils, elles mourussent
Impératif	viens	cueille	meurs
	venons, venez	cueillons, cueillez	mourons, mourez
Participe présent	venant	cueillant	mourant
Participe passé	venu, e	cueilli, e	mort, e

	43 partir	**44 revêtir**	**45 courir**
Indicatif présent	je pars tu pars il, elle part nous partons vous partez ils, elles partent	je revêts tu revêts il, elle revêt nous revêtons vous revêtez ils, elles revêtent	je cours tu cours il, elle court nous courons vous courez ils, elles courent
Indicatif imparfait	il, elle partait	il, elle revêtait	il, elle courait
Indicatif passé simple	il, elle partit ils, elles partirent	il, elle revêtit ils, elles revêtirent	il, elle courut ils, elles coururent
Indicatif futur	je partirai il, elle partira	je revêtirai il, elle revêtira	je courrai il, elle courra
Conditionnel présent	je partirais il, elle partirait	je revêtirais il, elle revêtirait	je courrais il, elle courrait
Subjonctif présent	que je parte qu'il, elle parte que nous partions qu'ils, elles partent	que je revête qu'il, elle revête que nous revêtions qu'ils, elles revêtent	que je coure qu'il, elle coure que nous courions qu'ils, elles courent
Subjonctif imparfait	qu'il, elle partît qu'ils, elles partissent	qu'il, elle revêtît qu'ils, elles revêtissent	qu'il, elle courût qu'ils, elles courussent
Impératif	pars partons, partez	revêts revêtons, revêtez	cours courons, courez
Participe présent	partant	revêtant	courant
Participe passé	parti, e	revêtu, e	couru, e

	46 faillir	**47 défaillir**	**48 bouillir**
Indicatif présent	je faillis, faux tu faillis, faux il, elle faillit, faut nous faillissons, faillons vous faillissez, faillez ils, elles faillissent, faillent	je défaille tu défailles il, elle défaille nous défaillons vous défaillez ils, elles défaillent	je bous tu bous il, elle bout nous bouillons vous bouillez ils, elles bouillent
Indicatif imparfait	il, elle faillissait, faillait	il, elle défaillait	il, elle bouillait
Indicatif passé simple	il, elle faillit ils, elles faillirent	il, elle défaillit ils, elles défaillirent	il, elle bouillit ils, elles bouillirent
Indicatif futur	je faillirai, faudrai il, elle faillira, faudra	je défaillirai, défaillerai il, elle défaillira, défaillera	je bouillirai il, elle bouillira
Conditionnel présent	je faillirais, faudrais il, elle faillirait, faudrait	je défaillirais, défaillerais il, elle défaillirait, défaillerait	je bouillirais il, elle bouillirait
Subjonctif présent	que je faillisse, faille qu'il, elle faillisse, faille que nous faillissions, faillions qu'ils, elles faillissent, faillent	que je défaille qu'il, elle défaille que nous défaillions qu'ils, elles défaillent	que je bouille qu'il, elle bouille que nous bouillions qu'ils, elles bouillent
Subjonctif imparfait	qu'il, elle faillît qu'ils, elles faillissent	qu'il, elle défaillît qu'ils, elles défaillissent	qu'il, elle bouillît qu'ils, elles bouillissent
Impératif	faillis, faux ; faillissons, faillons ; faillissez, faillez	défaille défaillons, défaillez	bous bouillons, bouillez
Participe présent	faillissant, faillant	défaillant	bouillant
Participe passé	failli	défailli	bouilli, e

	49 gésir *	**50 saillir**	**51 ouïr**
Indicatif présent	je gis tu gis il, elle gît nous gisons vous gisez ils, elles gisent	– – il, elle saille – – ils, elles saillent	j'ouïs, ois tu ouïs, ois il, elle ouït, oit nous ouïssons, oyons vous ouïssez, oyez ils, elles ouïssent, oient
Indicatif imparfait	il, elle gisait	il, elle saillait	il, elle ouïssait, oyait
Indicatif passé simple	–	il, elle saillit ils, elles saillirent	il, elle ouït ils, elles ouïrent
Indicatif futur	–	– il, elle saillera	j'ouïrai, orrais il, elle ouïra, orra
Conditionnel présent	–	– il, elle saillerait	j'ouïrais il, elle ouïrait, orrait
Subjonctif présent	–	qu'il, elle saille – qu'ils, elles saillent	que j'ouïsse, oie qu'il, elle ouïsse, oie que nous ouïssions, oyions qu'ils, elles ouïssent, oient
Subjonctif imparfait	–	qu'il, elle saillît qu'ils, elles saillissent	qu'il, elle ouït qu'ils, elles ouïssent
Impératif	–	–	ouïs, ois ; ouïssons, oyons ; ouïssez, oyez
Participe présent	gisant	saillant	oyant
Participe passé	–	sailli, e	ouï, e

* Gésir est défectif aux autres temps et modes.

	52 recevoir	**53 devoir**	**54 mouvoir**
Indicatif présent	je reçois tu reçois il, elle reçoit nous recevons vous recevez ils, elles reçoivent	je dois tu dois il, elle doit nous devons vous devez ils, elles doivent	je meus tu meus il, elle meut nous mouvons vous mouvez ils, elles meuvent
Indicatif imparfait	il, elle recevait	il, elle devait	il, elle mouvait
Indicatif passé simple	il, elle reçut ils, elles reçurent	il, elle dut ils, elles durent	il, elle mut ils, elles murent
Indicatif futur	je recevrai il, elle recevra	je devrai il, elle devra	je mouvrai il, elle mouvra
Conditionnel présent	je recevrais il, elle recevrait	je devrais il, elle devrait	je mouvrais il, elle mouvrait
Subjonctif présent	que je reçoive qu'il, elle reçoive que nous recevions qu'ils, elles reçoivent	que je doive qu'il, elle doive que nous devions qu'ils, elles doivent	que je meuve qu'il, elle meuve que nous mouvions qu'ils, elles meuvent
Subjonctif imparfait	qu'il, elle reçût qu'ils, elles reçussent	qu'il, elle dût qu'ils, elles dussent	qu'il, elle mût qu'ils, elles mussent
Impératif	reçois recevons, recevez	dois devons, devez	meus mouvons, mouvez
Participe présent	recevant	devant	mouvant
Participe passé	reçu, e	dû, due, dus, dues	mû, mue, mus, mues

	55 émouvoir	56 promouvoir	57 vouloir
Indicatif présent	j'émeus tu émeus il, elle émeut nous émouvons vous émouvez ils, elles émeuvent	je promeus tu promeus il, elle promeut nous promouvons vous promouvez ils, elles promeuvent	je veux tu veux il, elle veut nous voulons vous voulez ils, elles veulent
Indicatif imparfait	il, elle émouvait	il, elle promouvait	il, elle voulait
Indicatif passé simple	il, elle émut ils, elles émurent	il, elle promut ils, elles promurent	il, elle voulut ils, elles voulurent
Indicatif futur	j'émouvrai il, elle émouvra	je promouvrai il, elle promouvra	je voudrai il, elle voudra
Conditionnel présent	j'émouvrais il, elle émouvrait	je promouvrais il, elle promouvrait	je voudrais il, elle voudrait
Subjonctif présent	que j'émeuve qu'il, elle émeuve que nous émouvions qu'ils, elles émeuvent	que je promeuve qu'il, elle promeuve que nous promouvions qu'ils, elles promeuvent	que je veuille qu'il, elle veuille que nous voulions qu'ils, elles veuillent
Subjonctif imparfait	qu'il, elle émût qu'ils, elles émussent	qu'il, elle promût qu'ils, elles promussent	qu'il, elle voulût qu'ils, elles voulussent
Impératif	émeus émouvons, émouvez	promeus promouvons, promouvez	veux, veuille ; voulons, veuillons ; voulez, veuillez
Participe présent	émouvant	promouvant	voulant
Participe passé	ému, e	promu, e	voulu, e

	58 pouvoir	59 savoir	60 valoir
Indicatif présent	je peux, puis tu peux il peut nous pouvons vous pouvez ils, elles peuvent	je sais tu sais il, elle sait nous savons vous savez ils, elles savent	je vaux tu vaux il, elle vaut nous valons vous valez ils, elles valent
Indicatif imparfait	il, elle pouvait	il, elle savait	il, elle valait
Indicatif passé simple	il, elle put ils, elles purent	il, elle sut ils, elles surent	il, elle valut ils, elles valurent
Indicatif futur	je pourrai il, elle pourra	je saurai il, elle saura	je vaudrai il, elle vaudra
Conditionnel présent	je pourrais il, elle pourrait	je saurais il, elle saurait	je vaudrais il, elle vaudrait
Subjonctif présent	que je puisse qu'il, elle puisse que nous puissions qu'ils, elles puissent	que je sache qu'il, elle sache que nous sachions qu'ils, elles sachent	que je vaille qu'il, elle vaille que nous valions qu'ils, elles vaillent
Subjonctif imparfait	qu'il, elle pût qu'ils, elles pussent	qu'il, elle sût qu'ils, elles sussent	qu'il, elle valût qu'ils, elles valussent
Impératif	–	sache sachons, sachez	vaux valons, valez
Participe présent	pouvant	sachant	valant
Participe passé	pu	su, e	valu, e

	61 prévaloir	62 voir	63 prévoir
Indicatif présent	je prévaux	je vois	je prévois
	tu prévaux	tu vois	tu prévois
	il, elle prévaut	il, elle voit	il, elle prévoit
	nous prévalons	nous voyons	nous prévoyons
	vous prévalez	vous voyez	vous prévoyez
	ils, elles prévalent	ils, elles voient	ils, elles prévoient
Indicatif imparfait	il, elle prévalait	il, elle voyait	il, elle prévoyait
Indicatif passé simple	il, elle prévalut	il, elle vit	il, elle prévit
	ils, elles prévalurent	ils, elles virent	ils, elles prévirent
Indicatif futur	je prévaudrai	je verrai	je prévoirai
	il, elle prévaudra	il, elle verra	il, elle prévoira
Conditionnel présent	je prévaudrais	je verrais	jo prévoirais
	il, elle prévaudrait	il, elle verrait	il, elle prévoirait
Subjonctif présent	que je prévale	que je voie	que je prévoie
	qu'il, elle prévale	qu'il, elle voie	qu'il, elle prévoie
	que nous prévalions	que nous voyions	que nous prévoyions
	qu'ils, elles prévalent	qu'ils, elles voient	qu'ils, elles prévoient
Subjonctif imparfait	qu'il, elle prévalût	qu'il, elle vît	qu'il, elle prévît
	qu'ils, elles prévalussent	qu'ils, elles vissent	qu'ils, elles prévissent
Impératif	prévaux	vois	prévois
	prévalons, prévalez	voyons, voyez	prévoyons, prévoyez
Participe présent	prévalant	voyant	prévoyant
Participe passé	prévalu, e	vu, e	prévu, e

	64 pourvoir	65 asseoir	66 surseoir
Indicatif présent	je pourvois	j'assieds, j'assois	je sursois
	tu pourvois	tu assieds, assois	tu sursois
	il, elle pourvoit	il, elle assied, assoit	il, elle sursoit
	nous pourvoyons	nous asseyons, assoyons	nous sursoyons
	vous pourvoyez	vous asseyez, assoyez	vous sursoyez
	ils, elles pourvoient	ils, elles asseyent, assoient	ils, elles sursoient
Indicatif imparfait	il, elle pourvoyait	il, elle asseyait, assoyait	il, elle sursoyait
Indicatif passé simple	il, elle pourvut	il, elle assit	il, elle sursit
	ils, elles pourvurent	ils, elles assirent	ils, elles sursirent
Indicatif futur	je pourvoirai	j'assiérai, j'assoirai	je surseoirai
	il, elle pourvoira	il, elle assiéra, assoira	il, elle surseoira
Conditionnel présent	je pourvoirais	j'assiérais, j'assoirais	je surseoirais
	il, elle pourvoirait	il, elle assiérait, assoirait	il, elle surseoirait
Subjonctif présent	que je pourvoje	que j'asseye, j'assoie	que je sursoie
	qu'il, elle pourvoie	qu'il, elle asseye, assoie	qu'il, elle sursoie
	que nous pourvoyions	que nous asseyions, assoyions	que nous sursoyions
	qu'ils, elles pourvoient	qu'ils, elles asseyent, assoient	qu'ils, elles sursoient
Subjonctif imparfait	qu'il, elle pourvût	qu'il, elle assît	qu'il, elle sursît
	qu'ils, elles pourvussent	qu'ils, elles assissent	qu'ils, elles sursissent
Impératif	pourvois	assieds, assois ; asseyons,	sursois
	pourvoyons, pourvoyez	assoyons ; asseyez, assoyez	sursoyons, sursoyez
Participe présent	pourvoyant	asseyant, assoyant	sursoyant
Participe passé	pourvu, e	assis, e	sursis

	67 seoir	68 pleuvoir	69 falloir
Indicatif présent	– – il, elle sied – ils, elles siéent	– – il pleut – –	– – il faut – –
Indicatif imparfait	il, elle seyait	il pleuvait	il fallait
Indicatif passé simple	–	il plut –	il fallut –
Indicatif futur	– il, elle siéra	– il pleuvra	– il faudra
Conditionnel présent	– il, elle siérait	– il pleuvrait	– il faudrait
Subjonctif présent	– qu'il, elle siée – qu'ils, elles siéent	– qu'il pleuve – –	– qu'il faille – –
Subjonctif imparfait	–	qu'il plût –	qu'il fallût –
Impératif	–	–	–
Participe présent	seyant	pleuvant	–
Participe passé	–	plu	fallu

	70 échoir	71 déchoir	72 choir
Indicatif présent	– – il, elle échoit – – ils, elles échoient	je déchois tu déchois il, elle déchoit nous déchoyons vous déchoyez ils, elles déchoient	je chois tu chois il, elle choit – – ils, elles choient
Indicatif imparfait	il, elle échoyait	–	–
Indicatif passé simple	il, elle échut ils, elles échurent	il, elle déchut ils, elles déchurent	il, elle chut ils, elles churent
Indicatif futur	– il, elle échoira, écherra	je déchoirai il, elle déchoira	je choirai, cherrai il, elle choira, cherra
Conditionnel présent	– il, elle échoirait, écherrait	je déchoirais il, elle déchoirait	je choirais, cherrais il, elle choirait, cherrait
Subjonctif présent	– qu'il, elle échoie – qu'ils, elles échoient	que je déchoie qu'il, elle déchoie que nous déchoyions qu'ils, elles déchoient	–
Subjonctif imparfait	qu'il, elle échût qu'ils, elles échussent	qu'il, elle déchût qu'ils, elles déchussent	qu'il, elle chût –
Impératif	–	–	–
Participe présent	échéant	–	–
Participe passé	échu, e	déchu, e	chu, e

	73 vendre	74 répandre	75 répondre
Indicatif présent	je vends	je répands	je réponds
	tu vends	tu répands	tu réponds
	il, elle vend	il, elle répand	il, elle répond
	nous vendons	nous répandons	nous répondons
	vous vendez	vous répandez	vous répondez
	ils, elles vendent	ils, elles répandent	ils, elles répondent
Indicatif imparfait	il, elle vendait	il, elle répandait	il, elle répondait
Indicatif passé simple	il, elle vendit	il, elle répandit	il, elle répondit
	ils, elles vendirent	ils, elles répandirent	ils, elles répondirent
Indicatif futur	je vendrai	je répandrai	je répondrai
	il, elle vendra	il, elle répandra	il, elle répondra
Conditionnel présent	je vendrais	je répandrais	je répondrais
	il, elle vendrait	il, elle répandrait	il, elle répondrait
Subjonctif présent	que je vende	que je répande	que je réponde
	qu'il, elle vende	qu'il, elle répande	qu'il, elle réponde
	que nous vendions	que nous répandions	que nous répondions
	qu'ils, elles vendent	qu'ils, elles répandent	qu'ils, elles répondent
Subjonctif imparfait	qu'il, elle vendît	qu'il, elle répandît	qu'il, elle répondît
	qu'ils, elles vendissent	qu'ils, elles répandissent	qu'ils, elles répondissent
Impératif	vends	répands	réponds
	vendons, vendez	répandons, répandez	répondons, répondez
Participe présent	vendant	répandant	répondant
Participe passé	vendu, e	répandu, e	répondu, e

	76 mordre	77 perdre	78 rompre
Indicatif présent	je mords	je perds	je romps
	tu mords	tu perds	tu romps
	il, elle mord	il, elle perd	il, elle rompt
	nous mordons	nous perdons	nous rompons
	vous mordez	vous perdez	vous rompez
	ils, elles mordent	ils, elles perdent	ils, elles rompent
Indicatif imparfait	il, elle mordait	il, elle perdait	il, elle rompait
Indicatif passé simple	il, elle mordit	il, elle perdit	il, elle rompit
	ils, elles mordirent	ils, elles perdirent	ils, elles rompirent
Indicatif futur	je mordrai	je perdrai	je romprai
	il, elle mordra	il, elle perdra	il, elle rompra
Conditionnel présent	je mordrais	je perdrais	je romprais
	il, elle mordrait	il, elle perdrait	il, elle romprait
Subjonctif présent	que je morde	que je perde	que je rompe
	qu'il, elle morde	qu'il, elle perde	qu'il, elle rompe
	que nous mordions	que nous perdions	que nous rompions
	qu'ils, elles mordent	qu'ils, elles perdent	qu'ils, elles rompent
Subjonctif imparfait	qu'il, elle mordît	qu'il, elle perdît	qu'il, elle rompît
	qu'ils, elles mordissent	qu'ils, elles perdissent	qu'ils, elles rompissent
Impératif	mords	perds	romps
	mordons, mordez	perdons, perdez	rompons, rompez
Participe présent	mordant	perdant	rompant
Participe passé	mordu, e	perdu, e	rompu, e

	79 prendre	80 craindre	81 peindre
Indicatif présent	je prends tu prends il, elle prend nous prenons vous prenez ils, elles prennent	je crains tu crains il, elle craint nous craignons vous craignez ils, elles craignent	je peins tu peins il, elle peint nous peignons vous peignez ils, elles peignent
Indicatif imparfait	il, elle prenait	il, elle craignait	il, elle peignait
Indicatif passé simple	il, elle prit ils, elles prirent	il, elle craignit ils, elles craignirent	il, elle peignit ils, elles peignirent
Indicatif futur	je prendrai il, elle prendra	je craindrai il, elle craindra	je peindrai il, elle peindra
Conditionnel présent	je prendrais il, elle prendrait	je craindrais il, elle craindrait	je peindrais il, elle peindrait
Subjonctif présent	que je prenne qu'il, elle prenne que nous prenions qu'ils, elles prennent	que je craigne qu'il, elle craigne que nous craignions qu'ils, elles craignent	que je peigne qu'il, elle peigne que nous peignions qu'ils, elles peignent
Subjonctif imparfait	qu'il, elle prît qu'ils, elles prissent	qu'il, elle craignît qu'ils, elles craignissent	qu'il, elle peignît qu'ils, elles peignissent
Impératif	prends prenons, prenez	crains craignons, craignez	peins peignons, peignez
Participe présent	prenant	craignant	peignant
Participe passé	pris, e	craint, e	peint, e

	82 joindre	83 battre	84 mettre
Indicatif présent	je joins tu joins il, elle joint nous joignons vous joignez ils, elles joignent	je bats tu bats il, elle bat nous battons vous battez ils, elles battent	je mets tu mets il, elle met nous mettons vous mettez ils, elles mettent
Indicatif imparfait	il, elle joignait	il, elle battait	il, elle mettait
Indicatif passé simple	il, elle joignit ils, elles joignirent	il, elle battit ils, elles battirent	il, elle mit ils, elles mirent
Indicatif futur	je joindrai il, elle joindra	je battrai il, elle battra	je mettrai il, elle mettra
Conditionnel présent	je joindrais il, elle joindrait	je battrais il, elle battrait	je mettrais il, elle mettrait
Subjonctif présent	que je joigne qu'il, elle joigne que nous joignions qu'ils, elles joignent	que je batte qu'il, elle batte que nous battions qu'ils, elles battent	que je mette qu'il, elle mette que nous mettions qu'ils, elles mettent
Subjonctif imparfait	qu'il, elle joignît qu'ils, elles joignissent	qu'il, elle battît qu'ils, elles battissent	qu'il, elle mît qu'ils, elles missent
Impératif	joins joignons, joignez	bats battons, battez	mets mettons, mettez
Participe présent	joignant	battant	mettant
Participe passé	joint, e	battu, e	mis, e

	85 moudre	86 coudre	87 absoudre
Indicatif présent	je mouds tu mouds il, elle moud nous moulons vous moulez ils, elles moulent	je couds tu couds il, elle coud nous cousons vous cousez ils, elles cousent	j'absous tu absous il, elle absout nous absolvons vous absolvez ils, elles absolvent
Indicatif imparfait	il, elle moulait	il, elle cousait	il, elle absolvait
Indicatif passé simple	il, elle moulut ils, elles moulurent	il, elle cousit ils, elles cousirent	il, elle absolut ils, elles absolurent
Indicatif futur	je moudrai il, elle moudra	je coudrai il, elle coudra	j'absoudrai il, elle absoudra
Conditionnel présent	je moudrais il, elle moudrait	je coudrais il, elle coudrait	j'absoudrais il, elle absoudrait
Subjonctif présent	que je moule qu'il, elle moule que nous moulions qu'ils, elles moulent	que je couse qu'il, elle couse que nous cousions qu'ils, elles cousent	que j'absolve qu'il, elle absolve que nous absolvions qu'ils, elles absolvent
Subjonctif imparfait	qu'il, elle moulût qu'ils, elles moulussent	qu'il, elle cousît qu'ils, elles cousissent	qu'il, elle absolût qu'ils, elles absolussent
Impératif	mouds moulons, moulez	couds cousons, cousez	absous absolvons, absolvez
Participe présent	moulant	cousant	absolvant
Participe passé	moulu, e	cousu, e	absous, oute

	88 résoudre	89 suivre	90 vivre
Indicatif présent	je résous tu résous il, elle résout nous résolvons vous résolvez ils, elles résolvent	je suis tu suis il, elle suit nous suivons vous suivez ils, elles suivent	je vis tu vis il, elle vit nous vivons vous vivez ils, elles vivent
Indicatif imparfait	il, elle résolvait	il, elle suivait	il, elle vivait
Indicatif passé simple	il, elle résolut ils, elles résolurent	il, elle suivit ils, elles suivirent	il, elle vécut ils, elles vécurent
Indicatif futur	je résoudrai il, elle résoudra	je suivrai il, elle suivra	je vivrai il, elle vivra
Conditionnel présent	je résoudrais il, elle résoudrait	je suivrais il, elle suivrait	je vivrais il, elle vivrait
Subjonctif présent	que je résolve qu'il, elle résolve que nous résolvions qu'ils, elles résolvent	que je suive qu'il, elle suive que nous suivions qu'ils, elles suivent	que je vive qu'il, elle vive que nous vivions qu'ils, elles vivent
Subjonctif imparfait	qu'il, elle résolût qu'ils, elles résolussent	qu'il, elle suivît qu'ils, elles suivissent	qu'il, elle vécût qu'ils, elles vécussent
Impératif	résous résolvons, résolvez	suis suivons, suivez	vis vivons, vivez
Participe présent	résolvant	suivant	vivant
Participe passé	résolu, e	suivi, e	vécu, e

	91 paraître	92 naître	93 croître
Indicatif présent	je parais tu parais il, elle paraît nous paraissons vous paraissez ils, elles paraissent	je nais tu nais il, elle naît nous naissons vous naissez ils, elles naissent	je croîs tu croîs il, elle croît nous croissons vous croissez ils, elles croissent
Indicatif imparfait	il, elle paraissait	il, elle naissait	il, elle croissait
Indicatif passé simple	il, elle parut ils, elles parurent	il, elle naquit ils, elles naquirent	il, elle crût ils, elles crûrent
Indicatif futur	je paraîtrai il, elle paraîtra	je naîtrai il, elle naîtra	je croîtrai il, elle croîtra
Conditionnel présent	je paraîtrais il, elle paraîtrait	je naîtrais il, elle naîtrait	je croîtrais il, elle croîtrait
Subjonctif présent	que je paraisse qu'il, elle paraisse que nous paraissions qu'ils, elles paraissent	que je naisse qu'il, elle naisse que nous naissions qu'ils, elles naissent	que je croisse qu'il, elle croisse que nous croissions qu'ils, elles croissent
Subjonctif imparfait	qu'il, elle parût qu'ils, elles parussent	qu'il, elle naquît qu'ils, elles naquissent	qu'il, elle crût qu'ils, elles crûssent
Impératif	parais paraissons, paraissez	nais naissons, naissez	croîs croissons, croissez
Participe présent	paraissant	naissant	croissant
Participe passé	paru, e	né, e	crû, crue, crus, crues

	94 accroître	95 rire	96 conclure
Indicatif présent	j'accrois tu accrois il, elle accroît nous accroissons vous accroissez ils, elles accroissent	je ris tu ris il, elle rit nous rions vous riez ils, elles rient	je conclus tu conclus il, elle conclut nous concluons vous concluez ils, elles concluent
Indicatif imparfait	il, elle accroissait	il, elle riait	il, elle concluait
Indicatif passé simple	il, elle accrut ils, elles accrurent	il, elle rit ils, elles rirent	il, elle conclut ils, elles conclurent
Indicatif futur	j'accroîtrai il, elle accroîtra	je rirai il, elle rira	je conclurai il, elle conclura
Conditionnel présent	j'accroîtrais il, elle accroîtrait	je rirais il, elle rirait	je conclurais il, elle conclurait
Subjonctif présent	que j'accroisse qu'il, elle accroisse que nous accroissions qu'ils, elles accroissent	que je rie qu'il, elle rie que nous riions qu'ils, elles rient	que je conclue qu'il, elle conclue que nous concluions qu'ils, elles concluent
Subjonctif imparfait	qu'il, elle accrût qu'ils, elles accrussent	qu'il, elle rît qu'ils, elles rissent	qu'il, elle conclût qu'ils, elles conclussent
Impératif	accrois accroissons, accroissez	ris rions, riez	conclus concluons, concluez
Participe présent	accroissant	riant	concluant
Participe passé	accru, e	ri	conclu, e

	97 nuire	98 conduire	99 écrire
Indicatif présent	je nuis tu nuis il, elle nuit nous nuisons vous nuisez ils, elles nuisent	je conduis tu conduis il, elle conduit nous conduisons vous conduisez ils, elles conduisent	j'écris tu écris il, elle écrit nous écrivons vous écrivez ils, elles écrivent
Indicatif imparfait	il, elle nuisait	il, elle conduisait	il, elle écrivait
Indicatif passé simple	il, elle nuisit ils, elles nuisirent	il, elle conduisit ils, elles conduisirent	il, elle écrivit ils, elles écrivirent
Indicatif futur	je nuirai il, elle nuira	je conduirai il, elle conduira	j'écrirai il, elle écrira
Conditionnel présent	je nuirais il, elle nuirait	je conduirais il, elle conduirait	j'écrirais il, elle écrirait
Subjonctif présent	que je nuise qu'il, elle nuise que nous nuisions qu'ils, elles nuisent	que je conduise qu'il, elle conduise que nous conduisions qu'ils, elles conduisent	que j'écrive qu'il, elle écrive que nous écrivions qu'ils, elles écrivent
Subjonctif imparfait	qu'il, elle nuisît qu'ils, elles nuisissent	qu'il, elle conduisît qu'ils, elles conduisissent	qu'il, elle écrivît qu'ils, elles écrivissent
Impératif	nuis nuisons, nuisez	conduis conduisons, conduisez	écris écrivons, écrivez
Participe présent	nuisant	conduisant	écrivant
Participe passé	nui	conduit, e	écrit, e

	100 suffire	101 confire	102 dire
Indicatif présent	je suffis tu suffis il, elle suffit nous suffisons vous suffisez ils, elles suffisent	je confis tu confis il, elle confit nous confisons vous confisez ils, elles confisent	je dis tu dis il, elle dit nous disons vous dites ils, elles disent
Indicatif imparfait	il, elle suffisait	il, elle confisait	il, elle disait
Indicatif passé simple	il, elle suffit ils, elles suffirent	il, elle confit ils, elles confirent	il, elle dit ils, elles dirent
Indicatif futur	je suffirai il, elle suffira	je confirai il, elle confira	je dirai il, elle dira
Conditionnel présent	je suffirais il, elle suffirait	je confirais il, elle confirait	je dirais il, elle dirait
Subjonctif présent	que je suffise qu'il, elle suffise que nous suffisions qu'ils, elles suffisent	que je confise qu'il, elle confise que nous confisions qu'ils, elles confisent	que je dise qu'il, elle dise que nous disions qu'ils, elles disent
Subjonctif imparfait	qu'il, elle suffît qu'ils, elles suffissent	qu'il, elle confît qu'ils, elles confissent	qu'il, elle dît qu'ils, elles dissent
Impératif	suffis suffisons, suffisez	confis confisons, confisez	dis disons, dites
Participe présent	suffisant	confisant	disant
Participe passé	suffi	confit, e	dit, e

	103 contredire	104 maudire	105 bruire
Indicatif présent	je contredis tu contredis il, elle contredit nous contredisons vous contredisez ils, elles contredisent	je maudis tu maudis il, elle maudit nous maudissons vous maudissez ils, elles maudissent	je bruis tu bruis il, elle bruit – – –
Indicatif imparfait	il, elle contredisait	il, elle maudissait	il, elle bruyait
Indicatif passé simple	il, elle contredit ils, elles contredirent	il, elle maudit ils, elles maudirent	–
Indicatif futur	je contredirai il, elle contredira	je maudirai il, elle maudira	je bruirai il, elle bruira
Conditionnel présent	je contredirais il, elle contredirait	je maudirais il, elle maudirait	je bruirais il, elle bruirait
Subjonctif présent	que je contredise qu'il, elle contredise que nous contredisions qu'ils, elles contredisent	que je maudisse qu'il, elle maudisse que nous maudissions qu'ils, elles maudissent	–
Subjonctif imparfait	qu'il, elle contredît qu'ils, elles contredissent	qu'il, elle maudît qu'ils, elles maudissent	–
Impératif	contredis contredisons, contredisez	maudis maudissons, maudissez	–
Participe présent	contredisant	maudissant	–
Participe passé	contredit, e	maudit, e	bruit

	106 lire	107 croire	108 boire
Indicatif présent	je lis tu lis il, elle lit nous lisons vous lisez ils, elles lisent	je crois tu crois il, elle croit nous croyons vous croyez ils, elles croient	je bois tu bois il, elle boit nous buvons vous buvez ils, elles boivent
Indicatif imparfait	il, elle lisait	il, elle croyait	il, elle buvait
Indicatif passé simple	il, elle lut ils, elles lurent	il, elle crut ils, elles crurent	il, elle but ils, elles burent
Indicatif futur	je lirai il, elle lira	je croirai il, elle croira	je boirai il, elle boira
Conditionnel présent	je lirais il, elle lirait	je croirais il, elle croirait	je boirais il, elle boirait
Subjonctif présent	que je lise qu'il, elle lise que nous lisions qu'ils, elles lisent	que je croie qu'il, elle croie que nous croyions qu'ils, elles croient	que je boive qu'il, elle boive que nous buvions qu'ils, elles boivent
Subjonctif imparfait	qu'il, elle lût qu'ils, elles lussent	qu'il, elle crût qu'ils, elles crussent	qu'il, elle bût qu'ils, elles bussent
Impératif	lis lisons, lisez	crois croyons, croyez	bois buvons, buvez
Participe présent	lisant	croyant	buvant
Participe passé	lu, e	cru, e	bu, e

	109 faire	**110 plaire**	**111 taire**
Indicatif présent	je fais tu fais il, elle fait nous faisons vous faites ils, elles font	je plais tu plais il, elle plaît nous plaisons vous plaisez ils, elles plaisent	je tais tu tais il, elle tait nous taisons vous taisez ils, elles taisent
Indicatif imparfait	il, elle faisait	il, elle plaisait	il, elle taisait
Indicatif passé simple	il, elle fit ils, elles firent	il, elle plut ils, elles plurent	il, elle tut ils, elles turent
Indicatif futur	je ferai il, elle fera	je plairai il, elle plaira	je tairai il, elle taira
Conditionnel présent	je ferais il, elle ferait	je plairais il, elle plairait	je tairais il, elle tairait
Subjonctif présent	que je fasse qu'il, elle fasse que nous fassions qu'ils, elles fassent	que je plaise qu'il, elle plaise que nous plaisions qu'ils, elles plaisent	que je taise qu'il, elle taise que nous taisions qu'ils, elles taisent
Subjonctif imparfait	qu'il, elle fît qu'ils, elles fissent	qu'il, elle plût qu'ils, elles plussent	qu'il, elle tût qu'ils, elles tussent
Impératif	fais faisons, faites	plais plaisons, plaisez	tais taisons, taisez
Participe présent	faisant	plaisant	taisant
Participe passé	fait, e	plu	tu, e

	112 extraire	**113 clore**	**114 vaincre**
Indicatif présent	j'extrais tu extrais il, elle extrait nous extrayons vous extrayez ils, elles extraient	je clos tu clos il, elle clôt nous closons vous closez ils, elles closent	je vaincs tu vaincs il, elle vainc nous vainquons vous vainquez ils, elles vainquent
Indicatif imparfait	il, elle extrayait	–	il, elle vainquait
Indicatif passé simple	–	–	il, elle vainquit ils, elles vainquirent
Indicatif futur	j'extrairai il, elle extraira	je clorai il, elle clora	je vaincrai il, elle vaincra
Conditionnel présent	j'extrairais il, elle extrairait	je clorais il, elle clorait	je vaincrais il, elle vaincrait
Subjonctif présent	que j'extraie qu'il, elle extraie que nous extrayions qu'ils, elles extraient	que je close qu'il, elle close que nous closions qu'ils, elles closent	que je vainque qu'il, elle vainque que nous vainquions qu'ils, elles vainquent
Subjonctif imparfait	–	–	qu'il, elle vainquît qu'ils, elles vainquissent
Impératif	extrais extrayons, extrayez	clos –	vaincs vainquons, vainquez
Participe présent	extrayant	closant	vainquant
Participe passé	extrait, e	clos, e	vaincu, e

	115 frire	**116 foutre**
Indicatif présent	je fris tu fris il, elle frit – – –	je fous tu fous il, elle fout nous foutons vous foutez ils, elles foutent
Indicatif imparfait	–	il, elle foutait
Indicatif passé simple	–	–
Indicatif futur	je frirai il, elle frira	je foutrai il, elle foutra
Conditionnel présent	je frirais il, elle frirait	je foutrais il, elle foutrait
Subjonctif présent	–	que je foute qu'il, elle foute que nous foutions qu'ils, elles foutent
Subjonctif imparfait	–	–
Impératif	fris –	fous foutons, foutez
Participe présent	–	foutant
Participe passé	frit, e	foutu, e

ENGLISH IRREGULAR VERBS

Infinitive	Past Tense	Past Participle
arise	arose	arisen
awake	awoke	awoken
be	was, were	been
bear	bore	born(e)
beat	beat	beaten
become	became	become
begin	began	begun
bend	bent	bent
beseech	besought	besought
bet	bet (*also* betted)	bet (*also* betted)
bid	bid (*also* bade)	bid (*also* bidden)
bind	bound	bound
bite	bit	bitten
bleed	bled	bled
blow	blew	blown
break	broke	broken
breed	bred	bred
bring	brought	brought
build	built	built
burn	burnt (*also* burned)	burnt (*also* burned)
burst	burst	burst
buy	bought	bought
can	could	-
cast	cast	cast
catch	caught	caught
choose	chose	chosen
cling	clung	clung
come	came	come
cost	cost	cost
creep	crept	crept
cut	cut	cut
deal	dealt	dealt
dig	dug	dug
do	did	done
draw	drew	drawn
dream	dreamed (*also* dreamt)	dreamed (*also* dreamt)
drink	drank	drunk
drive	drove	driven
dwell	dwelt	dwelt
eat	ate	eaten
fall	fell	fallen
feed	fed	fed
feel	felt	felt
fight	fought	fought
find	found	found
flee	fled	fled
fling	flung	flung
fly	flew	flown
forbid	forbade	forbidden
forget	forgot	forgotten
forsake	forsook	forsaken
freeze	froze	frozen
get	got	got (*Am* gotten)
give	gave	given

Infinitive	Past Tense	Past Participle
go	went	gone
grind	ground	ground
grow	grew	grown
hang	hung (*also* hanged)	hung (*also* hanged)
have	had	had
hear	heard	heard
hide	hid	hidden
hit	hit	hit
hold	held	held
hurt	hurt	hurt
keep	kept	kept
kneel	knelt (*also* kneeled)	knelt (*also* kneeled)
know	knew	known
lay	laid	laid
lead	led	led
lean	leant (*also* leaned)	leant (*also* leaned)
leap	leapt (*also* leaped)	leapt (*also* leaped)
learn	learnt (*also* learned)	learnt (*also* learned)
leave	left	left
lend	lent	lent
let	let	let
lie	lay	lain
light	lit (*also* lighted)	lit (*also* lighted)
lose	lost	lost
make	made	made
may	might	-
mean	meant	meant
meet	met	met
mistake	mistook	mistaken
mow	mowed	mown (*also* mowed)
pay	paid	paid
put	put	put
quit	quit (*also* quitted)	quit (*also* quitted)
read	read	read
rend	rent	rent
rid	rid	rid
ride	rode	ridden
ring	rang	rung
rise	rose	risen
run	ran	run
saw	sawed	sawn
say	said	said
see	saw	seen
seek	sought	sought
sell	sold	sold
send	sent	sent
set	set	set
shake	shook	shaken
shall	should	
shear	sheared	shorn (*also* sheared)
shed	shed	shed
shine	shone	shone
shoot	shot	shot
show	showed	shown

Infinitive	Past Tense	Past Participle
shrink	shrank	shrunk
shut	shut	shut
sing	sang	sung
sink	sank	sunk
sit	sat	sat
slay	slew	slain
sleep	slept	slept
slide	slid	slid
sling	slung	slung
slit	slit	slit
smell	smelt (*also* smelled)	smelt (*also* smelled)
sow	sowed	sown (*also* sowed)
speak	spoke	spoken
speed	sped (*also* speeded)	sped (*also* speeded)
spell	spelt (*also* spelled)	spelt (*also* spelled)
spend	spent	spent
spill	spilt (*also* spilled)	spilt (*also* spilled)
spin	spun	spun
spit	spat	spat
split	split	split
spoil	spoiled (*also* spoilt)	spoiled (*also* spoilt)
spread	spread	spread
spring	sprang	sprung
stand	stood	stood
steal	stole	stolen
stick	stuck	stuck
sting	stung	stung
stink	stank	stunk
stride	strode	stridden
strike	struck	struck (*also* stricken)
strive	strove	striven
swear	swore	sworn
sweep	swept	swept
swell	swelled	swollen (*also* swelled)
swim	swam	swum
swing	swung	swung
take	took	taken
teach	taught	taught
tear	tore	torn
tell	told	told
think	thought	thought
throw	threw	thrown
thrust	thrust	thrust
tread	trod	trodden
wake	woke (*also* waked)	woken (*also* waked)
wear	wore	worn
weave	wove (*also* weaved)	woven (*also* weaved)
wed	wedded	wedded
weep	wept	wept
win	won	won
wind	wound	wound
wring	wrung	wrung
write	wrote	written

Achevé d'imprimer par l'Imprimerie
Maury-Eurolivres à Manchecourt
N° de projet 10078266 - 27,5 - OAB56°
N° de projet 10078267 - 8 - OAB56°
N° de projet 10075102 - 45 - OSB50°
Dépôt légal : janvier 2001 - N° d'imprimeur : 83410

Imprimé en France - (Printed in France)